Presented

TO

FROM

DATE

"All Scripture is God-breathed and is useful for teaching, rebuking, correcting and training in righteousness, so that the man of God may be thoroughly equipped for every good work."

2 TIMOTHY 3:16-17

New International Version

SPIRIT OF THE *Reformation* STUDY BIBLE

ZONDERVAN™

GRAND RAPIDS, MICHIGAN 49530

www.zondervan.com

ZONDERVAN™

NIV Spirit of the Reformation Study Bible

Published by Zondervan
Grand Rapids, Michigan 49530, U.S.A.

www.zondervan.com

Library of Congress Catalog Card Number 2002111445

Printed in the United States of America

03 04 05 06 07 08 09 10 /❖ DC/ 15 14 13 12 11 10 9 8 7 6 5 4 3 2 1

You will be pleased to know that a portion of the purchase price of your new NIV Bible has been provided to International Bible Society to help spread the gospel of Jesus Christ around the world!

CONTENTS

BIBLE BOOKS IN ALPHABETICAL ORDER

The books of the New Testament are indicated by *italics.*

INTRODUCTION

The *SPIRIT OF THE REFORMATION STUDY BIBLE* is a major revision and expansion of an earlier publication titled the *New Geneva Study Bible* (Thomas Nelson Publishers, 1995). Returning to the original contributions of over 58 highly respected Biblical and theological scholars, a team of editors reviewed, updated and expanded these contributions into their present form. Like its precursor, this study Bible represents an orientation toward Scripture characteristic of that branch of the church known as the Reformed tradition. These study notes and theological articles build on the Reformed doctrine of *Sola Scriptura*, an affirmation of the unquestionable authority of the infallible and inerrant Old and New Testament Scriptures as originally given by divine inspiration. The notes and articles also remain faithful to the system of theology contained in representative confessions and catechisms of the Reformed tradition.

The title, the *Spirit of the Reformation Study Bible*, reflects three central convictions that have guided this effort. First, we look back to the Protestant Reformation of the 16th century as a momentous work of the Holy Spirit in the church. At a time when the church had fallen into many serious false teachings and practices, the Protestant Reformers reaffirmed the authority and clarity of the Bible. This work of God's Spirit returned the people of God to the central truths of genuine Christian faith. For this reason this study Bible draws attention to classical expressions of Reformed theology by including in its appendices the full texts of several early confessions and catechisms: the Heidelberg Catechism, the Belgic Confession, the Canons of Dort, the Westminster Confession of Faith, the Westminster Larger Catechism and the Westminster Shorter Catechism. The study notes also incorporate a reverse index to all Scripture references contained in these documents.

Second, we recognize that the Holy Spirit has continued to bring reformation to the church. Through the Spirit's illumination many helpful insights into Scripture have come to be widely endorsed by those who have remained faithful to the central doctrinal perspectives of Reformed theology. In line with the claim that "the Reformed church is always reforming," this study Bible reflects many of these developments.

Third, it is our firm conviction that the Holy Spirit continues to reform the church today as his people devote themselves to faithful study and application of the Scriptures to all areas of life. For this reason, this study Bible has been designed to aid church leaders and lay people in their reading of the Word of God. Attention has been given to the historical backgrounds, major theological themes and literary qualities of each book of the Bible. This information not only guides readers toward an understanding of the original meaning of each portion of Scripture, but also points out ways in which the Scriptures are relevant for Christian life today.

Our sincere prayer is that followers of Christ will find the *Spirit of the Reformation Study Bible* to be a useful tool, but we also hope that no reader will ever confuse the fallible notes and confessional documents contained in this publication with the Scriptures themselves. We publish them all under one cover for your convenience, not to place Scripture and human interpretations on an equal footing. Only the original 66 books of sacred Scripture deserve our unqualified acceptance, for they alone are "God-breathed" (2Ti 3:16).

Richard L. Pratt, Jr.
General Editor

CONTRIBUTORS

EXECUTIVE DIRECTOR:
Luder G. Whitlock, Jr., D.Min.,
Excelsis

GENERAL EDITOR:
Richard L. Pratt, Jr. Th.D.,
Third Millennium Ministries,
Reformed Theological Seminary

OLD TESTAMENT EDITOR:
Bruce Waltke, Th.D., Ph.D.,
Reformed Theological Seminary

NEW TESTAMENT EDITORS:
Vern S. Poythress, Ph.D.,
Westminster Theological Seminary
Gregory K. Beale, Ph.D.,
Wheaton College Graduate School

THEOLOGICAL EDITORS:
John M. Frame, M.Phil.,
Reformed Theological Seminary
J.I. Packer, D.Phil.,
Regent College

ASSOCIATE EDITORS:
James Boice, D.Th. (deceased),
Tenth Presbyterian Church
Edmund P. Clowney, S.T.M., D.D.,
Westminster Theological Seminary
Roger R. Nicole, Ph.D.,
Reformed Theological Seminary

ASSOCIATE GENERAL EDITOR:
Ra McLaughlin, M.Div.,
Third Millennium Ministries

Old Testament Contributors
Carl E. Armerding, Ph.D., *Schloss Mittersill Study Centre*
Raymond B. Dillard, Ph.D. (deceased), *Westminster Theological Seminary*
William J. Dumbrell, Ph.D., *Moore Theological College*
Mark D. Futato, Ph.D., *Reformed Theological Seminary*
Graeme Goldsworthy, Ph.D., *Moore Theological College*
J. Alan Groves, Ph.D., *Westminster Theological Seminary*
R. Laird Harris, Ph.D. (emeritus), *Covenant Theological Seminary*
Kenneth J. Howell, Ph.D., *Reformed Theological Seminary*
M. M. Kline, Ph.D. (cand.), *Gordon-Conwell Theological Seminary*
Gary Knoppers, Ph.D., *Pennsylvania State University*
Donald A. Leggett, Ph.D., *Ontario Theological Seminary*
V. Phillips Long, Ph.D., *Regent College*
Tremper Longman III, Ph.D., *Westmont College*
Allan A. MacRae, Ph.D. (emeritus), *Biblical Theological Seminary*
J. Gordon McConville, Ph.D., *Wycliffe Hall, Oxford*
Jeffrey J. Niehaus, Ph.D., *Gordon-Conwell Theological Seminary*
Dirk H. Odendaal, Jr., Ph.D. (deceased), *University of Stellenbosch*
Raymond C. Ortlund, Ph.D., *First Presbyterian Church of Augusta, GA*
Gary D. Pratico, Th.D., *Gordon-Conwell Theological Seminary*
Richard L. Pratt, Jr., Th.D., *Third Millennium Ministries, Reformed Theological Seminary*
Elmer Smick, Ph.D. (deceased), *Reformed Theological Seminary*
Marion Ann Taylor, Ph.D., *Wycliffe College*
William A. VanGemeren, Ph.D., *Trinity Evangelical Divinity School*
J. Robert Vannoy, Th.D., *Biblical Theological Seminary*
Bruce K. Waltke, Th.D., Ph.D., *Reformed Theological Seminary*
Barry G. Webb, Ph.D., *Moore Theological College*
Gordon J. Wenham, Ph.D., *Cheltenham and Gloucester College of Higher Education*
John Woodhouse, Ph.D., *Moore Theological College*

New Testament Contributors
J. Knox Chamblin, Th.D. (emeritus), *Reformed Theological Seminary*
Karl J. Cooper, Th.M., *Providence, RI*
Sinclair B. Ferguson, Ph.D., *St. George Tron's Church, Glasgow, Scotland*
T. David Gordon, Ph.D., *Grove City College*
Wayne A. Grudem, Ph.D., *Phoenix Seminary*
Charles E. Hill, Ph.D., *Reformed Theological Seminary*
Kenneth J. Howell, Ph.D., *Reformed Theological Seminary*
Dennis J. Ireland, Ph.D., *Reformed Theological Seminary*
Dennis E. Johnson, Ph.D., *Northwestern Theological Seminary*
Peter R. Jones, Ph.D. *Westminster Theological Seminary in California*
Reggie M. Kidd, Ph.D., *Reformed Theological Seminary*
Simon J. Kistemaker, Th.D., *Reformed Theological Seminary*
W. Harold Mare, Ph.D., *Covenant Theological Seminary*
Dan G. McCartney, Ph.D., *Westminster Theological Seminary*
Leon Morris, Ph.D. (emeritus), *Ridley College*
Vern S. Poythress, D.Th., *Westminster Theological Seminary*
Moisés Silva, Ph.D., *New Testament Studies*
Frank S. Thielman, Ph.D., *The Beeson Divinity School*
Joseph Trafton, Ph.D., *Western Kentucky University*

Excelsis

Excelsis (formerly the Foundation for Reformation) exists to discover and promote that which is highest and best of Christianity within the church and to the world—to the glory of God. Excelsis established the vision for this study Bible and provided the financial resources for the project. Board of Directors: James M. Seneff, Jr., Ralph Veerman, Richard Hostetter and Luder G. Whitlock, Jr.

ABBREVIATIONS

Bible Books

Genesis	Ge
Exodus	Ex
Leviticus	Lev
Numbers	Nu
Deuteronomy	Dt
Joshua	Jos
Judges	Jdg
Ruth	Ru
1 Samuel	1Sa
2 Samuel	2Sa
1 Kings	1Ki
2 Kings	2Ki
1 Chronicles	1Ch
2 Chronicles	2Ch
Ezra	Ezr
Nehemiah	Neh
Esther	Est
Job	Job
Psalms	Ps
Proverbs	Pr
Ecclesiastes	Ecc
Song of Songs	SS
Isaiah	Isa
Jeremiah	Jer
Lamentations	La
Ezekiel	Eze
Daniel	Da
Hosea	Hos
Joel	Joel
Amos	Am
Obadiah	Ob
Jonah	Jnh
Micah	Mic
Nahum	Na
Habakkuk	Hab
Zephaniah	Zep
Haggai	Hag
Zechariah	Zec
Malachi	Mal
Matthew	Mt
Mark	Mk
Luke	Lk
John	Jn
Acts	Ac
Romans	Ro
1 Corinthians	1Co
2 Corinthians	2Co
Galatians	Gal
Ephesians	Eph
Philippians	Php
Colossians	Col
1 Thessalonians	1Th
2 Thessalonians	2Th
1 Timothy	1Ti
2 Timothy	2Ti
Titus	Tit
Philemon	Phm
Hebrews	Heb
James	Jas
1 Peter	1Pe
2 Peter	2Pe
1 John	1Jn
2 John	2Jn
3 John	3Jn
Jude	Jude
Revelation	Rev

General

c.	about, approximately
cf.	compare, confer
ch., chs.	chapter, chapters
e.g.	for example
etc.	and so on
ff.	following verse or verses
i.e.	that is
lit.	literally
NT	New Testament
OT	Old Testament
v., vv.	verse, verses

Reformed Doctrinal Standards and Other Historical Documents

ANF	*Ante-Nicene Fathers*
BC	Belgic Confession
CD	Canons of Dort
HC	Heidelberg Catechism
LBC	London Baptist Confession
NPNF	*Nicene and Post-Nicene Fathers*
WCF	Westminster Confession of Faith
ARP	Associate Reformed Presbyterian Church
EPC	Evangelical Presbyterian Church
OPC	Orthodox Presbyterian Church
PCA	Presbyterian Church in America
WLC	Westminster Larger Catechism
WSC	Westminster Shorter Catechism

The *HC, BC, CD, WCF, WLC* and *WSC* are historical doctrinal statements used by many Reformed traditions. All six documents are included in their entirety in the appendix to the *Spirit of the Reformation Study Bible*. The study notes throughout this volume indicate each time a passage of Scripture is footnoted by any of these historical standards. Such references are listed at the end of the notes in which they appear. Occasionally, note authors do reference these standards in passages that the standards have not footnoted. In these cases, the references are integrated into the note's text rather than being listed at the end of the note.

INDEX OF THEOLOGICAL ARTICLES

INDEX OF MAPS

INDEX OF CHARTS

NIV PREFACE

THE NEW INTERNATIONAL VERSION is a completely new translation of the Holy Bible made by over a hundred scholars working directly from the best available Hebrew, Aramaic and Greek texts. It had its beginning in 1965 when, after several years of exploratory study by committees from the Christian Reformed Church and the National Association of Evangelicals, a group of scholars met at Palos Heights, Illinois, and concurred in the need for a new translation of the Bible in contemporary English. This group, though not made up of official church representatives, was transdenominational. Its conclusion was endorsed by a large number of leaders from many denominations who met in Chicago in 1966.

Responsibility for the new version was delegated by the Palos Heights group to a self-governing body of fifteen, the Committee on Bible Translation, composed for the most part of biblical scholars from colleges, universities and seminaries. In 1967 the New York Bible Society (now the International Bible Society) generously undertook the financial sponsorship of the project—a sponsorship that made it possible to enlist the help of many distinguished scholars. The fact that participants from the United States, Great Britain, Canada, Australia and New Zealand worked together gave the project its international scope. That they were from many denominations—including Anglican, Assemblies of God, Baptist, Brethren, Christian Reformed, Church of Christ, Evangelical Free, Lutheran, Mennonite, Methodist, Nazarene, Presbyterian, Wesleyan and other churches—helped to safeguard the translation from sectarian bias.

How it was made helps to give the New International Version its distinctiveness. The translation of each book was assigned to a team of scholars. Next, one of the Intermediate Editorial Committees revised the initial translation, with constant reference to the Hebrew, Aramaic or Greek. Their work then went to one of the General Editorial Committees, which checked it in detail and made another thorough revision. This revision in turn was carefully reviewed by the Committee on Bible Translation, which made further changes and then released the final version for publication. In this way the entire Bible underwent three revisions, during each of which the translation was examined for its faithfulness to the original languages and for its English style.

All this involved many thousands of hours of research and discussion regarding the meaning of the texts and the precise way of putting them into English. It may well be that no other translation has been made by a more thorough process of review and revision from committee to committee than this one.

From the beginning of the project, the Committee on Bible Translation held to certain goals for the New International Version: that it would be an accurate translation and one that would have clarity and literary quality and so prove suitable for public and private reading, teaching, preaching, memorizing and liturgical use. The Committee also sought to preserve some measure of continuity with the long tradition of translating the Scriptures into English.

In working toward these goals, the translators were united in their commitment to the authority and infallibility of the Bible as God's Word in written form. They believe that it contains the divine answer to the deepest needs of humanity, that it sheds unique light on our path in a dark world, and that it sets forth the way to our eternal well-being.

The first concern of the translators has been the accuracy of the translation and its fidelity to the thought of the biblical writers. They have weighed the significance of the lexical and grammatical details of the Hebrew, Aramaic and Greek texts. At the same time, they have striven for more than a word-for-word translation. Because thought patterns and syntax differ from language to language, faithful communication of the meaning of the writers of the Bible demands frequent modifications in sentence structure and constant regard for the contextual meanings of words.

A sensitive feeling for style does not always accompany scholarship. Accordingly the Committee on Bible Translation submitted the developing version to a number of stylistic consultants. Two of them read every book of both Old and New Testaments twice—once before and once after the last major revision—and made invaluable suggestions. Samples of the translation were tested for clarity and ease of reading by various kinds of people—young and old, highly educated and less well educated, ministers and laymen.

Concern for clear and natural English—that the New International Version should be idiomatic but not idiosyncratic, contemporary but not dated—motivated the translators and consultants. At the same time, they tried to reflect the differing styles of the biblical writers. In view of the international use of English, the translators sought to avoid obvious Americanisms on the one hand and obvious Anglicisms on the other. A British edition reflects the comparatively few differences of significant idiom and of spelling.

As for the traditional pronouns "thou," "thee" and "thine" in reference to the Deity, the translators judged that to use these archaisms (along with the old verb forms such as "doest," "wouldest" and "hadst") would violate accuracy in translation. Neither Hebrew, Aramaic nor Greek uses special pronouns for the persons of the Godhead. A present-day translation is not enhanced by forms that in the time of the King James Version were used in everyday speech, whether referring to God or man.

For the Old Testament the standard Hebrew text, the Masoretic Text as published in the latest editions of *Biblia Hebraica*, was used throughout. The Dead Sea Scrolls contain material bearing on an earlier stage of the Hebrew text. They were consulted, as were the Samaritan Pentateuch and the ancient scribal traditions relating to textual changes. Sometimes a variant Hebrew reading in the margin of the Masoretic Text was followed instead of the text itself. Such instances, being variants within the Masoretic tradition, are not specified by footnotes. In rare cases, words in the consonantal text were divided differently from the way they appear in the Masoretic Text. Footnotes indicate this. The translators also consulted the more important early versions—the Septuagint; Aquila, Symmachus and Theodotion; the Vulgate; the Syriac Peshitta; the Targums; and for the Psalms the Juxta Hebraica of Jerome. Readings from these versions were occasionally followed where the Masoretic Text seemed doubtful and where accepted principles of textual criticism showed that one or more of these textual witnesses appeared to provide the correct reading. Such instances are footnoted. Sometimes vowel letters and vowel signs did not, in the judgment of the translators, represent the correct vowels for the original consonantal text. Accordingly some words were read with a different set of vowels. These instances are usually not indicated by footnotes.

The Greek text used in translating the New Testament was an eclectic one. No other piece of ancient literature has such an abundance of manuscript witnesses as does the New Testament. Where existing manuscripts differ, the translators made their choice of readings according to accepted principles of New Testament textual criticism. Footnotes call attention to places where there was uncertainty about what the original text was. The best current printed texts of the Greek New Testament were used.

There is a sense in which the work of translation is never wholly finished. This applies to all great literature and uniquely so to the Bible. In 1973 the New Testament in the New International Version was published. Since then, suggestions for corrections and revisions have been received from various sources. The Committee on Bible Translation carefully considered the suggestions and adopted a number of them. These were incorporated in the first printing of the entire Bible in 1978. Additional revisions were made by the Committee on Bible Translation in 1983 and appear in printings after that date.

As in other ancient documents, the precise meaning of the biblical texts is sometimes uncertain. This is more often the case with the Hebrew and Aramaic texts than with the Greek text. Although archaeological and linguistic discoveries in this century aid in understanding difficult passages, some uncertainties remain. The more significant of these have been called to the reader's attention in the footnotes.

In regard to the divine name *YHWH*, commonly referred to as the *Tetragrammaton*, the translators adopted the device used in most English versions of rendering that name as "Lord" in capital letters to distinguish it from Adonai, another Hebrew word rendered "Lord," for which small letters are used. Wherever the two names stand together in the Old Testament as a compound name of God, they are rendered "Sovereign Lord."

Because for most readers today the phrases "the LORD of hosts" and "God of hosts" have little meaning, this version renders them "the LORD Almighty" and "God Almighty." These renderings convey the sense of the Hebrew, namely, "he who is sovereign over all the 'hosts' (powers) in heaven and on earth, especially over the 'hosts' (armies) of Israel." For readers unacquainted with Hebrew this does not make clear the distinction between *Sabaoth* ("hosts" or "Almighty") and *Shaddai* (which can also be translated "Almighty"), but the latter occurs infrequently and is always footnoted. When *Adonai* and *YHWH Sabaoth* occur together, they are rendered "the LORD, the LORD Almighty."

As for other proper nouns, the familiar spellings of the King James Version are generally retained. Names traditionally spelled with "ch," except where it is final, are usually spelled in this translation with "k" or "c," since the biblical languages do not have the sound that "ch" frequently indicates in English—for example, in *chant*. For well-known names such as Zechariah, however, the traditional spelling has been retained. Variation in the spelling of names in the original languages has usually not been indicated. Where a person or place has two or more different names in the Hebrew, Aramaic or Greek texts, the more familiar one has generally been used, with footnotes where needed.

To achieve clarity the translators sometimes supplied words not in the original texts but required by the context. If there was uncertainty about such material, it is enclosed in brackets. Also for the sake of clarity or style, nouns, including some proper nouns, are sometimes substituted for pronouns, and vice versa. And though the Hebrew writers often shifted back and forth between first, second and third personal pronouns without change of antecedent, this translation often makes them uniform, in accordance with English style and without the use of footnotes.

Poetical passages are printed as poetry, that is, with indentation of lines and with separate stanzas. These are generally designed to reflect the structure of Hebrew poetry. This poetry is normally characterized by parallelism in balanced lines. Most of the poetry in the Bible is in the Old Testament, and scholars differ regarding the scansion of Hebrew lines. The translators determined the stanza divisions for the most part by analysis of the subject matter. The stanzas therefore serve as poetic paragraphs.

As an aid to the reader, italicized sectional headings are inserted in most of the books. They are not to be regarded as part of the NIV text, are not for oral reading, and are not intended to dictate the interpretation of the sections they head.

The footnotes in this version are of several kinds, most of which need no explanation. Those giving alternative translations begin with "Or" and generally introduce the alternative with the last word preceding it in the text, except when it is a single-word alternative; in poetry quoted in a footnote a slant mark indicates a line division. Footnotes introduced by "Or" do not have uniform significance. In some cases two possible translations were considered to have about equal validity. In other cases, though the translators were convinced that the translation in the text was correct, they judged that another interpretation was possible and of sufficient importance to be represented in a footnote.

In the New Testament, footnotes that refer to uncertainty regarding the original text are introduced by "Some manuscripts" or similar expressions. In the Old Testament, evidence for the reading chosen is given first and evidence for the alternative is added after a semicolon (for example: Septuagint; Hebrew *father*). In such notes the term "Hebrew" refers to the Masoretic Text.

It should be noted that minerals, flora and fauna, architectural details, articles of clothing and jewelry, musical instruments and other articles cannot always be identified with precision. Also measures of capacity in the biblical period are particularly uncertain (see the table of weights and measures following the text).

Like all translations of the Bible, made as they are by imperfect man, this one undoubtedly falls short of its goals. Yet we are grateful to God for the extent to which he has enabled us to realize these goals and for the strength he has given us and our colleagues to complete our task. We offer this version of the Bible to him in whose name and for whose glory it has been made. We pray that it will lead many into a better understanding of the Holy Scriptures and a fuller knowledge of Jesus Christ the incarnate Word, of whom the Scriptures so faithfully testify.

The Committee on Bible Translation

June 1978
(Revised Aug 1983)

Names of the translators and editors may be secured from the International Bible Society, translation sponsors of the New International Version, 1820 Jet Stream Drive, Colorado Springs, Colorado 08921-3696 U.S.A.

THE
OLD TESTAMENT

Introduction to the Pentateuch

THE first five books of the Bible (Genesis, Exodus, Leviticus, Numbers and Deuteronomy) are usually designated "the Law" or "the Pentateuch" (Greek *pentateuchos*, or "five-volume [book]"). They constitute the first and most important section of the Old Testament in both Jewish and Christian Bibles. The threefold division of the Hebrew Bible into Law, Prophets and Writings can be traced back to the New Testament (Lk 24:44) and to the prologue to the Apocryphal book of Ecclesiasticus (Sirach) (c. 130 B.C.). The division of the Old Testament in Christian Bibles, based on the Greek Old Testament (the Septuagint; c. 150 B.C.), also gives the Pentateuch pride of place.

AUTHOR AND DATE

References to the Pentateuch by such terms as "the Book of Moses" (2Ch 25:4; Ne 13:1), "the Book of the Law of Moses" (Ne 8:1), "the Law of the LORD" (1Ch 16:40; Ezr 7:10) and "the Book of the Law of God" (Ne 8:18) are largely restricted to the writings after the exile. (It is uncertain whether references to "the law [of Moses]" in the earlier books refer to the Pentateuch or to parts of it [e.g., Jos 1:8; 8:34; 2Ki 14:6; 22:8].) The New Testament uses similar designations for the Pentateuch (Mt 12:5; Mk 12:26; Lk 16:16; Jn 7:19; Gal 3:10). The attribution of these books to Moses underscored the binding authority of the Pentateuch. Mosaic authorship is indicated not only by these titles but also by the words of Jesus: "Moses . . . wrote about me" (Jn 5:46). Luke also asserts Mosaic authorship when he records that Jesus expounded the Scriptures "beginning with Moses" (Lk 24:27), and many other New Testament writers and characters do as well (Mt 8:4; 19:7–8; Mk 1:44; 7:10; 10:3–4; 12:19,26; Lk 16:29,31; 24:44; Jn 1:45; 8:5; Ac 15:21; 26:22; 28:23; Ro 10:5,19; 2Co 3:14–15). The Pentateuch itself tells of Moses' decisive contribution toward its composition: He wrote the great legal code, the Book of the Covenant (Ex 24:3–7), and his exposition of the law as recorded in the book of Deuteronomy (Dt 31:24–26).

During the past two centuries, however, most interpreters who do not accept the Bible's own witness about its authorship have attributed its final composition to editors after the exile who creatively pieced together at least four earlier literary documents. Their view is commonly called the documentary hypothesis. On the basis of varying divine names (e.g., "God" [*Elohim*] and "LORD" [*Yahweh*]), vocabulary (e.g., different Hebrew words for "maid servant"), duplicate stories (e.g., the jeopardizing of the matriarchs [Ge 12:10–20; 20:1–19; 26:1–11]) and laws (e.g., of the Passover [Ex 12:1–20,21–23; Dt 16:1–8]), and by the varying theologies, they regard the Pentateuch as essentially a composite of the Yahwist's narrative (*J* from German "Jahwist"; c. 950 B.C.); the Elohist's narrative (*E;* c. 850 B.C.); the Deuteronomist document, mostly Deuteronomy (*D;* c. 622 to 587 B.C.); and the Priestly document (*P;* c. 500 B.C.). During the second half of the twentieth century this point of view has been significantly modified. On the basis of literary forms and archaeological evidence, it became clear that all of the alleged documents contained much older material, some of which might even date back to Moses. Those who hold to the documentary hypothesis today generally believe that the writers of *J, E, D* and *P* were not authors but editors who collected and arranged earlier materials. Most recently a number of scholars, while still essentially recognizing these claimed documents in the Pentateuch, have called into question the goal and methods that led to the identification of these sources and have expressed admiration for the Pentateuch's unified structure.

To speak of Moses as the author of the Pentateuch is to say that he was its fundamental source and authority and that the books of the Pentateuch were originally composed, in largely the forms in which they exist today, during the life of Moses. We should readily admit, however, that, in conformity with known practices in the ancient Near East, Moses used literary sources. Sometimes these are clearly identified (e.g., Ge 5:1; Nu 21:14); at other times they may be inferred from changes in literary styles (cf. Ge 1:1—2:3 with Ge 2:4—2:25). Later inspired prophets, who succeeded Moses in mediating God's authoritative word (cf. Dt 18:15–20), kept the text up-to-date linguistically and historically and even added material such as Genesis 36:31 (See "Introduction to Genesis") and Moses' obituary (Dt 34:1–12). The NIV sometimes places non-Mosaic material in parenthesis (e.g., Ex 11:3; Nu 12:3).

UNITY

The Pentateuch is both a composite of individual books and a seamless narrative that renders a complete story from creation to the death of Moses. To read it as merely one or the other would distort its text. On the one hand, each book in its own way guided Israel through the exodus from Egypt toward the conquest of Canaan. Genesis is distinctive on the basis of its unique literary focus on the primeval and patriarchal periods, thereby setting the backdrop for the accounts of the exodus and the conquest. Exodus highlights Moses' leadership, the law and the tabernacle; Leviticus is a distinctly priestly manual to guide worship in Israel; Numbers focuses on Israel as the Lord's army marching toward Canaan; and Deuteronomy consists of three addresses by Moses on the plains of Moab, in which he expounded the law and directed covenant renewal.

At the same time these books are bound together into a continuous narrative. For example, Exodus is linked with Genesis by reference to the number of Israelites who went down to Egypt (Ge 46:26, 27; Ex 1:1). Moses, at the time of the exodus, quotes Joseph's deathbed request that the Israelites carry up his bones out of Egypt when God came to their aid (Ge 50:25; Ex 13:19). Leviticus 1–9 can almost be read as an appendix to Exodus 25–40. The latter text legitimates the building of the tabernacle and the former its ritual. The priest's ordination service is outlined in Exodus 29 but does not take place until Leviticus 8–9. The dietary restrictions in Leviticus are based on the story of the exodus (Lev 11:45). Numbers shares many connections with both Exodus and Leviticus. Large portions of the narratives of all three of these middle books take place in the wilderness of Sinai, and the books share similar liturgical regulations and concerns. At the beginning of his first address in Deuteronomy, Moses summarizes Israel's history from Sinai to Moab as recorded in Numbers, and in his second address he makes frequent allusions to Exodus, even repeating with slight modification the Ten Commandments and Israel's response (Ex 20; Dt 5).

THEME

The Pentateuch is primarily a blending of history and law. These themes are not unrelated: The narrative history explains the laws. For example, the law about circumcision is given in the recounting of God's announcement of his covenant with Abraham and Sarah (Ge 17:9–14), and breaking the Sabbath is made a capital offense in the story about the man who gathered sticks on that day (Nu 15:32–36). But, as noted above, the Pentateuch's big story relates to God's covenants with the patriarchs; his later deliverance of their descendants, now a nation, from Egypt; and their obligation to keep God's laws as delineated in the covenant to which they agreed at Sinai and that Moses expounded in Deuteronomy (Dt 6:20–25).

Genesis ends with Joseph's coffin in Egypt (Ge 50:26), Exodus with the Lord's guiding glory-cloud over the tabernacle in the wilderness of Sinai (Ex 40:34–38); Leviticus with the summary "These are the commands the LORD gave Moses on Mount Sinai for the Israelites" (Lev 27:34); Numbers with a similar summary but now "on the plains of Moab" (Nu 36:13); and Deuteronomy with the burial of Moses in Moab and provision for Joshua to succeed him (Dt 34). This spatial and temporal progression from Egypt to Sinai to Moab can be traced back to Abraham's call to leave his homeland, Ur of the Chaldees, and God's offer to make of him a great nation in its own land, one that would bless all the other nations of the earth (Ge 12:1–3). The Pentateuch is a story about God's gracious, unfolding covenants to form a priestly, holy nation that would bring salvation to all peoples.

Genesis focuses on God's covenants with its fathers, Abraham, Isaac and Jacob, which promise that God will make of their family a great nation. The narrative in Exodus through Deuteronomy deals with the nation's founder, Moses, and God's covenant mediated through him to make Israel a holy nation. That story and these covenants find their fulfillment in Christ and the new Israel as the sovereign God directs history toward its ultimate destiny.

GENESIS

Introduction

Overview

Author: Moses

Purpose: To teach the Israelites God's design for them as a nation through the background of early world history and the lives of their patriarchs

Date: c. 1446–1406 B.C.

Key Truths:

- Although sin corrupted the ideal world Israel's God had created, redemption would come through God's chosen people.
- The lives of Abraham, Isaac and Jacob provide many insights into the nature of God's covenant with his people and their hope for the future.
- The lives of Joseph and his brothers reveal the ways in which the people of God are to relate to each other and to the world.

Author

Because this book is part of the unified Pentateuch, establishing its authorship cannot be entirely separated from the composition of Exodus, Leviticus, Numbers and Deuteronomy (see "Introduction to the Pentateuch"). Evidences for Genesis itself suggest that, as is the case with the rest of the Pentateuch, Moses, under the Holy Spirit's inspiration, gave the book its essential substance; therefore, he may correctly be called its author. Later inspired editors modernized and supplemented it in a number of places to form the book as we have it today.

It would be arbitrary to exclude Genesis from the New Testament testimony that Moses authored the Pentateuch. More specifically, our Lord said, "Moses gave you circumcision" (Jn 7:22; see also Ac 15:1), a rite that was uniquely laid out in Genesis 17. It is not surprising that the founder of Israel's theocracy provided this masterful literary composition. Moses' superb training in the courts of Egypt, his exceptional spiritual gifts and his divine call uniquely qualified him to compose the essential content and shape of the Pentateuch. The founder of Israel's theocracy of necessity would have given Israel its prior history, meaning and destiny, as well as its laws. Nearly every significant political and/or religious community in the ancient world retained accounts of its defining origins. In much the same way, Genesis furnished the theological and ethical underpinnings of the Torah: Israel's unique covenantal relationship with God (Dt 9:5). Moreover, since creation myths were basic to pagan religions, it is reasonable to expect Israel's founder to have provided the Genesis creation account to counter them (see notes on 1:1—2:3).

This outlook is corroborated by evidence of the antiquity of Genesis. Its first 11 chapters share many continuities and conscious discontinuities with ancient Near Eastern myths that preceded the time of Moses and were certainly known to him (e.g., the *Enuma Elish,* the *Atrahasis* epic and the 11th tablet of the *Gilgamesh* epic—Mesopotamian accounts of the creation and flood). Names and customs in the narratives about the patriarchs (chs. 12–50) accurately reflect their era, suggesting an early author working from reliable documents. The Ebla texts (twenty-fourth century B.C.) mention Ebrium, very possibly the Eber of 10:21; and the Mari texts (eighteenth century B.C.) attest, among others, the names Abraham, Jacob and Amorite. The practice of granting a birthright (i.e., additional privileges to an eldest son; 25:5–6,32–34) was widespread in the ancient Near East, and the sale of an inheritance (25:29–34) is documented at different periods in this area. The adoption of one's own slave (15:3) is found in a Larsa letter from the Old Babylonian period, and the adoption of Ephraim and Manasseh by their grandfather (48:5) may be compared with a similar adoption of a grandson at Ugarit (fourteenth century B.C.). The gift of a female slave as part of a dowry and her presentation to her husband by an infertile wife (see 16:1–6 and their notes; see also 30:1–3) are attested in the Hammurapi Code (eighteenth century B.C.). In fact, some religious practices of the patriarchs antedate Moses. They worshiped God under such ancient names as *El Olam* ("the Eternal God"; 21:33) and *El Shaddai* (17:1). These names never recur in the Torah, except in Exodus 6:3, where the NIV translates *El Shaddai* as "God Almighty" (Nu 21:4 and Nu 24:16 employ *Shaddai* alone, translated "the Almighty"). Contrary to the Mosaic Law, and without the narrator's censure, Jacob erected a stone pillar (28:18–22), Abraham married his half sister (20:12), and Jacob simultaneously married sisters (29:15–30; cf. Dt 16:21–22; Lev 18:9,18, respectively). Moreover, of the 38 names by which the patriarchs and their families are called, 27 are never found again in the Bible. Only Genesis calls Hebron "Mamre," and only Genesis mentions Paddan Aram. These details indicate not only that Moses depended on earlier sources, but also that Genesis was written early in Israel's history, when there was little need to justify or condemn these earlier customs.

Time and Place of Writing

Given the evidence linking Genesis and its contents to Moses and his era, we may reasonably conclude that the book's essential form and content date from about 1400 B.C. Insofar as David (c. 1000 B.C.) set the creation account (Ge 1) to music (Ps 8), a date of composition in the second millennium B.C. is certified for chapter 1.

Although words known to have been used only in the middle of the second millennium B.C. occasionally turn up in the text (see note on "the older" at 25:23), readers should note that the grammar and the place names (see note on "Dan" at 14:14) of Genesis, like those of the rest of the Pentateuch, have been modernized. Also, the king list in 36:31–43 appears to be an addendum dating after the time of Saul.

There is not enough evidence to determine precisely when Moses wrote the book of Genesis. He may have composed it as a way of calling the first generation of the exodus away from Egypt or, more likely, in conjunction with the rest of the Pentateuch for the second generation of the exodus as the people prepared on the plains of Moab for the conquest of Canaan.

Original Audience

The book of Genesis was written to provide encouragement to the Israelites as they faced the manifold challenges of separating from their background of slavery in Egypt and moving forward toward the conquest of the promised land. The narratives provide a prologue for the responsibilities the nation faced in the days of Moses. For instance, Genesis explicitly focuses on the rite of circumcision (17:9–14) and Sabbath observance (2:2–3). More importantly, Genesis recounts the origins of Israel, reaching back to the beginnings of human history and to the conflict between the kingdom of God and the kingdom of the serpent—a conflict in which the nation of Israel was to play a crucial role. Genesis also recounts the election of Israel to a unique covenant relationship with the only God. According to that covenant, the descendants of the patriarchs would become a great nation in the land of promise, through whom the Gentiles would be blessed.

Purpose and Distinctives

Following the ancient custom of naming books by their first word(s), the Hebrew title is *bereshith,* "in the beginning." Based on the book's content, the Greek title is *geneseos,* meaning "origin." Both titles are appropriate since the book is about the origin of sacred history.

A study of the literary structure of Genesis discloses the following highlights. The prologue (1:1—2:3) is made apparent by a device at the book's beginning and conclusion: In the Hebrew text the word order of 1:1 (where "created" precedes "the heavens and the earth") is reversed in 2:1–3 (where "the heavens and the earth" precedes "the work of creating"). After the prologue, Genesis is divided into ten parts marked out by the formula "This is the account of . . ." This heading is followed by a genealogy of the person named and/or by stories involving the person's notable descendants. The first three "accounts" pertain to history before the flood; the last seven to times after the flood. The first three and the initial three of the seven parallel one another: They include stories about the developments of humanity universally at the creation out of the primordial, chaotic waters and at the re-creation after the flood (accounts one and four); the genealogy of the redemptive lines through Seth and Shem (accounts two and five); and the stories of the epochal covenant transactions with Noah and Abraham (accounts three and six). The final two pairs expand the Abrahamic line, contrasting narrative concerning his rejected offspring, Ishmael and Esau (accounts seven and nine) with stories about the elect, Isaac and Jacob (accounts eight and ten). The key to a story is often given in an opening revelation; e.g., the offer to Abraham (12:1–3), the prenatal sign of the rivalry between Jacob and Esau (25:22–23) and Joseph's dreams (37:1–11). A transitional section is found at the end of each account; e.g., 4:25–26, 6:1–8, 9:18–29 and 11:10–26 (see "Introduction: Outline"). The closing section of the last account contains strong links with Exodus, concluding with an oath Joseph elicited from his brothers to carry his embalmed body with them when God came to their aid to lead them back to Canaan (50:24–25; Ex 13:19).

The book's focus on the origins of Israel unfolds against a backdrop of concerns with matters that affect the world. Moses tells us that prior to God's election of the patriarchs (i.e., the fathers of Israel; chs. 12–50), humanity asserted its independence from God by defying his command (chs. 2–3). Human beings demonstrated their depravity by token religion, fratricide and unrestrained vengeance (as represented by Cain in chapter 4); by tyranny, harems and continuous evil thoughts (as represented by the wicked kings of 6:1–8); and by the erection of their own kingdom against God (as represented by Nimrod's infamous tower in 10:8–12; see note on 11:1–9). God's verdict about humanity stands: "Every inclination of his heart is evil from childhood" (8:21). Behind this dark history stands fallen humanity's spiritual father: the malevolent, cunning devil (ch. 3).

Just as miraculously and surely as God sovereignly transformed the dark, mysterious chaos at Earth's origins (1:2) into a glorious habitat for humanity and brought it to rest (1:3—2:3), so also God sovereignly elected his covenant people in Christ to conquer Satan (3:15) and to bless the depraved world (12:1–3). He unconditionally elected the patriarchs, Abraham, Isaac and Jacob, promising to make of their elect descendants the nation destined to bless the earth—a promise entailing an eternal seed, land and king (12:1–3,7; 13:14–17; 17:1–8; 26:2–6; 28:10–15). Before Jacob was born or had done either good or evil, God chose him rather than his older twin brother, Esau (25:21–23). God even used Judah's scandalous wrongs against Tamar, as he did Tamar's own daring ruse, to advance the Messianic line (ch. 38). The heavenly King displayed his glorious rule by miraculously preserving the matriarchs in pagan harems (12:10–20; 20:1–18) and by opening their barren wombs (17:15–22; 18:1–15; 21:1–7; 25:21; 29:31; 30:22). He overrode normal human practices time and again by choosing the younger, not the older, to inherit the blessing (see note on 25:23). Blatant prophecies and subtle types are sterling witnesses that God directs history. For example, Noah prophesied Shem's subjugation of Canaan (9:24–26), and Abraham prefigured the greater exodus led by Moses when God delivered Abraham and Sarah from the oppression of Egypt with wealth (see note on 12:10–20).

God inclined the hearts of his elect to trust his promises and obey his commands. Against all hope, Abraham counted on God to bless him with innumerable offspring, and the narrator says that God credited that faith as on a par with keeping the law (15:6). Confident of God's sure promises, Abraham gave up his rights to the land (ch. 13), and later on Jacob (subsequently called Israel), clinging only to God (32:9–12), symbolically gave back the birthright to Esau (ch. 33). At the beginning of the Joseph story, Judah sold Joseph as a slave (37:26–27), but at its end the former slave trader was willing to become a slave himself in the place of his brother (44:33–34). Secure in the truth that God's sovereign design included sins as heinous as his attempted murder and enslavement at the hands of his brothers, Joseph forgave them without recrimination (45:4–8; 50:24).

It must be admitted that there are a few difficulties in interpreting the book. The tension between Genesis and modern science regarding the origins of the universe and of species is largely resolved when it is recognized that the two are speaking from different perspectives. Genesis is concerned about who created them and why, not about how they were created and when. Science cannot answer the former questions, and Genesis is mute about the latter ones (see notes on 1:2,5,11).

The authorship of Genesis has also been called into question. For the past century, scholars have contended that it is composed of conflicting documents by different writers, usually identified as: *J* (for the writer or writers who referred to God as *Jahweh/Yahweh*, "the LORD"), *E* (for the writer or writers who referred to God as *Elohim*, "God"), *P* (for the writer or writers who were concerned with priestly matters) and *D* (for the writer or writers of Deuteronomy). Although this approach, commonly called the documentary hypothesis, is still widely accepted, few believe any longer that these documents can be used to reconstruct a history of Israel's religion, since all the alleged sources contain both early and late materials. To be sure, many documents were composed in the ancient Near East by combining earlier written sources, and Moses himself may have used them (see "Author"), but no criticism has successfully demonstrated that Moses himself could not have authorized or written from all four perspectives. Moreover, many scholars today question the criteria used for identifying these sources and emphasize instead the unity of the text in hand. For example, the flood story, a veritable textbook example of synthesis, according to the documentary hypothesis, is now conceded to have remarkable integrity (see note on 6:9—9:29). See the article "Introduction to the Pentateuch" on page 1.

Christ in Genesis

What was begun in Genesis is fulfilled in Christ. The genealogy begun in chapter 5 and advanced in chapter 11 is completed with the birth of Jesus Christ (Mt 1; Lk 3:23–38). He is the quintessential offspring promised to Abraham (17:15–16; Gal 3:16). The elect are blessed in him because he alone by his active obedience satisfied the law's demands and by his willingness to relinguish his rights of equality with God died in their stead. All who are baptized into him are Abraham's descendants (Gal 3:26–29). The bold prophecies and subtle types in Genesis show that God was writing a history that was to be completed in Jesus. On the threshold of Biblical prophecy, Noah predicted that the Japhethites would find salvation through the Semites (9:27), a prophecy fulfilled in the New Testament (Ro 11; cf. note on Ge 9:27), and God himself proclaimed that the woman's offspring would destroy Satan (3:15). That offspring is Christ and his church (Ro 16:20). The gift of the bride to Adam prefigured the gift of the church to Christ (2:18–26; Eph 5:22–32); Melchizedek's priesthood is like that of the Son of God (14:18–20; Heb 7). The paradise lost by the first Adam is restored by the last Adam. This marvelously unified sacred history certifies that the focus of Genesis is ultimately Christ.

Outline

I. The Primeval History (1:1—11:9)

During the early years of world history, God established an ideal order for his world. Humanity's sin brought ruin to God's world, but God began to redeem his creation in ways that led directly to Israel's exodus and conquest.

- A. Prologue: Creation of the Heavens and the Earth (1:1—2:3)
- B. Account of the Heavens and the Earth (2:4—4:26)
  1. Adam and Eve on Probation (2:4–25)
  2. The Fall and Its Consequences (3:1–24)
  3. Escalation of Sin in the Line of Cain (4:1–24)
  4. Godly Remnant (4:25–26)
- C. Account of Adam's Genealogy (5:1—6:8)
  1. Covenant Line of Seth (5:1–32)
  2. Escalation of Sin Before the Flood (6:1–8)
- D. Account of Noah (6:9—9:29)
  1. Preparation for the Flood (6:9—7:10)
  2. The Flood and Salvation (7:11—8:19)
  3. God's Covenant Not to Destroy (8:20—9:17)
  4. Prophecies About Noah's Sons (9:18–29)
- E. Account of Shem, Ham and Japheth (10:1—11:9)
  1. Table of Nations (10:1–32)
  2. Escalation of Evil in Babylon (11:1–9)

- II. The Early Patriarchal History (11:10—37:1)
  - A. Account of Shem (11:10–26)
  - B. Account of Abraham (11:27—25:11)
    1. Abraham's Genealogy (11:27–32)
    2. Abraham's Land and Descendants (12:1—22:19)
       - a. Migration to the Promised Land (12:1–9)
       - b. Deliverance From Egypt (12:10–20)
       - c. Lot's Separation From the Land (13:1–18)
       - d. Victory Over Eastern Kings (14:1–24)
       - e. Covenant Regarding the Land (15:1–21)
       - f. Hagar and Ishmael Rejected (16:1–16)
       - g. God's Covenant Regarding Seed and Land (17:1–27)
       - h. Sarah to Have a Son (18:1–15)
       - i. Abraham, Lot and Sodom (18:16—19:38)
         - (1) Justice and Intercession for Sodom (18:16–33)
         - (2) Lot's Rescue From Sodom (19:1–29)
         - (3) Lot and His Daughters (19:30–38)
       - j. Abraham's Intercession for Abimelech (20:1–18)
       - k. The Birth of Isaac (21:1–21)
       - l. Abraham's Treaty With Abimelech (21:22–34)
       - m. Abraham's Test and Assurance (22:1–19)
    3. Transition to Isaac (22:20—25:11)
       - a. Rebekah's Family Background (22:20–24)
       - b. The Death of Sarah (23:1–20)
       - c. The Gift of Rebekah to Isaac (24:1–67)
       - d. Isaac the Sole Heir (25:1–6)
       - e. The Death of Abraham (25:7–11)
  - C. Account of Ishmael (25:12–18)
  - D. Account of Isaac (25:19—35:29)
    1. Jacob in the Land (25:19—27:40)
       - a. Rivalry Between Jacob and Esau (25:19–34)
       - b. Isaac and Abimelech (26:1–35)
       - c. Jacob's Acquisition of Esau's Blessing (27:1–40)
    2. Jacob Outside the Land (27:41—33:17)
       - a. Jacob's Flight From Esau (27:41—28:9)
       - b. Divine Encounter While Fleeing (28:10–22)
       - c. Conflict With Laban (29:1–30)
       - d. Birth of Tribal Patriarchs (29:31—30:24)
       - e. Jacob's Departure From Laban (30:25—31:55)
       - f. Divine Encounter While Returning (32:1–32)
       - g. Esau's Reconciliation With Jacob (33:1–17)
    3. Jacob Back in the Land (33:18—35:29)
       - a. Crisis in Shechem (33:18—34:31)
       - b. Assurance at Bethel (35:1–15)
       - c. Closing Travels and Events (35:16–29)
  - E. Account of Esau (36:1—37:1)

The lives of Abraham, Isaac and Jacob provide many insights into the way in which God would later use Israel as his instrument for redemption. His covenant promises of land and numerous descendants were passed through the faithful in Israel from generation to generation.

III. The Joseph History (37:2—50:26)
   A. The Patriarchs Separated and Disharmonious (37:2—41:57)
      1. Joseph's Troubling Dreams (37:2–11)
      2. Joseph Sold Into Slavery (37:12–36)
      3. Patriarchal Corruption in Canaan (38:1–30)
      4. Joseph's Integrity in Potiphar's House (39:1–20a)
      5. Joseph's Unwavering Faith in Prison (39:20b—40:23)
      6. Joseph Exalted in Egypt (41:1–57)
   B. The Patriarchs Together in Harmony (42:1—47:28)
      1. Joseph's First Test of His Brothers (42:1–38)
      2. Joseph's Second Test of His Brothers (43:1–34)
      3. Joseph's Third Test of His Brothers (44:1–34)
      4. Joseph's Reunion With His Brothers (45:1–28)
      5. The Patriarchs' Full Migration to Egypt (46:1–30)
      6. The Patriarchs' Preservation in Goshen (46:31—47:28)
   C. The Patriarchs' Future in the Land (47:29—50:26)
      1. Jacob and the Land (47:29—50:14)
         a. Jacob's Burial Request (47:29–31)
         b. Jacob's Blessings on His Sons (48:1—49:28)
         c. Jacob's Death and Burial in Canaan (49:29—50:14)
      2. Joseph and the Land (50:15–26)
         a. Joseph's Reassurance (50:15–21)
         b. Joseph's Final Words and Death (50:22–26)

The experiences of Joseph and his brothers taught the tribes of Israel loyalty to God and to each other as they served as God's instruments of redemption.

The Beginning

1 In the beginning[a] God created the heavens and the earth.[b] 2Now the earth
was[a] formless and empty,[c] darkness was over the surface of the deep, and the
Spirit of God[d] was hovering over the waters.

a 2 Or possibly *became*

1:1 [a]Jn 1:1-2 [b]Job 38:4; Ps 90:2; Isa 42:5; 44:24; 45:12,18; Ac 17:24; Heb 11:3; Rev 4:11
1:2 [c]Jer 4:23 [d]Ps 104:30

■ **1:1—11:9** *The Primeval History.* The first major portion of the book concerns the earliest times. It divides into five major parts: a prologue (1:1—2:3) and accounts of the heavens and the earth (2:4—4:26); Adam (5:1—6:8); Noah (6:9—9:29); and Shem, Ham and Japheth (10:1—11:9).
1:1—2:25 See *HC* 26.
■ **1:1—2:3** *Prologue: Creation of the Heavens and the Earth.* This account of creation (cf. Job 38; Pss 8; 104; 136:1–9; 148; Pr 8:22–31) lays the foundation of Israel's understanding of God, humanity and the world.
1:1–31 See *WCF* 4.1; *WLC* 15; *WSC* 9.
1:1–2 See *HC* 53.
1:1 In the beginning. Genesis begins history with the first week of creation. **God.** The Hebrew word for "God"—the first subject of Genesis and the Bible—is formed as a plural to emphasize his majesty and/or divinity. There is no other god (Dt 4:39; Isa 40:21,28; 43:10; Jn 1:1; Col 1:17), and he is truth, the basis for all sound knowledge (Pr 1:7). God is personal: He speaks and acts. **created.** *Create* always has as its object the finished product, indicating that this verse summarizes the entire prologue. **the heavens and the earth.** This compound of opposites signifies the organized universe. Some think, however, that in this unique instance the reference is to two distinct spheres: the invisible heavens where God and his angels dwell and the "embryonic" earth (as in v. 2). See *BC* 10.
1:2 the earth . . . the deep. The primordial earth was without light and land. There had as yet been no word from God. The origins of darkness, of the abyss and of Satan (3:1–6) are not given in Genesis. Although their origins are a mystery, only God is eternal (Ps 90:2; Pr 8:22–31). In the new heavens and the new earth there will be no sea or darkness (Rev 21:1,25). **formless and empty.** This compound signifies "dreadful chaos." The earth was not only uninhabited but also uninhabitable. **darkness . . . deep.** These opposites of "light" and "land" (vv. 4,10) were associated with evil (Ex 15:8; Pr 2:13). They became the objects upon which God's creative ordering, and later his redemptive work, were focused. The image of this primordial chaos out of which God established a blessed place for humanity would appear again as a description of Egypt during Israel's captivity there (Dt 32:10). **Spirit of God.** The word rendered "Spirit" also means "wind," and some translate it "mighty wind" (cf. 8:1). Here God's Spirit moved against the primordial chaos, bringing God's order to the universe. God's Spirit

3 And God said,[e] "Let there be light," and there was light.[f] 4 God saw that the light was
good, and he separated the light from the darkness. 5 God called the light "day,"
and the darkness he called "night."[g] And there was evening, and there was morning—the first day.
6 And God said, "Let there be an expanse[h] between the waters to separate water from
water." 7 So God made the expanse and separated the water under the expanse
from the water above it.[i] And it was so. 8 God called the expanse "sky." And there
was evening, and there was morning—the second day.
9 And God said, "Let the water under the sky be gathered to one place,[j] and let dry
ground appear." And it was so. 10 God called the dry ground "land," and the gathered waters he called "seas." And God saw that it was good.
11 Then God said, "Let the land produce vegetation:[k] seed-bearing plants and
trees on the land that bear fruit with seed in it, according to their various kinds."
And it was so. 12 The land produced vegetation: plants bearing seed according to
their kinds and trees bearing fruit with seed in it according to their kinds. And God
saw that it was good. 13 And there was evening, and there was morning—the third
day.
14 And God said, "Let there be lights[l] in the expanse of the sky to separate the day from
the night, and let them serve as signs[m] to mark seasons[n] and days and years,
15 and let them be lights in the expanse of the sky to give light on the earth." And
it was so. 16 God made two great lights—the greater light to govern[o] the day and
the lesser light to govern[p] the night. He also made the stars.[q] 17 God set them in
the expanse of the sky to give light on the earth, 18 to govern the day and the night,[r]
and to separate light from darkness. And God saw that it was good. 19 And there
was evening, and there was morning—the fourth day.
20 And God said, "Let the water teem with living creatures, and let birds fly above the
earth across the expanse of the sky." 21 So God created the great creatures of the
sea and every living and moving thing with which the water teems,[s] according to

1:3 [e]Ps 33:6,9; 148:5; Heb 11:3 [f]2Co 4:6*
1:5 [g]Ps 74:16
1:6 [h]Jer 10:12
1:7 [i]Job 38:8-11,16; Ps 148:4
1:9 [j]Job 38:8-11; Ps 104:6-9; Pr 8:29; Jer 5:22; 2Pe 3:5
1:11 [k]Ps 65:9-13; 104:14
1:14 [l]Ps 74:16 [m]Jer 10:2 [n]Ps 104:19
1:16 [o]Ps 136:8 [p]Ps 136:9 [q]Job 38:7,31-32; Ps 8:3; Isa 40:26
1:18 [r]Jer 33:20,25
1:21 [s]Ps 104:25-26

---

gives life to all (see 6:17 and its note), and when God withdraws his Spirit, life ceases (see 6:3 and its note). He continues to give and withdraw life (Job 33:4; Ps 104:30; Ecc 12:7; Lk 23:46). The Spirit also created the places of God's abode: the cosmos (Ps 104:1–4), the tabernacle (35:31), the incarnation of Christ (Lk 1:35; cf. Jn 2:19) and the church, which he continues to build (1Co 3:16; Eph 2:22). **hovering over the waters.** Hovering like an eagle over the primordial abyss, the almighty Spirit converted the emerging earth into a habitat for human beings and then gave it a Sabbath rest. That same Spirit hovered over Israel as he led her toward rest in the promised land (Dt 32:11–12); later he would fill God's Son and his church to establish his final Sabbath (Isa 42:1; 61:1; Ac 2:14–36; 2Co 4:6). See *WCF* 4.1; *WLC* 11; *BC* 11.

1:3–31 The ordering of creation progresses over two triads of days, looking back respectively to "formless and empty" (v. 2).

Day 1: Light	Day 4: Luminaries
Day 2: Sky/Water	Day 5: Fish/Fowl
Day 3: Land/Vegetation	Day 6: Animals/Humanity

In the first triad God gave the earth *form* by separating the following elements: the light of day from the darkness of night, the sea below from the clouds above, and the dry land with its vegetation from the sea. In the second triad God *filled* these realms. Each triad, moving from sky to Earth, progressed from a single creative act (vv. 3–5, 14–19) to one creative act with two aspects (vv. 6–8,20–23) to two separate creative acts, each culminating in the earth bringing forth (vv. 9–13,24–31). The pattern of each day is similar: an announcement ("God said"), a command ("Let there be"), a report ("and it was so"), an evaluation ("good") and a chronological framework (e.g., "first day"). The Israelites who followed Moses had seen this ordering disrupted during the plagues on Egypt (Ex 7:14—11:10), but they were headed for a land that was good (see Dt 1:25), where nature would exhibit the bounty of God's blessed order.

1:3 God said. This figure (Ps 33:6) signifies the ease with which Israel's God conformed all of creation to his will. There was no primeval struggle with competing forces or gods.

1:4 light. God was the ultimate source of the daylight that alternated with darkness, with the sun as the immediate means (vv. 14–18; see also v. 5 and its note). Light symbolized life and blessing (Ps 56:13; Isa 9:2; Jn 1:4–5). **good.** It satisfied God's purpose and humanity's role in the world. Brought within God's constraints, even the sea (v. 10) was now good (see v. 2 and its note), serving God's benevolent purposes along with the darkness (Ps 104:19–26).

1:5 called. God showed that he was ruler of the cosmos by naming its spheres (17:5; cf. Nu 32:38; 2Ki 23:34; 24:17; Rev. 2:17). Even the darkness and the chaotic seas were under his dominion. By his words God gave existence and meaning to everything according to his eternal counsel. Though both the Creator and his creation are unfathomable to human beings (Job 28,38; Pr 25:2), there are no mysteries for God, and everything has coherence and meaning within his will. For this reason, the beginning of wisdom for humanity is the fear of the Lord (see Pr 1:7 and its note). **first day.** This anthropomorphic presentation of creation in the first week (Ex 20:11) enabled the covenant people to imitate the Creator in their weekly pattern of work and rest (Ex 31:13,17).

1:6–8 In days two and three the deep was structured into a benevolent system of rain clouds, springs and rivers.

1:6 expanse. The Hebrew here suggests something flat and hard (Job 37:18; Isa 40:22). The language is phenomenological; that is, the way things appear from an earthly, human perspective. In verses 6–8 "expanse" refers ambiguously to the atmosphere and/or the sky. Here it separated rain clouds from rivers and seas.

1:10 land. Signifies the sphere of life and security (see Pr 2:21–22).

1:11 various kinds. There are no species of life apart from God's design and creative acts. He intended the vegetation to serve as food for higher forms of life (vv. 29–30).

1:14 in . . . the sky. The language is phenomenological; that is, as it appears to the human eye. **as signs to mark seasons.** The Hebrew could be translated "for signs and for seasons" (see Isa 38:7,8).

1:16 two great lights. Moses did not even name the sun and moon, which were principal deities in pagan pantheons, because they were merely created luminaries that served the purposes of God. **govern.** The moving inhabitants of the second triad of days ruled over the spheres that housed and sheltered them (see note on vv. 3–31): The luminaries ruled over the day and night (Ps 136:7–9); the birds and fish over the sky and sea, respectively; and animals over the land and its vegetation, with man ruling over both the animals and the land. **stars.** Pagans often credited the stars in their pantheons with controlling human destiny. Here, mentioned almost as an afterthought, God simply assigned them, together with the sun and moon, the roles of marking off the calendar, of giving light on Earth, of ruling day and night as his surrogates and of separating light from darkness.

1:21 created. See verse 1. **creatures of the sea.** In Old Testament poetry these are the dreaded sea dragons of pagan mythology (Ps 74:13; Isa 27:1; 51:9). Hebrew poets adopted pagan imagery, but not pagan theology. In this antimythical polemic the aquatic animals are appreciated as part of God's creation.

their kinds, and every winged bird according to its kind. And God saw that it was
good. 22God blessed them and said, "Be fruitful and increase in number and fill the
water in the seas, and let the birds increase on the earth." [t] 23And there was evening, and there was morning—the fifth day.
24And God said, "Let the land produce living creatures according to their kinds: livestock,
creatures that move along the ground, and wild animals, each according to its
kind." And it was so. 25God made the wild animals [u] according to their kinds, the
livestock according to their kinds, and all the creatures that move along the
ground according to their kinds. And God saw that it was good.
26Then God said, "Let us [v] make man in our image, [w] in our likeness, and let
them rule [x] over the fish of the sea and the birds of the air, over the livestock, over
all the earth, [a] and over all the creatures that move along the ground."

27So God created man in his own image, [y]
in the image of God he created him;
male and female [z] he created them.

1:22 [t] ver 28; Ge 8:17
1:25 [u] Jer 27:5
1:26 [v] Ps 100:3 [w] Ge 9:6; Jas 3:9 [x] Ps 8:6-8
1:27 [y] 1Co 11:7 [z] Ge 5:2; Mt 19:4*; Mk 10:6*

[a] *26* Hebrew; Syriac *all the wild animals*

1:22 blessed. The Hebrew here entails the notion of multiplication for the purpose of ruling (22:18). The birds and fish rule their realms through multiplication (v. 22), while God rules over all as the great King. The Lord Jesus, who never married, blessed his disciples so they would multiply spiritually (Mt 28:18–20; Lk 24: 50–51).
1:24 livestock . . . wild animals. The contrast between wild and domesticated animals differentiates carnivores from cattle (the Hebrew here for "wild animals" is the same as that in Job 5:22; Ps 79:2; Eze 29:5; 32:4; 34:28).
1:26–29 See *WCF* 6.3; 19.1; *WLC* 20,92; *WSC* 10; *BC* 9,14; *HC* 6.
1:26 us. The use of the plural here is variously interpreted. Some view it as an indication of the Trinity. Others explain this usage in grammatical terms, either as plural in form to indicate majesty or emphasize divinity (see note on v. 1), or as a deliberative plural (in which God speaks to himself). Some also argue that God and his heavenly angelic court are in view (see note on Isa 6:8). **image.** Humans in their whole beings—body and soul—truly represent God (Ps 94:10), possess his life and so have the potential for intimacy with him (see note on 2:7). They also serve on Earth as his vice-regents (Ps 8). God's image is passed on to every human being, conferring upon each person divinely ordained dignity (see 5:3; 9:6; Pr 22:2 and their notes). This quality was marred, but not lost, through sin; it is restored only in Christ (Ro 8:29). See theological article "Human Beings in God's Image," below. **likeness.** This description may simply be a synonym for "image," or it could be used to ensure the understanding that human beings are not themselves somehow divine. In the ancient Near East, an image often served as the equivalent of the god itself. **rule.** God gave human beings the cultural mandate to rule the creation as benevolent monarchs (9:2; Ps 8:5–8; Heb 2:5–9). Man can rule the animal (v. 28) and plant (v. 29) kingdoms but has no jurisdiction over the heavenly powers, especially Satan (ch. 3; Eph 6:10–12). Only the last Adam, the express image of God's person (Col 1:15; Heb 1:3), along with those in him, can do that (3:15; Mt 4:1–11). See *WCF* 4.2, 9.2.
1:27 See theological article "Human Beings in God's Image," below. **created.** In this first poem in the Bible, which celebrates

Human Beings in God's Image: Who Am I?

ALTHOUGH God knew all that human beings would become and do, including our fall into sin, the first thing the Bible says about us (Ge 1:26–27, echoed in 5:1; 9:6; 1Co 11:7; Jas 3:9) is that we are like God in a way that is true of no other creatures. In Hebrew, the expression "in our image, in our likeness" (Ge 1:26) means that God made human beings to *be* his image and likeness. We are "image bearers," but not merely image bearers, as if this characteristic could be separated from us. Rather, we *are,* intrinsically and irrevocably, his image and likeness.

Traditionally, Reformed theology has stressed several important dimensions of what this means. John Calvin drew upon Paul's letters to stress that being the image of God is closely connected with becoming like Christ, "like God in true righteousness and holiness" (Eph 4:24). Believers have "put on the new self, which is being renewed in knowledge in the image of its Creator" (Col 3:10). True, we are corrupted images of God, defiled by sin, but in Christ we are restored to the original goodness that characterized Adam and Eve in the garden. Other Reformed theologians have stressed that all people are like God in that we are personal, rational, creative and moral creatures. There can be no doubt that all of these insights are true and valuable.

But the immediate context of Genesis 1:27–28 also has much more to teach us about the image of God. In the ancient historical context, to be an image of God was associated with the idea of being a royal son of God. Ancient kings were thought to be the sons of the gods, imbued with the honor of ensuring that the will of heaven be enforced on Earth. This concept was part of God's design for Israel's kings, who were also called sons of God (1Ch 28:6; Ps 2:7). In Genesis, however, a radical extension of this outlook of the son or image of God takes place: The term "image of God" is applied to every human being: "Male and female he created them" (Ge 1:27).

So, in the Biblical view, all human beings assume the honor and value once attributed only to royalty (Ps 8:3–8). All people have been set in the world to display the glory of the true and living God, the great King of the universe, by establishing his will on Earth. In Reformed theology, this role for human beings is often called the "cultural mandate," referring to our blessing and our responsibility to develop culture under the Lordship of Christ (Ge 1:28–30). This finds ultimate fulfillment in Jesus, who commanded the redeemed image of God (his faithful people) to fulfill the cultural mandate through the "gospel mandate" by proclaiming Christ's name throughout the world (Mt 28:18–20).

1:28 [a]Ge 9:1,7; Lev 26:9
1:29 [b]Ps 104:14
1:30 [c]Ps 104:14,27; 145:15
1:31 [d]Ps 104:24 [e]1Ti 4:4
2:2 [f]Ex 20:11; 31:17; Heb 4:4*
2:3 [g]Lev 23:3; Isa 58:13
2:5 [h]Ge 1:11 [i]Ps 65:9-10
2:7 [j]Ge 3:19 [k]Ps 103:14 [l]Job 33:4 [m]Ac 17:25 [n]1Co 15:45*

28 God blessed them and said to them, "Be fruitful and increase in number; fill
the earth [a] and subdue it. Rule over the fish of the sea and the birds of the air and
over every living creature that moves on the ground."
29 Then God said, "I give you every seed-bearing plant on the face of the whole
earth and every tree that has fruit with seed in it. They will be yours for food.[b]
30 And to all the beasts of the earth and all the birds of the air and all the creatures
that move on the ground—everything that has the breath of life in it—I give every green plant for food.[c]" And it was so.
31 God saw all that he had made,[d] and it was very good.[e] And there was evening, and there was morning—the sixth day.

2

Thus the heavens and the earth were completed in all their vast array.
2 By the seventh day God had finished the work he had been doing; so on the seventh
day he rested[a] from all his work.[f] 3 And God blessed the seventh day and made it
holy,[g] because on it he rested from all the work of creating that he had done.

Adam and Eve

4 This is the account of the heavens and the earth when they were created.

When the LORD God made the earth and the heavens— 5 and no shrub of the field had
yet appeared on the earth[b] and no plant of the field had yet sprung up,[h] for the LORD God
had not sent rain on the earth[b][i] and there was no man to work the ground, 6 but streams[c]
came up from the earth and watered the whole surface of the ground— 7 the LORD God
formed the man[d] from the dust[j] of the ground[k] and breathed into his nostrils the
breath[l] of life,[m] and the man became a living being.[n]

[a] *2* 2 Or *ceased*; also in verse 3 [b] 5 Or *land*; also in verse 6 [c] 6 Or *mist* [d] 7 The Hebrew for *man (adam)* sounds like and may be related to the Hebrew for *ground (adamah)*; it is also the name *Adam* (see Gen. 2:20).

the creation of man, the word "created" (cf. v. 1) is used three times. See theological article "Body and Soul in the Bible" at Genesis 2. See *WCF* 4.2; *WLC* 17.

1:28 blessed. See verse 22, 9:1 and their notes. The genealogies of chapters 5, 9, 11, 25, 36 and 46 bear silent testimony to its fulfillment. **Rule . . . ground.** Animals, as well as vegetation, were created suitable for the human diet (1Ti 4:3–5). Under divine blessing, people accomplished the cultural mandate (see note on v. 26) by naming the creatures (v. 5; 2:19–20). This creative activity expressed the reality of humans having been formed in the image of the Creator-King. Fallen human beings, however, have distorted this activity into self-deification and the exploitation of the creation. See *WCF* 4.2; *WLC* 17,20.

1:29–30 food. In Mesopotamian myths humanity was created as food for the gods.

1:31 See *HC* 6,9.

2:1 The concluding summary statement underscores that the Creator perfectly executed his will (v. 31).

2:2–3 No mention is made of "evening and morning" because the Sabbath continues forever, and people are exhorted to participate in it (Heb 4:3–11). See *WCF* 21.7; *WLC* 116,121; *WSC* 59.

2:2 seventh day. The Sabbath is as old as creation, but in pagan Mesopotamia the seventh, fourteenth, nineteenth, twenty-first and twenty-eighth days of each month were regarded by some as unlucky. See 7:2 and its note. The number of the seventh day is mentioned three times in verses 2–3, indicating its significance above all other days. **finished.** The establishment of the Sabbath prefigured Moses' goal for this book: to move the nation toward the gift of God's finished redemption, namely rest in the promised land (see note on Jos 6:3–4).

2:3 made it holy. In the Torah, the seventh day was the first recipient of God's holiness, and so he set it apart to himself (Ex 20:11). It summons humanity to imitate the pattern of the King and so confess God as Lord over all, and promises divine rest, both now and forever (Mt 11:28). See *WLC* 20.

■ **2:4—4:26** *Account of the Heavens and the Earth.* Moses' narration moves from the prologue concerning the creation of the heavens and the earth to the history (lit., "generations") of the heavens and the earth under humanity's rule. It sets forth the creation and probation of Adam and Eve in Paradise (2:4–25), their fall and its consequences (3:1–24), the escalation of sin in the ungodly line of Cain (4:1–24) and the preservation of a godly remnant in the line of Seth (4:25–26). This account displays humanity's worsening situation.

■ **2:4–25** *Adam and Eve on Probation.* This narrative presents the fall of Adam and Eve from innocence into sin. Although they were historical persons (1Ch 1:1; Mt 19:5; Lk 3:23–38; Ro 5:12–14; 1Co 15:45), these characters represented every man and woman in God's eyes (2:24; 3:16–19; Mt 19:6; Ro 5:12–14; 1Co 15:45). The chief actor throughout is God: He formed the man (v. 7; Job 10:8–12), planted the garden (Ps 87:1; Mt 16:18), sovereignly placed the man in it (v. 15; Eph 1:3–14), ordered his life (vv. 16–17; Ps 31:15), gave him his wife (vv. 18–25; Mt 19:6), judged them for sin and restored them (ch. 3; Heb 9:27–28).

2:4 This is the account of. These words often introduce a major new development in the narrative (see "Introduction: Purpose and Distinctives"), in this case a sequel to 1:1—2:3. **the heavens and the earth.** See 1:1. This account pertains to what the cosmos generated, not the generation of the cosmos. As the earth brought forth the first man (cf. Job 1:21; Ps 139:16), so in the last day it will bring forth the children of God (Ro 8:21–22). **LORD God.** These names for God are normally isolated: "God" represents him as sovereign Creator of all, and "LORD" signifies his unique commitment to Israel (Ex 3:14–15). Here they are combined to stress that the Creator is also Israel's covenant God.

2:5 no shrub . . . no plant of the field. Inedible growth, such as thorns (3:18), and cultivated grains (3:17), respectively. Because of the crucial role played by the garden, the trees and the cursed ground, the introduction focuses on plants, not animals. Animals are featured in verses 18–20.

2:7 See theological article "Body and Soul in the Bible" at Genesis 2. **formed.** This figure from pottery making represents God's activity in shaping each person (Job 10:8–12). **man from the dust of the ground.** The wordplay in Hebrew—"man" (Hebrew, *'adam*) and "ground" (Hebrew, *'adamah*)—shows man's close connection with the ground, for it was his cradle, his home, his grave (vv. 7,15; 3:19), and underlies Paul's commentary that the first Adam was fashioned in a natural body for an earthly existence. The heavenly Son of Man (Da 7:13) shared in this earthly state in order to secure for fallen humanity a spiritual body of imperishable glory in the resurrection (1Co 15:42–49). **living being.** Traditionally the Hebrew word is rendered "soul," but it is translated "living creature" in verse 19. The first man was not formed from preexistent life. He was created a living creature along with the animals, with drives and appetites. But humanity is differentiated from animal life, in that only human beings are formed in the image of God (see note on 1:26). Adam demonstrated his authority over the animals by naming them. See *WCF* 4.2; *WLC* 17; *BC* 7.

8Now the LORD God had planted a garden in the east, in Eden;[o] and there he put the
man he had formed. 9And the LORD God made all kinds of trees grow out of the ground—
trees that were pleasing to the eye and good for food. In the middle of the garden were
the tree of life[p] and the tree of the knowledge of good and evil.[q]
10A river watering the garden flowed from Eden; from there it was separated into four
headwaters. 11The name of the first is the Pishon; it winds through the entire land of Havilah, where there is gold. 12(The gold of that land is good; aromatic resin[a] and onyx are

2:8 [o]Ge 3:23,24; Isa 51:3

2:9 [p]Ge 3:22,24; Rev 2:7; 22:2,14,19 [q]Eze 47:12

[a] 12 Or *good; pearls*

2:8–17 The account of man's probation consists of his creation (v. 8), the stage (the paradisiacal garden; vv. 8–14) and the plot (the climactic test to keep the covenant stipulation; vv. 15–17). In this covenant arrangement God graciously offered life to human beings, but he demanded obedience to his command. The first Adam, representing all of humanity, failed to obey, thereby bringing death upon all. The active obedience of the last Adam, Jesus Christ, representing the elect, satisfied God's demands, thereby giving them eternal life (Ro 5:12–19; 1Co 15:45–49).
2:8–14 By providing the man with so many blessings, God pressed upon him the claims of his love and rendered the man's rebellion inexcusable (Ro 1:20).
2:8 garden. A garden is an enclosed area; here it is a sanctuary representing territorial space where God invited the first man to enjoy fellowship and peace with him. Cherubim protected the garden's sanctity (see note on 3:24; see also Ex 26:1; 2Ch 3:7), so that sin and death would be excluded (3:23; Rev 21:8). The garden prefigured the promised land and the temple, where fellowship between God and humanity was restored (28:12; Isa 51:3), which in turn prefigures the new heavens and the new earth (Rev 21:1–4). Faith and obedience are prerequisites for living in this center of the universe. **east.** In Biblical times the east (where the sun rises) represented life; the west represented death. **Eden.** Eden, probably meaning "pleasure, delight," was a mountain, as the outbound flow of the river in verse 10 indicates (Eze 28:13–14). This temple mountain established the axis between heaven and Earth. Here priestly humanity was to serve God in fellowship with him (Ex 15:17; Col 3:1–4; Heb 12:22). See *WLC* 20.
2:9 all kinds of trees . . . food. Life in the garden is represented as a banqueting table. **tree of life.** This tree represented life in its highest potency—eternal life, beyond the life granted all human beings. That life is now available only to the faithful who reenter the garden through the second Adam (3:22; Rev 22:14). Its counterpart today is found in sacramentally eating the flesh and drinking the blood of Jesus Christ (Jn 6:53). **tree of the knowledge of good and evil.** Good and evil, a compound of opposites like "the heavens and the earth" (1:1), is a figure for potentially unlimited knowledge. It was a good tree (3:22), but humanity was not to seize it or to partake of its fruit. Sin consisted of an illicit reach of unbelief, an assertion of human autonomy, the desire to know apart from God. We must live by faith in God's Word and not by a professed self-sufficiency of knowledge (Dt 8:3; Eze 28:6,15–17). The law makes wise the simple (Ps 19:7–9). See *WLC* 20.
2:10 A river. This river flowed from Eden through the temple-garden and then branched out to the four corners of the earth. It is the stream that will flow from the throne of the living God (Ps 36:8; Jer 17:13; Eze 47:1–12; Rev 22:1), recalled later in the prophetic Word of God flowing from the temple (see Mic 4:1–4) and the Spirit of God (Jn 7:37–39).
2:11–13 Pishon . . . Gihon. Their identities are uncertain. Compare the rivers of Eden with those of the promised land (see 25:18).
2:11 Havilah. Probably in Arabia (10:7,29; 25:18; 1Sa 15:7).

Body and Soul in the Bible: What Am I?

EACH human being in this world consists of an outward, material body animated by an inward, immaterial, personal core. Scripture calls this inward aspect of our self both "soul" and "spirit."

Reformed theology denies that man is "trichotomous" (made up of three distinct parts: body, soul and spirit). The notion that the soul is concerned with this-worldly awareness only, while the spirit is a distinct part of a person that can participate in communion with God and the supernatural world, is out of step both with Biblical teaching and with typical Hebrew and Greek word usage (both languages use "soul" and "spirit" interchangeably). Although a few passages seem to distinguish on the surface between the two (e.g., 1Th 5:23; Heb 4:12 and their notes), these passages do not intend to identify the constituent parts of human beings. Hebrews 4:12—arguably the passage quoted most often in defense of trichotomy—states that the Word of God "penetrates even to dividing soul and spirit" (see note on this verse). However, this passage attributes thoughts and attitudes neither to the spirit nor to the soul but to the heart. In this particular verse all three words—heart, soul and spirit—synonymously identify the non-corporeal part of human beings. In fact, if one were to insist that all the various terms associated with humankind's incorporeal aspects are distinct components of people (e.g., heart, soul, mind, spirit, inner parts, inmost place, inmost being), the attempt to subdivide would cause endless confusion.

Reformed theology has also stressed that our physical bodies are integral to God's design for humanity. There was nothing evil or corruptible about the body as God first created it, and had humankind not fallen into sin, the physical ailments and aging process that lead to death would have been no part of the human experience (Ge 2:17; 3:19,22; Ro 5:12). As a result, salvation in Christ is the salvation of the whole person– body and soul. Just as Jesus Christ rose from the dead both spiritually and physically, we are not fully delivered from sin's effects until we receive full inward and complete outward renewal. Before the return of Christ, we are constantly being renewed in our inward beings as our bodies continue to suffer corruption (2Co 4:16–18), but when Christ returns in glory we will receive our full adoption, including the redemption of our bodies (Ro 8:23).

At death and throughout the intermediate state as the dead await Christ's return, the soul and body are separated. This condition, however, is not our final destiny. The Christian hope is not redemption of the soul from the body, but redemption of the soul and body together. Although the Scriptures do not explain the exact nature of our future glorified bodies, we know that there will be sufficient continuity with our present bodies that we will maintain our unique identities (1Co 15:35–49; Php 3:20–21; Col 3:4).

also there.) [13]The name of the second river is the Gihon; it winds through the entire land
2:14 [r]Da 10:4 of Cush.[a] [14]The name of the third river is the Tigris;[r] it runs along the east side of Asshur.
And the fourth river is the Euphrates.
[15]The LORD God took the man and put him in the Garden of Eden to work it and take
care of it. [16]And the LORD God commanded the man, "You are free to eat from any tree
2:17 [s]Dt 30:15,19; Ro 5:12; 6:23; Jas 1:15 in the garden; [17]but you must not eat from the tree of the knowledge of good and evil,
for when you eat of it you will surely die."[s]
[18]The LORD God said, "It is not good for the man to be alone. I will make a helper suit-
2:18 [t]1Co 11:9 able for him."[t]
[19]Now the LORD God had formed out of the ground all the beasts of the field[u] and all
2:19 [u]Ps 8:7 [v]Ge 1:24 the birds of the air. He brought them to the man to see what he would name them; and
whatever the man called each living creature,[v] that was its name. [20]So the man gave
names to all the livestock, the birds of the air and all the beasts of the field.
But for Adam[b] no suitable helper was found. [21]So the LORD God caused the man to
2:22 [w]1Co 11:8,9,12 fall into a deep sleep; and while he was sleeping, he took one of the man's ribs[c] and
closed up the place with flesh. [22]Then the LORD God made a woman from the rib[d] [w] he
had taken out of the man, and he brought her to the man.
[23]The man said,

2:23 [x]Ge 29:14; Eph 5:28-30

"This is now bone of my bones
and flesh of my flesh;[x]
she shall be called 'woman,[e]'
for she was taken out of man."

2:24 [y]Mal 2:15 [z]Mt 19:5*; Mk 10:7-8*; 1Co 6:16*; Eph 5:31*
[24]For this reason a man will leave his father and mother and be united[y] to his wife, and
they will become one flesh.[z]
[25]The man and his wife were both naked,[a] and they felt no shame.

2:25 [a]Ge 3:7,10-11

The Fall of Man

3:1 [b]2Co 11:3; Rev 12:9; 20:2
3 Now the serpent[b] was more crafty than any of the wild animals the LORD God had
made. He said to the woman, "Did God really say, 'You must not eat from any tree
in the garden'?"
[2]The woman said to the serpent, "We may eat fruit from the trees in the garden, [3]but

a *13* Possibly southeast Mesopotamia b *20* Or *the man* c *21* Or *took part of the man's side*
d *22* Or *part* e *23* The Hebrew for *woman* sounds like the Hebrew for *man.*

2:15–17 See *WCF* 6.3; 9.2; *WLC* 20,22,141; *WSC* 16.
2:15 work it and take care of it. The Hebrew words behind this translation connote priestly activity in the holy garden. The latter task also entailed guarding it against the encroachment of enemies (see Nu 1:50,53; 3:8).
2:16 commanded. God's first words to man assumed humanity's ability to choose, as well as humankind's moral capacity and responsibility.
2:17 must not eat. This unique prohibition, an exception to humanity's dominion (1:29), asserted the Creator's rule. **surely die.** The heavenly King threatened a sentence of death (see notes on 3:7–13). See *WCF* 4.2; 6.2; 7.2; 19.1; *WLC* 20,27,92,193; *WSC* 12; *HC* 40.
2:18–25 The gift of the bride, representing marriage before the fall and therefore the ideal, provides the basis for the laws against adultery (Ex 20:14; Heb 13:4), a model for marriage, the basis for government in the home and church (1Co 11:3–12; 1Ti 2:12–13) and a type for Christ's relationship to his church (Eph 5:22–32). The focus in 1:26–27 is on a couple's sexuality as male and female; here it is on their social relationship as husband and wife.
2:18 not good. See note on 1:4. The one thing God concluded was not right with the world was Adam's lack of companionship. Devotion to God does not necessitate celibacy. In the Old Testament the most holy persons—the high priest (Lev 21:13) and the Nazirites—were not required to be celibate (Nu 6:1–4). **helper.** Adam needed Eve to help him fulfill the mandate given to humanity. This does not indicate Eve's inferiority, for elsewhere God is called "helper" (see Pss 27:9; 118:7). **suitable for him.** The expression indicates that what Adam lacked Eve supplied and vice versa. Both were uniquely fashioned in the image of God (1:26–27). See *WCF* 24.2; *WLC* 20.
2:19–20 God prepared Adam for the gift of his bride by making him aware of his loneliness and by fostering his leadership ability by assigning the task of naming the animals.
2:19 called. See 1:5 and its note. The image-of-God bearer carried out the cultural mandate (see 1:26; 1Ki 4:33 and their notes). The place of human beings is a little lower than that of the heavenly beings (Ps 8:5) and higher than that of the animals.
2:20–25 See theological article "Marriage and Divorce" at Matthew 19.
2:21 man's ribs. The first woman was derived from the man, giving him priority within the institution of marriage, but from that time forward men have been derived from women (see 1Co 11:3–12).
2:22 See *WLC* 17.
2:23 This . . . man. Adam's first poem—his only words recorded before his fall—celebrated his wife's kinship and equality with himself. **called woman.** See 1:5 and its note. Adam's naming of Eve expressed his authority, but paradoxically he named her "woman," implying that she was his equal.
2:24 leave. Once married, a man's priorities change. Obligations to his wife take precedence. **be united to.** This is the language of covenant commitment. Human beings are never more like the covenant-keeping God than when they pledge themselves in covenant to one another. Marriage depicts God's relationship to his people (Hos 2:14–23; Eph 5:22–32). **one flesh.** The complete unity and profound solidarity of the marriage relationship hints at God's intention that marriage be monogamous. See *WCF* 24.1.
2:25 no shame. Their nakedness without shame indicated their openness, respect and trust. With their loss of innocence, they felt shame and temptation, so they needed to protect their vulnerability by wearing clothes as barriers.
■ **3:1–24** *The Fall and Its Consequences.* As priestly guardians (see note on 2:15) of the sanctuary, the man and woman were now tested for their fidelity to their King. The test was administered under a covenant of works: Obedience entitled them to life with God; disobedience would bring death. Their failure pointed to their need for justification and sanctification through the covenant of grace to be established with and through Christ. See theological article "The Covenants of Works and Grace" at Genesis 6. See *HC* 7.
3:1 the serpent. In the Biblical world, snakes were symbolic of many things, but here it is significant that the god of chaos was sometimes likened to one (Job 26:12–13; Isa 27:1). This serpent was an incarnation of Satan, "the adversary" (cf. Rev 12:9; 20:2).

God did say, 'You must not eat fruit from the tree that is in the middle of the garden, and
you must not touch it, or you will die.' "
4"You will not surely die," the serpent said to the woman.[c] 5"For God knows that
when you eat of it your eyes will be opened, and you will be like God,[d] knowing good and
evil."
6When the woman saw that the fruit of the tree was good for food and pleasing to the
eye, and also desirable[e] for gaining wisdom, she took some and ate it. She also gave
some to her husband, who was with her, and he ate it.[f] 7Then the eyes of both of them
were opened, and they realized they were naked; so they sewed fig leaves together and
made coverings for themselves.
8Then the man and his wife heard the sound of the LORD God as he was walking[g] in
the garden in the cool of the day, and they hid[h] from the LORD God among the trees of
the garden. 9But the LORD God called to the man, "Where are you?"
10He answered, "I heard you in the garden, and I was afraid because I was naked; so
I hid."
11And he said, "Who told you that you were naked? Have you eaten from the tree that
I commanded you not to eat from?"
12The man said, "The woman you put here with me—she gave me some fruit from the
tree, and I ate it."
13Then the LORD God said to the woman, "What is this you have done?"
The woman said, "The serpent deceived me,[i] and I ate."
14So the LORD God said to the serpent, "Because you have done this,

"Cursed[j] are you above all the livestock
and all the wild animals!
You will crawl on your belly
and you will eat dust[k]
all the days of your life.

3:4 [c]Jn 8:44; 2Co 11:3
3:5 [d]Isa 14:14; Eze 28:2
3:6 [e]Jas 1:14-15; 1Jn 2:16 [f]1Ti 2:14
3:8 [g]Dt 23:14 [h]Job 31:33; Ps 139:7-12; Jer 23:24
3:13 [i]2Co 11:3; 1Ti 2:14
3:14 [j]Dt 28:15-20 [k]Isa 65:25; Mic 7:17

He was malevolent and more wily than Adam and Eve; he used speech to introduce confusion since he understood divine matters. He is later identified as one of the heavenly beings (v. 22; Lk 10:18–19; Jn 8:44; Rev 12:9), although he will ultimately be destroyed by Christ and his seed (see note on v. 15). **crafty.** Satan's embodiment matched his own malevolent brilliance; encroachment by deception (2Co 11:13–15). Satan's craftiness is seen in his cunning distortion of God's words. With subtle guise, the adversary speaks as a winsome angelic theologian. He can be withstood only by one's putting on God's splendid armor (Mt 4:1–11; Eph 6:10–20).
3:2–5 Satan tempted the first humans by emphasizing God's prohibition rather than his provision, by reducing God's command to a question, by casting doubt upon God's sincerity, by defaming God's motives and by denying the veracity of God's threat. Eve gradually yielded to Satan's denials and half-truths that disparaged her privileges and minimized the threat.
3:5 God, knowing. Or "divine beings, knowers of" (see "us" in v. 22). **good and evil.** See 2:9 and its note. See *WLC* 145.
3:6–8 See *WCF* 6.2; *WLC* 21; *WSC* 13.
3:6 Sin is essentially humanity's breach of trust in God, disbelief in God's word, an assertion of autonomy (see note on 2:16). True religion consists of communion with God based on trust, issuing into obedience (Jn 14:15). See theological article "Creation, Fall, Redemption" at Genesis 3. **fruit . . . wisdom.** The woman's decision was based on practical values, aesthetic appreciation and spiritual gratification. **took some and ate.** By this act she sealed an alliance with the prince of death and darkness. God's unconditional and irresistible election were now her only hope (see note on 3:15). **he ate it.** The man became a rebel. Surrounded with sufficient motives to trust and obey God, he chose disobedience (6:5; 8:21). By God's appointment Adam represented the human race as its covenant head and brought death upon all, just as Christ brings life to all who are in him (Ro 5:12–19). See *WCF* 4.2; 9.2; *WLC* 17; *WSC* 15; *HC* 9.
3:7–11 One result of sin was alienation—from one another (symbolized by the sewing together of fig leaves for clothing) and from God (symbolized by their hiding among the trees).
3:7 naked. The Hebrew term describes someone stripped of protective clothing in the sense of being defenseless, weak or humiliated (Dt 28:48; Job 1:21; Isa 58:7). The Hebrew for "naked" sounds like the Hebrew for "crafty" in 3:6. Ironically, the first couple sought to be shrewd and found themselves nude. The intimacy of marriage was shattered (see note on 2:24). The first experience of guilt was expressed in terms of an awareness of nakedness. Redemption is linked to God's providing a "covering" for human sin (see note on v. 21). **fig leaves.** Strong and broad enough for clothing. See *BC* 23.
3:8–11 See *WCF* 4.2; *BC* 17.
3:8 sound of the LORD. Their time of judgment by their God had come (Am 4:12). **walking.** The gardener did not abandon his garden. In his tabernacle God would walk with Israel (Lev 26:12; Dt 23:14; 2Sa 7:6–7). **cool of the day.** Literally, "wind" or "spirit" of the day. The wind/spirit is the symbol of God's presence (1:2). **hid.** Their consciences condemning them, the pair no longer desired the intimacy with God they had formerly enjoyed in the garden (Ro 2:12–16). Their expulsion from it matched their attitudes and actions. See *WLC* 20,27; *WSC* 19.
3:9–14 The just King does not pass judgment without careful investigation (4:9–10; 18:21).
3:9 Where . . . ? This rhetorical question incited them to come to him (4:9).
3:10 I heard you. Literally, "I heard your voice." Ironically, this is the Hebrew idiom for "to obey"—precisely what Adam did not do. See *WLC* 27; *WSC* 19.
3:11 Who . . . ? The rhetorical questions (see v. 13) prodded Adam and Eve to confess their guilt. God asked Satan no questions but simply consigned him to judgment (v. 14).
3:12–13 Adam and Eve demonstrated their allegiance to Satan by distorting the truth and accusing one another and ultimately God (Jas 1:13). Their efforts to conceal their sin only exposed it. See *WLC* 145; *WSC* 15.
3:13 deceived. See notes on 1 Timothy 2:12 and 14. See *WCF* 6.1; *WLC* 21; *WSC* 13; *HC* 9.
3:14–19 God's judgments against Satan (vv. 14–15), the woman (v. 16) and the man (vv. 17–19) contained within them promises of salvation.
3:14–15 The language refers both to serpents in general and to Satan in particular.
3:14 to the serpent. Satan, who had instigated this evil, was not questioned or given opportunity to explain. **Cursed.** The opposite of blessed (see note on 1:22), denoting a consignment to impotence. The serpent's seed does not have the promise of God upon it, and it cannot overcome final death or bring about eternal life. **eat dust all the days.** Dust is the symbol of abject humiliation (Pss 44:25; 72:9), and it will last forever. Satan's final defeat under the heel of the Messiah (v. 15) is being delayed to bring about God's program of redemption through the image of God. God left Satan to test the fidelity of each succeeding generation of God's covenant people (Jdg 2:20–22) and to teach them to "fight" against evil (Jdg 3:2).

15 And I will put enmity
between you and the woman,
and between your offspring[a] [l] and hers;[m]
he will crush[b] your head,[n]
and you will strike his heel."

16 To the woman he said,
"I will greatly increase your pains in childbearing;
with pain you will give birth to children.
Your desire will be for your husband,
and he will rule over you.[o]"

3:15 [l] Jn 8:44; Ac 13:10; 1Jn 3:8 [m] Isa 7:14; Mt 1:23; Rev 12:17 [n] Ro 16:20; Heb 2:14
3:16 [o] 1Co 11:3; Eph 5:22

a *15* Or *seed* b *15* Or *strike*

3:15 I will put enmity. In sovereign grace God converted the depraved woman's affections from Satan to himself. **your offspring and hers.** Humanity was, and still is, divided into two communities: the faithful, who love God, and the lost, who love self (Jn 8:44; 1Jn 3:8). This division found immediate expression in the hostility of Cain against Abel (ch. 4). **he . . . you.** The battle is a confrontation of champions. The decisive battle is won by Jesus Christ (Da 7:13–14; Ro 5:12–19; 16:20; 1Co 15:45–49; Gal 3:16,29; Heb 2:14; Rev 12). **crush . . . strike.** These two words translate the same Hebrew root (see NIV text note). The faithful must suffer to win the new community from the serpent's dominion before Christ's glorious victory (Isa 53:12; Lk 24:26,46; Ro 16:20; 1Pe 1:10–11). God's judgment reveals that suffering plays a part in the lives of those who identify with God's overcoming of the serpent (2Co 1:5–7; Col 1:24). **head . . . heel.** The suffering Christ is victorious. He has already won the victory at the cross by providing an atonement for redeemed saints (Col 2:13–15), and he will consummate his victory at his second coming (2Th 1:5–10). See *WCF* 7.3; 8.6; 25.2; *WLC* 32; *BC* 17; *HC* 19.

3:16–19 The woman would be frustrated in her natural relationships within the home and would endure painful labor in bearing children. The man would be frustrated in his attempt to provide food. Each would experience "pain" by these reversals. Constraint replaced freedom; coercion replaced cooperation.

Creation, Fall, Redemption: Why Is Everything So Bad?

ALTHOUGH some interpreters take the story of Adam and Eve as a figurative account, the Scriptures teach that there was an actual, individual man who fell into sin and brought God's curse on all of creation and humanity. In Genesis, Adam is linked to the patriarchs and with them to the rest of humanity by natural genealogy (chs. 5,10,11). This fact makes it clear that Adam was as much a part of space, time and history as were Abraham, Isaac and Jacob.

Beyond this, the apostle Paul traced the fallen condition of humanity back to the sin of the one actual man, Adam, whom he described as our common ancestor (Ac 17:26; Ro 5:12–14; cf. 1Co 15:22). This is the authoritative New Testament interpretation of the events recorded in Genesis 3, where we find the account of the fall, the original human lapse from God and righteousness into sin and death.

Reformed theology has depended heavily on the historical reality of the fall into sin. John Calvin structured much of his theology around the themes of creation, the fall and redemption, focusing on the parallels between Adam and Christ. Adam was originally created in righteousness but fell into a state of corruption and judgment, and now we find redemption from the curse of the fall by faith in the atoning work of Jesus Christ on our behalf. These motifs appear throughout Reformed creeds and catechisms (*WCF* 6,7; *WSC* 15–26; *WLC* 21–45; *BC* 14–17; *HC* 6–20).

The Scriptures teach at least five primary truths related to the fall:

1. God assigned the first man the role of representative for all of his posterity, just as he later ordained Jesus Christ as the representative for all God's elect (Ro 5:15–19 with 8:29–30; 9:22–26).
2. God set the first man in a state of unadulterated happiness and promised to continue this condition for him and his offspring if he would show fidelity by perfect obedience—specifically by refraining from eating the fruit of the tree of the knowledge of good and evil.
3. Adam and Eve's sin brought themselves and their descendents (all of humankind) under the grip of sin and guilt and made them and all people ashamed and fearful before God (Ge 3:7–11). The original human pair were cursed with expectations of pain and death and expelled from the paradise of Eden (Ge 3:14–24).
4. The entire creation was placed under a divine curse because of Adam and Eve's sin. The present disharmony of nature that often makes the world a hostile environment for all living things resulted from the fall (Ro 8:20–23).
5. God began even in the days of Adam and Eve to show mercy through his promise that the woman's seed would one day crush the serpent's head (Ge 3:15). This promise was fulfilled by Christ, who redeems his people and restores creation to its rightful order (Ro 8:20–21; Rev 21:1–5).

The narrative of the fall provides a convincing historical explanation of human perversion and the corruption of nature. Unless we believe in the veracity of this account in Genesis, we are seriously hindered in our understanding of Christ, whom the New Testament describes as the "last Adam" (1Co 15:45) because through his sacrificial death and resurrection he reverses the tragic effects of what the first Adam did (Ro 5:12–19; 1Co 15:22).

17 To Adam he said, "Because you listened to your wife and ate from the tree about
which I commanded you, 'You must not eat of it,'

"Cursed[p] is the ground because of you;
through painful toil you will eat of it
all the days of your life.[q]
18 It will produce thorns and thistles for you,
and you will eat the plants of the field.[r]
19 By the sweat of your brow
you will eat your food[s]
until you return to the ground,
since from it you were taken;
for dust you are
and to dust you will return."[t]

20 Adam[a] named his wife Eve,[b] because she would become the mother of all the living.
21 The LORD God made garments of skin for Adam and his wife and clothed them.
22 And the LORD God said, "The man has now become like one of us, knowing good and
evil. He must not be allowed to reach out his hand and take also from the tree of life[u]
and eat, and live forever." 23 So the LORD God banished him from the Garden of Eden[v] to
work the ground[w] from which he had been taken. 24 After he drove the man out, he
placed on the east side[c] of the Garden of Eden cherubim[x] and a flaming sword[y] flashing back and forth to guard the way to the tree of life.[z]

3:17 [p]Ge 5:29; Ro 8:20-22 [q]Job 5:7; 14:1; Ecc 2:23
3:18 [r]Ps 104:14
3:19 [s]2Th 3:10 [t]Ge 2:7; Ps 90:3; 104:29; Ecc 12:7
3:22 [u]Rev 22:14
3:23 [v]Ge 2:8 [w]Ge 4:2
3:24 [x]Ex 25:18-22 [y]Ps 104:4 [z]Ge 2:9

Cain and Abel

4 Adam[a] lay with his wife Eve, and she became pregnant and gave birth to Cain.[d] She
said, "With the help of the LORD I have brought forth[e] a man." 2 Later she gave birth
to his brother Abel.[a]

4:2 [a]Lk 11:51

[a] *20,1* Or *The man* [b] *20* *Eve* probably means *living*. [c] *24* Or *placed in front* [d] *1* *Cain* sounds like the Hebrew for *brought forth* or *acquired*. [e] *1* Or *have acquired*

3:16 childbearing. Despite her fallen condition, the woman was still to be involved in procreation (see 1:28). **desire.** The phrase "he will rule over you" and the parallel wording in 4:7 ("it desires to have you") suggest that the woman's desire to control would be met by male dominance. The marriage ordinance was to continue, but it would be frustrated by conflict between the sexes. **rule over you.** "To love and to cherish" (see 2:21–24 and its notes) was now replaced by "to dominate" (cf. Eph 5:25 29) this was another aspect of God's curse against sin, not a new and good design for marriage. The solution is found in a new life in Christ (Mt 20:25–28).
3:17–19 See *BC* 14.
3:17 To Adam. As with the others, God's punishment fit the crime. In response to Adam's sin of consumption, God's speech to him mentions eating no fewer than five times (vv. 17–19). Adam was also to suffer pain and frustration in natural relationships. **painful toil.** Human beings were to continue to exercise dominion over the earth, despite frustration (1:26). Work, although a blessing of the working God, would now be cursed by frustration. As humankind obeys God, God may respond by reducing the effects of the curse, making the earth's ecology partly dependent on human morality (4:12; 6:7; Lev 26; Dt 11:13–17; 28:1–68; Pr 30:21; Joel 1–2). See *WLC* 28,193.
3:18 thorns and thistles. The hostile creation that must be overcome by work serves as a parable for spiritual hostility that must be overcome by heavenly wisdom (Pr 24:30–34).
3:19 to the ground, since from it. Humanity's natural relationship to the ground—to rule over it—was now reversed; instead of submitting to human beings, it would resist and eventually swallow them (see note on 2:7). The earth, frustrated by the Creator's assignment to disharmony, longs for resurrection and restoration (Ro 8:20–22). **dust you will return.** Ironically, transgressing the divinely ordered boundaries did not bring human beings the elevated lives they had hoped for; instead it brought them chaos and death. As a result, physical death renders all activity vain. But it also delivers the redeemed from an eternal consignment to cursed lives on the earth and opens the way to an eternal salvation that outlasts the grave. See *WCF* 32.1; *WLC* 141.
3:20 named. See notes on 1:5 and 2:23. To the woman's generic designation, Adam added a personal name that defined her destiny. **Eve.** When Adam named his wife "woman," he implicitly declared her his equal (2:23). Here, by naming her Eve, Adam again exercised his authority over Eve by naming her, but the name he gave her honored her as the mother of all humankind. Adam twice used his authority to lift up his wife rather than to subjugate her. **living.** Adam showed his restoration to God by believing the promise that the woman would bear children, including the offspring who would defeat Satan.
3:21 garments of skin. The word "coverings" (v. 7) refers to loin cloths, which were inadequate to conceal their shame; "garments" means "tunics." God did for the couple what the two could not do for themselves. Humans cannot deal with their shame, but God can, will and does. His covering entailed killing an animal, implicitly a sacrifice for salvation (see note on 7:2). **clothed.** Through the Lord's adequate and durable covering, the alienated couple was restored to a measure of fellowship with him and with one another. This covering also prefigured the atoning suffering of the Messiah (see v. 15 and its note) insofar as his death permanently and perfectly reconciles sinners to God (Ro 5:8–10).
3:22 us. See verse 5, 1:26 and their notes. See *BC* 9.
3:23 banished. God cleansed his temple garden (Lk 10:18; Jn 2:12–17; Rev 21:27). See *WCF* 4.2.
3:24 east. See 2:8 and its note. Israel's tabernacle and temple, like the medieval cathedrals, faced toward the east. **cherubim.** These heavenly beings protected God's holiness, barring sinners from access to him (Ex 25:18; 2Ch 3:7; Eze 28:14). Here the angelic beings were delegated the role of preventing sinners from grasping at immortality. **to guard.** Access to Paradise was available only as God permitted. A measure of access was later conferred upon the Israelites under Moses as they entered the land of promise from the east after encountering a sword-bearing heavenly being (Jos 5:13). Yet Jesus, the last Adam, who reconciled sinners to God by his toil, sweat, thorns, conflict, death on a tree and descent into dust, regained the garden, tearing apart the veil of the temple on which images of the cherubim were sewn (see 2:8 and its note; Ex 26:1; Mt 27:51; Heb 6:19; 9:3). See *WLC* 27; *WSC* 19.
■ **4:1–24** *Escalation of Sin in the Line of Cain.* The prophesied hostility between the seed of the serpent and that of the woman (cf. 3:15) took shape immediately in the hostility of ungodly Cain against godly Abel (vv. 1–16). This distinction was followed by the conflict between Cain's ungodly offspring and the godly line of Seth (4:17—5:32). There was a horrendous escalation of sin during the period from Cain to Lamech.
4:1–16 The focus is on Cain, the archetype of Satan's followers. Cain revealed his kinship with the devil by his hostility toward God

Now Abel kept flocks, and Cain worked the soil. [3]In the course of time Cain brought
some of the fruits of the soil as an offering to the LORD.[b] [4]But Abel brought fat portions[c]
from some of the firstborn of his flock.[d] The LORD looked with favor on Abel and his offering,[e] [5]but on Cain and his offering he did not look with favor. So Cain was very angry,
and his face was downcast.
[6]Then the LORD said to Cain, "Why are you angry? Why is your face downcast? [7]If you
do what is right, will you not be accepted? But if you do not do what is right, sin is crouching at your door;[f] it desires to have you, but you must master it.[g]"
[8]Now Cain said to his brother Abel, "Let's go out to the field."[a] And while they were
in the field, Cain attacked his brother Abel and killed him.[h]
[9]Then the LORD said to Cain, "Where is your brother Abel?"
"I don't know," he replied. "Am I my brother's keeper?"
[10]The LORD said, "What have you done? Listen! Your brother's blood cries out to me
from the ground.[i] [11]Now you are under a curse and driven from the ground, which opened
its mouth to receive your brother's blood from your hand. [12]When you work the ground,
it will no longer yield its crops for you. You will be a restless wanderer on the earth."
[13]Cain said to the LORD, "My punishment is more than I can bear. [14]Today you are
driving me from the land, and I will be hidden from your presence;[j] I will be a restless
wanderer on the earth, and whoever finds me will kill me."[k]
[15]But the LORD said to him, "Not so[b]; if anyone kills Cain[l], he will suffer vengeance
seven times over.[m]" Then the LORD put a mark on Cain so that no one who found him

4:3 [b]Nu 18:12
4:4 [c]Lev 3:16 [d]Ex 13:2, 12 [e]Heb 11:4
4:7 [f]Nu 32:23 [g]Ro 6:16
4:8 [h]Mt 23:35; 1Jn 3:12
4:10 [i]Ge 9:5; Nu 35:33; Heb 12:24; Rev 6:9-10
4:14 [j]2Ki 17:18; Ps 51:11; 139:7-12; Jer 7:15; 52:3 [k]Ge 9:6; Nu 35:19, 21,27,33
4:15 [l]Eze 9:4,6 [m]ver 24; Ps 79:12

[a] *8* Samaritan Pentateuch, Septuagint, Vulgate and Syriac; Masoretic Text does not have *"Let's go out to the field."* [b] *15* Septuagint, Vulgate and Syriac; Hebrew *Very well*

(vv. 8–9), his murder of a good man (Mt 23:35; Heb 11:4) and his lies (v. 9; Jn 8:44; 1Jn 3:12).

4:1 lay with. Literally, "knew." The word involves a personal and intimate knowing. Here *knowing* refers to the closest and most hallowed relationship between a husband and his wife. **Cain.** His name may mean "acquire, get, possess," a foreshadowing of his primary proclivities. **help of the LORD.** Human beings, both originally (1:26–27) and derivatively, owe their existence to God.. **a man.** This unexpected term for a mature man, not a baby, may have been chosen to echo 2:23. Woman originally came from man; now man derives from woman. The sexes are mutually dependent on one another, and both are dependent on God (1Co 11:8–12).

4:2 Later. To emphasize the unconditional nature of his election, the Lord rejected the human principle that the firstborn son inherits the greatest blessings. **Abel.** The name means "perishable," a somber prophecy of what was to follow. **flocks . . . soil.** In spite of the fall, human beings still carried out the cultural mandate (1:26,28).

4:3 brought. The law, Sabbath (2:1–3), divine sanctuary (ch. 2) and sacrifice (3:21; 7:2) were given to humankind from the beginning. Because Cain failed at the altar, he would later fail in the field. Theology and ethics are inseparable.

4:4–5 offering. The Hebrew here is the common word for "tribute," the gift of an inferior to a superior (1Sa 10:27; 1Ki 4:21). In the Pentateuch the Hebrew term is used of a bloodless sacrifice (Lev 2:14; 1Ki 10:25). Each brother brought a gift appropriate to his vocation (cf. 32:13–21). Both came as priests, worshiped the same God and desired God's acceptance, but only Abel brought an acceptable tribute.

4:4 fat . . . firstborn. As the author and owner of life, God was entitled to the first share produced by plants ("firstfruits"; Dt 26:1–11), by animals ("firstborn"; Dt 12:6) and by people ("firstborn"; Ex 13:2,12; 34:19). He was also entitled to the best a worshiper had to offer ("fat"; Lev 3:14–16). Abel brought both the first and the best, while Cain brought "some." The implication of this contrast seems to be that Cain did not offer the firstfruits of his crop (cf. v. 7; Heb 11:4). The prophesied battle between the seed of the serpent (Cain; cf. Jn 8:44) and that of the woman was already apparent in their offspring. Even though Adam and Eve had been restored to God, they had two distinct seeds, even within the one family. **The LORD looked.** God saw the heart (cf. 1Sa 16:7). **Abel and his offering.** The worshiper and his offering were inseparable: By faith Abel was commended as a righteous man when God spoke well of his offerings; without faith neither Cain nor his token offering of some of his harvest was pleasing to God (Heb 11:4,6). See *WCF* 16.6; *BC* 24.

4:5 Cain was very angry. Fundamentally, the elect and non-elect are differentiated by their attitudes toward God. See *WCF* 16.7.

4:6 Why . . . ? God's rhetorical question allowed Cain to confess his failure (3:9).

4:7 If you do what is right. The narrative illustrates original sin. Cain had a consciousness of right and wrong, but he rebelled against right, choosing to yield to sin and anger. **will you not be accepted?** It takes faith to believe that God always does what is right. By leaving the question unanswered, Cain showed that he lacked the kind of faith that pleases God. **crouching.** The depiction of sin as a demon or a vicious animal lying in wait to devour is possibly an allusion to the serpent in 3:15 (cf. 1Pe 5:8). **master.** While human beings can master the ground and flocks, they cannot master sin. Only the last Adam and those in him can do that.

4:8 said to . . . Abel. Cain's answer to God's questioning is not recorded in his words to God but in his words and actions toward his brother. Abel is mentioned only for his birth, offering and death. **his brother.** The word "brother" occurs seven times in verses 2–11. **killed him.** Cain's bad feelings against God spilled over into irrational, jealous rage against his brother. Because Cain renounced God, he renounced God's image. The sundering of the familial bond begun in chapter 3 intensified to fratricide. Like his parents in the pride of their sin, he arrogated to himself divine sovereignty, even over life.

4:9 Am I my brother's keeper? His question was absurd. The sarcastic hypocrite had already determined his brother's fate. His play at innocence repeated his father's attempt at concealment. See *WLC* 145.

4:10–14 The murderer, alienated both from the ground and from society, would have no rest.

4:10 What . . . done? The question registered God's outrage. **cries out.** Whereas Abel's blood cried out for vengeance (Isa 26:21; Mt 23:35; Rev 6:10), Christ's blood cries out more loudly (Heb 12:24).

4:11 curse. God now linked Cain with the serpent (see 3:14), who was Satan (see note on 3:1). Cain's time of grace had ended; he was consigned to judgment (Heb 9:27; 10:27). Whereas in 3:17–19 the ground was cursed so as not to yield its produce without frustrating labor, here Cain was cursed to become a fugitive without a permanent place or security.

4:12 no longer yield. See 3:17.

4:13 more than I can bear. Cain responded with self-pity instead of repenting for his sin against God and man. He feared physical and social exposure but not the invisible God who had created him. See *WLC* 28,83,105.

4:14 hidden from your presence. Like Cain, unbelievers fail to believe that the God who fashioned them and sees their heart can also view their situation and prevent the world from dissolving into anarchy. **whoever.** Up to this point, the story has focused on Cain, not on Adam's other descendants (v. 17; 5:4). **kill me.** Cain accurately described his offspring's response: None would be "his keeper." He would be the next victim (see 6:11).

4:15 Not so. The long-suffering Lord shouldered Cain's implied request for a keeper (Isa 55:8–9). **vengeance seven times over.** "Seven" denotes a complete cycle and here represents perfect justice (see 9:5,6 and their notes). **mark.** Probably a protective tattoo that allowed Cain to live out his normal life span.

would kill him. 16 So Cain went out from the LORD's presence and lived in the land of Nod,[a] east of Eden.[n]

17 Cain lay with his wife, and she became pregnant and gave birth to Enoch. Cain was then building a city, and he named it after his son[o] Enoch. 18 To Enoch was born Irad, and Irad was the father of Mehujael, and Mehujael was the father of Methushael, and Methushael was the father of Lamech.

19 Lamech married two women, one named Adah and the other Zillah. 20 Adah gave birth to Jabal; he was the father of those who live in tents and raise livestock. 21 His brother's name was Jubal; he was the father of all who play the harp and flute. 22 Zillah also had a son, Tubal-Cain, who forged all kinds of tools out of[b] bronze and iron. Tubal-Cain's sister was Naamah.

23 Lamech said to his wives,

> "Adah and Zillah, listen to me;
> wives of Lamech, hear my words.
> I have killed[c][p] a man for wounding me,
> a young man for injuring me.
> 24 If Cain is avenged[q] seven times,[r]
> then Lamech seventy-seven times."

25 Adam lay with his wife again, and she gave birth to a son and named him Seth,[d][s] saying, "God has granted me another child in place of Abel, since Cain killed him."[t] 26 Seth also had a son, and he named him Enosh.

At that time men began to call on[e] the name of the LORD.[u]

From Adam to Noah

5 This is the written account of Adam's line.

When God created man, he made him in the likeness of God.[v] 2 He created them male and female[w] and blessed them. And when they were created, he called them "man.[f]"

4:16 [n]Ge 2:8
4:17 [o]Ps 49:11
4:23 [p]Ex 20:13; Lev 19:18
4:24 [q]Dt 32:35 [r]ver 15
4:25 [s]Ge 5:3 [t]ver 8
4:26 [u]Ge 12:8; 1Ki 18:24; Ps 116:17; Joel 2:32; Zep 3:9; Ac 2:21; 1Co 1:2
5:1 [v]Ge 1:27; Eph 4:24; Col 3:10
5:2 [w]Ge 1:27; Mt 19:4; Mk 10:6; Gal 3:28

[a] *16* Nod means *wandering* (see verses 12 and 14). [b] *22* Or *who instructed all who work in* [c] *23* Or *I will kill* [d] *25* *Seth* probably means *granted.* [e] *26* Or *to proclaim* [f] *2* Hebrew *adam*

4:16 land of Nod. This symbolic name means "wandering." The person alienated from God is a person without an abiding place.
4:17–24 The ambiguity of godless human culture is portrayed by paralleling advances in civilization, including the first metallurgy and the first city, with an increase in violence. Cain's lineage is symbolic of a human culture with great civilizations but no true God. The narrative silently polemicizes against pagan myths that attribute the advances of the cultural mandate to divine and semidivine figures.
4:17–18 Cain . . . Enoch . . . Irad . . . Mehujael . . . Methushael . . . Lamech. These names are similar to those in Seth's line (ch. 5) not because they represent variations of the same source but because they parallel and contrast two offspring of Adam. The seventh from Adam through both Cain and Seth—the ungodly Lamech (vv. 19–24) and the godly Enoch (5:24), respectively—stand in sharp contrast to one another. The former inflicted death; the latter escaped it.
4:17 with his wife. In common grace the family was instituted for unbelievers as well as for believers. No law at this time forbade marrying a sister (see 5:4). **city.** In the Biblical world, defensive walls were the hallmark of a great city. Cities were intended for religious and public purposes, not simply to be lived in. The earthly city provided both civilization and protection, but this development culminated in the building of a city that challenged God's supremacy (11:4). The city functioned as an alternative to wandering and as a protection against human retaliation. The faithful, by contrast, looked—and still look—for a heavenly city (Php 3:20; Col 3:1–4; Heb 11:10,16; 12:22; 13:14). **named it.** Instead of honoring God, the unbeliever honors human beings. This perverse direction gives rise to a self-idolizing, Machiavellian state (11:4).
4:19–24 Lamech. Lamech represented both a progressive hardening in sin—polygamy (cf. 2:24; Mt 19:5–6) and a grossly unjust vendetta—and the extension of the cultural mandate from animal husbandry (v. 20) to the arts (v. 21) and sciences (v. 22). He expressed his titanic tyranny in song (vv. 23–24).
4:19 two women. Bigamy represents an abuse of the marriage institution, in that God intended marriage to be monogamous (2:24).
4:20–22 See *WLC* 124.
4:21–22 Jubal . . . Tubal-Cain . . . Naamah. The name *Jubal* is connected with productivity, while *Naamah* means pleasant. This family line is a tragic image of sin's distortion and destruction. The arts and sciences, appropriate extensions of the divine cultural mandate, are here expressed as a means of self-assertion and violence in a depraved culture. This image climaxes with Lamech's song of tyranny.
4:21 harp and flute. Although invented by the godless, these instruments were and are rightly used by the godly to praise the Lord (1Sa 16:23).
4:24 seventy-seven times. Lamech was confident of even more divine protection than his ancestor had received (see 3:15). He flagrantly and abusively transformed the rightful prerogatives of the state for justice into tyranny (6:1–6).
■ **4:25–26** *Godly Remnant.* This brief episode provides a transition between the two accounts begun in 2:4 and 5:1.
4:25 Adam lay with his wife again. The line of Cain through tyrannical Lamech was presented to illustrate the consequences of the sin of revenge. Here the story flashes back to the birth of Seth to reveal hope in the progress of the godly seed. Despite the vicissitudes of history, God was keeping his promise to provide a seed to destroy the serpent (3:15). The comparison and contrast of verse 25 with verses 1 and 17 form the transition to the line of the godly offspring predicted in 3:15. **Seth.** His name, derived from the Hebrew verb translated "granted," expressed Eve's faith that God would continue the covenant family in spite of death and martyrdom (3:15).
4:26 call on the name of the LORD. The covenant family, by making its petition and voicing its praise in the name of the Lord, glorified God, not man (cf. v. 17). This practice later distinguished Israel from all other nations (see 12:8; 13:4). Thus Moses' original readers would rightly have identified themselves with Seth and his descendants.
■ **5:1—6:8** *Account of Adam's Genealogy.* These chapters begin the process of identifying the seed that would eventually rule the earth (1:26–28) and crush the serpent (3:15). This account traces that lineage from Adam to Noah (5:1–32). This material concludes with the rapid hardening of sin and the inability of the godly seed of the woman to reverse sin (6:1–8).
■ **5:1–32** *Covenant Line of Seth.* This chapter contains ten formally identical paragraphs, one for each generation in Adam's line through Seth. The Sumerian flood story mentions nine kings prior to the flood who together reigned for an exceptionally long time (up to 64,000 years). After the Sumerian account of the flood (cf. vv. 6–9), there is a list of shorter-lived kings (cf. ch. 11). More significant are the connections between chapters 5 and 4. Structural-

[3]When Adam had lived 130 years, he had a son in his own likeness, in his own image;[x] and he named him Seth. [4]After Seth was born, Adam lived 800 years and had other sons and daughters. [5]Altogether, Adam lived 930 years, and then he died.[y]
[6]When Seth had lived 105 years, he became the father[a] of Enosh. [7]And after he became the father of Enosh, Seth lived 807 years and had other sons and daughters. [8]Al-
together, Seth lived 912 years, and then he died.
[9]When Enosh had lived 90 years, he became the father of Kenan. [10]And after he became the father of Kenan, Enosh lived 815 years and had other sons and daughters. [11]Al-
together, Enosh lived 905 years, and then he died.
[12]When Kenan had lived 70 years, he became the father of Mahalalel. [13]And after he
became the father of Mahalalel, Kenan lived 840 years and had other sons and daughters. [14]Altogether, Kenan lived 910 years, and then he died.
[15]When Mahalalel had lived 65 years, he became the father of Jared. [16]And after he
became the father of Jared, Mahalalel lived 830 years and had other sons and daughters.
[17]Altogether, Mahalalel lived 895 years, and then he died.
[18]When Jared had lived 162 years, he became the father of Enoch.[z] [19]And after he became the father of Enoch, Jared lived 800 years and had other sons and daughters. [20]Al-
together, Jared lived 962 years, and then he died.
[21]When Enoch had lived 65 years, he became the father of Methuselah. [22]And after
he became the father of Methuselah, Enoch walked with God[a] 300 years and had other sons and daughters. [23]Altogether, Enoch lived 365 years. [24]Enoch walked with God;[b]
then he was no more, because God took him away.[c]
[25]When Methuselah had lived 187 years, he became the father of Lamech. [26]And after he became the father of Lamech, Methuselah lived 782 years and had other sons and
daughters. [27]Altogether, Methuselah lived 969 years, and then he died.
[28]When Lamech had lived 182 years, he had a son. [29]He named him Noah[b] and said,
"He will comfort us in the labor and painful toil of our hands caused by the ground the
LORD has cursed.[d]" [30]After Noah was born, Lamech lived 595 years and had other sons
and daughters. [31]Altogether, Lamech lived 777 years, and then he died.
[32]After Noah was 500 years old, he became the father of Shem, Ham and Japheth.

5:3 [x]Ge 1:26; 1Co 15:49
5:5 [y]Ge 3:19
5:18 [z]Jude 1:14
5:22 [a]ver 24; Ge 6:9; 17:1; 48:15; Mic 6:8; Mal 2:6
5:24 [b]ver 22 [c]2Ki 2:1, 11; Heb 11:5
5:29 [d]Ge 3:17; Ro 8:20

[a] 6 *Father* may mean *ancestor*; also in verses 7–26. [b] 29 *Noah* sounds like the Hebrew for *comfort.*

ly both genealogies begin in a linear fashion, focusing on one individual in each generation and concluding by segmenting the line into three sons (4:20–22; 5:32; cf. 11:10–26). But thematically they contrast sharply. Whereas the former presents the curse-laden line of Cain that ends with murderer begetting murderer (4:17–24), the latter links the founder of humanity, Adam, with its re-founder, Noah (see notes on 4:25–26). The Enoch and Lamech in Seth's line should not be confused with the first and last descendants in Cain's line. Enoch, the seventh in this list of Seth's line, "walked with God; then . . . God took him" (v. 24), and the Lamech in Seth's line named his son Noah, hoping the Lord would "comfort [them]" (v. 29). Cain's line died out in the flood, whereas Seth's lived through it.

5:1–3 The godly line of Seth, in contradistinction to that of Cain (4:17–24), was begun by linking it with the original creation: Verses 1–2 summarize 1:1—2:3, and especially 1:27–28, while verse 3 echoes both 1:27 and 4:25. God's intention for creation would be realized through Seth, not Cain.

5:1 This is the written account. See 2:4 and its note. The mention of a "written account" demonstrates the author's use of sources (11:10). **account of Adam's line.** This account pertains to Adam's sons and to the covenant line. **likeness.** This reference to the prologue of Genesis establishes a firm connection between Adam's line and God's intention for creation.

5:2 blessed. See 9:1 and its note. **called.** See 1:5 and its note. The pattern of birth and naming furthers humanity's connection to divine activity. The connection between God and the first parents and between the first parents and their children is established by the similarity between verses 1–2 and 1:26–28, by the naming of the "offspring" (see v. 2) and by the repetition of "likeness . . . image" (v. 3).

5:3 130 years. If the sums of (1) the years at the time of fathering and (2) the total life spans from Adam to Lamech are each divided by 60—the Babylonians used an arithmetic based on the number 60—and the remainders added together, the sum of the remainders is 365, perhaps representing the perfect or ideal life span. In light of the many ways ancient Near Eastern genealogies were designed, it is unlikely that Moses simply intended to give precise numbers of years for the descendants of Seth. **likeness . . . image.** The disobedience of the fall did not destroy God's image. The verbal linkage with 1:26–28 presents human procreation as the continuation of God's creative act. The order is reversed to mark the beginning and close of the frame. Although the breath/spirit of God is passed on seminally (see vv. 1–3), God gives his breath/spirit to all those who breathe and so creates each one (Ps 104:29–30). See *WCF* 6.3.

5:5 930 years. These large numbers indicate that God blessed Seth's line (see Ex 20:12; Dt 6:2). These ages may be related to astronomical periods known to the Babylonians (e.g., Enoch's 365 years [v. 23] = days of the year; Lamech's 777 years [v. 31] = synodic periods [the time it takes a planet to return to the same place in the sky] of Jupiter + Saturn; Jared's 962 years [v. 20] = synodic periods of Venus + Saturn). The cycles of a man's years may match the cycles of the heavenly spheres to show that their lives followed a meaningful pattern and ended with a completed cycle. **died.** See 3:19 and its note. In spite of this judgment, God's grace preserved the Messianic line (see 3:15 and its note), even while sin abounded in the earth (4:17–24).

5:21–24 In Biblical genealogies the seventh member is often favored (see note on vv. 1–32; Heb 11:5; Jude 14).

5:22 walked with God. This rare expression (used only in vv. 22,24; 6:9; Mal 2:6) signifies intimate fellowship with God, not merely having lived a pious life (3:8; 6:9).

5:23 365 years. Perhaps a symbolic number corresponding to the days of the solar year and signifying a life of special privilege.

5:24 he was no more. He did not die (Heb 11:5). **God took him away.** So also Elijah (2Ki 2:1,5,9–10). The same language is used of resurrection (Pss 49:15; 73:24).

5:29 He will comfort us. See NIV text note. Whereas the Cainite Lamech sought to redress wrong through unjust revenge (4:24), the Sethite Lamech looked to the Lord to provide the seed through whom would come deliverance from the curse.

5:32 500 years old. See note on 6:3. **father of Shem, Ham and Japheth.** See 9:18, where their story is resumed.

The Flood

6 When men began to increase in number on the earth[e] and daughters were born to
them, 2the sons of God saw that the daughters of men were beautiful, and they married any of them they chose. 3Then the LORD said, "My Spirit will not contend with[a] man
forever,[f] for he is mortal[b];[g] his days will be a hundred and twenty years."
4The Nephilim[h] were on the earth in those days—and also afterward—when the sons
of God went to the daughters of men and had children by them. They were the heroes
of old, men of renown.
5The LORD saw how great man's wickedness on the earth had become, and that every inclination of the thoughts of his heart was only evil all the time.[i] 6The LORD was
grieved[j] that he had made man on the earth, and his heart was filled with pain. 7So the
LORD said, "I will wipe mankind, whom I have created, from the face of the earth—men
and animals, and creatures that move along the ground, and birds of the air—for I am
grieved that I have made them." 8But Noah found favor in the eyes of the LORD.[k]

9This is the account of Noah.

Noah was a righteous man, blameless among the people of his time,[l] and he walked
with God.[m] 10Noah had three sons: Shem, Ham and Japheth.[n]

6:1 [e]Ge 1:28
6:3 [f]Isa 57:16 [g]Ps 78:39
6:4 [h]Nu 13:33
6:5 [i]Ge 8:21; Ps 14:1-3
6:6 [j]1Sa 15:11,35; Isa 63:10
6:8 [k]Ge 19:19; Ex 33:12,13,17; Lk 1:30; Ac 7:46
6:9 [l]Ge 7:1; Eze 14:14, 20; Heb 11:7; 2Pe 2:5 [m]Ge 5:22
6:10 [n]Ge 5:32

[a] 3 Or *My spirit will not remain in* [b] 3 Or *corrupt*

■ **6:1–8** *Escalation of Sin Before the Flood.* This section, by the mention of Noah (5:32; 6:8–9), forms the transition from the godly line of Seth to the flood story (6:9—9:17). It reaches back to the ominous situation at the end of the Cainite lineage (4:17–24).
6:1 daughters. See 5:4.
6:2 sons of God. They have been variously identified as the Sethites (the traditional Christian interpretation); as angels (the earliest Jewish interpretation, perhaps in agreement with 2Pe 2:4; Jude 6–7); and as royal tyrannical successors to Lamech (the interpretation of second-century A.D. rabbis). All three views can be defended linguistically. Superficially, the first interpretation best fits the immediate context, contrasting the curse-laden line of Cain with the godly line of Seth, but it fails to explain adequately why the phrase "daughters of men" refers to Cainite women. The second interpretation has the support of antiquity but seems to contradict Jesus' statement that angels do not marry (Mk 12:25). It also fails to explain why the focus is on mortals (v. 3) and the judgment on them (vv. 5–7). The third interpretation best explains the phrase "any of them they chose" (12:10–20; 20:1; 1Sa 11), but evidence for its existence prior to the second century A.D. is lacking. The best solution is probably a combination of the latter two interpretations. These tyrants were the offspring of Cain (3:15), empowered by evil (Dt 32:17). **beautiful . . . married.** The Hebrew words here mean "good" and "took." Their sin repeated the pattern of the original sin: "saw . . . good . . . took" (3:6). They were driven by lust, not by spiritual discernment. "Took" is not the normal word for "married" and may imply abduction or even rape—such a reading accords well with God's condemnation of their actions (vv. 5–7).
6:3 My Spirit. The Spirit of God is the source of natural life (Ps 104:29–30). When God withdraws his Spirit, his creatures die (see notes on 1:4; 2:7). **contend.** The unique Hebrew may mean "shield/protect" on the basis of an Akkadian cognate (see NIV text note). If so, the sense is that God's Spirit would not forever enliven those who disordered God's world (see note on 1:2). **a hundred and twenty years.** Probably the span of time between this proclamation and the ensuing flood (5:32; 7:6). Some have taken this as a reference to an individual's life span, but that premise seems to be contradicted by the age of the people living after the flood (ch. 11). God's judgment was seasoned by grace (cf. 1Pe 3:20). The delay allowed time for people to repent and provided testimony of the coming judgment through Noah and his building of the huge ark. See *BC* 15.
6:4 Nephilim. Also called "heroes." These vicious warriors, some of whom were the offspring of the "sons of God" (see note on v. 2) filled the earth with violence (v. 11; Nu 13:32–33). The Hebrew root means "to fall" and may suggest their fate (Isa 14:12) or their character (Gal 5:4). **and also afterward.** In this parenthetical remark Moses reminded his original readers that the same kind of powerful, evil people existed in their own day (Nu 13:33). **heroes.** The Hebrew here is also used for Nimrod and his bestial kingdom (10:8–11). This term is best understood as sarcasm (Isa 5:22) or as a simple reflection of popular opinion.
6:5 every inclination. A vivid portrayal of the depth and comprehensiveness of human depravity (cf. 8:21). The situation portends the end of history at the second coming of Christ (Lk 17:26–27; 18:8; 2Ti 3:1–5; Rev 20:7–10). **heart.** See Proverbs 4:23. See *WCF* 6.2; 6.4; *WLC* 25,149; *WSC* 82; *HC* 5,8; *CD* 3–4.IV.
6:6 was grieved. The Hebrew here is also translated "changed his mind," a reference to a change of attitude and action. This is not a reference to God's immutable character, eternal plan or covenant promises (see Nu 23:19; 1Sa 15:29). Instead, it refers to God's providential involvement in history. When people sin or repent of sin, God responds in a variety of ways (Ex 32:12,14; 1Sa 15:11; 2Sa 24:16; Jer 18:9–10; Am 7:3,6). **pain.** The Hebrew here means "indignant rage." See *WCF* 3.1; 3.2; *WLC* 12; *WSC* 7,8.
6:7 I will wipe. God's judgment of the first cosmos (lasting from creation to the flood) is a prophetic model of the coming second judgment on the second cosmos (lasting from the flood to the future destruction by fire; 2Pe 3:5–7). **animals . . . air.** As the ground endured the consequences of its rulers' sin, so also must the animals.
6:8 But Noah. See Hebrews 11:7. **found favor.** Noah found God's grace not only in spite of sin, but also because of his righteousness (v. 9). He is a type of Christ, for his righteousness secured salvation for his family.
■ **6:9—9:29** *Account of Noah.* Noah, who is listed exactly midway in the genealogies between Adam and Abraham, is a pivotal figure in chapters 1–11, and the account of Noah and his family records a pivotal event in that history. Moses raced through the millennia between Adam and Noah and between Noah and Abraham. Yet he significantly slowed the action for the six-hundredth year of Noah's life. In that year, through a cataclysmic flood, God wiped out the seed of the serpent (the wicked and faithless of humankind) but spared the righteous seed of the woman (Noah, and his family through him) and with them his creation in miniature.

Stories of a cataclysmic flood survive from all over the world, but none are as strikingly similar to this account as those of ancient Mesopotamia. In the Mesopotamian narratives, however, the petty gods brought the flood to control overpopulation and/or to rid the earth of the annoying noise of people. Once it came, they were frightened by it, and afterward, when their worshipers presented sacrifices to them, they gathered around hungrily to eat the offerings. In Genesis, however, God sovereignly brought about the flood because of humanity's wickedness. In response to Noah's sacrifices, however, God pledged never again to destroy the earth.

These chapters cover the provision for the flood with a divine monologue pertaining to God's covenant with Noah (6:9–22); the embarkation (7:1–10); the increasing waters (7:11–12); the prevailing waters (7:13–24); the decreasing waters (8:1–14); the disembarkation (8:15–19); and God's provisions after the flood with another divine monologue pertaining to his covenant with Noah (8:20—9:17). The sevenfold division revolves around the center of the story: "God remembered Noah" (8:1). The narratives in 6:1–8 and 9:18–29 serve as transitions between accounts (see notes on 4:25–26).

Many parallels exist between the histories before and after the flood: the creation of the cosmos out of chaotic waters (1:1—2:3; 8:1—9:16); the division of the founders' sons into elect and reprobate lines (4:1–26; 9:24–28); the actions of evil people, Cain and Nimrod, in building cities and making names for themselves (4:17–24; 10:8–12; 11:1–9); the preservation of godly lines (5:1–32; 11:10–26); and faithful agents of blessing, Noah and Abraham, in the fallen world (6:1–8; 11:27—12:9). The parallel judgment on the

6:11 [o]Eze 7:23; 8:17 **6:12** [p]Ps 14:1-3 **6:13** [q]ver 17; Eze 7:2-3

11Now the earth was corrupt in God's sight and was full of violence.[o] 12God saw how
corrupt the earth had become, for all the people on earth had corrupted their ways.[p] 13So
God said to Noah, "I am going to put an end to all people, for the earth is filled with violence because of them. I am surely going to destroy both them and the earth.[q] 14So

reprobate (6:9—7:24) will take place in the fire at the second coming of Jesus Christ (2Pe 3:13–17).

■ **6:9—7:10** *Preparation for the Flood.* Noah was chosen and proved faithful in all of his duties as he prepared for the great flood.

6:9–22 This section balances with 8:20—9:17. It features the covenant relationship between God and Noah. Noah was righteous (v. 9), obeying God's commands (see notes on 7:5,9,16), and God confirmed his covenant with him to preserve his creation (v. 18).

6:9 This is the account of. See note on 2:4. **righteous.** The word presupposes a relationship with God that included moral standards. These were revealed to Noah through nature (Ro 1:18–32) and special revelations. **blameless.** Literally means "whole, complete," signifying wholehearted commitment. "Blameless" denotes abstaining from sin but not being entirely without sin (see 9:20–23; 2Sa 22:24). The pairing of "blameless" and "righteous" suggests that Noah was wholly committed to righteousness (see Dt 32:4; Pss 18:30; 19:7–8). **walked with God.** See 5:22. Faith led to diverse consequences: Abel died, Enoch did not die and Noah saw almost everyone else die (Heb 11:4–7). But eventually all of the faithful will be raised from the dead and rewarded.

6:10 three sons. See 5:32; 9:18ff.

6:11 corrupt. This expression, which occurs seven times in the narrative, means "to spoil or disfigure." **violence.** From Cain's murder (4:1–16) to Lamech's murder (4:19–23) to the violation of women (vv. 1–8), the history leading up to Noah has been full of violence. As the Spirit brought the first cosmos out of the chaotic waters (see 1:2 and its note), so also the Spirit in connection with Noah would bring the second cosmos out of chaotic waters associated with violence (1Pe 3:18–20; 2Pe 3:5–7).

6:12 all the people. Literally, "all flesh." Here it may also refer to animals as well as people (6:19; 7:16; 8:17; 9:11,15–17).

6:13 destroy. The same Hebrew word lies behind the translations

The Covenants of Works and Grace: What Is Covenant Theology?

In the seventeenth century an outlook developed in Reformed theology that saw covenants between God and humanity as central to the teaching of Scripture. In older works this approach to the Bible was called *Federalism.* In our day, it is more common to speak of this perspective simply as *Covenant Theology.*

In traditional Covenant Theology, the whole history of the Bible was divided into two major covenant relationships: the *covenant of works* and the *covenant of grace.* Neither of these expressions appears in the Bible, but the distinctions form helpful theological categories that reflect the underlying unity of Scripture, much as the term "Trinity" summarizes one essential aspect of the truth of Scripture about God. This dual covenant approach to Scripture finds a clear expression in the Westminster Confession and Catechisms (*WCF* 7.1–5; 19.1,6; *WLC* 31–36,97).

In Reformed theology the term *covenant of works* refers to the arrangement God made between himself and Adam before humanity's fall into sin. It does not refer to the covenant made with Moses at Sinai, as other Christian traditions tend to use the term. In the covenant of works with Adam, God promised blessings to Adam if he obeyed the command of God (Ge 1:28–30), but judgment if he disobeyed (Ge 2:15–17). The determining factor was Adam's works, thus the term *covenant of works* (cf. Hos 6:7). In recent years, the value of describing Adam's relationship with God as a covenant of works has been questioned; many prefer simply to speak of a pre-redemptive arrangement or probation before the fall into sin. In all events, the Scriptures indicate that Adam failed to keep God's command. So God made a second covenant arrangement, the covenant of grace in Christ.

The terminology *covenant of grace* is used to describe God's relationship with his people throughout the rest of Scripture. Properly speaking, this covenant was ultimately made with Christ as the last Adam, the representative of redeemed humanity. It is designated a covenant of grace because it operates on the basis of divine grace offered through Christ's death and resurrection to all who believe in him. Some Reformed theologians have spoken of a heavenly, eternal covenant between the Father and the Son, which they have called the *covenant of redemption* (Jn 6:37). The covenant of grace is the historical expression of this eternal covenant.

The covenant of grace began with the promise made after the fall that the seed of the woman would one day crush the seed of the serpent (Ge 3:15). After this, the covenant of grace unfolded in five major stages of Biblical history. None of these covenant stages opposes any other. On the contrary, each subsequent stage builds upon the previous ones.

(1) After its initiation with God's grace offered to Adam (Ge 3:15), the covenant of grace developed through the covenant of nature's preservation given to Noah (Ge 6:18; 9:9–17). Noah's covenant focused on the stability of the present order of nature until the end of all things, thus providing a stable arena within which God's redemptive plan would unfold. (2) Next, God's covenant with Abraham (Ge 15; 17) began several stages of covenants made with the nation of Israel as God's special chosen people. God promised that Abraham's descendants would receive great blessings and would be the instrument of blessing to the entire human race. (3) Following this, the nation of Israel received Moses' covenant of law (Ex 19–24) during the exodus from Egypt, in order to guide the nation toward greater blessings in the land of promise. (4) When David became king, God then made a royal covenant with him (2Sa 7; Pss 89; 132), in which he promised to bless David's faithful sons and never to take the throne of Israel away from David's family. (5) Finally, the climax of the covenant of grace came through the new covenant established by Christ (Jer 31; Lk 22:20; 1Co 11:25; Heb 8:8–13). This covenant comes in three stages: the first coming of Christ, the history before his return and the consummation of his kingdom. As the covenant of grace unfolded in this manner, the various stages did not differ in substance but were "one and the same under various dispensations" (*WCF* 7.6).

make yourself an ark of cypress[a] wood;[r] make rooms in it and coat it with pitch[s] inside
and out. 15This is how you are to build it: The ark is to be 450 feet long, 75 feet wide and
45 feet high.[b] 16Make a roof for it and finish[c] the ark to within 18 inches[d] of the top. Put
a door in the side of the ark and make lower, middle and upper decks. 17I am going to
bring floodwaters on the earth to destroy all life under the heavens, every creature that

6:14 [r]Heb 11:7; 1Pe 3:20 [s]Ex 2:3

[a] *14* The meaning of the Hebrew for this word is uncertain. [b] *15* Hebrew *300 cubits long, 50 cubits wide and 30 cubits high* (about 140 meters long, 23 meters wide and 13.5 meters high) [c] *16* Or *Make an opening for light by finishing* [d] *16* Hebrew *a cubit* (about 0.5 meter)

"corrupt" and "corrupted" in verses 11–12. The punishment matched the crime: As humankind ruined the good earth, so God would spoil the good earth so that it would no longer feed and enrich humanity. Through its corruption, society set in motion the process of inevitable self-destruction.

6:14 make yourself. The Lord specified the construction of the ark. He did not entrust the means of salvation to human imagination. **ark.** This key word is used seven times in the instructions to build the ark and seven times in the report of the subsiding of the waters (8:1–4), but only once again in Scripture in the salvation of baby Moses (where "ark" is translated "basket" in Ex 2:3). Noah prefigured Moses, whom God also used to bring forth a new humanity from a world under judgment.

6:15 450 . . . 45. Its length and its dimensions, like those of modern ships, afforded it the necessary capacity for its cargo and rendered it seaworthy. By contrast, the ark described in a Babylonian story, though pitched within and without, would have been unable to float, as it was a 180-foot cube, about five times larger in volume than Noah's ark (see 7:4 and its note).

6:17 floodwaters. God sovereignly ruled over the flood (Ps

The stages of the covenant of grace manifested in God's Old Testament national covenants with Israel had the special role of preparing God's people for the coming of his Son, who would fulfill all of God's promises and give substance to the shadows cast by Old Testament types (Isa 40:10; Mal 3:1; Jn 1:14; Heb 7–10). In the new covenant the temporary arrangements for imparting those blessings are replaced by the realization of that which they anticipated, namely Jesus Christ, the Mediator of the new covenant, the Seed of Abraham and heir of his promises (Gal 3:16). Christ obeyed the law perfectly and offered himself as the true and final sacrifice for sin. As the royal son of David, he now reigns over the world as the inheritor of all the covenant blessings of pardon, peace, and fellowship with God in his renewed creation—blessings he now bestows upon believers (Ro 8:17). Christ's sending of the Spirit from the throne of his glory seals God's people as his own, even as he gives himself to them (2Co 1:22; Eph 1:13–14).

As Hebrews 7–10 explains, the new covenant is the supreme expression of God's one eternal covenant of grace with sinners (Heb 13:20)—a better stage of the covenant than those of the Old Testament, with better promises (Heb 8:6), based on a better sacrifice (Heb 9:23), offered by a better high priest in a better sanctuary (Heb 7:26—8:13) and guaranteeing a better hope than the former versions of the covenant ever made explicit. The fulfillment of the old national covenants in Christ brings to fruition the promise that the door of faith would be open to large numbers of Gentiles. To extend the kingdom of God throughout the world (see theological article "The Kingdom of God" at Mt 4), Gentiles and Jews alike become Abraham's seed by faith in Christ (Gal 3:26–29), while Jews and Gentiles outside of Christ are also outside the covenant of grace (Ro 4:9–17; 11:13–24).

Scripture describes the elements of God's covenants with his people in ways that parallel the international treaty arrangements of human emperors in the ancient Near East. Either explicitly or implicitly, four basic dynamics appear in each stage of the Biblical covenant: (1) God shows himself to be the benevolent King who initiates and sustains his chosen people throughout their covenant relationship with him. (2) God requires loyal gratitude from the people embraced by his covenants. (3) Judgments come against those who flagrantly violate his covenants. (4) Blessings come to those who are faithful to the covenants.

As the divine King of the universe (see theological article "The Kingdom of God" at Mt 4), God's covenantal dealings guided the kingdom forward toward its ultimate end: the gathering of a redeemed people "from every nation, tribe, people and language" (Rev 7:9), who will inhabit a renewed world order (Rev 21:1–5). Here the covenant relationship will find its fullest expression: "They will be his people, and God himself will be with them and be their God" (Rev 21:3). The kingdom of God still moves toward that goal in our day.

The dual framework of the covenants of works and grace describes the whole of God's sovereign dealings with humanity. Salvation comes to us because Christ fulfilled the requirements of the covenant of works through his perfect obedience. As a result, our salvation is covenant salvation: Justification and adoption, regeneration and sanctification are covenant mercies; election was God's choice of the members of his final, purified covenant community, the invisible church (see theological article "The Church: Visible and Invisible" at 1 Pe 4); baptism and the Lord's Supper, corresponding to circumcision and Passover, are covenant ordinances; God's law is covenant law, and keeping it is the truest expression of gratitude and loyalty in response to God's covenant grace. Renewing our covenant commitments to God in response to his faithfulness should be a regular devotional exercise for all believers, both in private and in public worship. An understanding of the covenant of grace guides us through and helps us to appreciate not only the diversity of Scripture, but its amazing unity as well.

has the breath of life in it. Everything on earth will perish.[t] 18But I will establish my covenant with you,[u] and you will enter the ark[v]—you and your sons and your wife and your
sons' wives with you. 19You are to bring into the ark two of all living creatures, male and
female, to keep them alive with you. 20Two[w] of every kind of bird, of every kind of animal and of every kind of creature that moves along the ground will come to you to be
kept alive. 21You are to take every kind of food that is to be eaten and store it away as
food for you and for them."
22Noah did everything just as God commanded him.[x]
7 The LORD then said to Noah, "Go into the ark, you and your whole family,[y] because
I have found you righteous[z] in this generation. 2Take with you seven[a] of every kind
of clean[a] animal, a male and its mate, and two of every kind of unclean animal, a male
and its mate, 3and also seven of every kind of bird, male and female, to keep their various kinds alive throughout the earth. 4Seven days from now I will send rain on the earth
for forty days and forty nights, and I will wipe from the face of the earth every living creature I have made."
5And Noah did all that the LORD commanded him.[b]
6Noah was six hundred years old when the floodwaters came on the earth. 7And Noah
and his sons and his wife and his sons' wives entered the ark to escape the waters of the
flood. 8Pairs of clean and unclean animals, of birds and of all creatures that move along
the ground, 9male and female, came to Noah and entered the ark, as God had commanded Noah. 10And after the seven days the floodwaters came on the earth.
11In the six hundredth year of Noah's life, on the seventeenth day of the second
month—on that day all the springs of the great deep[c] burst forth, and the floodgates of
the heavens[d] were opened. 12And rain fell on the earth forty days and forty nights.[e]
13On that very day Noah and his sons, Shem, Ham and Japheth, together with his wife

6:17 [t]Ge 7:4,21-23; 2Pe 2:5
6:18 [u]Ge 9:9-16 [v]Ge 7:1,7,13
6:20 [w]Ge 7:15
6:22 [x]Ge 7:5,9,16
7:1 [y]Mt 24:38 [z]Ge 6:9; Eze 14:14
7:2 [a]ver 8; Ge 8:20; Lev 10:10; 11:1-47
7:5 [b]Ge 6:22
7:11 [c]Eze 26:19 [d]Ge 8:2
7:12 [e]ver 4

[a] 2 Or *seven pairs*; also in verse 3

29:10), which both punished and purged the world. **earth . . . all life.** A worldwide flood seems to be in view (7:19–23; 8:21; 9:11,15; 2Pe 3:5–7). Yet comprehensive language can be used for limited situations (see 11:1; see 7:17–20 and its notes; Da 2:28; 4:22; 5:19). At the very least, the flood covered all of the populated regions of the earth, judging all of humanity except those in the ark. **breath.** The Hebrew here is translated "Spirit" in verse 3 (cf. 7:15). See 1:2 and its note.

6:18–20 God preserved his creation in miniature: human beings (v. 18), animals (v. 19), vegetables (v. 20). In that some of every sort were preserved, God's work here was a type of Christ's work of definite redemption (e.g., see Rev 5:9, where Christ is said to have purchased not all, but some from "every tribe and language and people and nation").

6:18 establish. The Hebrew here does not mean "to initiate" but rather "to confirm" preexisting terms (cf. 17:7,19,21; 26:3; Nu 23:19; 30:14). A covenant solemnized and confirmed a social relationship already in existence. Moses' readers knew from verse 8 that Noah enjoyed God's favor prior to this confirming covenant (see 5:29). In Noah's six-hundredth year, God more specifically obligated himself to preserve Noah through the imminent flood. After the flood, God would again confirm his covenant with Noah to preserve his creation in spite of sin (8:20–22; 9:9–17). **covenant.** This is the first appearance of this important term in the Bible (see theological article "Major Covenants in the Bible" on p. 25). The Hebrew word is closely related to the concept of "obligation." God graciously obliged himself to save those who worshiped him and to save his creation as well. That obligation was linked with Noah's righteousness (v. 9) and obedience (v. 22; see also 17:1–2). God's grant was worked out through Noah's building of the ark (vv. 14–16) and through his entering and provisioning it (vv. 19–21). **your sons . . . with you.** This refrain (7:7,13; 8:16,18; cf. 7:1) emphasizes that God preserved humanity in its basic family structure and that his salvation extended to the entire family, including children. As Noah's children were delivered because of Noah's righteousness (7:1), so the children of believers in all ages are the expected heirs of the divine covenants. Here the covenant relationship is secured in the midst of floodwater, a type of Christian baptism (1Pe 3:20–21).

6:20 of every kind. The connection of this verse to 1:20–23 is unmistakable (see note on vv. 18–20).

6:22 Noah did. These few words underscore that Noah lived by faith (Heb 11:7), but they hide the tremendous effort and investment involved. It must have taken Noah years of work to cut down the multitude of needed trees, convey them to his building site and fit and join the huge planks. Moreover, he must have spent a fortune building a boat of such a prodigious size and provisioning it with a sufficient and varied food supply for so many people and animals.

7:1–10 See note on 6:9—9:29. The gathering and preservation of this family is a prototype of God's salvation of his elect in the day of the Lord (Mt 3:12; 24:31; 2Th 2:1). This remnant, however, would prove itself a mixture of elect in Christ and non-elect (see notes on 9:20–27).

7:1 your whole family. See 6:18 and its note. **righteous.** See 6:9 and 18 and their notes.

7:2–3 These precise directives clarify, rather than contradict, those of 6:19–20.

7:2 seven. To keep them from extinction, additional clean animals were necessary because Noah needed them for sacrifice (8:20). **every kind.** See note on 6:20. **clean.** The Hebrew here means "pure" (i.e., "pure-formed"; see Lev 10:10; 11:1–47). Noah would have known of the distinction between pure and impure because he "walked with God" (5:22; see 6:9 and its note). Fundamental institutions of the law, Sabbath (2:1–3), divine sanctuary (ch. 2) and sacrifice (3:21; 4:3–5) reached back to the beginning. Earth's future depended on these sacrificial animals (see 8:20–22 and its notes).

7:4 Seven days. It took 120 years to build the ark (see 6:3 and its note) and one week to fill it. A Babylonian account seems to imagine seven days to build a ship much larger than Noah's (see 6:15 and its note) and a flood lasting seven days (vv. 11–12; 8:4). **forty.** A conventional number for a long time. It represents the introduction of a new age by Noah, Moses (Ex 24:18), Elijah (1Ki 19:8) and Christ (Ac 1:3), respectively. The 40 days are part of the 150 total days that Noah and his family lived in the ark (vv. 11–12; 8:4).

7:5–10 See note on 6:9—9:29.

7:5 commanded. This threefold repeated refrain (vv. 5,9,16) marks off the section (see note on 6:22).

7:6 six hundred years old. See note on 6:3. The precise day is given in verse 11.

7:7 flood. See 6:17 and its note.

7:9 came. See note on 6:20. **as God had commanded Noah.** See notes on verses 5 and 16.

■ **7:11—8:19** *The Flood and Salvation.* Moses took up the story of the deliverance of righteous Noah (6:9; 7:1) and his household by beginning with the account of increasing waters (see notes on 6:9—9:29; 7:11). In distinguishing grace, God shut Noah in safely behind the door of the ark, while shutting out the world of the wicked.

7:11 springs . . . floodgates. Poetic expressions for the unrestrained release of water (Ps 78:23; Isa 24:18; Mal 3:10). God returned the earth to primordial chaos by the release of the bound waters above and by the upsurge of the subterranean waters (see notes on 1:2,6–8; 8:2–5). God was about to re-create the world. **deep.** See note on 1:2.

and the wives of his three sons, entered the ark. 14They had with them every wild animal according to its kind, all livestock according to their kinds, every creature that moves
along the ground according to its kind and every bird according to its kind, everything
with wings. 15Pairs of all creatures that have the breath of life in them came to Noah and
entered the ark.[f] 16The animals going in were male and female of every living thing, as
God had commanded Noah. Then the LORD shut him in.
17For forty days[g] the flood kept coming on the earth, and as the waters increased they
lifted the ark high above the earth. 18The waters rose and increased greatly on the earth,
and the ark floated on the surface of the water. 19They rose greatly on the earth, and all
the high mountains under the entire heavens were covered.[h] 20The waters rose and covered the mountains to a depth of more than twenty feet.[a,b] 21Every living thing that
moved on the earth perished—birds, livestock, wild animals, all the creatures that
swarm over the earth, and all mankind.[i] 22Everything on dry land that had the breath of
life[j] in its nostrils died. 23Every living thing on the face of the earth was wiped out; men
and animals and the creatures that move along the ground and the birds of the air were
wiped from the earth.[k] Only Noah was left, and those with him in the ark.[l]
24The waters flooded the earth for a hundred and fifty days.[m]

8 But God remembered[n] Noah and all the wild animals and the livestock that were
with him in the ark, and he sent a wind over the earth,[o] and the waters receded.
2Now the springs of the deep and the floodgates of the heavens[p] had been closed, and
the rain had stopped falling from the sky. 3The water receded steadily from the earth. At
the end of the hundred and fifty days the water had gone down, 4and on the seventeenth
day of the seventh month the ark came to rest on the mountains of Ararat. 5The waters
continued to recede until the tenth month, and on the first day of the tenth month the
tops of the mountains became visible.
6After forty days Noah opened the window he had made in the ark 7and sent out a raven, and it kept flying back and forth until the water had dried up from the earth. 8Then
he sent out a dove to see if the water had receded from the surface of the ground. 9But
the dove could find no place to set its feet because there was water over all the surface
of the earth; so it returned to Noah in the ark. He reached out his hand and took the dove
and brought it back to himself in the ark. 10He waited seven more days and again sent
out the dove from the ark. 11When the dove returned to him in the evening, there in its
beak was a freshly plucked olive leaf! Then Noah knew that the water had receded from
the earth. 12He waited seven more days and sent the dove out again, but this time it did
not return to him.
13By the first day of the first month of Noah's six hundred and first year, the water had
dried up from the earth. Noah then removed the covering from the ark and saw that the

7:15 [f]Ge 6:19
7:17 [g]ver 4
7:19 [h]Ps 104:6
7:21 [i]Ge 6:7,13
7:22 [j]Ge 1:30
7:23 [k]Mt 24:39; Lk 17:27; 1Pe 3:20; 2Pe 2:5 [l]Heb 11:7
7:24 [m]Ge 8:3
8:1 [n]Ge 9:15; 19:29; Ex 2:24; 1Sa 1:11, 19 [o]Ex 14:21
8:2 [p]Ge 7:11

[a] 20 Hebrew *fifteen cubits* (about 6.9 meters) [b] 20 Or *rose more than twenty feet, and the mountains were covered*

7:13–16 See note on 6:18–20. The full roll call echoes chapter 1.
7:13 On that very day. This phrase connotes a memorable occasion (17:23,26; Ex 12:41,51; Dt 32:48).
7:15 breath. The Hebrew here is also translated "spirit." **came.** See note on 6:20.
7:16 the LORD shut. In a Babylonian account of the flood, the hero shuts the door. God is the chief actor throughout the Biblical account. So it will also be in the day of the Lord's coming (Mt 25:10–13).
7:17–24 In this climactic section (see note on 6:9—9:29) the chaotic waters multiply and triumph in destroying the creation. Contrast this scene with the meaning of "bless" (see note on 1:22).
7:17 forty. See note on verse 4.
7:18 rose. The Hebrew word, repeated three times, is a military term for triumphing in battle.
7:19 all. This key Hebrew word, variously translated "all" (vv. 19,21), "entire" (v. 19), "every" (vv. 21,23) and "everything" (v. 22), denotes the all-encompassing devastation and death inflicted by the flood.
7:20 twenty feet. The story assumes that the ark's draft was half its height.
7:21 The creatures are listed in the order in which they were created in chapter 1.
7:22 breath. See note on verse 15.
7:23 Only . . . the ark. See note on 6:18. The flood was the divine agent for punishing the old world and for purifying humanity for the new one.
8:1–14 See note on 6:9—9:29.
8:1 God remembered Noah. The Hebrew word translated "remembered," especially with reference to God, signifies an act that is taken based on a previous commitment (9:15; 19:29; 30:22; Ex 2:24; 6:5; Lk 1:72–73). **wind.** The Hebrew root for "wind" is translated "Spirit" in 1:2. This was God's first act in renewing the earth out of the chaotic waters (see notes on vv. 2–5,6–13,15–19; 9:1–3). He repeated this action in creating Israel (see note on Ex 14:21), who would also pass over on dry ground (see v. 13 and its note; Ex 14:16,22,29). **receded.** The militant waters now began to retreat (see notes on 7:18; Ex 14:26,28; Jos 4:18).
8:2–5 The return of the earth to chaos was stopped by the regathering of the lower and upper waters, God's second act in renewing the earth (see 1:6–8; 8:1 and their notes).
8:4 See 7:19–20. **mountains of Ararat.** In the area of ancient Urartu (2Ki 19:37), now part of eastern Turkey, Armenia, Azerbaijan and northwestern Iran. The reference is too imprecise to specify the exact mountain range.
8:6–12 In a Babylonian account of the flood, the hero sends out a dove, a swallow and a raven. The difference in the sequence profiles again the superiority of the Biblical account. The raven could have braved the storm, fed on carrion and, as the stronger bird, remained in flight much longer. The birds once again had dominion over the heavens, God's third act in renewing the earth (see 1:20–23; 8:1 and their notes).
8:6 forty. See 7:4 and its note.
8:9 brought it back to himself in the ark. The speed of the narrative, which has been racing through weeks in one verse, slows dramatically to provide this cameo of Noah, who models God's concern to preserve the creation (Pr 12:10). See note on 6:9.

surface of the ground was dry. 14 By the twenty-seventh day of the second month the
earth was completely dry.
15 Then God said to Noah, 16 "Come out of the ark, you and your wife and your sons
and their wives.[q] 17 Bring out every kind of living creature that is with you—the birds, the
animals, and all the creatures that move along the ground—so they can multiply on the
earth and be fruitful and increase in number upon it."[r]
18 So Noah came out, together with his sons and his wife and his sons' wives. 19 All the
animals and all the creatures that move along the ground and all the birds—everything
that moves on the earth—came out of the ark, one kind after another.
20 Then Noah built an altar to the LORD[s] and, taking some of all the clean animals and
clean[t] birds, he sacrificed burnt offerings[u] on it. 21 The LORD smelled the pleasing aroma[v]
and said in his heart: "Never again will I curse the ground[w] because of man, even
though[a] every inclination of his heart is evil from childhood.[x] And never again will I destroy all living creatures,[y] as I have done.

22 "As long as the earth endures,
seedtime and harvest,
cold and heat,
summer and winter,
day and night
will never cease."[z]

God's Covenant With Noah

9 Then God blessed Noah and his sons, saying to them, "Be fruitful and increase in
number and fill the earth.[a] 2 The fear and dread of you will fall upon all the beasts
of the earth and all the birds of the air, upon every creature that moves along the
ground, and upon all the fish of the sea; they are given into your hands. 3 Everything that
lives and moves will be food for you.[b] Just as I gave you the green plants, I now give you
everything.

8:16 [q]Ge 7:13
8:17 [r]Ge 1:22
8:20 [s]Ge 12:7-8; 13:18; 22:9 [t]Ge 7:8; Lev 11:1-47 [u]Ge 22:2,13; Ex 10:25
8:21 [v]Lev 1:9,13; 2Co 2:15 [w]Ge 3:17 [x]Ge 6:5; Ps 51:5; Jer 17:9 [y]Ge 9:11, 15; Isa 54:9
8:22 [z]Ge 1:14; Jer 33:20,25
9:1 [a]Ge 1:22
9:3 [b]Ge 1:29

[a] *21* Or *man, for*

8:13 ground . . . dry. The words for "dried up" and "dry" differ in Hebrew. Even after Noah saw that the earth had dried out, he waited patiently almost another two months until it was completely dry (v. 14), waiting for the divine word that it was safe to disembark. The reestablished earth was ready for its rulers once again; this constituted God's fourth act in renewing the earth (see notes on 1:10,11; 8:1).
8:14 See notes on 6:17–20.
8:15–19 See note on 6:19—9:29. The pattern is again command and obedience (6:13–22). The reentrance of the animals and of humankind onto the land marks God's fifth step in renewing the earth (see notes on 1:24–27; 8:1).
8:16 Come out. Since the flood is a type of Christian baptism (1Pe 3:20–21), the emergence of the covenant people out of the ark may be thought of as their rising out of the waters of death into a new life (see Jn 5:28–29; 11:43–44; Ro 6:3–5). Noah and the members of his family prefigure the new humanity who will prevail over evil (Rev 21:7). **your sons.** See note on 6:18.
8:17 Bring out. The Hebrew here is translated "produce(d)" in 1:11 and 24. See note on verses 15–19. **multiply.** This directive, matching 1:20–22, marks God's sixth act in renewing the earth (see note on v. 1).
8:18 So Noah came out. See notes on 6:9–22 and on 7:5, 9 and 16.
■**8:20—9:17** *God's Covenant Not to Destroy.* God promised not to judge again through a worldwide flood. See note at 6:9—9:29.
8:20–22 Whereas God had spared the earth on the basis of Noah's righteousness, now, on the basis of Noah's sacrifice, he resolved never again to destroy it in spite of humanity's sin (see notes on 6:9–22,18). Noah, the priest, and his sacrifice are a prototype of Israel's priests and their sacrifices (see Job 1:5; 42:8). They ultimately point to the great high priest Jesus Christ and to his sacrifice of himself (Isa 53; Heb 2:17).
8:20 altar . . . burnt offerings. Though mentioned for the first time, these aspects of the sacrificial system are presupposed. See note on 7:2. The burnt offering expressed both dependence and propitiation (Lev 1:4). See note on verse 21. Noah symbolically consecrated his kingdom to God, once again prefiguring Christ (1Co 15:28). **clean.** See note on 7:2.
8:21 pleasing. The sweet savor of the offerings soothed God's indignation against sin (6:6), prefiguring Christ's death (Isa 53:10). The Hebrew root used in Noah's name (5:29) recurs in this word. In the pagan flood account, the gods gather "like flies" around the sacrifice. **in his heart.** The Septuagint (the Greek translation of the OT) paraphrases the term as "having considered," apparently in order to explain clearly the connection between the soothing sacrifice and God's resolve (see note on v. 21; Lev 17:11). **Never again . . . curse the ground.** God was referencing his judgment by water, not the troubles that resulted from Adam's sin (see Heb 3:17 for different terminology regarding judgment on sin). **even though.** God mediated his mercy through Noah for the natural world, through Moses for Israel and through Christ for all the elect. **every inclination . . . from childhood.** The change from "all the time" (6:5) to "from childhood" emphasizes that human depravity is passed on biologically (Pss 51:5; 58:3). God saw that even the great flood was insufficient to do away with human depravity. **never again . . . destroy.** God's grace toward Noah was extended to humanity in general (6:8; 9:11). See *WCF* 6.4; *WLC* 149; *WSC* 82; *HC* 8.
8:22 As long as the earth endures. This expression qualifies "never again" in verse 21. God will preserve the earth and its ecology until the final judgment (2Pe 3:7,13); it will not end prematurely. See *WCF* 5.2.
9:1–17 See note on 6:9—9:29.
9:1–7 The repeated command to "be fruitful" (vv. 1,7) repeats 1:28–30 but modifies the food law (v. 3) and focuses on the sanctity of human life (4:1–24). This framework ordains the propagation of life (vv. 1,7), the protection of human life by curbing violence (vv. 2,4–6) and the sustenance of life (vv. 2–3). Before the flood the lack of capital punishment had led to blood vendettas (see ch. 4).
9:1–3 God's blessing on Noah—that he would be fruitful and have dominion—constitutes the seventh and climactic act in renewing the cosmos (1:28–30; see 8:1 and its note).
9:1 blessed. See 1:22 and its note. This is the third time God has blessed human beings (1:28; 5:2) and commanded them to be fruitful (1:28; v. 7).
9:2 fear and dread of you. This military term is probably stronger than "rule over" in 1:28. Human beings fear God, and animals fear human beings (Isa 8:12–13). **given into your hands.** Humanity holds the power of life and death over the animal kingdom.
9:3 Everything . . . everything. Perhaps because of a changed climate, the human diet was expanded. No distinction is here made between clean and unclean (contrast 7:2), a situation later restored under the new covenant (Mk 7:19; Ac 10:9–16; 1Ti 4:3–5). **that lives and moves.** Human beings may not eat a cadaver (Lev 11:40; Dt. 14:21) or blood (v. 4; Lev 17:10). **food.** See note on 1:29–30.

Major Covenants in the Bible

Covenants	References	Participants	Divine Benevolence	Human Loyalty
Covenant of Works	Ge 1:28–30; 2:15–17	Made with Adam as head of humanity.	Adam was created in God's image and given the role of expanding human vice-regency from Eden to the entire earth by means of multiplication and dominion.	Adam was required to pass the test of the forbidden fruit or he would bring the judgment of death to the entire human race.
Covenant of Grace	Ge 3:15; Isa 42:6	Made with Christ as head of redeemed humanity.	Christ received the promise of an elect people whom he redeemed from the Fall through the history of salvation culminating in his humiliation, exaltation and glorious return.	Christ fulfilled the obligations of human loyalty that Adam failed to keep and gives eternal life to the elect.
Noahic Covenant	Ge 6:18–22; 9:8–17	Made with Noah as father of humanity.	Noah was redeemed from the flood and granted a stable creation within which human vice-regency could extend through multiplication and dominion over the entire earth.	Noah and his descendants were required to observed God's moral requirements or suffer the judgment of death.
Abrahamic Covenant	Ge 15:9–21; 17:1–27	Made with Abraham as father of Israel.	Abraham was chosen to further the vice-regency of humanity first through the multiplication and dominion of his redeemed descendants in the land of Canaan and then through extending the blessing of redemption throughout the entire earth.	Abraham and Israel were required to live righteously and to observe circumcision, which symbolized judgment against those who violated God's moral requirements.
Mosaic Covenant	Ex 19–24	Made with Israel through Moses' mediation.	Israel was redeemed from slavery in Egypt and granted holy laws to guide their vice-regency as redeemed humanity first through multiplication and dominion in the land of Canaan and then in the entire earth.	Israel was required to observe the law of Moses or suffer the judgment from God which would culminate in defeat and exile from the land.
Davidic Covenant	2Sa 7:5–16; Ps 89; 132	Made with David as head of Israel's permanent royal dynasty.	David was promised a permanent dynasty to further the vice-regency of Israel as redeemed humanity first through multiplication and dominion in the land of Canaan and then in the entire earth.	The descendants of David were required to observe the law of Moses or suffer judgment from God culminating in temporary defeat and the exile from the throne of Israel.
New Covenant	Isa 54:10; Jer 31:31–34; Eze 34:25; 37:26	Made with Israel and Judah for the time of Christ after exile.	Israel was promised complete redemption from sin and unprecedented blessings in vice-regency through multiplication and dominion over the entire new creation.	All of God's people throughout the world will be fully redeemed from sin in Christ and will observe the law of God perfectly through the power of the Spirit of Christ.

[4]"But you must not eat meat that has its lifeblood still in it.[c] [5]And for your lifeblood
I will surely demand an accounting. I will demand an accounting from every animal.[d]
And from each man, too, I will demand an accounting for the life of his fellow man.[e]

[6]"Whoever sheds the blood of man,
by man shall his blood be shed;[f]
for in the image of God[g]
has God made man.

[7]As for you, be fruitful and increase in number; multiply on the earth and increase
upon it."[h]
[8]Then God said to Noah and to his sons with him: [9]"I now establish my covenant with
you[i] and with your descendants after you [10]and with every living creature that was with
you—the birds, the livestock and all the wild animals, all those that came out of the ark
with you—every living creature on earth. [11]I establish my covenant[j] with you: Never
again will all life be cut off by the waters of a flood; never again will there be a flood to
destroy the earth.[k]"
[12]And God said, "This is the sign of the covenant[l] I am making between me and you
and every living creature with you, a covenant for all generations to come: [13]I have set
my rainbow in the clouds, and it will be the sign of the covenant between me and the
earth. [14]Whenever I bring clouds over the earth and the rainbow appears in the clouds,
[15]I will remember my covenant[m] between me and you and all living creatures of every
kind. Never again will the waters become a flood to destroy all life. [16]Whenever the rainbow appears in the clouds, I will see it and remember the everlasting covenant[n] between
God and all living creatures of every kind on the earth."
[17]So God said to Noah, "This is the sign of the covenant[o] I have established between
me and all life on the earth."

The Sons of Noah

[18]The sons of Noah who came out of the ark were Shem, Ham and Japheth. (Ham was
the father of Canaan.)[p] [19]These were the three sons of Noah, and from them came the
people who were scattered over the earth.[q]
[20]Noah, a man of the soil, proceeded[a] to plant a vineyard. [21]When he drank some of

9:4 [c]Lev 3:17; 17:10-14; Dt 12:16,23-25; 1Sa 14:33
9:5 [d]Ex 21:28-32 [e]Ge 4:10
9:6 [f]Ge 4:14; Ex 21:12, 14; Lev 24:17; Mt 26:52 [g]Ge 1:26
9:7 [h]Ge 1:22
9:9 [i]Ge 6:18
9:11 [j]ver 16; Isa 24:5 [k]Ge 8:21; Isa 54:9
9:12 [l]ver 17; Ge 17:11
9:15 [m]Ex 2:24; Lev 26:42,45; Dt 7:9; Eze 16:60
9:16 [n]ver 11; Ge 17:7, 13,19; 2Sa 7:13; 23:5
9:17 [o]ver 12; Ge 17:11
9:18 [p]ver 25-27; Ge 10:6,15
9:19 [q]Ge 10:32

[a] *20* Or *soil, was the first*

9:4 not eat . . . lifeblood. See Leviticus 3:17, 7:27, 19:26, Deuteronomy 12:16 and 1 Samuel 14:32–34. This law reveals the connection between blood and life (2:7), a concept basic to the sacrificial system (Lev 17:11) and to the atoning work of Christ (Heb 9:14,22). The regulation also protected life against wanton abuse.
9:5 I will surely demand an accounting. This phrase for exacting compensation is emphatically repeated three times. An animal's blood could be shed for food, but homicidal blood was to be avenged. The Lord was its vindicator (2Ki 9:26; Ps 9:12; Heb 12:24). Human bloodshed invested the guilty with its pollution (Nu 35:33; Ps 106:38) and secured its expiation by the death of the murderer (v. 6; 1Ki 2:31–32) or through atonement (Dt 21:7–9). If these measures were not used, it brought the Lord's judgment on the land (Dt 19:13; 2Sa 21; 1Ki 2:9,31–33). **from every animal.** For example, see Exodus 21:28–29. **fellow man.** The Hebrew word used here is translated "brother" in 4:8–11. This legislation was designed to restrain the violence begun in the days of Cain and Abel. At that time God protected the murderer (4:15), but here he condemned murderers to execution.
9:6 by man. See note on verse 5. God's investment of human beings with this judicial authority shows that they stand in God's stead as rulers (1:26) and lays the foundation for government by the state (Ro 13:1–7). Exacting retribution is a societal obligation, not a personal matter. Since this time, society has rested on a more secure moral footing. **image.** In spite of their depravity, human beings remained God's image-bearers (see note on 1:26). This is why homicidal blood, in contrast to animal blood, was to be avenged. See theological article "Human Beings in God's Image" at Genesis 1. See *WLC* 136; *WSC* 69; *HC* 105.
9:9 I now establish. See 6:18 and its note. God unilaterally took full responsibility to preserve the earth and its complete ecology forever in order to sustain the human race (8:20–22). The covenant confirmed God's preexisting relationship with all creatures when he blessed them at the time of their creation. In 6:18 the covenant was exclusively with Noah; now it was extended to his descendants in common grace and to "every living creature" (v. 10). **covenant.** See notes on 6:9–22; 6:18. See theological article "Major Covenants in the Bible" on page 25.
9:12 sign. The rainbow "sign" forms a frame around verses 12–17. Covenants were usually certified by some visual symbols that were often already in existence: circumcision for Abraham's covenant (17:11), the Sabbath for Moses' covenant (Ex 31:13,17) and the cup for Christ's covenant (Lk 22:20). David's covenant required none, since his offspring were its visible token (2Sa 7:11–16).
9:13 rainbow. The Hebrew reads simply "bow," a battle weapon and a hunting instrument. As lightning bolts are the Lord's arrows (Ps 18:14), he also has a bow of war. Here the warrior's bow is hung up, pointed away from the earth, a sign of peace. The relaxed bow stretches from earth to heaven and extends from horizon to horizon, reminding God of his covenant commitment. See *BC* 33.
9:15 remember. See note on 8:1.
9:16 see. Contrast with 6:12. The transcendent God, who humbles himself to involve himself with people, deliberately chose to reflect on this colorful vision rather than on humanity's evil (see 6:12). **everlasting.** The Hebrew word may be relativized by the context, in this case by "as long as the earth endures" (8:22).
▪ **9:18–29** *Prophecies About Noah's Sons.* This transition is linked with Noah's covenant by continuing the prophetic overview of history and with the table of nations by focusing on Noah's three sons (10:1). Framed by the genealogical notes in verses 18 and following and 28 and following, this story illustrates the future piety and virtue of the Shemites and Japhethites and the moral degradation of the Hamites, who include the Egyptians, Babylonians and Canaanites. Noah's sons carried on both the seed of the serpent and the seed of the woman.
9:18 father of Canaan. This parenthetical statement prepares the audience for the important topic of the Canaanites. Ham's immoral action foreshadowed their spiritual degradation and established a ground for Israel's later conquest of Canaan.
9:20 soil. The Hebrew here is the same word translated "ground" in 5:29. It connects Noah with Adam, who was formed from the ground (2:7). **proceeded.** The Hebrew means "he began," implying a new, as opposed to a renewed, activity. **vineyard.** The vine came originally from Armenia, where the ark came to rest (see 8:4).

its wine, he became drunk and lay uncovered inside his tent. 22Ham, the father of Canaan, saw his father's nakedness and told his two brothers outside. 23But Shem and Japheth took a garment and laid it across their shoulders; then they walked in backward
and covered their father's nakedness. Their faces were turned the other way so that they
would not see their father's nakedness.

24When Noah awoke from his wine and found out what his youngest son had done
to him, 25he said,

"Cursed be Canaan![r]
The lowest of slaves
will he be to his brothers.[s]"

26He also said,

"Blessed be the LORD, the God of Shem!
May Canaan be the slave of Shem.[a]
27May God extend the territory of Japheth[b];
may Japheth live in the tents of Shem,
and may Canaan be his[c] slave."

28After the flood Noah lived 350 years. 29Altogether, Noah lived 950 years, and then
he died.

The Table of Nations

10 This is the account[t] of Shem, Ham and Japheth, Noah's sons, who themselves
had sons after the flood.

9:25 [r]ver 18 [s]Ge 25:23; Jos 9:23

10:1 [t]Ge 2:4

[a] *26* Or *be his slave* [b] *27* *Japheth* sounds like the Hebrew for *extend.* [c] *27* Or *their*

9:21 drank some of its wine. Scripture looks favorably on wine (Nu 15:5–10; Dt 14:26; Ps 104:15; Jn 2:1–11), but soberly warns of the dangers of its excess (Pr 21:17; 23:20–21,29–35; Isa 5:22; 28:7). Excessive consumption of wine causes moral laxity (Hab 2:15). Nazirites (Nu 6:3–4), officiating priests (Lev 10:9) and rulers responsible for making decisions (Pr 31:4–5) were to abstain from it. **lay uncovered.** Although Noah uncovered himself in private, his action occasioned his younger son's sin, and his older sons felt it necessary to cover their father's nakedness. See *WLC* 130.
9:22 saw his father's nakedness. See note on 3:1 The Hebrew word means "to look at (searchingly)" (see SS 1:6; 6:11). It is not altogether clear what Ham did. A number of interpretations have been offered: (1) Ham's voyeurism violated his father's dignity (see 3:7; Hab 2:15). If this was homosexual stimulation by visual means, it was worsened by the fact that it was committed against his father, whom he should have honored even above others (Ex 21:15,17; Dt 21:18–21; Mk 7:10). That Shem and Japheth covered Noah while averting their eyes (v. 23) accords well with this reading. (2) The Hebrew for uncovering someone's nakedness is a euphemism for having sex with that person (the NIV consistently translates this concept in terms of "sexual relations;" Lev 18:6–19; 20:11,17–21). This may indicate that Ham homosexually molested his father. This interpretation may explain Noah's extreme outrage at what Ham "had done to him" (v. 24). (3) On the basis that the Hebrew term for "father's nakedness" may also be identified with one's father's wife (see Lev 18:8, 20:11, where the NIV renders the Hebrew for "father's nakedness" in terms of dishonoring him), and in conjuction with the preceding argument that uncovering nakedness refers to sexual relations, some interpreters also suggest that Ham had sexual relations with his mother. **told.** If it is wrong to publicize another's sin (Pr 10:12; 17:9), how much more a father's? See *WLC* 145.
9:23 covered . . . nakedness. Because they behaved like God (3:22), God would bless them both (vv. 26–27). See *WLC* 127.
9:24–27 God's words in verses 1–23 pertained to human history in general, but they had particular importance for the nation of Israel as its people followed Moses toward the conquest of Canaan.
9:24 youngest. See note on verse 25.
9:25 Cursed. The Canaanites succeeded the Cainites as the curse-laden descendants of the serpent (see notes on 3:14–15; 4:11). **Canaan.** In light of Moses' immediate circumstance of facing conquest in Canaan, it is not strange that he focused on the curse of Canaan instead of on Ham individually (vv. 18,22). Ham's descendants included, in addition to the Canaanites, Israel's most dreaded enemies: Egypt, Philistia, Assyria and Babylon (10:6–13). **lowest of slaves.** By this curse God excluded the Canaanites as a people from the covenant of grace (Dt 7:3–6; Ro 9:12–13) and anticipated the conquest of the land of Canaan. Nevertheless, God elected some individuals even from among the cursed Canaanites (see notes on Jos 2:11–12). Moreover, when the Israelites behaved like the Canaanites, God rejected them and thrust them from his presence (see 2Ki 17:20).
9:26 Blessed. By this doxological benediction Noah acknowledged God as the author of life and extended the blessing to Shem (see 1:22 and its note; 14:19). **God of Shem!** God sovereignly committed himself to Shem's offspring for the Messiah's lineage (see 3:15; 4:26 and their notes). In the Old Testament God favored the descendants of Shem (especially Israel) over others, but as this passage indicates, his favor was for the purpose of sharing salvation with others. By the time of the New Testament, Israel had been exiled for over 500 years, and only a remnant believed. Later, the ministries of Christ and his apostles fulfilled the expectation that Israel's blessings would extend to the Gentiles. In Christ, God shows no racial favoritism (Ac 10:34–35) and reckons all who believe as Abraham's children (Gal 3:29).
9:27 live in the tents. The figure implies displacement (see Job 18:14–15). The promise was fulfilled in the New Testament (Ac 14:27; Ro 11).
9:28–29 The genealogy begun in 5:32 is now completed according to the pattern of chapter 5. Because of this, 6:9—9:27 may be seen as a parenthesis within 5:1—9:29.
■ **10:1—11:9** *Account of Shem, Ham and Japheth.* The narrative of Noah's family history includes the table of nations (ch. 10) and the tower of Babel (11:1–9). Chronologically the former follows the latter, for it assumes the story; but, whereas that story represents the nations as confused and scattered due to God's judgment, this catalog represents them as of one blood, multiplying under God's blessing (but see note on 9:25). The two sections are linked verbally by "scattered" (10:18; 11:4) and "Shinar" (10:10; 11:2).
■ **10:1–32** *Table of Nations.* This record is framed by the similarity of verses 1 and 32. The table presents a segmented genealogy of Noah's three sons to show the relationships of their descendants. It also includes two biographical notes on Nimrod and Peleg, both of which foreshadow the tower of Babel narrative. The table does not aim to give an exhaustive list of all peoples (see v. 5). Its intentions are theological, and its clear tripartite arrangement represents the threefold division of humanity (vv. 1,32): verses 2–5, verses 6–20 and verses 21–31 (see 9:24 27 and its note). The Japhethites migrated westward, the Hamites south by southwest and the Semites south by southeast. The number of nations is given as 70: 14 from Japheth, 30 from Ham and 26 from Shem. Israel's 70 sons are a microcosm of the nations (see 46:27 and its note). The number 70,

The Japhethites

2 The sons[a] of Japheth:
Gomer,[u] Magog,[v] Madai, Javan, Tubal,[w] Meshech and Tiras.
3 The sons of Gomer:
Ashkenaz,[x] Riphath and Togarmah.[y]
4 The sons of Javan:
Elishah, Tarshish,[z] the Kittim and the Rodanim.[b] 5 (From these the maritime
peoples spread out into their territories by their clans within their nations, each
with its own language.)

The Hamites

6 The sons of Ham:
Cush, Mizraim,[c] Put and Canaan.[a]
7 The sons of Cush:
Seba, Havilah, Sabtah, Raamah and Sabteca.
The sons of Raamah:
Sheba and Dedan.

8 Cush was the father[d] of Nimrod, who grew to be a mighty warrior on the earth. 9 He
was a mighty hunter before the LORD; that is why it is said, "Like Nimrod, a mighty hunter before the LORD." 10 The first centers of his kingdom were Babylon,[b] Erech, Akkad and
Calneh, in[e] Shinar.[f][c] 11 From that land he went to Assyria,[d] where he built Nineveh,[e] Rehoboth Ir,[g] Calah 12 and Resen, which is between Nineveh and Calah; that is the great city.

13 Mizraim was the father of
the Ludites, Anamites, Lehabites, Naphtuhites, 14 Pathrusites, Casluhites (from
whom the Philistines[f] came) and Caphtorites.

10:2 [u]Eze 38:6 [v]Eze 38:2; Rev 20:8 [w]Isa 66:19
10:3 [x]Jer 51:27 [y]Eze 27:14; 38:6
10:4 [z]Eze 27:12,25; Jnh 1:3
10:6 [a]ver 15; Ge 9:18
10:10 [b]Ge 11:9 [c]Ge 11:2
10:11 [d]Ps 83:8; Mic 5:6 [e]Jnh 1:2; 4:11; Na 1:1
10:14 [f]Ge 21:32,34; 26:1,8

[a] *2 Sons* may mean *descendants* or *successors* or *nations*; also in verses 3, 4, 6, 7, 20–23, 29 and 31. [b] *4* Some manuscripts of the Masoretic Text and Samaritan Pentateuch (see also Septuagint and 1 Chron. 1:7); most manuscripts of the Masoretic Text *Dodanim* [c] *6* That is, Egypt; also in verse 13 [d] *8 Father* may mean *ancestor* or *predecessor* or *founder*; also in verses 13, 15, 24 and 26. [e] *10* Or *Erech and Akkad—all of them in* [f] *10* That is, Babylonia [g] *11* Or *Nineveh with its city squares*

a multiple of seven and ten (connoting completeness and fullness), represents a large (Jdg 8:30; 2Ki 10:1) and complete number. Some names are personal (e.g., Japheth and Nimrod); others are place-names (e.g., Sidon and Sheba) or names of peoples (e.g., Ludim and Capthorim). This selective list is not always racial; the phrases "sons of" and "the father of" might refer to a political, geographical, social or linguistic relationship (4:20–21; 10:31). Some belong to more than one family because of early mixtures. All these families, with the exception of the cursed Canaanites (see 9:25 and its note; vv. 15–19), would be blessed through their brother Abraham (see 12:3 and its note). Jebus (v. 16) would become God's holy mountain and Jerusalem/Zion God's answer to Nimrod's Babylon (v. 10).
10:1 This is the account. See 2:4.
10:2 Japheth. See 9:27. **Gomer.** The later Cimmerians. **Magog.** Lydia. **Madai.** The later Medes. **Javan.** The Ionian Greeks. **Tubal.** Often mentioned with Meshech (Eze 27:13; 38:2). **Meshech.** Phrygia. **Tiras.** Turcsha (region of the Aegean Sea) or Thrace.
10:3 Ashkenaz. Scythians. **Riphath.** "Riphath" in 1 Chronicles 1:6; "Diphath" in NIV text note at 1 Chronicles 1:6. **Togarmah.** In the region of Armenia.
10:4 Elishah. Probably Cyprus. **Tarshish.** Proposals range from Carthage to Tartessus in southwestern Spain. **Kittim.** Southern Cyprus. **Rodanim.** Rhodes.
10:5 maritime. The Hebrew term means "islands." **spread out.** Occurred after the tower of Babel (11:1–9).
10:6–20 The Egyptians, Babylonians and Canaanites—Israel's most bitter adversaries and influential neighbors—are mentioned in this list (see note on 9:25).
10:6 Cush. The dark-skinned tribes south of Egypt. **Mizraim.** Egypt. **Put.** Libya. **Canaan.** The southern Levant from southern Syria, so including Phoenicia and the whole of the region much later known as Palestine, west of the Jordan.
10:7 sons of Cush. Most settled in southern Arabia. **Seba.** Northern Africa.
10:8–12 This break in the genealogy would be of great importance to later generations. It explains the racial and spiritual origins of the Assyrians and Babylonians, who conquered the Israelites and held them as exiles.
10:8 Nimrod. His name means "we shall rebel" (11:1–9). This hunter and warrior was an archetype of Mesopotamian ideals of kingship. Nimrod founded his empire on naked aggression. His might was so great that it became proverbial in Israel (v. 9). His empire included all of Mesopotamia, both Babylonia in the south (v. 10) and Assyria in the north (vv. 10–12). As the chief centers of his empire, he founded the great cities of Babylonia, most notably Babylon (v. 10), and subsequently, having moved to Assyria, the greater city of Nineveh (v. 11). Some interpreters have identified him with the known historical king Sargon I. **grew.** The Hebrew here means "began to be." It is used in 4:26, 6:1, 9:20 and 11:6 for other important innovations in history. **warrior.** Literally, "tyrant," a title that may link him with the infamous tyrants in 6:4.
10:9 before the LORD. Even in the Lord's estimation, Nimrod was a fearful warrior and tyrant.
10:10 first. The Hebrew may refer to chronological order and/or level prominence. **Babylon.** The political and religious antithesis to Jerusalem, it was in Israel's world what Rome was to the Middle Ages. The Babylonians later became the infamous destroyers of Judah. **Erech.** Modern Warka, in Iraq, the site at which archaeologists situate the birth of civilization (see 4:20–22). Assyria later deported the inhabitants of this area to Samaria (Ezr 4:9–10). **Akkad.** The home of the famous Sargon I. Its location is unknown. **Calneh.** Unidentified. **Shinar.** All of Mesopotamia.
10:11 Assyria. See note on "Asshur" at verse 22. The cruelest nation known in ancient history (see Mic 5:5). The Assyrians became the infamous destroyers of Israel's northern kingdom. **Calah.** Nimrud, in Iraq, 20 miles south of Nineveh.
10:12 great city. Calah or Nineveh (Jn 1:2; 3:2–3; 4:11).
10:13 Mizraim. Egypt, the infamous house of slavery. **Ludites.** See note on verse 22. Refers to the Lydians of North Africa, not those of Asia Minor. **Anamites.** Identification is uncertain; possibly Egyptian people. **Lehabites.** Unidentified. **Naphtuhites.** Inhabitants of Middle or Lower (i.e., northern) Egypt.
10:14 Pathrusites. People of Pathros. **Casluhites.** Unidentified. **Philistines.** Not one of the 70 nations, but mentioned parenthetically to identify another bitter foe of Israel. They may have migrated to Caphtor (Crete) and from there settled in southwest Canaan around 1200 B.C. (see Am 9:7). The references to the Philistines in 21:32 and 34 and 26:1–35 probably refer to smaller settlements of the Sea Peoples, who arrived during the patriarchal period and lived there intermittently. **Caphtorites.** Cretans.

[15]Canaan[g] was the father of
Sidon[h] his firstborn,[a] and of the Hittites,[i] [16]Jebusites,[j] Amorites, Girgashites,
[17]Hivites, Arkites, Sinites, [18]Arvadites, Zemarites and Hamathites.

Later the Canaanite[k] clans scattered [19]and the borders of Canaan[l] reached from Sidon[m] toward Gerar as far as Gaza, and then toward Sodom, Gomorrah, Admah and Zeboiim, as far as Lasha.
[20]These are the sons of Ham by their clans and languages, in their territories and nations.

The Semites

[21]Sons were also born to Shem, whose older brother was[b] Japheth; Shem was the ancestor of all the sons of Eber.[n]

[22]The sons of Shem:
Elam,[o] Asshur, Arphaxad,[p] Lud and Aram.
[23]The sons of Aram:
Uz,[q] Hul, Gether and Meshech.[c]
[24]Arphaxad was the father of[d] Shelah,
and Shelah the father of Eber.[r]
[25]Two sons were born to Eber:
One was named Peleg,[e] because in his time the earth was divided; his brother was named Joktan.
[26]Joktan was the father of
Almodad, Sheleph, Hazarmaveth, Jerah, [27]Hadoram, Uzal, Diklah, [28]Obal,
Abimael, Sheba, [29]Ophir, Havilah and Jobab. All these were sons of Joktan.

10:15 [g]ver 6; Ge 9:18 [h]Eze 28:21 [i]Ge 23:3,20
10:16 [j]1Ch 11:4
10:18 [k]Ge 12:6; Ex 13:11
10:19 [l]Ge 11:31; 13:12; 17:8 [m]ver 15
10:21 [n]ver 24; Nu 24:24
10:22 [o]Jer 49:34 [p]Lk 3:36
10:23 [q]Job 1:1
10:24 [r]ver 21

[a] *15* Or *of the Sidonians, the foremost* [b] *21* Or *Shem, the older brother of* [c] *23* See Septuagint and 1 Chron. 1:17; Hebrew *Mash* [d] *24* Hebrew; Septuagint *father of Cainan, and Cainan was the father of* [e] *25 Peleg* means *division.*

10:15–19 The area of Canaan, the curse-laden people (see note on 9:25), extended from modern southwest Syria to Gaza (Nu 34). **Hittites.** These pre-Israelites are not to be identified with the great Hittite Empire in Asia Minor; their Biblical names are Semitic, not Hittite. They were progenitors of Jerusalem (Eze 16:3), who lived in Judah's territory during the Patriarchal period (ch.23). Their immorality repulsed Isaac and Rebekah (27:46), but Esau intermarried with them (26:34–35).
10:16 Jebusites. See Judges 19:10 and 12 and 2 Samuel 5:6–9. Their names are Hurrian. **Amorites.** The Old Testament uses the term loosely (Dt 3:8; Jos 10:5; 11:3). Some of the most famous dynasties of Babylon came from these "westerners." They, too, were progenitors of Jerusalem (Eze 16:3); they were scattered through Israel's hill country on either side of the Jordan (48:22; Nu 13:29; Dt 3:8; Jos 10:5; Jdg 10:8; 11:21–23). **Girgashites.** See 15:18–21 (see also Dt 7:1–5; Jos 3:10–17).
10:17 Hivites. They lived in Lebanon and Syria (Jos 11:3; Jdg 3:3) and some in Shechem and Gibeon (34:2; Jos 9:1,7). **Arkites.** Residents of Arqad, northwest of Tripoli. **Sinites.** From the Ugarit (modern Ras Shamra) in Phoenicia.
10:18 Arvadites. Inhabitants of Ruad, 50 miles north of Byblos. **Zemarites.** They located about 12 miles south of Arwad. **Hamathites.** Hamath is modern Hama on the Orontes River (2Sa 8:9–10; 2Ki 18:34–35). It marked the northernmost boundary of the land of Canaan (Nu 34:7–9; Jos 13:5; 1Ki 8:65; 2Ki 14:25–28). **scattered.** This key word foreshadowed the punitive judgment on the tower builders.
10:19 borders of Canaan. Critical for identifying the land sworn to the patriarchs. **Gerar.** Modern Tell Abu Hureireh, located 11 miles southeast of Gaza. It sets the scene for chapters 20–21 and 26. **Sodom . . . Zeboiim.** These sites east or southeast of the Dead Sea set the scene for chapters 13–14 and 18–19. All four were overthrown when God rained down brimstone on them. **Lasha.** Perhaps the northern end of the Dead Sea.
10:21–31 The elect line is presented last (see note on vv. 1–32) and overlaps with the more specific lineage of the elect Eber (v. 21) in 11:10–26.
10:21 older brother. According to the NIV text note, the chronological order is Shem, Japheth and Ham (9:24). Ham is usually presented second for phonetic reasons (v. 1). **ancestor.** The Hebrew here is the same word translated elsewhere as "father"; Shem was at least Eber's great-great-grandfather (see v. 24; 11:13–14 and their NIV text notes). **Eber.** The background on the origin of this Hebrew word for *Hebrew* is uncertain. Traditionally, *Hebrew* has been identified from this proper name. More recently, interpreters have favored the source being the nomadic Habiru (see note on Ex 1:15). In the first case, Eber was the heir of God's blessing on Shem, even as Canaan, son of Ham, was the target of Noah's curse. The Ebla texts (2350 B.C.) mention Ebrium, possibly this Eber, as a king of Ebla, capital of the earliest empire known in history. See note on 14:13. The genealogy accents Eber by mentioning him out of order (see vv. 21,24), by repeating his name both as son of Shelah and as father of Peleg and Joktan and by mentioning at the outset that Shem is the father of all his sons.
10:22 Elam. Modern southwestern Iran (see 14:1,9; Ezr 4:9; Isa 11:11). **Asshur.** Possibly a northern Sinaitic tribe (25:3,18), not the dreaded Assyrians in Israel's later history (v. 11). **Arphaxad.** Territory is uncertain. **Lud.** See verse 13. Home of the Lydians of Asia Minor (Isa 66:19; Eze 27:10). **Aram.** As a place name it refers to the whole kingdom of the Aramean tribes or to diverse sites in Syria and Mesopotamia. Amos 9:7 traces the Arameans to Kir, perhaps in southern Babylonia in the vicinity of Elam (see Isa 22:6). The patriarchs had close relations with the Arameans (see 25:20; 31:20; Dt 26:5).
10:23 sons of Aram. Little is known about them. **Uz.** See 22:21; Job 1:1. **Hul, Gether.** Unidentified. **Meshech.** See NIV text note.
10:24–25 These verses are expanded in 11:12–17.
10:24 father of Shelah. See NIV text note for the Greek version; the Greek addition is found in Luke 3:36 in the lineage of Jesus Christ. Shelah means "sprout, branch or descendant." His identity is uncertain. **Eber.** See verse 21. He was the direct heir of God's blessing on Shem (see 9:26 and its note). Shem's lineage probably gave Eber's name (i.e., "Hebrew") to the patriarchs and to Israel (e.g., 14:13; 39:14; 40:15; 41:12; Ex 2:11; 3:18).
10:25 Peleg. See NIV text note and 11:18. His name, which means "division," probably prophesied the dispersal of the nations at Babel (see Lamech's prophecy in 5:29). It may also signify the separation of the elect from the non-elect line. **earth was divided.** Probably a reference to the division of the peoples into nations (11:8ff.). In Psalm 55:9 the same Hebrew word is translated "confound their speech." **Joktan.** Means "watchful." His non-elect branch would contrast with his brother's (11:16–26).
10:26–29 Joktan . . . Joktan. His descendants located in southern Arabia.
10:26 Almodad. Ancestor, region or tribe in Yemen. **Sheleph.** A Yemenite tribe. **Hazarmaveth.** The south Arabian region of Hadhramaut.
10:27 Hadoram. Arabian tribe Uzal. **Diklah.** South Arabian oasis meaning "palm land."
10:28 Obal. Between Hodeida and San'a in southwest Arabia.

30 The region where they lived stretched from Mesha toward Sephar, in the eastern hill
country.
31 These are the sons of Shem by their clans and languages, in their territories and nations.
10:32 [s]ver 1 [t]Ge 9:19
32 These are the clans of Noah's sons,[s] according to their lines of descent, within their
nations. From these the nations spread out over the earth[t] after the flood.

The Tower of Babel

11:2 [u]Ge 10:10
11 Now the whole world had one language and a common speech. 2 As men moved
eastward,[a] they found a plain in Shinar[b u] and settled there.
11:3 [v]Ex 1:14 [w]Ge 14:10
3 They said to each other, "Come, let's make bricks[v] and bake them thoroughly." They
used brick instead of stone, and tar[w] for mortar. 4 Then they said, "Come, let us build our-
11:4 [x]Dt 1:28; 9:1 [y]Ge 6:4 [z]Dt 4:27
selves a city, with a tower that reaches to the heavens,[x] so that we may make a name[y]
for ourselves and not be scattered over the face of the whole earth."[z]

[a] 2 Or *from the east*; or *in the east* [b] 2 That is, Babylonia

First Chronicles 1:22 and the Samaritan version read "Ebal." **Abimael.** Unidentified.

10:29 Ophir. Situated between Sheba and Havilah in southwest Arabia and identified as having gold in its wadis (seasonal river beds) (Job 22:24), it possibly included the coast of Africa on the opposing shore, which is called the land of Punt in Egyptian sources. **Havilah.** See verse 7. **Jobab.** In southern Arabia.

10:30 region where they lived. The reference to the region of Joktan's sons shows the importance of the Shemites to sacred history. **from Mesha.** Territory in northern Arabia. **toward Sephar.** Traditionally a city in the south of Hadhramaut or on a harbor in Oman or Yemen.

10:32 these the nations. The Greek and Samaritan versions read "these islands of the nations." **spread out.** The change from "sons" (v. 1) to "spread out" prepares the way for chapter 11.

■ **11:1–9** *Escalation of Evil in Babylon.* The story is framed by "language" (v. 1) and "the whole world" (v. 9). A Babylonian story celebrates the building of Babylon and its temple tower, and a Sumerian epic speaks of a time when all human beings spoke or would speak the same language (cf. Zep 3:8–9). The same overweening pride behind the attempts to overcome the boundaries ordained by God that inspired rebellious Eve and Adam to rival deity (3:5) and the ungodly Cain to name his city after man (4:17) now motivated "the whole earth" (v. 4). The city and tower were connected with Nimrod's anti-god kingdom (see 10:8–12 and its notes) by the mention of "Shinar" (10:10; 11:2) and "Babel" (= Babylon; 10:10; 11:9). See note on 10:1—11:9.

11:2 eastward. Here the word "eastward" marks separation. It connotes that the people of Babel were outside God's blessing (cf. 3:24; 4:16; 13:10–12; 25:6; 29:1). **Shinar.** See 10:10 and 14:1.

11:4 let us build. See Psalm 127:1. The Hebrew grammar underscores the builders' willful resolve. **city.** See note on 4:17. **tower.** The Hebrew, from the root "to be great," has a wide range of meanings. Here it designates the Mesopotamian ziggurat. The ziggurat was a massive, lofty, solid-brick, staircaselike structure. It was an inseparable part of a city, and sometimes the temple complex comprised the entire city. **that reaches to the heavens.** The ziggurat supposedly served as a gate to heaven (see note on 11:9; 28:12,17). It culminated in a small shrine at the top, often painted with blue enamel to make it blend with the celestial home of the gods. The addition "to the heavens" shows these people were vying with God himself (cf. 19:24; 21:17; 22:11,15; Dt 26:15; Ps 115:16). **make a name.** Since "name" connotes fame and progeny, these city builders were futilely attempting to find significance and immortality in their own achievements (see 6:4). Ironically, the people of Babel earned for themselves the ignominious name "confused" (see note on v. 9). In contrast, God gave an everlasting name (12:2) to Abraham, who magnified the Lord's name (4:26; 12:8; Isa 63:12,14). Abraham looked for the city the Lord will one day build. **not be scattered.** This skyscraper was a symbol of the

Table of Nations

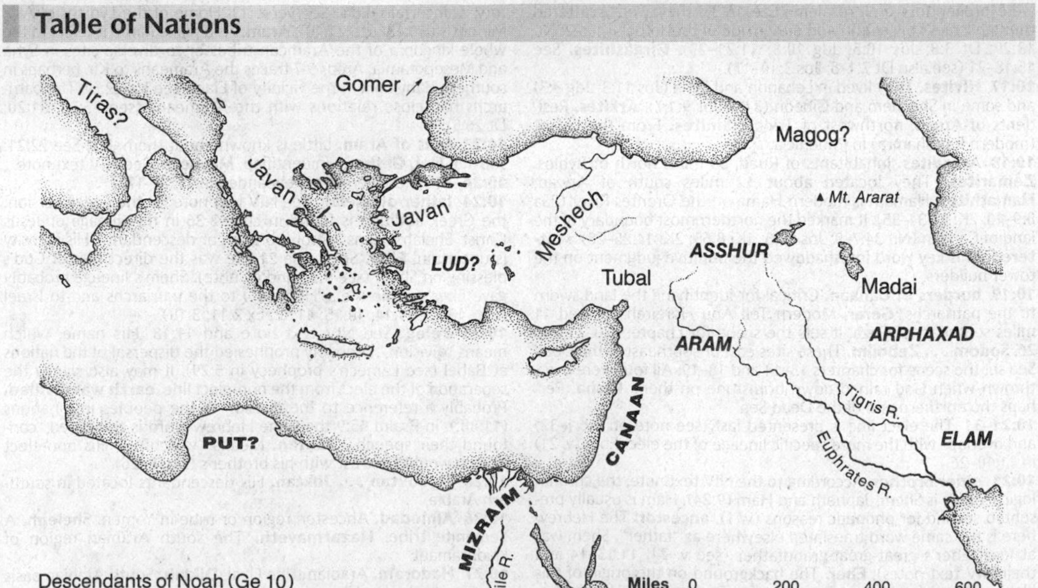

5But the LORD came down[a] to see the city and the tower that the men were building.
6The LORD said, "If as one people speaking the same language they have begun to do this,
then nothing they plan to do will be impossible for them. 7Come, let us[b] go down and
confuse their language so they will not understand each other."[c]

8So the LORD scattered them from there over all the earth,[d] and they stopped building the city. 9That is why it was called Babel[a][e]—because there the LORD confused the language of the whole world. From there the LORD scattered them over the face of the whole
earth.

From Shem to Abram

10This is the account of Shem.

Two years after the flood, when Shem was 100 years old, he became the father[b] of
Arphaxad. 11And after he became the father of Arphaxad, Shem lived 500 years and had
other sons and daughters.
12When Arphaxad had lived 35 years, he became the father of Shelah.[f] 13And after he
became the father of Shelah, Arphaxad lived 403 years and had other sons and daughters.[c]
14When Shelah had lived 30 years, he became the father of Eber. 15And after he became the father of Eber, Shelah lived 403 years and had other sons and daughters.
16When Eber had lived 34 years, he became the father of Peleg. 17And after he became
the father of Peleg, Eber lived 430 years and had other sons and daughters.
18When Peleg had lived 30 years, he became the father of Reu. 19And after he became
the father of Reu, Peleg lived 209 years and had other sons and daughters.
20When Reu had lived 32 years, he became the father of Serug.[g] 21And after he became the father of Serug, Reu lived 207 years and had other sons and daughters.
22When Serug had lived 30 years, he became the father of Nahor. 23And after he became the father of Nahor, Serug lived 200 years and had other sons and daughters.
24When Nahor had lived 29 years, he became the father of Terah.[h] 25And after he became the father of Terah, Nahor lived 119 years and had other sons and daughters.
26After Terah had lived 70 years, he became the father of Abram,[i] Nahor[j] and Haran.

11:5 [a]ver 7; Ge 18:21; Ex 3:8; 19:11,18, 20
11:7 [b]Ge 1:26 [c]Ge 42:23
11:8 [d]Ge 9:19; Lk 1:51
11:9 [e]Ge 10:10
11:12 [f]Lk 3:35
11:20 [g]Lk 3:35
11:24 [h]Lk 3:34
11:26 [i]Lk 3:34 [j]Jos 24:2

[a] *9* That is, Babylon; *Babel* sounds like the Hebrew for *confused.* [b] *10* *Father* may mean *ancestor;* also in verses 11–25. [c] *12,13* Hebrew; Septuagint (see also Luke 3:35,36 and note at Gen. 10:24) *35 years, he became the father of Cainan. 13And after he became the father of Cainan, Arphaxad lived 430 years and had other sons and daughters, and then he died. When Cainan had lived 130 years, he became the father of Shelah. And after he became the father of Shelah, Cainan lived 330 years and had other sons and daughters*

builders' arrogant self-assertion against God, who had commanded them to "fill the earth" (9:1). These proud sinners, like Cain, feared a loss of place in their isolation from God and perhaps from one another (4:14). Like Cain, they found their solution in an abiding city rivaling God (see 2:9; 3:6 and their notes).

11:5 came down. God thoroughly investigated the situation before giving a judicial sentence (3:8–13; 4:9–10; 18:21). Ironically, God had to come down to see the tower that the humans thought was so massive. **see.** See 1:4. The ziggurat towers were built as descending stairways for the gods to come down.

11:6 The LORD said. The language is a rhetorical accommodation to human beings (see 3:9 and its note). **begun.** See note on 9:20. **nothing they plan.** Note the power of linguistic communication, here in sin, elsewhere in grace (Rom. 1:16).

11:7 us. See 1:26 and its note. Angels superintend the nations (see notes on Dt 32:8; Da 10:13) and accompany the Lord in judgment (19:1ff.; 2Th 1:7).

11:8 scattered. Instead of attaining significance and immortality, they achieved alienation and dispersal. Expulsion was the earlier fate of Adam and Eve (3:23) and of Cain (4:12). But this act of judgment was also an act of salvation; in isolation the peoples were more likely to turn to God (12:3; Ac 17:26–27).

11:9 Babel. See NIV text notes. To the Babylonians the word meant "gate of god," not "confused." God's total victory over the great primeval tower of Babel assured Moses' original readers of God's victory over the Canaanite cities, whose walls they believed reached to heaven (Dt 1:28).

■ **11:10—37:1** *The Early Patriarchal History.* Moses turned to the history of the early patriarchs: Abraham, Isaac and Jacob. He carefully shaped his record of their lives in ways that were relevant for his original readers as they faced the challenges of the exodus and the conquest. These chapters divide into five parts: the accounts of Shem (11:10–26), Abraham (11:27—25:11), Ishmael (25:12–18), Isaac (25:19—35:29) and Esau (36:1—37:1).

■ **11:10–26** *Account of Shem.* Like 5:1–32, this genealogy is first linear and at the end segmented into three sons (see notes on 5:1–32; 8:1). It overlaps with 10:21–31 and forms a transition from primeval history to the story of Terah/Abraham, bridging the genealogy from the flood to Abraham. By tracing the lineage from the God-blessed Shem to Abraham, his legitimate heir, the genealogy presents God's gracious presence in the midst of prideful humanity. In the context of God's scattering rebellious humanity over the face of the earth (vv. 1–9), the Lord preserved the seed to whom he had committed himself. The events of chapters 9–11 cover less than three centuries. If this genealogy presents a precise historical account rather than a stylized, selective list, then all of Abraham's ancestors listed here were still living when he was born, and Shem outlived him by 14 years. The genealogy advances the Messianic line.

11:10 This is the account of. See note on 2:4. **Two years after the flood.** See 5:1–3 and 32, as well as 7:6.

11:12–35 In the Sumerian flood story, the ages of the kings are also reduced after the flood (see note on 5:1–32).

11:12 he became the father of Shelah. The Septuagint (Greek translation of the OT) reading is to be preferred (see NIV text note).

11:16–26 See note on 10:25.

11:16 Eber. See 10:21 and 24, Ex 1:15 and their notes. **Peleg.** See note on 10:25.

11:22 Serug. An Akkadian place name located approximately 45 miles west of Haran in northern Mesopotamia.

11:24 Terah. Attested as a place on the Balik River near Haran. Terah and his sons first migrated to Ur in southern Mesopotamia (v. 28) and then to Canaan (v. 31).

11:26 70 years. If Haran was the oldest son, the 135 years between his birth and his father Terah's death (v. 32) gives sufficient time for Nahor to have married his niece. **Abram.** His name means "exalted father," suggesting his noble lineage. It was later changed by God to "Abraham," meaning "father of many" (17:5). The name is known in other ancient Near Eastern literature span-

27 This is the account of Terah.

Terah became the father of Abram, Nahor and Haran. And Haran became the father
of Lot.[k] 28 While his father Terah was still alive, Haran died in Ur of the Chaldeans,[l] in
the land of his birth. 29 Abram and Nahor both married. The name of Abram's wife was
Sarai,[m] and the name of Nahor's wife was Milcah;[n] she was the daughter of Haran, the
father of both Milcah and Iscah. 30 Now Sarai was barren; she had no children.[o]
31 Terah took his son Abram, his grandson Lot son of Haran, and his daughter-in-law
Sarai, the wife of his son Abram, and together they set out from Ur of the Chaldeans[p] to
go to Canaan.[q] But when they came to Haran, they settled there.
32 Terah lived 205 years, and he died in Haran.

The Call of Abram

12 The LORD had said to Abram, "Leave your country, your people and your father's
household and go to the land I will show you.[r]

2 "I will make you into a great nation[s]
and I will bless you;[t]
I will make your name great,
and you will be a blessing.

11:27 [k]ver 31; Ge 12:4; 14:12; 19:1; 2Pe 2:7
11:28 [l]ver 31; Ge 15:7
11:29 [m]Ge 17:15 [n]Ge 22:20
11:30 [o]Ge 16:1; 18:11
11:31 [p]Ge 15:7; Ne 9:7; Ac 7:4 [q]Ge 10:19
12:1 [r]Ac 7:3*; Heb 11:8
12:2 [s]Ge 15:5; 17:2,4; 18:18; 22:17; Dt 26:5 [t]Ge 24:1, 35

ning a thousand years from the eighteenth century B.C. **Nahor.** See verse 24. In the ancient Near East, children were sometimes named after grandfathers.

■ **11:27—25:11** *Account of Abraham.* God's division of the world into nations (11:1–9) provides the backdrop for his selection of one particular nation from Shem's lineage from which to bring salvation to all the nations. The extensive but unified narrative of 11:27—25:11 presents God entering into a covenant with Abraham. With the call of Abraham, God commenced the story of creating Israel as his covenant people. God's original blessing on all humanity (1:28) would now find its fulfillment through Abraham and the nation that would spring from him. In this call of Abraham and subsequently of his chosen people, the Lord revealed his mercy and holiness in judgment against infidelity. For his part, Abraham, though not without flaws, was to live by faith, trusting that God would keep his promises. As Abraham's faith matured, God increasingly committed himself to Abraham. He began by offering to bless Abraham and to make him into a nation (12:2), and ultimately through him to bless the earth (12:2–3). God subsequently promised these same things to Abraham in the form of an immutable covenant (ch. 15); still later he confirmed his pledge to bless the nations through Abraham by confirming that covenant (ch. 17). Finally, the Lord swore to it (ch. 22).

11:27–32 *Abraham's Genealogy.* This introduction to the story identifies the main characters in Abraham's life: father, brother, wife, sister-in-law and nephew.

11:27 This is the account of Terah. See note on 2:4. Terah was steeped in idolatry (cf. 29:5; 31:19; Jos 24:2), most probably in the form of moon worship. Ur was associated with moon worship (cf. Jos 24:2,15), and the names Sarah and Milcah may be related to the names of the moon god Sin's wife, Sharratu ("princess") and daughter, Malkah ("queen"). After this introduction Terah is not mentioned again, most likely since he did not share Abraham's faith (15:6). **Nahor.** See 22:20–24.

11:28 Haran died. Haran's premature death explains the fate of his children in this close-knit family. Abraham adopted Lot (v. 31; 12:4), Haran's son, and Nahor married Milcah, Haran's daughter. **Ur of the Chaldeans.** Ur (modern Tell el-Muqayyar) was in southern Mesopotamia. "Chaldeans" is probably a modernization because the Chaldees penetrated into Ur (in modern southern Iraq) almost a millennium after the time of Abraham (see "Introduction: Time and Place of Writing").

11:29 Sarai. She was the daughter of Terah by a different mother than that of Abraham (20:2). Laws against this kind of incest were nonexistent in patriarchal times (Lev 18:9; 20:17; Dt 27:22). **Nahor's wife . . . daughter of Haran.** The law did not prohibit marrying one's niece.

11:30 barren. This reality, which symbolized human hopelessness, drives the whole story of Abraham; only a miraculous offspring from God could resolve Sarah's plight. (Abram and Sarai, whose names were later changed to Abraham and Sarah, are referred to throughout these notes by the latter names.) The theme of God's purposes overcoming symbolic barrenness (see Isa 54:1) recurs with Rebekah (25:21), Rachel (29:31; 30:22) and Hannah (1Sa 1:2,19–20) and foreshadows the virgin birth of Jesus (Lk 1:26–38). All these women actively committed themselves to God's grace.

11:31 Terah took. The migration to Canaan began not as a pilgrimage following a vision but as a family decision. Genesis 12:1 suggests that Abraham was instructed to depart for Canaan alone, but he did not separate himself from the larger family group until after his father had died. This introduction reveals Abraham as slow to believe. Likewise a heavenly vision would later transform Jacob from a fleeing fugitive to a pilgrim (28:10–22). **set out from Ur.** See Nehemiah 9:6. **settled there.** This was an act of unbelief on Abraham's part (15:7; Ac 7:4).

11:32 205 years. An early text reads "145" (cf. "70" [v. 26] and "75" [12:4]). This is probably the basis for Stephen's comment in Acts 7:4. Terah could have been 130 years of age when Abraham was born (v. 26).

■ **12:1—22:19** *Abraham's Land and Descendants.* These chapters contain many interconnected episodes that comprise the main description of the patriarch's life. They explain not only Abraham's covenant blessings of the promised land and many descendants, but also his interactions with other groups of people. These aspects of the patriarch's life were important to Moses as he wrote to teach his original readers about their own covenant blessings and relationships with other peoples. These chapters teach believers in every age the dynamics of covenant life with God.

■ **12:1–9** *Migration to the Promised Land.* God called Abraham to migrate to the promised land so that he would receive blessings of land and descendants and become a blessing to all nations. The patriarch responded in faithful obedience. His call and response modeled for the Israelites the kind of response they were to manifest as Moses led them. Believers in all ages may learn through the life and obedience of Abraham the purpose for God's calling to salvation and the proper response to his call.

12:1–3 The redemption that began with the setting apart of Abraham in c. 2000 B.C. (v. 1) continued with the making of Abraham into a nation in c. 1400 B.C. (v. 2) and climaxed in Jesus Christ and his church with the bringing of salvation to the world (v. 3; Gal 3:16,26–29). The call to Abraham was passed on to the other two patriarchs, Isaac (26:2–4) and Jacob (28:14). The nation would be formed from Jacob's 12 sons (ch. 49).

12:1 had said. The call came to Abraham in Ur, not in Haran, before his father had died (15:7; Ac 7:4). **Leave.** Literally, "Leave by yourself" (i.e., "disassociate yourself"). **land.** The Canaanite culture was depraved (v. 5; 15:16; Lev 18:3,28). The land of Abraham's ultimate destiny would be progressively defined (10:19; 12:7; 13:14–15; 15:18–21).

12:2 I will make you. Literally, "So that I might make you . . . bless you . . . make your name great." That this offer would later develop into a covenant is apparent from the structure. God sovereignly obligated himself to Abraham while assigning him a task. God's commands were fulfilled in Abraham's obedient faith in God's promise (vv. 1–9; 16:9–22; 17:1–2). **great.** Both in numbers and in significance. **nation.** A nation consists of offspring, land, constitution and king. Offspring and land are dominant concerns of the books of Genesis through Joshua; king is the concern of Judges through 2 Kings. See verse 7 and its note. **bless.** In chapters 1–11 "bless" occurs six times and "curse" five times. Their usage in verses 1–3 links these texts. The two nuances of "blessing"—potency and victory (see note on 1:22)—are spelled out in 22:17. **make your name great.** What

3 I will bless those who bless you,
and whoever curses you I will curse;[u]
and all peoples on earth
will be blessed through you.[v]"

4 So Abram left, as the LORD had told him; and Lot went with him. Abram was seventy-five years old when he set out from Haran.[w] 5 He took his wife Sarai, his nephew Lot,
all the possessions they had accumulated and the people[x] they had acquired in Haran,
and they set out for the land of Canaan, and they arrived there.
6 Abram traveled through the land[y] as far as the site of the great tree of Moreh[z] at Shechem. At that time the Canaanites[a] were in the land. 7 The LORD appeared to Abram[b] and
said, "To your offspring[a] I will give this land."[c] So he built an altar there to the LORD,[d]
who had appeared to him.
8 From there he went on toward the hills east of Bethel[e] and pitched his tent, with
Bethel on the west and Ai on the east. There he built an altar to the LORD and called on
the name of the LORD. 9 Then Abram set out and continued toward the Negev.[f]

Abram in Egypt

10 Now there was a famine in the land, and Abram went down to Egypt to live there
for a while because the famine was severe. 11 As he was about to enter Egypt, he said to
his wife Sarai, "I know what a beautiful woman you are. 12 When the Egyptians see you,
they will say, 'This is his wife.' Then they will kill me but will let you live. 13 Say you are
my sister,[g] so that I will be treated well for your sake and my life will be spared because
of you."
14 When Abram came to Egypt, the Egyptians saw that she was a very beautiful woman. 15 And when Pharaoh's officials saw her, they praised her to Pharaoh, and she was
taken into his palace. 16 He treated Abram well for her sake, and Abram acquired sheep
and cattle, male and female donkeys, menservants and maidservants, and camels.
17 But the LORD inflicted serious diseases on Pharaoh and his household[h] because of

12:3 [u]Ge 27:29; Ex 23:22; Nu 24:9 [v]Ge 18:18; 22:18; 26:4; Ac 3:25; Gal 3:8*
12:4 [w]Ge 11:31
12:5 [x]Ge 14:14; 17:23
12:6 [y]Heb 11:9 [z]Ge 35:4; Dt 11:30 [a]Ge 10:18
12:7 [b]Ge 17:1; 18:1; Ex 6:3 [c]Ge 13:15, 17; 15:18; 17:8; Ps 105:9-11 [d]Ge 13:4
12:8 [e]Ge 13:3
12:9 [f]Ge 13:1,3
12:13 [g]Ge 20:2; 26:7
12:17 [h]1Ch 16:21

[a] 7 Or *seed*

the city-builders at Babel sought in their own strength God here freely gave in sovereign grace (see note on 11:4). History validated God's offer. The great names of Abraham and David (2Sa 7:9) given in the Old Testament would be overshadowed by the name given to Jesus (Php 2:9–11). **blessing.** See Zechariah 8:13. Through one man's faith God mediated salvation to all nations.
12:3 See theological article "Major Covenants in the Bible" on page 25. **I will bless . . . I will curse.** God's greater intention was to bless, not curse. This is indicated in the Hebrew text by switching from a form indicating resolve ("I will bless") to a simple statement of fact ("I will curse") and by switching from the plural ("those who bless") to the singular ("whoever curses"). Compare 27:29 and Numbers 24:9. **those who bless.** That is, those who acknowledge Abraham and his offspring as God's agent of blessing. **you.** Abraham and his descendants played a representative role that prefigured Christ. The promise does not pertain to unbelieving, ethnic Israel (Ro 9:6–8; Gal 6:15) but to those who believe and are therefore in Christ (see v. 7; 13:16 and their notes; see also Gal 3:16,26–29; 6:16). **whoever curses . . . I will curse.** The Hebrew words for "curses" and "curse" differ here: The first means "to disdain"; the second "to weaken" (see 3:14). **all peoples.** This phrase is qualified by the phrase "those who bless you."
12:4 Lot. See 11:31. Lot agreed to accompany his uncle on this venture of faith. **seventy-five.** See note on 11:32.
12:5 possessions. See verse 16. **Canaan.** See 11:31.
12:6 great tree. Probably an oak tree whose great height made it a preferred place of worship (13:18; 14:13; 18:1; 21:33). Pagans worshiped fertility deities under such trees, but Abraham, who was looking for a heavenly city (Heb 11:10), sanctified this one to the Lord (v. 7), the one true God. Although Abraham worshiped according to the religious customs of his time, the content of his worship differed significantly from those around him. **Moreh.** The name means "teacher." It was probably a pagan site for oracles. The Lord sanctified it by appearing to Abraham (v. 7). **Shechem.** This site was regarded as lying in the heart of Canaan (Jos 20:7). **At that time.** It is likely that Moses actually pointed to the similarity between Abraham's circumstance and his original readers' situation to inspire them to follow Abraham's example. **the Canaanites were in the land.** A generic term for the pre-Israelite inhabitants. Two obstacles stood in the way of God's promised offspring and land: Sarah's barrenness (11:30) and the Canaanites in the land who prevented Abraham from settling down there.
12:7 appeared. The sojourning patriarchs were prophets (15:1,4; 17:1; 18:1; 20:7; 26:2,24; 28:10–15; 31:3; 35:9; 48:3). See Psalm 105:12–15. **offspring . . . land.** Here is the essence of God's promise to the patriarchs (see v. 2 and its note; 13:14–16; 26:4; 35:9–12). **offspring.** The child in view is Isaac who will be heir to Abraham's covenant and the representative father of all to whom it is passed in later generations. In this way, Isaac was a type of Christ, the great Son of Abraham (Gal 3:16). Because blessings of Abraham's covenant were passed to Christ, all who put their faith in him become heirs of Abraham. **land.** See verse 2, 13:16 and their notes. **built an altar.** By this act the father of the new nation consecrated the promised land to God (Ex 20:24; Jos 22:19). See verse 8, 13:18, 22:9, 26:25 and 35:7.
12:8 Bethel. Otherwise called Luz until 28:19. **called on the name of the LORD.** See note on 4:26.
12:9 Negev. Literally, "the dry land." It is located in the far south of the promised land. Its rainfall is too low to sustain cultivated grain and therefore settlement. Abraham traveled the entire length of the land, symbolizing that it belonged to him and to his descendants, who first read this narrative as they prepared to enter the land.
■ **12:10–20** *Deliverance From Egypt.* Abraham's departure from Egypt typified the nation's later exodus: God sent a famine (v. 10; 47:4). The Egyptians afflicted God's people (vv. 12–15; Ex 1:11–14). God plagued the Egyptians (v. 17; Ex 8–11). The Egyptians allowed God's people to depart after bestowing upon them great wealth (vv. 16,20; Ex 12:33–36). They returned to the land by stages through the wilderness (13:3; Ex 17:1). And they finally arrived back in the land, where they worshiped the Lord (13:3; Ex 15:17). See Psalm 105:14–15. Abraham's experience also guides the church through its sojourn toward the new heavens and the new earth (1Co 10:1–4).
12:13 Say. Literally, "please say." **sister.** See note on 11:29.
12:15 Pharaoh's officials . . . praised her to Pharaoh. This may have been more than Abraham had bargained for. Only the Lord could save him now. "Pharaoh" was a title, meaning "great house," rather than a personal name. **was taken.** The Hebrew here does not necessarily entail sexual intercourse (20:2,6).
12:16 He treated Abram well. In spite of the patriarch's failures of faith (see also 20:1–16; 26: 8–14), God extended grace. God plundered the real criminal, who would have killed Abraham to gratify his lust. **camels.** Archaeological evidence points to a limited domestication of the camel as early as 3000 B.C. Possession of this animal, which was rare at the time, signaled wealth and status (24:35).

Abram's wife Sarai. 18 So Pharaoh summoned Abram. "What have you done to me?"[i] he
said. "Why didn't you tell me she was your wife? 19 Why did you say, 'She is my sister,'
so that I took her to be my wife? Now then, here is your wife. Take her and go!" 20 Then
Pharaoh gave orders about Abram to his men, and they sent him on his way, with his
wife and everything he had.

Abram and Lot Separate

13 So Abram went up from Egypt to the Negev,[j] with his wife and everything he
had, and Lot went with him. 2 Abram had become very wealthy in livestock and
in silver and gold.

3 From the Negev he went from place to place until he came to Bethel,[k] to the place
between Bethel and Ai where his tent had been earlier 4 and where he had first built an
altar.[l] There Abram called on the name of the LORD.

5 Now Lot, who was moving about with Abram, also had flocks and herds and tents.
6 But the land could not support them while they stayed together, for their possessions
were so great that they were not able to stay together.[m] 7 And quarreling[n] arose between
Abram's herdsmen and the herdsmen of Lot. The Canaanites and Perizzites were also living in the land[o] at that time.

8 So Abram said to Lot, "Let's not have any quarreling between you and me,[p] or between
your herdsmen and mine, for we are brothers.[q] 9 Is not the whole land before you? Let's part
company. If you go to the left, I'll go to the right; if you go to the right, I'll go to the left."

10 Lot looked up and saw that the whole plain of the Jordan was well watered, like the
garden of the LORD,[r] like the land of Egypt, toward Zoar.[s] (This was before the LORD destroyed Sodom and Gomorrah.)[t] 11 So Lot chose for himself the whole plain of the Jordan
and set out toward the east. The two men parted company: 12 Abram lived in the land of
Canaan, while Lot lived among the cities of the plain[u] and pitched his tents near Sodom.[v] 13 Now the men of Sodom were wicked and were sinning greatly against the LORD.[w]

14 The LORD said to Abram after Lot had parted from him, "Lift up your eyes from
where you are and look north and south, east and west.[x] 15 All the land that you see I will
give to you and your offspring[a] forever.[y] 16 I will make your offspring like the dust of the
earth, so that if anyone could count the dust, then your offspring could be counted. 17 Go,
walk through the length and breadth of the land,[z] for I am giving it to you."

12:18 [i]Ge 20:9; 26:10
13:1 [j]Ge 12:9
13:3 [k]Ge 12:8
13:4 [l]Ge 12:7
13:6 [m]Ge 36:7
13:7 [n]Ge 26:20,21 [o]Ge 12:6
13:8 [p]Pr 15:18; 20:3 [q]Ps 133:1
13:10 [r]Ge 2:8-10; Isa 51:3 [s]Ge 19:22, 30 [t]Ge 14:8; 19:17-29
13:12 [u]Ge 19:17,25,29 [v]Ge 14:12
13:13 [w]Ge 18:20; Eze 16:49-50; 2Pe 2:8
13:14 [x]Ge 28:14; Dt 3:27
13:15 [y]Ge 12:7; Gal 3:16*
13:17 [z]ver 15; Nu 13:17-25

[a] *15* Or *seed;* also in verse 16

12:18 Why didn't you tell me . . . ? We may assume that Sarai informed the suspicious pharaoh of the true situation.

■ **13:1–18** *Lot's Separation From the Land.* Lot's separation from Abraham and his association with Sodom (v. 13) established that he was not to inherit the covenant blessing to be promised to Abraham. Yet Abraham's kindness to his nephew was evident as well. The Israelites following Moses encountered the descendants of Lot, the Moabites and Ammonites, as they traveled toward the promised land (see Dt 2:8–19). The developing covenant arrangement was again apparent. Abraham displayed his faith in worship (vv. 1–4) and in his self-effacing generosity (vv. 5–13), and the Lord responded by elaborating his offer of blessing (vv. 14–17). Abraham's kindness and faith are an example for all believers.

13:1 Lot. See note on 11:31; see also 12:4.

13:2 wealthy. The Hebrew here is translated "severe" in 12:10, highlighting a contrast in Abraham's situation before and after he went to Egypt (12:10–20).

13:4 altar. See note on 12:7. Abraham returned to a position of faith.

13:7 quarreling. See 26:12–33 and 36:6–7. **Perizzites.** This social, not ethnic, term refers to Canaanites who had been driven out of a town and were living in the open country (see Dt 3:5; 1Sa 6:18; Est 9:19). The Perizzites are not mentioned in 10:15–18 as descendants of Canaan. Their presence, along with that of the Canaanites, strained the land's ability to provide sustenance.

13:8–17 Lot and Abraham are compared and contrasted: Both looked around (vv. 10,14), were offered all the land (vv. 9,15–17) and traveled to their allotted portions (vv. 11–12,18), but Lot, who chose by sight (cf. 27:18–27), would escape twice by the skin of his teeth (14:12,16; 19:1–29), while Abraham would be enriched forever.

13:8 brothers. Abraham put peace with Lot before his own prosperity.

13:9 Let's part company. Sometimes relatives must separate for the sake of peace (Ac 15:39–40; 1Co 7:12–15). **If . . . left.** The social superior humbled himself before the social inferior in order to preserve peace. Faith in God's sovereignty gave Abraham the freedom to be generous. His generosity typified that of Israel to Moab and Ammon, Lot's descendants (Dt 2:8–19). God applauds the generous and the peacemakers (Lev 19:18; Ps 133; Mt 5:43–48; Jas 3:17–18).

13:10 plain of the Jordan. The edge of the promised land and/or possibly just beyond it (10:19; Nu 34:2–12). This plain is contrasted with Canaan in verse 12. **like the garden of the LORD.** A way of describing a place as paradise. **like the land of Egypt.** Lot's choice and its disastrous consequences foreshadowed the desire of the rebels to return to Egypt for the good things to be had there (Ex 16:3; Nu 11:5; 14:2–3). **Zoar.** Probably located on the southern end of the Dead Sea.

13:11 east. See 11:2.

13:12 pitched his tents. See note on 14:12. **Sodom.** The story anticipates the episodes of chapters 14 and 18–19.

13:13 wicked. See 6:5 and 8:21.

13:14 look . . . west. This may reflect the legal practice of transferring property rights by sight and intention. The Lord invited Moses to a similar panoramic overview of the land (Dt 34:1–4). In each case, the invitation was given to confirm the blessing to one who himself would not participate in dispossessing the Canaanites.

13:15 land . . . offspring. See 12:7. **land . . . forever.** See note on 12:1. The promises of land were fulfilled several times but never consummated. God fulfilled the promise through Joshua (Jos 21:43–45), but not completely (Jos 13:1–7)—and even more so through David and Solomon (1Ki 4:20–25; Ne 9:8), though still not completely (Ps 95:11; Heb 4:6–8; 11:39–40). As Israel's exodus from Egypt through the Passover (Ex 12:1) is a type of the church's exodus from the condemned world through Christ (1Co 5:7; 10:1–4), so also old Israel's life in the land is a type of new Israel's life in Christ. Both were and are a gift (15:7,18; Dt 1:8; Ro 6:23) received by faith alone (Nu 14:26–44; Jos 7 and Jn 3:16), and both uniquely possess(ed) the blessed presence, life and rest of God (Ex 23:20–31; Dt 11:12; 12:9–10; 28:1–14; Mt 11:28; Jn 1:51; 14:9) and demand(ed) persevering faith (Dt 28:15–19; Heb 6). The land promises will be consummated in the new heavens and the new earth (Heb 11:39–40; Rev 21:1—22:6).

13:16 offspring. See 12:7. **like the dust.** See 32:12. The promise of offspring also finds fulfillment in the old Israel (Nu 23:10; 1Ki

18So Abram moved his tents and went to live near the great trees of Mamre[a] at Hebron,[b] where he built an altar to the LORD.[c]

Abram Rescues Lot

14 At this time Amraphel king of Shinar,[a][d] Arioch king of Ellasar, Kedorlaomer
king of Elam and Tidal king of Goiim 2went to war against Bera king of Sodom,
Birsha king of Gomorrah, Shinab king of Admah, Shemeber king of Zeboiim,[e] and the
king of Bela (that is, Zoar).[f] 3All these latter kings joined forces in the Valley of Siddim
(the Salt Sea[b][g]). 4For twelve years they had been subject to Kedorlaomer, but in the thirteenth year they rebelled.
5In the fourteenth year, Kedorlaomer and the kings allied with him went out and defeated the Rephaites[h] in Ashteroth Karnaim, the Zuzites in Ham, the Emites[i] in Shaveh
Kiriathaim 6and the Horites[j] in the hill country of Seir,[k] as far as El Paran[l] near the desert. 7Then they turned back and went to En Mishpat (that is, Kadesh), and they conquered the whole territory of the Amalekites, as well as the Amorites who were living in
Hazazon Tamar.[m]
8Then the king of Sodom, the king of Gomorrah,[n] the king of Admah, the king of Zeboiim[o] and the king of Bela (that is, Zoar) marched out and drew up their battle lines in
the Valley of Siddim 9against Kedorlaomer king of Elam, Tidal king of Goiim, Amraphel
king of Shinar and Arioch king of Ellasar—four kings against five. 10Now the Valley of
Siddim was full of tar pits, and when the kings of Sodom and Gomorrah fled, some of the
men fell into them and the rest fled to the hills.[p] 11The four kings seized all the goods of
Sodom and Gomorrah and all their food; then they went away. 12They also carried off
Abram's nephew Lot and his possessions, since he was living in Sodom.
13One who had escaped came and reported this to Abram the Hebrew. Now Abram
was living near the great trees of Mamre[q] the Amorite, a brother[c] of Eshcol and Aner,
all of whom were allied with Abram. 14When Abram heard that his relative had been tak-
en captive, he called out the 318 trained men born in his household[r] and went in pursuit as far as Dan.[s] 15During the night Abram divided his men to attack them and he routed them, pursuing them as far as Hobah, north of Damascus. 16He recovered all the

13:18 [a]Ge 14:13,24; 18:1 [b]Ge 35:27 [c]Ge 8:20
14:1 [d]Ge 10:10
14:2 [e]Ge 10:19 [f]Ge 13:10
14:3 [g]Nu 34:3,12; Dt 3:17; Jos 3:16; 15:2,5
14:5 [h]Ge 15:20; Dt 2:11,20 [i]Dt 2:10
14:6 [j]Dt 2:12,22 [k]Dt 2:1,5,22 [l]Ge 21:21; Nu 10:12
14:7 [m]2Ch 20:2
14:8 [n]Ge 13:10; 19:17-29 [o]Dt 29:23
14:10 [p]Ge 19:17,30
14:13 [q]ver 24; Ge 13:18
14:14 [r]Ge 15:3 [s]Dt 34:1; Jdg 18:29

[a] *1* That is, Babylonia; also in verse 9   [b] *3* That is, the Dead Sea   [c] *13* Or *a relative;* or *an ally*

4:20; 2Ch 1:9) and consummation in the new Israel, which is composed of Jews and Gentiles (see note on 12:3; Ro 4:16–18; Gal 3:29; Rev 7:9).
13:17 Go, walk. Abraham was invited to possess the land both symbolically and legally (see 12:7 and its note; Jos 1:3; 18:4; 24:3).
13:18 great trees. The Hebrew word is the same as in 12:6. Several ancient textual witnesses read singular, as in 14:13 and 18:1. **Mamre.** The name of an Amorite who sought security in an alliance with Abraham. He would be blessed through Abraham (ch. 14). Here it is a place name. **built an altar.** A proper response to God's renewed promises (see note on 12:7).
▪**14:1–24** *Victory Over Eastern Kings.* Abraham displayed his obedient faith by risking war in order to deliver Lot. His victory was astonishing since the plundering confederacy of five kings had just conquered sundry Canaanites and a confederacy of five Dead Sea kings. This victory led to Abraham's blessing by Melchizedek, God's priest in Salem, and to Abraham's remaining separate from the Canaanites. The Israelites following Moses learned from Abraham's example to follow God in faith against seemingly overwhelming military odds, just as believers in the New Testament may learn to stand by faith in spiritual warfare.
14:1–2 None of these kings has been definitely identified in extrabiblical sources. One came from Elam (located in modern Iran), one from Babylon (located in modern Iraq) and two probably from Turkey.
14:1 Shinar. See 10:10 and its note, as well as 11:2.
14:2 war. For the first time in the Bible, tribes/nations war against each other due to the intensification of sin and the confusion from Babel. **Bera . . . Birsha . . . Shinab . . . Shemeber.** Note the alliterative pairs. These rulers were kings of regions located on the peninsula that juts into the Dead Sea on its southeastern side.
14:3 Valley of Siddim. This valley is today about 20 feet below the surface of the south end of the Dead Sea.
14:4 subject to. That is, they were compelled to give him whatever he demanded. Much of this story is about possessions. The eastern kings obtained them by war, and the king of Sodom was a pretentious benefactor. Abraham trusted God and was generous.
14:5 Rephaites. They inhabited Bashan (Dt 3:13). The Ammonites called them Zamzummites (Dt 2:20). **Ashteroth Karnaim.** Ashteroth, near Karnaim, was capital of Bashan, but its precise location is unknown. **Ham.** Nineteen miles east of Beth Shan. **Emites.** Means "terrors." The Emites were the original inhabitants of Moab. They were strong and numerous (Dt 2:10–11).
14:6 Horites. Their identity is uncertain. **Seir.** The hill country southeast of the Dead Sea along the Arabah. **El Paran.** Possible Elath.
14:7 Kadesh. Also known as Kadesh Barnea, a group of springs 46 miles south of Beersheba. **Amalekites.** A despicable seminomadic tribe living primarily in the Negev (Dt 25:17–18; 1Sa 27:8–11; 30:1–20).
14:10 the rest fled. The point seems to be that they, including the king of Sodom, escaped from the battle (v. 17).
14:12 living in Sodom. Note Lot's progressive identification with Sodom: He chose it (13:11), camped near it (13:12), lived in it and became a respected citizen within its boundaries (see note on 19:6; see also 19:1; Ps 1:1).
14:13 the Hebrew. See 10:21 (see also note on Ex. 1:15). **great trees of Mamre.** See notes on 12:6 and 18:1. **Amorite.** Sometimes a blanket term for the earlier inhabitants of the region only much later referred to as Palestine (48:22; Dt 1:44; Jos 2:10 and its note). The Amorites, who were "allied with Abraham" and accompanied him in battle (see v. 24), found blessing (see vv. 19–20; 12:3); not so the others (see v. 7). **allied.** The law forbade Israel from making treaties with the Amorites, for they might steal the covenant children away from Israel's faith. Here the Amorites seem to have recognized Abraham as a mediator of blessing. They accompanied him in battle (see v. 24) and found blessing (see vv. 19–20; 12:3).
14:14 relative. The Hebrew here is usually rendered "brother." The term explains Abraham's action: The godly display "loving loyalty" toward their kinsmen. **318.** A fighting force of 300 men was a sizable army in Abraham's time and a clear indication of Abraham's great wealth, even before he recovered the plunder. **trained.** The unique Hebrew here is cognate to an Egyptian word meaning "retainer." **men born in his household.** That is, his most reliable slaves. **Dan.** The name was modernized from "Laish" after the time of Moses (Jdg 18:29).

goods and brought back his relative Lot and his possessions, together with the women
and the other people.
17 After Abram returned from defeating Kedorlaomer and the kings allied with him,
the king of Sodom came out to meet him in the Valley of Shaveh (that is, the King's Valley).[t]
18 Then Melchizedek[u] king of Salem[a][v] brought out bread and wine. He was priest of
God Most High, 19 and he blessed Abram,[w] saying,

"Blessed be Abram by God Most High,
Creator[b] of heaven and earth.[x]
20 And blessed be[c] God Most High,[y]
who delivered your enemies into your hand."

Then Abram gave him a tenth of everything.[z]
21 The king of Sodom said to Abram, "Give me the people and keep the goods for yourself."
22 But Abram said to the king of Sodom, "I have raised my hand[a] to the LORD, God
Most High, Creator of heaven and earth,[b] and have taken an oath 23 that I will accept
nothing belonging to you,[c] not even a thread or the thong of a sandal, so that you will
never be able to say, 'I made Abram rich.' 24 I will accept nothing but what my men have
eaten and the share that belongs to the men who went with me—to Aner, Eshcol and
Mamre. Let them have their share."

God's Covenant With Abram

15 After this, the word of the LORD came to Abram[d] in a vision:

"Do not be afraid,[e] Abram.
I am your shield,[d][f]
your very great reward.[e]"

2 But Abram said, "O Sovereign LORD, what can you give me since I remain childless[g]

14:17 [t]2Sa 18:18
14:18 [u]Ps 110:4; Heb 5:6 [v]Ps 76:2; Heb 7:2
14:19 [w]Heb 7:6 [x]ver 22
14:20 [y]Ge 24:27 [z]Ge 28:22; Dt 26:12; Heb 7:4
14:22 [a]Ex 6:8; Da 12:7; Rev 10:5-6 [b]ver 19
14:23 [c]2Ki 5:16
15:1 [d]Da 10:1 [e]Ge 21:17; 26:24; 46:3; 2Ki 6:16; Ps 27:1; Isa 41:10, 13-14 [f]Dt 33:29; 2Sa 22:3,31; Ps 3:3
15:2 [g]Ac 7:5

[a] *18* That is, Jerusalem [b] *19* Or *Possessor*; also in verse 22 [c] *20* Or *And praise be to* [d] *1* Or *sovereign*
[e] *1* Or *shield; / your reward will be very great*

14:17 king of Sodom came out. In striking contrast to Melchizedek, he came out mute and empty-handed. **Shaveh.** Valley west of Jerusalem.
14:18 Then. The Hebrew text suggests that Melchizedek came out at the same time as the king of Sodom, in order to contrast the two. **Melchizedek.** See Hebrews 7. **king of Salem . . . priest of God.** In the Biblical world the political king was also the religious priest. Salem is probably a shortened form of Jerusalem (Ps 76:2). **bread and wine.** The combination implies a full dinner, a banquet. **priest.** Or "a priest," suggesting the existence of other priests of God. This is the first reference to priests in the Bible. **God Most High.** Israel later was required to acknowledge this truth (Dt 4:39; Jos 2:11). The Hebrew here is *El Elyon.* El, the supreme god in the Canaanite pantheon at the time of Abraham, had similar titles; e.g., *El Olam,* "Everlasting God." The patriarchs used these titles for the Lord, the true God, Creator of heaven and Earth. Abraham interpreted Melchizedek's praise in this way, repeating the same titles with reference to the Lord (see v. 22 and its note). A pagan priest could not meaningfully have "blessed" Abraham, nor would Abraham, who was consecrating the land to the Lord (12:7; 13:3), have given a "tithe" to a priest of the Canaanite god El. The Canaanite texts from c. 1400 B.C. portray El as terribly depraved.
14:19 blessed Abram. See 1:22 and its note. Melchizedek was greater than Abraham (Heb 7:7). **Blessed be.** Noah's doxological benediction on Shem is here specified to Abraham: The Japhethites would find salvation in him, and the Canaanites would become his slaves (see 9:26 and its note). **Creator of heaven and earth.** This title refers to God as the source of life and joy in the midst of trials of the day, not just as the source of the material universe (cf. Pss 115:15; 121:2; 124:8; 134:8; 146:6). In Psalms 121:2, 124:8 and 146:6 it is associated with "to help."
14:20 delivered. The Hebrew here is the same as that behind the word translated "shield" in 15:1. **tenth.** Tithing was an ancient practice in the Biblical world. See Numbers 18 and Leviticus 27:30–33. Kedorlaomer's tribute was paid as a tithe to the Lord. Melchizedek celebrated Abraham as God's warrior and blessed him, and Abraham recognized Melchizedek as the legitimate priest and king of his God. **everything.** That is, the spoils.
14:21 Give. The king of Sodom addressed Abraham with a command rather than with honor and praise. His attitude may have reflected an ungrateful heart. **keep.** His proposal was fair and probably generous. The victor who had risked his life and fortune to recover the plunder was due his share.
14:23 nothing belonging to you. Abraham would not be stained with the moral ambiguity of keeping a victim's plunder. **I made Abram rich.** Abraham wanted a clear, unambiguous moral claim to all his possessions.
14:24 to the men who went with me. The spoil was their rightful share (1Sa 30:16–25). This disposition of the goods emphasized Abraham's fairness and generosity.
▪ **15:1–21** *Covenant Regarding the Land.* After Abraham's expression of faith in God's reward (14:22–23), God certified his promises of offspring (vv. 1–6) and land (see 12:7 and its note) by making a covenant. The two night scenes (vv. 5,17) parallel each other: The Lord promised a reward (vv. 1,7), Abraham questioned the sovereign Lord about his inheritance (vv. 2–3,8) and the Lord responded with a visual act (vv.4–5,9–21). From this account Israel learned the nature of faith and the certainty of possessing the land. Through this same example, believers today may learn the nature of their own faith and the certainty of their inheritance in Christ.
15:1 word of the LORD came. This phrase typically introduces a revelation to a prophet (see note on 12:7). **vision.** Visions were an ancient mode of revelation, but the word itself is rare in the Old Testament (Nu 24:4,16; Eze 13:7). **shield.** The Lord confirmed Melchizedek's blessing (see note on 14:20). **reward.** Compensation for military service (14:22–23). It had the character of a royal grant given to an officer for faithful military service. Abraham's reward for faithful service was much greater than the tarnished booty the king of Sodom offered. Only God could reward Abraham with innumerable offspring and land that others now possessed.
15:2–3 God's people would not multiply by unaided natural generation, for Abraham's marriage had produced no children. As Adam and Noah were founders of the fallen race, Abraham was the father of the new race, which was symbolically raised from the dead (17:5; Heb 11:12).
15:2 Sovereign LORD. By this rare title Abraham showed that in

and the one who will inherit[a] my estate is Eliezer of Damascus?" 3And Abram said, "You
have given me no children; so a servant[h] in my household will be my heir."
4Then the word of the LORD came to him: "This man will not be your heir, but a son
coming from your own body will be your heir.[i]" 5He took him outside and said, "Look
up at the heavens and count the stars[j]—if indeed you can count them." Then he said to
him, "So shall your offspring be."[k]
6Abram believed the LORD, and he credited it to him as righteousness.[l]
7He also said to him, "I am the LORD, who brought you out of Ur of the Chaldeans to
give you this land to take possession of it."
8But Abram said, "O Sovereign LORD, how can I know[m] that I will gain possession of it?"
9So the LORD said to him, "Bring me a heifer, a goat and a ram, each three years old,
along with a dove and a young pigeon."
10Abram brought all these to him, cut them in two and arranged the halves opposite
each other;[n] the birds, however, he did not cut in half.[o] 11Then birds of prey came down
on the carcasses, but Abram drove them away.
12As the sun was setting, Abram fell into a deep sleep,[p] and a thick and dreadful darkness came over him. 13Then the LORD said to him, "Know for certain that your descendants
will be strangers in a country not their own, and they will be enslaved[q] and mistreated
four hundred years.[r] 14But I will punish the nation they serve as slaves, and afterward they
will come out[s] with great possessions.[t] 15You, however, will go to your fathers in peace
and be buried at a good old age.[u] 16In the fourth generation your descendants will come
back here, for the sin of the Amorites[v] has not yet reached its full measure."
17When the sun had set and darkness had fallen, a smoking firepot with a blazing
torch appeared and passed between the pieces.[w] 18On that day the LORD made a covenant with Abram and said, "To your descendants I give this land,[x] from the river[b] of
Egypt[y] to the great river, the Euphrates— 19the land of the Kenites, Kenizzites, Kad-

15:3 [h]Ge 24:2,34
15:4 [i]Gal 4:28
15:5 [j]Ps 147:4; Jer 33:22 [k]Ge 12:2; 22:17; Ex 32:13; Ro 4:18*; Heb 11:12
15:6 [l]Ps 106:31; Ro 4:3*,20-24*; Gal 3:6*; Jas 2:23*
15:8 [m]Lk 1:18
15:10 [n]ver 17; Jer 34:18 [o]Lev 1:17
15:12 [p]Ge 2:21
15:13 [q]Ex 1:11 [r]ver 16; Ex 12:40; Ac 7:6,17
15:14 [s]Ac 7:7* [t]Ex 12:32-38
15:15 [u]Ge 25:8
15:16 [v]1Ki 21:26
15:17 [w]ver 10
15:18 [x]Ge 12:7 [y]Nu 34:5

[a] *2* The meaning of the Hebrew for this phrase is uncertain. [b] *18* Or *Wadi*

his complaint he was not compromising his role of being the Lord's slave. He complained out of faith, not unbelief (see v. 6). **remain.** The Hebrew here means "going," a metaphor for either "living" or "passing away/dying." See 12:2 and 7 and 13:6. **childless.** Abraham understood that he had been created for the purpose of multiplying (1:28) and that God intended to bless him with progeny (12:1–3). The situation presented an opportunity for God to perform signs and wonders (Jdg 13:2; 1Sa 1:1—2:10; Isa 54:1–5). **the one who will inherit my estate.** The Hebrew expression is unexplained. The phrase "a servant in my household will be my heir" (v. 3) helps to interpret it. A letter from the Old Babylonian period mentions the adoption of a slave, and other tablets suggest that in Abraham's culture a childless man could adopt someone to be the guardian and heir of his estate as compensation for the person's performing the duties of a son.

15:3 servant. The practice of adopting one's own slave is found in only one letter from the Old Babylonian period.

15:5 offspring. See 12:7 and 13:16.

15:6 This verse contains the core doctrine of justification by faith, not works (Gal 3:6–14). Abraham believed the promise of the birth of an heir (Ro 4:17–21; Heb 11:11–12), and God counted Abraham to be righteous; that is, to have met his covenant demand. Abraham's faith became the model for all those who trust in the resurrection of Jesus Christ, who was God's sacrifice for sin, and rely on Christ's righteousness credited to us by faith (Ro 4:22–25). The divine reckoning qualified Abraham to become the recipient of a land grant to be transmitted to his descendants. **believed.** Abraham is the spiritual father of all those who believe (Ro 4:11; Gal 3:7). **righteousness.** See note on 6:9. Also see Hebrews 11:7. See *HC* 60.

15:7 I am the LORD, who brought you out. Ancient royal covenants included a historical prologue. The historical prologue in this covenant, together with "I am the LORD," foreshadowed the exodus and the Ten Commandments that would follow (Ex 20:2). Abraham's departure from his homeland and Israel's exodus from Egypt were two pivotal events in the formation of national Israel. **land.** See notes on 12:7 and 13:15. **take possession.** The Hebrew term connotes a sense of possession by dispossession.

15:8 how can I know . . . ? This request for a sign was motivated by faith (v. 6; Isa 7:10–14). Complaint and faith are not antithetical; complaint here was based on taking God seriously. **gain possession.** The Hebrew word here is the same one translated "heir" in verse 4.

15:9 heifer . . . pigeon. These are all the species that could be offered in sacrifice. **three years old.** These animals were fully grown and ready for service (see 1Sa 1:24).

15:11 birds of prey. The verbal root may mean "to fall upon with shouting" (cf. "pounce on" in 1Sa 15:19). The noun, denoting a powerful and swift bird of prey that swoops upon carrion, is used as a metaphor for a conqueror in Isaiah 46:11. **drove them away.** Abraham symbolically protected his promised inheritance against foreign attackers.

15:12–14 Israel would inherit Canaan through God's supernatural act of redemption from slavery.

15:12 As the sun was setting. This marks the beginning of the second encounter. The eerie scene of intensifying darkness matched Israel's darkening and declining fortunes in Egypt (see Ac 7:6–7).

15:13 four hundred years. A round number for a full four centuries (Ex 12:40–41; Ac 7:6; 13:20). God's people must learn to be patient (2Pe 3:8–10).

15:14 nation. Egypt (Ex 6:6; 7:4; 12:12; 15:13).

15:15 good old age. See 25:8. Since sorrow and sadness more commonly come to the elderly (42:38; 44:29,31; 1Ki 2:6,9; Ecc 12:1), "good" is added to denote a prosperous life (Jdg 8:32; 1Ch 29:28).

15:16 the sin of the Amorites has not yet reached its full measure. "Amorites" figuratively represent the ten nations listed in verses 19–21 (see Lev 18:24–28; 20:23). God did not send the flood until the earth was fully corrupt (6:5,12), and he would not destroy Sodom and Gomorrah until he had satisfied himself that not even a quorum of righteous remained in the city (18:22–33). Israel's conquest and settlement of Canaan were based on God's absolute justice, not on naked aggression. Later, when Israel's iniquities reached an intolerable level, God would drive even his elect nation from the land (Dt 28:36–37; 2Ki 24:14; 25:7). The Ugaritic texts (c. 1400 B.C.) claimed that the Canaanite gods degraded themselves in violent atrocities and in sexual promiscuity.

15:17 smoking firepot with a blazing torch. The smoke and fire reminded Moses' original audience of God's presence with them on their way to the promised land (Ex 13:21; 19:18; 20:18). **passed between the pieces.** To judge from ancient Near Eastern texts and from Jeremiah 34:18, God was invoking a curse upon himself if he did not keep his covenant. See Hebrews 6:13–20.

15:18 covenant. God's covenant with Abraham closely paralleled ancient Near Eastern royal land grants made by kings to loyal servants and to their descendants in perpetuity. Yet such land grants were never entirely unconditional, as chapter 17 makes clear. **from the river . . . Euphrates.** Delineation of borders constituted an important part of the royal land grants. **river of Egypt.** Probably

monites, 20Hittites, Perizzites, Rephaites, 21Amorites, Canaanites, Girgashites and Jebusites."

Hagar and Ishmael

16:1 [z]Ge 11:30; Gal 4:24-25 [a]Ge 21:9
16:2 [b]Ge 30:3-4, 9-10
16:3 [c]Ge 12:5
16:5 [d]Ge 31:53
16:7 [e]Ge 21:17; 22:11, 15; 31:11 [f]Ge 20:1
16:10 [g]Ge 13:16; 17:20

16 Now Sarai, Abram's wife, had borne him no children.[z] But she had an Egyptian
maidservant[a] named Hagar; 2so she said to Abram, "The LORD has kept me from
having children. Go, sleep with my maidservant; perhaps I can build a family through her."[b]
Abram agreed to what Sarai said. 3So after Abram had been living in Canaan[c] ten
years, Sarai his wife took her Egyptian maidservant Hagar and gave her to her husband
to be his wife. 4He slept with Hagar, and she conceived.
When she knew she was pregnant, she began to despise her mistress. 5Then Sarai
said to Abram, "You are responsible for the wrong I am suffering. I put my servant in your
arms, and now that she knows she is pregnant, she despises me. May the LORD judge between you and me."[d]
6"Your servant is in your hands," Abram said. "Do with her whatever you think
best." Then Sarai mistreated Hagar; so she fled from her.
7The angel of the LORD[e] found Hagar near a spring in the desert; it was the spring that
is beside the road to Shur.[f] 8And he said, "Hagar, servant of Sarai, where have you come
from, and where are you going?"
"I'm running away from my mistress Sarai," she answered.
9Then the angel of the LORD told her, "Go back to your mistress and submit to her."
10The angel added, "I will so increase your descendants that they will be too numerous
to count."[g]
11The angel of the LORD also said to her:

"You are now with child
and you will have a son.

---

one of the Nile's eastern branches. **Euphrates.** At its height the Davidic empire exercised political and economic control all the way to the Euphrates (2Sa 8:1; 1Ch 18), but Israel did not attempt to dispossess the people beyond the geographic boundaries of Canaan (10:19). Note the comparison with the boundaries of Eden (see 2:8–14 and its note).

15:19–21 In addition to its geographical boundaries, the land was defined by its occupants. See 10:15–18.

15:19 Kenites. The name suggests that they were metalworkers. They were located on the border of Judah with Edom, southeast of Arad. **Kenizzites.** A nomadic clan living around Hebron and Debir. **Kadmonites.** The Hebrew reads, literally, "easterners." This is the only reference to these people.

■ **16:1–16** *Hagar and Ishmael Rejected.* In her impatience, Sarah tried to fulfill the divine promise by means of her maidservant Hagar. The immediate result was strife, and its long-term consequence was the mixed blessing of numerous progeny who would inherit Hagar's defiant spirit. This natural generation did not bring peace; only the child granted by God's supernatural intervention could do that. The episode illustrates the contrast between trusting in God's promises and seeking salvation by human effort (Gal 4:21–31).

16:1 Abram's wife. This designation emphasized Sarah's rightful standing. The promised son should come from her. **maidservant.** A personal servant of the wife, not a slave girl. Her relationship to Sarah resembled Eliezer's to Abraham (see 15:2).

16:2 The LORD has kept me. Sarah had probably already reached menopause. She recognized the Lord as the Creator of life but did not interpret her infertility in terms of God's promise. Her complaint led her to seize the initiative from God's hands. **build a family through her.** Surrogate motherhood for an infertile wife through her maidservant was an accepted legal custom (30:3–12). According to an old Assyrian marriage contract, the chief wife could sell the surrogate mother, but this was not acceptable according to the Code of Hammurapi. **agreed to what Sarai said.** The Hebrew here occurs again only in 3:17. Like Adam, Abraham agreed to his wife's faithless suggestion.

16:3 ten years. See 12:4 and 16:16. **took . . . gave her to her husband.** See 3:6.

16:4 despise. This word is translated "curses" in 12:3. See Proverbs 30:23. Ancient Near Eastern law protected the first wife against this natural response. The narrator agreed with Sarah's evaluation (see v. 5). Because Hagar treated Sarah with disdain, she was alienated from the family of blessing.

16:5 You are responsible. Abraham alone had the judicial authority to effect a change, and up to now he had not acted to protect their marriage. **wrong.** The Hebrew term suggests a flagrant violation of law (see v. 11). The intractable Ishmael was the unruly son of a mother who chose the freedom of the wilderness over submission to the yoke of her mistress (v. 9). **I am suffering.** Sarah looked to Abraham as to a judge to right the injustice. **the LORD judge.** She appealed to a still higher court (31:53; Ex 5:21; 1Sa 24:12,15).

16:6 whatever you think. According to the Code of Hammurapi, the mistress (Sarah, in this situation) whom the maidservant despised could not sell her maidservant but could brand her with the slave mark and count her among the slaves. The Law of Ur-Nammu prescribed that an insolent concubine have "her mouth scoured with one quart of salt" (Hagar is not identified as Abraham's concubine, but see note on 21:12).

16:7 angel of the LORD. Like all angels (lit., "messengers"), this one was a heavenly being sent from the heavenly court to Earth as God's personal agent. In the ancient Near East, the royal messenger was treated as a surrogate of the king (Jdg 11:13; 2Sa 3:12–13; 1Ki 20:2–4). So the Lord's messenger was treated both as God and as distinct from God (21:17; 22:11; 31:11; Ex 3:2; 14:19; 23:20; 32:34). If he is equated with the "angel of the Lord" of the New Testament, he announced the births of both John the Baptist (Lk 1:11) and Jesus (Mt 1:20,24; Lk 2:9) and identified himself as Gabriel (Lk 1:19). **Shur.** The name means "wall," a reference to the Egyptian border forts.

16:8–13 The angel's announcement to Hagar bears striking similarities to the announcement to Mary (Lk 1:28–33,35–37): the greeting of the messenger (v. 8; Lk 1:28), the announcement of conception (v. 11; Lk 1:31) because of God's favor (v. 11; Lk 1:30), the name of the child with etymology (v. 11, Lk 1:31) and a rendition of the child's future achievements (v. 12, Lk 1:32), followed by the thankful response (v. 13; Lk 1:48).

16:8 Hagar. This is the only known instance in ancient Near Eastern literature in which the deity calls a woman by name. The greeting made a trusting response possible. God's concern for, and revelation to, this defiant Egyptian woman anticipated the way Jesus would deal with the sinful Samaritan woman (Jn 4). **where . . . ?** This rhetorical question elicited Hagar's participation (see 3:9 and its note).

16:9 Go back. The child legally belonged to Abraham. **submit.** A servant advanced not by discarding social boundaries, but by honoring them (Pr 17:2; 27:18). God did not condone Hagar's breach of legal relations.

16:10 increase your descendants. Abraham fathered many descendants, including both the covenant people of Israel and Ishmael's progeny. Both groups of descendants would be protected by God and made into great nations (17:20; 25:13–16).

You shall name him Ishmael,[a]
for the LORD has heard of your misery.[h]
12 He will be a wild donkey of a man;
his hand will be against everyone
and everyone's hand against him,
and he will live in hostility
toward[b] all his brothers.[i]"

13 She gave this name to the LORD who spoke to her: "You are the God who sees me,"
for she said, "I have now seen[c] the One who sees me."[j] 14 That is why the well was called
Beer Lahai Roi[d]; it is still there, between Kadesh and Bered.
15 So Hagar bore Abram a son,[k] and Abram gave the name Ishmael to the son she had
borne. 16 Abram was eighty-six years old when Hagar bore him Ishmael.

The Covenant of Circumcision

17 When Abram was ninety-nine years old, the LORD appeared to him and said, "I
am God Almighty[e];[l] walk before me and be blameless.[m] 2 I will confirm my covenant between me and you[n] and will greatly increase your numbers."
3 Abram fell facedown, and God said to him, 4 "As for me, this is my covenant with
you:[o] You will be the father of many nations.[p] 5 No longer will you be called Abram[f]; your
name will be Abraham,[g][q] for I have made you a father of many nations.[r] 6 I will make you
very fruitful;[s] I will make nations of you, and kings will come from you.[t] 7 I will establish
my covenant as an everlasting covenant between me and you and your descendants after you for the generations to come, to be your God[u] and the God of your descendants
after you.[v] 8 The whole land of Canaan,[w] where you are now an alien,[x] I will give as an
everlasting possession to you and your descendants after you;[y] and I will be their God."
9 Then God said to Abraham, "As for you, you must keep my covenant, you and your
descendants after you for the generations to come. 10 This is my covenant with you and
your descendants after you, the covenant you are to keep: Every male among you shall
be circumcised.[z] 11 You are to undergo circumcision,[a] and it will be the sign of the cov-

a 11 *Ishmael* means *God hears.* b 12 Or *live to the east / of* c 13 Or *seen the back of* d 14 *Beer Lahai Roi* means *well of the Living One who sees me.* e 1 Hebrew *El-Shaddai* f 5 *Abram* means *exalted father.* g 5 *Abraham* means *father of many.*

16:11 [h]Ex 2:24; 3:7,9
16:12 [i]Ge 25:18
16:13 [j]Ge 32:30
16:15 [k]Gal 4:22
17:1 [l]Ge 28:3; Ex 6:3 [m]Dt 18:13
17:2 [n]Ge 15:18
17:4 [o]Ge 15:18 [p]ver 16; Ge 12:2; 35:11; 48:19
17:5 [q]ver 15; Ne 9:7 [r]Ro 4:17*
17:6 [s]Ge 35:11 [t]Mt 1:6
17:7 [u]Ex 29:45,46 [v]Ro 9:8; Gal 3:16
17:8 [w]Ps 105:9,11 [x]Ge 23:4; 28:4; Ex 6:4 [y]Ge 12:7
17:10 [z]ver 23; Ge 21:4; Jn 7:22; Ac 7:8; Ro 4:11
17:11 [a]Ex 12:48; Dt 10:16

16:11 heard of your misery. The Lord looks after the oppressed (29:32; Ex 3:7; 4:31; Dt 26:7; 1Sa 1:11), redeems human error and protects the wronged.
16:12 wild donkey. The fearless and fleet-footed Syrian onager is a metaphor for an individualistic lifestyle unrestrained by social convention (Job 24:5–8; 39:5–8; Jer 2:24; Hos 8:9). Ishmael's blessing would occur away from the land of promise; he would live by his own resources. **hostility.** The fierce, aggressive ways of the Ishmaelites are contrasted with the nomadic lifestyle of the patriarchs.
16:14 still there. The site is uncertain, but it was known to Moses and Israel. **Kadesh.** See note on 14:7.
16:15 a son. The genealogy is given in 25:12–18.
■ **17:1–27** *God's Covenant Regarding Seed and Land.* God reaffirmed his covenant with Abraham (ch. 15) but added the feature of the promised seed. God would supernaturally give Abraham a royal offspring through Sarah. This chapter stresses the need for God's covenant people to fulfill the responsibility of loyal love for God.
17:1 ninety-nine. Ishmael, twelve or thirteen years old at this time, was entering young adulthood (16:16). God made clear to Abraham that Ishmael was not the child who would inherit his blessing. **God Almighty.** This name [*El Shaddai*] for God may signify his universal dominion. **walk before me and be blameless.** See 6:9. Faithfulness (not perfection) was a necessary condition to experiencing covenant blessings. To walk before God meant to orient one's entire life to his presence, promises and demands. The command was similar to the one given Solomon (1Ki 9:4–5) and Hezekiah (2Ki 20:3). Such a high standard was appropriately demanded of Abraham, who would become the father of kings (cf. 24:40; 48:15). See *WCF* 2.1; *WLC* 7.
17:2 I will confirm. Or "that I might give." The covenantal arrangement again surfaces: God committed himself to Abraham, and Abraham assumed the task of companionship with God and rejection of sin. **my covenant.** The three divisions of the covenant—"As for me . . ." (vv. 4–8), "As for you . . ." (vv. 9–14) and "As for Sarai . . ." (vv. 15–16)—recognize the obligations of all the partners.See theological article "Major Covenants in the Bible" on page 25.
17:3 Abram fell facedown. An act of worship.
17:5 called . . . your name. The name changes of the patriarch and matriarch showed that they were under God's rule (see notes on 1:5; 2:19) and were called to a new destiny and mission. **Abram . . . Abraham.** *Abraham* sounds like a Hebrew expression meaning "father of a multitude." His old name, which meant "exalted father," spoke of his noble ancestry; his new name spoke of his many offspring. He claimed his new name by faith. **father of many nations.** See 15:6, 28:3 and their notes. God's promise to make Abraham a father of many nations had both a biological (25:1–4,12–18; ch. 36) and a spiritual sense. The psalmist (Ps 87:4) and the apostle Paul (Ro 4:16–17; Gal 3:16,29) both interpreted the text as a reference to the Gentiles becoming Abraham's offspring. Uncircumcised Gentiles do not become Abraham's children through circumcision but through faith, because Abraham was justified prior to circumcision (Ro 4:11,16–17). Circumcision was added as a visible sign of the righteousness of faith Abraham already possessed (Ro 4:11,16–17).
17:6 kings. In primary view are Israel's kings (35:11; 49:10; 2Sa 7:8–16), but the greatest of these would be the Messiah (Heb 12:22–24). **will come from you.** A reference to physical offspring.
17:7 everlasting. God's covenant will endure forever because he does not change, and Jesus Christ fulfills every condition (2Co 1:20; Eph 2:12–13). This does not signify, however, that every person bound to God in Abraham's covenant will receive its blessings. It merely means that the purpose for which God gave this covenant (Abraham's land and offspring) would not fail. **your descendants.** See Romans 9:6–9. **to be your God.** That the faithful of Israel belonged to God and he to them guaranteed eternal life and final victory (Jer 31:33). See *WCF* 25.2; 27.1; 28.4; *WLC* 62,101,162,166, 177; *WSC* 92.
17:8 land . . . everlasting possession. See note on 13:15.
17:9–14 See *WCF* 28.4; *WLC* 166,177; *HC* 74,78.
17:10 circumcised. The symbolic significance of circumcision was manifold. First, it was a cutting ritual similar to the cutting of animals in other covenant ceremonies (see 15:10–11 and its notes). Thus it symbolized the curses that would come to a person who flagrantly broke covenant. Second, by submitting to this ritual, the organ of procreation was consecrated to God (Ex 6:12 [see NIV text note]; Lev 19:23 [see NIV text note]; 26:41). God wanted the

enant[b] between me and you. 12For the generations to come every male among you who
is eight days old must be circumcised,[c] including those born in your household or bought
with money from a foreigner—those who are not your offspring. 13Whether born in your
household or bought with your money, they must be circumcised. My covenant in your
flesh is to be an everlasting covenant. 14Any uncircumcised male, who has not been circumcised in the flesh, will be cut off from his people;[d] he has broken my covenant."
15God also said to Abraham, "As for Sarai your wife, you are no longer to call her Sarai; her name will be Sarah. 16I will bless her and will surely give you a son by her.[e] I will
bless her so that she will be the mother of nations;[f] kings of peoples will come from her."
17Abraham fell facedown; he laughed[g] and said to himself, "Will a son be born to a
man a hundred years old? Will Sarah bear a child at the age of ninety?" 18And Abraham
said to God, "If only Ishmael might live under your blessing!"
19Then God said, "Yes, but your wife Sarah will bear you a son,[h] and you will call him
Isaac.[a] I will establish my covenant with him[i] as an everlasting covenant for his descendants after him. 20And as for Ishmael, I have heard you: I will surely bless him; I will make
him fruitful and will greatly increase his numbers.[j] He will be the father of twelve rulers,[k]
and I will make him into a great nation.[l] 21But my covenant I will establish with Isaac,
whom Sarah will bear to you by this time next year."[m] 22When he had finished speaking with Abraham, God went up from him.
23On that very day Abraham took his son Ishmael and all those born in his household
or bought with his money, every male in his household, and circumcised them, as God
told him. 24Abraham was ninety-nine years old when he was circumcised,[n] 25and his son
Ishmael was thirteen; 26Abraham and his son Ishmael were both circumcised on that
same day. 27And every male in Abraham's household, including those born in his household or bought from a foreigner, was circumcised with him.

The Three Visitors

18 The LORD appeared to Abraham near the great trees of Mamre[o] while he was sitting at the entrance to his tent in the heat of the day. 2Abraham looked up and
saw three men[p] standing nearby. When he saw them, he hurried from the entrance of
his tent to meet them and bowed low to the ground.
3He said, "If I have found favor in your eyes, my lord,[b] do not pass your servant by.

17:11 [b]Ro 4:11
17:12 [c]Lev 12:3; Lk 2:21
17:14 [d]Ex 4:24-26
17:16 [e]Ge 18:10 [f]Ge 35:11; Gal 4:31
17:17 [g]Ge 18:12; 21:6
17:19 [h]Ge 18:14; 21:2 [i]Ge 26:3
17:20 [j]Ge 16:10 [k]Ge 25:12-16 [l]Ge 21:18
17:21 [m]Ge 21:2
17:24 [n]Ro 4:11
18:1 [o]Ge 13:18; 14:13
18:2 [p]ver 16,22; Ge 32:24; Jos 5:13; Jdg 13:6-11; Heb 13:2

a *19 Isaac* means *he laughs.* b *3* Or *O Lord*

heart and ear consecrated to himself (Dt 10:16; 30:6; Jer 4:4; 6:10 [see NIV text note]; Eze 44:7,9). It was understood by those under the old covenant that circumcision in the flesh was inadequate to please God (see notes on vv. 11–14; Dt 30:6; Jer 9:25–26). See *WCF* 27.1; 27.2; *WLC* 162; *WSC* 92,95.

17:11 sign. See 9:12 and its note. See *BC* 33,34; *HC* 66,74.

17:12 eight days old. See Luke 1:59 and 2:21, as well as Philippians 3:5. Other cultures circumcised their male children at puberty as a rite of passage from childhood to manhood. God employed the sign for infant boys to show that the children were "holy" (i.e., separated from the profane world and belonging to the covenant community; Ro 11:16; 1Co 7:14). God continues to use the family institution (5:1; Ac 16:31) as a means of growing his covenant community. The initiation rite into the covenant community today is baptism (Col 2:11–12; see theological article "Infant or Believer's Baptism" at Col 2). **born in your household.** See note on 14:14. **not your offspring.** The covenant's promises were extended to all within the family of faith. See *BC* 34.

17:13 everlasting covenant. The Hebrew word behind the term "everlasting" means "the most distant time," a concept whose interpretation is determined by the context. As long as God administered his nation by the people's physical lineage from Abraham, Isaac and Jacob, the sign of circumcision endured. Although the issue was for a time controversial in the first-century church, the apostles eventually affirmed that the rite of circumcision was no longer required after the coming of Christ (Ac 15). See theological article "Major Covenants on the Bible" on page 25.

17:14 will be cut off. God would sever the disloyal descendants from the covenant community and from its blessings. Instead, they would suffer the covenant curses (Lev 26:14–39).

17:15 Sarai . . . Sarah. Although the Septuagint (the Greek translation of the OT) associated the new name ("Sarah") with a Hebrew word meaning "strife," both names are probably dialectical variants meaning "princess." "Sarai," her birth name, probably looked back on her noble descent, whereas "Sarah," her covenantal name, looked ahead to her noble descendants (see v. 5 and its note). **your . . . call.** See note on 2:23.

17:16 bless. See notes on 1:22 and 12:2. **nations . . . kings.** See verse 6.

17:17 laughed. The Hebrew term appears here in the name "Isaac." Both Abraham and Sarah at first laughed in disbelief (18:12), but at Isaac's birth Sarah laughed in joy at this supernatural work of grace (21:1–7; Ro 4:19–21). Isaac's name was given in this latter connection.

17:19 my covenant. See verse 4.

17:20 twelve rulers. See 25:12–16.

17:21 with Isaac. By his own sovereign counsel, the Lord elected Isaac, not Ishmael. His chosen race would not come by natural generation but by supernatural grace. (Ro 9:6–13; Heb 11:11–12).

17:23 On that very day. Abraham showed himself faithful to the covenant by fulfilling his obligations immediately (see 22:2–3). **Ishmael.** Both Isaac and Ishmael received the sign of the covenant because they were both Abraham's sons.

■ **18:1–15** *Sarah to Have a Son.* Abraham solicitously entertained the Lord with a lavish nomad's banquet (vv. 1–8), and the Lord rewarded his hospitality with a gift, the announcement that Sarah would bear a son in the immediate future (vv. 9–10). The gift was so miraculous that Sarah responded not with joy, but with incredulity (vv. 11–15). God's reaction to Sarah's doubt demonstrated the need for trust that God would do everything he promised.

18:1 appeared. See 12:7 and its note. **great trees of Mamre.** See note on 13:18. **entrance to his tent.** Contrast with 19:1. **heat of the day.** The time when travelers sought shade and rest.

18:2 three men. The Lord (vv. 1,10,13–15) and two angels (19:1). The admonition to show hospitality in Hebrews 13:2 is based on the incidents recorded in chapters 18–19. **standing nearby.** The ancient equivalent to knocking at the door. **hurried.** Throughout the story Abraham was completely at their service. See theological article "Angels" at Zechariah 1:9.

18:3 found favor. This phrase was always addressed to one of higher rank. **my lord.** The Hebrew text should be translated "Lord," a title for God, as in verse 27 ("the Lord"). See NIV text note.

4 Let a little water be brought, and then you may all wash your feet[q] and rest under this
tree. 5 Let me get you something to eat,[r] so you can be refreshed and then go on your
way—now that you have come to your servant."
"Very well," they answered, "do as you say."
6 So Abraham hurried into the tent to Sarah. "Quick," he said, "get three seahs[a] of fine
flour and knead it and bake some bread."
7 Then he ran to the herd and selected a choice, tender calf and gave it to a servant, who
hurried to prepare it. 8 He then brought some curds and milk and the calf that had been prepared, and set these before them.[s] While they ate, he stood near them under a tree.
9 "Where is your wife Sarah?" they asked him.
"There, in the tent," he said.
10 Then the LORD[b] said, "I will surely return to you about this time next year, and Sarah your wife will have a son."[t]
Now Sarah was listening at the entrance to the tent, which was behind him. 11 Abraham and Sarah were already old and well advanced in years,[u] and Sarah was past the
age of childbearing.[v] 12 So Sarah laughed[w] to herself as she thought, "After I am worn
out and my master[c][x] is old, will I now have this pleasure?"
13 Then the LORD said to Abraham, "Why did Sarah laugh and say, 'Will I really have
a child, now that I am old?' 14 Is anything too hard for the LORD?[y] I will return to you at
the appointed time next year and Sarah will have a son."
15 Sarah was afraid, so she lied and said, "I did not laugh."
But he said, "Yes, you did laugh."

Abraham Pleads for Sodom

16 When the men got up to leave, they looked down toward Sodom, and Abraham
walked along with them to see them on their way. 17 Then the LORD said, "Shall I hide
from Abraham[z] what I am about to do?[a] 18 Abraham will surely become a great and powerful nation,[b] and all nations on earth will be blessed through him. 19 For I have chosen
him, so that he will direct his children[c] and his household after him to keep the way of
the LORD[d] by doing what is right and just, so that the LORD will bring about for Abraham
what he has promised him."
20 Then the LORD said, "The outcry against Sodom and Gomorrah is so great and their
sin so grievous 21 that I will go down[e] and see if what they have done is as bad as the outcry that has reached me. If not, I will know."

18:4 [q]Ge 19:2; 43:24
18:5 [r]Jdg 13:15
18:8 [s]Ge 19:3
18:10 [t]Ro 9:9*
18:11 [u]Ge 17:17 [v]Ro 4:19
18:12 [w]Ge 17:17; 21:6 [x]1Pe 3:6
18:14 [y]Jer 32:17,27; Zec 8:6; Mt 19:26; Lk 1:37; Ro 4:21
18:17 [z]Am 3:7 [a]Ge 19:24
18:18 [b]Gal 3:8*
18:19 [c]Dt 4:9-10; 6:7 [d]Jos 24:15; Eph 6:4
10:21 [e]Ge 11:5

[a] 6 That is, probably about 20 quarts (about 22 liters) [b] 10 Hebrew *Then he* [c] 12 Or *husband*

18:9 Where . . . ? This question was rhetorical. The Lord knew what Sarah was doing (vv. 13–15).
18:10 I will surely return. Only God could faithfully promise life out of barrenness and decay. **Sarah . . . son.** God's promise demanded faith (see 11:30; 15:2–4; 16:11; 17:15–16; Ro 9:9).
18:11 past the age of childbearing. Literally, Sarah "no longer experienced the cycle of women" (see Ro 4:19; Heb 11:11–12).
18:12 my master. See 1 Peter 3:6. **pleasure.** The Hebrew behind this term is unique; according to an ancient Aramaic translation, it means "conception."
18:14 too hard . . . ? Abraham knew the answer (15:4–6; Heb 11:11). His faith in God's ability was the means of his justification (15:6). See *HC* 26.
18:15 you did laugh. The historical fact remained and was worth pondering (17:17; 21:6). This was both a restorative rebuke (Pr 28:13) and an assuring sign: The one who read her thoughts could also open her womb.
■ **18:16—19:38** *Abraham, Lot and Sodom.* In a rather elaborate account, Moses described the roles of Abraham and Lot in relation to the destruction of Sodom. These chapters divide into three main parts: the events leading up to divine judgment on the city (18:16–33), the destruction and rescue (19:1–29), and the aftermath of the judgment (19:30–38). These chapters described to the Israelites how they should view Canaanite cities as well as their relatives, the Moabites and Ammonites. They also explain the manner in which God's people in all ages should seek the salvation of others while separating themselves from evil influences.
■ **18:16–33** *Justice and Intercession for Sodom.* The Lord's promise to Abraham of a miraculous birth anticipated that he would become a great and powerful nation to bless the earth. Such a nation had to learn justice, beginning with its father, Abraham (vv. 17–19). The Lord modeled justice to Abraham in his treatment of the Sodomites (vv. 20–33). Abraham also exemplified the proper role for himself and his descendants as he mediated for the righteous that might be in the cities of Canaan. The Israelites, hearing accounts of these events, would learn justice and mercy toward the righteous within Canaan, just as believers today should see the universal need for justice and mercy.
18:16 they looked down toward Sodom. The strangers served as the messengers of hope and life to Abraham and Sarah but of judgment and death to the people of Sodom and Gomorrah (Dt 32:39; 1Sa 2:6; Ps 76:7; Isa 45:7).
18:17 Shall I hide . . . ? God so esteemed his servants the prophets that he revealed his plan to them (20:7; Jer 23:16–22; Am 3:7; Jn 15:15). As a prophet, Abraham also interceded (Jer 15:1; 27:18), thereby standing in the prophetic train of Enoch (Jude 14) and Noah (2Pe 2:5). See *WLC* 156.
18:19 so that. God had known Abraham, had claimed him in his covenant and would fulfill his promises to him. Those promises claimed by Abraham in faith were also to be claimed by his descendents through their covenant faithfulness. Fidelity was to be shown in order for the purpose and promises of God to be realized (see notes on 17:2; 22:16–18; 26:4–5). **direct his children.** Israel's heritage was passed down through generations, primarily within the home (see Dt 6:8; Pr 1:8). There is no record of a school for children in Israel before the late intertestamental period. **way of the LORD.** A technical metaphor for right behavior that leads to a right destiny due to one's relationship with the Lord. **right and just.** Righteousness portrays living in a community in a way that promotes the life and well-bring of all its members. Justice portrays mending a broken community, especially by punishing the oppressors and delivering the oppressed. **so that.** The conditionality of the Abrahamic covenant is explicit here. Abraham had to teach future generations in order for the promises to be fulfilled (see 17:2; 22:15–18; 26:4–5). See *WLC* 99,156.
18:20 outcry. As the Judge of the earth, the Lord attends to all cries of wrongdoing (v. 25; 4:10; 16:6–7). **their sin.** See chapter 19 and Ezekiel 16:49–50.

22The men turned away and went toward Sodom,[f] but Abraham remained standing
before the LORD.[a] 23Then Abraham approached him and said: "Will you sweep away the
righteous with the wicked?[g] 24What if there are fifty righteous people in the city? Will you
really sweep it away and not spare[b] the place for the sake of the fifty righteous people
in it?[h] 25Far be it from you to do such a thing—to kill the righteous with the wicked, treating the righteous and the wicked alike. Far be it from you! Will not the Judge[c] of all the
earth do right?"[i]

26The LORD said, "If I find fifty righteous people in the city of Sodom, I will spare the
whole place for their sake.[j]"

27Then Abraham spoke up again: "Now that I have been so bold as to speak to the
Lord, though I am nothing but dust and ashes,[k] 28what if the number of the righteous
is five less than fifty? Will you destroy the whole city because of five people?"

"If I find forty-five there," he said, "I will not destroy it."

29Once again he spoke to him, "What if only forty are found there?"

He said, "For the sake of forty, I will not do it."

30Then he said, "May the Lord not be angry, but let me speak. What if only thirty can
be found there?"

He answered, "I will not do it if I find thirty there."

31Abraham said, "Now that I have been so bold as to speak to the Lord, what if only
twenty can be found there?"

He said, "For the sake of twenty, I will not destroy it."

32Then he said, "May the Lord not be angry, but let me speak just once more.[l] What
if only ten can be found there?"

He answered, "For the sake of ten,[m] I will not destroy it."

33When the LORD had finished speaking with Abraham, he left, and Abraham returned
home.

Sodom and Gomorrah Destroyed

19 The two angels arrived at Sodom[n] in the evening, and Lot was sitting in the
gateway of the city.[o] When he saw them, he got up to meet them and bowed
down with his face to the ground. 2"My lords," he said, "please turn aside to your servant's house. You can wash your feet[p] and spend the night and then go on your way early in the morning."

"No," they answered, "we will spend the night in the square."

3But he insisted so strongly that they did go with him and entered his house. He prepared a meal for them, baking bread without yeast, and they ate.[q] 4Before they had gone
to bed, all the men from every part of the city of Sodom—both young and old—surround-

18:22 [f]Ge 19:1
18:23 [g]Nu 16:22
18:24 [h]Jer 5:1
18:25 [i]Job 8:3,20; Ps 58:11; 94:2; Isa 3:10-11; Ro 3:6
18:26 [j]Jer 5:1
18:27 [k]Ge 2:7; 3:19; Job 30:19; 42:6
18:32 [l]Jdg 6:39 [m]Jer 5:1
19:1 [n]Ge 18:22 [o]Ge 18:1
19:2 [p]Ge 18:4; Lk 7:44
19:3 [q]Ge 18:6

[a] 22 Masoretic Text; an ancient Hebrew scribal tradition *but the LORD remained standing before Abraham*
[b] 24 Or *forgive*; also in verse 26 [c] 25 Or *Ruler*

18:21 go down and see. A figurative way of saying that God always investigates the crime before passing sentence (see notes on 3:11–13; 4:9–12; 11:5).
18:22 The men. The two angels attending the Lord (see note on v. 2) went in order to confirm the crime, just as the spies later investigated the promised land in pairs (Jos 1:2).
18:23 Will you sweep away the righteous with the wicked? The answer was no, but this was a truth that needed to be reaffirmed to the original readers of Genesis as they anticipated the conquest of the land. God called on his people to spare the righteous when he judged a nation; e.g., Rahab (Jos 2), Assyria (Jnh 3–4) and Israel (Eze 14:12–20). The situation differed considerably in cases of natural disaster that did not involve judicial judgments (Job 9:22; 12:4,16; Lk 13:4).
18:24 fifty. Half of a small city (Am 5:13).
18:25 Will not the Judge . . . do right? A deliberative prayer asserting faith in God's just character and exhibiting the commitment to justice that Israel was to have in her holy war.
18:26 I will spare. God sometimes spares the wicked for the sake of the righteous.
18:27 See *WCF* 21.3; *WLC* 185.
18:32 ten. Ten was still a community. Fewer than ten could be saved individually, as would happen later (ch. 19).
18:33 he left. It was now established that the judgment on Sodom and Gomorrah, a model for God's future judgments (cf. Lk 17:28–35), was just.
■ **19:1–29** *Lot's Rescue From Sodom.* The destruction of Sodom reveals the pattern of God's judgment on sin (2Pe 2:5). Ultimately, Lot was saved because of God's mercy to him (v. 16) and because of God's covenantal commitment to Abraham (v. 29). All believers should desire the rescue of others from God's judgment.
19:1–11 Judges 19:15–25 was written with this account in mind.
19:1 two angels. See 16:9, 18:2 and their notes, as well as the theological article "Angels" at Zec 1:9. The Lord himself did not appear after 18:33, although he would rain down the judgment from heaven (v. 24). **sitting in the gateway.** See 14:12. The elders and officials sat on stone benches in the gate to adjudicate legal matters and discuss local affairs. The gate was the physical symbol of collective authority and power. Curiously, Lot was apparently the only one sitting at this focal point of communal life when the angels arrived, suggesting that only he was concerned about the community's interests and well-being. Though politically one with the people of Sodom, Lot remained theologically distinct. Peter later referred to Lot as "a righteous man" (2Pe 2:7). **bowed down.** Throughout the story Lot demonstrated his righteousness by his hospitality to the strangers (see 18:2 and its note; 2Pe 2:6–7).
19:3 insisted so strongly. Lot anticipated the treachery of his neighbors. **meal.** The Hebrew term denotes a banquet, a sumptuous entertainment of guests with food and drink.
19:4 every part . . . young and old. These details are necessary to spell out that everyone who was destroyed was wicked (see 18:16–33 and its notes). See 6:5, 8:21 and Romans 1:26–32. **Sodom.** Here the city was said to be guilty of two crimes: violation of guests and unnatural lust. Elsewhere the sins of Sodom and Gomorrah are identified as social oppression (Isa 1:10); adultery, lying and abetting the criminal (Jer 23:14); and arrogance and complacency, showing no pity on the needy (Eze 16:49).

ed the house. 5They called to Lot, "Where are the men who came to you tonight? Bring
them out to us so that we can have sex with them."[r]
6Lot went outside to meet them[s] and shut the door behind him 7and said, "No, my
friends. Don't do this wicked thing. 8Look, I have two daughters who have never slept
with a man. Let me bring them out to you, and you can do what you like with them. But
don't do anything to these men, for they have come under the protection of my roof."[t]
9"Get out of our way," they replied. And they said, "This fellow came here as an alien,
and now he wants to play the judge![u] We'll treat you worse than them." They kept bringing pressure on Lot and moved forward to break down the door.
10But the men inside reached out and pulled Lot back into the house and shut the
door. 11Then they struck the men who were at the door of the house, young and old, with
blindness[v] so that they could not find the door.
12The two men said to Lot, "Do you have anyone else here—sons-in-law, sons or
daughters, or anyone else in the city who belongs to you?[w] Get them out of here, 13be-
cause we are going to destroy this place. The outcry to the LORD against its people is so
great that he has sent us to destroy it."[x]
14So Lot went out and spoke to his sons-in-law, who were pledged to marry[a] his
daughters. He said, "Hurry and get out of this place, because the LORD is about to destroy
the city![y]" But his sons-in-law thought he was joking.[z]
15With the coming of dawn, the angels urged Lot, saying, "Hurry! Take your wife and
your two daughters who are here, or you will be swept away[a] when the city is punished.[b]"
16When he hesitated, the men grasped his hand and the hands of his wife and of his two
daughters and led them safely out of the city, for the LORD was merciful to them. 17As soon
as they had brought them out, one of them said, "Flee for your lives![c] Don't look back,[d] and
don't stop anywhere in the plain! Flee to the mountains or you will be swept away!"
18But Lot said to them, "No, my lords,[b] please! 19Your[c] servant has found favor in
your[c] eyes, and you[c] have shown great kindness to me in sparing my life. But I can't flee
to the mountains; this disaster will overtake me, and I'll die. 20Look, here is a town near
enough to run to, and it is small. Let me flee to it—it is very small, isn't it? Then my life
will be spared."
21He said to him, "Very well, I will grant this request too; I will not overthrow the town
you speak of. 22But flee there quickly, because I cannot do anything until you reach it."
(That is why the town was called Zoar.[d])
23By the time Lot reached Zoar, the sun had risen over the land. 24Then the LORD
rained down burning sulfur on Sodom and Gomorrah[e]—from the LORD out of the heavens.[f] 25Thus he overthrew those cities and the entire plain, including all those living in
the cities—and also the vegetation in the land.[g] 26But Lot's wife looked back,[h] and she
became a pillar of salt.[i]

19:5 [r]Jdg 19:22; Isa 3:9; Ro 1:24-27
19:6 [s]Jdg 19:23
19:8 [t]Jdg 19:24
19:9 [u]Ex 2:14; Ac 7:27
19:11 [v]Dt 28:28-29; 2Ki 6:18; Ac 13:11
19:12 [w]Ge 7:1
19:13 [x]1Ch 21:15
19:14 [y]Nu 16:21 [z]Ex 9:21; Lk 17:28
19:15 [a]Nu 16:26 [b]Rev 18:4
19:17 [c]Jer 48:6 [d]ver 26
19:24 [e]Dt 29:23; Isa 1:9; 13:19 [f]Lk 17:29; 2Pe 2:6; Jude 7
19:25 [g]Ps 107:34; Eze 16:48
19:26 [h]ver 17 [i]Lk 17:32

[a] *14* Or *were married to* [b] *18* Or *No, Lord;* or *No, my lord* [c] *19* The Hebrew is singular. [d] *22 Zoar* means *small.*

19:6 shut the door behind him. An act of courage. Lot risked himself to protect his guests.
19:7 His offer stressed the seriousness of the crime and implicitly warned them of the consequences. **friends.** More literally, "brothers." He appealed to them as equals to win their goodwill (29:4). **this wicked thing.** Lot knew right from wrong through his conscience and through Abraham. His appeal assumed his righteousness (2Pe 2:6–7).
19:8 I have two daughters. Lot was confronted with a difficult choice. We cannot know what motivations may have guided him. Perhaps he merely sought to divert and delay the mob. He may also have reasoned that the angelic spies would have intervened on behalf of his daughters. In any event, this account in no way approves of Lot's endangering his daughters. According to the Mosaic Law, the violator of a betrothed woman's sanctity was subject to death by stoning (Dt 22:23–27).
19:9 This fellow. The ungrateful mob forgot that, 15 years earlier, they themselves had been rescued because of Lot's connection with Abraham (14:14–16). To Lot's credit he stood apart morally and spiritually (Lk 6:26). **the judge!** The Hebrew here is the same as that in 18:25.
19:10 shut the door. See 7:16 and its note.
19:11 blindness. The Hebrew term probably means "to dazzle," suggesting that they were blinded by a blazing light.
19:12 sons-in-law, sons or daughters. God was concerned with the salvation of the whole family (see 7:1). The mention of the in-laws before the children accented God's grace.
19:13 destroy. The Hebrew here is the same as that in 6:13.
19:14 joking. Lot's sons-in-law did not show themselves to be men of faith.
19:15 wife . . . daughters. The family was saved as a unit, but this family, like Noah's, would prove itself a mixture of those who persevered (Lot) and those who apostatized (Lot's wife [v. 26] and daughters [vv. 30–38]).
19:16 hesitated. Lot felt more secure inside a city with wicked persons than he did outside of it with God (vv. 18–21).
19:19 found favor. See note on 18:3. **this disaster.** Lot's fear illustrates the irrationality of unbelief.
19:20 very small. His argument betrayed a lack of faith, a jaded spiritual evaluation of justice and a taste for depraved urbanity.
19:21 I will not overthrow. God continued to show grace and patience toward his faltering servant.
19:23 the sun had risen. In the ancient Near East, court was held symbolically at the rising of the sun (see Job 38:12–15; Ps 5).
19:24 the LORD rained down burning sulfur. Deposits of asphalt and sulfur are still found on the edge of the Dead Sea (14:10). In an earthquake, gases from the earth can catch fire. Here the Scriptures describe the ultimate divine cause rather than the secondary created causes.
19:25 entire plain. See note on 13:10.
19:26 Lot's wife looked back. The death of Lot's wife is a sobering lesson against vacillating when God's judgment is at hand (Lk 17:28–37; 2Pe 2:6). **salt.** In the Biblical world, a site was strewn with salt to condemn it to perpetual barrenness and desolation (Dt

27 Early the next morning Abraham got up and returned to the place where he had
stood before the LORD.[j] 28 He looked down toward Sodom and Gomorrah, toward all the
land of the plain, and he saw dense smoke rising from the land, like smoke from a furnace.[k]
29 So when God destroyed the cities of the plain, he remembered Abraham, and he
brought Lot out of the catastrophe[l] that overthrew the cities where Lot had lived.

Lot and His Daughters

30 Lot and his two daughters left Zoar and settled in the mountains,[m] for he was afraid
to stay in Zoar. He and his two daughters lived in a cave. 31 One day the older daughter
said to the younger, "Our father is old, and there is no man around here to lie with us,
as is the custom all over the earth. 32 Let's get our father to drink wine and then lie with
him and preserve our family line through our father."
33 That night they got their father to drink wine, and the older daughter went in and
lay with him. He was not aware of it when she lay down or when she got up.
34 The next day the older daughter said to the younger, "Last night I lay with my father. Let's get him to drink wine again tonight, and you go in and lie with him so we can
preserve our family line through our father." 35 So they got their father to drink wine that
night also, and the younger daughter went and lay with him. Again he was not aware of
it when she lay down or when she got up.
36 So both of Lot's daughters became pregnant by their father. 37 The older daughter
had a son, and she named him Moab[a]; he is the father of the Moabites[n] of today. 38 The
younger daughter also had a son, and she named him Ben-Ammi[b]; he is the father of the
Ammonites[o] of today.

Abraham and Abimelech

20 Now Abraham moved on from there[p] into the region of the Negev and lived between Kadesh and Shur. For a while he stayed in Gerar,[q] 2 and there Abraham
said of his wife Sarah, "She is my sister.[r]" Then Abimelech king of Gerar sent for Sarah
and took her.[s]
3 But God came to Abimelech in a dream[t] one night and said to him, "You are as good
as dead because of the woman you have taken; she is a married woman."[u]
4 Now Abimelech had not gone near her, so he said, "Lord, will you destroy an innocent nation?[v] 5 Did he not say to me, 'She is my sister,' and didn't she also say, 'He is my
brother'? I have done this with a clear conscience and clean hands."
6 Then God said to him in the dream, "Yes, I know you did this with a clear conscience,
and so I have kept[w] you from sinning against me. That is why I did not let you touch her.

19:27 [j]Ge 18:22
19:28 [k]Rev 9:2; 18:9
19:29 [l]2Pe 2:7
19:30 [m]ver 19
19:37 [n]Dt 2:9
19:38 [o]Dt 2:19
20:1 [p]Ge 18:1 [q]Ge 26:1, 6,17
20:2 [r]ver 12; Ge 12:13; 26:7 [s]Ge 12:15
20:3 [t]Job 33:15; Mt 27:19 [u]Ps 105:14
20:4 [v]Ge 18:25
20:6 [w]1Sa 25:26,34

[a] *37 Moab* sounds like the Hebrew for *from father.* [b] *38 Ben-Ammi* means *son of my people.*

29:23; Jdg 9:45; Ps 107:34; Jer 17:6). This event would have captured the imaginations of the original readers. The salt deposits at the Dead Sea with which they would have associated this event would have been well known to the Israelites following Moses toward the promised land.

19:29 remembered. See 8:1. Twice Abraham had saved Lot (14:1–16; 19:1–29).

■ **19:30–38** *Lot and His Daughters.* Despite Lot's righteousness and God's sparing of him, Moses made it clear that Lot's line was of a morally questionable character (see note on 13:13). The Lord protected Lot's lineage and land (Dt 2:16–19) because of his faith and his relationship to Abraham. Yet the conclusion of this passage begins the story of the bitter animosity of Moab and Ammon against Israel (see Nu 23–25; 2Ki 3). It also warned Israel, as it does all believers, against the influences of evil.

19:30 cave. What a contrast to Lot's prosperity and prospects in 13:1–13!

19:31 said. She did what was right in her own eyes (cf. 18:18–19). Her evaluative standard was society at large, not the covenant community under God, and she made no mention of the Lord.

19:32 Let's get our father. Lot had taken no initiative to take care of the situation. The sexual immorality of his daughters later found expression in their daughters' seduction of Israel's men (Nu 25). **drink wine.** She conspired to usurp her father's authority. **preserve our family line.** No mention is made of the Lord, who opens the womb (cf. 16:2). The Moabites and Ammonites were largely rejected by God because of their mistreatment of Israel (Dt 23:3–6). Ruth, and so Jesus Christ, physically participated in this lineage (Ru 4:18–22; Mt 1:5), but through faith Ruth was reckoned among the tribe of Judah.

■ **20:1–18** *Abraham's Intercession for Abimelech.* Abraham interceded on behalf of a God-fearing Philistine king (see 21:32,34; 26:1,8,14–15,18). This event illustrates the intercessory role of believers.

20:1 Negev. See 12:9. **he stayed in Gerar.** This city was at the edge of Philistine land.

20:2 my sister. The reason is given in verse 11 and in 12:11–13. Abraham was without excuse, for he acted out of fear rather than faith. God had pledged that the promised seed would be through Sarah (17:18; 18:9–15). **Abimelech.** A common West Semitic name, meaning "My father is king" (see Jdg 8:31; Ps 34 title). He was probably the father or grandfather of a later king with the same name who faced a similar situation (26:1). **took.** See 12:15. On the brink of Isaac's conception (18:10–14; 21:1–2), the program of redemption was placed in jeopardy.

20:3 in a dream. Dreams were a mode of revelation sometimes given by God to those outside of the covenant (28:12; 31:24; 37:5–9; 40:5; 41:1; Nu 22:9,20). **You are as good as dead.** People recognized the sacred character of marriage (cf. Lev 20:22; Dt 22:22). Adultery was considered a "great sin" among many Semitic groups (see 26:10; 39:9).

20:4 Lord. Abimelech knew the true God but not his salvation through Abraham's seed. **will you destroy an innocent nation?** See 18:23. The answer is given in verse 6.

20:5 clear conscience. God judges people without the law by the standard of general revelation (see notes on 3:8; 6:9; Ro 2:14–15).

20:6 I know. God exonerated the king.

7 Now return the man's wife, for he is a prophet, and he will pray for you[x] and you will
live. But if you do not return her, you may be sure that you and all yours will die."
8 Early the next morning Abimelech summoned all his officials, and when he told them
all that had happened, they were very much afraid. 9 Then Abimelech called Abraham in
and said, "What have you done to us? How have I wronged you that you have brought
such great guilt upon me and my kingdom? You have done things to me that should not
be done.[y]" 10 And Abimelech asked Abraham, "What was your reason for doing this?"
11 Abraham replied, "I said to myself, 'There is surely no fear of God[z] in this place, and
they will kill me because of my wife.'[a] 12 Besides, she really is my sister, the daughter of
my father though not of my mother; and she became my wife. 13 And when God had me
wander from my father's household, I said to her, 'This is how you can show your love
to me: Everywhere we go, say of me, "He is my brother." ' "
14 Then Abimelech brought sheep and cattle and male and female slaves and gave
them to Abraham,[b] and he returned Sarah his wife to him. 15 And Abimelech said, "My
land is before you; live wherever you like."[c]
16 To Sarah he said, "I am giving your brother a thousand shekels[a] of silver. This is
to cover the offense against you before all who are with you; you are completely vindicated."
17 Then Abraham prayed to God,[d] and God healed Abimelech, his wife and his slave
girls so they could have children again, 18 for the LORD had closed up every womb in Abimelech's household because of Abraham's wife Sarah.[e]

The Birth of Isaac

21 Now the LORD was gracious to Sarah[f] as he had said, and the LORD did for Sarah what he had promised.[g] 2 Sarah became pregnant and bore a son[h] to Abraham in his old age,[i] at the very time God had promised him. 3 Abraham gave the name
Isaac[b][j] to the son Sarah bore him. 4 When his son Isaac was eight days old, Abraham circumcised him,[k] as God commanded him. 5 Abraham was a hundred years old when his
son Isaac was born to him.
6 Sarah said, "God has brought me laughter,[l] and everyone who hears about this will
laugh with me." 7 And she added, "Who would have said to Abraham that Sarah would
nurse children? Yet I have borne him a son in his old age."

Hagar and Ishmael Sent Away

8 The child grew and was weaned, and on the day Isaac was weaned Abraham held

20:7 [x]ver 17; 1Sa 7:5; Job 42:8
20:9 [y]Ge 12:18; 26:10; 34:7
20:11 [z]Ge 42:18; Ps 36:1 [a]Ge 12:12; 26:7
20:14 [b]Ge 12:16
20:15 [c]Ge 13:9
20:17 [d]Job 42:9
20:18 [e]Ge 12:17
21:1 [f]1Sa 2:21 [g]Ge 8:1; 17:16,21; Gal 4:23
21:2 [h]Ge 17:19 [i]Gal 4:22; Heb 11:11
21:3 [j]Ge 17:19
21:4 [k]Ge 17:10,12; Ac 7:8
21:6 [l]Ge 17:17; Isa 54:1

[a] 16 That is, about 25 pounds (about 11.5 kilograms) [b] 3 *Isaac* means *he laughs.*

20:7 prophet. This is the first time this term is used in the Bible. Abraham was a man of God who received revelations and interceded for others (see notes on 12:7; 15:1). **will die.** Abraham was an instrument of life and death (12:3; 2Co 2:14–16).

20:8 Early the next morning. Another example of prompt obedience (see 17:23).

20:11–13 In Abraham's attempt to mitigate his guilt, he tacitly admitted his own and exonerated Abimelech. Abraham's experience was probably intended to teach Moses' original audience about their relationships with Philistines as God's people approached the land of promise.

20:11 fear of God. This phrase should be distinguished from "fear of the LORD." The latter phrase refers to respect for the special revelation of Scripture, while "fear of God" involves general revelation, moral standards that are known by human beings through conscience. Human conscience also commends God's special revelation to the Gentiles (Dt 4:6; Mic 4:2; 2Co 4:2).

20:12 my sister. See 11:29 and 12:11–12. Even after the giving of the law (cf. Lev 18:8,11; Dt 2:22), violating the law against marrying one's sister was considered a lesser wrong than breaking some of the other laws (2Sa 13:13; Eze 22:11).

20:13 everywhere we go. Abraham intended no insult, particularly against Abimelech.

20:14–16 Abimelech gave gifts to Abraham (vv. 14–15) and to Sarah (v. 16) to honor God and their special relationship to him, not to compensate for his guilt (cf. 12:19–20). God not only delivered his elect out of dreadful peril, but he also rewarded them with unexpected riches (see 12:16 and its note). Abimelech opened his land to Abraham, a hopeful note for the original audience as they moved toward those territories.

20:16 giving your brother. Social convention demanded that the gift to Sarah be given through the male head of the family. **a thousand shekels.** A large sum. **cover the offense.** Abimelech aimed to restore Sarah's honor, which he had tarnished, in the eyes of others, even though he himself had not violated her.

20:17 Abraham prayed. In his role of intercessor for the Gentiles, Abraham fulfilled his grand historical significance (see 12:3) and prefigured Jesus Christ (Isa 53:12; Ro 8:34).

20:18 closed up. Abraham and Sarah had convincing proof that the Lord controls conception (see 16:2; 20:1–2 and their notes). Ironically, when she left, other wombs were opened, but she remained barren.

■ **21:1–21** *The Birth of Isaac.* The report of Isaac's birth concludes the story begun with Sarah's barrenness (11:27–32). The covenantal arrangement is underscored: God kept his promise to give Abraham a son through Sarah (vv. 1–2; 17:1–6,15–16; 18:1–15), and Abraham obeyed the Lord by naming him Isaac (v. 3; 17:16) and by circumcising him (vv. 4–5; 17:9–14), while Sarah responded with praise (vv. 6–7). This episode illustrates God's faithfulness to his promise to make Abraham's descendants numerous.

21:1 was gracious. More literally, "visited"; that is, God intervened to shape destiny. The Hebrew is translated "come to your aid" in 50:24. **as he had said.** This is matched by "as God commanded him" (v. 4).

21:2 in his old age, at the very time. See 17:17 and 24 and 18:11–14.

21:3 Abraham gave the name. In the naming of Isaac (see 17:19) and in the act of circumcision (v. 4; see 17:9–12), Abraham kept the covenant.

21:6 will laugh. Sarah's laughter of incredulity before the birth was changed afterward to that of joy .

21:7 children? The unexpected plural implies that Sarah was looking beyond Isaac to his offspring, who were destined to bless the earth.

21:8–11 The expulsion of Hagar and Ishmael removed any threat to Isaac's inheritance. The birth of Isaac and the removal of Ishma-

a great feast. 9But Sarah saw that the son whom Hagar the Egyptian had borne to Abraham[m] was mocking,[n] 10and she said to Abraham, "Get rid of that slave woman and her
son, for that slave woman's son will never share in the inheritance with my son Isaac."[o]
11The matter distressed Abraham greatly because it concerned his son.[p] 12But God
said to him, "Do not be so distressed about the boy and your maidservant. Listen to whatever Sarah tells you, because it is through Isaac that your offspring[a] will be reckoned.[q]
13I will make the son of the maidservant into a nation[r] also, because he is your offspring."
14Early the next morning Abraham took some food and a skin of water and gave them
to Hagar. He set them on her shoulders and then sent her off with the boy. She went on
her way and wandered in the desert of Beersheba.[s]
15When the water in the skin was gone, she put the boy under one of the bushes.
16Then she went off and sat down nearby, about a bowshot away, for she thought, "I cannot watch the boy die." And as she sat there nearby, she[b] began to sob.
17God heard the boy crying,[t] and the angel of God called to Hagar from heaven and
said to her, "What is the matter, Hagar? Do not be afraid; God has heard the boy crying
as he lies there. 18Lift the boy up and take him by the hand, for I will make him into a
great nation.[u]"
19Then God opened her eyes[v] and she saw a well of water. So she went and filled the
skin with water and gave the boy a drink.
20God was with the boy[w] as he grew up. He lived in the desert and became an archer.
21While he was living in the Desert of Paran, his mother got a wife for him[x] from Egypt.

The Treaty at Beersheba

22At that time Abimelech and Phicol the commander of his forces said to Abraham,
"God is with you in everything you do. 23Now swear[y] to me here before God that you will
not deal falsely with me or my children or my descendants. Show to me and the country where you are living as an alien the same kindness I have shown to you."
24Abraham said, "I swear it."
25Then Abraham complained to Abimelech about a well of water that Abimelech's
servants had seized.[z] 26But Abimelech said, "I don't know who has done this. You did not
tell me, and I heard about it only today."
27So Abraham brought sheep and cattle and gave them to Abimelech, and the two
men made a treaty.[a] 28Abraham set apart seven ewe lambs from the flock, 29and Abim-

21:9 [m]Ge 16:15 [n]Gal 4:29
21:10 [o]Gal 4:30*
21:11 [p]Ge 17:18
21:12 [q]Ro 9:7*; Heb 11:18*
21:13 [r]ver 18
21:14 [s]ver 31,32
21:17 [t]Ex 3:7
21:18 [u]ver 13
21:19 [v]Nu 22:31
21:20 [w]Ge 26:3,24; 28:15; 39:2,21,23
21:21 [x]Ge 24:4,38
21:23 [y]ver 31; Jos 2:12
21:25 [z]Ge 26:15,18,20-22
21:27 [a]Ge 26:28,31

[a] *12* Or *seed* [b] *16* Hebrew; Septuagint *the child*

el are linked by the Hebrew word for "laugh," which appears in verses 6 and 9 (see note), and, more importantly, by the word of the Lord assuring Isaac's birth (v. 1) and inheritance (v. 12). Once again Abraham received God's promise (v. 12) on the basis of his ready obedience (v. 14; see note on 20:8).

21:8 weaned. This rite of passage, which marked the passing of a child from the precarious stage of infancy to that of childhood, occurred at about three years of age.

21:9 Sarah saw. From her experience with Hagar (ch. 16), Sarah perceived the significance of Ishmael's disdain for Isaac and his threat to her son's inheritance. **mocking.** The Hebrew root means "laugh" (v. 6), but the form here signifies "to laugh malevolently." The son of the slave woman persecuted the son of the free woman (Gal 4:29). See *WLC* 145.

21:10 Get rid of. That is, disinherit (25:5–6).

21:11 distressed. Paternal love, not moral or legal concerns, explains Abraham's distress (see 16:6 and its note; see 17:18).

21:12 boy. The Hebrew term simply means "inexperienced," and so it could refer to any age. Even Solomon at forty years of age applied this term to himself (1Ki 3:7). The NIV renders two different Hebrew terms "boy": *na'ar* (vv. 12,17,18,19,20) and *yeled* (vv. 14,15, 16). The former suggests care and concern; the latter a biological relationship. **maidservant.** The same Hebrew word is translated "slave woman" in verse 10; a different word is translated "maidservant" in 16:1. Its use here identifies Hagar as married to Abraham; in verse 10 it signifies that she is Sarah's possession and laborer. **your offspring will be reckoned.** Everlasting blessing was pronounced only on those of the promise (see 17:7; Heb 11:17–19).

21:13 nation. That is, "a great nation" (v. 18; 16:10). Because of God's great love for Abraham, even his natural children would be blessed on Earth, although as a group the descendants of Ishmael were not heirs to the covenant promises made to Abraham.

21:14 skin of water. Approximately three gallons. **with the boy.** Literally, "He gave unto Hagar." He set the food and water on her shoulders and, together with the boy, sent her away.

21:15 put. Literally, "to throw"; that is, "to expose, abandon" (Jer 38:6; Eze 16:5).

21:17–19 God's common grace was extended beyond Isaac's line.

21:17 God heard. See 16:11. **the boy crying.** Ishmael had initially provoked their plight; here his cry led to their salvation.

21:20 archer. He would survive by his weapons.

21:21 Desert of Paran . . . wife. The persecutor's destiny was sealed forever: He would not inherit the divine promises of offspring and land. **Egypt.** See 16:1.

■ **21:22–34** *Abraham's Treaty With Abimelech.* This report of a Philistine king and his commander suing for a nonaggression pact in perpetuity between Abraham and his descendants provides concrete evidence of God's blessing on Abraham and assurance that he would possess the land. The naming of the site in commemoration of that covenant, the planting of a commemorative tree and the use of the name "Eternal God" (v. 33) guided the original readers as they anticipated encountering the descendants of Abimelech in the promised land.

21:22 At that time. The Philistine king's visit gave further assurance that Isaac would receive the promised inheritance. **Abimelech.** Abraham's first encounter with Abimelech pertained to offspring and grazing rights (20:1–18); this one to well rights (v. 25).

21:23 Now swear to me. The supernatural blessing on Abraham, an alien shepherd, could be measured by a king and his commander seeking a nonaggression pact with him (14:13; 23:6). **before God.** The oaths were in God's name (vv. 31,33). **my descendants.** The covenant was to endure in perpetuity, but it was no more reliable than any other human document (26:15–31). **kindness.** The Hebrew term denotes a voluntary commitment by a stronger party to meet the needs of a weaker.

21:24 See *HC* 101.

21:25 complained. That the shepherd responded to a king and the king backed down (v. 26) revealed Abraham's superiority over Abimelech.

elech asked Abraham, "What is the meaning of these seven ewe lambs you have set apart
by themselves?"
30He replied, "Accept these seven lambs from my hand as a witness[b] that I dug this well."
31So that place was called Beersheba,[a c] because the two men swore an oath there.
32After the treaty had been made at Beersheba, Abimelech and Phicol the commander of his forces returned to the land of the Philistines. 33Abraham planted a tamarisk tree in Beersheba, and there he called upon the name of the LORD,[d] the Eternal God.[e]
34And Abraham stayed in the land of the Philistines for a long time.

Abraham Tested

22 Some time later God tested[f] Abraham. He said to him, "Abraham!"
"Here I am," he replied.
2Then God said, "Take your son[g], your only son, Isaac, whom you love, and go to the
region of Moriah.[h] Sacrifice him there as a burnt offering on one of the mountains I will
tell you about."
3Early the next morning Abraham got up and saddled his donkey. He took with him
two of his servants and his son Isaac. When he had cut enough wood for the burnt offering, he set out for the place God had told him about. 4On the third day Abraham looked
up and saw the place in the distance. 5He said to his servants, "Stay here with the donkey while I and the boy go over there. We will worship and then we will come back to you."
6Abraham took the wood for the burnt offering and placed it on his son Isaac,[i] and
he himself carried the fire and the knife. As the two of them went on together, 7Isaac
spoke up and said to his father Abraham, "Father?"
"Yes, my son?" Abraham replied.
"The fire and wood are here," Isaac said, "but where is the lamb[j] for the burnt offering?"
8Abraham answered, "God himself will provide the lamb for the burnt offering, my
son." And the two of them went on together.
9When they reached the place God had told him about, Abraham built an altar there
and arranged the wood on it. He bound his son Isaac and laid him on the altar,[k] on top
of the wood. 10Then he reached out his hand and took the knife to slay his son. 11But the
angel of the LORD called out to him from heaven, "Abraham! Abraham!"
"Here I am," he replied.

21:30 [b]Ge 31:44,47,48,50,52
21:31 [c]Ge 26:33
21:33 [d]Ge 4:26 [e]Dt 33:27
22:1 [f]Dt 8:2,16; Heb 11:17; Jas 1:12-13
22:2 [g]ver 12,16; Jn 3:16; Heb 11:17; 1Jn 4:9 [h]2Ch 3:1
22:6 [i]Jn 19:17
22:7 [j]Lev 1:10
22:9 [k]Heb 11:17-19; Jas 2:21

a 31 *Beersheba* can mean *well of seven* or *well of the oath.*

21:30 Accept. By accepting the gift, Abimelech was obliged to acknowledge Abraham's right to the well. The covenant had to be ratified by witnesses and oaths (v. 31).
21:31 Beersheba. The name means either "well of oath" or "well of seven," a pun on the key word. **swore.** A verbal agreement of the covenant was not enough (v. 23). It had to be ratified by an oath.
21:33 tamarisk tree. The planting of this small tree in the Negev probably served as a landmark of God's grace, as a pledge that Abraham would stay in the land and perhaps as a symbol of God's shading presence (see note on 12:6). **called upon.** See 12:8 and its note. **Eternal God.** See 14:19 and its note.
21:34 stayed. The Hebrew here is elsewhere translated "for a while he stayed." Abraham's activities in the land of Philistia encouraged the original audience as the people anticipated their approaching conquest of those lands.
■ **22:1–19** *Abraham's Test and Assurance.* Having already graciously committed himself to Abraham, God tested Abraham's obedience. Abraham displayed his full commitment to the Lord by being willing to sacrifice his son Isaac. As a result of his fidelity, God assured Abraham that it would be through his son Isaac that all the promises of the covenant would be fulfilled. God's provision of the ram typifies the sacrifice of Jesus Christ, who died instead of the elect so that they would live (vv. 13–14). In taking an oath to bless Abraham and all nations through him, God guaranteed the promise to Abraham's offspring (vv. 15–19). See note on Hebrews 11:17–19.
22:1 tested. God tests his saints to prove the quality of their faith and obedience. Often this is done through adversity or hardship (Ex 20:20; Dt 8:2; 2Ch 32:31; 2Co 2:9; 8:8; 13:5; Jas 1:12; Rev 2:10; 3:10). The Hebrew here does not mean "to entice to do wrong." Satan tempts us to destroy us (Ro 6:2; Jas 1:15; 1Pe 5:8), but God tests us to strengthen us. **"Here I am."** A replay in ordinary speech, especially between persons related by intimacy or respect (Ex 3:4; 1Sa 3:4; Isa 6:8; Heb 10:7).
22:2 Take. The Hebrew grammar suggests the meaning "Since you are ready to obey me, take your son. **only.** Isaac was Abraham's special child, though Ishmael had also been born to him. Isaac's death would mean the end of the line of promise, a terrible catastrophe (Jer 6:26; Am 8:10; Zec 12:10; cf. Jdg 11:34). **son.** Repeated for emphasis (vv. 2,3,6,7,8,9,10,12,13,16). The test was monumental. **go to.** The Hebrew adds "by yourself," signifying God's determination to disassociate Abraham from his familiar surroundings. As Abraham had left all that he held dear to go to the land prescribed by the Lord (12:1), he also had to offer to the Lord what he held most dear and worship at the place of God's choosing (Dt 12:5,30–32). Faith is a lonely pilgrimage that demands no less than total commitment. **region of Moriah.** Later the site of Israel's temple (2Ch 3:1). **Sacrifice him.** God's command did not contradict his moral law. The firstborn belonged to the Lord (Ex 13:11–13; 22:29; 34:19–20), but God never intended for Abraham to carry through with the sacrifice. **burnt offering.** This offering symbolized consecration and atonement (Lev 1:3–9).
22:3 Early the next morning. Another example of Abraham's prompt obedience (see note on 20:8). **wood.** Since the exact destination was as yet unknown to Abraham, he split the wood before hand.
22:4 third day. A typical period of preparation for an important event (see 31:22; 42:18). Abraham proceeded with resolute faith.
22:5 we will come back. For interpretive comments, see Romans 4:16–25 and Hebrews 11:19.
22:6 wood . . . on his son. A son who could carry sufficient wood for a sacrifice on his back up a mountain could certainly resist his father. Isaac typified Christ, who bore the cross to Calvary (Mt 27:32).
22:8 provide the lamb. Abraham's faith in God's word enabled him to see God's command in the light of the promises.
22:9 laid him on the altar. This moment of great internal struggle by both Abraham and Isaac provides a poignant type of Christ's willing obedience to do his Father's will (Jn 1:29,36; Ro 8:32; Php 2:6–8; 1Pe 2:21–24).
22:11 angel of the LORD. See note on 16:7. **"Abraham! Abraham!"** The repetition connotes urgency (cf. 46:2; Ex 3:4; 1Sa 3:10; Ac 9:4).

12“Do not lay a hand on the boy,” he said. “Do not do anything to him. Now I know
that you fear God,[l] because you have not withheld from me your son, your only son.[m]”
13Abraham looked up and there in a thicket he saw a ram[a] caught by its horns. He
went over and took the ram and sacrificed it as a burnt offering instead of his son.[n] 14So
Abraham called that place The LORD Will Provide. And to this day it is said, “On the
mountain of the LORD it will be provided.[o]”
15The angel of the LORD called to Abraham from heaven a second time 16and said, “I
swear by myself,[p] declares the LORD, that because you have done this and have not withheld your son, your only son, 17I will surely bless you and make your descendants[q] as numerous as the stars in the sky[r] and as the sand on the seashore.[s] Your descendants will
take possession of the cities of their enemies,[t] 18and through your offspring[b] all nations
on earth will be blessed,[u] because you have obeyed me.”[v]
19Then Abraham returned to his servants, and they set off together for Beersheba.
And Abraham stayed in Beersheba.

Nahor's Sons

20Some time later Abraham was told, “Milcah is also a mother; she has borne sons
to your brother Nahor:[w] 21Uz the firstborn, Buz his brother, Kemuel (the father of Aram),
22Kesed, Hazo, Pildash, Jidlaph and Bethuel.” 23Bethuel became the father of Rebekah.[x]
Milcah bore these eight sons to Abraham's brother Nahor. 24His concubine, whose
name was Reumah, also had sons: Tebah, Gaham, Tahash and Maacah.

The Death of Sarah

23 Sarah lived to be a hundred and twenty-seven years old. 2She died at Kiriath
Arba[y] (that is, Hebron)[z] in the land of Canaan, and Abraham went to mourn for
Sarah and to weep over her.
3Then Abraham rose from beside his dead wife and spoke to the Hittites.[c] He said, 4“I
am an alien and a stranger[a] among you. Sell me some property for a burial site here so
I can bury my dead.”
5The Hittites replied to Abraham, 6“Sir, listen to us. You are a mighty prince[b] among

22:12 [l]1Sa 15:22; Jas 2:21-22 [m]ver 2; Jn 3:16
22:13 [n]Ro 8:32
22:14 [o]ver 8
22:16 [p]Lk 1:73; Heb 6:13
22:17 [q]Heb 6:14* [r]Ge 15:5 [s]Ge 26:24; 32:12 [t]Ge 24:60
22:18 [u]Ge 12:2,3; Ac 3:25*; Gal 3:8* [v]ver 10
22:20 [w]Ge 11:29
22:23 [x]Ge 24:15
23:2 [y]Jos 14:15 [z]ver 19; Ge 13:18
23:4 [a]Ge 17:8; 1Ch 29:15; Ps 105:12; Heb 11:9,13
23:6 [b]Ge 14:14-16; 24:35

[a] *13* Many manuscripts of the Masoretic Text, Samaritan Pentateuch, Septuagint and Syriac; most manuscripts of the Masoretic Text *a ram behind ⌊him⌋* [b] *18* Or *seed* [c] *3* Or *the sons of Heth*; also in verses 5, 7, 10, 16, 18 and 20

22:12 Now I know. God acknowledged the quality of Abraham's faith. It was not expressed in words, but in deeds (Jas 2:21–22). **fear God.** See note on 20:11.
22:14 The LORD Will Provide. Here providential provision is seen. The name by which Abraham commemorated the event shows that he perceived God's revelation of his saving purpose. “Provide” means “to see” or “to see to it” (vv. 4,8,13).
22:16 I swear by myself. For interpretive comment, see Hebrews 6:13–20, especially verse 17. **not withheld . . . your only son.** A type of God's consecration of Christ (Jn 3:16; Ro 8:32).
22:17 bless. See notes on 1:22 and 12:2. **descendants.** See 13:16 and 15:5.
22:18 offspring. See notes on 12:7, 13:16, 15:5 and 17:5,15 and 16. God reassured Abraham that the promises of the covenant would be fulfilled through Isaac. This fact provides the background for the transition to Isaac in the following chapters (see 22:20—25:11). **because you have obeyed me.** The promise was now grounded in both the will and purpose of the Lord and in the obedience of Abraham. Abraham's obedience prefigured the active obedience of Christ, who secured the covenantal blessings for Abraham's innumerable offspring who share his faith in the God who gives life to the dead (see note on 18:11; see also Ro 4:17,19–24). See *BC* 17,27; *HC* 19.
▪ **22:20—25:11** *Transition to Isaac.* This final section of the account of Terah provides a transition from the patriarchy of Abraham to that of Isaac. The narrative begins to shift to Isaac's headship. This section divides into five sections: Rebekah's family background (22:20–24); Sarah's death (23:1–20); Isaac's marriage to Rebekah (24:1–67); the dismissal of Abraham's other children, leaving Isaac the sole heir (25:1–6); and Abraham's death (25:7–11). This shift in focus to Isaac was important to the Israelites, as it is to all believers, because Isaac was the patriarch through whom God's covenant blessings would come.
▪ **22:20–24** *Rebekah's Family Background.* The 12 offspring of Nahor parallel the 12 tribes of Israel (49:28): Eight came from the principal wives and four from the secondary wives (30:1–24; 35:16–18). The purity of Israel's line is stressed.
22:20 was told. The report of his brother's children reminded Abraham of his unfinished task: securing the second generation of the promised family.
22:21 Buz. In northern or eastern Arabia.
22:22 Hazo. Modern Hasa, located on the Arabian coast opposite Bahrain. **Pildash, Jidlaph.** Unknown sites.
22:23 Rebekah. She was related to both of Abraham's brothers. Her father, Bethuel, was the son of Milcah, the daughter of Haran and the wife of Nahor (11:29). In the next generation, Leah and Rachel shared the same ancestry, for their father, Laban, was the brother of Rebekah (29:10).
22:24 concubine. A second-class wife who was acquired without payment of bride money or land; she possessed few legal rights (Dt 21:10–14).
▪ **23:1–20** *The Death of Sarah.* By firmly securing a piece of real estate in the land God had promised him, Abraham showed his unswerving commitment to the promise (22:17–18). Though he had no place to bury his dead (vv. 4,6,8,11,13,15; cf. v. 19), without wavering in his faith he purchased his first piece of property in the promised land: a cemetery plot. His faith exemplifies that of all believers who die without having obtained the promise (Heb 11:39–40), yet who believe that the meek will inherit the earth (Mt 5:5).
23:1 a hundred and twenty-seven years old. Sarah is the only woman in the Bible whose life span is recorded; this detail signifies her importance.
23:3–18 The narrative details demonstrate that Abraham held an impeccable legal claim to the field in Machpelah, near Mamre (50:13).
23:3 Hittites. See note on 10:15–19.
23:4 an alien and a stranger. This hendiadys (conjunction of two terms that function together with one meaning), meaning “resident alien,” underscores that Abraham owned no land. As a type of all saints, Abraham was dependent on God's gracious provisions (1Ch 29:15; Ps 39:12; Heb 11:13). **Sell me.** God's gift of the land would be fulfilled beyond the lifetimes of Abraham and Sarah.

us. Bury your dead in the choicest of our tombs. None of us will refuse you his tomb for
burying your dead."
7Then Abraham rose and bowed down before the people of the land, the Hittites. 8He
said to them, "If you are willing to let me bury my dead, then listen to me and intercede
with Ephron son of Zohar[c] on my behalf 9so he will sell me the cave of Machpelah, which
belongs to him and is at the end of his field. Ask him to sell it to me for the full price as
a burial site among you."
10Ephron the Hittite was sitting among his people and he replied to Abraham in the
hearing of all the Hittites who had come to the gate[d] of his city. 11"No, my lord," he said.
"Listen to me; I give[a][e] you the field, and I give[a] you the cave that is in it. I give[a] it to you
in the presence of my people. Bury your dead."
12Again Abraham bowed down before the people of the land 13and he said to Ephron
in their hearing, "Listen to me, if you will. I will pay the price of the field. Accept it from
me so I can bury my dead there."
14Ephron answered Abraham, 15"Listen to me, my lord; the land is worth four hundred shekels[b] of silver,[f] but what is that between me and you? Bury your dead."
16Abraham agreed to Ephron's terms and weighed out for him the price he had
named in the hearing of the Hittites: four hundred shekels of silver,[g] according to the
weight current among the merchants.
17So Ephron's field in Machpelah near Mamre[h]—both the field and the cave in it, and
all the trees within the borders of the field—was deeded 18to Abraham as his property
in the presence of all the Hittites who had come to the gate of the city. 19Afterward Abraham buried his wife Sarah in the cave in the field of Machpelah near Mamre (which is
at Hebron) in the land of Canaan. 20So the field and the cave in it were deeded[i] to Abraham by the Hittites as a burial site.

Isaac and Rebekah

24 Abraham was now old and well advanced in years, and the LORD had blessed
him in every way.[j] 2He said to the chief[c] servant in his household, the one in
charge of all that he had,[k] "Put your hand under my thigh.[l] 3I want you to swear by the
LORD, the God of heaven and the God of earth,[m] that you will not get a wife for my son[n]
from the daughters of the Canaanites,[o] among whom I am living, 4but will go to my country and my own relatives[p] and get a wife for my son Isaac."
5The servant asked him, "What if the woman is unwilling to come back with me to
this land? Shall I then take your son back to the country you came from?"
6"Make sure that you do not take my son back there," Abraham said. 7"The LORD, the
God of heaven, who brought me out of my father's household and my native land and
who spoke to me and promised me on oath, saying, 'To your offspring[d][q] I will give this
land'[r]—he will send his angel before you[s] so that you can get a wife for my son from

23:8 [c]Ge 25:9
23:10 [d]Ge 34:20-24; Ru 4:4
23:11 [e]2Sa 24:23
23:15 [f]Eze 45:12
23:16 [g]Jer 32:9; Zec 11:12
23:17 [h]Ge 25:9; 49:30-32; 50:13; Ac 7:16
23:20 [i]Jer 32:10
24:1 [j]ver 35
24:2 [k]Ge 39:4-6 [l]ver 9; Ge 47:29
24:3 [m]Ge 14:19 [n]Ge 28:1; Dt 7:3 [o]Ge 10:15-19
24:4 [p]Ge 12:1; 28:2
24:7 [q]Gal 3:16* [r]Ge 12:7; 13:15 [s]Ex 23:20,23

[a] *11* Or *sell* [b] *15* That is, about 10 pounds (about 4.5 kilograms) [c] *2* Or *oldest* [d] *7* Or *seed*

23:6 mighty prince. Or "a prince of God." They recognized God's blessing and protection on this alien (see note on 21:23). Abraham ranked himself at the bottom of society, but they placed him at the top. **tombs.** They changed the language from "property for a burial site" (v. 4) to "tomb," suggesting that they were reluctant to sell him a permanent possession.
23:7 people of the land. May refer to the men who were responsible for a region's political activity or who belonged to the upper class.
23:9 Machpelah. The name means "double cave" or "split cave."
23:10 Ephron . . . replied. Ephron's direct reply indicated that he had sold the cave and the field of his own free will, without social pressure, making Abraham's claim to the property even more incontestable. **in the hearing.** The details ensured that the transaction was proper and legal, with appropriate witnesses. **gate.** Legal transactions took place in the gate of the city (Ru 4:1).
23:11 I give. Alternatively, "I am going to give." His proposition was part of the exaggerated politeness of the bargaining.
23:15 four hundred shekels. The price seems high when compared with the field that Jeremiah bought for 17 shekels (Jer 32:9) and with the hill of Samaria that Omri purchased for 600 shekels (1Ki 16:24). Ephron took advantage of Abraham.
23:16 Abraham agreed. Abraham did not try to bargain; he wanted an indisputable sale.
23:19 buried . . . in the cave. Her impressive grave was a worthy memorial to a great woman, and it anchored Abraham's descendants in the promised land (24:6–9; 25:9; 49:30; 50:13; Heb 11:13–16).

■**24:1–67** *The Gift of Rebekah to Isaac.* God providentially arranged through a prayerful servant for Isaac, the promised heir, to meet, marry and grow in love with the matriarch whom God had chosen. God cared for his faithful people from generation to generation.
24:1 blessed. See 1:22, 12:2 and their notes. God's blessing was now proclaimed as realized.
24:2–9 See *WCF* 22.3.
24:2 chief. Abraham entrusted this important mission only to his most devoted manager. This servant, probably Eliezer (15:2–3), fully shared Abraham's faith and wonderfully participated in God's history of redemption (17:12–13). **Put your hand under my thigh.** One facing death secured his last will by an oath taken at the source of life, near the genitalia (see 47:29).
24:3 the LORD, the God of heaven and the God of earth. See 14:22. An appropriate title by which to swear an oath for one beginning a perilous journey to a distant land. **not get a wife for my son from the daughters of the Canaanites.** Abraham set an example for his descendants to secure wives from the blessed Semites, not from the cursed Canaanites (9:24–27; 15:16; 18:18–19; Dt 7:1–4).
24:4 my own relatives. Abraham's appeal was characterized by family loyalty (see notes on 11:27–32; 22:23; 31:50).
24:6 do not take my son back there. Abraham did not turn back on God's call to leave his homeland (see notes on 12:1,7; 23:19).
24:7 who brought me out. Abraham oriented his entire life, even at death, to God's promise (12:1–3,7). **To your offspring I will give this land.** The patriarch's last words expressed his enduring hope in God's promise (12:7). **his angel.** See note on 16:7.

there. 8If the woman is unwilling to come back with you, then you will be released from
this oath of mine. Only do not take my son back there." 9So the servant put his hand under the thigh[t] of his master Abraham and swore an oath to him concerning this matter.
10Then the servant took ten of his master's camels and left, taking with him all kinds
of good things from his master. He set out for Aram Naharaim[a] and made his way to the
town of Nahor. 11He had the camels kneel down near the well[u] outside the town; it was
toward evening, the time the women go out to draw water.[v]
12Then he prayed, "O LORD, God of my master Abraham,[w] give me success today, and
show kindness to my master Abraham. 13See, I am standing beside this spring, and the
daughters of the townspeople are coming out to draw water. 14May it be that when I say
to a girl, 'Please let down your jar that I may have a drink,' and she says, 'Drink, and I'll
water your camels too'—let her be the one you have chosen for your servant Isaac. By
this I will know[x] that you have shown kindness to my master."
15Before he had finished praying,[y] Rebekah[z] came out with her jar on her shoulder.
She was the daughter of Bethuel son of Milcah,[a] who was the wife of Abraham's brother Nahor.[b] 16The girl was very beautiful,[c] a virgin; no man had ever lain with her. She
went down to the spring, filled her jar and came up again.
17The servant hurried to meet her and said, "Please give me a little water from your
jar."
18"Drink,[d] my lord," she said, and quickly lowered the jar to her hands and gave him
a drink.
19After she had given him a drink, she said, "I'll draw water for your camels too,[e] until they have finished drinking." 20So she quickly emptied her jar into the trough, ran back
to the well to draw more water, and drew enough for all his camels. 21Without saying a
word, the man watched her closely to learn whether or not the LORD had made his journey successful.[f]
22When the camels had finished drinking, the man took out a gold nose ring[g] weighing a beka[b] and two gold bracelets weighing ten shekels.[c] 23Then he asked, "Whose
daughter are you? Please tell me, is there room in your father's house for us to spend the
night?"
24She answered him, "I am the daughter of Bethuel, the son that Milcah bore to Nahor.[h]" 25And she added, "We have plenty of straw and fodder, as well as room for you
to spend the night."
26Then the man bowed down and worshiped the LORD,[i] 27saying, "Praise be to the
LORD,[j] the God of my master Abraham, who has not abandoned his kindness and faithfulness[k] to my master. As for me, the LORD has led me on the journey[l] to the house of my
master's relatives."[m]
28The girl ran and told her mother's household about these things. 29Now Rebekah
had a brother named Laban,[n] and he hurried out to the man at the spring. 30As soon as
he had seen the nose ring, and the bracelets on his sister's arms, and had heard Rebekah tell what the man said to her, he went out to the man and found him standing by the
camels near the spring. 31"Come, you who are blessed by the LORD,"[o] he said. "Why are
you standing out here? I have prepared the house and a place for the camels."
32So the man went to the house, and the camels were unloaded. Straw and fodder
were brought for the camels, and water for him and his men to wash their feet.[p] 33Then

24:9 [t]ver 2
24:11 [u]Ex 2:15 [v]ver 13; 1Sa 9:11
24:12 [w]ver 27,42,48; Ge 26:24; Ex 3:6, 15,16
24:14 [x]Jdg 6:17,37
24:15 [y]ver 45 [z]Ge 22:23 [a]Ge 22:20 [b]Ge 11:29
24:16 [c]Ge 26:7
24:18 [d]ver 14
24:19 [e]ver 14
24:21 [f]ver 12
24:22 [g]ver 47
24:24 [h]ver 15
24:26 [i]ver 48,52; Ex 4:31
24:27 [j]Ex 18:10; Ru 4:14; 1Sa 25:32 [k]ver 49; Ge 32:10; Ps 98:3 [l]ver 21 [m]ver 12,48
24:29 [n]ver 4; Ge 29:5,12, 13
24:31 [o]Ge 26:29; Ru 3:10; Ps 115:15
24:32 [p]Ge 43:24; Jdg 19:21

[a] *10* That is, Northwest Mesopotamia [b] *22* That is, about 1/5 ounce (about 5.5 grams) [c] *22* That is, about 4 ounces (about 110 grams)

Abraham learned from his experience with Hagar not to trust the flesh to secure the promise but to expect God's supernatural provision (ch. 16).

24:10 Aram Naharaim. Means "Aram of the Two Rivers" (i.e., the Euphrates and Habor Rivers). **town of Nahor.** In the vicinity of Haran.

24:12 he prayed. The meeting was framed in prayer (vv. 26–27). This is the first recorded prayer for specific guidance in the Bible. **kindness.** The Hebrew here entails loyalty to a covenant relationship.

24:14 By this I will know. A request for a sign was appropriate because his mission was so important. He was conscious of the angel's invisible presence (v. 7).

24:15 Before he had finished praying. God's providential timing was key in this and other stories. **Rebekah.** See note on 22:23.

24:16 very beautiful. Many honored women in Scripture were noted for their beauty (12:11; 20:2; 29:17; 38:13–19; Jos 2:1; Ru 3:1–9; Ps 45:11–15). **a virgin.** To assure that her children would unquestionably be Isaac's.

24:22 took out a gold. To reward her, to win her goodwill and to impress her family.

24:26 worshiped the LORD. The meeting was framed by prayer and worship.

24:27 has led. The Hebrew term connotes leading through difficulty (Ex 13:17,21; 15:13; 32:34).

24:29 Laban. Laban took responsibility for the family, either because the family government was fratriarchal, not patriarchal, or because the father, Bethuel, was incapacitated (see v. 50; 20:16 and their notes).

24:30 As soon as he had seen. This picture of Laban racing after gold foreshadowed his dealings with Jacob.

24:33 I will not eat until. The servant put his mission before his need and comfort without displaying any sense of obligation to his host and hostess.

food was set before him, but he said, "I will not eat until I have told you what I have to
say."
"Then tell us," ⌊Laban⌋ said.
34So he said, "I am Abraham's servant. 35The LORD has blessed my master abundantly,[q] and he has become wealthy. He has given him sheep and cattle, silver and gold, menservants and maidservants, and camels and donkeys.[r] 36My master's wife Sarah has
borne him a son in her[a] old age,[s] and he has given him everything he owns.[t] 37And my
master made me swear an oath, and said, 'You must not get a wife for my son from the
daughters of the Canaanites, in whose land I live,[u] 38but go to my father's family and to
my own clan, and get a wife for my son.'[v]
39"Then I asked my master, 'What if the woman will not come back with me?'[w]
40"He replied, 'The LORD, before whom I have walked, will send his angel with you[x]
and make your journey a success, so that you can get a wife for my son from my own clan
and from my father's family. 41Then, when you go to my clan, you will be released from
my oath even if they refuse to give her to you—you will be released from my oath.'[y]
42"When I came to the spring today, I said, 'O LORD, God of my master Abraham, if you
will, please grant success[z] to the journey on which I have come. 43See, I am standing beside this spring;[a] if a maiden comes out to draw water and I say to her, "Please let me
drink a little water from your jar,"[b] 44and if she says to me, "Drink, and I'll draw water
for your camels too," let her be the one the LORD has chosen for my master's son.'
45"Before I finished praying in my heart,[c] Rebekah came out, with her jar on her
shoulder.[d] She went down to the spring and drew water, and I said to her, 'Please give
me a drink.'[e]
46"She quickly lowered her jar from her shoulder and said, 'Drink, and I'll water your
camels too.'[f] So I drank, and she watered the camels also.
47"I asked her, 'Whose daughter are you?'[g]
"She said, 'The daughter of Bethuel son of Nahor, whom Milcah bore to him.'[h]
"Then I put the ring in her nose and the bracelets on her arms,[i] 48and I bowed down
and worshiped the LORD.[j] I praised the LORD, the God of my master Abraham, who had
led me on the right road to get the granddaughter of my master's brother for his son.[k]
49Now if you will show kindness and faithfulness[l] to my master, tell me; and if not, tell
me, so I may know which way to turn."
50Laban and Bethuel answered, "This is from the LORD;[m] we can say nothing to you
one way or the other.[n] 51Here is Rebekah; take her and go, and let her become the wife
of your master's son, as the LORD has directed."
52When Abraham's servant heard what they said, he bowed down to the ground before the LORD.[o] 53Then the servant brought out gold and silver jewelry and articles of clothing and gave them to Rebekah; he also gave costly gifts[p] to her brother and to her mother. 54Then he and the men who were with him ate and drank and spent the night there.
When they got up the next morning, he said, "Send me on my way[q] to my master."
55But her brother and her mother replied, "Let the girl remain with us ten days or so;
then you[b] may go."
56But he said to them, "Do not detain me, now that the LORD has granted success to
my journey. Send me on my way so I may go to my master."
57Then they said, "Let's call the girl and ask her about it." 58So they called Rebekah
and asked her, "Will you go with this man?"
"I will go," she said.
59So they sent their sister Rebekah on her way, along with her nurse[r] and Abraham's
servant and his men. 60And they blessed Rebekah and said to her,

24:35 [q]ver 1 [r]Ge 13:2
24:36 [s]Ge 21:2,10 [t]Ge 25:5
24:37 [u]ver 3
24:38 [v]ver 4
24:39 [w]ver 5
24:40 [x]ver 7
24:41 [y]ver 8
24:42 [z]ver 12
24:43 [a]ver 13 [b]ver 14
24:45 [c]1Sa 1:13 [d]ver 15 [e]ver 17
24:46 [f]ver 18-19
24:47 [g]ver 23 [h]ver 24 [i]Eze 16:11-12
24:48 [j]ver 26 [k]ver 27
24:49 [l]Ge 47:29; Jos 2:14
24:50 [m]Ps 118:23 [n]Ge 31:7,24,29,42
24:52 [o]ver 26
24:53 [p]ver 10,22
24:54 [q]ver 56,59
24:59 [r]Ge 35:8

[a] *36* Or *his* [b] *55* Or *she*

24:36 in her old age. To assure them that Isaac was not too old. **he has given him everything he owns.** A detail indicating Isaac's wealth and importance (25:5–6).
24:42–48 The repetition of the story was necessary for Laban, Milcah and Rebekah to acknowledge the hand of the Lord.
24:50 Laban and Bethuel. The irregular sequence of mentioning the son before the father suggests that Bethuel may have been incapacitated. In verse 55, only the brother and mother are mentioned. **This is from the LORD.** They validated the hand of providence. **one way or the other.** The Hebrew here is translated "either good or bad" in 31:24.
24:53 brought out gold. The bride price was payment for the loss of the bride's services and potential offspring (34:12; Ex 22:16).
24:55 Let the girl remain. A similar event takes place in the Apocryphal book Tobit (Tobit 8:20), indicating that it was a customary practice.
24:57–58 See *WCF* 24.3.
24:57 about it. That is, the time of departure; the marriage was already arranged.
24:58 I will go. This is the most decisive remark in the narrative. In complying with the Lord's direction (v. 56), Rebekah acted in faith similarly to Abraham, leaving her own family (see 12:1,4).
24:59 her nurse. The wet nurse, after having suckled the child, had the responsibility of rearing her and serving as guardian.

"Our sister, may you increase
to thousands upon thousands;[s]
may your offspring possess
the gates of their enemies."[t]

61 Then Rebekah and her maids got ready and mounted their camels and went back
with the man. So the servant took Rebekah and left.
62 Now Isaac had come from Beer Lahai Roi,[u] for he was living in the Negev.[v] 63 He
went out to the field one evening to meditate,[a][w] and as he looked up, he saw camels approaching. 64 Rebekah also looked up and saw Isaac. She got down from her camel 65 and
asked the servant, "Who is that man in the field coming to meet us?"
"He is my master," the servant answered. So she took her veil and covered herself.
66 Then the servant told Isaac all he had done. 67 Isaac brought her into the tent of his
mother Sarah, and he married Rebekah.[x] So she became his wife, and he loved her;[y] and
Isaac was comforted after his mother's death.[z]

The Death of Abraham

25 Abraham took[b] another wife, whose name was Keturah. 2 She bore him Zimran,
Jokshan, Medan, Midian, Ishbak and Shuah.[a] 3 Jokshan was the father of Sheba and Dedan; the descendants of Dedan were the Asshurites, the Letushites and the Le-
ummites. 4 The sons of Midian were Ephah, Epher, Hanoch, Abida and Eldaah. All these
were descendants of Keturah.
5 Abraham left everything he owned to Isaac.[b] 6 But while he was still living, he gave
gifts to the sons of his concubines[c] and sent them away from his son Isaac[d] to the land
of the east.
7 Altogether, Abraham lived a hundred and seventy-five years. 8 Then Abraham
breathed his last and died at a good old age,[e] an old man and full of years; and he was
gathered to his people.[f] 9 His sons Isaac and Ishmael buried him[g] in the cave of Machpelah near Mamre, in the field of Ephron son of Zohar the Hittite,[h] 10 the field Abraham
had bought from the Hittites.[c][i] There Abraham was buried with his wife Sarah. 11 After
Abraham's death, God blessed his son Isaac, who then lived near Beer Lahai Roi.[j]

Ishmael's Sons

12 This is the account of Abraham's son Ishmael, whom Sarah's maidservant, Hagar[k]
the Egyptian, bore to Abraham.[l]

13 These are the names of the sons of Ishmael, listed in the order of their birth: Nebaioth the firstborn of Ishmael, Kedar, Adbeel, Mibsam, 14 Mishma, Dumah, Massa, 15 Hadad, Tema, Jetur, Naphish and Kedemah. 16 These were the sons of Ishmael, and these
are the names of the twelve tribal rulers[m] according to their settlements and camps. 17 Al-

24:60 [s]Ge 17:16 [t]Ge 22:17
24:62 [u]Ge 16:14; 25:11 [v]Ge 20:1
24:63 [w]Ps 1:2; 77:12; 119:15,27,48,97, 148; 143:5; 145:5
24:67 [x]Ge 25:20 [y]Ge 29:18,20 [z]Ge 23:1-2
25:2 [a]1Ch 1:32,33
25:5 [b]Ge 24:36
25:6 [c]Ge 22:24 [d]Ge 21:10,14
25:8 [e]Ge 15:15 [f]ver 17; Ge 35:29; 49:29, 33
25:9 [g]Ge 35:29 [h]Ge 50:13
25:10 [i]Ge 23:16
25:11 [j]Ge 16:14
25:12 [k]Ge 16:1 [l]Ge 16:15
25:16 [m]Ge 17:20

[a] 63 The meaning of the Hebrew for this word is uncertain. [b] 1 Or *had taken* [c] 10 Or *the sons of Heth*

24:60 increase . . . possess the gates of their enemies. See note on 22:17.

24:62 Beer Lahai Roi. The name means "Well of the Living One who sees me." It was significant that Isaac came from a well, a symbolic meeting place for marriages.

24:63 to meditate. The Hebrew term may mean "to come," enhancing the idea of providence.

24:64 got down. She dismounted to show respect to her husband.

24:65 covered herself. She comported herself as custom demanded.

24:66 told Isaac. If Abraham lived another 35 years (21:5; 25:7, 9,20), the narrative omits the servant's report to Abraham and focuses directly on the future patriarch.

24:67 the tent of his mother. Rebekah replaced Sarah in salvation history. **loved her.** The narrative closes with a scene of romantic fulfillment.

■ **25:1–6** *Isaac the Sole Heir.* The genealogies of Abraham's natural sons are a preface (vv. 1–4) to his death (vv. 7–11) and an appendage after it (vv. 12–18). They indicate that Abraham's other natural offspring were to be distinguished from Isaac, the father of Israel. All believers in all ages find salvation through Jesus, the descendant of Isaac.

25:1 took another wife. Elsewhere Keturah is called a concubine (1Ch 1:32). No attempt is made to date these secondary offspring of Abraham.

25:2–4 Some of these names can be identified in the region of the Syrian-Arabian Desert, east of the Jordan River.

25:5 left everything he owned to Isaac. See 24:36. Abraham dispossessed his descendants by Keturah, as he had done with Ishmael by Hagar (see note on 21:10).

25:6 while he was still living. Abraham legally secured Isaac's inheritance in the land. **gifts.** These gifts were their inheritance.

■ **25:7–11** *The Death of Abraham.* The patriarch passed from this life.

25:8 died. He died in faith, envisioning the promises from afar (Heb 11:10,13–16). **at a good old age.** See 15:15. **gathered to his people.** Abraham's being "gathered to his people" occurred between his death and burial. This phrase does not refer to his burial because Abraham was not buried with his ancestors (see Nu 20:26; Dt. 32:50). It therefore likely testifies to the early belief in human immortality. Death was looked upon as a transition to an afterlife where one was united with one's ancestors.

25:9 in the cave. See 23:1–20; 35:27–29; 49:29–32.

■ **25:12–18** *Account of Ishmael.* Moses traced the lines of Ishmael's descendants to distinguish them from the line of Isaac. God's people must always distinguish between their spiritual heritage and their physical heritage, even when the two are close and similar.

25:12 This is the account. See note on 2:4.

25:13–15 Some of these names are Arabic and others are attested in extrabiblical texts as being the names of tribes in northwestern Arabia.

25:16 twelve tribal rulers. See 17:20.

together, Ishmael lived a hundred and thirty-seven years. He breathed his last and
died, and he was gathered to his people.[n] 18 His descendants settled in the area from Havilah to Shur, near the border of Egypt, as you go toward Asshur. And they lived in hostility toward[a] all their brothers.[o]

Jacob and Esau

19 This is the account of Abraham's son Isaac.

Abraham became the father of Isaac, 20 and Isaac was forty years old[p] when he married Rebekah[q] daughter of Bethuel the Aramean from Paddan Aram[b] and sister of Laban[r] the Aramean.

21 Isaac prayed to the LORD on behalf of his wife, because she was barren. The LORD
answered his prayer,[s] and his wife Rebekah became pregnant. 22 The babies jostled each
other within her, and she said, "Why is this happening to me?" So she went to inquire
of the LORD.[t]

23 The LORD said to her,

> "Two nations[u] are in your womb,
>   and two peoples from within you will be separated;
> one people will be stronger than the other,
>   and the older will serve the younger.[v]"

24 When the time came for her to give birth, there were twin boys in her womb. 25 The
first to come out was red, and his whole body was like a hairy garment;[w] so they named
him Esau.[c] 26 After this, his brother came out, with his hand grasping Esau's heel;[x] so he
was named Jacob.[d][y] Isaac was sixty years old when Rebekah gave birth to them.

27 The boys grew up, and Esau became a skillful hunter, a man of the open country,[z]
while Jacob was a quiet man, staying among the tents. 28 Isaac, who had a taste for wild
game,[a] loved Esau, but Rebekah loved Jacob.[b]

25:17 [n]ver 8
25:18 [o]Ge 16:12
25:20 [p]ver 26; Ge 26:34 [q]Ge 24:67 [r]Ge 24:29
25:21 [s]1Ch 5:20; 2Ch 33:13; Ezr 8:23; Ps 127:3; Ro 9:10
25:22 [t]1Sa 9:9; 10:22
25:23 [u]Ge 17:4 [v]Ge 27:29,40; Mal 1:3; Ro 9:11-12*
25:25 [w]Ge 27:11
25:26 [x]Hos 12:3 [y]Ge 27:36
25:27 [z]Ge 27:3,5
25:20 [a]Ge 27:; 19 [b]Ge 27:6

[a] 18 Or *lived to the east of* [b] 20 That is, Northwest Mesopotamia [c] 25 *Esau* may mean *hairy*; he was also called Edom, which means *red.* [d] 26 *Jacob* means *he grasps the heel* (figuratively, *he deceives*).

25:18 lived in hostility toward all their brothers. See 16:12.

▪ **25:19—35:29** *Account of Isaac.* The covenant promise to Abraham (24:7) was passed on to Isaac and Jacob (28:3–4,13–15; 35:11–12). The promise was elaborated to include God's protective presence (28:15; 31:42; 32:9,12; 35:3). Overarching the entire story is God's sovereign good pleasure (Ro 9:10–12). He opened Rebekah's barren womb, established the supremacy of Jacob over Esau, contravened firstborn rights and overrode Isaac's patriarchal authority, Laban's social position and Esau's military might. The divine choice entailed the gift of faith to Jacob, not Esau (25:27–34). These chapters divide into three main sections: Jacob in the land (25:19—27:40), Jacob outside the land (27:41—33:17) and Jacob back in the land (33:18—35:29).

▪ **25:19—27:40** *Jacob in the Land.* The story of Jacob begins with him in the land. This material corresponds to the end of Jacob's life when he returns to the land (33:18—35:29). These chapters divide into three parts: the rivalry between Jacob and Esau (25:19–34), Isaac and Abimelech (26:1–35) and Jacob's acquisition of Esau's blessing (27:1–40).

▪ **25:19–34** *Rivalry Between Jacob and Esau.* The struggle for supremacy between Jacob and Esau in the womb and the Lord's sovereign choice form a fitting introduction to this account and set its tone. Israel learned that Moses' account was not only about Jacob and Esau, but that it also impacted their rivalry with the Edomites for the blessings of God. In this way the episode introduced the significance of Jacob and Esau for all ages.

25:19 This is the account. See note on 2:4. **of Abraham's son Isaac.** This account took place while Isaac was still patriarch. After reporting that Isaac tried to subvert God's blessing on Jacob (ch. 27), the account does not mention Isaac again until the event of his death (35:27–29).

25:20 Aramean. See Deuteronomy 26:5. The stage is being set for Jacob's flight to Paddan Aram and his conflict with Laban (chs. 28–31). **Paddan Aram.** Another name for Aram Naharaim (24:10).

25:21 prayed. See 20:7. The prayer secured Isaac's wife and offspring (24:12). Although the twins had been begotten by faith, only one had the gift of faith. **barren.** This next generation also had to learn that theirs was a supernatural seed, not a natural one (11:30; 17:15–16; 18:1–15; 21:1–7), and that the son of promise was sovereignly chosen by God (v. 23).

25:22 Why . . . ? This anguished question that is spread across the pages of human history finds its answer in accepting the truth that God's good pleasure stands behind all things (Jos 7:7). **to inquire of the LORD.** She consulted an oracle of some sort, probably at a patriarchal altar (see notes on 12:6,7).

25:23 The LORD said. By prophecies on the various thresholds of history, God displayed his sovereign control of Adam and Eve (3:15), Noah's descendants (9:25–27), Abraham's career (12:1–3), Jacob and Esau (27:27–29,39–40) and Joseph and his brothers (37:1–11). **to her.** This revelation came to Rebekah; it is not clear whether or not Isaac understood these matters. His later actions displayed his lack of awareness or his refusal to submit to this divine disclosure. Rebekah sought to accomplish what she was told would happen, but she did so by deceiving her husband rather than by following an honorable path. **Two nations.** These words indicate the significance of this account of Jacob and Esau for the original audience. The children represented two peoples, two nations: Israel and Edom. **the older.** The Hebrew used here for the eldest son has been found so far only in Akkadian literature from the middle of the second millennium B.C. **will serve the younger.** Jacob owed his supremacy to sovereign election, not to natural rights (Dt 21:15–17). This prophecy finds its fulfillment throughout Israel's history (2Sa 8:13).

25:25 hairy. The Hebrew word sounds like "Seir," where Esau lived (36:8).

25:26 Jacob. This name is probably a shortened form of a typical West Semitic name meaning "May El Protect/Reward." But Jacob tarnished his honorable name by adding misguided efforts to achieve God's good pleasure (27:33; Hos 12:3–4). For this reason the name was transformed by a pun on the meaning of the verbal root "to seize someone by the heel, to go behind someone, to betray or to supplant."

25:27–34 Esau was a profane, rough-and-ready man of the field who shortsightedly gratified his appetite and despised the family's future inheritance. Jacob had faith's farsightedness to value the inheritance, but he tarnished his actions by bartering to advantage himself and disadvantage his brother.

25:27 quiet. The Hebrew means "complete" and here connotes being civilized, fine. Jacob's "completeness" stood in opposition to Esau's particular skill of hunting.

25:28 Isaac . . . loved . . . but Rebekah loved. Parental favoritism further set the family at loggerheads. Isaac's favoritism was based on natural senses; Rebekah's on spiritual virtue (ch. 27).

29Once when Jacob was cooking some stew, Esau came in from the open country, famished. 30He said to Jacob, "Quick, let me have some of that red stew! I'm famished!" (That is why he was also called Edom.[a])

31Jacob replied, "First sell me your birthright."

32"Look, I am about to die," Esau said. "What good is the birthright to me?"

33But Jacob said, "Swear to me first." So he swore an oath to him, selling his birthright[c] to Jacob.

34Then Jacob gave Esau some bread and some lentil stew. He ate and drank, and then got up and left.

So Esau despised his birthright.

Isaac and Abimelech

26 Now there was a famine in the land[d]—besides the earlier famine of Abraham's time—and Isaac went to Abimelech king of the Philistines in Gerar.[e] 2The LORD appeared[f] to Isaac and said, "Do not go down to Egypt; live in the land where I tell you to live.[g] 3Stay in this land for a while,[h] and I will be with you and will bless you.[i] For to you and your descendants I will give all these lands[j] and will confirm the oath I swore to your father Abraham. 4I will make your descendants as numerous as the stars in the sky[k] and will give them all these lands, and through your offspring[b] all nations on earth will be blessed,[l] 5because Abraham obeyed me[m] and kept my requirements, my commands, my decrees and my laws." 6So Isaac stayed in Gerar.

7When the men of that place asked him about his wife, he said, "She is my sister,[n]" because he was afraid to say, "She is my wife." He thought, "The men of this place might kill me on account of Rebekah, because she is beautiful."

8When Isaac had been there a long time, Abimelech king of the Philistines looked down from a window and saw Isaac caressing his wife Rebekah. 9So Abimelech summoned Isaac and said, "She is really your wife! Why did you say, 'She is my sister'?"

25:33 [c]Ge 27:36; Heb 12:16
26:1 [d]Ge 12:10 [e]Ge 20:1
26:2 [f]Ge 12:7; 17:1; 18:1 [g]Ge 12:1
26:3 [h]Ge 20:1; 28:15 [i]Ge 12:2; 22:16-18 [j]Ge 12:7; 13:15; 15:18
26:4 [k]Ge 15:5; 22:17; Ex 32:13 [l]Ge 12:3; 22:18; Gal 3:8
26:5 [m]Ge 22:16
26:7 [n]Ge 12:13; 20:2, 12; Pr 29:25

[a] *30 Edom* means *red.* [b] *4* Or *seed*

God's sovereign grace had to prevail over Isaac's appetite and apathy, for Isaac had the legal authority to pass on the family's inheritance and blessing (24:36; 25:5). **Isaac, who had a taste for wild game.** Adam failed in eating, Noah in drinking and Isaac in tasting.
25:30 Quick, let me have. Esau was impulsive. **red stew!** The Hebrew here is coarse: "red stuff, this red stuff!"
25:31 sell me. Jacob exploited Esau's misery. His lack of compassion and hospitality stood in sharp contrast with Abraham's treatment of Lot (ch. 13) and would later be corrected (ch. 33). Jacob lacked the fraternal respect and brotherly love that creates community. **birthright.** The firstborn had the right to be the principal heir of the family's fortunes (27:33; Dt. 21:17; 1Ch 5:1–2). The father's inheritance was divided by the number of sons, and the firstborn always had the right to two of those portions. For example, if there were nine sons, the firstborn received two portions and the other eight split the remaining seven portions. If there were only two sons, the firstborn inherited both portions, leaving nothing for his brother. Accompanying the birthright was also the responsibility to be the family protector, the leader of the family. In the covenant family, that fortune included the Lord's promise to give Abraham an offspring in the land that would bless all nations. The birthright was transferable, as in the cases of Judah/Reuben, Ephraim/Manasseh and Solomon/Adonijah.
25:32 I am about to die. This was a gross exaggeration. Esau had the strength to travel to Jacob, the presence of mind to barter, the ability to feed himself and the constitution to leave once he had eaten. Esau had no faith in Abraham's God and lived for the moment.
25:34 ate and drank, and then got up and left. The staccato style represents Esau as being as crude and as non-reflective as his speech. **despised his birthright.** See Hebrews 12:16–17. God hates the man who holds his promises in contempt (Mal 1:3).
▪ **26:1–35** *Isaac and Abimelech.* An introduction to the account of Isaac (25:19–34) is linked with the covenant promises. Within two revelations of covenantal promises (vv. 2–6,23–24) occur two incidents of God's presence: the protection of the endangered ancestress (vv. 7–11) and Isaac's material greatness and protection against hostility, both in the fertile land (vv. 8–15) and in the steppe with wells (vv. 16–22). At Beersheba the Philistines renewed their nonaggression pact with Isaac, which finally resulted in a secure peace (vv. 25–32). All of these historical facts informed the Israelites following Moses about important dimensions of their own identity and their reactions to peoples whom they would surely encounter in the land, as they continue to guide all believers in their relations with others.
26:1 besides the earlier famine of Abraham's time. God confirmed his commitment to Isaac in a way so similar to that of his commitment to Abraham that the narrator felt it necessary to point out that these were distinct events. **Abimelech.** See 20:2. **Gerar.** Isaac may have been stopping at this place of royal pasturage (see 20:1) on his way to Egypt (see 12:10).
26:2–6 The Lord's command and promise to Isaac and Isaac's obedience are stylistically and substantively linked with his promise to Abraham and Abraham's obedience (see notes on 12:1–4). See *HC* 54.
26:3 Stay . . . and I will be. The promise of God is linked to the land of the promise, as in 12:1. **Stay in this land for a while.** The translation seeks to convey the meaning of "sojourn." The point is not that only a brief stay was commanded but that Isaac was to remain there as a "stranger" who did not yet possess the land. **I will be with you.** The immediate promise in the story of Abraham pertained to the supernatural birth of a son; in the story of Isaac it pertained to supernatural protection (vv. 3,24; 28:15,20; 31:3,5,42; 32:10). **bless.** See notes on 1:22 and 12:2. **give all these lands.** See note on 13:15. **confirm the oath.** See 15:18, 17:21 and especially 22:16–18 and its notes. The promise to Abraham was secure, but Isaac's participation required obedience on his own part.
26:4 stars in the sky. See note on 15:5. **offspring.** See note on 12:3. See *BC* 18.
26:5 because. See note on 22:18. **my commands, my decrees and my laws.** Moses described Abraham's obedience in terms of Israel's requirement to keep the law delivered at Sinai.
26:6 So Isaac stayed. See 12:4.
26:7–11 The narrative about the endangering of the ancestress Rebekah closely parallels similar accounts involving Sarah (see note on 20:1–18). Although father and son made the same mistake and were both protected, the stories differ enough that there is no reason to think, as some interpreters have suggested, that they represent the same event recounted twice.
26:7 sister. See 12:13 and 20:2. See *WLC* 145.
26:8 looked down from a window. Whereas Abraham was spared by a special revelation to Abimelech (20:3), Isaac was saved by providence. **caressing.** The Hebrew here means "play" and is from the same root as the name "Isaac." The same form is translated "mocking" in 21:9.
26:9 Abimelech. See note on 20:2. See *WLC* 145.

Isaac answered him, "Because I thought I might lose my life on account of her."
10 Then Abimelech said, "What is this you have done to us?[o] One of the men might
well have slept with your wife, and you would have brought guilt upon us."
11 So Abimelech gave orders to all the people: "Anyone who molests[p] this man or his
wife shall surely be put to death."
12 Isaac planted crops in that land and the same year reaped a hundredfold, because
the LORD blessed him.[q] 13 The man became rich, and his wealth continued to grow until
he became very wealthy.[r] 14 He had so many flocks and herds and servants[s] that the Philistines envied him.[t] 15 So all the wells[u] that his father's servants had dug in the time of
his father Abraham, the Philistines stopped up,[v] filling them with earth.
16 Then Abimelech said to Isaac, "Move away from us; you have become too powerful for us.[w]"
17 So Isaac moved away from there and encamped in the Valley of Gerar and settled
there. 18 Isaac reopened the wells[x] that had been dug in the time of his father Abraham,
which the Philistines had stopped up after Abraham died, and he gave them the same
names his father had given them.
19 Isaac's servants dug in the valley and discovered a well of fresh water there. 20 But
the herdsmen of Gerar quarreled with Isaac's herdsmen and said, "The water is ours!"[y]
So he named the well Esek,[a] because they disputed with him. 21 Then they dug another
well, but they quarreled over that one also; so he named it Sitnah.[b] 22 He moved on from
there and dug another well, and no one quarreled over it. He named it Rehoboth,[c] saying, "Now the LORD has given us room and we will flourish[z] in the land."
23 From there he went up to Beersheba. 24 That night the LORD appeared to him and
said, "I am the God of your father Abraham.[a] Do not be afraid,[b] for I am with you; I will
bless you and will increase the number of your descendants[c] for the sake of my servant
Abraham."[d]
25 Isaac built an altar[e] there and called on the name of the LORD. There he pitched his
tent, and there his servants dug a well.
26 Meanwhile, Abimelech had come to him from Gerar, with Ahuzzath his personal adviser and Phicol the commander of his forces.[f] 27 Isaac asked them, "Why have you come
to me, since you were hostile to me and sent me away?[g]"
28 They answered, "We saw clearly that the LORD was with you;[h] so we said, 'There
ought to be a sworn agreement between us'—between us and you. Let us make a treaty with you 29 that you will do us no harm, just as we did not molest you but always treated you well and sent you away in peace. And now you are blessed by the LORD."[i]
30 Isaac then made a feast[j] for them, and they ate and drank. 31 Early the next morning the men swore an oath[k] to each other. Then Isaac sent them on their way, and they
left him in peace.
32 That day Isaac's servants came and told him about the well they had dug. They said,

[a] 20 *Esek* means *dispute.* [b] 21 *Sitnah* means *opposition.* [c] 22 *Rehoboth* means *room.*

26:10 [o]Ge 20:9
26:11 [p]Ps 105:15
26:12 [q]ver 3; Job 42:12
26:13 [r]Pr 10:22
26:14 [s]Ge 24:36 [t]Ge 37:11
26:15 [u]Ge 21:30 [v]Ge 21:25
26:16 [w]Ex 1:9
26:18 [x]Ge 21:30
26:20 [y]Ge 21:25
26:22 [z]Ge 17:6; Ex 1:7
26:24 [a]Ge 24:12; Ex 3:6 [b]Ge 15:1 [c]ver 4 [d]Ge 17:7
26:25 [e]Ge 12:7,8; 13:4, 18; Ps 116:17
26:26 [f]Ge 21:22
26:27 [g]ver 16
26:28 [h]Ge 21:22
26:29 [i]Ge 24:31; Ps 115:15
26:30 [j]Ge 19:3
26:31 [k]Ge 21:31

26:10 One of the men. In the case of Sarah, the king took her for himself (20:2). Here the king was not guilty, and no compensatory gift was needed. **have brought guilt.** Abimelech feared God (see 20:9).
26:12 planted crops. Pastoral nomads in the ancient Near East occasionally engaged in small-scale agriculture. Isaac's success depended on rain from heaven. **hundredfold.** His obedience brought tremendous blessing. **the LORD blessed him.** God's good hand was as evident upon the chosen successor of God's promises as it had been upon his predecessor (21:22).
26:15 the Philistines stopped up. Now that Abraham was gone, the Philistines violated their nonaggression pact (see 21:23). They feared God but lacked faith that God had made enduring promises to Abraham and his descendants.
26:16 Move away. See 13:7. **too powerful for us.** See 21:23. This comment probably strengthened the wandering Israelites' faith centuries later as they faced challenges from other peoples.
26:17–22 Isaac retreated from the fertile land into the steppe, depending on wells. He moved from one successful well to another. The names of the wells commemorated God's provision and protection.
26:18 same names. Wells were given names to establish proprietary rights. By giving them the same names as his father had, Isaac aimed to make his ownership incontestable. This underscores the injustice (see 21:23–33) but also commemorates God's provision and protection.
26:22 Now the LORD has given us room. God's protection of Isaac during this rivalry over wells resembles his reward to Abraham in his controversy with Lot (ch. 13). It also encouraged the Israelite readers as they moved toward the promised land to believe that God would give them room as well.
26:23–33 Isaac returned to the site of Abraham's pact with the Philistines (21:22–34).
26:23 Beersheba. The commemorative tokens of God's blessing were still there (see 21:22–34 and its notes).
26:24 See notes on verses 2–6. **servant.** See note on 18:3.
26:25 built an altar. Like his father, Isaac constructed an altar in response to God's revelation (see 12:7,8; 21:33 and their notes). Abraham's sanctuary at Beersheba became Isaac's (21:32–33).
26:26 Ahuzzath his personal adviser. His presence added even greater weight to the negotiations.
26:28–29 the LORD was with you . . . you are blessed. Their statement validated the Lord's promise (vv. 3–4) and assured the Israelites to whom Moses wrote that they were the heirs of one who had been wonderfully blessed by God and that God was indeed present with them.
26:28 We saw clearly. They saw that Isaac had become a nomad without economic ruin because God had provided him with successful wells. **a sworn agreement.** See note on 21:23.
26:30–31 feast . . . oath. Isaac also was equal to a king (see 21:23). His faith led him to secure ground.
26:32 well. The reference to the well links Beersheba with God's provisions related in verses 17–22.

"We've found water!" [33]He called it Shibah,[a] and to this day the name of the town has been Beersheba.[b] [l]

[34]When Esau was forty years old,[m] he married Judith daughter of Beeri the Hittite, and also Basemath daughter of Elon the Hittite.[n] [35]They were a source of grief to Isaac and Rebekah.[o]

Jacob Gets Isaac's Blessing

27 When Isaac was old and his eyes were so weak that he could no longer see,[p] he called for Esau his older son[q] and said to him, "My son."

"Here I am," he answered.

[2]Isaac said, "I am now an old man and don't know the day of my death.[r] [3]Now then, get your weapons—your quiver and bow—and go out to the open country[s] to hunt some wild game for me. [4]Prepare me the kind of tasty food I like and bring it to me to eat, so that I may give you my blessing[t] before I die."

[5]Now Rebekah was listening as Isaac spoke to his son Esau. When Esau left for the open country to hunt game and bring it back, [6]Rebekah said to her son Jacob,[u] "Look, I overheard your father say to your brother Esau, [7]'Bring me some game and prepare me some tasty food to eat, so that I may give you my blessing in the presence of the LORD before I die.' [8]Now, my son, listen carefully and do what I tell you:[v] [9]Go out to the flock and bring me two choice young goats, so I can prepare some tasty food for your father, just the way he likes it. [10]Then take it to your father to eat, so that he may give you his blessing before he dies."

[11]Jacob said to Rebekah his mother, "But my brother Esau is a hairy man,[w] and I'm a man with smooth skin. [12]What if my father touches me?[x] I would appear to be tricking him and would bring down a curse on myself rather than a blessing."

[13]His mother said to him, "My son, let the curse fall on me.[y] Just do what I say;[z] go and get them for me."

[14]So he went and got them and brought them to his mother, and she prepared some tasty food, just the way his father liked it. [15]Then Rebekah took the best clothes[a] of Esau her older son, which she had in the house, and put them on her younger son Jacob. [16]She also covered his hands and the smooth part of his neck with the goatskins. [17]Then she handed to her son Jacob the tasty food and the bread she had made.

26:33 [l]Ge 21:14
26:34 [m]Ge 25:20 [n]Ge 28:9; 36:2
26:35 [o]Ge 27:46
27:1 [p]Ge 48:10; 1Sa 3:2 [q]Ge 25:25
27:2 [r]Ge 47:29
27:3 [s]Ge 25:27
27:4 [t]ver 10,25,31; Ge 49:28; Dt 33:1; Heb 11:20
27:6 [u]Ge 25:28
27:8 [v]ver 13,43
27:11 [w]Ge 25:25
27:12 [x]ver 22
27:13 [y]Mt 27:25 [z]ver 8
27:15 [a]ver 27

a *33 Shibah* can mean *oath* or *seven.* b *33 Beersheba* can mean *well of the oath* or *well of seven.*

26:33 name of the town has been Beersheba. The Lord's protection of Abraham at Beersheba was now linked with that of Isaac.
26:34–35 The story about Jacob's reception of the blessing is framed by the account of Esau's marriage to Hittite women and his parents' displeasure (27:46). This frame profiles the contrast between Abraham, who in faith provided for Isaac's future according to God's elective purposes (ch. 24), and Isaac, who tried to thwart the divine election (25:23).
26:34 married. Profane Esau demonstrated his disregard for the covenant blessings by marrying daughters of the land (see 24:3–4; 31:50 and their notes). By intermarrying with the Canaanites and so vexing his parents (27:46), he effectively sealed himself off from the sacred inheritance (21:21; 25:6). **Hittite.** They were reckoned as among the Canaanites (28:1).
■ **27:1–40** *Jacob's Acquisition of Esau's Blessing.* The interplay of human motives and divine purposes complicates this account. Jacob had been chosen by God (see 25:23) and was praised for desiring and obtaining God's covenant blessings (see 32:28). Even so, some of his methods were inappropriate. As the narrative reveals both sides of Jacob's actions, the Israelite readers were to exult in the outcome that they were the heirs of God's covenant with Abraham and Isaac. Yet they were also to learn humility toward Esau's descendants, the Edomites, as they encountered them. Believers in all ages should not only delight in receiving the grace of God in Christ but also recognize proper humility toward others, for their status before God is an act of divine grace alone.
27:1 eyes were so weak. Isaac's physical blindness matched his spiritual blindness. **called for Esau.** The blessing should have been a more public affair (49:1,28; 50:24–25; Dt 33:1).
27:2 don't know the day of my death. Although the already aged Isaac lived for another 80 years, it appears here that he was sick. The narrator introduced Isaac as old and blind, and his sons asked him to sit up (vv. 19,31). Esau assumed that his father's death was imminent (v. 41).
27:3–4 quiver and bow. Symbols of masculinity. **game . . . tasty food I like.** The word "game" is repeated eight times and "tasty food" six times in the account of Isaac. His sensuality may explain why he preferred Esau over Jacob (see note on vv. 18–27). If Isaac understood the prophecy given to Rebekah (see note on 25:23), then his sensuality led him to a conscious choice against the will of God. **give you my blessing.** See 1:27 and note on verse 28. In Esau's mind the birthright and blessing were separate, for he expected to receive the blessing even though he admitted that he had lost the birthright (v. 36). To God, however, the two were inseparable (Heb 12:17). Both pertained to the firstborn's rights to property, divine potency, prosperity and dominion (vv. 27–29). Together they made the inheritor the primary carrier of the family heritage.
27:5 Rebekah. Her desire to see the blessing extend to Jacob was in accordance with what God had revealed to her (see vv. 23,46; 26:35), but her method was deplorable (cf. Lev 19:14; Dt 27:18; cf. 2Co 4:2). She even accepted that there might be a curse to come upon her for suggesting that Jacob deceive his father (v. 13). **Esau left.** Although the birthright and blessing were not identical, they were related because both pertained to the inheritance. Esau reneged on the oath he had long ago made with Jacob (25:33), but his original act of unbelief in selling his inheritance was decisive (Heb 12:16–17).
27:7 my blessing. The family blessing in patriarchal times was given at a departure, at the start of a journey (24:60) or upon imminent death. It could be conferred upon only one person and could not be altered. The blessing was sanctioned because the Lord, using the legal social customs of those times, mediated it through the faith of the patriarch (Heb 11:20). After the law was given, God's blessing was mediated to all his people through the priest (Nu 6:22–27).
27:12 bring down a curse on myself. Jacob understood that his plan had the potential of bringing a divinely sanctioned curse from his father rather than the divine blessing he desired. The plan to deceive his father was morally problematic. He sought what was promised him, but he did so through deceptive means.
27:13 let the curse fall on me. Rebekah assured Jacob by expressing her willingness to accept whatever divine punishment might be meted out because of the deception.
27:15 clothes. Ironically, Jacob's sons deceived him as well by clothing (37:31–33).

18 He went to his father and said, "My father."
"Yes, my son," he answered. "Who is it?"
19 Jacob said to his father, "I am Esau your firstborn. I have done as you told me. Please
sit up and eat some of my game so that you may give me your blessing."[b]
20 Isaac asked his son, "How did you find it so quickly, my son?"
"The LORD your God gave me success,[c]" he replied.
21 Then Isaac said to Jacob, "Come near so I can touch you,[d] my son, to know whether you really are my son Esau or not."
22 Jacob went close to his father Isaac, who touched him and said, "The voice is the
voice of Jacob, but the hands are the hands of Esau." 23 He did not recognize him, for his
hands were hairy like those of his brother Esau;[e] so he blessed him. 24 "Are you really my
son Esau?" he asked.
"I am," he replied.
25 Then he said, "My son, bring me some of your game to eat, so that I may give you
my blessing."[f]
Jacob brought it to him and he ate; and he brought some wine and he drank. 26 Then
his father Isaac said to him, "Come here, my son, and kiss me."
27 So he went to him and kissed him[g]. When Isaac caught the smell of his clothes,[h]
he blessed him and said,

"Ah, the smell of my son
is like the smell of a field
that the LORD has blessed.[i]
28 May God give you of heaven's dew[j]
and of earth's richness[k]—
an abundance of grain and new wine.[l]
29 May nations serve you
and peoples bow down to you.[m]
Be lord over your brothers,
and may the sons of your mother bow down to you.[n]
May those who curse you be cursed
and those who bless you be blessed.[o]"

30 After Isaac finished blessing him and Jacob had scarcely left his father's presence,
his brother Esau came in from hunting. 31 He too prepared some tasty food and brought
it to his father. Then he said to him, "My father, sit up and eat some of my game, so that
you may give me your blessing."[p]
32 His father Isaac asked him, "Who are you?"[q]
"I am your son," he answered, "your firstborn, Esau."
33 Isaac trembled violently and said, "Who was it, then, that hunted game and brought
it to me? I ate it just before you came and I blessed him—and indeed he will be blessed![r]"
34 When Esau heard his father's words, he burst out with a loud and bitter cry[s] and
said to his father, "Bless me—me too, my father!"
35 But he said, "Your brother came deceitfully[t] and took your blessing."
36 Esau said, "Isn't he rightly named Jacob[a]?[u] He has deceived me these two times: He
took my birthright,[v] and now he's taken my blessing!" Then he asked, "Haven't you reserved any blessing for me?"
37 Isaac answered Esau, "I have made him lord over you and you have made all his rela

27:19 [b]ver 4
27:20 [c]Ge 24:12
27:21 [d]ver 12
27:23 [e]ver 16
27:25 [f]ver 4
27:27 [g]Heb 11:20 [h]SS 4:11 [i]Ps 65:9-13
27:28 [j]Dt 33:13 [k]ver 39 [l]Ge 45:18; Nu 18:12; Dt 33:28
27:29 [m]Isa 45:14,23; 49:7,23 [n]Ge 9:25; 25:23; 37:7 [o]Ge 12:3; Nu 24:9; Zep 2:8
27:31 [p]ver 4
27:32 [q]ver 18
27:33 [r]ver 29; Ge 28:3,4; Ro 11:29
27:34 [s]Heb 12:17
27:35 [t]Jer 9:4; 12:6
27:36 [u]Ge 25:26 [v]Ge 25:33

[a] 36 *Jacob* means *he grasps the heel* (figuratively, *he deceives*).

27:20 The LORD your God. Jacob compounded his misdeed by referring to God as he deceived his father.
27:26 kiss. This physical contact may have been a part of the ritual of passing along the blessing.
27:27 smell. What was perceived through the senses gave form to the blessing (cf. 3:14–15; Nu 24:5).
27:28–29 The blessing pertained to fertility (v. 28) and dominion (v. 29) as the descendants of Abraham are the chosen instruments through which the divinely ordained destiny of humanity will be fulfilled. See 1:22, 22:15–18, 48:15–19 and Numbers 24:3–9. The similarity to the prenatal oracle shows clearly that the Lord sovereignly rules history despite the failures of sinful humans.
27:28 earth's richness. This included rain. **grain and new wine.** The image of a banquet, which would be fulfilled when Israel settled in the promised land.
27:29 nations. The blessing of universal dominion ultimately falls on Christ and his church. **sons of your mother.** To include all her descendants through Esau (see 36:1–43). **May those . . . be cursed.** Repeated word for word in Numbers 24:9 (see 12:3).
27:33 indeed he will be blessed! Although Isaac had the wrong son in view, he still exercised faith and accomplished what God had planned.
27:34 a loud and bitter cry. See note on verse 5 (see also Heb 12:16–17).
27:35 deceitfully. Jacob would reap what he had sown (see 29:15–30). **took your blessing.** Isaac still refused to accept God's plan for his sons. Here as in other situations, however, God used human sin to effect his purposes: Compare Israel's choice of a king (1Sa 8:12), Assyria's boast (Isa 10) and Jesus' death (1Co 2:8).
27:36 Jacob. See note on 25:26. **He took.** See 31:1 and its note.

tives his servants, and I have sustained him with grain and new wine.[w] So what can I possibly do for you, my son?"
38Esau said to his father, "Do you have only one blessing, my father? Bless me too, my father!" Then Esau wept aloud.[x]
39His father Isaac answered him,

> "Your dwelling will be
> away from the earth's richness,
> away from the dew[y] of heaven above.
> 40You will live by the sword
> and you will serve[z] your brother.[a]
> But when you grow restless,
> you will throw his yoke
> from off your neck.[b]"

Jacob Flees to Laban

41Esau held a grudge[c] against Jacob[d] because of the blessing his father had given him.
He said to himself, "The days of mourning[e] for my father are near; then I will kill my
brother Jacob."[f]
42When Rebekah was told what her older son Esau had said, she sent for her younger son Jacob and said to him, "Your brother Esau is consoling himself with the thought
of killing you. 43Now then, my son, do what I say:[g] Flee at once to my brother Laban[h] in
Haran.[i] 44Stay with him for a while[j] until your brother's fury subsides. 45When your
brother is no longer angry with you and forgets what you did to him,[k] I'll send word for
you to come back from there. Why should I lose both of you in one day?"
46Then Rebekah said to Isaac, "I'm disgusted with living because of these Hittite
women. If Jacob takes a wife from among the women of this land, from Hittite women
like these, my life will not be worth living."[l]

28 So Isaac called for Jacob and blessed[a] him and commanded him: "Do not marry a Canaanite woman.[m] 2Go at once to Paddan Aram,[b] to the house of your
mother's father Bethuel.[n] Take a wife for yourself there, from among the daughters of
Laban, your mother's brother. 3May God Almighty[c][o] bless you and make you fruitful[p]
and increase your numbers until you become a community of peoples. 4May he give you
and your descendants the blessing given to Abraham,[q] so that you may take possession
of the land where you now live as an alien,[r] the land God gave to Abraham." 5Then Isaac
sent Jacob on his way, and he went to Paddan Aram,[s] to Laban son of Bethuel the Aramean, the brother of Rebekah,[t] who was the mother of Jacob and Esau.
6Now Esau learned that Isaac had blessed Jacob and had sent him to Paddan Aram
to take a wife from there, and that when he blessed him he commanded him, "Do not
marry a Canaanite woman,"[u] 7and that Jacob had obeyed his father and mother and had
gone to Paddan Aram. 8Esau then realized how displeasing the Canaanite women[v]

27:37 [w]ver 28
27:38 [x]Heb 12:17
27:39 [y]ver 28
27:40 [z]2Sa 8:14 [a]Ge 25:23 [b]2Ki 8:20-22
27:41 [c]Ge 37:4 [d]Ge 32:11 [e]Ge 50:4,10 [f]Ob 1:10
27:43 [g]ver 8 [h]Ge 24:29 [i]Ge 11:31
27:44 [j]Ge 31:38,41
27:45 [k]ver 35
27:46 [l]Ge 26:35
28:1 [m]Ge 24:3
28:2 [n]Ge 25:20
28:3 [o]Ge 17:1 [p]Ge 17:6
28:4 [q]Ge 12:2,3 [r]Ge 17:8
28:5 [s]Hos 12:12 [t]Ge 24:29
28:6 [u]ver 1
28:8 [v]Ge 24:3

[a] *1* Or *greeted* [b] *2* That is, Northwest Mesopotamia; also in verses 5, 6 and 7 [c] *3* Hebrew *El-Shaddai*

27:39–40 Esau inherited a curse; he was denied the earth's fertility and dominion over his brother (vv. 28–29).
27:40 You will live. Esau was to have a hard life, but he was to live. **throw his yoke.** This oracle was fulfilled in 2 Kings 8:20–22.
■ **27:41—33:17** *Jacob Outside the Land.* In fear, Jacob fled from his brother Esau. He faced difficulties along the way but was also protected and blessed by God. These chapters divide into six main parts: Jacob's flight (27:41—28:9), his divine encounter at Bethel (28:10–22), his struggle with Laban (29:1–30), his sons (29:31—30:24), his prosperity and flight (30:25—31:55) and his divine encounters while returning to Canaan (32:1–32). These chapters clearly illustrate the change that God's grace brings to his elect people.
■ **27:41—28:9** *Jacob's Flight From Esau.* Jacob left the land but was kept separate from the Canaanites. Esau, however, did not remain separate. The Israelites learned the importance of continuing to resist the corruption of the Canaanites, as all believers must resist the corruption of the world.
27:41–44 Rebekah learned that Esau had threatened to kill Jacob, so she sent Jacob away for a while.
27:45 I'll send word for you. Rebekah never carried out her wish. **lose both of you.** Although Rebekah evaded Esau's resolve, she would taste the bitter consequences of her deception: the loss of her beloved Jacob in exile.
27:46 Rebekah said. As Sarah had taken the initiative to provide for Isaac (see 21:10), so Rebekah acted on Jacob's behalf. **because of these Hittite women.** See 24:4, 26:34–35 and 31:50.
28:1–2 Do not marry . . . Take a wife. The negative and positive commands correspond to those of Abraham (see notes on 24:2–4).
28:1 blessed. The blessing in 27:27–29, given in the face of death, determined the patriarchal succession. This blessing at the farewell before a journey (see 24:60; 27:7 and their notes) linked the blessing with Abraham.
28:2 Paddan Aram. See 22:23 and 25:20.
28:3 God Almighty. See note on 17:1. This blessing was a fresh affirmation of the covenant with Abraham recorded in 17:1–8. **a community of peoples.** In 35:11 the expression means a community of peoples coming from the patriarch (see 17:6 and its note). The blessing was reversed against Israel under judgment: A community of peoples attacked her (Eze 23:24; 32:3).
28:4 take possession. The Hebrew here entails "to dispossess," introducing the concept of holy war against the Canaanites (15:16).
28:5 Then Isaac sent Jacob. After the blessings on Abraham and Isaac, they obeyed (12:1–4; 26:2–6), but after this blessing on Jacob, Isaac acted to send Jacob away.
28:6 Esau learned. Esau married out of rivalry, not out of obedience to God. Thus he disqualified himself further from inheriting his father's blessing.

were to his father Isaac;[w] 9so he went to Ishmael and married Mahalath, the sister of Nebaioth[x] and daughter of Ishmael son of Abraham, in addition to the wives he already
had.[y]

Jacob's Dream at Bethel

10Jacob left Beersheba and set out for Haran.[z] 11When he reached a certain place, he
stopped for the night because the sun had set. Taking one of the stones there, he put it
under his head and lay down to sleep. 12He had a dream[a] in which he saw a stairway[a]
resting on the earth, with its top reaching to heaven, and the angels of God were ascending and descending on it.[b] 13There above it[b] stood the LORD,[c] and he said: "I am the LORD,
the God of your father Abraham and the God of Isaac.[d] I will give you and your descendants the land[e] on which you are lying. 14Your descendants will be like the dust of the
earth, and you[f] will spread out to the west and to the east, to the north and to the south.[g]
All peoples on earth will be blessed through you and your offspring.[h] 15I am with you[i]
and will watch over you[j] wherever you go, and I will bring you back to this land. I will
not leave you[k] until I have done what I have promised you."[l]

16When Jacob awoke from his sleep, he thought, "Surely the LORD is in this place, and
I was not aware of it." 17He was afraid and said, "How awesome is this place![m] This is
none other than the house of God; this is the gate of heaven."

18Early the next morning Jacob took the stone he had placed under his head and set
it up as a pillar[n] and poured oil on top of it.[o] 19He called that place Bethel,[c] though the
city used to be called Luz.[p]

20Then Jacob made a vow,[q] saying, "If God will be with me and will watch over me[r]
on this journey I am taking and will give me food to eat and clothes to wear 21so that I
return safely[s] to my father's house, then the LORD[d] will be my God[t] 22and[e] this stone that
I have set up as a pillar will be God's house,[u] and of all that you give me I will give you
a tenth.[v]"

[a] *12* Or *ladder* [b] *13* Or *There beside him* [c] *19* *Bethel* means *house of God.* [d] *20,21* Or *Since God . . . father's house, the LORD* [e] *21,22* Or *house, and the LORD will be my God, 22then*

28:8 [w]Ge 26:35
28:9 [x]Ge 25:13 [y]Ge 26:34
28:10 [z]Ge 11:31
28:12 [a]Ge 20:3 [b]Jn 1:51
28:13 [c]Ge 12:7; 35:7,9; 48:3 [d]Ge 26:24 [e]Ge 13:15; 35:12
28:14 [f]Ge 26:4 [g]Ge 13:14 [h]Ge 12:3; 18:18; 22:18; Gal 3:8
28:15 [i]Ge 26:3; 48:21 [j]Nu 6:24; Ps 121:5, 7-8 [k]Dt 31:6,8 [l]Nu 23:19
28:17 [m]Ex 3:5; Jos 5:15
28:18 [n]Ge 35:14 [o]Lev 8:11
28:19 [p]Jdg 1:23,26
28:20 [q]Ge 31:13; Jdg 11:30; 2Sa 15:8 [r]ver 15
28:21 [s]Jdg 11:31 [t]Dt 26:17
28:22 [u]Ge 35:7,14 [v]Ge 14:20; Lev 27:30

28:9 so he went to Ishmael. Esau's journey parodied Jacob's, but Esau went to Ishmael, the natural offspring of Abraham who had been rejected as heir to the covenant promises. **in addition to the wives.** See note on 31:50.

■ **28:10–22** *Divine Encounter While Fleeing.* The Lord appeared to Jacob and gave him assurances at critical junctures in his life: on his flight from the land (vv. 10–22), in the face of the threat from Laban's sons (31:1–3), on his return to confront Esau (32:1–2, 22–32) and on his return from the Canaanites (35:1–15).

28:11, 17 See note on 13:4.

28:11 reached. The Hebrew here is translated "met" in 32:1, linking these two accounts. **a certain place.** Luz is not mentioned (v. 19) here because the place was unimportant until God revealed himself there. **sun had set.** Sunset and sunrise are common images of distress and deliverance (see 15:12,17; 19:1; Jn 13:30). The true "daybreak" for his soul would not come until the end of Jacob's twenty-year exile (32:26). **under his head.** The Hebrew here is translated "near his head" in 1 Samuel 26:7. It may have protected his head. An ordinary stone was transformed into a sanctuary.

28:12 dream. Jacob's dream was not a morbid review of a shameful past but the presentation of an alternative future with God. **a stairway.** This was not a wooden ladder but a vast stone ramp with steps. **top reaching to heaven.** This phrase repeats the description of the tower of Babel (11:4). Jacob may have seen a ziggurat structure. **angels of God.** The Hebrew here is unique to this verse and to 32:1. Angels guard (3:24), communicate (18:2) and protect (ch. 19). **ascending and descending on it.** Their activity underscored that this land was the axis between heaven and Earth. Bethel, the "house of God" (see NIV text note on v. 19), foreshadowed Jesus Christ (Jn 1:47–51), who gives "access to the Father by one Spirit" (Eph 2:18), is the only "mediator between God and men" (1Ti 2:5) and sends his angels as ministering spirits "to serve those who will inherit salvation" (Heb 1:14).

28:13 There above it stood. Alternatively, "There beside him stood" (see NIV text note). The same preposition is used in God's second revelation to Jacob at Bethel: "God went up from [beside] him at the place where he had talked with him" (35:13). God did not stand above the ladder, but over a sleeping Jacob. Note Jacob's response: "Surely the LORD is in this place" (v. 16). God came down the stairway. **I am the LORD.** See 15:7 and 26:2. The fact that the patriarchs knew the name *Yahweh* does not contradict Exodus 6:3 (see note). **descendants.** The Hebrew here is also translated "offspring" (see notes on v. 14; 12:3,7; 13:15). **on which you are lying.** The promise was adapted to the immediate situation.

28:14 will spread out. A fresh expansion of 13:16. The Hebrew here denotes "to break out" with destructive force but connotes holy war. **will be blessed.** See 12:3, 18:18, 22:18 and 27:27.

28:15 I am with you. See notes on 26:3 (see also Ex 3:12; Pss 23; 46; Heb 13:5). The three promises of this verse pertained to Jacob's own lifetime. **I will not leave you.** Pagan deities were often linked with particular lands. God would be with Jacob outside the promised land. **until I have done.** The Hebrew for "until" does not entail or expect a change in the situation after God had fulfilled this promise.

28:16 the LORD is in this place. See note on verse 13. **in this place.** A verbal link with "this is" in 32:2 (see note on 32:2).

28:17 He was afraid. While worshipful fear in God's presence is appropriate (Ex 19:16; Ps 2:11; Ac 5:11), Jacob's reaction contrasted with those of his fathers, who built altars and worshiped upon receiving a revelation from God (12:7; 26:24–25).

28:18 a pillar. As a witness (31:45–59) and a monument to draw attention to the importance of the place. **poured oil.** That is, to consecrate it (Ex 30:25–29).

28:19 He called that place. A verbal link with the same formula in 32:2.

28:20–22 This is the longest vow in the Old Testament. The journey had originated as a flight to avoid assassination and a trip to find a wife suitable to his parents. Now, however, Jacob's journey had become a religious pilgrimage. He traveled as a carrier of God's promises, with divine assurance of aid and committed to a destiny to meet God and worship him in the promised land. See *WCF* 22.6.

28:20 If. Whereas in the covenants with Abraham and Isaac the Lord had made the fulfillment of his promises conditional upon the obedience of the patriarchs, Jacob made his worship of the Lord at this site conditional upon the Lord's fulfillment of his promises. The Lord looks with favor upon well-considered, realistic vows (Lev 7:16; 30:1–15; 1Sa 1:10–20; Pss 16:12–13; 22:25; 50:14; 66:13–15; Isa 19:21). Jacob confessed God's presence in 31:5 and worshiped in 33:20. See *WLC* 193; *WSC* 104.

28:22 give you a tenth. See 14:20. Jacob would no longer be a grasper but a giver. This mention of the tithe demonstrates its importance even before the giving of the Mosaic Law.

Jacob Arrives in Paddan Aram

29:1 **29** Then Jacob continued on his journey and came to the land of the eastern peo-
[w]Jdg 6:3,33 ples.[w] [2]There he saw a well in the field, with three flocks of sheep lying near it
because the flocks were watered from that well. The stone over the mouth of the well was
large. [3]When all the flocks were gathered there, the shepherds would roll the stone away
from the well's mouth and water the sheep. Then they would return the stone to its place
over the mouth of the well.
29:4 [4]Jacob asked the shepherds, "My brothers, where are you from?"
[x]Ge 28:10 "We're from Haran,[x]" they replied.
[5]He said to them, "Do you know Laban, Nahor's grandson?"
"Yes, we know him," they answered.
[6]Then Jacob asked them, "Is he well?"
"Yes, he is," they said, "and here comes his daughter Rachel with the sheep."
[7]"Look," he said, "the sun is still high; it is not time for the flocks to be gathered. Water the sheep and take them back to pasture."
[8]"We can't," they replied, "until all the flocks are gathered and the stone has been
rolled away from the mouth of the well. Then we will water the sheep."
29:9 [y]Ex 2:16 [9]While he was still talking with them, Rachel came with her father's sheep,[y] for she
was a shepherdess. [10]When Jacob saw Rachel daughter of Laban, his mother's brother,
29:10 and Laban's sheep, he went over and rolled the stone away from the mouth of the well
[z]Ex 2:17 29:11 and watered his uncle's sheep.[z] [11]Then Jacob kissed Rachel and began to weep aloud.[a]
[a]Ge 33:4 29:12 [b]Ge 13:8; 14:14,16 [12]He had told Rachel that he was a relative[b] of her father and a son of Rebekah. So she
[c]Ge 24:28 ran and told her father.[c]
29:13 [d]Ge 24:29 [13]As soon as Laban[d] heard the news about Jacob, his sister's son, he hurried to meet
him. He embraced him and kissed him and brought him to his home, and there Jacob
29:14 [e]Ge 2:23; Jdg 9:2; 2Sa 19:12-13 told him all these things. [14]Then Laban said to him, "You are my own flesh and blood."[e]

Jacob Marries Leah and Rachel

After Jacob had stayed with him for a whole month, [15]Laban said to him, "Just because you are a relative of mine, should you work for me for nothing? Tell me what your
wages should be."
[16]Now Laban had two daughters; the name of the older was Leah, and the name of
the younger was Rachel. [17]Leah had weak[a] eyes, but Rachel was lovely in form, and
beautiful. [18]Jacob was in love with Rachel and said, "I'll work for you seven years in re-
29:18 [f]Hos 12:12 turn for your younger daughter Rachel."[f]
[19]Laban said, "It's better that I give her to you than to some other man. Stay here with
me." [20]So Jacob served seven years to get Rachel, but they seemed like only a few days
29:20 [g]SS 8:7; Hos 12:12 to him because of his love for her.[g]
[21]Then Jacob said to Laban, "Give me my wife. My time is completed, and I want to
29:21 [h]Jdg 15:1 lie with her.[h]"

[a] *17* Or *delicate*

■ **29:1–30** *Conflict With Laban.* Jacob experienced the blessings of providence in meeting Rachel (vv. 1–14), and in bitter irony the deceiver became the deceived (vv. 15–29). Behind the two scenes, the gracious and just hand of the sovereign God can be discerned. God cared for Jacob, but Jacob also learned hard lessons about himself from his encounters in the northern regions of Syria. The Israelites were to make discoveries about themselves and their trials from these episodes, as all believers must learn to see the providence of God in times of trouble.

29:2 well. The similarity of this meeting at the well with the encounter recorded in 24:11–33 suggests the benevolence of divine providence. **The stone . . . was large.** Cisterns and wells were covered with a broad, thick, flat stone with a round hole cut in the middle. This stone was then covered with another heavy stone that required several men to roll away. The enormous rock features prominently in this scene (vv. 2–3,8,10) and speaks particularly of Jacob's strength.

29:4 My brothers. The Hebrew here is rendered "friends" in 19:7; it was a gesture to win goodwill.

29:5 grandson. The Hebrew here also means "son."

29:7 it is not time. At what appeared to be the wrong time, Jacob providentially met the right people and the right woman.

29:8 until all the flocks are gathered. Since three shepherds with their flocks had already gathered there, the implication is that it took more than that many men to remove the large rock. These shepherds functioned as a foil to Jacob's ambition, energy and strength.

29:10 rolled the stone away. Jacob gained superhuman power in his service of love.

29:11 kissed. A customary greeting among relatives (v. 13–14; 31:55). **weep aloud.** Unlike Abraham's servant, he offered no praise, for he had made no petition.

29:13 he hurried to meet him. Earlier the gold jewelry of Abraham's servant had attracted Laban's attention (see 24:30); now Jacob's strength impressed Laban as he considered the service Jacob could render to his house.

29:15 wages. Laban would rather have given any wage than to confer upon Jacob the dignity and help due a relative. He degraded their blood relationship to an economic arrangement. While he should have helped Jacob start building a home (30:25–34), Laban treated him as nothing more than a laborer under contract, as Jacob bitterly complained in 31:38–42.

29:16 Leah . . . Rachel. Their names mean "cow" and "ewe," respectively. Sadly, Laban actually treated Leah and Rachel like shepherds' animals, as commodities for bargaining and trading (see 31:15).

29:17 weak. Literally, "soft." Leah's eyes lacked the fire and sparkle that people of that day prized as beauty.

29:18 in love. See note on 34:3.

29:19 I give her. Laban's answer was shrewdly ambiguous. He did not explicitly agree to give Rachel, and Jacob was not discerning enough either to see through his uncle's character or to detect the ambiguity of Laban's response.

[22]So Laban brought together all the people of the place and gave a feast.[i] [23]But when
evening came, he took his daughter Leah and gave her to Jacob, and Jacob lay with her.
[24]And Laban gave his servant girl Zilpah to his daughter as her maidservant.
[25]When morning came, there was Leah! So Jacob said to Laban, "What is this you
have done to me?[j] I served you for Rachel, didn't I? Why have you deceived me?[k]"
[26]Laban replied, "It is not our custom here to give the younger daughter in marriage
before the older one. [27]Finish this daughter's bridal week;[l] then we will give you the
younger one also, in return for another seven years of work."
[28]And Jacob did so. He finished the week with Leah, and then Laban gave him his
daughter Rachel to be his wife. [29]Laban gave his servant girl Bilhah[m] to his daughter Rachel as her maidservant.[n] [30]Jacob lay with Rachel also, and he loved Rachel more than
Leah.[o] And he worked for Laban another seven years.[p]

Jacob's Children

[31]When the LORD saw that Leah was not loved,[q] he opened her womb,[r] but Rachel
was barren. [32]Leah became pregnant and gave birth to a son. She named him Reuben,[a]
for she said, "It is because the LORD has seen my misery.[s] Surely my husband will love
me now."
[33]She conceived again, and when she gave birth to a son she said, "Because the LORD
heard that I am not loved, he gave me this one too." So she named him Simeon.[b][t]
[34]Again she conceived, and when she gave birth to a son she said, "Now at last my
husband will become attached to me,[u] because I have borne him three sons." So he was
named Levi.[c][v]
[35]She conceived again, and when she gave birth to a son she said, "This time I will
praise the LORD." So she named him Judah.[d][w] Then she stopped having children.

30

When Rachel saw that she was not bearing Jacob any children,[x] she became
jealous of her sister.[y] So she said to Jacob, "Give me children, or I'll die!"
[2]Jacob became angry with her and said, "Am I in the place of God, who has kept you
from having children?"[z]
[3]Then she said, "Here is Bilhah, my maidservant. Sleep with her so that she can bear
children for me and that through her I too can build a family."[a]
[4]So she gave him her servant Bilhah as a wife.[b] Jacob slept with her,[c] [5]and she be-

29:22 [i]Jdg 14:10; Jn 2:1-2
29:25 [j]Ge 12:18 [k]Ge 27:36
29:27 [l]Jdg 14:12
29:29 [m]Ge 30:3 [n]Ge 16:1
29:30 [o]ver 16 [p]Ge 31:41
29:31 [q]Dt 21:15-17 [r]Ge 11:30; 30:1; Ps 127:3
29:32 [s]Ge 16:11; 31:42; Ex 4:31; Dt 26:7; Ps 25:18
29:33 [t]Ge 34:25; 49:5
29:34 [u]Ge 30:20; 1Sa 1:2-4 [v]Ge 49:5-7
29:35 [w]Ge 49:8; Mt 1:2-3
30:1 [x]Ge 29:31; 1Sa 1:5-6 [y]Lev 18:18
30:2 [z]Ge 16:2; 20:18; 29:31
30:3 [a]Ge 16:2
30:4 [b]ver 9,18 [c]Ge 16:3-4

[a] 32 *Reuben* sounds like the Hebrew for *he has seen my misery*; the name means *see, a son.* [b] 33 *Simeon* probably means *one who hears.* [c] 34 *Levi* sounds like and may be derived from the Hebrew for *attached.* [d] 35 *Judah* sounds like and may be derived from the Hebrew for *praise.*

29:23 evening. As Jacob had taken advantage of his father's blindness in order to deceive him, so Laban used the cover of night to outwit Jacob. **he took his daughter Leah.** The custom of veiling the bride (24:65) and of marrying off the elder daughter first served Laban's selfish intentions.

29:24 maidservant. The custom of a father presenting his daughter with a maidservant at the time of her marriage is well attested in ancient Near Eastern sources.

29:25 deceived me. See 27:35. In dramatic irony, Jacob married the wrong woman. In yet another divine paradox, God would use the unloved daughter and wife to give birth to the tribal fathers of Levi and Judah (vv. 33–35), who were to become so important to the tribal arrangements in the days of Moses. Moreover, Jesus would come from the line of Leah through Judah.

29:26 not our custom. An honest man would have made this clear in the original contract, but Jacob was powerless and so said nothing. **to give the younger . . . before the older.** The enforcement of the custom by duplicity reflected in some ways Jacob's earlier acquisition of Isaac's blessing (ch. 27). God contravened the custom in the cases of Isaac, Jacob and Joseph.

29:27 bridal week. The week of feasting (v. 22) toasted Laban's wit and Jacob's humiliation, turning his marriage into an occasion for jest.

29:30 loved Rachel more than Leah. Isaac's marriage to Rebekah had brought peaceful love, but Jacob's marriages to Laban's daughters fomented strife and rivalry between the sisters (29:31—30:24). **worked.** A similar Hebrew expression is translated "serve" in 27:29.

■ **29:31—30:24** *Birth of Tribal Patriarchs.* God blessed Jacob with 12 sons in spite of his questionable character and the rivalry between Rachel and Leah, who competed for supremacy in their husband's affections by bearing him sons. The names the mothers gave their sons reflected this struggle and their recognition of God's assistance to them in their unloved or childless states (see NIV text notes). God graciously built up the nation of Israel, just as he had promised Abraham. Believers in all ages may gain assurance of God's mercy as they see for themselves the ways by which God increased the number of his people.

29:31–35 God graciously gave Leah, the unloved wife, the firstborn of Jacob's sons and several others, including the priestly line of Levi and the Messianic line of Judah.

29:31 opened. See 16:2 and 21:17. **barren.** See 25:21. There was no natural way for Rachel to have children.

29:32 the LORD has seen my misery. The first and last of the children born in Paddan Aram were given by the Lord to compensate a disgraced wife: the first to Leah, the last to Rachel (vv. 30:22–24).

29:34 attached to me. Her hope was not realized (30:15–16). **Levi.** His name took on greater significance when the tribe became attached to the ark (Nu 18:2).

29:35 Judah. The name means "he will be praised." Here the praise is of the Lord; in 49:8 it is of Judah himself. The unloved wife climactically concluded this stage of her childbearing with a resolve to praise the Lord. Judah became the tribe out of which issued the royal line of David, which eventually led to Jesus.

30:1 became jealous. Compare note on 25:21. Each woman wanted what the other had, and neither treasured what she herself had been given. **I'll die!** A hyperbole for her extreme grief (25:32; 27:46). Ironically, Rachel died in childbirth (vv. 35:16–18).

30:2 Am I in the place of God . . . ? His angry retort, though theologically sound, contrasted sharply with the prayer of Isaac on behalf of his childless wife (25:21).

30:3 Here is Bilhah. See note on 16:2. **for me.** Literally, "upon my knees." The ritual indicated some kind of recognized welcome or acceptance of a newborn child into the family that could be carried out by parents, grandparents or even great-grandparents.

30:4 as a wife. The terms *wife* and *concubine* were used somewhat loosely during the patriarchal period, but not after it (cf. 16:3; 25:1,6; 30:4; 35:22).

came pregnant and bore him a son. 6Then Rachel said, "God has vindicated me;[d] he has
listened to my plea and given me a son." Because of this she named him Dan.[a e]
7Rachel's servant Bilhah conceived again and bore Jacob a second son. 8Then Rachel
said, "I have had a great struggle with my sister, and I have won."[f] So she named him
Naphtali.[b g]
9When Leah saw that she had stopped having children, she took her maidservant Zilpah and gave her to Jacob as a wife.[h] 10Leah's servant Zilpah bore Jacob a son. 11Then
Leah said, "What good fortune!"[c] So she named him Gad.[d i]
12Leah's servant Zilpah bore Jacob a second son. 13Then Leah said, "How happy I am!
The women will call me[j] happy."[k] So she named him Asher.[e l]
14During wheat harvest, Reuben went out into the fields and found some mandrake
plants,[m] which he brought to his mother Leah. Rachel said to Leah, "Please give me
some of your son's mandrakes."
15But she said to her, "Wasn't it enough[n] that you took away my husband? Will you
take my son's mandrakes too?"
"Very well," Rachel said, "he can sleep with you tonight in return for your son's mandrakes."
16So when Jacob came in from the fields that evening, Leah went out to meet him.
"You must sleep with me," she said. "I have hired you with my son's mandrakes." So he
slept with her that night.
17God listened to Leah,[o] and she became pregnant and bore Jacob a fifth son. 18Then
Leah said, "God has rewarded me for giving my maidservant to my husband." So she
named him Issachar.[f p]
19Leah conceived again and bore Jacob a sixth son. 20Then Leah said, "God has presented me with a precious gift. This time my husband will treat me with honor, because
I have borne him six sons." So she named him Zebulun.[g q]
21Some time later she gave birth to a daughter and named her Dinah.
22Then God remembered Rachel;[r] he listened to her and opened her womb.[s] 23She
became pregnant and gave birth to a son[t] and said, "God has taken away my disgrace."[u] 24She named him Joseph,[h v] and said, "May the LORD add to me another son."[w]

Jacob's Flocks Increase

25After Rachel gave birth to Joseph, Jacob said to Laban, "Send me on my way[x] so I
can go back to my own homeland. 26Give me my wives and children, for whom I have
served you,[y] and I will be on my way. You know how much work I've done for you."
27But Laban said to him, "If I have found favor in your eyes, please stay. I have learned

30:6 [d]Ps 35:24; 43:1; La 3:59 [e]Ge 49:16-17
30:8 [f]Hos 12:3-4 [g]Ge 49:21
30:9 [h]ver 4
30:11 [i]Ge 49:19
30:13 [j]Ps 127:3 [k]Pr 31:28; Lk 1:48 [l]Ge 49:20
30:14 [m]SS 7:13
30:15 [n]Nu 16:9,13
30:17 [o]Ge 25:21
30:18 [p]Ge 49:14
30:20 [q]Ge 35:23; 49:13; Mt 4:13
30:22 [r]Ge 8:1; 1Sa 1:19-20 [s]Ge 29:31
30:23 [t]ver 6 [u]Isa 4:1; Lk 1:25
30:24 [v]Ge 35:24; 37:2; 39:1; 49:22-26 [w]Ge 35:17
30:25 [x]Ge 24:54
30:26 [y]Ge 29:20,30; Hos 12:12

a *6 Dan* here means *he has vindicated.* b *8 Naphtali* means *my struggle.* c *11* Or *"A troop is coming!"* d *11 Gad* can mean *good fortune* or *a troop.* e *13 Asher* means *happy.* f *18 Issachar* sounds like the Hebrew for *reward.* g *20 Zebulun* probably means *honor.* h *24 Joseph* means *may he add.*

30:6 God . . . has listened to my plea. To judge from Isaac's example, the husband had a responsibility to intercede with God for births within the family. Without a husband willing to mediate for her, Rachel, like Hannah after her, prayed on her own behalf.
30:8 great struggle. Literally, "a struggle of God."
30:11 "What good fortune!" Or "Good fortune has come."
30:14 mandrake plants. An aphrodisiac promoting fertility (SS 7:13). This is an honest recognition that Rachel was not free of the influences of her pagan background (see also note on 31:19).
30:16 hired you. Just as Jacob's relationship with Laban was changed from "flesh and blood" to "wages," so now his marriage to Leah was reduced to a commercial contract.
30:17–21 Ironically, Leah bore two more sons and a daughter without the aphrodisiac.
30:18 rewarded. The Hebrew word here is the same one translated "hired" in verse 16. Leah's pun summed up God's grace and Jacob's lamentable lack of leadership.
30:20 presented me with a precious gift. More literally, "endowed me with a good dowry."
30:21 Dinah. Dinah is the only named daughter of Jacob (46:7); she figures prominently in chapter 34.
30:22 remembered. This is the climax of 29:21—30:24 (see 8:1 and its note). Rachel credited the birth of Joseph not to the aphrodisiac, but to God.
■ **30:25—31:55** *Jacob's Departure From Laban.* Jacob departed from Laban to return to the promised land. These chapters divide into his preparations (30:25–43), the flight (31:1–21) and a final encounter with Laban (31:22–55). God's provision for Jacob's departure demonstrated his care for his covenant people.
30:25–43 God sovereignly blessed Jacob's flocks at Laban's expense in spite of the inexcusable cunning of both men (see note on 25:19—35:29). Jacob ultimately outmaneuvered Laban, obtaining his family (29:31—30:24) and wealth by God's grace.
30:25 After. After the birth of Joseph, Jacob felt free to leave Paddan Aram with his family, for Rachel was now bound to him by a child (cf. 31:1–16). **Send me on my way.** If a slave owner would send away an indentured slave with a liberal supply of flocks, grain and wine to get a new start for his own household (cf. Dt 12:12–14), how much more should Laban have sent off his own flesh and blood with generous provisions (31:28–42)?
30:26 Give me my wives. Jacob could have claimed his wives without Laban's consent (31:43), but Laban and his sons could have overtaken him with swords (31:22–25). Moreover, Jacob would have looked like a thief running away.
30:27 If I have found favor. A formula of courtesy in negotiations. **learned by divination.** Most of the extrabiblical texts from Mesopotamia pertain to divination. The practice was forbidden in Israel (Lev 19:26; Dt 18:10,14) because it presumed that human beings could manipulate the deity to serve them instead of depending in faith on God's good pleasure. Ironically, the Lord used even Laban's magic so that he confessed God's blessing on Jacob, even as the Philistine kings had acknowledged their blessings on Abraham (21:22) and Isaac (26:28–29). Once again, the original audience was encouraged to hear that another who was not their predecessor in the covenant recognized the blessing of God on their patriarch. **blessed.** See note on 1:22.

by divination that[a] the LORD has blessed me because of you."[z] 28 He added, "Name your
wages,[a] and I will pay them."
29 Jacob said to him, "You know how I have worked for you[b] and how your livestock
has fared under my care.[c] 30 The little you had before I came has increased greatly, and
the LORD has blessed you wherever I have been. But now, when may I do something for
my own household?[d]"
31 "What shall I give you?" he asked.
"Don't give me anything," Jacob replied. "But if you will do this one thing for me, I
will go on tending your flocks and watching over them: 32 Let me go through all your
flocks today and remove from them every speckled or spotted sheep, every dark-colored
lamb and every spotted or speckled goat.[e] They will be my wages. 33 And my honesty will
testify for me in the future, whenever you check on the wages you have paid me. Any goat
in my possession that is not speckled or spotted, or any lamb that is not dark-colored,
will be considered stolen."
34 "Agreed," said Laban. "Let it be as you have said." 35 That same day he removed all
the male goats that were streaked or spotted, and all the speckled or spotted female
goats (all that had white on them) and all the dark-colored lambs, and he placed them
in the care of his sons.[f] 36 Then he put a three-day journey between himself and Jacob,
while Jacob continued to tend the rest of Laban's flocks.
37 Jacob, however, took fresh-cut branches from poplar, almond and plane trees and
made white stripes on them by peeling the bark and exposing the white inner wood of the
branches. 38 Then he placed the peeled branches in all the watering troughs, so that they
would be directly in front of the flocks when they came to drink. When the flocks were in
heat and came to drink, 39 they mated in front of the branches. And they bore young that
were streaked or speckled or spotted. 40 Jacob set apart the young of the flock by themselves, but made the rest face the streaked and dark-colored animals that belonged to Laban. Thus he made separate flocks for himself and did not put them with Laban's animals.
41 Whenever the stronger females were in heat, Jacob would place the branches in the
troughs in front of the animals so they would mate near the branches, 42 but if the animals
were weak, he would not place them there. So the weak animals went to Laban and the
strong ones to Jacob. 43 In this way the man grew exceedingly prosperous and came to own
large flocks, and maidservants and menservants, and camels and donkeys.[g]

Jacob Flees From Laban

31 Jacob heard that Laban's sons were saying, "Jacob has taken everything our father owned and has gained all this wealth from what belonged to our father."
2 And Jacob noticed that Laban's attitude toward him was not what it had been.
3 Then the LORD said to Jacob, "Go back[h] to the land of your fathers and to your relatives, and I will be with you."[i]

30:27 [z]Ge 26:24; 39:3,5
30:28 [a]Ge 29:15
30:29 [b]Ge 31:6 [c]Ge 31:38-40
30:30 [d]1Ti 5:8
30:32 [e]Ge 31:8,12
30:35 [f]Ge 31:1
30:43 [g]ver 30; Ge 12:16; 13:2; 24:35; 26:13-14
31:3 [h]ver 13; Ge 32:9 [i]Ge 21:22; 26:3; 28:15

a 27 Or possibly *have become rich and*

30:28 Name your wages. Laban wanted to manipulate the Lord through Jacob to serve his own greed rather than to bless Jacob and so receive God's blessing (see 12:3; 20:14–18; 31:9 and their notes).
30:30 See *WSC* 74.
30:31 do this one thing. The success of Jacob's proposal depended on God (31:10–13). But Jacob had the faulty notion that vivid prenatal impressions affected the unborn. Despite Jacob's scheming, God's intention to bless Jacob was not thwarted (31:11–12).
30:32–33 The narrator clarified the verbal agreement in verse 35: Only the abnormally colored goats with white in them and the dark lambs were Jacob's.
30:34 Agreed. Laban's unhesitating acceptance of the offer highlights the unexpected and supernatural blessing on Jacob.
30:35–36 placed them . . . put a three-day journey. Laban's two precautionary measures validated the supernatural blessing.
30:35 That same day he removed. Laban was cheating. According to the agreement the unusually colored animals should have been Jacob's starting flock. Jacob began with none of these, highlighting the supernatural blessing on him.
30:39 And they bore. The scheme worked only because of God's sovereign grace, not on account of pagan magic (31:9).
30:43 grew exceedingly prosperous. God provided abundantly more than Jacob had requested (see 28:20). For more details, see 31:41.
31:1–55 Revealing himself in dreams, the Lord sovereignly led a chastened Jacob back to the promised land with great wealth at Laban's expense and resolved the conflict in a nonaggression pact between a victorious Jacob and a defeated Laban—all this in spite of the pagan idolatry in Jacob's household. Jacob confessed to his wives and to Laban that the Lord had been with him and was calling him to pay his vow at Bethel, and his wives resolutely turned their backs on their homeland.
31:1 Jacob has taken. Jacob's scheming, which denied the Lord his rightful praise, contrasted sharply with Abraham's dealings (14:23; 27:36). In the mouths of Laban's sons, however, the accusation was a lie. Laban had cheated Jacob, but it was the Lord who had plundered Laban (vv. 4–9). The Lord and Jacob's wives agreed with Jacob's interpretation of the situation, not with that of Laban's sons.
31:2 Laban's attitude. Laban's attitude is reminiscent of the Philistines' envy toward Isaac (26:14).
31:3 Go back to the land. The predecessors of the 12 tribes retraced Abraham's journey from Paddan Aram (see notes on 12:1–9) and later from Egypt, accompanied by great wealth, en route to the promised land (see notes on 12:10–20; 35:24). Their journey also foreshadowed Israel's exodus from Egypt (Dt 26:5–8; Hos 12:12–13): Jacob and his family departed in response to God's call (v. 3) to worship in the land of Canaan (vv. 13,17) after plundering their enemy of wealth and gods (vv. 17–21). The slow-moving procession was pursued and overtaken by superior forces (vv. 22–23) but delivered by divine intervention (v. 24). This also prefigures the pilgrimage of all of God's people to the new heavens and the new earth (1Co 10:1–4). **I will be with you.** See note on 28:15.

4 So Jacob sent word to Rachel and Leah to come out to the fields where his flocks
were. 5 He said to them, "I see that your father's attitude toward me is not what it was
before, but the God of my father has been with me.[j] 6 You know that I've worked for your
father with all my strength,[k] 7 yet your father has cheated me by changing my wages ten
times.[l] However, God has not allowed him to harm me.[m] 8 If he said, 'The speckled ones
will be your wages,' then all the flocks gave birth to speckled young; and if he said, 'The
streaked ones will be your wages,'[n] then all the flocks bore streaked young. 9 So God has
taken away your father's livestock and has given them to me.[o]

10 "In breeding season I once had a dream in which I looked up and saw that the male
goats mating with the flock were streaked, speckled or spotted. 11 The angel of God[p] said
to me in the dream, 'Jacob.' I answered, 'Here I am.' 12 And he said, 'Look up and see that
all the male goats mating with the flock are streaked, speckled or spotted, for I have seen
all that Laban has been doing to you.[q] 13 I am the God of Bethel,[r] where you anointed a
pillar and where you made a vow to me. Now leave this land at once and go back to your
native land.[s]' "

14 Then Rachel and Leah replied, "Do we still have any share in the inheritance of our
father's estate? 15 Does he not regard us as foreigners? Not only has he sold us, but he has
used up what was paid for us.[t] 16 Surely all the wealth that God took away from our father belongs to us and our children. So do whatever God has told you."

17 Then Jacob put his children and his wives on camels, 18 and he drove all his livestock
ahead of him, along with all the goods he had accumulated in Paddan Aram,[a] to go to
his father Isaac[u] in the land of Canaan.[v]

19 When Laban had gone to shear his sheep, Rachel stole her father's household
gods.[w] 20 Moreover, Jacob deceived[x] Laban the Aramean by not telling him he was running away.[y] 21 So he fled with all he had, and crossing the River,[b] he headed for the hill
country of Gilead.[z]

Laban Pursues Jacob

22 On the third day Laban was told that Jacob had fled. 23 Taking his relatives with him,
he pursued Jacob for seven days and caught up with him in the hill country of Gilead.
24 Then God came to Laban the Aramean in a dream at night and said to him,[a] "Be careful not to say anything to Jacob, either good or bad."[b]

25 Jacob had pitched his tent in the hill country of Gilead when Laban overtook him,
and Laban and his relatives camped there too. 26 Then Laban said to Jacob, "What have

31:5 [j]Ge 21:22; 26:3
31:6 [k]Ge 30:29
31:7 [l]ver 41; Job 19:3 [m]ver 52; Ps 37:28; 105:14
31:8 [n]Ge 30:32
31:9 [o]ver 1,16; Ge 30:42
31:11 [p]Ge 16:7; 48:16
31:12 [q]Ex 3:7
31:13 [r]Ge 28:10-22 [s]ver 3; Ge 32:9
31:15 [t]Ge 29:20
31:18 [u]Ge 35:27 [v]Ge 10:19
31:19 [w]ver 30,32,34-35; Ge 35:2; Jdg 17:5; 1Sa 19:13; Hos 3:4
31:20 [x]Ge 27:36 [y]ver 27
31:21 [z]Ge 37:25
31:24 [a]Ge 20:3; Job 33:15 [b]Ge 24:50

a *18* That is, Northwest Mesopotamia b *21* That is, the Euphrates

---

As the Lord had assured Jacob of his presence and protection on his initial flight from Esau, so now God confirmed his protecting presence upon the return.

31:4 So Jacob sent word. Jacob promptly obeyed the heavenly vision (cf. 12:4). His full speech demonstrated that he had finally taken spiritual leadership. He openly proclaimed his faith and gave all credit to God for his blessing. Jacob's speech began (v. 5), continued (vv. 6–7) and ended with proclamations of God's victories over Laban (vv. 8–9). **come out to the fields.** Where they could not be overheard.

31:5 the God of my father has been with me. Jacob was ready to fulfill his vow (v. 13; 28:20–22).

31:7 cheated me. See 29:23 and 30:25. Jacob's spoiling of Laban was justified (vv. 38–42). **ten.** The symbolic number for "time and again." Here it signified "enough is enough."

31:8 The speckled ones. See 30:31–35.

31:9 So God has taken away. This Aramaic legal term for the transfer and conveyance of property revealed Jacob's sober reflections on the happenings of the last several years. God cursed those who had cursed Abraham's seed (12:3; 27:29).

31:10 a dream. The narrator validated Jacob's defense by recounting God's revelation to Jacob affirming his presence with him (v. 3), by recording God's warning to Laban not to harm Jacob (v. 24) and by relating the agreement of both wives with Jacob against their father. God's revelation certified that his own blessings, not Jacob's scheme, had produced Jacob's prosperity at Laban's expense.

31:11 angel of God. See note on 16:7.

31:12 male goats mating with the flock are streaked. This, and not Jacob's cunning, was the real reason for Jacob's triumph over Laban (see note on 30:31). **I have seen.** The just God championed the cause of the oppressed (see 16:13; 29:31; 31:42; Ex 3:7,9; 4:31), and God decided the ethical issue between Laban and Jacob in Jacob's favor.

31:14 replied. Jacob's wives followed him in retaliation against their father (vv. 14–15) and in recognition of God's providence in the events described in 30:25–43 (see v. 16). In the past Laban had sold them, and at present he counted them as foreigners. Their future depended on their wealth—wealth that rightly belonged to them but that they feared Laban would steal.

31:15 he has used up. This phrase (lit., "to consume money") appears in identical contexts in the Nuzi tablets (c. 1500 B.C.). Legally the consummating sum given in marriage was to be passed on, at least in part, to the daughters.

31:16 took away. The Hebrew here is translated "plunder" in Exodus 12:36. **whatever God has told you.** They acknowledged God's blessing and were willing to risk a journey to the promised land.

31:18 Paddan Aram. See 25:20.

31:19 to shear his sheep. An ideal time to flee. Sheepshearing entailed large numbers of men working at great distances from their homes for an extended period of time. Laban and his men were far away and preoccupied. **stole her father's household gods.** Household gods were thought to provide protection and blessing. Their sizes and shapes were not uniform (cf. v. 34 with 1Sa 19:13,16). Unlike Sarah and Rebekah, who had embraced the God of the patriarchs upon coming to the promised land, Rachel had not given up her pagan idols or ethics (see 30:14 and its note).

31:20 deceived. The Hebrew term implies taking away a person's ability to discern and act appropriately. **Aramean.** The ethnic identification underscores the total alienation of Jacob and Laban and presages the treaty between them.

31:23 his relatives. The presence of his whole clan gave Laban military superiority (v. 29).

31:24 God came. God sovereignly protected Jacob, as he had Abraham (12:17; 20:3) and Isaac (26:8). **either good or bad.** God had earlier revealed himself to Laban through acts of providence (24:50); now he did so through a dream.

you done? You've deceived me,[c] and you've carried off my daughters like captives in war.[d]
27Why did you run off secretly and deceive me? Why didn't you tell me, so I could send you
away with joy and singing to the music of tambourines[e] and harps?[f] 28You didn't even let
me kiss my grandchildren and my daughters good-by.[g] You have done a foolish thing. 29I
have the power to harm you;[h] but last night the God of your father[i] said to me, 'Be careful not to say anything to Jacob, either good or bad.' 30Now you have gone off because you
longed to return to your father's house. But why did you steal my gods?[j]"
31Jacob answered Laban, "I was afraid, because I thought you would take your daughters away from me by force. 32But if you find anyone who has your gods, he shall not live.[k]
In the presence of our relatives, see for yourself whether there is anything of yours here
with me; and if so, take it." Now Jacob did not know that Rachel had stolen the gods.
33So Laban went into Jacob's tent and into Leah's tent and into the tent of the two maidservants, but he found nothing. After he came out of Leah's tent, he entered Rachel's tent.
34Now Rachel had taken the household gods and put them inside her camel's saddle and
was sitting on them. Laban searched[l] through everything in the tent but found nothing.
35Rachel said to her father, "Don't be angry, my lord, that I cannot stand up in your
presence;[m] I'm having my period." So he searched but could not find the household
gods.

31:26 [c]Ge 27:36 [d]1Sa 30:2-3
31:27 [e]Ex 15:20 [f]Ge 4:21
31:28 [g]ver 55
31:29 [h]ver 7 [i]ver 53
31:30 [j]ver 19; Jdg 18:24
31:32 [k]Ge 44:9
31:34 [l]ver 37; Ge 44:12
31:35 [m]Ex 20:12; Lev 19:3,32

31:31 Jacob answered. Jacob's future depended on this critical search.
31:32 he shall not live. Theft of temple property was a capital offense according to the Code of Hammurapi.
31:34 saddle. An archaeological discovery in northern Syria (c. 900 B.C.) shows a camel driver fully and securely seated on a box-like saddle. The box, about 18 inches long and 14 inches high, was bound by straps to the camel and served as both a riding saddle and a pack saddle. **sitting on them.** The contrast between Jacob's God and Laban's idols is laughable (Isa 46:1–2). **searched.** This word (which appears both here and in v. 37) is translated "touched" in 27:22. Trusting their senses, neither Isaac nor Laban uncovered the truth.
31:35 I'm having my period. The law later codified that women were ceremonially unclean at this time (Lev 15:19–30, especially v. 20). As in chapter 27, the younger child deceived the father.

Jacob's Journeys

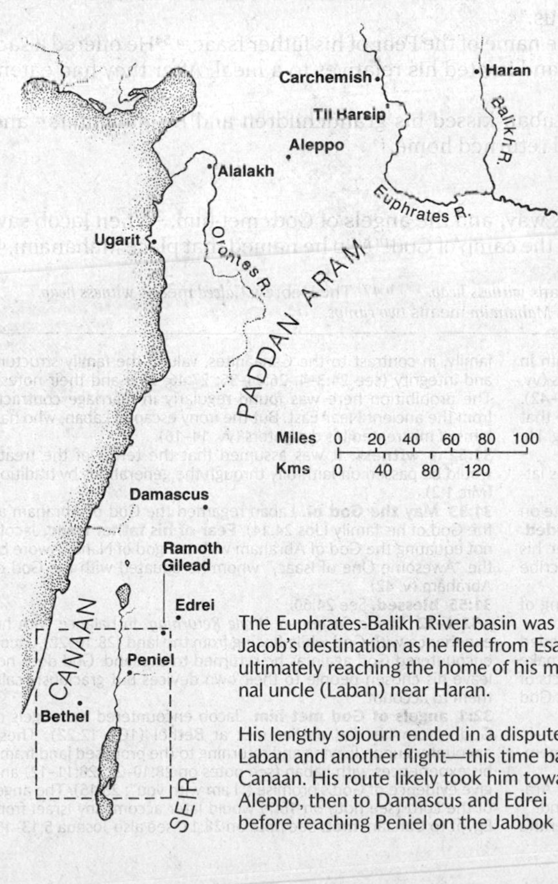

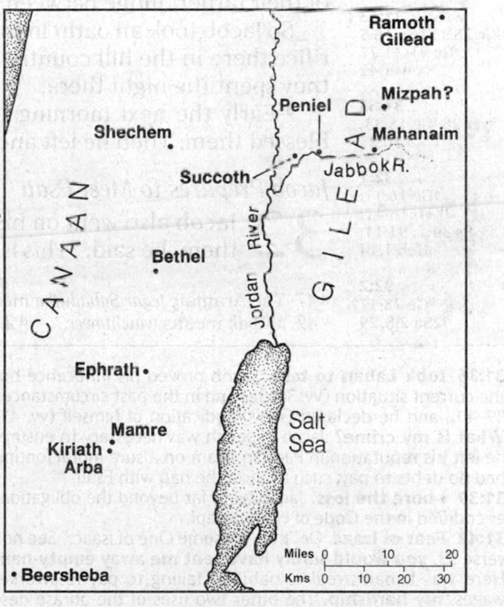

The Euphrates-Balikh River basin was Jacob's destination as he fled from Esau, ultimately reaching the home of his maternal uncle (Laban) near Haran.

His lengthy sojourn ended in a dispute with Laban and another flight—this time back to Canaan. His route likely took him toward Aleppo, then to Damascus and Edrei before reaching Peniel on the Jabbok River.

He and his dependents reached the hill country of Gilead before their caravan was overtaken by Laban. The covenant at Mizpah was celebrated on one of the hills later used as a border station between Aramean and Israelite territories.

Jacob tarried at Succoth, entered Canaan and proceeded to Shechem, where he erected an altar to the Lord.

36 Jacob was angry and took Laban to task. "What is my crime?" he asked Laban. "What sin have I committed that you hunt me down? 37 Now that you have searched through all my goods, what have you found that belongs to your household? Put it here in front of your relatives[n] and mine, and let them judge between the two of us.

38 "I have been with you for twenty years now. Your sheep and goats have not miscarried, nor have I eaten rams from your flocks. 39 I did not bring you animals torn by wild beasts; I bore the loss myself. And you demanded payment from me for whatever was stolen by day or night.[o] 40 This was my situation: The heat consumed me in the daytime and the cold at night, and sleep fled from my eyes. 41 It was like this for the twenty years I was in your household. I worked for you fourteen years for your two daughters[p] and six years for your flocks, and you changed my wages ten times.[q] 42 If the God of my father,[r] the God of Abraham and the Fear of Isaac,[s] had not been with me,[t] you would surely have sent me away empty-handed. But God has seen my hardship and the toil of my hands,[u] and last night he rebuked you."

43 Laban answered Jacob, "The women are my daughters, the children are my children, and the flocks are my flocks. All you see is mine. Yet what can I do today about these daughters of mine, or about the children they have borne? 44 Come now, let's make a covenant,[v] you and I, and let it serve as a witness between us."[w]

45 So Jacob took a stone and set it up as a pillar.[x] 46 He said to his relatives, "Gather some stones." So they took stones and piled them in a heap, and they ate there by the heap. 47 Laban called it Jegar Sahadutha,[a] and Jacob called it Galeed.[b]

48 Laban said, "This heap is a witness between you and me today." That is why it was called Galeed. 49 It was also called Mizpah,[c][y] because he said, "May the LORD keep watch between you and me when we are away from each other. 50 If you mistreat my daughters or if you take any wives besides my daughters, even though no one is with us, remember that God is a witness[z] between you and me."

51 Laban also said to Jacob, "Here is this heap, and here is this pillar[a] I have set up between you and me. 52 This heap is a witness, and this pillar is a witness,[b] that I will not go past this heap to your side to harm you and that you will not go past this heap and pillar to my side to harm me.[c] 53 May the God of Abraham[d] and the God of Nahor, the God of their father, judge between us."[e]

So Jacob took an oath[f] in the name of the Fear of his father Isaac.[g] 54 He offered a sacrifice there in the hill country and invited his relatives to a meal. After they had eaten, they spent the night there.

55 Early the next morning Laban kissed his grandchildren and his daughters[h] and blessed them. Then he left and returned home.[i]

Jacob Prepares to Meet Esau

32 Jacob also went on his way, and the angels of God[j] met him. 2 When Jacob saw them, he said, "This is the camp of God!"[k] So he named that place Mahanaim.[d][l]

31:37 [n]ver 23
31:39 [o]Ex 22:13
31:41 [p]Ge 29:30 [q]ver 7
31:42 [r]ver 5; Ex 3:15; 1Ch 12:17 [s]ver 53; Isa 8:13 [t]Ps 124:1-2 [u]Ge 29:32
31:44 [v]Ge 21:27; 26:28 [w]Jos 24:27
31:45 [x]Ge 28:18
31:49 [y]Jdg 11:29; 1Sa 7:5-6
31:50 [z]Jer 29:23; 42:5
31:51 [a]Ge 28:18
31:52 [b]Ge 21:30 [c]ver 7; Ge 26:29
31:53 [d]Ge 28:13 [e]Ge 16:5 [f]Ge 21:23,27 [g]ver 42
31:55 [h]ver 28 [i]Ge 18:33; 30:25
32:1 [j]Ge 16:11; 2Ki 6:16-17; Ps 34:7; 91:11; Heb 1:14
32:2 [k]Ge 28:17 [l]2Sa 2:8,29

[a] 47 The Aramaic *Jegar Sahadutha* means *witness heap.* [b] 47 The Hebrew *Galeed* means *witness heap.*
[c] 49 *Mizpah* means *watchtower.* [d] 2 *Mahanaim* means *two camps.*

31:36 took Laban to task. Jacob proved his innocence both in the current situation (vv. 36–38) and in the past circumstances (vv. 39–40), and he declared God's vindication of himself (vv. 41–42). **What is my crime?** Jacob's speech was necessary to ensure that he left his reputation in Paddan Aram on a sure moral footing. He had no debts to pay, such as those he had with Esau.
31:39 I bore the loss. Jacob went far beyond the obligations later codified in the Code of Hammurapi.
31:42 Fear of Isaac. Or "the Awesome One of Isaac." See note on verse 53. **you would surely have sent me away empty-handed.** Here was Laban's real culpability: failing to pay his worker his wages. **my hardship.** The other two uses of the phrase describe Egyptian oppression (Ex 3:7; Dt 26:7).
31:43 All you see is mine. He was a pretender, like the king of Sodom, claiming goods to which he had no title (14:21).
31:44 make a covenant. By proposing the pact, Laban conceded that he had lost the lawsuit. The Hebrew here is translated make "a treaty" in 21:27 and 26:28; it was like the nonaggression pacts of Abraham and Isaac with the Philistines, not like the covenant God had made with Abraham (15:8).
31:45 pillar. Jacob marked the end of each cycle of his life—in Canaan and now in Haran (Paddan Aram)—with a pillar commemorating God's presence and protection (28:18–19).
31:47 called it. By using the language of Canaan rather than Aramaic, Jacob decisively identified himself with the promised land.
31:50 if you take any wives besides my daughters. Terah's family, in contrast to the Canaanites, valued the family structure and integrity (see 24:3–4; 26:34–35; 27:46; 28:9 and their notes). The prohibition here was found regularly in marriage contracts from the ancient Near East. But the irony escaped Laban, who had himself mistreated his daughters (vv. 14–16).
31:52 a witness. It was assumed that the terms of the treaty would be passed on faithfully through the generations by tradition (Mic 1:2).
31:53 May the God of. Laban regarded the God of Abraham as the God of his family (Jos 24:14). **Fear of his father Isaac.** Jacob, not equating the God of Abraham with the god of Nahor, swore by the "Awesome One of Isaac," whom he equated with the God of Abraham (v. 42).
31:55 blessed. See 24:60.
■ **32:1–32** *Divine Encounter While Returning.* In balance with his experience with God while fleeing from the land (28:10–22), Jacob encountered God again as he returned to the land. God does not leave his chosen people to their own devices but graciously calls them to account.
32:1 angels of God met him. Jacob encountered the angels of God whom he had earlier met at Bethel (1Ch 12:22). These encounters upon leaving and returning to the promised land frame his experiences with Laban (see notes on 28:10–22; 28:11–12) and give evidence of God's promise ("I am with you"; 28:15). The angel of the Lord (see note on 16:7) would later accompany Israel from Egypt to Canaan. **met.** See note on 28:11; see also Joshua 5:13–15.

3 Jacob sent messengers ahead of him to his brother Esau[m] in the land of Seir, the
country of Edom.[n] 4 He instructed them: "This is what you are to say to my master
Esau: 'Your servant Jacob says, I have been staying with Laban and have remained
there till now. 5 I have cattle and donkeys, sheep and goats, menservants and maidservants.[o] Now I am sending this message to my lord, that I may find favor in your
eyes.[p]' "
6 When the messengers returned to Jacob, they said, "We went to your brother Esau,
and now he is coming to meet you, and four hundred men are with him."[q]
7 In great fear[r] and distress Jacob divided the people who were with him into two
groups,[a] and the flocks and herds and camels as well. 8 He thought, "If Esau comes and
attacks one group,[b] the group[b] that is left may escape."
9 Then Jacob prayed, "O God of my father Abraham, God of my father Isaac,[s] O LORD,
who said to me, 'Go back to your country and your relatives, and I will make you prosper,'[t] 10 I am unworthy of all the kindness and faithfulness[u] you have shown your servant.
I had only my staff when I crossed this Jordan, but now I have become two groups. 11 Save
me, I pray, from the hand of my brother Esau, for I am afraid he will come and attack
me,[v] and also the mothers with their children.[w] 12 But you have said, 'I will surely make
you prosper and will make your descendants like the sand[x] of the sea, which cannot be
counted.[y]' "
13 He spent the night there, and from what he had with him he selected a gift[z] for his
brother Esau: 14 two hundred female goats and twenty male goats, two hundred ewes and
twenty rams, 15 thirty female camels with their young, forty cows and ten bulls, and twenty female donkeys and ten male donkeys. 16 He put them in the care of his servants, each
herd by itself, and said to his servants, "Go ahead of me, and keep some space between
the herds."
17 He instructed the one in the lead: "When my brother Esau meets you and asks, 'To
whom do you belong, and where are you going, and who owns all these animals in front
of you?' 18 then you are to say, 'They belong to your servant[a] Jacob. They are a gift sent
to my lord Esau, and he is coming behind us.' "
19 He also instructed the second, the third and all the others who followed the herds:
"You are to say the same thing to Esau when you meet him. 20 And be sure to say, 'Your
servant Jacob is coming behind us.' " For he thought, "I will pacify him with these gifts
I am sending on ahead; later, when I see him, perhaps he will receive me."[b] 21 So Jacob's
gifts went on ahead of him, but he himself spent the night in the camp.

32:3 [m]Ge 27:41-42 [n]Ge 25:30; 36:8,9
32:5 [o]Ge 12:16; 30:43 [p]Ge 33:8,10,15
32:6 [q]Ge 33:1
32:7 [r]ver 11
32:9 [s]Ge 28:13; 31:42 [t]Ge 31:13
32:10 [u]Ge 24:27
32:11 [v]Ps 59:2 [w]Ge 27:41
32:12 [x]Ge 22:17 [y]Ge 28:13-15; Hos 1:10; Ro 9:27
32:13 [z]Ge 43:11,15,25, 26; Pr 18:16
32:18 [a]Ge 18:3
32:20 [b]Ge 33:10; Pr 21:14

[a] 7 Or *camps*; also in verse 10 [b] 8 Or *camp*

32:2 This is. Once again Jacob was surprised by the revelation of the angels' presence (see 28:15 and its note; see also 2Ki 6:17–18). **camp.** The Hebrew here is translated "group" in verses 7–8. Jacob may have been referring to the company of angels he had seen on the stairway (28:12). **named that place.** See note on 28:19. **Mahanaim.** The name means either "two camps" or simply "camp." If "two camps" was intended, Jacob may have had in mind both his camp and God's camp, which served as a heavenly shield and escort. As Bethel was the "house of God" (see NIV text note at 28:19), Mahanaim was God's camp on Earth. Its location is uncertain.

32:3–31 The scene of Jacob's preparation to meet Esau has an alternating structure: sending of messengers (vv. 3–6,13–21), dividing of his family (vv. 7–8,22–23) and prayer (vv. 9–12,24–32). Faithful to his promise, God had been with Jacob—not only protecting him but also reforming his character. The formerly prayerless and self-ambitious Jacob now became Israel, a limping, humble man who strove with God and man through prayer.

32:3 messengers. See note on 16:7. The Hebrew here is the same word translated "angels" in verse 1. **Seir.** During the 20 years of Jacob's exile from the land, Esau had dispossessed (or was in the process of dispossessing) the Horites at Seir (Dt 2:12). This suggested Esau's military might.

32:4 master . . . servant. Although this introductory greeting conformed to the customary epistolary style of the ancient Near East, through this courtesy Jacob began to right his wrong against his brother. He began to relinquish the rights of his election to the blessing (27:29), much as Abraham had done with Lot (ch. 13). The rivalry was almost over; Jacob was now in God's hand.

32:6 coming to meet you. The Hebrew expression may or may not denote hostility (cf. Jos 9:11; 1Ki 20:27; 2Ki 8:8–9; 2Ki 23:29 with 24:65). In fact, Esau ended up escorting Jacob (33:12). **four hundred men.** The round number for a standard militia. **great fear.** Jacob had reason to fear (14:14; 27:40), yet he had survived Laban's stronger forces (see 31:29).

32:9 Jacob prayed. Jacob's prayer (vv. 9–12), his first recorded in Scripture, stands in the center of the two embassies to Esau (vv. 3–8,13–21). This structure suggests that he trusted God to prosper his gifts to his brother. **Go back.** See 31:3.

32:10 I am unworthy. A spiritual transformation had taken place in Jacob: He submitted to Esau and recognized his unworthiness before God. **kindness and faithfulness.** These were typical words to express God's loyalty and faithfulness in keeping his covenants. Jacob now identified himself fully with God's covenants to Abraham and Isaac. **your servant.** Jacob was now a servant of the Lord, ready to serve others. **two groups.** God's past faithfulness served to bolster Jacob's faith in the new crisis. See *WLC* 185,193.

32:11 Save. The Hebrew root here is translated "spared" in verse 30. See *WLC* 183.

32:12 But you have said. Jacob based his future on God's promises. **make your descendants like the sand.** Jacob appropriated to himself God's covenantal promises to Abraham (22:17). He was concerned for the survival of his posterity, not just himself.

32:13 a gift. The Hebrew here connotes "tribute" (see 43:11); it is translated "offering" in 4:4–5. In 33:11 Jacob would call his present (in Hebrew) "the blessing." Jacob was ready to restore the blessing and recognize Esau as lord.

32:15–16 Jacob encircled Esau with extravagant gifts in a sincere attempt to win his favor.

32:19 the third and all the others who followed. The repetition that he was Esau's servant emphasized the genuineness of his statement.

32:20 pacify him. The Hebrew root here is translated "appease" in a similar context (Pr 16:17). It literally means "cover his face," an expression for covering guilt. **he will receive me.** Literally, "he will lift up my face," which may also connote "forgive me."

Jacob Wrestles With God

22 That night Jacob got up and took his two wives, his two maidservants and his elev-
en sons and crossed the ford of the Jabbok.[c] 23 After he had sent them across the stream,
he sent over all his possessions. 24 So Jacob was left alone, and a man[d] wrestled with him
till daybreak. 25 When the man saw that he could not overpower him, he touched the
socket of Jacob's hip[e] so that his hip was wrenched as he wrestled with the man. 26 Then
the man said, "Let me go, for it is daybreak."

But Jacob replied, "I will not let you go unless you bless me."[f]

27 The man asked him, "What is your name?"

"Jacob," he answered.

28 Then the man said, "Your name will no longer be Jacob, but Israel,[a][g] because you
have struggled with God and with men and have overcome."

29 Jacob said, "Please tell me your name."[h]

But he replied, "Why do you ask my name?"[i] Then he blessed[j] him there.

30 So Jacob called the place Peniel,[b] saying, "It is because I saw God face to face,[k] and
yet my life was spared."

31 The sun rose above him as he passed Peniel,[c] and he was limping because of his hip.
32 Therefore to this day the Israelites do not eat the tendon attached to the socket of the
hip, because the socket of Jacob's hip was touched near the tendon.

Jacob Meets Esau

33 Jacob looked up and there was Esau, coming with his four hundred men;[l] so he
divided the children among Leah, Rachel and the two maidservants. 2 He put the
maidservants and their children in front, Leah and her children next, and Rachel and Joseph in the rear. 3 He himself went on ahead and bowed down to the ground[m] seven
times as he approached his brother.

4 But Esau ran to meet Jacob and embraced him; he threw his arms around his neck
and kissed him. And they wept.[n] 5 Then Esau looked up and saw the women and children. "Who are these with you?" he asked.

Jacob answered, "They are the children God has graciously given your servant.[o]"

6 Then the maidservants and their children approached and bowed down. 7 Next, Leah

a *28* *Israel* means *he struggles with God.* b *30* *Peniel* means *face of God.* c *31* Hebrew *Penuel,* a variant of *Peniel*

32:22 [c]Dt 2:37; 3:16; Jos 12:2
32:24 [d]Ge 18:2
32:25 [e]ver 32
32:26 [f]Hos 12:4
32:28 [g]Ge 17:5; 35:10; 1Ki 18:31
32:29 [h]Jdg 13:17 [i]Jdg 13:18 [j]Ge 35:9
32:30 [k]Ge 16:13; Ex 24:11; Nu 12:8; Jdg 6:22; 13:22
33:1 [l]Ge 32:6
33:3 [m]Ge 18:2; 42:6
33:4 [n]Ge 45:14-15
33:5 [o]Ge 48:9; Ps 127:3; Isa 8:18

32:22–32 In God's wrestling with Jacob he appeared in human form and removed from Jacob his natural strength, but Jacob emerged the victor by clinging to God for blessing.
32:24 left alone. There was no one to deliver him. **a man.** The mysterious man was identified with the presence of God. Hosea called him an angel (Hos 12:4). **wrestled with him.** The Lord unexpectedly initiated the match.
32:25 could not overpower. Another example of Jacob's natural strength (see note on 29:10). This all-night wrestling scene symbolized Jacob's lifelong struggle with other people and with God (see note on 25:19—35:29). **touched the socket of Jacob's hip.** In sovereign grace and in severe mercy, God dislocated Jacob's hip, the wrestler's pivot of strength (v. 31), and Jacob's natural strength shriveled.
32:26 Let me go. The contest was still undecided, for Jacob held on. **for it is daybreak.** God reveals himself differently in Scripture for symbolic reasons. He revealed himself as fire in a bush that was not consumed in order to symbolize his purifying presence in Israel that did not consume his people. At other times, as here, his presence was dark and mysterious; he chose to appear as the hidden God. **I will not let you go.** Jacob desperately clung to the angel of God for blessing.
32:27 "What is your name?" The question forced Jacob to admit to his devious past and be purged from it by embracing his new name.
32:28 Your name. The assailant had authority to impart a new life. **Israel.** Jacob's new name represented a reorientation from supplanter and deceiver to prevailer. The transformation pertained to the way in which Jacob would prevail. Heretofore he had bested people by trickery. Now, as he had triumphed with God, so he would prevail with humans. This name, given to the victor, announced his true, maturing spiritual character and destiny. **God.** Jacob recognized that he had met one from heaven, but in his newfound humility he treated the encounter as a face-to-face experience with God.
32:29 "Why do you ask my name?" The heavenly wrestler knew that Jacob already understood who he was.
32:30 Peniel. Perhaps modern Tulul edh-Dhahab esh-Sherqiyeh, which stands on the bank of the Jabbok River, four miles east of Succoth. The exact site of Peniel (Penuel) is uncertain. **I saw God face to face.** "Face to face" is used only of direct divine-human encounters and does not necessarily reflect a visual perception. Jacob "saw" the invisible God not with his eyes (see v. 26) but in his experience. The encounter was both terrifying and intimate. **spared.** See verse 11. Jacob was preserved from death and emerged with power. His deliverance from God after meeting him face-to-face certified his salvation from Esau, whom he had yet to confront.
32:31 limping. The limp is the carriage of a saint who walks not in physical, but in spiritual strength.
32:32 to this day. This dietary restriction, mentioned elsewhere only in later Jewish literature, served as a perpetual reminder that when Jacob became weak in his struggle with God, Israel the victor emerged.
■**33:1–17** *Esau's Reconciliation With Jacob.* Esau was reconciled to a humbled Israel through God's grace, and Israel was established as God's chosen patriarch in the promised land. God blesses his humble people in all ages.
33:1 four hundred. See note on 32:6.
33:3 He himself went on ahead. See also 32:18. Jacob (Israel) had become a leader. **seven times.** Common practice in ancient court protocol.
33:4 But Esau. Jacob greeted Esau as a vassal greeted his patron, with the ceremony of a royal court—solemnity of approach as becomes rank (vv. 2–3,6–7), the sevenfold obeisance (v. 3), the submissive address of a "servant" (v. 5) to this "lord" (vv. 8,13) and the presentation of gifts of homage (vv. 10–11). But Esau greeted Jacob as one "brother" (v. 9) greets another after a long separation.
33:5 graciously given. As Jacob looked back over his troubled history, he confessed God's unmerited kindness in giving him children (29:31—30:24) and prosperity (v. 11; 30:25—31:55). **servant.** In the international diplomacy of that day, this was the unmistakable language of one submitting himself by treaty as a subject.

and her children came and bowed down. Last of all came Joseph and Rachel, and they
too bowed down.
[8]Esau asked, "What do you mean by all these droves I met?"[p]
"To find favor in your eyes, my lord,"[q] he said.
[9]But Esau said, "I already have plenty, my brother. Keep what you have for yourself."
[10]"No, please!" said Jacob. "If I have found favor in your eyes, accept this gift from me.
For to see your face is like seeing the face of God,[r] now that you have received me favorably.[s] [11]Please accept the present[t] that was brought to you, for God has been gracious
to me[u] and I have all I need." And because Jacob insisted, Esau accepted it.
[12]Then Esau said, "Let us be on our way; I'll accompany you."
[13]But Jacob said to him, "My lord knows that the children are tender and that I must
care for the ewes and cows that are nursing their young. If they are driven hard just one
day, all the animals will die. [14]So let my lord go on ahead of his servant, while I move
along slowly at the pace of the droves before me and that of the children, until I come
to my lord in Seir."[v]
[15]Esau said, "Then let me leave some of my men with you."
"But why do that?" Jacob asked. "Just let me find favor in the eyes of my lord."[w]
[16]So that day Esau started on his way back to Seir. [17]Jacob, however, went to Succoth,[x] where he built a place for himself and made shelters for his livestock. That is why
the place is called Succoth.[a]
[18]After Jacob came from Paddan Aram,[b][y] he arrived safely at the[c] city of Shechem[z]
in Canaan and camped within sight of the city. [19]For a hundred pieces of silver,[d] he
bought from the sons of Hamor, the father of Shechem, [a] the plot of ground[b] where he
pitched his tent. [20]There he set up an altar and called it El Elohe Israel.[e]

Dinah and the Shechemites

34 Now Dinah,[c] the daughter Leah had borne to Jacob, went out to visit the wom-
en of the land. [2]When Shechem son of Hamor the Hivite, the ruler of that area,
saw her, he took her and violated her. [3]His heart was drawn to Dinah daughter of Jacob,
and he loved the girl and spoke tenderly to her. [4]And Shechem said to his father Hamor,
"Get me this girl as my wife."
[5]When Jacob heard that his daughter Dinah had been defiled, his sons were in the
fields with his livestock; so he kept quiet about it until they came home.

33:8 [p]Ge 32:14-16 [q]Ge 24:9; 32:5
33:10 [r]Ge 16:13 [s]Ge 32:20
33:11 [t]1Sa 25:27 [u]Ge 30:43
33:14 [v]Ge 32:3
33:15 [w]Ge 34:11; 47:25; Ru 2:13
33:17 [x]Jos 13:27; Jdg 8:5, 6, 8, 14-16; Ps 60:6
33:18 [y]Ge 25:20; 28:2 [z]Jos 24:1; Jdg 9:1
33:19 [a]Jos 24:32 [b]Jn 4:5
34:1 [c]Ge 30:21

[a] *17 Succoth* means *shelters.* [b] *18* That is, Northwest Mesopotamia [c] *18* Or *arrived at Shalem, a* [d] *19* Hebrew *hundred kesitahs;* a kesitah was a unit of money of unknown weight and value. [e] *20 El Elohe Israel* can mean *God, the God of Israel* or *mighty is the God of Israel.*

33:8 To find favor. The Hebrew for "reconciliation," it is repeated three times (see also vv. 10,15).
33:9 I already have plenty. Accumulated by war, not by farming or shepherding (27:39–40; 32:3).
33:10 gift. See note on 32:13. **like seeing the face of God.** As at Peniel, when Jacob saw God's face and his life was mercifully spared (32:20), so now he scanned the dreaded face of Esau and saw only forgiveness and welcome. This is an illustration of how God graciously receives the elect because of Christ's gift of himself for their sins.
33:11 present. A deliberate and crucial change from "gift" in 32:18. The Hebrew here is the same word for "blessing" in 27:35–36, which was what Jacob had originally stolen. Israel (Jacob) humbly gave up his blessing so that Esau would be reconciled to him. The positive quality of this act is evident in the way Jesus later relinquished his right to equality with God in service to the world (2Co 5:16–21; Php 2:6–8). **insisted . . . accepted.** By declining to offer a gift in exchange, Esau indicated that he accepted Jacob's offering as payment for the wrong done to him.
33:13 knows. A caravan of 400 men would have moved at a different pace from one of flocks and family.
33:14 until I come to . . . Seir. Jacob may have been acting deceptively, but more probably Esau knew that this was Jacob's polite way of declining to contradict him; Jacob could not refuse Esau directly without offending him and risking his anger.
33:17 Succoth. The Hebrew means "shelters." **built a place for himself.** The patriarch now settled back into the promised land.
■ **33:18—35:29** *Jacob Back in the Land.* In balance with Jacob's earlier life in the land of promise (25:19—27:40), Moses reported events that transpired during the patriarch's latter days in Canaan. These chapters divide into three sections: a crisis in Shechem (33:18—34:31); divine reassurance at Bethel (35:1–15); and concluding travels and events, including the deaths of Rachel and Isaac and a listing of Jacob's progeny (35:16–29). Jacob learned, as every generation of God's people must, that God fulfills his covenant promises in his own timing.
■ **33:18—34:31** *Crisis in Shechem.* Safely in the land, all seemed settled for Jacob. In fact, his circumstance was so secure that he and his children too closely associated with the inhabitants of Shechem. A morally complex situation arose, creating difficulties for Jacob and his sons that made it impossible for them to live at peace with the inhabitants of the land. By this means God's people were kept distinct, but the full possession of the land was pushed back to later generations.
33:18 arrived safely. The danger in facing Esau was over.
33:19–20 bought . . . the plot of ground . . . altar. Jacob followed the example of his father. He purchased a plot in the land (see ch. 23) and set up an altar to God (12:6–7). Thus Jacob was confirmed as the true heir of Abraham's inheritance. See notes on 28:20–22 and 31:5.
34:1 daughter Leah had borne. This clarifies the roles of Levi and Simeon, Dinah's full brothers (vv. 13,25,27,31). **visit the women of the land.** Dinah's actions demonstrated that she and her family had become too familiar with the inhabitants of the land.
34:2 Hivite. See notes on 9:25 and 10:15–19. **saw . . . took.** See note on 6:2. **violated.** The Hebrew here is the same word translated "mistreated" in 15:13; it means "to humble, oppress, afflict." Dinah did not consent. The problem with their close association with the people of Canaan became evident.
34:3 was drawn. The Hebrew here suggests that he "remained true," but he made no apology and did not attempt to indemnify the family he had wronged. **loved.** The same natural emotion that motivated Jacob (29:18).
34:5 defiled. The rape rendered Dinah ritually unclean. **kept quiet.** The narrator censured Jacob's passivity in the face of his daughter's defilement by contrasting his reaction to that of his sons

6 Then Shechem's father Hamor went out to talk with Jacob.[d] 7 Now Jacob's sons had
come in from the fields as soon as they heard what had happened. They were filled with
grief and fury, because Shechem had done a disgraceful thing in[a] Israel[e] by lying with
Jacob's daughter—a thing that should not be done.[f]
8 But Hamor said to them, "My son Shechem has his heart set on your daughter.
Please give her to him as his wife. 9 Intermarry with us; give us your daughters and take
our daughters for yourselves. 10 You can settle among us;[g] the land is open to you.[h] Live
in it, trade[b] in it,[i] and acquire property in it."
11 Then Shechem said to Dinah's father and brothers, "Let me find favor in your eyes,
and I will give you whatever you ask. 12 Make the price for the bride[j] and the gift I am to
bring as great as you like, and I'll pay whatever you ask me. Only give me the girl as my
wife."
13 Because their sister Dinah had been defiled, Jacob's sons replied deceitfully as they
spoke to Shechem and his father Hamor. 14 They said to them, "We can't do such a thing;
we can't give our sister to a man who is not circumcised.[k] That would be a disgrace to
us. 15 We will give our consent to you on one condition only: that you become like us by
circumcising all your males.[l] 16 Then we will give you our daughters and take your
daughters for ourselves. We'll settle among you and become one people with you. 17 But
if you will not agree to be circumcised, we'll take our sister[c] and go."
18 Their proposal seemed good to Hamor and his son Shechem. 19 The young man, who
was the most honored of all his father's household, lost no time in doing what they said,
because he was delighted with Jacob's daughter.[m] 20 So Hamor and his son Shechem went
to the gate of their city[n] to speak to their fellow townsmen. 21 "These men are friendly toward us," they said. "Let them live in our land and trade in it; the land has plenty of room
for them. We can marry their daughters and they can marry ours. 22 But the men will consent to live with us as one people only on the condition that our males be circumcised,
as they themselves are. 23 Won't their livestock, their property and all their other animals
become ours? So let us give our consent to them, and they will settle among us."
24 All the men who went out of the city gate[o] agreed with Hamor and his son Shechem,
and every male in the city was circumcised.
25 Three days later, while all of them were still in pain, two of Jacob's sons, Simeon and
Levi, Dinah's brothers, took their swords[p] and attacked the unsuspecting city, killing every male.[q] 26 They put Hamor and his son Shechem to the sword and took Dinah from Shechem's house and left. 27 The sons of Jacob came upon the dead bodies and looted the city
where[d] their sister had been defiled. 28 They seized their flocks and herds and donkeys and
everything else of theirs in the city and out in the fields. 29 They carried off all their wealth
and all their women and children, taking as plunder everything in the houses.
30 Then Jacob said to Simeon and Levi, "You have brought trouble on me by making
me a stench[r] to the Canaanites and Perizzites, the people living in this land.[s] We are few
in number,[t] and if they join forces against me and attack me, I and my household will
be destroyed."
31 But they replied, "Should he have treated our sister like a prostitute?"

34:6 [d]Jdg 14:2-5
34:7 [e]Dt 22:21; Jdg 20:6; 2Sa 13:12 [f]Jos 7:15
34:10 [g]Ge 47:6,27 [h]Ge 13:9; 20:15 [i]Ge 42:34
34:12 [j]Ex 22:16; Dt 22:29; 1Sa 18:25
34:14 [k]Ge 17:14; Jdg 14:3
34:15 [l]Ex 12:48
34:19 [m]ver 3
34:20 [n]Ru 4:1; 2Sa 15:2
34:24 [o]Ge 23:10
34:25 [p]Ge 49:5 [q]Ge 49:7
34:30 [r]Ex 5:21; 1Sa 13:4 [s]Ge 13:7 [t]Ge 46:27; 1Ch 16:19; Ps 105:12

[a] *7* Or *against* [b] *10* Or *move about freely*; also in verse 21 [c] *17* Hebrew *daughter* [d] *27* Or *because*

(v. 7). **until they came home.** See 2 Samuel 13:20–21 and Psalm 127:5.
34:7 grief. The Hebrew here is used elsewhere only for God's reaction to human wickedness (6:6). **disgraceful thing.** The Hebrew term signifies serious disorderly and unruly action resulting in the break-up of an existing relationship. Those who committed a moral outrage of the vilest sort against the deepest realities and convictions of the community were to be punished to protect the fabric of the community (Dt 22:21; Jos 7:15; Jdg 19:23–24; 20:6,10; 2Sa 13:12; Jer 29:23). **that should not be done.** The author's comment put Shechem's crime and the brothers' outrage into perspective (2Sa 13:12).
34:9 Intermarry. What Abraham and Isaac had dreaded was now a near possibility because of the complexity of the situation.
34:10 acquire property. Israel had the opportunity to settle and possess the land through intermarriage with its inhabitants.
34:12 price for the bride. See 24:14. If a bride price was accepted, the marriage, even if not yet consummated, would have been legally in force.
34:13 deceitfully. Jacob reaped the whirlwind: His sons copied his deception (27:36), but killing was their goal. Once again, the moral complexity of the situation became evident: The brothers wanted to rescue their sister, but their methods were dishonorable. While deceit in war was expected by both parties, it was unacceptable under the terms of a peace treaty (cf. 2Ki 9:23). The Hebrew term here is not used for warfare situations.
34:14 See *WCF* 24.3; 27.1; *WLC* 162.
34:15 circumcising. They reprehensibly emptied the sign of the holy covenant of its religious significance (i.e., commitment by faith to Abraham's God) and abused it in order to inflict vengeance.
34:20 gate. See 23:18.
34:24 went out of the city. That is, "able-bodied men." **agreed.** They were willing to accept the sign of God's covenant with Israel.
34:27 looted. By their unbridled, faithless and rash revenge, Simeon and Levi lost leadership (49:6) and land in Israel (49:7; Mt 26:52).
34:30 Jacob said. Jacob scolded his sons for their imprudence; they in turn reproved him for his lack of moral indignation. **trouble on me.** Jacob recognized that his situation in the land was insecure. **will be destroyed.** The patriarchs had to survive in the land by faith, not by war (ch. 26).
34:31 our sister. Not "your daughter" (see v. 1). **like a prostitute?** The sons of Jacob had a legitimate question to raise against their father, but they, too, had acted immorally. The covenant people had fallen into the quagmire of too closely associating with the inhabitants of the land.

Jacob Returns to Bethel

35 Then God said to Jacob, "Go up to Bethel[u] and settle there, and build an altar
there to God, who appeared to you when you were fleeing from your brother
Esau."[v]
2 So Jacob said to his household[w] and to all who were with him, "Get rid of the foreign gods[x] you have with you, and purify yourselves and change your clothes.[y] 3 Then
come, let us go up to Bethel, where I will build an altar to God, who answered me in the
day of my distress[z] and who has been with me wherever I have gone.[a]" 4 So they gave Jacob all the foreign gods they had and the rings in their ears, and Jacob buried them under the oak at Shechem.[b] 5 Then they set out, and the terror of God[c] fell upon the towns
all around them so that no one pursued them.
6 Jacob and all the people with him came to Luz[d] (that is, Bethel) in the land of Canaan. 7 There he built an altar, and he called the place El Bethel,[a] because it was there
that God revealed himself to him[e] when he was fleeing from his brother.
8 Now Deborah, Rebekah's nurse,[f] died and was buried under the oak below Bethel.
So it was named Allon Bacuth.[b]
9 After Jacob returned from Paddan Aram,[c] God appeared to him again and blessed
him.[g] 10 God said to him, "Your name is Jacob,[d] but you will no longer be called Jacob;
your name will be Israel.[e]"[h] So he named him Israel.
11 And God said to him, "I am God Almighty[f];[i] be fruitful and increase in number. A
nation[j] and a community of nations will come from you, and kings will come from your
body.[k] 12 The land I gave to Abraham and Isaac I also give to you, and I will give this land
to your descendants after you.[l]"[m] 13 Then God went up from him[n] at the place where he
had talked with him.
14 Jacob set up a stone pillar at the place where God had talked with him, and he
poured out a drink offering on it; he also poured oil on it.[o] 15 Jacob called the place where
God had talked with him Bethel.[g][p]

The Deaths of Rachel and Isaac

16 Then they moved on from Bethel. While they were still some distance from Ephrath,
Rachel began to give birth and had great difficulty. 17 And as she was having great difficulty in childbirth, the midwife said to her, "Don't be afraid, for you have another son."[q]
18 As she breathed her last—for she was dying—she named her son Ben-Oni.[h] But his father named him Benjamin.[i]

35:1 [u]Ge 28:19 [v]Ge 27:43
35:2 [w]Ge 18:19; Jos 24:15 [x]Ge 31:19 [y]Ex 19:10,14
35:3 [z]Ge 32:7 [a]Ge 28:15,20-22; 31:3,42
35:4 [b]Jos 24:25-26
35:5 [c]Ex 15:16; 23:27; Jos 2:9
35:6 [d]Ge 28:19; 48:3
35:7 [e]Ge 28:13
35:8 [f]Ge 24:59
35:9 [g]Ge 32:29
35:10 [h]Ge 17:5
35:11 [i]Ge 17:1; Ex 6:3 [j]Ge 28:3; 48:4 [k]Ge 17:6
35:12 [l]Ge 13:15; 28:13 [m]Ge 12:7; 26:3
35:13 [n]Ge 17:22
35:14 [o]Ge 28:18
35:15 [p]Ge 28:19
35:17 [q]Ge 30:24

a 7 *El Bethel* means *God of Bethel.* b 8 *Allon Bacuth* means *oak of weeping.* c 9 That is, Northwest Mesopotamia; also in verse 26 d 10 *Jacob* means *he grasps the heel* (figuratively, *he deceives*). e 10 *Israel* means *he struggles with God.* f 11 Hebrew *El-Shaddai* g 15 *Bethel* means *house of God.* h 18 *Ben-Oni* means *son of my trouble.* i 18 *Benjamin* means *son of my right hand.*

■ **35:1–15** *Assurance at Bethel.* After the disappointing setback at Shechem, the Lord called Jacob back to Bethel to reassure him of his role as the heir of his forefathers' covenant with God. He returned to fulfill his vow at Bethel (vv. 1–8) and was confirmed as the successor to God's promises to Abraham (vv. 9–15).
35:1 Go up to Bethel. Jacob had a vow to fulfill. God's revelation there (vv. 9–13) repeated his covenant to Abraham, who in the beginning had worshiped at Bethel (see notes on 13:4,14–17).
35:2 Get rid of. The expression signifies the people's rededication of themselves to the Lord. Repentance involves renouncing whatever hinders or tarnishes the worship of God. See theological article "Repentance" at Psalm 51. The covenant's primary requirement was exclusive allegiance to the Lord (Ex 20:3–5; Jos 24:14; Jdg 10:16). **gods.** See 31:19 and Joshua 24:23. Jacob recognized the evil that still permeated his family. He called on his entire household to repent and to consecrate themselves to the Lord. **purify yourselves.** That is, to bathe their bodies, wash their clothes and abstain from sex (Lev 14:8–9; 22:6–7; Nu 8:7)—to effect passage from defilement of idols to purity before God (Dt. 7:25–26; Jer 2:23; 7:30).
35:4 they gave Jacob. He recovered his spiritual leadership. **oak at Shechem.** The sacred tree associated with Abraham (see 12:6 and its note; see also Hos 4:18).
35:5 terror of God. In contrast with the situation Jacob had faced as he associated too closely with inhabitants of the land (32:30), the divinely induced panic of holy war (Ex 23:27; Jos 2:9) validated Jacob's good confession of God's presence.
35:7 built an altar. By their worship, the covenant family retained their separation from the Canaanites, their witness to them and (symbolically) their claim to the land based on God's promises (see note on 12:7).
35:9–15 God's revelation to Jacob after his return from Paddan Aram to Bethel confirmed his promises to him (28:13–14). By closely paralleling his covenant with Abraham regarding nations, royalty and land (17:5–8), he directed his promises to Israel, the transformed Jacob (32:28) and indirectly to Jacob's 12 sons.
35:11 be fruitful. The common call of God for all humanity (1:28; 9:1,7) is focused particularly on the redeemed covenant community, which is God's instrument for bringing redemption to all nations (47:27; Ex 1:3). **a community of nations.** A fresh expression of 17:4.
35:12 land . . . descendants. See note on 12:7.
35:14 stone pillar. Perhaps by this ritual Jacob restored the original sanctuary at which he had vowed to return to the land (28:22).
■ **35:16–29** *Closing Travels and Events.* Moses closed this section by noting how Jacob moved from place to place in the land. Jacob endured the loss of Rachel at the birth of Benjamin (vv. 16–20) and learned that Reuben had committed incest (vv. 21–22). After this, Moses listed Jacob's 12 sons (vv. 23–26) and closed with Jacob's reunion with his father and brother in Mamre (vv. 27–29).
35:16 to give birth. The birth of Benjamin completed the 12 tribes.
35:17 another son. Her prayer was answered (30:24).
35:18 Ben-Oni. Rachel's weeping portended the anguished future of the nation as it gave birth to a new age (Jer 31:15–17; Mt 2:17–18). **Benjamin.** The name, meaning "son of my right hand" (see NIV text note), may refer to the south (the other sons were born in Paddan Aram, north of Canaan; cf. 1Sa 23:19,24; Ps 89:13). It may also refer to power and protection (cf. Ex 15:6,12; Isa 62:18) or symbolize good fortune (e.g., 48:12–14; Ps 109:31). The context, which contrasts the name Rachel chose (i.e., "misfortune") with the one Jacob selected (i.e., "good fortune"), favors the latter two interpretations.

[19]So Rachel died and was buried on the way to Ephrath (that is, Bethlehem[r]). [20]Over
her tomb Jacob set up a pillar, and to this day that pillar marks Rachel's tomb.[s]
[21]Israel moved on again and pitched his tent beyond Migdal Eder. [22]While Israel was
living in that region, Reuben went in and slept with his father's concubine[t] Bilhah,[u] and
Israel heard of it.

Jacob had twelve sons:
[23]The sons of Leah:
Reuben the firstborn[v] of Jacob,
Simeon, Levi, Judah,[w] Issachar and Zebulun.[x]
[24]The sons of Rachel:
Joseph[y] and Benjamin.[z]
[25]The sons of Rachel's maidservant Bilhah:
Dan and Naphtali.[a]
[26]The sons of Leah's maidservant Zilpah:
Gad[b] and Asher.[c]
These were the sons of Jacob, who were born to him in Paddan Aram.

[27]Jacob came home to his father Isaac in Mamre,[d] near Kiriath Arba[e] (that is, Hebron), where Abraham and Isaac had stayed. [28]Isaac lived a hundred and eighty years.[f]
[29]Then he breathed his last and died and was gathered to his people,[g] old and full of
years.[h] And his sons Esau and Jacob buried him.[i]

Esau's Descendants

36 This is the account of Esau (that is, Edom).[j]

[2]Esau took his wives from the women of Canaan:[k] Adah daughter of Elon the
Hittite,[l] and Oholibamah daughter of Anah[m] and granddaughter of Zibeon the Hivite— [3]also Basemath daughter of Ishmael and sister of Nebaioth.
[4]Adah bore Eliphaz to Esau, Basemath bore Reuel,[n] [5]and Oholibamah bore Jeush, Jalam and Korah. These were the sons of Esau, who were born to him in Canaan.
[6]Esau took his wives and sons and daughters and all the members of his
household, as well as his livestock and all his other animals and all the goods he
had acquired in Canaan,[o] and moved to a land some distance from his brother Jacob. [7]Their possessions were too great for them to remain together; the land
where they were staying could not support them both because of their livestock.[p]
[8]So Esau[q] (that is, Edom) settled in the hill country of Seir.[r]

[9]This is the account of Esau the father of the Edomites in the hill country of Seir.

[10]These are the names of Esau's sons:
Eliphaz, the son of Esau's wife Adah, and Reuel, the son of Esau's wife Basemath.
[11]The sons of Eliphaz:[s]
Teman,[t] Omar, Zepho, Gatam and Kenaz.

35:19 [r]Ge 48:7; Ru 1:1, 19; Mic 5:2; Mt 2:16
35:20 [s]1Sa 10:2
35:22 [t]Ge 49:4; 1Ch 5:1 [u]Ge 29:29; Lev 18:8
35:23 [v]Ge 46:8 [w]Ge 29:35 [x]Ge 30:20
35:24 [y]Ge 30:24 [z]ver 18
35:25 [a]Ge 30:8
35:26 [b]Ge 30:11 [c]Ge 30:13
35:27 [d]Ge 13:18; 18:1 [e]Jos 14:15
35:28 [f]Ge 25:7,20
35:29 [g]Ge 25:8; 49:33 [h]Ge 15:15 [i]Ge 25:9
36:1 [j]Ge 25:30
36:2 [k]Ge 28:8-9 [l]Ge 26:34 [m]ver 25
36:4 [n]1Ch 1:35
36:6 [o]Ge 12:5
36:7 [p]Ge 13:6; 17:8; 28:4
36:8 [q]Dt 2:4 [r]Ge 32:3
36:11 [s]ver 15-16; Job 2:11 [t]Am 1:12; Hab 3:3

35:21–26 In spite of Reuben's sin, God's blessing on Jacob would be manifested in the lives of his 12 sons, who embodied the promise of a great nation to come.

35:22 Israel was living. No mention is made of an altar at Migdal Eder, where Reuben sinned. **slept with his father's concubine.** Probably both to gratify his lusts and, according to known ancient Near Eastern cultural forms, to seize leadership from Jacob (2Sa 3:7–8; 12:7–8; 16:21–22; 1Ki 2:13–25; 16:15–23). Also, by defiling Bilhah, Rachel's maidservant, Reuben made certain that, with Rachel's death, Bilhah could not supplant Leah as his father's chief wife (cf. 2Sa 15:16; 16:22; 20:3). For his sin (Dt 22:30) Reuben, along with Simeon and Levi, was deprived of leadership (49:3–4). Judah, Leah's fourth son, would assume it. **Israel heard.** See 34:5. **twelve sons.** The 12 sons are here listed in a summary catalog (see also Mt 10:2–4; Rev 21:12–14).

35:24 Benjamin. See verses 16–18. This list is a stylized representation of the births of Jacob's sons rather than a strict historical accounting. It states that Benjamin, who was not born in Paddan Aram (v. 26), participated with his brothers in the move from the exile in Paddan Aram (v. 26) to the promised land (see note on 46:8). By this device, Moses may have been encouraging all the tribes of Israel during his own day to leave exile in Egypt and travel to the promised land in solidarity. See note on 31:3.

35:27 came home to . . . Isaac. The account of Isaac ends with Jacob's reconciliation to him.

35:28 hundred and eighty years. Isaac's life journey ended with a full length of years, but God had passed him by as patriarch after he had tried to thwart God's purpose in conferring the blessing (ch. 27).

■ **36:1—37:1** *Account of Esau.* The prophecies about Esau (25:23; 27:39–40) were fulfilled in such a way as to reinforce the greatness of Israel, who ruled over Edom (27:29).

36:1 account. See note on 2:4. **Edom.** As Jacob's personal name was transformed to the national name Israel, so also Esau's personal name was transformed into the national name Edom.

36:2–8 This genealogy focuses on Esau's Canaanite wives and the children born in Canaan prior to his migration to Mount Seir.

36:2 took his wives. See notes on 26:34 and 27:46. **from the women of Canaan.** See 9:25 and 10:15–19. This is a derogatory expression (26:34–35; 27:46; 28:1,6,8, 33:18). Canaan broadly covered the tribes in the land. **Adah.** The names of Esau's wives listed here differ from those delineated in 26:34 and 28:9. **granddaughter.** Some ancient texts and versions read "son."

36:6 moved to a land. Jacob's return to Mamre clinched Esau's decision to move permanently to Edom.

36:9–14 This genealogy focuses on Esau's 12 sons (vv. 2–8)—not including Amalek, the son of Timna, Eliphaz's concubine (v. 12).

12 Esau's son Eliphaz also had a concubine named Timna, who bore him Amalek.[u] These were grandsons of Esau's wife Adah.[v]
13 The sons of Reuel:
Nahath, Zerah, Shammah and Mizzah. These were grandsons of Esau's wife Basemath.
14 The sons of Esau's wife Oholibamah daughter of Anah and granddaughter of Zibeon, whom she bore to Esau:
Jeush, Jalam and Korah.
15 These were the chiefs[w] among Esau's descendants:
The sons of Eliphaz the firstborn of Esau:
Chiefs Teman,[x] Omar, Zepho, Kenaz,
16 Korah,[a] Gatam and Amalek. These were the chiefs descended from Eliphaz in Edom; they were grandsons of Adah.[y]
17 The sons of Esau's son Reuel:[z]
Chiefs Nahath, Zerah, Shammah and Mizzah. These were the chiefs descended from Reuel in Edom; they were grandsons of Esau's wife Basemath.
18 The sons of Esau's wife Oholibamah:
Chiefs Jeush, Jalam and Korah. These were the chiefs descended from Esau's wife Oholibamah daughter of Anah.
19 These were the sons of Esau (that is, Edom),[a] and these were their chiefs.
20 These were the sons of Seir the Horite,[b] who were living in the region:
Lotan, Shobal, Zibeon, Anah,
21 Dishon, Ezer and Dishan. These sons of Seir in Edom were Horite chiefs.
22 The sons of Lotan:
Hori and Homam.[b] Timna was Lotan's sister.
23 The sons of Shobal:
Alvan, Manahath, Ebal, Shepho and Onam.
24 The sons of Zibeon:
Aiah and Anah. This is the Anah who discovered the hot springs[c] in the desert while he was grazing the donkeys of his father Zibeon.
25 The children of Anah:
Dishon and Oholibamah daughter of Anah.
26 The sons of Dishon[d]:
Hemdan, Eshban, Ithran and Keran.
27 The sons of Ezer:
Bilhan, Zaavan and Akan.
28 The sons of Dishan:
Uz and Aran.
29 These were the Horite chiefs:
Lotan, Shobal, Zibeon, Anah,
30 Dishon, Ezer and Dishan. These were the Horite chiefs, according to their divisions, in the land of Seir.

The Rulers of Edom

31 These were the kings who reigned in Edom before any Israelite king[c] reigned[e]:
32 Bela son of Beor became king of Edom. His city was named Dinhabah.
33 When Bela died, Jobab son of Zerah from Bozrah[d] succeeded him as king.
34 When Jobab died, Husham from the land of the Temanites[e] succeeded him as king.
35 When Husham died, Hadad son of Bedad, who defeated Midian in the country of Moab,[f] succeeded him as king. His city was named Avith.
36 When Hadad died, Samlah from Masrekah succeeded him as king.
37 When Samlah died, Shaul from Rehoboth on the river[f] succeeded him as king.

36:12 [u]Ex 17:8,16; Nu 24:20; 1Sa 15:2 [v]ver 16
36:15 [w]Ex 15:15 [x]Job 2:11
36:16 [y]ver 12
36:17 [z]1Ch 1:37
36:19 [a]Ge 25:30
36:20 [b]Ge 14:6; Dt 2:12, 22; 1Ch 1:38
36:31 [c]Ge 17:6; 1Ch 1:43
36:33 [d]Jer 49:13,22
36:34 [e]Eze 25:13
36:35 [f]Ge 19:37; Nu 22:1; Dt 1:5; Ru 1:1,6

a *16* Masoretic Text; Samaritan Pentateuch (see also Gen. 36:11 and 1 Chron. 1:36) does not have *Korah.*
b *22* Hebrew *Hemam,* a variant of *Homam* (see 1 Chron. 1:39)
c *24* Vulgate; Syriac *discovered water;* the meaning of the Hebrew for this word is uncertain.
d *26* Hebrew *Dishan,* a variant of *Dishon*
e *31* Or *before an Israelite king reigned over them*
f *37* Possibly the Euphrates

36:15–19 This lists shows the transition of Esau's descendants from a family arrangement to a tribal one.
36:20–30 This genealogy acknowledges the aboriginal inhabitants of Mount Seir, whom the sons of Esau destroyed (Dt 2:22) or, in other cases, married (vv. 22,25). Esau emerged as a powerful overlord, but he was subservient to Israel (25:23).
36:31–39 This list shows the transition of Esau's descendants from a tribal arrangement to a designated kingship.
36:31 before any Israelite king reigned. See "Introduction: Time and Place of Writing."

38 When Shaul died, Baal-Hanan son of Acbor succeeded him as king.
39 When Baal-Hanan son of Acbor died, Hadad[a] succeeded him as king. His city was
named Pau, and his wife's name was Mehetabel daughter of Matred, the
daughter of Me-Zahab.

40 These were the chiefs descended from Esau, by name, according to their clans and
regions:
Timna, Alvah, Jetheth, 41 Oholibamah, Elah, Pinon, 42 Kenaz, Teman, Mibzar,
43 Magdiel and Iram. These were the chiefs of Edom, according to their settlements in the land they occupied.

This was Esau the father of the Edomites.

Joseph's Dreams

37:1 [g]Ge 17:8 [h]Ge 10:19

37 Jacob lived in the land where his father had stayed,[g] the land of Canaan.[h]
2 This is the account of Jacob.

37:2 [i]Ps 78:71 [j]Ge 35:25 [k]Ge 35:26 [l]1Sa 2:24

Joseph, a young man of seventeen, was tending the flocks[i] with his brothers, the sons
of Bilhah[j] and the sons of Zilpah,[k] his father's wives, and he brought their father a bad
report[l] about them.

37:3 [m]Ge 25:28 [n]Ge 44:20 [o]2Sa 13:18-19

3 Now Israel loved Joseph more than any of his other sons,[m] because he had been
born to him in his old age;[n] and he made a richly ornamented[b] robe[o] for him. 4 When his
brothers saw that their father loved him more than any of them, they hated him[p] and
could not speak a kind word to him.

37:4 [p]Ge 27:41; 49:22-23; Ac 7:9

5 Joseph had a dream,[q] and when he told it to his brothers, they hated him all the
more. 6 He said to them, "Listen to this dream I had: 7 We were binding sheaves of grain
out in the field when suddenly my sheaf rose and stood upright, while your sheaves gathered around mine and bowed down to it."[r]

37:5 [q]Ge 20:3; 28:12

37:7 [r]Ge 42:6,9; 43:26,28; 44:14; 50:18

8 His brothers said to him, "Do you intend to reign over us? Will you actually rule us?"[s]
And they hated him all the more because of his dream and what he had said.

37:8 [s]Ge 49:26

9 Then he had another dream, and he told it to his brothers. "Listen," he said, "I had
another dream, and this time the sun and moon and eleven stars were bowing down
to me."

37:10 [t]ver 5

10 When he told his father as well as his brothers,[t] his father rebuked him and said,
"What is this dream you had? Will your mother and I and your brothers actually come

[a] *39* Many manuscripts of the Masoretic Text, Samaritan Pentateuch and Syriac (see also 1 Chron. 1:50); most manuscripts of the Masoretic Text *Hadar* [b] *3* The meaning of the Hebrew for *richly ornamented* is uncertain; also in verses 23 and 32.

■ **37:2—50:26** *The Joseph History.* Although Joseph is the main character in these chapters, all the heads of Israel's 12 tribes are important to the story line. As the Israelites followed Moses toward the promised land, their tribal identities were based on their descent from Joseph's two sons (Ephraim and Manasseh) and Joseph's brothers. For this reason, what happened to these tribal patriarchs had much to teach the Israelites about their inter-tribal relations and their service to God, as these events also teach believers in all ages about their responsibilities toward each other. These chapters divide into three main parts: the period of disharmony among the brothers (37:2—41:57), the reunion of the brothers in harmony (42:1—47:28) and the future of the brothers (47:29—50:26).

■ **37:2—41:57** *The Patriarchs Separated and Disharmonious.* The story of Joseph begins with the patriarchs at odds and separated. This material unfolds in six basic steps: Joseph's problematic dream (37:2–11), his enslavement (37:12–36), a segue to the corruption of the patriarchs in Canaan (38:1–30), Joseph's contrasting moral integrity (39:1–20a), his unwavering faith in prison (39:20b—40:23) and his exaltation in Egypt (41:1–57).

■ **37:2–11** *Joseph's Troubling Dreams.* The story of the tribal patriarchs begins with Joseph's childhood dreams of rising above his brothers, mother and father. These dreams drove his brothers to jealousy and his father to serious contemplation.

37:2 account. See 2:4. **a young man.** Joseph would rule over his older brothers (25:23; 1Sa 16–17; see "Introduction: Time and Place of Writing"). **the sons of Bilhah and the sons of Zilpah.** Dan, Naphtali, Gad and Asher (30:4–13). **bad report.** Their evil was turned against Joseph. See also 35:22 and 38:1–26.

37:3 loved. Parental favoritism again promoted family discord, deception and the disappearance of the preferred son, yet God's grace again intervened despite these problems to achieve his good will (25:28). Nevertheless, the brothers' jealousy was wrong, and God would use Joseph to convert them (43:24). **richly ornamented robe.** By this apparently regal apparel (2Sa 13:18), Jacob publicly designated Joseph as the ruler over the family.

37:4 could not speak a kind word to him. Or "could not so much as greet him."

37:5 dream. The revelation at the beginning of the story shows that God was the director and that he chose Joseph as the hero in this drama of redemption (see 20:3 and its note; see also 28:12; 42:6; 43:26,28; 44:14).

37:7 bowed down. This was fulfilled in escalating stages (see 42:6; 43:26; 44:14).

37:8 rule. See 37:2 and its note, as well as Deuteronomy 33:16. Joseph received "the rights of the firstborn" (1Ch 5:2) (i.e., the double portion of the inheritance), since Jacob adopted Joseph's two sons as his own (48:5). The monarchy was coming into view, even as it developed in Edom (ch. 36). **hated.** Indirectly, the brothers hated not only Joseph but also the sovereign God who had given him the revelation, and they would go to any lengths to thwart his good program for them.

37:9 another dream. Throughout the Joseph story the dreams came in pairs (chs. 40–41) to demonstrate that the outcome of a particular matter was determined by God and would come quickly to fulfillment (see 41:32).

37:10 rebuked. Joseph's dream threatened to reverse the social order. **mother.** After the death of his mother, Rachel, one of Jacob's other wives possibly became Joseph's surrogate mother.

and bow down to the ground before you?" [u] 11His brothers were jealous of him, [v] but his
father kept the matter in mind. [w]

Joseph Sold by His Brothers

12Now his brothers had gone to graze their father's flocks near Shechem, 13and Israel said to Joseph, "As you know, your brothers are grazing the flocks near Shechem.
Come, I am going to send you to them."
"Very well," he replied.
14So he said to him, "Go and see if all is well with your brothers and with the flocks,
and bring word back to me." Then he sent him off from the Valley of Hebron. [x]
When Joseph arrived at Shechem, 15a man found him wandering around in the fields
and asked him, "What are you looking for?"
16He replied, "I'm looking for my brothers. Can you tell me where they are grazing
their flocks?"
17"They have moved on from here," the man answered. "I heard them say, 'Let's go
to Dothan.' [y]"
So Joseph went after his brothers and found them near Dothan. 18But they saw him
in the distance, and before he reached them, they plotted to kill him. [z]
19"Here comes that dreamer!" they said to each other. 20"Come now, let's kill him and
throw him into one of these cisterns [a] and say that a ferocious animal devoured him.
Then we'll see what comes of his dreams." [b]
21When Reuben heard this, he tried to rescue him from their hands. "Let's not take
his life," he said. [c] 22"Don't shed any blood. Throw him into this cistern here in the desert, but don't lay a hand on him." Reuben said this to rescue him from them and take him
back to his father.
23So when Joseph came to his brothers, they stripped him of his robe—the richly ornamented robe he was wearing— 24and they took him and threw him into the cistern. [d]
Now the cistern was empty; there was no water in it.
25As they sat down to eat their meal, they looked up and saw a caravan of Ishmaelites coming from Gilead. Their camels were loaded with spices, balm and myrrh, [e] and
they were on their way to take them down to Egypt. [f]
26Judah said to his brothers, "What will we gain if we kill our brother and cover up
his blood? [g] 27Come, let's sell him to the Ishmaelites and not lay our hands on him; after
all, he is our brother, [h] our own flesh and blood." His brothers agreed.
28So when the Midianite [i] merchants came by, his brothers pulled Joseph up out of the
cistern and sold him for twenty shekels[a] of silver to the Ishmaelites, who took him to
Egypt. [j]
29When Reuben returned to the cistern and saw that Joseph was not there, he tore
his clothes. [k] 30He went back to his brothers and said, "The boy isn't there! Where can I
turn now?" [l]
31Then they got Joseph's robe, [m] slaughtered a goat and dipped the robe in the blood.
32They took the ornamented robe back to their father and said, "We found this. Examine it to see whether it is your son's robe."
33He recognized it and said, "It is my son's robe! Some ferocious animal [n] has devoured him. Joseph has surely been torn to pieces." [o]
34Then Jacob tore his clothes, [p] put on sackcloth [q] and mourned for his son many
days. [r] 35All his sons and daughters came to comfort him, but he refused to be comfort-

[a] *28* That is, about 8 ounces (about 0.2 kilogram)

37:10 [u]ver 7; Ge 27:29
37:11 [v]Ac 7:9 [w]Lk 2:19, 51
37:14 [x]Ge 13:18; 35:27
37:17 [y]2Ki 6:13
37:18 [z]1Sa 19:1; Mk 14:1; Ac 23:12
37:20 [a]Jer 38:6,9 [b]Ge 50:20
37:21 [c]Ge 42:22
37:24 [d]Jer 41:7
37:25 [e]Ge 43:11 [f]ver 28
37:26 [g]ver 20; Ge 4:10
37:27 [h]Ge 42:21
37:28 [i]Ge 25:2; Jdg 6:1-3 [j]Ge 45:4-5; Ps 105:17; Ac 7:9
37:29 [k]ver 34; Ge 44:13; Job 1:20
37:30 [l]ver 22; Ge 42:13, 36
37:31 [m]ver 3,23
37:33 [n]ver 20 [o]Ge 44:20, 28
37:34 [p]ver 29 [q]2Sa 3:31 [r]Ge 50:3,10,11

37:11 kept the matter in mind. Jacob took the dream seriously. ▪ **37:12–36** *Joseph Sold Into Slavery.* In their jealousy, Joseph's brothers sold Joseph into slavery in Egypt, where he served in Potiphar's house.
37:14 if all is well. Jacob had reason to worry about his sons at Shechem (see ch. 34).
37:16 I'm looking for my brothers. This statement epitomized Joseph's career. He was the opposite of Cain (4:9) and was made of good leadership material.
37:17 I heard. Another providential act.
37:18 kill. The brothers behaved like Cain, the serpent's seed (4:8).
37:21–22 See *WLC* 135.
37:21 Reuben. As the eldest brother, Reuben assumed the role of the father while the brothers were away from home (vv. 13–14).
37:25 they sat down to eat their meal. In seeming indifference to their brother's cries (42:21), the ten went about their normal routine. Their next meal in Joseph's presence would be with Joseph at the head table (43:32–34). **Ishmaelites.** See 39:1; also called Midianites (v. 28) and Medanites (see NIV text note on v. 36). These three descendants of Abraham (25:2,18) intermarried (see 28:9).
37:27 sell him. Kidnapping was a capital offense in Mosaic Law (Ex 21:16). **our hands.** Behind the scene was the hand of God (45:5; Ps 105:17).
37:28 twenty shekels. The value of a growing boy (Lev 27:4–5).
37:30 turn. That is, away from his father's face, for he owed him an accounting.
37:31 goat. As Jacob had deceived his father with goatskins and Esau's clothing (27:9,16), so he would now be deceived with goat's blood and his son's cloak.
37:33 ferocious animal. Ironically, Jacob's heartless sons were the true animals.

ed. "No," he said, "in mourning will I go down to the grave[a][s] to my son." So his father
wept for him.
36 Meanwhile, the Midianites[b] sold Joseph in Egypt to Potiphar, one of Pharaoh's officials, the captain of the guard.[t]

Judah and Tamar

38 At that time, Judah left his brothers and went down to stay with a man of Adullam named Hirah. 2 There Judah met the daughter of a Canaanite man named
Shua.[u] He married her and lay with her; 3 she became pregnant and gave birth to a son,
who was named Er.[v] 4 She conceived again and gave birth to a son and named him Onan.
5 She gave birth to still another son and named him Shelah. It was at Kezib that she gave
birth to him.
6 Judah got a wife for Er, his firstborn, and her name was Tamar. 7 But Er, Judah's firstborn, was wicked in the LORD's sight; so the LORD put him to death.[w]
8 Then Judah said to Onan, "Lie with your brother's wife and fulfill your duty to her
as a brother-in-law to produce offspring for your brother."[x] 9 But Onan knew that the offspring would not be his; so whenever he lay with his brother's wife, he spilled his semen
on the ground to keep from producing offspring for his brother. 10 What he did was wicked in the LORD's sight; so he put him to death also.[y]
11 Judah then said to his daughter-in-law Tamar, "Live as a widow in your father's
house until my son Shelah grows up."[z] For he thought, "He may die too, just like his
brothers." So Tamar went to live in her father's house.
12 After a long time Judah's wife, the daughter of Shua, died. When Judah had recovered from his grief, he went up to Timnah,[a] to the men who were shearing his sheep, and
his friend Hirah the Adullamite went with him.
13 When Tamar was told, "Your father-in-law is on his way to Timnah to shear his
sheep," 14 she took off her widow's clothes, covered herself with a veil to disguise herself,
and then sat down at the entrance to Enaim, which is on the road to Timnah. For she saw
that, though Shelah[b] had now grown up, she had not been given to him as his wife.
15 When Judah saw her, he thought she was a prostitute, for she had covered her face.
16 Not realizing that she was his daughter-in-law,[c] he went over to her by the roadside
and said, "Come now, let me sleep with you."
"And what will you give me to sleep with you?" she asked.
17 "I'll send you a young goat[d] from my flock," he said.
"Will you give me something as a pledge[e] until you send it?" she asked.
18 He said, "What pledge should I give you?"
"Your seal[f] and its cord, and the staff in your hand," she answered. So he gave them

37:35 [s]Ge 42:38; 44:22, 29,31
37:36 [t]Ge 39:1
38:2 [u]1Ch 2:3
38:3 [v]ver 6; Ge 46:12; Nu 26:19
38:7 [w]ver 10; Ge 46:12; 1Ch 2:3
38:8 [x]Dt 25:5-6; Mt 22:24-28
38:10 [y]Ge 46:12; Dt 25:7-10
38:11 [z]Ru 1:13
38:12 [a]ver 14; Jos 15:10, 57
38:14 [b]ver 11
38:16 [c]Lev 18:15; 20:12
38:17 [d]Eze 16:33 [e]ver 20
38:18 [f]ver 25

a 35 Hebrew *Sheol* b 36 Samaritan Pentateuch, Septuagint, Vulgate and Syriac (see also verse 28); Masoretic Text *Medanites*

37:35 to the grave. The family peace was shattered. The brothers could eliminate the preferred son, but not a father's love or Jacob's painful grief over Joseph.
37:36 sold. See Amos 1:6–7. **Potiphar.** His name means "he whom Ra [the sun god] has given."
■ **38:1–30** *Patriarchal Corruption in Canaan.* The story of Joseph is interrupted to set up a contrast between Joseph and his brothers (especially Judah). Although Joseph's brothers remained in the land, they began to intermarry with the cursed Canaanites (12:3). This corruption stands in contrast with the moral purity that Joseph exemplified during the same time period (see note on 39:1–20a).
38:1 At that time, Judah left his brothers. The family, shattered by attempted fratricide, was further degenerated by disloyalty. The events of this scene cover a span of approximately 22 years, chronologically connecting the sale of Joseph to Judah's intermarriage with the Canaanites. **went down.** From Hebron's heights (35:27) to Canaan's lowlands. **Adullam.** A royal Canaanite city about three miles southwest of Bethlehem (Jos 12:15).
38:2 met . . . married. Literally, "saw . . . took." The conjunction of the two verbs has overtones of lust (3:6; 6:2; 12:15; 34:2). **Canaanite.** See notes on 9:26, 12:1 and 24:4. **married.** See notes on 24:3 and 26:34–35. This was the very thing that Abraham and Isaac had feared and that had contributed to the rejection of Esau. Possibly one reason God would lead the family into Egypt was to prevent their complete assimilation with the Canaanites while he waited for the sin of the Canaanites to increase (15:16).
38:7 the LORD put him to death. God carefully investigated the crime before passing a death sentence (18:21). This is the first text explicitly stating that God put someone to death.
38:8 Judah said. Having given Tamar to Er, Judah was responsible for her. **duty to her as a brother-in-law.** This duty was later codified in Israel's law (Dt 25:5–6; Ru 4:5,10,17). As Simeon and Levi had desecrated the rite of circumcision for vengeance (see 34:15 and its note), so Onan desecrated the duty of raising offspring for his brother in favor of self-gratification.
38:9 to keep from producing offspring for his brother. Like Cain, Onan abused both his brother's memory and his brother's wife (4:9). If his brother had no heir, Onan would inherit his father's whole estate.
38:11 For he thought. Judah, failing to perceive God's judgment on his own folly and on his wicked sons, superstitiously regarded Tamar as a wife who brought misfortune. See *WLC* 130.
38:12 After a long time. Literally, "after many days." Other chronological notices allow no more than a year. **died.** Death plagued Judah.
38:13 Tamar. Although she played on Judah's vice, Scripture commends Tamar for her daring ruse to redress Judah's wrong and to build up the family (v. 25; Ru 4:12).
38:14 she took off. Tamar's demand that her father-in-law sire a child by her, since he had refused to give her his son, was consistent with accepted ethical practices at that time. The Mosaic Law did not go this far, but her actions were consistent with the principle that the deceased brother's widow not marry outside the family (Dt 25:5). **clothes.** Once again clothes played a part in deception (37:33). **For she saw.** Tamar met trickery with trickery.
38:16 Not realizing. Judah was cleared of any charge of committing incest, assuring the legitimacy of these births.
38:18 Your seal and its cord. A cylinder seal, which was worn on

to her and slept with her, and she became pregnant by him. 19After she left, she took off
her veil and put on her widow's clothes[g] again.
20Meanwhile Judah sent the young goat by his friend the Adullamite in order to get
his pledge back from the woman, but he did not find her. 21He asked the men who lived
there, "Where is the shrine prostitute[h] who was beside the road at Enaim?"
"There hasn't been any shrine prostitute here," they said.
22So he went back to Judah and said, "I didn't find her. Besides, the men who lived
there said, 'There hasn't been any shrine prostitute here.' "
23Then Judah said, "Let her keep what she has, or we will become a laughingstock.
After all, I did send her this young goat, but you didn't find her."
24About three months later Judah was told, "Your daughter-in-law Tamar is guilty of
prostitution, and as a result she is now pregnant."
Judah said, "Bring her out and have her burned to death!"[i]
25As she was being brought out, she sent a message to her father-in-law. "I am pregnant by the man who owns these," she said. And she added, "See if you recognize
whose seal and cord and staff these are."[j]
26Judah recognized them and said, "She is more righteous than I,[k] since I wouldn't
give her to my son Shelah.[l]" And he did not sleep with her again.
27When the time came for her to give birth, there were twin boys in her womb.[m] 28As
she was giving birth, one of them put out his hand; so the midwife took a scarlet thread
and tied it on his wrist and said, "This one came out first." 29But when he drew back his
hand, his brother came out, and she said, "So this is how you have broken out!" And he
was named Perez.[a][n] 30Then his brother, who had the scarlet thread on his wrist, came
out and he was given the name Zerah.[b][o]

Joseph and Potiphar's Wife

39 Now Joseph had been taken down to Egypt. Potiphar, an Egyptian who was one
of Pharaoh's officials, the captain of the guard,[p] bought him from the Ishmaelites who had taken him there.[q]
2The LORD was with Joseph[r] and he prospered, and he lived in the house of his Egyptian master. 3When his master saw that the LORD was with him[s] and that the LORD gave
him success in everything he did,[t] 4Joseph found favor in his eyes and became his attendant. Potiphar put him in charge of his household, and he entrusted to his care everything he owned.[u] 5From the time he put him in charge of his household and of all that
he owned, the LORD blessed the household of the Egyptian because of Joseph.[v] The blessing of the LORD was on everything Potiphar had, both in the house and in the field. 6So
he left in Joseph's care everything he had; with Joseph in charge, he did not concern himself with anything except the food he ate.
Now Joseph was well-built and handsome,[w] 7and after a while his master's wife took
notice of Joseph and said, "Come to bed with me!"[x]
8But he refused.[y] "With me in charge," he told her, "my master does not concern himself with anything in the house; everything he owns he has entrusted to my care. 9No one

38:19 [g]ver 14
38:21 [h]Lev 19:29; Hos 4:14
38:24 [i]Lev 21:9; Dt 22:21,22
38:25 [j]ver 18
38:26 [k]1Sa 24:17 [l]ver 11
38:27 [m]Ge 25:24
38:29 [n]Ge 46:12; Nu 26:20,21; Ru 4:12,18; 1Ch 2:4; Mt 1:3
38:30 [o]1Ch 2:4
39:1 [p]Ge 37:36 [q]Ge 37:25; Ps 105:17
39:2 [r]Ge 21:20,22; Ac 7:9
39:3 [s]Ge 21:22; 26:28 [t]Ps 1:3
39:4 [u]ver 8,22; Ge 24:2
39:5 [v]Ge 26:24; 30:27
39:6 [w]1Sa 16:12
39:7 [x]2Sa 13:11; Pr 7:15-18
39:8 [y]Pr 6:23-24

[a] 29 *Perez* means *breaking out.* [b] 30 *Zerah* can mean *scarlet* or *brightness.*

a cord around the neck, was the insignia of a prominent man. When it was rolled across soft clay, it resulted in an impression that identified the owner of the object. **staff.** This symbol of authority had his mark of ownership etched on its top.
38:21 shrine prostitute. Judah's Canaanite friend elevated Tamar's social status from that of a common whore to a shrine prostitute that one would expect to find at a Canaanite festival.
38:24 Bring her out. Of the city (Dt 22:21,24). **burned to death.** Later this punishment for a priest's daughter who prostituted herself was codified as the law in Israel (Lev 21:9). See *WLC* 145.
38:25 recognize. The deceiver was again deceived, measure for measure (cf. ch. 29; 37:33).
38:26 She is more righteous than I. Or "She is righteous, not I." Tamar was a heroine in Israel because she risked her life for family fidelity. See *WLC* 130,139. **did not sleep with her again.** He was again cleared of incest.
38:29 broken out! See note on 28:13. Once again the younger brother was preferred over the older (25:23; 37:2). **Perez.** In the Messianic line (Ru 4:18–22; Mt 1:1–6; Lk 3:33).
■ **39:1–20a** *Joseph's Integrity in Potiphar's House.* Joseph's career was an expression of God's covenant faithfulness to preserve and prosper his people. God orchestrated the most unlikely set of circumstances into an astonishing chain of events that accomplished his design for Joseph's life. God's blessing was evident in Joseph's competence and unflinching loyalty.
39:1 officials . . . captain. See 37:36 and its note. **Ishmaelites.** See note on 37:25.
39:2 The Lord was with Joseph. See Acts 7:9. This is not only the theological entrance to the story as it unfolded in Egypt, but also the frame of the chapter (vv. 3,21,23) and the link between Joseph and the other patriarchs (28:15). God's beneficent presence was experienced even in slavery, outside the land of blessing.
39:4 put him in charge. That is, Joseph was installed as the official over Potiphar's entire estate. One often sees in Egyptian representations the chief steward of a royal household with a staff or papyrus in hand.
39:5 blessed. The Lord's power overflowed through the Semitic Joseph to the Hamitic Egyptians, as the Lord had foretold to Abraham (see note on 12:3).
39:6 the food he ate. A figure for his private affairs.
39:8–10 See *WLC* 138,139.
39:8 With me in charge. Joseph exemplified loyalty to his master. We can surmise that his reasons for refusing Potiphar's wife included unwillingness to sin against God, refusal to abuse a trust, refusal to violate her husband's marital rights and gratitude for Potiphar's generosity.

is greater in this house than I am.[z] My master has withheld nothing from me except you, because you are his wife. How then could I do such a wicked thing and sin against God?"[a] 10And though she spoke to Joseph day after day, he refused to go to bed with her or even be with her.

11One day he went into the house to attend to his duties, and none of the household servants was inside. 12She caught him by his cloak[b] and said, "Come to bed with me!" But he left his cloak in her hand and ran out of the house.

13When she saw that he had left his cloak in her hand and had run out of the house, 14she called her household servants. "Look," she said to them, "this Hebrew has been brought to us to make sport of us! He came in here to sleep with me, but I screamed.[c] 15When he heard me scream for help, he left his cloak beside me and ran out of the house."

16She kept his cloak beside her until his master came home. 17Then she told him this story:[d] "That Hebrew slave you brought us came to me to make sport of me. 18But as soon as I screamed for help, he left his cloak beside me and ran out of the house."

19When his master heard the story his wife told him, saying, "This is how your slave treated me," he burned with anger.[e] 20Joseph's master took him and put him in prison,[f] the place where the king's prisoners were confined.

But while Joseph was there in the prison, 21the LORD was with him; he showed him kindness and granted him favor in the eyes of the prison warden.[g] 22So the warden put Joseph in charge of all those held in the prison, and he was made responsible for all that was done there.[h] 23The warden paid no attention to anything under Joseph's care, because the LORD was with Joseph and gave him success in whatever he did.[i]

The Cupbearer and the Baker

40 Some time later, the cupbearer[j] and the baker of the king of Egypt offended their master, the king of Egypt. 2Pharaoh was angry[k] with his two officials, the chief cupbearer and the chief baker, 3and put them in custody in the house of the captain of the guard,[l] in the same prison where Joseph was confined. 4The captain of the guard assigned them to Joseph,[m] and he attended them.

After they had been in custody for some time, 5each of the two men—the cupbearer and the baker of the king of Egypt, who were being held in prison—had a dream the same night, and each dream had a meaning of its own.[n]

6When Joseph came to them the next morning, he saw that they were dejected. 7So he asked Pharaoh's officials who were in custody with him in his master's house, "Why are your faces so sad today?"[o]

8"We both had dreams," they answered, "but there is no one to interpret them."[p]

Then Joseph said to them, "Do not interpretations belong to God?[q] Tell me your dreams."

9So the chief cupbearer told Joseph his dream. He said to him, "In my dream I saw a vine in front of me, 10and on the vine were three branches. As soon as it budded, it blossomed, and its clusters ripened into grapes. 11Pharaoh's cup was in my hand, and I took the grapes, squeezed them into Pharaoh's cup and put the cup in his hand."

39:9 [z]Ge 41:33,40 [a]Ge 20:6; 42:18; 2Sa 12:13
39:12 [b]Pr 7:13
39:14 [c]Dt 22:24,27
39:17 [d]Ex 23:1,7; Ps 101:5
39:19 [e]Pr 6:34
39:20 [f]Ge 40:3; Ps 105:18
39:21 [g]Ex 3:21
39:22 [h]ver 4
39:23 [i]ver 3
40:1 [j]Ne 1:11
40:2 [k]Pr 16:14,15
40:3 [l]Ge 39:20
40:4 [m]Ge 39:4
40:5 [n]Ge 41:11
40:7 [o]Ne 2:2
40:8 [p]Ge 41:8,15 [q]Ge 41:16; Da 2:22,28,47

39:9 sin against God? Contrary to Judah (ch. 38), Joseph remained keenly aware of God's covenantal claims on his life.
39:14 this Hebrew. See notes on 10:21, 14:13 and 43:32. **to make sport of us!** As she was false to her husband with regard to Joseph, Potiphar's wife was now disloyal to his name before the domestic servants (cf. v. 17).
39:19 he burned with anger. Against Joseph or perhaps against his wife (see v. 20 and note).
39:20 put him in prison . . . where the king's prisoners were confined. Attempted rape was a capital offense. The milder punishment of placing Joseph with the king's prisoners suggests that Potiphar may not have believed his wife.
■ **39:20b—40:23** *Joseph's Unwavering Faith in Prison.* Joseph experienced God's blessing while in prison as he continued to have faith in God's good purposes. This narrative paralleled the imprisonment in Egypt of Moses' original audience.
39:21 he showed him kindness. God did not remove Joseph's suffering but remained at his side through it. **granted him favor.** The Hebrew here is the same as that used in the account of the exodus (Ex 3:21; 11:3; 12:36).
40:1–23 God continued to be with Joseph, enabling him to interpret two dreams. But the beneficiaries let him down. The closing of the prison doors, however, was designed by the Lord to open the doors to the palace (Ac 7:10).
40:2 chief cupbearer. Kings often feared being poisoned, so they entrusted cupbearers with their lives. In many cases these officials became confidants and favorites of the king and wielded political influence. **chief baker.** Both of Joseph's royal inmates had been trusted with preparing elements of Pharaoh's food, so both had experienced close access to Pharaoh and could have played a sinister role in a conspiracy against him.
40:3 custody. They were waiting for Pharaoh's sentence.
40:8 dreams. An important means of revelation (see notes on 20:3; 31:1–55; 41:25). The three sets of dreams—to Joseph (37:5–11), to the cupbearer and the baker (ch. 40) and to Pharaoh (ch. 41)—emphasized that God sovereignly controlled each individual's destiny (41:28). **no one to interpret them.** In ancient Egypt the interpretation of dreams was considered a specialized skill. **interpretations belong to God?** If interpretations belong to God and are not gained through manipulation, then God can confer them as gifts on whomever he pleases (41:16; Da 2:24–49). Although the Egyptians stood outside God's special covenant people, Joseph still assumed he could speak to them about the same God whom they both recognized (as one god among many, though they did not worship him). **Tell me.** Joseph recognized himself as a prophet (37:5–11). God was with Joseph not only in providential acts, but also in revealing to him dreams and their interpretations.

12“This is what it means,[r]” Joseph said to him. “The three branches are three days.
13Within three days Pharaoh will lift up your head and restore you to your position, and
you will put Pharaoh’s cup in his hand, just as you used to do when you were his cupbearer. 14But when all goes well with you, remember me[s] and show me kindness;[t] mention
me to Pharaoh and get me out of this prison. 15For I was forcibly carried off from the land
of the Hebrews,[u] and even here I have done nothing to deserve being put in a dungeon.”
16When the chief baker saw that Joseph had given a favorable interpretation, he said
to Joseph, “I too had a dream: On my head were three baskets of bread.[a] 17In the top basket were all kinds of baked goods for Pharaoh, but the birds were eating them out of the
basket on my head.”
18“This is what it means,” Joseph said. “The three baskets are three days.[v] 19Within
three days Pharaoh will lift off your head[w] and hang you on a tree.[b] And the birds will
eat away your flesh.”
20Now the third day was Pharaoh’s birthday,[x] and he gave a feast for all his officials.[y]
He lifted up the heads of the chief cupbearer and the chief baker in the presence of his
officials: 21He restored the chief cupbearer to his position, so that he once again put the
cup into Pharaoh’s hand,[z] 22but he hanged[c] the chief baker,[a] just as Joseph had said to
them in his interpretation.[b]
23The chief cupbearer, however, did not remember Joseph; he forgot him.[c]

Pharaoh’s Dreams

41 When two full years had passed, Pharaoh had a dream:[d] He was standing by the
Nile, 2when out of the river there came up seven cows, sleek and fat,[e] and they
grazed among the reeds.[f] 3After them, seven other cows, ugly and gaunt, came up out
of the Nile and stood beside those on the riverbank. 4And the cows that were ugly and
gaunt ate up the seven sleek, fat cows. Then Pharaoh woke up.
5He fell asleep again and had a second dream: Seven heads of grain, healthy and
good, were growing on a single stalk. 6After them, seven other heads of grain sprouted—
thin and scorched by the east wind. 7The thin heads of grain swallowed up the seven
healthy, full heads. Then Pharaoh woke up; it had been a dream.
8In the morning his mind was troubled,[g] so he sent for all the magicians[h] and wise
men of Egypt. Pharaoh told them his dreams, but no one could interpret them for him.
9Then the chief cupbearer said to Pharaoh, “Today I am reminded of my shortcomings. 10Pharaoh was once angry with his servants,[i] and he imprisoned me and the chief
baker in the house of the captain of the guard.[j] 11Each of us had a dream the same night,
and each dream had a meaning of its own.[k] 12Now a young Hebrew was there with us,
a servant of the captain of the guard. We told him our dreams, and he interpreted them
for us, giving each man the interpretation of his dream.[l] 13And things turned out exactly as he interpreted them to us: I was restored to my position, and the other man was
hanged.[c][m]”
14So Pharaoh sent for Joseph, and he was quickly brought from the dungeon.[n] When
he had shaved and changed his clothes, he came before Pharaoh.

40:12 [r]Ge 41:12,15,25; Da 2:36; 4:19
40:14 [s]Lk 23:42 [t]Jos 2:12; 1Sa 20:14,42; 1Ki 2:7
40:15 [u]Ge 37:26-28
40:18 [v]ver 12
40:19 [w]ver 13
40:20 [x]Mt 14:6-10 [y]Mk 6:21
40:21 [z]ver 13
40:22 [a]ver 19 [b]Ps 105:19
40:23 [c]Job 19:14; Ecc 9:15
41:1 [d]Ge 20:3
41:2 [e]ver 26 [f]Isa 19:6
41:8 [g]Da 2:1,3; 4:5,19 [h]Ex 7:11,22; Da 1:20; 2:2,27; 4:7
41:10 [i]Ge 40:2 [j]Ge 39:20
41:11 [k]Ge 40:5
41:12 [l]Ge 40:12
41:13 [m]Ge 40:22
41:14 [n]Ps 105:20; Da 2:25

a 16 Or *three wicker baskets* b 19 Or *and impale you on a pole* c 22,13 Or *impaled*

40:13 lift up . . . head. The Hebrew here is rendered “release” in 2 Kings 25:27, where it is used in a context of freeing from prison.
40:14 when all goes well. Joseph’s faith remained strong. **remember.** See note on 8:1. Joseph appealed to a higher tribunal and briefly supported his case for justice.
40:15 dungeon. Probably a hyperbole and a link to his first imprisonment. The Hebrew here is translated “cistern” in 37:24.
40:16 On my head. Egyptian art of this time period portrays a baker carrying a basket on his head.
40:17 birds were eating them. In the dream, the chief baker amazingly did nothing to protect his delicacies. This may have symbolized his failure to protect Pharaoh’s table.
40:20 lifted up the heads. A ritual by which the king singled out a servant.
40:23 did not remember. This was a self-centered moral lapse. The cupbearer’s ingratitude prefigured the later national ingratitude of the Egyptians to the enslaved Israelites.
■**41:1–57** *Joseph Exalted in Egypt.* God exalted faithful Joseph over all of Egypt and indirectly over the world by gifting him with supernatural wisdom (v. 33), including the ability to interpret dreams (v. 16), as well as statesmanship and savvy in national economics (v. 38). Joseph prefigured Moses at the founding of Israel and Daniel at the end of Israel’s monarchy. All three were oppressed captives who came to power in a hostile land by pitting God’s wisdom against that of this world. In so doing, they each displayed the superiority of God’s wisdom and his rule over the nations. They prefigured Jesus Christ, God’s ultimate Wisdom, who astonishingly was raised from the cross to rule the world (1Co 1:18—2:16; Rev 12:1–5).
41:1 dream. Royal dreams played a special role in the ancient Near East, indicating a bond between the king and his god (see 40:8 and its note; see also 1Ki 3:4–16; Pr 21:1). **Nile.** The source of Egypt’s fertility.
41:8 troubled. See Daniel 2:1 and 3. Joseph was probably troubled because Pharaoh attributed the bountiful harvests reaped during his reign to his good and magical relations to the grain god. **magicians.** Priests were occupied with magic and soothsaying (Ex 7–9; Da 2:2). **no one could interpret.** See 40:8 and its note.
41:9 I am reminded. Or “I must make mention.”
41:12 Hebrew. See note on 39:14.
41:13 exactly as he interpreted. Because it was the word of the Lord (see Ps 105:19). Joseph’s eyewitness testimony prepared Pharaoh and his officials to accept his interpretation as God’s word (see Ps 105:19).
41:14 changed his clothes. See 39:13 and 2 Kings 25:29.

15Pharaoh said to Joseph, "I had a dream, and no one can interpret it. But I have heard it said of you that when you hear a dream you can interpret it."[o]

16"I cannot do it," Joseph replied to Pharaoh, "but God will give Pharaoh the answer he desires."[p]

17Then Pharaoh said to Joseph, "In my dream I was standing on the bank of the Nile, 18when out of the river there came up seven cows, fat and sleek, and they grazed among the reeds. 19After them, seven other cows came up—scrawny and very ugly and lean. I had never seen such ugly cows in all the land of Egypt. 20The lean, ugly cows ate up the seven fat cows that came up first. 21But even after they ate them, no one could tell that they had done so; they looked just as ugly as before. Then I woke up.

22"In my dreams I also saw seven heads of grain, full and good, growing on a single stalk. 23After them, seven other heads sprouted—withered and thin and scorched by the east wind. 24The thin heads of grain swallowed up the seven good heads. I told this to the magicians, but none could explain it to me.[q]"

25Then Joseph said to Pharaoh, "The dreams of Pharaoh are one and the same. God has revealed to Pharaoh what he is about to do.[r] 26The seven good cows[s] are seven years, and the seven good heads of grain are seven years; it is one and the same dream. 27The seven lean, ugly cows that came up afterward are seven years, and so are the seven worthless heads of grain scorched by the east wind: They are seven years of famine.[t]

28"It is just as I said to Pharaoh: God has shown Pharaoh what he is about to do. 29Seven years of great abundance[u] are coming throughout the land of Egypt, 30but seven years of famine[v] will follow them. Then all the abundance in Egypt will be forgotten, and the famine will ravage the land.[w] 31The abundance in the land will not be remembered, because the famine that follows it will be so severe. 32The reason the dream was given to Pharaoh in two forms is that the matter has been firmly decided[x] by God, and God will do it soon.

33"And now let Pharaoh look for a discerning and wise man[y] and put him in charge of the land of Egypt. 34Let Pharaoh appoint commissioners over the land to take a fifth[z] of the harvest of Egypt during the seven years of abundance.[a] 35They should collect all the food of these good years that are coming and store up the grain under the authority of Pharaoh, to be kept in the cities for food.[b] 36This food should be held in reserve for the country, to be used during the seven years of famine that will come upon Egypt,[c] so that the country may not be ruined by the famine."

37The plan seemed good to Pharaoh and to all his officials.[d] 38So Pharaoh asked them, "Can we find anyone like this man, one in whom is the spirit of God[a]?"[e]

39Then Pharaoh said to Joseph, "Since God has made all this known to you, there is no one so discerning and wise as you. 40You shall be in charge of my palace, and all my people are to submit to your orders.[f] Only with respect to the throne will I be greater than you."

Joseph in Charge of Egypt

41So Pharaoh said to Joseph, "I hereby put you in charge of the whole land of Egypt."[g] 42Then Pharaoh took his signet ring[h] from his finger and put it on Joseph's finger. He dressed him in robes of fine linen and put a gold chain around his neck.[i] 43He had him ride in a chariot as his second-in-command,[b] and men shouted before him, "Make way[c]!"[j] Thus he put him in charge of the whole land of Egypt.

41:15 [o]Da 5:16
41:16 [p]Ge 40:8; Da 2:30; Ac 3:12; 2Co 3:5
41:24 [q]ver 8
41:25 [r]Da 2:45
41:26 [s]ver 2
41:27 [t]Ge 12:10; 2Ki 8:1
41:29 [u]ver 47
41:30 [v]ver 54; Ge 47:13 [w]ver 56
41:32 [x]Nu 23:19; Isa 46:10-11
41:33 [y]ver 39
41:34 [z]1Sa 8:15 [a]ver 48
41:35 [b]ver 48
41:36 [c]ver 56
41:37 [d]Ge 45:16
41:38 [e]Nu 27:18; Job 32:8; Da 4:8-9, 18; 5:11,14
41:40 [f]Ps 105:21-22; Ac 7:10
41:41 [g]Ge 42:6; Da 6:3
41:42 [h]Est 3:10 [i]Da 5:7, 16,29
41:43 [j]Est 6:9

[a] *38* Or *of the gods* [b] *43* Or *in the chariot of his second-in-command*; or *in his second chariot* [c] *43* Or *Bow down*

41:16 I cannot. See 2 Corinthians 3:5. **God.** See notes on 40:8 and 41:1–57.

41:25 one and the same. That is, the lean devoured the fat—one dream involved animal husbandry and the other agriculture. **revealed.** Both the dream and its interpretation were from God (40:8). Joseph was inspired by God and did not act as a magician. Neither Pharaoh nor his officials were in control; God and his servant were.

41:33 look for a discerning and wise man. Pharaoh had just discovered that he had no one in his service to fit this description. True wisdom is found only in God's people (Pr 9:10; 15:33).

41:38 spirit of God? Joseph pointed to God's action in giving the dream (v. 16), and Pharaoh acknowledged God's power at work in Joseph (vv. 1–57). God manifested his Spirit uniquely in certain elect individuals in the Old Testament, gifting them in extraordinary ways for the sacred task of establishing his kingdom (e.g., Ex 31:3; 35:31; Nu 11:17, 25; Jdg 6:34; 13:25; Isa 11:1–3; Mic 3:8).

41:39 no one so discerning and wise as you. Joseph had just defeated Egypt's most renowned wise men.

41:41–46 Joseph's installation as viceroy over Egypt consisted of a public act of installation (vv. 41–44), the family act of conferring a new name (v. 45) and the elevation to nobility by marriage (vv. 45–46).

41:41 put you in charge of the whole land. This reflected the Egyptian title "Chief of the Entire Land," an epithet applied to the vizier. Joseph allowed others to praise and exalt him, rather than praising himself (cf. Pr 27:2). He who had been faithful in little (39:4,22) was put in charge of much (Lk 16:10; 19:17).

41:42 Pharaoh took. Pharaoh's investiture of Joseph consisted of transferring his signet ring (to validate documents) to Joseph, dressing him in fine linen, placing a gold chain around his neck and parading him through the streets with pomp and ceremony in a chariot. These were all recognized symbols of investiture in Egypt. **robes.** See 39:13.

44 Then Pharaoh said to Joseph, "I am Pharaoh, but without your word no one will lift
hand or foot in all Egypt."[k] 45 Pharaoh gave Joseph the name Zaphenath-Paneah and
gave him Asenath daughter of Potiphera, priest of On,[a] to be his wife.[l] And Joseph went
throughout the land of Egypt.
46 Joseph was thirty years old[m] when he entered the service[n] of Pharaoh king of Egypt.
And Joseph went out from Pharaoh's presence and traveled throughout Egypt. 47 During
the seven years of abundance the land produced plentifully. 48 Joseph collected all the
food produced in those seven years of abundance in Egypt and stored it in the cities. In
each city he put the food grown in the fields surrounding it. 49 Joseph stored up huge
quantities of grain, like the sand of the sea; it was so much that he stopped keeping records because it was beyond measure.
50 Before the years of famine came, two sons were born to Joseph by Asenath daughter of Potiphera, priest of On.[o] 51 Joseph named his firstborn[p] Manasseh[b] and said, "It is
because God has made me forget all my trouble and all my father's household." 52 The
second son he named Ephraim[c][q] and said, "It is because God has made me fruitful[r] in
the land of my suffering."
53 The seven years of abundance in Egypt came to an end, 54 and the seven years of
famine began,[s] just as Joseph had said. There was famine in all the other lands, but in
the whole land of Egypt there was food. 55 When all Egypt began to feel the famine,[t] the
people cried to Pharaoh for food. Then Pharaoh told all the Egyptians, "Go to Joseph and
do what he tells you."[u]
56 When the famine had spread over the whole country, Joseph opened the storehouses and sold grain to the Egyptians, for the famine[v] was severe throughout Egypt. 57 And
all the countries came to Egypt to buy grain from Joseph,[w] because the famine was severe in all the world.

Joseph's Brothers Go to Egypt

42 When Jacob learned that there was grain in Egypt,[x] he said to his sons, "Why
do you just keep looking at each other?" 2 He continued, "I have heard that there
is grain in Egypt. Go down there and buy some for us, so that we may live and not die."[y]
3 Then ten of Joseph's brothers went down to buy grain from Egypt. 4 But Jacob did not
send Benjamin, Joseph's brother, with the others, because he was afraid that harm might
come to him.[z] 5 So Israel's sons were among those who went to buy grain,[a] for the famine was in the land of Canaan also.[b]
6 Now Joseph was the governor of the land,[c] the one who sold grain to all its people.
So when Joseph's brothers arrived, they bowed down to him with their faces to the
ground.[d] 7 As soon as Joseph saw his brothers, he recognized them, but he pretended to
be a stranger and spoke harshly to them.[e] "Where do you come from?" he asked.
"From the land of Canaan," they replied, "to buy food."

41:44 [k]Ps 105:22
41:45 [l]ver 50; Ge 46:20, 27
41:46 [m]Ge 37:2 [n]1Sa 16:21; Da 1:19
41:50 [o]Ge 46:20; 48:5
41:51 [p]Ge 48:14,18,20
41:52 [q]Ge 48:1,5; 50:23 [r]Ge 17:6; 28:3; 49:22
41:54 [s]ver 30; Ps 105:11; Ac 7:11
41:55 [t]Dt 32:24 [u]ver 41
41:56 [v]Ge 12:10
41:57 [w]Ge 42:5; 47:15
42:1 [x]Ac 7:12
42:2 [y]Ge 43:8
42:4 [z]ver 38
42:5 [a]Ge 41:57 [b]Ge 12:10; Ac 7:11
42:6 [c]Ge 41:41 [d]Ge 37:7-10
42:7 [e]ver 30

[a] *45* That is, Heliopolis; also in verse 50 [b] *51* *Manasseh* sounds like and may be derived from the Hebrew for *forget.* [c] *52* *Ephraim* sounds like the Hebrew for *twice fruitful.*

41:45 Zaphenath-Paneah. His unique name means "God speaks and lives." Joseph's role in Egypt was like that of Daniel in Babylon: Both accepted pagan names without accepting pagan religion. **Asenath.** Her name means "She belongs to [the goddess] Neith." She was not Canaanite, and therefore Joseph was free to marry her (see note on 38:2). **Potiphera.** For the meaning of this name, see note at 37:36. **On.** A temple for sun worship; its high priest was one of the most prominent in ancient Egypt.
41:46 thirty years old. See 37:2. Joseph had risen from slavery to become the king's second-in-command in a mere 13 years. See also 2 Samuel 5:4.
41:51 God. The names of both Joseph's sons praise God, first for preserving Joseph, then for blessing him (see 48:9 and its note). He gave his sons Hebrew, not Egyptian, names, showing that he had not forgotten his religious and cultural heritage.
41:52 fruitful. See 17:6 and 20, 28:3, 48:4 and Ps 105:23–24.
41:57 all the world. The salvation of the then-known world depended upon a descendant of the patriarchs, a type of Christ.
■ **42:1—47:28** *The Patriarchs Together in Harmony.* With Joseph exalted in Egypt, the narrative moves toward the reunion of the patriarchs under Joseph's authority in Egypt. These chapters divide into six main sections: three tests (42:1–38; 43:1–34; 44:1–34), an initial reconciliation (45:1–28), a full migration of the family (46:1–30) and the magnificent preservation in Goshen (46:31—47:28).
■ **42:1–38** *Joseph's First Test of His Brothers.* Joseph was able to use the circumstances of the providential famine and his own authority to help reconcile his shattered family. By confronting his brothers with life and death issues (vv. 18,20), he awakened their consciences so that they would confess their guilt (vv. 21–24), fear God (v. 28), take responsibility to retrieve Simeon from prison (vv. 19,24) and protect Benjamin from harm (v. 37).
42:1 Jacob. The patriarch was responsible for the entire family (see 37:21 and its note). **just keep looking at each other?** Perhaps they delayed because they had sold Joseph into Egypt or because they dreaded Pharaoh (12:12; 43:18; 46:3).
42:2 that we may live and not die. An event of this kind is attested several times in the Bible (12:10; 26:1–2) and particularly in Egypt.
42:3 ten. Whereas Abraham went down to Egypt alone, these ten men and their beasts of burden all made the journey, as each had his own family to support (43:8).
42:4 did not send Benjamin. Joseph's full brother had taken Joseph's place in his father's affections (see note on 37:3). The brothers' treatment of Benjamin and of their father would test whether there had been a spiritual change in them.
42:6 bowed down. To preserve their lives, the brothers had unwittingly fulfilled Joseph's divine boyhood dream (see note on 37:5).
42:7 he pretended to be a stranger and spoke harshly. Joseph retained the power inherent in his knowledge of the truth. He had no reason at this point to trust those who had sold him into slavery more than 20 years earlier.

8 Although Joseph recognized his brothers, they did not recognize him.[f] 9 Then he remembered his dreams[g] about them and said to them, "You are spies! You have come to
see where our land is unprotected."
10 "No, my lord," they answered. "Your servants have come to buy food. 11 We are all
the sons of one man. Your servants are honest men, not spies."
12 "No!" he said to them. "You have come to see where our land is unprotected."
13 But they replied, "Your servants were twelve brothers, the sons of one man, who
lives in the land of Canaan. The youngest is now with our father, and one is no more."[h]
14 Joseph said to them, "It is just as I told you: You are spies! 15 And this is how you will
be tested: As surely as Pharaoh lives,[i] you will not leave this place unless your youngest
brother comes here. 16 Send one of your number to get your brother; the rest of you will
be kept in prison, so that your words may be tested to see if you are telling the truth.[j] If
you are not, then as surely as Pharaoh lives, you are spies!" 17 And he put them all in custody[k] for three days.
18 On the third day, Joseph said to them, "Do this and you will live, for I fear God:[l] 19 If
you are honest men, let one of your brothers stay here in prison, while the rest of you go
and take grain back for your starving households. 20 But you must bring your youngest
brother to me,[m] so that your words may be verified and that you may not die." This they
proceeded to do.
21 They said to one another, "Surely we are being punished because of our brother.[n]
We saw how distressed he was when he pleaded with us for his life, but we would not
listen; that's why this distress[o] has come upon us."
22 Reuben replied, "Didn't I tell you not to sin against the boy?[p] But you wouldn't listen! Now we must give an accounting[q] for his blood."[r] 23 They did not realize that Joseph
could understand them, since he was using an interpreter.
24 He turned away from them and began to weep, but then turned back and spoke to
them again. He had Simeon taken from them and bound before their eyes.[s]
25 Joseph gave orders to fill their bags with grain,[t] to put each man's silver back in his
sack,[u] and to give them provisions for their journey.[v] After this was done for them, 26 they
loaded their grain on their donkeys and left.
27 At the place where they stopped for the night one of them opened his sack to get
feed for his donkey, and he saw his silver in the mouth of his sack.[w] 28 "My silver has been
returned," he said to his brothers. "Here it is in my sack."
Their hearts sank and they turned to each other trembling and said, "What is this that
God has done to us?"[x]
29 When they came to their father Jacob in the land of Canaan, they told him all that
had happened to them. They said, 30 "The man who is lord over the land spoke harshly
to us[y] and treated us as though we were spying on the land. 31 But we said to him, 'We

42:8 [f]Ge 37:2
42:9 [g]Ge 37:7
42:13 [h]Ge 37:30,33;; 44:20
42:15 [i]1Sa 17:55
42:16 [j]ver 11
42:17 [k]Ge 40:4
42:18 [l]Ge 20:11; Lev 25:43
42:20 [m]ver 15,34; Ge 43:5; 44:23
42:21 [n]Ge 37:26-28 [o]Hos 5:15
42:22 [p]Ge 37:21-22 [q]Ge 9:5 [r]1Ki 2:32; 2Ch 24:22; Ps 9:12
42:24 [s]ver 13; Ge 43:14, 23; 45:14-15
42:25 [t]Ge 43:2 [u]Ge 44:1, 8 [v]Ro 12:17,20-21
42:27 [w]Ge 43:21-22
42:28 [x]Ge 43:23
42:30 [y]ver 7

42:9–11 You are spies! Syntactically, verse 9 links Joseph's accusations with his memory of the dream. Joseph strategized to get Benjamin to join the other brothers. His actions brought about the fulfillment of his first dream (of all 11 brothers bowing down to him; 37:2–10). In order to test their sincerity while retaining his power over them, Joseph tried to get the brothers to admit that they had yet another brother (Benjamin, the youngest). To do this, he created the fiction that he thought them to be spies. Next he incarcerated one of them to force the rest to return with Benjamin from Canaan. Frontier guards at Egypt's Asian border routinely checked travelers to discover spies. **sons of one man.** It was unlikely that any man would have risked the lives of nearly all of his sons in the dangerous venture of spying. Ironically, their statement included Joseph.
42:12 No! This characteristic hammering of an accusation to unnerve defenseless spies was necessary both to make the ruse believable and to pound information out of them (43:7), so that the interrogator could take his next step.
42:13 they replied. The brothers evidently thought that adding details would make their story more believable.
42:15 As surely as Pharaoh lives. Ancients swore by the life of the king (2Sa 15:21).
42:18–20 you will live . . . that you may not die. Joseph threatened them with death.
42:18 On the third day. The brothers tasted for three days what Joseph had endured for 13 years. **fear God.** God implants in all people an innate moral conviction that it is right to provide for the hungry and to protect the defenseless (see 20:11 and its note). Joseph planted the thought that the brothers, too, should fear God.
42:21 we are being punished. That is, "we are guilty and are being punished." Though falsely accused of spying, the brothers saw Joseph as the tool of God's higher justice, matched their punishment with their real crime against him and so confessed their guilt. Without that response, they could not have participated in God's redemptive kingdom (see note on 44:16). **we would not listen.** A real conversion was taking place from their former hardness of heart to a new sense of guilt when they themselves were confronted with the possibility of death.
42:22 Reuben. Reuben may have been arguing that he should be excused from consideration because he had opposed harming Joseph in the first place. Until now Joseph had probably held his eldest brother responsible for casting him into the pit, not realizing that Reuben had opposed the scheme and had intended to rescue his younger brother. **an accounting for his blood.** See 9:5–6.
42:24 to weep. With their confession of guilt, reconciliation was possible (cf. Pr 28:13). **Simeon.** Joseph now understood that the second-eldest brother was responsible for selling him into slavery.
42:25 to put each man's silver back. The ten had previously attributed a higher value to money than to life. Joseph was now testing their loyalty to Simeon. To return with Benjamin would have been easy enough, but it would not be so easy if they appeared to be criminals.
42:28 Their hearts sank. The brothers would surely be accused as thieves. **that God has done to us?** This is the first record of their mentioning God. They rightly saw God at work behind their crime and punishment (vv. 21–22).

are honest men; we are not spies.[z] 32 We were twelve brothers, sons of one father. One
is no more, and the youngest is now with our father in Canaan.'
33 "Then the man who is lord over the land said to us, 'This is how I will know whether you are honest men: Leave one of your brothers here with me, and take food for your
starving households and go.[a] 34 But bring your youngest brother to me so I will know that
you are not spies but honest men. Then I will give your brother back to you, and you can
trade[a] in the land.[b]' "
35 As they were emptying their sacks, there in each man's sack was his pouch of silver! When they and their father saw the money pouches, they were frightened.[c] 36 Their
father Jacob said to them, "You have deprived me of my children. Joseph is no more and
Simeon is no more, and now you want to take Benjamin.[d] Everything is against me!"
37 Then Reuben said to his father, "You may put both of my sons to death if I do not
bring him back to you. Entrust him to my care, and I will bring him back."
38 But Jacob said, "My son will not go down there with you; his brother is dead[e] and
he is the only one left. If harm comes to him[f] on the journey you are taking, you will bring
my gray head down to the grave[b][g] in sorrow.[h]"

The Second Journey to Egypt

43 Now the famine was still severe in the land.[i] 2 So when they had eaten all the
grain they had brought from Egypt, their father said to them, "Go back and buy
us a little more food."
3 But Judah said to him, "The man warned us solemnly, 'You will not see my face again
unless your brother is with you.'[j] 4 If you will send our brother along with us, we will go
down and buy food for you. 5 But if you will not send him, we will not go down, because
the man said to us, 'You will not see my face again unless your brother is with you.[k]' "
6 Israel asked, "Why did you bring this trouble on me by telling the man you had another brother?"
7 They replied, "The man questioned us closely about ourselves and our family. 'Is
your father still living?'[l] he asked us. 'Do you have another brother?'[m] We simply answered his questions. How were we to know he would say, 'Bring your brother down
here'?"
8 Then Judah said to Israel his father, "Send the boy along with me and we will go at
once, so that we and you and our children may live and not die.[n] 9 I myself will guarantee his safety; you can hold me personally responsible for him. If I do not bring him back
to you and set him here before you, I will bear the blame before you all my life.[o] 10 As it
is, if we had not delayed, we could have gone and returned twice."
11 Then their father Israel said to them, "If it must be, then do this: Put some of the
best products of the land in your bags and take them down to the man as a gift[p]—a little balm[q] and a little honey, some spices[r] and myrrh, some pistachio nuts and almonds.
12 Take double the amount of silver with you, for you must return the silver that was put
back into the mouths of your sacks.[s] Perhaps it was a mistake. 13 Take your brother also

42:31 [z]ver 11
42:33 [a]ver 19,20
42:34 [b]Ge 34:10
42:35 [c]Ge 43:12,15,18
42:36 [d]Ge 43:14
42:38 [e]Ge 37:33 [f]ver 4 [g]Ge 37:35 [h]Ge 44:29,34
43:1 [i]Ge 12:10; 41:56-57
43:3 [j]Ge 42:15; 44:23
43:5 [k]Ge 42:15; 2Sa 3:13
43:7 [l]ver 27 [m]Ge 42:13
43:8 [n]Ge 42:2; Ps 33:18-19
43:9 [o]Ge 42:37; 44:32; Phm 1:18-19
43:11 [p]Ge 32:20; Pr 18:16 [q]Ge 37:25; Jer 8:22 [r]1Ki 10:2
43:12 [s]Ge 42:25

[a] *34* Or *move about freely* [b] *38* Hebrew *Sheol*

42:33 Leave one of your brothers. The remaining nine brothers gave their aged father the impression that Simeon was an honored guest, not a prisoner. Their attitude toward the grieving Jacob was now sensitive rather than callous.
42:34 you can trade in the land. In consideration for their father's feelings, they altered the wording of Joseph's death threat (vv. 18,20) to make it sound like a promise of economic opportunity.
42:37 You may put both of my sons to death. Reuben's proposal, which was not well thought-out, did not change Jacob's mind. Would Reuben really have put his half brother before his own sons? How would the murder of the patriarch's grandsons have consoled Jacob?
■ **43:1–34** *Joseph's Second Test of His Brothers.* Joseph's ruse was now at work, moving his brothers from indifference to integrity and loyalty toward one another (vv. 1–34). The merciful (v. 14), generous (v. 23) and gracious (v. 29) God of their fathers brought peace to the shattered family (vv. 23,26–28). The formerly heartless brothers now exhibited integrity and loving loyalty toward Jacob, Benjamin and Joseph (42:1–38).
43:3 Judah. Another brother had to step forward after Jacob's definitive refusal of Reuben's offer, although Judah could not overbid his older brother (42:37–38). Judah, the oldest son still in good standing with his father, now became the leader. His tribe would later become preeminent among the sons of Israel (49:8–10; Mt 1:2,17; Lk 3:23,33).
43:5 we will not go down. Judah acceded to his father's direction: "If you will send . . . if you will not send." But Judah laid down a definitive condition to match his father's refusal.
43:7 questioned us closely about ourselves and our family. This was how the brothers rightly interpreted Joseph's repeated assertion that they were spies (see note on 42:12).
43:8 Judah said. Judah did not overstep the patriarch's authority, but his approach was forthright, firm, sober and pointed. **boy.** The Hebrew term is flexible, referring to a male from infancy (Ex 2:6) to marriage (cf. 21:12,17–18; 34:19; 41:12). Benjamin was more than twenty-two years of age, but his social standing remained that of the youngest brother. **live and not die.** This phrase refers both to the famine and to Joseph's threat (see notes at 42:18–20,34).
43:9 you can hold me personally responsible. Judah was willing to surrender the family's fortune to Jacob, who could then do with it as he wished. **I will bear the blame.** He was willing to accept whatever penalty Jacob wished to inflict on him for the rest of his life—and we see later that the patriarch could treat his sons harshly (49:3–7).
43:11 gift. The Hebrew term refers to giving a token of submission (see notes on 4:4–5; 32:13). **honey.** A delightful sweet during a famine.
43:12–14 See *WLC* 193.
43:12 must return. The covenant family was to act ethically and to make restitution (see note on 42:9–11).

and go back to the man at once. 14 And may God Almighty[a] [t] grant you mercy before the
man so that he will let your other brother and Benjamin come back with you.[u] As for me,
if I am bereaved, I am bereaved."[v]
15 So the men took the gifts and double the amount of silver, and Benjamin also. They
hurried[w] down to Egypt and presented themselves[x] to Joseph. 16 When Joseph saw Benjamin with them, he said to the steward of his house,[y] "Take these men to my house,
slaughter an animal and prepare dinner;[z] they are to eat with me at noon."
17 The man did as Joseph told him and took the men to Joseph's house. 18 Now the men
were frightened[a] when they were taken to his house. They thought, "We were brought
here because of the silver that was put back into our sacks the first time. He wants to attack us and overpower us and seize us as slaves and take our donkeys."
19 So they went up to Joseph's steward and spoke to him at the entrance to the house.
20 "Please, sir," they said, "we came down here the first time to buy food.[b] 21 But at the
place where we stopped for the night we opened our sacks and each of us found his silver—the exact weight—in the mouth of his sack. So we have brought it back with us.[c]
22 We have also brought additional silver with us to buy food. We don't know who put our
silver in our sacks."
23 "It's all right," he said. "Don't be afraid. Your God, the God of your father, has giv-
en you treasure in your sacks;[d] I received your silver." Then he brought Simeon out to
them.[e]
24 The steward took the men into Joseph's house,[f] gave them water to wash their feet[g]
and provided fodder for their donkeys. 25 They prepared their gifts for Joseph's arrival at
noon, because they had heard that they were to eat there.
26 When Joseph came home, they presented to him the gifts[h] they had brought into
the house, and they bowed down before him to the ground.[i] 27 He asked them how they
were, and then he said, "How is your aged father you told me about? Is he still living?"[j]
28 They replied, "Your servant our father is still alive and well." And they bowed low
to pay him honor.[k]
29 As he looked about and saw his brother Benjamin, his own mother's son, he asked,
"Is this your youngest brother, the one you told me about?"[l] And he said, "God be gracious to you,[m] my son." 30 Deeply moved[n] at the sight of his brother, Joseph hurried out
and looked for a place to weep. He went into his private room and wept[o] there.
31 After he had washed his face, he came out and, controlling himself,[p] said, "Serve
the food."
32 They served him by himself, the brothers by themselves, and the Egyptians who ate
with him by themselves, because Egyptians could not eat with Hebrews,[q] for that is detestable to Egyptians.[r] 33 The men had been seated before him in the order of their ages,
from the firstborn to the youngest; and they looked at each other in astonishment.
34 When portions were served to them from Joseph's table, Benjamin's portion was five
times as much as anyone else's.[s] So they feasted and drank freely with him.

A Silver Cup in a Sack

44 Now Joseph gave these instructions to the steward of his house: "Fill the men's
sacks with as much food as they can carry, and put each man's silver in the

43:14 [t]Ge 17:1; 28:3; 35:11 [u]Ge 42:24 [v]Est 4:16
43:15 [w]Ge 45:9,13 [x]Ge 47:2,7
43:16 [y]Ge 44:1,4,12 [z]ver 31; Lk 15:23
43:18 [a]Ge 42:35
43:20 [b]Ge 42:3
43:21 [c]ver 15; Ge 42:27,35
43:23 [d]Ge 42:28 [e]Ge 42:24
43:24 [f]ver 16 [g]Ge 18:4; 24:32
43:26 [h]Mt 2:11 [i]Ge 37:7,10
43:27 [j]ver 7
43:28 [k]Ge 37:7
43:29 [l]Ge 42:13 [m]Nu 6:25; Ps 67:1
43:30 [n]Jn 11:33,38 [o]Ge 42:24; 45:2,14,15; 46:29
43:31 [p]Ge 45:1
43:32 [q]Gal 2:12 [r]Ge 46:34; Ex 8:26
43:34 [s]Ge 37:3; 45:22

a *14* Hebrew *El-Shaddai*

43:14 God Almighty. See note on 17:1.
43:18 frightened. Since they were singled out from other buyers, the frightened brothers interpreted Joseph's "good" providence as evil. **seize us as slaves.** An ironic reflection of their own earlier treatment of Joseph.
43:23 It's all right. Literally, "Peace to you." Rites of greetings established social status and relationship. "Peace," repeated three times, was the key word in the brothers' new relationship with Joseph (see vv. 27,28 and their notes). **Your God, the God of your father.** This turning point in the relationship of the brothers toward Joseph was ostensibly spoken by a foreigner who trusted in their God. **Then he brought Simeon out.** Simeon's restoration depended on the reinstatement of the money, not on the return with Benjamin. The unexpected connection validates the brothers' interpretation that Joseph had placed the money in their sack to test their fidelity to their brother.
43:26 bowed down. See 37:5 and its note. At their first meeting they bowed in submission (42:6); now they bowed in homage, with tribute in hand (v. 28; Mt 2:11).
43:27 how they were. The Hebrew here is "peace."
43:28 well. The Hebrew here is "peace."
43:29 God be gracious. This was not a common greeting (33:5,11). **my son.** An assurance that they were family.
43:30 private room. These are still seen in burial chambers of important persons.
43:31 Serve the food. See note on 37:25.
43:32 Hebrews. See note on 39:14. **detestable to Egyptians.** Herein lies the clue to the rationale for the Egyptian sojourn. Whereas the Canaanites were willing to integrate and absorb the sons of Israel, the Egyptians held them in contempt. Judah's intermarriage with the Canaanites (ch. 38) reflected the danger that the Canaanites presented to the patriarchs. The segregated culture of Egypt guaranteed that the Israelites would develop into a distinct, great nation within Egypt's borders. The Egyptian threat would later take the form of tyranny (Ex 1).
43:34 Benjamin's portion was five times as much. This preferential treatment is comparable to the favoritism Jacob had shown Joseph. The brothers' character was still being tested (see Pr 23:1–3). **feasted and drank.** They passed the test.
■ **44:1–34** *Joseph's Third Test of His Brothers.* The brothers proved that they were genuinely changing when Judah led them in accepting God's just punishment (v. 16) and offered to become a

mouth of his sack.[t] 2 Then put my cup, the silver one, in the mouth of the youngest one's
sack, along with the silver for his grain." And he did as Joseph said.
3 As morning dawned, the men were sent on their way with their donkeys. 4 They had
not gone far from the city when Joseph said to his steward, "Go after those men at once,
and when you catch up with them, say to them, 'Why have you repaid good with evil?[u]
5 Isn't this the cup my master drinks from and also uses for divination?[v] This is a wicked thing you have done.' "
6 When he caught up with them, he repeated these words to them. 7 But they said to
him, "Why does my lord say such things? Far be it from your servants to do anything like
that! 8 We even brought back to you from the land of Canaan the silver we found inside
the mouths of our sacks.[w] So why would we steal silver or gold from your master's
house? 9 If any of your servants is found to have it, he will die;[x] and the rest of us will become my lord's slaves."
10 "Very well, then," he said, "let it be as you say. Whoever is found to have it will become my slave; the rest of you will be free from blame."
11 Each of them quickly lowered his sack to the ground and opened it. 12 Then the steward proceeded to search, beginning with the oldest and ending with the youngest. And
the cup was found in Benjamin's sack.[y] 13 At this, they tore their clothes.[z] Then they all
loaded their donkeys and returned to the city.
14 Joseph was still in the house when Judah and his brothers came in, and they threw
themselves to the ground before him.[a] 15 Joseph said to them, "What is this you have
done? Don't you know that a man like me can find things out by divination?[b]"
16 "What can we say to my lord?" Judah replied. "What can we say? How can we prove
our innocence? God has uncovered your servants' guilt. We are now my lord's slaves[c]—
we ourselves and the one who was found to have the cup.[d]"
17 But Joseph said, "Far be it from me to do such a thing! Only the man who was found
to have the cup will become my slave. The rest of you, go back to your father in peace."
18 Then Judah went up to him and said: "Please, my lord, let your servant speak a word
to my lord. Do not be angry[e] with your servant, though you are equal to Pharaoh himself. 19 My lord asked his servants, 'Do you have a father or a brother?'[f] 20 And we answered, 'We have an aged father, and there is a young son born to him in his old age.[g]
His brother is dead,[h] and he is the only one of his mother's sons left, and his father loves
him.'[i]
21 "Then you said to your servants, 'Bring him down to me so I can see him for myself.'[j]
22 And we said to my lord, 'The boy cannot leave his father; if he leaves him, his father
will die.'[k] 23 But you told your servants, 'Unless your youngest brother comes down with
you, you will not see my face again.'[l] 24 When we went back to your servant my father,
we told him what my lord had said.
25 "Then our father said, 'Go back and buy a little more food.'[m] 26 But we said, 'We cannot go down. Only if our youngest brother is with us will we go. We cannot see the man's
face unless our youngest brother is with us.'
27 "Your servant my father said to us, 'You know that my wife bore me two sons.[n]

44:1 [t]Ge 42:25
44:4 [u]Ps 35:12
44:5 [v]Ge 30:27; Dt 18:10-14
44:8 [w]Ge 42:25; 43:21
44:9 [x]Ge 31:32
44:12 [y]ver 2
44:13 [z]Ge 37:29; Nu 14:6; 2Sa 1:11
44:14 [a]Ge 37:7,10
44:15 [b]ver 5; Ge 30:27
44:16 [c]ver 9; Ge 43:18 [d]ver 2
44:18 [e]Ge 18:30; Ex 32:22
44:19 [f]Ge 43:7
44:20 [g]Ge 37:3 [h]Ge 37:33 [i]Ge 42:13
44:21 [j]Ge 42:15
44:22 [k]Ge 37:35
44:23 [l]Ge 43:5
44:25 [m]Ge 43:2
44:27 [n]Ge 46:19

slave in Benjamin's stead to spare their father additional misery (vv. 33–34).
44:1 Joseph gave these instructions. As God had tested the reality of Abraham's faith (22:1), so Joseph tested the genuineness of his once hateful brothers' conversion.
44:2 put my cup. Joseph put the brothers to the final test of family fidelity. **in the mouth of the youngest one's sack.** If they had been motivated by selfish interests, not the good of the family, the brothers, aware that slavery was a real possibility (see 43:18), would have voiced every possible reason to free themselves from slavery and abandon Benjamin. **youngest one's sack.** The original crime pertained to the selling of Joseph, Rachel's young son and Jacob's favorite, into slavery. Joseph brilliantly recreated the same grouping.
44:5 divination? This was a necessary part of the ruse (42:12). In reality, Joseph received revelation from God alone (see notes on v. 15; 41:16).
44:10 will become my slave. Joseph's modification of the brother's proposal (v. 9) was also necessary: The test pertained to their attitude toward his making Benjamin a slave (see note on v. 17). See *HC* 19.
44:13 they tore their clothes. Their actions confirmed their character change. All of the brothers showed affection for both their father and youngest brother. **all . . . returned.** All nine passed the test; they did not abandon their brother.
44:14 threw themselves. This time they bowed before Joseph with entreaties for mercy (see note on 43:26).
44:15 divination? Joseph's words were not to be taken at face value any more than his feigned anger. Ironically, divination could not distinguish between the guilty and the innocent (v. 5).
44:16 Judah replied. Judah made three points: He protested the brothers' innocence with regard to the theft, attributed their dilemma to God's judgment for previous guilt and offered all of the brothers as slaves. In that way he undid the rash oath to kill the guilty and avoided having to face their father without Benjamin. **God has uncovered your servants' guilt.** Judah could not have been referring to the cup, for he had just asserted their innocence. He was probably referring to their crime against Joseph. If so, the brothers confessed their crime against Joseph twice in his presence (42:21).
44:17 Only the man. The situation was now reconstructed. Would the brothers show compassion on their father and loyalty to Joseph's brother, his surrogate in the reconstructed scenario? See note on verse 10.
44:18 Judah. Representing all of the brothers (see note on 43:3).
44:19 father. This is the key word (used 14 times) in Judah's speech. Judah's appeal to Joseph to show mercy to his father demonstrated how much this rash brother had changed.
44:20 loves him. Jacob had not changed. He still doted upon his youngest son. But the brothers had experienced a conversion of affections.

28 One of them went away from me, and I said, "He has surely been torn to pieces."[o] And
I have not seen him since. 29 If you take this one from me too and harm comes to him, you
will bring my gray head down to the grave[a] in misery.'[p]
30 "So now, if the boy is not with us when I go back to your servant my father and if
my father, whose life is closely bound up with the boy's life,[q] 31 sees that the boy isn't
there, he will die. Your servants will bring the gray head of our father down to the grave
in sorrow. 32 Your servant guaranteed the boy's safety to my father. I said, 'If I do not bring
him back to you, I will bear the blame before you, my father, all my life!'[r]
33 "Now then, please let your servant remain here as my lord's slave[s] in place of the
boy,[t] and let the boy return with his brothers. 34 How can I go back to my father if the boy
is not with me? No! Do not let me see the misery that would come upon my father."[u]

Joseph Makes Himself Known

45 Then Joseph could no longer control himself[v] before all his attendants, and he
cried out, "Have everyone leave my presence!" So there was no one with Joseph
when he made himself known to his brothers. 2 And he wept[w] so loudly that the Egyptians heard him, and Pharaoh's household heard about it.[x]
3 Joseph said to his brothers, "I am Joseph! Is my father still living?"[y] But his brothers were not able to answer him,[z] because they were terrified at his presence.
4 Then Joseph said to his brothers, "Come close to me." When they had done so, he
said, "I am your brother Joseph, the one you sold into Egypt![a] 5 And now, do not be distressed[b] and do not be angry with yourselves for selling me here,[c] because it was to save
lives that God sent me ahead of you.[d] 6 For two years now there has been famine in the
land, and for the next five years there will not be plowing and reaping. 7 But God sent me
ahead of you to preserve for you a remnant[e] on earth and to save your lives by a great
deliverance.[b][f]
8 "So then, it was not you who sent me here, but God. He made me father[g] to Pharaoh, lord of his entire household and ruler of all Egypt.[h] 9 Now hurry back to my father
and say to him, 'This is what your son Joseph says: God has made me lord of all Egypt.
Come down to me; don't delay.[i] 10 You shall live in the region of Goshen[j] and be near
me—you, your children and grandchildren, your flocks and herds, and all you have. 11 I
will provide for you there,[k] because five years of famine are still to come. Otherwise you
and your household and all who belong to you will become destitute.'
12 "You can see for yourselves, and so can my brother Benjamin, that it is really I who
am speaking to you. 13 Tell my father about all the honor accorded me in Egypt and about
everything you have seen. And bring my father down here quickly.[l]"
14 Then he threw his arms around his brother Benjamin and wept, and Benjamin embraced him, weeping. 15 And he kissed[m] all his brothers and wept over them. Afterward
his brothers talked with him.[n]
16 When the news reached Pharaoh's palace that Joseph's brothers had come,[o] Pharaoh and all his officials were pleased. 17 Pharaoh said to Joseph, "Tell your brothers, 'Do

[a] 29 Hebrew *Sheol;* also in verse 31 [b] 7 Or *save you as a great band of survivors*

44:28 [o]Ge 37:33
44:29 [p]Ge 42:38
44:30 [q]1Sa 18:1
44:32 [r]Ge 43:9
44:33 [s]Ge 43:18 [t]Jn 15:13
44:34 [u]Est 8:6
45:1 [v]Ge 43:31
45:2 [w]Ge 29:11 [x]ver 16; Ge 46:29
45:3 [y]Ac 7:13 [z]ver 15
45:4 [a]Ge 37:28
45:5 [b]Ge 42:21 [c]Ge 42:22 [d]ver 7-8; Ge 50:20; Ps 105:17
45:7 [e]2Ki 19:4,30,31; Isa 10:20,21; Mic 4:7; Zep 2:7 [f]Ex 15:2; Est 4:14; Isa 25:9
45:8 [g]Jdg 17:10 [h]Ge 41:41
45:9 [i]Ge 43:10
45:10 [j]Ge 46:28,34; 47:1
45:11 [k]Ge 47:12
45:13 [l]Ac 7:14
45:15 [m]Lk 15:20 [n]ver 3
45:16 [o]Ac 7:13

44:33 in place of the boy. This was a different Judah from the one who had sold his brother into slavery (37:26–27). Judah's self-sacrificing love—there is none greater—prefigured the vicarious atonement of Christ, who by his voluntary sufferings mended the breach between God and human beings.
44:34 see the misery. A formerly coldhearted Judah (see 37:34–35) was now compassionate. In fact, Judah's love excelled (see 43:3).
■ **45:1–28** *Joseph's Reunion With His Brothers.* By faith Joseph gave a theological basis for the brothers to forgive each other by interpreting sins within the context of God's eternal purpose.
45:1 before all his attendants. The Egyptian wisdom literature prized men who controlled their emotions. Now Egypt's wisest man gave expression to a higher wisdom of authentic passion. **"Have everyone leave my presence!"** Heretofore Joseph had talked privately with his Egyptian steward (44:1–15); now he spoke behind closed doors with his brothers. In doing so he affiliated himself with the struggling covenant family, not with the riches of Egypt (Heb 11:22).
45:2 wept so loudly. Joseph wept in preparation for revealing his true identity, hidden beneath the Egyptian veneer.
45:3 I am Joseph! See Acts 7:13. **Is my father still living?** His burning question revealed his love for the covenant family. **not able to answer him.** The family was moving toward true intimacy, but as long as the brothers lived in fear of the one they had wronged and until they allowed themselves to be embraced by forgiveness, they could not find such closeness.
45:5 do not be angry with yourselves. Joseph directed their gaze away from their sins to God's grace (50:19; Nu 21:8–9). **to save lives.** Joseph rightly believed that God was using him to save countless people from starvation. He not only blessed his own people, but many other nations as well. **God sent me.** This statement, repeated three times (vv. 5,7–8), is the theological heart of the Joseph narrative (50:19–21; Ac 7:9–10). God directs all of the maze of human guilt to achieve his good and set purposes (Ac 2:23; 4:28).
45:6 For two years. Joseph was now 39 years old (41:46,53).
45:7 remnant. Joseph, believing in the promises of God for the covenant people, knew that God would always preserve a remnant in spite of adverse circumstances (50:25; Isa 10:20; 35:9; 37:32; Mic 2:12–13). See *WCF* 5.1; *WLC* 18.
45:8 it was not you. Joseph alleviated the guilt and shame of his converted brothers by viewing their crime against the broader picture of God's sovereign plan (see note on 44:16). **ruler.** Joseph's faith was validated by the dream at the beginning of his story (37:8). See *WLC* 124; *BC* 13.
45:9 God has made me lord of all Egypt. God had truly made the impossible possible (v. 26).
45:11 See *WLC* 127.

this: Load your animals and return to the land of Canaan, 18 and bring your father and
your families back to me. I will give you the best of the land of Egypt[p] and you can enjoy the fat of the land.'[q]

19 "You are also directed to tell them, 'Do this: Take some carts[r] from Egypt for your
children and your wives, and get your father and come. 20 Never mind about your belongings, because the best of all Egypt will be yours.' "

21 So the sons of Israel did this. Joseph gave them carts, as Pharaoh had commanded, and he also gave them provisions for their journey.[s] 22 To each of them he gave new
clothing, but to Benjamin he gave three hundred shekels[a] of silver and five sets of
clothes.[t] 23 And this is what he sent to his father: ten donkeys loaded with the best things
of Egypt, and ten female donkeys loaded with grain and bread and other provisions for
his journey. 24 Then he sent his brothers away, and as they were leaving he said to them,
"Don't quarrel on the way!"[u]

25 So they went up out of Egypt and came to their father Jacob in the land of Canaan.
26 They told him, "Joseph is still alive! In fact, he is ruler of all Egypt." Jacob was stunned;
he did not believe them.[v] 27 But when they told him everything Joseph had said to them,
and when he saw the carts[w] Joseph had sent to carry him back, the spirit of their father
Jacob revived. 28 And Israel said, "I'm convinced! My son Joseph is still alive. I will go and
see him before I die."

Jacob Goes to Egypt

46 So Israel set out with all that was his, and when he reached Beersheba,[x] he offered sacrifices to the God of his father Isaac.[y]
2 And God spoke to Israel in a vision at night[z] and said, "Jacob! Jacob!"

"Here I am,"[a] he replied.

3 "I am God, the God of your father,"[b] he said. "Do not be afraid to go down to Egypt,
for I will make you into a great nation[c] there.[d] 4 I will go down to Egypt with you, and I
will surely bring you back again.[e] And Joseph's own hand will close your eyes.[f]"

5 Then Jacob left Beersheba, and Israel's sons took their father Jacob and their children and their wives in the carts[g] that Pharaoh had sent to transport him. 6 They also
took with them their livestock and the possessions they had acquired in Canaan, and Jacob and all his offspring went to Egypt.[h] 7 He took with him to Egypt his sons and grandsons and his daughters and granddaughters—all his offspring.[i]

8 These are the names of the sons of Israel[j] (Jacob and his descendants) who went to
Egypt:

Reuben the firstborn of Jacob.

9 The sons of Reuben:[k]

Hanoch, Pallu, Hezron and Carmi.

10 The sons of Simeon:[l]

Jemuel,[m] Jamin, Ohad, Jakin, Zohar and Shaul the son of a Canaanite woman.

11 The sons of Levi:[n]

Gershon, Kohath and Merari.

12 The sons of Judah:[o]

Er, Onan, Shelah, Perez and Zerah (but Er and Onan had died in the land of Canaan).

45:18 [p]Ge 27:28; 46:34; 47:6,11,27; Nu 18:12,29 [q]Ps 37:19
45:19 [r]Ge 46:5
45:21 [s]Ge 42:25
45:22 [t]Ge 37:3; 43:34
45:24 [u]Ge 42:21-22
45:26 [v]Ge 44:28
45:27 [w]ver 19
46:1 [x]Ge 21:14; 28:10 [y]Ge 26:24; 28:13; 31:42
46:2 [z]Ge 15:1; Job 33:14-15 [a]Ge 22:1; 31:11
46:3 [b]Ge 28:13 [c]Ge 12:2; Dt 26:5 [d]Ex 1:7
46:4 [e]Ge 28:15; 48:21; Ex 3:8 [f]Ge 50:1,24
46:5 [g]Ge 15:19
46:6 [h]Dt 26:5; Jos 24:4; Ps 105:23; Isa 52:4; Ac 7:15
46:7 [i]Ge 45:10
46:8 [j]Ex 1:1; Nu 26:4
46:9 [k]1Ch 5:3
46:10 [l]Ge 29:33; Nu 26:14 [m]Ex 6:15
46:11 [n]Ge 29:34; Nu 3:17
46:12 [o]Ge 29:35

a *22* That is, about 7 1/2 pounds (about 3.5 kilograms)

45:22 he gave new clothing. In striking contrast to the brothers' act of stripping off Joseph's robe (37:23).
45:24 Don't quarrel. The theme of harmony appears in Joseph's instruction. The brothers were not to make recriminations against one another regarding their crime, especially in explaining it to their father. If Joseph had forgiven them, how much more should they forgive one another (Mt 18:21–35)?
■ **46:1–30** *The Patriarchs' Full Migration to Egypt.* The patriarchs and their father migrated to Egypt in harmony and peace with each other and with God.
46:1 Beersheba. At the southern border of the promised land. This was a liturgical site of importance to Abraham (21:32–33), Isaac (26:23–25) and Jacob (28:10–15).
46:2 God spoke. Once again, upon Jacob's departure from the promised land, God repeated his promise to be with Israel and to bring the people back (28:15). **in a vision.** The patriarchs functioned from time to time as prophets (e.g., 15:1). Scripture does not record that any of Jacob's 12 sons ever received a vision directly addressed to him with promises about seed and land.
46:3 I am God. God repeated his assuring promises to Isaac (26:24) and Jacob (28:13–15). **Do not be afraid.** See note on 42:1. **I will make you into a great nation there.** An elaboration of the promises to the fathers (12:2; 15:13–14; 17:20; 18:18; 21:13,18). See Exodus 1:7 for its fulfillment.
46:4 I will surely bring you back. Joseph repeated the promise at his death (50:24). **close your eyes.** See 50:1.
46:8–27 This catalog of sons closes the patriarchal period in Canaan and forms a transition to the exodus out of Egypt (Ex 1:1–7).
46:8 who went to Egypt. This catalog includes the sons of Benjamin, who were probably born in Egypt (vv. 21,27), just as the listing of those born in Paddan Aram (35:23–26) included Benjamin, who had obviously been born in Canaan (35:16–18,22).
46:10 Ohad. This name is omitted in the Septuagint (the Greek translation of the OT), Numbers 26:12–13 and 1 Chronicles 4:24. Its deletion brings the number to 33 (v. 15).

46:12 [p]1Ch 2:5; Mt 1:3
46:13 [q]Ge 30:18 [r]1Ch 7:1
46:14 [s]Ge 30:20
46:16 [t]Ge 30:11 [u]Nu 26:15
46:17 [v]Ge 30:13; 1Ch 7:30-31
46:18 [w]Ge 30:10 [x]Ge 29:24
46:19 [y]Ge 44:27
46:20 [z]Ge 41:51 [a]Ge 41:52
46:21 [b]Nu 26:38-41; 1Ch 7:6-12; 8:1

The sons of Perez:[p]
Hezron and Hamul.
13 The sons of Issachar:[q]
Tola, Puah,[a r] Jashub[b] and Shimron.
14 The sons of Zebulun:[s]
Sered, Elon and Jahleel.
15 These were the sons Leah bore to Jacob in Paddan Aram,[c] besides his daughter Dinah. These sons and daughters of his were thirty-three in all.

16 The sons of Gad:[t]
Zephon,[d u] Haggi, Shuni, Ezbon, Eri, Arodi and Areli.
17 The sons of Asher:[v]
Imnah, Ishvah, Ishvi and Beriah.
Their sister was Serah.
The sons of Beriah:
Heber and Malkiel.
18 These were the children born to Jacob by Zilpah,[w] whom Laban had given to his
daughter Leah[x]—sixteen in all.
19 The sons of Jacob's wife Rachel:
Joseph and Benjamin.[y] 20 In Egypt, Manasseh[z] and Ephraim[a] were born to Joseph by Asenath daughter of Potiphera, priest of On.[e]
21 The sons of Benjamin:[b]
Bela, Beker, Ashbel, Gera, Naaman, Ehi, Rosh, Muppim, Huppim and Ard.
22 These were the sons of Rachel who were born to Jacob—fourteen in all.

23 The son of Dan:
Hushim.

[a] *13* Samaritan Pentateuch and Syriac (see also 1 Chron. 7:1); Masoretic Text *Puvah* [b] *13* Samaritan Pentateuch and some Septuagint manuscripts (see also Num. 26:24 and 1 Chron. 7:1); Masoretic Text *Iob* [c] *15* That is, Northwest Mesopotamia [d] *16* Samaritan Pentateuch and Septuagint (see also Num. 26:15); Masoretic Text *Ziphion* [e] *20* That is, Heliopolis

46:15 Paddan Aram. See 25:20. **thirty-three.** Leah and her children together bore half of the 66 children (v. 26).
46:20 The Septuagint (the Greek translation of the OT) adds to the record five sons and grandsons of Manasseh and Ephraim (see note on v. 27).
46:21 Naaman . . . Ard. These are listed as grandsons of Benjamin in the Septuagint (the Greek translation of the OT) and in Numbers 26:38–40.

The Tribes of Israel

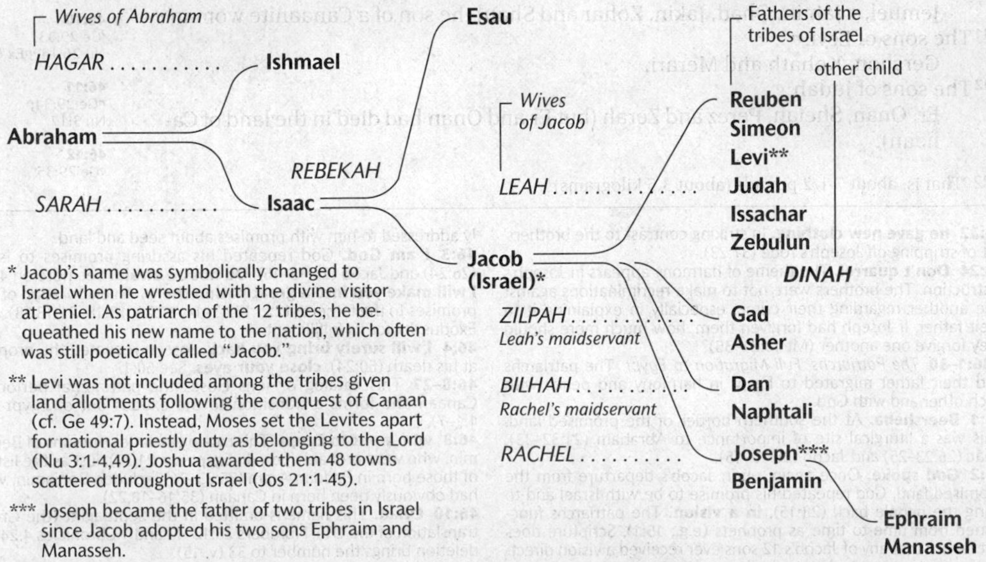

* Jacob's name was symbolically changed to Israel when he wrestled with the divine visitor at Peniel. As patriarch of the 12 tribes, he bequeathed his new name to the nation, which often was still poetically called "Jacob."

** Levi was not included among the tribes given land allotments following the conquest of Canaan (cf. Ge 49:7). Instead, Moses set the Levites apart for national priestly duty as belonging to the Lord (Nu 3:1-4,49). Joshua awarded them 48 towns scattered throughout Israel (Jos 21:1-45).

*** Joseph became the father of two tribes in Israel since Jacob adopted his two sons Ephraim and Manasseh.

24 The sons of Naphtali:
Jahziel, Guni, Jezer and Shillem.
25 These were the sons born to Jacob by Bilhah,[c] whom Laban had given to his daughter Rachel[d]—seven in all.

26 All those who went to Egypt with Jacob—those who were his direct descendants,
not counting his sons' wives—numbered sixty-six persons.[e] 27 With the two sons[a] who
had been born to Joseph in Egypt, the members of Jacob's family, which went to Egypt,
were seventy[b] in all.[f]

28 Now Jacob sent Judah ahead of him to Joseph to get directions to Goshen.[g] When
they arrived in the region of Goshen, 29 Joseph had his chariot made ready and went to
Goshen to meet his father Israel. As soon as Joseph appeared before him, he threw his
arms around his father[c] and wept for a long time.[h]
30 Israel said to Joseph, "Now I am ready to die, since I have seen for myself that you
are still alive."
31 Then Joseph said to his brothers and to his father's household, "I will go up and
speak to Pharaoh and will say to him, 'My brothers and my father's household, who were
living in the land of Canaan, have come to me.[i] 32 The men are shepherds; they tend livestock, and they have brought along their flocks and herds and everything they own.'
33 When Pharaoh calls you in and asks, 'What is your occupation?'[j] 34 you should answer,
'Your servants have tended livestock from our boyhood on, just as our fathers did.' Then
you will be allowed to settle in the region of Goshen,[k] for all shepherds are detestable
to the Egyptians.[l]"

47 Joseph went and told Pharaoh, "My father and brothers, with their flocks and
herds and everything they own, have come from the land of Canaan and are
now in Goshen."[m] 2 He chose five of his brothers and presented them before Pharaoh.
3 Pharaoh asked the brothers, "What is your occupation?"[n]
"Your servants are shepherds," they replied to Pharaoh, "just as our fathers were."
4 They also said to him, "We have come to live here awhile,[o] because the famine is severe in Canaan[p] and your servants' flocks have no pasture. So now, please let your servants settle in Goshen."[q]
5 Pharaoh said to Joseph, "Your father and your brothers have come to you, 6 and the
land of Egypt is before you; settle your father and your brothers in the best part of the
land.[r] Let them live in Goshen. And if you know of any among them with special ability,[s] put them in charge of my own livestock."
7 Then Joseph brought his father Jacob in and presented him before Pharaoh. After Jacob blessed[d] Pharaoh,[t] 8 Pharaoh asked him, "How old are you?"
9 And Jacob said to Pharaoh, "The years of my pilgrimage are a hundred and thirty.[u]
My years have been few and difficult,[v] and they do not equal the years of the pilgrimage
of my fathers.[w]" 10 Then Jacob blessed[e] Pharaoh[x] and went out from his presence.
11 So Joseph settled his father and his brothers in Egypt and gave them property in the
best part of the land, the district of Rameses,[y] as Pharaoh directed. 12 Joseph also pro-

46:25 [c]Ge 30:8 [d]Ge 29:29
46:26 [e]ver 5-7; Ex 1:5; Dt 10:22
46:27 [f]Ac 7:14
46:28 [g]Ge 45:10
46:29 [h]Ge 45:14-15; Lk 15:20
46:31 [i]Ge 47:1
46:33 [j]Ge 47:3
46:34 [k]Ge 45:10 [l]Ge 43:32; Ex 8:26
47:1 [m]Ge 46:31
47:3 [n]Ge 46:33
47:4 [o]Ge 15:13; Dt 26:5 [p]Ge 43:1 [q]Ge 46:34
47:6 [r]Ge 45:18 [s]Ex 18:21, 25
47:7 [t]ver 10; 2Sa 14:22
47:9 [u]Ge 25:7 [v]Heb 11:9, 13 [w]Ge 35:28
47:10 [x]ver 7
47:11 [y]Ex 1:11; 12:37

[a] 27 Hebrew; Septuagint *the nine children* [b] 27 Hebrew (see also Exodus 1:5 and footnote); Septuagint (see also Acts 7:14) *seventy-five* [c] 29 Hebrew *around him* [d] 7 Or *greeted* [e] 10 Or *said farewell to*

46:25 seven. The progeny of Rachel's maidservant Bilhah accounted for precisely half the number for Rachel (v. 22), as the number of Zilpah's descendants was about half the number for Leah's (v. 18).

46:26 sixty-six. Er and Onan, who died in Canaan (v. 12), and Manasseh and Ephraim, who were born in Egypt (v. 27), reduce the number of the 70 sons of Jacob to 66.

46:27 seventy. The family is represented ideally as consisting of 70, the multiple of two perfect numbers (see note on 10:1–32; see also 36:23–26; Ex 24:1; Dt 10:22; 32:8). In Acts 7:14 (based on the Septuagint, the Greek OT), the sum is 75 (see note on 46:20). To achieve the ideal number, Jacob and Joseph are excluded, and others are included.

■ **46:31—47:28** *The Patriarchs' Preservation in Goshen.* Through Joseph's wisdom God preserved Israel in Goshen, both physically (by providing food and land) and spiritually (by providing for the family's isolation from the Egyptians) until their exodus (Ps 105:16–22). Under Jacob's blessing on Pharaoh and Pharaoh's honoring of Israel, everyone prospered: Pharaoh gained control of all the property and people in Egypt, the Egyptians hailed Joseph as a savior and, remarkably, the Israelites prospered even more than the Egyptians. This mutual blessing and prosperity contrasts with the situation 400 years later, when another pharaoh cursed Israel and was himself cursed as a result.

46:32 shepherds. Joseph emphasized that his family members were shepherds in order to assure Pharaoh that they entertained no social or political ambitions under their brother's aegis and to preserve them from an alien way of life and intermarriage with the Egyptians (see note on 34:9). The latter threat was more acute in conjunction with the possession of property in Egypt (see v. 11).

47:6 put them in charge. Within their own trade they could advance socially in Pharaoh's court.

47:7 blessed. This word also appears in verse 10. See 1:22, 12:2, 24:60 and 28:1. The patriarch demonstrated his dignity, for the greater blessed the lesser (see note on 14:19). His blessing was fulfilled in verses 13–25.

47:9 pilgrimage. Jacob was on a pilgrimage to the city that will come from heaven (Dt 26:5; Heb 11:9–10), the city of God's kingdom in its full glory. **few and difficult.** He did not glory in the number of his years. Though blessed, he had endured his share of human afflictions.

47:11 gave them property in the best part of the land. This was more than they had asked for, and it remarkably differentiated the covenant people from the Egyptians (v. 27). **Rameses.** A mod-

vided his father and his brothers and all his father's household with food, according to the number of their children.[z]

Joseph and the Famine

13 There was no food, however, in the whole region because the famine was severe; both Egypt and Canaan wasted away because of the famine.[a] 14 Joseph collected all the money that was to be found in Egypt and Canaan in payment for the grain they were buying, and he brought it to Pharaoh's palace.[b] 15 When the money of the people of Egypt and Canaan was gone, all Egypt came to Joseph and said, "Give us food. Why should we die before your eyes?[c] Our money is used up."

16 "Then bring your livestock," said Joseph. "I will sell you food in exchange for your livestock, since your money is gone." 17 So they brought their livestock to Joseph, and he gave them food in exchange for their horses,[d] their sheep and goats, their cattle and donkeys. And he brought them through that year with food in exchange for all their livestock.

18 When that year was over, they came to him the following year and said, "We cannot hide from our lord the fact that since our money is gone and our livestock belongs to you, there is nothing left for our lord except our bodies and our land. 19 Why should we perish before your eyes—we and our land as well? Buy us and our land in exchange for food, and we with our land will be in bondage to Pharaoh. Give us seed so that we may live and not die, and that the land may not become desolate."

20 So Joseph bought all the land in Egypt for Pharaoh. The Egyptians, one and all, sold their fields, because the famine was too severe for them. The land became Pharaoh's, 21 and Joseph reduced the people to servitude,[a] from one end of Egypt to the other. 22 However, he did not buy the land of the priests, because they received a regular allotment from Pharaoh and had food enough from the allotment[e] Pharaoh gave them. That is why they did not sell their land.

23 Joseph said to the people, "Now that I have bought you and your land today for Pharaoh, here is seed for you so you can plant the ground. 24 But when the crop comes in, give a fifth[f] of it to Pharaoh. The other four-fifths you may keep as seed for the fields and as food for yourselves and your households and your children."

25 "You have saved our lives," they said. "May we find favor in the eyes of our lord;[g] we will be in bondage to Pharaoh."

26 So Joseph established it as a law concerning land in Egypt—still in force today—that a fifth of the produce belongs to Pharaoh. It was only the land of the priests that did not become Pharaoh's.[h]

27 Now the Israelites settled in Egypt in the region of Goshen. They acquired property there and were fruitful and increased greatly in number.[i]

28 Jacob lived in Egypt[j] seventeen years, and the years of his life were a hundred and forty-seven. 29 When the time drew near for Israel to die,[k] he called for his son Joseph and said to him, "If I have found favor in your eyes, put your hand under my thigh[l] and promise that you will show me kindness and faithfulness.[m] Do not bury me in Egypt, 30 but when I rest with my fathers, carry me out of Egypt and bury me where they are buried."[n]

"I will do as you say," he said.

47:12 [z]Ge 45:11
47:13 [a]Ge 41:30; Ac 7:11
47:14 [b]Ge 41:56
47:15 [c]ver 19; Ex 16:3
47:17 [d]Ex 14:9
47:22 [e]Dt 14:28-29; Ezr 7:24
47:24 [f]Ge 41:34
47:25 [g]Ge 32:5
47:26 [h]ver 22
47:27 [i]Ge 17:6; 46:3; Ex 1:7
47:28 [j]Ps 105:23
47:29 [k]Dt 31:14 [l]Ge 24:2 [m]Ge 24:49
47:30 [n]Ge 49:29-32; 50:5,13; Ac 7:15-16

[a] *21* Samaritan Pentateuch and Septuagint (see also Vulgate); Masoretic Text *and he moved the people into the cities*

---

ernization for Goshen (45:10), possibly named after Rameses II (c. 1300 B.C.). Also called the region of Zoan (Ps 78:12,43).

47:12 See *WLC* 127.

47:13–26 Because Pharaoh had obeyed the divine revelation (ch. 41) and blessed Joseph (see 12:3 and its note), Joseph brought all the money, cattle, land and people in Egypt under Pharaoh's control and preserved the Egyptians. Joseph's beneficent policies contrast sharply with the curse on the pharaoh who later oppressed Israel (Ex 1:8ff.).

47:14,20 See *WLC* 141; *WSC* 74.

47:25–26 saved our lives. The Egyptians regarded Joseph as a savior (45:7), not a tyrant.

47:27 They acquired property. The independence and prosperity of the Israelites stood in striking contrast to the fate of the Egyptians (see notes on vv. 13–26). **increased greatly.** A link with Exodus 1:7.

■ **47:29—50:26** *The Patriarchs' Future in the Land.* With the patriarchs safe and living harmoniously in Egypt, attention turns to the most important aspect of this story: the future relations of the patriarchs and their tribes. These materials divide into two parts: a focus on Jacob (47:29—50:14) and a focus on Joseph (50:15–26).

■ **47:29—50:14** *Jacob and the Land.* As Jacob reached the end of his life, his heart turned back to the promised land. He requested that he be buried there (47:29–31), predicted his sons' roles there (48:1—49:28) and was eventually laid to rest there (49:29—50:14).

■ **47:29–31** *Jacob's Burial Request.* Jacob insisted that he not be buried in Egypt. He had not given up on God's promise to establish his covenant people in the promised land.

47:29 Joseph. Jacob elaborated on the command to all his sons in 49:29–32, but Joseph was in charge. **put your hand under my thigh.** See note on 24:2. Jacob later enjoined the same wish upon Joseph's brothers (49:29–32). **kindness and faithfulness.** Covenant loyalty entailed that the party in the stronger social position do what was right by the weaker; in this case, that the living bury the dead according to the covenantal promises regarding the promised land.

47:30 where they are buried. By faith Jacob staked his destiny in the promised land, not in embalmment in the land of Egypt (v. 11; 50:2).

31 "Swear to me,"[o] he said. Then Joseph swore to him,[p] and Israel worshiped as he
leaned on the top of his staff.[a][q]

Manasseh and Ephraim

48 Some time later Joseph was told, "Your father is ill." So he took his two sons Manasseh and Ephraim[r] along with him. 2 When Jacob was told, "Your son Joseph
has come to you," Israel rallied his strength and sat up on the bed.
3 Jacob said to Joseph, "God Almighty[b] appeared to me at Luz[s] in the land of Canaan,
and there he blessed me[t] 4 and said to me, 'I am going to make you fruitful and will increase your numbers.[u] I will make you a community of peoples, and I will give this land
as an everlasting possession to your descendants after you.'
5 "Now then, your two sons born to you in Egypt[v] before I came to you here will be
reckoned as mine; Ephraim and Manasseh will be mine,[w] just as Reuben and Simeon are
mine. 6 Any children born to you after them will be yours; in the territory they inherit they
will be reckoned under the names of their brothers. 7 As I was returning from Paddan,[c]
to my sorrow Rachel died in the land of Canaan while we were still on the way, a little
distance from Ephrath. So I buried her there beside the road to Ephrath" (that is, Bethlehem).[x]
8 When Israel saw the sons of Joseph, he asked, "Who are these?"
9 "They are the sons God has given me here,"[y] Joseph said to his father.
Then Israel said, "Bring them to me so I may bless[z] them."
10 Now Israel's eyes were failing because of old age, and he could hardly see.[a] So Joseph brought his sons close to him, and his father kissed them[b] and embraced them.
11 Israel said to Joseph, "I never expected to see your face again, and now God has allowed me to see your children too."[c]
12 Then Joseph removed them from Israel's knees and bowed down with his face to the
ground. 13 And Joseph took both of them, Ephraim on his right toward Israel's left hand
and Manasseh on his left toward Israel's right hand,[d] and brought them close to him.
14 But Israel reached out his right hand and put it on Ephraim's head, though he was the
younger, and crossing his arms, he put his left hand on Manasseh's head, even though
Manasseh was the firstborn.[e]
15 Then he blessed[f] Joseph and said,

> "May the God before whom my fathers
> Abraham and Isaac walked,
> the God who has been my shepherd[g]
> all my life to this day,

47:31 [o]Ge 21:23 [p]Ge 24:3 [q]Heb 11:21 *fn* 1Ki 1:47
48:1 [r]Ge 41:52
48:3 [s]Ge 28:19 [t]Ge 28:13; 35:9-12
48:4 [u]Ge 17:6
48:5 [v]Ge 41:50-52; 46:20 [w]1Ch 5:1; Jos 14:4
48:7 [x]Ge 35:19
48:9 [y]Ge 33:5 [z]Ge 27:4
48:10 [a]Ge 27:1 [b]Ge 27:27
48:11 [c]Ge 50:23; Ps 128:6
48:13 [d]Ps 110:1
48:14 [e]Ge 41:51
48:15 [f]Ge 17:1 [g]Ge 49:24

[a] *31* Or *Israel bowed down at the head of his bed* [b] 3 Hebrew *El-Shaddai* [c] 7 That is, Northwest Mesopotamia

---

47:31 swore to him. For the fulfillment of his oath, see 50:1–14. **worshiped.** In thankful praise that his last wish would be fulfilled.

■ **48:1—49:28** *Jacob's Blessings on His Sons.* Jacob prepared his sons for future life in the land by pronouncing blessings on them.

48:1 So he took. Joseph would receive the rights of firstborn, the double portion, through Jacob's adoption and elevation of Joseph's two sons to the status of founding fathers among Israel's 12 tribes. The adoption ritual included Jacob's statement of authority (vv. 3–4), his intention to adopt Ephraim and Manasseh (vv. 5–7), his legal gestures (vv. 8–12) and his words of blessing (vv. 15–16).

48:3 God Almighty. See note on 17:1. **appeared.** Because of God's direct revelation to Jacob, not to Joseph, Jacob could legitimate Joseph's two sons as numbered among his own 12 sons. His preferential treatment of Joseph, giving him the double portion, reasserted God's sovereignty to do as he pleased with Israel. **at Luz.** See notes on 28:10–22. **blessed.** See 47:7 and 10. God's blessing on Jacob empowered him to bless the 12 tribes (48:5—49:28). Through these patriarchal blessings, characters in these chapters were linked to the original audience of Genesis.

48:4 community of peoples. See note on 28:3. **land . . . descendants.** See note on 12:7.

48:5 Ephraim and Manasseh. The younger was again preferred over the older (v. 20; 25:23). **Reuben and Simeon.** The first two sons of Leah are mentioned because they were bypassed by Jacob in order to give the double portion to Joseph, Rachel's firstborn. Reuben lost his rights because he had defiled his father's marriage bed (49:3–4).

48:6 will be yours. In contrast to Ephraim and Manasseh, who were now reckoned as Jacob's. **in the territory.** Joseph's double portion in the land, implemented by Jacob's adoption of his two sons, was grasped by faith.

48:7 Paddan. See 25:20. **Rachel.** Although Leah was buried in the family grave, Rachel was honored and memorialized in the double portion given her firstborn. **we were still on the way.** See note on 35:24.

48:8 Who are these? This question, which identified the beneficiaries, was part of the ritual.

48:9 God has given. Joseph gave the same answer as Jacob had given Esau to the same question; he shared his father's faith (see note on 33:5; see also 41:50–52).

48:10 kissed. The ritual of Isaac's blessing of Jacob was repeated between Jacob and Joseph's two sons (27:26).

48:11 God has allowed. In the blessing to be given, Jacob's perspective shifted from God's miraculous blessings on him in Egypt (see 45:26) to the greater blessings to come upon the 12 tribes upon their return to the promised land.

48:12 from Israel's knees. See note on 30:3. **bowed . . . to the ground.** The one equal to Pharaoh (44:18) humbled himself before the patriarch who mediated God's promises.

48:14 right hand. In the ancient Near East, oral statements were accompanied by the correct placement of the right hand, an action that functioned as a legal safeguard.

48:15 blessed. See verse 3. Later the blessing was mediated to all Israel through the priest (Nu 6:24–26). **Joseph.** He was represented through his two sons. In 49:22 Joseph was also blessed with fertility, but without distinguishing his two sons. **before whom my fathers . . . walked.** See note on 17:1.

7 Cursed be their anger, so fierce,
and their fury, so cruel!
I will scatter them in Jacob
and disperse them in Israel.[b]

8 "Judah,[a] your brothers will praise you;
your hand will be on the neck of your enemies;
your father's sons will bow down to you.[c]
9 You are a lion's[d] cub, O Judah;[e]
you return from the prey, my son.
Like a lion he crouches and lies down,
like a lioness—who dares to rouse him?
10 The scepter will not depart from Judah,[f]
nor the ruler's staff from between his feet,
until he comes to whom it belongs[b]
and the obedience of the nations is his.[g]
11 He will tether his donkey to a vine,
his colt to the choicest branch;
he will wash his garments in wine,
his robes in the blood of grapes.
12 His eyes will be darker than wine,
his teeth whiter than milk.[c]

13 "Zebulun[h] will live by the seashore
and become a haven for ships;
his border will extend toward Sidon.

14 "Issachar[i] is a rawboned[d] donkey
lying down between two saddlebags.[e]
15 When he sees how good is his resting place
and how pleasant is his land,
he will bend his shoulder to the burden
and submit to forced labor.

16 "Dan[f][j] will provide justice for his people
as one of the tribes of Israel.
17 Dan[k] will be a serpent by the roadside,
a viper along the path,
that bites the horse's heels
so that its rider tumbles backward.

18 "I look for your deliverance, O LORD.[l]

19 "Gad[g][m] will be attacked by a band of raiders,
but he will attack them at their heels.

49:7 [b]Jos 19:1,9; 21:1-42
49:8 [c]Dt 33:7; 1Ch 5:2
49:9 [d]Nu 24:9; Eze 19:5; Mic 5:8 [e]Rev 5:5
49:10 [f]Nu 24:17,19; Ps 60:7 [g]Ps 2:9; Isa 42:1,4
49:13 [h]Ge 30:20; Dt 33:18-19; Jos 19:10-11
49:14 [i]Ge 30:18
49:16 [j]Ge 30:6; Dt 33:22; Jdg 18:26-27
49:17 [k]Jdg 18:27
49:18 [l]Ps 119:166,174
49:19 [m]Ge 30:11; Dt 33:20; 1Ch 5:18

a *8 Judah* sounds like and may be derived from the Hebrew for *praise.* b *10* Or *until Shiloh comes;* or *until he comes to whom tribute belongs* c *12* Or *will be dull from wine, / his teeth white from milk* d *14* Or *strong* e *14* Or *campfires* f *16 Dan* here means *he provides justice.* g *19 Gad* can mean *attack* and *band of raiders.*

49:8 Judah. See note on 29:35. **father's sons will bow down to you.** As Esau did before Isaac (25:23; 27:29) and as the brothers did before Joseph (43:26), the tribes would bow down to Judah because of his heroic deeds (2Sa 5:1–3).
49:9 lion. The most powerful and daring beast of prey was a symbol of kingship in the ancient Near East. Judah's greatest royal descendant, Jesus Christ, is called "the Lion of the tribe of Judah" (Rev 5:5). **who dares to rouse him?** The lion inspires such fear (Nu 24:9).
49:10–12 The blessedness of the ideal ruler was evidenced in his victories (v. 10), fertility (v. 11) and beauty (v. 12; Ps 45).
49:10 scepter. See note on Numbers 24:17. **not depart.** This prophecy was confirmed by the Davidic covenant (2Sa 7:16). **until he comes to whom it belongs.** An ancient Aramaic translation interprets this as "until the Messiah comes, whose is the kingdom, and him shall the nations obey." This prediction was not fulfilled among David's descendants until the birth of Jesus Christ (Eze 21:27; Rev 5:5). God's plan for humanity to rule and exercise dominion (1:26–28) is fulfilled in Jesus. **obedience of the nations is his.** See 27:29 and its note. See *WCF* 19.4; *WLC* 45.
49:11 donkey. The king's mount (Zec 9:9). **vine.** Fertility was described under the imagery of the noble vine. **wine.** Jesus signified that the fulfillment of this prophecy was at hand by changing water into wine (Jn 2:1–11).
49:13 Zebulun. See 30:20, Joshua 19:10–16 and Judges 5:18.
49:14 Issachar. See 30:18. **saddlebags.** In Judges 5:16 the NIV reverses what appears here in the text and the text note. Some think that the Hebrew here means "cattle pens" or "sheepfolds."
49:15 forced labor. Although Issachar was praised in Judges 5:15, here the tribe was blamed for its willingness to trade its liberty for forced labor in order to enjoy material goods (Jos 16:10; Jdg 1:28, 30,33).
49:16 Dan. See 30:6. **provide justice.** That is, execute judgment.
49:17 a serpent. Though small, Dan was dangerous and later struck unexpectedly to overthrow larger nations (Jdg 18). Samson, who was from this tribe, single-handedly struck down the Philistines (Jdg 14–16).
49:18 Jacob's prayer stands in the middle of the oracles.
49:19 Gad. See 30:11. Four of the six Hebrew words here sound like *Gad,* using Hebrew roots meaning "fortune," "cut off" and "overcome/attack." Gad was constantly in danger from its southern and eastern neighbors.

20 “Asher’s[n] food will be rich;
he will provide delicacies fit for a king.

21 “Naphtali[o] is a doe set free
that bears beautiful fawns.[a]

22 “Joseph[p] is a fruitful vine,
a fruitful vine near a spring,
whose branches climb over a wall.[b]
23 With bitterness archers attacked him;
they shot at him with hostility.[q]
24 But his bow remained steady,
his strong arms[r] stayed[c] limber,
because of the hand of the Mighty One of Jacob,[s]
because of the Shepherd, the Rock of Israel,[t]
25 because of your father’s God,[u] who helps you,
because of the Almighty,[d] who blesses you
with blessings of the heavens above,
blessings of the deep that lies below,[v]
blessings of the breast and womb.
26 Your father’s blessings are greater
than the blessings of the ancient mountains,
than[e] the bounty of the age-old hills.
Let all these rest on the head of Joseph,
on the brow of the prince among[f] his brothers.[w]

27 “Benjamin[x] is a ravenous wolf;
in the morning he devours the prey,
in the evening he divides the plunder.”

28 All these are the twelve tribes of Israel, and this is what their father said to them
when he blessed them, giving each the blessing appropriate to him.

The Death of Jacob

29 Then he gave them these instructions:[y] “I am about to be gathered to my people.[z]
Bury me with my fathers[a] in the cave in the field of Ephron the Hittite, 30 the cave in the
field of Machpelah,[b] near Mamre in Canaan, which Abraham bought as a burial place
from Ephron the Hittite, along with the field.[c] 31 There Abraham[d] and his wife Sarah[e]
were buried, there Isaac and his wife Rebekah[f] were buried, and there I buried Leah.
32 The field and the cave in it were bought from the Hittites.[g]”
33 When Jacob had finished giving instructions to his sons, he drew his feet up into the
bed, breathed his last and was gathered to his people.[g]

50

Joseph threw himself upon his father and wept over him and kissed him.[h]
2 Then Joseph directed the physicians in his service to embalm his father Israel.
So the physicians embalmed him,[i] 3 taking a full forty days, for that was the time required
for embalming. And the Egyptians mourned for him seventy days.[j]

49:20 [n]Ge 30:13; Dt 33:24
49:21 [o]Ge 30:8; Dt 33:23
49:22 [p]Ge 30:24; Dt 33:13-17
49:23 [q]Ge 37:24
49:24 [r]Ps 18:34 [s]Ps 132:2,5; Isa 1:24; 41:10 [t]Isa 28:16
49:25 [u]Ge 28:13 [v]Ge 27:28
49:26 [w]Dt 33:15-16
49:27 [x]Ge 35:18; Jdg 20:12-13
49:29 [y]Ge 50:16 [z]Ge 25:8 [a]Ge 15:15; 47:30; 50:13
49:30 [b]Ge 23:9 [c]Ge 23:20
49:31 [d]Ge 25:9 [e]Ge 23:19 [f]Ge 35:29
49:33 [g]ver 29; Ge 25:8; Ac 7:15
50:1 [h]Ge 46:4
50:2 [i]ver 26; 2Ch 16:14
50:3 [j]Ge 37:34; Nu 20:29; Dt 34:8

[a] *21* Or *free; / he utters beautiful words* [b] *22* Or *Joseph is a wild colt, / a wild colt near a spring, / a wild donkey on a terraced hill* [c] *23,24* Or *archers will attack . . . will shoot . . . will remain . . . will stay* [d] *25* Hebrew *Shaddai* [e] *26* Or *of my progenitors, / as great as* [f] *26* Or *the one separated from* [g] *32* Or *the sons of Heth*

49:20 Asher’s. See 30:13. **food will be rich.** A reference to its fertile land (Dt 33:24; Jos 19:24–31).
49:21 Naphtali. See 30:8 and Joshua 19:32–38.
49:22 Joseph. See 30:24 and 48:15–20. **fruitful.** Barren Rachel would produce the most fruitful tribe (see 30:2,22; 41:52 and NIV text note). **climb over a wall.** For the expansion of their territory, see Joshua 17:14–18.
49:24–25 The multiplication of names and titles for God is striking.
49:24 Mighty One of Jacob. See Isaiah 49:26. **Shepherd.** See 48:15–16. **Rock.** Israel’s sure defense (Dt 32:4,15,18).
49:25 blesses. The Hebrew root for “bless/blessing” is used six times in this verse. The blessings were fertility of land fed by beneficent water from the heavens above and from the earth below (see 1:6–8 and its note) and fertility of body (“breast and womb”; see 1:22; Nu 24:5–7).
49:26 blessings of the ancient mountains. See Deuteronomy 33:15. **Let . . . brothers.** The movement of blessing was from God to the head of Joseph (repeated in Dt 33:16). **prince.** The Hebrew word here designates one who is consecrated to special acts; it is never used of a king.
49:27 Benjamin. See 35:18. **wolf.** It kills more than it can eat. **divides the plunder.** He was so successful he could share the prey.
49:28 See *WLC* 129.
■ **49:29—50:14** *Jacob’s Death and Burial in Canaan.* Believing in God’s promises to Abraham and Isaac to give them the promised land, Jacob arranged for his burial to be in Canaan, not in Egypt.
49:29 these instructions. See 47:29–31 and its notes. Two texts (47:29–31 and 49:29–33) form a frame around the blessing on the 12 tribes (which includes the adoption of Ephraim and Manasseh). The first announces Jacob’s death, while the second recounts it. **in the cave.** See note on 25:9.
49:31 All the patriarchs died in faith, none having yet obtained the promises (Heb 11:39–40).
49:33 drew his feet up into the bed. See 48:2, where the scene begins.
50:2 to embalm. The embalming assisted the journey.

4When the days of mourning had passed, Joseph said to Pharaoh's court, "If I have
found favor in your eyes, speak to Pharaoh for me. Tell him, 5'My father made me swear
an oath[k] and said, "I am about to die; bury me in the tomb I dug for myself[l] in the land
of Canaan."[m] Now let me go up and bury my father; then I will return.' "
6Pharaoh said, "Go up and bury your father, as he made you swear to do."
7So Joseph went up to bury his father. All Pharaoh's officials accompanied him—the
dignitaries of his court and all the dignitaries of Egypt— 8besides all the members of Joseph's household and his brothers and those belonging to his father's household. Only
their children and their flocks and herds were left in Goshen. 9Chariots and horsemen[a]
also went up with him. It was a very large company.
10When they reached the threshing floor of Atad, near the Jordan, they lamented
loudly and bitterly;[n] and there Joseph observed a seven-day period[o] of mourning for his
father. 11When the Canaanites who lived there saw the mourning at the threshing floor
of Atad, they said, "The Egyptians are holding a solemn ceremony of mourning." That
is why that place near the Jordan is called Abel Mizraim.[b]
12So Jacob's sons did as he had commanded them: 13They carried him to the land of
Canaan and buried him in the cave in the field of Machpelah, near Mamre, which Abraham had bought as a burial place from Ephron the Hittite, along with the field.[p] 14After
burying his father, Joseph returned to Egypt, together with his brothers and all the others who had gone with him to bury his father.

Joseph Reassures His Brothers

15When Joseph's brothers saw that their father was dead, they said, "What if Joseph
holds a grudge against us and pays us back for all the wrongs we did to him?"[q] 16So they
sent word to Joseph, saying, "Your father left these instructions before he died: 17'This
is what you are to say to Joseph: I ask you to forgive your brothers the sins and the
wrongs they committed in treating you so badly.' Now please forgive the sins of the servants of the God of your father." When their message came to him, Joseph wept.
18His brothers then came and threw themselves down before him.[r] "We are your
slaves,"[s] they said.
19But Joseph said to them, "Don't be afraid. Am I in the place of God?[t] 20You intended to harm me,[u] but God intended[v] it for good[w] to accomplish what is now being done,
the saving of many lives.[x] 21So then, don't be afraid. I will provide for you and your children.[y]" And he reassured them and spoke kindly to them.

The Death of Joseph

22Joseph stayed in Egypt, along with all his father's family. He lived a hundred and ten
years[z] 23and saw the third generation[a] of Ephraim's children. Also the children of Makir[b] son of Manasseh were placed at birth on Joseph's knees.[c]
24Then Joseph said to his brothers, "I am about to die.[c] But God will surely come to
your aid[d] and take you up out of this land to the land[e] he promised on oath to Abra-

50:5 [k]Ge 47:31 [l]2Ch 16:14; Isa 22:16 [m]Ge 47:31
50:10 [n]2Sa 1:17; Ac 8:2 [o]1Sa 31:13; Job 2:13
50:13 [p]Ge 23:20; Ac 7:16
50:15 [q]Ge 37:28; 42:21-22
50:18 [r]Ge 37:7 [s]Ge 43:18
50:19 [t]Ro 12:19; Heb 10:30
50:20 [u]Ge 37:20 [v]Mic 4:11-12 [w]Ro 8:28 [x]Ge 45:5
50:21 [y]Ge 45:11; 47:12
50:22 [z]Ge 25:7; Jos 24:29
50:23 [a]Job 42:16 [b]Nu 32:39,40
50:24 [c]Ge 48:21 [d]Ex 3:16-17 [e]Ge 15:14

[a] *9* Or *charioteers* [b] *11* *Abel Mizraim* means *mourning of the Egyptians.* [c] *23* That is, were counted as his

50:4 to Pharaoh's court. Perhaps he could not speak directly to Pharaoh because of the mourning rites.
50:5 I dug for myself. Joseph repeated Jacob's instructions in words that Pharaoh understood.
50:6 Go up. A rehearsal for their future exodus (v. 24).
50:7–11 The royal procession elevated Israel; he was buried like a king.
50:9 Chariots and horsemen. A striking contrast with the Mosaic exodus (Ex 14:9; 15:4–5).
50:14 returned to Egypt. The famine was not yet over and the iniquity of the Amorites not yet complete enough to bring down God's judgment (15:13–16).
■ **50:15–26** *Joseph and the Land.* After Jacob died, Joseph directed the attention of the tribal patriarchs toward the promised land. He reassured them of their safety in Egypt (vv. 15–21) and of their future in the land (vv. 22–26).
■ **50:15–21** *Joseph's Reassurance.* Joseph's brothers feared that Joseph would seek vengeance once their father had died. Joseph assured them of their safety.
50:17 servants of the God of your father. The brothers based their case for forgiveness on their worship of the same family God.
50:19 Don't be afraid. See 43:23 and 45:5. **Am I in the place of God?** Only God could have designed their evil in order to accomplish good. Joseph directed the nation's attention away from himself to the sovereign God who ruled their history, even when they lacked a charismatic leader such as Joseph or Moses.
50:20 You intended to harm me, but God intended it for good. A classic statement of God's sovereignty (see notes on 24:27; 45:5,7–8). **the saving of many lives.** In Egypt and Canaan. See *WCF* 5.4; *BC* 13.
50:21 I will provide. The famine was not yet over.
■ **50:22–26** *Joseph's Final Words and Death.* As he died, Joseph encouraged the Israelites in Egypt not to give up on God's promise of a return to the land of promise.
50:22 a hundred and ten years. Regarded in ancient Egypt as the ideal life span and so a sign of God's blessing.
50:23 third generation. That is, great-grandchildren; another sign of God's blessing. **on Joseph's knees.** See 30:3 and its note.
50:24 I am about to die. This link with the patriarchs (48:21) stresses the continuity of the generations in Israel. **come to your aid.** The book ends with the expectation of God's visitation. The Hebrew here ("to visit") connotes that God would change fortunes (see 21:1 and its note); it is translated "watched over" (Ex 3:16) and "was concerned about" (Ex 4:31) with reference to the exodus. A fuller visitation came in the birth of Jesus Christ (Lk 1:68), and the New Testament ends with the expectation of his visitation from heaven, at which time all believers will experience their exodus from death to eternal physical life (Rev 22:20). **take you up**

50:24 [f]Ge 12:7; 26:3; 28:13; 35:12
50:25 [g]Ge 47:29-30; Ex 13:19; Jos 24:32; Heb 11:22

ham, Isaac and Jacob."[f] 25 And Joseph made the sons of Israel swear an oath and said,
"God will surely come to your aid, and then you must carry my bones up from this
place."[g]
26 So Joseph died at the age of a hundred and ten. And after they embalmed him,[h] he
was placed in a coffin in Egypt.

50:26 [h]ver 2

out of this land. A technical phrase for the exodus from Egypt (15:13–14). **to the land he promised on oath.** The theme of the patriarchs was on Joseph's lips at the time of his death. **Abraham, Isaac and Jacob.** The first time these three patriarchs are mentioned together. Their era had passed, but not their hope.

50:25 carry my bones up. Moses fulfilled the oath to the dying Joseph (see Ex 13:19), and Joshua completed the burial. Joseph was buried at Shechem (Jos 24:32).

EXODUS

Introduction

Overview

Author: Moses

Purpose: To affirm the divine authority of Moses' leadership and of covenant law and worship regulations

Date: c. 1446–1406 B.C.

Key Truths:

- The Lord authorized Moses as Israel's leader to bring the blessing of deliverance from Egypt.
- The covenant laws given by Moses were divinely authorized to lead to blessings for God's people.
- Moses' regulations for worship at the tabernacle were divinely ordained to lead to blessings for God's people.

Author

Moses was the fundamental writer of Exodus (see "Introduction to Genesis: Author"). Some portions of the book explicitly declare their Mosaic origins. The Ten Commandments were originally "inscribed by the finger of God" on tablets of stone (31:18; see also 32:15–16; 34:1,28), but Moses delivered these laws to Israel. Moses also wrote the Book of the Covenant (i.e., 20:18—23:33; see 24:4,7; 34:27). Beyond this, Joshua 8:31 refers to the words of Exodus 20:25 as being "written in the Book of the Law of Moses." Moreover, Jesus called Exodus "the book of Moses" (see Mk 7:10; 12:26; Lk 2:22–23). It is likely that Moses employed scribes and that some later editing may have occurred, but the book itself and other Scripture support the traditional view that Moses was the author of this book.

The name *Exodus* is a Latin form of the Greek *exodos*, which means "exit" or "departure" (Lk 9:31). The book takes its name from the central event of Israel's departure from Egypt, which is recorded in the book's first 15 chapters. Exodus does not continue directly the narrative of Genesis 50, but its opening section, beginning with "These are the names . . . ," alludes to Genesis 46:8–27, where the names of the Israelites who went down to Egypt are listed. Exodus is a separate work, but it is part of the structure of the Pentateuch (Genesis through Deuteronomy).

Time and Place of Writing

Although the main plot of Exodus stretches from the time of the Israelites' enslavement in Egypt to their receiving God's law at Mount Sinai, at least two remarks indicate that the book of Exodus reached its final form at a later date. Exodus 16:35 states that the people "ate manna forty years, until they came to a land that was settled; they ate manna until they reached the border of Canaan" (see also Jos 5:10–12). Similarly, Exodus 40:38 states that "the cloud of the LORD was over the tabernacle by day, and fire was in the cloud by night, in the sight of all the house of Israel during all their travels." These references strongly suggest that Moses brought this book to its final form for the second generation of the exodus as the people waited on the plains of Moab (see Dt 1:5). For these reasons, the book should be dated about 1446–1406 B.C., the time of Israel's 40 years of wandering in the desert.

The date and route of the exodus have been subjects of considerable debate. Biblical chronology dates the exodus event at 480 years before the reign of Solomon (1Ki 6:1)—at about 1440 B.C. This early date is consistent with Judges 11:26, which declares that 300 years had elapsed since Israel had entered Canaan. The 1440 B.C. date is also supported by Exodus 12:40–41, where 430 years is specified as the duration of Israel's stay in Egypt. The pharaoh of the exodus probably would then have been Thutmose III or Amenhotep II.

Advocates of a much later date appeal to the name Rameses as one of the store cities built with Israelite labor (1:11). Rameses II (1290–1224 B.C.) is then taken to be the pharaoh of the exodus, thus setting the date as approximately 1270 B.C. This is held to be more consistent with the archaeology of cities destroyed in the region and with the lack of earlier settlement in Transjordan. More recent discoveries in Transjordan and a new evaluation of the destruction of Jericho have weakened the case for the later date.

The route of the exodus began at Rameses. Its exact location is the subject of considerable debate, although Tell el-Daba (modern Qantir) is the site most favored. From there the Hebrews journeyed south to Succoth (13:20). Here, apparently unable to move on, they turned northward (14:2). Three sites are mentioned: Baal Zephon, Migdol and Pi Hahiroth. Baal Zephon is associated with Tahpanhes, bordering Lake Menzaleh, one of the salt lakes between the Mediterranean and the Gulf of Suez. There were three possible routes of Israelite escape: The way of the land of the Philistines connected Egypt with Canaan by the heavily fortified coastal route. A second route, the way of Shur, began near the Wadi Tumilat in the delta area, crossed to Kadesh Barnea and branched off to Canaan. The Egyptian boundary wall of Shur may have been a major obstacle to this route. In leading the people south to southern Sinai, the Lord not only brought them to the mountain he had designated to Moses, but also distanced them from further contact with the Egyptians. The deliverance through the sea may have been on a southern extension of Lake Menzaleh.

The Sinai peninsula measures approximately 150 miles across at the top and 260 miles along the sides. It is flanked by two arms of the Red Sea: the Gulf of Suez and the Gulf of Aqaba (Elath). The Hebrews proceeded south along the west coast of the Sinai. The bitter waters of Marah (15:22–25) are usually identified with modern Ain Hawarah some 45–50 miles south of the tip of the Gulf of Suez, but perhaps Ayun Musa would be a better choice. Elim, with its many springs and trees, has been identified as Wadi Gharandel, the encampment by the Red Sea (Nu 33:10), about seven miles south of modern Ain Hawarah. The Desert of Sin would be best identified with Debbet er-Ramleh, a sandy plain along the edge of the Sinai plateau. If the location of Mount Sinai is the traditional one of Jebel Musa, then the Israelites would have turned inland by a series of valleys to Jebel Musa, traveling through the desert of Rephidim, where they fought against the Amalekites (17:8–16). Rephidim was the last encampment in the Desert of Sinai before their arrival at the sacred mountain. They proceeded to Mount Sinai (ch. 19), where they received the law. Deuteronomy 1:2 agrees with such a location of Sinai. They then traveled the way of the Paran to Kadesh (see map "The Exodus" at on page 121).

Purpose and Distinctives

The book of Exodus has several major themes. First, it tells how the Lord liberated Israel from Egypt to fulfill his covenant with the fathers. A second major element of the book is the covenant revelation at Sinai. The third theme is a result of the first two: the establishment of the tabernacle as the place of God's dwelling with Israel. Each of these themes presents a triumph of God's grace. The true God judged the gods and human rulers of Egypt as he delivered his people, came to speak with men at Sinai and identified his own presence with the tabernacle he instructed the people to build. The unfolding of these themes also reveals the Lord's holiness and grace in his covenant law and in the ceremonial symbolism of Israel's life and worship.

At the center of all of these divine actions is Moses, God's chosen servant. He mediated God's judgment against Egypt (4:1–17) and was the one through whom God delivered Israel at the Red Sea (14:31). Through Moses God gave his revelation at Sinai (20:19). Moses also received and delivered the regulations for the tabernacle (chs. 32–34). Although God's power and authority accomplished all these blessings for Israel, the book itself concentrates on Moses' role as God's servant.

Christ in Exodus

Christians may learn about Christ through the book of Exodus in many ways. First, on a large scale, the way in which Israel was delivered from the hardship of slavery in Egypt to the promised land of divine blessing presents a major metaphor for God's saving work throughout history. God redeemed his chosen people from the powers of evil to which they had become enslaved, and he judged those powers and claimed his people as his firstborn son, a holy nation of priests among whom he dwelled by his Spirit. The pattern of divine victory over enemies, the establishment of the divine dwelling place and the abundance of blessings find their greatest fulfillment in Christ's first and second advents (e.g., 1Co 10:1–13; Eph 2:14–22; Rev 20:11—22:5).

Second, the tabernacle and the services there pointed to Christ. In general terms, as the tabernacle was the place of approachable divine presence on Earth, so Jesus dwelled (lit., "tabernacled") among us (Jn 1:14,17). Beyond this, the provision of animal sacrifices as temporary remedies for Israel's sins anticipated the sacrifice of Christ's death, when sin was punished once and for all (24:8; Mt 26:27–28; Jn 1:29; Heb 12:24; 1Pe 1:2). Moreover, the important event of Passover is fulfilled in Christ (1Co 5:7).

The central role that Moses plays in this book also points to Christ. As the Israelites were "baptized into Moses" (1Co 10:2) when the people were led through the Red Sea, so Christians are baptized into Christ. Moses was the great servant of the Lord who received God's words directly. The Gospel of Matthew especially presents Jesus as the fulfillment of this role of Moses by portraying Jesus as One who underwent his own exodus (Mt 2:14–15), taught God's law on a mountainside (Mt 5:1) and stood in complete harmony with Moses on the Mount of Transfiguration (Mt 17). As Moses was willing to die for the sake of the people (32:10), so Jesus substituted himself for his people. The glory of God that reflected in the face of Moses (34:29; 2Co 3:8) is now reflected in those transformed by Christ's Spirit (2Co 3:18).

Outline

- I. God's Deliverance Led by Moses (1:1—18:27)
  - A. Leading From Egypt (1:1—15:21)
    - 1. Moses Born to Deliver (1:1—2:10)
      - a. The Background to Pharaoh's Plans (1:1–7)
      - b. Pharaoh's First Foiled Plan (1:8–14)
      - c. Pharaoh's Second Foiled Plan (1:15–21)
      - d. Pharaoh's Third Foiled Plan (1:22—2:10)
    - 2. Moses Called to Deliver (2:11—4:31)
      - a. Moses Flees From Egypt (2:11–25)
      - b. Moses Called at the Burning Bush (3:1—4:17)
      - c. Moses Returns to Egypt (4:18–31)

Moses' special birth and childhood anticipated his divine appointment as Israel's deliverer. Moses received a divine call to deliver Israel; he did not lead Israel for his own reasons. His divine authorization was evident when he led Israel from Egypt to the promised land. Moses executed many miraculous plagues against Egypt by God's power. The deliverance at the sea secured Israel's freedom from Egypt. Along the way to Sinai, Moses performed many services to Israel that showed his divine authorization.

3. Moses Is Successful in Deliverance (5:1—15:21)
    a. Refusal, Promise and Unbelief (5:1—6:12)
    b. Plagues Against Egypt (6:13—13:16)
        (1) Affirmation of Commission (6:13—7:7)
        (2) Miraculous Plagues (7:8—12:30)
        (3) Completion of Commission (12:31–41)
        (4) Future Observances (12:42—13:16)
    c. Final Deliverance at the Sea (13:17—15:21)
        (1) Passing Through the Sea (13:17—14:31)
        (2) Celebrating at the Sea (15:1–21)

B. Leading to Sinai (15:22—18:27)
1. Marah and Elim (15:22–27)
2. The Desert of Sin (16:1–36)
3. Rephidim (17:1–16)
    a. The Provision of Water (17:1–7)
    b. The Defeat of the Amalekites (17:8–16)
4. Near Sinai (18:1–27)

II. God's Covenant Mediated by Moses (19:1—24:18)

A. The Initiation of the Covenant (19:1–25)

B. The Codification of the Covenant (20:1—23:33)
1. The Ten Commandments (20:1–17)
2. The Book of the Covenant (20:18—23:33)
    a. Prologue (20:18–26)
    b. The Book (21:1—23:19)
    c. Epilogue (23:20–33)

C. The Finalization of the Covenant (24:1–18)

Moses served as the mediator of the covenant between God and Israel. The entire nation of Israel committed to the divine covenant mediated through Moses. The Mosaic covenant was codified in the Ten Commandments and the Book of the Covenant. Israel's acceptance of the covenant through Moses led to great blessings.

III. God's Tabernacle Erected by Moses (25:1—40:38)

A. Instructions Concerning the Tabernacle (25:1—31:18)
1. The Tabernacle and Its Priests (25:1—30:10)
    a. The Tabernacle and Its Furnishings (25:1—27:19)
        (1) Collection of Materials (25:1–9)
        (2) The Ark (25:10–22)
        (3) The Table (25:23–30)
        (4) The Gold Lampstand (25:31–40)
        (5) The Tabernacle (26:1–37)
        (6) The Altar (27:1–8)
        (7) The Courtyard (27:9–19)
    b. The Priests and Their Services (27:20—30:10)
        (1) Collection of Oil (27:20–21)
        (2) The Priestly Garments (28:1–43)
        (3) The Consecration of Priests (29:1–46)
        (4) The Altar of Incense (30:1–10)
2. Atonement Money (30:11–16)
3. The Bronze Basin (30:17–21)
4. Anointing Oil (30:22–33)

God authorized Moses' tabernacle regulations. Moses gave instructions from God for the construction of the tabernacle and the priestly services there. God cursed the Israelites when they violated Moses' worship regulations, and only Moses' intercession delivered them. The Israelites built the tabernacle just as the Lord and Moses had instructed, and they received great blessings for their faithfulness.

5. Incense (30:34–38)
6. Appointment of Craftsmen (31:1–11)
7. Sabbath Observance (31:12–18)

B. Israel's Failure and God's Forgiveness (32:1—34:35)
1. Israel's Violation and Moses' Intercession (32:1–29)
2. God's Threat and Moses' Intercession (32:30—33:23)
3. Renewal of the Covenant (34:1–35)

C. The Construction of the Tabernacle (35:1—40:38)
1. The Preparations (35:1—36:7)
 a. The Call to Contribute (35:1–19)
 b. Israel's Offerings (35:20–29)
 c. The Craftsmen (35:30—36:7)
2. The Construction (36:8—39:43)
 a. The Tabernacle (36:8–38)
 b. The Furnishings (37:1—38:8)
 c. The Courtyard (38:9–20)
 d. Summary of Amounts (38:21–31)
 e. The Priestly Garments (39:1–31)
 f. Moses' Blessing (39:32–43)
3. The Erection of the Tabernacle (40:1–38)
 a. The Tabernacle Built (40:1–33)
 b. Glory in the Tabernacle (40:34–38)

The Israelites Oppressed

1:1 [a]Ge 46:8
1 These are the names of the sons of Israel[a] who went to Egypt with Jacob, each with
1:5 [b]Ge 46:26 his family: **2**Reuben, Simeon, Levi and Judah; **3**Issachar, Zebulun and Benjamin;
4Dan and Naphtali; Gad and Asher. **5**The descendants of Jacob numbered seventy[a] in
1:6 [c]Ge 50:26 all;[b] Joseph was already in Egypt.
6Now Joseph and all his brothers and all that generation died,[c] **7**but the Israelites
1:7 [d]Ge 46:3; Dt 26:5; Ac 7:17 were fruitful and multiplied greatly and became exceedingly numerous,[d] so that the land
was filled with them.
1:9 [e]Ps 105:24-25 **8**Then a new king, who did not know about Joseph, came to power in Egypt. **9**"Look,"
he said to his people, "the Israelites have become much too numerous[e] for us. **10**Come,
1:10 [f]Ps 83:3 [g]Ac 7:17-19 we must deal shrewdly[f] with them or they will become even more numerous and, if war
breaks out, will join our enemies, fight against us and leave the country."[g]
1:11 [h]Ex 3:7 [i]Ge 15:13; Ex 2:11; 5:4; 6:6-7 [j]Ge 47:11 [k]1Ki 9:19; 2Ch 8:4 **11**So they put slave masters[h] over them to oppress them with forced labor,[i] and they
built Pithom and Rameses[j] as store cities[k] for Pharaoh. **12**But the more they were op-

[a] 5 Masoretic Text (see also Gen. 46:27); Dead Sea Scrolls and Septuagint (see also Acts 7:14 and note at Gen. 46:27) *seventy-five*

■ **1:1—18:27** *God's Deliverance Led by Moses.* The first section of Exodus presents Moses as the one who led Israel from its bondage in Egypt to the holy mountain of Sinai. These chapters divide into two main sections: the actual deliverance from Egypt (1:1—15:21) and God's gracious provisions while en route to Sinai (15:22—18:27).

■ **1:1—15:21** *Leading From Egypt.* The Israelites suffered the hardships of slavery in Egypt, but God sent his servant Moses to deliver them. These events divide into three sections: divine interventions culminating in Moses' birth (1:1—2:10), Moses' call to service (2:11—4:31) and Moses' success in delivering Israel (5:1—15:21).

■ **1:1—2:10** *Moses Born to Deliver.* Moses' birth and miraculous survival climaxed a series of events in which God protected his people by foiling the plans of the pharaoh. These verses divide into four sections: the introduction (1:1–7), the first foiled plan (1:8–14), the second foiled plan (1:15–21) and the third foiled plan (1:22—2:10).

■ **1:1–7** *The Background to Pharaoh's Plans.* The Israelites had entered Egypt 70 strong, but they multiplied so greatly that the land was filled with their descendants.

1:5 seventy. The number of the company as 70 persons (Ge 46:8–27) alludes to the 70 nations of Genesis 10. As the special chosen people of God, Israel embodied the hopes of humanity's future.

1:7 multiplied greatly. "Fruitful," "multiplied" and "the land was filled" all refer back to Genesis 1:26–28. Through Israel the mandate given to humanity in Genesis 1:28 was extended to the day when all nations would receive God's blessing. **the land.** Probably the land of Goshen in northeast Egypt, which is located in the Wadi Tumilat in the delta, a valley some 30–40 miles long (cf. Ge 47:4), though the area seems small for the numbers involved.

■ **1:8–14** *Pharaoh's First Foiled Plan.* Pharaoh's first attempt to control the multiplication of Israelites by increasing their labor was thwarted.

1:8 a new king. The beginning of a new era was marked by the advent of a new pharaoh. The pharaoh concerned may have been Ahmose I (c. 1552–1527 B.C.), the first king of the 18th dynasty, who expelled the Hyksos, Semitic rulers of Egypt from c. 1720–1580 B.C. See "Introduction: Time and Place of Writing."

1:9 too numerous for us. The decision to restrict population growth eventually ushered in the exodus and Egypt's defeat.

1:11 Pithom and Rameses. These store cities for agricultural provisions and military supplies were in the strategic delta region. Pithom was probably located at modern Tell er-Retabah or Tell el-Maskhuta, and Rameses is identified as modern Qantir. This comes

pressed, the more they multiplied and spread; so the Egyptians came to dread the Israelites **13**and worked them ruthlessly.[l] **14**They made their lives bitter with hard labor in
brick and mortar and with all kinds of work in the fields; in all their hard labor the Egyptians used them ruthlessly.[m]
15The king of Egypt said to the Hebrew midwives, whose names were Shiphrah and
Puah, **16**"When you help the Hebrew women in childbirth and observe them on the delivery stool, if it is a boy, kill him; but if it is a girl, let her live." **17**The midwives, however, feared[n] God and did not do what the king of Egypt had told them to do;[o] they let the
boys live. **18**Then the king of Egypt summoned the midwives and asked them, "Why have
you done this? Why have you let the boys live?"
19The midwives answered Pharaoh, "Hebrew women are not like Egyptian women;
they are vigorous and give birth before the midwives arrive."[p]
20So God was kind to the midwives[q] and the people increased and became even more
numerous. **21**And because the midwives feared God, he gave them families[r] of their own.
22Then Pharaoh gave this order to all his people: "Every boy that is born[a] you must
throw into the Nile, but let every girl live."[s]

The Birth of Moses

2 Now a man of the house of Levi married a Levite woman,[t] **2**and she became pregnant and gave birth to a son. When she saw that he was a fine child, she hid him
for three months.[u] **3**But when she could hide him no longer, she got a papyrus basket
for him and coated it with tar and pitch. Then she placed the child in it and put it among
the reeds along the bank of the Nile. **4**His sister[v] stood at a distance to see what would
happen to him.
5Then Pharaoh's daughter went down to the Nile to bathe, and her attendants were
walking along the river bank.[w] She saw the basket among the reeds and sent her slave
girl to get it. **6**She opened it and saw the baby. He was crying, and she felt sorry for him.
"This is one of the Hebrew babies," she said.
7Then his sister asked Pharaoh's daughter, "Shall I go and get one of the Hebrew
women to nurse the baby for you?"
8"Yes, go," she answered. And the girl went and got the baby's mother. **9**Pharaoh's
daughter said to her, "Take this baby and nurse him for me, and I will pay you." So the
woman took the baby and nursed him. **10**When the child grew older, she took him to
Pharaoh's daughter and he became her son. She named him Moses,[b] saying, "I drew him
out of the water."

1:13 [l]Dt 4:20
1:14 [m]Ex 2:23; 6:9; Nu 20:15; Ps 81:6; Ac 7:19
1:17 [n]ver 21; Pr 16:6 [o]Da 3:16-18; Ac 4:18-20; 5:29
1:19 [p]Jos 2:4-6; 2Sa 17:20
1:20 [q]ver 12; Pr 11:18; Isa 3:10
1:21 [r]1Sa 2:35; 2Sa 7:11,27-29; 1Ki 11:38
1:22 [s]Ac 7:19
2:1 [t]Ex 6:20; Nu 26:59
2:2 [u]Ac 7:20; Heb 11:23
2:4 [v]Ex 15:20; Nu 26:59
2:5 [w]Ex 7:15; 8:20

[a] *22* Masoretic Text; Samaritan Pentateuch, Septuagint and Targums *born to the Hebrews* [b] *10 Moses* sounds like the Hebrew for *draw out.*

too early in the oppression cycle to be identified as the work of Rameses II (1290–1224 B.C.), who is often identified as the pharaoh of the exodus. The only other pharaoh with the necessary 40-year reign was Thutmose III (1490–1436 B.C.). By the 19th dynasty, the term *pharaoh* ("great house") had become a royal title. Earlier it had been a synonym for public authority.

1:12 the more they multiplied and spread. By divine enablement, the Israelites were stronger than the Egyptians had anticipated (see 1:19).

1:14 See *WLC* 136.

■ **1:15–21** *Pharaoh's Second Foiled Plan.* Pharaoh's second attempt to control Israel's multiplication was frustrated by Hebrew midwives.

1:15 Hebrew. The term *Hebrew* is used in the Old Testament by foreigners of Israelites or by Israelites to identify themselves to foreigners. It is probably directly related to the Egyptian term *apiru* and the Babylonian *hab/piru,* terms used to describe a widely distributed social class of semi-nomads in the Near East in the second millennium who posed a threat to organized society. Groups of *habiru* are known to have been operating in the region when the Israelites moved in c. 1440 B.C. **midwives.** Two midwives seem far too few to service such a large population; they may have been guild leaders. Their names are Semitic, and their fear of God (v. 17) identifies them as Israelites.

1:16 delivery stool. These were the two stones on which women in labor squatted.

1:19 The midwives praised Israelite women and mocked Egyptian women. There may have been enough truth in what they said that their statement was considered true, but they probably exaggerated the situation.

1:20–21 Some interpreters have understood God's blessing as an indication of God's approval of their deception (v. 19), and they relate this action to Acts 5:29. Other interpreters, without approving of their deception, have argued that God blessed them because they feared him (v. 17). In any event, Pharaoh's second and stronger attempt to halt Israelite multiplication failed because of the midwives' action.

■ **1:22—2:10** *Pharaoh's Third Foiled Plan.* Pharaoh's third attempt to stop Israelite multiplication was hindered by God through the ironic rescue of Moses by Pharaoh's own daughter.

2:1–2 a man . . . a Levite woman . . . a son. The fate of Israel hung on one here unnamed Israelite couple and their unnamed son. We learn later that the son had an older sister (v. 4) and brother (7:7). His parents were Amram and Jochebed (6:20).

2:2 fine child. The child was healthy and likely to survive.

2:3 papyrus basket. Papyrus strips, when woven together and daubed with tar, made a navigable basket (see Job 9:26; Isa 18:2). Moses is depicted as a second Noah, since the Hebrew term for "basket" is used only one other time in the Old Testament, for Noah's craft in Genesis 6–9 (where it is translated "ark"). It is possible that the original readers also associated this event with the ancient legend that Sargon of Akkad (c. the twenty-fourth century B.C.) was exposed in a similar chest and left to float in the Euphrates. This association would have hinted at the grand significance of Moses.

2:5 Pharaoh's daughter. Some interpreters have suggested that this princess became the famous Hatshepsut, the queen of Thutmose II (1494–1490 B.C.).

2:8 the baby's mother. To indicate Moses' sanctity as Israel's leader, the narrative reports that he spent his early years (at least two) with his biological mother, an Israelite.

2:10 Moses. The choice of this name was particularly ironic. It is likely that the name *Moses* was chosen because it sounded like the Egyptian name meaning "is born" or "son," thus indicating to the Egyptians that Moses was the son of Pharaoh. At the same time,

Moses Flees to Midian

11 One day, after Moses had grown up, he went out to where his own people[x] were and
watched them at their hard labor. He saw an Egyptian beating a Hebrew, one of his own
people. 12 Glancing this way and that and seeing no one, he killed the Egyptian and hid
him in the sand. 13 The next day he went out and saw two Hebrews fighting. He asked the
one in the wrong, "Why are you hitting your fellow Hebrew?"[y]
14 The man said, "Who made you ruler and judge over us?[z] Are you thinking of killing me as you killed the Egyptian?" Then Moses was afraid and thought, "What I did
must have become known."
15 When Pharaoh heard of this, he tried to kill Moses, but Moses fled from Pharaoh
and went to live in Midian,[a] where he sat down by a well. 16 Now a priest of Midian[b] had
seven daughters, and they came to draw water[c] and fill the troughs to water their father's
flock. 17 Some shepherds came along and drove them away, but Moses got up and came
to their rescue and watered their flock.[d]
18 When the girls returned to Reuel[e] their father, he asked them, "Why have you returned so early today?"
19 They answered, "An Egyptian rescued us from the shepherds. He even drew water
for us and watered the flock."
20 "And where is he?" he asked his daughters. "Why did you leave him? Invite him to
have something to eat."[f]
21 Moses agreed to stay with the man, who gave his daughter Zipporah[g] to Moses in
marriage. 22 Zipporah gave birth to a son, and Moses named him Gershom,[a] saying, "I
have become an alien[h] in a foreign land."
23 During that long period,[i] the king of Egypt died. The Israelites groaned in their slavery and cried out, and their cry[j] for help because of their slavery went up to God. 24 God
heard their groaning and he remembered his covenant[k] with Abraham, with Isaac and
with Jacob. 25 So God looked on the Israelites and was concerned[l] about them.

Moses and the Burning Bush

3 Now Moses was tending the flock of Jethro[m] his father-in-law, the priest of Midian,
and he led the flock to the far side of the desert and came to Horeb,[n] the mountain[o]
of God. 2 There the angel of the LORD[p] appeared to him in flames of fire from within a
bush.[q] Moses saw that though the bush was on fire it did not burn up. 3 So Moses
thought, "I will go over and see this strange sight—why the bush does not burn up."

2:11 [x]Ac 7:23; Heb 11:24-26
2:13 [y]Ac 7:26
2:14 [z]Ac 7:27*
2:15 [a]Ac 7:29; Heb 11:27
2:16 [b]Ex 3:1 [c]Ge 24:11
2:17 [d]Ge 29:10
2:18 [e]Nu 10:29
2:20 [f]Ge 31:54
2:21 [g]Ex 18:2
2:22 [h]Ex 18:3-4; Heb 11:13
2:23 [i]Ac 7:30 [j]Ex 3:7,9; Dt 26:7; Jas 5:4
2:24 [k]Ex 6:5; Ps 105:10, 42
2:25 [l]Ex 3:7; 4:31
3:1 [m]Ex 2:18 [n]1Ki 19:8 [o]Ex 18:5
3:2 [p]Ge 16:7 [q]Dt 33:16; Mk 12:26; Ac 7:30

[a] *22 Gershom* sounds like the Hebrew for *an alien there.*

---

the name *Moses* sounded like Hebrew for "to draw out" (see NIV text note), indicating that Moses had been rescued from the Nile. From that point forward, the name of Israel's leader reminded Israelite readers that Pharaoh's plan to control Israel's multiplication had been obstructed by his own daughter's rescue of Moses. From the very beginning, God's plan was for Moses to undermine Pharaoh's control over the people of God.

■ **2:11—4:31** *Moses Called to Deliver.* Moses was not only rescued from death by God, but he was also called and equipped to deliver Israel from bondage in Egypt. This account divides into three main parts: Moses' departure from Egypt (2:11–25), his call at the burning bush (3:1—4:17) and his return to Egypt (4:18–31).

■ **2:11–25** *Moses Flees From Egypt.* Although Moses was raised in the courts of Pharaoh, he demonstrated that his heart was with the people of God and that he was not corrupted by the Egyptian court. He left Egypt not for his own political gain, but for having defended an Israelite.

2:11–15 Moses, then 40 (Ac 7:23), identified himself with God's people (Heb 11:24–27).

2:11–12 seeing no one. Moses' actions violated Egypt's laws (cf. Pharaoh's response in v. 15), but not God's (cf. Ac 7:24-25; see also Pss 72:4; 82:3).

2:14 Who made you ruler and judge over us? An Israelite raised doubts about Moses that would be voiced time and again. His doubts were balanced by the response of the Israelites upon Moses' return (4:31). The unspoken answer was that God himself had ordained Moses as Israel's ruler and judge.

2:15 Midian. Probably the name of an early tribal confederacy operating in the Arabian desert. Midian was a descendant of Abraham and Keturah (Ge 25:1–6); his descendants were a nomadic people (Nu 10:29–32; Jdg 6).

2:16 draw water. The text suggests that the women completed the difficult task of drawing water, but were not able to use the water they had drawn because they were driven off by the shepherds.

2:18 Reuel. The name means "Friend of God." He later became Moses' father-in-law. He is variously called Reuel, Jethro (3:1; 4:18) and Hobab (Nu 10:29). Hobab was also the name of Moses' son-in-law. Jethro and Reuel may be variant names; Reuel may be a clan name.

2:19 Moses was identified as an Egyptian by his clothing.

2:22 Gershom. See NIV text note. Moses expressed sadness over his homeless condition.

2:23–25 groaned . . . cried out . . . went up. The Israelites' anguish was intense, and their cries rose to God. Israel's cry was balanced by a fourfold description of God's response: God "heard . . . remembered . . . looked on . . . [and] was concerned." This summary prepares the reader for the call of Moses and shows that Moses' call was an act of divine grace toward Israel.

■ **3:1—4:17** *Moses Called at the Burning Bush.* While in the desert, God miraculously called and equipped Moses for his role as Israel's deliverer.

3:1 far side. That is, the west. **desert.** An uncultivated area but one capable of sustaining grazing. According to 34:3 and Numbers 10:11, the Desert of Sinai sustained Israel's flocks for a year. Horeb and Sinai are interchangeable terms used of the range/mountain (cf. Dt 4:15 with Ex 19:18,20). **mountain of God.** This term describes the mountain as a sanctuary, a designation that anticipates chapter 19. Moses was now 80 years old (7:7) and had been in Midian 40 years.

3:2 angel of the LORD. God's authoritative heavenly messenger (23:21; Ge 16:7; 21:17), whom some interpreters identify with Christ himself in his preincarnate state. **fire.** This is a frequent Biblical symbol for God's presence (13:21; 19:18; Ge 3:24; 1Ki 18:24,38), sometimes symbolizing (as here) the threat of his holiness (Heb 12:29).

3:3 bush. A real bush illumined with supernatural fire.

4When the LORD saw that he had gone over to look, God called to him from within the
bush, "Moses! Moses!"
And Moses said, "Here I am."
5"Do not come any closer," God said. "Take off your sandals, for the place where you
are standing is holy ground."[r] 6Then he said, "I am the God of your father, the God of
Abraham, the God of Isaac and the God of Jacob."[s] At this, Moses hid his face, because
he was afraid to look at God.
7The LORD said, "I have indeed seen the misery of my people in Egypt. I have heard
them crying out because of their slave drivers, and I am concerned[t] about their suffering. 8So I have come down[u] to rescue them from the hand of the Egyptians and to bring
them up out of that land into a good and spacious land, a land flowing with milk and
honey[v]—the home of the Canaanites, Hittites, Amorites, Perizzites, Hivites and Jebusites.[w] 9And now the cry of the Israelites has reached me, and I have seen the way the
Egyptians are oppressing[x] them. 10So now, go. I am sending you to Pharaoh to bring my
people the Israelites out of Egypt."[y]
11But Moses said to God, "Who am I,[z] that I should go to Pharaoh and bring the Israelites out of Egypt?"

3:5 [r]Ge 28:17; Jos 5:15; Ac 7:33*
3:6 [s]Ex 4:5; Mt 22:32*; Mk 12:26*; Lk 20:37*; Ac 7:32*
3:7 [t]Ex 2:25
3:8 [u]Ge 50:24 [v]ver 17; Ex 13:5; Dt 1:25 [w]Ge 15:18-21
3:9 [x]Ex 1:14; 2:23
3:10 [y]Mic 6:4
3:11 [z]Ex 6:12,30; 1Sa 18:18

3:5 Take off your sandals. An ancient custom ensuring that holy places were not defiled. **holy.** The spot was made sacred by God's presence (19:23; 24:2). The question of how to approach the holy God is central in Exodus. It is resolved in the symbolism of the tabernacle.
3:6 God of your father . . . Abraham . . . Isaac . . . Jacob. The mention of Abraham, Isaac and Jacob indicates that God called Moses because he remembered his covenant promises to these patriarchs (see Ge 26:24; 28:13; 31:42; 32:9). This suggestion is strengthened by the overlap of people groups listed in verses 8 and 17 with those in the land promised to Abraham's descendants (Ge 15:19–21).
3:8 Canaanites. Inhabitants of the Syro-Palestinian coastland. **Hittites.** Possibly an ethnic pocket in the region related to the great Asiatic power of c. 1400–1200 B.C. **Amorites.** Probably pre-Israelite inhabitants of the region, only much later known as Palestine. **Perizzites.** Possibly the peasantry located in the central part of the region (Jos 17:15). **Hivites.** The early inhabitants near Gibeon (Jos 9:7; 11:19) or Shechem (Ge 34:2). **Jebusites.** The original occupants of Jerusalem who were dispossessed by David (2Sa 5:6–9).
3:10 Pharaoh. Probably Thutmose III or Amenhotep II. See "Introduction: Time and Place of Writing."
3:11 Who am I . . . ? Moses felt inadequate for the task, as Gide-

God's Self-Disclosure: Does God Have a Name?

IN the modern world, a person's name is merely an identifying label. In Biblical times, however, personal names were often chosen to give information, describing in some way the character of a person or circumstances at the time of the birth. In a similar way, the Scriptures often speak of God's names as a way to reveal his character. The Old Testament constantly celebrates the fact that God has made his name known to Israel. Among the many names for God in the Old Testament, as rendered in the English language, are God Almighty (Ge 17:1; 35:11), Most High (Nu 24:16), God Most High (Ge 14:18–22), Creator (Ge 14:22), Holy One (Isa 43:15) and Holy One of Israel (Ps 89:18)

Without a doubt the most important name for God in the Old Testament is Yahweh, as modern scholars write it, Jehovah as it used to be rendered, or "the LORD" as in the NIV and many other modern translations. Although God revealed himself to the patriarchs as Yahweh before the days of Moses (Ge 15:7; 28:13), God declared to Moses that this name had special significance in his day and for the rest of Israel's history. When God spoke to Moses out of the burning bush, Moses asked God for his name. God first said, "I AM WHO I AM" (or, "I WILL BE WHAT I WILL BE"), then shortened it to "I AM" and finally called himself "The LORD (Hebrew *Yahweh*, a name related to the single Hebrew word translated "I AM"), the God of your fathers" (Ex 3:15).

Much mystery attaches to the name *Yahweh*. Traditionally, this name in all its forms was understood to focus on God's eternal, self-sustaining, self-determining, sovereign character—that supernatural mode of existence that the sign of the burning bush had signified. More recently, the name has been connected closely to the idea that God is a faithful, covenant-keeping God. When God first spoke from the burning bush, he revealed himself as the One who had made covenant promises to the patriarchs (Ex 3:6). This revelation prompted Moses to ask for his name. When God revealed his name as Yahweh, he announced that he was not merely the God of the past, but the God who remembers his covenant promises and moves on behalf of his people to keep them—as he was about to do for the Israelites in Egypt. Later in his life (Ex 33:18—34:7) Moses asked to see God's "glory," and in reply God proclaimed his name, Yahweh, in this way: "The LORD, the LORD, the compassionate and gracious God, slow to anger, abounding in love and faithfulness, maintaining love to thousands, and forgiving wickedness, rebellion and sin. Yet he does not leave the guilty unpunished . . ." God's faithfulness to acting on his covenants is often echoed in later Scriptures (Dt 7:9; Ne 9:7–8; Isa 61:8; Jer 31:31–34). This is all part of the disclosure of his nature, for which he is to be adored forever.

In this light, it is not difficult to see why the name of God is often associated with his ownership and authorization (Ex 23:21; Dt 18:19; 2Ch 7:14; Isa 43:7). It also stands as the invocable presence of God in Solomon's temple, where it is closely associated with God's watchful eyes, listening ears and responsive heart (2Ch 7:14–15). As such, the name of God is the object of prayer and praise (Pss 8:1; 113:1–3; 145:1–2; 148:5,13).

12 And God said, "I will be with you.[a] And this will be the sign to you that it is I who
have sent you: When you have brought the people out of Egypt, you[a] will worship God
on this mountain."
13 Moses said to God, "Suppose I go to the Israelites and say to them, 'The God of your
fathers has sent me to you,' and they ask me, 'What is his name?' Then what shall I tell
them?"
14 God said to Moses, "I AM WHO I AM.[b] This is what you are to say to the Israelites: 'I
AM[b] has sent me to you.' "
15 God also said to Moses, "Say to the Israelites, 'The LORD,[c] the God of your fathers—
the God of Abraham, the God of Isaac and the God of Jacob—has sent me to you.' This
is my name[c] forever, the name by which I am to be remembered from generation to generation.
16 "Go, assemble the elders[d] of Israel and say to them, 'The LORD, the God of your fathers—the God of Abraham, Isaac and Jacob—appeared to me and said: I have watched
over you and have seen what has been done to you in Egypt. 17 And I have promised to
bring you up out of your misery in Egypt[e] into the land of the Canaanites, Hittites, Amorites, Perizzites, Hivites and Jebusites—a land flowing with milk and honey.'
18 "The elders of Israel will listen[f] to you. Then you and the elders are to go to the king
of Egypt and say to him, 'The LORD, the God of the Hebrews, has met with us. Let us take
a three-day journey into the desert to offer sacrifices[g] to the LORD our God.' 19 But I know
that the king of Egypt will not let you go unless a mighty hand[h] compels him. 20 So I will
stretch out my hand[i] and strike the Egyptians with all the wonders[j] that I will perform
among them. After that, he will let you go.[k]
21 "And I will make the Egyptians favorably disposed[l] toward this people, so that when
you leave you will not go empty-handed.[m] 22 Every woman is to ask her neighbor and any
woman living in her house for articles of silver and gold[n] and for clothing, which you will
put on your sons and daughters. And so you will plunder[o] the Egyptians."

Signs for Moses

4 Moses answered, "What if they do not believe me or listen[p] to me and say, 'The LORD
did not appear to you'?"
2 Then the LORD said to him, "What is that in your hand?"
"A staff,"[q] he replied.

3:12 [a]Ge 31:3; Jos 1:5; Ro 8:31
3:14 [b]Ex 6:2-3; Jn 8:58; Heb 13:8
3:15 [c]Ps 135:13; Hos 12:5
3:16 [d]Ex 4:29
3:17 [e]Ge 15:16; Jos 24:11
3:18 [f]Ex 4:1,8,31 [g]Ex 5:1,3
3:19 [h]Ex 4:21; 5:2
3:20 [i]Ex 6:1,6; 9:15 [j]Dt 6:22; Ne 9:10; Ac 7:36 [k]Ex 12:31-33
3:21 [l]Ex 12:36 [m]Ps 105:37
3:22 [n]Ex 11:2 [o]Eze 39:10
4:1 [p]Ex 3:18; 6:30
4:2 [q]ver 17,20

a *12* The Hebrew is plural. b *14* Or *I WILL BE WHAT I WILL BE* c *15* The Hebrew for *LORD* sounds like and may be derived from the Hebrew for *I AM* in verse 14.

---

on (Jdg 6:15) and Jeremiah (Jer 1:6) later also did. This is the first of Moses' four objections (see 3:13; 4:1,10).
3:12 sign. God's call would be confirmed by his future action. God would be with Moses to bring him back to worship on this same mountain. The word translated "worship" means "serve" and implies that the Israelites, who served the Egyptians, would become God's servants in covenant worship.
3:13–22 God's name and presence confirmed his promise to Moses.
3:13 What is his name? Moses' second expression of reluctance (see 3:11; 4:1,10). He anticipated a question from the people that was also his own: Who is this God? What name is to be used to invoke him? The name Yahweh is the only name (as opposed to titles) of God used in Genesis when people call upon "the name of the LORD" (Ge 4:26; 12:8; 13:4; 21:33; 26:25). In ancient times, a personal name often was not merely a form of address, but also a description of character and personality.
3:14 I AM WHO I AM. Perhaps a purposefully mysterious, full liturgical name. It could also be translated "I will be who I will be." In this context it is closely associated with God's consistency in remembering and acting on his previous covenant commitments. It was shortened to "I am" ("I will be" [v. 14]) and "he is" ("he will be," or "*Yahweh*" [translated "the LORD" in v. 15]). See *WCF* 2.1; *WLC* 7,101; *WSC* 4.
3:15 The LORD. The Hebrew is *Yahweh*, the third person form of the verb "to be" ("he is/will be"), which corresponds to the first person form *'Ehyeh*, "I am." Note the parallels: "I AM has sent me" (v. 14) and "The LORD [*Yahweh*] . . . has sent me" (v. 15). **the name by which I am to be remembered.** This is the name upon which Israel must always call. English versions of the Old Testament usually render the Hebrew name *Yahweh* as "the LORD," following the practice of the New Testament and of the Jews in the time between the Testaments. The Jews thought *Yahweh* too holy to pronounce and when reading the text substituted *'adonay* ("my Lord"). The vowel signs from *'adonay* were later added to the consonants *YHWH* in order to indicate that *'adonay* should be the word spoken in place of *YHWH* when the text was read. Combining the consonants from *YHWH* with the vowels from *'adonay* produced the hybrid form *Yehowah* (or "Jehovah") in texts with written vowel signs (Hebrew is traditionally written without vowels). This last form was never so pronounced until centuries later when those who misunderstood the purpose of these vowels treated them as if they were part of the divine name. In the New Testament, the name Lord is applied to Jesus (see Ro 10:13, citing Joel 2:32).
3:16 elders. Literally, "bearded ones." These were family heads who represented Israel. They were to be assembled to hear of God's faithfulness.
3:17 milk and honey. A frequently used description of Canaan, indicating that the land was extraordinarily fertile. Animals' milk and bees' honey were so abundant that they were said to flow through the land like rivers.
3:18 three-day. A "three-day journey" may have been an expression for a short period of time. This request for a brief journey was to fulfill the promise of the sign of returning to the mountain (v. 12), but it would later be followed by the full liberation of the Israelites from slavery.
3:19 But I know. If a reasoned approach to Pharaoh were to fail, as indeed it would, the Lord would intervene.
3:20 wonders. The mention of extraordinary deeds anticipates the plagues.
3:21 not go empty-handed. God would see that their years of bondage were recompensed, as he had promised (see 12:36; Ge 15:14).
4:1 What if . . . ? This was Moses' third objection (see 3:11,13; 4:10). Israel had to be persuaded. This was to be a difficult task, even though God had ensured that many Israelites would initially accept Moses' leadership (3:18).
4:2 hand. Against the oppressive hand of Egypt (3:8; 14:30; 18:10), the mighty hand of God would be stretched out (3:19–20). God would use the hand of Moses to show his power. Moses' staff would become the staff of God (v. 20).

3 The LORD said, "Throw it on the ground."
Moses threw it on the ground and it became a snake, and he ran from it. 4 Then the
LORD said to him, "Reach out your hand and take it by the tail." So Moses reached out
and took hold of the snake and it turned back into a staff in his hand. 5 "This," said the
LORD, "is so that they may believe[r] that the LORD, the God of their fathers—the God of
Abraham, the God of Isaac and the God of Jacob—has appeared to you."
6 Then the LORD said, "Put your hand inside your cloak." So Moses put his hand into
his cloak, and when he took it out, it was leprous,[a] like snow.[s]
7 "Now put it back into your cloak," he said. So Moses put his hand back into his cloak,
and when he took it out, it was restored,[t] like the rest of his flesh.
8 Then the LORD said, "If they do not believe you or pay attention to the first miraculous sign, they may believe the second. 9 But if they do not believe these two signs or listen to you, take some water from the Nile and pour it on the dry ground. The water you
take from the river will become blood[u] on the ground."
10 Moses said to the LORD, "O Lord, I have never been eloquent, neither in the past nor
since you have spoken to your servant. I am slow of speech and tongue."[v]
11 The LORD said to him, "Who gave man his mouth? Who makes him deaf or mute?
Who gives him sight or makes him blind?[w] Is it not I, the LORD? 12 Now go; I will help you
speak and will teach you what to say."[x]
13 But Moses said, "O Lord, please send someone else to do it."
14 Then the LORD's anger burned against Moses and he said, "What about your brother, Aaron the Levite? I know he can speak well. He is already on his way to meet[y] you,
and his heart will be glad when he sees you. 15 You shall speak to him and put words in
his mouth;[z] I will help both of you speak and will teach you what to do. 16 He will speak
to the people for you, and it will be as if he were your mouth[a] and as if you were God to
him. 17 But take this staff[b] in your hand so you can perform miraculous signs[c] with it."

Moses Returns to Egypt

18 Then Moses went back to Jethro his father-in-law and said to him, "Let me go back
to my own people in Egypt to see if any of them are still alive."
Jethro said, "Go, and I wish you well."
19 Now the LORD had said to Moses in Midian, "Go back to Egypt, for all the men who
wanted to kill[d] you are dead."[e] 20 So Moses took his wife and sons, put them on a donkey and started back to Egypt. And he took the staff[f] of God in his hand.
21 The LORD said to Moses, "When you return to Egypt, see that you perform before
Pharaoh all the wonders[g] I have given you the power to do. But I will harden his heart[h]
so that he will not let the people go. 22 Then say to Pharaoh, 'This is what the LORD says:
Israel is my firstborn son,[i] 23 and I told you, "Let my son go,[j] so he may worship me." But
you refused to let him go; so I will kill your firstborn son.'"[k]
24 At a lodging place on the way, the LORD met ⌊Moses⌋[b] and was about to kill[l] him.

a 6 The Hebrew word was used for various diseases affecting the skin—not necessarily leprosy.
b 24 Or ⌊*Moses' son*⌋; Hebrew *him*

4:5 [r]Ex 19:9
4:6 [s]Nu 12:10; 2Ki 5:1, 27
4:7 [t]Nu 12:13-15; Dt 32:39; 2Ki 5:14; Mt 8:3
4:9 [u]Ex 7:17-21
4:10 [v]Ex 6:12; Jer 1:6
4:11 [w]Ps 94:9; Mt 11:5
4:12 [x]Isa 50:4; Jer 1:9; Mt 10:19-20; Mk 13:11; Lk 12:12; 21:14-15
4:14 [y]ver 27
4:15 [z]Nu 23:5,12,16
4:16 [a]Ex 7:1-2
4:17 [b]ver 2 [c]Ex 7:9-21
4:19 [d]Ex 2:15 [e]Ex 2:23
4:20 [f]Ex 17:9; Nu 20:8-9,11
4:21 [g]Ex 3:19,20 [h]Ex 7:3,13; 9:12, 35; 14:4,8; Dt 2:30; Isa 63:17; Jn 12:40; Ro 9:18
4:22 [i]Isa 63:16; 64:8; Jer 31:9; Hos 11:1; Ro 9:4
4:23 [j]Ex 5:1; 7:16 [k]Ex 11:5; 12:12,29
4:24 [l]Nu 22:22

4:3 snake. Knowing that the staff was only a rod, Moses recoiled from the serpent. The Hebrew term for "snake" is used for the poetic image of the primeval chaos dragon (Ps 74:13; Isa 27:1), which was a symbol for Egypt (Eze 29:3). Egyptian pharaohs wore a cobra made of metal on the front of their headdresses as a sign of authority. The powers of evil chaos were focused in Egypt, but Moses' rod in his hand would be adequate for the redemption of his people.
4:6 leprous. A general term for common skin diseases of the time. God showed his power to judge and to heal.
4:9 Nile. The Nile was revered as a god and was the source of Egypt's life.
4:10–14 See *WLC* 145.
4:10 slow of speech. The fourth objection (see 3:11,13; 4:1). It could refer to anything from a slight voice to a speech impediment to a lack of fluency in court Egyptian.
4:13–16 Left without excuse, Moses tried to decline his commission. But the Lord already had his brother Aaron on the way. The relation of Moses to Aaron illumines the nature of prophecy. Aaron would be a mouthpiece for Moses as a prophet is a mouthpiece for God (v. 16). See also 6:30 and 7:1.
4:17 signs. That is, miracles. The plagues are again anticipated. They would be initiated with this same staff.
■ **4:18–31** *Moses Returns to Egypt.* Having been called by God, Moses determined to carry through with his commission by returning to Egypt.
4:19 men . . . are dead. These men included Thutmose III if Amenhotep II is accepted as the pharaoh of the exodus (see "Introduction: Time and Place of Writing").
4:20 sons. Gershom (2:22) and Eliezer (18:4).
4:21–23 wonders. The series of miracles that Moses would perform before Pharaoh is here foreshadowed.
4:21 I will harden his heart. The Lord's hardening of Pharaoh's heart constituted sovereign, divine judgment on Pharaoh, who was also said to have hardened his own heart (8:15; Ro 9:17–18). God purposed to display his power over the stubborn hostility of the king so that his people might know that he was the Lord their Deliverer (6:6–8).
4:22 Israel is my firstborn son. The Lord put his claim upon Israel as his firstborn son, his beloved, a title that came to be realized in Jesus Christ, the royal representative of Israel (Mk 1:11). God's claim was the rationale for his deliverance and for the covenant to be sealed at Sinai ("so he [Israel] may worship me"; v. 23).
4:24–26 See *WCF* 28.5; *WLC* 109.
4:24 kill him. The Hebrew does not specify whether God intended to kill Moses or his firstborn son Gershom (see v. 23). That Gershom is not specifically introduced until after this statement lends support to the idea that it refers to Moses, since he has already been mentioned in this narrative. Some interpreters, however, believe that the sanction against uncircumcised males in Genesis 17:14 suggests that "him" refers to Gershom.

25 But Zipporah took a flint knife, cut off her son's foreskin[m] and touched ⌊Moses'⌋ feet
with it.[a] "Surely you are a bridegroom of blood to me," she said. 26 So the LORD let him
alone. (At that time she said "bridegroom of blood," referring to circumcision.)
27 The LORD said to Aaron, "Go into the desert to meet Moses." So he met Moses at the
mountain[n] of God and kissed[o] him. 28 Then Moses told Aaron everything the LORD had
sent him to say,[p] and also about all the miraculous signs he had commanded him to perform.
29 Moses and Aaron brought together all the elders[q] of the Israelites, 30 and Aaron told
them everything the LORD had said to Moses. He also performed the signs before the people, 31 and they believed.[r] And when they heard that the LORD was concerned[s] about
them and had seen their misery, they bowed down and worshiped.

Bricks Without Straw

5 Afterward Moses and Aaron went to Pharaoh and said, "This is what the LORD, the
God of Israel, says: 'Let my people go, so that they may hold a festival[t] to me in the
desert.' "
2 Pharaoh said, "Who is the LORD,[u] that I should obey him and let Israel go? I do not
know the LORD and I will not let Israel go."[v]
3 Then they said, "The God of the Hebrews has met with us. Now let us take a three-
day journey into the desert to offer sacrifices to the LORD our God, or he may strike us
with plagues[w] or with the sword."
4 But the king of Egypt said, "Moses and Aaron, why are you taking the people away
from their labor?[x] Get back to your work!" 5 Then Pharaoh said, "Look, the people of the
land are now numerous,[y] and you are stopping them from working."
6 That same day Pharaoh gave this order to the slave drivers and foremen in charge
of the people: 7 "You are no longer to supply the people with straw for making bricks; let
them go and gather their own straw. 8 But require them to make the same number of
bricks as before; don't reduce the quota. They are lazy; that is why they are crying out,
'Let us go and sacrifice to our God.' 9 Make the work harder for the men so that they keep
working and pay no attention to lies."
10 Then the slave drivers and the foremen went out and said to the people, "This is
what Pharaoh says: 'I will not give you any more straw. 11 Go and get your own straw
wherever you can find it, but your work will not be reduced at all.' " 12 So the people scattered all over Egypt to gather stubble to use for straw. 13 The slave drivers kept pressing
them, saying, "Complete the work required of you for each day, just as when you had
straw." 14 The Israelite foremen appointed by Pharaoh's slave drivers were beaten[z] and
were asked, "Why didn't you meet your quota of bricks yesterday or today, as before?"
15 Then the Israelite foremen went and appealed to Pharaoh: "Why have you treated

4:25 [m]Ge 17:14; Jos 5:2,3
4:27 [n]Ex 3:1 [o]ver 14
4:28 [p]ver 8-9,16
4:29 [q]Ex 3:16
4:31 [r]ver 8; Ex 3:18 [s]Ex 2:25
5:1 [t]Ex 3:18
5:2 [u]2Ki 18:35; Job 21:15 [v]Ex 3:19
5:3 [w]Ex 3:18
5:4 [x]Ex 1:11
5:5 [y]Ex 1:7,9
5:14 [z]Isa 10:24

[a] 25 Or *and drew near ⌊Moses'⌋ feet*

4:25 flint knife. Presumably a ceremonial instrument. Zipporah intervened to circumcise her son. Moses had to comply with the Abrahamic covenant by circumcising his son (Ge 17:10) before he could serve as Israel's deliverer. **bridegroom of blood.** The significance of these words is uncertain. It may have originally expressed Zipporah's disappointment with Moses and later been remembered positively as a title for Moses that indicated his rightful compliance with the rite of circumcision.
4:27 The LORD said. This may be translated "the LORD had said." The narrative steps back in time to the mountain of God, where Aaron had met Moses before he began his journey to Egypt. **he met Moses.** In Hebrew narrative style, this statement takes the reader back in time to explain Aaron's meeting with Moses before Moses left Sinai.
4:28–30 Moses' commission and promises were relayed to Aaron and then to the elders of Israel.
4:30 Aaron. Aaron would function as Moses' spokesman. See note on verses 13–16.
4:31 believed. The Israelites now believed as God had said they would (3:18). They worshiped, praising God for his care.
■ **5:1—15:21** *Moses Is Successful in Deliverance.* Moses delivered Israel from Egypt despite Pharaoh's resistance. These chapters divide into three main parts: Pharaoh's initial resistance (5:1—6:12), the plagues (6:13—13:16) and the final deliverance at the sea (13:17—15:21).
■ **5:1—6:12** *Refusal, Promise and Unbelief.* Pharaoh refused to let Israel go. His obstinacy led to discouragement and unbelief despite God's reaffirmation of his covenant promises.
5:1–14 Pharaoh increased Israel's oppression in response to God's demand for Israel's release.
5:1 Let my people go. The confrontation with Pharaoh began with God's demand. The people were his, not Pharaoh's. **festival.** A pilgrimage to a shrine where a feast was to be held (3:18). See *HC* 99,100.
5:2 Who is the LORD . . . ? Pharaoh's question would be answered by the plagues. See *WLC* 113.
5:3 After presenting God's demand, Moses and Aaron sought to reason with Pharaoh by saying that the Lord was the God of the Hebrews, that the distance would only require a three-day journey and that disobedience to God's command could seriously reduce Pharaoh's work force. Although the initial request was for a three-day journey, God knew that Pharaoh would not comply, to which God would respond by increasing his demands.
5:4 work. Pharaoh would not tolerate the loss of three days' work.
5:5 people of the land. Later this term came to mean the upper middle class in Israel, but here it means peasants attached to the land.
5:7 straw. The bricks of the time were much larger than bricks of today. They were molded of Nile mud with straw to increase their strength.
5:10–18 See *WLC* 130.
5:10 slave drivers. The slave masters and section leaders passed the order down through the ranks. During the events of verses 6–19, Moses and Aaron did not intervene. This crushing reply of Pharaoh highlights his human supremacy.

your servants this way? 16Your servants are given no straw, yet we are told, 'Make
bricks!' Your servants are being beaten, but the fault is with your own people."
17Pharaoh said, "Lazy, that's what you are—lazy![a] That is why you keep saying, 'Let
us go and sacrifice to the LORD.' 18Now get to work. You will not be given any straw, yet
you must produce your full quota of bricks."
19The Israelite foremen realized they were in trouble when they were told, "You are
not to reduce the number of bricks required of you for each day." 20When they left Pharaoh, they found Moses and Aaron waiting to meet them, 21and they said, "May the LORD
look upon you and judge you! You have made us a stench[b] to Pharaoh and his officials
and have put a sword in their hand to kill us."[c]

God Promises Deliverance

22Moses returned to the LORD and said, "O Lord, why have you brought trouble upon
this people?[d] Is this why you sent me? 23Ever since I went to Pharaoh to speak in your
name, he has brought trouble upon this people, and you have not rescued[e] your people
at all."

6 Then the LORD said to Moses, "Now you will see what I will do to Pharaoh: Because
of my mighty hand[f] he will let them go;[g] because of my mighty hand he will drive
them out of his country."[h]
2God also said to Moses, "I am the LORD. 3I appeared to Abraham, to Isaac and to Jacob as God Almighty,[a][i] but by my name[j] the LORD[b][k] I did not make myself known to
them.[c] 4I also established my covenant[l] with them to give them the land of Canaan,
where they lived as aliens.[m] 5Moreover, I have heard the groaning[n] of the Israelites,
whom the Egyptians are enslaving, and I have remembered my covenant.
6"Therefore, say to the Israelites: 'I am the LORD, and I will bring you out from under
the yoke of the Egyptians. I will free you from being slaves to them, and I will redeem[o]
you with an outstretched arm[p] and with mighty acts of judgment. 7I will take you as my
own people, and I will be your God.[q] Then you will know[r] that I am the LORD your God,
who brought you out from under the yoke of the Egyptians. 8And I will bring you to the
land[s] I swore with uplifted hand[t] to give to Abraham, to Isaac and to Jacob.[u] I will give
it to you as a possession. I am the LORD.' "
9Moses reported this to the Israelites, but they did not listen to him because of their
discouragement and cruel bondage.
10Then the LORD said to Moses, 11"Go, tell Pharaoh king of Egypt to let the Israelites
go out of his country."
12But Moses said to the LORD, "If the Israelites will not listen to me, why would Pharaoh listen to me, since I speak with faltering lips[d]?"[v]

Family Record of Moses and Aaron

13Now the LORD spoke to Moses and Aaron about the Israelites and Pharaoh king of
Egypt, and he commanded them to bring the Israelites out of Egypt.

5:17 [a]ver 8
5:21 [b]Ge 34:30 [c]Ex 14:11
5:22 [d]Nu 11:11
5:23 [e]Jer 4:10
6:1 [f]Ex 3:19 [g]Ex 3:20 [h]Ex 12:31,33,39
6:3 [i]Ge 17:1 [j]Ps 68:4; 83:18; Isa 52:6 [k]Ex 3:14
6:4 [l]Ge 15:18 [m]Ge 28:4,13
6:5 [n]Ex 2:23
6:6 [o]Dt 7:8; 1Ch 17:21 [p]Dt 26:8
6:7 [q]Dt 4:20; 2Sa 7:24 [r]Ex 16:12; Isa 41:20
6:8 [s]Ge 15:18; 26:3 [t]Ge 14:22 [u]Ps 136:21-22
6:12 [v]ver 30; Ex 1:10; Jer 1:6

[a] 3 Hebrew *El-Shaddai* [b] 3 See note at Exodus 3:15. [c] 3 Or *Almighty, and by my name the LORD did I not let myself be known to them?* [d] 12 Hebrew *I am uncircumcised of lips;* also in verse 30

5:15–21 The Israelites appealed to Pharaoh for relief and complained to Moses and Aaron about their plight.
5:21 the LORD . . . judge you! Not for the last time, leaders of Israel would curse Moses for obeying the command of the Lord.
5:22—6:8 God reaffirmed his covenant promise to the fathers in response to Pharaoh's refusal and Israel's disbelief.
5:22 Moses . . . said. To the people, Moses spoke God's word; to God he pleaded, "Where is God's promised deliverance?" This pattern is repeated throughout Exodus. God's reply (ch. 6) gave assurance that the apparently hopeless situation would be the occasion for his mighty action.
6:1 drive. The Lord's power would more than prevail. Pharaoh would not only let them go, but he would drive the Israelites out.
6:2 I am the LORD. This formula appears four times in logical progression: In verse 2 it reinforces the promises given to Abraham. In verse 6 it confirms God's new promise of redemption. In verse 7 it underscores God's intention to adopt Israel. In verse 8 it confirms the promise of the land as the goal of the exodus and concludes the message.
6:3 God Almighty. God had revealed himself to the patriarchs primarily as God Almighty (Hebrew, *El-Shaddai;* Ge 17:1; 28:3; 35:11). Genesis indicates that God had also revealed himself as Yahweh from the earliest times (Ge 4:26; 9:26; 12:8; 24:12). But in the days of Moses, God identified himself afresh as Yahweh, the God who would act in accordance with his promises and would redeem Israel by his powerful hand. See *WLC* 101.
6:4 my covenant. Yahweh is *El Shaddai,* the God of Abraham, Isaac and Jacob, and his covenant promise to them would now come to fruition. Verses 4–5 affirm the continuity between the covenants with Abraham and Moses.
6:5 remembered. When God "remembers," it means that he is about to act on his promises, not that he has forgotten in the sense of lacking omniscience.
6:6 redeem. The term *redeem* normally refers to the restoration of rights to a disadvantaged family member by the payment of a price or a ransom. Redemption was normally effected by the next of kin (Lev 25:25; cf. Ru 4). Israel, as Yahweh's son (4:22), was redeemed from Egypt to be God's own people.
6:7 my own people. This anticipates 19:5–6.
6:9–12 The discouragement of Israel and of Moses shows how completely the deliverance would be God's work. In spite of God's renewed promise, the people would not listen, and even Moses would not believe that he would succeed.
■ **6:13—13:16** *Plagues Against Egypt.* Moses and Aaron delivered Israel through God's miraculous intervention by bringing plagues against the Egyptians. This dramatic portion of the book divides into four main parts: an affirmation of Moses and Aaron (6:13—7:7), the miraculous plagues on Egypt (7:8—12:30), the fulfillment

14These were the heads of their families[a]:[w]

The sons of Reuben the firstborn son of Israel were Hanoch and Pallu, Hezron
and Carmi. These were the clans of Reuben.
15The sons of Simeon[x] were Jemuel, Jamin, Ohad, Jakin, Zohar and Shaul the
son of a Canaanite woman. These were the clans of Simeon.
16These were the names of the sons of Levi according to their records: Gershon,[y] Kohath and Merari.[z] Levi lived 137 years.
17The sons of Gershon, by clans, were Libni and Shimei.[a]
18The sons of Kohath were Amram, Izhar, Hebron and Uzziel.[b] Kohath lived
133 years.
19The sons of Merari were Mahli and Mushi.[c]
These were the clans of Levi according to their records.
20Amram married his father's sister Jochebed, who bore him Aaron and Moses.[d] Amram lived 137 years.
21The sons of Izhar[e] were Korah, Nepheg and Zicri.
22The sons of Uzziel were Mishael, Elzaphan[f] and Sithri.
23Aaron married Elisheba, daughter of Amminadab[g] and sister of Nahshon,
and she bore him Nadab and Abihu,[h] Eleazar[i] and Ithamar.[j]
24The sons of Korah[k] were Assir, Elkanah and Abiasaph. These were the Korahite clans.
25Eleazar son of Aaron married one of the daughters of Putiel, and she bore him
Phinehas.[l]

These were the heads of the Levite families, clan by clan.

26It was this same Aaron and Moses to whom the LORD said, "Bring the Israelites out
of Egypt by their divisions."[m] 27They were the ones who spoke to Pharaoh king of Egypt
about bringing the Israelites out of Egypt. It was the same Moses and Aaron.

Aaron to Speak for Moses

28Now when the LORD spoke to Moses in Egypt, 29he said to him, "I am the LORD.[n] Tell
Pharaoh king of Egypt everything I tell you."
30But Moses said to the LORD, "Since I speak with faltering lips,[o] why would Pharaoh
listen to me?"

7 Then the LORD said to Moses, "See, I have made you like God[p] to Pharaoh, and your
brother Aaron will be your prophet. 2You are to say everything I command you, and
your brother Aaron is to tell Pharaoh to let the Israelites go out of his country. 3But I will
harden Pharaoh's heart,[q] and though I multiply my miraculous signs and wonders in

a *14* The Hebrew for *families* here and in verse 25 refers to units larger than clans.

6:14 [w]Ge 46:9
6:15 [x]Ge 46:10; 1Ch 4:24
6:16 [y]Ge 46:11 [z]Nu 3:17
6:17 [a]1Ch 6:17
6:18 [b]1Ch 6:2,18
6:19 [c]Nu 3:20,33; 1Ch 6:19; 23:21
6:20 [d]Ex 2:1-2; Nu 26:59
6:21 [e]1Ch 6:38
6:22 [f]Lev 10:4; Nu 3:30
6:23 [g]Ru 4:19,20 [h]Lev 10:1 [i]Nu 3:2, 32 [j]Nu 26:60
6:24 [k]Nu 26:11
6:25 [l]Nu 25:7,11; Jos 24:33; Ps 106:30
6:26 [m]Ex 7:4; 12:17,41, 51
6:29 [n]ver 11; Ex 7:2
6:30 [o]ver 12; Ex 4:10
7:1 [p]Ex 4:16
7:3 [q]Ex 4:21; 11:9

---

of the commission (12:31–41) and future observances (12:42—13:16).

■ **6:13—7:7** *Affirmation of Commission.* The divine authorization of Moses' activities in Egypt is so important to this book that in this transitional section God's commission of Moses and Aaron is formally recapitulated in a genealogy (6:13–27) and in a summary of their compliance with their divine call (6:28—7:7).

6:13–27 Moses and Aaron were formally legitimated through a genealogy that begins with Reuben, Israel's oldest son, and then proceeds to Simeon, the second son, and to Levi. Levi's genealogy established the link to Moses and Aaron. Among the Levites Amram is singled out, then Aaron and Moses. The priestly line for Israel follows (Nu 25:10–13; 26:57–62). For Korah, see Numbers 16:1–35.

6:20 The record of the marriage of Amram to his paternal aunt would have been most unlikely in a fictitious genealogy. Such a marriage was later forbidden in the law (Lev 18:12). Three women are mentioned in tracing the line: Jochebed, Elisheba and a daughter of Putiel.

6:23 bore him. No descendant of Moses is named, but those of Aaron continue for the next two generations to establish priestly succession from Aaron through his successor Eleazar. The genealogy spans only four generations for the sojourn in Egypt and is clearly selective.

6:25 Putiel . . . Phinehas. Like Merari in verse 16, these are probably Egyptian names, which occurred fairly commonly among Levites.

6:26 divisions. Israel is portrayed as a holy army that God delivered through Moses. The mention of bringing out Israel's divisions here and in 7:4 is balanced by the accomplishment of the same at the end of this section (12:41,51).

6:28—7:7 This section reviews and restates Moses' commission after his hesitation (6:12,30). Moses and Aaron were specifically called to perform miracles.

7:1 prophet. The term means "one called." The function of Aaron in relation to Moses demonstrates that of a true prophet in relation to God. See note at 4:13–16.

7:2–5 The theological explanation of the plagues is given in the first five plagues. Pharaoh's obstinacy was self-motivated (7:22; 8:15,32; 9:7). God is said to have hardened Pharaoh's heart in plagues seven, eight and nine (10:1,20,27). In plague six, Pharaoh's obstinacy stemmed from Pharaoh himself (9:35), but God also claimed to have hardened Pharaoh (10:1). God's purpose was not simply judgment on Pharaoh, but manifestion of his power to save his people so that his name might be proclaimed in all the earth (9:16; Ro 9:17–18).

7:3 harden Pharaoh's heart. The term "heart" refers to the inner person—feeling, thinking and willing. Some interpreters suggest that the Lord caused Pharaoh's heart to become hard (lit., "difficult") by giving it over to its evil direction without restraint (Ro 1:24,26,28). Others assign a somewhat more active role to God by arguing that he actually removed from Pharaoh the ability to choose that which is outwardly good (Ro 9:19–22), similar to the way in which he removed from all people the ability to perform meritorious works after humankind's fall into sin. Neither view attributes evil to God, and both recognize the hardening of Pharaoh's heart as God's judgment against Pharaoh for his prior wickedness. As a result of the judgment, the Israelites experienced God's mercy and witnessed his power to save. **though I multiply.** Alternatively, "in order that I might multiply." **signs and wonders.** See note on 7:8—12:30. See *WCF* 5.6.

Egypt, 4 he will not listen[r] to you. Then I will lay my hand on Egypt and with mighty acts
of judgment[s] I will bring out my divisions, my people the Israelites. 5 And the Egyptians
will know that I am the LORD[t] when I stretch out my hand[u] against Egypt and bring the
Israelites out of it."
6 Moses and Aaron did just as the LORD commanded[v] them. 7 Moses was eighty years
old[w] and Aaron eighty-three when they spoke to Pharaoh.

Aaron's Staff Becomes a Snake

8 The LORD said to Moses and Aaron, 9 "When Pharaoh says to you, 'Perform a miracle,[x]' then say to Aaron, 'Take your staff and throw it down before Pharaoh,' and it will
become a snake."[y]
10 So Moses and Aaron went to Pharaoh and did just as the LORD commanded. Aaron
threw his staff down in front of Pharaoh and his officials, and it became a snake. 11 Pharaoh then summoned wise men and sorcerers, and the Egyptian magicians[z] also did the
same things by their secret arts:[a] 12 Each one threw down his staff and it became a snake.
But Aaron's staff swallowed up their staffs. 13 Yet Pharaoh's heart[b] became hard and he
would not listen to them, just as the LORD had said.

The Plague of Blood

14 Then the LORD said to Moses, "Pharaoh's heart is unyielding;[c] he refuses to let the
people go. 15 Go to Pharaoh in the morning as he goes out to the water. Wait on the bank
of the Nile to meet him, and take in your hand the staff that was changed into a snake.
16 Then say to him, 'The LORD, the God of the Hebrews, has sent me to say to you: Let my
people go, so that they may worship[d] me in the desert. But until now you have not listened. 17 This is what the LORD says: By this you will know that I am the LORD:[e] With the
staff that is in my hand I will strike the water of the Nile, and it will be changed into
blood.[f] 18 The fish in the Nile will die, and the river will stink; the Egyptians will not be
able to drink its water.' "[g]
19 The LORD said to Moses, "Tell Aaron, 'Take your staff and stretch out your hand[h]
over the waters of Egypt—over the streams and canals, over the ponds and all the reservoirs'—and they will turn to blood. Blood will be everywhere in Egypt, even in the
wooden buckets and stone jars."
20 Moses and Aaron did just as the LORD had commanded. He raised his staff in the
presence of Pharaoh and his officials and struck the water of the Nile,[i] and all the water was changed into blood.[j] 21 The fish in the Nile died, and the river smelled so bad that
the Egyptians could not drink its water. Blood was everywhere in Egypt.
22 But the Egyptian magicians did the same things by their secret arts,[k] and Pharaoh's
heart became hard; he would not listen to Moses and Aaron, just as the LORD had said.
23 Instead, he turned and went into his palace, and did not take even this to heart. 24 And
all the Egyptians dug along the Nile to get drinking water, because they could not drink
the water of the river.

7:4 [r]Ex 11:9 [s]Ex 3:20; 6:6
7:5 [t]ver 17; Ex 8:19,22 [u]Ex 3:20
7:6 [v]ver 2
7:7 [w]Dt 31:2; 34:7; Ac 7:23,30
7:9 [x]Isa 7:11; Jn 2:18 [y]Ex 4:2-5
7:11 [z]Ge 41:8; 2Ti 3:8 [a]ver 22; Ex 8:7,18
7:13 [b]Ex 4:21
7:14 [c]Ex 8:15,32; 10:1, 20,27
7:16 [d]Ex 3:18; 5:1,3
7:17 [e]Ex 5:2 [f]Ex 4:9; Rev 11:6; 16:4
7:18 [g]ver 21,24
7:19 [h]Ex 8:5-6,16; 9:22; 10:12,21; 14:21
7:20 [i]Ex 17:5 [j]Ps 78:44; 105:29
7:22 [k]ver 11

7:6 This summary completes the formal affirmation of Moses and Aaron as those divinely ordained to deliver Israel through miraculous plagues.

■ **7:8—12:30** *Miraculous Plagues.* The account of the plagues of Egypt begins with an initial miracle before Pharaoh (7:8–13), is followed by a series of nine plagues (7:14—10:29) and is culminated by the devastating plague of Passover night (11:1—12:30).

7:8–13 Moses and Aaron performed an initial miracle that directly confronted Pharaoh's authority.

7:9 snake. The word here (different from the word for "snake" in 4:3) refers to a sea reptile or river monster (see Ge 1:21; Eze 29:3; 32:2) but occasionally also to a land lizard (Dt 32:33). A young crocodile may be in view.

7:11 magicians. The term refers to one skilled in the use of a stylus, thus indicating a learned person. The Egyptian magicians relied on the familiar tricks of magic; Aaron relied on divine power. See note on 9:11.

7:13 became hard. The verb form indicates the subsequent state of Pharaoh's heart from that point onward. **as the LORD had said.** See 4:21; 7:3,22; 8:15,19).

7:14—10:29 The nine plagues were introduced by the sign in Pharaoh's court (7:8–13) and were closed by the plague against the firstborn (11:1—12:30). These plagues divide into three groups of three (7:14—8:19; 8:20—9:12; 9:13—10:29). The first plague of each group began with a warning to Pharaoh as he went down to the Nile in the mornings (7:14–15; 8:20; 9:13), the second with a warning to Pharaoh at an undisclosed place (8:1; 9:1; 10:1–2) and the third without a warning (8:16; 9:8; 10:21). The description of the first plague of each triplet reveals the theme of the triplet.

7:14—8:19 The first three plagues demonstrated the absolute superiority of the Lord over Pharaoh (7:16–17).

7:14–25 God raised his rod against the Nile, turning the water to blood. The Egyptians were unmoved by this sign and even mimicked it.

7:14 unyielding. Pharaoh's hardening was the necessary prerequisite for the display of divine power.

7:15 bank. The riverbank would be the expected meeting place. A theory of natural causation for the plagues does not do justice to the clear statements of the text. Moreover, the list of plagues in Psalms 78:44–51 and 105:28–36 differ in number and sequence, but the order stated here is essential for the naturalistic explanation that sees the plagues as natural events tied up with the inundation of the Nile.

7:17 I will strike. Aaron would strike, but the Lord would perform the miracle. The striking was by God's hand, by his rod. The deed of Aaron was owned by God no less than the word that God gave him through Moses was owned by him. **blood.** The red clay that comes down at inundation time from the Ethiopian highlands is not in view, for Hebrew never denotes red color in this way.

7:19 waters. All the natural waters of Egypt were involved, including the natural arms of the Nile, the irrigation canals and the pools formed by the overflowing inundation.

7:22 magicians. See note on 9:11.

The Plague of Frogs

8 25 Seven days passed after the LORD struck the Nile. 1 Then the LORD said to Moses,
"Go to Pharaoh and say to him, 'This is what the LORD says: Let my people go, so
that they may worship[l] me. 2 If you refuse to let them go, I will plague your whole country with frogs. 3 The Nile will teem with frogs. They will come up into your palace and your
bedroom and onto your bed, into the houses of your officials and on your people,[m] and
into your ovens and kneading troughs. 4 The frogs will go up on you and your people and
all your officials.' "
5 Then the LORD said to Moses, "Tell Aaron, 'Stretch out your hand with your staff[n]
over the streams and canals and ponds, and make frogs come up on the land of Egypt.' "
6 So Aaron stretched out his hand over the waters of Egypt, and the frogs[o] came up
and covered the land. 7 But the magicians did the same things by their secret arts;[p] they
also made frogs come up on the land of Egypt.
8 Pharaoh summoned Moses and Aaron and said, "Pray[q] to the LORD to take the frogs
away from me and my people, and I will let your people go to offer sacrifices[r] to the
LORD."
9 Moses said to Pharaoh, "I leave to you the honor of setting the time for me to pray
for you and your officials and your people that you and your houses may be rid of the
frogs, except for those that remain in the Nile."
10 "Tomorrow," Pharaoh said.
Moses replied, "It will be as you say, so that you may know there is no one like the
LORD our God.[s] 11 The frogs will leave you and your houses, your officials and your people; they will remain only in the Nile."
12 After Moses and Aaron left Pharaoh, Moses cried out to the LORD about the frogs he
had brought on Pharaoh. 13 And the LORD did what Moses asked. The frogs died in the
houses, in the courtyards and in the fields. 14 They were piled into heaps, and the land
reeked of them. 15 But when Pharaoh saw that there was relief, he hardened his heart[t]
and would not listen to Moses and Aaron, just as the LORD had said.

The Plague of Gnats

16 Then the LORD said to Moses, "Tell Aaron, 'Stretch out your staff and strike the dust
of the ground,' and throughout the land of Egypt the dust will become gnats." 17 They did
this, and when Aaron stretched out his hand with the staff and struck the dust of the
ground, gnats[u] came upon men and animals. All the dust throughout the land of Egypt
became gnats. 18 But when the magicians[v] tried to produce gnats by their secret arts,[w]
they could not. And the gnats were on men and animals.
19 The magicians said to Pharaoh, "This is the finger[x] of God." But Pharaoh's heart
was hard and he would not listen, just as the LORD had said.

The Plague of Flies

20 Then the LORD said to Moses, "Get up early in the morning[y] and confront Pharaoh
as he goes to the water and say to him, 'This is what the LORD says: Let my people go, so
that they may worship[z] me. 21 If you do not let my people go, I will send swarms of flies
on you and your officials, on your people and into your houses. The houses of the Egyptians will be full of flies, and even the ground where they are.
22 " 'But on that day I will deal differently with the land of Goshen, where my people
live;[a] no swarms of flies will be there, so that you will know[b] that I, the LORD, am in this
land. 23 I will make a distinction[a] between my people and your people. This miraculous
sign will occur tomorrow.' "

8:1 [l]Ex 3:12,18; 4:23
8:3 [m]Ex 10:6
8:5 [n]Ex 7:19
8:6 [o]Ps 78:45; 105:30
8:7 [p]Ex 7:11
8:8 [q]ver 28; Ex 9:28; 10:17 [r]ver 25
8:10 [s]Ex 9:14; Dt 4:35; 33:26; 2Sa 7:22; 1Ch 17:20; Ps 86:8; Isa 46:9; Jer 10:6
8:15 [t]Ex 7:14
8:17 [u]Ps 105:31
8:18 [v]Ex 9:11; Da 5:8 [w]Ex 7:11
8:19 [x]Ex 7:5; 10:7; Ps 8:3; Lk 11:20
8:20 [y]Ex 7:15; 9:13 [z]ver 1; Ex 3:18
8:22 [a]Ex 9:4,6,26; 10:23; 11:7 [b]Ex 7:5; 9:29

[a] *23* Septuagint and Vulgate; Hebrew *will put a deliverance*

8:1–15 God raised his rod against the waters, making them swarm with frogs. Again the sign was mimicked, after which it was removed.
8:2 frogs. Frogs were deified in the form of the goddess Heqt, who assisted women at childbirth. The theme of the gradual weakening of Pharaoh's resistance now begins. However, the plagues were not intended to soften his resistance (7:3) but to magnify Yahweh's power.
8:3 teem. The Nile would teem with frogs, as the delta did (1:7) with Israelites.
8:7 made frogs come up. Again the magicians could only add to the distress. See 7:22; see also 9:11 and its note.
8:15 would not listen. Yahweh's hand was in the plagues so that Israel might believe, not so that Pharaoh might be moved. Pharaoh, being personally affected, made his first concession. See *WCF* 5.6.
8:16–19 God raised his rod against the dust, turning it into a plague of gnats.
8:19 finger of God. The magicians now admitted that a divine intervention was directly involved (31:18; Ps 8:3). Pharaoh was not persuaded.
8:20—9:12 The second set of plagues was designed primarily to demonstrate God's love for his people in contrast to his harsh treatment of his enemies, the Egyptians (8:22).
8:20–32 God's rod brought a plague of flies on Egypt, sparing his own people and prompting Pharaoh's deceit.
8:21 swarms. The word occurs only here and in Psalms 78:45 and 105:31.

24 And the LORD did this. Dense swarms of flies poured into Pharaoh's palace and into
the houses of his officials, and throughout Egypt the land was ruined by the flies.[c]
25 Then Pharaoh summoned[d] Moses and Aaron and said, "Go, sacrifice to your God
here in the land."
26 But Moses said, "That would not be right. The sacrifices we offer the LORD our God
would be detestable to the Egyptians.[e] And if we offer sacrifices that are detestable in
their eyes, will they not stone us? 27 We must take a three-day journey into the desert to
offer sacrifices[f] to the LORD our God, as he commands us."
28 Pharaoh said, "I will let you go to offer sacrifices to the LORD your God in the desert, but you must not go very far. Now pray[g] for me."
29 Moses answered, "As soon as I leave you, I will pray to the LORD, and tomorrow the
flies will leave Pharaoh and his officials and his people. Only be sure that Pharaoh does
not act deceitfully[h] again by not letting the people go to offer sacrifices to the LORD."
30 Then Moses left Pharaoh and prayed to the LORD,[i] 31 and the LORD did what Moses
asked: The flies left Pharaoh and his officials and his people; not a fly remained. 32 But
this time also Pharaoh hardened his heart[j] and would not let the people go.

The Plague on Livestock

9 Then the LORD said to Moses, "Go to Pharaoh and say to him, 'This is what the LORD,
the God of the Hebrews, says: "Let my people go, so that they may worship[k] me."
2 If you refuse to let them go and continue to hold them back, 3 the hand[l] of the LORD will
bring a terrible plague on your livestock in the field—on your horses and donkeys and
camels and on your cattle and sheep and goats. 4 But the LORD will make a distinction between the livestock of Israel and that of Egypt,[m] so that no animal belonging to the Israelites will die.' "
5 The LORD set a time and said, "Tomorrow the LORD will do this in the land." 6 And the
next day the LORD did it: All the livestock[n] of the Egyptians died,[o] but not one animal belonging to the Israelites died. 7 Pharaoh sent men to investigate and found that not even
one of the animals of the Israelites had died. Yet his heart was unyielding and he would
not let the people go.[p]

The Plague of Boils

8 Then the LORD said to Moses and Aaron, "Take handfuls of soot from a furnace and
have Moses toss it into the air in the presence of Pharaoh. 9 It will become fine dust over
the whole land of Egypt, and festering boils[q] will break out on men and animals throughout the land."
10 So they took soot from a furnace and stood before Pharaoh. Moses tossed it into the
air, and festering boils broke out on men and animals. 11 The magicians[r] could not
stand before Moses because of the boils that were on them and on all the Egyptians.
12 But the LORD hardened Pharaoh's heart[s] and he would not listen to Moses and Aaron,
just as the LORD had said to Moses.

The Plague of Hail

13 Then the LORD said to Moses, "Get up early in the morning, confront Pharaoh and
say to him, 'This is what the LORD, the God of the Hebrews, says: Let my people go, so

8:24 [c]Ps 78:45; 105:31
8:25 [d]ver 8; Ex 9:27
8:26 [e]Ge 43:32; 46:34
8:27 [f]Ex 3:18
8:28 [g]ver 8; Ex 9:28; 1Ki 13:6
8:29 [h]ver 15
8:30 [i]ver 12
8:32 [j]ver 8, 15; Ex 4:21
9:1 [k]Ex 8:1
9:3 [l]Ex 7:4
9:4 [m]ver 26; Ex 8:22
9:6 [n]ver 19-21; Ex 11:5 [o]Ps 78:48-50
9:7 [p]Ex 7:14; 8:32
9:9 [q]Dt 28:27, 35; Rev 16:2
9:11 [r]Ex 8:18
9:12 [s]Ex 4:21

8:25 Under the swarms of flies, Pharaoh offered to negotiate by agreeing to less than the Lord had demanded. Moses refused to compromise: He would not worship in the land (or closer than a three-day journey away; v. 28) or leave behind the women and children (10:11) or the flocks and herds (10:24).
8:26 detestable. Egyptians deified the animals customarily sacrificed by the Israelites.
8:32 See *WCF* 5.6.
9:1–7 God's rod brought a plague of disease on Egypt's livestock, but not on Israel's.
9:3 hand. The Biblical account permits no naturalistic explanation; for example, anthrax, stemming from dead frogs. **horses.** The horse was brought into Egypt by the Hyksos about 1700 B.C. **camels.** The camel was in sporadic use in Egypt's early history, only appearing in general use much later. Perhaps camels of the merchant traders from Arabia and elsewhere are referred to here.
9:5 set a time. It would be clear that the plague had not come by coincidence. **Tomorrow.** That the Lord gave them a day's notice suggests that he was providing time for God-fearing Egyptians to put their livestock in a place of shelter (cf. vv. 18–19).
9:6 All the livestock. Since the next plague also affected livestock, this phrase must designate either all kinds of livestock or all the livestock referred to in verse 3; i.e., those in the field. Compare verses 18–19.
9:8–12 God's rod brought a plague of boils on Egypt.
9:8 handfuls. Perhaps one handful for each cardinal point was to be tossed. It was done before Pharaoh to make him aware that the event was of supernatural origin.
9:11 magicians. The defeat of the magicians was clear from the start: Aaron's staff-turned-serpent swallowed up the serpents the magicians produced (7:12). The magicians were able to imitate turning water to blood and producing frogs, but they could only add to, not reverse, these plagues (7:22; 8:7). When they could not imitate the production of gnats, they told Pharaoh the plagues were divine judgments, not magic (8:18–19). Ultimately the magicians were struck with boils and left the scene (9:11).
9:13—10:29 The third set of plagues was designed to show that God could have utterly destroyed Egypt at any moment but that in his mercy he had held back his fierce anger (9:15–16).
9:13–35 God raised his rod against Egypt in a hailstorm but again spared the Israelites.

that they may worship[t] me, 14 or this time I will send the full force of my plagues against
you and against your officials and your people, so you may know[u] that there is no one
like[v] me in all the earth. 15 For by now I could have stretched out my hand and struck you
and your people[w] with a plague that would have wiped you off the earth. 16 But I have
raised you up[a] for this very purpose,[x] that I might show you my power[y] and that my
name might be proclaimed in all the earth. 17 You still set yourself against my people and
will not let them go. 18 Therefore, at this time tomorrow I will send the worst hailstorm[z]
that has ever fallen on Egypt, from the day it was founded till now.[a] 19 Give an order now
to bring your livestock and everything you have in the field to a place of shelter, because
the hail will fall on every man and animal that has not been brought in and is still out
in the field, and they will die.' "

20 Those officials of Pharaoh who feared[b] the word of the LORD hurried to bring their
slaves and their livestock inside. 21 But those who ignored the word of the LORD left their
slaves and livestock in the field.

22 Then the LORD said to Moses, "Stretch out your hand toward the sky so that hail will
fall all over Egypt—on men and animals and on everything growing in the fields of
Egypt." 23 When Moses stretched out his staff toward the sky, the LORD sent thunder[c] and
hail,[d] and lightning flashed down to the ground. So the LORD rained hail on the land of
Egypt; 24 hail fell and lightning flashed back and forth. It was the worst storm in all the
land of Egypt since it had become a nation. 25 Throughout Egypt hail struck everything
in the fields—both men and animals; it beat down everything growing in the fields and
stripped every tree.[e] 26 The only place it did not hail was the land of Goshen,[f] where the
Israelites were.[g]

27 Then Pharaoh summoned Moses and Aaron. "This time I have sinned,"[h] he said to
them. "The LORD is in the right,[i] and I and my people are in the wrong. 28 Pray[j] to the
LORD, for we have had enough thunder and hail. I will let you go;[k] you don't have to stay
any longer."

29 Moses replied, "When I have gone out of the city, I will spread out my hands[l] in
prayer to the LORD. The thunder will stop and there will be no more hail, so you may
know that the earth[m] is the LORD's. 30 But I know that you and your officials still do not
fear the LORD God."

31 (The flax and barley[n] were destroyed, since the barley had headed and the flax was
in bloom. 32 The wheat and spelt, however, were not destroyed, because they ripen later.)

33 Then Moses left Pharaoh and went out of the city. He spread out his hands toward
the LORD; the thunder and hail stopped, and the rain no longer poured down on the land.
34 When Pharaoh saw that the rain and hail and thunder had stopped, he sinned again:
He and his officials hardened their hearts. 35 So Pharaoh's heart[o] was hard and he
would not let the Israelites go, just as the LORD had said through Moses.

The Plague of Locusts

10 Then the LORD said to Moses, "Go to Pharaoh, for I have hardened his heart[p]
and the hearts of his officials so that I may perform these miraculous signs[q] of
mine among them 2 that you may tell your children[r] and grandchildren how I dealt harshly with the Egyptians and how I performed my signs among them, and that you may
know that I am the LORD."

3 So Moses and Aaron went to Pharaoh and said to him, "This is what the LORD, the
God of the Hebrews, says: 'How long will you refuse to humble[s] yourself before me? Let
my people go, so that they may worship me. 4 If you refuse to let them go, I will bring locusts[t] into your country tomorrow. 5 They will cover the face of the ground so that it cannot be seen. They will devour what little you have left[u] after the hail, including every tree

[a] 16 *Or have spared you*

9:13 [t]Ex 8:20
9:14 [u]Ex 8:10 [v]2Sa 7:22; 1Ch 17:20; Ps 86:8; Isa 46:9; Jer 10:6
9:15 [w]Ex 3:20
9:16 [x]Pr 16:4 [y]Ro 9:17*
9:18 [z]ver 23 [a]ver 24
9:20 [b]Pr 13:13
9:23 [c]Ps 18:13 [d]Jos 10:11; Ps 78:47; 105:32; Isa 30:30; Eze 38:22; Rev 8:7; 16:21
9:25 [e]Ps 105:32-33
9:26 [f]ver 4 [g]Ex 8:22; 10:23; 11:7; 12:13
9:27 [h]Ex 10:16 [i]2Ch 12:6; Ps 129:4; La 1:18
9:28 [j]Ex 10:17 [k]Ex 8:8
9:29 [l]1Ki 8:22, 38; Ps 143:6; Isa 1:15 [m]Ex 19:5; Ps 24:1; 1Co 10:26
9:31 [n]Ru 1:22; 2:23
9:35 [o]Ex 4:21
10:1 [p]Ex 4:21 [q]Ex 7:3
10:2 [r]Ex 12:26-27; 13:8, 14; Dt 4:9; Ps 44:1; 78:4, 5; Joel 1:3
10:3 [s]1Ki 21:29; Jas 4:10; 1Pe 5:6
10:4 [t]Rev 9:3
10:5 [u]Ex 9:32; Joel 1:4

9:14 The plagues (lit., "blows" or "strokes") showed the power of God's hand in smiting Egypt (3:20; 7:25; 12:13). The last three plagues fell when the staff of the Lord was stretched out to heaven (v. 22), Earth (10:13) and again to heaven (10:21).
9:20–21 Some Egyptian officers had learned to fear God's word. See 10:7.
9:23 thunder. Literally, "voices." This was no natural hailstorm.
9:25 stripped every tree. The shattering of trees reminds us of the theophany recounted in Psalm 29.
9:27 This time. Implies the superficiality of Pharaoh's confession. Though not believing Pharaoh's feigned contrition, Moses sought occasion to showcase God's power over the earth in stopping the hail. **I have sinned.** Pharaoh confessed his guilt for the first time, but his literal statement was only "I have missed the way."
9:31–32 in bloom . . . ripen later. This information seems to set the time in January-February, a period when hailstorms are frequent in Egypt. Flax was in the bud in January, and barley was in the ear at that time; it would have been harvested in February.
10:1–20 God struck Egypt with a locust plague.
10:1 hardened his heart. Pharaoh's will was reversed four times in this one narrative (verses 8,10–11,16–17,20).
10:2 tell. The plagues were intended to teach the Israelites and to leave an indelible impression on their posterity. This verse is a clear statement of the divine plan involving Pharaoh.

that is growing in your fields. 6They will fill your houses and those of all your officials and all the Egyptians—something neither your fathers nor your forefathers have ever seen from the day they settled in this land till now.' " Then Moses turned and left Pharaoh.

7Pharaoh's officials said to him, "How long will this man be a snare[v] to us? Let the people go, so that they may worship the LORD their God. Do you not yet realize that Egypt is ruined?"[w]

8Then Moses and Aaron were brought back to Pharaoh. "Go, worship[x] the LORD your God," he said. "But just who will be going?"

9Moses answered, "We will go with our young and old, with our sons and daughters, and with our flocks and herds, because we are to celebrate a festival to the LORD."

10Pharaoh said, "The LORD be with you—if I let you go, along with your women and children! Clearly you are bent on evil.[a] 11No! Have only the men go; and worship the LORD, since that's what you have been asking for." Then Moses and Aaron were driven out of Pharaoh's presence.

12And the LORD said to Moses, "Stretch out your hand[y] over Egypt so that locusts will swarm over the land and devour everything growing in the fields, everything left by the hail."

13So Moses stretched out his staff over Egypt, and the LORD made an east wind blow across the land all that day and all that night. By morning the wind had brought the locusts;[z] 14they invaded all Egypt and settled down in every area of the country in great numbers. Never before had there been such a plague of locusts,[a] nor will there ever be again. 15They covered all the ground until it was black. They devoured[b] all that was left after the hail—everything growing in the fields and the fruit on the trees. Nothing green remained on tree or plant in all the land of Egypt.

16Pharaoh quickly summoned Moses and Aaron and said, "I have sinned[c] against the LORD your God and against you. 17Now forgive my sin once more and pray[d] to the LORD your God to take this deadly plague away from me."

18Moses then left Pharaoh and prayed to the LORD.[e] 19And the LORD changed the wind to a very strong west wind, which caught up the locusts and carried them into the Red Sea.[b] Not a locust was left anywhere in Egypt. 20But the LORD hardened Pharaoh's heart,[f] and he would not let the Israelites go.

The Plague of Darkness

21Then the LORD said to Moses, "Stretch out your hand toward the sky so that darkness[g] will spread over Egypt—darkness that can be felt." 22So Moses stretched out his hand toward the sky, and total darkness[h] covered all Egypt for three days. 23No one could see anyone else or leave his place for three days. Yet all the Israelites had light in the places where they lived.[i]

24Then Pharaoh summoned Moses and said, "Go, worship the LORD. Even your women and children[j] may go with you; only leave your flocks and herds behind."

25But Moses said, "You must allow us to have sacrifices and burnt offerings to present to the LORD our God. 26Our livestock too must go with us; not a hoof is to be left behind. We have to use some of them in worshiping the LORD our God, and until we get there we will not know what we are to use to worship the LORD."

27But the LORD hardened Pharaoh's heart,[k] and he was not willing to let them go. 28Pharaoh said to Moses, "Get out of my sight! Make sure you do not appear before me again! The day you see my face you will die."

29"Just as you say," Moses replied, "I will never appear[l] before you again."

The Plague on the Firstborn

11 Now the LORD had said to Moses, "I will bring one more plague on Pharaoh and on Egypt. After that, he will let you go from here, and when he does, he will drive you out completely. 2Tell the people that men and women alike are to ask their neigh-

10:7 [v]Ex 23:33; Jos 23:13; 1Sa 18:21; Ecc 7:26 [w]Ex 8:19
10:8 [x]Ex 8:8
10:12 [y]Ex 7:19
10:13 [z]Ps 105:34
10:14 [a]Ps 78:46; Joel 2:1-11,25
10:15 [b]ver 5; Ps 105:34-35
10:16 [c]Ex 9:27
10:17 [d]Ex 8:8
10:18 [e]Ex 8:30
10:20 [f]Ex 4:21; 11:10
10:21 [g]Dt 28:29
10:22 [h]Ps 105:28; Rev 16:10
10:23 [i]Ex 8:22
10:24 [j]ver 8-10
10:27 [k]ver 20; Ex 4:21
10:29 [l]Heb 11:27

[a] *10* Or *Be careful, trouble is in store for you!* [b] *19* Hebrew *Yam Suph*; that is, Sea of Reeds

10:9 festival. Moses' demand was that Israel's worship be unqualified and total. See note on 8:25.
10:11 only the men. Only adult males were necessary at Israel's later festivals (23:17; 34:23). Note the sarcasm of verse 10.
10:12–15 Goshen was presumably exempt.
10:16 quickly. Pharaoh's action underlined Egypt's peril. **I have sinned.** He declared his guilt before God and before Moses and Aaron. Pharaoh's tone was one of panic and conciliation.
10:21–29 God struck Egypt with impenetrable darkness but again spared the Israelites.
10:22 total darkness. This darkness was clearly more than a blinding sandstorm or an eclipse of the sun. It was an unnatural darkness, one usually associated in the Old Testament with the day of the Lord (Isa 8:22; 58:10; Joel 2:2; Am 5:20; Zep 1:15; cf. Dt 28:29).
11:1—12:41 The final plague of death for the firstborn echoed

bors for articles of silver and gold."[m] 3(The LORD made the Egyptians favorably disposed
toward the people, and Moses himself was highly regarded[n] in Egypt by Pharaoh's officials and by the people.)
4So Moses said, "This is what the LORD says: 'About midnight[o] I will go throughout
Egypt. 5Every firstborn[p] son in Egypt will die, from the firstborn son of Pharaoh, who sits
on the throne, to the firstborn son of the slave girl, who is at her hand mill, and all the
firstborn of the cattle as well. 6There will be loud wailing[q] throughout Egypt—worse than
there has ever been or ever will be again. 7But among the Israelites not a dog will bark
at any man or animal.' Then you will know that the LORD makes a distinction[r] between
Egypt and Israel. 8All these officials of yours will come to me, bowing down before me
and saying, 'Go,[s] you and all the people who follow you!' After that I will leave." Then
Moses, hot with anger, left Pharaoh.
9The LORD had said to Moses, "Pharaoh will refuse to listen[t] to you—so that my wonders may be multiplied in Egypt." 10Moses and Aaron performed all these wonders before Pharaoh, but the LORD hardened Pharaoh's heart,[u] and he would not let the Israelites go out of his country.

The Passover

12 The LORD said to Moses and Aaron in Egypt, 2"This month is to be for you the
first month,[v] the first month of your year. 3Tell the whole community of Israel
that on the tenth day of this month each man is to take a lamb[a] for his family, one for
each household. 4If any household is too small for a whole lamb, they must share one
with their nearest neighbor, having taken into account the number of people there are.
You are to determine the amount of lamb needed in accordance with what each person
will eat. 5The animals you choose must be year-old males without defect,[w] and you may
take them from the sheep or the goats. 6Take care of them until the fourteenth day of the
month,[x] when all the people of the community of Israel must slaughter them at twilight.[y]
7Then they are to take some of the blood and put it on the sides and tops of the doorframes of the houses where they eat the lambs. 8That same night[z] they are to eat the
meat roasted[a] over the fire, along with bitter herbs,[b] and bread made without yeast.[c]
9Do not eat the meat raw or cooked in water, but roast it over the fire—head, legs and
inner parts. 10Do not leave any of it till morning;[d] if some is left till morning, you must
burn it. 11This is how you are to eat it: with your cloak tucked into your belt, your sandals on your feet and your staff in your hand. Eat it in haste;[e] it is the LORD's Passover.[f]

11:2 [m]Ex 3:21,22
11:3 [n]Dt 34:11
11:4 [o]Ex 12:29
11:5 [p]Ex 4:23; Ps 78:51
11:6 [q]Ex 12:30
11:7 [r]Ex 8:22
11:8 [s]Ex 12:31-33
11:9 [t]Ex 7:4
11:10 [u]Ex 4:21; 10:20,27
12:2 [v]Ex 13:4; Dt 16:1
12:5 [w]Lev 22:18-21; Heb 9:14
12:6 [x]Lev 23:5; Nu 9:1-3,5,11 [y]Ex 16:12; Dt 16:4,6
12:8 [z]Ex 34:25; Nu 9:12 [a]Dt 16:7 [b]Nu 9:11 [c]Dt 16:3-4; 1Co 5:8
12:10 [d]Ex 23:18; 34:25
12:11 [e]Dt 16:3 [f]ver 13, 21,27,43; Dt 16:1

a 3 The Hebrew word can mean *lamb* or *kid*; also in verse 4.

---

the initial miracle that concluded with the deaths of the magicians' snakes (7:8–13). It resulted in Israel's release.

11:1–3 Israel was told to plunder Egypt (see 12:23–40).

11:1 plague. This word (lit., "stroke"; i.e., "a knock-out blow"), a different term for "plague," occurs only here in Exodus.

11:2 Tell. Literally, "Now tell . . ." The Hebrew emphatic particle is found in the Old Testament only four times of God speaking with a human being, and each time it refers to something that defies or transcends human understanding (Ge 13:14; 15:5; 22:2).

11:3 favorably disposed. All four versions of this narrative (3:21–22; 11:2–3; 12:35–36; Ps 105:36–38) emphasize that the Egyptians gave gladly because of the Lord's intervention.

11:4–10 Moses announced the final plague to come on Egypt: the death of the firstborn.

11:5 mill. The grinding of corn was menial work done by slaves and prisoners of war.

11:9 The LORD had said. Verses 9–10 summarize and conclude the accounts of the plagues.

12:1–51 See *WLC* 162; *WSC* 92.

12:1–28 The Lord instituted the Passover.

12:2 The first month of the year is Abib (March/April) on the spring calendar. Perhaps 12:2 reports the institution of this, a new religious calendar, stemming from the exodus. Abib is the first month since it commemorates Israel's liberation. An autumn calendar is attested at 23:16 and 34:22 (see also NIV text note). In the later Babylonian (spring) calendar, the month of Abib is called Nisan (Ne 2:1; Est 3:7).

12:5 males without defect. Like the sacrifices of Israel (e.g., Lev 1:3), the Passover lamb was to be symbolically perfect. Since the lamb died in the place of the firstborn, substitution was the key to the symbolism.

12:6 Deuteronomy 16:6 puts the slaughter at sunset. The act marked the beginning of the Passover. See *BC* 21.

12:7 blood. Blood symbolized the death of a victim, and thus the lamb's death here was substitutionary (Lev 17:11).

12:8 roasted. Roasting would deal with the fat and required no water. Bitter herbs were associated with suffering (La 3:15). **bread made without yeast.** Or more likely, without leaven. Yeast was not widely available except as a naturally occurring organism in fermentation. Leaven was a portion of a prior day's batch of dough that remained unbaked and had been allowed to ferment. It was added to fresh dough to introduce yeast into the whole batch. These cakes (the Hebrew is plural) were to be eaten as a reminder of the haste of the exit.

12:11 the LORD's Passover. Passover is the oldest of the Jewish festivals and was celebrated at twilight on the 14th day of the first month (v. 6) and for the seven succeeding days (the 15th through the 21st). On the tenth day of the first month, an unblemished male animal (normally a lamb) up to a year old was to be selected from each household's flocks or herds. It was to be killed at twilight on the 14th day (v. 6), and in the exodus account, a branch of hyssop dipped in the blood was to be used to sprinkle the sides and tops of the doorframes of each house. The animal was to be roasted whole with no bones broken and was to be eaten in haste with bitter herbs and unleavened bread. The later participants were to be garbed for travel to celebrate the hasty and anxious exit of Israel from Egypt on the night that the Lord defeated the gods of Egypt. What was not eaten was consumed by fire.

The Feast of Unleavened Bread lasted seven days, beginning on the 15th day of the month. Passover was the time when the family head recited the meaning of the festival to the children. Provision was later made (Nu 9:1–14) for a second, or minor, Passover to be celebrated one month later by members of the community who had missed the initial festival. The New Testament establishes a direct redemptive connection between this episode and the death of Jesus, the true Passover Lamb, who was sacrificed for us (1Co 5:7). See *HC* 78.

Hebrew Calendar and Selected Events

Number of Month		Hebrew Name	Modern Equivalent	Biblical References	Agriculture	Feasts**
1 Sacred sequence begins	7	**Abib; Nisan**	March–April	Ex 12:2; 13:4; 23:15; 34:18; Dt 16:1; Ne 2:1; Est 3:7	Spring (later) rains; barley and flax harvest begins	Passover; Unleavened Bread; Firstfruits
2	8	**Ziv (Iyyar)***	April–May	1Ki 6:1,37	Barley harvest; dry season begins	
3	9	**Sivan**	May–June	Est 8:9	Wheat harvest	Pentecost (Weeks)
4	10	**(Tammuz)***	June–July		Tending vines	
5	11	**(Ab)***	July–August		Ripening of grapes, figs and olives	
6	12	**Elul**	August–September	Ne 6:15	Processing grapes, figs and olives	
7	1 Civil sequence	**Ethanim (Tishri)***	September–October	1Ki 8:2	Autumn (early) rains begin; plowing	Trumpets; Day of Atonement; Tabernacles (Booths)
8	2	**Bul (Marcheshvan)***	October–November	1Ki 6:38	Sowing of wheat and barley	
9	3	**Kislev**	November–December	Ne 1:1; Zec 7:1	Winter rains begin (snow in some areas)	Hanukkah ("Dedication")
10	4	**Tebeth**	December–January	Est 2:16		
11	5	**Shebat**	January–February	Zec 1:7		
12	6	**Adar**	February–March	Ezr 6:15; Est 3:7,13; 8:12; 9:1,15,17,19,21	Almond trees bloom; citrus fruit harvest	Purim
		(Adar Sheni)* — Second Adar	This intercalary month was added about every three years so the lunar calendar would correspond to the solar year.			

*Names of months in parentheses are not in the Bible. **For more information on the feasts see chart, pp. 192–193.

12"On that same night I will pass through[g] Egypt and strike down every firstborn—
both men and animals—and I will bring judgment on all the gods[h] of Egypt. I am the
LORD.[i] 13The blood will be a sign for you on the houses where you are; and when I see
the blood, I will pass over you. No destructive plague will touch you when I strike Egypt.
14"This is a day you are to commemorate;[j] for the generations to come you shall celebrate it as a festival to the LORD—a lasting ordinance.[k] 15For seven days you are to eat
bread made without yeast.[l] On the first day remove the yeast from your houses, for whoever eats anything with yeast in it from the first day through the seventh must be cut off[m]
from Israel. 16On the first day hold a sacred assembly, and another one on the seventh
day. Do no work at all on these days, except to prepare food for everyone to eat—that
is all you may do.
17"Celebrate the Feast of Unleavened Bread, because it was on this very day that I
brought your divisions out of Egypt.[n] Celebrate this day as a lasting ordinance for the
generations to come. 18In the first month[o] you are to eat bread made without yeast, from
the evening of the fourteenth day until the evening of the twenty-first day. 19For seven
days no yeast is to be found in your houses. And whoever eats anything with yeast in it
must be cut off from the community of Israel, whether he is an alien or native-born. 20Eat
nothing made with yeast. Wherever you live, you must eat unleavened bread."
21Then Moses summoned all the elders of Israel and said to them, "Go at once and
select the animals for your families and slaughter the Passover[p] lamb. 22Take a bunch
of hyssop, dip it into the blood in the basin and put some of the blood[q] on the top and
on both sides of the doorframe. Not one of you shall go out the door of his house until
morning. 23When the LORD goes through the land to strike down the Egyptians, he will
see the blood[r] on the top and sides of the doorframe and will pass over[s] that doorway,
and he will not permit the destroyer[t] to enter your houses and strike you down.
24"Obey these instructions as a lasting ordinance for you and your descendants.
25When you enter the land that the LORD will give you as he promised, observe this ceremony. 26And when your children[u] ask you, 'What does this ceremony mean to you?'
27then tell them, 'It is the Passover[v] sacrifice to the LORD, who passed over the houses
of the Israelites in Egypt and spared our homes when he struck down the Egyptians.' "
Then the people bowed down and worshiped.[w] 28The Israelites did just what the LORD
commanded Moses and Aaron.
29At midnight[x] the LORD struck down all the firstborn[y] in Egypt, from the firstborn of
Pharaoh, who sat on the throne, to the firstborn of the prisoner, who was in the dungeon, and the firstborn of all the livestock[z] as well. 30Pharaoh and all his officials and all
the Egyptians got up during the night, and there was loud wailing[a] in Egypt, for there
was not a house without someone dead.

The Exodus

31During the night Pharaoh summoned Moses and Aaron and said, "Up! Leave my
people, you and the Israelites! Go, worship[b] the LORD as you have requested. 32Take your
flocks and herds,[c] as you have said, and go. And also bless me."
33The Egyptians urged the people to hurry and leave[d] the country. "For otherwise,"
they said, "we will all die!" 34So the people took their dough before the yeast was added, and carried it on their shoulders in kneading troughs wrapped in clothing. 35The Israelites did as Moses instructed and asked the Egyptians for articles of silver and gold[e]
and for clothing. 36The LORD had made the Egyptians favorably disposed toward the people, and they gave them what they asked for; so they plundered[f] the Egyptians.
37The Israelites journeyed from Rameses to Succoth.[g] There were about six hundred

12:12 [g]Ex 11:4; Am 5:17 [h]Nu 33:4 [i]Ex 6:2
12:14 [j]Ex 13:9 [k]ver 17, 24; Ex 13:5,10; 2Ki 23:21
12:15 [l]Ex 13:6-7; 23:15; 34:18; Lev 23:6; Dt 16:3 [m]Ge 17:14; Nu 9:13
12:17 [n]ver 41; Ex 13:3
12:18 [o]ver 2; Lev 23:5-8; Nu 28:16-25
12:21 [p]ver 11; Mk 14:12-16
12:22 [q]ver 7; Heb 11:28
12:23 [r]Rev 7:3 [s]ver 13 [t]1Co 10:10; Heb 11:28
12:26 [u]Ex 10:2; 13:8,14-15; Jos 4:6
12:27 [v]ver 11 [w]Ex 4:31
12:29 [x]Ex 11:4 [y]Ex 4:23; Ps 78:51 [z]Ex 9:6
12:30 [a]Ex 11:6
12:31 [b]Ex 8:8
12:32 [c]Ex 10:9,26
12:33 [d]Ps 105:38
12:35 [e]Ex 3:22
12:36 [f]Ex 3:22
12:37 [g]Nu 33:3-5

12:12 firstborn. The firstborn had the right of inheritance. No mere epidemic or accident could have been so selective.
12:13 sign. This is the only time when the symbolism for a use of blood is explained in the Old Testament. See *BC* 33; *HC* 78.
12:14 This is a day. That is, the day of the exodus. This regulation must have been fixed with later observance in view, for at the first Passover the 14th and 15th days were spent in flight.
12:15 yeast. See note on verse 8. See *WLC* 171.
12:19 cut off from the community of Israel. This implies physical exclusion from the camp, which would have meant death (see note on Lev 7:20). Resident aliens and native-born non-Israelites were expected to keep the law of the land.
12:22 hyssop. Hyssop was a species of marjoram used for purification (Lev 14:4–6; Nu 19:6,18; Ps 51:7). The richly textured branches and leaves could hold the necessary quantity of blood. **basin.** The word can also mean a threshold, where the blood may have collected in a hollow. The blood to be smeared was clearly protective. It would bar the way from the destroyer.
12:26 your children ask you. This command is still observed in Jewish circles today. The youngest child asks the question, and the events of the exodus are then recited.
12:29–30 The Lord struck down the firstborn in Egypt, both man and animal.
▪**12:31–41** *Completion of Commission.* Moses and Aaron completed the commission they had received to deliver Israel through miraculous plagues (see 6:13—7:7).
12:31 Up! . . . Go, worship. This threefold command underscored Pharaoh's urgency. He admitted defeat.
12:32 bless me. The blessing sought was presumably to countermand the dreadful curse that had devastated the land.
12:36 favorably disposed. Fulfills 11:1–3.
12:37 Rameses. See note on 1:11. **Succoth.** Cannot be precisely

thousand men[h] on foot, besides women and children. 38 Many other people[i] went up with
them, as well as large droves of livestock, both flocks and herds. 39 With the dough they
had brought from Egypt, they baked cakes of unleavened bread. The dough was without yeast because they had been driven out[j] of Egypt and did not have time to prepare
food for themselves.
40 Now the length of time the Israelite people lived in Egypt[a] was 430 years.[k] 41 At the
end of the 430 years, to the very day, all the LORD's divisions[l] left Egypt.[m] 42 Because the
LORD kept vigil that night to bring them out of Egypt, on this night all the Israelites are
to keep vigil to honor the LORD for the generations to come.[n]

Passover Restrictions

43 The LORD said to Moses and Aaron, "These are the regulations for the Passover:[o]
"No foreigner[p] is to eat of it. 44 Any slave you have bought may eat of it after you have
circumcised[q] him, 45 but a temporary resident and a hired worker[r] may not eat of it.
46 "It must be eaten inside one house; take none of the meat outside the house. Do not
break any of the bones.[s] 47 The whole community of Israel must celebrate it.
48 "An alien living among you who wants to celebrate the LORD's Passover must have
all the males in his household circumcised; then he may take part like one born in the
land.[t] No uncircumcised male may eat of it. 49 The same law applies to the native-born
and to the alien[u] living among you."
50 All the Israelites did just what the LORD had commanded Moses and Aaron. 51 And
on that very day the LORD brought the Israelites out of Egypt by their divisions.[v]

Consecration of the Firstborn

13 The LORD said to Moses, 2 "Consecrate to me every firstborn male.[w] The first offspring of every womb among the Israelites belongs to me, whether man or animal."
3 Then Moses said to the people, "Commemorate this day, the day you came out of
Egypt, out of the land of slavery, because the LORD brought you out of it with a mighty
hand.[x] Eat nothing containing yeast.[y] 4 Today, in the month of Abib,[z] you are leaving.
5 When the LORD brings you into the land of the Canaanites, Hittites, Amorites, Hivites
and Jebusites[a]—the land he swore to your forefathers to give you, a land flowing with
milk and honey—you are to observe this ceremony[b] in this month: 6 For seven days eat
bread made without yeast and on the seventh day hold a festival[c] to the LORD. 7 Eat unleavened bread during those seven days; nothing with yeast in it is to be seen among you,
nor shall any yeast be seen anywhere within your borders. 8 On that day tell your son,[d]
'I do this because of what the LORD did for me when I came out of Egypt.' 9 This observance will be for you like a sign on your hand and a reminder on your forehead[e] that the

12:37 [h]Ex 38:26; Nu 1:46; 11:13,21
12:38 [i]Nu 11:4
12:39 [j]ver 31-33; Ex 6:1; 11:1
12:40 [k]Ge 15:13; Ac 7:6; Gal 3:17
12:41 [l]ver 17; Ex 6:26 [m]Ex 3:10
12:42 [n]Ex 13:10; Dt 16:1,6
12:43 [o]ver 11 [p]ver 48; Nu 9:14
12:44 [q]Ge 17:12-13
12:45 [r]Lev 22:10
12:46 [s]Nu 9:12; Jn 19:36*
12:48 [t]Nu 9:14
12:49 [u]Nu 15:15-16,29; Gal 3:28
12:51 [v]ver 41; Ex 6:26
13:2 [w]ver 12,13,15; Ex 22:29; Nu 3:13; Dt 15:19; Lk 2:23*
13:3 [x]Ex 3:20; 6:1 [y]Ex 12:19
13:4 [z]Ex 12:2
13:5 [a]Ex 3:8 [b]Ex 12:25-26
13:6 [c]Ex 12:15-20
13:8 [d]ver 14; Ex 10:2; Ps 78:5-6
13:9 [e]ver 16; Dt 6:8; 11:18

[a] 40 Masoretic Text; Samaritan Pentateuch and Septuagint *Egypt and Canaan*

located, but must have been in the eastern delta and has been connected with Tell el-Maskhuta in the Wadi Tumilat. The coastal routes to Canaan (13:17) were shorter but well guarded. **six hundred thousand.** The number has been thought too large (but note Nu 11:21; 26:51). But four centuries could well have produced such numbers (1:7). As often suggested, the Hebrew word for "thousand" could be taken as "family" or some subsection of a tribe or clan, thus leading to an alternate translation of "600 families."

12:38 Many other people. Perhaps persecuted ethnic minorities or other slaves came with the Israelites, as well as other Semites (i.e., descendants of Shem; see Ge 10:21–31). Perhaps Egyptians who had intermarried with Israelites or even some who had concluded that the Lord was God were also included (cf. 9:19; 12:48; Isa 56:3).

12:40 430 years. The Greek and Samaritan Old Testament texts relate the figure to the period spent in both Canaan and Egypt since Abraham (Ge 15:13). Acts 13:20 renders the time frame as "about 450 years."

12:41 divisions. A technical term for military organization (see note on 6:26).

■ **12:42—13:16** *Future Observances.* These verses form a digression into some details of Passover restrictions, the consecration of the firstborn and the Feast of Unleavened Bread.

12:42 Because the LORD. God's grace shown to Israel was the basis for the future careful observance of Passover regulations.

12:43 The LORD said to Moses. The repetition of the Passover regulations that follows may have been due to the mention of non-Israelites with Israel (v. 38). Only covenant (circumcised) members were eligible.

12:46 inside one house. None of the meat was to be taken outside of the house, where non-covenant members could have had access to it. **bones.** No bones of the animal were to be broken, perhaps as a symbol of covenant unity.

12:48 alien. The resident-alien who lived permanently among the Israelites and who wished to come under their protection and join their covenant could eat. Slaves born in a house would have been circumcised and could participate. See *WCF* 27.1; *WLC* 162.

13:1–2 The LORD said to Moses. These verses form a heading to the exposition of verses 3–16; verses 3–10 parallel verses 11–16.

13:2 Consecrate. The word may mean either "consider as the Lord's" or "sacrifice." **firstborn male.** Firstborn humans and cattle were sacred to the Lord. Like the firstfruits of the harvest, the firstborn from the womb represented God's claim on all. The principle is enunciated here, and the details are given at 13:12–16, 22:29–30 and 34:19–20. Jesus was so presented as Mary's firstborn (Lk 2:22–23).

13:8 tell your son. The details were to be shared with the children.

13:9 sign . . . reminder. Later, in literal compliance, Jews bound sections of the law (vv. 1–16; Dt 6:4–9; 11:13–21) on their left arms and foreheads. The texts were written on strips of parchment and placed in two small leather boxes that were then strapped on their foreheads and left arms before morning prayers. They were called the tephillim, the phylacteries (protections) of later Judaism.

law of the LORD is to be on your lips. For the LORD brought you out of Egypt with his
mighty hand. 10 You must keep this ordinance[f] at the appointed time year after year.
11 "After the LORD brings you into the land of the Canaanites and gives it to you, as he
promised on oath to you and your forefathers, 12 you are to give over to the LORD the first
offspring of every womb. All the firstborn males of your livestock belong to the LORD.[g]
13 Redeem with a lamb every firstborn donkey, but if you do not redeem it, break its
neck.[h] Redeem every firstborn among your sons.[i]
14 "In days to come, when your son[j] asks you, 'What does this mean?' say to him, 'With
a mighty hand the LORD brought us out of Egypt, out of the land of slavery.[k] 15 When Pharaoh stubbornly refused to let us go, the LORD killed every firstborn in Egypt, both man
and animal. This is why I sacrifice to the LORD the first male offspring of every womb and
redeem each of my firstborn sons.'[l] 16 And it will be like a sign on your hand and a symbol on your forehead[m] that the LORD brought us out of Egypt with his mighty hand."

Crossing the Sea

17 When Pharaoh let the people go, God did not lead them on the road through the
Philistine country, though that was shorter. For God said, "If they face war, they might
change their minds and return to Egypt."[n] 18 So God led[o] the people around by the desert road toward the Red Sea.[a] The Israelites went up out of Egypt armed for battle.[p]
19 Moses took the bones of Joseph[q] with him because Joseph had made the sons of Israel swear an oath. He had said, "God will surely come to your aid, and then you must
carry my bones up with you from this place."[b r]
20 After leaving Succoth they camped at Etham on the edge of the desert.[s] 21 By day the
LORD went ahead of them in a pillar of cloud[t] to guide them on their way and by night
in a pillar of fire to give them light, so that they could travel by day or night. 22 Neither
the pillar of cloud by day nor the pillar of fire by night left its place in front of the people.
14 Then the LORD said to Moses, 2 "Tell the Israelites to turn back and encamp near
Pi Hahiroth, between Migdol[u] and the sea. They are to encamp by the sea, directly opposite Baal Zephon. 3 Pharaoh will think, 'The Israelites are wandering around
the land in confusion, hemmed in by the desert.' 4 And I will harden Pharaoh's heart,[v]
and he will pursue them. But I will gain glory[w] for myself through Pharaoh and all his
army, and the Egyptians will know that I am the LORD."[x] So the Israelites did this.
5 When the king of Egypt was told that the people had fled, Pharaoh and his officials
changed their minds about them and said, "What have we done? We have let the Isra-

13:10 [f]Ex 12:24-25
13:12 [g]Lev 27:26; Lk 2:23*
13:13 [h]Ex 34:20 [i]Nu 18:15
13:14 [j]Ex 10:2; 12:26-27; Dt 6:20 [k]ver 3,9
13:15 [l]Ex 12:29
13:16 [m]ver 9
13:17 [n]Ex 14:11; Nu 14:1-4; Dt 17:16
13:18 [o]Ps 136:16 [p]Jos 1:14
13:19 [q]Jos 24:32; Ac 7:16 [r]Ge 50:24-25
13:20 [s]Nu 33:6
13:21 [t]Ex 14:19,24; 33:9-10; Nu 9:16; Dt 1:33; Ne 9:12, 19; Ps 78:14; 99:7; 105:39; Isa 4:5; 1Co 10:1
14:2 [u]Nu 33:7; Jer 44:1
14:4 [v]Ex 4:21 [w]Ro 9:17, 22-23 [x]Ex 7:5

a *18* Hebrew *Yam Suph;* that is, Sea of Reeds b *19* See Gen. 50:25.

13:12 give over. Literally, "make to pass through." An animal from the flock or herd could be given to the Lord as a whole burnt offering. The firstborn son was to be redeemed (v. 13). (Note the pagan use of the firstborn as an offering in 2Ki 16:3.) **firstborn males.** The firstborn were the Lord's.

13:13 break its neck. If the donkey was not redeemed, its neck was to be broken. This would not involve the use of blood, and the animal would not be used as a sacrifice.

13:15–16 The Lord's judgment on the firstborn in Egypt is the explanation for his claim on the firstborn in Israel. His claim was made both as Creator and as Judge. Israel was not exempt from the death sentence on the firstborn in Egypt. The firstborn were spared only through the blood of the Passover lamb. Subsequent generations were also to be redeemed: either through the life consecration of the Levites, who were chosen by God in place of the firstborn (Nu 3:11–13), or through the redemption price of five shekels (Nu 3:46–51).

■ **13:17—15:21** *Final Deliverance at the Sea.* God delivered Israel from Pharaoh's armies, revealing himself as the Warrior and Shepherd of his people and demonstrating his favor toward Moses. This material divides into two main sections: Israel passes through the sea (13:17—14:31), and Israel celebrates (15:1–21).

■ **13:17—14:31** *Passing Through the Sea.* This is the account of Pharaoh's defeat and Israel's passing to safety through the sea.

13:17–22 God led Israel by way of the sea.

13:17 road. See "Introduction: Time and Place of Writing." The main caravan route ran practically parallel to the Mediterranean coast. This route was too strongly fortified. There was another route that led to Beersheba and to the south of the region much later known as Palestine, but the southeastern route toward the peninsula of Sinai was chosen.

13:18 Red Sea. Literally, "the Reed Sea" (the translation "Red Sea" came about by Greek and Latin versions). This was probably one of the lakes or the network of lakes (the Bitter Lakes) to the north of Suez. Perhaps it was the southern extension of Lake Menzaleh. Archeological evidence suggests that the Bitter Lakes system was joined to the Gulf of Suez and that it contained shallows. Recent research suggests that the Hebrew may mean "Sea of the End," an expression used to designate any remote ocean or sea, especially the Red Sea and the Gulfs of Aqaba (Elath) and Suez (1Ki 9:26; Jer 49:21).

13:19 bones of Joseph. Israel went out in military formation, disciplined and prepared to the extent that the bones of Joseph were taken (Ge 50:25).

13:20 Etham. The Israelites camped on the edge of the wilderness near what may have been an Egyptian fortress at Etham (since the name seems to be Egyptian). They turned back (14:1), perhaps to avoid a direct military confrontation with the Egyptian forces at Etham.

13:21 cloud . . . fire. Cloud and fire are customary symbols for the immediate presence of God (33:9–10; 40:34–38; Nu 9:15–22; 11:25; Pss 99:7; 105:39; see note on 3:2). God was not only present, but he also guided Israel day and night by his presence.

14:1–9 God set up Israel's camp by the sea, inviting Pharaoh's pursuit.

14:2 Pi Hahiroth. Israel turned back and camped at Pi Hahiroth, reputedly in the vicinity of Rameses (modern Qantir). **Migdol.** A general word for "fortification"; the site is impossible to pinpoint. **Baal Zephon.** This site ("Baal of the North") was reputed to be in the vicinity of Tahpanhes near Lake Menzaleh, about 20 miles east of Rameses.

14:4 Pharaoh's pursuit of his escaping slaves took place under God's sovereign direction. Again, God prepares to do a mighty work so that people (in this case the Egyptians, in their defeat) will "know that I am the Lord" (cf. 6:7; 7:5,17; 8:22; 10:2; 14:18; 16:12; 29:46; 31:13).

elites go and have lost their services!" 6So he had his chariot made ready and took his
army with him. 7He took six hundred of the best chariots, along with all the other chariots of Egypt, with officers over all of them. 8The LORD hardened the heart[y] of Pharaoh
king of Egypt, so that he pursued the Israelites, who were marching out boldly.[z] 9The
Egyptians—all Pharaoh's horses and chariots, horsemen[a] and troops—pursued the Israelites and overtook[a] them as they camped by the sea near Pi Hahiroth, opposite Baal
Zephon.

10As Pharaoh approached, the Israelites looked up, and there were the Egyptians,
marching after them. They were terrified and cried[b] out to the LORD. 11They said to Moses, "Was it because there were no graves in Egypt that you brought us to the desert to
die?[c] What have you done to us by bringing us out of Egypt? 12Didn't we say to you in
Egypt, 'Leave us alone; let us serve the Egyptians'? It would have been better for us to
serve the Egyptians than to die in the desert!"

13Moses answered the people, "Do not be afraid.[d] Stand firm and you will see[e] the deliverance the LORD will bring you today. The Egyptians you see today you will never see[f]
again. 14The LORD will fight[g] for you; you need only to be still."[h]

15Then the LORD said to Moses, "Why are you crying out to me? Tell the Israelites to
move on. 16Raise your staff[i] and stretch out your hand over the sea to divide the water[j]
so that the Israelites can go through the sea on dry ground. 17I will harden the hearts of
the Egyptians so that they will go in after them.[k] And I will gain glory through Pharaoh
and all his army, through his chariots and his horsemen. 18The Egyptians will know that
I am the LORD when I gain glory through Pharaoh, his chariots and his horsemen."

19Then the angel of God, who had been traveling in front of Israel's army, withdrew
and went behind them. The pillar of cloud[l] also moved from in front and stood behind
them, 20coming between the armies of Egypt and Israel. Throughout the night the cloud
brought darkness to the one side and light to the other side; so neither went near the other all night long.

21Then Moses stretched out his hand over the sea, and all that night the LORD drove
the sea back with a strong east wind[m] and turned it into dry land. The waters were divided,[n] 22and the Israelites went through the sea on dry ground,[o] with a wall of water
on their right and on their left.

23The Egyptians pursued them, and all Pharaoh's horses and chariots and horsemen followed them into the sea. 24During the last watch of the night the LORD looked down from
the pillar of fire and cloud[p] at the Egyptian army and threw it into confusion. 25He made
the wheels of their chariots come off[b] so that they had difficulty driving. And the Egyptians
said, "Let's get away from the Israelites! The LORD is fighting[q] for them against Egypt."

26Then the LORD said to Moses, "Stretch out your hand over the sea so that the waters may flow back over the Egyptians and their chariots and horsemen." 27Moses
stretched out his hand over the sea, and at daybreak the sea went back to its place.[r] The
Egyptians were fleeing toward[c] it, and the LORD swept them into the sea.[s] 28The water

14:8 [y]ver 4; Ex 11:10 [z]Nu 33:3; Ac 13:17
14:9 [a]Ex 15:9
14:10 [b]Jos 24:7; Ne 9:9; Ps 34:17
14:11 [c]Ps 106:7-8
14:13 [d]Ge 15:1 [e]2Ch 20:17; Isa 41:10,13-14 [f]ver 30
14:14 [g]ver 25; Ex 15:3; Dt 1:30; 3:22; 2Ch 20:29 [h]Ps 37:7; 46:10; Isa 30:15
14:16 [i]Ex 4:17; Nu 20:8-9,11 [j]Isa 10:26
14:17 [k]ver 4
14:19 [l]Ex 13:21
14:21 [m]Ex 15:8 [n]Ps 74:13; 114:5; Isa 63:12
14:22 [o]Ex 15:19; Ne 9:11; Ps 66:6; Heb 11:29
14:24 [p]Ex 13:21
14:25 [q]ver 14
14:27 [r]Jos 4:18 [s]Ex 15:1,21; Ps 78:53; 106:11

a 9 Or *charioteers;* also in verses 17, 18, 23, 26 and 28 b 25 Or *He jammed the wheels of their chariots* (see Samaritan Pentateuch, Septuagint and Syriac) c 27 Or *from*

14:6 chariot. The horse and chariot seem to have been introduced into Egypt by the Hyksos. The Egyptian chariot carried three men. **made ready.** Pharaoh was in earnest since his elite chariot force was deployed.
14:10–20 The Lord fought for Israel.
14:11 They said to Moses. Israel's rebellious complaints against God's leading are a continuing theme in Exodus (5:21; 15:24; 16:3; 17:2; 32:1).
14:13 Do not be afraid. The Israelites needed to understand that their salvation was entirely God's work, a point at the crux of Israel's deliverance. God's judgments on Egypt, his hardening of Pharaoh's heart, his leading Israel to this seemingly hopeless impasse of being pinned between Pharaoh's chariots and the sea—all these prepared for the climactic display of his saving power.
14:14 The LORD will fight. This phrase indicates the origin of the concept of the Lord as warrior, which chapter 15 celebrates. War in the ancient world was viewed as a sacred undertaking in which the honor of the deity was at stake. In Israel God was not only the "God of the armies of Israel" (1Sa 17:45) but also the "LORD of Hosts" (i.e., the Lord of the armies of heaven), the architect of Israel's victories and the inflicter of Israel's defeats. An early account of Israel's conquests under the Lord's leadership was called "the Book of the Wars of the LORD" (Nu 21:14). The theology of holy war (or Yahweh War) that arose as a result finds expression throughout both Testaments. At the exodus the Lord fought for Israel, drowning Egypt's army in the Red Sea.
14:15 crying. A prayer of Moses is to be understood.
14:16 Raise your staff. The rod of Moses that had been used in bringing God's judgments on Egypt would now bring salvation to his people.
14:19 angel . . . cloud. The angel of the Lord was identified with God's own presence in the cloud (23:20–22). The angel is mysteriously identified with God in Genesis (Ge 16:7,13; 18:2,16–17,22; 21:17,19; 32:24,30).
14:21–31 The Lord brought Israel victoriously through the sea.
14:21 east wind. God sent the wind to accomplish his purpose, but further supernatural power was needed to maintain the water on either side of the escape route and then return it with sufficient force to destroy Pharaoh's army.
14:24 last watch. The night was divided into three watches of four hours each; thus the last watch was from 2 A.M. to 6 A.M. This was often the time for a surprise attack (1Sa 11:11). It was the Lord who threw the Egyptian army into confusion.
14:25 wheels. Literally, "he took off the wheels." Probably the wheels first bogged down, then the horses plunged and the axles broke. **The LORD is fighting.** The Egyptians recognized the victory as God's. See verse 14.
14:27 Through God's power, Moses' outstretched hand/staff brought about the destruction of the pursuing army for Israel's deliverance.

flowed back and covered the chariots and horsemen—the entire army of Pharaoh that
had followed the Israelites into the sea. Not one of them survived.

14:29 [t]ver; 22

29 But the Israelites went through the sea on dry ground,[t] with a wall of water on their

14:30 [u]Ps 106:8,10,21

right and on their left. 30 That day the LORD saved[u] Israel from the hands of the Egyptians,
and Israel saw the Egyptians lying dead on the shore. 31 And when the Israelites saw the

14:31 [v]Ps 106:12; Jn 2:11

great power the LORD displayed against the Egyptians, the people feared the LORD and
put their trust[v] in him and in Moses his servant.

The Song of Moses and Miriam

15:1 [w]Rev 15:3 [x]Ps 106:12

15 Then Moses and the Israelites sang this song[w] to the LORD:

"I will sing[x] to the LORD,
for he is highly exalted.
The horse and its rider
he has hurled into the sea.

15:2 [y]Ps 59:17 [z]Ps 18:2, 46; Isa 12:2; Hab 3:18 [a]Ge 28:21 [b]Ex 3:6, 15-16; Isa 25:1

2 The LORD is my strength[y] and my song;
he has become my salvation.[z]
He is my God,[a] and I will praise him,
my father's God, and I will exalt[b] him.

15:3 [c]Ex 14:14; Ps 24:8; Rev 19:11 [d]Ex 6:2-3, 7-8; Ps 83:18

3 The LORD is a warrior;[c]
the LORD is his name.[d]

15:4 [e]Ex 14:6-7

4 Pharaoh's chariots and his army[e]
he has hurled into the sea.
The best of Pharaoh's officers
are drowned in the Red Sea.[a]

15:5 [f]ver 10; Ne 9:11

5 The deep waters have covered them;
they sank to the depths like a stone.[f]

15:6 [g]Ps 118:15

6 "Your right hand,[g] O LORD,
was majestic in power.
Your right hand, O LORD,
shattered the enemy.
7 In the greatness of your majesty
you threw down those who opposed you.

15:7 [h]Ps 78:49-50

You unleashed your burning anger;[h]
it consumed them like stubble.

15:8 [i]Ex 14:21 [j]Ps 78:13 [k]Ex 14:22

8 By the blast of your nostrils[i]
the waters piled up.[j]
The surging waters stood firm like a wall;[k]
the deep waters congealed in the heart of the sea.

15:9 [l]Ex 14:5-9 [m]Jdg 5:30; Isa 53:12

9 "The enemy boasted,
'I will pursue,[l] I will overtake them.
I will divide the spoils;[m]
I will gorge myself on them.
I will draw my sword
and my hand will destroy them.'

[a] *4* Hebrew *Yam Suph*; that is, Sea of Reeds; also in verse 22

14:30 the LORD saved Israel. Verses 29–31 summarize God's saving deed and its effect on Israel.

14:31 feared . . . put their trust in him and in Moses his servant. At this point, Israel trusted not only in the Lord, but in Moses as well. This fact touches on one of the main themes of the book of Exodus: the divine authorization of Moses. See *WLC* 104.

■ **15:1–21** *Celebrating at the Sea.* Moses and Israel sang of their deliverance and hope.

15:1–18 The poem of verses 1–18 is a victory song expressed in the first person singular as a song of Moses. It celebrates the Lord's majestic power in saving Israel at the sea (vv. 1–12) and claims his power in planting Israel in the land (vv. 13–18). The song contains many archaic expressions.

15:1 I will sing. So begins the song of Moses, which became the song of Israel. The Lord had shown his glory as he had promised, and it was the privilege of his people, led by his servant Moses, to praise the God of their salvation. The song of Moses anticipates the song of the Lamb (Rev 15:3). The praise of verse 2 is repeated in Psalm 118:14 and Isaiah 12:2.

15:2 strength. The word may mean "defender."

15:3 The Lord as Warrior now becomes a major Biblical image. See Isaiah 59:16–18.

15:5 deep waters. The sea (deep waters) is portrayed as the "chaos waters," ordered by God at creation (Ge 1:2). God's people were delivered from its power, but it destroyed God's enemies.

15:6 Your right hand. In Canaanite art the warrior god Baal was depicted with mace upheld. In Israel's deliverance the symbol of God's power was the outstretched hand of Moses grasping the rod of the Lord.

15:8 surging waters. Through the threatening waters of death, God brought his people to himself. The apostle Paul (with some support from Jewish traditions) later understood the Red Sea crossing as Israel's "baptism" (see 1Co 10:2).

15:9 I . . . I . . . I . . . I . . . I. The staccato repetition of these first person claims reveals an arrogance that was soon silenced.

The Exodus

The exodus and conquest narratives form the classic historical and spiritual drama of OT times. Subsequent ages looked back to this period as one of obedient and victorious living under divine guidance. Close examination of the environment and circumstances also reveals the strenuous exertions, human sin and bloody conflicts of the era.

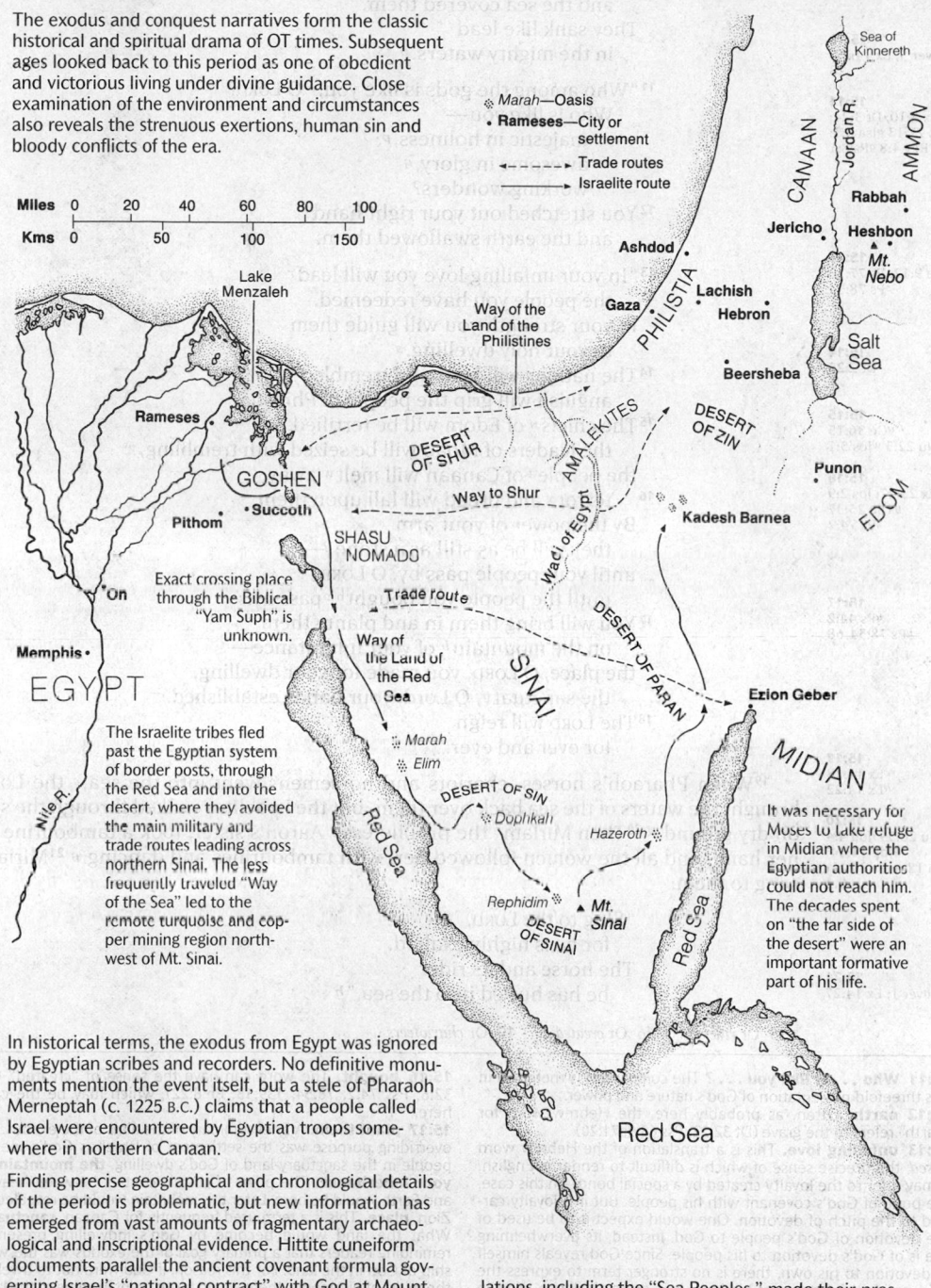

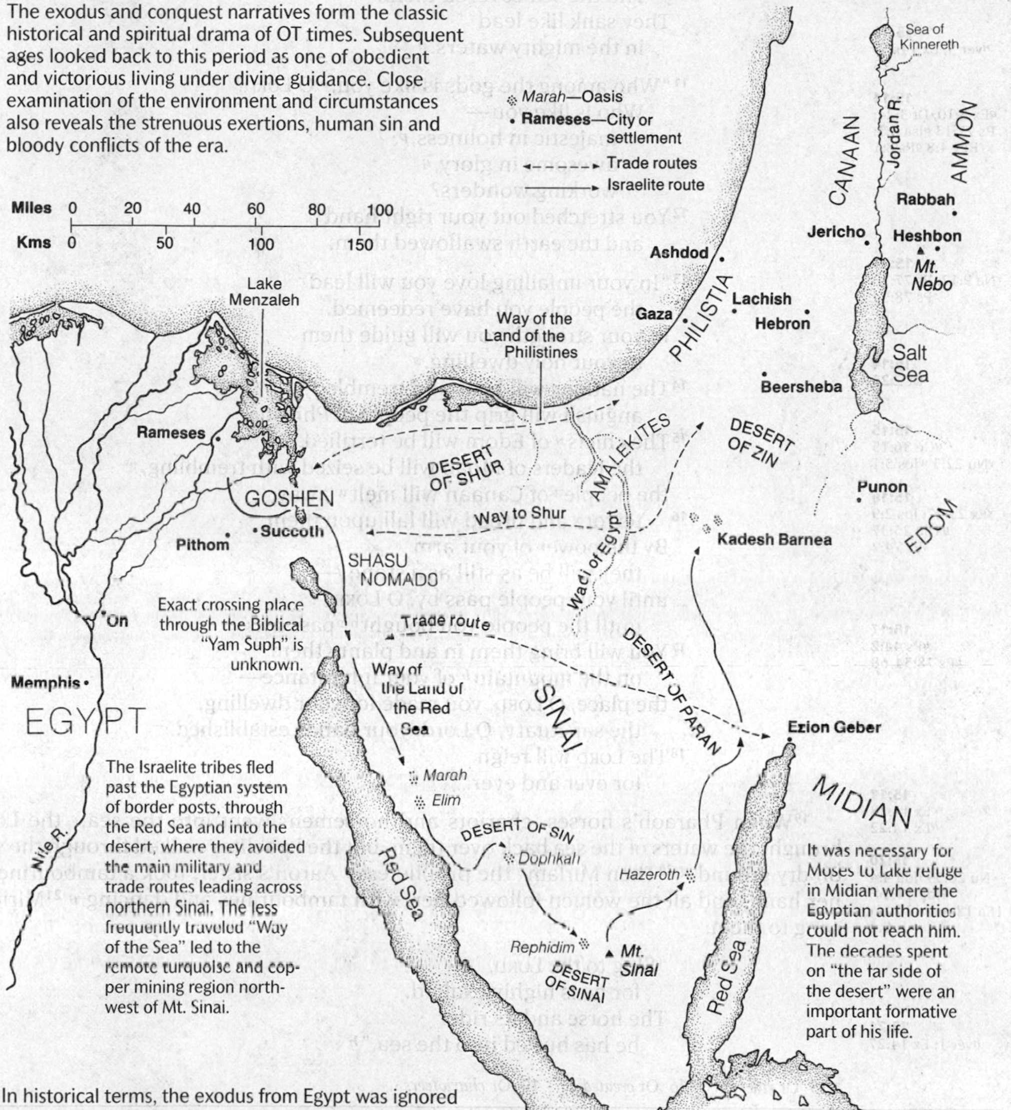

In historical terms, the exodus from Egypt was ignored by Egyptian scribes and recorders. No definitive monuments mention the event itself, but a stele of Pharaoh Merneptah (c. 1225 B.C.) claims that a people called Israel were encountered by Egyptian troops somewhere in northern Canaan.

Finding precise geographical and chronological details of the period is problematic, but new information has emerged from vast amounts of fragmentary archaeological and inscriptional evidence. Hittite cuneiform documents parallel the ancient covenant formula governing Israel's "national contract" with God at Mount Sinai.

The Late Bronze Age (c. 1550-1200 B.C.) was a time of major social migrations. Egyptian control over the Semites in the eastern Nile delta was harsh, with a system of brickmaking quotas imposed on the labor force, often the landless, low-class "Apiru." Numerous Canaanite towns were violently destroyed. New populations, including the "Sea Peoples," made their presence felt in Anatolia, Egypt, Canaan, Transjordan, and elsewhere in the eastern Mediterranean.

Correspondence from Canaanite town rulers to the Egyptian court in the time of Akhenaten (c. 1375 B.C.) reveals a weak structure of alliances, with an intermittent Egyptian military presence and an ominous fear of people called "Habiru" ("Apiru").

15:10 [n]ver 5; Ex 14:27-28
15:11 [o]Ex 8:10; Dt 3:24; Ps 77:13 [p]Isa 6:3; Rev 4:8 [q]Ps 8:1
15:13 [r]Ne 9:12; Ps 77:20 [s]Ps 78:54
15:14 [t]Dt 2:25
15:15 [u]Ge 36:15 [v]Nu 22:3 [w]Jos 5:1
15:16 [x]Ex 23:27; Jos 2:9 [y]1Sa 25:37 [z]Ps 74:2
15:17 [a]Ps 44:2 [b]Ps 78:54,68
15:19 [c]Ex 14:28 [d]Ex 14:22
15:20 [e]Nu 26:59 [f]Jdg 4:4 [g]Jdg 11:34; 1Sa 18:6; Ps 30:11; 150:4
15:21 [h]ver 1; Ex 14:27

10 But you blew with your breath,
and the sea covered them.
They sank like lead
in the mighty waters.[n]

11 "Who among the gods is like you,[o] O LORD?
Who is like you—
majestic in holiness,[p]
awesome in glory,[q]
working wonders?
12 You stretched out your right hand
and the earth swallowed them.

13 "In your unfailing love you will lead[r]
the people you have redeemed.
In your strength you will guide them
to your holy dwelling.[s]
14 The nations will hear and tremble;[t]
anguish will grip the people of Philistia.
15 The chiefs[u] of Edom will be terrified,
the leaders of Moab will be seized with trembling,[v]
the people[a] of Canaan will melt[w] away;
16 terror[x] and dread will fall upon them.
By the power of your arm
they will be as still as a stone[y]—
until your people pass by, O LORD,
until the people you bought[b][z] pass by.
17 You will bring them in and plant[a] them
on the mountain[b] of your inheritance—
the place, O LORD, you made for your dwelling,
the sanctuary, O Lord, your hands established.
18 The LORD will reign
for ever and ever."

19 When Pharaoh's horses, chariots and horsemen[c] went into the sea,[c] the LORD
brought the waters of the sea back over them, but the Israelites walked through the sea
on dry ground.[d] 20 Then Miriam[e] the prophetess,[f] Aaron's sister, took a tambourine in
her hand, and all the women followed her, with tambourines and dancing.[g] 21 Miriam
sang to them:

"Sing to the LORD,
for he is highly exalted.
The horse and its rider
he has hurled into the sea."[h]

[a] 15 Or *rulers* [b] 16 Or *created* [c] 19 Or *charioteers*

15:11 Who . . . is like you . . . ? The comparison is rhetorical in this threefold presentation of God's nature and power.
15:12 earth. Often, as probably here, the Hebrew word for "earth" refers to the grave (Dt 32:22; Pss 63:9; 71:20).
15:13 unfailing love. This is a translation of the Hebrew word *hesed,* the precise sense of which is difficult to render in English. It may refer to the loyalty created by a special bond—in this case, the bond of God's covenant with his people. But it is loyalty carried to the pitch of devotion. One would expect it to be used of the devotion of God's people to God. Instead, its overwhelming use is of God's devotion to his people. Since God reveals himself in devotion to his own, there is no stronger term to express the free and faithful grace of his love. It is dramatically so used in Hosea. (See "abounding in love" in 34:6; see also Ps 136.) **lead.** Literally, "shepherd," a common image of kingship in the ancient world.
15:14 tremble. The fear of the inhabitants of Canaan is here depicted. These people are presented in the rough order in which the Israelites met them when traveling northeast from Egypt. A paralysis of fear overtook them each time as Israel passed by, this time through "walls" of peoples, as God's people had previously passed through "walls" of water.
15:16 bought. The word can have the sense of "created" (Dt 32:6; Pss 74:2; 78:54; 139:13; Pr 8:22), which may be the case here.
15:17 plant them. A brief summary of the aims of the exodus. An overriding purpose was the settlement of Israel as God's special people in the sanctuary-land of God's dwelling. **the mountain of your inheritance.** The point of cosmic contact between heaven and Earth would be here. Later this mountain would be revealed as Zion. **place.** This is a term used frequently for Canaan. **sanctuary.** What the land would become by God's indwelling presence, reminding readers that a primary goal of the exodus was the worship of God in the land. For this reason, if God were not to dwell in the midst of his people, there would be no point in going to the land (33:15).
15:18 will reign. Although God is portrayed implicitly as King from the beginning of Scripture, this is the first explicit reference to him reigning as King in an earthly sanctuary (see note on 15:13). His victory over Egypt demonstrated his kingship over all (see Nu 23:21; Dt 33:5; see also 1Sa 8:6–9).
15:19–21 Miriam and all the other women sang and danced a variation of Moses' song at the sea. This detail indicates how widespread the celebration was.

The Waters of Marah and Elim

22Then Moses led Israel from the Red Sea and they went into the Desert of Shur. For
three days they traveled in the desert without finding water. 23When they came to Marah, they could not drink its water because it was bitter. (That is why the place is called
Marah.[a] [i]) 24So the people grumbled[j] against Moses, saying, "What are we to drink?"
25Then Moses cried out[k] to the LORD, and the LORD showed him a piece of wood. He
threw it into the water, and the water became sweet.
There the LORD made a decree and a law for them, and there he tested[l] them. 26He
said, "If you listen carefully to the voice of the LORD your God and do what is right in his
eyes, if you pay attention to his commands and keep all his decrees,[m] I will not bring on
you any of the diseases[n] I brought on the Egyptians, for I am the LORD, who heals[o] you."
27Then they came to Elim, where there were twelve springs and seventy palm trees,
and they camped[p] there near the water.

Manna and Quail

16 The whole Israelite community set out from Elim and came to the Desert of Sin,[q]
which is between Elim and Sinai, on the fifteenth day of the second month after they had come out of Egypt. 2In the desert the whole community grumbled[r] against
Moses and Aaron. 3The Israelites said to them, "If only we had died by the LORD's hand
in Egypt![s] There we sat around pots of meat and ate all the food[t] we wanted, but you
have brought us out into this desert to starve this entire assembly to death."
4Then the LORD said to Moses, "I will rain down bread from heaven[u] for you. The people are to go out each day and gather enough for that day. In this way I will test them
and see whether they will follow my instructions. 5On the sixth day they are to prepare
what they bring in, and that is to be twice[v] as much as they gather on the other days."
6So Moses and Aaron said to all the Israelites, "In the evening you will know that it
was the LORD who brought you out of Egypt,[w] 7and in the morning you will see the glory[x] of the LORD, because he has heard your grumbling[y] against him. Who are we, that
you should grumble against us?"[z] 8Moses also said, "You will know that it was the LORD
when he gives you meat to eat in the evening and all the bread you want in the morning, because he has heard your grumbling against him. Who are we? You are not grumbling against us, but against the LORD."[a]

15:23 [i]Nu 33:8
15:24 [j]Ex 14:12; 16:2
15:25 [k]Ex 14:10 [l]Jdg 3:4
15:26 [m]Dt 7:12 [n]Dt 28:27,58-60 [o]Ex 23:25-26
15:27 [p]Nu 33:9
16:1 [q]Nu 33:11,12
16:2 [r]Ex 14:11; 15:24; 1Co 10:10
16:3 [s]Ex 17:3 [t]Nu 11:4, 34
16:4 [u]Dt 8:3; Jn 6:31*
16:5 [v]ver 22
16:6 [w]Ex 6:6
16:7 [x]ver 10; Isa 35:2; 40:5 [y]ver 12; Nu 14:2,27,28 [z]Nu 16:11
16:8 [a]1Sa 8:7; Ro 13:2

[a] 23 *Marah* means *bitter.*

■ **15:22—18:27** *Leading to Sinai.* These chapters describe how the divine authorization of Moses and his laws was demonstrated as the people traveled from the sea to Sinai: at Marah and Elim (15:22–27), in the Desert of Sin (16:1–36), at Rephidim (17:1–16) and at Sinai (18:1–27). For the path of Israel's journey, see map "The Exodus" on page 121.
■ **15:22–27** *Marah and Elim.* The people challenged Moses' leadership, but God exalted Moses and the law that he mediated by providing water in response to Moses' prayer.
15:22 Desert. See 3:1. The word refers here to grazing land as opposed to cultivated land. **Shur.** See Genesis 16:7, 20:1 and 25:18. Shur was located north of the Sinai peninsula, between Egypt and the region much later known as Palestine.
15:23 Marah. The word means "bitterness." The suggested location is modern Ain Hawarah, inland and 50 miles south of the northern end of the Gulf of Suez. Apparently the Israelites went down the west coast of Sinai until they turned east to Mount Sinai.
15:24 grumbled. This note begins the grumbling theme that typified the Israelites' unbelief in the wilderness. The situation was critical. After nine days, their water skins were probably empty, and death from dehydration was an immediate threat. Further, their hopes were dashed when, upon finding water, they discovered it to be undrinkable. Their faith was tested and failed in the bitterness of disillusionment.
15:25 Moses cried out. The complaint of the people directed against Moses was also against God. Since Moses led at God's command (17:1), he appealed to the Lord. The people received good water because Moses mediated on their behalf; thus they owed their survival not only to God but also to Moses. Moses' continuing effectiveness as God's appointed leader and mediator reinforced the people's obligation to follow him. **tested them.** The faithfulness of Israel was tested during the wilderness travels (see Dt 8). The people had to listen to God's voice by obeying his laws given through Moses. Only then would God bless them.
15:26 any of the diseases . . . the LORD, who heals you. God promised not to bring covenant curses on his people if they would be faithful to the laws revealed by Moses (Dt 28:26,60–62; 7:15). **I am the LORD, who heals you.** God has the power (Dt 32:39) and the mercy to heal (Ps 103:3). He alone can heal in the peace of his salvation (2Ch 16:12; Isa 38:17). To the prayer of anguish (Jer 17:14) God responds (Jer 30:17; 33:6). Healing from the damage inflicted by sin and death comes through the Lord's Anointed, by whose wounds we are healed (Isa 53:5; 61:1–2; Mt 8:17).
15:27 Elim. The site is probably the Wadi Gharandel, seven miles south of modern Ain Hawarah. **twelve springs and seventy palm trees.** The correspondence of 12 springs to the 12 tribes of Israel and 70 palm trees to the 70 who first came to Egypt (1:5) demonstrates that the water at Elim was a gift from God specially designed for Israel, rather than a mere natural occurrence.
■ **16:1–36** *The Desert of Sin.* The Israelites again rebelled against Moses' leadership, but Moses interceded successfully on their behalf.
16:1 Desert of Sin. Situated in southwestern Sinai, this seems to be the modern region called Debbet er-Ramleh. The traditional site of Sinai is Jebel Musa, one of the three central peaks of the area. **fifteenth day of the second month.** The Israelites arrived in time to observe the Sabbath at Elim, and God appeared to them on the Sabbath (vv. 9–13). The chapter draws to a close (vv. 27–30) with rest on the following Sabbath. How Israel kept the Sabbath during the wilderness wanderings before Sinai is a major theme of the chapter.
16:2 grumbled against Moses. The Israelites were dissatisfied with God's provisions, but their dissatisfaction was directed at Moses, their leader (see 15:24; 17:2).
16:3 If only we had died. Hardship led to utter ingratitude for the Israelites' deliverance from slavery in Egypt.
16:4 bread. The people cried for bread and meat (v. 3), and God would give both (v. 8). Manna is elsewhere called the "bread of angels" (Ps 78:25). Jesus labeled himself as the true manna ("bread of life"; Jn 6:35), of which this provision in the desert was only a symbol and type.
16:7 glory. The word normally refers to the brilliant presence of God. Here the provision of the manna is in view because the manna displayed God's power and majesty.

9 Then Moses told Aaron, “Say to the entire Israelite community, ‘Come before the
LORD, for he has heard your grumbling.’ ”
10 While Aaron was speaking to the whole Israelite community, they looked toward
the desert, and there was the glory[b] of the LORD appearing in the cloud.[c]
11 The LORD said to Moses, 12 “I have heard the grumbling[d] of the Israelites. Tell them,
‘At twilight you will eat meat, and in the morning you will be filled with bread. Then you
will know that I am the LORD your God.’ ”
13 That evening quail[e] came and covered the camp, and in the morning there was a
layer of dew[f] around the camp. 14 When the dew was gone, thin flakes like frost[g] on the
ground appeared on the desert floor. 15 When the Israelites saw it, they said to each other, “What is it?” For they did not know what it was.
Moses said to them, “It is the bread[h] the LORD has given you to eat. 16 This is what the
LORD has commanded: ‘Each one is to gather as much as he needs. Take an omer[a][i] for
each person you have in your tent.’ ”
17 The Israelites did as they were told; some gathered much, some little. 18 And when
they measured it by the omer, he who gathered much did not have too much, and he who
gathered little did not have too little.[j] Each one gathered as much as he needed.
19 Then Moses said to them, “No one is to keep any of it until morning.”[k]
20 However, some of them paid no attention to Moses; they kept part of it until morning, but it was full of maggots and began to smell. So Moses was angry with them.
21 Each morning everyone gathered as much as he needed, and when the sun grew
hot, it melted away. 22 On the sixth day, they gathered twice[l] as much—two omers[b] for
each person—and the leaders of the community[m] came and reported this to Moses. 23 He
said to them, “This is what the LORD commanded: ‘Tomorrow is to be a day of rest, a holy
Sabbath[n] to the LORD. So bake what you want to bake and boil what you want to boil.
Save whatever is left and keep it until morning.’ ”
24 So they saved it until morning, as Moses commanded, and it did not stink or get
maggots in it. 25 “Eat it today,” Moses said, “because today is a Sabbath to the LORD. You
will not find any of it on the ground today. 26 Six days you are to gather it, but on the seventh day, the Sabbath,[o] there will not be any.”
27 Nevertheless, some of the people went out on the seventh day to gather it, but they
found none. 28 Then the LORD said to Moses, “How long will you[c] refuse to keep my commands[p] and my instructions? 29 Bear in mind that the LORD has given you the Sabbath;
that is why on the sixth day he gives you bread for two days. Everyone is to stay where
he is on the seventh day; no one is to go out.” 30 So the people rested on the seventh day.
31 The people of Israel called the bread manna.[d][q] It was white like coriander seed and
tasted like wafers made with honey. 32 Moses said, “This is what the LORD has commanded: ‘Take an omer of manna and keep it for the generations to come, so they can see the
bread I gave you to eat in the desert when I brought you out of Egypt.’ ”
33 So Moses said to Aaron, “Take a jar and put an omer of manna[r] in it. Then place it
before the LORD to be kept for the generations to come.”
34 As the LORD commanded Moses, Aaron put the manna in front of the Testimony,[s]
that it might be kept. 35 The Israelites ate manna[t] forty years,[u] until they came to a land
that was settled; they ate manna until they reached the border of Canaan.[v]
36 (An omer is one tenth of an ephah.)

16:10 [b]ver 7; Nu 16:19 [c]Ex 13:21; 1Ki 8:10
16:12 [d]ver 7
16:13 [e]Nu 11:31; Ps 78:27-28; 105:40 [f]Nu 11:9
16:14 [g]ver 31; Nu 11:7-9; Ps 105:40
16:15 [h]ver 4; Jn 6:31
16:16 [i]ver 32,36
16:18 [j]2Co 8:15*
16:19 [k]ver 23; Ex 12:10; 23:18
16:22 [l]ver 5 [m]Ex 34:31
16:23 [n]Ge 2:3; Ex 20:8; 23:12; Lev 23:3
16:26 [o]Ex 20:9-10
16:28 [p]2Ki 17:14; Ps 78:10; 106:13
16:31 [q]Nu 11:7-9
16:33 [r]Heb 9:4
16:34 [s]Ex 25:16,21,22; 40:20; Nu 17:4,10
16:35 [t]Jn 6:31,49 [u]Ne 9:21 [v]Jos 5:12

[a] *16* That is, probably about 2 quarts (about 2 liters); also in verses 18, 32, 33 and 36 [b] *22* That is, probably about 4 quarts (about 4.5 liters) (see verse 15). [c] *28* The Hebrew is plural. [d] *31* *Manna* means *What is it?*

16:9 before the LORD. Israel was to assemble at the place where the Lord would reveal himself.
16:12 Then you will know. God would confirm this claim on his people, and they would recognize his power and care.
16:13–36 The Lord met Israel's needs with quail and manna, but he regulated the provision according to his Sabbath laws. God's provision became a test of the faithfulness of Israel to his laws as mediated through Moses.
16:13 quail. A small game bird of the partridge family. As a migratory bird, it would have come from its winter habitat in Africa in the spring, alighting on the ground exhausted by flight. On a second occasion, the birds were brought by a strong east wind (Nu 11).
16:14 thin flakes. Manna seems to have been similar to a honeylike secretion of insects that infest the tamarisks of the area (called "manna" by the Arabs). It solidifies in the cold desert nights but must be gathered in early morning. If this is what "manna" refers to, then the miracle would have centered around God's control of the amount. The amount gathered was an omer (about two liters) per person, though the related Arabic word means a cupful; perhaps this is the meaning here.
16:22 See *WLC* 117.
16:23 holy Sabbath. The Hebrew word used here is an elevated term normally reserved for New Year's Day and holy festivals. The implication is that the weekly Sabbath was normally kept by Israel before Sinai. This reference indicates that the Sabbath ordinance in the Ten Commandments was a codification of Sabbath observance, not its inauguration. See *WCF* 21.8; *WLC* 121.
16:25–30 See *WCF* 21.8; *WLC* 117; *WSC* 60.
16:31 coriander. This seed is small, globular, grayish and aromatic, tasting like honey cake.
16:33 jar. This manna was set aside in what was called "the gold jar" (Heb 9:4).
16:35 forty years. The manna continued to be available each morning until the Israelites arrived in Canaan (Jos 5:10–12). When

Water From the Rock

17 The whole Israelite community set out from the Desert of Sin,[w] traveling from
place to place as the LORD commanded. They camped at Rephidim, but there
was no water[x] for the people to drink. 2So they quarreled with Moses and said, "Give us
water[y] to drink."
Moses replied, "Why do you quarrel with me? Why do you put the LORD to the test?"[z]
3But the people were thirsty for water there, and they grumbled[a] against Moses. They
said, "Why did you bring us up out of Egypt to make us and our children and livestock
die of thirst?"
4Then Moses cried out to the LORD, "What am I to do with these people? They are almost ready to stone[b] me."
5The LORD answered Moses, "Walk on ahead of the people. Take with you some of the
elders of Israel and take in your hand the staff with which you struck the Nile,[c] and go.
6I will stand there before you by the rock at Horeb. Strike the rock, and water[d] will come
out of it for the people to drink." So Moses did this in the sight of the elders of Israel. 7And
he called the place Massah[a] and Meribah[b][e] because the Israelites quarreled and because
they tested the LORD saying, "Is the LORD among us or not?"

The Amalekites Defeated

8The Amalekites[f] came and attacked the Israelites at Rephidim. 9Moses said to Joshua, "Choose some of our men and go out to fight the Amalekites. Tomorrow I will stand
on top of the hill with the staff[g] of God in my hands."
10So Joshua fought the Amalekites as Moses had ordered, and Moses, Aaron and Hur[h]
went to the top of the hill. 11As long as Moses held up his hands, the Israelites were winning,[i] but whenever he lowered his hands, the Amalekites were winning. 12When Moses' hands grew tired, they took a stone and put it under him and he sat on it. Aaron and
Hur held his hands up—one on one side, one on the other—so that his hands remained
steady till sunset. 13So Joshua overcame the Amalekite army with the sword.
14Then the LORD said to Moses, "Write[j] this on a scroll as something to be remembered and make sure that Joshua hears it, because I will completely blot out the memory of Amalek[k] from under heaven."
15Moses built an altar and called it The LORD is my Banner. 16He said, "For hands were

17:1 [w]Ex 16:1 [x]Nu 33:14
17:2 [y]Nu 20:2 [z]Dt 6:16; Ps 78:18,41; 1Co 10:9
17:3 [a]Ex 15:24; 16:2-3
17:4 [b]Nu 14:10; 1Sa 30:6
17:5 [c]Ex 7:20
17:6 [d]Nu 20:11; Ps 114:8; 1Co 10:4
17:7 [e]Nu 20:13,24; Ps 81:7
17:8 [f]Ge 36:12; Dt 25:17-19
17:9 [g]Ex 4:17
17:10 [h]Ex 21:11
17:11 [i]Jas 5:16
17:14 [j]Ex 24:4; 34:27; Nu 33:2 [k]1Sa 15:3; 30:17-18

[a] 7 *Massah* means *testing.* [b] 7 *Meribah* means *quarreling.*

they reached the Transjordanian country, there were fields, vineyards and wells of water (Nu 21:22), but the provision of manna seems to have continued. This information indicates that Exodus was written after the 40 years of wandering (see also 40:36).

■ **17:1–16** *Rephidim.* Two events took place at Rephidim during which Moses' leadership proved to be a blessing to Israel: the provision of water (vv. 1–7) and the defeat of the Amalekites (vv. 8–16).

■ **17:1–7** *The Provision of Water.* The Lord provided water through Moses.

17:1 Rephidim. This region, generally identified with the modern Wadi Refayid, about eight miles south of Jebel Musa, was the last stop before Sinai.

17:2 quarreled. The Hebrew for "quarreled" is *rib,* which also appears in the name Meribah (v. 7). This is a legal term that means "to bring a lawsuit" (Dt 25:1; Mic 6:1–2). The move to stone Moses (v. 4) was probably a threat to carry out an official execution. **quarrel with me . . . put the LORD to the test.** Challenging Moses in this way was equivalent to putting God himself on trial. "Testing" (Massah; v. 7) in this setting takes on a judicial meaning. Moses argued that the Israelites were not only challenging him but also accusing God of abandoning his people.

17:5 some of the elders. The elders were summoned as representative witnesses (cf. v. 6).

17:6 by the rock. Literally, "upon the rock." God stands on the rock and is identified with it. *Rock* is often a metaphor for royalty. Here the rock appears to represent divine kingship, and the water represents the good provisions of the divine King (see note on 1Co 10:4). God is the Rock in the song of Moses (Dt 32:4,15,18,31) and in the psalms that speak of Massah/Meribah (Pss 78:15,20,35; 95:1). **Strike the rock.** Moses struck the rock on which God stands and with which he is symbolically identified. By causing water to flow, God demonstrated that he was not guilty of mistreating his people. The solemnity of striking the rock is seen when Moses later did so unbidden and thereby dishonored the rule of God (Nu 20:9–12). **water.** The reference is to the water of life that flows from the throne of God (Eze 47:1–12; Zec 13:1; 14:8). Jesus offered this water in the temple, where water was symbolically poured out during the feast (see Jn 7:37). This rock was understood by the apostle Paul as a type of Christ (see note on 1Co 10:4).

17:7 See *WLC* 192.

■ **17:8–16** *The Defeat of the Amalekites.* The Lord used Moses to protect his people against the Amalekites.

17:8 Amalekites. The Amalekites, a nomadic group based in the southern portion of the region only recently known as Palestine, were descendants of Esau (Ge 36:12–16), which indicates the origin of the enmity. The Amalekites attacked from the rear (Dt 25:18).

17:9 Joshua. Joshua (an Ephraimite; Nu 13:8)—previously known as Hoshea ("salvation"; Nu 13:8,16), but later called Joshua ("Yahweh saves") as a result of this victory—is not formally introduced to the reader, nor is Hur the son of Caleb. **I will stand.** Joshua would choose men to fight, but they would do so under the uplifted staff, the sign of the Lord's victory.

17:10 Joshua fought. Holy war was waged by the sword of Joshua, but the Israelites prevailed only when Moses held up to heaven the staff that symbolized his authority (4:2; 9:23; 14:16). For the Israelites who were to follow Joshua forward into Canaan, it demonstrated that Joshua's leadership was dependent on Moses'. **Hur.** Attested in later tradition as the husband of Miriam, Moses' sister, he was possibly the grandfather of Bezalel, the famous artisan of the tabernacle (1Ch 2:19–20).

17:11 The victory of Israel over the Amalekites was directly connected to Moses' leadership, a central theme in this context.

17:12 Moses' hands. The hands (lit., "hand") that held aloft the rod. Moses' hands and the rod were identified in the plagues (7:19; 8:5).

17:14 Write this. One of the few references to writing in the Old Testament, although the practice was widespread at the time. It is linked with oral recitation here. The account was written, perhaps in "the Book of the Wars of the LORD," which is mentioned elsewhere (Nu 21:14). See *BC* 3.

17:15 The LORD is my Banner. The word for "banner" is that of the "staff" of verse 9 and that of the "pole" on which the bronze

lifted up to the throne of the LORD. The[a] LORD will be at war against the Amalekites from
generation to generation."

Jethro Visits Moses

18 Now Jethro, the priest of Midian[l] and father-in-law of Moses, heard of everything God had done for Moses and for his people Israel, and how the LORD had
brought Israel out of Egypt.
2 After Moses had sent away his wife Zipporah,[m] his father-in-law Jethro received her
3 and her two sons.[n] One son was named Gershom,[b] for Moses said, "I have become an
alien in a foreign land";[o] 4 and the other was named Eliezer,[c][p] for he said, "My father's
God was my helper; he saved me from the sword of Pharaoh."
5 Jethro, Moses' father-in-law, together with Moses' sons and wife, came to him in the
desert, where he was camped near the mountain[q] of God. 6 Jethro had sent word to him,
"I, your father-in-law Jethro, am coming to you with your wife and her two sons."
7 So Moses went out to meet his father-in-law and bowed down[r] and kissed[s] him.
They greeted each other and then went into the tent. 8 Moses told his father-in-law about
everything the LORD had done to Pharaoh and the Egyptians for Israel's sake and about
all the hardships they had met along the way and how the LORD had saved[t] them.
9 Jethro was delighted to hear about all the good things the LORD had done for Israel
in rescuing them from the hand of the Egyptians. 10 He said, "Praise be to the LORD,[u] who
rescued you from the hand of the Egyptians and of Pharaoh, and who rescued the people from the hand of the Egyptians. 11 Now I know that the LORD is greater than all other
gods,[v] for he did this to those who had treated Israel arrogantly."[w] 12 Then Jethro, Moses'
father-in-law, brought a burnt offering and other sacrifices to God, and Aaron came with
all the elders of Israel to eat bread with Moses' father-in-law in the presence[x] of God.
13 The next day Moses took his seat to serve as judge for the people, and they stood
around him from morning till evening. 14 When his father-in-law saw all that Moses was
doing for the people, he said, "What is this you are doing for the people? Why do you
alone sit as judge, while all these people stand around you from morning till evening?"
15 Moses answered him, "Because the people come to me to seek God's will.[y] 16 Whenever they have a dispute, it is brought to me, and I decide between the parties and inform them of God's decrees and laws."[z]
17 Moses' father-in-law replied, "What you are doing is not good. 18 You and these people who come to you will only wear yourselves out. The work is too heavy for you; you
cannot handle it alone.[a] 19 Listen now to me and I will give you some advice, and may
God be with you.[b] You must be the people's representative before God and bring their
disputes[c] to him. 20 Teach them the decrees and laws,[d] and show them the way to live[e]
and the duties they are to perform.[f] 21 But select capable men[g] from all the people—men
who fear God, trustworthy men who hate dishonest gain[h]—and appoint them as officials[i] over thousands, hundreds, fifties and tens. 22 Have them serve as judges for the people at all times, but have them bring every difficult case[j] to you; the simple cases they

18:1 [l]Ex 2:16; 3:1
18:2 [m]Ex 2:21; 4:25
18:3 [n]Ex 4:20; Ac 7:29 [o]Ex 2:22
18:4 [p]1Ch 23:15
18:5 [q]Ex 3:1
18:7 [r]Ge 43:28 [s]Ge 29:13
18:8 [t]Ex 15:6,16; Ps 81:7
18:10 [u]Ge 14:20; Ps 68:19-20
18:11 [v]Ex 12:12; 15:11; 2Ch 2:5 [w]Lk 1:51
18:12 [x]Dt 12:7
18:15 [y]Nu 9:6,8; Dt 17:8-13
18:16 [z]Lev 24:12
18:18 [a]Nu 11:11,14,17
18:19 [b]Ex 3:12 [c]Nu 27:5
18:20 [d]Dt 5:1 [e]Ps 143:8 [f]Dt 1:18
18:21 [g]Ac 6:3 [h]Dt 16:19; Ps 15:5; Eze 18:8 [i]Dt 1:13,15; 2Ch 19:5-10
18:22 [j]Dt 1:17-18

a *16* Or *"Because a hand was against the throne of the LORD, the* b *3* *Gershom* sounds like the Hebrew for *an alien there.* c *4* *Eliezer* means *my God is helper.*

serpent was later placed (Nu 21:8). Since *banner* suggests cloth to modern readers, this connection is lost. A spear could serve as a standard in battle, with or without bits of cloth tied to it. Later a staff might have a device on it to mark the rallying point for troops. In the ancient world these were sometimes images or signs of the gods. Moses' staff was the ensign to which Joshua's army could look and which symbolized God's saving power. Moses declared that God himself was the standard, the ensign of his people.

■ **18:1–27** *Near Sinai.* Before he narrated the covenant established at Sinai, Moses paused to report the blessing of an effective judicial system enacted near Sinai that had been given through him to Israel according to the will of God.

18:1–12 Jethro heard Moses' testimony of Israel's redemption from Egypt.

18:1 priest of Midian. Although not an Israelite, Jethro was a believer (v. 11) and worshiped the true God (v. 12).

18:2 sent away. Moses seems to have sent his family, including Zipporah, back to Jethro sometime after the incident of 4:24–26. This may have taken place after the exodus from Egypt.

18:4 Eliezer. The name means "My God is my help."

18:11 Now I know. This formula most likely indicates that Jethro's faith was being strengthened (1Ki 17:24). In any event, Jethro offered sacrifices and shared the communion meal, apparently as a leader, not simply as a supplicant.

18:12 burnt offering. The whole burnt offering as a dedication sacrifice came first. Fellowship sacrifices, shared by the worshipers, followed. Provision for sin and guilt offerings would complete the system later (in Leviticus). **Aaron came with all the elders.** The participation of Aaron and the elders showed their approval of Jethro as a priest who could sacrifice to the God of Israel. **in the presence of God.** Jethro participated in the experience of the holy presence of God in worship. He is shown again as a true priest of God as he offered counsel to Moses according to God's will.

18:13–27 Taking Jethro's counsel, Moses organized the government of Israel into a system of courts.

18:14 When his father-in-law saw. The judicial process exhausted Moses, and the people had to wait their turn. Jethro, after a day's observation, offered advice.

18:16 decrees and laws. The word "decrees" suggests statutes; "laws" suggests case decisions. They would be codified later.

18:19 people's representative. Moses was to represent the people to God, but the requirements and instructions were God's, not Moses'. See *WLC* 127.

18:20 See *BC* 36.

18:21 select capable men. Men were chosen here on moral, rather than intellectual, grounds to deal with simple matters. Difficult cases (or, presumably, those without precedent) were brought to Moses. This was how Israel's later legal system would function.

can decide themselves. That will make your load lighter, because they will share[k] it with
you. 23 If you do this and God so commands, you will be able to stand the strain, and all
these people will go home satisfied."
24 Moses listened to his father-in-law and did everything he said. 25 He chose capable
men from all Israel and made them leaders of the people, officials over thousands, hundreds, fifties and tens.[l] 26 They served as judges for the people at all times. The difficult
cases they brought to Moses, but the simple ones they decided themselves.[m]
27 Then Moses sent his father-in-law on his way, and Jethro returned to his own
country.[n]

At Mount Sinai

19 In the third month after the Israelites left Egypt—on the very day—they came
to the Desert of Sinai. 2 After they set out from Rephidim,[o] they entered the Desert of Sinai, and Israel camped there in the desert in front of the mountain.[p]
3 Then Moses went up to God, and the LORD called[q] to him from the mountain and
said, "This is what you are to say to the house of Jacob and what you are to tell the people of Israel: 4 'You yourselves have seen what I did to Egypt,[r] and how I carried you on
eagles' wings[s] and brought you to myself. 5 Now if you obey me fully[t] and keep my covenant,[u] then out of all nations you will be my treasured possession.[v] Although the
whole earth[w] is mine, 6 you[a] will be for me a kingdom of priests[x] and a holy nation.'[y]
These are the words you are to speak to the Israelites."
7 So Moses went back and summoned the elders of the people and set before them all
the words the LORD had commanded him to speak. 8 The people all responded together,
"We will do everything the LORD has said."[z] So Moses brought their answer back to the
LORD.
9 The LORD said to Moses, "I am going to come to you in a dense cloud,[a] so that the
people will hear me speaking[b] with you and will always put their trust in you." Then Moses told the LORD what the people had said.
10 And the LORD said to Moses, "Go to the people and consecrate[c] them today and tomorrow. Have them wash their clothes[d] 11 and be ready by the third day,[e] because on
that day the LORD will come down on Mount Sinai in the sight of all the people. 12 Put limits for the people around the mountain and tell them, 'Be careful that you do not go up
the mountain or touch the foot of it. Whoever touches the mountain shall surely be put
to death. 13 He shall surely be stoned[f] or shot with arrows; not a hand is to be laid on him.
Whether man or animal, he shall not be permitted to live.' Only when the ram's horn
sounds a long blast may they go up to the mountain."
14 After Moses had gone down the mountain to the people, he consecrated them, and
they washed their clothes. 15 Then he said to the people, "Prepare yourselves for the third
day. Abstain from sexual relations."

18:22 [k]Nu 11:17
18:25 [l]Dt 1:13-15
18:26 [m]ver 22
18:27 [n]Nu 10:29-30
19:2 [o]Ex 17:1 [p]Ex 3:1
19:3 [q]Ex 3:4; Ac 7:38
19:4 [r]Dt 29:2 [s]Isa 63:9
19:5 [t]Ex 15:26 [u]Dt 5:2 [v]Dt 14:2; Ps 135:4 [w]Ex 9:29; Dt 10:14
19:6 [x]1Pe 2:5 [y]Dt 7:6; 26:19; Isa 62:12
19:8 [z]Ex 24:3,7; Dt 5:27
19:9 [a]ver 16; Ex 24:15-16 [b]Dt 4:12,36
19:10 [c]Lev 11:44; Heb 10:22 [d]Ge 35:2
19:11 [e]ver 16
19:13 [f]Heb 12:20*

[a] 5,6 Or *possession, for the whole earth is mine.* 6 *You*

18:23 will go home satisfied. That is, the people would receive justice. Thus the judicial system enacted here was a great blessing from God through Moses.
18:24 See *WLC* 127.
■ **19:1—24:18** *God's Covenant Mediated by Moses.* The second way in which the book of Exodus affirms the divine authorization of Moses is in the covenant he mediated between God and Israel. These chapters divide into three main parts: initiating the covenant (19:1–25), the laws of the covenant (20:1—23:33) and finalizing the covenant (24:1–18). See theological article "Major Covenants in the Bible" on page 25.
■ **19:1–25** *The Initiation of the Covenant.* God offered a covenant relationship with Israel through Moses.
19:1 Desert of Sinai. Located in the southeast region of the Sinai peninsula.
19:3–6 This is what you are to say . . . These are the words. God's words began and ended with his instruction to Moses, who was presented as the mediator of God's covenant with Israel.
19:4 what I did. Divine deliverance is summarized as release from Egyptian oppression, guidance through the wilderness and worship at the holy mountain. God's deliverance from slavery was not just liberation. He brought his people out of Egypt and carried them through the wilderness to bring them to himself, to make them his own.
19:5 obey me fully and keep my covenant. The intention of the covenant is expressed by these equivalent phrases. The latter phrase (Ge 17:9–10; 1Ki 11:11; Pss 78:10; 103:18; 132:12; Eze 17:14) always refers to fidelity. God does not require perfection from his people, but faithfulness and sincere devotion. **treasured possession.** Israel would be his personal treasure within what is more generally owned by him (1Ch 29:3). Israel was separated and specially loved by God. **Although the whole earth is mine.** This sentence gives the reason for God's choice of Israel: In the seed of Abraham as a kingdom of priests, all the nations of the earth would be blessed (see Ge 12:3).
19:6 kingdom of priests and a holy nation. The two phrases are equivalents. Israel was to be "priestly royalty, a holy nation." That is, Israel was to be set apart from her world as a priest was set apart in ancient society. The emphasis falls on Israel's relation to God rather than on any priestly ministry to the nations. Verses 4–6 reflect the Abrahamic covenant of Genesis 15 and 17. What this passage prescribes for Israel is continued in the church, which consists of Jews and Gentiles in covenant with God (1Pe 2:9–10; Rev 1:6; 5:10; 20:6).
19:7 summoned the elders. Moses set this before Israel's elders, whose affirmative response represented the entire nation.
19:10 wash their clothes. The washing of clothes symbolized purification (Ge 35:2).
19:11 be ready by the third day. God set out the preparations necessary for the theophany on the mountain. Sinai was not to be directly approached.
19:12 See *HC* 99.
19:15 sexual relations. Sexual intercourse made the parties ritually unclean (Lev 15:16ff.; 1Sa 21:4).

16On the morning of the third day there was thunder and lightning, with a thick cloud
over the mountain, and a very loud trumpet blast.[g] Everyone in the camp trembled.[h]
17Then Moses led the people out of the camp to meet with God, and they stood at the foot
of the mountain. 18Mount Sinai was covered with smoke,[i] because the LORD descended
on it in fire.[j] The smoke billowed up from it like smoke from a furnace,[k] the whole mountain[a] trembled[l] violently, 19and the sound of the trumpet grew louder and louder. Then
Moses spoke and the voice[m] of God answered[n] him.[b]
20The LORD descended to the top of Mount Sinai and called Moses to the top of the
mountain. So Moses went up 21and the LORD said to him, "Go down and warn the people so they do not force their way through to see[o] the LORD and many of them perish.
22Even the priests, who approach[p] the LORD, must consecrate themselves, or the LORD
will break out against them."[q]
23Moses said to the LORD, "The people cannot come up Mount Sinai, because you
yourself warned us, 'Put limits[r] around the mountain and set it apart as holy.' "
24The LORD replied, "Go down and bring Aaron[s] up with you. But the priests and the
people must not force their way through to come up to the LORD, or he will break out
against them."
25So Moses went down to the people and told them.

The Ten Commandments

20 And God spoke all these words:

2"I am the LORD your God, who brought you out of Egypt, out of the land of slavery.[t]

3"You shall have no other gods before[c] me.[u]

4"You shall not make for yourself an idol[v] in the form of anything in heaven above
or on the earth beneath or in the waters below. 5You shall not bow down
to them or worship[w] them; for I, the LORD your God, am a jealous God,[x]
punishing the children for the sin of the fathers to the third and fourth gen-

19:16 [g]Heb 12:18-19; Rev 4:1 [h]Heb 12:21
19:18 [i]Ps 104:32 [j]Ex 3:2; 24:17; Dt 4:11; 2Ch 7:1; Ps 18:8; Heb 12:18 [k]Ge 19:28 [l]Jdg 5:5; Ps 68:8; Jer 4:24
19:19 [m]Ne 9:13 [n]Ps 81:7
19:21 [o]Ex 3:5; 1Sa 6:19
19:22 [p]Lev 10:3 [q]2Sa 6:7
19:23 [r]ver 12
19:24 [s]Ex 24:1,9
20:2 [t]Ex 13:3
20:3 [u]Dt 6:14; Jer 35:15
20:4 [v]Lev 26:1; Dt 4:15-19,23; 27:15
20:5 [w]Isa 44:15,17,19 [x]Ex 34:14; Dt 4:24

[a] *18* Most Hebrew manuscripts; a few Hebrew manuscripts and Septuagint *all the people* [b] *19* Or *and God answered him with thunder* [c] *3* Or *besides*

19:16 On the morning of the third day. God came as promised on the morning of the third day. No natural explanation of verses 16–19 is sufficient. This was a divine manifestation by storm and fire. The intensity rose to a crescendo: rumbling thunder, lightning and daybreak; then the mountain was covered with a cloud.
19:18 trembled violently. The violent quaking of the mountain represented the upheaval of the natural world that accompanied God's divine manifestation (see also Mic 1:3–4).
19:20 The LORD descended. Verses 20–22 constitute a summary introduction to the delivery of the Ten Commandments.
19:24 priests. Before the Aaronic priesthood was enacted (28:1), priestly functions were performed by men who were temporarily consecrated for the task (see 24:5). It is possible, however, that this statement anticipates the restrictions that would be placed on the Aaronic priests as well, once they were established.
■ **20:1—23:33** *The Codification of the Covenant.* The narrative is interrupted to give a record of the stipulations of the covenant that God made through Moses. These chapters divide between the Ten Commandments (20:1–17) and the Book of the Covenant (20:18—23:33).
■ **20:1–17** *The Ten Commandments.* God spoke the (ten) "words" of his covenant. These are expressions of the eternal law of God that transcend all cultures and times. The first several commandments describe how people are to relate to God: They are to serve him alone without idols, reverence his name and keep his Sabbath holy. The remaining commandments describe how God's people are to relate to one another: They are to respect parents, life, the marriage relationship, property and another's good name, living in contentment. See theological article "The Three Uses of the Law" at Psalm 119.

The Ten Commandments (also called The Decalogue) contain elements that are also found in ancient Near-Eastern covenants (i.e., treaties) made between a powerful king (suzerain) and a less powerful king or nation that served him (vassal). First is the preamble, which introduced the parties between whom the covenant was made: "I am the LORD your God" (v. 2). Next is the historical prologue, which recalled the good things the powerful king, the Lord, had done for his servant nation, Israel: ". . . who brought you out of Egypt." The commandments themselves are the covenant stipulations, those things Israel had to do in order to obtain the benefits of the covenant and avoid its penalties. These words were spoken in the hearing of all the people (19:9; 20:18–20; Dt 4:10–14; 5:22–27; 9:10; Ne 9:13). The absence of stated penalties indicates that the commandments are not a legal code but a foundational document. The legal code itself (i.e., the Book of the Covenant) follows in chapters 21–23. See *HC* 92. See theological article "The Law of God" on page 129.
20:1–2 See *WLC* 152.
20:1 words. What are here called "words" are elsewhere referred to as "commandments" (34:28; Dt 4:13 10:4). "Words" was the technical term for "stipulations" in the covenants of the time.
20:2 your God. God's claim came first. Israel was his by right of creation and redemption. The Lord's covenant commands were given as a way for those whom he had already delivered from slavery to express their grateful loyalty (19:4). They were never designed as a way of salvation. See *WLC* 101; *WSC* 43.
20:3 before me. That is, "before my face" or "in my presence." The Lord is a jealous God; he had already claimed Israel as his own and would tolerate no rivals. See *WLC* 103; *WSC* 45.
20:4–6 See *WCF* 21.1; *WLC* 107,110; *WSC* 49.
20:4 idol. The term "idol" means something hewn from wood or stone. The prohibited image may be that of the Lord, since other deities had been excluded by verse 2. On the other hand, the qualifying words "in the form of anything" suggest that pagan idols were in view.
20:5 jealous. When used of God, this term describes his passion for his holy name, a zeal that demands the exclusive devotion of his people. It is employed when that claim is threatened by allegiance to other deities (Dt 6:15; Jos 24:19). Also, God is jealous for his people (though never of them). In this connection, his jealousy is against other gods (34:14). **fourth generation.** This is the longest span of generations normally represented in a given household at any one time. The severity of God's judgment on the generations of those who hate him stands as a strong warning to those who love their children's children. **hate me.** In accordance with the language of ancient treaties, hatred for the divine king meant refusal to submit to him by joining him in the bonds of covenant.

eration[y] of those who hate me, [6]but showing love to a thousand[z] ⌊generations⌋ of those who love me and keep my commandments.
[7]"You shall not misuse the name of the LORD your God, for the LORD will not hold anyone guiltless who misuses his name.[a]
[8]"Remember the Sabbath[b] day by keeping it holy. [9]Six days you shall labor and do all your work,[c] [10]but the seventh day is a Sabbath to the LORD your God. On it you shall not do any work, neither you, nor your son or daughter, nor your manservant or maidservant, nor your animals, nor the alien within your

20:5 [y]Nu 14:18; Jer 32:18
20:6 [z]Dt 7:9
20:7 [a]Lev 19:12; Mt 5:33
20:8 [b]Ex 31:13-16; Lev 26:2
20:9 [c]Ex 34:21; Lk 13:14

20:6 showing love. God's love is shown in his devotion to his people. It is the bond forged by God's own faithfulness to the grace of his covenant. **a thousand generations.** See Deuteronomy 7:9. **who love me and keep my commandments.** Love for God and obedience to him are closely connected, but not identical. In ancient treaties, vassals were told to love their kings by offering them loyal devotion out of gratitude for what they had done. Love for God is the source of obedience (see Jn 14:15; 1Jn 5:3).

20:7 misuse the name. God's name was a gift of grace to Israel. By sincerely invoking the Name, Israel had access to God's special presence (see 1Ki 8). God's name is therefore to be revered. This command forbids the use of God's name in false worship, for incantations or divination, for attesting falsehood or for speaking blasphemy (Dt 28:58). Jesus taught his disciples to pray that God would hallow his name (Mt 6:9). See *WCF* 22.1; 22.2; 22.3; *WLC* 99,111,114; *WSC* 53.

20:8–11 See *WCF* 21.7; *WLC* 115,120; *WSC* 57,62.

20:8 Sabbath day. The underlying idea in the word "sabbath" is that which completes a sequence. The seventh day is that which completes and perfects a series of days (Ge 1:1—2:3). It was the day on which Israel was to remember her place within God's purposes for creation (v. 11; Ge 2:1–3). The Sabbath became the sign of the Sinai covenant (31:13), as circumcision was the sign of the Abrahamic covenant (Ge 17:11). In Deuteronomy 5:12–15 the Sabbath functioned as a reminder that God's covenant people were saved from physical bondage unto rest. The Sabbath is a type of the rest Christ brings (Mt 11:28; Col 2:16–17; Heb 4:1–13). See *WCF* 21.7; 21.8; *WLC* 117,121; *WSC* 60.

20:10 not do any work. The Sabbath, as the provision for servants and animals shows, is a time for rest and refreshment from hard labor (Dt 5:14). It is not designed as a burden, but as a release and a blessing (Mk 2:27). The holiness of the day separates it to the

The Law of God: What Is God's Law?

THE law of God is nothing less than an expression of God's holy and moral character (Jas 2:10–11). In this sense the law of God is eternal, just as God himself is eternal. Beyond this, God's law is his good gift to the human race (Ro 7:12). God designed humanity and the world to operate in ways that accord with his law. For this reason, when God's law is rightly understood and applied, it is our delight and joy, our path for successful living, neither a burden nor a curse (Jos 1:8–9; Pss 112:1; 119:14,16,47–48,97–113,127–128,163–167).

Rightly identifying, interpreting and applying the law of God, however, is a complex task requiring an appreciation for all of Scripture. God revealed his law to Adam and Eve in the form of their general responsibilities as his image-bearers (Ge 1:27–30) and in the prohibition regarding the forbidden fruit (Ge 2:15–17). God also revealed his law to Noah and to Israel's patriarchs in a variety of ways appropriate for their circumstances. In the days of Moses, God delineated his law in great detail in ways that were appropriate for that stage of salvation history and also inspired its codification for the first time. Further revelation conveyed to God's people by the Old Testament prophets also applied the eternal law of God to Israel, especially during the time of Israel's monarchy (2Sa 23:1–2; 24:11). Finally, the eternal law of God was revealed by Christ and his apostles, whose teachings are authoritatively summarized in the New Testament (e.g., Mt 5–7). Because God's character is immutable and never self-contradictory, at no time did the principles of conduct called for in one stage of revelation contradict those in another. Yet at no time were they precisely the same.

The most complex expression of God's eternal law in Biblical revelation comes from the period of Moses, Israel's great lawgiver. Traditionally, Reformed theology has divided the Mosaic Law into three parts: the moral law, the ceremonial law (rituals, worship, etc.) and the civil or judicial laws (criminal and social regulations). So long as we remember that these categories overlap in many ways, this threefold distinction is helpful.

The Ten Commandments expressed the basic moral principles of God's law in ten simple but all-encompassing rules. These laws are stated rather abstractly and can therefore be applied with relative ease to every person, place and time. The ceremonial and judicial laws, however, are closely tied to specific aspects of the circumstances of the time. The ceremonies were designed for tabernacle and temple worship and the judicial laws to guide Israel as a theocratic nation-state. These aspects of Moses' Law are relatively difficult to apply in the New Testament era because Old Testament ceremonies and the body politic of Israel have been fulfilled in Christ. Even so, the moral principles undergirding the ceremonial and judicial laws must still be applied in the present age.

Finally, the New Testament itself guides believers living after the earthly ministry of Christ by providing its own rules or laws. The Christian life is not without external laws. Jesus himself taught many moral principles and demonstrated time and again how his teachings were true applications of the Law of Moses (Mt 5–7; 12:11–12; Mk 2:23–28). The apostles also taught the church the commands of God (Jn 13:34; 1Co 14:37; 1Jn 2:7–8) and frequently demonstrated that these regulations were true applications of Old Testament revelation. For example, when Paul stated, "I am not free from God's law but am under Christ's law" (1Co 9:21), he meant that he was obligated to obey all of God's law as Christ and the apostles applied it to the circumstances the early church faced. Following the example of Jesus and his apostles, we too must discern the moral principles taught throughout Scripture and apply them carefully to the church and world of our day.

gates. 11 For in six days the LORD made the heavens and the earth, the sea,
and all that is in them, but he rested[d] on the seventh day. Therefore the
LORD blessed the Sabbath day and made it holy.
12 "Honor your father and your mother,[e] so that you may live long in the land the
LORD your God is giving you.
13 "You shall not murder.[f]
14 "You shall not commit adultery.[g]
15 "You shall not steal.[h]
16 "You shall not give false testimony against your neighbor.[i]
17 "You shall not covet[j] your neighbor's house. You shall not covet your neighbor's
wife, or his manservant or maidservant, his ox or donkey, or anything that
belongs to your neighbor."
18 When the people saw the thunder and lightning and heard the trumpet[k] and saw
the mountain in smoke, they trembled with fear. They stayed at a distance 19 and said to
Moses, "Speak to us yourself and we will listen. But do not have God speak to us or we
will die."[l]
20 Moses said to the people, "Do not be afraid. God has come to test you, so that the
fear[m] of God will be with you to keep you from sinning."[n]
21 The people remained at a distance, while Moses approached the thick darkness[o]
where God was.

Idols and Altars

22 Then the LORD said to Moses, "Tell the Israelites this: 'You have seen for yourselves
that I have spoken to you from heaven:[p] 23 Do not make any gods to be alongside me;[q]
do not make for yourselves gods of silver or gods of gold.[r]
24 " 'Make an altar of earth for me and sacrifice on it your burnt offerings and fellowship offerings,[a] your sheep and goats and your cattle. Wherever I cause my name[s] to be
honored, I will come to you and bless[t] you. 25 If you make an altar of stones for me, do
not build it with dressed stones, for you will defile it if you use a tool[u] on it. 26 And do not
go up to my altar on steps, lest your nakedness be exposed on it.'

20:11 [d]Ge 2:2
20:12 [e]Mt 15:4*; Mk 7:10*; Eph 6:2
20:13 [f]Mt 5:21*; Ro 13:9*
20:14 [g]Mt 19:18*
20:15 [h]Lev 19:11,13; Mt 19:18*
20:16 [i]Ex 23:1,7; Mt 19:18*
20:17 [j]Ro 7:7*; 13:9*; Eph 5:3
20:18 [k]Ex 19:16-19; Heb 12:18-19
20:19 [l]Dt 5:5,23-27; Gal 3:19
20:20 [m]Dt 4:10; Isa 8:13 [n]Pr 16:6
20:21 [o]Dt 5:22
20:22 [p]Ne 9:13
20:23 [q]ver 3 [r]Ex 32:4,8,31
20:24 [s]Dt 12:5; 16:6,11; 2Ch 6:6 [t]Ge 12:2
20:25 [u]Dt 27:5-6

[a] 24 Traditionally *peace offerings*

Lord so that it is enjoyed by sharing his rest, celebrating his finished work of creation and redemption (Dt 5:15). See *WCF* 21.7; *WLC* 99,117,118; *WSC* 60.

20:11 For in six days. Here the motivation for keeping the Sabbath is the imitation of God. In the version of this command found in Deuteronomy 5:15, the motivation is God's deliverance of Israel from the hardship of slavery in Egypt. See *WSC* 62; *HC* 26.

20:12 your father and your mother. The Ten Commandments begin with a call to reverence toward God. In the fifth commandment, the commands turn more toward human relations, beginning with the family. Honor toward parents not only anchors society but also joins children to parents in the continuance of faith. The promise and implied warning of this commandment are unique in this series. Disrespect for parents is a serious matter, for it translates to disrespect for the Lord. See *WLC* 99,123,133; *WSC* 63.

20:13 murder. The law distinguishes between manslaughter and premeditated murder. The verb used here is never applied to Israel at war. Capital punishment had already been authorized in Genesis 9:6 (cf. Lev 24:17; Nu 35:30–34). Human life is sacred because it bears God's image (Ge 9:6). See *WLC* 134; *WSC* 67.

20:14 adultery. Sexual intercourse with someone other than one's spouse is in view. Adultery is an attack upon the marriage relationship appointed by God (Ge 2:24; Mt 19:4–6). God's ordinance of exclusive love within the marriage bond prepares his people to understand the exclusive love of God's covenant, broken by Israel's spiritual adultery but restored in Christ (Eph 5:22–33). The vulnerability of human nature to sexual sin is indicated in that Leviticus 18 is devoted entirely to sexual offenses. See *WLC* 137; *WSC* 71.

20:15 not steal. Theft threatens the welfare of a neighbor. This law protected the rights of private property as God's people received their inheritance. See *WCF* 26.3; *WLC* 140; *WSC* 73.

20:16 false testimony. Integrity is demanded in matters of justice. One cannot use language merely to suit one's own ends. The command is directed against the willful perversion of truth. See *WLC* 143; *WSC* 76.

20:17 covet. This last commandment summarizes social relations in the covenant, as the first commandment had introduced the whole. "Covet" describes an attitude of mind that in itself is wrong, a discontented desire for that which cannot rightly be had. See *WLC* 146; *WSC* 79.

▪ **20:18—23:33** *The Book of the Covenant.* The Ten Commandments are followed by a summation of the more extensive case laws that God revealed to Moses to guide Israel in covenant life. These chapters divide into three parts: a prologue (20:18–26), the collection of laws (21:1—23:19) and an epilogue (23:20–33).

▪ **20:18–26** *Prologue.* The sequence of the narrative does not correspond to the actual order of events. The events of verse 18 most likely followed those of 19:25, and the Ten Commandments were likely given at the same time as the Book of the Covenant, "while Moses approached the thick darkness where God was" (v. 21). As it stands in the order of the narrative, verses 18–26 form a historical prologue to the Book of the Covenant.

20:18 they trembled with fear. The awe that comes from recognizing God's power and glory deters sin (v. 20). Such awe is greater in the reality of new covenant worship (Heb 12:28–29).

20:19 Speak to us yourself. The authority of Moses as God's mediator was acknowledged. God might have spoken all his law to all Israel, but the people could not have endured his dread voice. Moses, therefore, brought God's words to God's people. Thus Moses was exalted as the mediator of the covenant by the choice of the people, not by his own desire for power.

20:22 Then the LORD said. God continued to speak from heaven—his voice came from heaven or from the cloud (24:16).

20:24 Make an altar. God would reveal himself at the places he chose. There altars were to be built, and God would bless the people. There was no fixed, central sanctuary in Israel until the later move to Jerusalem. **burnt offerings and fellowship offerings.** Only two types of sacrifices are mentioned, but the list would be expanded later (in Leviticus). The fellowship offering ("peace offering") was a communion offering. Part of the sacrifice was burned on the altar; the remainder was eaten by the worshiper and the priests (18:12).

20:25 defile it. It is not entirely clear why this restriction was placed on the Israelites. Many altars of undressed stone have been discovered in archaeological sites. It is likely that the use of undressed stones in altars was commonly associated with holiness and therefore adopted by God for Israel.

20:26 This provision guards against immodest display.

16 the Angel who has delivered me from all harm
—may he bless these boys.[h]
May they be called by my name
and the names of my fathers Abraham and Isaac,[i]
and may they increase greatly
upon the earth."

17 When Joseph saw his father placing his right hand on Ephraim's head[j] he was displeased; so he took hold of his father's hand to move it from Ephraim's head to Manasseh's head. 18 Joseph said to him, "No, my father, this one is the firstborn; put your right hand on his head."

19 But his father refused and said, "I know, my son, I know. He too will become a people, and he too will become great.[k] Nevertheless, his younger brother will be greater than he,[l] and his descendants will become a group of nations." 20 He blessed them that day and said,

"In your[a] name will Israel pronounce this blessing:
'May God make you like Ephraim[m] and Manasseh.[n]' "

So he put Ephraim ahead of Manasseh.

21 Then Israel said to Joseph, "I am about to die, but God will be with you[b][o] and take you[b] back to the land of your[b] fathers.[p] 22 And to you, as one who is over your brothers,[q] I give the ridge of land[c][r] I took from the Amorites with my sword and my bow."

Jacob Blesses His Sons

49 Then Jacob called for his sons and said: "Gather around so I can tell you what will happen to you in days to come.[s]

2 "Assemble and listen, sons of Jacob;
listen to your father Israel.[t]

3 "Reuben, you are my firstborn,[u]
my might, the first sign of my strength,[v]
excelling in honor, excelling in power.
4 Turbulent as the waters,[w] you will no longer excel,
for you went up onto your father's bed,
onto my couch and defiled it.[x]

5 "Simeon and Levi are brothers—
their swords[d] are weapons of violence.[y]
6 Let me not enter their council,
let me not join their assembly,[z]
for they have killed men in their anger[a]
and hamstrung oxen as they pleased.

48:16 [h]Heb 11:21 [i]Ge 28:13
48:17 [j]ver 14
48:19 [k]Ge 17:20 [l]Ge 25:23
48:20 [m]Nu 2:18 [n]Nu 2:20; Ru 4:11
48:21 [o]Ge 26:3; 46:4 [p]Ge 28:13; 50:24
48:22 [q]Ge 37:8 [r]Jos 24:32; Jn 4:5
49:1 [s]Nu 24:14; Jer 23:20
49:2 [t]Ps 34:11
49:3 [u]Ge 29:32 [v]Dt 21:17; Ps 78:51
49:4 [w]Isa 57:20 [x]Ge 35:22; Dt 27:20
49:5 [y]Ge 34:25; Pr 4:17
49:6 [z]Pr 1:15; Eph 5:11 [a]Ge 34:26

[a] *20* The Hebrew is singular. [b] *21* The Hebrew is plural. [c] *22* Or *And to you I give one portion more than to your brothers—the portion* [d] *5* The meaning of the Hebrew for this word is uncertain.

48:16 the Angel. Jacob had learned through experience the reality of God's presence (28:12; 31:11; 32:1–3,22–32).
48:17 When Joseph saw. The explanatory notice (vv. 17–20) was appended to the ritual so as not to interrupt the narrative (see note on v. 1).
48:19 his father refused. The patriarch, empowered by God, was greater than the ruler of Egypt. **I know.** A deliberate and striking contrast with Jacob's long-ago deception of Isaac in order to secure the blessing. **his younger brother will be greater than he.** Against social convention, the younger was blessed, as in the cases of Isaac versus Ishmael, Jacob versus Esau and Joseph versus Reuben. In his sovereign grace God overrode the natural ways of people (Isa 55:8–9).
48:20 Ephraim ahead of Manasseh. Ephraim became the greatest of the ten northern tribes.
49:1–28 The blessings of the inspired patriarch prophesied the fate of the 12 tribes, based on praise or blame, mostly by plays on their names and through comparisons to animals. The names and/or actions of the 12 sons portend the destiny of each tribe (Mic 1:10–16). These prophetic blessings at the end of the patriarchal era, arranged by mothers—Leah's six (vv. 3–15), the maidservants' four (vv. 16–21) and Rachel's two (vv. 22–27)—exhibit the future roles of the patriarchs' tribes. These blessings closely parallel those of Moses (Dt 33) that were given near his death, demonstrating that the information here was of great importance to the Israelite readers as they prepared to begin the conquest of Canaan.
49:1 in days to come. See Numbers 24:14 (see also Dt 31:28–29; Isa 2:2; Mic 4:1). Jacob's prophecies embrace the entire history of Israel, from the conquest and distribution of the land to the consummate reign of Jesus Christ.
49:3–7 The prophecies about Leah's first three sons (Reuben, Simeon and Levi) pronounced punishments for crimes; they do not use animal comparisons. The sins of the fathers were visited upon the children (see Ex 20:5).
49:3 Reuben. See notes on 29:32 and 35:22. The alteration of a man's inheritance prospects in the ancient Near East was never subject to a father's arbitrary decision. In this instance, as in many other examples from history, it was brought about by serious sex offenses against one's own family.
49:4 Turbulent. That is, destructive. The Hebrew here connotes pride and presumption (1Ch 5:1–2).
49:5 Simeon and Levi. See 29:33–34 and 34:25. **swords.** The Hebrew here may connote "circumcision knives."

21

"These are the laws[v] you are to set before them:

Hebrew Servants

2"If you buy a Hebrew servant, he is to serve you for six years. But in the seventh year,
he shall go free,[w] without paying anything. 3If he comes alone, he is to go free alone; but
if he has a wife when he comes, she is to go with him. 4If his master gives him a wife and
she bears him sons or daughters, the woman and her children shall belong to her master, and only the man shall go free.
5"But if the servant declares, 'I love my master and my wife and children and do not
want to go free,'[x] 6then his master must take him before the judges.[a][y] He shall take him
to the door or the doorpost and pierce his ear with an awl. Then he will be his servant
for life.[z]
7"If a man sells his daughter as a servant, she is not to go free as menservants do. 8If
she does not please the master who has selected her for himself,[b] he must let her be redeemed. He has no right to sell her to foreigners, because he has broken faith with her.
9If he selects her for his son, he must grant her the rights of a daughter. 10If he marries
another woman, he must not deprive the first one of her food, clothing and marital
rights.[a] 11If he does not provide her with these three things, she is to go free, without any
payment of money.

Personal Injuries

12"Anyone who strikes a man and kills him shall surely be put to death.[b] 13However,
if he does not do it intentionally, but God lets it happen, he is to flee to a place[c] I will designate. 14But if a man schemes and kills another man deliberately,[d] take him away from
my altar and put him to death.[e]
15"Anyone who attacks[c] his father or his mother must be put to death.
16"Anyone who kidnaps another and either sells[f] him or still has him when he is
caught must be put to death.[g]
17"Anyone who curses his father or mother must be put to death.[h]
18"If men quarrel and one hits the other with a stone or with his fist[d] and he does not
die but is confined to bed, 19the one who struck the blow will not be held responsible if
the other gets up and walks around outside with his staff; however, he must pay the injured man for the loss of his time and see that he is completely healed.
20"If a man beats his male or female slave with a rod and the slave dies as a direct result, he must be punished, 21but he is not to be punished if the slave gets up after a day
or two, since the slave is his property.[i]

21:1 [v]Dt 4:14
21:2 [w]Jer 34:8,14
21:5 [x]Dt 15:16
21:6 [y]Ex 22:8-9 [z]Ne 5:5
21:10 [a]1Co 7:3-5
21:12 [b]Ge 9:6; Mt 26:52
21:13 [c]Nu 35:10-34; Dt 19:2-13; Jos 20:9; 1Sa 24:4, 10,18
21:14 [d]Heb 10:26 [e]Dt 19:11-12; 1Ki 2:28-34
21:16 [f]Ge 37:28 [g]Ex 22:4; Dt 24:7
21:17 [h]Lev 20:9-10; Mt 15:4*; Mk 7:10*
21:21 [i]Lev 25:44-46

[a] 6 Or *before God* [b] 8 Or *master so that he does not choose her* [c] 15 Or *kills* [d] 18 Or *with a tool*

■ **21:1—23:19** *The Book.* This book provided precedents, guiding principles determined by case decisions. These laws applied the foundation of the Ten Commandments (20:1–17) to rather specific situations. The derivative character of these laws suggests that they were delivered indirectly through Moses, rather than directly, as the Ten Commandments were. As in other law codes of the ancient Near East, these laws touch on many issues with little apparent organization. In general, civil and penal laws are presented in 21:1—22:15, laws controlling morality in 22:16–27 and 23:1–9 and laws of worship in 20:22–26, 22:28–30 and 23:10–19. The laws in 21:1—22:17 are in the form of case law ("If . . . then" laws with penalties). Laws forbidding certain behavior ("Do not . . .") follow in 22:18—23:19. The purpose of these social codes was to regulate Israelite life in the promised land. Such case law in the ancient world was a public declaration of the ruler's responsibility for justice in his land.
21:1–36 See *WCF* 19.4; *WLC* 136,151; *HC* 105.
21:2 Hebrew. This probably refers to an Israelite slave. A person could sell himself or his wife into slavery because of poverty or debt (2Ki 4:1; Ne 5:1–5; Am 2:6). An Israelite could also be sold by his father into slavery (v. 7). The law limits such servitude to six years. If the Year of Jubilee (the 50th year) came first, then the slave could go free before the end of the six-year limit. It was appropriate to commence with laws against slavery, for that had been Israel's position in Egypt.
21:6 before the judges. See NIV text note. The judges probably held court at God's sanctuary. Whether the door/doorpost was at the sanctuary or the home is not specified here, but Deuteronomy 15:17 favors the latter interpretation. The piercing of the ear was a public indication of permanent slavery.
21:7–11 The sale of a woman as a slave-wife seems intended for her protection. A slave could also be bought as a prospective daughter-in-law.
21:12 strikes. A premeditated blow (see v. 13).
21:13 not . . . intentionally. An unpremeditated blow is in mind. In this case, unlike that of a premeditated murder, the offender could flee to a sanctuary for protection. Sanctuary was extended until innocence or guilt could be proven (1Ki 1:50–53) or until the anger of the avenger had abated and compensation could be determined. See *WCF* 5.2.
21:15 attacks his father. Such actions transgress the fifth commandment. See *WLC* 128.
21:16 kidnaps. Kidnapping for slavery was common in the ancient world. It involved the sin of "man-stealing."
21:17 curses. A further transgression of the fifth commandment. Some have suggested that the word "curses" meant "repudiates" and may not have involved a spoken curse. See *HC* 104.
21:18 stone . . . fist. Less serious public actions are in view, and they seem unpremeditated; otherwise the assailant would have carried a weapon. The man who struck with a tool or a stone had an unfair advantage.
21:19 if . . . walks around outside with his staff. That is, if he is a convalescent.
21:20 slave. The slave, remarkably for the period, was considered a person. If the slave was confined to his bed temporarily, it was agreed that the master had disciplined him and had not meant to kill him.
21:21 his property. While the Law of Moses permitted indentured slavery, it went far beyond other cultures of the time to protect slaves from abuse. The New Testament does not repudiate these regulations but carries further the need for protection of

22"If men who are fighting hit a pregnant woman and she gives birth prematurely[a] but
there is no serious injury, the offender must be fined whatever the woman's husband demands[j] and the court allows. 23But if there is serious injury, you are to take life for life,[k]
24eye for eye, tooth for tooth,[l] hand for hand, foot for foot, 25burn for burn, wound for
wound, bruise for bruise.
26"If a man hits a manservant or maidservant in the eye and destroys it, he must let
the servant go free to compensate for the eye. 27And if he knocks out the tooth of a manservant or maidservant, he must let the servant go free to compensate for the tooth.
28"If a bull gores a man or a woman to death, the bull must be stoned to death,[m] and
its meat must not be eaten. But the owner of the bull will not be held responsible. 29If,
however, the bull has had the habit of goring and the owner has been warned but has
not kept it penned up and it kills a man or woman, the bull must be stoned and the owner also must be put to death. 30However, if payment is demanded of him, he may redeem
his life by paying whatever is demanded.[n] 31This law also applies if the bull gores a son
or daughter. 32If the bull gores a male or female slave, the owner must pay thirty shekels[b][o] of silver to the master of the slave, and the bull must be stoned.
33"If a man uncovers a pit or digs one and fails to cover it and an ox or a donkey falls
into it, 34the owner of the pit must pay for the loss; he must pay its owner, and the dead
animal will be his.
35"If a man's bull injures the bull of another and it dies, they are to sell the live one
and divide both the money and the dead animal equally. 36However, if it was known that
the bull had the habit of goring, yet the owner did not keep it penned up, the owner must
pay, animal for animal, and the dead animal will be his.

Protection of Property

22 "If a man steals an ox or a sheep and slaughters it or sells it, he must pay back[p]
five head of cattle for the ox and four sheep for the sheep.
2"If a thief is caught breaking in[q] and is struck so that he dies, the defender is not
guilty of bloodshed;[r] 3but if it happens[c] after sunrise, he is guilty of bloodshed.
"A thief must certainly make restitution, but if he has nothing, he must be sold[s] to
pay for his theft.
4"If the stolen animal is found alive in his possession—whether ox or donkey or
sheep—he must pay back double.[t]
5"If a man grazes his livestock in a field or vineyard and lets them stray and they graze
in another man's field, he must make restitution from the best of his own field or vineyard.
6"If a fire breaks out and spreads into thornbushes so that it burns shocks of grain or
standing grain or the whole field, the one who started the fire must make restitution.
7"If a man gives his neighbor silver or goods for safekeeping and they are stolen from
the neighbor's house, the thief, if he is caught, must pay back double.[u] 8But if the thief
is not found, the owner of the house must appear before the judges[d][v] to determine

21:22 [j]ver 30; Dt 22:18-19
21:23 [k]Lev 24:19; Dt 19:21
21:24 [l]Mt 5:38*
21:28 [m]ver 32; Ge 9:5
21:30 [n]ver 22; Nu 35:31
21:32 [o]Zec 11:12-13; Mt 26:15; 27:3,9
22:1 [p]2Sa 12:6; Pr 6:31; Lk 19:8
22:2 [q]Mt 6:19-20; 24:43 [r]Nu 35:27
22:3 [s]Ex 21:2; Mt 18:25
22:4 [t]Ge 43:12
22:7 [u]ver 4
22:8 [v]Ex 21:6; Dt 17:8-9; 19:17

[a] *22* Or *she has a miscarriage* [b] *32* That is, about 12 ounces (about 0.3 kilogram) [c] *3* Or *if he strikes him*
[d] *8* Or *before God*; also in verse 9

slaves and evaluates slavery as inappropriate (1Co 7:21). Moses' laws were frequently designed to restrain exploitation and oppression in recognition of the fact that the Israelites' "hearts were hard" (Mt 19:8), not to present God's absolute ideal for humanity as revealed before the fall into sin.

21:22 and she gives birth prematurely. Literally, "and children come forth." The plural is generic: any child whatever, male or female, one or two. The usual word for "children" is used (as in v. 4). The verb used describes the "coming forth" of a child, as in Genesis 25:26 and 38:28–30. If there was no lasting harm to either the mother or the child, compensation for the hurt inflicted, fixed by a third party, was to be paid to the husband. Otherwise, the penalty was proportionate to the injury to the mother or child, even to "life for life." Although the harm to the woman or child may not have been intentional, there was culpable negligence in disregarding their welfare. Apparently, only in the case of willful murder was it impossible to ransom the life under capital sentence (Nu 35:31).

21:24 eye for eye. The fundamental principle is that the wrongdoer was to suffer the same wrong he had inflicted (Lev 24:19–20; Dt 19:21). Jesus did not repudiate this law in Matthew 5:38, but he rejected its abuse by those who sought personal vengeance for wrongs committed.

21:28 If a bull gores. Harm done by an animal was the responsibility of the careless owner, and appropriate compensation was to be paid. Since the bull had been involved in blood guilt, its flesh could not be eaten.

21:32 thirty shekels of silver. The standard price for a slave (Zec 11:12).

21:33 falls into it. Livestock losses suffered by an owner whose animal was injured through negligence or theft.

22:1–29 See *WCF* 19.4; 22.3; *WLC* 136; *HC* 110.

22:1,4 pay back. It is not clear whether the return of the animal was in addition to, or part of, the compensation. More was required for an ox that had taken longer to rear.

22:3 after sunrise. In the daylight the thief is clearly identifiable and presumably perceived not to be a threat to life or health. Before sunrise the thief cannot be identified as seeking property only, and thus may rightly be killed in self-defense.

22:4 double. Restitution for a stolen animal found alive was less than that required for one that had been slaughtered or sold (v. 1).

22:5 make restitution. Restitution was to be made for harm done to crops through negligence.

22:6 thornbushes. Perhaps these acted as a hedge (Mic 7:4).

22:7 double. The law of exact compensation was strictly applied. The thief was not only to repay what he had stolen but to remit to the victim additional property of equal value, thereby suffering himself the harm he had inflicted on his neighbor.

22:8 before the judges. If the thief was not found, the one

whether he has laid his hands on the other man's property. [9]In all cases of illegal possession of an ox, a donkey, a sheep, a garment, or any other lost property about which somebody says, 'This is mine,' both parties are to bring their cases before the judges.[w] The one whom the judges declare[a] guilty must pay back double to his neighbor.

[10]"If a man gives a donkey, an ox, a sheep or any other animal to his neighbor for safekeeping and it dies or is injured or is taken away while no one is looking, [11]the issue between them will be settled by the taking of an oath[x] before the LORD that the neighbor did not lay hands on the other person's property. The owner is to accept this, and no restitution is required. [12]But if the animal was stolen from the neighbor, he must make restitution to the owner. [13]If it was torn to pieces by a wild animal, he shall bring in the remains as evidence and he will not be required to pay for the torn animal.[y]

[14]"If a man borrows an animal from his neighbor and it is injured or dies while the owner is not present, he must make restitution. [15]But if the owner is with the animal, the borrower will not have to pay. If the animal was hired, the money paid for the hire covers the loss.

Social Responsibility

[16]"If a man seduces a virgin[z] who is not pledged to be married and sleeps with her, he must pay the bride-price, and she shall be his wife. [17]If her father absolutely refuses to give her to him, he must still pay the bride-price for virgins.

[18]"Do not allow a sorceress[a] to live.

[19]"Anyone who has sexual relations with an animal[b] must be put to death.

[20]"Whoever sacrifices to any god other than the LORD must be destroyed.[b][c]

[21]"Do not mistreat an alien[d] or oppress him, for you were aliens[e] in Egypt.

[22]"Do not take advantage of a widow or an orphan.[f] [23]If you do and they cry out[g] to me, I will certainly hear their cry.[h] [24]My anger will be aroused, and I will kill you with the sword; your wives will become widows and your children fatherless.[i]

[25]"If you lend money to one of my people among you who is needy, do not be like a moneylender; charge him no interest.[c][j] [26]If you take your neighbor's cloak as a pledge,[k] return it to him by sunset, [27]because his cloak is the only covering he has for his body. What else will he sleep in? When he cries out to me, I will hear, for I am compassionate.[l]

[28]"Do not blaspheme God[d][m] or curse the ruler of your people.[n]

[29]"Do not hold back offerings[o] from your granaries or your vats.[e]

"You must give me the firstborn of your sons.[p] [30]Do the same with your cattle and your sheep.[q] Let them stay with their mothers for seven days, but give them to me on the eighth day.[r]

[31]"You are to be my holy people.[s] So do not eat the meat of an animal torn by wild beasts;[t] throw it to the dogs.

22:9 [w]ver 28; Dt 25:1
22:11 [x]Heb 6:16
22:13 [y]Ge 31:39
22:16 [z]Dt 22:28
22:18 [a]Lev 20:27; Dt 18:11; 1Sa 28:3
22:19 [b]Lev 18:23; Dt 27:21
22:20 [c]Dt 17:2-5
22:21 [d]Lev 19:33 [e]Dt 10:19
22:22 [f]Dt 24:6, 10, 12, 17
22:23 [g]Lk 18:7 [h]Dt 15:9; Ps 18:6
22:24 [i]Ps 69:24; 109:9
22:25 [j]Lev 25:35-37; Dt 23:20; Ps 15:5
22:26 [k]Dt 24:6
22:27 [l]Ex 34:6
22:28 [m]Lev 24:11, 16 [n]Ecc 10:20; Ac 23:5*
22:29 [o]Ex 23:15, 16, 19 [p]Ex 13:2
22:30 [q]Ex 13:12; Dt 15:19 [r]Lev 22:27
22:31 [s]Lev 19:2 [t]Eze 4:14

[a] 9 Or *whom God declares* [b] 20 The Hebrew term refers to the irrevocable giving over of things or persons to the LORD, often by totally destroying them. [c] 25 Or *excessive interest* [d] 28 Or *Do not revile the judges* [e] 29 The meaning of the Hebrew for this phrase is uncertain.

entrusted with the goods was to be brought to the sanctuary (see note on 21:6), where he would presumably swear an oath of innocence. In any dispute regarding ownership, both parties were to go to the sanctuary (v. 9–11).
22:12 was stolen. In this case the one entrusted with the goods was presumed to have been negligent.
22:14 make restitution. The burden of proof fell on the borrower. Where the animal concerned was on loan at the borrower's request, the borrower was liable, unless the owner had rented it for a fee.
22:15 The last sentence of this verse could be translated "If he was hiring, it comes out of his hire."
22:16 If a man seduces. Laws on premarital intercourse required full responsibility from the male for consequences. The exploited woman was to be protected. **bride-price.** Money paid to the family for the loss of the bride's services.
22:18 sorceress. Sorcery is not defined. Its practices were well known and condemned (Dt 18:9–13; 2Ki 21:6; Jer 27:9–10; Mic 5:12; Na 3:4). Sorcery was at least an attempt to circumvent the will of God. The future lay in God's hands alone.
22:19 sexual relations with an animal. Copulation with an animal (bestiality) may have been a fertility cult rite, since it was common in Canaan. The practice is condemned as perversion (Lev 18:23).
22:20 destroyed. Literally, "devoted to sacred use" or "put to the ban." If a sacred use was impossible, the item was destroyed, as it was here. In Israel's holy war—by which God's judgment was executed against the Canaanites—the spoils were under the ban, devoted to God (Nu 21:2–4; Jos 7:11).
22:21 alien. These individuals were temporary dwellers without family support, much as Israel had been in Egypt.
22:22 Do not take advantage of. Widows and orphans, who might lack family defenders, were God's special concern. He would hear their cry and avenge them (cf. Ps 82:3; Isa 1:17,23; Jer 5:28).
22:25 no interest. Loans made to them were made as to a member of God's covenant family, and no interest could be charged.
22:26 pledge. If a pledge was held, it was to be returned before hardship by its absence was experienced (Dt 24:10–11; Am 2:8).
22:28 blaspheme God. This text was cited by Paul (Ac 23:5). To question duly appointed authority is to question God's authority. Neither God nor the ruler whose authority comes from him is to be reviled (see notes on Ro 13:1–3).
22:29 Do not hold back. Covenant members were not to hold back the offerings of firstfruits, wine or oil, since the tithe indicated God's ownership of all.
22:31 torn by wild beasts. Since the blood would not have been properly drained.

Laws of Justice and Mercy

23 "Do not spread false reports.[u] Do not help a wicked man by being a malicious
witness.[v]
2 "Do not follow the crowd in doing wrong. When you give testimony in a lawsuit, do
not pervert justice[w] by siding with the crowd, 3 and do not show favoritism to a poor man
in his lawsuit.
4 "If you come across your enemy's ox or donkey wandering off, be sure to take it back
to him.[x] 5 If you see the donkey[y] of someone who hates you fallen down under its load,
do not leave it there; be sure you help him with it.
6 "Do not deny justice[z] to your poor people in their lawsuits. 7 Have nothing to do with
a false charge[a] and do not put an innocent or honest person to death, for I will not acquit the guilty.
8 "Do not accept a bribe,[b] for a bribe blinds those who see and twists the words of the
righteous.
9 "Do not oppress an alien;[c] you yourselves know how it feels to be aliens, because you
were aliens in Egypt.

Sabbath Laws

10 "For six years you are to sow your fields and harvest the crops, 11 but during the seventh year let the land lie unplowed and unused. Then the poor among your people may
get food from it, and the wild animals may eat what they leave. Do the same with your
vineyard and your olive grove.
12 "Six days do your work,[d] but on the seventh day do not work, so that your ox and
your donkey may rest and the slave born in your household, and the alien as well, may
be refreshed.
13 "Be careful[e] to do everything I have said to you. Do not invoke the names of other
gods; do not let them be heard on your lips.

The Three Annual Festivals

14 "Three times[f] a year you are to celebrate a festival to me.
15 "Celebrate the Feast of Unleavened Bread;[g] for seven days eat bread made without
yeast, as I commanded you. Do this at the appointed time in the month of Abib, for in
that month you came out of Egypt.
"No one is to appear before me empty-handed.[h]
16 "Celebrate the Feast of Harvest with the firstfruits[i] of the crops you sow in your field.
"Celebrate the Feast of Ingathering at the end of the year, when you gather in your
crops from the field.[j]
17 "Three times[k] a year all the men are to appear before the Sovereign LORD.
18 "Do not offer the blood of a sacrifice to me along with anything containing yeast.[l]
"The fat of my festival offerings must not be kept until morning.[m]

23:1 [u] Ex 20:16; Ps 101:5 [v] Ps 35:11; Ac 6:11
23:2 [w] Dt 16:19
23:4 [x] Dt 22:1-3
23:5 [y] Dt 22:4
23:6 [z] ver 2
23:7 [a] Eph 4:25
23:8 [b] Dt 10:17; 16:19; Pr 15:27
23:9 [c] Ex 22:21
23:12 [d] Ex 20:9
23:13 [e] 1Ti 4:16
23:14 [f] Ex 34:23,24
23:15 [g] Ex 12:17 [h] Ex 34:20
23:16 [i] Ex 34:22 [j] Dt 16:13
23:17 [k] Dt 16:16
23:18 [l] Ex 34:25 [m] Dt 16:4

23:1 malicious witness. One offering false or misleading testimony with unjust intent. See *WLC* 145.
23:2 siding. To be an accomplice or to succumb to group pressure is wrong.
23:4–5 See *WLC* 141; *WSC* 74; *HC* 107.
23:4 your enemy's. The covenant member was to refuse to take advantage of the misfortune of an enemy (perhaps a legal opponent here). Note how Jesus elaborated on this statute (Mt 5:43–48; see also Ro 12:20–21).
23:6 Do not deny justice. Verses 6–8 offer instructions for legal proceedings. Rules were not to be bent. Complaints were to be founded in truth. A bribe destroyed judicial integrity.
23:7 See *HC* 12.
23:9 alien. This verse repeats 22:21, but here the context is legal, not social.
23:11 seventh year. The poor were to eat the produce of the sabbath year. Unlike the rich, they would not have been able to make provision for the seventh year. The seventh year of release was patterned on the Sabbath concept. Leviticus 26:34–35 suggests that the sabbath year was not always observed. But it is clearly in place in Nehemiah 10:31 and 1 Maccabees 6:49 and 53 (an Apocryphal book). The sabbath-year laws preserved God's ownership of the land. **wild animals may eat.** This edict came from the Creator God who cares for the sparrows (Mt 10:29) and feeds the ravens (Lk 12:24).
23:12 See *WLC* 118.
23:14 Three times a year. Israel's three festivals were to be connected with the nation's ongoing agricultural life. The first harvest was the early barley harvest in the month of Abib (April/May), when the Feast of the Passover and Unleavened Bread took place. The harvest of other cereal crops occurred seven weeks later, giving rise to the Feast of the Harvest; i.e., Pentecost (50 days later, in June). The final harvest of all crops, celebrated by the Feast of the Ingathering, took place in the autumn (September).
23:15 Feast of Unleavened Bread. Passover and Unleavened Bread together constituted one feast. It is often argued that Unleavened Bread was simply an agricultural festival, but its connection with the exodus deliverance as beginning a new year is clear here. The Passover feast was the initial item in the celebration.
23:16 the Feast of Harvest. Also called the Feast of Weeks, since it occurred seven weeks after the Feast of Unleavened Bread. By New Testament times this feast had become associated with the giving of the law at Sinai. The new covenant counterpart is the gift of the Spirit (Ro 8:23) at Pentecost (Ac 2). **Feast of Ingathering.** Also known as the Feast of Tabernacles (Lev 23:34) or the Feast of Booths, since the Israelites had lived in temporary shelters during the exodus. It was celebrated at the end of the agricultural year, when the produce had been completely garnered. It commemorated the desert wanderings. **end of the year.** According to the Israelite calendar, the year ended in the fall. Only later, under Babylonian influence, was a calendar developed that began in the spring. Others suggest that there were always two calendars, one liturgical and one civil.
23:18 Do not offer. The detail of this verse has often been simply related to Passover, but it is better taken as general. Blood and visceral fat constituted the essence of life. Fat portions kept overnight would not have been fresh and thus were unworthy as an offering.

19"Bring the best of the firstfruits[n] of your soil to the house of the LORD your God.
"Do not cook a young goat in its mother's milk.[o]

God's Angel to Prepare the Way

20"See, I am sending an angel[p] ahead of you to guard you along the way and to bring
you to the place I have prepared.[q] 21Pay attention to him and listen[r] to what he says. Do
not rebel against him; he will not forgive your rebellion,[s] since my Name is in him. 22If
you listen carefully to what he says and do all that I say, I will be an enemy[t] to your enemies and will oppose those who oppose you. 23My angel will go ahead of you and bring
you into the land of the Amorites, Hittites, Perizzites, Canaanites, Hivites and Jebusites,[u]
and I will wipe them out. 24Do not bow down before their gods or worship[v] them or follow their practices.[w] You must demolish[x] them and break their sacred stones to pieces. 25Worship the LORD your God,[y] and his blessing[z] will be on your food and water. I will
take away sickness[a] from among you, 26and none will miscarry or be barren[b] in your
land. I will give you a full life span.[c]

27"I will send my terror[d] ahead of you and throw into confusion[e] every nation you encounter. I will make all your enemies turn their backs and run. 28I will send the hornet[f]
ahead of you to drive the Hivites, Canaanites and Hittites out of your way. 29But I will not
drive them out in a single year, because the land would become desolate and the wild
animals[g] too numerous for you. 30Little by little I will drive them out before you, until you
have increased enough to take possession of the land.

31"I will establish your borders from the Red Sea[a] to the Sea of the Philistines,[b] and
from the desert to the River.[c][h] I will hand over to you the people who live in the land and
you will drive them out[i] before you. 32Do not make a covenant[j] with them or with their
gods. 33Do not let them live in your land, or they will cause you to sin against me, because
the worship of their gods will certainly be a snare[k] to you."

The Covenant Confirmed

24 Then he said to Moses, "Come up to the LORD, you and Aaron, Nadab and Abihu,[l] and seventy of the elders[m] of Israel. You are to worship at a distance, 2but
Moses alone is to approach the LORD; the others must not come near. And the people may
not come up with him."

3When Moses went and told the people all the LORD's words and laws, they responded with one voice, "Everything the LORD has said we will do."[n] 4Moses then wrote[o] down
everything the LORD had said.

He got up early the next morning and built an altar at the foot of the mountain and

[a] *31* Hebrew *Yam Suph;* that is, Sea of Reeds [b] *31* That is, the Mediterranean [c] *31* That is, the Euphrates

23:19 [n]Ex 22:29; Dt 26:2, 10 [o]Dt 14:21
23:20 [p]Ex 14:19; 32:34 [q]Ex 15:17
23:21 [r]Nu 14:11; Dt 18:19 [s]Ps 78:8, 40,56
23:22 [t]Ge 12:3; Dt 30:7
23:23 [u]ver 20; Jos 24:8, 11
23:24 [v]Ex 20:5 [w]Dt 12:30-31 [x]Ex 34:13; Nu 33:52
23:25 [y]Dt 6:13; Mt 4:10 [z]Dt 7:12-15; 28:1-14 [a]Ex 15:26
23:26 [b]Dt 7:14; Mal 3:11 [c]Job 5:26
23:27 [d]Ex 15:14; Dt 2:25 [e]Dt 7:23
23:28 [f]Dt 7:20; Jos 24:12
23:29 [g]Dt 7:22
23:31 [h]Ge 15:18 [i]Jos 21:44; 24:12, 18
23:32 [j]Ex 34:12; Dt 7:2
23:33 [k]Dt 7:16; Ps 106:36
24:1 [l]Ex 6:23; Lev 10:1-2 [m]Nu 11:16
24:3 [n]Ex 19:8; Dt 5:27
24:4 [o]Dt 31:9

Leaven, representing the old harvest, was considered an impurity (see note on 12:8).
23:19 firstfruits. As representative of the entire harvest. This image is applied to Christ's resurrection (1Co 15:20). **Do not cook.** Perhaps this was a Canaanite practice. This is the Biblical source of the modern kosher practice of not consuming meat and dairy products at the same meal.
■ **23:20–33** *Epilogue.* These verses conclude the Book of the Covenant by relating it more directly to the historical circumstances of the exodus. They parallel to some extent 20:22–26. The devotion of Israel to the Lord and the rejection of all other gods are stressed.
23:20 an angel. The angel of God's presence was mysteriously distinguished from God and yet identified with him (see note on 14:19). The cloud that symbolized God's presence also marked the presence of the angel (14:19).
23:21 my Name is in him. God's powerful presence accompanied the angel who led the nation.
23:22 If you listen carefully. The details of this verse resemble the clauses of protection in the suzerainty treaties (see note on 20:1-17).
23:23 will wipe them out. They were to blot out every vestige of pagan worship in the promised land.
23:24 sacred stones. The Israelites were to break down sacred stones connected with Canaanite shrines.
23:25 his blessing. For the longer blessing list, see Deuteronomy 28:1–14.
23:27 my terror. One of the key terms of holy war is picked up here, reminding us of the panic that God would use to subdue the Canaanites (Jos 2:11).
23:28 hornet. The term may be used metaphorically, perhaps in relation to Egyptian military action.
23:29 I will not drive them out. The conquest would be gradual. The Israelites were not to be responsible for the whole land until they were able to defend it.
23:31 borders. These borders of the promised land were not established until David's time, when the conquest was formally completed. **Red Sea.** This apparently refers to the Gulf of Aqaba on the southeast, but see note on 13:18.
23:32 Do not make a covenant. Israel was quick to disobey this command (Jos 9).
■ **24:1–18** *The Finalization of the Covenant.* The text continues the narrative begun in 19:1–25. The covenant bond between God and Israel was finalized.
24:1–11 Moses presided over the ceremony of covenant ratification.
24:1 Then he said to Moses. Verses 1–2 provide a summary of the chapter and continue from 20:21. The mention of Aaron and his two sons speaks for the authenticity of the narrative, for the sons were later killed (Lev 10:1–2) for an offense against God. The 70 elders of 18:12 (or possibly the "capable" men of 18:21) perhaps represent the 70 descendants of Jacob. See *WCF* 19.2.
24:2 Moses alone is to approach. Once again Moses was exalted as the one who mediated this covenant. He had greater access to the divine presence than anyone else had.
24:3 words. The Ten Commandments. **laws.** Presumably the Book of the Covenant (20:22—23:19). This may mark its delivery, since all Israel had heard the Decalogue. **responded.** Israel responded with the formula of commitment that appears in 19:8 (see v. 7).
24:4 wrote down. The Ten Commandments and the Book of the Covenant were reduced to writing. The altar represented God, and

24:4 [p]Ge 28:18
24:6 [q]Heb 9:18
24:7 [r]Heb 9:19
24:8 [s]Heb 9:20*; 1Pe 1:2
24:9 [t]ver 1
24:10 [u]Mt 17:2; Jn 1:18; 6:46 [v]Eze 1:26 [w]Rev 4:3
24:11 [x]Ge 32:30; Ex 19:21
24:12 [y]Ex 32:15-16
24:13 [z]Ex 17:9 [a]Ex 3:1
24:15 [b]Ex 19:9
24:16 [c]Ex 16:10 [d]Ps 99:7
24:17 [e]Ex 3:2; Dt 4:36; Heb 12:18,29
24:18 [f]Dt 9:9 [g]Ex 34:28
25:2 [h]Ex 35:21; 1Ch 29:5,7,9; Ezr 2:68; 2Co 8:11-12; 9:7

set up twelve stone pillars[p] representing the twelve tribes of Israel. 5Then he sent young
Israelite men, and they offered burnt offerings and sacrificed young bulls as fellowship
offerings[a] to the LORD. 6Moses took half of the blood[q] and put it in bowls, and the other
half he sprinkled on the altar. 7Then he took the Book of the Covenant[r] and read it to
the people. They responded, "We will do everything the LORD has said; we will obey."
8Moses then took the blood, sprinkled it on the people and said, "This is the blood
of the covenant[s] that the LORD has made with you in accordance with all these words."
9Moses and Aaron, Nadab and Abihu, and the seventy elders[t] of Israel went up
10and saw[u] the God of Israel. Under his feet was something like a pavement made of sapphire,[b][v] clear as the sky[w] itself. 11But God did not raise his hand against these leaders
of the Israelites; they saw[x] God, and they ate and drank.
12The LORD said to Moses, "Come up to me on the mountain and stay here, and I will
give you the tablets of stone,[y] with the law and commands I have written for their instruction."
13Then Moses set out with Joshua[z] his aide, and Moses went up on the mountain[a] of
God. 14He said to the elders, "Wait here for us until we come back to you. Aaron and Hur
are with you, and anyone involved in a dispute can go to them."
15When Moses went up on the mountain, the cloud[b] covered it, 16and the glory[c] of
the LORD settled on Mount Sinai. For six days the cloud covered the mountain, and on
the seventh day the LORD called to Moses from within the cloud.[d] 17To the Israelites the
glory of the LORD looked like a consuming fire[e] on top of the mountain. 18Then Moses entered the cloud as he went on up the mountain. And he stayed on the mountain forty[f]
days and forty nights.[g]

Offerings for the Tabernacle

25 The LORD said to Moses, 2"Tell the Israelites to bring me an offering. You are to
receive the offering for me from each man whose heart prompts[h] him to give.

[a] 5 Traditionally *peace offerings* [b] *10* Or *lapis lazuli*

---

the 12 standing stones represented the tribes as witnesses to the agreement (Ge 31:51–54).

24:5 young Israelite men. Strength and agility were needed for this task, for there was no appointed priesthood as yet. The offerings sealed the covenant, indicating that God's acceptance of Israel was on the basis of atonement for sin.

24:6 half of the blood. The blood dashed on the altar signified God's acceptance of this as a covenant offering and thus of the covenant with Israel through the blood of atonement.

24:7 Book of the Covenant. Usually this phrase is applied to the social law of 20:2—23:19. In this context, however, it refers to everything that Moses had just written (v. 4), including the Ten Commandments and perhaps other passages such as 19:5–6. This is confirmed by the repetition of the phrase "everything the LORD has said" from verse 3, where it referred to both the Ten Commandments and the social laws. See *WLC* 157.

24:8 sprinkled it on the people. The people were sprinkled with "the blood of the covenant," the blood that put the covenant into effect (see Heb 9:18–19, noting that the Book of the Covenant, as well as the people, was sprinkled with blood). The blood signified cleansing from sin so that the people could enter into the covenant. It also marked the covenant relationship as accomplished only through atonement (Heb 9:21–22). Israel was consecrated to God's service. See also the ordination of Aaron, where blood accompanied anointing oil (Lev 8:23,30). Jesus proclaimed the fulfillment of this symbolism when he offered the cup at the supper, saying, "This is my blood of the covenant, which is poured out for many for the forgiveness of sins" (Mt 26:28). See *WLC* 174.

24:9 Moses and Aaron . . . seventy elders. The text resumes the narrative of verses 1–2.

24:10–17 See *HC* 99,100.

24:10 saw the God of Israel. Not a full revelation of God, but a partial, veiled one (see note on Jn 1:18). **feet.** The text concentrates on God's feet only. Perhaps the leaders were not permitted to look higher. **pavement.** Perhaps they saw the vault of the sky under the throne (cf. Eze 1:26). **sapphire.** This is lapis lazuli. It was available in a natural form from Cyprus and Scythia and in artificial form from Egypt.

24:11 hand. God did not manifest his "hand" (i.e., his awesome power) against the leaders (see 33:20; Ge 32:30). **ate and drank.** Not only did they see God, but they also ate and drank before him. Meals such as this, to celebrate the conclusion of a covenant, are recorded elsewhere (18:12; Ge 31:46; Mt 26:28). The wonder of this scene resulted from Israel's commitment to the covenant mediated through Moses. Thus the original readers were reminded of the great blessings that would come to those who continued their commitment to Moses and the covenant he administered.

24:12–18 Moses ascended Mount Sinai to receive the covenant tablets that contained the stipulations of the relationship into which Israel was entering with the Lord.

24:12 Come up to me. The narrative picks up the point of verse 2. Moses was to receive further instructions regarding the building of the tabernacle. God would give Moses tablets of stone upon which the Lord himself had written. The authority of God produced written, as well as spoken, words.

24:14 Wait here for us. This sets the scene for chapter 32.

24:16 glory. The term is used for manifestation of God's divine presence. God's "dwelling" with his people would become the primary topic for the rest of the book.

24:18 Moses entered the cloud. With the elders and even Joshua left behind, Moses walked into the fiery cloud of God's very presence (32:15). This unique access to God's presence exalted Moses as Israel's greatest leader.

■ **25:1—40:38** *God's Tabernacle Erected by Moses.* The third major section of Exodus concerns the importance of observing the regulations of worship God provided to Israel through the tabernacle and its services. The inauguration of the covenant established God's kingship over Israel. That kingship was to be appropriately recognized by the building of a residence for God as a symbol of his royal authority over Israel. These chapters divide into three main parts: instructions for the tabernacle (25:1—31:18), Israel's early failure to observe these instructions (32:1—34:35) and the blessings that followed the actual construction of the tabernacle (35:1—40:38).

As these chapters taught Israel the importance of seeking God's forgiveness and presence in the ways prescribed by Moses, Christians recall that Jesus came to fulfill the symbolism of the tabernacle and the temple (see Heb 8–10). As God dwelling with people (Jn 2:19,21), he told the Samaritan woman that the hour was coming when worship would no longer be centered around the earthly temple (Jn 4:21). He who is both the great high priest and the sacrifice brings us with himself into the true Most Holy Place in heaven.

■ **25:1—31:18** *Instructions Concerning the Tabernacle.* This section goes into great detail to exhibit the divine pattern for the place where the Lord himself would dwell among his people. These chapters divide into seven speeches of uneven length, each of which begins with the same formula: "The LORD said to Moses"

3These are the offerings you are to receive from them: gold, silver and bronze; 4blue, purple and scarlet yarn and fine linen; goat hair; 5ram skins dyed red and hides of sea cows[a];
acacia wood; 6olive oil[i] for the light; spices for the anointing oil and for the fragrant incense; 7and onyx stones and other gems to be mounted on the ephod[j] and breastpiece.[k]
8"Then have them make a sanctuary[l] for me, and I will dwell[m] among them. 9Make
this tabernacle and all its furnishings exactly like the pattern[n] I will show you.

The Ark

10"Have them make a chest[o] of acacia wood—two and a half cubits long, a cubit and
a half wide, and a cubit and a half high.[b] 11Overlay it with pure gold, both inside and out,
and make a gold molding around it. 12Cast four gold rings for it and fasten them to its
four feet, with two rings on one side and two rings on the other. 13Then make poles of
acacia wood and overlay them with gold. 14Insert the poles into the rings on the sides of
the chest to carry it. 15The poles are to remain in the rings of this ark; they are not to be
removed.[p] 16Then put in the ark the Testimony,[q] which I will give you.
17"Make an atonement cover[c r] of pure gold—two and a half cubits long and a cubit and
a half wide.[d] 18And make two cherubim out of hammered gold at the ends of the cover.
19Make one cherub on one end and the second cherub on the other; make the cherubim of
one piece with the cover, at the two ends. 20The cherubim are to have their wings spread
upward, overshadowing[s] the cover with them. The cherubim are to face each other, looking toward the cover. 21Place the cover on top of the ark[t] and put in the ark the Testimony,[u]
which I will give you. 22There, above the cover between the two cherubim[v] that are over the
ark of the Testimony, I will meet[w] with you and give you all my commands for the Israelites.

25:6 [i]Ex 27:20; 30:22-32
25:7 [j]Ex 28:4,6-14 [k]Ex 28:15-30
25:8 [l]Ex 36:1-5; Heb 9:1-2 [m]Ex 29:45; 1Ki 6:13; 2Co 6:16; Rev 21:3
25:9 [n]ver 40; Ac 7:44; Heb 8:5
25:10 [o]Dt 10:1-5; Heb 9:4
25:15 [p]1Ki 8:8
25:16 [q]Dt 31:26; Heb 9:4
25:17 [r]Ro 3:25
25:20 [s]1Ki 8:7; 1Ch 28:18; Heb 9:5
25:21 [t]Ex 26:34 [u]ver 16
25:22 [v]Nu 7:89; 1Sa 4:4; 2Sa 6:2; 2Ki 19:15; Ps 80:1; Isa 37:16 [w]Ex 29:42-43

[a] *5* That is, dugongs [b] *10* That is, about 3 3/4 feet (about 1.1 meters) long and 2 1/4 feet (about 0.7 meter) wide and high [c] *17* Traditionally *a mercy seat* [d] *17* That is, about 3 3/4 feet (about 1.1 meters) long and 2 1/4 feet (about 0.7 meter) wide

---

(25:1; 30:11,17,22,34; 31:1,12), thus stressing the divine origin of the tabernacle as well as Moses' mediation.

■ **25:1—30:10** *The Tabernacle and Its Priests.* God's first speech to Moses focused on the construction of the tabernacle itself (25:1—27:19) and the service of the priesthood (27:20—30:10).

■ **25:1—27:19** *The Tabernacle and Its Furnishings.* After the Lord called for contributions for building the tabernacle (25:1–9), he set forth the construction plans for the ark (25:10–22), the table (25:23–30) and the lampstand (25:31–40). Specifications follow for the tabernacle itself (26:1–37), the altar of burnt offerings (27:1–8) and the courtyard (27:9–19). See charts "The Tabernacle" at Exodus 26 and "Tabernacle Furnishings," also at Exodus 26.

■ **25:1–9** *Collection of Materials.* God first called for a collection of materials. It was Israel's responsibility to provide material support for the tabernacle.

25:1 The materials were to be gathered as freewill offerings from the treasures of the people.

25:3 gold, silver and bronze. The finest metals were required—the type used depended upon the proximity to the divine presence—as well as the finest fabrics, leathers, wood, oil, incense and semiprecious stones. Metals and colored yarns are listed here in descending order of value.

25:4 blue. That is, violet. Violet and purple dyes were obtained from shellfish; scarlet, from an insect of the cochineal type. All dyes were precious because they were expensive to make. There is no evidence that the colors were symbolic. **fine linen.** It was probably Egyptian. **goat hair.** Natural, undyed wool. It was used as a first covering for the tabernacle; over it other skins would be placed (26:14).

25:5 ram skins. Leather that was tanned or dyed or perhaps both. **sea cows.** The sea cow (native to the Red Sea) leather may have been cured only, in which case the list is in descending order of value. **acacia wood.** Acacia is a hard, long-lasting wood suitable for carving and for use as an overlay.

25:6 spices. Balsam spices were a mixture of three ingredients (30:34) that were added to pure frankincense and salt to create a special formula used only on the golden altar of incense.

25:7 onyx stones. The stones set in the two shoulder pieces of the ephod (28:9–12; 39:6–7) were of a substance such as carnelian, onyx or lapis lazuli, which could be engraved.

25:8 sanctuary. Literally, "holy place." This is a broader word than "tabernacle" and refers to any place where God is present in a special way (15:17; Jos 24:26; Eze 11:16).

25:9 tabernacle. The term means "residence" and designated a mobile, divine palace/temple. **pattern.** The pattern shown to Moses was a model or general blueprint of the tabernacle to be built. Compare the plan of the temple revealed to David (1Ch 28:19). This pattern was based on the heavenly palace of God (Heb 9:24), of which the tabernacle was a miniature replica. See Ezekiel 43:10–11.

■ **25:10–22** *The Ark.* The first item that is mentioned was the centerpiece of the tabernacle: the ark of the covenant.

25:10–12 chest. That is, the ark. It contained the Ten Commandments, the pot of manna and Aaron's rod (16:33; 25:16; Nu 17:10; Dt 10:1–5; Heb 9:4). The cover of the ark was viewed as the royal footstool of the Lord (1Ch 28:2). Thus the Lord was the One "enthroned between the cherubim" (1Sa 4:4; see Ex 29:43–46; 2Sa 6:2; 2Ki 19:15; Pss 80:1; 99:1; Isa 37:16). **cubit.** The cubit was a measure stretching in length from the tip of the middle finger to the elbow (about 18 inches).

25:13 make poles. The ark was carried on poles so that it could be moved without being touched. To touch the ark was to treat God's footstool as a common thing and thus to defy his holiness (2Sa 6:6).

25:16 Testimony. The tablets of stone of the Sinai covenant. God's written word was his witness to the terms of his covenant.

25:17 atonement. This term is the normal English translation for the Hebrew root that means "to wipe away" or perhaps "to cover" the guilt of sin from God's eyes so that believers may be reconciled to God. This act of propitiation was provided by God himself (Lev 17:11) and was effected by blood sacrifice in the Old Testament. Blood, the indication of the death of the sacrificial victim, dramatized the cost of forgiveness. Even so, blood effected forgiveness of sin only because God had divinely appointed it to do so (Lev 17:11). Paul (in Ro 3:25) and John (in 1Jn 2:2) both declared that Jesus has been made the atonement for our sins. The symbolism of the Day of Atonement in view here is fulfilled through Christ's death and session (Heb 9:11–12). **cover.** The ark cover. It was also called the "mercy seat" because of God's divine provision. The ark cover is sometimes distinguished from the ark itself as the place where atonement was made (Lev 16:14–15).

25:18 cherubim. The wings of the cherubim would touch each other (or perhaps be spread out) across the ark cover. The cherubim were usually connected with the throne of the Lord as guardians or bearers of the throne. In other cultures of the ancient world, cherubim were minor deities protective of palaces and temples; in Israel they symbolized angelic guardians (Ge 3:24).

25:22 I will meet. God would meet with Moses and speak with him from above the ark cover between the cherubim.

The Table

23“Make a table[x] of acacia wood—two cubits long, a cubit wide and a cubit and a half
high.[a] 24Overlay it with pure gold and make a gold molding around it. 25Also make
around it a rim a handbreadth[b] wide and put a gold molding on the rim. 26Make four gold
rings for the table and fasten them to the four corners, where the four legs are. 27The
rings are to be close to the rim to hold the poles used in carrying the table. 28Make the
poles of acacia wood, overlay them with gold and carry the table with them. 29And make
its plates and dishes of pure gold, as well as its pitchers and bowls for the pouring out
of offerings.[y] 30Put the bread of the Presence[z] on this table to be before me at all times.

The Lampstand

31“Make a lampstand[a] of pure gold and hammer it out, base and shaft; its flowerlike
cups, buds and blossoms shall be of one piece with it. 32Six branches are to extend from
the sides of the lampstand—three on one side and three on the other. 33Three cups
shaped like almond flowers with buds and blossoms are to be on one branch, three on
the next branch, and the same for all six branches extending from the lampstand. 34And
on the lampstand there are to be four cups shaped like almond flowers with buds and
blossoms. 35One bud shall be under the first pair of branches extending from the lampstand, a second bud under the second pair, and a third bud under the third pair—six
branches in all. 36The buds and branches shall all be of one piece with the lampstand,
hammered out of pure gold.

37“Then make its seven lamps[b] and set them up on it so that they light the space in
front of it. 38Its wick trimmers and trays are to be of pure gold. 39A talent[c] of pure gold
is to be used for the lampstand and all these accessories. 40See that you make them according to the pattern[c] shown you on the mountain.

25:23 [x]Heb 9:2
25:29 [y]Nu 4:7
25:30 [z]Lev 24:5-9
25:31 [a]1Ki 7:49; Zec 4:2; Heb 9:2; Rev 1:12
25:37 [b]Ex 27:21; Lev 24:3-4; Nu 8:2
25:40 [c]Ex 26:30; Nu 8:4; Ac 7:44; Heb 8:5*

The Tabernacle

26 “Make the tabernacle with ten curtains of finely twisted linen and blue, purple
and scarlet yarn, with cherubim worked into them by a skilled craftsman. 2All
the curtains are to be the same size—twenty-eight cubits long and four cubits wide.[d]
3Join five of the curtains together, and do the same with the other five. 4Make loops of
blue material along the edge of the end curtain in one set, and do the same with the end

[a] *23* That is, about 3 feet (about 0.9 meter) long and 1 1/2 feet (about 0.5 meter) wide and 2 1/4 feet (about 0.7 meter) high [b] *25* That is, about 3 inches (about 8 centimeters) [c] *39* That is, about 75 pounds (about 34 kilograms) [d] *2* That is, about 42 feet (about 12.5 meters) long and 6 feet (about 1.8 meters) wide

■ **25:23–30** *The Table.* The revelation of the earthly sanctuary pattern continues with instructions for the table upon which the bread of the Presence was to be placed.

25:23 Make a table. The table was called variously “the table of the Presence” (Nu 4:7), “the table of pure gold” (Lev 24:6, 2Ch 13:11) and “the golden table on which was the bread of the Presence” (1Ki 7:48). The table stood on the north side of the Holy Place (40:22).

25:29 make its plates. The table was equipped with containers of four kinds, all of pure gold: (1) a dish or a plate on which the bread of the Presence was to be placed; (2) a small pan onto which the frankincense was poured as an accompaniment offering with the bread of the Presence; (3) a pitcher for the wine libation, or drink offering; and (4) a bowl into which this offering was poured.

25:30 bread of the Presence. This special bread to be placed on the table each Sabbath was arranged in two rows of six loaves each (Lev 24:6). The 12 loaves represented the 12 tribes of Israel.

■ **25:31–40** *The Gold Lampstand.* The menorah was also set within the Holy Place.

25:31 lampstand. Standing opposite the table in the Holy Place, the lampstand was constructed of a talent (about 75 pounds) of hammered gold and was patterned to suggest a growing tree, perhaps an almond tree (the first tree to blossom in spring).

25:32 Six branches. It is probable that the six branches rose to the height of the central shaft. The pedestal and main upright constituted the trunk of the tree, and growing out of this on either side were three branches. The total, seven, indicated completeness.

25:33 Three cups. Each of these branches ended in a leafy base of a bud from which opened the petals of a flower. Into this was fixed a lamp holder or cup. This motif appeared four times on the trunk (v. 34) and three times on each branch (v. 33). The symbol of fruitfulness links with the cherubim to suggest paradise (Ge 3:24). In Zechariah’s vision the oil of the lampstand symbolized the anointing of the Spirit (Zec 4:6,12,14). John saw Jesus ministering among the lampstands (representing the churches) of the heavenly sanctuary (Rev 1:12,20). The light and the fire of the lamps were symbols related to God’s presence.

25:37 set them up. The lamps at the end of the trunk and the six branches were placed so as to provide a wide arc of light. The seven lamps rested on the topmost ornaments of the shaft and the branches.

25:38 wick trimmers. A special tool was to be made to adjust and remove the wicks. **trays.** Containers to receive the spent wicks.

■ **26:1–37** *The Tabernacle.* The tabernacle, as God’s holy dwelling in the midst of his sinful people, served at least two main functions. On the one hand, it separated the people from God’s holy presence. The curtains of the Most Holy Place, of the Holy Place and even of the courtyard stood between the people and the threat of God’s consuming holiness. Like the boundaries set at Sinai, the tabernacle protected the people from the danger of unauthorized intrusion. On the other hand, the tabernacle symbolized a way of approach to the Lord. Worshipers could enter the east gate, confess their sins, offer sacrifices and pray to God where his glory dwelled. The priests could carry their petitions into the Holy Place, and once a year the high priest could enter with the blood atonement into the very throne room of the Almighty. It was the “Tent of Meeting” where God dwelled; there he met with his redeemed people at the mercy seat.

26:1 tabernacle. The tabernacle, the structure enclosed by the inner curtains, was 45 feet long, 15 feet wide and 15 feet high and was to be covered with ten curtains woven of expensive fabrics adorned with cherubim. Two sets of five curtains, each 42 feet long and six feet wide and made of fine linen, were draped over the framework and connected so as to provide a continuous length and width. They were 60 feet long and 42 feet wide and made up the basic covering. The inner curtains ended one and one-half feet short of the ground on either side (vv. 1–6).

curtain in the other set. 5Make fifty loops on one curtain and fifty loops on the end curtain of the other set, with the loops opposite each other. 6Then make fifty gold clasps and
use them to fasten the curtains together so that the tabernacle is a unit.
7"Make curtains of goat hair for the tent over the tabernacle—eleven altogether. 8All
eleven curtains are to be the same size—thirty cubits long and four cubits wide.[a] 9Join
five of the curtains together into one set and the other six into another set. Fold the sixth
curtain double at the front of the tent. 10Make fifty loops along the edge of the end curtain in one set and also along the edge of the end curtain in the other set. 11Then make
fifty bronze clasps and put them in the loops to fasten the tent together as a unit. 12As
for the additional length of the tent curtains, the half curtain that is left over is to hang
down at the rear of the tabernacle. 13The tent curtains will be a cubit[b] longer on both
sides; what is left will hang over the sides of the tabernacle so as to cover it. 14Make for
the tent a covering of ram skins dyed red, and over that a covering of hides of sea cows.[c][d]
15"Make upright frames of acacia wood for the tabernacle. 16Each frame is to be ten cubits long and a cubit and a half wide,[d] 17with two projections set parallel to each other.

26:14 [d]Ex 36:19; Nu 4:25

[a] *8* That is, about 45 feet (about 13.5 meters) long and 6 feet (about 1.8 meters) wide [b] *13* That is, about 1 1/2 feet (about 0.5 meter) [c] *14* That is, dugongs [d] *16* That is, about 15 feet (about 4.5 meters) long and 2 1/4 feet (about 0.7 meter) wide

26:7 curtains of goat hair. As protection for the inner curtain, two sets of curtains of goat hair were to be joined by loops and clasps to make one curtain of 67 ½ feet from top to bottom and 99 feet from end to end, permitting an overlap at the front and back of the tabernacle.

26:13 a cubit longer. The outer curtains were three feet longer than the inner ones and would barely reach the ground.

26:14 a covering. Two further covers of ram hides and sea cow hides were to be made to protect the two inner sets. They were apparently arranged in that sequence.

26:15 upright frames. These provided the framework on which the curtains were draped. They were planks— or better, open frames—that were set vertically to provide the sides and back of the structure. They were stabilized with cross bars and anchored in silver sockets driven into the ground. There were 20 on each side and six at the back (west). The corners were braced together. Their height and width were 15 feet.

The Tabernacle

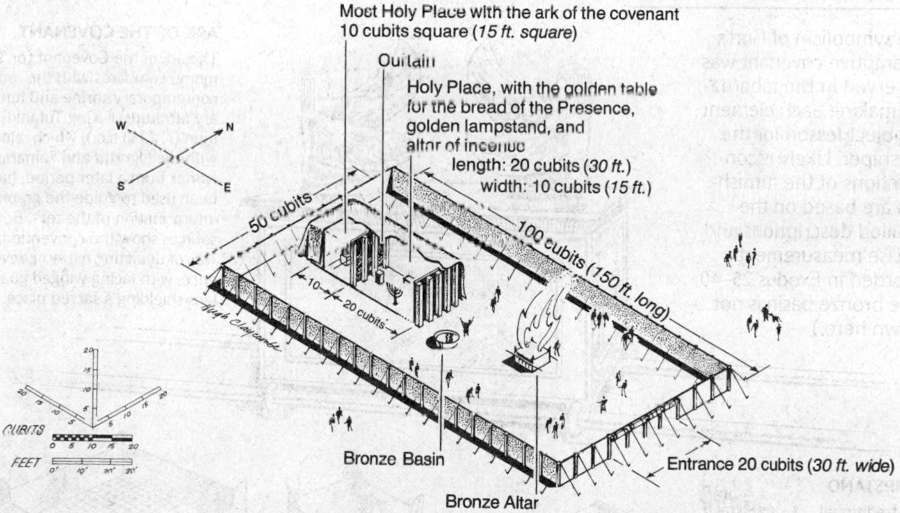

The new religious observances taught by Moses in the desert centered on rituals connected with the tabernacle, and amplified Israel's sense of separateness, purity and oneness under the Lordship of Yahweh.

A few desert shrines have been found in Sinai, notably at Serabit el-Khadem and at Timnah in the Negev, and show marked Egyptian influence.

Specific cultural antecedents to portable shrines carried on poles and covered with thin sheets of gold can be found in ancient Egypt as early as the Old Kingdom (2800-2250 B.C.), but were especially prominent in the 18th and 19th dynasties (1570-1180). The best examples come from the fabulous tomb of Tutankhamun, c. 1350.

Comparisons of construction details in the text of Ex 25-40 with the frames, shrines, poles, sheathing, draped fabric covers, gilt rosettes, and winged protective figures from the shrine of Tutankhamun are instructive. The period, the Late Bronze Age, is equivalent in all dating systems to the era of Moses and the exodus.

Make all the frames of the tabernacle in this way. 18 Make twenty frames for the south side
of the tabernacle 19 and make forty silver bases to go under them—two bases for each
frame, one under each projection. 20 For the other side, the north side of the tabernacle,
make twenty frames 21 and forty silver bases—two under each frame. 22 Make six frames for
the far end, that is, the west end of the tabernacle, 23 and make two frames for the corners
at the far end. 24 At these two corners they must be double from the bottom all the way to
the top, and fitted into a single ring; both shall be like that. 25 So there will be eight frames
and sixteen silver bases—two under each frame.
26 "Also make crossbars of acacia wood: five for the frames on one side of the tabernacle, 27 five for those on the other side, and five for the frames on the west, at the far end
of the tabernacle. 28 The center crossbar is to extend from end to end at the middle of the
frames. 29 Overlay the frames with gold and make gold rings to hold the crossbars. Also
overlay the crossbars with gold.
30 "Set up the tabernacle according to the plan[e] shown you on the mountain.
31 "Make a curtain[f] of blue, purple and scarlet yarn and finely twisted linen, with cherubim[g] worked into it by a skilled craftsman. 32 Hang it with gold hooks on four posts of
acacia wood overlaid with gold and standing on four silver bases. 33 Hang the curtain
from the clasps and place the ark of the Testimony behind the curtain.[h] The curtain will
separate the Holy Place from the Most Holy Place.[i] 34 Put the atonement cover[j] on the
ark of the Testimony in the Most Holy Place. 35 Place the table[k] outside the curtain on the
north side of the tabernacle and put the lampstand[l] opposite it on the south side.

26:30 [e]Ex 25:9,40; Ac 7:44; Heb 8:5
26:31 [f]2Ch 3:14; Mt 27:51; Heb 9:3 [g]Ex 36:35
26:33 [h]Ex 40:3,21; Lev 16:2 [i]Heb 9:2-3
26:34 [j]Ex 25:21; 40:20; Heb 9:5
26:35 [k]Heb 9:2 [l]Ex 40:22,24

26:26 make crossbars. The frames were supported by 15 beams overlaid with gold, five for each of the three closed sides, with the middle bar to run the length of each side. The entire structure could be dismantled or assembled in a minimum of time.
26:31 Make a curtain. The space formed internally by the tabernacle was to be subdivided by a veil (the "shielding curtain"; 39:34; 40:21; Nu 4:5), a tapestry (like the inner curtains) placed 30 feet from the entrance. This created an inner cube of 15 feet where the ark was kept. This was the Most Holy Place, the throne room where the Lord would meet with Israel's high priest on the Day of Atonement. The Holy Place, a royal antechamber, extended 30 feet from the veil to the entrance.

Tabernacle Furnishings

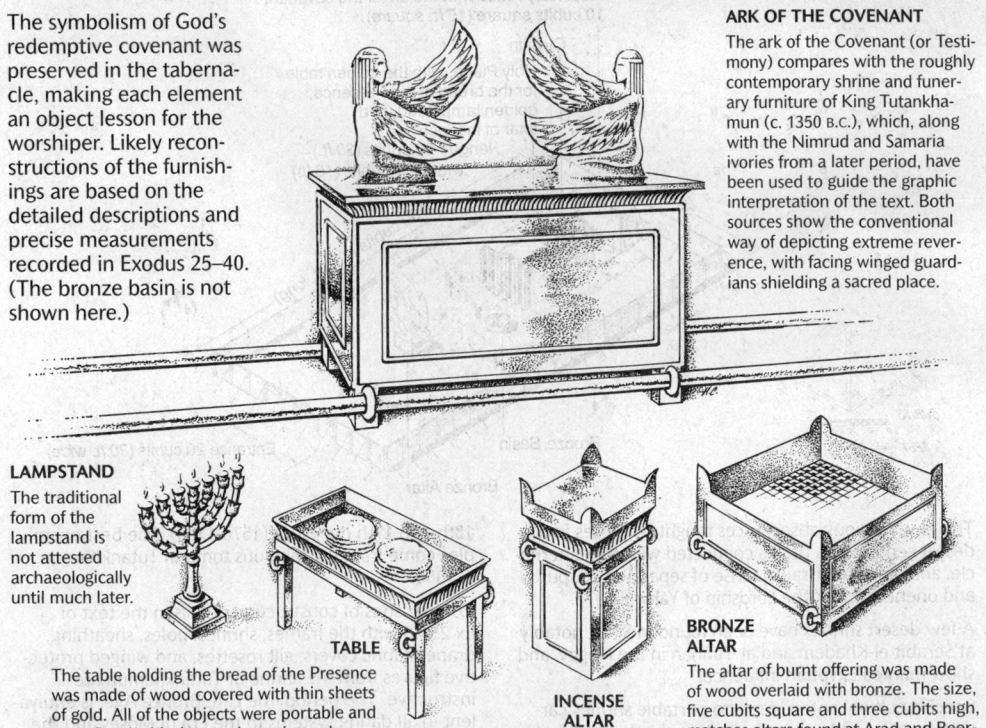

The symbolism of God's redemptive covenant was preserved in the tabernacle, making each element an object lesson for the worshiper. Likely reconstructions of the furnishings are based on the detailed descriptions and precise measurements recorded in Exodus 25–40. (The bronze basin is not shown here.)

ARK OF THE COVENANT
The ark of the Covenant (or Testimony) compares with the roughly contemporary shrine and funerary furniture of King Tutankhamun (c. 1350 B.C.), which, along with the Nimrud and Samaria ivories from a later period, have been used to guide the graphic interpretation of the text. Both sources show the conventional way of depicting extreme reverence, with facing winged guardians shielding a sacred place.

LAMPSTAND
The traditional form of the lampstand is not attested archaeologically until much later.

TABLE
The table holding the bread of the Presence was made of wood covered with thin sheets of gold. All of the objects were portable and were fitted with rings and carrying poles, practices typical of Egyptian ritual processions as early as the Old Kingdom.

INCENSE ALTAR

BRONZE ALTAR
The altar of burnt offering was made of wood overlaid with bronze. The size, five cubits square and three cubits high, matches altars found at Arad and Beersheba from the period of the monarchy.

36 “For the entrance to the tent make a curtain of blue, purple and scarlet yarn and
finely twisted linen—the work of an embroiderer. 37 Make gold hooks for this curtain and
five posts of acacia wood overlaid with gold. And cast five bronze bases for them.

The Altar of Burnt Offering

27 “Build an altar[m] of acacia wood, three cubits[a] high; it is to be square, five cubits — 27:1 [m]Eze 43:13
long and five cubits wide.[b] 2 Make a horn[n] at each of the four corners, so that the
horns and the altar are of one piece, and overlay the altar with bronze. 3 Make all its uten- — 27:2 [n]Ps 118:27
sils of bronze—its pots to remove the ashes, and its shovels, sprinkling bowls, meat forks and
firepans. 4 Make a grating for it, a bronze network, and make a bronze ring at each of the four
corners of the network. 5 Put it under the ledge of the altar so that it is halfway up the altar.
6 Make poles of acacia wood for the altar and overlay them with bronze. 7 The poles are to
be inserted into the rings so they will be on two sides of the altar when it is carried. 8 Make
the altar hollow, out of boards. It is to be made just as you were shown[o] on the mountain. — 27:8 [o]Ex 25:9,40

The Courtyard

9 “Make a courtyard for the tabernacle. The south side shall be a hundred cubits[c] long
and is to have curtains of finely twisted linen, 10 with twenty posts and twenty bronze bases and with silver hooks and bands on the posts. 11 The north side shall also be a hundred cubits long and is to have curtains, with twenty posts and twenty bronze bases and
with silver hooks and bands on the posts.

12 “The west end of the courtyard shall be fifty cubits[d] wide and have curtains, with
ten posts and ten bases. 13 On the east end, toward the sunrise, the courtyard shall also
be fifty cubits wide. 14 Curtains fifteen cubits[e] long are to be on one side of the entrance,
with three posts and three bases, 15 and curtains fifteen cubits long are to be on the other side, with three posts and three bases.

16 “For the entrance to the courtyard, provide a curtain twenty cubits[f] long, of blue,
purple and scarlet yarn and finely twisted linen—the work of an embroiderer—with four
posts and four bases. 17 All the posts around the courtyard are to have silver bands and
hooks, and bronze bases. 18 The courtyard shall be a hundred cubits long and fifty cubits
wide,[g] with curtains of finely twisted linen five cubits[h] high, and with bronze bases. 19 All
the other articles used in the service of the tabernacle, whatever their function, including all the tent pegs for it and those for the courtyard, are to be of bronze.

Oil for the Lampstand

20 “Command the Israelites to bring you clear oil of pressed olives for the light so that

[a] *1* That is, about 4 1/2 feet (about 1.3 meters) [b] *1* That is, about 7 1/2 feet (about 2.3 meters) long and wide [c] *9* That is, about 150 feet (about 46 meters); also in verse 11 [d] *12* That is, about 75 feet (about 23 meters); also in verse 13 [e] *14* That is, about 22 1/2 feet (about 6.9 meters); also in verse 15 [f] *16* That is, about 30 feet (about 9 meters) [g] *18* That is, about 150 feet (about 46 meters) long and 75 feet (about 23 meters) wide [h] *18* That is, about 7 1/2 feet (about 2.3 meters)

26:36 For the entrance. The open east end was to be enclosed by a screen with bronze bases. The screen was to be made of the same material as the inner curtains and the veil, but it was to be embroidered; it was not a tapestry, since it was further from the Presence. It was to be hung on the five columns of supports.

■ **27:1–8** *The Altar.* Following his previous pattern, God spoke first of the courtyard's furnishings and then of the courtyard area itself.

27:1 altar. The altar of burnt offering was to be made of acacia wood overlaid with bronze. The horns at the four corners were ritually important, for they were smeared with blood at the consecration of priests (29:12), as part of the sin offering (Lev 4:25,30) and on the Day of the Atonement (Lev 16:18). They provided sanctuary to anyone who laid hold of them (1Ki 1:50). The altar was hollow, to be filled, it would seem, with earth or stones (20:24).

27:3 its utensils. Accessories—a pot or pail and a shovel to remove ashes, a basin for dashing liquids, pronged meat forks and special pans for holding and removing coals—were all made of bronze, for they were outside of the tabernacle proper.

27:4 Make a grating. The details and function of the grate are obscure. The grate was placed halfway down the altar, running from below the ledge of the altar to the ground. Perhaps it was for ventilation for the altar fire. It is usually assumed that the "ledge" of verse 5 was for priests to stand on when offering sacrifices.

■ **27:9–19** *The Courtyard.* The dimensions and structures of the outer courtyard are explained.

27:9 Make a courtyard. The courtyard was a rectangle 150 feet long and 75 feet wide. It was enclosed by white linen hangings seven and one-half feet high (v. 18) that separated the courtyard from the surrounding camp of Israel.

27:16 For the entrance. A 30-foot opening on the east side was covered by a screen (v. 16). There were 56 pillars (20 each on the north and south sides, ten on the west side and three on either side of the entrance on the east side) in bronze bases to suspend the linen hangings. Another four pillars supported the screen. Their arrangement is not specified, nor is the placement of the tabernacle within the courtyard. Exodus 35:18 suggests that the pillars were held in place by pegs and guy ropes.

27:18 The courtyard. The courtyard apparently consisted of two equal squares of 75 feet each: one area held the tabernacle proper, and the other was open space before the tabernacle. The ark and the altar of burnt offering were the respective central objects. The purpose of the eastern half of the courtyard was to provide public space where sacrifices could be made and worshipers could gather. **five cubits high.** Since the height of the draperies was seven and one-half feet and the height of the tabernacle 15 feet, the tabernacle was not blocked from public view.

■ **27:20—30:10** *The Priests and Their Services.* The second major portion of God's first set of instructions to Moses focuses on the priesthood. It begins with another call to collect oil (27:20–21) and touches on the priests' garments (28:1–43), priestly consecration (29:1–46) and the priestly service at the altar of incense (30:1–10).

■ **27:20–21** *Collection of Oil.* This divine speech began with a call to collect building materials for the tabernacle; now God called for oil to be brought so the priests could perform their rites.

the lamps may be kept burning. **21** In the Tent of Meeting,[p] outside the curtain that is in front of the Testimony,[q] Aaron and his sons are to keep the lamps[r] burning before the LORD from evening till morning. This is to be a lasting ordinance[s] among the Israelites for the generations to come.

The Priestly Garments

28 "Have Aaron[t] your brother brought to you from among the Israelites, along with his sons Nadab and Abihu, Eleazar and Ithamar, so they may serve me as priests.[u] **2** Make sacred garments[v] for your brother Aaron, to give him dignity and honor. **3** Tell all the skilled men[w] to whom I have given wisdom[x] in such matters that they are to make garments for Aaron, for his consecration, so he may serve me as priest. **4** These are the garments they are to make: a breastpiece,[y] an ephod, a robe,[z] a woven tunic,[a] a turban and a sash. They are to make these sacred garments for your brother Aaron and his sons, so they may serve me as priests. **5** Have them use gold, and blue, purple and scarlet yarn, and fine linen.

The Ephod

6 "Make the ephod of gold, and of blue, purple and scarlet yarn, and of finely twisted linen—the work of a skilled craftsman. **7** It is to have two shoulder pieces attached to two of its corners, so it can be fastened. **8** Its skillfully woven waistband is to be like it—of one piece with the ephod and made with gold, and with blue, purple and scarlet yarn, and with finely twisted linen.

9 "Take two onyx stones and engrave on them the names of the sons of Israel **10** in the order of their birth—six names on one stone and the remaining six on the other. **11** Engrave the names of the sons of Israel on the two stones the way a gem cutter engraves a seal. Then mount the stones in gold filigree settings **12** and fasten them on the shoulder pieces of the ephod as memorial stones for the sons of Israel. Aaron is to bear the names on his shoulders as a memorial before the LORD. **13** Make gold filigree settings **14** and two braided chains of pure gold, like a rope, and attach the chains to the settings.

The Breastpiece

15 "Fashion a breastpiece for making decisions—the work of a skilled craftsman. Make it like the ephod: of gold, and of blue, purple and scarlet yarn, and of finely twisted linen. **16** It is to be square—a span[a] long and a span wide—and folded double. **17** Then mount four rows of precious stones on it. In the first row there shall be a ruby, a topaz and a beryl; **18** in the second row a turquoise, a sapphire[b] and an emerald; **19** in the third row a jacinth, an agate and an amethyst; **20** in the fourth row a chrysolite, an onyx and a jasper.[c] Mount them in gold filigree settings. **21** There are to be twelve stones, one for each of the names of the sons of Israel, each engraved like a seal with the name of one of the twelve tribes.

22 "For the breastpiece make braided chains of pure gold, like a rope. **23** Make two gold rings for it and fasten them to two corners of the breastpiece. **24** Fasten the two gold chains to the rings at the corners of the breastpiece, **25** and the other ends of the chains to the two settings, attaching them to the shoulder pieces of the ephod at the front. **26** Make two gold

27:21 [p]Ex 28:43 [q]Ex 26:31,33 [r]Ex 25:37; 30:8; 1Sa 3:3; 2Ch 13:11 [s]Ex 29:9; Lev 3:17; 16:34; Nu 18:23; 19:21
28:1 [t]Heb 5:4 [u]Nu 18:1-7; Heb 5:1
28:2 [v]Ex 29:5,29; 31:10; 39:1; Lev 8:7-9,30
28:3 [w]Ex 31:6; 36:1 [x]Ex 31:3
28:4 [y]ver 15-30 [z]ver 31-35 [a]ver 39

[a] *16* That is, about 9 inches (about 22 centimeters) [b] *18* Or *lapis lazuli* [c] *20* The precise identification of some of these precious stones is uncertain.

27:20 clear oil . . . for the light. Pure olive oil, which would provide a virtually smoke-free light, was to be extracted by pounding. Leviticus 24:1–4 supports the view that the lamp was the golden lampstand that stood on the south side of the Holy Place.
27:21 Tent of Meeting. The tabernacle was so named because God and Israel's priestly representatives met there as determined by liturgical regulation. It was to be associated with the tent of meeting outside the camp where God met Moses (33:7; Nu 12:4).
■ **28:1–43** *The Priestly Garments.* God told Moses how the priests were to dress as they performed their duties in the holy presence of God.
28:1 Nadab and Abihu. Later, these two sons of Aaron were slain for unlawful activity (Lev 10:1–2). **Eleazar.** Aaron's successor (Dt 10:6). **serve me as priests.** Priests (descendants of Aaron) officiated at sacrifices, were responsible for the care of the place of worship and operated as judges, dispensers of blessing, teachers, archivists and keepers of the sacred lots.
28:2 Make sacred garments. What Aaron would wear as the chief figure was vital. Vestments were to be beautiful and splendid, fashioned of the same expensive materials as those used for the tabernacle. Eight sacral vestments are listed in this chapter (four worn by Aaron alone). Six are listed in verse 4; two others later: the flowered plate at the front of the turban (vv. 36–38) and the undergarments of plain linen (vv. 42–43).
28:6 the ephod. The ephod of the high priest was to be distinguished from a simple ephod, which might have been just a linen loincloth (2Sa 6:14,20). The high priest's was made from costly material and reached from the breast to the hips. It had shoulder straps with two onyx stones engraved with the names of the tribes, as well as a waistband (39:2–7). The breastpiece that contained the Urim and Thummim (v. 30) was fastened to the ephod (v. 27; 1Sa 23:9–10).
28:15 a breastpiece. This was a single piece of fabric, folded double to form a square pouch. It had gemstones on its front bearing the names of the 12 tribes and held the Urim and Thummim within it.
28:22 braided chains. Ropes of twisted gold thread connected the breastpiece to the shoulder straps of the ephod.

rings and attach them to the other two corners of the breastpiece on the inside edge next to the ephod. 27Make two more gold rings and attach them to the bottom of the shoulder pieces on the front of the ephod, close to the seam just above the waistband of the ephod. 28The rings of the breastpiece are to be tied to the rings of the ephod with blue cord, connecting it to the waistband, so that the breastpiece will not swing out from the ephod.

29"Whenever Aaron enters the Holy Place,[b] he will bear the names of the sons of Israel over his heart on the breastpiece of decision as a continuing memorial before the LORD. 30Also put the Urim and the Thummim[c] in the breastpiece, so they may be over Aaron's heart whenever he enters the presence of the LORD. Thus Aaron will always bear the means of making decisions for the Israelites over his heart before the LORD.

Other Priestly Garments

31"Make the robe of the ephod entirely of blue cloth, 32with an opening for the head in its center. There shall be a woven edge like a collar[a] around this opening, so that it will not tear. 33Make pomegranates of blue, purple and scarlet yarn around the hem of the robe, with gold bells between them. 34The gold bells and the pomegranates are to alternate around the hem of the robe. 35Aaron must wear it when he ministers. The sound of the bells will be heard when he enters the Holy Place before the LORD and when he comes out, so that he will not die.

36"Make a plate of pure gold and engrave on it as on a seal: HOLY TO THE LORD.[d] 37Fasten a blue cord to it to attach it to the turban; it is to be on the front of the turban. 38It will be on Aaron's forehead, and he will bear the guilt[e] involved in the sacred gifts the Israelites consecrate, whatever their gifts may be. It will be on Aaron's forehead continually so that they will be acceptable to the LORD.

39"Weave the tunic of fine linen and make the turban of fine linen. The sash is to be the work of an embroiderer. 40Make tunics, sashes and headbands for Aaron's sons,[f] to give them dignity and honor. 41After you put these clothes on your brother Aaron and his sons, anoint[g] and ordain them. Consecrate them so they may serve me as priests.[h]

42"Make linen undergarments[i] as a covering for the body, reaching from the waist to the thigh. 43Aaron and his sons must wear them whenever they enter the Tent of Meeting[j] or approach the altar to minister in the Holy Place, so that they will not incur guilt and die.[k]

"This is to be a lasting ordinance[l] for Aaron and his descendants.

Consecration of the Priests

29 "This is what you are to do to consecrate them, so they may serve me as priests: Take a young bull and two rams without defect. 2And from fine wheat flour, without yeast, make bread, and cakes mixed with oil, and wafers spread with oil.[m] 3Put them in a basket and present them in it—along with the bull and the two rams. 4Then bring Aaron and his sons to the entrance to the Tent of Meeting and wash them with water.[n] 5Take the garments[o] and dress Aaron with the tunic, the robe of the ephod, the ephod itself and the breastpiece. Fasten the ephod on him by its skillfully woven waist-

[a] 32 The meaning of the Hebrew for this word is uncertain.

28:29 [b]ver 12
28:30 [c]Lev 8:8; Nu 27:21; Dt 33:8; Ezr 2:63; Ne 7:65
28:36 [d]Zec 14:20
28:38 [e]Lev 10:17; 22:9, 16; Nu 18:1; Heb 9:28; 1Pe 2:24
28:40 [f]ver 4; Ex 39:41
28:41 [g]Ex 29:7; Lev 10:7 [h]Ex 29:7-9; 30:30; 40:15; Lev 8:1-36; Heb 7:28
28:42 [i]Lev 6:10; 16:4, 23; Eze 44:18
28:43 [j]Ex 27:21 [k]Ex 20:26 [l]Lev 17:7
29:2 [m]Lev 2:1, 4; 6:19-23
29:4 [n]Ex 40:12; Heb 10:22
29:5 [o]Ex 28:2; Lev 8:7

28:29 Whenever Aaron enters. Aaron, on entering the Holy Place, carried this double reminder of Israel.
28:30 the Urim and the Thummim. Literally, "lights and perfections." These two Hebrew words begin with the first and last letters of the alphabet (cf. the Alpha and Omega of Rev 1:18). It is clear that whatever the Urim and Thummim were, they were used to receive oracles from God (Nu 27:21; Dt 33:8; 1Sa 23:6–13; 28:6; Ezr 2:63). There is no hint of how they functioned or what they were—perhaps stones of different colors or two small objects engraved with symbols or letters of the alphabet and cast as lots.
28:31 robe of the ephod. Aaron was to wear this blue robe under the breastpiece and the ephod. It was the robe of people of high social standing (1Sa 18:4; 24:4). Bells around the hem would identify and protect him when he entered a zone of sanctity.
28:36 HOLY TO THE LORD. On Aaron's turban was fastened a plate of pure gold. The same word is also translated "diadem" (29:6; 39:30; Lev 8:9) or "crown," which was worn by kings (2Sa 1:10; 2Ki 11:12; Ps 89:39). The plate was of pure gold and was inscribed with the words "HOLY TO THE LORD." This identified Aaron as set apart to the Lord as his representative to Israel.
28:38 See *WCF* 16.6; *WLC* 78.
28:40 Make tunics, sashes and headbands. The other priestly garments are only briefly described. The tunic seems to have been a long, shiftlike garment worn under the robe. This article of clothing was not restricted to the priesthood (2Sa 15:32). The sash was also part of the apparel of a high official or a king (Isa 22:21). These priestly garments were to be worn in God's presence. Ordinary priests were attired with plain tunics, less ornate sashes and headbands different from that of the high priest. Donning these special vestments was part of the three-stage process of vesting, anointing and ordination proper.
28:42 linen undergarments. The undergarment was common to the garb of all the priests. It was to be worn to avoid violation of 20:26. Ritual nakedness, so common in other ancient religions, was forbidden in Israel.
■ **29:1–46** *The Consecration of Priests.* The ceremony for the consecration of the priests and the altar is expounded.
29:1 consecrate. Literally, "make them holy"; i.e., set them apart from their fellow Israelites for God's service. **Take a young bull.** Moses was to bring to the tabernacle door the ingredients for the installation sacrifices.
29:2 bread . . . cakes . . . wafers. Three kinds of meal offerings were to be presented (Lev 2:10).
29:4 wash them with water. Aaron and his sons could not enter the tabernacle until (1) they had been ceremonially cleansed by washing and (2) sacrifice had been made for them (Heb 7:27).
29:5 Take the garments. Aaron and his sons were to be vested with sacred garments symbolic of their office. Only Aaron was anointed (and thereby authorized to act as chief priest).

band.[p] 6 Put the turban on his head and attach the sacred diadem[q] to the turban. 7 Take
the anointing oil[r] and anoint him by pouring it on his head. 8 Bring his sons and dress
them in tunics 9 and put headbands on them. Then tie sashes on Aaron and his sons.[a][s]
The priesthood is theirs by a lasting ordinance.[t] In this way you shall ordain Aaron and
his sons.

10 "Bring the bull to the front of the Tent of Meeting, and Aaron and his sons shall lay
their hands on its head. 11 Slaughter it in the LORD's presence at the entrance to the Tent
of Meeting. 12 Take some of the bull's blood and put it on the horns[u] of the altar with your
finger, and pour out the rest of it at the base of the altar. 13 Then take all the fat[v] around
the inner parts, the covering of the liver, and both kidneys with the fat on them, and burn
them on the altar. 14 But burn the bull's flesh and its hide and its offal outside the
camp.[w] It is a sin offering.

15 "Take one of the rams, and Aaron and his sons shall lay their hands on its head.
16 Slaughter it and take the blood and sprinkle it against the altar on all sides. 17 Cut the
ram into pieces and wash the inner parts and the legs, putting them with the head and
the other pieces. 18 Then burn the entire ram on the altar. It is a burnt offering to the LORD,
a pleasing aroma,[x] an offering made to the LORD by fire.

19 "Take the other ram,[y] and Aaron and his sons shall lay their hands on its head.
20 Slaughter it, take some of its blood and put it on the lobes of the right ears of Aaron and
his sons, on the thumbs of their right hands, and on the big toes of their right feet. Then
sprinkle blood against the altar on all sides. 21 And take some of the blood[z] on the altar
and some of the anointing oil[a] and sprinkle it on Aaron and his garments and on his sons
and their garments. Then he and his sons and their garments will be consecrated.[b]

22 "Take from this ram the fat, the fat tail, the fat around the inner parts, the covering of the liver, both kidneys with the fat on them, and the right thigh. (This is the ram
for the ordination.) 23 From the basket of bread made without yeast, which is before the
LORD, take a loaf, and a cake made with oil, and a wafer. 24 Put all these in the hands of
Aaron and his sons and wave them before the LORD as a wave offering.[c] 25 Then take them
from their hands and burn them on the altar along with the burnt offering for a pleasing aroma to the LORD, an offering made to the LORD by fire. 26 After you take the breast
of the ram for Aaron's ordination, wave it before the LORD as a wave offering, and it will
be your share.[d]

27 "Consecrate those parts of the ordination ram that belong to Aaron and his sons:[e]
the breast that was waved and the thigh that was presented. 28 This is always to be the
regular share from the Israelites for Aaron and his sons. It is the contribution the Israelites are to make to the LORD from their fellowship offerings.[b][f]

29 "Aaron's sacred garments will belong to his descendants so that they can be anointed and ordained in them.[g] 30 The son[h] who succeeds him as priest and comes to the Tent
of Meeting to minister in the Holy Place is to wear them seven days.

31 "Take the ram for the ordination and cook the meat in a sacred place. 32 At the entrance to the Tent of Meeting, Aaron and his sons are to eat the meat of the ram and the
bread[i] that is in the basket. 33 They are to eat these offerings by which atonement was
made for their ordination and consecration. But no one else may eat[j] them, because they
are sacred. 34 And if any of the meat of the ordination ram or any bread is left over till
morning,[k] burn it up. It must not be eaten, because it is sacred.

35 "Do for Aaron and his sons everything I have commanded you, taking seven days

29:5 [p]Ex 28:8
29:6 [q]Lev 8:9
29:7 [r]Ex 30:25,30,31; Lev 8:12; 21:10; Nu 35:25; Ps 133:2
29:9 [s]Ex 28:40 [t]Ex 40:15; Nu 3:10; 18:7; 25:13; Dt 18:5
29:12 [u]Ex 27:2
29:13 [v]Lev 3:3,5,9
29:14 [w]Lev 4:11-12,21; Heb 13:11
29:18 [x]Ge 8:21
29:19 [y]ver 3
29:21 [z]Heb 9:22 [a]Ex 30:25,31 [b]ver 1
29:24 [c]Lev 7:30
29:26 [d]Lev 7:31-34
29:27 [e]Lev 7:31,34; Dt 18:3
29:28 [f]Lev 10:15
29:29 [g]Nu 20:26,28
29:30 [h]Nu 20:28
29:32 [i]Mt 12:4
29:33 [j]Lev 10:14; 22:10,13
29:34 [k]Ex 12:10

a *9* Hebrew; Septuagint *on them* b *28* Traditionally *peace offerings*

29:9 ordain. Or "install"; literally, "fill the hand." This phrase is an ancient expression used to describe induction into office.
29:10 Bring the bull. Priests laid their hands on the bull calf to symbolize personal identification and substitution in this sin offering (v. 14). Blood was smeared on the horns of the altar, as was done for laymen, since Aaron and his sons were still unconsecrated (Lev 4:25,30). The remainder of the blood was to be poured at the bottom of the altar, as was done for a sin offering. Certain parts were to be burned on the altar (v. 13), but the remainder was to be burned outside the camp as unclean (v. 14).
29:15 one of the rams. One ram was offered for a dedicatory burnt offering.
29:19 Take the other ram. The other ram was to be offered as a fellowship offering.
29:20 put it on the lobes. The ears, hands and feet of the priests (extremities as parts for the whole) were cleansed from impurities as consecration for service.
29:21 some of the blood. By the sprinkling of blood on the persons and garments of the priests, they were set apart to their office.
29:22 the right thigh. Added to what was to be burned was the right thigh, which would normally have gone to the priest (Lev 7:32–33).
29:24 wave them. These, with a sample of each cereal offering from the basket, were then waved to and fro before the altar (as gifts to God) and then retained by the priest (Lev 7:30–31; 10:15).
29:26 your share. Moses, since he was acting as priest, was to have the breast and the thigh of the ram as his portion; thereafter the priests were to receive the breast and the right thigh (Lev 7:31–32). Moses was acting as priest on this occasion and was entitled to share the offering.
29:35 seven days. The ordination sacrifices were to be repeated for seven days, and the altar, since it was made with human hands, was to be cleansed by sin offerings for seven days during the consecration period. It would then be holy, and it would make anything that touched it holy as well (v. 37).

to ordain them. 36Sacrifice a bull each day[l] as a sin offering to make atonement. Purify
the altar by making atonement for it, and anoint it to consecrate[m] it. 37For seven days
make atonement for the altar and consecrate it. Then the altar will be most holy, and
whatever touches it will be holy.[n]
38"This is what you are to offer on the altar regularly each day:[o] two lambs a year old.
39Offer one in the morning and the other at twilight.[p] 40With the first lamb offer a tenth
of an ephah[a] of fine flour mixed with a quarter of a hin[b] of oil from pressed olives, and
a quarter of a hin of wine as a drink offering. 41Sacrifice the other lamb at twilight with
the same grain offering and its drink offering as in the morning—a pleasing aroma, an
offering made to the LORD by fire.
42"For the generations to come[q] this burnt offering is to be made regularly at the entrance to the Tent of Meeting before the LORD. There I will meet you and speak to you;[r]
43there also I will meet with the Israelites, and the place will be consecrated by my
glory.[s]
44"So I will consecrate the Tent of Meeting and the altar and will consecrate Aaron
and his sons to serve me as priests.[t] 45Then I will dwell[u] among the Israelites and be their
God.[v] 46They will know that I am the LORD their God, who brought them out of Egypt so
that I might dwell among them. I am the LORD their God.[w]

The Altar of Incense

30 "Make an altar[x] of acacia wood for burning incense.[y] 2It is to be square, a cubit long and a cubit wide, and two cubits high[c]—its horns[z] of one piece with it.
3Overlay the top and all the sides and the horns with pure gold, and make a gold molding around it. 4Make two gold rings for the altar below the molding—two on opposite
sides—to hold the poles used to carry it. 5Make the poles of acacia wood and overlay
them with gold. 6Put the altar in front of the curtain that is before the ark of the Testimony—before the atonement cover[a] that is over the Testimony—where I will meet
with you.
7"Aaron must burn fragrant incense[b] on the altar every morning when he tends the
lamps. 8He must burn incense again when he lights the lamps at twilight so incense will
burn regularly before the LORD for the generations to come. 9Do not offer on this altar any
other incense[c] or any burnt offering or grain offering, and do not pour a drink offering
on it. 10Once a year Aaron shall make atonement[d] on its horns. This annual atonement
must be made with the blood of the atoning sin offering for the generations to come. It
is most holy to the LORD."

Atonement Money

11Then the LORD said to Moses, 12"When you take a census[e] of the Israelites to count
them, each one must pay the LORD a ransom[f] for his life at the time he is counted. Then
no plague[g] will come on them when you number them. 13Each one who crosses over to
those already counted is to give a half shekel,[d] according to the sanctuary shekel,[h] which
weighs twenty gerahs. This half shekel is an offering to the LORD. 14All who cross over,
those twenty years old or more, are to give an offering to the LORD. 15The rich are not to
give more than a half shekel and the poor are not to give less[i] when you make the offer-

29:36 [l]Heb 10:11 [m]Ex 40:10
29:37 [n]Ex 30:28-29; 40:10; Mt 23:19
29:38 [o]Nu 28:3-8; 1Ch 16:40; Da 12:11
29:39 [p]Eze 46:13-15
29:42 [q]Ex 30:8 [r]Ex 25:22
29:43 [s]1Ki 8:11
29:44 [t]Lev 21:15
29:45 [u]Ex 25:8; Lev 26:12; Zec 2:10; Jn 14:17 [v]2Co 6:16; Rev 21:3
29:46 [w]Ex 20:2
30:1 [x]Ex 37:25 [y]Rev 8:3
30:2 [z]Ex 27:2
30:6 [a]Ex 25:22; 26:34
30:7 [b]ver 34-35; Ex 27:21; 1Sa 2:28
30:9 [c]Lev 10:1
30:10 [d]Lev 16:18-19,30
30:12 [e]Ex 38:25; Nu 1:2, 49; 2Sa 24:1 [f]Nu 31:50; Mt 20:28 [g]2Sa 24:13
30:13 [h]Nu 3:47; Mt 17:24
30:15 [i]Pr 22:2; Eph 6:9

[a] *40* That is, probably about 2 quarts (about 2 liters) [b] *40* That is, probably about 1 quart (about 1 liter)
[c] *2* That is, about 1 1/2 feet (about 0.5 meter) long and wide and about 3 feet (about 0.9 meter) high
[d] *13* That is, about 1/5 ounce (about 6 grams); also in verse 15

29:38–46 The requirements for the daily priestly offerings are reviewed.
29:38 regularly each day. Each day was to open and close with gifts to the Lord, to be made at the entrance to the tabernacle. God set apart by his presence the tabernacle and the altar, as well as Aaron and his sons. The whole of chapters 25–29 is brought to a conclusion.
29:43–46 I will meet . . . I will dwell. This passage states the goal of the exodus event (and of the book). God "brought them out of Egypt so that [he] might dwell among them" (v. 46). God's meeting with his people from his throne of atonement among them was the climax and purpose of his deliverance. To be their God, he had to be the Lord who was there with them. They were his "meeting" ("congregation") because they would encounter him at the Tent of Meeting through the blood of the covenant.
■ **30:1–10** *The Altar of Incense.* This section gives the plans for making the altar of incense, with a special focus on the priestly service rendered at the altar.
30:1 an altar . . . for burning incense. The altar was to be stationed before the veil at the entrance to the Most Holy Place (v. 6). It was lit by the high priest each morning and evening. The smoke that then covered the mercy seat protected the high priest from God's divine holiness (Lev 16:13).
■ **30:11–16** *Atonement Money.* Prescriptions for the collection of atonement money were given in this second speech of God to Moses about the tabernacle and its services (see note on 25:1—31:18).
30:12 take a census. The half shekel (the atonement money) that was to accompany each census witnessed to the Israelites' dependence on the Lord's mercy. Their lives were forfeit because of sin, and they needed to be redeemed. The lesson of the Passover and the redemption of the firstborn was applied to all Israel (13:15; 22:29; Nu 3:40–51). **ransom.** Literally, "atone." The payment served as an act of individual atonement and was an assertion of God's rights over Israel.
30:13 a half shekel. Nehemiah 10:32 shows that the amount was reduced during difficult times.

ing to the LORD to atone for your lives. 16 Receive the atonement money from the Israelites and use it for the service of the Tent of Meeting.[j] It will be a memorial for the Israelites before the LORD, making atonement for your lives."

Basin for Washing

17 Then the LORD said to Moses, 18 "Make a bronze basin,[k] with its bronze stand, for
washing. Place it between the Tent of Meeting and the altar, and put water in it. 19 Aaron and his sons are to wash their hands and feet[l] with water[m] from it. 20 Whenever they
enter the Tent of Meeting, they shall wash with water so that they will not die. Also, when
they approach the altar to minister by presenting an offering made to the LORD by fire,
21 they shall wash their hands and feet so that they will not die. This is to be a lasting ordinance[n] for Aaron and his descendants for the generations to come."

Anointing Oil

22 Then the LORD said to Moses, 23 "Take the following fine spices: 500 shekels[a] of liquid myrrh,[o] half as much (that is, 250 shekels) of fragrant cinnamon, 250 shekels of fragrant cane, 24 500 shekels of cassia[p]—all according to the sanctuary shekel—and a
hin[b] of olive oil. 25 Make these into a sacred anointing oil, a fragrant blend, the work of
a perfumer.[q] It will be the sacred anointing oil.[r] 26 Then use it to anoint[s] the Tent of Meeting, the ark of the Testimony, 27 the table and all its articles, the lampstand and its accessories, the altar of incense, 28 the altar of burnt offering and all its utensils, and the
basin with its stand. 29 You shall consecrate them so they will be most holy, and whatever touches them will be holy.[t]
30 "Anoint Aaron and his sons and consecrate[u] them so they may serve me as priests.
31 Say to the Israelites, 'This is to be my sacred anointing oil for the generations to come.
32 Do not pour it on men's bodies and do not make any oil with the same formula. It is
sacred, and you are to consider it sacred.[v] 33 Whoever makes perfume like it and whoever puts it on anyone other than a priest must be cut off[w] from his people.' "

Incense

34 Then the LORD said to Moses, "Take fragrant spices—gum resin, onycha and galba-
num—and pure frankincense, all in equal amounts, 35 and make a fragrant blend of incense, the work of a perfumer.[x] It is to be salted and pure and sacred. 36 Grind some of
it to powder and place it in front of the Testimony in the Tent of Meeting, where I will
meet with you. It shall be most holy[y] to you. 37 Do not make any incense with this formula for yourselves; consider it holy[z] to the LORD. 38 Whoever makes any like it to enjoy its
fragrance must be cut off[a] from his people."

Bezalel and Oholiab

31 Then the LORD said to Moses, 2 "See, I have chosen Bezalel[b] son of Uri, the son
of Hur, of the tribe of Judah, 3 and I have filled him with the Spirit of God, with
skill, ability and knowledge in all kinds of crafts[c]— 4 to make artistic designs for work in
gold, silver and bronze, 5 to cut and set stones, to work in wood, and to engage in all kinds
of craftsmanship. 6 Moreover, I have appointed Oholiab son of Ahisamach, of the tribe

30:16 [j]Ex 38:25-28
30:18 [k]Ex 38:8; 40:7,30
30:19 [l]Ex 40:31-32; Isa 52:11 [m]Ps 26:6
30:21 [n]Ex 27:21; 28:43
30:23 [o]Ge 37:25
30:24 [p]Ps 45:8
30:25 [q]Ex 37:29 [r]Ex 40:9
30:26 [s]Ex 40:9; Lev 8:10; Nu 7:1
30:29 [t]Ex 29:37
30:30 [u]Ex 29:7; Lev 8:2, 12,30
30:32 [v]ver 25,37
30:33 [w]ver 38; Ge 17:14
30:35 [x]ver 25
30:36 [y]ver 32; Ex 29:37; Lev 2:3
30:37 [z]ver 32
30:38 [a]ver 33
31:2 [b]Ex 36:1,2; 1Ch 2:20
31:3 [c]1Ki 7:14

[a] *23* That is, about 12 1/2 pounds (about 6 kilograms) [b] *24* That is, probably about 4 quarts (about 4 liters)

■ **30:17–21** *The Bronze Basin.* In his third speech (see note on 25:1—31:18), God required the making of a washing basin for priestly cleansing. The priests washed their hands and feet when they approached the altar or entered the tabernacle for ministry. No dimensions are given for the basin. Solomon's temple basins were massive. That neglecting to wash might cause death (v. 20) shows the intense reality of the presence of God.

■ **30:22–33** *Anointing Oil.* Stipulations for priestly anointing oil are presented in this fourth divine speech (see note on 25:1—31:18). The anointing oil to be made was used for sacred purposes (for consecration, as here, and also for healing and restoration). The anointed elements, as here, were then most holy and thus made holy all that they touched.

■ **30:34–38** *Incense.* Requirements for priestly incenses are set forth in this fifth divine speech (see note on 25:1—31:18). To make the sanctuary incense, four ingredients were used in equal proportions, and then the mixture was seasoned with a small amount of salt (Lev 2:13).

■ **31:1–11** *Appointment of Craftsmen.* In his sixth speech, God appointed artisans for the construction of the tabernacle (see note on 25:1—31:18). God granted Bezalel the gift of his Spirit, as well as three other gifts for the construction task: "skill" (the experienced hand to guide and accomplish the labor), "ability" (the talent for solving difficulties in the creation of the complex series of objects and materials) and "knowledge" (the gift needed to understand God's instructions [v. 3]). Included were a combination of theoretical, practical and planning activities. Bezalel had to design intricate patterns in three metals (gold, silver and copper), engrave gemstones and carve wood. The tabernacle was to be produced by divinely gifted men according to the divine design through the enablement of the Spirit. There was no room for human error. Interestingly, in 1 Corinthians 3:5–17, Paul represented himself and Apollos as the Bezalel and Oholiab of the new covenant temple at Corinth. In fact, when Paul described himself as "an expert builder" (1Co 3:10) and Apollos as "building on [the foundation Paul had laid]," he did so in terms borrowed from the Greek Old Testament description of Bezalel (v. 4; 35:32,34).

31:2 Bezalel. The name means "in *El's* [God's] shadow." Bezalel was a descendant of Caleb from the tribe of Judah (1Ch 2:20).

of Dan, to help him. Also I have given skill to all the craftsmen to make everything I have
commanded you: 7the Tent of Meeting,[d] the ark of the Testimony[e] with the atonement
cover[f] on it, and all the other furnishings of the tent— 8the table[g] and its articles, the
pure gold lampstand[h] and all its accessories, the altar of incense, 9the altar of burnt offering and all its utensils, the basin with its stand— 10and also the woven garments[i], both
the sacred garments for Aaron the priest and the garments for his sons when they serve
as priests, 11and the anointing oil[j] and fragrant incense for the Holy Place. They are to
make them just as I commanded you."

The Sabbath

12Then the LORD said to Moses, 13"Say to the Israelites, 'You must observe my Sabbaths.[k] This will be a sign[l] between me and you for the generations to come, so you may
know that I am the LORD, who makes you holy.[a][m]

14" 'Observe the Sabbath, because it is holy to you. Anyone who desecrates it must
be put to death;[n] whoever does any work on that day must be cut off from his people.
15For six days, work[o] is to be done, but the seventh day is a Sabbath of rest,[p] holy to the
LORD. Whoever does any work on the Sabbath day must be put to death. 16The Israelites
are to observe the Sabbath, celebrating it for the generations to come as a lasting covenant. 17It will be a sign[q] between me and the Israelites forever, for in six days the LORD
made the heavens and the earth, and on the seventh day he abstained from work and
rested.[r]' "

18When the LORD finished speaking to Moses on Mount Sinai, he gave him the two
tablets of the Testimony, the tablets of stone[s] inscribed by the finger of God.[t]

The Golden Calf

32 When the people saw that Moses was so long in coming down from the mountain,[u] they gathered around Aaron and said, "Come, make us gods[b] who will go
before us. As for this fellow Moses who brought us up out of Egypt, we don't know what
has happened to him."[v]

2Aaron answered them, "Take off the gold earrings[w] that your wives, your sons and
your daughters are wearing, and bring them to me." 3So all the people took off their earrings and brought them to Aaron. 4He took what they handed him and made it into an
idol cast in the shape of a calf,[x] fashioning it with a tool. Then they said, "These are your
gods,[c] O Israel, who brought you up out of Egypt."

5When Aaron saw this, he built an altar in front of the calf and announced, "Tomorrow there will be a festival[y] to the LORD." 6So the next day the people rose early and sacrificed burnt offerings and presented fellowship offerings.[d][z] Afterward they sat down to
eat and drink and got up to indulge in revelry.[a]

[a] 13 Or *who sanctifies you*; or *who sets you apart as holy* [b] 1 Or *a god*; also in verses 23 and 31
[c] 4 Or *This is your god*; also in verse 8 [d] 6 Traditionally *peace offerings*

31:7 [d]Ex 36:8-38 [e]Ex 37:1-5 [f]Ex 37:6
31:8 [g]Ex 37:10-16 [h]Ex 37:17-24
31:10 [i]Ex 28:2; 39:1,41
31:11 [j]Ex 30:22-32
31:13 [k]Ex 20:8; Lev 19:3, 30 [l]Eze 20:12,20 [m]Lev 11:44
31:14 [n]Nu 15:32-36
31:15 [o]Ex 20:8-11 [p]Ge 2:3; Ex 16:23
31:17 [q]ver 13 [r]Ge 2:2-3
31:18 [s]Ex 24:12 [t]Ex 32:15-16; 34:1, 28; Dt 4:13; 5:22
32:1 [u]Ex 24:18; Dt 9:9-12 [v]Ac 7:40*
32:2 [w]Ex 35:22
32:4 [x]Dt 9:16; Ne 9:18; Ps 106:19; Ac 7:41
32:5 [y]Lev 23:2,37; 2Ki 10:20
32:6 [z]Nu 25:2, Ac 7:41 [a]ver 17-19; 1Co 10:7*

31:6 Oholiab. Oholiab (which means "My tent is the father") was Bezalel's assistant.

■ **31:12–18** *Sabbath Observance.* The Sabbath commandment is reiterated as the finale of God's instructions for tabernacle worship. These instructions make up the climactic seventh address of the section (see note on 25:1—31:18) and form an appropriate conclusion to the worship provisions. To keep God's Sabbath was to keep the covenant, since the Sabbath was now a sign of the special relationship between God and Israel. To disregard God's Sabbath was to disregard God's purposes for creation through his redemption of Israel.

31:15–17 See *WCF* 21.8.

31:18 the two tablets of the Testimony. Reference to the Decalogue followed by way of conclusion, since God completed his revelation by giving Moses the two tablets. One copy belonged to each treaty partner and was to be stored in the respective sanctuaries. Since Israel's copy was to be kept in God's presence, both copies were placed in the ark. **finger of God.** See 8:19. See also *BC* 3.

■ **32:1—34:35** *Israel's Failure and God's Forgiveness.* Having reported the instructions he received regarding the tabernacle and its personnel and services, Moses described a failure in worship that took place at Sinai. These chapters divide into three parts: Moses' intercession at a time of failure (32:1–29), a second intercession (32:30—33:23) and Moses' leadership in covenant renewal (34:1–35). These accounts dramatically demonstrate the consequences for the Israelites when they rejected Moses' worship directives and the results when they exalted Moses once again as Israel's faithful leader and mediator.

■ **32:1–29** *Israel's Violation and Moses' Intercession.* While Moses remained on the mountain, the Israelites turned to idolatry, which would have resulted in near devastation had Moses not returned and intervened.

32:1–6 While Moses spent time with God on Sinai, Aaron and the Israelites engaged in idolatrous worship. Although they may not yet have received many details of God's requirements for worship, they had been clearly told that idolatry was not acceptable.

32:1 Notice the stark contrast between the unbelief expressed here and the faith previously professed at the sea (14:31).

32:4 calf. The bull as a symbol of deity was common in the ancient world. Perhaps a symbol of Apis, the Egyptian bull god, is meant. It would appear that Aaron identified the bull with the Lord, as he declared the day a "festival to the LORD" (v. 5). The people, however, declared, "These are your gods, O Israel, who brought you up out of Egypt." The shout of the people is reported here using the plural verb ("brought . . . up") with the noun *Elohim* ("God" or "gods"). The singular verb is always used with this noun when it refers to God. In gross parody of 20:2, the people were turning to a pantheon of gods, here represented by the bull god, to lead them.

32:5 festival. Perhaps this was represented as the festival to be celebrated at Sinai (3:18). The first, second, third and (possibly) seventh commandments were all violated, but the emphasis was upon the second. The golden calf signified the people's determination to have God on their own terms. The symbol of God's presence that they were demanding was at that very moment being given to Moses on the mountain. See *WLC* 109; *WSC* 51.

32:6 indulge in revelry. The people then rose from their meal to

7 Then the LORD said to Moses, "Go down, because your people, whom you brought
up out of Egypt,[b] have become corrupt.[c] 8 They have been quick to turn away from what
I commanded them and have made themselves an idol[d] cast in the shape of a calf. They
have bowed down to it and sacrificed[e] to it and have said, 'These are your gods, O Israel, who brought you up out of Egypt.'[f]
9 "I have seen these people," the LORD said to Moses, "and they are a stiff-necked[g] people. 10 Now leave me alone so that my anger may burn against them and that I may destroy them. Then I will make you into a great nation."[h]
11 But Moses sought the favor[i] of the LORD his God. "O LORD," he said, "why should your
anger burn against your people, whom you brought out of Egypt with great power and a
mighty hand?[j] 12 Why should the Egyptians say, 'It was with evil intent that he brought
them out, to kill them in the mountains and to wipe them off the face of the earth'?[k] Turn
from your fierce anger; relent and do not bring disaster on your people. 13 Remember[l] your
servants Abraham, Isaac and Israel, to whom you swore by your own self:[m] 'I will make
your descendants as numerous as the stars[n] in the sky and I will give your descendants
all this land[o] I promised them, and it will be their inheritance forever.' " 14 Then the LORD
relented[p] and did not bring on his people the disaster he had threatened.
15 Moses turned and went down the mountain with the two tablets of the Testimony[q]
in his hands.[r] They were inscribed on both sides, front and back. 16 The tablets were the
work of God; the writing was the writing of God, engraved on the tablets.[s]
17 When Joshua heard the noise of the people shouting, he said to Moses, "There is
the sound of war in the camp."
18 Moses replied:

"It is not the sound of victory,
it is not the sound of defeat;
it is the sound of singing that I hear."

19 When Moses approached the camp and saw the calf[t] and the dancing, his anger
burned and he threw the tablets out of his hands, breaking them to pieces[u] at the foot
of the mountain. 20 And he took the calf they had made and burned it in the fire; then he
ground it to powder, scattered it on the water[v] and made the Israelites drink it.
21 He said to Aaron, "What did these people do to you, that you led them into such
great sin?"
22 "Do not be angry, my lord," Aaron answered. "You know how prone these people
are to evil.[w] 23 They said to me, 'Make us gods who will go before us. As for this fellow
Moses who brought us up out of Egypt, we don't know what has happened to him.'[x] 24 So
I told them, 'Whoever has any gold jewelry, take it off.' Then they gave me the gold, and
I threw it into the fire, and out came this calf!"[y]
25 Moses saw that the people were running wild and that Aaron had let them get out of
control and so become a laughingstock to their enemies. 26 So he stood at the entrance to
the camp and said, "Whoever is for the LORD, come to me." And all the Levites rallied to him.

32:7 [b]ver 4,11 [c]Ge 6:11-12; Dt 9:12
32:8 [d]Ex 20:4 [e]Ex 22:20 [f]1Ki 12:28
32:9 [g]Ex 33:3,5; 34:9; Isa 48:4; Ac 7:51
32:10 [h]Nu 14:12; Dt 9:14
32:11 [i]Dt 9:18 [j]Dt 9:26
32:12 [k]Nu 14:13-16; Dt 9:28
32:13 [l]Ex 2:24 [m]Ge 22:16; Heb 6:13 [n]Ge 15:5; 26:4 [o]Ge 12:7
32:14 [p]2Sa 24:16; Ps 106:45
32:15 [q]Ex 31:18 [r]Dt 9:15
32:16 [s]Ex 31:18
32:19 [t]Dt 9:16 [u]Dt 9:17
32:20 [v]Dt 9:21
32:22 [w]Dt 9:24
32:23 [x]ver 1
32:24 [y]ver 4

---

what may have been sexual immorality (Ge 26:8; 39:14,17). This activity was in stark contrast to the holy meal (24:11).
32:7–29 Moses confronted the idolaters and imposed the divine punishment. Through Moses' intercession, Israel as a whole was not destroyed, but the people's idol was pulverized. Aaron's lame excuse for the escapade (vv. 22–24) was a vain effort to conceal the weakness of the Levitical priesthood (cf. Heb 5:2–3; 9:7).
32:7 your people. God was so enraged against Israel that he spoke of disowning his people and sarcastically attributed the exodus to Moses. But Moses refused to accept this explanation (v. 11).
32:8 See *WLC* 109; *WSC* 51.
32:10 leave me alone. Anticipating Moses' intercession, God proposed to destroy the obstinate, wicked apostates and to make a new nation of Moses. If he were to have done so, God would not have been setting aside his promises to Abraham, Isaac and Jacob, for Moses was their descendant (Ge 12:2; 26:4; 28:14). Even so, such a move would have been devastating and certainly was not anticipated in God's promises.
32:11 Moses rejected God's offer (v. 10). He pleaded with God, begging him to continue to own Israel as his people, for the honor of God's name and in faithfulness to his promises to the patriarchs (v. 13).
32:13 Israel. The normal sequence would have employed the name Jacob (2:24; 3:6,15,16; 4:5; 6:3,8; 33:1), but Moses substituted "Israel" (Jacob's new name; Ge 32:28) to emphasize that the entire nation of Israel was heir to the promises made to the patriarchs.
32:14 relented. Moses' prayer was eternally and immutably decreed by God. Yet God used this prayer to bring about a change in his own attitude toward his people. The Lord graciously decided to follow a different course of action, one in which judgment would be severe but only temporary, not disastrous and final. See verse 34 and its note.
32:16 work of God . . . writing of God. Attention is emphatically drawn to the divine origin of the tablets that would soon be smashed.
32:18 sound. Moses replied in a short, graphic poem with a threefold use of the word for "singing." The poem literally reads, "Not the sound of singing victory; not the sound of singing defeat; but the sound of singing I hear."
32:19 breaking them to pieces. The broken tablets powerfully pictured the broken covenant.
32:20 burned it. Perhaps the calf was made of wood, with a golden overlay. The Israelites were forced to drink their sin as a sign that they would have to bear it (cf. the water of bitterness that later was to be drunk by an adulteress [Nu 5:18–22]). Israel had been unfaithful to the Lord, her husband.
32:21–24 these people. Aaron's defense follows. He blamed the people for his own unfaithfulness and even suggested a miraculous origin for the calf. Aaron's conduct throughout this episode suggests that the Levitical priesthood was destined for failure from its inception.
32:26 Whoever is for the LORD. That is, whoever is the Lord's on

27Then he said to them, "This is what the LORD, the God of Israel, says: 'Each man
strap a sword to his side. Go back and forth through the camp from one end to the other, each killing his brother and friend and neighbor.' "[z] 28The Levites did as Moses commanded, and that day about three thousand of the people died. 29Then Moses said, "You
have been set apart to the LORD today, for you were against your own sons and brothers, and he has blessed you this day."

30The next day Moses said to the people, "You have committed a great sin.[a] But now
I will go up to the LORD; perhaps I can make atonement[b] for your sin."

31So Moses went back to the LORD and said, "Oh, what a great sin these people have
committed![c] They have made themselves gods of gold.[d] 32But now, please forgive their
sin—but if not, then blot me[e] out of the book[f] you have written."

33The LORD replied to Moses, "Whoever has sinned against me I will blot out[g] of my
book. 34Now go, lead the people to the place[h] I spoke of, and my angel[i] will go before
you. However, when the time comes for me to punish,[j] I will punish them for their sin."

35And the LORD struck the people with a plague because of what they did with the
calf[k] Aaron had made.

33 Then the LORD said to Moses, "Leave this place, you and the people you brought
up out of Egypt, and go up to the land I promised on oath to Abraham, Isaac and
Jacob, saying, 'I will give it to your descendants.'[l] 2I will send an angel[m] before you and
drive out the Canaanites, Amorites, Hittites, Perizzites, Hivites and Jebusites.[n] 3Go up to
the land flowing with milk and honey.[o] But I will not go with you, because you are a stiff-
necked[p] people and I might destroy[q] you on the way."

4When the people heard these distressing words, they began to mourn[r] and no one
put on any ornaments. 5For the LORD had said to Moses, "Tell the Israelites, 'You are a
stiff-necked people. If I were to go with you even for a moment, I might destroy you. Now
take off your ornaments and I will decide what to do with you.' " 6So the Israelites
stripped off their ornaments at Mount Horeb.

The Tent of Meeting

7Now Moses used to take a tent and pitch it outside the camp some distance away,
calling it the "tent of meeting."[s] Anyone inquiring of the LORD would go to the tent of
meeting outside the camp. 8And whenever Moses went out to the tent, all the people rose
and stood at the entrances to their tents,[t] watching Moses until he entered the tent. 9As
Moses went into the tent, the pillar of cloud[u] would come down and stay at the entrance,
while the LORD spoke[v] with Moses. 10Whenever the people saw the pillar of cloud stand-

32:27 [z]Nu 25:3,5; Dt 33:9
32:30 [a]1Sa 12:20 [b]Lev 1:4; Nu 25:13
32:31 [c]Dt 9:18 [d]Ex 20:23
32:32 [e]Ro 9:3 [f]Ps 69:28; Da 12:1; Php 4:3; Rev 3:5; 21:27
32:33 [g]Dt 29:20; Ps 9:5
32:34 [h]Ex 3:17 [i]Ex 23:20 [j]Dt 32:35; Ps 99:8; Ro 2:5-6
32:35 [k]ver 4
33:1 [l]Ge 12:7
33:2 [m]Ex 32:34 [n]Ex 23:27-31; Jos 24:11
33:3 [o]Ex 3:8 [p]Ex 32:9 [q]Ex 32:10
33:4 [r]Nu 14:39
33:7 [s]Ex 29:42-43
33:8 [t]Nu 16:27
33:9 [u]Ex 13:21 [v]Ex 31:18; Ps 99:7

---

the Lord's terms. Only the Levites, Moses' own tribe, answered his call to arms to put down the rebellion. We are not told how the Levites identified the apostates. They were prepared, however, to use God's sword of judgment against neighbors or even family members.
32:29 set apart. Literally, "fill the hand." See note on 29:9.
▪ **32:30—33:23** *God's Threat and Moses' Intercession.* In view of the Israelites' idolatry, God proposed to withdraw from them, lest he destroy them for their stubbornness. Upon Moses' intercession, however, he retracted this plan.
32:30 I will go up to the LORD. Although the rebellion had been put down, the guilt of Israel's sin still loomed. Moses again had to leave Israel and climb the mountain to meet the Lord.
32:32 blot me out of the book. As there was a register of Israel (cf. Nu 1:1–2), so God himself has a register of his people (Ps 56:8; Isa 4:3; Mal 3:16). If God would not forgive his people, Moses, far from desiring their replacement (v. 10), would ask to be cut off from God in their place. Compare the apostle Paul's plea (Ro 9:3).
32:33 Whoever has sinned. Moses could not atone for a sin of which he was not guilty—only God could do that. Israel's punishment was presented as certain but undefined.
32:34 I will punish them. The whole generation, save the remnant, eventually died in the wilderness.
32:35 plague. This direct judgment of God was added to the sword of the Levites. Although God did not cast off the Israelites as his covenant people, he cursed them with a plague. Additional punishments followed later.
33:1 Leave this place. The Israelites were to continue their march to the promised land, but without the Lord in their midst. **you brought up.** The word "you" suggests that God absolved himself of responsibility for Israel since his people had broken the covenant. They were instead the people Moses had brought up.
33:2 an angel. There is no sharp contrast between the Lord and the angel here, for the angel who was to go before Israel had already been identified with the Lord: God's name was in him (23:20–23). The angel, no less than the Lord, judged sin (23:21). The person of the angel would not make God's holiness less threatening to this "stiff-necked people" (v. 3). The key, then, to understanding God's proposal is in verse 3, which literally says, "I will not go in the midst of you." At issue was God's dwelling in their midst (29:44–46). If God were not to dwell in Israel's midst, but to go before her in his angel, then there was no point in Israel's building the tabernacle; indeed, Israel could "leave this place" (v. 1) without constructing God's house. God's promise would be kept—he would drive out the Canaanites and give his people the land—but he would not be the Lord who dwelled among them. Instead, another arrangement, one already in operation (described in vv. 7–11), would be continued. God would meet with Moses and with inquiring Israelites at a tent "outside the camp some distance away" (v. 7). This "tent of meeting" (v. 7) was not God's dwelling; Joshua lived there (v. 11). God only came to the entrance of the tent in the pillar of cloud to speak with Moses (vv. 9–10).
33:4 mourn. One might think that the Israelites would rejoice at the prospect of receiving their inheritance in the land without the threat of God's immediate presence. The Lord would still be available for consultation (v. 7). But at God's command, the people stripped off their ornaments and mourned as at a funeral. And well they should have, for no longer would Israel be a nation of priests, enjoying immediate fellowship with God (19:3–6; 29:45–46). This was the great crisis of the story of the exodus.
33:5 take off your ornaments. The people were to be stripped of the festive dress associated with idolatry (cf. Ge 35:4) and reduced to the state of mourners. But this was remorse, not true repentance. They were, and would continue to be, a stubborn people. Still, there was a note of hope in the words "I will decide what to do with you."
33:7 used to take a tent. The verbal forms are continuous, pointing to the customary practice during this period at Sinai. **outside . . . some distance away . . . outside.** The absence of God from the camp is emphasized. He was not in Israel's midst.

ing at the entrance to the tent, they all stood and worshiped, each at the entrance to his
tent. 11 The LORD would speak to Moses face to face,[w] as a man speaks with his friend.
Then Moses would return to the camp, but his young aide Joshua son of Nun did not
leave the tent.

Moses and the Glory of the LORD

12 Moses said to the LORD, "You have been telling me, 'Lead these people,'[x] but you
have not let me know whom you will send with me. You have said, 'I know you by name[y]
and you have found favor with me.' 13 If you are pleased with me, teach me your ways[z]
so I may know you and continue to find favor with you. Remember that this nation is
your people."[a]
14 The LORD replied, "My Presence[b] will go with you, and I will give you rest."[c]
15 Then Moses said to him, "If your Presence does not go with us, do not send us up
from here. 16 How will anyone know that you are pleased with me and with your people
unless you go with us?[d] What else will distinguish me and your people from all the other people on the face of the earth?"[e]
17 And the LORD said to Moses, "I will do the very thing you have asked, because I am
pleased with you and I know you by name."
18 Then Moses said, "Now show me your glory."
19 And the LORD said, "I will cause all my goodness to pass in front of you, and I will
proclaim my name, the LORD, in your presence. I will have mercy on whom I will have
mercy, and I will have compassion on whom I will have compassion.[f] 20 But," he said,
"you cannot see my face, for no one may see[g] me and live."
21 Then the LORD said, "There is a place near me where you may stand on a rock.
22 When my glory passes by, I will put you in a cleft in the rock and cover you with my
hand[h] until I have passed by. 23 Then I will remove my hand and you will see my back;
but my face must not be seen."

The New Stone Tablets

34 The LORD said to Moses, "Chisel out two stone tablets like the first ones, and I
will write on them the words that were on the first tablets,[i] which you broke.[j]
2 Be ready in the morning, and then come up on Mount Sinai.[k] Present yourself to me
there on top of the mountain. 3 No one is to come with you or be seen anywhere on the
mountain;[l] not even the flocks and herds may graze in front of the mountain."
4 So Moses chiseled out two stone tablets like the first ones and went up Mount Sinai
early in the morning, as the LORD had commanded him; and he carried the two stone tablets in his hands. 5 Then the LORD came down in the cloud and stood there with him and

33:11 [w]Nu 12:8; Dt 34:10
33:12 [x]Ex 3:10 [y]ver 17; Jn 10:14-15; 2Ti 2:19
33:13 [z]Ps 25:4; 86:11; 119:33 [a]Ex 34:9; Dt 9:26,29
33:14 [b]Isa 63:9 [c]Jos 21:44; 22:4
33:16 [d]Nu 14:14 [e]Ex 34:10
33:19 [f]Ro 9:15*
33:20 [g]Ge 32:30; Isa 6:5
33:22 [h]Ps 91:4
34:1 [i]Dt 10:2,4 [j]Ex 32:19
34:2 [k]Ex 19:11
34:3 [l]Ex 19:12-13,21

33:12 Moses said to the LORD. Moses responded to the dismaying threat of verses 1–3. He could not argue that Israel was not stiff-necked or that the golden calf was an uncharacteristic aberration. He could only plead God's grace. He did so by asking precisely for what the Lord was threatening to withdraw: his presence. Moses' request was expressed in three forms: Moses asked God to show him his ways so that he could know him (vv. 12–13), to maintain his presence with them (vv. 15–16) and to show him his glory (v. 18). **you have not let me know whom you will send with me.** Moses implied his objection to the angel's presence acting as a surrogate for God himself. This inquiry was not different in substance from his request to know God (v. 13). **You have said.** God had declared his electing knowledge of Moses (32:10; 33:11) and would repeat that assurance expressly (v. 17). Because the Lord knew Moses, Moses would know the Lord. God knew Moses by name—personally and intimately—and Moses would likewise know the Lord by name (34:5; see also 3:13).

33:13 your ways. Moses would know the Lord himself and his purposes for Israel. **your people.** God had not yet decided what to do with Israel. Moses interceded in the confidence that the Lord who had revealed his grace to him would also remember Israel.

33:14 Presence. Literally, "face." This referred to God's intimate presence. **give you rest.** The use of the singular pronoun "you" means that the promise of 3:13–15 for all Israel was now repeated for Moses alone.

33:15 with us. Moses prayed for God's presence with "us," linking Israel with himself. If God chose not to go with his people by dwelling among them, it would be useless for them to proceed to the land of promise. The goal was not milk and honey in Canaan, but a holy land where God would dwell with his people.

33:16 distinguish. God's presence made Israel distinct, and she would only remain so if his presence continued to be with her. Moses sought God's good pleasure for Israel as well as for himself.

33:17 I am pleased with you. God agreed to include Israel for Moses' sake; Israel was dependent upon Moses as mediator. Moses' intercession reveals him to be a type of Christ, the new covenant Mediator.

33:18–20 See theological article "The Glory of God" at Ezekiel 1.

33:18 show me your glory. As the Lord had sealed his covenant with Israel by revealing himself (24:9–11), so Moses would now seek a further revelation of God in his glory. His only hope for God's continuing mercy to Israel lay in God himself. Tasting God's mercy, Moses yearned for a full disclosure (Jn 14:8).

33:19 my goodness to pass in front of you. The full glory of God was more than Moses could bear (v. 20; cf. 40:34–35). But God's glory would pass before Moses, whose eyes would be shielded by God's hand, and Moses would see only God's back. **I will proclaim my name.** God's person and nature were revealed to Moses in his name. God, the "I AM" Lord (3:14), is sovereign in his purposes of mercy (Ro 9:14–16).

33:23 my back. The Lord's goodness withheld what Moses could not bear and revealed all that he could bear. In Jesus Christ the glory withheld from Moses is displayed to believers (Jn 1:14,18; 2Co 3:18) through the Spirit.

■ **34:1–35** *Renewal of the Covenant.* After the terrible events surrounding Israel's failure in worship, Moses led the people in renewing their commitment to their covenant with God.

34:1–4 See *WLC* 98.

34:1 two stone tablets. The replacement of the tablets signals the renewal of the covenant.

34:2 come up on Mount Sinai. The Exodus 19 encounter was to be repeated, but this time with Moses only.

34:5–8 See *WCF* 2.1; *WSC* 4; *HC* 10,11,122.

34:5 the LORD came down. Here is the revelation that was prom-

proclaimed his name, the LORD.[m] 6And he passed in front of Moses, proclaiming, "The
LORD, the LORD, the compassionate[n] and gracious God, slow to anger,[o] abounding in
love[p] and faithfulness,[q] 7maintaining love to thousands,[r] and forgiving wickedness, rebellion and sin.[s] Yet he does not leave the guilty unpunished;[t] he punishes the children
and their children for the sin of the fathers to the third and fourth generation."
8Moses bowed to the ground at once and worshiped. 9"O Lord, if I have found favor
in your eyes," he said, "then let the Lord go with us.[u] Although this is a stiff-necked people, forgive our wickedness and our sin, and take us as your inheritance."[v]
10Then the LORD said: "I am making a covenant[w] with you. Before all your people I will
do wonders never before done in any nation in all the world.[x] The people you live
among will see how awesome is the work that I, the LORD, will do for you. 11Obey what
I command you today. I will drive out before you the Amorites, Canaanites, Hittites, Perizzites, Hivites and Jebusites.[y] 12Be careful not to make a treaty with those who live in
the land where you are going, or they will be a snare[z] among you. 13Break down their
altars, smash their sacred stones and cut down their Asherah poles.[a][a] 14Do not worship
any other god,[b] for the LORD, whose name is Jealous, is a jealous God.[c]
15"Be careful not to make a treaty with those who live in the land; for when they prostitute[d] themselves to their gods and sacrifice to them, they will invite you and you will
eat their sacrifices.[e] 16And when you choose some of their daughters as wives[f] for your
sons and those daughters prostitute themselves to their gods,[g] they will lead your sons
to do the same.
17"Do not make cast idols.[h]
18"Celebrate the Feast of Unleavened Bread.[i] For seven days eat bread made without
yeast,[j] as I commanded you. Do this at the appointed time in the month of Abib,[k] for in
that month you came out of Egypt.
19"The first offspring[l] of every womb belongs to me, including all the firstborn males
of your livestock, whether from herd or flock. 20Redeem the firstborn donkey with a lamb,
but if you do not redeem it, break its neck.[m] Redeem all your firstborn sons.
"No one is to appear before me empty-handed.[n]
21"Six days you shall labor, but on the seventh day you shall rest;[o] even during the
plowing season and harvest you must rest.
22"Celebrate the Feast of Weeks with the firstfruits of the wheat harvest, and the Feast
of Ingathering[p] at the turn of the year.[b] 23Three times[q] a year all your men are to appear
before the Sovereign LORD, the God of Israel. 24I will drive out nations[r] before you and
enlarge your territory, and no one will covet your land when you go up three times each
year to appear before the LORD your God.
25"Do not offer the blood of a sacrifice to me along with anything containing yeast,[s]
and do not let any of the sacrifice from the Passover Feast remain until morning.[t]
26"Bring the best of the firstfruits of your soil to the house of the LORD your God.
"Do not cook a young goat in its mother's milk."[u]
27Then the LORD said to Moses, "Write[v] down these words, for in accordance with

34:5 [m]Ex 33:19
34:6 [n]Ps 86:15 [o]Nu 14:18; Ro 2:4 [p]Ne 9:17; Ps 103:8; Joel 2:13 [q]Ps 108:4
34:7 [r]Ex 20:6 [s]Ps 103:3; 130:4,8; Da 9:9; 1Jn 1:9 [t]Job 10:14; Na 1:3
34:9 [u]Ex 33:15 [v]Ps 33:12
34:10 [w]Dt 5:2-3 [x]Ex 33:16; Dt 4:32
34:11 [y]Ex 33:2
34:12 [z]Ex 23:32-33
34:13 [a]Ex 23:24; Dt 12:3; 2Ki 18:4
34:14 [b]Ex 20:3 [c]Ex 20:5; Dt 4:24
34:15 [d]Jdg 2:17 [e]Nu 25:2; 1Co 8:4
34:16 [f]Dt 7:3 [g]1Ki 11:4
34:17 [h]Ex 32:8
34:18 [i]Ex 12:17 [j]Ex 12:15 [k]Ex 12:2
34:19 [l]Ex 13:2
34:20 [m]Ex 13:13,15 [n]Ex 23:15; Dt 16:16
34:21 [o]Ex 20:9; Lk 13:14
34:22 [p]Ex 23:16
34:23 [q]Ex 23:14
34:24 [r]Ex 23:28; 33:2; Ps 78:55
34:25 [s]Ex 23:18 [t]Ex 12:8, 10
34:26 [u]Ex 23:19
34:27 [v]Ex 17:14; 24:4

[a] *13* That is, symbols of the goddess Asherah [b] *22* That is, in the fall

ised in 33:19–23: Yahweh passed by and proclaimed his name. Moses received an overwhelming answer to his prayer. God's own glory showed his compassion and grace.

34:6 the compassionate and gracious God. These are the famous 13 attributes of Israelite tradition (Nu 14:18; Ne 9:17; Pss 86:15; 103:8; 145:8; Joel 2:13; Jnh 4:2; Na 1:3). God's mercy was still proclaimed for Israel despite her dismal failure (Ge 8:21–22; Hos 11:8). **abounding in love and faithfulness.** God's love is revealed in his devotion to his people (see note on 15:13). His faithfulness reveals his integrity; he is true to his Name and his promises of mercy, but also to his judgment on sin (v. 7). Because of God's love and faithfulness, he would not abandon his people, but would dwell among them in his tabernacle. John cited this context in his Gospel: "The Word became flesh and made his dwelling [literally, 'tabernacled'] among us. We have seen his glory . . . full of grace and truth" (Jn 1:14). See *WLC* 7.

34:9 go with us. Literally, "go in the midst of us." This was what the Lord had said he would not do because the people were too sinful, too "stiff-necked" (33:3,5). Now Moses gave this as the reason for the presence of the merciful God. In effect, he was saying, "Let the Lord of grace dwell in his tabernacle among his people and forgive our wickedness and our sin." Then came the amazing petition: "Take us as your inheritance." It was not, "Give us our inheritance in the land" (33:2–3), but rather, "Take us as your treasured possession in your faithful love" (19:5).

34:10–35 The Lord renewed his covenant with Israel.

34:10 do wonders. God promised his mighty acts for Israel as he renewed his covenant.

34:11–16 God warned against apostate practices. The selection of cultic laws here points to the area in which Israel had sinned or was weak. Singular pronouns are used almost totally throughout, for God was making his covenant with Moses and with Israel through Moses (v. 27). As in chapters 19–20, Moses alone ascended the mountain and God came down. God announced what he would do and made a covenant on the basis of his words.

34:13–14 See *WLC* 110; *WSC* 52; *HC* 97.

34:13 Asherah. The name of the Canaanite goddess of fertility. **poles.** Cult objects representing Asherah, such as sacred trees or poles that stood beside the Baal altars (cf. Jdg 6:25). Israel was not to be compromised by the worship of pagan peoples in the land.

34:14–17 any other god. The theme continues with allusions to the first (vv. 14–16) and second commandments (v. 17). God began at the point of Israel's sin and with the Decalogue that his people had violated.

34:16–17 See *WCF* 24.3; *HC* 97.

34:18–26 This section parallels the laws in the Book of the Covenant (23:14–19). See *WLC* 121.

34:27 these words. That is, the stipulations of verses 12–26. See *BC* 3.

these words I have made a covenant with you and with Israel." 28Moses was there with
the LORD forty days and forty nights[w] without eating bread or drinking water. And he
wrote on the tablets[x] the words of the covenant—the Ten Commandments.[y]

The Radiant Face of Moses

29When Moses came down from Mount Sinai with the two tablets of the Testimony
in his hands,[z] he was not aware that his face was radiant[a] because he had spoken with
the LORD. 30When Aaron and all the Israelites saw Moses, his face was radiant, and they
were afraid to come near him. 31But Moses called to them; so Aaron and all the leaders
of the community came back to him, and he spoke to them. 32Afterward all the Israelites came near him, and he gave them all the commands[b] the LORD had given him on
Mount Sinai.

33When Moses finished speaking to them, he put a veil[c] over his face. 34But whenever he entered the LORD's presence to speak with him, he removed the veil until he came
out. And when he came out and told the Israelites what he had been commanded, 35they
saw that his face was radiant. Then Moses would put the veil back over his face until he
went in to speak with the LORD.

Sabbath Regulations

35 Moses assembled the whole Israelite community and said to them, "These are
the things the LORD has commanded[d] you to do: 2For six days, work is to be
done, but the seventh day shall be your holy day, a Sabbath[e] of rest to the LORD. Whoever does any work on it must be put to death. 3Do not light a fire in any of your dwellings on the Sabbath day.[f]"

Materials for the Tabernacle

4Moses said to the whole Israelite community, "This is what the LORD has commanded: 5From what you have, take an offering for the LORD. Everyone who is willing is to bring
to the LORD an offering of gold, silver and bronze; 6blue, purple and scarlet yarn and fine
linen; goat hair; 7ram skins dyed red and hides of sea cows[a]; acacia wood; 8olive oil for
the light; spices for the anointing oil and for the fragrant incense; 9and onyx stones and
other gems to be mounted on the ephod and breastpiece.

10"All who are skilled among you are to come and make everything the LORD has commanded:[g] 11the tabernacle[h] with its tent and its covering, clasps, frames, crossbars,
posts and bases; 12the ark[i] with its poles and the atonement cover and the curtain that
shields it; 13the table[j] with its poles and all its articles and the bread of the Presence;
14the lampstand[k] that is for light with its accessories, lamps and oil for the light; 15the
altar[l] of incense with its poles, the anointing oil[m] and the fragrant incense;[n] the curtain
for the doorway at the entrance to the tabernacle; 16the altar[o] of burnt offering with its
bronze grating, its poles and all its utensils; the bronze basin with its stand; 17the curtains of the courtyard with its posts and bases, and the curtain for the entrance to the

34:28 [w]Ge 7:4; Ex 24:18; Mt 4:2 [x]ver 1; Ex 31:18 [y]Dt 4:13; 10:4
34:29 [z]Ex 32:15 [a]Ps 34:5; Mt 17:2; 2Co 3:7, 13
34:32 [b]Ex 24:3
34:33 [c]2Co 3:13
35:1 [d]Ex 34:32
35:2 [e]Ex 20:9-10; 34:21; Lev 23:3
35:3 [f]Ex 16:23
35:10 [g]Ex 31:6
35:11 [h]Ex 26:1-37
35:12 [i]Ex 25:10-22
35:13 [j]Ex 25:23-30; Lev 24:5-6
35:14 [k]Ex 25:31
35:15 [l]Ex 30:1-6 [m]Ex 30:25 [n]Ex 30:34-38
35:16 [o]Ex 27:1-8

[a] 7 That is, dugongs; also in verse 23

34:28 he wrote. The Lord himself seems to be intended (v. 1).
34:29 was radiant. Literally, "sent out horns (of light?)." Although the Hebrew root usually refers to horns, it would seem that rays are in view here (cf. Hab 3:4). Moses' leadership was reestablished by the reflected light of God's glory.
34:30 they were afraid to come near him. The reaction of fear suggests the events of chapters 19–20. Only when the people drew near to Moses and conversed with him without harm were they reassured.
34:33 put a veil over his face. Only after Moses had finished speaking did he veil his face. In communicating God's words, he had to speak with open face (i.e., without a veil), and from that face God's reflected glory shone (see 2Co 3:12—4:6). So, too, Moses received revelation without a veil. The position of Moses as mediator was heightened by the covenant renewal, pointing to the need of a Mediator greater than Moses. As the Israelites reading this account were to respond to Moses, so new covenant believers should respond to Christ, the final and ultimate Mediator.
■ **35:1—40:38** *The Construction of the Tabernacle.* In accordance with the instructions given earlier (see 25:1—31:18), these chapters relate the actual building of the tabernacle. The crisis was past; construction could go forward. The details are recorded with precision in order to demonstrate that the tabernacle was built exactly to the stated specifications. These chapters divide into three main parts: gathering materials (35:1—36:7), the construction of the tabernacle (36:8—39:43) and the erection of the tabernacle (40:1–38).
■ **35:1—36:7** *The Preparations.* Moses led the Israelites in gathering materials for construction. These verses divide into three parts: Moses' call to collect offerings (35:1–19), the offerings themselves (35:20–29) and the craftsmen (35:30—36:7).
■ **35:1–19** *The Call to Contribute.* Moses called a national assembly and asked for contributions for the construction of the tabernacle.
35:1–3 The work started with an admonition to keep the Sabbath, just as the early instruction for the work (31:12–18) had concluded with such a reminder. The construction of the tabernacle was central to Israel's fulfillment of this commandment.
35:4—36:7 Israel responded to the call for materials to build the tabernacle.
35:5–9 gold, silver . . . acacia wood . . . onyx stones and other gems. Bezalel, Oholiab and their skilled coworkers on the tabernacle worked with building materials brought by the rest of the Israelite community. In a similar way, Paul, Apollos and their coworkers on the new covenant temple, the church, worked with building materials already present among the Christian community (1Co 3:10,12). In the context of the old covenant, the building materials were lifeless things. In the context of the new covenant, however, they were living persons, a fact made clear by Christ's identification as the foundation stone (1Co 3:11; Eph 2:20) and the church's identification as "living stones" (1Pe 2:4–5; cf. Eph 2:21–22).

courtyard;[p] 18the tent pegs for the tabernacle and for the courtyard, and their ropes;
19the woven garments worn for ministering in the sanctuary—both the sacred garments[q] for Aaron the priest and the garments for his sons when they serve as priests."
20Then the whole Israelite community withdrew from Moses' presence, 21and everyone who was willing and whose heart moved him came and brought an offering to the
LORD for the work on the Tent of Meeting, for all its service, and for the sacred garments.
22All who were willing, men and women alike, came and brought gold jewelry of all
kinds: brooches, earrings, rings and ornaments. They all presented their gold as a wave
offering to the LORD. 23Everyone who had blue, purple or scarlet yarn[r] or fine linen, or
goat hair, ram skins dyed red or hides of sea cows brought them. 24Those presenting an
offering of silver or bronze brought it as an offering to the LORD, and everyone who had
acacia wood for any part of the work brought it. 25Every skilled woman[s] spun with her
hands and brought what she had spun—blue, purple or scarlet yarn or fine linen. 26And
all the women who were willing and had the skill spun the goat hair. 27The leaders[t]
brought onyx stones and other gems to be mounted on the ephod and breastpiece.
28They also brought spices and olive oil for the light and for the anointing oil and for the
fragrant incense.[u] 29All the Israelite men and women who were willing[v] brought to the
LORD freewill offerings[w] for all the work the LORD through Moses had commanded them
to do.

Bezalel and Oholiab

30Then Moses said to the Israelites, "See, the LORD has chosen Bezalel son of Uri, the
son of Hur, of the tribe of Judah, 31and he has filled him with the Spirit of God, with skill,
ability and knowledge in all kinds of crafts[x]— 32to make artistic designs for work in gold,
silver and bronze, 33to cut and set stones, to work in wood and to engage in all kinds of
artistic craftsmanship. 34And he has given both him and Oholiab[y] son of Ahisamach, of
the tribe of Dan, the ability to teach[z] others. 35He has filled them with skill to do all kinds
of work[a] as craftsmen, designers, embroiderers in blue, purple and scarlet yarn and fine
36 linen, and weavers—all of them master craftsmen and designers. 1So Bezalel,
Oholiab and every skilled person[b] to whom the LORD has given skill and ability
to know how to carry out all the work of constructing the sanctuary[c] are to do the work
just as the LORD has commanded."
2Then Moses summoned Bezalel[d] and Oholiab[e] and every skilled person to whom the
LORD had given ability and who was willing[f] to come and do the work. 3They received
from Moses all the offerings[g] the Israelites had brought to carry out the work of constructing the sanctuary. And the people continued to bring freewill offerings morning after morning. 4So all the skilled craftsmen who were doing all the work on the sanctuary
left their work 5and said to Moses, "The people are bringing more than enough[h] for doing the work the LORD commanded to be done."
6Then Moses gave an order and they sent this word throughout the camp: "No man
or woman is to make anything else as an offering for the sanctuary." And so the people
were restrained from bringing more, 7because what they already had was more[i] than
enough to do all the work.

The Tabernacle

8All the skilled men among the workmen made the tabernacle with ten curtains of
finely twisted linen and blue, purple and scarlet yarn, with cherubim worked into them
by a skilled craftsman. 9All the curtains were the same size—twenty-eight cubits long and
four cubits wide.[a] 10They joined five of the curtains together and did the same with the
other five. 11Then they made loops of blue material along the edge of the end curtain in

35:17 [p]Ex 27:9
35:19 [q]Ex 28:2; 31:10; 39:1
35:23 [r]1Ch 29:8
35:25 [s]Ex 28:3
35:27 [t]1Ch 29:6; Ezr 2:68
35:28 [u]Ex 25:6
35:29 [v]ver 21; 1Ch 29:9 [w]ver 4-9; Ex 25:1-7; 36:3; 2Ki 12:4
35:31 [x]ver 35; 2Ch 2:7,14
35:34 [y]Ex 31:6 [z]2Ch 2:14
35:35 [a]ver 31; Ex 31:3,6; 1Ki 7:14
36:1 [b]Ex 28:3 [c]Ex 25:8
36:2 [d]Ex 31:2 [e]Ex 31:6 [f]Ex 25:2; 35:21,26; 1Ch 29:5
36:3 [g]Ex 35:29
36:5 [h]2Ch 24:14; 31:10; 2Co 8:2-3
36:7 [i]1Ki 7:47

[a] 9 That is, about 42 feet (about 12.5 meters) long and 6 feet (about 1.8 meters) wide

■ **35:20–29** *Israel's Offerings.* This is an extensive account of the generous contributions that were offered for the tabernacle.
35:22 women. Women are mentioned for the first time in the contexts of both the donation and preparation of materials.
35:29 all the work the LORD through Moses had commanded. The emphasis is twofold. On the one hand, enough was collected to satisfy God's command. On the other hand, this divine command came through Moses. Thus the blessings that would appear (39:32–40:33) would be the result of following the regulations delivered through Moses.
■ **35:30—36:7** *The Craftsmen.* The craftsmen who were going to work on the tabernacle are introduced. They also testified that the Israelites had brought enough materials for the construction (36:5).
■ **36:8—39:43** *The Construction.* The actual work of Bezalel, Oholiab and their crews of skilled laborers is recounted. The detail of the account underscores the attention the builders gave to the word of the Lord. The account divides into six parts: the tabernacle (36:8–38), its furnishings (37:1—38:8), the courtyard (38:9–20), a summary of amounts (38:21–31), the priestly garments (39:1–31) and Moses' blessing on the people for their work (39:32–43).
■ **36:8–38** *The Tabernacle.* The work on the sanctuary and its furnishings was completed according to God's instructions. See note on 26:1–37.

one set, and the same was done with the end curtain in the other set. 12They also made
fifty loops on one curtain and fifty loops on the end curtain of the other set, with the loops
36:13 opposite each other. 13Then they made fifty gold clasps and used them to fasten the two
[j]ver 18 sets of curtains together so that the tabernacle was a unit.[j]

14They made curtains of goat hair for the tent over the tabernacle—eleven altogether. 15All eleven curtains were the same size—thirty cubits long and four cubits wide.[a]
16They joined five of the curtains into one set and the other six into another set. 17Then
they made fifty loops along the edge of the end curtain in one set and also along the edge
36:18 of the end curtain in the other set. 18They made fifty bronze clasps to fasten the tent to-
[k]ver 13 gether as a unit.[k] 19Then they made for the tent a covering of ram skins dyed red, and
over that a covering of hides of sea cows.[b]

20They made upright frames of acacia wood for the tabernacle. 21Each frame was ten
cubits long and a cubit and a half wide,[c] 22with two projections set parallel to each other. They made all the frames of the tabernacle in this way. 23They made twenty frames
for the south side of the tabernacle 24and made forty silver bases to go under them—two
bases for each frame, one under each projection. 25For the other side, the north side of
the tabernacle, they made twenty frames 26and forty silver bases—two under each
frame. 27They made six frames for the far end, that is, the west end of the tabernacle,
28and two frames were made for the corners of the tabernacle at the far end. 29At these
two corners the frames were double from the bottom all the way to the top and fitted into
a single ring; both were made alike. 30So there were eight frames and sixteen silver bases—two under each frame.

31They also made crossbars of acacia wood: five for the frames on one side of the tabernacle, 32five for those on the other side, and five for the frames on the west, at the far
end of the tabernacle. 33They made the center crossbar so that it extended from end to
end at the middle of the frames. 34They overlaid the frames with gold and made gold
36:35 rings to hold the crossbars. They also overlaid the crossbars with gold.
[l]Ex 39:38; 35They made the curtain[l] of blue, purple and scarlet yarn and finely twisted linen,
Mt 27:51; with cherubim worked into it by a skilled craftsman. 36They made four posts of acacia
Lk 23:45; Heb 9:3 wood for it and overlaid them with gold. They made gold hooks for them and cast their
36:37 four silver bases. 37For the entrance to the tent they made a curtain of blue, purple and
[m]Ex 27:16 scarlet yarn and finely twisted linen—the work of an embroiderer;[m] 38and they made five
posts with hooks for them. They overlaid the tops of the posts and their bands with gold
and made their five bases of bronze.

37:1 *The Ark*

[n]Ex 31:2 [o]Ex 30:6; 39:35; Dt 10:3 **37** Bezalel[n] made the ark[o] of acacia wood—two and a half cubits long, a cubit and
37:2 a half wide, and a cubit and a half high.[d] 2He overlaid it with pure gold,[p] both
[p]ver 11,26 inside and out, and made a gold molding around it. 3He cast four gold rings for it and
fastened them to its four feet, with two rings on one side and two rings on the other.
4Then he made poles of acacia wood and overlaid them with gold. 5And he inserted the
37:6 poles into the rings on the sides of the ark to carry it.
[q]Ex 26:34; 31:7; 6He made the atonement cover[q] of pure gold—two and a half cubits long and a cu-
Heb 9:5 bit and a half wide.[e] 7Then he made two cherubim[r] out of hammered gold at the ends
37:7 of the cover. 8He made one cherub on one end and the second cherub on the other; at
[r]Eze 41:18 the two ends he made them of one piece with the cover. 9The cherubim had their wings
37:9 spread upward, overshadowing[s] the cover with them. The cherubim faced each other,
[s]Heb 9:5 [t]Dt 10:3 looking toward the cover.[t]

The Table

37:10
[u]Heb 9:2 10They[f] made the table[u] of acacia wood—two cubits long, a cubit wide, and a cubit
37:11 and a half high.[g] 11Then they overlaid it with pure gold[v] and made a gold molding around
[v]ver 2 it. 12They also made around it a rim a handbreadth[h] wide and put a gold molding on the
rim. 13They cast four gold rings for the table and fastened them to the four corners, where

[a] *15* That is, about 45 feet (about 13.5 meters) long and 6 feet (about 1.8 meters) wide [b] *19* That is, dugongs [c] *21* That is, about 15 feet (about 4.5 meters) long and 2 1/4 feet (about 0.7 meter) wide
[d] *1* That is, about 3 3/4 feet (about 1.1 meters) long and 2 1/4 feet (about 0.7 meter) wide and high
[e] *6* That is, about 3 3/4 feet (about 1.1 meters) long and 2 1/4 feet (about 0.7 meter) wide [f] *10* Or *He;* also in verses 11–29 [g] *10* That is, about 3 feet (about 0.9 meter) long, 1 1/2 feet (about 0.5 meter) wide, and 2 1/4 feet (about 0.7 meter) high [h] *12* That is, about 3 inches (about 8 centimeters)

■ **37:1—38:8** *The Furnishings.* The furnishings of the tabernacle were crafted precisely to God's specifications. See notes on 25:1-9, 27:1–8 and 30:1–10.

the four legs were. 14The rings[w] were put close to the rim to hold the poles used in carrying the table. 15The poles for carrying the table were made of acacia wood and were
overlaid with gold. 16And they made from pure gold the articles for the table—its plates
and dishes and bowls and its pitchers for the pouring out of drink offerings.

The Lampstand

17They made the lampstand[x] of pure gold and hammered it out, base and shaft; its
flowerlike cups, buds and blossoms were of one piece with it. 18Six branches extended
from the sides of the lampstand—three on one side and three on the other. 19Three cups
shaped like almond flowers with buds and blossoms were on one branch, three on the
next branch and the same for all six branches extending from the lampstand. 20And on
the lampstand were four cups shaped like almond flowers with buds and blossoms.
21One bud was under the first pair of branches extending from the lampstand, a second
bud under the second pair, and a third bud under the third pair—six branches in all.
22The buds and the branches were all of one piece with the lampstand, hammered out
of pure gold.[y]

23They made its seven lamps,[z] as well as its wick trimmers and trays, of pure gold.
24They made the lampstand and all its accessories from one talent[a] of pure gold.

The Altar of Incense

25They made the altar of incense[a] out of acacia wood. It was square, a cubit long and
a cubit wide, and two cubits high[b]—its horns[b] of one piece with it. 26They overlaid the
top and all the sides and the horns with pure gold, and made a gold molding around it.
27They made two gold rings[c] below the molding—two on opposite sides—to hold the
poles used to carry it. 28They made the poles of acacia wood and overlaid them with
gold.[d]

29They also made the sacred anointing oil[e] and the pure, fragrant incense[f]—the work
of a perfumer.

The Altar of Burnt Offering

38 They[c] built the altar of burnt offering of acacia wood, three cubits[d] high; it was
square, five cubits long and five cubits wide.[e] 2They made a horn at each of the
four corners, so that the horns and the altar were of one piece, and they overlaid the altar with bronze.[g] 3They made all its utensils[h] of bronze—its pots, shovels, sprinkling
bowls, meat forks and firepans. 4They made a grating for the altar, a bronze network, to
be under its ledge, halfway up the altar. 5They cast bronze rings to hold the poles for the
four corners of the bronze grating. 6They made the poles of acacia wood and overlaid
them with bronze. 7They inserted the poles into the rings so they would be on the sides
of the altar for carrying it. They made it hollow, out of boards.

Basin for Washing

8They made the bronze basin[i] and its bronze stand from the mirrors of the women[j]
who served at the entrance to the Tent of Meeting.

The Courtyard

9Next they made the courtyard. The south side was a hundred cubits[f] long and had
curtains of finely twisted linen, 10with twenty posts and twenty bronze bases, and with
silver hooks and bands on the posts. 11The north side was also a hundred cubits long and
had twenty posts and twenty bronze bases, with silver hooks and bands on the posts.

12The west end was fifty cubits[g] wide and had curtains, with ten posts and ten bases, with silver hooks and bands on the posts. 13The east end, toward the sunrise, was also
fifty cubits wide. 14Curtains fifteen cubits[h] long were on one side of the entrance, with
three posts and three bases, 15and curtains fifteen cubits long were on the other side of
the entrance to the courtyard, with three posts and three bases. 16All the curtains
around the courtyard were of finely twisted linen. 17The bases for the posts were bronze.

37:14 [w]ver 27
37:17 [x]Heb 9:2; Rev 1:12
37:22 [y]ver 17; Nu 8:4
37:23 [z]Ex 40:4,25
37:25 [a]Ex 30:34-36; Lk 1:11; Heb 9:4; Rev 8:3 [b]Ex 27:2; Rev 9:13
37:27 [c]ver 14
37:28 [d]Ex 25:13
37:29 [e]Ex 31:11 [f]Ex 30:1, 25; 39:38
38:2 [g]2Ch 1:5
38:3 [h]Ex 31:9
38:8 [i]Ex 30:18; 40:7 [j]Dt 23:17; 1Sa 2:22; 1Ki 14:24

[a] *24* That is, about 75 pounds (about 34 kilograms) [b] *25* That is, about 1 1/2 feet (about 0.5 meter) long and wide, and about 3 feet (about 0.9 meter) high [c] *1* Or *He*; also in verses 2–9 [d] *1* That is, about 4 1/2 feet (about 1.3 meters) [e] *1* That is, about 7 1/2 feet (about 2.3 meters) long and wide [f] *9* That is, about 150 feet (about 46 meters) [g] *12* That is, about 75 feet (about 23 meters) [h] *14* That is, about 22 1/2 feet (about 6.9 meters)

■ **38:9–20** *The Courtyard.* The courtyard was built in strict compliance with God's directions. See notes on 27:9–19.

The hooks and bands on the posts were silver, and their tops were overlaid with silver; so all the posts of the courtyard had silver bands.

[18]The curtain for the entrance to the courtyard was of blue, purple and scarlet yarn and finely twisted linen—the work of an embroiderer. It was twenty cubits[a] long and, like the curtains of the courtyard, five cubits[b] high, [19]with four posts and four bronze bases. Their hooks and bands were silver, and their tops were overlaid with silver. [20]All the tent pegs[k] of the tabernacle and of the surrounding courtyard were bronze.

The Materials Used

[21]These are the amounts of the materials used for the tabernacle, the tabernacle of the Testimony,[l] which were recorded at Moses' command by the Levites under the direction of Ithamar[m] son of Aaron, the priest. [22](Bezalel[n] son of Uri, the son of Hur, of the tribe of Judah, made everything the LORD commanded Moses; [23]with him was Oholiab[o] son of Ahisamach, of the tribe of Dan—a craftsman and designer, and an embroiderer in blue, purple and scarlet yarn and fine linen.) [24]The total amount of the gold from the wave offering used for all the work on the sanctuary[p] was 29 talents and 730 shekels,[c] according to the sanctuary shekel.[q]

[25]The silver obtained from those of the community who were counted in the census[r] was 100 talents and 1,775 shekels,[d] according to the sanctuary shekel— [26]one beka per person,[s] that is, half a shekel,[e] according to the sanctuary shekel,[t] from everyone who had crossed over to those counted, twenty years old or more,[u] a total of 603,550 men.[v] [27]The 100 talents[f] of silver were used to cast the bases[w] for the sanctuary and for the curtain—100 bases from the 100 talents, one talent for each base. [28]They used the 1,775 shekels[g] to make the hooks for the posts, to overlay the tops of the posts, and to make their bands.

[29]The bronze from the wave offering was 70 talents and 2,400 shekels.[h] [30]They used it to make the bases for the entrance to the Tent of Meeting, the bronze altar with its bronze grating and all its utensils, [31]the bases for the surrounding courtyard and those for its entrance and all the tent pegs for the tabernacle and those for the surrounding courtyard.

The Priestly Garments

39 From the blue, purple and scarlet yarn[x] they made woven garments for ministering in the sanctuary.[y] They also made sacred garments[z] for Aaron, as the LORD commanded Moses.

The Ephod

[2]They[i] made the ephod of gold, and of blue, purple and scarlet yarn, and of finely twisted linen. [3]They hammered out thin sheets of gold and cut strands to be worked into the blue, purple and scarlet yarn and fine linen—the work of a skilled craftsman. [4]They made shoulder pieces for the ephod, which were attached to two of its corners, so it could be fastened. [5]Its skillfully woven waistband was like it—of one piece with the ephod and made with gold, and with blue, purple and scarlet yarn, and with finely twisted linen, as the LORD commanded Moses.

[6]They mounted the onyx stones in gold filigree settings and engraved them like a seal with the names of the sons of Israel. [7]Then they fastened them on the shoulder pieces of the ephod as memorial[a] stones for the sons of Israel, as the LORD commanded Moses.

The Breastpiece

[8]They fashioned the breastpiece[b]—the work of a skilled craftsman. They made it like the ephod: of gold, and of blue, purple and scarlet yarn, and of finely twisted linen. [9]It

38:20 [k]Ex 35:18
38:21 [l]Nu 1:50,53; 8:24; 9:15; 10:11; 17:7; 1Ch 23:32; 2Ch 24:6; Ac 7:44; Rev 15:5 [m]Nu 4:28,33
38:22 [n]Ex 31:2
38:23 [o]Ex 31:6
38:24 [p]Ex 30:16 [q]Ex 30:13; Lev 27:25; Nu 3:47; 18:16
38:25 [r]Ex 30:12
38:26 [s]Ex 30:12 [t]Ex 30:13 [u]Ex 30:14 [v]Ex 12:37; Nu 1:46
38:27 [w]Ex 26:19
39:1 [x]Ex 35:23 [y]Ex 35:19 [z]ver 41; Ex 28:2
39:7 [a]Lev 24:7; Jos 4:7
39:8 [b]Lev 8:8

[a] *18* That is, about 30 feet (about 9 meters) [b] *18* That is, about 7 1/2 feet (about 2.3 meters) [c] *24* The weight of the gold was a little over one ton (about 1 metric ton). [d] *25* The weight of the silver was a little over 3 3/4 tons (about 3.4 metric tons). [e] *26* That is, about 1/5 ounce (about 5.5 grams) [f] *27* That is, about 3 3/4 tons (about 3.4 metric tons) [g] *28* That is, about 45 pounds (about 20 kilograms) [h] *29* The weight of the bronze was about 2 1/2 tons (about 2.4 metric tons). [i] *2* Or *He*; also in verses 7, 8 and 22

■ **38:21–31** *Summary of Amounts.* These verses were probably derived from an official treasurer's report.
38:25 100 talents and 1,775 shekels. Using the recognized 3,000 shekels to the talent, this equals 2,210 pounds of gold (see v. 24), 7,601 pounds of silver (see v. 27) and 5,350 pounds of copper (see v. 29). The amount of silver (a total of 301,175 shekels) is linked to the head count of the Israelites: half a shekel from all males over the age of twenty; i.e., 603,550 men of military age (Nu 1:46).

■ **39:1–31** *The Priestly Garments.* The work on the priestly garments and accessories was completed in conformity to the Lord's descriptions. See notes on 28:6–42.

was square—a span[a] long and a span wide—and folded double. 10Then they mounted
four rows of precious stones on it. In the first row there was a ruby, a topaz and a beryl;
11in the second row a turquoise, a sapphire[b] and an emerald; 12in the third row a jacinth,
an agate and an amethyst; 13in the fourth row a chrysolite, an onyx and a jasper.[c] They
were mounted in gold filigree settings. 14There were twelve stones, one for each of the
names of the sons of Israel, each engraved like a seal with the name of one of the twelve
tribes.[c]
15For the breastpiece they made braided chains of pure gold, like a rope. 16They made
two gold filigree settings and two gold rings, and fastened the rings to two of the corners
of the breastpiece. 17They fastened the two gold chains to the rings at the corners of the
breastpiece, 18and the other ends of the chains to the two settings, attaching them to the
shoulder pieces of the ephod at the front. 19They made two gold rings and attached them
to the other two corners of the breastpiece on the inside edge next to the ephod. 20Then
they made two more gold rings and attached them to the bottom of the shoulder pieces on the front of the ephod, close to the seam just above the waistband of the ephod.
21They tied the rings of the breastpiece to the rings of the ephod with blue cord, connecting it to the waistband so that the breastpiece would not swing out from the ephod—as
the LORD commanded Moses.

Other Priestly Garments

22They made the robe of the ephod entirely of blue cloth—the work of a weaver—
23with an opening in the center of the robe like the opening of a collar,[d] and a band
around this opening, so that it would not tear. 24They made pomegranates of blue, purple and scarlet yarn and finely twisted linen around the hem of the robe. 25And they
made bells of pure gold and attached them around the hem between the pomegranates.
26The bells and pomegranates alternated around the hem of the robe to be worn for ministering, as the LORD commanded Moses.
27For Aaron and his sons, they made tunics of fine linen[d]—the work of a weaver—
28and the turban[e] of fine linen, the linen headbands and the undergarments of finely
twisted linen. 29The sash was of finely twisted linen and blue, purple and scarlet yarn—
the work of an embroiderer—as the LORD commanded Moses.
30They made the plate, the sacred diadem, out of pure gold and engraved on it, like
an inscription on a seal: HOLY TO THE LORD. 31Then they fastened a blue cord to it to attach
it to the turban, as the LORD commanded Moses.

Moses Inspects the Tabernacle

32So all the work on the tabernacle, the Tent of Meeting, was completed. The Israelites did everything just as the LORD commanded Moses.[f] 33Then they brought the tabernacle to Moses: the tent and all its furnishings, its clasps, frames, crossbars, posts and
bases; 34the covering of ram skins dyed red, the covering of hides of sea cows[e] and the
shielding curtain; 35the ark of the Testimony[g] with its poles and the atonement cover;
36the table with all its articles and the bread of the Presence; 37the pure gold lampstand[h]
with its row of lamps and all its accessories, and the oil for the light; 38the gold altar,[i] the
anointing oil, the fragrant incense, and the curtain[j] for the entrance to the tent; 39the
bronze altar with its bronze grating, its poles and all its utensils; the basin with its stand;
40the curtains of the courtyard with its posts and bases, and the curtain for the entrance
to the courtyard;[k] the ropes and tent pegs for the courtyard; all the furnishings for the
tabernacle, the Tent of Meeting; 41and the woven garments worn for ministering in the
sanctuary, both the sacred garments for Aaron the priest and the garments for his sons
when serving as priests.
42The Israelites had done all the work just as the LORD had commanded Moses.[l] 43Mo-
ses inspected the work and saw that they had done it just as the LORD had commanded.
So Moses blessed[m] them.

39:14 [c]Rev 21:12
39:27 [d]Lev 6:10
39:28 [e]Ex 28:4
39:32 [f]ver 42-43; Ex 25:9
39:35 [g]Ex 30:6
39:37 [h]Ex 25:31
39:38 [i]Ex 30:1-10 [j]Ex 36:35
39:40 [k]Ex 27:9-19
39:42 [l]Ex 25:9
39:43 [m]Lev 9:22,23; Nu 6:23-27; 2Sa 6:18; 1Ki 8:14, 55; 2Ch 30:27

a *9* That is, about 9 inches (about 22 centimeters) b *11* Or *lapis lazuli* c *13* The precise identification of some of these precious stones is uncertain. d *23* The meaning of the Hebrew for this word is uncertain. e *34* That is, dugongs

39:30 sacred diadem. Note the mention of the golden plate of Aaron's turban (28:36) as a golden diadem.

■ **39:32–43** *Moses' Blessing.* Moses inspected the work that had been done on the tabernacle, as well as the priestly garments. He was pleased and blessed the people.

39:33 Then they brought . . . to Moses. The finished components were brought to Moses for inspection. Moses determined that all had been constructed to the specifications the Lord had provided.

39:42–43 just as the LORD . . . just as the LORD. The blessing that Moses pronounced, as well as that of divine presence to follow (see 40:1–38), resulted from the Israelites faithfully following the commands of God as they had been given through Moses. Thus the original readers understood the importance of remaining faithful to the tabernacle regulations as they were given through Moses.

Setting Up the Tabernacle

40 Then the LORD said to Moses: 2"Set up the tabernacle, the Tent of Meeting,[n] on
the first day of the first month.[o] 3Place the ark[p] of the Testimony in it and shield
the ark with the curtain. 4Bring in the table and set out what belongs on it.[q] Then bring
in the lampstand[r] and set up its lamps. 5Place the gold altar[s] of incense in front of the
ark of the Testimony and put the curtain at the entrance to the tabernacle.
6"Place the altar of burnt offering in front of the entrance to the tabernacle, the Tent
of Meeting; 7place the basin[t] between the Tent of Meeting and the altar and put water
in it. 8Set up the courtyard around it and put the curtain at the entrance to the courtyard.
9"Take the anointing oil and anoint[u] the tabernacle and everything in it; consecrate
it and all its furnishings, and it will be holy. 10Then anoint the altar of burnt offering and
all its utensils; consecrate[v] the altar, and it will be most holy. 11Anoint the basin and its
stand and consecrate them.
12"Bring Aaron and his sons to the entrance to the Tent of Meeting and wash them
with water.[w] 13Then dress Aaron in the sacred garments,[x] anoint him and consecrate[y]
him so he may serve me as priest. 14Bring his sons and dress them in tunics. 15Anoint
them just as you anointed their father, so they may serve me as priests. Their anointing
will be to a priesthood that will continue for all generations to come.[z]" 16Moses did everything just as the LORD commanded him.
17So the tabernacle[a] was set up on the first day of the first month[b] in the second year.
18When Moses set up the tabernacle, he put the bases in place, erected the frames, inserted the crossbars and set up the posts. 19Then he spread the tent over the tabernacle
and put the covering over the tent, as the LORD commanded him.
20He took the Testimony[c] and placed it in the ark, attached the poles to the ark and
put the atonement cover over it. 21Then he brought the ark into the tabernacle and hung
the shielding curtain[d] and shielded the ark of the Testimony, as the LORD commanded
him.
22Moses placed the table[e] in the Tent of Meeting on the north side of the tabernacle
outside the curtain 23and set out the bread[f] on it before the LORD, as the LORD commanded him.
24He placed the lampstand[g] in the Tent of Meeting opposite the table on the south side
of the tabernacle 25and set up the lamps[h] before the LORD, as the LORD commanded him.
26Moses placed the gold altar[i] in the Tent of Meeting in front of the curtain 27and
burned fragrant incense on it, as the LORD commanded[j] him. 28Then he put up the curtain[k] at the entrance to the tabernacle.
29He set the altar of burnt offering near the entrance to the tabernacle, the Tent of Meeting, and offered on it burnt offerings and grain offerings,[l] as the LORD commanded him.
30He placed the basin[m] between the Tent of Meeting and the altar and put water in
it for washing, 31and Moses and Aaron and his sons used it to wash their hands and feet.
32They washed whenever they entered the Tent of Meeting or approached the altar,[n] as
the LORD commanded Moses.
33Then Moses set up the courtyard[o] around the tabernacle and altar and put up the
curtain[p] at the entrance to the courtyard. And so Moses finished the work.

The Glory of the LORD

34Then the cloud[q] covered the Tent of Meeting, and the glory of the LORD filled the
tabernacle. 35Moses could not enter the Tent of Meeting because the cloud had settled
upon it, and the glory of the LORD filled the tabernacle.[r]

40:2 [n]Nu 1:1 [o]ver 17; Ex 12:2
40:3 [p]ver 21; Nu 4:5; Ex 26:33
40:4 [q]Ex 25:30 [r]ver 22-25; Ex 26:35
40:5 [s]ver 26; Ex 30:1
40:7 [t]ver 30; Ex 30:18
40:9 [u]Ex 30:26; Lev 8:10
40:10 [v]Ex 29:36
40:12 [w]Lev 8:1-13
40:13 [x]Ex 28:41 [y]Lev 8:12
40:15 [z]Ex 29:9; Nu 25:13
40:17 [a]Nu 7:1 [b]ver 2
40:20 [c]Ex 16:34; 25:16; Dt 10:5; 1Ki 8:9; Heb 9:4
40:21 [d]Ex 26:33
40:22 [e]Ex 26:35
40:23 [f]ver 4
40:24 [g]Ex 26:35
40:25 [h]ver 4; Ex 25:37
40:26 [i]ver 5; Ex 30:6
40:27 [j]Ex 30:7
40:28 [k]Ex 26:36
40:29 [l]ver 6; Ex 29:38-42
40:30 [m]ver 7
40:32 [n]Ex 30:20
40:33 [o]Ex 27:9 [p]ver 8
40:34 [q]Nu 9:15-23; 1Ki 8:12
40:35 [r]1Ki 8:11; 2Ch 5:13-14

■ **40:1–38** *The Erection of the Tabernacle.* All the preliminary work was finally done, and the Spirit-enabled people of God had finished their contribution. Taking all these elements that had been shaped and formed in accordance with the pattern shown to him by the Lord, the mediator now began his final work in this drama of redemption, covenant making and restoration, so that Israel could now live in the presence of God. These verses divide into two parts: the building of the tabernacle (vv. 1–33) and the arrival of God's divine glory over it (vv. 34–38).

■ **40:1–33** *The Tabernacle Built.* The Lord ordered Moses to complete the construction and to appoint the priests. Moses followed God's commands.

40:1–16 The Lord instructed Moses regarding the placement of the tabernacle furnishings (vv. 1–8). Then he commanded the consecration of the tabernacle and of the priests who would minister within it (vv. 9–16).

40:2 Set up the tabernacle. The tabernacle was set up approximately nine months after the Israelites' arrival at Sinai (v. 17; 12:2,6). Once the tabernacle had been erected, Moses was careful to follow the prescribed sequence in arranging the furnishings, beginning with the ark. Everything was to be anointed as holy (vv. 9–11; Lev 8:10–11).

40:17–33 Moses carried out the Lord's instructions, just as he had been commanded.

40:31 wash their hands and feet. Following the placement of the basin, Moses and Aaron complied with 30:19–21.

40:33 Moses finished the work. A number of interpreters have noted that several similarities between Genesis 1:1—2:3 and Exodus 39:1—40:33 suggest that Moses may have been describing this event as the beginning of the restructuring of the universe into the dwelling place of God.

■ **40:34–38** *Glory in the Tabernacle.* The glory of the Lord filling the tabernacle brings the book of Exodus to a climax. God, who had brought Israel out of Egypt, had renewed his covenant with his

36In all the travels of the Israelites, whenever the cloud lifted from above the tabernacle, they would set out;[s] 37but if the cloud did not lift, they did not set out—until the day it lifted. 38So the cloud[t] of the LORD was over the tabernacle by day, and
fire was in the cloud by night, in the sight of all the house of Israel during all their
travels.

40:36 [s]Nu 9:17-23; 10:13; Ne 9:19

40:38 [t]Ex 13:21; Nu 9:15; 1Co 10:1

people and made his dwelling in their midst. Verses 34–38 are a powerful reminder of the primary themes of the book. This tremendous blessing of God's presence resulted from faithfulness to God's instructions given through Moses.

40:35 Moses could not enter. Moses was to await an invitation to enter. Some interpreters believe that this invitation was originally given in Leviticus 1:1. Certainly by Leviticus 9:23 the invitation had been extended and accepted.

40:36 In all the travels. Israel's journeys are linked to the guiding presence. The covenant God at last was dwelling among his people and would lead them to the land he had promised them.

LEVITICUS

Introduction

Overview

Author: Moses

Purpose: To guide the Israelites in the ways of holiness, so they would be set apart from the world and receive blessings instead of judgment as they lived near the special presence of their holy God.

Date: c. 1446–1406 B.C.

Key Truths:

- God is holy, and he requires holiness from his people.
- God's people invariably failed to keep the requirements of holiness, but temporary atonement could be found in the sacrificial system.
- God called his people to pursue holiness in every aspect of their lives out of gratitude for the mercy he had shown to them.
- God offered wondrous blessings and threatened judgment so that his people would repent and offer vows of commitment to him.

Author

That Moses is the author of Leviticus is a conclusion derived from the book's date and occasion and from Old Testament and New Testament references to Moses as the author of the Pentateuch. See the article "Introduction to the Pentateuch" on page 1.

Time and Place of Writing

Leviticus reports the words of God to Moses and his brother, Aaron, but it never states when and how these words were written down. This makes the date of Leviticus somewhat uncertain. The majority of critical interpreters place the writing of Leviticus in the exilic era (c. the sixth century B.C.), many centuries after Moses. This view is improbable because the content of Leviticus does not fit such a late period: The worship of the second temple differed significantly from that enjoined in Leviticus, and Leviticus is presupposed or quoted by earlier books such as Deuteronomy, Amos and, most obviously, Ezekiel. The book reflects the ideals of worship and holiness that were accepted in Israel from the time of Moses to the fall of Jerusalem in 587 B.C.

The book of Leviticus reports events that took place for the most part at Mount Sinai. For this reason, Moses could have compiled this book for the first generation of the exodus. Yet it is likely that he brought this book to completion along with the rest of the Pentateuch on the plains of Moab in order to instruct the second generation of the exodus how to live in the promised land. For additional discussion, see the article "Introduction to the Pentateuch" on page 1.

Original Audience

Leviticus, the Latin form of the Greek title of the book, means "about Levites." The Levites were the tribe from whom the priests were drawn, and they had the responsibility for maintaining worship. The title is apt, because the book is primarily about worship and fitness for worship. However, it is addressed not solely to priests or Levites, but also to lay Israelites, telling them how to offer sacrifices and how to be pure, a requirement for entering the presence of God in worship.

Purpose and Distinctives

Perhaps no other Old Testament book represents a greater challenge to the modern reader than Leviticus, and imagination is required to picture the ceremonies and rites that form the bulk of the book. However, it is important to understand the rituals in Leviticus for two reasons. First, rituals in all societies enshrine, express and teach those values and ideas that society holds most dear. Although many aspects of the rituals of Leviticus seem obscure to modern readers, the Old Testament Israelites knew why particular sacrifices were offered on specific occasions and what certain gestures meant. By analyzing the ceremonies described in Leviticus, we can learn about the most important ideas of Old Testament Israel. Second, these same ideas were fundamental for the theology of the New Testament. The concepts of sin, sacrifice and atonement found in Leviticus are essential for interpreting the death of Jesus in the New Testament.

Leviticus is part of the covenant law given at Sinai. The ideas that inform the whole Mosaic covenant are also presupposed here, including God's sovereign grace in choosing Israel and his requirement of loyalty (see theological article "Major Covenants in the Bible" on p. 25). Certain themes are especially prominent in Leviticus. First, God is present with his people. Second, because God is holy, his people must also be holy. Third, atonement for sin through the offering of sacrifices is of paramount importance. These themes may be elaborated as follows:

1. *The divine presence.* Every act of worship took place "before the LORD" (e.g., 1:5), who dwelled with his people in the Tent of Meeting. Because of God's special presence in the Most Holy Place, entry was barred to all but the high priest, and he was allowed to enter only once a year on the Day of Atonement (16:17). Although God's presence is usually invisible, he did on special occasions (e.g., the ordination of the priests) become visible in a cloud of fire (9:23–24). It is the greatest of God's gifts that he deigns to dwell with his people (26:12).

2. *Holiness.* "Be holy, because I am holy" (11:45) is the theme of Leviticus. Human beings are meant to be like God in his character. That involves imitating God in daily life. The holiness of God involves his being the source of perfect life—life in its physical and moral dimensions. Animals offered to him in sacrifice were to be free of defect (1:3), and priests who represented God to Israel and Israel to God were to be free of physical disabilities (21:17–23). Those who suffered discharges (particularly of blood) or disfiguring skin diseases were barred from worship until they were cured (chs. 12–15). Physical health is seen to symbolize the perfection of divine life. But holiness is also an inward matter, one of attitudes issuing in moral behavior. The theme of holiness is especially emphasized in chapters 17–25—chapters that are chiefly concerned with personal ethical conduct—and is summed up in 19:18 with the command to "love your neighbor as yourself."

3. *Atonement through sacrifice.* Since no one was able to live in perfect accordance with God's law, a means of atonement was essential so that moral lapses and physical failings could be pardoned. To this end Leviticus gives the fullest descriptions of the sacrificial system (chs. 1–7), the role of the priests (chs. 8–10,21–22) and the great national festivals (chs. 16,23,25) introduced in the Old Testament. These great ceremonies were designed to make possible the coexistence of the holy God with his sinful people through temporary atonements for sin. These sacrifices had no power in and of themselves to atone for sin, but depended upon the merits of Christ's then future atonement (Jn 14:6; Heb 9:15; 10:11).

Christ in Leviticus

Through its symbols and rites, Leviticus paints a picture of God's character that is presupposed and deepened in the New Testament message about Christ. Leviticus teaches that God is the source of perfect life, loves his people and wants to dwell among them. In this we see a foreshadowing of the incarnation, when "the Word became flesh and made his dwelling among us" (Jn 1:14). Leviticus also clearly shows human sinfulness: No sooner were Aaron's sons ordained than they profaned their office and died in a fearful display of divine judgment (ch. 10). Those who were suffering from skin diseases or bodily discharges, as well as those with moral failures, were barred from worship because their imperfections were incompatible with a holy and perfect God (chs. 12–15). Here we see Leviticus teaching through symbolism the universality of human sin, a doctrine endorsed by Jesus (Mk 7:21–23) and Paul (Ro 3:23). Caught between divine holiness and human sinfulness, humanity's paramount need is for atonement. It is here that the book has the most to teach the Christian, for its ideas are fulfilled in the atoning work of Christ. He is the perfect sacrificial Lamb who takes away the sin of the world (Lev 1:10; 4:32; Jn 1:29). His death is the ransom for many (Mk 10:45), and his blood cleanses us from all sin (Lev 4; Heb 9:13–14; 1Jn 1:17). Above all, Jesus is the perfect high priest who enters not the earthly tabernacle once a year on the Day of Atonement (Lev 16), but the heavenly temple forever. He offered not merely a goat for the sins of his people, but his own life (Heb 9–10). The rending of the temple curtain when Jesus was crucified was a visible demonstration that his death opened up the way to God for fuller access by all believers (Mt 27:51; Heb 10:20). Furthermore, while Leviticus focuses on keeping Israel separate from surrounding peoples, the New Testament opens the kingdom to all nations and thus abrogates observing food laws (Mk 7; Ac 10), while at the same time insisting on the moral principles symbolized in the dietary regulations (Jn 17:16; 2Co 6:14—7:1). The holy God of Leviticus is shown in the Gospels to be Christ, who offers life, health and holiness to all who are willing to follow him.

Outline

- I. Laws on Sacrifice (1:1—7:38)

Moses explained how the laity and the priests were to participate in a variety of sacrifices in the presence of God at the tabernacle.

  - A. Introduction (1:1–2)
  - B. Instructions for the Laity (1:3—6:7)
    1. Burnt Offering (1:3–17)
    2. Grain Offering (2:1–16)
    3. Fellowship Offering (3:1–17)
    4. Sin Offering (4:1—5:13)
    5. Guilt Offering (5:14—6:7)
  - C. Instructions for the Priests (6:8—7:36)
    1. Burnt Offering (6:8–13)
    2. Grain Offering (6:14–18)
    3. Priest's Grain Offering (6:19–23)
    4. Sin Offering (6:24–30)
    5. Guilt Offering (7:1–10)
    6. Fellowship Offering (7:11–36)
  - D. Conclusion (7:37–38)

II. The Ordination of the Aaronic Priesthood (8:1—10:20)
   A. Moses Begins the Ceremonies (8:1–36)
      1. Moses Calls an Assembly (8:1–4)
      2. Moses Washes and Clothes (8:5–9)
      3. Moses Anoints With Oil (8:10–13)
      4. Moses Makes a Sin Offering (8:14–17)
      5. Moses Makes a Burnt Offering (8:18–21)
      6. Moses Makes an Ordination Offering (8:22–36)
   B. Aaron and His Sons Complete the Ceremonies (9:1–24)
      1. Moses Orders Sacrifices (9:1–7)
      2. Aaron Offers Sacrifices (9:8–23a)
      3. God Responds to the Sacrifices (9:23b–24)
   C. Aaron and His Sons Violate the Ceremonies (10:1–20)
      1. Nadab and Abihu (10:1–11)
      2. Eleazar and Ithamar (10:12–20)

Moses described how Aaron and his sons were ordained to be priests for Israel. Moses performed a number of ceremonies, and Aaron and his sons completed the ceremonies. In order to encourage priests not to violate their ordination, Moses then explained why two sons of Aaron had fallen under God's judgment while two others had been exonerated.

III. Uncleanness and Its Treatment (11:1—16:34)
   A. Unclean Animals (11:1–47)
   B. Childbirth (12:1–8)
   C. Skin Diseases and Mildew (13:1—14:57)
      1. Uncleanness Caused by Skin Diseases and Mildew (13:1–59)
      2. Cleansing From Uncleanness Caused by Skin Diseases and Mildew (14:1–57)
   D. Discharges (15:1–33)
   E. The Day of Atonement (16:1–34)

Moses described how to identify and deal with ritual uncleanness.

IV. The Practice of Holiness (17:1—27:34)
   A. Sacrifice and Food (17:1–16)
   B. Sexual Behavior (18:1–30)
   C. Holiness Toward God and Neighbor (19:1–37)
   D. Capital Crimes (20:1–27)
   E. Rules for Priests (21:1–24)
   F. Rules on Sacrifice (22:1–33)
   G. Holy Assemblies (23:1–44)
   H. Oil and Loaves (24:1–9)
   I. Blasphemy (24:10–23)
   J. Years of Release (25:1–55)
      1. Sabbath Year (25:1–7)
      2. Jubilee Year (25:8–55)
   K. Blessings and Curses (26:1–46)
   L. Vows to God (27:1–34)

Moses revealed the far-reaching implications of Israel's call to holiness by touching on how to remain holy in many different spheres of life.

1:1 [a]Ex 19:3; 25:22 [b]Nu 7:89
1:2 [c]Lev 22:18-19

The Burnt Offering

1 The LORD called to Moses[a] and spoke to him from the Tent of Meeting.[b] He said,
2 "Speak to the Israelites and say to them: 'When any of you brings an offering to the
LORD, bring as your offering an animal from either the herd or the flock.[c]

■ **1:1—7:38** *Laws on Sacrifice.* Moses begins this manual on worship at the tabernacle by recording the laws of sacrifice. Following a brief introduction (1:1–2), the laws are subdivided into sections addressed to the laity (1:3—6:7) and to the priests (6:8—7:36), concluding with a summary of the sacrifices (7:37–38). See *HC* 19.
■ **1:1–2** *Introduction.* Moses reported that the Lord required offerings from his people. Sacrifice in Israel involved the offering of selected domestic animals, wheat, oil and wine. All these products symbolized the worshiping Israelites, who, through the act of sacrifice, were presenting themselves to God in some way. In every animal offering, the worshiper placed his hand on the animal's head, thereby identifying himself with the animal and saying in effect, "This animal represents me." The animal sacrifices involved the animal's death, and so the sacrifices had an atoning function: The animal dying in the sinful worshiper's place temporarily saved the worshiper from the deserved penalty of death. There is then a common core of meaning and significance shared by all sacrifices. In addition to this common core, each type of sacrifice had its own distinctive ritual features and religious emphases. This is indicated by the different names of the sacrifices, which sometimes highlight

3[a] 'If the offering is a burnt offering from the herd, he is to offer a male without defect.[d] He must present it at the entrance to the Tent[e] of Meeting so that it[a] will be acceptable to the LORD. 4He is to lay his hand on the head[f] of the burnt offering, and it will
be accepted on his behalf to make atonement[g] for him. 5He is to slaughter[h] the young
bull before the LORD, and then Aaron's sons the priests shall bring the blood and sprinkle it against the altar on all sides[i] at the entrance to the Tent of Meeting. 6He is to skin[j]
the burnt offering and cut it into pieces. 7The sons of Aaron the priest are to put fire on
the altar and arrange wood[k] on the fire. 8Then Aaron's sons the priests shall arrange
the pieces, including the head and the fat,[l] on the burning wood that is on the altar. 9He
is to wash the inner parts and the legs with water, and the priest is to burn all of it on
the altar.[m] It is a burnt offering, an offering made by fire, an aroma pleasing to the
LORD.[n]

10[a] 'If the offering is a burnt offering from the flock, from either the sheep or the
goats,[o] he is to offer a male without defect. 11He is to slaughter it at the north side of
the altar before the LORD, and Aaron's sons the priests shall sprinkle its blood against
the altar on all sides.[p] 12He is to cut it into pieces, and the priest shall arrange them,
including the head and the fat, on the burning wood that is on the altar. 13He is to wash
the inner parts and the legs with water, and the priest is to bring all of it and burn it on
the altar. It is a burnt offering, an offering made by fire, an aroma pleasing to the LORD.

14[a] 'If the offering to the LORD is a burnt offering of birds, he is to offer a dove or a
young pigeon.[q] 15The priest shall bring it to the altar, wring off the head and burn it on
the altar; its blood shall be drained out on the side of the altar.[r] 16He is to remove the
crop with its contents[b] and throw it to the east side of the altar, where the ashes[s] are.
17He shall tear it open by the wings, not severing it completely,[t] and then the priest shall
burn it on the wood[u] that is on the fire on the altar. It is a burnt offering, an offering
made by fire, an aroma pleasing to the LORD.

The Grain Offering

2 " 'When someone brings a grain offering[v] to the LORD, his offering is to be of fine
flour. He is to pour oil[w] on it, put incense on it 2and take it to Aaron's sons the
priests. The priest shall take a handful of the fine flour[x] and oil, together with all the incense,[y] and burn this as a memorial portion[z] on the altar, an offering made by fire, an

1:3 [d]Ex 12:5; Dt 15:21; Heb 9:14; 1Pe 1:19 [e]Lev 17:9
1:4 [f]Ex 29:10,15; Lev 3:2 [g]2Ch 29:23-24
1:5 [h]Lev 3:2,8 [i]Heb 12:24; 1Pe 1:2
1:6 [j]Lev 7:8
1:7 [k]Lev 6:12
1:8 [l]ver 12
1:9 [m]Ex 29:18 [n]ver 13; Ge 8:21; Nu 15:8-10; Eph 5:2
1:10 [o]ver 3; Ex 12:5
1:11 [p]ver 5
1:14 [q]Ge 15:9; Lev 5:7; Lk 2:24
1:15 [r]Lev 5:9
1:16 [s]Lev 6:10
1:17 [t]Ge 15:10 [u]Lev 5:8
2:1 [v]Lev 6:14-18 [w]Nu 15:4
2:2 [x]Lev 5:11 [y]Lev 6:15; Isa 66:3 [z]ver 9,16; Lev 5:12; 6:15; 24:7; Ac 10:4

[a] 3 Or *he* [b] 16 Or *crop and the feathers*; the meaning of the Hebrew for this word is uncertain.

the ritual distinctiveness (e.g., "burnt offering") and sometimes highlight the theologically distinctive feature (e.g., "fellowship offering" or "guilt offering").

1:1 Tent of Meeting. The tent shrine or tabernacle described in Exodus 26.

1:2 Speak to the Israelites. Israel was to obey this manual of instruction on how to be fit to live in the presence of God. God, not humans, prescribes the way his people must live with him. **an offering to the LORD.** Unlike all other sacral communities in Israel's world, not only did the sacred personnel, such as the king and/or priests, have access to the sacred precincts or to ritual instructions, but all the covenant people also had access to intimacy with God. Although only the high priest could enter the Most Holy Place, in contrast to the practice of other religions, there was no mystery about it or the priest's functions. God clearly revealed them in Scripture. His people, with imagination and faith, could enter that heavenly sphere. **from either the herd or the flock.** Only valuable, unblemished (1:3) domesticated animals could be offered. Wild animals, which cost nothing, could not be offered.

■ **1:3—6:7** *Instructions for the Laity.* Sacrifice rituals were not the responsibility of the priests alone. The laity also participated in carefully regulated, yet significant, ways. These chapters touch on various aspects of five different kinds of sacrifices: burnt offerings (1:3–17), grain offerings (2:1–16), fellowship offerings (3:1–17), sin offerings (4:1—5:13) and guilt offerings (5:14—6:7).

■ **1:3–17** *Burnt Offering.* The burnt offering is first on the list of sacrifices because it was the sacrifice offered most frequently (cf. 6:8–13). The Hebrew term means "going up" because its distinctive feature is that the whole animal—except for the skin, which the officiating priest kept—was burned on the altar so that its smoke rose to God. This symbolized the total consecration of the worshiper to God's service and served as a ransom for him (see v. 4 and its note). The regulations begin by specifying the most expensive kind of animal that could be offered (the bull; vv. 3–9) and end with the cheapest (the young pigeon; vv. 14–17). Burnt offerings were offered at the tabernacle every morning and evening (Ex 29:39–42), and they were made on behalf of the entire nation. Double offerings were made on each Sabbath morning and evening (Nu 28:9–10). Special feasts also required additional burnt offerings. Individuals and families could offer burnt offerings at any time in addition to these regular offerings.

1:3 He. The layman offering the sacrifice (vv. 4–6,9) was to kill and butcher the animal, after which the priest was to bring it to God by putting the blood and flesh on the altar. **entrance to the Tent of Meeting.** Moses was referring to the passageway into the screened-off courtyard surrounding the Tent of Meeting. In the courtyard also stood the great altar and the basin for ritual washings (v. 9).

1:4 make atonement. Literally, "act as a ransom for him." The death of the animal was seen as a payment whereby the worshiper was set free from the penalty of his sin.

1:9 aroma pleasing to the LORD. The meaning of this phrase is seen most clearly in Genesis 8:21. Sacrifices soothed God's anger, making him look benevolently on the worshiper. Ephesians 5:2 speaks of the death of Christ in similar language.

1:10–13 Sheep and goats were sacrificed in the same way as bulls (vv. 3–9).

1:14–17 A simpler procedure was prescribed for doves or pigeons, the offering of the poor. The priest carried out the whole ceremony.

■ **2:1–16** *Grain Offering.* Instructions for the grain offering were given to the laity (cf. 6:14–23; 7:9–10).

2:1 grain offering. Usually offered in conjunction with an animal sacrifice (Nu 6:14–15,17; 28:3–6), it consisted of wheat flour mixed with olive oil, incense and salt. The mixture was baked, fried or cooked on a griddle. The Hebrew word for grain offering means "present" or "tribute," and like other sacrifices it symbolized the worshiper dedicating himself to God.

2:2 memorial portion. Only a handful of the grain offering was burned; the rest was to be eaten by the priest. Such offerings constituted an important part of their income.

aroma pleasing to the LORD. 3The rest of the grain offering belongs to Aaron and his sons;[a] it is a most holy part of the offerings made to the LORD by fire.

4" 'If you bring a grain offering baked in an oven, it is to consist of fine flour: cakes made without yeast and mixed with oil, or[a] wafers made without yeast and spread with oil.[b] 5If your grain offering is prepared on a griddle, it is to be made of fine flour mixed with oil, and without yeast. 6Crumble it and pour oil on it; it is a grain offering. 7If your grain offering is cooked in a pan,[c] it is to be made of fine flour and oil. 8Bring the grain offering made of these things to the LORD; present it to the priest, who shall take it to the altar. 9He shall take out the memorial portion[d] from the grain offering and burn it on the altar as an offering made by fire, an aroma pleasing to the LORD.[e] 10The rest of the grain offering belongs to Aaron and his sons;[f] it is a most holy part of the offerings made to the LORD by fire.

11" 'Every grain offering you bring to the LORD must be made without yeast,[g] for you are not to burn any yeast or honey in an offering made to the LORD by fire. 12You may bring them to the LORD as an offering of the firstfruits,[h] but they are not to be offered on the altar as a pleasing aroma. 13Season all your grain offerings with salt. Do not leave the salt of the covenant[i] of your God out of your grain offerings; add salt to all your offerings.

14" 'If you bring a grain offering of firstfruits[j] to the LORD, offer crushed heads of new grain roasted in the fire. 15Put oil and incense on it; it is a grain offering. 16The priest shall burn the memorial portion[k] of the crushed grain and the oil, together with all the incense, as an offering made to the LORD by fire.

The Fellowship Offering

3 " 'If someone's offering is a fellowship offering,[b] [l] and he offers an animal from the herd, whether male or female, he is to present before the LORD an animal without defect.[m] 2He is to lay his hand on the head[n] of his offering and slaughter it[o] at the entrance to the Tent of Meeting. Then Aaron's sons the priests shall sprinkle the blood against the altar on all sides. 3From the fellowship offering he is to bring a sacrifice made to the LORD by fire: all the fat[p] that covers the inner parts or is connected to them, 4both kidneys with the fat on them near the loins, and the covering of the liver, which he will remove with the kidneys. 5Then Aaron's sons[q] are to burn it on the altar on top of the burnt offering[r] that is on the burning wood, as an offering made by fire, an aroma pleasing to the LORD.

6" 'If he offers an animal from the flock as a fellowship offering[s] to the LORD, he is to offer a male or female without defect. 7If he offers a lamb, he is to present it before the LORD.[t] 8He is to lay his hand on the head of his offering and slaughter it[u] in front of the Tent of Meeting. Then Aaron's sons shall sprinkle its blood against the altar on all sides. 9From the fellowship offering he is to bring a sacrifice made to the LORD by fire: its fat, the entire fat tail cut off close to the backbone, all the fat that covers the inner parts or is connected to them, 10both kidneys with the fat on them near the loins, and the covering of the liver, which he will remove with the kidneys. 11The priest shall burn them on the altar[v] as food,[w] an offering made to the LORD by fire.

2:3 [a]ver 10; Lev 6:16; 10:12,13
2:4 [b]Ex 29:2
2:7 [c]Lev 7:9
2:9 [d]ver 2 [e]Ex 29:18; Lev 6:15
2:10 [f]ver 3
2:11 [g]Ex 23:18; 34:25; Lev 6:16
2:12 [h]Lev 7:13; 23:10
2:13 [i]Nu 18:19; Eze 43:24
2:14 [j]Lev 23:10
2:16 [k]ver 2
3:1 [l]Lev 7:11-34 [m]Lev 1:3; 22:21
3:2 [n]Ex 29:10,15 [o]Lev 1:5
3:3 [p]Ex 29:13
3:5 [q]Lev 7:29-34 [r]Ex 29:13,38-42
3:6 [s]ver 1
3:7 [t]Lev 17:8-9
3:8 [u]ver 2; Lev 1:5
3:11 [v]ver 5 [w]ver 16; Lev 21:6,17

[a] 4 Or *and* [b] 1 Traditionally *peace offering*; also in verses 3, 6 and 9

2:4–5 without yeast. Or "without leaven" (see note on Ex 12:8). This is mentioned 12 times in Leviticus. Leaven may have been omitted because it caused fermentation, which sometimes symbolized corruption (cf. Ex 12:7–20). Its omission may also have served to separate Israel from some now unknown pagan worship practices.
2:11 honey. See note at 2:4–5.
2:13 salt of the covenant. Salt was associated with the covenant in that it symbolized the permanence of the covenant between God and Israel (see Nu 18:19; 2Ch 13:5).
2:14 firstfruits. See 23:9–14 and Deuteronomy 26:1–11. The Israelite was expected to give the first of his harvest to God, and on this occasion the grain offering was prepared differently.
■ **3:1–17** *Fellowship Offering.* Moses instructed the laity on the fellowship offering (cf. 7:11–21,28–34).
3:1 fellowship offering. Alternatively, "peace offering" or "covenant offering." The term used seems to be connected to the Hebrew word *shalom,* which means "peace" or "well-being." Its precise meaning is unclear, but it indicated harmony and peace between God and the worshiper, a standing that enabled worshiping individuals to share in the sacrifice. This sacrifice was unique in that the worshiper and his family could eat much of the meat, with only a part being given to the priests or burned on the altar. It was a sacrifice brought when someone was seeking God's blessing or celebrating blessings received. It was offered (1) to underline a solemn prayer (such as a vow), (2) when such a prayer was answered or (3) out of simple gratitude (7:16). Because of this, many fellowship offerings were offered at Israel's annual feasts (see Ex 23:14–17). Leviticus 17:3 (see note) prescribes that every animal killed for food must be offered in sacrifice first, so at least in the wilderness period (see Dt 12:15–16 for regulations in the promised land), every meal involving meat was preceded by a "fellowship offering."
3:2 lay his hand on . . . Aaron's sons. The worshiper was symbolically to identify with the sacrifice and hand it over to the priest, who sprinkled the blood on all sides of the altar.
3:3–4 the fat . . . the kidneys. These were considered the choice parts of the carcass, so they were symbolically given to God by being burned.
3:11 as food. God did not literally eat the food burned on the altar (cf. Ps 50:12–14)—it was reduced to ash by the fire, and the ashes were discarded (4:12). The description of the burnt sacrifice as food metaphorically indicated that God was pleased with the sacrifice, just as human beings enjoy food. It also suggested God's intimacy with his people through the image of table fellowship.

Old Testament Sacrifices

Sacrifice	OT References	Elements	Purpose
BURNT OFFERING	Lev 1; 6:8-13; 8:18-21; 16:24	Bull, ram or male bird (dove or young pigeon for the poor); wholly consumed; no defect	Voluntary act of worship; atonement for unintentional sin in general; expression of devotion, commitment and complete surrender to God
GRAIN OFFERING	Lev 2; 6:14-23	Grain, fine flour, olive oil, incense, baked bread (cakes or wafers), salt; no yeast or honey; accompanied burnt offering and fellowship offering (along with drink offering)	Voluntary act of worship; recognition of God's goodness and provisions; devotion to God
FELLOWSHIP OFFERING	Lev 3; 7:11-34	Any animal without defect from herd or flock; variety of breads	Voluntary act of worship; thanksgiving and fellowship (it included a communal meal)
SIN OFFERING	Lev 4:1—5:13; 6:24-30; 8:14-17; 16:3-22	1. Young bull: for high priest and congregation 2. Male goat: for leader 3. Female goat or lamb: for common person 4. Dove or pigeon: for the poor 5. Tenth of an ephah of fine flour: for the very poor	Mandatory atonement for specific unintentional sin; confession of sin; forgiveness of sin; cleansing from defilement
GUILT OFFERING	Lev 5:14—6:7; 7:1-6	Ram	Mandatory atonement for unintentional sin requiring restitution; cleansing from defilement; make restitution; pay 20% fine

When more than one kind of offering was presented (as in Nu 7:16,17), the procedure was usually as follows: (1) sin offering or guilt offering, (2) burnt offering, (3) fellowship offering and grain offering (along with a drink offering). This sequence furnishes part of the spiritual significance of the sacrificial system. First, sin had to be dealt with (sin offering or guilt offering). Second, the worshipers committed themselves completely to God (burnt offering and grain offering). Third, fellowship or communion between the Lord, the priest and the worshiper (fellowship offering) was established. To state it another way, there were sacrifices of expiation (sin offerings and guilt offerings), consecration (burnt offerings and grain offerings) and communion (fellowship offerings—these included vow offerings, thank offerings and freewill offerings).

12 'If his offering is a goat, he is to present it before the LORD. 13 He is to lay his hand
on its head and slaughter it in front of the Tent of Meeting. Then Aaron's sons shall sprinkle[x] its blood against the altar on all sides. 14 From what he offers he is to make this offering to the LORD by fire: all the fat that covers the inner parts or is connected to them,
15 both kidneys with the fat on them near the loins, and the covering of the liver, which
he will remove with the kidneys. 16 The priest shall burn them on the altar as food, an offering made by fire, a pleasing aroma. All the fat is the LORD's.[y]
17 'This is a lasting ordinance for the generations to come,[z] wherever you live: You
must not eat any fat or any blood.[a]' "

The Sin Offering

4 The LORD said to Moses, 2 "Say to the Israelites: 'When anyone sins unintentionally[b] and does what is forbidden in any of the LORD's commands—
3 'If the anointed priest sins, bringing guilt on the people, he must bring to the LORD
a young bull[c] without defect as a sin offering[d] for the sin he has committed. 4 He is to present the bull at the entrance to the Tent of Meeting before the LORD.[e] He is to lay his hand
on its head and slaughter it before the LORD. 5 Then the anointed priest shall take some
of the bull's blood[f] and carry it into the Tent of Meeting. 6 He is to dip his finger into the
blood and sprinkle some of it seven times before the LORD, in front of the curtain of the
sanctuary. 7 The priest shall then put some of the blood on the horns of the altar of fragrant incense that is before the LORD in the Tent of Meeting. The rest of the bull's blood
he shall pour out at the base of the altar[g] of burnt offering[h] at the entrance to the Tent
of Meeting. 8 He shall remove all the fat[i] from the bull of the sin offering—the fat that covers the inner parts or is connected to them, 9 both kidneys with the fat on them near the
loins, and the covering of the liver, which he will remove with the kidneys[j]— 10 just as
the fat is removed from the ox[a] sacrificed as a fellowship offering.[b] Then the priest shall
burn them on the altar of burnt offering. 11 But the hide of the bull and all its flesh, as well
as the head and legs, the inner parts and offal[k]— 12 that is, all the rest of the bull—he
must take outside the camp[l] to a place ceremonially clean,[m] where the ashes are
thrown, and burn it in a wood fire on the ash heap.

13 'If the whole Israelite community sins unintentionally[n] and does what is forbidden in any of the LORD's commands, even though the community is unaware of the matter, they are guilty. 14 When they become aware of the sin they committed, the assembly
must bring a young bull[o] as a sin offering[p] and present it before the Tent of Meeting.
15 The elders of the community are to lay their hands on the bull's head[q] before the LORD,

a *10* The Hebrew word can include both male and female. b *10* Traditionally *peace offering*; also in verses 26, 31 and 35

3:13 [x]Ex 24:6
3:16 [y]1Sa 2:16
3:17 [z]Lev 6:18; 17:7 [a]Ge 9:4; Lev 7:25-26; 17:10-16; Dt 12:16; Ac 15:20
4:2 [b]Lev 5:15-18; Ps 19:12; Heb 9:7
4:3 [c]ver 14; Ps 66:15 [d]Lev 9:2-22; Heb 9:13-14
4:4 [e]Lev 1:3
4:5 [f]Lev 16:14
4:7 [g]ver 34; Lev 8:15 [h]ver 18, 30; Lev 5:9; 9:9; 16:18
4:8 [i]Lev 3:3-5
4:9 [j]Lev 3:4
4:11 [k]Ex 29:14; Lev 9:11; Nu 19:5
4:12 [l]Heb 13:11 [m]Lev 6:11
4:13 [n]ver 2; Lev 5:2-4, 17; Nu 15:24-26
4:14 [o]ver 3 [p]ver 23, 28
4:15 [q]Lev 1:4; 8:14, 22; Nu 8:10

3:17 fat or any blood. Fat from sacrificial animals belonged to God (v. 3). To "eat . . . blood" means to eat meat from which the blood had not been drained (1Sa 14:33). The reason for this ban is given in 17:11 (see Ge 9:4).

■ **4:1—5:13** *Sin Offering.* Moses introduced his instruction to the laity regarding the sin offering with the words "When anyone sins . . ." (4:2). While all sacrifices made atonement for sin to some extent, atonement was the dominant concern of the sin offering. Sin and uncleanness make a person unfit to be in God's presence and also pollute the sanctuary, making it unworthy of God's special presence. The sin offering was designed to cope with this aspect of sin by purifying both the sinner and the sanctuary. The distinctive feature of the sin offering was the use to which the sacrificial blood was put. In other sacrifices the animal's blood was splashed over the sides of the altar, but in the case of the sin offering the blood could be smeared on the horned corners of the altar or sprinkled inside the Tent of Meeting on the incense altar, on the veil or even inside the Most Holy Place. Through the means of these rites combined with faith (Ps 51:16–17), both the holy furniture and the Israelites were cleansed. But the sacrifices themselves were not the basis of forgiveness—they depended on the merit of Christ's coming atonement (Jn 14:6; Heb 9:15; 10:11). Believers in the new covenant (see theological article "Major Covenants in the Bible" on p. 25) can see the importance of dealing with various kinds of sin from this legislation. But we look to Christ as the fulfillment of sin offerings. When we fall into sin, we appeal through prayer to Jesus' one-time, all-sufficient sacrifice on the cross.

4:1–35 These verses deal with four hypothetical situations in which someone might do something without realizing that the act is sinful ("unintentionally"; v. 2).

4:3–12 Moses gave instructions on how to deal with the sin of the anointed priest.

4:3 anointed priest. That is, the high priest. His sin had the direct consequence of "bringing guilt on the people" because he represented them before God. For this reason, his sin offering was the most expensive: a bull. **he must bring.** The sin and guilt offerings (4:1—6:7) were compulsory for certain sins, whereas other offerings could sometimes be offered spontaneously, when the worshiper felt so inclined.

4:6 The serious effects of high priestly sin are shown by the need to purify "the curtain of the sanctuary"; that is, the curtain separating the Holy Place from the Most Holy Place (see Ex 26:31–35). Tangible items around the sinful priest were corrupted by his presence.

4:7 the altar of fragrant incense. This piece of sacred furniture stood in the front of the curtain leading into the Most Holy Place. The altar was cleansed by sprinkling it with blood, the holy cleansing agent, making the tent suitable for God to dwell in it. The high priest, who represented the nation, was cleansed at the same time.

4:12 outside the camp. Hebrews 13:11–13 compares Jesus' death to a sin offering. **ceremonially clean.** "Clean" and "unclean" in Leviticus refer to ritual acceptability, not to physical cleanliness. Many places outside the camp contained impurities that made the priest unfit to officiate in worship. He was to avoid these and put the ashes left from the burnt offering in a place designated as "clean."

4:13–21 Moses gave instructions on how to deal with an unintentional corporate sin (cf. Nu 15:22—26). A procedure like that found in verses 3–12 was prescribed, with the elders of the community representing the people at the altar (v. 15).

and the bull shall be slaughtered before the LORD. 16Then the anointed priest is to take
some of the bull's blood[r] into the Tent of Meeting. 17He shall dip his finger into the blood
and sprinkle it before the LORD[s] seven times in front of the curtain. 18He is to put some
of the blood on the horns of the altar that is before the LORD[t] in the Tent of Meeting. The
rest of the blood he shall pour out at the base of the altar of burnt offering at the entrance
to the Tent of Meeting. 19He shall remove all the fat[u] from it and burn it on the altar,
20and do with this bull just as he did with the bull for the sin offering. In this way the
priest will make atonement[v] for them, and they will be forgiven.[w] 21Then he shall take
the bull outside the camp and burn it as he burned the first bull. This is the sin offering
for the community.[x]

22“ ‘When a leader[y] sins unintentionally[z] and does what is forbidden in any of the
commands of the LORD his God, he is guilty. 23When he is made aware of the sin he committed, he must bring as his offering a male goat without defect. 24He is to lay his hand
on the goat's head and slaughter it at the place where the burnt offering is slaughtered
before the LORD. It is a sin offering. 25Then the priest shall take some of the blood of the
sin offering with his finger and put it on the horns of the altar of burnt offering and pour
out the rest of the blood at the base of the altar.[a] 26He shall burn all the fat on the altar
as he burned the fat of the fellowship offering. In this way the priest will make atonement
for the man's sin, and he will be forgiven.[b]

27“ ‘If a member of the community sins unintentionally[c] and does what is forbidden
in any of the LORD's commands, he is guilty. 28When he is made aware of the sin he committed, he must bring as his offering[d] for the sin he committed a female goat[e] without
defect. 29He is to lay his hand on the head[f] of the sin offering[g] and slaughter it at the
place of the burnt offering. 30Then the priest is to take some of the blood with his finger
and put it on the horns of the altar of burnt offering[h] and pour out the rest of the blood
at the base of the altar. 31He shall remove all the fat, just as the fat is removed from the
fellowship offering, and the priest shall burn it on the altar as an aroma pleasing to the
LORD.[i] In this way the priest will make atonement for him, and he will be forgiven.

32“ ‘If he brings a lamb as his sin offering, he is to bring a female without defect.[j] 33He
is to lay his hand on its head and slaughter it for a sin offering at the place where the
burnt offering is slaughtered.[k] 34Then the priest shall take some of the blood of the sin
offering with his finger and put it on the horns of the altar of burnt offering and pour out
the rest of the blood at the base of the altar.[l] 35He shall remove all the fat, just as the fat
is removed from the lamb of the fellowship offering, and the priest shall burn it on the
altar[m] on top of the offerings made to the LORD by fire. In this way the priest will make
atonement for him for the sin he has committed, and he will be forgiven.

5 “ ‘If a person sins because he does not speak up when he hears a public charge to
testify[n] regarding something he has seen or learned about, he will be held responsible.[o]

2“ ‘Or if a person touches anything ceremonially unclean—whether the carcasses of
unclean wild animals or of unclean livestock or of unclean creatures that move along the
ground[p]—even though he is unaware of it, he has become unclean and is guilty.

3“ ‘Or if he touches human uncleanness[q]—anything that would make him unclean—
even though he is unaware of it, when he learns of it he will be guilty.

4“ ‘Or if a person thoughtlessly takes an oath[r] to do anything, whether good or
evil—in any matter one might carelessly swear about—even though he is unaware of it,
in any case when he learns of it he will be guilty.

5“ ‘When anyone is guilty in any of these ways, he must confess[s] in what way he has
sinned 6and, as a penalty for the sin he has committed, he must bring to the LORD a fe-

4:16 [r]ver 5
4:17 [s]ver 6
4:18 [t]ver 7
4:19 [u]ver 8
4:20 [v]Heb 10:10-12 [w]Nu 15:25
4:21 [x]Lev 16:5,15
4:22 [y]Nu 31:13 [z]ver 2
4:25 [a]ver 7,18,30,34; Lev 9:9
4:26 [b]Lev 5:10
4:27 [c]ver 2; Nu 15:27
4:28 [d]ver 23 [e]ver 3
4:29 [f]ver 4,24 [g]Lev 1:4
4:30 [h]ver 7
4:31 [i]Ge 8:21
4:32 [j]ver 28
4:33 [k]ver 29
4:34 [l]ver 7
4:35 [m]ver 26,31
5:1 [n]Pr 29:24 [o]ver 17
5:2 [p]Lev 11:11,24-40; Dt 14:8
5:3 [q]Nu 19:11-16
5:4 [r]Nu 30:6,8
5:5 [s]Lev 16:21; 26:40; Nu 5:7; Pr 28:13

4:22–26 Moses gave instructions on the procedure for dealing with an unintentional sin by a community leader. A sin by a leader of a tribe or clan was not as serious as that of a high priest or of the entire community (vv. 3–21). This is reflected in that the leader was required to offer only a "male goat" (v. 23) and that its blood was smeared not within the tent, but outside on the altar of burnt offering (v. 25). It is apparent from the variations in sacrifices that some sins were considered worse than others (cf. *WLC* 150,151).

4:27–35 Moses gave instructions on the method for dealing with the unintentional sin of a community member. The ordinary sins of Israelites were treated similarly to those of leaders. However, they were allowed to offer a female goat instead of a male goat, and if they were poor, they could offer birds or grain (5:7–13).

5:1–6 These verses deal with a more serious kind of sin, one that had been committed knowingly or willfully, had been ignored after the fact and had finally started to trouble the conscience. The cases in view are the sins of (1) withholding evidence (v. 1), (2) contacting anything unclean (vv. 2–3) and (3) carelessly taking an oath (v. 4). See *WLC* 145.

5:2–3 unclean. For a more complete discussion, see chapters 11–15 and their notes.

5:5 These sins that had been previously ignored required confession to God in the presence of a priest and a sin offering for the forgiveness of the sinner (see 1Jn 1:7,9).

male lamb or goat from the flock as a sin offering;[t] and the priest shall make atonement
for him for his sin.
7 " 'If he cannot afford[u] a lamb, he is to bring two doves or two young pigeons to the
LORD as a penalty for his sin—one for a sin offering and the other for a burnt offering. 8 He
is to bring them to the priest, who shall first offer the one for the sin offering. He is to
wring its head from its neck,[v] not severing it completely,[w] 9 and is to sprinkle some of the
blood of the sin offering against the side of the altar; the rest of the blood must be drained
out at the base of the altar.[x] It is a sin offering. 10 The priest shall then offer the other as
a burnt offering in the prescribed way[y] and make atonement for him for the sin he has
committed, and he will be forgiven.[z]
11 " 'If, however, he cannot afford two doves or two young pigeons, he is to bring as
an offering for his sin a tenth of an ephah[a] of fine flour[a] for a sin offering. He must not
put oil or incense on it, because it is a sin offering. 12 He is to bring it to the priest, who
shall take a handful of it as a memorial portion and burn it on the altar on top of the offerings made to the LORD by fire. It is a sin offering. 13 In this way the priest will make
atonement[b] for him for any of these sins he has committed, and he will be forgiven. The
rest of the offering will belong to the priest,[c] as in the case of the grain offering.' "

The Guilt Offering

14 The LORD said to Moses: 15 "When a person commits a violation and sins unintentionally in regard to any of the LORD's holy things, he is to bring to the LORD as a penalty[d] a ram[e]
from the flock, one without defect and of the proper value in silver, according to the sanctuary shekel.[b][f] It is a guilt offering. 16 He must make restitution[g] for what he has failed to
do in regard to the holy things, add a fifth of the value[h] to that and give it all to the priest,
who will make atonement for him with the ram as a guilt offering, and he will be forgiven.
17 "If a person sins and does what is forbidden in any of the LORD's commands, even
though he does not know it,[i] he is guilty and will be held responsible. 18 He is to bring to
the priest as a guilt offering a ram from the flock, one without defect and of the proper
value. In this way the priest will make atonement for him for the wrong he has committed unintentionally, and he will be forgiven.[j] 19 It is a guilt offering; he has been guilty of[c]
wrongdoing against the LORD."

6 The LORD said to Moses: 2 "If anyone sins and is unfaithful to the LORD[k] by deceiving
his neighbor[l] about something entrusted to him or left in his care[m] or stolen, or if
he cheats him, 3 or if he finds lost property and lies about it,[n] or if he swears falsely, or if
he commits any such sin that people may do— 4 when he thus sins and becomes guilty,
he must return[o] what he has stolen or taken by extortion, or what was entrusted to him,
or the lost property he found, 5 or whatever it was he swore falsely about. He must make
restitution[p] in full, add a fifth of the value to it and give it all to the owner on the day he
presents his guilt offering.[q] 6 And as a penalty he must bring to the priest, that is, to the
LORD, his guilt offering,[r] a ram from the flock, one without defect and of the proper value. 7 In this way the priest will make atonement[s] for him before the LORD, and he will be
forgiven for any of these things he did that made him guilty."

The Burnt Offering

8 The LORD said to Moses: 9 "Give Aaron and his sons this command: 'These are the regulations for the burnt offering: The burnt offering is to remain on the altar hearth

5:6 [t]Lev 4:28
5:7 [u]Lev 12:8; 14:21
5:8 [v]Lev 1:15 [w]Lev 1:17
5:9 [x]Lev 4:7, 18
5:10 [y]Lev 1:14-17 [z]Lev 4:26
5:11 [a]Lev 2:1
5:13 [b]Lev 4:26 [c]Lev 2:3
5:15 [d]Lev 22:14 [e]Nu 5:8 [f]Ex 30:13
5:16 [g]Lev 6:4 [h]Lev 22:14; Nu 5:7
5:17 [i]ver 15; Lev 4:2
5:18 [j]ver 15
6:2 [k]Nu 5:6; Ac 5:4; Col 3:9 [l]Pr 24:28 [m]Ex 22:7
6:3 [n]Dt 22:1-3
6:4 [o]Lk 19:8
6:5 [p]Nu 5:7 [q]Lev 5:15
6:6 [r]Lev 5:15
6:7 [s]Lev 4:26

a *11* That is, probably about 2 quarts (about 2 liters) b *15* That is, about 2/5 ounce (about 11.5 grams)
c *19* Or *has made full expiation for his*

5:7–10 The poor man's sin offering was like the humblest burnt offering (1:14–17), except for the sprinkling of the blood (v. 9; see 1:15).

5:11–13 The items brought here as sin offerings resemble those of the grain offering of chapter 2, but no oil or incense is included.

■ **5:14—6:7** *Guilt Offering.* Moses gave instructions to the laity regarding guilt offerings. This type of sacrifice dealt with sins for which some type of restitution was required. For example, stolen property had to be restored with an added fine, along with the guilt offering. A ram was required in all cases. New Testament believers trust in Christ's death as their final and complete guilt offering. Believers stand forgiven because of Christ's finished work on the cross. However, when Christians sin in ways that allow for restitution, reparation to the offended should be encouraged (Phm 1:17–19).

5:16 holy things. Apparently these words refer to the theft of property dedicated to God (22:7,10,14; 27:28). **add a fifth.** In cases where a guilt offering was required, misappropriated property was also to be restored in full, plus 20 percent (see 6:5).

5:17–19 In view here is a guilt offering made either by someone who committed an unintentional sin or by someone with an uneasy conscience (an individual unsure of his or her guilt).

6:1–7 In view here are guilt offerings made on behalf of someone else who has intentionally sinned against a neighbor. The offender was required to make reparation (plus one fifth of the value of the lost or damaged property) on the day the offering was made. It is likely that Jesus had this kind of ceremony in mind when he instructed his disciples in Matthew 5:24. See *WLC* 141.

■ **6:8—7:36** *Instructions for the Priests.* Having addressed the laity concerning the laws of sacrifice, Moses here addressed the priests. His chief concern was that the priestly entitlement to portions of sacrifices not be abused. Moses sought to ensure that the priests did not fail in their duties, but he anticipated that they would do so. New covenant believers have Christ as their priest, and he per-

throughout the night, till morning, and the fire must be kept burning on the altar. 10 The priest shall then put on his linen clothes, with linen undergarments next to his body,[t] and shall remove the ashes of the burnt offering that the fire has consumed on the altar and place them beside the altar. 11 Then he is to take off these clothes and put on others, and carry the ashes outside the camp to a place that is ceremonially clean.[u] 12 The fire on the altar must be kept burning; it must not go out. Every morning the priest is to add firewood and arrange the burnt offering on the fire and burn the fat of the fellowship offerings[a] on it. 13 The fire must be kept burning on the altar continuously; it must not go out.

The Grain Offering

14 " 'These are the regulations for the grain offering:[v] Aaron's sons are to bring it before the LORD, in front of the altar. 15 The priest is to take a handful of fine flour and oil, together with all the incense on the grain offering,[w] and burn the memorial portion[x] on the altar as an aroma pleasing to the LORD. 16 Aaron and his sons[y] shall eat the rest[z] of it, but it is to be eaten without yeast[a] in a holy place;[b] they are to eat it in the courtyard of the Tent of Meeting. 17 It must not be baked with yeast; I have given it as their share of the offerings made to me by fire. Like the sin offering and the guilt offering, it is most holy.[c] 18 Any male descendant of Aaron may eat it.[d] It is his regular share of the offerings made to the LORD by fire for the generations to come. Whatever touches them will become holy.[b][e] ' "

19 The LORD also said to Moses, 20 "This is the offering Aaron and his sons are to bring to the LORD on the day he[c] is anointed: a tenth of an ephah[d][f] of fine flour as a regular grain offering,[g] half of it in the morning and half in the evening. 21 Prepare it with oil on a griddle;[h] bring it well-mixed and present the grain offering broken[e] in pieces as an aroma pleasing to the LORD. 22 The son who is to succeed him as anointed priest shall prepare it. It is the LORD's regular share and is to be burned completely. 23 Every grain offering of a priest shall be burned completely; it must not be eaten."

The Sin Offering

24 The LORD said to Moses, 25 "Say to Aaron and his sons: 'These are the regulations for the sin offering: The sin offering is to be slaughtered before the LORD[i] in the place[j] the burnt offering is slaughtered; it is most holy. 26 The priest who offers it shall eat it; it is to be eaten in a holy place,[k] in the courtyard[l] of the Tent of Meeting. 27 Whatever touches any of the flesh will become holy,[m] and if any of the blood is spattered on a garment, you must wash it in a holy place. 28 The clay pot[n] the meat is cooked in must be broken; but if it is cooked in a bronze pot, the pot is to be scoured and rinsed with water. 29 Any male in a priest's family may eat it;[o] it is most holy.[p] 30 But any sin offering whose blood is brought into the Tent of Meeting to make atonement in the Holy Place[q] must not be eaten; it must be burned.[r]

[a] *12* Traditionally *peace offerings* [b] *18* Or *Whoever touches them must be holy*; similarly in verse 27 [c] *20* Or *each* [d] *20* That is, probably about 2 quarts (about 2 liters) [e] *21* The meaning of the Hebrew for this word is uncertain.

6:10 [t]Ex 28:39-42,43; 39:28
6:11 [u]Lev 4:12
6:14 [v]Lev 2:1; 15:4
6:15 [w]Lev 2:9 [x]Lev 2:2
6:16 [y]Lev 2:3 [z]Eze 44:29 [a]Lev 2:11 [b]Lev 10:13
6:17 [c]ver 29; Ex 40:10; Nu 18:9,10
6:18 [d]ver 29; Nu 18:9-10 [e]ver 27
6:20 [f]Ex 16:36 [g]Ex 29:2
6:21 [h]Lev 2:5
6:25 [i]Lev 1:3 [j]Lev 1:5, 11
6:26 [k]ver 16 [l]Lev 10:17-18
6:27 [m]Ex 29:37
6:28 [n]Lev 11:33; 15:12
6:29 [o]ver 18 [p]ver 17
6:30 [q]Lev 4:18 [r]Lev 4:12

---

forms his priestly duties without flaw. These chapters discuss the following offerings: burnt (6:8–13), grain (6:14–18), priest's grain (6:19–23), sin (6:24–30), guilt (7:1–10) and fellowship (7:11–36).

■ **6:8–13** *Burnt Offering.* Compare 1:3–17. Christ, the high priest of the new covenant, offered the final burnt offering in his body: He was wholly consecrated to God, suffering death for sin and bringing about the believer's death to sin (Ro 6:2–7).

6:10 linen clothes. Being white, this apparel probably symbolized purity. Exodus 20:26 and Exodus 28:42–43 insist that priests must cover their private parts before approaching God (see Ge 3:7,21).

6:12 The fire . . . must be kept burning. This action was probably prescribed as a reminder of God's continual presence and of the people's need for continual atonement (see v. 13).

■ **6:14–18** *Grain Offering.* Compare 2:1–16. Christ symbolically offered the grain offering as he gave God honor and thanks in his perfect obedience. Here Moses described two types: the common grain offering (vv. 14–18) and the grain offering for the anointed priest (vv. 19–23).

6:18 Whatever touches them will become holy. See NIV text note for an alternative reading. People who approach God in worship must be careful not to offend him (10:3). This is a warning to laity not to touch food consecrated to God in sacrifice.

■ **6:19–23** *Priest's Grain Offering.* The priest's grain offering, mentioned here for the first time.

6:20 on the day he is anointed. That is, beginning on this day, but also continuing daily thereafter. **regular.** The priest's grain offering had to be offered daily (cf. Nu 28:3–10).

6:22 anointed priest. That is, the high priest.

■ **6:24–30** *Sin Offering.* Compare 4:1—5:13. Christ, the new covenant high priest, offered the final sin offering as he bore the once-for-all-time punishment for the believer's sins (Isa 53:5; 1Pe 2:24).

6:26 shall eat it. Most sin offerings were made at the altar of burnt offerings in the courtyard. Because it was sacred (see 7:6), the priest was to eat a portion of the offering only in the courtyard of the tabernacle.

6:30 atonement in the Holy Place. When the whole community sinned, even unintentionally, the blood of the sacrifice was to be placed on the altar within the Holy Place (4:18). The priest was not to eat any of this offering because of the magnitude of the sin for which it atoned.

The Guilt Offering

7 " 'These are the regulations for the guilt offering,[s] which is most holy: 2The guilt offering is to be slaughtered in the place where the burnt offering is slaughtered, and
its blood is to be sprinkled against the altar on all sides. 3All its fat[t] shall be offered: the
fat tail and the fat that covers the inner parts, 4both kidneys with the fat on them near
the loins, and the covering of the liver, which is to be removed with the kidneys. 5The
priest shall burn them on the altar as an offering made to the LORD by fire. It is a guilt offering. 6Any male in a priest's family may eat it,[u] but it must be eaten in a holy place; it
is most holy.[v]

7" 'The same law applies to both the sin offering and the guilt offering: They belong
to the priest[w] who makes atonement with them. 8The priest who offers a burnt offering
for anyone may keep its hide for himself. 9Every grain offering baked in an oven or
cooked in a pan or on a griddle[x] belongs to the priest who offers it, 10and every grain offering, whether mixed with oil or dry, belongs equally to all the sons of Aaron.

The Fellowship Offering

11" 'These are the regulations for the fellowship offering[a] a person may present to the
LORD:

12" 'If he offers it as an expression of thankfulness, then along with this thank offering[y] he is to offer cakes of bread made without yeast and mixed with oil, wafers[z] made
without yeast and spread with oil, and cakes of fine flour well-kneaded and mixed with
oil. 13Along with his fellowship offering of thanksgiving he is to present an offering with
cakes of bread made with yeast.[a] 14He is to bring one of each kind as an offering, a contribution to the LORD; it belongs to the priest who sprinkles the blood of the fellowship
offerings. 15The meat of his fellowship offering of thanksgiving must be eaten on the day
it is offered; he must leave none of it till morning.[b]

16" 'If, however, his offering is the result of a vow or is a freewill offering, the sacrifice shall be eaten on the day he offers it, but anything left over may be eaten on the next
day.[c] 17Any meat of the sacrifice left over till the third day must be burned up. 18If any
meat of the fellowship offering is eaten on the third day, it will not be accepted.[d] It will
not be credited[e] to the one who offered it, for it is impure; the person who eats any of it
will be held responsible.

19" 'Meat that touches anything ceremonially unclean must not be eaten; it must be
burned up. As for other meat, anyone ceremonially clean may eat it. 20But if anyone who
is unclean eats any meat of the fellowship offering belonging to the LORD, that person
must be cut off from his people.[f] 21If anyone touches something unclean[g]—whether human uncleanness or an unclean animal or any unclean, detestable thing—and then eats
any of the meat of the fellowship offering belonging to the LORD, that person must be cut
off from his people.' "

Eating Fat and Blood Forbidden

22The LORD said to Moses, 23"Say to the Israelites: 'Do not eat any of the fat of cattle,
sheep or goats.[h] 24The fat of an animal found dead or torn by wild animals[i] may be used
for any other purpose, but you must not eat it. 25Anyone who eats the fat of an animal
from which an offering by fire may be[b] made to the LORD must be cut off from his peo-

7:1 [s]Lev 5:14-6:7
7:3 [t]Ex 29:13; Lev 3:4,9
7:6 [u]Lev 6:18; Nu 18:9-10 [v]Lev 2:3
7:7 [w]Lev 6:17,26; 1Co 9:13
7:9 [x]Lev 2:5
7:12 [y]ver 13,15 [z]Lev 2:4; Nu 6:15
7:13 [a]Lev 23:17; Am 4:5
7:15 [b]Lev 22:30
7:16 [c]Lev 19:5-8
7:18 [d]Lev 19:7 [e]Nu 18:27
7:20 [f]Lev 22:3-7
7:21 [g]Lev 5:2; 11:24,28
7:23 [h]Lev 3:17; 17:13-14
7:24 [i]Ex 22:31

a *11* Traditionally *peace offering*; also in verses 13–37 b *25* Or *fire is*

■ **7:1–10** *Guilt Offering.* Compare 5:14—6:7. The relevance of the guilt offering to Christ's sacrifice is similar to that of the sin offering to Christ's sacrifice. See note at 6:24–30.

7:6 eaten in a holy place. The priest had a right to a portion of the guilt offering, but its holiness was to be acknowledged by consuming it only within the confines of the tabernacle courtyard (see 6:16).

■ **7:11–36** *Fellowship Offering.* Compare 3:1–17. Rules were given regarding the grain offerings that were to accompany fellowship offerings and the method by which the meat was to be eaten (vv. 15–16). Three types of fellowship offerings are described: thank (vv. 12–15), vow (vv. 16–17) and wave (vv. 30–31) offerings. For other regulations, see 22:18–23.

7:12 thank offering. One type of fellowship offering was the thank offering. It expressed appreciation to God for help in times of sorrow and hardship (see Ps 116:17).

7:16 vow. Another type of fellowship offering was associated with taking vows. In dire straits people made vows promising to give God something if he answered their prayers (Ge 28:20–22; 1Sa 1:11; 2:21,24). Such vows were usually accompanied by fellowship offerings at the time the vow was made and again when it was fulfilled. For more on vows, see *WCF* 22. **freewill offering.** This spontaneous offering probably included a broad variety of offerings made to show gratitude to God.

7:19 ceremonially unclean. For a definition of uncleanness, see chapters 11–15.

7:20 be cut off. This language is a general expression used to describe coming under the curses of the covenant, the exact meaning of which is determined by the context of Scripture. To make a covenant is literally "to cut a covenant" because of associated cutting rituals (see notes on Ge 15:1–18; 17:10,13–14). To be "cut off" is to receive the curses of the covenant symbolized in the cutting rituals. It may mean the penalty of execution (e.g., Ex 31:14–15) or of death without children (see Lev 18:14,29 with 20:20). In any event, God put the offender to death, with or without human agency.

7:25 fat. Compare 3:3 and 17.

ple. 26And wherever you live, you must not eat the blood[j] of any bird or animal. 27If anyone eats blood,[k] that person must be cut off from his people.' "

The Priests' Share

28The LORD said to Moses, 29"Say to the Israelites: 'Anyone who brings a fellowship offering to the LORD is to bring part of it as his sacrifice to the LORD. 30With his own hands
he is to bring the offering made to the LORD by fire; he is to bring the fat, together with
the breast, and wave the breast before the LORD as a wave offering.[l] 31The priest shall
burn the fat on the altar, but the breast belongs to Aaron and his sons.[m] 32You are to give
the right thigh of your fellowship offerings to the priest as a contribution.[n] 33The son of
Aaron who offers the blood and the fat of the fellowship offering shall have the right
thigh as his share. 34From the fellowship offerings of the Israelites, I have taken the
breast that is waved and the thigh[o] that is presented and have given them to Aaron the
priest and his sons[p] as their regular share from the Israelites.' "
35This is the portion of the offerings made to the LORD by fire that were allotted to Aaron and his sons on the day they were presented to serve the LORD as priests. 36On the day
they were anointed,[q] the LORD commanded that the Israelites give this to them as their
regular share for the generations to come.

37These, then, are the regulations for the burnt offering,[r] the grain offering,[s] the sin
offering, the guilt offering, the ordination offering[t] and the fellowship offering, 38which
the LORD gave Moses on Mount Sinai on the day he commanded the Israelites to bring
their offerings to the LORD,[u] in the Desert of Sinai.

The Ordination of Aaron and His Sons

8 The LORD said to Moses, 2"Bring Aaron and his sons, their garments, the anointing
oil,[v] the bull for the sin offering, the two rams and the basket containing bread
made without yeast,[w] 3and gather the entire assembly[x] at the entrance to the Tent of
Meeting." 4Moses did as the LORD commanded him, and the assembly gathered at the entrance to the Tent of Meeting.
5Moses said to the assembly, "This is what the LORD has commanded to be done."
6Then Moses brought Aaron and his sons forward and washed them with water.[y] 7He
put the tunic on Aaron, tied the sash around him, clothed him with the robe and put the
ephod on him. He also tied the ephod to him by its skillfully woven waistband; so it was
fastened on him.[z] 8He placed the breastpiece on him and put the Urim and Thummim[a]
in the breastpiece. 9Then he placed the turban on Aaron's head and set the gold plate,
the sacred diadem,[b] on the front of it, as the LORD commanded Moses.
10Then Moses took the anointing oil[c] and anointed[d] the tabernacle and everything
in it, and so consecrated them. 11He sprinkled some of the oil on the altar seven times,

7:26 [j]Ge 9:4
7:27 [k]Lev 17:10-24; Ac 15:20,29
7:30 [l]Ex 29:24; Nu 6:20
7:31 [m]ver 34
7:32 [n]ver 34; Lev 9:21; Nu 6:20
7:34 [o]Lev 10:15 [p]Ex 29:27; Nu 18:18-19
7:36 [q]Ex 40:13,15; Lev 8:12,30
7:37 [r]Lev 6:9 [s]Lev 6:14 [t]ver 1,11
7:38 [u]Lev 1:2
8:2 [v]Ex 30:23-25,30 [w]Ex 29:2-3
8:3 [x]Nu 8:9
8:6 [y]Ex 29:4; 30:19; Ps 26:6; Ac 22:16; 1Co 6:11; Eph 5:26
8:7 [z]Ex 28:4
8:8 [a]Ex 28:30
8:9 [b]Ex 28:36
8:10 [c]ver 2 [d]Ex 30:26

7:26 eat the blood. This phrase refers to eating meat from which the blood had not been drained (1Sa 14:33). The theological reason for this ban is given in 17:11 (see Ge 9:4).
7:30 wave offering. A wave offering was usually part of a larger ritual that involved the breast of the animal being waved (perhaps lifted up) before the altar by the priest and worshiper before it was given to the priest for eating (see Nu 5:25). It is mentioned ten times in Leviticus.
■ **7:37–38** *Conclusion.* This summary of the instructions on sacrifices balances with the introduction in 1:1–2.
7:37 ordination offering. This type of offering was not mentioned in the preceding instructions. It was a sacrifice offered when a priest was consecrated to holy service (8:14–36; Ex 29:1–35).
■ **8:1—10:20** *The Ordination of the Aaronic Priesthood.* These chapters consist primarily of narratives that depict the institution of the Aaronic priesthood. They report Moses' installation of the priests (8:1–36), their first sacrifices (9:1–24) and their severe failure (10:1–20). Through these accounts Moses demonstrated the central role of the Aaronic priesthood in Israel's faith, but he also warned that the priesthood was to submit to the law of God as it performed its all-important duties.
8:1—9:24 This passage repeats the instructions about the Levites' ordination given in Exodus 29. Following God's command, Moses ordained Aaron and his sons to the priesthood. Believers today can learn from these chapters how important God's chosen priesthood is for their faith as well. Unlike the corruptible Aaronic priesthood, Christ is our perfect high priest. We can also learn of the importance of our own daily priestly activities (such as prayer, worship, etc.) and the necessity of performing them in accordance with God's Word.

■ **8:1–36** *Moses Begins the Ceremonies.* Moses led the ceremony of ordination by carefully following God's law and preparing Aaron and his sons for making their own sacrifices. This material divides into six sections, each one detailing something Moses did in the ceremonies. Elaborate ceremonies continued for eight days and led to a grand display of God's approval of the Aaronic priesthood.
■ **8:1–4** Moses Calls an Assembly. Following the command of God, Moses called for Israel to gather in a sacred assembly.
8:2 their garments. The priests' garments separated them from common activities through a variety of symbolic elements. See Exodus 28:4–43. **anointing oil.** Ceremonial oil was used to consecrate holy things and holy people (vv. 10–12). The anointing oil represented the presence of God's Spirit (see 1Sa 16:13). **bull . . . without yeast.** Preparations for sacrificial ceremonies were made according to the instructions given in the preceding chapters (see 1:3—7:36).
8:3 at the entrance to the Tent of Meeting. That is, in the screened-off area surrounding the tabernacle.
■ **8:5–9** *Moses Washes and Clothes.* Moses' first step was to cleanse and clothe Aaron and his sons.
8:6 washed. Ritual washings were performed in the bronze basin of the courtyard (Ex 40:30). The priests' cleansing symbolized the removal of the moral corruption of the world and their consecration to the Lord's service. Many interpreters see these kinds of Old Testament washings as precursors of New Testament baptism (Ex 30:17–21).
8:7 ephod. See note on Exodus 28:6.
8:8 Urim and Thummim. See note on Exodus 28:30.
■ **8:10–13** *Moses Anoints With Oil.* Moses anointed the tabernacle, as well as Aaron and his sons, to symbolize God's Spirit on them.
8:10 consecrated them. The oil anointed common things with

8:11 anointing the altar and all its utensils and the basin with its stand, to consecrate them.[e]
[e]Ex 30:29 12He poured some of the anointing oil on Aaron's head and anointed[f] him to consecrate
8:12 [f]Lev 21:10,12 him.[g] 13Then he brought Aaron's sons forward, put tunics on them, tied sashes around
[g]Ex 30:30 them and put headbands on them, as the LORD commanded Moses.
8:14 14He then presented the bull[h] for the sin offering,[i] and Aaron and his sons laid their
[h]Lev 4:3 [i]Ps 66:15; hands on its head. 15Moses slaughtered the bull and took some of the blood, and with
Eze 43:19 his finger he put it on all the horns of the altar[j] to purify the altar.[k] He poured out the
8:15 rest of the blood at the base of the altar. So he consecrated it to make atonement for it.[l]
[j]Lev 4:7 [k]Heb 9:22 [l]Eze 43:20 16Moses also took all the fat around the inner parts, the covering of the liver, and both
8:17 kidneys and their fat, and burned it on the altar. 17But the bull with its hide and its flesh
[m]Lev 4:11 and its offal[m] he burned up outside the camp,[n] as the LORD commanded Moses.
[n]Lev 4:12 18He then presented the ram[o] for the burnt offering, and Aaron and his sons laid their
8:18 hands on its head. 19Then Moses slaughtered the ram and sprinkled the blood against
[o]ver 2 the altar on all sides. 20He cut the ram into pieces and burned the head, the pieces and
the fat. 21He washed the inner parts and the legs with water and burned the whole ram
on the altar as a burnt offering, a pleasing aroma, an offering made to the LORD by fire,
8:22 as the LORD commanded Moses.
[p]ver 2 22He then presented the other ram, the ram for the ordination,[p] and Aaron and his
sons laid their hands on its head. 23Moses slaughtered the ram and took some of its blood
and put it on the lobe of Aaron's right ear, on the thumb of his right hand and on the big
toe of his right foot. 24Moses also brought Aaron's sons forward and put some of the
8:24 blood on the lobes of their right ears, on the thumbs of their right hands and on the big
[q]Heb 9:18-22 toes of their right feet. Then he sprinkled blood against the altar on all sides.[q] 25He took
the fat, the fat tail, all the fat around the inner parts, the covering of the liver, both kidneys and their fat and the right thigh. 26Then from the basket of bread made without
yeast, which was before the LORD, he took a cake of bread, and one made with oil, and
a wafer; he put these on the fat portions and on the right thigh. 27He put all these in the
hands of Aaron and his sons and waved them before the LORD as a wave offering. 28Then
Moses took them from their hands and burned them on the altar on top of the burnt of-
8:29 fering as an ordination offering, a pleasing aroma, an offering made to the LORD by fire.
[r]Lev 7:31-34 29He also took the breast—Moses' share of the ordination ram[r]—and waved it before the
LORD as a wave offering, as the LORD commanded Moses.
30Then Moses took some of the anointing oil and some of the blood from the altar and
8:30 [s]Ex 28:2 [t]Nu 3:3 sprinkled them on Aaron and his garments[s] and on his sons and their garments. So he
consecrated[t] Aaron and his garments and his sons and their garments.
31Moses then said to Aaron and his sons, "Cook the meat at the entrance to the Tent
of Meeting and eat it there with the bread from the basket of ordination offerings, as I
commanded, saying,[a] 'Aaron and his sons are to eat it.' 32Then burn up the rest of the
meat and the bread. 33Do not leave the entrance to the Tent of Meeting for seven days,
8:34 until the days of your ordination are completed, for your ordination will last seven days.
[u]Heb 7:16 34What has been done today was commanded by the LORD[u] to make atonement for you.

[a] 31 Or *I was commanded:*

---

the presence of God, thus separating them to him and his service (see note on v. 2).

8:12 on Aaron's head. The consecration of Aaron through the anointing of oil on this day and that of his descendants in the future was celebrated in the worship of Israel (Ps 133). Thus the high priest could later be set alongside the king as one anointed (Zec 4:14).

■**8:14–17** *Moses Makes a Sin Offering.* Moses offered a bull as a sin offering to atone for the sins of Aaron and his sons (cf. 4:1—5:13 and 6:24–30).

8:14 laid their hands on its head. Placing hands on the animal symbolized the transference of guilt from the worshipers to the animal. Aaron and his sons needed forgiveness before they could minister to others.

8:15–16 Moses went through an elaborate ceremony in line with God's instructions for sin offerings. He put some of the blood on the altar "to purify" it and poured the rest at its base "to consecrate it to make atonement." He burned the required parts of the sacrifice on the altar to make atonement and burned up the rest of it outside the camp.

■**8:18–21** *Moses Makes a Burnt Offering.* Moses presented a ram as a burnt offering on behalf of Aaron and his sons (cf. 1:3–17; 6:8–13).

■**8:22–36** *Moses Makes an Ordination Offering.* Moses performed his last sacrifice (8:22–30). Then he ordered the priests to wait for seven days before proceeding to a more active priestly role.

8:22 ram for the ordination. See note on 7:37.

8:23–26 right. The right side was often associated with strength and high performance (Ge 48:13–18; Ex 15:6,12; Pss 16:11; 17:7). The right side symbolized the most important and best portion of the worshiper and the sacrifice (see 14:14–28).

8:23 lobe . . . thumb . . . big toe. Probably symbolizing that the whole body (from head to toe) was consecrated to God.

8:27–29 as a wave offering . . . as an ordination offering . . . as a wave offering. The portions Moses gave to Aaron and his sons were waved as though they were a wave offering (see Nu 18:18), but Moses took them back for burning as an ordination offering (v. 28). Then Moses took the breast, his rightful portion (see note on 7:30) and performed a normal wave offering.

8:30 anointing oil . . . blood . . . sprinkled. The sprinkling of oil and blood was to set the priests and their garments apart from ordinary use for the special use of service to the Lord (cf. Ex 24:6–7; Heb 9:13,19,21). These rituals are fulfilled in the consecration that occurs when Christ's blood is sprinkled on our hearts (Heb 10:22; 12:24).

8:33–35 Do not leave . . . for seven days . . . so you will not die. Aaron and his sons spent a full week without interruption in the presence of God in preparation for their service as priests. This full devotion to the Lord was so important that they would suffer death if they neglected it (cf. 10:1–3).

8:34 to make atonement for you. The purpose of all of Moses' activities up to this point was to atone for the sins of the priests.

35 You must stay at the entrance to the Tent of Meeting day and night for seven days and
do what the LORD requires,[v] so you will not die; for that is what I have been commanded." 36 So Aaron and his sons did everything the LORD commanded through Moses.

The Priests Begin Their Ministry

9 On the eighth day[w] Moses summoned Aaron and his sons and the elders of Israel.
2 He said to Aaron, "Take a bull calf for your sin offering and a ram for your burnt
offering, both without defect, and present them before the LORD. 3 Then say to the Israelites: 'Take a male goat for a sin offering, a calf and a lamb—both a year old and without defect—for a burnt offering, 4 and an ox[a] and a ram for a fellowship offering[b] to sacrifice before the LORD, together with a grain offering mixed with oil. For today the LORD
will appear to you.[x]' "

5 They took the things Moses commanded to the front of the Tent of Meeting, and the
entire assembly came near and stood before the LORD. 6 Then Moses said, "This is what
the LORD has commanded you to do, so that the glory of the LORD[y] may appear to you."

7 Moses said to Aaron, "Come to the altar and sacrifice your sin offering and your
burnt offering and make atonement for yourself and the people; sacrifice the offering
that is for the people and make atonement for them, as the LORD has commanded.[z]"

8 So Aaron came to the altar and slaughtered the calf as a sin offering[a] for himself.
9 His sons brought the blood to him,[b] and he dipped his finger into the blood and put it
on the horns of the altar; the rest of the blood he poured out at the base of the altar.[c]
10 On the altar he burned the fat, the kidneys and the covering of the liver from the sin
offering, as the LORD commanded Moses; 11 the flesh and the hide[d] he burned up outside
the camp.[e]

12 Then he slaughtered the burnt offering. His sons handed him the blood, and he
sprinkled it against the altar on all sides. 13 They handed him the burnt offering piece by
piece, including the head, and he burned them on the altar.[f] 14 He washed the inner parts
and the legs and burned them on top of the burnt offering on the altar.

15 Aaron then brought the offering that was for the people.[g] He took the goat for the
people's sin offering and slaughtered it and offered it for a sin offering as he did with the
first one.

16 He brought the burnt offering and offered it in the prescribed way.[h] 17 He also
brought the grain offering, took a handful of it and burned it on the altar in addition to
the morning's burnt offering.[i]

18 He slaughtered the ox and the ram as the fellowship offering for the people.[j] His
sons handed him the blood, and he sprinkled it against the altar on all sides. 19 But the
fat portions of the ox and the ram—the fat tail, the layer of fat, the kidneys and the covering of the liver— 20 these they laid on the breasts, and then Aaron burned the fat on
the altar. 21 Aaron waved the breasts and the right thigh before the LORD as a wave offering,[k] as Moses commanded.

22 Then Aaron lifted his hands toward the people and blessed them.[l] And having sacrificed the sin offering, the burnt offering and the fellowship offering, he stepped down.

23 Moses and Aaron then went into the Tent of Meeting. When they came out, they
blessed the people; and the glory of the LORD[m] appeared to all the people. 24 Fire[n] came

8:35 [v]Nu 3:7; 9:19; Dt 11:1; 1Ki 2:3; Eze 48:11
9:1 [w]Eze 43:27
9:4 [x]Ex 29:43
9:6 [y]ver 23; Ex 24:16
9:7 [z]Heb 5:1,3; 7:27
9:8 [a]Lev 4:1-12
9:9 [b]ver 12,18 [c]Lev 4:7
9:11 [d]Lev 4:11 [e]Lev 4:12; 8:17
9:13 [f]Lev 1:8
9:15 [g]Lev 4:27-31
9:16 [h]Lev 1:1-13
9:17 [i]Lev 2:1-2; 3:5
9:18 [j]Lev 3:1-11
9:21 [k]Ex 29:24,26; Lev 7:30-34
9:22 [l]Nu 6:23; Dt 21:5; Lk 24:50
9:23 [m]ver 6
9:24 [n]Jdg 6:21; 2Ch 7:1

[a] *4* The Hebrew word can include both male and female; also in verses 18 and 19. [b] *4* Traditionally *peace offering*; also in verses 18 and 22

■ **9:1–24** *Aaron and His Sons Complete the Ceremonies.* After a waiting period of seven days, Moses turned the practice of sacrificing over to Aaron and his sons. Moses ordered the sacrifices (vv. 1–7), they were offered (vv. 8–23a) and God responded positively (vv. 23b–24).

■ **9:1–7** *Moses Orders Sacrifices.* Moses commanded Aaron and his sons to prepare and perform sacrifices for themselves and for the people.

9:2 sin offering . . . burnt offering. These sacrifices were for the priests (see 6:8–13,24–30).

9:3–4 sin offering . . . burnt offering . . . fellowship offering . . . grain offering. These offerings were made on behalf of the people (see 1:3—5:13). **the LORD will appear.** Moses' expectation was fulfilled at the end of this narrative (vv. 23b–24).

9:6 so that the glory . . . may appear to you. The promise of a revelation of God's glory was so important that Moses repeated it before the people after first giving it to the priests (see vv. 4, 23b–24). Divine approval of these events exalted the careful observance of Moses' worship regulations as a model for generations to come. It also explains why the glory of God was shown at the resurrection and ascension of Christ (Mt 28:1–10,16–20; Lk 24; Ac 1:1–10; 2:1–12,29–36; Eph 1:18–21): It was a demonstration of God's approval of his atoning death.

9:7 The priests made atonement for themselves as well as for the people, thus the various regulations in 1:3—7:36. Hebrews 5:3 explains that the need to offer sacrifices for the priests shows the inferiority of the Aaronic priests to Christ, the great and final high priest who knew no sin. In this way these Old Testament regulations pointed to their own inadequacies and the need for a greater high priest to come.

■ **9:8–23a** *Aaron Offers Sacrifices.* Moses carefully recorded that Aaron and his sons did everything just as they had been instructed, in total compliance with the laws God had given (cf. 1:3—7:36). The blessings that followed resulted from this fidelity, as they did for generations to come.

9:22 blessed. The traditional priestly blessing is found in Numbers 6:23–26.

9:23 the glory of the LORD. Just as Moses had promised the priests (v. 4) and the people (v. 5), God's brilliant glory was revealed to them.

out from the presence of the LORD and consumed the burnt offering and the fat portions
on the altar. And when all the people saw it, they shouted for joy and fell facedown.[o]

The Death of Nadab and Abihu

10 Aaron's sons Nadab and Abihu[p] took their censers, put fire in them[q] and added incense; and they offered unauthorized fire before the LORD, contrary to his
command.[r] 2 So fire came out from the presence of the LORD and consumed them,[s] and
they died before the LORD. 3 Moses then said to Aaron, "This is what the LORD spoke of
when he said:

> " 'Among those who approach me[t]
> I will show myself holy;[u]
> in the sight of all the people
> I will be honored.[v]' "

Aaron remained silent.
4 Moses summoned Mishael and Elzaphan,[w] sons of Aaron's uncle Uzziel,[x] and said
to them, "Come here; carry your cousins outside the camp,[y] away from the front of the
sanctuary." 5 So they came and carried them, still in their tunics,[z] outside the camp, as
Moses ordered.
6 Then Moses said to Aaron and his sons Eleazar and Ithamar, "Do not let your hair
become unkempt,[a][a] and do not tear your clothes, or you will die and the LORD will be angry with the whole community.[b] But your relatives, all the house of Israel, may mourn
for those the LORD has destroyed by fire. 7 Do not leave the entrance to the Tent of Meeting or you will die, because the LORD's anointing oil[c] is on you." So they did as Moses said.
8 Then the LORD said to Aaron, 9 "You and your sons are not to drink wine[d] or other
fermented drink[e] whenever you go into the Tent of Meeting, or you will die. This is a lasting ordinance for the generations to come. 10 You must distinguish between the holy and
the common, between the unclean and the clean,[f] 11 and you must teach[g] the Israelites
all the decrees the LORD has given them through Moses.[h]"
12 Moses said to Aaron and his remaining sons, Eleazar and Ithamar, "Take the grain
offering left over from the offerings made to the LORD by fire and eat it prepared without
yeast beside the altar,[i] for it is most holy. 13 Eat it in a holy place, because it is your share
and your sons' share of the offerings made to the LORD by fire; for so I have been commanded. 14 But you and your sons and your daughters may eat the breast that was waved
and the thigh that was presented. Eat them in a ceremonially clean place;[j] they have been

9:24 [o]1Ki 18:39
10:1 [p]Ex 24:1; Nu 3:2-4; 26:61 [q]Lev 16:12 [r]Ex 30:9
10:2 [s]Nu 3:4; 16:35; 26:61
10:3 [t]Ex 19:22 [u]Ex 30:29; Lev 21:6; Eze 28:22 [v]Isa; 49:3
10:4 [w]Ex 6:22 [x]Ex 6:18 [y]Ac 5:6,9,10
10:5 [z]Lev 8:13
10:6 [a]Lev 21:10 [b]Nu 1:53; 16:22; Jos 7:1; 22:18; 2Sa 24:1
10:7 [c]Ex 28:41; Lev 21:12
10:9 [d]Hos 4:11 [e]Pr 20:1; Isa 28:7; Eze 44:21; Lk 1:15; Eph 5:18; 1Ti 3:3; Tit 1:7
10:10 [f]Lev 11:47; 20:25; Eze 22:26
10:11 [g]Mal 2:7 [h]Dt 24:8
10:12 [i]Lev 6:14-18; 21:22
10:14 [j]Ex 29:24,26-27; Lev 7:31,34; Nu 18:11

[a] 6 Or *Do not uncover your heads*

■ **9:23b–24** *God Responds to the Sacrifices.* God demonstrated his approval of the Aaronic priesthood by consuming the sacrifices with a miraculous fire from his holy presence.

9:24 Fire came out. This unusual display of God's glory confirmed his acceptance of Aaron and his sons (see 1Ki 18:38; 1Ch 21:26; 2Ch 7:1). By contrast, in the next narrative, fire from God destroyed in judgment (10:2; Heb 12:28–29).

■ **10:1–20** *Aaron and His Sons Violate the Ceremonies.* The dramatic display of God's approval through fire consuming the sacrifices (9:23b–24) led Moses to report God's judgment against Aaron's sons to explain the current state of the Aaronic priesthood and to warn against violations in the future. These first halting steps of the priests would characterize their history and lead to Malachi's prophecy of the need for a purified priesthood (Mal 3:1–5). This chapter looks first at the sin of Nadab and Abihu (vv. 1–11) and closes with violations by Eleazar and Ithamar (vv. 12–20).

■ **10:1–11** *Nadab and Abihu.* This passage recounts the sin of these two priests and God's judgment against them.

10:1–7 See *HC* 96.

10:1 censers. Vessels for burning incense (16:12–13; Rev 8:3–4). **unauthorized fire.** The priests did not carefully observe the regulations for offering incense. Apparently they used coals that were not from the altar (16:12; Ex 30:1–9). In light of the regulation that follows (vv. 8–11), it is likely that Nadab and Abihu fell into this serious error because they were intoxicated.

10:2 fire came out from the presence of the LORD. The same divine fire that had signaled God's approval of Aaron and his sons (9:24) engulfed those who encroached upon his altar in an unauthorized fashion. Under the new covenant, the divine wrath against sin that occasioned the death of Christ will blaze against those who reject that sacrifice yet still attempt to approach God in their sin (Heb 10:26–31; 12:14–28).

10:3 those who approach me . . . show myself holy. Although all of God's people in all times fail to honor him as they ought, God is exceedingly patient with his people (Joel 2:13). Even so, God expects the utmost regard for his holy character from those who draw near his special presence (see Nu 25:6–8; 2Sa 6:6–7). His intolerance of violations in this regard demonstrates his holiness. See *WLC* 152,174.

10:6 hair . . . unkempt . . . tear . . . clothes. These were marks of mourning (13:45; 21:10). Although the laity could mourn the deaths of Nadab and Abihu, the priests were forbidden to mourn (cf. 21:10–12)—in demonstration that their judgment was just.

10:8–11 This addendum to the story suggests that the cause of the violation was drunkenness.

10:10 holy . . . common . . . unclean . . . clean. The priests' job was to teach the people these basic religious distinctions. "Holy" applies to what is consecrated to God's service; "clean" to what is fit for him; "common" and "unclean" to what is unfit for God's presence. The care required to make these distinctions could not be exercised while a priest was intoxicated. See note on 11:1—16:34.

■ **10:12–20** *Eleazar and Ithamar.* Following the flagrant violation of Nadab and Abihu, Moses recorded a second case of violations of the ceremonies of worship. Aaron's other sons, Eleazar and Ithamar, also broke the rules of worship, but they were not destroyed. This passage indicates that they were in violation and yet continued to serve as priests. It begins with instructions regarding the priests' portions of sacrifices (vv. 12–15) and the discovery of a violation (vv. 16–20).

10:12–15 The priests and their families were to eat portions of sacrifices, but with certain limits. They were to eat only what was appropriate and that only in a holy place (see 7:28–36).

given to you and your children as your share of the Israelites' fellowship offerings.[a] 15The thigh[k] that was presented and the breast that was waved must be brought with the fat portions of the offerings made by fire, to be waved before the LORD as a wave offering. This will be the regular share for you and your children, as the LORD has commanded."

10:15
[k]Lev 7:34

a 14 Traditionally *peace offerings*

10:16–20 Moses discovered that Eleazar and Ithamar had violated the distinction between (1) a sin offering whose blood was sprinkled within the tabernacle and (2) one whose blood was sprinkled on the great altar in the courtyard. The priests were expected to eat the appropriate portions of the second type, but they did not.

God's Pattern for Worship: How Should I Worship God?

WORSHIP is the honoring and glorifying of God by gratefully acknowledging, in ways he has prescribed, the wonder of his attributes and actions. Distinctions may be made between private worship, including worship in a more general sense as a way of life (Ro 12:1; 1Co 10:31), and public worship, the corporate gathering of believers in the presence of God (2Ch 20:18; 29:28; Ne 8:6).

At all times, worship is a blend of awe and joy at the privilege of drawing near to the mighty Creator with radical humility and honest confession of sin and need. As worship is and will be central to life in the new heavens and the new earth (Isa 66:22–23; Rev 4:8–11, 5:9–14; 7:9–17; 11:15–18; 15:2–4; 19:1–10), so it must be central in the life of the church on Earth; worship should be one of the most important activities, both private and corporate, in each believer's life (Col 3:16–17).

The Law of Moses regulated worship much more specifically than it did any other aspect of life. Not only does this demonstrate that worship must be carefully regulated by the Word of God, but it also suggests that the Mosaic Law offers many insights into worship that is pleasing to God. Many aspects of Moses' regulations pointed forward to Christ and ceased to be valid after he had come, apart from the underlying moral principles they illustrated (see theological article "The Law of God" at Ex 20). Yet in the book of Psalms and a number of other Old Testament sources, God provided directions, hymns and prayers for use in Israel's worship. Christians rightly use these in worship today when they make proper applications in the light of the fuller revelation of the New Testament.

The primary features in the pattern for public worship that God gave to Israel were:

(1) The Sabbath, each seventh day following six days for labor, is to be set aside as a holy day of rest, to be observed as a memorial of creation (Ge 2:3; Ex 20:8–11) and redemption (Dt 5:12–15). God insisted on Sabbath-keeping (Ex 16:21–30; 20:8–9; 31:12–17; 34:21; 35:1–3; Lev 19:3,30; 23:3; cf. Isa 58:13–14) and declared Sabbath-breaking a capital offence (Ex 31:14; Nu 15:32–36).

(2) Three annual national feasts were instituted (Ex 23:14–17; 34:23; Dt 16:16), at which the people gathered at God's sanctuary, offered sacrifices celebrating his bounty, sought and acknowledged reconciliation and fellowship with him and ate and drank together as an expression of joy. The feasts of Passover and Unleavened Bread, held on the fourteenth day of the first month, commemorated the exodus (Ex 12; Lev 23:5–8; Nu 28:16–25; Dt 16:1–8). The Feast of Weeks, also called the Feast of Harvest and the day of Firstfruits, marked the end of the grain harvest and was held 50 days after the Sabbath that began Passover (Ex 23:16; 34:22; Lev 23:15–22; Nu 28:26–31; Dt 16:9–12). Finally, the Feast of Tabernacles or Booths, also called the Feast of Ingathering, held from the fifteenth to the twenty-second day of the seventh month, celebrated the end of the agricultural year and reminded the people of how God had led Israel through the desert (Lev 23:39–43; Nu 29:12–38, Dt 16:13–15).

(3) The Day of Atonement was held on the tenth day of the seventh month. On this important day in the annual calendar the high priest took blood into the central shrine of the sanctuary to atone for Israel's sins during the previous year, and the scapegoat went into the desert as a sign that those sins were now gone (Lev 16).

(4) The regular sacrificial system involved daily and monthly burnt offerings (Nu 28:1–15), plus a variety of personal sacrifices. The common features of these sacrifices were that anything offered must be flawless and that the blood of a sacrificial animal must be poured out on the altar of burnt offering to make atonement (Lev 17:11).

Rituals of personal purification (Lev 12–15; Nu 19) and devotion (e.g., consecration of the firstborn; Ex 13:1–16) were also part of the God-given pattern.

Under the new covenant, in which Old Testament types give way to their fulfillments, Christ's priesthood, sacrifice and intercession supersede the entire Mosaic system for atonement for sin (Heb 7–10). Baptism (Mt 28:19) and the Lord's Supper (Mt 26:26–29; 1Co 11:23–26) replace circumcision (Gal 2:3–5; 6:12–16) and Passover (1Co 5:7–8). Likewise, the Jewish festal calendar no longer binds believers (Gal 4:10; Col 2:16), and notions of ceremonial defilement and purification, imposed by God to enforce Old Testament awareness that some behaviors, conditions and exposures cut one off from God, cease to apply directly (Mk 7:19; 1Ti 4:3–4). Even the Sabbath has been renewed and is now observed on the first day of the week, the day of Jesus' resurrection, also referred to as "the Lord's day" (Ac 20:7; Rev 1:10). These changes were at first momentous, but the pattern of praise, thanksgiving, desire, trust, purity and service, which together comprise and embody true worship, continues unchanged to this day.

10:16 [l]Lev 9:3 16When Moses inquired about the goat of the sin offering[l] and found that it had been
burned up, he was angry with Eleazar and Ithamar, Aaron's remaining sons, and asked,
10:17 [m]Lev 6:24-30 17"Why didn't you eat the sin offering[m] in the sanctuary area? It is most holy; it was giv-
en to you to take away the guilt of the community by making atonement for them before
10:18 [n]Lev 6:26,30 the LORD. 18Since its blood was not taken into the Holy Place,[n] you should have eaten the
goat in the sanctuary area, as I commanded."

10:19 [o]Lev 9:12 19Aaron replied to Moses, "Today they sacrificed their sin offering and their burnt offering[o] before the LORD, but such things as this have happened to me. Would the LORD
have been pleased if I had eaten the sin offering today?" 20When Moses heard this, he
was satisfied.

Clean and Unclean Food

11:2 [p]Ac 10:12-14 **11** The LORD said to Moses and Aaron, 2"Say to the Israelites: 'Of all the animals
that live on land, these are the ones you may eat:[p] 3You may eat any animal that
has a split hoof completely divided and that chews the cud.

4" 'There are some that only chew the cud or only have a split hoof, but you must not
eat them. The camel, though it chews the cud, does not have a split hoof; it is ceremonially unclean for you. 5The coney,[a] though it chews the cud, does not have a split hoof;
it is unclean for you. 6The rabbit, though it chews the cud, does not have a split hoof; it
11:7 [q]Isa 65:4; 66:3,17 is unclean for you. 7And the pig,[q] though it has a split hoof completely divided, does not
11:8 chew the cud; it is unclean for you. 8You must not eat their meat or touch their carcass-
[r]Isa 52:11; Heb 9:10 es; they are unclean for you.[r]

9" 'Of all the creatures living in the water of the seas and the streams, you may eat
any that have fins and scales. 10But all creatures in the seas or streams that do not have
11:10 fins and scales—whether among all the swarming things or among all the other living
[s]Lev 7:18 creatures in the water—you are to detest.[s] 11And since you are to detest them, you must
not eat their meat and you must detest their carcasses. 12Anything living in the water that
does not have fins and scales is to be detestable to you.

13" 'These are the birds you are to detest and not eat because they are detestable: the
eagle, the vulture, the black vulture, 14the red kite, any kind of black kite, 15any kind of
raven, 16the horned owl, the screech owl, the gull, any kind of hawk, 17the little owl, the
cormorant, the great owl, 18the white owl, the desert owl, the osprey, 19the stork, any
11:20 kind of heron, the hoopoe and the bat.[b]
[t]Ac 10:14 20" 'All flying insects that walk on all fours are to be detestable to you.[t] 21There are,
however, some winged creatures that walk on all fours that you may eat: those that have

[a] 5 That is, the hyrax or rock badger [b] 19 The precise identification of some of the birds, insects and animals in this chapter is uncertain.

10:19 such things as this have happened. Given the literary context, this is almost certainly a reference to the deaths of Nadab and Abihu. Although Aaron and his sons had been forbidden to engage in traditional public displays of mourning over the deaths of Nadab and Abihu, and had been commanded to maintain the regular sacrifices, they were not forbidden to feel great sorrow and loss over these deaths. Eating their portion of the sacrifice was supposed to celebrate the atonement obtained through the sacrifice, but Aaron and his remaining sons were in no mood for rejoicing. Accordingly, they offered the sacrifices on behalf of the people, but did not eat the goat that had been given to them as their portion. Aaron's question implied that going through the motions of celebration on the day his sons had died would have been grossly insincere and inappropriate. Moses concurred with this conclusion. Since Aaron and his sons did not suffer divine judgment, God evidently agreed as well. David confirmed this type of reasoning in Psalm 51:16–17 when he expressed that a right heart is critical to the acceptability of godly sacrifice and rejoicing. Jesus also taught that extenuating circumstances sometimes make it appropriate to delay or alter normal forms of worship (Mt 5:23–24; cf. 2Ch 30:1–20).

▪ **11:1—16:34** *Uncleanness and Its Treatment.* In these chapters Moses explained the difference between clean and unclean. This was of vital importance for Israel's life with her holy God. "Clean" meant "fit for God's presence"; "unclean" "unfit for God's presence." Moses spoke of unclean animals (11:1–47), childbirth (12:1–8), skin diseases and mildew (13:1—14:57), bodily discharges (15:1–33) and the Day of Atonement (16:1–34). There were different categories of cleanliness when used to describe different objects. The reasons for many of these distinctions are unclear. At times, the Lord's regulations were very different from the ceremonial customs of cultures surrounding Israel. At other times, they were not entirely distinctive. In all cases, the chief purpose of observing these distinctions was that Israel be holy (11:44), separated from defiling practices. All who were unclean or who had come into contact with uncleanness had to abstain from public worship until they were cleansed.

▪ **11:1–47** *Unclean Animals.* Moses instructed the Israelites regarding clean and unclean animals. Although corpses of all animals were unclean (vv. 24,27,31–40), some perfectly healthy creatures were also declared unclean and were therefore not to be eaten. This classification was not justified by the Biblical writers based on health grounds (e.g., pigs as carriers of trichinosis) but on fundamental moral and theological principles. Carnivorous animals and birds of prey eat flesh with blood in it—a practice forbidden to God's people (7:26)—and they also approach corpses, which are unclean. Because of these practices, such animals were unclean. Others may have been considered unclean because they appeared to violate the natural order, such as in their mode of locomotion (e.g., winged creatures that walk instead of fly). Theologically, the clean creatures symbolize Israelites, while unclean animals symbolize Gentiles. Only domesticated clean animals were to be offered in sacrifice, for the sacrificial animal represented the worshiper. In restricting their diet to clean animals, the Israelites were reminded that God had chosen Israel alone among the nations. Only much later, when the new covenant widely included Gentiles among the people of God, were dietary restrictions lifted (Mk 7:19; Ac 10:15), even though their moral lessons still applied.

11:1–8 Cud-chewing (vegetarian), cloven-hoofed land animals were clean and so could be eaten. Other animals were unclean.

11:9–12 Only ordinary fish with fins and scales were clean. Other water creatures were unclean and therefore forbidden.

11:13–19 Birds of prey were unclean, but other birds were clean.

jointed legs for hopping on the ground. 22Of these you may eat any kind of locust,[u] katydid, cricket or grasshopper. 23But all other winged creatures that have four legs you are
to detest.
24" 'You will make yourselves unclean by these; whoever touches their carcasses will
be unclean till evening. 25Whoever picks up one of their carcasses must wash his
clothes,[v] and he will be unclean till evening.[w]
26" 'Every animal that has a split hoof not completely divided or that does not chew
the cud is unclean for you; whoever touches ⌊the carcass of⌋ any of them will be unclean.
27Of all the animals that walk on all fours, those that walk on their paws are unclean for
you; whoever touches their carcasses will be unclean till evening. 28Anyone who picks
up their carcasses must wash his clothes, and he will be unclean till evening. They are
unclean for you.
29" 'Of the animals that move about on the ground, these are unclean for you: the
weasel, the rat,[x] any kind of great lizard, 30the gecko, the monitor lizard, the wall lizard,
the skink and the chameleon. 31Of all those that move along the ground, these are unclean for you. Whoever touches them when they are dead will be unclean till evening.
32When one of them dies and falls on something, that article, whatever its use, will be
unclean, whether it is made of wood, cloth, hide or sackcloth.[y] Put it in water; it will be
unclean till evening, and then it will be clean. 33If one of them falls into a clay pot, everything in it will be unclean, and you must break the pot.[z] 34Any food that could be eat-
en but has water on it from such a pot is unclean, and any liquid that could be drunk
from it is unclean. 35Anything that one of their carcasses falls on becomes unclean; an
oven or cooking pot must be broken up. They are unclean, and you are to regard them
as unclean. 36A spring, however, or a cistern for collecting water remains clean, but anyone who touches one of these carcasses is unclean. 37If a carcass falls on any seeds that
are to be planted, they remain clean. 38But if water has been put on the seed and a carcass falls on it, it is unclean for you.
39" 'If an animal that you are allowed to eat dies, anyone who touches the carcass will
be unclean till evening. 40Anyone who eats some of the carcass must wash his clothes,
and he will be unclean till evening.[a] Anyone who picks up the carcass must wash his
clothes, and he will be unclean till evening.
41" 'Every creature that moves about on the ground is detestable; it is not to be eat-
en. 42You are not to eat any creature that moves about on the ground, whether it moves
on its belly or walks on all fours or on many feet; it is detestable. 43Do not defile yourselves by any of these creatures.[b] Do not make yourselves unclean by means of them or
be made unclean by them. 44I am the LORD your God;[c] consecrate yourselves[d] and be
holy,[e] because I am holy.[f] Do not make yourselves unclean by any creature that moves
about on the ground. 45I am the LORD who brought you up out of Egypt[g] to be your God;[h]
therefore be holy, because I am holy.[i]
46" 'These are the regulations concerning animals, birds, every living thing that
moves in the water and every creature that moves about on the ground. 47You must distinguish between the unclean and the clean, between living creatures that may be eat-
en and those that may not be eaten.[j] ' "

Purification After Childbirth

12 The LORD said to Moses, 2"Say to the Israelites: 'A woman who becomes pregnant and gives birth to a son will be ceremonially unclean for seven days, just
as she is unclean during her monthly period.[k] 3On the eighth day the boy is to be circumcised.[l] 4Then the woman must wait thirty-three days to be purified from her bleeding.
She must not touch anything sacred or go to the sanctuary until the days of her purifi-

11:22 [u]Mt 3:4; Mk 1:6
11:25 [v]Lev 14:8,47; 15:5 [w]ver 40; Nu 31:24
11:29 [x]Isa 66:17
11:32 [y]Lev 15:12
11:33 [z]Lev 6:28; 15:12
11:40 [a]Lev 17:15; 22:8; Eze 44:31
11:43 [b]Lev 20:25
11:44 [c]Ex 6:2,7; Isa 43:3; 51:15 [d]Lev 20:7 [e]Ex 19:6 [f]Lev 19:2; Ps 99:3; Eph 1:4; 1Th 4:7; 1Pe 1:15, 16*
11:45 [g]Lev 25:38,55; Ex 6:7; 20:2 [h]Ge 17:7 [i]Ex 19:6; 1Pe 1:16*
11:47 [j]Lev 10:10
12:2 [k]Lev 15:19; 18:19
12:3 [l]Ge 17:12; Lk 1:59; 2:21

11:20–23 Winged insects that walked could not be eaten, except for those that also had legs made for jumping.

11:24–45 Moses offered a list of animals that would defile Israelites if they were eaten or if their carcasses were touched.

11:24 till evening. Presumably the defilement took place after morning sacrifices (see note on 1:3–17). The evening sacrifices restored the cleanness of any who had become defiled during the day (vv. 24–25,27–28,31–32,39–40).

11:44–45 See *WLC* 95,152.

11:45 be holy. The word "holy" means "separate." Only God is intrinsically holy. He is holy in the sense of transcendence—by nature majestic and separate from his creation. He is also holy in the sense of moral purity. He has no sin, harbors no evil. Israel was to be holy as God is holy only in this latter sense. God's desire was that Israel be a "holy nation" that served him as priests (Ex 19:6). This holiness was attained by avoiding moral and ceremonial defilement. Such holiness is also important for those who now follow Jesus Christ, the Mediator of the new covenant (Heb 8:6; 9:15; 12:24). Christ also demands perfection (Mt 5:48) but provides the new Israel with holiness by his perfect sacrifice, which removed the sins of the elect forever (Heb 9–10), and by his Holy Spirit, who (among other things) inscribes God's moral law on their hearts (2Co 3:3). Without that holiness no one will see God (Heb 12:14).

■ **12:1–8** *Childbirth.* Moses instructed the Israelites regarding purification after childbirth.

12:2 unclean. It was the bleeding after childbirth that made a mother unclean (vv. 4–5,7). Similar regulations applied to the monthly period (v. 5; 15:19–27). It is possible that the bleeding in childbirth, like semen (15:16–18), was closely associated with fertility rituals in Canaan and was therefore unclean in Israel.

cation are over. 5 If she gives birth to a daughter, for two weeks the woman will be unclean, as during her period. Then she must wait sixty-six days to be purified from her bleeding.

6 " 'When the days of her purification for a son or daughter are over,[m] she is to bring to the priest at the entrance to the Tent of Meeting a year-old lamb[n] for a burnt offering and a young pigeon or a dove for a sin offering.[o] 7 He shall offer them before the LORD to make atonement for her, and then she will be ceremonially clean from her flow of blood.

" 'These are the regulations for the woman who gives birth to a boy or a girl. 8 If she cannot afford a lamb, she is to bring two doves or two young pigeons,[p] one for a burnt offering and the other for a sin offering.[q] In this way the priest will make atonement for her, and she will be clean.[r]' "

Regulations About Infectious Skin Diseases

13 The LORD said to Moses and Aaron, 2 "When anyone has a swelling[s] or a rash or a bright spot[t] on his skin that may become an infectious skin disease,[a][u] he must be brought to Aaron the priest[v] or to one of his sons[b] who is a priest. 3 The priest is to examine the sore on his skin, and if the hair in the sore has turned white and the sore appears to be more than skin deep,[c] it is an infectious skin disease. When the priest examines him, he shall pronounce him ceremonially unclean.[w] 4 If the spot[x] on his skin is white but does not appear to be more than skin deep and the hair in it has not turned white, the priest is to put the infected person in isolation for seven days.[y] 5 On the seventh day[z] the priest is to examine him,[a] and if he sees that the sore is unchanged and has not spread in the skin, he is to keep him in isolation another seven days. 6 On the seventh day the priest is to examine him again, and if the sore has faded and has not spread in the skin, the priest shall pronounce him clean;[b] it is only a rash. The man must wash his clothes,[c] and he will be clean.[d] 7 But if the rash does spread in his skin after he has shown himself to the priest to be pronounced clean, he must appear before the priest again.[e] 8 The priest is to examine him, and if the rash has spread in the skin, he shall pronounce him unclean; it is an infectious disease.

9 "When anyone has an infectious skin disease, he must be brought to the priest. 10 The priest is to examine him, and if there is a white swelling in the skin that has turned the hair white and if there is raw flesh in the swelling, 11 it is a chronic skin disease[f] and the priest shall pronounce him unclean. He is not to put him in isolation, because he is already unclean.

12 "If the disease breaks out all over his skin and, so far as the priest can see, it covers all the skin of the infected person from head to foot, 13 the priest is to examine him, and if the disease has covered his whole body, he shall pronounce that person clean. Since it has all turned white, he is clean. 14 But whenever raw flesh appears on him, he will be unclean. 15 When the priest sees the raw flesh, he shall pronounce him unclean. The raw flesh is unclean; he has an infectious disease.[g] 16 Should the raw flesh change and turn white, he must go to the priest. 17 The priest is to examine him, and if the sores

12:6 [m]Lk 2:22 [n]Ex 29:38; Lev 23:12; Nu 6:12,14; 7:15 [o]Lev 5:7
12:8 [p]Ge 15:9; Lev 14:22 [q]Lev 5:7; Lk 2:22-24* [r]Lev 4:26
13:2 [s]ver 10,19,28,43 [t]ver 4,38,39; Lev 14:56 [u]ver 3,9, 15; Ex 4:6; Lev 14:3,32; Nu 5:2; Dt 24:8 [v]Dt 24:8
13:3 [w]ver 8,11,20,30; Lev 21:1; Nu 9:6
13:4 [x]ver 2 [y]ver 5,21, 26,33,46; Lev 14:38; Nu 12:14,15; Dt 24:9
13:5 [z]Lev 14:9 [a]ver 27, 32,34,51
13:6 [b]ver 13,17,23,28, 34; Mt 8:3; Lk 5:12-14 [c]Lev 11:25 [d]Lev 11:25; 14:8,9, 20,48; 15:8; Nu 8:7
13:7 [e]Lk 5:14
13:11 [f]Ex 4:6; Lev 14:8; Nu 12:10; Mt 8:2
13:15 [g]ver 2

[a] *2* Traditionally *leprosy*; the Hebrew word was used for various diseases affecting the skin—not necessarily leprosy; also elsewhere in this chapter. [b] *2* Or *descendants* [c] *3* Or *be lower than the rest of the skin*; also elsewhere in this chapter

12:5 sixty-six days. It is not clear why a mother was unclean twice as long for the birth of a daughter (80 days total) as for the birth of a son (40 days total), though it may reflect the greater covenant status of males over females (males inherited hereditary land, had closer access to the presence of God in the sanctuary and in sacrifices, etc.). In Christ, such disparity between the genders with regard to covenant blessings is removed (Gal 3:28; see theological article "Union With Christ" at Gal 6).
12:6 See *BC* 34.
12:8 two doves or two young pigeons. These offerings were made after the birth of Jesus (Lk 2:24), thus depicting the poverty of Jesus' family. **burnt offering . . . sin offering.** Either or both were appropriate, depending on the circumstances of the mother (see notes on 1:3–17; 4:1—5:13).
■ **13:1—14:57** *Skin Diseases and Mildew.* These chapters contain God's laws concerning unclean skin diseases and mildew. These two forms of uncleanness are treated as one category (see 14:54–57) because of the apparent similarity between sores on the surface of the skin and mildew on other surfaces. The key principle in identifying a skin disease or mildew as unclean was whether or not it was progressing, suggesting active defilement. A disease affecting the whole body did not make a person unclean (13:12–13). Stable conditions were clean, but deteriorating ones were unclean (13:5–8,18–37). Similar principles applied to the diagnosis of uncleanness in clothing: Progressive mildews were unclean (13:47–52) but stable ones clean (13:53–58). These chapters divide into two main parts: identifying uncleanness caused by skin disease and mildew (13:1–59) and cleansing from such defilements (14:1–57).
■ **13:1–59** *Uncleanness Caused by Skin Diseases and Mildew.* Moses regulated the identification of skin diseases and mildew.
13:1–46 Moses described skin diseases that defile. As an alternative to the NIV's "infectious skin disease" and older translations' "leprosy," the notes here speak to "serious skin disease." Although modern physicians recognize the symptoms of various complaints here, the Biblical classification is didactic, not hygienic. After a preliminary discussion of the diseases in view (vv. 1–8), the passage deals with diseases exhibiting raw flesh (vv. 9–17), boils (vv. 18–23), burns (vv. 24–28), head sores (vv. 29–37), white spots (vv. 38–39) and baldness (vv. 40–44).

have turned white, the priest shall pronounce the infected person clean;[h] then he will be clean.

[18]"When someone has a boil[i] on his skin and it heals, [19]and in the place where the boil was, a white swelling or reddish-white[j] spot[k] appears, he must present himself to the priest. [20]The priest is to examine it, and if it appears to be more than skin deep and the hair in it has turned white, the priest shall pronounce him unclean. It is an infectious skin disease[l] that has broken out where the boil was. [21]But if, when the priest examines it, there is no white hair in it and it is not more than skin deep and has faded, then the priest is to put him in isolation for seven days. [22]If it is spreading in the skin, the priest shall pronounce him unclean; it is infectious. [23]But if the spot is unchanged and has not spread, it is only a scar from the boil, and the priest shall pronounce him clean.[m]

[24]"When someone has a burn on his skin and a reddish-white or white spot appears in the raw flesh of the burn, [25]the priest is to examine the spot, and if the hair in it has turned white, and it appears to be more than skin deep, it is an infectious disease that has broken out in the burn. The priest shall pronounce him unclean; it is an infectious skin disease.[n] [26]But if the priest examines it and there is no white hair in the spot and if it is not more than skin deep and has faded, then the priest is to put him in isolation for seven days.[o] [27]On the seventh day the priest is to examine him,[p] and if it is spreading in the skin, the priest shall pronounce him unclean; it is an infectious skin disease. [28]If, however, the spot is unchanged and has not spread in the skin but has faded, it is a swelling from the burn, and the priest shall pronounce him clean; it is only a scar from the burn.[q]

[29]"If a man or woman has a sore on the head[r] or on the chin, [30]the priest is to examine the sore, and if it appears to be more than skin deep and the hair in it is yellow and thin, the priest shall pronounce that person unclean; it is an itch, an infectious disease of the head or chin. [31]But if, when the priest examines this kind of sore, it does not seem to be more than skin deep and there is no black hair in it, then the priest is to put the infected person in isolation for seven days.[s] [32]On the seventh day the priest is to examine the sore,[t] and if the itch has not spread and there is no yellow hair in it and it does not appear to be more than skin deep, [33]he must be shaved except for the diseased area, and the priest is to keep him in isolation another seven days. [34]On the seventh day the priest is to examine the itch,[u] and if it has not spread in the skin and appears to be no more than skin deep, the priest shall pronounce him clean. He must wash his clothes, and he will be clean.[v] [35]But if the itch does spread in the skin after he is pronounced clean, [36]the priest is to examine him, and if the itch has spread in the skin, the priest does not need to look for yellow hair; the person is unclean.[w] [37]If, however, in his judgment it is unchanged and black hair has grown in it, the itch is healed. He is clean, and the priest shall pronounce him clean.

[38]"When a man or woman has white spots on the skin, [39]the priest is to examine them, and if the spots are dull white, it is a harmless rash that has broken out on the skin; that person is clean.

[40]"When a man has lost his hair and is bald,[x] he is clean. [41]If he has lost his hair from the front of his scalp and has a bald forehead, he is clean. [42]But if he has a reddish-white sore on his bald head or forehead, it is an infectious disease breaking out on his head or forehead. [43]The priest is to examine him, and if the swollen sore on his head or forehead is reddish-white like an infectious skin disease, [44]the man is diseased and is unclean. The priest shall pronounce him unclean because of the sore on his head.

[45]"The person with such an infectious disease must wear torn clothes,[y] let his hair be unkempt,[a] cover the lower part of his face[z] and cry out, 'Unclean! Unclean!'[a] [46]As long as he has the infection he remains unclean. He must live alone; he must live outside the camp.[b]

Regulations About Mildew

[47]"If any clothing is contaminated with mildew—any woolen or linen clothing, [48]any woven or knitted material of linen or wool, any leather or anything made of leather—[49]and if the contamination in the clothing, or leather, or woven or knitted material, or any leather article, is greenish or reddish, it is a spreading mildew and must be shown

13:17 [h]ver 6
13:18 [i]Ex 9:9
13:19 [j]ver 24,42; Lev 14:37 [k]ver 2
13:20 [l]ver 2
13:23 [m]ver 6
13:25 [n]ver 11
13:26 [o]ver 4
13:27 [p]ver 5
13:28 [q]ver 2
13:29 [r]ver 43,44
13:31 [s]ver 4
13:32 [t]ver 5
13:34 [u]ver 5 [v]Lev 11:25
13:36 [w]ver 30
13:40 [x]Lev 21:5; 2Ki 2:23; Isa 3:24; 15:2; 22:12; Eze 27:31; 29:18; Am 8:10; Mic 1:16
13:45 [y]Lev 10:6 [z]Eze 24:17,22; Mic 3:7 [a]Lev 5:2; La 4:15; Lk 17:12
13:46 [b]Nu 5:1-4; 12:14; 2Ki 7:3; 15:5; Lk 17:12

[a] 45 *Or clothes, uncover his head*

13:47–59 Moses described mildew that defiles. Mildew was a problem near the Mediterranean Sea and the Sea of Galilee throughout much of the year, but particularly during the rainy season (October through March). In sum, an item with mildew that continued to grow was pronounced unclean.

to the priest.[c] 50The priest is to examine the mildew[d] and isolate the affected article for seven days. 51On the seventh day he is to examine it,[e] and if the mildew has spread in the clothing, or the woven or knitted material, or the leather, whatever its use, it is a destructive mildew; the article is unclean.[f] 52He must burn up the clothing, or the woven or knitted material of wool or linen, or any leather article that has the contamination in it, because the mildew is destructive; the article must be burned up.[g]

53"But if, when the priest examines it, the mildew has not spread in the clothing, or the woven or knitted material, or the leather article, 54he shall order that the contaminated article be washed. Then he is to isolate it for another seven days. 55After the affected article has been washed, the priest is to examine it, and if the mildew has not changed its appearance, even though it has not spread, it is unclean. Burn it with fire, whether the mildew has affected one side or the other. 56If, when the priest examines it, the mildew has faded after the article has been washed, he is to tear the contaminated part out of the clothing, or the leather, or the woven or knitted material. 57But if it reappears in the clothing, or in the woven or knitted material, or in the leather article, it is spreading, and whatever has the mildew must be burned with fire. 58The clothing, or the woven or knitted material, or any leather article that has been washed and is rid of the mildew, must be washed again, and it will be clean."

59These are the regulations concerning contamination by mildew in woolen or linen clothing, woven or knitted material, or any leather article, for pronouncing them clean or unclean.

Cleansing From Infectious Skin Diseases

14 The LORD said to Moses, 2"These are the regulations for the diseased person at the time of his ceremonial cleansing, when he is brought to the priest:[h] 3The priest is to go outside the camp and examine him.[i] If the person has been healed of his infectious skin disease,[a] 4the priest shall order that two live clean birds and some cedar wood, scarlet yarn and hyssop be brought for the one to be cleansed.[j] 5Then the priest shall order that one of the birds be killed over fresh water in a clay pot. 6He is then to take the live bird and dip it, together with the cedar wood, the scarlet yarn and the hyssop, into the blood of the bird that was killed over the fresh water.[k] 7Seven times he shall sprinkle[l] the one to be cleansed of the infectious disease and pronounce him clean. Then he is to release the live bird in the open fields.

8"The person to be cleansed must wash his clothes,[m] shave off all his hair and bathe with water;[n] then he will be ceremonially clean.[o] After this he may come into the camp,[p] but he must stay outside his tent for seven days. 9On the seventh day he must shave off all his hair; he must shave his head, his beard, his eyebrows and the rest of his hair. He must wash his clothes and bathe himself with water, and he will be clean.

10"On the eighth day[q] he must bring two male lambs and one ewe lamb a year old, each without defect, along with three-tenths of an ephah[b] of fine flour mixed with oil for a grain offering,[r] and one log[c] of oil.[s] 11The priest who pronounces him clean shall present both the one to be cleansed and his offerings before the LORD at the entrance to the Tent of Meeting.

12"Then the priest is to take one of the male lambs and offer it as a guilt offering,[t] along with the log of oil; he shall wave them before the LORD as a wave offering.[u] 13He is to slaughter the lamb in the holy place[v] where the sin offering and the burnt offering are slaughtered. Like the sin offering, the guilt offering belongs to the priest;[w] it is most

13:49 [c]Mk 1:44
13:50 [d]Eze 44:23
13:51 [e]ver 5 [f]Lev 14:44
13:52 [g]ver 55,57
14:2 [h]Mt 8:2-4; Mk 1:40-44; Lk 5:12-14; 17:14
14:3 [i]Lev 13:46
14:4 [j]ver 6,49,51,52; Nu 19:6; Ps 51:7
14:6 [k]ver 4
14:7 [l]2Ki 5:10,14; Isa 52:15; Eze 36:25
14:8 [m]Lev 11:25; 13:6 [n]ver 9 [o]ver 20 [p]Nu 5:2,3; 12:14,15; 2Ch 26:21
14:10 [q]Mt 8:4; Mk 1:44; Lk 5:14 [r]Lev 2:1 [s]ver 12,15,21,24
14:12 [t]Lev 5:18; 6:6-7 [u]Ex 29:24
14:13 [v]Ex 29:11 [w]Lev 6:24-30; 7:7

[a] *3* Traditionally *leprosy;* the Hebrew word was used for various diseases affecting the skin—not necessarily leprosy; also elsewhere in this chapter. [b] *10* That is, probably about 6 quarts (about 6.5 liters) [c] *10* That is, probably about 2/3 pint (about 0.3 liter); also in verses 12, 15, 21 and 24

■ **14:1–57** *Cleansing From Uncleanness Caused by Skin Diseases and Mildew.* Moses regulated the ceremonies for cleansing of skin diseases and mildew.

14:1–32 This section details the process for ritual cleansing following relief from skin diseases.

14:2 cleansing. These ceremonies conducted by the priest did not cure skin diseases. Diseased people came to the priest *after* having been healed (Lk 5:14). The task of the priest was to make them ceremonially clean, so that they would no longer be excluded from the camp, from other people and from God. Through these ceremonies the individuals were cleansed and restored to the community of the people of God. The cleansing took place in two stages, occurring one week apart.

14:3–8 Stage one took place outside the camp (see 13:45–46). Those infected would wash themselves and their clothes and shave off all their hair. The restoration ceremony involved two birds, one of which was killed and its blood used to purify the person who had been infected. The bird's death portrayed the end of life outside the camp. The other bird was set free. Its flight to freedom pictured the person's liberation from the effects of the disease. After this rite the person was restored to fellowship inside the camp.

14:9–20 This passage shows the Israelite being brought back into full communion with God. The ceremonies depicted here are like those used during the ordination of the priest (ch. 8). The Israelite was daubed with blood and anointed with oil and thus linked to the altar, the symbol of God's presence. A variation on this restoration procedure is prescribed for the poor in verses 21–31.

holy. 14The priest is to take some of the blood of the guilt offering and put it on the lobe
of the right ear of the one to be cleansed, on the thumb of his right hand and on the big
toe of his right foot.[x] 15The priest shall then take some of the log of oil, pour it in the palm
of his own left hand, 16dip his right forefinger into the oil in his palm, and with his finger sprinkle some of it before the LORD seven times. 17The priest is to put some of the oil
remaining in his palm on the lobe of the right ear of the one to be cleansed, on the thumb
of his right hand and on the big toe of his right foot, on top of the blood of the guilt offering. 18The rest of the oil in his palm the priest shall put on the head of the one to be
cleansed and make atonement for him before the LORD.
19"Then the priest is to sacrifice the sin offering and make atonement for the one to
be cleansed from his uncleanness. After that, the priest shall slaughter the burnt offering 20and offer it on the altar, together with the grain offering, and make atonement for
him, and he will be clean.[y]
21"If, however, he is poor[z] and cannot afford these,[a] he must take one male lamb as
a guilt offering to be waved to make atonement for him, together with a tenth of an
ephah[a] of fine flour mixed with oil for a grain offering, a log of oil, 22and two doves or two
young pigeons,[b] which he can afford, one for a sin offering and the other for a burnt offering.
23"On the eighth day he must bring them for his cleansing to the priest at the entrance
to the Tent of Meeting, before the LORD.[c] 24The priest is to take the lamb for the guilt offering,[d] together with the log of oil,[e] and wave them before the LORD as a wave offering.[f]
25He shall slaughter the lamb for the guilt offering and take some of its blood and put it
on the lobe of the right ear of the one to be cleansed, on the thumb of his right hand and
on the big toe of his right foot.[g] 26The priest is to pour some of the oil into the palm of
his own left hand,[h] 27and with his right forefinger sprinkle some of the oil from his palm
seven times before the LORD. 28Some of the oil in his palm he is to put on the same places he put the blood of the guilt offering—on the lobe of the right ear of the one to be
cleansed, on the thumb of his right hand and on the big toe of his right foot. 29The rest
of the oil in his palm the priest shall put on the head of the one to be cleansed, to make
atonement for him before the LORD.[i] 30Then he shall sacrifice the doves or the young pigeons, which the person can afford,[j] 31one[b] as a sin offering and the other as a burnt offering,[k] together with the grain offering. In this way the priest will make atonement before the LORD on behalf of the one to be cleansed.[l]"
32These are the regulations for anyone who has an infectious skin disease[m] and who
cannot afford the regular offerings[n] for his cleansing.

Cleansing From Mildew

33The LORD said to Moses and Aaron, 34"When you enter the land of Canaan,[o] which
I am giving you as your possession,[p] and I put a spreading mildew in a house in that land,
35the owner of the house must go and tell the priest, 'I have seen something that looks
like mildew in my house.' 36The priest is to order the house to be emptied before he goes
in to examine the mildew, so that nothing in the house will be pronounced unclean. After this the priest is to go in and inspect the house. 37He is to examine the mildew on the
walls, and if it has greenish or reddish[q] depressions that appear to be deeper than the
surface of the wall, 38the priest shall go out the doorway of the house and close it up for
seven days.[r] 39On the seventh day[s] the priest shall return to inspect the house. If the mildew has spread on the walls, 40he is to order that the contaminated stones be torn out
and thrown into an unclean place outside the town.[t] 41He must have all the inside walls
of the house scraped and the material that is scraped off dumped into an unclean place
outside the town. 42Then they are to take other stones to replace these and take new clay
and plaster the house.
43"If the mildew reappears in the house after the stones have been torn out and the
house scraped and plastered, 44the priest is to go and examine it and, if the mildew has
spread in the house, it is a destructive mildew; the house is unclean.[u] 45It must be torn
down—its stones, timbers and all the plaster—and taken out of the town to an unclean
place.

14:14 [x]Ex 29:20; Lev 8:23
14:20 [y]ver 8
14:21 [z]Lev 5:7; 12:8 [a]ver 22,32
14:22 [b]Lev 5:7
14:23 [c]ver 10,11
14:24 [d]Nu 6:14 [e]ver 10 [f]ver 12
14:25 [g]ver 14; Ex 29:20
14:26 [h]ver 15
14:29 [i]ver 18
14:30 [j]Lev 5:7
14:31 [k]ver 22; Lev 5:7; 15:15,30 [l]ver 18, 19
14:32 [m]Lev 13:2 [n]ver 21
14:34 [o]Ge 12:5; Ex 6:4; Nu 13:2 [p]Ge 17:8; 48:4; Nu 27:12; 32:22; Dt 3:27; 7:1; 32:49
14:37 [q]Lev 13:19
14:38 [r]Lev 13:4
14:39 [s]Lev 13:5
14:40 [t]ver 45
14:44 [u]Lev 13:51

[a] *21* That is, probably about 2 quarts (about 2 liters) [b] *31* Septuagint and Syriac; Hebrew *31such as the person can afford, one*

14:33–57 This law adapts the principles of diagnosis (13:47–58) of uncleanness and of its cleansing (vv. 1–7) to the problems of mildew in houses. This is an issue that would have arisen in the settlement of Canaan rather than during the wilderness wanderings.

46"Anyone who goes into the house while it is closed up will be unclean till evening.[v]
47Anyone who sleeps or eats in the house must wash his clothes.[w]
48"But if the priest comes to examine it and the mildew has not spread after the house
has been plastered, he shall pronounce the house clean,[x] because the mildew is gone.
49To purify the house he is to take two birds and some cedar wood, scarlet yarn and hyssop.[y] 50He shall kill one of the birds over fresh water in a clay pot.[z] 51Then he is to take
the cedar wood, the hyssop,[a] the scarlet yarn and the live bird, dip them into the blood
of the dead bird and the fresh water, and sprinkle the house seven times.[b] 52He shall purify the house with the bird's blood, the fresh water, the live bird, the cedar wood, the
hyssop and the scarlet yarn. 53Then he is to release the live bird in the open fields[c] outside the town. In this way he will make atonement for the house, and it will be clean.[d]"
54These are the regulations for any infectious skin disease,[e] for an itch, 55for mildew[f]
in clothing or in a house, 56and for a swelling, a rash or a bright spot,[g] 57to determine
when something is clean or unclean.
These are the regulations for infectious skin diseases and mildew.[h]

Discharges Causing Uncleanness

15 The LORD said to Moses and Aaron, 2"Speak to the Israelites and say to them:
'When any man has a bodily discharge,[i] the discharge is unclean. 3Whether it
continues flowing from his body or is blocked, it will make him unclean. This is how his
discharge will bring about uncleanness:
4" 'Any bed the man with a discharge lies on will be unclean, and anything he sits on
will be unclean. 5Anyone who touches his bed must wash his clothes[j] and bathe with water,[k] and he will be unclean till evening.[l] 6Whoever sits on anything that the man with
a discharge sat on must wash his clothes and bathe with water, and he will be unclean
till evening.
7" 'Whoever touches the man[m] who has a discharge[n] must wash his clothes and
bathe with water, and he will be unclean till evening.
8" 'If the man with the discharge spits[o] on someone who is clean, that person must
wash his clothes and bathe with water, and he will be unclean till evening.
9" 'Everything the man sits on when riding will be unclean, 10and whoever touches
any of the things that were under him will be unclean till evening; whoever picks up
those things[p] must wash his clothes and bathe with water, and he will be unclean till
evening.
11" 'Anyone the man with a discharge touches without rinsing his hands with water
must wash his clothes and bathe with water, and he will be unclean till evening.
12" 'A clay pot[q] that the man touches must be broken, and any wooden article[r] is to
be rinsed with water.
13" 'When a man is cleansed from his discharge, he is to count off seven days[s] for his
ceremonial cleansing; he must wash his clothes and bathe himself with fresh water, and
he will be clean.[t] 14On the eighth day he must take two doves or two young pigeons[u] and
come before the LORD to the entrance to the Tent of Meeting and give them to the priest.
15The priest is to sacrifice them, the one for a sin offering[v] and the other for a burnt offering.[w] In this way he will make atonement before the LORD for the man because of his
discharge.[x]
16" 'When a man has an emission of semen,[y] he must bathe his whole body with water, and he will be unclean till evening.[z] 17Any clothing or leather that has semen on it
must be washed with water, and it will be unclean till evening. 18When a man lies with
a woman and there is an emission of semen,[a] both must bathe with water, and they will
be unclean till evening.
19" 'When a woman has her regular flow of blood, the impurity of her monthly period[b] will last seven days, and anyone who touches her will be unclean till evening.
20" 'Anything she lies on during her period will be unclean, and anything she sits on
will be unclean. 21Whoever touches her bed must wash his clothes and bathe with wa-

14:46 [v]Lev 11:24
14:47 [w]Lev 11:25
14:48 [x]Lev 13:6
14:49 [y]ver 4; 1Ki 4:33; ver 4
14:50 [z]ver 5
14:51 [a]ver 6; Ps 51:7 [b]ver 4,7
14:53 [c]ver 7 [d]ver 20
14:54 [e]Lev 13:2,30
14:55 [f]Lev 13:47-52
14:56 [g]Lev 13:2
14:57 [h]Lev 10:10
15:2 [i]ver 16,32; Lev 22:4; Nu 5:2; 2Sa 3:29; Mt 9:20
15:5 [j]Lev 11:25 [k]Lev 14:8 [l]Lev 11:24
15:7 [m]ver 19; Lev 22:5 [n]ver 16; Lev 22:4
15:8 [o]Nu 12:14
15:10 [p]Nu 19:10
15:12 [q]Lev 6:28 [r]Lev 11:32
15:13 [s]Lev 8:33 [t]ver 5
15:14 [u]Lev 14:22
15:15 [v]Lev 5:7 [w]Lev 14:31 [x]Lev 14:18,19
15:16 [y]ver 2; Lev 22:4; Dt 23:10 [z]ver 5; Dt 23:11
15:18 [a]1Sa 21:4
15:19 [b]ver 24; Lev 12:2

■ **15:1–33** *Discharges.* This chapter deals with the uncleanness caused by the following bodily discharges: (1) long-term male discharges (e.g., gonorrhea; vv. 2–15); (2) short-term male discharges (vv. 16–18); (3) short-term female discharges (i.e., menstruation; vv. 19–24); and (4) long-term female discharges (vv. 25–30). The association of discharges caused by illness with uncleanness is not difficult to understand. Yet healthy processes like semen emission (vv. 16–17), sexual intercourse (v. 18) or menstruation also made someone unclean; that is, unfit to worship in the special presence of God at the tabernacle. In some cases the inability to distinguish between these normal experiences and diseases with similar symptoms may have necessitated these regulations. Moreover, it may have been necessary to regulate normal, healthy sexual experiences in these ways to guard against the encroachment into Israel's worship of fertility rituals so widespread in Canaanite culture. A designation of "unclean" forced significant separation between sexual experiences and worship at the tabernacle (see 18:3).

ter, and he will be unclean till evening.[c] 22Whoever touches anything she sits on must
wash his clothes and bathe with water, and he will be unclean till evening. 23Whether it
is the bed or anything she was sitting on, when anyone touches it, he will be unclean till
evening.
24" 'If a man lies with her and her monthly flow[d] touches him, he will be unclean for
seven days; any bed he lies on will be unclean.
25" 'When a woman has a discharge of blood for many days at a time other than her
monthly period[e] or has a discharge that continues beyond her period, she will be unclean as long as she has the discharge, just as in the days of her period. 26Any bed she
lies on while her discharge continues will be unclean, as is her bed during her monthly
period, and anything she sits on will be unclean, as during her period. 27Whoever touches them will be unclean; he must wash his clothes and bathe with water, and he will be
unclean till evening.
28" 'When she is cleansed from her discharge, she must count off seven days, and after that she will be ceremonially clean. 29On the eighth day she must take two doves or
two young pigeons[f] and bring them to the priest at the entrance to the Tent of Meeting.
30The priest is to sacrifice one for a sin offering and the other for a burnt offering. In this
way he will make atonement for her before the LORD for the uncleanness of her discharge.[g]
31" 'You must keep the Israelites separate from things that make them unclean, so
they will not die in their uncleanness for defiling my dwelling place,[a][h] which is among
them.' "
32These are the regulations for a man with a discharge, for anyone made unclean by
an emission of semen,[i] 33for a woman in her monthly period, for a man or a woman with
a discharge, and for a man who lies with a woman who is ceremonially unclean.[j]

The Day of Atonement

16 The LORD spoke to Moses after the death of the two sons of Aaron who died
when they approached the LORD.[k] 2The LORD said to Moses: "Tell your brother
Aaron not to come whenever he chooses[l] into the Most Holy Place[m] behind the curtain
in front of the atonement cover on the ark, or else he will die, because I appear[n] in the
cloud[o] over the atonement cover.
3"This is how Aaron is to enter the sanctuary area:[p] with a young bull for a sin offer-

15:21 [c]ver 27
15:24 [d]ver 19; Lev 12:2; 18:19; 20:18; Eze 18:6
15:25 [e]Mt 9:20; Mk 5:25; Lk 8:43
15:29 [f]Lev 14:22
15:30 [g]Lev 5:10; 14:20, 31; 18:19; 2Sa 11:4; Mk 5:25; Lk 8:43
15:31 [h]Lev 20:3; Nu 5:3; 19:13,20; 2Sa 15:25; 2Ki 21:7; Ps 33:14; 74:7; 76:2; Eze 5:11; 23:38
15:32 [i]ver 2
15:33 [j]ver 19,24,25
16:1 [k]Lev 10:1
16:2 [l]Ex 30:10, Heb 9:7 [m]Heb 9:25; 10:19 [n]Ex 25:22 [o]Ex 40:34
16:3 [p]Heb 9:24,25

[a] 31 Or *my tabernacle*

16:1–34 *The Day of Atonement.* This was the holiest day in the Old Testament calendar. It fell in the seventh month (October) and involved the offering of various sacrifices; the entry of the high priest into the Most Holy Place; and the dispatch of a goat, symbolically carrying the people's sins, into the wilderness. For a summary of the sacrifices mentioned here, see notes on chapters 1, 4 and 5. A summary of the rites is given in verses 6–10 and fuller details in verses 11–28.

The Day of Atonement proceeded according to the following steps: (1) The high priest washed and dressed (v. 4). (2) He sacrificed a bull as a sin offering for himself (v. 6; cf. v. 11). (3) He entered the Most Holy Place and sprinkled the ark with blood (vv. 12–14). (4) He took two goats and by lot chose one to be the scapegoat and the other a sin offering (vv. 7–8). (5) He sacrificed one goat as a sin offering (vv. 9,15). (6) He reentered the Most Holy Place and sprinkled the ark with blood (v. 15). (7) He went out to the outer part of the Tent of Meeting and sprinkled the blood (v. 16). (8) He went out into the courtyard of the tabernacle and sprinkled the main altar with blood (vv. 18–19). (9) He confessed the sins of the Israelites as he laid his hands on the scapegoat's head (v. 21). (10) He sent the scapegoat into the desert (vv. 21–22). (11) With the scapegoat gone, the high priest changed into his regular garments and washed (vv. 23–24). (12) He offered burnt offerings for himself and for the people (vv. 24–25).

For the high priest the most important aspects of the ceremony were his entry into the Most Holy Place with the blood of the sin offerings and the dispatch of the scapegoat into the desert. These actions atoned for the sins of repentant Israelites (vv. 16,19,21–22). All sin offerings served to cleanse both the earthly sanctuary and the worshipers, but on other occasions the high priest entered only the Holy Place, not the Most Holy Place. Because the ark was housed in the Most Holy Place and served as God's throne, entry into the Most Holy Place was rare and perilous (v. 2). That the high priest entered on this one day of the year indicated the depth of atonement being made.

The scapegoat ceremony is unique to this day. By placing his hands on the goat's head and confessing the nation's sins, the high priest transferred the people's sins, which he normally bore, to the goat. The goat then symbolically carried the people's sins away into the desert.

Christians have long regarded the scapegoat as a type of Christ. The New Testament letter to the Hebrews (7:26–27; 9:6—10:19) makes many comparisons between the Day of Atonement and the death of Jesus. That Christ was delivered to the Gentiles and killed outside the walls of Jerusalem indicated that he was sent "outside the camp" like the scapegoat of old.

16:1 sons of Aaron who died. Compare 10:1–3.

16:2 atonement cover. The top of the ark, the atonement cover, was just beneath the throne of God (1Sa 4:4; 2Sa 6:2), as he was flanked by two cherubim (Ex 25:17–22). There God appeared and Aaron sprinkled the blood on the Day of Atonement; hence the renderings "atonement cover" or "mercy seat." God symbolically revealed the gospel through this cover on the ark. The ark itself contained the two stone tablets on which the very finger of God had inscribed the Ten Commandments (Ex 20; Dt 5; 10:1–6), which summarize God's law. Since all humans have violated this law, the righteousness of God demands death for all (Eze 18:20; Ro 6:23). God provided that the only means of atonement be the atoning blood on the ark's cover. That blood-splattered cover was the meeting point of the holy God with his unholy people. This earthly symbol pointed to the throne of the Majesty in heaven, where Christ has entered by his own blood (Heb 8:1; 9:12), blood that is efficacious for all the sins of the faithful—past, present and future (Ro 3:21–26; Heb 7:25; 9:15).

16:3 Aaron was to offer a bull as a sin offering for himself and his family before offering a goat for the people (v. 5). By contrast, Jesus Christ, the Mediator of the new and eternal covenant, was without sin and therefore offered sacrifice for his people only (Heb 7:26–27).

ing and a ram for a burnt offering. 4He is to put on the sacred linen tunic, with linen undergarments next to his body; he is to tie the linen sash around him and put on the lin-
en turban.[q] These are sacred garments;[r] so he must bathe himself with water[s] before
he puts them on. 5From the Israelite community[t] he is to take two male goats[u] for a sin
offering and a ram for a burnt offering.
6"Aaron is to offer the bull for his own sin offering to make atonement for himself and
his household.[v] 7Then he is to take the two goats and present them before the LORD at
the entrance to the Tent of Meeting. 8He is to cast lots for the two goats—one lot for the
LORD and the other for the scapegoat.[a] 9Aaron shall bring the goat whose lot falls to the
LORD and sacrifice it for a sin offering. 10But the goat chosen by lot as the scapegoat shall
be presented alive before the LORD to be used for making atonement[w] by sending it into
the desert as a scapegoat.
11"Aaron shall bring the bull for his own sin offering to make atonement for himself
and his household,[x] and he is to slaughter the bull for his own sin offering. 12He is to take
a censer full of burning coals[y] from the altar before the LORD and two handfuls of finely ground fragrant incense[z] and take them behind the curtain. 13He is to put the incense
on the fire before the LORD, and the smoke of the incense will conceal the atonement cover above the Testimony, so that he will not die.[a] 14He is to take some of the bull's
blood[b] and with his finger sprinkle it on the front of the atonement cover; then he shall
sprinkle some of it with his finger seven times before the atonement cover.[c]
15"He shall then slaughter the goat for the sin offering for the people[d] and take its
blood behind the curtain[e] and do with it as he did with the bull's blood: He shall sprinkle it on the atonement cover and in front of it. 16In this way he will make atonement[f] for
the Most Holy Place because of the uncleanness and rebellion of the Israelites, whatever their sins have been. He is to do the same for the Tent of Meeting, which is among them
in the midst of their uncleanness. 17No one is to be in the Tent of Meeting from the time
Aaron goes in to make atonement in the Most Holy Place until he comes out, having made
atonement for himself, his household and the whole community of Israel.
18"Then he shall come out to the altar[g] that is before the LORD and make atonement
for it. He shall take some of the bull's blood and some of the goat's blood and put it on
all the horns of the altar.[h] 19He shall sprinkle some of the blood on it with his finger sev-
en times to cleanse it and to consecrate it from the uncleanness of the Israelites.[i]
20"When Aaron has finished making atonement for the Most Holy Place, the Tent of
Meeting and the altar, he shall bring forward the live goat. 21He is to lay both hands on
the head of the live goat and confess[j] over it all the wickedness and rebellion of the Israelites—all their sins—and put them on the goat's head. He shall send the goat away
into the desert in the care of a man appointed for the task. 22The goat will carry on itself
all their sins[k] to a solitary place; and the man shall release it in the desert.
23"Then Aaron is to go into the Tent of Meeting and take off the linen garments he
put on before he entered the Most Holy Place, and he is to leave them there.[l] 24He shall
bathe himself with water in a holy place and put on his regular garments.[m] Then he shall
come out and sacrifice the burnt offering for himself and the burnt offering for the people, to make atonement for himself and for the people. 25He shall also burn the fat of the
sin offering on the altar.
26"The man who releases the goat as a scapegoat must wash his clothes[n] and bathe
himself with water; afterward he may come into the camp. 27The bull and the goat for
the sin offerings, whose blood was brought into the Most Holy Place to make atonement,
must be taken outside the camp;[o] their hides, flesh and offal are to be burned up. 28The
man who burns them must wash his clothes and bathe himself with water; afterward he
may come into the camp.
29"This is to be a lasting ordinance for you: On the tenth day of the seventh month you
must deny yourselves[b][p] and not do any work—whether native-born or an alien living

16:4 [q]Ex 28:39 [r]Ex 28:42 [s]ver 24; Heb 10:22
16:5 [t]Lev 4:13-21 [u]2Ch 29:23
16:6 [v]Lev 9:7; Heb 5:3; 7:27; 9:7,12
16:10 [w]Isa 53:4-10; Ro 3:25; 1Jn 2:2
16:11 [x]Heb 7:27; 9:7
16:12 [y]Lev 10:1 [z]Ex 30:34-38
16:13 [a]Ex 28:43; Lev 22:9
16:14 [b]Lev 4:5; Heb 9:7, 13,25 [c]Lev 4:6
16:15 [d]Heb 9:7,12 [e]Heb 9:3
16:16 [f]Ex 29:36
16:18 [g]Lev 4:7 [h]Lev 4:25
16:19 [i]Eze 43:20
16:21 [j]Lev 5:5
16:22 [k]Isa 53:12
16:23 [l]Eze 42:14; 44:19
16:24 [m]ver 3-5
16:26 [n]Lev 11:25
16:27 [o]Lev 4:12,21; Heb 13:11
16:29 [p]Lev 23:27,32; Nu 29:7; Isa 58:3

[a] 8 That is, the goat of removal; Hebrew *azazel*; also in verses 10 and 26 [b] 29 Or *must fast*; also in verse 31

16:8 one lot for the LORD. That is, one to be sacrificed.
16:12 take a censer. The incense prevented the high priest from seeing God, which would have resulted in his death (v. 13; Ex 33:20). As a form of atonement, it also averted God's wrath (Nu 16:46–50).
16:16 for the Most Holy Place. The atonement was not only for the people, but also for the sanctuary itself, which was defiled by them. The earthly sanctuary was a copy of the heavenly sanctuary that the blood of Christ also cleansed (Heb 9:23–24). **which is among them.** Literally, "which camps among them." The verb connotes impermanence. God's presence was not finalized in this arrangement. His tent dwelling foreshadowed his "camping" among his people in his incarnation in Jesus Christ (see Jn 1:14). Today he still dwells among the church, which is his temple (1Co 3:16). His final and complete dwelling with his people will occur in the new heavens and the new earth (Rev 21:1–4). His presence sustains and guides his people, and the "dwelling places" of God are sanctified by the blood of Christ and by his Spirit.

among you— 30 because on this day atonement will be made for you, to cleanse you.
Then, before the LORD, you will be clean from all your sins.[q] 31 It is a sabbath of rest, and
you must deny yourselves;[r] it is a lasting ordinance. 32 The priest who is anointed and ordained to succeed his father as high priest is to make atonement. He is to put on the sacred linen garments[s] 33 and make atonement for the Most Holy Place, for the Tent of
Meeting and the altar, and for the priests and all the people of the community.[t]
34 "This is to be a lasting ordinance for you: Atonement is to be made once a year[u] for
all the sins of the Israelites."
And it was done, as the LORD commanded Moses.

Eating Blood Forbidden

17 The LORD said to Moses, 2 "Speak to Aaron and his sons and to all the Israelites
and say to them: 'This is what the LORD has commanded: 3 Any Israelite who sacrifices an ox,[a] a lamb or a goat in the camp or outside of it 4 instead of bringing it to the
entrance to the Tent of Meeting to present it as an offering to the LORD in front of the tabernacle of the LORD[v]—that man shall be considered guilty of bloodshed; he has shed
blood and must be cut off from his people.[w] 5 This is so the Israelites will bring to the LORD
the sacrifices they are now making in the open fields. They must bring them to the priest,
that is, to the LORD, at the entrance to the Tent of Meeting and sacrifice them as fellowship offerings.[b] 6 The priest is to sprinkle the blood against the altar of the LORD[x] at the
entrance to the Tent of Meeting and burn the fat as an aroma pleasing to the LORD.[y]
7 They must no longer offer any of their sacrifices to the goat idols[c][z] to whom they prostitute themselves.[a] This is to be a lasting ordinance for them and for the generations to
come.'
8 "Say to them: 'Any Israelite or any alien living among them who offers a burnt offering or sacrifice 9 and does not bring it to the entrance to the Tent of Meeting[b] to sacrifice it to the LORD—that man must be cut off from his people.
10 " 'Any Israelite or any alien living among them who eats any blood—I will set my
face against that person who eats blood[c] and will cut him off from his people. 11 For the
life of a creature is in the blood,[d] and I have given it to you to make atonement for yourselves on the altar; it is the blood that makes atonement for one's life.[e] 12 Therefore I say
to the Israelites, "None of you may eat blood, nor may an alien living among you eat
blood."
13 " 'Any Israelite or any alien living among you who hunts any animal or bird that may
be eaten must drain out the blood and cover it with earth,[f] 14 because the life of every
creature is its blood. That is why I have said to the Israelites, "You must not eat the blood
of any creature, because the life of every creature is its blood; anyone who eats it must
be cut off."[g]

16:30 [q]Jer 33:8; Eph 5:26
16:31 [r]Isa 58:3,5
16:32 [s]ver 4; Nu 20:26, 28
16:33 [t]ver 11,16-18
16:34 [u]Heb 9:7,25
17:4 [v]Dt 12:5-21 [w]Ge 17:14
17:6 [x]Lev 3:2 [y]Nu 18:17
17:7 [z]Ex 22:20; 2Ch 11:15 [a]Ex 32:8; 34:15; Dt 32:17; 1Co 10:20
17:9 [b]ver 4
17:10 [c]Ge 9:4; Lev 3:17; Dt 12:16,23; 1Sa 14:33
17:11 [d]ver 14; Ge 9:4 [e]Heb 9:22
17:13 [f]Lev 7:26; Dt 12:16
17:14 [g]ver 11; Ge 9:4

[a] 3 The Hebrew word can include both male and female. [b] 5 Traditionally *peace offerings*
[c] 7 Or *demons*

16:29,31 deny yourselves. Literally, "afflict yourselves." An ordinary Israelite had to show penitence for his sins by refraining from work, by fasting and possibly by wearing sackcloth (Ps 35:13). Failure to observe the day made him liable unto death (23:28–30). The Day of Atonement is the only holy day to which this warning was attached.

16:30 atonement will be made for you. The ritual of the Day of Atonement was God's gracious gift to his people. God ordained a procedure for making them "at-one" with him. He not only gave commandments to his people on how to live, but also offered them a sacrifice by which their covenantal relationship might be retained, despite their sin. While this Old Testament procedure had only temporary and incomplete results, the atonement of Christ is eternal and complete. **to cleanse you . . . from all your sins.** The reason for placing the Day of Atonement at the end of this section on uncleanness (11:1—16:34) is that the ceremony was not only designed to remove the people's guilt but also to make the entire nation ritually clean so that the people might draw near to God in worship.

16:34 once a year. By contrast, Jesus Christ offered the final sacrifice for sin once for all time to come (Heb 9:11—10:14).

■ **17:1—27:34** *The Practice of Holiness.* The Lord's demands for holiness clearly reached into every aspect of Israel's life. In 12 sections God revealed his will to Moses on topics as diverse as sexual behavior and jubilee years, capital crimes and tabernacle loaves. In all of these areas the Lord stated his claim that Israel must imitate his holiness.

■ **17:1–16** *Sacrifice and Food.* The Lord instructed the people regarding the prohibitions against offering sacrifices anywhere but the tabernacle (vv. 3–9) and against eating animal flesh with blood in it (vv. 10–16).

17:3 sacrifices. Literally, "slaughters." In the wilderness period, animals could be killed only at the tabernacle, even for ordinary meals. This was probably to prevent secret sacrifices to idols (v. 7). In all likelihood, the Israelites did not commonly eat meat in the wilderness, since they continued to rely on manna for their daily sustenance (Ex 16:35; Nu 11:4–6) and because they did not have the resources to raise large numbers of animals. Thus, the number of slaughtered animals was probably low. Once the people entered Canaan, this rule was relaxed (Dt 12:15–16).

17:4 has shed blood. That is, has committed a transgression as bad as that involving bloodshed (e.g, murder). **cut off.** See note on 7:20.

17:11 This is one of the most important statements in Leviticus. Life is sacred because it belongs to God. As a mark of respect for life and for its Creator, no Israelite could eat meat with blood in it, "for the life of the creature is in the blood" (see Ge 9:4–6) and "it is the blood that makes atonement for one's life." That is, the blood of animals shed in sacrifice took the place of, and symbolically redeemed the life of, the worshiper. Animal blood was the sign of salvation. Because animal blood symbolically atoned for human sin, people were not to consume it. **I have given it to you.** Atonement is a gift of God, not a human invention.

[15]“ ‘Anyone, whether native-born or alien, who eats anything found dead or torn by
wild animals[h] must wash his clothes and bathe with water, and he will be ceremonially unclean till evening; then he will be clean. [16]But if he does not wash his clothes and
bathe himself, he will be held responsible.’ ”

Unlawful Sexual Relations

18 The LORD said to Moses, [2]“Speak to the Israelites and say to them: ‘I am the LORD
your God.[i] [3]You must not do as they do in Egypt, where you used to live, and you
must not do as they do in the land of Canaan, where I am bringing you. Do not follow
their practices.[j] [4]You must obey my laws and be careful to follow my decrees. I am the
LORD your God.[k] [5]Keep my decrees and laws, for the man who obeys them will live by
them.[l] I am the LORD.
[6]“ ‘No one is to approach any close relative to have sexual relations. I am the LORD.
[7]“ ‘Do not dishonor your father[m] by having sexual relations with your mother.[n] She
is your mother; do not have relations with her.
[8]“ ‘Do not have sexual relations with your father’s wife;[o] that would dishonor your
father.[p]
[9]“ ‘Do not have sexual relations with your sister,[q] either your father’s daughter or
your mother’s daughter, whether she was born in the same home or elsewhere.
[10]“ ‘Do not have sexual relations with your son’s daughter or your daughter’s daughter; that would dishonor you.
[11]“ ‘Do not have sexual relations with the daughter of your father’s wife, born to your
father; she is your sister.
[12]“ ‘Do not have sexual relations with your father’s sister;[r] she is your father’s close
relative.
[13]“ ‘Do not have sexual relations with your mother’s sister, because she is your mother’s close relative.
[14]“ ‘Do not dishonor your father’s brother by approaching his wife to have sexual relations; she is your aunt.[s]
[15]“ ‘Do not have sexual relations with your daughter-in-law.[t] She is your son’s wife;
do not have relations with her.
[16]“ ‘Do not have sexual relations with your brother’s wife;[u] that would dishonor your
brother.
[17]“ ‘Do not have sexual relations with both a woman and her daughter.[v] Do not have
sexual relations with either her son’s daughter or her daughter’s daughter; they are her
close relatives. That is wickedness.
[18]“ ‘Do not take your wife’s sister as a rival wife and have sexual relations with her
while your wife is living.
[19]“ ‘Do not approach a woman to have sexual relations during the uncleanness of her
monthly period.[w]
[20]“ ‘Do not have sexual relations with your neighbor’s wife[x] and defile yourself with her.
[21]“ ‘Do not give any of your children[y] to be sacrificed[a] to Molech,[z] for you must not
profane the name of your God.[a] I am the LORD.
[22]“ ‘Do not lie with a man as one lies with a woman;[b] that is detestable.

17:15 [h]Ex 22:31; Dt 14:21
18:2 [i]Ex 6:7; Lev 11:44; Eze 20:5
18:3 [j]ver 24-30; Ex 23:24; Lev 20:23
18:4 [k]ver 2
18:5 [l]Eze 20:11; Ro 10:5*; Gal 3:12*
18:7 [m]Lev 20:11 [n]Eze 22:10
18:8 [o]1Co 5:1 [p]Lev 20:11
18:9 [q]Lev 20:17
18:12 [r]Lev 20:19
18:14 [s]Lev 20:20
18:15 [t]Lev 20:12
18:16 [u]Lev 20:21
18:17 [v]Lev 20:14
18:19 [w]Lev 15:24; 20:18
18:20 [x]Ex 20:14; Lev 20:10; Mt 5:27,28; 1Co 6:9; Heb 13:4
18:21 [y]Dt 12:31 [z]Lev 20:2-5 [a]Lev 19:12; 21:6; Eze 36:20
18:22 [b]Lev 20:13; Dt 23:18; Ro 1:27

[a] *21 Or to be passed through* ⌊*the fire*⌋

■ **18:1–30** *Sexual Behavior.* Moses instructed Israel concerning unlawful practices linked to sex and family, including incest (vv. 6–18), adultery (6:20), child sacrifice (v. 21), homosexuality (v. 22) and bestiality (v. 23). Israel’s neighbors were much less restrained in their sexual attitudes and behaviors. They permitted closer intermarriage than God allowed. They also allowed homosexuality in cases where there was mutual consent (cf. v. 22). Some forms of bestiality were acceptable as well (cf. v. 23). The fundamental principles of Biblical sexuality are set forth in Genesis 1–2. The creation of one man partnered with one woman set the normative pattern for all to follow in sexual relationships. As for male-female unions, this set of laws presupposed that an Israelite would normally marry another Israelite. However, unions between relatives of the first degree (brother-sister, father-daughter) and the second degree (father-granddaughter, nephew-aunt) were prohibited. Although the text directly speaks to men who might engage in improper unions, it implicitly prohibits women from engaging in such relationships as well. In marriage, husband and wife become one flesh so that each becomes part of the spouse’s family (Ge 2:24; Lev 18:7–8). For this reason, unions to close family members of one’s spouse were forbidden just as were unions to one’s own close family members. See *WCF* 24.4.

18:1–21 See *WLC* 139.

18:3 Do not follow their practices. The Lord was very concerned that Israel follow the standards of his law rather than the customs of the Canaanites. See *HC* 108.

18:4 See *HC* 91.

18:8 your father’s wife. Not your own mother (v. 7), but your father’s second wife (cf. 1Co 5:1).

18:9 your sister. A full or half sister.

18:11 your sister. A stepsister.

18:16 Deuteronomy 25:5–6 encouraged a man to marry his widowed sister-in-law if her first marriage had been childless. This shows the importance in Old Testament Israelite society of preserving the family inheritance by perpetuating the family line.

18:17 her daughter. The daughter of the woman would be the man’s stepdaughter or step-granddaughter.

18:18 See the account of Leah and Rachel (Ge 29:23—30:24).

18:19 Do not approach a woman. See note on 15:1–33.

18:21 Molech. The custom of sacrificing children was known among the Phoenicians and is occasionally mentioned in the Old Testament (Dt 12:31; 2Ki 23:10).

23 " 'Do not have sexual relations with an animal and defile yourself with it. A woman must not present herself to an animal to have sexual relations with it; that is a perversion.[c]
24 " 'Do not defile yourselves in any of these ways, because this is how the nations that
I am going to drive out before you[d] became defiled.[e] 25 Even the land was defiled; so I
punished it for its sin,[f] and the land vomited out its inhabitants.[g] 26 But you must keep
my decrees and my laws. The native-born and the aliens living among you must not do
any of these detestable things, 27 for all these things were done by the people who lived
in the land before you, and the land became defiled. 28 And if you defile the land, it will
vomit you out as it vomited out the nations that were before you.
29 " 'Everyone who does any of these detestable things—such persons must be cut off
from their people. 30 Keep my requirements[h] and do not follow any of the detestable customs that were practiced before you came and do not defile yourselves with them. I am
the LORD your God.[i]' "

Various Laws

19 The LORD said to Moses, 2 "Speak to the entire assembly of Israel and say to
them: 'Be holy because I, the LORD your God, am holy.[j]
3 " 'Each of you must respect his mother and father,[k] and you must observe my Sabbaths. I am the LORD your God.[l]
4 " 'Do not turn to idols or make gods of cast metal for yourselves.[m] I am the LORD your
God.
5 " 'When you sacrifice a fellowship offering[a] to the LORD, sacrifice it in such a way that
it will be accepted on your behalf. 6 It shall be eaten on the day you sacrifice it or on the
next day; anything left over until the third day must be burned up. 7 If any of it is eaten
on the third day, it is impure and will not be accepted. 8 Whoever eats it will be held responsible because he has desecrated what is holy to the LORD; that person must be cut
off from his people.
9 " 'When you reap the harvest of your land, do not reap to the very edges of your field
or gather the gleanings of your harvest.[n] 10 Do not go over your vineyard a second time
or pick up the grapes that have fallen. Leave them for the poor and the alien. I am the
LORD your God.
11 " 'Do not steal.[o]
" 'Do not lie.[p]
" 'Do not deceive one another.
12 " 'Do not swear falsely by my name[q] and so profane the name of your God. I am the
LORD.
13 " 'Do not defraud your neighbor or rob him.[r]
" 'Do not hold back the wages of a hired man overnight.[s]
14 " 'Do not curse the deaf or put a stumbling block in front of the blind,[t] but fear your
God. I am the LORD.
15 " 'Do not pervert justice;[u] do not show partiality[v] to the poor or favoritism to the
great, but judge your neighbor fairly.
16 " 'Do not go about spreading slander[w] among your people.
" 'Do not do anything that endangers your neighbor's life.[x] I am the LORD.
17 " 'Do not hate your brother in your heart.[y] Rebuke your neighbor frankly[z] so you
will not share in his guilt.
18 " 'Do not seek revenge[a] or bear a grudge[b] against one of your people, but love your
neighbor as yourself.[c] I am the LORD.
19 " 'Keep my decrees.

a 5 Traditionally *peace offering*

18:23 [c]Ex 22:19; Lev 20:15; Dt 27:21
18:24 [d]ver 3,27,30 [e]Dt 18:12
18:25 [f]Lev 20:23; Dt 9:5; 18:12 [g]ver 28; Lev 20:22
18:30 [h]Dt 11:1 [i]ver 2
19:2 [j]1Pe 1:16*; Lev 11:44
19:3 [k]Ex 20:12 [l]Lev 11:44
19:4 [m]Ex 20:4,23; 34:17; Lev 26:1; Ps 96:5; 115:4-7
19:9 [n]Lev 23:10,22; Dt 24:19-22
19:11 [o]Ex 20:15 [p]Eph 4:25
19:12 [q]Ex 20:7; Mt 5:33
19:13 [r]Ex 22:15,25-27 [s]Dt 24:15; Jas 5:4
19:14 [t]Dt 27:18
19:15 [u]Ex 23:2,6 [v]Dt 1:17
19:16 [w]Ps 15:3; Eze 22:9 [x]Ex 23:7
19:17 [y]1Jn 2:9; 3:15 [z]Mt 18:15; Lk 17:3
19:18 [a]Ro 12:19 [b]Ps 103:9 [c]Mt 5:43*; 19:16*; 22:39*; Mk 12:31*; Lk 10:27*; Jn 13:34; Ro 13:9*; Gal 5:14*; Jas 2:8*

18:25 the land was defiled. Uncleanness and sin were contagious, infecting everything that came into contact with them, including the sanctuary (see note on 16:16) and the land. **vomited.** This personification of the land underscores the poisonous contagion of uncleanness and sin.
18:29 cut off. See note on 7:20.
18:30 See *WLC* 101.
■ **19:1–37** *Holiness Toward God and Neighbor.* The theme of holiness was elaborated as God instructed the people on what holiness meant in daily life with regard to God and others. The mixing of concern for God and other people illustrates how love for God and neighbor go hand in hand.
19:3 See *WLC* 127.
19:5 fellowship offering. See note on 3:1 (cf. 7:16–18).
19:9–10 Compare Deuteronomy 24:19–21 and Ruth 2.
19:11–12 See *WCF* 22.1; *WLC* 114,145; *HC* 112.
19:13 wages of a hired man. Compare Deuteronomy 24:14–15.
19:15 See *WLC* 144,145.
19:16 See *WLC* 145; *WSC* 78.
19:17–18 See *WLC* 99,136,145; *HC* 105.
19:18 love your neighbor. "Neighbor" applied to anyone with whom one came into contact, whether an Israelite (v. 17) or an alien who resided with the people of God (v. 34). Jesus considered this the second greatest commandment (see Mt 22:39–40; Mk 12:31; Lk 10:27), and both Paul (Ro 13:9; Gal 5:14) and James (Jas 2:8) referred to its importance as well. See *HC* 4.

" 'Do not mate different kinds of animals.

" 'Do not plant your field with two kinds of seed.[d]

" 'Do not wear clothing woven of two kinds of material.[e]

20" 'If a man sleeps with a woman who is a slave girl promised to another man but who has not been ransomed or given her freedom, there must be due punishment. Yet they are not to be put to death, because she had not been freed. 21The man, however, must bring a ram to the entrance to the Tent of Meeting for a guilt offering to the LORD.[f] 22With the ram of the guilt offering the priest is to make atonement for him before the LORD for the sin he has committed, and his sin will be forgiven.

23" 'When you enter the land and plant any kind of fruit tree, regard its fruit as forbidden.[a] For three years you are to consider it forbidden[a]; it must not be eaten. 24In the fourth year all its fruit will be holy,[g] an offering of praise to the LORD. 25But in the fifth year you may eat its fruit. In this way your harvest will be increased. I am the LORD your God.

26" 'Do not eat any meat with the blood still in it.[h]

" 'Do not practice divination or sorcery.[i]

27" 'Do not cut the hair at the sides of your head or clip off the edges of your beard.[j]

28" 'Do not cut your bodies for the dead or put tattoo marks on yourselves. I am the LORD.

29" 'Do not degrade your daughter by making her a prostitute,[k] or the land will turn to prostitution and be filled with wickedness.

30" 'Observe my Sabbaths and have reverence for my sanctuary. I am the LORD.[l]

31" 'Do not turn to mediums or seek out spiritists,[m] for you will be defiled by them. I am the LORD your God.

32" 'Rise in the presence of the aged, show respect for the elderly[n] and revere your God. I am the LORD.

33" 'When an alien lives with you in your land, do not mistreat him. 34The alien living with you must be treated as one of your native-born.[o] Love him as yourself, for you were aliens in Egypt.[p] I am the LORD your God.

35" 'Do not use dishonest standards when measuring length, weight or quantity. 36Use honest scales and honest weights, an honest ephah[b] and an honest hin.[c][q] I am the LORD your God, who brought you out of Egypt.

37" 'Keep all my decrees and all my laws and follow them. I am the LORD.' "

Punishments for Sin

20 The LORD said to Moses, 2"Say to the Israelites: 'Any Israelite or any alien living in Israel who gives[d] any of his children to Molech must be put to death. The people of the community are to stone him. 3I will set my face against that man and I will cut him off from his people; for by giving his children to Molech, he has defiled my sanctuary[r] and profaned my holy name.[s] 4If the people of the community close their eyes when that man gives one of his children to Molech and they fail to put him to death,[t] 5I will set my face against that man and his family and will cut off from their people both him and all who follow him in prostituting themselves to Molech.

6" 'I will set my face against the person who turns to mediums and spiritists to prostitute himself by following them, and I will cut him off from his people.[u]

7" 'Consecrate yourselves and be holy,[v] because I am the LORD your God. 8Keep my decrees and follow them. I am the LORD, who makes you holy.[e][w]

19:19 [d]Dt 22:9 [e]Dt 22:11
19:21 [f]Lev 5:15
19:24 [g]Pr 3:9
19:26 [h]Lev 17:10 [i]Dt 18:10
19:27 [j]Lev 21:5
19:29 [k]Dt 23:18
19:30 [l]Lev 26:2
19:31 [m]Lev 20:6; Isa 8:19
19:32 [n]1Ti 5:1
19:34 [o]Ex 12:48 [p]Dt 10:19
19:36 [q]Dt 25:13-15
20:3 [r]Lev 15:31 [s]Lev 18:21
20:4 [t]Dt 17:2-5
20:6 [u]Lev 19:31
20:7 [v]Eph 1:4; 1Pe 1:16*
20:8 [w]Ex 31:13

[a] *23* Hebrew *uncircumcised* [b] *36* An ephah was a dry measure. [c] *36* A hin was a liquid measure.
[d] *2* Or *sacrifices*; also in verses 3 and 4 [e] *8* Or *who sanctifies you*; or *who sets you apart as holy*

19:19 It is likely that these regulations portrayed the kind of care all Israelites were to take in every aspect of life to keep their hearts as pure as possible.
19:21–22 guilt offering. See 5:14—6:7 and its note.
19:24 Firstfruits, like firstborn creatures, were to be given to God (Ex 22:29–30; 23:19), for Israel was God's firstborn and so was consecrated to him (Ex 4:22).
19:27–28 These regulations may be in reaction to the practices of other cultures from which God wanted Israel to be distinct. Egyptians, for instance, characteristically trimmed their beards in these ways. Cutting the edge of a beard appears in 21:5 as part of ritual mourning.
19:29 See *WLC* 139.
19:31 See *HC* 94.
19:32 See *WLC* 127.
19:37 See *WLC* 101.
■ **20:1–27** *Capital Crimes.* The Lord's instructions here go over many of the same points as found in chapters 18–19, but in addition to merely stating commands, this passage also lays down penalties. The death penalty was appropriate punishment for many offenses. From Biblical examples, however, we know that the death penalty was in fact a maximum sentence rather than a mandatory sentence.
20:2–5 See 18:21.
20:3 cut him off. See note on 7:20.
20:6 See Deuteronomy 18:10–11 and 1 Samuel 28:9. See also *WLC* 105.
20:7–8 See *WLC* 95.

9 " 'If anyone curses his father or mother,[x] he must be put to death.[y] He has cursed
his father or his mother, and his blood will be on his own head.[z]
10 " 'If a man commits adultery with another man's wife[a]—with the wife of his neighbor—both the adulterer and the adulteress must be put to death.
11 " 'If a man sleeps with his father's wife, he has dishonored his father.[b] Both the man
and the woman must be put to death; their blood will be on their own heads.
12 " 'If a man sleeps with his daughter-in-law,[c] both of them must be put to death.
What they have done is a perversion; their blood will be on their own heads.
13 " 'If a man lies with a man as one lies with a woman, both of them have done what
is detestable.[d] They must be put to death; their blood will be on their own heads.
14 " 'If a man marries both a woman and her mother,[e] it is wicked. Both he and they
must be burned in the fire, so that no wickedness will be among you.[f]
15 " 'If a man has sexual relations with an animal,[g] he must be put to death, and you
must kill the animal.
16 " 'If a woman approaches an animal to have sexual relations with it, kill both the
woman and the animal. They must be put to death; their blood will be on their own
heads.
17 " 'If a man marries his sister[h], the daughter of either his father or his mother, and
they have sexual relations, it is a disgrace. They must be cut off before the eyes of their
people. He has dishonored his sister and will be held responsible.
18 " 'If a man lies with a woman during her monthly period[i] and has sexual relations
with her, he has exposed the source of her flow, and she has also uncovered it. Both of
them must be cut off from their people.
19 " 'Do not have sexual relations with the sister of either your mother or your father,[j]
for that would dishonor a close relative; both of you would be held responsible.
20 " 'If a man sleeps with his aunt,[k] he has dishonored his uncle. They will be held responsible; they will die childless.
21 " 'If a man marries his brother's wife,[l] it is an act of impurity; he has dishonored his
brother. They will be childless.
22 " 'Keep all my decrees and laws and follow them, so that the land[m] where I am
bringing you to live may not vomit you out. 23 You must not live according to the customs
of the nations[n] I am going to drive out before you.[o] Because they did all these things, I
abhorred them. 24 But I said to you, "You will possess their land; I will give it to you as
an inheritance, a land flowing with milk and honey."[p] I am the LORD your God, who has
set you apart from the nations.[q]
25 " 'You must therefore make a distinction between clean and unclean animals and
between unclean and clean birds.[r] Do not defile yourselves by any animal or bird or anything that moves along the ground—those which I have set apart as unclean for you.
26 You are to be holy to me[a] because I, the LORD, am holy,[s] and I have set you apart from
the nations to be my own.
27 " 'A man or woman who is a medium or spiritist among you must be put to death.[t]
You are to stone them; their blood will be on their own heads.' "

Rules for Priests

21 The LORD said to Moses, "Speak to the priests, the sons of Aaron, and say to
them: 'A priest must not make himself ceremonially unclean for any of his people who die,[u] 2 except for a close relative, such as his mother or father, his son or daughter, his brother, 3 or an unmarried sister who is dependent on him since she has no hus-

[a] 26 Or *be my holy ones*

20:9 [x]Dt 27:16 [y]Ex 21:17; Mt 15:4*; Mk 7:10* [z]ver 11; 2Sa 1:16
20:10 [a]Ex 20:14; Dt 5:18; 22:22
20:11 [b]Lev 18:7; Dt 27:23
20:12 [c]Lev 18:15
20:13 [d]Lev 18:22
20:14 [e]Lev 18:17 [f]Dt 27:23
20:15 [g]Lev 18:23
20:17 [h]Lev 18:9
20:18 [i]Lev 15:24; 18:19
20:19 [j]Lev 18:12-13
20:20 [k]Lev 18:14
20:21 [l]Lev 18:16
20:22 [m]Lev 18:25-28
20:23 [n]Lev 18:3 [o]Lev 18:24, 27, 30
20:24 [p]Ex 3:8; 13:5; 33:3 [q]Ex 33:16
20:25 [r]Lev 11:1-47; Dt 14:3-21
20:26 [s]Lev 19:2
20:27 [t]Lev 19:31
21:1 [u]Eze 44:25

20:9 Jesus quoted this text in Mark 7:10, thus demonstrating that these rules for holiness are not cast aside in the New Testament period (cf. Mt 5:17–20).
20:10 See 18:20.
20:11 See 18:8.
20:12 See 18:15.
20:13 See 18:22.
20:14 See 18:17.
20:15–16 See 18:23. See also *WLC* 139.
20:17 See 18:9.
20:18 See 18:19.
20:19–21 See *WCF* 24.4.
20:19–20 See 18:12–14.
20:21 See 18:16.
20:25 See chapter 11 and its notes.
20:27 See 20:6.
■ **21:1–24** *Rules for Priests.* Moses recorded in this chapter God's rules for priests. Verses 1–9 cover rules for priests in general, while verses 10–15 cover rules specifically for the high priest. All priests represented others when they were near God's special presence; therefore, they had to show God's holiness in their character and in their bodies. Holiness ultimately involves perfection and health (fullness of life and freedom from mortality, perishability, decay), so a priest whose physical condition did not reflect these ideals was not to offer sacrifices (vv. 17–21), although he could still enjoy a full share of priestly dues (v. 22).
21:1 unclean for any of his people who die. Touching a corpse or entering the home of a dead person defiled an individual (Nu 19:11,14). For this reason, priests were to involve themselves with death only as it applied to their closest relatives (vv. 2–3).

band—for her he may make himself unclean. 4 He must not make himself unclean for
people related to him by marriage,[a] and so defile himself.
5 " 'Priests must not shave their heads or shave off the edges of their beards[v] or cut
their bodies.[w] 6 They must be holy to their God and must not profane the name of their
God.[x] Because they present the offerings made to the LORD by fire,[y] the food of their God,
they are to be holy.
7 " 'They must not marry women defiled by prostitution or divorced from their husbands,[z] because priests are holy to their God.[a] 8 Regard them as holy,[b] because they offer up the food of your God. Consider them holy, because I the LORD am holy—I who
make you holy.[b]
9 " 'If a priest's daughter defiles herself by becoming a prostitute, she disgraces her father; she must be burned in the fire.[c]
10 " 'The high priest, the one among his brothers who has had the anointing oil
poured on his head and who has been ordained to wear the priestly garments,[d] must not
let his hair become unkempt[c] or tear his clothes.[e] 11 He must not enter a place where
there is a dead body.[f] He must not make himself unclean,[g] even for his father or mother, 12 nor leave the sanctuary of his God or desecrate it, because he has been dedicated
by the anointing oil[h] of his God. I am the LORD.
13 " 'The woman he marries must be a virgin.[i] 14 He must not marry a widow, a divorced
woman, or a woman defiled by prostitution, but only a virgin from his own people, 15 so
he will not defile his offspring among his people. I am the LORD, who makes him holy.[d]' "
16 The LORD said to Moses, 17 "Say to Aaron: 'For the generations to come none of your
descendants who has a defect may come near to offer the food of his God.[j] 18 No man who
has any defect[k] may come near: no man who is blind or lame, disfigured or deformed;
19 no man with a crippled foot or hand, 20 or who is hunchbacked or dwarfed, or who has
any eye defect, or who has festering or running sores or damaged testicles.[l] 21 No descendant of Aaron the priest who has any defect is to come near to present the offerings made
to the LORD by fire. He has a defect; he must not come near to offer the food of his God.
22 He may eat the most holy food of his God,[m] as well as the holy food; 23 yet because of
his defect, he must not go near the curtain or approach the altar, and so desecrate my
sanctuary. I am the LORD, who makes them holy.[e]' "
24 So Moses told this to Aaron and his sons and to all the Israelites.

22

The LORD said to Moses, 2 "Tell Aaron and his sons to treat with respect the sacred offerings the Israelites consecrate to me, so they will not profane my holy
name. I am the LORD.
3 "Say to them: 'For the generations to come, if any of your descendants is ceremonially unclean and yet comes near the sacred offerings that the Israelites consecrate to the
LORD, that person must be cut off from my presence.[n] I am the LORD.
4 " 'If a descendant of Aaron has an infectious skin disease[f] or a bodily discharge,[o] he
may not eat the sacred offerings until he is cleansed. He will also be unclean if he
touches something defiled by a corpse[p] or by anyone who has an emission of semen, 5 or
if he touches any crawling thing[q] that makes him unclean, or any person[r] who makes
him unclean, whatever the uncleanness may be. 6 The one who touches any such thing
will be unclean till evening. He must not eat any of the sacred offerings unless he has
bathed himself with water. 7 When the sun goes down, he will be clean, and after that he
may eat the sacred offerings, for they are his food.[s] 8 He must not eat anything found
dead[t] or torn by wild animals,[u] and so become unclean[v] through it. I am the LORD.
9 " 'The priests are to keep my requirements so that they do not become guilty and
die[w] for treating them with contempt. I am the LORD, who makes them holy.[g]
10 " 'No one outside a priest's family may eat the sacred offering, nor may the guest

21:5 [v]Eze 44:20 [w]Lev 19:28; Dt 14:1
21:6 [x]Lev 18:21 [y]Lev 3:11
21:7 [z]ver 13,14 [a]Eze 44:22
21:8 [b]ver 6
21:9 [c]Ge 38:24; Lev 19:29
21:10 [d]Lev 16:32 [e]Lev 10:6
21:11 [f]Nu 19:11,13,14 [g]Lev 19:28
21:12 [h]Ex 29:6-7; Lev 10:7
21:13 [i]Eze 44:22
21:17 [j]ver 6
21:18 [k]Lev 22:19-25
21:20 [l]Dt 23:1; Isa 56:3
21:22 [m]1Co 9:13
22:3 [n]Lev 7:20,21; Nu 19:13
22:4 [o]Lev 14:1-32; 15:2-15 [p]Lev 11:24-28,39
22:5 [q]Lev 11:24-28,43 [r]Lev 15:7
22:7 [s]Nu 18:11
22:8 [t]Lev 11:39 [u]Ex 22:31; Lev 17:15 [v]Lev 11:40
22:9 [w]ver 16; Ex 28:43

a 4 Or *unclean as a leader among his people* b 8 Or *who sanctify you*; or *who set you apart as holy* c 10 Or *not uncover his head* d 15 Or *who sanctifies him*; or *who sets him apart as holy* e 23 Or *who sanctifies them*; or *who sets them apart as holy* f 4 Traditionally *leprosy*; the Hebrew word was used for various diseases affecting the skin—not necessarily leprosy. g 9 Or *who sanctifies them*; or *who sets them apart as holy*; also in verse 16

21:5 Mourning customs involving disfigurement of the body were also banned because priests, as holy men, had to have whole bodies.
21:10–12 The high priest, as a representative of humanity restored to fellowship with God, was obligated to avoid all contact with death. Compare 10:6–7.
21:13–15 His wife was also required to be above reproach (v. 9). He could marry only a virgin, not a widow or a divorced woman, to ensure the purity of his offspring (v. 15).

■ **22:1–33** *Rules on Sacrifice.* The Lord instructed the priests concerning proper treatment of the sacrifices.
22:3 Any unclean person who ate holy food from a sacrifice risked death (7:20–21).
22:4–9 This principle also applied to the priests if they were to become unclean.
22:10–13 These verses define which dependents of the priests were allowed to eat sacrificial food.

of a priest or his hired worker eat it. 11 But if a priest buys a slave with money, or if a slave
is born in his household, that slave may eat his food.[x] 12 If a priest's daughter marries anyone other than a priest, she may not eat any of the sacred contributions. 13 But if a priest's
daughter becomes a widow or is divorced, yet has no children, and she returns to live
in her father's house as in her youth, she may eat of her father's food. No unauthorized
person, however, may eat any of it.

14 " 'If anyone eats a sacred offering by mistake, he must make restitution to the priest
for the offering and add a fifth of the value[y] to it. 15 The priests must not desecrate the
sacred offerings the Israelites present to the LORD[z] 16 by allowing them to eat the sacred
offerings and so bring upon them guilt requiring payment.[a] I am the LORD, who makes
them holy.' "

Unacceptable Sacrifices

17 The LORD said to Moses, 18 "Speak to Aaron and his sons and to all the Israelites and
say to them: 'If any of you—either an Israelite or an alien living in Israel—presents a gift[b]
for a burnt offering to the LORD, either to fulfill a vow or as a freewill offering, 19 you must
present a male without defect[c] from the cattle, sheep or goats in order that it may be accepted on your behalf. 20 Do not bring anything with a defect,[d] because it will not be accepted on your behalf. 21 When anyone brings from the herd or flock a fellowship offering[a][e]
to the LORD to fulfill a special vow or as a freewill offering, it must be without defect or
blemish to be acceptable. 22 Do not offer to the LORD the blind, the injured or the maimed,
or anything with warts or festering or running sores. Do not place any of these on the altar as an offering made to the LORD by fire. 23 You may, however, present as a freewill offering an ox[b] or a sheep that is deformed or stunted, but it will not be accepted in fulfillment of a vow. 24 You must not offer to the LORD an animal whose testicles are bruised,
crushed, torn or cut.[f] You must not do this in your own land, 25 and you must not accept
such animals from the hand of a foreigner and offer them as the food of your God.[g] They
will not be accepted on your behalf, because they are deformed and have defects.' "

26 The LORD said to Moses, 27 "When a calf, a lamb or a goat is born, it is to remain with
its mother for seven days.[h] From the eighth day on, it will be acceptable as an offering made
to the LORD by fire. 28 Do not slaughter a cow or a sheep and its young on the same day.[i]

29 "When you sacrifice a thank offering[j] to the LORD, sacrifice it in such a way that it
will be accepted on your behalf. 30 It must be eaten that same day; leave none of it till
morning.[k] I am the LORD.

31 "Keep[l] my commands and follow them. I am the LORD. 32 Do not profane my holy
name.[m] I must be acknowledged as holy by the Israelites.[n] I am the LORD, who makes[c]
you holy[d] 33 and who brought you out of Egypt to be your God.[o] I am the LORD."

23

The LORD said to Moses, 2 "Speak to the Israelites and say to them: 'These are my
appointed feasts,[p] the appointed feasts of the LORD, which you are to proclaim
as sacred assemblies.[q]

The Sabbath

3 " 'There are six days when you may work,[r] but the seventh day is a Sabbath of rest,[s]
a day of sacred assembly. You are not to do any work; wherever you live, it is a Sabbath
to the LORD.

The Passover and Unleavened Bread

4 " 'These are the LORD's appointed feasts, the sacred assemblies you are to proclaim
at their appointed times: 5 The LORD's Passover begins at twilight on the fourteenth day

22:11 [x]Ge 17:13; Ex 12:44
22:14 [y]Lev 5:15
22:15 [z]Nu 18:32
22:16 [a]ver 9
22:18 [b]Lev 1:2
22:19 [c]Lev 1:3
22:20 [d]Dt 15:21; 17:1; Mal 1:8,14; Heb 9:14; 1Pe 1:19
22:21 [e]Lev 3:6; Nu 15:3,8
22:24 [f]Lev 21:20
22:25 [g]Lev 21:6
22:27 [h]Ex 22:30
22:28 [i]Dt 22:6,7
22:29 [j]Lev 7:12; Ps 107:22
22:30 [k]Lev 7:15
22:31 [l]Dt 4:2,40; Ps 105:45
22:32 [m]Lev 18:21 [n]Lev 10:3
22:33 [o]Lev 11:45
23:2 [p]ver 4,37,44; Nu 29:39 [q]ver 21,27
23:3 [r]Ex 20:9 [s]Ex 20:10; 31:13-17; Lev 19:3; Dt 5:13; Heb 4:9,10

a *21* Traditionally *peace offering* b *23* The Hebrew word can include both male and female.
c *32* Or *made* d *32* Or *who sanctifies you*; or *who sets you apart as holy*

22:14 Moses prescribed a penalty of restitution for non-priests who ate the priestly portions of the sacrifices.
22:17–25 Only unblemished animals were to be sacrificed because God was not to be given anything but the best (Mal 1:8) and because sacrifices were holy and holiness was symbolized by an unblemished appearance (see 21:17–21).
22:23 In the case of the optional "freewill offering," a kind of fellowship offering (ch. 3), minor blemishes could be tolerated.
22:27–28 To kill an animal too soon after birth showed little respect for life and therefore was incompatible with holiness. Killing an animal and its young on the same day was viewed similarly. Compare Deuteronomy 14:21 and 22:6–7.

■ **23:1–44** *Holy Assemblies.* The Lord turned his attention to the calendar of holy days and the responsibilities of the laity. (See chart "Old Testament Feasts and Other Sacred Days" on page 192.) God told the nation what to do on the different days (cf. Nu 28–29). These verses divide into nine sections: an introduction (vv. 1–2), the weekly Sabbath (v. 3), Passover and the Feast of Unleavened Bread (vv. 4–8), Firstfruits (vv. 9–14), the Feast of Weeks (vv. 15–22), the Feast of Trumpets (vv. 23–25), the Day of Atonement (vv. 26–32), the Feast of Tabernacles (vv. 33–43) and a conclusion (v. 44).
23:3 See *WLC* 117.
23:4–8 See Exodus 12–13.

23:5 [t]Ex 12:18-19; Nu 28:16-17; Dt 16:1-8
23:7 [u]ver 3,8
23:10 [v]Ex 23:16,19; 34:26
23:11 [w]Ex 29:24
23:13 [x]Lev 2:14-16; 6:20
23:14 [y]Ex 34:26 [z]Nu 15:21

of the first month.[t] 6On the fifteenth day of that month the LORD's Feast of Unleavened
Bread begins; for seven days you must eat bread made without yeast. 7On the first day
hold a sacred assembly[u] and do no regular work. 8For seven days present an offering
made to the LORD by fire. And on the seventh day hold a sacred assembly and do no regular work.' "

Firstfruits

9The LORD said to Moses, 10"Speak to the Israelites and say to them: 'When you enter the land I am going to give you and you reap its harvest, bring to the priest a sheaf[v]
of the first grain you harvest. 11He is to wave the sheaf before the LORD[w] so it will be accepted on your behalf; the priest is to wave it on the day after the Sabbath. 12On the day
you wave the sheaf, you must sacrifice as a burnt offering to the LORD a lamb a year old
without defect, 13together with its grain offering[x] of two-tenths of an ephah[a] of fine flour
mixed with oil—an offering made to the LORD by fire, a pleasing aroma—and its drink
offering of a quarter of a hin[b] of wine. 14You must not eat any bread, or roasted or new
grain, until the very day you bring this offering to your God.[y] This is to be a lasting ordinance for the generations to come,[z] wherever you live.

Feast of Weeks

15" 'From the day after the Sabbath, the day you brought the sheaf of the wave offering, count off seven full weeks. 16Count off fifty days up to the day after the seventh Sab-

[a] *13* That is, probably about 4 quarts (about 4.5 liters); also in verse 17 [b] *13* That is, probably about 1 quart (about 1 liter)

23:9–14 See 1 Corinthians 15:23.

Old Testament Feasts and Other Sacred Days

Name	Old Testament References	OT Time	Modern Equivalent
SABBATH	Ex 20:8-11; 31:12-17; Lev 23:3; Dt 5:12-15	7th day	Same
SABBATH YEAR	Ex 23:10-11; Lev 25:1-7	7th year	Same
YEAR OF JUBILEE	Lev 25:8-55; 27:17-24; Nu 36:4	50th year	Same
PASSOVER	Ex 12:1-14; Lev 23:5; Nu 9:1-14; 28:16; Dt 16:1-3a,4b-7	1st month (Abib) 14	Mar.–Apr.
UNLEAVENED BREAD	Ex 12:15-20; 13:3-10; 23:15; 34:18; Lev 23:6-8; Nu 28:17-25; Dt 16:3b,4a,8	1st month (Abib) 15-21	Mar.–Apr.
FIRSTFRUITS	Lev 23:9-14	1st month (Abib) 16	Mar.–Apr.
WEEKS (Pentecost) (Harvest)	Ex 23:16a; 34:22a; Lev 23:15-21; Nu 28:26-31; Dt 16:9-12	3rd month (Sivan) 6	May–June
TRUMPETS (Later: Rosh Hashanah–New Year's Day)	Lev 23:23-25; Nu 29:1-6	7th month (Tishri) 1	Sept.–Oct.
DAY OF ATONEMENT (Yom Kippur)	Lev 16; 23:26-32; Nu 29:7-11	7th month (Tishri) 10	Sept.–Oct.
TABERNACLES (Booths) (Ingathering)	Ex 23:16b; 34:22b; Lev 23:33-36a,39-43; Nu 29:12-34; Dt 16:13-15; Zec 14:16-19	7th month (Tishri) 15-21	Sept.–Oct.
SACRED ASSEMBLY	Lev 23:36b; Nu 29:35-38	7th month (Tishri) 22	Sept.–Oct.
PURIM	Est 9:18-32	12th month (Adar) 14,15	Feb.–Mar.

On Kislev 25 (mid-December) Hanukkah, the feast of dedication or festival of lights, commemorated the purification of the temple and altar in the Maccabean period (165/4 B.C.). This feast is mentioned in Jn 10:22 (see note there).

bath,[a] and then present an offering of new grain to the LORD. 17From wherever you live,
bring two loaves made of two-tenths of an ephah of fine flour, baked with yeast, as a
wave offering of firstfruits[b] to the LORD. 18Present with this bread seven male lambs, each
a year old and without defect, one young bull and two rams. They will be a burnt offering to the LORD, together with their grain offerings and drink offerings—an offering made
by fire, an aroma pleasing to the LORD. 19Then sacrifice one male goat for a sin offering
and two lambs, each a year old, for a fellowship offering.[a] 20The priest is to wave the two
lambs before the LORD as a wave offering, together with the bread of the firstfruits. They
are a sacred offering to the LORD for the priest. 21On that same day you are to proclaim
a sacred assembly[c] and do no regular work.[d] This is to be a lasting ordinance for the generations to come, wherever you live.

22" 'When you reap the harvest[e] of your land, do not reap to the very edges of your
field or gather the gleanings of your harvest.[f] Leave them for the poor and the alien. I am
the LORD your God.' "

Feast of Trumpets

23The LORD said to Moses, 24"Say to the Israelites: 'On the first day of the seventh
month you are to have a day of rest, a sacred assembly commemorated with trumpet
blasts.[g] 25Do no regular work,[h] but present an offering made to the LORD by fire.' "

Day of Atonement

26The LORD said to Moses, 27"The tenth day of this seventh month[i] is the Day of Atone-

23:16 [a]Nu 28:26; Ac 2:1
23:17 [b]Ex 34:22; Lev 2:12
23:21 [c]ver 2 [d]ver 3
23:22 [e]Lev 19:9 [f]Lev 19:10; Dt 24:19-21; Ru 2:15
23:24 [g]Lev 25:9; Nu 10:9, 10; 29:1
23:25 [h]ver 21
23:27 [i]Lev 16:29

[a] *19* Traditionally *peace offering*

23:26–32 See 16:2–34.

Description	**Purpose**	**New Testament References**
Day of rest; no work	Rest for people and animals	Mt 12:1-14; 28:1; Lk 4:16; Jn 5:9–10; Ac 13:42; Col 2:16; Heb 4:1-11
Year of rest; fallow fields	Rest for land	
Canceled debts; liberation of slaves and indentured servants; land returned to original family owners	Help for poor; stabilize society	
Slaying and eating a lamb, together with bitter herbs and bread made without yeast, in every household	Remember Israel's deliverance from Egypt	Mt 26:17; Mk 14:12-26; Jn 2:13; 11:55; 1Co 5:7; Heb 11:28
Eating bread made without yeast; holding several assemblies; making designated offerings	Remember how the Lord brought the Israelites out of Egypt in haste	Mk 14:1; Ac 12:3; 1Co 5:6-8
Presenting a sheaf of the first of the barley harvest as a wave offering; making a burnt offering and a grain offering	Recognize the Lord's bounty in the land	Ro 8:23; 1Co 15:20-23
A festival of joy; mandatory and voluntary offerings, including the firstfruits of the wheat harvest	Show joy and thankfulness for the Lord's blessing of harvest	Ac 2:1-4; 20:16; 1Co 16:8
An assembly on a day of rest commemorated with trumpet blasts and sacrifices	Present Israel before the Lord for his favor	
A day of rest, fasting and sacrifices of atonement for priests and people and atonement for the tabernacle and altar	Atone for the sins of priests and people and purify the Holy Place	Ro 3:24-26; Heb 9:7; 10:3,19-22
A week of celebration for the harvest; living in booths and offering sacrifices	Memorialize the journey from Egypt to Canaan; give thanks for the productivity of Canaan	Jn 7:2,37
A day of convocation, rest and offering sacrifices	Commemorate the closing of the cycle of feasts	
A day of joy and feasting and giving presents	Remind the Israelites of their national deliverance in the time of Esther	

In addition, new moons were often special feast days (Nu 10:10; 1Ch 23:31; Ezr 3:5; Ne 10:33; Ps 81:3; Isa 1:13-14; 66:23; Hos 5:7; Am 8:5; Col 2:16).

ment.[j] Hold a sacred assembly[k] and deny yourselves,[a] and present an offering made to the LORD by fire. [28]Do no work on that day, because it is the Day of Atonement, when atonement is made for you before the LORD your God. [29]Anyone who does not deny himself on that day must be cut off from his people.[l] [30]I will destroy from among his people[m] anyone who does any work on that day. [31]You shall do no work at all. This is to be a lasting ordinance for the generations to come, wherever you live. [32]It is a sabbath of rest for you, and you must deny yourselves. From the evening of the ninth day of the month until the following evening you are to observe your sabbath."

Feast of Tabernacles

[33]The LORD said to Moses, [34]"Say to the Israelites: 'On the fifteenth day of the seventh month the LORD's Feast of Tabernacles[n] begins, and it lasts for seven days. [35]The first day is a sacred assembly; do no regular work. [36]For seven days present offerings made to the LORD by fire, and on the eighth day hold a sacred assembly[o] and present an offering made to the LORD by fire. It is the closing assembly; do no regular work.

[37]("'These are the LORD's appointed feasts, which you are to proclaim as sacred assemblies for bringing offerings made to the LORD by fire—the burnt offerings and grain offerings, sacrifices and drink offerings[p] required for each day. [38]These offerings are in addition to those for the LORD's Sabbaths[q] and[b] in addition to your gifts and whatever you have vowed and all the freewill offerings you give to the LORD.)

[39]"'So beginning with the fifteenth day of the seventh month, after you have gathered the crops of the land, celebrate the festival to the LORD for seven days;[r] the first day is a day of rest, and the eighth day also is a day of rest. [40]On the first day you are to take choice fruit from the trees, and palm fronds, leafy branches and poplars,[s] and rejoice before the LORD your God for seven days. [41]Celebrate this as a festival to the LORD for seven days each year. This is to be a lasting ordinance for the generations to come; celebrate it in the seventh month. [42]Live in booths[t] for seven days: All native-born Israelites are to live in booths [43]so your descendants will know[u] that I had the Israelites live in booths when I brought them out of Egypt. I am the LORD your God.'"

[44]So Moses announced to the Israelites the appointed feasts of the LORD.

Oil and Bread Set Before the LORD

24 The LORD said to Moses, [2]"Command the Israelites to bring you clear oil of pressed olives for the light so that the lamps may be kept burning continually. [3]Outside the curtain of the Testimony in the Tent of Meeting, Aaron is to tend the lamps before the LORD from evening till morning, continually. This is to be a lasting ordinance for the generations to come. [4]The lamps on the pure gold lampstand[v] before the LORD must be tended continually.

[5]"Take fine flour and bake twelve loaves of bread,[w] using two-tenths of an ephah[c] for each loaf. [6]Set them in two rows, six in each row, on the table of pure gold[x] before the LORD. [7]Along each row put some pure incense as a memorial portion[y] to represent the bread and to be an offering made to the LORD by fire. [8]This bread is to be set out before the LORD regularly,[z] Sabbath after Sabbath,[a] on behalf of the Israelites, as a lasting covenant. [9]It belongs to Aaron and his sons,[b] who are to eat it in a holy place, because it is a most holy part of their regular share of the offerings made to the LORD by fire."

A Blasphemer Stoned

[10]Now the son of an Israelite mother and an Egyptian father went out among the Israelites, and a fight broke out in the camp between him and an Israelite. [11]The son of the Israelite woman blasphemed the Name[c] with a curse; so they brought him to Moses. (His mother's name was Shelomith, the daughter of Dibri the Danite.) [12]They put him in custody until the will of the LORD should be made clear to them.[d]

23:27 [j]Ex 30:10 [k]Nu 29:7
23:29 [l]Ge 17:14; Nu 5:2
23:30 [m]Lev 20:3
23:34 [n]Ex 23:16; Dt 16:13; Ezr 3:4; Ne 8:14; Zec 14:16; Jn 7:2
23:36 [o]2Ch 7:9; Ne 8:18; Jn 7:37
23:37 [p]ver 2,4
23:38 [q]Eze 45:17
23:39 [r]Ex 23:16; Dt 16:13
23:40 [s]Ne 8:14-17
23:42 [t]Ne 8:14-16
23:43 [u]Dt 31:13; Ps 78:5
24:4 [v]Ex 25:31; 31:8
24:5 [w]Ex 25:30
24:6 [x]Ex 25:23-30; 1Ki 7:48
24:7 [y]Lev 2:2
24:8 [z]Nu 4:7; 1Ch 9:32; 2Ch 2:4 [a]Mt 12:5
24:9 [b]Lev 8:31; Mt 12:4; Mk 2:26; Lk 6:4
24:11 [c]Ex 3:15
24:12 [d]Ex 18:16; Nu 15:34

[a] *27* Or *and fast*; also in verses 29 and 32 [b] *38* Or *These feasts are in addition to the LORD's Sabbaths, and these offerings are* [c] *5* That is, probably about 4 quarts (about 4.5 liters)

23:33-43 See Deuteronomy 16:13–17.
■ **24:1-9** *Oil and Loaves.* Moses passed along the Lord's requirements regarding lamp oil and tabernacle bread. See chart "Tabernacle Furnishings" at Exodus 26.
24:2 the lamps. They formed part of the seven-branched candlestick that stood in the Holy Place, the outer part of the tabernacle. For a description, see Exodus 25:31–40. Shaped like a tree in bloom, the lampstand symbolized the life- and light-giving power of God.
24:5 Opposite the lampstand in the Holy Place was a small table on which were placed 12 large loaves that symbolized the 12 tribes of Israel. This arrangement symbolized Israel as being constantly in the light of God's care and blessing.
■ **24:10-23** *Blasphemy.* To impress upon the Israelites the seriousness of these holiness regulations, Moses recounted an incident of blasphemy and its deadly consequence.
24:10 Egyptian father. After many years of slavery in Egypt, cases of intermarriage must have been common.
24:11 blasphemed. See Exodus 20:7. See *WLC* 113.

13Then the LORD said to Moses: 14"Take the blasphemer outside the camp. All those
who heard him are to lay their hands on his head, and the entire assembly is to stone
him.[e] 15Say to the Israelites: 'If anyone curses his God,[f] he will be held responsible; 16any-
one who blasphemes the name of the LORD must be put to death.[g] The entire assembly
must stone him. Whether an alien or native-born, when he blasphemes the Name, he
must be put to death.
17" 'If anyone takes the life of a human being, he must be put to death.[h] 18Anyone who
takes the life of someone's animal must make restitution[i]—life for life. 19If anyone injures
his neighbor, whatever he has done must be done to him: 20fracture for fracture, eye for
eye, tooth for tooth.[j] As he has injured the other, so he is to be injured. 21Whoever kills
an animal must make restitution, but whoever kills a man must be put to death.[k] 22You
are to have the same law for the alien[l] and the native-born.[m] I am the LORD your God.' "
23Then Moses spoke to the Israelites, and they took the blasphemer outside the
camp and stoned him. The Israelites did as the LORD commanded Moses.

The Sabbath Year

25 The LORD said to Moses on Mount Sinai, 2"Speak to the Israelites and say to
them: 'When you enter the land I am going to give you, the land itself must observe a sabbath to the LORD. 3For six years sow your fields, and for six years prune your
vineyards and gather their crops.[n] 4But in the seventh year the land is to have a sabbath
of rest, a sabbath to the LORD. Do not sow your fields or prune your vineyards. 5Do not
reap what grows of itself or harvest the grapes of your untended vines. The land is to have
a year of rest. 6Whatever the land yields during the sabbath year[o] will be food for you—
for yourself, your manservant and maidservant, and the hired worker and temporary resident who live among you, 7as well as for your livestock and the wild animals in your
land. Whatever the land produces may be eaten.

The Year of Jubilee

8" 'Count off seven sabbaths of years—seven times seven years—so that the seven
sabbaths of years amount to a period of forty-nine years. 9Then have the trumpet[p]
sounded everywhere on the tenth day of the seventh month; on the Day of Atonement
sound the trumpet throughout your land. 10Consecrate the fiftieth year and proclaim liberty[q] throughout the land to all its inhabitants. It shall be a jubilee[r] for you; each one
of you is to return to his family property and each to his own clan. 11The fiftieth year shall
be a jubilee for you; do not sow and do not reap what grows of itself or harvest the untended vines. 12For it is a jubilee and is to be holy for you; eat only what is taken directly from the fields.
13" 'In this Year of Jubilee[s] everyone is to return to his own property.
14" 'If you sell land to one of your countrymen or buy any from him, do not take advantage of each other.[t] 15You are to buy from your countryman on the basis of the number of years[u] since the Jubilee. And he is to sell to you on the basis of the number of years
left for harvesting crops. 16When the years are many, you are to increase the price, and

24:14 [e]Lev 20:27; Dt 13:9; 17:5,7; 21:21
24:15 [f]Ex 22:28
24:16 [g]1Ki 21:10,13; Mt 26:66
24:17 [h]Ge 9:6; Ex 21:12; Nu 35:30-31; Dt 27:24
24:18 [i]ver 21
24:20 [j]Ex 21:24; Mt 5:38*
24:21 [k]ver 17
24:22 [l]Ex 12:49 [m]Nu 9:14; 15:16
25:3 [n]Ex 23:10
25:6 [o]ver 20
25:9 [p]Lev 23:24
25:10 [q]Isa 61:1; Jer 34:8, 15,17; Lk 4:19 [r]Nu 36:4
25:13 [s]ver 10
25:14 [t]Lev 19:13; 1Sa 12:3,4
25:15 [u]Lev 27:18,23

24:14 lay their hands on his head. This action probably was taken to rid them of the guilt they had contracted by hearing his blasphemy.
24:16 See *WCF* 23.3.
24:17–22 An elaboration on the legal principles behind the execution order.
24:20 eye for eye, tooth for tooth. Expressed the principle that punishment was to be proportionate to the offense. This was designed to curb exaggerated revenge, such as anger that led to murder (Ge 4:24), but it was not always enforced literally (Ex 21:26–27). As with other legal penalties, this was a statement of maximum liability rather than of mandatory retribution or compensation. Jesus (and the apostles) affirmed this principle and encouraged that its application be tempered by love (19:18; see Mt 7:12). So for the sake of the kingdom, Jesus encouraged his disciples to deny self, to forbear and to forgive, rather than to seek revenge (Mt 5:38–42), recognizing that God will judge people on the last day by their works (Mt 25:31–46).
■ **25:1–55** *Years of Release.* The Lord asserted his royal ownership of the promised land by presenting laws to prevent the exploitation of his land and subjects. This chapter divides into two sections: the Sabbath year (vv. 1–7) and the Jubilee year (vv. 8–55).
■ **25:1–7** *Sabbath Year.* Just as man needed a day of rest, land without fertilizers needed to lie fallow for a time. Similar regulations appear in Exodus 23:10–11.
25:4 Do not sow. In the absence of crop rotation, the Sabbath year allowed the land to be replenished with nutrients, which would be needed by crops in the coming years.
25:7 may be eaten. Eating whatever grew on its own during the Sabbath year was permitted. The purpose of the year was not to produce hunger, but to give rest to the land.
■ **25:8–55** *Jubilee Year.* A year of liberation and restoration that was to take place every fiftieth year. It was to be more than a fallow year. All the poor who had fallen into debt were to be given a fresh start. Loans were to be written off. Land that had been sold was to be returned to its original, hereditary owner. Slaves were to be released. The evidence suggests that Israel never put these commands into practice. The Lord warned that the regular neglect of the Sabbath year and Jubilee would eventually lead to exile from the promised land (26:34–35), and in fact this ultimately came to pass (2Ch 36:21). Recognizing their failing in this area, those who returned from exile to participate in the restoration efforts vowed to maintain the Sabbath year, and even to apply some of the commands of Jubilee, such as the forgiving of debts (Ne 10:31), to every Sabbath year.
25:13 return to his own property. God protected his gift to each family within the covenant community. In this way he protected the family structure, provided life in perpetuity for its members and prevented commercial exploitation of his gift.

when the years are few, you are to decrease the price,[v] because what he is really selling
you is the number of crops. 17 Do not take advantage of each other,[w] but fear your
God.[x] I am the LORD your God.[y]
18 " 'Follow my decrees and be careful to obey my laws, and you will live safely in the
land.[z] 19 Then the land will yield its fruit,[a] and you will eat your fill and live there in safety. 20 You may ask, "What will we eat in the seventh year[b] if we do not plant or harvest
our crops?" 21 I will send you such a blessing[c] in the sixth year that the land will yield
enough for three years. 22 While you plant during the eighth year, you will eat from the
old crop and will continue to eat from it until the harvest of the ninth year comes in.[d]
23 " 'The land must not be sold permanently, because the land is mine[e] and you are
but aliens[f] and my tenants. 24 Throughout the country that you hold as a possession, you
must provide for the redemption of the land.
25 " 'If one of your countrymen becomes poor and sells some of his property, his
nearest relative[g] is to come and redeem[h] what his countryman has sold. 26 If, however,
a man has no one to redeem it for him but he himself prospers and acquires sufficient
means to redeem it, 27 he is to determine the value for the years since he sold it and re-
fund the balance to the man to whom he sold it; he can then go back to his own property. 28 But if he does not acquire the means to repay him, what he sold will remain in the
possession of the buyer until the Year of Jubilee. It will be returned in the Jubilee, and
he can then go back to his property.[i]
29 " 'If a man sells a house in a walled city, he retains the right of redemption a full year
after its sale. During that time he may redeem it. 30 If it is not redeemed before a full year
has passed, the house in the walled city shall belong permanently to the buyer and his
descendants. It is not to be returned in the Jubilee. 31 But houses in villages without walls
around them are to be considered as open country. They can be redeemed, and they are
to be returned in the Jubilee.
32 " 'The Levites always have the right to redeem their houses in the Levitical towns,[j]
which they possess. 33 So the property of the Levites is redeemable—that is, a house sold
in any town they hold—and is to be returned in the Jubilee, because the houses in the
towns of the Levites are their property among the Israelites. 34 But the pastureland belonging to their towns must not be sold; it is their permanent possession.[k]
35 " 'If one of your countrymen becomes poor[l] and is unable to support himself among
you, help him[m] as you would an alien or a temporary resident, so he can continue to live
among you. 36 Do not take interest[n] of any kind[a] from him, but fear your God, so that your
countryman may continue to live among you. 37 You must not lend him money at interest or sell him food at a profit. 38 I am the LORD your God, who brought you out of Egypt
to give you the land of Canaan and to be your God.[o]
39 " 'If one of your countrymen becomes poor among you and sells himself to you, do
not make him work as a slave.[p] 40 He is to be treated as a hired worker or a temporary
resident among you; he is to work for you until the Year of Jubilee. 41 Then he and his children are to be released, and he will go back to his own clan and to the property[q] of his
forefathers. 42 Because the Israelites are my servants, whom I brought out of Egypt, they
must not be sold as slaves. 43 Do not rule over them ruthlessly,[r] but fear your God.
44 " 'Your male and female slaves are to come from the nations around you; from them
you may buy slaves. 45 You may also buy some of the temporary residents living among
you and members of their clans born in your country, and they will become your property. 46 You can will them to your children as inherited property and can make them
slaves for life, but you must not rule over your fellow Israelites ruthlessly.
47 " 'If an alien or a temporary resident among you becomes rich and one of your coun-

25:16 [v]ver 27,51,52
25:17 [w]Pr 22:22; Jer 7:5, 6; 1Th 4:6 [x]Lev 19:14 [y]Lev 19:32
25:18 [z]Lev 26:4,5; Dt 12:10; Ps 4:8; Jer 23:6
25:19 [a]Lev 26:4
25:20 [b]ver 4
25:21 [c]Dt 28:8,12; Hag 2:19; Mal 3:10
25:22 [d]Lev 26:10
25:23 [e]Ex 19:5 [f]Ge 23:4; 1Ch 29:15; Ps 39:12; Heb 11:13; 1Pe 2:11
25:25 [g]Ru 2:20; Jer 32:7 [h]Lev 27:13,19,31; Ru 4:4
25:28 [i]ver 10
25:32 [j]Nu 35:1-8; Jos 21:2
25:34 [k]Nu 35:2-5
25:35 [l]Dt 24:14,15 [m]Dt 15:8; Ps 37:21,26; Lk 6:35
25:36 [n]Ex 22:25; Dt 23:19-20
25:38 [o]Ge 17:7; Lev 11:45
25:39 [p]Ex 21:2; Dt 15:12; 1Ki 9:22
25:41 [q]ver 28
25:43 [r]Ex 1:13; Eze 34:4; Col 4:1

[a] *36* Or *take excessive interest*; similarly in verse 37

25:17 See *WLC* 142.
25:23 land is mine. Although God gave Israel the land as a good gift to be enjoyed (Dt 6:10–12; 8:10–13), he retained its final ownership and so could terminate the lease should the Israelites prove undesirable tenants. The people did not possess the land as an inalienable right but did so within the structures of a covenantal relationship with God. The land was not private property to be bought and sold. It symbolized life with God (see note on Ge 12:7).
25:25 All the sales described here took place because of hardship. Land could not be sold permanently (v. 23) from family to family (see 1Ki 19). **his nearest relative.** It was hoped that a relative would buy a poor man's land and return it to him. In any event, the poor man was to receive it back in the Year of Jubilee.
25:29 a house in a walled city. Reversion to hereditary owners applied only to land grants, not to property in general. The sale of houses in walled cities became permanent (v. 30) if the houses were not redeemed within a year.
25:35 See *WLC* 141; *WSC* 74.
25:36 interest. At the minimum, this text forbids the charging of excessive interest on loans to the poor (see NIV text note). It may also forbid all forms of interest on loans to the poor (v. 37; Ex 22:25; Ps 15:5).
25:39 sells himself. If a man sold a son or a daughter into slavery because of debt, he or she was released after seven years (Ex 21:2–11; Dt 15:12–18). This text deals with an even worse debt: After having presumably sold his land, a man and his whole family (v. 41) were sold as slaves. In this case they were to be released in the Year of Jubilee.

bath,[a] and then present an offering of new grain to the LORD. 17From wherever you live, bring two loaves made of two-tenths of an ephah of fine flour, baked with yeast, as a wave offering of firstfruits[b] to the LORD. 18Present with this bread seven male lambs, each a year old and without defect, one young bull and two rams. They will be a burnt offering to the LORD, together with their grain offerings and drink offerings—an offering made by fire, an aroma pleasing to the LORD. 19Then sacrifice one male goat for a sin offering and two lambs, each a year old, for a fellowship offering.[a] 20The priest is to wave the two lambs before the LORD as a wave offering, together with the bread of the firstfruits. They are a sacred offering to the LORD for the priest. 21On that same day you are to proclaim a sacred assembly[c] and do no regular work.[d] This is to be a lasting ordinance for the generations to come, wherever you live.

22" 'When you reap the harvest[e] of your land, do not reap to the very edges of your field or gather the gleanings of your harvest.[f] Leave them for the poor and the alien. I am the LORD your God.' "

Feast of Trumpets

23The LORD said to Moses, 24"Say to the Israelites: 'On the first day of the seventh month you are to have a day of rest, a sacred assembly commemorated with trumpet blasts.[g] 25Do no regular work,[h] but present an offering made to the LORD by fire.' "

Day of Atonement

26The LORD said to Moses, 27"The tenth day of this seventh month[i] is the Day of Atone-

23:16 [a]Nu 28:26; Ac 2:1
23:17 [b]Ex 34:22; Lev 2:12
23:21 [c]ver 2 [d]ver 3
23:22 [e]Lev 19:9 [f]Lev 19:10; Dt 24:19-21; Ru 2:15
23:24 [g]Lev 25:9; Nu 10:9,10; 29:1
23:25 [h]ver 21
23:27 [i]Lev 16:29

[a] *19* Traditionally *peace offering*

23:26–32 See 16:2–34.

Description	Purpose	New Testament References
Day of rest; no work	Rest for people and animals	Mt 12:1-14; 28:1; Lk 4:16; Jn 5:9–10; Ac 13:42; Col 2:16; Heb 4:1-11
Year of rest; fallow fields	Rest for land	
Canceled debts; liberation of slaves and indentured servants; land returned to original family owners	Help for poor; stabilize society	
Slaying and eating a lamb, together with bitter herbs and bread made without yeast, in every household	Remember Israel's deliverance from Egypt	Mt 26:17; Mk 14:12-26; Jn 2:13; 11:55; 1Co 5:7; Heb 11:28
Eating bread made without yeast; holding several assemblies; making designated offerings	Remember how the Lord brought the Israelites out of Egypt in haste	Mk 14:1; Ac 12:3; 1Co 5:6-8
Presenting a sheaf of the first of the barley harvest as a wave offering; making a burnt offering and a grain offering	Recognize the Lord's bounty in the land	Ro 8:23; 1Co 15:20-23
A festival of joy; mandatory and voluntary offerings, including the firstfruits of the wheat harvest	Show joy and thankfulness for the Lord's blessing of harvest	Ac 2:1-4; 20:16; 1Co 16:8
An assembly on a day of rest commemorated with trumpet blasts and sacrifices	Present Israel before the Lord for his favor	
A day of rest, fasting and sacrifices of atonement for priests and people and atonement for the tabernacle and altar	Atone for the sins of priests and people and purify the Holy Place	Ro 3:24-26; Heb 9:7; 10:3,19-22
A week of celebration for the harvest; living in booths and offering sacrifices	Memorialize the journey from Egypt to Canaan; give thanks for the productivity of Canaan	Jn 7:2,37
A day of convocation, rest and offering sacrifices	Commemorate the closing of the cycle of feasts	
A day of joy and feasting and giving presents	Remind the Israelites of their national deliverance in the time of Esther	

In addition, new moons were often special feast days (Nu 10:10; 1Ch 23:31; Ezr 3:5; Ne 10:33; Ps 81:3; Isa 1:13-14; 66:23; Hos 5:7; Am 8:5; Col 2:16).

ment.[j] Hold a sacred assembly[k] and deny yourselves,[a] and present an offering made to
the LORD by fire. 28Do no work on that day, because it is the Day of Atonement, when
atonement is made for you before the LORD your God. 29Anyone who does not deny himself on that day must be cut off from his people.[l] 30I will destroy from among his people[m]
anyone who does any work on that day. 31You shall do no work at all. This is to be a lasting ordinance for the generations to come, wherever you live. 32It is a sabbath of rest for
you, and you must deny yourselves. From the evening of the ninth day of the month until the following evening you are to observe your sabbath."

Feast of Tabernacles

33The LORD said to Moses, 34"Say to the Israelites: 'On the fifteenth day of the seventh
month the LORD's Feast of Tabernacles[n] begins, and it lasts for seven days. 35The first day
is a sacred assembly; do no regular work. 36For seven days present offerings made to the
LORD by fire, and on the eighth day hold a sacred assembly[o] and present an offering made
to the LORD by fire. It is the closing assembly; do no regular work.

37(" 'These are the LORD's appointed feasts, which you are to proclaim as sacred assemblies for bringing offerings made to the LORD by fire—the burnt offerings and grain
offerings, sacrifices and drink offerings[p] required for each day. 38These offerings are in
addition to those for the LORD's Sabbaths[q] and[b] in addition to your gifts and whatever
you have vowed and all the freewill offerings you give to the LORD.)

39" 'So beginning with the fifteenth day of the seventh month, after you have gathered
the crops of the land, celebrate the festival to the LORD for seven days;[r] the first day is a
day of rest, and the eighth day also is a day of rest. 40On the first day you are to take
choice fruit from the trees, and palm fronds, leafy branches and poplars,[s] and rejoice before the LORD your God for seven days. 41Celebrate this as a festival to the LORD for sev-
en days each year. This is to be a lasting ordinance for the generations to come; celebrate
it in the seventh month. 42Live in booths[t] for seven days: All native-born Israelites are
to live in booths 43so your descendants will know[u] that I had the Israelites live in booths
when I brought them out of Egypt. I am the LORD your God.' "

44So Moses announced to the Israelites the appointed feasts of the LORD.

Oil and Bread Set Before the LORD

24 The LORD said to Moses, 2"Command the Israelites to bring you clear oil of
pressed olives for the light so that the lamps may be kept burning continually.
3Outside the curtain of the Testimony in the Tent of Meeting, Aaron is to tend the lamps
before the LORD from evening till morning, continually. This is to be a lasting ordinance
for the generations to come. 4The lamps on the pure gold lampstand[v] before the LORD
must be tended continually.

5"Take fine flour and bake twelve loaves of bread,[w] using two-tenths of an ephah[c] for
each loaf. 6Set them in two rows, six in each row, on the table of pure gold[x] before the
LORD. 7Along each row put some pure incense as a memorial portion[y] to represent the
bread and to be an offering made to the LORD by fire. 8This bread is to be set out before
the LORD regularly,[z] Sabbath after Sabbath,[a] on behalf of the Israelites, as a lasting covenant. 9It belongs to Aaron and his sons,[b] who are to eat it in a holy place, because it is
a most holy part of their regular share of the offerings made to the LORD by fire."

A Blasphemer Stoned

10Now the son of an Israelite mother and an Egyptian father went out among the Israelites, and a fight broke out in the camp between him and an Israelite. 11The son of the
Israelite woman blasphemed the Name[c] with a curse; so they brought him to Moses. (His
mother's name was Shelomith, the daughter of Dibri the Danite.) 12They put him in custody until the will of the LORD should be made clear to them.[d]

23:27 [j]Ex 30:10 [k]Nu 29:7
23:29 [l]Ge 17:14; Nu 5:2
23:30 [m]Lev 20:3
23:34 [n]Ex 23:16; Dt 16:13; Ezr 3:4; Ne 8:14; Zec 14:16; Jn 7:2
23:36 [o]2Ch 7:9; Ne 8:18; Jn 7:37
23:37 [p]ver 2,4
23:38 [q]Eze 45:17
23:39 [r]Ex 23:16; Dt 16:13
23:40 [s]Ne 8:14-17
23:42 [t]Ne 8:14-16
23:43 [u]Dt 31:13; Ps 78:5
24:4 [v]Ex 25:31; 31:8
24:5 [w]Ex 25:30
24:6 [x]Ex 25:23-30; 1Ki 7:48
24:7 [y]Lev 2:2
24:8 [z]Nu 4:7; 1Ch 9:32; 2Ch 2:4 [a]Mt 12:5
24:9 [b]Lev 8:31; Mt 12:4; Mk 2:26; Lk 6:4
24:11 [c]Ex 3:15
24:12 [d]Ex 18:16; Nu 15:34

[a] *27* Or *and fast;* also in verses 29 and 32 [b] *38* Or *These feasts are in addition to the LORD's Sabbaths, and these offerings are* [c] *5* That is, probably about 4 quarts (about 4.5 liters)

23:33–43 See Deuteronomy 16:13–17.
■ **24:1–9** *Oil and Loaves.* Moses passed along the Lord's requirements regarding lamp oil and tabernacle bread. See chart "Tabernacle Furnishings" at Exodus 26.
24:2 the lamps. They formed part of the seven-branched candlestick that stood in the Holy Place, the outer part of the tabernacle. For a description, see Exodus 25:31–40. Shaped like a tree in bloom, the lampstand symbolized the life- and light-giving power of God.
24:5 Opposite the lampstand in the Holy Place was a small table on which were placed 12 large loaves that symbolized the 12 tribes of Israel. This arrangement symbolized Israel as being constantly in the light of God's care and blessing.
■ **24:10–23** *Blasphemy.* To impress upon the Israelites the seriousness of these holiness regulations, Moses recounted an incident of blasphemy and its deadly consequence.
24:10 Egyptian father. After many years of slavery in Egypt, cases of intermarriage must have been common.
24:11 blasphemed. See Exodus 20:7. See *WLC* 113.

trymen becomes poor and sells himself to the alien living among you or to a member of
the alien's clan, 48he retains the right of redemption after he has sold himself. One of his
relatives[s] may redeem him: 49An uncle or a cousin or any blood relative in his clan may
redeem him. Or if he prospers,[t] he may redeem himself. 50He and his buyer are to count
the time from the year he sold himself up to the Year of Jubilee. The price for his release
is to be based on the rate paid to a hired man[u] for that number of years. 51If many years
remain, he must pay for his redemption a larger share of the price paid for him. 52If only
a few years remain until the Year of Jubilee, he is to compute that and pay for his redemption accordingly. 53He is to be treated as a man hired from year to year; you must see to
it that his owner does not rule over him ruthlessly.

54" 'Even if he is not redeemed in any of these ways, he and his children are to be released in the Year of Jubilee, 55for the Israelites belong to me as servants. They are my
servants, whom I brought out of Egypt. I am the LORD your God.

Reward for Obedience

26 " 'Do not make idols[v] or set up an image or a sacred stone[w] for yourselves, and
do not place a carved stone[x] in your land to bow down before it. I am the LORD
your God.

2" 'Observe my Sabbaths and have reverence for my sanctuary.[y] I am the LORD.

3" 'If you follow my decrees and are careful to obey[z] my commands, 4I will send you
rain[a] in its season, and the ground will yield its crops and the trees of the field their fruit.[b]
5Your threshing will continue until grape harvest and the grape harvest will continue until planting, and you will eat all the food you want[c] and live in safety in your land.[d]

6" 'I will grant peace in the land,[e] and you will lie down[f] and no one will make you
afraid.[g] I will remove savage beasts[h] from the land, and the sword will not pass through
your country. 7You will pursue your enemies, and they will fall by the sword before you.
8Five of you will chase a hundred, and a hundred of you will chase ten thousand, and
your enemies will fall by the sword before you.[i]

9" 'I will look on you with favor and make you fruitful and increase your numbers,[j]
and I will keep my covenant[k] with you. 10You will still be eating last year's harvest when
you will have to move it out to make room for the new.[l] 11I will put my dwelling place[a][m]
among you, and I will not abhor you. 12I will walk[n] among you and be your God, and you
will be my people.[o] 13I am the LORD your God, who brought you out of Egypt so that you
would no longer be slaves to the Egyptians; I broke the bars of your yoke[p] and enabled
you to walk with heads held high.

Punishment for Disobedience

14" 'But if you will not listen to me and carry out all these commands,[q] 15and if you
reject my decrees and abhor my laws and fail to carry out all my commands and so violate my covenant, 16then I will do this to you: I will bring upon you sudden terror, wasting diseases and fever[r] that will destroy your sight and drain away your life.[s] You will
plant seed in vain, because your enemies will eat it.[t] 17I will set my face[u] against you so
that you will be defeated by your enemies; those who hate you will rule over you,[v] and
you will flee even when no one is pursuing you.[w]

18" 'If after all this you will not listen to me, I will punish you for your sins seven times
over.[x] 19I will break down your stubborn pride[y] and make the sky above you like iron and

[a] *11* Or *my tabernacle*

25:48 [s]Ne 5:5
25:49 [t]ver 26
25:50 [u]Job 7:1; Isa 16:14; 21:16
26:1 [v]Ex 20:4; Lev 19:4; Dt 5:8 [w]Ex 23:24 [x]Nu 33:52
26:2 [y]Lev 19:30
26:3 [z]Dt 7:12; 11:13,22; 28:1,9
26:4 [a]Dt 11:14 [b]Ps 67:6
26:5 [c]Dt 11:15; Joel 2:19,26; Am 9:13 [d]Lev 25:18
26:6 [e]Ps 29:11; 85:8; 147:14 [f]Ps 4:8 [g]Zep 3:13 [h]ver 22
26:8 [i]Dt 32:30; Jos 23:10
26:9 [j]Ge 17:6; Ne 9:23 [k]Ge 17:7
26:10 [l]Lev 25:22
26:11 [m]Ex 25:8; Ps 76:2; Eze 37:27
26:12 [n]Ge 3:8 [o]2Co 6:16*
26:13 [p]Eze 34:27
26:14 [q]Dt 28:15-68; Mal 2:2
26:16 [r]Dt 28:22,35 [s]1Sa 2:33 [t]Job 31:8
26:17 [u]Lev 17:10 [v]Ps 106:41 [w]ver 36,37; Dt 28:7,25; Ps 53:5
26:18 [x]ver 21
26:19 [y]Isa 25:11

■ **26:1–46** *Blessings and Curses.* The Lord's instructions to the Israelites culminated in a reaffirmation of the importance of proper tabernacle worship (vv. 1–2), followed by offers of blessings for obedience (vv. 3–13) and warnings of curses for disobedience (vv. 14–39).

26:1–14 See *WCF* 19.6.

26:1–2 The centrality of proper tabernacle worship is evident throughout this book. Here the focus is on idolatry and Sabbath observance.

26:2 have reverence for my sanctuary. Expresses the purpose for the many regulations of worship in this book.

26:3–13 Biblical covenants exhibit a dynamic of blessings and curses as given by the benevolent, divine King in correspondence with human loyalty and disloyalty. See theological article "Major Covenants in the Bible" on page 25. Moses first spoke of blessings that would follow upon fidelity (see Ex 20:12; Dt 28:1–14; Mt 6:4).

26:4–5 rain . . . food. God would reward his faithful people with blessings in nature.

26:6–8 peace . . . sword. God would reward his faithful people with victory in war.

26:9–13 favor . . . walk among you . . . your God. The full presence of God among his people would come as the blessings i[n] nature and war were fully realized. God offered all of this to hi[s] faithful people.

26:14–39 Moses spoke of the terrible consequences of infidel[ity] in balance with his preceding description of covenant blessi[ngs] (see note on 26:3–13). The sacrificial system described through[out] this book was designed to bring renewal upon repentance, [but] Moses anticipated the possibility that sin would increase to suc[h an] extent that Israel would be sent into exile (vv. 27–35). Is[rael's] prophets depended heavily on these verses (see also Dt 28:[15–68]) as they warned of divine judgment and called for repentanc[e].

26:18,21,24,28 seven times. God threatened at each s[tage] of the Israelites' increasing rebellion to increase their curse[s seven] times. The end of this increase would result in utter de[struction] and

the ground beneath you like bronze.[z] 20Your strength will be spent in vain,[a] because your
soil will not yield its crops, nor will the trees of the land yield their fruit.[b]
21"'If you remain hostile toward me and refuse to listen to me, I will multiply your afflictions seven times over,[c] as your sins deserve. 22I will send wild animals[d] against you,
and they will rob you of your children, destroy your cattle and make you so few in number that your roads will be deserted.
23"'If in spite of these things you do not accept my correction[e] but continue to be hostile toward me, 24I myself will be hostile toward you and will afflict you for your sins seven
times over. 25And I will bring the sword upon you to avenge the breaking of the covenant.
When you withdraw into your cities, I will send a plague[f] among you, and you will be giv-
en into enemy hands. 26When I cut off your supply of bread,[g] ten women will be able to
bake your bread in one oven, and they will dole out the bread by weight. You will eat, but
you will not be satisfied.
27"'If in spite of this you still do not listen to me but continue to be hostile toward me,
28then in my anger I will be hostile toward you, and I myself will punish you for your sins
seven times over. 29You will eat the flesh of your sons and the flesh of your daughters.[h]
30I will destroy your high places,[i] cut down your incense altars[j] and pile your dead bodies on the lifeless forms of your idols,[k] and I will abhor you. 31I will turn your cities into
ruins and lay waste your sanctuaries,[l] and I will take no delight in the pleasing aroma
of your offerings. 32I will lay waste the land,[m] so that your enemies who live there will
be appalled. 33I will scatter you among the nations[n] and will draw out my sword and pursue you. Your land will be laid waste, and your cities will lie in ruins. 34Then the land will
enjoy its sabbath years all the time that it lies desolate and you are in the country of your
enemies;[o] then the land will rest and enjoy its sabbaths. 35All the time that it lies desolate, the land will have the rest it did not have during the sabbaths you lived in it.
36"'As for those of you who are left, I will make their hearts so fearful in the lands of
their enemies that the sound of a windblown leaf will put them to flight.[p] They will run
as though fleeing from the sword, and they will fall, even though no one is pursuing
them. 37They will stumble over one another as though fleeing from the sword, even
though no one is pursuing them. So you will not be able to stand before your enemies.[q]
38You will perish among the nations; the land of your enemies will devour you.[r] 39Those
of you who are left will waste away in the lands of their enemies because of their sins;
also because of their fathers' sins they will waste away.[s]
40"'But if they will confess their sins and the sins of their fathers[t]—their treachery
against me and their hostility toward me, 41which made me hostile toward them so that
I sent them into the land of their enemies—then when their uncircumcised hearts[u] are
humbled and they pay for their sin, 42I will remember my covenant with Jacob[v] and my
covenant with Isaac[w] and my covenant with Abraham, and I will remember the land.
43For the land will be deserted by them and will enjoy its sabbaths while it lies desolate
without them. They will pay for their sins because they rejected my laws and abhorred
my decrees. 44Yet in spite of this, when they are in the land of their enemies, I will not
reject them or abhor[x] them so as to destroy them completely,[y] breaking my covenant[z]
with them. I am the LORD their God. 45But for their sake I will remember[a] the covenant
with their ancestors whom I brought out of Egypt[b] in the sight of the nations to be their
God. I am the LORD.'"
46These are the decrees, the laws and the regulations that the LORD established on
Mount Sinai between himself and the Israelites through Moses.[c]

Redeeming What Is the LORD's

27 The LORD said to Moses, 2"Speak to the Israelites and say to them: 'If anyone
makes a special vow[d] to dedicate persons to the LORD by giving equivalent values, 3set the value of a male between the ages of twenty and sixty at fifty shekels[a] of sil-

26:19 [z]Dt 28:23
26:20 [a]Ps 127:1; Isa 17:11 [b]Dt 11:17
26:21 [c]ver 18
26:22 [d]Dt 32:24
26:23 [e]Jer 2:30; 5:3
26:25 [f]Nu 14:12; Eze 5:17
26:26 [g]Ps 105:16; Isa 3:1; Mic 6:14
26:29 [h]Dt 28:53
26:30 [i]2Ch 34:3; Eze 6:3 [j]Eze 6:6 [k]Eze 6:13
26:31 [l]Ps 74:3-7
26:32 [m]Jer 9:11
26:33 [n]Dt 4:27; Eze 12:15; 20:23; Zec 7:14
26:34 [o]ver 43; 2Ch 36:21
26:36 [p]Eze 21:7
26:37 [q]Jos 7:12
26:38 [r]Dt 4:26
26:39 [s]Eze 4:17
26:40 [t]Jer 3:12-15; Lk 15:18; 1Jn 1:9
26:41 [u]Eze 44:7,9; Ac 7:51
26:42 [v]Ge 22:15-18; 28:15 [w]Ge 26:5
26:44 [x]Ro 11:2 [y]Dt 4:31; Jer 30:11 [z]Jer 33:26
26:45 [a]Ge 17:7 [b]Ex 6:8; Lev 25:38
26:46 [c]Lev 7:38; 27:34
27:2 [d]Nu 6:2

a 3 That is, about 1 1/4 pounds (about 0.6 kilogram); also in verse 16

xile (vv. 27–35). This was the problem Daniel faced as he yearned r Israel's return from exile in Daniel 9. The people in exile had t repented. So on the basis of the "seven times" pattern estab- ed here, God declared that the 70 years of exile would be eased sevenfold (see Da 9:24).

25 See *WLC* 151.

2 **if they will confess.** Even in exile there was hope of restora- tio the exiles would repent (see also vv. 44–45; Dt 30:1–10).

■27:34 *Vows to God.* The subject of vows forms an appropriate ending for the book. In light of the offer of blessing and the warning of exile sounded by the previous chapter, this final chapter anticipates that some readers of this book would make significant vows of repentance and devotion to God. Later they might wish to redeem the property vowed. This chapter shows when and how this could be done.

27:2 persons. It was possible to offer oneself or a member of one's family to the full-time service of God in the temple (1Sa 1:11). But only Levites could serve God in this way; other vowed persons had

ver, according to the sanctuary shekel[a]; [e] 4and if it is a female, set her value at thirty shekels.[b] 5If it is a person between the ages of five and twenty, set the value of a male at twenty shekels[c] and of a female at ten shekels.[d] 6If it is a person between one month and five
years, set the value of a male at five shekels[e] [f] of silver and that of a female at three shekels[f] of silver. 7If it is a person sixty years old or more, set the value of a male at fifteen
shekels[g] and of a female at ten shekels. 8If anyone making the vow is too poor to pay[g]
the specified amount, he is to present the person to the priest, who will set the value[h]
for him according to what the man making the vow can afford.

9" 'If what he vowed is an animal that is acceptable as an offering to the LORD, such
an animal given to the LORD becomes holy. 10He must not exchange it or substitute a
good one for a bad one, or a bad one for a good one;[i] if he should substitute one animal
for another, both it and the substitute become holy. 11If what he vowed is a ceremonially unclean animal—one that is not acceptable as an offering to the LORD—the animal
must be presented to the priest, 12who will judge its quality as good or bad. Whatever
value the priest then sets, that is what it will be. 13If the owner wishes to redeem[j] the animal, he must add a fifth to its value.

14" 'If a man dedicates his house as something holy to the LORD, the priest will judge
its quality as good or bad. Whatever value the priest then sets, so it will remain. 15If the
man who dedicates his house redeems it,[k] he must add a fifth to its value, and the house
will again become his.

16" 'If a man dedicates to the LORD part of his family land, its value is to be set according to the amount of seed required for it—fifty shekels of silver to a homer[h] of barley
seed. 17If he dedicates his field during the Year of Jubilee, the value that has been set remains. 18But if he dedicates his field after the Jubilee, the priest will determine the value according to the number of years that remain[l] until the next Year of Jubilee, and its
set value will be reduced. 19If the man who dedicates the field wishes to redeem it, he
must add a fifth to its value, and the field will again become his. 20If, however, he does
not redeem the field, or if he has sold it to someone else, it can never be redeemed.
21When the field is released in the Jubilee,[m] it will become holy, like a field devoted to
the LORD;[n] it will become the property of the priests.[i]

22" 'If a man dedicates to the LORD a field he has bought, which is not part of his family land, 23the priest will determine its value up to the Year of Jubilee, and the man must
pay its value on that day as something holy to the LORD. 24In the Year of Jubilee the field
will revert to the person from whom he bought it,[o] the one whose land it was. 25Every
value is to be set according to the sanctuary shekel,[p] twenty gerahs[q] to the shekel.

26" 'No one, however, may dedicate the firstborn of an animal, since the firstborn already belongs to the LORD;[r] whether an ox[j] or a sheep, it is the LORD's. 27If it is one of the
unclean animals,[s] he may buy it back at its set value, adding a fifth of the value to it. If
he does not redeem it, it is to be sold at its set value.

28" 'But nothing that a man owns and devotes[k] [t] to the LORD—whether man or animal
or family land—may be sold or redeemed; everything so devoted is most holy to the LORD.

29" 'No person devoted to destruction[l] may be ransomed; he must be put to death.

30" 'A tithe[u] of everything from the land, whether grain from the soil or fruit from the
trees, belongs to the LORD; it is holy to the LORD. 31If a man redeems any of his tithe, he
must add a fifth of the value to it. 32The entire tithe of the herd and flock—every tenth
animal that passes under the shepherd's rod[v]—will be holy to the LORD. 33He must not
pick out the good from the bad or make any substitution.[w] If he does make a substitution, both the animal and its substitute become holy and cannot be redeemed.' "

34These are the commands the LORD gave Moses on Mount Sinai for the Israelites.[x]

27:3 [e]Ex 30:13; Nu 3:47; 18:16
27:6 [f]Nu 18:16
27:8 [g]Lev 5:11 [h]ver 12, 14
27:10 [i]ver 33
27:13 [j]ver 15,19; Lev 25:25
27:15 [k]ver 13,20
27:18 [l]Lev 25:15
27:21 [m]Lev 25:10 [n]ver 28; Nu 18:14; Eze 44:29
27:24 [o]Lev 25:28
27:25 [p]Ex 30:13; Nu 18:16 [q]Nu 3:47; Eze 45:12
27:26 [r]Ex 13:2,12
27:27 [s]ver 11
27:28 [t]Nu 18:14; Jos 6:17-19
27:30 [u]Ge 28:22; 2Ch 31:6; Mal 3:8
27:32 [v]Jer 33:13; Eze 20:37
27:33 [w]ver 10
27:34 [x]Lev 26:46; Dt 4:5

[a] *3* That is, about 2/5 ounce (about 11.5 grams); also in verse 25 [b] *4* That is, about 12 ounces (about 0.3 kilogram) [c] *5* That is, about 8 ounces (about 0.2 kilogram) [d] *5* That is, about 4 ounces (about 110 grams); also in verse 7 [e] *6* That is, about 2 ounces (about 55 grams) [f] *6* That is, about 1 1/4 ounces (about 35 grams) [g] *7* That is, about 6 ounces (about 170 grams) [h] *16* That is, probably about 6 bushels (about 220 liters) [i] *21* Or *priest* [j] *26* The Hebrew word can include both male and female. [k] *28* The Hebrew term refers to the irrevocable giving over of things or persons to the LORD. [l] *29* The Hebrew term refers to the irrevocable giving over of things or persons to the LORD, often by totally destroying them.

to be redeemed according to the tariffs described in verses 3–8.
27:9–10 Once vowed, sacrificial animals could not be withdrawn.
27:11–13 Unclean animals had to be redeemed for their value, plus a fifth.
27:28 devotes. See NIV text note. To devote (vv. 28–29) and to dedicate (v. 26) were not the same thing. The former was a solemn, irrevocable vow (see Nu 21:2; 1Sa 15); the latter allowed for redemption (vv. 15,19).
27:30 tithe. A tenth of all agricultural produce was given to God; that is, to the priestly tribe of Levi (Nu 18:21–29; Dt 12:6–18; 14:22–29). Any redemption of animals, grain or fruit was to include its value, plus a fifth.

NUMBERS

Introduction

Overview

Author: Moses

Purpose: To call the second generation of the exodus to serve God as his holy army in the conquest of the promised land by avoiding the failures of the past and by remaining faithful to God's directives

Date: c. 1406 B.C.

Key Truths:

- God fully prepared his people to serve him and to succeed in the conquest of the promised land.
- The members of the first generation failed to succeed because they were ungrateful for the grace God had shown them and feared the power of the Canaanites.
- God raised up another generation for the conquest of the promised land, but they also had to remain faithful to the Lord in order to succeed.

Author

Like the rest of the Pentateuch, Numbers was written by Moses, although a few portions may have been added at later times. See the article "Introduction to the Pentateuch" on page 1 for further discussion of the authorship of the Pentateuch and of Numbers.

Time and Place of Writing

We may date the book in the period after the wilderness wandering and before the death of Moses around 1406 B.C. The book begins with the preparations for the march across the desert and ends with the preparation for entering Canaan (see 22:1; 26:3,63; 31:12; 33:48,50; 34:15; 35:1; 36:13). Numbers was written for the generation of Israelites born in the desert as they waited in the plains of Moab across from Jericho. Moses encouraged them to persevere in faith and obedience, which their parents had not. As the Israelites prepared for the conquest of Canaan, this book called them to move forward as the Lord's holy army.

Purpose and Distinctives

The title of this book in the Hebrew Bible derives from the fifth Hebrew word of the first verse, which is translated "in the desert"—a good description of the book's content. When the Old Testament was translated into Greek (the Septuagint), its books were given Greek names. In this case, a Greek word that actually describes only the lists of fighting men was adopted: *Arithmoi*, or "Numbers."

At least three themes are vital to the message of Numbers. First, Numbers vividly describes the mercy and faithfulness of God toward his people. It shows God directing his people as they prepared for their journey through the wilderness, comforting them in their difficulties, dealing with their fears and punishing them only after extending them much patience. The failures of the Israelites—even those of the best of them, including Aaron, Miriam and Moses—are contrasted with the perfection of the ever-faithful, covenant God.

A second major theme of Numbers is the sovereign power of God to accomplish his purposes. This book reveals the utter failure of the members of the first generation and God's severe judgment against them. Yet it also offered hope to the second generation of the exodus: God was still directing history toward his goal of bringing Israel into the promised land. God's purposes will not fail, even if his people do.

The third vital theme is the responsibility of God's people to be faithful to the calling God has given them. The book ends abruptly with the second generation preparing to enter the land. No record is given of the battles they faced across the Jordan. This book was written to call the second generation to move forward into the conquest as God's holy army.

One of the most controversial matters that arise when interpreting this book is the large numbers of soldiers listed (see chs. 1,26). The total population would have been over two million if these numbers are taken literally. Archeological difficulties arise when the sizes of Canaanite cities at the time are compared with this figure. Moreover, other numbers (such as that of the firstborn in 3:43) present difficulties in comparison to such a large total figure.

In the history of interpretation, those who maintain belief in the veracity of Scripture have taken at least five major views regarding this problem:

1. The numbers are taken literally despite the apparent difficulties.
2. The current numbers in the Hebrew Bible are explained as resulting from corruptions of the texts during the history of transmission.
3. The Hebrew word translated "thousand" may be a technical term referring to units considerably less than a thousand.
4. The Hebrew word translated "thousand" may be emended to read "chiefs."
5. The numbers are taken as hyperboles, exaggerations intended by the writer and understood by the first generation readers to highlight the astounding grace God had shown to Israel.

Christ in Numbers

Numbers gives a historical portrait that points forward to Christ in at least five major ways. First, in general terms, as the book describes Israel preparing, failing and preparing again for holy war in Canaan, Christian readers are reminded of the final stages of holy war through which Christ will win the new heavens and the new earth. Christ began the last battle against the enemies of God when he died and rose from the dead (Col 2:15; Heb 2:14–15). He continues this war through the preaching of the gospel by the church today (Ac 15:15–17; Eph 6:10–18). Finally, when Christ returns, the battle for the world will be complete (Rev 19:11–21; 21:1–5). Second, the repeated focus of the book on the faithfulness of God's people reminds Christians not only of the salvation that comes through Christ's perfect obedience (2Co 5:19) but also of his call for those who follow him to seek holiness (Heb 12:14). Third, Christ is also revealed in some specific types in Numbers. For example, the work of Christ is foreshadowed by the typology of the red heifer (ch. 19; Heb 9:13), by the bringing of water from the rock (20:11; 1Co 10:4), and by the raised serpent that brought life out of death (21:4–9; Jn 3:14–15). Fourth, the specific prophecy of the conquests of David, who would defeat Israel's enemies (24:15–19), foreshadows Christ, who as the great son of David will one day be universally recognized as the greatest King of all. Finally, the centrality of the tabernacle also foreshadows Christ. Jesus came to dwell (lit., "tabernacle") among humanity in his first coming (Jn 1:14), and by his death and resurrection he opened up the way for all who believe to enter the very presence of God (Mk 15:38; Heb 6:19; 10:20). The apostle Paul taught that the church is the temple of God and that individual Christians are also temples of God (1Co 3:16; 6:19–20; Eph 2:19–22). At the second advent, the dwelling of God will be with humanity in fullness, and believers will no longer need a temple for the Lord God, for the Lamb will be the temple (Rev. 21:3,22).

Outline

- I. The Preparation of the First-Generation Army (1:1—9:14)
  - A. The Count and Arrangement of the Army (1:1—4:49)
    1. The Count of the Men of War (1:1–54)
    2. Positions for the Tribes (2:1–34)
    3. The Numbers and Duties of the Levites (3:1—4:49)
  - B. The Central Tabernacle (5:1—9:14)
    1. The Importance of the Tabernacle (5:1—6:27)
       - a. Exclusion of the Unclean (5:1–4)
       - b. Cases of Restitution (5:5–10)
       - c. The Law of Jealousy (5:11–31)
       - d. Nazirites (6:1–21)
       - e. The Aaronic Blessing (6:22–27)
    2. Offerings for the Tabernacle (7:1—8:4)
    3. Other Important Aspects of the Tabernacle (8:5—9:14)
       - a. The Levites (8:5–26)
       - b. The Passover (9:1–14)

Through the leadership of Moses and Aaron, God prepared the first generation of the exodus with everything it needed to be a holy army ready to possess the promised land.

- II. The Failed March of the First-Generation Army (9:15—25:18)
  - A. Introduction to the March (9:15—10:10)
    1. The Leading Cloud (9:15–23)
    2. The Silver Trumpets (10:1–10)
  - B. The Early Travels (10:11—12:16)
    1. The March Ensues (10:11–36)
    2. Complaints About Hardships (11:1–3)
    3. Complaints About Meat (11:4–35)
    4. Complaints About Moses' Authority (12:1–16)
  - C. The Period of Wandering (13:1—19:22)
    1. The Rebellion at Kadesh Barnea (13:1—14:45)
    2. Remembering the Offerings (15:1–41)
    3. The Great Rebellion Against Moses and Aaron (16:1–50)

The first generation of the exodus began the march toward the promised land with great hope, but complaints and rebellion led to the demise of nearly the entire generation. Yet, in his mercy, God began to prepare a second generation to move forward.

4. Reaffirmation of Aaronic Priesthood (17:1—19:22)
    a. Aaron's Staff (17:1–13)
    b. Priests and Levites (18:1–32)
    c. Arrangements for Cleansing (19:1–22)

D. The Later Travels (20:1—25:18)
1. Changing Generations (20:1—21:35)
    a. Moses' Sin at Meribah (20:1–13)
    b. Troubles With Edom (20:14–21)
    c. Aaron's Death (20:22–29)
    d. Victory Over Arad (21:1–3)
    e. The Bronze Snake (21:4–9)
    f. Blessings on the Way to Moab (21:10–20)
    g. Victory Over Sihon and Og (21:21–35)
2. Israel and the Moabites (22:1—25:18)
    a. The Summoning of Balaam (22:1–40)
    b. Balaam's Prophecies (22:41—24:24)
    c. The Aftermath of the Balaam Incident (24:25—25:18)

III. The Preparation of the Second-Generation Army (26:1—36:13)

God prepared the second generation of the exodus to move forward as his holy army. God demonstrated his love for Israel by restoring their numbers and reaffirming holy leadership for the nation. He also gave instructions that would guide the people as they conquered the land.

A. The Count and Continuity of the Generations (26:1—27:23)
1. The New Count of the Men of War (26:1–51)
2. Distribution of the Land (26:52–56)
3. The Levites (26:57–65)
4. A Problem With Land Inheritance (27:1–11)
5. The New Leader of the Army (27:12–23)

B. The Centrality of the Tabernacle Reaffirmed (28:1—31:54)
1. Daily Observances (28:1–8)
2. Weekly Observances (28:9–10)
3. Monthly Observances (28:11–15)
4. Annual Observances (28:16—29:40)
5. Rules About Vows (30:1–16)
6. Tributes of Holy War (31:1–54)

C. Looking Ahead to the Conquest (32:1—36:13)
1. The Transjordan Controversy (32:1–42)
2. Israel's Travels and Call to Conquest (33:1–56)
3. The Boundaries of the Land (34:1–15)
4. The Distributors of the Land (34:16–29)
5. Levite Towns and Cities of Refuge (35:1–34)
6. An Additional Thought Concerning Inheritances (36:1–13)

The Census

1:1 [a]Ex 40:2 [b]Ex 19:1 [c]Ex 40:17

1:2 [d]Ex 30:11-16; Nu 26:2

1 The LORD spoke to Moses in the Tent of Meeting[a] in the Desert of Sinai[b] on the first
day of the second month[c] of the second year after the Israelites came out of Egypt.
He said: 2"Take a census[d] of the whole Israelite community by their clans and families,
listing every man by name, one by one. 3You and Aaron are to number by their divisions

■ **1:1—9:14** *The Preparation of the First-Generation Army.* After the completion of the tabernacle (Ex 35:4—40:38), the Lord began to prepare his people for the conquest of the land promised to their fathers. This section exhibits this preparation in two parts: the numbers and arrangements of the tribes of Israel's army (1:1—4:49) and the centrality of the tabernacle (5:1—9:14). In these chapters Moses stressed not only the provisions from God but also the requirement of holiness.

■ **1:1—4:49** *The Count and Arrangement of the Army.* The army of the first generation was numbered by tribes, and the tribes were

all the men in Israel twenty years old or more[e] who are able to serve in the army. 4One
man from each tribe, each the head of his family,[f] is to help you.[g] 5These are the names
of the men who are to assist you:

from Reuben,[h] Elizur son of Shedeur;
6from Simeon, Shelumiel son of Zurishaddai;
7from Judah,[i] Nahshon son of Amminadab;[j]
8from Issachar,[k] Nethanel son of Zuar;
9from Zebulun,[l] Eliab son of Helon;
10from the sons of Joseph:
from Ephraim,[m] Elishama son of Ammihud;
from Manasseh, Gamaliel son of Pedahzur;
11from Benjamin, Abidan son of Gideoni;
12from Dan,[n] Ahiezer son of Ammishaddai;
13from Asher,[o] Pagiel son of Ocran;
14from Gad, Eliasaph son of Deuel;[p]
15from Naphtali,[q] Ahira son of Enan."

16These were the men appointed from the community, the leaders[r] of their ancestral
tribes. They were the heads of the clans of Israel.[s]
17Moses and Aaron took these men whose names had been given, 18and they called
the whole community together on the first day of the second month.[t] The people indicated their ancestry[u] by their clans and families, and the men twenty years old or more
were listed by name, one by one, 19as the LORD commanded Moses. And so he counted
them in the Desert of Sinai:

20From the descendants of Reuben[v] the firstborn son of Israel:
All the men twenty years old or more who were able to serve in the army were listed by name, one by one, according to the records of their clans and families. 21The number from the tribe of Reuben was 46,500.

22From the descendants of Simeon:[w]
All the men twenty years old or more who were able to serve in the army were counted and listed by name, one by one, according to the records of their clans and families. 23The number from the tribe of Simeon was 59,300.

24From the descendants of Gad:[x]
All the men twenty years old or more who were able to serve in the army were listed by name, according to the records of their clans and families. 25The number from the tribe of Gad was 45,650.

26From the descendants of Judah:[y]
All the men twenty years old or more who were able to serve in the army were listed by name, according to the records of their clans and families. 27The number from the tribe of Judah was 74,600.

28From the descendants of Issachar:[z]
All the men twenty years old or more who were able to serve in the army were

1:3 [e]Ex 30:14
1:4 [f]ver 16 [g]Ex 18:21; Dt 1:15
1:5 [h]Ge 29:32; Dt 33:6; Rev 7:5
1:7 [i]Ge 29:35; Ps 78:68 [j]Ru 4:20; 1Ch 2:10; Lk 3:32
1:8 [k]Ge 30:18
1:9 [l]ver 30
1:10 [m]ver 32
1:12 [n]ver 38
1:13 [o]ver 40
1:14 [p]Nu 2:14
1:15 [q]ver 42
1:16 [r]Ex 18:25 [s]ver 4; Ex 18:21; Nu 7:2
1:18 [t]ver 1 [u]Ezr 2:59; Heb 7:3
1:20 [v]Nu 26:5-11; Rev 7:5
1:22 [w]Nu 26:12-14; Rev 7:7
1:24 [x]Ge 30:11; Nu 26:15-18; Rev 7:5
1:26 [y]Ge 29:35; Nu 26:19-22; Mt 1:2; Rev 7:5
1:28 [z]Nu 26:23-25; Rev 7:7

---

arranged around the tabernacle. These chapters consist of three main parts: the men of war (1:1–54), the positioning of the tribes (2:1–34) and the numbers and duties of the Levites (3:1—4:49).

■ **1:1–54** *The Count of the Men of War.* While Israel was at Sinai, God ordered a census of the fighting men to be taken. This count depicted the army as great in number in order to display the blessings God had shown the nation.

1:1 The LORD spoke to Moses. This phrase and others indicating that the Lord communicated directly with Moses occur continually throughout Numbers. Moses was the preeminent prophet. In contrast to the prophets with whom God spoke in visions and dreams, God spoke with Moses face-to-face (cf. 12:8), giving him greater authority. Of all those who have lived on Earth, only Christ has greater authority than Moses possessed. **the Tent of Meeting.** Here and in most of its uses, another name for the tabernacle (see note on Ex 27:21). This term occurs frequently in the Pentateuch and occasionally in later books. Here God would reveal himself to his spokesman. **of the second year.** Numbers begins 13 months after the exodus from Egypt and relates events that occurred during the following 39 years.

1:2 Take a census. God later judged David for doing the very thing he had ordered Moses to do here (2Sa 24:1–25; 1Ch 21:1—22:1). The difference was probably in their motivations. David's census was not directed by God and was probably motivated by David's desire to secure himself militarily. This census was designed to demonstrate how God had blessed his people and prepared them for the conquest of the land.

1:5–16 The heads of all the tribes except the Levites (who had been set apart for the service of the tabernacle) are listed here and also in chapters 2, 7 and 10. The two tribes of Ephraim and Manasseh are listed under Joseph (v. 10). The number 12 is preserved, without counting the Levites. As God prepared his army for conquest, the unity of the nation was stressed. All tribes participated in the war.

1:20–43 These verses list the number of fighting men in each tribe. Except for the differences in the numbers, the verses follow a strict formula that involves much repetition. The tribes are listed in the same order as that of verses 1–15, except that the tribe of Gad is mentioned third instead of eleventh.

listed by name, according to the records of their clans and families. 29The number from the tribe of Issachar was 54,400.

1:30 [a]Nu 26:26-27; Rev 7:8

30From the descendants of Zebulun:[a]

All the men twenty years old or more who were able to serve in the army were listed by name, according to the records of their clans and families. 31The number from the tribe of Zebulun was 57,400.

1:32 [b]Nu 26:35-37

32From the sons of Joseph:

From the descendants of Ephraim:[b]

All the men twenty years old or more who were able to serve in the army were listed by name, according to the records of their clans and families. 33The number from the tribe of Ephraim was 40,500.

1:34 [c]Nu 26:28-34; Rev 7:6

34From the descendants of Manasseh:[c]

All the men twenty years old or more who were able to serve in the army were listed by name, according to the records of their clans and families. 35The number from the tribe of Manasseh was 32,200.

1:36 [d]Nu 26:38-41; 2Ch 17:17; Rev 7:8

36From the descendants of Benjamin:[d]

All the men twenty years old or more who were able to serve in the army were listed by name, according to the records of their clans and families. 37The number from the tribe of Benjamin was 35,400.

1:38 [e]Ge 30:6; Nu 26:42-43

38From the descendants of Dan:[e]

All the men twenty years old or more who were able to serve in the army were listed by name, according to the records of their clans and families. 39The number from the tribe of Dan was 62,700.

1:40 [f]Nu 26:44-47; Rev 7:6

40From the descendants of Asher:[f]

All the men twenty years old or more who were able to serve in the army were listed by name, according to the records of their clans and families. 41The number from the tribe of Asher was 41,500.

1:42 [g]Nu 26:48-50; Rev 7:6

42From the descendants of Naphtali:[g]

All the men twenty years old or more who were able to serve in the army were listed by name, according to the records of their clans and families. 43The number from the tribe of Naphtali was 53,400.

1:44 [h]Nu 26:64
1:46 [i]Ex 12:37; 38:26; Nu 2:32; 26:51
1:47 [j]Nu 2:33; 26:57 [k]Nu 4:3,49
1:50 [l]Ex 38:21; Ac 7:44
1:51 [m]Nu 3:38; 4:1-33
1:52 [n]Nu 2:2; Ps 20:5
1:53 [o]Lev 10:6; Nu 16:46; 18:5 [p]Nu 18:2-4

44These were the men counted by Moses and Aaron[h] and the twelve leaders of Israel, each one representing his family. 45All the Israelites twenty years old or more who were able to serve in Israel's army were counted according to their families. 46The total number was 603,550.[i]

47The families of the tribe of Levi,[j] however, were not counted[k] along with the others. 48The LORD had said to Moses: 49"You must not count the tribe of Levi or include them in the census of the other Israelites. 50Instead, appoint the Levites to be in charge of the tabernacle of the Testimony[l]—over all its furnishings and everything belonging to it. They are to carry the tabernacle and all its furnishings; they are to take care of it and encamp around it. 51Whenever the tabernacle is to move, the Levites are to take it down, and whenever the tabernacle is to be set up, the Levites shall do it.[m] Anyone else who goes near it shall be put to death. 52The Israelites are to set up their tents by divisions, each man in his own camp under his own standard.[n] 53The Levites, however, are to set up their tents around the tabernacle of the Testimony so that wrath will not fall[o] on the Israelite community. The Levites are to be responsible for the care of the tabernacle of the Testimony.[p]"

54The Israelites did all this just as the LORD commanded Moses.

The Arrangement of the Tribal Camps

2:2 [q]Nu 1:52; Ps 74:4; Isa 31:9

2 The LORD said to Moses and Aaron: 2"The Israelites are to camp around the Tent of Meeting some distance from it, each man under his standard[q] with the banners of his family."

1:44–46 These two verses provide a total for the census, while repeating much of the same formula.

1:47–54 As in the rest of the book, the Levites were not counted with the others, for they were set apart to care for the tabernacle and were therefore exempt from military service. Their numbers appear later (3:1—4:49).

■ **2:1–34** *Positions for the Tribes.* This chapter gives regulations for arranging the tribes in the camp and for their order on the march. Little rationale is given for these arrangements. The Lord demonstrated his kingship by ordering them as he wished, just as he would later distribute portions of the land however he chose. The people were divided into four camps, each one consisting of three tribes:

3On the east, toward the sunrise, the divisions of the camp of Judah are to encamp under their standard. The leader of the people of Judah is Nahshon son of
Amminadab.[r] 4His division numbers 74,600.
5The tribe of Issachar will camp next to them. The leader of the people of Issachar is Nethanel son of Zuar.[s] 6His division numbers 54,400.
7The tribe of Zebulun will be next. The leader of the people of Zebulun is Eliab son of Helon.[t] 8His division numbers 57,400.
9All the men assigned to the camp of Judah, according to their divisions, number 186,400. They will set out first.[u]

10On the south will be the divisions of the camp of Reuben under their standard. The leader of the people of Reuben is Elizur son of Shedeur.[v] 11His division
numbers 46,500.
12The tribe of Simeon will camp next to them. The leader of the people of Simeon is Shelumiel son of Zurishaddai.[w] 13His division numbers 59,300.
14The tribe of Gad will be next. The leader of the people of Gad is Eliasaph son
of Deuel.[a][x] 15His division numbers 45,650.
16All the men assigned to the camp of Reuben,[y] according to their divisions,
number 151,450. They will set out second.

17Then the Tent of Meeting and the camp of the Levites[z] will set out in the middle of the camps. They will set out in the same order as they encamp, each in his
own place under his standard.

18On the west will be the divisions of the camp of Ephraim[a] under their standard. The leader of the people of Ephraim is Elishama son of Ammihud.[b] 19His division numbers 40,500.
20The tribe of Manasseh will be next to them. The leader of the people of Manasseh is Gamaliel son of Pedahzur.[c] 21His division numbers 32,200.
22The tribe of Benjamin will be next. The leader of the people of Benjamin is
Abidan son of Gideoni.[d] 23His division numbers 35,400.

2:3 [r]Nu 10:14; Ru 4:20; 1Ch 2:10
2:5 [s]Nu 1:8
2:7 [t]Nu 1:9
2:9 [u]Nu 10:14
2:10 [v]Nu 1:5
2:12 [w]Nu 1:6
2:14 [x]Nu 1:14
2:16 [y]Nu 10:18
2:17 [z]Nu 1:53; 10:21
2:18 [a]Ge 48:20; Jer 31:18-20 [b]Nu 1:10
2:20 [c]Nu 1:10
2:22 [d]Nu 1:11; Ps 68:27

[a] 11 Many manuscripts of the Masoretic Text, Samaritan Pentateuch and Vulgate (see also Num. 1:14); most manuscripts of the Masoretic Text *Reuel*

Judah (with Issachar and Zebulun), Reuben (with Simeon and Gad), Ephraim (with Manasseh and Benjamin) and Dan (with Asher and Naphtali). The tribes are named in the same order as that found in the latter part of chapter 1. In camp, the Levites were to be stationed around the tabernacle (1:50,53), and the four camps were to be positioned on the east, south, west and north sides of the Levites in the order in which they were listed. See chart "Encampment of the Tribes of Israel," below. The most important aspect of these arrangements was the centrality of the tabernacle in the camp. It signified the dependence of the tribes on the presence of God. A similar arrangement appears in the foursquare city of Revelation 21:16, the final dwelling place of God on Earth.

Encampment of the Tribes of Israel

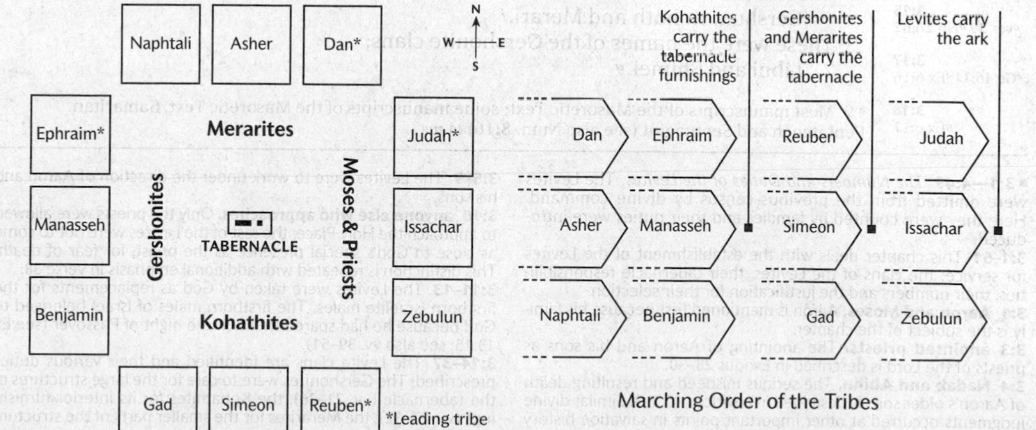

24 All the men assigned to the camp of Ephraim,[e] according to their divisions,
number 108,100. They will set out third.[f]

25 On the north will be the divisions of the camp of Dan, under their standard.
The leader of the people of Dan is Ahiezer son of Ammishaddai.[g] 26 His division
numbers 62,700.
27 The tribe of Asher will camp next to them. The leader of the people of Asher
is Pagiel son of Ocran.[h] 28 His division numbers 41,500.
29 The tribe of Naphtali will be next. The leader of the people of Naphtali is Ahira son of Enan.[i] 30 His division numbers 53,400.
31 All the men assigned to the camp of Dan number 157,600. They will set out
last,[j] under their standards.

32 These are the Israelites, counted according to their families. All those in the
camps, by their divisions, number 603,550.[k] 33 The Levites, however, were not
counted[l] along with the other Israelites, as the LORD commanded Moses.

34 So the Israelites did everything the LORD commanded Moses; that is the way they
encamped under their standards, and that is the way they set out, each with his clan and
family.

The Levites

3 This is the account of the family of Aaron and Moses[m] at the time the LORD talked
with Moses on Mount Sinai.
2 The names of the sons of Aaron were Nadab the firstborn and Abihu, Eleazar and Ithamar.[n] 3 Those were the names of Aaron's sons, the anointed priests,[o] who were ordained to serve as priests. 4 Nadab and Abihu, however, fell dead before the LORD[p] when
they made an offering with unauthorized fire before him in the Desert of Sinai.[q] They had
no sons; so only Eleazar and Ithamar served as priests during the lifetime of their father
Aaron.[r]
5 The LORD said to Moses, 6 "Bring the tribe of Levi[s] and present them to Aaron the
priest to assist him.[t] 7 They are to perform duties for him and for the whole community
at the Tent of Meeting by doing the work[u] of the tabernacle. 8 They are to take care of
all the furnishings of the Tent of Meeting, fulfilling the obligations of the Israelites by doing the work of the tabernacle. 9 Give the Levites to Aaron and his sons;[v] they are the Israelites who are to be given wholly to him.[a] 10 Appoint Aaron and his sons to serve as
priests;[w] anyone else who approaches the sanctuary must be put to death."[x]
11 The LORD also said to Moses, 12 "I have taken the Levites[y] from among the Israelites
in place of the first male offspring[z] of every Israelite woman. The Levites are mine,[a] 13 for
all the firstborn are mine.[b] When I struck down all the firstborn in Egypt, I set apart for
myself every firstborn in Israel, whether man or animal. They are to be mine. I am the
LORD."
14 The LORD said to Moses in the Desert of Sinai, 15 "Count[c] the Levites by their families and clans. Count every male a month old or more."[d] 16 So Moses counted them, as
he was commanded by the word of the LORD.
17 These were the names of the sons of Levi:[e]
Gershon, Kohath and Merari.[f]
18 These were the names of the Gershonite clans:
Libni and Shimei.[g]

2:24 [e]Nu 10:22 [f]Ps 80:2
2:25 [g]Nu 1:12
2:27 [h]Nu 1:13
2:29 [i]Nu 1:15
2:31 [j]Nu 10:25
2:32 [k]Ex 38:26; Nu 1:46
2:33 [l]Nu 1:47; 26:57-62
3:1 [m]Ex 6:27
3:2 [n]Ex 6:23; Nu 26:60
3:3 [o]Ex 28:41
3:4 [p]Lev 10:2 [q]Lev 10:1 [r]1Ch 24:1
3:6 [s]Dt 10:8; 31:9; 1Ch 15:2 [t]Nu 8:6-22; 18:1-7; 2Ch 29:11
3:7 [u]Lev 8:35; Nu 1:50
3:9 [v]Nu 8:19; 18:6
3:10 [w]Ex 29:9 [x]Nu 1:51
3:12 [y]Mal 2:4 [z]ver 41; Nu 8:16,18 [a]Ex 13:2
3:13 [b]Ex 13:12
3:15 [c]ver 39 [d]Nu 26:62
3:17 [e]Ge 46:11 [f]Ex 6:16
3:18 [g]Ex 6:17

[a] 9 Most manuscripts of the Masoretic Text; some manuscripts of the Masoretic Text, Samaritan Pentateuch and Septuagint (see also Num. 8:16) *to me*

■ **3:1—4:49** *The Numbers and Duties of the Levites.* The Levites were omitted from the previous census by divine command. Here they were counted by families and their duties were introduced.

3:1–51 This chapter deals with the establishment of the Levites for service: the clans of the Levites, their tabernacle responsibilities, their numbers and the justification for their selection.

3:1 Aaron and Moses. Aaron is mentioned first because his family is the subject of the chapter.

3:3 anointed priests. The anointing of Aaron and his sons as priests of the Lord is described in Exodus 28–30.

3:4 Nadab and Abihu. The serious misdeed and resulting death of Aaron's older sons is described in Leviticus 10:1–3. Similar divine judgments occurred at other important points in salvation history (cf. Jos 7; 2Sa 6:7; Ac 5:1–11; see also 2Ch 26:16–21).

3:5–9 The Levites were to work under the direction of Aaron and his sons.

3:10 anyone else who approaches. Only the priests were allowed to approach the Holy Place; the rest of the Levites were not to come as close to God's special presence as the priest, for fear of death. This distinction is repeated with additional emphasis in verse 38.

3:11–13 The Levites were taken by God as replacements for the firstborn Israelite males. The firstborn males of Israel belonged to God because he had spared them on the night of Passover (see Ex 13:15; see also vv. 39–51).

3:14–37 The Levite clans are identified and their various duties prescribed. The Gershonites were to care for the large structures of the tabernacle (vv. 21–26); the Kohathites for its interior furnishings (vv. 27–32); the Merarites for the smaller parts of the structure (vv. 33–37).

19 The Kohathite clans:
Amram, Izhar, Hebron and Uzziel.[h]
20 The Merarite clans:[i]
Mahli and Mushi.[j]
These were the Levite clans, according to their families.

21 To Gershon belonged the clans of the Libnites and Shimeites;[k] these were the Gershonite clans. 22 The number of all the males a month old or more who were counted
was 7,500. 23 The Gershonite clans were to camp on the west, behind the tabernacle.
24 The leader of the families of the Gershonites was Eliasaph son of Lael. 25 At the Tent of
Meeting the Gershonites were responsible for the care of the tabernacle[l] and tent, its
coverings,[m] the curtain at the entrance[n] to the Tent of Meeting, 26 the curtains of the
courtyard[o], the curtain at the entrance to the courtyard surrounding the tabernacle and
altar, and the ropes[p]—and everything related to their use.

27 To Kohath belonged the clans of the Amramites, Izharites, Hebronites and Uzzielites;[q] these were the Kohathite clans. 28 The number of all the males a month old or more
was 8,600.[a] The Kohathites were responsible for the care of the sanctuary. 29 The Kohathite clans were to camp on the south side[r] of the tabernacle. 30 The leader of the families
of the Kohathite clans was Elizaphan son of Uzziel. 31 They were responsible for the care
of the ark,[s] the table,[t] the lampstand,[u] the altars,[v] the articles of the sanctuary used in
ministering, the curtain,[w] and everything related to their use.[x] 32 The chief leader of the
Levites was Eleazar son of Aaron, the priest. He was appointed over those who were responsible for the care of the sanctuary.

33 To Merari belonged the clans of the Mahlites and the Mushites;[y] these were the Merarite clans. 34 The number of all the males a month old or more who were counted
was 6,200. 35 The leader of the families of the Merarite clans was Zuriel son of Abihail;
they were to camp on the north side of the tabernacle.[z] 36 The Merarites were appointed[a] to take care of the frames of the tabernacle, its crossbars, posts, bases, all its equipment, and everything related to their use, 37 as well as the posts of the surrounding courtyard with their bases, tent pegs and ropes.

38 Moses and Aaron and his sons were to camp to the east[b] of the tabernacle, toward
the sunrise, in front of the Tent of Meeting.[c] They were responsible for the care of the
sanctuary[d] on behalf of the Israelites. Anyone else who approached the sanctuary was
to be put to death.[e]

39 The total number of Levites counted at the LORD's command by Moses and Aaron
according to their clans, including every male a month old or more, was 22,000.[f]

40 The LORD said to Moses, "Count all the firstborn Israelite males who are a month old
or more[g] and make a list of their names. 41 Take the Levites for me in place of all the firstborn of the Israelites,[h] and the livestock of the Levites in place of all the firstborn of the
livestock of the Israelites. I am the LORD."
42 So Moses counted all the firstborn of the Israelites, as the LORD commanded him.
43 The total number of firstborn males a month old or more, listed by name, was 22,273.[i]
44 The LORD also said to Moses, 45 "Take the Levites in place of all the firstborn of Israel, and the livestock of the Levites in place of their livestock. The Levites are to be mine.
I am the LORD. 46 To redeem[j] the 273 firstborn Israelites who exceed the number of the
Levites, 47 collect five shekels[b][k] for each one, according to the sanctuary shekel,[l] which
weighs twenty gerahs.[m] 48 Give the money for the redemption of the additional Israelites
to Aaron and his sons."
49 So Moses collected the redemption money from those who exceeded the number
redeemed by the Levites. 50 From the firstborn of the Israelites he collected silver weigh-

3:19 [h]Ex 6:18
3:20 [i]Ge 46:11 [j]Ex 6:19
3:21 [k]Ex 6:17
3:25 [l]Ex 25:9 [m]Ex 26:14 [n]Ex 26:36; Nu 4:25
3:26 [o]Ex 27:9 [p]Ex 35:18
3:27 [q]1Ch 26:23
3:29 [r]Nu 1:53
3:31 [s]Ex 25:10-22 [t]Ex 25:23 [u]Ex 25:31 [v]Ex 27:1; 30:1 [w]Ex 26:33 [x]Nu 4:15
3:33 [y]Ex 6:19
3:35 [z]Nu 1:53; 2:25
3:36 [a]Nu 4:32
3:38 [b]Nu 2:3 [c]Nu 1:53 [d]ver 7; Nu 18:5 [e]ver 10, Nu 1:51
3:39 [f]Nu 26:62
3:40 [g]ver 15
3:41 [h]ver 12
3:43 [i]ver 39
3:46 [j]Ex 13:13; Nu 18:15
3:47 [k]Lev 27:6 [l]Ex 30:13 [m]Lev 27:25

[a] *28* Hebrew; some Septuagint manuscripts *8,300* [b] *47* That is, about 2 ounces (about 55 grams)

3:38 Moses and the priests were to camp in front of the Tent of Meeting and were to have exclusive approach to the sanctuary.
3:39–49 Firstborn Israelite males belonged to God (see note on 3:11–13). The firstborn (22,273 total in v. 43) were redeemed from full tabernacle service by God's taking of the Levites (22,000 total in v. 39) into his service. Money was to be paid for all firstborn males who exceeded the number of Levites (a total of 237; v. 46).

ing 1,365 shekels,[a][n] according to the sanctuary shekel. 51 Moses gave the redemption money to Aaron and his sons, as he was commanded by the word of the LORD.

The Kohathites

4 The LORD said to Moses and Aaron: 2 "Take a census[o] of the Kohathite branch of the Levites by their clans and families. 3 Count all the men from thirty to fifty years of age[p] who come to serve in the work in the Tent of Meeting.

4 "This is the work of the Kohathites in the Tent of Meeting: the care of the most holy things.[q] 5 When the camp is to move, Aaron and his sons are to go in and take down the shielding curtain[r] and cover the ark of the Testimony with it.[s] 6 Then they are to cover this with hides of sea cows,[b] spread a cloth of solid blue over that and put the poles[t] in place.

7 "Over the table of the Presence[u] they are to spread a blue cloth and put on it the plates, dishes and bowls, and the jars for drink offerings; the bread that is continually there[v] is to remain on it. 8 Over these they are to spread a scarlet cloth, cover that with hides of sea cows and put its poles in place.

9 "They are to take a blue cloth and cover the lampstand that is for light, together with its lamps, its wick trimmers and trays,[w] and all its jars for the oil used to supply it. 10 Then they are to wrap it and all its accessories in a covering of hides of sea cows and put it on a carrying frame.

11 "Over the gold altar[x] they are to spread a blue cloth and cover that with hides of sea cows and put its poles in place.

12 "They are to take all the articles used for ministering in the sanctuary, wrap them in a blue cloth, cover that with hides of sea cows and put them on a carrying frame.

13 "They are to remove the ashes from the bronze altar[y] and spread a purple cloth over it. 14 Then they are to place on it all the utensils used for ministering at the altar, including the firepans, meat forks,[z] shovels and sprinkling bowls.[a] Over it they are to spread a covering of hides of sea cows and put its poles[b] in place.

15 "After Aaron and his sons have finished covering the holy furnishings and all the holy articles, and when the camp is ready to move, the Kohathites are to come to do the carrying.[c] But they must not touch the holy things or they will die.[d] The Kohathites are to carry those things that are in the Tent of Meeting.

16 "Eleazar[e] son of Aaron, the priest, is to have charge of the oil for the light,[f] the fragrant incense, the regular grain offering[g] and the anointing oil. He is to be in charge of the entire tabernacle and everything in it, including its holy furnishings and articles."

17 The LORD said to Moses and Aaron, 18 "See that the Kohathite tribal clans are not cut off from the Levites. 19 So that they may live and not die when they come near the most holy things,[h] do this for them: Aaron and his sons are to go into the sanctuary and assign to each man his work and what he is to carry. 20 But the Kohathites must not go in to look[i] at the holy things, even for a moment, or they will die."

The Gershonites

21 The LORD said to Moses, 22 "Take a census also of the Gershonites by their families and clans. 23 Count all the men from thirty to fifty years of age[j] who come to serve in the work at the Tent of Meeting.

24 "This is the service of the Gershonite clans as they work and carry burdens: 25 They are to carry the curtains of the tabernacle,[k] the Tent of Meeting,[l] its covering[m] and the outer covering of hides of sea cows, the curtains for the entrance to the Tent of Meeting, 26 the curtains of the courtyard surrounding the tabernacle and altar, the curtain for the entrance, the ropes and all the equipment used in its service. The Gershonites are to do all that needs to be done with these things. 27 All their service, whether carrying or doing other work, is to be done under the direction of Aaron and his sons. You shall assign to them as their responsibility all they are to carry. 28 This is the service of the Gershonite clans[n] at the Tent of Meeting. Their duties are to be under the direction of Ithamar son of Aaron, the priest.

3:50 [n]ver 46-48
4:2 [o]Ex 30:12
4:3 [p]ver 23; Nu 8:25; 1Ch 23:3,24,27; Ezr 3:8
4:4 [q]ver 19
4:5 [r]Ex 26:31,33 [s]Ex 25:10,16
4:6 [t]Ex 25:13-15; 1Ki 8:7; 2Ch 5:8
4:7 [u]Ex 25:23,29; Lev 24:6 [v]Ex 25:30
4:9 [w]Ex 25:31,37,38
4:11 [x]Ex 30:1
4:13 [y]Ex 27:1-8
4:14 [z]2Ch 4:16 [a]Jer 52:18 [b]Ex 27:6
4:15 [c]Nu 7:9 [d]Nu 1:51; 2Sa 6:6,7
4:16 [e]Lev 10:6 [f]Ex 25:6 [g]Ex 29:41; Lev 6:14-23
4:19 [h]ver 15
4:20 [i]Ex 19:21; 1Sa 6:19
4:23 [j]ver 3; 1Ch 23:3, 24,27
4:25 [k]Ex 27:10-18; Nu 3:26 [l]Nu 3:25 [m]Ex 26:14
4:28 [n]Nu 7:7

[a] *50* That is, about 35 pounds (about 15.5 kilograms) [b] *6* That is, dugongs; also in verses 8, 10, 11, 12, 14 and 25

4:1–33 The work of the Levite families is explained. The arrangements already described in chapter 3 are repeated here in greater detail: Kohathites (vv. 1–15), Gershonites (vv. 21–28) and Merarites (vv. 29–33). In verses 16–20 Eleazar, son of Aaron the priest, was assigned supervision of the entire tabernacle, but all Kohathites, except the descendants of Aaron, were forbidden direct access to the holy things.

The Merarites

29"Count the Merarites by their clans and families.[o] 30Count all the men from thirty to fifty years of age who come to serve in the work at the Tent of Meeting. 31This is their duty as they perform service at the Tent of Meeting: to carry the frames of the tabernacle, its crossbars, posts and bases,[p] 32as well as the posts of the surrounding courtyard with their bases, tent pegs, ropes, all their equipment and everything related to their use. Assign to each man the specific things he is to carry. 33This is the service of the Merarite clans as they work at the Tent of Meeting under the direction of Ithamar son of Aaron, the priest."

The Numbering of the Levite Clans

34Moses, Aaron and the leaders of the community counted the Kohathites[q] by their clans and families. 35All the men from thirty to fifty years of age who came to serve in the work in the Tent of Meeting, 36counted by clans, were 2,750. 37This was the total of all those in the Kohathite clans[r] who served in the Tent of Meeting. Moses and Aaron counted them according to the LORD's command through Moses.

38The Gershonites[s] were counted by their clans and families. 39All the men from thirty to fifty years of age who came to serve in the work at the Tent of Meeting, 40counted by their clans and families, were 2,630. 41This was the total of those in the Gershonite clans who served at the Tent of Meeting. Moses and Aaron counted them according to the LORD's command.

42The Merarites were counted by their clans and families. 43All the men from thirty to fifty years of age who came to serve in the work at the Tent of Meeting, 44counted by their clans, were 3,200. 45This was the total of those in the Merarite clans.[t] Moses and Aaron counted them according to the LORD's command through Moses.

46So Moses, Aaron and the leaders of Israel counted all the Levites by their clans and families. 47All the men from thirty to fifty years of age[u] who came to do the work of serving and carrying the Tent of Meeting 48numbered 8,580.[v] 49At the LORD's command through Moses, each was assigned his work and told what to carry.

Thus they were counted,[w] as the LORD commanded Moses.

The Purity of the Camp

5 The LORD said to Moses, 2"Command the Israelites to send away from the camp anyone who has an infectious skin disease[a][x] or a discharge[y] of any kind, or who is ceremonially unclean[z] because of a dead body. 3Send away male and female alike; send them outside the camp so they will not defile their camp, where I dwell among them.[a]" 4The Israelites did this; they sent them outside the camp. They did just as the LORD had instructed Moses.

Restitution for Wrongs

5The LORD said to Moses, 6"Say to the Israelites: 'When a man or woman wrongs another in any way[b] and so is unfaithful[b] to the LORD, that person is guilty[c] 7and must confess[d] the sin he has committed. He must make full restitution[e] for his wrong, add one fifth to it and give it all to the person he has wronged. 8But if that person has no close relative to whom restitution can be made for the wrong, the restitution belongs to the LORD and must be given to the priest, along with the ram with which atonement is made for him.[f] 9All the sacred contributions the Israelites bring to a priest will belong to him.[g]

4:29 [o]Ge 46:11
4:31 [p]Nu 3:36
4:34 [q]ver 2
4:37 [r]Nu 3:27
4:38 [s]Ge 46:11
4:45 [t]ver 29
4:47 [u]ver 3
4:48 [v]Nu 3:39
4:49 [w]Nu 1:47
5:2 [x]Lev 13:10 [y]Lev 15:2; Mt 9:20 [z]Lev 13:3; Nu 9:6-10
5:3 [a]Lev 26:12; Nu 35:34; 2Co 6:16
5:6 [b]Lev 6:2 [c]Lev 5:14-6:7
5:7 [d]Lev 5:5; 26:40; Jos 7:19; Lk 19:8 [e]Lev 6:5
5:8 [f]Lev 6:6, 7; 7:7
5:9 [g]Lev 6:17; 7:6-14

[a] *2* Traditionally *leprosy;* the Hebrew word was used for various diseases affecting the skin—not necessarily leprosy. [b] *6* Or *woman commits any wrong common to mankind*

4:34–49 The tribe of Levi had been excluded from the previous count (1:1–54), but now its numbers are recorded. The census of the men from 30 to 50 years of age in all the Levite families is presented.

■ **5:1—9:14** *The Central Tabernacle.* Having already established that the tribes of Israel's army were to camp around the tabernacle, with the tabernacle in the camp's center (2:1–34), Moses focused on the role of the tabernacle and its priests. These chapters divide into three main parts: examples of the tabernacle's importance (5:1—6:27), contributions made for the tabernacle (7:1—8:4) and other examples of the tabernacle's importance (8:5—9:14).

■ **5:1—6:27** *The Importance of the Tabernacle.* Moses listed ways in which the tabernacle and its priesthood were central in Israel's life. He touched on five matters: the exclusion of the unclean (5:1–4), restitution (5:1–10), the law of jealousy (5:11–31), Nazirites (6:1–21) and the priestly national blessing (6:22–27).

■ **5:1–4** *Exclusion of the Unclean.* Persons physically or ceremonially unclean were sent outside the camp because the area surrounding the tabernacle was too sacred to harbor them.

5:2 infectious skin disease. See Leviticus 13:1–46 and 14:1–32. **discharge of any kind.** See Leviticus 15. **dead body.** See Leviticus 21:11. These and other defilements were dealt with on the Day of Atonement as well (Lev 16).

■ **5:5–10** *Cases of Restitution.* The centrality of the tabernacle is again in view. Moses spoke of the ceremony of the guilt offering. When someone wronged another person, restitution was to be made, plus an additional 20 percent, and the offender was required to go to the tabernacle to make a guilt offering. If the wronged person was unavailable and had no relative to whom restitution could be made, restitution was to be given to the priest, as representing the Lord (Lev 5:14—6:7).

10 Each man's sacred gifts are his own, but what he gives to the priest will belong to the priest.[h]' "

The Test for an Unfaithful Wife

11 Then the LORD said to Moses, 12 "Speak to the Israelites and say to them: 'If a man's wife goes astray[i] and is unfaithful to him 13 by sleeping with another man,[j] and this is hidden from her husband and her impurity is undetected (since there is no witness against her and she has not been caught in the act), 14 and if feelings of jealousy[k] come over her husband and he suspects his wife and she is impure—or if he is jealous and suspects her even though she is not impure— 15 then he is to take his wife to the priest. He must also take an offering of a tenth of an ephah[a] [l] of barley flour[m] on her behalf. He must not pour oil on it or put incense on it, because it is a grain offering for jealousy, a reminder[n] offering to draw attention to guilt.

16 " 'The priest shall bring her and have her stand before the LORD. 17 Then he shall take some holy water in a clay jar and put some dust from the tabernacle floor into the water. 18 After the priest has had the woman stand before the LORD, he shall loosen her hair[o] and place in her hands the reminder offering, the grain offering for jealousy, while he himself holds the bitter water that brings a curse. 19 Then the priest shall put the woman under oath and say to her, "If no other man has slept with you and you have not gone astray[p] and become impure while married to your husband, may this bitter water that brings a curse not harm you. 20 But if you have gone astray[q] while married to your husband and you have defiled yourself by sleeping with a man other than your husband"— 21 here the priest is to put the woman under this curse of the oath[r]—"may the LORD cause your people to curse and denounce you when he causes your thigh to waste away and your abdomen to swell.[b] 22 May this water[s] that brings a curse[t] enter your body so that your abdomen swells and your thigh wastes away.[c]"

" 'Then the woman is to say, "Amen. So be it.[u]"

23 " 'The priest is to write these curses on a scroll[v] and then wash them off into the bitter water. 24 He shall have the woman drink the bitter water that brings a curse, and this water will enter her and cause bitter suffering. 25 The priest is to take from her hands the grain offering for jealousy, wave it before the LORD[w] and bring it to the altar. 26 The priest is then to take a handful of the grain offering as a memorial offering and burn it on the altar; after that, he is to have the woman drink the water. 27 If she has defiled herself and been unfaithful to her husband, then when she is made to drink the water that brings a curse, it will go into her and cause bitter suffering; her abdomen will swell and her thigh waste away,[d] and she will become accursed[x] among her people. 28 If, however, the woman has not defiled herself and is free from impurity, she will be cleared of guilt and will be able to have children.

29 " 'This, then, is the law of jealousy when a woman goes astray[y] and defiles herself while married to her husband, 30 or when feelings of jealousy come over a man because he suspects his wife. The priest is to have her stand before the LORD and is to apply this entire law to her. 31 The husband will be innocent of any wrongdoing, but the woman will bear the consequences[z] of her sin.' "

The Nazirite

6 The LORD said to Moses, 2 "Speak to the Israelites and say to them: 'If a man or woman wants to make a special vow[a], a vow of separation to the LORD as a Nazirite,[b] 3 he

5:10 [h]Lev 10:13
5:12 [i]Ex 20:14
5:13 [j]Lev 18:20; 20:10
5:14 [k]Pr 6:34; SS 8:6
5:15 [l]Ex 16:36 [m]Lev 6:20 [n]Eze 29:16
5:18 [o]Lev 10:6; 1Co 11:6
5:19 [p]ver 12,29
5:20 [q]ver 12
5:21 [r]Jos 6:26; 1Sa 14:24; Ne 10:29
5:22 [s]Ps 109:18 [t]ver 18 [u]Dt 27:15
5:23 [v]Jer 45:1
5:25 [w]Lev 8:27
5:27 [x]Isa 43:28; 65:15; Jer 26:6; 29:18; 42:18; 44:12,22; Zec 8:13
5:29 [y]ver 19
5:31 [z]Lev 5:1; 20:17
6:2 [a]Ge 28:20; Ac 21:23 [b]Jdg 13:5; 16:17; Am 2:11,12

[a] *15* That is, probably about 2 quarts (about 2 liters) [b] *21* Or *causes you to have a miscarrying womb and barrenness* [c] *22* Or *body and cause you to be barren and have a miscarrying womb* [d] *27* Or *suffering; she will have barrenness and a miscarrying womb*

■ **5:11–31** *The Law of Jealousy.* A procedure described as "the law of jealousy" (v. 29) was performed by a priest to determine the guilt or innocence of a woman accused of unfaithfulness. If she was guilty, God would make her sick and unable to bear children (v. 27); if innocent, she would be able to bear children (v. 28). In cases like this, the priest and his service at the tabernacle were obviously indispensable.

5:19,21 See *WCF* 22.3.

■ **6:1–21** *Nazirites.* The Nazirite vow involved a special type of voluntary devotion to God. A man or woman could take a special vow of separation, usually for a limited period of time. During that time people so separated could not eat or drink anything that came from the grapevine, nor could they cut their hair (including the beard, in the case of men). The grapevine was the source of many of the physical pleasures then available, and abstention from it represented a life given over to God. Allowing the hair to grow wild signified abstention from human adornment. This legislation demonstrates the importance of the tabernacle and the priesthood to Israel because during the period for which the vow was taken, the Nazirite was to be careful to avoid becoming ceremonially unclean (v. 7). If someone died suddenly in the presence of one who had taken a Nazirite vow, the individual who had taken the vow would have to make certain prescribed offerings at the tabernacle (vv. 10–12), shave his or her head and start the period of separation all over again (v. 12), repeating all the original stipulations. A special tabernacle ceremony for the ending of the period of Nazirite separation is described in verses 13–21.

must abstain from wine[c] and other fermented drink and must not drink vinegar[d] made
from wine or from other fermented drink. He must not drink grape juice or eat grapes
or raisins. 4As long as he is a Nazirite, he must not eat anything that comes from the
grapevine, not even the seeds or skins.

5" 'During the entire period of his vow of separation no razor[e] may be used on his
head.[f] He must be holy until the period of his separation to the LORD is over; he must let
the hair of his head grow long. 6Throughout the period of his separation to the LORD he
must not go near a dead body.[g] 7Even if his own father or mother or brother or sister dies,
he must not make himself ceremonially unclean[h] on account of them, because the
symbol of his separation to God is on his head. 8Throughout the period of his separation
he is consecrated to the LORD.

9" 'If someone dies suddenly in his presence, thus defiling the hair he has dedicated,[i]
he must shave his head on the day of his cleansing[j]—the seventh day. 10Then on the
eighth day he must bring two doves or two young pigeons[k] to the priest at the entrance
to the Tent of Meeting. 11The priest is to offer one as a sin offering and the other as a
burnt offering[l] to make atonement[m] for him because he sinned by being in the presence
of the dead body. That same day he is to consecrate his head. 12He must dedicate himself to the LORD for the period of his separation and must bring a year-old male lamb as
a guilt offering. The previous days do not count, because he became defiled during his
separation.

13" 'Now this is the law for the Nazirite when the period of his separation is over.[n] He
is to be brought to the entrance to the Tent of Meeting. 14There he is to present his offerings to the LORD: a year-old male lamb without defect for a burnt offering, a year-old
ewe lamb without defect for a sin offering,[o] a ram without defect for a fellowship offering,[a] 15together with their grain offerings and drink offerings,[p] and a basket of bread
made without yeast—cakes made of fine flour mixed with oil, and wafers spread with
oil.[q]

16" 'The priest is to present them before the LORD and make the sin offering and the
burnt offering. 17He is to present the basket of unleavened bread and is to sacrifice the
ram as a fellowship offering to the LORD, together with its grain offering and drink offering.

18" 'Then at the entrance to the Tent of Meeting, the Nazirite must shave off the hair
that he dedicated.[r] He is to take the hair and put it in the fire that is under the sacrifice
of the fellowship offering.

19" 'After the Nazirite has shaved off the hair of his dedication, the priest is to place
in his hands a boiled shoulder of the ram, and a cake and a wafer from the basket, both
made without yeast. 20The priest shall then wave them before the LORD as a wave offering; they are holy and belong to the priest, together with the breast that was waved and
the thigh that was presented. After that, the Nazirite may drink wine.[s]

21" 'This is the law of the Nazirite who vows his offering to the LORD in accordance
with his separation, in addition to whatever else he can afford. He must fulfill the vow
he has made, according to the law of the Nazirite.' "

The Priestly Blessing

22The LORD said to Moses, 23"Tell Aaron and his sons, 'This is how you are to bless[t]
the Israelites. Say to them:

24" ' "The LORD bless you[u]
and keep you;[v]
25the LORD make his face shine upon you[w]
and be gracious to you;[x]
26the LORD turn his face[y] toward you
and give you peace."[z] '

27"So they will put my name[a] on the Israelites, and I will bless them."

a 14 Traditionally *peace offering*; also in verses 17 and 18

6:3 [c]Lk 1:15 [d]Ru 2:14; Ps 69:21; Pr 10:26
6:5 [e]Ps 52:2; 57:4; 59:7; Isa 7:20; Eze 5:1 [f]1Sa 1:11
6:6 [g]Lev 21:1-3; Nu 19:11-22
6:7 [h]Nu 9:6
6:9 [i]ver 18 [j]Lev 14:9
6:10 [k]Lev 5:7; 14:22
6:11 [l]Ge 8:20 [m]Ex 29:36
6:13 [n]Ac 21:26
6:14 [o]Lev 14:10; Nu 15:27
6:15 [p]Nu 15:1-7 [q]Ex 29:2; Lev 2:4
6:18 [r]ver 9; Ac 21:24
6:20 [s]Ecc 9:7
6:23 [t]Dt 21:5; 1Ch 23:13
6:24 [u]Dt 28:3-6; Ps 28:9 [v]1Sa 2:9; Ps 17:8
6:25 [w]Job 29:24; Ps 31:16; 80:3; 119:135 [x]Ge 43:29; Ps 25:16; 86:16
6:26 [y]Ps 4:6; 44:3 [z]Ps 29:11; 37:11, 37; Jn 14:27
6:27 [a]Dt 28:10; 2Sa 7:23; 2Ch 7:14; Ne 9:10; Jer 25:29

■ **6:22–27** *The Aaronic Blessing.* This well-known benediction is a fitting end to this section that demonstrates the importance of the priesthood and the tabernacle for Israel. Great blessings came through the mediation of Aaron and his sons.

6:25 make his face shine upon you. A vivid picture of God looking favorably upon his worshipers. The closer one's access to the face of God, the greater the blessing.

Offerings at the Dedication of the Tabernacle

7 When Moses finished setting up the tabernacle,[b] he anointed it and consecrated it
and all its furnishings.[c] He also anointed and consecrated the altar and all its
utensils.[d] **2**Then the leaders of Israel,[e] the heads of families who were the tribal leaders
in charge of those who were counted, made offerings. **3**They brought as their gifts before
the LORD six covered carts and twelve oxen—an ox from each leader and a cart from every two. These they presented before the tabernacle.
4The LORD said to Moses, **5**"Accept these from them, that they may be used in the work
at the Tent of Meeting. Give them to the Levites as each man's work requires."
6So Moses took the carts and oxen and gave them to the Levites. **7**He gave two carts
and four oxen to the Gershonites,[f] as their work required, **8**and he gave four carts and
eight oxen to the Merarites,[g] as their work required. They were all under the direction
of Ithamar son of Aaron, the priest. **9**But Moses did not give any to the Kohathites, because they were to carry on their shoulders[h] the holy things, for which they were responsible.
10When the altar was anointed,[i] the leaders brought their offerings for its dedication[j]
and presented them before the altar. **11**For the LORD had said to Moses, "Each day one
leader is to bring his offering for the dedication of the altar."
12The one who brought his offering on the first day was Nahshon son of Amminadab of
the tribe of Judah.
13His offering was one silver plate weighing a hundred and thirty shekels,[a] and one
silver sprinkling bowl weighing seventy shekels,[b] both according to the sanctuary
shekel,[k] each filled with fine flour mixed with oil as a grain offering;[l] **14**one gold
dish weighing ten shekels,[c] filled with incense;[m] **15**one young bull,[n] one ram and
one male lamb a year old, for a burnt offering;[o] **16**one male goat for a sin offering;[p]
17and two oxen, five rams, five male goats and five male lambs a year old, to be
sacrificed as a fellowship offering.[d][q] This was the offering of Nahshon son of Amminadab.[r]
18On the second day Nethanel son of Zuar,[s] the leader of Issachar, brought his offering.
19The offering he brought was one silver plate weighing a hundred and thirty shekels, and one silver sprinkling bowl weighing seventy shekels, both according to the
sanctuary shekel, each filled with fine flour mixed with oil as a grain offering; **20**one
gold dish[t] weighing ten shekels, filled with incense; **21**one young bull, one ram and
one male lamb a year old, for a burnt offering; **22**one male goat for a sin offering;
23and two oxen, five rams, five male goats and five male lambs a year old, to be
sacrificed as a fellowship offering. This was the offering of Nethanel son of Zuar.
24On the third day, Eliab son of Helon,[u] the leader of the people of Zebulun, brought his
offering.
25His offering was one silver plate weighing a hundred and thirty shekels, and one
silver sprinkling bowl weighing seventy shekels, both according to the sanctuary
shekel, each filled with fine flour mixed with oil as a grain offering; **26**one gold dish
weighing ten shekels, filled with incense; **27**one young bull, one ram and one male
lamb a year old, for a burnt offering; **28**one male goat for a sin offering; **29**and two
oxen, five rams, five male goats and five male lambs a year old, to be sacrificed as
a fellowship offering. This was the offering of Eliab son of Helon.

7:1 [b]Ex 40:17 [c]Ex 40:9 [d]ver 84,88; Ex 40:10
7:2 [e]Nu 1:5-16
7:7 [f]Nu 4:24-26,28
7:8 [g]Nu 4:31-33
7:9 [h]Nu 4:15
7:10 [i]ver 1 [j]2Ch 7:9
7:13 [k]Ex 30:13; Nu 3:47 [l]Lev 2:1
7:14 [m]Ex 30:34
7:15 [n]Ex 24:5; 29:3; Nu 28:11 [o]Lev 1:3
7:16 [p]Lev 4:3,23
7:17 [q]Lev 3:1 [r]Nu 1:7
7:18 [s]Nu 1:8
7:20 [t]ver 14
7:24 [u]Nu 1:9

[a] *13* That is, about 3 1/4 pounds (about 1.5 kilograms); also elsewhere in this chapter [b] *13* That is, about 1 3/4 pounds (about 0.8 kilogram); also elsewhere in this chapter [c] *14* That is, about 4 ounces (about 110 grams); also elsewhere in this chapter [d] *17* Traditionally *peace offering*; also elsewhere in this chapter

---

■ **7:1—8:4** *Offerings for the Tabernacle.* Moses reviewed the offerings made at the dedication of the tabernacle. The enthusiastic participation of so many Israelites showed the readers that the people of God understood the centrality of the tabernacle at that time. This passage divides into four sections: an introduction (vv. 1–11); the list of offerings that were brought for 12 days, one day for each of the 12 tribes (vv. 12–83); a summary of the offerings (vv. 84–88); and the final touches on setting up the lamps (7:89—8:4).

7:1–11 The carts and oxen were presented. The tribal leaders joined together in providing carts, as well as oxen to pull them, for the use of two of the Levitical clans in carrying the parts of the tabernacle that had been assigned to them. See 3:21–26 and 33–37, as well as 4:21–33. No cart was given to the Kohathites, who were expected to carry the holy things on their shoulders (v. 9).

7:12–83 Each of the 12 tribal leaders was assigned a day on which he was to bring a number of expensive gifts and specified offerings. These gifts and offerings are mentioned in precise detail in each case, though all the lists are identical—a vivid reminder that God is interested in every part of the spiritual service rendered by his people. Thus, in the beginning, the first-generation army was fully committed to the centrality of the tabernacle.

30 On the fourth day Elizur son of Shedeur,[v] the leader of the people of Reuben, brought 7:30 [v]Nu 1:5
his offering.
31 His offering was one silver plate weighing a hundred and thirty shekels, and one
silver sprinkling bowl weighing seventy shekels, both according to the sanctuary
shekel, each filled with fine flour mixed with oil as a grain offering; 32 one gold dish
weighing ten shekels, filled with incense; 33 one young bull, one ram and one male
lamb a year old, for a burnt offering; 34 one male goat for a sin offering; 35 and two
oxen, five rams, five male goats and five male lambs a year old, to be sacrificed as
a fellowship offering. This was the offering of Elizur son of Shedeur.

36 On the fifth day Shelumiel son of Zurishaddai,[w] the leader of the people of Simeon, 7:36 [w]Nu 1:6
brought his offering.
37 His offering was one silver plate weighing a hundred and thirty shekels, and one
silver sprinkling bowl weighing seventy shekels, both according to the sanctuary
shekel, each filled with fine flour mixed with oil as a grain offering; 38 one gold dish
weighing ten shekels, filled with incense; 39 one young bull, one ram and one male
lamb a year old, for a burnt offering; 40 one male goat for a sin offering; 41 and two
oxen, five rams, five male goats and five male lambs a year old, to be sacrificed as
a fellowship offering. This was the offering of Shelumiel son of Zurishaddai.

42 On the sixth day Eliasaph son of Deuel,[x] the leader of the people of Gad, brought his 7:42 [x]Nu 1:14
offering.
43 His offering was one silver plate weighing a hundred and thirty shekels, and one
silver sprinkling bowl weighing seventy shekels, both according to the sanctuary
shekel, each filled with fine flour mixed with oil as a grain offering; 44 one gold dish
weighing ten shekels, filled with incense; 45 one young bull, one ram and one male
lamb a year old, for a burnt offering; 46 one male goat for a sin offering; 47 and two
oxen, five rams, five male goats and five male lambs a year old, to be sacrificed as
a fellowship offering. This was the offering of Eliasaph son of Deuel.

48 On the seventh day Elishama son of Ammihud,[y] the leader of the people of Ephraim, 7:48 [y]Nu 1:10
brought his offering.
49 His offering was one silver plate weighing a hundred and thirty shekels, and one
silver sprinkling bowl weighing seventy shekels, both according to the sanctuary
shekel, each filled with fine flour mixed with oil as a grain offering; 50 one gold dish
weighing ten shekels, filled with incense; 51 one young bull, one ram and one male
lamb a year old, for a burnt offering; 52 one male goat for a sin offering; 53 and two
oxen, five rams, five male goats and five male lambs a year old, to be sacrificed as
a fellowship offering. This was the offering of Elishama son of Ammihud.[z] 7:53 [z]Nu 1:10

54 On the eighth day Gamaliel son of Pedahzur,[a] the leader of the people of Manasseh, 7:54 [a]Nu 1:10; 2:20
brought his offering.
55 His offering was one silver plate weighing a hundred and thirty shekels, and one
silver sprinkling bowl weighing seventy shekels, both according to the sanctuary
shekel, each filled with fine flour mixed with oil as a grain offering; 56 one gold dish
weighing ten shekels, filled with incense; 57 one young bull, one ram and one male
lamb a year old, for a burnt offering; 58 one male goat for a sin offering; 59 and two
oxen, five rams, five male goats and five male lambs a year old, to be sacrificed as
a fellowship offering. This was the offering of Gamaliel son of Pedahzur.

60 On the ninth day Abidan son of Gideoni,[b] the leader of the people of Benjamin, 7:60 [b]Nu 1:11
brought his offering.
61 His offering was one silver plate weighing a hundred and thirty shekels, and one
silver sprinkling bowl weighing seventy shekels, both according to the sanctuary
shekel, each filled with fine flour mixed with oil as a grain offering; 62 one gold dish
weighing ten shekels, filled with incense; 63 one young bull, one ram and one male
lamb a year old, for a burnt offering; 64 one male goat for a sin offering; 65 and two
oxen, five rams, five male goats and five male lambs a year old, to be sacrificed as
a fellowship offering. This was the offering of Abidan son of Gideoni.

66 On the tenth day Ahiezer son of Ammishaddai,[c] the leader of the people of Dan, 7:66 [c]Nu 1:12; 2:25
brought his offering.
67 His offering was one silver plate weighing a hundred and thirty shekels, and one
silver sprinkling bowl weighing seventy shekels, both according to the sanctuary
shekel, each filled with fine flour mixed with oil as a grain offering; 68 one gold dish

weighing ten shekels, filled with incense; 69one young bull, one ram and one male
lamb a year old, for a burnt offering; 70one male goat for a sin offering; 71and two
oxen, five rams, five male goats and five male lambs a year old, to be sacrificed as
a fellowship offering. This was the offering of Ahiezer son of Ammishaddai.

7:72 [d]Nu 1:13
72On the eleventh day Pagiel son of Ocran,[d] the leader of the people of Asher, brought
his offering.
73His offering was one silver plate weighing a hundred and thirty shekels, and one
silver sprinkling bowl weighing seventy shekels, both according to the sanctuary
shekel, each filled with fine flour mixed with oil as a grain offering; 74one gold dish
weighing ten shekels, filled with incense; 75one young bull, one ram and one male
lamb a year old, for a burnt offering; 76one male goat for a sin offering; 77and two
oxen, five rams, five male goats and five male lambs a year old, to be sacrificed as
a fellowship offering. This was the offering of Pagiel son of Ocran.

7:78 [e]Nu 1:15; 2:29
78On the twelfth day Ahira son of Enan,[e] the leader of the people of Naphtali, brought
his offering.
79His offering was one silver plate weighing a hundred and thirty shekels, and one
silver sprinkling bowl weighing seventy shekels, both according to the sanctuary
shekel, each filled with fine flour mixed with oil as a grain offering; 80one gold dish
weighing ten shekels, filled with incense; 81one young bull, one ram and one male
lamb a year old, for a burnt offering; 82one male goat for a sin offering; 83and two
oxen, five rams, five male goats and five male lambs a year old, to be sacrificed as
a fellowship offering. This was the offering of Ahira son of Enan.

7:84 [f]ver 1,10 [g]Nu 4:14 [h]ver 14
84These were the offerings of the Israelite leaders for the dedication of the altar
when it was anointed:[f] twelve silver plates, twelve silver sprinkling bowls[g] and twelve
gold dishes.[h] 85Each silver plate weighed a hundred and thirty shekels, and each sprinkling bowl seventy shekels. Altogether, the silver dishes weighed two thousand four hundred shekels,[a] according to the sanctuary shekel. 86The twelve gold dishes filled with incense weighed ten shekels each, according to the sanctuary shekel. Altogether, the gold
dishes weighed a hundred and twenty shekels.[b] 87The total number of animals for the
burnt offering came to twelve young bulls, twelve rams and twelve male lambs a year old,
together with their grain offering. Twelve male goats were used for the sin offering. 88The
total number of animals for the sacrifice of the fellowship offering came to twenty-four
7:88 [i]ver 1,10
oxen, sixty rams, sixty male goats and sixty male lambs a year old. These were the offerings for the dedication of the altar after it was anointed.[i]

7:89 [j]Ex 25:21,22; 33:9, 11 [k]Ps 80:1; 99:1
89When Moses entered the Tent of Meeting to speak with the LORD,[j] he heard the
voice speaking to him from between the two cherubim above the atonement cover[k] on
the ark of the Testimony. And he spoke with him.

Setting Up the Lamps

8:2 [l]Ex 25:37; Lev 24:2,4
8 The LORD said to Moses, 2"Speak to Aaron and say to him, 'When you set up the sev-
en lamps, they are to light the area in front of the lampstand.[l]' "
3Aaron did so; he set up the lamps so that they faced forward on the lampstand, just
8:4 [m]Ex 25:18,36; 25:18 [n]Ex 25:9
as the LORD commanded Moses. 4This is how the lampstand was made: It was made of
hammered gold[m]—from its base to its blossoms. The lampstand was made exactly like
the pattern[n] the LORD had shown Moses.

The Setting Apart of the Levites

8:6 [o]Lev 22:2; Isa 1:16; 52:11
5The LORD said to Moses: 6"Take the Levites from among the other Israelites and make
them ceremonially clean.[o] 7To purify them, do this: Sprinkle the water of cleansing[p] on

8:7 [p]Nu 19:9,17

[a] *85* That is, about 60 pounds (about 28 kilograms) [b] *86* That is, about 3 pounds (about 1.4 kilograms)

7:89—8:4 This conclusion illustrates that although Moses was in charge of mediating the commands of God, Aaron was responsible for implementing them. There was no division between obedience to Moses and submission to the tabernacle personnel.
7:89 God spoke to Moses in the Tent of Meeting. **the atonement cover.** This designation of the ornate cover of the ark represents one Hebrew word (lit., "atonement"). See notes on Exodus 25:17–22.
8:1–4 See Exodus 25:31–39.
■ **8:5—9:14** *Other Important Aspects of the Tabernacle.* Moses closed this section on the centrality of the tabernacle by reporting two other important dimensions of its services. He referred first to the appointment of Levites alongside Aaron and his sons (8:5–26) and then to the role of the tabernacle personnel in the Passover celebration (9:1–14).
■ **8:5–26** *The Levites.* The Aaronic priests had already been ordained. Now the Levites were cleansed for service. First they were purified (vv. 6–7), then the offering was made (v. 8), the laying on of hands took place (vv. 9–10) and finally they were presented before the Lord (vv. 11–14). The Levites were taken "from among the other Israelites" (v. 6), and their dependence on and service to the tabernacle were defined. This account explains how

them; then have them shave their whole bodies[q] and wash their clothes,[r] and so purify themselves. 8 Have them take a young bull with its grain offering of fine flour mixed
with oil;[s] then you are to take a second young bull for a sin offering. 9 Bring the Levites
to the front of the Tent of Meeting[t] and assemble the whole Israelite community.[u]
10 You are to bring the Levites before the LORD, and the Israelites are to lay their hands
on them.[v] 11 Aaron is to present the Levites before the LORD as a wave offering[w] from the
Israelites, so that they may be ready to do the work of the LORD.

12 "After the Levites lay their hands on the heads of the bulls,[x] use the one for a sin
offering to the LORD and the other for a burnt offering, to make atonement[y] for the Levites. 13 Have the Levites stand in front of Aaron and his sons and then present them as
a wave offering to the LORD. 14 In this way you are to set the Levites apart from the other
Israelites, and the Levites will be mine.[z]

15 "After you have purified the Levites and presented them as a wave offering,[a] they
are to come to do their work at the Tent of Meeting. 16 They are the Israelites who are to
be given wholly to me. I have taken them as my own in place of the firstborn, the first
male offspring[b] from every Israelite woman. 17 Every firstborn male in Israel, whether
man or animal,[c] is mine. When I struck down all the firstborn in Egypt, I set them apart
for myself.[d] 18 And I have taken the Levites in place of all the firstborn sons in Israel.[e] 19 Of
all the Israelites, I have given the Levites as gifts to Aaron and his sons[f] to do the work
at the Tent of Meeting on behalf of the Israelites[g] and to make atonement for them[h] so
that no plague will strike the Israelites when they go near the sanctuary."

20 Moses, Aaron and the whole Israelite community did with the Levites just as the
LORD commanded Moses. 21 The Levites purified themselves and washed their clothes.[i]
Then Aaron presented them as a wave offering before the LORD and made atonement for
them to purify them.[j] 22 After that, the Levites came to do their work at the Tent of Meet-
ing under the supervision of Aaron and his sons. They did with the Levites just as the
LORD commanded Moses.

23 The LORD said to Moses, 24 "This applies to the Levites: Men twenty-five years old or
more[k] shall come to take part in the work at the Tent of Meeting,[l] 25 but at the age of fifty, they must retire from their regular service and work no longer. 26 They may assist their
brothers in performing their duties at the Tent of Meeting, but they themselves must not
do the work. This, then, is how you are to assign the responsibilities of the Levites."

The Passover

9 The LORD spoke to Moses in the Desert of Sinai in the first month[m] of the second year
after they came out of Egypt.[n] He said, 2 "Have the Israelites celebrate the Passover
at the appointed time. 3 Celebrate it at the appointed time, at twilight on the fourteenth
day of this month, in accordance with all its rules and regulations.[o]"

4 So Moses told the Israelites to celebrate the Passover, 5 and they did so in the Desert of Sinai at twilight on the fourteenth day of the first month.[p] The Israelites did everything just as the LORD commanded Moses.

6 But some of them could not celebrate the Passover on that day because they were
ceremonially unclean[q] on account of a dead body. So they came to Moses and Aaron[r]
that same day 7 and said to Moses, "We have become unclean because of a dead body,
but why should we be kept from presenting the LORD's offering with the other Israelites
at the appointed time?"

8 Moses answered them, "Wait until I find out what the LORD commands concerning
you."[s]

9 Then the LORD said to Moses, 10 "Tell the Israelites: 'When any of you or your descendants are unclean because of a dead body or are away on a journey, they may still celebrate[t] the LORD's Passover. 11 They are to celebrate it on the fourteenth day of the sec-

8:7 [q]Lev 14:9; Dt 21:12 [r]Lev 14:8
8:8 [s]Lev 2:1; Nu 15:8-10
8:9 [t]Ex 40:12 [u]Lev 8:3
8:10 [v]Ac 6:6
8:11 [w]Lev 7:30
8:12 [x]Ex 29:10 [y]Ex 29:36
8:14 [z]Nu 3:12
8:15 [a]Ex 29:24
8:16 [b]Nu 3:12
8:17 [c]Ex 4:23 [d]Ex 13:2; Lk 2:23
8:18 [e]Nu 3:12
8:19 [f]Nu 3:9 [g]Nu 1:53 [h]Nu 16:46
8:21 [i]ver 7 [j]ver 12
8:24 [k]1Ch 23:3 [l]Ex 38:21; Nu 4:3
9:1 [m]Ex 40:2 [n]Nu 1:1
9:3 [o]Ex 12:2-11,43-49; Lev 23:5-8; Dt 16:1-8
9:5 [p]Ex 12:1-13; Jos 5:10
9:6 [q]Lev 5:3 [r]Ex 18:15; Nu 27:2
9:8 [s]Ex 18:15; Nu 27:5,21; Ps 85:8
9:10 [t]2Ch 30:2

---

the Levites were to mediate for the people, even though they were not directly involved with the tabernacle sacrifices.

8:15–26 The Levites were to do the work of the sanctuary under the direction of the priests. Later violations of this regulation brought great hardship on God's people (see Jdg 17:12).

8:18 in place of all the firstborn. The Levites represented the tribes at the tabernacle. See 3:40–45.

8:24–25 twenty-five . . . age of fifty. In chapter 4 the Levites "from thirty to fifty years of age" were counted. Perhaps there was a period of apprenticeship before actual service was to commence. A Levite was to remain among the tribes until his 25th birthday, serve at the tabernacle for 25 years and then retire, unless he desired to assist the younger Levites (vv. 25–26).

■ **9:1–14** *The Passover.* Passover was originally observed in the homes of Israelites in Egypt, but later it was centralized and celebrated at the tabernacle/temple (Dt 16:2). These special rules for Passover focus again on the centrality of the tabernacle for preparation of Israel's holy army.

9:1–5 The second celebration of the Passover is recalled.

9:6–13 A special problem was presented to Moses, and God's answer was given: One who was unclean or on a journey at the regular time for celebrating Passover could celebrate Passover exactly one month later. No others could postpone its observance. Even the postponed observance was to be done according to all the regulations of Moses, including observance at the tabernacle/temple.

ond month at twilight. They are to eat the lamb, together with unleavened bread and bitter herbs.[u] 12 They must not leave any of it till morning[v] or break any of its bones.[w] When
they celebrate the Passover, they must follow all the regulations. 13 But if a man who is
ceremonially clean and not on a journey fails to celebrate the Passover, that person must
be cut off from his people[x] because he did not present the LORD's offering at the appointed time. That man will bear the consequences of his sin.
14 " 'An alien[y] living among you who wants to celebrate the LORD's Passover must do
so in accordance with its rules and regulations. You must have the same regulations for
the alien and the native-born.' "

The Cloud Above the Tabernacle

15 On the day the tabernacle, the Tent of the Testimony, was set up, the cloud[z] covered it. From evening till morning the cloud above the tabernacle looked like fire.[a] 16 That
is how it continued to be; the cloud covered it, and at night it looked like fire. 17 Whenever the cloud lifted from above the Tent, the Israelites set out; wherever the cloud settled, the Israelites encamped.[b] 18 At the LORD's command the Israelites set out, and at his
command they encamped. As long as the cloud stayed over the tabernacle, they remained in camp. 19 When the cloud remained over the tabernacle a long time, the Israelites obeyed the LORD's order and did not set out. 20 Sometimes the cloud was over the
tabernacle only a few days; at the LORD's command they would encamp, and then at his
command they would set out. 21 Sometimes the cloud stayed only from evening till
morning, and when it lifted in the morning, they set out. Whether by day or by night,
whenever the cloud lifted, they set out. 22 Whether the cloud stayed over the tabernacle
for two days or a month or a year, the Israelites would remain in camp and not set out;
but when it lifted, they would set out. 23 At the LORD's command they encamped, and at
the LORD's command they set out. They obeyed the LORD's order, in accordance with his
command through Moses.

The Silver Trumpets

10 The LORD said to Moses: 2 "Make two trumpets[c] of hammered silver, and use
them for calling the community[d] together and for having the camps set out.
3 When both are sounded, the whole community is to assemble before you at the entrance to the Tent of Meeting. 4 If only one is sounded, the leaders[e]—the heads of the
clans of Israel—are to assemble before you. 5 When a trumpet blast is sounded, the tribes
camping on the east are to set out.[f] 6 At the sounding of a second blast, the camps on the
south are to set out.[g] The blast will be the signal for setting out. 7 To gather the assembly, blow the trumpets,[h] but not with the same signal.[i]
8 "The sons of Aaron, the priests, are to blow the trumpets. This is to be a lasting ordinance for you and the generations to come.[j] 9 When you go into battle in your own land
against an enemy who is oppressing you,[k] sound a blast on the trumpets. Then you will
be remembered[l] by the LORD your God and rescued from your enemies.[m] 10 Also at your
times of rejoicing—your appointed feasts and New Moon festivals[n]—you are to sound
the trumpets[o] over your burnt offerings and fellowship offerings,[a] and they will be a memorial for you before your God. I am the LORD your God."

9:11 [u]Ex 12:8
9:12 [v]Ex 12:10,43 [w]Ex 12:46; Jn 19:36*
9:13 [x]Ge 17:14; Ex 12:15
9:14 [y]Ex 12:48,49
9:15 [z]Ex 40:34 [a]Ex 13:21
9:17 [b]Ex 40:36-38; Nu 10:11,12; 1Co 10:1
10:2 [c]Ne 12:35; Ps 47:5 [d]Jer 4:5,19; 6:1; Hos 5:8; Joel 2:1, 15; Am 3:6
10:4 [e]Ex 18:21; Nu 1:16; 7:2
10:5 [f]ver 14
10:6 [g]ver 18
10:7 [h]Eze 33:3; Joel 2:1 [i]1Co 14:8
10:8 [j]Nu 31:6
10:9 [k]Jdg 2:18; 6:9; 1Sa 10:18; Ps 106:42 [l]Ge 8:1 [m]Ps 106:4
10:10 [n]Ps 81:3 [o]Lev 23:24

[a] *10* Traditionally *peace offerings*

9:14 A resident alien could observe Passover but was to do so in the regular, prescribed way, including prior circumcision (Ex 12:48).

■ **9:15—25:18** *The Failed March of the First-Generation Army.* The people of Israel moved from Sinai toward the promised land as an army marching toward battle. God blessed them with his presence to lead them, but they failed to remain faithful to him. After much patience, the Lord forsook the first generation and allowed its members to die in the wilderness. These chapters divide into four main sections: an introduction (9:15—10:10), the early travels (10:11—12:16), the time of wandering (13:1—19:22) and the later travels (20:1—25:18).

■ **9:15—10:10** *Introduction to the March.* With the centrality of the tabernacle established, Moses introduced the march of Israel toward the promised land as a matter of following the presence of God associated with the tabernacle. He provided an overview (9:15–23) and gave a more detailed description of the manner in which the army was to move forward (10:1–10). Two kinds of guidance were arranged for this "people on the march": supernatural guidance by the cloud (9:15–23) and orders given by blowing trumpets (10:1–10).

■ **9:15–23** *The Leading Cloud.* The glory cloud of God's presence would at times rest on the tabernacle and at other times rise from the tent to indicate that Israel should move forward. This was the process followed throughout Israel's travels.

9:15 the cloud. This was no ordinary cloud; it was the cloud of God's glorious presence that led the people of Israel (see Ex 13:21).

9:23 They obeyed the LORD's order. The first-generation army began its march in good order, in compliance with the commands of God.

■ **10:1–10** *The Silver Trumpets.* Special trumpets were made to control the movements of Israel's marching army.

10:2 calling the community . . . having the camps set out. The trumpets were used mainly to call for holy assemblies of the heads of the tribes (when both trumpets sounded; v. 3) and to summon the fighting men to move forward toward battle (when only one trumpet sounded; vv. 5–6).

10:8–10 Moses discussed other uses to which the trumpets were put.

The Israelites Leave Sinai

11On the twentieth day of the second month of the second year,[p] the cloud lifted[q]
from above the tabernacle of the Testimony. 12Then the Israelites set out from the Desert of Sinai and traveled from place to place until the cloud came to rest in the Desert of
Paran. 13They set out, this first time, at the LORD's command through Moses.[r]
14The divisions of the camp of Judah went first, under their standard.[s] Nahshon son
of Amminadab[t] was in command. 15Nethanel son of Zuar was over the division of the
tribe of Issachar, 16and Eliab son of Helon was over the division of the tribe of Zebulun.
17Then the tabernacle was taken down, and the Gershonites and Merarites, who carried
it, set out.[u]
18The divisions of the camp of Reuben went next, under their standard.[v] Elizur son
of Shedeur was in command. 19Shelumiel son of Zurishaddai was over the division of the
tribe of Simeon, 20and Eliasaph son of Deuel was over the division of the tribe of Gad.
21Then the Kohathites set out, carrying the holy things.[w] The tabernacle was to be set
up before they arrived.[x]
22The divisions of the camp of Ephraim[y] went next, under their standard. Elishama
son of Ammihud was in command. 23Gamaliel son of Pedahzur was over the division of
the tribe of Manasseh, 24and Abidan son of Gideoni was over the division of the tribe of
Benjamin.
25Finally, as the rear guard[z] for all the units, the divisions of the camp of Dan set out,
under their standard. Ahiezer son of Ammishaddai was in command. 26Pagiel son of Ocran was over the division of the tribe of Asher, 27and Ahira son of Enan was over the division of the tribe of Naphtali. 28This was the order of march for the Israelite divisions
as they set out.
29Now Moses said to Hobab[a] son of Reuel[b] the Midianite, Moses' father-in-law,[c] "We
are setting out for the place about which the LORD said, 'I will give it to you.'[d] Come with
us and we will treat you well, for the LORD has promised good things to Israel."
30He answered, "No, I will not go;[e] I am going back to my own land and my own people."
31But Moses said, "Please do not leave us. You know where we should camp in the
desert, and you can be our eyes.[f] 32If you come with us, we will share with you[g] whatever good things the LORD gives us.[h]"
33So they set out[i] from the mountain of the LORD and traveled for three days. The ark
of the covenant of the LORD[j] went before them during those three days to find them a place
to rest. 34The cloud of the LORD was over them by day when they set out from the camp.[k]
35Whenever the ark set out, Moses said,

"Rise up, O LORD!
May your enemies be scattered;[l]
may your foes flee before you.[m]"

36Whenever it came to rest, he said,

"Return,[n] O LORD,
to the countless thousands of Israel.[o]"

Fire From the LORD

11 Now the people complained about their hardships in the hearing of the LORD,
and when he heard them his anger was aroused. Then fire from the LORD
burned among them[p] and consumed some of the outskirts of the camp. 2When the people cried out to Moses, he prayed to the LORD[q] and the fire died down. 3So that place was
called Taberah,[a][r] because fire from the LORD had burned among them.

a 3 *Taberah* means *burning.*

10:11 [p]Ex 40:17 [q]Nu 9:17
10:13 [r]Dt 1:6
10:14 [s]Nu 2:3-9 [t]Nu 1:7
10:17 [u]Nu 4:21-32
10:18 [v]Nu 2:10-16
10:21 [w]Nu 4:20 [x]ver 17
10:22 [y]Nu 2:24
10:25 [z]Nu 2:31; Jos 6:9
10:29 [a]Jdg 4:11 [b]Ex 2:18 [c]Ex 3:1 [d]Ge 12:7
10:30 [e]Mt 21:29
10:31 [f]Job 29:15
10:32 [g]Dt 10:18 [h]Ps 22:27-31; 67:5-7
10:33 [i]ver 12; Dt 1:33 [j]Jos 3:3
10:34 [k]Nu 9:15-23
10:35 [l]Ps 68:1 [m]Dt 7:10; 32:41; Ps 68:2; Isa 17:12-14
10:36 [n]Isa 63:17 [o]Dt 1:10
11:1 [p]Lev 10:2
11:2 [q]Nu 21:7
11:3 [r]Dt 9:22

■ **10:11—12:16** *The Early Travels.* This section begins with the Lord's guidance of the people toward the area of Kadesh (10:12; 12:16; 13:3,26). The travels began well (10:11–36) but quickly deteriorated as the people voiced complaints and opposition to what God had done for Israel through Moses (11:1–3,4–35; 12:1–16).

■ **10:11–36** *The March Ensues.* The nation departed Sinai in a positive manner.

10:14–28 Here the order of the march, already prescribed in chapter 2, was followed without change, showing that the first-generation army began its march as prescribed.

10:29–32 Another element of guidance was found. Moses asked his brother-in-law, a man familiar with the desert, to function as the army's "eyes" (v. 31).

10:33–34 The first three days of travel.

10:35–36 This was Moses' prayer at the start and finish of each part of the journey. **Rise up . . . your enemies . . . your foes.** The forward movement of the ark (and thus of the people) was a movement into battle.

10:36 countless thousands. The large number of Israelites shows how greatly God had blessed them (see notes on Ge 1:28–29; Ex 1:7).

■ **11:1–3** *Complaints About Hardships.* Immediately upon moving forward, the Israelites grumbled for the first time, and the Lord responded by sending fire to destroy the outskirts of the camp.

Quail From the LORD

4The rabble with them began to crave other food,[s] and again the Israelites started wailing[t] and said, "If only we had meat to eat! 5We remember the fish we ate in Egypt at no cost—also the cucumbers, melons, leeks, onions and garlic.[u] 6But now we have lost our appetite; we never see anything but this manna!"

7The manna was like coriander seed[v] and looked like resin.[w] 8The people went around gathering it, and then ground it in a handmill or crushed it in a mortar. They cooked it in a pot or made it into cakes. And it tasted like something made with olive oil. 9When the dew[x] settled on the camp at night, the manna also came down.

10Moses heard the people of every family wailing, each at the entrance to his tent. The LORD became exceedingly angry, and Moses was troubled. 11He asked the LORD, "Why have you brought this trouble on your servant? What have I done to displease you that you put the burden of all these people on me?[y] 12Did I conceive all these people? Did I give them birth? Why do you tell me to carry them in my arms, as a nurse carries an infant,[z] to the land you promised on oath to their forefathers?[a] 13Where can I get meat for all these people?[b] They keep wailing to me, 'Give us meat to eat!' 14I cannot carry all these people by myself; the burden is too heavy for me.[c] 15If this is how you are going to treat me, put me to death[d] right now[e]—if I have found favor in your eyes—and do not let me face my own ruin."

16The LORD said to Moses: "Bring me seventy of Israel's elders who are known to you as leaders and officials among the people. Have them come to the Tent of Meeting, that they may stand there with you. 17I will come down and speak with you there, and I will take of the Spirit that is on you and put the Spirit on them.[f] They will help you carry the burden of the people so that you will not have to carry it alone.[g]

18"Tell the people: 'Consecrate yourselves[h] in preparation for tomorrow, when you will eat meat. The LORD heard you when you wailed,[i] "If only we had meat to eat! We were better off in Egypt!"[j] Now the LORD will give you meat, and you will eat it. 19You will not eat it for just one day, or two days, or five, ten or twenty days, 20but for a whole month—until it comes out of your nostrils and you loathe it[k]—because you have rejected the LORD,[l] who is among you, and have wailed before him, saying, "Why did we ever leave Egypt?" ' "

21But Moses said, "Here I am among six hundred thousand men[m] on foot, and you say, 'I will give them meat to eat for a whole month!' 22Would they have enough if flocks and herds were slaughtered for them? Would they have enough if all the fish in the sea were caught for them?"[n]

23The LORD answered Moses, "Is the LORD's arm too short?[o] You will now see whether or not what I say will come true for you.[p]"

24So Moses went out and told the people what the LORD had said. He brought together seventy of their elders and had them stand around the Tent. 25Then the LORD came down in the cloud[q] and spoke with him,[r] and he took of the Spirit[s] that was on him and put the Spirit on the seventy elders.[t] When the Spirit rested on them, they prophesied,[u] but they did not do so again.[a]

26However, two men, whose names were Eldad and Medad, had remained in the camp. They were listed among the elders, but did not go out to the Tent. Yet the Spirit also rested on them, and they prophesied in the camp. 27A young man ran and told Moses, "Eldad and Medad are prophesying in the camp."

[a] *25* Or *prophesied and continued to do so*

11:4 [s]Ex 12:38 [t]Ps 78:18; 1Co 10:6
11:5 [u]Ex 16:3
11:7 [v]Ex 16:31 [w]Ge 2:12
11:9 [x]Ex 16:13
11:11 [y]Ex 5:22
11:12 [z]Isa 40:11; 49:23 [a]Ex 13:5
11:13 [b]Jn 6:5-9
11:14 [c]Ex 18:18
11:15 [d]Ex 32:32 [e]1Ki 19:4; Jnh 4:3
11:17 [f]ver 25,29; 1Sa 10:6; 2Ki 2:9, 15; Joel 2:28 [g]Ex 18:18
11:18 [h]Ex 19:10 [i]Ex 16:7 [j]ver 5; Ac 7:39
11:20 [k]Ps 78:29; 106:14, 15 [l]Jos 24:27; 1Sa 10:19
11:21 [m]Ex 12:37
11:22 [n]Mt 15:33
11:23 [o]Isa 50:2; 59:1 [p]Nu 23:19; Eze 12:25; 24:14
11:25 [q]Nu 12:5 [r]ver 17 [s]1Sa 10:6 [t]Ac 2:17 [u]1Sa 10:10

11:1 complained. See also "started wailing" (v. 4) and "began to talk against" (12:1). It is important to distinguish legitimate lament that God welcomes from complaint that stirs his wrath. The former involves situations of injustice, untimely death, defeat in war and prolonged suffering. Such are the psalms of lament or complaint (see "Introduction to the Psalms" on p. 718). Here the people's complaints regarding hardships demonstrated a lack of gratitude for the wondrous deliverance they had just received. In their second complaint (v. 6) they grumbled about having to eat the miraculous manna instead of meat. In their third complaint Aaron and Miriam grumbled about Moses having authority over them (12:2). In all of these situations, people who had been wonderfully blessed complained that God had not blessed them in the ways they preferred. Thus their ingratitude stirred God's wrath. **in the hearing of the LORD.** It was bad enough that the people were ungrateful for the kindness God had shown. They added to this lack of appreciation complaints at the tabernacle. This particularly defiant act was met with fire.

11:2 cried out to Moses, he prayed. The mediatory role of Moses appears repeatedly in the stories of Israel's march. God had mercy on Israel many times because of Moses' prayers (e.g., see 14:13–19; 16:22,45–48; 21:7; Ex 8:30; 10:18; 32:1–14).

11:3 Taberah. Means "burning." The place was so named because of the fire that consumed some of the camp.

■ **11:4–35** *Complaints About Meat.* Further complaints—about lack of meat (vv. 4–6)—were aired, and punishment resulted.

11:4 The rabble with them. These were non-Israelites who had come out from Egypt with the Israelites.

11:11–12 See *WLC* 125.

11:25–29 prophesied. In these verses the various forms of the word *prophesy* indicate the utterance of statements praising God and expressing divine truth, whether already known or supernaturally revealed (cf. 1Sa 10:10; 19:24). See *WLC* 128,145.

[28]Joshua son of Nun, who had been Moses' aide[v] since youth, spoke up and said,
"Moses, my lord, stop them!"[w]
[29]But Moses replied, "Are you jealous for my sake? I wish that all the LORD's people
were prophets[x] and that the LORD would put his Spirit on them!" [30]Then Moses and the
elders of Israel returned to the camp.
[31]Now a wind went out from the LORD and drove quail[y] in from the sea. It brought
them[a] down all around the camp to about three feet[b] above the ground, as far as a day's
walk in any direction. [32]All that day and night and all the next day the people went out
and gathered quail. No one gathered less than ten homers.[c] Then they spread them out
all around the camp. [33]But while the meat was still between their teeth[z] and before it
could be consumed, the anger of the LORD burned against the people, and he struck them
with a severe plague.[a] [34]Therefore the place was named Kibroth Hattaavah,[d][b] because
there they buried the people who had craved other food.
[35]From Kibroth Hattaavah the people traveled to Hazeroth[c] and stayed there.

Miriam and Aaron Oppose Moses

12 Miriam and Aaron began to talk against Moses because of his Cushite wife,[d] for
he had married a Cushite. [2]"Has the LORD spoken only through Moses?" they
asked. "Hasn't he also spoken through us?"[e] And the LORD heard this.[f]
[3](Now Moses was a very humble man,[g] more humble than anyone else on the face
of the earth.)
[4]At once the LORD said to Moses, Aaron and Miriam, "Come out to the Tent of Meeting, all three of you." So the three of them came out. [5]Then the LORD came down in a pillar of cloud;[h] he stood at the entrance to the Tent and summoned Aaron and Miriam.
When both of them stepped forward, [6]he said, "Listen to my words:

"When a prophet of the LORD is among you,
I reveal myself to him in visions,[i]
I speak to him in dreams.[j]
[7]But this is not true of my servant Moses;[k]
he is faithful in all my house.[l]
[8]With him I speak face to face,
clearly and not in riddles;[m]
he sees the form of the LORD.[n]
Why then were you not afraid
to speak against my servant Moses?"

[9]The anger of the LORD burned against them, and he left them.[o]
[10]When the cloud lifted from above the Tent, there stood Miriam—leprous,[e] like

11:28 [v]Ex 33:11; Jos 1:1 [w]Mk 9:38-40
11:29 [x]1Co 14:5
11:31 [y]Ex 16:13; Ps 78:26-28
11:33 [z]Ps 78:30 [a]Ps 106:15
11:34 [b]Dt 9:22
11:35 [c]Nu 33:17
12:1 [d]Ex 2:21
12:2 [e]Nu 16:3 [f]Nu 11:1
12:3 [g]Mt 11:29
12:5 [h]Nu 11:25
12:6 [i]Ge 15:1; 46:2 [j]Ge 31:10; 1Ki 3:5; Heb 1:1
12:7 [k]Jos 1:1-2; Ps 105:26 [l]Heb 3:2,5
12:8 [m]Dt 34:10 [n]Ex 20:4; Ps 17:15
12:9 [o]Ge 17:22

a *31* Or *They flew* b *31* Hebrew *two cubits* (about 1 meter) c *32* That is, probably about 60 bushels (about 2.2 kiloliters) d *34* *Kibroth Hattaavah* means *graves of craving.* e *10* The Hebrew word was used for various diseases affecting the skin—not necessarily leprosy.

11:31 about three feet above the ground. The quail were not piled to a depth of three feet but were flying blindly at a level at which they could easily be seized or struck down.
11:34 Kibroth Hattaavah. Means "graves of craving."
11:35 The people arrived at Hazeroth.
■ **12:1–16** *Complaints About Moses' Authority.* The complaints continued as Miriam and Aaron, Moses' sister and brother, confronted Moses about his Cushite wife.
12:1 his Cushite wife. If this is a reference to Zipporah (Ex 2:15–22), then it is a pejorative reflection on her Midianite heritage. It is also possible that Moses had married a second wife who was descended from Cush, the eldest son of Ham (Ge 10:6). Whatever the case, Miriam and Aaron had allowed ethnic prejudice to turn them against Moses.
12:2 spoken only through Moses? The deeper reason for their criticism comes to view: jealousy of Moses. Perhaps they referred to a controversy over which of them understood God's will regarding Moses' marriage. Miriam and Aaron had important places in God's plans for Israel (cf. Mic 6:4), but their jealousy of Moses, if not corrected, would greatly hinder the outworking of this plan. See *WLC* 132.
12:3 This statement about Moses may have been added by someone other than Moses. One of the unusual features of the Bible is its accurate representations of both the good and bad qualities of its characters. The use of secretaries by Moses may also explain this reference to his humility.
12:4–9 The Lord intervened on Moses' behalf. The jealousy of Miriam and Aaron threatened the success of the whole expedition. In this case the very future of God's people was threatened, and God acted vigorously to preserve it.
12:6–8 The Lord summoned Moses and his two accusers to the Tent of Meeting. There he rebuked Aaron and Miriam for their arrogance and lack of fear in opposing Moses. In light of the clarity and directness of God's self-revelation to Moses, they should have recognized their subordination to Moses' unique status and supported him.
12:7 my servant Moses. Miriam, Aaron and the rest of the Israelites should have been terrified about the consequences of speaking against God's servant. To how much greater an extent should those in the church be careful not to speak against Jesus, the Son over God's house (Heb 3:1–6)?
12:8–9 See *WLC* 151.
12:8 face to face. Contrast the way God revealed his will even to Elijah (cf. 1Ki 19:9–18). Except for Jesus Christ, no one else has been privileged to experience a relationship to God such as Moses enjoyed (see note on Jn 1:18). The hope of the believer is to see Christ "face to face" (1Co 13:12; see Rev 22:4).
12:10–15 Miriam's punishment was meted out.
12:10 leprous. The Hebrew word can include various skin diseases. It was clear to anyone who saw Miriam that God had condemned her attitude. Aaron shared the humiliation. It was evident to all that he was being condemned for joining her in claiming that the two were as great as Moses, but God did not make Aaron leprous, probably since his position as high priest, second in impor-

snow.[p] Aaron turned toward her and saw that she had leprosy;[q] 11and he said to Moses,
"Please, my lord, do not hold against us the sin we have so foolishly committed.[r] 12Do
not let her be like a stillborn infant coming from its mother's womb with its flesh half eat-
en away."
13So Moses cried out to the LORD, "O God, please heal her![s]"
14The LORD replied to Moses, "If her father had spit in her face,[t] would she not have
been in disgrace for seven days? Confine her outside the camp[u] for seven days; after that
she can be brought back." 15So Miriam was confined outside the camp for seven days,
and the people did not move on till she was brought back.
16After that, the people left Hazeroth[v] and encamped in the Desert of Paran.

Exploring Canaan

13 The LORD said to Moses, 2"Send some men to explore[w] the land of Canaan,
which I am giving to the Israelites. From each ancestral tribe send one of its
leaders."
3So at the LORD's command Moses sent them out from the Desert of Paran. All of them
were leaders of the Israelites. 4These are their names:

from the tribe of Reuben, Shammua son of Zaccur;
5from the tribe of Simeon, Shaphat son of Hori;
6from the tribe of Judah, Caleb son of Jephunneh;[x]
7from the tribe of Issachar, Igal son of Joseph;
8from the tribe of Ephraim, Hoshea son of Nun;
9from the tribe of Benjamin, Palti son of Raphu;
10from the tribe of Zebulun, Gaddiel son of Sodi;
11from the tribe of Manasseh (a tribe of Joseph), Gaddi son of Susi;
12from the tribe of Dan, Ammiel son of Gemalli;
13from the tribe of Asher, Sethur son of Michael;
14from the tribe of Naphtali, Nahbi son of Vophsi;
15from the tribe of Gad, Geuel son of Maki.

16These are the names of the men Moses sent to explore the land. (Moses gave Hoshea
son of Nun[y] the name Joshua.)[z]
17When Moses sent them to explore Canaan, he said, "Go up through the Negev[a] and
on into the hill country.[b] 18See what the land is like and whether the people who live
there are strong or weak, few or many. 19What kind of land do they live in? Is it good or
bad? What kind of towns do they live in? Are they unwalled or fortified? 20How is the soil?
Is it fertile or poor? Are there trees on it or not? Do your best to bring back some of the
fruit of the land.[c]" (It was the season for the first ripe grapes.)
21So they went up and explored the land from the Desert of Zin[d] as far as Rehob,[e] toward Lebo[a] Hamath.[f] 22They went up through the Negev and came to Hebron, where
Ahiman, Sheshai and Talmai,[g] the descendants of Anak,[h] lived. (Hebron had been built

12:10 [p]Ex 4:6; Dt 24:9 [q]2Ki 5:1,27
12:11 [r]2Sa 19:19; 24:10
12:13 [s]Isa 30:26; Jer 17:14
12:14 [t]Dt 25:9; Job 17:6; 30:9-10; Isa 50:6 [u]Lev 13:46; Nu 5:2-3
12:16 [v]Nu 11:35
13:2 [w]Dt 1:22
13:6 [x]ver 30; Nu 14:6, 24; 34:19; Jdg 1:12-15
13:16 [y]ver 8 [z]Dt 32:44
13:17 [a]Ge 12:9 [b]Jdg 1:9
13:20 [c]Dt 1:25
13:21 [d]Nu 20:1; 27:14; 33:36; Jos 15:1 [e]Jos 19:28 [f]Jos 13:5
13:22 [g]Jos 15:14 [h]Jos 15:13

[a] *21* Or *toward the entrance to*

tance only to that of Moses, needed to be safeguarded (cf. 16:6—17:11). Later on Uzziah, a beloved king of Judah, when he tried to assume the prerogatives of the high priest, was smitten with leprosy (see 2Ch 26:16–21), as Miriam was here.

12:14–15 The whole nation waited seven days for Miriam's disgrace to be ended.

12:16 This transitional verse moves the narrative to its next major stage: the move to the Desert of Paran, the region southwest of the promised land.

■ **13:1—19:22** *The Period of Wandering.* Moses' narrative turns next to the period of time during which the Israelites were condemned to wander and die in the desert. His account divides into four sections that alternate between Israel's failures and the importance of the tabernacle services and the priesthood. They include: failure and condemnation at Kadesh Barnea (13:1—14:45), remembering the offerings (15:1–41), the great rebellion against Moses and Aaron (16:1–50) and the reaffirmation of the Aaronic priesthood (17:1—19:22).

■ **13:1—14:45** *The Rebellion at Kadesh Barnea.* At Kadesh Barnea Moses sent spies into the land in preparation for the conquest. Most of them brought back pessimistic reports, and the people refused to move forward. God judged his people by condemning the first-generation army to die in the wilderness.

13:1–25 Spies were sent out to explore Canaan. God commanded Moses to use human means to prepare for the conquest of Canaan. An additional reason for the divine command was the need to make it evident that the nation was not yet ready to make the conquest. There is no contradiction in Moses' statement recorded in Deuteronomy 1:22–23 that the people asked that spies be sent.

13:3 Desert of Paran. See note on 12:16.

13:4–15 The names of the men selected to explore the land are cited. Although these were individuals who had shown leadership qualities, none of them were among the tribal leaders mentioned in chapters 1, 2, 7 and 10. Robust and vigorous younger leaders were needed for the arduous task of spying out the land.

13:16 Hoshea . . . Joshua. *Hoshea* means "salvation," while *Joshua* means "The LORD saves." It was desirable that the man who would later succeed Moses as leader of the nation bear a name that specifically pointed to the Lord as the source of both the exodus and coming conquest (see notes on Ex 3:13–22; 6:2–8).

13:22 Hebron. This city was significant for several reasons: (1) It was prominent in the lives of the patriarchs (Ge 13:14–18; 14:13; 23:2; 25:9; 35:27–29; 50:13). (2) It had a long history, having been built seven years before one of the famous capital cities of Egypt (v. 22). (3) Its land was exceptionally fertile (vv. 23–24). (4) Its inhabitants had great strength (v. 22; cf. vv. 28–29). After Joshua conquered Canaan, Hebron would become a significant Israelite city, later serving as David's capital during the first seven years of his reign (2Sa 5:5). **Anak.** The ancestor of a clan of powerful men (vv. 28,33; see also Dt 1:28; 2:10–11; 9:2; Jos 11:21–22; 14:12,15; 15:13–14; 21:11; Jdg 1:20).

seven years before Zoan in Egypt.)[i] 23When they reached the Valley of Eshcol,[a] they cut off a branch bearing a single cluster of grapes. Two of them carried it on a pole between them, along with some pomegranates and figs. 24That place was called the Valley of Eshcol because of the cluster of grapes the Israelites cut off there. 25At the end of forty days they returned from exploring the land.

Report on the Exploration

26They came back to Moses and Aaron and the whole Israelite community at Kadesh in the Desert of Paran. There they reported to them[j] and to the whole assembly and showed them the fruit of the land. 27They gave Moses this account: "We went into the land to which you sent us, and it does flow with milk and honey![k] Here is its fruit.[l] 28But the people who live there are powerful, and the cities are fortified and very large.[m] We even saw descendants of Anak there. 29The Amalekites live in the Negev; the Hittites, Jebusites and Amorites live in the hill country; and the Canaanites live near the sea and along the Jordan."

30Then Caleb silenced the people before Moses and said, "We should go up and take possession of the land, for we can certainly do it."

31But the men who had gone up with him said, "We can't attack those people; they are stronger than we are."[n] 32And they spread among the Israelites a bad report[o] about the land they had explored. They said, "The land we explored devours[p] those living in it. All the people we saw there are of great size.[q] 33We saw the Nephilim[r] there (the descendants of Anak[s] come from the Nephilim). We seemed like grasshoppers in our own eyes, and we looked the same to them."

The People Rebel

14 That night all the people of the community raised their voices and wept aloud. 2All the Israelites grumbled against Moses and Aaron, and the whole assembly said to them, "If only we had died in Egypt! Or in this desert![t] 3Why is the LORD bringing us to this land only to let us fall by the sword? Our wives and children will be taken as plunder. Wouldn't it be better for us to go back to Egypt?" 4And they said to each other, "We should choose a leader and go back to Egypt.[u]"

5Then Moses and Aaron fell facedown[v] in front of the whole Israelite assembly gathered there. 6Joshua son of Nun and Caleb son of Jephunneh, who were among those who had explored the land, tore their clothes 7and said to the entire Israelite assembly, "The land we passed through and explored is exceedingly good.[w] 8If the LORD is pleased with us,[x] he will lead us into that land, a land flowing with milk and honey,[y] and will give it to us. 9Only do not rebel[z] against the LORD. And do not be afraid of the people of the land,[a] because we will swallow them up. Their protection is gone, but the LORD is with us. Do not be afraid of them."

10But the whole assembly talked about stoning[b] them. Then the glory of the LORD[c] appeared at the Tent of Meeting to all the Israelites. 11The LORD said to Moses, "How long will these people treat me with contempt? How long will they refuse to believe in me,[d] in spite of all the miraculous signs I have performed among them? 12I will strike them down with a plague and destroy them, but I will make you into a nation[e] greater and stronger than they."

13Moses said to the LORD, "Then the Egyptians will hear about it! By your power you brought these people up from among them.[f] 14And they will tell the inhabitants of this land about it. They have already heard[g] that you, O LORD, are with these people and that you, O LORD, have been seen face to face, that your cloud stays over them, and that you go before them in a pillar of cloud by day and a pillar of fire by night.[h] 15If you put these people to death all at one time, the nations who have heard this report about you will say, 16'The LORD was not able to bring these people into the land he promised them on oath; so he slaughtered them in the desert.'[i]

13:22 [i]Ps 78:12,43; Isa 19:11,13
13:26 [j]Nu 32:8
13:27 [k]Ex 3:8 [l]Dt 1:25
13:28 [m]Dt 1:28; 9:1,2
13:31 [n]Dt 1:28; 9:1; Jos 14:8
13:32 [o]Nu 14:36,37 [p]Eze 36:13,14 [q]Am 2:9
13:33 [r]Ge 6:4 [s]Dt 1:28
14:2 [t]Nu 11:1
14:4 [u]Ne 9:17
14:5 [v]Nu 16:4,22,45
14:7 [w]Nu 13:27; Dt 1:25
14:8 [x]Dt 10:15 [y]Nu 13:27
14:9 [z]Dt 1:26; 9:7,23,24 [a]Dt 1:21; 7:18; 20:1
14:10 [b]Ex 17:4 [c]Lev 9:23
14:11 [d]Ps 78:22; 106:24
14:12 [e]Ex 32:10
14:13 [f]Ex 32:11-14; Ps 106:23
14:14 [g]Ex 15:14 [h]Ex 13:21
14:16 [i]Jos 7:7

[a] *23 Eshcol* means *cluster*; also in verse 24.

13:33 Nephilim. This term designates vicious, powerful warriors, not a group of people with a common race or ancestry. It is used in Genesis 6:4 to describe a number of strong and wicked men who lived on the earth before the flood. The presence of such men in Canaan suggests its ripeness for judgment. It may also help to explain the terror felt by the ten spies as they remembered seeing the strong sons of Anak (vv. 22,28,33).

14:1–45 The experience of the exodus generation is an example of apostasy that the psalmist (Ps 95:7–11) and the New Testament authors (1Co 10:5; Heb 3:12—4:13) would use to warn later generations against turning from the Lord's commands.

14:2 See *WLC* 192.

14:5–9 Joshua, the representative of the tribe of Ephraim, joined with Caleb in urging the people to trust that God would enable them to take the land.

14:13–19 Moses again interceded for the nation (see 11:2; 16:22, 45–48; 21:7).

17 "Now may the Lord's strength be displayed, just as you have declared: 18 'The LORD
is slow to anger, abounding in love and forgiving sin and rebellion.[j] Yet he does not leave
the guilty unpunished; he punishes the children for the sin of the fathers to the third and
fourth generation.'[k] 19 In accordance with your great love, forgive[l] the sin of these people,[m] just as you have pardoned them from the time they left Egypt until now."[n]
20 The LORD replied, "I have forgiven them,[o] as you asked. 21 Nevertheless, as surely as
I live[p] and as surely as the glory of the LORD fills the whole earth,[q] 22 not one of the men
who saw my glory and the miraculous signs I performed in Egypt and in the desert but
who disobeyed me and tested me ten times[r]— 23 not one of them will ever see the land
I promised on oath[s] to their forefathers. No one who has treated me with contempt will
ever see it.[t] 24 But because my servant Caleb has a different spirit and follows me wholeheartedly,[u] I will bring him into the land he went to, and his descendants will inherit it.[v]
25 Since the Amalekites and Canaanites are living in the valleys, turn[w] back tomorrow
and set out toward the desert along the route to the Red Sea.[a]"
26 The LORD said to Moses and Aaron: 27 "How long will this wicked community grumble against me? I have heard the complaints of these grumbling Israelites.[x] 28 So tell
them, 'As surely as I live,[y] declares the LORD, I will do to you the very things I heard you
say: 29 In this desert your bodies will fall[z]—every one of you twenty years old or more[a]
who was counted in the census and who has grumbled against me. 30 Not one of you will
enter the land I swore with uplifted hand to make your home, except Caleb son of Jephunneh and Joshua son of Nun. 31 As for your children that you said would be taken as
plunder, I will bring them in to enjoy the land you have rejected.[b] 32 But you—your bodies will fall[c] in this desert. 33 Your children will be shepherds here for forty years, suffering for your unfaithfulness, until the last of your bodies lies in the desert. 34 For forty
years—one year for each of the forty days you explored the land[d]—you will suffer for
your sins and know what it is like to have me against you.' 35 I, the LORD, have spoken,
and I will surely do these things[e] to this whole wicked community, which has banded together against me. They will meet their end in this desert; here they will die."
36 So the men Moses had sent[f] to explore the land, who returned and made the
whole community grumble against him by spreading a bad report[g] about it— 37 these
men responsible for spreading the bad report[h] about the land were struck down and
died of a plague[i] before the LORD. 38 Of the men who went to explore the land, only Joshua son of Nun and Caleb son of Jephunneh survived.[j]
39 When Moses reported this to all the Israelites, they mourned[k] bitterly. 40 Early the
next morning they went up toward the high hill country. "We have sinned[l]," they said.
"We will go up to the place the LORD promised."
41 But Moses said, "Why are you disobeying the LORD's command? This will not succeed![m] 42 Do not go up, because the LORD is not with you. You will be defeated by your
enemies,[n] 43 for the Amalekites and Canaanites will face you there. Because you have
turned away from the LORD, he will not be with you and you will fall by the sword."
44 Nevertheless, in their presumption they went up[o] toward the high hill country,
though neither Moses nor the ark of the LORD's covenant moved from the camp.[p] 45 Then
the Amalekites and Canaanites who lived in that hill country came down and attacked
them and beat them down all the way to Hormah.[q]

Supplementary Offerings

15 The LORD said to Moses, 2 "Speak to the Israelites and say to them: 'After you enter the land I am giving you[r] as a home 3 and you present to the LORD offerings
made by fire, from the herd or the flock,[s] as an aroma pleasing to the LORD[t]—whether

[a] *25* Hebrew *Yam Suph*; that is, Sea of Reeds

14:18 [j]Ex 34:6; Ps 145:8; Jnh 4:2 [k]Ex 20:5
14:19 [l]Ex 34:9 [m]Ps 106:45 [n]Ps 78:38
14:20 [o]Ps 106:23; Mic 7:18-20
14:21 [p]Dt 32:40; Isa 49:18 [q]Ps 72:19; Isa 6:3; Hab 2:14
14:22 [r]Ex 14:11; 32:1; 1Co 10:5
14:23 [s]Nu 32:11 [t]Heb 3:18
14:24 [u]ver 6-9; Jos 14:8, 14 [v]Nu 32:12
14:25 [w]Dt 1:40
14:27 [x]Ex 16:12
14:28 [y]ver 21
14:29 [z]Nu 26:65 [a]Nu 1:45
14:31 [b]Ps 106:24
14:32 [c]1Co 10:5
14:34 [d]Nu 13:25
14:35 [e]Nu 23:19
14:36 [f]Nu 13:4-16 [g]Nu 13:32
14:37 [h]1Co 10:10 [i]Nu 16:49
14:38 [j]Jos 14:6
14:39 [k]Ex 33:4
14:40 [l]Dt 1:41
14:41 [m]2Ch 24:20
14:42 [n]Dt 1:42
14:44 [o]Dt 1:43 [p]Nu 31:6
14:45 [q]Nu 21:3; Dt 1:44; Jdg 1:17
15:2 [r]Lev 23:10
15:3 [s]Lev 1:2 [t]ver 24; Ge 8:21; Ex 29:18

14:22 See *WLC* 151.
14:36–38 The unfaithful spies were killed by a plague.
14:39–45 The Israelites, realizing that they had committed a serious sin, made a futile attempt to enter Canaan. Despite Moses' opposition, they entered and were driven back.
14:43 sword. Compare verse 3. As the presumptuous Israelites fell by the sword of the Amalekites and Canaanites for disobeying God's command through Moses, so also will those who disobey the word God has spoken through Christ fall under judgment (Heb 1:1–2; 4:12).
14:45 Hormah. A place of some importance in later history (see 21:1–3; Jos 15:30; 19:4; Jdg 1:17; 1Sa 30:26–30).
■ **15:1–41** *Remembering the Offerings.* This book has already stressed the centrality of the tabernacle and its priests and ceremonies for the holiness and success of the first-generation army of Israel (see note on 5:1—9:14). This chapter continues this orientation by focusing on the importance of the same in the future, when Israel would successfully conquer the land. This chapter divides into three sections, discussing additional instructions on offerings (vv. 1–16), offerings for unintentional and intentional sins (vv. 17–36) and the wearing of tassels (vv. 37–41).
15:2 After you enter the land I am giving you. This is the keynote of the chapter. Moses was concerned that his readers, the second generation from the exodus, who were about to enter the land, understand the importance of the legislation he was about to give. See verses 14, 17, 21 and 37.
15:3–16 Some details of these procedures for offerings of fire are set forth here for the first time (see notes on Lev 1:1—7:38).

burnt offerings[u] or sacrifices, for special vows or freewill offerings[v] or festival offerings[w]—
4then the one who brings his offering shall present to the LORD a grain offering[x] of a tenth
of an ephah[a] of fine flour mixed with a quarter of a hin[b] of oil. 5With each lamb for the burnt
offering or the sacrifice, prepare a quarter of a hin of wine[y] as a drink offering.
6" 'With a ram[z] prepare a grain offering[a] of two-tenths of an ephah[c] of fine flour
mixed with a third of a hin[d] of oil,[b] 7and a third of a hin of wine as a drink offering. Offer it as an aroma pleasing to the LORD.
8" 'When you prepare a young bull as a burnt offering or sacrifice, for a special vow
or a fellowship offering[e][c] to the LORD, 9bring with the bull a grain offering of three-tenths
of an ephah[f][d] of fine flour mixed with half a hin[g] of oil. 10Also bring half a hin of wine as
a drink offering. It will be an offering made by fire, an aroma pleasing to the LORD. 11Each
bull or ram, each lamb or young goat, is to be prepared in this manner. 12Do this for each
one, for as many as you prepare.
13" 'Everyone who is native-born[e] must do these things in this way when he brings an
offering made by fire as an aroma pleasing to the LORD. 14For the generations to come,
whenever an alien or anyone else living among you presents an offering made by fire as
an aroma pleasing to the LORD, he must do exactly as you do. 15The community is to have
the same rules for you and for the alien living among you; this is a lasting ordinance for
the generations to come.[f] You and the alien shall be the same before the LORD: 16The
same laws and regulations will apply both to you and to the alien living among you.[g]' "
17The LORD said to Moses, 18"Speak to the Israelites and say to them: 'When you enter the land to which I am taking you 19and you eat the food of the land,[h] present a portion as an offering to the LORD. 20Present a cake from the first of your ground meal[i] and
present it as an offering from the threshing floor.[j] 21Throughout the generations to come
you are to give this offering to the LORD from the first of your ground meal.[k]

Offerings for Unintentional Sins

22" 'Now if you unintentionally fail to keep any of these commands the LORD gave Moses[l]— 23any of the LORD's commands to you through him, from the day the LORD gave
them and continuing through the generations to come— 24and if this is done unintentionally without the community being aware of it,[m] then the whole community is to offer a young bull for a burnt offering[n] as an aroma pleasing to the LORD, along with its prescribed grain offering and drink offering, and a male goat for a sin offering.[o] 25The priest
is to make atonement for the whole Israelite community, and they will be forgiven,[p] for
it was not intentional and they have brought to the LORD for their wrong an offering made
by fire and a sin offering. 26The whole Israelite community and the aliens living among
them will be forgiven, because all the people were involved in the unintentional wrong.[q]
27" 'But if just one person sins unintentionally,[r] he must bring a year-old female goat
for a sin offering. 28The priest is to make atonement before the LORD for the one who
erred by sinning unintentionally, and when atonement has been made for him, he will
be forgiven.[s] 29One and the same law applies to everyone who sins unintentionally,
whether he is a native-born Israelite or an alien.
30" 'But anyone who sins defiantly,[t] whether native-born or alien,[u] blasphemes the
LORD, and that person must be cut off from his people. 31Because he has despised the
LORD's word and broken his commands,[v] that person must surely be cut off; his guilt remains on him.[w]' "

The Sabbath-Breaker Put to Death

32While the Israelites were in the desert, a man was found gathering wood on the Sabbath day.[x] 33Those who found him gathering wood brought him to Moses and Aaron and

15:3 [u]Nu 28:19,27 [v]Lev 22:18,21; Ezr 1:4 [w]Lev 23:1-44
15:4 [x]Lev 2:1; 6:14
15:5 [y]Nu 28:7,14
15:6 [z]Lev 5:15 [a]Nu 28:12 [b]Eze 46:14
15:8 [c]Lev 1:3; 3:1
15:9 [d]Lev 14:10
15:13 [e]Lev 16:29
15:15 [f]ver 29; Nu 9:14
15:16 [g]Nu 9:14
15:19 [h]Jos 5:11,12
15:20 [i]Ex 34:26; Lev 23:14; Dt 26:2,10 [j]Lev 2:14
15:21 [k]Ro 11:16
15:22 [l]Lev 4:2
15:24 [m]Lev 5:15 [n]Lev 4:14 [o]Lev 4:3
15:25 [p]Lev 4:20; Ro 3:25; Heb 2:17
15:26 [q]ver 24
15:27 [r]Lev 4:27
15:28 [s]Lev 4:35
15:30 [t]Nu 14:40-44; Dt 1:43; 17:13; Ps 19:13 [u]ver 14
15:31 [v]2Sa 12:9; Ps 119:126; Pr 13:13 [w]Lev 5:1; Eze 18:20
15:32 [x]Ex 31:14,15; 35:2,3

[a] *4* That is, probably about 2 quarts (about 2 liters) [b] *4* That is, probably about 1 quart (about 1 liter); also in verse 5 [c] *6* That is, probably about 4 quarts (about 4.5 liters) [d] *6* That is, probably about 1 1/4 quarts (about 1.2 liters); also in verse 7 [e] *8* Traditionally *peace offering* [f] *9* That is, probably about 6 quarts (about 6.5 liters) [g] *9* That is, probably about 2 quarts (about 2 liters); also in verse 10

15:21 The first of the ground meal was to be offered to the Lord to symbolize gratitude for his provision and the expectation of further blessings in the final crop.
15:22–36 Moses differentiated between offerings for unintentional sins (vv. 17–29) and punishment for defiant sins (vv. 30–36).
15:22–29 Procedures were established to deal with cases of unintentional sins committed by the whole community (vv. 22–26), as well as of those committed by an individual (vv. 27–29).
15:30–36 The treatment of an individual who sinned defiantly was presented: The rule was given (vv. 30–31) along with an illustration of a Sabbath-breaker (vv. 32–36). See *WLC* 151.
15:33 gathering wood. This case illustrated defiant sin (see note on 15:30–36). It is unlikely that this man gathered wood to provide for an emergency or as an act of mercy; Jesus made it clear that the Sabbath commandment was not intended to prohibit such efforts (Mt 12:10–12; Mk 2:27). Instead, this man flagrantly defied the fourth commandment, perhaps for his own convenience, and deserved his judgment (Ex 20:8–11; 31:15; 35:2).

the whole assembly, 34 and they kept him in custody, because it was not clear what should be done to him.[y] 35 Then the LORD said to Moses, "The man must die.[z] The whole assembly must stone him outside the camp.[a]" 36 So the assembly took him outside the camp and stoned him to death, as the LORD commanded Moses.

Tassels on Garments

37 The LORD said to Moses, 38 "Speak to the Israelites and say to them: 'Throughout the generations to come you are to make tassels on the corners of your garments,[b] with a blue cord on each tassel. 39 You will have these tassels to look at and so you will remember[c] all the commands of the LORD, that you may obey them and not prostitute yourselves by going after the lusts of your own hearts and eyes. 40 Then you will remember to obey all my commands and will be consecrated to your God.[d] 41 I am the LORD your God, who brought you out of Egypt to be your God. I am the LORD your God.' "

Korah, Dathan and Abiram

16 Korah[e] son of Izhar, the son of Kohath, the son of Levi, and certain Reubenites—Dathan and Abiram, sons of Eliab,[f] and On son of Peleth—became insolent[a] 2 and rose up against Moses. With them were 250 Israelite men, well-known community leaders who had been appointed members of the council.[g] 3 They came as a group to oppose Moses and Aaron[h] and said to them, "You have gone too far! The whole community is holy,[i] every one of them, and the LORD is with them.[j] Why then do you set yourselves above the LORD's assembly?"[k]

4 When Moses heard this, he fell facedown.[l] 5 Then he said to Korah and all his followers: "In the morning the LORD will show who belongs to him and who is holy,[m] and he will have that person come near him. The man he chooses[n] he will cause to come near him. 6 You, Korah, and all your followers are to do this: Take censers 7 and tomorrow put fire and incense in them before the LORD. The man the LORD chooses will be the one who is holy. You Levites have gone too far!"

8 Moses also said to Korah, "Now listen, you Levites! 9 Isn't it enough for you that the God of Israel has separated you from the rest of the Israelite community and brought you near himself to do the work at the LORD's tabernacle and to stand before the community and minister to them?[o] 10 He has brought you and all your fellow Levites near himself, but now you are trying to get the priesthood too.[p] 11 It is against the LORD that you and all your followers have banded together. Who is Aaron that you should grumble[q] against him?[r]"

12 Then Moses summoned Dathan and Abiram, the sons of Eliab. But they said, "We will not come! 13 Isn't it enough that you have brought us up out of a land flowing with milk and honey to kill us in the desert?[s] And now you also want to lord it over us?[t] 14 Moreover, you haven't brought us into a land flowing with milk and honey[u] or given us an inheritance of fields and vineyards.[v] Will you gouge out the eyes of[b] these men?[w] No, we will not come!"

15 Then Moses became very angry and said to the LORD, "Do not accept their offering. I have not taken so much as a donkey[x] from them, nor have I wronged any of them."

16 Moses said to Korah, "You and all your followers are to appear before the LORD tomorrow—you and they and Aaron.[y] 17 Each man is to take his censer and put incense in it—250 censers in all—and present it before the LORD. You and Aaron are to present your censers also." 18 So each man took his censer, put fire and incense in it, and stood with

15:34 [y]Nu 9:8
15:35 [z]Ex 31:14, 15; Dt 21:21 [a]Lev 20:2; 24:14; Ac 7:58
15:38 [b]Dt 22:12; Mt 23:5
15:39 [c]Dt 4:23; 6:12; Ps 73:27
15:40 [d]Lev 11:44; Ro 12:1; Col 1:22; 1Pe 1:15
16:1 [e]Jude 1:11 [f]Nu 26:8; Dt 11:6
16:2 [g]Nu 1:16; 26:9
16:3 [h]ver 7; Ps 106:16 [i]Ex 19:6 [j]Nu 14:14 [k]Nu 12:2
16:4 [l]Nu 14:5
16:5 [m]Lev 10:3; 2Ti 2:19* [n]Nu 17:5; Ps 65:4
16:9 [o]Nu 3:6; Dt 10:8
16:10 [p]Nu 3:10; 18:7
16:11 [q]1Co 10:10 [r]Ex 16:7
16:13 [s]Nu 14:2 [t]Ac 7:27, 35
16:14 [u]Lev 20:24 [v]Ex 22:5; 23:11; Nu 20:5 [w]Jdg 16:21; 1Sa 11:2
16:15 [x]1Sa 12:3
16:16 [y]ver 6

[a] *1* Or *Peleth—took ⌞men⌟* [b] *14* Or *you make slaves of;* or *you deceive*

15:37–41 The centrality of the ceremonies of worship and sacrifice are stressed. Moses instructed the Israelites to wear tassels with blue cords affixed to their garments as reminders to keep God's commands. See *WLC* 109.

■ **16:1–50** *The Great Rebellion Against Moses and Aaron.* This chapter describes a complicated series of events. Two separate movements combined in a rebellion against Moses and Aaron.

16:1 Kohath . . . On. One rebellious group, made up of men from the tribe of Reuben, was led by Dathan, Abiram and On. These men were jealous of the leadership that God had established, and they incited resistance against Moses and Aaron. The other faction was made up of Kohathites, the very group to which Moses and Aaron belonged (6:16–20). Only the Kohathites had direct access to the most sacred parts of the tabernacle.

16:4–11 Moses dealt first with the Levite opposition, instructing the Levites to put fire and incense in censers to present before the Lord, after which God would show them who was holy. Moses pointed out that their opposition was actually against the Lord rather than against Aaron (v. 11). This affirmation of Aaron fits well within the larger context, which alternates between accounts of rebellion and discussion of the Aaronic priesthood (see note on 13:1—19:22).

16:12–14 Moses next summoned Dathan and Abiram, but they refused to come, blaming Moses for having led them out of Egypt, which they ironically called "a land flowing with milk and honey" (see note on Ex 3:17).

16:18–21 Korah and his 250 associates took censers and stood with Moses and Aaron at the entrance to the tabernacle. The glory of the Lord appeared to the whole assembly, not only to the men at the tabernacle entrance. God instructed Moses and Aaron to separate themselves from the assembly so that all the rest might be destroyed.

Moses and Aaron at the entrance to the Tent of Meeting. 19When Korah had gathered
all his followers in opposition to them[z] at the entrance to the Tent of Meeting, the glory of the LORD[a] appeared to the entire assembly. 20The LORD said to Moses and Aaron,
21"Separate yourselves from this assembly so I can put an end to them at once."[b]
22But Moses and Aaron fell facedown[c] and cried out, "O God, God of the spirits of all
mankind,[d] will you be angry with the entire assembly when only one man sins?"[e]
23Then the LORD said to Moses, 24"Say to the assembly, 'Move away from the tents of
Korah, Dathan and Abiram.'"
25Moses got up and went to Dathan and Abiram, and the elders of Israel followed him.
26He warned the assembly, "Move back from the tents of these wicked men![f] Do not
touch anything belonging to them, or you will be swept away[g] because of all their sins."
27So they moved away from the tents of Korah, Dathan and Abiram. Dathan and Abiram
had come out and were standing with their wives, children and little ones at the entrances to their tents.
28Then Moses said, "This is how you will know that the LORD has sent me[h] to do all
these things and that it was not my idea: 29If these men die a natural death and experience only what usually happens to men, then the LORD has not sent me.[i] 30But if the LORD
brings about something totally new, and the earth opens its mouth and swallows them,
with everything that belongs to them, and they go down alive into the grave,[a][j] then you
will know that these men have treated the LORD with contempt."
31As soon as he finished saying all this, the ground under them split apart[k] 32and the
earth opened its mouth and swallowed them,[l] with their households and all Korah's men
and all their possessions. 33They went down alive into the grave, with everything they
owned; the earth closed over them, and they perished and were gone from the community. 34At their cries, all the Israelites around them fled, shouting, "The earth is going to
swallow us too!"
35And fire came out from the LORD[m] and consumed[n] the 250 men who were offering
the incense.
36The LORD said to Moses, 37"Tell Eleazar son of Aaron, the priest, to take the censers
out of the smoldering remains and scatter the coals some distance away, for the censers
are holy— 38the censers of the men who sinned at the cost of their lives.[o] Hammer the
censers into sheets to overlay the altar, for they were presented before the LORD and have
become holy. Let them be a sign[p] to the Israelites."
39So Eleazar the priest collected the bronze censers brought by those who had been
burned up, and he had them hammered out to overlay the altar, 40as the LORD directed
him through Moses. This was to remind the Israelites that no one except a descendant
of Aaron should come to burn incense[q] before the LORD,[r] or he would become like Korah and his followers.[s]
41The next day the whole Israelite community grumbled against Moses and Aaron.
"You have killed the LORD's people," they said.
42But when the assembly gathered in opposition[t] to Moses and Aaron and turned toward the Tent of Meeting, suddenly the cloud covered it and the glory of the LORD appeared. 43Then Moses and Aaron went to the front of the Tent of Meeting, 44and the LORD
said to Moses, 45"Get away from this assembly so I can put an end to them at once." And
they fell facedown.
46Then Moses said to Aaron, "Take your censer and put incense in it, along with fire
from the altar, and hurry to the assembly[u] to make atonement[v] for them. Wrath has
come out from the LORD; the plague[w] has started." 47So Aaron did as Moses said, and ran
into the midst of the assembly. The plague had already started among the people,[x] but
Aaron offered the incense and made atonement for them. 48He stood between the living
and the dead, and the plague stopped.[y] 49But 14,700 people died from the plague, in ad-

a *30* Hebrew *Sheol*; also in verse 33

16:19 [z]ver 42 [a]Ex 16:7; Nu 14:10; 20:6
16:21 [b]Ex 32:10
16:22 [c]Nu 14:5 [d]Nu 27:16; Job 12:10; Heb 12:9 [e]Ge 18:23
16:26 [f]Isa 52:11 [g]Ge 19:15
16:28 [h]Ex 3:12; Jn 5:36; 6:38
16:29 [i]Ecc 3:19
16:30 [j]ver 33; Ps 55:15
16:31 [k]Mic 1:3-4
16:32 [l]Nu 26:11; Dt 11:6; Ps 106:17
16:35 [m]Nu 11:1-3; 26:10 [n]Lev 10:2
16:38 [o]Pr 20:2 [p]Nu 26:10; Eze 14:8; 2Pe 2:6
16:40 [q]Ex 30:7-10; Nu 1:51 [r]2Ch 26:18 [s]Nu 3:10
16:42 [t]ver 19; Nu 20:6
16:46 [u]Lev 10:6 [v]Nu 18:5; 25:13; Dt 9:22 [w]Nu 8:19; Ps 106:29
16:47 [x]Nu 25:6-8
16:48 [y]Nu 25:8; Ps 106:30

16:22 Moses and Aaron acted as intercessors for the assembly (see notes on 11:2; 14:13–19; 16:45–48; 21:7).
16:23–27 Other people were warned to move away from the tents of the leaders of the uprising.
16:28–30 Moses rested his claim of being God's messenger on the prediction that the Lord would bring about "something totally new"—that he would cause the earth to open its mouth and swallow up these men with everything that belonged to them.
16:31–35 Moses' predictions were fulfilled: The households were swallowed up, the other people were terrified, and the 250 men who were offering incense were consumed by fire.
16:36–40 God ordered the censers to be removed from the burnt debris and hammered into sheets to overlay the altar as a permanent reminder that none but Aaron's descendants were to act as priests.
16:41–45 The rest of the assembly criticized Moses and Aaron, and God threatened to destroy them all.
16:45–48 Moses and Aaron again acted as intercessors (11:2; 14:13–19; 16:22,45–48; 21:7).
16:49–50 The plague stopped, but only after many had died.

dition to those who had died because of Korah.[z] 50 Then Aaron returned to Moses at the entrance to the Tent of Meeting, for the plague had stopped.

The Budding of Aaron's Staff

17 The LORD said to Moses, 2 "Speak to the Israelites and get twelve staffs from them, one from the leader of each of their ancestral tribes. Write the name of each man on his staff. 3 On the staff of Levi write Aaron's name,[a] for there must be one staff for the head of each ancestral tribe. 4 Place them in the Tent of Meeting in front of the Testimony,[b] where I meet with you.[c] 5 The staff belonging to the man I choose[d] will sprout, and I will rid myself of this constant grumbling against you by the Israelites."

6 So Moses spoke to the Israelites, and their leaders gave him twelve staffs, one for the leader of each of their ancestral tribes, and Aaron's staff was among them. 7 Moses placed the staffs before the LORD in the Tent of the Testimony.[e]

8 The next day Moses entered the Tent of the Testimony and saw that Aaron's staff, which represented the house of Levi, had not only sprouted but had budded, blossomed and produced almonds.[f] 9 Then Moses brought out all the staffs from the LORD's presence to all the Israelites. They looked at them, and each man took his own staff.

10 The LORD said to Moses, "Put back Aaron's staff in front of the Testimony, to be kept as a sign to the rebellious.[g] This will put an end to their grumbling against me, so that they will not die." 11 Moses did just as the LORD commanded him.

12 The Israelites said to Moses, "We will die! We are lost, we are all lost![h] 13 Anyone who even comes near the tabernacle of the LORD will die.[i] Are we all going to die?"

Duties of Priests and Levites

18 The LORD said to Aaron, "You, your sons and your father's family are to bear the responsibility for offenses against the sanctuary,[j] and you and your sons alone are to bear the responsibility for offenses against the priesthood. 2 Bring your fellow Levites from your ancestral tribe to join you and assist you when you and your sons minister[k] before the Tent of the Testimony. 3 They are to be responsible to you and are to perform all the duties of the Tent,[l] but they must not go near the furnishings of the sanctuary or the altar, or both they and you will die.[m] 4 They are to join you and be responsible for the care of the Tent of Meeting—all the work at the Tent—and no one else may come near where you are.

5 "You are to be responsible for the care of the sanctuary and the altar,[n] so that wrath will not fall on the Israelites again. 6 I myself have selected your fellow Levites from among the Israelites as a gift to you,[o] dedicated to the LORD to do the work at the Tent of Meeting. 7 But only you and your sons may serve as priests in connection with everything at the altar and inside the curtain.[p] I am giving you the service of the priesthood as a gift.[q] Anyone else who comes near the sanctuary must be put to death.[r]"

Offerings for Priests and Levites

8 Then the LORD said to Aaron, "I myself have put you in charge of the offerings presented to me; all the holy offerings the Israelites give me I give to you and your sons as your portion and regular share.[s] 9 You are to have the part of the most holy offerings that is kept from the fire. From all the gifts they bring me as most holy offerings, whether

16:49 [z]ver 32
17:3 [a]Nu 1:3
17:4 [b]ver 7 [c]Ex 25:22
17:5 [d]Nu 16:5
17:7 [e]Ex 38:21; Ac 7:44
17:8 [f]Eze 17:24; Heb 9:4
17:10 [g]Dt 9:24
17:12 [h]Isa 6:5
17:13 [i]Nu 1:51
18:1 [j]Ex 28:38
18:2 [k]Nu 3:10
18:3 [l]Nu 1:51 [m]ver 7; Nu 4:15
18:5 [n]Nu 16:46
18:6 [o]Nu 3:9
18:7 [p]Heb 9:3,6 [q]ver 20; Ex 29:9 [r]Nu 3:10
18:8 [s]Lev 6:16; 7:6,31-34,36

■ **17:1—19:22** *Reaffirmation of Aaronic Priesthood.* Having just described another rebellion within Israel that focused not only on Moses, but on Aaron as well, the narrative turns to affirm the importance of Aaron and his sons. These chapters divide into three parts: the budding of Aaron's staff (17:1–13), the division of labor between priests and Levites (18:1–32) and the arrangements for cleansing (19:1–22).

■ **17:1–13** *Aaron's Staff.* Further evidence of Aaron's unique priesthood was given. The head of each tribe was directed to present a staff bearing his name and that of his tribe, with the name of Aaron on the staff of the tribe of Levi.

17:4 in front of the Testimony. Compare verses 8 and 10. This phrase is another designation for "in front of the ark." God had promised that the staff of the man he had chosen would sprout (v. 5). The Lord ordered that Aaron's rod be permanently kept in front of the ark as a lasting witness (vv. 10–11).

17:8 not only sprouted but had budded. This development exceeded what God had indicated would happen (v. 5), demonstrating God's enthusiastic endorsement of the Aaronic priesthood.

17:12–13 Instead of praising God for his power and goodness, the generation that was to die in the desert expressed terror. In context, their terror indicated their absolute need for the ministry of appointed mediators who could come near to God at appointed times.

■ **18:1–32** *Priests and Levites.* This section sets out the rules concerning priests and Levites. As the rebellion of Korah already indicated (16:28–40), only Aaron and his family were to go near the furnishings of the sanctuary or the altar; the other Levites were to be responsible to them and were to do all the work at the Tent of Meeting (vv. 1–7). The males of Aaron's family were to receive the part of the most holy offerings that were kept from the fire (vv. 8–10). All members of his family who were ceremonially clean were to share the wave offerings (cf. 5:25; 6:20; 18:11,18; Ex 29:24–27; Lev 7:30–34; 8:27–29; 9:21; 10:14–15; 14:12,24; 23:11–12, 15,17,20), as well as the firstfruits (vv. 12–13; cf. 28:26; Ex 23:16–19; 34:22–26; Lev 2:12–14; 23:10,17,20; Dt 18:4; 26:10). Further, everything that was "devoted to the LORD" was to be theirs (v. 14). The firstborn of both people and animals belonged to the priests, but they were to redeem every firstborn male (v. 15) at a set price (v. 16). The firstborn of oxen, sheep or goats were not to be redeemed but were to be sacrificed (v. 17) and the meat given to the priests and their families (vv. 18–19).

grain[t] or sin[u] or guilt offerings,[v] that part belongs to you and your sons. 10Eat it as something most holy; every male shall eat it.[w] You must regard it as holy.
11"This also is yours: whatever is set aside from the gifts of all the wave offerings[x] of
the Israelites. I give this to you and your sons and daughters as your regular share. Everyone in your household who is ceremonially clean[y] may eat it.
12"I give you all the finest olive oil and all the finest new wine and grain they give the
LORD as the firstfruits of their harvest.[z] 13All the land's firstfruits that they bring to the
LORD will be yours.[a] Everyone in your household who is ceremonially clean may eat it.
14"Everything in Israel that is devoted[a] to the LORD[b] is yours. 15The first offspring of
every womb, both man and animal, that is offered to the LORD is yours.[c] But you must
redeem[d] every firstborn son and every firstborn male of unclean animals.[e] 16When they
are a month old, you must redeem them at the redemption price set at five shekels[b][f] of
silver, according to the sanctuary shekel,[g] which weighs twenty gerahs.
17"But you must not redeem the firstborn of an ox, a sheep or a goat; they are holy.[h]
Sprinkle their blood[i] on the altar and burn their fat as an offering made by fire, an aroma pleasing to the LORD. 18Their meat is to be yours, just as the breast of the wave offering[j] and the right thigh are yours. 19Whatever is set aside from the holy offerings the Israelites present to the LORD I give to you and your sons and daughters as your regular
share. It is an everlasting covenant of salt[k] before the LORD for both you and your offspring."
20The LORD said to Aaron, "You will have no inheritance in their land, nor will you
have any share among them;[l] I am your share and your inheritance[m] among the Israelites.
21"I give to the Levites all the tithes[n] in Israel as their inheritance[o] in return for the
work they do while serving at the Tent of Meeting. 22From now on the Israelites must not
go near the Tent of Meeting, or they will bear the consequences of their sin and will die.[p]
23It is the Levites who are to do the work at the Tent of Meeting and bear the responsibility for offenses against it. This is a lasting ordinance for the generations to come. They
will receive no inheritance[q] among the Israelites. 24Instead, I give to the Levites as their
inheritance the tithes that the Israelites present as an offering to the LORD. That is why
I said concerning them: 'They will have no inheritance among the Israelites.' "
25The LORD said to Moses, 26"Speak to the Levites and say to them: 'When you receive
from the Israelites the tithe I give you[r] as your inheritance, you must present a tenth of
that tithe as the LORD's offering.[s] 27Your offering will be reckoned to you as grain from
the threshing floor or juice from the winepress. 28In this way you also will present an offering to the LORD from all the tithes[t] you receive from the Israelites. From these tithes
you must give the LORD's portion to Aaron the priest. 29You must present as the LORD's
portion the best and holiest part of everything given to you.'
30"Say to the Levites: 'When you present the best part, it will be reckoned to you as
the product of the threshing floor or the winepress.[u] 31You and your households may eat
the rest of it anywhere, for it is your wages for your work at the Tent of Meeting. 32By presenting the best part[v] of it you will not be guilty in this matter; then you will not defile
the holy offerings[w] of the Israelites, and you will not die.' "

The Water of Cleansing

19 The LORD said to Moses and Aaron: 2"This is a requirement of the law that the
LORD has commanded: Tell the Israelites to bring you a red heifer[x] without defect or blemish[y] and that has never been under a yoke.[z] 3Give it to Eleazar[a] the priest;
it is to be taken outside the camp[b] and slaughtered in his presence. 4Then Eleazar the
priest is to take some of its blood on his finger and sprinkle[c] it seven times toward the

a *14* The Hebrew term refers to the irrevocable giving over of things or persons to the LORD. b *16* That is, about 2 ounces (about 55 grams)

18:9 [t]Lev 2:1 [u]Lev 6:25 [v]Lev 5:15; 7:7
18:10 [w]Lev 6:16
18:11 [x]Ex 29:26 [y]Lev 22:1-16
18:12 [z]Ex 23:19; Ne 10:35
18:13 [a]Ex 22:29; 23:19
18:14 [b]Lev 27:28
18:15 [c]Ex 13:2 [d]Nu 3:46 [e]Ex 13:13
18:16 [f]Lev 27:6 [g]Ex 30:13
18:17 [h]Dt 15:19 [i]Lev 3:2
18:18 [j]Lev 7:30
18:19 [k]Lev 2:13; 2Ch 13:5
18:20 [l]Dt 12:12 [m]Dt 10:9; 14:27; 18:1-2; Jos 13:33; Eze 44:28
18:21 [n]Dt 14:22; Mal 3:8 [o]Lev 27:30-33; Heb 7:5
18:22 [p]Lev 22:9; Nu 1:51
18:23 [q]ver 20
18:26 [r]ver 21 [s]Ne 10:38
18:28 [t]Mal 3:8
18:30 [u]ver 27
18:32 [v]Lev 22:15 [w]Lev 19:8
19:2 [x]Ge 15:9; Heb 9:13 [y]Lev 22:19 25 [z]Dt 21:3; 1Sa 6:7
19:3 [a]Nu 3:4 [b]Lev 4:12, 21; Heb 13:11
19:4 [c]Lev 4:17

18:19 an everlasting covenant of salt. This phrase likely indicates the permanent nature of God's promise: It was based on the apparent indestructibility of coarse salt, which does not burn. The priests (Aaron's descendants) were to have no inheritance in the land (v. 20), nor were the rest of the Levites (vv. 23–24). In place of land, they were to receive the tithes (vv. 21,24), in return for which they were to maintain the Tent of Meeting (v. 22) and its surrounding grounds.
18:25–32 The tithes of the Levites are discussed. The Levites were to give to the priests a tenth of all that they received. The tithes were to be taken from the best and holiest parts (vv. 29–32).
■ **19:1–22** *Arrangements for Cleansing.* Under the direction of Eleazar, the priest, a red heifer that was without defect or blemish (v. 2) was to be taken outside the camp and killed (v. 3). This prefigured the Messiah who would be taken outside the city to be slain as the Sin-bearer (Heb 13:11–13). The priest was to perform a prescribed ceremony (v. 4), and the heifer was to be burned (vv. 5–6; cf. Heb 9:11–13). The priest and the man who burned the heifer were then to bathe and wash their clothes, after which they would remain unclean until evening (vv. 7–8). Then a man who was clean was to gather up the ashes and put them in a ceremonially clean place outside the camp, to be preserved for later use in the water of cleansing (vv. 9–10).

front of the Tent of Meeting. 5 While he watches, the heifer is to be burned—its hide,
flesh, blood and offal.[d] 6 The priest is to take some cedar wood, hyssop[e] and scarlet wool[f]
and throw them onto the burning heifer. 7 After that, the priest must wash his clothes and
bathe himself with water.[g] He may then come into the camp, but he will be ceremonially unclean till evening. 8 The man who burns it must also wash his clothes and bathe
with water, and he too will be unclean till evening.
9 "A man who is clean shall gather up the ashes of the heifer[h] and put them in a ceremonially clean place outside the camp. They shall be kept by the Israelite community
for use in the water of cleansing;[i] it is for purification from sin. 10 The man who gathers
up the ashes of the heifer must also wash his clothes, and he too will be unclean till evening. This will be a lasting ordinance both for the Israelites and for the aliens living
among them.
11 "Whoever touches the dead body[j] of anyone will be unclean for seven days.[k] 12 He
must purify himself with the water on the third day and on the seventh day;[l] then he will
be clean. But if he does not purify himself on the third and seventh days, he will not be
clean. 13 Whoever touches the dead body[m] of anyone and fails to purify himself defiles
the LORD's tabernacle.[n] That person must be cut off from Israel.[o] Because the water of
cleansing has not been sprinkled on him, he is unclean;[p] his uncleanness remains on
him.
14 "This is the law that applies when a person dies in a tent: Anyone who enters the
tent and anyone who is in it will be unclean for seven days, 15 and every open container
without a lid fastened on it will be unclean.
16 "Anyone out in the open who touches someone who has been killed with a sword
or someone who has died a natural death,[q] or anyone who touches a human bone or a
grave,[r] will be unclean for seven days.
17 "For the unclean person, put some ashes[s] from the burned purification offering into
a jar and pour fresh water over them. 18 Then a man who is ceremonially clean is to take
some hyssop,[t] dip it in the water and sprinkle the tent and all the furnishings and the
people who were there. He must also sprinkle anyone who has touched a human bone
or a grave or someone who has been killed or someone who has died a natural death.
19 The man who is clean is to sprinkle the unclean person on the third and seventh days,
and on the seventh day he is to purify him.[u] The person being cleansed must wash his
clothes and bathe with water, and that evening he will be clean. 20 But if a person who
is unclean does not purify himself, he must be cut off from the community, because he
has defiled the sanctuary of the LORD. The water of cleansing has not been sprinkled on
him, and he is unclean. 21 This is a lasting ordinance for them.
"The man who sprinkles the water of cleansing must also wash his clothes, and anyone who touches the water of cleansing will be unclean till evening. 22 Anything that an
unclean[v] person touches becomes unclean, and anyone who touches it becomes unclean till evening."

Water From the Rock

20 In the first month the whole Israelite community arrived at the Desert of Zin,[w]
and they stayed at Kadesh.[x] There Miriam[y] died and was buried.

19:5 [d]Ex 29:14
19:6 [e]ver 18; Ps 51:7 [f]Lev 14:4
19:7 [g]Lev 11:25; 16:26, 28; 22:6
19:9 [h]Heb 9:13 [i]ver 13; Nu 8:7
19:11 [j]Lev 21:1; Nu 5:2 [k]Nu 31:19
19:12 [l]ver 19; Nu 31:19
19:13 [m]Lev 20:3 [n]Lev 15:31; 2Ch 36:14 [o]Lev 7:20; 22:3 [p]Hag 2:13
19:16 [q]Nu 31:19 [r]Mt 23:27
19:17 [s]ver 9
19:18 [t]ver 6
19:19 [u]Eze 36:25; Heb 10:22
19:22 [v]Lev 5:2; Hag 2:13, 14
20:1 [w]Nu 13:21 [x]Nu 33:36 [y]Ex 15:20

19:9 outside the camp. Christ "suffered outside the city gate to make the people holy through his own blood" (Heb 13:12). The ceremonies for cleansing and purification prefigured his death. Anyone who touched a dead body became unclean and had to be sprinkled with the water of cleansing on the third and seventh days (vv. 11–13). Situations that would make a person unclean for seven days were listed (vv. 14–16), and the procedure for cleansing from ceremonial uncleanness was prescribed (vv. 17–21).

19:20 cut off from the community. The exact Hebrew phrase these words translate occurs nowhere else in the Old Testament. But "cut off from Israel" occurs twice (19:13; Ex 12:15); "cut off from his people" six times (9:13; 15:30; Lev 17:10; 20:3,6; 23:29); "cut off from their people" appears in Leviticus 20:5; and "cut off from my people" in Ezekiel 14:8. Compare John 9:34–35. On the meaning of "cut off," see note on Leviticus 7:20. Other circumstances that made one ceremonially unclean until evening are listed in verses 21–22. See New Testament uses of this language in Acts 3:23, Romans 9:3 and 11:22.

■ **20:1—25:18** *The Later Travels.* The narrative moves to the final stages of Israel's journey. The first generation began to recede to the background and the new generation to emerge. These chapters divide into two main sections: transitional incidents as the generations changed (20:1—21:35) and Israel's encounters with the Moabites (22:1—25:18).

■ **20:1—21:35** *Changing Generations.* A number of events took place as Israel moved from Kadesh to Moab. These chapters divide into seven sections: Moses' sin at Meribah (20:1–13), the encounter with the Edomites (20:14–21), the death of Aaron (20:22–29), the defeat of Arad (21:1–3), the bronze snake (21:4–9), travels to Moab (21:10–20) and the defeat of Sihon and Og (21:21–35).

■ **20:1–13** *Moses' Sin at Meribah.* In his exasperation with Israel, Moses failed to honor the holiness of God and was prohibited from entering the promised land.

20:1 the first month. That is, of the fortieth year (cf. vv. 22–29; 33:38). The 40 years of wandering in the desert were nearing their end. Most of those who had been at least 20 years old when they came out of Egypt had died, and it was time for a new generation to begin the next phase of God's plan: entrance into Canaan and conquest of the promised land. **Miriam died.** Moses' sister was a godly woman. When Moses was a baby she had helped in preserving him from destruction (Ex 2:4–10). After the deliverance at the Red Sea, she had led the victory celebration (Ex 15:20–21). Yet chapter 12 reveals her serious sin (v. 1) and the resulting punishment (12:5–15).

2Now there was no water for the community,[z] and the people gathered in opposition[a]
to Moses and Aaron. 3They quarreled[b] with Moses and said, "If only we had died when
our brothers fell dead before the LORD![c] 4Why did you bring the LORD's community into
this desert, that we and our livestock should die here?[d] 5Why did you bring us up out of
Egypt to this terrible place? It has no grain or figs, grapevines or pomegranates.[e] And
there is no water to drink!"
6Moses and Aaron went from the assembly to the entrance to the Tent of Meeting and
fell facedown,[f] and the glory of the LORD[g] appeared to them. 7The LORD said to Moses,
8"Take the staff,[h] and you and your brother Aaron gather the assembly together. Speak
to that rock before their eyes and it will pour out its water.[i] You will bring water out of
the rock for the community so they and their livestock can drink."
9So Moses took the staff from the LORD's presence,[j] just as he commanded him. 10He
and Aaron gathered the assembly together in front of the rock and Moses said to them,
"Listen, you rebels, must we bring you water out of this rock?"[k] 11Then Moses raised his
arm and struck the rock twice with his staff. Water[l] gushed out, and the community and
their livestock drank.
12But the LORD said to Moses and Aaron, "Because you did not trust in me enough to
honor me as holy[m] in the sight of the Israelites, you will not bring this community into
the land I give them."[n]
13These were the waters of Meribah,[a][o] where the Israelites quarreled[p] with the LORD
and where he showed himself holy among them.

Edom Denies Israel Passage

14Moses sent messengers from Kadesh[q] to the king of Edom,[r] saying:
"This is what your brother Israel says: You know[s] about all the hardships that
have come upon us. 15Our forefathers went down into Egypt,[t] and we lived there
many years.[u] The Egyptians mistreated[v] us and our fathers, 16but when we cried
out to the LORD, he heard our cry[w] and sent an angel[x] and brought us out of Egypt.
"Now we are here at Kadesh, a town on the edge of your territory. 17Please let
us pass through your country. We will not go through any field or vineyard, or
drink water from any well. We will travel along the king's highway and not turn
to the right or to the left until we have passed through your territory.[y]"

18But Edom answered:

"You may not pass through here; if you try, we will march out and attack you
with the sword."

19The Israelites replied:

"We will go along the main road, and if we or our livestock[z] drink any of your
water, we will pay for it.[a] We only want to pass through on foot—nothing else."

20Again they answered:

"You may not pass through."

Then Edom came out against them with a large and powerful army. 21Since Edom refused to let them go through their territory, Israel turned away from them.[b]

20:2 [z]Ex 17:1 [a]Nu 16:19
20:3 [b]Ex 17:2 [c]Nu 14:2; 16:31-35
20:4 [d]Ex 14:11; 17:3; Nu 14:3; 16:13
20:5 [e]Nu 16:14
20:6 [f]Nu 14:5 [g]Nu 16:19
20:8 [h]Ex 4:17,20 [i]Ex 17:6; Isa 43:20
20:9 [j]Nu 17:10
20:10 [k]Ps 106:32,33
20:11 [l]Ex 17:6; Dt 8:15; Ps 78:16; Isa 48:2; 1Co 10:4
20:12 [m]Nu 27:14 [n]ver 24; Dt 1:37; 3:27
20:13 [o]Ex 17:7 [p]Dt 33:8; Ps 95:8; 106:32
20:14 [q]Jdg 11:16-17 [r]Dt 2:4 [s]Jos 2:11; 9:9
20:15 [t]Ge 46:6 [u]Ge 15:13; Ex 12:40 [v]Ex 1:11; Dt 26:6
20:16 [w]Ex 2:23; 3:7 [x]Ex 14:19
20:17 [y]Nu 21:22
20:19 [z]Ex 12:38 [a]Dt 2:6, 28
20:21 [b]Dt 2:8; Jdg 11:18

a 13 *Meribah* means *quarreling.*

20:2–5 The people complained again—an echo of previous episodes of grumbling. Compare 16:12–14.
20:2 no water. Water was the greatest need in desert travel (cf. Ge 21:14–19; Ex 17:1–7).
20:9–11 After years of dedicated service and unparalleled patience, Moses fell at the point of his strongest trait—his humility—by (1) speaking in anger; (2) usurping the place of God, asking, "Must we bring you water out of this rock?" (v. 10); and (3) acting violently, striking the rock twice, when God had instructed him only to speak to it.
20:12 Moses and Aaron would not lead the people into the promised land. In part, this punishment demonstrated that even as great a man as Moses could fail at the area of his greatest strength. It also recognized that Moses had completed his great work and soon would turn over the leadership to others.
20:13 Meribah. This name, which means "quarreling," was also used on the first occasion of bringing water from the rock (Ex 17:7). That location was also called "Massah," meaning "testing" (cf. Ps 95:8).
■ **20:14–21** *Troubles With Edom.* Edom showed an unbrotherly attitude toward Israel. The Edomites were descendants of Jacob's brother Esau (Ge 25:25–34; 27:1–42; 28:5–9; 32:3—33:16; 35:29; 36:1–43). Moses made a courteous request of them, asking permission to travel peacefully through their territory, paying for anything the Israelites might need along the way. Since the Israelites were not given this permission and did not want to fight their way through Edomite territory, they could not reach the promised land without first making a long and arduous march through a particularly inhospitable part of the desert. In this way, the encounter with Edom was a humbling experience for the emerging generation of Israelites.
20:14 your brother Israel. In their youth, Jacob (later called Israel; Ge 32:28) and his brother Esau had quarreled, but in their latter years they had been reconciled (Ge 33:9–16; 35:29).

The Death of Aaron

22 The whole Israelite community set out from Kadesh and came to Mount Hor.[c] 23 At
Mount Hor, near the border of Edom,[d] the LORD said to Moses and Aaron, 24 "Aaron will
be gathered to his people.[e] He will not enter the land I give the Israelites, because both
of you rebelled against my command[f] at the waters of Meribah. 25 Get Aaron and his son
Eleazar and take them up Mount Hor.[g] 26 Remove Aaron's garments and put them on his
son Eleazar, for Aaron will be gathered to his people;[h] he will die there."
27 Moses did as the LORD commanded: They went up Mount Hor in the sight of the
whole community. 28 Moses removed Aaron's garments and put them on his son Eleazar.[i]
And Aaron died there[j] on top of the mountain. Then Moses and Eleazar came down from
the mountain, 29 and when the whole community learned that Aaron had died, the entire house of Israel mourned for him[k] thirty days.

Arad Destroyed

21 When the Canaanite king of Arad,[l] who lived in the Negev,[m] heard that Israel
was coming along the road to Atharim, he attacked the Israelites and captured
some of them. 2 Then Israel made this vow to the LORD: "If you will deliver these people
into our hands, we will totally destroy[a] their cities." 3 The LORD listened to Israel's plea
and gave the Canaanites over to them. They completely destroyed them and their towns;
so the place was named Hormah.[b]

The Bronze Snake

4 They traveled from Mount Hor[n] along the route to the Red Sea,[c] to go around
Edom. But the people grew impatient on the way;[o] 5 they spoke against God[p] and against
Moses, and said, "Why have you brought us up out of Egypt to die in the desert?[q] There
is no bread! There is no water! And we detest this miserable food!"[r]
6 Then the LORD sent venomous snakes[s] among them; they bit the people and many
Israelites died.[t] 7 The people came to Moses[u] and said, "We sinned when we spoke
against the LORD and against you. Pray that the LORD[v] will take the snakes away from us."
So Moses prayed[w] for the people.
8 The LORD said to Moses, "Make a snake and put it up on a pole;[x] anyone who is bitten can look at it and live." 9 So Moses made a bronze snake[y] and put it up on a pole.
Then when anyone was bitten by a snake and looked at the bronze snake, he lived.[z]

The Journey to Moab

10 The Israelites moved on and camped at Oboth.[a] 11 Then they set out from Oboth and
camped in Iye Abarim, in the desert that faces Moab[b] toward the sunrise. 12 From there
they moved on and camped in the Zered Valley.[c] 13 They set out from there and camped
alongside the Arnon[d], which is in the desert extending into Amorite territory. The Arnon
is the border of Moab, between Moab and the Amorites. 14 That is why the Book of the
Wars of the LORD says:

> ". . . Waheb in Suphah[d] and the ravines,
> the Arnon 15 and[e] the slopes of the ravines

20:22 [c]Nu 33:37
20:23 [d]Nu 33:37
20:24 [e]Ge 25:8 [f]ver 10
20:25 [g]Nu 33:38
20:26 [h]ver 24
20:28 [i]Ex 29:29 [j]Nu 33:38; Dt 10:6; 32:50
20:29 [k]Dt 34:8
21:1 [l]Nu 33:40; Jos 12:14 [m]Jdg 1:9, 16
21:4 [n]Nu 20:22 [o]Dt 2:8; Jdg 11:18
21:5 [p]Ps 78:19 [q]Nu 14:2, 3 [r]Nu 11:6
21:6 [s]Dt 8:15; Jer 8:17 [t]1Co 10:9
21:7 [u]Ps 78:34; Hos 5:15 [v]Ex 8:8; Ac 8:24 [w]Nu 11:2
21:8 [x]Jn 3:14
21:9 [y]2Ki 18:4 [z]Jn 3:14-15
21:10 [a]Nu 33:43
21:11 [b]Nu 33:44
21:12 [c]Dt 2:13, 14
21:13 [d]Nu 22:36; Jdg 11:13, 18

[a] *2* The Hebrew term refers to the irrevocable giving over of things or persons to the LORD, often by totally destroying them; also in verse 3. [b] *3* *Hormah* means *destruction.* [c] *4* Hebrew *Yam Suph*; that is, Sea of Reeds [d] *14* The meaning of the Hebrew for this phrase is uncertain. [e] *14,15* Or *"I have been given from Suphah and the ravines / of the Arnon* 15 *to*

■ **20:22–29** *Aaron's Death.* First Miriam (v. 1) and now Aaron had died. He, too, was prohibited from entering the promised land. His priestly authority, however, passed to Eleazar.
20:22–29 Aaron died, but the priesthood did not. Eleazar succeeded his father as priest. Moses' original readers were now to transfer all the authority that had been affirmed for Aaron to Eleazar.
■ **21:1–3** *Victory Over Arad.* The Israelites' first victory against the Canaanites was over Arad. This was the first triumph enjoyed by the second generation, which was to be more successful in war than the first. This victory indicates another way the narratives are shifting focus from the adults of the exodus generation to their descendants.
■ **21:4–9** *The Bronze Snake.* The emerging generation began to rebel as the first generation had. God moved swiftly to purify the new army. An Israelite who had been bitten by one of the poisonous snakes could do nothing to save his or her own life, but through the grace of God he or she could be saved from the effect of the deadly venom simply by looking at the uplifted bronze snake. The incident of the bronze serpent provides a vivid illustration of salvation by faith, as alluded to by Jesus in John 3:14–15.
21:7 Moses prayed for the people, as before (11:2; 14:13–19; 16:22, 45–48).
■ **21:10–20** *Blessings on the Way to Moab.* The nation experienced God's blessing as it marched to Pisgah.
21:14 the Book of the Wars of the LORD. This is the only Biblical reference to this book of victory songs that may have been widely circulated in the land of Israel in the years before the Babylonian exile. Perhaps it is another name for the Book of Jashar, which is quoted in Joshua 10:12–13 and 2 Samuel 1:19–27. It may have contained the song mentioned in verses 17–18. The reference to this ancient book that celebrates the Lord's victories may indicate that the nation at this time was full of joy in the blessings of God. **Arnon.** This perennial stream flowed into the Dead Sea from the east, through a deep ravine. It formed the border between the territory of Moab and the kingdom of Sihon (vv. 21–31). References for occurrences of other place names in this section can be found

that lead to the site of Ar[e]
and lie along the border of Moab."

16 From there they continued on to Beer,[f] the well where the LORD said to Moses, "Gather the people together and I will give them water."

17 Then Israel sang this song:[g]

"Spring up, O well!
Sing about it,
18 about the well that the princes dug,
that the nobles of the people sank—
the nobles with scepters and staffs."

Then they went from the desert to Mattanah, 19 from Mattanah to Nahaliel, from Nahaliel to Bamoth, 20 and from Bamoth to the valley in Moab where the top of Pisgah overlooks the wasteland.

Defeat of Sihon and Og

21 Israel sent messengers to say to Sihon[h] king of the Amorites:

22 "Let us pass through your country. We will not turn aside into any field or vineyard, or drink water from any well. We will travel along the king's highway until we have passed through your territory.[i]"

23 But Sihon would not let Israel pass through his territory.[j] He mustered his entire army and marched out into the desert against Israel. When he reached Jahaz,[k] he fought with Israel. 24 Israel, however, put him to the sword[l] and took over his land from the Arnon to the Jabbok, but only as far as the Ammonites,[m] because their border was fortified. 25 Israel captured all the cities of the Amorites[n] and occupied them, including Heshbon and all its surrounding settlements. 26 Heshbon was the city of Sihon[o] king of the Amorites, who had fought against the former king of Moab and had taken from him all his land as far as the Arnon.

27 That is why the poets say:

"Come to Heshbon and let it be rebuilt;
let Sihon's city be restored.

28 "Fire went out from Heshbon,
a blaze from the city of Sihon.[p]
It consumed Ar[q] of Moab,
the citizens of Arnon's heights.[r]
29 Woe to you, O Moab![s]
You are destroyed, O people of Chemosh![t]
He has given up his sons as fugitives[u]
and his daughters as captives[v]
to Sihon king of the Amorites.

30 "But we have overthrown them;
Heshbon is destroyed all the way to Dibon.[w]
We have demolished them as far as Nophah,
which extends to Medeba."

31 So Israel settled in the land of the Amorites.

32 After Moses had sent spies to Jazer,[x] the Israelites captured its surrounding settlements and drove out the Amorites who were there. 33 Then they turned and went up along the road toward Bashan,[y, z] and Og king of Bashan and his whole army marched out to meet them in battle at Edrei.[a]

34 The LORD said to Moses, "Do not be afraid of him, for I have handed him over to you, with his whole army and his land. Do to him what you did to Sihon king of the Amorites, who reigned in Heshbon.[b]"

35 So they struck him down, together with his sons and his whole army, leaving them no survivors. And they took possession of his land.

21:15 [e]ver 28; Dt 2:9,18
21:16 [f]Jdg 9:21
21:17 [g]Ex 15:1
21:21 [h]Dt 1:4; 2:26-27; Jdg 11:19-21
21:22 [i]Nu 20:17
21:23 [j]Nu 20:21 [k]Dt 2:32; Jdg 11:20
21:24 [l]Dt 2:33; Ps 135:10-11; Am 2:9 [m]Dt 2:37
21:25 [n]Nu 13:29; Jdg 10:11; Am 2:10
21:26 [o]Dt 29:7; Ps 135:11
21:28 [p]Jer 48:45 [q]ver 15 [r]Nu 22:41; Isa 15:2
21:29 [s]Isa 25:10; Jer 48:46 [t]Jdg 11:24; 1Ki 11:7,33; 2Ki 23:13; Jer 48:7,46 [u]Isa 15:5 [v]Isa 16:2
21:30 [w]Nu 32:3; Isa 15:2; Jer 48:18,22
21:32 [x]Nu 32:1,3,35; Jer 48:32
21:33 [y]Dt 3:3 [z]Dt 3:4 [a]Dt 1:4; 3:1,10; Jos 13:12,31
21:34 [b]Dt 3:2

---

in connection with the list of stages in Israel's journey (ch. 33).

■ **21:21–35** *Victory Over Sihon and Og.* Moses narrated Israel's conquest of Heshbon and Bashan. Both of these kingdoms were to the east, across the Jordan from Canaan.

Balak Summons Balaam

22 Then the Israelites traveled to the plains of Moab and camped along the Jordan across from Jericho.[a][c]

2 Now Balak son of Zippor[d] saw all that Israel had done to the Amorites, 3 and Moab was terrified because there were so many people. Indeed, Moab was filled with dread[e] because of the Israelites.

4 The Moabites said to the elders of Midian, "This horde is going to lick up everything around us, as an ox licks up the grass of the field."

So Balak son of Zippor, who was king of Moab at that time, 5 sent messengers to summon Balaam son of Beor,[f] who was at Pethor, near the River,[b] in his native land. Balak said:

> "A people has come out of Egypt; they cover the face of the land and have settled next to me. 6 Now come and put a curse[g] on these people, because they are too powerful for me. Perhaps then I will be able to defeat them and drive them out of the country. For I know that those you bless are blessed, and those you curse are cursed."

7 The elders of Moab and Midian left, taking with them the fee for divination.[h] When they came to Balaam, they told him what Balak had said.

8 "Spend the night here," Balaam said to them, "and I will bring you back the answer the LORD gives me.[i]" So the Moabite princes stayed with him.

9 God came to Balaam[j] and asked,[k] "Who are these men with you?"

10 Balaam said to God, "Balak son of Zippor, king of Moab, sent me this message: 11 'A people that has come out of Egypt covers the face of the land. Now come and put a curse on them for me. Perhaps then I will be able to fight them and drive them away.' "

12 But God said to Balaam, "Do not go with them. You must not put a curse on those people, because they are blessed.[l]"

13 The next morning Balaam got up and said to Balak's princes, "Go back to your own country, for the LORD has refused to let me go with you."

14 So the Moabite princes returned to Balak and said, "Balaam refused to come with us."

15 Then Balak sent other princes, more numerous and more distinguished than the first. 16 They came to Balaam and said:

> "This is what Balak son of Zippor says: Do not let anything keep you from coming to me, 17 because I will reward you handsomely[m] and do whatever you say. Come and put a curse[n] on these people for me."

18 But Balaam answered them, "Even if Balak gave me his palace filled with silver and gold, I could not do anything great or small to go beyond the command of the LORD my God.[o] 19 Now stay here tonight as the others did, and I will find out what else the LORD will tell me.[p]"

20 That night God came to Balaam[q] and said, "Since these men have come to summon you, go with them, but do only what I tell you."[r]

[a] *1* Hebrew *Jordan of Jericho*; possibly an ancient name for the Jordan River [b] *5* That is, the Euphrates

22:1 [c]Nu 33:48
22:2 [d]Jdg 11:25
22:3 [e]Ex 15:15
22:5 [f]Dt 23:4; Jos 13:22; 24:9; Ne 13:2; Mic 6:5; 2Pe 2:15
22:6 [g]ver 12,17; Nu 23:7,11,13
22:7 [h]Nu 23:23; 24:1
22:8 [i]ver 19
22:9 [j]Ge 20:3 [k]ver 20
22:12 [l]Ge 12:2; 22:17; Nu 23:20
22:17 [m]ver 37; Nu 24:11 [n]ver 6
22:18 [o]ver 38; Nu 23:12, 26; 24:13; 1Ki 22:14; 2Ch 18:13; Jer 42:4
22:19 [p]ver 8
22:20 [q]Ge 20:3 [r]ver 35, 38; Nu 23:5,12,16, 26; 24:13; 2Ch 18:13

■ **22:1—25:18** *Israel and the Moabites.* This unique series of events is a major signal of the Lord's loving plan for his covenant people. He would keep his promises to the fathers and his covenanted love for their seed. They would be a blessing to the nations, and those nations who threatened this purpose would be cursed. The Lord would not allow the pagan prophet Balaam (22:6) to speak a word against Israel. During the course of his prophecies, the Lord revealed important future plans for the nation, particularly regarding that royal person to come out of Jacob (24:8,17,19). In spite of this, Balaam persuaded the women of Moab to seduce the men of Israel by inviting them to their sacrifices (31:16). This event resulted in the destruction of the last members of that first generation of soldiers who had rebelled against the Lord (26:63–65). In addition, during the course of this narrative, Balaam established himself as a prime example of a false prophet/teacher (2Pe 2:15; Jude 11). These chapters divide into three main parts: the summoning of Balaam (22:1–40), Balaam's prophecies (22:41—24:24) and the aftermath of the Balaam incident (24:25—25:18).

■ **22:1–40** *The Summoning of Balaam.* The king of Moab feared the approaching Israelites and called on Balaam to put a curse on the nation.

22:1 After the conquests of Heshbon (vv. 21–26) and Bashan (vv. 33–35), the Israelites moved back to the area that was across the Jordan from Jericho and north of the territory of Moab.

22:2 When the Moabites saw the great number of Israelites, they were "filled with dread."

22:4–7 Balak, king of Moab, had heard of a man named Balaam, who lived at Pethor, near the Euphrates River, and who had a reputation for having supernatural powers. Balak sent messengers to ask Balaam to come and curse Israel.

22:4 The Moabites made an alliance with the Midianite leaders to oppose Israel (cf. 22:7; 25:6–18; 31:1–12).

22:8–12 Balaam had the emissaries stay overnight so that he might see what message the Lord would give him. God came to him (v. 9) and told him not to put a curse on "those people, because they are blessed" (v. 12).

22:13–18 When the messengers returned to Balak and told him that Balaam had refused to come, Balak sent more distinguished emissaries, promising great rewards to Balaam if he would come and curse Israel.

Balaam's Donkey

21 Balaam got up in the morning, saddled his donkey and went with the princes of Moab.
22 But God was very angry[s] when he went, and the angel of the LORD[t] stood in the road to
oppose him. Balaam was riding on his donkey, and his two servants were with him. 23 When
the donkey saw the angel of the LORD standing in the road with a drawn sword[u] in his hand,
she turned off the road into a field. Balaam beat her[v] to get her back on the road.
24 Then the angel of the LORD stood in a narrow path between two vineyards, with
walls on both sides. 25 When the donkey saw the angel of the LORD, she pressed close to
the wall, crushing Balaam's foot against it. So he beat her again.
26 Then the angel of the LORD moved on ahead and stood in a narrow place where
there was no room to turn, either to the right or to the left. 27 When the donkey saw the
angel of the LORD, she lay down under Balaam, and he was angry[w] and beat her with his
staff. 28 Then the LORD opened the donkey's mouth,[x] and she said to Balaam, "What have
I done to you to make you beat me these three times?[y]"
29 Balaam answered the donkey, "You have made a fool of me! If I had a sword in my
hand, I would kill you right now.[z]"
30 The donkey said to Balaam, "Am I not your own donkey, which you have always ridden, to this day? Have I been in the habit of doing this to you?"
"No," he said.
31 Then the LORD opened Balaam's eyes,[a] and he saw the angel of the LORD standing
in the road with his sword drawn. So he bowed low and fell facedown.
32 The angel of the LORD asked him, "Why have you beaten your donkey these three
times? I have come here to oppose you because your path is a reckless one before me.[a]
33 The donkey saw me and turned away from me these three times. If she had not turned
away, I would certainly have killed you by now,[b] but I would have spared her."
34 Balaam said to the angel of the LORD, "I have sinned.[c] I did not realize you were
standing in the road to oppose me. Now if you are displeased, I will go back."
35 The angel of the LORD said to Balaam, "Go with the men, but speak only what I tell
you." So Balaam went with the princes of Balak.
36 When Balak heard that Balaam was coming, he went out to meet him at the Moabite town on the Arnon[d] border, at the edge of his territory. 37 Balak said to Balaam,
"Did I not send you an urgent summons? Why didn't you come to me? Am I really not
able to reward you?"
38 "Well, I have come to you now," Balaam replied. "But can I say just anything? I must
speak only what God puts in my mouth."[e]
39 Then Balaam went with Balak to Kiriath Huzoth. 40 Balak sacrificed cattle and
sheep,[f] and gave some to Balaam and the princes who were with him. 41 The next morning Balak took Balaam up to Bamoth Baal,[g] and from there he saw part of the people.[h]

Balaam's First Oracle

23 Balaam said, "Build me seven altars here, and prepare seven bulls and seven
rams[i] for me." 2 Balak did as Balaam said, and the two of them offered a bull and
a ram on each altar.[j]
3 Then Balaam said to Balak, "Stay here beside your offering while I go aside. Perhaps
the LORD will come to meet with me.[k] Whatever he reveals to me I will tell you." Then he
went off to a barren height.
4 God met with him,[l] and Balaam said, "I have prepared seven altars, and on each altar I have offered a bull and a ram."
5 The LORD put a message in Balaam's mouth[m] and said, "Go back to Balak and give
him this message."[n]
6 So he went back to him and found him standing beside his offering, with all the
princes of Moab.[o] 7 Then Balaam[p] uttered his oracle:[q]

"Balak brought me from Aram,
the king of Moab from the eastern mountains.

[a] *32* The meaning of the Hebrew for this clause is uncertain.

22:22 [s]Ex 4:14 [t]Ge 16:7; Ex 23:20; Jdg 13:3, 6, 13
22:23 [u]Jos 5:13 [v]ver 25, 27
22:27 [w]Nu 11:1; Jas 1:19
22:28 [x]2Pe 2:16 [y]ver 32
22:29 [z]Dt 25:4; Pr 12:10; 27:23-27; Mt 15:19
22:31 [a]Ge 21:19
22:33 [b]ver 29
22:34 [c]Ge 39:9; Nu 14:40; 1Sa 15:24, 30; 2Sa 12:13; 24:10; Job 33:27; Ps 51:4
22:36 [d]Nu 21:13
22:38 [e]Nu 23:5, 16, 26
22:40 [f]Nu 23:1, 14, 29; Eze 45:23
22:41 [g]Nu 21:28 [h]Nu 23:13
23:1 [i]Nu 22:40
23:2 [j]ver 14, 30
23:3 [k]ver 15
23:4 [l]ver 16
23:5 [m]Dt 18:18; Jer 1:9 [n]Nu 22:20
23:6 [o]ver 17
23:7 [p]Nu 22:5 [q]ver 18; Nu 24:3, 21

22:21–35 In this remarkable account, the Lord took extraordinary steps to strengthen Balaam's resolve to say nothing except what God himself might direct.
■ **22:41—24:24** *Balaam's Prophecies.* Balaam offered prophecies about Israel that proclaimed God's blessing on the nation.
22:41—23:6 Balaam followed rituals that were common in the cultures of that day. Sets of seven were considered complete or wonderfully full. God met with Balaam and instructed him what to say about Israel.
23:7–10 In his first oracle, Balaam declared that he could not curse those whom God had not cursed.

'Come,' he said, 'curse Jacob for me;
come, denounce Israel.'[r]
8 How can I curse
those whom God has not cursed?[s]
How can I denounce
those whom the LORD has not denounced?
9 From the rocky peaks I see them,
from the heights I view them.
I see a people who live apart
and do not consider themselves one of the nations.[t]
10 Who can count the dust of Jacob[u]
or number the fourth part of Israel?
Let me die the death of the righteous,[v]
and may my end be like theirs![w]"

11 Balak said to Balaam, "What have you done to me? I brought you to curse my enemies, but you have done nothing but bless them!"[x]
12 He answered, "Must I not speak what the LORD puts in my mouth?"[y]

Balaam's Second Oracle

13 Then Balak said to him, "Come with me to another place where you can see them; you will see only a part but not all of them. And from there, curse them for me." 14 So he took him to the field of Zophim on the top of Pisgah, and there he built seven altars and offered a bull and a ram on each altar.[z]
15 Balaam said to Balak, "Stay here beside your offering while I meet with him over there."
16 The LORD met with Balaam and put a message in his mouth[a] and said, "Go back to Balak and give him this message."
17 So he went to him and found him standing beside his offering, with the princes of Moab. Balak asked him, "What did the LORD say?"
18 Then he uttered his oracle:

"Arise, Balak, and listen;
hear me, son of Zippor.
19 God is not a man,[b] that he should lie,
nor a son of man, that he should change his mind.[c]
Does he speak and then not act?
Does he promise and not fulfill?
20 I have received a command to bless;
he has blessed,[d] and I cannot change it.[e]

21 "No misfortune is seen in Jacob,[f]
no misery observed in Israel.[a][g]
The LORD their God is with them;[h]
the shout of the King[i] is among them.
22 God brought them out of Egypt;[j]
they have the strength of a wild ox.[k]
23 There is no sorcery against Jacob,
no divination[l] against Israel.
It will now be said of Jacob
and of Israel, 'See what God has done!'
24 The people rise like a lioness;[m]
they rouse themselves like a lion[n]
that does not rest till he devours his prey
and drinks the blood of his victims."

25 Then Balak said to Balaam, "Neither curse them at all nor bless them at all!"
26 Balaam answered, "Did I not tell you I must do whatever the LORD says?"

23:7 [r]Nu 22:6; Dt 23:4
23:8 [s]Nu 22:12
23:9 [t]Ex 33:16; Dt 32:8; 33:28
23:10 [u]Ge 13:16 [v]Ps 116:15; Isa 57:1 [w]Ps 37:37
23:11 [x]Nu 24:10; Ne 13:2
23:12 [y]Nu 22:20, 38
23:14 [z]ver 2
23:16 [a]Nu 22:38
23:19 [b]Isa 55:9; Hos 11:9 [c]1Sa 15:29; Mal 3:6; Tit 1:2; Jas 1:17
23:20 [d]Ge 22:17; Nu 22:12 [e]Isa 43:13
23:21 [f]Ps 32:2, 5; Ro 4:7-8 [g]Isa 40:2; Jer 50:20 [h]Ex 29:45, 46; Ps 145:18 [i]Dt 33:5; Ps 89:15-18
23:22 [j]Nu 24:8 [k]Dt 33:17; Job 39:9
23:23 [l]Nu 24:1; Jos 13:22
23:24 [m]Na 2:11 [n]Ge 49:9

a *21* Or *He has not looked on Jacob's offenses / or on the wrongs found in Israel.*

23:11–17 Just as the prophet Balaam had refused to listen to the word of God coming from the mouth of his donkey, so Balak refused to listen to God's word coming from the mouth of Balaam.
23:18–24 Balaam's second oracle reaffirmed God's determination to bless the Israelites by giving them victory over the Moabites.
23:25–30 At first Balak feared that there would be further blessing for Israel, but then he decided to see whether another viewpoint or additional sacrifices could bring a better answer.

Balaam's Third Oracle

27Then Balak said to Balaam, "Come, let me take you to another place.[o] Perhaps it
will please God to let you curse them for me from there." 28And Balak took Balaam to the
top of Peor,[p] overlooking the wasteland.
29Balaam said, "Build me seven altars here, and prepare seven bulls and seven rams
for me." 30Balak did as Balaam had said, and offered a bull and a ram on each altar.
24 Now when Balaam saw that it pleased the LORD to bless Israel, he did not resort
to sorcery[q] as at other times, but turned his face toward the desert.[r] 2When Balaam looked out and saw Israel encamped tribe by tribe, the Spirit of God came upon
him[s] 3and he uttered his oracle:

"The oracle of Balaam son of Beor,
the oracle of one whose eye sees clearly,
4the oracle of one who hears the words of God,[t]
who sees a vision from the Almighty,[a][u]
who falls prostrate, and whose eyes are opened:

5"How beautiful are your tents, O Jacob,
your dwelling places, O Israel!

6"Like valleys they spread out,
like gardens beside a river,
like aloes[v] planted by the LORD,
like cedars beside the waters.[w]
7Water will flow from their buckets;
their seed will have abundant water.

"Their king will be greater than Agag;[x]
their kingdom will be exalted.[y]

8"God brought them out of Egypt;
they have the strength of a wild ox.
They devour hostile nations
and break their bones in pieces;[z]
with their arrows they pierce them.[a]
9Like a lion they crouch and lie down,
like a lioness[b]—who dares to rouse them?

"May those who bless you be blessed
and those who curse you be cursed!"[c]

10Then Balak's anger burned against Balaam. He struck his hands together[d] and said
to him, "I summoned you to curse my enemies, but you have blessed them[e] these three
times.[f] 11Now leave at once and go home! I said I would reward you handsomely,[g] but
the LORD has kept you from being rewarded."
12Balaam answered Balak, "Did I not tell the messengers you sent me,[h] 13'Even if Balak gave me his palace filled with silver and gold, I could not do anything of my own accord, good or bad, to go beyond the command of the LORD[i]—and I must say only what
the LORD says'?[j] 14Now I am going back to my people, but come, let me warn you of what
this people will do to your people in days to come."[k]

Balaam's Fourth Oracle

15Then he uttered his oracle:

"The oracle of Balaam son of Beor,
the oracle of one whose eye sees clearly,

23:27 [o]ver 13
23:28 [p]Ps 106:28
24:1 [q]Nu 23:23 [r]Nu 23:28
24:2 [s]Nu 11:25, 26; 1Sa 10:10; 19:20; 2Ch 15:1
24:4 [t]Nu 22:20 [u]Ge 15:1
24:6 [v]Ps 45:8 [w]Ps 1:3; 104:16
24:7 [x]2Sa 15:8 [y]2Sa 5:12; 1Ch 14:2; Ps 145:11-13
24:8 [z]Ps 2:9; Jer 50:17 [a]Ps 45:5
24:9 [b]Ge 49:9; Nu 23:24 [c]Ge 12:3
24:10 [d]Eze 21:14 [e]Nu 23:11 [f]Ne 13:2
24:11 [g]Nu 22:17
24:12 [h]Nu 22:18
24:13 [i]Nu 22:18 [j]Nu 22:20
24:14 [k]Ge 49:1; Nu 31:8, 16; Da 2:28; Mic 6:5

[a] 4 Hebrew *Shaddai*; also in verse 16

24:1–9 Balaam's third oracle pictured the blessings that God planned for Israel, ending with a curse from God's words to Abraham (Ge 12:2), and from Isaac's blessing on Jacob (Ge 27:29), regarding those who cursed Israel.
24:7 greater than Agag. In 1 Samuel 15:32–33 there is an account of the death of a king of the Amalekites who bore this name. Perhaps it refers here to a contemporary king of the Amalekites bearing the same personal name. It is also possible that this was a title representing each of many Amalekite kings, just as the title *pharaoh* was used by Egyptian rulers.
24:10–14 Balak, angry at Balaam's inability to curse Israel, denied the prophet his "wages of wickedness" (2Pe 2:15). Balaam replied by affirming his inability to overrule the Lord's word and by introducing his fourth oracle.
24:15–19 In his fourth oracle, Balaam predicted the coming, a few centuries later ("but not near"; v. 17), of David, the great conqueror: "A scepter will rise out of Israel. He will crush the foreheads of Moab . . . Edom will be conquered" (vv. 17–18). The fulfillment of these predictions is found in 2 Samuel 8:2–14, which recounts how David overcame the Moabites and the Edomites. His

16 the oracle of one who hears the words of God,
who has knowledge from the Most High,
who sees a vision from the Almighty,
who falls prostrate, and whose eyes are opened:

17 "I see him, but not now;
I behold him, but not near.[l]
A star will come out of Jacob;[m]
a scepter will rise out of Israel.[n]
He will crush the foreheads of Moab,[o]
the skulls[a] of[b] all the sons of Sheth.[c]
18 Edom[p] will be conquered;
Seir, his enemy, will be conquered,
but Israel will grow strong.
19 A ruler will come out of Jacob[q]
and destroy the survivors of the city."

Balaam's Final Oracles

20 Then Balaam saw Amalek[r] and uttered his oracle:

"Amalek was first among the nations,
but he will come to ruin at last."

21 Then he saw the Kenites[s] and uttered his oracle:

"Your dwelling place is secure,
your nest is set in a rock;
22 yet you Kenites will be destroyed
when Asshur[t] takes you captive."

23 Then he uttered his oracle:

"Ah, who can live when God does this?[d]
24 Ships will come from the shores of Kittim;[u]
they will subdue Asshur and Eber,[v]
but they too will come to ruin."[w]

25 Then Balaam[x] got up and returned home and Balak went his own way.

Moab Seduces Israel

25 While Israel was staying in Shittim,[y] the men began to indulge in sexual immorality[z] with Moabite women,[a] 2 who invited them to the sacrifices[b] to their
gods.[c] The people ate and bowed down before these gods. 3 So Israel joined in worshiping the Baal of Peor.[d] And the LORD's anger burned against them.
4 The LORD said to Moses, "Take all the leaders of these people, kill them and expose
them in broad daylight before the LORD,[e] so that the LORD's fierce anger[f] may turn away
from Israel."
5 So Moses said to Israel's judges, "Each of you must put to death[g] those of your men
who have joined in worshiping the Baal of Peor."
6 Then an Israelite man brought to his family a Midianite woman right before the eyes
of Moses and the whole assembly of Israel while they were weeping at the entrance to
the Tent of Meeting. 7 When Phinehas son of Eleazar, the son of Aaron, the priest, saw

24:17 [l]Rev 1:7 [m]Mt 2:2 [n]Ge 49:10 [o]Nu 21:29; Isa 15:1-16:14
24:18 [p]Am 9:12
24:19 [q]Ge 49:10; Mic 5:2
24:20 [r]Ex 17:14
24:21 [s]Ge 15:19
24:22 [t]Ge 10:22
24:24 [u]Ge 10:4 [v]Ge 10:21 [w]ver 20
24:25 [x]Nu 31:8
25:1 [y]Jos 2:1; Mic 6:5 [z]1Co 10:8; Rev 2:14 [a]Nu 31:16
25:2 [b]Ex 34:15 [c]Ex 20:5; Dt 32:38; 1Co 10:20
25:3 [d]Ps 106:28; Hos 9:10
25:4 [e]Dt 4:3 [f]Dt 13:17
25:5 [g]Ex 32:27

[a] *17* Samaritan Pentateuch (see also Jer. 48:45); the meaning of the word in the Masoretic Text is uncertain. [b] *17* Or possibly *Moab, / batter* [c] *17* Or *all the noisy boasters* [d] *23* Masoretic Text; with a different word division of the Hebrew *A people will gather from the north.*

accomplishments prefigure the greater conquests of Christ over the entire world (e.g., 1Co 15:25–26; Col 2:15; Rev 20:10,14).

24:20–25 In his final oracles, Balaam predicted the downfall of the other nations in the area.

24:22 Asshur. The Assyrians of northern Mesopotamia were already an important military power, but their greatest conquests would be made several centuries later (cf. Isa 36).

24:24 Kittim. Perhaps this was originally a term for Cyprus, but it soon came to represent any area beyond the eastern border of the Mediterranean Sea. In Daniel 11:30, where this word is used in a prediction of the effects of Roman naval power, the NIV translates it as "western coastlands."

■**24:25—25:18** *The Aftermath of the Balaam Incident.* A plague of divine judgment was stopped by the forthright action of Aaron's grandson Phinehas. While the Israelites were staying in Shittim, their worship of false gods was joined with immorality (25:1–3,6). Moses ordered summary capital punishment (25:4–5), but intervention by Phinehas brought the plague to a standstill (25:6–9), and Phinehas was rewarded (25:10–13). The names of the principal people involved were made public (25:14–15), and the Midianites were condemned (25:16–18; cf. ch. 31). Balaam was behind this event (see 31:8,16).

25:1 Shittim. Another name for the region across the Jordan from Jericho (cf. Jos 2:1).

25:6–7 See *WLC* 151.

25:7 Phinehas. As this book has presented a number of times,

this, he left the assembly, took a spear in his hand 8and followed the Israelite into the
tent. He drove the spear through both of them—through the Israelite and into the woman's body. Then the plague against the Israelites was stopped;[h] 9but those who died in
the plague[i] numbered 24,000.[j]
10The LORD said to Moses, 11"Phinehas son of Eleazar, the son of Aaron, the priest, has
turned my anger away from the Israelites;[k] for he was as zealous as I am for my honor[l]
among them, so that in my zeal I did not put an end to them. 12Therefore tell him I am
making my covenant of peace[m] with him. 13He and his descendants will have a covenant
of a lasting priesthood,[n] because he was zealous for the honor of his God and made
atonement[o] for the Israelites."
14The name of the Israelite who was killed with the Midianite woman was Zimri son
of Salu, the leader of a Simeonite family. 15And the name of the Midianite woman who
was put to death was Cozbi[p] daughter of Zur, a tribal chief of a Midianite family.[q]
16The LORD said to Moses, 17"Treat the Midianites[r] as enemies and kill them, 18be-
cause they treated you as enemies when they deceived you in the affair of Peor[s] and their
sister Cozbi, the daughter of a Midianite leader, the woman who was killed when the
plague came as a result of Peor."

The Second Census

26 After the plague the LORD said to Moses and Eleazar son of Aaron, the priest,
2"Take a census[t] of the whole Israelite community by families—all those twenty years old or more who are able to serve in the army[u] of Israel." 3So on the plains of
Moab[v] by the Jordan across from Jericho,[a][w] Moses and Eleazar the priest spoke with
them and said, 4"Take a census of the men twenty years old or more, as the LORD commanded Moses."

These were the Israelites who came out of Egypt:

5The descendants of Reuben, the firstborn son of Israel, were:
through Hanoch,[x] the Hanochite clan;
through Pallu,[y] the Palluite clan;
6through Hezron, the Hezronite clan;
through Carmi, the Carmite clan.
7These were the clans of Reuben; those numbered were 43,730.
8The son of Pallu was Eliab, 9and the sons of Eliab[z] were Nemuel, Dathan and Abiram. The same Dathan and Abiram were the community[a] officials who rebelled against

25:8 [h]Nu 16:46-48; Ps 106:30
25:9 [i]Nu 14:37; 1Co 10:8 [j]Nu 31:16
25:11 [k]Ps 106:30 [l]Ex 20:5; Dt 32:16, 21; Ps 78:58
25:12 [m]Isa 54:10; Eze 34:25; Mal 2:4,5
25:13 [n]Ex 29:9 [o]Nu 16:46
25:15 [p]ver 18 [q]Nu 31:8; Jos 13:21
25:17 [r]Nu 31:1-3
25:18 [s]Nu 31:16
26:2 [t]Ex 30:11-16; 38:25-26; Nu 1:2 [u]Nu 1:3
26:3 [v]Nu 33:48 [w]Nu 22:1
26:5 [x]Ge 46:9 [y]1Ch 5:3
26:9 [z]Nu 16:1 [a]Nu 1:16

a 3 Hebrew *Jordan of Jericho*; possibly an ancient name for the Jordan River; also in verse 63

the priests took a central role in the life of Israel (see note at 13:1—19:22). Here Phinehas halted the plague (v. 8). This passage explicitly connects Phinehas to Aaron through his father Eleazar (see Ex 6:25; cf. 1Ch 6:4; Ezr 7:5).

25:9 24,000. The number who died here exceeds that of all other occurrences of deaths in the wilderness (cf. 16:49). Thus Moses indicated that this was the culmination of the judgment against the first generation.

25:11 See *WLC* 104.

25:12–13 my covenant of peace . . . a covenant of a lasting priesthood. The priesthood was passed from Eleazar to the family of Phinehas as a reward for the younger man's zeal. Phinehas would appear again as a leader of God's people (see 31:6; Jos 22:13–14).

■ **26:1—36:13** *The Preparation of the Second-Generation Army.* The final section of Numbers begins again with the plans for conquest and with a second census of the people for military and inheritance purposes; this time, however, the listing of the clans is included. As in chapter 1, the Levites were not counted. The individual sections take up matters germane to serving the Lord in the land, with peculiar particular stress on the questions of inheritance (chs. 33–34) and holiness. The daughters of Zelophehad, for example, are involved in two questions concerning inheritance. The common thread woven throughout this section is the loss of one's inheritance, either by losing a family name (ch. 26) or by losing the land to another tribe (ch. 36). More laws concerning sacrifices expanded the meaning of Israel's life with God in the land (chs. 28–30). The account of the war against Midian (ch. 31) was concerned more with the handling of the plunder of war in a fashion that preserved the holiness of God and the acceptability of the nation than it was with the curse against Midian for leading Israel astray. Detail of the Transjordan settlement (ch. 32) appears to be included because it involved a major threat to the conquest, as had the original rebellion at Kadesh (ch. 14). God's covenant with Israel still required obedience.

■ **26:1—27:23** *The Count and Continuity of the Generations.* In balance with the opening chapters of the book, this section focuses on the ways in which the second generation was in continuity with the first. These younger Israelites were afforded all the opportunities that God had offered the first generation leaving Egypt. These chapters divide into five main subjects: the new count (26:1–51), the rules of land allotment (26:52–56), the numbers of Levites (26:57–65), an affirmation of tribal continuity (27:1–11) and the new leader of Israel (27:12–23).

■ **26:1–51** *The New Count of the Men of War.* Like the census taken 38 years earlier (ch. 1), this second census counted only males aged 20 or older, those able to serve in the army (v. 2). It records only the total number for each tribe, although in each case it includes the names of the tribe's subdivisions. The tribe of Jacob's eldest son, Reuben, is listed first. Although it had suffered great losses because of the rebellion of Dathan and Abiram (vv. 8–10), it had recovered sufficiently to be almost as numerous as it had been at the time of the first census. Korah (of the tribe of Levi) is mentioned here because of his association with Dathan and Abiram, and it is observed that his line did not die out (v. 11). Simeon is listed next (vv. 12–14); its numbers had declined far more than those of any other tribe (from nearly 60,000 to a little over 22,000), probably an indication that the death of one of its leaders shortly before this census was taken (25:14) was only one of thousands that had resulted from the Midianite seduction (25:1–18). The variations in the numbers of the other tribes are much smaller, with Ephraim showing a rather marked decrease; Gad and Naphtali substantial decreases; Judah, Zebulon and Dan small increases; Issachar and Asher substantial increases; and Manasseh and Benjamin even greater increases. The total number of fighting men was almost identical to that of the earlier census.

Moses and Aaron and were among Korah's followers when they rebelled against the
LORD.[b] 10 The earth opened its mouth and swallowed them along with Korah, whose followers died when the fire devoured the 250 men. And they served as a warning sign.[c]
11 The line of Korah,[d] however, did not die out.[e]

12 The descendants of Simeon by their clans were:
through Nemuel, the Nemuelite clan;
through Jamin,[f] the Jaminite clan;
through Jakin, the Jakinite clan;
13 through Zerah,[g] the Zerahite clan;
through Shaul, the Shaulite clan.
14 These were the clans of Simeon; there were 22,200 men.[h]

15 The descendants of Gad by their clans were:
through Zephon,[i] the Zephonite clan;
through Haggi, the Haggite clan;
through Shuni, the Shunite clan;
16 through Ozni, the Oznite clan;
through Eri, the Erite clan;
17 through Arodi,[a] the Arodite clan;
through Areli, the Arelite clan.
18 These were the clans of Gad;[j] those numbered were 40,500.

19 Er and Onan were sons of Judah, but they died[k] in Canaan.
20 The descendants of Judah by their clans were:
through Shelah,[l] the Shelanite clan;
through Perez, the Perezite clan;
through Zerah, the Zerahite clan.[m]
21 The descendants of Perez were:
through Hezron,[n] the Hezronite clan;
through Hamul, the Hamulite clan.
22 These were the clans of Judah;[o] those numbered were 76,500.

23 The descendants of Issachar by their clans were:
through Tola,[p] the Tolaite clan;
through Puah, the Puite[b] clan;
24 through Jashub,[q] the Jashubite clan;
through Shimron, the Shimronite clan.
25 These were the clans of Issachar;[r] those numbered were 64,300.

26 The descendants of Zebulun by their clans were:
through Sered, the Seredite clan;
through Elon, the Elonite clan;
through Jahleel, the Jahleelite clan.
27 These were the clans of Zebulun;[s] those numbered were 60,500.

28 The descendants of Joseph by their clans through Manasseh and Ephraim were:
29 The descendants of Manasseh:
through Makir,[t] the Makirite clan (Makir was the father of Gilead[u]);
through Gilead, the Gileadite clan.
30 These were the descendants of Gilead:
through Iezer,[v] the Iezerite clan;
through Helek, the Helekite clan;
31 through Asriel, the Asrielite clan;
through Shechem, the Shechemite clan;
32 through Shemida, the Shemidaite clan;
through Hepher, the Hepherite clan.
33 (Zelophehad[w] son of Hepher had no sons; he had only daughters, whose
names were Mahlah, Noah, Hoglah, Milcah and Tirzah.)[x]

26:9 [b]Nu 16:2
26:10 [c]Nu 16:35,38
26:11 [d]Ex 6:24 [e]Nu 16:33; Dt 24:16
26:12 [f]1Ch 4:24
26:13 [g]Ge 46:10
26:14 [h]Nu 1:23
26:15 [i]Ge 46:16
26:18 [j]Nu 1:25; Jos 13:24-28
26:19 [k]Ge 38:2-10; 46:12
26:20 [l]1Ch 2:3 [m]Jos 7:17
26:21 [n]Ru 4:19; 1Ch 2:9
26:22 [o]Nu 1:27
26:23 [p]Ge 46:13; 1Ch 7:1
26:24 [q]Ge 46:13
26:25 [r]Nu 1:29
26:27 [s]Nu 1:31
26:29 [t]Jos 17:1 [u]Jdg 11:1
26:30 [v]Jos 17:2; Jdg 6:11
26:33 [w]Nu 27:1 [x]Nu 36:11

[a] 17 Samaritan Pentateuch and Syriac (see also Gen. 46:16); Masoretic Text *Arod* [b] 23 Samaritan Pentateuch, Septuagint, Vulgate and Syriac (see also 1 Chron. 7:1); Masoretic Text *through Puvah, the Punite*

26:19 Er and Onan. See Genesis 38:1–10.
26:33 Zelophehad . . . had no sons. This fact is mentioned in anticipation of the question of his representation in Israel in future generations. See 27:1–11 and 36:1–12.

34 These were the clans of Manasseh; those numbered were 52,700.[y]

35 These were the descendants of Ephraim by their clans:
through Shuthelah, the Shuthelahite clan;
through Beker, the Bekerite clan;
through Tahan, the Tahanite clan.
36 These were the descendants of Shuthelah:
through Eran, the Eranite clan.
37 These were the clans of Ephraim;[z] those numbered were 32,500.

These were the descendants of Joseph by their clans.

38 The descendants of Benjamin[a] by their clans were:
through Bela, the Belaite clan;
through Ashbel, the Ashbelite clan;
through Ahiram, the Ahiramite clan;
39 through Shupham,[a] the Shuphamite clan;
through Hupham, the Huphamite clan.
40 The descendants of Bela through Ard[b] and Naaman were:
through Ard,[b] the Ardite clan;
through Naaman, the Naamite clan.
41 These were the clans of Benjamin;[c] those numbered were 45,600.

42 These were the descendants of Dan by their clans:
through Shuham,[d] the Shuhamite clan.
These were the clans of Dan: 43 All of them were Shuhamite clans; and those numbered
were 64,400.

44 The descendants of Asher by their clans were:
through Imnah, the Imnite clan;
through Ishvi, the Ishvite clan;
through Beriah, the Beriite clan;
45 and through the descendants of Beriah:
through Heber, the Heberite clan;
through Malkiel, the Malkielite clan.
46 (Asher had a daughter named Serah.)
47 These were the clans of Asher;[e] those numbered were 53,400.

48 The descendants of Naphtali[f] by their clans were:
through Jahzeel, the Jahzeelite clan;
through Guni, the Gunite clan;
49 through Jezer, the Jezerite clan;
through Shillem, the Shillemite clan.
50 These were the clans of Naphtali;[g] those numbered were 45,400.

51 The total number of the men of Israel was 601,730.[h]

52 The LORD said to Moses, 53 "The land is to be allotted to them as an inheritance based
on the number of names.[i] 54 To a larger group give a larger inheritance, and to a smaller group a smaller one; each is to receive its inheritance according to the number[j] of
those listed. 55 Be sure that the land is distributed by lot.[k] What each group inherits will
be according to the names for its ancestral tribe. 56 Each inheritance is to be distributed
by lot among the larger and smaller groups."

57 These were the Levites[l] who were counted by their clans:
through Gershon, the Gershonite clan;

26:34 [y]Nu 1:35
26:37 [z]Nu 1:33
26:38 [a]Ge 46:21; 1Ch 7:6
26:40 [b]Ge 46:21; 1Ch 8:3
26:41 [c]Nu 1:37
26:42 [d]Ge 46:23
26:47 [e]Nu 1:41
26:48 [f]Ge 46:24; 1Ch 7:13
26:50 [g]Nu 1:43
26:51 [h]Ex 12:37; 38:26; Nu 1:46; 11:21
26:53 [i]Jos 11:23; 14:1; Eze 45:8
26:54 [j]Nu 33:54
26:55 [k]Nu 34:14
26:57 [l]Ge 46:11; Ex 6:16-19

a *39* A few manuscripts of the Masoretic Text, Samaritan Pentateuch, Vulgate and Syriac (see also Septuagint); most manuscripts of the Masoretic Text *Shephupham* b *40* Samaritan Pentateuch and Vulgate (see also Septuagint); Masoretic Text does not have *through Ard.*

■ **26:52–56** *Distribution of the Land.* Moses' concern with the second generation turned to the distribution of land in order to assure the original audience that, just as all of the tribes were represented in the new army, all of them would receive their land inheritance. The rules for distribution of the promised land are expounded here: The land was to be divided in proportion to the size of each group, with locations decided by lot.

■ **26:57–65** *The Levites.* The count of the Levites is given. The narrative covers the list of clans (vv. 57–58), the family of Moses and Aaron (vv. 59–61) and the census of Levites over a month old (v. 62). The figure—23,000—may be compared with 22,000 at the earlier census (3:39). Both numbers are extremely small when compared with those of other tribes.

through Kohath, the Kohathite clan;
through Merari, the Merarite clan.

58 These also were Levite clans:
the Libnite clan,
the Hebronite clan,
the Mahlite clan,
the Mushite clan,
the Korahite clan.
(Kohath was the forefather of Amram;[m] 59 the name of Amram's wife was Jochebed,[n] a descendant of Levi, who was born to the Levites[a] in Egypt. To Amram she bore Aaron, Moses[o] and their sister Miriam. 60 Aaron was the father of Nadab and Abihu, Eleazar and Ithamar.[p] 61 But Nadab and Abihu[q] died when they made an offering before the LORD with unauthorized fire.)[r]

62 All the male Levites a month old or more numbered 23,000.[s] They were not counted[t] along with the other Israelites because they received no inheritance[u] among them.[v]

63 These are the ones counted by Moses and Eleazar the priest when they counted the Israelites on the plains of Moab[w] by the Jordan across from Jericho. 64 Not one of them was among those counted[x] by Moses and Aaron the priest when they counted the Israelites in the Desert of Sinai. 65 For the LORD had told those Israelites they would surely die in the desert,[y] and not one of them was left except Caleb son of Jephunneh and Joshua son of Nun.[z]

Zelophehad's Daughters

27 The daughters of Zelophehad[a] son of Hepher,[b] the son of Gilead, the son of Makir,[c] the son of Manasseh, belonged to the clans of Manasseh son of Joseph. The names of the daughters were Mahlah, Noah, Hoglah, Milcah and Tirzah. They approached 2 the entrance to the Tent of Meeting and stood before Moses, Eleazar the priest, the leaders and the whole assembly, and said, 3 "Our father died in the desert.[d] He was not among Korah's followers, who banded together against the LORD,[e] but he died for his own sin and left no sons.[f] 4 Why should our father's name disappear from his clan because he had no son? Give us property among our father's relatives."

5 So Moses brought their case[g] before the LORD[h] 6 and the LORD said to him, 7 "What Zelophehad's daughters are saying is right. You must certainly give them property as an inheritance[i] among their father's relatives and turn their father's inheritance over to them.[j]

8 "Say to the Israelites, 'If a man dies and leaves no son, turn his inheritance over to his daughter. 9 If he has no daughter, give his inheritance to his brothers. 10 If he has no brothers, give his inheritance to his father's brothers. 11 If his father had no brothers, give his inheritance to the nearest relative in his clan, that he may possess it. This is to be a legal requirement[k] for the Israelites, as the LORD commanded Moses.' "

Joshua to Succeed Moses

12 Then the LORD said to Moses, "Go up this mountain in the Abarim range[l] and see the land[m] I have given the Israelites. 13 After you have seen it, you too will be gathered to your people,[n] as your brother Aaron[o] was, 14 for when the community rebelled at the waters in the Desert of Zin, both of you disobeyed my command to honor me as holy[p] before their eyes." (These were the waters of Meribah[q] Kadesh, in the Desert of Zin.)

15 Moses said to the LORD, 16 "May the LORD, the God of the spirits of all mankind,[r] appoint a man over this community 17 to go out and come in before them, one who will lead

26:58 [m]Ex 6:20
26:59 [n]Ex 2:1 [o]Ex 6:20
26:60 [p]Nu 3:2
26:61 [q]Lev 10:1-2 [r]Nu 3:4
26:62 [s]Nu 3:39 [t]Nu 1:47 [u]Nu 18:23 [v]Nu 2:33; Dt 10:9
26:63 [w]ver 3
26:64 [x]Nu 14:29; Dt 2:14-15; Heb 3:17
26:65 [y]Nu 14:28; 1Co 10:5 [z]Jos 14:6-10
27:1 [a]Nu 26:33 [b]Jos 17:2,3 [c]Nu 36:1
27:3 [d]Nu 26:65 [e]Nu 16:2 [f]Nu 26:33
27:5 [g]Ex 18:19 [h]Nu 9:8
27:7 [i]Job 42:15 [j]Jos 17:4
27:11 [k]Nu 35:29
27:12 [l]Nu 33:47; Jer 22:20 [m]Dt 3:23-27; 32:48-52
27:13 [n]Nu 31:2 [o]Nu 20:28
27:14 [p]Nu 20:12 [q]Ex 17:7; Dt 32:51; Ps 106:32
27:16 [r]Nu 16:22

[a] 59 Or *Jochebed, a daughter of Levi, who was born to Levi*

26:63–65 Note that, with the exception of Caleb and Joshua, there were no survivors from the time of the earlier census (cf. 14:30).

■ **27:1–11** *A Problem With Land Inheritance.* The rules for inheritance of the land are set forth in the context of the problem of Zelophehad's daughters (vv. 1–4; cf. 26:33). God's answer (vv. 5–7), along with the general rule of inheritance, is stated (vv. 8–11).

27:1 They approached. In an act of great courage, Zelophehad's daughters sought a determination regarding what would happen to land allotted to fathers who had no sons and who had died in the wilderness (v. 3).

27:11 a legal requirement. Although the case of Zelophehad's daughters was specifically concerned with the circumstances posed by the deaths of so many in the wilderness, its resolution settled similar cases for all generations.

■ **27:12–23** *The New Leader of the Army.* Moses was not permitted to enter the promised land but only to view it from a distance. This was punishment for his failure at Meribah (see note at 20:9–11). Joshua became his successor to lead the newly formed army. God reminded Moses that he would not enter the land (vv. 12–14), and Moses asked him to appoint a successor (vv. 15–17). God ordered that Joshua be commissioned (vv. 18–21), and Moses complied (vv. 22–23). Now the second-generation army was fully constituted.

them out and bring them in, so the LORD's people will not be like sheep without a shepherd."[s]
18 So the LORD said to Moses, "Take Joshua son of Nun, a man in whom is the spirit,[a][t]
and lay your hand on him.[u] 19 Have him stand before Eleazar the priest and the entire assembly and commission him[v] in their presence.[w] 20 Give him some of your authority so
the whole Israelite community will obey him.[x] 21 He is to stand before Eleazar the priest,
who will obtain decisions for him by inquiring[y] of the Urim[z] before the LORD. At his command he and the entire community of the Israelites will go out, and at his command they
will come in."
22 Moses did as the LORD commanded him. He took Joshua and had him stand before
Eleazar the priest and the whole assembly. 23 Then he laid his hands on him and commissioned him, as the LORD instructed through Moses.

Daily Offerings

28 The LORD said to Moses, 2 "Give this command to the Israelites and say to them:
'See that you present to me at the appointed time the food[a] for my offerings
made by fire, as an aroma pleasing to me.' 3 Say to them: 'This is the offering made by fire
that you are to present to the LORD: two lambs a year old without defect, as a regular
burnt offering each day.[b] 4 Prepare one lamb in the morning and the other at twilight,
5 together with a grain offering of a tenth of an ephah[b] of fine flour mixed with a quarter of a hin[c] of oil[c] from pressed olives. 6 This is the regular burnt offering instituted at
Mount Sinai[d] as a pleasing aroma, an offering made to the LORD by fire. 7 The accompanying drink offering[e] is to be a quarter of a hin of fermented drink with each lamb. Pour
out the drink offering to the LORD at the sanctuary.[f] 8 Prepare the second lamb at twilight,
along with the same kind of grain offering and drink offering that you prepare in the
morning. This is an offering made by fire, an aroma pleasing to the LORD.[g]

Sabbath Offerings

9 " 'On the Sabbath[h] day, make an offering of two lambs a year old without defect, together with its drink offering and a grain offering of two-tenths of an ephah[d][i] of fine flour
mixed with oil. 10 This is the burnt offering for every Sabbath, in addition to the regular
burnt offering[j] and its drink offering.

Monthly Offerings

11 " 'On the first of every month,[k] present to the LORD a burnt offering of two young
bulls, one ram and seven male lambs a year old, all without defect.[l] 12 With each bull
there is to be a grain offering[m] of three-tenths of an ephah[e][n] of fine flour mixed with
oil; with the ram, a grain offering of two-tenths of an ephah of fine flour mixed with oil;
13 and with each lamb, a grain offering[o] of a tenth of an ephah of fine flour mixed with
oil. This is for a burnt offering, a pleasing aroma, an offering made to the LORD by fire.
14 With each bull there is to be a drink offering[p] of half a hin[f] of wine; with the ram, a
third of a hin[g]; and with each lamb, a quarter of a hin. This is the monthly burnt offering to be made at each new moon[q] during the year. 15 Besides the regular burnt offering[r] with its drink offering, one male goat is to be presented to the LORD as a sin
offering.[s]

27:17 [s]Dt 31:2; 1Ki 22:17; Eze 34:5; Zec 10:2; Mt 9:36; Mk 6:34
27:18 [t]Ge 41:38; Nu 11:25-29 [u]ver 23; Dt 34:9
27:19 [v]Dt 3:28; 31:14,23 [w]Dt 31:7
27:20 [x]Jos 1:16,17
27:21 [y]Jos 9:14 [z]Ex 28:30
28:2 [a]Lev 3:11
28:3 [b]Ex 29:38
28:5 [c]Lev 2:1; Nu 15:4
28:6 [d]Ex 19:3
28:7 [e]Ex 29:41 [f]Lev 3:7
28:8 [g]Lev 1:9
28:9 [h]Ex 20:10 [i]Lev 23:13
28:10 [j]ver 3
28:11 [k]Nu 10:10 [l]Lev 1:3
28:12 [m]Nu 15:6 [n]Nu 15:9
28:13 [o]Lev 6:14
28:14 [p]Nu 15:7 [q]Ezr 3:5
28:15 [r]ver 3,23,24 [s]Lev 4:3

a *18* Or *Spirit* b *5* That is, probably about 2 quarts (about 2 liters); also in verses 13, 21 and 29 c *5* That is, probably about 1 quart (about 1 liter); also in verses 7 and 14 d *9* That is, probably about 4 quarts (about 4.5 liters); also in verses 12, 20 and 28 e *12* That is, probably about 6 quarts (about 6.5 liters); also in verses 20 and 28 f *14* That is, probably about 2 quarts (about 2 liters) g *14* That is, probably about 1 1/4 quarts (about 1.2 liters)

■ **28:1—31:54** *The Centrality of the Tabernacle Reaffirmed.* The functions, services and personnel of the tabernacle were central to the first-generation army (see note on 5:1—9:14), and Moses reaffirmed their importance for the second generation as well. These materials divide into descriptions of daily (28:1–8), weekly (28:9–10), monthly (28:11–15) and annual offerings (28:16—29:40), as well as a discussion of holy vows (30:1–16). This section closes with a narrative illustrating the importance of tributes to the tabernacle services from plunder gained through holy war (31:1–54).

■ **28:1–8** *Daily Observances.* The regular morning and evening sacrifices are listed. Constant repetition of these sacrifices emphasized the continual need for atonement. Jesus' once-for-all-time sacrifice eliminated forever the need for such daily rituals (Heb 10:11–12).

■ **28:9–10** *Weekly Observances.* Additional sacrifices punctuated the weekly cycle.

■ **28:11–15** *Monthly Observances.* At the beginning of each month much larger and more expensive sacrifices were offered.

■ **28:16—29:40** *Annual Observances.* Rules for the following observances and offerings at special feasts are presented: the Passover (28:16–25; cf. the rules for the associated Feast of Unleavened Bread in Ex 12:14–20; Lev 23:4–8; Dt 16:1–8), the Feast of Weeks (28:26–31; cf. Lev 23:15–22; Dt 16:9–12), the Feast of Trumpets (29:1–6; cf. Lev 23:23–25), the Day of Atonement (29:7–11; cf. Lev 16:2–34; 23:26–32), and the Feast of Tabernacles (29:12–39; cf. Lev 23:33–43; Dt 16:13–17). Since the Feast of Weeks came 50 days after Passover, the Greek-speaking Jews in later times called it "Pentecost," meaning "fifty" (cf. Ac 2:1).

The Passover

16“ ‘On the fourteenth day of the first month the LORD’s Passover[t] is to be held. 17On
the fifteenth day of this month there is to be a festival; for seven days[u] eat bread made
without yeast.[v] 18On the first day hold a sacred assembly and do no regular work.[w] 19Pre-
sent to the LORD an offering made by fire, a burnt offering of two young bulls, one ram
and seven male lambs a year old, all without defect. 20With each bull prepare a grain offering of three-tenths of an ephah[x] of fine flour mixed with oil; with the ram, two-
tenths; 21and with each of the seven lambs, one-tenth. 22Include one male goat as a sin
offering[y] to make atonement for you.[z] 23Prepare these in addition to the regular morning burnt offering. 24In this way prepare the food for the offering made by fire every day
for seven days as an aroma pleasing to the LORD; it is to be prepared in addition to the
regular burnt offering and its drink offering. 25On the seventh day hold a sacred assembly and do no regular work.

Feast of Weeks

26“ ‘On the day of firstfruits,[a] when you present to the LORD an offering of new grain
during the Feast of Weeks,[b] hold a sacred assembly and do no regular work.[c] 27Present
a burnt offering of two young bulls, one ram and seven male lambs a year old as an aroma pleasing to the LORD. 28With each bull there is to be a grain offering of three-tenths
of an ephah of fine flour mixed with oil; with the ram, two-tenths; 29and with each of the
seven lambs, one-tenth.[d] 30Include one male goat to make atonement for you. 31Prepare
these together with their drink offerings, in addition to the regular burnt offering[e] and
its grain offering. Be sure the animals are without defect.

Feast of Trumpets

29 “ ‘On the first day of the seventh month hold a sacred assembly and do no regular work.[f] It is a day for you to sound the trumpets. 2As an aroma pleasing to
the LORD,[g] prepare a burnt offering of one young bull, one ram and seven male lambs a
year old, all without defect.[h] 3With the bull prepare a grain offering of three-tenths of an
ephah[a] of fine flour mixed with oil; with the ram, two-tenths[b]; 4and with each of the sev-
en lambs, one-tenth.[c] 5Include one male goat[i] as a sin offering to make atonement for
you. 6These are in addition to the monthly[j] and daily burnt offerings[k] with their grain
offerings and drink offerings as specified. They are offerings made to the LORD by fire—
a pleasing aroma.

Day of Atonement

7“ ‘On the tenth day of this seventh month hold a sacred assembly. You must deny
yourselves[d] [l] and do no work.[m] 8Present as an aroma pleasing to the LORD a burnt offering of one young bull, one ram and seven male lambs a year old, all without defect. 9With
the bull prepare a grain offering[n] of three-tenths of an ephah of fine flour mixed with oil;
with the ram, two-tenths; 10and with each of the seven lambs, one-tenth.[o] 11Include one
male goat as a sin offering, in addition to the sin offering for atonement and the regular
burnt offering[p] with its grain offering, and their drink offerings.

Feast of Tabernacles

12“ ‘On the fifteenth day of the seventh[q] month,[r] hold a sacred assembly and do no
regular work. Celebrate a festival to the LORD for seven days. 13Present an offering made
by fire as an aroma pleasing to the LORD, a burnt offering of thirteen young bulls, two
rams and fourteen male lambs a year old, all without defect. 14With each of the thirteen
bulls prepare a grain offering[s] of three-tenths of an ephah of fine flour mixed with oil;
with each of the two rams, two-tenths; 15and with each of the fourteen lambs, one-tenth.
16Include one male goat as a sin offering, in addition to the regular burnt offering with
its grain offering and drink offering.[t]
17“ ‘On the second day[u] prepare twelve young bulls, two rams and fourteen male
lambs a year old, all without defect.[v] 18With the bulls, rams and lambs, prepare their
grain offerings[w] and drink offerings[x] according to the number specified.[y] 19Include one
male goat as a sin offering,[z] in addition to the regular burnt offering with its grain offering, and their drink offerings.
20“ ‘On the third day prepare eleven bulls, two rams and fourteen male lambs a year

28:16 [t]Ex 12:6, 18; Lev 23:5; Dt 16:1
28:17 [u]Ex 12:19 [v]Ex 23:15; 34:18; Lev 23:6; Dt 16:3-8
28:18 [w]Ex 12:16; Lev 23:7
28:20 [x]Lev 14:10
28:22 [y]Ro 8:3 [z]Nu 15:28
28:26 [a]Ex 34:22 [b]Ex 23:16 [c]ver 18; Dt 16:10
28:29 [d]ver 13
28:31 [e]ver 3, 19
29:1 [f]Lev 23:24
29:2 [g]Nu 28:2 [h]Nu 28:3
29:5 [i]Nu 28:15
29:6 [j]Nu 28:11 [k]Nu 28:3
29:7 [l]Ac 27:9 [m]Ex 31:15; Lev 16:29; 23:26-32
29:9 [n]ver 3, 18
29:10 [o]Nu 28:13
29:11 [p]Lev 16:3; Nu 28:3
29:12 [q]1Ki 8:2 [r]Lev 23:24
29:14 [s]ver 3
29:16 [t]ver 6
29:17 [u]Lev 23:36 [v]Nu 28:3
29:18 [w]ver 9 [x]Nu 28:7 [y]Nu 15:4-12
29:19 [z]Nu 28:15

[a] 3 That is, probably about 6 quarts (about 6.5 liters); also in verses 9 and 14 [b] 3 That is, probably about 4 quarts (about 4.5 liters); also in verses 9 and 14 [c] 4 That is, probably about 2 quarts (about 2 liters); also in verses 10 and 15 [d] 7 Or *must fast*

old, all without defect.[a] 21 With the bulls, rams and lambs, prepare their grain offerings
and drink offerings according to the number specified.[b] 22 Include one male goat as a sin
offering, in addition to the regular burnt offering with its grain offering and drink offering.
23 " 'On the fourth day prepare ten bulls, two rams and fourteen male lambs a year old,
all without defect. 24 With the bulls, rams and lambs, prepare their grain offerings and
drink offerings according to the number specified. 25 Include one male goat as a sin offering, in addition to the regular burnt offering with its grain offering and drink offering.
26 " 'On the fifth day prepare nine bulls, two rams and fourteen male lambs a year old,
all without defect. 27 With the bulls, rams and lambs, prepare their grain offerings and
drink offerings according to the number specified. 28 Include one male goat as a sin offering, in addition to the regular burnt offering with its grain offering and drink offering.
29 " 'On the sixth day prepare eight bulls, two rams and fourteen male lambs a year
old, all without defect. 30 With the bulls, rams and lambs, prepare their grain offerings
and drink offerings according to the number specified. 31 Include one male goat as a sin
offering, in addition to the regular burnt offering with its grain offering and drink offering.
32 " 'On the seventh day prepare seven bulls, two rams and fourteen male lambs a year
old, all without defect. 33 With the bulls, rams and lambs, prepare their grain offerings
and drink offerings according to the number specified. 34 Include one male goat as a sin
offering, in addition to the regular burnt offering with its grain offering and drink offering.
35 " 'On the eighth day hold an assembly[c] and do no regular work. 36 Present an offering made by fire as an aroma pleasing to the LORD,[d] a burnt offering of one bull, one ram
and seven male lambs a year old,[e] all without defect. 37 With the bull, the ram and the
lambs, prepare their grain offerings and drink offerings according to the number specified. 38 Include one male goat as a sin offering, in addition to the regular burnt offering
with its grain offering and drink offering.
39 " 'In addition to what you vow[f] and your freewill offerings, prepare these for the
LORD at your appointed feasts:[g] your burnt offerings,[h] grain offerings, drink offerings and
fellowship offerings.[a]' "
40 Moses told the Israelites all that the LORD commanded him.

Vows

30 Moses said to the heads of the tribes of Israel:[i] "This is what the LORD commands: 2 When a man makes a vow to the LORD or takes an oath to obligate himself by a pledge, he must not break his word but must do everything he said.[j]
3 "When a young woman still living in her father's house makes a vow to the LORD or
obligates herself by a pledge 4 and her father hears about her vow or pledge but says
nothing to her, then all her vows and every pledge by which she obligated herself will
stand.[k] 5 But if her father forbids her when he hears about it, none of her vows or the
pledges by which she obligated herself will stand; the LORD will release her because her
father has forbidden her.
6 "If she marries after she makes a vow[l] or after her lips utter a rash promise by which
she obligates herself 7 and her husband hears about it but says nothing to her, then her
vows or the pledges by which she obligated herself will stand. 8 But if her husband[m] forbids her when he hears about it, he nullifies the vow that obligates her or the rash promise by which she obligates herself, and the LORD will release her.
9 "Any vow or obligation taken by a widow or divorced woman will be binding on her.
10 "If a woman living with her husband makes a vow or obligates herself by a pledge
under oath 11 and her husband hears about it but says nothing to her and does not forbid her, then all her vows or the pledges by which she obligated herself will stand. 12 But

29:20 [a]ver 17
29:21 [b]ver 18
29:35 [c]Lev 23:36
29:36 [d]Lev 1:9 [e]ver 2
29:39 [f]Nu 6:2 [g]Lev 23:2 [h]Lev 1:3; 1Ch 23:31; 2Ch 31:3
30:1 [i]Nu 1:4
30:2 [j]Dt 23:21-23; Jdg 11:35; Job 22:27; Ps 22:25; 50:14; 116:14; Pr 20:25; Ecc 5:4,5; Jnh 1:16
30:4 [k]ver 7
30:6 [l]Lev 5:4
30:8 [m]Ge 3:16

a 39 Traditionally *peace offerings*

■ **30:1–16** *Rules About Vows.* God gave Israel laws about keeping vows "to the LORD" (v. 2). These regulations appear here because of the role of priests in these affairs. Ordinarily every person was obliged to fulfill any vow or obligation that he or she had made, even including a rash promise (v. 6). This was true whether the person was head of a household (v. 2), a young woman living in her father's house (vv. 3–4), a widow or divorced person (v. 9) or a married woman, regardless of whether the obligation had been assumed before or after she had become a wife (vv. 6–7,10–11,14). If one was a subordinate member of a household and the head of the house heard about the obligation that had been assumed, the head of the house could annul it (vv. 5,8,12–13,15). If the head of the household heard of it but did not cancel it, the person who had made the vow was obligated to fulfill it. In Deuteronomy 23:21–23 Moses urged his people not to make rash vows but declared that if one did make a vow, one was obligated to fulfill it. For a tragic instance of making a rash vow, see Judges 11:30–40 and its notes.
30:5,8,12–13 See *WCF* 22.7.

30:12 [n]Eph 5:22; Col 3:18
31:2 [o]Ge 25:2 [p]Nu 20:26; 27:13
31:3 [q]Jdg 11:36; 1Sa 24:12; 2Sa 4:8; 22:48; Ps 94:1; 149:7
31:6 [r]Nu 14:44 [s]Nu 10:9
31:7 [t]Dt 20:13; Jdg 21:11; 1Ki 11:15,16
31:8 [u]Jos 13:21 [v]Nu 25:15 [w]Jos 13:22
31:10 [x]Ge 25:16; 1Ch 6:54; Ps 69:25; Eze 25:4
31:11 [y]Dt 20:14
31:12 [z]Nu 27:2
31:14 [a]ver 48; Ex 18:21; Dt 1:15

if her husband nullifies them when he hears about them, then none of the vows or pledges that came from her lips will stand.[n] Her husband has nullified them, and the LORD will
release her. 13Her husband may confirm or nullify any vow she makes or any sworn
pledge to deny herself. 14But if her husband says nothing to her about it from day to day,
then he confirms all her vows or the pledges binding on her. He confirms them by saying nothing to her when he hears about them. 15If, however, he nullifies them some time
after he hears about them, then he is responsible for her guilt."
16These are the regulations the LORD gave Moses concerning relationships between
a man and his wife, and between a father and his young daughter still living in his house.

Vengeance on the Midianites

31 The LORD said to Moses, 2"Take vengeance on the Midianites[o] for the Israelites.
After that, you will be gathered to your people.[p]"
3So Moses said to the people, "Arm some of your men to go to war against the Midianites and to carry out the LORD's vengeance[q] on them. 4Send into battle a thousand
men from each of the tribes of Israel." 5So twelve thousand men armed for battle, a thousand from each tribe, were supplied from the clans of Israel. 6Moses sent them into battle, a thousand from each tribe, along with Phinehas son of Eleazar, the priest, who took
with him articles from the sanctuary[r] and the trumpets[s] for signaling.
7They fought against Midian, as the LORD commanded Moses, and killed every man.[t]
8Among their victims were Evi, Rekem, Zur, Hur and Reba[u]—the five kings of Midian.[v]
They also killed Balaam son of Beor with the sword.[w] 9The Israelites captured the Midianite women and children and took all the Midianite herds, flocks and goods as plunder. 10They burned all the towns where the Midianites had settled, as well as all their
camps.[x] 11They took all the plunder and spoils, including the people and animals,[y] 12and
brought the captives, spoils and plunder to Moses and Eleazar the priest and the Israelite assembly[z] at their camp on the plains of Moab, by the Jordan across from Jericho.[a]
13Moses, Eleazar the priest and all the leaders of the community went to meet them
outside the camp. 14Moses was angry with the officers of the army[a]—the commanders
of thousands and commanders of hundreds—who returned from the battle.

a *12* Hebrew *Jordan of Jericho*; possibly an ancient name for the Jordan River

▪ **31:1–54** *Tributes of Holy War.* To close out his focus on the centrality of the tabernacle for the second generation, Moses gave an account of how the plunder of victory over the Midianites was handled.
31:3–6 Twelve thousand men were sent to fight against the Midianites.
31:6 Phinehas . . . articles from the sanctuary and the trumpets. The active role of this heroic priest highlights the focus of this narrative on the priesthood (see 25:6–13). **Eleazar.** Aaron's successor is mentioned 11 times in this narrative to draw attention to the role of the priesthood in this event.
31:7–12 Israel was victorious over Midian and its five kings, killing all its men.
31:8 Balaam. See chapters 22–24.
31:13–18 Moses became angry when the women were spared, for they were an enticement to the men of Israel to sexual immorality and idolatry (cf. 25:1).

Honesty, Oaths, and Vows: Should I Swear?

TRUTH in relationships, especially between and among Christians, is divinely commanded (Eph 4:25; Col 3:9), and truth-telling is specified as integral to authentic godliness (Ps 15:1–3). God forbids lying, deception and malicious misrepresentation (Ex 20:16; Lev 19:11), and Jesus traces lying back to Satan (Jn 8:44). Those who, like Satan, tell untruths in order to deceive and/or damage the reputation of others are condemned in Scripture as being ungodly in a particularly detestable way (Pss 5:9; 12:1–4; 52:2–5; Jer 9:3–6; Rev 22:15). One way of acknowledging the dignity of our neighbor, who like ourselves is God's image-bearer, is to recognize that he or she generally has a right to the truth. Truth-telling, which demonstrates proper respect for facts, for our neighbor and, above all, for God, thus becomes a fundamental element in true religion and in the true expression of love of one's neighbor.

Oaths are solemn declarations that invoke God as a witness of one's statements and promises, inviting punishment for the liar. Scripture approves oath-taking as appropriate on solemn occasions (Ge 24:1–9; Ezr 10:5; Ne 5:12; cf. 2Co 1:23; Heb 6:13–17). At the time of the Reformation, the Anabaptists rejected all oath-taking as part of their repudiation of involvement in the secular world. They appealed to Jesus' condemnation of oaths, failing to recognize that Jesus argued against the abuse of oaths, not against legitimate oath-taking (Mt 5:33–37; cf. Jas 5:12).

Vows to God are the devotional equivalent of oaths and, like oaths, must be treated with the utmost seriousness (Dt 23:21; Ecc 5:4–6). Whatever one swears or vows to do must be done (Ps 15:4; cf. Jos 9:15–19). God requires us not only to take his words seriously, but to take our own seriously as well. Vows must never be used to excuse us from fulfilling the word of God (Mk 7:11). See *WCF* 21.5; 22:1–5; *WLC* 13; *HC* 101.

15"Have you allowed all the women to live?" he asked them. 16"They were the ones who followed Balaam's advice[b] and were the means of turning the Israelites away from the LORD in what happened at Peor,[c] so that a plague struck the LORD's people. 17Now kill all the boys. And kill every woman who has slept with a man,[d] 18but save for yourselves every girl who has never slept with a man.

19"All of you who have killed anyone or touched anyone who was killed[e] must stay outside the camp seven days. On the third and seventh days you must purify yourselves[f] and your captives. 20Purify every garment[g] as well as everything made of leather, goat hair or wood."

21Then Eleazar the priest said to the soldiers who had gone into battle, "This is the requirement of the law that the LORD gave Moses: 22Gold, silver, bronze, iron,[h] tin, lead 23and anything else that can withstand fire must be put through the fire,[i] and then it will be clean. But it must also be purified with the water of cleansing.[j] And whatever cannot withstand fire must be put through that water. 24On the seventh day wash your clothes and you will be clean.[k] Then you may come into the camp."

Dividing the Spoils

25The LORD said to Moses, 26"You and Eleazar the priest and the family heads of the community are to count all the people[l] and animals that were captured. 27Divide[m] the spoils between the soldiers who took part in the battle and the rest of the community. 28From the soldiers who fought in the battle, set apart as tribute for the LORD[n] one out of every five hundred, whether persons, cattle, donkeys, sheep or goats. 29Take this tribute from their half share and give it to Eleazar the priest as the LORD's part. 30From the Israelites' half, select one out of every fifty, whether persons, cattle, donkeys, sheep, goats or other animals. Give them to the Levites, who are responsible for the care of the LORD's tabernacle.[o]" 31So Moses and Eleazar the priest did as the LORD commanded Moses.

32The plunder remaining from the spoils that the soldiers took was 675,000 sheep, 3372,000 cattle, 3461,000 donkeys 35and 32,000 women who had never slept with a man.

36The half share of those who fought in the battle was:

337,500 sheep, 37of which the tribute for the LORD[p] was 675;
38 36,000 cattle, of which the tribute for the LORD was 72;
39 30,500 donkeys, of which the tribute for the LORD was 61;
40 16,000 people, of which the tribute for the LORD was 32.

41Moses gave the tribute to Eleazar the priest as the LORD's part,[q] as the LORD commanded Moses.

42The half belonging to the Israelites, which Moses set apart from that of the fighting men— 43the community's half—was 337,500 sheep, 4436,000 cattle, 4530,500 donkeys 46and 16,000 people. 47From the Israelites' half, Moses selected one out of every fifty persons and animals, as the LORD commanded him, and gave them to the Levites, who were responsible for the care of the LORD's tabernacle.

48Then the officers who were over the units of the army—the commanders of thousands and commanders of hundreds—went to Moses 49and said to him, "Your servants have counted the soldiers under our command, and not one is missing.[r] 50So we have brought as an offering to the LORD the gold articles each of us acquired—armlets, bracelets, signet rings, earrings and necklaces—to make atonement for ourselves[s] before the LORD."

51Moses and Eleazar the priest accepted from them the gold—all the crafted articles. 52All the gold from the commanders of thousands and commanders of hundreds that Moses and Eleazar presented as a gift to the LORD weighed 16,750 shekels.[a] 53Each soldier had taken plunder[t] for himself. 54Moses and Eleazar the priest accepted the gold from

31:16 [b]2Pe 2:15; Rev 2:14 [c]Nu 25:1-9
31:17 [d]Dt 7:2; 20:16-18; Jdg 21:11
31:19 [e]Nu 19:16 [f]Nu 19:12
31:20 [g]Nu 19:19
31:22 [h]Jos 6:19; 22:8
31:23 [i]1Co 3:13 [j]Nu 19:9,17
31:24 [k]Lev 11:25
31:26 [l]Nu 1:19
31:27 [m]Jos 22:8; 1Sa 30:24
31:28 [n]Nu 18:21
31:30 [o]Nu 3:7; 18:3
31:37 [p]ver 38-41
31:41 [q]Nu 5:9; 18:8
31:49 [r]Jer 23:4
31:50 [s]Ex 30:16
31:53 [t]Dt 20:14

[a] *52* That is, about 420 pounds (about 190 kilograms)

31:16 Balaam's advice. Compare Deuteronomy 23:4–5 (see also Jos 13:22; 24:9–10; Ne 13:2; Mic 6:5; 2Pe 2:15; Jude 11; Rev 2:14).
31:19–24 Ceremonial purification of soldiers, captives and property are the central concerns of this event. Moses instructed the second-generation army on the importance of following the cleansing rituals of the tabernacle.
31:25–47 Israel divided the Midianite spoils: Half went to the soldiers and half to the community (vv. 25–27). As a tribute to the Lord, one of every 500 people and animals from the soldier's half and one of every 50 from the community's half were to be given to the Levites (vv. 28–31,41). Enumeration of the portions follows (vv. 32–47). These details point again to the support of the tabernacle as a major focus of this narrative.
31:48–54 To express their joy that no Israelite soldier was missing (v. 49), the commanders of thousands and the commanders of hundreds brought all the gold they had acquired to Moses and Eleazar, who in turn brought it into the Tent of Meeting. Such willing and voluntary commitment to the tabernacle was exemplary, illustrating the devotion that all believers in all ages are to have to the joyful support of God's work.

the commanders of thousands and commanders of hundreds and brought it into the Tent of Meeting as a memorial[u] for the Israelites before the LORD.

The Transjordan Tribes

32 The Reubenites and Gadites, who had very large herds and flocks, saw that the lands of Jazer[v] and Gilead were suitable for livestock.[w] 2 So they came to Moses and Eleazar the priest and to the leaders of the community, and said, 3 "Ataroth,[x] Dibon, Jazer, Nimrah,[y] Heshbon, Elealeh,[z] Sebam, Nebo and Beon[a]— 4 the land the LORD subdued[b] before the people of Israel—are suitable for livestock,[c] and your servants have livestock. 5 If we have found favor in your eyes," they said, "let this land be given to your servants as our possession. Do not make us cross the Jordan."

6 Moses said to the Gadites and Reubenites, "Shall your countrymen go to war while you sit here? 7 Why do you discourage the Israelites from going over into the land the LORD has given them?[d] 8 This is what your fathers did when I sent them from Kadesh Barnea to look over the land.[e] 9 After they went up to the Valley of Eshcol[f] and viewed the land, they discouraged the Israelites from entering the land the LORD had given them. 10 The LORD's anger was aroused[g] that day and he swore this oath: 11 'Because they have not followed me wholeheartedly, not one of the men twenty years old or more[h] who came up out of Egypt will see the land I promised on oath[i] to Abraham, Isaac and Jacob[j]— 12 not one except Caleb son of Jephunneh the Kenizzite and Joshua son of Nun, for they followed the LORD wholeheartedly.'[k] 13 The LORD's anger burned against Israel[l] and he made them wander in the desert forty years, until the whole generation of those who had done evil in his sight was gone.[m]

14 "And here you are, a brood of sinners, standing in the place of your fathers and making the LORD even more angry with Israel.[n] 15 If you turn away from following him, he will again leave all this people in the desert, and you will be the cause of their destruction.[o]"

16 Then they came up to him and said, "We would like to build pens here for our livestock[p] and cities for our women and children. 17 But we are ready to arm ourselves and go ahead of the Israelites[q] until we have brought them to their place.[r] Meanwhile our women and children will live in fortified cities, for protection from the inhabitants of the land. 18 We will not return to our homes until every Israelite has received his inheritance.[s] 19 We will not receive any inheritance with them on the other side of the Jordan, because our inheritance has come to us on the east side of the Jordan."[t]

20 Then Moses said to them, "If you will do this—if you will arm yourselves before the LORD for battle,[u] 21 and if all of you will go armed over the Jordan before the LORD until he has driven his enemies out before him— 22 then when the land is subdued before the LORD, you may return[v] and be free from your obligation to the LORD and to Israel. And this land will be your possession before the LORD.[w]

23 "But if you fail to do this, you will be sinning against the LORD; and you may be sure that your sin will find you out.[x] 24 Build cities for your women and children, and pens for your flocks,[y] but do what you have promised.[z]"

25 The Gadites and Reubenites said to Moses, "We your servants will do as our lord commands. 26 Our children and wives, our flocks and herds will remain here in the cities of Gilead.[a] 27 But your servants, every man armed for battle, will cross over to fight before the LORD, just as our lord says."

28 Then Moses gave orders about them[b] to Eleazar the priest and Joshua son of Nun and to the family heads of the Israelite tribes. 29 He said to them, "If the Gadites and Reubenites, every man armed for battle, cross over the Jordan with you before the LORD, then when the land is subdued before you, give them the land of Gilead as their possession.

31:54 [u]Ex 28:12
32:1 [v]Nu 21:32 [w]Ex 12:38
32:3 [x]ver 34 [y]ver 36 [z]ver 37; Isa 15:4; 16:9; Jer 48:34 [a]ver 38; Jos 13:17; Eze 25:9
32:4 [b]Nu 21:34 [c]Ex 12:38
32:7 [d]Nu 13:27-14:4
32:8 [e]Nu 13:3,26; Dt 1:19-25
32:9 [f]Nu 13:23; Dt 1:24
32:10 [g]Nu 11:1
32:11 [h]Ex 30:14 [i]Nu 14:23 [j]Nu 14:28-30
32:12 [k]Nu 14:24,30; Dt 1:36; Ps 63:8
32:13 [l]Ex 4:14 [m]Nu 14:28-35; 26:64,65
32:14 [n]ver 10; Dt 1:34; Ps 78:59
32:15 [o]Dt 30:17-18; 2Ch 7:20
32:16 [p]Ex 12:38; Dt 3:19
32:17 [q]Jos 4:12,13 [r]Nu 22:4; Dt 3:20
32:18 [s]Jos 22:1-4
32:19 [t]Jos 12:1
32:20 [u]Dt 3:18
32:22 [v]Jos 22:4 [w]Dt 3:18-20
32:23 [x]Ge 4:7; 44:16; Isa 59:12
32:24 [y]ver 1,16 [z]Nu 30:2
32:26 [a]Jos 1:14
32:28 [b]Dt 3:18-20; Jos 1:13

■ **32:1—36:13** *Looking Ahead to the Conquest.* This last section of the book turns to the future challenges of the second-generation army. After establishing the hopeful note that the second generation did not shrink from conquest as the first generation had (32:1–42), Moses summarized how Israel's journey had brought the nation to the point of being called to enter Canaan (33:1–56). Discussion ensued regarding the boundaries of the land (34:1–15), the authorities to distribute the land (34:16–29), cities of refuge (35:1–34) and an additional matter concerning tribal inheritances (36:1–13).

■ **32:1–42** *The Transjordan Controversy.* The tribes of Reuben and Gad, possessors of much livestock, requested permission to settle in territory in the Transjordan that had already been conquered (vv. 1–5; cf. 21:24–26,31–35). At the heart of this narrative is the connection Moses made between this desire to settle in Transjordan and the sin of the spies (vv. 6–15). Moses warned those involved that similar unbelief would suffer the same consequences. The men wishing to settle in Transjordan offered to leave their wives and children in fortified cities while they themselves took part in entering and conquering Canaan, and they promised to do this without asking that they be given any part of the land west of the Jordan (vv. 16–19). Moses accepted the offer but declared that if they did not keep their promise, their sin would find them out (vv. 20–24). This agreement was reiterated and accepted by both parties (vv. 25–33). As a result, all 12 tribes of Israel were ready to begin the conquest of the land.

30 But if they do not cross over with you armed, they must accept their possession with
you in Canaan."
31 The Gadites and Reubenites answered, "Your servants will do what the LORD has
said.[c] 32 We will cross over before the LORD into Canaan armed, but the property we inherit will be on this side of the Jordan."
33 Then Moses gave to the Gadites,[d] the Reubenites and the half-tribe of Manasseh
son of Joseph the kingdom of Sihon king of the Amorites[e] and the kingdom of Og king
of Bashan—the whole land with its cities and the territory around them.[f]
34 The Gadites built up Dibon, Ataroth, Aroer,[g] 35 Atroth Shophan, Jazer,[h] Jogbehah,
36 Beth Nimrah[i] and Beth Haran as fortified cities, and built pens for their flocks. 37 And
the Reubenites rebuilt Heshbon, Elealeh and Kiriathaim, 38 as well as Nebo[j] and Baal
Meon (these names were changed) and Sibmah. They gave names to the cities they rebuilt.
39 The descendants of Makir[k] son of Manasseh went to Gilead, captured it and drove
out the Amorites who were there. 40 So Moses gave Gilead to the Makirites,[l] the descendants of Manasseh, and they settled there. 41 Jair, a descendant of Manasseh, captured
their settlements and called them Havvoth Jair.[a][m] 42 And Nobah captured Kenath and its
surrounding settlements and called it Nobah after himself.[n]

Stages in Israel's Journey

33 Here are the stages in the journey of the Israelites when they came out of
Egypt[o] by divisions under the leadership of Moses and Aaron.[p] 2 At the LORD's
command Moses recorded the stages in their journey. This is their journey by stages:

3 The Israelites set out from Rameses on the fifteenth day of the first month, the
day after the Passover.[q] They marched out boldly[r] in full view of all the Egyptians,
4 who were burying all their firstborn, whom the LORD had struck down among
them; for the LORD had brought judgment on their gods.[s]
5 The Israelites left Rameses and camped at Succoth.[t]
6 They left Succoth and camped at Etham, on the edge of the desert.[u]
7 They left Etham, turned back to Pi Hahiroth, to the east of Baal Zephon,[v] and
camped near Migdol.[w]
8 They left Pi Hahiroth[b] and passed through the sea[x] into the desert, and when
they had traveled for three days in the Desert of Etham, they camped at Marah.[y]
9 They left Marah and went to Elim, where there were twelve springs and seventy palm trees, and they camped[z] there.
10 They left Elim and camped by the Red Sea.[c]
11 They left the Red Sea and camped in the Desert of Sin.[a]
12 They left the Desert of Sin and camped at Dophkah.
13 They left Dophkah and camped at Alush.
14 They left Alush and camped at Rephidim, where there was no water for the
people to drink.
15 They left Rephidim[b] and camped in the Desert of Sinai.[c]
16 They left the Desert of Sinai and camped at Kibroth Hattaavah.[d]
17 They left Kibroth Hattaavah and camped at Hazeroth.[e]
18 They left Hazeroth and camped at Rithmah.
19 They left Rithmah and camped at Rimmon Perez.
20 They left Rimmon Perez and camped at Libnah.[f]

[a] *41* Or *them the settlements of Jair* [b] *8* Many manuscripts of the Masoretic Text, Samaritan Pentateuch and Vulgate; most manuscripts of the Masoretic Text *left from before Hahiroth* [c] *10* Hebrew *Yam Suph*; that is, Sea of Reeds; also in verse 11

32:31 [c]ver 29
32:33 [d]Jos 13:24-28; 1Sa 13:7 [e]Dt 2:26 [f]Nu 21:24; Jos 12:6
32:34 [g]Dt 2:36; Jdg 11:26
32:35 [h]ver 3
32:36 [i]ver 3
32:38 [j]ver 3; Isa 15:2; Jer 48:1,22
32:39 [k]Ge 50:23
32:40 [l]Dt 3:15; Jos 17:1
32:41 [m]Dt 3:14; Jos 13:30; Jdg 10:4; 1Ch 2:23
32:42 [n]2Sa 18:18; Ps 49:11
33:1 [o]Mic 6:4 [p]Ps 77:20
33:3 [q]Ex 13:4 [r]Ex 14:8
33:4 [s]Ex 12:12
33:5 [t]Ex 12:37
33:6 [u]Ex 13:20
33:7 [v]Ex 14:9 [w]Ex 14:2
33:8 [x]Ex 14:22 [y]Ex 15:23
33:9 [z]Ex 15:27
33:11 [a]Ex 16:1
33:15 [b]Ex 17:1 [c]Ex 19:1
33:16 [d]Nu 11:34
33:17 [e]Nu 11:35
33:20 [f]Jos 10:29

32:33 the half-tribe of Manasseh. It seems that many from this tribe joined the Reubenites and Gadites in wishing to live east of the Jordan. During the time in the wilderness, the number of men in the tribe of Manasseh able to go to war had increased from 32,200 to 52,700 (cf. 1:35 and 26:34). Reuben and Gad settled territory already conquered (vv. 33–38), but the half-tribe of Manasseh went farther north and made new conquests (vv. 39–42).

■ **33:1–56** *Israel's Travels and Call to Conquest.* Moses reviewed the stages of the Israelites' journey from Egypt to Abel Shittim. Then he issued the call to enter and take possession of Canaan.

33:3–4 These verses provide a vivid summary of the manner in which the Israelites had left Egypt.

33:4 all their firstborn. See Exodus 12:29–33.

33:5–48 Many of the names in this list may represent desert camps that have since disappeared.

33:5 Rameses. See Genesis 47:11 and Exodus 12:37. **Succoth.** See Exodus 12:37 and 13:20.

33:6 Etham. See Exodus 13:20.

33:7 Pi Hahiroth. See Exodus 14:2.

33:8 Marah. See Exodus 15:23.

33:9 Elim. See Exodus 15:27—16:1.

33:11 Desert of Sin. See Exodus 16:1—17:1.

33:14 Rephidim. See Exodus 17:1—19:2.

33:16 Kibroth Hattaavah. See 11:34–35 and Deuteronomy 9:22.

33:17 Hazeroth. See 11:35 and 12:16.

21They left Libnah and camped at Rissah.
22They left Rissah and camped at Kehelathah.
23They left Kehelathah and camped at Mount Shepher.
24They left Mount Shepher and camped at Haradah.
25They left Haradah and camped at Makheloth.
26They left Makheloth and camped at Tahath.
27They left Tahath and camped at Terah.
28They left Terah and camped at Mithcah.
29They left Mithcah and camped at Hashmonah.
30They left Hashmonah and camped at Moseroth.[g]
31They left Moseroth and camped at Bene Jaakan.
32They left Bene Jaakan and camped at Hor Haggidgad.
33They left Hor Haggidgad and camped at Jotbathah.[h]
34They left Jotbathah and camped at Abronah.
35They left Abronah and camped at Ezion Geber.[i]
36They left Ezion Geber and camped at Kadesh, in the Desert of Zin.[j]
37They left Kadesh and camped at Mount Hor,[k] on the border of Edom.[l] 38At the
LORD's command Aaron the priest went up Mount Hor, where he died[m] on the first
day of the fifth month of the fortieth year after the Israelites came out of Egypt.[n]
39Aaron was a hundred and twenty-three years old when he died on Mount Hor.
40The Canaanite king of Arad,[o] who lived in the Negev of Canaan, heard that
the Israelites were coming.
41They left Mount Hor and camped at Zalmonah.
42They left Zalmonah and camped at Punon.
43They left Punon and camped at Oboth.[p]
44They left Oboth and camped at Iye Abarim, on the border of Moab.[q]
45They left Iyim[a] and camped at Dibon Gad.
46They left Dibon Gad and camped at Almon Diblathaim.
47They left Almon Diblathaim and camped in the mountains of Abarim,[r] near
Nebo.
48They left the mountains of Abarim and camped on the plains of Moab by the
Jordan across from Jericho.[b] [s] 49There on the plains of Moab they camped along the
Jordan from Beth Jeshimoth to Abel Shittim.[t]

50On the plains of Moab by the Jordan across from Jericho the LORD said to Moses,
51"Speak to the Israelites and say to them: 'When you cross the Jordan into Canaan,[u]
52drive out all the inhabitants of the land before you. Destroy all their carved images and
their cast idols, and demolish all their high places.[v] 53Take possession of the land and
settle in it, for I have given you the land to possess.[w] 54Distribute the land by lot, according to your clans.[x] To a larger group give a larger inheritance, and to a smaller group a
smaller one. Whatever falls to them by lot will be theirs. Distribute it according to your
ancestral tribes.
55" 'But if you do not drive out the inhabitants of the land, those you allow to remain
will become barbs in your eyes and thorns[y] in your sides. They will give you trouble in
the land where you will live. 56And then I will do to you what I plan to do to them.' "

Boundaries of Canaan

34 The LORD said to Moses, 2"Command the Israelites and say to them: 'When you
enter Canaan, the land that will be allotted to you as an inheritance[z] will have
these boundaries:[a]

33:30 [g]Dt 10:6
33:33 [h]Dt 10:7
33:35 [i]Dt 2:8; 1Ki 9:26; 22:48
33:36 [j]Nu 20:1
33:37 [k]Nu 20:22 [l]Nu 20:16; 21:4
33:38 [m]Dt 10:6 [n]Nu 20:25-28
33:40 [o]Nu 21:1
33:43 [p]Nu 21:10
33:44 [q]Nu 21:11
33:47 [r]Nu 27:12
33:48 [s]Nu 22:1
33:49 [t]Nu 25:1
33:51 [u]Jos 3:17
33:52 [v]Ex 23:24; 34:13; Lev 26:1; Dt 7:2,5; 12:3; Jos 11:12; Ps 106:34-36
33:53 [w]Dt 11:31; Jos 21:43
33:54 [x]Nu 26:54
33:55 [y]Jos 23:13; Jdg 2:3; Ps 106:36
34:2 [z]Ge 17:8; Dt 1:7-8; Ps 78:54-55 [a]Eze 47:15

a *45* That is, Iye Abarim b *48* Hebrew *Jordan of Jericho*; possibly an ancient name for the Jordan River; also in verse 50

33:30 Moseroth. See Deuteronomy 10:6.
33:31 Bene Jaakan. See Deuteronomy 10:6.
33:33 Jotbathah. See Deuteronomy 30:7.
33:35 Ezion Geber. See Deuteronomy 2:8 (see also 1Ki 9:26; 22:48; 2Ch 8:17; 20:36).
33:36 Desert of Zin. See 13:21.
33:37 Mount Hor. See 20:22–28.
33:40 Arad. See 21:1. **Negev.** See 21:1 and Genesis 12:9.
33:43 Oboth. See 21:10–11.
33:44 Iye Abarim. See 27:12.
33:50–56. Moses called upon the Israelites to take the land of Canaan, to drive out all its inhabitants and to utterly destroy all vestiges of their idolatrous worship.
33:52 drive out all the inhabitants. God ordered the complete extermination of the Canaanites and the destruction of all symbols of idolatry, as had been done in the case of the Midianites (ch. 31).
33:53 settle in it. God set forth rules for settlement, summarizing the earlier directives in 26:52–56.
33:55 if you do not. The terrible results of disobedience are predicted (vv. 55–56). Sadly, the Israelites did not fulfill Moses' command, and his warning proved valid.
■**34:1–15** *The Boundaries of the Land.* These boundaries of Israel's inheritance demonstrate how much God had given to his people and how much area they had to enter and possess.

3" 'Your southern side will include some of the Desert of Zin[b] along the border of
Edom. On the east, your southern boundary will start from the end of the Salt Sea,[a][c]
4cross south of Scorpion[b] Pass,[d] continue on to Zin and go south of Kadesh Barnea.[e]
Then it will go to Hazar Addar and over to Azmon, 5where it will turn, join the Wadi of
Egypt[f] and end at the Sea.[c]
6" 'Your western boundary will be the coast of the Great Sea. This will be your
boundary on the west.
7" 'For your northern boundary,[g] run a line from the Great Sea to Mount Hor 8and
from Mount Hor to Lebo[d] Hamath.[h] Then the boundary will go to Zedad, 9continue to
Ziphron and end at Hazar Enan. This will be your boundary on the north.
10" 'For your eastern boundary, run a line from Hazar Enan to Shepham. 11The
boundary will go down from Shepham to Riblah[i] on the east side of Ain and continue
along the slopes east of the Sea of Kinnereth.[e][j] 12Then the boundary will go down along
the Jordan and end at the Salt Sea.
" 'This will be your land, with its boundaries on every side.' "
13Moses commanded the Israelites: "Assign this land by lot as an inheritance.[k] The
LORD has ordered that it be given to the nine and a half tribes, 14because the families of
the tribe of Reuben, the tribe of Gad and the half-tribe of Manasseh have received their
inheritance.[l] 15These two and a half tribes have received their inheritance on the east
side of the Jordan of Jericho,[f] toward the sunrise."
16The LORD said to Moses, 17"These are the names of the men who are to assign the
land for you as an inheritance: Eleazar the priest and Joshua[m] son of Nun. 18And appoint
one leader from each tribe to help[n] assign the land. 19These are their names:

Caleb[o] son of Jephunneh,
from the tribe of Judah;[p]
20 Shemuel son of Ammihud,
from the tribe of Simeon;[q]
21 Elidad son of Kislon,
from the tribe of Benjamin;[r]
22 Bukki son of Jogli,
the leader from the tribe of Dan;
23 Hanniel son of Ephod,
the leader from the tribe of Manasseh son of Joseph;
24 Kemuel son of Shiphtan,
the leader from the tribe of Ephraim son of Joseph;
25 Elizaphan son of Parnach,
the leader from the tribe of Zebulun;
26 Paltiel son of Azzan,
the leader from the tribe of Issachar;
27 Ahihud son of Shelomi,
the leader from the tribe of Asher;[s]
28 Pedahel son of Ammihud,
the leader from the tribe of Naphtali."

29These are the men the LORD commanded to assign the inheritance to the Israelites
in the land of Canaan.

Towns for the Levites

35 On the plains of Moab by the Jordan across from Jericho,[g] the LORD said to Moses,
2"Command the Israelites to give the Levites towns to live in[t] from the inheritance
the Israelites will possess. And give them pasturelands around the towns. 3Then they will
have towns to live in and pasturelands for their cattle, flocks and all their other livestock.

34:3 [b]Jos 15:1-3 [c]Ge 14:3
34:4 [d]Jos 15:3 [e]Nu 32:8
34:5 [f]Ge 15:18; Jos 15:4
34:7 [g]Eze 47:15-17
34:8 [h]Nu 13:21; Jos 13:5
34:11 [i]2Ki 23:33; Jer 39:5 [j]Dt 3:17; Jos 11:2; 13:27
34:13 [k]Jos 14:1-5
34:14 [l]Nu 32:33; Jos 14:3
34:17 [m]Jos 14:1
34:18 [n]Nu 1:4, 16
34:19 [o]Nu 26:65 [p]Ge 29:35; Dt 33:7
34:20 [q]Ge 49:5
34:21 [r]Ge 49:27; Ps 68:27
34:27 [s]Nu 1:40
35:2 [t]Lev 25:32-34; Jos 14:3, 4

[a] *3* That is, the Dead Sea; also in verse 12 [b] *4* Hebrew *Akrabbim* [c] *5* That is, the Mediterranean; also in verses 6 and 7 [d] *8* Or *to the entrance to* [e] *11* That is, Galilee [f] *15* *Jordan of Jericho* was possibly an ancient name for the Jordan River. [g] *1* Hebrew *Jordan of Jericho*; possibly an ancient name for the Jordan River

34:13–15 The territory already assigned in Transjordan is included with the other boundaries (see ch. 32).

■ **34:16–29** *The Distributors of the Land.* The Lord designated men to assign the portions of the land of Canaan: Eleazar the priest (20:25–26) and Joshua the commander (27:18–23) were to be in charge, together with a leader from each of the ten tribes that had not yet been given their inheritance. None of these ten names is included in earlier lists of leaders (1:5–15; 2:3–29; 7:12–78), nor is any one of them the son of a man included in those lists. This list of leaders provided Moses' original audience with an authoritative way of determining who would receive what portion of land.

■ **35:1–34** *Levite Towns and Cities of Refuge.* The Levites were to be assigned 48 towns, along with surrounding pasture land, including six "cities of refuge." They did not possess a tribal land (1:47–53) but were spread throughout the tribal territories.

4 "The pasturelands around the towns that you give the Levites will extend out fifteen hundred feet[a] from the town wall. 5 Outside the town, measure three thousand feet[b] on the east side, three thousand on the south side, three thousand on the west and three thousand on the north, with the town in the center. They will have this area as pastureland for the towns.

Cities of Refuge

6 "Six of the towns you give the Levites will be cities of refuge, to which a person who has killed someone may flee.[u] In addition, give them forty-two other towns. 7 In all you must give the Levites forty-eight towns, together with their pasturelands. 8 The towns you give the Levites from the land the Israelites possess are to be given in proportion to the inheritance of each tribe: Take many towns from a tribe that has many, but few from one that has few."[v]

9 Then the LORD said to Moses: 10 "Speak to the Israelites and say to them: 'When you cross the Jordan into Canaan,[w] 11 select some towns to be your cities of refuge, to which a person who has killed someone[x] accidentally[y] may flee. 12 They will be places of refuge from the avenger,[z] so that a person accused of murder may not die before he stands trial before the assembly. 13 These six towns you give will be your cities of refuge. 14 Give three on this side of the Jordan and three in Canaan as cities of refuge. 15 These six towns will be a place of refuge for Israelites, aliens and any other people living among them, so that anyone who has killed another accidentally can flee there.

16 " 'If a man strikes someone with an iron object so that he dies, he is a murderer; the murderer shall be put to death.[a] 17 Or if anyone has a stone in his hand that could kill, and he strikes someone so that he dies, he is a murderer; the murderer shall be put to death. 18 Or if anyone has a wooden object in his hand that could kill, and he hits someone so that he dies, he is a murderer; the murderer shall be put to death. 19 The avenger of blood shall put the murderer to death; when he meets him, he shall put him to death.[b] 20 If anyone with malice aforethought shoves another or throws something at him intentionally[c] so that he dies 21 or if in hostility he hits him with his fist so that he dies, that person shall be put to death; he is a murderer. The avenger of blood shall put the murderer to death when he meets him.

22 " 'But if without hostility someone suddenly shoves another or throws something

35:6 [u]Jos 20:7-9; 21:3, 13
35:8 [v]Nu 26:54; 33:54; Jos 21:1-42
35:10 [w]Jos 20:2
35:11 [x]ver 22-25 [y]Ex 21:13; Dt 19:1-13
35:12 [z]Dt 19:6; Jos 20:3
35:16 [a]Ex 21:12; Lev 24:17
35:19 [b]ver 21
35:20 [c]Ge 4:8; Ex 21:14; Dt 19:11; 2Sa 3:27; 20:10

[a] 4 Hebrew *a thousand cubits* (about 450 meters) [b] 5 Hebrew *two thousand cubits* (about 900 meters)

35:9–33 Six cities of refuge were to be established for those who might accidentally kill someone (see notes on Jos 20:1–9).
35:12 the avenger. A member of the victim's family was customarily designated to avenge the victim's death by executing the accused killer.
35:16–21 The avenger was to put a murderer to death. See *WLC* 136.

Cities of Refuge

The idea of providing cities of refuge (Jos 20:1-9) for capital offenses is rooted in the tension between customary tribal law (retaliation or revenge, in which the blood relative is obligated to execute vengeance) and civil law (carried out less personally by an assembly according to a standard code of justice).

Blood feuds are usually associated with nomadic groups; legal procedures, with villages and towns. Israel, a society in the process of sedentarization, found it necessary to adopt an intermediate step regulating manslaughter, so that an innocent person would not be killed before standing trial. Absolution was possible only by being cleared by the assembly, and by the eventual death of the high priest (when there would be general amnesty).

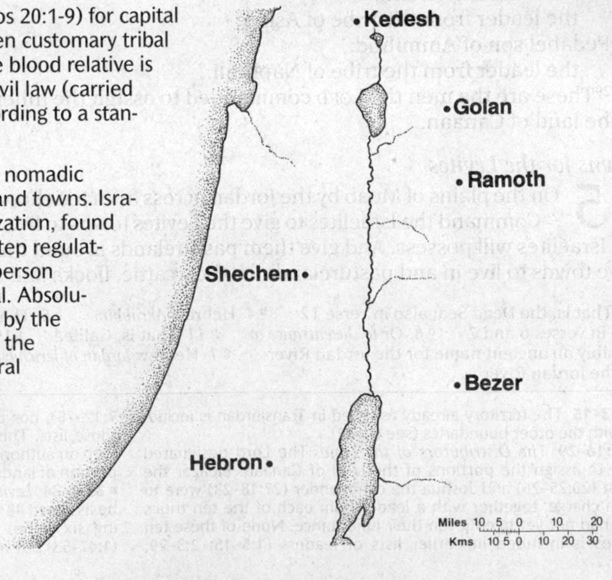

at him unintentionally[d] 23or, without seeing him, drops a stone on him that could kill him, and he dies, then since he was not his enemy and he did not intend to harm him, 24the assembly[e] must judge between him and the avenger of blood according to these regulations. 25The assembly must protect the one accused of murder from the avenger of blood and send him back to the city of refuge to which he fled. He must stay there until the death of the high priest, who was anointed with the holy oil.[f]

26" 'But if the accused ever goes outside the limits of the city of refuge to which he has fled 27and the avenger of blood finds him outside the city, the avenger of blood may kill the accused without being guilty of murder. 28The accused must stay in his city of refuge until the death of the high priest; only after the death of the high priest may he return to his own property.

29" 'These are to be legal requirements[g] for you throughout the generations to come, wherever you live.

30" 'Anyone who kills a person is to be put to death as a murderer only on the testimony of witnesses. But no one is to be put to death on the testimony of only one witness.[h]

31" 'Do not accept a ransom for the life of a murderer, who deserves to die. He must surely be put to death.

32" 'Do not accept a ransom for anyone who has fled to a city of refuge and so allow him to go back and live on his own land before the death of the high priest.

33" 'Do not pollute the land where you are. Bloodshed pollutes the land,[i] and atonement cannot be made for the land on which blood has been shed, except by the blood of the one who shed it. 34Do not defile the land[j] where you live and where I dwell,[k] for I, the LORD, dwell among the Israelites.' "

Inheritance of Zelophehad's Daughters

36 The family heads of the clan of Gilead[l] son of Makir, the son of Manasseh, who were from the clans of the descendants of Joseph, came and spoke before Moses and the leaders,[m] the heads of the Israelite families. 2They said, "When the LORD commanded my lord to give the land as an inheritance to the Israelites by lot, he ordered you to give the inheritance of our brother Zelophehad[n] to his daughters. 3Now suppose they marry men from other Israelite tribes; then their inheritance will be taken from our ancestral inheritance and added to that of the tribe they marry into. And so part of the inheritance allotted to us will be taken away. 4When the Year of Jubilee[o] for the Israelites comes, their inheritance will be added to that of the tribe into which they marry, and their property will be taken from the tribal inheritance of our forefathers."

5Then at the LORD's command Moses gave this order to the Israelites: "What the tribe of the descendants of Joseph is saying is right. 6This is what the LORD commands for Zelophehad's daughters: They may marry anyone they please as long as they marry within the tribal clan of their father. 7No inheritance[p] in Israel is to pass from tribe to tribe, for every Israelite shall keep the tribal land inherited from his forefathers. 8Every daughter who inherits land in any Israelite tribe must marry someone in her father's tribal clan,[q] so that every Israelite will possess the inheritance of his fathers. 9No inheritance may pass from tribe to tribe, for each Israelite tribe is to keep the land it inherits."

10So Zelophehad's daughters did as the LORD commanded Moses. 11Zelophehad's daughters—Mahlah, Tirzah, Hoglah, Milcah and Noah[r]—married their cousins on their father's side. 12They married within the clans of the descendants of Manasseh son of Joseph, and their inheritance remained in their father's clan and tribe.

13These are the commands and regulations the LORD gave through Moses[s] to the Israelites on the plains of Moab by the Jordan across from Jericho.[a][t]

35:22 [d]ver 11; Ex 21:13
35:24 [e]ver 12; Jos 20:6
35:25 [f]Ex 29:7
35:29 [g]Nu 27:11
35:30 [h]ver 16; Dt 17:6; 19:15; Mt 18:16; Jn 7:51; 2Co 13:1; Heb 10:28
35:33 [i]Ge 9:6; Ps 106:38; Mic 4:11
35:34 [j]Lev 18:24,25 [k]Ex 29:45
36:1 [l]Nu 26:29 [m]Nu 27:2
36:2 [n]Nu 26:33; 27:1,7
36:4 [o]Lev 25:10
36:7 [p]1Ki 21:3
36:8 [q]1Ch 23:22
36:11 [r]Nu 26:33; 27:1
36:13 [s]Lev 26:46; 27:34 [t]Nu 22:1

a 13 Hebrew *Jordan of Jericho*; possibly an ancient name for the Jordan River

---

35:22–28 The assembly (of judges) was to protect the accused killer by sending him to a city of refuge for the lifetime of the current high priest (vv. 22–25). Departure from the city of refuge would mean that "the avenger of blood" could avenge the death of his family member by executing the accused killer.

35:25 until the death of the high priest. See also verse 28. The death of the high priest resulted in a change in the legal status of the accused killer: He was no longer liable for manslaughter.

35:30 No one was to be put to death on the evidence of only one witness.

35:31–32 Accepting a ransom payment was forbidden in cases of murder and manslaughter.

35:31,33 See *WLC* 136.

35:33–34 Pollution of the land by bloodshed was removed only by the shedding of the blood of the killer.

■**36:1–13** *An Additional Thought Concerning Inheritances.* In what may be a post-Mosaic addition to the book, the family heads of a clan of Manasseh brought a problem to Moses because of the earlier decision (27:8) that if a man had no son, a daughter could receive his inheritance. They feared that this would result in transferring land from one tribe to another (v. 4).

36:4 the Year of Jubilee. During Jubilee, land reverted to its ancestral owners. See the full discussion in Leviticus 25 and 27. "At the LORD's command" (v. 5), Moses ordered that "no inheritance may pass from tribe to tribe" (v. 9). Subsequently, Zelophehad's daughters, whose situation had originally raised the question of female inheritance (27:1–11), married within their father's clan (vv. 11–12).

DEUTERONOMY

Introduction

Overview

Author: Moses
Purpose: To encourage a renewal of the covenant mediated by Moses as Israel was about to enter the promised land under Joshua's leadership
Date: c. 1406 B.C.
Key Truths:

- The Israelites on the plains of Moab were to learn the importance of loyalty to the covenant from the experiences of the previous generation.
- The laws of Moses were designed to benefit the people of God as they moved into the promised land under Joshua's leadership.
- Loyalty to the covenant would be rewarded with blessings, and disobedience would be punished with curses.
- The Israelites were to renew their commitment to the covenant as they waited on the plains of Moab and after they entered the promised land.

Author

Deuteronomy, like the rest of the Pentateuch, is substantially the work of Moses. It is apparent that some portions of the book were later additions (e.g., the account of the death of Moses in ch. 34) and that other portions underwent later editing. Nevertheless, the book should be read as coming from the time of Moses. See "Introduction to the Pentateuch" on page 1.

Time and Place of Writing

Deuteronomy was probably largely written on the plains of Moab, c. 1406 B.C., as the Israelites prepared to enter the promised land, though it probably was not completed until the days of Joshua, when such elements as the account of Moses' death (ch. 34) were likely added. See "Introduction to the Pentateuch" on page 1.

Original Audience

Moses wrote to the second generation of the exodus. Their faithless parents had all died in the wilderness as a punishment from God (Nu 32:10–13), but God had spared the children in order to preserve his holy people and maintain his promises to their forefathers. Since Moses would not be allowed to lead them into the promised land (Dt 1:37–38), he restated God's law in order to guide them in covenant renewal under Joshua. See "Introduction to the Pentateuch" at on page 1.

Purpose and Distinctives

With the first generation of the exodus gone, Moses needed to exhort the new generation to avoid the sins of their parents and to commit to the law so that blessings would come in the future. Deuteronomy consists mainly of three great speeches and a legal compendium given by Moses at the end of his life. The book summarizes addresses he made to the nation as he called the people to renew their covenant commitment to God both before, and after entering the land. It has been noted that Deuteronomy's content resembles the main elements of ancient Near Eastern treaties. Treaties between great kings (suzerains) and their vassals typically contained a number of elements, and the book follows this well-attested pattern: the preamble (1:1–4), the historical prologue (1:5—4:43), the stipulations (4:44—26:19), ratification (27:1—30:20) and leadership succession (31:1—34:12). Some interpreters have made too much of these connections, for these sections of Deuteronomy only roughly resemble the elements of treaties. Yet because these descriptions are helpful orientations, they have been included in the outline and in the study notes for the book.

Deuteronomy is better understood as a series of addresses that have been joined together in their present form. The opening address (1:5—4:43) recounts the experiences of Israel under Moses' leadership. Deuteronomy does not speak of how Moses confronted Pharaoh or of how the miracles of the ten plagues forced Pharaoh to let the people go, but it does allude to the exodus repeatedly (five times in the first address; 1:27,30; 4:20,34,37). Moses recounted God's providential and miraculous care for the people during the journey from Egypt to Horeb. Then he detailed their defeat both spiritually and militarily at Kadesh Barnea. There are references here to events recorded in Numbers. Like the record in Numbers, practically nothing is said about events during the 40 years of wandering. The journey around Edom toward Transjordan is mentioned, and the defeat of Sihon and Og is recorded in fuller detail than in Numbers. Then the allocation of land in Transjordan for Reuben, Gad and the half-tribe of Manasseh is described (cf. Nu 32). The narrative ends with reference to Moses' personal plea to enter Canaan, which God disallowed (cf. Nu 27:12–23). Moses concluded this address with exhortations to be loyal to the Lord.

The first part of the second address (4:44—11:32) is composed of exhortations and begins with the Ten Commandments. The Ten Commandments were given directly by the voice of God, but the rest of the law was mediated through Moses. Chapters 6–11 set out the great issues that inform a covenant relationship with God. Chapter 6 records the famous Shema—"Hear, O Israel: The LORD our God, the LORD is one" (v. 4)—with the exhortation to love God with all one's heart (v. 5), which is followed by an exhortation to teach, remember and obey (vv. 6–25). The following chapters are sprinkled with examples of God's care and judgments since leaving Egypt—all allusions to material in Exodus and Numbers. These examples served to warn the Israelites to trust the Lord rather than themselves. These chapters then lead to a promise of success in the coming wars of Canaan.

The laws of the second part of the second address (12:1—26:19) include regulations for worship, clean foods, slaves and debts, annual feasts, judges, cities of refuge and various other matters of conduct. Most of these laws have parallels in the previous books of the Pentateuch.

The third address (27:1—30:20) is a powerful exhortation to Israel to obey the laws of the Lord. It includes the instructions for the solemn ceremony that would be held in the valley between Mount Ebal and Mount Gerizim, near Shechem, after Israel had secured a foothold in Canaan. This ceremony is reminiscent of the covenant ceremony of Exodus 20:1—24:8 and was duly carried out by Joshua (Jos 8:30–35). Some interpreters hold that this address, with its instructions about the altar and its recitation of blessings and curses, is really a conclusion to the previous one, which is viewed as being in the form of a treaty-covenant. Whatever the case, these laws and exhortations were given by Moses with tremendous emphasis on Israel's obligation before God to hear and obey the law of the Lord.

The final sections of the book are equally important and powerful (31:1—34:2). They include the investiture of Joshua as Moses' successor; the song of Moses, which celebrates the greatness of God and his care for his covenant people (ch. 32); Moses' blessing of the 12 tribes, which is similar to Jacob's blessing of his 12 sons (Ge 49); and the obituary describing Moses' death (ch. 34).

The book received its title from the Septuagint (the Greek translation of the OT), which called it *Deuteronomion,* "the second law." A better sense of its meaning would be "the repetition of the law."

Christ in Deuteronomy

Moses, the founder of Israel's theocracy, mediated the old covenant and as such foreshadowed Jesus Christ, the Son of God, who mediated the new covenant (Jer 31:31–34). The moral substance of the covenants is the same, but their forms of administration differ significantly. This substantial identity is evident in the way Paul connected his gospel message with Moses' appeal for Israel to renew the covenant (see note on 30:11–14). In Deuteronomy, grace precedes the human obligation of faith, and human obedience is the proof of genuine faith. The same is true in the teaching of the New Testament.

Even so, Deuteronomy represented a stage of God's covenant dealings that foreshadowed the greater realities of Christ's covenant (see notes on Heb 8:6–13; see also theological article "The Covenants of Works and Grace" at Ge 6). The old covenant was effected with the blood of animals; the everlasting new covenant with the efficacious blood of Christ (Jer 32:40; Heb 9:11–28). Moses called for a religion of the heart (6:6; 30:6), but it failed through human weakness and became obsolete (Ro 8:3; Heb 8:13). Jesus Christ through the Holy Spirit changes human hearts (see note on 10:16; cf. Jn 3:1–15).

Christ is also anticipated in Deuteronomy by a number of its specific concerns. He is the Passover Lamb (see 16:1–17 and its notes) and the coming Prophet (see note on 18:15–22). Deuteronomy's concern with the establishment of one sanctuary (ch. 12) anticipates the New Testament's outlook on Christ as the only One who can bring salvation. The details of the sacrificial system anticipate Jesus' sacrifice of himself. The emphasis of Deuteronomy on life in the promised land anticipates the hope of the new heavens and the new earth that Christ offers to all who believe in him. As Moses called the Israelites to fidelity so that they could enter the land to take possession of it, so also Christ calls us to fidelity to himself so that we may enter the world to come and enjoy its eternal blessings.

Outline

I. The Introduction [The Preamble] (1:1–4)

Moses identified himself as the mediator of Israel's covenant renewal on the plains of Moab.

II. Moses' First Address [The Historical Prologue] (1:5—4:43)

The Israelites were to learn gratitude and loyalty to the Lord from their experiences and from the experiences of the previous generation.

- A. Recital of History (1:5—3:29)
  1. Introduction (1:5)
  2. The Call to Leave Sinai (1:6–8)
  3. Establishment of Judges (1:9–18)
  4. At Kadesh Barnea (1:19–46)
  5. The Wanderings (2:1–23)
  6. The Transjordan Victories (2:24—3:20)
  7. Joshua as Leader (3:21–29)
- B. The Call to Fidelity (4:1–40)
  1. The Contours of Fidelity (4:1–2)
  2. Lessons From the Past (4:3–24)
     - a. Baal Peor (4:3–9)
     - b. Sinai (4:10–20)
     - c. Meribah (4:21–24)
  3. Threats and Hope in the Future (4:25–31)
  4. Summation (4:32–40)
- C. A Note on Cities of Refuge in Transjordan (4:41–43)

III. Moses' Second Address [The Stipulations] (4:44—26:19)
- A. Introduction (4:44–49)
- B. Orientation Toward the Stipulations (5:1—11:32)
  - 1. Laws From God and Moses (5:1–33)
    - a. The Ten Commandments From God (5:1–22)
    - b. Moses the Mediator (5:23–33)
  - 2. Fidelity in the Future in Light of the Past (6:1—11:25)
    - a. The Priorities of Fidelity (6:1–9)
    - b. Testing the Lord (6:10–25)
    - c. Requirements of Holy War (7:1–26)
    - d. Prosperity and Pride (8:1–20)
    - e. Self-Righteousness (9:1—10:11)
    - f. Circumcision of the Heart (10:12—11:25)
  - 3. Call to Renewal (11:26–32)
- C. Detailed Stipulations (12:1—26:15)
- D. Conclusion (26:16–19)

Loving loyalty to the Lord required obedience to his many laws. These laws were his kind gift to his people. In the future, Israel was to be even more firmly committed to the law.

IV. Moses' Third Address [Ratification: Curses and Blessings] (27:1—30:20)
- A. The Ratification to Come at Ebal and Gerizim (27:1–26)
- B. The Covenant Renewal in Moab (28:1—30:20)
  - 1. Blessings (28:1–14)
  - 2. Curses (28:15—29:1)
  - 3. Appeal for Renewal (29:2—30:20)
    - a. Prologue (29:2–8)
    - b. Stipulations (29:9–18)
    - c. Curses (29:19–29)
    - d. Blessings (30:1–10)
    - e. Offer (30:11–18)
    - f. Witnesses (30:19–20)

Israel was to renew her commitment to the covenant in the promised land. She was also to recommit on the plains of Moab. The wonderful blessings and fearful curses of the covenant required such commitments. Even if the curse of exile occurred, God promised to return his people to the land and to his rich blessings.

V. The Conclusion of Moses' Ministry [Leadership Succession] (31:1—34:12)
- A. Transfer of Leadership to Joshua (31:1–29)
- B. The Song of Moses (31:30—32:47)
- C. The Blessing of Moses (32:48—33:29)
- D. The Death of Moses (34:1–12)

Moses transferred his authority to Joshua. He left God's people with lessons learned from the past and with high hopes for the future.

The Command to Leave Horeb

1 These are the words Moses spoke to all Israel in the desert east of the Jordan—that is,
in the Arabah—opposite Suph, between Paran and Tophel, Laban, Hazeroth and Dizahab. 2 (It takes eleven days to go from Horeb[a] to Kadesh Barnea[b] by the Mount Seir road.)

1:2 [a]Ex 3:1 [b]Nu 13:26; Dt 9:23

■ **1:1–4** *The Introduction.* These introductory verses identify the author, Moses, and the circumstances of his addresses to the people just before his death and their crossing of the Jordan. This section resembles the preambles of suzerain-vassal treaties in which the king identified himself to those with whom he was about to make the treaty. In this case, however, Moses identified himself as the one who mediated Israel's covenant with God.

1:1 east of the Jordan. Some have translated this phrase "across [or beyond] the Jordan" because the Hebrew for the words "east of" comes from the root meaning "cross over" or "travel." But the word is used of either side of the river, sometimes in the same verse (see "Introduction: Author" regarding later additions/editing). **Suph . . . Paran . . . Tophel, Laban, Hazeroth and Dizahab.** *Suph,* meaning "reeds," is often used in the phrase *Yam suph,* translated "Red Sea." The expression "Red Sea" in ancient times clearly included the Gulf of Aqaba (1Ki 9:26). Perhaps the word as used here refers to the Gulf of Aqaba, but the feminine form *supha* is used in Numbers 21:14 as an otherwise unknown place near the Arnon River. The Desert of Paran is mentioned as being located somewhere in the Sinai peninsula (Nu 10:12; 12:16). Mount Paran is named in connection with the theophany at Mount Sinai (33:2; Hab 3:3). Paran was located somewhere to the south, and therefore Tophel was to the north. Laban and Dizahab are not mentioned elsewhere, and nothing is known of them. Hazeroth is indicated as a stop on the march from Sinai to Kadesh Barnea (Nu 11:35; 12:16; see also 33:17–18). One meaning of the word *Hazeroth* is "villages," and there may have been two or more places by that name. Because of our lack of information about these loca-

3 In the fortieth year,[c] on the first day of the eleventh month, Moses proclaimed[d] to
the Israelites all that the LORD had commanded him concerning them. 4 This was after he
had defeated Sihon[e] king of the Amorites, who reigned in Heshbon,[f] and at Edrei had
defeated Og[g] king of Bashan, who reigned in Ashtaroth.
5 East of the Jordan in the territory of Moab, Moses began to expound this law, saying:

6 The LORD our God said to us[h] at Horeb,[i] "You have stayed long enough at this mountain. 7 Break camp and advance into the hill country of the Amorites; go to all the neighboring peoples in the Arabah, in the mountains, in the western foothills, in the Negev[j]
and along the coast, to the land of the Canaanites and to Lebanon,[k] as far as the great
river, the Euphrates. 8 See, I have given you this land. Go in and take possession of the
land that the LORD swore[l] he would give to your fathers—to Abraham, Isaac and Jacob—
and to their descendants after them."

The Appointment of Leaders

9 At that time I said to you, "You are too heavy a burden for me to carry alone.[m] 10 The
LORD your God has increased your numbers so that today you are as many[n] as the stars
in the sky.[o] 11 May the LORD, the God of your fathers, increase you a thousand times and
bless you as he has promised![p] 12 But how can I bear your problems and your burdens
and your disputes all by myself? 13 Choose some wise, understanding and respected men[q]
from each of your tribes, and I will set them over you."
14 You answered me, "What you propose to do is good."
15 So I took[r] the leading men of your tribes, wise and respected men, and appointed
them to have authority over you—as commanders of thousands, of hundreds, of fifties
and of tens and as tribal officials. 16 And I charged your judges at that time: Hear the disputes between your brothers and judge fairly,[s] whether the case is between brother Israelites or between one of them and an alien.[t] 17 Do not show partiality[u] in judging; hear

1:3 [c]Nu 33:38 [d]Dt 4:1-2
1:4 [e]Nu 21:21-26 [f]Nu 21:25 [g]Nu 21:33-35; Jos 13:12
1:6 [h]Nu 10:13 [i]Ex 3:1
1:7 [j]Jos 10:40 [k]Dt 11:24
1:8 [l]Ge 12:7; 15:18; 17:7-8; 26:4; 28:13
1:9 [m]Ex 18:18
1:10 [n]Ge 15:5 [o]Dt 10:22; 28:62
1:11 [p]Ge 22:17; Ex 32:13
1:13 [q]Ex 18:21
1:15 [r]Ex 18:25
1:16 [s]Dt 16:18; Jn 7:24 [t]Lev 24:22
1:17 [u]Lev 19:15; Dt 16:19; Pr 24:23; Jas 2:1

---

tions, most of our knowledge about them comes from the descriptions in Joshua (Jos 2:1; 3:1,19).

1:2 eleven days. From Horeb to Kadesh Barnea is about 150 miles in a straight line. The Israelites went by way of the Mount Seir road, which probably means that they traveled part of the time along the valley north of Ezion Geber, a journey of 175 miles or more. They made good time if the whole nation arrived in 11 days. But the mention of 11 days could refer to this as the normal time it would have taken a traveler. The whole camp, with families and animals, could have taken longer.

1:3 the fortieth year. That this is a real number and not an approximation for "a generation" is shown by 2:14, which states that the company reached the brook Zered near the southern end of the Dead Sea after 38 years. This left two years for the conquest of Transjordan.

1:4 Sihon . . . Og. The conquest of Transjordan is detailed in 2:24—3:20.

■ **1:5—4:43** *Moses' First Address.* The first portion of Deuteronomy serves in many respects as a historical prologue, like the portion of a suzerain-vassal treaty that rehearsed the benevolence the great king had shown to those with whom he was entering into a treaty relationship. Moses' first speech reviews the history of Israel from the time of Sinai. Moses provided a travelogue of the nation's movements from the Sinai region to Hormah, on to the Arnon and into the Transjordan area. He concluded this segment of the book with an overview of the requirements of the covenant given in the past that were to be renewed now with the generation born in the wilderness. These chapters divide into three main parts: a rehearsal of history (1:5—3:29), a call to faithfulness (4:1–40) and a note on cities of refuges (4:41–43).

■ **1:5—3:29** *Recital of History.* Moses began his address to the nation by recalling some of the notable ways in which God had blessed Israel. This rehearsal was designed to set forth gratitude for God's blessings as the basis of obedience. After an introduction (1:5), he described the call to leave Sinai (1:6–8), the establishment of leaders (1:9–18), events at Kadesh Barnea (1:19–46), the wanderings (2:1–23), the Transjordan victories (2:24—3:20) and the establishment of Joshua as Israel's leader (3:21–29).

■ **1:5** *Introduction.* The historical setting of Moses' speech is presented.

1:5 in the territory of Moab. The Israelites are said to have camped in the plains of Moab (Nu 22:1; 26:2,68) or in the land of Moab (29:1; 32:49). Israel was not to fight with Moab (2:8), so the people stayed north of the Arnon, which formed the northern border of Moab. Moab had earlier held the northern territory but had been driven south of the Arnon by the Amorite king Sihon (Nu 21:26). Jephthah rehearsed this history in Judges 11:14–27. He claimed that Israel had captured this area not from the Moabites or Ammonites, but from Sihon. **this law.** The collection of laws associated with the Mosaic covenant; that is, the Ten Commandments and the Book of the Covenant (see Ex 19–24).

■ **1:6–8** *The Call to Leave Sinai.* In his mercy, God called Israel to move forward to the promised land.

1:6 Horeb. Another name for Sinai. It was apparently used to describe the area around Mount Sinai. The name "Sinai" is nearly always used with the designation "Mount" or "Desert." Horeb is used only once with the designation "Mount" (Ex 33:6).

1:7 the land of the Canaanites. These borders of the promised land roughly correspond to those declared to Abraham (Ge 15:18–19). The promise included driving out the Canaanites and the other inhabitants of the land.

1:8 Go in and take possession. Moses recalled how he had called Israel to move forward into the conquest. **the LORD swore.** God's solemn oath to give the land to Abraham's descendants was the basis upon which the nation could move forward with confidence (see, e.g., Ge 15:18; 17:8; 26:3). This aspect of God's covenant promise to Israel was fulfilled in part in the conquest of the promised land by Joshua and further by the much later conquests of David and Solomon. Yet the promised land was but the beginning of the full gift of land for God's people: the whole world (Ro 4:13). This promise will be ultimately fulfilled in the new heavens and the new earth, which followers of Christ will receive when Christ returns (Rev 21:1–3).

■ **1:9–18** *Establishment of Judges.* God's mercy to Israel is also seen in the provision of an effective judicial system.

1:9 At that time. Moses was referring to the events of Exodus 18, which took place at Mount Sinai.

1:10 increased your numbers . . . as many as the stars. Moses declared that the establishment of the entire judicial system was a great gift from God that added to his blessing of multiplying their numbers, just as God had promised Abraham (Ge 15:4–5; 22:17).

1:13 Choose some wise . . . men. Moses took the good advice of Jethro, his father-in-law. During the year at Mount Sinai, Moses, under God's authority, organized the nation's judicial system, military power and worship. For the establishment of judges, see 16:18, 17:8 and 19:17.

1:14 good. Moses did not tyrannically impose his laws or judicial system on the people. The people enthusiastically endorsed them (see notes on Ex 19:7; 24:7).

1:15–18 Moses described the benefits of Israel's judicial system. See *BC* 36.

both small and great alike. Do not be afraid of any man,[v] for judgment belongs to God. Bring me any case too hard for you, and I will hear it.[w] **18**And at that time I told you everything you were to do.

Spies Sent Out

19Then, as the LORD our God commanded us, we set out from Horeb and went toward the hill country of the Amorites through all that vast and dreadful desert[x] that you have seen, and so we reached Kadesh Barnea.[y] **20**Then I said to you, "You have reached the hill country of the Amorites, which the LORD our God is giving us. **21**See, the LORD your God has given you the land. Go up and take possession of it as the LORD, the God of your fathers, told you. Do not be afraid;[z] do not be discouraged."

22Then all of you came to me and said, "Let us send men ahead to spy out the land for us and bring back a report about the route we are to take and the towns we will come to."

23The idea seemed good to me; so I selected[a] twelve of you, one man from each tribe. **24**They left and went up into the hill country, and came to the Valley of Eshcol[b] and explored it. **25**Taking with them some of the fruit of the land, they brought it down to us and reported,[c] "It is a good land that the LORD our God is giving us."

Rebellion Against the LORD

26But you were unwilling to go up;[d] you rebelled against the command of the LORD your God. **27**You grumbled[e] in your tents and said, "The LORD hates us; so he brought us out of Egypt to deliver us into the hands of the Amorites to destroy us. **28**Where can we go? Our brothers have made us lose heart. They say, 'The people are stronger and taller[f] than we are; the cities are large, with walls up to the sky. We even saw the Anakites[g] there.' "

29Then I said to you, "Do not be terrified; do not be afraid of them. **30**The LORD your God, who is going before you, will fight[h] for you, as he did for you in Egypt, before your very eyes, **31**and in the desert. There you saw how the LORD your God carried[i] you, as a father carries his son, all the way you went until you reached this place."

32In spite of this, you did not trust[j] in the LORD your God, **33**who went ahead of you on your journey, in fire by night and in a cloud by day,[k] to search[l] out places for you to camp and to show you the way you should go.

34When the LORD heard what you said, he was angry and solemnly swore:[m] **35**"Not a man of this evil generation shall see the good land[n] I swore to give your forefathers, **36**except Caleb son of Jephunneh. He will see it, and I will give him and his descendants the land he set his feet on, because he followed the LORD wholeheartedly.[o]"

37Because of you the LORD became angry[p] with me also and said, "You shall not enter[q] it, either. **38**But your assistant, Joshua[r] son of Nun, will enter it. Encourage[s] him, because he will lead[t] Israel to inherit it. **39**And the little ones that you said would be taken captive,[u] your children who do not yet know[v] good from bad—they will enter the land. I will give it to them and they will take possession of it. **40**But as for you, turn around and set out toward the desert along the route to the Red Sea.[a][w]"

41Then you replied, "We have sinned against the LORD. We will go up and fight, as the

[a] *40* Hebrew *Yam Suph;* that is, Sea of Reeds

1:17 [v]2Ch 19:6 [w]Ex 18:26
1:19 [x]Dt 8:15; Jer 2:2,6 [y]ver 2; Nu 13:26
1:21 [z]Jos 1:6,9,18
1:23 [a]Nu 13:1-3
1:24 [b]Nu 13:21-25
1:25 [c]Nu 13:27
1:26 [d]Nu 14:1-4
1:27 [e]Dt 9:28; Ps 106:25
1:28 [f]Nu 13:32 [g]Nu 13:33; Dt 9:1-3
1:30 [h]Ex 14:14; Dt 3:22; Ne 4:20
1:31 [i]Dt 32:10-12; Isa 46:3-4; 63:9; Hos 11:3; Ac 13:18
1:32 [j]Ps 106:24; Jude 1:5
1:33 [k]Ex 13:21; Ps 78:14 [l]Nu 10:33
1:34 [m]Nu 14:23,28-30
1:35 [n]Ps 95:11
1:36 [o]Nu 14:24; Jos 14:9
1:37 [p]Dt 3:26; 4:21 [q]Nu 20:12
1:38 [r]Nu 14:30 [s]Dt 31:7 [t]Dt 3:28
1:39 [u]Nu 14:3 [v]Isa 7:15-16
1:40 [w]Nu 14:25

■ **1:19–46** *At Kadesh Barnea.* Moses rehearsed Israel's rebellion at Kadesh Barnea (cf. Nu 13:1—14:45), which stood in striking contrast to the blessings God had shown to the nation.

1:19 Kadesh Barnea. This city is called simply Kadesh in the account of the spies' negative report (Nu 13:26). The original inhabitants of Kadesh (meaning "holy place") doubtless gave it its name due to the many supposedly sacred places located there. It was called Kadesh Barnea to distinguish it from other places named Kadesh or Kedesh (e.g., in Naphtali [Jdg 4:6] and in Judah [Jos 15:23]).

1:26 you rebelled. This account of the debacle at Kadesh parallels extensively that of Numbers 13. Both reports mention the following: the 12 spies, the report of a good land, the power of the Amorites, the fidelity of Caleb, the exhortation to trust God, the doom befalling the present generation, the people's change of heart and their desire to fight, Moses' warning, their defeat, and the flight as far as the place called Hormah.

1:28 the Anakites. Egyptian texts of the early second millennium B.C. list a man named Anak as a ruler in the region later called Palestine. That Anak was probably related to the Biblical Anak, whose descendants lived in Hebron (Nu 13:22). The terrified spies reported that these people were taller than the Israelites and that they were feared for their prowess (Nu 13:27–33). Joshua conquered them, and their remnants merged with the Philistines (Jos 12:21–22).

1:29–30 Do not be terrified . . . The LORD . . . will fight. The Israelites' confidence in the conquest should have been based on the fact that God would fight for them. The same assurance was given to Joshua (Jos 1:6–9). The conquest of Canaan was no mere human war; it was a supernatural war fought by God himself, as was displayed in its miraculous character.

1:33 in fire by night. Refers to Exodus 13:21, which describes how the pillar guided the people out of Egypt, and especially to Numbers 9:15–23, which recounts the Lord's guidance through the entire wilderness journey.

1:37 the LORD became angry with me. Mentioning the doom befalling the lost generation brought to mind God's rejection of Moses and refusal to allow him to enter Canaan. The reason is given in 32:51 (see also Nu 20:1–13; 27:14). Moses (and Aaron) had brought water from the rock in their own name, without giving glory to God. Joshua, a faithful spy, would carry on as leader (Nu 27:12–23).

LORD our God commanded us." So every one of you put on his weapons, thinking it easy to go up into the hill country.

42But the LORD said to me, "Tell them, 'Do not go up and fight, because I will not be with you. You will be defeated by your enemies.' "[x]

43So I told you, but you would not listen. You rebelled against the LORD's command and in your arrogance you marched up into the hill country. 44The Amorites who lived in those hills came out against you; they chased you like a swarm of bees[y] and beat you down from Seir all the way to Hormah. 45You came back and wept before the LORD, but he paid no attention to your weeping and turned a deaf ear to you. 46And so you stayed in Kadesh[z] many days—all the time you spent there.

Wanderings in the Desert

2 Then we turned back and set out toward the desert along the route to the Red Sea,[a][a] as the LORD had directed me. For a long time we made our way around the hill country of Seir.

2Then the LORD said to me, 3"You have made your way around this hill country long enough; now turn north. 4Give the people these orders:[b] 'You are about to pass through the territory of your brothers the descendants of Esau, who live in Seir. They will be afraid of you, but be very careful. 5Do not provoke them to war, for I will not give you any of their land, not even enough to put your foot on. I have given Esau the hill country of Seir as his own.[c] 6You are to pay them in silver for the food you eat and the water you drink.' "

7The LORD your God has blessed you in all the work of your hands. He has watched[d] over your journey through this vast desert. These forty years the LORD your God has been with you, and you have not lacked anything.

8So we went on past our brothers the descendants of Esau, who live in Seir. We turned from the Arabah road, which comes up from Elath and Ezion Geber,[e] and traveled along the desert road of Moab.[f]

9Then the LORD said to me, "Do not harass the Moabites or provoke them to war, for I will not give you any part of their land. I have given Ar[g] to the descendants of Lot[h] as a possession."

10(The Emites[i] used to live there—a people strong and numerous, and as tall as the Anakites.[j] 11Like the Anakites, they too were considered Rephaites, but the Moabites called them Emites. 12Horites used to live in Seir, but the descendants of Esau drove them out. They destroyed the Horites from before them and settled in their place, just as Israel did[k] in the land the LORD gave them as their possession.)

13And the LORD said, "Now get up and cross the Zered Valley." So we crossed the valley.

14Thirty-eight years passed from the time we left Kadesh Barnea[l] until we crossed the Zered Valley. By then, that entire generation[m] of fighting men had perished from the camp, as the LORD had sworn to them.[n] 15The LORD's hand was against them until he had completely eliminated[o] them from the camp.

1:42 [x]Nu 14:41-43
1:44 [y]Ps 118:12
1:46 [z]Nu 20:1; Jdg 11:17
2:1 [a]Nu 21:4
2:4 [b]Nu 20:14-21
2:5 [c]Ge 36:8; Jos 24:4
2:7 [d]Dt 8:2-4
2:8 [e]1Ki 9:26 [f]Jdg 11:18
2:9 [g]Nu 21:15 [h]Ge 19:36-38
2:10 [i]Ge 14:5 [j]Nu 13:22, 33
2:12 [k]ver 22
2:14 [l]Nu 13:26 [m]Nu 14:29-35 [n]Dt 1:34-35
2:15 [o]Ps 106:26

[a] *1* Hebrew *Yam Suph*; that is, Sea of Reeds

1:45 paid no attention . . . deaf ear. The Israelites had flagrantly violated the requirement of covenant loyalty (see theological article "Major Covenants in the Bible" on p. 25).

■ **2:1–23** *The Wanderings.* Moses summarized the major events of the wilderness wanderings to remind the Israelites not only of their failures but also of God's continuing mercy.

2:1 the Red Sea. As in 1:40, this name can include the Gulf of Aqaba, and here it probably does. The valley north of Ezion Geber toward the Dead Sea included some springs that would be vital to the support of the people. Regarding the possibility of this large number of people surviving in the Desert of Sinai, note that a slight shift in the storm track would have brought significant precipitation to this area, which has high mountains that would hold the snow of the rainy season, as the mountains of Lebanon do today. In addition, the Lord miraculously supplied the Israelites with manna and with water from the rock.

2:4 your brothers the descendants of Esau. The Edomites refused peaceful passage, so Israel circumvented their territory (v. 8; Nu 20:14–21). Deuteronomy adds to the Numbers account by stating that this was the Lord's command. According to archaeological study, the Edomites of Moses' day were apparently not sedentary. They were brothers to Israel in nomadic life as well as in ancestry (Ge 25:25–26).

2:9–23 The Israelites moved on to the area of Moab, east of the Jordan.

2:10–12 The Emites . . . Rephaites . . . Horites. Little is known of these former inhabitants of Transjordan, but their names occur in Genesis 14, which reports the raid of eastern kings throughout this area in the days of Abraham. Verses 10–12 and 20–23 tell us that the Emites, also called Rephaites, lived where Moab later lived; that Zamzummites, also called Rephaites, lived where the Ammonites later lived; and that the Horites preceded the Edomites. The remark that the Emites and Zamzummites were tall like the Anakites (yet had been conquered) would have helped the morale of the Israelites, for they had yet to conquer the Anakites. The Horites are a puzzle. An important early people in Mesopotamia were called Hurrians (an equivalent of the Hebrew "Horite"). Some Horites in Canaan seem to have Hurrian names. But there is no other evidence that these eastern Horites were related. Rephaites are mentioned elsewhere (1Ch 20:4 as descendants of Rapha), but they may not have been related.

2:12 the land the LORD gave them. This may have been inserted later by someone after Israel conquered Canaan, but it could as easily have been spoken by Moses after the significant conquest of the Transjordan and the settlement of the two and one-half tribes there.

2:14 Thirty-eight years. See note on 1:3. **as the LORD had sworn.** Another clear reference to Numbers, where God swore by himself that the faithless generation would die in the wilderness (Nu 14:21–23).

16 Now when the last of these fighting men among the people had died, 17 the LORD said to me, 18 "Today you are to pass by the region of Moab at Ar. 19 When you come to the Ammonites,[p] do not harass them or provoke them to war, for I will not give you possession of any land belonging to the Ammonites. I have given it as a possession to the descendants of Lot.[q]"

20 (That too was considered a land of the Rephaites, who used to live there; but the Ammonites called them Zamzummites. 21 They were a people strong and numerous, and as tall as the Anakites.[r] The LORD destroyed them from before the Ammonites, who drove them out and settled in their place. 22 The LORD had done the same for the descendants of Esau, who lived in Seir,[s] when he destroyed the Horites from before them. They drove them out and have lived in their place to this day. 23 And as for the Avvites[t] who lived in villages as far as Gaza, the Caphtorites[u] coming out from Caphtor[a][v] destroyed them and settled in their place.)

Defeat of Sihon King of Heshbon

24 "Set out now and cross the Arnon Gorge.[w] See, I have given into your hand Sihon the Amorite, king of Heshbon, and his country. Begin to take possession of it and engage him in battle. 25 This very day I will begin to put the terror[x] and fear[y] of you on all the nations under heaven. They will hear reports of you and will tremble[z] and be in anguish because of you."

26 From the desert of Kedemoth I sent messengers to Sihon king of Heshbon offering peace and saying, 27 "Let us pass through your country. We will stay on the main road; we will not turn aside to the right or to the left.[a] 28 Sell us food to eat and water to drink for their price in silver. Only let us pass through on foot[b]— 29 as the descendants of Esau, who live in Seir, and the Moabites, who live in Ar, did for us—until we cross the Jordan into the land the LORD our God is giving us." 30 But Sihon king of Heshbon refused to let us pass through. For the LORD[c] your God had made his spirit stubborn[d] and his heart obstinate in order to give him into your hands, as he has now done.

31 The LORD said to me, "See, I have begun to deliver Sihon and his country over to you. Now begin to conquer and possess his land."[e]

32 When Sihon and all his army came out to meet us in battle[f] at Jahaz, 33 the LORD our God delivered him over to us and we struck him down,[g] together with his sons and his whole army. 34 At that time we took all his towns and completely destroyed[b][h] them—men, women and children. We left no survivors. 35 But the livestock and the plunder from the towns we had captured we carried off for ourselves. 36 From Aroer[i] on the rim of the Arnon Gorge, and from the town in the gorge, even as far as Gilead, not one town was too strong for us. The LORD our God gave[j] us all of them. 37 But in accordance with the command of the LORD our God,[k] you did not encroach on any of the land of the Ammonites,[l] neither the land along the course of the Jabbok[m] nor that around the towns in the hills.

Defeat of Og King of Bashan

3 Next we turned and went up along the road toward Bashan, and Og king of Bashan with his whole army marched out to meet us in battle at Edrei.[n] 2 The LORD said to

2:19 [p]Ge 19:38 [q]ver 9
2:21 [r]ver 10
2:22 [s]Ge 36:8
2:23 [t]Jos 13:3 [u]Ge 10:14 [v]Am 9:7
2:24 [w]Nu 21:13-14; Jdg 11:13,18
2:25 [x]Dt 11:25 [y]Jos 2:9, 11 [z]Ex 15:14-16
2:27 [a]Nu 21:21-22
2:28 [b]Nu 20:19
2:30 [c]Jos 11:20 [d]Ex 4:21; Nu 21:23; Ro 9:18
2:31 [e]Dt 1:8
2:32 [f]Nu 21:23
2:33 [g]Dt 29:7
2:34 [h]Dt 3:6; 7:2
2:36 [i]Dt 3:12; 4:48; Jos 13:9 [j]Ps 44:3
2:37 [k]ver 18-19 [l]Nu 21:24 [m]Ge 32:22; Dt 3:16
3:1 [n]Nu 21:33

[a] *23* That is, Crete [b] *34* The Hebrew term refers to the irrevocable giving over of things or persons to the LORD, often by totally destroying them.

2:19 the Ammonites. The kinship with Ammon, as with Moab and Edom, was long remembered (Ge 19:37–38).

2:23 the Caphtorites. If Caphtor means Crete, as it usually does, then the reference is to an early, and probably local, Philistine conquest (before the great Philistine invasion of 1180 B.C.).

■ **2:24—3:20** *The Transjordan Victories.* Moses recalled how God had blessed the nation with victories in the land east of the Jordan. These experiences encouraged gratitude for God's mercy so that obedience would follow.

2:24–37 Moses reminded the Israelites of their victory over Sihon.

2:25 the . . . fear of you. The Israelites were now to begin the conquest, but they were to remember that God went before them. This was to be the emphasis of God's people ever after (cf. Ps 44:3).

2:27 Let us pass through. The same offer was given as had been made earlier to Edom and Moab. But there was no way around the kingdom of Og. In this instance it was God's will for Israel to conquer the territory.

2:30 made his spirit stubborn and his heart obstinate. Sihon refused Moses' offer, but God was in sovereign control, as he had been with Pharaoh (Ex 4:21). God hardened Sihon so that his land would be given into Israel's hands. See *WCF* 5.6.

2:32 at Jahaz. Located about seven miles south of Heshbon. Here Sihon was beaten and his territory conquered. The cities were put under the ban; that is, Israel left no survivors. The calculated effect of the ban in ancient times was to make the inhabitants flee an area without putting up resistance. The Israelites were commanded not to use this procedure except in their conquest of Canaan and the Transjordan (20:10–15), where the holy nation would have been corrupted by the influence of the remaining pagan cultures. Israel also failed here (Ps 106:34–39). The immoral values and lifestyles of the surviving peoples to some extent corrupted the victors.

3:1–11 Moses recalled Israel's victory over Og.

3:1 Og king of Bashan. Bashan is the fertile territory east of the Sea of Galilee. The storms that come from the west over Galilee do not encounter mountains as they do farther south, so some of their moisture is dropped across the Jordan in Bashan. It is wheat country today, but in ancient times it was known for its cattle and flocks (32:14; Ps 22:12). Og understandably feared the invaders who had conquered Sihon, so he attacked Israel. But the Lord gave victory here too. The spoil of this area must have been a great treasure in the eyes of the nomadic Israelites.

me, "Do not be afraid[o] of him, for I have handed him over to you with his whole army
and his land. Do to him what you did to Sihon king of the Amorites, who reigned in Heshbon."
3So the LORD our God also gave into our hands Og king of Bashan and all his army.
We struck them down, leaving no survivors.[p] 4At that time we took all his cities. There
was not one of the sixty cities that we did not take from them—the whole region of Argob, Og's kingdom in Bashan.[q] 5All these cities were fortified with high walls and with
gates and bars, and there were also a great many unwalled villages. 6We completely destroyed[a] them, as we had done with Sihon king of Heshbon, destroying[a r] every city—
men, women and children. 7But all the livestock and the plunder from their cities we carried off for ourselves.
8So at that time we took from these two kings of the Amorites the territory east of the
Jordan, from the Arnon Gorge as far as Mount Hermon. 9(Hermon is called Sirion[s] by the
Sidonians; the Amorites call it Senir.)[t] 10We took all the towns on the plateau, and all Gilead, and all Bashan as far as Salecah[u] and Edrei, towns of Og's kingdom in Bashan.
11(Only Og king of Bashan was left of the remnant of the Rephaites.[v] His bed[b] was made
of iron and was more than thirteen feet long and six feet wide.[c] It is still in Rabbah[w] of
the Ammonites.)

Division of the Land

12Of the land that we took over at that time, I gave the Reubenites and the Gadites
the territory north of Aroer[x] by the Arnon Gorge, including half the hill country of Gilead, together with its towns. 13The rest of Gilead and also all of Bashan, the kingdom of
Og, I gave to the half tribe of Manasseh. (The whole region of Argob in Bashan used to
be known as a land of the Rephaites. 14Jair,[y] a descendant of Manasseh, took the whole
region of Argob as far as the border of the Geshurites and the Maacathites; it was
named after him, so that to this day Bashan is called Havvoth Jair.[d]) 15And I gave Gilead to Makir.[z] 16But to the Reubenites and the Gadites I gave the territory extending from
Gilead down to the Arnon Gorge (the middle of the gorge being the border) and out to
the Jabbok River,[a] which is the border of the Ammonites. 17Its western border was the
Jordan in the Arabah, from Kinnereth[b] to the Sea of the Arabah (the Salt Sea[e c]), below
the slopes of Pisgah.
18I commanded you at that time: "The LORD your God has given you this land to take
possession of it. But all your able-bodied men, armed for battle, must cross over ahead
of your brother Israelites.[d] 19However, your wives, your children and your livestock (I
know you have much livestock) may stay in the towns I have given you, 20until the LORD
gives rest to your brothers as he has to you, and they too have taken over the land that
the LORD your God is giving them, across the Jordan. After that, each of you may go back
to the possession I have given you."

Moses Forbidden to Cross the Jordan

21At that time I commanded Joshua: "You have seen with your own eyes all that the
LORD your God has done to these two kings. The LORD will do the same to all the king-

3:2 [o]Nu 21:34
3:3 [p]Nu 21:35
3:4 [q]1Ki 4:13
3:6 [r]Dt 2:24,34
3:9 [s]Dt 4:48; Ps 29:6 [t]1Ch 5:23
3:10 [u]Jos 13:11
3:11 [v]Ge 14:5 [w]2Sa 12:26; Jer 49:2
3:12 [x]Nu 32:32-38; Dt 2:36; Jos 13:8-13
3:14 [y]Nu 32:41; 1Ch 2:22
3:15 [z]Nu 32:39-40
3:16 [a]Nu 21:24
3:17 [b]Nu 34:11; Jos 13:27 [illegible]; Jos 12:3
3:18 [d]Nu 32:17

[a] *6* The Hebrew term refers to the irrevocable giving over of things or persons to the LORD, often by totally destroying them. [b] *11* Or *sarcophagus* [c] *11* Hebrew *nine cubits long and four cubits wide* (about 4 meters long and 1.8 meters wide) [d] *14* Or *called the settlements of Jair* [e] *17* That is, the Dead Sea

3:8 east of the Jordan. This territory was in extent more than half as large as Canaan proper. From the Arnon to Mount Hermon is about 150 miles. It includes much of the arable land of modern-day Jordan. But at God's command, Ammon and Moab were exempted from the war.

3:9 Sirion . . . Senir. Both forms of the name *Hermon* are witnessed in ancient Canaanite and Mesopotamian texts. Ancient Canaan was multilingual; as a result, words were used that are difficult to translate with precision.

3:11 His bed was made of iron. Og's 13-foot bedstead may suggest that he and his people, the Rephaites, were extremely tall. The NIV text note is probably correct in suggesting that this bedstead was actually a sarcophagus or casket. The ancients were not particular about their beds, but their tombs were important. The word "bed" could here have been used euphemistically for a sarcophagus, which would have been large enough also to hold tomb objects. If so, its size would not necessarily indicate that Og was abnormally tall. That it was "made of iron" need only mean that it was joined or trimmed with iron, which was a new material at this time (iron came into general use in the Iron Age, which began c. 1200 B.C.).

3:12–20 Moses described the granting of the Transjordan to Reuben, Gad and the half-tribe of Manasseh.

3:12 the Reubenites and the Gadites. These tribes received the southern part of the area. Today this territory is sparsely settled, but it was more thickly populated in earlier times.

3:13 the half tribe of Manasseh. The northern half of Gilead, beginning near Zarethan, as well as all of Bashan, went to half of the tribe of Manasseh.

3:14–15 Jair . . . Makir. Within Manasseh's land in the Transjordan, the clan of Jair received a large allotment in the east and the clan of Makir a sizable portion in the west. The account of Jair's conquest of his cities is given in Numbers 32:41.

3:18 your able-bodied men, armed for battle. Moses insisted that the nation remain unified in its holy war. None could settle until all had conquered (see Nu 32). Compare the fulfillment of the pledge in Joshua 22.

■ **3:21–29** *Joshua as Leader.* These verses recount two items. First, Moses prayed to enter the land personally but was refused. Second, Moses appointed Joshua as his replacement, climaxing all of the events rehearsed in the preceding verses. The original audi-

doms over there where you are going. 22 Do not be afraid[e] of them; the LORD your God
himself will fight[f] for you."
23 At that time I pleaded with the LORD: 24 "O Sovereign LORD, you have begun to show
to your servant your greatness[g] and your strong hand. For what god[h] is there in heav-
en or on earth who can do the deeds and mighty works[i] you do?[j] 25 Let me go over and
see the good land[k] beyond the Jordan—that fine hill country and Lebanon."
26 But because of you the LORD was angry[l] with me and would not listen to me. "That
is enough," the LORD said. "Do not speak to me anymore about this matter. 27 Go up to
the top of Pisgah and look west and north and south and east. Look at the land with your
own eyes, since you are not going to cross this Jordan.[m] 28 But commission[n] Joshua, and
encourage and strengthen him, for he will lead this people across[o] and will cause them
to inherit the land that you will see." 29 So we stayed in the valley near Beth Peor.[p]

Obedience Commanded

4 Hear now, O Israel, the decrees and laws I am about to teach you. Follow them so
that you may live[q] and may go in and take possession of the land that the LORD, the
God of your fathers, is giving you. 2 Do not add[r] to what I command you and do not subtract from it, but keep the commands of the LORD your God that I give you.
3 You saw with your own eyes what the LORD did at Baal Peor.[s] The LORD your God destroyed from among you everyone who followed the Baal of Peor, 4 but all of you who held
fast to the LORD your God are still alive today.
5 See, I have taught you decrees and laws as the LORD my God commanded me, so that
you may follow them in the land you are entering to take possession of it. 6 Observe them
carefully, for this will show your wisdom[t] and understanding to the nations, who will
hear about all these decrees and say, "Surely this great nation is a wise and understanding people."[u] 7 What other nation is so great[v] as to have their gods near[w] them the way
the LORD our God is near us whenever we pray to him? 8 And what other nation is so great
as to have such righteous decrees and laws as this body of laws I am setting before you
today?
9 Only be careful,[x] and watch yourselves closely so that you do not forget the things
your eyes have seen or let them slip from your heart as long as you live. Teach[y] them to
your children[z] and to their children after them. 10 Remember the day you stood before
the LORD your God at Horeb,[a] when he said to me, "Assemble the people before me to
hear my words so that they may learn to revere me as long as they live in the land and
may teach them to their children." 11 You came near and stood at the foot of the moun-

3:22 [e]Dt 1:29 [f]Ex 14:14; Dt 20:4
3:24 [g]Dt 11:2 [h]Ex 15:11; Ps 86:8 [i]Ps 71:16, 19 [j]2Sa 7:22
3:25 [k]Dt 4:22
3:26 [l]Dt 1:37; 31:2
3:27 [m]Nu 27:12
3:28 [n]Nu 27:18-23 [o]Dt 31:3,23
3:29 [p]Dt 4:46; 34:6
4:1 [q]Dt 5:33; 8:1; 16:20; 30:15-20; Eze 20:11; Ro 10:5
4:2 [r]Dt 12:32; Jos 1:7; Rev 22:18-19
4:3 [s]Nu 25:1-9; Ps 106:28
4:6 [t]Dt 30:19-20; Ps 19:7; Pr 1:7 [u]Job 28:28
4:7 [v]2Sa 7:23 [w]Ps 46:1; Isa 55:6
4:9 [x]Pr 4:23 [y]Ge 18:19; Eph 6:4 [z]Ps 78:5-6
4:10 [a]Ex 19:9,16

---

ence of Deuteronomy was to receive God's provision of leadership in the light of their history.

3:21 I commanded Joshua. The events of Numbers 20:1–13 are assumed here.

3:22 the LORD your God himself will fight for you. As Moses passed along the command to Joshua, he underlined the promise: The Lord will give victory (see 1:29).

3:23–29 Moses recounted how he had prayed to enter the land but had been told to encourage Joshua instead. Moses' prayer is instructive. He knew of the Lord's anger because of his sin at Meribah (Nu 20:12) but also realized that God does not "harbor his anger forever" (Ps 103:9). He recognized God's sovereign power and asked for great mercy, but he was satisfied with the Lord's negative answer. It was time for Joshua to take over. Moses' work was done. He was still strong, but the new phase of action, which would go on for many years, demanded a new leader.

3:28 encourage and strengthen him. Moses may have written Deuteronomy at least partially in response to this command, encouraging and strengthening Joshua in the promised land through the book's history and instruction.

■ **4:1–40** *The Call to Fidelity.* The blessings of God's care for the nation from Sinai to the Transjordan established the basis for Moses' call for loyal service to God. This call divides into four main parts: the basic contours of fidelity (vv. 1–2), lessons from the past (vv. 3–24), threats and hopes for the future (vv. 25–31) and a summation (vv. 32–40).

■ **4:1–2** *The Contours of Fidelity.* Moses presented the basic pattern of fidelity to the nation. Obedience to all the law of God would lead to life and victory in the land. This outlook does not amount to salvation by works. As Moses himself noted elsewhere, the ability to obey is itself a gracious gift from God (see note on 8:17–18).

4:1 that you may live and may go in and take possession. Although the grace of God is the source of all blessings, God normally grants his blessings in accordance with the faithfulness of his people.

4:2 Do not add. See 12:32. This does not mean that Moses wanted no more words from God, but rather that the words God was giving were to be treated as sacred and kept inviolate. A similar certification appears in Revelation 22:18–19, which is quite possibly modeled on this portion of Deuteronomy. See *WLC* 109.

■ **4:3–24** *Lessons From the Past.* Moses explained further the kind of fidelity required of Israel by pointing to lessons from the nation's past. He mentioned events at Baal Peor (vv. 3–9), Sinai (vv. 10–20) and Meribah (vv. 21–24).

■ **4:3–9** *Baal Peor.* This event dramatically demonstrated that turning from God would lead to terrible consequences.

4:3 Baal Peor. Refers to Israel's idolatry at Baal Peor, which God judged by killing 24,000 people (see Nu 25). Those who remained faithful survived, but now they faced another test of their faith as Moses called them to further obedience in the light of this event.

4:5–6 See *BC* 7.

4:5 See . . . to take possession. Moses applied the event at Baal Peor to Israel's current and future circumstances.

4:6 the nations. Israel's fidelity would be a testimony to a watching world. The testimony was to be that God was near his people and that Israel had received wisdom from God. The laws of Moses were not arbitrary regulations, nor were they designed merely to reveal sin. Obedience to the law also demonstrates an enviable wisdom (see theological article "The Three Uses of the Law" at Ps 119).

4:8–9 See *WLC* 99.

4:9 Teach them to your children. Deuteronomy strongly emphasizes the fact that Biblical faith is to be passed from generation to generation (see note on 6:7). The salvation of believers' children is not guaranteed, but it is to be the goal of many efforts and prayers.

■ **4:10–20** *Sinai.* Moses demonstrated that the critical events at Mount Sinai also taught the second generation of Israelites after the exodus lessons about their own need to remain faithful to God.

4:10 Remember. Refers to the great theophany at Mount Sinai (Ex 19:9—20:19)—a never-to-be-forgotten experience.

tain while it blazed with fire[b] to the very heavens, with black clouds and deep darkness.
12Then the LORD spoke[c] to you out of the fire. You heard the sound of words but saw no
form; there was only a voice. 13He declared to you his covenant,[d] the Ten Commandments,[e] which he commanded you to follow and then wrote them on two stone tablets.
14And the LORD directed me at that time to teach you the decrees and laws you are to follow in the land that you are crossing the Jordan to possess.

Idolatry Forbidden

15You saw no form[f] of any kind the day the LORD spoke to you at Horeb out of the fire.
Therefore watch yourselves very carefully,[g] 16so that you do not become corrupt and
make for yourselves an idol,[h] an image of any shape, whether formed like a man or a
woman, 17or like any animal on earth or any bird that flies in the air, 18or like any creature that moves along the ground or any fish in the waters below. 19And when you look
up to the sky and see the sun,[i] the moon and the stars—all the heavenly array[j]—do not
be enticed into bowing down to them and worshiping things the LORD your God has apportioned to all the nations under heaven. 20But as for you, the LORD took you and
brought you out of the iron-smelting furnace,[k] out of Egypt, to be the people of his inheritance,[l] as you now are.

21The LORD was angry with me[m] because of you, and he solemnly swore that I would
not cross the Jordan and enter the good land the LORD your God is giving you as your inheritance. 22I will die in this land; I will not cross the Jordan; but you are about to cross
over and take possession of that good land.[n] 23Be careful not to forget the covenant[o] of
the LORD your God that he made with you; do not make for yourselves an idol[p] in the form
of anything the LORD your God has forbidden. 24For the LORD your God is a consuming
fire,[q] a jealous God.

25After you have had children and grandchildren and have lived in the land a long
time—if you then become corrupt and make any kind of idol, doing evil[r] in the eyes of
the LORD your God and provoking him to anger, 26I call heaven and earth as witnesses
against you[s] this day that you will quickly perish from the land that you are crossing the
Jordan to possess. You will not live there long but will certainly be destroyed. 27The LORD
will scatter[t] you among the peoples, and only a few of you will survive among the nations
to which the LORD will drive you. 28There you will worship man-made gods[u] of wood and
stone, which cannot see or hear or eat or smell.[v] 29But if from there you seek[w] the LORD
your God, you will find him if you look for him with all your heart[x] and with all your
soul.[y] 30When you are in distress and all these things have happened to you, then in later days[z] you will return to the LORD your God and obey him. 31For the LORD your God is

4:11 [b]Ex 19:18; Heb 12:18-19
4:12 [c]Ex 20:22; Dt 5:4, 22
4:13 [d]Dt 9:9, 11 [e]Ex 24:12; 31:18; 34:28
4:15 [f]Isa 40:18 [g]Jos 23:11
4:16 [h]Ex 20:4-5; 32:7; Dt 5:8; Ro 1:23
4:19 [i]Dt 17:3; Job 31:26 [j]2Ki 17:16; 21:3; Ro 1:25
4:20 [k]1Ki 8:51; Jer 11:4 [l]Ex 19:5; Dt 9:29
4:21 [m]Nu 20:12; Dt 1:37
4:22 [n]Dt 3:25
4:23 [o]ver 9, 16 [p]Ex 20:4
4:24 [q]Ex 24:17; Dt 9:3; Heb 12:29
4:25 [r]2Ki 17:2, 17
4:26 [s]Dt 30:18-19; Isa 1:2; Mic 6:2
4:27 [t]Lev 26:33; Dt 28:36, 64; Ne 1:8
4:28 [u]Dt 28:36, 64; 1Sa 26:19; Jer 16:13 [v]Ps 115:4-8; 135:15-18
4:29 [w]2Ch 15:4; Isa 55:6 [x]Jer 29:13 [y]Dt 30:1-3, 10
4:30 [z]Dt 31:29; Jer 23:20; Hos 3:5

4:13 the Ten Commandments. This title is also used in 10:4 and in Exodus 34:28. Protestants usually divide the list into four commandments that stipulate one's duty to God (5:7–15) and six that designate one's duty to humans (5:16–21). Roman Catholics and Lutherans unite the first and second and divide the tenth so as to get a division of three and seven. Jewish tradition translates "Ten Words" rather than "Ten Commandments," and many within this tradition count the prologue (5:6) as the first word, uniting the first and second without dividing the tenth. The command regarding the Sabbath is pivotal, as it makes reference to God and is also for the benefit of both people and animals (Mk 2:27). As Protestants count them, the first three commandments primarily concern God, and the last six primarily concern humans.

4:15–31 One of the chief concerns of Deuteronomy is the judgment of God that comes against idolatry. This emphasis is reflected in Joshua, Judges, 1 and 2 Samuel and 1 and 2 Kings, all of which rely heavily on Deuteronomy.

4:15–20 See *WCF* 2.1; 21.1; *WLC* 109; *WSC* 51; *HC* 96.

4:15 You saw no form. It was common practice in the ancient Near East to portray gods in specific forms. Moses stressed that images of the Lord were entirely unacceptable as objects of worship because God revealed himself through amorphous fire. See notes on Exodus 20:4–6.

4:20 the iron-smelting furnace. A very hot furnace used to smelt iron. This is a strong metaphor for Egypt as a place of great affliction and refinement (see 1Ki 8:51; Jer 11:4).

■ **4:21–24** *Meribah.* Moses recalled the events at Meribah, where he was forbidden to enter the promised land because of his infidelity. The Israelites were to learn the importance of faithfulness from this event. Rebellion could also keep them from entering the land.

4:21 angry with me because of you. Compare 1:37. The passage presupposes knowledge of Numbers 20:1–13. Moses placed part of the blame on the nation, because the people's complaining had led him to strike the rock.

4:24 a consuming fire. An allusion to the fact that God appeared as fire on the mountain (v. 15); taken further it indicates that God is wrathful against those who turn from him to idolatry. The writer of Hebrews used this passage as a warning against apostasy in the Christian church, much as Moses used it here for Israel (Heb 12:29). **a jealous God.** *Zealous* and *jealous* come from the same root word. *Jealous,* as used here, does not include the meaning of envy but that of energy and single-minded purpose. See note at Exodus 20:5. See also *BC* 26.

■ **4:25–31** *Threats and Hope in the Future.* Moses turned from lessons from the past to warn and encourage the Israelites about their future once they possessed the land.

4:25–29 Moses warned that, even after Israel entered the land, future generations would suffer severely if they turned to idolatry. Here in brief summary is found the warning embodied in the curses of 28:15–68.

4:27 The LORD will scatter you. Exile from the land was the greatest curse God threatened to bring against his people (see Lev 26). The northern kingdom was exiled by the Assyrians in 722 B.C., and Judah went into Babylonian captivity in 586 B.C.

4:29 all your heart. See note on 6:5.

4:30 later days. This phrase can refer to any general future time of apostasy and renewal. This general meaning is like that of the phrase "in days to come" (31:29), which is parallel to "after my death" (31:29). The prophets took this expression in a technical sense as a way of referring to the days at the end of the exile or to the time when the exile was to be brought to completion (see note on Hos 3:5). God promised that, despite the sinfulness of his people, their exile would not continue forever (cf. Lev 26). This guarantee was the basis of prophetic hopes for return from exile, and of the New Testament promise of the consummation of the kingdom

a merciful[a] God; he will not abandon or destroy you or forget the covenant with your
forefathers, which he confirmed to them by oath.

The LORD Is God

32 Ask[b] now about the former days, long before your time, from the day God created
man on the earth;[c] ask from one end of the heavens to the other.[d] Has anything so great
as this ever happened, or has anything like it ever been heard of? 33 Has any other people heard the voice of God[a] speaking out of fire, as you have, and lived?[e] 34 Has any god
ever tried to take for himself one nation out of another nation,[f] by testings, by miraculous signs[g] and wonders,[h] by war, by a mighty hand and an outstretched arm,[i] or by
great and awesome deeds,[j] like all the things the LORD your God did for you in Egypt before your very eyes?
35 You were shown these things so that you might know that the LORD is God; besides
him there is no other.[k] 36 From heaven he made you hear his voice[l] to discipline you. On
earth he showed you his great fire, and you heard his words from out of the fire. 37 Because he loved[m] your forefathers and chose their descendants after them, he brought
you out of Egypt by his Presence and his great strength,[n] 38 to drive out before you nations greater and stronger than you and to bring you into their land to give it to you for
your inheritance,[o] as it is today.
39 Acknowledge and take to heart this day that the LORD is God in heaven above and
on the earth below. There is no other.[p] 40 Keep[q] his decrees and commands, which I am
giving you today, so that it may go well[r] with you and your children after you and that
you may live long[s] in the land the LORD your God gives you for all time.

Cities of Refuge

41 Then Moses set aside three cities east of the Jordan, 42 to which anyone who had
killed a person could flee if he had unintentionally killed his neighbor without malice
aforethought. He could flee into one of these cities and save his life. 43 The cities were
these: Bezer in the desert plateau, for the Reubenites; Ramoth in Gilead, for the Gadites;
and Golan in Bashan, for the Manassites.

Introduction to the Law

44 This is the law Moses set before the Israelites. 45 These are the stipulations, decrees
and laws Moses gave them when they came out of Egypt 46 and were in the valley near
Beth Peor east of the Jordan, in the land of Sihon[t] king of the Amorites, who reigned in
Heshbon and was defeated by Moses and the Israelites as they came out of Egypt.
47 They took possession of his land and the land of Og king of Bashan, the two Amorite
kings east of the Jordan. 48 This land extended from Aroer[u] on the rim of the Arnon Gorge
to Mount Siyon[b][v] (that is, Hermon), 49 and included all the Arabah east of the Jordan, as
far as the Sea of the Arabah,[c] below the slopes of Pisgah.

4:31 [a] 2Ch 30:9; Ne 9:31; Ps 116:5; Jnh 4:2
4:32 [b] Dt 32:7; Job 8:8 [c] Ge 1:27 [d] Mt 24:31
4:33 [e] Ex 20:22; Dt 5:24-26
4:34 [f] Ex 6:6 [g] Ex 7:3 [h] Dt 7:19; 26:8 [i] Ex 13:3 [j] Dt 34:12
4:35 [k] Dt 32:39; 1Sa 2:2; Isa 45:5,18
4:36 [l] Ex 19:9,19
4:37 [m] Dt 10:15 [n] Ex 13:3,9,14
4:38 [o] Dt 7:1; 9:5
4:39 [p] ver 35; Jos 2:11
4:40 [q] Lev 22:31; Dt 5:33 [r] Dt 5:16 [s] Dt 6:3,18; Eph 6:2-3
4:46 [t] Nu 21:26; Dt 3:29
4:48 [u] Dt 2:36 [v] Dt 3:9

[a] *33* Or *of a god* [b] *48* Hebrew; Syriac (see also Deut. 3:9) *Sirion* [c] *49* That is, the Dead Sea

---

of God when Jesus returns (see theological articles "The Plan of the Ages" at Heb 7 and "Kingdom of God" at Mt 4).

4:31 a merciful God. God was forgiving to his people during the period of the old covenant, just as he is during the period of the new covenant. This may be an allusion to the name of God given in Exodus 34:6 (the word translated "merciful" here is there translated "compassionate"). **the covenant with your forefathers.** See 1:8.

■ **4:32–40** *Summation.* Moses brought together the principles he had outlined in the previous verses.

4:32 the day God created man. A reference to the early chapters of Genesis.

4:34 in Egypt. Refers to the deliverance from Egypt. Deuteronomy does not tell the story of the exodus but refers to it repeatedly and in detail.

4:37 his Presence. Probably refers to the event recounted in Exodus 33:14.

■ **4:41–43** *A Note on Cities of Refuge in Transjordan.* This section is an aside that notes the names of the cities of refuge for the Transjordan. It forms a transition between Moses' first and second speeches. The principle of having cities of refuge was given in Exodus 21:13. That there were to be six was stated in Numbers 35:6. This section names the three for the Transjordan, and Deuteronomy 19 states that there should be three in Canaan. Joshua 20 completes the list by naming all six.

■ **4:44—26:19** *Moses' Second Address.* This portion of Deuteronomy roughly corresponds to the series of rules and stipulations that appear in suzerain-vassal treaties. It contains Moses' second address, which focuses on the origin and content of the laws of the Sinai covenant and the need for Moses' audience to reaffirm their loyalty to these laws. These chapters divide into four sections: an introduction (4:44–49), a general orientation toward the stipulations (5:1—11:32), a more detailed list of laws (12:1—26:15) and a conclusion (26:16–19).

■ **4:44–49** *Introduction.* Moses provided a historical setting for the giving of God's law to this generation.

4:45 stipulations, decrees and laws. This is covenantal language. Those who emphasize the treaty form of the book compare this language with the stipulation section of ancient treaties, especially those of the second millennium B.C.

4:48 Mount Siyon. This is perhaps a fourth name for Mount Hermon (3:9). There is still a fifth name used today: Jebel es Sheikh, "Old Man Mountain," named so for its white summit. But the name "Siyon" is not attested elsewhere. It is possible that it is a copying mistake for "Sirion," which it closely resembles, but only the Syriac translation reads "Sirion" here.

4:49 the slopes of Pisgah. See 3:17.

The Ten Commandments

5 Moses summoned all Israel and said:
Hear, O Israel, the decrees and laws I declare in your hearing today. Learn them and
be sure to follow them. 2 The LORD our God made a covenant[w] with us at Horeb. 3 It was
not with our fathers that the LORD made this covenant, but with us, with all of us who
are alive here today.[x] 4 The LORD spoke[y] to you face to face out of the fire on the mountain. 5 (At that time I stood between[z] the LORD and you to declare to you the word of the
LORD, because you were afraid[a] of the fire and did not go up the mountain.) And he said:

6 "I am the LORD your God, who brought you out of Egypt, out of the land of
slavery.
7 "You shall have no other gods before[a] me.
8 "You shall not make for yourself an idol in the form of anything in heaven above
or on the earth beneath or in the waters below. 9 You shall not bow down
to them or worship them; for I, the LORD your God, am a jealous God, punishing the children for the sin of the fathers to the third and fourth generation of those who hate me,[b] 10 but showing love to a thousand ⌊generations⌋
of those who love me and keep my commandments.[c]
11 "You shall not misuse the name of the LORD your God, for the LORD will not hold
anyone guiltless who misuses his name.[d]
12 "Observe the Sabbath day by keeping it holy,[e] as the LORD your God has commanded you. 13 Six days you shall labor and do all your work, 14 but the seventh day[f]
is a Sabbath to the LORD your God. On it you shall not do any work, neither
you, nor your son or daughter, nor your manservant or maidservant, nor
your ox, your donkey or any of your animals, nor the alien within your
gates, so that your manservant and maidservant may rest, as you do. 15 Remember that you were slaves in Egypt and that the LORD your God brought
you out of there with a mighty hand and an outstretched arm.[g] Therefore the
LORD your God has commanded you to observe the Sabbath day.
16 "Honor your father and your mother,[h] as the LORD your God has commanded you,
so that you may live long[i] and that it may go well with you in the land the
LORD your God is giving you.
17 "You shall not murder.[j]
18 "You shall not commit adultery.[k]
19 "You shall not steal.
20 "You shall not give false testimony against your neighbor.

a 7 Or *besides*

5:2 [w]Ex 19:5
5:3 [x]Heb 8:9
5:4 [y]Dt 4:12,33,36
5:5 [z]Gal 3:19 [a]Ex 20:18,21
5:9 [b]Ex 34:7
5:10 [c]Jer 32:18
5:11 [d]Lev 19:12; Mt 5:33-37
5:12 [e]Ex 20:8
5:14 [f]Ge 2:2; Heb 4:4
5:15 [g]Dt 4:34
5:16 [h]Ex 20:12; Lev 19:3; Dt 27:16; Eph 6:2-3*; Col 3:20 [i]Dt 4:40
5:17 [j]Mt 5:21-22*
5:18 [k]Mt 5:27-30, Lk 18:20*; Jas 2:11*

■ **5:1—11:32** *Orientation Toward the Stipulations.* Moses set forth a number of basic concepts concerning the origin and importance of the covenant stipulations. He touched on three matters: how the laws originated with God but came through him (5:1–33), future fidelity in light of the past (6:1—11:25) and God's call for covenant renewal (11:26–32).
■ **5:1–33** *Laws From God and Moses.* Moses set forth the two main sources of the laws for Israel: the Ten Commandments, which came directly from God (vv. 1–22), and the other laws, which came from Moses (vv. 23–33).
■ **5:1–22** *The Ten Commandments From God.* Moses recounted how the Lord had given Israel the Ten Commandments from Mount Sinai (cf. Ex 20).
5:1–3 See *WLC* 93.
5:1 Hear, O Israel. This solemn form of address to Israel is found only in Deuteronomy (here, in the Shema of 6:4 and in the exhortation of 9:1–3). Its use is also prescribed in 20:3 as part of the priestly exhortation before battle.
5:3 not with our fathers. Moses was differentiating this covenant in Horeb from the promise of the land made to the patriarchs, Abraham, Isaac and Jacob. The Israelites of Moses' day, not the patriarchs, received the Mosaic covenant.
5:6–21 See *HC* 92.
5:6 I am the LORD your God. This preface to the Ten Commandments is identical to that used in Exodus 20:2. It may be likened to the historical preamble to an ancient treaty covenant, with stipulations to follow. **brought you out of Egypt.** This phrase roughly parallels the historical prologue of a suzerain-vassal treaty in which the king rehearsed the benevolence he had shown toward his vassals. Israel received laws, but those laws were to be obeyed out of gratitude for the grace God had shown Israel, not out of a desire to earn salvation.
5:7 no other gods. The Lord had done so much for his people that he demanded exclusive loyalty. The high ethical monotheism of this commandment and of the whole Old Testament was unique in ancient times. There are no other gods (4:39), but depraved humans worship "what is no god" (32:21). The worship of anything other than God is forbidden.
5:8 an idol. See 4:15. The prohibition is not against making statues or objects for use in worship, but against making and worshiping images. God himself commanded that certain crafted images be used in tabernacle worship (Ex 25:18–22,31–36; 26:1,31; 28:33–34).
5:10 a thousand generations. Whereas God's anger extends only to the third and fourth generation, his love extends to a thousand generations.
5:12–15 See *WLC* 116,121; *WSC* 58.
5:12 Observe the Sabbath day. Most of the commandments in Deuteronomy parallel almost verbatim those in Exodus 20, with obvious interdependence. Deuteronomy changes the explanation for this command. Whereas Exodus cites God's work of creation as a basis (see Ex 20:11), Deuteronomy focuses on the experience of slavery in Egypt.
5:16 so that you may live long. See 5:33 and 30:18 and 20. A comparison of 22:7 and 25:15 suggests that this clause may primarily be a promise of settled conditions and long peace for the people in the land, which would also include freedom from early death due to war, famine and plagues. Paul referred to this command, changing the expression "the land the LORD your God is giving you" to "the earth" (Eph 6:2–3). This was an appropriate adjustment for the New Testament age. Ultimately the fulfillment of this promise will take place when Christ returns and those who love him are brought into the eternal life of the new heavens and the new earth. See *WLC* 133; *WSC* 66.

21 "You shall not covet your neighbor's wife. You shall not set your desire on your
neighbor's house or land, his manservant or maidservant, his ox or donkey,
or anything that belongs to your neighbor."[l]

22 These are the commandments the LORD proclaimed in a loud voice to your whole
assembly there on the mountain from out of the fire, the cloud and the deep darkness;
and he added nothing more. Then he wrote them on two stone tablets[m] and gave them
to me.
23 When you heard the voice out of the darkness, while the mountain was ablaze with
fire, all the leading men of your tribes and your elders came to me. 24 And you said, "The
LORD our God has shown us his glory and his majesty, and we have heard his voice from
the fire. Today we have seen that a man can live even if God speaks with him.[n] 25 But now,
why should we die? This great fire will consume us, and we will die if we hear the voice
of the LORD our God any longer.[o] 26 For what mortal man has ever heard the voice of the
living God speaking out of fire, as we have, and survived?[p] 27 Go near and listen to all that
the LORD our God says. Then tell us whatever the LORD our God tells you. We will listen
and obey."
28 The LORD heard you when you spoke to me and the LORD said to me, "I have heard
what this people said to you. Everything they said was good.[q] 29 Oh, that their hearts
would be inclined to fear me[r] and keep all my commands[s] always, so that it might go
well with them and their children forever![t]
30 "Go, tell them to return to their tents. 31 But you stay here[u] with me so that I may
give you all the commands, decrees and laws you are to teach them to follow in the land
I am giving them to possess."
32 So be careful to do what the LORD your God has commanded you; do not turn aside
to the right or to the left.[v] 33 Walk in all the way that the LORD your God has commanded you,[w] so that you may live and prosper and prolong your days[x] in the land that you
will possess.

Love the LORD Your God

6 These are the commands, decrees and laws the LORD your God directed me to teach
you to observe in the land that you are crossing the Jordan to possess, 2 so that you,
your children and their children after them may fear[y] the LORD your God as long as you
live by keeping all his decrees and commands that I give you, and so that you may enjoy long life. 3 Hear, O Israel, and be careful to obey so that it may go well with you and
that you may increase greatly[z] in a land flowing with milk and honey,[a] just as the LORD,
the God of your fathers, promised you.
4 Hear, O Israel: The LORD our God, the LORD is one.[a][b] 5 Love[c] the LORD your God with
all your heart and with all your soul and with all your strength.[d] 6 These commandments

5:21 [l]Ro 7:7*; 13:9*
5:22 [m]Ex 24:12; 31:18; Dt 4:13
5:24 [n]Ex 19:19
5:25 [o]Dt 18:16
5:26 [p]Dt 4:33
5:28 [q]Dt 18:17
5:29 [r]Ps 81:8,13 [s]Dt 11:1; Isa 48:18 [t]Dt 4:1,40
5:31 [u]Ex 24:12
5:32 [v]Dt 17:11,20; 28:14; Jos 1:7; 23:6; Pr 4:27
5:33 [w]Jer 7:23 [x]Dt 4:40
6:2 [y]Ex 20:20; Dt 10:12-13
6:3 [z]Dt 5:33 [a]Ex 3:8
6:4 [b]Mk 12:29*; 1Co 8:4
6:5 [c]Mt 22:37*; Mk 12:30*; Lk 10:27* [d]Dt 10:12

[a] 4 Or *The LORD our God is one LORD;* or *The LORD is our God, the LORD is one;* or *The LORD is our God, the LORD alone*

5:21 See *WLC* 148; *WSC* 81.
5:22 and he added nothing more. The Hebrew simply says, "and he did not add," which may be an idiom meaning that he did not after this point speak directly to the people. **two stone tablets.** In Exodus the tablets are mentioned in 24:12 and again in 31:18, where they are called "the two tablets of the Testimony . . . inscribed by the finger of God." Exodus 32:15 states that the writing was on both sides, inscribed by God. These tablets were broken (Ex 32:19), but new ones were made (Ex 34:1–4,27). They were called "the Testimony" and were placed inside "the ark of the Testimony" (see Ex 25:16; 40:20). The ark was called both "the ark of the Testimony" (Ex 40:3) and "the ark of the covenant" (Nu 10:33). In some contexts "testimony" and "covenant" are synonyms; both are treaty or covenant terms. The Ten Commandments were a significant part of God's covenant. See *BC* 3.
■ **5:23–33** *Moses the Mediator.* Moses recalled how he had been chosen to mediate the other laws of God. The people of Israel had asked him to be the mediator of the law. He fulfilled this role in Israel with God's authority and the people's approval.
5:29 See *WLC* 110.
5:31 you stay here. Moses remained in the presence of God to receive many more commands that he would later deliver to the people so that they would know how to live in God's blessing in the land.
5:31,33 See *WLC* 93.
■ **6:1—11:25** *Fidelity in the Future in Light of the Past.* After providing the background to the laws he had given to Israel, Moses called on the Israelites to love God and to pass their love for God on to their children by remembering and recounting important lessons from the past. He first noted the basic pattern of fidelity (6:1–9) and addressed a number of issues that would arise in the future: testing the Lord (6:10–25), holy war (7:1–26), prosperity and pride (8:1–20), self-righteousness (9:1—10:11) and the need to circumcise the heart (10:12—11:25).
■ **6:1–9** *The Priorities of Fidelity.* Moses set forth the highest priorities of the covenant: loving God in the present and passing on that love to future generations.
6:2 long life. See note at 5:16. Here also it may be understood as "long life in the land."
6:3 Hear, O Israel. These words do not translate the same Hebrew phrase as 5:1, 6:4 and 9:1, but they are emphatic.
6:4–9 See *WCF* 21.6; *WLC* 99,129,156,160; *HC* 103.
6:4 Hear, O Israel. The Hebrew word is *shema;* hence the common Jewish designation of this verse as the Shema. The importance of this command was echoed by Christ (Mk 12:29). See *WCF* 2.1; *WLC* 8; *WSC* 5; *BC* 1; *BC* 7; *HC* 25.
6:5 all . . . all . . . all. This repetition emphasizes totality. The reading of Mark 12:30 ("mind and . . . strength") probably resulted from consolidating different translations of the terms in various Septuagint (the Greek translation of the OT) traditions. This is the language of wholehearted devotion. God does not merely demand obedience to a law or fidelity to a covenant. His word is this: "My son, give me your heart" (Pr 23:26) and "The sacrifices of God are a broken spirit; a broken and contrite heart, O God, you will not despise" (Ps 51:17). **with all your heart and with all your soul.** This and similar terminology express the ideal of perfect devotion

that I give you today are to be upon your hearts.[e] 7Impress them on your children. Talk
about them when you sit at home and when you walk along the road, when you lie down
and when you get up.[f] 8Tie them as symbols on your hands and bind them on your foreheads.[g] 9Write them on the doorframes of your houses and on your gates.[h]
10When the LORD your God brings you into the land he swore to your fathers, to Abraham,
Isaac and Jacob, to give you—a land with large, flourishing cities you did not build,[i] 11hous-
es filled with all kinds of good things you did not provide, wells you did not dig, and vineyards and olive groves you did not plant—then when you eat and are satisfied,[j] 12be careful that you do not forget the LORD, who brought you out of Egypt, out of the land of slavery.
13Fear the LORD[k] your God, serve him only[l] and take your oaths in his name. 14Do not
follow other gods, the gods of the peoples around you; 15for the LORD your God[m], who
is among you, is a jealous God and his anger will burn against you, and he will destroy
you from the face of the land. 16Do not test the LORD your God[n] as you did at Massah. 17Be
sure to keep the commands of the LORD your God and the stipulations and decrees he has
given you.[o] 18Do what is right and good in the LORD's sight, so that it may go well[p] with
you and you may go in and take over the good land that the LORD promised on oath to
your forefathers, 19thrusting out all your enemies before you, as the LORD said.
20In the future, when your son asks you,[q] "What is the meaning of the stipulations, decrees and laws the LORD our God has commanded you?" 21tell him: "We were slaves of
Pharaoh in Egypt, but the LORD brought us out of Egypt with a mighty hand. 22Before our
eyes the LORD sent miraculous signs and wonders—great and terrible—upon Egypt and
Pharaoh and his whole household. 23But he brought us out from there to bring us in and
give us the land that he promised on oath to our forefathers. 24The LORD commanded us
to obey all these decrees and to fear the LORD our God,[r] so that we might always prosper
and be kept alive, as is the case today.[s] 25And if we are careful to obey all this law before
the LORD our God, as he has commanded us, that will be our righteousness.[t]"

Driving Out the Nations

7 When the LORD your God brings you into the land you are entering to possess and
drives out before you many nations[u]—the Hittites, Girgashites, Amorites, Canaanites, Perizzites, Hivites and Jebusites, seven nations larger and stronger than you—
2and when the LORD your God has delivered them over to you and you have defeated
them, then you must destroy them totally.[a] Make no treaty[v] with them, and show them

[a] 2 The Hebrew term refers to the irrevocable giving over of things or persons to the LORD, often by totally destroying them; also in verse 26.

6:6 [e]Dt 11:18
6:7 [f]Dt 4:9; 11:19; Eph 6:4
6:8 [g]Ex 13:9,16; Dt 11:18
6:9 [h]Dt 11:20
6:10 [i]Jos 24:13
6:11 [j]Dt 8:10
6:13 [k]Dt 10:20 [l]Mt 4:10*; Lk 4:8*
6:15 [m]Dt 4:24
6:16 [n]Ex 17:7; Mt 4:7*; Lk 4:12*
6:17 [o]Dt 11:22; Ps 119:4
6:18 [p]Dt 4:40
6:20 [q]Ex 13:14
6:24 [r]Dt 10:12; Jer 32:39 [s]Ps 41:2
6:25 [t]Dt 24:13; Ro 10:3,5
7:1 [u]Dt 31:3; Ac 13:19
7:2 [v]Ex 23:32

(see 4:29; 10:12; 11:13; 13:3; 26:16; 30:2,6,10), but when people are described as actually having this quality, it expresses their deep-seated and sincere, however imperfect, loyalty (see 2Ki 20:3; 1Ch 28:9; 29:19). See *WLC* 99,104; *HC* 4,94.

6:7 Impress them on your children. Biblical faith is deeply concerned with passing the truths of God from generation to generation. This process is one dimension of fulfilling the original mandate for humanity to multiply (Ge 1:28–29). When sin entered the world, it became necessary to teach future generations the ways of God to ensure that knowledge of the Lord is not lost.

6:8 bind them on your foreheads. The phrases in this section are heaped up expressions to emphasize the overall importance of God's law. Since the time of Christ some Jews have taken these verses literally, tying little boxes (phylacteries) containing these verses on their arms and foreheads and fastening them on their doorposts.

■ **6:10–25** *Testing the Lord.* At Massah the people of Israel lost sight of how much goodness God had shown to them. Out of ingratitude they tested the Lord. Moses called on his readers to avoid such ingratitude.

6:10–12 Moses knew that it would be easy for the Israelites to forget that their good lives in the land were the result of God's grace. So he reminded them to remind themselves constantly. Forgetting God's goodness is one of the first steps toward rebellion against him.

6:10 the land he swore to your fathers. See 5:3. This is one of many references to God's solemn promise to the patriarchs.

6:11 you did not. One of the great blessings to be enjoyed in the promised land was God's gracious provision. Because of this, life and work would be much easier there (cf. 11:10–11).

6:12 brought you out of Egypt. See note on 5:6.

6:13 serve him only. Jesus referred to this command (Mt 4:10; Lk 4:12) as he resisted Satan's temptations (see note on v. 16). **take your oaths in his name.** The third commandment does not forbid taking an oath but prohibits false oaths and oath breaking. Here Moses meant that the people of God were not to swear in the names of other gods, thereby giving their allegiance to them instead of to the Lord. See *WCF* 21.5, 22.2; *WLC* 99,108; *HC* 94,101.

6:15 a jealous God. See 4:24.

6:16 Massah. See Exodus 17:7. *Massah* means "testing." Apparently King Ahaz alluded to this verse insincerely to get rid of the prophet Isaiah (Isa 7:12). Jesus quoted this passage (Mt 4:7; Lk 4:12) in response to Satan's temptation (see note on v. 13).

6:18 go well . . . go in . . . take over. Faithfulness to the Lord was necessary for the success of the conquest.

6:20–25 See *HC* 103.

6:20 when your son asks you. The focus on future generations appears again (see note on v. 7).

6:24 to obey . . . and to fear the LORD. For a summary of this section, see John 14:23.

6:25 our righteousness. Here righteousness simply means right living, not the fuller concept of perfect justification by God as developed in the New Testament. Moses encouraged Israel to obey the law in the same way as the New Testament encourages believers to obey God—as an expression of gratitude (see note at 5:6).

■ **7:1–26** *Requirements of Holy War.* Moses turned the people's attention to the next major event in Israel's national life: the conquest of the land. He assured them of victory but also warned them against apostasy once they were in the land.

7:1 drives out. See 2:32. **seven nations.** Canaan was evidently not ruled by a single power. These seven nations are hard to identify, and the names are fluid. In 20:17 only six nations are mentioned, as is also true five times in Exodus (Ex 3:8,17; 23:23; 33:2; 34:11). In these six places, the Girgashites are omitted. The Jebusites are said to inhabit Jebus, another name for Jerusalem. There is some indication that the Jebusites were Hurrians (see note on 2:10–12). Amorites are known from ancient Mesopotamia. Hammurapi was an Amorite, as were Og and Sihon, kings of the Transjordan. The word "Canaanite" seems sometimes to include them all.

7:2 destroy them totally. See note on 2:32. God had told Abraham that conquest of the land would not take place until "the sin of the

no mercy.[w] [3]Do not intermarry with them.[x] Do not give your daughters to their sons or
take their daughters for your sons, [4]for they will turn your sons away from following me
to serve other gods, and the LORD's anger will burn against you and will quickly destroy[y]
you. [5]This is what you are to do to them: Break down their altars, smash their sacred
stones, cut down their Asherah poles[a] and burn their idols in the fire.[z] [6]For you are a people holy[a] to the LORD your God.[b] The LORD your God has chosen[c] you out of all the peoples on the face of the earth to be his people, his treasured possession.
[7]The LORD did not set his affection on you and choose you because you were more numerous than other peoples, for you were the fewest of all peoples.[d] [8]But it was because
the LORD loved[e] you and kept the oath he swore[f] to your forefathers that he brought you
out with a mighty hand and redeemed you from the land of slavery,[g] from the power of
Pharaoh king of Egypt. [9]Know therefore that the LORD your God is God;[h] he is the faithful God,[i] keeping his covenant of love[j] to a thousand generations of those who love him
and keep his commands. [10]But

those who hate him he will repay to their face by destruction;
he will not be slow to repay to their face those who hate him.

[11]Therefore, take care to follow the commands, decrees and laws I give you today.
[12]If you pay attention to these laws and are careful to follow them, then the LORD your
God will keep his covenant of love with you, as he swore to your forefathers.[k] [13]He will
love you and bless you[l] and increase your numbers. He will bless the fruit of your
womb, the crops of your land—your grain, new wine and oil—the calves of your herds
and the lambs of your flocks in the land that he swore to your forefathers to give you.[m]
[14]You will be blessed more than any other people; none of your men or women will be
childless, nor any of your livestock without young.[n] [15]The LORD will keep you free from
every disease.[o] He will not inflict on you the horrible diseases you knew in Egypt, but he
will inflict them on all who hate you. [16]You must destroy all the peoples the LORD your
God gives over to you. Do not look on them with pity[p] and do not serve their gods, for
that will be a snare[q] to you.
[17]You may say to yourselves, "These nations are stronger than we are. How can we
drive them out?[r]" [18]But do not be afraid[s] of them; remember well what the LORD your
God did to Pharaoh and to all Egypt.[t] [19]You saw with your own eyes the great trials, the
miraculous signs and wonders, the mighty hand and outstretched arm, with which the
LORD your God brought you out. The LORD your God will do the same to all the peoples
you now fear.[u] [20]Moreover, the LORD your God will send the hornet[v] among them until

7:2 [w]Dt 13:8
7:3 [x]Ex 34:15-16; Ezr 9:2
7:4 [y]Dt 6:15
7:5 [z]Ex 23:24; Dt 12:2-3
7:6 [a]Ex 19:5-6; 1Pe 2:9 [b]Ps 50:5; Jer 2:3 [c]Dt 14:2
7:7 [d]Dt 10:22
7:8 [e]Dt 10:15 [f]Ex 32:13 [g]Ex 13:14
7:9 [h]Dt 4:35 [i]1Co 1:9; 2Ti 2:13 [j]Ne 1:5; Da 9:4
7:12 [k]Lev 26:3-13; Dt 28:1-14; Ps 105:8-9
7:13 [l]Jn 14:21 [m]Dt 28:4
7:14 [n]Ex 23:26
7:15 [o]Ex 15:26
7:16 [p]ver 2; Ex 23:33 [q]Jdg 8:27
7:17 [r]Nu 33:53
7:18 [s]Dt 31:6 [t]Ps 105:5
7:19 [u]Dt 4:34
7:20 [v]Ex 23:28; Jos 24:12

a 5 That is, symbols of the goddess Asherah; here and elsewhere in Deuteronomy

Amorites . . . reached its full measure" (Ge 15:16). God was just in ordering the conquest both because the sins of the Canaanites were extreme and because their sin defiled the promised land, the region where God's special presence dwelled. Canaanite religious poems describe their gods as worse than even those of the Greeks and Assyrians. God commanded holy war as the means of destroying these pagan idolators. Far from ethnocentric, the Biblical concept of holy war is one of war against evil. This is evident in the fact that if the Israelites turned away from God, they too would perish (28:15–68).

7:3–4 See *WCF* 24.3.

7:3 Do not intermarry. Marriage is the closest of human ties. Its sacredness was guarded in Old Testament law. This verse was not a prohibition against racial or ethnic intermarriage. Instead, it banned religious intermarriage (see notes on Ezr 9:1–15). The same rule appears in the New Testament (1Co 7:39).

7:5 Break down their altars. Israel was, by God's design and command, a theocracy. God had promised his grace to his people. He would not tolerate pagan religion. These kinds of rules apply today to the church, which is to be a pure body in a godless world. Believers today should not attack pagan shrines because the new covenant church is not to achieve its purposes by the sword of war (Mt 26:52) but through the sword of the Spirit, which is the Word of God (Eph 6:17, Heb 4:12). The example of Jesus and the apostles is consistent in this regard—while none of them tolerated pagan religions, all refrained from violence against them. Nevertheless, the call for separation from unbelieving worship is still just as emphatic (see 2Co 6:15). See *WLC* 108.

7:6 chosen you. Moses looked to the past and pointed out that God had chosen his people to be holy, separate from the Canaanites. Moses had in mind the election of the nation of Israel to be in a covenant relationship with God, not election to salvation.

7:8 because the LORD loved you. The election of the nation of Israel (vv. 6–7) was grounded in God's covenant of love with the nation's forebears and not in any intrinsic value or goodness of the nation of his choice (see v. 7). **swore to your forefathers.** See 6:10. God's election of Israel was based on his oath to Abraham, Isaac and Jacob. In New Testament times, his election of the church is based on his oath to Jesus, the son of Abraham and the Son of God (Ps 110:4; Heb 7:20–28).

7:9–11 See *HC* 11.

7:9 a thousand generations. See note on 5:10.

7:13 He will bless the fruit of your womb. This phrase is practically the same as that found in 28:4, where it heads a liturgy of blessings. Israel furthered the fulfillment of humanity's call to multiply and fill the earth (Ge 1:26–29; see note on Ex 1:7). **grain, new wine and oil.** The word here translated "wine" is not the common word associated with drunkenness but the word describing the product as it came fresh from the wine presses (Pr 3:10). The word "oil" refers to the olive oil used for cooking and in lamps. The call to dominion was also offered to Israel (Ge 1:26–29).

7:15 the horrible diseases you knew in Egypt. The same promise is given in Exodus 15:26; the opposite is given as a curse in Deuteronomy 28:60.

7:17 You may say to yourselves. Moses anticipated that his listeners would be afraid as they faced the conquest. To assure them, he referred to the past defeat of Egypt (vv. 18–19).

7:19 You saw with your own eyes. See note on 5:3.

7:20 God will send the hornet. The Hebrew word translated "hornet" is from the same root word rendered as "skin disease" in Leviticus 14. Possibly it means "God will send distress." But the figure of stinging insects chasing the enemy is used elsewhere (1:44; Isa 7:18), and that of a hornet is quite appropriate. God promised to fight for his people with the same power that their forebears had witnessed in the exodus.

even the survivors who hide from you have perished. 21 Do not be terrified by them, for
the LORD your God, who is among you,[w] is a great and awesome God.[x] 22 The LORD your
God will drive out those nations before you, little by little.[y] You will not be allowed to
eliminate them all at once, or the wild animals will multiply around you. 23 But the LORD
your God will deliver them over to you, throwing them into great confusion until they are
destroyed. 24 He will give their kings into your hand, and you will wipe out their names
from under heaven. No one will be able to stand up against you;[z] you will destroy them.
25 The images of their gods you are to burn[a] in the fire. Do not covet[b] the silver and gold
on them, and do not take it for yourselves, or you will be ensnared[c] by it, for it is detestable[d] to the LORD your God. 26 Do not bring a detestable thing into your house or you, like
it, will be set apart for destruction.[e] Utterly abhor and detest it, for it is set apart for destruction.

Do Not Forget the LORD

8 Be careful to follow every command I am giving you today, so that you may live[f] and
increase and may enter and possess the land that the LORD promised on oath to your
forefathers. 2 Remember how the LORD your God led[g] you all the way in the desert these
forty years, to humble you and to test you in order to know what was in your heart,
whether or not you would keep his commands. 3 He humbled you, causing you to hunger and then feeding you with manna,[h] which neither you nor your fathers had known,
to teach you that man does not live on bread alone but on every word that comes from
the mouth of the LORD.[i] 4 Your clothes did not wear out and your feet did not swell during these forty years.[j] 5 Know then in your heart that as a man disciplines his son, so the
LORD your God disciplines you.[k]

6 Observe the commands of the LORD your God, walking in his ways and revering him.[l]
7 For the LORD your God is bringing you into a good land—a land with streams and pools
of water, with springs flowing in the valleys and hills;[m] 8 a land with wheat and barley,
vines and fig trees, pomegranates, olive oil and honey; 9 a land where bread will not be
scarce and you will lack nothing; a land where the rocks are iron and you can dig copper out of the hills.

10 When you have eaten and are satisfied,[n] praise the LORD your God for the good land
he has given you. 11 Be careful that you do not forget the LORD your God, failing to observe
his commands, his laws and his decrees that I am giving you this day. 12 Otherwise, when
you eat and are satisfied, when you build fine houses and settle down,[o] 13 and when your
herds and flocks grow large and your silver and gold increase and all you have is multiplied, 14 then your heart will become proud and you will forget[p] the LORD your God, who
brought you out of Egypt, out of the land of slavery. 15 He led you through the vast and
dreadful desert,[q] that thirsty and waterless land, with its venomous snakes[r] and scorpions. He brought you water out of hard rock.[s] 16 He gave you manna to eat in the des-

7:21 [w]Jos 3:10 [x]Dt 10:17; Ne 9:32
7:22 [y]Ex 23:28-30
7:24 [z]Jos 23:9
7:25 [a]Ex 32:20; 1Ch 14:12 [b]Jos 7:21 [c]Jdg 8:27 [d]Dt 17:1
7:26 [e]Lev 27:28-29
8:1 [f]Dt 4:1
8:2 [g]Am 2:10
8:3 [h]Ex 16:12,14,35 [i]Ex 16:2-3; Mt 4:4*; Lk 4:4*
8:4 [j]Dt 29:5; Ne 9:21
8:5 [k]2Sa 7:14; Pr 3:11-12; Heb 12:5-11; Rev 3:19
8:6 [l]Dt 5:33
8:7 [m]Dt 11:9-12
8:10 [n]Dt 6:10-12
8:12 [o]Hos 13:6
8:14 [p]Ps 106:21
8:15 [q]Jer 2:6 [r]Nu 21:6 [s]Nu 20:11; Ps 78:15; 114:8

7:26 it is set apart for destruction. Another call for total hatred of idolatry. But since the idols were often made of gold, they were valuable. The precious metal was under the ban calling for total destruction; the idols themselves were to be destroyed, but what could pass through the fire (e.g., gold and other precious metals) was to be given to the Lord (Jos 6:18–19).

■ **8:1–20** *Prosperity and Pride.* Moses addressed Israel's future temptation to pride and self-dependence by reminding his listeners of the tests the nation had undergone in the wilderness. The difficulties faced in the desert had proved that the nation could succeed only by God's mercy.

8:2 to test you. The Lord had determined to test the nation through the hardships of the travels from Egypt to Canaan. This testing was intended to show the condition of their hearts through their responses to his commandments. The faith of God's covenant people is tested in every age (see 1Co 3:13; 2Co 2:9; 8:8; 13:5–7; Jas 1:12).

8:3 manna. The first giving of manna is recorded in Exodus 16:15, and its cessation in Joshua 5:12. The remark may mean that prior to the events of Exodus 16:15 the first and second generations of the exodus had not been familiar with manna. It is also possible that Moses had in mind those who had been born in the wilderness and had always eaten manna as their staple food. Alternatively, the somewhat similar setting in 5:3 suggests that the word "fathers" here is a reference to the patriarchs, indicating that they had not known manna either—even though they had suffered famine. See verse 16. **man does not live on bread alone.** Bread is used by God to feed his people, but God's Word is the power behind the bread his people eat. To rely on bread alone for life is to be shortsighted; God's people must rely in the first place on God's Word by obeying it. Jesus referred to this passage as he faced the devil's temptation (see Mt 4:4; Lk 4:4). See *WLC* 193; *HC* 125.

8:4 Your clothes did not wear out. This miraculous preservation is mentioned again in 29:5.

8:5 as a man disciplines his son. Verse 3 told how God allowed his people to suffer hunger in order that he might show them his food supply. Discipline usually begins with difficulty and ends with blessing. This teaching is elaborated in Proverbs 3:11–12 (quoted in Heb 12:5–6). Here Israel is called God's son; this is part of the background to the New Testament teaching on divine adoption (e.g., Eph 1:5).

8:7–9 a good land . . . iron . . . copper. This description is more extensive than the familiar "flowing with milk and honey" description found in Exodus, in Leviticus and frequently in Deuteronomy. Assyrian art from c. 800 B.C. confirms (see also 11:9–12) that, while arid today, ancient Israel was filled with a variety of flora and fauna.

8:9 the rocks are iron. The Iron Age came to Canaan after the time of Moses (c. 1200 B.C.), but iron was known before then. Inventories in ancient Ugarit (c. 1400 B.C.) mention two talents of iron. The copper mines of the Sinai peninsula and the area of south Transjordan were a valuable resource in antiquity, probably a source of some of Solomon's wealth.

8:10-11 praise the LORD . . . do not forget. Moses warned the people that after they had received all these blessings from God they would be tempted to grow prideful. Rather than forgetting the God who had provided these blessings, they were to offer him thanks. Their response to God at that time would determine whether or not God would allow them to continue to receive his blessings. See *HC* 28.

ert, something your fathers had never known,[t] to humble and to test you so that in the end it might go well with you. 17 You may say to yourself,[u] "My power and the strength of my hands have produced this wealth for me." 18 But remember the LORD your God, for it is he who gives you the ability to produce wealth,[v] and so confirms his covenant, which he swore to your forefathers, as it is today.

19 If you ever forget the LORD your God and follow other gods and worship and bow down to them, I testify against you today that you will surely be destroyed.[w] 20 Like the nations the LORD destroyed before you, so you will be destroyed for not obeying the LORD your God.

Not Because of Israel's Righteousness

9 Hear, O Israel. You are now about to cross the Jordan to go in and dispossess nations greater and stronger than you,[x] with large cities that have walls up to the sky.[y] 2 The people are strong and tall—Anakites! You know about them and have heard it said: "Who can stand up against the Anakites?"[z] 3 But be assured today that the LORD your God is the one who goes across ahead of you[a] like a devouring fire.[b] He will destroy them; he will subdue them before you. And you will drive them out and annihilate them quickly,[c] as the LORD has promised you.

4 After the LORD your God has driven them out before you, do not say to yourself,[d] "The LORD has brought me here to take possession of this land because of my righteousness." No, it is on account of the wickedness of these nations[e] that the LORD is going to drive them out before you. 5 It is not because of your righteousness or your integrity[f] that you are going in to take possession of their land; but on account of the wickedness of these nations, the LORD your God will drive them out before you, to accomplish what he swore[g] to your fathers, to Abraham, Isaac and Jacob. 6 Understand, then, that it is not because of your righteousness that the LORD your God is giving you this good land to possess, for you are a stiff-necked people.[h]

The Golden Calf

7 Remember this and never forget how you provoked the LORD your God to anger in the desert. From the day you left Egypt until you arrived here, you have been rebellious against the LORD. 8 At Horeb you aroused the LORD's wrath so that he was angry enough to destroy you.[i] 9 When I went up on the mountain to receive the tablets of stone, the tablets of the covenant that the LORD had made with you, I stayed on the mountain forty days and forty nights; I ate no bread and drank no water.[j] 10 The LORD gave me two stone tablets inscribed by the finger of God.[k] On them were all the commandments the LORD proclaimed to you on the mountain out of the fire, on the day of the assembly.

11 At the end of the forty days and forty nights, the LORD gave me the two stone tablets, the tablets of the covenant. 12 Then the LORD told me, "Go down from here at once, because your people whom you brought out of Egypt have become corrupt.[l] They have turned away quickly[m] from what I commanded them and have made a cast idol for themselves."

13 And the LORD said to me, "I have seen this people[n], and they are a stiff-necked people indeed! 14 Let me alone,[o] so that I may destroy them and blot out[p] their name from

8:16 [t]Ex 16:15
8:17 [u]Dt 9:4,7,24
8:18 [v]Pr 10:22; Hos 2:8
8:19 [w]Dt 4:26; 30:18
9:1 [x]Dt 4:38; 11:23,31 [y]Dt 1:28
9:2 [z]Nu 13:22,28,32-33
9:3 [a]Dt 31:3; Jos 3:11 [b]Dt 4:24; Heb 12:29 [c]Ex 23:31; Dt 7:23-24
9:4 [d]Dt 8:17 [e]Lev 18:21,24-30; Dt 18:9-14
9:5 [f]Tit 3:5 [g]Ge 12:7; 13:15; 15:7; 17:8; 26:4
9:6 [h]ver 13; Ex 32:9; Dt 31:27
9:8 [i]Ex 32:7-10; Ps 106:19
9:9 [j]Ex 24:12,15,18; 34:28
9:10 [k]Ex 31:18; Dt 4:13
9:12 [l]Ex 32:7-8; Dt 31:29 [m]Jdg 2:17
9:13 [n]ver 6; Ex 32:9; Dt 10:16
9:14 [o]Ex 32:10 [p]Nu 14:12; Dt 29:20

8:17–18 My power and the strength of my hands. The temptation toward pride and self-reliance is in view here. **gives you the ability . . . and so confirms his covenant.** Moses made it clear that when God's people kept his covenant to the point that they received the reward of wealth, it was actually God's power that had given them their ability. The conditional character of Moses' covenant does not imply that God's blessings are earned by human merit, for God's grace is behind every human accomplishment and divine reward. See *WLC* 105,193.

8:19 If you ever forget. Continuing fidelity was the requirement for blessing. To turn to other gods was to incite divine wrath. Even so, God would keep his covenant with the fathers and save a remnant chosen by grace (v. 18; Ro 9:27; 11:28–29).

■ **9:1—10:11** *Self-Righteousness.* Moses addressed a future temptation of the people: believing that their success was the direct result of their own righteousness. He countered this false idea by pointing to Israel's idolatry at Sinai.

9:1 Hear, O Israel. See note on 5:1. **stronger than you.** In human terms, the armies of Canaan were to be feared. God assured his people that they would conquer because of his might. **walls up to the sky.** A way of saying that the cities seemed invincible. Perhaps an allusion to the tower of Babel, the prototype of evil cities raised up against God (see Ge 11:1–9).

9:2 Anakites. See 1:28 and 2:21. It was the Anakites who had frightened the faithless spies 40 years earlier (Nu 13:22,28).

9:4 because of my righteousness. Here is the heart of the matter Moses addressed. Victory was not because of Israel's goodness, but because the nations of Canaan were so much worse than Israel (vv. 4–5). As a result, God would use the Israelites to execute judgment on the Canaanites. The Israelites were too "stiff-necked" to be granted victory over Canaan as a result of their own righteousness (v. 7). Whatever righteousness the Israelites possessed had been given to them by God, and his blessings on the nation were entirely gracious (see note on 8:17–18).

9:7 Remember this. Moses warned the Israelites not to forget how close they had come to complete destruction when they had worshiped the golden calf.

9:9 I went up on the mountain. Moses retold the story given in Exodus. Verses 9–10 are a contraction of Exodus 24:12 and 18. Verses 12–14 are similar in content to Exodus 32:7–10, and verses 15–21 recall the same data given in Exodus 32:15–20. All of these texts emphasize Moses' role as the mediator for Israel and God's mercy to the nation through Moses. Here the focus is on how the nation was barely spared from the wrath of God.

under heaven. And I will make you into a nation stronger and more numerous than they."

15 So I turned and went down from the mountain while it was ablaze with fire. And the two tablets of the covenant were in my hands.[a][q] 16 When I looked, I saw that you had sinned against the LORD your God; you had made for yourselves an idol cast in the shape of a calf.[r] You had turned aside quickly from the way that the LORD had commanded you. 17 So I took the two tablets and threw them out of my hands, breaking them to pieces before your eyes.

18 Then once again I fell[s] prostrate before the LORD for forty days and forty nights; I ate no bread and drank no water, because of all the sin you had committed, doing what was evil in the LORD's sight and so provoking him to anger. 19 I feared the anger and wrath of the LORD, for he was angry enough with you to destroy you.[t] But again the LORD listened to me.[u] 20 And the LORD was angry enough with Aaron to destroy him, but at that time I prayed for Aaron too. 21 Also I took that sinful thing of yours, the calf you had made, and burned it in the fire. Then I crushed it and ground it to powder as fine as dust and threw the dust into a stream that flowed down the mountain.[v]

22 You also made the LORD angry at Taberah,[w] at Massah[x] and at Kibroth Hattaavah.[y]

23 And when the LORD sent you out from Kadesh Barnea, he said, "Go up and take possession of the land I have given you." But you rebelled against the command of the LORD your God. You did not trust[z] him or obey him. 24 You have been rebellious against the LORD ever since I have known you.[a]

25 I lay prostrate before the LORD those forty days and forty nights because the LORD had said he would destroy you.[b] 26 I prayed to the LORD and said, "O Sovereign LORD, do not destroy your people, your own inheritance that you redeemed by your great power and brought out of Egypt with a mighty hand.[c] 27 Remember your servants Abraham, Isaac and Jacob. Overlook the stubbornness of this people, their wickedness and their sin. 28 Otherwise, the country from which you brought us will say, 'Because the LORD was not able to take them into the land he had promised them, and because he hated them, he brought them out to put them to death in the desert.'[d] 29 But they are your people, your inheritance[e] that you brought out by your great power and your outstretched arm.[f]"

Tablets Like the First Ones

10 At that time the LORD said to me, "Chisel out two stone tablets[g] like the first ones and come up to me on the mountain. Also make a wooden chest.[b] 2 I will write on the tablets the words that were on the first tablets, which you broke. Then you are to put them in the chest."[h]

3 So I made the ark out of acacia wood[i] and chiseled[j] out two stone tablets like the first ones, and I went up on the mountain with the two tablets in my hands. 4 The LORD wrote on these tablets what he had written before, the Ten Commandments he had proclaimed[k] to you on the mountain, out of the fire, on the day of the assembly. And the LORD gave them to me. 5 Then I came back down the mountain[l] and put the tablets in the ark[m] I had made, as the LORD commanded me, and they are there now.[n]

6 (The Israelites traveled from the wells of the Jaakanites to Moserah.[o] There Aaron died and was buried, and Eleazar his son succeeded him as priest.[p] 7 From there they traveled to Gudgodah and on to Jotbathah, a land with streams of water.[q] 8 At that time

9:15 [q]Ex 19:18; 32:15
9:16 [r]Ex 32:19
9:18 [s]Ex 34:28
9:19 [t]Ex 32:10-11,14 [u]Dt 10:10
9:21 [v]Ex 32:20
9:22 [w]Nu 11:3 [x]Ex 17:7 [y]Nu 11:34
9:23 [z]Ps 106:24
9:24 [a]ver 7; Dt 31:27
9:25 [b]ver 18
9:26 [c]Ex 32:11
9:28 [d]Ex 32:12; Nu 14:16
9:29 [e]Dt 4:20; 1Ki 8:51 [f]Dt 4:34; Ne 1:10
10:1 [g]Ex 25:10; 34:1-2
10:2 [h]Ex 25:16,21; Dt 4:13
10:3 [i]Ex 25:5,10; 37:1-9 [j]Ex 34:4
10:4 [k]Ex 20:1
10:5 [l]Ex 34:29 [m]Ex 40:20 [n]1Ki 8:9
10:6 [o]Nu 33:30-31,38 [p]Nu 20:25-28
10:7 [q]Nu 33:32-34

[a] 15 Or *And I had the two tablets of the covenant with me, one in each hand* [b] 1 That is, an ark

9:21 a stream that flowed down the mountain. No stream flows down from Mount Sinai today. The ground has some moisture and low bushes grow there, but the mention of a stream indicates that there was more rainfall in Moses' time than there is today.
9:22 Taberah. See Numbers 11:3. **Massah.** See 6:16 and Exodus 17:7. **Kibroth Hattaavah.** See Numbers 11:34.
9:23 you rebelled. Moses recounted the rebellion at Kadesh Barnea. Then he spoke again of the sin surrounding the incident of the golden calf and of his prayer on Mount Sinai (the second period of 40 days and nights). Moses' great petition pleaded God's covenant with the patriarchs and his redemption of Israel as his own inheritance.
10:1–5 Moses tied together the receiving of the commandments and the building of the ark by summarizing the material of Exodus 34:1–4 and 40:20. Moses met God twice on Mount Sinai. The first time he received the directions for the tabernacle and its furniture, which were actually constructed after Moses had descended the mountain for the second time. The tablets were put in the ark when the tabernacle was set up (Ex 40:20).
10:1 two stone tablets. The meaning of the word "two" has recently been questioned. In the past, it was assumed that one copy of the Ten Commandments extended to both tablets. More recent research has led some scholars to suspect that there may have been two tablets, one for each party, each tablet bearing the entire law; this would reflect the practices of ancient covenants and treaties.
10:4 the Ten Commandments. See 4:13. See also *WCF* 19.2; *WLC* 98; *WSC* 41.
10:6–9 This parenthetical section seems out of place, but it may be included to clarify the timing of the giving of the laws surrounding the Levitical ministry. While Aaron was alive, the tablets and the ark (10:5) had been under his care. After Aaron's death, the blessings and responsibilities of caring for the ark and its contents were given to the Levites alone by direct command of God and under the oversight of Aaron's son.

the LORD set apart the tribe of Levi[r] to carry the ark of the covenant of the LORD, to stand
before the LORD to minister[s] and to pronounce blessings[t] in his name, as they still do today. 9 That is why the Levites have no share or inheritance among their brothers; the LORD
is their inheritance,[u] as the LORD your God told them.)
10 Now I had stayed on the mountain forty days and nights, as I did the first time, and
the LORD listened to me at this time also. It was not his will to destroy you.[v] 11 "Go," the
LORD said to me, "and lead the people on their way, so that they may enter and possess
the land that I swore to their fathers to give them."

Fear the LORD

12 And now, O Israel, what does the LORD your God ask of you[w] but to fear the LORD
your God, to walk in all his ways, to love him,[x] to serve the LORD your God with all your
heart[y] and with all your soul, 13 and to observe the LORD's commands and decrees that
I am giving you today for your own good?
14 To the LORD your God belong the heavens, even the highest heavens,[z] the earth and
everything in it.[a] 15 Yet the LORD set his affection on your forefathers and loved[b] them,
and he chose you, their descendants, above all the nations, as it is today. 16 Circumcise[c]
your hearts, therefore, and do not be stiff-necked[d] any longer. 17 For the LORD your God
is God of gods[e] and Lord of lords, the great God, mighty and awesome, who shows no
partiality[f] and accepts no bribes. 18 He defends the cause of the fatherless and the widow,[g] and loves the alien, giving him food and clothing. 19 And you are to love those who
are aliens, for you yourselves were aliens in Egypt.[h] 20 Fear the LORD your God and serve
him.[i] Hold fast[j] to him and take your oaths in his name.[k] 21 He is your praise;[l] he is your
God, who performed for you those great and awesome wonders[m] you saw with your own
eyes. 22 Your forefathers who went down into Egypt were seventy in all,[n] and now the
LORD your God has made you as numerous as the stars in the sky.[o]

Love and Obey the LORD

11 Love[p] the LORD your God and keep his requirements, his decrees, his laws and
his commands always.[q] 2 Remember today that your children were not the ones
who saw and experienced the discipline of the LORD your God:[r] his majesty, his mighty
hand, his outstretched arm; 3 the signs he performed and the things he did in the heart
of Egypt, both to Pharaoh king of Egypt and to his whole country; 4 what he did to the
Egyptian army, to its horses and chariots, how he overwhelmed them with the waters of
the Red Sea[a][s] as they were pursuing you, and how the LORD brought lasting ruin on
them. 5 It was not your children who saw what he did for you in the desert until you arrived at this place, 6 and what he did[t] to Dathan and Abiram, sons of Eliab the Reubenite, when the earth opened its mouth right in the middle of all Israel and swallowed them

a 4 Hebrew *Yam Suph*; that is, Sea of Reeds

10:8 [r]Nu 3:6 [s]Dt 18:5 [t]Dt 21:5
10:9 [u]Nu 18:20; Dt 18:1-2; Eze 44:28
10:10 [v]Ex 33:17; 34:28; Dt 9:18-19,25
10:12 [w]Mic 6:8 [x]Dt 5:33; 6:13; Mt 22:37 [y]Dt 6:5
10:14 [z]1Ki 8:27 [a]Ex 19:5
10:15 [b]Dt 4:37
10:16 [c]Jer 4:4 [d]Dt 9:6
10:17 [e]Jos 22:22; Da 2:47 [f]Ac 10:34; Ro 2:11; Eph 6:9
10:18 [g]Ps 68:5
10:19 [h]Lev 19:34
10:20 [i]Mt 4:10 [j]Dt 11:22 [k]Ps 63:11
10:21 [l]Ex 15:2; Jer 17:14 [m]Ps 106:21-22
10:22 [n]Ge 46:26-27 [o]Ge 15:5; Dt 1:10
11:1 [p]Dt 10:12 [q]Zec 3:7
11:2 [r]Dt 5:24; 8:5
11:4 [s]Ex 14:27
11:6 [t]Nu 16:1-35

■ **10:12—11:25** *Circumcision of the Heart.* Moses called on the people to serve God from the heart. They needed to undergo a radical change in order to love and obey God as they ought.
10:11 to their fathers. That is, to the patriarchs. The reference is clearly to the promise of the land made to the patriarchs (9:5; Ex 33:1).
10:12 what does the LORD your God ask of you . . . ? The form of this rhetorical question is similar to that of Micah 6:8, which exhorts us to do right and walk with God in humility (see also Mt 23:23). To walk with God is at the very least to love him with all our being and to keep his commandments. According to Jesus, love and obedience go together (Jn 14:23). To love God with our whole being is the greatest commandment (6:5; Mk 12:29–34). **all your heart.** See note on 6:5.
10:14–15 See *CD* 1.IX.
10:15 Yet. The contrast is noble: It exalts the Lord's majesty (v. 14) in order to highlight the tremendous grace and honor he granted to the patriarchs and the nation of Israel by setting his electing love upon them.
10:16 Circumcise your hearts, therefore. This verse (along with others such as 30:6 and Jer 4:4) demonstrates that Old Testament faith was not a religion of mere outward form. Circumcision was a symbol, a sacrament, an outward sign of an inward grace. Circumcision was commanded for infant boys in Israel to bring them into covenant relationship with God in the hope that in time they would circumcise their own hearts (Ge 17:9–14).
10:18 He defends. The high theology of the previous verse is balanced by the tender care that the great God has for the needy—the fatherless, the widow and the alien. In this also, he is our example.
10:20 See *WCF* 22.1; *HC* 101.
10:22 seventy. The number of those who originally traveled to Egypt is given to emphasize the great love of God in increasing their numbers. While Exodus 1:5 counts 70 in Jacob's family, the NIV text note there indicates that the Dead Sea Scrolls of Exodus, the Septuagint (the Greek translation of the OT) and Acts 7:14 all record 75 as the number. The actual names are given in Genesis 46. Counting men only, and including Jacob, the group as delineated there did number 70. But at this point the Septuagint adds 5 previously unnamed descendants of Joseph. By this reckoning, the number totals 75. Both versions of Genesis 46 accurately count the men they list. It should be remembered that the total of 75 includes only men. With women and children, the group would likely have numbered well over 150. **as numerous as the stars.** See note on 1:9.
11:1–7 Moses reminded his listeners of events from the past that demonstrated the importance of circumcised hearts and of serving God wholeheartedly.
11:6 Dathan and Abiram. Moses here distinguished Dathan and Abiram from Korah. Likewise, Psalm 106:17 does not include Korah with those buried alive. According to Numbers 16:16–35, Korah was at the tabernacle among the 250 men with censers. These men were burned by fire from the Lord. Dathan and Abiram, who were not Levites, were in front of their tents when the earth swallowed them up. Much of Korah's family was engulfed with the other, but some escaped (Nu 26:11).

up with their households, their tents and every living thing that belonged to them. 7But
it was your own eyes that saw all these great things the LORD has done.
8Observe therefore all the commands I am giving you today, so that you may have the
strength to go in and take over the land that you are crossing the Jordan to possess,[u]
9and so that you may live long[v] in the land that the LORD swore[w] to your forefathers to
give to them and their descendants, a land flowing with milk and honey.[x] 10The land you
are entering to take over is not like the land of Egypt, from which you have come,
where you planted your seed and irrigated it by foot as in a vegetable garden. 11But the
land you are crossing the Jordan to take possession of is a land of mountains and valleys
that drinks rain from heaven.[y] 12It is a land the LORD your God cares for; the eyes[z] of the
LORD your God are continually on it from the beginning of the year to its end.
13So if you faithfully obey[a] the commands I am giving you today—to love[b] the LORD
your God and to serve him with all your heart and with all your soul— 14then I will send
rain[c] on your land in its season, both autumn and spring rains,[d] so that you may gather in your grain, new wine and oil. 15I will provide grass[e] in the fields for your cattle, and
you will eat and be satisfied.[f]
16Be careful, or you will be enticed to turn away and worship other gods and bow
down to them.[g] 17Then the LORD's anger[h] will burn against you, and he will shut[i] the
heavens so that it will not rain and the ground will yield no produce, and you will soon
perish[j] from the good land the LORD is giving you. 18Fix these words of mine in your
hearts and minds; tie them as symbols on your hands and bind them on your foreheads.[k]
19Teach them to your children,[l] talking about them when you sit at home and when you
walk along the road, when you lie down and when you get up.[m] 20Write them on the
doorframes of your houses and on your gates,[n] 21so that your days and the days of your
children may be many[o] in the land that the LORD swore to give your forefathers, as many
as the days that the heavens are above the earth.[p]
22If you carefully observe[q] all these commands I am giving you to follow—to love the
LORD your God, to walk in all his ways and to hold fast[r] to him— 23then the LORD will drive
out all these nations before you, and you will dispossess nations larger and stronger than
you.[s] 24Every place where you set your foot will be yours:[t] Your territory will extend from
the desert to Lebanon, and from the Euphrates River to the western sea.[a] 25No man will
be able to stand against you. The LORD your God, as he promised you, will put the terror and fear of you on the whole land, wherever you go.[u]
26See, I am setting before you today a blessing and a curse[v]— 27the blessing[w] if you
obey the commands of the LORD your God that I am giving you today; 28the curse if you
disobey[x] the commands of the LORD your God and turn from the way that I command
you today by following other gods, which you have not known. 29When the LORD your
God has brought you into the land you are entering to possess, you are to proclaim on
Mount Gerizim the blessings, and on Mount Ebal the curses.[y] 30As you know, these
mountains are across the Jordan, west of the road,[b] toward the setting sun, near the
great trees of Moreh,[z] in the territory of those Canaanites living in the Arabah in the vicinity of Gilgal.[a] 31You are about to cross the Jordan to enter and take possession[b] of
the land the LORD your God is giving you. When you have taken it over and are living
there, 32be sure that you obey all the decrees and laws I am setting before you today.

11:8 [u]Jos 1:7
11:9 [v]Dt 4:40; Pr 10:27 [w]Dt 9:5 [x]Ex 3:8
11:11 [y]Dt 8:7
11:12 [z]1Ki 9:3
11:13 [a]Dt 6:17 [b]Dt 10:12
11:14 [c]Lev 26:4; Dt 28:12 [d]Joel 2:23; Jas 5:7
11:15 [e]Ps 104:14 [f]Dt 6:11
11:16 [g]Dt 8:19; 29:18; Job 31:9,27
11:17 [h]Dt 6:15 [i]1Ki 8:35; 2Ch 6:26 [j]Dt 4:26
11:18 [k]Dt 6:6-8
11:19 [l]Dt 6:7 [m]Dt 4:9-10
11:20 [n]Dt 6:9
11:21 [o]Pr 3:2; 4:10 [p]Ps 72:5
11:22 [q]Dt 6:17 [r]Dt 10:20
11:23 [s]Dt 4:38; 9:1
11:24 [t]Ge 15:18; Ex 23:31; Jos 1:3; 14:9
11:25 [u]Ex 23:27; Dt 7:24
11:26 [v]Dt 30:1,15,19
11:27 [w]Dt 28:1-14
11:28 [x]Dt 28:15
11:29 [y]Dt 27:12-13; Jos 8:33
11:30 [z]Ge 12:6 [a]Jos 4:19
11:31 [b]Dt 9:1; Jos 1:11

[a] *24* That is, the Mediterranean [b] *30* Or *Jordan, westward*

11:9 live long in the land. See 5:16.
11:10 irrigated it by foot. Egypt depended heavily on irrigation because it had little to no rainfall. Water was channeled from the Nile and its branches in the delta. Moving the water from one canal to another was done in various ways. Perhaps irrigation "by foot" refers to the burdensome practice of walking up a bank with a bucket. In Canaan and the surrounding region there was also irrigation for the dry summer season, but because of the hilly country, it could often be done using gravity. See 8:7.
11:13 with all your heart. See note on 6:5.
11:14 grain, new wine and oil. See 7:13.
11:19 Teach them to your children. See the similar exhortations and metaphors in 6:6–9.
11:24 where you set your foot. The same expression and the same boundaries of Canaan are repeated in Joshua 1:3–5. The phrase "from the desert to Lebanon" is unclear. Since the boundaries needed to include a southern limit, the "desert" probably means the Desert of Sinai. The boundaries included all of modern Israel and Lebanon and part of modern Syria.
■ **11:26–32** *Call to Renewal.* Having warned the Israelites not to repeat the sins they had committed and observed in the past, Moses closed this section by telling his audience that they had to prepare for a covenant renewal to take place after they had crossed the Jordan.
11:26 a blessing and a curse. The two ways in which God reacted to his covenant people: Blessings came to those who were faithful and curses to those who were unfaithful. Recalling blessings and curses was an important part of renewing covenant commitments.
11:29 Mount Gerizim . . . Mount Ebal. This area and this ceremony are described in detail in chapters 27–28. Everything was done by Joshua according to Moses' direction (Jos 8:30–35). These mountains are said to be "across the Jordan, west of the road, toward the setting sun" (v. 30). What road is intended is not specified. Perhaps the NIV text note is better: ". . . across the Jordan, westward, toward the setting sun." This simply gives their location as being in Canaan. They are further said to be "near the great trees of Moreh" (v. 30), which are near Shechem (Ge 12:6). Although the location of these mountains is not entirely clear, there is no reason to doubt their usual identification as the two that are astride the main north-south road near Shechem.

The One Place of Worship

12 These are the decrees and laws you must be careful to follow in the land that
the LORD, the God of your fathers, has given you to possess—as long as you live
in the land.[c] 2Destroy completely all the places on the high mountains and on the hills
and under every spreading tree[d] where the nations you are dispossessing worship their
gods. 3Break down their altars, smash[e] their sacred stones and burn their Asherah
poles in the fire; cut down the idols of their gods and wipe out their names from those
places.
4You must not worship the LORD your God in their way. 5But you are to seek the place
the LORD your God will choose from among all your tribes to put his Name there for his
dwelling.[f] To that place you must go; 6there bring your burnt offerings and sacrifices,
your tithes[g] and special gifts, what you have vowed to give and your freewill offerings,
and the firstborn of your herds and flocks. 7There, in the presence of the LORD your God,
you and your families shall eat and shall rejoice[h] in everything you have put your hand
to, because the LORD your God has blessed you.
8You are not to do as we do here today, everyone as he sees fit, 9since you have not
yet reached the resting place and the inheritance the LORD your God is giving you. 10But
you will cross the Jordan and settle in the land the LORD your God is giving[i] you as an inheritance, and he will give you rest from all your enemies around you so that you will live
in safety. 11Then to the place the LORD your God will choose as a dwelling for his Name[j]—
there you are to bring everything I command you: your burnt offerings and sacrifices,
your tithes and special gifts, and all the choice possessions you have vowed to the LORD.
12And there rejoice[k] before the LORD your God, you, your sons and daughters, your menservants and maidservants, and the Levites from your towns, who have no allotment or
inheritance[l] of their own. 13Be careful not to sacrifice your burnt offerings anywhere you
please. 14Offer them only at the place the LORD will choose[m] in one of your tribes, and
there observe everything I command you.
15Nevertheless, you may slaughter your animals in any of your towns and eat as much
of the meat as you want, as if it were gazelle or deer,[n] according to the blessing the LORD
your God gives you. Both the ceremonially unclean and the clean may eat it. 16But you
must not eat the blood;[o] pour it out on the ground like water.[p] 17You must not eat in your
own towns the tithe of your grain and new wine and oil, or the firstborn of your herds
and flocks, or whatever you have vowed to give, or your freewill offerings or special gifts.
18Instead, you are to eat[q] them in the presence of the LORD your God at the place the LORD
your God will choose[r]—you, your sons and daughters, your menservants and maidservants, and the Levites from your towns—and you are to rejoice[s] before the LORD your
God in everything you put your hand to. 19Be careful not to neglect the Levites[t] as long
as you live in your land.
20When the LORD your God has enlarged your territory[u] as he promised[v] you, and you
crave meat and say, "I would like some meat," then you may eat as much of it as you
want. 21If the place where the LORD your God chooses to put his Name is too far away

12:1 [c]Dt 4:9-10; 1Ki 8:40
12:2 [d]2Ki 16:4; 17:10
12:3 [e]Nu 33:52; Dt 7:5; Jdg 2:2
12:5 [f]ver 11,13; 2Ch 7:12,16
12:6 [g]Dt 14:22-23
12:7 [h]ver 12,18; Lev 23:40; Dt 14:26
12:10 [i]Dt 11:31
12:11 [j]ver 5; Dt 15:20; 16:2
12:12 [k]ver 7 [l]Dt 10:9; 14:29
12:14 [m]ver 11
12:15 [n]ver 20-23; Dt 14:5; 15:22
12:16 [o]Ge 9:4; Lev 7:26; 17:10-12 [p]Dt 15:23
12:18 [q]Dt 14:23 [r]ver 5 [s]ver 7,12
12:19 [t]Dt 14:27
12:20 [u]Dt 19:8 [v]Ge 15:18; Dt 11:24

■ **12:1—26:15** *Detailed Stipulations.* After providing a relatively general orientation toward the requirement of obedience to the laws of God, Moses listed a number of specific regulations that were to be observed in the land. These chapters resemble the Book of the Covenant (Ex 21:1—23:33) in many ways. As in other codes of the ancient Near East, these regulations do not appear in clearly discernable order. The laws are especially concerned with the purity of worship, but they touch on other subjects as well.

12:1 as long as you live in the land. This statement probably goes with the first part of the verse. The meaning is: "Follow these laws all the time as [closer to the Hebrew than 'as long as'] you live in the land, the land the LORD God of your forefathers has given you."

12:2 Destroy completely. The high places and other places of worship, which Moses here said were to be destroyed, were not scattered places of worship of the Lord; rather, they were specified as the places of Asherah worship and of other idolatry. This was not a program for centralization of worship but a requirement for pure worship. No compromise with idolatry was to be tolerated.

12:5–12 See *HC* 103.

12:5 the place the LORD your God will choose. From the time of Moses' praise at the crossing at the sea, the Israelites knew that God would lead them to a particular place where he would erect his mountain sanctuary in the land (Ex 15:17–18). It would be some time before Jerusalem would clearly be the place of God's sanctuary. For other references to the one central worship location, see 12:5, 11, 14, 18, 21 and 26, 14:23–25, 15:20, 16:2, 6–7, 11 and 15–16, 17:8 and 10, 18:6, 26:2 and 31:11.

12:7 eat and . . . rejoice. The burnt offerings were totally burned. Of the other sacrifices, some were burned; some were partially eaten by the priests; and some, especially the fellowship offerings, were shared by the priests and the worshipers (see chart "Old Testament Sacrifices" at 165). The worship of Israel was holy, reverent and joyful. Worship involved repentance and cleansing. But the redeemed heart was full of joy and praise. Many of the psalms express such joyful devotion.

12:12 no . . . inheritance. The gifts of the worshipers were given, in part, to support the priests and Levites.

12:15 slaughter . . . in any of your towns. Verses 20–21 give the same rule. The people could slaughter for meat anywhere, but they could sacrifice and eat from the tithe of their grain only at the place God would use for worship. Deuteronomy 15:22 gives instructions that allow for the eating anywhere of imperfect animals. Leviticus 17:3–12 has similar instructions. The NIV has rightly translated Leviticus 17:3 as "sacrifice," saying that sacrifices were to be offered only at the central place of worship. The law of Leviticus thus interpreted is in conformity with the commandment in Deuteronomy. In 15:22, it is clear that domestic animals unfit for sacrifice were to be eaten at home with the usual restriction against eating blood. It follows that 12:15 also allowed for butchering.

12:21 If the place . . . is too far away. See 14:24–26 for further rules.

from you, you may slaughter animals from the herds and flocks the LORD has given you,
as I have commanded you, and in your own towns you may eat as much of them as you
want. 22Eat them as you would gazelle or deer.[w] Both the ceremonially unclean and the
clean may eat. 23But be sure you do not eat the blood,[x] because the blood is the life, and
you must not eat the life with the meat. 24You must not eat the blood; pour it out on the
ground like water. 25Do not eat it, so that it may go well[y] with you and your children after you, because you will be doing what is right[z] in the eyes of the LORD.
26But take your consecrated things and whatever you have vowed to give,[a] and go to
the place the LORD will choose. 27Present your burnt offerings[b] on the altar of the LORD
your God, both the meat and the blood. The blood of your sacrifices must be poured beside the altar of the LORD your God, but you may eat the meat. 28Be careful to obey all
these regulations I am giving you, so that it may always go well[c] with you and your children after you, because you will be doing what is good and right in the eyes of the LORD
your God.
29The LORD your God will cut off[d] before you the nations you are about to invade and
dispossess. But when you have driven them out and settled in their land, 30and after they
have been destroyed before you, be careful not to be ensnared by inquiring about their
gods, saying, "How do these nations serve their gods? We will do the same." 31You must
not worship the LORD your God in their way, because in worshiping their gods, they do
all kinds of detestable things the LORD hates.[e] They even burn their sons[f] and daughters
in the fire as sacrifices to their gods.
32See that you do all I command you; do not add[g] to it or take away from it.

Worshiping Other Gods

13 If a prophet,[h] or one who foretells by dreams, appears among you and announces to you a miraculous sign or wonder, 2and if the sign or wonder of which he
has spoken takes place, and he says, "Let us follow other gods"[i] (gods you have not
known) "and let us worship them," 3you must not listen to the words of that prophet or
dreamer. The LORD your God is testing[j] you to find out whether you love him with all your
heart and with all your soul. 4It is the LORD your God you must follow,[k] and him you must
revere. Keep his commands and obey him; serve him and hold fast[l] to him. 5That prophet or dreamer must be put to death, because he preached rebellion against the LORD your
God, who brought you out of Egypt and redeemed you from the land of slavery; he has
tried to turn you from the way the LORD your God commanded you to follow. You must
purge the evil[m] from among you.
6If your very own brother, or your son or daughter, or the wife you love, or your closest friend secretly entices[n] you, saying, "Let us go and worship other gods" (gods that
neither you nor your fathers have known, 7gods of the peoples around you, whether near
or far, from one end of the land to the other), 8do not yield[o] to him or listen to him. Show
him no pity. Do not spare him or shield him. 9You must certainly put him to death.[p] Your
hand must be the first in putting him to death, and then the hands of all the people.
10Stone him to death, because he tried to turn you away from the LORD your God, who
brought you out of Egypt, out of the land of slavery. 11Then all Israel will hear and be
afraid,[q] and no one among you will do such an evil thing again.
12If you hear it said about one of the towns the LORD your God is giving you to live in

12:22 [w]ver 15
12:23 [x]ver 16; Ge 9:4; Lev 17:11,14
12:25 [y]Dt 4:40; Isa 3:10 [z]Ex 15:26; Dt 13:18; 1Ki 11:38
12:26 [a]ver 17; Nu 5:9-10
12:27 [b]Lev 1:5,9,13
12:28 [c]ver 25; Dt 4:40
12:29 [d]Jos 23:4
12:31 [e]Dt 9:5 [f]Dt 18:10; Jer 32:35
12:32 [g]Dt 4:2; Jos 1:7; Rev 22:18-19
13:1 [h]Mt 24:24; Mk 13:22; 2Th 2:9
13:2 [i]ver 6,13
13:3 [j]Dt 8:2,16
13:4 [k]2Ki 23:3; 2Ch 34:31 [l]Dt 10:20
13:5 [m]Dt 17:7,12; 1Co 5:13
13:6 [n]Dt 17:2-7; 29:18
13:8 [o]Pr 1:10
13:9 [p]Dt 17:5,7
13:11 [q]Dt 19:20

12:23 the blood is the life. The same principle is given in Genesis 9:4 and Leviticus 17:10–14. The treatment of the blood in the sacrificial system reflected the fact that blood stood for the life of the animal. When the blood was gone, the life was gone. When blood was sprinkled on the altar, innocent life was shed for a guilty sinner. The Old Testament sacrifices symbolized a theology of substitution of the innocent for the guilty. This theology was incomplete because no animal, no matter how perfect, was of enough value to redeem the soul (Mic 6:6–7). The resolution is stated most clearly in Isaiah 53:10, where it is predicted that the innocent son of David would die as a sin offering.

12:30–32 See *WLC* 109; *WSC* 51.

12:31 They even burn their sons and daughters. Child sacrifice was common in ancient times but was especially excessive in the later Phoenician colony of Carthage in North Africa. In a time of great need, Jephthah offered God his daughter (Jdg 11:30–35), and the king of Moab offered his firstborn son (2Ki 3:27). In later years some of the Israelites, by leaving God to follow the customs of other nations, condemned their own children to die in child sacrifice (Ps 106:34–39).

12:32 do not add. See 4:2. See *WCF* 21.1; *BC* 7; *HC* 91.

13:1—14:2 Moses issued warnings against idolatry. The first warning (vv. 1–5) concerned false prophets. The other warnings concerned a near relative who tempted others to apostasy (vv. 6–11), the apostasy of a whole town (vv. 12–18) and participation in pagan death rituals (14:1–2).

13:1–5 The caution against a false prophet was given to emphasize that even though a prophet seemed to carry impressive credentials, the theological test was still crucial. No true prophet could possibly advance a false religion, since Israel's God was the true and only God; all other gods were the creations of humans. Those who followed and worshiped them were to be destroyed.

13:3 all your heart. See note on 6:5.

13:5–12 See *WCF* 20.4; 23.3; *WLC* 109,145.

13:6–11 The second instance of seduction to apostasy.

13:6 your very own brother. The closest ties on Earth do not dissolve one's obligation to remain faithful to the true and only God. The New Testament calls for a husband or wife to remain married to an unbelieving partner unless they are rejected (1Co 7:12–16). The hope is that the unbelieving spouse may be saved. In any case, the believing partner's strongest obligation is to remain true to God. See 21:18.

13:10 See theological article "The Three Uses of the Law" at Psalm 119.

13:13 [r]ver 2,6; 1Jn 2:19
13:16 [s]Jos 6:24 [t]Jos 8:28; Jer 49:2
13:17 [u]Nu 25:4 [v]Dt 30:3 [w]Dt 7:13 [x]Ge 22:17; 26:4, 24; 28:14
13:18 [y]Dt 12:25,28
14:1 [z]Lev 19:28; 21:5; Jer 16:6; 41:5; Ro 8:14; 9:8; Gal 3:26
14:2 [a]Lev 20:26 [b]Dt 7:6; 26:18-19
14:3 [c]Eze 4:14
14:4 [d]Lev 11:2-45; Ac 10:14
14:8 [e]Lev 11:26-27
14:21 [f]Lev 17:15; 22:8 [g]ver 2 [h]Ex 23:19; 34:26
14:22 [i]Lev 27:30; Dt 12:6,17; Ne 10:37

13 that wicked men[r] have arisen among you and have led the people of their town astray,
saying, "Let us go and worship other gods" (gods you have not known), 14 then you must
inquire, probe and investigate it thoroughly. And if it is true and it has been proved that
this detestable thing has been done among you, 15 you must certainly put to the sword
all who live in that town. Destroy it completely,[a] both its people and its livestock. 16 Gather all the plunder of the town into the middle of the public square and completely burn
the town and all its plunder as a whole burnt offering to the LORD your God.[s] It is to remain a ruin[t] forever, never to be rebuilt. 17 None of those condemned things[a] shall be
found in your hands, so that the LORD will turn from his fierce anger;[u] he will show you
mercy, have compassion[v] on you, and increase your numbers,[w] as he promised[x] on oath
to your forefathers, 18 because you obey the LORD your God, keeping all his commands
that I am giving you today and doing what is right[y] in his eyes.

Clean and Unclean Food

14 You are the children[z] of the LORD your God. Do not cut yourselves or shave the
front of your heads for the dead, 2 for you are a people holy to the LORD your
God.[a] Out of all the peoples on the face of the earth, the LORD has chosen you to be his
treasured possession.[b]

3 Do not eat any detestable thing.[c] 4 These are the animals you may eat:[d] the ox, the
sheep, the goat, 5 the deer, the gazelle, the roe deer, the wild goat, the ibex, the antelope
and the mountain sheep.[b] 6 You may eat any animal that has a split hoof divided in two
and that chews the cud. 7 However, of those that chew the cud or that have a split hoof
completely divided you may not eat the camel, the rabbit or the coney.[c] Although they
chew the cud, they do not have a split hoof; they are ceremonially unclean for you. 8 The
pig is also unclean; although it has a split hoof, it does not chew the cud. You are not to
eat their meat or touch their carcasses.[e]

9 Of all the creatures living in the water, you may eat any that has fins and scales. 10 But
anything that does not have fins and scales you may not eat; for you it is unclean.

11 You may eat any clean bird. 12 But these you may not eat: the eagle, the vulture, the
black vulture, 13 the red kite, the black kite, any kind of falcon, 14 any kind of raven, 15 the
horned owl, the screech owl, the gull, any kind of hawk, 16 the little owl, the great owl,
the white owl, 17 the desert owl, the osprey, the cormorant, 18 the stork, any kind of heron, the hoopoe and the bat.

19 All flying insects that swarm are unclean to you; do not eat them. 20 But any winged
creature that is clean you may eat.

21 Do not eat anything you find already dead.[f] You may give it to an alien living in any
of your towns, and he may eat it, or you may sell it to a foreigner. But you are a people
holy to the LORD your God.[g]

Do not cook a young goat in its mother's milk.[h]

Tithes

22 Be sure to set aside a tenth[i] of all that your fields produce each year. 23 Eat the tithe

a *15,17* The Hebrew term refers to the irrevocable giving over of things or persons to the LORD, often by totally destroying them. b *5* The precise identification of some of the birds and animals in this chapter is uncertain. c *7* That is, the hyrax or rock badger

---

13:12–18 In the third instance of danger from apostasy, the case of a whole town is considered. First, an investigation was to be undertaken (vv. 12–14). If the allegation was true, the town was to be destroyed (vv. 14–15). Note that the plunder of the town was not to be taken for private gain (vv. 16–18). The thought of gain might have clouded the judgment of those who investigated the accusation. The awfulness of the apostasy of a whole town is here affirmed. The town was to become a ruin.

14:1 Do not cut yourselves . . . for the dead. See Leviticus 19:27–28, where the same rules are given. The details of this practice are unknown, but it doubtless concerned behaviors associated with ancestor worship and pagan mourning rituals. The Israelites were to drop all pagan religion and the associated rituals and be different. They belonged to God (v. 2). He had chosen them as his special possession (26:18), and they were called to be faithful to him.

14:3–21 This section, Leviticus 11–15 and Numbers 5:1–4 are the main references to the legislation of clean and unclean things. Although some connections can be established between these ceremonial dietary regulations and modern concerns for physical health, the main concern was ceremonial cleanness. Most of these distinctions probably stemmed more from a reaction to common practices among the cultures surrounding Israel than from health considerations. See note on Leviticus 11:1–47.

14:11 any clean bird. No easy formula is explicitly given to identify clean birds. In general the scavenger birds were unclean. The identification of these birds is somewhat uncertain (see NIV text note), but the list in Deuteronomy is almost exactly like that found in Leviticus 11:13–19. The interdependence of the two passages is obvious.

14:20 any winged creature that is clean. In Leviticus 11:22 the locust, katydid, cricket and grasshopper are mentioned explicitly as clean insects.

14:21 a young goat in its mother's milk. This prohibition is not fully explained. It appears also in Exodus 23:19 and 34:26. It is the basis for the practice among orthodox Jews of not eating milk and meat products together. The prohibition may be similar to 22:6, which forbids taking the mother bird with its young. There, the idea is to preserve the mother and nest so as to have more birds for the future. Some have claimed that there is evidence in Canaanite poetry for cooking a goat in milk; if so, God's prohibition would distance the Israelites from such practices with pagan implications. However, this evidence comes from a damaged tablet and is therefore uncertain.

of your grain, new wine and oil, and the firstborn of your herds and flocks in the presence of the LORD your God at the place he will choose as a dwelling for his Name,[j] so that
you may learn[k] to revere the LORD your God always. 24But if that place is too distant and
you have been blessed by the LORD your God and cannot carry your tithe (because the
place where the LORD will choose to put his Name is so far away), 25then exchange your
tithe for silver, and take the silver with you and go to the place the LORD your God will
choose. 26Use the silver to buy whatever you like: cattle, sheep, wine or other fermented drink, or anything you wish. Then you and your household shall eat there in the presence of the LORD your God and rejoice.[l] 27And do not neglect the Levites[m] living in your
towns, for they have no allotment or inheritance of their own.[n]
28At the end of every three years, bring all the tithes of that year's produce and store
it in your towns,[o] 29so that the Levites (who have no allotment[p] or inheritance of their
own) and the aliens,[q] the fatherless and the widows who live in your towns may come
and eat and be satisfied, and so that the LORD your God may bless[r] you in all the work
of your hands.

The Year for Canceling Debts

15 At the end of every seven years you must cancel debts.[s] 2This is how it is to be
done: Every creditor shall cancel the loan he has made to his fellow Israelite. He
shall not require payment from his fellow Israelite or brother, because the LORD's time
for canceling debts has been proclaimed. 3You may require payment from a foreigner,[t]
but you must cancel any debt your brother owes you. 4However, there should be no poor
among you, for in the land the LORD your God is giving you to possess as your inheritance,
he will richly bless[u] you, 5if only you fully obey the LORD your God and are careful to follow[v] all these commands I am giving you today. 6For the LORD your God will bless you
as he has promised, and you will lend to many nations but will borrow from none. You
will rule over many nations but none will rule over you.[w]
7If there is a poor man among your brothers in any of the towns of the land that the
LORD your God is giving you, do not be hardhearted or tightfisted[x] toward your poor
brother. 8Rather be openhanded[y] and freely lend him whatever he needs. 9Be careful not
to harbor this wicked thought: "The seventh year, the year for canceling debts,[z] is
near," so that you do not show ill will[a] toward your needy brother and give him nothing. He may then appeal to the LORD against you, and you will be found guilty of sin.[b]
10Give generously to him and do so without a grudging heart;[c] then because of this the
LORD your God will bless[d] you in all your work and in everything you put your hand to.
11There will always be poor people in the land. Therefore I command you to be openhanded toward your brothers and toward the poor and needy in your land.[e]

14:23 [j]Dt 12:5 [k]Dt 4:10
14:26 [l]Dt 12:7-8
14:27 [m]Dt 12:19 [n]Nu 18:20
14:28 [o]Dt 26:12
14:29 [p]ver 27 [q]Dt 26:12 [r]Dt 15:10; Mal 3:10
15:1 [s]Dt 31:10
15:3 [t]Dt 23:20
15:4 [u]Dt 28:8
15:5 [v]Dt 28:1
15:6 [w]Dt 28:12-13,44
15:7 [x]1Jn 3:17
15:8 [y]Mt 5:42; Lk 6:34
15:9 [z]ver 1 [a]Mt 20:15 [b]Dt 24:15
15:10 [c]2Co 9:5 [d]Dt 14:29; 24:19
15:11 [e]Mt 26:11; Mk 14:7; Jn 12:8

14:22 a tenth. The law of the tithe was expressed as early as the time of Abraham (Ge 14:20; 28:22). Leviticus 27:30–33 specifies that the tithe of animals was not to be selective but was to include what "pass[ed] under the shepherd's rod." As specified in 12:17, the tithe was to be taken to the sanctuary, as were the firstfruits. The command to eat the tithe and firstfruits does not mean that the worshiper was to eat it all (which would destroy the purpose of the tithe) but that the worshiper was to eat some in fellowship with the priests, the Levites and the poor.
14:24 if that place is too distant. Travel was not easy. Carrying a large load a long distance was harder still. A practical consideration allowed for goods to be converted to money.
14:28 At the end of every three years. The third-year tithe is mentioned again only in 26:12. It is not clear how it was handled, but apparently it was a special gift for the Levites and the poor. It seems clear that the regular tithe went primarily to the Levites and that the Levites did not work at the sanctuary all the time. The Levitical cities were scattered throughout Israel (Jos 21), so there was a point in not taking all the tithes all the time to the central place of worship. It would seem that this third-year tithe was not an extra tithe but a regular tithe in the third year, perhaps staggered in some way not made explicit.
15:1 every seven years you must cancel debts. The Sabbath year was established and described in Exodus 23:10–11 and Leviticus 25:1–7. Both of those passages say that the land was to lie fallow during the seventh year. Deuteronomy 15:1–11 adds the point that debts were also to be forgiven in that year. The same verbal root used to describe allowing land to lie fallow is also used for allowing debts to be released. For this reason, the Jews often call the seventh year the *Shemita* instead of the Sabbath year. It is difficult to assess this arrangement, because so little is known about ancient lending practices. The question is raised whether Leviticus 25:36–37 forbids interest per se (see NIV text) or only exorbitant interest, or usury (see NIV text note; see also 23:19). In either case, the rule set forth here and in Leviticus 25 applies only to a fellow Israelite. Interest or usury could be required of an alien. If a loan was arranged a short time before the Sabbath year, it amounted to a gift. For this reason verses 7–11 warn against refusing to lend to the poor under these circumstances.
15:4 However, there should be no poor. As translated in the NIV, this verse indicates that if the Israelites obey God in the promised land, there will be no poor, and thus no need for loans. By this reading, verse 11 indicates that the people will never obey God sufficiently to eliminate poverty. Alternatively, this verse may be translated with the force "unless there are no poor," such that the provisions of verses 1–3 are suspended when there are no poor, perhaps implying that they also do not apply when the borrower is not poor, regardless of the wealth of the rest of the nation. The idea that the obligation to forgive debts depended on the real need of the debtor seems to agree with the observation of verse 11 that there would always be some poor and therefore always a need for generosity. It is probable that long-term loans for house mortgages or foreign trade were not used, or perhaps if used were not covered by this provision, which would have applied more naturally to personal loans. The Sabbath-year and the Jubilee-year provisions (Lev 25:8–34) are interesting examples of a system that seems to minimize (not prevent) aggrandizement and the accumulation of great wealth.

Freeing Servants

12 If a fellow Hebrew, a man or a woman, sells himself to you and serves you six years, in the seventh year you must let him go free.[f] 13 And when you release him, do not send him away empty-handed. 14 Supply him liberally from your flock, your threshing floor and your winepress. Give to him as the LORD your God has blessed you. 15 Remember that you were slaves[g] in Egypt and the LORD your God redeemed you.[h] That is why I give you this command today.

16 But if your servant says to you, "I do not want to leave you," because he loves you and your family and is well off with you, 17 then take an awl and push it through his ear lobe into the door, and he will become your servant for life. Do the same for your maidservant.

18 Do not consider it a hardship to set your servant free, because his service to you these six years has been worth twice as much as that of a hired hand. And the LORD your God will bless you in everything you do.

The Firstborn Animals

19 Set apart for the LORD your God every firstborn male[i] of your herds and flocks. Do not put the firstborn of your oxen to work, and do not shear the firstborn of your sheep. 20 Each year you and your family are to eat them in the presence of the LORD your God at the place he will choose.[j] 21 If an animal has a defect, is lame or blind, or has any serious flaw, you must not sacrifice it to the LORD your God.[k] 22 You are to eat it in your own towns. Both the ceremonially unclean and the clean may eat it, as if it were gazelle or deer.[l] 23 But you must not eat the blood; pour it out on the ground like water.[m]

Passover

16 Observe the month of Abib[n] and celebrate the Passover of the LORD your God, because in the month of Abib he brought you out of Egypt by night. 2 Sacrifice as the Passover to the LORD your God an animal from your flock or herd at the place the LORD will choose as a dwelling for his Name.[o] 3 Do not eat it with bread made with yeast, but for seven days eat unleavened bread, the bread of affliction,[p] because you left Egypt in haste[q]—so that all the days of your life you may remember the time of your departure from Egypt.[r] 4 Let no yeast be found in your possession in all your land for seven days. Do not let any of the meat you sacrifice on the evening of the first day remain until morning.[s]

5 You must not sacrifice the Passover in any town the LORD your God gives you 6 except in the place he will choose as a dwelling for his Name. There you must sacrifice the Passover in the evening, when the sun goes down, on the anniversary[a][t] of your departure

15:12 [f]Ex 21:2; Lev 25:39; Jer 34:14
15:15 [g]Dt 5:15 [h]Dt 16:12
15:19 [i]Ex 13:2
15:20 [j]Dt 12:5-7,17,18; 14:23
15:21 [k]Lev 22:19-25
15:22 [l]Dt 12:15,22
15:23 [m]Dt 12:16
16:1 [n]Ex 12:2; 13:4
16:2 [o]Dt 12:5,26
16:3 [p]Ex 12:8,39; 34:18 [q]Ex 12:11,15,19 [r]Ex 13:3,6-7
16:4 [s]Ex 12:10; 34:25
16:6 [t]Ex 12:6; Dt 12:5

[a] 6 Or *down, at the time of day*

15:12 If a fellow Hebrew . . . sells. Exodus 21:2–6 delineates the same law but adds the detail that if the master had supplied a wife, the wife and any children were to stay with the master. This stipulation seems harsh, except that the husband could also choose to stay; if he did elect to leave, he could in due time redeem his wife and children. Because this law of servitude is placed in close proximity to that of the Sabbath year, it might be assumed that the Sabbath year freed all slaves. But that is not explicitly stated. Rather, the period of servitude was six years for every slave, and in his seventh year he was to go free. The slave's situation in Israel was similar to that of an indentured servant during the American colonial period, but quite different from that of an American slave. The slave in ancient Israel had his rights. He was not to be beaten to death (Ex 21:20–21); if he ran away, he was not to be returned (23:15–16). The provision here is generous: A freed slave was to be given provisions with which to start fresh. The Israelite attitude toward slaves was to be based on God's rescue of the Hebrews from their hard servitude in Egypt. The seven-year period of servitude here described does not contradict the provision for freedom in the Year of Jubilee (Lev 25:39–43). That specification probably involved the case of a slave who had nowhere to go if freed, for his ancestral home was gone. When the Year of Jubilee came, his home would be restored and he could go to it.
15:19 Set apart . . . every firstborn. See 12:15–19. **do not shear.** The firstborn ox was not to be worked nor the firstborn sheep to be shorn, because they were to be given to the Lord while still young.
15:21 a defect. See 17:1.
16:1–17 These verses deal with the three pilgrimage festivals, so called because all grown males were required to celebrate them at the sanctuary. These feasts are mentioned briefly in Exodus 23:14–17, ending with the same charge given in Deuteronomy 16:16 (using practically the same wording): Every man was to bring his offering. The feasts are listed again in Exodus 34:18–23, where (as in Ex 23:15) the Passover is called the Feast of Unleavened Bread. All five major feasts are listed more fully in Leviticus 23; they are listed with their specified offerings in Numbers 28–29.
16:1 the month of Abib. When the Feast of Unleavened Bread and the Passover were instituted, they were stipulated to be celebrated in the "first month" (Ex 12:2,18). Later (Ex 23; 34) this month was called Abib. In Leviticus and Numbers, it is referred to simply as "the first month." Apparently Abib was a Canaanite name for the first month. The Babylonian name was Nisan, but Babylonian names were used only in Old Testament books written during the exilic period. **celebrate the Passover.** The Passover symbolized substitution. On that fateful night in Egypt, the firstborn in every household was to be killed by the Lord. If the Israelites were to mark their houses with the blood of the Passover sacrifice, however, their houses would be "passed over" and the firstborn son spared. The lamb would die, but the son would live. Like all other animal sacrifices, the lamb was a sacramental symbol. The argument in Hebrews 10:1–4 is based on common sense. The blood of animals could not redeem. If it could, sacrifices would not have to have been offered repeatedly. As the kingship typified Christ's kingly office, so the sacrifices symbolized Christ's mediatorial work. Israel therefore expected a dying Savior as well as a righteous King. Psalm 22 speaks of the death of the innocent one, and Isaiah 53:10 calls this death a "guilt offering." So Paul was fully justified in stating that "Christ, our Passover lamb, has been sacrificed" (1Co 5:7). It was at the last true Passover feast that Jesus said "This is my body . . . This cup is the new covenant in my blood" (Lk 22:19–20).
16:3 unleavened bread. Unleavened bread was used because the Israelites had to eat in haste on the night they left Egypt (see Ex 12:34).
16:6 in the place he will choose. See note on 12:5. The people

from Egypt. 7Roast[u] it and eat it at the place the LORD your God will choose. Then in the
morning return to your tents. 8For six days eat unleavened bread and on the seventh day
hold an assembly[v] to the LORD your God and do no work.

Feast of Weeks

9Count off seven weeks[w] from the time you begin to put the sickle to the standing
grain.[x] 10Then celebrate the Feast of Weeks to the LORD your God by giving a freewill offering in proportion to the blessings the LORD your God has given you. 11And rejoice[y] before the LORD your God at the place he will choose as a dwelling for his Name—you, your
sons and daughters, your menservants and maidservants, the Levites[z] in your towns,
and the aliens, the fatherless and the widows living among you. 12Remember that you
were slaves in Egypt,[a] and follow carefully these decrees.

Feast of Tabernacles

13Celebrate the Feast of Tabernacles for seven days after you have gathered the produce of your threshing floor[b] and your winepress.[c] 14Be joyful[d] at your Feast—you, your
sons and daughters, your menservants and maidservants, and the Levites, the aliens, the
fatherless and the widows who live in your towns. 15For seven days celebrate the Feast
to the LORD your God at the place the LORD will choose. For the LORD your God will bless
you in all your harvest and in all the work of your hands, and your joy[e] will be complete.
16Three times a year all your men must appear before the LORD your God at the place
he will choose: at the Feast of Unleavened Bread, the Feast of Weeks and the Feast of
Tabernacles.[f] No man should appear before the LORD empty-handed:[g] 17Each of you
must bring a gift in proportion to the way the LORD your God has blessed you.

Judges

18Appoint judges[h] and officials for each of your tribes in every town the LORD your God
is giving you, and they shall judge the people fairly. 19Do not pervert justice[i] or show partiality.[j] Do not accept a bribe,[k] for a bribe blinds the eyes of the wise and twists the words
of the righteous. 20Follow justice and justice alone, so that you may live and possess the
land the LORD your God is giving you.

Worshiping Other Gods

21Do not set up any wooden Asherah pole[a][l] beside the altar you build to the LORD your
God,[m] 22and do not erect a sacred stone,[n] for these the LORD your God hates.

17 Do not sacrifice to the LORD your God an ox or a sheep that has any defect[o] or
flaw in it, for that would be detestable to him.[p]

[a] *21* Or *Do not plant any tree dedicated to Asherah*

16:7 [u]Ex 12:8; 2Ch 35:13
16:8 [v]Ex 12:16; 13:6; Lev 23:8
16:9 [w]Ex 34:22; Lev 23:15 [x]Ex 23:16; Nu 28:26
16:11 [y]Dt 12:7 [z]Dt 12:12
16:12 [a]Dt 15:15
16:13 [b]Lev 23:34 [c]Ex 23:16
16:14 [d]ver 11
16:15 [e]Lev 23:39
16:16 [f]Ex 23:14,16 [g]Ex 34:20
16:18 [h]Dt 1:16
16:19 [i]Ex 23:2,8 [j]Lev 19:15; Dt 1:17 [k]Ecc 7:7
16:21 [l]Dt 7:5 [m]Ex 34:13; 2Ki 17:16; 21:3; 2Ch 33:3
16:22 [n]Lev 26:1
17:1 [o]Mal 1:8,13 [p]Dt 15:21

were to "go up three times each year to appear before the LORD" (see Ex 34:23); one of those times was to celebrate Passover. They were to bring the offering from wherever they lived (Lev 23:17). It is obvious that the first Passover meal, when the Israelites were leaving Egypt, was cooked in haste in their homes. But every other time that the matter is mentioned, the celebration is said to have taken place not at home, but at the sanctuary.

16:7 in the morning return to your tents. There is no contradiction between this regulation and the following statement that there was to be an assembly on the seventh day after the Passover evening (v. 8). The picture is this: The lamb or goat was to be slaughtered at the sanctuary at sundown, roasted in that area for hours and then eaten at midnight. After a long night, the people would return to their tents in the morning. In the wilderness they lived in tents. In later years when they assembled at the central sanctuary, the majority surely again lived in tents. In modern times the Samaritan Passover on Mount Gerizim is conducted in precisely this way.

16:9–12 The Passover was always celebrated on the fourteenth day of the first spring month. The Israelites used the lunar month, so there was always a full moon on Passover. Associated with Passover was the presentation of the first ripe sheaf of grain (Lev 23:9). On the day after the seventh Sabbath after that presentation (Lev 23:15–16) was the one-day celebration of the Feast of Weeks (v. 10). Because of the calculation used to determine the date of the celebration of the Feast of Weeks (50 days; see Lev 23:16), the Feast of Weeks is called Pentecost in the New Testament (the Greek word *pentekoste* means "fiftieth"). On the first Pentecost after Jesus' ascension, the Holy Spirit was poured out in power on the apostles (Ac 2:1–4). There was an argument as to the calculation to be used in determining the day of celebration for the Feast of Weeks. The Pharisees held that the 50-day count should begin on Passover and end on the fiftieth day, regardless of what day of the week it fell on. The Sadducees held that the count should begin on a Sabbath; therefore, the Feast of Weeks would always fall on a Sunday. It seems that this is the meaning of Leviticus 23:15–16.

16:13–17 The Feast of Tabernacles (v. 13) was also called the Feast of Sukkoth (Booths) because the Israelites were to gather at the sanctuary and live in temporary structures for a week. The feast began on the fifteenth day of the seventh lunar month (in the fall). It occurred at the end of the agricultural season after the grain had been threshed and the grapes harvested. Naturally, the tithe of the harvest was to be brought at this feast. God authorized that this feast was to memorialize Israel's pilgrim experience after leaving Egypt (Lev 23:43) and was to be a time of reading the law (31:10–13; see also Ezr 8).

16:18 Appoint judges and officials. Moses had earlier appointed judges at Sinai (1:13); this section specifies that such an organization should continue. Moreover, the high ideal of justice, and justice alone, was to guide their conduct (see note on 19:16).

16:19 a bribe blinds. This obvious fact is often emphasized (Ex 23:8; Pr 17:23; see *BC* 36).

16:21 Asherah pole. Asherah was the name of a Canaanite deity, and her pole was "repulsive" (2Ch 15:16). It probably consisted at least partially of wood, since it could be burned (2Ch 15:16), and may have had an overlay of precious metal, since it could also be broken up or crushed (2Ch 15:16). It was periodically decorated with woven hangings by the women worshipers of Asherah (2Ki 23:7). Asherah, the wife of El, was a goddess associated with fertility.

17:1 any defect. Any flaw or defect would make an animal unsuitable for sacrifice (15:21; Lev 22:19–25; Nu 19:2). Also, any

2 If a man or woman living among you in one of the towns the LORD gives you is found
doing evil in the eyes of the LORD your God in violation of his covenant,[q] 3 and contrary
to my command[r] has worshiped other gods, bowing down to them or to the sun[s] or the
moon or the stars of the sky, 4 and this has been brought to your attention, then you must
investigate it thoroughly. If it is true and it has been proved that this detestable thing has
been done in Israel,[t] 5 take the man or woman who has done this evil deed to your city
gate and stone that person to death.[u] 6 On the testimony of two or three witnesses a man
shall be put to death, but no one shall be put to death on the testimony of only one witness.[v] 7 The hands of the witnesses must be the first in putting him to death, and then
the hands of all the people. You must purge the evil[w] from among you.

Law Courts

8 If cases come before your courts that are too difficult for you to judge—whether
bloodshed, lawsuits or assaults[x]—take them to the place the LORD your God will
choose.[y] 9 Go to the priests, who are Levites, and to the judge who is in office at that time.
Inquire of them and they will give you the verdict.[z] 10 You must act according to the decisions they give you at the place the LORD will choose. Be careful to do everything they
direct you to do. 11 Act according to the law they teach you and the decisions they give
you. Do not turn aside from what they tell you, to the right or to the left.[a] 12 The man who
shows contempt[b] for the judge or for the priest who stands ministering there to the LORD
your God must be put to death. You must purge the evil from Israel. 13 All the people will
hear and be afraid, and will not be contemptuous again.[c]

The King

14 When you enter the land the LORD your God is giving you and have taken possession of it and settled in it, and you say, "Let us set a king over us like all the nations
around us,"[d] 15 be sure to appoint over you the king the LORD your God chooses. He must
be from among your own brothers.[e] Do not place a foreigner over you, one who is not a
brother Israelite. 16 The king, moreover, must not acquire great numbers of horses for
himself[f] or make the people return to Egypt[g] to get more of them,[h] for the LORD has told
you, "You are not to go back that way again."[i] 17 He must not take many wives,[j] or his
heart will be led astray. He must not accumulate large amounts of silver and gold.
18 When he takes the throne of his kingdom, he is to write[k] for himself on a scroll a
copy of this law, taken from that of the priests, who are Levites. 19 It is to be with him, and
he is to read it all the days of his life[l] so that he may learn to revere the LORD his God and
follow carefully all the words of this law and these decrees 20 and not consider himself
better than his brothers and turn from the law[m] to the right or to the left.[n] Then he and
his descendants will reign a long time over his kingdom in Israel.

Offerings for Priests and Levites

18 The priests, who are Levites—indeed the whole tribe of Levi—are to have no allotment or inheritance with Israel. They shall live on the offerings made to the

17:2 [q]Dt 13:6-11
17:3 [r]Jer 7:22-23 [s]Job 31:26
17:4 [t]Dt 13:12-14
17:5 [u]Lev 24:14
17:6 [v]Nu 35:30; Dt 19:15; Jos 7:25; Mt 18:16; Jn 8:17; 2Co 13:1; 1Ti 5:19; Heb 10:28
17:7 [w]Dt 13:5,9
17:8 [x]2Ch 19:10 [y]Dt 12:5; Hag 2:11
17:9 [z]Dt 19:17; Eze 44:24
17:11 [a]Dt 25:1
17:12 [b]Nu 15:30
17:13 [c]Dt 13:11; 19:20
17:14 [d]Dt 11:31; 1Sa 8:5, 19-20
17:15 [e]Jer 30:21
17:16 [f]1Ki 4:26; 10:26 [g]Isa 31:1; Hos 11:5 [h]1Ki 10:28; Eze 17:15 [i]Ex 13:17
17:17 [j]1Ki 11:3
17:18 [k]Dt 31:22,24
17:19 [l]Jos 1:8
17:20 [m]1Ki 15:5 [n]Dt 5:32

priest who had a physical deformity was not to officiate (Lev 21:16–23). The symbolism is clear: God is holy (Lev 21:23) and demands perfection. The Old Testament sacrificial system, with its demand for a sacrifice without defect, was symbolic of the coming perfect Savior and his worthy sacrifice.

17:2–7 The idea of "doing evil" (v. 2) is general, but verse 3 makes it clear that the specific transgression in mind is violating God's covenant by worshiping other gods. This case of the apostasy of an individual is to be compared to chapter 13, which considers the apostasy of a prophet, a close relative or a whole town. The penalty here, as there, is death. This case is slightly different, because here it was not a public matter, and witnesses were to be sought. Condemnation was not to take place on the basis of rumor. Instead, two or three witnesses had to agree (v. 6; 19:15–19; Nu 35:30), and the witnesses had to be sincere and convinced enough of the person's guilt to take part in the stoning, knowing that the penalty for acting as a false witness was also stoning. The net result was not rehabilitation or restitution, which were allowed for other types of crimes, but the purging of idolatry from Israel.

17:8 If cases come before your courts. We do not know the details of the Israelite court system (see note on 19:16), but we are aware that there were different courts to handle the more difficult cases (Ex 18:21–26). Evidently there were priests who judged and also other judges, but how a particular case was allocated we do not know. The main points were that the judges were to judge in the fear of God and that their verdicts were to be accepted—those who rejected the judges' verdicts were liable unto death (v. 12).

17:10 See *WLC* 157.

17:14–17 This passage assumes that Israel, like every other known ancient nation, would one day have a king (see Ge 49:10). This presumption was never denied, although it was stated regularly and emphatically that God was Israel's King (33:5; see note on 1Sa 8:7). On the basis of the references to horses, wives and wealth, critics have argued that this section was written long after Solomon by one of his detractors, but there is no persuasive evidence of this. Warnings against choosing an alien king (v. 16) would seem to disprove this criticism, since Solomon was a native Israelite.

17:17 See *WLC* 130.

17:18–20 See *WLC* 108,156,157; *BC* 36.

17:18 this law. Ancient Israel was a constitutional monarchy, and God was the author of the constitution. God's law ("this law," of which Deuteronomy is a part) was to be placed by the priests beside the ark of the covenant (31:26) and used by them in public instruction (31:11). The king was to make a copy of it, read it and follow it.

18:1 The priests, who are Levites. Aaron and his sons (the priests) were to have no inheritance in Canaan because the Lord

LORD by fire, for that is their inheritance.[o] 2They shall have no inheritance among their
brothers; the LORD is their inheritance, as he promised them.
3This is the share due the priests from the people who sacrifice a bull or a sheep: the
shoulder, the jowls and the inner parts.[p] 4You are to give them the firstfruits of your
grain, new wine and oil, and the first wool from the shearing of your sheep,[q] 5for the LORD
your God has chosen them[r] and their descendants out of all your tribes to stand and minister[s] in the LORD's name always.
6If a Levite moves from one of your towns anywhere in Israel where he is living, and
comes in all earnestness to the place the LORD will choose,[t] 7he may minister in the name
of the LORD his God like all his fellow Levites who serve there in the presence of the LORD.
8He is to share equally in their benefits, even though he has received money from the sale
of family possessions.[u]

Detestable Practices

9When you enter the land the LORD your God is giving you, do not learn to imitate[v]
the detestable ways of the nations there. 10Let no one be found among you who sacrifices his son or daughter in[a] the fire, who practices divination[w] or sorcery, interprets
omens, engages in witchcraft,[x] 11or casts spells, or who is a medium or spiritist or who
consults the dead. 12Anyone who does these things is detestable to the LORD, and because
of these detestable practices the LORD your God will drive out those nations before
you.[y] 13You must be blameless before the LORD your God.

The Prophet

14The nations you will dispossess listen to those who practice sorcery or divination.
But as for you, the LORD your God has not permitted you to do so. 15The LORD your God
will raise up for you a prophet like me from among your own brothers.[z] You must listen
to him. 16For this is what you asked of the LORD your God at Horeb on the day of the assembly when you said, "Let us not hear the voice of the LORD our God nor see this great
fire anymore, or we will die."[a]
17The LORD said to me: "What they say is good. 18I will raise up for them a prophet like
you from among their brothers; I will put my words[b] in his mouth, and he will tell them
everything I command him.[c] 19If anyone does not listen to my words that the prophet
speaks in my name, I myself will call him to account.[d] 20But a prophet who presumes to
speak in my name anything I have not commanded him to say, or a prophet who speaks
in the name of other gods,[e] must be put to death."[f]
21You may say to yourselves, "How can we know when a message has not been spoken by the LORD?" 22If what a prophet proclaims in the name of the LORD does not take
place or come true, that is a message the LORD has not spoken.[g] That prophet has spoken presumptuously.[h] Do not be afraid of him.

Cities of Refuge

19 When the LORD your God has destroyed the nations whose land he is giving you,
and when you have driven them out and settled in their towns and houses,[i]
2then set aside for yourselves three cities centrally located in the land the LORD your God

18:1 [o]Dt 10:9; 1Co 9:13
18:3 [p]Lev 7:28-34
18:4 [q]Ex 22:29; Nu 18:12
18:5 [r]Ex 28:1 [s]Dt 10:8
18:6 [t]Nu 35:2-3
18:8 [u]2Ch 31:4; Ne 12:44,47
18:9 [v]Dt 12:29-31
18:10 [w]Dt 12:31 [x]Lev 19:31
18:12 [y]Lev 18:24; Dt 9:4
18:15 [z]Jn 1:21; Ac 3:22*; 7:37*
18:16 [a]Ex 20:19; Dt 5:23-27
18:18 [b]Isa 51:16; Jn 17:8 [c]Jn 4:25-26; 8:28; 12:49-50
18:19 [d]Ac 3:23*
18:20 [e]Jer 14:14 [f]Dt 13:1-5
18:22 [g]Jer 28:9 [h]ver 20
19:1 [i]Dt 12:29

a 10 *Or who makes his son or daughter pass through*

was their inheritance (Nu 18:20). The expression "the priests, who are Levites" is unusual, but it emphasizes their tribal relationship. The expression is also used in Joshua 3:3 of those who carried the ark across the Jordan (see also Jos 3:14,17; Eze 43:19). **indeed the whole tribe of Levi.** No Levite was to receive an inheritance of land (10:9; Nu 26:62).The implication is that Levites were not to have farms on which to base their livelihood. Moses specifically allotted the tribe 42 cities, six of which were to be designated as cities of refuge (Nu 35:2–8). In due time these cities were allocated by Joshua (Jos 21).

18:3 the share due the priests. See Leviticus 7:32. The exact cuts of meat intended are obscure, for little is known of ancient butchering practices. Leviticus specifies the right thigh, using a word that is also applied to the human leg. Deuteronomy speaks of the shoulder, using a word that is also applied to the human arm. These two Hebrew words are applied exclusively to the hind legs and forelegs, respectively, of animals. It might be that either quarter was allowed. Likewise, the Leviticus passage speaks of the breast, while Deuteronomy specifies the jowls. Exactly what these Hebrew words include and exclude is hard to determine. It is safe to say that the priest would get a right leg and a right side.

18:6 If a Levite moves. There is a problem as to where the conclusion of the sentence should come. The NIV places it at the beginning of verse 7, such that verses 6–7 instruct that if a Levite were to sell his house and move to the central sanctuary, he was to receive the provisions that others received. The conclusion, however, might also be placed at the beginning of verse 8. By this reading, a Levite who sold his house and moved to the sanctuary could receive provisions only if he also ministered.

18:9–14 See *WLC* 113; *HC* 94.

18:9 the detestable ways of the nations. These "detestable ways" were not merely magical methods by which to forecast the future. They were integral parts of the pagan religions that had corrupted Canaan and the rest of the ancient world.

18:15–22 With Moses about to die, there was a need to restate the credentials of the true prophets to come. The tests were accomplished by observing the predictive (1Ki 13:12; 22:28), theological (13:1–2) and supernatural (Ex 4:30–31) natures of a prophet's ministry. Acts 3:22 and 7:37 refer to this section as pointing to Christ, of whom Moses and all the prophets were but types.

18:15 See *HC* 31.

18:18 See "Introduction to the Prophets" at 1064.

is giving you to possess. 3 Build roads to them and divide into three parts the land the LORD your God is giving you as an inheritance, so that anyone who kills a man may flee there.

4 This is the rule concerning the man who kills another and flees there to save his life—one who kills his neighbor unintentionally, without malice aforethought. 5 For instance, a man may go into the forest with his neighbor to cut wood, and as he swings his ax to fell a tree, the head may fly off and hit his neighbor and kill him. That man may flee to one of these cities and save his life. 6 Otherwise, the avenger of blood[j] might pursue him in a rage, overtake him if the distance is too great, and kill him even though he is not deserving of death, since he did it to his neighbor without malice aforethought. 7 This is why I command you to set aside for yourselves three cities.

8 If the LORD your God enlarges your territory, as he promised on oath to your forefathers, and gives you the whole land he promised them, 9 because you carefully follow all these laws I command you today—to love the LORD your God and to walk always in his ways[k]—then you are to set aside three more cities. 10 Do this so that innocent blood will not be shed in your land, which the LORD your God is giving you as your inheritance, and so that you will not be guilty of bloodshed.[l]

11 But if a man hates his neighbor and lies in wait for him, assaults and kills him,[m] and then flees to one of these cities, 12 the elders of his town shall send for him, bring him back from the city, and hand him over to the avenger of blood to die. 13 Show him no pity.[n] You must purge from Israel the guilt of shedding innocent blood,[o] so that it may go well with you.

14 Do not move your neighbor's boundary stone set up by your predecessors in the inheritance you receive in the land the LORD your God is giving you to possess.[p]

Witnesses

15 One witness is not enough to convict a man accused of any crime or offense he may have committed. A matter must be established by the testimony of two or three witnesses.[q]

16 If a malicious witness[r] takes the stand to accuse a man of a crime, 17 the two men involved in the dispute must stand in the presence of the LORD before the priests and the judges[s] who are in office at the time. 18 The judges must make a thorough investigation, and if the witness proves to be a liar, giving false testimony against his brother, 19 then do to him as he intended to do to his brother.[t] You must purge the evil from among you. 20 The rest of the people will hear of this and be afraid,[u] and never again will such an evil thing be done among you. 21 Show no pity:[v] life for life, eye for eye, tooth for tooth, hand for hand, foot for foot.[w]

Going to War

20 When you go to war against your enemies and see horses and chariots and an army greater than yours,[x] do not be afraid[y] of them,[z] because the LORD your

19:6 [j]Nu 35:12
19:9 [k]Jos 20:7-8
19:10 [l]Nu 35:33; Dt 21:1-9
19:11 [m]Nu 35:16
19:13 [n]Dt 7:2 [o]1Ki 2:31
19:14 [p]Dt 27:17; Pr 22:28; Hos 5:10
19:15 [q]Nu 35:30; Dt 17:6; Mt 18:16*; Jn 8:17; 2Co 13:1*; 1Ti 5:19; Heb 10:28
19:16 [r]Ex 23:1; Ps 27:12
19:17 [s]Dt 17:9
19:19 [t]Pr 19:5,9
19:20 [u]Dt 17:13; 21:21
19:21 [v]ver 13 [w]Ex 21:24; Lev 24:20; Mt 5:38*
20:1 [x]Ps 20:7; Isa 31:1 [y]Dt 31:6,8 [z]2Ch 32:7-8

19:2 three cities. These cities of refuge were to be set aside in Canaan. The three cities of refuge for the Transjordan had already been named and set aside. See 4:41–43 for the sequence of establishing these cities.
19:4 one who kills his neighbor unintentionally. The law against manslaughter is given first in Exodus 21:13 and more fully detailed in Numbers 35:6–28. The passage here repeats some provisions stated in Numbers and adds other stipulations, such as the requirement for roads to each city of refuge to make the city readily accessible. This passage also specifies three extra cities in Canaan if the nation's territory were to be greatly enlarged. But it is plain in both Numbers and Deuteronomy that a man guilty of premeditated murder was to die. This regulation does not reflect a disrespect for life but an intense respect for the life of the innocent victim, who like all other people had been created in the image of God (Ge 9:6).
19:5 See *WCF* 15.2; *BC* 13.
19:9 to love the LORD your God and to walk always in his ways. See note on 6:5.
19:14 your neighbor's boundary stone. This law was intended to prevent encroachment and theft of land (27:17; Pr 22:28; 23:20). See *WLC* 142.
19:15 One witness. See 17:6.
19:16 a malicious witness. In the jurisprudence of the ancient Near East, much responsibility was given to the judge. He did not compare an offense to a particular law and thereby pronounce a verdict but instead compared the case with the principles of the law and with typical cases and gave a decision in accordance with justice and equity (1:13; 16:18; 17:8). All witnesses were to be thoroughly examined. A false witness was to suffer the penalty that the accused would have suffered if he had been found guilty.
19:21 eye for eye. This saying occurs three times in the Pentateuch (here; Ex 21:24; Lev 24:20). In each case, the verse is part of a legal context. This most likely idiomatic statement delineated a principle of public justice: The penalty was to fit the crime. We have no evidence that eyes were actually put out or teeth knocked out in judgment. Indeed, the penalty for assault was a payment of damages (Ex 21:18). If an owner were to destroy the tooth or eye of a slave, the owner's penalty was the slave's freedom (Ex 21:26–27). No prisons are envisaged in Moses' laws, though indentured servitude was allowed in the case of those who could not afford to make restitution for their crimes (Ex 22:3). The punishment for serious civil or religious offenses was death; for theft the penalty was restitution with a fine. The only corporal consequence mentioned is flogging, and that was limited to 40 strokes (25:3). See notes on Exodus 21:24 and Leviticus 24:20. Jesus quoted this verse when he opposed the misunderstandings of the hypocrites (Mt 5:38—6:2), who were construing it as an excuse for personal vengeance. Christ instructed them, in effect, to "turn the other cheek."
20:1–20 See *WLC* 136.
20:1 do not be afraid. Verses 1–9 deal with morale in the army. The main thrust is on reliance on the Lord, who had displayed his might in Israel's great deliverance from Egypt. Relying on the Lord, Israel's soldiers would fight with a will and, trusting in him, would win. The question may be raised as to whether the man recently

God, who brought you up out of Egypt, will be with you. 2When you are about to go into
battle, the priest shall come forward and address the army. 3He shall say: "Hear, O Israel, today you are going into battle against your enemies. Do not be fainthearted[a] or
afraid; do not be terrified or give way to panic before them. 4For the LORD your God is the
one who goes with you to fight[b] for you against your enemies to give you victory."
5The officers shall say to the army: "Has anyone built a new house and not dedicated[c] it? Let him go home, or he may die in battle and someone else may dedicate it. 6Has
anyone planted a vineyard and not begun to enjoy it? Let him go home, or he may die
in battle and someone else enjoy it. 7Has anyone become pledged to a woman and not
married her? Let him go home, or he may die in battle and someone else marry her.[d]"
8Then the officers shall add, "Is any man afraid or fainthearted? Let him go home so that
his brothers will not become disheartened too."[e] 9When the officers have finished speaking to the army, they shall appoint commanders over it.
10When you march up to attack a city, make its people an offer of peace.[f] 11If they accept and open their gates, all the people in it shall be subject to forced labor[g] and shall
work for you. 12If they refuse to make peace and they engage you in battle, lay siege to
that city. 13When the LORD your God delivers it into your hand, put to the sword all the
men in it.[h] 14As for the women, the children, the livestock[i] and everything else in the city,
you may take these as plunder for yourselves. And you may use the plunder the LORD
your God gives you from your enemies. 15This is how you are to treat all the cities that
are at a distance from you and do not belong to the nations nearby.
16However, in the cities of the nations the LORD your God is giving you as an inheritance, do not leave alive anything that breathes.[j] 17Completely destroy[a] them—the Hittites, Amorites, Canaanites, Perizzites, Hivites and Jebusites—as the LORD your God has
commanded you. 18Otherwise, they will teach you to follow all the detestable things they
do in worshiping their gods,[k] and you will sin[l] against the LORD your God.
19When you lay siege to a city for a long time, fighting against it to capture it, do not
destroy its trees by putting an ax to them, because you can eat their fruit. Do not cut
them down. Are the trees of the field people, that you should besiege them?[b] 20Howev-
er, you may cut down trees that you know are not fruit trees and use them to build siege
works until the city at war with you falls.

Atonement for an Unsolved Murder

21 If a man is found slain, lying in a field in the land the LORD your God is giving you
to possess, and it is not known who killed him, 2your elders and judges shall go
out and measure the distance from the body to the neighboring towns. 3Then the elders
of the town nearest the body shall take a heifer that has never been worked and has never worn a yoke 4and lead her down to a valley that has not been plowed or planted and
where there is a flowing stream. There in the valley they are to break the heifer's neck.
5The priests, the sons of Levi, shall step forward, for the LORD your God has chosen them
to minister and to pronounce blessings[m] in the name of the LORD and to decide all cases of dispute and assault.[n] 6Then all the elders of the town nearest the body shall wash
their hands[o] over the heifer whose neck was broken in the valley, 7and they shall declare:
"Our hands did not shed this blood, nor did our eyes see it done. 8Accept this atonement
for your people Israel, whom you have redeemed, O LORD, and do not hold your people

20:3 [a]Jos 23:10
20:4 [b]Dt 1:30; 3:22; Jos 23:10
20:5 [c]Ne 12:27
20:7 [d]Dt 24:5
20:8 [e]Jdg 7:3
20:10 [f]Lk 14:31-32
20:11 [g]1Ki 9:21
20:13 [h]Nu 31:7
20:14 [i]Jos 8:2; 22:8
20:16 [j]Ex 23:31-33; Nu 21:2-3; Dt 7:2; Jos 11:14
20:18 [k]Ex 34:16; Dt 7:4; 12:30-31 [l]Ex 23:33
21:5 [m]1Ch 23:13 [n]Dt 17:8-11
21:6 [o]Mt 27:24

[a] *17* The Hebrew term refers to the irrevocable giving over of things or persons to the LORD, often by totally destroying them. [b] *19* Or *down to use in the siege, for the fruit trees are for the benefit of man.*

---

married or involved in building, planting, etc., was actually excused from military service, but the principle is that anyone whose heart was not in the fight was not to take part in it. Israel's was a voluntary army that fought under the banner of the Lord. The natural result of such an attitude was an extraordinarily high level of morale, which would itself contribute to victory.

20:10 an offer of peace. Most cities relied on their walls for defense and could withstand a siege for perhaps a year, hoping for relief from some friendly power. Because the attackers preferred to forestall a siege, an offer of peace was attractive to them. An offer of peace was often attractive to the defending city, as well, since it averted the threat of the total slaughter of its soldiers.

20:17 Completely destroy. The Hebrew word means "to put under the ban" (i.e., to devote everything to the Lord). This stipulation in the case of Jericho, for example, meant that the Israelites were to kill all the people and livestock, but give all the gold and silver to the Lord (see note on 7:26; see also 2:32–34; 7:1,3,5,26). The sparing of individuals and families who converted to Israel's faith is not in view here, although God did approve this exception (see Jos 2–6).

20:19 do not destroy its trees. The reference is clearly to fruit trees, as the following verse specifies that non-fruit trees could be freely cut to help in the siege. There is a question about the last sentence of verse 19. The Hebrew could either be read, "Are the fruit trees men?" (as in the NIV text) or "The fruit trees are for men" (as in the NIV text note). The text note's translation may better fit the context.

21:1 If a man is found slain. Murder was to be avenged by the next of kin. If a murderer claimed asylum, he could be pried even from the altar for execution (Ex 21:14). This particular case concerned an unsolved murder. The responsible elders from the nearest town were to take an oath of innocence and ignorance. A young heifer, never used for work, was to be killed violently in a desolate, out-of-the-way place while the oath was taken. The symbolism is clear. The heifer was to die in place of the murderer, the one who ought to die. Thus the land would be purged of serious guilt.

guilty of the blood of an innocent man." And the bloodshed will be atoned for.[p] 9So you
will purge[q] from yourselves the guilt of shedding innocent blood, since you have done
what is right in the eyes of the LORD.

Marrying a Captive Woman

10When you go to war against your enemies and the LORD your God delivers them into
your hands[r] and you take captives, 11if you notice among the captives a beautiful woman and are attracted to her, you may take her as your wife. 12Bring her into your home
and have her shave her head,[s] trim her nails 13and put aside the clothes she was wearing when captured. After she has lived in your house and mourned her father and
mother for a full month,[t] then you may go to her and be her husband and she shall be
your wife. 14If you are not pleased with her, let her go wherever she wishes. You must
not sell her or treat her as a slave, since you have dishonored her.[u]

The Right of the Firstborn

15If a man has two wives, and he loves one but not the other, and both bear him sons
but the firstborn is the son of the wife he does not love,[v] 16when he wills his property to
his sons, he must not give the rights of the firstborn to the son of the wife he loves in preference to his actual firstborn, the son of the wife he does not love.[w] 17He must acknowledge the son of his unloved wife as the firstborn by giving him a double share of all he
has. That son is the first sign of his father's strength.[x] The right of the firstborn belongs
to him.[y]

A Rebellious Son

18If a man has a stubborn and rebellious son who does not obey his father and mother[z] and will not listen to them when they discipline him, 19his father and mother shall
take hold of him and bring him to the elders at the gate of his town. 20They shall say to
the elders, "This son of ours is stubborn and rebellious. He will not obey us. He is a profligate and a drunkard." 21Then all the men of his town shall stone him to death. You must
purge the evil[a] from among you. All Israel will hear of it and be afraid.[b]

Various Laws

22If a man guilty of a capital offense[c] is put to death and his body is hung on a tree,
23you must not leave his body on the tree overnight.[d] Be sure to bury him that same day,
because anyone who is hung on a tree is under God's curse.[e] You must not desecrate[f]
the land the LORD your God is giving you as an inheritance.

22 If you see your brother's ox or sheep straying, do not ignore it but be sure to take
it back to him.[g] 2If the brother does not live near you or if you do not know who
he is, take it home with you and keep it until he comes looking for it. Then give it back
to him. 3Do the same if you find your brother's donkey or his cloak or anything he loses. Do not ignore it.

4If you see your brother's donkey[h] or his ox fallen on the road, do not ignore it. Help
him get it to its feet.

21:8 [p]Nu 35:33-34
21:9 [q]Dt 19:13
21:10 [r]Jos 21:44
21:12 [s]Lev 14:9; Nu 6:9
21:13 [t]Ps 45:10
21:14 [u]Ge 34:2
21:15 [v]Ge 29:33
21:16 [w]1Ch 26:10
21:17 [x]Ge 49:3 [y]Ge 25:31
21:18 [z]Pr 1:8; Isa 30:1; Eph 6:1-3
21:21 [a]Dt 19:19; 1Co 5:13* [b]Dt 13:11
21:22 [c]Dt 22:26; Mk 14:64; Ac 23:29
21:23 [d]Jos 8:29; 10:27; Jn 19:31 [e]Gal 3:13* [f]Lev 18:25; Nu 35:34
22:1 [g]Ex 23:4-5
22:4 [h]Ex 23:5

21:11 among the captives a beautiful woman. It was common for soldiers to take captive women as wives and then to cast them off. Here the Law of Moses protected these women. A soldier could take a captive woman, but he was to wait a month, both for her sake and for his own. She was not chattel and deserved an opportunity to adjust, to grieve her lost family and possibly to grow into love. If he married her after this waiting period, he was not to divorce her or sell her as a slave. She was a wife.

21:15 two wives. Polygamy was not ruled out in Israel. As divorce was allowed because the people's "hearts were hard" (Mt 19:8), so polygamy was given some status, but its harsher evils were mitigated. The unloved wife had rights. And the son of an unloved wife, if he were the firstborn, could not be dispossessed. The laws had been somewhat different during the patriarchal period (i.e., Ge 12-50). For example, the birthright could be sold in Esau's day (just as was done in the Nuzi culture of Mesopotamia), and Ishmael, Abraham's firstborn son, was disinherited.

21:18–20 See *WLC* 128.

21:18 a stubborn and rebellious son. The precise meaning of this phrase is not given. But in verse 20 such a son is called "a profligate and a drunkard." These terms occur together again in Proverbs 23:21. The implication is probably a life of abandon, one lived in drunkenness and deep sin. A similar concept is expressed in the law governing the case of a son who was a false prophet (Zec 13:2–3). In such a situation, even the parent was not supposed to shield the son. If the son (probably not a mere child) was living a life of evil and crime, the parent was in fact to bring him to justice. The text is not a license for parental severity, child abuse or infanticide, but an insistence on loyalty and fidelity to God above all others.

21:22 hung on a tree. This law does not refer to a person being hanged; execution by hanging is not referred to in the Old Testament. The practice in view is the exposure of the corpse of a criminal or an enemy after his death, as when Saul's body was hung on the walls of Beth Shan by the Philistines (1Sa 31:10–13).

21:23 not leave . . . overnight. This stipulation lay behind the request of the Pharisees to have the body of Jesus taken off the cross before nightfall, for the next day was "a special Sabbath" (Jn 19:31). See *HC* 39.

22:1–5 See *WLC* 141; *WSC* 74.

22:1 take it back. This law concerning lost property required that an effort be made to locate the owner of a stray animal or missing property so that the owner's property could be returned to him. If the owner could not be found, the property was to be kept for him until he was located. Note the emphasis on the rightful ownership of private property. The property even of one's enemy was to be returned (Ex 23:4).

22:4 his ox fallen. Again, accidental loss of private property was to be prevented if possible. Jesus quoted this verse to justify his

5A woman must not wear men's clothing, nor a man wear women's clothing, for the
LORD your God detests anyone who does this.
6If you come across a bird's nest beside the road, either in a tree or on the ground,
and the mother is sitting on the young or on the eggs, do not take the mother with the
young.[i] 7You may take the young, but be sure to let the mother go, so that it may go well
with you and you may have a long life.[j]
8When you build a new house, make a parapet around your roof so that you may not
bring the guilt of bloodshed on your house if someone falls from the roof.
9Do not plant two kinds of seed in your vineyard;[k] if you do, not only the crops you
plant but also the fruit of the vineyard will be defiled.[a]
10Do not plow with an ox and a donkey yoked together.[l]

22:6 [i]Lev 22:28
22:7 [j]Dt 4:40
22:9 [k]Lev 19:19
22:10 [l]2Co 6:14

[a] 9 Or *be forfeited to the sanctuary*

healing of a man on the Sabbath. The Pharisees did allow the provision that permitted helping a fallen animal to supersede their rules for Sabbath keeping, but they had little pity for a man in serious need (Lk 14:5). This law also parallels one in Exodus 23:5.
22:5 A woman must not wear men's clothing, nor a man wear women's clothing. There are perhaps a number of reasons for this law. The Hebrew for "wear women's clothing" is more likely to mean "use women's implements," which might refer to such things as distaffs or mirrors, which were used in Canaanite spells. The word for men's clothing may also refer to implements. Even the word for "man" is not the typical one, being associated with men able to make war. A man's sword and bow were used in fertility and heroism rituals. Any such ritual was, of course, detestable to the Lord. That each gender is forbidden to use those things typically employed by the other suggests that this law primarily instructs men and women to fulfill their appointed roles, perhaps with special emphasis on wartime in expectation of the holy wars to be waged in Canaan (e.g., men should be the warriors; cf. Jdg 9:54; Isa 19:16; Jer 51:30). It is also possible that this law refers to transvestite practices.
22:6 See 14:21.
22:8 a parapet around your roof. Roofs in ancient Israel were flat and often accessible by an outside stairway. The roof was used for work (Jos 2:6) or leisure. To prevent accidental injury or death from falling, a parapet, or fence, was to be placed around the roof. This was a law against criminal negligence. See *WLC* 135.
22:9–11 These verses speak of three prohibited mixtures. Leviticus 19:19 also forbids three mixtures, two of which (crops and clothing) are clearly the same as those mentioned here. But the third mixture seems to be different. In the matter of mixed seed, it is unclear whether two kinds of seed refers to such a mixture as wheat and barley or to a mixture of good seed with weed seed. If the former is intended, it is difficult to see how the vineyard would be harmed. If the reference is to impure seed, both the crop and the vineyard would indeed be affected. The Hebrew for "two kinds" is not specific enough to decide the matter.
22:10 an ox and a donkey yoked together. The reason for this prohibition is obvious. It would be inhumane to compel a donkey to pull an ox's load or to force an ox to move at the faster pace of the donkey. The apostle Paul, on the basis of this principle, later forbade the union of believers and unbelievers (2Co 6:14). But the

Major Social Concerns in the Covenant

1. **Personhood**
   Everyone's person is to be secure (Ex 20:13; Dt 5:17; Ex 21:16-21,26-32; Lev 19:14; Dt 24:7; 27:18).

2. **False Accusation**
   Everyone is to be secure against slander and false accusation (Ex 20:16; Dt 5:20; Ex 23:1-3,6-8; Lev 19:16; Dt 19:15-21).

3. **Woman**
   No woman is to be taken advantage of within her subordinate status in society (Ex 21:7-11,20,26-32; 22:16-17; Dt 21:10-14; 22:13-30; 24:1-5).

4. **Punishment**
   Punishment for wrongdoing shall not be excessive so that the culprit is dehumanized (Dt 25:1-5).

5. **Dignity**
   Every Israelite's dignity and right to be God's servant are to be honored and safeguarded (Ex 21:2,5-6; Lev 25; Dt 15:12-18).

6. **Inheritance**
   Every Israelite's inheritance in the promised land is to be secure (Lev 25; Nu 27:5-7; 36:1-9; Dt 25:5-10).

7. **Property**
   Everyone's property is to be secure (Ex 20:15; Dt 5:19; Ex 21:33-36; 22:1-15; 23:4-5; Lev 19:35-36; Dt 22:1-4; 25:13-15).

8. **Fruit of Labor**
   Everyone is to receive the fruit of their labors (Lev 19:13; Dt 24:14; 25:4).

9. **Fruit of the Ground**
   Everyone is to share the fruit of the ground (Ex 23:10-11; Lev 19:9-10; 23:22; 25:3-55; Dt 14:28-29; 24:19-21).

10. **Rest on Sabbath**
    Everyone, down to the humblest servant and the resident alien, is to share in the weekly rest of God's Sabbath (Ex 20:8-11; Dt 5:12-15; Ex 23:12).

11. **Marriage**
    The marriage relationship is to be kept inviolate (Ex 20:14; Dt 5:18; see also Lev 18:6-23; 20:10-21; Dt 22:13-30).

12. **Exploitation**
    No one, however disabled, impoverished or powerless, is to be oppressed or exploited (Ex 22:21-27; Lev 19:14,33-34; 25:35-36; Dt 23:19; 24:6,12-15,17; 27:18).

13. **Fair Trial**
    Everyone is to have free access to the courts and is to be afforded a fair trial (Ex 23:6-8; Lev 19:15; Dt 1:17; 10:17-18; 16:18-20; 17:8-13; 19:15-21).

14. **Social Order**
    Every person's God-given place in the social order is to be honored (Ex 20:12; Dt 5:16; Ex 21:15,17; 22:28; Lev 19:3,32; 20:9; Dt 17:8-13; 21:15-21; 27:16).

15. **Law**
    No one shall be above the law, not even the king (Dt 17:18-20).

16. **Animals**
    Concern for the welfare of other creatures is to be extended to the animal world (Ex 23:5,11; Lev 25:7; Dt 22:4,6-7; 25:4).

22:11 [11]Do not wear clothes of wool and linen woven together.[m]
[m]Lev 19:19 [12]Make tassels on the four corners of the cloak you wear.[n]
22:12
[n]Nu 15:37-41;

Mt 23:5 *Marriage Violations*

22:13 [13]If a man takes a wife and, after lying with her[o], dislikes her [14]and slanders her and
[o]Dt 24:1 gives her a bad name, saying, "I married this woman, but when I approached her, I did
not find proof of her virginity," [15]then the girl's father and mother shall bring proof that
she was a virgin to the town elders at the gate. [16]The girl's father will say to the elders,
"I gave my daughter in marriage to this man, but he dislikes her. [17]Now he has slandered
her and said, 'I did not find your daughter to be a virgin.' But here is the proof of my
22:18 daughter's virginity." Then her parents shall display the cloth before the elders of the
[p]Ex 18:21 town, [18]and the elders[p] shall take the man and punish him. [19]They shall fine him a hundred shekels of silver[a] and give them to the girl's father, because this man has given an
Israelite virgin a bad name. She shall continue to be his wife; he must not divorce her
as long as he lives.
[20]If, however, the charge is true and no proof of the girl's virginity can be found, [21]she
22:21 shall be brought to the door of her father's house and there the men of her town shall
[q]Ge 34:7; Dt 13:5; 23:17-18; Jdg 20:6; stone her to death. She has done a disgraceful thing[q] in Israel by being promiscuous
2Sa 13:12 while still in her father's house. You must purge the evil from among you.
22:22 [22]If a man is found sleeping with another man's wife, both the man who slept with
[r]Lev 20:10; Jn 8:5 her and the woman must die.[r] You must purge the evil from Israel.
[23]If a man happens to meet in a town a virgin pledged to be married and he sleeps
with her, [24]you shall take both of them to the gate of that town and stone them to
22:24 death—the girl because she was in a town and did not scream for help, and the man be-
[s]ver 21-22; 1Co 5:13* cause he violated another man's wife. You must purge the evil from among you.[s]
[25]But if out in the country a man happens to meet a girl pledged to be married and
rapes her, only the man who has done this shall die. [26]Do nothing to the girl; she has
committed no sin deserving death. This case is like that of someone who attacks and
murders his neighbor, [27]for the man found the girl out in the country, and though the
betrothed girl screamed, there was no one to rescue her.
22:28 [28]If a man happens to meet a virgin who is not pledged to be married and rapes her
[t]Ex 22:16 and they are discovered,[t] [29]he shall pay the girl's father fifty shekels of silver.[b] He must
22:30 marry the girl, for he has violated her. He can never divorce her as long as he lives.
[u]Lev 18:8; 20:11; 18:8; Dt 27:20; [30]A man is not to marry his father's wife; he must not dishonor his father's bed.[u]
1Co 5:1

Exclusion From the Assembly

23 No one who has been emasculated by crushing or cutting may enter the assembly of the LORD.

[a] *19* That is, about 2 1/2 pounds (about 1 kilogram) [b] *29* That is, about 1 1/4 pounds (about 0.6 kilogram)

case seems different in Leviticus 19:19, where the following is stated: "Do not mate different kinds of animals." This prohibition is not as clear. Obviously sheep will not mate with cows nor goats with sheep. But does the law in this verse forbid hybridization of horses with asses in order to get mules? This interpretation seems unlikely since kings rode on mules (1Ki 1:33). Perhaps the rule prohibited, for example, mating Egyptian cattle with desert cattle in order to keep the breed pure. It is not unlikely, however, that the word for "mate" in Leviticus is actually an Aramaic form for "crouching down" under a load, like the similar Hebrew word in Exodus 23:5, such that the law in Leviticus also prohibits yoking together an ox and a donkey.

22:11 clothes of wool and linen. Both Leviticus 19:19 and this verse use the Hebrew word translated "woven" in the NIV. It is not used elsewhere. Deuteronomy explains the Leviticus passage in that this word means woven with a mixture of wool and linen. It is unclear why this practice was proscribed, but one suggestion is that the differing materials would shrink at varying rates and that the fabric would therefore not wash well. Another suggestion is that through eating pure foods (14:3–21) and declining to mix their seeds (v. 9), their draft animals (v. 10) or the materials of their garments, the Israelites were reminded that they were to be a pure people (see 7:2–5 and its notes).

22:12 Make tassels. We do not know what these tassels were. The word can refer to twisted ornaments or to any ornament designating glory or status. Pictures of ancient clothing do show some such tassels on men's skirtlike garments. These may have been a special kind of tassel to identify the wearers as Israelites.

22:14 proof of her virginity. The situation is generally clear. A man disliked his new wife and slandered her, claiming that she was not a virgin. If the report were false, he was to be given a heavy fine and would not be allowed to divorce her. However, if the accusation were true, she was to be killed for her adultery. The details of the ancient methods of proving virginity at the time of marriage are unknown, but generally they were related to appraising the preservation of the hymen.

22:22 sleeping with another man's wife. Verses 22–29 discuss adultery and rape in various situations. Adultery carried a maximum sentence of death (Lev 18:20; 20:10). Verse 23 specifies that if the sexual relations were with a betrothed girl, the act still constituted adultery, and both partners were to die. There was no difference in treatment between the sexes: Both were guilty and each had to pay the extreme penalty. If the sexual act occurred in a town, it was presumed to be adultery and not rape, because the girl could have screamed for help. However, if it occurred in the country, it was presumed to be a case of rape, for no help would have been available. In such a case, the girl was considered innocent, but the rapist had to die. If the girl was a virgin and not betrothed (whether or not she was compliant), the man had to pay a heavy fine, marry her and never divorce her. This law parallels that of Exodus 22:16–17. See *WLC* 151.

22:28–29 See *WLC* 151.

22:30 A man is not to marry his father's wife. This prohibition parallels laws against incest given in Leviticus 18:7–8 and 20:11. In Leviticus 18 the law is categorically given; in Leviticus 20 it is repeated with the penalty specified as death.

2No one born of a forbidden marriage[a] nor any of his descendants may enter the assembly of the LORD, even down to the tenth generation.
3No Ammonite or Moabite or any of his descendants may enter the assembly of the
LORD, even down to the tenth generation.[v] 4For they did not come to meet you with bread
and water on your way when you came out of Egypt, and they hired Balaam[w] son of Beor
from Pethor in Aram Naharaim[b] to pronounce a curse on you. 5However, the LORD your
God would not listen to Balaam but turned the curse[x] into a blessing for you, because the
LORD your God loves you. 6Do not seek a treaty of friendship with them as long as you live.[y]
7Do not abhor an Edomite, for he is your brother.[z] Do not abhor an Egyptian, because
you lived as an alien in his country.[a] 8The third generation of children born to them may
enter the assembly of the LORD.

Uncleanness in the Camp

9When you are encamped against your enemies, keep away from everything impure.
10If one of your men is unclean because of a nocturnal emission, he is to go outside the
camp and stay there.[b] 11But as evening approaches he is to wash himself, and at sunset
he may return to the camp.
12Designate a place outside the camp where you can go to relieve yourself. 13As part
of your equipment have something to dig with, and when you relieve yourself, dig a hole
and cover up your excrement. 14For the LORD your God moves[c] about in your camp to
protect you and to deliver your enemies to you. Your camp must be holy,[d] so that he will
not see among you anything indecent and turn away from you.

Miscellaneous Laws

15If a slave has taken refuge with you, do not hand him over to his master.[e] 16Let him
live among you wherever he likes and in whatever town he chooses. Do not oppress[f] him.
17No Israelite man[g] or woman is to become a shrine prostitute.[h] 18You must not bring
the earnings of a female prostitute or of a male prostitute[c] into the house of the LORD your
God to pay any vow, because the LORD your God detests them both.
19Do not charge your brother interest, whether on money or food or anything else that
may earn interest.[i] 20You may charge a foreigner interest, but not a brother Israelite, so
that the LORD your God may bless[j] you in everything you put your hand to in the land you
are entering to possess.
21If you make a vow to the LORD your God, do not be slow to pay it, for the LORD your
God will certainly demand it of you and you will be guilty of sin.[k] 22But if you refrain from
making a vow, you will not be guilty. 23Whatever your lips utter you must be sure to do,
because you made your vow freely to the LORD your God with your own mouth.
24If you enter your neighbor's vineyard, you may eat all the grapes you want, but do
not put any in your basket. 25If you enter your neighbor's grainfield, you may pick kernels with your hands, but you must not put a sickle to his standing grain.[l]
24 If a man marries a woman who becomes displeasing to him[m] because he finds
something indecent about her, and he writes her a certificate of divorce,[n] gives

23:3 [v]Ne 13:2
23:4 [w]Nu 22:5-6; 23:7; 2Pe 2:15
23:5 [x]Pr 26:2
23:6 [y]Ezr 9:12
23:7 [z]Ge 25:26; Ob 1:10,12 [a]Ex 22:21; 23:9; Lev 19:34; Dt 10:19
23:10 [b]Lev 15:16
23:14 [c]Lev 26:12 [d]Ex 3:5
23:15 [e]1Sa 30:15
23:16 [f]Ex 22:21
23:17 [g]Ge 19:25; 2Ki 23:7 [h]Lev 19:29; Dt 22:21
23:19 [i]Ex 22:25; Lev 25:35-37
23:20 [j]Dt 15:10; 28:12
23:21 [k]Nu 30:1-2; Ecc 5:4-5; Mt 5:33
23:25 [l]Mt 12:1; Mk 2:23; Lk 6:1
24:1 [m]Dt 22:13 [n]Mt 5:31*; 19:7-9; Mk 10:4-5

[a] 2 Or *one of illegitimate birth* [b] 4 That is, Northwest Mesopotamia [c] 18 Hebrew *of a dog*

23:1 the assembly of the LORD. This expression is used in this section six times but elsewhere in the Old Testament only five times, one of which is a reference to this passage (Ne 13:1). The most common expression is the "congregation of Israel." It is unknown whether the phrase refers to the whole congregation of Israel or to a particular group holding special privileges or responsibilities within the nation. In 1 Chronicles 28:8 David charged the people "in the sight of all Israel and of the assembly of the LORD, and in the hearing of [their] God." Here, too, the phrase "assembly of the LORD" could refer to a special group.

23:3 the tenth generation. There is a question as to whether this should be counted as exactly 400 years (assuming that a generation comprises 40 years) or interpreted simply as a long time. Actually, the Hebrew adds the expression "forever," apparently interpreting the words "tenth generation" in this way. Nehemiah 13:1–3, referring to this section, takes the term to mean "forever" and assumes from it the exclusion of foreigners from the whole congregation of Israel. The law apparently does not have in view foreigners who converted to the worship of Yahweh, such as the Moabitess Ruth, ancestor of David.

23:4 Balaam. Note the clear reference to details in Numbers 22–24.

23:13 dig a hole. This is perhaps the first time in history that soldiers were instructed to dig a latrine. The reason given: God was present, and the camp was to be holy. This reason does not exclude the suggestion that the law was given for the benefit of the health of the men. That which caused illness for his people was also of concern to God.

23:14 anything indecent. This expression at the conclusion of this section about the war-camp (vv. 9–14) seems to have the same meaning as "everything impure," which is used in the section's introduction (v. 9). Both expressions pertain to preserving the camp's holiness.

23:15 If a slave has taken refuge. See 16:12.

23:17–18 See *WLC* 113,139.

23:17 a shrine prostitute. The Hebrew words concerned are the masculine and feminine versions of "holy one." This is an implicit commentary on the religion of the Canaanites, in that prostitution was a part of their sacred ritual. The Lord detested the practice.

23:19 interest. See note on 15:1.

23:21–23 See *WCF* 22.6.

23:21 a vow to the LORD. Such a vow was given voluntarily. This was a serious matter, and a valid vow had to be kept (see Lev 27; Nu 30).

24:1–4 See theological article "Marriage and Divorce" at Matthew 19. See *WCF* 24.6.

it to her and sends her from his house, 2and if after she leaves his house she becomes
the wife of another man, 3and her second husband dislikes her and writes her a certificate of divorce, gives it to her and sends her from his house, or if he dies, 4then her first
husband, who divorced her, is not allowed to marry her again after she has been defiled.
That would be detestable in the eyes of the LORD. Do not bring sin upon the land the
LORD[o] your God is giving you as an inheritance.
5If a man has recently married, he must not be sent to war or have any other duty laid
on him. For one year he is to be free to stay at home and bring happiness to the wife he
has married.[p]
6Do not take a pair of millstones—not even the upper one—as security for a debt, because that would be taking a man's livelihood as security.
7If a man is caught kidnapping one of his brother Israelites and treats him as a slave
or sells him, the kidnapper must die.[q] You must purge the evil from among you.
8In cases of leprous[a] diseases be very careful to do exactly as the priests, who are Levites, instruct you. You must follow carefully what I have commanded them.[r] 9Remem-
ber what the LORD your God did to Miriam along the way after you came out of Egypt.[s]
10When you make a loan of any kind to your neighbor, do not go into his house to get
what he is offering as a pledge. 11Stay outside and let the man to whom you are making
the loan bring the pledge out to you. 12If the man is poor, do not go to sleep with his
pledge in your possession. 13Return his cloak to him by sunset[t] so that he may sleep in
it. Then he will thank you, and it will be regarded as a righteous act in the sight of the
LORD your God.[u]
14Do not take advantage of a hired man who is poor and needy, whether he is a brother Israelite or an alien living in one of your towns.[v] 15Pay him his wages each day before
sunset, because he is poor[w] and is counting on it.[x] Otherwise he may cry to the LORD
against you, and you will be guilty of sin.[y]
16Fathers shall not be put to death for their children, nor children put to death for
their fathers; each is to die for his own sin.[z]
17Do not deprive the alien or the fatherless of justice,[a] or take the cloak of the widow as a pledge. 18Remember that you were slaves in Egypt and the LORD your God redeemed you from there. That is why I command you to do this.
19When you are harvesting in your field and you overlook a sheaf, do not go back to
get it.[b] Leave it for the alien, the fatherless and the widow, so that the LORD your God may
bless[c] you in all the work of your hands. 20When you beat the olives from your trees, do
not go over the branches a second time.[d] Leave what remains for the alien, the fatherless and the widow. 21When you harvest the grapes in your vineyard, do not go over the
vines again. Leave what remains for the alien, the fatherless and the widow. 22Remem-
ber that you were slaves in Egypt. That is why I command you to do this.[e]

24:4 [o]Jer 3:1
24:5 [p]Dt 20:7
24:7 [q]Ex 21:16
24:8 [r]Lev 13:1-46; 14:2
24:9 [s]Nu 12:10
24:13 [t]Ex 22:26 [u]Dt 6:25; Da 4:27
24:14 [v]Lev 25:35-43; Dt 15:12-18
24:15 [w]Jer 22:13 [x]Lev 19:13 [y]Dt 15:9; Jas 5:4
24:16 [z]2Ki 14:6; 2Ch 25:4; Jer 31:29-30; Eze 18:20
24:17 [a]Dt 1:17; 10:17-18; 16:19
24:19 [b]Lev 19:9; 23:22 [c]Pr 19:17
24:20 [d]Lev 19:10
24:22 [e]ver 18

[a] *8* The Hebrew word was used for various diseases affecting the skin—not necessarily leprosy.

24:1 a certificate of divorce. For the grammatical structure of the clause, see note on 18:6. Two questions may be raised: Where is the grammatical conclusion, and what are legitimate grounds for divorce? Some see the conclusion early: ". . . then let him write her a bill of divorcement." The Pharisees apparently interpreted the provision this way, for they asked, "Why . . . did Moses command . . . ?" (Mt 19:7). This interpretation sanctions granting a divorce for some unspecified cause—the phrase "something indecent" (v. 1) is the same as "anything indecent" (23:14) and is rather general. The NIV and the Septuagint (the Greek translation of the OT) place the conclusion late, at the beginning of verse 4. By this reading, the law recognized the fact of divorce but prohibited remarriage of the first couple after an intervening marriage. A husband might be tempted to sell his wife in time of need and then to buy her back when it became convenient. This law kept the marriage vow sacred. By this reading, there is no mention of allowable grounds of divorce. Adultery as a ground for divorce is apparently not in view, for that was punishable by death. See theological article "Marriage and Divorce" at Matthew 19.
24:5 recently married. A one-year exemption for the newly married would not only benefit the home but would also fortify the morale of the army. See note on 20:1.
24:6 security for a debt. Although the customs of making loans are hard to interpret due to our ignorance of ancient general practices, major references to the subject are available (see vv. 6,10–13,17; Ex 22:26–27; Job 22:6; 24:3,9; Am 2:8). It seems probable that the practice does not refer to offering collateral of equivalent value for the debt, but rather to registering some personal possession at the city gate as a token of the promise to pay. A cloak would do, but it was to be returned before sundown, as it would be needed for a cover during the night (v. 13; Ex 22:26–27). Millstones would not work, as they were needed every day in food preparation. The choice of a pledge was at the convenience of the debtor; the lender could not go through the debtor's house to select the collateral (vv. 10–11). It is notable that the interests of the poor were protected.
24:7 kidnapping. The chief objective of kidnapping was enslavement. This kind of slavery was forbidden on pain of death. The law allowed for indentured slavery, but, as mentioned earlier (15:12), it was mitigated in ancient Israel in several important ways. Paul also condemned those who traded in slaves procured through kidnapping (1Ti 1:9–10).
24:8 leprous diseases. As the NIV text note specifies, this category covered not only leprosy, but any disease with an observable rash (e.g., measles or small pox, which were highly communicable). The details for handling such diseases were left in the hands of the priests (see Lev 13–14). The reference to Miriam's judgment (v. 9) is found in Numbers 12:10. As has often been seen, Deuteronomy presupposes the existence of the rest of the Pentateuch (see "Introduction to the Pentateuch" at on p. 1).
24:14 a hired man who is poor. See Leviticus 19:13.
24:16 Fathers shall not be put to death for their children. This law is cited in almost exactly the same Hebrew words in 2 Kings 14:6 and 2 Chronicles 25:4. In each case the quote is said to be from "the Book of the Law of Moses" (2Ki 14:6) or from "the Law, in the Book of Moses" (2Ch 25:4).
24:19 When you are harvesting. See Leviticus 23:22. The practical results of gleaning are revealed in touching language in Ruth 2.

25 When men have a dispute, they are to take it to court and the judges will decide
the case,[f] acquitting the innocent and condemning the guilty.[g] 2If the guilty
man deserves to be beaten,[h] the judge shall make him lie down and have him flogged
in his presence with the number of lashes his crime deserves, 3but he must not give him
more than forty lashes.[i] If he is flogged more than that, your brother will be degraded
in your eyes.[j]
4Do not muzzle an ox while it is treading out the grain.[k]
5If brothers are living together and one of them dies without a son, his widow must
not marry outside the family. Her husband's brother shall take her and marry her and
fulfill the duty of a brother-in-law to her.[l] 6The first son she bears shall carry on the name
of the dead brother so that his name will not be blotted out from Israel.[m]
7However, if a man does not want to marry his brother's wife, she shall go to the elders at the town gate and say, "My husband's brother refuses to carry on his brother's
name in Israel. He will not fulfill the duty of a brother-in-law to me."[n] 8Then the elders
of his town shall summon him and talk to him. If he persists in saying, "I do not want to
marry her," 9his brother's widow shall go up to him in the presence of the elders, take
off one of his sandals,[o] spit in his face and say, "This is what is done to the man who will
not build up his brother's family line." 10That man's line shall be known in Israel as The
Family of the Unsandaled.
11If two men are fighting and the wife of one of them comes to rescue her husband
from his assailant, and she reaches out and seizes him by his private parts, 12you shall
cut off her hand. Show her no pity.[p]
13Do not have two differing weights in your bag—one heavy, one light.[q] 14Do not have
two differing measures in your house—one large, one small. 15You must have accurate
and honest weights and measures, so that you may live long[r] in the land the LORD your
God is giving you. 16For the LORD your God detests anyone who does these things, anyone who deals dishonestly.[s]
17Remember what the Amalekites[t] did to you along the way when you came out of
Egypt. 18When you were weary and worn out, they met you on your journey and cut off
all who were lagging behind; they had no fear of God.[u] 19When the LORD your God gives
you rest from all the enemies around you in the land he is giving you to possess as an inheritance, you shall blot out the memory of Amalek[v] from under heaven. Do not forget!

Firstfruits and Tithes

26 When you have entered the land the LORD your God is giving you as an inheritance and have taken possession of it and settled in it, 2take some of the firstfruits[w] of all that you produce from the soil of the land the LORD your God is giving you
and put them in a basket. Then go to the place the LORD your God will choose as a dwelling for his Name[x] 3and say to the priest in office at the time, "I declare today to the LORD
your God that I have come to the land the LORD swore to our forefathers to give us." 4The
priest shall take the basket from your hands and set it down in front of the altar of the
LORD your God. 5Then you shall declare before the LORD your God: "My father was a wandering Aramean,[y] and he went down into Egypt with a few people[z] and lived there and
became a great nation, powerful and numerous. 6But the Egyptians mistreated us and
made us suffer,[a] putting us to hard labor. 7Then we cried out to the LORD, the God of our

25:1 [f]Dt 19:17 [g]Dt 1:16-17
25:2 [h]Lk 12:47-48
25:3 [i]2Co 11:24 [j]Job 18:3
25:4 [k]Pr 12:10; 1Co 9:9*; 1Ti 5:18*
25:5 [l]Mt 22:24; Mk 12:19; Lk 20:28
25:6 [m]Ge 38:9; Ru 4:5, 10
25:7 [n]Ru 4:1-2, 5-6
25:9 [o]Ru 4:7-8, 11
25:12 [p]Dt 19:13
25:13 [q]Lev 19:35-37; Pr 11:1; Eze 45:10; Mic 6:11
25:15 [r]Ex 20:12
25:16 [s]Pr 11:1
25:17 [t]Ex 17:8
25:18 [u]Ps 36:1; Ro 3:18
25:19 [v]1Sa 15:2-3
26:2 [w]Ex 22:29; 23:16, 19; Nu 18:13; Pr 3:9 [x]Dt 12:5
26:5 [y]Hos 12:12 [z]Ge 43:1-2; 45:7, 11; 46:27; Dt 10:22
26:6 [a]Ex 1:11, 14

25:3 forty lashes. This is the background of the Jewish practice of giving "forty lashes minus one" (2Co 11:24). The Jews were concerned that someone might miscount, so they decided to err on the side of mercy. See *WLC* 130.
25:4 Do not muzzle an ox. This provision for oxen is quoted twice by Paul in the New Testament (1Co 9:9–12; 1Ti 5:18). It seems to be significant that in the first instance Paul argued that if this principle applied to oxen, it would apply much more to Christian preachers. In the latter instance, the apostle briefly quoted Deuteronomy and sealed the argument by a verbatim quotation from Luke 10:7.
25:5 Her husband's brother. This law of levirate (from the Latin *levir,* meaning "husband's brother") marriage is expressed only here and with little detail. Did it apply to an unmarried brother only? Probably so, because the reference is to brothers who were "living together" (see also Ge 38:8–11). But in practice it is doubtful whether this limitation held. The obvious purpose of the arrangement was to keep property within the family (see the book of Ruth). That the first son of the second marriage had the name of the first husband meant that the son would inherit his stepfather's portion. It also provided that the young widow with no family would be cared for. Examples of the operation of the levirate custom come from patriarchal times, from the book of Ruth and from the New Testament (Mt 22:23–28; Mk 12:18–23; Lk 20:27–33).
25:13–16 See *HC* 110.
25:13 differing weights. See Leviticus 19:35–36 for the same law. Deuteronomy notes the divine displeasure at dishonest dealings in business (see Pr 11:1; 16:21; 20:10,23; Mic 6:11).
25:17 when you came out of Egypt. See Exodus 17:8–16.
26:2 the firstfruits. At first glance, this passage appears to refer only to the original firstfruits offering to be given upon entering Canaan. But it likely constitutes a liturgy that was to be used every year. The firstfruits ordinance given in connection with Passover (Lev 23) is said to be a perpetual ordinance, and this is a suitable liturgy for every year. See the law concerning firstborn animals (Dt 15:19–22). These also were to be brought to the Lord once a year. **the place the LORD your God will choose.** See 12:5.
26:5 a wandering Aramean. The allusion is doubtless to Jacob's many vicissitudes in his flight to and from Aram and in his retreat from Shechem (Ge 35:1). He was almost a fugitive at times. The reference to his Aramean roots clearly depends on Genesis.

fathers, and the LORD heard our voice[b] and saw[c] our misery, toil and oppression. 8So the
LORD brought us out of Egypt with a mighty hand and an outstretched arm, with great
terror and with miraculous signs and wonders.[d] 9He brought us to this place and gave
us this land, a land flowing with milk and honey;[e] 10and now I bring the firstfruits of the
soil that you, O LORD, have given me." Place the basket before the LORD your God and bow
down before him. 11And you and the Levites[f] and the aliens among you shall rejoice[g] in
all the good things the LORD your God has given to you and your household.
12When you have finished setting aside a tenth[h] of all your produce in the third year,
the year of the tithe,[i] you shall give it to the Levite, the alien, the fatherless and the widow, so that they may eat in your towns and be satisfied. 13Then say to the LORD your God:
"I have removed from my house the sacred portion and have given it to the Levite, the
alien, the fatherless and the widow, according to all you commanded. I have not turned
aside from your commands nor have I forgotten any of them.[j] 14I have not eaten any of
the sacred portion while I was in mourning, nor have I removed any of it while I was unclean,[k] nor have I offered any of it to the dead. I have obeyed the LORD my God; I have
done everything you commanded me. 15Look down from heaven,[l] your holy dwelling
place, and bless your people Israel and the land you have given us as you promised on
oath to our forefathers, a land flowing with milk and honey."

Follow the LORD's Commands

16The LORD your God commands you this day to follow these decrees and laws; carefully observe them with all your heart and with all your soul.[m] 17You have declared this
day that the LORD is your God and that you will walk in his ways, that you will keep his
decrees, commands and laws, and that you will obey him. 18And the LORD has declared
this day that you are his people, his treasured possession[n] as he promised, and that you
are to keep all his commands. 19He has declared that he will set you in praise, fame and
honor high above all the nations[o] he has made and that you will be a people holy[p] to the
LORD your God, as he promised.

The Altar on Mount Ebal

27 Moses and the elders of Israel commanded the people: "Keep all these commands that I give you today. 2When you have crossed the Jordan into the land
the LORD your God is giving you, set up some large stones and coat them with plaster.[q]
3Write on them all the words of this law when you have crossed over to enter the land
the LORD your God is giving you, a land flowing with milk and honey,[r] just as the LORD,
the God of your fathers, promised you. 4And when you have crossed the Jordan, set up
these stones on Mount Ebal,[s] as I command you today, and coat them with plaster.
5Build there an altar[t] to the LORD your God, an altar of stones. Do not use any iron tool[u]
upon them. 6Build the altar of the LORD your God with fieldstones and offer burnt offerings on it to the LORD your God. 7Sacrifice fellowship offerings[a] there, eating them and

26:7 [b]Ex 2:23-25 [c]Ex 3:9
26:8 [d]Dt 4:34
26:9 [e]Ex 3:8
26:11 [f]Dt 12:7 [g]Dt 16:11
26:12 [h]Lev 27:30 [i]Nu 18:24; Dt 14:28-29; Heb 7:5,9
26:13 [j]Ps 119:141,153, 176
26:14 [k]Lev 7:20; Hos 9:4
26:15 [l]Isa 63:15; Zec 2:13
26:16 [m]Dt 4:29
26:18 [n]Ex 6:7; 19:5; Dt 7:6; 14:2; 28:9
26:19 [o]Dt 4:7-8; 28:1,13, 44 [p]Ex 19:6; Dt 7:6; 1Pe 2:9
27:2 [q]Jos 8:31
27:3 [r]Dt 26:9
27:4 [s]Dt 11:29
27:5 [t]Jos 8:31 [u]Ex 20:25

[a] 7 Traditionally *peace offerings*

26:12 a tenth. See notes on 14:22 and 28 for a discussion of the tithe and the third-year tithe.
26:13 the sacred portion. Here we see God's estimate of the tithe. The tithe was to be given to the Levite and the poor, and the worshiper was to feast with them when he brought his tithe (14:23). The worshiper was to remember that this was a sacred feast that was not to be eaten in any illegitimate way.
26:15 Look down from heaven. This phrase was adapted by Solomon in his great prayer at the dedication of the temple: "Hear from heaven, your dwelling place" (1Ki 8:30).
■ **26:16–19** *Conclusion.* This concluding section is a solemn enforcement of the laws of God just laid out in chapters 12–26. Some would emphasize the idea of covenant ratification here. Moses stated that the Israelites had here accepted God as their sovereign and his laws as their rule of obedience. The Lord, for his part, had called the Israelites his special people ("his treasured possession") and had promised them the high honor of his special grace. In an eloquent climax, Moses assured the Israelites that God would keep them as his holy people, according to his promise. In similar fashion, Moses had sprinkled the blood of the covenant on the altar, on the Book of the Covenant and on the people at Sinai (Ex 24:6–8), and the people had responded with a pledge of obedience (Ex 24:7). It is possible that, instead of this section being a conclusion to the preceding laws, these verses serve as an introduction to the solemn ratification ceremony detailed in chapter 27.
26:16 all your heart. See note on 6:5.
26:17 See *WLC* 104; *WSC* 46.
■ **27:1—30:20** *Moses' Third Address.* These chapters focus on the ratification of the Mosaic covenant, much as an ancient Near Eastern suzerain-vassal treaty used blessings and curses in its ratification. Moses called for a ratification of the covenant in Canaan (27:1–26) and commitment to the covenant at that moment (28:1—30:20).
■ **27:1–26** *The Ratification to Come at Ebal and Gerizim.* Moses described how the nation was to recommit to the Mosaic covenant once the people had entered the land. The laws were to be published, the liturgy was to be impressive, the people were to add their Amen, and a long list of blessings and curses was to be announced.
27:1 Moses . . . commanded. Moses and the elders set up a ceremony of dedication to be held after the Israelites had entered the land.
27:2 coat them with plaster. The Egyptians had walls covered with inscriptions. Hammurapi had 282 laws engraved on his famous stele long before the time of Moses. These stones were coated with clay plaster and the laws inscribed in the plaster.
27:4 when you have crossed the Jordan. Verse 4 repeats much of verse 2, adding the detail of location.
27:5 any iron tool. There is no suggestion here that iron was a new, untried and taboo metal that should not be used in religious worship. A similar provision was given in Exodus 20:25; it does not mention an iron tool but does specify uncut, undressed stones. Joshua built such an altar from "uncut stones [the same Hebrew

rejoicing in the presence of the LORD your God. 8And you shall write very clearly all the
words of this law on these stones you have set up."

Curses From Mount Ebal

9Then Moses and the priests, who are Levites, said to all Israel, "Be silent, O Israel,
and listen! You have now become the people of the LORD your God.[v] 10Obey the LORD your
God and follow his commands and decrees that I give you today."

11On the same day Moses commanded the people:

12When you have crossed the Jordan, these tribes shall stand on Mount Gerizim[w] to
bless the people: Simeon, Levi, Judah, Issachar, Joseph and Benjamin.[x] 13And these
tribes shall stand on Mount Ebal to pronounce curses: Reuben, Gad, Asher, Zebulun,
Dan and Naphtali.

14The Levites shall recite to all the people of Israel in a loud voice:

15"Cursed is the man who carves an image or casts an idol[y]—a thing detestable to the LORD, the work of the craftsman's hands—and sets it up in secret."
Then all the people shall say, "Amen!"

16"Cursed is the man who dishonors his father or his mother."[z]
Then all the people shall say, "Amen!"

17"Cursed is the man who moves his neighbor's boundary stone."[a]
Then all the people shall say, "Amen!"

18"Cursed is the man who leads the blind astray on the road."[b]
Then all the people shall say, "Amen!"

19"Cursed is the man who withholds justice from the alien,[c] the fatherless or
the widow."[d]
Then all the people shall say, "Amen!"

20"Cursed is the man who sleeps with his father's wife, for he dishonors his father's bed."[e]
Then all the people shall say, "Amen!"

21"Cursed is the man who has sexual relations with any animal."[f]
Then all the people shall say, "Amen!"

22"Cursed is the man who sleeps with his sister, the daughter of his father or
the daughter of his mother."[g]
Then all the people shall say, "Amen!"

23"Cursed is the man who sleeps with his mother-in-law."[h]
Then all the people shall say, "Amen!"

24"Cursed is the man who kills[i] his neighbor secretly."
Then all the people shall say, "Amen!"

25"Cursed is the man who accepts a bribe to kill an innocent person."[j]
Then all the people shall say, "Amen!"

26"Cursed is the man who does not uphold the words of this law by carrying
them out."[k]
Then all the people shall say, "Amen!"

27:9 [v]Dt 26:18
27:12 [w]Dt 11:29 [x]Jos 8:35
27:15 [y]Ex 20:4; 34:17; Lev 19:4; 26:1; Dt 4:16,23; 5:8; Isa 44:9
27:16 [z]Ex 20:12; 21:17; Lev 19:3; 20:9
27:17 [a]Dt 19:14; Pr 22:28
27:18 [b]Lev 19:14
27:19 [c]Ex 22:21; Dt 24:19 [d]Dt 10:18
27:20 [e]Lev 18:7; Dt 22:30
27:21 [f]Lev 18:23
27:22 [g]Lev 18:9; 20:17
27:23 [h]Lev 20:14
27:24 [i]Lev 24:17; Nu 35:31
27:25 [j]Ex 23:7-8; Dt 10:17; Eze 22:12
27:26 [k]Jer 11:3; Gal 3:10*

---

word is translated "fieldstones" in Dt 27:6], on which no iron tool had been used" (Jos 8:31).

27:12 these tribes . . . on Mount Gerizim to bless. The division of the tribes given here follows no known order. Perhaps that is best, for surely the tribes that pronounced curses were not given their task because of their lowly condition. Here Levi was included among the regular tribes (indeed, among the six that blessed), although some of the Levites were to recite the curses to which the people would answer. The tribe of Joseph united Manasseh and Ephraim, so the enumeration followed that of the 12 patriarchs rather than that of the later tribal divisions.

27:14–26 Some have noted that the 12 curses listed here tend to address the kinds of offenses people are liable to commit in secret, such as sexual sins, bribery, private idolatry and murder. Whether or not these secret sins are ever brought to public light, God knows them, and none escape his judgment.

27:15 the man who carves an image. The first curse concerned idolatry. **Amen!** The Hebrew word means "so be it," and it is so translated in its first occurrence (Nu 5:22).

27:16 who dishonors. The second curse concerned the fifth commandment.

27:17 boundary stone. The third curse was against stealing land (19:14).

27:18 leads the blind astray. Leviticus 19:14 commands care for the disabled.

27:19 withholds justice. God upholds the cause of the helpless (10:18).

27:20 sleeps with his father's wife. See note on 22:30.

27:21 sexual relations with any animal. The penalty for this perversion was death (Ex 22:19; Lev 18:23; 20:15).

27:22 who sleeps with his sister. This curse concerned both a full sister and a half sister. See Leviticus 18:11 and 20:17.

27:23 sleeps with his mother-in-law. The penalty was death (Lev 18:17; 20:14).

27:24 kills his neighbor secretly. Secret murder was as bad as open violence.

27:25 accepts a bribe to kill. Murder for hire, being premeditated, was worse than murder committed in a moment of anger.

27:26 who does not uphold the words of this law. The final curse covered all the rest of God's commandments. Paul later quoted this verse in Galatians 3:10 as a total condemnation of righteousness by works, for measured by God's standards all have sinned and fall short of the glory of God (Ro 3:23). But this does not remit the obligation of the believer to obey the moral laws of God through the Spirit's enabling. See *BC* 23; *HC* 62.

Blessings for Obedience

28 If you fully obey the LORD your God and carefully follow all his commands[l] I give
you today, the LORD your God will set you high above all the nations on earth.[m]
2All these blessings will come upon you[n] and accompany you if you obey the LORD your
God:

3You will be blessed[o] in the city and blessed in the country.[p]
4The fruit of your womb will be blessed, and the crops of your land and the
young of your livestock—the calves of your herds and the lambs of your flocks.[q]
5Your basket and your kneading trough will be blessed.
6You will be blessed when you come in and blessed when you go out.[r]

7The LORD will grant that the enemies who rise up against you will be defeated before
you. They will come at you from one direction but flee from you in seven.[s]
8The LORD will send a blessing on your barns and on everything you put your hand
to. The LORD your God will bless you in the land he is giving you.
9The LORD will establish you as his holy people,[t] as he promised you on oath, if you
keep the commands of the LORD your God and walk in his ways. 10Then all the peoples
on earth will see that you are called by the name[u] of the LORD, and they will fear you.
11The LORD will grant you abundant prosperity—in the fruit of your womb, the young of
your livestock and the crops of your ground—in the land he swore to your forefathers
to give you.[v]
12The LORD will open the heavens, the storehouse of his bounty, to send rain[w] on your
land in season and to bless all the work of your hands. You will lend to many nations but
will borrow from none.[x] 13The LORD will make you the head, not the tail. If you pay attention to the commands of the LORD your God that I give you this day and carefully follow them,
you will always be at the top, never at the bottom. 14Do not turn aside from any of the commands I give you today, to the right or to the left,[y] following other gods and serving them.

Curses for Disobedience

15However, if you do not obey[z] the LORD your God and do not carefully follow all his
commands and decrees I am giving you today, all these curses will come upon you and
overtake you:[a]

16You will be cursed in the city and cursed in the country.
17Your basket and your kneading trough will be cursed.
18The fruit of your womb will be cursed, and the crops of your land, and the
calves of your herds and the lambs of your flocks.
19You will be cursed when you come in and cursed when you go out.

20The LORD will send on you curses,[b] confusion and rebuke[c] in everything you put
your hand to, until you are destroyed and come to sudden ruin[d] because of the evil you
have done in forsaking him.[a] 21The LORD will plague you with diseases until he has destroyed you from the land you are entering to possess.[e] 22The LORD will strike you with
wasting disease, with fever and inflammation, with scorching heat and drought,[f] with
blight and mildew, which will plague you until you perish.[g] 23The sky over your head will
be bronze, the ground beneath you iron.[h] 24The LORD will turn the rain of your country
into dust and powder; it will come down from the skies until you are destroyed.

a *20* Hebrew *me*

28:1 [l]Ex 15:26; Lev 26:3; Dt 7:12-26 [m]Dt 26:19
28:2 [n]Zec 1:6
28:3 [o]Ps 128:1,4 [p]Ge 39:5
28:4 [q]Ge 49:25; Pr 10:22
28:6 [r]Ps 121:8
28:7 [s]Lev 26:8,17
28:9 [t]Ex 19:6; Dt 7:6
28:10 [u]2Ch 7:14
28:11 [v]Dt 30:9; Pr 10:22
28:12 [w]Lev 26:4 [x]Dt 15:3,6
28:14 [y]Dt 5:32
28:15 [z]Lev 26:14 [a]Jos 23:15; Da 9:11; Mal 2:2
28:20 [b]Mal 2:2 [c]Isa 51:20; 66:15 [d]Dt 4:26
28:21 [e]Lev 26:25; Jer 24:10
28:22 [f]Lev 26:16 [g]Am 4:9
28:23 [h]Lev 26:19

■ **28:1—30:20** *The Covenant Renewal in Moab.* After describing what was to be done upon entering the land, Moses turned to the people before him and called them to covenant renewal. He listed the blessings (28:1–14) and the curses (28:15—29:1) and made an appeal for the people to recommit (29:2—30:20) to the covenant.

■ **28:1–14** *Blessings.* Moses described the kinds of blessings that God offered his listeners for fidelity to the covenant.

28:4 The fruit of your womb. The children, the crops and the cattle would be blessed. For an agricultural people, these were basics.

28:5 Your basket and your kneading trough. Probably a summary of household tasks.

28:6 when you come in. "To come in . . . and go out" probably means "to come in and out of the city gate"—to conduct non-home-related business. "To go out" may also sometimes mean "to go to battle." God would bless an obedient people in every way.

28:11 in the land. The blessings detailed above would come to fruition in the land of promise—a major part of the blessing.

28:12 will open the heavens. Such expressions are figurative and should not to be made the basis for cosmology. It is clear that the ancients knew from observation that rain comes from clouds (1Ki 18:44; Isa 5:6).

■ **28:15—29:1** *Curses.* True to the dynamics of the covenant, Moses listed the curses that would come upon the nation if flagrant violations were to continue.

28:15–68 See *WLC* 28,152,193.

28:16 cursed in the city. The curses of verses 16–19 are the exact opposite of the blessings of verses 3–6.

28:23 The sky . . . will be bronze. Interestingly, this metaphor finds expression as a simile in Leviticus 26:19, another chapter of threats: "The sky . . . like iron and the ground . . . like bronze." Whatever figure is used, the thought of rainless skies and waterless land was frightful to a people totally dependent on rain and soil.

25The LORD will cause you to be defeated before your enemies. You will come at them
from one direction but flee from them in seven,[i] and you will become a thing of horror
to all the kingdoms on earth.[j] 26Your carcasses will be food for all the birds of the air and
the beasts of the earth, and there will be no one to frighten them away.[k] 27The LORD will
afflict you with the boils of Egypt[l] and with tumors, festering sores and the itch, from
which you cannot be cured. 28The LORD will afflict you with madness, blindness and confusion of mind. 29At midday you will grope[m] about like a blind man in the dark. You will
be unsuccessful in everything you do; day after day you will be oppressed and robbed,
with no one to rescue you.

30You will be pledged to be married to a woman, but another will take her and rav-
ish her.[n] You will build a house, but you will not live in it.[o] You will plant a vineyard, but
you will not even begin to enjoy its fruit.[p] 31Your ox will be slaughtered before your eyes,
but you will eat none of it. Your donkey will be forcibly taken from you and will not be
returned. Your sheep will be given to your enemies, and no one will rescue them. 32Your
sons and daughters will be given to another nation,[q] and you will wear out your eyes
watching for them day after day, powerless to lift a hand. 33A people that you do not
know will eat what your land and labor produce, and you will have nothing but cruel oppression all your days.[r] 34The sights you see will drive you mad. 35The LORD will afflict
your knees and legs with painful boils[s] that cannot be cured, spreading from the soles
of your feet to the top of your head.

36The LORD will drive you and the king[t] you set over you to a nation unknown to you
or your fathers.[u] There you will worship other gods, gods of wood and stone.[v] 37You will
become a thing of horror and an object of scorn and ridicule to all the nations where the
LORD will drive you.[w]

38You will sow much seed in the field but you will harvest little,[x] because locusts will
devour[y] it. 39You will plant vineyards and cultivate them but you will not drink the wine
or gather the grapes, because worms will eat them.[z] 40You will have olive trees throughout your country but you will not use the oil, because the olives will drop off.[a] 41You will
have sons and daughters but you will not keep them, because they will go into captivity.[b] 42Swarms of locusts will take over all your trees and the crops of your land.

43The alien who lives among you will rise above you higher and higher, but you will
sink lower and lower.[c] 44He will lend to you, but you will not lend to him.[d] He will be the
head, but you will be the tail.[e]

45All these curses will come upon you. They will pursue you and overtake you until
you are destroyed,[f] because you did not obey the LORD your God and observe the commands and decrees he gave you. 46They will be a sign and a wonder to you and your descendants forever.[g] 47Because you did not serve[h] the LORD your God joyfully and gladly[i] in the time of prosperity, 48therefore in hunger and thirst, in nakedness and dire
poverty, you will serve the enemies the LORD sends against you. He will put an iron yoke[j]
on your neck until he has destroyed you.

49The LORD will bring a nation against you from far away, from the ends of the earth,[k]
like an eagle[l] swooping down, a nation whose language you will not understand, 50a
fierce-looking nation without respect for the old[m] or pity for the young. 51They will devour the young of your livestock and the crops of your land until you are destroyed. They
will leave you no grain, new wine or oil, nor any calves of your herds or lambs of your
flocks until you are ruined.[n] 52They will lay siege to all the cities throughout your land
until the high fortified walls in which you trust fall down. They will besiege all the cities
throughout the land the LORD your God is giving you.[o]

53Because of the suffering that your enemy will inflict on you during the siege, you will
eat the fruit of the womb, the flesh of the sons and daughters the LORD your God has giv-

28:25 [i]Isa 30:17 [j]Jer 15:4; 24:9; Eze 23:46
28:26 [k]Jer 7:33; 16:4; 34:20
28:27 [l]ver 60-61; 1Sa 5:6
28:29 [m]Job 5:14; Isa 59:10
28:30 [n]Job 31:10; Jer 8:10 [o]Am 5:11 [p]Jer 12:13
28:32 [q]ver 41
28:33 [r]Jer 5:15-17
28:35 [s]ver 27
28:36 [t]2Ki 17:4,6; 24:12, 14; 25:7,11 [u]Jer 16:13 [v]Dt 4:28
28:37 [w]Jer 24:9
28:38 [x]Mic 6:15; Hag 1:6,9 [y]Joel 1:4
28:39 [z]Isa 5:10; 17:10-11
28:40 [a]Mic 6:15
28:41 [b]ver 32
28:43 [c]ver 13
28:44 [d]ver 12 [e]ver 13
28:45 [f]ver 15
28:46 [g]Isa 8:18; Eze 14:8
28:47 [h]Dt 32:15 [i]Ne 9:35
28:48 [j]Jer 28:13-14
28:49 [k]Jer 5:15; 6:22 [l]La 4:19; Hos 8:1
28:50 [m]Isa 47:6
28:51 [n]ver 33
28:52 [o]Jer 10:18; Zep 1:14-16,17

28:25 defeated before your enemies. The expression is the reverse of the blessing in verse 7, with the added horror that their corpses would be exposed with none to give them decent burial.
28:27 the boils of Egypt. The various diseases mentioned in this verse cannot be identified with any exactitude. They may be included under the "diseases of Egypt" (v. 60), which were dreaded. God had promised to deliver them from these maladies (7:15; Ex 15:26) if they would obey his laws.
28:35 from the soles of your feet to the top of your head. This expression was used to describe Job's boils (Job 2:7).
28:36 you and the king you set over you. Only here and in 17:14–17 is a king over Israel mentioned. In chapter 17 a monarchy is mentioned only as a possibility, and here the translation could as well be "the king you will set over you" or "the king you may set over you."
28:44 He will lend to you. This curse, like several in this section, is the opposite of the corresponding blessing (vv. 12–13).
28:49 from the ends of the earth. This figurative expression was based on the way the eye perceives the earth: It appears to have end points at those places on the horizon beyond which the eye cannot see. The figure is explained here in the phrase "from far away." A similar expression is used also in 13:7: ". . . whether near or far, from one end of the land to the other." Such expressions were used by the kings of Assyria, who called themselves "kings of the four quarters," even though they knew of the lands of Egypt and the Orient that lay beyond their domain.
28:53 eat the fruit of the womb. Cannibalism was a dreadful accompaniment of ancient sieges. The frightful details are given here. Even the most sensitive and delicate people would resort to the most abnormal extremes near the end of a siege.

en you.[p] [54]Even the most gentle and sensitive man among you will have no compassion
on his own brother or the wife he loves or his surviving children, [55]and he will not give
to one of them any of the flesh of his children that he is eating. It will be all he has left
because of the suffering your enemy will inflict on you during the siege of all your cities.
[56]The most gentle and sensitive[q] woman among you—so sensitive and gentle that she
would not venture to touch the ground with the sole of her foot—will begrudge the husband she loves and her own son or daughter [57]the afterbirth from her womb and the children she bears. For she intends to eat them secretly during the siege and in the distress
that your enemy will inflict on you in your cities.

[58]If you do not carefully follow all the words of this law, which are written in this book,
and do not revere[r] this glorious and awesome name[s]—the LORD your God— [59]the LORD
will send fearful plagues on you and your descendants, harsh and prolonged disasters,
and severe and lingering illnesses. [60]He will bring upon you all the diseases of Egypt[t] that
you dreaded, and they will cling to you. [61]The LORD will also bring on you every kind of
sickness and disaster not recorded in this Book of the Law, until you are destroyed.[u]
[62]You who were as numerous as the stars in the sky[v] will be left but few in number, because you did not obey the LORD your God. [63]Just as it pleased[w] the LORD to make you
prosper and increase in number, so it will please[x] him to ruin and destroy you. You will
be uprooted[y] from the land you are entering to possess.

[64]Then the LORD will scatter[z] you among all nations,[a] from one end of the earth to the
other. There you will worship other gods—gods of wood and stone, which neither you
nor your fathers have known. [65]Among those nations you will find no repose, no resting
place for the sole of your foot. There the LORD will give you an anxious mind, eyes weary with longing, and a despairing heart.[b] [66]You will live in constant suspense, filled with
dread both night and day, never sure of your life. [67]In the morning you will say, "If only
it were evening!" and in the evening, "If only it were morning!"—because of the terror
that will fill your hearts and the sights that your eyes will see.[c] [68]The LORD will send you
back in ships to Egypt on a journey I said you should never make again. There you will
offer yourselves for sale to your enemies as male and female slaves, but no one will buy
you.

Renewal of the Covenant

29 These are the terms of the covenant the LORD commanded Moses to make with
the Israelites in Moab, in addition to the covenant he had made with them at
Horeb.[d]

[2]Moses summoned all the Israelites and said to them:

Your eyes have seen all that the LORD did in Egypt to Pharaoh, to all his officials and
to all his land.[e] [3]With your own eyes you saw those great trials, those miraculous signs
and great wonders.[f] [4]But to this day the LORD has not given you a mind that understands
or eyes that see or ears that hear.[g] [5]During the forty years that I led you through the desert, your clothes did not wear out, nor did the sandals on your feet.[h] [6]You ate no bread
and drank no wine or other fermented drink. I did this so that you might know that I am
the LORD your God.[i]

[7]When you reached this place, Sihon[j] king of Heshbon and Og king of Bashan came

28:53 [p]Lev 26:29; 2Ki 6:28-29; Jer 19:9; La 2:20; 4:10
28:56 [q]ver 54
28:58 [r]Mal 1:14 [s]Ex 6:3
28:60 [t]ver 27
28:61 [u]Dt 4:25-26
28:62 [v]Dt 4:27; 10:22; Ne 9:23
28:63 [w]Jer 32:41 [x]Pr 1:26 [y]Jer 12:14; 45:4
28:64 [z]Lev 26:33; Dt 4:27 [a]Ne 1:8
28:65 [b]Lev 26:16,36
28:67 [c]ver 34; Job 7:4
29:1 [d]Dt 5:2-3
29:2 [e]Ex 19:4
29:3 [f]Dt 4:34; 7:19
29:4 [g]Isa 6:10; Ac 28:26-27; Ro 11:8*; Eph 4:18
29:5 [h]Dt 8:4
29:6 [i]Dt 8:3
29:7 [j]Dt 2:32; 3:1

28:58–59 See *WLC* 114; *WSC* 56.
28:58 this glorious and awesome name. Compare the high theology of 10:14–21 and contrast it with the foolish and sinful gods of pagan antiquity. See *WLC* 112; *WSC* 54.
28:61 this Book of the Law. See verse 58. The king they might set over them was to have a scroll (the same Hebrew word translated "Book" here) of the law copied from the priest's copy (17:18). The scroll was to include the curses enumerated here. It was to incorporate "the words of this law from beginning to end" (31:24), and there is no good reason to deny that it included at least all of Deuteronomy.
28:64 will scatter you. This threat does not indicate an exilic date for the writing of Deuteronomy; it is a far more general threat of widespread dispersion, expressed generally as "from the ends of the earth" (v. 49). This curse was experienced by the northern kingdom in 722 B.C. and by Judah in 586 B.C. (see 2Ki 17:6; 25:21).
28:68 but no one will buy you. Compare with the striking emphasis of verse 29, which predicts that there will be "no one to rescue you." The aggregation of curses in this chapter is overwhelming. The chapter should be compared with the similar, but shorter, sequence of curses found in Leviticus 26, which ends with the opportunity for confession and restoration. In the present case, the possibility of restoration is delayed until chapter 30.
29:1 the covenant . . . in Moab. It is likely that the phrase "these are the terms" refers to the preceding verses.
▪ **29:2—30:20** *Appeal for Renewal.* Moses called the nation to recommit to the covenant first made at Sinai. His address follows the typical pattern for covenant making: the prologue (29:2–8), the stipulations (29:9–18), the curses (29:19–29), the blessings (30:1–10), the offer (30:11–18) and the witnesses (30:19–20).
▪ **29:2–8** *Prologue.* Moses began with a review of the mercy God had shown his people in the past.
29:2 in Egypt. The deliverance from Egypt, which occupies a third of the book of Exodus, is alluded to in Deuteronomy briefly but frequently; see especially 11:2–7. See *BC* 18.
29:4 the LORD has not given you . . . eyes that see. Paul combined this verse with Isaiah 29:10 and applied both verses to the Jews of his day (Ro 11:8). See *WCF* 5.6.
29:5 During the forty years. The special preservation of clothes was mentioned in 8:4. The additional point is given here that the Israelites drank no wine or other fermented drink, as there were no grapes in the desert. They also had no bread, but God supplied them with manna as the staple of their diet.
29:7 Sihon . . . and Og. The Transjordan conquest was a major

out to fight against us, but we defeated them.[k] 8 We took their land and gave it as an inheritance to the Reubenites, the Gadites and the half-tribe of Manasseh.[l]
9 Carefully follow[m] the terms of this covenant, so that you may prosper in everything
you do.[n] 10 All of you are standing today in the presence of the LORD your God—your leaders and chief men, your elders and officials, and all the other men of Israel, 11 together
with your children and your wives, and the aliens living in your camps who chop your
wood and carry your water.[o] 12 You are standing here in order to enter into a covenant
with the LORD your God, a covenant the LORD is making with you this day and sealing with
an oath, 13 to confirm you this day as his people,[p] that he may be your God[q] as he promised you and as he swore to your fathers, Abraham, Isaac and Jacob. 14 I am making this
covenant,[r] with its oath, not only with you 15 who are standing here with us today in the
presence of the LORD our God but also with those who are not here today.[s]
16 You yourselves know how we lived in Egypt and how we passed through the countries on the way here. 17 You saw among them their detestable images and idols of wood
and stone, of silver and gold.[t] 18 Make sure there is no man or woman, clan or tribe
among you today whose heart turns away from the LORD our God to go and worship the
gods of those nations; make sure there is no root among you that produces such bitter
poison.[u]
19 When such a person hears the words of this oath, he invokes a blessing on himself
and therefore thinks, "I will be safe, even though I persist in going my own way." This
will bring disaster on the watered land as well as the dry.[a] 20 The LORD will never be willing to forgive him; his wrath and zeal[v] will burn[w] against that man. All the curses written in this book will fall upon him, and the LORD will blot[x] out his name from under heav-
en. 21 The LORD will single him out from all the tribes of Israel for disaster, according to
all the curses of the covenant written in this Book of the Law.
22 Your children who follow you in later generations and foreigners who come from
distant lands will see the calamities that have fallen on the land and the diseases with
which the LORD has afflicted it.[y] 23 The whole land will be a burning waste[z] of salt[a] and
sulfur—nothing planted, nothing sprouting, no vegetation growing on it. It will be like
the destruction of Sodom and Gomorrah,[b] Admah and Zeboiim, which the LORD overthrew in fierce anger. 24 All the nations will ask: "Why has the LORD done this to this
land?[c] Why this fierce, burning anger?"
25 And the answer will be: "It is because this people abandoned the covenant of the
LORD, the God of their fathers, the covenant he made with them when he brought them
out of Egypt. 26 They went off and worshiped other gods and bowed down to them, gods
they did not know, gods he had not given them. 27 Therefore the LORD's anger burned
against this land, so that he brought on it all the curses written in this book.[d] 28 In furious anger and in great wrath the LORD uprooted[e] them from their land and thrust them
into another land, as it is now."

29:7 [k]Nu 21:21-24,33-35
29:8 [l]Nu 32:33; Dt 3:12-13
29:9 [m]Dt 4:6; Jos 1:7 [n]1Ki 2:3
29:11 [o]Jos 9:21,23,27
29:13 [p]Dt 28:9 [q]Ge 17:7; Ex 6:7
29:14 [r]Jer 31:31
29:15 [s]Ac 2:39
29:17 [t]Dt 28:36
29:18 [u]Dt 11:16; Heb 12:15
29:20 [v]Eze 23:25 [w]Ps 74:1; 79:5 [x]Ex 32:33; Dt 9:14
29:22 [y]Jer 19:8
29:23 [z]Isa 34:9 [a]Jer 17:6 [b]Ge 19:24,25; Zep 2:9
29:24 [c]1Ki 9:8; Jer 22:8-9
29:27 [d]Da 9:11,13,14
29:28 [e]1Ki 14:15; 2Ch 7:20; Ps 52:5; Pr 2:22

[a] 19 *Or way, in order to add drunkenness to thirst.*

---

victory, but Moses mentioned it only briefly, as he wanted to move quickly to giving the charge.

■ **29:9–18** *Stipulations.* In light of God's mercy in the past, Moses called on the Israelites to commit themselves to the covenant.

29:12 to enter into a covenant. This refers back to the Sinai covenant, to which a new generation was committing. All those men who were over 20 years old at Sinai had perished in the wilderness. Many of those who had been under 20 at the time (i.e., between 40 and 60 now) had seen these great events but had not taken part in them. Now they, too, were to affirm the covenant.

■ **29:19–29** *Curses.* In typical fashion the curses for covenant violations were listed (cf. 27:14–26; 28:15–68).

29:19 This will bring disaster . . . The meaning of this sentence is difficult. The three key Hebrew words can be taken in two ways. The first word can mean "to sweep away"; that is, "to bring disaster" or "to add." The next word can refer either to saturation by water or to intoxication. The last word can refer to dry land or to thirst. The NIV text takes the former interpretation in each case, with the idea that the sinful man goes his own way and brings destruction on everything. The NIV text note takes the second interpretation in each case, with the idea that the already sinful man sinks further into sin, adding drunkenness to his thirst. The Septuagint (the Greek translation of the OT) refers to the sinner going on in sin. A decision regarding interpretation is difficult, but the context seems to favor the translation given in the NIV text note. See *WCF* 8.1.

29:21 this Book of the Law. Note the frequent reference not to a section or to a subject, but to the written record of God's law (e.g., 28:58,61; 29:19,20,26; 30:10; 31:9,11,24,26). See Joshua 1:7–8.

29:23 Sodom. The four cities of the plain that had been destroyed in Abraham's day are named. Genesis 14 mentions five cities of the plain, but does not allude to their destruction. Genesis 19 mentions Sodom and Gomorrah, and the whole area is said to be destroyed (although Zoar is spared). Deuteronomy puts the two records together and lists the four destroyed cities. Hosea 11:8 refers to the destruction of Admah and Zeboiim. As the cities were destroyed c. 2000 B.C. and never rebuilt, it would seem that Hosea got his information from Deuteronomy, unless he made the same synthesis of the Genesis accounts. In any event, the judgment of Sodom was a prophetic model of divine wrath. Like Moses, Isaiah compared the judgment of Israel to that of Sodom (Isa 1:10). Jesus also compared the judgment to come at his return to that of Sodom (Lk 17:28–35), as did Peter (2Pe 2:6).

29:25 because this people abandoned the covenant. The assumption is that the nation would have followed the example of the sinful man of verse 19 and abandoned the covenant, bringing destruction upon itself. This destruction would be so awful that surrounding peoples would be astonished and would ask the reason for it. The answer would be based on Moses' solemn warning of the bitter fruits of turning away from the Lord and his covenant and going after the idols of the heathen.

29:28 as it is now. This would be said from the perspective of people observing the event after it had happened.

29The secret things belong to the LORD our God, but the things revealed belong to us
and to our children forever, that we may follow all the words of this law.

Prosperity After Turning to the LORD

30 When all these blessings and curses[f] I have set before you come upon you and
you take them to heart wherever the LORD your God disperses you among the
nations,[g] 2and when you and your children return[h] to the LORD your God and obey him
with all your heart and with all your soul according to everything I command you today,
3then the LORD your God will restore your fortunes[a] [i] and have compassion on you and
gather[j] you again from all the nations where he scattered you.[k] 4Even if you have been
banished to the most distant land under the heavens, from there the LORD your God will
gather you and bring you back.[l] 5He will bring[m] you to the land that belonged to your
fathers, and you will take possession of it. He will make you more prosperous and numerous than your fathers. 6The LORD your God will circumcise your hearts and the
hearts of your descendants,[n] so that you may love him with all your heart and with all
your soul, and live. 7The LORD your God will put all these curses on your enemies who
hate and persecute you.[o] 8You will again obey the LORD and follow all his commands I
am giving you today. 9Then the LORD your God will make you most prosperous in all the
work of your hands and in the fruit of your womb, the young of your livestock and the
crops of your land.[p] The LORD will again delight in you and make you prosperous, just
as he delighted in your fathers, 10if you obey the LORD your God and keep his commands
and decrees that are written in this Book of the Law and turn to the LORD your God with
all your heart and with all your soul.[q]

The Offer of Life or Death

11Now what I am commanding you today is not too difficult for you or beyond your
reach.[r] 12It is not up in heaven, so that you have to ask, "Who will ascend into heaven
to get it and proclaim it to us so we may obey it?"[s] 13Nor is it beyond the sea, so that you
have to ask, "Who will cross the sea to get it and proclaim it to us so we may obey it?"
14No, the word is very near you; it is in your mouth and in your heart so you may obey it.

30:1 [f]ver 15,19; Dt 11:26 [g]Lev 26:40-45; Dt 28:64; 29:28; 1Ki 8:47
30:2 [h]Dt 4:30; Ne 1:9
30:3 [i]Ps 126:4 [j]Ps 147:2; Jer 32:37; Eze 34:13 [k]Jer 29:14
30:4 [l]Ne 1:8-9; Isa 43:6
30:5 [m]Jer 29:14
30:6 [n]Dt 10:16; Jer 32:39
30:7 [o]Dt 7:15
30:9 [p]Dt 28:11; Jer 31:28; 32:41
30:10 [q]Dt 4:29
30:11 [r]Isa 45:19,23
30:12 [s]Ro 10:6*

[a] 3 Or *will bring you back from captivity*

29:29 The secret things. This verse is traditionally used to defend the idea of the secret (decretive) will of God as opposed to his revealed (prescriptive) will (see theological article "The Will of God" at Eze 18). However, the text is unclear as to what the "secret things" are. Perhaps it refers to the unknown future of Israel after Moses. If this is the case, the use of this verse as a proof text for the categories of God's will seems appropriate. See *WCF* 3.8; *WLC* 105,113.

■ **30:1–10** *Blessings.* Moses looked beyond the time when the curse of the exile would occur. He spoke of the promise of an eventual return to the land and to God's blessing (see note on 4:30). This renewal would be accompanied by a redemptive victory of the Lord over the enemies of his people (v. 7), not unlike the redemptive victory he had accomplished through Moses in the exodus. But whereas the former victory delivered God's people from slavery to Egypt, the future triumph would deliver them from slavery to sin (vv. 2,6,8). Old Testament prophets depended on this passage when they spoke of the return from exile as a time of a new covenant with unprecedented blessings (e.g., Jer 31:31–34; Eze 36–37). The New Testament teaches that this expectation of final covenant renewal and blessing was ultimately fulfilled in Jesus.

30:1–2 The future covenant renewal would take place when a remnant in exile repented of their sins and returned to the Lord to obey his commandments.

30:2 with all your heart and with all your soul. Moses referred again to the great commandment of 6:5, holding out the hope of repentance despite apostasy and judgment.

30:4–5 The measure of God's compassion in restoration would be the measure of his wrath in exile. This expectation of exceedingly blessed restoration is the basis for the New Testament's hope that the blessings of Christ's consummated kingdom will far surpass those realized in the Old Testament.

30:6 The LORD . . . will circumcise your hearts. See note on 10:16. The promised restoration and renewal would result from a sovereign work of God in the hearts of his elect people. By circumcising their hearts, he would replace their total inability and stubbornness (5:29; 10:16; 29:4) with the humility and repentance they needed (cf. vv. 1–2), thereby purifying for himself a people who would love and obey him. **all your heart.** See note on 6:5. See *WCF* 10.1; *WLC* 67; *HC* 66.

30:7 on your enemies. The future restoration would bring a fulfillment of the promise made to Abraham and his seed ("whoever curses you I will curse"; Ge 12:3). Moses thus linked the restoration pictured in verses 3–10 to another judgment by God against the enemies of his people.

30:8–9 Moses considered again the blessings he had mentioned earlier (vv. 4–5), but they were now to be understood as the result of God's victory for his people (v. 7). God's blessings on work and womb (v. 9) would signal the reversal of the curses he had imposed in Genesis 3:16–19. In addition, the delight that God (the covenant Lord) had taken in humankind (his covenant servant) at creation (Ge 1:26–28) would be restored.

30:10 The blessings of the renewed covenant would be inseparable from, but not based on, the obedience of the restored remnant to their Lord's commandments (cf., e.g., Mt 7:21). Christ's obedience, which won the victory over sin in which the remnant would share by faith, is the only meritorious basis of all such blessings. **all your heart.** See note on 6:5.

■ **30:11–18** *Offer.* Moses offered the covenant renewal and encouraged the nation to enter it.

30:11–14 This is one of the clearest expressions of the continuity between the covenant with Moses and the new covenant in Christ. Recalling his words in 6:6, Moses maintained that the commandments God had revealed through him and the righteousness they required were readily accessible to, and attainable by, the Israelites (v. 11). He insisted that righteousness was found "in [their] mouth and in [their] heart" (v. 14). In other words, God did not expect perfection from his people. They did have to recommit themselves sincerely ("in [their] mouth") to the covenant and give their hearts to God faithfully and lovingly ("in [their] heart"). The sacrificial system was an integral part of the Mosaic covenant and was designed to deal with the failures that were sure to come. Paul later referred to this passage in much the same way, identifying the preaching of the gospel with Moses' offer of the covenant (see Ro 10:6–11). The requirements of the new covenant in Christ are not difficult either. One merely needs to profess faith with the mouth and believe in the heart. The death of Jesus has fully and permanently atoned for the sins of all those who trust in him.

15 See, I set before you today life and prosperity, death and destruction.[t] 16 For I command you today to love the LORD your God, to walk in his ways, and to keep his commands, decrees and laws; then you will live and increase, and the LORD your God will bless you in the land you are entering to possess.

17 But if your heart turns away and you are not obedient, and if you are drawn away to bow down to other gods and worship them, 18 I declare to you this day that you will certainly be destroyed.[u] You will not live long in the land you are crossing the Jordan to enter and possess.

19 This day I call heaven and earth as witnesses against you[v] that I have set before you life and death, blessings and curses.[w] Now choose life, so that you and your children may live 20 and that you may love[x] the LORD your God, listen to his voice, and hold fast to him. For the LORD is your life,[y] and he will give you many years in the land he swore to give to your fathers, Abraham, Isaac and Jacob.

Joshua to Succeed Moses

31 Then Moses went out and spoke these words to all Israel: 2 "I am now a hundred and twenty years old[z] and I am no longer able to lead you.[a] The LORD has said to me, 'You shall not cross the Jordan.'[b] 3 The LORD your God himself will cross[c] over ahead of you.[d] He will destroy these nations before you, and you will take possession of their land. Joshua also will cross[e] over ahead of you, as the LORD said. 4 And the LORD will do to them what he did to Sihon and Og, the kings of the Amorites, whom he destroyed along with their land. 5 The LORD will deliver[f] them to you, and you must do to them all that I have commanded you. 6 Be strong and courageous.[g] Do not be afraid or terrified[h] because of them, for the LORD your God goes with you;[i] he will never leave you[j] nor forsake[k] you."

7 Then Moses summoned Joshua and said[l] to him in the presence of all Israel, "Be strong and courageous, for you must go with this people into the land that the LORD swore to their forefathers to give them, and you must divide it among them as their inheritance. 8 The LORD himself goes before you and will be with you;[m] he will never leave you nor forsake you. Do not be afraid; do not be discouraged."

The Reading of the Law

9 So Moses wrote down this law and gave it to the priests, the sons of Levi, who carried[n] the ark of the covenant of the LORD, and to all the elders of Israel. 10 Then Moses commanded them: "At the end of every seven years, in the year for canceling debts,[o] during the Feast of Tabernacles,[p] 11 when all Israel comes to appear[q] before the LORD your God at the place he will choose, you shall read this law[r] before them in their hearing. 12 Assemble the people—men, women and children, and the aliens living in your towns—so they can listen and learn[s] to fear the LORD your God and follow carefully all the words

30:15 [t]Dt 11:26
30:18 [u]Dt 8:19
30:19 [v]Dt 4:26 [w]ver 1
30:20 [x]Dt 6:5; 10:20 [y]Ps 27:1; Jn 11:25
31:2 [z]Dt 34:7 [a]Nu 27:17; 1Ki 3:7 [b]Dt 3:23,26
31:3 [c]Nu 27:18 [d]Dt 9:3 [e]Dt 3:28
31:5 [f]Dt 7:2
31:6 [g]Jos 10:25; 1Ch 22:13 [h]Dt 7:18 [i]Dt 1:29; 20:4 [j]Jos 1:5 [k]Heb 13:5*
31:7 [l]Dt 1:38; 3:28
31:8 [m]Ex 13:21; 33:14
31:9 [n]ver 25; Nu 4:15; Jos 3:3
31:10 [o]Dt 15:1 [p]Lev 23:34
31:11 [q]Dt 16:16 [r]Jos 8:34-35; 2Ki 23:2
31:12 [s]Dt 4:10

30:15 I set before you. Moses called for a decision. The people had but two choices: life or death, God's blessing or his sure judgment. They were encouraged to choose life (v. 20). Joshua would later give the identical alternatives (Jos 24:15). Jesus, who is greater than either Moses or Joshua, called his disciples to take the narrow path that leads to life (Mt 7:13–14).

■ **30:19–20** *Witnesses.* The mention of witnesses is similar to the form of ancient treaty documents that included a list of witnesses (often the names of the pagan gods) at the end. In the Scriptures, God's creation was called to witness against his people (Isa 1:2; Mic 1:2). See *WCF* 9.1.

■ **31:1—34:12** *The Conclusion of Moses' Ministry.* These closing chapters resemble the processes of succession that appear in suzerain-vassal treaties. Moses made provision for a smooth transition in covenant administration after his death (31:1–29). Also included is the song of Moses (31:30—32:47), Moses' blessing of the tribes (32:48—33:29) and the record of his death (34:1–12).

■ **31:1–29** *Transfer of Leadership to Joshua.* Moses commissioned Joshua to lead the people into the promised land.

31:1 Moses went out and spoke. This brief exhortation (vv. 1–8) can hardly be called another address, but it includes details regarding Moses' final affairs and the transfer of authority to Joshua, his lieutenant.

31:2 a hundred and twenty years old. Moses had spent 40 years in Midian tending sheep (Ac 7:30). This time was not at all wasted, for he had learned the geography and climate of the Sinai peninsula in preparation for leading the Israelites in that area for another 40 years. That leaves 40 years for Moses' youth and training in Egypt. God saw to it that Moses was prepared for his great task.

31:3 Joshua also will cross over ahead of you. See notes on 1:37 and 3:23–29. It seems that Moses was reconciled to the fact that he would not be crossing into Canaan. He had attained a great age, and although his powers had not abated (34:7), the conquest of Canaan would require a period of some years, and it was time for a younger man to take over. The most important thing was that the Lord would lead Moses' successor, as he had guided Moses (Ex 33:14–15).

31:6 Be strong and courageous. These and the following words are similar to the encouragement God would give Joshua after Moses' death (Jos 1:9).

31:7 Moses summoned Joshua. Moses wisely, and at God's command, elevated Joshua in the presence of the people. Further commissioning would follow.

31:9 Moses wrote down this law. Repeatedly in Deuteronomy and in Exodus Moses is said to have written down the law or laws of the Lord. In Leviticus most of the chapters begin with the words, "The LORD said to Moses." God used Moses preeminently to speak and write his will and word for Israel. In verse 24 Moses is said to have finished writing. That verse may refer to the continuation of the work of verse 9. Verse 9 specifies that Moses gave the law to the priests, and verse 26 stipulates that they should retain a copy of it beside the ark. See *WLC* 156.

31:10 during the Feast of Tabernacles. This weeklong feast occurred in the fall after the fieldwork was done. In the year of canceling debts (see note on 15:1), the people had free time during this week. The priests were to use this time to instruct them. This was a practical arrangement to teach the law to all who were present for the feast.

31:11–13 See *WLC* 156.

of this law. 13 Their children,[t] who do not know this law, must hear it and learn to fear
the LORD your God as long as you live in the land you are crossing the Jordan to possess."

Israel's Rebellion Predicted

14 The LORD said to Moses, "Now the day of your death[u] is near. Call Joshua and present yourselves at the Tent of Meeting, where I will commission him." So Moses and Joshua came and presented themselves at the Tent of Meeting.
15 Then the LORD appeared at the Tent in a pillar of cloud, and the cloud stood over
the entrance to the Tent.[v] 16 And the LORD said to Moses: "You are going to rest with your
fathers, and these people will soon prostitute[w] themselves to the foreign gods of the land
they are entering. They will forsake[x] me and break the covenant I made with them. 17 On
that day I will become angry[y] with them and forsake[z] them; I will hide[a] my face from
them, and they will be destroyed. Many disasters and difficulties will come upon them,
and on that day they will ask, 'Have not these disasters come upon us because our God
is not with us?'[b] 18 And I will certainly hide my face on that day because of all their wickedness in turning to other gods.
19 "Now write down for yourselves this song and teach it to the Israelites and have
them sing it, so that it may be a witness for me against them. 20 When I have brought
them into the land flowing with milk and honey, the land I promised on oath to their
forefathers,[c] and when they eat their fill and thrive, they will turn to other gods[d] and
worship them, rejecting me and breaking my covenant.[e] 21 And when many disasters and
difficulties come upon them,[f] this song will testify against them, because it will not be
forgotten by their descendants. I know what they are disposed to do,[g] even before I bring
them into the land I promised them on oath." 22 So Moses wrote[h] down this song that day
and taught it to the Israelites.
23 The LORD gave this command[i] to Joshua son of Nun: "Be strong and courageous,[j]
for you will bring the Israelites into the land I promised them on oath, and I myself will
be with you."
24 After Moses finished writing in a book the words of this law from beginning to end,
25 he gave this command to the Levites who carried the ark of the covenant of the LORD:
26 "Take this Book of the Law and place it beside the ark of the covenant of the LORD your
God. There it will remain as a witness against you.[k] 27 For I know how rebellious and stiff-
necked[l] you are. If you have been rebellious against the LORD while I am still alive and
with you, how much more will you rebel after I die! 28 Assemble before me all the elders
of your tribes and all your officials, so that I can speak these words in their hearing and
call heaven and earth to testify against them.[m] 29 For I know that after my death you are
sure to become utterly corrupt[n] and to turn from the way I have commanded you. In days
to come, disaster[o] will fall upon you because you will do evil in the sight of the LORD and
provoke him to anger by what your hands have made."

The Song of Moses

30 And Moses recited the words of this song from beginning to end in the hearing of
the whole assembly of Israel:

32

Listen, O heavens,[p] and I will speak;
hear, O earth, the words of my mouth.
2 Let my teaching fall like rain
and my words descend like dew,[q]
like showers[r] on new grass,
like abundant rain on tender plants.
3 I will proclaim the name of the LORD.[s]
Oh, praise the greatness[t] of our God!

31:13 [t]Dt 11:2; Ps 78:6-7
31:14 [u]Nu 27:13; Dt 32:49-50
31:15 [v]Ex 33:9
31:16 [w]Jdg 2:12 [x]Jdg 10:6,13
31:17 [y]Jdg 2:14,20 [z]Jdg 6:13; 2Ch 15:2 [a]Dt 32:20; Isa 1:15; 8:17 [b]Nu 14:42
31:20 [c]Dt 6:10-12 [d]Dt 32:15-17 [e]ver 16
31:21 [f]ver 17 [g]Hos 5:3
31:22 [h]ver 19
31:23 [i]ver 7 [j]Jos 1:6
31:26 [k]ver 19
31:27 [l]Ex 32:9; Dt 9:6,24
31:28 [m]Dt 4:26; 30:19; 32:1
31:29 [n]Dt 32:5; Jdg 2:19 [o]Dt 28:15
32:1 [p]Isa 1:2
32:2 [q]Isa 55:11 [r]Ps 72:6
32:3 [s]Ex 33:19 [t]Dt 3:24

31:14 the Tent of Meeting. In Deuteronomy the tent is mentioned only here and in verse 15. It was at the entrance to the Tent of Meeting that Joshua was commissioned as the Lord appeared in the pillar of cloud, as he had done with Moses (Ex 40:35; Nu 12:4–12).
31:19 write down for yourselves this song. God knew the future unfaithfulness of the people but also the power of song in worship and in memory. He commanded Moses to write a song that would bear testimony to himself and his work in future days. Moses had written a song of deliverance from Egypt (Ex 15:1–18), and there are other brief songs by him in Numbers. Psalm 90 is also credited to Moses.

31:22 this song. The song of verses 30–43.
■ **31:30—32:47** *The Song of Moses.* Moses recited his song before the people so they could learn it and so that future generations, to whom they would pass it along, would not forget the goodness of God and the covenant he had established with them.
32:1 heavens . . . earth. Moses had called heaven and Earth as witnesses at the end of the covenant renewal in 30:19.
32:3 proclaim the name of the LORD. This song was to be a future witness to the Lord, to his goodness and to his saving work for Israel (31:19).

4 He is the Rock,[u] his works are perfect,[v]
and all his ways are just.
A faithful God[w] who does no wrong,
upright and just is he.

5 They have acted corruptly toward him;
to their shame they are no longer his children,
but a warped and crooked generation.[a x]
6 Is this the way you repay[y] the LORD,
O foolish and unwise people?[z]
Is he not your Father,[a] your Creator,[b]
who made you and formed you?[b]

7 Remember the days of old;
consider the generations long past.
Ask your father and he will tell you,
your elders, and they will explain to you.[c]
8 When the Most High gave the nations their inheritance,
when he divided all mankind,[d]
he set up boundaries for the peoples
according to the number of the sons of Israel.[c]
9 For the LORD's portion[e] is his people,
Jacob his allotted inheritance.[f]

10 In a desert[g] land he found him,
in a barren and howling waste.
He shielded him and cared for him;
he guarded him as the apple of his eye,[h]
11 like an eagle that stirs up its nest
and hovers over its young,[i]
that spreads its wings to catch them
and carries them on its pinions.
12 The LORD alone led him;
no foreign god was with him.[j]

13 He made him ride on the heights[k] of the land
and fed him with the fruit of the fields.
He nourished him with honey from the rock,
and with oil[l] from the flinty crag,
14 with curds and milk from herd and flock
and with fattened lambs and goats,
with choice rams of Bashan
and the finest kernels of wheat.[m]
You drank the foaming blood of the grape.[n]

15 Jeshurun[d] grew fat[o] and kicked;
filled with food, he became heavy and sleek.
He abandoned[p] the God who made him
and rejected the Rock[q] his Savior.

32:4 [u]ver 15,18,30 [v]2Sa 22:31 [w]Dt 7:9
32:5 [x]Dt 31:29
32:6 [y]Ps 116:12 [z]Ps 74:2 [a]Dt 1:31; Isa 63:16 [b]ver 15
32:7 [c]Ex 13:14
32:8 [d]Ge 11:8; Ac 17:26
32:9 [e]Jer 10:16 [f]1Ki 8:51,53
32:10 [g]Jer 2:6 [h]Ps 17:8; Zec 2:8
32:11 [i]Ex 19:4
32:12 [j]ver 39
32:13 [k]Isa 58:14 [l]Job 29:6
32:14 [m]Ps 81:16; 147:14 [n]Ge 49:11
32:15 [o]Dt 31:20 [p]ver 6; Isa 1:4,28 [q]ver 4

[a] 5 Or *Corrupt are they and not his children, / a generation warped and twisted to their shame* [b] 6 Or *Father, who bought you* [c] 8 Masoretic Text; Dead Sea Scrolls (see also Septuagint) *sons of God* [d] 15 *Jeshurun* means *the upright one,* that is, Israel.

32:4 Rock. This is the first instance of the use of the word "Rock" as a name for God. The usage is common in the Psalms and in other poetic passages. It was a royal metaphor, indicating reliability and strength. See *WLC* 7.
32:5 to their shame. Note the sharp contrast between the most holy God (v. 4) and the corrupt nation (v. 5). This passage could be translated "no longer his children, a shameful, warped and crooked generation."
32:6 See *WLC* 151.
32:8 their inheritance. God, by ancient decree, had given the promised land to Israel in a grant to the patriarchs (v. 7). He had arranged the nations in accordance with this decree. The Lord had elected Jacob (a name used also for the sons of Jacob, the nation of Israel) to be his own portion, his heritage. See *BC* 16.
32:10 apple of his eye. The Hebrew word here for "apple" is a figure for a most precious thing.
32:11 hovers over its young. Pictures an eagle teaching its young to fly. The Lord did the same for Israel. The poetic figures of this song of Moses are powerful expressions of God's dealings with his people. See note on Genesis 1:2.
32:14 rams of Bashan. See note at 3:1.
32:15 Jeshurun. See NIV text note. In verse 4 God is called "upright" (Hebrew, *yashar,* anglicized to "Jashar"). Israel is called Jeshurun (which derives from *yashar*) also in 33:5 and 26 and in Isaiah 44:2. The Book of Jashar (Jos 10:13; 2Sa 1:18) was presumably an early book of chronicles of the nation, like the later chronicles of the kings of Israel and Judah. There is an extant book called the Book of Jashar, but it is clearly non-canonical. **grew fat and kicked.** Israel is aptly described in this telling picture of a well-fed ox. See *WLC* 105.

32:16 [r]1Co 10:22 [s]Ps 78:58
32:17 [t]Dt 28:64 [u]Jdg 5:8
32:18 [v]Isa 17:10
32:19 [w]Jer 44:21-23 [x]Ps 106:40
32:20 [y]Dt 31:17,29 [z]ver 5
32:21 [a]1Co 10:22 [b]1Ki 16:13,26 [c]Ro 10:19*
32:22 [d]Ps 18:7-8; Jer 15:14; La 4:11
32:23 [e]Dt 29:21 [f]Ps 7:13; Eze 5:16
32:24 [g]Dt 28:22 [h]Ps 91:6 [i]Lev 26:22 [j]Am 5:18-19
32:25 [k]Eze 7:15 [l]2Ch 36:17; La 2:21
32:26 [m]Dt 4:27 [n]Ps 34:16
32:27 [o]Isa 10:13
32:29 [p]Dt 5:29; Ps 81:13
32:30 [q]Lev 26:8 [r]Ps 44:12

16 They made him jealous[r] with their foreign gods
and angered[s] him with their detestable idols.
17 They sacrificed to demons, which are not God—
gods they had not known,[t]
gods that recently appeared,[u]
gods your fathers did not fear.
18 You deserted the Rock, who fathered you;
you forgot[v] the God who gave you birth.

19 The LORD saw this and rejected them[w]
because he was angered by his sons and daughters.[x]
20 "I will hide my face[y] from them," he said,
"and see what their end will be;
for they are a perverse generation,[z]
children who are unfaithful.
21 They made me jealous[a] by what is no god
and angered me with their worthless idols.[b]
I will make them envious by those who are not a people;
I will make them angry by a nation that has no
understanding.[c]
22 For a fire has been kindled by my wrath,
one that burns to the realm of death[a] below.[d]
It will devour the earth and its harvests
and set afire the foundations of the mountains.

23 "I will heap calamities[e] upon them
and spend my arrows[f] against them.
24 I will send wasting famine against them,
consuming pestilence[g] and deadly plague;[h]
I will send against them the fangs of wild beasts,[i]
the venom of vipers[j] that glide in the dust.
25 In the street the sword will make them childless;
in their homes terror will reign.[k]
Young men and young women will perish,
infants and gray-haired men.[l]
26 I said I would scatter[m] them
and blot out their memory from mankind,[n]
27 but I dreaded the taunt of the enemy,
lest the adversary misunderstand
and say, 'Our hand has triumphed;
the LORD has not done all this.'"[o]

28 They are a nation without sense,
there is no discernment in them.
29 If only they were wise and would understand this[p]
and discern what their end will be!
30 How could one man chase a thousand,
or two put ten thousand to flight,[q]
unless their Rock had sold them,
unless the LORD had given them up?[r]
31 For their rock is not like our Rock,
as even our enemies concede.

[a] 22 Hebrew *to Sheol*

32:16–20 See *WLC* 110.
32:21 god . . . idols. The foreign gods of verse 16 are here called "no god" and these "detestable idols" (v. 16) referred to as "worthless" (or "things of a mere breath"). In the contrast within this verse, the "no god" the Israelites espoused would make them "not a people," and just as they had angered God, he would anger them. See Romans 10:19.
32:22 a fire has been kindled . . . to the realm of death. For the figure of God's consuming fire, see Jeremiah 15:14. "The realm of death" is "Sheol" (see NIV text note), the grave. Job 31:12 uses the figure of a "fire that burns to Destruction." "Destruction" in Psalm 88:11 is in poetic parallel with the usual word for "grave." The poetic figure here is satisfactorily understood to represent God's wrath as an all-devouring fire that burns to the deepest grave, consumes the surface of the earth and reaches to the roots of the mountains.
32:30 one man chase a thousand. It has been called divine arithmetic—that few could do the work of many if they were faithful to the Lord. A similar figure was used in Leviticus 26, where five would chase 100, and 100 would in turn chase 10,000. On the other hand, in the case of disobedience, they would flee when no one pursued them (Lev 26:17). See also Psalm 91:7.

32 Their vine comes from the vine of Sodom
and from the fields of Gomorrah.
Their grapes are filled with poison,
and their clusters with bitterness.
33 Their wine is the venom of serpents,
the deadly poison of cobras.[s]

34 "Have I not kept this in reserve
and sealed it in my vaults?[t]
35 It is mine to avenge; I will repay.[u]
In due time their foot will slip;[v]
their day of disaster is near
and their doom rushes upon them.[w]"

36 The LORD will judge his people
and have compassion on his servants[x]
when he sees their strength is gone
and no one is left, slave or free.
37 He will say: "Now where are their gods,
the rock they took refuge in,[y]
38 the gods who ate the fat of their sacrifices
and drank the wine of their drink offerings?
Let them rise up to help you!
Let them give you shelter!

39 "See now that I myself am He![z]
There is no god besides me.[a]
I put to death and I bring to life,[b]
I have wounded and I will heal,[c]
and no one can deliver out of my hand.[d]
40 I lift my hand to heaven and declare:
As surely as I live forever,
41 when I sharpen my flashing sword[e]
and my hand grasps it in judgment,
I will take vengeance on my adversaries
and repay those who hate me.[f]
42 I will make my arrows drunk with blood,[g]
while my sword devours flesh:[h]
the blood of the slain and the captives,
the heads of the enemy leaders."

43 Rejoice,[i] O nations, with his people,[a,b]
for he will avenge the blood of his servants;[j]
he will take vengeance on his enemies
and make atonement for his land and people.[k]

44 Moses came with Joshua[c][l] son of Nun and spoke all the words of this song in the
hearing of the people. 45 When Moses finished reciting all these words to all Israel, 46 he
said to them, "Take to heart all the words I have solemnly declared to you this day,[m] so
that you may command your children to obey carefully all the words of this law. 47 They

32:33 [s]Ps 58:4
32:34 [t]Jer 2:22; Hos 13:12
32:35 [u]Ro 12:19*; Heb 10:30* [v]Jer 23:12 [w]Eze 7:8-9
32:36 [x]Dt 30:1-3; Ps 135:14; Joel 2:14
32:37 [y]Jdg 10:14; Jer 2:28
32:39 [z]Isa 41:4 [a]Isa 45:5 [b]1Sa 2:6; Ps 68:20 [c]Hos 6:1 [d]Ps 50:22
32:41 [e]Isa 34:6; 66:16; Eze 21:9-10 [f]Jer 50:29
32:42 [g]ver 23 [h]Jer 46:10, 14
32:43 [i]Ro 15:10* [j]2Ki 9:7 [k]Ps 65:3; 85:1; Rev 19:2
32:44 [l]Nu 13:8,16
32:46 [m]Eze 40:4

a 43 Or *Make his people rejoice, O nations* b 43 Masoretic Text; Dead Sea Scrolls (see also Septuagint) *people, / and let all the angels worship him /* c 44 Hebrew *Hoshea,* a variant of *Joshua*

32:32 the vine of Sodom. False gods brought evil deeds and poisonous fruit. Sodom was a symbol of awful destruction (see note on 29:23).
32:35 It is mine to avenge; I will repay. There is no serious question about the translation of the first phrase, although the Septuagint (the Greek translation of the OT) translates it slightly differently. The last phrase represents one Hebrew word. In this exact form, it does not occur elsewhere as a noun. With slight variation of the first vowel, it can be taken as an infinitive and translated "I will repay" (NIV; Septuagint). The NIV depends on the Hebrew for the first phrase and on the Septuagint for the last, and this is how it is quoted in the New Testament (Ro 12:19; Heb 10:30). **avenge.** See note on Micah 5:13.
32:36 have compassion. These words suggest that their parallel ("judge") means "vindicate," not "punish" (cf. v. 43). Still, the Israelites needed to see that they had no help apart from the one true God.
32:39 I myself am He! The Hebrew emphasizes by repetition: "I, I am He." This whole stanza is a towering expression of the uniqueness of God in his being, power, providence and judgment. **no one can deliver out of my hand.** Quoted verbatim in Isaiah 43:13. Because we know a God of justice, we can be sure that evil will at last be destroyed. The ultimate cry in heaven is "Hallelujah! Salvation and glory and power belong to our God, for true and just are his judgments" (Rev 19:1–2).
32:43 he will avenge the blood of his servants. Again, the New Testament echo is "He has avenged . . . the blood of his servants" (Rev 19:2).

32:47 [n]Dt 30:20

are not just idle words for you—they are your life.[n] By them you will live long in the land you are crossing the Jordan to possess."

32:49 [o]Nu 27:12
32:50 [p]Ge 25:8
32:51 [q]Nu 20:11-13 [r]Nu 27:14
32:52 [s]Dt 34:1-3 [t]Dt 1:37

Moses to Die on Mount Nebo

48 On that same day the LORD told Moses, 49 "Go up into the Abarim[o] Range to Mount Nebo in Moab, across from Jericho, and view Canaan, the land I am giving the Israelites as their own possession. 50 There on the mountain that you have climbed you will die[p] and be gathered to your people, just as your brother Aaron died on Mount Hor and was gathered to his people. 51 This is because both of you broke faith with me in the presence of the Israelites at the waters of Meribah Kadesh in the Desert of Zin[q] and because you did not uphold my holiness among the Israelites.[r] 52 Therefore, you will see the land only from a distance;[s] you will not enter[t] the land I am giving to the people of Israel."

33:1 [u]Jos 14:6
33:2 [v]Ex 19:18; Ps 68:8 [w]Jdg 5:4 [x]Hab 3:3 [y]Da 7:10; Ac 7:53; Rev 5:11
33:3 [z]Hos 11:1 [a]Dt 14:2 [b]Lk 10:39
33:4 [c]Jn 1:17 [d]Ps 119:111
33:7 [e]Ge 49:10
33:8 [f]Ex 28:30

Moses Blesses the Tribes

33 This is the blessing that Moses the man of God[u] pronounced on the Israelites before his death. 2 He said:

"The LORD came from Sinai[v]
and dawned over them from Seir;[w]
he shone forth from Mount Paran.[x]
He came with[a] myriads of holy ones[y]
from the south, from his mountain slopes.[b]
3 Surely it is you who love[z] the people;
all the holy ones are in your hand.[a]
At your feet they all bow down,[b]
and from you receive instruction,
4 the law that Moses gave us,[c]
the possession of the assembly of Jacob.[d]
5 He was king over Jeshurun[c]
when the leaders of the people assembled,
along with the tribes of Israel.

6 "Let Reuben live and not die,
nor[d] his men be few."

7 And this he said about Judah:[e]

"Hear, O LORD, the cry of Judah;
bring him to his people.
With his own hands he defends his cause.
Oh, be his help against his foes!"

8 About Levi he said:

"Your Thummim and Urim[f] belong
to the man you favored.

[a] 2 Or *from* [b] 2 The meaning of the Hebrew for this phrase is uncertain. [c] 5 *Jeshurun* means *the upright one,* that is, Israel; also in verse 26. [d] 6 Or *but let*

32:46–47 See *WLC* 108; *WSC* 50.
32:47 they are your life. Moses emphasized again that obedience from the heart to God's commands is a matter of life—eternal life—and death.
■ **32:48—33:29** *The Blessing of Moses.* This chapter includes a narrative introduction (32:48–52) that is followed by Moses' blessing (33:1–29).
32:49 Mount Nebo. Like Mount Sinai, the location of this mountain is not known with certainty. This place is known only to God, who called Moses up to Mount Sinai for 80 days and later summoned him up to Mount Nebo to stay. Moses saw the promised land from afar (34:1–3), but because of his sin at Meribah (Nu 20:12) could not enter.
33:1 Moses the man of God. This expression is used customarily for prophets and is applied to Moses only here and in the title of Psalm 90. Moses' blessing of the tribes is to be compared with Jacob's blessing of his sons (Ge 49). In the case of Jacob's blessing, the order had a logical reason: Leah's children came first, then the children of the handmaidens and finally Rachel's children. Here there is no discernible order. Levi is counted, Manasseh and Ephraim are counted as Joseph, but Simeon is omitted, perhaps to keep the number of tribes at 12.
33:2 The LORD came from Sinai. This introduction to the blessing pictures the Lord as coming in a theophany to reveal himself to the people who had received his instruction at the hand of Moses. There is a similar passage at the beginning of the poem in Habakkuk 3, where God is said to come from Teman and from Paran. Teman is an area to the south and may be compared to "from the south" in the verse here. **Paran.** See 1:1.
33:3 See *WLC* 157.
33:5 He was king over Jeshurun. God was King over his people, whereas Moses was never called a king. **Jeshurun.** See 32:15 and its note.
33:6 nor his men be few. This is best read with the NIV text note ("but let his men be few"). It is a reminder of the curse on Reuben (Ge 49:3).
33:7 about Judah. The blessing on Judah is surprisingly short in view of the promise of rulership to Judah (Ge 49:8–12) and in consideration of Judah's large part in later history.
33:8 About Levi. The blessing on Levi reflects Levi's fidelity at the time of the golden-calf incident, when the tribe of Levi rallied to Moses' side. Note that the teaching of the law was the province of

You tested him at Massah;
    you contended with him at the waters of Meribah.[g]
9 He said of his father and mother,[h]
    'I have no regard for them.'
He did not recognize his brothers
    or acknowledge his own children,
but he watched over your word
    and guarded your covenant.[i]
10 He teaches your precepts to Jacob
    and your law to Israel.[j]
He offers incense before you
    and whole burnt offerings on your altar.[k]
11 Bless all his skills, O LORD,
    and be pleased with the work of his hands.[l]
Smite the loins of those who rise up against him;
    strike his foes till they rise no more."

12 About Benjamin he said:

"Let the beloved of the LORD rest secure in him,[m]
    for he shields him all day long,
    and the one the LORD loves rests between his
        shoulders.[n]"

13 About Joseph[o] he said:

"May the LORD bless his land
    with the precious dew from heaven above
    and with the deep waters that lie below;[p]
14 with the best the sun brings forth
    and the finest the moon can yield;
15 with the choicest gifts of the ancient mountains[q]
    and the fruitfulness of the everlasting hills;
16 with the best gifts of the earth and its fullness
    and the favor of him who dwelt in the burning bush.[r]
Let all these rest on the head of Joseph,
    on the brow of the prince among[a] his brothers.
17 In majesty he is like a firstborn bull;
    his horns are the horns of a wild ox.[s]
With them he will gore[t] the nations,
    even those at the ends of the earth.
Such are the ten thousands of Ephraim;
    such are the thousands of Manasseh."

18 About Zebulun[u] he said:

"Rejoice, Zebulun, in your going out,
    and you, Issachar, in your tents.
19 They will summon peoples to the mountain[v]
    and there offer sacrifices of righteousness;[w]
they will feast on the abundance of the seas,[x]
    on the treasures hidden in the sand."

20 About Gad[y] he said:

"Blessed is he who enlarges Gad's domain!
    Gad lives there like a lion,
    tearing at arm or head.

33:8 [g]Ex 17:7
33:9 [h]Ex 32:26-29 [i]Mal 2:5
33:10 [j]Lev 10:11; Dt 31:9-13 [k]Ps 51:19
33:11 [l]2Sa 24:23
33:12 [m]Dt 12:10 [n]Ex 28:12
33:13 [o]Ge 49:25 [p]Ge 27:28
33:15 [q]Hab 3:6
33:16 [r]Ex 3:2
33:17 [s]Nu 23:22 [t]1Ki 22:11; Ps 44:5
33:18 [u]Ge 49:13-15
33:19 [v]Ex 15:17; Isa 2:3 [w]Ps 4:5 [x]Isa 60:5, 11
33:20 [y]Ge 49:19

[a] 16 Or *of the one separated from*

the Levites (v. 10). Mention of the Urim and Thummim is probably an allusion to Exodus 28:30, although they are mentioned also in Leviticus 8:8.
33:16 who dwelt in the burning bush. Moses was alluding to Exodus 3:4. **prince among his brothers.** The word "prince" translates the Hebrew word used also for a Nazirite. It can mean "separated from" (see NIV text note) or "one of high station." The same word with the same ambiguity is applied to Joseph (Ge 49:26) with similar mention of blessings of heaven, deep waters and ancient hills. Because of the reference to blessings, the meaning "prince" may be preferred. The ten thousands of Ephraim, being larger than the thousands of Manasseh, did not fit the numbers then current, for Ephraim was at the time much smaller than Manasseh. Ephraim would soon, however, become more important.

[21] He chose the best land for himself;[z]
the leader's portion was kept for him.
When the heads of the people assembled,
he carried out the LORD's righteous will,[a]
and his judgments concerning Israel."

[22] About Dan[b] he said:

"Dan is a lion's cub,
springing out of Bashan."

[23] About Naphtali he said:

"Naphtali is abounding with the favor of the LORD
and is full of his blessing;
he will inherit southward to the lake."

[24] About Asher[c] he said:

"Most blessed of sons is Asher;
let him be favored by his brothers,
and let him bathe his feet in oil.[d]
[25] The bolts of your gates will be iron and bronze,
and your strength will equal your days.[e]

[26] "There is no one like the God of Jeshurun,[f]
who rides on the heavens to help you[g]
and on the clouds in his majesty.
[27] The eternal God is your refuge,[h]
and underneath are the everlasting arms.
He will drive out your enemy before you,[i]
saying, 'Destroy him!'[j]
[28] So Israel will live in safety alone;[k]
Jacob's spring is secure
in a land of grain and new wine,
where the heavens drop dew.[l]
[29] Blessed are you, O Israel![m]
Who is like you,[n]
a people saved by the LORD?[o]
He is your shield and helper[p]
and your glorious sword.
Your enemies will cower before you,
and you will trample down their high places.[a][q]"

The Death of Moses

34 Then Moses climbed Mount Nebo from the plains of Moab to the top of Pisgah,
across from Jericho.[r] There the LORD showed[s] him the whole land—from Gilead to Dan, [2] all of Naphtali, the territory of Ephraim and Manasseh, all the land of Judah
as far as the western sea,[b][t] [3] the Negev and the whole region from the Valley of Jericho,
the City of Palms,[u] as far as Zoar. [4] Then the LORD said to him, "This is the land I promised on oath[v] to Abraham, Isaac and Jacob when I said, 'I will give it[w] to your descendants.' I have let you see it with your eyes, but you will not cross[x] over into it."
[5] And Moses the servant of the LORD[y] died[z] there in Moab, as the LORD had said. [6] He
buried him[c] in Moab, in the valley opposite Beth Peor,[a] but to this day no one knows
where his grave is.[b] [7] Moses was a hundred and twenty years old[c] when he died, yet his

33:21 [z]Nu 32:1-5,31-32 [a]Jos 4:12; 22:1-3
33:22 [b]Ge 49:16
33:24 [c]Ge 49:21 [d]Ge 49:20; Job 29:6
33:25 [e]Dt 4:40; 32:47
33:26 [f]Ex 15:11 [g]Ps 104:3
33:27 [h]Ps 90:1 [i]Jos 24:18 [j]Dt 7:2
33:28 [k]Nu 23:9; Jer 23:6 [l]Ge 27:28
33:29 [m]Ps 144:15 [n]Ps 18:44 [o]2Sa 7:23 [p]Ps 115:9-11 [q]Dt 32:13
34:1 [r]Dt 32:49 [s]Dt 32:52
34:2 [t]Dt 11:24
34:3 [u]Jdg 1:16; 3:13; 2Ch 28:15
34:4 [v]Ge 28:13 [w]Ge 12:7 [x]Dt 3:27
34:5 [y]Nu 12:7 [z]Dt 32:50; Jos 1:1-2
34:6 [a]Dt 3:29 [b]Jude 1:9
34:7 [c]Dt 31:2

[a] *29* Or *will tread upon their bodies* [b] *2* That is, the Mediterranean [c] *6* Or *He was buried*

33:22 a lion's cub, springing out of Bashan. The meaning is that Dan was as strong as the lions that came from the forests near the Jordan in Bashan. The tribe of Dan was not located near Bashan.
33:24 let him bathe his feet in oil. Olive oil was a valued commodity, both for food and for burning in the saucer-shaped lamps that were a main source of illumination.
33:26 the God of Jeshurun. See 32:15 and its note. This final stanza has blessed the hearts of multitudes of God's people through the ages. God is the majestic God (v. 26), the eternal God (v. 27), the protecting and providing God (v. 28), and the great blessing conferred upon the Israelites was that he was their God. Such a song of praise can perhaps only be matched by such verses in the New Testament as "the song of Moses the servant of God and the song of the Lamb" (Rev 15:3–4).
■ **34:1–12** *The Death of Moses.* This account of Moses' death reports a past event. This section was added after the book of Deuteronomy had been substantially written in the days of Moses.
34:1 from Gilead to Dan. The descriptions here and in verse 2 name the areas in terms of the land allotted by Joshua to the tribes who settled in Canaan.

eyes were not weak[d] nor his strength gone. 8 The Israelites grieved for Moses in the plains
of Moab thirty days, until the time of weeping and mourning[e] was over.
9 Now Joshua son of Nun was filled with the spirit[a] of wisdom[f] because Moses had laid
his hands on him.[g] So the Israelites listened to him and did what the LORD had commanded Moses.
10 Since then, no prophet has risen in Israel like Moses,[h] whom the LORD knew face
to face,[i] 11 who did all those miraculous signs and wonders[j] the LORD sent him to do in
Egypt—to Pharaoh and to all his officials[k] and to his whole land. 12 For no one has ever
shown the mighty power or performed the awesome deeds that Moses did in the sight
of all Israel.

a 9 Or *Spirit*

34:7 [d]Ge 27:1
34:8 [e]Ge 50:3, 10; 2Sa 11:27
34:9 [f]Ge 41:38; Isa 11:2; Da 6:3 [g]Nu 27:18, 23
34:10 [h]Dt 18:15, 18 [i]Ex 33:11; Nu 12:6, 8; Dt 5:4
34:11 [j]Dt 4:34 [k]Dt 7:19

34:8 The Israelites grieved for Moses . . . thirty days. The Egyptian period of embalming was 40 days (Ge 50:3), and Joseph mourned seven days for Jacob (Ge 50:10). The Bible gives no minimum or maximum time period for mourning.
34:9 Moses had laid his hands on him. As the worshiper placed his hands on the head of the sacrifice to symbolize the transfer of guilt, so Moses had laid his hand on Joshua to symbolize the transfer of the Spirit for leadership.
34:10 Since then. These words imply that generations had passed since Moses' death. The book of Joshua does not mention prophets, and Judges does not refer to any by name. To compare Moses with Nathan or Gad would not greatly elevate Moses. For his evaluation to be significant, the writer must have been comparing Moses with Israel's great prophets, such as Elijah, Elisha and the writing prophets preserved in Scripture. Moses' miracles, his clarity of revelation and his access to God were unique (Nu 12:6–8). In Jesus, a prophet like (but superior to) Moses arose and performed signs and wonders before the kings and rulers of the people—indeed in the sight of all Israel (cf. Mt 4:23–25; Ac 2:22).

Introduction to the Historical Books

Introduction

THE arrangement of the English Bible is based on the Septuagint (Greek translation of the OT). In this arrangement Joshua through Esther are counted as historical books. For the most part, these historical books divide into two groups.

1. The Deuteronomic History: Joshua through Kings (excluding Ruth)
2. The Chronistic History: Chronicles, Ezra, Nehemiah

This arrangement differs from that of the Hebrew Bible, which counts the Deuteronomic History under the heading *Former Prophets* and includes Ezra, Nehemiah and Chronicles in "the other books" of *The Writings.* Ruth and Esther stand apart from these two edited histories both in modern scholarly discussions and in the Hebrew Bible, where they are included in the five *Rolls.* Because they are best studied separately from the other historical books, they will not be introduced here (see their introductions).

The Deuteronomic History is so called because Deuteronomy introduces the collection. Although the various works of this history were originally authored at different times (see the introductions to each of the books), the collection appears to have been edited as a unit shortly after 562 B.C., which is the latest date in Kings. This editorial work addressed a crisis of faith among the exiled Judahites who were living in servitude under King Nebuchadnezzar in Babylon at the time. To them it seemed as though God had forgotten his promises of an eternal land to Israel and an everlasting throne to David and his descendants.

The later collection, Chronicles, Ezra and Nehemiah, was edited as a unit for the Judahites who had been restored to the promised land after the Babylonian exile. Although they were back in the land and the line of David had survived, Judah was now but one of many provinces in the Persian Empire. These books gave hope and practical guidance to this dispirited community of returnees.

Both collections contain true history written by inspired authors and subsequently finalized by inspired editors. Neither the writers nor the editors fabricated events. They cited their sources (Jos 10:13; 1Ki 11:41; 2Ki 16:19; 1Ch 4:22; 5:17; 2Ch 9:29; Ezr 6:1,2) and followed a relentless chronological order. At the same time, it is apparent that each book and collection was written and edited for theological purposes, not simply to preserve a historical record.

The Deuteronomic History (Joshua, Judges, Samuel and Kings)

Literary unity. The coupling of Joshua with Deuteronomy is especially convincing. For example, the Lord's promises and exhortations that introduce Joshua (1:1–9) consist entirely of expressions from Moses' speeches in Deuteronomy. Joshua 1:2 corresponds to Deuteronomy 10:11; Joshua 1:3–5a is a virtual quotation of Deuteronomy 11:23–25; Joshua 1:5b–7a and 9 largely repeats Deuteronomy 31:6–8 and 23; Joshua 1:7b–8 is reminiscent of a series of texts in Deuteronomy that identify that book as the "Book of the Law" and stress the importance of meditation and obedience (Dt 5:32–33; 17:18–19; 30:10).

Likewise, Judges is linked with Joshua. After the introduction to Judges (1:2—2:5), its main body of material (2:6—16:31) is introduced by referring back to Joshua (Jdg 2:6–10). In Judges, each episode and section in the book employs verbal repetition, historical paralleling and quotations from Joshua.

Samuel, in turn, is related to Judges. Judges prepares its audience for the establishment of the Davidic monarchy by raising the question of proper leadership and strongly affirming that God chose Judah, not Benjamin, to lead his nation. Samuel records the actual failure of Benjamite kingship under Saul and the successful establishment of the Judahite monarchy under David. Even the refrain in Judges "in those days Israel had no king" might be applied to the early chapters of 1 Samuel prior to Saul's kingship. Finally, Samuel's summary treatment of the history of the judges (1Sa 12:9–11) sounds like an application of the editor's summary of that history (Jdg 2:6–19).

Kings is so closely related to Samuel that some scholars see a common source running from 2 Samuel 9–20 through 1 Kings 2. In those chapters one finds a narrative treating, among other concerns, the succession to David's throne, beginning with the birth of Solomon and climaxing with his coronation.

Thematic unity. To meet the exiles' crisis of faith, several themes that are emphasized in Deuteronomy are featured throughout the rest of the Deuteronomic History.

First, Deuteronomy lays down a firm foundation for the office of prophet and provides the test of a true prophet: that his words come to pass (Dt 18:14–22). The distinct office of prophet is instituted in 1 Samuel 9. Jewish tradition, as noted above, was so impressed with the important role prophets played in the Deuteronomic History that they labeled it *Former Prophets.* Beyond this many specific prophetic elements connect the books of this history. For example, Joshua's prophecy that whoever undertook to rebuild Jericho would do so at the cost of his firstborn (Jos 6:26) is fulfilled in 1 Kings 16:34. Solomon interprets his reign and his building the temple (1Ki 8:20) as a fulfillment of the Lord's promise to David (2Sa 7:12–13). Kings reassures the exiles of the truth of the prophetic word that God would give his people an eternal land and throne.

Second, the concept of "covenant," so important in Deuteronomy, informs this entire history. On the divine side the focus is on promise. God swore to the patriarchs and their descendants that he would be their God and never forsake them (Dt 4:31; 29:12–13; Jos 1:6; Jdg 2:1; 2Ki 13:23). Out of his inscrutable love God chose the Israelites and obliged himself to give them the land he swore to the fathers. That promise, repeated about 30 times in Deuteronomy (e.g., Dt 1:8; 34:4), is remembered in the rest of the history (e.g., Jos 1:2; 24:13; Jdg 1:2; 1Ki 4:21; 8:34). On the human side the focus is on trust and obedience. Possession of the land, this history repeats again and again, depends on Israel's covenant faithfulness. The Lord's promises and Israel's obligations are featured in the sermons of its heroes such as Moses (Dt 1–4; 5–11,27–28), Joshua (Jos 24:1–27), Samuel (1Sa 12) and David (1Ki 2:1–4). The Lord clearly annunciated the conditions to Solomon with reference to kingship (1Ki 9:1–9).

Israel's obligations are concentrated in the first two of the Ten Commandments: Worship no other gods and do not make idols. Or, in the language of this history, the nation is to "love," "serve" and "hold fast to" the Lord, to "walk before him," to "follow him," and "not to forget him" (Dt 6:5; Jos 1:7–8; 24:14–15; Jdg 2:6–10; 1Sa 12:20,24; 1Ki 2:4; 3:6; 8:23–25; 11:4–5). The command is fundamentally a matter of faith, not of strict obedience to an external code. For example, particular commandments, such as the requirement to worship only at Jerusalem, did not serve bureaucratic legalism but thwarted the temptation to idolatry. This history is not so much concerned with individual commands as with loyalty to God. Failure to obey specific commandments is symptomatic of a more pervasive problem: disloyalty to God. God's election of Israel and his saving actions on its behalf constituted the relationship. Trust in the Lord derived from the bond God had already established. Joshua 1 exhibits the connection. The Lord had committed himself to the Israelites, and the land was theirs for the taking. They needed only trust (Jos 1:1–9). On the other hand, if they failed to trust and so disobeyed the command to love God and put away other gods, then the guilty would be judged (Dt 28; Jos 24:19–20; Jdg 2:10–15; 1Sa 12:5–15; 2Ki 17:7–20). The key question raised by the exiles in Babylon is articulated in Deuteronomy 29:24 and 1 Kings 9:8: "Why has the LORD done such a thing to this land and to this temple?" This history answers unambiguously: "God did not fail; Israel failed." Nevertheless, God's promises are everlasting (Dt 30:1–9; Jdg 2:1; 1Sa 12:22; 2Sa 7:16).

Third, Deuteronomy also lays down a firm foundation for kingship and its regulation (Dt 17:14–20). Israel's merciful and faithful God is an endless source of blessing, even though the people have been faithless (Dt 9:4–6). In spite of Israel's sin, the compassionate God takes new initiatives and raises up leaders in times of crisis: Joshua, the judges, Saul and finally the house of David. His covenant with David's house, like all covenants with Israel, invariably moves the kingdom of God forward but presents conditions that regulate participation in that kingdom. God will continue to raise up a "son" in the house of David, but he will discipline unfaithful ones (2Sa 7:14–16). The history ends with sinful King Jehoiakin in exile; nevertheless, he is elevated to a seat of honor higher than those of other captive kings in Babylon. That glimmer of hope will not be extinguished but will shine ever brighter until the coming of the greater son of David, the true Son of God, Jesus Christ. See theological article "Major Covenants in the Bible" on page 25.

Finally, the theme of repentance in this history rests on God's eternal promises (Dt 4:29–31; Jos 7; Jdg 2:18; 2Sa 12:13; 1Ki 8:46–51). The hope of relief from divine judgment, even a return to God's blessings once the judgment of exile occurs, is tied to repentance (Dt 30:1–10; 1Ki 8:58). Thus John the Baptist and Jesus came offering the kingdom of God to all who repent (Mt 3:2; 4:17; Mk 1:15).

The Chronistic History (Chronicles, Ezra and Nehemiah)

As noted in the introduction to Ezra, Ezra-Nehemiah was originally one book. Chronicles and Ezra-Nehemiah are linked together as a connected piece of literature by introducing the latter with the conclusion of the former (2Ch 36:22–23; Ezr 1:1–3). In addition, the two works share many of the same religious interests and ideology. For example, they describe the preparation for building the first and second temples in parallel ways (1Ch 22:2,4,15; 2Ch 2:9,15–16; Ezr 3:7); both temples are endowed by the heads of ancestral houses (1Ch 26:26; Ezr 2:68); both show great interest in sacred vessels (1Ch 28:13–19; 2Ch 5:1; Ezr 1:7; 7:19; 8:25–30,33–34); and both present the order of sacrifices (2Ch 2:4; 8:13; Ezr 3:4–6) and the enumeration of sacrificial materials (1Ch 29:21; 2Ch 29:21,32; Ezr 6:9,17; 7:17,22; 8:35–36) in practically identical ways. Just as the Deuteronomic History consists of distinct books edited into a common history, this postexilic history is composed by locking disparate works together.

This later group of works covers much the same ground as the Deuteronomic History but continues beyond the point at which the first concludes to take in the constitution of Israel after the exile. Whereas the former is based primarily on Deuteronomy, this history is based on the entire Pentateuch, tracing its history back to Adam. It centers, however, on Israel's history from the First Temple period to the Second, the latter anticipated in the final verses of Chronicles and narrated fully in Ezra 1–6.

Chronicles, Ezra and Nehemiah were written to encourage the dispirited Judahites after exile. These books reminded the people of their glorious heritage in the Davidic dynasty and the temple. The history taught the returnees that they had to keep covenant and repent of their sins (2Ch 7:14). Nevertheless, it did not focus on failure but featured the greatness of David's dynasty and the glory of the temple. David is depicted as the founder of Israel's worship, and those kings who restored Israel's liturgy after dark periods of disorder and neglect are singled out for special attention: Hezekiah following Ahaz, and Josiah following Manasseh and Amon both serve as models to the Judahites who survived the dark chaos of the Babylonian exile. Following these emphases, the New Testament presents Jesus as the rightful and perfect heir of David's covenant (Mt 1:1; 22:42; Lk 1:31–33) and the One in whom the temple is fulfilled (Jn 2:19–22; Rev 21:22).

JOSHUA

Introduction

Overview

Author: Unknown

Purpose: To present the fulfillments of God's promises in the days of Joshua and to teach future generations in Israel how to serve the Lord—in battle, in distributing the promised land among the tribes and in renewing their covenant with the Lord

Date: c. 1000–561 B.C.

Key Truths:

- Through Joshua God blessed Israel with many victories in the promised land, but there were many battles yet to be fought.
- Through Joshua God distributed the land in the way it was to be maintained in the future.
- The covenant renewal that took place in Joshua's day provides a model for renewal in future generations.

Author

The author of the book of Joshua is unknown, and attempts to associate him with a particular time period depend on the interpretation of certain clues within the book. Theories range from the view that the book was largely composed by Joshua himself (the tradition of the Talmud) to the hypothesis that it was written by someone late in the postexilic period. It is likely that its final form resulted from a compiler or compilers working with an earlier version of the book, but it is difficult and unprofitable to try to separate these various strata. See "Introduction to the Historical Books" on page 304.

Time and Place of Writing

The time of the composition of the book of Joshua is unclear. Comments within the book itself, such as notices that something is true "to this day," suggest that many of its sources originated from a time between the death of Joshua (24:29–31) and the time of Samuel (c. 1050 B.C.). Because Sidon was still reckoned as Phoenicia's leading city (11:8; 19:28), some would date the book no later than 1200 B.C.; after that time Tyre gained the ascendancy. Jerusalem was as yet unconquered by the Israelites (15:63), a feat that would be accomplished by David (2Sa 5:6–10), and Gezer was not as yet under Solomon's rule (16:10; 1Ki 9:16). The notice about Rahab in 6:25 may refer to her descendants, and a reliable Hebrew tradition reads 5:1 as "they," not "we." The "we/us" in 5:6 may have been used by a later generation out of a sense of solidarity with the generation that had entered the land.

A number of passages indicate that the final composition was later than the days of Joshua. Updated equivalents for older place names are given (15:9,49,54), and several events recorded in the book probably took place after Joshua's lifetime, such as Caleb's conquest of Hebron (15:13; Jdg 1:8–10), Othniel's victory over Debir (15:15–17; Jdg 1:11–13) and the northward migration of the Danites (19:47; Jdg 18:27–29). It is also possible that 11:21 distinguishes between Judah and Israel in ways that would have been appropriate only after the national division into the northern and southern kingdoms. The last chapter certainly extends to the elders who outlived Joshua (24:31). We may therefore conclude that the book came to its final form no earlier than a generation or so after Joshua. In fact, the prominence given to the tribe of Judah (see notes on ch. 15) may indicate that the Davidic throne had already been established (c. 1000 B.C.) by the time of final composition. If this earlier orientation is correct, we may assume that the book was compiled in the promised land to encourage the nation to continue the work that Joshua had begun.

The latest likely date is established by 1 Kings 16:34, which alludes to Joshua's curse (6:26). The book of Kings may be firmly dated (see "Introduction to Kings: Time and Place of Writing") between the release of Jehoiachin (561 B.C.) and the Cyrus edict (538 B.C.). If the book is to be dated this late, it was compiled during the Babylonian exile to encourage the exiles to complete Joshua's work after they had returned to the land.

A number of difficulties arise when relating archaeological data to the Biblical record of Joshua's conquest. In addition to disputes over the locations of specific sites, the larger question of the date of Joshua's conquest has been problematic.

Among interpreters who hold to the veracity of the Biblical presentation, some have argued in recent years that archaeological data (such as the destruction of Canaanite cities and occupation patterns) point to a violent and successful Israelite invasion of Canaan around 1250 B.C. Others argue that there is archaeological evidence (such as that at Jericho) to support the more traditional view that the conquest took place earlier, around 1400 B.C. This view coincides more closely with other passages (e.g., Ex 12:40; Jdg 11:26; 1Ki 6:1). Difficulties continue, however, due to uncertainties over the identification of ancient sites, disputes over the dating of archaeological data and disagreements over the interpretation of Biblical, chronological references.

Original Audience

See "Time and Place of Writing."

Purpose and Distinctives

The main theological idea in the book of Joshua is that just as Israel under Joshua's leadership was to serve the Lord with gratitude for his fulfilled promises, so the readers were to continue grateful service in the light of the divine promises fulfilled. The book testifies to God's faithfulness to his promises by recounting the successful entry of the Israelites into the land (2:1—5:12), the dispossession of its inhabitants (5:13—12:24; see notes on Ge 15:13–16), the allocation of the territory to the 12 tribes (chs. 13–21) and the renewal of the covenant between the Lord and Israel (chs. 22–24).

The book of Joshua indicates that much of what God had promised was yet to be realized (e.g., 13:1; 23:5; Ge 13:5) and that the possibility of losing the land through disobedience was real (e.g., 23:12–13,15–16). This implied to the original readers that much still had to be done. As a result, they were to imitate the obedience of Joshua and Israel and reject the disobedience reflected in the failures recorded in the book.

Joshua should be understood in relation to the Pentateuch. God made a wondrous promise to Abraham, delivered his people from Egypt to Mount Sinai and blessed them along their journey through the wilderness. Because the first generation of the exodus flagrantly violated the covenant with the Lord, the Pentateuch ends with the people still outside the promised land. The great hope of taking possession of Canaan still remained to be fulfilled. The book of Joshua brings that promise to fulfillment.

Joshua should also be understood in relation to what follows it, namely, the continuing history of Israel in the land, which is recorded in Judges, Samuel and Kings. This story is a tragic one as far as Israel is concerned. The nation failed to follow the Lord wholeheartedly and was all but destroyed by God's judgment through the successive assaults of the Assyrians in the eighth century B.C. (2Ki 17) and the Babylonians in the sixth century B.C. (2Ki 25). The book of Joshua begins this history with the account of God's rich blessings toward Israel in the conquest. The rebellion that led to exile occurred in the face of the fulfillment of gracious, divine promises.

Christ in Joshua

The book of Joshua points to Christ in many different ways. As the first portion of the book presents Joshua as a warrior leading the conquest of Canaan, the New Testament speaks of Christ as the great Warrior who leads his people to take possession of the new heavens and the new earth. What Joshua merely began, Christ has fulfilled in his defeat of the devil in his first coming (Eph 4:8–9; Col 2:15; Heb 2:14–15), is continuing to fulfill in the spiritual holy war now being waged through the church (Ac 15:15–17; Eph 6:10–18) and will ultimately fulfill in his second coming (Rev 19:11–21; 21:1–5).

As the second portion of the book focuses on the allotment of Israel's inheritance to every tribe as God had designed, the New Testament explains that Christ gives his people their inheritance. In his resurrection and ascension, Christ received many blessings from God that he distributes to his people in the gifts of the Spirit (Eph 4:4–13). Thus the Spirit is the deposit guaranteeing our inheritance to come (Eph 1:13–14). When Christ returns in glory, he will grant his people their full and eternal inheritance: to reign with him eternally over the new heavens and the new earth (Rev 5:10; 22:5).

As the third portion of the book focuses on the necessity of faithful covenant living, the New Testament teaches that Christ fulfilled all covenant obligations for those who trust in him so that they become the righteousness of God (2Co 5:21). He perfectly fulfilled all of God's holy law, and his righteousness is imputed to those who believe (Ro 3:21–24; 4:3–13; Gal 2:16). At the same time, however, life in covenant with God remains a time of testing, for we prove the faith that we profess by conforming our lives to the requirements of God's covenant with us (Mt 24:12–14; Php 2:12–13; Heb 3:14; 10:15–39; Rev 2:7,11,17,26,28; 3:21).

Outline

- I. The Conquest of the Land (1:1—12:24)
  - A. The Divine Commission to Begin War (1:1–18)
  - B. Contrasting Early Battles (2:1—8:29)
    - 1. The Positive Model of the Battle at Jericho (2:1—6:27)
      - a. The Covenant Made With Rahab (2:1–24)
      - b. Consecration for Battle (3:1—5:12)
        - (1) Crossing the Jordan (3:1—4:24)
        - (2) Circumcision and Passover at Gilgal (5:1–12)
      - c. The Fall of Jericho (5:13—6:21)
      - d. The Covenant With Rahab Fulfilled (6:22–27)
    - 2. The Negative Model of the Battle at Ai (7:1—8:29)
      - a. Israel's Failures (7:1–26)
      - b. The Fall of Ai (8:1–29)
  - C. The Covenant Renewal (8:30–35)

God fulfilled his promises to give Israel the land. Israel learned how to fight for the land from Joshua's actions in a variety of battles.

- D. Later Expansive Battles (9:1—11:15)
  1. The Alliances Formed Against Israel (9:1–2)
  2. Victory Over Southern Territories (9:3—10:43)
     - a. The Gibeonite Deception (9:3–27)
     - b. Victory at Gibeon (10:1–15)
     - c. The Execution of Five Kings (10:16–28)
     - d. Victories Over Southern Cities (10:29–39)
     - e. Summary of Southern Territories (10:40–43)
  3. Victory Over Northern Territories (11:1–15)
- E. The Whole Land Taken (11:16–23)
- F. The List of Conquered Kings and Territories (12:1–24)

II. The Distribution of the Promised Land (13:1—21:45)

God directed Joshua in the initial distribution of the land and indicated that the land was not to be violated.

- A. The Divine Commission to Allocate the Land (13:1–7)
- B. East of the Jordan (13:8–33)
- C. West of the Jordan (14:1—19:51)
  1. Introduction (14:1–5)
  2. Caleb's Special Allotment (14:6–15)
  3. Judah's Allotment (15:1–63)
  4. Joseph's Allotment (16:1—17:18)
  5. Allotments for Other Tribes (18:1—19:48)
  6. Joshua's Special Allotment (19:49–50)
  7. Conclusion (19:51)
- D. Cities of Refuge (20:1–9)
- E. Levi's Allotment (21:1–42)
- F. Summation (21:43–45)

III. Covenant Loyalty in the Land (22:1—24:33)

Joshua led the entire nation in exemplary covenant renewal.

- A. The Unity of Israel (22:1–34)
  1. The Transjordan Tribes Released (22:1–9)
  2. The Controversy Over an Altar (22:10–34)
- B. The Requirement of Covenant Loyalty (23:1–16)
  1. All Israel Summoned (23:1–2a)
  2. First Exhortation (23:2b–8)
  3. Second Exhortation (23:9–13)
  4. Third Exhortation (23:14–16)
- C. The Covenant Renewal at Shechem (24:1–28)
  1. All Israel Summoned (24:1–2a)
  2. Historical Reflections (24:2b–13)
  3. Renewed Commitments to the Covenant (24:14–24)
  4. The Covenant Document (24:25–28)
- D. Notices of Deaths and Burials (24:29–33)

1:1 [a]Nu 12:7; Dt 34:5 [b]Ex 24:13; Dt 1:38
1:2 [c]ver 11

The LORD Commands Joshua

1 After the death of Moses the servant of the LORD,[a] the LORD said to Joshua[b] son of
Nun, Moses' aide: 2 "Moses my servant is dead. Now then, you and all these people,
get ready to cross the Jordan River[c] into the land I am about to give to them—to the Is-

---

■ **1:1—12:24** *The Conquest of the Land.* The first major portion of the book concerns the manner in which Joshua successfully waged holy war in the conquest of Canaan. The account of this topic divides into six major parts: God's commission to begin the war (1:1–18), examples of proper and improper ways to conduct a battle (2:1—8:29), the covenant renewal in the midst of war (8:30–35),

raelites. 3I will give you every place where you set your foot,[d] as I promised Moses. 4Your
territory will extend from the desert to Lebanon, and from the great river, the Euphrates[e]—all the Hittite country—to the Great Sea[a] on the west.[f] 5No one will be able to
stand up against you[g] all the days of your life. As I was with[h] Moses, so I will be with you;
I will never leave you nor forsake[i] you.
6"Be strong and courageous, because you will lead these people to inherit the land I
swore to their forefathers[j] to give them. 7Be strong and very courageous. Be careful to
obey all the law my servant Moses gave you; do not turn from it to the right or to the left,[k]
that you may be successful wherever you go.[l] 8Do not let this Book of the Law depart
from your mouth; meditate on it day and night, so that you may be careful to do everything written in it. Then you will be prosperous and successful.[m] 9Have I not commanded you? Be strong and courageous. Do not be terrified;[n] do not be discouraged, for the
LORD your God will be with you wherever you go."[o]
10So Joshua ordered the officers of the people: 11"Go through the camp and tell the
people, 'Get your supplies ready. Three days from now you will cross the Jordan here to
go in and take possession[p] of the land the LORD your God is giving you for your own.'"

[a] *4* That is, the Mediterranean

1:3 [d]Dt 11:24
1:4 [e]Ge 15:18 [f]Nu 34:2-12
1:5 [g]Dt 7:24 [h]Jos 3:7; 6:27 [i]Dt 31:6-8
1:6 [j]Dt 31:23
1:7 [k]Dt 5:32; 28:14 [l]Jos 11:15
1:8 [m]Dt 29:9; Ps 1:1-3
1:9 [n]Ps 27:1 [o]ver 7; Dt 31:7-8; Jer 1:8
1:11 [p]Joel 3:2

Joshua's victories over Canaanite alliances (9:1—11:15), the whole land taken (11:16–23) and an appended summary of conquered kings and territories (12:1–24).

■ **1:1–18** *The Divine Commission to Begin War.* The book begins with God calling Joshua to move forward into the conquest of the promised land. This section balances with the closing of the war in 11:16–23. Moses' death concluded the judgment of God on the generation that had come out of Egypt (5:4–6; Dt 1:35; 32:51). This chapter makes it plain that "after the death of Moses" (v. 1) the Lord remained faithful to his promises to give the land to Israel. This record divides into four parts: the call to Joshua (vv. 1–9), Joshua's orders to the people through their officers (vv. 10–11), Joshua's orders to two and one-half tribes in particular (vv. 12–15) and the people's response (vv. 16–18). The divine word that called and assured Joshua was recorded here to call and assure the original readers as they faced the reality of continuing holy war in their own day.

1:1–9 God's word to Joshua "after the death of Moses" (v. 1) is dominated by the promise of God first made to Abraham, namely, the giving of the land to the Israelites (Ge 12:7; 13:15). This promise is affirmed in verses 2–5, and the consequences for Joshua are spelled out in verses 6–9. The recollection of God's promises precedes the announcement of Joshua's responsibilities (see note on 23:3–8).

1:1 the servant of the LORD. This honorific title, which was also given to Abraham (Ge 26:24) and would later be applied to Joshua at the time of his death (24:29), suggests the special role of Moses in God's purposes. **Joshua.** Joshua's name was changed from Hoshea ("salvation") to Joshua ("the LORD is salvation") by Moses (Nu 13:16). Joshua functioned as Moses' assistant as early as Exodus 17. He was one of the men sent from Kadesh Barnea to explore the land (Nu 13:8), and he joined Caleb in calling on the Israelites to trust the Lord and not rebel against him (Nu 14:6–9). Therefore he, like Caleb (Dt 1:36), was exempted from the judgment that fell on the exodus generation because of its refusal to obey God at Kadesh Barnea. The book that bears Joshua's name presents him as the successor of Moses, as had been anticipated before Moses' death (Nu 27:12–23; Dt 3:28; 31:1–8). Joshua's role, however, continued to be subordinate to that of Moses. This was expressed in his submission to the Book of the Law (v. 8) and his obedience to the commands of Moses, which the book repeatedly emphasizes (e.g., v. 7; 8:31; 11:12,15; 14:2,5; 20:2). The transition to Joshua's leadership after the death of Moses marks a continuity in that the purpose of God for Israel persisted, but it also marks a discontinuity in that the era of Moses remained unique and a standard of comparison for future generations.

1:2 to cross the Jordan. The people were east of the river (Dt 1:1), which, with its deep valley, formed the formidable boundary between them and the land God had promised. See 3:15. **about to give.** The dominant theme of this book is God's gift of the land to the Israelites in faithfulness to his promise to Abraham (see vv. 3,6). Note the elaboration of this idea in 24:13, which echoes Deuteronomy 6:10–11. The land was an expression of divine mercy and grace. See note on 21:43.

1:3 I will give. Or "I have given," emphasizing the certainty of the promise. **your foot.** The second person pronoun is plural here and in verse 4, indicating that the promise was addressed to all Israel. See note on verses 12–15. **as I promised Moses.** The promise to Moses was a reaffirmation of the promise to Abraham. See verse 6 and Exodus 3:16–17.

1:4 The extent of the land promised here exceeds what was actually assimilated in the days of Joshua and corresponds to the dimensions of David's and Solomon's kingdoms (1Ki 4:21). For all the emphasis on fulfillment in Joshua (see note on 21:45), the book sees the promise as still pointing to the future (see notes on 13:1; 23:5,12–13).

1:5–9 The second person pronouns in verses 5–9 are singular (cf. v. 3), applying the promise of God to Joshua in particular as the successor of Moses and as the one who would lead Israel into the fulfillment of the promises. Joshua's speech to all Israel in chapter 23 (see note on 1:12–15) would later apply these ideas to the people in the light of the faithfulness of God that this book proclaims. See notes on 23:1–16.

1:5 I will be with you. See Genesis 26:3 and Exodus 3:12. The divine presence here is not God's general omnipresence but his special, accessible and powerful presence. Sometimes his presence was revealed to Joshua in the tabernacle and in the ministry of the priesthood. Some interpreters believe that God also sometimes appeared as the angel of the Lord (5:14). Compare the promise of Jesus in connection with the progress of the gospel in Matthew 28:20.

1:6 Be strong and courageous. In human terms, Joshua had every reason to be afraid. Yet the promise of God gave him the needed strength and courage for the warfare ahead (vv. 9,18; 8:1; 10:8,25; 11:6). **inherit.** This important term, as well as the cognate noun "inheritance," is often used in the book of Joshua for the receiving of the land. It reflected the fact that Israel's divine King had given the nation the land through a covenant. The major section of this book focuses much on inheritance (see 13:1—21:45). **forefathers.** That is, Abraham, Isaac and Jacob.

1:7 obey. The essential relationship between faith and obedience is illustrated here. Faith is confidence based on God's promise (v. 6), which issues in obedience (v. 7). In this respect, the process of salvation is not presented differently from one Testament to the other. **law.** The Hebrew word is broader in meaning than the English word *law* and could here be translated "teaching." The concept may include promises and commands, as well as records of God's activity, although here the emphasis is on the commands. **gave.** Literally, "commanded." **successful.** Success is here understood in terms of what God had promised. This success cannot be understood simply as a reward earned by obedience, because the promise preceded obedience. It would be more accurate to understand the promised success as that which could be forfeited by disobedience.

1:8 Book of the Law. See 8:34–35, 23:6, 24:26 and Deuteronomy 31:24–26. This book functioned as Scripture: the Word of God (promises, threats, commands, etc.) under which Joshua and the Israelites were to live. **mouth.** Compare Psalms 19:10, 119:103, Jeremiah 15:16 and Ezekiel 3:1–3. **meditate.** Compare Psalm 1:2. Obedience and success flow from meditation on the Book of the Law.

1:10–11 Joshua ordered his officers in response to the Lord's command.

1:11 Three days. Not all of the narrative in the book of Joshua is arranged in a strictly chronological manner. It is possible that the command of verse 11 was spoken after 3:1 but is recorded here to indicate Joshua's ongoing role as the one who would lead the people by the promise of God. Alternatively, "three days" may not be a precise expression but a colloquial way of saying "a few days."

1:12 [q]Nu 32:20-22
12But to the Reubenites, the Gadites and the half-tribe of Manasseh,[q] Joshua said,
13"Remember the command that Moses the servant of the LORD gave you: 'The LORD your
1:13 [r]Dt 3:18-20
God is giving you rest[r] and has granted you this land.' 14Your wives, your children and
your livestock may stay in the land that Moses gave you east of the Jordan, but all your
fighting men, fully armed, must cross over ahead of your brothers. You are to help your
brothers 15until the LORD gives them rest, as he has done for you, and until they too have
taken possession of the land that the LORD your God is giving them. After that, you may
1:15 [s]Jos 22:1-4
go back and occupy your own land, which Moses the servant of the LORD gave you east
of the Jordan toward the sunrise."[s]
16Then they answered Joshua, "Whatever you have commanded us we will do, and
1:17 [t]ver 5,9
wherever you send us we will go. 17Just as we fully obeyed Moses, so we will obey you.[t]
Only may the LORD your God be with you as he was with Moses. 18Whoever rebels
against your word and does not obey your words, whatever you may command them, will
be put to death. Only be strong and courageous!"

Rahab and the Spies

2:1 [u]Jas 2:25 [v]Nu 25:1; Jos 3:1 [w]Heb 11:31
2 Then Joshua son of Nun secretly sent two spies[u] from Shittim.[v] "Go, look over the
land," he said, "especially Jericho." So they went and entered the house of a prostitute[a] named Rahab[w] and stayed there.
2The king of Jericho was told, "Look! Some of the Israelites have come here tonight
to spy out the land." 3So the king of Jericho sent this message to Rahab: "Bring out the
men who came to you and entered your house, because they have come to spy out the
whole land."
2:4 [x]2Sa 17:19-20
4But the woman had taken the two men and hidden them.[x] She said, "Yes, the men
came to me, but I did not know where they had come from. 5At dusk, when it was time
to close the city gate, the men left. I don't know which way they went. Go after them
quickly. You may catch up with them." 6(But she had taken them up to the roof and hid-

[a] *1* Or possibly *an innkeeper*

take possession. The promise that God had given (v. 2) demanded the human act of taking possession, which depended on obedient faith. See note on 18:3.
1:12–15 Numbers 32 records the circumstances that led up to the Reubenites, Gadites and the half-tribe of Manasseh (see note on 13:8) receiving their portion of land east of the Jordan River. It was understood, however, that these tribes would be fully involved in Israel's taking of the promised land (Nu 32:16–32; Dt 3:18–20). Time and again this book stresses that all of the tribes were to act together and that the people would be held responsible as a whole; this would inspire national unity in future generations (see 1:12; 3:7,17; 4:14; 7:24–25; 8:15,21,24,33,35; 9:18; 10:15,24,29,31,34,36,38,43; 18:1; 22:12,16; 23:2; 24:1). There is a dramatic sequel in chapter 22. See notes at 12:1, 13:8–33 and 22:1–34. The New Testament similarly stresses the importance of the unity of the church.
1:13 rest. See also verse 15. The goal of God's gift of the land is often referred to as rest (e.g., 11:23; 21:44; 22:4; 23:1), a concept that links the land with God's purposes in the six days of ordering the world (Ge 2:2–3). For the New Testament extension of this idea, see Hebrews 3:7—4:11.
1:16–18 The people's obedient response to Joshua, and therefore to God, is echoed and elaborated at the end of the book (24:16–24). The essential connection between faith and obedience is implicit here. The obedience of the people was unambiguous evidence that they believed the promise. The necessary qualities for Joshua's leadership were that God be with him (v. 5) and that he be a man of faith (v. 6).
■ **2:1—8:29** *Contrasting Early Battles.* This first major section of the book describes the earliest battles Israel fought in the promised land, highlighting their contrasts. Israel first fought at Jericho (2:1—6:27) and later at Ai (7:1—8:29). The former battle is presented as an ideal event, with not a single shortcoming noted. The latter is presented as a series of errors and sins. The juxtaposition of these battles provided the original readers with positive and negative examples of how holy war was to be conducted in their own day.
■ **2:1—6:27** *The Positive Model of the Battle at Jericho.* The opening battle of Joshua's conquest is presented as a flawless encounter. Its idealization was important because the battle entailed some actions that would have raised questions in the minds of the original readers. These chapters divide into four main parts: the covenant established between the spies and Rahab (2:1–24), the consecration of Israel's army (3:1—5:12), the fall of Jericho (5:13—6:21) and the fulfillment of the covenant between the spies and Rahab (6:22–27).
■ **2:1–24** *The Covenant Made With Rahab.* Before the expected sequel to chapter 1 (namely, 3:1), there is the surprising story of the spies who returned to Joshua proclaiming the promise of God (v. 24; cf. 1:2–5). It is remarkable that this book, which describes in graphic detail the destruction of the Canaanites (chs. 6–12), gives such a prominent place to Rahab who, as a pagan prostitute, may have been regarded as a typical Canaanite (see Lev 18:24). It is from her lips that the spies heard testimony to the promise and the power of God (vv. 9–11), in the light of which she sought (v. 12) and found (v. 14) "kindness." Rahab was spared from the coming judgment (6:22–23) and found a place among the people of God (6:25). This focus on Rahab speaks of the mercy of God toward those outside the nation of Israel who repent. The chapter has a structure in which the central section is climactic: (*a*) the spies sent by Joshua (v. 1a); (*b*) the spies get into a dangerous situation (vv. 1b–7); (*c*) Rahab's faith (vv. 8–14); (*d*) the spies escape and return (vv. 15–23); (*e*) the spies report to Joshua (v. 24).
2:1 spies. The role of these spies is as unusual as the conquest that follows their report. Both were shaped by the promise of God. See their report in verse 24 (cf. Nu 13:17–20). **Shittim.** This site is a reminder of an earlier instance of Israelite prostitution (both physical and spiritual; Nu 25:1–3), which this book has not forgotten (22:17). **prostitute.** The narrative is silent about the reason for the spies' choice of a prostitute's house. If their intentions had been immoral, it is unlikely that this detail would have been mentioned in this otherwise idealized account. **Rahab.** She is remembered in the New Testament as an ancestress of Christ (Mt 1:5) and as an example both of faith (Heb 11:31) and of good works (Jas 2:25).
2:2–3 The skillfully narrated story creates a moment of tense crisis before informing the reader that the men have been hidden (v. 4).
2:2 king. At the time Canaan was made up of city-states, each with its own king.
2:4–5 I did not know. Compare "I know" in verse 9. This text neither justifies nor condemns Rahab's deception (see notes on Ex 1:15–21; 1Sa 16:2). Some interpreters admit that she violated God's commandment (Ex 20:16) but argue that God blessed her despite her lie. Others state that deception is a necessary tactic in war and that it was therefore not a violation of the commandment. James approves her action without explanation (Jas 2:25). The text's interest is in why she protected the spies (vv. 9–11).
2:6 But she had taken . . . and hidden them. Note the narrative style used here; information is often given out of chronological sequence.

den them under the stalks of flax[y] she had laid out on the roof.)[z] 7So the men set out in
pursuit of the spies on the road that leads to the fords of the Jordan, and as soon as the
pursuers had gone out, the gate was shut.
8Before the spies lay down for the night, she went up on the roof 9and said to them,
"I know that the LORD has given this land to you and that a great fear[a] of you has fallen
on us, so that all who live in this country are melting in fear because of you. 10We have
heard how the LORD dried up[b] the water of the Red Sea[a] for you when you came out of
Egypt,[c] and what you did to Sihon and Og,[d] the two kings of the Amorites east of the Jordan, whom you completely destroyed.[b] 11When we heard of it, our hearts melted and everyone's courage failed because of you,[e] for the LORD your God is God in heaven above
and on the earth[f] below. 12Now then, please swear to me by the LORD that you will show
kindness to my family, because I have shown kindness to you. Give me a sure sign[g] 13that
you will spare the lives of my father and mother, my brothers and sisters, and all who belong to them, and that you will save us from death."
14"Our lives for your lives!" the men assured her. "If you don't tell what we are doing,
we will treat you kindly and faithfully[h] when the LORD gives us the land."
15So she let them down by a rope through the window,[i] for the house she lived in was
part of the city wall. 16Now she had said to them, "Go to the hills so the pursuers will not
find you. Hide yourselves there three days[j] until they return, and then go on your way."[k]
17The men said to her, "This oath[l] you made us swear will not be binding on us 18un-
less, when we enter the land, you have tied this scarlet cord in the window through
which you let us down, and unless you have brought your father and mother, your broth
ers and all your family[m] into your house. 19If anyone goes outside your house into the
street, his blood will be on his own head;[n] we will not be responsible. As for anyone who
is in the house with you, his blood will be on our head[o] if a hand is laid on him. 20But if
you tell what we are doing, we will be released from the oath you made us swear."
21"Agreed," she replied. "Let it be as you say." So she sent them away and they de
parted. And she tied the scarlet cord in the window.
22When they left, they went into the hills and stayed there three days, until the pursuers had searched all along the road and returned without finding them. 23Then the two
men started back. They went down out of the hills, forded the river and came to Joshua
son of Nun and told him everything that had happened to them. 24They said to Joshua,
"The LORD has surely given the whole land into our hands;[p] all the people are melting
in fear because of us."

Crossing the Jordan

3 Early in the morning Joshua and all the Israelites set out from Shittim[q] and went to
the Jordan, where they camped before crossing over. 2After three days the officers

[a] *10* Hebrew *Yam Suph*; that is, Sea of Reeds [b] *10* The Hebrew term refers to the irrevocable giving over of things or persons to the LORD, often by totally destroying them.

2:6 [y]Jas 2:25 [z]Ex 1:17, 19; 2Sa 17:19
2:9 [a]Ge 35:5; Ex 23:27; Dt 2:25
2:10 [b]Ex 14:21 [c]Nu 23:22 [d]Nu 21:21, 24, 34-35
2:11 [e]Ex 15:14; Jos 5:1; 7:5; Ps 22:14; Isa 13:7 [f]Dt 4:39
2:12 [g]ver 18
2:14 [h]Jdg 1:24; Mt 5:7
2:15 [i]Ac 9:25
2:16 [j]Jas 2:25 [k]Heb 11:31
2:17 [l]Ge 24:8
2:18 [m]ver 12; Jos 6:23
2:19 [n]Eze 33:4 [o]Mt 27:25
2:24 [p]ver 9; Jos 6:2
3:1 [q]Jos 2:1

2:7 the gate was shut. The suspense intensifies, as there was no apparent way of escape for the spies (the information in v. 15 has not yet been given to the reader).
2:8–14 These verses are the center and focus of the chapter.
2:9 I know. Rahab already recognized what God wanted Israel to understand (3:10)—namely, that the promise of God was true. **a great fear.** This is the inevitable response of those who find themselves on the wrong side of what God has promised to do. Contrast 1:6. In holy war God sent a panic upon his enemies (5:1; 9:24; 10:2; Ex 15:14–16; Dt 2:25).
2:10 We have heard. The cause of Rahab's knowledge and of the Canaanites' terror was the news of what God had already done for Israel in faithfulness to his promises. See note on 9:3. **Sihon and Og.** See note on 12:2–5. **Amorites.** The term is flexible, sometimes referring to all the peoples of Canaan (e.g., 24:15), sometimes more specifically to those in the hill country (e.g., 5:1) and at other times more specifically still to those distinguished from the Jebusites, who also occupied the hill country (e.g., 3:10). **completely destroyed.** See notes on 6:17 and 18.
2:11 the LORD your God is God in heaven above and on the earth below. Rahab made the acknowledgment of God that was required of Israel (Dt 4:39).
2:12 kindness. The Hebrew word often refers to God's mercy to Israel in accordance with his promises. Rahab had shown mercy and now sought mercy. **sign.** Probably the oath itself (v. 14).
2:13 save us from death. The mercy sought presupposed the certainty of God's promise. It was no less than deliverance from the coming wrath (see 1Th 1:10).
2:14 when the LORD gives us the land. The certainty of the promise was again assumed.
2:15 she let them down . . . for the house . . . was part of the city wall. The suspense that was created in verses 2–3 and 7 is now resolved.
2:16–21 This conversation probably took place before verse 15, as the translation "had said" (v. 16) suggests.
2:18 scarlet cord. The cord is not mentioned in chapter 6. Although it is unlikely that symbolic significance should be attached to the color, some have compared it with the blood of the Passover lamb and of Christ.
2:21 So . . . they departed. This notice may pick up the narrative again from verse 15.
2:24 The LORD has surely given. The spies returned with the news that the promise of God was indeed certain (1:2)—news they have learned, ironically, from Rahab, the Jericho prostitute.
■ **3:1—5:12** *Consecration for Battle.* Joshua prepared the army of Israel for the first battle in the promised land by consecrating the fighting men to God. Before he entered the conquest, he called for the removal of idols, memorialized the events, circumcised his army and celebrated Passover. This devotion of the army divides into two sections: the crossing of the Jordan River and the memorial at Gilgal (3:1—4:24) and the rites of circumcision and Passover at Gilgal (5:1–12). These extensive preparations of Joshua's army demonstrated that all future soldiers were also to be consecrated before entering holy war.
■ **3:1—4:24** *Crossing the Jordan.* The crossing of the boundary (the Jordan River) between the desert and the promised land was

went throughout the camp,[r] 3giving orders to the people: "When you see the ark of the
covenant[s] of the LORD your God, and the priests,[t] who are Levites, carrying it, you are
to move out from your positions and follow it. 4Then you will know which way to go,
since you have never been this way before. But keep a distance of about a thousand
yards[a] between you and the ark; do not go near it."
5Joshua told the people, "Consecrate yourselves,[u] for tomorrow the LORD will do
amazing things among you."
6Joshua said to the priests, "Take up the ark of the covenant and pass on ahead of the
people." So they took it up and went ahead of them.
7And the LORD said to Joshua, "Today I will begin to exalt you[v] in the eyes of all Israel, so they may know that I am with you as I was with Moses.[w] 8Tell the priests[x] who carry the ark of the covenant: 'When you reach the edge of the Jordan's waters, go and stand
in the river.' "
9Joshua said to the Israelites, "Come here and listen to the words of the LORD your
God. 10This is how you will know that the living God[y] is among you and that he will certainly drive out before you the Canaanites, Hittites, Hivites, Perizzites, Girgashites, Amorites and Jebusites.[z] 11See, the ark of the covenant of the Lord of all the earth[a] will go
into the Jordan ahead of you. 12Now then, choose twelve men[b] from the tribes of Israel,
one from each tribe. 13And as soon as the priests who carry the ark of the LORD—the Lord
of all the earth[c]—set foot in the Jordan, its waters flowing downstream[d] will be cut off
and stand up in a heap.[e]"
14So when the people broke camp to cross the Jordan, the priests carrying the ark
of the covenant[f] went ahead[g] of them. 15Now the Jordan is at flood stage[h] all during
harvest. Yet as soon as the priests who carried the ark reached the Jordan and their
feet touched the water's edge, 16the water from upstream stopped flowing.[i] It piled up
in a heap a great distance away, at a town called Adam in the vicinity of Zarethan,[j]
while the water flowing down[k] to the Sea of the Arabah[l] (the Salt Sea[b][m]) was com-

[a] *4* Hebrew *about two thousand cubits* (about 900 meters) [b] *16* That is, the Dead Sea

3:2 [r]Jos 1:11
3:3 [s]Nu 10:33 [t]Dt 31:9
3:5 [u]Ex 19:10,14; Lev 20:7; Jos 7:13; 1Sa 16:5; Joel 2:16
3:7 [v]Jos 4:14; 1Ch 29:25 [w]Jos 1:5
3:8 [x]ver 3
3:10 [y]Dt 5:26; 1Sa 17:26,36; 2Ki 19:4,16; Hos 1:10; Mt 16:16; 1Th 1:9 [z]Ex 33:2; Dt 7:1
3:11 [a]ver 13; Job 41:11; Zec 6:5
3:12 [b]Jos 4:2,4
3:13 [c]ver 11 [d]ver 16 [e]Ex 15:8; Ps 78:13
3:14 [f]Ps 132:8 [g]Ac 7:44-45
3:15 [h]Jos 4:18; 1Ch 12:15
3:16 [i]Ps 66:6; 74:15 [j]1Ki 4:12; 7:46 [k]ver 13 [l]Dt 1:1 [m]Ge 14:3

an occasion characterized by "amazing things" (3:5), comparable in wonder and significance to the crossing of the Red Sea (4:23; cf. 3:7; 4:14). The great significance of these wonders is indicated in 4:24. They were to remain a testimony for all peoples and for all time that the hand of the Lord is powerful. The prominence of the ark of the covenant (3:3) speaks of the power of God in faithfulness to his promises. Chapter 3 traces the events basically in chronological order, while chapter 4 elaborates on several points: the memorial stones (vv. 1–9), crossing the river (vv. 10–14), exiting the river (vv. 15–18) and again the memorial stones (vv. 19–24).

3:1 crossing over. A key word in chapters 3–4 is the verb "to cross over." It occurs more than 20 times (variously rendered in the NIV) and usually refers to the crossing of the boundary into the promised land. See 1:2.

3:2 three days. See note on 1:11.

3:3 the ark of the covenant of the LORD your God. See Exodus 25:10–22 and Deuteronomy 10:5. The ark plays a prominent role in chapters 3–4, in chapter 6 and again in 8:30–35. It not only signified the presence of the Lord (Nu 10:33–36) but also contained within it a written record of his covenant with Israel, his promises and Israel's consequent obligations. See notes on 1:5 and 24:25. **priests, who are Levites.** See Deuteronomy 10:8.

3:4 Then you will know which way . . . But keep a distance . . . do not go near it. The order of phrases in the Hebrew is "But keep a distance of about a thousand yards between you and the ark; do not go near it so that you may know the way to go since you have never been this way before." This suggests that the required distance was necessary so that the ark would be visible to the maximum number of people, enhancing its symbolic function. See 4:11.

3:5 Consecrate yourselves. The verb means "to make holy" (see note on 5:15) and refers to physical actions, such as washing, which symbolized the sanctification of the people at particular times. Compare the same requirement when God came down to the people at Mount Sinai (Ex 19:10,14–15). **amazing things.** The Hebrew word, sometimes translated "wonders," is used of the plagues in Egypt (Ex 3:20; Jdg 6:13; Ps 78:11; Mic 7:15) and the conquest of Canaan (Ex 34:10; 1Ch 16:9–24; cf. Jer 21:2).

3:6 they took it up and went ahead. Apparently this refers to the "tomorrow" of verse 5.

3:7–13 The events of these verses probably preceded in time those of verse 6.

3:7 I will . . . exalt you. By repeating the wonders done through Moses at the Red Sea, the Lord validated Joshua's leadership. The God of Moses was the God of Joshua. See note on 4:14. **all Israel.** See note on 1:12–15. **so they may know.** God's acts are often said to have the purpose of bringing about knowledge (e.g., Ex 8:10; Dt 4:35; 2Ki 19:19; Isa 45:6). Such knowledge is never merely cognitive. It is, however, attainable through hearing the news of God's acts, as well as by seeing them (2:9–10; 4:24). Here the object of knowledge is the presence of God with Joshua (see note on 1:5; cf. Ex 14:31), which the people would know experientially in the faithfulness of God to his promises. See notes on verse 10 and on 4:24.

3:9 listen to the words of the LORD. This is the fundamental activity of the people of God. See 1:8 and 24:2.

3:10 This. The reference is probably to the whole miracle of the crossing, but attention is focused on the role of the ark (v. 11). **know.** That is, "know by experience" (see note on v. 7). What the people would know was the presence of God with Israel to bring his promise to certain fulfillment. Remarkably, Rahab had already attained this knowledge (2:9). **living God.** Israel's God is here opposed to and contrasted with lifeless idols (Dt 32:21). **Canaanites . . . Jebusites.** One of several ways of listing the inhabitants of Canaan (Ge 15:18–21; Dt 7:1). See note on 2:10.

3:11 the ark of the covenant of the Lord of all the earth. Literally, "the ark of the covenant, the LORD of all the earth." Not only the symbol of the covenant, but the Lord himself would go ahead of his people. The reminder that he is Lord of all the earth suggests that the events that were to follow would have a purpose that reached beyond Israel (4:24; cf. 2:11; Ge 12:3; Ex 19:5–6).

3:12 choose twelve men. The command of this verse anticipates the main subject of chapter 4 (see 4:2).

3:13 cut off and stand up in a heap. This language has similarities to Exodus 15:8 and Psalm 78:13, which describe the crossing of the Red Sea (4:23). The God of the exodus was the God of the conquest.

3:14 the people broke camp. This verse picks up the action from verse 6. **the ark of the covenant.** Literally, "the ark, the covenant." The ark was virtually identified with the covenant. See note on verse 3.

3:15 Now the Jordan . . . harvest. This vital piece of information was withheld by the narrator until the last possible moment, taking the reader by surprise. The crossing would be even more remarkable than verse 13 had indicated. Throughout verses 14–17, the crossing is, by implication, compared to the exodus (cf. v. 15 and Ex 15:8).

3:16–17 The "amazing things" (v. 5) are described at last.

pletely cut off. So the people crossed over opposite Jericho. 17The priests who carried
the ark of the covenant of the LORD stood firm on dry ground in the middle of the Jordan, while all Israel passed by until the whole nation had completed the crossing on
dry ground.[n]

4 When the whole nation had finished crossing the Jordan,[o] the LORD said to Joshua,
2"Choose twelve men[p] from among the people, one from each tribe, 3and tell them
to take up twelve stones[q] from the middle of the Jordan from right where the priests
stood and to carry them over with you and put them down at the place where you stay
tonight.[r]"
4So Joshua called together the twelve men he had appointed from the Israelites, one
from each tribe, 5and said to them, "Go over before the ark of the LORD your God into the
middle of the Jordan. Each of you is to take up a stone on his shoulder, according to the
number of the tribes of the Israelites, 6to serve as a sign among you. In the future, when
your children ask you, 'What do these stones mean?'[s] 7tell them that the flow of the Jordan was cut off[t] before the ark of the covenant of the LORD. When it crossed the Jordan,
the waters of the Jordan were cut off. These stones are to be a memorial[u] to the people
of Israel forever."
8So the Israelites did as Joshua commanded them. They took twelve stones from the
middle of the Jordan, according to the number of the tribes of the Israelites, as the LORD
had told Joshua;[v] and they carried them over with them to their camp, where they put
them down. 9Joshua set up the twelve stones[w] that had been[a] in the middle of the Jordan at the spot where the priests who carried the ark of the covenant had stood. And they
are there to this day.
10Now the priests who carried the ark remained standing in the middle of the Jordan
until everything the LORD had commanded Joshua was done by the people, just as Moses had directed Joshua. The people hurried over, 11and as soon as all of them had
crossed, the ark of the LORD and the priests came to the other side while the people
watched. 12The men of Reuben, Gad and the half-tribe of Manasseh crossed over, armed,
in front of the Israelites,[x] as Moses had directed them. 13About forty thousand armed for
battle crossed over before the LORD to the plains of Jericho for war.
14That day the LORD exalted[y] Joshua in the sight of all Israel; and they revered him all
the days of his life, just as they had revered Moses.
15Then the LORD said to Joshua, 16"Command the priests carrying the ark of the Testimony[z] to come up out of the Jordan."
17So Joshua commanded the priests, "Come up out of the Jordan."
18And the priests came up out of the river carrying the ark of the covenant of the LORD.
No sooner had they set their feet on the dry ground than the waters of the Jordan returned to their place and ran at flood stage[a] as before.
19On the tenth day of the first month the people went up from the Jordan and camped
at Gilgal[b] on the eastern border of Jericho. 20And Joshua set up at Gilgal the twelve

3:17 [n]Ex 14:22,29
4:1 [o]Dt 27:2
4:2 [p]Jos 3:12
4:3 [q]ver 20 [r]ver 19
4:6 [s]ver 21; Ex 12:26, 13:14
4:7 [t]Jos 3:13 [u]Ex 12:14
4:8 [v]ver 20
4:9 [w]Ge 28:18; Jos 24:26; 1Sa 7:12
4:12 [x]Nu 32:27
4:14 [y]Jos 3:7
4:16 [z]Ex 25:22
4:18 [a]Jos 3:15
4:19 [b]Jos 5:9

a 9 Or *Joshua also set up twelve stones*

3:17 the ark of the covenant. Still the center of attention, the ark transforms the account from a miracle story to a recounting of God's powerful faithfulness to his covenant promises. **all Israel.** See note on 1:12–15. **nation.** This word is not commonly applied to Israel; "people" is more usual, but see 4:1, 5:8 and 10:13. "Nation" is perhaps significantly reminiscent of Genesis 12:2 and Exodus 19:6.
4:2 twelve. All Israel was to be represented (see note on 1:12–15).
4:6 sign. The importance of the sign lay in what was signified. This testimony for future generations to God's faithfulness to his promises is the first of several memorials in Joshua (7:26; 8:29). See note on verse 9. **What do these stones mean?** Compare Exodus 12:26–27 and Deuteronomy 6:20–25. The stones would provide the occasion for the story to be told (v. 7).
4:7 the ark of the covenant of the LORD. As the ark was prominent in the account recorded in chapter 3, so it was to be central to the retelling of the story to future generations. See notes on 3:3 and 17. **memorial.** The purpose of the "sign" and the explanation of its meaning was that future generations might remember God's wonderful faithfulness to his promises. On the importance of such remembering for Israel, see Deuteronomy 8:1–20 (see also 1Co 11:25; 2Ti 2:8).
4:8 the Israelites. That is, the 12 representatives of all Israel (v. 4).
4:9 Joshua set up the twelve stones. The Hebrew of the verse could be taken to mean that Joshua set up another pile of stones in the middle of the Jordan; the NIV text note gives this understanding, which is also followed by the Septuagint (the Greek translation of the OT) and other ancient versions. **to this day.** That is, the day of the narrator. This expression occurs frequently in the book of Joshua (5:9; 6:25; 7:26; 8:28–29; 9:27; 10:27; 13:13; 14:14; 15:63; 16:10) and indicates that at least portions of the book were written by someone living near the events.
4:10–13 This portion of the chapter does not follow the chronology of events but elaborates on 3:17, with the usual emphasis on the role of the ark.
4:12 men of Reuben, Gad and . . . Manasseh. See 1:12–15.
4:13 About forty thousand. Some interpreters suggest that the word translated "thousand" may mean a military unit of unspecified size, a "contingent" (see note on 1Ch 12:23–37).
4:14 the LORD exalted Joshua . . . and they revered him. Joshua's exaltation was in fulfillment of 3:7. See Exodus 14:31. God's powerful faithfulness to his promises had the effect of exalting the one whose leadership was based on those promises. **all Israel.** See note on 1:12–15.
4:15–18 The conclusion of the miracle is described, with the focus still on the ark.
4:16 the ark of the Testimony. The Ten Commandments, contained within the ark, were known as "the Testimony" (Ex 25:16,21–22; 31:18; 32:15; 40:20) because they testified to the covenant between the Lord and Israel.
4:19 the tenth day of the first month. This was the day the Passover lamb was to be chosen (Ex 12:3), underlining the connection between the crossing and the exodus. See verse 23 and 5:10.

stones[c] they had taken out of the Jordan. 21 He said to the Israelites, "In the future when
your descendants ask their fathers, 'What do these stones mean?'[d] 22 tell them, 'Israel
crossed the Jordan on dry ground.'[e] 23 For the LORD your God dried up the Jordan before
you until you had crossed over. The LORD your God did to the Jordan just what he had
done to the Red Sea[a] when he dried it up before us until we had crossed over.[f] 24 He did
this so that all the peoples of the earth might know[g] that the hand of the LORD is powerful[h] and so that you might always fear the LORD your God.[i]"

Circumcision at Gilgal

5 Now when all the Amorite kings west of the Jordan and all the Canaanite kings
along the coast[j] heard how the LORD had dried up the Jordan before the Israelites
until we had crossed over, their hearts melted[k] and they no longer had the courage to
face the Israelites.
2 At that time the LORD said to Joshua, "Make flint knives[l] and circumcise the Israelites again." 3 So Joshua made flint knives and circumcised the Israelites at Gibeath Haaraloth.[b]
4 Now this is why he did so: All those who came out of Egypt—all the men of military
age—died in the desert on the way after leaving Egypt.[m] 5 All the people that came out
had been circumcised, but all the people born in the desert during the journey from
Egypt had not. 6 The Israelites had moved about in the desert forty years[n] until all the
men who were of military age when they left Egypt had died, since they had not obeyed
the LORD. For the LORD had sworn to them that they would not see the land that he had
solemnly promised their fathers to give us,[o] a land flowing with milk and honey.[p] 7 So he
raised up their sons in their place, and these were the ones Joshua circumcised. They
were still uncircumcised because they had not been circumcised on the way. 8 And after
the whole nation had been circumcised, they remained where they were in camp until
they were healed.[q]
9 Then the LORD said to Joshua, "Today I have rolled away the reproach of Egypt from
you." So the place has been called Gilgal[c] to this day.
10 On the evening of the fourteenth day of the month,[r] while camped at Gilgal on the
plains of Jericho, the Israelites celebrated the Passover. 11 The day after the Passover, that
very day, they ate some of the produce of the land:[s] unleavened bread and roasted

4:20 [c]ver 3,8 **4:21** [d]ver 6 **4:22** [e]Jos 3:17 **4:23** [f]Ex 14:21 **4:24** [g]1Ki 8:42-43; 2Ki 19:19; Ps 106:8; Jer 10:7 [h]Ex 15:16; 1Ch 29:12; Ps 89:13 [i]Ex 14:31 **5:1** [j]Nu 13:29 [k]Jos 2:9-11 **5:2** [l]Ex 4:25 **5:4** [m]Dt 2:14 **5:6** [n]Dt 2:7 [o]Nu 14:23, 29-35; Dt 2:14 [p]Ex 3:8 **5:8** [q]Ge 34:25 **5:10** [r]Ex 12:6 **5:11** [s]Nu 15:19

[a] 23 Hebrew *Yam Suph*; that is, Sea of Reeds [b] 3 *Gibeath Haaraloth* means *hill of foreskins.* [c] 9 *Gilgal* sounds like the Hebrew for *roll.*

4:22 tell. The Hebrew verb means "cause to know." See notes on 3:7 and 10.

4:23–24 If the quotation mark at the end of verse 22 is placed at the end of verse 24, the pronoun "you" in verses 23–24 identifies the later generations with the earlier great acts of God, as Moses did (Dt 4:9–24; 5:2–5) and as Joshua would later do (24:5–10; see note on 24:7). This way of understanding later believers' participation in the redemptive events of the past is also found in the New Testament concept of dying and rising "with" Christ (e.g., Ro 6:8; Gal 2:20; Eph 2:6; Col 3:1).

4:24 all the peoples of the earth. The wonders of chapters 3–4 would have effects far beyond not only the immediate generation, but also the Israelite people in the longer term (2:10; 5:1). Compare Genesis 12:3. The wonderful works of God in the Bible were to affect those who heard about them as powerfully as they affected those who saw them (see Ex 10:2; Jn 20:30–31). See notes on 2:9 and 10. The Hebrew word for "earth" can also mean "land" (e.g., 5:6), but in the light of 3:11 and 13 the meaning here should not be so restricted. **know.** The knowledge of God and his purposes had previously been the objective of these wonders (see notes on 3:7,10; 4:22). This goal was now shown to apply to all peoples. This knowledge did not necessarily imply salvation (Ex 14:18). **fear the LORD.** A common Old Testament expression for true faith (e.g., Ps 128:1). See note on 24:14.

■**5:1–12** *Circumcision and Passover at Gilgal.* This highly significant moment for the Israelites (v. 9)—with the desert behind them and the new life in the land of promise before them (vv. 11–12)—was marked by two symbolic actions: circumcision (vv. 2–8) and the Passover (v. 10). Circumcision was the sign of the covenant with Abraham (see notes on Ge 17:9–14) and was required for participation in the Passover (Ex 12:48). Circumcision marked the people as the children of Abraham, while the Passover celebrated their redemption from Egypt. Both the promise to Abraham and the redemption from Egypt looked forward to this day (Ge 17:8; Ex 3:8).

5:1 when all the . . . kings . . . heard . . . their hearts melted. This verse may be the conclusion to chapters 3–4 and certainly illustrates 4:24. See note on 2:9. **Amorite.** See note on 2:10. **heard.** See note on 9:3.

5:2–9 The structure is: (*a*) word from God (v. 2); (*b*) circumcision performed (v. 3); (*c*) explanation (vv. 4–7); (*d*) circumcision complete (v. 8); (*e*) word from God (v. 9).

5:2 circumcise . . . again. This injunction is to be understood in the light of verse 5. Joshua's faith in the word of God was evident in that he circumcised his fighting men just before battle.

5:4–7 This is a detailed explanation of the necessity for this circumcision, with an obvious implied lesson. This circumcision was needed for two reasons: (1) The circumcised generation that came out of Egypt had fallen under God's judgment, and (2) the second generation had not yet been circumcised. Thus the new generation had to be separated from the world and joined to the Lord by this covenant sign. Physical circumcision was an outward covenant sign indicating the necessity of an inward circumcision of the heart (see notes at Ge 17; Dt 10:16; 30:6).

5:6 they had not obeyed the LORD. This is the simplest description of the behavior that brought judgment. The reference is to Numbers 14 (see also Dt 1:32,43). **the LORD had sworn.** The promise of God could apply negatively.

5:9 Today I have rolled away the reproach of Egypt. These words indicate the great significance of this moment. The redemption from Egypt came to completion only with the entry into the promised land. See the promise of the exodus and its goal (Ex 3:8). Had that goal not been reached, the reproach, or scorn, of Egypt would have remained (see, e.g., Dt 9:28). **to this day.** See note on 4:9.

5:10 Passover. For details, see Exodus 12.

5:11–12 they ate some of the produce of the land . . . The manna stopped. This was another indication that a new era had begun and that the first major section of the book was concluded. On manna and its significance, see Exodus 16 and Deuteronomy 8:3.

grain.[t] 12 The manna stopped the day after[a] they ate this food from the land; there was
no longer any manna for the Israelites, but that year they ate of the produce of Canaan.[u]

The Fall of Jericho

13 Now when Joshua was near Jericho, he looked up and saw a man[v] standing in front
of him with a drawn sword[w] in his hand. Joshua went up to him and asked, "Are you for
us or for our enemies?"
14 "Neither," he replied, "but as commander of the army of the LORD I have now
come." Then Joshua fell facedown[x] to the ground in reverence, and asked him, "What
message does my Lord[b] have for his servant?"
15 The commander of the LORD's army replied, "Take off your sandals, for the place
where you are standing is holy."[y] And Joshua did so.

6 Now Jericho[z] was tightly shut up because of the Israelites. No one went out and no
one came in.
2 Then the LORD said to Joshua, "See, I have delivered[a] Jericho into your hands, along
with its king and its fighting men. 3 March around the city once with all the armed men.
Do this for six days. 4 Have seven priests carry trumpets of rams' horns in front of the ark.
On the seventh day, march around the city seven times, with the priests blowing the
trumpets.[b] 5 When you hear them sound a long blast[c] on the trumpets, have all the people give a loud shout;[d] then the wall of the city will collapse and the people will go up,
every man straight in."
6 So Joshua son of Nun called the priests and said to them, "Take up the ark of the covenant of the LORD and have seven priests carry trumpets in front of it." 7 And he ordered
the people, "Advance[e]! March around the city, with the armed guard going ahead of the
ark of the LORD."
8 When Joshua had spoken to the people, the seven priests carrying the seven trumpets before the LORD went forward, blowing their trumpets, and the ark of the LORD's cov-

5:11 [t]Lev 23:14
5:12 [u]Ex 16:35
5:13 [v]Ge 18:2; 32:24 [w]Nu 22:23
5:14 [x]Ge 17:3
5:15 [y]Ex 3:5; Ac 7:33
6:1 [z]Jos 24:11
6:2 [a]Dt 7:24; Jos 2:9, 24; 8:1
6:4 [b]Lev 25:9; Nu 10:8
6:5 [c]Ex 19:13 [d]ver 20; 1Sa 4:5; Ps 42:4; Isa 42:13
6:7 [e]Ex 14:15

[a] *12* Or *the day* [b] *14* Or *lord*

5:13—6:21 *The Fall of Jericho.* With the army of Israel consecrated to the Lord, God's people were ready to complete the first victory at Jericho. The destruction that appears here and elsewhere was the true and just judgment of God on flagrant sinners who lived in the holiest place on the earth (Ge 15:16; cf. Lev 18:24–27; Dt 9:4–5). God used the destruction to fulfill his gracious promises to Israel. Because the world is full of evil people opposed to the ways of God, salvation cannot take place in its fullness without judgment (see 14:13–14; Rev 19:1–2). These accounts of destruction therefore testify to God's faithfulness to his promises and prefigure his future judgment on those who reject his grace when Christ returns to make a new and holy creation (Mt 25:46; Heb 9:27; 10:26–31).
5:13–15 The account of the conquest begins with this appearance of the "commander of the army of the LORD" (v. 14), which indicates (1) God's sovereign freedom (v. 14a); (2) that the ensuing action was ultimately God's, not Joshua's (v. 14b); and (3) that all of this was a piece of that which had begun with Moses at the burning bush (v. 15; cf. Ex 3:5).
5:14 Neither. This surprising answer is powerfully illustrated in the subsequent chapters in the examples of Rahab (6:25) and Achan (ch. 7). God was bound neither to destroy all Canaanites nor to deliver all Israelites. He could not be categorized in the simple terms of Joshua's question in verse 13. See note on 6:17–18. **commander of the army of the LORD.** The commander was apparently an angel. Some interpreters have suggested the he was an appearance of the pre-incarnate Son of God (see note on 1:5). The divine warrior and his army were prepared for war.
5:15 Take off . . . holy. These are the precise words of Exodus 3:5. The continuity between what began with Moses and what would ensue under Joshua is thus indicated: Joshua was in effect a new Moses, and the land of Canaan was as holy as Mount Sinai. Holiness is fundamentally a quality of God. The Bible describes people (see note on 3:5) or things (as here) as "holy" when they belong to God in some special way.
6:1–27 The destruction of the Canaanites, no less than the crossing of the Jordan, was the powerful work of God in faithfulness to the covenant. Compare the role of the ark of the covenant in chapters 3–4 and 6 (see notes on 3:3,11,14,17; 4:16; 6:4). The fearful judgment of God in securing the promised deliverance of his people is an important Biblical theme (e.g., Ex 14:13–14; Rev 19:1–2). Furthermore, that the grace of God was not restricted to Israel (Ge 12:3) is evidenced by the example of Rahab and her household (v. 25). God was not simply anti-Canaanite (cf. "neither" in 5:14).
6:1 Jericho. Its name probably means "Moon City," a center for moon worship. **was tightly shut up.** All visible evidence indicated the impenetrability of Jericho, which provides for the paradox of "see" in verse 2.
6:2 the LORD. Although this is sometimes taken to refer to the figure in 5:13–15, the latter verses are more likely a separate episode that introduced the whole of the conquest. **See, I have delivered.** This is a striking paradox since all that could be seen were the shut gates of Jericho (v. 1). The promise of God created possibilities not inherent in the situation. A similar contrast between present circumstances and what God has promised is frequently found in the Bible and in the experience of believers (see, e.g., Ge 15:2–5; Isa 65:17; Ro 8:18).
6:3–4 From the additional details in verses 8–9, the procession was to consist of an "armed guard" (v. 9), seven priests blowing their trumpets, the ark of the covenant (carried by priests) and finally a "rear guard" (v. 9). **six days . . . the seventh day.** The numbers suggest a parallel to the work of creation (underlined by the many sevens in this chapter). Just as the work of creation reached its goal in the seventh day (Ge 2:1–3), so the work of redemption from Egypt reached its goal in the taking of possession of the promised land. Note that Sabbath rest is connected to both creation and redemption in Exodus 20:8–11 and Deuteronomy 5:12–15, respectively. The parallel between creation and redemption is suggested elsewhere in Joshua by the term "rest" (see note on 1:13) and is related to the ultimate goal of God's promises in Hebrews 3:7—4:11.
6:4 the ark. The ark is given its fuller title, and therefore its fuller significance, in verse 6. See note on 3:3. The procession, with the ark as its central feature, symbolically applied the covenant promises of God to Jericho. For Jericho the covenant promises would mean judgment. The parallel between the role of the ark in the crossing of the Jordan (chs. 3–4) and the conquest of Canaan (typified here in the fall of Jericho) is illuminated by Exodus 15:1–18, where the crossing of the Red Sea and the conquest are described in similar terms. All of these events were powerful acts of God in accordance with his covenant, directed to the goal of bringing his people to their promised rest. **trumpets.** Military instruments.
6:5 straight in. The complete collapse of the wall would allow access from every direction. Compare verse 1.
6:6 the ark of the covenant of the LORD. The ark is mentioned first to indicate its preeminent role.
6:8 before the LORD. As in 3:11 (see its note), the presence of the Lord's covenant (the ark) was identified with the presence of the Lord himself. See note on 1:5.

enant followed them. 9The armed guard marched ahead of the priests who blew the
trumpets, and the rear guard[f] followed the ark. All this time the trumpets were sounding. 10But Joshua had commanded the people, "Do not give a war cry, do not raise your
voices, do not say a word until the day I tell you to shout. Then shout![g]" 11So he had the
ark of the LORD carried around the city, circling it once. Then the people returned to
camp and spent the night there.

12Joshua got up early the next morning and the priests took up the ark of the LORD. 13The
seven priests carrying the seven trumpets went forward, marching before the ark of the
LORD and blowing the trumpets. The armed men went ahead of them and the rear guard
followed the ark of the LORD, while the trumpets kept sounding. 14So on the second day they
marched around the city once and returned to the camp. They did this for six days.

15On the seventh day, they got up at daybreak and marched around the city seven
times in the same manner, except that on that day they circled the city seven times.[h]
16The seventh time around, when the priests sounded the trumpet blast, Joshua commanded the people, "Shout! For the LORD has given you the city! 17The city and all that
is in it are to be devoted[a][i] to the LORD. Only Rahab the prostitute[b] and all who are with
her in her house shall be spared, because she hid[j] the spies we sent. 18But keep away
from the devoted things,[k] so that you will not bring about your own destruction by taking any of them. Otherwise you will make the camp of Israel liable to destruction[l] and
bring trouble[m] on it. 19All the silver and gold and the articles of bronze and iron[n] are sacred to the LORD and must go into his treasury."

20When the trumpets sounded,[o] the people shouted, and at the sound of the trumpet,
when the people gave a loud shout,[p] the wall collapsed; so every man charged straight in,
and they took the city.[q] 21They devoted the city to the LORD and destroyed[r] with the sword
every living thing in it—men and women, young and old, cattle, sheep and donkeys.

22Joshua said to the two men who had spied out the land, "Go into the prostitute's
house and bring her out and all who belong to her, in accordance with your oath to
her.[s]" 23So the young men who had done the spying went in and brought out Rahab, her
father and mother and brothers and all who belonged to her.[t] They brought out her entire family and put them in a place outside the camp of Israel.

24Then they burned the whole city and everything in it, but they put the silver and gold
and the articles of bronze and iron[u] into the treasury of the LORD's house. 25But Joshua
spared Rahab the prostitute,[v] with her family and all who belonged to her, because she hid
the men Joshua had sent as spies to Jericho[w]—and she lives among the Israelites to this day.

26At that time Joshua pronounced this solemn oath: "Cursed before the LORD is the
man who undertakes to rebuild this city, Jericho:

"At the cost of his firstborn son
will he lay its foundations;
at the cost of his youngest
will he set up its gates."[x]

27So the LORD was with Joshua,[y] and his fame spread[z] throughout the land.

6:9 [f]ver 13; Isa 52:12
6:10 [g]ver 20
6:15 [h]1Ki 18:44
6:17 [i]Lev 27:28; Dt 20:17 [j]Jos 2:4
6:18 [k]Jos 7:1 [l]Jos 7:12 [m]Jos 7:25,26
6:19 [n]ver 24; Nu 31:22
6:20 [o]Jdg 6:34; Jer 4:21; Am 2:2 [p]ver 5 [q]Heb 11:30
6:21 [r]Dt 20:16
6:22 [s]Jos 2:14; Heb 11:31
6:23 [t]Jos 2:13
6:24 [u]ver 19
6:25 [v]Heb 11:31 [w]Jos 2:6
6:26 [x]1Ki 16:34
6:27 [y]Ge 39:2; Jos 1:5 [z]Jos 9:1

[a] *17* The Hebrew term refers to the irrevocable giving over of things or persons to the LORD, often by totally destroying them; also in verses 18 and 21. [b] *17* Or possibly *innkeeper*; also in verses 22 and 25

6:11 he had the ark . . . carried around the city. The whole procession could be summed up with reference to the ark only. **returned to camp.** At Gilgal (5:10).
6:15–19 The description of the seventh day is expanded with a report of Joshua's speech. In accordance with the narrative style noted elsewhere (see 1:11; 2:6,16–21; 3:7–13; 4:10–13), the words of verses 17–19 may have been spoken earlier, but they are recorded here for dramatic effect.
6:17–18 These verses provide a concise expression of the principles that underlie the narratives of chapters 6–7 and are a vivid elaboration of the meaning of "neither" in 5:14. Jericho would fall under God's judgment, but Rahab would find mercy, and the Israelites would face judgment if they were disobedient.
6:17 devoted. See NIV text note. The same Hebrew word is translated "completely destroyed" in 2:10. It was the Lord's victory, so the booty belonged to him. The meaning is seen in verse 21. The term conveys the horrifying reality of the judgment that was coming not only on Jericho, but on the whole of Canaan (11:11–12,14,20; Lev 27:28–29; Dt 13:16; 20:10–18). **Only Rahab . . . and all who are with her.** Even here judgment did not exclude grace. The mercy sought in 2:12 was to be given. **in her house.** See note on 2:19.
6:18 devoted things . . . them . . . liable to destruction. The same Hebrew term (translated "devoted" in v. 17) occurs three times here, indicating that Israel could fall under the same judgment as the Canaanites. Chapter 7 demonstrates the reality of this statement.
6:19 sacred. Or "holy." See note on 5:15.
6:20–21 The fall of Jericho is briefly described. Further details may be deduced from verse 24, 8:2, 10:1 and 24:11.
■ **6:22–27** *The Covenant With Rahab Fulfilled.* These verses are the sequel to chapter 2. They indicate that the interaction of the spies with Rahab was good in the eyes of God.
6:23 her entire family. The mercy given to Rahab was extended to "all who belonged to her." Perhaps they had already come to share Rahab's faith. Certainly the implication of verse 25 is that they came to be included among the covenant people as they lived permanently "among the Israelites." **outside the camp.** The phrase describes a temporary state of affairs (v. 25) due to ceremonial uncleanness (e.g., Lev 13:46).
6:24 the LORD's house. See note on 9:23.
6:25 among the Israelites. Rahab was included in the people of God (see Mt 1:5; Heb 11:31; Jas 2:25). **to this day.** See note on 4:9.
6:26 Cursed . . . who undertakes to rebuild. Jericho was to remain under God's curse, presumably as a sign of the judgment of

Achan's Sin

7 But the Israelites acted unfaithfully in regard to the devoted things[a]; [a] Achan son of
Carmi, the son of Zimri,[b] the son of Zerah,[b] of the tribe of Judah, took some of them.
So the LORD's anger burned against Israel.
2Now Joshua sent men from Jericho to Ai, which is near Beth Aven[c] to the east of
Bethel, and told them, "Go up and spy out the region." So the men went up and spied
out Ai.
3When they returned to Joshua, they said, "Not all the people will have to go up
against Ai. Send two or three thousand men to take it and do not weary all the people,
for only a few men are there." 4So about three thousand men went up; but they were
routed by the men of Ai,[d] 5who killed about thirty-six of them. They chased the Israelites from the city gate as far as the stone quarries[c] and struck them down on the slopes.
At this the hearts of the people melted[e] and became like water.
6Then Joshua tore his clothes[f] and fell facedown to the ground before the ark of the
LORD, remaining there till evening. The elders of Israel did the same, and sprinkled dust[g]
on their heads. 7And Joshua said, "Ah, Sovereign LORD, why did you ever bring this people across the Jordan to deliver us into the hands of the Amorites to destroy us?[h] If only
we had been content to stay on the other side of the Jordan! 8O Lord, what can I say, now
that Israel has been routed by its enemies? 9The Canaanites and the other people of the
country will hear about this and they will surround us and wipe out our name from the
earth.[i] What then will you do for your own great name?"
10The LORD said to Joshua, "Stand up! What are you doing down on your face? 11Is-
rael has sinned; they have violated my covenant,[j] which I commanded them to keep.
They have taken some of the devoted things; they have stolen, they have lied,[k] they have
put them with their own possessions. 12That is why the Israelites cannot stand against
their enemies;[l] they turn their backs and run because they have been made liable to destruction.[m] I will not be with you anymore unless you destroy whatever among you is devoted to destruction.
13"Go, consecrate the people. Tell them, 'Consecrate yourselves[n] in preparation for

7:1 [a]Jos 6:18 [b]Jos 22:20
7:2 [c]Jos 18:12; 1Sa 13:5; 14:23
7:4 [d]Lev 26:17; Dt 28:25
7:5 [e]Lev 26:36; Jos 2:9, 11; Eze 21:7; Na 2:10
7:6 [f]Ge 37:29 [g]1Sa 4:12; 2Sa 13:19; Ne 9:1; Job 2:12; La 2:10; Rev 18:19
7:7 [h]Ex 5:22
7:9 [i]Ex 32:12; Dt 9:28
7:11 [j]Jos 6:17-19 [k]Ac 5:1-2
7:12 [l]Nu 14:45; Jdg 2:14 [m]Jos 6:18
7:13 [n]Jos 3:5; 6:18

a *1* The Hebrew term refers to the irrevocable giving over of things or persons to the LORD, often by totally destroying them; also in verses 11, 12, 13 and 15. b *1* See Septuagint and 1 Chron. 2:6; Hebrew *Zabdi*; also in verses 17 and 18. c *5* Or *as far as Shebarim*

God that had fallen on the Canaanites and that could fall on Israel (see 1Ki 16:34).

6:27 the LORD was with Joshua. See note on 4:14.

■ **7:1—8:29** *The Negative Model of the Battle at Ai.* As the account of Jericho was described as an exemplary holy-war battle, this battle is depicted as a fiasco. Like the previous chapter, chapter 7 illustrates the meaning of "neither" in 5:14 (see note on 6:17–18). The incident and its implications for Israel are recalled in 22:18–20. These chapters divide into two parts: Israel's failures (7:1–26) and the eventual victory over Ai (8:1–29).

■ **7:1–26** *Israel's Failures.* In striking contrast to the battle at Jericho, the Israelites violated the Law of Moses for the conquest of Ai—and consequently suffered defeat.

7:1 the Israelites. Although the offense was committed by one man, all Israel was involved and affected (see note on 1:12–15). See verse 11 and 22:18. The facts stated in verse 1 only gradually became known to the Israelites. **devoted things.** See 6:18, as well as the note on 6:17. **the LORD's anger.** The anger (wrath) of God is his personal, righteous hostility to actual evil. Unlike ancient pagan conceptions of divine wrath, God's wrath in the Bible is never arbitrary or capricious.

7:2–5 In contrast to the situation with respect to the spies in chapter 2 and the conquest of Jericho in chapter 6, Israel was now (unknowingly) under God's anger, and the outcome therefore would be different.

7:2 from Jericho to Ai. The movement was westward and up into the central hill country. **Beth Aven.** The name means "house of nothingness" or "house of wickedness." It may have been used disparagingly for Bethel (as in Hos 4:15; 10:5). **spy out.** Compare 2:1.

7:3 Not all the people will have to go up. Contrast the report of the spies in 2:24. In this battle, the divine design of all Israel fighting together was set aside out of false confidence in an easy victory (see notes on 1:12–15; 8:2).

7:5 thirty-six. The number of casualties was not great by normal standards, underlining that the fear and dismay of the people was related to the Lord's anger rather than simply to the human tragedy of the defeat. **the hearts of the people melted.** Disobedience in Israel had brought about a great reversal. The Israelites now found themselves in the situation of the Canaanites in 2:11 and 5:1.

7:6 tore his clothes . . . sprinkled dust on their heads. Customary expressions of grief (see Job 1:20; 2:12). **the ark of the LORD.** The cause of the grief was the apparent failure of the covenant promises, the symbol of which was the ark. See notes on 3:3 and 17, 4:16 and 6:4. Joshua's prayer (vv. 7–9) would appeal to those promises. See note on 10:6.

7:7–9 Joshua prayed for Israel, as Moses had done in similar circumstances (see Nu 14:13–19).

7:7 why. This is a recurring question on the lips of those who find their experience at odds with their understanding of the promises of God. It can be a rebellious question (as in Nu 14:3), but it can also express faith that is perplexed by circumstances (as in Ps 22:1). **Amorites.** See note on 2:10.

7:9 will hear. See note on 9:3. **our name.** The promise to Abraham included a "great name" (Ge 12:2). Joshua's prayer was based on the promises of God. **your own great name?** God's own name (reputation) was at stake (Ex 32:12; Nu 14:13–16; Eze 36:16–23).

7:11 Israel. The corporate unity of Israel is stressed throughout the chapter: The sin of one man (v. 15) brought guilt on the community of which he was a part. Compare 22:18. **violated my covenant.** This is a further indication of the nature of the sin. The concept of God's covenant includes his commitment to his promises and the consequent obligations on the recipients of those promises. See note on 3:3. It was God's covenant because he had set its terms. **devoted things.** See 6:18 and note on 6:17.

7:12 because they have been made liable to destruction. The cause of Israel's defeat at Ai was not a failure of God's promises (see note on v. 6) but disobedience that had made Israel like the Canaanites; that is, "devoted to destruction." **I will not be with you anymore.** This terrible reversal of 1:5 brings the first half of chapter 7 to a climax. The second half elaborates the words "unless you destroy whatever among you is devoted to destruction."

7:13 consecrate. See note on 3:5. In contrast to chapter 3, this refers to preparation to meet God's judgment.

tomorrow; for this is what the LORD, the God of Israel, says: That which is devoted is
7:14 among you, O Israel. You cannot stand against your enemies until you remove it.
[o]Pr 16:33 14" 'In the morning, present yourselves tribe by tribe. The tribe that the LORD takes[o]
shall come forward clan by clan; the clan that the LORD takes shall come forward family by family; and the family that the LORD takes shall come forward man by man. 15He
7:15 who is caught with the devoted things shall be destroyed by fire, along with all that be-
[p]1Sa 14:39 [q]ver 11 [r]Ge 34:7 longs to him.[p] He has violated the covenant[q] of the LORD and has done a disgraceful
thing in Israel!' "[r]
7:17 16Early the next morning Joshua had Israel come forward by tribes, and Judah was
[s]Nu 26:20 taken. 17The clans of Judah came forward, and he took the Zerahites.[s] He had the clan
of the Zerahites come forward by families, and Zimri was taken. 18Joshua had his family come forward man by man, and Achan son of Carmi, the son of Zimri, the son of Ze-
7:19 rah, of the tribe of Judah, was taken.
[t]1Sa 6:5; Jer 13:16; 19Then Joshua said to Achan, "My son, give glory[t] to the LORD,[a] the God of Israel, and
Jn 9:24* [u]1Sa 14:43 give him the praise.[b] Tell[u] me what you have done; do not hide it from me."
20Achan replied, "It is true! I have sinned against the LORD, the God of Israel. This is
7:21 what I have done: 21When I saw in the plunder a beautiful robe from Babylonia,[c] two
[v]Dt 7:25; Eph 5:5; hundred shekels[d] of silver and a wedge of gold weighing fifty shekels,[e] I coveted[v] them
1Ti 6:10 and took them. They are hidden in the ground inside my tent, with the silver underneath."
22So Joshua sent messengers, and they ran to the tent, and there it was, hidden in his
tent, with the silver underneath. 23They took the things from the tent, brought them to
Joshua and all the Israelites and spread them out before the LORD.
24Then Joshua, together with all Israel, took Achan son of Zerah, the silver, the robe,
7:24 the gold wedge, his sons and daughters, his cattle, donkeys and sheep, his tent and all
[w]ver 26; Jos 15:7 that he had, to the Valley of Achor.[w] 25Joshua said, "Why have you brought this trouble[x]
7:25 on us? The LORD will bring trouble on you today."
[x]Jos 6:18 [y]Dt 17:5 Then all Israel stoned him,[y] and after they had stoned the rest, they burned them.
7:26 26Over Achan they heaped up a large pile of rocks, which remains to this day. Then the
[z]Nu 25:4; Dt 13:17 LORD turned from his fierce anger.[z] Therefore that place has been called the Valley of
[a]ver 24; Isa 65:10; Hos 2:15 Achor[f][a] ever since.

Ai Destroyed

8:1
[b]Dt 31:6 [c]Dt 1:21; 8 Then the LORD said to Joshua, "Do not be afraid;[b] do not be discouraged.[c] Take the
7:18; Jos 1:9 whole army[d] with you, and go up and attack Ai. For I have delivered[e] into your
[d]Jos 10:7 [e]Jos 6:2 hands the king of Ai, his people, his city and his land. 2You shall do to Ai and its king as
8:2 you did to Jericho and its king, except that you may carry off their plunder and livestock
[f]ver 27; Dt 20:14 for yourselves.[f] Set an ambush behind the city."
3So Joshua and the whole army moved out to attack Ai. He chose thirty thousand of
his best fighting men and sent them out at night 4with these orders: "Listen carefully. You

[a] *19* A solemn charge to tell the truth [b] *19* Or *and confess to him* [c] *21* Hebrew *Shinar* [d] *21* That is, about 5 pounds (about 2.3 kilograms) [e] *21* That is, about 1 1/4 pounds (about 0.6 kilogram) [f] *26* *Achor* means *trouble.*

7:14 that the LORD takes. The actual procedure may have been by the Urim and Thummim (see note on Ex 28:30).
7:15 a disgraceful thing in Israel. Such an act was contrary to the nature of Israel as the covenant people, and it was therefore an act of folly. Elsewhere this expression is used of sexual perversions prohibited in Israel (Ge 34:7; Dt 22:21; Jdg 20:6,10; 2Sa 13:12; Jer 29:23).
7:19 give glory to the LORD . . . give him the praise. The expressions are virtually synonymous. See NIV text notes. The praise of God means here the acknowledgment of God. Achan's sin and its concealment had been a failure to accept God's rule, whereas confession of sin would have been an open acknowledgment of God (v. 20). See *WCF* 15.6; *WLC* 144.
7:21 saw . . . coveted . . . took. There may be an allusion here to Genesis 3:6, where these three verbs occur in the same order (NIV, "saw . . . desirable . . . took"). The pattern of the garden of Eden was repeated in the promised land: No sooner was the gift of God given than the recipients found desirable, and appropriated, that which was forbidden. See *WLC* 151.
7:23 before the LORD. Presumably, before the ark. See note on 6:8.
7:24 all Israel. Israel had been implicated in Achan's sin (v. 11) but now purged herself (see note on 1:12–15). **all that he had.** Just as mercy extended from Rahab to her family (6:23), the punishment of Achan reached his family as well. Possibly his family members were implicated in his crime (Dt 24:16). **Valley of Achor.** See NIV text note on verse 26.
7:26 to this day . . . ever since. These phrases translate the same phrase in Hebrew. See note on 4:9. **turned from his fierce anger.** God's wrath, being righteous, ceases when sin has been dealt with. This is fundamental to the New Testament teaching about the death of Christ as an atoning, or propitiatory, sacrifice (see, e.g., Ro 3:25–26).
■ **8:1–29** *The Fall of Ai.* Although Israel had suffered for sinning against the Lord in this holy war, God was merciful to his people and led them to ultimate victory over the city of Ai.
8:1 Do not be afraid; do not be discouraged. Compare 7:5. This call to faith (see 1:6,7,9) based on the promises of God despite visible circumstances, was a common expression of God's favor (cf. Ge 15:1). It confirmed that the Lord's anger (7:1) had ceased toward Israel (7:26). **the whole army.** Contrast 7:3. **Ai.** See note on 7:2. **delivered.** Literally, "given." The promise of 1:2–3 was applied to Ai.
8:2 as you did to Jericho. See 6:21 and note on 6:17. **except.** Just as there had been an exception to the total destruction of Jericho (6:17), so God in his sovereign freedom made another exception to that requirement here. He gave the spoils to his warriors.
8:3 thirty thousand. See note on 4:13.

are to set an ambush behind the city. Don't go very far from it. All of you be on the alert.
5 I and all those with me will advance on the city, and when the men come out against
us, as they did before, we will flee from them. 6 They will pursue us until we have lured
them away from the city, for they will say, 'They are running away from us as they did
before.' So when we flee from them, 7 you are to rise up from ambush and take the city.
The LORD your God will give it into your hand.[g] 8 When you have taken the city, set it on
fire.[h] Do what the LORD has commanded.[i] See to it; you have my orders."
9 Then Joshua sent them off, and they went to the place of ambush[j] and lay in wait between Bethel and Ai, to the west of Ai—but Joshua spent that night with the people.
10 Early the next morning[k] Joshua mustered his men, and he and the leaders of Israel[l]
marched before them to Ai. 11 The entire force that was with him marched up and approached the city and arrived in front of it. They set up camp north of Ai, with the valley
between them and the city. 12 Joshua had taken about five thousand men and set them in
ambush between Bethel and Ai, to the west of the city. 13 They had the soldiers take up
their positions—all those in the camp to the north of the city and the ambush to the west
of it. That night Joshua went into the valley.
14 When the king of Ai saw this, he and all the men of the city hurried out early in the
morning to meet Israel in battle at a certain place overlooking the Arabah.[m] But he did
not know[n] that an ambush had been set against him behind the city. 15 Joshua and all
Israel let themselves be driven back[o] before them, and they fled toward the desert.[p] 16 All
the men of Ai were called to pursue them, and they pursued Joshua and were lured
away[q] from the city. 17 Not a man remained in Ai or Bethel who did not go after Israel.
They left the city open and went in pursuit of Israel.
18 Then the LORD said to Joshua, "Hold out toward Ai the javelin[r] that is in your hand,[s]
for into your hand I will deliver the city." So Joshua held out his javelin[t] toward Ai. 19 As
soon as he did this, the men in the ambush rose quickly[u] from their position and rushed
forward. They entered the city and captured it and quickly set it on fire.[v]
20 The men of Ai looked back and saw the smoke of the city rising against the sky,[w]
but they had no chance to escape in any direction, for the Israelites who had been fleeing toward the desert had turned back against their pursuers. 21 For when Joshua and all
Israel saw that the ambush had taken the city and that smoke was going up from the city,
they turned around and attacked the men of Ai. 22 The men of the ambush also came out
of the city against them, so that they were caught in the middle, with Israelites on both
sides. Israel cut them down, leaving them neither survivors nor fugitives.[x] 23 But they took
the king of Ai alive[y] and brought him to Joshua.
24 When Israel had finished killing all the men of Ai in the fields and in the desert where
they had chased them, and when every one of them had been put to the sword, all the Israelites returned to Ai and killed those who were in it. 25 Twelve thousand men and wom-
en fell that day—all the people of Ai.[z] 26 For Joshua did not draw back the hand that held
out his javelin until he had destroyed[a] [a] all who lived in Ai.[b] 27 But Israel did carry off for
themselves the livestock and plunder of this city, as the LORD had instructed Joshua.[c]
28 So Joshua burned[d] Ai[e] and made it a permanent heap of ruins,[f] a desolate place to
this day.[g] 29 He hung the king of Ai on a tree and left him there until evening. At sunset,[h]
Joshua ordered them to take his body from the tree and throw it down at the entrance
of the city gate. And they raised a large pile of rocks[i] over it, which remains to this day.

The Covenant Renewed at Mount Ebal

30 Then Joshua built on Mount Ebal[j] an altar[k] to the LORD, the God of Israel, 31 as Mo-

[a] *26* The Hebrew term refers to the irrevocable giving over of things or persons to the LORD, often by totally destroying them.

8:7 [g]Jdg 7:7; 1Sa 23:4
8:8 [h]Jdg 20:29-38 [i]ver 19
8:9 [j]2Ch 13:13
8:10 [k]Ge 22:3 [l]Jos 7:6
8:14 [m]Dt 1:1 [n]Jdg 20:34
8:15 [o]Jdg 20:36 [p]Jos 15:61; 16:1; 18:12
8:16 [q]Jdg 20:31
8:18 [r]Job 41:26; Ps 35:3 [s]Ex 4:2; 14:16; 17:9-12 [t]ver 26
8:19 [u]Jdg 20:33 [v]ver 8
8:20 [w]Jdg 20:40
8:22 [x]Dt 7:2; Jos 10:1
8:23 [y]1Sa 15:8
8:25 [z]Dt 20:16-18
8:26 [a]Nu 21:2 [b]Ex 17:12
8:27 [c]ver 2
8:28 [d]Nu 31:10 [e]Jos 7:2; Jer 49:3 [f]Dt 13:16; Jos 10:1 [g]Ge 35:20
8:29 [h]Dt 21:23; Jn 19:31 [i]2Sa 18:17
8:30 [j]Dt 11:29 [k]Ex 20:24

8:5 as they did before. See 7:5.
8:7 give. See notes on 1:2 and 3 and 8:1.
8:12 five thousand. The apparent discrepancy with the "thirty thousand" in verse 3 may indicate that there were two units assigned to different aspects of the ambush.
8:14 the Arabah. The Jordan Valley.
8:15 all Israel. Compare verses 15, 21, 24, 33 and 35. See note on 1:12–15. **the desert.** The uncultivated land to the east of Ai, not the desert on the other side of the Jordan Valley (v. 24).
8:17 or Bethel. The sudden inclusion of Bethel is not explained or elaborated, but see 12:9 and 16.
8:18 the javelin. See Moses' action in Exodus 14:16 and 17:9.
8:26 destroyed. See NIV text note and notes on 6:17 and 18.
8:28–29 to this day. See note on 4:9.
8:29 hung . . . on a tree. This action was a sign of the curse of God (see note on Dt 21:22–23; Gal 3:13).
■ **8:30–35** *The Covenant Renewal.* This record of the assembly at Mount Ebal and Mount Gerizim to hear God's promise of blessing and his warning of curses separates the two main portions that focus on battles (2:1—8:29; 9:1—11:23). This assembly, which had been commanded by Moses (Dt 11:29; 27:1–13), presents a clear picture of the nature of the people of Israel: The nation's life was centered on the covenant (v. 33) and was lived under the word of God (v. 34).
8:30 Mount Ebal. Just north of Shechem. This is the important location of the assembly in 24:1. At Shechem Abraham had received the promise—"To your offspring I will give this land" (Ge 12:7)—and had built an altar. **altar.** Abraham's altar had symboli-

ses the servant of the LORD had commanded the Israelites. He built it according to what
8:31 is written in the Book of the Law of Moses—an altar of uncut stones, on which no iron
[l]Ex 20:25 [m]Dt 27:6-7 tool[l] had been used. On it they offered to the LORD burnt offerings and sacrificed fellowship offerings.[a][m] 32There, in the presence of the Israelites, Joshua copied on stones the
8:32 [n]Dt 27:8 law of Moses, which he had written.[n] 33All Israel, aliens and citizens[o] alike, with their
elders, officials and judges, were standing on both sides of the ark of the covenant of the
8:33 [o]Lev 16:29 LORD, facing those who carried it—the priests, who were Levites.[p] Half of the people
[p]Dt 31:12 stood in front of Mount Gerizim and half of them in front of Mount Ebal,[q] as Moses the
[q]Dt 11:29; 27:11-14 servant of the LORD had formerly commanded when he gave instructions to bless the people of Israel.
8:34 34Afterward, Joshua read all the words of the law—the blessings and the curses—just
[r]Dt 28:61; 31:11; Jos 1:8 as it is written in the Book of the Law.[r] 35There was not a word of all that Moses had commanded that Joshua did not read to the whole assembly of Israel, including the women
8:35 [s]Ex 12:38; Dt 31:12 and children, and the aliens who lived among them.[s]

[a] *31* Traditionally *peace offerings*

cally laid claim to the land promised; Joshua's altar represented the promise realized.
8:31 Moses the servant of the LORD. See note on 1:1. **commanded.** See Deuteronomy 27:5–6. **the Book of the Law.** See note on 1:8–9. Here the reference is to Deuteronomy 27:5 (cf. Ex 20:25). **uncut stones.** To show that it belonged to the Lord (see note on Ex 20:25). **burnt offerings.** See Leviticus 1. **fellowship offerings.** See Leviticus 3.
8:32 in the presence of the Israelites . . . the law of Moses. The word of God was set before the people. See note on 1:8. **stones.** These could have been the stones of the altar (but see Dt 27:1–8).
8:33 All Israel. This is a comprehensive concept that included "aliens" such as Rahab (6:25). See note on 1:12–15. **the ark of the covenant.** See notes on 3:3, 6:4 and 7:6. At the center of the assembly of Israel was the symbol of the covenant that had made them the people of God and on the basis of which they had received the land. **to bless the people of Israel.** Although blessings and curses would be read (v. 34), blessing had priority in the purposes of God toward his covenant people (see Ge 12:3).
8:34 the blessings and the curses. This phrase highlights both sides of the covenant of God, which had already been experienced in the land: blessing (ch. 6; 8:1–29) and cursing (ch. 7). See Deuteronomy 27–28.
8:35 whole assembly. This assembly of all the people of God (see Dt 9:10) under the word of God has important similarities to the New Testament concept of the church. See note on 1:12–15.

Conquest of Canaan: Entry Into Canaan and Central Campaign

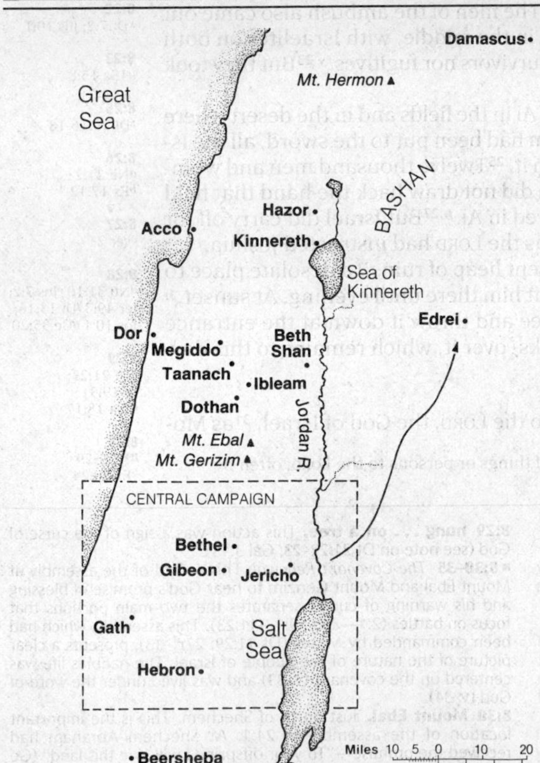

ENTRY INTO CANAAN

When the Israelite tribes approached Canaan after four decades of desert existence, they had to overcome the two Amorite kingdoms on the Medeba plateau and in Bashan. Under Moses' leadership, they also subdued the Midianites in order to consolidate their control over the Transjordanian region.

The conquest of Canaan followed a course that in retrospect appears as though it had been planned by a brilliant strategist. Taking Jericho gave Israel control of its strategic plains, fords and roads as a base of operations. When Israel next gained control of the Bethel, Gibeon and Upper Beth Horon region, it dominated the center of the north-south Palestinian ridge. Subsequently, Israel was able to break the power of the allied urban centers in separate campaigns south and north.

THE CENTRAL CAMPAIGN

The destruction of both Jericho and Ai led to a major victory against the Canaanites in the Valley of Aijalon—the "battle of the long day" which then allowed Joshua to proceed against the cities of the western foothills.

The Gibeonite Deception

9 Now when all the kings west of the Jordan heard about these things—those in the
hill country, in the western foothills, and along the entire coast of the Great Sea[a t]
as far as Lebanon (the kings of the Hittites, Amorites, Canaanites, Perizzites, Hivites and
Jebusites)[u]— 2they came together to make war against Joshua and Israel.
3However, when the people of Gibeon[v] heard what Joshua had done to Jericho and
Ai, 4they resorted to a ruse: They went as a delegation whose donkeys were loaded[b] with

9:1 [t]Nu 34:6 [u]Ex 3:17; Jos 3:10

9:3 [v]ver 17; Jos 10:2; 2Sa 2:12; 2Ch 1:3; Isa 28:21

[a] *1* That is, the Mediterranean [b] *4* Most Hebrew manuscripts; some Hebrew manuscripts, Vulgate and Syriac (see also Septuagint) *They prepared provisions and loaded their donkeys*

▪ **9:1—11:15** *Later Expansive Battles.* The record of Joshua's conquest turns to the manner in which he conquered many Canaanites and possessed much of the promised land. These chapters divide into three main parts: the formation of alliances against Israel (9:1–2), Joshua's victories in the south (9:3—10:43) and those in the north (11:1–15).

▪ **9:1–2** *The Alliances Formed Against Israel.* These verses form the background for the events that follow. The fear of the Israelites that had immobilized the Canaanites in 5:1 here united the Canaanites against Joshua and Israel.

9:1 heard. See note on verse 3. **Hittites . . . Jebusites.** See note on 3:10.

▪ **9:3—10:43** *Victory Over Southern Territories.* Through several intertwined events Joshua led Israel to great victories over large portions of the southern lands. This account records the Gibeonite deception (9:3–27), the victory at Gibeon (10:1–15), the execution of five kings (10:16–28), the victories over southern cities (10:29–39) and a summary of southern territories conquered (10:40–43).

▪ **9:3–27** *The Gibeonite Deception.* Chapter 9 provides a detailed account of the unusual circumstances that resulted in the people of Gibeon not being killed (note the requirements of Dt 7:1–6) but becoming subject to the Israelites. Like Rahab, the Gibeonites had heard of God's deeds (vv. 9–10; cf. 2:9–11) and received a measure of mercy (v. 26; cf. 6:25). However, unlike Rahab (who deceived Israel's enemies; 2:4–5), the Gibeonites deceived Israel. While they were delivered from destruction, they became servants of the people of God (v. 23; 6:25).

9:3 Gibeon. The action taken by the people of Gibeon (approximately eight miles north of Jerusalem) was in contrast to the general pattern taken by other peoples throughout Canaan (see 11:19). **heard.** The effect of the news of God's powerful faithfulness to his promises is an important theme in the account of the conquest (2:10–11; 5:1; 9:1,9; 10:1; 11:1; cf. 7:9). For the Canaanites this news was terrifying, for it meant that the God of heaven and Earth (2:11) would destroy them. In many respects the Canaanites' hearing of the victories brought by God's intervention corresponds to the hearing of the Christian gospel and its announcement of victory accomplished by Christ (see Isa 52:7; Ro 2:16).

9:4 a ruse. This deception would save the Gibeonites from annihilation, but it would also bring a curse on them (v. 23). Their actions stand in contrast to Rahab's toward the representatives of Israel in chapter 2.

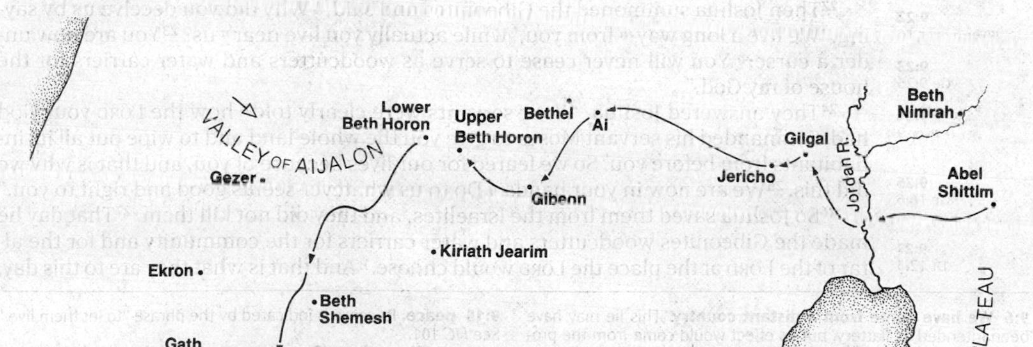

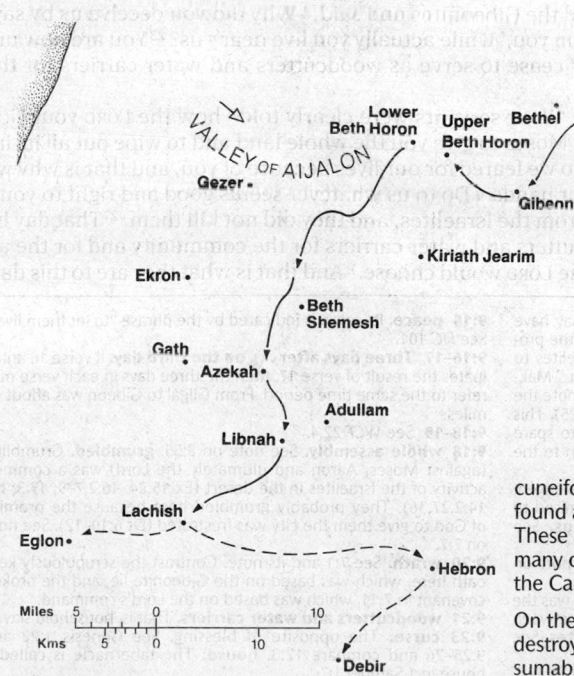

Archaeological evidence for the conquest is mixed, in part because the chronological problems are unsolved. On the one hand, clay tablets containing cuneiform letters to the Egyptian court have been found at Tell el-Amarna in Egypt from c. 1375 B.C. These mention bands of Habiru who threaten many of the cities of Canaan and create fear among the Canaanite inhabitants.

On the other hand, numerous towns were destroyed c. 1230 B.C. by unknown assailants, presumably the "Sea Peoples," but possibly including the Israelites as well. The Biblical chronology based on 1Ki 6:1 seems to demand an even earlier dating, near the end of the 15th century (see Introduction to Joshua: Historical Setting).

worn-out sacks and old wineskins, cracked and mended. 5The men put worn and
patched sandals on their feet and wore old clothes. All the bread of their food supply was
dry and moldy. 6Then they went to Joshua in the camp at Gilgal[w] and said to him and
the men of Israel, "We have come from a distant country; make a treaty with us."

7The men of Israel said to the Hivites,[x] "But perhaps you live near us. How then can
we make a treaty[y] with you?"

8"We are your servants,[z]" they said to Joshua.

But Joshua asked, "Who are you and where do you come from?"

9They answered: "Your servants have come from a very distant country[a] because of
the fame of the LORD your God. For we have heard reports[b] of him: all that he did in
Egypt, 10and all that he did to the two kings of the Amorites east of the Jordan—Sihon
king of Heshbon, and Og king of Bashan,[c] who reigned in Ashtaroth.[d] 11And our elders
and all those living in our country said to us, 'Take provisions for your journey; go and
meet them and say to them, "We are your servants; make a treaty with us." ' 12This bread
of ours was warm when we packed it at home on the day we left to come to you. But now
see how dry and moldy it is. 13And these wineskins that we filled were new, but see how
cracked they are. And our clothes and sandals are worn out by the very long journey."

14The men of Israel sampled their provisions but did not inquire[e] of the LORD. 15Then
Joshua made a treaty of peace[f] with them to let them live, and the leaders of the assembly ratified it by oath.

16Three days after they made the treaty with the Gibeonites, the Israelites heard that
they were neighbors, living near them. 17So the Israelites set out and on the third day
came to their cities: Gibeon, Kephirah, Beeroth[g] and Kiriath Jearim.[h] 18But the Israelites did not attack them, because the leaders of the assembly had sworn an oath[i] to them
by the LORD, the God of Israel.

The whole assembly grumbled[j] against the leaders, 19but all the leaders answered,
"We have given them our oath by the LORD, the God of Israel, and we cannot touch them
now. 20This is what we will do to them: We will let them live, so that wrath will not fall
on us for breaking the oath we swore to them." 21They continued, "Let them live,[k] but
let them be woodcutters and water carriers[l] for the entire community." So the leaders'
promise to them was kept.

22Then Joshua summoned the Gibeonites and said, "Why did you deceive us by saying, 'We live a long way[m] from you,' while actually you live near[n] us? 23You are now under a curse:[o] You will never cease to serve as woodcutters and water carriers for the
house of my God."

24They answered Joshua, "Your servants were clearly told[p] how the LORD your God
had commanded his servant Moses to give you the whole land and to wipe out all its inhabitants from before you. So we feared for our lives because of you, and that is why we
did this. 25We are now in your hands.[q] Do to us whatever seems good and right to you."

26So Joshua saved them from the Israelites, and they did not kill them. 27That day he
made the Gibeonites woodcutters and water carriers for the community and for the altar of the LORD at the place the LORD would choose.[r] And that is what they are to this day.

9:6 [w]Jos 5:10
9:7 [x]ver 1; Jos 11:19 [y]Ex 23:32; Dt 7:2
9:8 [z]Dt 20:11; 2Ki 10:5
9:9 [a]Dt 20:15 [b]ver 24; Jos 2:9
9:10 [c]Nu 21:33 [d]Nu 21:24,35
9:14 [e]Nu 27:21
9:15 [f]Ex 23:32; Jos 11:19; 2Sa 21:2
9:17 [g]Jos 18:25 [h]1Sa 7:1-2
9:18 [i]Ps 15:4 [j]Ex 15:24
9:21 [k]ver 15 [l]Dt 29:11
9:22 [m]ver 6 [n]ver 16
9:23 [o]Ge 9:25
9:24 [p]ver 9
9:25 [q]Ge 16:6
9:27 [r]Dt 12:5

9:6 We have come from a distant country. This lie may have been intended as flattery, but its effect would come from the provision of Deuteronomy 20:10–18, which allowed the Israelites to offer terms of peace to distant cities. **treaty.** Or "covenant." Making a covenant was a means of formalizing a relationship (note the Gibeonite claim "We are your servants" in vv. 8,11; cf. 24:25). This covenant would have specified a commitment by Israel to spare the Gibeonites in exchange for the Gibeonites' submission to the Israelites.

9:7 Hivites. This ethnic group, to which the Gibeonites belonged, was identified as one of the groups whom God had promised to drive out of Canaan (3:10). **perhaps you live near us.** See Deuteronomy 7:1–2 and 20:15–18.

9:9 fame. Literally, "name." See note on 7:9. **heard.** See note on verse 3.

9:10 all that he did. The news the Gibeonites had heard was the same as that confessed by Rahab (see 2:10). The contrast between their behavior toward Israel and hers is suggested. **Amorites.** See note on 2:10.

9:14 did not inquire of the LORD. The manner of the inquiry they should have made is unclear, but it likely involved seeking divine direction from the priests. As in 5:6 and 7:1, Israel's failure was a failure to be obedient to, literally, "the mouth of the LORD" (Dt 8:3). To his detriment, Joshua neglected to seek guidance from the Lord.

9:15 peace. Its sense is indicated by the phrase "to let them live." See *HC* 101.

9:16–17 Three days after . . . on the third day. If verse 16 anticipates the result of verse 17, then the three days in each verse may refer to the same time period. From Gilgal to Gibeon was about 19 miles.

9:18–19 See *WCF* 22.4.

9:18 whole assembly. See note on 8:35. **grumbled.** Grumbling (against Moses, Aaron and ultimately the Lord) was a common activity of the Israelites in the desert (Ex 15:24; 16:2,7–9; 17:3; Nu 14:2,27,36). They probably grumbled here because the promise of God to give them the city was frustrated (Dt 6:10–12). See note on 7:7.

9:20 wrath. See 7:1 and its note. Contrast the scrupulously kept oath here, which was based on the Gibeonite lie, and the broken covenant in 7:11, which was based on the Lord's command.

9:21 woodcutters and water carriers. That is, household slaves.

9:23 curse. The opposite of blessing. See Genesis 1:22 and 9:25–26 and compare 12:3. **house.** The tabernacle is called a house in 1 Samuel 1:7.

9:24 feared. See note on 2:9.

9:26 Joshua saved them. This chapter explains why Joshua delivered a group of Canaanites from destruction.

9:27 the place the LORD would choose. See Deuteronomy 12 and compare Exodus 20:24. **to this day.** See note on 4:9.

The Sun Stands Still

10 Now Adoni-Zedek king of Jerusalem[s] heard that Joshua had taken Ai[t] and totally destroyed[a][u] it, doing to Ai and its king as he had done to Jericho and its king,
and that the people of Gibeon had made a treaty of peace[v] with Israel and were living near
them. 2He and his people were very much alarmed at this, because Gibeon was an important city, like one of the royal cities; it was larger than Ai, and all its men were good fighters. 3So Adoni-Zedek king of Jerusalem appealed to Hoham king of Hebron,[w] Piram king
of Jarmuth, Japhia king of Lachish[x] and Debir king of Eglon. 4"Come up and help me attack Gibeon," he said, "because it has made peace[y] with Joshua and the Israelites."
5Then the five kings of the Amorites[z]—the kings of Jerusalem, Hebron, Jarmuth, Lachish and Eglon—joined forces. They moved up with all their troops and took up positions against Gibeon and attacked it.
6The Gibeonites then sent word to Joshua in the camp at Gilgal: "Do not abandon
your servants. Come up to us quickly and save us! Help us, because all the Amorite kings
from the hill country have joined forces against us."
7So Joshua marched up from Gilgal with his entire army,[a] including all the best fighting men. 8The LORD said to Joshua, "Do not be afraid[b] of them; I have given them into
your hand. Not one of them will be able to withstand you."
9After an all-night march from Gilgal, Joshua took them by surprise. 10The LORD
threw them into confusion before Israel,[c] who defeated them in a great victory at Gibeon. Israel pursued them along the road going up to Beth Horon[d] and cut them down all
the way to Azekah[e] and Makkedah. 11As they fled before Israel on the road down from
Beth Horon to Azekah, the LORD hurled large hailstones[f] down on them from the sky, and
more of them died from the hailstones than were killed by the swords of the Israelites.
12On the day the LORD gave the Amorites[g] over to Israel, Joshua said to the LORD in
the presence of Israel:

> "O sun, stand still over Gibeon,
> O moon, over the Valley of Aijalon.[h]"
> 13So the sun stood still,[i]
> and the moon stopped,
> till the nation avenged itself on[b] its enemies,

as it is written in the Book of Jashar.[j]
The sun stopped[k] in the middle of the sky and delayed going down about a full day.
14There has never been a day like it before or since, a day when the LORD listened to a
man. Surely the LORD was fighting[l] for Israel!
15Then Joshua returned with all Israel to the camp at Gilgal.[m]

10:1 [s]Jdg 1:7 [t]Jos 8:1 [u]Dt 20:16; Jos 8:22 [v]Jos 9:15
10:3 [w]Ge 13:18 [x]2Ch 11:9; 25:27; Ne 11:30; Isa 36:2; 37:8; Jer 34:7; Mic 1:13
10:4 [y]Jos 9:15
10:5 [z]Nu 13:29
10:7 [a]Jos 8:1
10:8 [b]Dt 3:2; Jos 1:9
10:10 [c]Dt 7:23 [d]Jos 16:3, 5 [e]Jos 15:35
10:11 [f]Ps 18:12; Isa 28:2, 17
10:12 [g]Am 2:9 [h]Jdg 1:35; 12:12
10:13 [i]Hab 3:11 [j]2Sa 1:18
10:13 [k]Isa 38:8
10:14 [l]ver 42; Ex 14:14; Dt 1:30; Ps 106:43; 136:24
10:15 [m]ver 43

[a] *1* The Hebrew term refers to the irrevocable giving over of things or persons to the LORD, often by totally destroying them; also in verses 28, 35, 37, 39 and 40. [b] *13* Or *nation triumphed over*

■ **10:1–15** *Victory at Gibeon.* The hostility anticipated in 9:1–2 begins to emerge. In chapter 10 the hostile nations to the south are overthrown by remarkable divine intervention. The scheming of the five kings (v. 4) and their destruction (vv. 26,40–42) demonstrate the great power of God to fulfill his promises. This battle follows the pattern for holy war. It was not fought by Israel but by God (v. 14; Dt 20:4) in faithfulness to his covenant promises (v. 8). There are six sections to chapter 10: the threat to Gibeon from the five kings of the Amorites (vv. 1–5); Israel's victory over the kings (vv. 6–11); a description of the intervention of God for Israel (vv. 12–15); an account of the killing of the five kings (vv. 16–27); a brief account of further destruction of cities in southern Canaan (vv. 28–39); and a concluding summary (vv. 40–43).
10:1 Adoni-Zedek. His name means "My Lord is righteous." Compare his name with that of Melchizedek, an earlier king in Jerusalem (Ge 14:18). **Jerusalem.** The first occurrence of this full name in the Bible (but see Ge 14:18). **heard.** See note on 9:3. The news concerned the events recorded in chapters 8–9. **totally destroyed.** See notes on 6:17 and 18. **treaty of peace.** See 9:15.
10:2 alarmed. Or "afraid." See note on 2:9. **an important city, like one of the royal cities.** Gibeon did not have a king (9:11), but it was comparable to the Canaanite city-states, which had monarchical governments.
10:3 Hoham . . . Debir. These were the kings of five southern Canaanite cities.
10:5 Amorites. See note on 2:10.
10:6 save us! Help us. The covenant (treaty) relationship between Gibeon and Israel (9:15) gave grounds for the former to appeal for help from the stronger covenant partner.
10:8 Do not be afraid . . . I have given. The particular actions in this chapter took place under the promises of God introduced in chapter 1. See notes on 1:2, 3, 5–9 and 8:1.
10:9 all-night march. Gibeon, on top of the mountain, was about 20 miles west of Gilgal, which was at the bottom of the Jordan Valley.
10:10 threw them into confusion. Similar Hebrew expressions often appear in descriptions of battles in which the Lord was the fighter (2:9; Ex 14:24; 23:27; Jdg 4:15; 1Sa 7:10; 2Sa 22:15; cf. Jer 51:34). The inexplicable confusion of the enemy was a demonstration that God was at work.
10:11 more of them died from the hailstones. This phrase emphasizes that this victory was "given" to Israel (v. 8). Experiences like this illuminate the use of storm phenomena in poetic descriptions of God's judgment (e.g., Ps 18:7–16; Isa 30:30).
10:12 On the day the LORD gave. This account may be a flashback; the chronological order of events in this context is not clear. **"O sun . . . moon."** These rhetorical words are not actually addressed to the sun and moon, but to the Lord.
10:13 the sun stood still. This action is understood as quite literal in the following sentence. **the Book of Jashar.** A work no longer in existence, possibly celebrating the lives of Israelite heroes (2Sa 1:18). The extent of the quotation from the Book of Jashar is not certain; it may extend as far as the end of verse 15.
10:14 never been a day like it. This was a day of unparalleled answer to prayer. **the LORD was fighting for Israel!** See Deuteronomy 20, especially verse 4; see also Exodus 14:14.
10:15 all Israel. See verses 24, 29, 31, 34, 36, 38 and 43. See also note on 1:12–15. **to the camp at Gilgal.** This is possibly an anticipation of verse 43.

Five Amorite Kings Killed

16 Now the five kings had fled and hidden in the cave at Makkedah. 17 When Joshua
was told that the five kings had been found hiding in the cave at Makkedah, 18 he said,
"Roll large rocks up to the mouth of the cave, and post some men there to guard it. 19 But
don't stop! Pursue your enemies, attack them from the rear and don't let them reach
10:20 their cities, for the LORD your God has given them into your hand."
[n]Dt 20:16 20 So Joshua and the Israelites destroyed them completely[n]—almost to a man—but
the few who were left reached their fortified cities. 21 The whole army then returned safely to Joshua in the camp at Makkedah, and no one uttered a word against the Israelites.
22 Joshua said, "Open the mouth of the cave and bring those five kings out to me." 23 So
they brought the five kings out of the cave—the kings of Jerusalem, Hebron, Jarmuth, Lachish and Eglon. 24 When they had brought these kings to Joshua, he summoned all the
men of Israel and said to the army commanders who had come with him, "Come here
10:24 [o]Mal 4:3 [p]Ps 110:1 and put your feet[o] on the necks of these kings." So they came forward and placed their
feet[p] on their necks.
25 Joshua said to them, "Do not be afraid; do not be discouraged. Be strong and cou-
10:25 [q]Dt 31:6 rageous.[q] This is what the LORD will do to all the enemies you are going to fight." 26 Then
Joshua struck and killed the kings and hung them on five trees, and they were left hang-
10:27 ing on the trees until evening.
[r]Dt 21:23; Jos 8:9, 29 27 At sunset[r] Joshua gave the order and they took them down from the trees and threw
them into the cave where they had been hiding. At the mouth of the cave they placed
large rocks, which are there to this day.
10:28 28 That day Joshua took Makkedah. He put the city and its king to the sword and to-
[s]Dt 20:16 [t]Jos 6:21 tally destroyed everyone in it. He left no survivors.[s] And he did to the king of Makkedah
as he had done to the king of Jericho.[t]

Southern Cities Conquered

29 Then Joshua and all Israel with him moved on from Makkedah to Libnah and attacked it. 30 The LORD also gave that city and its king into Israel's hand. The city and everyone in it Joshua put to the sword. He left no survivors there. And he did to its king as
he had done to the king of Jericho.
31 Then Joshua and all Israel with him moved on from Libnah to Lachish; he took up
positions against it and attacked it. 32 The LORD handed Lachish over to Israel, and Joshua took it on the second day. The city and everyone in it he put to the sword, just as he
10:33 had done to Libnah. 33 Meanwhile, Horam king of Gezer[u] had come up to help Lachish,
[u]Jos 16:3, 10; Jdg 1:29; 1Ki 9:15 but Joshua defeated him and his army—until no survivors were left.
34 Then Joshua and all Israel with him moved on from Lachish to Eglon; they took up
positions against it and attacked it. 35 They captured it that same day and put it to the
sword and totally destroyed everyone in it, just as they had done to Lachish.
10:36 36 Then Joshua and all Israel with him went up from Eglon to Hebron[v] and attacked it.
[v]Jos 14:13; 15:13; Jdg 1:10 37 They took the city and put it to the sword, together with its king, its villages and everyone in it. They left no survivors. Just as at Eglon, they totally destroyed it and everyone in it.
10:38 38 Then Joshua and all Israel with him turned around and attacked Debir.[w] 39 They
[w]Jos 15:15; Jdg 1:11 took the city, its king and its villages, and put them to the sword. Everyone in it they totally destroyed. They left no survivors. They did to Debir and its king as they had done
10:40 to Libnah and its king and to Hebron.
[x]Ge 12:9; Jos 12:8 40 So Joshua subdued the whole region, including the hill country, the Negev,[x] the

---

■ **10:16–28** *The Execution of Five Kings.* Another flashback returns the narrative to the pursuit of verse 10 in order to recount the fate of the five kings introduced in verse 5.
10:19 for the LORD . . . has given. The action of God (in terms of his promise) still dominates the account. See verses 8, 10 and 14.
10:20 destroyed them completely. The Hebrew words here are different from those in verse 1, but the idea is essentially the same.
10:21 no one uttered a word. Not even a word, let alone a more substantial resistance, could be raised against God's army.
10:24 feet on the necks. A vivid demonstration of the defeat of their enemies. Defeated enemies were often said to be "under the feet" of the victor (1Ki 5:3; Ps 110:1; cf. 1Co 15:25), and ancient Egyptian royal footstools depict the pharaoh's feet on the necks of his enemies.
10:25 Do not be afraid. See note on verse 8.
10:26 hung them on five trees. See note on 8:29.
10:27 to this day. See note on 4:9.
■ **10:29–39** *Victories Over Southern Cities.* These verses are a summary account of the victories over the cities in southern Canaan. The theological perspective of the account is indicated by a number of repeated or similar expressions. Those expressions include "totally destroyed" and/or "no survivors" in verses 28, 30, 33, 35, 37 and 39 (see notes on 6:17,18; cf. NIV text note at 10:1) and "as he [they] had done to . . ." in verses 28, 30, 32, 35, 37 and 39. The destruction throughout the region had the same fundamental character as that already seen in the defeat of Jericho; namely, it was the judgment of God. Another repeated expression is "Joshua and all Israel" (vv. 29,31,34,36,38). The emphasis of this phrase is the unity of Israel (see note on 1:12–15) under Joshua's leadership (1:1–9). Finally, the phrase "the LORD gave" (or some variation) is repeated in verses 30 and 32 to show that the destruction of the Canaanite cities was granted by God to Israel (1:2).
■ **10:40–43** *Summary of Southern Territories.* Summarizing the account of the southern campaign, these verses emphasize the totality of the destruction under God's command (see v. 40; NIV text note at v. 1; see also notes on 6:17,18) and show that all this

western foothills and the mountain slopes,[y] together with all their kings.[z] He left no survivors. He totally destroyed all who breathed, just as the LORD, the God of Israel, had
commanded.[a] 41Joshua subdued them from Kadesh Barnea[b] to Gaza[c] and from the
whole region of Goshen[d] to Gibeon. 42All these kings and their lands Joshua conquered
in one campaign, because the LORD, the God of Israel, fought[e] for Israel.
43Then Joshua returned with all Israel to the camp at Gilgal.[f]

Northern Kings Defeated

11 When Jabin[g] king of Hazor[h] heard of this, he sent word to Jobab king of Madon,
to the kings of Shimron[i] and Acshaph, 2and to the northern kings who were in
the mountains, in the Arabah[j] south of Kinnereth,[k] in the western foothills and in Naphoth Dor[a][l] on the west; 3to the Canaanites in the east and west; to the Amorites, Hittites, Perizzites and Jebusites in the hill country; and to the Hivites[m] below Hermon in
the region of Mizpah.[n] 4They came out with all their troops and a large number of horses and chariots—a huge army, as numerous as the sand on the seashore.[o] 5All these
kings joined forces[p] and made camp together at the Waters of Merom, to fight against
Israel.
6The LORD said to Joshua, "Do not be afraid of them, because by this time tomorrow
I will hand all of them over[q] to Israel, slain. You are to hamstring[r] their horses and burn
their chariots."

a 2 Or *in the heights of Dor*

10:40 [y]Dt 1:7 [z]Dt 7:24 [a]Dt 20:16-17
10:41 [b]Ge 14:7 [c]Ge 10:19 [d]Jos 11:16; 15:51
10:42 [e]ver 14
10:43 [f]ver 15; Jos 5:9
11:1 [g]Jdg 4:2,7,23 [h]ver 10; 1Sa 12:9 [i]Jos 19:15
11:2 [j]Jos 12:3 [k]Nu 34:11 [l]Jos 17:11; Jdg 1:27; 1Ki 4:11
11:3 [m]Dt 7:1; Jdg 3:3,5; 1Ki 9:20 [n]Ge 31:49; Jos 15:38; 18:26
11:4 [o]Jdg 7:12; 1Sa 13:5
11:5 [p]Jdg 5:19
11:6 [q]Jos 10:8 [r]2Sa 8:4

was the work of God for Israel (v. 42; see note on v. 14). See note on 21:45.
■ **11:1–15** *Victory Over Northern Territories.* The account of the conquest of the northern region is similar in its emphases to the report of the southern victories in chapter 10 and brings the book's record of Israel's taking of the land to a conclusion.
11:1–4 Compare the reaction of the Canaanite kings in 10:1–5.
11:1 Jabin king of Hazor. Hazor was an important city in northern Canaan (v. 10). Jabin was possibly a hereditary title (Jdg 4:2). **heard.** See note on 9:3.
11:2 the Arabah. The Jordan Valley. **Kinnereth.** Probably near the Sea of Galilee (12:3). **Dor.** On the Mediterranean coast.
11:3 Canaanites . . . Jebusites. See note on 3:10.
11:4 a huge army. The enormous threat posed by the Canaanites is vividly presented as the background to the promise in verse 6.
11:5 to fight against Israel. This is possibly an ironic contrast to 10:14, where the one who could stop the sun in the middle of the sky was said to be fighting for Israel.
11:6 Do not be afraid. The promise of God (1:2–3,9) provided the basis for confidence. See notes at 6:2, 8:1 and 10:8. **I will hand . . . over.** The Hebrew wording is emphatic and may be translated

Conquest of Canaan: Southern Campaign

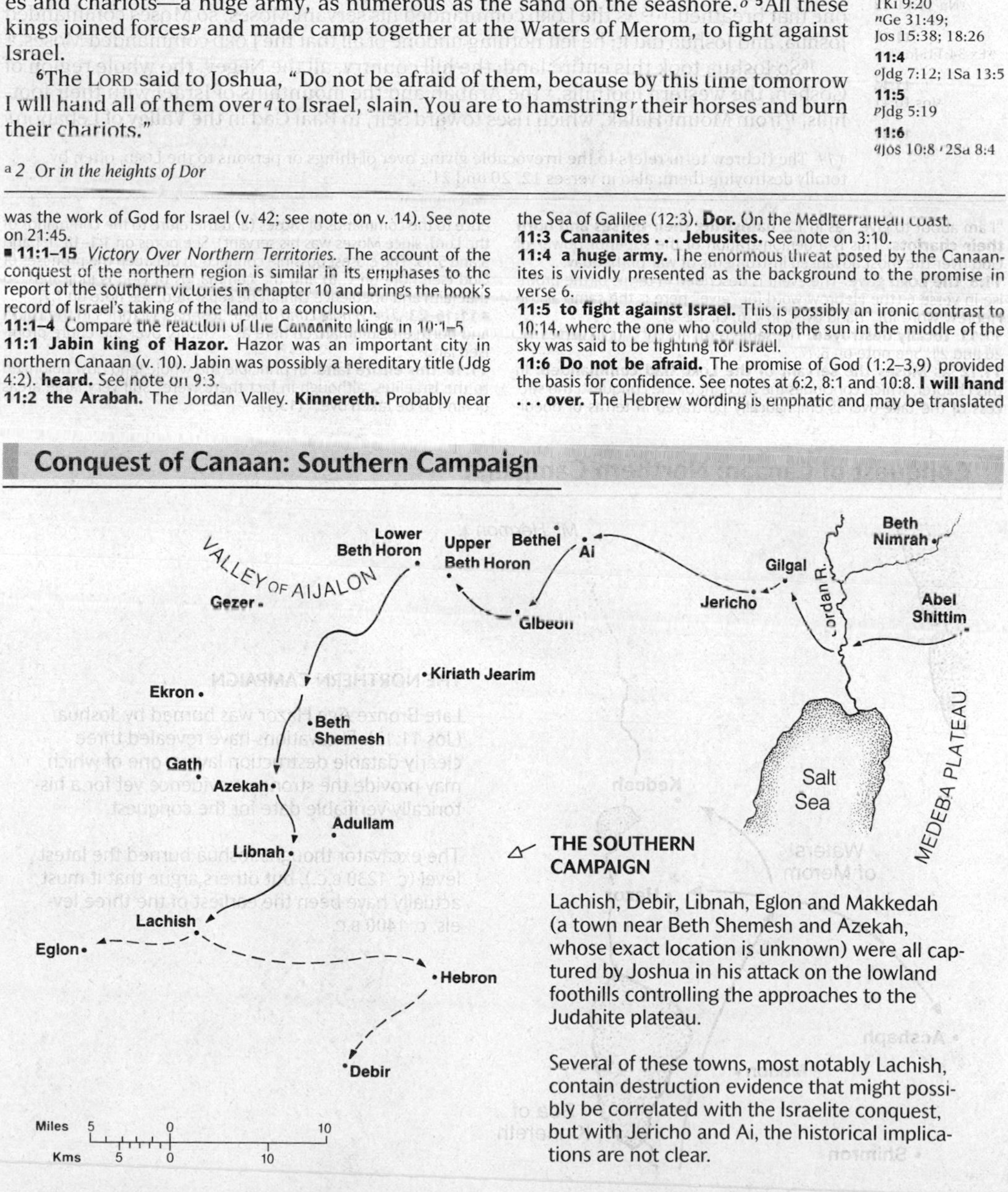

THE SOUTHERN CAMPAIGN

Lachish, Debir, Libnah, Eglon and Makkedah (a town near Beth Shemesh and Azekah, whose exact location is unknown) were all captured by Joshua in his attack on the lowland foothills controlling the approaches to the Judahite plateau.

Several of these towns, most notably Lachish, contain destruction evidence that might possibly be correlated with the Israelite conquest, but with Jericho and Ai, the historical implications are not clear.

11:8 [s]Jos 13:6
11:11 [t]Dt 20:16-17
11:12 [u]Nu 33:50-52; Dt 7:2
11:14 [v]Nu 31:11-12
11:15 [w]Ex 34:11; Jos 1:7
11:16 [x]Jos 10:41
11:17 [y]Jos 12:7

7 So Joshua and his whole army came against them suddenly at the Waters of Merom
and attacked them, 8 and the LORD gave them into the hand of Israel. They defeated them
and pursued them all the way to Greater Sidon, to Misrephoth Maim,[s] and to the Valley of Mizpah on the east, until no survivors were left. 9 Joshua did to them as the LORD
had directed: He hamstrung their horses and burned their chariots.

10 At that time Joshua turned back and captured Hazor and put its king to the sword.
(Hazor had been the head of all these kingdoms.) 11 Everyone in it they put to the sword.
They totally destroyed[a] them, not sparing anything that breathed,[t] and he burned up Ha-
zor itself.

12 Joshua took all these royal cities and their kings and put them to the sword. He totally destroyed them, as Moses the servant of the LORD had commanded.[u] 13 Yet Israel did
not burn any of the cities built on their mounds—except Hazor, which Joshua burned.
14 The Israelites carried off for themselves all the plunder and livestock of these cities, but
all the people they put to the sword until they completely destroyed them, not sparing anyone that breathed.[v] 15 As the LORD commanded his servant Moses, so Moses commanded
Joshua, and Joshua did it; he left nothing undone of all that the LORD commanded Moses.[w]

16 So Joshua took this entire land: the hill country, all the Negev, the whole region of
Goshen, the western foothills,[x] the Arabah and the mountains of Israel with their foothills, 17 from Mount Halak, which rises toward Seir, to Baal Gad in the Valley of Lebanon[y]

[a] *11* The Hebrew term refers to the irrevocable giving over of things or persons to the LORD, often by totally destroying them; also in verses 12, 20 and 21.

"I am about to give," as in 1:2. **hamstring their horses and burn their chariots.** This is a demonstration of the superior power of God over the most advanced instruments of war of that day.
11:8 the LORD gave. The event is described in terms of the promise in verse 6 (the Hebrew word for "give" here is the same as the Hebrew word for "hand over" in v. 6; cf. 1:2–3).
11:11 totally destroyed. The same term also occurs in verses 12, 20 and 21. See note on 6:17.
11:12 as Moses the servant of the LORD had commanded. In this chapter, which concludes the account of the conquest, the success of the take-over is emphatically portrayed in terms of obedience to the commands of Moses (and therefore to the commands of the Lord, since Moses was his servant). See notes on 1:1–18, 1:1 and 3 and 5:15. The closest possible connection between the promises of God (see note on v. 6) and the commands of God is indicated, so that faith and obedience cannot be separated. See note on 1:7.
■ **11:16–23** *The Whole Land Taken.* Joshua's victories in the south and north are summarized here as a victory over the entire promised land.
11:16 this entire land. In principle the whole land now belonged to the Israelites, although in fact there were "still very large areas of land to be taken over" (13:1).

Conquest of Canaan: Northern Campaign

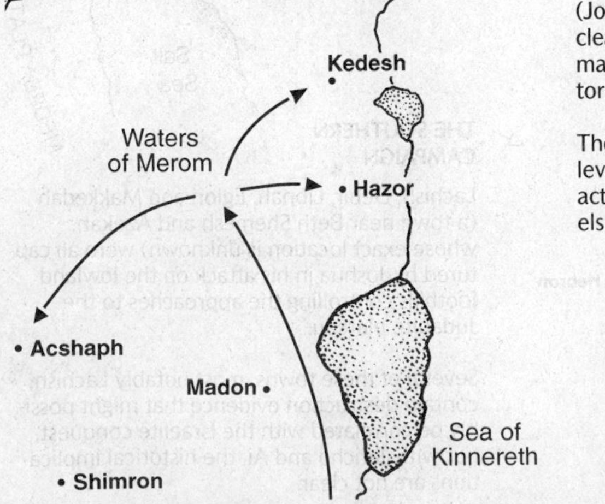

THE NORTHERN CAMPAIGN

Late Bronze Age Hazor was burned by Joshua (Jos 11:13). Excavations have revealed three clearly datable destruction layers, one of which may provide the strongest evidence yet for a historically verifiable date for the conquest.

The excavator thought Joshua burned the latest level (c. 1230 B.C.), but others argue that it must actually have been the earliest of the three levels, c. 1400 B.C.

below Mount Hermon. He captured all their kings and struck them down, putting them
to death.[z] 18 Joshua waged war against all these kings for a long time. 19 Except for the Hivites living in Gibeon,[a] not one city made a treaty of peace with the Israelites, who took
them all in battle. 20 For it was the LORD himself who hardened their hearts[b] to wage war
against Israel, so that he might destroy them totally, exterminating them without mercy, as the LORD had commanded Moses.[c]
21 At that time Joshua went and destroyed the Anakites[d] from the hill country: from
Hebron, Debir and Anab, from all the hill country of Judah, and from all the hill country of Israel. Joshua totally destroyed them and their towns. 22 No Anakites were left in
Israelite territory; only in Gaza, Gath[e] and Ashdod[f] did any survive. 23 So Joshua took the
entire land,[g] just as the LORD had directed Moses, and he gave it as an inheritance[h] to
Israel according to their tribal divisions.[i]
Then the land had rest from war.[j]

List of Defeated Kings

12 These are the kings of the land whom the Israelites had defeated and whose territory they took over east of the Jordan, from the Arnon Gorge to Mount Hermon,[k] including all the eastern side of the Arabah:

2 Sihon king of the Amorites,
who reigned in Heshbon. He ruled from Aroer on the rim of the Arnon Gorge—
from the middle of the gorge—to the Jabbok River, which is the border of the Ammonites. This included half of Gilead.[l] 3 He also ruled over the eastern Arabah from
the Sea of Kinnereth[a][m] to the Sea of the Arabah (the Salt Sea[b]), to Beth Jeshimoth,[n] and then southward below the slopes of Pisgah.

4 And the territory of Og king of Bashan,[o]
one of the last of the Rephaites, who reigned in Ashtaroth[p] and Edrei. 5 He ruled
over Mount Hermon, Salecah,[q] all of Bashan to the border of the people of Geshur[r] and Maacah,[s] and half of Gilead to the border of Sihon king of Heshbon.

6 Moses, the servant of the LORD, and the Israelites conquered them. And Moses the
servant of the LORD gave their land to the Reubenites, the Gadites and the half-tribe of
Manasseh to be their possession.[t]
7 These are the kings of the land that Joshua and the Israelites conquered on the west
side of the Jordan, from Baal Gad in the Valley of Lebanon[u] to Mount Halak, which rises toward Seir (their lands Joshua gave as an inheritance to the tribes of Israel according to their tribal divisions— 8 the hill country, the western foothills, the Arabah, the
mountain slopes, the desert and the Negev[v]—the lands of the Hittites, Amorites, Canaanites, Perizzites, Hivites and Jebusites):

9 the king of Jericho[w]	one
the king of Ai[x] (near Bethel)	one

11:17 [z]Dt 7:24
11:19 [a]Jos 9:3
11:20 [b]Ex 14:17; Ro 9:18 [c]Dt 7:16; Jdg 14:4
11:21 [d]Nu 13:22, 33; Dt 9:2
11:22 [e]1Sa 17:4; 1Ki 2:39; 1Ch 8:13 [f]1Sa 5:1; Isa 20:1
11:23 [g]Jos 21:43-45 [h]Dt 1:38; 12:9-10; 25:19 [i]Nu 26:53 [j]Jos 14:15
12:1 [k]Dt 3:8
12:2 [l]Dt 2:36
12:3 [m]Jos 11:2 [n]Jos 13:20
12:4 [o]Nu 21:21, 33; Dt 3:11 [p]Dt 1:4
12:5 [q]Dt 3:10 [r]1Sa 27:8 [s]Dt 3:14
12:6 [t]Nu 32:29, 33; Jos 13:8
12:7 [u]Jos 11:17
12:8 [v]Jos 11:16
12:9 [w]Jos 6:2 [x]Jos 8:29

a 3 That is, Galilee b 3 That is, the Dead Sea

11:18 a long time. This is an indication that the preceding chapters presented a greatly condensed account of the events.
11:19 a treaty of peace. See 9:6 and 15.
11:20 the LORD himself who hardened their hearts. The relationship between divine sovereignty and human responsibility is illustrated by the divine hardening of hearts to achieve God's purposes. God's sovereign act does not, however, overthrow either God's justice or human responsibility (cf. Ex 10:1–2; Ro 9:14–29).
11:21–22 Anakites. The inhabitants of Canaan who had frightened the Israelites into disobedience a generation earlier (Nu 13:26–33; Dt 1:26–28). Their destruction concludes the account of the obedient conquest under Joshua. See also 14:12 and 15:14.
11:23 an inheritance . . . according to their tribal divisions. This is an anticipatory summary of chapters 13–21. See note on 1:6. **The land had rest from war.** Although much land still needed to be taken (see note on 13:1), God had accomplished so much through Joshua that his victory could be considered completed. These words sum up the success of the conquest and, therefore, the fulfillment of God's promise given in 1:2–5. See notes on 1:13 and 21:45.
■ **12:1–24** *The List of Conquered Kings and Territories.* This chapter provides a summary of the entire conquest in the form of a list of defeated kings and their territories. It functions as an elaboration of 11:17, a striking resolution to 9:1–2 and a testimony to the truth of the promise in 1:5. It is a chapter that praises God for his powerful faithfulness to his promises. The summary begins with the kings and their territories east of the Jordan that were defeated in the days of Moses (vv. 1–6; see note on 1:12–15) and ends with a review of the conquest west of the Jordan under Joshua (vv. 7–24).
12:1 the land. The territory east of the Jordan was clearly included in the land given by God to Israel (v. 7). See notes on 1:12–15, 13:8–33 and 22:1–34. **Arnon Gorge.** This runs into the Dead Sea from the east and marks the southern boundary of the land. **Mount Hermon.** Located northeast of the Sea of Galilee. **the Arabah.** The Jordan Valley.
12:2–5 See Numbers 21:21–35 and Deuteronomy 2:24—3:11. The defeat of Sihon and Og marked the beginning of the conquest and was remembered as a testimony to God's power and faithfulness (see Dt 29:7–8; 31:4; Jos 2:10; 9:10; Ne 9:22; Pss 135:11; 136:19–20).
12:6 Moses, the servant of the LORD. This designation (or a shorter form of it) is applied to Moses five times (1:1,2,7,13,15). See note on 1:1.
12:7 Joshua gave as an inheritance to the tribes. These words anticipate chapters 13–21.
12:9–24 The list approximates the order of the account in earlier chapters, but with additions, indicating the incomplete and representative nature of the preceding accounts.

12:10 [y]Jos 10:23
12:12 [z]Jos 10:33
12:14 [a]Nu 21:1
12:16 [b]Jos 7:2
12:17 [c]1Ki 4:10
12:18 [d]Jos 13:4
12:20 [e]Jos 11:1
12:22 [f]Jos 19:37; 20:7; 21:32 [g]1Sa 15:12
12:23 [h]Jos 11:2
12:24 [i]Ps 135:11; Dt 7:24

10 the king of Jerusalem[y]	one
the king of Hebron	one
11 the king of Jarmuth	one
the king of Lachish	one
12 the king of Eglon	one
the king of Gezer[z]	one
13 the king of Debir	one
the king of Geder	one
14 the king of Hormah	one
the king of Arad[a]	one
15 the king of Libnah	one
the king of Adullam	one
16 the king of Makkedah	one
the king of Bethel[b]	one
17 the king of Tappuah	one
the king of Hepher[c]	one
18 the king of Aphek[d]	one
the king of Lasharon	one
19 the king of Madon	one
the king of Hazor	one
20 the king of Shimron Meron	one
the king of Acshaph[e]	one
21 the king of Taanach	one
the king of Megiddo	one
22 the king of Kedesh[f]	one
the king of Jokneam in Carmel[g]	one
23 the king of Dor (in Naphoth Dor[a] [h])	one
the king of Goyim in Gilgal	one
24 the king of Tirzah	one

thirty-one kings in all.[i]

Land Still to Be Taken

13:1 [j]Ge 24:1; Jos 14:10
13:3 [k]Jer 2:18 [l]Jdg 1:18 [m]Jdg 3:3 [n]Dt 2:23
13:4 [o]Jos 12:18; 19:30 [p]Am 2:10
13:5 [q]1Ki 5:18; Ps 83:7; Eze 27:9 [r]Jos 12:7
13:6 [s]Jos 11:8 [t]Nu 33:54
13:7 [u]Jos 11:23; Ps 78:55

13 When Joshua was old and well advanced in years,[j] the LORD said to him, "You
are very old, and there are still very large areas of land to be taken over.

2 "This is the land that remains: all the regions of the Philistines and Geshurites:
3 from the Shihor River[k] on the east of Egypt to the territory of Ekron[l] on the north,
all of it counted as Canaanite (the territory of the five Philistine rulers[m] in Gaza,
Ashdod, Ashkelon, Gath and Ekron—that of the Avvites);[n]
4 from the south, all the
land of the Canaanites, from Arah of the Sidonians as far as Aphek,[o] the region
of the Amorites,[p]
5 the area of the Gebalites[b];[q] and all Lebanon[r] to the east, from
Baal Gad below Mount Hermon to Lebo[c] Hamath.

6 "As for all the inhabitants of the mountain regions from Lebanon to Misrephoth
Maim,[s] that is, all the Sidonians, I myself will drive them out before the Israelites. Be sure
to allocate this land to Israel for an inheritance, as I have instructed you,[t]
7 and divide it
as an inheritance[u] among the nine tribes and half of the tribe of Manasseh."

[a] 23 Or *in the heights of Dor* [b] 5 That is, the area of Byblos [c] 5 Or *to the entrance to*

■ **13:1—21:45** *The Distribution of the Promised Land.* This second major division of the book primarily concerns the divine authorization of the distribution of the promised land among the tribes. The many details included would later help to settle disputes that would arise after the days of Joshua. These chapters divide into six main sections: the divine commission (13:1–7), allocations east of the Jordan (13:8–33), allocations west of the Jordan (14:1—19:51), cities of refuge (20:1–9), towns for the Levites (21:1–42) and a concluding summary (21:43–45).

■ **13:1–7** *The Divine Commission to Allocate the Land.* The long description of the allocation of the land to the tribes of Israel (chs. 13–21) is introduced by a word from God to Joshua indicating Joshua's advanced age (v. 1a), the incompleteness of the conquest (vv. 1b–5), God's promise to finish it (v. 6a) and the command to Joshua to allocate the land in the meantime (vv. 6b–7).

13:1 Joshua was old. The implication is that further conquest would not take place under him. **still very large areas of land.** The book of Joshua speaks of both the complete fulfillment of God's promises (e.g., 11:23; 21:45) and the incompleteness of the actual possession of the land (e.g., v. 1; 23:4–5). Compare the New Testament perspective of the completeness of what has been given in Christ and the future expectation that remains (e.g., Eph 1:3,14). While the book of Joshua testifies to Israel's experience of the Lord's complete faithfulness, the promise still pointed forward to the future. See notes on 1:4, 21:45 and Genesis 13:15.

13:3 all of it counted as Canaanite. The Philistines were not strictly Canaanites, but their territory was in Canaan and was therefore included in God's promise to Israel. **rulers.** The Hebrew here is derived from a Greek term for "tyrant," suggesting the Hellenic background of the Philistines (cf. Am 9:7).

13:4 Amorites. See note on 2:10.

13:6 allocate. The Hebrew word (lit., "cause to fall") suggests allocation by lot (14:2; note on 15:1; 18:6; 19:51). **inheritance.** See also verse 8 and note on 1:6.

Division of the Land East of the Jordan

8The other half of Manasseh,[a] the Reubenites and the Gadites had received the inheritance that Moses had given them east of the Jordan, as he, the servant of the LORD, had
assigned[v] it to them.

9It extended from Aroer[w] on the rim of the Arnon Gorge, and from the town in the
middle of the gorge, and included the whole plateau[x] of Medeba as far as Dibon,[y]
10and all the towns of Sihon king of the Amorites, who ruled in Heshbon, out to
the border of the Ammonites.[z] 11It also included Gilead, the territory of the people of Geshur and Maacah, all of Mount Hermon and all Bashan as far as Salecah[a]— 12that is, the whole kingdom of Og in Bashan,[b] who had reigned in Ashtaroth[c] and Edrei and had survived as one of the last of the Rephaites.[d] Moses had
defeated them and taken over their land. 13But the Israelites did not drive out the
people of Geshur[e] and Maacah,[f] so they continue to live among the Israelites to
this day.

14But to the tribe of Levi he gave no inheritance, since the offerings made by fire to
the LORD, the God of Israel, are their inheritance, as he promised them.[g]

15This is what Moses had given to the tribe of Reuben, clan by clan:

16The territory from Aroer[h] on the rim of the Arnon Gorge, and from the town in
the middle of the gorge, and the whole plateau past Medeba[i] 17to Heshbon and
all its towns on the plateau, including Dibon,[j] Bamoth Baal, Beth Baal Meon,[k]
18Jahaz,[l] Kedemoth, Mephaath,[m] 19Kiriathaim,[n] Sibmah, Zereth Shahar on the
hill in the valley, 20Beth Peor,[o] the slopes of Pisgah, and Beth Jeshimoth 21—all the
towns on the plateau and the entire realm of Sihon king of the Amorites, who
ruled at Heshbon. Moses had defeated him and the Midianite chiefs,[p] Evi, Rekem,
Zur, Hur and Reba[q]—princes allied with Sihon—who lived in that country. 22In
addition to those slain in battle, the Israelites had put to the sword Balaam son
of Beor,[r] who practiced divination. 23The boundary of the Reubenites was the
bank of the Jordan. These towns and their villages were the inheritance of the Reubenites, clan by clan.

24This is what Moses had given to the tribe of Gad, clan by clan:

25The territory of Jazer,[s] all the towns of Gilead and half the Ammonite country as
far as Aroer, near Rabbah; 26and from Heshbon[t] to Ramath Mizpah and Betonim,
and from Mahanaim to the territory of Debir;[u] 27and in the valley, Beth Haram,
Beth Nimrah, Succoth[v] and Zaphon with the rest of the realm of Sihon king of
Heshbon (the east side of the Jordan, the territory up to the end of the Sea of Kinnereth[b][w]). 28These towns and their villages were the inheritance of the Gadites,[x]
clan by clan.

29This is what Moses had given to the half-tribe of Manasseh, that is, to half the family
of the descendants of Manasseh, clan by clan:

30The territory extending from Mahanaim[y] and including all of Bashan, the entire
realm of Og king of Bashan—all the settlements of Jair[z] in Bashan, sixty towns,
31half of Gilead, and Ashtaroth and Edrei (the royal cities of Og in Bashan). This

13:8 [v]Jos 12:6
13:9 [w]ver 16; Jdg 11:26 [x]Jer 48:8,21 [y]Nu 21:30
13:10 [z]Nu 21:24
13:11 [a]Jos 12:5
13:12 [b]Dt 3:11 [c]Jos 12:4 [d]Ge 14:5
13:13 [e]Jos 12:5 [f]Dt 3:14
13:14 [g]ver 33; Dt 18:1-2
13:16 [h]ver 9; Jos 12:2 [i]Nu 21:30
13:17 [j]Nu 32:3 [k]1Ch 5:8
13:18 [l]Nu 21:23 [m]Jer 48:21
13:19 [n]Nu 32:37
13:20 [o]Dt 3:29
13:21 [p]Nu 25:15 [q]Nu 31:8
13:22 [r]Nu 22:5; 31:8
13:25 [s]Nu 21:32; Jos 21:39
13:26 [t]Nu 21:25; Jer 49:3 [u]Jos 10:3
13:27 [v]Ge 33:17 [w]Nu 34:11
13:28 [x]Nu 32:33
13:30 [y]Ge 32:2 [z]Nu 32:41

[a] *8* Hebrew *With it* (that is, with the other half of Manasseh)   [b] *27* That is, Galilee

■ **13:8–33** *East of the Jordan.* As the summary of the conquest in chapter 12 began with the kings and their territories east of the Jordan (12:1–6; cf. 1:12–15), so the account of the distribution of the land also begins with the allocation of these territories to the tribes of Reuben (vv. 15–23), Gad (vv. 24–28) and the half-tribe of Manasseh (vv. 29–31). In this way Joshua completed what Moses had begun, and the unity of all Israel was affirmed (see note on 1:12–15), despite the geographical boundary of the Jordan (22:25) and the historical separation of the work of Moses and Joshua. See chapter 22.

13:8 Manasseh. The elder of Joseph's two sons. See Genesis 48 and its notes. **Reubenites.** Reuben was Jacob's eldest son, born to Leah (see Ge 29:32; 35:22; 49:3,4 and their notes). **Gadites.** Gad was Jacob's seventh son, his first by Zilpah (Ge 30:9–11; see 49:19 and its note).

13:13 the Israelites did not drive out the people. The significance of this failure of the Israelites becomes clearer in the book of Judges (e.g., Jdg 1:27–36; 2:20—3:6). **to this day.** See note on 4:9.

13:14 the tribe of Levi. Levi was Jacob's third son, born to Leah (see Ge 29:34; 34:25; 49:5 and their notes). That Levi received no allotment of land from either Moses or Joshua is explained here and in verse 33 (see also 14:3–4; 18:7; Dt 18:1–8). The 12-tribe structure of Israel is enumerated in various ways in the Old Testament. In the allotment of the land in these chapters, there were still 12 tribal territories, since the descendants of Joseph were treated as two tribes, Ephraim and Manasseh (14:4; Ge 48:5).

13:22 Balaam son of Beor. See Numbers 31:8. Balaam was associated with "the sin of Peor" (see Nu 31:16), which is referred to in 22:17. Balaam's evil influence was long remembered (2Pe 2:15; Rev 2:14). **divination.** An attempt to attain knowledge by supernatural means. It was commonly practiced among pagan peoples but forbidden in Israel (Lev 19:26; Dt 18:9–14; 1Sa 15:23; cf. 2Ki 17:17; 21:6; Isa 2:6; Eze 13:23).

was for the descendants of Makir[a] son of Manasseh—for half of the sons of Makir, clan by clan.

32 This is the inheritance Moses had given when he was in the plains of Moab across
the Jordan east of Jericho. 33 But to the tribe of Levi, Moses had given no inheritance; the
LORD, the God of Israel, is their inheritance,[b] as he promised them.[c]

Division of the Land West of the Jordan

14 Now these are the areas the Israelites received as an inheritance in the land of
Canaan, which Eleazar the priest, Joshua son of Nun and the heads of the tribal clans of Israel allotted to them.[d] 2 Their inheritances were assigned by lot[e] to the nine-
and-a-half tribes, as the LORD had commanded through Moses. 3 Moses had granted the
two-and-a-half tribes their inheritance east of the Jordan[f] but had not granted the Levites an inheritance among the rest,[g] 4 for the sons of Joseph had become two tribes—
Manasseh and Ephraim.[h] The Levites received no share of the land but only towns to live
in, with pasturelands for their flocks and herds. 5 So the Israelites divided the land, just
as the LORD had commanded Moses.[i]

Hebron Given to Caleb

6 Now the men of Judah approached Joshua at Gilgal, and Caleb son of Jephunneh[j] the
Kenizzite said to him, "You know what the LORD said to Moses the man of God at Kadesh
Barnea[k] about you and me. 7 I was forty years old when Moses the servant of the LORD
sent me from Kadesh Barnea to explore the land.[l] And I brought him back a report according to my convictions,[m] 8 but my brothers who went up with me made the hearts of
the people melt with fear.[n] I, however, followed the LORD my God wholeheartedly.[o] 9 So
on that day Moses swore to me, 'The land on which your feet have walked will be your
inheritance and that of your children[p] forever, because you have followed the LORD my
God wholeheartedly.'[a]

10 "Now then, just as the LORD promised,[q] he has kept me alive for forty-five years
since the time he said this to Moses, while Israel moved about in the desert. So here I am
today, eighty-five years old! 11 I am still as strong[r] today as the day Moses sent me out;
I'm just as vigorous to go out to battle now as I was then. 12 Now give me this hill country that the LORD promised me that day. You yourself heard then that the Anakites[s] were
there and their cities were large and fortified,[t] but, the LORD helping me, I will drive them
out just as he said."

13 Then Joshua blessed[u] Caleb son of Jephunneh and gave him Hebron[v] as his inheritance.[w] 14 So Hebron has belonged to Caleb son of Jephunneh the Kenizzite ever since,
because he followed the LORD, the God of Israel, wholeheartedly. 15 (Hebron used to be
called Kiriath Arba[x] after Arba,[y] who was the greatest man among the Anakites.)
Then the land had rest[z] from war.

13:31 [a]Ge 50:23
13:33 [b]Nu 18:20 [c]ver 14; Jos 18:7
14:1 [d]Nu 34:17-18
14:2 [e]Nu 26:55
14:3 [f]Nu 32:33 [g]Jos 13:14
14:4 [h]Ge 41:52; 48:5
14:5 [i]Nu 34:13; 35:2; Jos 21:2
14:6 [j]Nu 13:6; 14:30 [k]Nu 13:26
14:7 [l]Nu 13:17 [m]Nu 13:30; 14:6-9
14:8 [n]Nu 13:31 [o]Nu 14:24
14:9 [p]Nu 14:24; Dt 1:36
14:10 [q]Nu 14:30
14:11 [r]Dt 34:7
14:12 [s]Nu 13:33 [t]Nu 13:28
14:13 [u]Jos 22:6,7 [v]Jos 10:36 [w]Jdg 1:20; 1Ch 6:56
14:15 [x]Ge 23:2 [y]Jos 15:13 [z]Jos 11:23

a 9 Deut. 1:36

13:33 the tribe of Levi. See note on verse 14.
▪ **14:1—19:51** *West of the Jordan.* These chapters detail the allotment of territory to the tribes west of the Jordan. There is a correspondence of vocabulary between 14:1 and 19:51 that marks the beginning and end of this section. These materials divide into seven sections: an introduction (14:1–5), Caleb's special allotment (14:6–15), Judah's allotment (15:1–63), the allotment for Ephraim and Manasseh (16:1—17:18), the allotments for the other tribes (18:1—19:48), Joshua's special allotment (19:49–50) and a conclusion (19:51).
▪ **14:1–5** *Introduction.* This introduction to the description of the territories allotted to the tribes west of the Jordan relates what follows once again to the tribes east of the Jordan, and it explains again the situation of the Levites. A major purpose of this description was to keep the audience's attention focused on the unity of all Israel (see notes on 1:12–15; 13:8–33).
14:1 inheritance. See note on 1:6. **Canaan.** The word here means the land west of the Jordan. **Eleazar the priest.** Eleazar was the son of Aaron the high priest (Ex 6:23). He took precedence over Joshua here, possibly because of his role in the casting of the lots (Ex 28:30; 1Sa 2:28).
14:2 lot. See note on 15:1.
14:3 the Levites. See note on 13:14.
14:4 Manasseh and Ephraim. See note on 13:14.
▪ **14:6–15** *Caleb's Special Allotment.* The story of Caleb receiving his inheritance stands at the beginning of the account of the allotment of the land and balances with the story of Joshua receiving his inheritance (19:49–50). These two men were given special treatment because of their faithfulness at Kadesh Barnea (see note on v. 6).
14:6 Gilgal. Probably the same as the one mentioned in 10:43. It was located to the east of Jericho. **Caleb.** He was the representative of Judah among the 12 men sent by Moses from Kadesh Barnea to spy out the land (Nu 13:6). Caleb and Joshua (the representative of Ephraim on the same mission; Nu 13:8) were the only two spies to believe the promise of God (Nu 13:30; 14:6–9,24,30,38; Dt 1:36).
14:7 a report according to my convictions. Literally, "a word according to what was with my heart." Caleb's report had expressed his trust in God's promise. See Numbers 14:6–9.
14:8–9 followed the LORD my God wholeheartedly. Caleb's obedient faith was exemplary.
14:8 hearts . . . melt with fear. The people's reaction was the opposite of Caleb's faith (v. 7; see note on 7:5).
14:9 Moses swore to me. This oath is not recorded in Numbers 14 or Deuteronomy 1.
14:12 Anakites. See note on 11:21–22. **the LORD helping me.** Literally, "the LORD with me," as in the promise of 1:5. **I will drive them out.** Caleb's faith in God's promise was not expressed in human passivity, but in active obedience. See notes on 1:6 and 7 and 17:15.
14:13 blessed. See note on 8:33.
14:14 ever since. Literally, "to this day." See note on 4:9.
14:15 the land had rest from war. See note on 11:23.

Allotment for Judah

15 The allotment for the tribe of Judah, clan by clan, extended down to the territory of Edom,[a] to the Desert of Zin[b] in the extreme south.
2Their southern boundary started from the bay at the southern end of the Salt
Sea,[a] 3crossed south of Scorpion[b] Pass,[c] continued on to Zin and went over to the
south of Kadesh Barnea. Then it ran past Hezron up to Addar and curved around
to Karka. 4It then passed along to Azmon[d] and joined the Wadi of Egypt,[e] ending
at the sea. This is their[c] southern boundary.
5The eastern boundary[f] is the Salt Sea as far as the mouth of the Jordan.
The northern boundary[g] started from the bay of the sea at the mouth of the Jordan, 6went up to Beth Hoglah[h] and continued north of Beth Arabah to the Stone
of Bohan[i] son of Reuben. 7The boundary then went up to Debir from the Valley
of Achor[j] and turned north to Gilgal, which faces the Pass of Adummim south of
the gorge. It continued along to the waters of En Shemesh and came out at En Rogel.[k] 8Then it ran up the Valley of Ben Hinnom along the southern slope of the Jebusite[l] city (that is, Jerusalem). From there it climbed to the top of the hill west of
the Hinnom Valley at the northern end of the Valley of Rephaim. 9From the hilltop the boundary headed toward the spring of the waters of Nephtoah,[m] came out
at the towns of Mount Ephron and went down toward Baalah[n] (that is, Kiriath Jearim). 10Then it curved westward from Baalah to Mount Seir, ran along the northern slope of Mount Jearim (that is, Kesalon), continued down to Beth Shemesh
and crossed to Timnah.[o] 11It went to the northern slope of Ekron, turned toward
Shikkeron, passed along to Mount Baalah and reached Jabneel.[p] The boundary
ended at the sea.
12The western boundary is the coastline of the Great Sea.[d][q]
These are the boundaries around the people of Judah by their clans.

13In accordance with the LORD's command to him, Joshua gave to Caleb son of Jephunneh a portion in Judah—Kiriath Arba, that is, Hebron. (Arba was the forefather of
Anak.)[r] 14From Hebron Caleb drove out the three Anakites[s]—Sheshai, Ahiman and Talmai[t]—descendants of Anak.[u] 15From there he marched against the people living in Debir (formerly called Kiriath Sepher). 16And Caleb said, "I will give my daughter Acsah[v]
in marriage to the man who attacks and captures Kiriath Sepher." 17Othniel[w] son of Kenaz, Caleb's brother, took it; so Caleb gave his daughter Acsah to him in marriage.
18One day when she came to Othniel, she urged him[e] to ask her father for a field.
When she got off her donkey, Caleb asked her, "What can I do for you?"
19She replied, "Do me a special favor. Since you have given me land in the Negev, give
me also springs of water." So Caleb gave her the upper and lower springs.
20This is the inheritance of the tribe of Judah, clan by clan:

21The southernmost towns of the tribe of Judah in the Negev toward the boundary of
Edom were:
Kabzeel, Eder,[x] Jagur, 22Kinah, Dimonah, Adadah, 23Kedesh, Hazor, Ithnan,
24Ziph,[y] Telem, Bealoth, 25Hazor Hadattah, Kerioth Hezron (that is, Hazor),
26Amam, Shema, Moladah,[z] 27Hazar Gaddah, Heshmon, Beth Pelet, 28Hazar Shual, Beersheba,[a] Biziothiah, 29Baalah,[b] Iim, Ezem, 30Eltolad,[c] Kesil, Hormah, 31Zik-

a *2* That is, the Dead Sea; also in verse 5 b *3* Hebrew *Akrabbim* c *4* Hebrew *your* d *12* That is, the Mediterranean; also in verse 47 e *18* Hebrew and some Septuagint manuscripts; other Septuagint manuscripts (see also note at Judges 1:14) *Othniel, he urged her*

15:1 [a]Nu 34:3 [b]Nu 33:36
15:3 [c]Nu 34:4
15:4 [d]Nu 34:5 [e]Ge 15:18
15:5 [f]Nu 34:10 [g]Jos 18:15-19
15:6 [h]Jos 18:19,21 [i]Jos 18:17
15:7 [j]Jos 7:24 [k]2Sa 17:17; 1Ki 1:9
15:8 [l]ver 63; Jos 18:16, 28; Jdg 1:21; 19:10
15:9 [m]Jos 18:15 [n]1Ch 13:6
15:10 [o]Ge 38:12; Jdg 14:1
15:11 [p]Jos 19:33
15:12 [q]Nu 34:6
15:13 [r]Jos 14:13-15
15:14 [s]Nu 13:33 [t]Nu 13:22 [u]Jdg 1:10,20
15:16 [v]Jdg 1:12
15:17 [w]Jdg 3:9,11
15:21 [x]Ge 35:21
15:24 [y]1Sa 23:14
15:26 [z]1Ch 4:28
15:28 [a]Ge 21:31
15:29 [b]ver 9
15:30 [c]Jos 19:4

■ **15:1–63** *Judah's Allotment.* The first and most detailed description of the territory allotted to the tribes west of the Jordan is that of Judah, reflecting the later importance of Judah in the history of Israel as the tribe of David (and subsequently of the expected Messiah; Isa 11:1). This importance may reflect a date of final composition for the book during or after the time of David. Judah was Jacob's fourth son, born to Leah (Ge 29:35). He received special blessing from his father (Ge 49:8–12). In this and subsequent chapters many of the place names cannot today be identified with certainty. Furthermore, the allocation does not necessarily correspond in every detail to the actual territory subsequently occupied by the tribes, since the promise was never fully realized in Israel's Old Testament experience.

15:1–12 The four boundaries of Judah's territory are described here.

15:1 allotment. Or "lot" (cf. 14:2; 18:6). The method of casting lots is not specified, but the important point is that the allocation of the land was not a matter of human decision (Pr 16:33; 18:18).

15:8 Jerusalem. Jerusalem lay outside Judah's territory as it is described here.

15:13–19 The story of Caleb receiving what was promised him (14:6–15) is brought to its conclusion here, underlining again the vindication of his trust in God.

15:14 Anakites. See note on 11:21–22.

15:17 Othniel. See Judges 3:7–11 for his later role as a judge.

15:19 special favor. Literally, "blessing." See 14:13 and note on 8:33.

15:20–62 These verses provide a detailed list of the towns in the territory allotted to Judah. Although many of these towns cannot today be identified with confidence, the extensive enumeration is a tangible representation of the promise of God (21:45).

15:20 inheritance. See note on 1:6.

lag,[d] Madmannah, Sansannah, [32]Lebaoth, Shilhim, Ain and Rimmon[e]—a total of
twenty-nine towns and their villages.

[33]In the western foothills:

Eshtaol,[f] Zorah, Ashnah, [34]Zanoah,[g] En Gannim, Tappuah, Enam, [35]Jarmuth,[h]
Adullam,[i] Socoh, Azekah, [36]Shaaraim, Adithaim and Gederah[j] (or Gederothaim)[a]—fourteen towns and their villages.

[37]Zenan, Hadashah, Migdal Gad, [38]Dilean, Mizpah, Joktheel,[k] [39]Lachish,[l] Bozkath,[m] Eglon, [40]Cabbon, Lahmas, Kitlish, [41]Gederoth, Beth Dagon, Naamah and
Makkedah[n]—sixteen towns and their villages.

[42]Libnah, Ether, Ashan,[o] [43]Iphtah, Ashnah, Nezib, [44]Keilah, Aczib[p] and Mareshah[q]—nine towns and their villages.

[45]Ekron, with its surrounding settlements and villages; [46]west of Ekron, all that
were in the vicinity of Ashdod, together with their villages; [47]Ashdod,[r] its surrounding settlements and villages; and Gaza, its settlements and villages, as far
as the Wadi of Egypt[s] and the coastline of the Great Sea.[t]

[48]In the hill country:

Shamir, Jattir,[u] Socoh, [49]Dannah, Kiriath Sannah (that is, Debir[v]), [50]Anab, Esh-
temoh,[w] Anim, [51]Goshen,[x] Holon and Giloh—eleven towns and their villages.

[52]Arab, Dumah,[y] Eshan, [53]Janim, Beth Tappuah, Aphekah, [54]Humtah, Kiriath
Arba (that is, Hebron) and Zior—nine towns and their villages.

[55]Maon, Carmel,[z] Ziph, Juttah, [56]Jezreel,[a] Jokdeam, Zanoah, [57]Kain, Gibeah[b]
and Timnah—ten towns and their villages.

[58]Halhul, Beth Zur,[c] Gedor, [59]Maarath, Beth Anoth and Eltekon—six towns
and their villages.

[60]Kiriath Baal (that is, Kiriath Jearim[d]) and Rabbah[e]—two towns and their villages.

[61]In the desert:

Beth Arabah, Middin, Secacah, [62]Nibshan, the City of Salt and En Gedi[f]—six
towns and their villages.

[63]Judah could not[g] dislodge the Jebusites[h], who were living in Jerusalem; to this day
the Jebusites live there with the people of Judah.

Allotment for Ephraim and Manasseh

16 The allotment for Joseph began at the Jordan of Jericho,[b] east of the waters of Jericho, and went up from there through the desert[i] into the hill
country of Bethel. [2]It went on from Bethel (that is, Luz[j]),[c] crossed over to the territory of the Arkites in Ataroth, [3]descended westward to the territory of the Japh-
letites as far as the region of Lower Beth Horon[k] and on to Gezer,[l] ending at the sea.
[4]So Manasseh and Ephraim, the descendants of Joseph, received their inheritance.[m]

[5]This was the territory of Ephraim, clan by clan:

The boundary of their inheritance went from Ataroth Addar[n] in the east to Upper Beth Horon [6]and continued to the sea. From Micmethath[o] on the north it
curved eastward to Taanath Shiloh, passing by it to Janoah on the east. [7]Then it
went down from Janoah to Ataroth[p] and Naarah, touched Jericho and came out
at the Jordan. [8]From Tappuah the border went west to the Kanah Ravine[q] and
ended at the sea. This was the inheritance of the tribe of the Ephraimites, clan by
clan. [9]It also included all the towns and their villages that were set aside for the
Ephraimites within the inheritance of the Manassites.

15:31 [d]1Sa 27:6
15:32 [e]Jdg 20:45
15:33 [f]Jdg 13:25; 16:31
15:34 [g]1Ch 4:18; Ne 3:13
15:35 [h]Jos 10:3 [i]1Sa 22:1
15:36 [j]1Ch 12:4
15:38 [k]2Ki 14:7
15:39 [l]Jos 10:3; 2Ki 14:19 [m]2Ki 22:1
15:41 [n]Jos 10:10
15:42 [o]1Sa 30:30
15:44 [p]Jdg 1:31 [q]Mic 1:15
15:47 [r]Jos 11:22 [s]ver 4 [t]Nu 34:6
15:48 [u]1Sa 30:27
15:49 [v]Jos 10:3
15:50 [w]Jos 21:14
15:51 [x]Jos 10:41; 11:16
15:52 [y]Ge 25:14
15:55 [z]Jos 12:22
15:56 [a]Jos 17:16
15:57 [b]Jos 18:28; Jdg 19:12
15:58 [c]1Ch 2:45
15:60 [d]Jos 18:14 [e]Dt 3:11
15:62 [f]1Sa 23:29
15:63 [g]Jdg 1:21 [h]2Sa 5:6
16:1 [i]Jos 8:15; 18:12
16:2 [j]Jos 18:13
16:3 [k]2Ch 8:5 [l]Jos 10:33; 1Ki 9:15
16:4 [m]Jos 17:14
16:5 [n]Jos 18:13
16:6 [o]Jos 17:7
16:7 [p]1Ch 7:28
16:8 [q]Jos 17:9

[a] *36* Or *Gederah and Gederothaim* [b] *1* *Jordan of Jericho* was possibly an ancient name for the Jordan River.
[c] *2* Septuagint; Hebrew *Bethel to Luz*

15:63 Judah could not dislodge the Jebusites. This brief note on Judah's failure (see Dt 7:1) is another reminder that the experience of the fulfillment of God's promises (21:45) was incomplete. See note on 21:45. **Jebusites.** The victory over the Jebusites recorded in Judges 1:8 apparently was not permanent (see Jdg 1:21). **to this day.** See note on 4:9.

■ **16:1—17:18** *Joseph's Allotment.* These two chapters outline the allotment to the two tribes of Joseph. Joseph was Jacob's eleventh son, his first by Rachel (Ge 30:22–24). Joseph received the double portion of the firstborn: His two sons, Ephraim and Manasseh (Ge 41:50–52; see note on Jos 13:14), were counted as tribal fathers (Ge 48). Half of the tribe of Manasseh had already received its land east of the Jordan (17:1). A general description of the boundary (16:1–4) is followed by details for the tribes of Ephraim (16:5–10) and Manasseh (17:1–13) and an account of their complaint (17:14–18).

16:1 allotment. See note on 15:1.

16:4 Manasseh and Ephraim. Here they are mentioned in the order of their birth, not their priority (Ge 48:12–20). **inheritance.** See note on 1:6.

16:5–10 Ephraim was Joseph's younger son (Ge 41:52). Ephraim's territory is described before Manasseh's, probably reflecting the precedence given Ephraim (Ge 48:12–20).

10They did not dislodge the Canaanites living in Gezer; to this day the Canaanites live
among the people of Ephraim but are required to do forced labor.[r]

17 This was the allotment for the tribe of Manasseh as Joseph's firstborn,[s] that is,
for Makir,[t] Manasseh's firstborn. Makir was the ancestor of the Gileadites,
who had received Gilead and Bashan because the Makirites were great soldiers. 2So this
allotment was for the rest of the people of Manasseh—the clans of Abiezer,[u] Helek, Asriel, Shechem, Hepher and Shemida. These are the other male descendants of Manasseh son of Joseph by their clans.
3Now Zelophehad son of Hepher,[v] the son of Gilead, the son of Makir, the son of Manasseh, had no sons but only daughters,[w] whose names were Mahlah, Noah, Hoglah,
Milcah and Tirzah. 4They went to Eleazar the priest, Joshua son of Nun, and the leaders
and said, "The LORD commanded Moses to give us an inheritance among our brothers."
So Joshua gave them an inheritance along with the brothers of their father, according
to the LORD's command.[x] 5Manasseh's share consisted of ten tracts of land besides Gilead and Bashan east of the Jordan, 6because the daughters of the tribe of Manasseh received an inheritance among the sons. The land of Gilead belonged to the rest of the descendants of Manasseh.
7The territory of Manasseh extended from Asher to Micmethath[y] east of Shechem.[z] The boundary ran southward from there to include the people living at En
Tappuah. 8(Manasseh had the land of Tappuah, but Tappuah[a] itself, on the
boundary of Manasseh, belonged to the Ephraimites.) 9Then the boundary continued south to the Kanah Ravine.[b] There were towns belonging to Ephraim lying among the towns of Manasseh, but the boundary of Manasseh was the northern side of the ravine and ended at the sea. 10On the south the land belonged to
Ephraim, on the north to Manasseh. The territory of Manasseh reached the sea
and bordered Asher on the north and Issachar[c] on the east.
11Within Issachar and Asher, Manasseh also had Beth Shan,[d] Ibleam and the
people of Dor,[e] Endor,[f] Taanach and Megiddo,[g] together with their surrounding
settlements (the third in the list is Naphoth[a]).
12Yet the Manassites were not able[h] to occupy these towns, for the Canaanites were determined to live in that region. 13However, when the Israelites grew stronger, they subjected the Canaanites to forced labor but did not drive them out completely.[i]
14The people of Joseph said to Joshua, "Why have you given us only one allotment and
one portion for an inheritance? We are a numerous people and the LORD has blessed us
abundantly."[j]
15"If you are so numerous," Joshua answered, "and if the hill country of Ephraim is
too small for you, go up into the forest and clear land for yourselves there in the land of
the Perizzites and Rephaites."[k]
16The people of Joseph replied, "The hill country is not enough for us, and all the Canaanites who live in the plain have iron chariots,[l] both those in Beth Shan and its settlements and those in the Valley of Jezreel."
17But Joshua said to the house of Joseph—to Ephraim and Manasseh—"You are numerous and very powerful. You will have not only one allotment 18but the forested hill
country as well. Clear it, and its farthest limits will be yours; though the Canaanites have
iron chariots[m] and though they are strong, you can drive them out."

a *11* That is, Naphoth Dor

16:10 [r]Jos 17:13; Jdg 1:28-29; 1Ki 9:16
17:1 [s]Ge 41:51 [t]Ge 50:23
17:2 [u]Nu 26:30; 1Ch 7:18
17:3 [v]Nu 27:1 [w]Nu 26:33
17:4 [x]Nu 27:5-7
17:7 [y]Jos 16:6 [z]Ge 12:6; Jos 21:21
17:8 [a]Jos 16:8
17:9 [b]Jos 16:8
17:10 [c]Ge 30:18
17:11 [d]1Sa 31:10; 1Ki 4:12; 1Ch 7:29 [e]Jos 11:2 [f]1Sa 28:7; Ps 83:10 [g]1Ki 9:15
17:12 [h]Jdg 1:27
17:13 [i]Jos 16:10
17:14 [j]Nu 26:28-37
17:15 [k]Ge 14:5
17:16 [l]Jdg 1:19; 4:3,13
17:18 [m]ver 16

16:10 They did not dislodge the Canaanites. See note on 15:63. **to this day.** See note on 4:9.
17:1 This was the allotment. The reference is to the allotment to the half-tribe of Manasseh east of the Jordan (13:29–31). **Manasseh.** Manasseh was the elder, but subordinate, of Joseph's two sons (Ge 41:50–51; 48:12–20). **Joseph's firstborn.** See note on 16:5–10. **Manasseh's firstborn.** See Genesis 50:23.
17:2 this allotment. This reference is to the allotment to the other half of the tribe of Manasseh west of the Jordan. **allotment.** See note on 15:1.
17:3–6 A detail of the promise of God (namely, that the daughters of a man with no son would receive his inheritance) is here applied (see Nu 27:1–11, especially v. 8).
17:12–13 not able to occupy . . . did not drive them out completely. See notes on 15:63 and 21:45.
17:14–18 The people's complaining request of Joshua (v. 14) and their fear of the Canaanites (v. 16) stand in contrast to Caleb's faith and courage (14:6–12).
17:14 one allotment. The territory of Manasseh on both sides of the Jordan and that of Ephraim is here (as in 16:1) treated as one allotment, or lot (see note on 15:1). **numerous people . . . blessed.** See note on 8:33. Growth in numbers is an aspect of the promise to Abraham (e.g., Ge 15:5).
17:15 go up . . . and clear land for yourselves. Faith in the promise of God ought to be expressed in courageous, obedient action. See notes on 1:6 and 7 and 14:12.
17:16 not enough . . . the Canaanites. Their fear and unwillingness to obey were expressions of unbelief in the promise of God. **iron chariots.** Possibly iron-plated chariots.
17:18 though they are strong, you can drive them out. The fears of the people of Joseph were met by an application of the promise of God (cf. 1:5).

Division of the Rest of the Land

18 The whole assembly of the Israelites gathered at Shiloh[n] and set up the Tent of Meeting[o] there. The country was brought under their control, 2 but there were still seven Israelite tribes who had not yet received their inheritance.

3 So Joshua said to the Israelites: "How long will you wait before you begin to take possession of the land that the LORD, the God of your fathers, has given you? 4 Appoint three men from each tribe. I will send them out to make a survey of the land and to write a description of it, according to the inheritance of each.[p] Then they will return to me. 5 You are to divide the land into seven parts. Judah is to remain in its territory on the south[q] and the house of Joseph in its territory on the north.[r] 6 After you have written descriptions of the seven parts of the land, bring them here to me and I will cast lots[s] for you in the presence of the LORD our God. 7 The Levites, however, do not get a portion among you, because the priestly service of the LORD is their inheritance.[t] And Gad, Reuben and the half-tribe of Manasseh have already received their inheritance on the east side of the Jordan. Moses the servant of the LORD gave it to them.[u]"

8 As the men started on their way to map out the land, Joshua instructed them, "Go and make a survey of the land and write a description of it. Then return to me, and I will cast lots for you here at Shiloh[v] in the presence of the LORD." 9 So the men left and went through the land. They wrote its description on a scroll, town by town, in seven parts, and returned to Joshua in the camp at Shiloh. 10 Joshua then cast lots[w] for them in Shiloh in the presence[x] of the LORD, and there he distributed the land to the Israelites according to their tribal divisions.[y]

Allotment for Benjamin

11 The lot came up for the tribe of Benjamin, clan by clan. Their allotted territory lay between the tribes of Judah and Joseph:

12 On the north side their boundary began at the Jordan, passed the northern slope of Jericho and headed west into the hill country, coming out at the desert[z] of Beth Aven.[a] 13 From there it crossed to the south slope of Luz[b] (that is, Bethel[c]) and went down to Ataroth Addar[d] on the hill south of Lower Beth Horon.

14 From the hill facing Beth Horon[e] on the south the boundary turned south along the western side and came out at Kiriath Baal (that is, Kiriath Jearim), a town of the people of Judah. This was the western side.

15 The southern side began at the outskirts of Kiriath Jearim on the west, and the boundary came out at the spring of the waters of Nephtoah.[f] 16 The boundary went down to the foot of the hill facing the Valley of Ben Hinnom, north of the Valley of Rephaim. It continued down the Hinnom Valley[g] along the southern slope of the Jebusite city and so to En Rogel.[h] 17 It then curved north, went to En Shemesh, continued to Geliloth, which faces the Pass of Adummim, and ran down to the Stone of Bohan[i] son of Reuben. 18 It continued to the northern slope of Beth Arabah[a][j] and on down into the Arabah. 19 It then went to the northern slope of

18:1 [n]Jos 19:51; 21:2; Jdg 18:31; 21:12, 19; 1Sa 1:3; 4:3; Jer 7:12; 26:6 [o]Ex 27:21
18:4 [p]Mic 2:5
18:5 [q]Jos 15:1 [r]Jos 16:1-4
18:6 [s]Jos 14:2
18:7 [t]Jos 13:33 [u]Jos 13:8
18:8 [v]ver 1
18:10 [w]Nu 34:13 [x]ver 1; Jer 7:12 [y]Nu 33:54; Jos 19:51
18:12 [z]Jos 16:1 [a]Jos 7:2
18:13 [b]Ge 28:19 [c]Jdg 1:23 [d]Jos 16:5
18:14 [e]Jos 10:10
18:15 [f]Jos 15:9
18:16 [g]Jos 15:8; 2Ki 23:10 [h]Jos 15:7
18:17 [i]Jos 15:6
18:18 [j]Jos 15:6

a *18* Septuagint; Hebrew *slope facing the Arabah*

■ **18:1—19:48** *Allotments for Other Tribes.* These chapters delineate the allotment of land for the remaining seven tribes. The assembly took place at Shiloh.
18:1–10 The account of the assembly at Shiloh, which was for the purpose of completing the allotment of land, underlines several important theological aspects of this occasion in Israel's history.
18:1 The whole assembly . . . gathered. This vocabulary has similarities to 8:35 and 9:15. See also note on 1:12–15. **Shiloh.** Located in the territory of Ephraim (16:6), Shiloh had not been featured previously in Biblical history, but here it became "the place the LORD your God will choose" (Dt 12:5,11,18; cf. Jer 7:12). In the days of David this role would be transferred to Jerusalem. For the role of Shiloh in Israel's history, see 22:12 (see also Jdg 18:31; 21:19; 1Sa 1:3,24; 2:14; 3:21; 4:3; 14:3; 1Ki 2:27; 11:29; 14:2; Ps 78:60; Jer 7:12,14; 26:6,9). **Tent of Meeting.** The book of Joshua uses this designation for the tabernacle only here and in 19:51 ("tabernacle" is used in 22:19,29 and "his sanctuary" in 22:27; cf. 6:24; 9:23), though the term is a common name for the tabernacle in the Pentateuch (e.g., Ex 39:32,40; 40:2,6,29,35; Lev 17:4; Nu 3:7–8,25; 4:25,31). The "meeting" was God's meeting with his people (see note on 1:5). The importance of this tent, or tabernacle, was largely derived from the ark it housed (see notes on 3:3,4,11,14,17; 4:7; 6:4,8; 7:6; 8:33); the ark in turn contained the "Testimony" (see 4:16). See Exodus 25:10–22. **country.** Or "land."
18:2 inheritance. See verses 4 and 28; see also note on 1:6.
18:3 take possession. This verb refers to the complete occupation of the land, which included more than the initial conquest (1:11,15; 13:1 ["taken over"]; 21:43). It was an act of obedient faith because it was based on the promise of God (see 1:11), hence the note of rebuke in Joshua's question. See note on 21:45. **the God of your fathers.** This is an allusion to the promises to the fathers (see note on 1:1–9). **has given.** See notes on 1:2, 3 and 11.
18:6 lots. See note on 15:1. **the presence of the LORD.** God's "presence" was represented by the tent (also in vv. 8,10; 19:51). Note the relationship between the ark and the presence of God in 3:11 and 7:23.
18:7 The Levites . . . do not get a portion . . . And Gad, Reuben and . . . Manasseh have already received. Two facts that focus attention on the 12-tribe structure of Israel are again explained. See notes on 13:8–33 and 13:14.
18:11–28 These verses furnish details regarding the territory allotted to Benjamin. Benjamin was Jacob's twelfth (and youngest) son, his second by Rachel (see notes on Ge 35:16–18; 49:27). A description of the boundaries (vv. 12–20) is followed by a list of cities (vv. 21–28).

Beth Hoglah and came out at the northern bay of the Salt Sea,[a][k] at the mouth of the Jordan in the south. This was the southern boundary.

20 The Jordan formed the boundary on the eastern side.

These were the boundaries that marked out the inheritance of the clans of Benjamin on all sides.[l]

21 The tribe of Benjamin, clan by clan, had the following cities:

Jericho, Beth Hoglah, Emek Keziz, 22 Beth Arabah, Zemaraim, Bethel,[m] 23 Avvim, Parah, Ophrah, 24 Kephar Ammoni, Ophni and Geba[n]—twelve towns and their villages.

25 Gibeon,[o] Ramah,[p] Beeroth,[q] 26 Mizpah,[r] Kephirah, Mozah, 27 Rekem, Irpeel, Taralah, 28 Zelah,[s] Haeleph, the Jebusite city[t] (that is, Jerusalem[u]), Gibeah[v] and Kiriath—fourteen towns and their villages.

This was the inheritance of Benjamin for its clans.

Allotment for Simeon

19 The second lot came out for the tribe of Simeon, clan by clan. Their inheritance lay within the territory of Judah.[w] 2 It included:

Beersheba[x] (or Sheba),[b] Moladah, 3 Hazar Shual, Balah, Ezem, 4 Eltolad, Bethul, Hormah, 5 Ziklag, Beth Marcaboth, Hazar Susah, 6 Beth Lebaoth and Sharuhen—thirteen towns and their villages;

7 Ain, Rimmon, Ether and Ashan[y]—four towns and their villages— 8 and all the villages around these towns as far as Baalath Beer (Ramah in the Negev).[z]

This was the inheritance of the tribe of the Simeonites, clan by clan. 9 The inheritance of the Simeonites was taken from the share of Judah,[a] because Judah's portion was more than they needed. So the Simeonites received their inheritance within the territory of Judah.[b]

Allotment for Zebulun

10 The third lot came up for Zebulun,[c] clan by clan:

The boundary of their inheritance went as far as Sarid. 11 Going west it ran to Maralah, touched Dabbesheth, and extended to the ravine near Jokneam.[d] 12 It turned east from Sarid toward the sunrise to the territory of Kisloth Tabor and went on to Daberath and up to Japhia. 13 Then it continued eastward to Gath Hepher and Eth Kazin; it came out at Rimmon[e] and turned toward Neah. 14 There the boundary went around on the north to Hannathon and ended at the Valley of Iphtah El. 15 Included were Kattath, Nahalal, Shimron, Idalah and Bethlehem.[f] There were twelve towns and their villages.

16 These towns and their villages were the inheritance of Zebulun,[g] clan by clan.[h]

Allotment for Issachar

17 The fourth lot came out for Issachar,[i] clan by clan. 18 Their territory included:

Jezreel,[j] Kesulloth, Shunem,[k] 19 Hapharaim, Shion, Anaharath, 20 Rabbith, Kishion, Ebez, 21 Remeth, En Gannim, En Haddah and Beth Pazzez. 22 The boundary touched Tabor,[l] Shahazumah and Beth Shemesh,[m] and ended at the Jordan. There were sixteen towns and their villages.

23 These towns and their villages were the inheritance of the tribe of Issachar,[n] clan by clan.[o]

Allotment for Asher

24 The fifth lot came out for the tribe of Asher,[p] clan by clan. 25 Their territory included:

Helkath, Hali, Beten, Acshaph, 26 Allammelech, Amad and Mishal. On the west the boundary touched Carmel[q] and Shihor Libnath. 27 It then turned east toward

18:19 [k]Ge 14:3
18:20 [l]Jos 21:4,17; 1Sa 9:1
18:22 [m]Jos 16:1
18:24 [n]Isa 10:29
18:25 [o]Jos 9:3 [p]Jdg 4:5 [q]Jos 9:17
18:26 [r]Jos 11:3
18:28 [s]2Sa 21:14 [t]Jos 15:8 [u]Jos 10:1 [v]Jos 15:57
19:1 [w]ver 9; Ge 49:7
19:2 [x]Ge 21:14; 1Ki 19:3
19:7 [y]Jos 15:42
19:8 [z]Jos 10:40
19:9 [a]Ge 49:7 [b]Eze 48:24
19:10 [c]Jos 21:7,34
19:11 [d]Jos 12:22
19:13 [e]Jos 15:32
19:15 [f]Ge 35:19
19:16 [g]ver 10; Jos 21:7 [h]Eze 48:26
19:17 [i]Ge 30:18
19:18 [j]Jos 15:56 [k]1Sa 28:4; 2Ki 4:8
19:22 [l]Jdg 4:6,12; Ps 89:12 [m]Jos 15:10
19:23 [n]Jos 17:10 [o]Ge 49:15; Eze 48:25
19:24 [p]Jos 17:7
19:26 [q]Jos 12:22

a *19* That is, the Dead Sea b *2* Or *Beersheba, Sheba*; 1 Chron. 4:28 does not have *Sheba*.

19:1–9 These verses delineate a list of towns allotted to Simeon. Simeon was Jacob's second son, born to Leah (Ge 29:33).
19:1 within the territory of Judah. Simeon's territory lay within that of Judah (cf. Ge 49:7). Judah and Simeon acted together in Judges 1:3 and 17. At some point the tribe of Simeon seems to have lost its distinct identity.
19:8–9 inheritance. See verses 16, 23, 31, 39 and 48, as well as note on 1:6.
19:10–16 The boundary (vv. 10–14) and towns (vv. 15–16) allotted to Zebulun are given here. Zebulun was Jacob's tenth son, his sixth by Leah (Ge 30:19–20; see note on 49:13).
19:15 twelve. The list apparently is incomplete.
19:17–23 These verses give a list of towns allotted to Issachar (vv. 18–21) and a brief comment on the boundary (v. 22). Issachar was Jacob's ninth son, his fifth by Leah (Ge 30:18; note on 49:14–15).
19:24–31 This passage lists the towns allotted to Asher. He was Jacob's eighth son, his second by Zilpah (Ge 30:12–13; see note on 49:20).

Beth Dagon, touched Zebulun[r] and the Valley of Iphtah El, and went north to Beth
Emek and Neiel, passing Cabul[s] on the left. 28It went to Abdon,[a] Rehob,[t] Hammon[u] and Kanah, as far as Greater Sidon.[v] 29The boundary then turned back toward Ramah[w] and went to the fortified city of Tyre,[x] turned toward Hosah and
came out at the sea in the region of Aczib,[y] 30Ummah, Aphek and Rehob. There
were twenty-two towns and their villages.
31These towns and their villages were the inheritance of the tribe of Asher,[z] clan by clan.

Allotment for Naphtali

32The sixth lot came out for Naphtali, clan by clan:
33Their boundary went from Heleph and the large tree in Zaanannim, passing
Adami Nekeb and Jabneel to Lakkum and ending at the Jordan. 34The boundary
ran west through Aznoth Tabor and came out at Hukkok. It touched Zebulun on
the south, Asher on the west and the Jordan[b] on the east. 35The fortified cities were
Ziddim, Zer, Hammath, Rakkath, Kinnereth,[a] 36Adamah, Ramah,[b] Hazor,[c] 37Ke-
desh, Edrei,[d] En Hazor, 38Iron, Migdal El, Horem, Beth Anath and Beth Shemesh.
There were nineteen towns and their villages.
39These towns and their villages were the inheritance of the tribe of Naphtali, clan by clan.[e]

Allotment for Dan

40The seventh lot came out for the tribe of Dan, clan by clan. 41The territory of their inheritance included:
Zorah, Eshtaol, Ir Shemesh, 42Shaalabbin, Aijalon,[f] Ithlah, 43Elon, Timnah,[g]
Ekron, 44Eltekeh, Gibbethon, Baalath, 45Jehud, Bene Berak, Gath Rimmon,[h] 46Me
Jarkon and Rakkon, with the area facing Joppa.[i]
47(But the Danites had difficulty taking possession of their territory,[j] so they went up
and attacked Leshem[k], took it, put it to the sword and occupied it. They settled in Leshem and named it Dan after their forefather.)[l]
48These towns and their villages were the inheritance of the tribe of Dan,[m] clan by clan.

Allotment for Joshua

49When they had finished dividing the land into its allotted portions, the Israelites
gave Joshua son of Nun an inheritance among them, 50as the LORD had commanded.
They gave him the town he asked for—Timnath Serah[c][n] in the hill country of Ephraim.
And he built up the town and settled there.
51These are the territories that Eleazar the priest, Joshua son of Nun and the heads
of the tribal clans of Israel assigned by lot at Shiloh in the presence of the LORD at the entrance to the Tent of Meeting. And so they finished dividing the land.[o]

Cities of Refuge

20 Then the LORD said to Joshua: 2"Tell the Israelites to designate the cities of refuge, as I instructed you through Moses, 3so that anyone who kills a person accidentally and unintentionally[p] may flee there and find protection from the avenger of
blood.[q]

19:27 [r]ver 10 [s]1Ki 9:13
19:28 [t]Jdg 1:31 [u]1Ch 6:76 [v]Ge 10:19; Jos 11:8
19:29 [w]Jos 18:25 [x]2Sa 5:11; 24:7; Isa 23:1; Jer 25:22; Eze 26:2 [y]Jdg 1:31
19:31 [z]Ge 30:13; Eze 48:2
19:35 [a]Jos 11:2
19:36 [b]Jos 18:25 [c]Jos 11:1
19:37 [d]Nu 21:33
19:39 [e]Dt 33:23; Eze 48:3
19:42 [f]Jdg 1:35
19:43 [g]Ge 38:12
19:45 [h]Jos 21:24; 1Ch 6:69
19:46 [i]2Ch 2:16; Jnh 1:3
19:47 [j]Jdg 18:1 [k]Jdg 18:7,14 [l]Jdg 18:27,29
19:48 [m]Ge 30:6
19:50 [n]Jos 24:30
19:51 [o]Jos 14:1; 18:10; Ac 13:19
20:3 [p]Lev 4:2 [q]Nu 35:12

[a] *28* Some Hebrew manuscripts (see also Joshua 21:30); most Hebrew manuscripts *Ebron*
[b] *34* Septuagint; Hebrew *west, and Judah, the Jordan,*
[c] *50* Also known as *Timnath Heres* (see Judges 2:9)

19:30 twenty-two. There are more than 22 towns mentioned, but some may be noted as a way of indicating the approximate position of the boundary.
19:32–39 These verses review the territory allotted to Naphtali. He was Jacob's sixth son, his second by Bilhah (Ge 30:7–8; see note on 49:21).
19:38 nineteen. The list apparently is incomplete.
19:39 inheritance. See note on 1:6.
19:40–48 This passage covers the allotment granted to Dan, Jacob's fifth son, his first by Bilhah (Ge 30:3–6; see note on 49:16–17).
19:47 the Danites had difficulty taking possession of their territory. Or "the territory of the Danites was lost to them." There is a more detailed account of the Danites' capture and renaming of Leshem (or Laish) in Judges 18.
■ **19:49–50** *Joshua's Special Allotment.* Like Caleb, Joshua was rewarded for his faithfulness (see notes on 14:6–15).
19:50 as the LORD had commanded. This divine command is not recorded (cf. note on 14:9). See Numbers 14:30. **Timnath Serah.** This would also be the site of Joshua's burial (24:30).
■ **19:51** *Conclusion.* The vocabulary of this verse ("These are the territories . . ."), which has connections with 14:1, marks the verse as the conclusion of these chapters.
19:51 Eleazar. See note on 14:1. **Shiloh.** See note on 18:1. **the presence of the LORD.** See note on 18:6. **Tent of Meeting.** See note on 18:1.
■ **20:1–9** *Cities of Refuge.* The record of the allocation of the land promised to the tribes of Israel (chs. 13–19) is immediately followed by the locations of the cities of refuge that were scattered throughout the promised land.
20:2 cities of refuge. These were places where certain offenders (v. 3) could seek a fair trial and escape unjust vengeance. These cities would be given to the Levites (21:13,21,27,32,36,38; Nu 35:6). **as I instructed you through Moses.** See Exodus 21:12–14 (see also Nu 35:6–34; Dt 19:1–13).
20:3 accidentally and unintentionally. Unintentional sin received specific treatment in the law (Lev 4:2,13,22,27; 5:15,18; Nu 15:22–29; 35:22; Dt 4:42; 19:4; Eze 45:20; cf. Heb 9:7). **avenger of blood.** This was probably the victim's nearest male relative or possibly an official of the city in which the killing occurred (Nu 35:19–21).

4"When he flees to one of these cities, he is to stand in the entrance of the city gate[r]
and state his case before the elders[s] of that city. Then they are to admit him into their
city and give him a place to live with them. 5If the avenger of blood pursues him, they
must not surrender the one accused, because he killed his neighbor unintentionally and
without malice aforethought. 6He is to stay in that city until he has stood trial before the
assembly[t] and until the death of the high priest who is serving at that time. Then he may
go back to his own home in the town from which he fled."
7So they set apart Kedesh[u] in Galilee in the hill country of Naphtali, Shechem[v] in the
hill country of Ephraim, and Kiriath Arba (that is, Hebron[w]) in the hill country of Judah.[x]
8On the east side of the Jordan of Jericho[a] they designated Bezer[y] in the desert on the
plateau in the tribe of Reuben, Ramoth in Gilead[z] in the tribe of Gad, and Golan in Bashan in the tribe of Manasseh. 9Any of the Israelites or any alien living among them who
killed someone accidentally could flee to these designated cities and not be killed by the
avenger of blood prior to standing trial before the assembly.[a]

Towns for the Levites

21 Now the family heads of the Levites approached Eleazar the priest, Joshua son
of Nun, and the heads of the other tribal families of Israel[b] 2at Shiloh[c] in Canaan
and said to them, "The LORD commanded through Moses that you give us towns to live
in, with pasturelands for our livestock."[d] 3So, as the LORD had commanded, the Israelites
gave the Levites the following towns and pasturelands out of their own inheritance:
4The first lot came out for the Kohathites, clan by clan. The Levites who were descendants of Aaron the priest were allotted thirteen towns from the tribes of Judah, Simeon
and Benjamin.[e] 5The rest of Kohath's descendants were allotted ten towns from the clans
of the tribes of Ephraim, Dan and half of Manasseh.[f]
6The descendants of Gershon were allotted thirteen towns from the clans of the tribes
of Issachar,[g] Asher, Naphtali and the half-tribe of Manasseh in Bashan.
7The descendants of Merari,[h] clan by clan, received twelve towns from the tribes of
Reuben, Gad and Zebulun.[i]
8So the Israelites allotted to the Levites these towns and their pasturelands, as the
LORD had commanded through Moses.
9From the tribes of Judah and Simeon they allotted the following towns by name 10(these
towns were assigned to the descendants of Aaron who were from the Kohathite clans of
the Levites, because the first lot fell to them):
11They gave them Kiriath Arba (that is, Hebron[j]), with its surrounding pastureland, in the hill country of Judah. (Arba was the forefather of Anak.) 12But the fields
and villages around the city they had given to Caleb son of Jephunneh as his possession.
13So to the descendants of Aaron the priest they gave Hebron (a city of refuge
for one accused of murder), Libnah,[k] 14Jattir,[l] Eshtemoa,[m] 15Holon,[n] Debir, 16Ain,
Juttah[o] and Beth Shemesh,[p] together with their pasturelands—nine towns from
these two tribes.

a 8 *Jordan of Jericho* was possibly an ancient name for the Jordan River.

20:4 [r]Ru 4:1; Jer 38:7 [s]Jos 7:6
20:6 [t]Nu 35:12
20:7 [u]Jos 21:32; 1Ch 6:76 [v]Ge 12:6 [w]Jos 10:36; 21:11 [x]Lk 1:39
20:8 [y]Jos 21:36; 1Ch 6:78 [z]Jos 12:2
20:9 [a]Ex 21:13; Nu 35:15
21:1 [b]Jos 14:1
21:2 [c]Jos 18:1 [d]Nu 35:2-3
21:4 [e]ver 19
21:5 [f]ver 26
21:6 [g]Ge 30:18
21:7 [h]Ex 6:16 [i]Jos 19:10
21:11 [j]Jos 15:13; 1Ch 6:55
21:13 [k]Jos 15:42; 1Ch 6:57
21:14 [l]Jos 15:48 [m]Jos 15:50
21:15 [n]Jos 15:51
21:16 [o]Jos 15:55 [p]Jos 15:10

20:4 city gate. This was the usual place for legal transactions to take place (see Ru 4:1–12). **elders.** Apparently the elders held a preliminary hearing of the accused man's case.

20:5 they must not surrender the one accused. There was a presumption in favor of the accused.

20:6 assembly. See note on 8:35. **death of the high priest.** His death marked the end of an era and provided a convenient limitation to the provisions made here.

20:7 set apart. The Hebrew verb can also be translated "sanctified." The cities chosen provided access from various parts of the land.

20:8 the east side. See Deuteronomy 4:41–43.

20:9 alien. Concern for the foreigner in Israel was a common feature of the law (e.g., Ex 12:48–49; 20:10; 22:21; 23:9,12).

■ **21:1–42** *Levi's Allotment.* The last aspect of the elaborate description of the allotment of the land in chapters 13–21 is the assignment of towns for the Levites, whose lack of an inheritance in the land was mentioned in 13:14 (see its note), 13:33, 14:3–4 and 18:7. These towns were to remain the possession of the tribes to which they had already been allotted, but they were provided, along with adjoining pasturelands, for the Levites "to live in" (v. 2). This chapter reports the Levites' request (vv. 1–3), the assignment of towns to them by lot (vv. 4–8), a list of the towns (vv. 9–40) and a conclusion (vv. 41–42).

21:1 Eleazar. See note on 14:1.

21:2 Shiloh. See note on 18:1. **The LORD commanded through Moses.** The reference is to Numbers 35:1–8. The request of the Levites, like that of Caleb in 14:6–12, was an expression of faith in the promise of God.

21:3 inheritance. See note on 1:6.

21:4 lot. See note on 15:1. **Kohathites.** Kohath was Levi's second son (Ex 6:16; Nu 3:17), but his descendants were given precedence here because his was the family from which the priestly line descended via Aaron. **Aaron.** Aaron was a grandson of Kohath and son of Amram (Ex 6:18,20). Aaron and his sons were chosen by God to serve as priests (Ex 28:1; Lev 8:1–36). **Judah, Simeon and Benjamin.** The towns allotted from these tribes were in the vicinity of Jerusalem, where the temple would later be built, although Jerusalem itself is not mentioned in this chapter.

21:6 Gershon. Levi's first son (Ex 6:16; Nu 3:17).

21:7 Merari. Levi's third son (Ex 6:16; Nu 3:17).

21:10 the first lot. The precedence of the priestly line is emphasized (v. 4).

21:12 Caleb. See note on 14:6.

21:13 city of refuge. See note on 20:2.

17 And from the tribe of Benjamin they gave them Gibeon, Geba,[q] 18 Anathoth
and Almon, together with their pasturelands—four towns.
19 All the towns for the priests, the descendants of Aaron, were thirteen, together with
their pasturelands.

20 The rest of the Kohathite clans of the Levites were allotted towns from the tribe of
Ephraim:
21 In the hill country of Ephraim they were given Shechem[r] (a city of refuge for
one accused of murder) and Gezer, 22 Kibzaim and Beth Horon,[s] together with
their pasturelands—four towns.[t]
23 Also from the tribe of Dan they received Eltekeh, Gibbethon, 24 Aijalon and
Gath Rimmon,[u] together with their pasturelands—four towns.
25 From half the tribe of Manasseh they received Taanach and Gath Rimmon,
together with their pasturelands—two towns.
26 All these ten towns and their pasturelands were given to the rest of the Kohathite clans.

27 The Levite clans of the Gershonites were given:
from the half-tribe of Manasseh,
Golan in Bashan[v] (a city of refuge for one accused of murder[w]) and Be Eshtarah,
together with their pasturelands—two towns;
28 from the tribe of Issachar,[x]
Kishion, Daberath, 29 Jarmuth and En Gannim, together with their pasturelands—
four towns;
30 from the tribe of Asher,[y]
Mishal, Abdon, 31 Helkath and Rehob, together with their pasturelands—four
towns;
32 from the tribe of Naphtali,
Kedesh[z] in Galilee (a city of refuge for one accused of murder[a]), Hammoth Dor
and Kartan, together with their pasturelands—three towns.
33 All the towns of the Gershonite[b] clans were thirteen, together with their pasturelands.

34 The Merarite clans (the rest of the Levites) were given:
from the tribe of Zebulun,[c]
Jokneam, Kartah, 35 Dimnah and Nahalal, together with their pasturelands—four
towns;
36 from the tribe of Reuben,
Bezer,[d] Jahaz, 37 Kedemoth and Mephaath, together with their pasturelands—four
towns;
38 from the tribe of Gad,
Ramoth[e] in Gilead (a city of refuge for one accused of murder), Mahanaim,[f]
39 Heshbon and Jazer, together with their pasturelands—four towns in all.
40 All the towns allotted to the Merarite clans, who were the rest of the Levites, were
twelve.
41 The towns of the Levites in the territory held by the Israelites were forty-eight in all,
together with their pasturelands.[g] 42 Each of these towns had pasturelands surrounding
it; this was true for all these towns.

43 So the LORD gave Israel all the land he had sworn to give their forefathers,[h] and they
took possession[i] of it and settled there.[j] 44 The LORD gave them rest[k] on every side, just
as he had sworn to their forefathers. Not one of their enemies[l] withstood them; the LORD
handed all their enemies[m] over to them.[n] 45 Not one of all the LORD's good promises[o] to
the house of Israel failed; every one was fulfilled.

21:17 [q]Jos 18:24
21:21 [r]Jos 17:7; 20:7
21:22 [s]Jos 10:10 [t]1Sa 1:1
21:24 [u]Jos 19:45
21:27 [v]Jos 12:5 [w]Nu 35:6
21:28 [x]Ge 30:18
21:30 [y]Jos 17:7
21:32 [z]Jos 12:22 [a]Nu 35:6; Jos 20:7
21:33 [b]ver 6
21:34 [c]Jos 19:10; 1Ch 6:77
21:36 [d]Jos 20:8
21:38 [e]Dt 4:43 [f]Ge 32:2
21:41 [g]Nu 35:7
21:43 [h]Dt 34:4 [i]Dt 11:31 [j]Dt 17:14
21:44 [k]Ex 33:14; Jos 1:13 [l]Dt 6:19 [m]Ex 23:31 [n]Dt 7:24; 21:10
21:45 [o]Jos 23:14; Ne 9:8

21:17 Gibeon. See note on 9:3. The Gibeonites were to serve in the house of God (see note on 9:23).

■ **21:43–45** *Summation.* This concluding summary is a concise review of the theology of the whole book (not just chs. 13–21). Verse 43 sums up chapters 13–21, verse 44 reflects on chapters 1–12 and verse 45 expresses the idea that dominates the entire book; namely, the faithfulness of God to his promises.

21:43 the LORD gave. A persistent theme of the book is the land as God's gift to Israel. See note on 1:2. **sworn to give their forefathers.** The faithfulness of God to which this book testifies is faithfulness to the promises made to Abraham, Isaac and Jacob. From the perspective of the New Testament, these promises can be identified with the promises of the gospel (see "Introduction: Christ in Joshua" and Gal 3:8). **took possession.** See notes on 1:11 and 18:3.

21:44 rest. See note on 1:13. **Not one . . . withstood.** This statement sums up chapters 1–12 and testifies to the validity of the promise in 1:5. **enemies.** See note on 23:1.

21:45 the LORD's good promises. Literally, "the good word that the Lord spoke." **the house of Israel.** Israel was considered one united entity (see notes on 1:12–15 and 13:8–33). **failed.** Literally, "fell." Without any sense of contradiction, the book of Joshua speaks of both the complete faithfulness of God to his promise—in terms of the completeness of the conquest (10:40–42; 11:23; 21:43–45 and its note; 23:1,14)—and the incompleteness of the occupation of the land in the days of Joshua (13:1–7; 15:63; 17:12–13; 18:3; 23:5). A contradiction is seen here only if the reader presses the statements about completeness beyond their intended meaning (i.e., although there was much land yet to be

Eastern Tribes Return Home

22 Then Joshua summoned the Reubenites, the Gadites and the half-tribe of Manasseh 2and said to them, "You have done all that Moses the servant of the LORD
commanded,[p] and you have obeyed me in everything I commanded. 3For a long time
now—to this very day—you have not deserted your brothers but have carried out the
mission the LORD your God gave you. 4Now that the LORD your God has given your
brothers rest as he promised, return to your homes[q] in the land that Moses the servant
of the LORD gave you on the other side of the Jordan.[r] 5But be very careful to keep the
commandment[s] and the law that Moses the servant of the LORD gave you: to love the
LORD your God, to walk in all his ways, to obey his commands,[t] to hold fast to him and
to serve him with all your heart and all your soul.[u]"
6Then Joshua blessed[v] them and sent them away, and they went to their homes. 7(To
the half-tribe of Manasseh Moses had given land in Bashan,[w] and to the other half of the
tribe Joshua gave land on the west side[x] of the Jordan with their brothers.) When Joshua sent them home, he blessed them, 8saying, "Return to your homes with your great
wealth—with large herds of livestock,[y] with silver, gold, bronze and iron, and a great
quantity of clothing—and divide[z] with your brothers the plunder[a] from your enemies."
9So the Reubenites, the Gadites and the half-tribe of Manasseh left the Israelites at
Shiloh in Canaan to return to Gilead,[b] their own land, which they had acquired in accordance with the command of the LORD through Moses.
10When they came to Geliloth near the Jordan in the land of Canaan, the Reubenites,
the Gadites and the half-tribe of Manasseh built an imposing altar there by the Jordan.
11And when the Israelites heard that they had built the altar on the border of Canaan at
Geliloth near the Jordan on the Israelite side, 12the whole assembly of Israel gathered at
Shiloh[c] to go to war against them.
13So the Israelites sent Phinehas[d] son of Eleazar,[e] the priest, to the land of Gilead—to
Reuben, Gad and the half-tribe of Manasseh. 14With him they sent ten of the chief men, one
for each of the tribes of Israel, each the head of a family division among the Israelite clans.[f]
15When they went to Gilead—to Reuben, Gad and the half-tribe of Manasseh—they
said to them: 16"The whole assembly of the LORD says: 'How could you break faith[g] with
the God of Israel like this? How could you turn away from the LORD and build yourselves
an altar in rebellion[h] against him now? 17Was not the sin of Peor[i] enough for us? Up to

22:2 [p]Nu 32:25
22:4 [q]Nu 32:22; Dt 3:20 [r]Nu 32:18; Jos 1:13-15
22:5 [s]Isa 43:22 [t]Dt 5:29 [u]Dt 6:6,17
22:6 [v]Ex 39:43
22:7 [w]Nu 32:33; Jos 12:5 [x]Jos 17:2,5
22:8 [y]Dt 20:14 [z]Nu 31:27 [a]Ge 49:27; 1Sa 30:16; Isa 9:3
22:9 [b]Nu 32:26, 29
22:12 [c]Jos 18:1
22:13 [d]Nu 25:7 [e]Nu 3:32; Jos 24:33
22:14 [f]Nu 1:4
22:16 [g]Dt 13:14 [h]Dt 12:13-14
22:17 [i]Nu 25:1-9

---

taken over in the days of Joshua, God had proven himself completely faithful to all his promises). See note on 13:1.

▪ **22:1—24:33** *Covenant Loyalty in the Land.* The book closes with three chapters that take up the matter of Israel's faithfulness in the light of God's faithfulness to his promises (the main subject of the book; see 21:43–45 and its note). The recurring theme of these final chapters is the human response demanded by God's remarkable grace (e.g., each chapter begins with the statement that Joshua "summoned" the people; 22:1; 23:1–2; 24:1). These chapters focus on four main matters: the unity of Israel before God (22:1–34), the demand for covenant loyalty (23:1–16), the covenant renewal at Shechem (24:1–28) and the notices of deaths and burials (24:29–33).

▪ **22:1–34** *The Unity of Israel.* The two and one-half tribes whose land lay east of the Jordan had been faithful to their brothers, as Joshua had commanded them in 1:12–15, for they recognized the unity of Israel under the promises of God. This chapter dramatically presents the basis of that unity (v. 34) and the nature of the ever-present threat to it; namely, "turning away from the LORD" (v. 18), which would bring God's wrath on Israel, as had the unfaithfulness of Achan (v. 20; ch. 7).

▪ **22:1–9** *The Transjordan Tribes Released.* Joshua released the Transjordan tribes from their obligations and sent them home with his blessing.

22:1–5 Joshua commended the two and one-half tribes (vv. 1–3) for their obedience to the commands of 1:12–15, allowed them to return to their land east of the Jordan (v. 4) and exhorted them to continue their obedience to the Lord (v. 5).

22:1 Reubenites . . . Manasseh. See note on 13:8–33.

22:4 rest. See 21:44; see 1:13 and its note.

22:5 be very careful to keep the commandment . . . to love . . . to walk . . . to obey . . . with all your heart and . . . soul. The various expressions used here to portray the proper human response to the grace of God are found in Deuteronomy (see notes on 4:9,29; 6:5; 10:12–13; 11:13). They describe wholehearted, glad, willing and confident love and obedience. See note on 23:11. For the connection between love and obedience, see note on 1:7 and especially John 14:23.

22:6–7 blessed. See 14:13; also see note on 8:33.

22:8 Return. Joshua's words of blessing were in the form of imperatives (compare Ge 1:28). Joshua not only pronounced blessing on the people, but also commanded them to obey the will of God.

22:9 Shiloh. See note on 18:1. **Gilead.** The term is general, referring to the whole land east of the Jordan. **in accordance with . . . Moses.** The unity of the eastern tribes with the rest of Israel was again stressed (see note on 13:8–33).

▪ **22:10–34** *The Controversy Over an Altar.* The faithfulness of the Transjordan tribes was questioned and investigated because they had built an altar as they returned to their lands. The main concern of this passage is that these tribes remain united with Israel and loyal to the Law of Moses.

22:10 Geliloth. Or possibly "Gilgal," as understood in the Septuagint (the Greek translation of the OT). **an imposing altar.** Literally, "great in appearance," which is consistent with the claim that it was to serve as a monument (v. 27).

22:12 the whole assembly of Israel gathered. See notes on 1:12–15 and 18:1. **to go to war.** The reaction of the Israelites can be understood in the light of the injunction to erect no rival altars to the one at the central sanctuary (Lev 17:8–9). The law demanded that disciplinary action be taken against apostasy (Dt 13:12–18).

22:13 Phinehas. His role on the occasion of "the sin of Peor" (v. 17; Nu 25:7–8) added solemnity to his choice for this mission.

22:16 The whole assembly . . . says. The unity of Israel has been emphasized throughout the book. Geographical boundaries and differences in historical experience were transcended by the one God under whose promises all Israel comprised one united people (see note on 13:8–33). Now the one thing that could break that unity was revealed: apostasy and rebellion against God. See notes on 1:12–15 and 18:1. **break faith.** The same expression was used in 7:1 ("acted unfaithfully"). It refers to a violation of trust. **turn away from the LORD.** This expression for apostasy recurs in verses 23 (in part) and 29 (see also 23:12; Nu 14:43; 32:15; 1Sa 15:11; 1Ki 9:6). It is the opposite of repentance, which is returning to God (1Ki 8:33; Jer 3:7; Hos 6:1). **build yourselves an altar in rebellion.** The building of an altar was understood by the rest of Israel in the light of the teaching of Leviticus 17:8–9 and Deuteronomy 12. Their accusation was rash, for the law prescribed careful investigation before taking disciplinary action (Dt 13:12–14).

22:17 the sin of Peor. The reference is to the occasion of great

this very day we have not cleansed ourselves from that sin, even though a plague fell on
the community of the LORD! 18 And are you now turning away from the LORD?
"'If you rebel against the LORD today, tomorrow he will be angry with the whole community[j] of Israel. 19 If the land you possess is defiled, come over to the LORD's land, where
the LORD's tabernacle stands, and share the land with us. But do not rebel against the
LORD or against us by building an altar for yourselves, other than the altar of the LORD
our God. 20 When Achan son of Zerah acted unfaithfully regarding the devoted things,[a][k]
did not wrath[l] come upon the whole community of Israel? He was not the only one who
died for his sin.'"[m]

21 Then Reuben, Gad and the half-tribe of Manasseh replied to the heads of the clans
of Israel: 22 "The Mighty One, God, the LORD! The Mighty One, God,[n] the LORD![o] He
knows![p] And let Israel know! If this has been in rebellion or disobedience to the LORD,
do not spare us this day. 23 If we have built our own altar to turn away from the LORD and
to offer burnt offerings and grain offerings,[q] or to sacrifice fellowship offerings[b] on it,
may the LORD himself call us to account.[r]

24 "No! We did it for fear that some day your descendants might say to ours, 'What do
you have to do with the LORD, the God of Israel? 25 The LORD has made the Jordan a boundary between us and you—you Reubenites and Gadites! You have no share in the LORD.'
So your descendants might cause ours to stop fearing the LORD.

26 "That is why we said, 'Let us get ready and build an altar—but not for burnt offerings or sacrifices.' 27 On the contrary, it is to be a witness[s] between us and you and the
generations that follow, that we will worship the LORD at his sanctuary with our burnt
offerings, sacrifices and fellowship offerings.[t] Then in the future your descendants will
not be able to say to ours, 'You have no share in the LORD.'

28 "And we said, 'If they ever say this to us, or to our descendants, we will answer:
Look at the replica of the LORD's altar, which our fathers built, not for burnt offerings and
sacrifices, but as a witness between us and you.'

29 "Far be it from us to rebel[u] against the LORD and turn away from him today by building an altar for burnt offerings, grain offerings and sacrifices, other than the altar of the
LORD our God that stands before his tabernacle."[v]

30 When Phinehas the priest and the leaders of the community—the heads of the clans
of the Israelites—heard what Reuben, Gad and Manasseh had to say, they were pleased.
31 And Phinehas son of Eleazar, the priest, said to Reuben, Gad and Manasseh, "Today
we know that the LORD is with us,[w] because you have not acted unfaithfully toward the
LORD in this matter. Now you have rescued the Israelites from the LORD's hand."

32 Then Phinehas son of Eleazar, the priest, and the leaders returned to Canaan from their
meeting with the Reubenites and Gadites in Gilead and reported to the Israelites. 33 They
were glad to hear the report and praised God.[x] And they talked no more about going to war
against them to devastate the country where the Reubenites and the Gadites lived.
34 And the Reubenites and the Gadites gave the altar this name: A Witness[y] Between
Us that the LORD is God.

22:18 [j]Lev 10:6; Nu 16:22
22:20 [k]Jos 7:1 [l]Ps 7:11 [m]Jos 7:5
22:22 [n]Dt 10:17 [o]Ps 50:1 [p]1Ki 8:39; Job 10:7; Ps 44:21; Jer 17:10
22:23 [q]Jer 41:5 [r]Dt 12:11; 18:19; 1Sa 20:16
22:27 [s]Ge 21:30; Jos 24:27 [t]Dt 12:6
22:29 [u]Jos 24:16 [v]Dt 12:13-14
22:31 [w]Lev 26:11-12; 2Ch 15:2
22:33 [x]1Ch 29:20; Da 2:19; Lk 2:28
22:34 [y]Ge 21:30

[a] *20* The Hebrew term refers to the irrevocable giving over of things or persons to the LORD, often by totally destroying them. [b] *23* Traditionally *peace offerings*; also in verse 27

apostasy prior to the entry into the land (Nu 25; see note on "Shittim" at Jos 2:1). **not cleansed ourselves.** For the idea of cleansing, see Leviticus 11–16. More than ceremonial cleansing is implied here, however. The Israelites were not yet rid of the tendency displayed at Peor.
22:18 angry. See note on 7:1. **community.** The same word is translated "assembly" in verses 12 and 16.
22:19 If the land you possess is defiled. That is, if the land east of the Jordan was not sanctified by God's presence. The book of Joshua, as well as the outcome of the present episode, emphasizes that this land, like that west of the Jordan, was also the gift of God (see 13:8–33). **the LORD's land.** Limiting this expression to the western territories would only have been appropriate if the eastern land had been defiled. **tabernacle.** See note on 18:1. **or against us.** Apostasy is an offense not only against God, but also against the people of God.
22:20 Achan. See chapter 7. **wrath.** See note on 7:1. **not the only one who died.** See 7:5. See *WLC* 151.
22:22 The Mighty One, God, the LORD! Or "God, God the LORD." **If this has been in rebellion . . . do not spare us.** The accusation of rebellion was taken with great seriousness, but the rebellion was denied.
22:23 If we have built . . . may the LORD. The teaching of passages such as Leviticus 17:8–9 and Deuteronomy 12 was accepted by both groups (see note on v. 16). **burnt offerings.** See Leviticus 1. **grain offerings.** See Leviticus 2. **fellowship offerings.** See Leviticus 3.
22:25 the Jordan a boundary between us. The book of Joshua has repeatedly rejected the idea of disunity (see note on 13:8–33). The idea was suggested in verse 19. **no share in the LORD.** To deny that their land was God's land (v. 19) was to deny that they shared in God's promise.
22:27 witness. The altar was to function as a testimony (cf. the stones at Gilgal; 4:20–24), not as a place of sacrifice. **his sanctuary.** That is, the tabernacle (see note on 18:1).
22:30 pleased. Contrast Phinehas's reaction to actual apostasy (Nu 25:7–8).
22:31 we know that the LORD is with us. The fears of verse 18 would not be realized because the suspected unfaithfulness had not occurred. **rescued.** This was an unusual way of making an important point: By not turning from God, they had saved Israel from God's wrath.
22:34 name. By its name the altar witnessed (v. 27) to the one reality that united all Israel, and by implication to the one offense that could destroy Israel (v. 16). See note on 1:12–15.

Joshua's Farewell to the Leaders

23 After a long time had passed and the LORD had given Israel rest[z] from all their enemies around them, Joshua, by then old and well advanced in years,[a] **2**summoned all Israel—their elders,[b] leaders, judges and officials[c]—and said to them: "I am old
and well advanced in years. **3**You yourselves have seen everything the LORD your God has
done to all these nations for your sake; it was the LORD your God who fought for you.[d] **4**Remember how I have allotted[e] as an inheritance for your tribes all the land of the nations
that remain—the nations I conquered—between the Jordan and the Great Sea[a][f] in the
west. **5**The LORD your God himself will drive them out of your way. He will push them out
before you, and you will take possession of their land, as the LORD your God promised you.[g]
6"Be very strong; be careful to obey all that is written in the Book of the Law of Moses, without turning aside to the right or to the left.[h] **7**Do not associate with these nations
that remain among you; do not invoke the names of their gods or swear[i] by them. You
must not serve them or bow down[j] to them. **8**But you are to hold fast to the LORD[k] your
God, as you have until now.
9"The LORD has driven out before you great and powerful nations;[l] to this day no one
has been able to withstand you.[m] **10**One of you routs a thousand,[n] because the LORD your
God fights for you,[o] just as he promised. **11**So be very careful to love the LORD[p] your God.
12"But if you turn away and ally yourselves with the survivors of these nations that
remain among you and if you intermarry with them[q] and associate with them,[r] **13**then
you may be sure that the LORD your God will no longer drive out these nations before you.
Instead, they will become snares[s] and traps for you, whips on your backs and thorns in
your eyes,[t] until you perish from this good land, which the LORD your God has given you.
14"Now I am about to go the way of all the earth.[u] You know with all your heart and
soul that not one of all the good promises the LORD your God gave you has failed. Every
promise has been fulfilled; not one has failed.[v] **15**But just as every good promise of the
LORD your God has come true, so the LORD will bring on you all the evil he has threatened,

[a] *4* That is, the Mediterranean

23:1 [z]Dt 12:9; Jos 21:44 [a]Jos 13:1
23:2 [b]Jos 7:6 [c]Jos 24:1
23:3 [d]Ex 14:14
23:4 [e]Jos 19:51 [f]Nu 34:6
23:5 [g]Ex 23:30; Nu 33:53
23:6 [h]Dt 5:32; Jos 1:7
23:7 [i]Ex 23:13; Ps 16:4; Jer 5:7 [j]Ex 20:5
23:8 [k]Dt 10:20
23:9 [l]Dt 11:23 [m]Dt 7:24
23:10 [n]Lev 26:8 [o]Ex 14:14; Dt 3:22
23:11 [p]Jos 22:5
23:12 [q]Dt 7:3 [r]Ex 34:16; Ps 106:34-35
23:13 [s]Ex 23:33 [t]Nu 33:55
23:14 [u]1Ki 2:2 [v]Jos 21:45

▪ **23:1–16** *The Requirement of Covenant Loyalty.* An assembly of all Israel, probably at Shiloh (18:1; 19:51; 21:2), was addressed by Joshua in his old age (vv. 1–2,14). This and the following chapter take up the major hortatory themes of chapter 1 and apply them to Israel in the light of the substantial fulfillment of God's promises. The framework of the book (chs. 1,23–24) conveys the purpose of the whole; namely, an exhortation to faithful obedience based on the complete faithfulness of God to his promises. An introduction (vv. 1–2a) is followed by three calls to faithfulness (vv. 2b–8,9–13,14–16). Each section describes the blessing of God and follows with exhortations. In this way the imperatives of this chapter are set very clearly in the context of grace. In covenant renewal ceremonies a historical prologue citing the sovereign's benefits to the people was brought up to date.

▪ **23:1–2a** *All Israel Summoned.* Joshua called the nation together to give the people his final exhortations.

23:1 rest. See note on 1:13. **enemies.** The perspective that sees these nations as Israel's enemies must be understood in theological, not simply in nationalistic, terms. While Israel, representing God's kingship to the world (Ex 19:5–6), would ultimately bring blessing to the nations (Ge 12:3), the nations' hostility to Israel expressed their hostility to God (cf. notes on Ge 3:15; Ex 23:22). The experience of "rest from all their enemies," which was here partially realized, would become part of Israel's hope (Dt 12:10; 2Sa 7:11; 1Ch 22:9; cf. Mic 5:9; Lk 1:71). **old.** Joshua died at the age of 110 (see note on 24:29).

23:2a all Israel. The words that follow suggest that "all Israel" should probably here be understood representatively. See note on 1:12–15.

▪ **23:2b–8** *First Exhortation.* These verses report the first of three calls to faithful obedience that make up Joshua's speech.

23:3 God who fought for you. See note on 10:14.

23:4 allotted. Literally, "caused to fall." See note on 13:6. **inheritance.** See note on 1:6. **nations that remain.** The affirmation of the complete faithfulness of God to his promises and the incompleteness of the actual conquest stand side by side in this chapter (see note on 21:45).

23:5 God himself will drive them out . . . as the LORD your God promised you. The faithfulness of God to his promises, which had been the experience of Israel under Joshua, would continue into the future.

23:6 Be very strong. The consequences of God's promises that were applied to Joshua in 1:6 (see its note) are here applied to all Israel. See note on 1:12–15. **obey.** See note on 1:7. **Book of the Law.** See note on 1:8.

23:7 Do not associate. The Hebrew suggests a close connection between verses 6 and 7. Faithful obedience to the Book of the Law was the way in which the Israelites were to avoid the kind of association with the pagan nations described here.

23:8 hold fast to. See note on 22:5. **as you have until now.** Contrast the previous generation, which rebelled in the wilderness, with the succeeding generations (cf. 24:31).

▪ **23:9–13** *Second Exhortation.* This section introduces a note of warning in verses 12–13. See note on verses 3–8.

23:9 no one has been able to withstand you. The promise to Joshua in 1:5 had also been the experience of the Israelites (Dt 7:24; 11:25).

23:11 be very careful to love. In the Bible love can be commanded. This does not mean that such love lacks emotional depth, but it does mean that it is more than mere emotion. Love is to be expressed in glad and willing obedience (cf. note on 22:5).

23:12–13 The tragedy recorded in the books of Judges through 2 Kings reveals that these verses anticipate all too accurately the ensuing history of the people of Israel (2Ki 17:7–23).

23:12 turn away. See note on 22:16. **intermarry.** See notes on Genesis 26:34 and 35, 34:1–31 and 38:1–30.

23:13 God will no longer drive out. Although the validity of God's promise (v. 5) is not dependent on human cooperation (the history of Israel is ample testimony to this truth, as is the rest of the Bible's story, culminating in the work of Christ), the promise will not benefit those who reject the grace of God. This indeed was part of the promise from the beginning (Ge 12:3). **perish from this good land.** As the gift of the land had been the content of God's promise and the expression of his faithfulness, so the loss of the land would be proof of his displeasure and the manner of his judgment.

▪ **23:14–16** *Third Exhortation.* In this final section of Joshua's speech, the exhortation is again based on a reminder of God's faithfulness, but it consists entirely of warnings regarding the consequences of turning away from the Lord. See note on verses 3–8.

23:14 know with all your heart and soul. Knowledge of God's faithfulness can never be merely cognitive; it will shape every aspect of a person. **not one . . . has failed.** See note on 21:45.

23:15 just as . . . so. There are two sides to God's faithfulness because there are two sides to his covenant: "good" promises (v. 5) and stern warnings (vv. 12–13). He can be trusted to fulfill the latter as fully as he can be trusted to keep the former.

until he has destroyed you from this good land he has given you.[w] 16If you violate the covenant of the LORD your God, which he commanded you, and go and serve other gods and
bow down to them, the LORD's anger will burn against you, and you will quickly perish
from the good land he has given you.[x]"

The Covenant Renewed at Shechem

24 Then Joshua assembled all the tribes of Israel at Shechem. He summoned the
elders, leaders, judges and officials of Israel,[y] and they presented themselves
before God.
2Joshua said to all the people, "This is what the LORD, the God of Israel, says: 'Long
ago your forefathers, including Terah the father of Abraham and Nahor, lived beyond the
River[a] and worshiped other gods.[z] 3But I took your father Abraham from the land beyond
the River and led him throughout Canaan[a] and gave him many descendants.[b] I gave him
Isaac,[c] 4and to Isaac I gave Jacob and Esau.[d] I assigned the hill country of Seir[e] to Esau,
but Jacob and his sons went down to Egypt.[f]
5" 'Then I sent Moses and Aaron,[g] and I afflicted the Egyptians by what I did there,
and I brought you out. 6When I brought your fathers out of Egypt, you came to the sea,
and the Egyptians pursued them with chariots and horsemen[b][h] as far as the Red Sea.[c]
7But they cried to the LORD for help, and he put darkness[i] between you and the Egyptians; he brought the sea over them and covered them.[j] You saw with your own eyes
what I did to the Egyptians. Then you lived in the desert for a long time.[k]
8" 'I brought you to the land of the Amorites who lived east of the Jordan. They fought
against you, but I gave them into your hands. I destroyed them from before you, and you
took possession of their land.[l] 9When Balak son of Zippor,[m] the king of Moab, prepared
to fight against Israel, he sent for Balaam son of Beor to put a curse on you.[n] 10But I
would not listen to Balaam, so he blessed you[o] again and again, and I delivered you out
of his hand.

23:15 [w]Lev 26:17; Dt 28:15
23:16 [x]Dt 4:25-26
24:1 [y]Jos 23:2
24:2 [z]Ge 11:32
24:3 [a]Ge 12:1 [b]Ge 15:5 [c]Ge 21:3
24:4 [d]Ge 25:26 [e]Dt 2:5 [f]Ge 46:5-6
24:5 [g]Ex 3:10
24:6 [h]Ex 14:9
24:7 [i]Ex 14:20 [j]Ex 14:28 [k]Dt 1:46
24:8 [l]Nu 21:31
24:9 [m]Nu 22:2 [n]Nu 22:6
24:10 [o]Nu 23:11; Dt 23:5

[a] *2* That is, the Euphrates; also in verses 3, 14 and 15 [b] *6* Or *charioteers* [c] *6* Hebrew *Yam Suph*; that is, Sea of Reeds

---

23:16 violate the covenant. The expression is virtually synonymous with "turn away" in verse 12. See note on 7:11. **anger.** See note on 7:1. **perish from the good land.** See note on verse 13.

■ **24:1–28** *The Covenant Renewal at Shechem.* Joshua led Israel in a reaffirmation of the covenant near the end of his life, as Moses had done before him. Like Deuteronomy, there are analogies between this covenant renewal and the formalizing of relationships between ancient suzerains (sovereigns) and vassal (servant) states by means of treaties (see "Introduction to Deuteronomy: Purpose and Distinctives"). Such treaties commonly included elements analogous to some features of the present chapter, such as a historical prologue reviewing the sovereign's dealings with the servant (vv. 2–13), stipulations (vv. 14–15), rites of commitment (vv. 16–24) and the provision of a treaty document (vv. 25–26). There are, however, also marked differences between this chapter and ancient treaty documents. The assembly described here should be compared to that in 8:30–35.

■ **24:1–2a** *All Israel Summoned.* As in 23:1–2a, Joshua called an assembly.

24:1 all the tribes of Israel. See notes on 1:12–15 and 23:2a. **Shechem.** The very place at which God had first explicitly promised the land to the descendants of Abraham (Ge 12:6–7) was the place where those descendants were now assembled after having received the land. See note on 8:30. **before God.** This does not necessarily imply the movement of the tabernacle from Shiloh (19:51) to Shechem for the occasion. The presence of God was not restricted to the tabernacle (cf. 1Ki 8:27) any more than it was guaranteed by the physical possession of the ark (1Sa 4:3–11).

24:2a the LORD . . . says. The people of God assembled to hear the word of God. See notes on 8:30–35. Joshua spoke with the authority of Moses (Dt 5:27) and with that of a prophet (Dt 18:15–19).

■ **24:2b–13** *Historical Reflections.* The word of God to the people on this occasion was not a new one. The books of Genesis (vv. 2b–4), Exodus (vv. 5–7), Numbers (vv. 8–10) and Joshua (vv. 11–13) are reviewed in a rehearsal of God's dealings with this people since the days of Abraham, culminating in the gift of the land promised to Abraham and now received by his descendants. The significance of this moment is shown in terms of its place in the unfolding history of God's faithfulness to his promises.

24:2b–4 The review began with a digest of Genesis 11:27—50:26. The earlier material (Ge 1–11) was not summarized because the history that climaxed with the receiving of the land began with the initial offer to Abraham (Ge 12:1,7).

24:2b beyond the River. The reference is presumably to Ur (Ge 11:28) or Haran (Ge 11:31). **worshiped.** See note on verse 14. **other gods.** The pagan beginning underlines the grace of God to which this history testifies, and it also provides the background for the exhortation in verse 14.

24:3 But I. God is the dominant subject of the verbs in verses 3–13. **many descendants.** The promise of multiple offspring to Abraham is the preeminent concern of Genesis 12–50 (see notes on Ge 12:2; 15:5; 17:2) and is related to the content of God's blessing on human beings in Genesis 1:26–18 (cf. note on Ex 1:7).

24:4 Esau, but Jacob. The principle of divine election was explicit in the choice of Jacob over Esau (see Ge 25:23; note on Ro 9:11), as was the reality that God's promises are often in apparent conflict with the course of history ("Jacob . . . went down to Egypt").

24:5–7 Joshua's summary of the book of Exodus is remarkable for its lack of mention of Israel's experience at Mount Sinai. This may be because this greatly condensed account presents God's saving acts—the exodus in particular—as culminating in the occupation of the promised land, and it therefore passes as quickly as possible to that end (see note on v. 7).

24:5 I brought you out. The great act of redemption that became the reference point for the Lord's relationship with Israel (Ex 20:2) had as its goal the gift of the promised land (see note on Ex 15:17). **you.** See note on verse 7.

24:6 the Red Sea. See note on Exodus 13:18.

24:7 they . . . you . . . your own eyes. The people of Joshua's day were spoken of as having participated in the redemptive events of the past. This emphasizes that they must have seen the goodness of God toward them not only in their contemporary experience, but also in the history here recounted. See note on 4:23–24. **you lived in the desert for a long time.** These few words summarized everything (including the experience at Mount Sinai), from the crossing of the sea to the arrival at the land to be given to the tribes east of the Jordan. See note on verses 5–7.

24:8–10 Joshua's summary of the book of Numbers omits mention of the rebellions that took place in the desert (Nu 14; 25), probably because the emphasis of the historical review is on the deeds of God.

24:8 Amorites. See note on 2:10.

24:9 Balaam. See Numbers 22–24, as well as the note on Joshua 13:22.

24:10 he blessed you. Balaam illustrated God's complete power over those who would bring harm to his people.

[11]" 'Then you crossed the Jordan[p] and came to Jericho.[q] The citizens of Jericho
fought against you, as did also the Amorites, Perizzites, Canaanites, Hittites, Girgashites,
Hivites and Jebusites, but I gave them into your hands.[r] [12]I sent the hornet[s] ahead of you,
which drove them out before you—also the two Amorite kings. You did not do it with
your own sword and bow. [13]So I gave you a land on which you did not toil and cities you
did not build; and you live in them and eat from vineyards and olive groves that you did
not plant.'[t]
[14]"Now fear the LORD and serve him with all faithfulness.[u] Throw away the gods[v] your
forefathers worshiped beyond the River and in Egypt,[w] and serve the LORD. [15]But if serv-

24:11 [p]Jos 3:16-17 [q]Jos 6:1 [r]Ex 23:23; Dt 7:1
24:12 [s]Ex 23:28; Dt 7:20; Ps 44:3,6-7
24:13 [t]Dt 6:10-11
24:14 [u]Dt 10:12; 18:13; 1Sa 12:24; 2Co 1:12 [v]ver 23 [w]Eze 23:3

24:11–13 These verses are Joshua's summary of the contents of the present book.
24:11 Amorites . . . Jebusites. See 3:10 and its note.
24:12 hornet. This is possibly a metaphor for sudden panic (2:9; 5:1; Ex 23:28). **You did not do it.** The Israelites received the land as a gift; its acquisition was not to be understood as being based on their own achievement (see note on 1:2; cf. Eph 2:8).
24:13 gave. See note on 1:2.
▪**24:14 24** *Renewed Commitments to the Covenant.* Joshua called on the nation to become fully committed to the Lord. After challenging the sincerity of their expressed desire to do so, Joshua led the people in renewing their commitments to the covenant.
24:14 fear the LORD. Compare 4:24. This response was demanded by the history of God's faithfulness to his promises in verses 2–13. This fear of God was therefore associated with knowledge of his grace (cf. Ps 130:4) and was fully compatible with love for God (Dt 10:12–13). Contrast 2:9 (where the Canaanites feared God because of his coming judgment) and 7:5 (where the Israelites experienced his anger). **faithfulness.** That is, integrity and trustworthiness. **Throw away the gods.** This may refer literally to dis-

The Freedom and Bondage of the Will: Do I Have a Free Will to Believe?

REFORMED theology is often thought to deny free will for human beings and to run counter to passages that emphasize the importance of the human choice in the process of salvation. In reality, however, Reformed theology has always recognized the positive activities of the human will in salvation. See *WCF* 9.4 and *CD* 3–4.10–12.

While the term "free will" never appears in the Scriptures in a technical, philosophical or theological sense, it is fair to say that in different ways the Bible both affirms and denies that people have free will. Reformed theologians have often approached this matter by distinguishing among human free agency, moral free will and absolute freedom. See *WCF* 3,5,9.

Free agency simply acknowledges that human beings are volitional or willful creatures. In distinction from rocks, trees, mountains and other aspects of creation, human beings make moral choices. All humans are free agents in the sense that they make decisions as to what they will do, and each individual is morally responsible for his or her voluntary choices. This was true of Adam, both before and after he sinned; it is so now, and it will be so for glorified believers—this fact is reflected throughout the Bible. All people are called upon to make right and responsible choices (Jos 24:15; 2Sa 12:1–10; Jn 7:24; Ro 1:18–32; 14:13). Free agency, however, does not include the ability to make any given moral choice in any given circumstance or the ability to choose contrary to one's nature. Since obeying and believing the gospel is contrary to fallen humanity's nature (Ro 8:4–8), the concept of free agency does not affirm that a fallen person possesses the free will to do these things.

Moral free will is an ability to choose from among all the moral options a situation presents. Many Christian theologians from the second century on (e.g., Clement of Alexandria, Origen), taught that fallen human beings possess such a will. They denied that human beings are restrained by their fallen moral condition, insisting instead that fallen humans are capable of making choices in any direction they wish, including choosing of their own power and volition to obey and believe the gospel. This view is in stark contrast to Scripture. Augustine and Reformed theologians after him have rightly affirmed that although humankind possessed moral free will before the fall, original sin has robbed us of it.

Having been born in Adam, we have no natural ability to discern and choose God's way or to believe the gospel because we have no natural inclination toward God. Our hearts are in bondage to sin, and only the grace of regeneration can liberate us from that slavery. This is why Paul taught in Romans 6:16–23 that only people freed from the dominion of sin are able freely and heartily to opt for righteousness. An inclination of the heart toward pleasing God is one aspect of the freedom that Christ gives his followers (Jn 8:34-36; Gal 5:1,13). See *WCF* 9; *CD* 3–4.

There have been and still are Christian theologians who have argued in a variety of ways that human choices to be significant must be absolutely free from God's sovereign decrees. Reformed theology has categorically rejected this error. In the first place, it is obvious that many physical and mental limitations are placed on us by the natural order God has ordained for his world. We do not have absolute freedom in any area. Beyond this, the Scriptures teach that God has an immutable plan that includes all events that come to pass, from the greatest to the least (Isa 46:10; Mt 10:29–31). Human choices are included in that plan, but they can never thwart or circumvent what God has decreed (Isa 8:10, 14:26–27). Thus, as surely as we know that no fallen human has the moral ability to choose to believe the gospel, we can be confident that no one has the ability to overturn the good purposes of God or the salvation he has ordained for us in Christ (Ro 8:28–30). All whom he has predestined to salvation will be effectually called and regenerated, and will choose to believe. Far from comprising a fatalism that diminishes the importance of human choice, this limitation on our freedom is in reality a wonderful affirmation of our important place in God's world. See *WCF* 9; *CD* 3–4.

ing the LORD seems undesirable to you, then choose for yourselves this day whom you
will serve, whether the gods your forefathers served beyond the River, or the gods of the
Amorites,[x] in whose land you are living. But as for me and my household, we will serve
the LORD."[y]
16 Then the people answered, "Far be it from us to forsake the LORD to serve other
gods! 17 It was the LORD our God himself who brought us and our fathers up out of Egypt,
from that land of slavery, and performed those great signs before our eyes. He protected us on our entire journey and among all the nations through which we traveled. 18 And
the LORD drove out before us all the nations, including the Amorites, who lived in the
land. We too will serve the LORD, because he is our God."
19 Joshua said to the people, "You are not able to serve the LORD. He is a holy God;[z]
he is a jealous God.[a] He will not forgive your rebellion[b] and your sins. 20 If you forsake
the LORD[c] and serve foreign gods, he will turn[d] and bring disaster on you and make an
end of you,[e] after he has been good to you."
21 But the people said to Joshua, "No! We will serve the LORD."
22 Then Joshua said, "You are witnesses against yourselves that you have chosen[f] to
serve the LORD."
"Yes, we are witnesses," they replied.
23 "Now then," said Joshua, "throw away the foreign gods[g] that are among you and
yield your hearts[h] to the LORD, the God of Israel."
24 And the people said to Joshua, "We will serve the LORD our God and obey him."[i]
25 On that day Joshua made a covenant[j] for the people, and there at Shechem he drew
up for them decrees and laws.[k] 26 And Joshua recorded these things in the Book of the
Law of God.[l] Then he took a large stone[m] and set it up there under the oak near the holy
place of the LORD.
27 "See!" he said to all the people. "This stone will be a witness[n] against us. It has
heard all the words the LORD has said to us. It will be a witness against you if you are untrue to your God."

Buried in the Promised Land

28 Then Joshua sent the people away, each to his own inheritance.
29 After these things, Joshua son of Nun, the servant of the LORD, died at the age of a

24:15 [x]Jdg 6:10; Ru 1:15 [y]Ru 1:16; 1Ki 18:21
24:19 [z]Lev 19:2; 20:26 [a]Ex 20:5 [b]Ex 23:21
24:20 [c]1Ch 28:9,20 [d]Ac 7:42 [e]Jos 23:15
24:22 [f]Ps 119:30,173
24:23 [g]ver 14 [h]1Ki 8:58; Ps 119:36; 141:4
24:24 [i]Ex 19:8; 24:3,7; Dt 5:27
24:25 [j]Ex 24:8 [k]Ex 15:25
24:26 [l]Dt 31:24 [m]Ge 28:18
24:27 [n]Jos 22:27

carding idols, metaphorically to abandoning allegiance to other gods or to both. The goodness of God to Israel (vv. 2–13) demanded exclusive allegiance, which was summed up by the first commandment (Ex 20:3). **worshiped.** The same Hebrew verb is translated "serve" in the next clause and in verse 15. **beyond the River.** See note on verse 2b. **and in Egypt.** Israel's idolatry in Egypt would be recalled by Ezekiel (Eze 20:7–10; 23:3–8,19–21,27). See *WCF* 21.1.

24:15 choose . . . this day whom you will serve. There is apparent irony in the presentation of the choice available if the Lord were to be rejected. The choice in that event would have been between the gods Abraham had left behind (vv. 2–3) and the gods of the dispossessed Amorites (v. 12). **Amorites.** See note on 2:10. **me and my household.** See 6:25, 7:24 and Acts 16:15. See *WLC* 99,104,118.

24:16–18 The people's response to the call of verse 14 consisted of (*a*) their repudiation of other gods (v. 16), (*b*) their acknowledgment of God's acts from the exodus to the conquest and their participation in them (vv. 17–18a; see note on v. 7) and (*c*) their submission to the Lord as their God (v. 18b).

24:19 You are not able to serve the LORD. This paradoxical statement would all too soon be tragically proven true (see notes on v. 31; 7:1–26; 23:12–13; see also Dt 31:16; Jdg 2:7,10–13; 2Ki 17:7–23). It is based on two realities: God's holiness (which means he cannot be served easily, after the manner of other gods) and the people's rebelliousness (which has been displayed far too often already; see 22:17 and its note). **holy.** Only a holy people (separated from pagan ways; Lev 18:3; 20:26) can serve the God who is holy (separate from other gods; Lev 19:2). **jealous.** See Exodus 20:5 and its note. **will not forgive.** The rebellion in view here refers to the apostasy described in the following verse.

24:20 If you forsake . . . he will. Or "For you will forsake . . . and he will." The latter translation provides the basis for the preceding harsh remarks and is consistent with, for example, the prediction in Deuteronomy 31:16–18. **foreign gods.** These Gods had no place in Israel. The contrast was with the Lord, "the God of Israel" (vv. 2,23). Compare Deuteronomy 32:12. **he will turn.** God's manner of acting would change from grace to judgment (Ge 6:7). In another sense, God never changes (1Sa 15:29), since his promise always included the threat of judgment (see notes on 23:15; Ge 6:6). **disaster.** See 22:15–18.

24:21 We will serve the LORD. The emphasis is on "the LORD" as opposed to "foreign gods" (v. 20). The people rejected the possibility envisaged (or predicted) in verse 20.

24:22 witnesses against yourselves. When they would later be accused of forsaking the Lord, the case against them would be supported by their decision on this occasion, for their choice to serve the Lord was an affirmation of the truth of God's claim to their undivided allegiance (vv. 16–18). See *WLC* 104.

24:23 throw away . . . and yield. See note on verse 14.

■ **24:25–28** *The Covenant Document.* As part of the ratification of this renewal, Joshua wrote down the terms of Israel's submission to the Lord.

24:25 made a covenant. This expression refers to the formalizing of the relationship (cf. Ge 15:18; Dt 4:23; 29:1). See notes on 3:3 and 9:6. **decrees and laws.** These would specify the content of Israel's obedience to the Lord.

24:26 Book of the Law of God. This is probably to be identified with the Book of the Law in 1:8, 8:31 and 23:6. **oak.** Compare Genesis 12:6, 35:4 and Judges 9:6.

24:27 witness. Compare the way in which the stones at Gilgal were to provide a testimony to what God had done (see 4:20–24). **if you are untrue.** Or "lest you should be untrue."

24:28 each to his own inheritance. These words are a fitting conclusion to the book that tells of God's giving the promised inheritance to Israel. Similar words occur, after a different period, at the end of the book of Judges (21:24). See note on 1:6.

■ **24:29–33** *Notices of Deaths and Burials.* The deaths of Joshua and Eleazar mark the end of the period that has been the subject of this book. Their burials, along with that of the bones of Joseph, in the land that was now Israel's possession symbolized God's faithful fulfillment of his promises to the patriarchs.

24:29 servant of the LORD. See note on 1:1. **a hundred and ten.** This ideal age is the same as Joseph's at his death (see Ge 50:22 and its note). Such long lives signified God's blessing (cf. Dt 34:7).

hundred and ten.[o] 30And they buried him in the land of his inheritance, at Timnath Serah[a][p] in the hill country of Ephraim, north of Mount Gaash.
31Israel served the LORD throughout the lifetime of Joshua and of the elders[q] who outlived him and who had experienced everything the LORD had done for Israel.
32And Joseph's bones, which the Israelites had brought up from Egypt,[r] were buried
at Shechem in the tract of land[s] that Jacob bought for a hundred pieces of silver[b] from
the sons of Hamor, the father of Shechem. This became the inheritance of Joseph's descendants.
33And Eleazar son of Aaron[t] died and was buried at Gibeah, which had been allotted
to his son Phinehas[u] in the hill country of Ephraim.

24:29 [o]Jdg 2:8
24:30 [p]Jos 19:50
24:31 [q]Jdg 2:7
24:32 [r]Ge 50:25; Ex 13:19 [s]Ge 33:19; Jn 4:5; Ac 7:16
24:33 [t]Jos 22:13 [u]Ex 6:25

[a] *30* Also known as *Timnath Heres* (see Judges 2:9) [b] *32* Hebrew *hundred kesitahs*; a kesitah was a unit of money of unknown weight and value.

24:30 his inheritance. See 19:49–50. Unlike Abraham, who had to purchase land for a burial plot (Ge 23:4; cf. Ge 33:19), Joshua was buried in what was now his own land.
24:31 Israel served the LORD throughout the lifetime. The faithfulness of the generation of Joshua and the elders was testimony to the power of everything that the Lord had done for Israel. That such faithfulness was so short-lived supports Joshua's assertion in verses 19–20 (see their notes; see also Jdg 2:7,10–13).
24:32 Joseph's bones. The promise that Joseph had believed (see Ge 50:24–25 and their notes) had come to fulfillment. **land that Jacob bought.** See Genesis 33:19. The new situation of possession of the land is again contrasted to that of the patriarchs, who had only the promise.
24:33 Eleazar. See note on 14:1. **Phinehas.** See note on 22:13.

JUDGES

Introduction

Overview
Author: Unknown
Purpose: To establish Israel's need for a godly king from the line of David
Date: c. 1000–538 B.C.
Key Truths:

- The tribes of Israel failed to complete the conquest of the land and suffered from this failure.
- God's provision of judges could at best only temporarily bring blessings to the people of God.
- God's provision of the Levites also failed to bring effective leadership to God's people.
- The people of God must have a godly king from Judah, not from Benjamin, to lead them.

Author
The author of the book of Judges is unknown, and attempts to identify his era depend on clues within the book. Opinions range from the view that the book was composed by Samuel to the hypothesis that it was written late in the postexilic period. It is possible that its final form resulted from a compiler or compilers completing an earlier version of the book. See "Introduction to the Historical Books" on page 304.

Time and Place of Writing
Much evidence in the book suggests that the original author of Judges lived and wrote in Judah during the early period of David's reign at Hebron. The favor shown toward Judah and the negative characterization of the tribe of Benjamin that permeate the book (see "Purpose and Distinctives") fit best during the period in which there was still a debate about whether the house of David or the house of Saul would rule. That tension existed especially when David was king in Hebron and Saul's son Ish-Bosheth ruled in the north.

Nevertheless, there are some indications that the book may have come to its final form at a later time. The attention to false worship in Dan (18:30) reflects interests well-suited to the time after Jeroboam II had established his false worship in the northern kingdom (c. 930 B.C.). Some interpreters have also suggested that "until . . . the captivity of the land" (18:30) refers to the captivity of the northern kingdom in 722 B.C. Although earlier defeats in battle may have been in mind (see note on 18:30), this later possibility cannot be ruled out completely. The patterning of the narrative of Samuel's birth after that of Samson's birth in 13:2 (see note on 1 Sa 1:1) strongly suggests that at least a preliminary form of the book of Judges was completed by the time 1 and 2 Samuel were written.

Original Audience
See "Time and Place of Writing."

Purpose and Distinctives
Judges is named for the 12 characters God raised up prior to the time of Samuel to deliver Israel from assorted oppressors. They were designated with the title "judge" in 2:11–19. Apart from this introduction, the judges were called "deliverers," not "judges" (see 3:9,15; note on "he became Israel's judge" at 3:10). The Hebrew word *shaphat,* "to judge," is also translated "to lead" (see 10:2–3; 12:7–8,11,13; 15:20; 16:31). The task of these deliverers was military (2:16–19; 3:7—16:31) rather than judicial (Dt 17:8–13). Only Deborah is mentioned as having functioned in an explicitly judicial fashion (4:5).

The events narrated in the book span the approximately 350-year period from the conquest of Canaan (c. 1400 B.C.) until just prior to the time of Samuel, who anointed Israel's first king (c. 1050 B.C.). Othniel, the first judge, belonged to the generation after Joshua, and Samson, the final judge, was more or less contemporary with Samuel. During this period the Israelites were oppressed by enemies from within (the Canaanites) and without (the Arameans, Moabites, Midianites, Ammonites, Amalekites, Amorites and Philistines).

In general terms, the author of Judges evaluated the events of this period in Israel's history by using the theological concerns of Deuteronomy. Time and again covenant violations highlighted in Deuteronomy were identified and the corresponding covenant judgments pronounced (see 2:1–5; 6:7–10; 8:27; 9:56; 10:11–13; 21:25; "Introduction to the Historical Books" on page 304).

More specifically, however, the book of Judges established the importance of godly Davidic kingship. This point of view was advanced in the book in a number of ways. (1) The author pointed out that in the past the people of God had sinned because their appointed leaders had failed. He recorded that parents (2:6–10; 6:11–32, especially vv. 13,22–25), priests (ch. 17), judges (4:9; 8:27; 11:39; 14:3) and Israel's first king (8:33—9:57) had not led the people of God to faithful observance of God's law. In his view only a covenant-keeping king from Judah could lead the people into covenant obedience and correlative blessing and prevent new oppression. (2) Recalling the Lord's saving acts (2:10; 6:13) and refraining from the worship of false gods were the chief challenges Israel confronted in the book of Judges in terms of keeping covenant. As in Deuteronomy, seeking other gods was the sin synonymous with covenant disobedience (2:11–12; 3:7,12;

8:33; 10:6,10; Dt 4:23). The repeated cycles with the repeated refrains of "The Israelites did evil in the eyes of the LORD" (e.g., 3:7,12; 4:1) and "everyone did as he saw fit" (17:6; 21:25; see also Dt 12:8; 31:16–17) served as a stiff warning to the Israelites in the early part of David's reign concerning their peril if they failed to choose a covenant-keeping king. (3) Even though Judges never mentions David's name, it purposefully and prominently plays Judah and Benjamin against one another, probably at a time when a debate raged over which tribe would produce Israel's king. The writer of Judges affirmed Judah's leadership (1:1–2; 1:3–20) and rejected any reliance on leadership from the tribe of Benjamin (see note on 1:21).

Christ in Judges

The emphasis of the book of Judges on the need for a righteous kingship from the line of David points to the role that Jesus Christ would later fulfill as king. Jesus was of the family of David and the rightful heir of David's throne (Mt 1:1–17; Lk 3:1–37), and he was David's unique son in that he never failed to keep the law of God perfectly (Mt 5:17). As a result, God raised Christ from the dead, seated him on his heavenly throne (1Co 15:25) and established the kingdom that will never end (Isa 9:6–9). Although Christ is King already, all will recognize him as such when he returns in glory and rules over the new heavens and the new earth (Rev 22:1–3). The success of Jesus' kingship stands in sharp contrast to the failing leadership others have provided for the people of God. Like the judges and Levites of Israel, sinful leaders cannot fulfill the need for a perfectly righteous king. Only Christ can meet that need.

Outline

I. Faltering Conquest (1:1—2:5)

God chose Judah to be the leading tribe of Israel, but the conquest faltered for lack of a unified leadership.

- A. Judah as Leader (1:1–2)
- B. Judah's Success Contrasted With Benjamin's Failure (1:3–21)
- C. Joseph's Success at Bethel (1:22–26)
- D. The Failures by the Remaining Tribes (1:27–36)
- E. The Resulting Divine Judgment (2:1–5)

II. The Cycles of the Judges (2:6—16:31)

The judges provided some leadership to Israel, but they failed to guide the nation into ongoing loyalty to the covenant.

- A. The Pattern of the Cycles (2:6—3:6)
  1. Israel in Joshua's Day (2:6–9)
  2. Introduction of the Cycles (2:10–19)
  3. The Purpose of God's Judgment (2:20–23)
  4. The Instruments of God's Judgment (3:1–6)
- B. The Twelve Cycles (3:7—16:31)
  1. Othniel (3:7–11)
  2. Ehud (3:12–30)
  3. Shamgar (3:31)
  4. Deborah (4:1—5:31)
  5. Gideon (6:1—8:32)
     - a. Introduction to Gideon: The Evil Situation at the Time of His Call (6:1–10)
     - b. Gideon's Call to Deliver (6:11–32)
     - c. Gideon's Struggle to Believe God's Promise (6:33–7:18)
     - d. Gideon Delivers Israel From Midian (7:19—8:21)
     - e. Conclusion to Gideon: The Evil Situation When He Died (8:22–32)
     - f. Abimelech (8:33—9:57)
  6. Tola (10:1–2)
  7. Jair (10:3–5)
  8. Jephthah (10:6—12:7)
  9. Ibzan (12:8–10)
  10. Elon (12:11–12)
  11. Abdon (12:13–15)

12. Samson (13:1—16:31)
    a. Introduction to Samson (13:1)
    b. Samson's Birth (13:2–25)
    c. Samson's Career (14:1—16:31)
        (1) A Wife and Trouble With the Philistines (14:1—15:20)
        (2) Delilah and Trouble With the Philistines (16:1–30)
    d. Death and Burial (16:31)

III. The Failures of the Levites (17:1—21:25)
   A. A Levite and Idolatry in Israel (17:1—18:31)
      1. Micah and the Levite (17:1–13)
      2. The Danites and the Levite (18:1–31)
   B. A Levite and Violence in Israel (19:1—21:25)
      1. The Violence by the Men of Gibeah (19:1–30)
      2. The Violence Against the Men of Gibeah (20:1–48)
      3. The Violence Against Jabesh Gilead (21:1–25)

The Levites were unable to lead the nation into righteousness; Israel needed a godly, Davidic king.

Israel Fights the Remaining Canaanites

1 After the death[a] of Joshua, the Israelites asked the LORD, "Who will be the first[b] to
go up and fight for us against the Canaanites?[c]"
2 The LORD answered, "Judah[d] is to go; I have given the land into their hands.[e]"
3 Then the men of Judah said to the Simeonites their brothers, "Come up with us into
the territory allotted to us, to fight against the Canaanites. We in turn will go with you
into yours." So the Simeonites[f] went with them.
4 When Judah attacked, the LORD gave the Canaanites and Perizzites[g] into their hands
and they struck down ten thousand men at Bezek.[h] 5 It was there that they found Adoni-Bezek and fought against him, putting to rout the Canaanites and Perizzites. 6 Adoni-
Bezek fled, but they chased him and caught him, and cut off his thumbs and big toes.
7 Then Adoni-Bezek said, "Seventy kings with their thumbs and big toes cut off have
picked up scraps under my table. Now God has paid me back[i] for what I did to them."
They brought him to Jerusalem, and he died there.
8 The men of Judah attacked Jerusalem[j] also and took it. They put the city to the sword
and set it on fire.
9 After that, the men of Judah went down to fight against the Canaanites living in the
hill country,[k] the Negev[l] and the western foothills. 10 They advanced against the Canaanites living in Hebron[m] (formerly called Kiriath Arba[n]) and defeated Sheshai, Ahiman and
Talmai.[o]

1:1 [a]Jos 24:29 [b]Nu 27:21 [c]ver 27; Jdg 3:1-6
1:2 [d]Ge 49:8 [e]ver 4; Jdg 3:28
1:3 [f]ver 17
1:4 [g]Ge 13:7; Jos 3:10 [h]1Sa 11:8
1:7 [i]Lev 24:19
1:8 [j]ver 21; Jos 15:63
1:9 [k]Nu 13:17 [l]Nu 21:1
1:10 [m]Ge 13:18 [n]Ge 35:27 [o]Jos 15:14

■ **1:1—2:5** *Faltering Conquest.* This first portion of the book raises the issue of leadership among the tribes and the failures of Israel when there was no united, godly leadership. The successes and failures of the various tribes are recounted (see 1:3–36), along with God's judgment on Israel for covenant failure in letting the Canaanites live in the land (see Dt 7:1–2; 20:16–20). The space and detail given to Judah's successes (1:3–20) contrast strongly with the brief and formulaic accounts of the failures of the rest of the tribes (1:21–36), except that the house of Joseph is treated positively (1:22–26). These verses divide into five main sections: Judah as leader (1:1–2), Judah's success contrasted with Benjamin's failure (1:1–21), Joseph's success at Bethel (1:22–26), the failures of the remaining tribes (1:27–36) and the resulting divine judgment (2:1–5).

■ **1:1–2** *Judah as Leader.* The book opens with its central concern. God's appointment of Judah as Israel's leading tribe foreshadowed the choice of David as king over Israel.

1:1 After. The book of Joshua opens with the almost identical words "After the death of Moses" (see Jos 1:1). **Who . . . ?** Important to the anti-Benjamin theme of Judges, the Israelites ask an almost identical question at the end of the book: "Who of us shall go first to fight against the Benjamites?" (20:18; see "Introduction: Purpose and Distinctives). **Canaanites?** The Canaanites were one of the seven groups inhabiting Canaan that the Israelites were commanded to annihilate (Dt 7:1–2; 20:16–20). Obedience in holy war is a central issue of this entire section (1:1—2:5).

1:2 Judah. God also appointed Judah in response to Israel's later request for leadership (see 20:18), but that later dispute was with the Benjamites, not the Canaanites.

■ **1:3–21** *Judah's Successes Contrasted With Benjamin's Failure.* With Judah established as the leading tribe, the success of Judah in the conquest is contrasted with Benjamin's failure. In this way the author introduced his stand in favor of Judahite leadership and in opposition to Benjamite leadership for the nation.

1:8 sword. Judah kept covenant by destroying the prior inhabitants of the land (Dt 7:1–2; 20:16–20) but did not occupy Jerusalem at this point (see v. 21).

1:10–15 These verses, which describe the victories of Caleb and Othniel, also appear in Joshua 15:13–19 (see note on v. 20). These events actually occurred after the death of Joshua (see v. 1), which makes it clear that the account in Joshua was taken out of chronological order to frame the settlement of the land with narratives of the heroes of the conquest: Caleb (Jos 15:13–19) and Joshua (Jos 19:49–51).

11 From there they advanced against the people living in Debir[p] (formerly called Kiriath Sepher). 12 And Caleb said, "I will give my daughter Acsah in marriage to the man
who attacks and captures Kiriath Sepher." 13 Othniel son of Kenaz, Caleb's younger
brother, took it; so Caleb gave his daughter Acsah to him in marriage.
14 One day when she came to Othniel, she urged him[a] to ask her father for a field.
When she got off her donkey, Caleb asked her, "What can I do for you?"
15 She replied, "Do me a special favor. Since you have given me land in the Negev, give
me also springs of water." Then Caleb gave her the upper and lower springs.
16 The descendants of Moses' father-in-law,[q] the Kenite,[r] went up from the City of
Palms[b][s] with the men of Judah to live among the people of the Desert of Judah in the
Negev near Arad.[t]
17 Then the men of Judah went with the Simeonites[u] their brothers and attacked the
Canaanites living in Zephath, and they totally destroyed[c] the city. Therefore it was
called Hormah.[d][v] 18 The men of Judah also took[e] Gaza,[w] Ashkelon and Ekron—each city
with its territory.
19 The LORD was with[x] the men of Judah. They took possession of the hill country, but
they were unable to drive the people from the plains, because they had iron chariots.[y]
20 As Moses had promised, Hebron[z] was given to Caleb, who drove from it the three sons
of Anak.[a] 21 The Benjamites, however, failed[b] to dislodge the Jebusites, who were living
in Jerusalem;[c] to this day the Jebusites live there with the Benjamites.
22 Now the house of Joseph attacked Bethel, and the LORD was with them. 23 When they
sent men to spy out Bethel (formerly called Luz),[d] 24 the spies saw a man coming out of
the city and they said to him, "Show us how to get into the city and we will see that you
are treated well.[e]" 25 So he showed them, and they put the city to the sword but spared[f]
the man and his whole family. 26 He then went to the land of the Hittites, where he built
a city and called it Luz, which is its name to this day.
27 But Manasseh did not drive out the people of Beth Shan or Taanach or Dor or Ibleam[g] or Megiddo and their surrounding settlements, for the Canaanites[h] were determined to live in that land. 28 When Israel became strong, they pressed the Canaanites into
forced labor but never drove them out completely. 29 Nor did Ephraim drive out the Canaanites living in Gezer,[i] but the Canaanites continued to live there among them.[j]
30 Neither did Zebulun drive out the Canaanites living in Kitron or Nahalol, who remained
among them; but they did subject them to forced labor. 31 Nor did Asher drive out those
living in Acco or Sidon or Ahlab or Aczib[k] or Helbah or Aphek or Rehob, 32 and because
of this the people of Asher lived among the Canaanite inhabitants of the land. 33 Neither
did Naphtali drive out those living in Beth Shemesh or Beth Anath[l]; but the Naphtalites
too lived among the Canaanite inhabitants of the land, and those living in Beth Shemesh
and Beth Anath became forced laborers for them. 34 The Amorites[m] confined the Danites to the hill country, not allowing them to come down into the plain. 35 And the Amo-

1:11 [p]Jos 15:15
1:16 [q]Nu 10:29 [r]Ge 15:19; Jdg 4:11 [s]Dt 34:3; Jdg 3:13 [t]Nu 21:1
1:17 [u]ver 3 [v]Nu 21:3
1:18 [w]Jos 11:22
1:19 [x]ver 2 [y]Jos 17:16
1:20 [z]Jos 14:9; 15:13-14 [a]ver 10; Jos 14:13
1:21 [b]Jos 15:63 [c]ver 8
1:23 [d]Ge 28:19
1:24 [e]Jos 2:12,14
1:25 [f]Jos 6:25
1:27 [g]Jos 17:11 [h]ver 1
1:29 [i]1Ki 9:16 [j]Jos 16:10
1:31 [k]Jdg 10:6
1:33 [l]Jos 19:38
1:34 [m]Ex 3:17

[a] *14* Hebrew; Septuagint and Vulgate *Othniel, he urged her* [b] *16* That is, Jericho [c] *17* The Hebrew term refers to the irrevocable giving over of things or persons to the LORD, often by totally destroying them. [d] *17* *Hormah* means *destruction.* [e] *18* Hebrew; Septuagint *Judah did not take*

1:12 Caleb. Caleb, though of Kenizzite ancestry (Ge 15:19; Nu 32:12), belonged to the tribe of Judah, as evidenced by his selection to represent Judah among the 12 men sent to spy out Canaan (Nu 13:6).
1:13 Othniel. See Joshua 15:17–19. Verses 12–15 provide a straightforward picture of this first judge. He simply obeyed and took the land. The parallel in Joshua 15:17 does not mention that Othniel was Caleb's younger brother. This addition forges a stronger relationship with David, who was also a youngest son in Judah.
1:19 The LORD was with the men of Judah. God fulfilled his covenant by his presence with Judah in battle (see note on v. 22). With the exception of the house of Joseph, the exploits of the rest of the tribes are dealt with in terse fashion as their failures are described (see note on vv. 27–36). **iron chariots.** These chariots, with their wooden wheels overlaid with iron, made formidable weapons of battle, especially in the flat area of the plains. In effect, the tribe of Judah was excused for its failure to dislodge the Canaanites in this area.
1:20 promised. See Numbers 14:24 (see also Dt 1:36; Jos 14:9). **Caleb.** Caleb is an example of covenant keeping leadership from the tribe of Judah. Deuteronomy 1:36–37 uses Caleb as an example of someone who was rewarded for an obedience that flowed from faith in God's promise.
1:21 The Benjamites. This verse provides a first critical clue into the contrast between King David and King Saul. It is quoted from Joshua 15:63, with the crucial difference that "Benjamin" has replaced "Judah" as the tribe that failed to dislodge the Jebusites. Jerusalem was on the boundary between these tribes (Jos 15:63; 18:28), so either one could have been held responsible for taking the city. The writer sharply contrasted Judah and Benjamin, as do the later narratives surrounding David and Saul. Benjamin and Saul failed in giving Israel its capital, whereas Judah and David succeeded. **Jebusites.** The Benjamites failed to keep covenant in that they did not annihilate the Jebusites (Dt 7:1–2; 20:16–20). See note on "Canaanites" at verse 1; contrast Judah's obedience in fighting holy war at Jerusalem (v. 8).
▪ **1:22–26** *Joseph's Success at Bethel.* Apart from Judah, only the family of Joseph is portrayed in a positive manner. While certainly historical fact, this complimentary assessment may have been mentioned to solicit support from these tribes for the leadership of Judah.
1:22 the LORD was with them. With the exception of Judah (see v. 19), the presence of God is mentioned only with regard to Joseph's tribes. The presence of God in holy war was essential to success because he fought for his people (see note on Jos 1:5).
▪ **1:27–36** *The Failures of the Remaining Tribes.* Having already mentioned Judah, Benjamin and Joseph, the author presents in a highly structured manner the progressive failures of the other tribes (Dt 7:1–2; 20:16–20).
1:34 Danites. See chapters 17–18.

1:35 ⁿJos 19:42
1:36 ᵒJos 15:3
2:1 ᵖJdg 6:11 ᵠver 5 ʳEx 20:2 ˢGe 17:8 ᵗLev 26:42-44; Dt 7:9
2:2 ᵘEx 23:32; 34:12; Dt 7:2 ᵛEx 34:13
2:3 ʷJos 23:13 ˣNu 33:55 ʸDt 7:16; Jdg 3:6; Ps 106:36

rites were determined also to hold out in Mount Heres, Aijalon[n] and Shaalbim, but when
the power of the house of Joseph increased, they too were pressed into forced labor.
36 The boundary of the Amorites was from Scorpion[a] Pass[o] to Sela and beyond.

The Angel of the LORD at Bokim

2 The angel of the LORD[p] went up from Gilgal to Bokim[q] and said, "I brought you up
out of Egypt[r] and led you into the land that I swore to give to your forefathers.[s] I said,
'I will never break my covenant with you,[t] 2 and you shall not make a covenant with the
people of this land,[u] but you shall break down their altars.[v]' Yet you have disobeyed me.
Why have you done this? 3 Now therefore I tell you that I will not drive them out before
you;[w] they will be ⌊thorns⌋[x] in your sides and their gods will be a snare[y] to you."

a 36 Hebrew *Akrabbim*

■ **2:1–5** *The Resulting Divine Judgment.* These verses summarize Judges' introduction (1:1—2:5). Similar language in 2:20—3:6 forges a link between this section's finale and the beginning of the cycles of the judges (2:6—16:31). The covenantal language gives the episode a prophetic focus. The covenant parties are identified and the covenant agreement reviewed. Because the Israelites had violated God's commands, judgment was pronounced upon them. See Numbers 33:50–56, Deuteronomy 7:1–16 and Joshua 23:1–16. **2:1 The angel of the LORD.** See 6:11–24 and 13:2–23. The words of God's preeminent messenger (see 6:11–24; Ex 3:1–17) are those of the Lord. The "angel of the LORD," also known as the "angel of his presence," had led the Israelites out of captivity in Egypt and had fought for them (Ex 14:19; 23:20–23; 33:2; Nu 20:16). **Gilgal.** The ark of the covenant was there (see Jos 5:1–12). **I brought you up out of Egypt.** The Ten Commandments begin in the same way (Ex 20:2; Dt 5:6), serving as a reminder that God's mercy always provides the basis upon which he gives his people commands. The angel's statement set the covenant context (see note on 2:1–5) and focused first on God's covenant keeping (see Dt 7:8,12–13). **and led you into the land that I swore.** God kept his oath (see Jos 23:3–16). **I will never break my covenant.** See Deuteronomy 7:9. **2:2 not make a covenant with the people.** See Exodus 34:12–14, Deuteronomy 7:2–4 and Joshua 3:5–6. **you shall break down their altars.** See Numbers 33:52. Idolatry embodied covenant breaking (see v. 11; Ex 34:13; Dt 7:5; 12:3; Jos 23:16). **disobeyed me.** Israel made covenants with the people of the land (see 3:5–6) and failed to tear down their altars (see 6:25–32). **2:3 not drive them out before you.** Israel was dependent on God, not on its own strength, for its victories. Because Israel had disobeyed (v. 2), God determined not to help his people drive out the Canaanites (see Nu 33:52,55; Jos 23:13). **thorns . . . a snare.** Intermarriage and all other relationships with the Canaanites had been forbidden because such contact would (and did) lead to idolatry (see Ex 34:12; Nu 33:55; Dt 7:16; Jos 23:13). If the Israelites fla-

Five Cities of the Philistines

Gaza, Ashkelon, Ashdod, Ekron and Gath comprise a list of familiar Biblical names. Each of these cities was a commercial emporium with important connections both north (as far as Mesopotamia) and south (as far as Egypt) by way of the coastal highway that served as one of the major highways of the ancient world. Also the ships of Phoeniecia, Cyprus, Crete and the Aegean called at Philistia's seaports. Among these seaports was a place today called Tell Qasile on the Yarkon River (the "Kanah Ravine" of Jos 16:8, 17:9) just north of Modern Tel Aviv. A Philistine temple has been found at Tell Qasile.

The Philistine plain itself was an arid, loam-covered lowland between the Mediterranean Sea and the foothills of the Judahite plateau on the east. To the south lay a stretch of undulating sand dunes adjacent to the sea. No area in Biblical history was more frequently contested than the western foothills, lying on the border between Judah and Philistia. Originally a part of Judah's tribal allotment, the coastal area was never totally wrested away from the Philistines. Beth Shemesh, Timnah, Azekah and Ziklag were among the towns coveted by both Israelites and Philistines, and they figure in the stories of Samson, Goliath and David. The area to the north of Philistia, the plain of Sharon, was also contested at various periods. During Saul's reign the Philistines even held Beth Shan and the Valley of Jezreel. Later, from about the time of Baasha on, a long border war was conducted by the Israelites at Gibbethon.

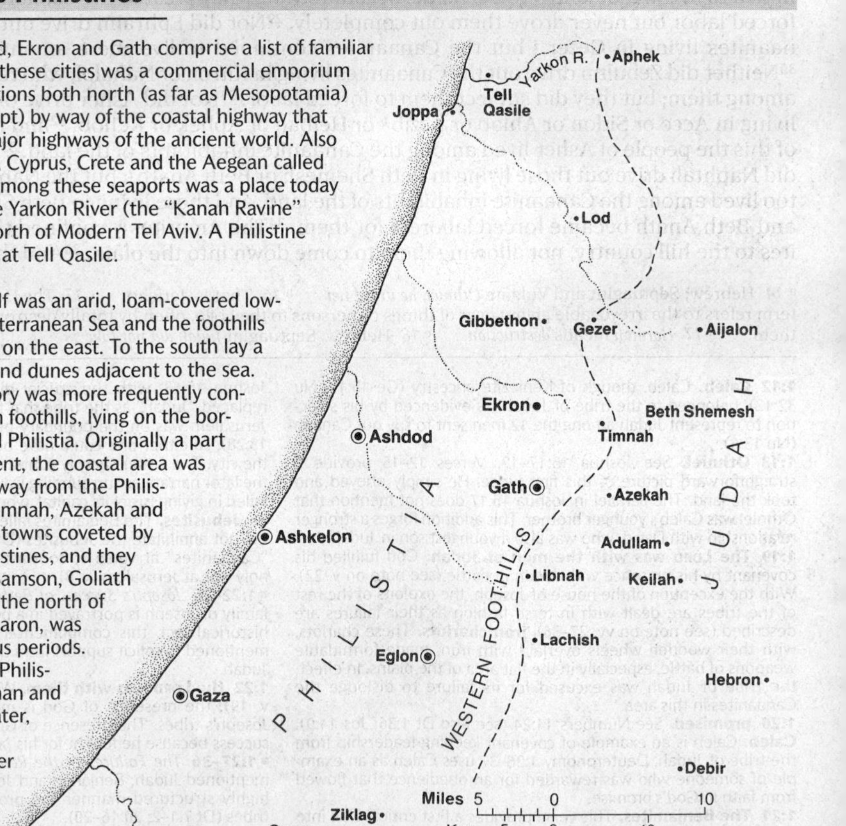

4When the angel of the LORD had spoken these things to all the Israelites, the people
wept aloud, 5and they called that place Bokim.[a] There they offered sacrifices to the LORD.

Disobedience and Defeat

6After Joshua had dismissed the Israelites, they went to take possession of the land,
each to his own inheritance. 7The people served the LORD throughout the lifetime of Joshua and of the elders who outlived him and who had seen all the great things the LORD
had done for Israel.

8Joshua son of Nun, the servant of the LORD, died at the age of a hundred and ten.
9And they buried him in the land of his inheritance, at Timnath Heres[b][z] in the hill country of Ephraim, north of Mount Gaash.

10After that whole generation had been gathered to their fathers, another generation
grew up, who knew neither the LORD nor what he had done for Israel.[a] 11Then the Israelites did evil in the eyes of the LORD[b] and served the Baals.[c] 12They forsook the LORD, the
God of their fathers, who had brought them out of Egypt. They followed and worshiped
various gods[d] of the peoples around them.[e] They provoked the LORD to anger 13because
they forsook him and served Baal and the Ashtoreths.[f] 14In his anger[g] against Israel the
LORD handed them over[h] to raiders who plundered them. He sold them[i] to their enemies
all around, whom they were no longer able to resist.[j] 15Whenever Israel went out to fight,
the hand of the LORD was against them to defeat them, just as he had sworn to them.
They were in great distress.

16Then the LORD raised up judges,[c][k] who saved[l] them out of the hands of these raiders. 17Yet they would not listen to their judges but prostituted[m] themselves to other gods
and worshiped them. Unlike their fathers, they quickly turned from the way in which
their fathers had walked, the way of obedience to the LORD's commands.[n] 18Whenever
the LORD raised up a judge for them, he was with the judge and saved them out of the
hands of their enemies as long as the judge lived; for the LORD had compassion[o] on them
as they groaned[p] under those who oppressed and afflicted them. 19But when the judge
died, the people returned to ways even more corrupt[q] than those of their fathers, following other gods and serving and worshiping them.[r] They refused to give up their evil practices and stubborn ways.

20Therefore the LORD was very angry[s] with Israel and said, "Because this nation has
violated the covenant that I laid down for their forefathers and has not listened to me,
21I will no longer drive out[t] before them any of the nations Joshua left when he died. 22I
will use them to test[u] Israel and see whether they will keep the way of the LORD and walk

2:9 [z]Jos 19:50
2:10 [a]Ex 5:2; 1Sa 2:12; 1Ch 28:9; Gal 4:8
2:11 [b]Jdg 3:12; 4:1; 6:1; 10:6 [c]Jdg 3:7; 8:33
2:12 [d]Ps 106:36 [e]Dt 31:16; Jdg 10:6
2:13 [f]Jdg 10:6
2:14 [g]Dt 31:17 [h]Ps 106:41 [i]Dt 32:30; Jdg 3:8 [j]Dt 28:25
2:16 [k]Ac 13:20 [l]Ps 106:43
2:17 [m]Ex 34:15 [n]ver 7
2:18 [o]Dt 32:36; Jos 1:5 [p]Ps 106:44
2:19 [q]Jdg 3:12 [r]Jdg 4:1; 8:33
2:20 [s]ver 14; Jos 23:16
2:21 [t]Jos 23:13
2:22 [u]Dt 8:2,16; Jdg 3:1,14

[a] 5 *Bokim* means *weepers.* [b] 9 Also known as *Timnath Serah* (see Joshua 19:50 and 24:30)
[c] 16 Or *leaders*; similarly in verses 17–19

grantly violated the covenant, they would receive Canaan's punishment: removal from the land (see Nu 33:56; Jos 23:13).

■ **2:6—16:31** *The Cycles of the Judges.* This second major portion of the book reports the cycles of sin, judgment, and deliverance that Israel experienced during the period of the judges. These chapters divide into two main parts: an explanation of the pattern of the cycles (2:6—3:6) and 12 examples of that pattern (3:7—16:31).

■ **2:6—3:6** *The Pattern of the Cycles.* The author introduced and explained the pattern of Israel's history during this period. These verses divide into four sections: the days of Joshua (2:6–9), an introduction to the cycles (2:10–19), the purpose of God's judgments (2:20–23) and the instruments of those judgments (3:1–6).

■ **2:6–9** *Israel in Joshua's Day.* This section, which is quoted from Joshua 24:28–31, presents the background to the cycles of the judges (see notes on 2:6—16:31 and on 2:10–19).

2:6 After Joshua. See 1:1.

2:7 The people served the LORD. See Joshua 24:16–18, 21–22 and 31. Covenant obedience led to blessing in the land for that generation. **had seen all the great things.** See verse 10 (see also Dt 4:9; 6:22; 7:19; 11:2–7; Jos 23:3).

■ **2:10–19** *Introduction of the Cycles.* These verses explain the pattern that undergirds chapters 3–16 and reveal God sovereignly at work in covenant judgment. It was God who judged his people and raised up deliverers. Idolatry was the primary sin on account of which God was angry (vv. 11–13,17,19) and punished Israel. 1 Samuel 12:9–11 and Psalm 106:34–46 elaborate on these verses.

2:10 who knew neither the LORD nor what he had done for Israel. One generation was to declare God's wonders to the next (Dt 4:9; 6:1–6), but the Israelites did not fulfill this responsibility. If God's people had remembered what he had done, they would have understood why they should have obeyed the commands of his covenant.

2:11 served the Baals. Israel's evil is summed up by the worship of false gods (see note on v. 2). The people chose Baal, the Canaanite storm god who was considered crucial to the agricultural cycle, and rejected the Lord, who had brought them through the Red Sea and was the true Lord of the storm. "Baals" is plural because Baal was worshiped differently in each Canaanite locality.

2:13 Ashtoreths. The goddess of fertility (also plural).

2:14 the LORD handed them over. See Deuteronomy 28:48 and 1 Samuel 12:9. Israel's enemies and oppressors had no power over God's people unless God allowed it.

2:15 the hand of the LORD was against them. The "hand of the LORD" refers to mighty, divine action. Often it was synonymous with salvation (see Ex 3:20; 6:1; 13:3; Dt 4:34), but here that same hand was turned against the Israelites in punishment. The Lord was faithful both to bless and to judge.

2:16 judges. The role of the judges was primarily to deliver (see 3:9,15; 1Sa 12:11).

2:17 not listen to their judges. Apparently at least some judges told the people to keep covenant, but this book illustrates that the judges themselves often failed to act as models of covenant keeping. **prostituted themselves.** Israel violated her covenant "marriage" with God by following other gods (see 8:33; Dt 31:16; the book of Hosea).

2:18 had compassion. See Deuteronomy 4:30–31, 30:3 and 32:43.

2:19 They refused. Neither the judges (v. 17) nor their deliverances brought consistent obedience (see v. 10).

■ **2:20–23** *The Purpose of God's Judgment.* The purpose of God in permitting these cycles was to test his people.

in it as their forefathers did." 23The LORD had allowed those nations to remain; he did not
drive them out at once by giving them into the hands of Joshua.

3 These are the nations the LORD left to test[v] all those Israelites who had not experienced any of the wars in Canaan 2(he did this only to teach warfare to the descendants of the Israelites who had not had previous battle experience): 3the five[w] rulers of
the Philistines, all the Canaanites, the Sidonians, and the Hivites living in the Lebanon
mountains from Mount Baal Hermon to Lebo[a] Hamath. 4They were left to test[x] the Israelites to see whether they would obey the LORD's commands, which he had given their
forefathers through Moses.

5The Israelites lived[y] among the Canaanites, Hittites, Amorites, Perizzites, Hivites and
Jebusites. 6They took their daughters in marriage and gave their own daughters to their
sons, and served their gods.[z]

Othniel

7The Israelites did evil in the eyes of the LORD; they forgot the LORD[a] their God and
served the Baals and the Asherahs.[b] 8The anger of the LORD burned against Israel so that
he sold[c] them into the hands of Cushan-Rishathaim king of Aram Naharaim,[b] to whom
the Israelites were subject for eight years. 9But when they cried out[d] to the LORD, he raised
up for them a deliverer, Othniel[e] son of Kenaz, Caleb's younger brother, who saved
them. 10The Spirit of the LORD came upon him,[f] so that he became Israel's judge[c] and went
to war. The LORD gave Cushan-Rishathaim king of Aram into the hands of Othniel, who
overpowered him. 11So the land had peace for forty years, until Othniel son of Kenaz died.

Ehud

12Once again the Israelites did evil in the eyes of the LORD,[g] and because they did this
evil the LORD gave Eglon king of Moab[h] power over Israel. 13Getting the Ammonites and
Amalekites to join him, Eglon came and attacked Israel, and they took possession of the
City of Palms.[d][i] 14The Israelites were subject to Eglon king of Moab for eighteen years.
15Again the Israelites cried out to the LORD, and he gave them a deliverer[j]—Ehud, a
left-handed man, the son of Gera the Benjamite. The Israelites sent him with tribute to
Eglon king of Moab. 16Now Ehud had made a double-edged sword about a foot and a
half[e] long, which he strapped to his right thigh under his clothing. 17He presented the

[a] *3* Or *to the entrance to* [b] *8* That is, Northwest Mesopotamia [c] *10* Or *leader* [d] *13* That is, Jericho
[e] *16* Hebrew *a cubit* (about 0.5 meter)

3:1 [v]Jdg 2:21-22
3:3 [w]Jos 13:3
3:4 [x]Dt 8:2; Jdg 2:22
3:5 [y]Ps 106:35
3:6 [z]Ex 34:16; Dt 7:3-4
3:7 [a]Dt 4:9 [b]Ex 34:13; Jdg 2:11,13
3:8 [c]Jdg 2:14
3:9 [d]ver 15; Jdg 6:6,7; 10:10; Ps 106:44 [e]Jdg 1:13
3:10 [f]Nu 11:25,29; 24:2; Jdg 6:34; 11:29; 13:25; 14:6, 19; 1Sa 11:6
3:12 [g]Jdg 2:11,14 [h]1Sa 12:9
3:13 [i]Jdg 1:16
3:15 [j]ver 9; Ps 78:34; 107:13

2:22 to test Israel. Verses 20–22 and 3:1–4 explain that God allowed the Canaanites to remain in the land in order to test his people. By testing his people God proved the true nature of their professed commitments to him and the covenant (see note on Ge 22:1; see also 2Co 13:5).

2:23 allowed. See Deuteronomy 7:22–23 and Joshua 13:1–7. These verses explain why there were still Canaanites in the land during a period when Israel had been faithful (see vv. 6–9).

■ **3:1–6** *The Instruments of God's Judgment.* The writer explained which nations God used to test his people.

3:1 to test. See note on 2:22. **not experienced.** See 2:10. Even God's judgment is gracious. The testing was not temptation but an opportunity for the members of a generation who had not seen the Lord work on their behalf to exercise faith and see his might with their own eyes (see v. 2).

3:2 to teach warfare. War against the Canaanites tested covenant faithfulness.

3:3 Philistines, all the Canaanites, the Sidonians, and the Hivites. The Canaanites and the Hivites were to be utterly destroyed (see 1:1). David was the Israelite leader who would ultimately defeat or destroy these enemies.

3:5 among the Canaanites . . . Jebusites. All of these nations were supposed to be destroyed (see 1:1). By living among these people and not destroying them, Israel broke covenant.

3:6 They took their daughters. The Israelites were led astray (see Ex 34:16; Dt 7:4). The result of forging covenants with the Canaanites rather than destroying them is repeatedly pictured in the following narrative cycles (see 2:2).

■ **3:7—16:31** *The Twelve Cycles.* Having explained the basic pattern of Israel's history during the time of the judges, the author gave 12 examples of the cycles of judges. These chapters divide in this manner: Othniel (3:7–11), Ehud (3:12–30), Shamgar (3:31), Deborah (4:1—5:31), Gideon (6:1—8:32), Tola (10:1–2), Jair (10:3–5), Jephthah (10:6—12:7), Ibzan (12:8–10), Elon (12:11–12), Abdon (12:13–15) and Samson (13:1—16:31).

■ **3:7–11** *Othniel.* The first judge, Othniel, belonged to the generation of the faithful (see 2:7,22).

3:7 did evil. See 2:11. **the Baals and the Asherahs.** See 2:11 and 13.

3:9 cried out. Israel's crying out is not part of the pattern structure used in the introductory model of 2:11–19. It is, however, included in all of the accounts of the major judges, except for Samson (13:1—16:31). See Deuteronomy 4:30–31 and 1 Samuel 12:10. **a deliverer.** See 2:16 and 3:10. **Othniel.** See note on 1:13. The prominence of the role of Judah in Israelite leadership was highlighted by the fact that the first judge was from Judah. This was a subtle argument in favor of Judahite leadership and David's kingship.

3:10 Spirit of the LORD came upon him. This language is also used of Gideon (6:34), Jephthah (11:29) and Samson (14:6,19; 15:14). By the gift of the Spirit, the judge was empowered to deliver the people. **he became Israel's judge.** Elsewhere in Judges, this Hebrew clause is rendered "he led Israel."

3:11 the land had peace for forty years. Though the pattern in 2:11–19 does not mention the length of this period of peace, each story ends with a comment on the prevalence or lack of peace (see v. 30; 5:31; 8:28; 12:7; 15:20; 16:31).

■ **3:12–30** *Ehud.* The story of Ehud pokes subtle fun at the oppressor of God's people and at the deliverer whom God raised up to bring the oppressor down (see notes on vv. 12,15,20,22,24–25). The juxtaposition of Othniel, the judge from Judah, and the second judge, who was from Benjamin, underscores the priority of leadership of Judah over that of Benjamin.

3:12 the Israelites did evil in the eyes of the LORD. See 2:11. **Eglon king of Moab.** See 1 Samuel 12:9.

3:15 cried out. See note on verse 9. **a deliverer.** See 2:16, as well as note on 3:9. **a left-handed man.** Literally, "a man wounded in his right hand." This is not the common Hebrew expression for left-handedness, which is used only in 20:16, also with regard to the men of Benjamin. Because Benjamin can mean "son of the right hand," the writer probably made a derogatory pun about a left-handed son of the right hand. In this way he revealed his opposition to Benjamite leadership again.

tribute to Eglon king of Moab, who was a very fat man.[k] 18After Ehud had presented the
tribute, he sent on their way the men who had carried it. 19At the idols[a] near Gilgal he
himself turned back and said, "I have a secret message for you, O king."
The king said, "Quiet!" And all his attendants left him.
20Ehud then approached him while he was sitting alone in the upper room of his summer palace[b] and said, "I have a message from God for you." As the king rose from his
seat, 21Ehud reached with his left hand, drew the sword from his right thigh and plunged
it into the king's belly. 22Even the handle sank in after the blade, which came out his
back. Ehud did not pull the sword out, and the fat closed in over it. 23Then Ehud went
out to the porch[c]; he shut the doors of the upper room behind him and locked them.
24After he had gone, the servants came and found the doors of the upper room locked.
They said, "He must be relieving himself[l] in the inner room of the house." 25They waited
to the point of embarrassment,[m] but when he did not open the doors of the room, they
took a key and unlocked them. There they saw their lord fallen to the floor, dead.
26While they waited, Ehud got away. He passed by the idols and escaped to Seirah.
27When he arrived there, he blew a trumpet[n] in the hill country of Ephraim, and the Israelites went down with him from the hills, with him leading them.
28"Follow me," he ordered, "for the LORD has given Moab, your enemy, into your
hands.[o]" So they followed him down and, taking possession of the fords of the Jordan[p]
that led to Moab, they allowed no one to cross over. 29At that time they struck down
about ten thousand Moabites, all vigorous and strong; not a man escaped. 30That day
Moab was made subject to Israel, and the land had peace[q] for eighty years.

Shamgar

31After Ehud came Shamgar son of Anath,[r] who struck down six hundred[s] Philistines
with an oxgoad. He too saved Israel.

Deborah

4 After Ehud died, the Israelites once again did evil[t] in the eyes of the LORD. 2So the
LORD sold them into the hands of Jabin, a king of Canaan, who reigned in Hazor.[u]
The commander of his army was Sisera,[v] who lived in Harosheth Haggoyim. 3Because
he had nine hundred iron chariots[w] and had cruelly oppressed[x] the Israelites for twenty years, they cried to the LORD for help.
4Deborah, a prophetess, the wife of Lappidoth, was leading[d] Israel at that time. 5She
held court under the Palm of Deborah between Ramah and Bethel[y] in the hill country
of Ephraim, and the Israelites came to her to have their disputes decided. 6She sent for
Barak son of Abinoam[z] from Kedesh in Naphtali and said to him, "The LORD, the God of
Israel, commands you: 'Go, take with you ten thousand men of Naphtali and Zebulun
and lead the way to Mount Tabor. 7I will lure Sisera, the commander of Jabin's army, with
his chariots and his troops to the Kishon River[a] and give him into your hands.' "
8Barak said to her, "If you go with me, I will go; but if you don't go with me, I won't go."
9"Very well," Deborah said, "I will go with you. But because of the way you are going
about this,[e] the honor will not be yours, for the LORD will hand Sisera over to a woman."

3:17 [k]ver 12
3:24 [l]1Sa 24:3
3:25 [m]2Ki 2:17; 8:11
3:27 [n]Jdg 6:34; 1Sa 13:3
3:28 [o]Jdg 7:9,15 [p]Jos 2:7; Jdg 7:24; 12:5
3:30 [q]ver 11
3:31 [r]Jdg 5:6 [s]Jos 23:10
4:1 [t]Jdg 2:19
4:2 [u]Jos 11:1 [v]ver 13, 16; 1Sa 12:9; Ps 83:9
4:3 [w]Jdg 1:19 [x]Ps 106:42
4:5 [y]Ge 35:8
4:6 [z]Heb 11:32
4:7 [a]Ps 83:9

[a] *19* Or *the stone quarries;* also in verse 26 [b] *20* The meaning of the Hebrew for this phrase is uncertain. [c] *23* The meaning of the Hebrew for this word is uncertain. [d] *4* Traditionally *judging* [e] *9* Or *But on the expedition you are undertaking*

3:20 I have a message from God for you. The secret message of verse 19 here became the true word of God against the very rod that God had raised up to punish his people. Eglon had exceeded the bounds of God's wrath and thus received it back upon himself.
3:26 passed by the idols. This expression is ambiguous. It may simply indicate that Ehud went past idols; it may also imply that he worshiped there as he was escaping.
3:28 the LORD has given. Each major judge, except for the silent Othniel, verbally acknowledged God's control in Israel's victories (4:14; 7:15; 11:21–30; 15:18; 16:28).
3:30 peace for eighty years. See note on verse 11.
■ **3:31** *Shamgar.* Shamgar is mentioned only here and in the song of Deborah (5:6). Since Anath was a Canaanite goddess of war, perhaps "son of Anath" was this war hero's nickname.
3:31 six hundred Philistines with an oxgoad. Compare Samson, who slew 1,000 Philistines with the jawbone of a donkey (15:15–17).
■ **4:1–5:31** *Deborah.* The narrative concerning Deborah is unique in that she is the only woman deliverer of Israel in the book. Deborah is exalted as a woman of faith and courage.
4:1 did evil. See 2:11.
4:2 the LORD sold. See 2:14. **Jabin.** A descendent of the Jabin mentioned in Joshua 11:1–9.
4:3 cried. See note on 3:9.
4:4 Deborah, a prophetess, the wife of Lappidoth. Literally, "a woman, a prophetess, the wife of Lappidoth." Deborah is exalted as a prophetess (vv. 6–7,9,14).
4:5 held court. That is, she handed down legal decisions. Deborah is the only judge who is described as holding court.
4:6 Barak. The military leader whom God raised up (see 2:16; 3:9–10; 1Sa 12:11). **Mount Tabor.** A rounded hillock standing isolated on the north side of the plain in the Jezreel Valley. Barak's later hesitancy to go up is readily understandable from a military point of view; Sisera's 900 chariots could have easily surrounded the hill, preventing any means of escape.
4:7 Kishon River. This river was near the base of Mount Tabor and was virtually dry for much of the year (see v. 15).
4:8 If you go. Barak, the chosen deliverer and judge, lacked faith in God's word. From his perspective the mission was suicidal (see note on v. 6). Yet, he had such high regard for Deborah that he was willing to go if she were to accompany him.

So Deborah went with Barak to Kedesh,[b] 10 where he summoned[c] Zebulun and Naphtali. Ten thousand men followed him, and Deborah also went with him.
11 Now Heber the Kenite had left the other Kenites,[d] the descendants of Hobab,[e] Moses' brother-in-law,[a] and pitched his tent by the great tree in Zaanannim[f] near Kedesh.
12 When they told Sisera that Barak son of Abinoam had gone up to Mount Tabor,
13 Sisera gathered together his nine hundred iron chariots[g] and all the men with him,
from Harosheth Haggoyim to the Kishon River.
14 Then Deborah said to Barak, "Go! This is the day the LORD has given Sisera into your
hands. Has not the LORD gone ahead[h] of you?" So Barak went down Mount Tabor, followed by ten thousand men. 15 At Barak's advance, the LORD routed[i] Sisera and all his
chariots and army by the sword, and Sisera abandoned his chariot and fled on foot. 16 But
Barak pursued the chariots and army as far as Harosheth Haggoyim. All the troops of Sisera fell by the sword; not a man was left.[j]
17 Sisera, however, fled on foot to the tent of Jael, the wife of Heber the Kenite, because
there were friendly relations between Jabin king of Hazor and the clan of Heber the Kenite.
18 Jael went out to meet Sisera and said to him, "Come, my lord, come right in. Don't
be afraid." So he entered her tent, and she put a covering over him.
19 "I'm thirsty," he said. "Please give me some water." She opened a skin of milk,[k] gave
him a drink, and covered him up.
20 "Stand in the doorway of the tent," he told her. "If someone comes by and asks you,
'Is anyone here?' say 'No.' "
21 But Jael, Heber's wife, picked up a tent peg and a hammer and went quietly to him
while he lay fast asleep, exhausted. She drove the peg through his temple into the
ground, and he died.[l]
22 Barak came by in pursuit of Sisera, and Jael went out to meet him. "Come," she said,
"I will show you the man you're looking for." So he went in with her, and there lay Sisera with the tent peg through his temple—dead.
23 On that day God subdued[m] Jabin, the Canaanite king, before the Israelites. 24 And
the hand of the Israelites grew stronger and stronger against Jabin, the Canaanite king,
until they destroyed him.

The Song of Deborah

5 On that day Deborah and Barak son of Abinoam sang this song:[n]

2 "When the princes in Israel take the lead,
when the people willingly offer[o] themselves—
praise the LORD![p]

3 "Hear this, you kings! Listen, you rulers!
I will sing to[b] the LORD, I will sing;
I will make music to[c] the LORD, the God of Israel.[q]

4 "O LORD, when you went out from Seir,[r]
when you marched from the land of Edom,
the earth shook, the heavens poured,
the clouds poured down water.[s]
5 The mountains quaked[t] before the LORD, the One of Sinai,
before the LORD, the God of Israel.

4:9 [b]ver 21; Jdg 2:14
4:10 [c]ver 14; Jdg 5:15, 18
4:11 [d]Jdg 1:16 [e]Nu 10:29 [f]Jos 19:33
4:13 [g]ver 3
4:14 [h]Dt 9:3; 2Sa 5:24; Ps 68:7
4:15 [i]Jos 10:10; Ps 83:9-10
4:16 [j]Ps 83:9
4:19 [k]Jdg 5:25
4:21 [l]Jdg 5:26
4:23 [m]Ne 9:24; Ps 18:47
5:1 [n]Ex 15:1
5:2 [o]2Ch 17:16; Ps 110:3 [p]ver 9
5:3 [q]Ps 27:6
5:4 [r]Dt 33:2 [s]Ps 68:8
5:5 [t]Ex 19:18; Ps 68:8; 97:5; Isa 64:3

[a] 11 Or *father-in-law* [b] 3 Or *of* [c] 3 Or / *with song I will praise*

4:9 the honor will not be yours. Barak was punished for doubting (see v. 8). **for the LORD will hand Sisera over to a woman.** Not just another person, but a woman. In those times, a warrior would have been greatly shamed to have his honor given to a woman who fought in his place, for this would have revealed his lack of courage and ability.
4:10 Zebulun and Naphtali. See 5:13–18.
4:13 Kishon River. See verses 7 and 15.
4:15 the LORD routed. From Deborah's song we learn that the Lord sent rain to mire down the chariots and cause flash flooding (see 5:4–5,20–21). **abandoned his chariot.** Sisera's chariot became stuck in the mud (5:20–21).
4:18–21 See 5:24–27.
4:22 I will show you the man. The main concern at this point was that a woman performed this act. According to the customs of warfare at the time, Sisera was mocked for dying at the hand of a woman (see 9:53–54), and Barak was shamed for failing to demonstrate the courage to fulfill his calling (see note on v. 9).
5:1–31 Following the prose account (4:1–24), the story of Deborah is celebrated in poetry. Deborah is exalted again by this unique feature of the record of her leadership.
5:2 the princes in Israel take the lead. This raises the issue of leadership, a major theme in the book (see note on vv. 1–31).
5:4–5 from Seir, when you marched from the land of Edom. Mount Seir was the main mountain ridge running through Edom, Israel's point of departure for the battles of conquest (see Dt 33:2). God is pictured as the mighty warrior going before his people. **the earth shook . . . before the LORD.** God's approach in battle is often conveyed in terms of cosmic upheaval (see notes on Mic 1:3–7). The particular portrayal of God as Lord of the storm is especially appropriate here. By defeating Sisera with a cloudburst (v. 20), God refuted Baal's claim to being lord of the storm.

6 "In the days of Shamgar son of Anath,[u]
in the days of Jael,[v] the roads[w] were abandoned;
travelers took to winding paths.
7 Village life[a] in Israel ceased,
ceased until I,[b] Deborah, arose,
arose a mother in Israel.
8 When they chose new gods,[x]
war came to the city gates,
and not a shield or spear was seen
among forty thousand in Israel.
9 My heart is with Israel's princes,
with the willing volunteers[y] among the people.
Praise the LORD!

10 "You who ride on white donkeys,[z]
sitting on your saddle blankets,
and you who walk along the road,
consider 11 the voice of the singers[c] at the watering places.
They recite the righteous acts[a] of the LORD,
the righteous acts of his warriors[d] in Israel.

"Then the people of the LORD
went down to the city gates.[b]
12 'Wake up,[c] wake up, Deborah!
Wake up, wake up, break out in song!
Arise, O Barak!
Take captive your captives,[d] O son of Abinoam.'

13 "Then the men who were left
came down to the nobles;
the people of the LORD
came to me with the mighty.
14 Some came from Ephraim, whose roots were in Amalek;[e]
Benjamin was with the people who followed you.
From Makir captains came down,
from Zebulun those who bear a commander's staff.
15 The princes of Issachar were with Deborah;[f]
yes, Issachar was with Barak,
rushing after him into the valley.
In the districts of Reuben
there was much searching of heart.
16 Why did you stay among the campfires[e]
to hear the whistling for the flocks?[g]
In the districts of Reuben
there was much searching of heart.
17 Gilead stayed beyond the Jordan.
And Dan, why did he linger by the ships?
Asher remained on the coast[h]
and stayed in his coves.
18 The people of Zebulun risked their very lives;
so did Naphtali on the heights of the field.[i]

19 "Kings came[j], they fought;
the kings of Canaan fought

5:6 [u]Jdg 3:31 [v]Jdg 4:17 [w]Isa 33:8
5:8 [x]Dt 32:17
5:9 [y]ver 2
5:10 [z]Jdg 10:4; 12:14
5:11 [a]1Sa 12:7; Mic 6:5 [b]ver 8
5:12 [c]Ps 57:8 [d]Ps 68:18; Eph 4:8
5:14 [e]Jdg 3:13
5:15 [f]Jdg 4:10
5:16 [g]Nu 32:1
5:17 [h]Jos 19:29
5:18 [i]Jdg 4:6, 10
5:19 [j]Jos 11:5; Jdg 4:13

[a] 7 Or *Warriors* [b] 7 Or *you* [c] 11 Or *archers*; the meaning of the Hebrew for this word is uncertain. [d] 11 Or *villagers* [e] 16 Or *saddlebags*

5:6–7 the roads . . . ceased. Israel's failed leadership had led to chaos and foreign domination. The roads were abandoned because they were not safe for travel due to foreign oppressors and thieves.
5:7 a mother in Israel. A woman was raised up to lead Israel—a sad commentary on the fear that had gripped Barak.
5:8 chose new gods, war came to the city gates. This is a poetic representation of the cycle of sin and punishment (see 2:11–19).
5:9 volunteers. See verses 13–23 for listings of the tribes that came gladly or not at all.
5:10 ride on white donkeys. Donkeys were ridden by nobility; therefore the song is addressed to the princes mentioned in verses 2 and 9.
5:11 the righteous acts of the LORD, the righteous acts of his warriors. In keeping covenant and defeating his enemies, God acted righteously (see 2:10).
5:15 In . . . Reuben there was much searching of heart. The failures of Reuben, Gilead, Dan and Asher (v. 17) to participate reflected the problem of disunity in Israel.

5:19 [k]Jdg 1:27 [l]ver 30
5:20 [m]Jos 10:11
5:21 [n]Jdg 4:7

at Taanach by the waters of Megiddo,[k]
 but they carried off no silver, no plunder.[l]
20 From the heavens[m] the stars fought,
 from their courses they fought against Sisera.
21 The river Kishon[n] swept them away,
 the age-old river, the river Kishon.
 March on, my soul; be strong!
22 Then thundered the horses' hoofs—
 galloping, galloping go his mighty steeds.
23 'Curse Meroz,' said the angel of the LORD.
 'Curse its people bitterly,
because they did not come to help the LORD,
 to help the LORD against the mighty.'

5:24 [o]Jdg 4:17
5:25 [p]Jdg 4:19
5:26 [q]Jdg 4:21

24 "Most blessed of women be Jael,[o]
 the wife of Heber the Kenite,
 most blessed of tent-dwelling women.
25 He asked for water, and she gave him milk;[p]
 in a bowl fit for nobles she brought him curdled milk.
26 Her hand reached for the tent peg,
 her right hand for the workman's hammer.
She struck Sisera, she crushed his head,
 she shattered and pierced his temple.[q]
27 At her feet he sank,
 he fell; there he lay.
At her feet he sank, he fell;
 where he sank, there he fell—dead.

5:28 [r]Pr 7:6
5:30 [s]Ex 15:9; 1Sa 30:24

28 "Through the window peered Sisera's mother;
 behind the lattice she cried out,[r]
'Why is his chariot so long in coming?
 Why is the clatter of his chariots delayed?'
29 The wisest of her ladies answer her;
 indeed, she keeps saying to herself,
30 'Are they not finding and dividing the spoils:[s]
 a girl or two for each man,
 colorful garments as plunder for Sisera,
 colorful garments embroidered,
 highly embroidered garments for my neck—
all this as plunder?'

5:31 [t]2Sa 23:4; Ps 19:4; 89:36 [u]Jdg 3:11

31 "So may all your enemies perish, O LORD!
 But may they who love you be like the sun[t]
 when it rises in its strength."

Then the land had peace[u] forty years.

6:1 [v]Jdg 2:11 [w]Nu 25:15-18; 31:1-3

Gideon

6 Again the Israelites did evil in the eyes of the LORD,[v] and for seven years he gave them into the hands of the Midianites.[w] 2 Because the power of Midian was so op-

5:20 the stars fought. Again, the act of the divine warrior was cast in terms of cosmic upheaval (see note on v. 4).
5:23 Curse Meroz. A city of uncertain location, it was cursed for failing to participate in the battle against Sisera.
5:24–27 This section of the song closely parallels the narrative of 4:18–22.
5:31 Then the land had peace forty years. This standard conclusion ties Deborah and Barak's song to chapter 4 (see note on 3:11). The duration of peace indicated the relative effectiveness of Deborah's leadership.
■ **6:1—8:32** *Gideon.* With Gideon the characterizations of the judges significantly shift from "better" (i.e., positive/strong) to "worse" (i.e., negative/weak). By the end of the book, it is tragically clear that judges could neither lead nor deliver; a new kind of leader (i.e., one who would keep covenant) and a new mode of leadership (i.e., kingship) were needed.

Gideon was an exceptional judge in many ways. His account is the longest in the book. The Lord is more visibly active in his story than in any of the others. The angel of the Lord is recorded as appearing to Gideon but not to any other judge (vv. 11–24), either before or after him. Centuries later Isaiah remembered Gideon's defeat of Midian as a significant victory (Isa 9:4; 10:26). Gideon (Jerub-Baal) is listed first in Samuel's roster of deliverers (1Sa 12:11), and he is compared with Moses (see note on 6:11–24). The people sought to make Gideon king (8:22–23). Indeed, he lived like a king (8:26–27,30,32), and one of his sons briefly became Israel's first king (see ch. 9).

Yet for all of this, Gideon failed. He cynically expressed disappointment with God (6:13) and was reluctant to accept God's call (6:15). He tore down God's altar at night for fear of his own countrymen (6:27). The fleece incident revealed Gideon's lack of faith in God's word (6:36ff.). He took extreme vengeance against fellow

pressive,[x] the Israelites prepared shelters for themselves in mountain clefts, caves and
strongholds.[y] 3Whenever the Israelites planted their crops, the Midianites, Amalekites[z]
and other eastern peoples invaded the country. 4They camped on the land and ruined
the crops[a] all the way to Gaza and did not spare a living thing for Israel, neither sheep
nor cattle nor donkeys. 5They came up with their livestock and their tents like swarms
of locusts.[b] It was impossible to count the men and their camels;[c] they invaded the land
to ravage it. 6Midian so impoverished the Israelites that they cried out[d] to the LORD for
help.
7When the Israelites cried to the LORD because of Midian, 8he sent them a prophet,
who said, "This is what the LORD, the God of Israel, says: I brought you up out of Egypt,[e]
out of the land of slavery. 9I snatched you from the power of Egypt and from the hand of
all your oppressors. I drove them from before you and gave you their land.[f] 10I said to
you, 'I am the LORD your God; do not worship[g] the gods of the Amorites,[h] in whose land
you live.' But you have not listened to me."
11The angel of the LORD[i] came and sat down under the oak in Ophrah that belonged
to Joash the Abiezrite,[j] where his son Gideon[k] was threshing wheat in a winepress to
keep it from the Midianites. 12When the angel of the LORD appeared to Gideon, he said,
"The LORD is with you,[l] mighty warrior."
13"But sir," Gideon replied, "if the LORD is with us, why has all this happened to us?
Where are all his wonders that our fathers told[m] us about when they said, 'Did not the
LORD bring us up out of Egypt?' But now the LORD has abandoned[n] us and put us into the
hand of Midian."
14The LORD turned to him and said, "Go in the strength you have[o] and save Israel out
of Midian's hand. Am I not sending you?"
15"But Lord,[a]" Gideon asked, "how can I save Israel? My clan is the weakest in Manasseh, and I am the least in my family.[p]"
16The LORD answered, "I will be with you,[q] and you will strike down all the Midianites together."
17Gideon replied, "If now I have found favor in your eyes, give me a sign[r] that it is really you talking to me. 18Please do not go away until I come back and bring my offering and
set it before you."
And the LORD said, "I will wait until you return."
19Gideon went in, prepared a young goat, and from an ephah[b] of flour he made bread
without yeast. Putting the meat in a basket and its broth in a pot, he brought them out
and offered them to him under the oak.[s]
20The angel of God said to him, "Take the meat and the unleavened bread, place them
on this rock,[t] and pour out the broth." And Gideon did so. 21With the tip of the staff that
was in his hand, the angel of the LORD touched the meat and the unleavened bread.[u] Fire
flared from the rock, consuming the meat and the bread. And the angel of the LORD dis-

6:2 [x]1Sa 13:6; Isa 8:21 [y]Heb 11:38
6:3 [z]Jdg 3:13
6:4 [a]Lev 26:16; Dt 28:30, 51
6:5 [b]Jdg 7:12 [c]Jdg 8:10
6:6 [d]Jdg 3:9
6:8 [e]Jdg 2:1
6:9 [f]Ps 44:2
6:10 [g]2Ki 17:35 [h]Jer 10:2
6:11 [i]Ge 16:7 [j]Jos 17:2 [k]Heb 11:32
6:12 [l]Jos 1:5; Jdg 13:3; Lk 1:11, 28
6:13 [m]Ps 44:1 [n]2Ch 15:2
6:14 [o]Heb 11:34
6:15 [p]Ex 3:11; 1Sa 9:21
6:16 [q]Ex 3:12; Jos 1:5
6:17 [r]ver 36-37; Ge 24:14; Isa 38:7-8
6:19 [s]Ge 18:7-8
6:20 [t]Jdg 13:19
6:21 [u]Lev 9:24

a *15* Or *sir* b *19* That is, probably about 3/5 bushel (about 22 liters)

Israelites and was the first judge to turn the sword against his compatriots (8:16–17). Gideon caused Israel to play the harlot by his ephod (8:27). He declined kingship but outwardly coveted its rewards: plunder (8:23–29) and a harem (8:30–31). Although the angel of the Lord promised Gideon that he would be with him and that Gideon would defeat the Midianites (6:15), Gideon was full of fear (6:27).

Gideon's narrative divides into five balanced episodes followed by an attached account of his son, Abimelech: the evil situation at the time (6:1–10), Gideon's call to deliver (6:11–32), his struggle to believe God's promise (6:33—7:18), his deliverance of Israel from Midian (7:19—8:21) and the evil situation when he died (8:22–32).

■ **6:1–10** *Introduction to Gideon: The Evil Situation at the Time of His Call.* The account of Gideon begins with a description of the terrible condition of God's people at that time.

6:1 did evil. See 2:11. **he gave.** See 2:14.

6:2 the power of Midian was so oppressive. None of the other stories in Judges devotes such attention to the details of the oppression as this one. Homes, crops and livestock were subject to the covenant curse (see Dt 28:30–33,38–42). The Midianite oppression was so great that Isaiah mentioned it centuries later (Isa 9:4; 10:26).

6:5 swarms of locusts. Locusts are one of the covenant curses (see Dt 28:42–43). Here the image is used metaphorically of the Midianite oppression (see notes on Joel 1:2–4).

6:6 impoverished. Literally, "made Israel small." The covenant curse was a reversal of God's promise to Abraham (Ge 15:5; 22:17; see Dt 28:62; Ps 107:38ff.). **cried out.** See note on 3:9.

6:8–9 a prophet. The prophet constantly reminded the people of God's covenant obligations. The words of this unnamed prophet are virtually identical to those of the angel of the Lord in 2:1–5. As in Deborah's story, at the point in the narrative at which God normally raises up the deliverer, he first sends a prophet (see note on 4:4). **I brought . . . snatched . . . drove them . . . gave you.** Remembering these saving actions of God was the first part of covenant keeping.

■ **6:11–32** *Gideon's Call to Deliver.* This passages lies at the heart of the Gideon narrative: His call parallels Moses' call (Ex 3). He asked the question that is central to the book's message (v. 13).

6:11 angel of the LORD came. See 2:1 and 13:1.

6:13 why . . . ? This question is central to the book of Judges. The angel did not answer it, for it had already been answered by the prophet (vv. 8–10; see Dt 28:47–52; 29:24–26; 31:17). Various psalms raise similar issues (Pss 44:20; 74:9,11). **Where . . . ?** Recalling and teaching what God had done was essential to covenant keeping (see 2:10; 6:8–10). Gideon had heard about God's wonders but had failed to grasp their significance, perhaps because of a lack of modeling by his father (see vv. 25–27).

6:14 Go in the strength you have. See verse 34 and 7:2 and 7. God was his strength, although Gideon did not yet realize that fact.

6:15 weakest. When asked about kingship, Saul would use similar words (see 1Sa 9:21).

appeared. 22 When Gideon realized[v] that it was the angel of the LORD, he exclaimed, "Ah,
Sovereign LORD! I have seen the angel of the LORD face to face!"[w]
23 But the LORD said to him, "Peace! Do not be afraid.[x] You are not going to die."
24 So Gideon built an altar to the LORD there and called[y] it The LORD is Peace. To this
day it stands in Ophrah[z] of the Abiezrites.
25 That same night the LORD said to him, "Take the second bull from your father's herd,
the one seven years old.[a] Tear down your father's altar to Baal and cut down the Asherah pole[b][a] beside it. 26 Then build a proper kind of[c] altar to the LORD your God on the top
of this height. Using the wood of the Asherah pole that you cut down, offer the second[d]
bull as a burnt offering."
27 So Gideon took ten of his servants and did as the LORD told him. But because he was
afraid of his family and the men of the town, he did it at night rather than in the daytime.
28 In the morning when the men of the town got up, there was Baal's altar,[b] demolished, with the Asherah pole beside it cut down and the second bull sacrificed on the
newly built altar!
29 They asked each other, "Who did this?"
When they carefully investigated, they were told, "Gideon son of Joash did it."
30 The men of the town demanded of Joash, "Bring out your son. He must die, because
he has broken down Baal's altar and cut down the Asherah pole beside it."
31 But Joash replied to the hostile crowd around him, "Are you going to plead Baal's
cause? Are you trying to save him? Whoever fights for him shall be put to death by morning! If Baal really is a god, he can defend himself when someone breaks down his altar."
32 So that day they called Gideon "Jerub-Baal,[e][c]" saying, "Let Baal contend with him," because he broke down Baal's altar.
33 Now all the Midianites, Amalekites and other eastern peoples[d] joined forces and
crossed over the Jordan and camped in the Valley of Jezreel.[e] 34 Then the Spirit of the LORD
came upon[f] Gideon, and he blew a trumpet,[g] summoning the Abiezrites to follow him.
35 He sent messengers throughout Manasseh, calling them to arms, and also into Asher,
Zebulun and Naphtali,[h] so that they too went up to meet them.
36 Gideon said to God, "If you will save[i] Israel by my hand as you have promised—
37 look, I will place a wool fleece on the threshing floor.[j] If there is dew only on the fleece
and all the ground is dry, then I will know[k] that you will save Israel by my hand, as you
said." 38 And that is what happened. Gideon rose early the next day; he squeezed the
fleece and wrung out the dew—a bowlful of water.
39 Then Gideon said to God, "Do not be angry with me. Let me make just one more request.[l] Allow me one more test with the fleece. This time make the fleece dry and the
ground covered with dew." 40 That night God did so. Only the fleece was dry; all the
ground was covered with dew.

Gideon Defeats the Midianites

7 Early in the morning, Jerub-Baal[m] (that is, Gideon) and all his men camped at the
spring of Harod. The camp of Midian was north of them in the valley near the hill
of Moreh.[n] 2 The LORD said to Gideon, "You have too many men for me to deliver Midian into their hands. In order that Israel may not boast against me that her own strength[o]
has saved her, 3 announce now to the people, 'Anyone who trembles with fear may turn
back and leave Mount Gilead.[p]' " So twenty-two thousand men left, while ten thousand
remained.

6:22 [v]Jdg 13:16,21 [w]Ge 32:30; Ex 33:20; Jdg 13:22
6:23 [x]Da 10:19
6:24 [y]Ge 22:14 [z]Jdg 8:32
6:25 [a]Ex 34:13; Dt 7:5
6:28 [b]1Ki 16:32
6:32 [c]Jdg 7:1; 8:29,35; 1Sa 12:11
6:33 [d]ver 3 [e]Jos 17:16
6:34 [f]Jdg 3:10; 1Ch 12:18; 2Ch 24:20 [g]Jdg 3:27
6:35 [h]Jdg 4:6
6:36 [i]ver 14
6:37 [j]Ex 4:3-7 [k]Ge 24:14
6:39 [l]Ge 18:32
7:1 [m]Jdg 6:32 [n]Ge 12:6
7:2 [o]Dt 8:17; 2Co 4:7
7:3 [p]Dt 20:8

[a] 25 Or *Take a full-grown, mature bull from your father's herd* [b] 25 That is, a symbol of the goddess Asherah; here and elsewhere in Judges [c] 26 Or *build with layers of stone an* [d] 26 Or *full-grown*; also in verse 28 [e] 32 *Jerub-Baal* means *let Baal contend.*

6:22 I have seen . . . face. See 13:22.
6:25–32 This episode in Gideon's life reveals how he came to be known as Jerub-Baal (see v. 32). His father's idolatry is especially ironic in light of verse 13.
6:25–26 Take . . . Tear down . . . cut down . . . build . . . offer. See Deuteronomy 12:3.
6:25 your father's altar to Baal. While Gideon's father may have taught his son the facts concerning the wonders of God (v. 13), he failed to demonstrate faith in God. He was an idolater.
6:26 proper kind of altar. That is, an altar to the Lord.
6:27 he was afraid of his family. Gideon's fear is ironic in that he was called a mighty warrior by God himself (see vv. 11,17,22).
6:32 Jerub-Baal . . . Let Baal contend with him. Joash called Gideon this name to mock the powerlessness of Baal to resist Gideon, who was empowered by the Spirit of God (see v. 34). Gideon is called by this name many times in the narrative.
■ **6:33—7:18** *Gideon's Struggle to Believe God's Promise.* As Gideon faced the challenge of fulfilling God's call, he sought assurance that God would keep his promise.
6:36–49 Gideon's request for a fleece was a mark of his unbelief in God's promise, not of his faith (see vv. 36–37). His sinful preoccupation with signs led him into idolatry (see 8:27; Lk 11:29).
6:36 If you will save. Even though the Spirit had come upon him, Gideon still struggled with lack of faith (see notes on 3:10; 6:17,27).
7:1–8 The drastic reduction of troops demonstrated God's power to save Israel and brought him glory. It also challenged Gideon and encouraged Israel to trust God.

4But the LORD said to Gideon, "There are still too many[q] men. Take them down to the water, and I will sift them for you there. If I say, 'This one shall go with you,' he shall go; but if I say, 'This one shall not go with you,' he shall not go." 5So Gideon took the men down to the water. There the LORD told him, "Separate those who lap the water with their tongues like a dog from those who kneel down to drink." 6Three hundred men lapped with their hands to their mouths. All the rest got down on their knees to drink.

7The LORD said to Gideon, "With the three hundred men that lapped I will save you and give the Midianites into your hands. Let all the other men go, each to his own place."[r] 8So Gideon sent the rest of the Israelites to their tents but kept the three hundred, who took over the provisions and trumpets of the others.

Now the camp of Midian lay below him in the valley. 9During that night the LORD said to Gideon, "Get up, go down against the camp, because I am going to give it into your hands.[s] 10If you are afraid to attack, go down to the camp with your servant Purah 11and listen to what they are saying. Afterward, you will be encouraged to attack the camp." So he and Purah his servant went down to the outposts of the camp. 12The Midianites, the Amalekites[t] and all the other eastern peoples had settled in the valley, thick as locusts.[u] Their camels[v] could no more be counted than the sand on the seashore.[w]

13Gideon arrived just as a man was telling a friend his dream. "I had a dream," he was saying. "A round loaf of barley bread came tumbling into the Midianite camp. It struck the tent with such force that the tent overturned and collapsed."

14His friend responded, "This can be nothing other than the sword of Gideon son of Joash, the Israelite. God has given the Midianites and the whole camp into his hands."

15When Gideon heard the dream and its interpretation, he worshiped God.[x] He returned to the camp of Israel and called out, "Get up! The LORD has given the Midianite camp into your hands." 16Dividing the three hundred men[y] into three companies,[z] he placed trumpets and empty jars in the hands of all of them, with torches inside.

17"Watch me," he told them. "Follow my lead. When I get to the edge of the camp, do exactly as I do. 18When I and all who are with me blow our trumpets,[a] then from all around the camp blow yours and shout, 'For the LORD and for Gideon.' "

19Gideon and the hundred men with him reached the edge of the camp at the beginning of the middle watch, just after they had changed the guard. They blew their trumpets and broke the jars that were in their hands. 20The three companies blew the trumpets and smashed the jars. Grasping the torches in their left hands and holding in their right hands the trumpets they were to blow, they shouted, "A sword[b] for the LORD and for Gideon!" 21While each man held his position around the camp, all the Midianites ran, crying out as they fled.[c]

22When the three hundred trumpets sounded,[d] the LORD caused the men throughout the camp to turn on each other[e] with their swords. The army fled to Beth Shittah toward Zererah as far as the border of Abel Meholah[f] near Tabbath. 23Israelites from Naphtali, Asher and all Manasseh were called out,[g] and they pursued the Midianites. 24Gideon sent messengers throughout the hill country of Ephraim, saying, "Come down against the Midianites and seize the waters of the Jordan[h] ahead of them as far as Beth Barah."

So all the men of Ephraim were called out and they took the waters of the Jordan as far as Beth Barah. 25They also captured two of the Midianite leaders, Oreb and Zeeb[i]. They killed Oreb at the rock of Oreb,[j] and Zeeb at the winepress of Zeeb. They pursued the Midianites and brought the heads of Oreb and Zeeb to Gideon, who was by the Jordan.[k]

Zebah and Zalmunna

8 Now the Ephraimites asked Gideon, "Why have you treated us like this? Why didn't you call us when you went to fight Midian?"[l] And they criticized him sharply.[m]

2But he answered them, "What have I accomplished compared to you? Aren't the gleanings of Ephraim's grapes better than the full grape harvest of Abiezer? 3God gave

7:4 [q]1Sa 14:6
7:7 [r]1Sa 14:6
7:9 [s]Jos 2:24; 10:8; 11:6
7:12 [t]Jdg 8:10 [u]Jdg 6:5 [v]Jer 49:29 [w]Jos 11:4
7:15 [x]1Sa 15:31
7:16 [y]Ge 14:15 [z]2Sa 18:2
7:18 [a]Jdg 3:27
7:20 [b]ver 14
7:21 [c]2Ki 7:7
7:22 [d]Jos 6:20 [e]1Sa 14:20; 2Ch 20:23 [f]1Ki 4:12; 19:16
7:23 [g]Jdg 6:35
7:24 [h]Jdg 3:28
7:25 [i]Jdg 8:3; Ps 83:11 [j]Isa 10:26 [k]Jdg 8:4
8:1 [l]Jdg 12:1 [m]2Sa 19:41

7:12 thick as locusts. See note on 6:5.
7:15–18 Gideon was a changed man ready for battle. He had moved from fear to faith, and he now repeated the Lord's promise. All of the struggles in the book of Judges are due to a lack of faith, and God was looking for a leader who would simply worship him and take him at his word. God had brought Gideon to a holy moment—a moment at which, with all human confidence stripped away, God's chosen instrument sat in silent and humble dependence on God as the One who is everything and who is totally sufficient against all odds to accomplish his will.
7:17 Watch me. Echoed by Gideon's son Abimelech (9:48–49).
■ **7:19—8:21** *Gideon Delivers Israel From Midian.* God fulfilled his promise to Gideon by using him to deliver Israel from Midianite oppression.
7:24 Gideon sent messengers. See 12:1–3.
7:25 at the rock of Oreb. See 6:1—8:32 and Isaiah 10:26.
8:1–3 A similar conflict between Ephraim and Jephthah appears in 12:1–6. See *WLC* 135.

Oreb and Zeeb,[n] the Midianite leaders, into your hands. What was I able to do compared
to you?" At this, their resentment against him subsided.
4Gideon and his three hundred men, exhausted yet keeping up the pursuit, came to
the Jordan[o] and crossed it. 5He said to the men of Succoth,[p] "Give my troops some bread;
they are worn out, and I am still pursuing Zebah and Zalmunna,[q] the kings of Midian."
6But the officials of Succoth said, "Do you already have the hands of Zebah and Zalmunna in your possession? Why should we give bread[r] to your troops?"[s]
7Then Gideon replied, "Just for that, when the LORD has given Zebah and Zalmunna[t]
into my hand, I will tear your flesh with desert thorns and briers."
8From there he went up to Peniel[a][u] and made the same request of them, but they answered as the men of Succoth had. 9So he said to the men of Peniel, "When I return in
triumph, I will tear down this tower."[v]
10Now Zebah and Zalmunna were in Karkor with a force of about fifteen thousand
men, all that were left of the armies of the eastern peoples; a hundred and twenty thousand swordsmen had fallen.[w] 11Gideon went up by the route of the nomads east of Nobah[x] and Jogbehah[y] and fell upon the unsuspecting army. 12Zebah and Zalmunna, the
two kings of Midian, fled, but he pursued them and captured them, routing their entire
army.
13Gideon son of Joash then returned from the battle by the Pass of Heres. 14He caught
a young man of Succoth and questioned him, and the young man wrote down for him the
names of the seventy-seven officials of Succoth, the elders of the town. 15Then Gideon
came and said to the men of Succoth, "Here are Zebah and Zalmunna, about whom you

8:3 [n]Jdg 7:25; Pr 15:1
8:4 [o]Jdg 7:25
8:5 [p]Ge 33:17 [q]Ps 83:11
8:6 [r]1Sa 25:11 [s]ver 15
8:7 [t]Jdg 7:15
8:8 [u]Ge 32:30; 1Ki 12:25
8:9 [v]ver 17
8:10 [w]Jdg 6:5; 7:12; Isa 9:4
8:11 [x]Nu 32:42 [y]Nu 32:35

[a] *8* Hebrew *Penuel,* a variant of *Peniel;* also in verses 9 and 17

8:4–21 Gideon had problems with Succoth and Peniel and ultimately punished both for failing to help him in his pursuit of the Midianite leaders.

Gideon's Battles

The story of Gideon begins with a graphic portrayal of one of the most striking facts of life in the Fertile Crescent: the periodic migration of nomadic people from the Aramean desert into the settled areas of Canaan. Each spring the tents of the bedouin herdsmen appeared overnight almost as if by magic, scattered on the hills and fields of the farming districts. Conflict between these two ways of life (herdsmen and farmers) was inevitable.

In the Biblical period, the vast numbers and warlike practice of the herdsmen reduced the village people to near vassalage. God's answer was twofold: (1) religious reform, starting with Gideon's own family; and (2) military action, based on a coalition of northern Israelite tribes. The location of Gideon's hometown, "Ophrah of the Abiezrites," is not known with certainty, but probably was ancient Aper (modern Afula) in the Valley of Jezreel.

The battle at the spring of Harod is justly celebrated for its strategic brilliance. Denied the use of the only local water source, the Midianites camped in the valley and fell victim to the small band of Israelites, who attacked them from the heights of the hill of Moreh.

The main battle took place north of the hill near the village of Endor at the foot of Mount Tabor. Fleeing by way of the Jordan Valley, the Midianites were trapped when the Ephraimites seized the fords of the Jordan from below Beth Shan to Beth Barah near Adam.

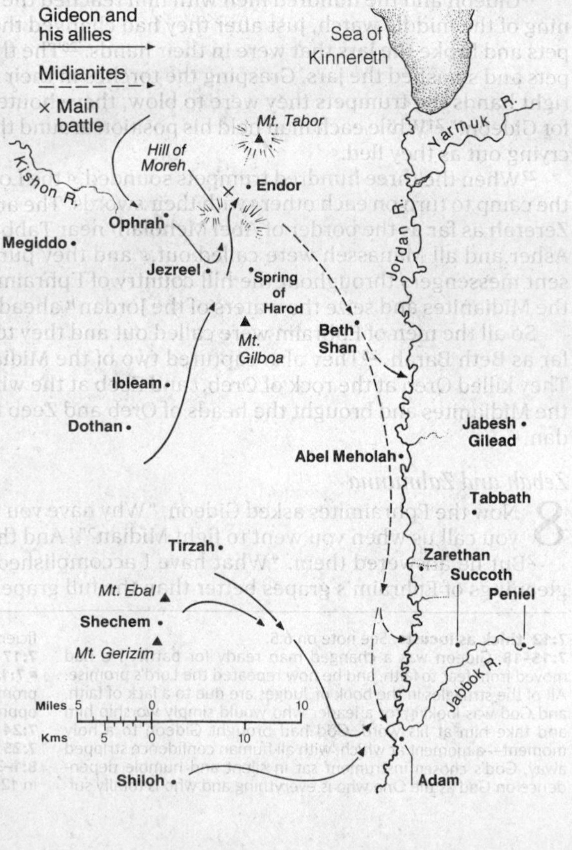

taunted me by saying, 'Do you already have the hands of Zebah and Zalmunna in your
possession? Why should we give bread to your exhausted men?[z]' " 16 He took the elders
of the town and taught the men of Succoth a lesson[a] by punishing them with desert thorns
and briers. 17 He also pulled down the tower of Peniel and killed the men of the town.[b]
18 Then he asked Zebah and Zalmunna, "What kind of men did you kill at Tabor?[c]"
"Men like you," they answered, "each one with the bearing of a prince."
19 Gideon replied, "Those were my brothers, the sons of my own mother. As surely as
the LORD lives, if you had spared their lives, I would not kill you." 20 Turning to Jether, his
oldest son, he said, "Kill them!" But Jether did not draw his sword, because he was only
a boy and was afraid.
21 Zebah and Zalmunna said, "Come, do it yourself. 'As is the man, so is his strength.' "
So Gideon stepped forward and killed them, and took the ornaments[d] off their camels'
necks.

Gideon's Ephod

22 The Israelites said to Gideon, "Rule over us—you, your son and your grandson—
because you have saved us out of the hand of Midian."
23 But Gideon told them, "I will not rule over you, nor will my son rule over you. The
LORD will rule[e] over you." 24 And he said, "I do have one request, that each of you give me
an earring from your share of the plunder." (It was the custom of the Ishmaelites[f] to wear
gold earrings.)
25 They answered, "We'll be glad to give them." So they spread out a garment, and each
man threw a ring from his plunder onto it. 26 The weight of the gold rings he asked for came
to seventeen hundred shekels,[a] not counting the ornaments, the pendants and the purple
garments worn by the kings of Midian or the chains that were on their camels' necks. 27 Gideon made the gold into an ephod,[g] which he placed in Ophrah, his town. All Israel prostituted themselves by worshiping it there, and it became a snare[h] to Gideon and his family.

Gideon's Death

28 Thus Midian was subdued before the Israelites and did not raise its head again. During Gideon's lifetime, the land enjoyed peace[i] forty years.
29 Jerub-Baal[j] son of Joash went back home to live. 30 He had seventy sons[k] of his own,
for he had many wives. 31 His concubine, who lived in Shechem, also bore him a son,
whom he named Abimelech.[l] 32 Gideon son of Joash died at a good old age[m] and was buried in the tomb of his father Joash in Ophrah of the Abiezrites.
33 No sooner had Gideon died than the Israelites again prostituted themselves to the
Baals.[n] They set up Baal-Berith[o] as their god[p] and 34 did not remember[q] the LORD their
God, who had rescued them from the hands of all their enemies on every side. 35 They
also failed to show kindness to the family of Jerub-Baal (that is, Gideon) for all the good
things he had done for them.[r]

a *26* That is, about 43 pounds (about 19.5 kilograms)

8:15 [z]ver 6
8:16 [a]ver 7
8:17 [b]ver 9
8:18 [c]Jos 19:22; Jdg 4:6
8:21 [d]ver 26; Ps 83:11
8:23 [e]Ex 16:8; 1Sa 8:7; 10:19; 12:12
8:24 [f]Ge 25:13
8:27 [g]Jdg 17:5; 18:14 [h]Dt 7:16; Ps 106:39
8:28 [i]Jdg 5:31
8:29 [j]Jdg 7:1
8:30 [k]Jdg 9:2,5,18,24
8:31 [l]Jdg 9:1
8:32 [m]Ge 25:8
8:33 [n]Jdg 2:11,13,19 [o]Jdg 9:4 [p]Jdg 9:27,46
8:34 [q]Jdg 3:7; Dt 4:9; Ps 78:11,42
8:35 [r]Jdg 9:16

8:16–17 There are strong parallels between the actions of Abimelech and those of Gideon (see 9:45–52).
■ **8:22–32** *Conclusion to Gideon: The Evil Situation When He Died.* Once Gideon had delivered Israel from the Midianites, the people immediately turned from God.
8:22 Rule over us. The Israelites wrongly credited Gideon, not God, with the victory. Note the parallel with Saul (1Sa 8:5; 9:21).
8:23 The LORD will rule. Gideon refused to exercise comprehensive leadership, but the narrative immediately discounts his answer by portraying him as desiring only the pleasures of kingship without its responsibilities. Gideon gathered jewelry and royal garments from his people (vv. 24–26), made and used an ephod (v. 27), established a harem (vv. 30–31) and named his most prominent son Abimelech (which means "My father [is] king"). The people of Shechem assumed that his son would succeed him. For the problem of human kingship in Israel see note on 1 Samuel 8:7. This book is not opposed to kingship per se (see 17:6; 18:1; 19:1; 21:25).
8:27 ephod. Usually this word designates various priestly garments (see Ex 28:4ff; 39:2; 1Sa 2:18; 22:18; 2Sa 6:14). As in several other passages, it is not clear precisely what this ephod was, other than that it was an object associated with idol worship (see 17:5; 18:14; Hos 3:4). **prostituted.** Gideon was unable to lead the people in keeping covenant (see 2:17).
8:30 many wives. See note on verse 23.
8:31 Abimelech. Strikingly, this son is named Abimelech ("My father [is] king"), notwithstanding all of Gideon's claims to the contrary. See verse 24.
■ **8:33—9:57** *Abimelech.* The story of Abimelech is appended to the account of Gideon to demonstrate the disasters that the wrong kind of king can bring to Israel. Abimelech was the opposite of a deliverer; he oppressed the people. This story focuses a number of times on the question of who should be king (9:2,8–20,28–29). In light of this question, it is significant that Saul and Abimelech are linked by strikingly similar episodes (see 9:23 and 54). These links reflect negatively on Saul's kingship, for they imply that he was the same sort of king as Abimelech. The message to the original audience of Judges was that the people should not want a son of Saul as their king because Saul's house is like that of Abimelech, the son of Gideon.
8:33 Gideon. See note on 6:32. **the Israelites again prostituted themselves.** While this language is similar to other introductions to major judges, it departs from the usual formula "the Israelites did evil in the eyes of the LORD." Perhaps the reason for this omission was to focus attention on Abimelech, the king. **Baal-Berith.** Literally, "Baal [lord] of the covenant," a counterfeit of the Lord God (see 9:4). The irony of the narrative is heightened by the use of Gideon's other name (Jerub-Baal ["let Baal contend"]). The people trusted in Baal-Berith (v. 33; 9:4,46), and this use of Gideon's name was a reminder of the powerlessness of Baal, in whom the apostate Israelites were trusting (see note on 6:32).
8:34 did not remember. Recalling God's saving wonders was the first step toward covenant obedience (see 2:12; note on 2:10).
8:35 failed to show kindness. See 9:5 and 16–19.

Abimelech

9 Abimelech[s] son of Jerub-Baal went to his mother's brothers in Shechem and said
to them and to all his mother's clan, 2 "Ask all the citizens of Shechem, 'Which is better for you: to have all seventy of Jerub-Baal's sons rule over you, or just one man?' Remember, I am your flesh and blood.[t]"
3 When the brothers repeated all this to the citizens of Shechem, they were inclined
to follow Abimelech, for they said, "He is our brother." 4 They gave him seventy shekels[a]
of silver from the temple of Baal-Berith,[u] and Abimelech used it to hire reckless adventurers,[v] who became his followers. 5 He went to his father's home in Ophrah and on one
stone murdered his seventy brothers,[w] the sons of Jerub-Baal. But Jotham, the youngest
son of Jerub-Baal, escaped by hiding.[x] 6 Then all the citizens of Shechem and Beth Millo gathered beside the great tree at the pillar in Shechem to crown Abimelech king.
7 When Jotham was told about this, he climbed up on the top of Mount Gerizim[y] and
shouted to them, "Listen to me, citizens of Shechem, so that God may listen to you. 8 One day
the trees went out to anoint a king for themselves. They said to the olive tree, 'Be our king.'
9 "But the olive tree answered, 'Should I give up my oil, by which both gods and men
are honored, to hold sway over the trees?'
10 "Next, the trees said to the fig tree, 'Come and be our king.'
11 "But the fig tree replied, 'Should I give up my fruit, so good and sweet, to hold sway
over the trees?'
12 "Then the trees said to the vine, 'Come and be our king.'
13 "But the vine answered, 'Should I give up my wine,[z] which cheers both gods and
men, to hold sway over the trees?'
14 "Finally all the trees said to the thornbush, 'Come and be our king.'
15 "The thornbush said to the trees, 'If you really want to anoint me king over you,
come and take refuge in my shade;[a] but if not, then let fire come out[b] of the thornbush
and consume the cedars of Lebanon!'[c]
16 "Now if you have acted honorably and in good faith when you made Abimelech
king, and if you have been fair to Jerub-Baal and his family, and if you have treated him
as he deserves— 17 and to think that my father fought for you, risked his life to rescue you
from the hand of Midian 18 (but today you have revolted against my father's family, murdered his seventy sons[d] on a single stone, and made Abimelech, the son of his slave girl,
king over the citizens of Shechem because he is your brother)— 19 if then you have acted honorably and in good faith toward Jerub-Baal and his family today, may Abimelech
be your joy, and may you be his, too! 20 But if you have not, let fire come out[e] from Abimelech and consume you, citizens of Shechem and Beth Millo, and let fire come out from
you, citizens of Shechem and Beth Millo, and consume Abimelech!"
21 Then Jotham fled, escaping to Beer, and he lived there because he was afraid of his
brother Abimelech.
22 After Abimelech had governed Israel three years, 23 God sent an evil spirit[f] between Abimelech and the citizens of Shechem, who acted treacherously against Abimelech. 24 God did this in order that the crime against Jerub-Baal's seventy sons, the shedding[g] of their blood, might be avenged[h] on their brother Abimelech and on the citizens
of Shechem, who had helped him[i] murder his brothers. 25 In opposition to him these citizens of Shechem set men on the hilltops to ambush and rob everyone who passed by,
and this was reported to Abimelech.
26 Now Gaal son of Ebed moved with his brothers into Shechem, and its citizens put

[a] 4 That is, about 1 3/4 pounds (about 0.8 kilogram)

9:1 [s] Jdg 8:31
9:2 [t] Ge 29:14; Jdg 8:30
9:4 [u] Jdg 8:33 [v] Jdg 11:3; 2Ch 13:7
9:5 [w] ver 2; Jdg 8:30 [x] 2Ki 11:2
9:7 [y] Dt 11:29; 27:12; Jn 4:20
9:13 [z] Ecc 2:3
9:15 [a] Isa 30:2 [b] ver 20 [c] Isa 2:13
9:18 [d] ver 5-6; Jdg 8:30
9:20 [e] ver 15
9:23 [f] 1Sa 16:14,23; 18:10; 1Ki 22:22; Isa 19:14; 33:1
9:24 [g] Nu 35:33; 1Ki 2:32 [h] ver 56-57 [i] Dt 27:25

9:2–3 See the ironic parallel in verses 27–29.
9:4 Baal-Berith. See verse 46 and 8:33. Baal-Berith is portrayed as having "bought" the Israelites and having placed them into the hands of an oppressive Israelite king, the son of Gideon (see 2:14).
9:5 on one stone . . . his seventy brothers. In the royal propaganda of other cultures, kings looked upon success in murdering their brothers as proof of divine approval for their rise to power. In the perspective of the writer, however, Abimelech's actions were deplorable.
9:6 crown. See 1 Samuel 12:13, where the people also crowned the man of their choice and suffered the consequences.
9:7–21 Jotham's fable is full of irony. The bramble was worthless, even harmful; it assumed the kingship, while the fruitful trees, which could have fulfilled the people's needs, refused. The fable assumes the just desire of the people that the good trees become kings, as well as the excellent qualifications of the good trees to reign.
9:7 Mount Gerizim. Ironically, the mount of blessing (Dt 27:12) was used for a curse during the reign of Abimelech (see notes on 8:33—9:57; 8:33).
9:14 thornbush. The product of idolatry (v. 4), Abimelech's kingship would be a thorn to the Israelites (see note on 2:3).
9:20 let fire. The fulfillment of Jotham's curse is found in verses 45–52.
9:23 an evil spirit. When God acted in Abimelech's story, he sent an evil spirit (see v. 56). The parallel with Saul was not accidental; it promoted the author's purpose of opposing Benjamite rule. Both Abimelech and Saul had an evil spirit come upon them at the point at which they began to lose their kingdoms (1Sa 15:23; 16:14). See notes on verse 54 and 8:33—9:57; see also "Introduction: Purpose and Distinctives."
9:26–29 Note parallels with verses 1–3.
9:26 Gaal. A descendant of Hamor, the father of Shechem (v. 28). He also sought the right to rule by virtue of his ancestry.

their confidence in him. 27After they had gone out into the fields and gathered the grapes and trodden[j] them, they held a festival in the temple of their god.[k] While they were eating and drinking, they cursed Abimelech. 28Then Gaal son of Ebed said, "Who[l] is Abimelech, and who is Shechem, that we should be subject to him? Isn't he Jerub-Baal's son, and isn't Zebul his deputy? Serve the men of Hamor,[m] Shechem's father! Why should we serve Abimelech? 29If only this people were under my command![n] Then I would get rid of him. I would say to Abimelech, 'Call out your whole army!' "[a]

30When Zebul the governor of the city heard what Gaal son of Ebed said, he was very angry. 31Under cover he sent messengers to Abimelech, saying, "Gaal son of Ebed and his brothers have come to Shechem and are stirring up the city against you. 32Now then, during the night you and your men should come and lie in wait[o] in the fields. 33In the morning at sunrise, advance against the city. When Gaal and his men come out against you, do whatever your hand finds to do.[p]"

34So Abimelech and all his troops set out by night and took up concealed positions near Shechem in four companies. 35Now Gaal son of Ebed had gone out and was standing at the entrance to the city gate just as Abimelech and his soldiers came out from their hiding place.[q]

36When Gaal saw them, he said to Zebul, "Look, people are coming down from the tops of the mountains!"

Zebul replied, "You mistake the shadows of the mountains for men."

37But Gaal spoke up again: "Look, people are coming down from the center of the land, and a company is coming from the direction of the soothsayers' tree."

38Then Zebul said to him, "Where is your big talk now, you who said, 'Who is Abimelech that we should be subject to him?' Aren't these the men you ridiculed?[r] Go out and fight them!"

39So Gaal led out[b] the citizens of Shechem and fought Abimelech. 40Abimelech chased him, and many fell wounded in the flight—all the way to the entrance to the gate. 41Abimelech stayed in Arumah, and Zebul drove Gaal and his brothers out of Shechem.

42The next day the people of Shechem went out to the fields, and this was reported to Abimelech. 43So he took his men, divided them into three companies[s] and set an ambush in the fields. When he saw the people coming out of the city, he rose to attack them. 44Abimelech and the companies with him rushed forward to a position at the entrance to the city gate. Then two companies rushed upon those in the fields and struck them down. 45All that day Abimelech pressed his attack against the city until he had captured it and killed its people. Then he destroyed the city[t] and scattered salt[u] over it.

46On hearing this, the citizens in the tower of Shechem went into the stronghold of the temple[v] of El-Berith. 47When Abimelech heard that they had assembled there, 48he and all his men went up Mount Zalmon.[w] He took an ax and cut off some branches, which he lifted to his shoulders. He ordered the men with him, "Quick! Do what you have seen me do!" 49So all the men cut branches and followed Abimelech. They piled them against the stronghold and set it on fire over the people inside. So all the people in the tower of Shechem, about a thousand men and women, also died.

50Next Abimelech went to Thebez[x] and besieged it and captured it. 51Inside the city, however, was a strong tower, to which all the men and women—all the people of the city—fled. They locked themselves in and climbed up on the tower roof. 52Abimelech went to the tower and stormed it. But as he approached the entrance to the tower to set it on fire, 53a woman dropped an upper millstone on his head and cracked his skull.[y]

54Hurriedly he called to his armor-bearer, "Draw your sword and kill me,[z] so that they can't say, 'A woman killed him.' " So his servant ran him through, and he died. 55When the Israelites saw that Abimelech was dead, they went home.

9:27 [j]Am 9:13 [k]Jdg 8:33
9:28 [l]1Sa 25:10; 1Ki 12:16 [m]Ge 34:2,6
9:29 [n]2Sa 15:4
9:32 [o]Jos 8:2
9:33 [p]1Sa 10:7
9:35 [q]Ps 32:7; Jer 49:10
9:38 [r]ver 28-29
9:43 [s]Jdg 7:16
9:45 [t]ver 20; 2Ki 3:25 [u]Dt 29:23
9:46 [v]Jdg 8:33
9:48 [w]Ps 68:14
9:50 [x]2Sa 11:21
9:53 [y]2Sa 11:21
9:54 [z]1Sa 31:4; 2Sa 1:9

[a] *29* Septuagint; Hebrew *him." Then he said to Abimelech, "Call out your whole army!"* [b] *39* Or *Gaal went out in the sight of*

9:28 Shechem's father! See note on verse 26.
9:45 scattered salt over it. That is, rendered it infertile.
9:46 El-Berith. Literally, "God of the covenant." See note on verse 4. El was the father of all gods in the Canaanite pantheon. His temple was probably one and the same with the temple of Baal-Berith, Baal having become the more prominent god in later years. Note the irony that money from the temple of Baal-Berith was used to "liberate" the people of Shechem from the rule of Gideon's sons (vv. 4–5), whereas now the temple of El-Berith failed to afford a refuge from the hand of Abimelech, "the deliverer."
9:48 Do what you have seen me do! Abimelech imitated his father Gideon (see note on 7:17).
9:49 set it on fire. This fulfilled Jotham's curse (v. 20).
9:53 an upper millstone. A stone figured prominently in Abimelech's death, as it did in the murder of Gideon's other sons (see note on v. 5).
9:54 Draw your sword and kill me. Saul tried to die in much the same way while in battle against the Philistines (1Sa 31:4). This incident, coupled with the presence of an evil spirit from God (v. 23), forged strong links between the stories of Saul and Abimelech and discredited any Benjamite claim to royal authority (see note on v. 23). **A woman killed him.** A shameful death (see note on 4:22).

56 Thus God repaid the wickedness that Abimelech had done to his father by murdering his seventy brothers. 57 God also made the men of Shechem pay for all their wickedness.[a] The curse of Jotham son of Jerub-Baal came on them.

Tola

10 After the time of Abimelech a man of Issachar,[b] Tola son of Puah,[c] the son of
Dodo, rose to save[d] Israel. He lived in Shamir, in the hill country of Ephraim. 2 He
led[a] Israel twenty-three years; then he died, and was buried in Shamir.

Jair

3 He was followed by Jair of Gilead, who led Israel twenty-two years. 4 He had thirty
sons, who rode thirty donkeys. They controlled thirty towns in Gilead, which to this day
are called Havvoth Jair.[b] [e] 5 When Jair died, he was buried in Kamon.

Jephthah

6 Again the Israelites did evil in the eyes of the LORD.[f] They served the Baals and the
Ashtoreths,[g] and the gods of Aram, the gods of Sidon, the gods of Moab, the gods of the
Ammonites and the gods of the Philistines.[h] And because the Israelites forsook the LORD[i]
and no longer served him, 7 he became angry[j] with them. He sold them[k] into the hands
of the Philistines and the Ammonites, 8 who that year shattered and crushed them. For
eighteen years they oppressed all the Israelites on the east side of the Jordan in Gilead,
the land of the Amorites. 9 The Ammonites also crossed the Jordan to fight against Judah,
Benjamin and the house of Ephraim; and Israel was in great distress. 10 Then the Israelites cried out to the LORD, "We have sinned against you, forsaking our God and serving
the Baals."[l]

11 The LORD replied, "When the Egyptians,[m] the Amorites, the Ammonites,[n] the Philistines,[o] 12 the Sidonians, the Amalekites and the Maonites[c] oppressed you[p] and you
cried to me for help, did I not save you from their hands? 13 But you have forsaken me and
served other gods, so I will no longer save you. 14 Go and cry out to the gods you have chosen. Let them save you when you are in trouble![q]"

15 But the Israelites said to the LORD, "We have sinned. Do with us whatever you think
best,[r] but please rescue us now." 16 Then they got rid of the foreign gods among them and
served the LORD.[s] And he could bear Israel's misery[t] no longer.[u]

9:57 [a]ver 20
10:1 [b]Ge 30:18 [c]Ge 46:13 [d]Jdg 2:16; 6:14
10:4 [e]Nu 32:41
10:6 [f]Jdg 2:11 [g]Jdg 2:13 [h]Jdg 2:12 [i]Dt 32:15
10:7 [j]Dt 31:17 [k]Dt 32:30; Jdg 2:14; 1Sa 12:9
10:10 [l]1Sa 12:10
10:11 [m]Ex 14:30 [n]Nu 21:21; Jdg 3:13 [o]Jdg 3:31
10:12 [p]Ps 106:42
10:14 [q]Dt 32:37
10:15 [r]1Sa 3:18; 2Sa 15:26
10:16 [s]Jos 24:23; Jer 18:8 [t]Isa 63:9 [u]Dt 32:36; Ps 106:44-45

[a] 2 Traditionally *judged;* also in verse 3 [b] 4 Or *called the settlements of Jair* [c] 12 Hebrew; some Septuagint manuscripts *Midianites*

9:56 Thus God repaid. God has not been much of a visible participant in this narrative (see v. 23). Here he is said to have repaid Abimelech for killing his brothers.

■ **10:1–2** *Tola.* One of the minor judges whose actions are briefly mentioned (see 3:31; 12:8–15). The minor judges are mentioned without details simply to provide 12 examples of judges. The number 12 is probably reminiscent of the 12 tribes of Israel and demonstrates the total inadequacy of the office of judge to provide leadership for the tribes.

10:1 Tola. Tola is not mentioned elsewhere in Scripture. **rose to save Israel.** See 2:16.

10:2 led. That is, judged.

■ **10:3–5** *Jair.* Another minor judge who receives little attention (see note on vv. 1–2).

10:3 Jair. Like Tola, Jair is not mentioned anywhere else in the Bible. **led.** See verse 2.

10:4 who rode thirty donkeys. His 30 sons, 30 donkeys and control of 30 towns all speak of his wealth and power (see 5:10).

■ **10:6—12:7** *Jephthah.* Jephthah's story marks the first account of the last two major judges; his work is characterized in a largely negative light. The list of idols that Israel followed had grown (10:6), the Lord rebuked Jephthah in 10:10–16 and inter-tribal tensions had escalated (see note on 12:1). Jephthah's characterization as a "mighty warrior" (11:1) hardly commends him spiritually for the role of savior in Israel. This ostracized son of a harlot and leader of a band of brigands in the mountains of Gilead was an unlikely leader (11:1–3). Although his bargaining with the Ammonites reflects political astuteness and faith in Israel's God (11:12–28), he was motivated by opportunistic ambition (11:9–11). His rash vow, which preceded his battle with the Ammonites, was similar to the vows of pagan warriors (11:30–31). Jephthah brought only six years of peace instead of a generation (12:7; see note on 3:11). Even so, he is mentioned by the writer of Hebrews as a man of faith (Heb 11:32).

A number of parallels appear between the narratives of Jephthah and Saul: Each was made a leader in Mizpah (11:11; 1Sa 10:17), faced the Ammonites as his principle adversaries (11:12–29; 1Sa 11:1–11), made a vow threatening the life of his first-born (11:30–40; 1Sa 14:24–45) and made an inappropriate sacrifice (11:30–40; 1Sa 13:8–14). By these parallels the writer discredited the claim to kingship from Saul's family (see Introduction: "Purpose and Distinctives").

10:6–10 The first part of the introduction follows the stereotypical frame: The Israelites served seven false gods (v. 6), the Lord delivered them into the hands of the Philistines and Ammonites (vv. 7–9) and Israel cried out for deliverance (v. 10).

10:6 gods. In the previous accounts only the Baals and Ashtoreths were mentioned (2:11,13; 3:7). The longer listing of gods indicates the further corruption of Israel's worship (see also vv. 11–12).

10:11–16 The second part of the introduction (vv. 11–16) features the Lord's past faithfulness to deliver from seven nations (vv. 11–12); his current refusal to deliver (vv. 13–14); Israel's true repentance ("We have sinned"; v. 15) and removal of the foreign gods; and the Lord's compassion on his people in their misery (vv. 15–16). This is the only account in the book of Judges in which the Israelites are said to have repented (see 1Sa 12:10). Elsewhere they simply cried out to the Lord, and he delivered them (see note on 3:9).

10:10 forsaking our God and serving the Baals. This is the same language used in the people's indictment (see v. 6).

10:11–12 When . . . oppressed you. The list of gods in verse 6 coincides almost identically with that of the nations that oppressed Israel. The Israelites rejected the God who had saved them and followed the pitiless gods of their oppressors.

10:13 no longer. See Deuteronomy 8:19–20 and 31:16–17 (see also 2:3; Nu 33:55–56; Jos 23:13).

10:14 cry out to the gods you have chosen. See Deuteronomy 32:37–38. God gave his people over to the futility of their sinful ways. The same taunt is made in Jeremiah 2:28 and 11:12–13.

10:16 could bear Israel's misery no longer. The importance of repentance and persistent prayer is illustrated in the fact that God finally responded to Israel despite his previous refusal (see Lk 18:1–8).

17When the Ammonites were called to arms and camped in Gilead, the Israelites assembled and camped at Mizpah.[v] 18The leaders of the people of Gilead said to each other, "Whoever will launch the attack against the Ammonites will be the head[w] of all those
living in Gilead."

11

Jephthah[x] the Gileadite was a mighty warrior.[y] His father was Gilead; his mother was a prostitute. 2Gilead's wife also bore him sons, and when they were
grown up, they drove Jephthah away. "You are not going to get any inheritance in our
family," they said, "because you are the son of another woman." 3So Jephthah fled from
his brothers and settled in the land of Tob,[z] where a group of adventurers[a] gathered
around him and followed him.
4Some time later, when the Ammonites[b] made war on Israel, 5the elders of Gilead
went to get Jephthah from the land of Tob. 6"Come," they said, "be our commander, so
we can fight the Ammonites."
7Jephthah said to them, "Didn't you hate me and drive me from my father's house?[c]
Why do you come to me now, when you're in trouble?"
8The elders of Gilead said to him, "Nevertheless, we are turning to you now; come
with us to fight the Ammonites, and you will be our head[d] over all who live in Gilead."
9Jephthah answered, "Suppose you take me back to fight the Ammonites and the
LORD gives them to me—will I really be your head?"
10The elders of Gilead replied, "The LORD is our witness;[e] we will certainly do as you
say." 11So Jephthah went with the elders of Gilead, and the people made him head and
commander over them. And he repeated all his words before the LORD in Mizpah.[f]
12Then Jephthah sent messengers to the Ammonite king with the question: "What do
you have against us that you have attacked our country?"
13The king of the Ammonites answered Jephthah's messengers, "When Israel came
up out of Egypt, they took away my land from the Arnon to the Jabbok,[g] all the way to
the Jordan. Now give it back peaceably."
14Jephthah sent back messengers to the Ammonite king, 15saying:

"This is what Jephthah says: Israel did not take the land of Moab[h] or the land of the
Ammonites.[i] 16But when they came up out of Egypt, Israel went through the desert to the Red Sea[a][j] and on to Kadesh.[k] 17Then Israel sent messengers[l] to the king
of Edom, saying, 'Give us permission to go through your country,'[m] but the king of
Edom would not listen. They sent also to the king of Moab, and he refused.[n] So Israel stayed at Kadesh.
18"Next they traveled through the desert, skirted the lands of Edom[o] and
Moab, passed along the eastern side[p] of the country of Moab, and camped on the
other side of the Arnon.[q] They did not enter the territory of Moab, for the Arnon
was its border.
19"Then Israel sent messengers to Sihon king of the Amorites, who ruled in
Heshbon, and said to him, 'Let us pass through your country to our own place.'[r]
20Sihon, however, did not trust Israel[b] to pass through his territory. He mustered
all his men and encamped at Jahaz and fought with Israel.[s]

10:17 [v]Ge 31:49; Jdg 11:29
10:18 [w]Jdg 11:8,9
11:1 [x]Heb 11:32 [y]Jdg 6:12
11:3 [z]2Sa 10:6,8 [a]Jdg 9:4
11:4 [b]Jdg 10:9
11:7 [c]Ge 26:27
11:8 [d]Jdg 10:18
11:10 [e]Ge 31:50; Jer 42:5
11:11 [f]Jos 11:3; Jdg 10:17; 20:1; 1Sa 10:17
11:13 [g]Ge 32:22; Nu 21:24
11:15 [h]Dt 2:9 [i]Dt 2:19
11:16 [j]Nu 14:25; Dt 1:40 [k]Nu 20:1
11:17 [l]Nu 20:14 [m]Nu 20:18,21 [n]Jos 24:9
11:18 [o]Nu 21:4 [p]Dt 2:8 [q]Nu 21:13
11:19 [r]Nu 21:21-22; Dt 2:26-27
11:20 [s]Nu 21:23; Dt 2:32

a 16 Hebrew *Yam Suph*; that is, Sea of Reeds b 20 Or *however, would not make an agreement for Israel*

10:17—11:11 In this section Jephthah was raised up by the Lord as the deliverer to lead Israel, even though there is no explicit mention of the Lord acting (see 2:16).
11:1 a mighty warrior. With this designation Jephthah is linked to Gideon (6:12). **his mother was a prostitute.** His heritage made him a social outcast (see v. 2).
11:2 inheritance. Lack of inheritance meant poverty. **son of another woman.** Like Abimelech, Jephthah was alienated from his family on account of his mother (see 8:31; 9:18).
11:3 adventurers. Another similarity between Jephthah and Abimelech (see 9:4) that discredits Jephthah.
11:5–10 In order to protect their power (vv. 4–6) the self-serving elders offered Jephthah the position of (military) commander for the duration of the war, but Jephthah negotiated to become their "head," first in a verbal agreement (vv. 7–8) and then by treaty (vv. 9–10). The "head" or "tribal chief" was the highest kinship head and the person on whom the kingdom was established—a precarious recognition of tribal headship. Jephthah was not called a king, but he was sheikh of the highest status. Also irregular for the period was the manner in which the bestowal of this position was rendered. The elders relegated the Lord to the position of confirming their selection of the person to be the "head."
11:9 the LORD gives. Jephthah exhibited faith that it was God who brought victory.
11:10 The LORD is our witness. The elders were swearing an oath in order to confirm a covenant.
11:11 he repeated all his words before the LORD in Mizpah. The covenant was confirmed before the Lord in Mizpah. Years later the people would make Saul king before the Lord at Mizpah (1Sa 10:17; see note on 10:6—12:7).
11:12–29 For the historical background to this conflict, see Numbers 20:14–21, 21:10–35 and Deuteronomy 2:16—3:11. At the time of Jephthah the Ammonites were seeking to expand their territory into land that had once been Amorite holdings but had been possessed by Israel for the previous 300 years. Jephthah countered the Ammonite demands by rehearsing the history of the region to indicate that the Israelites had taken only the land that the God of Israel had given them. God had forbidden their taking any territory from Ammon (see Dt 2:18–19). In his treaty-breach lawsuit against Ammon, Jephthah emerged as a man of faith who proclaimed salvation history in terms of the Lord's victories (see 2:1–12; 5:4; 6:8–9; 11:13–24; 19:30), as well as a skillful leader in politics as well as in war.
11:12 Ammonite king. Like Saul, Jephthah's first adversary was the Ammonites (see 1Sa 11:1–11). Gilead was the region threatened in Saul's story as well (see note on 10:6—12:7).

21 "Then the LORD, the God of Israel, gave Sihon and all his men into Israel's
hands, and they defeated them. Israel took over all the land of the Amorites who
lived in that country, 22 capturing all of it from the Arnon to the Jabbok and from
the desert to the Jordan.[t]
23 "Now since the LORD, the God of Israel, has driven the Amorites out before
his people Israel, what right have you to take it over? 24 Will you not take what
your god Chemosh[u] gives you? Likewise, whatever the LORD our God has given
us, we will possess. 25 Are you better than Balak son of Zippor,[v] king of Moab? Did
he ever quarrel with Israel or fight with them?[w] 26 For three hundred years Israel occupied[x] Heshbon, Aroer, the surrounding settlements and all the towns
along the Arnon. Why didn't you retake them during that time? 27 I have not
wronged you, but you are doing me wrong by waging war against me. Let the
LORD, the Judge,[a][y] decide[z] the dispute this day between the Israelites and the
Ammonites."

28 The king of Ammon, however, paid no attention to the message Jephthah sent him.
29 Then the Spirit[a] of the LORD came upon Jephthah. He crossed Gilead and Manasseh, passed through Mizpah of Gilead, and from there he advanced against the Ammonites. 30 And Jephthah made a vow[b] to the LORD: "If you give the Ammonites into my hands,
31 whatever comes out of the door of my house to meet me when I return in triumph from
the Ammonites will be the LORD's, and I will sacrifice it as a burnt offering."
32 Then Jephthah went over to fight the Ammonites, and the LORD gave them into his
hands. 33 He devastated twenty towns from Aroer to the vicinity of Minnith,[c] as far as Abel
Keramim. Thus Israel subdued Ammon.
34 When Jephthah returned to his home in Mizpah, who should come out to meet him
but his daughter, dancing to the sound of tambourines![d] She was an only child. Except
for her he had neither son nor daughter. 35 When he saw her, he tore his clothes and
cried, "Oh! My daughter! You have made me miserable and wretched, because I have
made a vow to the LORD that I cannot break."[e]
36 "My father," she replied, "you have given your word to the LORD. Do to me just as
you promised,[f] now that the LORD has avenged you of your enemies,[g] the Ammonites.
37 But grant me this one request," she said. "Give me two months to roam the hills and
weep with my friends, because I will never marry."
38 "You may go," he said. And he let her go for two months. She and the girls went into
the hills and wept because she would never marry. 39 After the two months, she returned
to her father and he did to her as he had vowed. And she was a virgin.
From this comes the Israelite custom 40 that each year the young women of Israel go
out for four days to commemorate the daughter of Jephthah the Gileadite.

[a] *27 Or Ruler*

11:22 [t]Dt 2:36
11:24 [u]Nu 21:29; Jos 3:10; 1Ki 11:7
11:25 [v]Nu 22:2 [w]Jos 24:9
11:26 [x]Nu 21:25
11:27 [y]Ge 18:25 [z]Ge 16:5; 31:53; 1Sa 24:12,15
11:29 [a]Nu 11:25; Jdg 3:10; 6:34; 14:6,19; 15:14; 1Sa 11:6; 16:13; Isa 11:2
11:30 [b]Ge 28:20
11:33 [c]Eze 27:17
11:34 [d]Ex 15:20; Jer 31:4
11:35 [e]Nu 30:2; Ecc 5:2,4,5
11:36 [f]Lk 1:38 [g]2Sa 18:19

11:23 the LORD, the God of Israel. Warfare was viewed as a battle between the gods of the opposing forces. If Israel won, it was because the God of Israel had accomplished the indisputable victory (see v. 24). See verse 21.
11:27 Let the LORD, the Judge, decide. See verses 21 and 23. Jephthah declared that God was the Judge over all peoples and gods. Here "judge" was used in a judicial sense, as in handing down a decision, although God would ultimately take on the deliverer role as well (see vv. 32–33). Judges affirms that God is both the true King (8:23) and the true Judge, who alone could solve Israel's woes.
11:29 Spirit of the LORD. See note on 3:10.
11:30–40 Jephthah defeated the Ammonites but in the process made a rash vow to the Lord, on the basis of which he was compelled to sacrifice his beloved daughter to the Lord as a burnt offering. Unlike the pagan gods, God was not to be worshiped by human sacrifice (Dt 32:17; Ps 106:37–38). Jephthah's ill-advised vow demonstrated his dearth of "leadership" faith; lacking that kind of faith, his house could not endure.
11:31 whatever comes out. Literally, "the one who comes out." It is unlikely that Jephthah expected an animal to emerge from the door of his house to greet him after a victory. His expectation was that a human being would come out (cf. 5:28; 1Sa 18:6),
11:35 tore his clothes. The sign of mourning over death. **made me miserable and wretched.** Literally, "You have troubled me." Jephthah pitied himself, not his only daughter. **made a vow.** Although he had made a vow, most interpreters still consider Jephthah's action to have been improper. The issue is complicated. The Law (Lev 18:21; 20:2) and the Prophets (Jer 19:5; Eze 20:30–31; 23:37,39) condemned child sacrifice, especially in the context of idolatry. Indeed, this reprehensible practice was an abomination promoted in the worship of Chemosh, the god against whom Jephthah was fighting (see v. 21). At the same time the Law required that every firstborn child and firstborn animal be given to the Lord. Most firstborn animals were to be sacrificed, but firstborn humans were to be redeemed (Ex 13:2,12–15). Implicitly, the sacrifices of redemption for human children were substitutionary, indicating that child sacrifice was the root concept of the practice. Human sacrifice is most clearly seen to be acceptable in God's eyes in the sacrifice of Jesus on the cross. Jephthah's actions must also be judged by laws pertaining to vows. With a few exceptions, rash vows (Nu 30) and even vows taken in the wake of deception (Jos 9) must be honored. It is difficult to know precisely what options were available to Jephthah. Perhaps he could have redeemed his daughter with another sacrifice, in which case his actions would have been clearly reprehensible. If this was not an option, however, his foolish vow placed him in the position of offering a questionable sacrifice or breaking an oath sworn to God himself.
11:39 he did to her. Some interpreters suggest that Jephthah did not sacrifice his daughter but merely dedicated her to the Lord. Though stated delicately, it is best to understand that Jephthah sacrificed his daughter as a burnt offering. The issue was not celibacy, but sacrifice.

Jephthah and Ephraim

12 The men of Ephraim called out their forces, crossed over to Zaphon and said to
Jephthah, "Why did you go to fight the Ammonites without calling us to go with
you?[h] We're going to burn down your house over your head."
2Jephthah answered, "I and my people were engaged in a great struggle with the Ammonites, and although I called, you didn't save me out of their hands. 3When I saw that
you wouldn't help, I took my life in my hands[i] and crossed over to fight the Ammonites,
and the LORD gave me the victory over them. Now why have you come up today to
fight me?"
4Jephthah then called together the men of Gilead and fought against Ephraim. The
Gileadites struck them down because the Ephraimites had said, "You Gileadites are renegades from Ephraim and Manasseh." 5The Gileadites captured the fords of the Jordan[j]
leading to Ephraim, and whenever a survivor of Ephraim said, "Let me cross over," the
men of Gilead asked him, "Are you an Ephraimite?" If he replied, "No," 6they said, "All
right, say 'Shibboleth.' " If he said, "Sibboleth," because he could not pronounce the
word correctly, they seized him and killed him at the fords of the Jordan. Forty-two thousand Ephraimites were killed at that time.
7Jephthah led[a] Israel six years. Then Jephthah the Gileadite died, and was buried in
a town in Gilead.

Ibzan, Elon and Abdon

8After him, Ibzan of Bethlehem led Israel. 9He had thirty sons and thirty daughters.
He gave his daughters away in marriage to those outside his clan, and for his sons he
brought in thirty young women as wives from outside his clan. Ibzan led Israel seven
years. 10Then Ibzan died, and was buried in Bethlehem.
11After him, Elon the Zebulunite led Israel ten years. 12Then Elon died, and was buried in Aijalon in the land of Zebulun.
13After him, Abdon son of Hillel, from Pirathon, led Israel. 14He had forty sons and
thirty grandsons,[k] who rode on seventy donkeys.[l] He led Israel eight years. 15Then Abdon son of Hillel died, and was buried at Pirathon in Ephraim, in the hill country of the
Amalekites.[m]

The Birth of Samson

13 Again the Israelites did evil in the eyes of the LORD, so the LORD delivered them
into the hands of the Philistines[n] for forty years.
2A certain man of Zorah,[o] named Manoah, from the clan of the Danites, had a wife

12:1 [h]Jdg 8:1
12:3 [i]1Sa 19:5; 28:21; Job 13:14
12:5 [j]Jos 22:11; Jdg 3:28
12:14 [k]Jdg 10:4 [l]Jdg 5:10
12:15 [m]Jdg 5:14
13:1 [n]Jdg 2:11; 1Sa 12:9
13:2 [o]Jos 15:33; 19:41

[a] 7 Traditionally *judged*; also in verses 8–14

12:1–7 The tribe of Ephraim again fell because of its arrogance (cf. 1:29; 7:24; 8:1; 17:1,8; 18:2,13; 19:1,16,18). This fall was an indication of Jephthah's greatness as a leader. He and his Gileadite "renegades" were superior in strength to the whole tribe of Ephraim. Psalm 78 (especially vv. 9–11,67) reflects on Ephraim's failure to fight (see also 8:1–5). This psalm explains God's rejection of Ephraim as Israel's leading tribe. Judah (i.e., David; Ps 78:68–72), not Ephraim, was to lead Israel.
12:1 men of Ephraim. Like Gideon, Jephthah had his problems with Ephraim (see 8:1–5). Unlike the story of Gideon, however, civil war resulted. Unity was sorely lacking in Israel. **Why . . . ?** See 8:1 for an almost identical question put to Gideon.
12:4 from Ephraim and Manasseh. The Gileadites, who lived on the eastern side of the Jordan, were descendants of Joseph, as were Ephraim and Manasseh, who lived on the western side of the Jordan.
12:7 Jephthah led Israel six years. See note on 3:11. Previous judges had typically led for 40–80 years, and the ensuing peace generally lasted for one or two generations. The mention of Jephthah's abbreviated rule indicated the writer's largely negative assessment of his leadership.
■ **12:8–10** *Ibzan.* A minor judge about whom little is said (see note on 10:1–2).
■ **12:11–12** *Elon.* Another minor judge (see note on 10:1–2).
■ **12:13–15** *Abdon.* Another minor judge (see note on 10:1–2).
12:14 He had forty sons and thirty grandsons, who rode on seventy donkeys. Abdon wielded nearly royal power and possessed comparable wealth (see 10:4).
■ **13:1—16:31** *Samson.* Samson's story is the last in the cycles of the judges. At first he showed great promise. His birth was a miraculous gift to barren parents (13:2–25). As in the case of the great judge Gideon, the angel of the Lord appeared at Samson's calling (13:21). Unlike any other judge, he was called from the womb (13:5), and more than any other judge he experienced the Spirit coming upon him (13:25; 14:6,19; 15:14). Yet of all the judges Samson was least disciplined. Having been devoted from birth to be a Nazirite (see 13:4–5,7,14; 16:17; Nu 6:1–22), he kept only the provision of leaving his hair uncut. He repeatedly broke covenant and repudiated his vow by seeking foreign wives, sleeping with prostitutes, touching dead things and drinking wine. He showed no interest in delivering Israel. Moreover, Samson offered the Israelites no years of peace (16:31; see note on 3:11). The fanfare of his calling and the miracles surrounding his birth (compare the births of Samuel, Isaac, Jacob and Joseph) and life only heighten the tragedy of his life and showcase the depths to which Israel had descended. But God had raised up Samson to deliver Israel from Philistia (v. 5), and the Lord used even Samson's sins to conquer the Philistines (see 14:4). Despite his failures, Samson is counted among the examples of faith in Hebrews 11:32.
Samson's account divides into three main parts: an introduction (13:1), his birth (13:2–25), his career (14:1—16:31) and his death and burial (16:31).
■ **13:1** *Introduction to Samson.* The formulaic structure for the cycles of the judges is especially abbreviated in this introduction to the Samson narrative (see 2:11–19). **delivered . . . Philistines.** See 2:14 and 1 Samuel 12:9.
■ **13:2–25** *Samson's Birth.* The author signaled Samson's potential greatness by recounting one of the rare, wonderful birth stories in the Old Testament (vv. 2–24; cf. Ge 11:30; 25:21; 1Sa 1:2), prominently featuring the angel of the Lord. However, as the people slipped farther and farther into sin, the spiritual character of their judges continued to deteriorate.

who was sterile and remained childless. 3The angel of the LORD[p] appeared to her[q] and
said, "You are sterile and childless, but you are going to conceive and have a son.[r] 4Now
see to it that you drink no wine or other fermented drink and that you do not eat anything unclean,[s] 5because you will conceive and give birth to a son. No razor[t] may be used
on his head, because the boy is to be a Nazirite,[u] set apart to God from birth, and he will
begin[v] the deliverance of Israel from the hands of the Philistines."
6Then the woman went to her husband and told him, "A man of God[w] came to me.
He looked like an angel of God,[x] very awesome. I didn't ask him where he came from,
and he didn't tell me his name. 7But he said to me, 'You will conceive and give birth to
a son. Now then, drink no wine or other fermented drink and do not eat anything unclean, because the boy will be a Nazirite of God from birth until the day of his death.' "
8Then Manoah prayed to the LORD: "O Lord, I beg you, let the man of God you sent
to us come again to teach us how to bring up the boy who is to be born."
9God heard Manoah, and the angel of God came again to the woman while she was
out in the field; but her husband Manoah was not with her. 10The woman hurried to tell
her husband, "He's here! The man who appeared to me the other day!"
11Manoah got up and followed his wife. When he came to the man, he said, "Are you
the one who talked to my wife?"
"I am," he said.
12So Manoah asked him, "When your words are fulfilled, what is to be the rule for the
boy's life and work?"
13The angel of the LORD answered, "Your wife must do all that I have told her. 14She must
not eat anything that comes from the grapevine, nor drink any wine or other fermented
drink[y] nor eat anything unclean.[z] She must do everything I have commanded her."
15Manoah said to the angel of the LORD, "We would like you to stay until we prepare
a young goat[a] for you."
16The angel of the LORD replied, "Even though you detain me, I will not eat any of your
food. But if you prepare a burnt offering,[b] offer it to the LORD." (Manoah did not realize
that it was the angel of the LORD.)
17Then Manoah inquired of the angel of the LORD, "What is your name,[c] so that we
may honor you when your word comes true?"
18He replied, "Why do you ask my name?[d] It is beyond understanding.[a]" 19Then Manoah took a young goat, together with the grain offering, and sacrificed it on a rock[e] to
the LORD. And the LORD did an amazing thing while Manoah and his wife watched: 20As
the flame[f] blazed up from the altar toward heaven, the angel of the LORD ascended in the
flame. Seeing this, Manoah and his wife fell with their faces to the ground.[g] 21When the
angel of the LORD did not show himself again to Manoah and his wife, Manoah realized[h]
that it was the angel of the LORD.
22"We are doomed[i] to die!" he said to his wife. "We have seen[j] God!"
23But his wife answered, "If the LORD had meant to kill us, he would not have accepted a burnt offering and grain offering from our hands, nor shown us all these things or
now told us this."[k]
24The woman gave birth to a boy and named him Samson.[l] He grew[m] and the LORD
blessed him,[n] 25and the Spirit of the LORD began to stir[o] him while he was in Mahaneh
Dan,[p] between Zorah and Eshtaol.

a *18* Or *is wonderful*

13:3 [p]ver 6,8; Jdg 6:12 [q]ver 10 [r]Lk 1:13
13:4 [s]ver 14; Nu 6:2-4; Lk 1:15
13:5 [t]Nu 6:5; 1Sa 1:11 [u]Nu 6:2,13 [v]1Sa 7:13
13:6 [w]ver 8; 1Sa 2:27; 9:6 [x]ver 17-18; Mt 28:3
13:14 [y]Nu 6:4 [z]ver 4
13:15 [a]ver 3; Jdg 6:19
13:16 [b]Jdg 6:20
13:17 [c]Ge 32:29
13:18 [d]Isa 9:6
13:19 [e]Jdg 6:20
13:20 [f]Lev 9:24 [g]1Ch 21:16; Eze 1:28; Mt 17:6
13:21 [h]ver 16; Jdg 6:22
13:22 [i]Dt 5:26 [j]Ge 32:30; Jdg 6:22
13:23 [k]Ps 25:14
13:24 [l]Heb 11:32 [m]1Sa 3:19 [n]Lk 1:80
13:25 [o]Jdg 3:10 [p]Jdg 18:12

13:3–14 This section includes the birth announcement, the focus of which is the identity of the angel of the Lord, who announced the birth. His revelation guaranteed the validity and significance of the announcement. The story faults Manoah's wife for her lack of faith and Manoah for his spiritual blindness.

13:3 The angel of the LORD. See 2:1, 6:11–24 and note on 13:1—16:31.

13:5 Nazirite . . . from birth. According to the law (Nu 6:1–22) a Nazirite man or woman voluntarily accepted three prohibitions: abstention from grapes (i.e., wine), no cutting of the hair and no proximity to a corpse. However, God and Samson's parents consecrated Samson before his birth. Throughout his life Samson, like Israel, would struggle with his involuntary conscription. See 14:1 and 9–10; see also 16:17.

13:6–7 The woman went to her husband. Her report of the angel's wonderful appearance (v. 6) left her without excuse for failing to train her son. Probably she asked no questions because she knew she was in the presence of an angel.

13:9 angel of God came again. The second appearance of the angel in answer to Manoah's prayer also indicates that Samson's birth was certain and imminent.

13:13–14 angel of the LORD answered. The angel repeated to the man the instructions he had already given for the woman, but not those for the boy.

13:17–18 What is your name . . . Why do you ask my name? A similar exchange occurred when Jacob wrestled at Jabbok (Ge 32:29). Manoah should already have recognized by this time that he was dealing with the angel of the Lord.

13:19–22 These incidents parallel those in 6:20–22 (see also Ge 32:30).

13:23 But his wife answered. She recognized a purpose behind the theophany, but Manoah apparently never quite understood. The Lord had accepted their offering, allowed them to witness the events and announced to them the coming birth.

13:24 He grew and the LORD blessed him. The blessings of God on Samson in his early life highlight the severity of his failures later in life.

13:25 the Spirit of the LORD. The Spirit worked in Samson

Samson's Marriage

14 Samson went down to Timnah[q] and saw there a young Philistine woman.
2When he returned, he said to his father and mother, "I have seen a Philistine
woman in Timnah; now get her for me as my wife."[r]
3His father and mother replied, "Isn't there an acceptable woman among your relatives or among all our people?[s] Must you go to the uncircumcised[t] Philistines to get a
wife?[u]"
But Samson said to his father, "Get her for me. She's the right one for me." 4(His parents did not know that this was from the LORD, who was seeking an occasion to confront
the Philistines;[v] for at that time they were ruling over Israel.)[w] 5Samson went down to
Timnah together with his father and mother. As they approached the vineyards of Timnah, suddenly a young lion came roaring toward him. 6The Spirit of the LORD came upon
him in power[x] so that he tore the lion apart with his bare hands as he might have torn
a young goat. But he told neither his father nor his mother what he had done. 7Then he
went down and talked with the woman, and he liked her.
8Some time later, when he went back to marry her, he turned aside to look at the lion's carcass. In it was a swarm of bees and some honey, 9which he scooped out with his
hands and ate as he went along. When he rejoined his parents, he gave them some, and
they too ate it. But he did not tell them that he had taken the honey from the lion's carcass.
10Now his father went down to see the woman. And Samson made a feast there, as
was customary for bridegrooms. 11When he appeared, he was given thirty companions.
12"Let me tell you a riddle,[y] Samson said to them. "If you can give me the answer
within the seven days of the feast,[z] I will give you thirty linen garments and thirty sets
of clothes.[a] 13If you can't tell me the answer, you must give me thirty linen garments and
thirty sets of clothes."
"Tell us your riddle," they said. "Let's hear it."
14He replied,

> "Out of the eater, something to eat;
> out of the strong, something sweet."

For three days they could not give the answer.
15On the fourth[a] day, they said to Samson's wife, "Coax[b] your husband into explaining the riddle for us, or we will burn you and your father's household to death.[c] Did you
invite us here to rob us?"
16Then Samson's wife threw herself on him, sobbing, "You hate me! You don't really love me.[d] You've given my people a riddle, but you haven't told me the answer."
"I haven't even explained it to my father or mother," he replied, "so why should I explain it to you?" 17She cried the whole seven days[e] of the feast. So on the seventh day he

14:1 [q]Ge 38:12
14:2 [r]Ge 21:21; 34:4
14:3 [s]Ge 24:4 [t]Dt 7:3 [u]Ex 34:16
14:4 [v]Jos 11:20 [w]Jdg 13:1
14:6 [x]Jdg 3:10; 13:25
14:12 [y]1Ki 10:1; Eze 17:2 [z]Ge 29:27 [a]Ge 45:22; 2Ki 5:5
14:15 [b]Jdg 16:5; Ecc 7:26 [c]Jdg 15:6
14:16 [d]Jdg 16:15
14:17 [e]Est 1:5

[a] 15 Some Septuagint manuscripts and Syriac; Hebrew *seventh*

---

even before his public career. See 3:10, 14:6,19, 15:14 and note on 13:1—16:31.

■ **14:1—16:31** *Samson's Career.* Samson's work divides into two parallel narratives (14:1—15:20; 16:1–31). Both began with dissolute entanglements with Philistine women that led to unwelcome involvements with Philistine men, leading to their deaths (14:1,19 [cf. 15:1,8]; 16:1,4,30). In addition, the two narratives incorporated numerous other parallel elements: Both included a prank involving a display of strength (14:5–6; 16:3); taunting for the answer to a secret/riddle (14:15; 16:5); a challenge from Philistine leaders accompanied by a threat for noncompliance and the promise for submission (14:15 [cf. 15:6]; 16:5,18); manipulation by a wife/woman (14:16; 16:15); pressure from a woman resulting in a turning point in the action (14:17; 16:16–17); the handing over of Samson to a third party (15:13; 16:19); binding of the strong man (15:14–15; 16:20); the motivation of revenge (15:3 for wife; 16:28 for eyes); a prayer for life/death (15:18; 16:28); and the concluding stereotypical frame (15:20; 16:31).

■ **14:1—15:20** *A Wife and Trouble with the Philistines.* This narrative revolves around the pursuit and loss of Samson's Philistine wife and the consequences for Samson and Philistia. In the course of these events, Samson broke aspects of his Nazirite vow by touching something dead (vv. 8–9) and by drinking wine (v. 10). All that remained was for him to shave his hair. Three times the Spirit of the Lord came upon him, and he killed numerous Philistines. Samson led Israel for 20 years (15:20). Normally this would be the end of the narrative. But Samson was relentless in his pursuit of foreign women, and the story concludes with the tale of his demise as a result of this lust (ch. 16).

14:2 I have seen a Philistine woman . . . get her for me as my wife. Israelite men, and Nazirites in particular, were not to marry foreign wives (see 3:1–6; 14:3; Dt 7:3–4; 1Ki. 11:1–6; Ezr 9–10).

14:4 this was from the LORD. While Samson's desire was sinful, God sovereignly used it for his own purposes to bring judgment on the Philistines. Although God's providence incorporates evil and moral ambiguities, it does not justify wrongdoing.

14:6 The Spirit of the LORD. See notes on 3:10, 13:1—16:31 and 13:25. **he told.** Samson's "telling" is a key motif in this scene, reflecting his gradual rejection of his parents and identification with Philistines: "he said to his father and mother" (v. 2); "he told neither his father nor his mother" (v. 6); "he did not tell them" (v. 9); "I haven't even explained it to my father or mother . . . so why should I explain it to you?" (v. 16).

14:8 the lion's carcass. Part of the Nazirite vow included avoiding close proximity to a dead body (Nu 6:6). Samson actually touched the carcass, which should have required him to shave his head and break his vow. Instead he chose not to tell his parents. On the surface the audience is led to believe that this happened for the sake of his riddle, but the irony is that his silence actually hid the violation of his vow.

14:10 made a feast. The Hebrew word entails drinking wine, whereas a Nazirite was to abstain from fermented drink (see notes on 13:1—16:31; 13:2–25).

finally told her, because she continued to press him. She in turn explained the riddle to her people.

18 Before sunset on the seventh day the men of the town said to him,

> "What is sweeter than honey?
> What is stronger than a lion?"[f]

Samson said to them,

> "If you had not plowed with my heifer,
> you would not have solved my riddle."

19 Then the Spirit of the LORD came upon him in power.[g] He went down to Ashkelon, struck down thirty of their men, stripped them of their belongings and gave their clothes to those who had explained the riddle. Burning with anger,[h] he went up to his father's house. 20 And Samson's wife was given to the friend[i] who had attended him at his wedding.

14:18 [f]ver 14
14:19 [g]Nu 11:25; Jdg 3:10; 6:34; 11:29; 13:25; 15:14; 1Sa 11:6; 16:13; 1Ki 18:46; 2Ch 24:20; Isa 11:2 [h]1Sa 11:6
14:20 [i]Jdg 15:2,6; Jn 3:29

Samson's Vengeance on the Philistines

15 Later on, at the time of wheat harvest, Samson took a young goat[j] and went to visit his wife. He said, "I'm going to my wife's room." But her father would not let him go in.

2 "I was so sure you thoroughly hated her," he said, "that I gave her to your friend.[k] Isn't her younger sister more attractive? Take her instead."

3 Samson said to them, "This time I have a right to get even with the Philistines; I will really harm them." 4 So he went out and caught three hundred foxes and tied them tail to tail in pairs. He then fastened a torch to every pair of tails, 5 lit the torches and let the foxes loose in the standing grain of the Philistines. He burned up the shocks and standing grain, together with the vineyards and olive groves.

6 When the Philistines asked, "Who did this?" they were told, "Samson, the Timnite's son-in-law, because his wife was given to his friend."

So the Philistines went up and burned her and her father to death.[l] 7 Samson said to them, "Since you've acted like this, I won't stop until I get my revenge on you." 8 He attacked them viciously and slaughtered many of them. Then he went down and stayed in a cave in the rock of Etam.

9 The Philistines went up and camped in Judah, spreading out near Lehi.[m] 10 The men of Judah asked, "Why have you come to fight us?"

"We have come to take Samson prisoner," they answered, "to do to him as he did to us."

11 Then three thousand men from Judah went down to the cave in the rock of Etam and said to Samson, "Don't you realize that the Philistines are rulers over us?[n] What have you done to us?"

He answered, "I merely did to them what they did to me."

12 They said to him, "We've come to tie you up and hand you over to the Philistines."

Samson said, "Swear to me that you won't kill me yourselves."

13 "Agreed," they answered. "We will only tie you up and hand you over to them. We will not kill you." So they bound him with two new ropes and led him up from the rock. 14 As he approached Lehi, the Philistines came toward him shouting. The Spirit of the LORD came upon him in power.[o] The ropes on his arms became like charred flax, and the bindings dropped from his hands. 15 Finding a fresh jawbone of a donkey, he grabbed it and struck down a thousand men.[p]

16 Then Samson said,

> "With a donkey's jawbone
> I have made donkeys of them.[a]

15:1 [j]Ge 38:17
15:2 [k]Jdg 14:20
15:6 [l]Jdg 14:15
15:9 [m]ver 14,17,19
15:11 [n]Jdg 13:1; 14:4; Ps 106:40-42
15:14 [o]Jdg 3:10; 14:19; 1Sa 11:6
15:15 [p]Lev 26:8; Jos 23:10; Jdg 3:31

[a] 16 Or *made a heap or two*; the Hebrew for *donkey* sounds like the Hebrew for *heap.*

14:18 my heifer. A metaphor for his wife (see v. 15).
14:19 the Spirit of the LORD. See 3:11, 14:6, 15:14 and note on 13:1—16:31.
14:20 was given to the friend. This was not a custom but an attempt by an embarrassed father to save face (15:1–2). Even the Philistines continued to refer to Samson as the "Timnite's son-in-law" (15:6).
15:1 at the time of wheat harvest. A dry time when fields burned easily (see vv. 4–5). **his wife.** Legally she was Samson's wife.
15:2 I gave her to your friend. See 14:20.
15:3 harm. Literally, "do evil to." In chapter 15 "doing" for personal revenge, not for the saving of Israel, is a key motif (vv. 3,6–7,10–11).
15:5 grain. Dagon, the Philistine god, was a grain deity.
15:6 Samson, the Timnite's son-in-law. See 14:20.
15:11 Philistines are rulers over us? The Judahites, who were supposed to lead Israel (1:2; 20:18), had accepted their subjugation. They were merely agents in this narrative.
15:13 bound him with two new ropes. See 16:11–12.
15:14 The Spirit of the LORD. See notes on 3:10, 13:1—16:31 and 13:25. See also 14:6 and 19.
15:15 a fresh jawbone . . . a thousand men. Note the parallel with Shamgar, son of Anath (3:31).

With a donkey's jawbone
I have killed a thousand men."

17When he finished speaking, he threw away the jawbone; and the place was called Ramath Lehi.[a]
18Because he was very thirsty, he cried out to the LORD,[q] "You have given your servant this great victory. Must I now die of thirst and fall into the hands of the uncircumcised?" 19Then God opened up the hollow place in Lehi, and water came out of it. When
Samson drank, his strength returned and he revived.[r] So the spring was called En Hakkore,[b] and it is still there in Lehi.
20Samson led[c] Israel for twenty years[s] in the days of the Philistines.

Samson and Delilah

16 One day Samson went to Gaza, where he saw a prostitute. He went in to spend
the night with her. 2The people of Gaza were told, "Samson is here!" So they surrounded the place and lay in wait for him all night at the city gate.[t] They made no move
during the night, saying, "At dawn we'll kill him."
3But Samson lay there only until the middle of the night. Then he got up and took
hold of the doors of the city gate, together with the two posts, and tore them loose, bar
and all. He lifted them to his shoulders and carried them to the top of the hill that faces
Hebron.[u]
4Some time later, he fell in love[v] with a woman in the Valley of Sorek whose name
was Delilah. 5The rulers of the Philistines[w] went to her and said, "See if you can lure[x]
him into showing you the secret of his great strength and how we can overpower him so
we may tie him up and subdue him. Each one of us will give you eleven hundred shekels[d] of silver."[y]
6So Delilah said to Samson, "Tell me the secret of your great strength and how you
can be tied up and subdued."
7Samson answered her, "If anyone ties me with seven fresh thongs[e] that have not
been dried, I'll become as weak as any other man."
8Then the rulers of the Philistines brought her seven fresh thongs that had not been
dried, and she tied him with them. 9With men hidden in the room,[z] she called to him,
"Samson, the Philistines are upon you!" But he snapped the thongs as easily as a piece
of string snaps when it comes close to a flame. So the secret of his strength was not discovered.
10Then Delilah said to Samson, "You have made a fool of me;[a] you lied to me. Come
now, tell me how you can be tied."
11He said, "If anyone ties me securely with new ropes[b] that have never been used, I'll
become as weak as any other man."
12So Delilah took new ropes and tied him with them. Then, with men hidden in the
room, she called to him, "Samson, the Philistines are upon you!" But he snapped the
ropes off his arms as if they were threads.
13Delilah then said to Samson, "Until now, you have been making a fool of me and
lying to me. Tell me how you can be tied."
He replied, "If you weave the seven braids of my head into the fabric ⌞on the loom⌟
and tighten it with the pin, I'll become as weak as any other man." So while he was sleep-

15:18 [q]Jdg 16:28
15:19 [r]Ge 45:27; Isa 40:29
15:20 [s]Jdg 13:1; 16:31; Heb 11:32
16:2 [t]1Sa 23:26; Ps 118:10-12; Ac 9:24
16:3 [u]Jos 10:36
16:4 [v]Ge 24:67
16:5 [w]Jos 13:3 [x]Ex 10:7; Jdg 14:15 [y]ver 18
16:9 [z]ver 12
16:10 [a]ver 13
16:11 [b]Jdg 15:13

[a] 17 *Ramath Lehi* means *jawbone hill.* [b] 19 *En Hakkore* means *caller's spring.* [c] 20 Traditionally *judged*
[d] 5 That is, about 28 pounds (about 13 kilograms) [e] 7 Or *bowstrings;* also in verses 8 and 9

15:18 he cried out. Samson is said to have spoken to the Lord only twice: once to spare his life and once for the strength to take it (see 16:28). **Must I now die of thirst . . . ?** Like the Israelites who had experienced miracle upon miracle in the wilderness, Samson complained to God after seeing God do great things in his life. The parallel is further strengthened by the cry for water and the miraculous manner in which God supplied it (Ex 17:1–7; Nu 20:1–13). With Israel and with Samson, God in his mercy and compassion met the need (10:10–16).
15:19 Lehi. See verses 16–17. In both episodes at Lehi Samson was being handed over to Philistines; in both instances the Lord saved him, and each episode at Lehi ends with an identification of a place name.
15:20 for twenty years. Ordinarily a statement of this nature would signal the end of a judge's story (see note on 14:1—15:20). Like Jephthah, Samson did not lead Israel for long.
■ **16:1–30** *Delilah and Trouble with the Philistines.* This account shows Samson's continuing sinful attraction to women, his prodigious strength and the efforts by which the Philistines captured him. In the preceding account Samson outwitted the Philistines, but not so here. God judged Samson's continual covenant breaking; he was captured by the Philistines and his eyes gouged out (vv. 23–31). Delilah's repeated and obvious attempts to snare Samson portray him as a fool. The Spirit of God left Samson after his hair had been cut, having remained with him through all of the earlier instances of his covenant breaking. God was patient with Samson until the last stipulation of his vow had been broken; then God moved decisively to judge him.
16:1 a prostitute. Samson once again broke covenant (see 14:2).
16:4 fell in love. This is the first time Samson is reported to have loved a woman.
16:5 give you eleven hundred shekels. The story derides Delilah's character; her loyalties were for sale.
16:11 new ropes. See 15:13.
16:13 seven braids. Since Samson had never had a haircut, his hair was luxuriant.

ing, Delilah took the seven braids of his head, wove them into the fabric **14**and[a] tightened
it with the pin.
Again she called to him, "Samson, the Philistines are upon you!"[c] He awoke from his
sleep and pulled up the pin and the loom, with the fabric.
15Then she said to him, "How can you say, 'I love you,'[d] when you won't confide in
me? This is the third time[e] you have made a fool of me and haven't told me the secret of
your great strength."[f] **16**With such nagging she prodded him day after day until he was
tired to death.
17So he told her everything.[g] "No razor has ever been used on my head," he said, "because I have been a Nazirite[h] set apart to God since birth. If my head were shaved, my
strength would leave me, and I would become as weak as any other man."
18When Delilah saw that he had told her everything, she sent word to the rulers of the
Philistines[i], "Come back once more; he has told me everything." So the rulers of the Philistines returned with the silver in their hands. **19**Having put him to sleep on her lap, she
called a man to shave off the seven braids of his hair, and so began to subdue him.[b] And
his strength left him.[j]
20Then she called, "Samson, the Philistines are upon you!"
He awoke from his sleep and thought, "I'll go out as before and shake myself free."
But he did not know that the LORD had left him.[k]
21Then the Philistines[l] seized him, gouged out his eyes[m] and took him down to
Gaza. Binding him with bronze shackles, they set him to grinding[n] in the prison. **22**But
the hair on his head began to grow again after it had been shaved.

The Death of Samson

23Now the rulers of the Philistines assembled to offer a great sacrifice to Dagon[o] their
god and to celebrate, saying, "Our god has delivered Samson, our enemy, into our hands."
24When the people saw him, they praised their god,[p] saying,

"Our god has delivered our enemy
into our hands,[q]
the one who laid waste our land
and multiplied our slain."

25While they were in high spirits,[r] they shouted, "Bring out Samson to entertain us."
So they called Samson out of the prison, and he performed for them.
When they stood him among the pillars, **26**Samson said to the servant who held his
hand, "Put me where I can feel the pillars that support the temple, so that I may lean
against them." **27**Now the temple was crowded with men and women; all the rulers of the
Philistines were there, and on the roof[s] were about three thousand men and women
watching Samson perform. **28**Then Samson prayed to the LORD,[t] "O Sovereign LORD, remember me. O God, please strengthen me just once more, and let me with one blow get
revenge[u] on the Philistines for my two eyes." **29**Then Samson reached toward the two
central pillars on which the temple stood. Bracing himself against them, his right hand
on the one and his left hand on the other, **30**Samson said, "Let me die with the Philistines!" Then he pushed with all his might, and down came the temple on the rulers and
all the people in it. Thus he killed many more when he died than while he lived.
31Then his brothers and his father's whole family went down to get him. They brought
him back and buried him between Zorah and Eshtaol in the tomb of Manoah[v] his father.
He had led[c][w] Israel twenty years.[x]

16:14 [c]ver 9,20
16:15 [d]Jdg 14:16 [e]Nu 24:10 [f]ver 5
16:17 [g]Mic 7:5 [h]Nu 6:2, 5; Jdg 13:5
16:18 [i]Jos 13:3; 1Sa 5:8
16:19 [j]Pr 7:26-27
16:20 [k]Nu 14:42; Jos 7:12; 1Sa 16:14; 18:12; 28:15
16:21 [l]Jer 47:1 [m]Nu 16:14 [n]Job 31:10; Isa 47:2
16:23 [o]1Sa 5:2; 1Ch 10:10
16:24 [p]Da 5:4 [q]1Sa 31:9; 1Ch 10:9
16:25 [r]Jdg 9:27; Ru 3:7; Est 1:10
16:27 [s]Dt 22:8; Jos 2:8
16:28 [t]Jdg 15:18 [u]Jer 15:15
16:31 [v]Jdg 13:2 [w]Ru 1:1; 1Sa 4:18 [x]Jdg 15:20

[a] *13,14* Some Septuagint manuscripts; Hebrew "*˻I can˼ if you weave the seven braids of my head into the fabric ˻on the loom˼." 14So she* [b] *19* Hebrew; some Septuagint manuscripts *and he began to weaken* [c] *31* Traditionally *judged*

16:15 How can you say . . . ? See 14:16–17.
16:17 since birth. See 13:5. **If my head were shaved.** Samson had habitually ignored the other aspects of his vow (see note on 13:1—16:31). His true strength was the Spirit of the Lord (v. 20).
16:20 the LORD had left him. That is, the Spirit of the Lord had departed from him (see 13:25; 14:6,19; 15:14). The Lord had graciously remained with Samson until the final sign of his vow was gone (see note on vv. 1–21). Like Saul (cf. v. 14 with 1Sa 15:23), Samson had lost the Spirit of the Lord because of his disobedience. God, not magic associated with long hair, had all along been the source of his power.
16:21 grinding. The Philistines shamed Samson because in the ancient world grinding grain was the labor of slaves and women.
16:23 Our god has delivered. Throughout Judges God was the Judge who delivered his people over to oppressors on account of their sins (v. 20). It was never the power of the gods of the nations that enabled them to overcome Israel (see 2:14–15).
16:28 O God . . . for my two eyes. See 15:18. Although Samson had selfish motives (i.e., revenge for the loss of his eyes), God heard his cry of faith. The grace of God was apparent in his acceptance of Samson's prayer (see 10:10–16; 15:18).
16:30 he killed many more when he died than while he lived. Despite Samson's many failures, he accomplished a great feat by killing so many enemies of Israel. See note on 13:1—16:31.
■**16:31** *Death and Burial.* Samson died after having served as judge for 20 years.
16:31 He had led Israel twenty years. See note on 15:20.

Micah's Idols

17 Now a man named Micah[y] from the hill country of Ephraim 2 said to his mother, "The eleven hundred shekels[a] of silver that were taken from you and about
which I heard you utter a curse—I have that silver with me; I took it."
Then his mother said, "The LORD bless you,[z] my son!"
3 When he returned the eleven hundred shekels of silver to his mother, she said, "I solemnly consecrate my silver to the LORD for my son to make a carved image and a cast
idol.[a] I will give it back to you."
4 So he returned the silver to his mother, and she took two hundred shekels[b] of silver
and gave them to a silversmith, who made them into the image and the idol.[b] And they
were put in Micah's house.
5 Now this man Micah had a shrine,[c] and he made an ephod[d] and some idols[e] and installed[f] one of his sons as his priest.[g] 6 In those days Israel had no king;[h] everyone did
as he saw fit.[i]
7 A young Levite from Bethlehem in Judah,[j] who had been living within the clan of Judah, 8 left that town in search of some other place to stay. On his way[c] he came to Micah's
house in the hill country of Ephraim.
9 Micah asked him, "Where are you from?"
"I'm a Levite from Bethlehem in Judah," he said, "and I'm looking for a place to stay."
10 Then Micah said to him, "Live with me and be my father and priest,[k] and I'll give
you ten shekels[d] of silver a year, your clothes and your food." 11 So the Levite agreed to
live with him, and the young man was to him like one of his sons. 12 Then Micah installed[l]
the Levite, and the young man became his priest and lived in his house. 13 And Micah
said, "Now I know that the LORD will be good to me, since this Levite has become my
priest."

Danites Settle in Laish

18 In those days Israel had no king.[m]
And in those days the tribe of the Danites was seeking a place of their own
where they might settle, because they had not yet come into an inheritance among the
tribes of Israel.[n] 2 So the Danites[o] sent five warriors from Zorah and Eshtaol to spy out
the land and explore it. These men represented all their clans. They told them, "Go, explore the land."[p]
The men entered the hill country of Ephraim and came to the house of Micah,[q] where
they spent the night. 3 When they were near Micah's house, they recognized the voice of
the young Levite; so they turned in there and asked him, "Who brought you here? What
are you doing in this place? Why are you here?"
4 He told them what Micah had done for him, and said, "He has hired me and I am his
priest.[r]"

17:1 [y]Jdg 18:2,13
17:2 [z]Ru 2:20; 1Sa 15:13; 2Sa 2:5
17:3 [a]Ex 20:4,23; 34:17; Lev 19:4
17:4 [b]Ex 32:4; Isa 17:8
17:5 [c]Isa 44:13; Eze 8:10 [d]Jdg 8:27 [e]Ge 31:19; Jdg 18:14 [f]Nu 16:10 [g]Ex 29:9; Jdg 18:24
17:6 [h]Jdg 18:1; 19:1; 21:25 [i]Dt 12:8
17:7 [j]Jdg 19:1; Ru 1:1-2; Mic 5:2; Mt 2:1
17:10 [k]Jdg 18:19
17:12 [l]Nu 16:10
18:1 [m]Jdg 17:6; 19:1 [n]Jos 19:47
18:2 [o]Jdg 13:25 [p]Jos 2:1 [q]Jdg 17:1
18:4 [r]Jdg 17:12

[a] *2* That is, about 28 pounds (about 13 kilograms) [b] *4* That is, about 5 pounds (about 2.3 kilograms)
[c] *8* Or *To carry on his profession* [d] *10* That is, about 4 ounces (about 110 grams)

▪ **17:1—21:25** *The Failures of the Levites.* Having demonstrated that the judges were unable to provide adequate leadership for Israel, the author turned to events showing that the Levites had also failed to lead Israel properly. The repeated phrase "In those days Israel had no king; everyone did as he saw fit" (17:6) joins this section to the last section of the narrative cycles (19:1—21:25). This statement describes the depth to which the people had sunk without a king. These chapters divide into two lengthy accounts which have as their common element a prominent role for a Levite: a Levite and idolatry (17:1—18:31) and a Levite and violence in Israel (19:1—21:25).

▪ **17:1—18:31** *A Levite and Idolatry in Israel.* The first account focuses on a Levite's involvement in idolatry as a reason for not entrusting the leadership of God's people to the Levites. This story divides into two large episodes: the accounts of Micah and the Levite (17:1–13) and the Danites and the Levite (18:1–31).

▪ **17:1–31** *Micah and the Levite.* An Ephraimite named Micah hired a Levite to begin his own form of false worship.

17:2 eleven hundred shekels of silver. The amount each Philistine ruler had given to Delilah (16:5).

17:3 consecrate . . . to the LORD . . . to make a carved image and a cast idol. A highly ironic statement. However well intentioned, consecrating this silver violated the second commandment (see note on 17:1—18:31; Dt 5:8).

17:5 an ephod. See note on 8:27.

17:6 In those days Israel had no king; everyone did as he saw fit. See 18:1, 19:1 and 21:25. The repeated refrain functions here as a comment on the actions of Micah and his mother (consecrating silver to make idols, making an ephod and installing Micah's son as priest). Micah was doing what he pleased in the absence of a covenant-keeping authority to challenge him to turn from his sin.

17:7 Levite. The Levites' inheritance was to serve the Lord at his dwelling place, the tabernacle.

17:10 be my father. That is, in a religious sense.

17:11 like one of his sons. The cozy atmosphere belied the grave apostasy and idolatry going on. A Levite had abandoned the Lord to minister before idols.

17:13 good to me. This statement is highly ironic (see note on 17:1—18:31).

▪ **18:1–31** *The Danites and the Levite.* Men from the tribe of Dan took Micah's Levite and established false worship in their new northern territory.

18:1 In those days Israel had no king. See note on 17:6. **in those days the tribe of the Danites.** The similarity in language between the first sentence in the verse and 17:6 subtly indicates from the outset that the Danites were doing "as [they] saw fit" (17:6). **they had not yet come into an inheritance.** Their failure was a covenant violation (see 1:34–36). The Danites would go anywhere else rather than where God had given them land to inherit.

18:2 to spy out the land. They were imitating their forefathers (see note on vv. 1–31).

18:3 they recognized the voice. The accent of the young man from the south of Israel was distinctive (see note on 12:6).

18:5 [s]1Ki 22:5
18:6 [t]1Ki 22:6
18:7 [u]Jos 19:47 [v]ver 28
18:9 [w]Nu 13:30; 1Ki 22:3
18:10 [x]ver 7,27; Dt 8:9 [y]1Ch 4:40
18:11 [z]ver 16,17 [a]Jdg 13:2
18:12 [b]Jdg 13:25
18:14 [c]Ge 31:19; Jdg 17:5
18:16 [d]ver 11
18:17 [e]Ge 31:19; Mic 5:13
18:18 [f]Isa 46:2; Jer 43:11; Hos 10:5
18:19 [g]Job 21:5; 29:9; 40:4; Mic 7:16 [h]Jdg 17:10
18:26 [i]Ps 18:17; 35:10
18:27 [j]ver 7,10

5Then they said to him, "Please inquire of God[s] to learn whether our journey will be successful."

6The priest answered them, "Go in peace[t]. Your journey has the LORD's approval."

7So the five men left and came to Laish,[u] where they saw that the people were living in safety, like the Sidonians, unsuspecting and secure. And since their land lacked nothing, they were prosperous.[a] Also, they lived a long way from the Sidonians[v] and had no relationship with anyone else.[b]

8When they returned to Zorah and Eshtaol, their brothers asked them, "How did you find things?"

9They answered, "Come on, let's attack them! We have seen that the land is very good. Aren't you going to do something? Don't hesitate to go there and take it over.[w] **10**When you get there, you will find an unsuspecting people and a spacious land that God has put into your hands, a land that lacks nothing[x] whatever.[y]"

11Then six hundred men[z] from the clan of the Danites,[a] armed for battle, set out from Zorah and Eshtaol. **12**On their way they set up camp near Kiriath Jearim in Judah. This is why the place west of Kiriath Jearim is called Mahaneh Dan[c][b] to this day. **13**From there they went on to the hill country of Ephraim and came to Micah's house.

14Then the five men who had spied out the land of Laish said to their brothers, "Do you know that one of these houses has an ephod, other household gods, a carved image and a cast idol?[c] Now you know what to do." **15**So they turned in there and went to the house of the young Levite at Micah's place and greeted him. **16**The six hundred Danites,[d] armed for battle, stood at the entrance to the gate. **17**The five men who had spied out the land went inside and took the carved image, the ephod, the other household gods[e] and the cast idol while the priest and the six hundred armed men stood at the entrance to the gate.

18When these men went into Micah's house and took[f] the carved image, the ephod, the other household gods and the cast idol, the priest said to them, "What are you doing?"

19They answered him, "Be quiet![g] Don't say a word. Come with us, and be our father and priest.[h] Isn't it better that you serve a tribe and clan in Israel as priest rather than just one man's household?" **20**Then the priest was glad. He took the ephod, the other household gods and the carved image and went along with the people. **21**Putting their little children, their livestock and their possessions in front of them, they turned away and left.

22When they had gone some distance from Micah's house, the men who lived near Micah were called together and overtook the Danites. **23**As they shouted after them, the Danites turned and said to Micah, "What's the matter with you that you called out your men to fight?"

24He replied, "You took the gods I made, and my priest, and went away. What else do I have? How can you ask, 'What's the matter with you?' "

25The Danites answered, "Don't argue with us, or some hot-tempered men will attack you, and you and your family will lose your lives." **26**So the Danites went their way, and Micah, seeing that they were too strong for him,[i] turned around and went back home.

27Then they took what Micah had made, and his priest, and went on to Laish, against a peaceful and unsuspecting people.[j] They attacked them with the sword and burned

[a] 7 The meaning of the Hebrew for this clause is uncertain. [b] 7 Hebrew; some Septuagint manuscripts *with the Arameans* [c] 12 *Mahaneh Dan* means *Dan's camp.*

18:5 inquire of God. Priests used an ephod to seek the will of the Lord (see 8:27; 17:5).

18:6 Your journey has the LORD's approval. The highly ironic nature of this story—the Levite ministering to idols, Micah's erroneous assumption (see 17:13) and the subsequent behavior of the Danites—suggests that the Lord had not approved at all.

18:7 unsuspecting and secure. Their peaceful, defenseless nature is emphasized by verbal repetitions (vv. 10, 27–28; Dt 20:10–11). The battle would be easy because the people were unsuspecting (vv. 7,10) and not warlike.

18:14 an ephod, other household gods, a carved image and a cast idol? This list is repeated (see 17:5) for emphasis in its entirety three more times in the next six verses (vv. 17–18,20) and is referred to generally two more times (vv. 27,30–31).

18:16 six hundred Danites, armed for battle, stood at the entrance. Once again the Danites parodied covenant obedience in their conquest. They went in the strength of their overwhelming numbers against a single household, rather than in the strength of the Lord. The presence of the armed men is made more prominent by the repeated mention of their proximity (v. 17).

18:19 be our father and priest. See note on 17:10.

18:20 Then the priest was glad. First he served idols. Now he was happy for advancement. Everyone was doing what was right in his own eyes. No covenant-keeping authority was encouraging people to faith and obedience. **He took the ephod . . . carved image.** See verse 14. The priest did not flee from idolatry but would lead Dan in false worship.

18:21 in front of them. That is, to protect the defenseless from the attack that might be mounted against them from behind.

18:24 How can you ask, "What's the matter with you?" Micah was a pathetic figure who believed that God would bless obedience in any way that he chose to offer it (see 17:13). God was not with him or with the Danites in their battle.

18:27 they took what Micah had made. See verse 14. **against a peaceful and unsuspecting people.** See verse 7. The Israelites were to destroy only the seven proscribed Canaanite nations (see Dt 7:1), but to other peoples they were first to offer peace (see Dt 20:10–18). Dan failed to inquire about who these people were (see Jos 9:1–27) and may have destroyed an uncensured people without first offering them peace. Moreover, God had not allotted the

down their city.[k] 28There was no one to rescue them because they lived a long way from
Sidon[l] and had no relationship with anyone else. The city was in a valley near Beth Rehob.[m]
The Danites rebuilt the city and settled there. 29They named it Dan[n] after their forefather Dan, who was born to Israel—though the city used to be called Laish.[o] 30There the
Danites set up for themselves the idols, and Jonathan son of Gershom,[p] the son of Moses,[a] and his sons were priests for the tribe of Dan until the time of the captivity of the
land. 31They continued to use the idols Micah had made, all the time the house of God[q]
was in Shiloh.[r]

A Levite and His Concubine

19 In those days Israel had no king.
Now a Levite who lived in a remote area in the hill country of Ephraim[s] took a
concubine from Bethlehem in Judah.[t] 2But she was unfaithful to him. She left him and
went back to her father's house in Bethlehem, Judah. After she had been there four
months, 3her husband went to her to persuade her to return. He had with him his servant and two donkeys. She took him into her father's house, and when her father saw
him, he gladly welcomed him. 4His father-in-law, the girl's father, prevailed upon him
to stay; so he remained with him three days, eating and drinking,[u] and sleeping there.
5On the fourth day they got up early and he prepared to leave, but the girl's father said
to his son-in-law, "Refresh yourself[v] with something to eat; then you can go." 6So the two
of them sat down to eat and drink together. Afterward the girl's father said, "Please stay
tonight and enjoy yourself.[w]" 7And when the man got up to go, his father-in-law persuaded him, so he stayed there that night. 8On the morning of the fifth day, when he rose to
go, the girl's father said, "Refresh yourself. Wait till afternoon!" So the two of them ate
together.
9Then when the man, with his concubine and his servant, got up to leave, his father-
in-law, the girl's father, said, "Now look, it's almost evening. Spend the night here; the
day is nearly over. Stay and enjoy yourself. Early tomorrow morning you can get up and
be on your way home." 10But, unwilling to stay another night, the man left and went toward Jebus[x] (that is, Jerusalem), with his two saddled donkeys and his concubine.
11When they were near Jebus and the day was almost gone, the servant said to his
master, "Come, let's stop at this city of the Jebusites[y] and spend the night."
12His master replied, "No. We won't go into an alien city, whose people are not Israelites. We will go on to Gibeah." 13He added, "Come, let's try to reach Gibeah or Ramah[z]
and spend the night in one of those places." 14So they went on, and the sun set as they

18:27 [k]Ge 49:17; Jos 19:47
18:28 [l]ver 7 [m]Nu 13:21; 2Sa 10:6
18:29 [n]Ge 14:14 [o]Jos 19:47; 1Ki 15:20
18:30 [p]Ex 2:22; Jdg 17:3, 5
18:31 [q]Jdg 19:18 [r]Jos 18:1; Jer 7:14
19:1 [s]Jdg 18:1 [t]Ru 1:1
19:4 [u]Ex 32:6
19:5 [v]ver 8; Ge 18:5
19:6 [w]ver 9, 22; Jdg 16:25
19:10 [x]Ge 10:16; Jos 15:8; 1Ch 11:4-5
19:11 [y]Jos 3:10
19:13 [z]Jos 18:25

[a] *30* An ancient Hebrew scribal tradition, some Septuagint manuscripts and Vulgate; Masoretic Text *Manasseh*

Danites this land (see Jos 19:47). Dan parodied covenant "obedience" in this conquest (see note on vv. 1–31).

18:30 set up for themselves the idols. Another expression for "everyone did as he saw fit" (17:6) in the absence of a covenant-keeping king (see v. 14; 17:6). **Jonathan son of Gershom, the son of Moses.** The situation had deteriorated so badly that even the direct descendants of Moses were involved in idolatry. **until the time of the captivity of the land.** In the light of verse 31, this expression probably refers to the incident of the Philistines capturing the ark and ruling Israel, not to the later defeat of the northern kingdom by the Assyrians (see Introduction: "Time and Place of Writing").

18:31 They continued to use the idols. Even though Israel had a central place to worship at the time at Shiloh, the Danites persisted in their wicked ways. **house of God.** That is, the tabernacle, which was at Shiloh up to the time of Samuel. **Shiloh.** The period of time that the ark was in Shiloh preceded David's reign. The ark was taken by Eli's sons from Shiloh into battle and was lost to the Philistines (1Sa 4:4–11). After that time it was never again in Shiloh.

■ **19:1—21:25** *A Levite and Violence in Israel.* The situation in Israel had declined so badly that there were those among God's people who behaved similarly to the earlier inhabitants of the doomed Sodom and Gomorrah. Civil war among the tribes resulted. This final, sordid story in Judges clearly blames the covenant failures of Israel on the lack of a covenant keeping king (17:6; 18:1; 19:1; 21:25). In this particular narrative, Benjamin was the tribe that sinned. More particularly, the men of Saul's hometown (Gibeah) behaved as the people of Sodom had. Highlighting the Levite's action of cutting his concubine into 12 pieces in order to summon Israel (clearly a parallel to Saul's action in 1Sa 11:6–8) reflected negatively on both Benjamin and Saul. Ultimately Judah, the tribe of David, was the Lord's choice to lead against the Benjamites (cf. 1:1–2 and 20:18), who were virtually viewed as Canaanites.

These chapters divide into three parts: violence by the men of Gibeah (19:1–30), violence against the men of Gibeah (20:1–48) and violence against Jabesh Gilead (21:1–25).

■ **19:1–30** *The Violence by the Men of Gibeah.* The first portion of this last section of the book begins a process of repeated violence that began with an event involving a Levite and his concubine in the territory of Benjamin.

19:1 In those days Israel had no king. See 17:6. **Levite.** From the tribe that served the Lord as his priests. **concubine.** Concubines were recognized companions but enjoyed fewer legal rights than wives (see 8:31 and 9:18).

19:2 she was unfaithful to him. The law demanded the stoning of adulterers (Dt 22:22). Yet, once again, "everyone did as he saw fit" (17:6; 21:25).

19:3–10 The repeated focus on the father-in-law's hospitality underscores the nature of hospitality in the ancient Near East and contrasts strongly with the failure of the Benjamites in Gibeah to provide hospitality in the narrative that follows (see notes on 6:19; 13:15).

19:10 Jebus (that is, Jerusalem). See 1:21.

19:12 We won't go into an alien city. Ironically, the two declined to lodge with the foreign Jebusites but were then treated with a wickedness comparable to that of Sodom and Gomorrah by their fellow Israelites in Gibeah (see note on 19:1—21:25). **Gibeah.** When the book of Judges was written, Gibeah would have been known as Saul's hometown (see note on 19:1—21:25).

19:14—20:48 The account of what happened to the Levite in Gibeah of Benjamin is reminiscent of the story of Sodom and Gomor-

neared Gibeah in Benjamin.[a] 15 There they stopped to spend the night. They went and
sat in the city square,[b] but no one took them into his home for the night.
16 That evening[c] an old man from the hill country of Ephraim,[d] who was living in Gibeah (the men of the place were Benjamites), came in from his work in the fields. 17 When
he looked and saw the traveler in the city square, the old man asked, "Where are you going? Where did you come from?"[e]
18 He answered, "We are on our way from Bethlehem in Judah to a remote area in the
hill country of Ephraim where I live. I have been to Bethlehem in Judah and now I am
going to the house of the LORD.[f] No one has taken me into his house. 19 We have both
straw and fodder[g] for our donkeys and bread and wine[h] for ourselves your servants—
me, your maidservant, and the young man with us. We don't need anything."
20 "You are welcome at my house," the old man said. "Let me supply whatever you
need. Only don't spend the night in the square." 21 So he took him into his house and fed
his donkeys. After they had washed their feet, they had something to eat and drink.[i]
22 While they were enjoying themselves,[j] some of the wicked men[k] of the city surrounded the house. Pounding on the door, they shouted to the old man who owned the
house, "Bring out the man who came to your house so we can have sex with him.[l]"
23 The owner of the house went outside[m] and said to them, "No, my friends, don't be
so vile. Since this man is my guest, don't do this disgraceful thing.[n] 24 Look, here is my
virgin daughter,[o] and his concubine. I will bring them out to you now, and you can use
them and do to them whatever you wish. But to this man, don't do such a disgraceful
thing."
25 But the men would not listen to him. So the man took his concubine and sent her
outside to them, and they raped her and abused her[p] throughout the night, and at dawn
they let her go. 26 At daybreak the woman went back to the house where her master was
staying, fell down at the door and lay there until daylight.
27 When her master got up in the morning and opened the door of the house and
stepped out to continue on his way, there lay his concubine, fallen in the doorway of the
house, with her hands on the threshold. 28 He said to her, "Get up; let's go." But there was
no answer. Then the man put her on his donkey and set out for home.
29 When he reached home, he took a knife[q] and cut up his concubine, limb by limb,
into twelve parts and sent them into all the areas of Israel.[r] 30 Everyone who saw it said,
"Such a thing has never been seen or done, not since the day the Israelites came up out
of Egypt.[s] Think about it! Consider it! Tell us what to do![t]"

Israelites Fight the Benjamites

20 Then all the Israelites[u] from Dan to Beersheba[v] and from the land of Gilead
came out as one man[w] and assembled[x] before the LORD in Mizpah. 2 The leaders of all the people of the tribes of Israel took their places in the assembly of the peo-

19:14 [a]1Sa 10:26; Isa 10:29
19:15 [b]Ge 19:2
19:16 [c]Ps 104:23 [d]ver 1
19:17 [e]Ge 29:4
19:18 [f]Jdg 18:31
19:19 [g]Ge 24:25 [h]Ge 14:18
19:21 [i]Ge 24:32-33; Lk 7:44
19:22 [j]Jdg 16:25 [k]Dt 13:13 [l]Ge 19:4-5; Jdg 20:5; Ro 1:26-27
19:23 [m]Ge 19:6 [n]Ge 34:7; Lev 19:29; Dt 22:21; Jdg 20:6; 2Sa 13:12; Ro 1:27
19:24 [o]Ge 19:8; Dt 21:14
19:25 [p]1Sa 31:4
19:29 [q]Ge 22:6 [r]Jdg 20:6; 1Sa 11:7
19:30 [s]Hos 9:9 [t]Jdg 20:7; Pr 13:10
20:1 [u]Jdg 21:5 [v]1Sa 3:20; 2Sa 3:10; 1Ki 4:25 [w]1Sa 11:7 [x]1Sa 7:5

---

rah (Ge 19:1–13). Gibeah's sin was similar to that of Sodom and Gomorrah, and hence the Benjamites were to be destroyed. This event served to reflect negatively on Saul and his descendants.

19:15 sat in the city square. In this manner travelers advertised their need for hospitality (see vv. 16–20).

19:16 an old man from the hill country of Ephraim. It took an old man from another tribe to show hospitality.

19:18 to the house of the LORD. The tabernacle in Shiloh (see 18:31). **No one has taken me into his house.** See verse 15.

19:20 in the square. See verse 15.

19:22 Bring out the man. See note on 19:1—21:25.

19:23 don't do this disgraceful thing. See verse 24.

19:24 here is my virgin daughter, and his concubine . . . don't do such a disgraceful thing. See verse 23. Judges does not condone the Ephraimite's offer. Rather, the offer is to be seen as an expression of the moral decay of Israel at the time. The Levite omitted these details in his retelling of the story (see 20:5). While ancient Near Eastern hospitality demanded that one defend one's guests, this offer was not part of the expectation.

19:25 So the man. The moral depravity of the Levite is evident in that he voluntarily gave his concubine to the men.

19:26 lay there until daylight. The Levite was so unconcerned with his concubine that he did not even wait for her return.

19:28 Get up; let's go. The Levite showed absolutely no sympathy for the concubine, even though he knew what had happened to her during the night. **But there was no answer.** An ironic manner of stating the horrible reality that she was dead.

19:29 twelve parts. This defilement of the woman's body once again revealed the hardened heart of the Levite. Her dismemberment was a perversion of a common ritual of cursing. It had the significance of threatening a similar fate for any tribe that did not respond to the call to war (see notes on Ge 15:10; 1Sa 11:6–8; Jer 34:18). The original audience of Judges would have been well aware of Saul's later action in cutting up a pair of oxen into 12 pieces in order to summon Israel to fight against the Ammonites (1Sa 11:6–8). This association again reflected negatively on Saul.

19:30 Such a thing. The sending of body parts for a sign. **since the day the Israelites came up out of Egypt.** Yet another highly ironic statement: Israel had been guilty of gross sin, idolatry and many other infractions against God's law since coming out of Egypt, yet the Israelites of that time viewed this event as the most shocking of all. For similar blindness to the state of affairs, see Gideon's critical question in 6:13.

20:1–48 *The Violence Against the Men of Gibeah.* Civil war between all Israel and Benjamin resulted from the attack upon the Levite and his concubine. Benjamin was legitimately punished for its sin (see notes on the parallel with Sodom and Gomorrah at 19:14—21:25 and the statement of the Lord's role in vv. 23–28).

20:1 from Dan to Beersheba. The extreme northern and southern boundaries of Israel, respectively. **came out as one man.** For the first time the Israelites were united, but the purpose was to wage war against their brothers. **before the LORD in Mizpah.** See note on 11:11. Saul was made king at Mizpah—again by association a negative reflection on him (see notes on 19:29; 20:1–48).

20:2 in the assembly of the people of God. The repeated cycles of sin, judgment and deliverance and these concluding stories of ironic and heinous sins are evidence of God's mercy, for Israel is still called the people of God.

ple of God, four hundred thousand soldiers[y] armed with swords. 3(The Benjamites
heard that the Israelites had gone up to Mizpah.) Then the Israelites said, "Tell us how
this awful thing happened."
4So the Levite, the husband of the murdered woman, said, "I and my concubine came
to Gibeah[z] in Benjamin to spend the night.[a] 5During the night the men of Gibeah came
after me and surrounded the house, intending to kill me.[b] They raped my concubine, and
she died.[c] 6I took my concubine, cut her into pieces and sent one piece to each region
of Israel's inheritance,[d] because they committed this lewd and disgraceful act[e] in Israel. 7Now, all you Israelites, speak up and give your verdict.[f]"
8All the people rose as one man, saying, "None of us will go home. No, not one of us
will return to his house. 9But now this is what we'll do to Gibeah: We'll go up against it
as the lot directs.[g] 10We'll take ten men out of every hundred from all the tribes of Israel, and a hundred from a thousand, and a thousand from ten thousand, to get provisions
for the army. Then, when the army arrives at Gibeah[a] in Benjamin, it can give them what
they deserve for all this vileness done in Israel." 11So all the men of Israel got together
and united as one man[h] against the city.
12The tribes of Israel sent men throughout the tribe of Benjamin, saying, "What
about this awful crime that was committed among you? 13Now surrender those wicked
men[i] of Gibeah so that we may put them to death and purge the evil from Israel.[j]"
But the Benjamites would not listen to their fellow Israelites. 14From their towns they
came together at Gibeah to fight against the Israelites. 15At once the Benjamites mobilized twenty-six thousand swordsmen from their towns, in addition to seven hundred
chosen men from those living in Gibeah. 16Among all these soldiers there were seven
hundred chosen men who were left-handed,[k] each of whom could sling a stone at a hair
and not miss.
17Israel, apart from Benjamin, mustered four hundred thousand swordsmen, all of
them fighting men.
18The Israelites went up to Bethel[b] and inquired of God.[l] They said, "Who of us shall
go first to fight[m] against the Benjamites?"
The LORD replied, "Judah shall go first."
19The next morning the Israelites got up and pitched camp near Gibeah. 20The men
of Israel went out to fight the Benjamites and took up battle positions against them at
Gibeah. 21The Benjamites came out of Gibeah and cut down twenty-two thousand Israelites[n] on the battlefield that day. 22But the men of Israel encouraged one another and
again took up their positions where they had stationed themselves the first day. 23The
Israelites went up and wept before the LORD until evening,[o] and they inquired of the
LORD. They said, "Shall we go up again to battle[p] against the Benjamites, our brothers?"
The LORD answered, "Go up against them."
24Then the Israelites drew near to Benjamin the second day. 25This time, when the
Benjamites came out from Gibeah to oppose them, they cut down another eighteen
thousand Israelites,[q] all of them armed with swords.
26Then the Israelites, all the people, went up to Bethel, and there they sat weeping
before the LORD.[r] They fasted that day until evening and presented burnt offerings and
fellowship offerings[c] to the LORD.[s] 27And the Israelites inquired of the LORD. (In those days
the ark of the covenant of God[t] was there, 28with Phinehas son of Eleazar,[u] the son of
Aaron, ministering before it.)[v] They asked, "Shall we go up again to battle with Benjamin our brother, or not?"
The LORD responded, "Go, for tomorrow I will give them into your hands.[w]"
29Then Israel set an ambush[x] around Gibeah. 30They went up against the Benjamites
on the third day and took up positions against Gibeah as they had done before. 31The

20:2 [y]Jdg 8:10
20:4 [z]Jos 15:57 [a]Jdg 19:15
20:5 [b]Jdg 19:22 [c]Jdg 19:25-26
20:6 [d]Jdg 19:29 [e]Jos 7:15; Jdg 19:23
20:7 [f]Jdg 19:30
20:9 [g]Lev 16:8
20:11 [h]ver 1
20:13 [i]Dt 13:13; Jdg 19:22 [j]Dt 17:12
20:16 [k]Jdg 3:15; 1Ch 12:2
20:18 [l]ver 26-27; Nu 27:21 [m]ver 23, 28
20:21 [n]ver 25
20:23 [o]Jos 7:6 [p]ver 18
20:25 [q]ver 21
20:26 [r]ver 23 [s]Jdg 21:4
20:27 [t]Jos 18:1
20:28 [u]Jos 24:33 [v]Dt 18:5 [w]Jdg 7:9
20:29 [x]Jos 8:2,4

[a] *10* One Hebrew manuscript; most Hebrew manuscripts *Geba*, a variant of *Gibeah* [b] *18* Or *to the house of God*; also in verse 26 [c] *26* Traditionally *peace offerings*

20:5 They raped my concubine. See 19:23–24. The Levite omitted the details of his own culpability (see notes on 19:25,26,28).
20:6 because they committed this lewd and disgraceful act in Israel. Yet the Ephraimite and the Levite behaved little better.
20:13 purge the evil. Ironically, the Israelites were missing the point that evil had pervaded their tribes as well.
20:16 were left-handed. See note on 3:15.
20:18 to Bethel. The ark of the Lord and the priest with the ephod were at Bethel at this time (see v. 27). **Who of us shall go first to fight against the Benjamites?** This is the same language that was used at the beginning of Judges when the question was asked as to who would lead the Israelites against the Canaanites (1:1). **Judah.** The Lord gave the same answer here as in 1:2, even though the circumstances were different.
20:23 wept. Their failure to succeed on their first attempt reflected God's judgment on the Israelites, who were certainly not without sin (see v. 26). **inquired of the LORD.** See verses 18 and 27–28. **the Benjamites, our brothers?** See verses 18 and 28. After their initial failure, note how the Israelites added "our brothers" to the repetition of their inquiry (see v. 18).
20:28 Benjamin our brother. See verse 23.

20:31 [y]Jos 8:16 Benjamites came out to meet them and were drawn away[y] from the city. They began to
inflict casualties on the Israelites as before, so that about thirty men fell in the open field
and on the roads—the one leading to Bethel and the other to Gibeah.
20:32 [z]ver 39 [32]While the Benjamites were saying, "We are defeating them as before,"[z] the Israelites were saying, "Let's retreat and draw them away from the city to the roads."
[33]All the men of Israel moved from their places and took up positions at Baal Tamar,
20:33 [a]Jos 8:19 and the Israelite ambush charged out of its place[a] on the west[a] of Gibeah.[b] [34]Then ten
thousand of Israel's finest men made a frontal attack on Gibeah. The fighting was so
20:34 [b]Jos 8:14 [c]Isa 47:11 heavy that the Benjamites did not realize[b] how near disaster was.[c] [35]The LORD defeated
20:35 [d]1Sa 9:21 Benjamin[d] before Israel, and on that day the Israelites struck down 25,100 Benjamites,
all armed with swords. [36]Then the Benjamites saw that they were beaten.
20:36 [e]Jos 8:15 Now the men of Israel had given way[e] before Benjamin, because they relied on the
ambush they had set near Gibeah. [37]The men who had been in ambush made a sudden
20:37 [f]Jos 8:19 dash into Gibeah, spread out and put the whole city to the sword.[f] [38]The men of Israel
20:38 [g]Jos 8:20 had arranged with the ambush that they should send up a great cloud of smoke[g] from
the city, [39]and then the men of Israel would turn in the battle.
The Benjamites had begun to inflict casualties on the men of Israel (about thirty), and
20:39 [h]ver 32 they said, "We are defeating them as in the first battle."[h] [40]But when the column of
smoke began to rise from the city, the Benjamites turned and saw the smoke of the whole
20:40 [i]Jos 8:20 city going up into the sky.[i] [41]Then the men of Israel turned on them, and the men of Benjamin were terrified, because they realized that disaster had come upon them. [42]So they
fled before the Israelites in the direction of the desert, but they could not escape the battle. And the men of Israel who came out of the towns cut them down there. [43]They surrounded the Benjamites, chased them and easily[c] overran them in the vicinity of Gibe-
20:44 [j]Ps 76:5 ah on the east. [44]Eighteen thousand Benjamites fell, all of them valiant fighters.[j] [45]As
20:45 [k]Jos 15:32; Jdg 21:13 they turned and fled toward the desert to the rock of Rimmon,[k] the Israelites cut down
five thousand men along the roads. They kept pressing after the Benjamites as far as Gi-
dom and struck down two thousand more.
[46]On that day twenty-five thousand Benjamite swordsmen fell, all of them valiant
fighters. [47]But six hundred men turned and fled into the desert to the rock of Rimmon,
where they stayed four months. [48]The men of Israel went back to Benjamin and put all
20:48 [l]Jdg 21:23 the towns to the sword, including the animals and everything else they found. All the
towns they came across they set on fire.[l]

Wives for the Benjamites

21:1 [m]Jos 9:18 [n]Jdg 20:1 [o]ver 7, 18 **21** The men of Israel had taken an oath[m] at Mizpah:[n] "Not one of us will give[o] his
daughter in marriage to a Benjamite."
[2]The people went to Bethel,[d] where they sat before God until evening, raising their
voices and weeping bitterly. [3]"O LORD, the God of Israel," they cried, "why has this happened to Israel? Why should one tribe be missing from Israel today?"
[4]Early the next day the people built an altar and presented burnt offerings and fellow-
21:4 [p]Jdg 20:26; 2Sa 24:25 ship offerings.[e p]
[5]Then the Israelites asked, "Who from all the tribes of Israel[q] has failed to assemble
21:5 [q]Jdg 5:23; 20:1 before the LORD?" For they had taken a solemn oath that anyone who failed to assemble
before the LORD at Mizpah should certainly be put to death.
[6]Now the Israelites grieved for their brothers, the Benjamites. "Today one tribe is cut
21:7 [r]ver 1 off from Israel," they said. [7]"How can we provide wives for those who are left, since we
have taken an oath[r] by the LORD not to give them any of our daughters in marriage?"
21:8 [s]1Sa 11:1; 31:11 [8]Then they asked, "Which one of the tribes of Israel failed to assemble before the LORD
at Mizpah?" They discovered that no one from Jabesh Gilead[s] had come to the camp for
the assembly. [9]For when they counted the people, they found that none of the people of
Jabesh Gilead were there.
[10]So the assembly sent twelve thousand fighting men with instructions to go to Jabesh
Gilead and put to the sword those living there, including the women and children.

[a] *33* Some Septuagint manuscripts and Vulgate; the meaning of the Hebrew for this word is uncertain.
[b] *33* Hebrew *Geba,* a variant of *Gibeah* [c] *43* The meaning of the Hebrew for this word is uncertain.
[d] *2* Or *to the house of God* [e] *4* Traditionally *peace offerings*

20:48 put all the towns to the sword. The rest of the Israelites treated the Benjamites like Canaanites (see v. 18; 1:8).

■**21:1–25** *The Violence Against Jabesh Gilead.* By slaughtering the Gileadites for their failure to support the summons, the Israelites compounded their sinful resolution of the dilemma of how to restore a seed to Benjamin without breaking their vow.

21:8 Jabesh Gilead. Saul's first act as king was to defend Jabesh Gilead. Since he was a Benjamite from Gibeah, his grandmother or great-grandmother may have been one of these women from Jabesh Gilead.

11“This is what you are to do,” they said. “Kill every male and every woman who is not
a virgin.[t]” 12They found among the people living in Jabesh Gilead four hundred young
women who had never slept with a man, and they took them to the camp at Shiloh[u] in
Canaan.
13Then the whole assembly sent an offer of peace[v] to the Benjamites at the rock of
Rimmon.[w] 14So the Benjamites returned at that time and were given the women of Jabesh Gilead who had been spared. But there were not enough for all of them.
15The people grieved for Benjamin,[x] because the LORD had made a gap in the tribes
of Israel. 16And the elders of the assembly said, “With the women of Benjamin destroyed, how shall we provide wives for the men who are left? 17The Benjamite survivors
must have heirs,” they said, “so that a tribe of Israel will not be wiped out. 18We can’t give
them our daughters as wives, since we Israelites have taken this oath: ‘Cursed be anyone who gives[y] a wife to a Benjamite.’ 19But look, there is the annual festival of the LORD
in Shiloh,[z] to the north of Bethel, and east of the road that goes from Bethel to Shechem,
and to the south of Lebonah.”
20So they instructed the Benjamites, saying, “Go and hide in the vineyards 21and
watch. When the girls of Shiloh come out to join in the dancing,[a] then rush from the
vineyards and each of you seize a wife from the girls of Shiloh and go to the land of Benjamin. 22When their fathers or brothers complain to us, we will say to them, ‘Do us a
kindness by helping them, because we did not get wives for them during the war, and
you are innocent, since you did not give[b] your daughters to them.’ ”
23So that is what the Benjamites did. While the girls were dancing, each man caught
one and carried her off to be his wife. Then they returned to their inheritance and rebuilt
the towns and settled in them.[c]
24At that time the Israelites left that place and went home to their tribes and clans,
each to his own inheritance.
25In those days Israel had no king; everyone did as he saw fit.[d]

21:11 [t]Nu 31:17-18
21:12 [u]Jos 18:1
21:13 [v]Dt 20:10 [w]Jdg 20:47
21:15 [x]ver 6
21:18 [y]ver 1
21:19 [z]Jos 18:1; Jdg 18:31; 1Sa 1:3
21:21 [a]Ex 15:20; Jdg 11:34
21:22 [b]ver 1,18
21:23 [c]Jdg 20:48
21:25 [d]Dt 12:8; Jdg 17:6; 18:1; 19:1

21:15–23 The Israelites’ entanglement in sin had left them unable to unravel themselves from their predicament. Their attempt at a solution was as evil as the actions that had brought them to this point. Ironically, this series of tragic events began with the violation of a woman (19:1–30) and ended with a further violation of women as all the tribes approved of the kidnappings of the virgins.

21:22 you are innocent. The declaration of innocence reveals once again how corrupt the Israelites had become.

21:25 In those days Israel had no king; everyone did as he saw fit. See note on 17:6. The conclusion to these accounts of violence points one final time to Israel’s need for a righteous king. Although history proved that Israel’s kings themselves led the people into rebellion against God, this book repeatedly affirms that godly kingship is the only hope for the law of God to be enforced in the land. See *BC* 36.

RUTH

Introduction

Overview

Author: Unknown
Purpose: To demonstrate the legitimacy of David's kingship despite his Moabite ancestress, Ruth
Date: c. 1000 B.C.
Key Truths:

- God's providence is sometimes harsh, but in the end he works for the blessing of his people.
- Familial love and devotion that are guided by God's law bring joy and happiness.
- David's family was God's chosen, honorable, royal line.

Author

The author of the book of Ruth, which is named after its principal character, is unknown. Rabbinic tradition holds that the prophet Samuel wrote Ruth, as well as Judges and 1 and 2 Samuel. There is little evidence to commend this view, however.

Time and Place of Writing

The book of Ruth reports events that took place during the period of the judges, but the explanation of a forgotten custom in 4:7 indicates that the book was written significantly later than that time period. The two references to David (4:17,22) point to a time after the beginning of his reign as the earliest possible date for final composition.

Establishing the latest possible date for completion is more difficult. Some interpreters have pointed to linguistic evidence as indicating a postexilic date (after 500 B.C.), but this evidence has been strongly disputed. It is likely that the genealogy of 4:18–22 extended to the king who ruled at the time of the book's composition; i.e., to David. For this reason, it is probably safe to conclude that Ruth was written during David's reign.

Purpose and Distinctives

Various interpreters have proposed different central themes for the book. Among other possible purposes, Ruth has been understood as an explanation that (1) a proselyte (even a Moabite) could be truly faithful to the Lord and gain full acceptance within Israel; (2) qualities of loyalty and covenant faithfulness exemplified by a foreigner could serve as a model for Israel's response to the Lord; and (3) the Lord as Redeemer would redeem and restore the exiled family of Israel to its land.

All of these proposals reflect some of the major themes of the book. Yet in light of the reference to David in 4:17 and the genealogical reference to him (4:18–22), the major objective seems inextricably tied to the support of David as king. The legitimacy of David and his house is established despite the presence of a Moabitess in his line. The Law of Moses insisted that Israel's king come "from among [their] own brothers" (Dt 17:15), and Moses had warned against Moabite women (see Nu 25:1; 31:13–18). To address these potential problems with David's lineage, the book portrays Ruth as a woman of noble character (see note on 3:11) and as a true convert (1:16), who entered Israel through the providence of God (1:1–7) and the legal practice of levirate marriage (3:1–8). Moreover, God approved of her by bestowing his blessing on her (4:13–17).

A number of issues that have fascinated interpreters arise directly from enigmas in the narrative. These may be divided into the following categories: (1) questions about purpose that are related to difficulties in dating and origin; (2) inability to understand the background of various legal customs—especially the relationship between levirate marriage (Dt 25:5–10) and kinsman-redemption responsibilities (Lev 25)—and how each was practiced in Israel (cf. Ge 38; Nu 27; 36; Jer 32); and (3) internal difficulties, such as the relationship between 4:12 and 17 and the genealogy in 4:18–22. A wealth of literature addresses each of these areas, with little agreement at times. A remarkable phenomenon of Biblical research is that such important and even divisive debate does little to blunt the powerful impact of this simple account on every generation of its readers.

The book of Ruth may be described as a unified short story. It consists of the story itself and an attached genealogy that associates the story with David's house (4:18–22). The five parts of the main plot form a discernable and intentional symmetry. "Naomi's Bitterness and Emptiness" (1:1–22) is counterbalanced by "Naomi's Blessing" (4:13–17); "Ruth Discovers Her Kinsman-Redeemer" (2:1–23) is offset by "Boaz Becomes Ruth's Kinsman-Redeemer" (4:1–12); and the centerpiece of the story is "Boaz Promises Ruth a Kinsman-Redeemer" (3:1–18). Within each of these segments many other such structures appear. See "Introduction: Outline."

Although clearly an important historical document of its period, the narrative of Ruth is told with dramatic intensity and movement combined with light touches of the best of the Hebrew storyteller's art. Moving quickly and succinctly through various stages, each part of the account is spiced with elements of irony and suspense, which contribute to the symphony of divine, providential fulfillment. Although the Lord is specifically cited as acting only twice (1:6; 4:13), the reader is left with no doubt as to his presence in inspiring Naomi's return, Ruth's covenant faithfulness and Boaz's righteous adherence to the law.

Christ in Ruth

Christ is revealed in the book of Ruth primarily in the way in which the book witnesses to the legitimacy of David's kingship. First, as this book legitimates David, it legitimates Christ as the great Messiah. Jesus acquired the throne of Israel because he was the perfectly faithful son of David (Mk 10:47–48; Ac 2:22–36; Ro 1:2–4). Because the Gospel writers Matthew and Luke were deeply concerned with Jesus' genealogy (Mt 1:1–17; Lk 3:23–38), followers of Christ can be assured of the New Testament claim that Jesus is the Messiah. Jesus inaugurated David's kingdom in his ministry on Earth, he now reigns over and extends that kingdom and he will one day return to bring worldwide dominion to the house of David (Am 9:11; Ac 15:14–19).

Second, the interest the book shows in the inclusion of Ruth, a Gentile, anticipates the expansion of the kingdom of God to Gentiles during the New Testament period. Because Ruth exhibited the faith of Abraham as she left country and relatives to travel under the Lord's care to a foreign land, she found the blessing promised to all the nations in Abraham's seed (Ge 12:3). As Ruth became one with Israel, Gentiles and Jews are now reconciled to God in one body through their union with Christ (Eph 2:16; 3:6).

Third, the ideal portrait of Boaz, Ruth's kinsman-redeemer, provides substance to the New Testament declaration that the church is the bride of Christ (Eph 5:25–27; Rev 19:1–8; 22:17). Boaz demonstrated ardent, selfless love for two helpless widows, Ruth and Naomi. This characterization of Boaz offers insight into how Christ ardently and selflessly loves his dependent bride, the church.

Outline

I. Naomi's Bitterness and Emptiness (1:1–22)
  - A. Naomi in Moab Without Husband or Sons (1:1–5)
  - B. Naomi and Daughters-in-law Set Out (1:6–7)
  - C. Daughters-in-law Make Choices (1:8–18)
  - D. Naomi and Ruth Travel Toward Bethlehem (1:19a)
  - E. Naomi With Ruth in Bethlehem Without Husbands (1:19b–22)

Ruth became a full convert to Israel's faith. She lovingly journeyed to Judah with Naomi as she faced bitterness and emptiness.

II. Ruth Discovers Her Kinsman-Redeemer (2:1–23)
  - A. Ruth Goes From Home to Work in the Field (2:1–3)
  - B. Boaz Inquires of His Men About Ruth (2:4–7)
  - C. Boaz Gives Protection and Blessing to Ruth (2:8–14)
  - D. Boaz Instructs His Men About Ruth (2:15–16)
  - E. Ruth Returns Home From Working in the Field (2:17–23)

As she gathered food, Ruth came upon Boaz, a near kinsman who showed her kindness and protection.

III. Boaz Promises Ruth a Kinsman-Redeemer (3:1–18)
  - A. Ruth Goes From Home to the Threshing Floor (3:1–6)
  - B. Ruth Meets Boaz at the Threshing Floor (3:7)
  - C. Ruth Requests a Kinsman-Redeemer and Boaz Commits (3:8–13)
  - D. Ruth Receives a Gift From Boaz (3:14–15)
  - E. Ruth Returns Home From the Threshing Floor (3:16–18)

Ruth received assurance from Boaz that she would have a kinsman-redeemer: either her nearer kinsman or he would care for her.

IV. Boaz Becomes Ruth's Kinsman-Redeemer (4:1–12)
  - A. Boaz Clears the Way to Become Ruth's Kinsman-Redeemer (4:1–8)
  - B. Boaz Publicly Announces His Commitment to Ruth (4:9–10)
  - C. Boaz Is Blessed as Ruth's Kinsman-Redeemer (4:11–12)

Boaz followed all legal means and found approval from the elders and the people to receive Ruth as his wife.

V. Naomi's Blessing (4:13–17) A. Boaz and Ruth Have a Son (4:13) B. Naomi Blessed by the Son (4:14–17a) C. Boaz and Ruth Name the Son (4:17b)	*Boaz and Ruth had a child who brought relief from Naomi's emptiness and became the ancestor of David.*
VI. Genealogical Appendix (4:18–22)	*The genealogy of David includes Obed, the child born to Ruth and Boaz.*

Naomi and Ruth

1:1 [a]Jdg 2:16-18 [b]Ge 12:10; Ps 105:16 [c]Jdg 3:30
1 In the days when the judges ruled,[a] [a] there was a famine in the land,[b] and a man
from Bethlehem in Judah, together with his wife and two sons, went to live for a
while in the country of Moab.[c] 2 The man's name was Elimelech, his wife's name Nao-
1:2 [d]Ge 35:19
mi, and the names of his two sons were Mahlon and Kilion. They were Ephrathites from
Bethlehem,[d] Judah. And they went to Moab and lived there.
1:4 [e]Mt 1:5
3 Now Elimelech, Naomi's husband, died, and she was left with her two sons. 4 They
married Moabite women, one named Orpah and the other Ruth.[e] After they had lived
there about ten years, 5 both Mahlon and Kilion also died, and Naomi was left without
her two sons and her husband.
1:6 [f]Ex 4:31; Jer 29:10; Zep 2:7 [g]Ps 132:15; Mt 6:11
6 When she heard in Moab that the LORD had come to the aid of his people[f] by providing food[g] for them, Naomi and her daughters-in-law prepared to return home from
there. 7 With her two daughters-in-law she left the place where she had been living and
set out on the road that would take them back to the land of Judah.
8 Then Naomi said to her two daughters-in-law, "Go back, each of you, to your moth-
1:8 [h]Ru 2:20; 2Ti 1:16 [i]ver 5
er's home. May the LORD show kindness[h] to you, as you have shown to your dead[i] and
to me. 9 May the LORD grant that each of you will find rest[j] in the home of another husband."
1:9 [j]Ru 3:1
Then she kissed them and they wept aloud 10 and said to her, "We will go back with
you to your people."
11 But Naomi said, "Return home, my daughters. Why would you come with me? Am I
1:11 [k]Ge 38:11; Dt 25:5
going to have any more sons, who could become your husbands?[k] 12 Return home, my

[a] *1* Traditionally *judged*

■ **1:1–22** *Naomi's Bitterness and Emptiness.* The story of Ruth opens with a description of her mother-in-law's extreme bitterness and emptiness (vv. 20–21). This episode divides into five parts: Naomi in Moab (vv. 1–5), leaving Moab (vv. 6–7), facing the choices of her daughters-in-law (vv. 8–18), traveling toward Bethlehem (v. 19a) and bitterness and emptiness in Bethlehem (vv. 19b–22). This episode stands in sharp contrast with the closing event (4:13–17) in which Naomi is blessed and fulfilled.

■ **1:1–5** *Naomi in Moab Without Husband or Sons.* Naomi faced the difficulty not only of living outside the promised land but also of losing her husband and sons.

1:1 In the days when the judges ruled. In Hebrew, this phrase is a standard formula that serves as an opening to a historical book: "And it happened . . ." is coupled with specific historical information. The period of the judges was clearly known to the original audience as a time of instability and apostasy. **a famine.** Much of the drama of the book of Ruth hinges on the curse of famine and its corresponding reversal in blessing. In Scripture famines are not always identified as the consequence of divine displeasure, but the general spiritual conditions at the time of the judges and the comments by the narrator (v. 6) and Naomi (v. 21) suggest that this was the case here. God's sovereign hand is not always explicit in this drama, but he must be viewed as constantly present and active (Am 3:6). **country of Moab.** Literally, "fields of Moab." Moabites, who were near relatives of Israel through Lot (see Ge 19:37), at various times occupied parts of central Transjordan that had been protected by God from the incoming Israelite conquerors (Dt 2:9). The Moabites were subjugated by both Saul (1Sa 14:47) and David (2Sa 8:2). See also Deuteronomy 23:3. But there were also periods of friendly relations and times of considerable cultural and economic interchange, as demonstrated by David's placement of his parents with the king of Moab while he was a fugitive (1Sa 22:3). Elimelech's sojourn in Moab took place during one such period.

1:2 Elimelech. Although the story revolves around Elimelech's family and might have climaxed with God's provision of an heir after Elimelech's death, the drama focuses initially on God's blessing for Naomi (4:14,16) and later on the lineage of David through Boaz (4:17–22). **Naomi.** Literally, "pleasant(ness)" (see vv. 20–21). The meaning of her name is ironic at the beginning of the book but fitting in the end (see 4:14–17). Along with Ruth, Naomi becomes a central, and initially tragic, figure.

1:4 They married Moabite women. This action was to be expected and was in no Biblical sense forbidden, although Deuteronomy 23:3–6 would have restricted temple participation, at least among male descendants. The irony would have been seen in the provision of an heir, an ancestor of the great king David, through one of these foreigners.

1:5 Naomi was left. As an elderly woman, beyond the age of child-bearing, alone in a foreign country except for two alien and childless daughters-in-law, Naomi was an unlikely prospect for any significant role in the Lord's covenantal history.

■ **1:6–7** *Naomi and Daughters-in-law Set Out.* Naomi's love for her Moabite daughters-in-law and her faithfulness to the Lord despite her bitter treatment at his hand dominates this scene of the drama.

1:6 she heard in Moab that the LORD . . . his people. A note of hope was sounded: The famine had run its course. The story never loses sight of God, whose covenant love ultimately determined the course of action. **prepared to return home from there.** It would appear that all three fully intended to go back to Judah. Along the way, however, Naomi had second thoughts about her daughters-in-law returning with her.

■ **1:8–18** *Daughters-in-law Make Choices.* Out of genuine concern, Naomi offered to make the journey to Judah alone. Orpah returned home, but Ruth insisted on accompanying Naomi.

1:9–10 they wept . . . and said. The initial pledge by both women heightens the dramatic tension. They were already "on the road . . . to . . . Judah" (v. 7), and the closer they got, the greater the stakes became.

1:11 Am I going to have any more sons . . . ? This is a vague allusion to the levirate (Latin, *levir,* "brother-in-law") law, under which a brother would be obligated to provide an heir for the dead man (Dt 25:5–6). Whether the levirate custom or the custom of the

daughters; I am too old to have another husband. Even if I thought there was still hope
for me—even if I had a husband tonight and then gave birth to sons— 13 would you wait
until they grew up? Would you remain unmarried for them? No, my daughters. It is more
bitter for me than for you, because the LORD's hand has gone out against me![l]"
14 At this they wept again. Then Orpah kissed her mother-in-law[m] good-by, but Ruth
clung to her.[n]
15 "Look," said Naomi, "your sister-in-law is going back to her people and her gods.[o]
Go back with her."
16 But Ruth replied, "Don't urge me to leave you[p] or to turn back from you. Where you
go I will go, and where you stay I will stay. Your people will be my people and your God
my God.[q] 17 Where you die I will die, and there I will be buried. May the LORD deal with
me, be it ever so severely,[r] if anything but death separates you and me." 18 When Naomi realized that Ruth was determined to go with her, she stopped urging her.[s]
19 So the two women went on until they came to Bethlehem. When they arrived in
Bethlehem, the whole town was stirred[t] because of them, and the women exclaimed,
"Can this be Naomi?"
20 "Don't call me Naomi,[a]" she told them. "Call me Mara,[b] because the Almighty[c][u] has
made my life very bitter.[v] 21 I went away full, but the LORD has brought me back empty.[w] Why
call me Naomi? The LORD has afflicted[d] me; the Almighty has brought misfortune upon me."
22 So Naomi returned from Moab accompanied by Ruth the Moabitess, her daughter-
in-law, arriving in Bethlehem as the barley harvest[x] was beginning.[y]

1:13 [l]Jdg 2:15; Job 4:5; 19:21; Ps 32:4
1:14 [m]Ru 2:11 [n]Pr 17:17; 18:24
1:15 [o]Jos 24:14; Jdg 11:24
1:16 [p]2Ki 2:2 [q]Ru 2:11, 12
1:17 [r]1Sa 3:17; 25:22; 2Sa 19:13; 2Ki 6:31
1:18 [s]Ac 21:14
1:19 [t]Mt 21:10
1:20 [u]Ex 6:3 [v]ver 13; Job 6:4
1:21 [w]Job 1:21
1:22 [x]Ex 9:31; Ru 2:23 [y]2Sa 21:9

[a] *20* Naomi means *pleasant*; also in verse 21. [b] *20* Mara means *bitter*. [c] *20* Hebrew *Shaddai*; also in verse 21 [d] *21* Or *has testified against*

kinsman redeemer determined the action of Boaz is still debated among scholars. In any event, Naomi realized that it was too late for her. She had nothing to offer Orpah and Ruth.

1:13 the LORD's hand . . . against me! There is no hint of any reason God may have treated Naomi harshly. As far as the book is concerned, her bereavement and subsequent trials were certainly not the direct result of any personal sin on her part. The absence of any explanation was no doubt designed to create tension in the original readers as they awaited clarification and resolution. In the end it becomes apparent that God's purpose in Naomi's difficulties was for the sake of Ruth and her descendants (see notes on 4:17,18–22).

1:15 her gods. A new element is introduced. Heretofore the readers had probably assumed that the daughters had effectively become worshipers of the Lord. Now they learn what the choice of homeland implied. Orpah's choice and Ruth's declaration (vv. 16–17) represented, respectively, their faith commitments.

1:16 Your people will be my people and your God my God. Ruth's words represented her complete conversion. She committed herself not only to Naomi, but also to Israel and to Israel's God (cf. 2Sa 15:21).

1:18 she stopped urging her. Resolution was achieved. The reader had suspected that redemption would come through this foreign woman; now it was almost certain.

■ **1:19a** *Naomi and Ruth Travel Toward Bethlehem.* This brief scene counterbalances the travels away from Moab (see vv. 6–7).

■ **1:19b–22** *Naomi With Ruth in Bethlehem Without Husbands.* Without husbands the women are left without a family provider or legal protector.

1:19–21 Naomi? . . . Mara . . . full . . . empty. The women's question (v. 19) expressed their amazement that this woman, whose earlier circumstances had reflected her name ("pleasant"), had fallen upon such hard times. Both sides agreed that this was the Lord's doing (see note on v. 13).

The Book of Ruth

Set in the dark and bloody days of the judges, the story of Ruth is silent about the underlying hostility and suspicion the two peoples—Judahites and Moabites—felt for each other. The original onslaught of the invading Israelite tribes against towns that were once Moabite had never been forgotten or forgiven, while the Hebrew prophets denounced Moab's pride and arrogance for trying to bewitch, seduce and oppress Israel from the time of Balaam on. The Mesha Stele (c. 830 B.C.) boasts of the massacre of entire Israelite towns.

Moab encompassed the expansive, grain-filled plateau between the Dead Sea and the eastern desert on both sides of the enormous rift of the Arnon River gorge. Much of eastern Moab was steppeland—semi-arid wastes not profitable for cultivation, but excellent for grazing flocks of sheep and goats. The tribute Moab paid to Israel in the days of Ahab was 100,000 lambs and the wool of 100,000 rams (see 2Ki 3:4 and note).

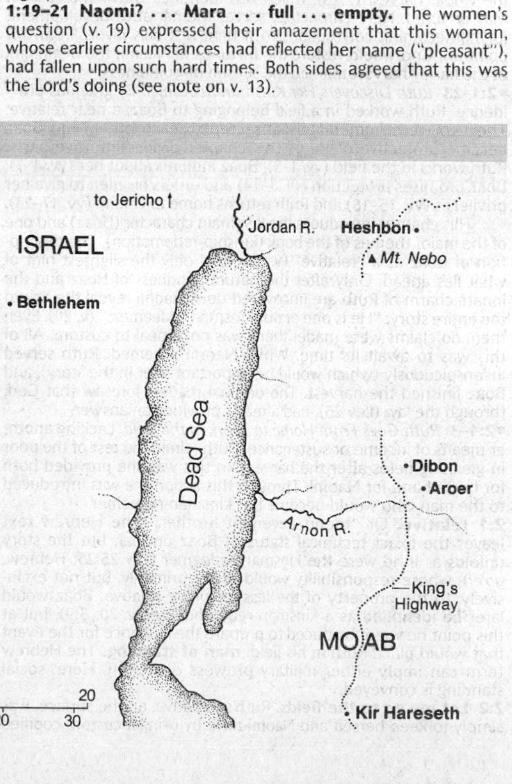

Ruth Meets Boaz

2:1 [z]Ru 3:2,12 [a]Ru 1:2 [b]Ru 4:21
2:2 [c]ver 7; Lev 19:9; 23:22; Dt 24:19
2:4 [d]Jdg 6:12; Lk 1:28; 2Th 3:16 [e]Ps 129:7-8
2:6 [f]Ru 1:22

2 Now Naomi had a relative[z] on her husband's side, from the clan of Elimelech,[a] a
man of standing, whose name was Boaz.[b]
2 And Ruth the Moabitess said to Naomi, "Let me go to the fields and pick up the left-
over grain[c] behind anyone in whose eyes I find favor."
Naomi said to her, "Go ahead, my daughter." 3 So she went out and began to glean
in the fields behind the harvesters. As it turned out, she found herself working in a field
belonging to Boaz, who was from the clan of Elimelech.
4 Just then Boaz arrived from Bethlehem and greeted the harvesters, "The LORD be
with you![d]"
"The LORD bless you![e]" they called back.
5 Boaz asked the foreman of his harvesters, "Whose young woman is that?"
6 The foreman replied, "She is the Moabitess[f] who came back from Moab with Naomi. 7 She said, 'Please let me glean and gather among the sheaves behind the harvesters.' She went into the field and has worked steadily from morning till now, except for
a short rest in the shelter."
8 So Boaz said to Ruth, "My daughter, listen to me. Don't go and glean in another field
and don't go away from here. Stay here with my servant girls. 9 Watch the field where the
men are harvesting, and follow along after the girls. I have told the men not to touch you.
And whenever you are thirsty, go and get a drink from the water jars the men have filled."

1:22 Ruth the Moabitess. For the purpose of the story it was crucial that Ruth be identified and remembered as a foreigner (v. 4; 2:2,6,21; 4:5,10; especially 2:10). Also, no one from the original audience would have heard the story of Ruth the Moabitess without making an association with the incestuous beginnings of the Moabite nation (Ge 19:30–38). The narrator hereafter offers a number of subtle comparisons between Ruth and Lot's daughters (see notes on 2:20; 3:1,4,15). **the barley harvest was beginning.** Earliest calendars, like the Gezer calendar from the tenth century B.C., reckoned months by the agricultural cycle. The barley harvest, which later in Jewish tradition was identified with Passover, took place in April and opened the period of the cereal harvest. Three months of the annual cycle were marked by rejoicing before God and with one another and recalling the needs of the poor. This period closed with the wheat harvest (2:23), which was identified with Pentecost (in May or June). Here chronology serves the narrative development, for homecoming corresponds to a time of God's favor. From this point on, God would restore the fortunes of Naomi; the beginning of the barley harvest marked the season of fruitfulness.

■ **2:1–23** *Ruth Discovers Her Kinsman-Redeemer.* By gracious providence, Ruth worked in a field belonging to Boaz, a near relative. The two were immediately attracted to each other, and Boaz became protective of Ruth. This chapter divides into five parts: Ruth works in the field (vv. 1–3); Boaz inquires about her (vv. 4–7), Boaz promises protection (vv. 8–14) and orders his men to give her privileges (vv. 15–16) and Ruth returns home to Naomi (vv. 17–23).

This chapter introduces the last main character (Boaz) and one of the major themes of the book (kinship-redemption). The description of Boaz as a "relative" (v. 1) offers only the slightest hint of what lies ahead. Only after the natural kindness of Boaz and the innate charm of Ruth are uncovered does Naomi reveal the key to the entire story: "He is one of our kinsman-redeemers" (v. 20). Even then, no claims were made; there was no appeal to custom. All of this was to await its time. While Naomi schemed, Ruth served inconspicuously (which would be important later in the story), and Boaz finished the harvest. The original readers foresaw that God, through the law (Lev 25), had already provided an answer.

■ **2:1–3** *Ruth Goes From Home to Work in the Field.* Lacking another means of income or sustenance, Ruth joined the rest of the poor in gleaning fields after the harvest. In this way she provided both for herself and for Naomi. Through this action she was introduced to the man who would become her kinsman-redeemer.

2:1 relative. Or "friend/covenant brother." The Hebrew text leaves the exact technical status of Boaz unclear, but the story unfolds as if he were the kinsman-redeemer (Lev 25:25; Hebrew, *go'el*), whose responsibility would relate primarily, but not exclusively, to the property of the less-fortunate relative. Boaz would later be identified as a kinsman-redeemer (see v. 20; 3:9), but at this point he was introduced to prepare the audience for the event that would place Ruth in his field. **man of standing.** The Hebrew term can imply either military prowess or wealth. Here, social standing is conveyed.

2:2 Let me go to the fields. Ruth's initiative, on the surface, was simply to keep herself and Naomi alive by using a custom codified in the laws of both Leviticus (19:9–10; 23:22) and Deuteronomy (24:19). As poor people she and Naomi were to be given consideration, but much more was about to come their way. A narrative hint is given in Ruth's plaintive suggestion that she would glean "behind anyone in whose eyes [she found] favor." **Naomi said . . . "Go ahead . . . "** Did Naomi, with the original audience, think ahead to the possibilities? Was she plotting? The suspense is heightened. **my daughter.** The use of this form of address is an important way in which the narrator revealed Ruth's character and that of those around her. Naomi called Ruth her daughter five separate times within this brief narrative (vv. 2,22; 3:1,16,18), indicating her maternal affection and Ruth's full acceptance into Naomi's family. Boaz used the identical term for Ruth three times (v. 8; 3:10,11). His use of the phrase not only acknowledged Ruth's young age but also revealed his paternal feelings, which would deepen into romantic affection. In all cases, the address indicated that Ruth was a chaste, humble, loving and loveable young woman. This characterization was essential to the purpose of demonstrating that Ruth did not fit the Israelite stereotype of a Moabitess.

2:3 As it turned out, she found herself. The Hebrew expression stresses that this occurred without Ruth's planning it. Ruth may not have intended to meet Boaz, but God had arranged that this would happen (*WCF* 5.1–3).

■ **2:4–7** *Boaz Inquires of His Men About Ruth.* Boaz noticed Ruth and asked about her. Possibly to his surprise, the harvesters had positive things to say about her.

2:4 Just then. What appeared to be a coincidence actually manifested the impeccable timing of divine providence. **The LORD be with you . . . bless you!** This exchange of greetings was recorded to create an atmosphere of piety. Boaz and his men were righteous and upstanding.

2:5 Whose young woman is that? It was rare in the culture of the time to find a young woman of marriageable age who was not already married. Boaz may also have been asking to which harvester she belonged.

2:6 the Moabitess. See note on 1:22. The harvesters were impressed by the behavior of this woman from Moab. She was in all likelihood not what they would have expected.

2:7 let me . . . among the sheaves. Although it was her right by law (Dt 24:19–21), Ruth requested permission to gather from among the cut piles left behind by the reapers. She behaved honorably, and the men recognized this as an indicator of her character. **worked steadily.** This phrase could be translated "has stood [waiting]"; i.e., she refrained from gleaning until she received a response to her request. Whatever the case, Ruth's character was above reproach—again, most likely not what an Israelite expected from a Moabitess (v. 6).

■ **2:8–14** *Boaz Gives Protection and Blessing to Ruth.* Boaz now spoke directly to Ruth.

2:8–9 Boaz acceded to her request and offered full protection and provision.

2:8 My daughter. Ruth was significantly younger than Boaz (see v. 5; 3:10). Already in his first words to her, Boaz expressed affection (see note on v. 2).

10 At this, she bowed down with her face to the ground.[g] She exclaimed, "Why have
I found such favor in your eyes that you notice me[h]—a foreigner?[i]"
11 Boaz replied, "I've been told all about what you have done for your mother-in-law[j]
since the death of your husband—how you left your father and mother and your homeland and came to live with a people you did not know before.[k] 12 May the LORD repay you
for what you have done. May you be richly rewarded by the LORD,[l] the God of Israel, under whose wings[m] you have come to take refuge.[n]"
13 "May I continue to find favor in your eyes, my lord," she said. "You have given me
comfort and have spoken kindly to your servant—though I do not have the standing of
one of your servant girls."
14 At mealtime Boaz said to her, "Come over here. Have some bread and dip it in the
wine vinegar."
When she sat down with the harvesters, he offered her some roasted grain. She ate all
she wanted and had some left over.[o] 15 As she got up to glean, Boaz gave orders to his men,
"Even if she gathers among the sheaves, don't embarrass her. 16 Rather, pull out some
stalks for her from the bundles and leave them for her to pick up, and don't rebuke her."
17 So Ruth gleaned in the field until evening. Then she threshed the barley she had
gathered, and it amounted to about an ephah.[a] 18 She carried it back to town, and her
mother-in-law saw how much she had gathered. Ruth also brought out and gave her
what she had left over[p] after she had eaten enough.
19 Her mother-in-law asked her, "Where did you glean today? Where did you work?
Blessed be the man who took notice of you![q]"
Then Ruth told her mother-in-law about the one at whose place she had been working. "The name of the man I worked with today is Boaz," she said.
20 "The LORD bless him!" Naomi said to her daughter-in-law. "He has not stopped
showing his kindness[r] to the living and the dead." She added, "That man is our close relative; he is one of our kinsman-redeemers.[s]"
21 Then Ruth the Moabitess said, "He even said to me, 'Stay with my workers until they
finish harvesting all my grain.'"
22 Naomi said to Ruth her daughter-in-law, "It will be good for you, my daughter, to
go with his girls, because in someone else's field you might be harmed."
23 So Ruth stayed close to the servant girls of Boaz to glean until the barley and
wheat harvests[t] were finished. And she lived with her mother-in-law.

Ruth and Boaz at the Threshing Floor

3 One day Naomi her mother-in-law said to her, "My daughter, should I not try to find
a home[b][u] for you, where you will be well provided for? 2 Is not Boaz, with whose ser-

2:10 [g]1Sa 25:23 [h]Ps 41:1 [i]Dt 15:3
2:11 [j]Ru 1:14 [k]Ru 1:16-17
2:12 [l]1Sa 24:19 [m]Ps 17:8; 36:7; 57:1; 61:4; 63:7; 91:4 [n]Ru 1:16
2:14 [o]ver 18
2:18 [p]ver 14
2:19 [q]ver 10; Ps 41:1
2:20 [r]Ru 3:10; 2Sa 2:5; Pr 17:17 [s]Ru 3:9, 12; 4:1,14
2:23 [t]Dt 16:9
3:1 [u]Ru 1:9

[a] 17 That is, probably about 3/5 bushel (about 22 liters) [b] 1 Hebrew *find rest* (see Ruth 1:9)

2:10 a foreigner? Ruth again demonstrated an unassuming character. She acknowledged herself as unworthy of his favor.
2:11–12 Boaz declared that he already knew much about Ruth. He recognized that she was no ordinary foreigner. She had come to take refuge under God's wings and would be "richly rewarded by the LORD" (v. 12). As the book explains later, Ruth's recompense would constitute a great reward for all of Israel and, ultimately, for all the world (see notes on 4:18–22).
2:13 your servant . . . one of your servant girls. Again, Ruth is portrayed as humble, acknowledging her lowly station in life.
2:14–16 Boaz extended himself to Ruth far beyond what might have been expected of him.
2:14 wine vinegar. This was probably a sour but refreshing drink or dip (cf. Nu 6:3).
■ **2:15–16** *Boaz Instructs His Men About Ruth.* In balance with an earlier conversation with his men about Ruth, Boaz ordered them to watch over and care for her.
■ **2:17–23** *Ruth Returns Home From Working in the Field.* Ruth returned to Naomi and reported what had happened that day. Naomi rightly interpreted the event as God's gracious provision for herself and Ruth.
2:17 threshed . . . an ephah. Threshing, or separating the kernels from the husks, chaff and stalks, was ordinarily done on a larger scale on a threshing floor. Here it was accomplished by hand. Reference to the ephah (see NIV text note) emphasizes the large amount.
2:18 what she had left over. This refers to what remained from the noon meal (v. 14).
2:20 He has not stopped showing his kindness. Naomi rightly viewed this series of events as evidence of the kindness of the Lord. The blessing would spread from Boaz to Ruth to Naomi and, eventually, to all of God's people through David, Ruth's descendant. **one of our kinsman-redeemers.** See note at verse 1. The law of redemption moves to center stage in the drama. According to this provision, it was the right and obligation of the nearest living male blood relative to defend his family's name and to preserve its possessions. This took several forms: (1) avenging the death of a family member (Nu 35:19–21); (2) buying back family property that had been sold to pay a debt (Lev 25:25); (3) buying back the nearest relative who had sold himself into slavery to pay a debt (Lev 25:47–49); and/or (4) marrying the widow of a deceased relative (Dt 25:5–10). These laws applied to family relatives according to the order specified in Leviticus 25:49 (first the paternal uncle, then his son, then other relatives). These rights/obligations apparently could be renounced or declined without much blame if there were others who were willing to take the responsibility (see 3:12; 4:1–8). That Boaz was "one of [their] kinsman-redeemers" (hinted at already in v. 1) sets the course of the action in the book. Ruth herself would proceed according to the law (of levirate marriage), unlike her ancestress, Lot's daughter, who had preserved her family by incest with her father (Ge 19:30–38; see note on 1:22).
2:22 my daughter. See note on verse 2.
2:23 barley and wheat harvests were finished. The two-month delay both heightened the drama and allowed the relationship and/or longing between Boaz and Ruth to develop sufficiently for the coming threshing-floor incident (ch. 3). **lived with her mother-in-law.** This was a reminder that the resourceful and clever Naomi was working in the background.
■ **3:1–18** *Boaz Promises Ruth a Kinsman-Redeemer.* This third major segment of the book serves as a turning point by intensifying the action and quickening the pace toward resolution. In a daring mid-

3:2 [v]Dt 25:5-10; Ru 2:1
3:3 [w]2Sa 14:2
3:5 [x]Eph 6:1; Col 3:20
3:7 [y]Jdg 19:6,9,22; 2Sa 13:28; 1Ki 21:7; Est 1:10
3:9 [z]Eze 16:8 [a]ver 12; Ru 2:20
3:11 [b]Pr 12:4; 31:10
3:12 [c]ver 9 [d]Ru 4:1
3:13 [e]Dt 25:5; Ru 4:5; Mt 22:24 [f]Jdg 8:19; Jer 4:2

vant girls you have been, a kinsman[v] of ours? Tonight he will be winnowing barley on
the threshing floor. [3]Wash and perfume yourself,[w] and put on your best clothes. Then
go down to the threshing floor, but don't let him know you are there until he has finished
eating and drinking. [4]When he lies down, note the place where he is lying. Then go and
uncover his feet and lie down. He will tell you what to do."
[5]"I will do whatever you say,"[x] Ruth answered. [6]So she went down to the threshing
floor and did everything her mother-in-law told her to do.
[7]When Boaz had finished eating and drinking and was in good spirits,[y] he went over
to lie down at the far end of the grain pile. Ruth approached quietly, uncovered his feet
and lay down. [8]In the middle of the night something startled the man, and he turned and
discovered a woman lying at his feet.
[9]"Who are you?" he asked.
"I am your servant Ruth," she said. "Spread the corner of your garment[z] over me,
since you are a kinsman-redeemer.[a]"
[10]"The LORD bless you, my daughter," he replied. "This kindness is greater than that
which you showed earlier: You have not run after the younger men, whether rich or poor.
[11]And now, my daughter, don't be afraid. I will do for you all you ask. All my fellow townsmen know that you are a woman of noble character.[b] [12]Although it is true that I am near
of kin, there is a kinsman-redeemer[c] nearer than[d] I. [13]Stay here for the night, and in the
morning if he wants to redeem,[e] good; let him redeem. But if he is not willing, as surely as the LORD lives[f] I will do it. Lie here until morning."

---

night drama, with sufficient intrigue to ensure the rapt attention of the readers, Ruth both fulfilled and expanded upon Naomi's plan, putting her own reputation and, as it turned out, the future of Israel's royal heritage, on the line. That she emerged undefiled is perfectly plausible, for both hero and heroine were among Israel's finest, and from the beginning God's activity behind the scenes has been evident. But even at this moment, the solution must be delayed; there is a nearer kinsman (v. 12), and Boaz, a man of outstanding rectitude, must deal with him first. This portion of the story divides into five parts: Ruth goes to the threshing floor (vv. 1–6), meets Boaz (v. 7), requests and receives a commitment from Boaz (vv. 8–13), receives a gift from Boaz (vv. 14–15) and returns home (vv. 16–18).

■ **3:1–6** *Ruth Goes From Home to the Threshing Floor.* Naomi and Ruth had carefully worked out the detail of how to win Boaz's affection and commitment, and Ruth began to execute the plan.

3:1 As was the circumstance with Lot's daughters (Ge 19:31–32), Ruth, bereft of husband, acted to preserve her family line (see note on 1:22). **My daughter.** See note on 2:2. **find a home.** See NIV text note. Included in Ruth's "rest" (see NIV text note) would be "rest" (future fulfillment and provision) for all concerned.

3:2 kinsman. Naomi avoided the word "redeemer" (see 2:20); the Hebrew term she employed shares a common root with "relative" (2:1). Just which custom or law was invoked is not altogether clear, but kinship carried with it certain duties, and Naomi built on those.

3:3–4 Naomi gave Ruth instructions that raise morally intriguing questions for modern readers. Whatever the precise meaning of her directives, the narrator made it clear that Ruth was "a woman of noble character" (v. 11). Today's readers must remember that courtship and marriage customs in ancient agrarian cultures were different from those of today.

3:3 Wash and perfume yourself . . . best clothes. Naomi was concerned that Ruth be her most attractive. **the threshing floor.** This was probably located on a breezy slope a bit below and away from the town. The threshing floor was a place of harlotry during harvest festivals (Hos 9:1), suggesting the moral risk in Naomi's plan. This association may have motivated Boaz later to insist that this event not be told in public (v. 14).

3:4 uncover his feet. It is unclear what precisely happened between Ruth and Boaz. It has been suggested that the term "feet" may be a euphemism for male genitalia, but this is not necessarily the case here. The narrator's intent to contrast Ruth with her ancestress, Lot's daughter, may clarify the scene (see note on 1:22). Ruth's act of "uncovering" is described with an expression that resembles the idiom for incest: "uncover the nakedness of" (the NIV reads "have sexual relations with"; Lev 18:6–20). Nevertheless, the narrator may have modified the idiom to "uncover his feet" in order to preserve Ruth's purity in contrast to the perversity of Lot's daughter. **lie down.** This terminology also may have sexual connotations; on the other hand, it may simply mean to recline. **He will tell you what to do.** Boaz was an older man of good reputation (see 2:5,8; 3:10), and he would be able to advise Ruth.

■ **3:7** *Ruth Meets Boaz at the Threshing Floor.* Ruth followed through with Naomi's plan.

3:7 in good spirits. Like Lot (Ge 19:33), Boaz had been drinking, although here the text does not necessarily indicate overindulgence. The combination of work, harvest festivity and time of night led Boaz to "the far end of the grain pile," providentially and privately positioned for the next event. **Ruth . . . lay down.** Lot's daughter had sought out her father (Ge 19:33), and Ruth sought out Boaz here. See notes on verse 4.

■ **3:8–13** *Ruth Requests a Kinsman-Redeemer and Boaz Commits.* The purpose of the preceding events is specified in the conversation between Ruth and Boaz. Ruth honored Boaz and requested that he marry her. Boaz responded with a commitment that she would have a kinsman-redeemer.

3:8 something startled the man. The narrator may have been implying that Boaz remained asleep until startled, even though Ruth had been lying next to him for some time (see v. 7).

3:9 Spread the corner of your garment over me. Ezekiel 16:8 explains the idiom. Ruth was requesting marriage. **you are a kinsman-redeemer.** Nowhere does the law specify marriage as a responsibility of such redemption, though such an extension of Leviticus 25 can readily be envisioned. That Mahlon's name was to be preserved with his property (4:10) has overtones of the levirate marriage, but it remains difficult to see how Deuteronomy 25:5–6 could be strictly applied. The issue was Naomi's (or Mahlon's) property, which included Ruth. See "Introduction: Purpose and Distinctives," as well as the note on 2:20.

3:10 my daughter. See note on 2:2. **kindness.** Literally, "covenant love." Throughout the book God's covenant love (1:8; 2:20) is mirrored by Ruth's love (1:8,16–17). Here her fidelity was proven by (1) her invoking of the kinsman-redeemer duties and (2) her refusal to seek after one of the young men. The phrase "this kindness" is apparently a reference to her willingness to invoke a custom that would provide an heir for Naomi. **showed earlier.** That is, in Ruth's devotion to Naomi.

3:11 my daughter. Boaz's deepening affections were displayed in the repetition of this tender address (see note on 2:2). **woman of noble character.** The Hebrew is a feminine equivalent of "man of standing" (2:1). Ruth had risen from Moabitess and servant to an attractive and viable candidate for marriage to Boaz. Although there are some ambiguities regarding what actually transpired during the night, here the narrator's concern was that his readers acknowledge Ruth's dignity and honor.

3:12 a kinsman-redeemer nearer than I. The narrative introduces an unexpected element that could have derailed the scheme. Further, if Naomi had envisioned a kinship solution, why had the nearer relative not been introduced earlier? The dramatic tension is heightened. Protection and redemption now appeared to pose a threat, and the engagement was put on hold.

3:13 Stay here for the night. The intent of Boaz's instruction was to avoid recognition and shame. How this intent would have been achieved is not disclosed, but, if the plan was to work, Ruth's integrity could not be impugned. **if he wants to redeem, good . . . I will do it.** Boaz did not know what the outcome would be, other than the fact that, one way or the other, Ruth would have a kinsman-redeemer to care for her. Either he or the nearer kinsman would come to her aid.

[14]So she lay at his feet until morning, but got up before anyone could be recognized;
and he said, "Don't let it be known that a woman came to the threshing floor."[g]
[15]He also said, "Bring me the shawl you are wearing and hold it out." When she did
so, he poured into it six measures of barley and put it on her. Then he[a] went back to
town.
[16]When Ruth came to her mother-in-law, Naomi asked, "How did it go, my daughter?"
Then she told her everything Boaz had done for her [17]and added, "He gave me these
six measures of barley, saying, 'Don't go back to your mother-in-law empty-handed.' "
[18]Then Naomi said, "Wait, my daughter, until you find out what happens. For the man
will not rest until the matter is settled today."[h]

3:14 [g]Ro 14:16; 2Co 8:21

3:18 [h]Ps 37:3-5

Boaz Marries Ruth

4 Meanwhile Boaz went up to the town gate and sat there. When the kinsman-redeemer he had mentioned[i] came along, Boaz said, "Come over here, my friend, and
sit down." So he went over and sat down.
[2]Boaz took ten of the elders[j] of the town and said, "Sit here," and they did so. [3]Then
he said to the kinsman-redeemer, "Naomi, who has come back from Moab, is selling the
piece of land that belonged to our brother Elimelech. [4]I thought I should bring the matter to your attention and suggest that you buy it in the presence of these seated here and
in the presence of the elders of my people. If you will redeem it, do so. But if you[b] will
not, tell me, so I will know. For no one has the right to do it except you,[k] and I am next
in line."
"I will redeem it," he said.
[5]Then Boaz said, "On the day you buy the land from Naomi and from Ruth the Moabitess, you acquire[c] the dead man's widow, in order to maintain the name of the dead
with his property."[l]
[6]At this, the kinsman-redeemer said, "Then I cannot redeem[m] it because I might endanger my own estate. You redeem it yourself. I cannot do it."
[7](Now in earlier times in Israel, for the redemption and transfer of property to become
final, one party took off his sandal and gave it to the other. This was the method of le-
galizing transactions in Israel.)[n]
[8]So the kinsman-redeemer said to Boaz, "Buy it yourself." And he removed his sandal.
[9]Then Boaz announced to the elders and all the people, "Today you are witnesses that

4:1 [i]Ru 3:12

4:2 [j]1Ki 21:8; Pr 31:23

4:4 [k]Lev 25:25; Jer 32:7-8

4:5 [l]Ge 38:8; Dt 25:5-6; Ru 3:13; Mt 22:24

4:6 [m]Lev 25:25; Ru 3:13

4:7 [n]Dt 25:7-9

[a] *15* Most Hebrew manuscripts; many Hebrew manuscripts, Vulgate and Syriac *she* [b] *4* Many Hebrew manuscripts, Septuagint, Vulgate and Syriac; most Hebrew manuscripts *he* [c] *5* Hebrew; Vulgate and Syriac *Naomi, you acquire Ruth the Moabitess,*

■ **3:14–15** *Ruth Receives a Gift From Boaz.* After rising in the morning Boaz gave Ruth a gift of barley before returning to town.
3:15 six measures of barley. In verse 17 this barley was evidence of Boaz's magnanimity toward Ruth and a symbol of Naomi's changed estate (1:21).
■ **3:16–18** *Ruth Returns Home From the Threshing Floor.* In balance with the beginning of this episode (see vv. 1–6), Ruth returned home and received encouragement from Naomi.
3:16 my daughter? See note on 2:2.
3:17 He gave me . . . Don't go back . . . empty-handed. Ruth described the solicitous care Boaz had shown her. Her enthusiasm was matched only by Naomi's confidence about Boaz's future actions (v. 18).
3:18 my daughter. Like Boaz (vv. 10–11) Naomi addressed Ruth twice in this way, indicating her intense maternal feelings for her. **the man will not rest until the matter is settled today.** Based on Ruth's report, Naomi was convinced that Boaz would carry through with his commitment on that very day. Her prediction turned out to be accurate.
■ **4:1–12** *Boaz Becomes Ruth's Kinsman-Redeemer.* In this fourth step in Ruth's story, Ruth moved toward the anticipated resolution. In a touch of irony, a piece of property, rather than the widow, was the basis for the bargain. Ruth, however, was still the key participant, and eventually the deal turned on what seemed to be a combination of a levirate marriage (Dt 25:5–10) and kinsman-redemption (Lev 25). Boaz cleared the way to marry Ruth (vv. 1–8), publicly announced his commitment to her (vv. 9–10) and received hearty approval as blessings for fruitfulness were invoked (vv. 11–12).
■ **4:1–8** *Boaz Clears the Way to Become Ruth's Kinsman-Redeemer.* Boaz kept his word to Ruth. He approached her nearer kinsman and received his permission to act as the kinsman-redeemer.
4:1 the town gate. This was the usual place for legal and commercial transactions to take place. A citizen, like the near relative, would have customarily passed through the gate en route to his fields. **my friend.** The Hebrew is literally "so and so." As Boaz would hardly have addressed the kinsman in this language, the narrator seems to be taking pains to avoid naming the self-interested relative.
4:2 took ten of the elders. No legal requirement specified any set number of elders as determinative in local government. Later Jewish religious practices in which ten males constituted a quorum for worship may have derived from this incident. In a largely illiterate, rural culture, the presence of official witnesses was imperative for an oral contract.
4:3 Naomi . . . is selling the . . . land. This was a surprising new element, no hint of which had been given, although property, not marriage, was the subject of redemption laws in Leviticus (see Lev 25). Not even the relative knew that Ruth was the real "property." Why, and under what circumstances, Naomi was selling was obviously irrelevant to the narrator's purpose.
4:5 On the day . . . you acquire the dead man's widow. Here the so-called levirate marriage (see note on 3:9) seems to be considered in combination with kinsman-redemption. In an explication of Old Testament law not elsewhere given, obligations for posterity and property are tied together.
4:7 took off his sandal and gave it. Little is known of the specific symbolism of the sandal custom, which by the time of the writing of this book needed to be explained. The point, however, is clear: The transaction was thereby legalized (cf. Dt 25:9–10; Am 8:6).
■ **4:9–10** *Boaz Publicly Announces His Commitment to Ruth.* To finalize the arrangement, Boaz called publicly for witnesses to his commitment to Ruth.

I have bought from Naomi all the property of Elimelech, Kilion and Mahlon. [10]I have also
acquired Ruth the Moabitess, Mahlon's widow, as my wife, in order to maintain the
name of the dead with his property, so that his name will not disappear from among his
family or from the town records.[o] Today you are witnesses!"
[11]Then the elders and all those at the gate said, "We are witnesses.[p] May the LORD
make the woman who is coming into your home like Rachel and Leah,[q] who together
built up the house of Israel. May you have standing in Ephrathah[r] and be famous in Bethlehem. [12]Through the offspring the LORD gives you by this young woman, may your family be like that of Perez,[s] whom Tamar bore to Judah."

The Genealogy of David

[13]So Boaz took Ruth and she became his wife. Then he went to her, and the LORD enabled her to conceive,[t] and she gave birth to a son. [14]The women[u] said to Naomi:
"Praise be to the LORD, who this day has not left you without a kinsman-redeemer. May
he become famous throughout Israel! [15]He will renew your life and sustain you in your
old age. For your daughter-in-law, who loves you and who is better to you than seven
sons,[v] has given him birth."
[16]Then Naomi took the child, laid him in her lap and cared for him. [17]The women living there said, "Naomi has a son." And they named him Obed. He was the father of Jesse,[w] the father of David.
[18]This, then, is the family line of Perez[x]:

Perez was the father of Hezron,
[19]Hezron the father of Ram,
Ram the father of Amminadab,[y]
[20]Amminadab the father of Nahshon,
Nahshon the father of Salmon,[a]
[21]Salmon the father of Boaz,[z]
Boaz the father of Obed,
[22]Obed the father of Jesse,
and Jesse the father of David.

4:10 [o]Dt 25:6
4:11 [p]Dt 25:9 [q]Ps 127:3; 128:3 [r]Ge 35:16
4:12 [s]ver 18; Ge 38:29
4:13 [t]Ge 29:31; 33:5; Ru 3:11
4:14 [u]Lk 1:58
4:15 [v]Ru 1:16-17; 2:11-12; 1Sa 1:8
4:17 [w]ver 22; 1Sa 16:1, 18; 1Ch 2:12,13
4:18 [x]Mt 1:3-6
4:19 [y]Ex 6:23
4:21 [z]Ru 2:1

[a] *20* A few Hebrew manuscripts, some Septuagint manuscripts and Vulgate (see also verse 21 and Septuagint of 1 Chron. 2:11); most Hebrew manuscripts *Salma*

4:9 to the elders and all the people. The scene of this dramatic moment was enlarged beyond that of the ten elders (v. 2) to include the entire town.

4:10 to maintain the name of the dead with his property. For one's name to disappear was a curse to be avoided (1Sa 24:21; 2Sa 14:7). Whether it was Elimelech's or Mahlon's name that was to be preserved is academic.

▪ 4:11–12 *Boaz Is Blessed as Ruth's Kinsman-Redeemer.* The elders and townspeople affirmed Ruth's marriage to Boaz and prayed for Boaz to be blessed through fathering children.

4:11 like Rachel and Leah. These were the two wives of Jacob (Israel) who had mothered—personally or by proxy through their maids Zilpah and Bilhah—the heads of the tribes of Israel. The blessing on Ruth was, in reality, a blessing on Boaz. **have standing in Ephrathah and be famous in Bethlehem.** These two Hebrew idioms bespeak the enduring distinction with which God would bless the union. As in 1:1–2, these place names, which are associated with David, are given unusual prominence because of the book's purpose.

4:12 be like . . . Perez. Perez, who was born to Judah because Onan refused to honor his levirate obligation (Ge 38:29), was an ancestor of Boaz (vv. 18–22) and a model of fruitful offspring. As Perez was to Judah, so the child of Boaz (born because another kinsman-redeemer refused to honor his obligation) would become to the Davidic line. Thus the elders and the entire crowd at the gate publicly affirmed the legitimacy of Ruth's place in David's lineage. Any question concerning this matter should have been put to rest by this scene. See *WCF* 21.4.

▪ 4:13–17 *Naomi's Blessing.* Three elements appear in these verses: the child's birth (v. 13), Naomi's blessed condition (vv. 14–17a) and the child's naming (v. 17b). Usually, the naming of a child followed directly after the birth (cf. Ge 4:25; 5:3; Ex 2:10; 1Sa 1:20). Here the narrator interrupted these two elements by his attention to Naomi. The effect of this technique was to set Naomi's condition alongside the birth as an essential element in the closing of the story. This concern balances with the attention to Naomi at the opening of the book (1:1–22).

▪ 4:13 *Boaz and Ruth Have a Son.* The marital union of Boaz and Ruth produced a son who would be heir of Naomi's (and Ruth's) inheritance.

▪ 4:14–17a *Naomi Blessed by the Son.* These verses stress the fulfillment of God's covenant love to Naomi. As the women of the town had noticed her bleak situation when she had first arrived (1:19), they now recognized the extent to which God had blessed her. First, Ruth, the daughter-in-law, was better than seven sons (v. 15). Second, while Ruth "gave birth to a son" (v. 13), Naomi "[had] a son" (v. 17).

4:16 Naomi took . . . cared for him. Literally, "Then Naomi took the child, laid him on her breast, and she became his nurse [or foster mother]." This may possibly indicate a formal adoption procedure. Whatever the case, this closing scene dramatically climaxed what was in a very real way Naomi's story. She who had returned empty (1:21) had been filled.

4:17 Obed . . . Jesse . . . David. Until now, the concern of the book with the house of David had been revealed only subtly, through tribal and territorial references. Now the connection was made explicit. The drama that had just unfolded was designed to demonstrate that David's Moabite ancestress had received full approval and acceptance by God and his people.

▪ 4:17b *Boaz and Ruth Name the Son.* This closing element not only completes the birth-naming announcement but also indicates the importance of this birth for the purpose of the book.

▪ 4:18–22 *Genealogical Appendix.* The closing genealogy shifts the focus from Naomi back to Boaz and reinforces the larger purpose of the narrative. Judah's history began with a breach (Perez; Ge 38:29; see NIV text note), but through the generations a kinsman-redeemer was born, and finally through the great King David God would redeem all Israel. For Christian readers, this genealogy points to Christ, the great son of David, the only Savior.

1 SAMUEL

Introduction

Overview

Author: Unknown

Purpose: To explain that David's dynasty remained Israel's hope for the future in spite of the curses that David and his house had brought upon the nation

Date: 930–538 B.C.

Key Truths:

- God wanted his people to have the king he would choose.
- God carefully prepared the way for the king of his choice.
- God chose the house of David as the royal family forever.
- Despite the weakness of David's kingdom, the hope for God's people still remained in his family.

Author

The books of Samuel were originally one work that was later divided into two. This book offers no clear guidance on the question of authorship. It seems likely that the attachment of Samuel's name simply reflects the role he played in the early chapters of the book. Samuel is described as an old man in 1 Samuel 8:1 and as dead in 1 Samuel 25:1, which would have been long before many of the events of 1 and 2 Samuel took place. However, 1 Chronicles 29:29 attaches the names of Samuel and of his prophetic successors Nathan and Gad to certain written sources, some of which may well have been incorporated into this written history of Israel as it took shape.

Time and Place of Writing

The book of Samuel offers several clues as to its date of final composition. The writer relied on a number of prophetic and royal sources for his history, but the earliest likely date for the book is indicated by the fact that it looks back on "the last words of David" (2Sa 23:1); i.e., David's final official words before his death. Also, 1 Samuel 27:6 remarks that Ziklag remained under the control of "the kings of Judah," which probably acknowledges the division of Judah and Israel in 930 B.C. If so, the book could not have been written until after the division of the nation that resulted from the failures of David and his house. If Samuel was written at this time, the book affirmed hope in David's line despite the troubles of the divided monarchy.

The latest likely date for final composition is the return from exile in 538 B.C. The writer of Chronicles used Samuel as one of his most important sources (see "Introduction to 1 Chronicles: Author"). Moreover, the book of Kings appears to pick up the history of Israel's throne where Samuel left off (see 2Sa 23:1–7; 1Ki 1:1), and 1 Kings 2:27 refers to the fulfillment of 1 Samuel 2:27–36. Therefore, Samuel was probably written before Kings, which is dated between 561 and 538 B.C. (see "Introduction to 1 Kings: Time and Place of Writing"). If Samuel was written at this time, the book declared hope in David's line despite the exile, which largely resulted from the disobedience of David's royal sons.

It is impossible to arrive at firm dates for many of the events that are described in 1 and 2 Samuel. There is broad consensus that David had consolidated his rule over the tribes shortly before 1000 B.C. (Judah c. 1010 B.C. and Israel c. 1003 B.C.). David's lifetime extended from c. 1040 to c. 970 B.C.

Purpose and Distinctives

The title of the book has varied throughout the centuries. The Septuagint (the Greek translation of the OT) groups 1 and 2 Samuel together with 1 and 2 Kings as the "First, Second, Third and Fourth Books of Reigns" (or "Kingdoms"). Similarly, the Vulgate (the Latin translation of the Bible) refers to these books as "First, Second, Third and Fourth Kings." Most modern versions reflect the Hebrew tradition of distinguishing between the books of Samuel and those of Kings. Until the fifteenth century, Hebrew tradition treated 1 and 2 Samuel as a single book.

It was during the latter half of the eleventh century B.C., a time when the empires of the ancient Near East were not at full strength, that God transformed Israel from a loosely knit tribal confederacy into a united monarchy. Although the institution of the monarchy marked a significant political and religious development, it was not a new idea in Israel. A fundamental tenet of Israelite faith was that the Lord himself was Israel's sovereign, the great King (e.g., 8:7; 12:12; Nu 23:21; Ps 5:2; Mal 1:14). Nevertheless, the opening books of the Bible contain various indications that Israel, in accordance with the divine will, would one day have a human monarch (Ge 49:10; Nu 24:7,17–19; cf. Ge 17:6,16; 35:11). In Deuteronomy 17:14 Moses anticipated a time when Israel would be settled in the land of promise and would desire a king, and he gave instructions to regulate kingship at such time as the monarchy would be instituted (vv. 15–20; cf. 28:36). This time period is the subject of the book of Samuel.

As a result, the narrator of the book of Samuel had at least two main purposes. First, he was determined to chronicle a true historical account of the birth and early development of the Israelite monarchy. This history is highly selective and evaluative, but it is historically accurate nonetheless. Second, the manner in which the narrator selected and evaluated the historical events alerts us to his complex theological purposes. The centerpiece of these theological interests was the theology of Davidic kingship. The book records the rise, successes and failures of David's rule, but it does so in order to teach a theology of kingship for the sake of future generations who would be led by David's royal sons.

Like Joshua, Judges and 1 and 2 Kings, the theology of 1 and 2 Samuel is deeply influenced by Deuteronomy (see "Introduction to the Historical Books" on page 304). The emphases of Deuteronomy on covenant blessings and curses, the centralization of worship and authority, the evils of idolatry, the necessary righteousness of the king, the role of prophets, etc., form a theological backdrop to the perspectives guiding the book of Samuel. When the writer of Samuel applied the theology of Deuteronomy to the development of Israel's early monarchy, he explained what future kings should learn from David's successes and failures and why David's dynasty remained Israel's hope despite the covenant curses that David's house had brought on the nation.

These theological purposes seldom come to explicit expression in the book of Samuel. Like most of the narrative portions of the Old Testament, Samuel tends to present dramatic narration. The characters act and interact, as it were, on stage. Relying on characters to *show* rather than the narrator to *tell* the readers how to evaluate events engages readers' interests and powers of moral discernment.

In keeping with the dramatic mode of narration, Samuel was written concisely, with the narrator employing a variety of sophisticated techniques to express his theological evaluations: key words (see note on 2:29); comparative or contrastive characterizations (e.g., Saul and Jonathan in chs. 13–14 [see notes on 13:22; 14:6] and David and Uriah in 2Sa 11); repetition with variation (e.g., Saul's two confessions in 15:24–25,30); and narrative analogy (e.g., Nabal as a surrogate of Saul in ch. 25). Sensitivity to these literary features will lead the reader to increased theological understanding.

The content of 1 Samuel is so complex that it is helpful to summarize the material. The plot of 1 Samuel divides into four main parts (and an appendix) that feature the intersecting lives of Samuel, Saul and David. Chapters 1–7 describe events leading up to the appearance of Saul, the first king of Israel. The first half of this material (chs. 1–3) recounts the birth narrative of Samuel (ch. 1). Chapter 2 opens with Hannah's song of praise for the birth of Samuel (vv. 1–10). Hannah's song and David's poetic compositions (2Sa 22; 23) frame the books of Samuel and introduce themes that prove fundamental to the theology of the books: the sovereignty and holiness of God, divine reversal of human fortunes, divine deliverance and the futility of trusting in human strength. Even kingship is anticipated in a reference to the Lord's "anointed," his king (2:10). The remainder of chapter 2 tells the story of the downfall of the priestly house of Eli, introducing yet another important theme in Samuel: divine rejection and its causes. Chapter 3 reiterates the rejection of the house of Eli, this time in the words of the Lord through the fledgling prophet Samuel, who henceforth would serve as God's man in the transition to kingship.

First Samuel 4:1—7:1 constitutes what is often called "the ark narrative." These chapters strikingly demonstrate the Lord's power, first in his resistance to Israel's attempt to manipulate the ark as a source of magical power and second in his devastating tour of Philistine cities, a virtual victory march. First Samuel 7:2–17 provides a climax to the preceding two sections, as God's power to deliver Israel and defeat Israel's enemies is displayed through God's man, the prophet Samuel.

Against this backdrop, the sinfulness of the people's demand for a human ruler (chs. 8–12) is most clearly seen. It was not that Israel was never to have a human monarch, for a king had long been anticipated. Rather it was objectionable that the people wanted a king "such as all the other nations [had]" (8:5), for this connoted a rejection of the great King, God himself (8:7). Despite the offensiveness and folly of the people's request, God was nevertheless willing to grant it—provided that they first heard warnings concerning the potential abuses of kingship and that the king himself did not seek autonomy but was willing to submit himself to an authority structure whereby God's rule would continue.

It is in this latter regard that Israel's first appointed king proved deficient. Saul is introduced in 9:2 as an impressive individual of striking proportions, presumably what the people had in mind. Nevertheless, it soon becomes apparent that this superb specimen was lacking in qualities necessary to be a successful king in Israel. A primary indication of Saul's unsuitability was his repeated failure to obey the word of the Lord as related by Samuel. While the better-known instances of Saul's disobedience are found in chapters 13 and 15, the first occurrence appears already in chapter 10. On the occasion of Saul's anointing by Samuel, three signs were given to serve as confirmation. When the third and last had been fulfilled, Saul was to "do whatever [his] hand [found] to do" (according to Samuel's charge in 10:7), after which (according to Samuel's further directive in 10:8) Saul was to return to Gilgal to await additional instructions regarding the Philistine battle that his first action would surely provoke. Had Saul adhered to this scheme, he would have demonstrated his willingness to submit himself to God's rule and would have confirmed his suitability to be king. He would also have moved a step closer to the throne, following the three-part pattern of designation (by anointing), demonstration (by a deed of valor; i.e., "whatever [his] hand [found] to do" [see 10:7 and its note]) and confirmation (by the people and the prophet). Unfortunately, Saul shrank back from the charge of 10:7 and forestalled the accession process. While Saul's victory over the Ammonites (ch. 11) was sufficient to satisfy the people, it was apparent from the tone of Samuel's speech (ch. 12) that, in Samuel's mind at least, Saul had yet to pass the test in terms of suitability for kingship.

In chapter 13 Jonathan, not Saul, did what Saul's hand should have done, thus throwing down the gauntlet to the Philistines. Apparently recognizing that the charge of 10:7 was now fulfilled, albeit by Jonathan, Saul immediately went down to Gilgal (in accordance with 10:8) to await Samuel's arrival. When Samuel was slow in coming, Saul proceeded to offer pre-battle sacrifices in Samuel's absence, judging that the military situation precluded further delay. No sooner had Saul begun than Samuel arrived and, after hearing Saul's excuses, announced that Saul had acted foolishly and that his kingdom would not endure. Commentators sometimes seek to justify, or at least to trivialize, Saul's actions and to criticize Samuel's reaction as overly harsh. But in the light of the significance of the charge issued in 10:7–8 as a test of Saul's fitness, such interpretations must be rejected. On this occasion of Saul's initial rejection, as also on the occasion of his second (ch. 15), Saul's specific deeds of disobedience were but symptomatic of his fundamental inability to accommodate himself to the necessary requirements of theocratic kingship.

After his definitive rejection in chapter 15, Saul was no longer the rightful king in God's eyes (though he remained on the throne for some years), and God turned his attention to another: David, "a man after his own heart" (13:14). Chapters 16–31 trace Saul's emotional and psychological disintegration—a disintegration exacerbated by his fear of David, whom he sensed to be God's choice for king. After failing in many attempts to take David's life, Saul eventually took his own. David was providentially, if circuitously, guided toward the throne. Beginning with his anointing in chapter 16, the account of David's rise was punctuated by reminders that "the LORD [was] with him" (16:18 and its note).

Christ in 1 and 2 Samuel

Christ stands in contrast to the many examples of the sinful leaders of Israel who appear in the book. More than this, however, Jesus is the heir of David's throne, and David's career anticipated the person and work of Christ. Both David and Jesus had prophetic sanction, David by Samuel (3:20; 16:13) and Jesus by John the Baptist (Mt 14:5; Jn 1:29–31; 5:31–35). The Spirit of the Lord came upon both (16:13; Mk 1:9–11), and both did mighty works (ch. 17; Mt 11:4–5), were involved in holy war (ch. 17; Col 1:20), and were rejected by jealous kings (18:9; Mt 2:16) and warned to flee for their lives (ch. 20; Mt 2:13–15). Rejected by their own people without just cause (23:12; Jn 19:15), both learned in exile to depend on God. Both interceded on behalf of God's people (2Sa 21; 24; Jn 17), and both were highly exalted by God (2Sa 23:1–8; Isa 52:13; Php 2:9). In these and many other ways, David's life foreshadowed the accomplishments of Christ, his son.

Outline

God chose Samuel to replace Eli and his sons as the recognized authority in Israel so that he could anoint Israel's king.

- I. Eli and Samuel: God's Preparations for Kingship (1:1—7:17)
  - A. Samuel's Miraculous Birth (1:1—2:10)
    - 1. Hannah's Struggle and Exaltation (1:1–28)
    - 2. Hannah's Praise for God's Power (2:1–10)
  - B. Samuel Rises as Eli and His Sons Fall (2:11—7:17)
    - 1. In the Divine Presence at Shiloh (2:11–21)
      - a. Eli's Sons' Evil at Shiloh (2:11–17)
      - b. Samuel Blessed at Shiloh (2:18–21)
    - 2. In Disapproval and Approval (2:22–26)
      - a. Eli's Sons Receive Human and Divine Disapproval (2:22–25)
      - b. Samuel Matures With Human and Divine Approval (2:26)
    - 3. In Divine Judgment and Blessing (2:27—4:1a)
      - a. Eli and Sons Are Judged by God (2:27–36)
      - b. Samuel Called and Blessed by God (3:1—4:1a)
    - 4. In Conflict With the Philistines (4:1b—7:17)
      - a. Eli's Sons Lead to Defeat and the Loss of the Ark (4:1b–22)
      - b. The Ark Brings Curses to the Philistines (5:1–12)
      - c. The Ark Is Returned by the Philistines (6:1—7:1)
      - d. Samuel Leads to Victory (7:2–17)

- II. Samuel and Saul: Saul's Rise and His Failed Kingship (8:1—15:35)

  Samuel anointed Saul, but also rejected him when he sinned.

  - A. Saul's Rise (8:1—12:25)
    - 1. Samuel Hears and God Grants the Request for a King (8:1–22)
    - 2. Saul Becomes King (9:1—11:15)
    - 3. Saul's Anointing by Samuel (9:1—10:16)
      - a. Saul's Public Selection by Lot at Mizpah (10:17–27)
      - b. Saul's Rescue of Jabesh Gilead (11:1–15)
    - 4. Samuel Warns and Encourages Israel (12:1–25)
  - B. Saul's Failed Kingship (13:1—15:35)
    - 1. Saul Is Rejected Initially (13:1–22)
    - 2. Saul's Character Exposed by Jonathan (14:1–46)
    - 3. Saul's Unending Philistine Warfare (14:47–52)
    - 4. Saul's Definitive Rejection (15:1–35)
- III. Saul and David: David's Rise and Saul's Fall (16:1—2Sa 1:27)

  God chose David to replace Saul as the king of Israel.

  - A. David's Success and Troubles in Saul's Service (16:1—18:30)
    - 1. David's Anointing by Samuel (16:1–23)
    - 2. David's Success and Saul's Initial Approval (17:1—18:5)
    - 3. David's Success and Saul's Jealousy (18:6–16)
    - 4. David's Success and Saul's Snare (18:17–30)
  - B. David's Help as He Flees From Saul (19:1—22:5)
    - 1. David's Initial Flight (19:1–10)
    - 2. David Aided by Michal (19:11–17)
    - 3. David Aided by Samuel (19:18–24)
    - 4. David Aided by Jonathan (20:1–42)
    - 5. David Aided by Ahimelech (21:1–9)
    - 6. David Aided by Achish (21:10–15)
    - 7. David Aided by the King of Moab and by Gad (22:1–5)
  - C. David's Innocence and Saul's Guilt (22:6—2Sa 1:27)
    - 1. Toward Other Israelites (22:6—23:6)
      - a. Saul Kills the Priests at Nob (22:6–23)
      - b. David Protects Keilah (23:1–6)
    - 2. Toward Each Other (23:7—26:25)
      - a. David Barely Escapes Saul (23:7–29)
      - b. David Spares Saul for the First Time (24:1–22)
      - c. David Kept From Bloodguilt (25:1–44)
      - d. David Spares Saul a Second Time (26:1–25)
    - 3. Toward the Philistines (27:1—2Sa 1:27)
      - a. David Fools the Philistines (27:1—28:2)
      - b. Saul Sins for Fear of the Philistines (28:3–25)
      - c. David Is Feared and Victorious (29:1—30:31)
      - d. Saul and His Sons Die in Battle With the Philistines (31:1–13)

e. David Reacts Innocently to Saul's Death (2Sa 1:1–27)
(1) David Avenges Saul and Jonathan (1:1–16)
(2) David Laments Saul and Jonathan (1:17–27)

IV. David: David's Full Kingship (2:1—20:26)
A. David's Kingship Under Divine Blessing (2:1—10:19)
1. David's Rise to Kingship (2:1—5:5)
a. David Becomes King Over Judah at Hebron (2:1–7)
b. David Becomes King Over All Israel (2:8—5:5)
(1) Resistance From Saul's House (2:8—3:5)
(2) Abner Is Murdered (3:6–39)
(3) Ish-Bosheth Is Murdered (4:1–12)
(4) David Becomes the King Over All Tribes at Hebron (5:1–5)
2. David's Throne Is Established Forever in Jerusalem (5:6—10:19)
a. Jerusalem Is Established (5:6—6:23)
(1) David Captures Jerusalem (5:6–16)
(2) David Conquers the Philistines (5:17–25)
(3) David Brings the Ark of God to Jerusalem (6:1–23)
b. God Promises David an Everlasting Dynasty (7:1–29)
(1) God's Promises (7:1–17)
(2) David's Response (7:18–29)
c. God's Blessings (8:1—10:19)
(1) Military Successes (8:1–18)
(2) Kindness to Mephibosheth (9:1–13)
(3) Kindness to Hanun (10:1–19)
B. David's Kingship Under Divine Curse (11:1—20:26)
1. David's Sins (11:1—12:25)
a. David and Bathsheba (11:1–27)
b. David and Nathan (12:1–25)
2. David's Consequences (12:26—20:26)
a. David's Weakness as a Warrior (12:26–31)
b. Rape and Murder (13:1—14:33)
(1) Amnon's Sexual Sin (13:1–22)
(2) Absalom's Revenge (13:23–39)
(3) Absalom's Reconciliation (14:1–33)
c. Absalom's Rebellion (15:1—19:40)
(1) Absalom Gains Victory (15:1–12)
(2) David Flees (15:13–31)
(3) Encounters Along the Way (15:32—16:14)
(4) Absalom's Two Counselors (16:15—17:23)
(5) Battle Against Absalom (17:24—19:8a)
(6) David's Return (19:8b–15a)
(7) Encounters Along the Way (19:15b–40)
d. Sheba's Rebellion (19:41—20:26)

David rose to establish a permanent dynasty over Israel. David's kingdom increased under God's blessing, but suffered under his curse.

V. Conclusion: Continuing Hope in David's House (21:1—24:25)
   A. David's Intercession Stops a Famine (21:1–14)
   B. David's Military Accomplishments (21:15–22)
   C. David's Praise and Confidence (22:1–51)
   D. David's Declaration About the Future (23:1–7)
   E. David's Military Accomplishments (23:8–39)
   F. David's Intercession Stops a Plague (24:1–25)

In spite of all the troubles David's disobedience brought upon himself, his house was still the hope of God's people in the future.

The Birth of Samuel

1 There was a certain man from Ramathaim, a Zuphite[a] from the hill country[a] of
Ephraim, whose name was Elkanah[b] son of Jeroham, the son of Elihu, the son of
Tohu, the son of Zuph, an Ephraimite. **2**He had two wives;[c] one was called Hannah and
the other Peninnah. Peninnah had children, but Hannah had none.
3Year after year[d] this man went up from his town to worship[e] and sacrifice to the LORD
Almighty at Shiloh,[f] where Hophni and Phinehas, the two sons of Eli, were priests of the
LORD. **4**Whenever the day came for Elkanah to sacrifice,[g] he would give portions of the
meat to his wife Peninnah and to all her sons and daughters. **5**But to Hannah he gave a
double portion because he loved her, and the LORD had closed her womb.[h] **6**And because
the LORD had closed her womb, her rival kept provoking her in order to irritate her.[i] **7**This
went on year after year. Whenever Hannah went up to the house of the LORD, her rival
provoked her till she wept and would not eat. **8**Elkanah her husband would say to her,
"Hannah, why are you weeping? Why don't you eat? Why are you downhearted? Don't
I mean more to you than ten sons?[j]"
9Once when they had finished eating and drinking in Shiloh, Hannah stood up. Now
Eli the priest was sitting on a chair by the doorpost of the LORD's temple.[b][k] **10**In bitter-

1:1 [a]Jos 17:17-18 [b]1Ch 6:27,34
1:2 [c]Dt 21:15-17; Lk 2:36
1:3 [d]ver 21; Ex 23:14; 34:23; Lk 2:41 [e]Dt 12:5-7 [f]Jos 18:1
1:4 [g]Dt 12:17-18
1:5 [h]Ge 16:1; 30:2
1:6 [i]Job 24:21
1:8 [j]Ru 4:15
1:9 [k]1Sa 3:3

[a] 1 Or *from Ramathaim Zuphim* [b] 9 That is, tabernacle

■ **1:1—7:17** *Eli and Samuel: God's Preparations for Kingship.* God prepared his people for the time of the monarchy by raising the greatest judge in Israel's history: Samuel. The exaltation of Samuel is essential to the purpose of this book. Samuel anointed Saul (ch. 10), reversed the anointing of Saul (ch. 13), anointed David (ch. 16) and announced the permanence of David's dynasty (2Sa 7). He played such a formative role that his status is firmly established in these chapters, which divide into two parts: Samuel's miraculous birth (1:1—2:10) and his rise to leadership (2:11—7:17).

■ **1:1—2:10** *Samuel's Miraculous Birth.* Samuel was no ordinary child. God exalted his humble mother, Hannah, through his miraculous birth (ch. 1), and that birth inspired her to sing (pray) a song of thanksgiving for God's power in history that would eventually lead to Israel's king (2:1–10).

■ **1:1–28** *Hannah's Struggle and Exaltation.* A touching account is given of the miraculous birth of Hannah's son Samuel. This episode reveals a basic principle guiding the theology of the book (which appears explicitly in 2:1–10): God exalts the humble and brings down the proud. This theme is also seen in the presentations of Samuel, Eli and his sons, and Saul and David.

1:1 certain man. This expression and the rather full genealogical notice suggest that Elkanah was a man of standing. These features, along with the reference to a barren wife (v. 2), are reminiscent of the introduction of Samson's birth narrative (Jdg 13:2). **Ephraimite.** If the genealogies of 1 Chronicles 6:16–30 and 33–37 are taken into account, "Ephraimite" would refer to Elkanah's tribal residence, not his tribal ancestry.

1:2 two wives. Polygamy is first mentioned in Genesis 4:19 and is recognized and regulated (although not endorsed) in Deuteronomy 21:15–17. **children.** Hannah was childless and was provoked by her prolific rival (vv. 6–7). The motif of a barren, although favored, wife to whom God granted a significant offspring is not uncommon in the Old Testament (e.g., Ge 18:1–15; 25:21–26; 30:22–24; Jdg 13:2–5; cf. Lk 1:5–25). Though strife is present in this account, this is the most benign example of polygamy in Scripture.

1:3 Year after year this man went up. Perhaps in observance of "the annual festival of the LORD in Shiloh" (Jdg 21:19) or simply for a family ceremony (20:6). Several times in the Pentateuch reference is made to three annual pilgrim-festivals (Ex 23:14–17; 34:18–23; Dt 16:1–17). **LORD Almighty.** This title occurs here for the first time in the Old Testament. The first word, *Yahweh* in Hebrew, is the personal name of the God of Israel; the second term has traditionally been understood as a military term meaning "hosts" or "armies." In this sense, the reference would seem to encompass the hosts of Israel (17:45), the cosmic hosts (i.e., the celestial bodies; Dt 4:19) and the angelic hosts (Jos 5:14). The title would then be expressive of the Lord's sovereignty over all earthly and heavenly powers to use them to carry out his will against opposition. Alternatively, but with similar effect, some have taken the second term as an abstract noun, yielding "LORD of Might" or "LORD, the Almighty." **Shiloh.** Located midway between Shechem and Bethel, Shiloh was an important Israelite religious center during the period before the monarchy (Jos 18:1; Jdg 21:19). The destruction of at least the sanctuary there (Jer 7:12) may have been at the hand of the Philistines in the aftermath of the battle of Aphek (4:1–11). **Hophni and Phinehas.** Both are Egyptian names, the latter being also the name of Aaron's grandson (Nu 25:7). **Eli.** As with some other well-known characters in the Old Testament (cf. Joshua [Ex 17:9] and Jonathan [1Sa 13:2]), Eli is first introduced by name only, without further description. The writer expected his readers to be familiar with this character.

1:5 double portion. The Hebrew is difficult and has elicited suggestions of an especially honorable portion. The Septuagint (the Greek translation of the OT) offers an alternative reading: "to Hannah he would give a single portion, still it was Hannah he loved." In any case, Elkanah's attempts to lessen Hannah's sorrow by expressions of his own love (v. 8) were ineffectual. **the LORD had closed her womb.** Hannah's barrenness was neither by chance nor a form of divine punishment (cf. 2Sa 6:23) but was under the Lord's sovereign control and intended ultimately for her good (see Ge 50:19–20; Ro 8:28).

1:6 her rival. See note on 1:2.

1:7 would not eat. Hannah refused to eat until the Lord promised a resolution to her problem (cf. David's actions in 2Sa 12:16–20 and Saul's in 1Sa 28:23–25). Fasting often accompanied serious dealings with the Lord during the New Testament period as well (e.g., Ac 13:2–3; 14:23).

1:9 temple. The reference here and in 3:3 is to the tabernacle (see NIV text note), although mention of doorposts here and doors in 3:15, as well as sleeping quarters in 3:2–3, may suggest elements of a more permanent structure to which the tabernacle may have

ness of soul[l] Hannah wept much and prayed to the LORD. 11 And she made a vow, saying,
"O LORD Almighty, if you will only look upon your servant's misery and remember[m] me,
and not forget your servant but give her a son, then I will give him to the LORD for all the
days of his life, and no razor[n] will ever be used on his head."
12 As she kept on praying to the LORD, Eli observed her mouth. 13 Hannah was praying
in her heart, and her lips were moving but her voice was not heard. Eli thought she was
drunk 14 and said to her, "How long will you keep on getting drunk? Get rid of your wine."
15 "Not so, my lord," Hannah replied, "I am a woman who is deeply troubled. I have
not been drinking wine or beer; I was pouring[o] out my soul to the LORD. 16 Do not take
your servant for a wicked woman; I have been praying here out of my great anguish and
grief."
17 Eli answered, "Go in peace,[p] and may the God of Israel grant you what you have
asked of him.[q]"
18 She said, "May your servant find favor in your eyes.[r]" Then she went her way and
ate something, and her face was no longer downcast.[s]
19 Early the next morning they arose and worshiped before the LORD and then went
back to their home at Ramah. Elkanah lay with Hannah his wife, and the LORD remembered[t] her. 20 So in the course of time Hannah conceived and gave birth to a son. She
named[u] him Samuel,[a] saying, "Because I asked the LORD for him."

Hannah Dedicates Samuel

21 When the man Elkanah went up with all his family to offer the annual[v] sacrifice to
the LORD and to fulfill his vow,[w] 22 Hannah did not go. She said to her husband, "After
the boy is weaned, I will take him and present[x] him before the LORD, and he will live there
always."
23 "Do what seems best to you," Elkanah her husband told her. "Stay here until you
have weaned him; only may the LORD make good[y] his[b] word." So the woman stayed at
home and nursed her son until she had weaned him.
24 After he was weaned, she took the boy with her, young as he was, along with a
three-year-old bull,[c z] an ephah[d] of flour and a skin of wine, and brought him to the
house of the LORD at Shiloh. 25 When they had slaughtered the bull, they brought the boy
to Eli, 26 and she said to him, "As surely as you live, my lord, I am the woman who stood
here beside you praying to the LORD. 27 I prayed[a] for this child, and the LORD has granted me what I asked of him. 28 So now I give him to the LORD. For his whole life[b] he will
be given over to the LORD." And he worshiped the LORD there.

1:10 [l]Job 7:11
1:11 [m]Ge 8:1; 28:20; 29:32 [n]Nu 6:1-21; Jdg 13:5
1:15 [o]Ps 42:4; 62:8; La 2:19
1:17 [p]Jdg 18:6; 1Sa 25:35; 2Ki 5:19; Mk 5:34 [q]Ps 20:3-5
1:18 [r]Ru 2:13 [s]Ecc 9:7; Ro 15:13
1:19 [t]Ge 4:1; 30:22
1:20 [u]Ge 41:51-52; Ex 2:10,22; Mt 1:21
1:21 [v]ver 3 [w]Dt 12:11
1:22 [x]ver 11,28; Lk 2:22
1:23 [y]ver 17; Nu 30:7
1:24 [z]Nu 15:8-10; Dt 12:5; Jos 18:1
1:27 [a]ver 11-13; Ps 66:19-20
1:28 [b]ver 11,22; Ge 24:26,52

[a] *20* *Samuel* sounds like the Hebrew for *heard of God.* [b] *23* Masoretic Text; Dead Sea Scrolls, Septuagint and Syriac *your* [c] *24* Dead Sea Scrolls, Septuagint and Syriac; Masoretic Text *with three bulls*
[d] *24* That is, probably about 3/5 bushel (about 22 liters)

been attached in some manner. Other designations of the structure in Samuel are "the house of the LORD" (v. 7; 3:15) and "the Tent of Meeting" (2:22). Psalm 27:4–5 employs "house of the LORD," "temple," "dwelling" and "tabernacle" as virtual synonyms, and 2 Samuel 7:6 makes it clear that the Lord's dwelling prior to the time of David was a tent and not a house in the strict sense (cf. Ps 78:60).
1:11 vow. On the making of vows by married women and the husbands' responsibility to confirm or nullify, see Numbers 30:6–15. **remember me.** In prayer. For God to remember was for him to act on that person's behalf. See note on Genesis 8:1. **no razor.** Hannah's vow on her son's behalf reflected the second of the three stipulations of the Nazirite vow described in Numbers 6:1–21. The stipulations were (1) abstinence from the fruit of the vine, (2) no haircuts and (3) avoidance of dead bodies. The Septuagint (the Greek translation of the OT) and probably also the Dead Sea Scrolls include the first element in the Samuel context. While such vows were generally made for a limited period of time, Hannah's was for "all the days" of her son's life. In this respect, there is a reminder of the Nazirite charge included in the annunciation of Samson's birth in Judges 13:3–7, where we also note that the order to abstain from wine or other fermented drink was extended to the mother. See *WCF* 22.6.
1:13–15 See *WLC* 145.
1:13 drunk. Whether by virtue of his failing eyesight (3:2; 4:15) or his unfamiliarity with the posture of fervent prayer, Eli's misapprehension of Hannah as being in a drunken state introduces an unsettling element into the narrative portrayal of the priest.
1:15 pouring out my soul. To Eli's insinuation that she has been imbibing, or pouring down, wine or beer, Hannah insisted that she had instead been pouring out her soul before the Lord. See *WLC* 185.
1:16 wicked. See note on 2:12.
1:18 her face was no longer downcast. Hannah's actions upon hearing the priestly benediction of verse 17 gave evidence of her believing response.
1:20 Samuel. Various meanings of the name Samuel have been suggested, including "heard of God" (see NIV text note), "he who is from God," "name of God" and even "son of God" (in the sense of "given" or "promised" by God).
1:21 vow. See Leviticus 7:16 and its note.
1:22 weaned. In the ancient Near East a child was weaned rather later than is customary today. This is suggested not only by the present context but also by a reference in an Apocryphal book, 2 Maccabees 7:27: "I carried you nine months in the womb, suckled you three years."
1:23 his word. "Your word" is probably to be preferred here (see NIV text note). Elkanah, as Hannah's husband (see note on v. 11), invoked the Lord's assistance in Hannah's fulfillment of her vow.
1:24 three-year-old bull . . . skin of wine. According to Numbers 15:8–10, the fulfillment of a special vow like this one was to be accompanied by an offering of three things: a young bull, fine flour and wine. Hannah brought all three, although in larger measure than stipulated in Numbers.
1:27 what I asked. See note on verse 20.

2:1
[c]Lk 1:46-55
[d]Ps 9:14; 13:5
[e]Ps 89:17,24; 92:10; Isa 12:2-3

2:2
[f]Ex 15:11; Lev 19:2
[g]Dt 32:30-31; 2Sa 22:2,32

2:3
[h]Pr 8:13 [i]1Sa 16:7; 1Ki 8:39 [j]Pr 16:2; 24:11-12

2:4
[k]Ps 37:15

2:5
[l]Ps 113:9; Jer 15:9

2:6
[m]Dt 32:39
[n]Isa 26:19

2:7
[o]Dt 8:18 [p]Job 5:11; Ps 75:7

2:8
[q]Ps 113:7-8
[r]Job 36:7 [s]Job 38:4

2:9
[t]Ps 91:12 [u]Mt 8:12
[v]Ps 33:16-17

Hannah's Prayer

2 Then Hannah prayed and said:[c]

"My heart rejoices[d] in the LORD;
in the LORD my horn[a e] is lifted high.
My mouth boasts over my enemies,
for I delight in your deliverance.

2 "There is no one holy[b f] like the LORD;
there is no one besides you;
there is no Rock[g] like our God.

3 "Do not keep talking so proudly
or let your mouth speak such arrogance,[h]
for the LORD is a God who knows,
and by him deeds[i] are weighed.[j]

4 "The bows of the warriors are broken,[k]
but those who stumbled are armed with strength.
5 Those who were full hire themselves out for food,
but those who were hungry hunger no more.
She who was barren[l] has borne seven children,
but she who has had many sons pines away.

6 "The LORD brings death and makes alive;[m]
he brings down to the grave[c] and raises up.[n]
7 The LORD sends poverty and wealth;[o]
he humbles and he exalts.[p]
8 He raises[q] the poor from the dust
and lifts the needy from the ash heap;
he seats them with princes
and has them inherit a throne of honor.[r]
"For the foundations[s] of the earth are the LORD's;
upon them he has set the world.
9 He will guard the feet[t] of his saints,
but the wicked will be silenced in darkness.[u]
"It is not by strength[v] that one prevails;

[a] *1 Horn* here symbolizes strength; also in verse 10. [b] *2* Or *no Holy One* [c] *6* Hebrew *Sheol*

2:1–10 *Hannah's Praise for God's Power.* Hannah accompanied the fulfillment of her vow with a jubilant song of thanksgiving. Focusing in hymnic fashion on the Lord's judgment of the proud and his grace to the humble, Hannah anticipated dominant themes throughout 1 and 2 Samuel. These themes are reiterated in David's own song of thanksgiving near the end of 2 Samuel (ch. 22). Thus the two songs together provide a poetic frame for 1 and 2 Samuel. Moreover, these themes extend far beyond the book of Samuel, reaching all the way to the New Testament. Mary's song of praise (the "Magnificat") reflects Hannah's song; e.g., both Hannah's and Mary's songs open with jubilation over the Lord's deliverance (v. 1; Lk 1:46–48), both extol the Lord's uniqueness and holiness (v. 2; Lk 1:49–50), both condemn proud boasting (v. 3; Lk 1:51), both point to reversals of human fortune as the result of interventions by the sovereign Lord (vv. 4–8; Lk 1:52–53) and both express the Lord's faithful care for his own (v. 9; Lk 1:54–55). In its final verses, Hannah's song includes also the assertion that while human strength is no match for the Lord's, the Lord himself will give strength to his anointed (vv. 9–10).
2:1 Hannah prayed. The text gives no indication as to whether the song was Hannah's own composition or simply appropriated by her. Like most of Israel's psalms, Hannah's song was composed largely in general, rather than particular, terms. Nevertheless, much of what she said was appropriate to Hannah's particular situation. **horn.** The Hebrew word for "horn," which was used to describe the horns of various animals (rams, wild oxen and even the tusks of elephants), is also used metaphorically in the Old Testament to symbolize pride and strength. As Psalm 75:10 makes clear, it is God who exalts the horns of the righteous but cuts off the horns of the wicked. In 2 Samuel 22:3, David extolled the Lord as his "shield and the horn of [his] salvation." See note on verse 10. See also *WLC* 185.
2:2 Rock. As a designation of divine kingship, this term is concentrated in poetic passages such as the song of Moses (Dt 32), the song of David (2Sa 22), Psalms and Isaiah. In its various locations it is suggestive of God's strength and sovereignty and of the security, stability and salvation of those who trust in him. In the present context the focus is on the uniqueness of the one true Rock as opposed, presumably, to false sources of security (cf. Isa 44:8 with Dt 32:31,37, where false gods are called "rock"). This theme is elaborated in relation to Christ in the New Testament (Ro 9:33; 1Pe 2:8). For other significant instances of rock imagery, see notes on Genesis 49:24, Isaiah 8:14, Daniel 2:34–35 and 45, Matthew 21:44 and 1 Corinthians 10:4.
2:3 a God who knows. The verb "to know" in Hebrew includes but goes beyond the notion of mere cognition. At times it may mean "to have regard for," "to pay attention to" or even "to choose" or "to select" (see Ge 18:19). In the present context God's "knowledge" certainly connotes awareness of the true nature of people's deeds (Jos 22:22; Pss 44:21; 94:11).
2:5 seven children. That Hannah bore a total of six children (v. 21), not seven, is best understood in the light of the general character of her song (see note on v. 1). The number seven represented ideal completeness (Ru 4:15).
2:6 The LORD . . . brings down . . . and raises up. Compare Deuteronomy 32:39 and Psalm 30:3.
2:9 It is not by strength that one prevails. The subsequent narratives eloquently confirm that it is not physical prowess but the Lord's accompanying presence that brings success. This theme appears many times in the book. Even without the assistance of human agents, God made his heavy hand felt by the captors of the ark, the Philistines (5:6). Other examples include the Lord's victory through Samuel (ch. 7); the contrasting successes of Saul and Jonathan (chs. 13–14); the selection of David, the smallest of Jesse's sons (ch. 16); and David's victory over Goliath, the largest of the Philistines (ch. 17).

10 those who oppose the LORD will be shattered.[w]
He will thunder[x] against them from heaven;
the LORD will judge[y] the ends of the earth.

"He will give strength[z] to his king
and exalt the horn[a] of his anointed."

11Then Elkanah went home to Ramah, but the boy ministered[b] before the LORD under Eli the priest.

2:10 [w]Ps 2:9 [x]Ps 18:13 [y]Ps 96:13 [z]Ps 21:1 [a]Ps 89:24

2:11 [b]ver 18; 1Sa 3:1

Eli's Wicked Sons

12Eli's sons were wicked men; they had no regard[c] for the LORD. 13Now it was the practice of the priests with the people that whenever anyone offered a sacrifice and while the
meat[d] was being boiled, the servant of the priest would come with a three-pronged fork
in his hand. 14He would plunge it into the pan or kettle or caldron or pot, and the priest
would take for himself whatever the fork brought up. This is how they treated all the Israelites who came to Shiloh. 15But even before the fat was burned, the servant of the
priest would come and say to the man who was sacrificing, "Give the priest some meat
to roast; he won't accept boiled meat from you, but only raw."
16If the man said to him, "Let the fat be burned up first, and then take whatever you
want," the servant would then answer, "No, hand it over now; if you don't, I'll take it by
force."
17This sin of the young men was very great in the LORD's sight, for they[a] were treating the LORD's offering with contempt.[e]
18But Samuel was ministering[f] before the LORD—a boy wearing a linen ephod.[g]
19Each year his mother made him a little robe and took it to him when she went up with
her husband to offer the annual[h] sacrifice. 20Eli would bless Elkanah and his wife, say-

2:12 [c]Jer 2:8; 9:6

2:13 [d]Lev 7:29-34

2:17 [e]Mal 2:7-9

2:18 [f]ver 11; 1Sa 3:1 [g]ver 28

2:19 [h]1Sa 1:3

[a] 17 Or *men*

2:10 his king. The reference to the Lord's king here at the end of Hannah's song touches on the central event of the book of Samuel; namely, the institution of the monarchy. The idea of kingship, properly conceived, was not wrong. Various passages in the Pentateuch anticipated that Israel would one day have a human king (see notes on v. 35; Ge 49:10; Nu 24:7,17–19; Dt 17:14 20). **horn.** The song ends as it began, with a reference to the Lord's exalting the horn, or strength (see note on v. 1), first of Hannah (v. 1) and then of the king (here). This framing of the song has theological as well as rhetorical significance inasmuch as the well-being of the people of Israel was intimately linked to the faithfulness of their leaders. **his anointed.** Sacral anointing was widely practiced in ancient Israel, applying both to religious objects and to personnel (Ex 30:22–33). When a person was called "the anointed," with rare exception (see 1Ch 16:22; Zec 4:14) this was a royal designation. The theological significance of anointing, especially when applied to persons, seems to include consecration to and authorization for divine service and a promise of divine empowerment for the service to be rendered. References to the king as the Lord's anointed are most prevalent in the book of Samuel (e.g., 2:35; 12:3,5; 16:6; 24:6) and in the Psalter (e.g., Pss 2:2; 18:50). The present passage represents the first such reference, though the general notion of anointing a king was evidenced already in Jotham's fable (Jdg 9:8,15). It is from the Hebrew word for "anointed" that we derive the term "Messiah" and from the Greek word for "anointed" that we derive "Christ." Hannah's celebration culminated in thoughts of the king, much as Christians find their hope in the exaltation of Christ.

■ **2:11—7:17** *Samuel Rises as Eli and His Sons Fall.* By contrasting Eli and his sons with Samuel, the writer explained how and why God rejected the house of Eli from priestly service and exalted Samuel as the leader of Israel. These contrasts appear in three stages: in service at Shiloh (2:11–21), in the disapprovals and approvals they received (2:22–26), in the revelation of divine judgment and blessing (2:27—4:1a) and in conflict with the Philistines (4:1b—7:17). These materials explained why the original readers should accept the directions for the nation that Samuel had established; namely, the rejection of Saul and the permanence of David's dynasty, despite its failings.

■ **2:11–21** *In the Divine Presence at Shiloh.* These verses set up a subtle contrast between Eli's sons and Samuel. On the one hand, Eli's sons sinned greatly by treating the Lord's offerings with contempt (vv. 11–17). On the other hand, Hannah continued to enjoy the grace of God, and Samuel grew up in God's presence (vv. 18–26).

■ **2:11–17** *Eli's Sons' Evil at Shiloh.* Eli's sons terribly abused their authority during sacrifices at Shiloh, inciting God's anger against themselves.

2:12 wicked men. The Hebrew term connotes worthlessness and vileness. It is used of scoundrels and troublemakers, those who incite others to idolatry (Dt 13:13) or insurrection (10:27; 2Sa 16:7; 20:1), the sexually immoral (Jdg 19:22) and liars (1Ki 21:10,13). **no regard.** The Hebrew word is the verb "to know" (see note on v. 3). Use of this term here and in 3:7 reinforces the contrast between Eli's sons and Samuel. See *WLC* 114; *WSC* 56.

2:13 practice of the priests. The practice described in verses 13–14 differs from the prescriptions of Leviticus 7:28–36 and Deuteronomy 18:3. The priests' procedure may be taken to be abusive or may simply be a local variation. Yet verses 15–17 leave no doubt that the sons of Eli were "treating the LORD's offering with contempt" (v. 17).

2:15 before the fat was burned. Since the time of Abel's pleasing offering of "fat portions from some of the firstborn of his flock" (Ge 4:4), the fat represented the best portion and, as such, belonged to the Lord. The priest was assigned the duty of burning the fat on the altar as a pleasing aroma to the Lord (Lev 3:16; 7:31). The fat, like the blood with which it is often associated, was strictly forbidden for human consumption (Lev 3:17; cf. Lev 7:33; Eze 39:19; 44:7,15), and anyone who committed such an offensive act was to be "cut off from his people" (Lev 7:25).

2:17 See *WLC* 114; *WSC* 56.

■ **2:18–21** *Samuel Blessed at Shiloh.* In contrast to the sons of Eli, Hannah continued to be blessed by God, and Samuel grew up accepted in the presence of the Lord.

2:18 But Samuel. The behavior not only of Samuel, who ministered faithfully before the Lord, but also of the aged priest Eli, who regularly blessed Elkanah and his wife (v. 20), stood in stark contrast to the abuses by Eli's sons. **linen ephod.** A loincloth or inner garment of some sort. It was associated with priestly service (22:18) and was worn also by King David on the occasion of his bringing the ark of the covenant to Jerusalem (2Sa 6:14). Thus Samuel was designated as a child devoted to the service of God. See also the note on verse 28.

2:19 robe. An outer garment of some sort to be worn over the linen ephod. Mention of the significance of Samuel's robe is not confined to this early stage. In 15:27–28 Samuel interpreted Saul's tearing of his robe as a symbol of God's tearing the kingdom from Saul. And in 28:14 Saul was apparently able to recognize Samuel merely on the basis of a description of him as an old man wearing a robe. See also note on 19:24.

ing, "May the LORD give you children by this woman to take the place of the one she
prayed[i] for and gave to the LORD." Then they would go home. 21And the LORD was gracious to Hannah;[j] she conceived and gave birth to three sons and two daughters. Meanwhile, the boy Samuel grew[k] up in the presence of the LORD.
22Now Eli, who was very old, heard about everything his sons were doing to all Israel and how they slept with the women[l] who served at the entrance to the Tent of Meeting. 23So he said to them, "Why do you do such things? I hear from all the people about
these wicked deeds of yours. 24No, my sons; it is not a good report that I hear spreading
among the LORD's people. 25If a man sins against another man, God[a] may mediate for
him; but if a man sins against the LORD, who will[m] intercede[n] for him?" His sons, however, did not listen to their father's rebuke, for it was the LORD's will to put them to death.
26And the boy Samuel continued to grow[o] in stature and in favor with the LORD and
with men.

Prophecy Against the House of Eli

27Now a man of God[p] came to Eli and said to him, "This is what the LORD says: 'Did I
not clearly reveal myself to your father's house when they were in Egypt under Pharaoh?
28I chose[q] your father out of all the tribes of Israel to be my priest, to go up to my altar,
to burn incense, and to wear an ephod[r] in my presence. I also gave your father's house
all the offerings made with fire by the Israelites. 29Why do you[b] scorn my sacrifice and
offering[s] that I prescribed for my dwelling?[t] Why do you honor your sons more than me
by fattening yourselves on the choice parts of every offering made by my people Israel?'
30"Therefore the LORD, the God of Israel, declares: 'I promised that your house and
your father's house would minister before me forever.[u]' But now the LORD declares: 'Far
be it from me! Those who honor me I will honor,[v] but those who despise[w] me will be disdained. 31The time is coming when I will cut short your strength and the strength of your
father's house, so that there will not be an old man in your family line[x] 32and you will

2:20 [i]1Sa 1:11,27-28; Lk 2:34
2:21 [j]Ge 21:1 [k]ver 26; Jdg 13:24; 1Sa 3:19; Lk 2:40
2:22 [l]Ex 38:8
2:25 [m]Nu 15:30; Jos 11:20 [n]Dt 1:17; 1Sa 3:14; Heb 10:26
2:26 [o]ver 21; Lk 2:52
2:27 [p]Ex 4:14-16; 1Ki 13:1
2:28 [q]Ex 28:1 [r]Lev 8:7-8
2:29 [s]ver 12-17 [t]Dt 12:5; Mt 10:37
2:30 [u]Ex 29:9 [v]Ps 50:23; 91:15 [w]Mal 2:9
2:31 [x]1Sa 4:11-18; 22:16-20

[a] *25* Or *the judges* [b] *29* The Hebrew is plural.

2:21 in the presence of the LORD. Or "with the LORD." The same Hebrew expression is used in verse 26, where it is translated "in favor with the LORD and with men." More than a statement of fact, this description of Samuel indicated Samuel's acceptance by God.
■ **2:22–26** *In Disapproval and Approval.* The contrast continued: Both Eli and the Lord severely disapproved of Eli's sons (vv. 22–25), but Samuel matured in the favor of God and of the people around him (v. 26). This exalted Samuel once again as God's favored man for the time.
■ **2:22–25** *Eli's Sons Receive Human and Divine Disapproval.* The sins of Eli's sons were so great that the two received severe disapproval and condemnation both from their father and from God.
2:22–24 See *WLC* 114,145,151.
2:22 Now Eli. Again the focus shifts back to the house of Eli (2:12—4:22). **heard.** Eli must have overheard what was apparently widely observed by others (v. 23). This is an unsettling reminder that Eli was not as attentive to duty as his position required. His advanced age may have accounted in part for his failure, but this did not excuse his true offense, which ran much deeper (v. 29). **slept with the women who served at the entrance to the Tent of Meeting.** On "the Tent of Meeting," see note on 1:9. On "the women who served," see note on Exodus 38:8. Though explicitly condemned by the Lord (Dt 23:17–18), cultic prostitution was practiced among Israel's Canaanite populations and was a constant temptation for the Israelites (1Ki 14:23–24; 15:12; 2Ki 23:7; Hos 4:14). See *WLC* 114; *WSC* 56.
2:25 God may mediate. The same verbal root is used here for mediation (or arbitration) in the case of sins against one's fellow man and, later in the verse, for intercession on behalf of one who had sinned against the Lord. Eli's point was that while God (or his representative; see NIV text note) may have intervened in the former case, in the latter case, where brazen sin against God himself had been committed, the offender was without hope (except in the most unusual of circumstances, such as those recorded in Ex 32:7–14). Eli's sons sinned first and foremost against the Lord (v. 17), and, as their own response to their father's rebuke confirmed, their doom was sure. **the LORD's will to put them to death.** This clear statement by the narrator of God's sovereignty in the affairs of the wicked in no way diminished their responsibility. Parallel references to the interplay between divine sovereignty and human responsibility appear in the hardening of Pharaoh's heart. About half the time, Pharaoh is said to have hardened his own heart; the rest of the time the hardening was ascribed to God (Ex 4:21; Ro 9:17–18). God sometimes punishes persistent, willful sin with a loss of ability to reform even in temporal, non-salvific ways (Jos 11:20; Ro 1:24,26,28). See *WCF* 7.1; *WLC* 128,151; *BC* 13.
■ **2:26** *Samuel Matures With Human and Divine Approval.* In contrast to Eli's sons, Samuel was approved by people and by God. The turn of phrase was picked up in Luke 2:52 as an apt description of the maturing of Jesus (cf. Pr 3:4).
■ **2:27—4:1a** *In Divine Judgment and Blessing.* The contrast between Eli's sons and Samuel increased further as they received revelation from God. Eli and his sons were judged by God's word (2:27–36), but Samuel was blessed by it (3:1—4:1a).
■ **2:27–36** *Eli and Sons Are Judged by God.* In these verses the words of the man of God to Eli exhibit features typical of prophetic judgment speeches: an accusation and an announcement of judgment. Other examples of prophetic speeches of this general type appear in the book of Samuel (1Sa 13; 15; 2Sa 12:7–12).
2:27 man of God. In the Old Testament this designation is often used interchangeably with "prophet" (see 9:8–11; 1Ki 13:15–18; 2Ki 5:8; 6:10–12) or even with "messenger [angel]" (Jdg 13:3–6). **father's house . . . in Egypt.** Although Eli's genealogy is nowhere recorded in the Old Testament, verse 28 implies that he was a descendant of Aaron. The assertion that the Lord revealed himself and selected Eli's house as far back as the period of Israelite servitude in Egypt brings to mind God's mercy even prior to the exodus and Sinai events and underscores the ingratitude of the house of Eli.
2:28 wear an ephod. Or perhaps "bear" the ephod. The ephod mentioned here is the high priestly ephod (Ex 28:4–30), not the linen ephod of verse 18. To it was attached "a breastpiece for making decisions" (Ex 28:15; see Ex 28:15–30), which contained the Urim and the Thummim, divinely ordained devices for discovering God's will (Ex 28:30).
2:29–31 See *WLC* 130
2:29 honor. As father and high priest, Eli should have confronted his sons with more than mere words (vv. 23–25). His failure to take action was interpreted as honoring his sons above the Lord (v. 30). See *WLC* 105; *WSC* 56.
2:30 forever. Not in the sense of "eternally," but rather "for the duration." The same expression is used of Samuel in 1:22: "He will live there always" (see also 13:13). **disdained.** Those who honor the Lord will be honored by him, but those who despise him will be "disdained"; i.e., lightly esteemed (lit., "be small, of little account").
2:31 will not be an old man in your family line. The decimation of Eli's house began with the death of his sons (4:11) and his own death (4:18), continued with Saul's massacre of the priests of

see distress in my dwelling. Although good will be done to Israel, in your family line there
will never be an old man.[y] 33 Every one of you that I do not cut off from my altar will be
spared only to blind your eyes with tears and to grieve your heart, and all your descendants will die in the prime of life.
34 " 'And what happens to your two sons, Hophni and Phinehas, will be a sign to you—
they will both die[z] on the same day.[a] 35 I will raise up for myself a faithful priest,[b] who
will do according to what is in my heart and mind. I will firmly establish his house, and
he will minister before my anointed[c] one always. 36 Then everyone left in your family line
will come and bow down before him for a piece of silver and a crust of bread and plead,
"Appoint me to some priestly office so I can have food to eat.[d]" ' "

The LORD Calls Samuel

3 The boy Samuel ministered[e] before the LORD under Eli. In those days the word of the
LORD was rare;[f] there were not many visions.[g]
2 One night Eli, whose eyes[h] were becoming so weak that he could barely see, was lying down in his usual place. 3 The lamp[i] of God had not yet gone out, and Samuel was
lying down in the temple[a] of the LORD, where the ark of God was. 4 Then the LORD called
Samuel.

Samuel answered, "Here I am.[j]" 5 And he ran to Eli and said, "Here I am; you
called me."

But Eli said, "I did not call; go back and lie down." So he went and lay down.
6 Again the LORD called, "Samuel!" And Samuel got up and went to Eli and said, "Here
I am; you called me."

"My son," Eli said, "I did not call; go back and lie down."
7 Now Samuel did not yet know the LORD: The word of the LORD had not yet been revealed[k] to him.
8 The LORD called Samuel a third time, and Samuel got up and went to Eli and said,
"Here I am; you called me."

Then Eli realized that the LORD was calling the boy. 9 So Eli told Samuel, "Go and lie
down, and if he calls you, say, 'Speak, LORD, for your servant is listening.' " So Samuel
went and lay down in his place.
10 The LORD came and stood there, calling as at the other times, "Samuel! Samuel!"

Then Samuel said, "Speak, for your servant is listening."

2:32 [y]1Ki 2:26-27; Zec 8:4
2:34 [z]1Sa 4:11 [a]1Ki 13:3
2:35 [b]1Sa 12:3; 1Ki 2:35 [c]1Sa 16:13; 2Sa 7:11,27; 1Ki 11:38
2:36 [d]1Ki 2:27
3:1 [e]1Sa 2:11 [f]Ps 74:9 [g]Am 8:11
3:2 [h]1Sa 4:15
3:3 [i]Lev 24:1-4
3:4 [j]Isa 6:8
3:7 [k]Ac 19:12

[a] 3 That is, tabernacle

Nob (22:17–19) and culminated in Solomon's removal of Abiathar from the priesthood (1Ki 2:26–27).

2:32 distress in my dwelling. The Hebrew of verse 32a is difficult. In fact, verses 31b–32a are lacking in the Septuagint (the Greek translation of the OT) and in the Dead Sea Scrolls. If the reference to "distress in my dwelling" is original and correctly translated, then the allusion would be to the capture of the ark (4:1–11), the destruction of the Lord's dwelling in Shiloh (Jer 7:12–14) and its relocation to Nob (21:1).

2:34 sign. Prophetic utterances were often confirmed by signs (see note on vv. 27–36; cf. 10:7,9; 1Ki 13:3,5; 2Ki 19:29; 20:8–9).

2:35 faithful priest. Faithfulness (lit., "firmness") would be rewarded with a faithful ("firm") house. The original readers may have been tempted to see Samuel as the fulfillment of this prediction (see 3:20), but the clearer fulfillment came in Zadok, who served as priest alongside Abiathar under David (2Sa 8:17) and came to preeminence under Solomon (see notes on v. 31; 1Ki 2:35). The descendants of Zadok held the high priesthood in both the Solomonic temple and the second temple. Even after the priesthood was transferred to Menelaus (c. 171 B.C.; 2 Maccabees 4:27 [an Apocryphal book]), loyalty to the Zadokite line persisted, at least in the Qumran community. **anointed one.** This is a second allusion to the coming king in this chapter (see note on v. 10).

2:36 crust of bread . . . food to eat. Prophetic judgment speeches were characterized by a correspondence between crime and punishment (see note on vv. 27–36). The ironic logic of the threat of hunger in this verse is unmistakable when compared with the earlier descriptions of the crimes (especially v. 29, "fattening yourselves"; see also vv. 12–17).

▪ **3:1—4:1a** *Samuel Called and Blessed by God.* In contrast to the prophetic condemnation of the preceding episode, this passage reports that Samuel received a call to service and blessing directly from God.

3:1 word of the LORD was rare. This notice accords well with what we know of the general time period as described in the book of Judges (e.g., Jdg 17:6). The Lord's withholding of his word was often a sign of his displeasure (14:37; Ps 74:9; La 2:9; Am 8:11–12). Conversely, his communication to Samuel in the following episode may be understood as a sign of the dawning of a new day, the day of the monarchy. **visions.** This was one of the primary means by which God communicated his word in the Old Testament (e.g., Ge 15:1). Despite the usual rendering "visions," the Hebrew word often denotes an auditory encounter rather than a visual one.

3:3 lamp of God had not yet gone out. This notice may have been intended simply as a time reference, suggesting the early morning hours (Ex 27:20–21; Lev 24:1–4). In view of the metaphorical uses of "lamp" elsewhere, however, it may have suggested hope and promise or someone in whom these things resided (e.g., 2Sa 21:17; 22:29; 1Ki 11:36; 15:4; Job 18:5; Ps 132:17; Pr 13:9). The possibility of such in the present context is worthy of consideration. With Samuel on the scene, there was still a "flicker" of hope. **temple.** See note on 1:9. **ark of God.** Elsewhere called "the ark of the Testimony" and "the ark of the covenant," this portable chest of acacia wood overlaid with gold is first mentioned in Exodus 25:10–22, where it heads the list of tabernacle furnishings. The ark figures significantly in chapters 4–6 and again in 2 Samuel 6.

3:7 Samuel did not yet know the LORD. The similarity in terminology with the statement in 2:12 serves only to highlight the flexibility of the expression. As the contexts of the respective verses make clear, the "not knowing" of Eli's sons signified wicked disregard, while Samuel's "not knowing" simply connoted unfamiliarity, since "the word of the LORD had not yet been revealed to him."

3:8 Then Eli realized. Eli's slowness in recognizing who had been calling Samuel may be partially excused on account of the rarity of visions (v. 1), his age and infirmity (2:22) or even the hour. Nevertheless, it also recalls earlier instances of misperception (1:12–16) and lack of awareness (2:22) and contributes to Eli's portrait as an aged priest who had grown dim-sighted (v. 2) in more ways than one.

11 And the LORD said to Samuel: "See, I am about to do something in Israel that will
make the ears of everyone who hears of it tingle.[l] 12 At that time I will carry out against
Eli everything[m] I spoke against his family—from beginning to end. 13 For I told him that
I would judge his family forever because of the sin he knew about; his sons made themselves contemptible,[a] and he failed to restrain[n] them. 14 Therefore, I swore to the house
of Eli, 'The guilt of Eli's house will never be atoned[o] for by sacrifice or offering.' "
15 Samuel lay down until morning and then opened the doors of the house of the LORD.
He was afraid to tell Eli the vision, 16 but Eli called him and said, "Samuel, my son."
Samuel answered, "Here I am."
17 "What was it he said to you?" Eli asked. "Do not hide it from me. May God deal with
you, be it ever so severely,[p] if you hide from me anything he told you." 18 So Samuel told
him everything, hiding nothing from him. Then Eli said, "He is the LORD; let him do what
is good in his eyes."[q]
19 The LORD was with[r] Samuel as he grew[s] up, and he let none[t] of his words fall to the
ground. 20 And all Israel from Dan to Beersheba[u] recognized that Samuel was attested
as a prophet of the LORD. 21 The LORD continued to appear at Shiloh, and there he revealed[v] himself to Samuel through his word.
4 And Samuel's word came to all Israel.

The Philistines Capture the Ark

Now the Israelites went out to fight against the Philistines. The Israelites camped at
Ebenezer,[w] and the Philistines at Aphek.[x] 2 The Philistines deployed their forces to meet
Israel, and as the battle spread, Israel was defeated by the Philistines, who killed about
four thousand of them on the battlefield. 3 When the soldiers returned to camp, the elders of Israel asked, "Why[y] did the LORD bring defeat upon us today before the Philistines? Let us bring the ark[z] of the LORD's covenant from Shiloh, so that it[b] may go with
us and save us from the hand of our enemies."

3:11 [l]2Ki 21:12; Jer 19:3
3:12 [m]1Sa 2:27-36
3:13 [n]1Sa 2:12,17,22, 29-31
3:14 [o]Lev 15:30-31; 1Sa 2:25; Isa 22:14
3:17 [p]Ru 1:17; 2Sa 3:35
3:18 [q]Job 2:10; Isa 39:8
3:19 [r]Ge 21:22; 39:2 [s]1Sa 2:21 [t]1Sa 9:6
3:20 [u]Jdg 20:1
3:21 [v]ver 10
4:1 [w]1Sa 7:12 [x]Jos 12:18; 1Sa 29:1
4:3 [y]Jos 7:7 [z]Nu 10:35; Jos 6:7

[a] *13* Masoretic Text; an ancient Hebrew scribal tradition and Septuagint *sons blasphemed God* [b] *3* Or *he*

3:12 everything I spoke. In view are the words spoken by the Lord through the man of God in 2:27–36. The succinct repetition to Samuel of the rejection oracle against Eli served both to confirm the earlier oracle and to establish Samuel as a prophet of the Lord (v. 20).
3:13 made themselves contemptible. The more likely reading is "cursed or blasphemed God" (see NIV text note). Cursing God was an offense deserving death (Lev 24:15–16). **failed to restrain them.** This verse confirms the notion introduced in the note on 2:29 that Eli, in view of his position, should have taken action to restrain his sons once verbal rebuke had proved ineffective (see note on 2Sa 13:21). See *WLC* 114,130; *WSC* 56.
3:14 never be atoned for by sacrifice or offering. While provision was made for the atonement of unintentional priestly sins (Lev 4:1–12), the sins of Eli's house were clearly of the defiant variety (Nu 15:30–31). The possibility of atonement was further precluded in that it was precisely the normal means of atonement (i.e., sacrifice and offering) that Eli's family had scorned (2:17,29).
3:18 He is the LORD; let him do what is good in his eyes. Whatever his failings arising from passivity and misperception, Eli comes off well in this humble acceptance. His words establish a benchmark by which later characters in the narrative are to be judged (e.g., Saul [20:30–31] and David [2Sa 15:25–26]).
3:19 LORD was with Samuel. From the perspective of the book of Samuel, God's presence makes the difference between success and failure. The Lord was with David on a continuing basis (e.g., 16:18; 18:12,14,28), but only once are we told that he was with Saul (20:13). Similar language is used to explain Joseph's rise to prominence in Egypt (see note on Ge 39:2). **let none of his words fall to the ground.** See 9:6. Samuel thus passed the test of a true prophet (see notes on Dt 18:21–22; Jer 18:1–9).
3:20 Dan to Beersheba . . . prophet of the LORD. While Samuel's responsibilities as judge took him on a circuit of certain sites in the central hill country (7:15–17), his reputation as a prophet (see note on Ge 20:7) spread throughout all Israel from Dan to Beersheba (see note on Jdg 20:1; see also 2Sa 3:10; 17:11; 24:2,25; 1Ki 4:25).
3:21 Shiloh. See note on 1:3.
4:1a Samuel's word came to all Israel. The episode that began with a notice of the rarity of the word of the Lord (3:1) concludes with a comment on the changed situation brought about by the selection of Samuel to be "a prophet of the LORD" (see 3:20 and its note). Hannah's hope for the life of the nation of Israel was beginning to be felt in Samuel (1:11).
■ **4:1b—7:17** *In Conflict With the Philistines.* The contrast between Eli and his sons and Samuel reaches its climax in conflict with the Philistines. The ark of the covenant played a significant role in this event, demonstrating God's utter disapproval of Eli and his sons, as well as God's power to overcome his enemies and to exalt whomever he pleases. These chapters divide into four main parts: the defeat and the loss of the ark (4:1b–22), the ark among the Philistines (5:1–12), the ark returned by the Philistines (6:1—7:1) and Samuel's victory over the Philistines (7:2–17). This contrast left no doubt that the Lord approved of Samuel and the direction he would later give to the nation.
■ **4:1b–22** *Eli's Sons Lead to Defeat and the Loss of the Ark.* The Philistines defeated Israel and captured the ark of God when Israel and Eli's sons tried to use it in battle. God's judgment against them became clear when severe tragedies struck the house of Eli.
4:1b Philistines. Mentioned previously in the Pentateuch (e.g., Ge 10:14; 21:32,34; 26:1), the Philistines were a Mediterranean people included among the "Sea Peoples" named in Egyptian texts from the time of Rameses III. At least by the time of the judges, the Philistines were resident along the coastlands of southern Canaan (Jdg 3:31; 13:1—16:31). Although they are consistently associated with the so-called Philistine pentapolis (five-city area) comprising Ashdod, Ashkelon, Ekron, Gath and Gaza (6:17; Jdg 3:3), the Philistines expanded to other territories during the time of Samuel and the early monarchy and came into direct conflict with their Israelite neighbors to the north and east. **Ebenezer.** A site of uncertain location. Ebenezer (meaning "stone of help") is mentioned again in 5:1. The Ebenezer of 7:12 recalls this earlier reference, but its location near Mizpah indicates that it should not be identified with this earlier site. **Aphek.** First mentioned in the Old Testament among the cities conquered by Joshua (Jos 12:18), Aphek was located at the southern end of the plain of Sharon, about nine miles inland from the Mediterranean along the Yarkon River (29:1).
4:3–5 See *WLC* 113.
4:3 Why did the LORD bring defeat . . . ? The Israelite elders' question was appropriate insofar as it reflected the belief that "the battle is the LORD's" (17:47). They awaited no answer to their question, however, but proceeded immediately to take matters into their own hands. **Let us bring the ark.** The magical understanding of the Lord's presence and activity evident in the elders' proposal to manipulate the ark to their benefit betrays a perspective not far, if at all, removed from that of the Philistines (vv. 7–9).

4So the people sent men to Shiloh, and they brought back the ark of the covenant of
the LORD Almighty, who is enthroned between the cherubim.[a] And Eli's two sons, Hophni and Phinehas, were there with the ark of the covenant of God.
5When the ark of the LORD's covenant came into the camp, all Israel raised such a
great shout[b] that the ground shook. 6Hearing the uproar, the Philistines asked, "What's
all this shouting in the Hebrew camp?"
When they learned that the ark of the LORD had come into the camp, 7the Philistines
were afraid.[c] "A god has come into the camp," they said. "We're in trouble! Nothing like
this has happened before. 8Woe to us! Who will deliver us from the hand of these mighty
gods? They are the gods who struck the Egyptians with all kinds of plagues in the desert. 9Be strong, Philistines! Be men, or you will be subject to the Hebrews, as they[d] have
been to you. Be men, and fight!"
10So the Philistines fought, and the Israelites were defeated[e] and every man fled to
his tent. The slaughter was very great; Israel lost thirty thousand foot soldiers. 11The ark
of God was captured, and Eli's two sons, Hophni and Phinehas, died.[f]

Death of Eli

12That same day a Benjamite ran from the battle line and went to Shiloh, his clothes
torn and dust[g] on his head. 13When he arrived, there was Eli[h] sitting on his chair by the
side of the road, watching, because his heart feared for the ark of God. When the man
entered the town and told what had happened, the whole town sent up a cry.
14Eli heard the outcry and asked, "What is the meaning of this uproar?"
The man hurried over to Eli, 15who was ninety-eight years old and whose eyes[i] were
set so that he could not see. 16He told Eli, "I have just come from the battle line; I fled
from it this very day."
Eli asked, "What happened, my son?"
17The man who brought the news replied, "Israel fled before the Philistines, and the
army has suffered heavy losses. Also your two sons, Hophni and Phinehas, are dead, and
the ark of God has been captured."
18When he mentioned the ark of God, Eli fell backward off his chair by the side of the
gate. His neck was broken and he died, for he was an old man and heavy. He had led[a][j]
Israel forty years.
19His daughter-in-law, the wife of Phinehas, was pregnant and near the time of delivery. When she heard the news that the ark of God had been captured and that her father-in-law and her husband were dead, she went into labor and gave birth, but was

4:4 [a]Ex 25:22; 2Sa 6:2
4:5 [b]Jos 6:5,10
4:7 [c]Ex 15:14
4:9 [d]Jdg 13:1; 1Co 16:13
4:10 [e]ver 2; Dt 28:25; 2Sa 18:17; 2Ki 14:12
4:11 [f]1Sa 2:34; Ps 78:61,64
4:12 [g]Jos 7:6; 2Sa 1:2; 15:32; Ne 9:1; Job 2:12
4:13 [h]ver 18; 1Sa 1:9
4:15 [i]1Sa 3:2
4:18 [j]ver 13

[a] *18* Traditionally *judged*

4:4 LORD Almighty. See note on 1:3. **enthroned between the cherubim.** See Exodus 25:17–22 and Numbers 7:89. **Hophni and Phinehas.** With his two wicked sons (2:12–17,27–36) in charge of the ark, it is not surprising that Eli's "heart feared for the ark of God" (v. 13).
4:6 Hebrew. This word first occurs in Genesis 14:13 as a description of Abram. It is most natural, from the perspective of Biblical genealogy, to link this designation with "sons of Eber" (see note on Ge 10:21). Eber was a great-grandson of Shem and an ancestor of Abram (Ge 11:10–27). The attestation in extra biblical documents of the second millennium B.C. of a diverse and widespread people called "Habiru" has caused considerable debate as to whether these might not refer to the Biblical Hebrews. The Habiru appear most often to have been a landless class of aliens or refugees who survived either by hiring themselves out (e.g., as soldiers or agricultural workers) or by plundering others as bandits. While it may be that the Biblical Hebrews were sometimes regarded as Habiru by their neighbors (suggested by the fact that the word "Hebrew" was most often found on the lips of non-Israelites), it now seems clear that the Habiru were far too widespread in the ancient Near East to allow a simple equation with the Biblical Hebrews.
4:7–9 See *WLC* 105.
4:8 mighty gods . . . who struck the Egyptians. The Philistines' cry of woe betrays not only their polytheistic perspective, but also their garbled understanding of the circumstances surrounding the Israelite exodus from Egypt. Nevertheless, it leaves little doubt of the impact that that event had on surrounding nations (6:6; Jos 2:9–11).
4:10 thirty thousand. Far from bringing relief, the Israelites' attempt to manipulate the Lord for their own ends resulted in even greater defeat (v. 2).
4:11 The ark of God was captured. An event as astonishing as it was disastrous, the loss of the ark must surely have made ears "tingle" (3:11). **Hophni and Phinehas** These sons of Eli died in fulfillment of 2:34 and 3:12.
4:13 his heart feared for the ark of God. Earlier rebuked for honoring his sons more than the Lord (2:29), Eli now showed a concern for the ark of God that surpassed even his concern for his own sons. The apparent spiritual rehabilitation of the old priest is further evidenced by his reaction to the report of battle losses in verses 17–18. There may even be a hint of the same in the narrator's report that Eli, although now physically blind (v. 15), was "watching" beside the road (v. 13).
4:15 could not see. See note on verse 13.
4:18 When he mentioned the ark. Neither at the news of the heavy losses suffered by the Israelite army nor even at the report of the deaths of his own sons (v. 17), but only at the announcement that the ark of God had been captured did Eli reel backward, with the result that his neck was broken under his own weight. **heavy.** It is ironic that Eli, charged in 2:29 with honoring his sons above the Lord by "fattening" himself (along with them) on the Lord's offering, should lose his life under his own heaviness. The irony is even more pointed in the Hebrew, where "honor" and "heavy" are derived from the same root. **He had led Israel.** Or "judged" (see NIV text note). There is no contradiction in the description of Eli as both priest and judge (e.g., Nu 25:5–8; Dt 17:8–12; 19:17; 1Ch 23:2–4; 2Ch 19:8; Eze 44:24). His designation as a judge brings him into association with the leaders whom God raised up during the period between the death of Joshua and the institution of kingship. **forty years.** Eli's 40-year tenure of leadership (the Septuagint, the Greek translation of the OT, records this as 20 years) would have overlapped with the exploits of Samson (Jdg 13–16) and possibly also with the judges mentioned in Judges 12:7–15.

overcome by her labor pains. **20**As she was dying, the women attending her said, "Don't
despair; you have given birth to a son." But she did not respond or pay any attention.
21She named the boy Ichabod,[a][k] saying, "The glory[l] has departed from Israel"—because of the capture of the ark of God and the deaths of her father-in-law and her husband. **22**She said, "The glory has departed from Israel, for the ark of God has been
captured."

The Ark in Ashdod and Ekron

5 After the Philistines had captured the ark of God, they took it from Ebenezer[m] to Ashdod.[n] **2**Then they carried the ark into Dagon's temple and set it beside Dagon.[o]
3When the people of Ashdod rose early the next day, there was Dagon, fallen[p] on his face
on the ground before the ark of the LORD! They took Dagon and put him back in his place.
4But the following morning when they rose, there was Dagon, fallen on his face on the
ground before the ark of the LORD! His head and hands had been broken[q] off and were
lying on the threshold; only his body remained. **5**That is why to this day neither the priests
of Dagon nor any others who enter Dagon's temple at Ashdod step on the threshold.[r]
6The LORD's hand[s] was heavy upon the people of Ashdod and its vicinity; he brought
devastation[t] upon them and afflicted them with tumors.[b][u] **7**When the men of Ashdod
saw what was happening, they said, "The ark of the god of Israel must not stay here with
us, because his hand is heavy upon us and upon Dagon our god." **8**So they called together all the rulers of the Philistines and asked them, "What shall we do with the ark of the
god of Israel?"

They answered, "Have the ark of the god of Israel moved to Gath.[v]" So they moved
the ark of the God of Israel.
9But after they had moved it, the LORD's hand was against that city, throwing it into
a great panic.[w] He afflicted the people of the city, both young and old, with an outbreak
of tumors.[c] **10**So they sent the ark of God to Ekron.

4:21 [k]Ge 35:18 [l]Ps 26:8; Jer 2:11
5:1 [m]1Sa 4:1; 7:12 [n]Jos 13:3
5:2 [o]Jdg 16:23
5:3 [p]Isa 19:1; 46:7
5:4 [q]Eze 6:6; Mic 1:7
5:5 [r]Zep 1:9
5:6 [s]ver 7; Ex 9:3; Ps 32:4; Ac 13:11 [t]ver 11; Ps 78:66 [u]Dt 28:27; 1Sa 6:5
5:8 [v]ver 11
5:9 [w]ver 6,11; Dt 2:15; 1Sa 7:13; Ps 78:66

[a] *21* *Ichabod* means *no glory.* [b] *6* Hebrew; Septuagint and Vulgate *tumors. And rats appeared in their land, and death and destruction were throughout the city* [c] *9* Or *with tumors in the groin* (see Septuagint)

4:21 Ichabod . . . The glory has departed. Phinehas's dying wife named their newborn son Ichabod, which means either "No glory" or "Where is the glory?" As verse 22 makes clear, the "glory" to which she referred was not the house of Eli but the ark of God, which at this time had departed (or "gone into exile"). See also note on 14:3.

▪ **5:1–12** *The Ark Brings Curses to the Philistines.* It seemed as if the Philistines had conquered not only Israel, but Israel's God as well. Yet God demonstrated his power against the Philistines and led to the exaltation of Samuel over Eli and his sons.

5:1 the Philistines had captured the ark of God. Such is the seemingly disastrous result of the events of chapter 4. As chapter 5 unfolds, however, it becomes apparent that the God of Israel had not, in any real sense, fallen into the hands of the Philistines; rather, the Philistines had fallen into his. **Ebenezer.** See note on 4:1. **Ashdod.** One of the cities of the Philistine five-city region (see note on 4:1), Ashdod lay about 27 miles south of Ebenezer and 2.5 miles inland from the Mediterranean. According to Ugaritic sources, Ashdod was an important commercial center in the fourteenth and thirteenth centuries B.C., specializing in the production of textiles and purple dye. Philistine occupation of the site is attested archaeologically for the twelfth and eleventh centuries B.C.

5:2 set it beside Dagon. It was standard procedure in the ancient Near East for the victorious army to carry off the gods of the vanquished and to deposit them in the temple of their own gods as adjunct deities and/or as a sign of the inferiority and subordination of the captured gods. Though not an idol, the ark of God was treated as such by the Philistines. **Dagon.** Not only a prominent deity among the Philistines, but worshiped also in Mesopotamia, Syria and Phoenicia from as early as the middle of the third millennium B.C., Dagon was once thought to be a fish deity because of the similarity between the name and the Hebrew word for "fish." It now appears far more likely that the name should be associated with the Hebrew word for "grain," thus making Dagon a fertility deity. Dagon seems to have headed the Philistine pantheon (Jdg 16:23; 1Ch 10:10), which would also have included the goddess Ashtoreth (31:8–10) and Baal-Zebul ("Baal the prince"). The latter was worshiped at Ekron, and his name was intentionally distorted by the Israelite faithful to Baal-Zebub ("lord of the flies"; 2Ki 1:1–6,16). The worship of Dagon is attested as late as the Maccabean period (second century B.C.; 1 Maccabees 10:83–85 [Apocryphal book]).

5:3 Dagon, fallen on his face. In a most surprising reversal of expectation (at least to the Philistines), the next morning the supposedly victorious deity was found lying on his face, paying homage to the ostensibly vanquished one.

5:4 head and hands. Dagon's losses in the present context should be understood in light of the common practice in antiquity of removing head and hands from dead enemies (17:54; 31:9; Jdg 7:25; 8:6; 2Sa 4:12). Their own god was now handless, and the Philistines would soon experience the heavy hand of the God whom they thought they had captured (vv. 6–9).

5:5 to this day. This notice suggests a significant interval of time between the event and the present account of it (cf. 6:18). **step on the threshold.** Thresholds were often invested with special significance, and the avoidance of stepping on the threshold of a sacred precinct was known, if not approved, in Israel (Zep 1:9). The point of linking this practice of the priests of Dagon with this humiliating incident may be more to ridicule than to convey information.

5:6 tumors. The longer reading of the Septuagint (the Greek translation of the OT), which is partially rendered in the NIV text note, anticipates 6:4, 11 and 18. As to the nature of the tumors, the most common explanation is also the most plausible; namely, that they were symptomatic of an outbreak of bubonic plague (transmitted by rodents).

5:8 rulers of the Philistines. The reference is apparently to the rulers of the Philistine pentapolis (see note on 4:1), who acted in concert from time to time. **Have the ark of the god of Israel moved to Gath.** This proposed solution to the problem could imply that not all the Philistines were convinced of a direct link between the distress in Ashdod and the location of the ark there (6:9). Skeptics may well have cited, as a natural explanation, the fact that plagues of the sort spread by rodent infestation were endemic to coastal areas, where shipping allowed easy transport of the infected carriers. The Septuagint (the Greek translation of the OT) of verse 6 makes reference to rodents swarming in Philistine ships. **Gath.** The location of Gath is debated, but the best candidate is Tell es-Safi, a site about 12 miles east of Ashdod. Quite likely the Philistine plan was to relocate the ark at an inland site in the hopes of demonstrating that it was mere coincidence that plague had broken out while the ark was in Ashdod. This hope was dramatically dashed (v. 9).

5:9 panic. The Lord's interventions in holy war typically aroused panic among the enemy (7:10; 14:15,20; Ex 14:23–25; Dt 7:23; Jos 10:10).

5:10 So they sent the ark of God to Ekron . . . the people of Ekron cried out. "They" most naturally refers to the citizens of

As the ark of God was entering Ekron, the people of Ekron cried out, "They have
brought the ark of the god of Israel around to us to kill us and our people." 11So they
called together all the rulers[x] of the Philistines and said, "Send the ark of the god of Israel away; let it go back to its own place, or it[a] will kill us and our people." For death had
filled the city with panic; God's hand was very heavy upon it. 12Those who did not die
were afflicted with tumors, and the outcry of the city went up to heaven.

The Ark Returned to Israel

6 When the ark of the LORD had been in Philistine territory seven months, 2the Philistines called for the priests and the diviners[y] and said, "What shall we do with the
ark of the LORD? Tell us how we should send it back to its place."
3They answered, "If you return the ark of the god of Israel, do not send it away empty,[z] but by all means send a guilt offering[a] to him. Then you will be healed, and you will
know why his hand[b] has not been lifted from you."
4The Philistines asked, "What guilt offering should we send to him?"
They replied, "Five gold tumors and five gold rats, according to the number[c] of the
Philistine rulers, because the same plague has struck both you and your rulers. 5Make
models of the tumors[d] and of the rats that are destroying the country, and pay honor[e]
to Israel's god. Perhaps he will lift his hand from you and your gods and your land. 6Why
do you harden[f] your hearts as the Egyptians and Pharaoh did? When he[b] treated them
harshly, did they[g] not send the Israelites out so they could go on their way?
7"Now then, get a new cart[h] ready, with two cows that have calved and have never
been yoked.[i] Hitch the cows to the cart, but take their calves away and pen them up.
8Take the ark of the LORD and put it on the cart, and in a chest beside it put the gold objects you are sending back to him as a guilt offering. Send it on its way, 9but keep watching it. If it goes up to its own territory, toward Beth Shemesh,[j] then the LORD has brought
this great disaster on us. But if it does not, then we will know that it was not his hand
that struck us and that it happened to us by chance."
10So they did this. They took two such cows and hitched them to the cart and penned up
their calves. 11They placed the ark of the LORD on the cart and along with it the chest con-

5:11 [x]ver 6,8-9
6:2 [y]Ge 41:8; Ex 7:11; Isa 2:6
6:3 [z]Ex 23:15; Dt 16:16 [a]Lev 5:15 [b]ver 9
6:4 [c]ver 17-18; Jos 13:3; Jdg 3:3
6:5 [d]1Sa 5:6-11 [e]Jos 7:19; Isa 42:12; Jn 9:24; Rev 14:7
6:6 [f]Ex 7:13; 8:15; 9:34; 14:17 [g]Ex 12:31,33
6:7 [h]2Sa 6:3 [i]Nu 19:2
6:9 [j]ver 3; Jos 15:10; 21:16

[a] *11* Or *he* [b] *6* That is, God

Gath. After the failed experiment in Gath, the people of Ekron, at least, were no longer skeptical regarding the link between the ark and the pestilence (see note on v. 8) and were in no mood to have the experiment repeated in their own city. Ekron lay about 5.5 miles due north of the assumed site of Gath and was the closest of the Philistines' major cities to Israelite territory.

5:11 Send the ark of the god of Israel away. Unable to bear up under the heavy hand of the Lord (v. 6), the Ekronites pleaded that the ark's travels be culminated by returning the ark "to its own place."

5:12 the outcry of the city went up to heaven. This phrase finds an appropriate conceptual parallel in the wailing of the Egyptians foretold in Exodus 11:6 and fulfilled in 12:30.

■ **6:1—7:1** *The Ark Is Returned by the Philistines.* In desperate fear of the power of God, the Philistines returned the ark to Israel. God thereby moved the situation closer to his goal of contrasting Samuel's exaltation with the demise of Eli and his sons.

6:1 seven months. The events recorded in the previous chapter took place over a period of months, not days. The numeral seven may at times signify completeness or a significant period of time.

6:2 diviners. Associated with witchcraft, sorcery and the like (Nu 23:23), divination was explicitly and frequently condemned in Israel (Dt 18:10,14; Jer 27:9; Eze 13:23), but it was apparently approved by some of Israel's neighbors (e.g., Nu 22:7; Eze 21:21). **What shall we do . . . ? Tell us how we should send it back to its place.** These questions recall the earlier one asked by the people of Ashdod (5:8). Attempts to alleviate the problem by moving the ark from place to place within Philistine territory had failed, and it was now obvious that the only solution was to send it back to its own place.

6:3 guilt offering. The offering was intended both to acknowledge guilt and to provide some compensation for the offense of taking the ark (v. 4; see notes on Lev 5:14—6:7). **and you will know.** The Septuagint (the Greek translation of the OT) and the Dead Sea Scrolls attest a different reading, one that speaks of atonement or reconciliation; i.e., "and he will be reconciled to you" or "and it will be atoned for you."

6:5 Make models of the tumors. As was often the case in ritual matters, the procedure adopted by the Philistines was designed to accomplish several purposes. The gold of which the models were fashioned implied compensation (v. 4), while the forms of models (representing the agents and symptoms of the plague) were suggestive of sympathetic magic. The explicitly stated purpose, however, was to pay honor to Israel's God. With this statement by the Philistines, the account of the adventures of the ark comes almost full circle. It was over the issue of honor, and specifically over Israel's failure to accord proper honor to the Lord and the ark (as a visible sign of his presence; e.g., 2:29; 4:3), that the Lord had withdrawn the ark from his people and sent it into exile. Here Israel's archenemies "pay honor to Israel's god." **Perhaps he will lift his hand from you and your gods.** The Lord's oppressive treatment of the gods of the Philistines was reminiscent of his similar treatment of "the gods of Egypt" (Ex 12:12). As the next verse indicates, the force of the comparison was not lost on the Philistines themselves.

6:6 Why do you harden your hearts as the Egyptians and Pharaoh did? The word translated "harden" in this sentence is the same key word encountered often in the chapters dealing with the rejection of the priesthood of Eli's house and the loss of the ark. Elsewhere this word is variously rendered "honor" (v. 5), "heavy" (4:18) and "glory" (4:21). See note on 2:29. On the Egyptians' hardening, see Exodus 4:21 and 8:15. **treated them harshly.** Or "mocked them," "made fools of them" or "abused them." The same expression is used in 31:4, Exodus 10:2 and Jeremiah 38:19.

6:7–9 An old Hittite ritual text shows partial parallels to the procedure described in these verses. In the Hittite ritual, relief from a plague thought to have been caused by an enemy god was sought by first ceremonially crowning a ram to pacify the enemy god and then driving the ram along a road leading to enemy territory. In the Philistine version, they apparently chose cows that had never been yoked, and locked away their calves to remove all doubt (should the cows in such unlikely circumstances nevertheless proceed in the direction of Israel) that Israel's God, and not chance (v. 9), was the cause of the plague.

6:9 Beth Shemesh. One of several sites in Israel with this name, this city has been identified with Tell er-Rumeileh, about seven miles east of Ekron (see note on 5:10). The route of the ark would have been through the Valley of Sorek. Beth Shemesh was a border city (v. 12; Jos 15:10) that was frequently disputed by the Philistines and Israelites (2Ch 28:18).

taining the gold rats and the models of the tumors. 12 Then the cows went straight up toward
Beth Shemesh, keeping on the road and lowing all the way; they did not turn to the right or
to the left. The rulers of the Philistines followed them as far as the border of Beth Shemesh.
13 Now the people of Beth Shemesh were harvesting their wheat in the valley, and
when they looked up and saw the ark, they rejoiced at the sight. 14 The cart came to the
field of Joshua of Beth Shemesh, and there it stopped beside a large rock. The people
chopped up the wood of the cart and sacrificed the cows as a burnt offering[k] to the LORD.
15 The Levites[l] took down the ark of the LORD, together with the chest containing the gold
objects, and placed them on the large rock. On that day the people of Beth Shemesh offered burnt offerings and made sacrifices to the LORD. 16 The five rulers of the Philistines
saw all this and then returned that same day to Ekron.
17 These are the gold tumors the Philistines sent as a guilt offering to the LORD—one
each[m] for Ashdod, Gaza, Ashkelon, Gath and Ekron. 18 And the number of the gold rats
was according to the number of Philistine towns belonging to the five rulers—the fortified towns with their country villages. The large rock, on which[a] they set the ark of the
LORD, is a witness to this day in the field of Joshua of Beth Shemesh.
19 But God struck down[n] some of the men of Beth Shemesh, putting seventy[b] of them to
death because they had looked[o] into the ark of the LORD. The people mourned because of
the heavy blow the LORD had dealt them, 20 and the men of Beth Shemesh asked, "Who can
stand[p] in the presence of the LORD, this holy[q] God? To whom will the ark go up from here?"
21 Then they sent messengers to the people of Kiriath Jearim,[r] saying, "The Philistines
have returned the ark of the LORD. Come down and take it up to your place." 7 1 So the
men of Kiriath Jearim came and took up the ark of the LORD. They took it to Abinadab's[s] house on the hill and consecrated Eleazar his son to guard the ark of the LORD.

Samuel Subdues the Philistines at Mizpah

2 It was a long time, twenty years in all, that the ark remained at Kiriath Jearim, and
all the people of Israel mourned and sought after the LORD. 3 And Samuel said to the
whole house of Israel, "If you are returning[t] to the LORD with all your hearts, then rid[u]
yourselves of the foreign gods and the Ashtoreths[v] and commit[w] yourselves to the LORD
and serve him only,[x] and he will deliver you out of the hand of the Philistines." 4 So the
Israelites put away their Baals and Ashtoreths, and served the LORD only.
5 Then Samuel said, "Assemble all Israel at Mizpah[y] and I will intercede with the LORD
for you." 6 When they had assembled at Mizpah, they drew water and poured[z] it out before the LORD. On that day they fasted and there they confessed, "We have sinned
against the LORD." And Samuel was leader[c][a] of Israel at Mizpah.

6:14 [k]2Sa 24:22; 1Ki 19:21
6:15 [l]Jos 3:3
6:17 [m]ver 4
6:19 [n]2Sa 6:7 [o]Ex 19:21; Nu 4:5, 15,20
6:20 [p]2Sa 6:9; Mal 3:2; Rev 6:17 [q]Lev 11:45
6:21 [r]Jos 9:17; 15:9,60; 1Ch 13:5-6
7:1 [s]2Sa 6:3
7:3 [t]Dt 30:10; Isa 55:7; Hos 6:1 [u]Ge 35:2; Jos 24:14 [v]Jdg 2:12-13; 1Sa 31:10 [w]Joel 2:12 [x]Dt 6:13; Mt 4:10; Lk 4:8
7:5 [y]Jdg 20:1
7:6 [z]Ps 62:8; La 2:19 [a]Jdg 10:10; Ne 9:1; Ps 106:6

[a] 18 A few Hebrew manuscripts (see also Septuagint); most Hebrew manuscripts *villages as far as Greater Abel, where* [b] 19 A few Hebrew manuscripts; most Hebrew manuscripts and Septuagint *50,070*
[c] 6 Traditionally *judge*

6:12 lowing all the way. Apparently not happy to be leaving their calves behind, the cows nevertheless did not deviate from their divinely directed path.
6:13 harvesting their wheat. See note on 12:17.
6:14 Joshua of Beth Shemesh. Although this Joshua is not mentioned elsewhere in the Bible, his field and the prominent rock located in it were apparently well known at the time this account was written (v. 18). **sacrificed.** The means of the ark's transport, the cart and cows, were taken by the residents of Beth Shemesh and converted into material for sacrifice. **burnt offering.** See note on 10:8.
6:15 Levites. Beth Shemesh was included among the cities assigned to the Levites (specifically, the descendants of Aaron) in Joshua 21:16. **placed them on the large rock.** The large rock served as a resting place for the ark and the gold objects, not as an impromptu altar.
6:18 to this day. See note on verse 14.
6:19 looked into the ark. See Numbers 4:5 and 20. There is a noteworthy comparison between the events surrounding the ark's removal from Israel and its return. Presumptuous handling of the ark led to the former, and the same offense was to be purged on the occasion of the latter. The problem would arise again (see 2Sa 6).
6:20 Who can stand . . . ? Compare Exodus 9:11.
6:21 Kiriath Jearim. Located about nine miles northeast of Beth Shemesh, Kiriath Jearim is elsewhere called Kiriath Baal (Jos 15:60; 18:14), Baalah (Jos 15:9) and Baalah of Judah (2Sa 6:2).
■ **7:2–17** *Samuel Leads to Victory.* In contrast with Israel's earlier defeat (see 4:1b–22), the people of Israel repented of their idolatry, Samuel interceded and God gave them victory over the Philistines at Mizpah. Through this event Samuel was exalted once again over Eli and his sons. God ordained him as the leader of his people.
7:2 twenty years . . . sought after the LORD. In light of Samuel's somewhat skeptical response in the next verse and his reference to "foreign gods" among the Israelites, it is clear that it was not throughout the 20-year period, but only at its close, that Israel began to seek the Lord.
7:3 commit yourselves to the LORD . . . and he will deliver you. The cycle of apostasy, oppression, repentance and deliverance so typical of the book of Judges (e.g., Jdg 3:7–9) also provides the appropriate frame of reference for the events of this chapter. If Israel would put away foreign gods and return to the Lord with all her heart, then deliverance was assured, for as preceding chapters had shown, no one could stand before "the LORD, this holy God" (6:20).
7:4 Baals and Ashtoreths. See notes on 5:2 and Judges 2:13.
7:5 Mizpah. A town in Benjamin about 7.5 miles north of Jerusalem and 7.5 miles northeast of Kiriath Jearim. Mizpah played a prominent role in Israel before the monarchy (10:17; Jdg 20:1; 21:1,5,8) and became one of the regular stops in Samuel's circuit (v. 16). The name, which means something like "place of watching," implies a high vantage point and was, not surprisingly, applied to a number of sites in addition to the one in view here (e.g., 22:3).
7:6 they drew water and poured it out before the LORD. Although the precise significance of this action cannot be determined by any specific parallel elsewhere in Scripture, it does seem to signify sorrow and, along with the fasting also mentioned in this verse, a desire to do serious business with God. This recalls Hannah's confession in 1:15: "I am a woman who is deeply troubled . . . I was pouring out my soul to the LORD" (cf. also Ps 62:8; La 2:19). David's action in 2 Samuel 23:16 occurred in a different context and had a

7When the Philistines heard that Israel had assembled at Mizpah, the rulers of the
Philistines came up to attack them. And when the Israelites heard of it, they were
afraid[b] because of the Philistines. 8They said to Samuel, "Do not stop crying[c] out to the
LORD our God for us, that he may rescue us from the hand of the Philistines." 9Then Samuel[d] took a suckling lamb and offered it up as a whole burnt offering to the LORD. He cried
out to the LORD on Israel's behalf, and the LORD answered him.[e]
10While Samuel was sacrificing the burnt offering, the Philistines drew near to engage
Israel in battle. But that day the LORD thundered[f] with loud thunder against the Philistines and threw them into such a panic[g] that they were routed before the Israelites. 11The
men of Israel rushed out of Mizpah and pursued the Philistines, slaughtering them
along the way to a point below Beth Car.
12Then Samuel took a stone[h] and set it up between Mizpah and Shen. He named it
Ebenezer,[a] saying, "Thus far has the LORD helped us." 13So the Philistines were subdued[i]
and did not invade Israelite territory again.
Throughout Samuel's lifetime, the hand of the LORD was against the Philistines.
14The towns from Ekron to Gath that the Philistines had captured from Israel were restored to her, and Israel delivered the neighboring territory from the power of the Philistines. And there was peace between Israel and the Amorites.
15Samuel[j] continued as judge over Israel all the days of his life. 16From year to year
he went on a circuit from Bethel to Gilgal to Mizpah, judging Israel in all those places.
17But he always went back to Ramah,[k] where his home was, and there he also judged
Israel. And he built an altar[l] there to the LORD.

Israel Asks for a King

8 When Samuel grew old, he appointed[m] his sons as judges for Israel. 2The name of
his firstborn was Joel and the name of his second was Abijah, and they served at Beersheba.[n] 3But his sons did not walk in his ways. They turned aside after dishonest gain
and accepted bribes[o] and perverted justice.
4So all the elders of Israel gathered together and came to Samuel at Ramah.[p] 5They
said to him, "You are old, and your sons do not walk in your ways; now appoint a king[q]
to lead[b] us, such as all the other nations have."

7:7 [b]1Sa 17:11
7:8 [c]1Sa 12:19, 23; Isa 37:4; Jer 15:1
7:9 [d]Ps 99:6 [e]Jer 15:1
7:10 [f]1Sa 2:10; 2Sa 22:14-15 [g]Jos 10:10
7:12 [h]Ge 35:14; Jos 4:9
7:13 [i]Jdg 13:1,5; 1Sa 13:5
7:15 [j]ver 6; 1Sa 12:11
7:17 [k]1Sa 1:19; 8:4 [l]Jdg 21:4
8:1 [m]Dt 16:18-19
8:2 [n]Ge 22:19, 1Ki 19:3; Am 5:4-5
8:3 [o]Ex 23:8; Dt 16:19; Ps 15:5
8:4 [p]1Sa 7:17
8:5 [q]Dt 17:14-20

[a] 12 *Ebenezer* means *stone of help.* [b] 5 Traditionally *judge*; also in verses 6 and 20

different significance (see note on 2Sa 23:16). **We have sinned against the LORD.** The words and actions of the Israelites gave evidence of true repentance (v. 4). The time was ripe for the Lord to deliver his people from their Philistine oppressors. God's supreme power and autonomy had been amply demonstrated during the sojourn of his ark among the Philistines (chs. 5–6). His chosen human agent, Samuel, was present and confirmed (3:19–21). All that was yet required was the right opportunity. This was brought about by the Philistines' response to the convocation at Mizpah (v. 7).
7:8 crying out to the LORD. In the book of Judges, the act of "crying out to the LORD" typically preceded deliverance, which would then be accomplished through a deliverer whom the Lord would raise up (e.g., Jdg 3:9,15). In the present instance, Samuel functioned as intercessor and intermediary, while the victory was clearly the Lord's doing (v. 10).
7:9 burnt offering. See note on 10:8.
7:10 the LORD thundered . . . against the Philistines. This statement dramatically recalls the earlier words of Hannah: "Those who oppose the LORD will be shattered. He will thunder against them from heaven" (2:10; cf. 2Sa 22:14). In the song of Hannah, these words are immediately preceded by the programmatic statement that "it is not by strength that one prevails" (2:9). If the adventures with the ark in chapters 4–6 had taught anything, it was that human strength is of little consequence when the Lord decides to act.
7:12 Ebenezer. Not to be identified with the site of the same name mentioned in 4:1 and 5:1, this Ebenezer nevertheless does recall that earlier episode in which the Israelites sought to manipulate their God and suffered a resounding defeat at the hands of their Philistine enemies. Now that the Israelites had (for the time being) learned their lesson (vv. 4,6,8), God had given them a great victory over those same enemies. Samuel's setting up of a memorial stone with the name Ebenezer, meaning "stone of help," not only commemorated the present victory but also served as an oblique reminder of the strikingly different results brought about by presumption on the one hand and penitence on the other. **Thus far has the LORD helped us.** This statement may have had both a spatial and a temporal sense. In terms of the former sense, Samuel was proclaiming that the Lord had given Israel victory up to a certain geographical location. The latter sense ("up to this point in time the LORD has helped us"), however, takes on particular significance as background to the next chapter. In chapter 8 the Israelites sought help elsewhere; namely, in the person of a human king "such as all the other nations [had]" (8:5; see 8:6,19–20).
7:13 did not invade Israelite territory again. The reference is to the immediate, temporary battle situation (cf. 2Ki 6:23–24; see also 2Sa 2:28 with 2Sa 3:1). The Philistines were convincingly defeated and attempted no counterattack, but this in no way ruled out subsequent Philistine aggression (9:16; 10:5; 13:3; 14:52). **the hand of the LORD was against the Philistines.** What God had accomplished during the tenure of the ark in Philistine territory (5:1,4,11; 6:5) he now also accomplished through the leadership of Samuel. As this verse indicates, throughout Samuel's lifetime God continued to give Israel the upper hand, although the fighting at times was bitter (14:52). The defeat recounted in chapter 31 came only after Samuel's death (25:1).
■ **8:1—15:35** *Samuel and Saul: Saul's Rise and His Failed Kingship.* Having demonstrated that Samuel was God's chosen leader for his people, the writer turned next to Samuel's role in supporting and opposing Saul as Israel's first king. These chapters divide into two main parts: Saul's rise as king (8:1—12:25) and his failed kingship (13:1—15:35).
■ **8:1—12:25** *Saul's Rise.* Saul became king over Israel under questionable circumstances. These beginnings appear in three steps: the people's request for a king (8:1–22); Saul's initial rise to power (9:1—11:15) and Samuel's warnings and encouragements to Israel (12:1–25).
■ **8:1–22** *Samuel Hears and God Grants the Request for a King.* The Israelites demanded a king and, after having warned them of the potential abuses of kingship, God authorized Samuel to grant their request.
8:5 now appoint a king. The elders' stated reasons for wanting a king, although valid in themselves (as confirmed by the narrator's own words in vv. 1–3), turned out to be but pretexts. Their fundamental motivation was to become like "other nations" (see v. 20). **to lead us.** Or "to judge us" (see NIV text note).

8:6 [r]1Sa 15:11
8:7 [s]Ex 16:8; 1Sa 10:19

6But when they said, "Give us a king to lead us," this displeased[r] Samuel; so he
prayed to the LORD. 7And the LORD told him: "Listen to all that the people are saying to
you; it is not you they have rejected, but they have rejected me as their king.[s] 8As they

8:7 it is not you they have rejected. Since the elders couched their request in terms of a "king to lead [or judge] us" (v. 5 and its note), Samuel initially interpreted their overture as a personal affront to his own leadership (v. 6). As the Lord pointed out, however, the affront was far graver than that. **they have rejected me as their king.** The offense of the elders' request was not in their

Human Kingship: Was It Wrong to Have a Human King?

MANY Christian traditions assert that divine kingship was incompatible with human kingship in Israel. This widespread view ordinarily rests on 1 Samuel 8:1–22, where the people of Israel entreated Samuel, "Give us a king" (1Sa 8:6), and God responded to Samuel, "It is not you they have rejected, but they have rejected me as their king" (1Sa 8:7). The belief of many well-intentioned Christians is that God's ideal for Israel was that he should remain Israel's only king throughout history and that the appointment of human kings was at best God's concession to his people's sinfulness.

In reality, divine and human kingship in Israel were quite compatible, so long as the human monarchs remained God's faithful vice-regents. Human kings in Israel, like human magistrates in all places and times, were required to be obedient to the Lord, and the obligation of service to them was always subject to their compliance with his commands. In fact, the kings of Israel could so violate their roles as God's vice-regents that they lost their authority over the people of God (1Sa 15:26–28; 1Ki 2:1–4). Nevertheless, the Scriptures consistently present human kingship over Israel as a blessing that God sovereignly ordained for his people (Ge 17:16; Ecc 10:17; Hos 3:4–5).

First, the Scriptures indicate that prior to the events of 1 Samuel 8, God had already indicated his will for his people to have the right kind of human king at the right time. (1) As early as Genesis 17:6 God blessed Abraham by promising, "kings will come from you." God gave Abraham a vision of the future that included royalty among his descendants. (2) When Jacob blessed his sons, he explained that the tribe of Judah was ordained to be the royal family of Israel: "The scepter will not depart from Judah, nor the ruler's staff from between his feet, until he comes to whom it belongs and the obedience of the nations is his" (Ge 49:10). (3) Mosaic Law anticipated a king (Dt 17:14–20), regulating rather than forbidding human kingship in Israel. The king must be chosen by God, must be an Israelite, must have neither many horses nor many wives and must not amass great wealth. He must be diligent to keep the Law of Moses, in this regard considering himself the peer of his fellow Israelites. Moses promised that if Israel's kings would follow these regulations they would reign for a long time. (4) When Hannah praised the Lord for the birth of her son, Samuel, she closed with the hope that the Lord would "give strength to his king and exalt the horn of his anointed" (1Sa 2:10). (5) From the time of God's covenant with David and his descendants (2Sa 7; 1Ch 17; Pss 89; 132), these passages indicate that from the earliest times human kingship had been at the heart of God's plan for his people.

Second, the record of 1 Samuel 8:1–22 indicates that the problem with human kingship in Samuel's day was that the people of Israel were violating the divine regulations for kingship. They preferred not to wait for God to choose a king for them in his timing but demanded one immediately, demonstrating their lack of trust of God's ability and adequacy to care for them. Samuel warned that their request would bring them a king who would violate nearly all the regulations of Deuteronomy 17:14–20. God was not forbidding human kingship *per se* but was warning against the troubles that would come to Israel for seeking a king from the wrong motives, at the wrong time and without regard for the law of God. God's warnings proved to be accurate: Even the best of Israel's monarchs failed miserably. Their violations of God's law brought much trouble to Israel and eventually led to the exile of God's people.

Third, human kingship culminates in the human kingship of Christ—an incomparable blessing. As the son of David, Jesus fulfilled the awesome promises given to David's dynasty (2Sa 7; 1Ch 17). David's monarchy was decimated during the exile, but Jesus came to re-establish David's throne and to usher in the kingdom of God and ultimately bring it to its grand finale (Mt 1:1). In fact, by the time of the New Testament, the title *christ* ("anointed one") had come to be virtually synonymous with *king* (Mk 15:32; Lk 23:2). Jesus was the long-awaited, perfect King who would sit forever on the throne of David (Lk 1:30-33). Through his resurrection and ascension into heaven, Jesus began his unending reign as King over all the world (Eph 1:20–23; Rev 2:26–27). He will continue to reign from heaven until all of his enemies have been relegated to a position beneath his feet (1Co 15:25). After that time the end will come, and he, along with all of his faithful servants, will reign together in the new heavens and the new earth (2Ti 2:12; Rev 11:15; 22:5). This human kingship of Jesus is neither a mistake nor a divine concession to human weakness. King Jesus is the glorious fulfillment of the hopes of God's people since the days of Abraham.

The fact that Jesus is both human and divine resolves any tension between human and divine kingship. As the Son of God, Jesus has an eternal right to reign over all for all time. As the sinless son of David, Jesus gained the right to reign forever as a human being, to be his people's Messiah and to inherit the blessings of God's covenant on behalf of his people. In Christ, divine and human kingship are brought into perfect harmony.

have done from the day I brought them up out of Egypt until this day, forsaking me and
serving other gods, so they are doing to you. 9Now listen to them; but warn them solemnly and let them know[t] what the king who will reign over them will do."
10Samuel told all the words of the LORD to the people who were asking him for a king.
11He said, "This is what the king who will reign over you will do: He will take[u] your sons
and make them serve with his chariots and horses, and they will run in front of his chariots.[v] 12Some he will assign to be commanders[w] of thousands and commanders of fifties,
and others to plow his ground and reap his harvest, and still others to make weapons of
war and equipment for his chariots. 13He will take your daughters to be perfumers and
cooks and bakers. 14He will take the best of your[x] fields and vineyards[y] and olive groves
and give them to his attendants. 15He will take a tenth of your grain and of your vintage
and give it to his officials and attendants. 16Your menservants and maidservants and the
best of your cattle[a] and donkeys he will take for his own use. 17He will take a tenth of your
flocks, and you yourselves will become his slaves. 18When that day comes, you will cry out
for relief from the king you have chosen, and the LORD will not answer[z] you in that day."
19But the people refused[a] to listen to Samuel. "No!" they said. "We want a king over
us. 20Then we will be like all the other nations,[b] with a king to lead us and to go out before us and fight our battles."
21When Samuel heard all that the people said, he repeated[c] it before the LORD. 22The
LORD answered, "Listen[d] to them and give them a king."
Then Samuel said to the men of Israel, "Everyone go back to his town."

Samuel Anoints Saul

9 There was a Benjamite, a man of standing, whose name was Kish[e] son of Abiel, the
son of Zeror, the son of Becorath, the son of Aphiah of Benjamin. 2He had a son
named Saul, an impressive young man without equal[f] among the Israelites—a head taller[g] than any of the others.
3Now the donkeys belonging to Saul's father Kish were lost, and Kish said to his son
Saul, "Take one of the servants with you and go and look for the donkeys." 4So he passed

8:9 [t]ver 11-18; 1Sa 10:25
8:11 [u]1Sa 10:25; 14:52 [v]Dt 17:16; 2Sa 15:1
8:12 [w]1Sa 22:7
8:14 [x]Eze 46:18 [y]1Ki 21:7,15
8:18 [z]Pr 1:28; Isa 1:15; Mic 3:4
8:19 [a]Isa 66:4; Jer 44:16
8:20 [b]ver 5
8:21 [c]Jdg 11:11
8:22 [d]ver 7
9:1 [e]1Sa 14:51; 1Ch 8:33; 9:39
9:2 [f]1Sa 10:24 [g]1Sa 10:23

[a] 16 Septuagint; Hebrew *young men*

desire for human kingship per se, for kingship in Israel had long been anticipated (see note on 2:10). As the Lord himself disclosed in this verse and in the next, it was the elders' desire to displace God as their king and to replace him with a human monarch (contrast Gideon's refusal in Jdg 8:23) that constituted their sin (10:17–19; 12:12,17–20). See *WLC* 128.

8:9 Now listen to them. See note on verse 22. The Lord instructed Samuel to accede to the elders' request, but not without first sternly warning them about "what the king . . . [would] do." The latter expression, though verbally quite similar to the phrase rendered "regulations of the kingship" in 10:25, is nevertheless distinct in sense. The focus here is on what could be anticipated regarding the king's behavior or misbehavior (vv. 11–17).

8:10 who were asking him for a king. For the second time in 1 Samuel, the Israelites "asked for" (see 12:14) an individual. The person given in response to their first request was Samuel (see note on 1:20), and Saul would be given in response to their second.

8:11 This is what the king . . . will do. See note on verse 9. The harsh practices described in verses 11–17 had analogies both among Israel's Canaanite neighbors and among subsequent Israelite kings. **chariots.** See 2 Samuel 8:4, 15:1, 1 Kings 4:26 and 10:26–29. **run in front.** See Absalom's actions in 2 Samuel 15:1 and Adonijah's in 1 Kings 1:5.

8:12–14 commanders of thousands . . . fields and vineyards. See note on 22:7.

8:15,17 tenth. The demands of the king would either encroach upon what was rightfully due the Lord (e.g., Lev 27:30–32; Dt 14:22,28) or create a tax burden for his subjects.

8:18 the king you have chosen. See 12:13; contrast 16:1. **the LORD will not answer you.** Judging by the consequences, Israel's rejection of the Lord in favor of a human king was the moral and religious equivalent of forsaking the Lord to serve other gods (Jdg 10:10–14). The request of chapter 8 and its predicted consequences were particularly evil in light of the fact that the Lord had been ready to answer in chapter 7.

8:20 like all the other nations. See note on verse 5. **fight our battles.** Contrast "the LORD's battles" (25:28; see also 18:17).

8:22 Listen to them and give them a king. The Lord's concession to the people's sinful request is, at this point in the account, perplexing. If their desire for a king was tantamount to rejection of God as king (see v. 7 and its note; v. 18 and its note), how could God grant it? The answer is in the standards of acceptable kingship that the Lord would establish through the auspices of his servant Samuel. God was graciously willing to grant the people a king and even to bless him, but not a king of the sort they envisaged (see notes on 10:1; 10:7,8). Nevertheless, because they seized kingship in unbelief, they would suffer under a king like those of the other nations. **Everyone go back to his town.** Samuel's dismissal of the men of Israel implied that the appointing of a king was not something to be undertaken on the spot, but would require some preparation. The nature of the preparation was related in the chapters that follow.

■ **9:1—11:15** *Saul Becomes King.* Saul rose to power by being privately anointed by Samuel (9:1—10:16) and publicly selected at Mizpah (10:17–21), and by rescuing Jabesh Gilead from the Ammonites (ch. 11).

■ **9:1—10:16** *Saul's Anointing by Samuel.* Samuel privately anointed Saul as Israel's first king.

9:1 There was a Benjamite, a man of standing. The opening verse of the account of Saul's adventures is formally similar to the beginning of the birth narrative of Samuel (1:1). In both instances the father of the principal is introduced with sufficient genealogical references to suggest a man of standing. In Samuel's introduction we are also told of the father's faithful religious observances (1:3–5). In the present account we are introduced immediately to Saul (v. 2), and the focus remains exclusively on external qualities. Perhaps the closest parallel to Saul's introduction is that of Absalom (2Sa 14:25–26).

9:2 an impressive young man. The emphasis in the description of Saul is on physical stature and impressiveness, not on age per se. In particular, the word here translated "young" might better be rendered "choice," referring to a select individual in the prime of manhood (see NIV rendering of the same word as "chosen" in 24:2; Jdg 20:15–16; "finest" in Jdg 20:34). **head taller.** In the midst of the air of expectancy created by the events of chapter 8, Saul's kingly proportions cannot go unnoticed. Nevertheless, the lack of any reference to internal qualities (such as are mentioned in the introduction of Saul's eventual successor in 16:18) is a bit troubling in light of the programmatic song of Hannah; i.e., that "it is not by strength that one prevails" (2:9; see also note on 7:10).

9:3 Take one of the servants. That Kish addressed Saul directly regarding the problem of the lost donkeys suggests that Saul was

9:4 [h]Jos 24:33 [i]2Ki 4:42
9:5 [j]1Sa 1:1 [k]1Sa 10:2
9:6 [l]Dt 33:1; 1Ki 13:1 [m]1Sa 3:19
9:7 [n]1Ki 14:3; 2Ki 5:5, 15; 8:8
9:9 [o]2Sa 24:11; 2Ki 17:13; 1Ch 9:22; 26:28; 29:29; Isa 30:10; Am 7:12
9:11 [p]Ge 24:11,13
9:12 [q]Nu 28:11-15; 1Sa 7:17 [r]Ge 31:54; 1Sa 10:5; 1Ki 3:2
9:16 [s]1Sa 10:1 [t]Ex 3:7-9
9:17 [u]1Sa 16:12

through the hill[h] country of Ephraim and through the area around Shalisha,[i] but they
did not find them. They went on into the district of Shaalim, but the donkeys were not
there. Then he passed through the territory of Benjamin, but they did not find them.
5 When they reached the district of Zuph,[j] Saul said to the servant who was with him,
"Come, let's go back, or my father will stop thinking about the donkeys and start worrying[k] about us."
6 But the servant replied, "Look, in this town there is a man of God;[l] he is highly respected, and everything[m] he says comes true. Let's go there now. Perhaps he will tell us
what way to take."
7 Saul said to his servant, "If we go, what can we give the man? The food in our sacks
is gone. We have no gift[n] to take to the man of God. What do we have?"
8 The servant answered him again. "Look," he said, "I have a quarter of a shekel[a] of
silver. I will give it to the man of God so that he will tell us what way to take." 9 (Formerly in Israel, if a man went to inquire of God, he would say, "Come, let us go to the seer,"
because the prophet of today used to be called a seer.)[o]
10 "Good," Saul said to his servant. "Come, let's go." So they set out for the town where
the man of God was.
11 As they were going up the hill to the town, they met some girls coming out to draw[p]
water, and they asked them, "Is the seer here?"
12 "He is," they answered. "He's ahead of you. Hurry now; he has just come to our
town today, for the people have a sacrifice[q] at the high place.[r] 13 As soon as you enter the
town, you will find him before he goes up to the high place to eat. The people will not
begin eating until he comes, because he must bless the sacrifice; afterward, those who
are invited will eat. Go up now; you should find him about this time."
14 They went up to the town, and as they were entering it, there was Samuel, coming
toward them on his way up to the high place.
15 Now the day before Saul came, the LORD had revealed this to Samuel: 16 "About this
time tomorrow I will send you a man from the land of Benjamin. Anoint[s] him leader over
my people Israel; he will deliver[t] my people from the hand of the Philistines. I have
looked upon my people, for their cry has reached me."
17 When Samuel caught sight of Saul, the LORD said to him, "This[u] is the man I spoke
to you about; he will govern my people."

[a] *8* That is, about 1/10 ounce (about 3 grams)

not a mere youth but was old enough to take the lead. Neither is youthfulness implied by Saul's still being under his father's authority, for it was commonplace for the Hebrew household during the Biblical period to comprise several generations (e.g., Ge 42:1–2,37).

9:5 Come, let's go back. Discouraged by their lack of success, and concerned that his father might begin to worry, Saul suggested forfeiting any opportunity of recovering the animals by returning home. The servant, however, was more persistent (v. 6).

9:6 Look, in this town there is a man of God. Here for the first time, but not the last, the servant took the initiative, informing Saul of the man of God (see note on 2:27) resident in "this town" (probably Ramah; see note on 1:1). It is vaguely unsettling that Saul was unaware of the man of God or had simply not thought of consulting him. **everything he says comes true.** A further indication that the man of God was in fact Samuel (see note on 3:19).

9:7 We have no gift to take to the man of God. Josephus (*Antiquities*, 6.4.1) interpreted Saul's words as a sign of ignorance of the fact that Israel's true prophets accepted no reward. The matter is uncertain, however, for there is no mention of payment when Saul finally does meet Samuel. Israel's literary prophets at times expressed disdain for those who prophesied for money (Am 7:12; Mic 3:5,11), yet there are various references to goods being exchanged in return for prophetic favors (e.g., 1Ki 13:7–9; 14:3; 2Ki 4:42; 5:15–16; 8:8). In two instances, however, payment was explicitly refused (1Ki 13:7–9; 2Ki 5:15–16); in the only instance of accepted payment, the goods did not benefit the prophet personally but were distributed among the people (2Ki 4:42).

9:8 The servant answered him again. The servant continued to take the lead (v. 6), countering Saul's hesitation with the reply that he had money and would give it to the man of God.

9:9 prophet of today used to be called a seer. The designations are synonymous (2Sa 24:11), and the point of the notice is simply that the more commonly used term was "seer" in the time of Saul but "prophet" by the time of the composition of the present account. This does not imply that either term was unknown in either period, but it is mentioned to point out a shift in popular usage. Samuel was confirmed as a prophet in 3:20, and it may be that both the mention of "prophet" in the present verse and the various wordplays on the term in the immediate context (e.g., the Hebrew for "can we give" in v. 7 sounds exactly like the Hebrew for "prophet") provide the reader with additional hints that the man of God whom Saul would encounter was in fact Samuel (see notes on vv. 5,6).

9:12 they answered. The pronoun "they" refers to the girls whom Saul and his servant encountered coming to draw water (v. 11). In the Hebrew, verses 12–13 suggest an excited and animated state as the girls urged Saul to "hurry" to the city, for he had arrived just in time to meet Samuel. **high place.** The term in the Old Testament may refer either to "heights" in a literal sense or to "hill shrines." Although such "high places" (often sites of Canaanite worship) posed a clear danger to the purity of Israelite worship (e.g., Lev 26:30; Nu 33:52; Dt 12:2–3; Jer 2:20), it is apparent from passages such as this one that worship of Yahweh was sometimes conducted at these sites, especially during the period of the early monarchy (10:5; 1Ki 3:2–4). Such worship may have been made necessary by the loss of the sanctuary at Shiloh (see note on 1:3). After the division of the kingdom, worship at "high places" constituted a severe problem both in the north (1Ki 12:31–32; 13:32–34) and in the south (1Ki 14:22–24). Removal of the "high places" became a major goal of reform movements under southern kings such as Hezekiah (e.g., 2Ki 18:4) and Josiah (e.g., 2Ki 23:5).

9:14 there was Samuel. The reader's deduction from earlier hints (see notes on vv. 5,6,9) is here explicitly confirmed; the man of God was Samuel.

9:16 I will send. That Saul's search for the lost donkeys was being providentially directed toward another end, which was suspected already in verse 5 (see its note), is here confirmed. **Anoint him.** See note on 2:10. **leader.** More specifically, the term appears to denote a "designated one." The designate's assignment in the immediate context was to deliver Israel from the hand of the Philistines. Against the background of chapter 8, the logical assumption was that he would go on to become king. **Philistines.** See notes on 4:1 and 7:13.

18 Saul approached Samuel in the gateway and asked, "Would you please tell me
where the seer's house is?"
19 "I am the seer," Samuel replied. "Go up ahead of me to the high place, for today you
are to eat with me, and in the morning I will let you go and will tell you all that is in your
heart. 20 As for the donkeys[v] you lost three days ago, do not worry about them; they have
been found. And to whom is all the desire[w] of Israel turned, if not to you and all your father's family?"
21 Saul answered, "But am I not a Benjamite, from the smallest tribe[x] of Israel, and
is not my clan the least of all the clans of the tribe of Benjamin?[y] Why do you say such
a thing to me?"
22 Then Samuel brought Saul and his servant into the hall and seated them at the head
of those who were invited—about thirty in number. 23 Samuel said to the cook, "Bring
the piece of meat I gave you, the one I told you to lay aside."
24 So the cook took up the leg[z] with what was on it and set it in front of Saul. Samuel
said, "Here is what has been kept for you. Eat, because it was set aside for you for this
occasion, from the time I said, 'I have invited guests.' " And Saul dined with Samuel that
day.
25 After they came down from the high place to the town, Samuel talked with Saul on
the roof[a] of his house. 26 They rose about daybreak and Samuel called to Saul on the roof,
"Get ready, and I will send you on your way." When Saul got ready, he and Samuel went
outside together. 27 As they were going down to the edge of the town, Samuel said to Saul,
"Tell the servant to go on ahead of us"—and the servant did so—"but you stay here
awhile, so that I may give you a message from God."

10 Then Samuel took a flask[b] of oil and poured it on Saul's head and kissed him,
saying, "Has not the LORD anointed[c] you leader over his inheritance?[a] [d] 2 When
you leave me today, you will meet two men near Rachel's tomb,[e] at Zelzah on the border of Benjamin. They will say to you, 'The donkeys[f] you set out to look for have been
found. And now your father has stopped thinking about them and is worried[g] about you.
He is asking, "What shall I do about my son?" '
3 "Then you will go on from there until you reach the great tree of Tabor. Three men
going up to God at Bethel[h] will meet you there. One will be carrying three young goats,
another three loaves of bread, and another a skin of wine. 4 They will greet you and offer you two loaves of bread, which you will accept from them.
5 "After that you will go to Gibeah of God, where there is a Philistine outpost.[i] As you
approach the town, you will meet a procession of prophets coming down from the high

9:20 [v]ver 3 [w]1Sa 8:5; 12:13
9:21 [x]1Sa 15:17 [y]Jdg 20:35,46
9:24 [z]Lev 7:32-34; Nu 18:18
9:25 [a]Dt 22:8; Ac 10:9
10:1 [b]1Sa 16:13; 2Ki 9:1,3,6 [c]Ps 2:12 [d]Dt 32:9; Ps 78:62,71
10:2 [e]Ge 35:20 [f]1Sa 9:4 [g]1Sa 9:5
10:3 [h]Ge 28:22; 35:7-8
10:5 [i]1Sa 13:3

[a] 1 Hebrew; Septuagint and Vulgate *over his people Israel? You will reign over the LORD's people and save them from the power of their enemies round about. And this will be a sign to you that the LORD has anointed you leader over his inheritance:*

9:18 Saul approached Samuel. That Saul did not recognize Samuel (as indicated by his question) is disconcerting, especially after the elaborate briefing by the girls at the well (vv. 12–13; cf. also note on v. 6). For the attentive reader, who even before the disclosure of verse 14 has deduced that the man of God was Samuel, Saul's failure to do so is a troubling hint of spiritual insensitivity and inattentiveness that would increasingly characterize him.

9:20 all the desire of Israel. Although the Hebrew is sometimes rendered "all that is desirable in Israel," referring to the immense wealth that kingship would bring, the NIV rendering seems preferable and may be taken to suggest that Saul was just the kind of king desired by the people in chapter 8.

9:24 took up the leg . . . set it in front of Saul. The special treatment given Saul evidenced not only Saul's newly elevated status but also Samuel's divinely enabled anticipation of his arrival (vv. 15–16).

9:25 Samuel talked with Saul. Samuel is not explicitly named in the Hebrew, and the Septuagint (the Greek translation of the OT) reading "they spread a bed for Saul" may well reflect the original text.

10:1 anointed you leader. See notes on 9:16. **his inheritance?** See 9:16 ("my people Israel"), 2 Samuel 20:19 and its note and Deuteronomy 32:9. The Lord's willingness to grant the people a human king does not at all imply a forfeiture of his divine rights as great King over his inheritance (or "possession"), Israel. The appointed king was to serve as vice-regent within an authority structure that the Lord himself would stipulate (v. 25). During the period of the judges, the hero-deliverer typically received the Lord's commission and carried out the military task. With the institution of kingship, however, these two functions were divided: The prophet became the recipient and mediator of the divine commission, and the king became the standing military agent (9:16). This two-tiered structure is not only evidenced in the first charge given to Saul (see notes on vv. 7,8), but also provides the essential background for an understanding of the eventual rift between Samuel and Saul and the ultimate rejection of the latter.

10:2–6 In the Septuagint (the Greek translation of the OT) the latter part of verse 1 states that a sign would be given Saul to confirm his anointing (see NIV text note). Actually, the confirmation comprised three signs: The first confirmed the truth of Samuel's words (v. 2; cf. 9:20), the second Saul's special status (vv. 3–4) and the third the availability of the Spirit of God to empower Saul (vv. 5–6).

10:5 Gibeah of God. Quite possibly the same location that is called simply "Geba" in 13:2 (see its note). Others have suggested identifying "Gibeah of God" with "Gibeah of Saul" (see v. 26; 11:4). In fact, recent research suggests that Gibeah of Saul may not have been a distinct site, but may have been an alternate name for "Geba" (modern Veba). **where there is a Philistine outpost.** It is difficult to decide between the rendering "outpost [garrison]" and the equally possible "governor [prefect]." The presence of the one would likely imply that of the other. The juxtaposition of Gibeah of God and a Philistine outpost draws attention to the task ahead for the one designated to deliver the people of God from the hand of the Philistines (9:16). On the stationing of garrisons in subject territories, see David's practice in 2 Samuel 8:6. **procession of prophets.** Samuel is associated with a group of prophets in 19:20, where he is described as their leader. Note the similar association of Elisha with the "company [lit., 'sons'] of the prophets" in 2 Kings 2:3, 5, 7 and 15, 6:1 and 9:1. These prophetic bands appear to have been made up of zealous defenders of true religion in times of

place[j] with lyres, tambourines, flutes and harps[k] being played before them, and they will
be prophesying.[l] 6 The Spirit[m] of the LORD will come upon you in power, and you will
prophesy with them; and you will be changed into a different person. 7 Once these signs
are fulfilled, do whatever[n] your hand finds to do, for God is with[o] you.
8 "Go down ahead of me to Gilgal.[p] I will surely come down to you to sacrifice burnt
offerings and fellowship offerings,[a] but you must wait seven days until I come to you and
tell you what you are to do."

Saul Made King

9 As Saul turned to leave Samuel, God changed[q] Saul's heart, and all these signs were
fulfilled that day. 10 When they arrived at Gibeah, a procession of prophets met him; the
Spirit of God came upon him in power, and he joined in their prophesying.[r] 11 When all
those who had formerly known him saw him prophesying with the prophets, they asked
each other, "What is this[s] that has happened to the son of Kish? Is Saul also among the
prophets?"[t]
12 A man who lived there answered, "And who is their father?" So it became a saying:
"Is Saul also among the prophets?" 13 After Saul stopped prophesying, he went to the high
place.
14 Now Saul's uncle[u] asked him and his servant, "Where have you been?"
"Looking for the donkeys," he said. "But when we saw they were not to be found, we
went to Samuel."
15 Saul's uncle said, "Tell me what Samuel said to you."
16 Saul replied, "He assured us that the donkeys[v] had been found." But he did not tell
his uncle what Samuel had said about the kingship.
17 Samuel summoned the people of Israel to the LORD at Mizpah[w] 18 and said to them,

10:5 [j]1Sa 9:12 [k]2Ki 3:15 [l]1Sa 19:20; 1Co 14:1
10:6 [m]ver 10; Nu 11:25; 1Sa 19:23-24
10:7 [n]Ecc 9:10 [o]Jos 1:5; Jdg 6:12; Heb 13:5
10:8 [p]1Sa 11:14-15
10:9 [q]ver 6
10:10 [r]ver 5-6; 1Sa 19:20
10:11 [s]Mt 13:54; Jn 7:15 [t]1Sa 19:24
10:14 [u]1Sa 14:50
10:16 [v]1Sa 9:20
10:17 [w]Jdg 20:1; 1Sa 7:5

[a] 8 Traditionally *peace offerings*

---

widespread apostasy and spiritual indifference. **prophesying.** Prophecy in the Old Testament is often, though not exclusively, associated with the giving of a message (e.g., Aaron's role as Moses' "prophet" or spokesman in Ex 6:28—7:2; cf. 1Ki 22:22; Jer 14:14; Eze 21:9; Am 3:8). God's prophets were his messengers (2Sa 7:1–5; 12:1; 24:11–12). In some Biblical contexts, prophecy seems to suggest strange behavior (e.g., 18:10; 1Ki 18:29), while in others it is particularly associated with music (e.g., Ex 15:20–21; 1Ch 25:1). The prophesying in view throughout the present chapter seems to be of the latter sort; i.e., praising and exhorting with musical accompaniment.

10:6 Spirit of the LORD will come upon you in power. See verse 10; see also 11:6 and its note. The activity of the Spirit upon Samson is expressed in identical terms (Jdg 14:6,19; 15:14). Only of David is it said that his endowment with the Spirit was permanent (16:13); Saul's would ultimately be reversed (cf. 16:14; 18:10). On the concept of the "Spirit of God/the LORD" in the Old Testament, see, for example, Genesis 1:2, 41:38, Judges 3:10 and their notes. Frequently in the Old Testament, the bestowal of the divine Spirit connotes God's empowering an individual for the accomplishment of a particular task. At other times, God's Spirit may prevent action (19:23). In addition, God sometimes sent a lying spirit (1Ki 22:23), an evil (tormenting) spirit (16:14–16,23; 18:10; 19:9; Jdg 9:23). **different person.** In context, Samuel's words should not be understood as referring to regeneration or any kind of permanent spiritual conversion in Saul. Rather, the sense seems to be that Saul was temporarily changed from his former self in order that the signs could be fulfilled (see v. 9; also note the astonishment in v. 11 of those who had formerly known Saul).

10:7 do whatever your hand finds to do. "Whatever" is attested by the Septuagint (the Greek translation of the OT), but the Hebrew text is better rendered simply, "Do what your hand finds to do." In light of Saul's general commission to deliver Israel from the Philistines (9:16) and of Samuel's specific mention of a visible symbol of Philistine domination at the site of the third and final sign (v. 5), the implication of Samuel's words here is that Saul should have responded to his anointing by attacking the Philistine outpost (or by assassinating the governor; see note on v. 5), thereby issuing a challenge to the Philistines.

10:8 Go down ahead of me to Gilgal. Envisioned in the preceding verse is a defiant gesture that would surely provoke a retaliatory response from the Philistines. Thus, Samuel here issued a second charge that was contingent upon the fulfillment of the first. When Saul had done what his "hand [found] to do," he was to rendezvous with Samuel in Gilgal, so the latter could consecrate the battle with sacrifices and give Saul further instructions. On Samuel's role in Saul's kingship, see note on verse 1. **burnt offerings.** The first Biblical record of a burnt offering is in Genesis 8:20. A full description of a burnt offering can be found in Leviticus 1:3–17. In addition to the present verse, burnt offerings are mentioned in 1 Samuel 6:14–15, 7:9–10, 13:9 and 12, 15:22, 2 Samuel 6:17–18 and 24:22–25. **fellowship offerings.** The fellowship offering is described in Leviticus 3 and is first mentioned in Exodus 20:24. Other references in Samuel to fellowship offerings are 11:15, 13:9, 2 Samuel 6:17–18 and 24:25.

10:9 God changed Saul's heart. See verse 6 and its note.

10:11 Is Saul also among the prophets? Or "Is even Saul among the prophets?" This "saying" (v. 12) seemed to imply surprise at seeing someone acting out of character. Whatever is to be assumed regarding their specific attitude toward prophets (see note on v. 12), the onlookers who had known Saul before were surprised to find him associating with religious enthusiasts. Had the Saul they knew changed, or was he simply acting very much out of character? The ironic repetition of the saying under very different circumstances in 19:24 suggests that the latter was the case.

10:12 who is their father? Since leaders of prophetic bands were sometimes called "father" (e.g., 2Ki 2:12; 6:21), this question may simply have been asking who led this particular band. Alternatively, assuming a generally positive attitude toward prophecy on the part of the onlookers, the point of the question may have been that any band that would include Saul would be under dubious leadership. If, on the other hand, the onlookers did not think highly of prophecy, their surprise may have been occasioned by the sight of a man of standing from a good family, such as Saul, associating with such "madmen" (cf. 2Ki 9:11). A fourth possibility is simply that since the gift of prophecy is not based on heredity, Saul was as eligible to receive it as anyone else was.

10:14–16 After the completion of the third sign (see note on vv. 2–6), Saul apparently did not do what his "hand [found] to do" (see v. 7 and its note; 13:3 and its note) but soon found himself in a conversation with his "uncle" or "kinsman" (possibly Abner). The significance of this conversation has long puzzled commentators. Some have understood Saul's reticence to mention the kingship (v. 16) as a sign of laudable humility. In view of the interpretation of verse 7 that is offered in the notes above, and in light of Saul's apparent hesitation to get on with it, it seems more likely that Saul's silence before the person who would later become his general (14:50) was a sign of timidity and faithlessness (see v. 22 and its note).

■ **10:17–27** *Saul's Public Selection by Lot at Mizpah.* After a relatively private anointing, Samuel called the people together to rebuke them and to give them the kind of king they desired.

"This is what the LORD, the God of Israel, says: 'I brought Israel up out of Egypt, and I delivered you from the power of Egypt and all the kingdoms that oppressed[x] you.' [19]But you
have now rejected your God, who saves you out of all your calamities and distresses. And
you have said, 'No, set a king[y] over us.' So now present[z] yourselves before the LORD by
your tribes and clans."

[20]When Samuel brought all the tribes of Israel near, the tribe of Benjamin was chosen. [21]Then he brought forward the tribe of Benjamin, clan by clan, and Matri's clan was
chosen. Finally Saul son of Kish was chosen. But when they looked for him, he was not
to be found. [22]So they inquired[a] further of the LORD, "Has the man come here yet?"

And the LORD said, "Yes, he has hidden himself among the baggage."

[23]They ran and brought him out, and as he stood among the people he was a head
taller[b] than any of the others. [24]Samuel said to all the people, "Do you see the man the
LORD has chosen?[c] There is no one like him among all the people."

Then the people shouted, "Long live[d] the king!"

[25]Samuel explained to the people the regulations[e] of the kingship. He wrote them
down on a scroll and deposited it before the LORD. Then Samuel dismissed the people,
each to his own home.

[26]Saul also went to his home in Gibeah,[f] accompanied by valiant men whose hearts
God had touched. [27]But some troublemakers[g] said, "How can this fellow save us?" They
despised him and brought him no gifts.[h] But Saul kept silent.

Saul Rescues the City of Jabesh

11 Nahash[i] the Ammonite went up and besieged Jabesh Gilead.[j] And all the men
of Jabesh said to him, "Make a treaty[k] with us, and we will be subject to you."

[2]But Nahash the Ammonite replied, "I will make a treaty with you only on the condition that I gouge[l] out the right eye of every one of you and so bring disgrace[m] on all
Israel."

[3]The elders of Jabesh said to him, "Give us seven days so we can send messengers
throughout Israel; if no one comes to rescue us, we will surrender to you."

[4]When the messengers came to Gibeah[n] of Saul and reported these terms to the people, they all wept[o] aloud. [5]Just then Saul was returning from the fields, behind his oxen,
and he asked, "What is wrong with the people? Why are they weeping?" Then they repeated to him what the men of Jabesh had said.

10:18 [x]Jdg 6:8-9
10:19 [y]1Sa 8:5-7; 12:12 [z]Jos 7:14; 24:1
10:22 [a]1Sa 23:2,4,9-11
10:23 [b]1Sa 9:2
10:24 [c]Dt 17:15; 2Sa 21:6 [d]1Ki 1:25,34,39
10:25 [e]Dt 17:14-20; 1Sa 8:11-18
10:26 [f]1Sa 11:4
10:27 [g]Dt 13:13 [h]1Ki 10:25; 2Ch 17:5
11:1 [i]1Sa 12:12 [j]Jdg 21:8 [k]1Ki 20:34; Eze 17:13
11:2 [l]Nu 16:14 [m]1Sa 17:26
11:4 [n]1Sa 10:5,26; 15:34 [o]Jdg 2:4; 1Sa 30:4

10:17 Samuel summoned the people. Since Saul failed to attract public attention by following the command of verse 7, Samuel devised another means of making God's designee known. Samuel's opening words to the people (v. 18) resemble those of a judgment speech (see note on 2:27–36), and the method he employed to reveal Saul closely resembles that used elsewhere to discover a guilty party (e.g., ch. 14; Jos 7).

10:20 Benjamin was chosen. Casting lots was probably the method of selection (see Lev 16:8–10; Nu 26:55). This may have involved the Urim and the Thummim (see note on 2:28; see Ex 28:30 and its note; Nu 27:21; Dt 33:8 and its note).

10:22 he has hidden himself among the baggage. The context is more suggestive of unhealthy bashfulness than of humility (see note on vv. 14–16).

10:25 regulations of the kingship. Although the Lord, through his spokesman Samuel, had appointed a king, God himself remained the great King. For kingship to succeed, both the king-designate and the people needed to abide by the prescribed regulations of the kingship (Dt 17:18–20; 2Ki 11:12). **deposited it before the LORD.** Compare Deuteronomy 31:26 and Joshua 24:26.

10:27 How can this fellow save us? Those who posed this question were rightly labeled "troublemakers," because they called into question the Lord's selection process. Nevertheless, their complaint was not entirely unjustified, inasmuch as Saul had as yet done nothing to distinguish himself. See *WLC* 128.

■ **11:1–15** *Saul's Rescue of Jabesh Gilead.* Saul rescued Jabesh Gilead from Ammonite attackers (vv. 1–11) and was confirmed as king at Gilgal (vv. 12–15).

11:1 Nahash the Ammonite. The Ammonites were a Semitic people (descended from Lot, according to Ge 19:38; Dt 2:19) whose kingdom lay in Transjordan, south of the Jabbok River. While they were sometimes on friendly terms with Israel (2Sa 10:2), the Ammonites' territorial ambitions often caused them to exert pressure on Israel's eastern border (e.g., Jdg 3:13; 11:4–32), as the Philistines did on Israel's western border. According to the Dead Sea Scrolls (on 10:27) and Josephus (*Antiquities,* 6.5.1), the siege of Jabesh Gilead was but part of a larger campaign by Nahash to subjugate Israel's Transjordanian holdings. **Jabesh Gilead.** A principal city of Gilead in what would probably have been the territory of Gad, Jabesh Gilead is commonly identified with a site 22 miles southeast of the Sea of Galilee in Transjordan.

11:2 gouge out the right eye. While the stated reason for such treatment was to "bring disgrace on all Israel," Josephus (*Antiquities,* 6.5.1) remarked that the loss of the right eye would also have rendered the injured party unfit for military service, since the left eye would typically have been screened by the shield.

11:3 we will surrender to you. Literally, "we will go out to you." While the Jabeshite elders clearly intended Nahash to understand their words in terms of surrender, the Hebrew verb employed is often used in a military sense of soldiers "going out" to battle (e.g., 8:20; 18:30; 2Sa 18:2–4,6). When the elders again promised to "go out" to the Ammonites (see v. 10), the situation was rich in irony, for while the Ammonites were still thinking "surrender," the Jabeshites, having just learned of their impending deliverance, intended "battle."

11:4 the messengers came to Gibeah of Saul. Unless we assume that the elders were speaking honestly to Nahash in verse 3 when they proposed sending "messengers throughout Israel," there is nothing to suggest that the messengers did not come directly to Gibeah of Saul (10:5,26). This seems to make the best sense in terms of the time frame. It is conceivable that Saul could have been able to send messengers "throughout Israel" and muster troops before the end of the seven days (vv. 7–9). But it would have been virtually impossible for messengers from Jabesh Gilead to have traveled "throughout Israel" prior to reaching Saul and for Saul subsequently to have sent his own messengers "throughout Israel" (v. 7) and mustered troops within that amount of time. As to the reason the Jabeshites should have sought help from Gibeah, familial ties between them and the Benjamites (Jdg 21) are often cited. In view of the present textual context and of the specific mention of "Gibeah of Saul" (as opposed to "Benjamin" more generally), it seems more likely that knowledge of Saul's recent designation as Israel's deliverer may have prompted the Jabeshites' action.

11:5 Saul was returning from the fields. To this point, Saul had attempted nothing that would have provided an answer to the troublemakers' question, "How can this fellow save us?" (10:27).

6 When Saul heard their words, the Spirit[p] of God came upon him in power, and he
burned with anger. 7 He took a pair of oxen, cut them into pieces, and sent the pieces by
messengers throughout Israel,[q] proclaiming, "This is what will be done to the oxen of
anyone[r] who does not follow Saul and Samuel." Then the terror of the LORD fell on the
people, and they turned out as one man. 8 When Saul mustered[s] them at Bezek,[t] the men
of Israel numbered three hundred thousand and the men of Judah thirty thousand.
9 They told the messengers who had come, "Say to the men of Jabesh Gilead, 'By the
time the sun is hot tomorrow, you will be delivered.' " When the messengers went and
reported this to the men of Jabesh, they were elated. 10 They said to the Ammonites, "Tomorrow we will surrender[u] to you, and you can do to us whatever seems good to you."
11 The next day Saul separated his men into three divisions;[v] during the last watch of
the night they broke into the camp of the Ammonites and slaughtered them until the
heat of the day. Those who survived were scattered, so that no two of them were left together.

Saul Confirmed as King

12 The people then said to Samuel, "Who[w] was it that asked, 'Shall Saul reign over us?'
Bring these men to us and we will put them to death."
13 But Saul said, "No one shall be put to death today,[x] for this day the LORD has rescued[y] Israel."
14 Then Samuel said to the people, "Come, let us go to Gilgal[z] and there reaffirm the
kingship.[a]" 15 So all the people went to Gilgal[b] and confirmed Saul as king in the presence of the LORD. There they sacrificed fellowship offerings[a] before the LORD, and Saul
and all the Israelites held a great celebration.

Samuel's Farewell Speech

12 Samuel said to all Israel, "I have listened[c] to everything you said to me and have
set a king[d] over you. 2 Now you have a king as your leader.[e] As for me, I am old
and gray, and my sons are here with you. I have been your leader from my youth until
this day. 3 Here I stand. Testify against me in the presence of the LORD and his anointed.[f]
Whose ox have I taken? Whose donkey[g] have I taken? Whom have I cheated? Whom

11:6 [p]Jdg 3:10; 6:34; 13:25; 14:6; 1Sa 10:10; 16:13
11:7 [q]Jdg 19:29 [r]Jdg 21:5
11:8 [s]Jdg 20:2 [t]Jdg 1:4
11:10 [u]ver 3
11:11 [v]Jdg 7:16
11:12 [w]1Sa 10:27; Lk 19:27
11:13 [x]2Sa 19:22 [y]Ex 14:13; 1Sa 19:5
11:14 [z]1Sa 10:8 [a]1Sa 10:25
11:15 [b]1Sa 10:8,17
12:1 [c]1Sa 8:7 [d]1Sa 10:24; 11:15
12:2 [e]1Sa 8:5
12:3 [f]1Sa 10:1; 24:6; 2Sa 1:14 [g]Nu 16:15

[a] *15* Traditionally *peace offerings*

11:6 Spirit of God came upon him in power. The phrase recalls the activity of the Spirit upon Samson (see note on 10:6).
11:7 sent the pieces by messengers throughout Israel. Saul's action here roughly parallels that of the Levite in Judges 19 (especially v. 29). Yet in this case the ceremony involved a dead animal, not a human body. The analogy may not be entirely complimentary inasmuch as the Levite had lived during the period when "Israel had no king" and "everyone did as he saw fit" (Jdg 17:6; 21:25).
11:8 men of Israel . . . men of Judah. Even before the division of the kingdom (1Ki 12), a distinction was often made between the northern and southern tribes (17:52; 18:16; Jos 11:21; 2Sa 2:10; 3:10; 5:5; 11:11; 12:8; 19:11,40–43; 20:2; 21:2; 24:1,9).
11:10 we will surrender to you. See note on verse 3.
11:11 three divisions. See 13:17, Judges 7:16, 9:43 and 2 Samuel 18:2. **during the last watch of the night.** That is, between approximately 2:00 and 6:00 A.M., thereby taking advantage of the element of surprise.
11:12 Bring these men to us. The reference likely includes, but may not be limited to, the "troublemakers" of 10:27.
11:13 the LORD has rescued Israel. Although this confession marks a high point for Saul, one might query the propriety of his responding to a question that had properly been addressed to Samuel (v. 12). Some commentators have suggested that Saul's pardon evidenced his carelessness in matters of sacral law.
11:14 let us go to Gilgal and there reaffirm the kingship. On one level the process of Saul's accession to the throne could now be resumed (see note on v. 15), but on a deeper level, the continued reign of the Lord, albeit within a newly defined authority structure (see notes on 8:22; 10:1), must now be reaffirmed (ch. 12). **Gilgal.** See note on 13:4.
11:15 confirmed Saul as king. Recent studies have indicated that an individual's rise to leadership in ancient Israel often followed a three-step pattern: (1) designation as the Lord's choice (through a personal encounter with God or, as in Saul's case, a prophetic mediation); (2) demonstration of the individual's valor and of the Lord's empowering through some heroic feat; and (3) confirmation by the people of the individual's right to lead. According to the reading of the Saul narratives thus far, the originally envisioned progress of events would have been as follows: (1) designation of Saul by Samuel (see 9:16; 10:1 and their notes); (2) demonstration of Saul's mettle through an attack on the Philistine outpost in Gibeah (see 10:5,7,8 and their notes); and (3) confirmation of Saul by the people. Saul's failure to execute stage two (see note on 10:14–16), however, arrested the process, making it necessary for Samuel to convene an assembly at Mizpah in order to bring Saul to public attention (10:17–27). Nevertheless, some people questioned the appointment of Saul, who as yet had done nothing to prove himself (10:27). In chapter 11 Saul's bold leadership rectified this deficiency, and the way was clear to execute stage three: the confirmation of Saul as king. **fellowship offerings.** See note on 10:8. **Saul and all the Israelites held a great celebration.** Samuel would strike a more somber tone in chapter 12 as he issued a final warning regarding the conditions under which kingship in Israel could succeed.
■ **12:1–25** *Samuel Warns and Encourages Israel.* Samuel addressed Israel for the last time, exhorting both king and people to obey God and warning them of judgment if they did not.
12:1 I have listened. See 8:7 and 22.
12:2 you have a king as your leader. Despite some faltering on Saul's part (see note on 11:15), the process of accession to the throne had now run its course, and the time had come for Saul to be installed. While Samuel's speech in chapter 12 marks the end of the period of the judges, Samuel himself did not retire but adopted adjusted responsibilities (see v. 23 and its note) in line with the two-tiered authority structure prescribed for the monarchy (see note on 10:1). **I have been your leader from my youth.** By employing phraseology similar to the preceding verse, Samuel set up a contrast between the king (whose abusive practices had already been described in 8:9–18) and himself, the prophet and judge (vv. 3–5).
12:3–15 Concerned that kingship begin properly and be given every opportunity to succeed, Samuel advanced a three-pronged argument designed to bring the people to a proper recognition of their guilt for requesting a king. First, Samuel expounded his own innocence of avarice or injustice (v. 3) and elicited a confession from the people that his leadership had been blameless (vv. 4–5). Second, he pointed out that in the past the Lord had always appointed Isra-

have I oppressed? From whose hand have I accepted a bribe[h] to make me shut my eyes?
If I have done[i] any of these, I will make it right."
4"You have not cheated or oppressed us," they replied. "You have not taken anything
from anyone's hand."
5Samuel said to them, "The LORD is witness against you, and also his anointed is witness this day, that you have not found anything[j] in my hand.[k]"
"He is witness," they said.
6Then Samuel said to the people, "It is the LORD who appointed Moses and Aaron and
brought[l] your forefathers up out of Egypt. 7Now then, stand here, because I am going
to confront[m] you with evidence before the LORD as to all the righteous acts performed
by the LORD for you and your fathers.
8"After Jacob entered Egypt, they cried[n] to the LORD for help, and the LORD sent[o] Moses and Aaron, who brought your forefathers out of Egypt and settled them in this
place.
9"But they forgot[p] the LORD their God; so he sold them into the hand of Sisera,[q] the
commander of the army of Hazor, and into the hands of the Philistines[r] and the king of
Moab,[s] who fought against them. 10They cried out to the LORD and said, 'We have
sinned; we have forsaken[t] the LORD and served the Baals and the Ashtoreths.[u] But now
deliver us from the hands of our enemies, and we will serve you.' 11Then the LORD sent
Jerub-Baal,[a][v] Barak,[b][w] Jephthah[x] and Samuel,[c] and he delivered you from the hands of
your enemies on every side, so that you lived securely.
12"But when you saw that Nahash[y] king[z] of the Ammonites was moving against you,
you said to me, 'No, we want a king to rule[a] over us'—even though the LORD your God
was your king. 13Now here is the king[b] you have chosen, the one you asked[c] for; see, the
LORD has set a king over you. 14If you fear[d] the LORD and serve and obey him and do not
rebel against his commands, and if both you and the king who reigns over you follow the
LORD your God—good! 15But if you do not obey the LORD, and if you rebel against[e] his
commands, his hand will be against you, as it was against your fathers.
16"Now then, stand still and see[f] this great thing the LORD is about to do before your
eyes! 17Is it not wheat harvest[g] now? I will call[h] upon the LORD to send thunder and rain.[i]
And you will realize what an evil[j] thing you did in the eyes of the LORD when you asked
for a king."
18Then Samuel called upon the LORD, and that same day the LORD sent thunder and
rain. So all the people stood in awe[k] of the LORD and of Samuel.

12:3 [h]Dt 16:19 [i]Ac 20:33
12:5 [j]Ac 23:9; 24:20 [k]Ex 22:4
12:6 [l]Ex 6:26; Mic 6:4
12:7 [m]Isa 1:18; Mic 6:1-5
12:8 [n]Ex 2:23 [o]Ex 3:10; 4:16
12:9 [p]Jdg 3:7 [q]Jdg 4:2 [r]Jdg 10:7; 13:1 [s]Jdg 3:12
12:10 [t]Jdg 10:10,15 [u]Jdg 2:13
12:11 [v]Jdg 6:14,32 [w]Jdg 4:6 [x]Jdg 11:1
12:12 [y]1Sa 11:1 [z]1Sa 8:5 [a]Jdg 8:23; 1Sa 8:6, 19
12:13 [b]1Sa 8:5; Hos 13:11 [c]1Sa 10:24
12:14 [d]Jos 24:14
12:15 [e]ver 9; Jos 24:20; Isa 1:20
12:16 [f]Ex 14:13
12:17 [g]1Sa 7:9-10 [h]Jas 5:18 [i]Pr 26:1 [j]1Sa 8:6-7
12:18 [k]Ex 14:31

a *11* Also called *Gideon* b *11* Some Septuagint manuscripts and Syriac; Hebrew *Bedan* c *11* Hebrew; some Septuagint manuscripts and Syriac *Samson*

el's leaders (v. 6) and that these leaders had always proved fully adequate (vv. 7–8). Third, he emphasized that even when the Israelites "forgot the LORD their God" (v. 9), the Lord had acted graciously. The pattern had replayed itself repeatedly: First the Lord had subjected them to enemy oppression (v. 9) and then responded to their confessions of sin and cries for deliverance (v. 10) by raising up judges, among whom Samuel himself was to be counted (v. 11). Against this background of the sufficiency of the Lord's provision, the people's request for a human king, "even though the LORD [their] God was [their] king" (v. 12), could be seen for what it was (8:7). Despite the people's sin in asking for a king, the Lord had graciously responded and had "set a king over [them]" (v. 13), albeit without relinquishing his own authority (see 8:22; 10:1; 10:25 and their notes). Kingship could succeed, but only if both king and people "fear[ed] the LORD and serve[d] and obey[ed] him and [did] not rebel against his commands" (v. 14).

12:3 his anointed. See note on 2:10. Saul's anointing was ordered in 9:16 and effected in 10:1. **Whose ox . . . ? Whose donkey have I taken?** These were valuable possessions in Biblical times. Oxen and donkeys are specifically mentioned in the tenth commandment, which prohibits covetousness (Ex 20:17; Dt 5:21).

12:7 Now then, stand. Samuel called the people to attention so that he could present the case against them. Identical words occur at the beginning of verse 16, as Samuel introduced the sign meant to bring the people to a full realization of their sin in asking for a king. **confront you with evidence.** After first taking the stand himself as the defendant and being acquitted (vv. 3–5), Samuel now became the prosecutor and the people the defendants. Their crime: seeking a king in total disregard for "all the righteous acts performed by the LORD for [them] and [their] fathers" throughout the periods of the exodus, the settlement (v. 8) and the judges (vv. 9–11).

12:12 when you saw that Nahash king of the Ammonites was moving against you. Although not explicitly mentioned in chapter 8, it is possible that the Ammonite threat was already of concern at the time (see note on 11:1). Alternatively, Samuel may have simply been citing the Ammonite affair as the most recent example of the people's faithless tendency to seek help from men rather than from God.

12:13 the king you have chosen. See 8:18 and contrast 16:1. **the one you asked for.** See 8:10 and its note.

12:14 fear the LORD. A fundamental prerequisite for covenant blessing—not only in Moses' day (Dt 6:2,24; 10:12; 31:12–13) and Joshua's days (Jos 4:24; 24:14) but also now in the new era of the monarchy. The phrase implies standing in awe of the Lord and according him the reverence, honor and obedience that are his due as our gracious God.

12:15 as it was against your fathers. The Hebrew reads literally "and against your fathers." The Septuagint (the Greek translation of the OT) reading—"and against your king [to destroy you]"—may preserve the more original text.

12:16–19 Having made his case against the people in verses 3–15, Samuel now invoked a dramatic sign to drive home the point of their guilt: "And you will realize what an evil thing you did in the eyes of the LORD when you asked for a king" (v. 17). The sign achieved the desired result, and the people repented for having "added to all [their] other sins the evil of asking for a king" (v. 19). On signs accompanying prophetic utterances, see 2:34 and its note. Signs also served other functions, such as providing visible reminders of God's covenant (e.g., Ge 9:12–13,17).

12:17 wheat harvest. The wheat harvest probably took place in May and June, early in Israel's dry season, which was characterized by almost complete drought.

12:19 [l]ver 23; Ex 9:28; Jas 5:18; 1Jn 5:16
12:21 [m]Isa 41:24,29; Jer 16:19; Hab 2:18 [n]Dt 11:16
12:22 [o]Ps 106:8 [p]Jos 7:9; [q]1Ki 6:13 [r]Dt 7:7; 1Pe 2:9
12:23 [s]Ro 1:9-10; Col 1:9; 2Ti 1:3 [t]1Ki 8:36; Ps 34:11; Pr 4:11
12:24 [u]Ecc 12:13 [v]Isa 5:12 [w]Dt 10:21
12:25 [x]1Sa 31:1-5 [y]Jos 24:20
13:2 [z]1Sa 10:26
13:3 [a]1Sa 10:5
13:4 [b]Ge 34:30

19 The people all said to Samuel, "Pray[l] to the LORD your God for your servants so that
we will not die, for we have added to all our other sins the evil of asking for a king."
20 "Do not be afraid," Samuel replied. "You have done all this evil; yet do not turn away
from the LORD, but serve the LORD with all your heart. 21 Do not turn away after useless[m]
idols.[n] They can do you no good, nor can they rescue you, because they are useless. 22 For
the sake[o] of his great name[p] the LORD will not reject[q] his people, because the LORD was
pleased to make[r] you his own. 23 As for me, far be it from me that I should sin against the
LORD by failing to pray[s] for you. And I will teach[t] you the way that is good and right. 24 But
be sure to fear[u] the LORD and serve him faithfully with all your heart; consider[v] what
great[w] things he has done for you. 25 Yet if you persist[x] in doing evil, both you and your
king will be swept[y] away."

Samuel Rebukes Saul

13 Saul was ⌊thirty⌋[a] years old when he became king, and he reigned over Israel
⌊forty-⌋[b] two years.
2 Saul[c] chose three thousand men from Israel; two thousand were with him at Micmash and in the hill country of Bethel, and a thousand were with Jonathan at Gibeah[z]
in Benjamin. The rest of the men he sent back to their homes.
3 Jonathan attacked the Philistine outpost[a] at Geba, and the Philistines heard about it.
Then Saul had the trumpet blown throughout the land and said, "Let the Hebrews hear!"
4 So all Israel heard the news: "Saul has attacked the Philistine outpost, and now Israel has
become a stench[b] to the Philistines." And the people were summoned to join Saul at Gilgal.

[a] *1* A few late manuscripts of the Septuagint; Hebrew does not have *thirty.* [b] *1* See the round number in Acts 13:21; Hebrew does not have *forty-.* [c] *1,2* Or *and when he had reigned over Israel two years, 2he*

12:20–25 In response to the people's repentance, Samuel comforted them, saying, "Do not be afraid" (v. 20). Then he challenged them to renewed commitment, counseling them: "Do not turn away from the LORD" (v. 20). The solution to sin never involves distancing oneself from God or seeking help from sources other than God (vv. 20–21). The Lord had a stake in his people's welfare, for his name was associated with them (v. 22). Samuel, too, continued to have their interests at heart (v. 23). Nevertheless, wholehearted commitment to the Lord was required (v. 24), and persistence in doing evil would cause both king and people to be "swept away" (v. 25).
12:22 See *BC* 16.
12:23 pray for you . . . teach you. Samuel's responsibilities within the new monarchical structure would include intercession and instruction (see note on v. 1; cf. Samuel's duties as envisioned in 10:8). See *WLC* 129.
12:24 fear the LORD. See note on verse 14. **with all your heart.** See verse 20, 13:14 and 16:7.
▪ **13:1—15:35** *Saul's Failed Kingship.* Now that the three-part accession process had run its course (see note on 11:15) and Samuel's final exhortations had been delivered (ch. 12), Saul's reign could officially begin. The narrative immediately displays the failure of that reign: Saul encroached on the priestly office (13:1–22), threatened his son because of a foolish vow (14:1–46), received many blessings from God (14:47–52) and then showed ingratitude by sparing some of the Amalekites (ch. 15).
▪ **13:1–22** *Saul Is Rejected Initially.* Jonathan's attack on the Philistines provoked war. Fearful of the Philistines, Saul offered sacrifices himself rather than waiting for a priest. Consequently, God rejected him as king.
13:1 thirty years old . . . reigned over Israel forty-two years. The words "thirty" and "forty-" do not appear in the Hebrew text (see NIV text notes). The Hebrew reads, "Saul was a year old [lit., 'son of a year'] when he became king, and he reigned over Israel two [lit., 'and two'] years." This reading yields an impossible sense, unless it is assumed that the narrator was not speaking of Saul's physical age but of something else. One possibility is that there was a year between Saul's anointing (when he was "changed into a different person"; see 10:6 and its note) and his confirmation as king (11:15—13:1). The two years may then refer to the length of Saul's reign up to his definitive rejection by God in chapter 15 (see especially vv. 23 and 29 and their notes). It is also possible that the "and" before "two" indicates that another number (such as "twenty," see below) has been lost through textual transmission. After chapter 15, Saul remained on the throne but was no longer the rightful king in God's eyes. As to the actual length of Saul's reign, the only Biblical statement comes in Acts 13:21. There, however, the "forty years" may well refer to the administrations of both Samuel and Saul (just as the "450 years" in Ac 13:20 seems to refer to the time in Egypt, the wilderness wandering and at least the start of the conquest of Canaan [vv. 17–19] or, according to another textual tradition, to the period of judges up to, but not including, Samuel). The NIV's rendering of Acts 13:21 gives the impression that the "forty years" refers unambiguously to Saul's reign by adding the words "who ruled" before "forty years." These words ("who ruled") are, however, lacking in the Greek text, and the difficulty of interpreting the relevant verses in Acts 13 is generally recognized. With what indirect Biblical evidence is available, a reign of about 20 years would seem to make sense for Saul. The following facts are known: David was 30 years old when he became king in Hebron and 37 1/2 years old when he became king over all Israel after the death of Ish-Bosheth (2Sa 5:4–5). Ish-Bosheth was 40 years old when he became king over the northern tribes, and he reigned only two years before he was assassinated (2Sa 2:10). Logically, then, Ish-Bosheth must have been at least five years older than David. Assuming that Jonathan was older than his brother Ish-Bosheth (cf. 20:31), he may have been about ten years older than David. If we are to understand the events of 1 Samuel 13 as taking place at the beginning of Saul's reign, then Jonathan, who was a commander of troops in 13:2, must have been at least 20 years old when Saul began to reign. Saul would have been at least 40 years old and David about 10 years old. Since David became king at 30 years old, just after the death of Saul, a simple subtraction leaves Saul a reign of about 20 years. This agrees with the figure for Saul's reign given by Josephus in *Antiquities,* 10.8.4. This historian, in *Antiquities,* 6.14.9, stated that Saul reigned 18 years during Samuel's lifetime and "two and twenty" thereafter, but the "twenty" is very doubtful on text-critical, as well as logical, grounds (it would make David only eight years old at the time of Samuel's death).
13:2 Micmash. The site was situated some four miles south-southeast of Bethel on the north side of the Wadi Suwenet, a seasonal river valley often used for travel between the Jordan Valley and the central hill country. **Gibeah in Benjamin.** The traditional identification of Gibeah with Tell el-Ful, to the north of Jerusalem, is questioned by some, noting that "Gibeah" and "Geba" (v. 3) may simply be variant spellings of the same site, namely, a village facing Micmash from the south side of the Wadi Suwenet.
13:3 Jonathan attacked the Philistine outpost at Geba. Jonathan performed the deed that, according to the interpretation offered so far in the notes, should have been what Saul's "hand [found] to do" at the time of his anointing (see 10:7; 10:14–16; 11:15 and their notes). The effect of this action, as anticipated, was to provoke the Philistines into retaliating. **had the trumpet blown.** The trumpet was used in warfare as a signaling device (e.g., 2Sa 2:28; 18:16; 20:1). **Hebrews.** See note on 4:6.
13:4 Gilgal. Saul immediately responded to the crisis precipitated by Jonathan (v. 3) by repairing to Gilgal in accordance with Samuel's instructions in 10:8. Gilgal's location in the Jordan Valley in the vicinity of Jericho placed it outside immediate Philistine control and in reasonable proximity to Transjordan, thus making it a strategic site for a general muster. Gilgal also figured prominently

5The Philistines assembled to fight Israel, with three thousand[a] chariots, six thousand
charioteers, and soldiers as numerous as the sand[c] on the seashore. They went up and
camped at Micmash, east of Beth Aven. 6When the men of Israel saw that their situation
was critical and that their army was hard pressed, they hid in caves and thickets, among
the rocks, and in pits and cisterns.[d] 7Some Hebrews even crossed the Jordan to the land
of Gad[e] and Gilead.
Saul remained at Gilgal, and all the troops with him were quaking with fear. 8He waited seven[f] days, the time set by Samuel; but Samuel did not come to Gilgal, and Saul's
men began to scatter. 9So he said, "Bring me the burnt offering and the fellowship offerings.[b]" And Saul offered[g] up the burnt offering. 10Just as he finished making the offering, Samuel[h] arrived, and Saul went out to greet him.
11"What have you done?" asked Samuel.
Saul replied, "When I saw that the men were scattering, and that you did not come
at the set time, and that the Philistines were assembling at Micmash,[i] 12I thought, 'Now
the Philistines will come down against me at Gilgal, and I have not sought the LORD's favor.[j]' So I felt compelled to offer the burnt offering."
13"You acted foolishly,[k]" Samuel said. "You have not kept[l] the command the LORD
your God gave you; if you had, he would have established your kingdom over Israel for
all time. 14But now your kingdom[m] will not endure; the LORD has sought out a man after his own heart[n] and appointed[o] him leader of his people, because you have not kept
the LORD's command."
15Then Samuel left Gilgal[c] and went up to Gibeah[p] in Benjamin, and Saul counted the
men who were with him. They numbered about six hundred.

Israel Without Weapons

16Saul and his son Jonathan and the men with them were staying in Gibeah[d] in Benjamin, while the Philistines camped at Micmash. 17Raiding[q] parties went out from the
Philistine camp in three detachments. One turned toward Ophrah[r] in the vicinity of Shual, 18another toward Beth Horon,[s] and the third toward the borderland overlooking the
Valley of Zeboim[t] facing the desert.
19Not a blacksmith[u] could be found in the whole land of Israel, because the Philistines had said, "Otherwise the Hebrews will make swords or spears!" 20So all Israel went
down to the Philistines to have their plowshares, mattocks, axes and sickles[e] sharpened.
21The price was two thirds of a shekel[f] for sharpening plowshares and mattocks, and a
third of a shekel[g] for sharpening forks and axes and for repointing goads.
22So on the day of the battle not a soldier with Saul and Jonathan[v] had a sword or
spear[w] in his hand; only Saul and his son Jonathan had them.

13:5 [c]Jos 11:4
13:6 [d]Jdg 6:2
13:7 [e]Nu 32:33
13:8 [f]1Sa 10:8
13:9 [g]2Sa 24:25; 1Ki 3:4
13:10 [h]1Sa 15:13
13:11 [i]ver 2,5,16,23
13:12 [j]Jer 26:19
13:13 [k]2Ch 16:9 [l]1Sa 15:23,24
13:14 [m]1Sa 15:28 [n]Ac 7:46; 13:22 [o]2Sa 6:21
13:15 [p]1Sa 14:2
13:17 [q]1Sa 14:15 [r]Jos 18:23
13:18 [s]Jos 18:13-14 [t]Ne 11:34
13:19 [u]2Ki 24:14; Jer 24:1
13:22 [v]1Ch 9:39 [w]Jdg 5:8

a *5* Some Septuagint manuscripts and Syriac; Hebrew *thirty thousand* b *9* Traditionally *peace offerings*
c *15* Hebrew; Septuagint *Gilgal and went his way; the rest of the people went after Saul to meet the army, and they went out of Gilgal* d *16* Two Hebrew manuscripts; most Hebrew manuscripts *Geba,* a variant of *Gibeah*
e *20* Septuagint; Hebrew *plowshares* f *21* Hebrew *pim;* that is, about 1/4 ounce (about 8 grams)
g *21* That is, about 1/8 ounce (about 4 grams)

in Israel's earlier history (e.g., 7:16; 11:14; Jos 4:19–20; 5:10; 9:6; 10:6–15,43).
13:7 all the troops. "All" should be understood in the qualified sense described in the note on 15:8. The reference here is to the people summoned in verse 4, not to the troops already deployed in verse 2.
13:8 the time set by Samuel. The reference is to 10:8.
13:9 burnt offering . . . fellowship offerings. See note on 10:8.
13:11–12 See *WLC* 109.
13:11 What have you done? See 2:27–36 and its note, as well as 14:43 (see also Ge 3:13; Jos 7:19). **When I saw.** From a purely human perspective, Saul's excuses would seem to carry some weight, but not from the divine perspective, as Jonathan's testimony in 14:6 confirms.
13:12 I felt compelled. Or perhaps, "I pulled myself together" (even though everyone else was falling apart).
13:13 You acted foolishly. This expression in Hebrew implies both mental and moral failure. For a similar confrontation between a prophet and a king, see 2 Chronicles 16:7–9. **You have not kept the command the LORD your God gave you.** "Command" refers to the "commission" of 10:8 (for this rendering, see Nu 27:19,23; Dt 3:28; 31:14). The full gravity of Saul's failure can be seen in light of the significance of that first commission as a test of his willingness to conform to a truly theocratic monarchy (see notes on 10:1; 12:3–15).
13:14 your kingdom will not endure. Saul's hopes of establishing a dynasty were dashed, though Saul himself had not as yet been deposed (15:23). **a man after his own heart.** The phrase might also be rendered "a man of his own choosing" or "the man he wants," placing the accent on the Lord's sovereign election. Nevertheless, in light of passages such as 2:35 and 16:7, the notion of the Lord's chosen one (i.e., David) as "a man after [God's] heart" in the sense of being committed to God's will and purposes, should not be diminished (cf. 14:7).
13:15 Then Samuel left. Because of Saul's foolish action, Samuel apparently departed without giving Saul any further instructions (10:8). The longer reading attested by the Septuagint (the Greek translation of the OT; see NIV text note) is probably to be preferred, suggesting that after Samuel's departure, Saul rejoined Jonathan at Geba (see notes on vv. 2,16).
13:16 Gibeah. See NIV text note. "Geba" is the more likely reading (see note on v. 2).
13:17 Raiding parties went out . . . in three detachments. Although the reader is not told this explicitly, the purpose of the raiding parties—which traveled roughly north, west and east—may have been to plunder, terrorize, reconnoiter and, by controlling important routes, prevent surprise attack from an unexpected direction.
13:19–21 This brief digression serves to emphasize the extent of the Israelites' predicament. They were without arms and dependent on the Philistines, even for the fashioning and maintenance of their tools. Archaeological evidence suggests that the Philistines led their neighbors in ironwork technology.

13:23 [x]1Sa 14:4
14:2 [y]1Sa 13:15 [z]Isa 10:28
14:3 [a]1Sa 4:21 [b]1Sa 22:11,20 [c]1Sa 2:28
14:4 [d]1Sa 13:23
14:6 [e]1Sa 17:26,36; Jer 9:26 [f]Heb 11:34 [g]Jdg 7:4 [h]1Sa 17:46-47
14:10 [i]Ge 24:14; Jdg 6:36-37
14:11 [j]1Sa 13:6
14:12 [k]1Sa 17:43-44 [l]2Sa 5:24
14:15 [m]Ge 35:5; 2Ki 7:5-7 [n]1Sa 13:17

Jonathan Attacks the Philistines

14 23 Now a detachment of Philistines had gone out to the pass[x] at Micmash. 1 One
day Jonathan son of Saul said to the young man bearing his armor, "Come, let's
go over to the Philistine outpost on the other side." But he did not tell his father.
2 Saul was staying on the outskirts of Gibeah[y] under a pomegranate tree in Migron.[z]
With him were about six hundred men, 3 among whom was Ahijah, who was wearing an
ephod. He was a son of Ichabod's[a] brother Ahitub[b] son of Phinehas, the son of Eli,[c] the
LORD's priest in Shiloh. No one was aware that Jonathan had left.
4 On each side of the pass[d] that Jonathan intended to cross to reach the Philistine outpost was a cliff; one was called Bozez, and the other Seneh. 5 One cliff stood to the north
toward Micmash, the other to the south toward Geba.
6 Jonathan said to his young armor-bearer, "Come, let's go over to the outpost of those
uncircumcised[e] fellows. Perhaps the LORD will act in our behalf. Nothing[f] can hinder the
LORD from saving, whether by many[g] or by few.[h]"
7 "Do all that you have in mind," his armor-bearer said. "Go ahead; I am with you
heart and soul."
8 Jonathan said, "Come, then; we will cross over toward the men and let them see us.
9 If they say to us, 'Wait there until we come to you,' we will stay where we are and not
go up to them. 10 But if they say, 'Come up to us,' we will climb up, because that will be
our sign[i] that the LORD has given them into our hands."
11 So both of them showed themselves to the Philistine outpost. "Look!" said the Philistines. "The Hebrews are crawling out of the holes they were hiding[j] in." 12 The men of
the outpost shouted to Jonathan and his armor-bearer, "Come up to us and we'll teach
you a lesson.[k]"
So Jonathan said to his armor-bearer, "Climb up after me; the LORD has given them
into the hand[l] of Israel."
13 Jonathan climbed up, using his hands and feet, with his armor-bearer right behind
him. The Philistines fell before Jonathan, and his armor-bearer followed and killed behind him. 14 In that first attack Jonathan and his armor-bearer killed some twenty men
in an area of about half an acre.[a]

Israel Routs the Philistines

15 Then panic[m] struck the whole army—those in the camp and field, and those in the
outposts and raiding[n] parties—and the ground shook. It was a panic sent by God.[b]

[a] *14* Hebrew *half a yoke*; a "yoke" was the land plowed by a yoke of oxen in one day. [b] *15* Or *a terrible panic*

13:22 only Saul and his son Jonathan had them. This notice pins the hopes of Israel on these two individuals in particular, and the following chapter develops the comparisons and contrasts between king and crown prince in such a way as to highlight the failures of the former and the successes of the latter.

■ **14:1–46** *Saul's Character Exposed by Jonathan.* Jonathan led Israel to victory over the Philistines, but he did so in a way that revealed Saul's true character.

14:1 But he did not tell his father. Jonathan's decision not to tell his father of his daring plan may imply that Jonathan lacked confidence in Saul (cf. Abigail's similar action in response to her husband Nabal in 25:19). This decision would not have been surprising given Saul's poor performance in the preceding chapter.

14:2–5 The narrator digressed briefly in these verses to describe Saul's position (vv. 2–3) and to stress the challenge facing Jonathan (vv. 4–5).

14:3 wearing an ephod. The presence of the oracular instrument (see note on 2:28) in the camp of Saul encourages the expectation that Saul might enlist it to receive the Lord's guidance, as David later did on several occasions (23:9–12; 30:7–8). In this instance, however, Saul's passivity or timidity left it to Jonathan to discover the Lord's will (see v. 10 and its note). In verse 19 (see note) Saul demonstrated a lack of respect for the ephod; later he savagely turned against those whose task it was to oversee its care and use (22:18; cf. 21:9). In the end, the ephod, along with the other means of discovering the Lord's will, simply mocked Saul's attempt to inquire of God (see 28:6 and its note). **son of Ichabod's brother Ahitub.** The presence of a member of the rejected priestly house of Eli (2:30) in Saul's camp is an unsettling reminder of the recent rejection of Saul's own royal house (13:14). In addition, the rather odd formulation of Ahijah's genealogy so as to mention his uncle Ichabod, whose name means "no glory" (see note on 4:21), serves obliquely to recall that Saul's glory was also vastly dimmed after the events of chapter 13.

14:4 Bozez . . . Seneh. The meanings of these names have not been determined with certainty, but if the suggestions of "slippery" for the former and "thorny" for the latter are correct, then explicit mention of the names in this context may serve to dramatize the challenge that was facing Jonathan.

14:6 After the brief digression of verses 2–5, verse 6 picks up where verse 1 left off. **uncircumcised fellows.** Elsewhere in 1 Samuel this term of disparagement occurs only in the contexts of David's confession of confidence in the Lord (17:26,36) and of Saul's contemplation of suicide (31:4). The uncircumcised were those who, like the Philistines, stood outside God's special covenant people (e.g., Ge 17:14; Ex 12:48; Jdg 14:3; 15:18). **Nothing can hinder the LORD from saving.** Compare David's confidence in 17:47. Although the inspired narrator made no explicit criticism of Saul's excuse in 13:11 (that "the men were scattering," etc.), Jonathan's bold confession in the present context functions literarily as an oblique commentary on the theological inadequacy of that excuse.

14:7 heart and soul. Literally, "after your heart." Compare 13:14 and its note.

14:10 our sign. Jonathan was loath to move ahead without the Lord's approval. In this regard also he proved more faithful than his father, who seemed to exhibit a declining commitment to obtaining divine guidance (13:8–15; 14:18; 14:19 and its note; 14:36 and its note).

14:11 Hebrews. See note on 4:6. **holes.** See 13:6.

14:15 a panic sent by God. The Hebrew may be rendered as expressing divine agency or as a superlative—"a divine panic" (cf. NIV text note)—similar to the English expression "You look simply divine." Both senses are appropriate to the present context. For other examples of God's intervention in warfare, see 7:10 and Joshua 10:11–14.

16Saul's lookouts[o] at Gibeah in Benjamin saw the army melting away in all directions.
17Then Saul said to the men who were with him, "Muster the forces and see who has left
us." When they did, it was Jonathan and his armor-bearer who were not there.
18Saul said to Ahijah, "Bring[p] the ark of God." (At that time it was with the Israelites.)[a]
19While Saul was talking to the priest, the tumult in the Philistine camp increased more
and more. So Saul said to the priest,[q] "Withdraw your hand."
20Then Saul and all his men assembled and went to the battle. They found the Philistines in total confusion, striking[r] each other with their swords. **21**Those Hebrews who
had previously been with the Philistines and had gone up with them to their camp went[s]
over to the Israelites who were with Saul and Jonathan. **22**When all the Israelites who had
hidden[t] in the hill country of Ephraim heard that the Philistines were on the run, they
joined the battle in hot pursuit. **23**So the LORD rescued[u] Israel that day, and the battle
moved on beyond Beth Aven.[v]

Jonathan Eats Honey

24Now the men of Israel were in distress that day, because Saul had bound the people under an oath,[w] saying, "Cursed be any man who eats food before evening comes,
before I have avenged myself on my enemies!" So none of the troops tasted food.
25The entire army[b] entered the woods, and there was honey on the ground. **26**When
they went into the woods, they saw the honey oozing out, yet no one put his hand to his
mouth, because they feared the oath. **27**But Jonathan had not heard that his father had
bound the people with the oath, so he reached out the end of the staff that was in his hand
and dipped it into the honeycomb.[x] He raised his hand to his mouth, and his eyes brightened.[c] **28**Then one of the soldiers told him, "Your father bound the army under a strict
oath, saying, 'Cursed be any man who eats food today!' That is why the men are faint."
29Jonathan said, "My father has made trouble[y] for the country. See how my eyes
brightened[d] when I tasted a little of this honey. **30**How much better it would have been
if the men had eaten today some of the plunder they took from their enemies. Would not
the slaughter of the Philistines have been even greater?"
31That day, after the Israelites had struck down the Philistines from Micmash to Aijalon,[z] they were exhausted. **32**They pounced on the plunder[a] and, taking sheep, cattle
and calves, they butchered them on the ground and ate them, together with the blood.[b]
33Then someone said to Saul, "Look, the men are sinning against the LORD by eating meat
that has blood in it."

"You have broken faith," he said. "Roll a large stone over here at once." **34**Then he
said, "Go out among the men and tell them, 'Each of you bring me your cattle and sheep,
and slaughter them here and eat them. Do not sin against the LORD by eating meat with
blood still in it.' "

So everyone brought his ox that night and slaughtered it there. **35**Then Saul built an
altar[c] to the LORD; it was the first time he had done this.

14:16 [o]2Sa 18:24
14:18 [p]1Sa 30:7
14:19 [q]Nu 27:21
14:20 [r]Jdg 7:22; 2Ch 20:23
14:21 [s]1Sa 29:4
14:22 [t]1Sa 13:6
14:23 [u]Ex 14:30; Ps 44:6-7 [v]1Sa 13:5
14:24 [w]Jos 6:26
14:27 [x]ver 43; 1Sa 30:12
14:29 [y]Jos 7:25; 1Ki 18:18
14:31 [z]Jos 10:12
14:32 [a]1Sa 15:19 [b]Ge 9:4; Lev 3:17; 7:26; 17:10-14; 19:26; Dt 12:16, 23-24
14:35 [c]1Sa 7:17

[a] *18* Hebrew; Septuagint *"Bring the ephod." (At that time he wore the ephod before the Israelites.)*
[b] *25* Or *Now all the people of the land* [c] *27* Or *his strength was renewed* [d] *29* Or *my strength was renewed*

14:18 ark of God. See NIV text note.
14:19 Withdraw your hand. In ordering the priest to withdraw his hand from the oracular instrument by which the will of the Lord could have been determined, Saul in essence took matters back into his own hands, as he had already done once before (13:9).
14:21 Hebrews. See note on 4:6.
14:24 in distress that day. "In distress" is rendered "hard pressed" in 13:6. It is linguistically appropriate and logically preferable to read verse 24 as a re-enactment of something that took place earlier that day—after Jonathan's departure and initial attack on the Philistine outpost (vv. 13–14) but prior to Saul's joining the fray (v. 20). As far as the people would have known at that time, little had changed militarily since 13:6, and the rift between Saul and Samuel (13:13–14) would have only heightened their anxiety. **because Saul.** Or "so Saul," viewing Saul's binding of the people under an oath as a response to, not as the cause of, the people's distress (see note on "in distress that day," above). **before I have avenged myself on my enemies!** Saul's emphasis on avenging himself on his enemies sounds rather profane when compared with the later description of David as the one who fought "the LORD's battles" (25:28; cf. 17:45; 18:17; 30:26).
14:27 But Jonathan had not heard. Jonathan's ignorance of his father's oath is best explained in terms of the interpretation of verse 24 suggested above (see note on v. 24).
14:29 My father has made trouble for the country. The lack of confidence implicit in Jonathan's exclusion of his father from his counsel in verse 1 now issued in an outright condemnation of his father's foolish action in binding the people under an oath. Charging Saul with "troubling" the land, Jonathan unwittingly anticipated and reversed the effect of the lot-casting procedure that would come later in the chapter (vv. 38–42). As in the case of Achan (Jos 7:16–18), for example, lots were often cast in order to discover a guilty party, a "troubler" of the land. Achan, it should be remembered, was stoned in the Valley of "Trouble," and in Hebrew his name even sounds like "troubler" (see Jos 7:25–26). In this chapter, the lot would eventually fall upon Jonathan as the offender, strictly speaking (v. 42), but the real "troubler" of Israel, as Jonathan's own words anticipated and as the people would come to realize, was Saul.
14:31 Aijalon. The site is located about 15 miles west of Micmash in the direction of Philistine territory and lies in the Valley of Aijalon, through which the Philistines seem to have fled.
14:33 eating meat that has blood in it. The Old Testament contains many prohibitions against eating blood (e.g., Ge 9:4; Lev 3:17; 7:26–27; 17:10,12; 19:26; Dt 15:23; Eze 33:25).
14:35 first time he had done this. No other altars are ever mentioned. The Hebrew of this clause is difficult and might possibly be rendered, "He began to build it . . . an altar to the LORD." A few commentators have suggested that Saul began building an altar using the stone mentioned in verse 33 as a cornerstone, but that

36 Saul said, "Let us go down after the Philistines by night and plunder them till dawn,
and let us not leave one of them alive."
"Do whatever seems best to you," they replied.
But the priest said, "Let us inquire of God here."
37 So Saul asked God, "Shall I go down after the Philistines? Will you give them into
Israel's hand?" But God did not answer[d] him that day.
38 Saul therefore said, "Come here, all you who are leaders of the army, and let us find
out what sin has been committed[e] today. 39 As surely as the LORD who rescues Israel
lives,[f] even if it lies with my son Jonathan, he must die." But not one of the men said a
word.
40 Saul then said to all the Israelites, "You stand over there; I and Jonathan my son will
stand over here."
"Do what seems best to you," the men replied.
41 Then Saul prayed to the LORD, the God of Israel, "Give[g] me the right[h] answer."[a] And
Jonathan and Saul were taken by lot, and the men were cleared. 42 Saul said, "Cast the
lot between me and Jonathan my son." And Jonathan was taken.
43 Then Saul said to Jonathan, "Tell me what you have done."[i]
So Jonathan told him, "I merely tasted a little honey[j] with the end of my staff. And
now must I die?"
44 Saul said, "May God deal with me, be it ever so severely,[k] if you do not die, Jonathan.[l]"
45 But the men said to Saul, "Should Jonathan die—he who has brought about this
great deliverance in Israel? Never! As surely as the LORD lives, not a hair[m] of his head will
fall to the ground, for he did this today with God's help." So the men rescued[n] Jonathan,
and he was not put to death.
46 Then Saul stopped pursuing the Philistines, and they withdrew to their own land.
47 After Saul had assumed rule over Israel, he fought against their enemies on every
side: Moab, the Ammonites,[o] Edom, the kings[b] of Zobah,[p] and the Philistines. Wherever he turned, he inflicted punishment on them.[c] 48 He fought valiantly and defeated the
Amalekites,[q] delivering Israel from the hands of those who had plundered them.

Saul's Family

49 Saul's sons were Jonathan, Ishvi and Malki-Shua.[r] The name of his older daughter
was Merab, and that of the younger was Michal.[s] 50 His wife's name was Ahinoam daughter of Ahimaaz. The name of the commander of Saul's army was Abner son of Ner, and
Ner was Saul's uncle. 51 Saul's father Kish[t] and Abner's father Ner were sons of Abiel.
52 All the days of Saul there was bitter war with the Philistines, and whenever Saul saw
a mighty or brave man, he took[u] him into his service.

The LORD Rejects Saul as King

15 Samuel said to Saul, "I am the one the LORD sent to anoint[v] you king over his
people Israel; so listen now to the message from the LORD. 2 This is what the LORD
Almighty says: 'I will punish the Amalekites[w] for what they did to Israel when they way-

14:37 [d] 1Sa 10:22; 28:6, 15
14:38 [e] Jos 7:11; 1Sa 10:19
14:39 [f] 2Sa 12:5
14:41 [g] Ac 1:24 [h] Pr 16:33
14:43 [i] Jos 7:19 [j] ver 27
14:44 [k] Ru 1:17 [l] ver 39
14:45 [m] 1Ki 1:52; Lk 21:18; Ac 27:34 [n] 2Sa 14:11
14:47 [o] 1Sa 11:1-13 [p] ver 52; 2Sa 10:6
14:48 [q] 1Sa 15:2,7
14:49 [r] 1Sa 31:2; 1Ch 8:33 [s] 1Sa 18:17-20
14:51 [t] 1Sa 9:1
14:52 [u] 1Sa 8:11
15:1 [v] 1Sa 9:16
15:2 [w] Ex 17:8-14; Nu 24:20; Dt 25:17-19

[a] *41* Hebrew; Septuagint *"Why have you not answered your servant today? If the fault is in me or my son Jonathan, respond with Urim, but if the men of Israel are at fault, respond with Thummim."* [b] *47* Masoretic Text; Dead Sea Scrolls and Septuagint *king* [c] *47* Hebrew; Septuagint *he was victorious*

---

he discontinued the construction in order to resume the pursuit of the Philistines.

14:36 But the priest said. As has often been observed, it was unusual for the priest—here probably Ahijah (v. 3)—to take the initiative. But this notice fits well with the pattern of Saul's declining commitment to obtaining the Lord's guidance (see note on v. 10).

14:39 But not one of the men said a word. The passive compliance evidenced in verse 36 ("Do whatever seems best to you") became passive resistance when Saul suggested the possibility that Jonathan might have to die.

14:45 Never! When forced by Saul's obduracy (vv. 39,44) to choose between Saul and his son, the people chose Jonathan, whom they clearly recognized as the one through whom the Lord had worked that day. Saul's foolish behavior, which in chapter 13 had resulted in a rift between Saul and Samuel, continued in chapter 14 until Saul found himself alienated from everyone around him, even his own men. His isolation would not be permanent, however, for Jonathan would later become his confidant again (20:2), the people would show signs of renewed loyalty (e.g., 23:19; 24:1) and even Samuel would have further dealings with him (ch. 15). See *WLC* 135.

■ **14:47–52** *Saul's Unending Philistine Warfare.* This section provides a summary of Saul's military accomplishments (vv. 47–48) and a portrayal of his family and chief military officer (vv. 49–51). A comparison of this section with the lengthier summary of David's victories and officers in 2 Samuel 8 reveals a number of similarities but also a telling difference: Nowhere in Saul's summary is there anything akin to the statement repeated in David's that "the LORD gave [him] victory wherever he went" (2Sa 8:6,14). Although it is apparent that Saul had much success, this success was counterbalanced by the ironic closing remark of verse 52.

14:52 All the days of Saul. As opposed to Samuel (see 7:13) and David (2Sa 3:18; 8:1), Saul was unable to gain victory over the Philistines. In fact, the Philistines would ultimately kill Saul and his sons in battle (ch. 31). **bitter war.** Saul's unending struggle with the Philistines was not simply war, but hard, or difficult, war.

■ **15:1–35** *Saul's Definitive Rejection.* Saul disobeyed God's command to destroy the Amalekites totally, and he was rejected as king for a second and final time.

laid them as they came up from Egypt. 3 Now go, attack the Amalekites and totally[x] destroy[a] everything that belongs to them. Do not spare them; put to death men and wom-
en, children and infants, cattle and sheep, camels and donkeys.' "
4 So Saul summoned the men and mustered them at Telaim—two hundred thousand
foot soldiers and ten thousand men from Judah. 5 Saul went to the city of Amalek and set
an ambush in the ravine. 6 Then he said to the Kenites,[y] "Go away, leave the Amalekites
so that I do not destroy you along with them; for you showed kindness to all the Israelites when they came up out of Egypt." So the Kenites moved away from the Amalekites.
7 Then Saul attacked the Amalekites[z] all the way from Havilah to Shur,[a] to the east
of Egypt. 8 He took Agag king of the Amalekites alive,[b] and all his people he totally destroyed with the sword. 9 But Saul and the army spared[c] Agag and the best of the sheep
and cattle, the fat calves[b] and lambs—everything that was good. These they were unwilling to destroy completely, but everything that was despised and weak they totally destroyed.
10 Then the word of the LORD came to Samuel: 11 "I am grieved[d] that I have made Saul
king, because he has turned[e] away from me and has not carried out my instructions."[f]
Samuel was troubled,[g] and he cried out to the LORD all that night.
12 Early in the morning Samuel got up and went to meet Saul, but he was told, "Saul
has gone to Carmel.[h] There he has set up a monument in his own honor and has turned
and gone on down to Gilgal."
13 When Samuel reached him, Saul said, "The LORD bless you! I have carried out the
LORD's instructions."
14 But Samuel said, "What then is this bleating of sheep in my ears? What is this lowing of cattle that I hear?"
15 Saul answered, "The soldiers brought them from the Amalekites; they spared the
best of the sheep and cattle to sacrifice to the LORD your God, but we totally destroyed
the rest."
16 "Stop!" Samuel said to Saul. "Let me tell you what the LORD said to me last night."
"Tell me," Saul replied.

15:3 [x]Nu 24:20; Dt 20:16-18; Jos 6:17; 1Sa 22:19
15:6 [y]Ex 18:10,19; Nu 10:29-32; 24:22; Jdg 1:16; 4:1
15:7 [z]1Sa 14:48 [a]Ge 16:7; 25:17-18; Ex 15:22
15:8 [b]1Sa 30:1
15:9 [c]ver 3,15
15:11 [d]Ge 6:6; 2Sa 24:16 [e]Jos 22:16 [f]1Sa 13:13; 1Ki 9:6-7 [g]ver 35
15:12 [h]Jos 15:55

[a] *3* The Hebrew term refers to the irrevocable giving over of things or persons to the LORD, often by totally destroying them; also in verses 8, 9, 15, 18, 20 and 21. [b] *9* Or *the grown bulls;* the meaning of the Hebrew for this phrase is uncertain.

15:1 I am the one the LORD sent to anoint you. After Saul's weak performance in chapters 13–14, Samuel here justifiably belabored the vital importance of his own role as mediator of God's orders to Saul (see note on 10:1). **so listen now to the message from the LORD.** Literally, "hear/listen to the sound/voice of the words of the LORD." The Hebrew words here translated "message" and "listen" recur several times in this chapter (e.g., vv. 14, 19–20,22,24) and underscore the central thematic significance of obedience.
15:2 Amalekites. Descendants of Esau (see Ge 36:12,16), the Amalekites appear to have been a nomadic tribe generally to be found in the Judean Negev. They frequently came into conflict with Israel. In addition to the references in the following note, see Judges 3:13, 6:3–5 and 33, 7:12 and 10:12. **for what they did to Israel.** See Exodus 17:8–13 and Numbers 14:43 and 45.
15:3 totally destroy. See NIV text note. With respect to the Amalekites, see Exodus 17:14–16 and Deuteronomy 25:17–19. **men and women, children and infants.** See note on 22:19.
15:4 Telaim. This is probably to be equated with Telem, which is listed in Joshua 15:24 as one of the cities of Judah. The Septuagint (the Greek translation of the OT) mentions Gilgal instead, which some have suggested may have been the site of Samuel's instructions to Saul (vv. 1–3).
15:6 Kenites. Kenites (Ge 15:19; Jdg 1:16) and Amalekites are associated in Numbers 24:20–22. **for you showed kindness.** This is perhaps an allusion to the kindness of Moses' Kenite father-in-law (Jdg 1:16), recorded in Exodus 18.
15:7 Havilah to Shur. See Genesis 25:18. Shur was located inside the boundary of the territory of the Amalekites (27:8), near the eastern border of Egypt. The location of Havilah remains uncertain, but the general sense of the reference is that Saul's victory was extensive.
15:8 Agag. This is either a personal name or a title (cf. "Pharaoh"); see Numbers 24:7 and compare "Agagite" in Esther 3:1. **all his people.** It is apparent from verses like Judges 7:7 (where the Hebrew reads lit., "all the men," and the NIV rightly understands this as "all the other men," as distinct from the 300 men retained by Gideon) that "all" in Hebrew does not always mean "all" in an absolute sense. Here the reference is to all the Amalekites who fell into Saul's hands (see further references to Amalekites in 27:8; 30:1,18). For this qualified sense of "all," compare 13:7 and 31:6.
15:9 Saul and the army spared . . . unwilling to destroy completely. These actions were in direct contradiction to the Lord's command recorded in verse 3. A desire to profit materially from the victory may have underlain their unwillingness to destroy anything that was good (cf. Achan's sin in retaining goods that had been devoted to destruction in Jos 7:1). The reader is not told Saul's motive for sparing Agag, but it may have been politics (cf. Ahab's sparing of Ben-Hadad in 1Ki 20:30–34) or Saul's desire to parade Agag as a trophy of war. Saul's erection of a victory monument "in his own honor" (v. 12) may imply the latter alternative.
15:11 grieved. See note on verse 29. **turned away from me and has not carried out my instructions.** This is a damning indictment in view of 12:14, where obedience and following the Lord are named as the essential requirements for a successful reign. **Samuel was troubled.** Literally, "Samuel became angry" (cf., e.g., 18:8; 2Sa 6:8, where the same Hebrew expression is used). Though the reader is not told directly, Samuel's anger was probably over Saul's latest misdeeds, which surely grieved and frustrated the prophet greatly. **he cried out to the LORD all that night.** That is, in exasperation and, perhaps, intercession; clearly Samuel took no pleasure in Saul's rejection (v. 35; 16:1).
15:12 Carmel. Situated about 7.5 miles south of Hebron (25:2; Jos 15:55), Carmel should not be confused with Mount Carmel in the north. **monument in his own honor.** The closest conceptual parallel is 2 Samuel 18:18, where Absalom erected "a monument to himself" that his name might be remembered.
15:14–23 These verses display the standard features of a prophetic judgment speech to an individual (see note on 2:27–36) but with the difference that in this instance the accused, Saul, vigorously contested the charges.
15:15 The soldiers brought them . . . to sacrifice. In response to Samuel's accusing questions in verse 14, Saul offered a dual defense: (1) The soldiers, rather than Saul himself, were responsible; and (2) the animals were to have been sacrificed anyway. Samuel would deal with these excuses in order.

[17]Samuel said, "Although you were once small[i] in your own eyes, did you not become
the head of the tribes of Israel? The LORD anointed you king over Israel. [18]And he sent you
on a mission, saying, 'Go and completely destroy those wicked people, the Amalekites;
make war on them until you have wiped them out.' [19]Why did you not obey the LORD?
Why did you pounce on the plunder[j] and do evil in the eyes of the LORD?"
[20]"But I did obey[k] the LORD," Saul said. "I went on the mission the LORD assigned me.
I completely destroyed the Amalekites and brought back Agag their king. [21]The soldiers
took sheep and cattle from the plunder, the best of what was devoted to God, in order
to sacrifice them to the LORD your God at Gilgal."
[22]But Samuel replied:

"Does the LORD delight in burnt offerings and sacrifices
as much as in obeying the voice of the LORD?
To obey is better than sacrifice,[l]
and to heed is better than the fat of rams.
[23]For rebellion is like the sin of divination,[m]
and arrogance like the evil of idolatry.
Because you have rejected[n] the word of the LORD,
he has rejected you as king."

[24]Then Saul said to Samuel, "I have sinned.[o] I violated the LORD's command and your
instructions. I was afraid[p] of the people and so I gave in to them. [25]Now I beg you, forgive[q] my sin and come back with me, so that I may worship the LORD."
[26]But Samuel said to him, "I will not go back with you. You have rejected[r] the word
of the LORD, and the LORD has rejected you as king over Israel!"
[27]As Samuel turned to leave, Saul caught hold of the hem of his robe, and it tore.[s]
[28]Samuel said to him, "The LORD has torn[t] the kingdom of Israel from you today and has
given it to one of your neighbors—to one better than you. [29]He who is the Glory of Israel does not lie[u] or change[v] his mind; for he is not a man, that he should change his
mind."
[30]Saul replied, "I have sinned. But please honor[w] me before the elders of my people

15:17 [i]1Sa 9:21
15:19 [j]1Sa 14:32
15:20 [k]ver 13
15:22 [l]Ps 40:6-8; 51:16; Isa 1:11-15; Jer 7:22; Hos 6:6; Mic 6:6-8; Mt 12:7; Mk 12:33; Heb 10:6-9
15:23 [m]Dt 18:10 [n]1Sa 13:13
15:24 [o]2Sa 12:13 [p]Pr 29:25; Isa 51:12-13
15:25 [q]Ex 10:17
15:26 [r]1Sa 13:14
15:27 [s]1Ki 11:11,31
15:28 [t]1Sa 28:17; 1Ki 11:31
15:29 [u]1Ch 29:11; Tit 1:2 [v]Nu 23:19; Eze 24:14
15:30 [w]Isa 29:13; Jn 5:44; 12:43

15:17 small in your own eyes. Whatever Saul's feelings of impotence in the face of public pressure, Samuel renounced in the strongest terms Saul's attempt to minimize his personal responsibility for the Amalekite affair. **did you not become the head of the tribes of Israel?** Saul's "headship" implied nothing if not leadership responsibility. "The LORD anointed you" and "sent you on a mission" (vv. 17–18), declared Samuel, and it simply would not do to try to shift the blame to the people.
15:19 pounce on the plunder. This wording shows that Samuel clearly discounted Saul's claim that the animals were spared only because they were to have been sacrificed. That the charge was directed against Saul personally does not prove that he initiated or even participated in the taking of booty, although he may have; rather, it underscores that, as the "head," Saul was ultimately responsible (see note on v. 17). For a discussion of the verb rendered "pounce," see note on 25:14.
15:20–21 Despite Samuel's refusal to accept Saul's excuses, Saul was not yet willing to relinquish them, and he reiterated them adamantly. He also took the opportunity to couch the delicate matter of the survival of Agag between two strong assertions of obedience (in the Hebrew of v. 20, Agag is mentioned after reference to the mission and prior to the reference to the Amalekites).
15:21–23 See *WCF* 16.1; *WLC* 109.
15:22–23 The elevated diction of these two verses indicates their climactic importance in the episode. See *HC* 96.
15:22 burnt offerings. See note on 10:8. **To obey is better than sacrifice.** Although Samuel clearly disbelieved Saul's sacrifice excuse (see note on v. 19), he here seemed to grant it validity, but only for the sake of argument, in order to make the point that ritual performance was worthless when unaccompanied by a sincere and submissive spirit. For later prophetic denunciations of empty ritual, see Isaiah 1:10–17 (see also Jer 6:19–20; 7:21–26; Hos 6:6; Am 5:21–24; Mic 6:6–8; cf. also Ps 51:16–17; Pr 15:8; 21:3,27). See *WLC* 91; *WSC* 39; *HC* 91.
15:23 For rebellion is like the sin of divination. Here Samuel explained the logic of what he had just said in verse 22. If, as 12:15 indicates, disobedience is in essence rebellion, and if rebellion is like divination or magic (both involve a rejection of the Lord in an attempt to gain personal power), then the offering of sacrifices under such circumstances was similar to idolatry. **Because you have rejected . . . he has rejected.** As Samuel came at last to the announcement of judgment upon Saul, he uttered it in a manner that made plain the justice of God's verdict. There is a correspondence between offense and punishment (see note on 2:27–36). While Saul's failure in chapter 13 spelled the end of any dynastic hopes (13:14), his disobedience in the present context signified the end, in God's eyes, of his right to be king. The very next chapter recounts the anointing of David and the departure of the Spirit of the Lord from Saul (16:14).
15:24–25 At last Saul began to accept responsibility ("I have sinned"; v. 24), although he still blamed the people for initiating the unfortunate events ("I gave in to them"; v. 24). On the surface, Saul's confession sounded adequate, but against the background of Samuel's warnings in 12:14–15, his admissions implied not so much the possibility of reconciliation as the certainty of being "swept away" (12:25). Saul would utter a second, more candid confession in verse 30.
15:26 I will not go back with you. That Samuel responded only to Saul's request that he return with him suggests that Samuel discounted the sincerity of the remainder of the confession (see v. 30 and its note).
15:27 Saul caught hold of the hem of his robe. His arguments having failed and his request having been refused, Saul made a last-ditch effort to rescue the situation by restraining Samuel physically; Samuel's robe, however, tore. On Samuel's association with special robes, see note on 2:19.
15:28 torn the kingdom. Samuel seized upon the tearing of the robe as a fitting symbol of the Lord's having "torn the kingdom" from Saul. For another incident involving a prophet and a torn robe, see 1 Kings 11:29–33 (cf. 19:24 and David's action in 24:4–5).
15:29 Glory of Israel. In this context, "Glory of Israel" is a title for God (cf. Mic 1:15, where a different Hebrew word for "glory" is used). **does not lie or change his mind.** Saul's rejection was final, and no attempt to mitigate its consequences would avail. There is no contradiction between this statement and the notices in verses 11 and 35 that the Lord was "grieved" for having made Saul king, even though "grieved" translates the same Hebrew word as is here rendered "change his mind." The point in this verse, as in Numbers 23:19, is that when the Lord makes a pronouncement intended to be final, he cannot, like a human being, be talked out of it.
15:30 please honor me. Saul's real concern was made clear in this, his second, confession (cf. vv. 24–25 and its note). As Samuel already seemed to have perceived (see note on v. 26), Saul was less concerned with being reconciled to the Lord than with being hon-

and before Israel; come back with me, so that I may worship the LORD your God." 31So
Samuel went back with Saul, and Saul worshiped the LORD.
32Then Samuel said, "Bring me Agag king of the Amalekites."
Agag came to him confidently,[a] thinking, "Surely the bitterness of death is past."
33But Samuel said,

"As your sword has made women childless,
so will your mother be childless among women."[x]

And Samuel put Agag to death before the LORD at Gilgal.
34Then Samuel left for Ramah,[y] but Saul went up to his home in Gibeah[z] of Saul.
35Until the day Samuel[a] died, he did not go to see Saul again, though Samuel mourned[b]
for him. And the LORD was grieved that he had made Saul king over Israel.

Samuel Anoints David

16 The LORD said to Samuel, "How long will you mourn[c] for Saul, since I have rejected[d] him as king over Israel? Fill your horn with oil[e] and be on your way; I am
sending you to Jesse[f] of Bethlehem. I have chosen[g] one of his sons to be king."
2But Samuel said, "How can I go? Saul will hear about it and kill me."
The LORD said, "Take a heifer with you and say, 'I have come to sacrifice to the LORD.'
3Invite Jesse to the sacrifice, and I will show[h] you what to do. You are to anoint[i] for me
the one I indicate."
4Samuel did what the LORD said. When he arrived at Bethlehem,[j] the elders of the
town trembled when they met him. They asked, "Do you come in peace?[k]"
5Samuel replied, "Yes, in peace; I have come to sacrifice to the LORD. Consecrate[l]
yourselves and come to the sacrifice with me." Then he consecrated Jesse and his sons
and invited them to the sacrifice.
6When they arrived, Samuel saw Eliab[m] and thought, "Surely the LORD's anointed
stands here before the LORD."
7But the LORD said to Samuel, "Do not consider his appearance or his height, for I
have rejected him. The LORD does not look at the things man looks at. Man looks at the
outward appearance,[n] but the LORD looks at the heart."[o]
8Then Jesse called Abinadab[p] and had him pass in front of Samuel. But Samuel said,

15:33 [x]Ge 9:6; Jdg 1:7
15:34 [y]1Sa 7:17 [z]1Sa 11:4
15:35 [a]1Sa 19:24 [b]1Sa 16:1
16:1 [c]1Sa 15:35 [d]1Sa 15:23 [e]2Ki 9:1 [f]Ru 4:17; 1Sa 9:16 [g]Ps 78:70; Ac 13:22
16:3 [h]Ex 4:15 [i]Dt 17:15; 1Sa 9:16
16:4 [j]Ge 48:7; Lk 2:4 [k]1Ki 2:13; 2Ki 9:17
16:5 [l]Ex 19:10,22
16:6 [m]1Sa 17:13
16:7 [n]Ps 147:10 [o]1Ki 8:39; 1Ch 28:9; Isa 55:8
16:8 [p]1Sa 17:13

[a] *32 Or him trembling, yet*

ored before the elders of his ["my"] people. In return, Saul offered to do obeisance before the Lord ["your"] God.

15:31 Samuel went back. Several reasons for Samuel's reversal of his earlier decision (v. 26) may be suggested: (1) Saul had at last issued a candid confession; (2) there was no danger after verses 28–29 that Saul might interpret Samuel's actions as a mitigation of his rejection; (3) Samuel still needed to deal with Agag. **worshiped.** The Hebrew may also be rendered "bowed/prostrated himself" (cf. 20:41). The outward action need not imply an inward disposition of true worship.

15:32 bitterness of death is past. Or perhaps, with the Septuagint (the Greek translation of the OT), "Would death have been as bitter as this?"

15:35 Samuel mourned for him. See notes on verse 11.

■ **16:1—2 Samuel 1:27** *Saul and David: David's Rise and Saul's Fall.* These chapters narrate in three large sections David's rise to power and Saul's fall from power and his death: (1) David's successes and trials in Saul's court (16:1—18:30), David's support as he fled from Saul (19:1—22:5) and David's innocence in contrast with Saul's guilt (22:6—2Sa 1:27). These chapters demonstrate that God replaced Saul with David.

■ **16:1—18:30** *David's Success and Troubles in Saul's Service.* In an ironic twist, Saul's own family liked David. Saul was isolated in his jealousy, but he still caused David much trouble. These chapters consist of four parts: David's anointing (16:1–23), Saul's initial approval of him (17:1—18:5), Saul's growing jealousy of him (18:6–16) and Saul's failed attempt to trap David (18:17–30). The characters of Saul and David are polarized to draw attention to God's choice of David and rejection of Saul.

■ **16:1–23** *David's Anointing by Samuel.* David was anointed Israel's next king by Samuel and was introduced to Saul. God had authorized Samuel to support this change in leadership from Saul to David (chs. 1–3).

16:1 Bethlehem. First mentioned in Genesis 35:19, Bethlehem was David's hometown (17:12,15) and the village to which God sent Samuel to anoint the new king. On the significance of this site for the Messiah ("the Anointed One"), see, for example, Micah 5:2, Matthew 2:5–6 and John 7:42. **I have chosen.** The Hebrew verb used here is not the most common word for "choose," and it also carries the meanings "see," "perceive," "get to know" and "select." The Hebrew speaks of choosing a king "for myself [the LORD]," which sets up a contrast with the choice of a king for "them [the people]" in 8:22 (cf. 8:18; 12:13).

16:2 Saul will . . . kill me. The latter stages of Samuel's recent debate with Saul gave Samuel adequate reason to fear such action (see 15:27 and its note). **say, "I have come to sacrifice."** While true insofar as it went, this statement did not disclose the fundamental reason for Samuel's journey to Bethlehem (v. 1). There may well be an ironic tone in the Lord's instruction to Samuel, coming as it does on the heels of Saul's adamant claim in chapter 15 to have spared Amalekite livestock only "to sacrifice" them (15:15, 21). Although it is a fair observation that in war, as in a chess game, one deceives his opponent in order to defeat him, care must be taken to assess each case of deception in terms of its own particular circumstances (see notes on 19:14; 20:6; 21:2; 27:10; Jos 2:2–7; 2Sa 16:17–19).

16:3 anoint. See note on 2:10.

16:4 the elders of the town trembled. See the similar response of Ahimelech upon David's arrival alone in Nob (21:1). The cause of the elders' trembling here is not stated, although it may have had to do with Samuel's prophetic function as an instrument of God's judgment. Perhaps the apparent failure of the experiment of kingship, which had been initiated by "the elders" (ch. 8), lay behind their trepidation.

16:5 Consecrate yourselves. See Exodus 19:10–22. The outward rituals of cleansing symbolized inward spiritual preparation.

16:7 height, for I have rejected him. The reference to "height" as a false measure of an individual's royal qualification, along with the notice that this son of Jesse was "rejected," cannot help but recall the recently rejected Saul, who was also notable for his height (9:2; 10:23) but was now rejected (15:23,26). **the LORD looks at the heart.** God's standards are of a different order than human criteria; they focus on inward, not outward, qualities (see note on 13:14).

"The LORD has not chosen this one either." [9]Jesse then had Shammah pass by, but Samuel said, "Nor has the LORD chosen this one." [10]Jesse had seven of his sons pass before
16:11 Samuel, but Samuel said to him, "The LORD has not chosen these." [11]So he asked Jesse,
[q]1Sa 17:12 "Are these all[q] the sons you have?"
"There is still the youngest," Jesse answered, "but he is tending the sheep."
16:12 Samuel said, "Send for him; we will not sit down[a] until he arrives."
[r]1Sa 9:17 [12]So he[r] sent and had him brought in. He was ruddy, with a fine appearance and
[s]Ge 39:6; 1Sa 17:42 handsome[s] features.
Then the LORD said, "Rise and anoint him; he is the one."
[13]So Samuel took the horn of oil and anointed him in the presence of his brothers, and
16:13 [t]Nu 27:18; Jdg 11:29 from that day on the Spirit of the LORD[t] came upon David in power.[u] Samuel then went
[u]1Sa 10:1,6,9-10; 11:6 to Ramah.

David in Saul's Service

16:14 [v]Jdg 16:20 [14]Now the Spirit of the LORD had departed[v] from Saul, and an evil[b] spirit[w] from the
[w]Jdg 9:23; 1Sa 18:10 LORD tormented him.

[a] *11* Some Septuagint manuscripts; Hebrew *not gather around* [b] *14* Or *injurious*; also in verses 15, 16 and 23

16:9–11 See *WLC* 135.
16:11 youngest. The Hebrew, which also connotes "smallest," sets up a contrast not only with the "height" (v. 7) of the first brother, who was rejected, but also, by implication, of the first king, who also was rejected (see v. 7 and its note). **tending the sheep.** As Jesus would later take fishermen and make them "fishers of men" (Mt 4:19), the Lord here took a shepherd and made him a "shepherd" for his people (see note on 2Sa 5:2).
16:13 in the presence of his brothers. It is likely that the elders also witnessed David's anointing (vv. 4–5). The emphasis on the brothers' witnessing of the event may be intended to shed light on Eliab's behavior in 17:28. **Spirit of the LORD came upon David in power.** See notes on 10:6 and 11:6. The sense of permanence in David's endowment with the Spirit "from that day on" sets him apart from Saul (and Samson), upon whom the Spirit descended only sporadically to empower or overpower (cf. 19:23).
16:14 Spirit of the LORD had departed from Saul. The empowering and validating presence of God's Spirit must have been

David's Family Tree

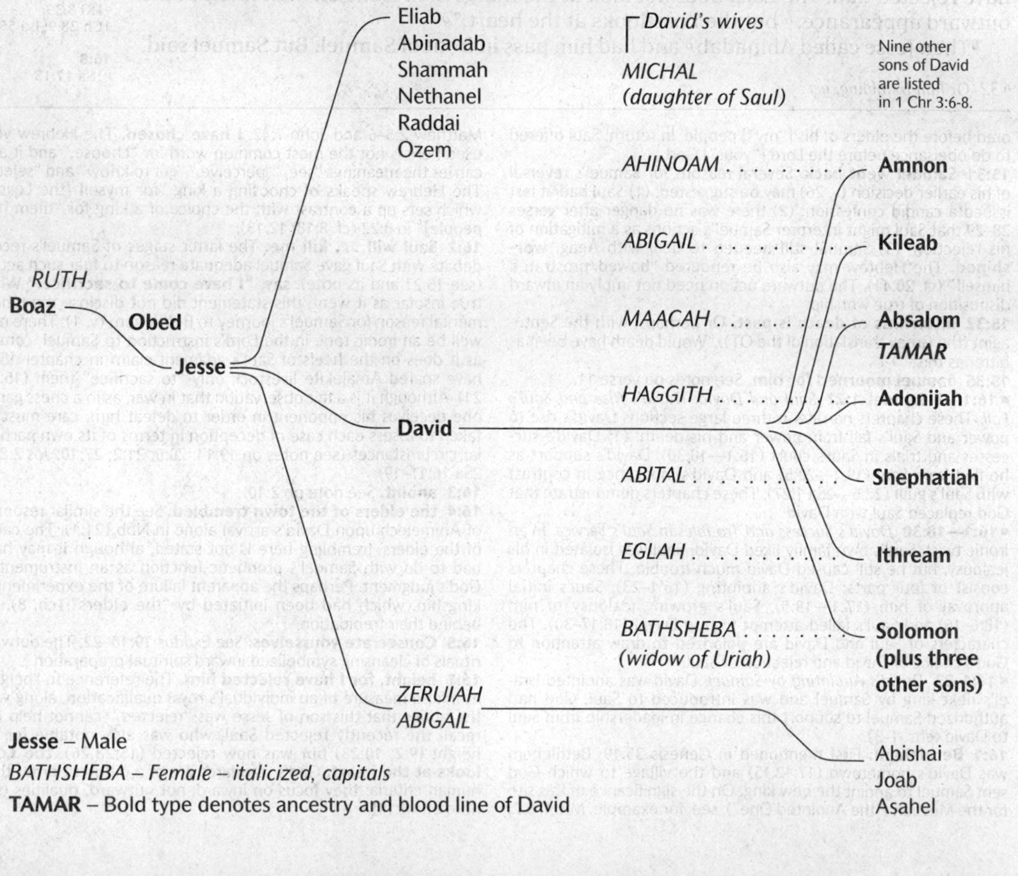

15 Saul's attendants said to him, "See, an evil spirit from God is tormenting you. 16 Let
our lord command his servants here to search for someone who can play the harp.[x] He
will play when the evil spirit from God comes upon you, and you will feel better."
17 So Saul said to his attendants, "Find someone who plays well and bring him to me."
18 One of the servants answered, "I have seen a son of Jesse of Bethlehem who knows
how to play the harp. He is a brave man and a warrior. He speaks well and is a fine-look-
ing man. And the LORD is with[y] him."
19 Then Saul sent messengers to Jesse and said, "Send me your son David, who is with
the sheep." 20 So Jesse took a donkey loaded with bread,[z] a skin of wine and a young goat
and sent them with his son David to Saul.
21 David came to Saul and entered his service.[a] Saul liked him very much, and David
became one of his armor-bearers. 22 Then Saul sent word to Jesse, saying, "Allow David
to remain in my service, for I am pleased with him."
23 Whenever the spirit from God came upon Saul, David would take his harp and play.
Then relief would come to Saul; he would feel better, and the evil spirit[b] would leave him.

David and Goliath

17 Now the Philistines gathered their forces for war and assembled[c] at Socoh in Judah. They pitched camp at Ephes Dammim, between Socoh[d] and Azekah. 2 Saul
and the Israelites assembled and camped in the Valley of Elah[e] and drew up their battle line to meet the Philistines. 3 The Philistines occupied one hill and the Israelites another, with the valley between them.
4 A champion named Goliath,[f] who was from Gath, came out of the Philistine camp.
He was over nine feet[a] tall. 5 He had a bronze helmet on his head and wore a coat of scale
armor of bronze weighing five thousand shekels[b]; 6 on his legs he wore bronze greaves,
and a bronze javelin[g] was slung on his back. 7 His spear shaft was like a weaver's rod,[h]
and its iron point weighed six hundred shekels.[c] His shield bearer[i] went ahead of him.
8 Goliath stood and shouted to the ranks of Israel, "Why do you come out and line up
for battle? Am I not a Philistine, and are you not the servants of Saul? Choose[j] a man and
have him come down to me. 9 If he is able to fight and kill me, we will become your subjects; but if I overcome him and kill him, you will become our subjects and serve us."
10 Then the Philistine said, "This day I defy[k] the ranks of Israel! Give me a man and let
us fight each other." 11 On hearing the Philistine's words, Saul and all the Israelites were
dismayed and terrified.
12 Now David was the son of an Ephrathite named Jesse,[l] who was from Bethlehem[m]

16:16 [x]ver 23; 1Sa 18:10; 19:9; 2Ki 3:15
16:18 [y]1Sa 3:19; 17:32-37
16:20 [z]1Sa 10:27; Pr 18:16
16:21 [a]Ge 41:46; Pr 22:29
16:23 [b]ver 14-16
17:1 [c]1Sa 13:5 [d]Jos 15:35; 2Ch 28:18
17:2 [e]1Sa 21:9
17:4 [f]Jos 11:21-22; 2Sa 21:19
17:6 [g]ver 45
17:7 [h]2Sa 21:19 [i]ver 41
17:8 [j]1Sa 8:17
17:10 [k]ver 26,45; 2Sa 21:21
17:12 [l]Ru 4:17; 1Ch 2:13-15 [m]Ge 35:19

[a] 4 Hebrew *was six cubits and a span* (about 3 meters) [b] 5 That is, about 125 pounds (about 57 kilograms) [c] 7 That is, about 15 pounds (about 7 kilograms)

---

removed from Saul at least as early as his definitive rejection in chapter 15 (cf. 16:1). **evil spirit.** See NIV text note (cf. 1Ki 22:21 23). The Hebrew word does not always mean "evil" in an absolute moral sense, but it may describe something that is troubling, annoying or harmful.

16:18 warrior. Literally, "man of war." Some see a contradiction between this statement and Saul's concern in 17:33 that David, who was but a boy (lit., "youth" or "young man"), would be no match for Goliath, the seasoned Philistine champion. In response the following should be recognized: (1) The servant's recommendation of David to Saul in verse 18 may have been no less given to hyperbole than a typical modern letter of reference; and (2) David's age did not necessarily disqualify him as a soldier. **the LORD is with him.** This fact, more than any human quality, would account for David's irresistible, if circuitous, rise to power. Saul's increasing recognition of this would play no small part in his own psychological disintegration (see 3:19 and its note; 17:37 and its note; 18:12,13–16 and their notes; 18:28–29 and its note; 20:13 and its note; 2Sa 7:9 and its note).

16:19 Send me your son David, who is with the sheep. Saul unwittingly invited his eventual replacement to enter his court. In this notice, the reader has but one of many evidences that David's rise to power was providentially directed and was not the result of human effort or grasping for power.

16:21 Saul liked him. The sense is appropriate and perhaps likely (note the similar response to David by Jonathan [18:1,3; 20:17], Michal [18:20,28], the people of Israel [18:16] and possibly even Saul's own servants [18:22]). The Hebrew is ambiguous, stating only that "he loved him very much." Elsewhere in this verse, David is consistently the grammatical subject. It is possible to read it as "He [David] loved him [Saul] and became one of his armor-bearers."

■ **17:1—18:5** *David's Success and Saul's Initial Approval.* David defeated Goliath, and Israel routed the disheartened Philistine army. This episode contrasts David and Saul as warrior-kings.

17:1 Ephes Dammim, between Socoh and Azekah. The Judean town of Socoh (Khirbet Abbad) lay almost 15 miles west of Bethlehem near the Philistine border. Azekah (Tell ez–Zakariyeh) lay 2.5 miles northwest of Socoh, and Ephes Dammim must have been located somewhere between the two.

17:2 Valley of Elah. The Hebrew name is retained to this day and means "Valley of the Terebinth." The valley (known in Arabic as the Wadi es-Sant) descends from east to west, passing just north of Socoh and Azekah.

17:4 champion. Trial by single combat—in which the outcome of a fight-to-the-death between two champions (representatives of the warring parties) was taken as the will of the gods—is rare in the Old Testament (cf., to a limited degree, 2Sa 2:14–16). It is well attested, however, among some of Israel's neighbors. **nine feet tall.** See NIV text note. The Septuagint (the Greek translation of the OT), Dead Sea Scrolls and Josephus (*Antiquities*, 6.9.1) all record four cubits instead of six cubits, making Goliath over six and a half feet tall, still "gigantic" by ancient standards.

17:5–7 The detailed description of Goliath's armor and weapons is striking in view of the generally compact style of Old Testament narrative. The description was likely intended to increase the wonder of David's victory (v. 50).

17:11 Saul and all the Israelites were dismayed and terrified. The Philistine's challenge to the "servants of Saul" (v. 8) had been to "choose a man" (v. 8). The logical choice, if Israel was to match giant for giant, would have been Saul (9:2; 10:23–24), but Saul, like everyone else, was terrified.

17:12 Ephrathite. See Genesis 35:19 and 48:7 (see also Ru 1:2; 4:11; 1Ch 4:4; Mic 5:2).

17:12 [n]1Sa 16:11 in Judah. Jesse had eight[n] sons, and in Saul's time he was old and well advanced in years.
13 Jesse's three oldest sons had followed Saul to the war: The firstborn was Eliab;[o] the sec-
17:13 [o]1Sa 16:6 ond, Abinadab; and the third, Shammah.[p] 14 David was the youngest. The three oldest
[p]1Sa 16:9 followed Saul, 15 but David went back and forth from Saul to tend his father's sheep[q] at
Bethlehem.
17:15 [q]1Sa 16:19 16 For forty days the Philistine came forward every morning and evening and took his
stand.
17:17 [r]1Sa 25:18 17 Now Jesse said to his son David, "Take this ephah[a] of roasted grain[r] and these ten
loaves of bread for your brothers and hurry to their camp. 18 Take along these ten chees-
17:18 [s]Ge 37:14 es to the commander of their unit.[b] See how your brothers[s] are and bring back some assurance[c] from them. 19 They are with Saul and all the men of Israel in the Valley of Elah,
fighting against the Philistines."
20 Early in the morning David left the flock with a shepherd, loaded up and set out, as
Jesse had directed. He reached the camp as the army was going out to its battle positions,
shouting the war cry. 21 Israel and the Philistines were drawing up their lines facing each
other. 22 David left his things with the keeper of supplies, ran to the battle lines and greet-
17:23 [t]ver 8-10 ed his brothers. 23 As he was talking with them, Goliath, the Philistine champion from
Gath, stepped out from his lines and shouted his usual[t] defiance, and David heard it.
24 When the Israelites saw the man, they all ran from him in great fear.
25 Now the Israelites had been saying, "Do you see how this man keeps coming out?
He comes out to defy Israel. The king will give great wealth to the man who kills him. He
17:25 [u]Jos 15:16; will also give him his daughter[u] in marriage and will exempt his father's family from tax-
1Sa 18:17 es in Israel."
17:26 26 David asked the men standing near him, "What will be done for the man who kills
[v]1Sa 11:2 [w]1Sa 14:6 [x]ver 10 this Philistine and removes this disgrace[v] from Israel? Who is this uncircumcised[w] Phi-
[y]Dt 5:26 listine that he should defy[x] the armies of the living[y] God?"
27 They repeated to him what they had been saying and told him, "This is what will
be done for the man who kills him."
17:28 28 When Eliab, David's oldest brother, heard him speaking with the men, he burned
[z]Ge 37:4,8,11; Pr 18:19; Mt 10:36 with anger[z] at him and asked, "Why have you come down here? And with whom did you
leave those few sheep in the desert? I know how conceited you are and how wicked your
heart is; you came down only to watch the battle."
29 "Now what have I done?" said David. "Can't I even speak?" 30 He then turned away
to someone else and brought up the same matter, and the men answered him as before.
17:32 31 What David said was overheard and reported to Saul, and Saul sent for him.
[a]Dt 20:3; 1Sa 16:18 32 David said to Saul, "Let no one lose heart[a] on account of this Philistine; your servant will go and fight him."
17:33 [b]Nu 13:31 33 Saul replied,[b] "You are not able to go out against this Philistine and fight him; you
are only a boy, and he has been a fighting man from his youth."
17:34 34 But David said to Saul, "Your servant has been keeping his father's sheep. When a
[c]Jer 49:19; Am 3:12 lion[c] or a bear came and carried off a sheep from the flock, 35 I went after it, struck it and
rescued the sheep from its mouth. When it turned on me, I seized it by its hair, struck it

a *17* That is, probably about 3/5 bushel (about 22 liters) b *18* Hebrew *thousand* c *18* Or *some token;* or *some pledge of spoils*

17:15 David went back and forth from Saul. This notice recalls the previous chapter in which David was inducted into Saul's service and suggests that his time was split between duties to his king and to his father. The detailed review of Jesse's sons (vv. 12–14) may serve a similar linking function, reminding the reader of the anointing episode in 16:1–13 and encouraging him or her to judge Eliab's angry interaction with David (v. 28) against that background. **17:19 fighting against the Philistines.** The disparity between Jesse's reasonable assumption (men at war should be engaging the enemy) and the reality of the situation (v. 11) subtly reinforces the reader's sense of the faithlessness of Saul and his troops. **17:25 The king will give.** Compare 8:14–18 and 22:7. **his daughter in marriage.** Compare Joshua 15:16; see also note on 18:20–27. **17:26 uncircumcised Philistine.** See note on 14:6. **17:28 Eliab . . . burned with anger at him.** The vehemence of Eliab's disparaging and critical reaction to David may be understood as that of a man who did not feel big enough to meet the challenge of the giant and who would have felt deeply resentful of being shown up by his little brother. His reaction was even more comprehensible against the background of David's anointing (cf. the attitude of Jacob's sons toward their younger brother Joseph, who also had received indications of future greatness [Ge 37:2–11] and who also was abused by his brothers when he was sent on a fact-finding mission by his father [Ge 37:12–19]). The falsity of Eliab's criticisms is clear from the context (see the following notes on this verse). **with whom did you leave those few sheep . . . ?** Verses 20 and 22 make it clear that, whatever his excitement about the battle, David acted responsibly in regard to his more mundane duties, placing both the sheep and his supplies in capable hands before proceeding to the battle lines. **how conceited.** Or "how presumptuous" or "how arrogant." Compare Genesis 37:19. **how wicked your heart is.** The focus on Eliab's height recalls that of Saul in 16:6–7. Eliab's radical misjudgment of the condition of David's heart contrasts with "man after [God's] own heart" (13:14) and "the LORD looks at the heart" (16:7). See *WLC* 145; *WSC* 78. **17:32 Let no one.** The Septuagint (the Greek translation of the OT) reads "Let not my lord." In Hebrew, "man" and "lord" look and sound much alike. **17:33–37** The conversation between Saul and David vividly illustrates the radical difference in their perspectives. Saul continued to think in terms of the humanly possible, warning, "You are not able" (v. 33), while David was confident in the Lord, asserting that "The LORD . . . will deliver me" (v. 37).

and killed it. 36 Your servant has killed both the lion and the bear; this uncircumcised Philistine will be like one of them, because he has defied the armies of the living God. 37 The
LORD who delivered[d] me from the paw of the lion[e] and the paw of the bear will deliver
me from the hand of this Philistine."
Saul said to David, "Go, and the LORD be with[f] you."
38 Then Saul dressed David in his own tunic. He put a coat of armor on him and a
bronze helmet on his head. 39 David fastened on his sword over the tunic and tried walking around, because he was not used to them.
"I cannot go in these," he said to Saul, "because I am not used to them." So he took
them off. 40 Then he took his staff in his hand, chose five smooth stones from the stream,
put them in the pouch of his shepherd's bag and, with his sling in his hand, approached
the Philistine.
41 Meanwhile, the Philistine, with his shield bearer in front of him, kept coming closer to David. 42 He looked David over and saw that he was only a boy, ruddy and handsome,[g] and he despised[h] him. 43 He said to David, "Am I a dog,[i] that you come at me with
sticks?" And the Philistine cursed David by his gods. 44 "Come here," he said, "and I'll give
your flesh to the birds of the air and the beasts of the field![j]"
45 David said to the Philistine, "You come against me with sword and spear and javelin, but I come against you in the name[k] of the LORD Almighty, the God of the armies
of Israel, whom you have defied.[l] 46 This day the LORD will hand you over to me, and I'll
strike you down and cut off your head. Today I will give the carcasses[m] of the Philistine
army to the birds of the air and the beasts of the earth, and the whole world[n] will know
that there is a God in Israel.[o] 47 All those gathered here will know that it is not by sword[p]
or spear that the LORD saves;[q] for the battle[r] is the LORD's, and he will give all of you into
our hands."
48 As the Philistine moved closer to attack him, David ran quickly toward the battle
line to meet him. 49 Reaching into his bag and taking out a stone, he slung it and struck
the Philistine on the forehead. The stone sank into his forehead, and he fell facedown
on the ground.
50 So David triumphed over the Philistine with a sling[s] and a stone; without a sword
in his hand he struck down the Philistine and killed him.
51 David ran and stood over him. He took hold of the Philistine's sword and drew it
from the scabbard. After he killed him, he cut[t] off his head with the sword.[u]
When the Philistines saw that their hero was dead, they turned and ran. 52 Then the
men of Israel and Judah surged forward with a shout and pursued the Philistines to the
entrance of Gath[a] and to the gates of Ekron.[v] Their dead were strewn along the Shaaraim[w] road to Gath and Ekron. 53 When the Israelites returned from chasing the Philistines, they plundered their camp. 54 David took the Philistine's head and brought it to Jerusalem, and he put the Philistine's weapons in his own tent.
55 As Saul watched David[x] going out to meet the Philistine, he said to Abner, commander of the army, "Abner, whose son is that young man?"

17:37 [d]2Co 1:10 [e]2Ti 4:17 [f]1Sa 20:13; 1Ch 22:11,16
17:42 [g]1Sa 16:12 [h]Ps 123:3-4; Pr 16:18
17:43 [i]1Sa 24:14; 2Sa 3:8; 9:8; 2Ki 8:13
17:44 [j]1Ki 20:10-11
17:45 [k]2Sa 22:33,35; 2Ch 32:8; Ps 124:8; Heb 11:32-34 [l]ver 10
17:46 [m]Dt 28:26 [n]Jos 4:24; 1Ki 8:43; Isa 52:10 [o]1Ki 18:36; 2Ki 19:19; Isa 37:20
17:47 [p]Hos 1:7; Zec 4:6 [q]1Sa 14:6; 2Ch 14:11 [r]2Ch 20:15; Ps 44:6-7
17:50 [s]2Sa 23:21
17:51 [t]Heb 11:34 [u]1Sa 21:9
17:52 [v]Jos 15:11 [w]Jos 15:36
17:55 [x]1Sa 16:21

[a] 52 Some Septuagint manuscripts; Hebrew *a valley*

17:36 uncircumcised Philistine. See note on 14:6.
17:37 the LORD be with you. David's rise to power continued to be furthered, if unwittingly, by Saul. Having brought him into his court (see note on 16:19), Saul now sent him to fight his battle. Most ironic of all, Saul invoked upon David that which most clearly distinguished them and would account for David's ultimate success: "The LORD be with you" (see note on 16:18).
17:38–39 David's rejection of Saul's armor and weapons accords well with the point of the narrative: "It is not by sword or spear that the LORD saves; for the battle is the LORD's" (v. 47; see note on vv. 5–7). Thus David is shown to be God's choice as king.
17:43 See *WLC* 113.
17:45 in the name of the LORD Almighty. See note on 1:3. David came "in the name" of God, that is, "as the instrument of God" and "in the power of all that his name connotes." On the significance of God's name as more than just a label, but connoting his very character, see Exodus 34:5–7.
17:46 carcasses of the Philistine army. David either did not believe or did not accept the terms of Goliath's challenge (v. 9), and he bettered Goliath's threat (v. 44) by extending his counter-threat to encompass the entire Philistine army.
17:47 the battle is the LORD's. See notes on verses 38–39 and 14:6.
17:49 forehead. In Hebrew the word "forehead" sounds much like the bronze "greaves" (pieces of armor for the shins) mentioned in verse 6. Unless this similarity is a mere coincidence, the narrator's choice of words here may obliquely reinforce the point, made explicitly in verse 50, that mere armor and weaponry were insufficient to protect even a giant from the man in whom God was at work. Greaves and armor notwithstanding, Goliath's forehead was still vulnerable.
17:50 without a sword. This verse marks the climax of the contest between Goliath, who physically speaking had all the advantages, and David, who, with God on his side, was able to triumph even "without a sword in his hand" (cf. vv. 45–47). **killed.** That is, dealt him the mortal wound (v. 51).
17:51 killed. A different form of the Hebrew verb is used here from that in verse 50. The sense is "dispatched," as in 14:13.
17:52 Gath and Ekron. See notes on 4:1 and 5:8 and 10.
17:54 brought it to Jerusalem. Jerusalem was at this time in Jebusite, not Israelite, hands (2Sa 5:6–9). It is therefore perhaps best to understand this notice as referring to a later time. It has also been conjectured that David, even prior to his capture of Jerusalem, may have taunted the Jebusites by displaying Goliath's head before their city as a warning of their own impending defeat. See note on 2 Samuel 5:6.
17:55 whose son is that young man? At first glance, Saul's question and Abner's response appear to be incongruous with the

Abner replied, "As surely as you live, O king, I don't know."
56 The king said, "Find out whose son this young man is."
57 As soon as David returned from killing the Philistine, Abner took him and brought
him before Saul, with David still holding the Philistine's head.
58 "Whose son are you, young man?" Saul asked him.
David said, "I am the son of your servant Jesse[y] of Bethlehem."

Saul's Jealousy of David

18 After David had finished talking with Saul, Jonathan became one in spirit with
David, and he loved[z] him as himself.[a] 2 From that day Saul kept David with him
and did not let him return to his father's house. 3 And Jonathan made a covenant[b] with
David because he loved him as himself. 4 Jonathan took off the robe[c] he was wearing and
gave it to David, along with his tunic, and even his sword, his bow and his belt.
5 Whatever Saul sent him to do, David did it so successfully[a] that Saul gave him a high
rank in the army. This pleased all the people, and Saul's officers as well.
6 When the men were returning home after David had killed the Philistine, the wom-
en came out from all the towns of Israel to meet King Saul with singing and dancing,[d]
with joyful songs and with tambourines[e] and lutes. 7 As they danced, they sang:[f]

"Saul has slain his thousands,
and David his tens[g] of thousands."

8 Saul was very angry; this refrain galled him. "They have credited David with tens of
thousands," he thought, "but me with only thousands. What more can he get but the
kingdom?[h]" 9 And from that time on Saul kept a jealous eye on David.
10 The next day an evil[b] spirit[i] from God came forcefully upon Saul. He was prophesying in his house, while David was playing the harp, as he usually[j] did. Saul had a spear
in his hand 11 and he hurled it, saying to himself,[k] "I'll pin David to the wall." But David
eluded[l] him twice.
12 Saul was afraid[m] of David, because the LORD[n] was with[o] David but had left Saul.
13 So he sent David away from him and gave him command over a thousand men, and
David led[p] the troops in their campaigns.[q] 14 In everything he did he had great success,[c][r]
because the LORD was with[s] him. 15 When Saul saw how successful[d] he was, he was afraid
of him. 16 But all Israel and Judah loved David, because he led them in their campaigns.[t]
17 Saul said to David, "Here is my older daughter[u] Merab. I will give her to you in mar-

17:58 [y]ver 12
18:1 [z]2Sa 1:26 [a]Ge 44:30
18:3 [b]1Sa 20:8,16,17, 42
18:4 [c]Ge 41:42
18:6 [d]Ex 15:20 [e]Jdg 11:34; Ps 68:25
18:7 [f]Ex 15:21 [g]1Sa 21:11; 29:5
18:8 [h]1Sa 15:8
18:10 [i]1Sa 16:14 [j]1Sa 19:7
18:11 [k]1Sa 20:7,33 [l]1Sa 19:10
18:12 [m]ver 15,29 [n]1Sa 16:13 [o]1Sa 28:15
18:13 [p]ver 16; Nu 27:17 [q]2Sa 5:2
18:14 [r]Ge 39:3 [s]Ge 39:2, 23; Jos 6:27; 1Sa 16:18
18:16 [t]ver 5
18:17 [u]1Sa 17:25

a 5 Or *wisely* b 10 Or *injurious* c 14 Or *he was very wise* d 15 Or *wise*

---

events described in 16:18–22. If a chronological relationship between chapters 16 and 17 is assumed (as verses such as 17:15 and 18:2 would seem to warrant), three points may be made in explanation of the apparent incongruity. First, despite the fact that Saul had been informed at least once of the name of David's father (16:18) and that David had been made one of Saul's armor-bearers (16:21), Saul's knowledge of him and his background may yet have been minimal (Saul's dealings with Jesse were consistently handled through messengers; 16:19,22). Second, in light of Saul's promises to the one who should defeat Goliath (v. 25), Saul's question may have been prompted by much deeper concerns that a mere desire to hear Jesse's name reiterated (i.e., Saul may have meant, Who is this man who is about to become my son-in-law? Whose family is to be exempt from taxes in Israel?). Third, the intensity of Saul's interest may also reflect his knowledge that the kingdom would ultimately be given to "one of [his] neighbors—to one better than [he]" (15:28; i.e., Saul may have wondered, Could this astonishing young man be the one?). See 18:8 and its note.

18:2 did not let him return. See note on 17:15.

18:3 covenant. The nature of the covenant is not explicitly stated, but see the note on verse 4. Further references to the covenant between Jonathan and David include 20:8,13–17 and 42, 22:8 and 23:18.

18:4 Jonathan took off the robe. As crown prince, Jonathan would likely have entertained the expectation that he would succeed his father as king (20:31). In 13:22 Jonathan and Saul had been distinguished from the rest of the people by their possession of swords and spears. Here Jonathan's transference of his robe and weaponry to David not only signified his self-giving loyalty but also implied that, even at this early stage, he recognized David as God's choice for the next king. See Jonathan's explicit confession in 23:17 (see note on 2Sa 1:10).

18:5 Whatever Saul sent him to do, David did it . . . successfully. Military success continued to be David's hallmark, and Saul gave David a rank in the army commensurate with his accomplishments, a move that pleased not only the people, but even Saul's own officers.

■ **18:6–16** *David's Success and Saul's Jealousy.* David's fame spread through Israel, and he was considered a greater warrior than Saul. Saul was enraged with jealousy, tried to kill him and finally demoted him.

18:7 David his tens of thousands. See 21:11 and 29:5. It is a common feature of Hebrew poetry to "step up" one or more terms in the second half of a poetic couplet (for the "thousand"/"ten thousand" intensification, see Dt 32:30; Pss 91:7; 144:13; Mic 6:7). Nevertheless, the women probably intended the comparison to reflect more than mere poetic convention, and Saul, at any rate, certainly took it that way (v. 8).

18:8 What more can he get but the kingdom? Saul rightly sensed that David might be the "neighbor" (15:28) who would replace him (see note on 17:55).

18:10 evil spirit. See note on 16:14. **prophesying.** For the sense of the Hebrew term in this context, see the note on 10:5 (see also 1Ki 18:29).

18:12 the LORD was with David. See 16:18 and its note. **had left Saul.** See 16:14 and its note.

18:13–16 Saul's removal of David from the court, with an accompanying demotion in military rank, may have been intended to decrease David's visibility (and hence popularity) and to increase the risk of his dying in battle. The effect of Saul's scheming, however, as throughout this chapter, was actually the reverse. David was brought into closer contact with the general populace, so that "all Israel and Judah loved David, because he led them in their campaigns" (v. 16).

■ **18:17–30** *David's Success and Saul's Snare.* In view of David's immense popularity, Saul could not stall forever in fulfilling his

riage; only serve me bravely and fight the battles[v] of the LORD." For Saul said to himself,[w]
"I will not raise a hand against him. Let the Philistines do that!"
18 But David said to Saul, "Who am I,[x] and what is my family or my father's clan in Israel, that I should become the king's son-in-law?[y]" 19 So[a] when the time came for Merab,[z]
Saul's daughter, to be given to David, she was given in marriage to Adriel of Meholah.[a]
20 Now Saul's daughter Michal[b] was in love with David, and when they told Saul about
it, he was pleased. 21 "I will give her to him," he thought, "so that she may be a snare[c] to
him and so that the hand of the Philistines may be against him." So Saul said to David,
"Now you have a second opportunity to become my son-in-law."
22 Then Saul ordered his attendants: "Speak to David privately and say, 'Look, the king
is pleased with you, and his attendants all like you; now become his son-in-law.' "
23 They repeated these words to David. But David said, "Do you think it is a small matter to become the king's son-in-law? I'm only a poor man and little known."
24 When Saul's servants told him what David had said, 25 Saul replied, "Say to David,
'The king wants no other price[d] for the bride than a hundred Philistine foreskins, to take
revenge on his enemies.' " Saul's plan[e] was to have David fall by the hands of the Philistines.
26 When the attendants told David these things, he was pleased to become the king's
son-in-law. So before the allotted time elapsed, 27 David and his men went out and
killed two hundred Philistines. He brought their foreskins and presented the full number to the king so that he might become the king's son-in-law. Then Saul gave him his
daughter Michal[f] in marriage.
28 When Saul realized that the LORD was with David and that his daughter Michal loved
David, 29 Saul became still more afraid of him, and he remained his enemy the rest of his
days.
30 The Philistine commanders continued to go out to battle, and as often as they did,
David met with more success[b][g] than the rest of Saul's officers, and his name became well
known.

Saul Tries to Kill David

19 Saul told his son Jonathan[h] and all the attendants to kill[i] David. But Jonathan
was very fond of David 2 and warned him, "My father Saul is looking for a
chance to kill you. Be on your guard tomorrow morning; go into hiding and stay there.
3 I will go out and stand with my father in the field where you are. I'll speak[j] to him about
you and will tell you what I find out."
4 Jonathan spoke[k] well of David to Saul his father and said to him, "Let not the king

a *19* Or *However,* b *30* Or *David acted more wisely*

18:17 [v]Nu 21:14; 1Sa 25:28 [w]ver 25
18:18 [x]1Sa 9:21; 2Sa 7:18 [y]ver 23
18:19 [z]2Sa 21:8 [a]Jdg 7:22
18:20 [b]ver 28
18:21 [c]ver 17,26
18:25 [d]Ge 34:12; Ex 22:17; 1Sa 14:24 [e]ver 17
18:27 [f]ver 13; 2Sa 3:14
18:30 [g]ver 5; 2Sa 11:1
19:1 [h]1Sa 18:1 [i]1Sa 18:9
19:3 [j]1Sa 20:12
19:4 [k]1Sa 20:32; Pr 31:8,9; Jer 18:20

promise of 17:25. Nevertheless, he added a further condition (that David "fight the battles of the LORD") in the hope that, having failed to kill David with his own hand (vv. 10–11), he might deliver him into the hand of the Philistines (v. 17; cf. vv. 21,25). Ironically, this was also how David later murdered Uriah the Hittite (2Sa 11:14–17). The illogic of supposing that lesser Philistines might fell one who had triumphed over Goliath seems not to have occurred to Saul. David hesitated (v. 18), as was generally appropriate in such circumstances (cf. 9:21), but certainly did not do so out of any hesitancy to fight the Lord's battles (25:28). At the last minute, however, Saul reneged (perhaps on the excuse that David had hesitated), and Merab was given to another.

18:20–27 When Saul's second daughter, Michal, fell in love with David, Saul again offered David a chance to become his son-in-law (vv. 20–21). This time it seems Saul was not so concerned with the promise of 17:25, which he may have regarded as having been fulfilled by the offer of Merab (vv. 17–19), so he heightened the conditions of David's eligibility to almost suicidal proportions (v. 25). Perhaps not wishing to repeat the misadventure of verse 19, David wasted no time (v. 26) in meeting Saul's requirement twice over, and he became the king's son-in-law (v. 27).

18:21 she may be a snare to him. Although Saul expected Michal to work on his behalf against David, she did not do so because she loved David (v. 28).

18:28 the LORD was with David. Having determined to hang on to his kingship, Saul's increasing fear of David (v. 29) was in a certain sense well-founded, for everywhere in chapter 18 it is apparent that the Lord was with David (vv. 12,14). All of Saul's attempts to lessen David's popularity or to eliminate him by his own hand or by the hand of the Philistines had rebounded to his own disadvantage. The chapter that begins with Jonathan's love for David (v. 1) ends with the love of another of Saul's offspring, Michal, for David (v. 28). Between these statements of love the reader learns of David's ever-increasing popularity with all the people, including Saul's own officers. Had Saul, like Jonathan, been willing to accept his rejection with equanimity, David's successes would not have proved so distressing. Saul was clearly unwilling to accept such rejection, however, and the reader is told in verse 29 that Saul "remained [David's] enemy the rest of his days."

▪ **19:1—22:5** *David's Help as He Flees From Saul.* As tensions rose between Saul and David, David fled for his life. All during his flight, however, various people came to his aid. At first Jonathan tried to protect David, but could not (19:1–10). Then David was helped by Michal (19:11–17), Samuel (19:18–24), Jonathan (20:1–42), Ahimelech (21:1–9), Achish (21:10–15), the king of Moab (22:1–4) and Gad (22:5). Those who aided David as he fled should be seen as God's provision and his approval of David as king.

▪ **19:1–10** *David's Initial Flight.* Although Jonathan convinced Saul that David's success had actually enhanced Saul's glory, when an evil spirit came over Saul, he came very close to killing David. As a result David fled.

19:1 Saul told his son Jonathan and all the attendants to kill David. When his covert attempts to eliminate David proved to be of no avail (ch. 18), Saul decided to take the direct approach.

19:4–5 See *WLC* 135,144.

19:4 Jonathan spoke well of David. Jonathan's magnanimity toward David stands in stark contrast to Saul's malevolence, continuing the unfavorable comparison of father and son noted earlier (see notes on 13:22; 14:1,6,10,29). It seems likely that Jonathan's loyalty to David stemmed not from naivete regarding the latter's destiny but rather from a willing acceptance of it (see notes on 18:4,28–29; 23:17).

do wrong[l] to his servant David; he has not wronged you, and what he has done has benefited you greatly. 5 He took his life in his hands when he killed the Philistine. The LORD
won a great victory[m] for all Israel, and you saw it and were glad. Why then would you
do wrong to an innocent[n] man like David by killing him for no reason?"
6 Saul listened to Jonathan and took this oath: "As surely as the LORD lives, David will
not be put to death."
7 So Jonathan called David and told him the whole conversation. He brought him to
Saul, and David was with Saul as before.[o]
8 Once more war broke out, and David went out and fought the Philistines. He struck
them with such force that they fled before him.
9 But an evil[a] spirit[p] from the LORD came upon Saul as he was sitting in his house with
his spear in his hand. While David was playing the harp, 10 Saul tried to pin him to the
wall with his spear, but David eluded[q] him as Saul drove the spear into the wall. That
night David made good his escape.
11 Saul sent men to David's house to watch[r] it and to kill him in the morning. But Michal, David's wife, warned him, "If you don't run for your life tonight, tomorrow you'll
be killed." 12 So Michal let David down through a window,[s] and he fled and escaped.
13 Then Michal took an idol[b] and laid it on the bed, covering it with a garment and putting some goats' hair at the head.
14 When Saul sent the men to capture David, Michal said,[t] "He is ill."
15 Then Saul sent the men back to see David and told them, "Bring him up to me in
his bed so that I may kill him." 16 But when the men entered, there was the idol in the bed,
and at the head was some goats' hair.
17 Saul said to Michal, "Why did you deceive me like this and send my enemy away so
that he escaped?"
Michal told him, "He said to me, 'Let me get away. Why should I kill you?' "
18 When David had fled and made his escape, he went to Samuel at Ramah[u] and told
him all that Saul had done to him. Then he and Samuel went to Naioth and stayed there.
19 Word came to Saul: "David is in Naioth at Ramah"; 20 so he sent men to capture him.
But when they saw a group of prophets[v] prophesying, with Samuel standing there as
their leader, the Spirit of God came upon[w] Saul's men and they also prophesied.[x] 21 Saul
was told about it, and he sent more men, and they prophesied too. Saul sent men a third
time, and they also prophesied. 22 Finally, he himself left for Ramah and went to the great
cistern at Secu. And he asked, "Where are Samuel and David?"
"Over in Naioth at Ramah," they said.
23 So Saul went to Naioth at Ramah. But the Spirit of God came even upon him, and
he walked along prophesying[y] until he came to Naioth. 24 He stripped[z] off his robes and

19:4 [l]Ge 42:22; Pr 17:13
19:5 [m]1Sa 11:13; 17:49-50; 1Ch 11:14 [n]Dt 19:10-13; 1Sa 20:32; Mt 27:4
19:7 [o]1Sa 16:21; 18:2, 13
19:9 [p]1Sa 16:14; 18:10-11
19:10 [q]1Sa 18:11
19:11 [r]Ps 59 Title
19:12 [s]Jos 2:15; Ac 9:25
19:14 [t]Jos 2:4
19:18 [u]1Sa 7:17
19:20 [v]ver 11,14; Jn 7:32,45 [w]Nu 11:25 [x]1Sa 10:5; Joel 2:28
19:23 [y]1Sa 10:13
19:24 [z]2Sa 6:20; Isa 20:2; Mic 1:8

[a] 9 Or *injurious* [b] 13 Hebrew *teraphim*; also in verse 16

19:6 oath. Saul's record in keeping oaths was not one to inspire confidence (14:24,39,44–45).
19:9 evil spirit. See note on 16:14.
19:10 Saul tried to pin him to the wall. Perhaps again galled by David's military success (v. 8; 18:8), Saul resorted to one of his old tricks (18:10–11). **made good his escape.** David had served faithfully and at much risk for many years. Now he sought safety away from Saul.
■ **19:11–17** *David Aided by Michal.* Saul searched for David in the morning, but Michal helped David by lying to Saul's men.
19:11 Michal, David's wife, warned him. As Saul's designs on David's life became increasingly intense and overt, David was warned first by Saul's son (v. 2) and then by his daughter.
19:12 down through a window. See Joshua 2:15 and Acts 9:25. **he fled and escaped.** Henceforth David would be on the run from Saul.
19:13 idol. The NIV renders the Hebrew term as "household gods." Compare Genesis 31:19, 34–35 and Judges 18:14. The Genesis references imply small objects, while the present reference suggests something larger.
19:14 He is ill. Michal's deception here and again in verse 17 should probably be attributed not to perversity, but to self-preservation. From the perspective of Saul's later behavior (20:32–33), Michal's concern to protect herself from her father seems warranted (see note on 16:2).
19:17 He said to me. See note on verse 14.
■ **19:18–24** *David Aided by Samuel.* When Saul followed David to Ramah, he met Samuel. The two of them went to Naioth, where the Holy Spirit fell on Saul so that he could not pursue David.
19:18 Ramah. See note on 1:1. **Naioth.** This word, which occurs only in the present context, is associated with the place name Ramah and is quite possibly not a proper noun but a descriptive noun signifying "camps" in which the prophets at Ramah were active (possibly cf. the prophets' lodge in 2Ki 6:1–2).
19:20 group of prophets prophesying. See notes on 10:5 and 18:10.
19:22 great cistern at Secu. Secu is otherwise unknown, but it has been tentatively identified with a site about two miles north of Ramah. Alternatively, some have suggested reconstructing the difficult Hebrew (on the basis of the Septuagint, the OT Greek translation) to read "cistern of the threshing floor on the bare height." This site may have been a familiar landmark, such as those that are mentioned fairly frequently in Samuel (20:19; 2Sa 15:17,23; 20:8). **Where are Samuel and David?** See verse 19 and note on 9:18.
19:23 the Spirit of God came even upon him. Having set out to destroy David, Saul in chapter 19 has been repeatedly frustrated by Jonathan, Michal and Samuel, Now God himself frustrated Saul, as the Spirit of God overpowered him (v. 24).
19:24 He stripped off his robes. Robes in the book of Samuel seem to carry a symbolic significance (see note on 2:19), often pertaining to the kingship (see notes on 15:27,28; 18:4; 24:4,5,6). While Jonathan's transference of his robe to David in 18:4 was voluntary, Saul's involuntary divestment here was under the compulsion of God's Spirit (see preceding note). **Is Saul also among the prophets?** Any ambiguity that was present at the first occurrence of this saying (see 10:11 and its note) is effectively removed by the context of this second saying. Saul was in no true sense "among the prophets," but he became so only when overpowered by the Spirit of God (10:6,9).

also prophesied in Samuel's presence. He lay that way all that day and night. This is why
people say, "Is Saul also among the prophets?"[a]

David and Jonathan

20 Then David fled from Naioth at Ramah and went to Jonathan and asked, "What
have I done? What is my crime? How have I wronged[b] your father, that he is trying to take my life?"
2"Never!" Jonathan replied. "You are not going to die! Look, my father doesn't do anything, great or small, without confiding in me. Why would he hide this from me? It's
not so!"
3But David took an oath[c] and said, "Your father knows very well that I have found favor in your eyes, and he has said to himself, 'Jonathan must not know this or he will be
grieved.' Yet as surely as the LORD lives and as you live, there is only a step between me
and death."
4Jonathan said to David, "Whatever you want me to do, I'll do for you."
5So David said, "Look, tomorrow is the New Moon festival,[d] and I am supposed to
dine with the king; but let me go and hide[e] in the field until the evening of the day after
tomorrow. 6If your father misses me at all, tell him, 'David earnestly asked my permission to hurry to Bethlehem,[f] his hometown, because an annual[g] sacrifice is being made
there for his whole clan.' 7If he says, 'Very well,' then your servant is safe. But if he loses his temper,[h] you can be sure that he is determined to harm me. 8As for you, show
kindness to your servant, for you have brought him into a covenant[i] with you before the
LORD. If I am guilty, then kill[j] me yourself! Why hand me over to your father?"
9"Never!" Jonathan said. "If I had the least inkling that my father was determined to
harm you, wouldn't I tell you?"
10David asked, "Who will tell me if your father answers you harshly?"
11"Come," Jonathan said, "let's go out into the field." So they went there together.
12Then Jonathan said to David: "By the LORD, the God of Israel, I will surely sound out
my father by this time the day after tomorrow! If he is favorably disposed toward you, will
I not send you word and let you know? 13But if my father is inclined to harm you, may
the LORD deal with me, be it ever so severely,[k] if I do not let you know and send you away
safely. May the LORD be with[l] you as he has been with my father. 14But show me unfailing kindness like that of the LORD as long as I live, so that I may not be killed, 15and do
not ever cut off your kindness from my family[m]—not even when the LORD has cut off every one of David's enemies from the face of the earth."
16So Jonathan made a covenant[n] with the house of David, saying, "May the LORD call
David's enemies to account." 17And Jonathan had David reaffirm his oath[o] out of love for
him, because he loved him as he loved himself.
18Then Jonathan said to David: "Tomorrow is the New Moon festival. You will be
missed, because your seat will be empty.[p] 19The day after tomorrow, toward evening, go
to the place where you hid[q] when this trouble began, and wait by the stone Ezel. 20I will

19:24 [a]1Sa 10:11
20:1 [b]1Sa 24:9
20:3 [c]Dt 6:13
20:5 [d]Nu 10:10; 28:11 [e]1Sa 19:2
20:6 [f]1Sa 17:58 [g]Dt 12:5
20:7 [h]1Sa 25:17
20:8 [i]1Sa 18:3; 23:18 [j]2Sa 14:32
20:13 [k]Ru 1:17; 1Sa 3:17 [l]Jos 1:5; 1Sa 17:37; 18:12; 1Ch 22:11, 16
20:15 [m]2Sa 9:7
20:16 [n]1Sa 25:22
20:17 [o]1Sa 18:3
20:18 [p]ver 5,25
20:19 [q]1Sa 19:2

■ **20:1–42** *David Aided by Jonathan.* Jonathan aided and encouraged David by informing him of Saul's determination to kill him.
20:1 Naioth. See 19:18 and its note.
20:2 Never! Apparently Jonathan was unaware of the most recent attempts on David's life (19:9–24) and assumed that the oath of 19:6 still stood.
20:3 Jonathan must not know. David readily recognized that Saul's refusal to take Jonathan into his confidence (v. 2) stemmed from Saul's awareness of the radical difference between his own and his son's intentions toward David.
20:5 the New Moon festival. This festival was a time of rejoicing at the beginning of each month. It was marked by the sounding of trumpets (Nu 10:10; Ps 81:3) and by special sacrifices (Nu 28:11–15). This festival is often mentioned in conjunction with the Sabbath (2Ki 4:23; 1Ch 23:31; Ne 10:33; Isa 66:23; Eze 46:3) and may have been subject to similar regulations (Am 8:5). The New Moon celebration is mentioned once in the New Testament (Col 2:16).
20:6 tell him. Jonathan went along with David's pretext in verses 28–29. In evaluating the ethics of such actions, one might compare the Lord's instructions to Samuel in 16:2 (see its note), although in that context the excuse consisted in a half-truth and not, as it seems to be here, in an outright untruth. **Bethlehem.** See note on 16:1. **annual sacrifice.** See notes on 1:3 and 1:21.
20:7 your servant. This address expressed humility and deference (e.g., 1:11,16; 3:10; 17:32; 22:15; 23:10; 25:24).
20:8 covenant. See 18:3–4 and their notes. Pledges of friendship and loyalty would be reiterated in verses 13–17 and 42.
20:13 May the LORD be with you as he has been with my father. This single exception to the lack of reference to the Lord being "with Saul" should be understood in a limited sense relating to the kingship. Recognizing that David was now God's man (see 18:4 and its note; 23:17 and its note), Jonathan gave allegiance to David, which superseded even his allegiance to his own father (v. 16).
20:15 do not ever cut off your kindness. For the fulfillment of this request see 2 Samuel 9:1–8 and 21:7.
20:16 enemies to account. See note on verse 13. Since David himself would be accountable to keep covenant with Jonathan, "enemies" was probably a euphemistic reference to Saul, Jonathan's father (cf. 25:22 [see NIV text note] and 2Sa 12:14).
20:17 oath. See note on verse 8. **he loved him.** See 18:3 and its note, as well as 2 Samuel 1:26 and its note.
20:18 New Moon festival. See note on verse 5.
20:19 stone Ezel. The site is otherwise unattested, and the Septuagint (the Greek translation of the OT) suggests a different reading: "this mound." If the Hebrew text is retained, however, the sense may be something like "departure stone" or "hiding stone," since a verbal root containing the consonants of Ezel is attested in Hebrew (e.g., 9:7; Dt 32:36; Pr 20:14) and in Aramaic (e.g., Ezr 5:15; Da 2:17) with the meanings "go away; disappear." This stone may have been a familiar landmark on the way out of town or known as a good place to hide or disappear. For other such landmarks mentioned in Samuel, see 19:22, 2 Samuel 15:17 and 23, as well as 20:8.

shoot three arrows to the side of it, as though I were shooting at a target. [21]Then I will
send a boy and say, 'Go, find the arrows.' If I say to him, 'Look, the arrows are on this
side of you; bring them here,' then come, because, as surely as the LORD lives, you are
safe; there is no danger. [22]But if I say to the boy, 'Look, the arrows are beyond[r] you,' then
you must go, because the LORD has sent you away. [23]And about the matter you and I discussed—remember, the LORD is witness[s] between you and me forever."
[24]So David hid in the field, and when the New Moon festival came, the king sat down
to eat. [25]He sat in his customary place by the wall, opposite Jonathan,[a] and Abner sat
next to Saul, but David's place was empty.[t] [26]Saul said nothing that day, for he thought,
"Something must have happened to David to make him ceremonially unclean—surely
he is unclean.[u]" [27]But the next day, the second day of the month, David's place was empty again. Then Saul said to his son Jonathan, "Why hasn't the son of Jesse come to the
meal, either yesterday or today?"
[28]Jonathan answered, "David earnestly asked me for permission[v] to go to Bethlehem.
[29]He said, 'Let me go, because our family is observing a sacrifice in the town and my
brother has ordered me to be there. If I have found favor in your eyes, let me get away
to see my brothers.' That is why he has not come to the king's table."
[30]Saul's anger flared up at Jonathan and he said to him, "You son of a perverse and
rebellious woman! Don't I know that you have sided with the son of Jesse to your own
shame and to the shame of the mother who bore you? [31]As long as the son of Jesse lives
on this earth, neither you nor your kingdom will be established. Now send and bring him
to me, for he must die!"
[32]"Why[w] should he be put to death? What[x] has he done?" Jonathan asked his father.
[33]But Saul hurled his spear at him to kill him. Then Jonathan knew that his father intended[y] to kill David.

20:22 [r]ver 37
20:23 [s]ver 14-15; Ge 31:50
20:25 [t]ver 18
20:26 [u]Lev 7:20-21; 15:5; 1Sa 16:5
20:28 [v]ver 6
20:32 [w]1Sa 19:4; Mt 27:23 [x]Ge 31:36; Lk 23:22
20:33 [y]ver 7; 1Sa 18:11, 17

[a] *25* Septuagint; Hebrew *wall. Jonathan arose*

20:23 the LORD is witness between you and me. See Genesis 31:50 and 53.
20:24 New Moon festival. See note on verse 5.
20:25 Abner. Saul's kinsman and military commander (14:50).
20:26 ceremonially unclean. For the present circumstance, see Leviticus 7:21. Laws of cleanliness are covered most fully in Leviticus 11–15, though references to clean and unclean are frequent throughout the Pentateuch (Ge 7:2; Lev 5:2; Nu 5:2; Dt 14:3–21; etc.). The focus was not on physical but on ritual, or religious, uncleanness. In the New Testament, see Hebrews 9:13.
20:28–29 See note on verse 6.
20:30 son of a perverse and rebellious woman! The aspersion, as in modern "son of . . ." expressions, is upon Jonathan, and not necessarily upon his mother.
20:31 neither you nor your kingdom will be established. Despite Samuel's words in 13:14, Saul still clung to dynastic aspirations (cf. 18:8 and its note). Contrast Jonathan's ready acceptance of the Lord's will (see notes on 18:4; 20:13; 23:17). It may be inferred from Saul's words that Jonathan was his firstborn and thus in line for the throne.
20:33 Saul hurled his spear at him. That Saul's and Jonathan's opposite reactions to David had driven a wedge between them was dramatically confirmed by Saul's attempt on Jonathan's life, which matched his earlier attempts on David's life (18:11; 19:10).

David the Fugitive

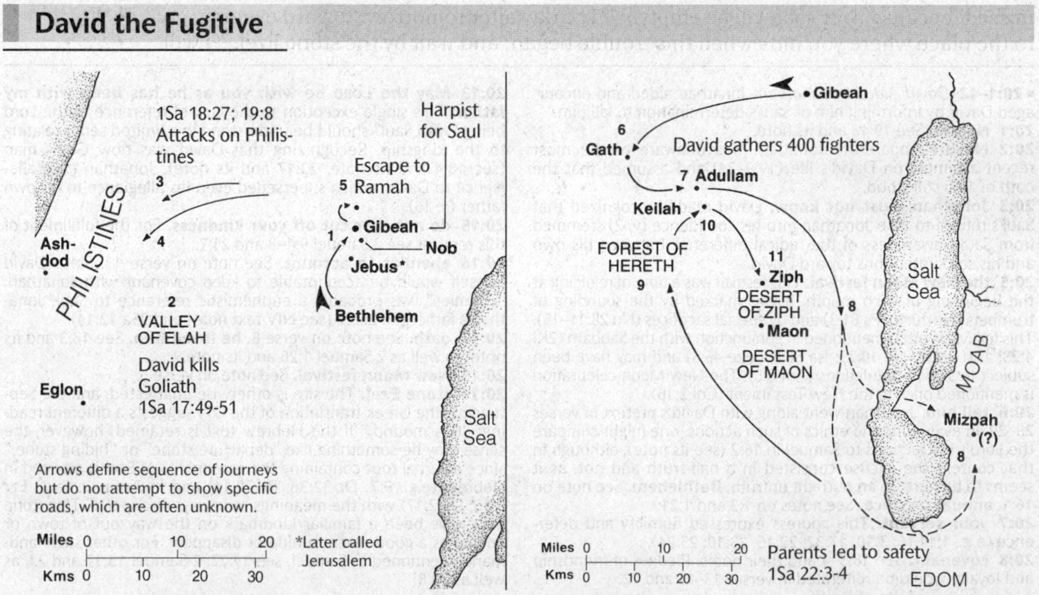

34 Jonathan got up from the table in fierce anger; on that second day of the month he
did not eat, because he was grieved at his father's shameful treatment of David.
35 In the morning Jonathan went out to the field for his meeting with David. He had a
small boy with him, 36 and he said to the boy, "Run and find the arrows I shoot." As the
boy ran, he shot an arrow beyond him. 37 When the boy came to the place where Jonathan's arrow had fallen, Jonathan called out after him, "Isn't the arrow beyond[z] you?"
38 Then he shouted, "Hurry! Go quickly! Don't stop!" The boy picked up the arrow and returned to his master. 39 (The boy knew nothing of all this; only Jonathan and David knew.)
40 Then Jonathan gave his weapons to the boy and said, "Go, carry them back to town."
41 After the boy had gone, David got up from the south side ⌊of the stone⌋ and bowed
down before Jonathan three times, with his face to the ground. Then they kissed each
other and wept together—but David wept the most.
42 Jonathan said to David, "Go in peace,[a] for we have sworn friendship[b] with each other in the name of the LORD, saying, 'The LORD is witness between you and me, and between your descendants and my descendants forever.' " Then David left, and Jonathan
went back to the town.

David at Nob

21 David went to Nob,[c] to Ahimelech the priest. Ahimelech trembled[d] when he met
him, and asked, "Why are you alone? Why is no one with you?"
2 David answered Ahimelech the priest, "The king charged me with a certain matter
and said to me, 'No one is to know anything about your mission and your instructions.'
As for my men, I have told them to meet me at a certain place. 3 Now then, what do you
have on hand? Give me five loaves of bread, or whatever you can find."
4 But the priest answered David, "I don't have any ordinary bread[e] on hand; however, there is some consecrated[f] bread here—provided the men have kept[g] themselves
from women."
5 David replied, "Indeed women have been kept from us, as usual whenever[a] I set out.
The men's things[b] are holy[h] even on missions that are not holy. How much more so today!" 6 So the priest gave him the consecrated bread,[i] since there was no bread there except the bread of the Presence that had been removed from before the LORD and replaced
by hot bread on the day it was taken away.
7 Now one of Saul's servants was there that day, detained before the LORD; he was
Doeg[j] the Edomite,[k] Saul's head shepherd.
8 David asked Ahimelech, "Don't you have a spear or a sword here? I haven't brought
my sword or any other weapon, because the king's business was urgent."
9 The priest replied, "The sword[l] of Goliath the Philistine, whom you killed in the Valley of Elah,[m] is here; it is wrapped in a cloth behind the ephod. If you want it, take it;
there is no sword here but that one."
David said, "There is none like it; give it to me."

David at Gath

10 That day David fled from Saul and went[n] to Achish king of Gath. 11 But the servants

20:37 [z]ver 22
20:42 [a]ver 22; 1Sa 1:17 [b]2Sa 1:26; Pr 18:24
21:1 [c]1Sa 14:3; 22:9, 19; Ne 11:32; Isa 10:32 [d]1Sa 16:4
21:4 [e]Lev 24:8-9 [f]Ex 25:30; Mt 12:4 [g]Ex 19:15
21:5 [h]1Th 4:4
21:6 [i]Lev 24:8-9; Mt 12:3-4; Mk 2:25-28; Lk 6:1-5
21:7 [j]1Sa 22:9,22 [k]1Sa 14:47; Ps 52 Title
21:9 [l]1Sa 17:51 [m]1Sa 17:2
21:10 [n]1Sa 27:2

[a] 5 Or *from us in the past few days since* [b] 5 Or *bodies*

20:42 sworn friendship. See note on verse 8.
■ **21:1–9** *David Aided by Ahimelech.* David persuaded Ahimelech, the priest at Nob, to give him bread and the sword of Goliath.
21:1 Nob. Probably to be associated with a site lying less than two miles northeast of Jerusalem (Isa 10:32), Nob became "the town of the priests" (22:19) sometime after the disaster that befell Shiloh (see notes on 1:3; 2:32) at the hands of the Philistines (4:1–11). **Ahimelech.** Either Ahijah's brother or simply another name for Ahijah (14:3), Ahimelech here occupied the position of high priest, which had once been held by his great-grandfather Eli (1:9). See also Mark 2:26 and its note.
21:2 king charged me. Having employed a pretext to good advantage not long before (see note on 20:6), David did so again, perhaps unnecessarily and with disastrous results for Ahimelech and the priests at Nob (22:6–19). While it is sometimes suggested that David's action may have been well-intentioned (e.g., to protect Ahimelech from the charge of complicity by not forcing a choice between loyalty to Saul or to David), David himself would tell another story in 22:22.
21:4 consecrated bread. That is, "the bread of the Presence" (v. 6; Ex 25:30; 35:13; Lev 24:5–9; 1Ch 9:32). See Jesus' reference to this episode (Mt 12:3–4; Mk 2:25–26; Lk 6:3–4). **kept themselves from women.** This statement does not reflect a negative view of sex but should be understood against the background of ritual cleanliness as a necessary part of consecration prior to battle or other auspicious occasions (Ex 19:15; Lev 15:18; Dt 23:9–14; Jos 3:5; 2Sa 11:11–12).
21:6 bread of the Presence. See verse 4 and its note.
21:7 Doeg the Edomite. That one of Saul's servants was witness to the transaction between David and Ahimelech arouses apprehensions in the reader and apparently also did so in David (22:22). These apprehensions later proved well-founded (22:9–10,18–19). Doeg is also mentioned in the title to Psalm 52.
21:9 sword of Goliath. See note on verse 10; see also 17:51 and 54. **ephod.** See note on 2:28.
■ **21:10–15** *David Aided by Achish.* David proceeded to Gath, where he received help from Achish.
21:10 Achish. See 27:2–12, 29:1–11 and the title to Psalm 34, where "Abimelech" may have been a name for Philistine kings. **Gath.** On the city in general, see notes on 4:1 and 5:8. That David went to Goliath's hometown (17:4) with the very sword of that defeated champion in his hand was either very courageous or very foolish. David's subsequent actions (v. 13) seem to rule out the first option and to confirm the impression that, in contrast to his com-

of Achish said to him, "Isn't this David, the king of the land? Isn't he the one they sing
about in their dances:

> " 'Saul has slain his thousands,
> and David his tens of thousands'?"[o]

12David took these words to heart and was very much afraid of Achish king of Gath.
13So he pretended to be insane[p] in their presence; and while he was in their hands he
acted like a madman, making marks on the doors of the gate and letting saliva run down
his beard.
14Achish said to his servants, "Look at the man! He is insane! Why bring him to me?
15Am I so short of madmen that you have to bring this fellow here to carry on like this
in front of me? Must this man come into my house?"

David at Adullam and Mizpah

22 David left Gath and escaped to the cave[q] of Adullam. When his brothers and his
father's household heard about it, they went down to him there. 2All those who
were in distress or in debt or discontented gathered[r] around him, and he became their
leader. About four hundred men were with him.
3From there David went to Mizpah in Moab and said to the king of Moab, "Would you
let my father and mother come and stay with you until I learn what God will do for me?"
4So he left them with the king of Moab, and they stayed with him as long as David was
in the stronghold.
5But the prophet Gad[s] said to David, "Do not stay in the stronghold. Go into the land
of Judah." So David left and went to the forest of Hereth.

Saul Kills the Priests of Nob

6Now Saul heard that David and his men had been discovered. And Saul, spear in hand,
was seated[t] under the tamarisk[u] tree on the hill at Gibeah, with all his officials standing
around him. 7Saul said to them, "Listen, men of Benjamin! Will the son of Jesse give all of
you fields and vineyards? Will he make all of you commanders[v] of thousands and commanders of hundreds? 8Is that why you have all conspired against me? No one tells me
when my son makes a covenant[w] with the son of Jesse. None of you is concerned[x] about
me or tells me that my son has incited my servant to lie in wait for me, as he does today."
9But Doeg[y] the Edomite, who was standing with Saul's officials, said, "I saw the son
of Jesse come to Ahimelech son of Ahitub at Nob.[z] 10Ahimelech inquired[a] of the LORD for
him; he also gave him provisions[b] and the sword of Goliath the Philistine."

21:11 [o]1Sa 18:7; 29:5; Ps 56 Title
21:13 [p]Ps 34 Title
22:1 [q]2Sa 23:13; Ps 57 Title; 142 Title
22:2 [r]1Sa 23:13; 25:13; 2Sa 15:20
22:5 [s]2Sa 24:11; 1Ch 21:9; 29:29; 2Ch 29:25
22:6 [t]Jdg 4:5 [u]Ge 21:33
22:7 [v]1Sa 8:14
22:8 [w]1Sa 18:3; 20:16 [x]1Sa 23:21
22:9 [y]1Sa 21:7; Ps 52 Title [z]1Sa 21:1
22:10 [a]Nu 27:21; 1Sa 10:22 [b]1Sa 21:6

---

manding first performance against the Philistines "without a sword" (17:50), this episode did not represent David's finest hour.

21:11 David, the king. Even outside Israel, David's royal destiny seems to have been recognized, even if the Philistines' statement is best understood as popular exaggeration. To have a kingly reputation in another king's domain would have been life-endangering, as David knew (v. 12). **David his tens of thousands.** See note on 18:7.

■ **22:1–5** *David Aided by the King of Moab and by Gad.* In rapid succession the narrator described how David received aid from the king of Moab and from the prophet Gad. David was also idealized as one who cared for his family.

■ **22:6—2 Samuel 1:27** *David's Innocence and Saul's Guilt.* In a series of contrasting episodes and groups of episodes, the writer demonstrated that God exalted David because he was innocent and judged Saul for his guilt. These chapters touch on how David and Saul were innocent and guilty, respectively, toward other Israelites (22:6—23:6), toward each other (23:7—26:25) and toward the Philistines (27:1—2Sa 1:27). These contrasts support the theme that David's house was God's choice over the house of Saul.

■ **22:6—23:6** *Toward Other Israelites.* David and Saul are contrasted in the ways they treated other Israelites. Saul killed a priest (22:6–23), while David protected Keilah (23:1–6). David treated his fellow Israelites as their king should have.

■ **22:6–23** *Saul Kills the Priests at Nob.* Saul sought revenge against the priests at Nob who had helped David earlier (see 21:1–9). David showed kindness to a survivor of the event.

22:1 cave of Adullam. Adullam, the meaning of which may be "refuge," has been identified with a site some 17 miles southwest of Jerusalem, midway between Gath and Hebron. (See also 2Sa 23:13; Jos 12:15; cf. titles to Pss 57; 142.) **father's household . . . went down to him.** The vehemence that drove Saul to attack even his own family (20:33) left David's family with little reason to feel secure.

22:3 Mizpah in Moab. The specific location of the present site is unknown. On the name Mizpah ("watchtower"), see note on 7:5. **king of Moab.** Moab had a king as early as Judges 3:12. **stay with you.** David's decision to seek sanctuary in Moab may have been based not only on the assumption that a nation at odds with Saul (14:47) might well wish to side with a rival, but also on David's familial ties with the Moabites (Ru 4:13–17). **what God will do for me?** While taking whatever practical measures were at his disposal, David nevertheless saw God as sovereignly in control of his situation (2Sa 15:25–26).

22:4 the stronghold. See note on 23:14.

22:5 prophet Gad. This prophet would later serve as King David's seer (2Sa 24:11; 2Ch 29:25; cf. 1Ch 29:29). Gad's presence in David's entourage at this point is a reminder that David's destiny was divinely appointed and that he was under the Lord's protection. At the end of this chapter, David would also be joined by a priest (vv. 20–23). **forest of Hereth.** This site, not otherwise mentioned in the Old Testament, must have been located somewhere in Judah.

22:6 spear in hand. The mention of Saul's spear here may be a reminder of his violent temperament (18:10–11; 19:10; 20:33), which would come to full expression later in this chapter. **under the tamarisk tree.** Compare Saul's posture in 14:2–3.

22:7 men of Benjamin. After apparently surrounding himself with members of his own tribe (9:1–2; 10:21), Saul sought to reinforce their loyalty with an appeal to self-interest: Would David, a Judahite, likely show favoritism to Benjamites? **Will the son of Jesse give all of you fields and vineyards?** The reproachful questions addressed by Saul to his officials in this verse suggest that he engaged in at least some of the abusive royal practices that had been the focus of Samuel's warning about kingship in 8:10–18.

22:8 son makes a covenant. See notes on 18:3 and 4.

22:9–14 See *WLC* 135,145.

22:9 Doeg the Edomite. See 21:7 and its note. **Ahimelech son of Ahitub at Nob.** See 21:1 and its note.

11 Then the king sent for the priest Ahimelech son of Ahitub and his father's whole family, who were the priests at Nob, and they all came to the king. 12 Saul said, "Listen now, son of Ahitub."

"Yes, my lord," he answered.

13 Saul said to him, "Why have you conspired[c] against me, you and the son of Jesse, giving him bread and a sword and inquiring of God for him, so that he has rebelled against me and lies in wait for me, as he does today?"

14 Ahimelech answered the king, "Who[d] of all your servants is as loyal as David, the king's son-in-law, captain of your bodyguard and highly respected in your household? 15 Was that day the first time I inquired of God for him? Of course not! Let not the king accuse your servant or any of his father's family, for your servant knows nothing at all about this whole affair."

16 But the king said, "You will surely die, Ahimelech, you and your father's whole family."

17 Then the king ordered the guards at his side: "Turn and kill the priests of the LORD, because they too have sided with David. They knew he was fleeing, yet they did not tell me."

But the king's officials were not willing[e] to raise a hand to strike the priests of the LORD.

18 The king then ordered Doeg, "You turn and strike down the priests." So Doeg the Edomite turned and struck them down. That day he killed eighty-five men who wore the linen ephod.[f] 19 He also put to the sword[g] Nob, the town of the priests, with its men and women, its children and infants, and its cattle, donkeys and sheep.

20 But Abiathar,[h] a son of Ahimelech son of Ahitub, escaped and fled to join David.[i] 21 He told David that Saul had killed the priests of the LORD. 22 Then David said to Abiathar: "That day, when Doeg[j] the Edomite was there, I knew he would be sure to tell Saul. I am responsible for the death of your father's whole family. 23 Stay with me; don't be afraid; the man who is seeking your life[k] is seeking mine also. You will be safe with me."

David Saves Keilah

23 When David was told, "Look, the Philistines are fighting against Keilah[l] and are looting the threshing floors," 2 he inquired[m] of the LORD, saying, "Shall I go and attack these Philistines?"

The LORD answered him, "Go, attack the Philistines and save Keilah."

3 But David's men said to him, "Here in Judah we are afraid. How much more, then, if we go to Keilah against the Philistine forces!"

4 Once again David inquired of the LORD, and the LORD answered him, "Go down to Keilah, for I am going to give the Philistines into your hand.[n]" 5 So David and his men went to Keilah, fought the Philistines and carried off their livestock. He inflicted heavy losses on the Philistines and saved the people of Keilah. 6 (Now Abiathar[o] son of Ahimelech had brought the ephod down with him when he fled to David at Keilah.)

22:13 [c]ver 8
22:14 [d]1Sa 19:4
22:17 [e]Ex 1:17
22:18 [f]1Sa 2:18,31
22:19 [g]1Sa 15:3
22:20 [h]1Sa 23:6,9; 30:7; 1Ki 2:22,26,27 [i]1Sa 2:32
22:22 [j]1Sa 21:7
22:23 [k]1Ki 2:26
23:1 [l]Jos 15:44
23:2 [m]ver 4,12; 1Sa 30:8; 2Sa 5:19,23
23:4 [n]Jos 8:7; Jdg 7:7
23:6 [o]1Sa 22:20

22:13 conspired against me. Saul's assumption that Ahimelech had plotted with David against the king was baseless; Ahimelech had simply been misled by David (see note on 21:2). **rebelled against me and lies in wait for me.** Saul's assumption of hostile motives on David's part was as ill-founded as his own supposition about Ahimelech.
22:14 as loyal as David. Saul had reason to fear for the security of his kingship, not because of David, whose record of loyalty was impeccable, but because of his own failures, which had elicited the Lord's rebuke and rejection (13:13–14; 15:23,26). See *WLC* 144.
22:17 not willing . . . to strike the priests. The sense of evil and irrationality in Saul's command to slaughter the priests of the Lord was heightened by his own men's refusal to carry it out. Saul's men had found it necessary to go against his orders at least once before (see note on 14:45).
22:18 killed eighty-five men. See note on 2:31. **linen ephod.** See note on 2:18.
22:19 men and women, its children and infants. With an irony extremely damaging to Saul's image, the description of the total slaughter of the inhabitants of Nob, "the town of the priests," matches almost verbatim the order that had been given for the slaughter of the Amalekites (15:3) a directive that Saul had failed to carry out.
22:20 Abiathar . . . fled to join David. Support for David continued to build, chiefly as a result of Saul's own misguided attempts at self-preservation. Saul's slaughter of the priests at Nob not only deprived him of what residual priestly backing he might have enjoyed, but also drove the sole surviving priest into David's camp. David now had the support of both prophet (v. 5) and priest. The latter, Abiathar, brought the ephod to David (23:6). It was a means of inquiring of the Lord (see notes on 2:28; 14:3). There can be no doubt that God was sovereignly at work behind the scenes, assuring that the kingdom of the man "after his own heart" (13:14) would be established (see note on 13:14).
22:22 I am responsible. It would have been easy for David to gain from the massacre at Nob by simply condemning Saul. Instead, he readily admitted his own share of responsibility for the disaster (see note on 21:2). In this admission the reader glimpses one of the major differences between David and his predecessor, neither of whom was faultless. This difference was in the quality of their repentance (see notes on 15:24–25,26; 15:30; 2Sa 12:13).
■ **23:1–6** *David Protects Keilah.* In striking contrast to Saul's previous actions, David risked his life for the sake of others, thus demonstrating the qualities of a righteous leader of God's people.
23:1 Keilah. Located about three miles south of Adullam (22:1) near Philistine territory, Keilah is also mentioned in Joshua 15:44. **looting the threshing floors.** Compare Judges 6:3–6.
23:5 saved the people of Keilah. David's liberation of the city of Keilah was in marked contrast to Saul's decimation of the city of Nob in the preceding chapter.
23:6 ephod. Not "the linen ephod" of 22:18, but the ephod that was associated with divine inquiry (see note on 2:28).

Saul Pursues David

7 Saul was told that David had gone to Keilah, and he said, "God has handed him over
to me, for David has imprisoned himself by entering a town with gates and bars." 8 And
Saul called up all his forces for battle, to go down to Keilah to besiege David and his men.
9 When David learned that Saul was plotting against him, he said to Abiathar[p] the
priest, "Bring the ephod." 10 David said, "O LORD, God of Israel, your servant has heard
definitely that Saul plans to come to Keilah and destroy the town on account of me. 11 Will
the citizens of Keilah surrender me to him? Will Saul come down, as your servant has
heard? O LORD, God of Israel, tell your servant."
And the LORD said, "He will."
12 Again David asked, "Will the citizens of Keilah surrender[q] me and my men to
Saul?"
And the LORD said, "They will."
13 So David and his men,[r] about six hundred in number, left Keilah and kept moving
from place to place. When Saul was told that David had escaped from Keilah, he did not
go there.
14 David stayed in the desert strongholds and in the hills of the Desert of Ziph.[s] Day
after day Saul searched[t] for him, but God did not[u] give David into his hands.
15 While David was at Horesh in the Desert of Ziph, he learned that Saul had come out
to take his life. 16 And Saul's son Jonathan went to David at Horesh and helped him find
strength[v] in God. 17 "Don't be afraid," he said. "My father Saul will not lay a hand on you.
You will be king[w] over Israel, and I will be second to you. Even my father Saul knows
this." 18 The two of them made a covenant[x] before the LORD. Then Jonathan went home,
but David remained at Horesh.
19 The Ziphites[y] went up to Saul at Gibeah and said, "Is not David hiding among us[z]
in the strongholds at Horesh, on the hill of Hakilah,[a] south of Jeshimon? 20 Now, O king,
come down whenever it pleases you to do so, and we will be responsible for handing[b]
him over to the king."
21 Saul replied, "The LORD bless you for your concern[c] for me. 22 Go and make further
preparation. Find out where David usually goes and who has seen him there. They tell
me he is very crafty. 23 Find out about all the hiding places he uses and come back to me
with definite information.[a] Then I will go with you; if he is in the area, I will track him
down among all the clans of Judah."
24 So they set out and went to Ziph ahead of Saul. Now David and his men were in the
Desert of Maon,[d] in the Arabah south of Jeshimon. 25 Saul and his men began the search,
and when David was told about it, he went down to the rock and stayed in the Desert of
Maon. When Saul heard this, he went into the Desert of Maon in pursuit of David.

23:9 [p]ver 6; 1Sa 22:20; 30:7
23:12 [q]ver 20
23:13 [r]1Sa 22:2; 25:13
23:14 [s]Jos 15:24,55 [t]Ps 54:3-4 [u]Ps 32:7
23:16 [v]1Sa 30:6
23:17 [w]1Sa 20:31; 24:20
23:18 [x]1Sa 18:3; 20:16, 42; 2Sa 9:1; 21:7
23:19 [y]1Sa 26:1 [z]Ps 54 Title [a]1Sa 26:3
23:20 [b]ver 12
23:21 [c]1Sa 22:8
23:24 [d]Jos 15:55; 1Sa 25:2

[a] *23* Or *me at Nacon*

▪ **23:7—26:25** *Toward Each Other.* Four instances are described to contrast the ways in which David and Saul treated each other. After David barely escaped death by Saul's hand (23:7–29), he spared Saul's life (24:1–22). David was kept from bloodguilt in another situation, even when he did not plan it (25:1–44), and then he spared Saul a second time (26:1–25). Again, David was shown to be a righteous man, as opposed to Saul.

▪ **23:7–29** *David Barely Escapes Saul.* Saul ruthlessly pursued David and would have killed him except that he was hindered by a report of Philistine attacks.

23:7 God has handed him over to me. Saul's theologizing of events was without foundation, as the narrator's diametrically opposed assertion makes clear: "God did not give David into his hands" (v. 14).

23:11–12 See *WCF* 3.2.

23:12 Will the citizens of Keilah surrender me . . . ? In view of Saul's ruthless treatment of the city of Nob, it is perhaps fair to understand the behavior of the Keilahites as reflecting fear, not ingratitude toward David.

23:13 men, about six hundred. The growth of David's company from 400 (22:2) to 600 was but another indication of his increasing strength (see note on 22:20).

23:14 desert strongholds. The term "strongholds" suggests a geographical area and not a single location (cf. 22:4; 2Sa 5:17; 23:14). **Desert of Ziph.** The village of Ziph was located about ten miles southeast of Keilah and four miles southeast of Hebron. The reference would be to the desert area in that vicinity, south of Hebron. Ziph is mentioned in Joshua 15:55, along with Maon (v. 24) and Carmel (15:12; 25:2), among the hill country villages of Judah. **God did not give David into his hands.** No matter how concealed his actions at times, God was clearly in sovereign control of David's destiny. See notes on verse 7 and 22:20.

23:16 Saul's son Jonathan . . . helped him find strength in God. No longer ignorant of his father's malevolence toward David (cf. 20:2), Jonathan acted as a true friend, not by playing down the difficulties, but by aiding David in finding strength where true strength could alone be found. See 30:6, where David, again in dire straits, once more found "strength in the LORD his God."

23:17 I will be second to you. Although in point of fact Jonathan would not survive to become second to David (31:2), his readiness to relinquish personal ambitions in the interest of God's man (18:4; 20:13) continued to function as a foil to Saul's desperate efforts to hang on to a kingdom that was no longer his (15:23). **Saul knows this.** See 20:30–31. Saul's refusal to accept his rejection gracefully (cf. Eli's response under similar circumstances in 3:18) cannot be excused on the grounds that he did not know to whom the kingdom should go.

23:18 covenant. See notes on 18:3 and 4.

23:19 Ziphites. See notes on 23:14 and 26:1. **Gibeah.** This was Saul's hometown (10:26; see notes on 10:5; 13:2). **hill of Hakilah, south of Jeshimon?** The location of this site is uncertain (v. 24; 26:1,3).

23:24 Desert of Maon. Situated some eight miles south of Hebron, Maon is mentioned in 25:2 as the hometown of Nabal. **Arabah.** This name is given to dry, desert regions, especially in the rift valley both north and south of the Dead Sea (which is sometimes called the Sea of the Arabah; Jos 3:16; 12:3; etc.).

26 Saul[e] was going along one side of the mountain, and David and his men were on
the other side, hurrying to get away from Saul. As Saul and his forces were closing in on
David and his men to capture them, 27 a messenger came to Saul, saying, "Come quickly! The Philistines are raiding the land." 28 Then Saul broke off his pursuit of David and
went to meet the Philistines. That is why they call this place Sela Hammahlekoth.[a] 29 And
David went up from there and lived in the strongholds of En Gedi.[f]

David Spares Saul's Life

24 After Saul returned from pursuing the Philistines, he was told, "David is in the
Desert of En Gedi.[g]" 2 So Saul took three thousand chosen men from all Israel
and set out to look[h] for David and his men near the Crags of the Wild Goats.
3 He came to the sheep pens along the way; a cave[i] was there, and Saul went in to relieve[j] himself. David and his men were far back in the cave. 4 The men said, "This is the
day the LORD spoke[k] of when he said[b] to you, 'I will give your enemy into your hands for
you to deal with as you wish.' "[l] Then David crept up unnoticed and cut off a corner of
Saul's robe.
5 Afterward, David was conscience-stricken[m] for having cut off a corner of his robe.
6 He said to his men, "The LORD forbid that I should do such a thing to my master, the
LORD's anointed,[n] or lift my hand against him; for he is the anointed of the LORD." 7 With
these words David rebuked his men and did not allow them to attack Saul. And Saul left
the cave and went his way.
8 Then David went out of the cave and called out to Saul, "My lord the king!" When
Saul looked behind him, David bowed down and prostrated himself with his face to the
ground.[o] 9 He said to Saul, "Why do you listen when men say, 'David is bent on harming
you'? 10 This day you have seen with your own eyes how the LORD delivered you into my
hands in the cave. Some urged me to kill you, but I spared you; I said, 'I will not lift my
hand against my master, because he is the LORD's anointed.' 11 See, my father, look at this
piece of your robe in my hand! I cut off the corner of your robe but did not kill you. Now
understand and recognize that I am not guilty[p] of wrongdoing or rebellion. I have not
wronged you, but you are hunting[q] me down to take my life. 12 May the LORD judge[r] between you and me. And may the LORD avenge[s] the wrongs you have done to me, but my
hand will not touch you. 13 As the old saying goes, 'From evildoers come evil deeds,'[t] so
my hand will not touch you.
14 "Against whom has the king of Israel come out? Whom are you pursuing? A dead
dog?[u] A flea?[v] 15 May the LORD be our judge[w] and decide between us. May he consider
my cause and uphold[x] it; may he vindicate[y] me by delivering[z] me from your hand."
16 When David finished saying this, Saul asked, "Is that your voice,[a] David my son?"
And he wept aloud. 17 "You are more righteous than I,"[b] he said. "You have treated me

23:26 [e]Ps 17:9
23:29 [f]2Ch 20:2
24:1 [g]1Sa 23:28-29
24:2 [h]1Sa 26:2
24:3 [i]Ps 57 Title; 142 Title [j]Jdg 3:24
24:4 [k]1Sa 25:28-30 [l]1Sa 23:17; 26:8
24:5 [m]2Sa 24:10
24:6 [n]1Sa 26:11
24:8 [o]1Sa 25:23-24
24:11 [p]Ps 7:3 [q]1Sa 23:14,23; 1Sa 26:20
24:12 [r]Ge 16:5; 31:53; Job 5:8 [s]Jdg 11:27; 1Sa 26:10
24:13 [t]Mt 7:20
24:14 [u]1Sa 17:43; 2Sa 9:8 [v]1Sa 26:20
24:15 [w]ver 12 [x]Ps 35:1, 23; Mic 7:9 [y]Ps 43:1 [z]Ps 119:134,154
24:16 [a]1Sa 26:17
24:17 [b]Ge 38:26; 1Sa 26:21

[a] *28 Sela Hammahlekoth* means *rock of parting.* [b] *4* Or *"Today the LORD is saying*

23:27 Philistines are raiding the land. The providential timing of this Philistine incursion is hard to overlook.
23:28 Saul broke off his pursuit. It was to Saul's credit that in this instance he sacrificed personal concerns in the interest of national security.
23:29 strongholds of En Gedi. Deriving its name, "goat's spring," from a large spring issuing from the steep western shore of the Dead Sea, En Gedi and its vicinity afforded David provision and protection in his continued efforts to elude Saul.
■ **24:1–22** *David Spares Saul for the First Time.* The first episode that demonstrated David's innocence of unjust killing occurred in a cave at En Gedi.
24:1 Desert of En Gedi. See note on 23:29.
24:4 This is the day the LORD spoke of when he said to you. While it is more providential than coincidental that Saul chose to seek relief in the same cave in which David and his men were hiding, there has been no hint to this point that God intended David to lift a hand against Saul. The suggestion by David's men that he do so was presumably based on their own incorrect inference drawn from the present propitious circumstances, possibly in conjunction with knowledge of David's anointed status and royal destiny. Or it may simply betray a desire to exploit an advantage, regardless of theological scruple (cf. David's action in v. 6). **cut off a corner of Saul's robe.** David resisted the prompting of his men to do Saul physical harm (v. 7), restricting himself to a more symbolic act (see note on v. 5).
24:5 David was conscience-stricken for having cut off a corner of his robe. Although David would later display the corner of Saul's robe as evidence of his goodwill toward Saul (v. 11), his pangs of conscience (cf. 2Sa 24:10) suggest that a desire to secure a visible testimonial may not have been his initial, and certainly not his sole, motivation for his action. In view of the symbolic significance of robes (see notes on 15:27,28; 18:4; 19:24), David's remorse may have stemmed from what he now perceived to be an inappropriate, albeit symbolic, grasping after the kingship and an act of aggression toward the Lord's anointed (v. 6).
24:6 for he is the anointed of the LORD. Despite Saul's misbehavior, David recognized and safeguarded the sanctity of the Lord's anointed (26:9; cf. note on 2:10), while leaving judgment and vengeance to the Lord (v. 12).
24:12 And may the LORD avenge ... but my hand will not touch you. David's refusal to avenge himself implied neither his indifference to justice nor an insensitivity to the wrongs he had suffered, but was a recognition that vengeance is the Lord's prerogative (Dt 32:35; Ps 94:1; Ro 12:19). See *WLC* 135.
24:13 old saying. David's point seems to be akin to the New Testament teaching that "by their fruit you will recognize them" (Mt 7:16,20). David was vindicated by his restraint in not killing Saul, while Saul's own evil was proven by his efforts to do David evil.
24:14 A dead dog? David abased himself before Saul, as Mephibosheth would later do before David (2Sa 9:8). The expression "dead dog" occurs only three times in the Old Testament, the third occurrence being in 2 Samuel 16:9. "Dog" is also used as a term of abasement (e.g., in 17:43; 2Sa 3:8; 2Ki 8:13). **A flea?** The Hebrew reads "A single flea?" See 26:20.
24:17 You are more righteous than I. Having just escaped with

well,[c] but I have treated you badly. 18You have just now told me of the good you did to
me; the LORD delivered[d] me into your hands, but you did not kill me. 19When a man finds
his enemy, does he let him get away unharmed? May the LORD reward you well for the
way you treated me today. 20I know that you will surely be king[e] and that the kingdom[f]
of Israel will be established in your hands. 21Now swear[g] to me by the LORD that you will
not cut off my descendants or wipe out my name from my father's family.[h]"
22So David gave his oath to Saul. Then Saul returned home, but David and his men
went up to the stronghold.[i]

David, Nabal and Abigail

25 Now Samuel died,[j] and all Israel assembled and mourned[k] for him; and they
buried him at his home in Ramah.[l]
Then David moved down into the Desert of Maon.[a] 2A certain man in Maon,[m] who
had property there at Carmel, was very wealthy. He had a thousand goats and three
thousand sheep, which he was shearing in Carmel. 3His name was Nabal and his wife's
name was Abigail.[n] She was an intelligent and beautiful woman, but her husband, a Calebite,[o] was surly and mean in his dealings.
4While David was in the desert, he heard that Nabal was shearing sheep. 5So he sent
ten young men and said to them, "Go up to Nabal at Carmel and greet him in my name.
6Say to him: 'Long life to you! Good health[p] to you and your household! And good health
to all that is yours![q]
7" 'Now I hear that it is sheep-shearing time. When your shepherds were with us, we
did not mistreat[r] them, and the whole time they were at Carmel nothing of theirs was
missing. 8Ask your own servants and they will tell you. Therefore be favorable toward my
young men, since we come at a festive time. Please give your servants and your son David whatever[s] you can find for them.' "
9When David's men arrived, they gave Nabal this message in David's name. Then they
waited.
10Nabal answered David's servants, "Who[t] is this David? Who is this son of Jesse?
Many servants are breaking away from their masters these days. 11Why should I take my
bread[u] and water, and the meat I have slaughtered for my shearers, and give it to men
coming from who knows where?"
12David's men turned around and went back. When they arrived, they reported every word. 13David said to his men, "Put on your swords!" So they put on their swords, and
David put on his. About four hundred men went[v] up with David, while two hundred
stayed with the supplies.[w]
14One of the servants told Nabal's wife Abigail: "David sent messengers from the desert to give our master his greetings,[x] but he hurled insults at them. 15Yet these men were
very good to us. They did not mistreat[y] us, and the whole time we were out in the fields
near them nothing was missing.[z] 16Night and day they were a wall[a] around us all the

24:17 [c]Mt 5:44
24:18 [d]1Sa 26:23
24:20 [e]1Sa 23:17 [f]1Sa 13:14
24:21 [g]Ge 21:23; 2Sa 21:1-9 [h]1Sa 20:14-15
24:22 [i]1Sa 23:29
25:1 [j]1Sa 28:3 [k]Nu 20:29; Dt 34:8 [l]Ge 21:21; 2Ch 33:20
25:2 [m]Jos 15:55; 1Sa 23:24
25:3 [n]Pr 31:10 [o]Jos 15:13
25:6 [p]Ps 122:7; Lk 10:5 [q]1Ch 12:18
25:7 [r]ver 15
25:8 [s]Ne 8:10
25:10 [t]Jdg 9:28
25:11 [u]Jdg 8:6
25:13 [v]1Sa 23:13 [w]1Sa 30:24
25:14 [x]1Sa 13:10
25:15 [y]ver 7 [z]ver 21
25:16 [a]Ex 14:22; Job 1:10

a *1* Some Septuagint manuscripts; Hebrew *Paran*

his life, Saul experienced a rare moment of remorse and objectivity. His testimony to David's superior righteousness provides an important element in the defense of David's eventual rule; even David's predecessor, in this moment of lucidity, acknowledged that David did not gain power by illicit means.

24:20 I know . . . that the kingdom of Israel will be established in your hands. Contrast Samuel's rebuke of Saul in 13:14, "But now your kingdom will not endure." In essence, Saul here recognized that David, who had refused to take matters into his own hands but had trusted God, was destined to accomplish what Saul had forfeited by his own opposite actions in 13:8–10. It is worth noting, however, that in contrast to Jonathan's action in 18:4 (see its note), Saul gave no sign of relinquishing the throne to David. See also 26:25 and its note.

24:21 not cut off my descendants. See 20:14–15.

■ **25:1–44** *David Kept From Bloodguilt.* Abigail wisely protected David from his own impulsivity because of her belief in his royal future.

25:1 Now Samuel died. The death of Samuel signals the passing of an era and sets the stage for Saul's misdeeds in chapter 28 (28:3). **all Israel . . . mourned for him.** This was a sign of Samuel's prominence as a leader. Compare the mourning that accompanied the deaths of Jacob (Ge 50:3,10), Aaron (Nu 20:29) and Moses (Dt 34:8). **Ramah.** See 1:1, 7:17 and 9:6 and their notes. **Desert of Maon.** See note on 23:24.

25:2 Carmel. This is the same Carmel at which Saul had erected a monument in his own honor (see 15:12 and its note). The setting of this chapter in the vicinity of Maon, and Carmel is the first of many reminders of Saul in the chapter, although the narrative is, strictly speaking, about David's altercation with Nabal.

25:3 Nabal. In verse 25 Abigail expounded this name as connoting "folly." If it seems unlikely that parents would have named a child "fool," it may simply be that this was a disparaging play on a name that sounded like "fool." **Abigail.** Abigail's character was as dissimilar to her husband's as was her name to his: "Abigail" means something like "my father rejoices." **Calebite.** On Calebite tribal holdings, see Joshua 14:13 and 15:13. The similarity of the name "Caleb" to the Hebrew word for "dog" may account for the inclusion of this particular detail in the introduction of Nabal, whose brutishness is one of the main points of the chapter.

25:8 your son David. Compare the filial posture adopted by David in addressing Saul as "my father" in 24:11.

25:14 he hurled insults at them. Nabal's attack on David's messengers was vicious. The Hebrew verb here rendered "hurled insults" means literally "to shriek at" or "to fly at" and is closely related to the Hebrew noun for "bird[s] of prey." The same verb was used of Saul in 15:19 to describe his unrestrained "pounc[ing]" upon the Amalekite spoils (cf. 14:32).

25:16 they were a wall around us. Not only had David's men refrained from inflicting harm (v. 7), but their presence had actually provided protection for the herds and herders of Nabal (v. 21).

time we were herding our sheep near them. 17Now think it over and see what you can
do, because disaster is hanging over our master and his whole household. He is such a
wicked[b] man that no one can talk to him."
18Abigail lost no time. She took two hundred loaves of bread, two skins of wine, five
dressed sheep, five seahs[a] of roasted grain, a hundred cakes of raisins[c] and two hundred
cakes of pressed figs, and loaded them on donkeys.[d] 19Then she told her servants, "Go
on ahead;[e] I'll follow you." But she did not tell her husband Nabal.
20As she came riding her donkey into a mountain ravine, there were David and his
men descending toward her, and she met them. 21David had just said, "It's been useless—all my watching over this fellow's property in the desert so that nothing of his was
missing. He has paid[f] me back evil for good. 22May God deal with David,[b] be it ever so
severely,[g] if by morning I leave alive one male[h] of all who belong to him!"
23When Abigail saw David, she quickly got off her donkey and bowed down before David with her face to the ground.[i] 24She fell at his feet and said: "My lord, let the blame
be on me alone. Please let your servant speak to you; hear what your servant has to say.
25May my lord pay no attention to that wicked man Nabal. He is just like his name—his
name is Fool,[j] and folly goes with him. But as for me, your servant, I did not see the men
my master sent.
26"Now since the LORD has kept you, my master, from bloodshed[k] and from avenging[l] yourself with your own hands, as surely as the LORD lives and as you live, may your
enemies and all who intend to harm my master be like Nabal.[m] 27And let this gift,[n] which
your servant has brought to my master, be given to the men who follow you. 28Please forgive[o] your servant's offense, for the LORD will certainly make a lasting[p] dynasty for my
master, because he fights the LORD's battles.[q] Let no wrongdoing[r] be found in you as long
as you live. 29Even though someone is pursuing you to take your life, the life of my master will be bound securely in the bundle of the living by the LORD your God. But the lives
of your enemies he will hurl[s] away as from the pocket of a sling. 30When the LORD has
done for my master every good thing he promised concerning him and has appointed
him leader[t] over Israel, 31my master will not have on his conscience the staggering burden of needless bloodshed or of having avenged himself. And when the LORD has brought
my master success, remember[u] your servant."
32David said to Abigail, "Praise[v] be to the LORD, the God of Israel, who has sent you
today to meet me. 33May you be blessed for your good judgment and for keeping me from
bloodshed[w] this day and from avenging myself with my own hands. 34Otherwise, as surely as the LORD, the God of Israel, lives, who has kept me from harming you, if you had not
come quickly to meet me, not one male belonging to Nabal would have been left alive
by daybreak."
35Then David accepted from her hand what she had brought him and said, "Go
home in peace. I have heard your words and granted[x] your request."

25:17 [b]1Sa 20:7
25:18 [c]1Ch 12:40 [d]2Sa 16:1
25:19 [e]Ge 32:20
25:21 [f]Ps 109:5
25:22 [g]1Sa 3:17; 20:13 [h]1Ki 14:10; 21:21; 2Ki 9:8
25:23 [i]1Sa 20:41
25:25 [j]Pr 14:16
25:26 [k]ver 33 [l]Heb 10:30 [m]2Sa 18:32
25:27 [n]Ge 33:11; 1Sa 30:26
25:28 [o]ver 24 [p]2Sa 7:11, 26 [q]1Sa 18:17 [r]1Sa 24:11
25:29 [s]Jer 10:18
25:30 [t]1Sa 13:14
25:31 [u]Ge 40:14
25:32 [v]Ge 24:27; Ex 18:10; Lk 1:68
25:33 [w]ver 26
25:35 [x]Ge 19:21; 1Sa 20:42; 2Ki 5:19

[a] *18* That is, probably about a bushel (about 37 liters) [b] *22* Some Septuagint manuscripts; Hebrew *with David's enemies*

25:17 He is such a wicked man that no one can talk to him. Nabal's plight was a function of his own wickedness. His lack of knowledge was a refusal to know.
25:19 But she did not tell her husband Nabal. In refusing to confide in her husband, Abigail expressed her lack of confidence in him, which is not at all surprising in light of Nabal's churlishness (v. 17). See Jonathan's similar action in 14:1 (see its note). In view of Abigail's remarkable insight into the Lord's choice of David (see v. 28 and its note), her decision to go against her husband's wishes seems to fall under the category of obeying "God rather than men" (Ac 5:29).
25:22 if by morning I leave alive one male. Unrestrained by any special status of the man Nabal, David, in contrast to his behavior in the preceding chapter, was intent upon exacting personal revenge. See *WCF* 22.4; *WLC* 113.
25:23 bowed down before David. Abigail adopted a posture similar to that of David before Saul in the preceding chapter (24:8).
25:25 He is just like his name. See note on verse 3. The play on words in English, "fool"/"folly," nicely reflects the Hebrew.
25:28 lasting dynasty. Abigail's perception of the Lord's plans for David (see 2Sa 7:11–16) was as remarkable as her husband's lack thereof (vv. 10–11). **he fights the LORD's battles.** See note on 14:24. Abigail's words insinuate the difference between David's proper military role and the personal vendetta upon which he had now embarked. Righteous engagement in conflict involves boldly standing for God, while leaving personal injury and insult to be dealt with by the Lord. **Let no wrongdoing be found in you.** While David had scrupulously avoided lifting a hand against the Lord's anointed (24:6,10), he seems to have felt no such compunction when it came to individuals not enjoying that special status. Had David taken personal revenge on an enemy, even a person like Nabal, he would have shown himself to have been little better than Saul, and David later praised the Lord for using Abigail to deter him from such a transgression (v. 32).
25:29 Even though someone is pursuing you to take your life. This was a hard-to-miss reminder of Saul's hostility toward David, so clearly evidenced in the two chapters that surround the present one. **bound securely in the bundle.** The pairing of "bound" with "bundle" provides an apt English equivalent to a metaphorical wordplay in the Hebrew that pictures the security of one who is willing to trust fully in God. See following note. **hurl away as from the pocket of a sling.** A second metaphorical wordplay (see preceding note on "bound securely in the bundle") that describes the fate of David's, and hence God's, enemies. It may be rendered, "The lives of your enemies he will sling away as from the pocket of a sling."
25:32–34 See *WCF* 22.4; *WLC* 113.
25:32 Praise be to the LORD . . . who has sent you today to meet me. David recognized God's providential hand in Abigail's intervention to prevent him from taking personal vengeance, and he praised the Lord, as well as blessed Abigail, for her good judgment (v. 33).

36 When Abigail went to Nabal, he was in the house holding a banquet like that of a
king. He was in high[y] spirits and very drunk.[z] So she told[a] him nothing until daybreak.
37 Then in the morning, when Nabal was sober, his wife told him all these things, and his
heart failed him and he became like a stone. 38 About ten days later, the LORD struck[b] Nabal and he died.
39 When David heard that Nabal was dead, he said, "Praise be to the LORD, who has
upheld my cause against Nabal for treating me with contempt. He has kept his servant
from doing wrong and has brought Nabal's wrongdoing down on his own head."
Then David sent word to Abigail, asking her to become his wife. 40 His servants went
to Carmel and said to Abigail, "David has sent us to you to take you to become his wife."
41 She bowed down with her face to the ground and said, "Here is your maidservant,
ready to serve you and wash the feet of my master's servants." 42 Abigail[c] quickly got on
a donkey and, attended by her five maids, went with David's messengers and became his
wife. 43 David had also married Ahinoam[d] of Jezreel, and they both were his wives.[e] 44 But
Saul had given his daughter Michal, David's wife, to Paltiel[a][f] son of Laish, who was from
Gallim.[g]

David Again Spares Saul's Life

26 The Ziphites[h] went to Saul at Gibeah and said, "Is not David hiding[i] on the hill
of Hakilah, which faces Jeshimon?"
2 So Saul went down to the Desert of Ziph, with his three thousand chosen men of Israel, to search[j] there for David. 3 Saul made his camp beside the road on the hill of Hakilah facing Jeshimon, but David stayed in the desert. When he saw that Saul had followed him there, 4 he sent out scouts and learned that Saul had definitely arrived.[b]
5 Then David set out and went to the place where Saul had camped. He saw where
Saul and Abner[k] son of Ner, the commander of the army, had lain down. Saul was lying
inside the camp, with the army encamped around him.
6 David then asked Ahimelech the Hittite and Abishai son of Zeruiah,[l] Joab's brother, "Who will go down into the camp with me to Saul?"
"I'll go with you," said Abishai.
7 So David and Abishai went to the army by night, and there was Saul, lying asleep inside the camp with his spear stuck in the ground near his head. Abner and the soldiers
were lying around him.
8 Abishai said to David, "Today God has delivered your enemy into your hands. Now
let me pin him to the ground with one thrust of my spear; I won't strike him twice."
9 But David said to Abishai, "Don't destroy him! Who can lay a hand on the LORD's
anointed[m] and be guiltless?[n] 10 As surely as the LORD lives," he said, "the LORD himself
will strike[o] him; either his time[p] will come and he will die,[q] or he will go into battle and
perish. 11 But the LORD forbid that I should lay a hand on the LORD's anointed. Now get
the spear and water jug that are near his head, and let's go."
12 So David took the spear and water jug near Saul's head, and they left. No one saw
or knew about it, nor did anyone wake up. They were all sleeping, because the LORD had
put them into a deep sleep.[r]
13 Then David crossed over to the other side and stood on top of the hill some distance

25:36 [y] 2Sa 13:23 [z] Pr 20:1; Isa 5:11, 22; Hos 4:11 [a] ver 19
25:38 [b] 1Sa 26:10; 2Sa 6:7
25:42 [c] Ge 24:61-67
25:43 [d] Jos 15:56 [e] 1Sa 27:3; 30:5
25:44 [f] 2Sa 3:15 [g] Isa 10:30
26:1 [h] 1Sa 23:19 [i] Ps 54 Title
26:2 [j] 1Sa 13:2; 24:2
26:5 [k] 1Sa 14:50; 17:55
26:6 [l] Jdg 7:10-11; 1Ch 2:16
26:9 [m] 2Sa 1:14 [n] 1Sa 24:5
26:10 [o] 1Sa 25:38; Ro 12:19 [p] Ge 47:29; Dt 31:14; Ps 37:13 [q] 1Sa 31:6; 2Sa 1:1
26:12 [r] Ge 2:21; 15:12

[a] *44* Hebrew *Palti,* a variant of *Paltiel* [b] *4* Or *had come to Nacon*

25:36 a banquet like that of a king. This notice provides yet another hint that Nabal was meant to remind the reader of Saul, the king.
25:37 when Nabal was sober. Literally, "when the wine had gone out of Nabal." "Nabal" sounds a lot like the Hebrew word for "storage jar" (for wine, among other things), which suggests a further disparaging pun on the culprit's name.
25:39 Praise be to the LORD. Though it would have been wrong for David to have taken matters into his own hands, this was not because Nabal was undeserving of punishment. Having now heard of the Lord's dealing with Nabal, David offered double praise to God for preventing him from personal wrongdoing, while at the same time upholding his cause.
25:40–44 Abigail . . . Ahinoam . . . Michal. David now had three wives: Michal, daughter of Saul, who in David's absence had been given to another; Ahinoam, who remarkably had the same name as Saul's wife (14:50); and Abigail, the former wife of Nabal, Saul's "alter ego" in chapter 25. See also 2 Samuel 2:2 and 3:2–3.
■ **26:1–25** *David Spares Saul a Second Time.* For a second time David showed his commitment not to harm Saul.
26:1 Ziphites went to Saul. See notes on 23:19.
26:6 Ahimelech. Inasmuch as Ahimelech the Hittite, not otherwise mentioned in the Bible, did not accompany David on his clandestine foray into Saul's camp, the explicit reference to him here is somewhat puzzling. Perhaps the narrator included this detail to recollect Saul's slaughter of a different Ahimelech in chapter 22 in order that David's clemency in the present chapter might capture the reader's attention all the more by comparison. **Hittite.** The first Biblical mention of Hittites is in Genesis 10:15. There is some uncertainty whether all references to Hittites refer to the same group. **Abishai son of Zeruiah, Joab's brother.** See notes on 2 Samuel 2:18.
26:8 Today God has delivered. See note on 24:4.
26:9 Who can lay a hand on the LORD's anointed and be guiltless? See 24:6 and its note.
26:10 the LORD himself will strike him. David's words reveal an assurance gained, or at least reinforced, by his recent experience of the Lord's dealings with Nabal in chapter 25.
26:12 the LORD had put them into a deep sleep. This is yet another indication that David's survival and ultimate success were divinely overseen and directed (see also 30:2,19).

away; there was a wide space between them. 14He called out to the army and to Abner
son of Ner, "Aren't you going to answer me, Abner?"
Abner replied, "Who are you who calls to the king?"
15David said, "You're a man, aren't you? And who is like you in Israel? Why didn't you
guard your lord the king? Someone came to destroy your lord the king. 16What you have
done is not good. As surely as the LORD lives, you and your men deserve to die, because
you did not guard your master, the LORD's anointed. Look around you. Where are the
king's spear and water jug that were near his head?"
17Saul recognized David's voice and said, "Is that your voice,[s] David my son?"
David replied, "Yes it is, my lord the king." 18And he added, "Why is my lord pursuing his servant? What have I done, and what wrong[t] am I guilty of? 19Now let my lord the
king listen to his servant's words. If the LORD has incited you against me, then may he
accept an offering.[u] If, however, men have done it, may they be cursed before the LORD!
They have now driven me from my share in the LORD's inheritance[v] and have said, 'Go,
serve other gods.' 20Now do not let my blood fall to the ground far from the presence of
the LORD. The king of Israel has come out to look for a flea[w]—as one hunts a partridge
in the mountains."
21Then Saul said, "I have sinned.[x] Come back, David my son. Because you considered
my life precious[y] today, I will not try to harm you again. Surely I have acted like a fool
and have erred greatly."
22"Here is the king's spear," David answered. "Let one of your young men come over
and get it. 23The LORD rewards[z] every man for his righteousness[a] and faithfulness. The
LORD delivered you into my hands today, but I would not lay a hand on the LORD's
anointed. 24As surely as I valued your life today, so may the LORD value my life and deliver[b] me from all trouble."
25Then Saul said to David, "May you be blessed, my son David; you will do great
things and surely triumph."
So David went on his way, and Saul returned home.

26:17 [s]1Sa 24:16
26:18 [t]1Sa 24:9,11-14
26:19 [u]2Sa 16:11 [v]2Sa 14:16
26:20 [w]1Sa 24:14
26:21 [x]Ex 9:27; 1Sa 15:24 [y]1Sa 24:17
26:23 [z]Ps 62:12 [a]Ps 7:8; 18:20,24
26:24 [b]Ps 54:7

26:15–16 See *WLC* 127.
26:19 LORD's inheritance. See note on 2 Samuel 20:19. **Go, serve other gods.** David was indicating not his own theological understanding, but that of his presumed opponents.
26:20 far from the presence of the LORD. That is, far from the center of the worship of the Lord. **a flea.** See 24:14. **a partridge in the mountains.** The partridge, whose name in Hebrew means "caller," is a cleverly chosen analogue to David, who himself stood upon the crest of a mountain and "called" (vv. 13–14).
26:21 I have sinned. Come back. David's response to Saul's confession and invitation indicated that he doubted Saul's sincerity (v. 22). Compare Samuel's response to a similar invitation by Saul in 15:21–26. **Surely I have acted like a fool.** Although a different word is used here, Saul's admission of folly draws the knot of comparison between himself and the fool of the preceding chapter yet tighter (see notes on 25:2,14,25,36).
26:25 May you be blessed, my son David. Saul's behavior was erratic, and David found neither his confessions nor his blessings sufficiently reassuring to do anything but keep a safe distance (27:1). See note on 24:20.

Exploits of David

Arrows show directions and sequence of journeys but do not attempt to define specific roads, which are largely unknown.

Numerals follow in sequence from the previous map, found at 1 Samuel 20.

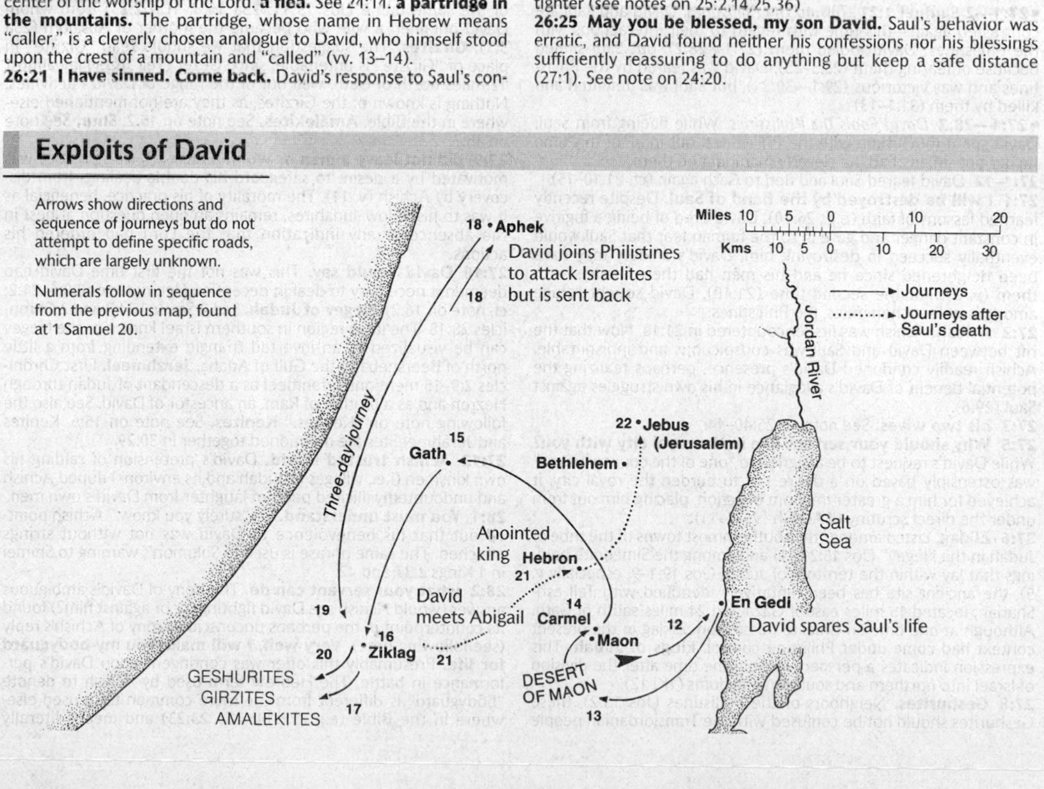

David Among the Philistines

27 But David thought to himself, "One of these days I will be destroyed by the hand
of Saul. The best thing I can do is to escape to the land of the Philistines. Then
Saul will give up searching for me anywhere in Israel, and I will slip out of his hand."
2 So David and the six hundred men[c] with him left and went[d] over to Achish[e] son of
Maoch king of Gath. 3 David and his men settled in Gath with Achish. Each man had his
family with him, and David had his two wives:[f] Ahinoam of Jezreel and Abigail of Carmel, the widow of Nabal. 4 When Saul was told that David had fled to Gath, he no longer searched for him.
5 Then David said to Achish, "If I have found favor in your eyes, let a place be assigned
to me in one of the country towns, that I may live there. Why should your servant live in
the royal city with you?"
6 So on that day Achish gave him Ziklag,[g] and it has belonged to the kings of Judah
ever since. 7 David lived[h] in Philistine territory a year and four months.
8 Now David and his men went up and raided the Geshurites,[i] the Girzites and the Amalekites.[j] (From ancient times these peoples had lived in the land extending to Shur[k] and
Egypt.) 9 Whenever David attacked an area, he did not leave a man or woman alive,[l] but
took sheep and cattle, donkeys and camels, and clothes. Then he returned to Achish.
10 When Achish asked, "Where did you go raiding today?" David would say, "Against
the Negev of Judah" or "Against the Negev of Jerahmeel[m]" or "Against the Negev of the
Kenites.[n]" 11 He did not leave a man or woman alive to be brought to Gath, for he
thought, "They might inform on us and say, 'This is what David did.' " And such was his
practice as long as he lived in Philistine territory. 12 Achish trusted David and said to himself, "He has become so odious to his people, the Israelites, that he will be my servant
forever."

27:2 [c]1Sa 25:13 [d]1Sa 21:10 [e]1Ki 2:39
27:3 [f]1Sa 25:43; 30:3
27:6 [g]Jos 15:31; 19:5; Ne 11:28
27:7 [h]1Sa 29:3
27:8 [i]Jos 13:2,13 [j]Ex 17:8; 1Sa 15:7-8 [k]Ex 15:22
27:9 [l]1Sa 15:3
27:10 [m]1Sa 30:29; 1Ch 2:9,25 [n]Jdg 1:16

Saul and the Witch of Endor

28 In those days the Philistines gathered[o] their forces to fight against Israel. Achish
said to David, "You must understand that you and your men will accompany me
in the army."
2 David said, "Then you will see for yourself what your servant can do."
Achish replied, "Very well, I will make you my bodyguard for life."

28:1 [o]1Sa 29:1

■ **27:1—2 Samuel 1:27** *Toward the Philistines.* David and Saul are contrasted again—this time with regard to their interactions with the Philistines. David fooled them (27:1—28:2), but Saul sinned because of fearing them (28:3–25). David was feared by the Philistines and was victorious (29:1—30:31), but Saul was defeated and killed by them (31:1–13)

■ **27:1—28:2** *David Fools the Philistines.* While fleeing from Saul, David spent much time with the Philistines, but in all of this time he did not sin. Instead, he cleverly manipulated them.

27:1–12 David feared Saul and fled to Gath again (cf. 21:10–15).

27:1 I will be destroyed by the hand of Saul. Despite recently learned lessons of faith (e.g., 26:10), David tired of being a fugitive in constant danger and gave in to the human fear that Saul would eventually succeed in destroying him. David's anxiety may have been heightened since he and his men had their families with them (v. 3). For the second time (21:10), David sought refuge among Israel's archenemies, the Philistines.

27:2 Achish. Achish was first encountered in 21:10. Now that the rift between David and Saul was conspicuous and indisputable, Achish readily condoned David's presence, perhaps realizing the potential benefit of David's allegiance in his own struggles against Saul (29:6).

27:3 his two wives. See note on 25:40–44.

27:5 Why should your servant live in the royal city with you? While David's request to be assigned to "one of the country towns" was ostensibly based on a desire not to burden the royal city, it achieved for him a greater freedom of action, placing him out from under the direct scrutiny of Achish (vv. 8–11).

27:6 Ziklag. Listed among "the southernmost towns of the tribe of Judah in the Negev" (Jos 15:21,31) and among the Simeonite holdings that lay within the territory of Judah (Jos 19:1–9, especially v. 5), the ancient site has been tentatively identified with Tell esh-Shariah, located 15 miles east of Gaza and 24 miles south of Gath. Although at one time an Israelite possession, Ziklag in the present context had come under Philistine control. **kings of Judah.** This expression indicates a perspective from the time after the division of Israel into northern and southern kingdoms (1Ki 12).

27:8 Geshurites. Neighbors of the Philistines (Jos 13:2), these Geshurites should not be confused with the Transjordanian people of the same name (Jos 13:11; 2Sa 15:8; 1Ch 2:23) from whom David obtained a wife who became the mother of Absalom (2Sa 3:3). **Girzites.** The suggestion that we should read "Gizrite" in place of "Girzite" is untenable, since Gezer (Tell Jezer) lay almost 12 miles north of Gath, well out of the range of David's activities. Nothing is known of the Girzites, as they are not mentioned elsewhere in the Bible. **Amalekites.** See note on 15:2. **Shur.** See note on 15:7.

27:9 did not leave a man or woman alive. David's practice was motivated by a desire to safeguard his double-dealings from discovery by Achish (v. 11). The morality of his practice, beneficial as it was to his fellow Judahites, remains an open question at best in the absence of any indication that the Lord had ordered his actions.

27:10 David would say. This was not the first time David had deemed it necessary to deal in deception (see notes on 20:6; 21:2; cf. note on 16:2). **Negev of Judah.** See 2 Samuel 24:7 and 2 Chronicles 28:18. The large region in southern Israel known as the Negev can be visualized as an inverted triangle extending from a little north of Beersheba to the Gulf of Aqaba. **Jerahmeel.** First Chronicles 2:9–15 mentions Jerahmeel as a descendant of Judah through Hezron and as a brother of Ram, an ancestor of David. See also the following note on "Kenites." **Kenites.** See note on 15:6. Kenites and Jerahmeelites are mentioned together in 30:29.

27:12 Achish trusted David. David's pretension of raiding his own kinsmen (i.e., villages in Judah and its environs) duped Achish and undoubtedly illicited peals of laughter from David's own men.

28:1 You must understand. Or "surely you know." Achish pointed out that his benevolence to David was not without strings attached. The same phrase is used in Solomon's warning to Shimei in 1 Kings 2:37 and 42.

28:2 what your servant can do. The irony of David's ambiguous answer (would Achish see David fighting for or against him?) found its counterpoint in the perhaps unconscious irony of Achish's reply (see following note). **Very well, I will make you my bodyguard for life.** Presumably this offer was contingent upon David's performance in battle. The Hebrew term used by Achish to denote "bodyguard" is different from the more common term used elsewhere in the Bible (e.g., 22:14; 2Sa 23:23) and means literally

3Now Samuel was dead,[p] and all Israel had mourned for him and buried him in his
own town of Ramah.[q] Saul had expelled the mediums and spiritists[r] from the land.
4The Philistines assembled and came and set up camp at Shunem,[s] while Saul gathered all the Israelites and set up camp at Gilboa.[t] 5When Saul saw the Philistine army,
he was afraid; terror filled his heart. 6He inquired[u] of the LORD, but the LORD did not answer him by dreams[v] or Urim[w] or prophets. 7Saul then said to his attendants, "Find me
a woman who is a medium,[x] so I may go and inquire of her."
"There is one in Endor,[y]" they said.
8So Saul disguised[z] himself, putting on other clothes, and at night he and two men
went to the woman. "Consult[a] a spirit for me," he said, "and bring up for me the one I
name."
9But the woman said to him, "Surely you know what Saul has done. He has cut off[b]
the mediums and spiritists from the land. Why have you set a trap for my life to bring
about my death?"
10Saul swore to her by the LORD, "As surely as the LORD lives, you will not be punished
for this."
11Then the woman asked, "Whom shall I bring up for you?"
"Bring up Samuel," he said.
12When the woman saw Samuel, she cried out at the top of her voice and said to Saul,
"Why have you deceived me? You are Saul!"
13The king said to her, "Don't be afraid. What do you see?"
The woman said, "I see a spirit[a] coming up out of the ground."
14"What does he look like?" he asked.
"An old man wearing a robe[c] is coming up," she said.
Then Saul knew it was Samuel, and he bowed down and prostrated himself with his
face to the ground.
15Samuel said to Saul, "Why have you disturbed me by bringing me up?"
"I am in great distress," Saul said. "The Philistines are fighting against me, and God
has turned[d] away from me. He no longer answers me, either by prophets or by dreams.
So I have called on you to tell me what to do."
16Samuel said, "Why do you consult me, now that the LORD has turned away from you
and become your enemy? 17The LORD has done what he predicted through me. The LORD
has torn[e] the kingdom out of your hands and given it to one of your neighbors—to Da-

28:3 [p]1Sa 25:1 [q]1Sa 7:17 [r]Ex 22:18; Lev 19:31; 20:27; Dt 18:10-11; 1Sa 15:23
28:4 [s]Jos 19:18; 2Ki 4:8 [t]1Sa 31:1,3
28:6 [u]1Sa 14:37; 1Ch 10:13-14; Pr 1:28 [v]Nu 12:6 [w]Ex 28:30; Nu 27:21
28:7 [x]Ac 16:16 [y]Jos 17:11
28:8 [z]2Ch 18:29; 35:22 [a]Dt 18:10-11; 1Ch 10:13; Isa 8:19
28:9 [b]ver 3
28:14 [c]1Sa 15:27; 24:8
28:15 [d]ver 6; 1Sa 18:12
28:17 [e]1Sa 15:28

[a] 13 Or *see spirits*; or *see gods*

"keeper of my head," a most unfortunate choice of words in view of David's treatment of an earlier Philistine's head (17:49–54).

■ **28:3–25** *Saul Sins for Fear of the Philistines.* Under attack by the Philistines and deserted by God, Saul consulted a medium at Endor to seek the counsel of the deceased prophet Samuel. Samuel told Saul of his (Saul's) imminent death, as well as of his sons' deaths.

28:3 Samuel was dead. See 25:1 and its note. **Saul had expelled the mediums and spiritists.** Although Saul's expulsion of mediums (lit., "[possessors of] ghosts, spirits"; v. 7) and spiritists (those who make contact with the spirit world) was fully in keeping with Mosaic Law (Lev 19:31; 20:6,27; Dt 18:11), it was not a sufficient proof of his zeal for the religion of Israel, since such actions were known to have sometimes been taken by non-Israelite kings as well (e.g., by Gudea, the Sumerian king of Lagash, who had ruled a thousand years before Saul). Whatever the case, Saul's turning to a medium in his time of need (v. 7) was indicative of the depths to which he had fallen. First Chronicles 10:13 cites Saul's consultation of a medium as a clear indication of his unfaithfulness and disobedience, while Leviticus 20:6 states that such a person was to be "cut . . . off from his people."

28:4 Shunem. Located just southwest of the hill of Moreh and some 16 miles southwest of the southern end of the Sea of Galilee, Shunem was the site of the Philistine camp on the eve of the battle of Mount Gilboa, the confrontation in which Saul would meet his end (ch. 31). **Gilboa.** This refers either to the mountain range that begins about five miles south of Shunem and extends southward along the eastern edge of the plain of Jezreel or to the village of the same name located in the heart of the Gilboa range some 11 miles south of Shunem. The latter seems the less likely option in view of the distances involved. Earlier positions of both Israelite and Philistine troops are given in 29:1 (see its note).

28:5 terror filled his heart. See 17:11 and its note.

28:6 the LORD did not answer him. Saul's inquiry was prompted by anxiety (v. 5), not piety, and the Lord's refusal to answer was reminiscent of the threat of 8:18. **dreams or Urim or prophets.** Having rejected the Lord and, as a consequence, been rejected by the Lord (see 15:23 and its note), Saul was cut off from the usual means of divine inquiry. For instance, while David had in his retinue the prophet Gad (22:5), it was not at all likely that a true prophet accompanied Saul. Moreover, the authentic ephod containing the Urim and the Thummim (see note on 2:28) had come into David's possession through Abiathar (23:6).

28:7 Find me a woman who is a medium. His purge of the land notwithstanding (see note on v. 3), Saul seems to have had no doubt that a medium could still be found and that his attendants could name one immediately. **Endor.** Joshua 17:11–12 attest to a persistent Canaanite influence at Endor, which lay less than five miles northeast of Shunem (see note on v. 4). Saul's recourse to Endor took him behind Philistine lines. See *WLC* 105.

28:11 See *WLC* 105.

28:12 When the woman saw Samuel, she cried out at the top of her voice. Is this the real Samuel or a mere apparition? The former is the more likely option for the following reasons: (1) The consternation of the medium upon seeing Samuel indicates that his appearance had nothing to do with her magical arts (which may not even have commenced) nor with such "familiar spirits" as were within her experience; (2) the narrator himself referred to the figure simply as "Samuel" (see also v. 14); and (3) the subsequent words of Samuel were fully in keeping with his pronouncements while alive (especially in ch. 15). It seems very likely, therefore, that the real Samuel appeared, although his return could not in any sense be credited to the necromancer, but could only be the result of the Lord's sovereign action.

28:14 Saul knew it was Samuel. Apparently Saul recognized Samuel on the basis of the woman's description of an "old man wearing a robe" (cf. note on 2:19). Robes have symbolized the fate of Saul's kingship in a variety of ways, and mention of Samuel's robe recollects the devastating pronouncement of 15:28 (see also 18:4; 19:24; 24:4–6).

28:18 [f]1Sa 15:20 [g]1Ki 20:42
28:19 [h]1Sa 31:2

vid. [18]Because you did not obey[f] the LORD or carry out his fierce wrath[g] against the Amalekites, the LORD has done this to you today. [19]The LORD will hand over both Israel and you to the Philistines, and tomorrow you and your sons[h] will be with me. The LORD will also hand over the army of Israel to the Philistines."

[20]Immediately Saul fell full length on the ground, filled with fear because of Samuel's words. His strength was gone, for he had eaten nothing all that day and night.

28:21 [i]Jdg 12:3; 1Sa 19:5; Job 13:14
28:23 [j]2Ki 5:13

[21]When the woman came to Saul and saw that he was greatly shaken, she said, "Look, your maidservant has obeyed you. I took my life[i] in my hands and did what you told me to do. [22]Now please listen to your servant and let me give you some food so you may eat and have the strength to go on your way."

[23]He refused[j] and said, "I will not eat."

But his men joined the woman in urging him, and he listened to them. He got up from the ground and sat on the couch.

[24]The woman had a fattened calf at the house, which she butchered at once. She took some flour, kneaded it and baked bread without yeast. [25]Then she set it before Saul and his men, and they ate. That same night they got up and left.

Achish Sends David Back to Ziklag

29:1 [k]1Sa 28:1 [l]Jos 12:18; 1Sa 4:1 [m]2Ki 9:30
29:2 [n]1Sa 28:2
29:3 [o]1Sa 27:7; Da 6:5

29 The Philistines gathered[k] all their forces at Aphek,[l] and Israel camped by the spring in Jezreel.[m] [2]As the Philistine rulers marched with their units of hundreds and thousands, David and his men were marching at the rear[n] with Achish. [3]The commanders of the Philistines asked, "What about these Hebrews?"

Achish replied, "Is this not David, who was an officer of Saul king of Israel? He has already been with me for over a year,[o] and from the day he left Saul until now, I have found no fault in him."

29:4 [p]1Ch 12:19 [q]1Sa 14:21

[4]But the Philistine commanders were angry with him and said, "Send[p] the man back, that he may return to the place you assigned him. He must not go with us into battle, or he will turn[q] against us during the fighting. How better could he regain his master's favor than by taking the heads of our own men? [5]Isn't this the David they sang about in their dances:

29:5 [r]1Sa 18:7; 21:11

" 'Saul has slain his thousands,
and David his tens of thousands'?"[r]

29:6 [s]1Sa 27:8-12 [t]ver 3

[6]So Achish called David and said to him, "As surely as the LORD lives, you have been reliable, and I would be pleased to have you serve with me in the army. From the day[s] you came to me until now, I have found no fault in you, but the rulers[t] don't approve of you. [7]Turn back and go in peace; do nothing to displease the Philistine rulers."

[8]"But what have I done?" asked David. "What have you found against your servant from the day I came to you until now? Why can't I go and fight against the enemies of my lord the king?"

29:9 [u]2Sa 14:17,20; 19:27 [v]ver 4

[9]Achish answered, "I know that you have been as pleasing in my eyes as an angel[u] of God; nevertheless, the Philistine commanders[v] have said, 'He must not go up with us

---

28:19 you and your sons will be with me. That is, with Samuel among the dead (31:2–4).
28:23 I will not eat. See note on 1:7.
28:24 fattened calf. Much had changed since Saul's first encounter with Samuel, when he had been designated as the one to deliver Israel from the Philistines (9:16) and had been treated to a festal meal by the prophet (9:22–24). Now, on the occasion of his last encounter with Samuel and on the eve of his own death and the crushing defeat of Israel by the Philistines, Saul was treated by a medium to a fattened calf and trimmings.
■ **29:1—30:31** *David Is Feared and Victorious.* Suspicious of David's loyalty, the Philistine rulers prohibited him and his men from marching with them against Israel. Yet this only made David stronger and more victorious.
29:1 The Philistines gathered all their forces. This notice resumes the account initiated in 28:1–2 but suspended in order to include the account of Saul's visit with the medium (28:3–25). **Aphek.** Probably the same Aphek mentioned in 4:1 (see its note). The site lay some 28 miles north of Gath and Ashdod and was the place at which the Philistines assembled their forces before continuing their northward march in concert (v. 2). **Jezreel.** This site lay north of Mount Gilboa, a few miles south of Shunem and some 40 miles northeast of Aphek. Israel's presence at Jezreel already at the time of the Philistine muster in Aphek suggests that the first move in the conflict that would lead to his death was made by Saul.
29:3 Hebrews. See note on 4:6. **I have found no fault in him.** This judgment was a measure of Achish's gullibility, not of David's sincerity (27:8–12).
29:4 he will turn against us during the fighting. The other Philistine commanders were less gullible than Achish and perhaps still carried painful memories of mid-battle defection in an earlier war with Israel (14:21).
29:5 Isn't this the David they sang about . . . ? See notes on 18:7 and 21:11.
29:8 But what have I done? A protest of genuine innocence when David had earlier posed the same question to Saul (26:18), it was now no more than a ruse. David had indeed done much (27:8–12), but Achish had not been clever enough to discover it. **Why can't I go and fight against the enemies of my lord the king?** As in 28:2, David again dealt in ambiguities apparent to the reader, even if not to Achish. The ambiguity in this instance revolved around the identity of "my lord the king"—Achish? Saul? or possibly the Lord himself?
29:9 you have been as pleasing in my eyes as an angel of God. Achish's grossly misplaced confidence made him appear almost as much a fool as Nabal (ch. 25), although without the malevolence. On the expression "angel of God," see 2 Samuel 14:17 and 20 and 19:27.

into battle.' 10 Now get up early, along with your master's servants who have come with you, and leave[w] in the morning as soon as it is light."

11 So David and his men got up early in the morning to go back to the land of the Philistines, and the Philistines went up to Jezreel.

David Destroys the Amalekites

30 David and his men reached Ziklag[x] on the third day. Now the Amalekites[y] had raided the Negev and Ziklag. They had attacked Ziklag and burned it, 2 and had taken captive the women and all who were in it, both young and old. They killed none of them, but carried them off as they went on their way.

3 When David and his men came to Ziklag, they found it destroyed by fire and their wives and sons and daughters taken captive. 4 So David and his men wept aloud until they had no strength left to weep. 5 David's two wives[z] had been captured—Ahinoam of Jezreel and Abigail, the widow of Nabal of Carmel. 6 David was greatly distressed because the men were talking of stoning[a] him; each one was bitter in spirit because of his sons and daughters. But David found strength[b] in the LORD his God.

7 Then David said to Abiathar[c] the priest, the son of Ahimelech, "Bring me the ephod.[d]" Abiathar brought it to him, 8 and David inquired[e] of the LORD, "Shall I pursue this raiding party? Will I overtake them?"

"Pursue them," he answered. "You will certainly overtake them and succeed[f] in the rescue."

9 David and the six hundred men[g] with him came to the Besor Ravine, where some stayed behind, 10 for two hundred men were too exhausted[h] to cross the ravine. But David and four hundred men continued the pursuit.

11 They found an Egyptian in a field and brought him to David. They gave him water to drink and food to eat— 12 part of a cake of pressed figs and two cakes of raisins. He ate and was revived,[i] for he had not eaten any food or drunk any water for three days and three nights.

13 David asked him, "To whom do you belong, and where do you come from?"

He said, "I am an Egyptian, the slave of an Amalekite. My master abandoned me when I became ill three days ago. 14 We raided the Negev of the Kerethites[j] and the territory belonging to Judah and the Negev of Caleb.[k] And we burned[l] Ziklag."

15 David asked him, "Can you lead me down to this raiding party?"

He answered, "Swear to me before God that you will not kill me or hand me over to my master, and I will take you down to them."

16 He led David down, and there they were, scattered over the countryside, eating, drinking and reveling[m] because of the great amount of plunder[n] they had taken from the land of the Philistines and from Judah. 17 David fought[o] them from dusk until the evening of the next day, and none of them got away, except four hundred young men who rode off on camels and fled.[p] 18 David recovered[q] everything the Amalekites had taken, including his two wives. 19 Nothing was missing: young or old, boy or girl, plunder or anything else they had taken. David brought everything back. 20 He took all the flocks and

29:10 [w]1Ch 12:19
30:1 [x]1Sa 29:4,11 [y]1Sa 15:7; 27:8
30:5 [z]1Sa 25:43; 2Sa 2:2
30:6 [a]Ex 17:4; Jn 8:59 [b]Ps 27:14; 56:3-4, 11; Ro 4:20
30:7 [c]1Sa 22:20 [d]1Sa 23:9
30:8 [e]1Sa 23:2 [f]ver 18
30:9 [g]1Sa 27:2
30:10 [h]ver 9,21
30:12 [i]Jdg 15:19
30:14 [j]2Sa 8:18; 1Ki 1:38,44; Eze 25:16; Zep 2:5 [k]ver 16; Jos 14:13; 15:13 [l]ver 1
30:16 [m]Lk 12:19 [n]ver 14
30:17 [o]1Sa 11:11 [p]1Sa 15:3
30:18 [q]Ge 14:16

30:1–31 David recovered what had been taken from him and his men by an Amalekite raiding party.

30:1 Ziklag. See note on 27:6. **Amalekites had raided.** See notes on 15:2 and 8. Having earlier been the victims of David's forays (27:8), the Amalekites had now taken the opportunity of David's absence from Ziklag to retaliate. **Negev.** See note on 27:10.

30:2 They killed none of them. A remarkable evidence of the Lord's providential protection of David (v. 19; 26:12), whose own practice had been quite different (27:9).

30:3 their wives and sons and daughters taken captive. This turn of events is especially poignant, inasmuch as concern for the safety of their families may have motivated the retreat of David and his men to Philistine territory in the first place (see note on 27:1).

30:6 David found strength in the LORD his God. See 23:16 and its note.

30:7 Abiathar. See note on 22:20. **ephod.** See note on 2:28.

30:9 Besor Ravine. Wadis (seasonal rivers) from the vicinity of Beersheba and southward converged to form the Brook Besor, which then ran northwestward to empty into the Mediterranean. David and his men would have come to the ravine some 13 miles south of Ziklag.

30:10 two hundred men were too exhausted to cross. Their exhaustion was not surprising after a march of over 60 miles from Aphek (29:1–11) to the Besor Ravine.

30:14 Negev of the Kerethites. On "Negev" generally, see note on 27:10. The Kerethites (or Cherethites) were an ethnic people, probably from Crete, who are often mentioned alongside the Philistines (e.g., Eze 25:16; Zep 2:5–6; numerous other places if "Pelethites" is understood as a linguistic variation of "Philistines" [e.g., 2Sa 8:18]). The "Kerethites and Pelethites" (2Sa 8:18) served under the command of Benaiah son of Jehoiada as professional troops loyal to David (see 2Sa 8:18; 15:18; 20:7,23) and, for a short time at least, to Solomon (1Ki 1:44). Their particular function seems to have been as the king's bodyguard (2Sa 23:20,23). **Negev of Caleb.** Caleb son of Jephunneh is first mentioned in Numbers 13:6 as one of the spies chosen to scout out the land of Canaan. He was commended in Numbers 14:24 as one who followed the Lord "wholeheartedly" and who, therefore, was to have an inheritance in the promised land. That inheritance included Hebron and its environs (Jos 14:13–14; Jdg 1:20). Nabal's designation as a Calebite (25:3) and his association with Carmel and Maon (25:2), seven and eight miles south of Hebron, respectively, suggest that these and possibly other cities south of Hebron were to be included in Calebite territory.

30:19 Nothing was missing. This is a further, striking evidence of the Lord's watchful care over David's affairs (v. 2).

herds, and his men drove them ahead of the other livestock, saying, "This is David's plunder."

21 Then David came to the two hundred men who had been too exhausted[r] to follow him and who were left behind at the Besor Ravine. They came out to meet David and the people with him. As David and his men approached, he greeted them. 22 But all the evil men and troublemakers among David's followers said, "Because they did not go out with us, we will not share with them the plunder we recovered. However, each man may take his wife and children and go."

23 David replied, "No, my brothers, you must not do that with what the LORD has given us. He has protected us and handed over to us the forces that came against us. 24 Who will listen to what you say? The share of the man who stayed with the supplies is to be the same as that of him who went down to the battle. All will share alike.[s]" 25 David made this a statute and ordinance for Israel from that day to this.

26 When David arrived in Ziklag, he sent some of the plunder to the elders of Judah, who were his friends, saying, "Here is a present for you from the plunder of the LORD's enemies."

27 He sent it to those who were in Bethel,[t] Ramoth[u] Negev and Jattir;[v] 28 to those in Aroer,[w] Siphmoth, Eshtemoa[x] 29 and Racal; to those in the towns of the Jerahmeelites[y] and the Kenites;[z] 30 to those in Hormah,[a] Bor Ashan,[b] Athach 31 and Hebron;[c] and to those in all the other places where David and his men had roamed.

Saul Takes His Life

31 Now the Philistines fought against Israel; the Israelites fled before them, and many fell slain on Mount Gilboa.[d] 2 The Philistines pressed hard after Saul and his sons, and they killed his sons Jonathan, Abinadab and Malki-Shua. 3 The fighting grew fierce around Saul, and when the archers overtook him, they wounded[e] him critically.

4 Saul said to his armor-bearer, "Draw your sword and run me through,[f] or these uncircumcised[g] fellows will come and run me through and abuse me."

But his armor-bearer was terrified and would not do it; so Saul took his own sword and fell on it. 5 When the armor-bearer saw that Saul was dead, he too fell on his sword and died with him. 6 So Saul and his three sons and his armor-bearer and all his men died together that same day.

7 When the Israelites along the valley and those across the Jordan saw that the Israelite army had fled and that Saul and his sons had died, they abandoned their towns and fled. And the Philistines came and occupied them.

8 The next day, when the Philistines came to strip the dead, they found Saul and his three sons fallen on Mount Gilboa. 9 They cut off his head and stripped off his armor, and they sent messengers throughout the land of the Philistines to proclaim the news[h] in the

30:21 [r]ver 10
30:24 [s]Nu 31:27; Jos 22:8
30:27 [t]Jos 7:2 [u]Jos 19:8 [v]Jos 15:48
30:28 [w]Jos 13:16 [x]Jos 15:50
30:29 [y]1Sa 27:10 [z]Jdg 1:16; 1Sa 15:6
30:30 [a]Nu 14:45; Jdg 1:17 [b]Jos 15:42
30:31 [c]Jos 14:13; 2Sa 2:1,4
31:1 [d]1Sa 28:4; 1Ch 10:1-12
31:3 [e]2Sa 1:6
31:4 [f]Jdg 9:54; 2Sa 1:6,10 [g]1Sa 14:6
31:9 [h]2Sa 1:20

30:21 Besor Ravine. See note on verse 9.
30:22 troublemakers. See note on 2:12, where the same Hebrew expression is used.
30:23 what the LORD has given us. David recognized that the successful rescue was not his doing, but the Lord's (see notes on vv. 2,19). Even David's forced return from following Achish into war (29:8–9) was now seen, in hindsight, as a merciful turn of events, since any further delay would have surely made the rescue operation far more difficult, if not impossible. With these things in mind, David rejected the notion that the front line troops had any more right to the spoils of victory than those who stayed behind.
30:26 he sent some of the plunder to the elders of Judah. The probable motivation for this generosity was gratitude for the help he had received in escaping from Saul (v. 31), although it is not without significance that it was also in this area that David's kingship was first officially recognized (2Sa 2:1–4).
30:27–31 As verse 31 states, the cities mentioned here were within the general range of David's wanderings during his fugitive period. All of them belonged to the southern part of Judah; thus Bethel (v. 27), for instance, should not be confused with a more northerly city of the same name (7:16).
■ **31:1–13** *Saul and His Sons Die in Battle With the Philistines.* Saul and his sons died in battle on Mount Gilboa. The Philistines so pressed Saul in battle that he shamefully took his own life.
31:1 many fell slain. In Hebrew this phrase recalls an earlier one in 17:52, which could be rendered "the Philistines fell slain." Its use here thus underscored the regression of Israel's fortunes under the leadership of Saul. Ironically, even the pinnacle of Israel's successes against the Philistines during Saul's reign came as a result of David's, not Saul's, performance (17:51–54; 18:6–7). **Mount Gilboa.** See 28:4 and its note.
31:2 his sons Jonathan, Abinadab and Malki-Shua. First Samuel 14:49 omits Abinadab but includes Ishvi, who is probably to be identified with Ish-Bosheth, the only son of Saul to survive the decimation of the house of Saul on Mount Gilboa. Though Ish-Bosheth would have been of age, at least 35 (see note on 13:1; see also 2Sa 2:10), it is not stated whether he took part in the battle. For a listing of all four sons of Saul, see 1 Chronicles 8:33. The Chronicles' reference gives the name Esh-Baal, which was probably the original name that was altered to Ish-Bosheth ("man of shame") to avoid any association with the Canaanite god Baal (cf. "Mephibosheth" [2Sa 4:4]; Jerub-Besheth [2Sa 11:21]).
31:3 they wounded him critically. Unlike David, Saul was subject to defeat and death at the hands of the Philistines. See note on "many fell slain" in verse 1.
31:4 uncircumcised fellows. See note on 14:6. **Saul took his own sword and fell on it.** While some laud Saul's action as worthy of a tragic hero seeking to gain mastery of his own fate even in death, the tenor of the book of Samuel points in another direction. To be commended are those who in times of distress, like David, find strength in God (23:16; 30:6) and who, like Jonathan, yield fully to his will (e.g., see notes on 18:4,28–29; 19:4; 20:31; 23:17).
31:6 all his men died together. On the qualified sense of "all," see the notes on 13:7 and 15:8.
31:7–10 These verses continue the description of Israel's defeats (see note on v. 1). While David had lifted the head of the Philistines' giant in 17:51, it was now Israel's "tallest" who received similar treatment (v. 9).

temple of their idols and among their people.[i] 10They put his armor in the temple of the
Ashtoreths[j] and fastened his body to the wall of Beth Shan.[k]
11When the people of Jabesh Gilead[l] heard of what the Philistines had done to Saul,
12all their valiant men journeyed through the night to Beth Shan. They took down the
bodies of Saul and his sons from the wall of Beth Shan and went to Jabesh, where they
burned[m] them. 13Then they took their bones[n] and buried them under a tamarisk[o] tree
at Jabesh, and they fasted[p] seven days.[q]

31:9 [i]Jdg 16:24
31:10 [j]Jdg 2:12-13; 1Sa 7:3 [k]Jos 17:11; 2Sa 21:12
31:11 [l]1Sa 11:1
31:12 [m]2Sa 2:4-7; 2Ch 16:14; Am 6:10 **31:13** [n]2Sa 21:12-14 [o]1Sa 22:6 [p]2Sa 1:12 [q]Ge 50:10

31:10 temple of the Ashtoreths. See note on 7:4. **Beth Shan.** Located in the Jordan Valley some 16 miles south of the Sea of Galilee, this border city of the territory of Manasseh is listed (Jos 17:11,16; Jdg 1:27) among those cities that resisted Israelite occupation and remained Canaanite and, as is seen here, Philistine strongholds.

31:11 Jabesh Gilead. See note on 11:1.

31:12 They took down the bodies. This courageous action by the "valiant men" of Jabesh Gilead is best understood as an expression of gratitude for their own rescue by Saul in chapter 11. Nevertheless, it serves in the present context as yet another illustration of Saul's demise, as the formerly rescued became the rescuers.

2 SAMUEL

Introduction

Overview
See "Introduction to 1 Samuel: Overview."

Author
See "Introduction to 1 Samuel: Author."

Time and Place of Writing
See "Introduction to 1 Samuel: Time and Place of Writing."

Purpose and Distinctives
With Saul dead (1Sa 31), the way was open for David to take the throne without lifting his hand against the Lord's anointed. Second Samuel 2:1—5:5 records the steps by which David became king, first over Judah and then over all Israel. Although his ascendancy over the former proceeded smoothly, blood was spilled before the way was clear for him to become king over the latter. The narratives are careful to make the point, however, that David was as innocent in relation to the deaths of Abner, Saul's former general, and Ish-Bosheth, Saul's surviving son, as he was in relation to the deaths of Saul and Jonathan.

With David king over a united Israel, chapters 5–10 summarize the transactions, both political and theological, by which David's throne was established. Chapters 5–6 recount David's acquisition of a capital city, his resounding defeat of the Philistines (Israel's archenemy from whom Saul had failed to deliver the people) and his transference of the ark of God to his newly established capital. Chapter 7 records the very significant Davidic promise (or "dynastic oracle") in which the Lord, after refusing David's offer to build the temple ("house" in Hebrew), promised to build David a dynasty (also "house" in Hebrew) that would endure forever. This promise to David marks the continuation and specification of the divine promise of blessing made to the patriarchs and is a major new development in the Messianic hope that finds its ultimate fulfillment in Christ (see note on 7:4–17). Chapters 8–10 summarize some of David's principal achievements; e.g., his victories and his covenant faithfulness to Jonathan in showing kindness to Mephibosheth.

The Davidic promise of chapter 7 establishes, beyond all doubt, that the purposes of God for the house of David were sure. This in no way implies, however, that David or his descendants would not forfeit some of the temporal benefits of their privileged position if they were to fall into sin. Chapters 11–20 depict the domestic and political chaos that followed in the wake of David's sins of adultery and murder (ch. 11). When confronted by Nathan in chapter 12, David's repentance was genuine and God's forgiveness immediate, but sin still had its consequences. With his ability to exercise proper authority impaired (perhaps by a sense of guilt), David witnessed his own sins replicated in the lives of his sons (see note on 13:21). Not until he had experienced two rebellions, the first by Absalom and the second by Sheba, son of Bicri, did David's reign regain a measure of equilibrium.

Chapters 21–24, which together form a kind of epilogue, provide thematic closure for the book of Samuel. These chapters recount a collection of events that took place at different points in David's life. At the heart of these chapters are two Davidic poems celebrating the two fundamental reasons for David's blessedness: The Lord (1) was his deliverer who (2) had made an "everlasting covenant" with him (23:5). Framing this central core are two lists of Davidic champions, the human agents of David's success. Finally, bracketing both the poems and the lists are two accounts of how David's intercession relieved Israel from divine judgment for Saul's and for his own sin. These chapters left the original readers with clear pictures of the hope they could have in the house of David despite the troubles that David and his sons had brought upon God's people.

Christ in 2 Samuel
See "Introduction to 1 Samuel: Christ in 1 and 2 Samuel."

Outline
See "Introduction to 1 Samuel: Outline."

David Hears of Saul's Death

1 After the death[a] of Saul, David returned from defeating[b] the Amalekites and stayed
in Ziklag two days. 2 On the third day a man[c] arrived from Saul's camp, with his
clothes torn and with dust on his head.[d] When he came to David, he fell to the ground
to pay him honor.
3 "Where have you come from?" David asked him.
He answered, "I have escaped from the Israelite camp."
4 "What happened?" David asked. "Tell me."
He said, "The men fled from the battle. Many of them fell and died. And Saul and his
son Jonathan are dead."
5 Then David said to the young man who brought him the report, "How do you know
that Saul and his son Jonathan are dead?"
6 "I happened to be on Mount Gilboa,[e]" the young man said, "and there was Saul,
leaning on his spear, with the chariots and riders almost upon him. 7 When he turned
around and saw me, he called out to me, and I said, 'What can I do?'
8 "He asked me, 'Who are you?'
" 'An Amalekite,[f] I answered.
9 "Then he said to me, 'Stand over me and kill me! I am in the throes of death, but I'm
still alive.'
10 "So I stood over him and killed him, because I knew that after he had fallen he could
not survive. And I took the crown[g] that was on his head and the band on his arm and
have brought them here to my lord."
11 Then David and all the men with him took hold of their clothes and tore[h] them.
12 They mourned and wept and fasted till evening for Saul and his son Jonathan, and for
the army of the LORD and the house of Israel, because they had fallen by the sword.
13 David said to the young man who brought him the report, "Where are you from?"
"I am the son of an alien, an Amalekite,[i]" he answered.
14 David asked him, "Why were you not afraid to lift your hand to destroy the LORD's
anointed?[j]"
15 Then David called one of his men and said, "Go, strike him down!"[k] So he struck him
down, and he died.[l] 16 For David had said to him, "Your blood be on your own head.[m] Your
own mouth testified against you when you said, 'I killed the LORD's anointed.' "

David's Lament for Saul and Jonathan

17 David took up this lament[n] concerning Saul and his son Jonathan, 18 and ordered that
the men of Judah be taught this lament of the bow (it is written in the Book of Jashar):[o]

1:1 [a]1Sa 31:6 [b]1Sa 30:17
1:2 [c]2Sa 4:10 [d]1Sa 4:12
1:6 [e]1Sa 28:4; 31:2-4
1:8 [f]1Sa 15:2; 30:13, 17
1:10 [g]Jdg 9:54; 2Ki 11:12
1:11 [h]Ge 37:29; 2Sa 3:31; 13:31
1:13 [i]ver 8
1:14 [j]1Sa 24:6; 26:9
1:15 [k]2Sa 4:12 [l]2Sa 4:10
1:16 [m]Lev 20:9; 2Sa 3:28-29; 1Ki 2:32; Mt 27:24-25; Ac 18:6
1:17 [n]2Ch 35:25
1:18 [o]Jos 10:13; 1Sa 31:3

■ **1:1–27** *David Reacts Innocently to Saul's Death.* Although Saul had tried to kill David numerous times, when David received word of Saul's death he did not rejoice. Instead, he executed the gloating Amalekite who had brought the news and claimed to have killed Saul personally (vv. 1–16), after which he mourned for Saul and Jonathan (vv. 17–27). David's qualification for kingship is again evident.
■ **1:1–16** *David Avenges Saul and Jonathan.* David demonstrated the sincerity of his commitment to Saul by his reaction to the news of Saul's death. His love for Jonathan is also evident here.
1:1 After the death of Saul. See 1 Samuel 31:4–6. **returned from defeating the Amalekites.** See 1 Samuel 30:16–19. **Ziklag.** See 1 Samuel 30:1; see also note on 1 Samuel 27:6.
1:2 clothes torn and with dust on his head. In the wake of Israel's devastating defeat (1Sa 31:1), the messenger apparently deemed it appropriate to take on the appearance of mourning (cf. Jos 7:6; 1Sa 4:12). His claim to have had a hand in Saul's death (v. 10), however, shows that he expected at least this item of news to please David. In this he was mistaken, and his misjudgment would cost him his life (see note on v. 14).
1:6 chariots and riders almost upon him. Chariots often served as mobile firing platforms for archers (cf. Saul's injury according to 1Sa 31:3).
1:9–10 See *WLC* 145.
1:9 Stand over me and kill me! Those who would harmonize the Amalekite's account of Saul's demise with that of 1 Samuel 31 postulate that Saul must have bungled his suicide attempt, with the result that he required further assistance. Details in the text, however, speak against such a reconstruction of events: (1) The Amalekite's claim that Saul was found "leaning on his spear" (v. 6) is in conflict with the clear statement of 1 Samuel 31:4 that Saul fell on his sword; (2) 1 Samuel 31:5 leaves no doubt that the suicide of Saul's armor-bearer, which surely preceded the arrival of the Amalekite, occurred only after it was certain that Saul was dead. The more likely case is that the Amalekite must have preceded the Philistines in discovering Saul's body and, in the hopes of receiving a reward from David, fabricated a part for himself in Saul's death.
1:10 crown . . . band. The crown in view is presumably a lighter version of the heavy state crown. The manner in which Saul's royal insignia came into David's possession stands in stark contrast to Jonathan's voluntary surrender of his robe and weaponry to David at an earlier time (see note on 1Sa 18:4). This contrast epitomizes the radically different responses of Saul and Jonathan to the divine will with respect to David and the house of Saul (e.g., 1Sa 18:28–29; 19:4; 20:30–31; 23:17–18).
1:14 the LORD's anointed. In failing or refusing to share David's conviction of the sacrosanct status of "the LORD's anointed" (1Sa 24:6; 26:9), the Amalekite signed his own death warrant (vv. 15–16).
1:15–16 See *WLC* 145.
1:15 Go, strike him down! David's severe reaction to the Amalekite's story serves as yet another evidence that he was not involved in Saul's death (see David's own interpretation of the event in 4:10). David's execution of the offender also suggests a telling contrast between the piety of David, who scrupulously safeguarded the sacred office of kingship, and the impiety of Saul, who not only took his own life (1Sa 31:4–5) but had also displayed utter contempt for Israel's other sacred office when he ordered the killing of the priests of Nob (1Sa 22:17–19).
■ **1:17–27** *David Laments Saul and Jonathan.* This beautiful song of lament reveals plainly that David was sincere in his affections and loyalties toward these men.
1:17 David took up this lament. David's lament is a funerary dirge different in form from the laments found in the book of Psalms. Its basic structure is concentric. Verses 19 and 25 parallel each other and enclose a central section that likewise begins and ends on a similar note, with verse 20 referring to "the daughters of the Philistines" and verse 24 addressing the "daughters of Israel."

1:19 [p]ver 27

[19] "Your glory, O Israel, lies slain on your heights.
How the mighty have fallen![p]

1:20 [q]Mic 1:10 [r]1Sa 31:8 [s]Ex 15:20; 1Sa 18:6

[20] "Tell it not in Gath,[q]
proclaim it not in the streets of Ashkelon,
lest the daughters of the Philistines[r] be glad,
lest the daughters of the uncircumcised rejoice.[s]

1:21 [t]ver 6; 1Sa 31:1 [u]Eze 31:15 [v]Isa 21:5

[21] "O mountains of Gilboa,[t]
may you have neither dew nor rain,
nor fields that yield offerings[u] ⌞of grain⌟.
For there the shield of the mighty was defiled,
the shield of Saul—no longer rubbed with oil.[v]

1:22 [w]Isa 34:3,7 [x]Dt 32:42; 1Sa 18:4

[22] From the blood[w] of the slain,
from the flesh of the mighty,
the bow[x] of Jonathan did not turn back,
the sword of Saul did not return unsatisfied.

[23] "Saul and Jonathan—
in life they were loved and gracious,
and in death they were not parted.

1:23 [y]Dt 28:49; Jer 4:13 [z]Jdg 14:18

They were swifter than eagles,[y]
they were stronger than lions.[z]

[24] "O daughters of Israel,
weep for Saul,
who clothed you in scarlet and finery,
who adorned your garments with ornaments of gold.

[25] "How the mighty have fallen in battle!
Jonathan lies slain on your heights.

1:26 [a]1Sa 20:42 [b]1Sa 18:1

[26] I grieve for you, Jonathan my brother;[a]
you were very dear to me.
Your love for me was wonderful,[b]
more wonderful than that of women.

1:27 [c]ver 19,25; 1Sa 2:4

[27] "How the mighty have fallen!
The weapons of war have perished!"[c]

David Anointed King Over Judah

2:1 [d]1Sa 23:2,11-12

2 In the course of time, David inquired[d] of the LORD. "Shall I go up to one of the towns of Judah?" he asked.

David's final words were reserved for his beloved friend Jonathan (v. 26), after which the mournful refrain of verses 19 and 25, "How the mighty have fallen," is intoned one last time (v. 27).

1:18 lament of the bow. "Bow" is missing in the Septuagint (the Greek translation of the OT), but if retained, it may refer to Jonathan (whose bow is mentioned in v. 22) and serve as a title for the lament. Note the closing line of the lament, where "weapons of war" (v. 27) probably stands for Saul and Jonathan (cf. the designation of Elijah and Elisha in 2Ki 13:14 as "the chariots and horsemen of Israel"). **Book of Jashar.** See note on Joshua 10:13.

1:19–27 See note on verse 17.

1:19 How the mighty have fallen! This phrase, which refers to Saul and Jonathan (v. 17), is repeated as a sort of refrain in verses 25 and 27. **mighty.** Occurs also in verse 21 as parallel to "Saul."

1:20 Tell it not in Gath. Compare Micah 1:10. David implored his listeners not to let the news be heard among the Philistine cities, lest the daughters of the Philistines rejoice over Israel's defeat, as the daughters of Israel had earlier rejoiced over the defeat of the Philistines (1Sa 18:7).

1:21 no longer rubbed with oil. It was customary in the ancient Near East to condition and preserve leather shields by rubbing them with oil (Isa 21:5). It may be more than coincidental, however, that the phraseology employed has a certain royal ring to it—the word translated "rubbed" is elsewhere rendered "anointed" (from which comes "Messiah"; see note on 1Sa 2:10), while the word "shield" seems sometimes in the Old Testament to mean "sovereign" or "chieftain" (see NIV text note on Ps 7:10). Lurking beneath the literal meaning of the words is perhaps the whisper, "Sovereign Saul, no longer anointed with oil."

1:22 the sword of Saul did not return unsatisfied. Although the intent of this line is certainly to praise Saul's military prowess, the reader can appreciate a subtle, if perhaps unintended, irony upon recall of the final use to which Saul's sword was put (1Sa 31:4).

1:23 loved and gracious. It is a measure of David's own graciousness that he mentioned only positive aspects of Israel's fallen heroes in his elegy, despite having experienced much that was negative at the hands of Saul.

1:26 more wonderful than that of women. While there can be no doubt that David had experienced more joy from Jonathan than from Michal (Jonathan's sister and David's wife), David's praise of Jonathan's love (cf. 1Sa 18:3) was not intended to suggest that love between friends is inherently superior to marital love. Rather, the point seems to be to underscore the astonishingly selfless quality of Jonathan's love for David. If David was generalizing about different kinds of love at all, then his point may have been that love that involves loyalty and commitment, whether between friends or marriage partners, is far more profound, ultimately, than mere erotic attraction between the sexes. Interpretations that read a homosexual nuance into David's words are neither warranted by the text nor admissible in terms of the wider Biblical context (Lev 18:22; 20:13).

■ **2:1—20:26** *David: David's Full Kingship.* Once Saul had passed from the scene, David took full control over Israel's throne. Yet even David did not remain faithful, and his kingdom came under the discipline of God. As a result, David's time of reigning over God's people can be divided into two periods: the time under God's blessing (2:1—10:19) and the period under his curse (11:1—20:26).

The LORD said, "Go up."
David asked, "Where shall I go?"
"To Hebron,"[e] the LORD answered.
2 So David went up there with his two wives,[f] Ahinoam of Jezreel and Abigail,[g] the
widow of Nabal of Carmel. 3 David also took the men who were with him,[h] each with his
family, and they settled in Hebron and its towns. 4 Then the men of Judah came to Hebron[i] and there they anointed[j] David king over the house of Judah.
When David was told that it was the men of Jabesh Gilead[k] who had buried Saul, 5 he
sent messengers to the men of Jabesh Gilead to say to them, "The LORD bless[l] you for
showing this kindness to Saul your master by burying him. 6 May the LORD now show you
kindness and faithfulness,[m] and I too will show you the same favor because you have
done this. 7 Now then, be strong and brave, for Saul your master is dead, and the house
of Judah has anointed me king over them."

War Between the Houses of David and Saul

8 Meanwhile, Abner[n] son of Ner, the commander of Saul's army, had taken Ish-Bosheth son of Saul and brought him over to Mahanaim.[o] 9 He made him king over Gilead,[p]
Ashuri[a][q] and Jezreel, and also over Ephraim, Benjamin and all Israel.[r]
10 Ish-Bosheth son of Saul was forty years old when he became king over Israel, and
he reigned two years. The house of Judah, however, followed David. 11 The length of time
David was king in Hebron over the house of Judah was seven years and six months.[s]
12 Abner son of Ner, together with the men of Ish-Bosheth son of Saul, left Mahanaim and went to Gibeon.[t] 13 Joab[u] son of Zeruiah and David's men went out and met them
at the pool of Gibeon. One group sat down on one side of the pool and one group on the
other side.
14 Then Abner said to Joab, "Let's have some of the young men get up and fight hand
to hand in front of us."
"All right, let them do it," Joab said.
15 So they stood up and were counted off—twelve men for Benjamin and Ish-Bosheth
son of Saul, and twelve for David. 16 Then each man grabbed his opponent by the head
and thrust his dagger into his opponent's side, and they fell down together. So that place
in Gibeon was called Helkath Hazzurim.[b]

2:1 [e]Ge 13:18; 1Sa 30:31
2:2 [f]1Sa 25:43; 30:5 [g]1Sa 25:42
2:3 [h]1Sa 27:2; 30:9
2:4 [i]1Sa 30:31 [j]1Sa 2:35; 2Sa 5:3-5 [k]1Sa 31:11-13
2:5 [l]1Sa 23:21
2:6 [m]Ex 34:6; 1Ti 1:16
2:8 [n]1Sa 14:50 [o]Ge 32:2
2:9 [p]Nu 32:26 [q]Jdg 1:32 [r]1Ch 12:29
2:11 [s]2Sa 5:5
2:12 [t]Jos 18:25
2:13 [u]2Sa 8:16; 1Ch 2:16; 11:6

[a] 9 Or *Asher* [b] 16 *Helkath Hazzurim* means *field of daggers* or *field of hostilities.*

■ **2:1—10:19** *David's Kingship Under Divine Blessing.* David's reign began with much success due to God's blessings. These blessings appear in two main ways: David's rise to kingship (2:1—5:5) and his throne in Jerusalem (5:6—8:18).

■ **2:1—5:5** *David's Rise to Kingship.* Although David had been privately anointed earlier (1Sa 16), he was here about to be acknowledged by the entire nation. This recognition took place first over Judah at Hebron (2:1–7), then over all Israel (2:8—5:5) and again at Hebron (5:1–5).

■ **2:1–7** *David Becomes King Over Judah at Hebron.* It stands to reason that David would first be acknowledged as king by his own tribe, Judah.

2:1 David inquired of the LORD. Although fully aware of his divine appointment to become Israel's next king, David was nevertheless not presumptuous with respect to the steps along the way, and so he sought the Lord's guidance, as he had done so often before (e.g., 1Sa 23:2,4,9–12; 30:7–8). **Hebron.** Situated 19 miles south-southwest of Jerusalem, Hebron has the highest elevation of any town in Israel and for various reasons was a site strategically well suited for the inauguration of David's rule over Judah. Hebron had been a Canaanite royal city at the time of the arrival of the Israelites from Egypt (Jos 10:3), but its links with the people of God extend all the way back to the patriarchs (e.g., Ge 13:18; 23:2,19; 35:27).

2:2 Ahinoam . . . Abigail. See note on 1 Samuel 25:40–44. **Jezreel.** Listed in Joshua 15:55–56 as one of the hill country villages south of Hebron, this Jezreel is not to be confused with the better known Jezreel to the north. **Carmel.** See notes on 1 Samuel 15:12 and 25:2.

2:4 anointed David king. On the significance of anointing, see 1 Samuel 2:10 and its note. Having earlier been anointed by Samuel (1Sa 16:3,12–13), David was now anointed a second time, as king over the house of Judah. David would be anointed yet a third time in 5:3, as king over all Israel.

2:5 The LORD bless you. David's commendation of the Jabeshites for showing kindness to Saul accomplished two things: (1) It attested to his lack of malice toward the now-deceased king, and (2) it set the stage for his own bid for leadership over the Gileadites in Transjordan.

■ **2:8—5:5** *David Becomes King Over All Israel.* The struggle between the houses of Saul and David culminated with David becoming king over all Israel. These chapters divide into four parts: resistance from Saul's house (2:8—3:5), Abner's murder (3:6–39), Ish-Bosheth's murder (4:1–12) and David's becoming king over all the tribes of Israel at Hebron (5:1–5).

■ **2:8—3:5** *Resistance From Saul's House.* Those remaining in Saul's house still resisted David's claims and asserted the right to rule. Abner's installation of Saul's son Ish-Bosheth as king over Israel resulted in war between the houses of Saul and David.

2:8 Ish-Bosheth. See note on 1 Samuel 31:2. As will become apparent as the narrative progresses, this last surviving son of Saul was little more than a pawn in the hand of Abner. **brought him over to Mahanaim.** Abner probably brought Ish-Bosheth over the Jordan into Transjordan in an effort to escape Philistine pressure. Two sites near the Jabbok River have been suggested: one about seven miles and the other about 17 miles east of the Jordan River.

2:9 king over Gilead . . . all Israel. Ish-Bosheth's claim to jurisdiction over the territories listed was probably, in some cases at least, more a matter of optimistic projection than one of factual reality.

2:11 seven years and six months. See note on 5:4–5.

2:12 Gibeon. A Benjamite town identified with modern El-Jib, located about five miles north of Jerusalem.

2:13 Joab son of Zeruiah. See note on verse 18. **pool of Gibeon.** See Jeremiah 41:12. Whether this pool should be identified with the large cylindrical cistern excavated at Gibeon remains uncertain.

2:14 Let's have some of the young men get up and fight. Abner suggested a form of representative combat somewhat similar to the earlier contest between David and Goliath (see note on 1Sa 17:4). In the present case, as in the earlier one, large-scale bloodshed was not thereby avoided (vv. 17,31).

2:17 [v]2Sa 3:1
2:18 [w]2Sa 3:39 [x]2Sa 3:30 [y]1Sa 26:6 [z]1Ch 2:16 [a]1Ch 12:8
2:22 [b]2Sa 3:27
2:23 [c]2Sa 3:27; 4:6 [d]2Sa 20:12
2:26 [e]Dt 32:42; Jer 46:10,14
2:28 [f]2Sa 18:16 [g]Jdg 3:27
2:29 [h]ver 8
2:32 [i]Ge 49:29
3:1 [j]1Ki 14:30 [k]2Sa 5:10 [l]2Sa 2:17
3:2 [m]1Sa 25:43; 1Ch 3:1-3
3:3 [n]1Sa 25:42 [o]2Sa 13:1,28 [p]1Sa 27:8; 2Sa 13:37; 14:32; 15:8

17 The battle that day was very fierce, and Abner and the men of Israel were defeated[v] by David's men.
18 The three sons of Zeruiah[w] were there: Joab,[x] Abishai[y] and Asahel.[z] Now Asahel was
as fleet-footed as a wild gazelle.[a] 19 He chased Abner, turning neither to the right nor to
the left as he pursued him. 20 Abner looked behind him and asked, "Is that you, Asahel?"
"It is," he answered.
21 Then Abner said to him, "Turn aside to the right or to the left; take on one of the
young men and strip him of his weapons." But Asahel would not stop chasing him.
22 Again Abner warned Asahel, "Stop chasing me! Why should I strike you down? How
could I look your brother Joab in the face?"[b]
23 But Asahel refused to give up the pursuit; so Abner thrust the butt of his spear into Asahel's stomach,[c] and the spear came out through his back. He fell there and died on the spot.
And every man stopped when he came to the place where Asahel had fallen and died.[d]
24 But Joab and Abishai pursued Abner, and as the sun was setting, they came to the
hill of Ammah, near Giah on the way to the wasteland of Gibeon. 25 Then the men of Benjamin rallied behind Abner. They formed themselves into a group and took their stand
on top of a hill.
26 Abner called out to Joab, "Must the sword devour[e] forever? Don't you realize that
this will end in bitterness? How long before you order your men to stop pursuing their
brothers?"
27 Joab answered, "As surely as God lives, if you had not spoken, the men would have
continued the pursuit of their brothers until morning.[a]"
28 So Joab[f] blew the trumpet,[g] and all the men came to a halt; they no longer pursued
Israel, nor did they fight anymore.
29 All that night Abner and his men marched through the Arabah. They crossed the
Jordan, continued through the whole Bithron[b] and came to Mahanaim.[h]
30 Then Joab returned from pursuing Abner and assembled all his men. Besides Asahel, nineteen of David's men were found missing. 31 But David's men had killed three
hundred and sixty Benjamites who were with Abner. 32 They took Asahel and buried him
in his father's tomb[i] at Bethlehem. Then Joab and his men marched all night and arrived
at Hebron by daybreak.

3 The war between the house of Saul and the house of David lasted a long time.[j] David grew stronger and stronger,[k] while the house of Saul grew weaker and weaker.[l]
2 Sons were born to David in Hebron:

His firstborn was Amnon the son of Ahinoam[m] of Jezreel;
3 his second, Kileab the son of Abigail[n] the widow of Nabal of Carmel;
the third, Absalom[o] the son of Maacah daughter of Talmai king of Geshur;[p]

a 27 Or *spoken this morning, the men would not have taken up the pursuit of their brothers*; or *spoken, the men would have given up the pursuit of their brothers by morning* b 29 Or *morning*; or *ravine*; the meaning of the Hebrew for this word is uncertain.

2:18 three sons of Zeruiah. According to 1 Chronicles 2:16, Zeruiah was one of David's two sisters, which would make her three sons David's nephews. **Joab.** Joab played a significant role throughout David's reign, serving as commander of David's forces (8:16). Although ardently supportive of David, Joab at times proved to be uncontrollable (3:39), acting independently in his own interests (3:26–27) and even defying David's orders (18:5,9–14). Joab's excesses and misdeeds eventually led to his execution under King Solomon (1Ki 2:28–35). **Abishai.** Abishai served alongside Joab in David's army (10:10; 18:2) and is described in 23:18 as "chief of the Three." **Asahel.** Also listed among David's mighty men (23:24), Asahel's relentless pursuit of Abner in the present episode would lead to his untimely and grisly demise (v. 23).

2:22 How could I look your brother Joab in the face? Abner's attempts to avoid the necessity of striking down Asahel may have been motivated not simply by a fear of reprisals from Joab, but also by a desire not to erect unnecessary barriers to an eventual compromise with David. See note on verse 26. See *WLC* 135.

2:26 order your men to stop pursuing their brothers? Abner's reference to "their brothers" may suggest a shift in a more conciliatory direction. Perhaps Abner sensed that David's ascendancy over all Israel could not long be denied.

2:28 trumpet. See note on 1 Samuel 13:3.

2:29 Arabah. See note on 1 Samuel 23:24.

2:30–31 The disparity between the number of casualties suffered by David's troops and those inflicted on the Benjamites is a token of things to come.

3:1 war between the house of Saul and the house of David. At least as far as the northern tribes of Israel were concerned, the transference of power to David after the death of Saul did not proceed without opposition. A key figure in the continued pro-Saulite sentiment was Abner, Saul's former military commander and the one who had installed Saul's surviving son, Ish-Bosheth, as king in Mahanaim (2:8–9). The momentum, however, was decidedly in David's favor (see note on 2:30–31). The hints seen already in chapter 2 that Abner knew this (vv. 22,26) finds further confirmation in the events of the present chapter (e.g., v. 17).

3:2–11 The list of six sons born to David (vv. 2–5) serves to amplify the statement in verse 1 that "David grew stronger and stronger," while the wrangling between Abner and Ish-Bosheth over a concubine (vv. 6–11) dramatizes the final statement in verse 1 that "the house of Saul grew weaker and weaker."

3:2 Sons were born to David in Hebron. As the list that follows reveals, David took additional wives. In 5:13–16, after David's arrival in Jerusalem, yet more wives, along with concubines, would be added and at least 11 more children would be born to David (see the cumulative list in 1Ch 3:1–9). While the Biblical narrator offers no explicit evaluation of David's "royal" behavior (i.e., ancient Near Eastern kings commonly multiplied wives and children), it was less than ideal according to the standards of Deuteronomy 17:17. **Amnon.** In chapter 13 Amnon would rape his half sister Tamar and indirectly contribute to the alienation of David from Absalom, who would in turn avenge Tamar's disgrace by killing Amnon (13:28–29).

3:3 Absalom. See chapters 13–18; see note on v. 2. **Maacah daughter of Talmai king of Geshur.** David's taking of a foreign

4 the fourth, Adonijah[q] the son of Haggith;
the fifth, Shephatiah the son of Abital;
5 and the sixth, Ithream the son of David's wife Eglah.
These were born to David in Hebron.

Abner Goes Over to David

6 During the war between the house of Saul and the house of David, Abner had been
strengthening his own position in the house of Saul. 7 Now Saul had had a concubine[r]
named Rizpah[s] daughter of Aiah. And Ish-Bosheth said to Abner, "Why did you sleep
with my father's concubine?"
8 Abner was very angry because of what Ish-Bosheth said and he answered, "Am I a
dog's head[t]—on Judah's side? This very day I am loyal to the house of your father Saul and
to his family and friends. I haven't handed you over to David. Yet now you accuse me of an
offense involving this woman! 9 May God deal with Abner, be it ever so severely, if I do not
do for David what the LORD promised[u] him on oath 10 and transfer the kingdom from the
house of Saul and establish David's throne over Israel and Judah from Dan to Beersheba."[v]
11 Ish-Bosheth did not dare to say another word to Abner, because he was afraid of him.
12 Then Abner sent messengers on his behalf to say to David, "Whose land is it?
Make an agreement with me, and I will help you bring all Israel over to you."
13 "Good," said David. "I will make an agreement with you. But I demand one thing
of you: Do not come into my presence unless you bring Michal daughter of Saul when
you come to see me."[w] 14 Then David sent messengers to Ish-Bosheth son of Saul, demanding, "Give me my wife Michal,[x] whom I betrothed to myself for the price of a hundred Philistine foreskins."
15 So Ish-Bosheth gave orders and had her taken away from her husband[y] Paltiel[z] son
of Laish. 16 Her husband, however, went with her, weeping behind her all the way to Bahurim.[a] Then Abner said to him, "Go back home!" So he went back.
17 Abner conferred with the elders[b] of Israel and said, "For some time you have wanted to make David your king. 18 Now do it! For the LORD promised David, 'By my servant
David I will rescue my people Israel from the hand of the Philistines[c] and from the hand
of all their enemies.[d]' "
19 Abner also spoke to the Benjamites in person. Then he went to Hebron to tell David everything that Israel and the whole house of Benjamin[e] wanted to do. 20 When Abner, who had twenty men with him, came to David at Hebron, David prepared a feast for
him and his men. 21 Then Abner said to David, "Let me go at once and assemble all Israel for my lord the king, so that they may make a compact[f] with you, and that you may
rule over all that your heart desires."[g] So David sent Abner away, and he went in peace.

Joab Murders Abner

22 Just then David's men and Joab returned from a raid and brought with them a great
deal of plunder. But Abner was no longer with David in Hebron, because David had sent

3:4 [q]1Ki 1:5,11
3:7 [r]2Sa 16:21-22 [s]2Sa 21:8-11
3:8 [t]1Sa 24:14; 2Sa 9:8; 16:9
3:9 [u]1Sa 15:28; 1Ki 19:2
3:10 [v]Jdg 20:1; 1Sa 3:20
3:13 [w]Ge 43:5; 1Sa 18:20
3:14 [x]1Sa 18:27
3:15 [y]Dt 24:1-4 [z]1Sa 25:44
3:16 [a]2Sa 16:5; 19:16
3:17 [b]Jdg 11:11
3:18 [c]1Sa 9:16 [d]1Sa 15:28; 2Sa 8:6
3:19 [e]1Sa 10:20-21; 1Ch 12:2,16,29
3:21 [f]ver 10,12 [g]1Ki 11:37

---

wife from the small Aramean kingdom of Geshur may have been politically motivated; i.e., it gave him an ally north of Ish-Bosheth's shaky realm.

3:4 Adonijah. See 1 Kings 1–2.

■ **3:6–39** *Abner Is Murdered.* Abner defected to David but was murdered by Joab without David's knowledge or approval. David lamented Abner's death.

3:7 Rizpah. She is mentioned again in 21:7–13. **Why did you sleep with my father's concubine?** Abner's appropriation of Saul's concubine would have been tantamount to laying claim to the throne (see 12:8 and its note; 16:21 and its note; 1Ki 2:22). The reader is not told whether Ish-Bosheth's suspicion was well-founded or based in the paranoia so typical of his father, Saul. Whatever the case, Abner jumped at the chance to shift his allegiance to David (vv. 8–10).

3:9 what the LORD promised him on oath. See 1 Samuel 13:14, 15:28, 24:20, 25:28, 2 Samuel 5:2 and their notes.

3:10 Dan to Beersheba. See note on Judges 20:1.

3:11 Ish-Bosheth . . . was afraid of him. Ish-Bosheth's reaction indicates that Abner was in a position not only to make a threat, but also to carry it out.

3:12 Whose land is it? The expected answer was that it was either Abner's or David's.

3:13 bring Michal daughter of Saul. The return to David of his wife Michal (1Sa 18:27) would not only have righted the wrong of Saul's having given her to another in David's absence (1Sa 25:44), but it would also have somewhat strengthened his claim to the throne over Saul's former realm. The restrictions of Deuteronomy 24:1–4 did not apply in David's situation, since his separation from Michal was involuntary.

3:14 David sent messengers to Ish-Bosheth. The insecurity of Ish-Bosheth's position is evident not only in his fear of Abner (v. 11) but also in his inability to resist David's orders. **a hundred Philistine foreskins.** David referred to the bride-price that Saul had set for Michal (1Sa 18:25); his payment had actually been twice the amount (1Sa 18:27).

3:16 Her husband, however, went with her, weeping. Saul's misdeeds brought suffering not only upon himself, but also upon others (see note on v. 13). **Bahurim.** Tentatively identified with Ras et-Tumeim, about 1.5 miles east of Jerusalem in what would have been Benjamite territory, Bahurim was also the hometown of Shimei, son of Gera (16:5; 1Ki 2:8).

3:17 you have wanted to make David your king. See note on verse 1. Apparently Ish-Bosheth and, more importantly, Abner were all that had stood in the way of a reestablishment of harmonious relations between Israel and David. Abner here stepped aside, and Ish-Bosheth would not long stand without him (ch. 4).

3:18 By my servant David I will rescue my people Israel from the . . . Philistines. David was now recognized as the recipient of a commission like that first given to Saul (1Sa 9:16).

3:21 that they may make a compact with you. See 5:3. **in peace.** The repetition of this phrase twice more in verses 22–23 underscores that David was not involved in Abner's death (see also vv. 26,28–29,37).

him away, and he had gone in peace. 23 When Joab and all the soldiers with him arrived,
he was told that Abner son of Ner had come to the king and that the king had sent him
away and that he had gone in peace.
24 So Joab went to the king and said, "What have you done? Look, Abner came to you.
Why did you let him go? Now he is gone! 25 You know Abner son of Ner; he came to deceive you and observe your movements and find out everything you are doing."

3:27 [h]2Sa 2:8 [i]2Sa 2:22; 20:9-10; 1Ki 2:5

26 Joab then left David and sent messengers after Abner, and they brought him back
from the well of Sirah. But David did not know it. 27 Now when Abner[h] returned to Hebron, Joab took him aside into the gateway, as though to speak with him privately. And
there, to avenge the blood of his brother Asahel, Joab stabbed him in the stomach, and
he died.[i]

3:28 [j]ver 37; Dt 21:9

3:29 [k]Lev 20:9 [l]1Ki 2:31-33 [m]Lev 15:2

28 Later, when David heard about this, he said, "I and my kingdom are forever innocent[j] before the LORD concerning the blood of Abner son of Ner. 29 May his blood[k] fall
upon the head of Joab and upon all his father's house![l] May Joab's house never be without someone who has a running sore[m] or leprosy[a] or who leans on a crutch or who falls
by the sword or who lacks food."
30 (Joab and his brother Abishai murdered Abner because he had killed their brother
Asahel in the battle at Gibeon.)

3:31 [n]2Sa 1:2, 11; Ps 30:11; Isa 20:2 [o]Ge 37:34

3:32 [p]Nu 14:1; Pr 24:17

3:33 [q]2Sa 1:17

31 Then David said to Joab and all the people with him, "Tear your clothes and put on
sackcloth[n] and walk in mourning[o] in front of Abner." King David himself walked behind
the bier. 32 They buried Abner in Hebron, and the king wept[p] aloud at Abner's tomb. All
the people wept also.
33 The king sang this lament[q] for Abner:

"Should Abner have died as the lawless die?
34 Your hands were not bound,
your feet were not fettered.
You fell as one falls before wicked men."

And all the people wept over him again.

3:35 [r]Ru 1:17; 1Sa 3:17 [s]1Sa 31:13; 2Sa 1:12; 12:17; Jer 16:7

3:37 [t]ver 28

3:38 [u]2Sa 1:19

3:39 [v]2Sa 2:18 [w]2Sa 19:5-7 [x]1Ki 2:5-6, 33-34; Ps 41:10; 101:8

35 Then they all came and urged David to eat something while it was still day; but David took an oath, saying, "May God deal with me, be it ever so severely,[r] if I taste bread[s]
or anything else before the sun sets!"
36 All the people took note and were pleased; indeed, everything the king did pleased
them. 37 So on that day all the people and all Israel knew that the king had no part[t] in
the murder of Abner son of Ner.
38 Then the king said to his men, "Do you not realize that a prince and a great man
has fallen[u] in Israel this day? 39 And today, though I am the anointed king, I am weak,
and these sons of Zeruiah[v] are too strong for me.[w] May the LORD repay[x] the evildoer according to his evil deeds!"

Ish-Bosheth Murdered

4:1 [y]2Sa 3:27; Ezr 4:4

4:2 [z]Jos 9:17; 18:25

4 When Ish-Bosheth son of Saul heard that Abner[y] had died in Hebron, he lost courage, and all Israel became alarmed. 2 Now Saul's son had two men who were leaders of raiding bands. One was named Baanah and the other Recab; they were sons of
Rimmon the Beerothite from the tribe of Benjamin—Beeroth[z] is considered part of

[a] *29* The Hebrew word was used for various diseases affecting the skin—not necessarily leprosy.

3:24 What . . . ? Look . . . Why . . . ? Now he is gone! Joab's agitation at the thought of Abner's peaceful departure was apparent in his words to David.
3:26 well of Sirah. Possibly located a few miles north of Hebron. **But David did not know it.** This notice is yet another confirmation of David's innocence in the death of Abner (vv. 21–23, 28–29,37).
3:27 to avenge the blood of his brother Asahel. See also verse 30. In 2:18–23 Abner's slaying of Asahel is depicted as essentially a matter of self-defense, and the battle context of Abner's action makes it doubtful that Joab had the right to act as an "avenger of blood" (see Nu 35:16–25; Dt 19:11–13; Jos 20:3; 2Sa 14:11). Joab's treacherous murder of Abner may well have found further motivation in a desire to eliminate a potential rival in David's court (see his murder of Amasa in 20:10).
3:28 I and my kingdom are forever innocent. See verses 21–23, 26 and 37.
3:29 May his blood fall upon the head of Joab. David's decision to content himself with uttering a curse upon Joab's house, in lieu of taking direct disciplinary action, may have arisen in part from the slightly ambiguous circumstances of Joab's crime. But it was more likely related to such factors as Joab's considerable power and reputation and his familial relationship with David. Ultimately, however, Joab's crime did not go unpunished (1Ki 2:5–6,28–35).
3:33 lawless. The word is that from which the name Nabal, "fool," is derived in 1 Samuel 25:3, etc.
3:39 too strong. That is, "too hard" or "ruthless." See note on verse 29; compare 16:10 and 19:22.
■ **4:1–12** *Ish-Bosheth Is Murdered.* Some of Ish-Bosheth's own men murdered him. The resistance of the house of Saul grew weaker and weaker (3:1).
4:1 Abner had died. The death of Abner affected Ish-Bosheth and "all Israel" in the same way, but for different reasons. Ish-Bosheth "lost courage" because he knew that Abner's death meant the loss of the backbone of his government. Israel, on the other hand, "became alarmed" by what may have appeared as a rejection of its friendly overture to David (3:17–21).
4:2 from the tribe of Benjamin. The Benjamite origin of Ish-

Benjamin, 3because the people of Beeroth fled to Gittaim[a] and have lived there as
aliens to this day.
4(Jonathan[b] son of Saul had a son who was lame in both feet. He was five years old
when the news[c] about Saul and Jonathan came from Jezreel. His nurse picked him up
and fled, but as she hurried to leave, he fell and became crippled.[d] His name was Mephibosheth.)[e]
5Now Recab and Baanah, the sons of Rimmon the Beerothite, set out for the house
of Ish-Bosheth,[f] and they arrived there in the heat of the day while he was taking his
noonday rest. 6They went into the inner part of the house as if to get some wheat, and
they stabbed[g] him in the stomach. Then Recab and his brother Baanah slipped away.
7They had gone into the house while he was lying on the bed in his bedroom. After
they stabbed and killed him, they cut off his head. Taking it with them, they traveled all
night by way of the Arabah. 8They brought the head of Ish-Bosheth to David at Hebron
and said to the king, "Here is the head of Ish-Bosheth son of Saul,[h] your enemy, who
tried to take your life. This day the LORD has avenged my lord the king against Saul and
his offspring."
9David answered Recab and his brother Baanah, the sons of Rimmon the Beerothite, "As surely as the LORD lives, who has delivered[i] me out of all trouble, 10when a man
told me, 'Saul is dead,' and thought he was bringing good news, I seized him and put him
to death in Ziklag.[j] That was the reward I gave him for his news! 11How much more—
when wicked men have killed an innocent man in his own house and on his own bed—
should I not now demand his blood[k] from your hand and rid the earth of you!"
12So David gave an order to his men, and they killed them.[l] They cut off their hands
and feet and hung the bodies by the pool in Hebron. But they took the head of Ish-Bosheth and buried it in Abner's tomb at Hebron.

David Becomes King Over Israel

5 All the tribes of Israel[m] came to David at Hebron and said, "We are your own flesh
and blood.[n] 2In the past, while Saul was king over us, you were the one who led Israel on their military campaigns.[o] And the LORD said to you, 'You will shepherd[p] my people Israel, and you will become their ruler.[q]' "
3When all the elders of Israel had come to King David at Hebron, the king made a compact[r] with them at Hebron before the LORD, and they anointed[s] David king over Israel.

4:3 [a]Ne 11:33
4:4 [b]1Sa 18:1 [c]1Sa 31:1-4 [d]Lev 21:18 [e]2Sa 9:3,6; 1Ch 8:34; 9:40
4:5 [f]2Sa 2:8
4:6 [g]2Sa 2:23
4:8 [h]1Sa 24:4; 25:29
4:9 [i]Ge 48:16; 1Ki 1:29
4:10 [j]2Sa 1:2-16
4:11 [k]Ge 9:5; Ps 9:12
4:12 [l]2Sa 1:15
5:1 [m]2Sa 19:43 [n]1Ch 11:1
5:2 [o]1Sa 18:5,13,16 [p]1Sa 16:1; 2Sa 7:7 [q]1Sa 25:30
5:3 [r]2Sa 3:21 [s]2Sa 2:4

Bosheth's soon-to-be assassins is stressed (two verses are dedicated to establishing it), perhaps in order to show that disenchantment with the house of Saul extended even into his own tribal area. See also the following note.

4:3 people of Beeroth fled to Gittaim. Although, according to Joshua 9:17, Beeroth was one of the four major cities of the Gibeonites (an Amorite people who had duped Joshua into making a peace treaty with them), Joshua 18:25 indicates that the town was allotted to Benjamin at the time of the division of the land. King Saul, according to 2 Samuel 21:1–2, attempted during his reign to annihilate the Gibeonites, and it is not unreasonable to suppose that this act of aggression may explain the flight of the people of Beeroth to Gittaim (location unknown). Presumably, the evacuated city of Beeroth would have been resettled by Benjamites. Whether Ish-Bosheth's assassins were from the original Beerothites or from the resettlers remains unclear.

4:4 news about Saul and Jonathan. That is, of their deaths (1Sa 31; 2Sa 1). **Mephibosheth.** Mention of Mephibosheth and his crippled condition at this point in the narrative emphasizes the debilitated condition of the house of Saul—apart from Ish-Bosheth, who was soon to die. Mephibosheth would appear again later (9:6–13; 16:1–4; 19:24–30; 21:7; 21:8 mentions a different Mephibosheth). In light of 1 Chronicles 8:34 and 9:40, his name seems originally to have been Merib-Baal, in which case the present form may have arisen through a transformation similar to that explained in the note on 1 Samuel 31:2.

4:7 This verse elaborates on the murder and escape described more briefly in verse 6. **Arabah.** See note on 1 Samuel 23:24.

4:9 who has delivered me out of all trouble. Whereas Recab and Baanah tried to portray themselves as pious agents of the Lord's judgment against Saul (v. 8), David's response was couched in such a way as to make it clear that, with the Lord as his deliverer, David had no need of human assistance.

4:12 So David gave an order. David showed none of the hesitation to act in this instance that he had shown in the case of Joab (see note on 3:29). **cut off their hands and feet.** Though mutilation of this sort was not uncommon in the ancient Near East, it may have had a special significance here: removal of the offending members—hands that had committed the murder and feet that had brought the news. **pool in Hebron.** This was undoubtedly a public spot. **Abner's tomb.** See 3:32.

■ **5:1–5** *David Becomes the King Over All Tribes at Hebron.* David succeeded in becoming king over all Israel.

5:1 All the tribes of Israel. That is, their leaders. Compare "all the elders" in verse 3. It has been suggested that the Hebrew word here translated "tribes" may also mean "rulers." **your own flesh and blood.** This is an expression of kinship (19:12–13; Ge 29:14; Jdg 9:2), and it was the first of three reasons given by the Israelites in verses 1–2 for wanting to make David king. See notes on "you were the one who led Israel on their military campaigns" and "the LORD said to you" at verse 2.

5:2 you were the one who led Israel on their military campaigns. The second reason for wanting to make David king (see note on "your own flesh and blood" at v. 1) is David's military leadership (1Sa 17:32,45–47; 18:7,13,16; 25:28). **the LORD said to you.** The third reason (see previous note; see note on "your own flesh and blood" at v. 1) for wanting to make David king was David's divine appointment (see 1Sa 16:1 and its note). **shepherd.** This designation is most often used metaphorically in the Bible, either for God the Father (Ge 48:15; 49:24; Pss 23:1; 80:1; etc.), for his Son Jesus (Jn 10:11; Heb 13:20; 1Pe 5:4; Rev 7:17; etc.) or, as in this case and frequently, for God's appointed human leaders (Nu 27:15–17; 2Sa 7:7; etc.). The image invoked is one of intimate, caring leadership. See verse 12 and its note. **ruler.** The same word is rendered "leader" in 1 Samuel 9:16 (see its note).

5:3 the king made a compact. See 3:21. The compact establishing David's rule over the northern tribes quite likely comprised regulations for the kingship (perhaps cf. 1Sa 10:25), including the rights and responsibilities of the respective parties to one another and to the Lord (2Ki 11:17). That David's compact was unable to erase entirely the separate sense of identity felt by the northern and southern tribes is evident in the revolt of Sheba (20:1) and particularly in the dissolution of the united kingdom under Rehoboam (1Ki 12:16). **they anointed David.** See note on 2:4.

4David was thirty years old[t] when he became king, and he reigned[u] forty[v] years. 5In
Hebron he reigned over Judah seven years and six months,[w] and in Jerusalem he reigned
over all Israel and Judah thirty-three years.

David Conquers Jerusalem

6The king and his men marched to Jerusalem[x] to attack the Jebusites,[y] who lived
there. The Jebusites said to David, "You will not get in here; even the blind and the lame
can ward you off." They thought, "David cannot get in here." 7Nevertheless, David captured the fortress of Zion, the City of David.[z]
8On that day, David said, "Anyone who conquers the Jebusites will have to use the
water shaft[a] to reach those 'lame and blind' who are David's enemies.[b]" That is why they
say, "The 'blind and lame' will not enter the palace."
9David then took up residence in the fortress and called it the City of David. He built
up the area around it, from the supporting terraces[c][a] inward. 10And he became more and
more powerful,[b] because the LORD God Almighty was with him.

5:4 [t]Lk 3:23 [u]1Ki 2:11; 1Ch 3:4 [v]1Ch 26:31; 29:27
5:5 [w]2Sa 2:11; 1Ch 3:4
5:6 [x]Jdg 1:8 [y]Jos 15:8
5:7 [z]2Sa 6:12,16; 1Ki 2:10
5:9 [a]ver 7; 1Ki 9:15,24
5:10 [b]2Sa 3:1

a *8* Or *use scaling hooks* b *8* Or *are hated by David* c *9* Or *the Millo*

5:4–5 In the Old Testament, a regnal formula often introduces the account of a king's official tenure in office (e.g., 1Sa 13:1; 2Sa 2:10; 1Ki 14:21; 22:42; etc.). In this case it appropriately marks David's assumption of power over all Israel.

■ **5:6—10:19** *David's Throne Is Established Forever in Jerusalem.* God's blessing on David is reflected in the acquisition of Jerusalem as the capital city (5:6—6:23), in the promise of an everlasting dynasty (7:1–29) and in a number of other achievements (8:1—10:19).

■ **5:6—6:23** *Jerusalem Is Established.* David established Jerusalem as his capital city. He captured the city (5:6–16), conquered the Philistines (5:17–25) and brought the ark of God into the city (6:1–23).

■ **5:6–16** *David Captures Jerusalem.* David captured Jerusalem from the Jebusites and expanded the city as his residence and capital (vv. 6–16).

5:6 Jerusalem. A city of venerable antiquity (occupied as early as the third millennium B.C.), Jerusalem was located in what was by the time of David the tribal territory of Benjamin, close to the northern border of Judah. The city had earlier been conquered by Judah (Jdg 1:8), but neither Judah nor Benjamin had been successful in permanently dislodging its Jebusite inhabitants (Jos 15:63; Jdg 1:21). David may well have recognized that Jerusalem's strategic location and relatively independent status made the city ideally suited to the establishment of a national capital that would not imply favoritism to any particular region. **Jebusites said to David.** The Jebusites' taunt, whether suggestive of overconfidence or simply of a determination to fight to the last man (even be he blind or lame), seems to fit into a pattern of ongoing hostility between the Jebusites and their Bethlehemite neighbor David (see v. 8, where David's enmity against the Jebusites is mentioned; see also note on 1Sa 17:54).

5:7 fortress of Zion. This marks the first occurrence of "Zion" in the Bible and the only one in Samuel. The name, the meaning of which is uncertain, originally designated a fortified mound located in what is now southeast Jerusalem. Eventually the name came to be used in an extended sense for Jerusalem itself (e.g., 2Ki 19:21; Isa 2:3) and even for the entire nation of Israel (e.g., Ps 149:2; Isa 46:13). The name occurs frequently in Israel's poetic and prophetic literature, where it is often presented as the locus of God's mighty acts of salvation and judgment (e.g., Ps 14:7; Isa 4:4; La 4:11).

5:10 he became more and more powerful. Just as chapters 3–4 detail the manner in which "the house of Saul grew weaker and weaker" (3:1; see notes on 3:2–11; 4:1–12), so chapter 5 and following show David growing "stronger and stronger" (3:1). The fundamental reason for David's success now, as from the start, was

The City of the Jebusites/David's Jerusalem

Substantial historical evidence, both Biblical and extra-Biblical, places the temple of Solomon on the holy spot where King David built an altar to the Lord. David had purchased the land from Araunah the Jebusite, who was using the exposed bedrock as a threshing floor (2Sa 24:18-25). Tradition claims a much older sanctity for the site, associating it with the altar of Abraham on Mount Moriah (Ge 22:1-19). The writer of Genesis equates Moriah with "the mountain of the LORD" (Ge 22:14).

c. 1000 B.C.

Less than 11 acres in size, Jebus, a Canaanite city, could well defend itself against attack, with walls atop steep canyons and shafts reaching an underground water source. David captured the stronghold c. 1000 B.C. and made it his capital.

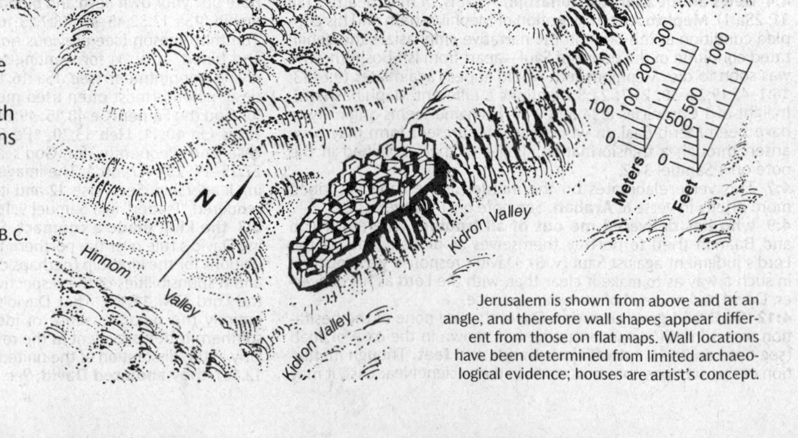

Jerusalem is shown from above and at an angle, and therefore wall shapes appear different from those on flat maps. Wall locations have been determined from limited archaeological evidence; houses are artist's concept.

11 Now Hiram[c] king of Tyre sent messengers to David, along with cedar logs and carpenters and stonemasons, and they built a palace for David. 12 And David knew that the
LORD had established him as king over Israel and had exalted his kingdom for the sake
of his people Israel.
13 After he left Hebron, David took more concubines and wives[d] in Jerusalem, and
more sons and daughters were born to him. 14 These are the names of the children born
to him there:[e] Shammua, Shobab, Nathan, Solomon, 15 Ibhar, Elishua, Nepheg, Japhia,
16 Elishama, Eliada and Eliphelet.

David Defeats the Philistines

17 When the Philistines heard that David had been anointed king over Israel, they
went up in full force to search for him, but David heard about it and went down to the
stronghold.[f] 18 Now the Philistines had come and spread out in the Valley of Rephaim;[g]
19 so David inquired[h] of the LORD, "Shall I go and attack the Philistines? Will you hand
them over to me?"

The LORD answered him, "Go, for I will surely hand the Philistines over to you."
20 So David went to Baal Perazim, and there he defeated them. He said, "As waters
break out, the LORD has broken out against my enemies before me." So that place was
called Baal Perazim.[a][i] 21 The Philistines abandoned their idols there, and David and his
men carried them off.[j]
22 Once more the Philistines came up and spread out in the Valley of Rephaim; 23 so
David inquired of the LORD, and he answered, "Do not go straight up, but circle around
behind them and attack them in front of the balsam trees. 24 As soon as you hear the
sound[k] of marching in the tops of the balsam trees, move quickly, because that will mean
the LORD has gone out in front[l] of you to strike the Philistine army." 25 So David did as the
LORD commanded him, and he struck down the Philistines all the way from Gibeon[b][m] to
Gezer.[n]

The Ark Brought to Jerusalem

6 David again brought together out of Israel chosen men, thirty thousand in all. 2 He
and all his men set out from Baalah[o] of Judah[c] to bring up from there the ark[p] of
God, which is called by the Name,[d][q] the name of the LORD Almighty, who is enthroned[r]
between the cherubim[s] that are on the ark. 3 They set the ark of God on a new cart[t] and
brought it from the house of Abinadab, which was on the hill. Uzzah and Ahio, sons of

5:11 [c]1Ki 5:1,18; 1Ch 14:1
5:13 [d]Dt 17:17; 1Ch 3:9
5:14 [e]1Ch 3:5
5:17 [f]2Sa 23:14; 1Ch 11:16
5:18 [g]Jos 15:8; 17:15; 18:16
5:19 [h]1Sa 23:2; 2Sa 2:1
5:20 [i]Isa 28:21
5:21 [j]Dt 7:5; 1Ch 14:12; Isa 46:2
5:24 [k]2Ki 7:6 [l]Jdg 4:14
5:25 [m]Isa 28:21 [n]1Ch 14:16
6:2 [o]Jos 15:9 [p]1Sa 4:4; 7:1 [q]Lev 24:16; Isa 63:14 [r]Ps 99:1 [s]Ex 25:22; 1Ch 13:5-6
6:3 [t]Nu 7:4-9; 1Sa 6:7

[a] 20 *Baal Perazim* means *the lord who breaks out.* [b] 25 Septuagint (see also 1 Chron. 14:16); Hebrew *Geba* [c] 2 That is, Kiriath Jearim; Hebrew *Baale Judah,* a variant of *Baalah of Judah* [d] 2 Hebrew; Septuagint and Vulgate do not have *the Name.*

---

that the Lord God Almighty was with him. See 1 Samuel 16:18 and its note.

5:11 Hiram king of Tyre. Tyre was a Phoenician port city located about 30 miles north of Mount Carmel and 25 miles south of Sidon. Hiram's generosity to David may have been motivated in part by the impressiveness of David's recent accomplishments, but it doubtless also involved an element of self-interest; namely, a concern that David not deny Hiram access to inland trade routes and necessary agricultural produce (note the goods supplied to Sidon and Tyre in Ezr 3:7). Hiram's friendship with Israel continued well into Solomon's reign (1Ki 5:1–12; 9:11; etc.).

5:12 the LORD had established him as king. See note on verse 10. **for the sake of his people Israel.** David understood not only that his kingship was dependent entirely upon God, but also that it was designed for the benefit of God's people rather than for his own self-gratification. See verse 2 and 8:15.

5:13–16 See 3:2 note and the slightly longer list in 1 Chronicles 14:3–7.

■ **5:17–25** *David Conquers the Philistines.* Before having had the time to organize the nation as he desired, David had to quell the Philistine threat.

5:17 When the Philistines heard . . . they went up in full force. While David's reign over Judah had not been contested by the Philistines, the extension of his domain to include the northern tribes posed a threat to Philistine interests that they could not ignore. **stronghold.** See note on 1 Samuel 23:14.

5:18 Valley of Rephaim. This valley begins just a few miles southwest of Jerusalem and descends in a westward direction toward Philistine territory. See also Joshua 15:8, 18:16, 2 Samuel 23:13 and especially the note on 21:16.

5:19 David inquired of the LORD. See note on 2:1.

5:20 So that place was called Baal Perazim. See NIV text note. Baal Perazim has been tentatively identified with a site three miles southwest of Jerusalem.

5:21 Philistines abandoned their idols. David inflicted upon the Philistines a loss of glory similar to that suffered by Israel with the capture of the ark in 1 Samuel 4 (especially v. 22). **carried them off.** See note on "set it beside" at 1 Samuel 5:2. First Chronicles 14:12 states that "David gave orders to burn them in the fire."

5:24 the sound of marching. Compare the divinely induced "sound of chariots and horses and a great army" in 2 Kings 7:6. **the LORD has gone out in front of you.** The Lord is a warrior (Ex 15:3) who goes before his people to fight for them (Ex 14:14; Dt 1:30).

5:25 Gibeon to Gezer. David's rout of the Philistines was more extensive and far more decisive than was Jonathan's in 1 Samuel 14:31. That David's defeat of this particular foe (8:1) was of special significance is reflected in the words of the people in 19:9 and in the Chronicler's summation in 1 Chronicles 14:17, and it is understandable in the light of verses such as 1 Samuel 9:16 and 2 Samuel 3:18.

■ **6:1–23** *David Brings the Ark of God to Jerusalem.* After an aborted first attempt, David brought the ark of God to Jerusalem.

6:2 Baalah of Judah. See note on 1 Samuel 6:21. **ark of God.** See note on 1 Samuel 3:3. **the Name.** See note on 1 Samuel 17:45 (see also Dt 12:5,11,21). **LORD Almighty.** See note on 1 Samuel 1:3.

6:3 new cart. This mode of transporting the ark recalls the Philistine precedent set in 1 Samuel 6:7, but it neglected the divine directive that the ark, equipped with rings and poles (e.g., Ex 25:12–14; 37:5), was to be carried, not carted (Nu 4:15,19; 7:9; Dt 10:8; Jos 3:8; etc.). **house of Abinadab.** See 1 Samuel 7:1–2. **Uzzah and Ahio.** While attempts have been made to identify one or the other of these with Eleazar of 1 Samuel 7:1, it is more likely that the two sons mentioned here were brothers of Eleazar or possibly even grandsons of Abinadab. The Hebrew word "son" can also mean "descendant."

Abinadab, were guiding the new cart 4 with the ark of God on it,[a] and Ahio was walking
in front of it. 5 David and the whole house of Israel were celebrating with all their might
before the LORD, with songs[b] and with harps, lyres, tambourines, sistrums and cymbals.[u]
6 When they came to the threshing floor of Nacon, Uzzah reached out and took hold
of[v] the ark of God, because the oxen stumbled. 7 The LORD's anger burned against Uzzah
because of his irreverent act;[w] therefore God struck him down[x] and he died there beside the ark of God.
8 Then David was angry because the LORD's wrath[y] had broken out against Uzzah, and
to this day that place is called Perez Uzzah.[c][z]
9 David was afraid of the LORD that day and said, "How[a] can the ark of the LORD ever
come to me?" 10 He was not willing to take the ark of the LORD to be with him in the City
of David. Instead, he took it aside to the house of Obed-Edom[b] the Gittite. 11 The ark of
the LORD remained in the house of Obed-Edom the Gittite for three months, and the LORD
blessed him and his entire household.[c]
12 Now King David[d] was told, "The LORD has blessed the household of Obed-Edom and
everything he has, because of the ark of God." So David went down and brought up the
ark of God from the house of Obed-Edom to the City of David with rejoicing. 13 When
those who were carrying the ark of the LORD had taken six steps, he sacrificed[e] a bull and
a fattened calf. 14 David, wearing a linen ephod,[f] danced[g] before the LORD with all his
might, 15 while he and the entire house of Israel brought up the ark of the LORD with
shouts and the sound of trumpets.[h]
16 As the ark of the LORD was entering the City of David,[i] Michal daughter of Saul
watched from a window. And when she saw King David leaping and dancing before the
LORD, she despised him in her heart.
17 They brought the ark of the LORD and set it in its place inside the tent that David had
pitched for it,[j] and David sacrificed burnt offerings[k] and fellowship offerings[d] before the
LORD. 18 After he had finished sacrificing[l] the burnt offerings and fellowship offerings, he
blessed the people in the name of the LORD Almighty. 19 Then he gave a loaf of bread, a
cake of dates and a cake of raisins[m] to each person in the whole crowd of Israelites, both
men and women.[n] And all the people went to their homes.
20 When David returned home to bless his household, Michal daughter of Saul came
out to meet him and said, "How the king of Israel has distinguished himself today, disrobing[o] in the sight of the slave girls of his servants as any vulgar fellow would!"
21 David said to Michal, "It was before the LORD, who chose me rather than your father

6:5 [u] 1Sa 18:6-7; Ezr 3:10; Ps 150:5
6:6 [v] Nu 4:15,19-20; 1Ch 13:9
6:7 [w] 1Ch 15:13-15 [x] Ex 19:22; 1Sa 6:19
6:8 [y] Ps 7:11 [z] Ge 38:29
6:9 [a] Ps 119:120
6:10 [b] 1Ch 13:13; 26:4-5
6:11 [c] Ge 30:27; 39:5
6:12 [d] 1Ki 8:1; 1Ch 15:25
6:13 [e] 1Ki 8:5,62
6:14 [f] Ex 19:6; 1Sa 2:18 [g] Ex 15:20
6:15 [h] Ps 47:5; 98:6
6:16 [i] 2Sa 5:7
6:17 [j] 1Ch 15:1; 2Ch 1:4 [k] Lev 1:1-17; 1Ki 8:62-64
6:18 [l] 1Ki 8:22
6:19 [m] Hos 3:1 [n] Ne 8:10
6:20 [o] ver 14,16

[a] *3,4* Dead Sea Scrolls and some Septuagint manuscripts; Masoretic Text *cart 4and they brought it with the ark of God from the house of Abinadab, which was on the hill* [b] *5* See Dead Sea Scrolls, Septuagint and 1 Chronicles 13:8; Masoretic Text *celebrating before the LORD with all kinds of instruments made of pine.* [c] *8* *Perez Uzzah* means *outbreak against Uzzah.* [d] *17* Traditionally *peace offerings*; also in verse 18

6:6 threshing floor of Nacon. Whether or not Nacon is to be considered a proper name or an adjectival construction, its meaning in Hebrew is something like "stable" or "secure"; see renderings of this word as "definite" (1Sa 23:23; 26:4) and as "established" (2Sa 7:16,26), the latter rendering referring to David's throne and house. It is a fine irony that the oxen should stumble (see note on "stumbled," below) and the ark begin to totter just at this place of assumed "stability." **stumbled.** More literally rendered, the Hebrew has the oxen "letting [the ark] fall." Not oxen, of course, but Levites should have been carrying the ark (see note on v. 3).
6:7 because of his irreverent act. The Hebrew here is difficult and may be an abbreviation of the phrase "because he had put his hand on the ark" (1Ch 13:10). It is also possible that the Chronicler simply paraphrased the text here in order to specify what the irreverent act had been. Either way, it seems that the punishment inflicted relates not only to Uzzah's reflex action to steady the ark, but, more importantly, to the unprescribed manner of the ark's transport (see note on v. 3; see also 1Ch 15:13–15).
6:8 Then David was angry. The reader is not told whether the cause of David's vexation was the Lord's apparent severity, Uzzah's recklessness or, as seems most likely, his own cavalier handling of the ark. Possibly one should think of it as being a combination of factors, with an emphasis on the latter. Compare note on "Samuel was troubled" at 1 Samuel 15:11.
6:10 Obed-Edom the Gittite. That is, a man of Gath. The ark was deposited in Gath under dreadful circumstances for the second time (1Sa 5:8), but with opposite results (v. 11; 1Sa 5:9). Whether the reference is to the Philistine city of Gath (see notes on 1Sa 4:1; 5:8; 5:10) or to Gath Rimmon (a Levitical city within the tribe of Dan or Manasseh; Jos 21:23–25) is uncertain. Obed-Edom, whose name means "servant of Edom" (cf. "Obadiah," which means "servant of Yah[weh]"), is frequently referred to as a Levite in Chronicles (e.g., 1Ch 15:17–25; 16:5,38; 26:4–5,8,15; 2Ch 25:24).
6:13 carrying the ark. This time the ark was transported in accordance with the Mosaic legislation (see notes on vv. 3,7). **six steps.** That is, after the first six steps, not every six steps. **he sacrificed.** David's sacrifice was perhaps a symbol of thanksgiving and intercession—thanksgiving that the procession had begun (six steps) apparently with God's blessing and intercession that it would so continue. **a bull and a fattened calf.** Or perhaps "a fattened bull." 1 Chronicles 15:26 mentions the sacrifice of seven bulls and seven rams, though it does not explicitly state that these were sacrificed after six steps (see above). What remains of 2 Samuel 6:13 in the Dead Sea Scrolls seems to follow the Chronicles version.
6:14 linen ephod. See note on 1 Samuel 2:18.
6:16 Michal daughter of Saul. The epithet "daughter of Saul" is apt here, for Michal showed as little regard for the ark and its significance as had her father during his reign (1Ch 13:3). As for David, "she despised him in her heart" for his exuberant display.
6:17 burnt offerings and fellowship offerings. See note on 1 Samuel 10:8.
6:18 See *WCF* 21.6.
6:20 How the king of Israel has distinguished himself. Or "honored himself." The Hebrew root is used as a key word elsewhere in Samuel (see note on 1Sa 2:29). Michal's comment was heavy with sarcasm, but David would turn it to his own advantage (v. 22). **disrobing.** David had laid aside his kingly garments and had worn only a linen ephod (v. 14). See *WCF* 21.6.
6:21 It was before the LORD. David would not accept Michal's indictment. It was not before the "slave girls" (v. 20)—that is, for their benefit—but "before the LORD" that he had celebrated.

or anyone from his house when he appointed[p] me ruler over the LORD's people Israel—I will
celebrate before the LORD. 22 I will become even more undignified than this, and I will be humiliated in my own eyes. But by these slave girls you spoke of, I will be held in honor."
23 And Michal daughter of Saul had no children to the day of her death.

God's Promise to David

7 After the king was settled in his palace[q] and the LORD had given him rest from all
his enemies around him, 2 he said to Nathan the prophet, "Here I am, living in a palace[r] of cedar, while the ark of God remains in a tent."[s]
3 Nathan replied to the king, "Whatever you have in mind, go ahead and do it, for the
LORD is with you."
4 That night the word of the LORD came to Nathan, saying:
5 "Go and tell my servant David, 'This is what the LORD says: Are you[t] the one
to build me a house to dwell in?[u] 6 I have not dwelt in a house from the day I
brought the Israelites up out of Egypt to this day. I have been moving from place
to place with a tent[v] as my dwelling.[w] 7 Wherever I have moved with all the Israelites,[x] did I ever say to any of their rulers whom I commanded to shepherd[y] my
people Israel, "Why have you not built me a house of cedar?[z]" '
8 "Now then, tell my servant David, 'This is what the LORD Almighty says: I took
you from the pasture and from following the flock[a] to be ruler[b] over my people Israel.[c] 9 I have been with you wherever you have gone,[d] and I have cut off all your
enemies from before you.[e] Now I will make your name great, like the names of the
greatest men of the earth. 10 And I will provide a place for my people Israel and will
plant[f] them so that they can have a home of their own and no longer be disturbed.
Wicked[g] people will not oppress them anymore,[h] as they did at the beginning
11 and have done ever since the time I appointed leaders[a][i] over my people Israel.
I will also give you rest from all your enemies.[j]
" 'The LORD declares to you that the LORD himself will establish[k] a house[l] for you:

6:21 [p]1Sa 13:14; 15:28
7:1 [q]1Ch 17:1
7:2 [r]2Sa 5:11 [s]Ex 26:1; Ac 7:45-46
7:5 [t]1Ki 8:19; 1Ch 22:8 [u]1Ki 5:3-5
7:6 [v]Ex 40:18,34 [w]1Ki 8:16
7:7 [x]Dt 23:14 [y]2Sa 5:2 [z]Lev 26:11-12
7:8 [a]1Sa 16:11 [b]2Sa 6:21 [c]Ps 78:70-72; 2Co 6:18*
7:9 [d]2Sa 5:10 [e]Ps 18:37-42
7:10 [f]Ex 15:17; Isa 5:1-7 [g]Ps 89:22-23 [h]Isa 60:18
7:11 [i]Jdg 2:16; 1Sa 12:9-11 [j]ver 1 [k]1Sa 25:28 [l]ver 27

a *11* Traditionally *judges*

6:22 I will become even more undignified than this. Literally, "I will humble myself even more than this." Unlike Eli and his sons (see 1Sa 2:29–30 and their notes) and Michal's own father Saul (see 1Sa 15:12,30 and their notes), David was willing to be abased that the Lord might receive the honor due him. Michal's vexation suggests that she, like her father, was not in sympathy with this spirit of kingly submission. This spirit was, however, precisely what was required of Israel's kings (see notes on 1Sa 10:1; 12:3–15; 13:13). **by these slave girls you spoke of, I will be held in honor.** David concluded his response to Michal's rebuke by repeating her own words (v. 20), but without the sarcasm. The notion that, although he had humbled himself in his own eyes, he would be held in honor by those more discerning than Michal, is in keeping with the general Biblical truth that in the Lord's economy "the lowly will be exalted and the exalted will be brought low" (Eze 21:26; see also 1Sa 2:7–8; Mt 23:12; Lk 14:10–11; 18:14).

6:23 Michal daughter of Saul had no children. The reader is not told whether Michal's childlessness resulted from David's decision or the Lord's, although the latter seems the more likely. Contrast 1 Chronicles 26:4–5, where the eight sons of Obed-Edom are listed as an indication of the Lord's blessing upon this one who had received the ark honorably (vv. 10–12).

■ **7:1–29** *God Promises David an Everlasting Dynasty.* David's reign reached its high point as he received a divine promise that his family would always be Israel's only legitimate royal family. This chapter divides into God's promise (vv. 1–17) and David's response (vv. 18–29).

■ **7:1–17** *God's Promises.* Refusing David's offer to build a temple for him, God promised David an everlasting dynasty instead. The ultimate fulfillment of this promise, based in God's promise of blessing to the patriarchs, is found in Jesus Christ, David's greater son.

7:1 rest from all his enemies. See notes on verses 6 and 9 (see also v. 11; Dt 12:10; 25:19; Jos 23:1).

7:2 Nathan. Mentioned here for the first time in the Old Testament, Nathan the prophet would also play a significant role in chapter 12 and 1 Kings 1. Further references to him include 1 Chronicles 29:29, 2 Chronicles 9:29 and 29:25. **while the ark of God remains in a tent.** David apparently viewed his palace as in some sense symbolic of his now-established rule (5:11–12), and he deemed it inappropriate that God's rulership not be similarly symbolized by a permanent dwelling for the ark. This focus on the ark links the present chapter with the immediately preceding one, which recounted David's bringing the ark to Jerusalem.

7:3 go ahead and do it. David's plan seemed reasonable enough to Nathan, but he was quick to reverse himself when so ordered by the Lord (v. 4). Nathan was no flatterer (12:7–14).

7:4–17 The theological and historical significance of the divine promise to David recorded in these verses (1Ch 17:3–15) can hardly be overstated. Indeed, the promise of an enduring Davidic kingdom has been called the ideological summit of the entire Old Testament. Looking back, it takes up the promises of blessing made to Abraham and his elect seed in Genesis (Ge 17:16) and brings them to rest on David (especially vv. 5,9–10,12). Looking forward, it sets the stage for the Messianic hope that would become a dominant thread in the fabric of Israel's faith both before and after the exile (e.g., Isa 11:1; Jer 23:5–6; Zec 3:8; 6:12). This hope would culminate ultimately in the coming of Jesus, the Christ (Isa 9:1–7; Lk 1:32–33,69–70; Ac 2:30–31; 13:22–23; Ro 1:1–4; 2Ti 2:8; Rev 22:16).

7:5 my servant David. Compare 3:18 and Psalm 89:3. The Lord's reference to David as "my servant" places David in a very select company, which includes Abraham (Ge 26:24), Moses (Nu 12:7–8; Dt 34:5), Caleb (Nu 14:24) and Joshua (Jos 24:29).

7:6 I have not dwelt in a house. God's concern had been to accompany his elect people throughout their wanderings (vv. 6–7). Not until he had planted them in their place (v. 10) and they had enjoyed a "rest" (v. 11) that in some sense exceeded that which they had already experienced under David (v. 1) would he deem it appropriate to allow a permanent house to be built for his name (v. 13).

7:9 I have been with you. See note on 1 Samuel 16:18. **I have cut off all your enemies.** See verses 1 and 11. In light of verse 11, this statement should not be taken to mean that David no longer had enemies with whom to contend, but rather that, in the case of each enemy encountered so far, God had given him the victory. **I will make your name great.** The shift here from past to future tense indicates that, as great as David's achievements had been to this point, God had yet more in store for him. The promise of a great name recalls the divine declaration made to the patriarch Abraham in Genesis 12:2. Compare 8:13, where David "became famous."

7:10 I will provide a place. As in the preceding verse, a comparison with the Abrahamic promise is in order (Ge 12:7; 15:18; 17:8).

7:11 rest from all your enemies. See notes on verses 1, 6 and 9. **the LORD himself will establish a house for you.** Having declined David's offer to build him a "house" (temple; v. 5), the

12 When your days are over and you rest[m] with your fathers, I will raise up your offspring to succeed you, who will come from your own body,[n] and I will establish his
kingdom. 13 He is the one who will build a house for my Name,[o] and I will establish
the throne of his kingdom forever.[p] 14 I will be his father, and he will be my son.[q]
When he does wrong, I will punish him with the rod[r] of men, with floggings inflicted by men. 15 But my love will never be taken away from him, as I took it away from
Saul,[s] whom I removed from before you. 16 Your house and your kingdom will endure forever before me[a]; your throne[t] will be established forever.[u]' "

17 Nathan reported to David all the words of this entire revelation.

David's Prayer

18 Then King David went in and sat before the LORD, and he said:

"Who am I,[v] O Sovereign LORD, and what is my family, that you have brought
me this far? 19 And as if this were not enough in your sight, O Sovereign LORD, you
have also spoken about the future of the house of your servant. Is this your usual way of dealing with man,[w] O Sovereign LORD?
20 "What more can David say to you? For you know[x] your servant,[y] O Sovereign
LORD. 21 For the sake of your word and according to your will, you have done this
great thing and made it known to your servant.
22 "How great[z] you are,[a] O Sovereign LORD! There is no one like you, and there
is no God[b] but you, as we have heard with our own ears.[c] 23 And who is like your
people Israel[d]—the one nation on earth that God went out to redeem as a people
for himself, and to make a name for himself, and to perform great and awesome
wonders[e] by driving out nations and their gods from before your people, whom
you redeemed[f] from Egypt?[b] 24 You have established your people Israel as your
very own[g] forever, and you, O LORD, have become their God.[h]
25 "And now, LORD God, keep forever the promise you have made concerning
your servant and his house. Do as you promised, 26 so that your name will be great
forever. Then men will say, 'The LORD Almighty is God over Israel!' And the house
of your servant David will be established before you.
27 "O LORD Almighty, God of Israel, you have revealed this to your servant, saying, 'I will build a house for you.' So your servant has found courage to offer you
this prayer. 28 O Sovereign LORD, you are God! Your words are trustworthy,[i] and
you have promised these good things to your servant. 29 Now be pleased to bless
the house of your servant, that it may continue forever in your sight; for you,
O Sovereign LORD, have spoken, and with your blessing[j] the house of your servant
will be blessed forever."

7:12 [m]1Ki 2:1 [n]Ps 132:11-12
7:13 [o]1Ki 5:5; 8:19,29 [p]Isa 9:7
7:14 [q]Ps 89:26; Heb 1:5* [r]Ps 89:30-33
7:15 [s]1Sa 15:23,28
7:16 [t]Ps 89:36-37 [u]ver 13
7:18 [v]Ex 3:11; 1Sa 18:18
7:19 [w]Isa 55:8-9
7:20 [x]Jn 21:17 [y]1Sa 16:7
7:22 [z]Ps 48:1; 86:10; Jer 10:6 [a]Dt 3:24 [b]Ex 15:11 [c]Ex 10:2; Ps 44:1
7:23 [d]Dt 4:32-38 [e]Dt 10:21 [f]Dt 9:26; 15:15
7:24 [g]Dt 26:18 [h]Ex 6:6-7; Ps 48:14
7:28 [i]Ex 34:6; Jn 17:17
7:29 [j]Nu 6:23-27

[a] *16* Some Hebrew manuscripts and Septuagint; most Hebrew manuscripts *you* [b] *23* See Septuagint and 1 Chron. 17:21; Hebrew *wonders for your land and before your people, whom you redeemed from Egypt, from the nations and their gods.*

Lord countered with the astonishingly gracious announcement that he would instead establish a "house" (dynasty) for David.
7:12–16 See *BC* 27; *HC* 35.
7:12 your offspring. That is, Solomon; compare verse 13. **who will come from your own body.** This is a verbatim repetition of words spoken to Abraham in Genesis 15:4. See *BC* 18.
7:13 a house. That is, a temple, as implied in verses 5–7. **for my Name.** It was "for the sake of his great name" (1Sa 12:22) that the Lord had refused to reject his people after their sinful request for a king. Now he announced that David's own son, who would succeed him as king, would build a house "for [the LORD's] Name." For an explication of the significance of God's name, see Exodus 34:5–7 (see also note on 1Sa 17:45).
7:14–16 his father . . . my son. The full significance of this promise, which is expressive of the special relationship that the Lord established with the Davidic kings (Pss 2:7; 89:18–37), was ultimately realized in Christ (e.g., Mk 1:11; Ac 13:33; Heb 1:5). **I will punish him.** As a father, the Lord would discipline his royal son when he did wrong, but his covenantal love would never be taken away from him. Although the punishment might be severe, extending even to the temporary loss of land, throne and temple (1Ki 9:6–9), God's promise to establish forever the throne of David would not fail. In the course of time this promise would increasingly come to be understood in Messianic terms (Isa 9:7; 11:1–5; Jer 33:14–26; Mic 5:1–5).
■ **7:18–29** *David's Response.* David humbly accepted God's plan for bringing about great blessings for David's family.
7:18 David went in and sat before the LORD. Presumably David entered the tent mentioned in 6:17 and sat before the ark. The ark served as a token of the Lord's presence (see, e.g., Ex 25:22; 30:6; Dt 10:8; Jos 6:8; 1Sa 6:20; 2Sa 6:16–17). **Who am I . . . that you have brought me this far?** Having set out to honor God by building him a house, David was overwhelmed by the generosity of the Lord's declaration that he intended, rather, to build David a house. The humility evident in David's "Who am I?" is consonant with his recognition that it was the sovereign Lord who had been with him (see note on 1Sa 16:18) to bring him this far.
7:19 Is this your usual way of dealing with man . . . ? The Hebrew of this phrase is compact and its sense somewhat ambiguous. It reads literally, "and this [is] the torah [= law, instruction] of man." The NIV takes the sentence as a question, but another possibility is to understand David as stating a matter of fact: "and this [shall be] the charter of humankind." The parallel verse in 1 Chronicles 17:17 reads quite differently: "You have looked on me as though I were the most exalted of men."
7:22–24 David was moved by the consideration of his own unique status and that of his house (vv. 18–21) to contemplate the uniqueness of his God. The Lord is the only true God, and his unmerited favor had been exhibited in the election not only of David, but also of the nation of Israel itself to be the people through whom God's great name would become known (Ex 15:11–13; Dt 7:6–8).
7:29 See *WCF* 21.4; *WLC* 183.

David's Victories

8 In the course of time, David defeated the Philistines and subdued them, and he took
Metheg Ammah from the control of the Philistines.
2 David also defeated the Moabites.[k] He made them lie down on the ground and measured them off with a length of cord. Every two lengths of them were put to death, and
the third length was allowed to live. So the Moabites became subject to David and
brought tribute.
3 Moreover, David fought Hadadezer[l] son of Rehob, king of Zobah,[m] when he went
to restore his control along the Euphrates River. 4 David captured a thousand of his chariots, seven thousand charioteers[a] and twenty thousand foot soldiers. He hamstrung[n] all
but a hundred of the chariot horses.
5 When the Arameans of Damascus[o] came to help Hadadezer king of Zobah, David
struck down twenty-two thousand of them. 6 He put garrisons in the Aramean kingdom
of Damascus, and the Arameans became subject to him and brought tribute. The LORD
gave David victory wherever he went.[p]
7 David took the gold shields[q] that belonged to the officers of Hadadezer and brought
them to Jerusalem. 8 From Tebah[b] and Berothai,[r] towns that belonged to Hadadezer,
King David took a great quantity of bronze.
9 When Tou[c] king of Hamath[s] heard that David had defeated the entire army of Hadadezer, 10 he sent his son Joram[d] to King David to greet him and congratulate him on his
victory in battle over Hadadezer, who had been at war with Tou. Joram brought with him
articles of silver and gold and bronze.
11 King David dedicated[t] these articles to the LORD, as he had done with the silver and
gold from all the nations he had subdued: 12 Edom[e] and Moab,[u] the Ammonites[v] and the
Philistines,[w] and Amalek.[x] He also dedicated the plunder taken from Hadadezer son of
Rehob, king of Zobah.
13 And David became famous[y] after he returned from striking down eighteen thousand Edomites[f] in the Valley of Salt.[z]

8:2 [k]Ge 19:37; Nu 24:17
8:3 [l]2Sa 10:16,19 [m]1Sa 14:47
8:4 [n]Jos 11:9
8:5 [o]1Ki 11:24
8:6 [p]ver 14; 2Sa 3:18; 7:9
8:7 [q]1Ki 10:16
8:8 [r]Eze 47:16
8:9 [s]1Ki 8:65; 2Ch 8:4
8:11 [t]1Ki 7:51; 1Ch 26:26
8:12 [u]ver 2 [v]2Sa 10:14 [w]2Sa 5:25 [x]1Sa 27:8
8:13 [y]2Sa 7:9 [z]2Ki 14:7; 1Ch 18:12

[a] *4* Septuagint (see also Dead Sea Scrolls and 1 Chron. 18:4); Masoretic Text *captured seventeen hundred of his charioteers* [b] *8* See some Septuagint manuscripts (see also 1 Chron. 18:8); Hebrew *Betah.* [c] *9* Hebrew *Toi,* a variant of *Tou;* also in verse 10 [d] *10* A variant of *Hadoram* [e] *12* Some Hebrew manuscripts, Septuagint and Syriac (see also 1 Chron. 18:11); most Hebrew manuscripts *Aram* [f] *13* A few Hebrew manuscripts, Septuagint and Syriac (see also 1 Chron. 18:12); most Hebrew manuscripts *Aram* (that is, Arameans)

■ **8:1—10:19** *God's Blessings.* These chapters reflect God's blessing on David by summarizing a number of David's achievements and actions: his victories and officers (ch. 8), his kindness to Mephibosheth (ch. 9) and his kindness to Hanun (ch. 10).

■ **8:1–18** *Military Successes.* David's victories (vv. 1–14) and officers (vv. 15–18) were evidences of God's blessing.

8:1 David defeated the Philistines and subdued them. In the summary of David's victories presented in this chapter, pride of place is given to his victory over the Philistines. Throughout the book of Samuel they have appeared as the archenemy of Israel (e.g., 1Sa 9:16; 2Sa 3:18), and against them David's successes have far outshone those of his predecessor, Saul (1Sa 14:52). See also note on 5:25. **Metheg Ammah.** This site is otherwise unattested (but see "hill of Ammah" in 2:24). It may be that the words should be understood as common, not proper, nouns. The words mean literally "the reins of the forearm," and this may connote control or supremacy: Thus, "and he gained supremacy over the Philistines." Alternatively, the text may be emended to read "the common lands": Thus, "and he took the common lands from the hand of the Philistines." The parallel phrase in 1 Chronicles 18:1 reads "Gath and its surrounding villages [or daughters]." Early rabbinic scholars sought to bring the two readings together by proposing that Gath was preeminent among the Philistine cities, so that to take Gath was to gain supremacy over the Philistines.

8:2 Moabites. See Genesis 19:37 and 1 Samuel 22:3 and its notes. **Every two lengths of them were put to death.** By this means David lessened the number of his Moabite opponents by two-thirds and reduced the Moabites to tributary status. The cause of David's ruthless treatment of this people whom he had earlier trusted (1Sa 22:3) is not stated. For a similar association of destruction with the "measuring line" (different Hebrew word), see 2 Kings 21:13.

8:3 Hadadezer. This name appears to be a compound of "Hadad," the Syrian storm god (equivalent to Baal), and "ezer," meaning "help": "Hadad is [my] helper." Although solidly defeated by David in the present chapter, Hadadezer would later lend support to the Ammonites in their opposition to David (10:15–19). **Zobah.** An Aramean region lying north of Israel and stretching from Damascus to as far north as Hamath. Already in Saul's reign there had been conflict between Israel and the "kings of Zobah" (1Sa 14:47).

8:4 hamstrung all but a hundred of the chariot horses. See Joshua 11:6 and its note. Israelite kings were not to "acquire great numbers of horses" (Dt 17:16). Nevertheless, two sons of David, Absalom and Adonijah, would later dramatize their bids for the throne by preparing chariots and horses and having 50 men run before them (15:1; 1Ki 1:5; see Samuel's warning in 1Sa 8:11). A third son, Solomon, would become particularly well known for his chariot forces (1Ki 4:26–28; 9:22; 10:26–29).

8:5 Arameans. See Genesis 10:22–23, 25:20 and Deuteronomy 26:5.

8:6 garrisons. See verse 14. The establishment of garrisons in enemy territory was a sign of domination (see note on "where there is a Philistine outpost" at 1Sa 10:5).**The LORD gave David victory wherever he went.** This statement, repeated in verse 14, sets the summary of David's victories apart from that of Saul's (see note on 1Sa 14:47–52). See note on "the LORD is with him" at 1 Samuel 16:18.

8:8 bronze. First Chronicles 18:8 adds a note that Solomon used this bronze in the construction of the temple.

8:11 King David dedicated these articles to the LORD. David's action was perhaps in preparation for the temple that would be built by Solomon (1Ch 22:1–5,14; 29:1–5,16–19).

8:13 David became famous. Literally, "made a name." See the promise of a great name in 7:9. **Valley of Salt.** The slaughter of 18,000 Edomites in the Valley of Salt, located somewhere south or southwest of the Dead Sea, is credited to Abishai (1Ch 18:12). Unless this divergent tradition is attributed to the vicissitudes of textual transmission, the best explanation may be that Abishai received credit as one of David's generals. If the title to Psalm 60 is taken as pertaining to the same battle (though only 12,000 dead are mentioned), then credit would also be shared with Abishai's brother Joab.

[14]He put garrisons throughout Edom, and all the Edomites[a] became subject to David.[b] The LORD gave David victory wherever he went.[c]

David's Officials

[15]David reigned over all Israel, doing what was just and right for all his people.
[16]Joab[d] son of Zeruiah was over the army; Jehoshaphat[e] son of Ahilud was recorder; [17]Za-
dok[f] son of Ahitub and Ahimelech son of Abiathar were priests; Seraiah was secretary;[g]
[18]Benaiah[h] son of Jehoiada was over the Kerethites[i] and Pelethites; and David's sons
were royal advisers.[a]

David and Mephibosheth

9 David asked, "Is there anyone still left of the house of Saul to whom I can show kindness for Jonathan's sake?"[j]
[2]Now there was a servant of Saul's household named Ziba.[k] They called him to appear before David, and the king said to him, "Are you Ziba?"
"Your servant," he replied.
[3]The king asked, "Is there no one still left of the house of Saul to whom I can show
God's kindness?"
Ziba answered the king, "There is still a son of Jonathan;[l] he is crippled[m] in both feet."
[4]"Where is he?" the king asked.
Ziba answered, "He is at the house of Makir[n] son of Ammiel in Lo Debar."
[5]So King David had him brought from Lo Debar, from the house of Makir son of Ammiel.
[6]When Mephibosheth son of Jonathan, the son of Saul, came to David, he bowed
down to pay him honor.[o]
David said, "Mephibosheth!"
"Your servant," he replied.
[7]"Don't be afraid," David said to him, "for I will surely show you kindness for the sake
of your father Jonathan. I will restore to you all the land that belonged to your grandfather Saul, and you will always eat at my table."[p]

8:14 [a]Nu 24:17-18 [b]Ge 27:29,37-40 [c]ver 6
8:16 [d]2Sa 19:13; 1Ch 11:6 [e]2Sa 20:24; 1Ki 4:3
8:17 [f]2Sa 15:24,29; 1Ch 16:39; 24:3 [g]1Ki 4:3; 2Ki 12:10
8:18 [h]2Sa 20:23; 1Ki 1:8,38; 1Ch 18:17 [i]1Sa 30:14
9:1 [j]1Sa 20:14-17,42
9:2 [k]2Sa 16:1-4; 19:17,26,29
9:3 [l]1Sa 20:14 [m]2Sa 4:4
9:4 [n]2Sa 17:27-29
9:6 [o]2Sa 16:4; 19:24-30
9:7 [p]ver 1,3; 2Sa 12:8; 19:28; 1Ki 2:7; 2Ki 25:29

a *18* Or *were priests*

8:14 He put garrisons . . . The LORD gave David victory wherever he went. See verse 6 and its note.
8:15 doing what was just and right. As the prototypical theocratic king, David's rule, like that of God himself, was characterized not only by subjugation of Israel's enemies (vv. 1–14), but also by "just and right" action, as measured presumably by, e.g., "the regulations of the kingship" (1Sa 10:25) and "the Law of Moses" (1Ki 2:3; cf. Ne 9:13). On the Lord's just and right rule, see Psalms 89:14 and 99:4. Although subsequent Davidic kings would not always follow their father David's example, despite prophetic exhortation to do so (Jer 22:3), and would ultimately witness the ruin of Jerusalem (foretold in, e.g., Jer 22:5; cf. 52:12–14), there would arise already before the fall of Jerusalem a hope in a "righteous Branch" (Jer 23:5; 33:15) from the line of David, "a King who [would] reign wisely and do what [was] just and right in the land" (Jer 23:5). On the Messianic expectation, see notes on 7:4–17. **for all his people.** See 5:12 and its note.
8:16 Joab. See note on 2:18. **Jehoshaphat . . . recorder.** The specific nature of the office of recorder, here mentioned for the first time in the Old Testament, is difficult to ascertain from the available evidence. Conjectures include "keeper of state records," "secretary of state" and, perhaps the most plausible, "royal herald." Jehoshaphat continued to hold this office under the Solomonic administration (1Ki 4:3).
8:17 Zadok son of Ahitub. A Levite of the line of Aaron through Eleazar (1Ch 6:3–8,50–53), Zadok is here mentioned for the first time in the Bible. Along with Abiathar, grandson of a different Ahitub (1Sa 22:20), Zadok is listed in the present verse as one of David's two priests. Under Solomon's rule, Abiathar would be removed from the priestly office because of his support for Adonijah in his bid for the throne (1Ki 1:7–8), and he would be replaced by Zadok (1Ki 2:35), fulfilling the judgment on the house of Eli foretold in 1 Samuel 2:31 (see its note). The importance attached to the Zadokite line is further evidenced by later references (e.g., Ezr 7:1–2; Eze 40:46; 43:19; 44:15). **Seraiah was secretary.** Variations in the recording of this individual's name (20:25; 1Ch 18:16; possibly 1Ki 4:3) may suggest a non-Israelite origin—perhaps Egyptian (scribal and administrative traditions were well established in Egypt). The secretary would have been among the highest-ranking civil servants (2Ki 12:10; 25:19).
8:18 Benaiah. A man of outstanding military credentials (23:20–22), Benaiah would have occasion to demonstrate his intense loyalty to David and Solomon (1Ki 1:8,36–37), and, after carrying out Solomon's order to execute Joab, he would become commander in chief over Solomon's army (1Ki 2:34–35; 4:4). **Kerethites and Pelethites.** See 1 Samuel 30:14 and its note. **royal advisers.** See NIV text note. The Hebrew text reads "priests," which is thought to be problematic, unless it can be assumed that David partook of a priest-king tradition in Jerusalem along the lines of Melchizedek, who was both "king of Salem" and "priest of God Most High" (Ge 14:18; cf. Ps 110:4). The parallel phrase "chief officials at the king's side" (1Ch 18:17) could be approximated in the present verse by a moderate textual emendation of the Hebrew to read "stewards."
■ **9:1–13** *Kindness to Mephibosheth.* David showed kindness to Mephibosheth for the sake of Jonathan. David's generosity speaks not only of his character but also of his security during this time of God's blessing. He felt he had nothing to fear from Saul's family.
9:1 house of Saul. On the progressive decline of the house of Saul, see note on 5:10. **kindness for Jonathan's sake.** On the covenant between David and Jonathan, see 1 Samuel 18:3–4, 20:15 and their notes.
9:2 Ziba. See also 16:1–4 and 19:17–30.
9:4 Makir son of Ammiel. Mentioned also in 17:27, Makir appears to have been a wealthy man in a good position to host a descendant of Israel's first king. According to Joshua 17:1, an earlier Makir, son of Manasseh, had been the ancestor of the Gileadites. **Lo Debar.** This city has been tentatively located in Gilead about ten miles north of Mahanaim, Ish-Bosheth's short-lived capital in Transjordan (see note on 2:8).
9:6 Mephibosheth. See note on 4:4.
9:7 land that belonged to your grandfather Saul. For Jonathan's sake David restored to Mephibosheth both property (which may well have been substantial; see note on v. 10) and honor (see note on "you will always eat at my table," to follow). **you will always eat at my table.** David offered Mephibosheth a place of honor at his own table (on the practice, cf. 2Ki 25:29). It has been suggested that David's motivation was at least partially self-serving, as the arrangement would have enabled him to keep Mephibosheth under surveillance. But this seems unlikely for several reasons: (1) The text offers no hint of such a motive; (2) Mephibo-

[8]Mephibosheth bowed down and said, "What is your servant, that you should notice
a dead dog[q] like me?"

[9]Then the king summoned Ziba, Saul's servant, and said to him, "I have given your
master's grandson everything that belonged to Saul and his family. [10]You and your sons
and your servants are to farm the land for him and bring in the crops, so that your master's grandson[r] may be provided for. And Mephibosheth, grandson of your master, will
always eat at my table." (Now Ziba had fifteen sons and twenty servants.)

[11]Then Ziba said to the king, "Your servant will do whatever my lord the king commands his servant to do." So Mephibosheth ate at David's[a] table like one of the king's
sons.[s]

[12]Mephibosheth had a young son named Mica, and all the members of Ziba's household were servants of Mephibosheth.[t] [13]And Mephibosheth lived in Jerusalem, because
he always ate at the king's table, and he was crippled in both feet.

9:8 [q]2Sa 16:9

9:10 [r]ver 7,11,13; 2Sa 19:28

9:11 [s]Job 36:7; Ps 113:8

9:12 [t]1Ch 8:34

David Defeats the Ammonites

10 In the course of time, the king of the Ammonites died, and his son Hanun succeeded him as king. [2]David thought, "I will show kindness to Hanun son of Nahash,[u] just as his father showed kindness to me." So David sent a delegation to express
his sympathy to Hanun concerning his father.

When David's men came to the land of the Ammonites, [3]the Ammonite nobles said
to Hanun their lord, "Do you think David is honoring your father by sending men to you
to express sympathy? Hasn't David sent them to you to explore the city and spy it out and
overthrow it?" [4]So Hanun seized David's men, shaved off half of each man's beard,[v] cut
off their garments in the middle at the buttocks,[w] and sent them away.

[5]When David was told about this, he sent messengers to meet the men, for they were
greatly humiliated. The king said, "Stay at Jericho till your beards have grown, and then
come back."

[6]When the Ammonites realized that they had become a stench[x] in David's nostrils,
they hired twenty thousand Aramean[y] foot soldiers from Beth Rehob[z] and Zobah, as well
as the king of Maacah[a] with a thousand men, and also twelve thousand men from Tob.

[7]On hearing this, David sent Joab out with the entire army of fighting men. [8]The Ammonites came out and drew up in battle formation at the entrance to their city gate,
while the Arameans of Zobah and Rehob and the men of Tob and Maacah were by themselves in the open country.

[9]Joab saw that there were battle lines in front of him and behind him; so he selected
some of the best troops in Israel and deployed them against the Arameans. [10]He put the
rest of the men under the command of Abishai his brother and deployed them against
the Ammonites. [11]Joab said, "If the Arameans are too strong for me, then you are to come
to my rescue; but if the Ammonites are too strong for you, then I will come to rescue you.
[12]Be strong[b] and let us fight bravely for our people and the cities of our God. The LORD
will do what is good in his sight."[c]

10:2 [u]1Sa 11:1

10:4 [v]Lev 19:27; Isa 15:2; Jer 48:37 [w]Isa 20:4

10:6 [x]Ge 34:30 [y]2Sa 8:5 [z]Jdg 18:28 [a]Dt 3:14

10:12 [b]Dt 31:6; 1Co 16:13; Eph 6:10 [c]Jdg 10:15; 1Sa 3:18; Ne 4:14

a *11* Septuagint; Hebrew *my*

sheth's crippled condition would have made him an unlikely candidate for the throne; and (3) David would surely have known from his own experience that the presence at court of a rival could prove disadvantageous (note also 16:3).

9:8 dead dog. See note on 1 Samuel 24:14.

9:10 fifteen sons and twenty servants. That so many could be put to work farming the former landholdings of Saul shows that the properties returned to Mephibosheth were fairly extensive. The notice also indicates Ziba's own personal strength and his potential threat to Mephibosheth (see 19:26 and its note).

9:12 a young son named Mica. See also the genealogies of 1 Chronicles 8:34–35 and 9:40–41. This notice is perhaps intended to show that David's beneficence "for Jonathan's sake" (v. 1) was not limited to Mephibosheth.

■ **10:1–19** *Kindness to Hanun.* The strength of David's reign is evident both in his ability to relate to Hanun with kindness and in his devastating military power.

10:1 Ammonites. See note on 1 Samuel 11:1.

10:2 show kindness to Hanun son of Nahash. The phrase "show kindness" suggests that a treaty or covenant relationship had existed between David and Nahash, even though it had been the latter's aggression toward Israel that had in part contributed to Saul's rise to power (1Sa 11:1–11; 12:12). The friendly relationship between David and Nahash may have been established during David's fugitive period from Saul.

10:3 the city. Presumably this is a reference to the capital city, Rabbah (see note on 11:1). See *WLC* 145.

10:4 shaved off half of each man's beard. Beards were sometimes shaved off as an expression of mourning (cf. Isa 15:2; Jer 41:5; 48:37). It may be that Hanun was making a mockery of David's intention "to express his sympathy to Hanun concerning his father" (v. 2).

10:5 Jericho. The first site west of the Jordan River that would have been reached by the delegation returning from Rabbah. On Jericho, see, e.g., Numbers 22:1, Joshua 2:1, 6:26 and 1 Kings 16:34.

10:6 Aramean foot soldiers from Beth Rehob and Zobah. See 8:3 and 5 and their notes. Beth Rehob lay southwest of Zobah (cf. Nu 13:21; Jdg 18:28). **Maacah.** Situated in Transjordan, north of Lake Hulah (Dt 3:14; Jos 13:11–13; cf. Ge 22:20–24; 2Sa 3:3; perhaps 20:14). **Tob.** Tentatively identified with a site southeast of Maacah in Transjordan, Tob lay some 48 miles north of Rabbah (11:1 note; Jdg 11:3,5).

10:7 Joab. See note on 2:18.

10:10 Abishai. See note on 2:18.

10:12 Be strong . . . The LORD will do what is good in his sight. Finding himself in the difficult military position of having to fight on two fronts, Joab, like the Philistines earlier (1Sa 4:9), urged courage, but he also recognized that the outcome of the conflict would depend ultimately on "what [was] good in his [the LORD's] sight" (cf. David's words in 15:26).

13Then Joab and the troops with him advanced to fight the Arameans, and they fled
before him. 14When the Ammonites saw that the Arameans were fleeing, they fled before Abishai and went inside the city. So Joab returned from fighting the Ammonites and
came to Jerusalem.
15After the Arameans saw that they had been routed by Israel, they regrouped.
16Hadadezer had Arameans brought from beyond the River[a]; they went to Helam, with
Shobach the commander of Hadadezer's army leading them.
17When David was told of this, he gathered all Israel, crossed the Jordan and went to Helam. The Arameans formed their battle lines to meet David and fought against him. 18But
they fled before Israel, and David killed seven hundred of their charioteers and forty thousand of their foot soldiers.[b] He also struck down Shobach the commander of their army, and
he died there. 19When all the kings who were vassals of Hadadezer saw that they had been
defeated by Israel, they made peace with the Israelites and became subject[d] to them.
So the Arameans[e] were afraid to help the Ammonites anymore.

David and Bathsheba

11 In the spring,[f] at the time when kings go off to war, David sent Joab[g] out with
the king's men and the whole Israelite army.[h] They destroyed the Ammonites
and besieged Rabbah.[i] But David remained in Jerusalem.
2One evening David got up from his bed and walked around on the roof[j] of the palace. From the roof he saw[k] a woman bathing. The woman was very beautiful, 3and David sent someone to find out about her. The man said, "Isn't this Bathsheba,[l] the daughter of Eliam[m] and the wife of Uriah[n] the Hittite?" 4Then David sent messengers to get
her.[o] She came to him, and he slept[p] with her. (She had purified herself from her uncleanness.)[q] Then[c] she went back home. 5The woman conceived and sent word to David, saying, "I am pregnant."
6So David sent this word to Joab: "Send me Uriah[r] the Hittite." And Joab sent him to
David. 7When Uriah came to him, David asked him how Joab was, how the soldiers were
and how the war was going. 8Then David said to Uriah, "Go down to your house and
wash your feet."[s] So Uriah left the palace, and a gift from the king was sent after him.

10:19 [d]2Sa 8:6 [e]1Ki 11:25; 2Ki 5:1
11:1 [f]1Ki 20:22,26 [g]2Sa 2:18 [h]1Ch 20:1 [i]2Sa 12:26-28
11:2 [j]Dt 22:8; Jos 2:8 [k]Mt 5:28
11:3 [l]1Ch 3:5 [m]2Sa 23:34 [n]2Sa 23:39
11:4 [o]Lev 20:10; Ps 51 Title; Jas 1:14-15 [p]Dt 22:22 [q]Lev 15:25-30; 18:19
11:6 [r]1Ch 11:41
11:8 [s]Ge 18:4; 43:24; Lk 7:44

[a] *16* That is, the Euphrates [b] *18* Some Septuagint manuscripts (see also 1 Chron. 19:18); Hebrew *horsemen* [c] *4* Or *with her. When she purified herself from her uncleanness,*

10:14 So Joab returned. Apparently he did not capture the city of Rabbah on this occasion (11:1; 12:26–29).
10:16 Hadadezer. See 8:3 and its note. **Helam.** This site lay about 12 miles north of Tob (see note on v. 6).
10:19 Arameans were afraid to help the Ammonites anymore. The door was thus opened to a second campaign against the Ammonites, which is launched in the following chapter.
■ **11:1—20:26** *David's Kingship Under Divine Curse.* David seriously sinned (11:1—12:25) and suffered the consequences (12:1—20:26).
■ **11:1—12:25** *David's Sins.* The subject of David's moral failure divides into two parts: the sin with Bathsheba (11:1–27) and Nathan's response to it (12:1–25).
■ **11:1–27** *David and Bathsheba.* David committed adultery with Bathsheba and arranged to have her husband, Uriah, killed at the hands of the Ammonites. David's violation of God's law brought much shame to the reputation of Israel's God.
11:1 In the spring . . . when kings go off to war. See 1 Kings 20:22 and 26. In the ancient Near East, springtime offered a logical time for military undertakings, since the rains of winter would have ceased and the labor-intensive harvest would not yet have begun. **David sent Joab.** This was not the first time that David had sent Joab on a military expedition (10:7), but the framing notices in the present verse—that it was the time when "kings [went] off to war" and yet "David remained in Jerusalem"—suggest an implicit criticism of David for remaining behind. See also verse 2 and its note. **besieged Rabbah.** Called "Rabbah of the Ammonites" (12:26; 17:27; Dt 3:11; Jer 49:2; Eze 21:20), this city was the ancient capital of Ammon (Am 1:13–15) and was located 24 miles east of the Jordan River just north of the latitude of Jericho. In New Testament times the city was called Philadelphia, and today it is called Amman. See also note on 10:14.
11:2 One evening David got up from his bed. David's leisurely existence is in marked contrast to the activities of Joab and his men (v. 1). **roof of the palace.** There is a subtle sense of justice expressed here since the flat roof of the palace, where David succumbed to the temptation to take another man's wife, was the very place at which his own concubines would be taken by Absalom (16:22) in fulfillment of the words of the Lord spoken through Nathan in 12:11–12.
11:3 Bathsheba. Not until 12:24 is the name *Bathsheba* mentioned again. In the intervening verses the reference is to "the woman" (v. 5), "Uriah's wife" (v. 26; 12:15) or "the wife of Uriah" (12:10). The focus, in other words, is not on Bathsheba as an individual in her own right, but on her as a beautiful woman (v. 2) and the wife of another man. Further references to Bathsheba include 1 Kings 1:11, 2:13 and Psalm 51 (title). **Eliam.** If Bathsheba's father is the same as "Eliam son of Ahithophel" (23:34), this may help explain Ahithophel's later betrayal of David in favor of Absalom's conspiracy (15:12; 16:15), which then would ostensibly have been motivated by a sense of David's injustice (15:4,6). Notice especially the nature of Ahithophel's advice in 16:20–21. **Uriah.** A Hebrew name meaning "the Lord is my light." Uriah may have received a Hebrew name as a result of having been born in Israel or by having chosen it for himself. **Hittite.** See note on 1 Samuel 26:6.
11:4 She came to him. No protest is mentioned. **her uncleanness.** If the reference is to the uncleanness of menstruation (Lev 15:19–30), as seems likely, then the point of the notice here would be to remove all doubt that David was responsible for Bathsheba's pregnancy (v. 5).
11:5 I am pregnant. According to Israelite law, the penalty for adultery was the death of both parties (Lev 20:10; Dt 22:22). Bathsheba left it to David to resolve the difficulty.
11:8 wash your feet. At the very least David was encouraging Uriah to relax and refresh himself at home with his wife (cf. Ge 18:4; 19:2). It has also been suggested that the expression may refer euphemistically to sexual intercourse; Uriah, at any rate, understood David to be suggesting as much (v. 11). If sexual abstinence was a requirement for soldiers on active duty, as may be inferred from 1 Samuel 21:5 (cf. Dt 23:10), David may have been seeking to entrap Uriah in a ritual infraction, thereby giving legal grounds for eliminating him. It is also possible that David was attempting to make it appear that Uriah was the father of Bathsheba's unborn child. **a gift.** This was perhaps a portion of food from the king's table (cf. Ge 43:34) that was intended to ply Uriah with

9But Uriah slept at the entrance to the palace with all his master's servants and did not
go down to his house.
10When David was told, "Uriah did not go home," he asked him, "Haven't you just
come from a distance? Why didn't you go home?"
11Uriah said to David, "The ark[t] and Israel and Judah are staying in tents, and my
master Joab and my lord's men are camped in the open fields. How could I go to my
house to eat and drink and lie with my wife? As surely as you live, I will not do such a
thing!"
12Then David said to him, "Stay here one more day, and tomorrow I will send you
back." So Uriah remained in Jerusalem that day and the next. 13At David's invitation, he
ate and drank with him, and David made him drunk. But in the evening Uriah went out
to sleep on his mat among his master's servants; he did not go home.
14In the morning David wrote a letter[u] to Joab and sent it with Uriah. 15In it he wrote,
"Put Uriah in the front line where the fighting is fiercest. Then withdraw from him so he
will be struck down[v] and die.[w]"
16So while Joab had the city under siege, he put Uriah at a place where he knew the
strongest defenders were. 17When the men of the city came out and fought against Joab,
some of the men in David's army fell; moreover, Uriah the Hittite died.
18Joab sent David a full account of the battle. 19He instructed the messenger: "When
you have finished giving the king this account of the battle, 20the king's anger may flare
up, and he may ask you, 'Why did you get so close to the city to fight? Didn't you know
they would shoot arrows from the wall? 21Who killed Abimelech[x] son of Jerub-Besheth[a]?
Didn't a woman throw an upper millstone on him from the wall,[y] so that he died in Thebez? Why did you get so close to the wall?' If he asks you this, then say to him, 'Also, your
servant Uriah the Hittite is dead.' "
22The messenger set out, and when he arrived he told David everything Joab had sent
him to say. 23The messenger said to David, "The men overpowered us and came out
against us in the open, but we drove them back to the entrance to the city gate. 24Then
the archers shot arrows at your servants from the wall, and some of the king's men died.
Moreover, your servant Uriah the Hittite is dead."
25David told the messenger, "Say this to Joab: 'Don't let this upset you; the sword devours one as well as another. Press the attack against the city and destroy it.' Say this to
encourage Joab."
26When Uriah's wife heard that her husband was dead, she mourned for him. 27After
the time of mourning was over, David had her brought to his house, and she became his
wife and bore him a son. But the thing David had done displeased[z] the LORD.

11:11 [t]2Sa 7:2
11:14 [u]1Ki 21:8
11:15 [v]2Sa 12:9 [w]2Sa 12:12
11:21 [x]Jdg 8:31 [y]Jdg 9:50-54
11:27 [z]2Sa 12:9; Ps 51:4-5

[a] *21* Also known as *Jerub-Baal* (that is, Gideon)

sumptuous fare (as David would later do with wine; v. 13), so that he would lower his guard.

11:9 But Uriah . . . did not go down to his house. Despite David's efforts, Uriah was not to be manipulated. Although it is not impossible that Uriah could have learned of the wrong he had suffered at David's hands (e.g., the messengers of v. 4 might have informed him), this seems unlikely in view of his willingness to bear a letter (unbeknownst to him containing his death warrant) from David to Joab (v. 14). Moreover, Uriah explicitly stated his motivation in verse 11.

11:11 The ark and Israel and Judah. Uriah's insistence that he would not fare better than his fellow combatants underscores by way of contrast the reprehensible nature of David's sin. Even though the Lord himself (as symbolized by the presence of the ark) had taken to the field of battle, the king has been content to take his ease in Jerusalem (vv. 1–2). **lie with my wife?** See notes on verse 8.

11:13 David made him drunk. See note on verse 8. Even so, Uriah remained faithful to his duty and did not go home. Contrast Genesis 19:32–36.

11:15 Put Uriah in the front line . . . so he will be struck down and die. Uriah having resisted David's more subtle attempts to cloud the paternity issue (vv. 8–13), David now felt compelled to take direct action, and Joab, not surprisingly (see notes on 2:18; 3:26,27; 20:8,9,10), was willing to help.

11:21 Abimelech. The allusion is to Judges 9 (especially vv. 52–53). **Jerub-Besheth.** See NIV text note and Judges 6:32. On the "Besheth" element in the name, see notes on "Ish-Bosheth" at 2:8 (see also note on 1Sa 31:2) and "Mephibosheth" at 4:4.

11:22 everything Joab had sent him to say. The Septuagint (the Greek translation of the OT) attests a longer reading in which this line is followed by an angry response from David along the lines anticipated by Joab in verses 20–21.

11:25 Don't let this upset you. Feigning consolation of Joab, where congratulations would have been more in keeping with the spirit of verse 15, David said, literally, "Don't let this matter be evil in your eyes." The final assessment of the matter, however, comes in verse 27, which reads literally, "But the matter that David had done was evil in the eyes of the LORD." **the sword devours one as well as another.** David's observation that warfare takes its casualties arbitrarily was, in view of verse 15, outrageously hypocritical.

11:27 After the time of mourning. Although the reader can only guess at Bathsheba's true feelings for Uriah, she did observe the customary period of mourning for her husband (probably seven days; Ge 50:10; 1Sa 31:13). National leaders were sometimes mourned for longer periods (e.g., 30 days for Aaron [Nu 20:29] and Moses [Dt 34:8]; cf. also the 70 days the Egyptians mourned for Jacob [Ge 50:3]). **she became his wife.** She was not by any means his first wife (see note on 3:2). **bore him a son.** See 12:14. **the thing David had done displeased the LORD.** Literally, "was evil in the eyes of the LORD" (see note on v. 25). David had in fact broken at least four of the Ten Commandments (Ex 20:2–17; Dt 5:6–21), namely, the sixth (murder), seventh (adultery), ninth (false testimony) and tenth (coveting one's neighbor's wife). See *WCF* 17.3.

Nathan Rebukes David

12 The LORD sent Nathan[a] to David.[b] When he came to him,[c] he said, "There were
two men in a certain town, one rich and the other poor. 2 The rich man had a very
large number of sheep and cattle, 3 but the poor man had nothing except one little ewe
lamb he had bought. He raised it, and it grew up with him and his children. It shared his
food, drank from his cup and even slept in his arms. It was like a daughter to him.
4 "Now a traveler came to the rich man, but the rich man refrained from taking one
of his own sheep or cattle to prepare a meal for the traveler who had come to him. Instead, he took the ewe lamb that belonged to the poor man and prepared it for the one
who had come to him."
5 David[d] burned with anger against the man and said to Nathan, "As surely as the
LORD lives, the man who did this deserves to die! 6 He must pay for that lamb four times
over,[e] because he did such a thing and had no pity."
7 Then Nathan said to David, "You are the man! This is what the LORD, the God of Israel, says: 'I anointed[f] you[g] king over Israel, and I delivered you from the hand of Saul.
8 I gave your master's house to you,[h] and your master's wives into your arms. I gave you
the house of Israel and Judah. And if all this had been too little, I would have given you
even more. 9 Why did you despise[i] the word of the LORD by doing what is evil in his eyes?
You struck down[j] Uriah the Hittite with the sword and took his wife to be your own. You
killed him with the sword of the Ammonites. 10 Now, therefore, the sword[k] will never depart from your house, because you despised me and took the wife of Uriah the Hittite to
be your own.'
11 "This is what the LORD says: 'Out of your own household I am going to bring calamity upon you.[l] Before your very eyes I will take your wives and give them to one who is
close to you, and he will lie with your wives in broad daylight. 12 You did it in secret,[m] but
I will do this thing in broad daylight[n] before all Israel.' "
13 Then David said to Nathan, "I have sinned[o] against the LORD."
Nathan replied, "The LORD has taken away[p] your sin.[q] You are not going to die.[r] 14 But
because by doing this you have made the enemies of the LORD show utter contempt,[a][s]
the son born to you will die."

a 14 Masoretic Text; an ancient Hebrew scribal tradition *this you have shown utter contempt for the LORD*

12:1 [a]2Sa 7:2; 1Ki 20:35-41 [b]Ps 51 Title [c]2Sa 14:4
12:5 [d]1Ki 20:40
12:6 [e]Ex 22:1; Lk 19:8
12:7 [f]1Sa 16:13 [g]1Ki 20:42
12:8 [h]2Sa 9:7
12:9 [i]Nu 15:31; 1Sa 15:19 [j]2Sa 11:15
12:10 [k]2Sa 13:28; 18:14-15; 1Ki 2:25
12:11 [l]Dt 28:30; 2Sa 16:21-22
12:12 [m]2Sa 11:4-15 [n]2Sa 16:22
12:13 [o]Ge 13:13; Nu 22:34; 1Sa 15:24; 2Sa 24:10 [p]Ps 32:1-5; 51:1,9; 103:12; Zec 3:4,9 [q]Pr 28:13; Mic 7:18-19 [r]Lev 20:10; 24:17
12:14 [s]Isa 52:5; Ro 2:24

■ **12:1–25** *David and Nathan.* When confronted with and exposed by Nathan's parable, David repented and was forgiven. Yet he still would endure the consequences of his sin. Nathan informed David that his illegitimate child would die and that David would experience calamity at the hands of his own family.

12:1 The LORD sent Nathan. On the prophets' role as intermediaries between the Lord and Israel's kings, see notes on 1 Samuel 10:1 and 15:1. Among the prophetic functions were the election, instruction, rebuke and even rejection of kings. Nathan is first mentioned in 2 Samuel 7:2 (see its note). **one rich and the other poor.** In at least two respects the rich man in Nathan's parable resembled David: First, he ignored the much that he possessed and helped himself to the little that the poor man owned. Second, he followed up the first offense with an audaciously hypocritical performance (i.e., his apparent show of hospitality in v. 4).

12:3 like a daughter to him. Nathan's choice of words may represent a subtle allusion to David's sin: "Daughter" (Hebrew, *bat*) is the first element in the name *Bathsheba.* See also note on verse 6.

12:5 the man who did this deserves to die! Nathan's parable succeeded. In pronouncing judgment on the rich man, David unwittingly condemned himself. In the light of verse 6, it is uncertain whether David actually intended the death penalty or was simply uttering the ancient equivalent of "He ought to be shot."

12:6 four times over. Exodus 22:1 mandates fourfold restitution for theft of sheep. Some commentators would detect here a hint of David's subsequent loss of four sons: the first son of Bathsheba (vv. 14,18), Amnon (13:28–29), Absalom (18:14–15) and Adonijah (1Ki 2:24–25). On the other hand, the Septuagint (the Greek translation of the OT) reads "sevenfold" restitution (instead of fourfold), suggesting perhaps another subtle reminder of Bathsheba (see note on v. 3), since "seven" is or sounds like the second element in the name *Bathsheba.*

12:7–12 In a manner typical of prophetic judgment speeches (see note on 1Sa 2:27–36), Nathan began with an accusation (including a description of the Lord's beneficence [vv. 7–8] and an accusing question and indictment [v. 9]) and ended with an announcement of judgment (involving a correspondence of offense and punishment [vv. 10–12]). The death of the son born of the illicit relationship between David and Bathsheba (v. 14) served not only as a punishment, but perhaps also as a sign confirming Nathan's words. See *WLC* 151.

12:7 I anointed you. See note on 2:4; see also the way Samuel began his indictment of Saul in 1 Samuel 15:17. **I delivered you from the hand of Saul.** See 1 Samuel 16–31 (especially the note on 1Sa 16:18 ["the LORD is with him"]).

12:8 your master's wives. It is uncertain whether this statement is to be taken literally (only one wife and one concubine of Saul are ever mentioned [1Sa 14:50; 2Sa 3:7]) or is meant simply to indicate the inclusiveness of David's inheritance of the kingdom that once was Saul's. On the general issue, see 3:7, 16:21 and 1 Kings 2:13–25.

12:9 despise the word of the LORD. See Numbers 15:31 and 1 Samuel 2:30. **evil in his eyes?** See note on 11:27. **You killed him.** Because David had engineered Uriah's death in battle, he was as guilty as if he had murdered him with his own hand. **with the sword.** This expression is to be taken figuratively, as in 11:25. The implication of 11:24 is that archers felled Uriah. See *WLC* 105.

12:10–12 The consequences of David's sin parallel his crimes. Having taken life by the sword, he would find his own house plagued by the sword; having taken another man's wife in secret, he would endure having another man take his own wives (actually concubines) in broad daylight.

12:10 the sword will never depart from your house. Subsequent history confirms that the house of David was plagued by domestic violence: Absalom killed Amnon (13:28–29), Joab killed Absalom (18:14–15) and Solomon ordered the deaths of Adonijah (1Ki 2:24–25) and Joab (1Ki 2:29–34). See also 2 Kings 11:1 and its note.

12:11 I am going to bring calamity. The predicted calamity came about through the rebellion of Absalom (chs. 15–16). **lie with your wives in broad daylight.** This prediction would be fulfilled in 16:21–22; see note on 11:2.

12:13 I have sinned against the LORD. When charged by God's prophet, David responded with an immediate and unqualified confession (cf. Saul's confessions in 1Sa 15:24–25,30; see also their notes). Psalm 51, according to its superscription, offers a fuller picture of David's contrition in the present circumstance. **You are not going to die.** See notes on 11:5 and 12:5.

12:14 you have made the enemies of the LORD show utter

David's Conquests

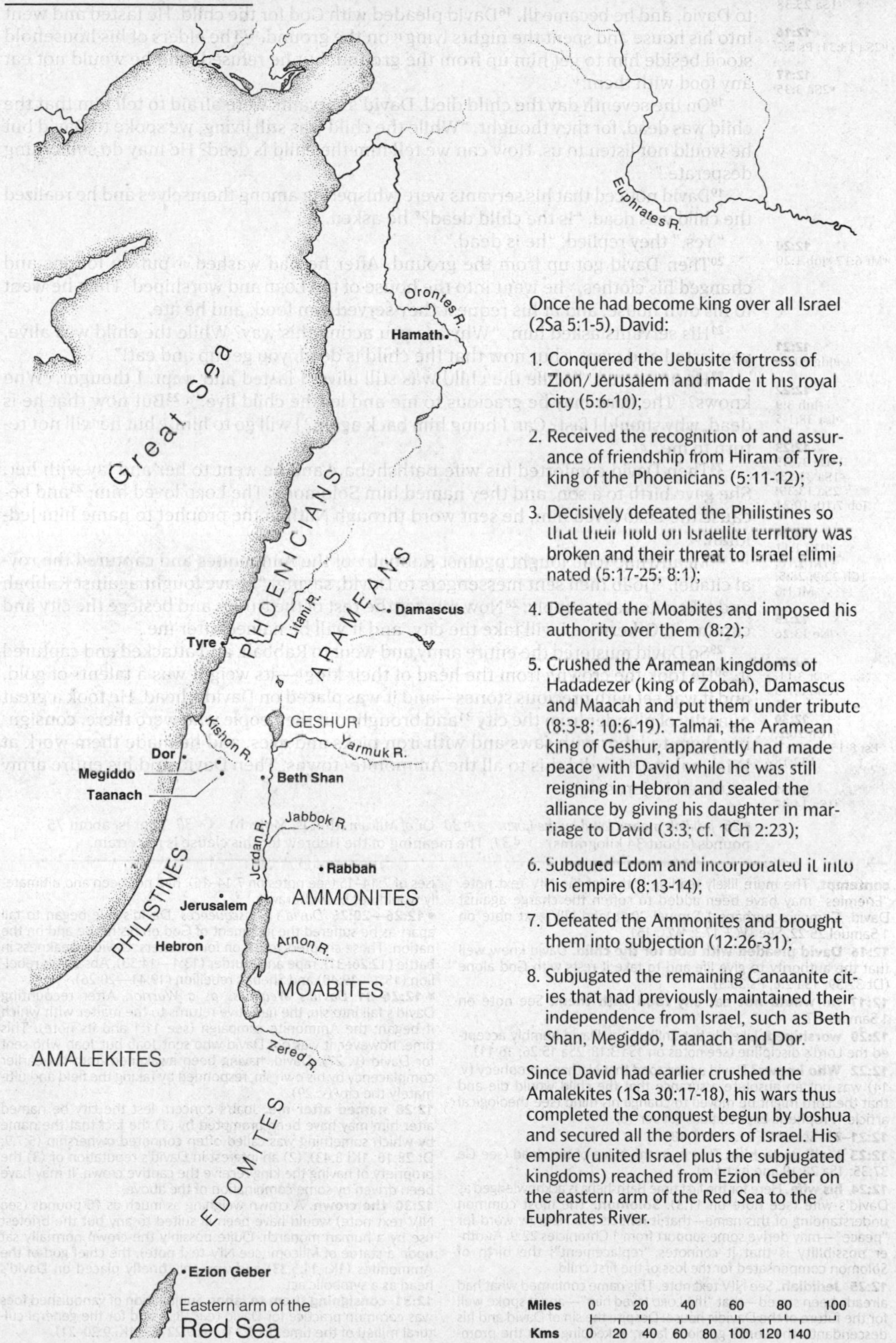

Once he had become king over all Israel (2Sa 5:1-5), David:

1. Conquered the Jebusite fortress of Zion/Jerusalem and made it his royal city (5:6-10);

2. Received the recognition of and assurance of friendship from Hiram of Tyre, king of the Phoenicians (5:11-12);

3. Decisively defeated the Philistines so that their hold on Israelite territory was broken and their threat to Israel eliminated (5:17-25; 8:1);

4. Defeated the Moabites and imposed his authority over them (8:2);

5. Crushed the Aramean kingdoms of Hadadezer (king of Zobah), Damascus and Maacah and put them under tribute (8:3-8; 10:6-19). Talmai, the Aramean king of Geshur, apparently had made peace with David while he was still reigning in Hebron and sealed the alliance by giving his daughter in marriage to David (3:3; cf. 1Ch 2:23);

6. Subdued Edom and incorporated it into his empire (8:13-14);

7. Defeated the Ammonites and brought them into subjection (12:26-31);

8. Subjugated the remaining Canaanite cities that had previously maintained their independence from Israel, such as Beth Shan, Megiddo, Taanach and Dor.

Since David had earlier crushed the Amalekites (1Sa 30:17-18), his wars thus completed the conquest begun by Joshua and secured all the borders of Israel. His empire (united Israel plus the subjugated kingdoms) reached from Ezion Geber on the eastern arm of the Red Sea to the Euphrates River.

15After Nathan had gone home, the LORD struck[t] the child that Uriah's wife had borne
to David, and he became ill. 16David pleaded with God for the child. He fasted and went
into his house and spent the nights lying[u] on the ground. 17The elders of his household
stood beside him to get him up from the ground, but he refused, and he would not eat
any food with them.[v]
18On the seventh day the child died. David's servants were afraid to tell him that the
child was dead, for they thought, "While the child was still living, we spoke to David but
he would not listen to us. How can we tell him the child is dead? He may do something
desperate."
19David noticed that his servants were whispering among themselves and he realized
the child was dead. "Is the child dead?" he asked.
"Yes," they replied, "he is dead."
20Then David got up from the ground. After he had washed,[w] put on lotions and
changed his clothes,[x] he went into the house of the LORD and worshiped. Then he went
to his own house, and at his request they served him food, and he ate.
21His servants asked him, "Why are you acting this way? While the child was alive,
you fasted and wept,[y] but now that the child is dead, you get up and eat!"
22He answered, "While the child was still alive, I fasted and wept. I thought, 'Who
knows?[z] The LORD may be gracious to me and let the child live.'[a] 23But now that he is
dead, why should I fast? Can I bring him back again? I will go to him,[b] but he will not return to me."[c]
24Then David comforted his wife Bathsheba,[d] and he went to her and lay with her.
She gave birth to a son, and they named him Solomon.[e] The LORD loved him; 25and because the LORD loved him, he sent word through Nathan the prophet to name him Jedidiah.[a][f]
26Meanwhile Joab fought against Rabbah[g] of the Ammonites and captured the royal citadel. 27Joab then sent messengers to David, saying, "I have fought against Rabbah
and taken its water supply. 28Now muster the rest of the troops and besiege the city and
capture it. Otherwise I will take the city, and it will be named after me."
29So David mustered the entire army and went to Rabbah, and attacked and captured
it. 30He took the crown[h] from the head of their king[b]—its weight was a talent[c] of gold,
and it was set with precious stones—and it was placed on David's head. He took a great
quantity of plunder from the city 31and brought out the people who were there, consigning them to labor with saws and with iron picks and axes, and he made them work at
brickmaking.[d] He did this to all the Ammonite[i] towns. Then David and his entire army
returned to Jerusalem.

12:15 [t]1Sa 25:38
12:16 [u]2Sa 13:31; Ps 5:7
12:17 [v]2Sa 3:35
12:20 [w]Mt 6:17 [x]Job 1:20
12:21 [y]Jdg 20:26
12:22 [z]Jnh 3:9 [a]Isa 38:1-5
12:23 [b]Ge 37:35 [c]1Sa 31:13; 2Sa 13:39; Job 7:10; 10:21
12:24 [d]1Ki 1:11 [e]1Ki 1:10; 1Ch 22:9; 28:5; Mt 1:6
12:25 [f]Ne 13:26
12:26 [g]Dt 3:11; 1Ch 20:1-3
12:30 [h]1Ch 20:2; Est 8:15; Ps 21:3; 132:18
12:31 [i]1Sa 14:47

[a] *25 Jedidiah* means *loved by the LORD.* [b] *30* Or *of Milcom* (that is, Molech) [c] *30* That is, about 75 pounds (about 34 kilograms) [d] *31* The meaning of the Hebrew for this clause is uncertain.

---

contempt. The more likely reading is that of the NIV text note. "Enemies" may have been added to soften the charge against David. Compare perhaps 1 Samuel 20:16 and NIV text note on 1 Samuel 25:22. See *WCF* 17.3; *WLC* 151.

12:16 David pleaded with God for the child. David knew well that the authority to give life and to take it rests with God alone (Dt 32:39; 1Sa 2:6; Ps 30:3).

12:17 he would not eat any food with them. See note on 1 Samuel 1:7.

12:20 worshiped. Like Eli, but unlike Saul, David humbly accepted the Lord's discipline (see notes on 1Sa 3:18; 2Sa 15:26; 16:11).

12:22 Who knows? David understood that Nathan's prophecy (v. 14) was not an absolute assurance that the child would die and that the Lord might be moved to change his mind (see theological article "Prophetic Expectations" at Jer 18).

12:21–23 See *WCF* 21.4; *WLC* 183.

12:23 I will go to him. That is, in the place of the dead (see Ge 37:35; 1Sa 28:19 and its note).

12:24 his wife. Here for the first time Bathsheba is acknowledged as David's wife (see note on 11:3). **Solomon.** The most common understanding of this name—that it reflects the Hebrew word for "peace"—may derive some support from 1 Chronicles 22:9. Another possibility is that it connotes "replacement"; the birth of Solomon compensated for the loss of the first child.

12:25 Jedidiah. See NIV text note. This name confirmed what had already been stated—that "the LORD loved him"—and it spoke well for the future of the Davidic house. Despite the sin of David and his descendants, the Lord's gracious favor, in keeping with the promises of 7:14–15 (see notes on 7:14–16), had not been and ultimately would not be withdrawn.

■ **12:26—20:26** *David's Consequences.* David's rule began to fall apart as he suffered the judgment of God on his house and on the nation. These chapters touch on four matters: David's weakness in battle (12:26–31), rape and murder (13:1—14:33), Absalom's rebellion (15:1—19:40) and Sheba's rebellion (19:41—20:26).

■ **12:26–31** *David's Weakness as a Warrior.* After recounting David's fall into sin, the narrative returns to the matter with which it began: the Ammonite campaign (see 11:1 and its note). This time, however, it was not David who sent Joab but Joab who sent for David (v. 27). David, having been awakened from his earlier complacency by his own sin, responded by taking the field and ultimately the city (v. 29).

12:28 named after me. Joab's concern lest the city be named after him may have been prompted by (1) the fact that the name by which something was called often connoted ownership (5:7,9; Dt 28:10; 1Ki 8:43), (2) an interest in David's reputation or (3) the propriety of having the king receive the captive crown. It may have been driven by some combination of the above.

12:30 the crown. A crown weighing as much as 75 pounds (see NIV text note) would have been ill suited to any but the briefest use by a human monarch. Quite possibly the crown normally sat upon a statue of Milcom (see NIV text note), the chief god of the Ammonites (1Ki 11:5,33) and was only briefly placed on David's head as a symbolic act.

12:31 consigning them to labor. Subjugation of vanquished foes was common practice for David (e.g., 8:2) and for the general cultural milieu of the time (Ex 1:11; Jos 9:22–27; 1Ki 9:20–21).

Amnon and Tamar

13 In the course of time, Amnon[j] son of David fell in love with Tamar,[k] the beautiful sister of Absalom[l] son of David.

2 Amnon became frustrated to the point of illness on account of his sister Tamar, for she was a virgin, and it seemed impossible for him to do anything to her.

3 Now Amnon had a friend named Jonadab son of Shimeah,[m] David's brother. Jonadab was a very shrewd man. 4 He asked Amnon, "Why do you, the king's son, look so haggard morning after morning? Won't you tell me?"

Amnon said to him, "I'm in love with Tamar, my brother Absalom's sister."

5 "Go to bed and pretend to be ill," Jonadab said. "When your father comes to see you, say to him, 'I would like my sister Tamar to come and give me something to eat. Let her prepare the food in my sight so I may watch her and then eat it from her hand.' "

6 So Amnon lay down and pretended to be ill. When the king came to see him, Amnon said to him, "I would like my sister Tamar to come and make some special bread in my sight, so I may eat from her hand."

7 David sent word to Tamar at the palace: "Go to the house of your brother Amnon and prepare some food for him." 8 So Tamar went to the house of her brother Amnon, who was lying down. She took some dough, kneaded it, made the bread in his sight and baked it. 9 Then she took the pan and served him the bread, but he refused to eat.

"Send everyone out of here,"[n] Amnon said. So everyone left him. 10 Then Amnon said to Tamar, "Bring the food here into my bedroom so I may eat from your hand." And Tamar took the bread she had prepared and brought it to her brother Amnon in his bedroom. 11 But when she took it to him to eat, he grabbed[o] her and said, "Come to bed with me, my sister."[p]

12 "Don't, my brother!" she said to him. "Don't force me. Such a thing should not be done in Israel![q] Don't do this wicked thing.[r] 13 What about me?[s] Where could I get rid of my disgrace? And what about you? You would be like one of the wicked fools in Israel. Please speak to the king; he will not keep me from being married to you." 14 But he refused to listen to her, and since he was stronger than she, he raped her.[t]

15 Then Amnon hated her with intense hatred. In fact, he hated her more than he had loved her. Amnon said to her, "Get up and get out!"

16 "No!" she said to him. "Sending me away would be a greater wrong than what you have already done to me."

But he refused to listen to her. 17 He called his personal servant and said, "Get this woman out of here and bolt the door after her." 18 So his servant put her out and bolted the door after her. She was wearing a richly ornamented[a] robe,[u] for this was the kind of garment the virgin daughters of the king wore. 19 Tamar put ashes[v] on her head and

13:1 [j]2Sa 3:2 [k]2Sa 14:27; 1Ch 3:9 [l]2Sa 3:3
13:3 [m]1Sa 16:9
13:9 [n]Ge 45:1
13:11 [o]Ge 39:12 [p]Ge 38:16
13:12 [q]Lev 20:17; Jdg 20:6 [r]Ge 34:7; Jdg 19:23
13:13 [s]Ge 20:12; Lev 18:9; Dt 22:21, 23 24
13:14 [t]Ge 34:2, Dt 22:25; Eze 22:11
13:18 [u]Ge 37:23; Jdg 5:30
13:19 [v]Jos 7:6; 1Sa 4:12; 2Sa 1:2; Est 4:1; Da 9:3

[a] *18* The meaning of the Hebrew for this phrase is uncertain.

■ **13:1—14:33** *Rape and Murder.* David's sin was replicated in his sons. These chapters divide into three parts: Amnon's sin (13:1–22), Absalom's revenge against him (13:23–39) and Absalom's reconciliation (14:1–33).

■ **13:1–22** *Amnon's Sexual Sin.* David's sons followed their father's example of adultery.

13:1 Amnon son of David fell in love with Tamar. Reference to a son of David with an illicit longing for a beautiful woman cannot help but recall the events of chapters 11–12. **Absalom son of David.** The order of the words in Hebrew emphasizes "Absalom," suggesting that he would somehow play an important role in the episode. Absalom is also mentioned in verses 4, 20 and 22.

13:3 Jonadab. While Jonadab must surely bear responsibility for his reprehensible advice, the meaning of his name (something like "he whom the LORD impels") might offer a hint that the prophesied calamity of the house of David (12:10–12) was beginning.

13:5 in my sight so I may watch her. This emphasis (also in vv. 6,8) is suggestive of a lustful aspect to Amnon's request.

13:6 make some special bread. The words used for the "special bread" and the making of it both relate to the Hebrew word for "heart" and may carry a subtly amorous connotation (cf. SS 4:9, where the phrase "stolen my heart" translates the same form of the verb that is here rendered "make"). This usage may be contrasted with the more general word for food used by Jonadab in verse 5 and by David himself in verse 7. Unfortunately, David seems to have missed the innuendo in Amnon's overture. **in my sight.** See notes on verse 5.

13:12–14 Tamar's desperate appeal to Amnon pointed first to the distinctive moral standards of Israel ("Such a thing should not be done in Israel!"; v. 12), then to the claims of simple human decency and compassion ("What about me?"; v. 13), next to Amnon's own self-interest ("And what about you?"; v. 13) and finally to marriage as a more legitimate means of Amnon getting what he wanted (v. 13). All her reasoning was to no avail (v. 14). See *WLC* 139,145.

13:12 Don't force me. The Hebrew translated "force" is elsewhere rendered "violate" (Ge 34:2; Dt 22:24,29), "use" (Jdg 19:24) and "rape" (13:14; Jdg 20:5).

13:13 he will not keep me from being married to you. It is uncertain whether David would, in fact, have allowed such a thing, which would have been in contravention of Leviticus 20:17 (see also Lev 18:9,11; Dt 27:22), or whether Tamar was simply trying every possible means of dissuasion.

13:15 he hated her more than he had loved her. With keen psychological insight, the narrator notes that Amnon had no sooner finished violating Tamar than he was suddenly repulsed by the victim of his crime. **Get up and get out!** Amnon's terse dismissal of Tamar comprises only two short words in Hebrew. Despite Tamar's further pleading (v. 16), Amnon would have nothing more to say to her before having her summarily tossed out and the door bolted behind her (v. 17–18).

13:16 Sending me away would be a greater wrong. See Exodus 22:16 and Deuteronomy 22:13–29.

13:17 this woman. This impersonal and abrupt reference (one word in Hebrew) is yet another indication of Amnon's callousness.

13:18 richly ornamented robe. A garment of similar description to that provided for Joseph in Genesis 37:3.

tore the ornamented[a] robe she was wearing. She put her hand on her head and went away, weeping aloud as she went.

[20]Her brother Absalom said to her, "Has that Amnon, your brother, been with you? Be quiet now, my sister; he is your brother. Don't take this thing to heart." And Tamar lived in her brother Absalom's house, a desolate woman.

[21]When King David heard all this, he was furious.[w] [22]Absalom never said a word to Amnon, either good or bad;[x] he hated[y] Amnon because he had disgraced his sister Tamar.

Absalom Kills Amnon

[23]Two years later, when Absalom's sheepshearers[z] were at Baal Hazor near the border of Ephraim, he invited all the king's sons to come there. [24]Absalom went to the king and said, "Your servant has had shearers come. Will the king and his officials please join me?"

[25]"No, my son," the king replied. "All of us should not go; we would only be a burden to you." Although Absalom urged him, he still refused to go, but gave him his blessing.

[26]Then Absalom said, "If not, please let my brother Amnon come with us."

The king asked him, "Why should he go with you?" [27]But Absalom urged him, so he sent with him Amnon and the rest of the king's sons.

[28]Absalom[a] ordered his men, "Listen! When Amnon is in high[b] spirits from drinking wine and I say to you, 'Strike Amnon down,' then kill him. Don't be afraid. Have not I given you this order? Be strong and brave."[c] [29]So Absalom's men did to Amnon what Absalom had ordered. Then all the king's sons got up, mounted their mules and fled.

[30]While they were on their way, the report came to David: "Absalom has struck down all the king's sons; not one of them is left." [31]The king stood up, tore[d] his clothes and lay down on the ground; and all his servants stood by with their clothes torn.

[32]But Jonadab son of Shimeah, David's brother, said, "My lord should not think that they killed all the princes; only Amnon is dead. This has been Absalom's expressed intention ever since the day Amnon raped his sister Tamar. [33]My lord the king should not be concerned about the report that all the king's sons are dead. Only Amnon is dead."

[34]Meanwhile, Absalom had fled.

Now the man standing watch looked up and saw many people on the road west of him, coming down the side of the hill. The watchman went and told the king, "I see men in the direction of Horonaim, on the side of the hill."[b]

[35]Jonadab said to the king, "See, the king's sons are here; it has happened just as your servant said."

13:21 [w]Ge 34:7
13:22 [x]Ge 31:24 [y]Lev 19:17-18; 1Jn 2:9-11
13:23 [z]1Sa 25:7
13:28 [a]2Sa 3:3 [b]Jdg 19:6, 9,22; Ru 3:7; 1Sa 25:36 [c]2Sa 12:10
13:31 [d]Nu 14:6; 2Sa 1:11; 12:16

[a] *19* The meaning of the Hebrew for this word is uncertain. [b] *34* Septuagint; Hebrew does not have this sentence.

13:20 Has that Amnon, your brother, been with you? Absalom's use of what is apparently a diminutive form of Amnon's name (not apparent in English) may imply disdain. At any rate, his ability to anticipate the wrong suffered by Tamar suggests that Amnon's infatuation with Tamar was not an entirely secret matter. **Be quiet now . . . Don't take this thing to heart.** Though he sought to calm his sister, Absalom himself took the matter to heart, as subsequent events would prove.

13:21 David . . . was furious. That David was furious at Amnon's violation of Tamar is understandable; that he took no disciplinary action is not (cf. 1Sa 3:13 and its note). The Septuagint (the Greek translation of the OT) and the Dead Sea Scrolls add "but he would not hurt Amnon because he was his eldest son and he loved him." Whether or not this sentence is original, it accurately highlights a weakness in David's handling of his sons that is seen also in 14:24 and 33 and in 1 Kings 1:6 (see their notes). Perhaps David felt morally crippled by his own recent adultery and homicide, but it nevertheless remained his duty as father and as king to do "what was just and right for all his people" (see 8:15 and its note). His failure to do so in the present context contributed to the greatest political and domestic crisis of his life; namely, Absalom's rebellion, which, it is worth noting, was fueled by Absalom's complaint that David had withheld justice (cf. 15:4–6).

■ **13:23–39** *Absalom's Revenge.* Absalom murdered Amnon for raping Tamar.

13:23 Two years later. Perhaps because of precautions taken by Amnon (note the 50-man escort employed by later royal contenders in 15:1 and 1Ki 1:5), two years elapsed before Absalom found opportunity to avenge his sister. **Baal Hazor.** Not to be confused with the better-known Hazor in Galilee, this site, probably situated some five miles northeast of Bethel, may have been chosen by Absalom to facilitate his imminent escape to relatives in Geshur, in Transjordan (v. 37). **near the border of Ephraim.** "Border" is lacking in the Hebrew. Possibly the reference is to the city of Ephron, four miles northeast of Bethel. **he invited all the king's sons.** Ostensibly, the reason for the invitation was to participate in the feasting that accompanied the shearing of sheep (1Sa 25:4–8).

13:26 let my brother Amnon come with us. Even if one assumes a certain reasonableness in Absalom's request that the eldest son and crown prince accompany them (perhaps as representative of the king, who had declined to come), his singling out of Amnon almost certainly must have aroused suspicion. David did, in fact, query the request: "Why should he go with you?"

13:27 But Absalom urged him. Upon Absalom's urging, David sent not only Amnon, but also the rest of his sons, perhaps counting on strength in numbers should Absalom try anything.

13:28 kill him. In one stroke Absalom would both avenge his sister Tamar and move himself one step closer to the throne (3:3; 15:1–6). He would also become guilty of a calculated murder and, in so doing, complete (together with Amnon) the reduplication of the sins of the father among the sons; i.e., sexual immorality and murder. See *WLC* 130.

13:29 mounted their mules. See note on 18:9.

13:32 only Amnon is dead. The shrewd Jonadab was probably simply deducing Absalom's action on the basis of the earlier crime of Amnon (v. 22). **expressed.** Absalom may well have stated his intention to avenge Tamar to others (but not "to Amnon" [v. 22]).

36 As he finished speaking, the king's sons came in, wailing loudly. The king, too, and
all his servants wept very bitterly.
37 Absalom fled and went to Talmai[e] son of Ammihud, the king of Geshur. But King
David mourned for his son every day.
38 After Absalom fled and went to Geshur, he stayed there three years. 39 And the spirit of the king[a] longed to go to Absalom,[f] for he was consoled[g] concerning Amnon's
death.

Absalom Returns to Jerusalem

14 Joab[h] son of Zeruiah knew that the king's heart longed for Absalom. 2 So Joab
sent someone to Tekoa[i] and had a wise woman[j] brought from there. He said to
her, "Pretend you are in mourning. Dress in mourning clothes, and don't use any cosmetic lotions.[k] Act like a woman who has spent many days grieving for the dead. 3 Then
go to the king and speak these words to him." And Joab[l] put the words in her mouth.
4 When the woman from Tekoa went[b] to the king, she fell with her face to the ground
to pay him honor, and she said, "Help me, O king!"
5 The king asked her, "What is troubling you?"
She said, "I am indeed a widow; my husband is dead. 6 I your servant had two sons.
They got into a fight with each other in the field, and no one was there to separate them.
One struck the other and killed him. 7 Now the whole clan has risen up against your servant; they say, 'Hand over the one who struck his brother down, so that we may put him
to death[m] for the life of his brother whom he killed; then we will get rid of the heir[n] as
well.' They would put out the only burning coal I have left,[o] leaving my husband neither
name nor descendant on the face of the earth."
8 The king said to the woman, "Go home,[p] and I will issue an order in your behalf."
9 But the woman from Tekoa said to him, "My lord the king, let the blame[q] rest on me
and on my father's family,[r] and let the king and his throne be without guilt.[s]"
10 The king replied, "If anyone says anything to you, bring him to me, and he will not
bother you again."
11 She said, "Then let the king invoke the LORD his God to prevent the avenger[t] of
blood from adding to the destruction, so that my son will not be destroyed."
"As surely as the LORD lives," he said, "not one hair[u] of your son's head will fall to the
ground.[v]"
12 Then the woman said, "Let your servant speak a word to my lord the king."
"Speak," he replied.
13 The woman said, "Why then have you devised a thing like this against the people
of God? When the king says this, does he not convict himself,[w] for the king has not
brought back his banished son?[x] 14 Like water[y] spilled on the ground, which cannot be
recovered, so we must die.[z] But God does not take away life; instead, he devises ways
so that a banished person[a] may not remain estranged from him.
15 "And now I have come to say this to my lord the king because the people have made
me afraid. Your servant thought, 'I will speak to the king; perhaps he will do what his ser-

13:37 [e]ver 34; 2Sa 3:3; 14:23,32
13:39 [f]2Sa 14:13 [g]2Sa 12:19-23
14:1 [h]2Sa 2:18
14:2 [i]2Ch 11:6; Ne 3:5; Jer 6:1; Am 1:1 [j]2Sa 20:16 [k]Ru 3:3; 2Sa 12:20; Isa 1:6
14:3 [l]ver 19
14:7 [m]Nu 35:19 [n]Mt 21:38 [o]Dt 19:10-13
14:8 [p]1Sa 25:35
14:9 [q]1Sa 25:24 [r]Mt 27:25 [s]1Sa 25:28; 1Ki 2:33
14:11 [t]Nu 35:12,21 [u]Mt 10:30 [v]1Sa 14:45
14:13 [w]2Sa 12:7; 1Ki 20:40 [x]2Sa 13:38-39
14:14 [y]Job 14:11; Ps 58:7; Isa 19:5 [z]Job 10:8; 17:13; 30:23; Ps 22:15; Heb 9:27 [a]Nu 35:15,25-28; Job 34:15

[a] *39* Dead Sea Scrolls and some Septuagint manuscripts; Masoretic Text *But ⌞the spirit of⌟ David the king*
[b] *4* Many Hebrew manuscripts, Septuagint, Vulgate and Syriac; most Hebrew manuscripts *spoke*

13:37 Talmai. Absalom's maternal grandfather (3:3). **Geshur.** See notes on verse 23 and 3:3.

■ **14:1–33** *Absalom's Reconciliation.* Although he arrived, he was not fully reconciled to David.

14:2 Tekoa. Later to become the birthplace of the prophet Amos (Am 1:1), Tekoa was situated some ten miles south of Jerusalem. **wise woman.** See 20:16 and 22 and Proverbs 14:1.

14:7 the whole clan has risen up against your servant. By the manner in which the wise woman concocted her tale, she raised not only the issue of blood revenge (v. 11; Nu 35:16–25; Dt 19:11–13; Jos 20:3; 2Sa 3:27) but also that of the continuance of her family line on its ancestral property, for the clan proposed to get rid of the heir as well. As she pointed out, this would have left her and her dead husband with neither name nor descendant, something that Israelite law sought to avoid (Dt 25:5–10). The woman skillfully introduced, in her fictional story, the same general dilemma with which David would have struggled; namely, his duty to avenge the blood of Amnon and his desire that Absalom, now presumably the crown prince (nothing more is known of Kileab than what is said in 3:3), not be cut off.

14:9 let the blame rest on me. The woman was either expressing her willingness to shoulder whatever blame might arise should the king's defense of her surviving son be adjudged unlawful, or she was requesting, in polite language, permission to speak further (1Sa 25:24).

14:11 invoke the LORD his God. The woman requested and secured an oath from David, in the name of the Lord, to prevent "the avenger of blood from adding to the destruction." As was the case in Nathan's parable (12:1–6), a judgment was elicited from David's own mouth that would then be turned and applied to his own case (see v. 13, "does he not convict himself . . . ?").

14:14 God does not take away life; instead, he devises ways. Taken in an absolute sense, this statement would represent a distortion of the truth of God's sovereignty over human life, which is eloquently affirmed in, e.g., Deuteronomy 32:39 and 1 Samuel 2:6 (cf. 2Sa 12:16). Although such a distortion cannot be discounted in the context of the woman's persuasive speech, the transposition of only one letter in the Hebrew text would yield a more appropriate sense: "God will not take away the life of the one who devises . . ."

14:15–16 While the woman had digressed in verses 13–14 to speak of David's banished son, she now returned immediately to the matter of her own endangered son, perhaps hoping that David would continue to believe her story and not discover that she and Joab had conspired together (vv. 1–3).

vant asks. 16 Perhaps the king will agree to deliver his servant from the hand of the man
who is trying to cut off both me and my son from the inheritance[b] God gave us.'
17 "And now your servant says, 'May the word of my lord the king bring me rest, for
my lord the king is like an angel[c] of God in discerning[d] good and evil. May the LORD your
God be with you.' "
18 Then the king said to the woman, "Do not keep from me the answer to what I am
going to ask you."
"Let my lord the king speak," the woman said.
19 The king asked, "Isn't the hand of Joab[e] with you in all this?"
The woman answered, "As surely as you live, my lord the king, no one can turn to the
right or to the left from anything my lord the king says. Yes, it was your servant Joab who
instructed me to do this and who put all these words into the mouth of your servant.
20 Your servant Joab did this to change the present situation. My lord has wisdom[f] like
that of an angel of God—he knows everything that happens in the land.[g]"
21 The king said to Joab, "Very well, I will do it. Go, bring back the young man Absalom."
22 Joab fell with his face to the ground to pay him honor, and he blessed the king.[h]
Joab said, "Today your servant knows that he has found favor in your eyes, my lord the
king, because the king has granted his servant's request."
23 Then Joab went to Geshur and brought Absalom back to Jerusalem. 24 But the king
said, "He must go to his own house; he must not see my face." So Absalom went to his
own house and did not see the face of the king.
25 In all Israel there was not a man so highly praised for his handsome appearance as
Absalom. From the top of his head to the sole of his foot there was no blemish in him.
26 Whenever he cut the hair of his head[i]—he used to cut his hair from time to time when
it became too heavy for him—he would weigh it, and its weight was two hundred shekels[a] by the royal standard.
27 Three sons[j] and a daughter were born to Absalom. The daughter's name was Tamar,[k] and she became a beautiful woman.
28 Absalom lived two years in Jerusalem without seeing the king's face. 29 Then Absalom sent for Joab in order to send him to the king, but Joab refused to come to him. So
he sent a second time, but he refused to come. 30 Then he said to his servants, "Look, Joab's field is next to mine, and he has barley[l] there. Go and set it on fire." So Absalom's
servants set the field on fire.
31 Then Joab did go to Absalom's house and he said to him, "Why have your servants
set my field on fire?[m]"
32 Absalom said to Joab, "Look, I sent word to you and said, 'Come here so I can send
you to the king to ask, "Why have I come from Geshur?[n] It would be better for me if I
were still there!" ' Now then, I want to see the king's face, and if I am guilty of anything,
let him put me to death."[o]
33 So Joab went to the king and told him this. Then the king summoned Absalom, and
he came in and bowed down with his face to the ground before the king. And the king
kissed[p] Absalom.

14:16 [b]Ex 34:9; 1Sa 26:19
14:17 [c]ver 20; 1Sa 29:9; 2Sa 19:27 [d]1Ki 3:9; Da 2:21
14:19 [e]ver 3
14:20 [f]1Ki 3:12,28; Isa 28:6 [g]ver 17; 2Sa 18:13; 19:27
14:22 [h]Ge 47:7
14:26 [i]2Sa 18:9; Eze 44:20
14:27 [j]2Sa 18:18 [k]2Sa 13:1
14:30 [l]Ex 9:31
14:31 [m]Jdg 15:5
14:32 [n]2Sa 3:3 [o]1Sa 20:8
14:33 [p]Ge 33:4; Lk 15:20

[a] *26* That is, about 5 pounds (about 2.3 kilograms)

14:17 angel of God. Or "emissary/messenger of God." Somewhat ironically, considering the circumstances, the woman flattered David by ascribing to him superhuman abilities in administering justice. See also verse 20, 19:27 and 1 Samuel 29:9. See *WLC* 16.
14:18–20 See *WLC* 144.
14:23 Geshur. See 13:37 and its note.
14:24 he must not see my face. David allowed Absalom to return to Jerusalem, but he did not allow a face-to-face encounter, which might have effected a reconciliation between father and son. The estrangement continued, and the question of whether Absalom would be allowed to "see the king's face" continued unanswered until the end of the chapter (vv. 28,32).
14:25–26 As with Saul before him, Absalom is described in exclusively external terms (cf. 1Sa 9:1,2 and their notes). The description of the hair-cutting and hair-weighing procedure not only offers a hint of Absalom's vanity, but it is also possibly an ironic foreshadowing of the manner of his death (18:9–15).
14:27 Three sons. See note on 18:18. **daughter's name was Tamar.** That only the daughter's name is recorded is sometimes taken to imply that Absalom's sons all died young, but the significance of this notice may lie elsewhere. Absalom's decision to name his daughter Tamar may have been not only an evidence of how strongly he felt about the wrong his sister Tamar had suffered at the hands of Amnon, but also a sign of his determination to keep the memory of the offense ever before him until the offender had been dealt with.
14:32 if I am guilty of anything, let him put me to death. It is unlikely that Absalom was actually willing to risk his life. Rather, his challenge may have been motivated by one or both of the following convictions: (1) that his killing of Amnon could be defended—after all, it was in accordance with justice and came only after it was clear that David intended no disciplinary action; and/or (2) that David would not take a strong stand in Absalom's case, since he had not done so in that of Amnon (see 13:21 and its note).
14:33 And the king kissed Absalom. The narrative comes rather abruptly to an end. Though David's action is sometimes referred to as the "kiss of reconciliation," it is doubtful that any true reconciliation was effected. Subsequent events would appear to belie such a notion. True reconciliation would have required words of repentance and forgiveness from both David (for having failed to punish Amnon) and Absalom (for having taken matters into his own hands), but the text gives no evidence that such words were ever exchanged. The kiss having failed to produce true reconciliation, it is ironic that with a kiss Absalom stole away the hearts of the people and launched his rebellion against his father (15:5–6).

Absalom's Conspiracy

15 In the course of time,[q] Absalom provided himself with a chariot[r] and horses and
with fifty men to run ahead of him. [2]He would get up early and stand by the side
of the road leading to the city gate.[s] Whenever anyone came with a complaint to be
placed before the king for a decision, Absalom would call out to him, "What town are
you from?" He would answer, "Your servant is from one of the tribes of Israel." [3]Then Absalom would say to him, "Look, your claims are valid and proper, but there is no representative of the king to hear you."[t] [4]And Absalom would add, "If only I were appointed
judge in the land![u] Then everyone who has a complaint or case could come to me and
I would see that he gets justice."

[5]Also, whenever anyone approached him to bow down before him, Absalom would
reach out his hand, take hold of him and kiss him. [6]Absalom behaved in this way toward
all the Israelites who came to the king asking for justice, and so he stole the hearts[v] of
the men of Israel.

[7]At the end of four[a] years, Absalom said to the king, "Let me go to Hebron and fulfill
a vow I made to the LORD. [8]While your servant was living at Geshur[w] in Aram, I made this
vow:[x] 'If the LORD takes me back to Jerusalem, I will worship the LORD in Hebron.[b]' "

[9]The king said to him, "Go in peace." So he went to Hebron.

[10]Then Absalom sent secret messengers throughout the tribes of Israel to say, "As
soon as you hear the sound of the trumpets,[y] then say, 'Absalom is king in Hebron.' "
[11]Two hundred men from Jerusalem had accompanied Absalom. They had been invited
as guests and went quite innocently, knowing nothing about the matter. [12]While Absalom was offering sacrifices, he also sent for Ahithophel[z] the Gilonite, David's counsel-
or,[a] to come from Giloh,[b] his hometown. And so the conspiracy gained strength, and Absalom's following kept on increasing.[c]

David Flees

[13]A messenger came and told David, "The hearts of the men of Israel are with Absalom."

[14]Then David said to all his officials who were with him in Jerusalem, "Come! We must
flee,[d] or none of us will escape from Absalom.[e] We must leave immediately, or he will
move quickly to overtake us and bring ruin upon us and put the city to the sword."

[15]The king's officials answered him, "Your servants are ready to do whatever our lord
the king chooses."

[16]The king set out, with his entire household following him; but he left ten concubines[f] to take care of the palace. [17]So the king set out, with all the people following him,
and they halted at a place some distance away. [18]All his men marched past him, along
with all the Kerethites[g] and Pelethites; and all the six hundred Gittites who had accompanied him from Gath marched before the king.

15:1 [q]2Sa 12:11 [r]1Sa 8:11; 1Ki 1:5
15:2 [s]Ge 23:10; 2Sa 19:8
15:3 [t]Pr 12:2
15:4 [u]Jdg 9:29
15:6 [v]Ro 16:18
15:8 [w]2Sa 3:3; 13:37-38 [x]Ge 28:20
15:10 [y]1Ki 1:34,39; 2Ki 9:13
15:12 [z]ver 31,34; 2Sa 16:15,23; 1Ch 27:33 [a]Job 19:14; Ps 41:9; 55:13; Jer 9:4 [b]Jos 15:51 [c]Ps 3:1
15:14 [d]2Sa 12:11; 1Ki 2:26; Ps 132:1; Ps 3 Title [e]2Sa 19:9
15:16 [f]2Sa 16:21-22; 20:3
15:18 [g]1Sa 30:14; 2Sa 8:18; 20:7,23; 1Ki 1:38,44; 1Ch 18:17

[a] 7 Some Septuagint manuscripts, Syriac and Josephus; Hebrew *forty* [b] 8 Some Septuagint manuscripts; Hebrew does not have *in Hebron.*

■ **15:1—19:40** *Absalom's Rebellion.* The third major curse brought upon David was the rebellion of his own son. The record of this event divides into seven interconnected parts: Absalom's victory (15:1–12), David's flight (15:13–31), David's encounters as he fled (15:32—16:14), Absalom's two counselors (16:15—17:23), Absalom's defeat (17:24—19:8a), David's return (19:8b–15a), and David's encounters on his return (19:15b–40).
■ **15:1–12** *Absalom Gains Victory.* Absalom took over Jerusalem. See *WLC* 128.
15:1 a chariot and horses and with fifty men to run ahead of him. See notes on 8:4 and 1 Samuel 8:11.
15:2 from one of the tribes of Israel. Despite the direct quotation marks in the English translation (which are nonexistent in the Hebrew), it is best to understand the sentence as an indirect statement intended to suggest a variety of individual, specific responses. An appropriate paraphrase might be "from such and such a tribe in Israel." For other such generalized assertions where specific information was probably given, see 17:6 ("this advice"), 17:15 ("such and such . . . so and so"), 17:21, 1 Kings 14:5 and 2 Kings 6:8.
15:4 I would see that he gets justice. See note on 13:21.
15:7 end of four years. This was presumably four years after the quasi reconciliation of 14:33 (see its note), making it six years after Absalom's return from Geshur (14:28). Given this rather prolonged time lag, it is surprising that Absalom's story was not queried by David. Surely, he could not have forgotten the disastrous outcome of an earlier proposal by Absalom (13:23–29). **Hebron.** See note on 2:1. Hebron was Absalom's birthplace (3:2–3) and, perhaps more significantly, the place where David had been anointed king, first over Judah (2:4) and subsequently over all Israel (5:3).
15:8 Geshur. See 3:3, 13:23 and 37 and their notes.
15:9 Go in peace. Though employing a standard expression (e.g., 1Sa 1:17; 20:42; 29:7), David's bidding of Absalom to go in peace adds a touch of irony to the narration, given the circumstances (v. 10).
15:10 Absalom is king in Hebron. See note on verse 7.
15:12 Ahithophel. See note on "Eliam" at 11:3. **Giloh.** A town of uncertain location in the hill country of Judah (Jos 15:48,51), Giloh was perhaps not too far from Hebron.
■ **15:13–31** *David Flees.* David fled for safety away from Jerusalem.
15:17 some distance away. While this rendering is defensible, the Hebrew reads more literally "the last house" or "the Far House," perhaps denoting a well-known landmark on the outskirts of the city. For possible analogies, see notes on verse 23 and 20:8; see also 1 Samuel 19:22, 20:19 and their notes.
15:18 Kerethites and Pelethites. See note on 1 Samuel 30:14. **six hundred.** This expression, which occurs frequently in military contexts (e.g., Jdg 3:31; 18:11; 20:47; 1Sa 13:15), may designate a standard military unit. **Gittites.** Perhaps David won the loyalty of these troops during his sojourn in the Philistine region ruled by Achish of Gath (1Sa 27:1–12).
15:19 Ittai the Gittite. This foreigner was soon to become one of David's trusted military commanders, alongside Joab and Abishai (vv. 21–22; 18:2,5,12).

15:19 [h]2Sa 18:2 [i]Ge 31:15
15:20 [j]1Sa 23:13 [k]2Sa 2:6
15:21 [l]Ru 1:16-17; Pr 17:17
15:23 [m]2Ch 29:16
15:24 [n]2Sa 8:17 [o]Nu 4:15 [p]1Sa 22:20
15:25 [q]Ex 15:13; Ps 43:3; Jer 25:30
15:26 [r]1Sa 3:18; 2Sa 22:20; 1Ki 10:9
15:27 [s]1Sa 9:9 [t]2Sa 17:17
15:28 [u]2Sa 17:16
15:30 [v]2Sa 19:4; Ps 126:6 [w]Est 6:12; Isa 20:2-4
15:31 [x]ver 12; 2Sa 16:23; 17:14,23
15:32 [y]Jos 16:2 [z]2Sa 1:2
15:33 [a]2Sa 19:35
15:34 [b]2Sa 16:19
15:35 [c]2Sa 17:15-16
15:36 [d]ver 27; 2Sa 17:17
15:37 [e]2Sa 16:16-17; 1Ch 27:33 [f]2Sa 16:15

19 The king said to Ittai[h] the Gittite, "Why should you come along with us? Go back
and stay with King Absalom. You are a foreigner,[i] an exile from your homeland. 20 You
came only yesterday. And today shall I make you wander[j] about with us, when I do not
know where I am going? Go back, and take your countrymen. May kindness and faithfulness[k] be with you."

21 But Ittai replied to the king, "As surely as the LORD lives, and as my lord the king
lives, wherever my lord the king may be, whether it means life or death, there will your
servant be."[l]

22 David said to Ittai, "Go ahead, march on." So Ittai the Gittite marched on with all
his men and the families that were with him.

23 The whole countryside wept aloud as all the people passed by. The king also
crossed the Kidron Valley,[m] and all the people moved on toward the desert.

24 Zadok[n] was there, too, and all the Levites who were with him were carrying the ark[o]
of the covenant of God. They set down the ark of God, and Abiathar[p] offered sacrifices[a]
until all the people had finished leaving the city.

25 Then the king said to Zadok, "Take the ark of God back into the city. If I find favor
in the LORD's eyes, he will bring me back and let me see it and his dwelling place[q] again.
26 But if he says, 'I am not pleased with you,' then I am ready; let him do to me whatever seems good to him.[r]"

27 The king also said to Zadok the priest, "Aren't you a seer?[s] Go back to the city in
peace, with your son Ahimaaz and Jonathan[t] son of Abiathar. You and Abiathar take
your two sons with you. 28 I will wait at the fords[u] in the desert until word comes from
you to inform me." 29 So Zadok and Abiathar took the ark of God back to Jerusalem and
stayed there.

30 But David continued up the Mount of Olives, weeping[v] as he went; his head[w] was
covered and he was barefoot. All the people with him covered their heads too and were
weeping as they went up. 31 Now David had been told, "Ahithophel[x] is among the conspirators with Absalom." So David prayed, "O LORD, turn Ahithophel's counsel into foolishness."

32 When David arrived at the summit, where people used to worship God, Hushai the
Arkite[y] was there to meet him, his robe torn and dust[z] on his head. 33 David said to him,
"If you go with me, you will be a burden[a] to me. 34 But if you return to the city and say
to Absalom, 'I will be your servant, O king; I was your father's servant in the past, but
now I will be your servant,'[b] then you can help me by frustrating Ahithophel's advice.
35 Won't the priests Zadok and Abiathar be there with you? Tell them anything you hear
in the king's palace.[c] 36 Their two sons, Ahimaaz son of Zadok and Jonathan[d] son of Abiathar, are there with them. Send them to me with anything you hear."

37 So David's friend Hushai[e] arrived at Jerusalem as Absalom[f] was entering the city.

[a] *24* Or *Abiathar went up*

15:20 yesterday. Presumably this is to be understood metaphorically, not literally (see note on v. 18).
15:21 there will your servant be. It is remarkable, in view of the defections among Israelite ranks, that David should have commanded such loyalty from even a foreigner.
15:23 Kidron Valley. A valley running from north to south along the eastern side of Jerusalem and separating Jerusalem from the Mount of Olives. **moved on toward the desert.** The Hebrew is difficult here, and the Septuagint (the Greek translation of the OT) offers a slightly different reading that is suggestive of another presumably familiar landmark: "the Olive Way in the wilderness" (see note on v. 17).
15:24 Zadok . . . Abiathar. See note on 8:17. **ark of the covenant of God.** See notes on 1 Samuel 3:3 and 4:3.
15:25–26 See *WLC* 192.
15:25 Take the ark of God back. David clearly resisted any mechanistic understanding of the ark's power (contrast the elders of Israel in 1Sa 4:3). Rather, he cast himself upon the Lord's mercy. See *WSC* 103.
15:26 let him do to me whatever seems good to him. David humbly accepted the Lord's sovereign will (cf. Eli's words in 1Sa 3:18; see 2Sa 10:12 and its note), but this in no way prevented him from taking whatever steps he could to secure his survival (vv. 27–28,32–36). See 1 Samuel 22:3 and its note on "what God will do for me."
15:27 Go back . . . with your son Ahimaaz and Jonathan son of Abiathar. Zadok, Abiathar and their sons would prove useful to David's cause in 17:15–21.
15:28 fords in the desert. The reference is presumably to fords across the Jordan River (see 17:16).
15:30 Mount of Olives. See note on verse 23. **head was covered . . . barefoot.** These were signs of grief and sorrow (Est 6:12; Isa 20:2–4; Jer 14:3–4; Mic 1:8).
15:31 turn Ahithophel's counsel into foolishness. David implored the Lord to turn the counsel of this former friend into foolishness. Interestingly, the name Ahithophel sounds like "brother of folly" (perhaps having arisen from a transformation of an original Ahi-Baal; cf. note on 1Sa 31:2). It may be that Ahithophel's betrayal of David elicited David's lament of Psalm 41:9, which would later be applied to Judas's betrayal of the greater son of David (Jn 13:18). See also Psalm 3, which is ascribed to David, "when he fled from his son Absalom" (title).
■ **15:32—16:14** *Encounters Along the Way.* David met several people as he left Jerusalem.
15:32 Hushai. No sooner had David prayed that Ahithophel's counsel be confounded than he was presented, in the person of Hushai, with the means of accomplishing that objective. Other than in chapters 15–17, Hushai is mentioned only in 1 Kings 4:16 (if the same) and in 1 Chronicles 27:33, where he is described (as in v. 37 of the present chapter) as King David's "friend." The latter description apparently connotes more than just a personal friend but an official personal adviser to the king. **the Arkite.** The Arkites were of Canaanite descent (Ge 10:15–17), and their territory lay west of Bethel (Jos 16:2).
15:37 David's friend Hushai. See note on verse 32.

David and Ziba

16 When David had gone a short distance beyond the summit, there was Ziba,[g] the
steward of Mephibosheth, waiting to meet him. He had a string of donkeys saddled and loaded with two hundred loaves of bread, a hundred cakes of raisins, a hundred cakes of figs and a skin of wine.[h]
2 The king asked Ziba, "Why have you brought these?"
Ziba answered, "The donkeys are for the king's household to ride on, the bread and
fruit are for the men to eat, and the wine is to refresh[i] those who become exhausted in
the desert."
3 The king then asked, "Where is your master's grandson?"[j]
Ziba said to him, "He is staying in Jerusalem, because he thinks, 'Today the house of
Israel will give me back my grandfather's kingdom.' "
4 Then the king said to Ziba, "All that belonged to Mephibosheth is now yours."
"I humbly bow," Ziba said. "May I find favor in your eyes, my lord the king."

Shimei Curses David

5 As King David approached Bahurim,[k] a man from the same clan as Saul's family
came out from there. His name was Shimei[l] son of Gera, and he cursed[m] as he came out.
6 He pelted David and all the king's officials with stones, though all the troops and the
special guard were on David's right and left. 7 As he cursed, Shimei said, "Get out, get out,
you man of blood, you scoundrel! 8 The LORD has repaid you for all the blood you shed
in the household of Saul, in whose place you have reigned.[n] The LORD has handed the
kingdom over to your son Absalom. You have come to ruin because you are a man of
blood!"
9 Then Abishai[o] son of Zeruiah said to the king, "Why should this dead dog curse my
lord the king? Let me go over and cut off his head."[p]
10 But the king said, "What do you and I have in common, you sons of Zeruiah?[q] If he
is cursing because the LORD said to him, 'Curse David,' who can ask, 'Why do you do
this?' "[r]
11 David then said to Abishai and all his officials, "My son,[s] who is of my own flesh, is
trying to take my life. How much more, then, this Benjamite! Leave him alone; let him
curse, for the LORD has told him to.[t] 12 It may be that the LORD will see my distress[u] and
repay me with good[v] for the cursing I am receiving today.[w]"
13 So David and his men continued along the road while Shimei was going along the
hillside opposite him, cursing as he went and throwing stones at him and showering him
with dirt. 14 The king and all the people with him arrived at their destination exhausted.[x]
And there he refreshed himself.

The Advice of Hushai and Ahithophel

15 Meanwhile, Absalom[y] and all the men of Israel came to Jerusalem, and Ahithophel[z]
was with him. 16 Then Hushai[a] the Arkite, David's friend, went to Absalom and said to
him, "Long live the king! Long live the king!"

16:1 [g]2Sa 9:1-13 [h]1Sa 25:18
16:2 [i]2Sa 17:27-29
16:3 [j]2Sa 9:9-10; 19:26-27
16:5 [k]2Sa 3:16 [l]2Sa 19:16-23; 1Ki 2:8-9,36,44 [m]Ex 22:28
16:8 [n]2Sa 21:9
16:9 [o]2Sa 9:8 [p]Ex 22:28; Lk 9:54
16:10 [q]2Sa 19:22 [r]Ro 9:20
16:11 [s]2Sa 12:11 [t]Ge 45:5
16:12 [u]Ps 4:1; 25:18 [v]Dt 23:5; Ro 8:28 [w]Ps 109:28
16:14 [x]2Sa 17:2
16:15 [y]2Sa 15:37 [z]2Sa 15:12
16:16 [a]2Sa 15:37

16:1 Ziba. See 9:2. **Mephibosheth.** See note on 4:4.
16:3 See *WLC* 145.
16:4 All that belonged to Mephibosheth is now yours. While David here appeared to believe Ziba's tale of Mephibosheth's treachery, he would later revise his ruling after hearing Mephibosheth's side of the story (19:24–30).
16:5 Bahurim. See note on 3:16. **Shimei.** As a kinsman of Saul, Shimei may have held David responsible for the deaths of Abner and Ish-Bosheth (vv. 7–8). On David's innocence, see notes on 3:21, 26, 28 and 37 and on 4:9 and 12. He may also have resented David's permitting the execution of seven of Saul's descendants by the Gibeonites (21:1–14). As a resident of Bahurim, moreover, Shimei may have been deeply vexed by David's treatment of Michal, Saul's daughter, for it was at Bahurim that Paltiel, Michal's second husband, had been ordered to cease following after his wife as she was being forcibly returned to David (3:16). Finally, of course, David had taken the throne that had once been Saul's. **Gera.** See Genesis 46:21, Judges 3:15 and 1 Chronicles 8:3, 5 and 7. That Shimei is consistently introduced as the "son of Gera" (19:16,18; 1Ki 2:8) may reflect that Shimei was a fairly common name (e.g., 1Ki 4:18; 1Ch 4:26). See *WLC* 113.
16:8 The LORD has repaid you. Shimei was correct that divine retribution played a part in David's present distress, but he was mistaken in linking this with any injustice on David's part to the house of Saul. It was, rather, as a result of David's sin against Uriah and Bathsheba that the Lord had announced, "Out of your own household I am going to bring calamity upon you" (12:11).
16:9 Abishai son of Zeruiah. See notes on 2:18. **dead dog.** See note on 1 Samuel 24:14.
16:10 What do you and I have in common, you sons of Zeruiah? See 19:22, as well as 3:39 and its note. See *WCF* 5.4; *BC* 13.
16:11 let him curse. David refused to silence Shimei for several reasons: (1) It may have been that the Lord had prompted him to curse (v. 10); (2) even his own son wanted to kill him, how much more a kinsman of Saul; (3) if the cursing was unjustified, the Lord would repay David with good (see note on v. 12). David's ready submission to God's judgment was consistent with his character (12:20; 15:26) and reminiscent of Eli in one of his better moments (see note on 1Sa 3:18).
16:12 repay me with good. In verse 8 Shimei gloated that David was being repaid by the Lord for wrongs he had inflicted on the household of Saul. Here, conversely, David expressed hope that the Lord would repay him with good for the wrongs inflicted on him by Shimei, a member of the household of Saul.
■ **16:15—17:23** *Absalom's Two Counselors.* Hushai and Ahithophel advised Absalom.
16:15 Ahithophel. See note on "Eliam" at 11:3.
16:16 Hushai the Arkite. See note on 15:32.

17 Absalom asked Hushai, "Is this the love you show your friend? Why didn't you go
with your friend?"[b]
18 Hushai said to Absalom, "No, the one chosen by the LORD, by these people, and by
all the men of Israel—his I will be, and I will remain with him. 19 Furthermore, whom
should I serve? Should I not serve the son? Just as I served your father, so I will serve
you."[c]
20 Absalom said to Ahithophel, "Give us your advice. What should we do?"
21 Ahithophel answered, "Lie with your father's concubines whom he left to take care
of the palace. Then all Israel will hear that you have made yourself a stench in your father's nostrils, and the hands of everyone with you will be strengthened." 22 So they
pitched a tent for Absalom on the roof, and he lay with his father's concubines in the
sight of all Israel.[d]
23 Now in those days the advice[e] Ahithophel gave was like that of one who inquires
of God. That was how both David[f] and Absalom regarded all of Ahithophel's advice.

17 Ahithophel said to Absalom, "I would[a] choose twelve thousand men and set out
tonight in pursuit of David. 2 I would[b] attack him while he is weary and weak.[g]
I would[b] strike him with terror, and then all the people with him will flee. I would[b] strike
down only the king[h] 3 and bring all the people back to you. The death of the man you seek
will mean the return of all; all the people will be unharmed." 4 This plan seemed good to
Absalom and to all the elders of Israel.
5 But Absalom said, "Summon also Hushai[i] the Arkite, so we can hear what he has
to say." 6 When Hushai came to him, Absalom said, "Ahithophel has given this advice.
Should we do what he says? If not, give us your opinion."
7 Hushai replied to Absalom, "The advice Ahithophel has given is not good this time.
8 You know your father and his men; they are fighters, and as fierce as a wild bear robbed
of her cubs.[j] Besides, your father is an experienced fighter;[k] he will not spend the night
with the troops. 9 Even now, he is hidden in a cave or some other place.[l] If he should attack your troops first,[c] whoever hears about it will say, 'There has been a slaughter
among the troops who follow Absalom.' 10 Then even the bravest soldier, whose heart is
like the heart of a lion,[m] will melt[n] with fear, for all Israel knows that your father is a
fighter and that those with him are brave.[o]
11 "So I advise you: Let all Israel, from Dan to Beersheba[p]—as numerous as the sand[q]
on the seashore—be gathered to you, with you yourself leading them into battle. 12 Then
we will attack him wherever he may be found, and we will fall on him as dew settles on
the ground. Neither he nor any of his men will be left alive. 13 If he withdraws into a city,
then all Israel will bring ropes to that city, and we will drag it down to the valley[r] until
not even a piece of it can be found."
14 Absalom and all the men of Israel said, "The advice[s] of Hushai the Arkite is better
than that of Ahithophel."[t] For the LORD had determined to frustrate[u] the good advice of
Ahithophel in order to bring disaster[v] on Absalom.[w]

16:17 [b]2Sa 19:25
16:19 [c]2Sa 15:34
16:22 [d]2Sa 12:11-12; 15:16
16:23 [e]2Sa 17:14,23 [f]2Sa 15:12
17:2 [g]2Sa 16:14 [h]1Ki 22:31; Zec 13:7
17:5 [i]2Sa 15:32
17:8 [j]Hos 13:8 [k]1Sa 16:18
17:9 [l]Jer 41:9
17:10 [m]1Ch 12:8 [n]Jos 2:9,11; Eze 21:15 [o]2Sa 23:8; 1Ch 11:11
17:11 [p]Jdg 20:1 [q]Ge 12:2; 22:17; Jos 11:4
17:13 [r]Mic 1:6
17:14 [s]2Sa 16:23 [t]2Sa 15:12 [u]2Sa 15:34; Ne 4:15 [v]Ps 9:16 [w]2Ch 10:8

[a] *1* Or *Let me* [b] *2* Or *will* [c] *9* Or *When some of the men fall at the first attack*

16:17–19 Absalom's apparent suspicion of David's "friend" (v. 16; 15:37) elicited from Hushai a clever reply to the effect that he whom the Lord and all Israel had chosen would have Hushai's loyalty as well, it being a natural thing for one who had served the father to serve also the son. For the role of deception in war, see note on "say, 'I have come to sacrifice'" at 1 Samuel 16:2.
16:21 Lie with your father's concubines. Lest there be any thought among Absalom's followers of a reconciliation with David, Ahithophel counseled Absalom to lie with David's concubines who had been left behind in 15:16 (David's acquisition of concubines is first mentioned in 5:13). The effect of such an action would be to make irreversible Absalom's claim to the throne (see notes on 3:7; 12:8; see also 1Ki 2:22). Whatever the motivation, such behavior is detestable to God and rightly deserving of judgment (Lev 18).
16:22 on the roof. See note on 11:2. **he lay with his father's concubines in the sight of all Israel.** This action thus fulfilled the judgment announced by Nathan in 12:11–12. See *WLC* 151.
17:1–4 Ahithophel's plan "seemed good to Absalom and to all the elders of Israel" (v. 4), and it was indeed good, as the narrator declared in verse 14. Decisive for the outcome, however, was the Lord's determination to "frustrate the good advice of Ahithophel" (v. 14).
17:5 Hushai the Arkite. See 15:32 and its note.
17:6 this advice. If Hushai was not included initially in the war council, as can be deduced from the summons of verse 5, then "this advice" must be a covering term for a more detailed communication to Hushai of Ahithophel's counsel. See note on 15:2.
17:7–13 After declaring Ahithophel's advice "not good" (v. 7), Hushai offered an alternative plan, the key to which would be not quick action but overpowering numbers (vv. 11–13). The suggestion that "all Israel" (v. 11) be mustered may have appealed to Absalom's vanity, and it certainly served Hushai's purpose of gaining time for David and all those with him to cross the Jordan (vv. 16,22).
17:10 even the bravest soldier . . . will melt. Hushai began his lengthy speech with a description of the well-known military prowess of David and his men (vv. 8–9), as well as a warning that Absalom could rapidly lose support should a hasty attack on David suffer even a minor setback. In this way Hushai predisposed his hearers to accept his more time-consuming, but ostensibly more certain, plan (see note on vv. 7–13).
17:11 from Dan to Beersheba. See Judges 20:1, 1 Samuel 3:20 and their notes.
17:12 we will fall on him as dew settles on the ground. Hushai's simile, unusual for a military context, not only evoked a sense of the all-encompassing and irresistible nature of a "blanketing" mass attack, but it also tended, by its use of serene imagery, to lessen the sense of military urgency and to suggest that the victory would be effortless.
17:14 the LORD had determined. Though the Lord did not overtly intervene in the present circumstance, he was far from inactive (see note on vv. 1–4). **to frustrate the good advice.** This was an answer to David's prayer in 15:31 (see its note).

15 Hushai told Zadok and Abiathar, the priests, "Ahithophel has advised Absalom and
the elders of Israel to do such and such, but I have advised them to do so and so. 16 Now
send a message immediately and tell David, 'Do not spend the night at the fords in the
desert;[x] cross over without fail, or the king and all the people with him will be swallowed up.[y]' "
17 Jonathan[z] and Ahimaaz were staying at En Rogel.[a] A servant girl was to go and inform them, and they were to go and tell King David, for they could not risk being seen
entering the city. 18 But a young man saw them and told Absalom. So the two of them left
quickly and went to the house of a man in Bahurim.[b] He had a well in his courtyard, and
they climbed down into it. 19 His wife took a covering and spread it out over the opening
of the well and scattered grain over it. No one knew anything about it.[c]
20 When Absalom's men came to the woman[d] at the house, they asked, "Where are
Ahimaaz and Jonathan?"

The woman answered them, "They crossed over the brook."[a] The men searched but
found no one, so they returned to Jerusalem.
21 After the men had gone, the two climbed out of the well and went to inform King
David. They said to him, "Set out and cross the river at once; Ahithophel has advised
such and such against you." 22 So David and all the people with him set out and crossed
the Jordan. By daybreak, no one was left who had not crossed the Jordan.
23 When Ahithophel saw that his advice[e] had not been followed, he saddled his donkey and set out for his house in his hometown. He put his house in order[f] and then
hanged himself. So he died and was buried in his father's tomb.
24 David went to Mahanaim,[g] and Absalom crossed the Jordan with all the men of Israel. 25 Absalom had appointed Amasa[h] over the army in place of Joab. Amasa was the
son of a man named Jether,[b][i] an Israelite[c] who had married Abigail,[d] the daughter of Nahash and sister of Zeruiah the mother of Joab. 26 The Israelites and Absalom camped in
the land of Gilead.
27 When David came to Mahanaim, Shobi son of Nahash[j] from Rabbah[k] of the Ammonites, and Makir[l] son of Ammiel from Lo Debar, and Barzillai[m] the Gileadite[n] from
Rogelim 28 brought bedding and bowls and articles of pottery. They also brought wheat
and barley, flour and roasted grain, beans and lentils,[e] 29 honey and curds, sheep, and
cheese from cows' milk for David and his people to eat.[o] For they said, "The people have
become hungry and tired and thirsty in the desert.[p]"

Absalom's Death

18 David mustered the men who were with him and appointed over them commanders of thousands and commanders of hundreds. 2 David sent the troops

17:16 [x]2Sa 15:28 [y]2Sa 15:35
17:17 [z]2Sa 15:27,36 [a]Jos 15:7; 18:16
17:18 [b]2Sa 3:16; 16:5
17:19 [c]Jos 2:6
17:20 [d]Ex 1:19; Jos 2:3-5; 1Sa 19:12-17
17:23 [e]2Sa 15:12; 16:23 [f]2Ki 20:1; Mt 27:5
17:24 [g]Ge 32:2; 2Sa 2:8
17:25 [h]2Sa 19:13; 20:4, 9-12; 1Ki 2:5,32; 1Ch 12:18 [i]1Ch 2:13-17
17:27 [j]1Sa 11:1 [k]Dt 3:11; 2Sa 10:1-2; 12:26, 29 [l]2Sa 9:4 [m]2Sa 19:31-39; 1Ki 2:7 [n]2Sa 19:31; Ezr 2:61
17:29 [o]1Ch 12:40 [p]2Sa 16:2; Ro 12:13

[a] *20* Or *"They passed by the sheep pen toward the water."* [b] *25* Hebrew *Ithra,* a variant of *Jether*
[c] *25* Hebrew and some Septuagint manuscripts; other Septuagint manuscripts (see also 1 Chron. 2:17) *Ishmaelite* or *Jezreelite* [d] *25* Hebrew *Abigal,* a variant of *Abigail* [e] *28* Most Septuagint manuscripts and Syriac; Hebrew *lentils, and roasted grain*

17:15 Zadok and Abiathar. In 15:27–29 David had sent these two, along with their sons Ahimaaz and Jonathan, back to Jerusalem in order that they might gather and convey information for him (15:35–36). For general information on Zadok and Abiathar, see note on 8:17. **such and such . . . so and so.** This is generalized narration intended to summarize a more specific briefing (see note on 15:2).

17:16 fords in the desert. See 15:28.

17:17 Jonathan and Ahimaaz. See note on verse 15. **En Rogel.** This was the name of a spring outside the walls of Jerusalem, probably at the southeastern end of the city. **servant girl was to go and inform them.** Reticent to enter the city, Jonathan and Ahimaaz stationed themselves near a spring, where a maidservant could bring them messages without arousing suspicion, since it was customary for young women to go frequently to such places to draw water.

17:18 went to the house of a man in Bahurim. David's recent passage through Bahurim, the site of Shimei's cursing (16:5–14), would have afforded him opportunity to confirm who his friends were, and he apparently passed this information on to Jonathan and Ahimaaz. On Bahurim, see note on 3:16.

17:21 such and such. See note on 15:2.

17:23 his hometown. See 15:12 and its note. **hanged himself.** Ahithophel's suicide was presumably prompted not only by the slight he had received in having his most recent advice ignored, but also by his awareness of how slim now were Absalom's chances of success. His earlier advice having been followed (16:21–22), Ahithophel knew that reconciliation with David was now impossible.

■ **17:24—19:8a** *Battle Against Absalom.* David's men killed Absalom, and David mourned his death.

17:24 Mahanaim. See note on 2:8.

17:25 Amasa. According to 1 Chonicles 2:13–17, Amasa was a nephew of David, and Amasa's mother, Abigail, was at least a half sister of David. This would have made Amasa a cousin of both Absalom and Joab. In this verse Absalom appointed Amasa to replace Joab as commander of the army, and David would later do the same (19:13). Amasa's ascendancy would be short-lived, however, for Joab had never been slow in dealing with a competitor (20:9–10). **Abigail.** This woman is not to be confused with the widow of Nabal (1Sa 25) who became David's wife (see note on 1Sa 25:40–44). **Nahash.** This is presumably a different Nahash than the Ammonite "Nahash from Rabbah" in verse 27.

17:27 Shobi son of Nahash. Like Hanun, Shobi was a member of the Ammonite royal family (10:1–2), but unlike Hanun he was friendly toward David and may even have been David's appointee to govern the city of Rabbah after its capture in 12:26–31. **Rabbah of the Ammonites.** See note on 11:1. **Makir.** See note on 9:4. **Barzillai.** For more on this benefactor of David and an account of David's attempt to reward him, see 19:31–39 and 1 Kings 2:7. Further references to him include Ezra 2.61 and Nehemiah 7:63.

18:1–33 Absalom was killed by Joab against David's orders (vv. 1–18), and he was mourned by David (vv. 19–33).

18:1 thousands . . . hundreds. These refer to standard military units (e.g., Ex 18:21; Nu 31:14; Dt 1:15; 1Sa 8:12; 22:7; 29:2).

out[q]—a third under the command of Joab, a third under Joab's brother Abishai[r] son of
Zeruiah, and a third under Ittai[s] the Gittite. The king told the troops, "I myself will surely march out with you."
3But the men said, "You must not go out; if we are forced to flee, they won't care
about us. Even if half of us die, they won't care; but you are worth ten[t] thousand of us.[a]
It would be better now for you to give us support from the city."[u]
4The king answered, "I will do whatever seems best to you."
So the king stood beside the gate while all the men marched out in units of hundreds
and of thousands. 5The king commanded Joab, Abishai and Ittai, "Be gentle with the
young man Absalom for my sake." And all the troops heard the king giving orders concerning Absalom to each of the commanders.
6The army marched into the field to fight Israel, and the battle took place in the forest[v] of Ephraim. 7There the army of Israel was defeated by David's men, and the casualties that day were great—twenty thousand men. 8The battle spread out over the whole
countryside, and the forest claimed more lives that day than the sword.
9Now Absalom happened to meet David's men. He was riding his mule, and as the
mule went under the thick branches of a large oak, Absalom's head[w] got caught in the
tree. He was left hanging in midair, while the mule he was riding kept on going.
10When one of the men saw this, he told Joab, "I just saw Absalom hanging in an oak
tree."
11Joab said to the man who had told him this, "What! You saw him? Why didn't you
strike[x] him to the ground right there? Then I would have had to give you ten shekels[b]
of silver and a warrior's belt.[y]"
12But the man replied, "Even if a thousand shekels[c] were weighed out into my hands,
I would not lift my hand against the king's son. In our hearing the king commanded you
and Abishai and Ittai, 'Protect the young man Absalom for my sake.[d]' 13And if I had put
my life in jeopardy[e]—and nothing is hidden from the king[z]—you would have kept your
distance from me."
14Joab[a] said, "I'm not going to wait like this for you." So he took three javelins in his
hand and plunged them into Absalom's heart while Absalom was still alive in the oak
tree. 15And ten of Joab's armor-bearers surrounded Absalom, struck him and killed him.[b]
16Then Joab[c] sounded the trumpet, and the troops stopped pursuing Israel, for Joab
halted them. 17They took Absalom, threw him into a big pit in the forest and piled up[d]
a large heap of rocks[e] over him. Meanwhile, all the Israelites fled to their homes.
18During his lifetime Absalom had taken a pillar and erected it in the King's Valley[f]
as a monument[g] to himself, for he thought, "I have no son[h] to carry on the memory of

18:2 [q]Jdg 7:16; 1Sa 11:11 [r]1Sa 26:6 [s]2Sa 15:19
18:3 [t]1Sa 18:7 [u]2Sa 21:17
18:6 [v]Jos 17:18
18:9 [w]2Sa 14:26
18:11 [x]2Sa 3:39 [y]1Sa 18:4
18:13 [z]2Sa 14:19-20
18:14 [a]2Sa 2:18; 14:30
18:15 [b]2Sa 12:10
18:16 [c]2Sa 2:28; 20:22
18:17 [d]Jos 7:26 [e]Jos 8:29
18:18 [f]Ge 14:17 [g]Ge 50:5; Nu 32:42; 1Sa 15:12 [h]2Sa 14:27

[a] *3* Two Hebrew manuscripts, some Septuagint manuscripts and Vulgate; most Hebrew manuscripts *care; for now there are ten thousand like us* [b] *11* That is, about 4 ounces (about 115 grams) [c] *12* That is, about 25 pounds (about 11 kilograms) [d] *12* A few Hebrew manuscripts, Septuagint, Vulgate and Syriac; most Hebrew manuscripts may be translated *Absalom, whoever you may be.* [e] *13* Or *Otherwise, if I had acted treacherously toward him*

18:2 a third. It was a conventional practice to divide troops into three sections (see 1Sa 11:11). **Abishai.** See notes on 2:18. **Ittai.** This Gittite is first mentioned in 15:19–22.
18:3 You must not go out. In response to David's emphatic pronouncement in verse 2—"I myself will surely march out with you"—the troops were adamant that he not do so. Perhaps they feared that David's feelings for Absalom (v. 5; 18:33—19:7) or simply his advancing age (21:15–17) might prove a liability to the success of the campaign. They recognized, moreover, that the death of David would mean sure defeat, as Ahithophel had earlier pointed out to Absalom (17:2–3). See *WLC* 127.
18:4 beside the gate. That is, in Mahanaim (17:24,27). See note on 19:8.
18:6 forest of Ephraim. Although the tribal territory of Ephraim lay west of the Jordan, the present context implies that the forest of Ephraim must have been in Transjordan, perhaps in the vicinity of Mahanaim. Judges 12:4 indicates that Ephraim was not always at peace with its Transjordanian neighbors, and the forest under discussion may have simply reflected Ephraimite expansionism east of the Jordan.
18:8 the forest claimed more lives that day than the sword. Whether through actual casualties (the forest apparently posed various natural dangers; e.g., vv. 9,17) or through the temptation to desertion (facilitated by the thick cover), the forest contributed to the success of David's cause. Outnumbered but well-trained troops often fare best in difficult terrain. For another instance in which nature was enlisted on behalf of the side with divine approval, see Joshua 10:11–14 (see also Jdg 5:20–21; 1Sa 2:10; 7:10; 12:17–18; 14:15; 2Sa 5:24; 22:8–16).
18:9 riding his mule. Mules were the royal mount of choice (13:29; 1Ki 1:33). **Absalom's head got caught in the tree.** The text does not specifically state that Absalom's celebrated hair contributed to his predicament, although this seems likely in view of 14:25–26 (see its note). An alternative conjecture is that Absalom was suddenly caught up and suspended in midair when the disturbance caused by his passage released branches previously pinned in a flexed position by other branches. Whatever the case, to be hung on a tree signified God's curse (Dt 21:23).
18:11 Then I would have had to give you. Joab was either chiding the man for forfeiting a reward already proffered for the one who should dispatch Absalom or was seeking to induce him even now to do the deed. Clearly Joab had no qualms about violating David's expressed command (v. 5).
18:12–13 The man obviously did not share Joab's cavalier attitude toward David's orders. Moreover, he astutely concluded that, should he kill Absalom, Joab would surely deny having any part in the affair and leave him to take full blame.
18:16 sounded the trumpet. See note on 1 Samuel 13:3.
18:17 large heap of rocks over him. A burial often reserved for criminals or enemies (Jos 7:26; 8:29).
18:18 King's Valley. This was presumably in the vicinity of Jerusalem (Ge 14:17). **monument to himself.** Compare Saul's action in 1 Samuel 15:12. The mention of Absalom's monument in the same breath with the "large heap of rocks" (v. 17) offers a

my name." He named the pillar after himself, and it is called Absalom's Monument to this
day.

David Mourns

19Now Ahimaaz[i] son of Zadok said, "Let me run and take the news to the king that
the LORD has delivered him from the hand of his enemies.[j]"
20"You are not the one to take the news today," Joab told him. "You may take the
news another time, but you must not do so today, because the king's son is dead."
21Then Joab said to a Cushite, "Go, tell the king what you have seen." The Cushite
bowed down before Joab and ran off.
22Ahimaaz son of Zadok again said to Joab, "Come what may, please let me run behind the Cushite."
But Joab replied, "My son, why do you want to go? You don't have any news that will
bring you a reward."
23He said, "Come what may, I want to run."
So Joab said, "Run!" Then Ahimaaz ran by way of the plain[a] and outran the Cushite.
24While David was sitting between the inner and outer gates, the watchman[k] went
up to the roof of the gateway by the wall. As he looked out, he saw a man running alone.
25The watchman called out to the king and reported it.
The king said, "If he is alone, he must have good news." And the man came closer and
closer.
26Then the watchman saw another man running, and he called down to the gatekeeper, "Look, another man running alone!"
The king said, "He must be bringing good news,[l] too."
27The watchman said, "It seems to me that the first one runs like[m] Ahimaaz son of
Zadok."
"He's a good man," the king said. "He comes with good news."
28Then Ahimaaz called out to the king, "All is well!" He bowed down before the king
with his face to the ground and said, "Praise be to the LORD your God! He has delivered
up the men who lifted their hands against my lord the king."
29The king asked, "Is the young man Absalom safe?"
Ahimaaz answered, "I saw great confusion just as Joab was about to send the king's
servant and me, your servant, but I don't know what it was."
30The king said, "Stand aside and wait here." So he stepped aside and stood there.
31Then the Cushite arrived and said, "My lord the king, hear the good news! The LORD
has delivered you today from all who rose up against you."
32The king asked the Cushite, "Is the young man Absalom safe?"
The Cushite replied, "May the enemies of my lord the king and all who rise up to harm
you be like that young man."[n]
33The king was shaken. He went up to the room over the gateway and wept. As he
went, he said: "O my son Absalom! My son, my son Absalom! If only I had died[o] instead
of you—O Absalom, my son, my son!"[p]

18:19 [i]2Sa 15:36 [j]ver 31; Jdg 11:36

18:24 [k]1Sa 14:16; 2Sa 19:8; 2Ki 9:17; Jer 51:12

18:26 [l]1Ki 1:42; Isa 52:7; 61:1

18:27 [m]2Ki 9:20

18:32 [n]Jdg 5:31; 1Sa 25:26

18:33 [o]Ex 32:32 [p]Ge 43:14; 2Sa 19:4; Ro 9:3

[a] 23 That is, the plain of the Jordan

telling irony. In life Absalom had envisioned for himself a king's career and had erected a pillar of remembrance in his own honor; in death he was branded a traitor and was laid to rest under a pile of rubble. "Absalom's Monument" is not to be confused with the late Hellenistic "Tomb of Absalom," which is still intact today in the Kidron Valley. **no son.** Absalom's three sons, mentioned but not named in 14:27, presumably were not yet born or were already deceased at the time Absalom erected his monument.

18:19 Ahimaaz. Ahimaaz had previously served as a messenger for David (15:27,36; 17:15–21) and wished to do so again.

18:20 You are not the one to take the news today. It can be inferred from verse 27 that there was a correlation between the messenger chosen and the content of the message, whether good, bad or mixed. Joab's disinclination to send Ahimaaz may have been prompted not simply by concern for Ahimaaz's safety, given David's likely reaction to the news, but also by a desire that he not appear to be taking too much pleasure in Absalom's demise (v. 22).

18:21 Cushite. See Genesis 10:6–7, Numbers 12:1 and their notes.

18:23 way of the plain. See NIV text note. The point seems to be that Ahimaaz took a less direct, but less taxing, route, arriving before the Cushite.

18:25 alone, he must have good news. Were he fleeing or bringing bad news, he would not likely have been alone, nor would he have been approaching so energetically and openly (cf. 19:3, which speaks of men "who are ashamed when they flee from battle" and so steal into the city).

18:27 good man . . . good news. See note on verse 20.

18:29 I saw great confusion . . . but I don't know what it was. By arriving before the Cushite messenger, Ahimaaz could claim to know only the good news of David's victory but no details of Absalom's welfare, when in fact he knew that Absalom was dead (v. 20).

18:32 like that young man. Unlike Ahimaaz (v. 29), the Cushite made no attempt to conceal Absalom's death, but he offered a conventionally phrased response (1Sa 25:26), which David readily understood (v. 33).

18:33 O my son Absalom! David's fivefold repetition of "my son" and threefold repetition of "Absalom" movingly conveyed his deep sense of anguish at the loss of his son (19:4). In spite of the harm that Absalom had caused and more that he had intended, David's grief was such that it virtually blinded him to all other considerations (see note on 19:5).

19 Joab was told, "The king is weeping and mourning for Absalom." 2And for the
whole army the victory that day was turned into mourning, because on that day
the troops heard it said, "The king is grieving for his son." 3The men stole into the city
that day as men steal in who are ashamed when they flee from battle. 4The king covered
his face and cried aloud, "O my son Absalom! O Absalom, my son, my son!"
5Then Joab went into the house to the king and said, "Today you have humiliated all
your men, who have just saved your life and the lives of your sons and daughters and the
lives of your wives and concubines. 6You love those who hate you and hate those who
love you. You have made it clear today that the commanders and their men mean nothing to you. I see that you would be pleased if Absalom were alive today and all of us were
dead. 7Now go out and encourage your men. I swear by the LORD that if you don't go out,
19:7 not a man will be left with you by nightfall. This will be worse for you than all the calam-
[q]Pr 14:28 ities that have come upon you from your youth till now."[q]
19:8 8So the king got up and took his seat in the gateway. When the men were told, "The
[r]2Sa 15:2 king is sitting in the gateway,[r]" they all came before him.

David Returns to Jerusalem

Meanwhile, the Israelites had fled to their homes. 9Throughout the tribes of Israel, the
people were all arguing with each other, saying, "The king delivered us from the hand of
19:9 [s]2Sa 8:1-14 our enemies; he is the one who rescued us from the hand of the Philistines.[s] But now he
[t]2Sa 15:14 has fled the country because of Absalom;[t] 10and Absalom, whom we anointed to rule over
19:11 us, has died in battle. So why do you say nothing about bringing the king back?"
[u]2Sa 15:24 11King David sent this message to Zadok[u] and Abiathar, the priests: "Ask the elders
of Judah, 'Why should you be the last to bring the king back to his palace, since what is
being said throughout Israel has reached the king at his quarters? 12You are my broth-
19:13 ers, my own flesh and blood. So why should you be the last to bring back the king?' 13And
[v]2Sa 17:25 say to Amasa,[v] 'Are you not my own flesh and blood?[w] May God deal with me, be it ever
[w]Ge 29:14 [x]Ru 1:17; 1Ki 19:2; so severely,[x] if from now on you are not the commander of my army in place of Joab.[y]' "
8:16 [y]2Sa 2:13 14He won over the hearts of all the men of Judah as though they were one man. They
19:15 sent word to the king, "Return, you and all your men." 15Then the king returned and
[z]Jos 5:9; 1Sa 11:15 went as far as the Jordan.
19:16 Now the men of Judah had come to Gilgal[z] to go out and meet the king and bring him
[a]2Sa 16:5-13; 1Ki 2:8 across the Jordan. 16Shimei[a] son of Gera, the Benjamite from Bahurim, hurried down
19:17 with the men of Judah to meet King David. 17With him were a thousand Benjamites,
[b]2Sa 9:2; 16:1-2 along with Ziba,[b] the steward of Saul's household,[c] and his fifteen sons and twenty ser-
[c]Ge 43:16 vants. They rushed to the Jordan, where the king was. 18They crossed at the ford to take
the king's household over and to do whatever he wished.
19:19 When Shimei son of Gera crossed the Jordan, he fell prostrate before the king 19and
[d]1Sa 22:15; 2Sa 16:6-8 said to him, "May my lord not hold me guilty. Do not remember how your servant did
19:21 wrong on the day my lord the king left Jerusalem.[d] May the king put it out of his mind.
[e]1Sa 26:6 [f]Ex 22:28 20For I your servant know that I have sinned, but today I have come here as the first of
[g]1Sa 12:3; 26:9; 2Sa 16:7-8 the whole house of Joseph to come down and meet my lord the king."
21Then Abishai[e] son of Zeruiah said, "Shouldn't Shimei be put to death for this? He
19:22 cursed[f] the LORD's anointed."[g]
[h]2Sa 2:18; 16:10 22David replied, "What do you and I have in common, you sons of Zeruiah?[h] This day
[i]1Sa 11:13 you have become my adversaries! Should anyone be put to death in Israel today?[i] Do I

19:5 you have humiliated all your men. What might, under different circumstances, have been an understandable display of fatherly grief was, as Joab forcefully asserted, totally unacceptable when the father was also the king. Joab minced no words in declaring to David the demoralizing effect his behavior was having on those who had just saved his life. If the behavior of later usurpers is any indication, Absalom's success might well have cost the lives of David and his whole household (e.g., 1Ki 15:29; 16:11–12; 2Ki 10:6–7,17).

19:7 not a man will be left with you. Joab as much as threatened to lead a rebellion himself if David did not correct his behavior and show his troops proper honor.

19:8a the king . . . took his seat in the gateway. It was near a different gateway in Jerusalem, however, that the rebellion was first incited (15:2–6), and it was to Jerusalem that David was yet to return (19:9—20:2).

■ **19:8b–15a** *David's Return.* David returned to Jerusalem to reestablish his kingdom.

19:13 Amasa. See note on 17:25. **commander of my army in place of Joab.** David's promotion of Amasa ahead of Joab appears to have been politically astute and astonishingly gracious, since Amasa had sided with Absalom and was deserving of a traitor's death. In reality, however, to be appointed Joab's replacement was not all that different from receiving a death sentence (20:8–10; see Joab's earlier murder of Abner at 3:27).

■ **19:15b–40** *Encounters Along the Way.* David encountered people along the way to Jerusalem, as he had earlier on the way out of Jerusalem (see 15:32—16:14).

19:15b Gilgal. See 1 Samuel 7:16 and note on 13:4.

19:16 Shimei son of Gera. See 16:5–14 and notes on 16:5, 8, 11 and 12. **Bahurim.** See note on 3:16.

19:20 house of Joseph. Strictly speaking, the house of Joseph included only the descendants of Joseph's two sons, Ephraim and Manasseh (Ge 48:5,20; Jos 17:17). The expression was frequently used, however, as it was here, to describe all the northern tribes (Jos 18:5; 1Ki 11:28; Am 5:6; Zec 10:6). In the present context, even Benjamin, Shimei's tribe, was included.

19:21 cursed the LORD's anointed. This was a grave offense. See note on 1 Samuel 2:10.

19:22 What do you and I have in common, you sons of Zeruiah? This is a verbatim repetition of 16:10 (see its note). **Should**

not know that today I am king over Israel?" 23So the king said to Shimei, "You shall not
die." And the king promised him on oath.[j]
24Mephibosheth,[k] Saul's grandson, also went down to meet the king. He had not tak-
en care of his feet or trimmed his mustache or washed his clothes from the day the king
left until the day he returned safely. 25When he came from Jerusalem to meet the king,
the king asked him, "Why didn't you go with me,[l] Mephibosheth?"
26He said, "My lord the king, since I your servant am lame,[m] I said, 'I will have my donkey saddled and will ride on it, so I can go with the king.' But Ziba[n] my servant betrayed
me. 27And he has slandered your servant to my lord the king. My lord the king is like an
angel[o] of God; so do whatever pleases you. 28All my grandfather's descendants deserved
nothing but death[p] from my lord the king, but you gave your servant a place among those
who eat at your table.[q] So what right do I have to make any more appeals to the king?"
29The king said to him, "Why say more? I order you and Ziba to divide the fields."
30Mephibosheth said to the king, "Let him take everything, now that my lord the king
has arrived home safely."
31Barzillai[r] the Gileadite also came down from Rogelim to cross the Jordan with the
king and to send him on his way from there. 32Now Barzillai was a very old man, eighty
years of age. He had provided for the king during his stay in Mahanaim, for he was a very
wealthy[s] man. 33The king said to Barzillai, "Cross over with me and stay with me in Jerusalem, and I will provide for you."
34But Barzillai answered the king, "How many more years will I live, that I should go
up to Jerusalem with the king? 35I am now eighty[t] years old. Can I tell the difference between what is good and what is not? Can your servant taste what he eats and drinks? Can
I still hear the voices of men and women singers?[u] Why should your servant be an added[v] burden to my lord the king? 36Your servant will cross over the Jordan with the king
for a short distance, but why should the king reward me in this way? 37Let your servant
return, that I may die in my own town near the tomb of my father[w] and mother. But here
is your servant Kimham.[x] Let him cross over with my lord the king. Do for him whatever pleases you."
38The king said, "Kimham shall cross over with me, and I will do for him whatever
pleases you. And anything you desire from me I will do for you."
39So all the people crossed the Jordan, and then the king crossed over. The king kissed
Barzillai and gave him his blessing,[y] and Barzillai returned to his home.
40When the king crossed over to Gilgal, Kimham crossed with him. All the troops of
Judah and half the troops of Israel had taken the king over.
41Soon all the men of Israel were coming to the king and saying to him, "Why did our
brothers, the men of Judah, steal the king away and bring him and his household across
the Jordan, together with all his men?"[z]
42All the men of Judah answered the men of Israel, "We did this because the king is
closely related to us. Why are you angry about it? Have we eaten any of the king's provisions? Have we taken anything for ourselves?"
43Then the men of Israel[a] answered the men of Judah, "We have ten shares in the
king; and besides, we have a greater claim on David than you have. So why do you treat
us with contempt? Were we not the first to speak of bringing back our king?"
But the men of Judah responded even more harshly than the men of Israel.

19:23 [j]1Ki 2:8,42
19:24 [k]2Sa 4:4; 9:6-10
19:25 [l]2Sa 16:17
19:26 [m]Lev 21:18 [n]2Sa 9:2
19:27 [o]1Sa 29:9; 2Sa 14:17,20
19:28 [p]2Sa 16:8; 21:6-9 [q]2Sa 9:7,13
19:31 [r]2Sa 17:27-29; 1Ki 2:7
19:32 [s]1Sa 25:2; 2Sa 17:27
19:35 [t]Ps 90:10 [u]2Ch 35:25; Ezr 2:65; Ecc 2:8; 12:1; Isa 5:11-12 [v]2Sa 15:33
19:37 [w]Ge 49:29; 1Ki 2:7 [x]ver 40; Jer 41:17
19:39 [y]Ge 31:55; Ge 47:7
19:41 [z]Jdg 8:1; 12:1
19:43 [a]2Sa 5:1

anyone be put to death in Israel today? For a similar sentiment under similar circumstances, see 1 Samuel 11:13.

19:23 You shall not die. Although David would remember his oath, he would not forget Shimei's offense and would later remind Solomon of it on his deathbed (1Ki 2:8–9).

19:24 Mephibosheth. See note on 4:4. **had not taken care of his feet.** Mephibosheth's discontinuation of normal personal hygiene signified his distress over David's predicament and may also have been intended to serve as evidence of his loyalty when and if David were to return.

19:26 Ziba my servant betrayed me. See 16:3.

19:27 angel of God. See note on 14:17.

19:29 divide the fields. David was either unwilling to call Ziba to account for his betrayal or uncertain of the veracity of Mephibosheth's version of events, so he settled for a compromise arrangement.

19:31–33 On Barzillai's material support of David during the latter's stay in Mahanaim, see 17:27–29.

19:35 Can I tell the difference between what is good and what is not? Barzillai was not saying that he had lost the capacity for ethical judgment but that age had robbed him of the potential fully to experience life's pleasures.

19:37 Kimham. In light of the circumstances and of David's words in 1 Kings 2:7, it is reasonable to assume that Kimham was a son of Barzillai. Elsewhere in the Old Testament, the name Kimham occurs only in Jeremiah 41:17, where "Geruth [lodging of?] Kimham near Bethlehem" may suggest that a land grant was part of Kimham's reward.

■ **19:41—20:26** *Sheba's Rebellion.* Another consequence of David's sin was division between the northern and southern tribes, leading to northern rebellion against David's royal authority.

19:43 ten shares in the king. The point is that the northern tribes, later to become the northern kingdom of Israel, were ten in number, while the southern tribes were only two, Judah and Simeon. It is ironic that within the space of a few short verses the northerners went from claiming ten shares in David to disavowing any (20:1). **men of Judah responded even more harshly than the men of Israel.** The north-south hostility so much in evidence in the present account would in the short term fuel Sheba's revolt (ch. 20) and eventually contribute to the division of the kingdom (1Ki 12). See note on 1 Samuel 11:8.

Sheba Rebels Against David

20:1 [b]Ge 31:14 [c]Ge 29:14; 1Ki 12:16 [d]1Sa 22:7-8; 2Ch 10:16

20 Now a troublemaker named Sheba son of Bicri, a Benjamite, happened to be
there. He sounded the trumpet and shouted,

"We have no share[b] in David,[c]
no part in Jesse's son![d]
Every man to his tent, O Israel!"

20:3 [e]2Sa 15:16; 16:21-22

2 So all the men of Israel deserted David to follow Sheba son of Bicri. But the men of
Judah stayed by their king all the way from the Jordan to Jerusalem.
3 When David returned to his palace in Jerusalem, he took the ten concubines[e] he had
left to take care of the palace and put them in a house under guard. He provided for
them, but did not lie with them. They were kept in confinement till the day of their death,
living as widows.

20:4 [f]2Sa 17:25; 19:13

4 Then the king said to Amasa,[f] "Summon the men of Judah to come to me within
three days, and be here yourself." 5 But when Amasa went to summon Judah, he took longer than the time the king had set for him.

20:6 [g]2Sa 21:17

6 David said to Abishai,[g] "Now Sheba son of Bicri will do us more harm than Absalom
did. Take your master's men and pursue him, or he will find fortified cities and escape

20:7 [h]1Sa 30:14; 2Sa 8:18; 15:18; 1Ki 1:38

from us." 7 So Joab's men and the Kerethites[h] and Pelethites and all the mighty warriors
went out under the command of Abishai. They marched out from Jerusalem to pursue
Sheba son of Bicri.

20:8 [i]Jos 9:3 [j]2Sa 2:18

8 While they were at the great rock in Gibeon,[i] Amasa came to meet them. Joab[j] was
wearing his military tunic, and strapped over it at his waist was a belt with a dagger in
its sheath. As he stepped forward, it dropped out of its sheath.

20:10 [k]Jdg 3:21; 2Sa 2:23; 3:27 [l]1Ki 2:5

9 Joab said to Amasa, "How are you, my brother?" Then Joab took Amasa by the beard
with his right hand to kiss him. 10 Amasa was not on his guard against the dagger[k] in Joab's[l] hand, and Joab plunged it into his belly, and his intestines spilled out on the
ground. Without being stabbed again, Amasa died. Then Joab and his brother Abishai
pursued Sheba son of Bicri.

20:12 [m]2Sa 2:23

11 One of Joab's men stood beside Amasa and said, "Whoever favors Joab, and whoever is for David, let him follow Joab!" 12 Amasa lay wallowing in his blood in the middle
of the road, and the man saw that all the troops came to a halt[m] there. When he realized that everyone who came up to Amasa stopped, he dragged him from the road into
a field and threw a garment over him. 13 After Amasa had been removed from the road,
all the men went on with Joab to pursue Sheba son of Bicri.
14 Sheba passed through all the tribes of Israel to Abel Beth Maacah[a] and through the

[a] *14* Or *Abel, even Beth Maacah*; also in verse 15

20:1–26 Sheba attempted to lead a secession, but it failed when he was killed.
20:1 troublemaker. See note on 1 Samuel 2:12, where the same Hebrew word is rendered "wicked men." **Sheba son of Bicri, a Benjamite.** Of the same tribe as Saul, Sheba may even have been a near relative if Bicri can legitimately be linked with the Becorath named in Saul's genealogy in 1 Samuel 9:1. **trumpet.** See note on 1 Samuel 13:3. **no share in David.** See 19:43 and its note. Not only the aggressive behavior of the men of Judah in the preceding chapter, but also residual pro-Saul sentiments must have played a part in the mass withdrawal of support for David among the northern tribes. **Every man to his tent.** This archaic turn of phrase, which recalls Israel's earlier history, should not be taken literally to imply that the Israelites in the current context were still tent-dwellers. See Judges 20:8 and 2 Kings 14:12, where the NIV renders the Hebrew word for "tent" simply as "home."
20:3 ten concubines. See 15:16 and notes on 16:21 and 22.
20:4 Amasa. See 17:25, 19:13 and their notes. **three days.** This was a limited, though not impossible, amount of time for the task set by David (see 1Sa 11:3,4 and their notes).
20:5 he took longer. The reason for Amasa's tardiness is not stated. Perhaps he did not feel entirely sympathetic toward David's cause or, alternatively, was unable to gain an immediate following among the Judahites, whose sympathies may still have lain with Joab (see v. 11 and its note).
20:6 said to Abishai. Though Amasa was proving unsatisfactory, David was still unwilling to reinstate Joab (19:13), so he addressed Joab's brother Abishai instead. By the end of the episode, however, Joab would have retaken his former position, regardless of David's wishes. **your master's men.** They are called "Joab's men" in verse 7.
20:7 Kerethites and Pelethites. See note on 1 Samuel 30:14. **mighty warriors.** They are presumably the same as those listed in 23:8–39.
20:8 the great rock. This was possibly a well-known landmark similar to those mentioned elsewhere in Samuel (1Sa 19:22; 20:19; 2Sa 15:17,23). The great rock may have served as an altar (cf. 1Sa 14:33–34), and some have even suggested a link with the "high place" in Gibeon (1Ki 3:4). **Gibeon.** See note on 2:12. **it dropped out of its sheath.** It is not stated whether it dropped to the ground or into the folds of Joab's tunic that was girded up for marching. See note on verse 10.
20:9 took Amasa by the beard. This was a normal gesture in administering the kiss of greeting and was not likely to arouse suspicion.
20:10 the dagger in Joab's hand. It is uncertain whether this was the dagger that had fallen and was retrieved, either from the ground or from the folds of Joab's tunic (see note on v. 8), or whether it was a second dagger that had been concealed on Joab's person (in which case the dropped dagger was a decoy). At any rate, Joab was able to catch Amasa completely off guard and thereby eliminate a rival, as he had done at least once before (3:27).
20:11 Whoever favors Joab . . . David. Two things might be inferred from this summons: (1) that Joab continued to enjoy the personal loyalty of at least some of the troops, despite his having been ousted by David (19:13); and (2) that Amasa's loyalty to David may not have been beyond question. See note on verse 5.
20:14 Abel Beth Maacah. This site is mentioned also in 1 Kings 15:20 and 2 Kings 15:29. On the kingdom of Maacah, see 10:6 and its note. Abel is perhaps to be associated with modern Tell Abil, which lies about 12 miles north of Lake Hulah and four miles west of Dan. **Berites.** This name is found nowhere else in the Old Testa-

entire region of the Berites,[n] who gathered together and followed him. [15]All the troops
with Joab came and besieged Sheba in Abel Beth Maacah.[o] They built a siege ramp[p] up
to the city, and it stood against the outer fortifications. While they were battering the wall
to bring it down, [16]a wise woman[q] called from the city, "Listen! Listen! Tell Joab to come
here so I can speak to him." [17]He went toward her, and she asked, "Are you Joab?"
"I am," he answered.
She said, "Listen to what your servant has to say."
"I'm listening," he said.
[18]She continued, "Long ago they used to say, 'Get your answer at Abel,' and that settled it. [19]We are the peaceful[r] and faithful in Israel. You are trying to destroy a city that
is a mother in Israel. Why do you want to swallow up the LORD's inheritance?"[s]
[20]"Far be it from me!" Joab replied, "Far be it from me to swallow up or destroy! [21]That
is not the case. A man named Sheba son of Bicri, from the hill country of Ephraim, has
lifted up his hand against the king, against David. Hand over this one man, and I'll withdraw from the city."
The woman said to Joab, "His head[t] will be thrown to you from the wall."
[22]Then the woman went to all the people with her wise advice,[u] and they cut off the
head of Sheba son of Bicri and threw it to Joab. So he sounded the trumpet, and his men
dispersed from the city, each returning to his home. And Joab went back to the king in
Jerusalem.
[23]Joab[v] was over Israel's entire army; Benaiah son of Jehoiada was over the Kerethites and Pelethites; [24]Adoniram[a][w] was in charge of forced labor; Jehoshaphat[x] son of
Ahilud was recorder; [25]Sheva was secretary; Zadok[y] and Abiathar were priests; [26]and Ira
the Jairite was David's priest.

The Gibeonites Avenged

21 During the reign of David, there was a famine[z] for three successive years; so David sought[a] the face of the LORD. The LORD said, "It is on account of Saul and his
blood-stained house; it is because he put the Gibeonites to death."

20:14 [n]Nu 21:16
20:15 [o]1Ki 15:20; 2Ki 15:29 [p]2Ki 19:32; Isa 37:33; Jer 6:6; 32:24
20:16 [q]2Sa 14:2
20:19 [r]Dt 2:26 [s]1Sa 26:19; 2Sa 21:3
20:21 [t]2Sa 4:8
20:22 [u]Ecc 9:13
20:23 [v]2Sa 2:28; 8:16-18; 24:2
20:24 [w]1Ki 4:6; 5:14; 12:18; 2Ch 10:18 [x]2Sa 8:16; 1Ki 4:3
20:25 [y]1Sa 2:35; 2Sa 8:17
21:1 [z]Ge 12:10; Dt 32:24 [a]Ex 32:11

[a] *24* Some Septuagint manuscripts (see also 1 Kings 4:6 and 5:14); Hebrew *Adoram*

---

ment, and some have suggested reading "Bicrites" (cf. "Sheba son of Bicri" in v. 1).
20:16 wise woman. See 14:2.
20:19 city that is a mother in Israel. In Hebrew perception, cities and countries were thought of figuratively as mothers of their inhabitants. The expression here, which can also be read "a city and a mother in Israel," may also point to any wise women who, like Deborah in Judges 5:7, could be called "a mother in Israel." **the LORD's inheritance?** That is, Israel—its land and its people, as a whole and in its parts (see 1Sa 10:1 and its note; 26:19; 2Sa 20:19; 21:3).
20:21 hill country of Ephraim. Either this name applies to a geographical area that extended into Benjamite territory or it is to be understood that Sheba, of Benjamite ancestry (v. 1), was resident in Ephraim.
20:22 sounded the trumpet. See verse 1 and note on 1 Samuel 13:3.
20:23–26 This summary of David's officers parallels the earlier listing in 8:15–18, although with several differences. The phrase "David reigned over all Israel" (8:15) is lacking, as is any mention of David's sons (this latter omission is hardly surprising in view of the foregoing events). "Seraiah" (8:17) is here called "Sheva" (v. 25), and two new names are added to the list: Adoniram and Ira (vv. 24,26). 1 Kings 4:1–6 indicates that many of David's officers continued in their duties during at least the early part of Solomon's reign.
20:23 Joab was over Israel's entire army. See note on verse 6. Having regained his former position, apparently without protest from David, Joab retained it until he was executed by Solomon for treason (1Ki 1:7; 2:22,28–35). **Benaiah . . . Kerethites and Pelethites.** See note on 8:18.
20:24 Adoniram. After serving as overseer of the forced labor not only under David, but also under Solomon (1Ki 4:6), Adoniram would be stoned by "all Israel" during the early days of King Rehoboam (1Ki 12:18). **forced labor.** This expression is used to describe both the hard labor into which subjugated peoples were sometimes pressed (e.g., the Israelites in Egypt [Ex 1:11] and the surviving Canaanites after the Israelite conquest [Jos 16:10; Jdg 1:28]) and the labor done by conscripts from Israel itself on, e.g., Solomonic building projects (1Ki 9:15). Neither Adoniram nor forced laborers are included in the first summary of David's government (8:15–18), which may suggest that forced labor was not introduced until partway through David's reign (cf. perhaps 12:31).
Jehoshaphat . . . recorder. Perhaps a "royal herald" (see note on 8:16).
20:25 Sheva was secretary. He was a high-ranking official, perhaps akin to "secretary of state" (see note on 8:17). **Zadok and Abiathar.** See note on 8:17.
20:26 Ira. Ira is otherwise not mentioned in the Old Testament, unless he can be identified with "Ira son of Ikkesh" (23:26) or, slightly more plausibly, "Ira the Ithrite" (23:38), who are both listed among David's "thirty" mighty men (23:24–39). **Jairite.** Some have attempted to link "Ira the Jairite" with the Levitical city of "Jattir" (Jos 21:14), while others perceive here a reference to "Jair, a descendant of Manasseh" (Nu 32:41; Dt 3:14) or "Jair of Gilead" (Jdg 10:3).
▪ **21:1—24:25** *Conclusion: Continuing Hope in David's House.* Without the occurrences in these last chapters, David's reign would have ended in utter disarray. As it stands, however, the writer added a selection of events taken from different times in David's life to show what hope the people of God could have in David's house despite the troubles that David had brought. These chapters are formed out of balanced pairs that touch on different subjects: David's effective intercessions (21:1–14; 24:1–25), his mighty army (21:15–22; 23:8–39) and his words (22:1–51; 23:1–7).
▪ **21:1–14** *David's Intercession Stops a Famine.* A famine resulting from Saul's sin was stopped when David prayed and discovered the reason for the drought. Afterward, prayer healed the land. The readers were to learn that despite David's failures and troubles, God listened to his prayers; his intercessions were effective.
21:1 During the reign of David. The time frame is stated quite generally; literally, "in the days of David." Perhaps the famine should be placed after the induction of Mephibosheth into David's court (v. 7; ch. 9) and before Absalom's rebellion (16:8), but this is uncertain. **there was a famine.** Not uncommon in the land of Canaan (Ge 12:10; 26:1; Ru 1:1), famine was often recognized in the Bible as a manifestation of God's judgment (e.g., Dt 32:24; 2Sa 24:13; 1Ki 17:1; 2Ki 8:1; Ps 105:16; Isa 14:30; Jer 11:22; Eze 14:21; Rev 6:8). Conversely, rain in the ancient Near East was often attributed to a king's good relations with his god. **Saul and his blood-stained house.** Verse 2 reveals that Saul had tried to annihilate the Gibeonites, though obviously with only partial success. For possible evidence of Saul's aggression, see 4:3 and its note. See *WCF* 22.4.

21:2 [b]Jos 9:15 2 The king summoned the Gibeonites[b] and spoke to them. (Now the Gibeonites were
not a part of Israel but were survivors of the Amorites; the Israelites had sworn to ⌊spare⌋
them, but Saul in his zeal for Israel and Judah had tried to annihilate them.) 3 David asked
21:3 the Gibeonites, "What shall I do for you? How shall I make amends so that you will bless
[c]1Sa 26:19; 2Sa 20:19 the LORD's inheritance?"[c]
21:4 4 The Gibeonites answered him, "We have no right to demand silver or gold from Saul
[d]Nu 35:33-34 or his family, nor do we have the right to put anyone in Israel to death."[d]
"What do you want me to do for you?" David asked.
5 They answered the king, "As for the man who destroyed us and plotted against us
so that we have been decimated and have no place anywhere in Israel, 6 let seven of his
21:6 [e]Nu 25:4 male descendants be given to us to be killed and exposed[e] before the LORD at Gibeah of
[f]1Sa 10:24 Saul—the LORD's chosen[f] one."
21:7 So the king said, "I will give them to you."
[g]2Sa 4:4 7 The king spared Mephibosheth[g] son of Jonathan, the son of Saul, because of the
[h]1Sa 18:3; 20:8, 15; 2Sa 9:7 oath[h] before the LORD between David and Jonathan son of Saul. 8 But the king took Ar-
21:8 moni and Mephibosheth, the two sons of Aiah's daughter Rizpah,[i] whom she had borne
[i]2Sa 3:7 [j]1Sa 18:19 to Saul, together with the five sons of Saul's daughter Merab,[a] whom she had borne to
Adriel son of Barzillai the Meholathite.[j] 9 He handed them over to the Gibeonites, who
killed and exposed them on a hill before the LORD. All seven of them fell together; they
21:9 were put to death[k] during the first days of the harvest, just as the barley harvest was be-
[k]2Sa 16:8 [l]Ru 1:22 ginning.[l]
10 Rizpah daughter of Aiah took sackcloth and spread it out for herself on a rock. From
21:10 the beginning of the harvest till the rain poured down from the heavens on the bodies,
[m]ver 8; Dt 21:23; she did not let the birds of the air touch them by day or the wild animals by night.[m]
1Sa 17:44 11 When David was told what Aiah's daughter Rizpah, Saul's concubine, had done, 12 he
21:12 [n]1Sa 31:11-13 went and took the bones of Saul[n] and his son Jonathan from the citizens of Jabesh Gil-
[o]Jos 17:11 ead. (They had taken them secretly from the public square at Beth Shan,[o] where the Phi-
[p]1Sa 31:10 listines had hung[p] them after they struck Saul down on Gilboa.) 13 David brought the
bones of Saul and his son Jonathan from there, and the bones of those who had been
killed and exposed were gathered up.
21:14 14 They buried the bones of Saul and his son Jonathan in the tomb of Saul's father
[q]Jos 18:28 Kish, at Zela[q] in Benjamin, and did everything the king commanded. After that,[r] God an-
[r]Jos 7:26 [s]2Sa 24:25 swered prayer[s] in behalf of the land.

Wars Against the Philistines

21:15 [t]2Sa 5:25 15 Once again there was a battle between the Philistines[t] and Israel. David went
down with his men to fight against the Philistines, and he became exhausted. 16 And Ishbi-Benob, one of the descendants of Rapha, whose bronze spearhead weighed three hun-

[a] *8* Two Hebrew manuscripts, some Septuagint manuscripts and Syriac (see also 1 Samuel 18:19); most Hebrew and Septuagint manuscripts *Michal*

21:2 the Israelites had sworn. Israel's oath to the Gibeonites is recorded in Joshua 9. Although Israel had been remiss in swearing an oath without inquiring of the Lord (Jos 9:14), the oath still had to be honored (Jos 9:19). **in his zeal for Israel and Judah.** Saul's attempt to annihilate the Gibeonites was motivated by nationalistic, not religious, zeal. Politically, he may have wished to rid his home tribe, Benjamin, of unwanted Amorite survivors. For Saul's ancestral association with Gibeon, see 1 Chronicles 8:29 and 9:35.
21:3 LORD's inheritance? See note on 20:19.
21:6 seven. This number symbolizes completeness, not the number of Gibeonites slain by Saul. **Gibeah of Saul—the LORD's chosen one.** The text should perhaps read "Gibeon—on the mountain of the LORD" (an emendation partially supported by the Septuagint, the Greek translation of the OT). Compare "on a hill before the LORD" in verse 9 and "the most important high place" at Gibeon in 1 Kings 3:4.
21:7 spared Mephibosheth. See notes on verse 1 and on chapter 9. **oath before the LORD between David and Jonathan.** See notes on 1 Samuel 18:3 and 4 and on 20:15.
21:8 Mephibosheth. This Mephibosheth was a son of Saul and should not be confused with the son of Jonathan (4:4). **Rizpah.** See verses 10–11, as well as 3:7. **Merab . . . Adriel.** See 1 Samuel 18:19. Adriel's father, Barzillai the Meholathite, should not be confused with the Gileadite of the same name (17:27; 19:31; 1Ki 2:7).
21:9 barley harvest was beginning. That is, in April (see note on Ru 1:22).
21:10 till the rain poured down from the heavens on the bodies. Since the "early rains" do not begin until October, an unseasonable shower signaling the end of the period of famine is probably in view here (v. 1). **she did not let the birds of the air touch them.** It was considered a disgrace when the bodies of the slain were allowed to become carrion for birds and beasts, with no one to frighten them away (Dt 28:26; 1Sa 17:44,46; Ps 79:2; Isa 18:6; Jer 7:33; 16:4). Rizpah's intent was to safeguard the bodies until they could be given proper burial (vv. 11–14).
21:11–14 David was prompted by Rizpah's vigil to gather up the bones not only of the recently slain, but also of Saul and Jonathan and to accord them a decent burial in the tomb of Kish, Saul's father.
21:14 God answered prayer in behalf of the land. An almost identical statement occurs in 24:25 at the end of the book, after the lifting of the plague brought about by David's taking of a census. The implication is that this was David's prayer and that his intercession is the common element between chapters 21 and 24.
■ **21:15–22** *David's Military Accomplishments.* These verses describe briefly the defeat of four Philistine champions at the hands of David and his men. While it is difficult to locate these events chronologically with any precision, their literary placement provides a fitting preface to David's song of praise, which follows immediately in chapter 22. From these examples of David's military accomplishments, the readers were to see the king whose house God would bless in war.
21:16 descendants of Rapha. "Rapha" is probably best understood not as the name of a deity in Gath, as some have suggested, but as a collective noun to be associated with the Rephaites, pre-Israelite inhabitants of the land of Canaan (Ge 14:5; 15:20; Dt 2:20;

dred shekels[a] and who was armed with a new ⌊sword⌋, said he would kill David. 17 But
Abishai[u] son of Zeruiah came to David's rescue; he struck the Philistine down and
killed him. Then David's men swore to him, saying, "Never again will you go out with us
to battle, so that the lamp[v] of Israel will not be extinguished.[w]"

18 In the course of time, there was another battle with the Philistines, at Gob. At that
time Sibbecai[x] the Hushathite killed Saph, one of the descendants of Rapha.

19 In another battle with the Philistines at Gob, Elhanan son of Jaare-Oregim[b] the Bethlehemite killed Goliath[c] the Gittite, who had a spear with a shaft like a weaver's rod.[y]

20 In still another battle, which took place at Gath, there was a huge man with six fingers on each hand and six toes on each foot—twenty-four in all. He also was descended from Rapha. 21 When he taunted Israel, Jonathan son of Shimeah,[z] David's brother,
killed him.

22 These four were descendants of Rapha in Gath, and they fell at the hands of David
and his men.

David's Song of Praise

22 David sang[a] to the LORD the words of this song when the LORD delivered him
from the hand of all his enemies and from the hand of Saul. 2 He said:

"The LORD is my rock,[b] my fortress[c] and my deliverer;[d]
3 my God is my rock, in whom I take refuge,[e]
my shield[f] and the horn[d][g] of my salvation.
He is my stronghold,[h] my refuge and my savior—
from violent men you save me.
4 I call to the LORD, who is worthy[i] of praise,
and I am saved from my enemies.

5 "The waves[j] of death swirled about me;
the torrents of destruction overwhelmed me.
6 The cords of the grave[e][k] coiled around me;
the snares of death confronted me.

21:17 [u]2Sa 20:6 [v]1Ki 11:36 [w]2Sa 18:3
21:18 [x]1Ch 11:29; 20:4; 27:11
21:19 [y]1Sa 17:7
21:21 [z]1Sa 16:9
22:1 [a]Ex 15:1; Jdg 5:1; Ps 18:2-50
22:2 [b]Dt 32:4; Ps 71:3 [c]Ps 31:3; 91:2 [d]Ps 144:2
22:3 [e]Dt 32:37; Jer 16:19 [f]Ge 15:1 [g]Lk 1:69 [h]Ps 9:9
22:4 [i]Ps 48:1; 96:4
22:5 [j]Ps 69:14-15; 93:4; Jnh 2:3
22:6 [k]Ps 116:3

[a] *16* That is, about 7 1/2 pounds (about 3.5 kilograms) [b] *19* Or *son of Jair the weaver* [c] *19* Hebrew and Septuagint; 1 Chron. 20:5 *son of Jair killed Lahmi the brother of Goliath* [d] *3* *Horn* here symbolizes strength. [e] *6* Hebrew *Sheol*

Jos 17:15). The term *Rephaites* is sometimes applied to such peoples as the Emites, Zamzummites and Anakites (Dt 2:10–11,20–21), all peoples distinguished for their strength and stature. According to Joshua 11:21–22, the Anakites were driven from the hill country of Israel and Judah by Joshua but were able to survive in the cities of Gaza, Gath and Ashdod, thus in the general area in view in the following verses. **three hundred shekels.** See NIV text note. Goliath's spearhead had weighed twice as much (1Sa 17:7).

21:17 Abishai. See notes on 2:18. **lamp of Israel.** This is a metaphor reflecting that, in a unique way, Israel's hope and promise of blessing resided in David and his house (see note on 1Sa 3:3).

21:18 Rapha. See note on verse 16.

21:19 Elhanan . . . killed Goliath. This text appears to credit someone other than David with the death of Goliath. The corresponding verse in 1 Chronicles 20:5 (see NIV text note at 2 Samuel 21:19) neatly resolves the difficulty, stating that Elhanan killed "Lahmi the brother of Goliath," and for that reason the Samuel text is held suspect by a majority of commentators. Some have sought to explain the Samuel text by suggesting that "Elhanan" might simply be another name for David (cf. 12:25, where Solomon bears the additional name "Jedidiah"). While this explanation eases the tension in the Samuel text, it entails the awkward and perhaps unacceptable assumption that the Chronicles reading is a misguided attempt at harmonization. On the other hand, it may be that Chronicles preserves the more original reading and that the Samuel reading contains an alteration of the original. In favor of the originality of the Chronicles reading, the following observations can be made: (1) There is clear evidence that the Samuel text, in some respects at least, is altered here (e.g., "Oregim" appears to be an inadvertent duplication of the same word, translated "weaver's," at the end of the verse); (2) "Bethlehemite" in Hebrew differs only slightly from "Lahmi" when it is preceded by "'eth," the Hebrew sign of the direct object, so that the Samuel reading could have arisen when a scribe (perhaps under the influence of "Elhanan son of Dodo from Bethlehem" in 23:24) mistook the rarer "'eth Lahmi" for the more common "Bethlehemite"; (3) with the loss of "Lahmi" as the direct object of the sentence, "the brother of Goliath" may have been altered, by a slight change of the Hebrew to simply "Goliath" (preceded by the sign of the direct object).

21:20 Rapha. See note on verse 16.

21:22 at the hands of David and his men. David was involved not only indirectly by virtue of being king, but also directly in the encounter with Ishbi-Benob (vv. 16–17).

■ **22:1–51** *David's Praise and Confidence.* David sang a song of praise to God for delivering him from his enemies. Together with 23:1-7, this chapter forms the heart of 21:1—24:25. David expressed confidence and trust in the Lord for the future of his kingdom. The readers were to share this optimism about the house of David.

22:1 this song. David's song of praise (which appears also in Ps 18 [see its notes] with minor variations) forms, together with the prayer of Hannah, a fitting frame for the books of 1 and 2 Samuel (see note on 1Sa 2:1–10). This song focuses on the Lord's deliverance of David, to which chapter 23 then adds a celebration of the dynasty of David. The song of chapter 22 may be outlined as follows: introductory praise of God as savior (vv. 2–4); the psalmist's distress (vv. 5–6), the psalmist's petition (v. 7); the Lord's response in cosmic demonstration (vv. 8–16) and personal rescue (vv. 17–20); the psalmist's innocence (vv. 21–25) and the Lord's faithfulness (vv. 26–30); the Lord's deliverance (vv. 31–37) and the psalmist's resultant victories (vv. 38–46); and concluding praise of God as savior (vv. 47–51). Psalm 144, which is ascribed to David, shows many similarities in theme and language. **all his enemies.** See 8:1–14 (cf. 1Sa 25:26; 2Sa 5:8; 7:1,9,11; 18:32). **from the hand of Saul.** See 12:7 and 1 Samuel 18–31 (especially 18:9–11; 19:2,10–11,15–16).

22:3 rock. See also verses 32 and 47, as well as note on 1 Samuel 2:2. **shield.** See also verses 31 and 36. See note on Genesis 15:1, in which the Lord refers to himself as Abram's "shield" (or possibly "sovereign"). Compare Moses' declaration of Israel's blessedness in having a God who was its "shield and helper and [its] glorious sword" (Dt 33:29). **horn.** See 1 Samuel 2:1 and 10 and their notes.

22:5 waves . . . torrents. See verse 17. The image of whelming or engulfing waters recurs frequently in Old Testament poetry as a symbol of distress and destruction (e.g., Pss 30:1; 32:6; 69:1–2,14; 144:7; Isa 43:2; Jnh 2:5).

22:6 cords of the grave. Compare "cords of affliction" (Job 36:8); "cords of death" (Pss 18:4; 116:3); "cords of his sin" (Pr 5:22); and

22:7 [l]Ps 120:1 [m]Ps 34:6,15; 116:4

7 In my distress[l] I called[m] to the LORD;
I called out to my God.
From his temple he heard my voice;
my cry came to his ears.

22:8 [n]Jdg 5:4; Ps 97:4 [o]Ps 77:18 [p]Job 26:11

8 "The earth[n] trembled and quaked,[o]
the foundations[p] of the heavens[a] shook;
they trembled because he was angry.

22:9 [q]Ps 97:3; Heb 12:29

9 Smoke rose from his nostrils;
consuming fire[q] came from his mouth,
burning coals blazed out of it.

22:10 [r]1Ki 8:12; Na 1:3

10 He parted the heavens and came down;
dark clouds[r] were under his feet.

22:11 [s]Ps 104:3

11 He mounted the cherubim and flew;
he soared[b] on the wings of the wind.[s]
12 He made darkness his canopy around him—
the dark[c] rain clouds of the sky.

22:13 [t]ver 9

13 Out of the brightness of his presence
bolts of lightning[t] blazed forth.

22:14 [u]1Sa 2:10

14 The LORD thundered[u] from heaven;
the voice of the Most High resounded.

22:15 [v]Dt 32:23

15 He shot arrows[v] and scattered ⌊the enemies⌋,
bolts of lightning and routed them.
16 The valleys of the sea were exposed
and the foundations of the earth laid bare

22:16 [w]Na 1:4

at the rebuke[w] of the LORD,
at the blast of breath from his nostrils.

22:17 [x]Ps 144:7 [y]Ex 2:10

17 "He reached down from on high[x] and took hold of me;
he drew[y] me out of deep waters.
18 He rescued me from my powerful enemy,
from my foes, who were too strong for me.

22:19 [z]Ps 23:4

19 They confronted me in the day of my disaster,
but the LORD was my support.[z]

22:20 [a]Ps 31:8 [b]Ps 118:5 [c]Ps 22:8 [d]2Sa 15:26

20 He brought me out into a spacious[a] place;
he rescued[b] me because he delighted[c] in me.[d]

22:21 [e]1Sa 26:23 [f]Ps 24:4

21 "The LORD has dealt with me according to my righteousness;[e]
according to the cleanness of my hands[f] he has
rewarded me.

22:22 [g]Ge 18:19; Ps 128:1; Pr 8:32

22 For I have kept[g] the ways of the LORD;
I have not done evil by turning from my God.

22:23 [h]Dt 6:4-9; Ps 119:30-32 [i]Ps 119:102

23 All his laws are before me;[h]
I have not turned[i] away from his decrees.

22:24 [j]Ge 6:9; Eph 1:4

24 I have been blameless[j] before him
and have kept myself from sin.

[a] *8* Hebrew; Vulgate and Syriac (see also Psalm 18:7) *mountains* [b] *11* Many Hebrew manuscripts (see also Psalm 18:10); most Hebrew manuscripts *appeared* [c] *12* Septuagint and Vulgate (see also Psalm 18:11); Hebrew *massed*

"cords of deceit" (Isa 5:18). Contrast "I led them with cords of human kindness, with ties of love" (Hos 11:4).

22:7 In my distress. In Hebrew the concept of distress is expressed in terms of being in a narrow or tightly confined space. In verse 20 (see its note) relief is described as being brought into a "spacious place." **From his temple.** This is probably to be understood as God's heavenly sanctuary (1Ki 8:27,38–39; Ps 11:4; Isa 6:1; Jnh 2:7; Rev 11:19; 14:17; 15:5).

22:8–20 The Lord's response to David's petition (v. 7) is described first in powerful, cosmic terms (vv. 8–16; see descriptions of the Lord's appearing in Ex 19:16–19; Jdg 5:4–5; Na 1:5; etc.) and then in terms of his personal rescue of David (vv. 17–20). For the combination of cosmic demonstration and personal rescue, see Joel 3:16.

22:9 Smoke rose from his nostrils. See the imagery used to describe the awesome power of the leviathan in Job 41:18–21.

22:11 mounted the cherubim and flew. See Exodus 25:17–22, Numbers 7:89 and Ezekiel 10:19 and 11:22.

22:14 The LORD thundered. See 1 Samuel 2:10 and 7:10. The Lord's voice is often likened to thunder (e.g., Job 37:4–5; 40:9; Pss 29:3; 68:33; Isa 33:3). **Most High.** See Genesis 14:18–22 and its notes.

22:15 He shot arrows. For similar imagery, see Deuteronomy 32:23 and 42, Job 6:4 and Psalm 64:7. Lightning is sometimes described as the Lord's arrows (Ps 77:17; cf. Hab 3:11; Zec 9:14).

22:17–20 See note on verses 8–20.

22:17 deep waters. See note on verse 5.

22:20 spacious place. This signals, in the Hebrew way of thinking, relief from distress or, in today's idiom, release from a "tight spot" (see note on v. 7). **because he delighted in me.** See 15:25–26.

22:21–25 In these verses David was not laying claim to righteousness or sinlessness in any absolute sense but was rather asserting his blamelessness with respect to his enemies and his confidence that the Lord rewards those who seek to be faithful to him (cf. v. 26 and David's declaration to Saul in 1Sa 26:23). If this were not the case, David would surely be classed among "the haughty" (v. 28).

25 The LORD has rewarded me according to my righteousness,[k]
according to my cleanness[a] in his sight.

26 "To the faithful you show yourself faithful,
to the blameless you show yourself blameless,
27 to the pure[l] you show yourself pure,
but to the crooked you show yourself shrewd.[m]
28 You save the humble,[n]
but your eyes are on the haughty to bring them low.[o]
29 You are my lamp,[p] O LORD;
the LORD turns my darkness into light.
30 With your help I can advance against a troop[b];
with my God I can scale a wall.

31 "As for God, his way is perfect;[q]
the word of the LORD is flawless.[r]
He is a shield
for all who take refuge in him.
32 For who is God besides the LORD?
And who is the Rock[s] except our God?
33 It is God who arms me with strength[c]
and makes my way perfect.
34 He makes my feet like the feet of a deer;[t]
he enables me to stand on the heights.[u]
35 He trains my hands[v] for battle;
my arms can bend a bow of bronze.
36 You give me your shield[w] of victory;
you stoop down to make me great.
37 You broaden the path[x] beneath me,
so that my ankles do not turn.

38 "I pursued my enemies and crushed them;
I did not turn back till they were destroyed.
39 I crushed[y] them completely, and they could not rise;
they fell beneath my feet.
40 You armed me with strength for battle;
you made my adversaries bow at my feet.[z]
41 You made my enemies turn their backs[a] in flight,
and I destroyed my foes.
42 They cried for help,[b] but there was no one to save them—[c]
to the LORD, but he did not answer.
43 I beat them as fine as the dust of the earth;
I pounded and trampled[d] them like mud[e] in the streets.

44 "You have delivered[f] me from the attacks of my people;
you have preserved[g] me as the head of nations.
People[h] I did not know are subject to me,
45 and foreigners come cringing[i] to me;
as soon as they hear me, they obey me.
46 They all lose heart;
they come trembling[d][j] from their strongholds.

22:25 [k]ver 21
22:27 [l]Mt 5:8 [m]Lev 26:23-24
22:28 [n]Ex 3:8; Ps 72:12-13 [o]Isa 2:12, 17; 5:15
22:29 [p]Ps 27:1
22:31 [q]Dt 32:4; Mt 5:48 [r]Ps 12:6; 119:140; Pr 30:5-6
22:32 [s]1Sa 2:2
22:34 [t]Hab 3:19 [u]Dt 32:13
22:35 [v]Ps 144:1
22:36 [w]Eph 6:16
22:37 [x]Pr 4:11
22:39 [y]Mal 4:3
22:40 [z]Ps 44:5
22:41 [a]Ex 23:27
22:42 [b]Isa 1:15 [c]Ps 50:22
22:43 [d]Mic 7:10 [e]Isa 10:6; Mic 7:10
22:44 [f]2Sa 3:1 [g]Dt 28:13 [h]2Sa 8:1-14; Isa 55:3-5
22:45 [i]Ps 66:3; 81:15
22:46 [j]Mic 7:17

[a] *25* Hebrew; Septuagint and Vulgate (see also Psalm 18:24) *to the cleanness of my hands* [b] *30* Or *can run through a barricade* [c] *33* Dead Sea Scrolls, some Septuagint manuscripts, Vulgate and Syriac (see also Psalm 18:32); Masoretic Text *who is my strong refuge* [d] *46* Some Septuagint manuscripts and Vulgate (see also Psalm 18:45); Masoretic Text *they arm themselves.*

22:27 shrewd. The psalmist here broke the pattern of verbal correspondence exhibited in the three preceding lines, since there is no sense in which God could be described as "crooked." The Hebrew rendered "shrewd" might also be translated "tortuous" and could be understood in the sense that, in the economy of God's justice, those who take "crooked" paths find the way "tortuous" indeed (see Isa 59:8).
22:28 humble . . . haughty. See the theme of divine reversal of fortunes in Hannah's prayer (see 1Sa 2:1–10 and its note, especially v. 7).
22:29 my lamp. See notes on 21:17 and 1 Samuel 3:3.
22:31 word . . . shield. See note on verse 3. Much of verse 31 is repeated almost verbatim by Agur in Proverbs 30:5. See also Psalm 119:114.
22:32 Rock. See verses 3 and 47 (see also note on 1Sa 2:2).
22:36 shield. See note on verse 3.
22:42 to the LORD, but he did not answer. See note on 1 Samuel 8:18.
22:44 my people. This is possibly a reference to the many perils that David had experienced at the hands of Saul, Absalom and other Israelites. The corresponding verse in Psalm 18:43, however, reads simply "the people," as does the Septuagint (the Greek translation of the OT) of the present verse.

47 "The LORD lives! Praise be to my Rock!
Exalted be God, the Rock, my Savior![k]
48 He is the God who avenges me,[l]
who puts the nations under me,
49 who sets me free from my enemies.[m]
You exalted me above my foes;
from violent men you rescued me.
50 Therefore I will praise you, O LORD, among the nations;
I will sing praises to your name.[n]
51 He gives his king great victories;[o]
he shows unfailing kindness to his anointed,[p]
to David[q] and his descendants forever."[r]

The Last Words of David

23 These are the last words of David:

"The oracle of David son of Jesse,
the oracle of the man exalted[s] by the Most High,
the man anointed[t] by the God of Jacob,
Israel's singer of songs[a]:
2 "The Spirit[u] of the LORD spoke through me;
his word was on my tongue.
3 The God of Israel spoke,
the Rock[v] of Israel said to me:
'When one rules over men in righteousness,[w]
when he rules in the fear of God,[x]
4 he is like the light of morning at sunrise[y]
on a cloudless morning,
like the brightness after rain
that brings the grass from the earth.'
5 "Is not my house right with God?
Has he not made with me an everlasting covenant,[z]
arranged and secured in every part?
Will he not bring to fruition my salvation
and grant me my every desire?
6 But evil men are all to be cast aside like thorns,[a]
which are not gathered with the hand.

22:47 [k]Ps 89:26
22:48 [l]Ps 94:1; 144:2; 1Sa 25:39
22:49 [m]Ps 140:1,4
22:50 [n]Ro 15:9*
22:51 [o]Ps 144:9-10 [p]Ps 89:20 [q]2Sa 7:13 [r]Ps 89:24,29
23:1 [s]2Sa 7:8-9; Ps 78:70-71; 89:27 [t]1Sa 16:12-13; Ps 89:20
23:2 [u]Mt 22:43; 2Pe 1:21
23:3 [v]Dt 32:4; 2Sa 22:2, 32 [w]Ps 72:2 [x]2Ch 19:7,9; Isa 11:1-5
23:4 [y]Jdg 5:31; Ps 89:36
23:5 [z]Ps 89:29; Isa 55:3
23:6 [a]Mt 13:40-41

a *1* Or *Israel's beloved singer*

22:47–51 These concluding verses recapitulate the themes and much of the vocabulary of the opening lines of the psalm.
22:50 among the nations. See Romans 15:9.
22:51 his king . . . anointed. The mention of the Lord's "king" and his "anointed" is reminiscent of the closing verse of Hannah's prayer in 1 Samuel 2:10, but with the added feature that David now, after the dynastic promise of 2 Samuel 7:5–16, could speak confidently of God's unfailing kindness even to "his descendants forever." This introduction of the dynastic theme provides a transition to "the last words of David" in the next chapter. In chapter 23 David celebrated the "everlasting covenant" (23:5) that the Lord had made with him.
■ **23:1–7** *David's Declaration About the Future.* In balance with the preceding praise and confidence expressed by David, this oracle of David focuses on the direction that was to be taken by his house in the future and the confidence the nation could have in his dynasty.
23:1 last words of David. See note on 22:51. First Kings 2:1–10 records what must also be considered the "last words" of David; namely, his final instructions to Solomon on the eve of his death. The designation "last words" in the present context may imply either that this was the last poetic composition by David or simply that David was speaking, as it were, the "last word" on the subject of his dynasty. **oracle.** Or "declaration" (cf. "declares" in 1Sa 2:30). The word is often, although not exclusively, associated with prophecy (e.g., Nu 24:3–4; 2Ki 9:25–26), a connection not foreign to David (see v. 2 and its note; Ac 2:30; perhaps 2Ch 29:25). **Israel's singer of songs.** See NIV text note. An alternative and equally plausible rendering of the Hebrew is "the beloved of Israel's Protector."
23:2–4 To David the Lord had revealed the essential character and glorious benefits of the ideal theocratic king. Only in the Christ, the greater son of David, would such qualities of character be fully displayed and such benefits be fully realized (see note on 7:4–17).
23:2 The Spirit of the LORD spoke through me. Further references to David as acting or speaking under divine inspiration include 1 Chronicles 28:11–12, Matthew 22:43 and Acts 1:16 and 4:25. David's empowering with the Spirit is recounted in 1 Samuel 16:13.
23:3 Rock. See notes on 22:3 and 32 (see also 1Sa 2:2). **When one rules over men in righteousness . . . in the fear of God.** Righteous rule is possible only for one who lives in right relationship to God. On what it means to "fear" God, see note on 1 Samuel 12:14. See *WCF* 23.2.
23:4 light of morning . . . brightness after rain that brings the grass. The benefits of righteous rule are enlightenment, refreshment and fruitfulness. For a fuller development of similar themes, see Psalm 72.
23:5 Is not my house right with God? David's confidence rested not in his own righteousness, but, as the next line reveals, in the everlasting covenant a gracious God had made with him (7:11–16; 2Ch 13:5; 21:7; Ps 89:3–4,28–29; Isa 55:3; Eze 37:25–26). **arranged and secured in every part?** This covenant was, as it were, a fully accomplished action. See *WLC* 79.
23:6 evil men. The Hebrew term is "Belial" (see note on 1Sa 2:12). The focus here may be on those who had opposed the rule of David.

[7]Whoever touches thorns
uses a tool of iron or the shaft of a spear;
they are burned up where they lie."

David's Mighty Men

[8]These are the names of David's mighty men:
Josheb-Basshebeth,[a] a Tahkemonite,[b] was chief of the Three; he raised his spear
against eight hundred men, whom he killed[c] in one encounter.
[9]Next to him was Eleazar son of Dodai[b] the Ahohite.[c] As one of the three mighty men,
he was with David when they taunted the Philistines gathered ⌊at Pas Dammim⌋[d] for battle. Then the men of Israel retreated, [10]but he stood his ground and struck down the Philistines till his hand grew tired and froze to the sword. The LORD brought about a great
victory that day. The troops returned to Eleazar, but only to strip the dead.
[11]Next to him was Shammah son of Agee the Hararite. When the Philistines banded
together at a place where there was a field full of lentils, Israel's troops fled from them.
[12]But Shammah took his stand in the middle of the field. He defended it and struck the
Philistines down, and the LORD brought about a great victory.
[13]During harvest time, three of the thirty chief men came down to David at the cave of
Adullam,[d] while a band of Philistines was encamped in the Valley of Rephaim.[e] [14]At that
time David was in the stronghold,[f] and the Philistine garrison was at Bethlehem.[g] [15]Da-
vid longed for water and said, "Oh, that someone would get me a drink of water from the
well near the gate of Bethlehem!" [16]So the three mighty men broke through the Philistine
lines, drew water from the well near the gate of Bethlehem and carried it back to David.
But he refused to drink it; instead, he poured[h] it out before the LORD. [17]"Far be it from me,
O LORD, to do this!" he said. "Is it not the blood[i] of men who went at the risk of their lives?"
And David would not drink it.
Such were the exploits of the three mighty men.
[18]Abishai[j] the brother of Joab son of Zeruiah was chief of the Three.[e] He raised his
spear against three hundred men, whom he killed, and so he became as famous as the
Three. [19]Was he not held in greater honor than the Three? He became their commander, even though he was not included among them.
[20]Benaiah[k] son of Jehoiada was a valiant fighter from Kabzeel,[l] who performed great
exploits. He struck down two of Moab's best men. He also went down into a pit on a
snowy day and killed a lion. [21]And he struck down a huge Egyptian. Although the Egyptian had a spear in his hand, Benaiah went against him with a club. He snatched the
spear from the Egyptian's hand and killed him with his own spear. [22]Such were the exploits of Benaiah son of Jehoiada; he too was as famous as the three mighty men. [23]He
was held in greater honor than any of the Thirty, but he was not included among the
Three. And David put him in charge of his bodyguard.

[24]Among the Thirty were:
Asahel[m] the brother of Joab,
Elhanan son of Dodo from Bethlehem,

23:9 [b]1Ch 27:4 [c]1Ch 8:4
23:13 [d]1Sa 22:1 [e]2Sa 5:18
23:14 [f]1Sa 22:4-5 [g]Ru 1:19
23:16 [h]Ge 35:14
23:17 [i]Lev 17:10-12
23:18 [j]2Sa 10:10, 14; 1Ch 11:20
23:20 [k]2Sa 8:18; 20:23 [l]Jos 15:21
23:24 [m]2Sa 2:18

[a] *8* Hebrew; some Septuagint manuscripts suggest *Ish-Bosheth,* that is, *Esh-Baal* (see also 1 Chron. 11:11 *Jashobeam*). [b] *8* Probably a variant of *Hacmonite* (see 1 Chron. 11:11) [c] *8* Some Septuagint manuscripts (see also 1 Chron. 11:11); Hebrew and other Septuagint manuscripts *Three; it was Adino the Eznite who killed eight hundred men* [d] *9* See 1 Chron. 11:13; Hebrew *gathered there.* [e] *18* Most Hebrew manuscripts (see also 1 Chron. 11:20); two Hebrew manuscripts and Syriac *Thirty*

■ **23:8–39** *David's Military Accomplishments.* The presentation of David's mighty men in these verses forms a counterpart to the much shorter description of Davidic champions in 21:15–22. Again, the purpose of this material was to illustrate what potential the house of David had militarily. According to verse 39, the warriors introduced in the present passage should total 37. This seems to assume two sets of "three" (vv. 8–12 and vv. 13–17) plus Abishai (vv. 18–19) and Benaiah (vv. 20–23), as well as the 29 listed in verses 24–39. There are various textual and other difficulties, however, such as the fact that the "three" of verses 13–17 are apparently to be counted among "the Thirty" and not separately. By some reckonings, this chapter lists 36 mighty men, to whom Joab could be added to make the total 37. First Chronicles 11:10–47 offers a somewhat divergent list to which more than 15 additional names are appended, and no summary total is given.

23:8 eight hundred. First Chronicles 11:11 reads "three hundred." See NIV text note.

23:10 The LORD brought about a great victory that day. This statement, which is repeated in verse 12, serves as a reminder that, whatever the heroic qualities (or lack thereof) of the human agent, it was the Lord who ultimately brought victory (e.g., 8:6,14; 1Sa 14:15,23; 19:5).

23:11 field full of lentils. Enemy incursions often sought to debilitate their foe by causing agricultural damage (e.g., Jdg 6:3–6,11).

23:13 cave of Adullam. See note on 1 Samuel 22:1. **Valley of Rephaim.** See note on 5:18.

23:14 stronghold. See note on 1 Samuel 23:14.

23:16 poured it out before the LORD. The brave exploit of the three men was a testimony to their devotion to David, while David's refusal to drink (v. 17) what had been procured at such risk to his loyal followers was testimony to his love for them.

23:18 Abishai. See notes on 2:18.

23:20 Benaiah son of Jehoiada. See note on 8:18.

23:23 bodyguard. David's bodyguard was presumably comprised of the Kerethites and Pelethites (see note on 1Sa 30:14).

23:24 the Thirty. "Thirty" may be a round number. Not surprisingly, more of David's men were from the tribe of Judah than from

25 Shammah the Harodite,[n]
Elika the Harodite,
26 Helez[o] the Paltite,
Ira son of Ikkesh from Tekoa,
27 Abiezer from Anathoth,[p]
Mebunnai[a] the Hushathite,
28 Zalmon the Ahohite,
Maharai[q] the Netophathite,[r]
29 Heled[b] son of Baanah the Netophathite,
Ithai son of Ribai from Gibeah[s] in Benjamin,
30 Benaiah the Pirathonite,[t]
Hiddai[c] from the ravines of Gaash,[u]
31 Abi-Albon the Arbathite,
Azmaveth the Barhumite,[v]
32 Eliahba the Shaalbonite,
the sons of Jashen,
Jonathan 33 son of[d] Shammah the Hararite,
Ahiam son of Sharar[e] the Hararite,
34 Eliphelet son of Ahasbai the Maacathite,
Eliam[w] son of Ahithophel[x] the Gilonite,
35 Hezro the Carmelite,[y]
Paarai the Arbite,
36 Igal son of Nathan from Zobah,[z]
the son of Hagri,[f]
37 Zelek the Ammonite,
Naharai the Beerothite, the armor-bearer of Joab son of Zeruiah,
38 Ira the Ithrite,[a]
Gareb the Ithrite
39 and Uriah[b] the Hittite.
There were thirty-seven in all.

David Counts the Fighting Men

24 Again[c] the anger of the LORD burned against Israel, and he incited David against them, saying, "Go and take a census of[d] Israel and Judah."
2 So the king said to Joab[e] and the army commanders[g] with him, "Go throughout the

23:25 [n]Jdg 7:1; 1Ch 11:27
23:26 [o]1Ch 27:10
23:27 [p]Jos 21:18
23:28 [q]1Ch 27:13 [r]2Ki 25:23; Ne 7:26
23:29 [s]Jos 15:57
23:30 [t]Jdg 12:13 [u]Jos 24:30
23:31 [v]2Sa 3:16
23:34 [w]2Sa 11:3 [x]2Sa 15:12
23:35 [y]Jos 12:22
23:36 [z]1Sa 14:47
23:38 [a]2Sa 20:26; 1Ch 2:53
23:39 [b]2Sa 11:3
24:1 [c]Jos 9:15 [d]1Ch 27:23
24:2 [e]2Sa 20:23

[a] *27* Hebrew; some Septuagint manuscripts (see also 1 Chron. 11:29) *Sibbecai* [b] *29* Some Hebrew manuscripts and Vulgate (see also 1 Chron. 11:30); most Hebrew manuscripts *Heleb* [c] *30* Hebrew; some Septuagint manuscripts (see also 1 Chron. 11:32) *Hurai* [d] *33* Some Septuagint manuscripts (see also 1 Chron. 11:34); Hebrew does not have *son of.* [e] *33* Hebrew; some Septuagint manuscripts (see also 1 Chron. 11:35) *Sacar* [f] *36* Some Septuagint manuscripts (see also 1 Chron. 11:38); Hebrew *Haggadi* [g] *2* Septuagint (see also verse 4 and 1 Chron. 21:2); Hebrew *Joab the army commander*

any other. **Asahel.** See note on 2:18. **Elhanan.** He is not to be confused with the Elhanan of 21:19 (see its note).
23:27 Mebunnai. See NIV text note, as well as 21:18.
23:29 Gibeah in Benjamin. David received support even from Saul's hometown (1Sa 10:26; 11:4).
23:30 Benaiah. He is not the same as the Benaiah of verses 20–23.
23:34 Eliam son of Ahithophel. See note on 11:3.
23:36 Zobah. See note on 8:3.
23:37 Beerothite. See note on 4:3.
23:39 Uriah the Hittite. By concluding the list of David's mighty men with Uriah, the victim of David's great sin in chapter 11, the chapter ends with a poignant reminder that, despite all God had accomplished for and through him, David was, like all men, a sinner in need of God's forgiveness (ch. 12). This theme is continued in the next chapter. **There were thirty-seven in all.** See note on verses 8–39.
■ **24:1–25** *David's Intercession Stops a Plague.* The events described in this final chapter provide a fitting conclusion to the book of Samuel. David is shown for what he was, a sinner—but a sinner who knew how to repent genuinely and to cast himself upon God's mercy (see 12:13 and its note). In this matter of repentance, David was quite unlike his predecessor Saul (see 1Sa 15:24–31 and their associated notes), and this distinction may account in part for the dissimilar fates of the two kings. Of far greater significance is the divine election of David, as expressed most strikingly in the dynastic promise of 7:11–16. A further reason for the choice of this chapter to conclude the book of Samuel may have been the association of the threshing floor of Araunah (vv. 18–25) with the future site of the temple (1Ch 22:1); namely, Mount Moriah, according to 2 Chronicles 3:1 (cf. Ge 22:2). The readers were to see in these events the effectiveness of intercession from David's sons, even as they dealt with the consequences of their own sins. David and his sons had taken the nation into troubled times, but David and his son were the ones to bring them out of it as well.
24:1 Again. If a specific earlier occasion was in view, the most likely candidate was the famine of 21:1. In the overall structure of chapters 21–24, the famine/plague accounts of 21:1–14 and chapter 24 serve as corresponding units that frame the intervening material (see "Introduction: Purpose and Distinctives"). **he incited David.** The natural grammatical antecedent of "he" is the Lord (on the Lord inciting someone, cf. 1Sa 26:19). According to 1 Chronicles 21:1, however, it was Satan who incited David. At issue here is the mystery of the presence and practice of evil. While Scripture makes it unambiguously clear that the holy God does not do evil or tempt others to do evil (Jas 1:13–15), it also reflects that not even the wicked acts of men and of Satan fall outside God's sovereign jurisdiction (Ex 4:21; 1Ki 22:20–23; Job 1:12; Eze 14:9; Ac 4:27–28; see also 1Sa 2:25 and its note on "the LORD's will to put them to death"). God and Satan are not coequal powers. Satan is always subordinate to the sovereignty of God. **take a census.** The taking of a census does not appear to have been wrong in itself (Nu 1:1–2; 4:1–2; 26:1–4), but see Exodus 30:11–12. The offense here, as in the matter of Israel's demand for a king (1Sa 8), must have lain in the area of motive. While the text is not explicit, David's order that "the fighting men" (v. 2) be numbered may have been prompted by a desire to take pride in, or find security in, the extent of his

tribes of Israel from Dan to Beersheba[f] and enroll the fighting men, so that I may know
how many there are."
3But Joab replied to the king, "May the LORD your God multiply the troops a hundred
times over,[g] and may the eyes of my lord the king see it. But why does my lord the king
want to do such a thing?"
4The king's word, however, overruled Joab and the army commanders; so they left the
presence of the king to enroll the fighting men of Israel.
5After crossing the Jordan, they camped near Aroer,[h] south of the town in the gorge,
and then went through Gad and on to Jazer.[i] 6They went to Gilead and the region of Tah-
tim Hodshi, and on to Dan Jaan and around toward Sidon.[j] 7Then they went toward the
fortress of Tyre[k] and all the towns of the Hivites and Canaanites. Finally, they went on
to Beersheba[l] in the Negev[m] of Judah.
8After they had gone through the entire land, they came back to Jerusalem at the end
of nine months and twenty days.
9Joab reported the number of the fighting men to the king: In Israel there were eight
hundred thousand able-bodied men who could handle a sword, and in Judah five hundred thousand.[n]
10David was conscience-stricken[o] after he had counted the fighting men, and he said
to the LORD, "I have sinned[p] greatly in what I have done. Now, O LORD, I beg you, take
away the guilt of your servant. I have done a very foolish thing.[q]"
11Before David got up the next morning, the word of the LORD had come to Gad[r] the
prophet, David's seer:[s] 12"Go and tell David, 'This is what the LORD says: I am giving you
three options. Choose one of them for me to carry out against you.'"
13So Gad went to David and said to him, "Shall there come upon you three[a] years of
famine[t] in your land? Or three months of fleeing from your enemies while they pursue
you? Or three days of plague[u] in your land? Now then, think it over and decide how I
should answer the one who sent me."
14David said to Gad, "I am in deep distress. Let us fall into the hands of the LORD, for
his mercy[v] is great; but do not let me fall into the hands of men."
15So the LORD sent a plague on Israel from that morning until the end of the time designated, and seventy thousand of the people from Dan to Beersheba died.[w] 16When the
angel stretched out his hand to destroy Jerusalem, the LORD was grieved[x] because of the
calamity and said to the angel who was afflicting the people, "Enough! Withdraw your
hand." The angel of the LORD[y] was then at the threshing floor of Araunah the Jebusite.
17When David saw the angel who was striking down the people, he said to the LORD,

24:2 [f]Jdg 20:1; 2Sa 3:10
24:3 [g]Dt 1:11
24:5 [h]Dt 2:36; Jos 13:9 [i]Nu 21:32
24:6 [j]Ge 10:19; Jos 19:28; Jdg 1:31
24:7 [k]Jos 19:29 [l]Ge 21:22-33 [m]Dt 1:7; Jos 11:3
24:9 [n]Nu 1:44-46; 1Ch 21:5
24:10 [o]1Sa 24:5 [p]2Sa 12:13 [q]Nu 12:11; 1Sa 13:13
24:11 [r]1Sa 22:5 [s]1Sa 9:9; 1Ch 29:29
24:13 [t]Dt 28:38-42, 48; Eze 14:21 [u]Lev 26:25
24:14 [v]Ne 9:28; Ps 51:1; 103:8, 13; 130:4
24:15 [w]1Ch 27:24
24:16 [x]Ge 6:6; 1Sa 15:11 [y]Ex 12:23; Ac 12:23

a *13* Septuagint (see also 1 Chron. 21:12); Hebrew *seven*

kingdom or perhaps even by a desire to extend his borders beyond those granted him by the Lord. **Israel and Judah.** See note on 1 Samuel 11:8. See *WCF* 5.4; 5.5.
24:2 Dan to Beersheba. See note on Judges 20:1.
24:3 But why . . . do such a thing? The reason for Joab's reluctance is not stated; it may as easily have been political as religious, since a census might have been interpreted by the populace as a sign that David intended more stringent taxation or military conscription.
24:4 king's word, however, overruled. That David simply forced his will, without stating his rationale in response to Joab's query, may be an indication that his motives were questionable (see note on v. 1).
24:5–7 These verses, although uncertain due to textual difficulties, are sufficiently clear to indicate that the census was begun in southern Transjordan and continued in a counterclockwise direction throughout the full extent of the land, ending in Beersheba.
24:8 nine months and twenty days. The vast majority of this time was needed for the census taking. The travel alone could have been accomplished in a matter of weeks (see note on 1Sa 11:4).
24:9 In Israel . . . eight hundred thousand . . . in Judah five hundred thousand. First Chronicles 21:5 reads "one million one hundred thousand" and "four hundred and seventy thousand," respectively. On this difference, see notes on 1 Chronicles 21:5 and 6.
24:10 conscience-stricken. See 1 Samuel 24:5. **I have sinned greatly.** See verse 17. **take away the guilt.** If sincerely offered, David's plea for forgiveness may have been granted by God already before the arrival of Gad (vv. 11–13). Nevertheless, as in the case of David's sin against Uriah and Bathsheba, forgiveness did not mean that David's sin would have no further consequences (v. 13; 12:13–14). **foolish thing.** See 1 Samuel 13:13 and its note.
24:11 Gad. See 1 Samuel 22:5 and its note. **the prophet, David's seer.** See note on 1 Samuel 9:9.
24:12 Go and tell David. The Lord sent Gad to confront David, as he had earlier sent the prophet Nathan (see 12:1 and its note).
24:13 famine . . . enemies . . . plague. Implicit in the threat of pursuit by "enemies" was loss of life by the sword, as 1 Chronicles 21:12 makes explicit: "three months of being swept away before your enemies, with their swords overtaking you." Famine, sword and plague constitute the Old Testament's triad of woes commonly threatened for obdurate covenant breaking (e.g., Lev 26:23–26; Dt 28:21–26; 32:24–25; 1Ki 8:37; 2Ch 20:9; Isa 51:19; Jer 14:12; Eze 6:11–12). **decide.** Perhaps mercifully (see preceding note), the Lord allowed David to choose one of the three potential punishments.
24:14 Let us fall into the hands of the LORD. Technically, this would have allowed either the first or third option; i.e., famine or plague (although 1Ch 21:12 describes plague as the "sword of the LORD"). The inference sometimes drawn that David's choice was a selfish one fails to recognize that all three options, including flight before enemies, would have cost lives (see note on v. 13). David's motivation was entirely different, for he had learned a marvelous truth; namely, that the Lord's mercy is great (v. 16; cf. Ex 34:6–7; Ne 9:17; Pss 30:5; 86:14–16; 103:8–10; Isa 54:7–8; 60:10; Hos 11:8–9; Joel 2:13).
24:15 Dan to Beersheba. See verse 2.
24:16 Enough! God mercifully stayed the hand of the destroying angel (see note on v. 14). **angel of the LORD.** See note on Genesis 16:7. On the Lord's angels as agents of judgment, see Exodus 33:2 (see also Pss 35:5–6; 78:49; Mt 13:41; Ac 12:23). **threshing floor of Araunah.** See note on 24:1–25.

24:17 [z]Ps 74:1 [a]Jnh 1:12

"I am the one who has sinned and done wrong. These are but sheep.[z] What have they
done? Let your hand fall upon me and my family."[a]

David Builds an Altar

[18]On that day Gad went to David and said to him, "Go up and build an altar to the
LORD on the threshing floor of Araunah the Jebusite." [19]So David went up, as the LORD had
commanded through Gad. [20]When Araunah looked and saw the king and his men coming toward him, he went out and bowed down before the king with his face to the
ground.

[21]Araunah said, "Why has my lord the king come to his servant?"

"To buy your threshing floor," David answered, "so I can build an altar to the LORD,
that the plague on the people may be stopped."[b]

24:21 [b]Nu 16:44-50

[22]Araunah said to David, "Let my lord the king take whatever pleases him and offer
it up. Here are oxen[c] for the burnt offering, and here are threshing sledges and ox yokes
for the wood. [23]O king, Araunah gives[d] all this to the king." Araunah also said to him,
"May the LORD your God accept you."

24:22 [c]1Sa 6:14; 1Ki 19:21

24:23 [d]Eze 20:40-41

[24]But the king replied to Araunah, "No, I insist on paying you for it. I will not sacrifice to the LORD my God burnt offerings that cost me nothing."[e]

24:24 [e]Mal 1:13-14

So David bought the threshing floor and the oxen and paid fifty shekels[a] of silver for
them. [25]David built an altar[f] to the LORD there and sacrificed burnt offerings and fellowship offerings.[b] Then the LORD answered prayer[g] in behalf of the land, and the plague on
Israel was stopped.

24:25 [f]1Sa 7:17 [g]2Sa 21:14

[a] *24* That is, about 1 1/4 pounds (about 0.6 kilogram) [b] *25* Traditionally *peace offerings*

24:17 Let your hand fall upon me. The heart of David, like the heart of God (v. 16), was grieved by the suffering he saw among his people, his "sheep." As their shepherd-king, he was moved to compassion and, not realizing that God in his mercy had already stayed his hand (vv. 16,21), asked that the hand of judgment fall upon him alone. Although David deserved punishment for his own sin, in his self-sacrificial willingness to suffer in the place of his "sheep" the reader may detect a faint glimmer of the greater Shepherd-King to come (Mt 2:6; 25:32–34), who would go so far as to lay down his life for his sheep (Jn 10:11; cf. Ro 5:8; 6:23; 1Co 15:3; Php 2:8; Heb 9:15; 12:2; 1Pe 3:18).

24:22 burnt offering. See note on 1 Samuel 10:8.

24:24 I will not sacrifice to the LORD my God burnt offerings that cost me nothing. While God's grace and forgiveness are free, David understood that proper worship of God is never to be cheap or careless (cf. Mal 1:6–14; 2Co 8:1–5). The consistent testimony of Scripture is that God deserves our best, the "firstfruits" (Nu 18:12; Dt 18:3–5; 26:10; Ne 12:44; Pr 3:9). **fifty shekels of silver.** First Chronicles 21:25 records the much larger sum of 600 shekels of gold (see note on 1Ch 21:25).

24:25 burnt offerings and fellowship offerings. See note on 1 Samuel 10:8. **the LORD answered prayer in behalf of the land.** An almost identical statement is made in 21:14 after the lifting of the famine brought about by Saul's mistreatment of the Gibeonites.

1 KINGS

Introduction

Overview

Author: Unknown

Purpose: To demonstrate the justice of the exile, to affirm continuing hope in David's house and to call for repentance so that Israel might return from exile

Date: c. 560–550 B.C.

Key Truths:

- Despite the severity of the exile of Israel and Judah, God was fully justified in his wrath because of the repeated and severe apostasy of the nation.
- God's promises to David's family continued despite his sons' failures.
- God called for his exiled people to repent of their sins.
- Restoration from exile was offered to Israel upon condition of repentance.

Author

The books of 1 and 2 Kings were originally one book whose author is not identified. Indications are that he was a compiler of historical sources who worked during the Babylonian exile.

Time and Place of Writing

Second Kings ends with the last king of Judah, Jehoiachin, being accorded special favors by the king of Babylon while in exile (2Ki 25:27–30). Since the book ends at that point and there is no mention of the return of the people from exile in 538 B.C., it may be inferred that the final composition of this work dates to the midpoint of the Babylonian exile (560–550 B.C.).

Not all of the material in Kings stems from the exilic period. First, the author had access to a variety of sources, both royal and prophetic. Three of these sources are explicitly named: "the book of the annals of Solomon" (1Ki 11:41), "the book of the annals of the kings of Israel" (1Ki 14:19) and "the book of the annals of the kings of Judah" (1Ki 14:29). Second, statements scattered throughout the book of Kings depict actions or institutions that the writer said continued "to this day" (e.g., 1Ki 9:21; 12:19; 2Ki 8:22) but that had disappeared or ended by the time of final composition. These and similar statements indicate the perspectives of sources that were incorporated into the text of Kings. Third, the last two chapters of the book of Kings are distinguished by their detailed chronology of events by day, month and year. As some interpreters have argued, it is possible that before the exile an earlier form of this book existed and formed the basis of the canonical form as we have it. If this is so, the book still offers a unified perspective.

Purpose and Distinctives

The book of Kings is concerned with the history and demise of the monarchy in Israel from the last days of David (c. 970 B.C.) until the exile to Babylon almost four centuries later (c. 586 B.C.). The books of 1 and 2 Kings comprise one unit within a larger group of books—Joshua, Judges, 1 and 2 Samuel, 1 and 2 Kings—designated traditionally as the Former Prophets and more recently as the Deuteronomistic (or Deuteronomic) History. Since these books naturally follow one another, the recognition of an essential unity is justified.

The books of 1 and 2 Kings were originally one book. Whereas in older Hebrew manuscripts, 1 and 2 Kings are one literary work (like 1 and 2 Samuel and 1 and 2 Chronicles), in the Septuagint (the Greek translation of the OT), the Vulgate (Latin translation) and most other versions, the work is divided into two books. The division is artificial, occasioned more by how much papyrus roll could fit on an ancient scroll than by dictates of content. The reigns of Ahaziah (1Ki 22:51–53; 2Ki 1:1–18) and Jehoshaphat (1Ki 22:41–50; 2Ki 3:1–27) overlap both books. Similarly, the prophetic ministry of Elijah appears in both volumes (1Ki 17–19; 2Ki 1–2).

Kings as History. Characteristic of this Biblical writer is a fondness for recording in detail many features of his nation's past. This genuine interest in the dates, figures and institutions of monarchial Israel is manifest in his careful recording of the preparations for the temple (1Ki 5), its dimensions (1Ki 7:1–12) and the furniture and vessels placed within it (1Ki 7:13–51). The writer's penchant for detail is also manifest in his presentation of individual reigns. Not only did he state the length of reign for monarchs in both kingdoms, but he also frequently synchronized their reigns.

The book of Kings is filled with chronological data. The author dated the building of the temple 480 years after the exodus (see note on 1Ki 6:1). Aside from providing figures for the length of David's and Solomon's reigns, the author gave explicit information on the tenures of all the Judahite and Israelite kings. During the period of the divided kingdom, he synchronized the start of each king's reign with the regnal year of the king in the other kingdom. Finally, for kings of Judah the author listed the king's age upon accession and the name of his mother.

The author's organization and periodization of Israel's experience with the monarchy reveal his concern to provide an orderly and meaningful account of his nation's past. Beginning by characterizing and evaluating the united monarchy under Solomon (1Ki 1–11), he carefully depicted its dissolution (1Ki 12:1–25) and the formation of two separate entities: Israel in the north and Judah in the south. He then proceeded to present the parallel, yet independent, history of each realm until the fall of the northern kingdom in 722 B.C. (2Ki 17). This consistent alternation between the northern kingdom (usually called "Israel") and the southern kingdom (usually called "Judah") can be confusing, but it is central to the author's purpose to present a unified history of all the Israelite tribes.

Creating a written record of two kingdoms that existed simultaneously presented complex challenges to the writer. To set events that occurred concurrently in a text, he chose to alternate between events in the north and in the south. The pattern for this alternation is evident from the following chart:

In Israel	*(930–909 B.C.)*	*(1Ki 12:25—14:20)*
In Judah	*(930–869 B.C.)*	*(14:21—15:24)*
In Israel	*(909–853 B.C.)*	*(15:25—22:40)*
In Judah	*(869–848 B.C.)*	*(22:41–50)*
In Israel	*(853–841 B.C.)*	*(22:51—2Ki 8:15)*
In Judah	*(848–841 B.C.)*	*(8:16–29)*
In Israel	*(841–814 B.C.)*	*(9:1—10:36)*
In Judah	*(841–796 B.C.)*	*(11–12)*
In Israel	*(814–782 B.C.)*	*(13:1–25)*
In Judah	*(796–767 B.C.)*	*(14:1–22)*
In Israel	*(793–753 B.C.)*	*(14:23–29)*
In Judah	*(792–740 B.C.)*	*(15:1–7)*
In Israel	*(753–732 B.C.)*	*(15:8–31)*
In Judah	*(750–715 B.C.)*	*(15:32—16:20)*
In Israel	*(732–722 B.C.)*	*(17:1–6)*

This chart indicates that the writer shifted from one kingdom to the other each time he reached the end of a king's reign in one kingdom that extended beyond the end of the reign of the last king previously mentioned in the other kingdom. For instance, Pekah of Israel reigned from 740–732 B.C. (2Ki 15:27–31); his reign extended beyond the first year of Jotham of Judah from 750–735 B.C. (2Ki 15:32–38), so the writer shifted to Judah at that point. Ahaz of Judah, who followed Jotham, ruled from 735–715 B.C. (15:32—16:20), and his reign extended beyond the end of Pekah's reign of Israel from 740–732 B.C. (15:27–31). For this reason, the writer shifted back to Israel and began with Hoshea of Israel, who reigned from 732–722 B.C. (2Ki 17:1–6).

In portraying the divided kingdom the Biblical writer points out important differences between the two realms. Whereas kingship in Judah was relatively stable, the throne never departing from the descendants of David, kingship in the northern kingdom was characterized by instability and a succession of dynasties. Nine different families and 20 kings ruled over the northern kingdom during its approximately 200-year existence. In contrast, one family and 20 kings ruled over the southern kingdom through approximately three and a half centuries. The Biblical writer concluded his coverage of the northern kingdom with a lengthy commentary on what he saw as its major shortcomings (2Ki 17:7–23). The author then chronicled the last 150 years of Judah's history alone.

The historical value of Kings should not be underestimated. In composing a coherent and meaningful account of his nation's past, the Biblical writer provided an invaluable service to anyone wishing to understand this momentous era in Israelite history.

Kings as Theology. Aside from manifesting a profound interest in Israel's past, Kings is also a work of theology, a reflection on God's ways with the people he had delivered from the "iron-smelting furnace" of Egypt to be his "own inheritance" (1Ki 8:51–53). In composing a work of theological history, the writer drew lessons from the past that served God's people in his present and future. There are a number of central tenets that undergird the overall perspective of the book of Kings.

1. *The People as God's Elect.* Central to the theology of Kings is the assertion that Israel (and later Judah) was not in itself better than any other nation. The Israelites did not first choose God; rather, God "singled them out from all the nations of the world" according to his unfathomable grace (1Ki 8:53). Holiness resulted not from any intrinsic merit on their part, but from God's election (1Ki 8:51,53; Dt 7:6; 26:18–19).

There is also an emphasis in Kings on the solidarity of Israel. In his coverage, the writer exhibited a concern for all Israelite tribes. Although he severely critiqued the northern kingdom and its monarchs for their pervasive idolatry, the writer still considered these tribes among the covenant people and demonstrated a sustained interest in their history. Even after the northern tribes were exiled by the Assyrians, the author did not lose interest in their fate, commending Josiah for reforming Samaria.

2. *The Prophetic Word.* Prophets play a major role in this history of the Israelite monarchy. In writing about the prophets, the historian expressed interest in their message and ministry as bearers of God's word. The prophets passionately and uncompromisingly insisted on total and undivided allegiance to the Lord, steadfastly opposing any alliance or political posture that might jeopardize the distinctive attributes of Israelite religion. Not surprisingly, this strict adherence to the covenant often set the prophets against kings and queens who were willing to compromise politically and religiously with Israel's neighbors. Although he devoted most of his attention to the ministries of Elijah and Elisha, the writer mentioned the activities of many other prophets throughout the era of the monarchy: Nathan (1Ki 1:22), Ahijah (1Ki 11:26–39; 14:1–18), Shemaiah (1Ki 12:21–24), Micaiah (1Ki 22:8–28), Jonah (2Ki 14:25), Isaiah (2Ki 19:1–7, 20:1–14) and Huldah (2Ki 22:14–20).

3. *One God, One Sanctuary.* According to this history, Yahweh is Lord of the cosmos and ruler over the kingdoms of the earth (2Ki 19:15–16). God led his people into battle, answered the prayers they directed toward the temple, honored their sacrifices and displayed a special concern for the poor and oppressed, the widow and the orphan. Exclusive devotion to God is a hallmark of the covenant (1Ki 18:21,39).

Correlative to the existence of only one supreme God is the writer's commitment to the belief that there could only be one central sanctuary in Israel (Dt 12). The construction of the temple by Solomon marked a major event in Israelite history. Accordingly, much space was devoted in 1 Kings to the preparations for, and construction of, this edifice, including detailed coverage of its dimensions and furnishings.

Consistent with this emphasis on one God and one temple is the prohibition against idolatry and worshiping at other cult sites. As Kings depicts the deterioration in devotion toward God during the course of the divided kingdom, the problem was not so much a wholesale abandonment of Yahweh for other gods as it was the combined worship of Yahweh and foreign deities. The influence of Canaanite worship was especially pronounced in northern Israel, which through the aegis of its monarchs promoted the use of Canaanite rituals, beliefs and idols. Such syncretism was also a serious problem in Judah. The writer cited the worship of other gods as a major reason for the defeat and exile of both Israel and Judah (2Ki 17:7,16,19; 21:3–5).

The author also gave extensive coverage to loyalty toward God as manifested by unwavering support of the temple in Jerusalem. Of the eight southern kings who received praise, only Hezekiah and Josiah were singled out for their incomparable devotion to Yahweh (2Ki 18:5; 23:25). Hezekiah earned highest praise for removing the high places in Judah and for his unwavering trust in God during Sennacherib's invasion (2Ki 18:3–7). The author accorded highest honor to Josiah for his refurbishment of the temple and for his sweeping reforms in both the south and the north (2Ki 22:2; 23:25). Among the northern kings only Jehu won any commendation, which he received because he purged Israel of Baal worship (2Ki 10:30).

4. *Covenant and Kingship.* Two major covenants figure prominently in Kings: the Mosaic and the Davidic covenants. The writer evaluated the conduct of king and people alike on the basis of the covenant established at Mount Sinai.

Viewing the relationship between God and Israel as covenantal meant that no human institution attained an absolute status. Every institution was subject to the authority of God. Hence, although the monarchy was God ordained, its power was by no means absolute. King and people alike were responsible for keeping covenant with their God. Each king (or queen) was evaluated according to whether he or she kept the Torah (or law).

The writer of Kings was also committed to the principles of the Davidic covenant. In effect, the Davidic covenant (2Sa 7; Pss 89; 132) identified David's dynasty as the permanent royal family for God's people. Although individual kings would be punished severely for covenant violations, the family of David would never be permanently removed from power. God's love for David prompted divine patience toward his descendants (see 1Kgs 15:4), and it explained the grand significance of the last scene of the book—when Jehoiachin was released from prison in Babylon—as a hopeful sign that God had not given up on David's royal house (2Ki 25:27–30).

Christ in Kings

The history of Kings points to Christ in a number of ways. At least two matters come to the foreground in the book of Kings. First, the history stressed the family of David as the centerpiece of Israel. All hopes of victory and salvation—even return from exile—were found in God's mercy shown to and through David's royal house. The New Testament teaches that Christ is the great son of David through whom God fulfilled all the promises he made to David and his sons (Mt 1:1–17; Ac 2:22–36).

Second, kingship and temple worship stood together in the center of this history. In fact, the kings of Israel and Judah were judged largely in terms of their loyalty or disloyalty to the temple in Jerusalem and to the purity of worship there. This motif is also fulfilled in Christ. The New Testament teaches that he is the eternal high priest for God's people (Heb. 3:1; 4:14–15), whose own blood atoned for their sins (Heb. 2:17; 9:25–28). He brings his people together into a holy sanctuary on Earth (1Pe 2:4–5,9) as he ministers in the heavenly palace of God (Heb. 6:19–20; 8:1–2; 9:24). The importance of exclusive fidelity to worship in Solomon's temple corresponds to Christ's call for his followers to rely on his priestly mediation alone for their salvation (Jn 14:6; Ac 4:12), as he ministers in the heavenly sanctuary now and ultimately replaces the earthly sanctuary in the new earth (Rev 21:22).

Outline

I. The Reign of Solomon (1:1—11:43)
   A. Solomon's Succession to the Throne (1:1—2:12)
      1. Solomon Becomes King Against Opposition (1:1–53)
      2. David's Charge to Solomon (2:1–9)
      3. David's Death and Burial (2:10–12)
   B. Solomon's Blessing of Consolidation (2:13–46)
      1. Adonijah (2:13–25)
      2. Abiathar (2:26–27)
      3. Joab (2:28–35)
      4. Shimei (2:36–46)
   C. Solomon's Establishment of Worship (3:1—9:25)
      1. Sacrificing Before Temple Construction (3:1–3)

God granted Solomon wisdom to lead the people of Israel. His greatest act of wisdom was to establish temple worship in Jerusalem. When Solomon himself desecrated worship, God severely judged him.

Outline

2. Solomon's Astounding Wisdom (3:4—4:34)
   a. Solomon's Gift of Wisdom (3:4–15)
   b. Solomon's Judicial Wisdom (3:16–28)
   c. Solomon's Domestic Political Wisdom (4:1–28)
   d. Solomon's International Wisdom (4:29–34)
3. Solomon's Temple and Palace (5:1—9:23)
   a. Those Serving Solomon in Preparations (5:1–18)
      (1) Hiram (5:1–12)
      (2) Conscripted Laborers (5:13–18)
   b. Construction of the Temple and Palace (6:1—7:51)
      (1) The Temple Construction (6:1–38)
      (2) The Palace Construction (7:1–12)
      (3) Furnishings for the Temple (7:13–51)
   c. Dedication of the Temple (8:1—9:9)
      (1) Solomon's Worship (8:1–66)
         (a) Solomon's Opening Ceremonies and Speech (8:1–21)
         (b) Solomon's Prayer (8:22–53)
         (c) Solomon's Closing Ceremonies and Speech (8:54–66)
      (2) God's Response (9:1–9)
   d. Those Who Served Solomon After Construction (9:10–23)
      (1) Hiram (9:10–14)
      (2) Conscripted Laborers (9:15–23)
4. Sacrificing After Temple Construction (9:24–25)

D. Solomon's Desecration of Worship (9:26—11:13)
1. Solomon's International Involvements (9:26—10:29)
   a. The Queen of Sheba (9:26—10:13)
   b. Solomon's Wealth From International Relations (10:14–29)
2. Solomon's Idolatry in the Temple (11:1–13)
   a. Solomon's Foreign Wives and Idolatry (11:1–8)
   b. God's Response of Judgment (11:9–13)

E. Solomon's Curse of Rebellions (11:14–40)
1. Hadad's Rebellion (11:14–22)
2. Rezon's Rebellion (11:23–25)
3. Jeroboam's Rebellion (11:26–40)

F. Solomon's Death and Burial (11:41–43)

II. The Divided Monarchy (12:1—2 Kings 17:41)

A. The Secession of the Northern Tribes (12:1–24)

B. In Israel (930–909 B.C.): Jeroboam I of Israel (12:25—14:20)
1. Jeroboam's False Worship Centers (12:25–33)
2. A Confirmed Prophetic Condemnation (13:1–34)

The history of the northern and southern kingdoms demonstrates the kindness of God toward his people and his requirement of loyalty. The line of David remained the chosen royal family. The corruption and reform of worship played a decisive role in the relationship between Israel and God. God severely punished the northern kingdom for idolatry and other evils.

Outline

3. A Second Prophetic Condemnation (14:1–18)
4. Closing of Reign (14:19–20)

C. In Judah (930–869 B.C.) (14:21—15:24)
   1. Rehoboam of Judah (930–913 B.C.) (14:21–31)
      a. Opening of the Reign (14:21)
      b. Corruption of Worship (14:22–24)
      c. Judgment of Shishak Invasion (14:25–28)
      d. Closure of the Reign (14:29–31)
   2. Abijah of Judah (913–910 B.C.) (15:1–8)
   3. Asa of Judah (910–869 B.C.) (15:9–24)

D. In Israel (909–853 B.C.) (15:25—22:40)
   1. Nadab of Israel (909–908 B.C.) (15:25–32)
   2. Baasha of Israel (908–886 B.C.) (15:33—16:7)
   3. Elah of Israel (886–885 B.C.) (16:8–14)
   4. Zimri of Israel (885 B.C.) (16:15–20)
   5. Omri of Israel (885–874 B.C.) (16:21–28)
   6. Ahab of Israel (874–853 B.C.) (16:29—22:40)
      a. Opening of the Reign (16:29–30)
      b. A Summary of Ahab's Sins (16:31–34)
      c. Ahab and Prophetic Condemnation (17:1—22:38)
         (1) Elijah's Early Ministry (17:1–24)
         (2) Elijah's Confrontation With the Prophets of Baal (18:1–46)
         (3) Elijah's Encounter With the Lord at Horeb (19:1–21)
         (4) Ahab's War With Aram and Prophetic Condemnation (20:1–43)
         (5) Naboth's Vineyard and Prophetic Condemnation (21:1–29)
         (6) Ahab's War With Aram and Micaiah's Prophetic Condemnation (22:1–38)
      d. Closure of the Reign (22:39–40)

E. In Judah (869–848 B.C.): Jehoshaphat of Judah (22:41–50)

F. In Israel (853–841 B.C.) (22:51—2 Kings 8:15)
   1. Ahaziah (853–852 B.C.) (22:51—2 Kings 1:18)
      a. Opening of the Reign (22:51–53)
      b. Ahaziah's Prophetic Condemnation (2 Kings1:1–17a)
         (1) Ahaziah Seeks the Baal (1:1–2)
         (2) Elijah Intervenes (1:3–8)
         (3) Elijah Sends Fire From Heaven (1:9–17a)
      c. Closure of the Reign (1:17b–18)
   2. The Transfer of Prophetic Ministry to Elisha (2:1–25)
      a. Elijah Succeeded by Elisha (2:1–18)
      b. Elisha's First Miracles (2:19–25)
   3. Joram (852–841 B.C.) (3:1—8:15)
      a. Opening of Reign (3:1–3)
      b. Elisha's Service in Moabite War (3:4–27)
      c. Elisha's Ministry to the Needy (4:1–44)

Outline

III. Judah Alone (715–586 B.C.) (18:1—25:30)
  A. Hezekiah (715–686 B.C.) (18:1—20:21)
    1. Opening of the Reign (18:1–4)
    2. Summary of Hezekiah's Reign (18:5–8)
    3. Assyrian Invasions (18:9—20:19)
      a. The Fall of Samaria (18:9–12)
      b. Sennacherib's Invasion of Judah (18:13—20:19)
        (1) The Invasion of Judah (18:13–16)
        (2) The Attack on Jerusalem (18:17–37)
        (3) Divine Deliverance (19:1–37)
        (4) Hezekiah's Healing (20:1–11)
        (5) The Babylonian Envoys (20:12–19)
    4. Closure of the Reign (20:20–21)
  B. Manasseh (686–642 B.C.) (21:1–18)
  C. Amon (642–640 B.C.) (21:19–26)
  D. Josiah (640–609 B.C.) (22:1—23:30)
    1. Opening of the Reign (22:1–2)
    2. Repairing the Temple (22:3–20)
    3. Reforms in Jerusalem, Judah and Samaria (23:1–20)
    4. Passover (23:21–27)
    5. Closure and Battle With Neco (23:28–30)
  E. Jehoahaz (609 B.C.) (23:31–35)
  F. Jehoiakim (609–598 B.C.) (23:36—24:7)
  G. Jehoiachin (598–597 B.C.) (24:8–17)
  H. Zedekiah (597–586 B.C.) (24:18—20a)
  I. The Exile of Judah (24:20b—25:30)
    1. Jerusalem's Destruction (24:20b—25:21)
    2. The Assassination of Gedaliah (25:22–26)
    3. Jehoiachin's Release (25:27–30)

The final years of Judah revealed how wonderfully God rewarded faithfulness and severely judged even the house of David for flagrant apostasy. Yet the history closes with a subtle reminder that God had promised to restore the house of David after exile.

Adonijah Sets Himself Up as King

1 When King David was old and well advanced in years, he could not keep warm even
when they put covers over him. 2So his servants said to him, "Let us look for a young
virgin to attend the king and take care of him. She can lie beside him so that our lord the
king may keep warm."
3Then they searched throughout Israel for a beautiful girl and found Abishag, a Shunammite,[a] and brought her to the king. 4The girl was very beautiful; she took care of the
king and waited on him, but the king had no intimate relations with her.
5Now Adonijah,[b] whose mother was Haggith, put himself forward and said, "I will be
king." So he got chariots[c] and horses[a] ready, with fifty men to run ahead of him. 6(His

1:3 [a]Jos 19:18
1:5 [b]2Sa 3:4 [c]2Sa 15:1

[a] 5 Or *charioteers*

■ **1:1—11:43** *The Reign of Solomon.* These chapters recount the details of the reign of Solomon, David's son and successor. They focus especially on his role as the one who established Israel's temple worship and whose desecration of that worship led to the division of the nation. This record of his reign divides into six balanced parts: Solomon's succession to the throne (1:1—2:12), his blessing of political consolidation (2:13–46), his establishment of worship at the temple (3:1—9:25), his desecration of worship (9:26—11:13), his curse of political opposition (11:14–40) and his death and burial (11:41–43).

■ **1:1—2:12** *Solomon's Succession to the Throne.* These chapters report in three steps how Solomon rose to be David's legitimate successor: Solomon's struggle with Adonijah for David's throne (1:1–53), David's charge to Solomon as his successor (2:1–9) and David's death and burial (2:10–12). These chapters explained to the original audience that Solomon and his descendants were the rightful heirs of David's throne because Solomon was so obviously blessed and authorized both by David and by God.

■ **1:1–53** *Solomon Becomes King Against Opposition.* Although Adonijah made a bid for the throne, events made it clear that Solomon was God's choice for David's successor.

1:1–4 The author of Kings introduced David's relationship with Abishag, because the status of Abishag would figure prominently in the subsequent struggle for the throne between two of David's sons, Solomon and Adonijah (see 2Sa 12:10–11; 14:25—18:33; 20:1–26).

1:1 old and well advanced in years. David was about 70 years old here (2Sa 5:4–5; 1Ki 2:11).

1:3 Abishag, a Shunammite. This means that Abishag came from Shunem, in the plain of Esdraelon near Mount Gilboa (Jos 19:18; 1Sa 28:4; 2Ki 4:8,12,25,36).

1:4 the king had no intimate relations with her. Since David did not have sexual or marital relations with Abishag, Adonijah's later request that he be allowed to marry her (2:17) did not contravene the law of Deuteronomy 22:30.

1:5 Adonijah. Probably the eldest living son of David (2Sa 3:2–5; 13:28; 18:14). As such, he may have presumed that he would succeed his father. At this time, however, apart from David's own wishes, there was no custom or law dictating who would be his successor (vv. 13,17,20,30; 2Ch 22:9–10). **chariots and horses.** Like Absalom before him (2Sa 15:1), Adonijah signaled his ambitions and positioned himself to usurp the throne.

father had never interfered[d] with him by asking, "Why do you behave as you do?" He was
also very handsome and was born next after Absalom.)
[7]Adonijah conferred with Joab[e] son of Zeruiah and with Abiathar[f] the priest, and they
gave him their support. [8]But Zadok[g] the priest, Benaiah[h] son of Jehoiada, Nathan[i] the
prophet, Shimei[j] and Rei[a] and David's special guard[k] did not join Adonijah.
[9]Adonijah then sacrificed sheep, cattle and fattened calves at the Stone of Zoheleth
near En Rogel.[l] He invited all his brothers, the king's sons, and all the men of Judah who
were royal officials, [10]but he did not invite Nathan the prophet or Benaiah or the special
guard or his brother Solomon.[m]
[11]Then Nathan asked Bathsheba,[n] Solomon's mother, "Have you not heard that Adonijah,[o] the son of Haggith, has become king without our lord David's knowing it?
[12]Now then, let me advise[p] you how you can save your own life and the life of your son
Solomon. [13]Go in to King David and say to him, 'My lord the king, did you not swear[q] to
me your servant: "Surely Solomon your son shall be king after me, and he will sit on my
throne"? Why then has Adonijah become king?' [14]While you are still there talking to the
king, I will come in and confirm what you have said."
[15]So Bathsheba went to see the aged king in his room, where Abishag[r] the Shunammite was attending him. [16]Bathsheba bowed low and knelt before the king.
"What is it you want?" the king asked.
[17]She said to him, "My lord, you yourself swore[s] to me your servant by the LORD your
God: 'Solomon your son shall be king after me, and he will sit on my throne.' [18]But now
Adonijah has become king, and you, my lord the king, do not know about it. [19]He has
sacrificed[t] great numbers of cattle, fattened calves, and sheep, and has invited all the
king's sons, Abiathar the priest and Joab the commander of the army, but he has not invited Solomon your servant. [20]My lord the king, the eyes of all Israel are on you, to learn
from you who will sit on the throne of my lord the king after him. [21]Otherwise, as soon
as my lord the king is laid to rest[u] with his fathers, I and my son Solomon will be treated as criminals."
[22]While she was still speaking with the king, Nathan the prophet arrived. [23]And they
told the king, "Nathan the prophet is here." So he went before the king and bowed with
his face to the ground.
[24]Nathan said, "Have you, my lord the king, declared that Adonijah shall be king after you, and that he will sit on your throne? [25]Today he has gone down and sacrificed
great numbers of cattle, fattened calves, and sheep. He has invited all the king's sons,
the commanders of the army and Abiathar the priest. Right now they are eating and
drinking with him and saying, 'Long live King Adonijah!' [26]But me your servant, and Zadok the priest, and Benaiah son of Jehoiada, and your servant Solomon he did not in-

1:6 [d]2Sa 3:3-4
1:7 [e]1Ki 2:22,28; 1Ch 11:6 [f]1Sa 22:20; 2Sa 20:25
1:8 [g]2Sa 20:25 [h]2Sa 8:18 [i]2Sa 12:1 [j]1Ki 4:18 [k]2Sa 23:8
1:9 [l]2Sa 17:17
1:10 [m]2Sa 12:24
1:11 [n]2Sa 12:24 [o]2Sa 3:4
1:12 [p]Pr 15:22
1:13 [q]ver 30; 1Ch 22:9-13
1:15 [r]ver 1
1:17 [s]ver 13,30
1:19 [t]ver 9
1:21 [u]Dt 31:16; 1Ki 2:10

[a] *8* Or *and his friends*

1:6 never interfered. As in dealing with his other rebellious sons, David made no attempt either to question or to discipline Adonijah. His neglect only seemed to spawn further rebellion (2Sa 13:21; 14:33; 18:5). **very handsome.** Attractive features were an asset for someone aspiring to the throne (1Sa 9:2; 16:12; 2Sa 14:25–26). See *WLC* 130,145.

1:7 Joab son of Zeruiah. Joab was one of David's longstanding, but not necessarily closest, supporters (1Sa 26:6; 2Sa 2:13; 8:16; 18:2; 19:13; 20:10,23; 1Ki 2:5–6). He joined with Adonijah and would later be judged for doing so (2:28–35). **Abiathar the priest.** He and Zadok were the two high priests appointed by David (1Sa 14:3; 22:20–22; 2Sa 8:17). He also joined with Adonijah (vv. 19:25,42) and would later be cursed for doing so (2:26).

1:8 Benaiah son of Jehoiada. Benaiah was the commander of the Kerethites and Pelethites, who functioned in large measure as David's royal guard (2Sa 8:18; 15:18; 20:7; 23:20; 1Ch 18:17). **Nathan the prophet.** The most prominent prophet during David's reign (2Sa 7:1–17; 12:1–15). **Shimei.** A different Shimei from the one in 2 Samuel 16:5–8 and 1 Kings 2:8 and 46. Perhaps this Shimei is to be identified with "Shimei, son of Ela" (4:18). **David's special guard.** See 2Sa 23:8–39.

1:9 sacrificed. Again, Adonijah followed the example of Absalom (2Sa 15:7–12; 1:5 note). **En Rogel.** Meaning "spring of Rogel," it was located southeast of the city and was considered an appropriate place for such an important activity (2Sa 17:17; cf. 1:33).

1:11 Bathsheba, Solomon's mother. Queen mothers could play an influential role in the affairs of state (2:19; 15:13; 2Ki 10:13; 2Ch 15:16). As the mother of Solomon, Bathsheba had a major interest in seeing that Adonijah was thwarted in his plans to become king (2Sa 12:25).

1:12 save your own life and the life of your son. Since pretenders to the throne in the ancient Near East sometimes sought to consolidate their own position by eliminating all potential rivals, Nathan's advice expressed urgency (15:29; 2Ki 10:11; 11:1).

1:13 Why then has Adonijah become king? Nathan's advice played on the ambiguity and instability inherent during a coup attempt. Actually David was still king, but Nathan's words underscored the fact that Adonijah had also publicly claimed this status (vv. 5,9). By telling Bathsheba to speak with David and then speaking himself to "the aged king" (v. 15), Nathan emphasized the gravity of the situation.

1:17 you yourself swore. In ancient Israel oaths taken in the Lord's name constituted sacred obligations and were, with a few exceptions, considered inviolable (Ex 20:7; Lev 19:12; Jos 9:15, 18,20; Jdg 11:30,35; Ecc 5:4–7).

1:20 learn from you who will sit on the throne. Only a public declaration that Solomon would succeed David as king would suffice to turn back Adonijah's revolt.

1:21 laid to rest with his fathers. This way of speaking was a conventional euphemism for death (2:10; 11:43; 14:20,31).

1:24–27 Have you . . . declared . . . ? Nathan incisively attacked the issue. Either David had privately affirmed Adonijah as heir apparent (and hence Nathan, Zadok and Benaiah had been shunned), or David had not done so (and hence Adonijah had rebelled against his own father).

vite.[v] 27Is this something my lord the king has done without letting his servants know
who should sit on the throne of my lord the king after him?"

David Makes Solomon King

28Then King David said, "Call in Bathsheba." So she came into the king's presence
and stood before him.
29The king then took an oath: "As surely as the LORD lives, who has delivered me out
of every trouble,[w] 30I will surely carry out today what I swore[x] to you by the LORD, the
God of Israel: Solomon your son shall be king after me, and he will sit on my throne in
my place."
31Then Bathsheba bowed low with her face to the ground and, kneeling before the
king, said, "May my lord King David live forever!"
32King David said, "Call in Zadok the priest, Nathan the prophet and Benaiah son of
Jehoiada." When they came before the king, 33he said to them: "Take your lord's servants
with you and set Solomon my son on my own mule[y] and take him down to Gihon.[z]
34There have Zadok the priest and Nathan the prophet anoint[a] him king over Israel. Blow
the trumpet[b] and shout, 'Long live King Solomon!' 35Then you are to go up with him, and
he is to come and sit on my throne and reign in my place. I have appointed him ruler over
Israel and Judah."
36Benaiah son of Jehoiada answered the king, "Amen! May the LORD, the God of my
lord the king, so declare it. 37As the LORD was with my lord the king, so may he be with[c]
Solomon to make his throne even greater[d] than the throne of my lord King David!"
38So Zadok[e] the priest, Nathan the prophet, Benaiah son of Jehoiada, the Kerethites[f]
and the Pelethites went down and put Solomon on King David's mule and escorted him
to Gihon.[g] 39Zadok the priest took the horn of oil[h] from the sacred tent and anointed Solomon. Then they sounded the trumpet and all the people shouted,[i] "Long live King Solomon!" 40And all the people went up after him, playing flutes and rejoicing greatly, so
that the ground shook with the sound.
41Adonijah and all the guests who were with him heard it as they were finishing their
feast. On hearing the sound of the trumpet, Joab asked, "What's the meaning of all the
noise in the city?"
42Even as he was speaking, Jonathan[j] son of Abiathar the priest arrived. Adonijah
said, "Come in. A worthy man like you must be bringing good news."[k]
43"Not at all!" Jonathan answered. "Our lord King David has made Solomon king.
44The king has sent with him Zadok the priest, Nathan the prophet, Benaiah son of Jehoiada, the Kerethites and the Pelethites, and they have put him on the king's mule,
45and Zadok the priest and Nathan the prophet have anointed him king at Gihon. From
there they have gone up cheering, and the city resounds[l] with it. That's the noise you
hear. 46Moreover, Solomon has taken his seat on the royal throne. 47Also, the royal officials have come to congratulate our lord King David, saying, 'May your God make Solomon's name more famous than yours and his throne greater[m] than yours!' And the king
bowed in worship on his bed 48and said, 'Praise be to the LORD, the God of Israel, who
has allowed my eyes to see a successor[n] on my throne today.'"
49At this, all Adonijah's guests rose in alarm and dispersed. 50But Adonijah, in fear

1:26 [v]ver 8,10
1:29 [w]2Sa 4:9
1:30 [x]ver 13,17
1:33 [y]2Sa 20:6-7 [z]2Ch 32:30; 33:14
1:34 [a]1Sa 10:1; 16:3, 13; 1Ki 19:16; 2Ki 9:3,13 [b]ver 25; 2Sa 5:3; 15:10
1:37 [c]Jos 1:5,17; 1Sa 20:13 [d]ver 47
1:38 [e]ver 8 [f]2Sa 8:18 [g]ver 33
1:39 [h]Ex 30:23-32; Ps 89:20 [i]ver 34; 1Sa 10:24
1:42 [j]2Sa 15:27,36 [k]2Sa 18:26
1:45 [l]ver 40
1:47 [m]ver 37; Ge 47:31
1:48 [n]2Sa 7:12; 1Ki 3:6

1:29–30 See *HC* 101.
1:30 Solomon your son shall be king after me. Solomon would be the "offspring" through whom God would continue his promise of establishing for David's son "the throne of his kingdom forever" (2Sa 7:12–13).
1:33 set Solomon my son on my own mule. Mules and donkeys were used as mounts of royalty (Jdg 10:4; 2Sa 13:29; 18:9; Zec 9:9). David was therefore making a public declaration that Solomon was his designated heir. **Gihon.** The Gihon spring, located a short distance north of En Rogel (v. 9), served as a major supply of water for Jerusalem (2Ki 20:20; 2Ch 32:30; 33:14). Due to topography, En Rogel is not visible from Gihon; however, the two are close enough to each other that one is within earshot of the other (v. 41).
1:34 anoint him king over Israel. Priests (Ex 28:41; 29:4–9; Lev. 4:3,5,16), kings (1Sa 2:10; 9:16; 10:1) and occasionally prophets (19:16) were anointed in ancient Israel. The term "anointed one" usually had royal connotations (see note at 1Sa 2:10). **Blow the trumpet and shout, "Long live King Solomon!"** A public celebration of Solomon's new status as crown prince (cf. 1Sa 10:24; 2Sa 15:10; 16:16; 20:1; 2Ki 9:13; 11:12).
1:35 ruler. This term usually refers to someone designated crown prince or heir apparent (1Sa 9:16; 13:14; 25:30) and therefore is appropriate in a context in which David is still reigning. **Israel and Judah.** Although made up of 12 tribes originally, the nation was composed of two major units, Israel in the north and Judah in the south. When David became king, he had to win assent from both Judah (2Sa 2:4) and Israel (2Sa 5:3). Heir to the Davidic legacy, Solomon became king of both regions at once.
1:37 even greater. Benaiah expressed an enthusiastic wish that Solomon would have the best possible reign; that is, better than even the best so far (David).
1:38 Kerethites and the Pelethites. See note on verse 8.
1:39 Zadok the priest. In ancient Israel both priests and prophets could officiate at the anointing of a king (1Sa 9:16; 16:12; 2Ki 9:1–3; 11:12). **the horn of oil.** The oil used was probably olive (1Sa 16:13). **sacred tent.** This is a reference to the tent that David pitched to house the ark of the covenant (Ex 37:1–9; 2Sa 6:17), not to be confused with the tabernacle (Ex 35:4–29; 36:8–38; 1Ki 3:4).
1:41 Adonijah and all the guests . . . heard it. See note on verse 33.
1:42 Jonathan son of Abiathar. See 2 Samuel 15:27 and 36 and 17:17–21.
1:47 Solomon's name more famous . . . and his throne greater. See note on verse 37. **And the king bowed in worship.** David praised God because his prayer for succession had been granted (see Ge 47:31).

of Solomon, went and took hold of the horns[o] of the altar. [51]Then Solomon was told, "Adonijah is afraid of King Solomon and is clinging to the horns of the altar. He says, 'Let
King Solomon swear to me today that he will not put his servant to death with the
sword.' "
[52]Solomon replied, "If he shows himself to be a worthy man, not a hair[p] of his head
will fall to the ground; but if evil is found in him, he will die." [53]Then King Solomon sent
men, and they brought him down from the altar. And Adonijah came and bowed down
to King Solomon, and Solomon said, "Go to your home."

David's Charge to Solomon

2 When the time drew near for David to die,[q] he gave a charge to Solomon his son.
[2]"I am about to go the way of all the earth,"[r] he said. "So be strong,[s] show yourself
a man, [3]and observe[t] what the LORD your God requires: Walk in his ways, and keep his
decrees and commands, his laws and requirements, as written in the Law of Moses, so
that you may prosper[u] in all you do and wherever you go, [4]and that the LORD may keep
his promise[v] to me: 'If your descendants watch how they live, and if they walk faithfully[w] before me with all their heart and soul, you will never fail to have a man on the
throne of Israel.'
[5]"Now you yourself know what Joab[x] son of Zeruiah did to me—what he did to the
two commanders of Israel's armies, Abner[y] son of Ner and Amasa[z] son of Jether. He
killed them, shedding their blood in peacetime as if in battle, and with that blood
stained the belt around his waist and the sandals on his feet. [6]Deal with him according
to your wisdom,[a] but do not let his gray head go down to the grave[a] in peace.
[7]"But show kindness to the sons of Barzillai[b] of Gilead and let them be among those
who eat at your table.[c] They stood by me when I fled from your brother Absalom.
[8]"And remember, you have with you Shimei[d] son of Gera, the Benjamite from Bahurim, who called down bitter curses on me the day I went to Mahanaim. When he came
down to meet me at the Jordan, I swore[e] to him by the LORD: 'I will not put you to death
by the sword.' [9]But now, do not consider him innocent. You are a man of wisdom;[f] you
will know what to do to him. Bring his gray head down to the grave in blood."
[10]Then David rested with his fathers and was buried[g] in the City of David.[h] [11]He had
reigned[i] forty years over Israel—seven years in Hebron and thirty-three in Jerusalem.
[12]So Solomon sat on the throne[j] of his father David, and his rule was firmly established.[k]

[a] *6* Hebrew *Sheol*; also in verse 9

1:50 [o]1Ki 2:28
1:52 [p]1Sa 14:45; 2Sa 14:11
2:1 [q]Ge 47:29; Dt 31:14
2:2 [r]Jos 23:14 [s]Dt 31:7, 23; Jos 1:6
2:3 [t]Dt 17:14-20; Jos 1:7 [u]1Ch 22:13
2:4 [v]2Sa 7:13, 25; 1Ki 8:25 [w]2Ki 20:3; Ps 132:12
2:5 [x]2Sa 2:18; 18:5, 12, 14 [y]2Sa 3:27 [z]2Sa 20:10
2:6 [a]ver 9
2:7 [b]2Sa 17:27; 19:31-39 [c]2Sa 9:7
2:8 [d]2Sa 16:5-13 [e]2Sa 19:18-23
2:9 [f]ver 6
2:10 [g]Ac 2:29; 13:36 [h]2Sa 5:7
2:11 [i]2Sa 5:4,5
2:12 [j]1Ch 29:23 [k]2Ch 1:1

1:50 horns of the altar. These were projections resembling horns at the four corners on the top of the altar (Ex 27:2; 29:12; Lev 4:7,18,25,30,34; Ps 118:27). Since this place of sacrifice was considered sacred, Adonijah threw himself on the mercy of God in the hope that he would not be killed (Ex 21:12–14; 1Ki 2:28–34).
1:52 If he shows himself. Solomon spared Adonijah on the condition that he conduct himself as a loyal citizen of Solomon's kingdom.
■ **2:1–9** *David's Charge to Solomon.* The writer included David's charge to Solomon to remind the readers of the standards that would justify Solomon's actions to follow. Solomon was to obey the laws of God (vv. 1–4) and to deal decisively with Joab and Shimei (vv. 5–9), who had troubled David.
2:1 he gave a charge. David, like Jacob (Ge 49), Moses (Dt 31:1–8), Joshua (Jos 23:1–16) and Samuel (1Sa 12:1–25) before him, gave a final speech before his death. These speeches mark the transition from one era to another, as well as the passing on of authority.
2:2 the way of all the earth. That is, the grave (Jos 23:14). **be strong, show yourself a man.** These instructions were suitable either before a warrior went into battle or before a person undertook a very difficult task (e.g., Dt 31:7,23; Jos 1:6–7,9,18; 1Sa 4:9).
2:3 Walk in his ways, and keep his decrees and commands. David admonished Solomon to be faithful to God by observing God's laws and so experience blessing (cf. Dt 6:2; 8:6,11; 10:12–23; 11:22). Should Solomon prove unfaithful to the instruction given to him, he and the nation would inevitably suffer dire consequences (Dt 4:40,44–45). **the Law of Moses.** Solomon and his sons were obligated to the stipulations of the Mosaic covenant, to which all Israel assented (Ex 19:3–8; 24:1–11; Dt 5:27).
2:4 If your descendants watch how they live. David's instructions to Solomon echo in part the promises of God as relayed to David by the prophet Nathan in 2 Samuel 7:7–16 and reaffirmed in David's prayer in 2 Samuel 7:18–29. David, however, here underscored the need for covenant fidelity. **with all their heart and soul.** These words are a quotation of Deuteronomy 4:29 and 6:5. When Jesus was asked to identify the greatest commandment, he also quoted, in part, this phrase from Deuteronomy 6:5 (Mt 22:35–40). See also 1 Kings 8:25–26 and 9:4–5.
2:5–9 David charged Solomon to rectify a number of wrongs that had gone unpunished during his own reign.
2:5 Joab son of Zeruiah. Joab was one of David's most successful but most unscrupulous generals (see note on "Joab" at 1:7). David called on Solomon to see to it that the crimes Joab had perpetrated against his rivals Abner (2Sa 3:22–30) and Amasa (2Sa 20:4–10) did not go unpunished. The manner in which Joab first tricked and then murdered Abner and Amasa ("shedding their blood in peacetime") was unlawful (Dt 19:1–13; 21:1–9). Joab had also supported Adonijah (1:7), an allegiance that would become a special concern for Solomon.
2:7 the sons of Barzillai. See 2 Samuel 17:27–29 and 19:31–40. **eat at your table.** That is, enjoy a position of honor in the court and share in the beneficence of the state (cf. 2Sa 9:7; 19:28; 2Ki 25:29; Ne 5:17).
2:8 Shimei son of Gera. Not the Shimei mentioned in 1:8. This Shimei had earlier cursed and thrown stones at David when the king was fleeing his son Absalom (2Sa 16:5–8). Shimei later begged for pardon, and David promised that he would not die (2Sa 19:16–23).
2:9 do not consider him innocent. The Mosaic covenant forbade cursing a ruler (Ex 22:28; cf. 1Ki 21:10). Evidently David had not pardoned Shimei but had only granted him a stay of execution.
■ **2:10–12** *David's Death and Burial.* David's reign was completed and Solomon's began.
2:10 rested with his fathers. See note at 1:21. **the City of David.** One of David's major accomplishments had been the capture of Jerusalem, which had become the nation's capital. The city subsequently bore David's name in his honor (2Sa 5:7).
2:11 He had reigned forty years. David ruled from approximately 1010–970 B.C. During his last years he may have shared a coregency with Solomon (1:38–40). **seven years in Hebron and thirty-three in Jerusalem.** Before conquering Jerusalem, David had ruled for seven years from the city of Hebron.

Solomon's Throne Established

[13]Now Adonijah, the son of Haggith, went to Bathsheba, Solomon's mother. Bathsheba asked him, "Do you come peacefully?"[l] 2:13
He answered, "Yes, peacefully." [14]Then he added, "I have something to say to you." [l]1Sa 16:4
"You may say it," she replied.
[15]"As you know," he said, "the kingdom was mine. All Israel looked to me as their
king. But things changed, and the kingdom has gone to my brother; for it has come to
him from the LORD. [16]Now I have one request to make of you. Do not refuse me."
"You may make it," she said.
[17]So he continued, "Please ask King Solomon—he will not refuse you—to give me Ab- 2:17
ishag[m] the Shunammite as my wife." [m]1Ki 1:3
[18]"Very well," Bathsheba replied, "I will speak to the king for you."
[19]When Bathsheba went to King Solomon to speak to him for Adonijah, the king
stood up to meet her, bowed down to her and sat down on his throne. He had a throne
brought for the king's mother,[n] and she sat down at his right hand.[o] 2:19
[20]"I have one small request to make of you," she said. "Do not refuse me." [n]1Ki 15:13 [o]Ps 45:9
The king replied, "Make it, my mother; I will not refuse you." 2:21
[21]So she said, "Let Abishag[p] the Shunammite be given in marriage to your brother [p]1Ki 1:3
Adonijah."
[22]King Solomon answered his mother, "Why do you request Abishag[q] the Shunam- 2:22 [q]2Sa 12:8; 1Ki 1:3
mite for Adonijah? You might as well request the kingdom for him—after all, he is my [r]1Ch 3:2
older brother[r]—yes, for him and for Abiathar the priest and Joab son of Zeruiah!"
[23]Then King Solomon swore by the LORD: "May God deal with me, be it ever so severely,[s] if Adonijah does not pay with his life for this request! [24]And now, as surely as the LORD 2:23
lives—he who has established me securely on the throne of my father David and has [s]Ru 1:17

■ **2:13–46** *Solomon's Blessing of Consolidation.* God blessed Solomon with the ability to consolidate his power by executing or exiling enemies, among them Adonijah (vv. 13–25), Abiathar (vv. 26–27), Joab (vv. 28–35) and Shimei (vv. 36–46).
■ **2:13–25** *Adonijah.* Solomon realized that Adonijah had not entirely given up on attaining David's throne.
2:15 All Israel looked to me as their king. This was wishful thinking on Adonijah's part (1:7–10). **it has come to him from the LORD.** Adonijah claimed to recognize the sanctity of Solomon's reign, but his request for Abishag demonstrated otherwise.
2:17 give me Abishag the Shunammite. In the ancient Near East, a large court and family were signs of royal glory. Abishag remained a virgin while she stayed with David (1:1–4), so Adonijah would not technically break the law by marrying her (Dt 22:30). Nonetheless, should Adonijah prove successful in luring Abishag away from Solomon's court, this would constitute an open affront to Solomon's power (cf. 2Sa 3:6–7; 12:8; 16:20–24).
2:18–20 Bathsheba acceded to Adonijah's request. It is unclear whether she was taken in by Adonijah's ruse or was merely playing along, confident of Solomon's response.
2:19 his right hand. The "right hand" was a position of high honor (Ps 110:1; Mt 20:21). See *WLC* 127.
2:23 Solomon swore by the LORD. Solomon invoked a curse upon himself should Adonijah go unpunished for this flagrant grab for power (see note on 1:17).
2:24 established me securely. See verse 12. **a dynasty for me as he promised.** According to 1 Kings 11:42 and 14:21, Rehobo-

Solomon's Jerusalem

c. 950 B.C.

Solomon extended the city northward from the original site and there built his magnificent temple.

His royal residence was nearby; however, its architecture and location are unknown.

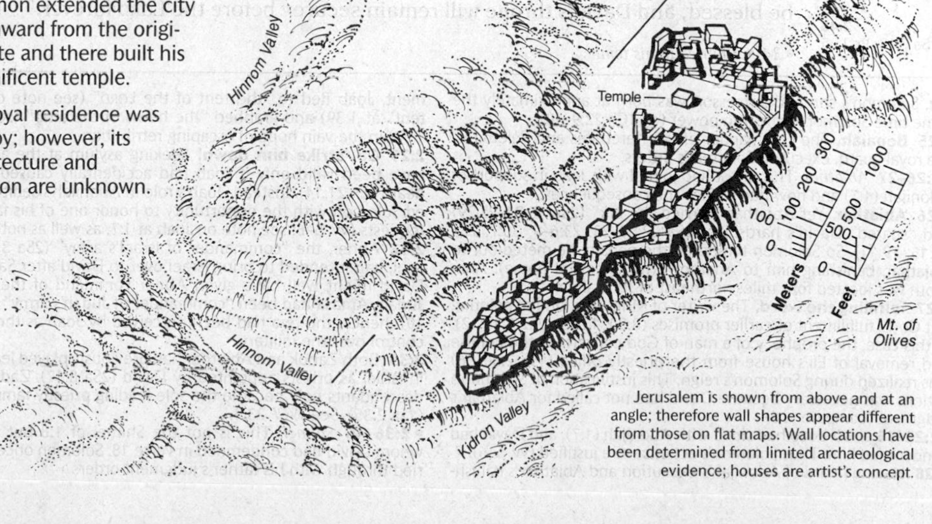

Jerusalem is shown from above and at an angle; therefore wall shapes appear different from those on flat maps. Wall locations have been determined from limited archaeological evidence; houses are artist's concept.

founded a dynasty for me as he promised[t]—Adonijah shall be put to death today!" [25]So
King Solomon gave orders to Benaiah[u] son of Jehoiada, and he struck down Adonijah
and he died.
[26]To Abiathar[v] the priest the king said, "Go back to your fields in Anathoth.[w] You deserve to die, but I will not put you to death now, because you carried the ark[x] of the Sovereign LORD before my father David and shared all my father's hardships."[y] [27]So Solomon
removed Abiathar from the priesthood of the LORD, fulfilling[z] the word the LORD had spoken at Shiloh about the house of Eli.
[28]When the news reached Joab, who had conspired with Adonijah though not with
Absalom, he fled to the tent of the LORD and took hold of the horns[a] of the altar. [29]King
Solomon was told that Joab had fled to the tent of the LORD and was beside the altar.
Then Solomon ordered Benaiah[b] son of Jehoiada, "Go, strike him down!"
[30]So Benaiah entered the tent of the LORD and said to Joab, "The king says, 'Come
out![c]'"
But he answered, "No, I will die here."
Benaiah reported to the king, "This is how Joab answered me."
[31]Then the king commanded Benaiah, "Do as he says. Strike him down and bury him,
and so clear me and my father's house of the guilt of the innocent blood[d] that Joab shed.
[32]The LORD will repay[e] him for the blood he shed,[f] because without the knowledge of my
father David he attacked two men and killed them with the sword. Both of them—Abner son of Ner, commander of Israel's army, and Amasa[g] son of Jether, commander of
Judah's army—were better[h] men and more upright than he. [33]May the guilt of their
blood rest on the head of Joab and his descendants forever. But on David and his descendants, his house and his throne, may there be the LORD's peace forever."
[34]So Benaiah son of Jehoiada went up and struck down Joab and killed him, and he
was buried on his own land[a] in the desert. [35]The king put Benaiah[i] son of Jehoiada over
the army in Joab's position and replaced Abiathar with Zadok[j] the priest.
[36]Then the king sent for Shimei[k] and said to him, "Build yourself a house in Jerusalem and live there, but do not go anywhere else. [37]The day you leave and cross the Kidron Valley,[l] you can be sure you will die; your blood will be on your own head."[m]
[38]Shimei answered the king, "What you say is good. Your servant will do as my lord
the king has said." And Shimei stayed in Jerusalem for a long time.
[39]But three years later, two of Shimei's slaves ran off to Achish[n] son of Maacah, king
of Gath, and Shimei was told, "Your slaves are in Gath." [40]At this, he saddled his donkey and went to Achish at Gath in search of his slaves. So Shimei went away and
brought the slaves back from Gath.
[41]When Solomon was told that Shimei had gone from Jerusalem to Gath and had returned, [42]the king summoned Shimei and said to him, "Did I not make you swear by the
LORD and warn you, 'On the day you leave to go anywhere else, you can be sure you will
die'? At that time you said to me, 'What you say is good. I will obey.' [43]Why then did you
not keep your oath to the LORD and obey the command I gave you?"
[44]The king also said to Shimei, "You know in your heart all the wrong[o] you did to my
father David. Now the LORD will repay you for your wrongdoing. [45]But King Solomon will
be blessed, and David's throne will remain secure[p] before the LORD forever."

2:24 [t]2Sa 7:11; 1Ch 22:10
2:25 [u]2Sa 8:18
2:26 [v]1Sa 22:20 [w]Jos 21:18 [x]2Sa 15:24 [y]1Sa 23:6
2:27 [z]1Sa 2:27-36
2:28 [a]1Ki 1:7,50
2:29 [b]ver 25
2:30 [c]Ex 21:14
2:31 [d]Nu 35:33; Dt 19:13; 21:8-9
2:32 [e]Jdg 9:57; Ps 7:16 [f]Jdg 9:24 [g]2Sa 3:27; 20:10 [h]2Ch 21:13
2:35 [i]1Ki 4:4 [j]ver 27; 1Ch 29:22
2:36 [k]ver 8; 2Sa 16:5
2:37 [l]2Sa 15:23 [m]Lev 20:9; Jos 2:19; 2Sa 1:16
2:39 [n]1Sa 27:2
2:44 [o]1Sa 25:39; 2Sa 16:5-13; Eze 17:19
2:45 [p]2Sa 7:13; Pr 25:5

[a] *34* Or *buried in his tomb*

---

am, Solomon's son and successor, was born at approximately the same time Solomon came into power (cf. 1Ch 22:9–10).

2:25 Benaiah. The commander of the Kerethites and Pelethites, the royal guard, executed Solomon's orders.

■ **2:26–27** *Abiathar.* This priest had joined with Joab in support of Adonijah (1:7) and now had to face the consequences.

2:26 Abiathar. Yet Abiathar "carried the ark" (2Sa 15:24–25,29) and "shared" David's hardships (1Sa 22:20–23; 23:6–9; 30:7; 2Sa 17:15; 19:11). So Solomon tempered the penalty he meted out to Abiathar, banishing him to Anathoth (his ancestral home). Anathoth was located four miles northeast of Jerusalem.

2:27 fulfilling the word. The writer of Kings was fond of pointing out God's fulfillment of earlier promises (8:20; 12:15; 15:29; 16:12). In this case, the prophecy of a man of God concerning the demise and removal of Eli's house from the priestly office (1Sa 2:30–36) was realized during Solomon's reign. This justification of Solomon's actions was necessary because David had not called for Abiathar's judgment (compare v. 6).

■ **2:28–35** *Joab.* Joab had sided with Adonijah (1:7), and David had condemned him. Thus Solomon's actions were justified (vv. 5–6).

2:28 Having heard of Adonijah's execution and Abiathar's banishment, Joab fled to "the tent of the LORD" (see note on "sacred tent" at 1:39) and grabbed "the horns of the altar" (see note on 1:50) in the vain hope of escaping retribution.

2:29 Go, strike him down! Seeking asylum at the altar would have been valid only if Joab had accidentally caused another's death (Ex 21:14). Instead, Joab's role in Adonijah's sedition provided Solomon with the opportunity to honor one of his father's last requests (vv. 5–6; see note on Joab at 1:7, as well as note on 2:32).

2:32 Abner, the "commander of Israel's army" (2Sa 3:27) under Saul, had intended to bring Israel over to David after Saul's death. David might well have given Abner command of the armies of Judah. Amasa had been "commander of Judah's army" (2Sa 20:8–10); hence, the two had been perceived by Joab as threats to his control over the military.

2:35 Both Zadok and Abiathar had previously played leading roles in Israel as priests appointed by David (2Sa 8:17). Zadok and his descendants now became the sole leading priestly family in Israel (1Sa 2:35). See *WCF* 23.4.

■ **2:36–46** *Shimei.* This is not the Shimei of 1:8 but is the one whom David had condemned in verse 18. Solomon once again carried through with his father's judgment orders.

46 Then the king gave the order to Benaiah son of Jehoiada, and he went out and
struck Shimei down and killed him.
The kingdom was now firmly established[q] in Solomon's hands.

Solomon Asks for Wisdom

3 Solomon made an alliance with Pharaoh king of Egypt and married[r] his daughter.[s]
He brought her to the City of David[t] until he finished building his palace[u] and the temple of the LORD, and the wall around Jerusalem. 2 The people, however, were still sacrificing at the high places,[v] because a temple had not yet been built for the Name of the LORD.
3 Solomon showed his love[w] for the LORD by walking according to the statutes[x] of his father
David, except that he offered sacrifices and burned incense on the high places.
4 The king went to Gibeon[y] to offer sacrifices, for that was the most important high
place, and Solomon offered a thousand burnt offerings on that altar. 5 At Gibeon the LORD
appeared[z] to Solomon during the night in a dream,[a] and God said, "Ask for whatever
you want me to give you."
6 Solomon answered, "You have shown great kindness to your servant, my father David, because he was faithful[b] to you and righteous and upright in heart. You have continued this great kindness to him and have given him a son[c] to sit on his throne this very
day.
7 "Now, O LORD my God, you have made your servant king in place of my father David. But I am only a little child[d] and do not know how to carry out my duties. 8 Your servant is here among the people you have chosen,[e] a great people, too numerous to
count or number.[f] 9 So give your servant a discerning[g] heart to govern your people and
to distinguish[h] between right and wrong. For who is able[i] to govern this great people of
yours?"
10 The Lord was pleased that Solomon had asked for this. 11 So God said to him,
"Since you have asked[j] for this and not for long life or wealth for yourself, nor have asked
for the death of your enemies but for discernment in administering justice, 12 I will do

2:46 [q]ver 12; 2Ch 1:1
3:1 [r]1Ki 7:8 [s]1Ki 9:24 [t]2Sa 5:7 [u]1Ki 7:1; 9:15,19
3:2 [v]Lev 17:3-5; Dt 12:2,4-5; 1Ki 22:43
3:3 [w]Dt 6:5; Ps 31:23; 1Co 8:3 [x]1Ki 2:3; 9:4; 11:4,6,38
3:4 [y]1Ch 16:39
3:5 [z]1Ki 9:2 [a]Nu 12:6; Mt 1:20
3:6 [b]1Ki 2:4; 9:4 [c]1Ki 1:48
3:7 [d]Nu 27:17; 1Ch 29:1
3:8 [e]Dt 7:6 [f]Ge 15:5
3:9 [g]2Sa 14:17; Jas 1:5 [h]Pr 2:3-9; Heb 5:14 [i]Ps 72:1-2
3:11 [j]Jas 4:3

■ **3:1—9:25** *Solomon's Establishment of Worship.* This lengthy section includes a variety of subjects united by the theme of Solomon's success in establishing temple worship in Jerusalem. These chapters begin and end with notices about Pharaoh's daughter and the place at which sacrifices were made (3:1–3; 9:24–25). The remaining chapters divide between accounts of Solomon's wisdom (3:3—4:34) and the temple and palace he constructed (5:1—9:9).

■ **3:1–3** *Sacrificing Before Temple Construction.* This notation of sacrificial practices before the building of the temple, along with the mention of Pharaoh's daughter, parallels the similar notice of worship after temple construction in 9:24–25. These two notations frame this material, focusing on how Solomon established as the norm that sacrifices were to be offered only at the temple in Jerusalem.

3:1 an alliance with Pharaoh. The precise identity of the pharaoh whose daughter Solomon married is unknown. Since the founder of the twenty-second Egyptian dynasty, Sheshonk I (Biblical Shishak), later invaded the territory of Solomon's son and successor, Rehoboam (1Ki 14:25–26), the pharaoh mentioned here might be either Siamun (978–959 B.C.) or Psusennes II (959–945), the last monarchs of the twenty-first Egyptian dynasty. This marriage alliance attests to Israel's international prominence during the united kingdom period but also foreshadows Solomon's later downfall (see notes on ch. 11). **his daughter.** Pharaoh's daughter is mentioned here at the beginning of construction, at the time of construction of the palace (7:8) and after the construction is completed (9:24–26). Her movement from the city of David to the palace is set alongside Solomon's sacrificial practices and serves to frame the narrative about the temple's construction.

3:2 sacrificing at the high places. That is, at hilltop shrines. When the Israelites entered the land of Canaan, they were supposed to abolish all the high places of the Canaanites (Nu 33:52; Dt 7:5; 12:3) and to build their own centers of worship or altars at divinely approved sites (Ex 20:24; Jdg 6:24; 13:19; 1Sa 7:17; 9:12–13). Such worship at certain sanctioned sites was deemed acceptable until the time when the central sanctuary, spoken about at length in Deuteronomy 12, would be built. See *WCF* 21.1

3:3 the statutes. That is, the stipulations of the Mosaic covenant (see note on "the law of Moses" at 2:3). **except that.** The fact that there was as yet no temple made Solomon's practice understandable, but, from the writer's point of view, it was still not ideal. The author would return to this exception later in Solomon's reign (11:1–13) because, even after the temple was built, Solomon never completely stopped worshiping at the high places.

■ **3:4—4:34** *Solomon's Astounding Wisdom.* Solomon's wisdom served the writer's larger interest in the establishment of temple worship. The construction of the temple was the epitome of Solomon's wisdom at work. The writer idealized Solomon in four episodes: his gift of wisdom (3:4–15), his judicial wisdom (3:16–28), his domestic political wisdom (4:1–28) and his international renown for his wisdom (4:29–34).

■ **3:4–15** *Solomon's Gift of Wisdom.* God granted Solomon wisdom because he was a humble man, not seeking blessings for himself but wisdom for the benefit of Israel. Thus the programs Solomon established on the basis of this wisdom were to be received as God's blessing to his people.

3:4 Gibeon. For the story of how Gibeon came into Israelite hands, see Joshua 9. **the most important high place.** The tabernacle and ancient bronze altar were located at Gibeon (1Ch 21:29; 2Ch 1:2–6). **burnt offerings.** The most common type of offering in Israelite worship, used for either thanksgiving or atonement. The animal was completely burned except for the hide, which was taken by the priest (Lev 7:8).

3:5 dream. This dream sets the stage for the first major period in Solomon's tenure as king. For dreams as vehicles of revelation elsewhere in the Bible, see Genesis 26:24, 28:11–12, 31:11, 46:2, Numbers 12:6, Judges 7:13, 1 Samuel 3:11–14, Daniel 2:4, 7:1 and Matthew 1:20 and 2:12 and 22.

3:7 little child. If Solomon was born early in David's reign in Jerusalem (2Sa 5:14) and David ruled in Jerusalem for 33 years, Solomon would have been approximately thirty years old at his accession. This must be a reference to his perceived suitability for ruling Israel, not to his age. **do not know.** Solomon was relatively young and inexperienced and was humble enough to admit it (cf. Jer 1:6).

3:8 a great people. Since the sojourn in and exodus from Egypt, the Israelites had grown in population to the point that the promises to Abraham (Ge 12:2; 13:16; 22:17–18) and Jacob (Ge 32:12) were being realized. Because of this population surge, the challenges facing a leader, such as Solomon, would be considerable.

3:9 a discerning heart. Solomon asked for wisdom to govern justly (cf. Dt 1:9–18). **distinguish between right and wrong.** See Genesis 3:22, 31:24 and 29 and 2 Samuel 13:22.

3:10 The LORD was pleased. Solomon did not ask for the usual wishes of an ancient king: long life, wealth or the death of his enemies (v. 11).

3:12 [k]1Jn 5:14-15 [l]1Ki 4:29,30,31; 5:12; 10:23; Ecc 1:16
3:13 [m]Mt 6:33; Eph 3:20 [n]1Ki 4:21-24; Pr 3:1-2,16 [o]1Ki 10:23
3:14 [p]ver 6; Pr 3:1-2,16 [q]Ps 61:6; 91:16
3:15 [r]Ge 41:7 [s]1Ki 8:65 [t]Mk 6:21 [u]Est 1:3, 9; Da 5:1
3:26 [v]Ge 43:30; Isa 49:15; Jer 31:20; Hos 11:8
3:28 [w]ver 9,11-12; Col 2:3
4:2 [x]1Ch 6:10
4:3 [y]2Sa 8:16
4:4 [z]1Ki 2:35 [a]1Ki 2:27

what you have asked.[k] I will give you a wise[l] and discerning heart, so that there will never have been anyone like you, nor will there ever be. 13 Moreover, I will give you what you
have not[m] asked for—both riches and honor[n]—so that in your lifetime you will have no
equal[o] among kings. 14 And if you walk[p] in my ways and obey my statutes and commands
as David your father did, I will give you a long life."[q] 15 Then Solomon awoke[r]—and he
realized it had been a dream.

He returned to Jerusalem, stood before the ark of the Lord's covenant and sacrificed
burnt offerings[s] and fellowship offerings.[a][t] Then he gave a feast[u] for all his court.

A Wise Ruling

16 Now two prostitutes came to the king and stood before him. 17 One of them said, "My
lord, this woman and I live in the same house. I had a baby while she was there with me.
18 The third day after my child was born, this woman also had a baby. We were alone;
there was no one in the house but the two of us.

19 "During the night this woman's son died because she lay on him. 20 So she got up
in the middle of the night and took my son from my side while I your servant was
asleep. She put him by her breast and put her dead son by my breast. 21 The next morning, I got up to nurse my son—and he was dead! But when I looked at him closely in the
morning light, I saw that it wasn't the son I had borne."

22 The other woman said, "No! The living one is my son; the dead one is yours."

But the first one insisted, "No! The dead one is yours; the living one is mine." And so
they argued before the king.

23 The king said, "This one says, 'My son is alive and your son is dead,' while that one
says, 'No! Your son is dead and mine is alive.' "

24 Then the king said, "Bring me a sword." So they brought a sword for the king.
25 He then gave an order: "Cut the living child in two and give half to one and half to
the other."

26 The woman whose son was alive was filled with compassion[v] for her son and said
to the king, "Please, my lord, give her the living baby! Don't kill him!"

But the other said, "Neither I nor you shall have him. Cut him in two!"

27 Then the king gave his ruling: "Give the living baby to the first woman. Do not kill
him; she is his mother."

28 When all Israel heard the verdict the king had given, they held the king in awe, because they saw that he had wisdom[w] from God to administer justice.

Solomon's Officials and Governors

4 So King Solomon ruled over all Israel. 2 And these were his chief officials:

Azariah[x] son of Zadok—the priest;
3 Elihoreph and Ahijah, sons of Shisha—secretaries;
Jehoshaphat[y] son of Ahilud—recorder;
4 Benaiah[z] son of Jehoiada—commander in chief;
Zadok[a] and Abiathar—priests;

a *15* Traditionally *peace offerings*

3:12 anyone like you, nor will there ever be. Solomon's wisdom was incomparable in the history of Israel (4:29–34; 5:7; 9:23–24; 10:6–9). See note at 2 Kings 18:5.

3:13 riches and honor. God was so delighted with Solomon's unselfish request that he promised to grant an abundance of the blessings for which Solomon did not ask (cf. 10:23).

3:14 if you walk in my ways . . . I will give you a long life. Longevity was contingent upon Solomon's continuing faithfulness to God, a condition he would fail to fulfill (11:1–13).

3:15 In gratitude to God, Solomon returned to Jerusalem; stood before "the ark," a central symbol of God's relationship with Israel (Ex 37:1–9); and offered burnt offerings (see note on "burnt offerings" at v. 4) and fellowship offerings (Lev 3).

■ **3:16–28** *Solomon's Judicial Wisdom.* This episode provides the first example of Solomon's wisdom: his ruling in a dispute over a baby.

3:16 prostitutes Because the two women were "prostitutes," determining the child's identity through similarity to the father would not be possible. **came to the king.** In the ancient Near East a king was expected under certain circumstances to adjudicate special cases and appeals (2Sa 14:4–21; 15:1–6; 19:8). In this manner, a monarch was directly responsible to the people.

3:25 give half to one and half to the other. A legal tradition in the ancient Near East stipulated that if a judge could not determine who owned a disputed piece of property, he should divide it evenly between the two contestants (cf. Ex 21:35). Solomon's application of this tradition in this case was brilliant, because the prospect of its implementation revealed the identity of the true mother.

3:28 they held the king in awe. Solomon's insightful ruling demonstrated that God had indeed given him "discernment in administering justice" (v. 11; cf. Pr. 16:10). See *WLC* 129.

■ **4:1–28** *Solomon's Domestic Political Wisdom.* A second example of Solomon's remarkable wisdom was the way in which he organized the bureaucracy of Israel so that the entire nation benefited. These verses consist of lists of his officers (vv. 1–19) and his provisions (vv. 20–28). See *WLC* 127–128.

4:1 all Israel. Solomon, like David before him, ruled over a united kingdom (see note on "Israel and Judah" at 1:35).

4:2 son. In Hebrew, the word can mean "descendent" (Ge 31:28, 43; Jos 22:24,25,27). In this case, Azariah was likely the grandson of Zadok, the son of Ahimaaz (2Sa 15:27,36; 1Ch 6:8–9).

4:4 Zadok and Abiathar. These were the two leading priests during David's reign and the beginning of Solomon's. Solomon deposed Abiathar for joining Adonijah in his sedition (1:7; 2:27),

[5] Azariah son of Nathan—in charge of the district officers;
Zabud son of Nathan—a priest and personal adviser to the king;
[6] Ahishar—in charge of the palace;
Adoniram son of Abda—in charge of forced labor.

[7] Solomon also had twelve district governors over all Israel, who supplied provisions
for the king and the royal household. Each one had to provide supplies for one month
in the year. [8] These are their names:

Ben-Hur—in the hill country[b] of Ephraim;
[9] Ben-Deker—in Makaz, Shaalbim,[c] Beth Shemesh[d] and Elon Bethhanan;
[10] Ben-Hesed—in Arubboth (Socoh[e] and all the land of Hepher[f] were his);
[11] Ben-Abinadab—in Naphoth Dor[a][g] (he was married to Taphath daughter of Solomon);
[12] Baana son of Ahilud—in Taanach and Megiddo, and in all of Beth Shan[h] next to Zarethan[i] below Jezreel, from Beth Shan to Abel Meholah[j] across to Jokmeam;[k]
[13] Ben-Geber—in Ramoth Gilead (the settlements of Jair[l] son of Manasseh in Gilead were his, as well as the district of Argob in Bashan and its sixty large walled cities[m] with bronze gate bars);
[14] Ahinadab son of Iddo—in Mahanaim;[n]
[15] Ahimaaz[o]—in Naphtali (he had married Basemath daughter of Solomon);
[16] Baana son of Hushai[p]—in Asher and in Aloth;
[17] Jehoshaphat son of Paruah—in Issachar;
[18] Shimei[q] son of Ela—in Benjamin;
[19] Geber son of Uri—in Gilead (the country of Sihon king of the Amorites and the country of Og[r] king of Bashan). He was the only governor over the district.

Solomon's Daily Provisions

[20] The people of Judah and Israel were as numerous as the sand[s] on the seashore; they
ate, they drank and they were happy. [21] And Solomon ruled[t] over all the kingdoms from
the River[b][u] to the land of the Philistines, as far as the border of Egypt.[v] These countries
brought tribute[w] and were Solomon's subjects all his life.
[22] Solomon's daily provisions were thirty cors[c] of fine flour and sixty cors[d] of meal,
[23] ten head of stall-fed cattle, twenty of pasture-fed cattle and a hundred sheep and goats,
as well as deer, gazelles, roebucks and choice fowl. [24] For he ruled over all the kingdoms
west of the River, from Tiphsah[x] to Gaza, and had peace[y] on all sides. [25] During Solomon's lifetime Judah and Israel, from Dan to Beersheba,[z] lived in safety,[a] each man under his own vine and fig tree.[b]
[26] Solomon had four[e] thousand stalls for chariot horses,[c] and twelve thousand
horses.[f]

4:8 [b]Jos 24:33
4:9 [c]Jdg 1:35 [d]Jos 21:16
4:10 [e]Jos 15:35 [f]Jos 12:17
4:11 [g]Jos 11:2
4:12 [h]Jos 17:11; Jdg 5:19 [i]Jos 3:16 [j]1Ki 19:16 [k]1Ch 6:68
4:13 [l]Nu 32:41 [m]Dt 3:4
4:14 [n]Jos 13:26
4:15 [o]2Sa 15:27
4:16 [p]2Sa 15:32
4:18 [q]1Ki 1:8
4:19 [r]Dt 3:8-10
4:20 [s]Ge 22:17; 32:12; 1Ki 3:8
4:21 [t]2Ch 9:26; Ps 72:11 [u]Jos 1:4; Ps 72:8 [v]Ge 15:18 [w]Ps 68:29
4:24 [x]Ps 72:11 [y]1Ch 22:9
4:25 [z]Jdg 20:1 [a]Jer 23:6 [b]Mic 4:4; Zec 3:10
4:26 [c]1Ki 10:26; 2Ch 1:14

[a] *11* Or *in the heights of Dor* [b] *21* That is, the Euphrates; also in verse 24 [c] *22* That is, probably about 185 bushels (about 6.6 kiloliters) [d] *22* That is, probably about 375 bushels (about 13.2 kiloliters) [e] *26* Some Septuagint manuscripts (see also 2 Chron. 9:25); Hebrew *forty*
[f] *26* Or *charioteers*

while Azariah succeeded Zadok as priest during the reign of Solomon (v. 2).
4:5 Nathan. His identity is unclear. Possibilities include the prophet Nathan (2Sa 7:2–17; 12:1–15; 1Ki 1:11) and Nathan, the son of David.
4:6 in charge of the palace. Administered the palace and oversaw the king's properties (16:9; 18:3; 2Ki 18:18,37; 19:2). **Adoniram.** Or "Adoram" (see NIV text note on 2Sa 20:24; 1Ki 12:18), was in charge of forced labor during the reigns of David, Solomon and Rehoboam. **forced labor.** This work was performed primarily, but not exclusively, by captives of war from defeated nations (5:13–16; 9:15–23; Nu 31:25–47; Jos 9:23).
4:7 twelve district governors. These new administrative districts do not wholly conform with the old Israelite tribal boundaries, possibly because the tribes greatly varied in population and land holdings and Solomon desired a steady monthly income for his government. This arrangement may also have contributed to a sentiment of nationalism over one of tribalism.
4:19 Geber . . . Gilead On the Israelite conquest of Sihon, king of the Amorites (whose land lay east of the Dead Sea), see Numbers 32:33 and Deuteronomy 2:24–37. After the capture of Sihon's territory, the Israelites defeated Og, king of Bashan, and captured all his lands (to the east of the Sea of Kinnereth). See Numbers 32:33 and Deuteronomy 3:1–11. Geber was, therefore, governor over a large district east of the Jordan.
4:20 numerous as the sand on the seashore. Fulfillment of the promises to the patriarchs (Ge 22:17; 32:12; cf. v. 29 and see note on 3:8). This demonstrated that God was continuing to fulfill the original destiny of humanity through Israel (see note at Ge 1:28–29). **they ate, they drank and they were happy.** A picture of idyllic contentment.
4:21 from the River. The Euphrates. **as far as the border of Egypt.** The borders of Solomon's kingdom correspond with the borders promised to Abraham (see Ge 15:18; 17:8; Dt 1:7; 11:24; Jos 1:4 and their notes). Hence, Kings presents Solomon's rule over an empire that represented the long-awaited fulfillment of the patriarchal promises (cf. vv. 24–25).
4:22 daily provisions. These were for Solomon's court, palace and extended family.
4:24 Tiphsah. Located on the western bank of the Euphrates. **Gaza.** On the southern Mediterranean coast. **peace on all sides.** David had been compelled to fight many wars to secure the kingdom, and Solomon enjoyed the benefits. Peaceful conditions were necessary for embarking on the major building projects of a temple and a palace (2Sa 7:10–11; 1Ki 5:3–5).
4:26 stalls for chariot horses. It is unclear from the available

4:27 [d]ver 7

27 The district officers,[d] each in his month, supplied provisions for King Solomon and
all who came to the king's table. They saw to it that nothing was lacking. 28 They also
brought to the proper place their quotas of barley and straw for the chariot horses and
the other horses.

Solomon's Wisdom

4:29 [e]1Ki 3:12
4:30 [f]Ge 25:6 [g]Ac 7:22
4:31 [h]1Ki 3:12; 1Ch 2:6; 6:33; 15:19; Ps 89 Title
4:32 [i]Pr 1:1; Ecc 12:9 [j]SS 1:1
4:34 [k]1Ki 10:1; 2Ch 9:23

29 God gave Solomon wisdom[e] and very great insight, and a breadth of understanding as measureless as the sand on the seashore. 30 Solomon's wisdom was greater than
the wisdom of all the men of the East,[f] and greater than all the wisdom of Egypt.[g] 31 He
was wiser[h] than any other man, including Ethan the Ezrahite—wiser than Heman, Calcol and Darda, the sons of Mahol. And his fame spread to all the surrounding nations.
32 He spoke three thousand proverbs[i] and his songs[j] numbered a thousand and five. 33 He
described plant life, from the cedar of Lebanon to the hyssop that grows out of walls. He
also taught about animals and birds, reptiles and fish. 34 Men of all nations came to listen to Solomon's wisdom, sent by all the kings[k] of the world, who had heard of his wisdom.

Preparations for Building the Temple

5:1 [l]ver 10, 18; 2Sa 5:11; 1Ch 14:1
5:3 [m]1Ch 22:8; 28:3
5:4 [n]1Ki 4:24; 1Ch 22:9
5:5 [o]1Ch 17:12 [p]2Sa 7:13; 1Ch 22:10

5 When Hiram[l] king of Tyre heard that Solomon had been anointed king to succeed
his father David, he sent his envoys to Solomon, because he had always been on
friendly terms with David. 2 Solomon sent back this message to Hiram:

3 "You know that because of the wars[m] waged against my father David from all
sides, he could not build a temple for the Name of the LORD his God until the LORD
put his enemies under his feet. 4 But now the LORD my God has given me rest[n] on
every side, and there is no adversary or disaster. 5 I intend, therefore, to build a
temple[o] for the Name of the LORD my God, as the LORD told my father David, when
he said, 'Your son whom I will put on the throne in your place will build the temple for my Name.'[p]

6 "So give orders that cedars of Lebanon be cut for me. My men will work with
yours, and I will pay you for your men whatever wages you set. You know that we
have no one so skilled in felling timber as the Sidonians."

Biblical source documents how many stalls Solomon had for chariot horses (see NIV text note). First Kings 10:26 states that Solomon owned 1400 chariots. Regular, ample provisions supplied Solomon's chariot force and his bureaucracy (vv. 27–28).

■ **4:29–34** *Solomon's International Wisdom.* Solomon's wisdom is described in superlative terms. He was renowned throughout the world for this gift he had received from God.

4:30 the East. That is, Mesopotamia to the northeast (Ge 29:1) and Arabia to the east (Jer 49:28; Eze 25:4,10). **Egypt.** South of Israel. Examples of wisdom literature from both Mesopotamia and Egypt have been discovered and translated (see "Introduction to Proverbs").

4:31 Ethan the Ezrahite. See the titles of Psalms 88 and 89. **Heman, Calcol and Darda.** Descendants of Zerah, a son of the patriarch Judah (1Ch 2:6–7).

4:32 proverbs . . . songs. Solomon was not only a lover and cultivator of wisdom literature but an accomplished author in his own right.

4:33 plant life . . . animals and birds. Solomon took a special interest in the natural world. By coining proverbs, he gave order to social relations; by listing fauna and flora he attributed order to the natural elements of his kingdom. **taught.** Or simply "spoke."

4:34 Men of all nations. Solomon acquired an international reputation for wisdom and attracted a wide following. The monarchs of various nations sent emissaries to learn from his erudition. This does not appear to have been unprecedented. The Ebla texts (c. 2350 B.C.) mention that learned men from many nations "lectured" in Ebla.

■ **5:1—9:23** *Solomon's Temple and Palace.* Having established that Solomon was acting with astounding wisdom from God, the writer revealed the most important act in Solomon's life, the building of the temple for the worship of God. The temple was a central theme from the writer's theological perspective. He wanted his readers to recall its importance for them during their exile and after their return to the land (see notes on 8:23–52). His record of this project divides into four balanced sections: a listing of those serving Solomon in preparation (5:1–18), the actual construction of the temple and the palace (6:1—7:51), the dedication of the temple (8:1—9:9) and a record of those who served Solomon after construction (9:10–23).

■ **5:1–18** *Those Serving Solomon in Preparations.* Solomon employed his wisdom in bringing together people to prepare for the building project. These verses parallel 9:1–23; together the two passages frame the topic of the temple. The writer mentioned both Hiram (vv. 1–12; 9:11–14) and the conscripted laborers (vv. 13–18; 9:15–21).

■ **5:1–12** *Hiram.* Hiram played an important role in preparing materials for Solomon's temple. He was not an Israelite but was still under Solomon's authority (cf. 4:21,24).

5:1 Hiram king of Tyre. Tyre is a city on the northern Mediterranean coast in the region of modern Lebanon. Since Hiram ruled from 978–944 B.C., his reign overlapped the tenures of both David and Solomon. **friendly terms with David.** Hiram had supplied both timber and workers when David built himself a palace (2Sa 5:11).

5:3 the wars waged against my father David. Although David wished to build the temple himself, he spent much of his reign expanding and consolidating the kingdom (2Sa 7:10–11). In a play on the Hebrew word *bet* (which can mean either "temple" or "dynasty"), God, through the prophet Nathan, informed David that God would build him a *bet* (dynasty), while David's offspring would build a *bet* (temple) for God (2Sa 7:11–16). Through God's grace, Solomon implemented the promise made to his father David.

5:4 rest on every side. The rest that many of Israel's leaders had long hoped and longed for (Ex 33:14; Dt 25:19; Jos 1:13,15; 2Sa 7:11) had become a reality.

5:5 the Name of the LORD. In Old Testament times a name often revealed something of a person's character and identity (Ge 2:19; 17:5; 32:28; Ex 3:13–14; 6:2–3; 20:24; Dt 12:5). See *WCF* 22.2 **Your son.** Solomon explicitly referred to God's promise in 2 Samuel 7:12–13.

5:6 cedars of Lebanon. Trees famous in the ancient Near East and often used in building royal palaces and temples. **no one so skilled.** The Israelites lacked the requisite craftsmen and artisans to begin construction of the temple by themselves. **Sidonians.** In a narrow sense, the residents of the port city of Sidon, north of Tyre. Here the term probably refers collectively to all the inhabitants of Tyre, Gebal (Byblos) and Sidon (these people were later called the Phoenicians).

7When Hiram heard Solomon's message, he was greatly pleased and said, "Praise be
to the LORD today, for he has given David a wise son to rule over this great nation."
8So Hiram sent word to Solomon:

"I have received the message you sent me and will do all you want in providing the cedar and pine logs. 9My men will haul them down from Lebanon to the
sea[q], and I will float them in rafts by sea to the place you specify. There I will separate them and you can take them away. And you are to grant my wish by providing food[r] for my royal household."

10In this way Hiram kept Solomon supplied with all the cedar and pine logs he wanted, 11and Solomon gave Hiram twenty thousand cors[a] of wheat as food for his household,
in addition to twenty thousand baths[b,c] of pressed olive oil. Solomon continued to do this
for Hiram year after year. 12The LORD gave Solomon wisdom,[s] just as he had promised
him. There were peaceful relations between Hiram and Solomon, and the two of them
made a treaty.[t]

13King Solomon conscripted laborers[u] from all Israel—thirty thousand men. 14He sent
them off to Lebanon in shifts of ten thousand a month, so that they spent one month in
Lebanon and two months at home. Adoniram[v] was in charge of the forced labor. 15Sol-
omon had seventy thousand carriers and eighty thousand stonecutters in the hills, 16as
well as thirty-three hundred[d] foremen[w] who supervised the project and directed the
workmen. 17At the king's command they removed from the quarry[x] large blocks of
quality stone[y] to provide a foundation of dressed stone for the temple. 18The craftsmen
of Solomon and Hiram and the men of Gebal[e][z] cut and prepared the timber and stone
for the building of the temple.

Solomon Builds the Temple

6 In the four hundred and eightieth[f] year after the Israelites had come out of Egypt,
in the fourth year of Solomon's reign over Israel, in the month of Ziv, the second
month, he began to build the temple of the LORD.[a]
2The temple[b] that King Solomon built for the LORD was sixty cubits long, twenty wide
and thirty high.[g] 3The portico at the front of the main hall of the temple extended the
width of the temple, that is twenty cubits,[h] and projected ten cubits[i] from the front of the

5:9 [q]Ezr 3:7 [r]Eze 27:17; Ac 12:20
5:12 [s]1Ki 3:12 [t]Am 1:9
5:13 [u]1Ki 9:15
5:14 [v]1Ki 4:6; 2Ch 10:18
5:16 [w]1Ki 9:23
5:17 [x]1Ki 6:7 [y]1Ch 22:2
5:18 [z]Jos 13:5
6:1 [a]Ac 7:47
6:2 [b]Eze 41:1

[a] *11* That is, probably about 125,000 bushels (about 4,400 kiloliters) [b] *11* Septuagint (see also 2 Chron. 2:10); Hebrew *twenty cors* [c] *11* That is, about 115,000 gallons (about 440 kiloliters) [d] *16* Hebrew; some Septuagint manuscripts (see also 2 Chron. 2:2,18) *thirty-six hundred* [e] *18* That is, Byblos [f] *1* Hebrew; Septuagint *four hundred and fortieth* [g] *2* That is, about 90 feet (about 27 meters) long and 30 feet (about 9 meters) wide and 45 feet (about 13.5 meters) high [h] *3* That is, about 30 feet (about 9 meters) [i] *3* That is, about 15 feet (about 4.5 meters)

5:7 Praise be to the LORD today. Even a non-Israelite king acknowledged the accomplishments of Israel's God through King Solomon (cf. 10:6–9).
5:9 food for my royal household. In exchange for the help Hiram granted, Solomon was expected to supply food for Hiram's court (v. 11) and wages for his workers (v. 6).
5:11 pressed olive oil. This was a high-quality resource.
5:12 The LORD gave Solomon wisdom. Solomon's administrative and political talents are again associated with God's gift of wisdom. (cf. Dt 1:15; Isa 11:2–4). **made a treaty.** Solomon and Hiram solidified their relationship by establishing a formal covenant between their two states.
■ **5:13–18** *Conscripted Laborers.* Solomon also forced laborers to work on the preparations for and construction of the temple.
5:13 conscripted laborers from all Israel. According to Mosaic Law (Lev 25:39), Israelites were not to be used as forced laborers. Solomon distinguished between Israelites and foreigners in this regard (see notes on 9:20,22), but this policy still caused considerable indignation among (northern) Israelites and contributed in no small way to the division of the kingdom following Solomon's death (see notes on 12:4,16).
5:14 Adoniram. See note on Adoniram at 4:6.
5:15 seventy thousand carriers. These porters hauled the material the stone cutters quarried.
5:18 the men of Gebal. Gebal (or Byblos) was internationally recognized for its trade in papyrus, the ancient form of paper.
■ **6:1—7:51** *Construction of the Temple and Palace.* Solomon undertook two main building projects: the temple and his own palace. Attention to the temple (6:1–38) and its furnishings (7:13–51) frames the notice of his palace construction (7:1–12).
■ **6:1–38** *The Temple Construction.* Solomon built the temple for God in seven years.
6:1 four hundred and eightieth year. See NIV text note. The author's chronology reflects how momentous the construction of the temple was for Israel's life. The building of the temple under Solomon represents the culmination of a long series of events that began with the deliverance from Egypt. The great love the Israelites had for the temple is evident in the meticulous detail with which the author describes it. **fourth year of Solomon's reign.** Approximately 966 B.C. (see "Introduction: Characteristics and Themes"), placing the exodus in 1446 B.C. Some interpreters believe that the exodus did not occur until the thirteenth century B.C. They understand the "four hundred and eightieth year" in one of two ways. Some hold 480 to be a figurative number representing 12 generations of approximately 40 years each (the actual length of a generation may vary). Others, on the basis of ancient Near Eastern techniques of recording chronology, argue that the figure represents the total of a sequence of periods, some of which may have been partially concurrent. **month of Ziv.** In the spring (April–May).
6:2 temple. There are a number of similarities between the tabernacle and the temple, although the temple was approximately double the tabernacle in size (Ex 26:15–30; 36:20–34). Both were divided into three main sections: the portico, the Holy Place (main hall) and the Most Holy Place (inner sanctuary). This tripartite structure was common in ancient Near Eastern temples. Israel's sanctuary radically differed from a pagan sanctuary, however, having at its center the ark of the covenant with the Ten Commandments—the moral will of God that ordered Israel's life—rather than an idol, representing some force of nature, that the people manipulated (Dt 10:4–5; 1Ki 8:6–9).

temple. 4He made narrow clerestory windows[c] in the temple. 5Against the walls of the
main hall and inner sanctuary he built a structure around the building, in which there
were side rooms.[d] 6The lowest floor was five cubits[a] wide, the middle floor six cubits[b] and
the third floor seven.[c] He made offset ledges around the outside of the temple so that
nothing would be inserted into the temple walls.
7In building the temple, only blocks dressed[e] at the quarry were used, and no hammer, chisel or any other iron tool[f] was heard at the temple site while it was being built.
8The entrance to the lowest[d] floor was on the south side of the temple; a stairway led up
to the middle level and from there to the third. 9So he built the temple and completed it, roofing it with beams and cedar[g] planks. 10And he built the side rooms all along the temple. The
height of each was five cubits, and they were attached to the temple by beams of cedar.
11The word of the LORD came to Solomon: 12"As for this temple you are building, if you
follow my decrees, carry out my regulations and keep all my commands and obey them,
I will fulfill through you the promise[h] I gave to David your father. 13And I will live among
the Israelites and will not abandon[i] my people Israel."

6:4 [c]Eze 40:16; 41:16
6:5 [d]ver 16,19-21; Eze 41:5-6
6:7 [e]Ex 20:25 [f]Dt 27:5
6:9 [g]ver 14,38
6:12 [h]2Sa 7:12-16; 1Ki 2:4; 9:5
6:13 [i]Ex 25:8; Lev 26:11; Dt 31:6; Heb 13:5

[a] *6* That is, about 7 1/2 feet (about 2.3 meters); also in verses 10 and 24 [b] *6* That is, about 9 feet (about 2.7 meters) [c] *6* That is, about 10 1/2 feet (about 3.1 meters) [d] *8* Septuagint; Hebrew *middle*

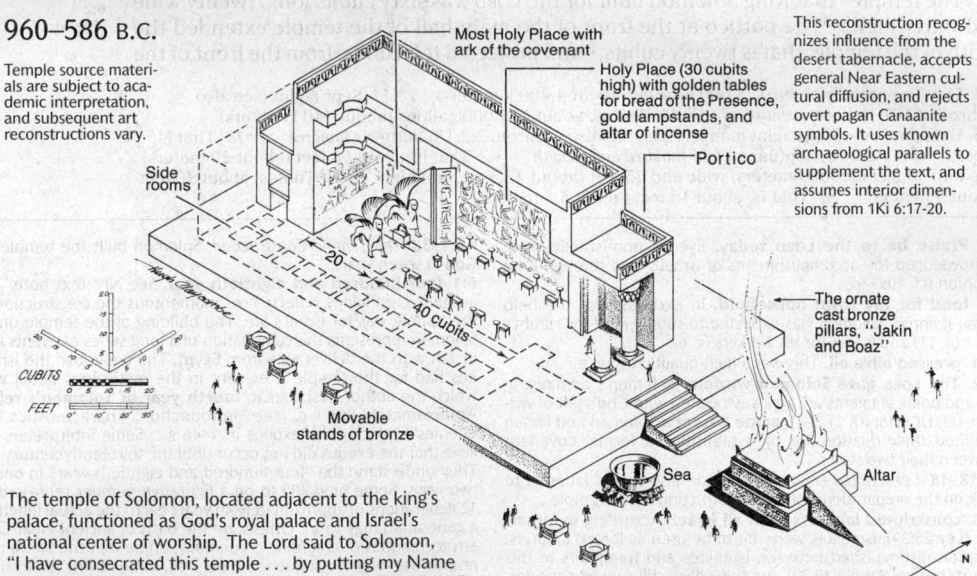

6:4 narrow clerestory windows. Wide on the inner side of the wall, these windows would gradually slope to form a slit on the outer wall.
6:5 side rooms. Rooms that surrounded the Most Holy Place and the Holy Place, but not the portico, and were used for storage.
6:6 The lowest floor. The height of these three stories of side rooms was less than that of the main temple.
6:8 entrance to the lowest floor. That is, to the side rooms.
6:11 The word of the LORD came to Solomon. God characteristically spoke to Solomon not through other prophets but directly, as though Solomon himself were a prophet (3:5,11–14; 9:2–9; 11:11–13).
6:12 if you follow my decrees. With special reference to the building of the temple, God reiterated to Solomon that the continuance and fulfillment of the promises to David required covenant fidelity on Solomon's part (see notes on 2:2–4).
6:13 will not abandon my people. The existence of the temple did not in and of itself vouchsafe the presence of God with Israel. Loyalty to the covenant was the main issue in the people's relationship with God (see note on 2:2; see 9:6–9).

Solomon's Temple

960–586 B.C.

Temple source materials are subject to academic interpretation, and subsequent art reconstructions vary.

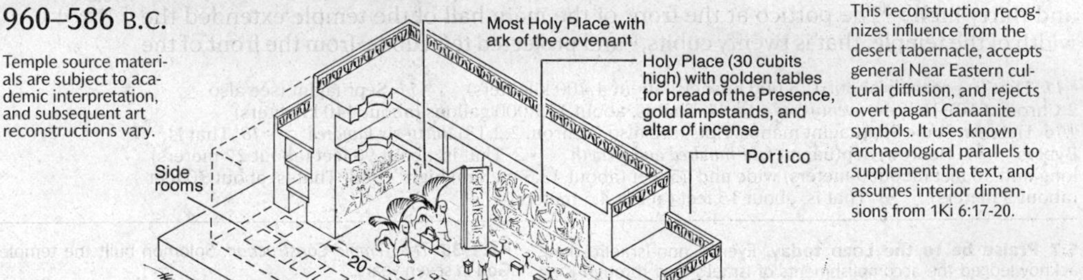

This reconstruction recognizes influence from the desert tabernacle, accepts general Near Eastern cultural diffusion, and rejects overt pagan Canaanite symbols. It uses known archaeological parallels to supplement the text, and assumes interior dimensions from 1Ki 6:17-20.

The temple of Solomon, located adjacent to the king's palace, functioned as God's royal palace and Israel's national center of worship. The Lord said to Solomon, "I have consecrated this temple . . . by putting my Name there forever. My eyes and my heart will always be there" (1Ki 9:3). By its cosmological and royal symbolism, the sanctuary taught the absolute sovereignty of the Lord over the whole creation and his special headship over Israel.

The floor plan is a type that has a long history in Semitic religion, particularly among the West Semites. An early example of the tripartite division into portico, main hall and inner sanctuary has been found at Syrian Ebla (c. 2300 B.C.) and, much later but more contemporaneous with Solomon, at Tell Tainat in the Orontes basin (c. 900 B.C.). Like Solomon's, the temple at Tell Tainat had three divisions, had two columns supporting the entrance, and was located adjacent to the royal palace.

Many archaeological parallels can be drawn to the methods of construction used in the temple, e.g., the "stone and cedar beam" technique described in 1Ki 6:36. Interestingly, evidence for the largest bronze-casting industry ever found in the Holy Land comes from the same locale and period as that indicated in Scripture: Zarethan in the Jordan Valley c. 1000 B.C.

14 So Solomon built the temple and completed[j] it. 15 He lined its interior walls with cedar boards, paneling them from the floor of the temple to the ceiling,[k] and covered the
floor of the temple with planks of pine. 16 He partitioned off twenty cubits[a] at the rear of
the temple with cedar boards from floor to ceiling to form within the temple an inner
sanctuary, the Most Holy Place.[l] 17 The main hall in front of this room was forty cubits[b]
long. 18 The inside of the temple was cedar,[m] carved with gourds and open flowers. Everything was cedar; no stone was to be seen.
19 He prepared the inner sanctuary[n] within the temple to set the ark of the covenant[o] of the LORD there. 20 The inner sanctuary[p] was twenty cubits long, twenty wide
and twenty high.[c] He overlaid the inside with pure gold, and he also overlaid the altar
of cedar. 21 Solomon covered the inside of the temple with pure gold, and he extended
gold chains across the front of the inner sanctuary, which was overlaid with gold. 22 So
he overlaid the whole interior with gold. He also overlaid with gold the altar that belonged to the inner sanctuary.
23 In the inner sanctuary he made a pair of cherubim[q] of olive wood, each ten cubits[d]
high. 24 One wing of the first cherub was five cubits long, and the other wing five cubits—
ten cubits from wing tip to wing tip. 25 The second cherub also measured ten cubits, for
the two cherubim were identical in size and shape. 26 The height of each cherub was ten
cubits. 27 He placed the cherubim[r] inside the innermost room of the temple, with their
wings spread out. The wing of one cherub touched one wall, while the wing of the other touched the other wall, and their wings touched each other in the middle of the room.
28 He overlaid the cherubim with gold.
29 On the walls all around the temple, in both the inner and outer rooms, he carved
cherubim,[s] palm trees and open flowers. 30 He also covered the floors of both the inner
and outer rooms of the temple with gold.
31 For the entrance of the inner sanctuary he made doors of olive wood with five sid
ed jambs. 32 And on the two olive wood doors he carved cherubim, palm trees and open
flowers, and overlaid the cherubim and palm trees with beaten gold. 33 In the same way
he made four-sided jambs of olive wood for the entrance to the main hall. 34 He also made
two pine doors, each having two leaves that turned in sockets. 35 He carved cherubim,
palm trees and open flowers on them and overlaid them with gold hammered evenly over
the carvings.
36 And he built the inner courtyard of three courses[t] of dressed stone and one course
of trimmed cedar beams.
37 The foundation of the temple of the LORD was laid in the fourth year, in the month
of Ziv. 38 In the eleventh year in the month of Bul, the eighth month, the temple was finished in all its details according to its specifications.[u] He had spent seven years building it.

Solomon Builds His Palace

7 It took Solomon thirteen years, however, to complete the construction of his palace.[v] 2 He built the Palace[w] of the Forest of Lebanon[x] a hundred cubits long, fifty

6:14 [j]ver 9,38
6:15 [k]1Ki 7:7
6:16 [l]Ex 26:33; Lev 16:2; 1Ki 8:6
6:18 [m]1Ki 7:24; Ps 74:6
6:19 [n]1Ki 8:6 [o]1Sa 3:3
6:20 [p]Eze 41:3-4
6:23 [q]Ex 37:1-9
6:27 [r]Ex 25:20; 37:9; 1Ki 8:7; 2Ch 5:8
6:29 [s]ver 32,35
6:36 [t]1Ki 7:12; Ezr 6:4
6:38 [u]Heb 8:5
7:1 [v]1Ki 9:10; 2Ch 8:1
7:2 [w]2Sa 7:2 [x]1Ki 10:17; 2Ch 9:16

[a] *16* That is, about 30 feet (about 9 meters) [b] *17* That is, about 60 feet (about 18 meters) [c] *20* That is, about 30 feet (about 9 meters) long, wide and high [d] *23* That is, about 15 feet (about 4.5 meters)

6:16 an inner sanctuary, the Most Holy Place. The Most Holy Place, a perfect cube of about 30 feet in each direction (v. 20), was the most sacred area of the temple. It contained the "ark of the covenant" (v. 19) and the cherubim. Only the high priest was allowed to enter this room and then only on one day each year, the Day of Atonement (Hebrew, *Yom Kippur;* Lev 16; 23:26–32; Nu 29:7–11). The inner sanctuary of the tabernacle was also called the Most Holy Place (Ex 26:33; Lev 16:2,16–17,20,23). See Hebrews 9:12 and 14.
6:19 the ark of the covenant of the LORD. A central religious symbol of the Israelite people's communion with God, the ark contained the two tablets of the covenant (Dt 9:9), which structured the divine-human relationship. The ark had moved about with the people as they journeyed from Sinai to the promised land (Ex 25:21; Dt 10:5; 1Sa 4:11; 7:2; 2Sa 7:6–7). Now that a stationary sanctuary had been built, it was appropriate for Solomon to place the ark there permanently.
6:20 overlaid the inside with pure gold. Egyptian, Babylonian and Assyrian kings were also fond of plating the interior of the temples they built with silver and gold. The lavishly decorated interior of the temple in Jerusalem made it both aesthetically impressive and economically valuable. In its glory and beauty, it was a symbol of God's heavenly temple (8:36,39; Heb 9:11).
6:22 the altar that belonged to the inner sanctuary. This was probably an incense altar (7:48; Ex 30:1,6; 37:25–28; Heb 9:3–4).
6:23 pair of cherubim. These were winged, symbolic figures, with human faces (cf. Ge 3:24; 1Ki 8:6–7; Eze 41:8–9). The two cherubim stood as guardians on either side of the ark (8:6–7; 2Ch 3:10–13). The tips of their unfolded wings reached ten cubits high, or half the height of the Most Holy Place itself (v. 16). In ancient Canaan, kings were sometimes depicted as sitting upon thrones supported by cherubim. In Israel, where making an image of God was expressly forbidden, there is no such image of the heavenly King (Ex 20:4). God was not represented by an idol but was visibly present with his people and associated himself in a special way with this place of worship (1Sa 4:4; 6:2; 1Ki 8:10–13; 2Ki 19:15; Pss 80:1; 99:1).
6:29 cherubim, palm trees and open flowers. Images reminiscent of the Garden of Eden in Genesis 2–3. Although humanity had been expelled from Paradise because of its rebellion against God (Ge 3:24), communion with God was and is still possible through his grace.
6:36 the inner courtyard. Part of the forecourt of the temple, where the great altar and the molten Sea were situated (cf. 7:23–26). **three courses.** For each three layers of stone, there was one layer of cedar beams (cf. Ex 6:4). Similar constructions have been unearthed at Megiddo.
6:37 the fourth year. That is, of Solomon's reign (v. 1).
■ **7:1–12** *The Palace Construction.* Solomon built a palace for himself. This project displayed his wisdom and glory but also hinted at his mixed motivations.

wide and thirty high,[a] with four rows of cedar columns supporting trimmed cedar
beams. 3 It was roofed with cedar above the beams that rested on the columns—forty-five
beams, fifteen to a row. 4 Its windows were placed high in sets of three, facing each other. 5 All the doorways had rectangular frames; they were in the front part in sets of three,
facing each other.[b]
6 He made a colonnade fifty cubits long and thirty wide.[c] In front of it was a portico,
and in front of that were pillars and an overhanging roof.
7 He built the throne hall, the Hall of Justice, where he was to judge,[y] and he covered
it with cedar from floor to ceiling.[d][z] 8 And the palace in which he was to live, set farther
back, was similar in design. Solomon also made a palace like this hall for Pharaoh's
daughter, whom he had married.[a]
9 All these structures, from the outside to the great courtyard and from foundation to
eaves, were made of blocks of high-grade stone cut to size and trimmed with a saw on
their inner and outer faces. 10 The foundations were laid with large stones of good quality, some measuring ten cubits[e] and some eight.[f] 11 Above were high-grade stones, cut
to size, and cedar beams. 12 The great courtyard was surrounded by a wall of three
courses[b] of dressed stone and one course of trimmed cedar beams, as was the inner
courtyard of the temple of the LORD with its portico.

The Temple's Furnishings

13 King Solomon sent to Tyre and brought Huram,[g][c] 14 whose mother was a widow
from the tribe of Naphtali and whose father was a man of Tyre and a craftsman in bronze.
Huram was highly skilled[d] and experienced in all kinds of bronze work. He came to King
Solomon and did all[e] the work assigned to him.
15 He cast two bronze pillars,[f] each eighteen cubits high and twelve cubits around,[h]
by line. 16 He also made two capitals[g] of cast bronze to set on the tops of the pillars; each
capital was five cubits[i] high. 17 A network of interwoven chains festooned the capitals on
top of the pillars, seven for each capital. 18 He made pomegranates in two rows[j] encircling
each network to decorate the capitals on top of the pillars.[k] He did the same for each capital. 19 The capitals on top of the pillars in the portico were in the shape of lilies, four cubits[l] high. 20 On the capitals of both pillars, above the bowl-shaped part next to the network, were the two hundred pomegranates[h] in rows all around. 21 He erected the pillars
at the portico of the temple. The pillar to the south he named Jakin[m] and the one to the
north Boaz.[n][i] 22 The capitals on top were in the shape of lilies. And so the work on the
pillars was completed.
23 He made the Sea[j] of cast metal, circular in shape, measuring ten cubits[e] from rim

7:7 [y]Ps 122:5; Pr 20:8 [z]1Ki 6:15
7:8 [a]1Ki 3:1; 2Ch 8:11
7:12 [b]1Ki 6:36
7:13 [c]2Ch 2:13
7:14 [d]Ex 31:2-5; 35:31; 36:1; 2Ch 2:14 [e]2Ch 4:11,16
7:15 [f]2Ki 25:17; 2Ch 3:15; 4:12; 52:17,21
7:16 [g]2Ki 25:17
7:20 [h]2Ch 3:16; 4:13; Jer 52:23
7:21 [i]1Ki 6:3; 2Ch 3:17
7:23 [j]2Ki 25:13; 1Ch 18:8; Jer 52:17

[a] *2* That is, about 150 feet (about 46 meters) long, 75 feet (about 23 meters) wide and 45 feet (about 13.5 meters) high [b] *5* The meaning of the Hebrew for this verse is uncertain. [c] *6* That is, about 75 feet (about 23 meters) long and 45 feet (about 13.5 meters) wide [d] *7* Vulgate and Syriac; Hebrew *floor* [e] *10,23* That is, about 15 feet (about 4.5 meters) [f] *10* That is, about 12 feet (about 3.6 meters) [g] *13* Hebrew *Hiram,* a variant of *Huram;* also in verses 40 and 45 [h] *15* That is, about 27 feet (about 8.1 meters) high and 18 feet (about 5.4 meters) around [i] *16* That is, about 7 1/2 feet (about 2.3 meters); also in verse 23 [j] *18* Two Hebrew manuscripts and Septuagint; most Hebrew manuscripts *made the pillars, and there were two rows* [k] *18* Many Hebrew manuscripts and Syriac; most Hebrew manuscripts *pomegranates* [l] *19* That is, about 6 feet (about 1.8 meters); also in verse 38 [m] *21* *Jakin* probably means *he establishes.* [n] *21* *Boaz* probably means *in him is strength.*

7:1 thirteen years. It took Solomon almost twice as long to build his palace as it did to construct the temple. This may be a subtle foreshadowing of Solomon's later preoccupation with his own splendor at the cost of desecrating worship at the temple (see note on 9:26—11:13).
7:2 the Palace of the Forest of Lebanon. Probably so named because of the extensive use of Lebanon cedar inside. This complex was probably located immediately south of the temple. **a hundred cubits long, fifty wide and thirty high.** Although the same height as the temple, Solomon's palace was considerably longer and more than twice as wide (6:2).
7:6 colonnade. Two-thirds the length of the palace and of the same width (v. 2), this colonnade probably served as an impressive entrance hall to the palace.
7:7 the Hall of Justice. The place where Solomon formally carried out his duties as administrator of God's holy kingdom. See note on "came to the king" at 3:16.
■ **7:13–51** *Furnishings for the Temple.* The author's keen interest in the temple over the palace is evident in the way he returned to the theme of the temple (see note at 6:1–38).
7:13 Solomon sent to Tyre. Although this account is placed after that of the construction of the temple and the palace, this arrangement is partly structural and not chronological. Solomon began making arrangements for equipping the temple with furniture before its actual completion (2Ch 2:7,13–14). **Huram.** His full name was Huram-abi (2Ch 2:12–13), and he should not be confused with Hiram, the king of Tyre, with whom Solomon ratified a treaty (5:1–12).
7:15 two bronze pillars. The pillars were erected on either side of the temple's entrance (v. 21). Although these pillars made the temple impressive to behold, it is unclear whether they were freestanding or supported a roof structure that possibly comprised a portico of the temple.
7:18–20 capitals. It was common in the ancient Near East to lavish capitals with ornate decoration.
7:21 The pillar to the south . . . the one to the north. Hence, the temple faced east. For the names of the two pillars, see the NIV text note.
7:23 the Sea of cast metal. A huge circular basin holding up to 12,000 gallons of water. According to the Chronicler, the Sea was used for priestly cleansing (2Ch 4:6). The symbolic significance of this object is disputed. Some scholars highlight the positive

to rim and five cubits high. It took a line of thirty cubits[a] to measure around it. [24]Below
the rim, gourds encircled it—ten to a cubit. The gourds were cast in two rows in one
piece with the Sea.
[25]The Sea stood on twelve bulls,[k] three facing north, three facing west, three facing
south and three facing east. The Sea rested on top of them, and their hindquarters were
toward the center. [26]It was a handbreadth[b] in thickness, and its rim was like the rim of
a cup, like a lily blossom. It held two thousand baths.[c]
[27]He also made ten movable stands[l] of bronze; each was four cubits long, four wide
and three high.[d] [28]This is how the stands were made: They had side panels attached to
uprights. [29]On the panels between the uprights were lions, bulls and cherubim—and on
the uprights as well. Above and below the lions and bulls were wreaths of hammered
work. [30]Each stand[m] had four bronze wheels with bronze axles, and each had a basin
resting on four supports, cast with wreaths on each side. [31]On the inside of the stand
there was an opening that had a circular frame one cubit[e] deep. This opening was round,
and with its basework it measured a cubit and a half.[f] Around its opening there was engraving. The panels of the stands were square, not round. [32]The four wheels were under
the panels, and the axles of the wheels were attached to the stand. The diameter of each

7:25 [k]2Ch 4:4-5; Jer 52:20
7:27 [l]ver 38; 2Ch 4:14
7:30 [m]2Ki 16:17

[a] *23* That is, about 45 feet (about 13.5 meters) [b] *26* That is, about 3 inches (about 8 centimeters)
[c] *26* That is, probably about 11,500 gallons (about 44 kiloliters); the Septuagint does not have this sentence. [d] *27* That is, about 6 feet (about 1.8 meters) long and wide and about 4 1/2 feet (about 1.3 meters) high [e] *31* That is, about 1 1/2 feet (about 0.5 meter) [f] *31* That is, about 2 1/4 feet (about 0.7 meter); also in verse 32

attributes of water as life-giving, while others argue that God's triumph over the unruly and chaotic sea is in view. While "sea" is deified among some of Israel's neighbors, the sea is depicted merely as God's passive instrument in the defeat of the Egyptians (Ex 15:4-10). The molten Sea would thus commemorate God's power over the forces of chaos (cf. Ge 1:2), typified by the sea. See Revelation 21:1.
7:25 twelve bulls. The Sea rested upon four triads of bulls arranged according to the four points of the compass. In the ancient Near East, bulls symbolized physical and reproductive potency. Their arrangement indicated God's universal lordship.
7:27 ten movable stands of bronze. These portable and highly decorated wagons held water basins (v. 38). The priests used the water from these stands to wash sections of animals that had been slaughtered for burnt offerings (Lev 1:9,13; 2Ch 4:6).

Temple Furnishings

Glimpses of the rich ornamentation of Solomon's temple can be gained through recent discoveries that illumine the text of 1Ki 6-7.

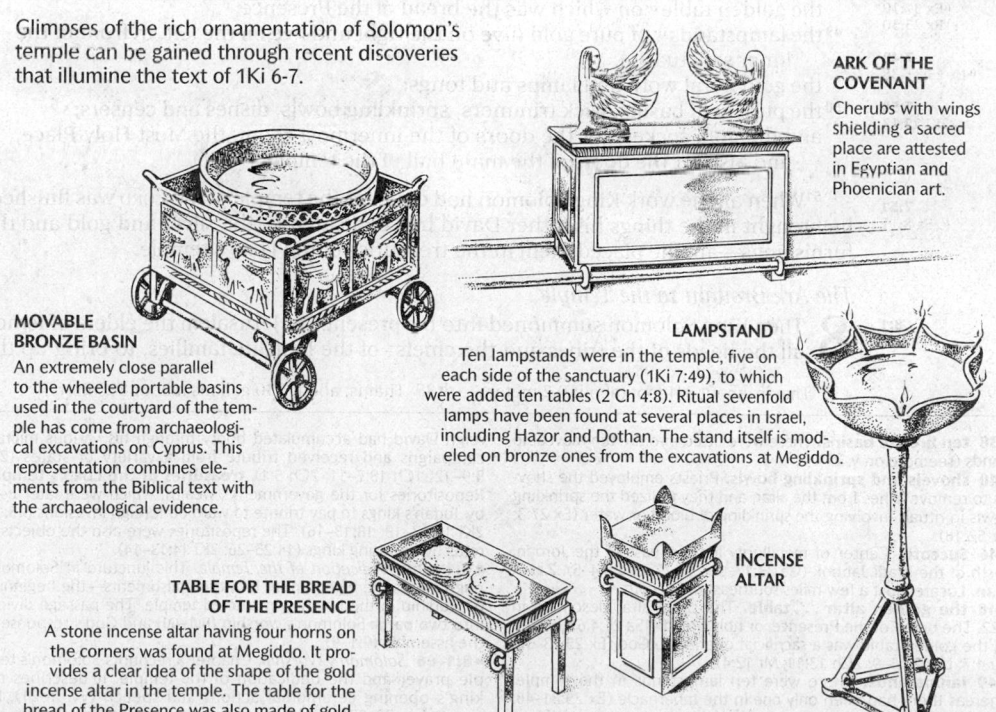

ARK OF THE COVENANT
Cherubs with wings shielding a sacred place are attested in Egyptian and Phoenician art.

MOVABLE BRONZE BASIN
An extremely close parallel to the wheeled portable basins used in the courtyard of the temple has come from archaeological excavations on Cyprus. This representation combines elements from the Biblical text with the archaeological evidence.

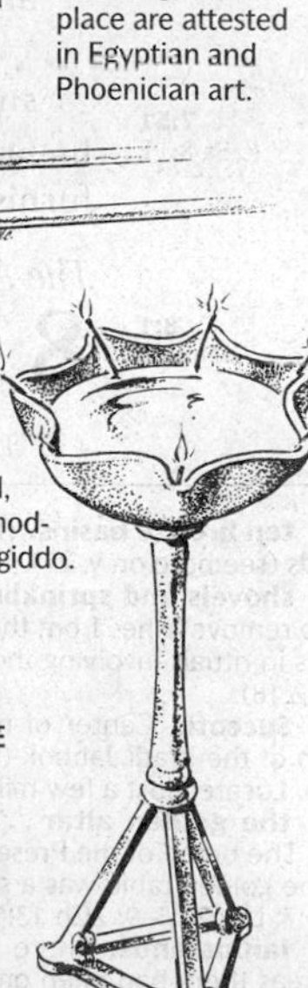

LAMPSTAND
Ten lampstands were in the temple, five on each side of the sanctuary (1Ki 7:49), to which were added ten tables (2 Ch 4:8). Ritual sevenfold lamps have been found at several places in Israel, including Hazor and Dothan. The stand itself is modeled on bronze ones from the excavations at Megiddo.

INCENSE ALTAR

TABLE FOR THE BREAD OF THE PRESENCE
A stone incense altar having four horns on the corners was found at Megiddo. It provides a clear idea of the shape of the gold incense altar in the temple. The table for the bread of the Presence was also made of gold.

wheel was a cubit and a half. 33 The wheels were made like chariot wheels; the axles,
rims, spokes and hubs were all of cast metal.
34 Each stand had four handles, one on each corner, projecting from the stand. 35 At
the top of the stand there was a circular band half a cubit[a] deep. The supports and panels were attached to the top of the stand. 36 He engraved cherubim, lions and palm trees
on the surfaces of the supports and on the panels, in every available space, with wreaths
all around. 37 This is the way he made the ten stands. They were all cast in the same molds
7:38 [n]Ex 30:18; 2Ch 4:6 and were identical in size and shape.
38 He then made ten bronze basins,[n] each holding forty baths[b] and measuring four cubits across, one basin to go on each of the ten stands. 39 He placed five of the stands on
the south side of the temple and five on the north. He placed the Sea on the south side,
at the southeast corner of the temple. 40 He also made the basins and shovels and sprinkling bowls.
So Huram finished all the work he had undertaken for King Solomon in the temple
of the LORD:

41 the two pillars;
the two bowl-shaped capitals on top of the pillars;
the two sets of network decorating the two bowl-shaped capitals on top of the pillars;
7:42 [o]ver 20 42 the four hundred pomegranates for the two sets of network (two rows of pomegranates for each network, decorating the bowl-shaped capitals[o] on top of the
pillars);
43 the ten stands with their ten basins;
7:45 [p]Ex 27:3 44 the Sea and the twelve bulls under it;
45 the pots, shovels and sprinkling bowls.[p]

7:46 [q]2Ch 4:17 [r]Ge 33:17; Jos 13:27 [s]Jos 3:16 All these objects that Huram made for King Solomon for the temple of the LORD were
of burnished bronze. 46 The king had them cast in clay molds in the plain[q] of the Jordan
between Succoth[r] and Zarethan.[s] 47 Solomon left all these things unweighed,[t] because
there were so many; the weight of the bronze was not determined.
7:47 [t]1Ch 22:3 48 Solomon also made all the furnishings that were in the LORD's temple:

7:48 [u]Ex 37:10 [v]Ex 25:30 the golden altar;
the golden table[u] on which was the bread of the Presence;[v]
49 the lampstands[w] of pure gold (five on the right and five on the left, in front of the
7:49 [w]Ex 25:31-38 inner sanctuary);
the gold floral work and lamps and tongs;
7:50 [x]2Ki 25:13 50 the pure gold basins, wick trimmers, sprinkling bowls, dishes and censers;[x]
and the gold sockets for the doors of the innermost room, the Most Holy Place,
and also for the doors of the main hall of the temple.

7:51 [y]2Sa 8:11 51 When all the work King Solomon had done for the temple of the LORD was finished,
he brought in the things his father David had dedicated[y]—the silver and gold and the
furnishings—and he placed them in the treasuries of the LORD's temple.

The Ark Brought to the Temple

8:1 [z]Nu 7:2 8 Then King Solomon summoned into his presence at Jerusalem the elders of Israel,
all the heads of the tribes and the chiefs[z] of the Israelite families, to bring up the

[a] *35* That is, about 3/4 foot (about 0.2 meter) [b] *38* That is, about 230 gallons (about 880 liters)

7:38 ten bronze basins. These were fitted into the ten moveable stands (see note on v. 27).
7:40 shovels and sprinkling bowls. Priests employed the shovels to remove ashes from the altar, and they utilized the sprinkling bowls in rituals involving the sprinkling of blood or water (Ex 27:3; Jer 52:18).
7:46 Succoth. Center of metallurgy located east of the Jordan, north of the Wadi Jabbok (Ge 33:17; Jos 13:27; Jdg 8:4–5). **Zarethan.** Located just a few miles southeast of Succoth.
7:48 the golden altar . . . table. The same altar described in 6:22. The bread of the Presence, or holy bread (1Sa 21:4,6), placed on the golden table was a sacrificial offering to God (Ex 25:23–30; Nu 4:7; Lev 24:5–9; 2Ch 13:11; Mt 12:4).
7:49 lampstands. There were ten lampstands in the temple, whereas there had been only one in the tabernacle (Ex 25:31–40; 26:35).
7:51 the things his father David had dedicated. During his reign David had accumulated booty through his various military campaigns and received tribute from a variety of states (2Sa 8:9–12; 1Ch 18:7–11; 2Ch 5:1). **treasuries of the LORD's temple.** Repositories for the government's wealth, which were later used by Judah's kings to pay tribute to ward off foreign invasions (15:18; 2Ki 12:17–18; 18:13–16). The repositories were also the objects of raids by opposing kings (14:25–26; 2Ki 14:13–14).
■ **8:1—9:9** *Dedication of the Temple.* This juncture in Solomon's reign marks the highpoint of his accomplishments—the beginning of worship in the newly constructed temple. The passage divides into two parts: Solomon's worship (8:1–66) and God's response to the assembly (9:1–9).
■ **8:1–66** *Solomon's Worship.* Chapter 8 recounts Solomon's temple prayer and the dedication of the temple. It describes the king's opening ceremonial actions and speech (vv. 1–21), his prayer (vv. 22–53) and his closing ceremonial actions and speech (vv. 54–66).

ark[a] of the LORD's covenant from Zion, the City of David.[b] 2All the men of Israel came together to King Solomon at the time of the festival[c] in the month of Ethanim, the seventh
month.[d]
3When all the elders of Israel had arrived, the priests[e] took up the ark, 4and they
brought up the ark of the LORD and the Tent of Meeting[f] and all the sacred furnishings
in it. The priests and Levites carried them up, 5and King Solomon and the entire assembly of Israel that had gathered about him were before the ark, sacrificing[g] so many sheep
and cattle that they could not be recorded or counted.
6The priests then brought the ark of the LORD's covenant[h] to its place in the inner
sanctuary of the temple, the Most Holy Place, and put it beneath the wings of the cherubim.[i] 7The cherubim spread their wings over the place of the ark and overshadowed the
ark and its carrying poles. 8These poles were so long that their ends could be seen from
the Holy Place in front of the inner sanctuary, but not from outside the Holy Place; and
they are still there today.[j] 9There was nothing in the ark except the two stone tablets[k]
that Moses had placed in it at Horeb, where the LORD made a covenant with the Israelites after they came out of Egypt.
10When the priests withdrew from the Holy Place, the cloud[l] filled the temple of the
LORD. 11And the priests could not perform their service because of the cloud, for the glory of the LORD filled his temple.
12Then Solomon said, "The LORD has said that he would dwell in a dark cloud;[m] 13I
have indeed built a magnificent temple for you, a place for you to dwell[n] forever."
14While the whole assembly of Israel was standing there, the king turned around and
blessed[o] them. 15Then he said:

"Praise be to the LORD,[p] the God of Israel, who with his own hand has fulfilled
what he promised with his own mouth to my father David. For he said, 16'Since the
day I brought my people Israel out of Egypt, I have not chosen a city in any tribe
of Israel to have a temple built for my Name[q] to be there, but I have chosen[r] David[s] to rule my people Israel.'
17"My father David had it in his heart to build a temple[t] for the Name of the
LORD, the God of Israel. 18But the LORD said to my father David, 'Because it was in
your heart to build a temple for my Name, you did well to have this in your heart.
19Nevertheless, you[u] are not the one to build the temple, but your son, who is your
own flesh and blood—he is the one who will build the temple for my Name.'[v]
20"The LORD has kept the promise he made: I have succeeded David my father
and now I sit on the throne of Israel, just as the LORD promised, and I have built[w]
the temple for the Name of the LORD, the God of Israel. 21I have provided a place
there for the ark, in which is the covenant of the LORD that he made with our fathers when he brought them out of Egypt."

Solomon's Prayer of Dedication

22Then Solomon stood before the altar of the LORD in front of the whole assembly of
Israel, spread out his hands[x] toward heaven 23and said:

8:1 [a]2Sa 6:17 [b]2Sa 5:7
8:2 [c]2Ch 7:8 [d]Lev 23:34
8:3 [e]Nu 7:9; Jos 3:3
8:4 [f]1Ki 3:4; 2Ch 1:3
8:5 [g]2Sa 6:13
8:6 [h]2Sa 6:17 [i]1Ki 6:19,27
8:8 [j]Ex 25:13-15
8:9 [k]Ex 24:7-8; 25:21; 40:20; Dt 10:2-5; Heb 9:4
8:10 [l]Ex 40:34-35; 2Ch 7:1-2
8:12 [m]Ps 18:11; 97:2
8:13 [n]Ex 15:17; 2Sa 7:13; Ps 132:13
8:14 [o]2Sa 6:18
8:15 [p]2Sa 7:12-13; 1Ch 29:10,20; Ne 9:5; Lk 1:68
8:16 [q]Dt 12:5 [r]1Sa 16:1 [s]2Sa 7:4-6,8
8:17 [t]2Sa 7:2; 1Ch 17:1
8:19 [u]2Sa 7:5 [v]2Sa 7:13; 1Ki 5:3,5
8:20 [w]1Ch 28:6
8:22 [x]Ex 9:29; Ezr 9:5

■ **8:1–21** *Solomon's Opening Ceremonies and Speech.* Solomon opened the assembly of the people at the temple.
8:1 the elders of Israel. Senior local leaders in charge of local government and justice throughout Old Testament history (Ex 18:13–17; Nu 11:16–30; Jdg 21:16–24; 1Sa 8:1–9). **Zion, the city of David.** This was south of the temple in the southeastern section of the city. David had earlier brought up the ark from the house of Obed-Edom to Zion (2Sa 6:1–19).
8:2 the festival. Solomon apparently waited 11 months to dedicate the temple (6:38) in order to make the dedication a part of the Feast of Tabernacles in the New Year, which was commemorated during the seventh month (Lev 23:34; Dt 16:13–15). **Ethanim.** That is, Tishri, in the autumn (September–October).
8:4 the Tent of Meeting. The tabernacle, along with all its furnishings, was brought, presumably from Gibeon (1Sa 7:1; 1Ki 3:4), by the appropriate priests and the Levites.
8:6 beneath the wings of the cherubim. See note on 6:23.
8:8 poles. These were used to carry the ark. **today.** Statements to the effect of "they are still there today" or "to this day" (9:13,21; 10:12; 12:19) were written from the perspective of a writer who lived before the destruction of the temple in 586 B.C. See "Introduction: Author."
8:9 the two stone tablets. The two copies of the covenant (cf. v. 21; Ex 25:16,21; 31:18; 34:1; 40:20). **a covenant with the Israelites.** At Mount Sinai (Ex 19:1–9; 24:1–11).
8:10 the cloud filled the temple of the LORD. After the exodus from Egypt, God had led his people through the desert by a pillar of cloud by day and a pillar of fire by night (Ex 13:21; 14:24; 16:10; 33:10; Lev 16:2; Dt 4:11; 5:22; Ps 18:10–11). At Mount Sinai God had revealed himself in a cloud (Ex 19:9; 24:15–18) and upon the construction of the tabernacle had shown his approval by covering it with the cloud of his glory. Now God revealed his approval of the newly constructed sanctuary.
8:12 dwell in a dark cloud. No one can see God and live, but God can reveal himself and manifest his love toward his people in indirect ways (see note on v. 10).
8:13 a place for you to dwell forever. The temple, as a divinely sanctioned place for prayer and sacrifice, constituted a special sign of God's presence among his people (Pss 76:2; 132:13–14; Isa 8:18; Am 1:2).
8:15 what he promised . . . to my father David. See 2 Samuel 7:1–16.
■ **8:22–53** *Solomon's Prayer.* Solomon stood before God with requests about the future role of the temple in Israel's life. The writer of Kings expressed what he hoped his readers would expect from prayers directed toward the ruins of the temple and in the rebuilt temple after the exile.
8:22 spread out his hands. This gesture signified prayer (Ex 9:29; Isa 1:15; 1Ti 2:8).

"O LORD, God of Israel, there is no God like[y] you in heaven above or on earth
below—you who keep your covenant of love[z] with your servants who continue
wholeheartedly in your way. **24**You have kept your promise to your servant David
my father; with your mouth you have promised and with your hand you have fulfilled it—as it is today.
25"Now LORD, God of Israel, keep for your servant David my father the promises[a] you made to him when you said, 'You shall never fail to have a man to sit before me on the throne of Israel, if only your sons are careful in all they do to walk
before me as you have done.' **26**And now, O God of Israel, let your word that you
promised[b] your servant David my father come true.
27"But will God really dwell[c] on earth? The heavens, even the highest heaven,
cannot contain[d] you. How much less this temple I have built! **28**Yet give attention
to your servant's prayer and his plea for mercy, O LORD my God. Hear the cry and
the prayer that your servant is praying in your presence this day. **29**May your eyes
be open[e] toward[f] this temple night and day, this place of which you said, 'My
Name[g] shall be there,' so that you will hear the prayer your servant prays toward
this place. **30**Hear the supplication of your servant and of your people Israel when
they pray toward this place. Hear from heaven, your dwelling place, and when you
hear, forgive.[h]
31"When a man wrongs his neighbor and is required to take an oath and he
comes and swears the oath[i] before your altar in this temple, **32**then hear from
heaven and act. Judge between your servants, condemning the guilty and bringing down on his own head what he has done. Declare the innocent not guilty, and
so establish his innocence.[j]
33"When your people Israel have been defeated[k] by an enemy because they
have sinned[l] against you, and when they turn back to you and confess your
name, praying and making supplication to you in this temple, **34**then hear from
heaven and forgive the sin of your people Israel and bring them back to the land
you gave to their fathers.
35"When the heavens are shut up and there is no rain[m] because your people have
sinned against you, and when they pray toward this place and confess your name
and turn from their sin because you have afflicted them, **36**then hear from heaven
and forgive the sin of your servants, your people Israel. Teach[n] them the right way[o]
to live, and send rain on the land you gave your people for an inheritance.
37"When famine[p] or plague comes to the land, or blight[q] or mildew, locusts or
grasshoppers, or when an enemy besieges them in any of their cities, whatever disaster or disease may come, **38**and when a prayer or plea is made by any of your
people Israel—each one aware of the afflictions of his own heart, and spreading
out his hands toward this temple— **39**then hear from heaven, your dwelling place.
Forgive and act; deal with each man according to all he does, since you know[r] his

8:23 [y]1Sa 2:2; 2Sa 7:22 [z]Dt 7:9,12; Ne 1:5; 9:32; Da 9:4
8:25 [a]1Ki 2:4
8:26 [b]2Sa 7:25
8:27 [c]Ac 7:48 [d]2Ch 2:6; Ps 139:7-16; Isa 66:1; Jer 23:24
8:29 [e]2Ch 7:15; Ne 1:6 [f]Da 6:10 [g]Dt 12:11
8:30 [h]Ps 85:2
8:31 [i]Ex 22:11
8:32 [j]Dt 25:1
8:33 [k]Lev 26:17; Dt 28:25 [l]Lev 26:39
8:35 [m]Lev 26:19; Dt 28:24
8:36 [n]1Sa 12:23; Ps 25:4; 94:12 [o]Ps 5:8; 27:11; Jer 6:16
8:37 [p]Lev 26:26 [q]Dt 28:22
8:39 [r]1Sa 16:7; 1Ch 28:9; Ps 11:4; Jer 17:10; Jn 2:24; Ac 1:24

8:23 there is no God like you. The incomparability of God is a prominent theme throughout the Scriptures (Ex 15:11; Dt 4:39; Ps 86:8; Mk 12:29; Eph 4:6; Rev 19:6). God's fidelity is not temporary (3:6; 8:16; Dt 7:9,12; Ps 52:8; Heb 13:8), nor is his power limited to a specific country (vv. 41–43; Jnh 1–4).
8:25 if only your sons are careful. Solomon reiterated a condition regarding the fulfillment of the promises to David of an everlasting dynasty over all of Israel—his sons were to remain faithful to God (2:2–4; 6:11–13; 9:4–9; 11:11–13). See *WLC* 133.
8:26 let your word . . . come true. God did not simply grant Solomon's request but rather held the question in abeyance, contingent upon Solomon's continuing loyalty (9:4–9).
8:27 The heavens . . . cannot contain you. Although the temple is a divinely approved location for worship, the heavens and earth cannot contain the God of the universe. See *WCF* 2.1; *WLC* 7.
8:29 My Name shall be there. Because God had promised to be present in a special way in the Jerusalem temple, Solomon implored him to be especially attentive to the prayers directed toward the temple. See the note on God's name at 5:5.
8:30 toward this place. Because in many cases Israelites were unable to travel to the temple, Solomon asked God to hear the requests of those who pray toward "this place" (Jnh 2:4; Da 6:10; 9:4,17). This included the readers of this book who lived in exile.
8:31 When a man wrongs his neighbor. In trial cases, when there was insufficient evidence to prosecute a suspect, the suspect might be required to take an oath of innocence at the sanctuary to corroborate his defense (Ex 22:7–12; Nu 5:11–31). Because the suspect took an oath, it was hoped that ensuing events (good or bad) would prove him or her either honest or dishonest. Solomon prayed that God, through his actions in the suspects' lives, would condemn the guilty and acquit the innocent (v. 32). See *WCF* 22.2.
8:33 because they have sinned against you. God's involvement with his people brought both blessings and curses (cf. Lev 26). Defeat by an enemy was not a defeat by that enemy's god but rather by God himself due to Israel's own infidelity (Dt 28:25; Jos 7; 2Ch 36:15–19; La 2:1–8).
8:34 bring them back to the land. It was not unusual for the members of a vanquished army or people to be deported to another land; hence Solomon prayed for God's mercy and restoration to those who would ask his forgiveness. This request fit well with the experience of the original readers.
8:35 When the heavens are shut up. Just as God directs wars, so also he controls the world of nature. Drought, like war (Dt 28:25), was one of the curses of the covenant (Dt 28:22–24; 1Ki 17:1; Am 4:7–8).
8:36 Teach them the right way. Solomon not only prayed that God would forgive his penitent people and heal the land, but also that the people might learn from their mistakes and be led by God into a more faithful lifestyle.
8:37 famine . . . disease. Solomon mentioned a variety of other afflictions that might befall the people: famine, (Lev 26:26), plague (Dt 28:21–22), locusts or grasshoppers (Dt 28:38,42), an enemy (Dt 28:52), disaster (Dt 28:61; 31:29; 32:23–25) and disease (Dt 28:22).
8:39 deal with each man according to all he does. Solomon prayed that God would use his infinite knowledge to establish justice among his people. See *WLC* 179.

heart (for you alone know the hearts of all men), 40so that they will fear[s] you all
the time they live in the land you gave our fathers.
41"As for the foreigner who does not belong to your people Israel but has
come from a distant land because of your name— 42for men will hear of your great
name and your mighty hand[t] and your outstretched arm—when he comes and
prays toward this temple, 43then hear from heaven, your dwelling place, and do
whatever the foreigner asks of you, so that all the peoples of the earth may know[u]
your name and fear[v] you, as do your own people Israel, and may know that this
house I have built bears your Name.
44"When your people go to war against their enemies, wherever you send
them, and when they pray to the LORD toward the city you have chosen and the
temple I have built for your Name, 45then hear from heaven their prayer and their
plea, and uphold their cause.
46"When they sin against you—for there is no one who does not sin[w]—and you

8:40 [s]Ps 130:4
8:42 [t]Dt 3:24
8:43 [u]1Sa 17:46; 2Ki 19:19 [v]Ps 102:15
8:46 [w]Pr 20:9; Ecc 7:20; Ro 3:9; 1Jn 1:8-10

8:41 As for the foreigner. Because the Lord's reputation extended beyond Israel's borders, foreigners would be attracted to Jerusalem to pay homage to God.
8:43 so that all the peoples of the earth may know your name. Solomon prayed that one day all peoples would commit their lives to God. Later, the prophets predicted that this would happen after restoration from exile, and the New Testament proclaimed the same through the ministry of the gospel (cf. Isa 56:6–8; Zec 8:3; Mt 28:19).
8:44 When your people go to war. Solomon referred to military endeavors taken at divine behest (20:13–30; Lev 26:7; Dt 20:1–20; 21:10; 1Sa 23:2,4; 2Sa 5:19,24).

The Presence of God: Where Are You, God?

WHERE is God? As simple as this question may appear at first, it is one of the most profound we can ask. It is a traditional theological query that Scripture answers in terms of God's being, God's providence and the experiences of encountering and worshiping God.

In a traditional, theological sense, we may say that God is everywhere. He is omnipresent, existing in all places at all times. As pure spirit he pervades all things in a relationship of immanence that is beyond anything we limited physical creatures can comprehend. He is present everywhere in the fullness of all he is and all the powers he possesses. Because God is omnipresent, nothing escapes his notice. He is able to devote his boundless attention to every situation and individual at the same time. Belief in God's omnipresence in this sense is reflected in Psalm 139:7–10, Jeremiah 23:23–24 and Acts 17:2–28. In terms of his general omnipresence, it is impossible for God to be far away and equally unfeasible for a human being not to be in his presence. In this sense, even Satan himself is constantly in the presence of God.

Scripture also speaks of God's presence as his special, providential care for certain people and places. In this sense, God's presence is his display of particular interest and concern at any given time for some more than for others. When God promised to be with his people, he did not mean that he would be where they were—he was already there because he is omnipresent. Rather, he meant that he would give more intense attention to their needs and cares. He promised to protect, provide for, stand with and support them. This aspect of divine presence is explicated in Genesis 31:3, Isaiah 7:14, 2 Chronicles 13:12 and Matthew 28:20. At times God withdraws from his people, leaving them temporarily to their own devices (2Ch 12:5; Eze 29:5). He distances himself because of sin and disloyalty by removing his blessings (Mic 2:8–10). When this kind of presence is not evident, believers should seek the favor of God; when God does manifest this degree of care, believers should thank him with all their hearts.

A third sense in which God is present in the world involves dramatic encounters with his people. Although God is forever omnipresent and often gives special providential care to his people, on rare occasions God encounters people with his even more intense presence. At times he does this to bless (Ge 32:24–32) and in other instances to judge them (2Ch 20:9). The premiere example of one who encountered God in such a way was Jesus during his earthly ministry (Jn 1:14; Heb 1:1–4).

A fourth sense of God's presence is his intimacy with his people during times of worship. In the garden of Eden God was with Adam and Eve in the sense of personal communion (Ge 1:27–31; 2:7–25). God also made his glorious presence known on Mount Sinai (Ex 24:15–18), in the tabernacle (Ex 40:33–35) and in the temple (1Ki 8:10–13). Paul hoped that unbelievers leaving a Christian worship service would be convinced that God had indeed been present (1Co 14:25). These experiences are holy moments of life when we draw near to God and he to us (James 4:8).

Christians fall into serious error when they fail to remember these ways in which God is present in the world. No matter where we go or what we do, we may rest assured that our kind and faithful God is with us. As his special, covenant people we can take heart from the fact that God cares for us providentially, looking after us and protecting us from harm. Although we should not expect dramatic encounters with God such as those of Biblical days until Christ returns in glory, our Christian life is deeply impoverished if we do not sincerely draw near to God and experience intimacy with him in worship, which will renew our hearts and empower us for faithful living.

become angry with them and give them over to the enemy, who takes them captive[x] to his own land, far away or near; 47and if they have a change of heart in the
land where they are held captive, and repent and plead[y] with you in the land of
their conquerors and say, 'We have sinned, we have done wrong, we have acted
wickedly';[z] 48and if they turn back to you with all their heart[a] and soul in the land
of their enemies who took them captive, and pray[b] to you toward the land you
gave their fathers, toward the city you have chosen and the temple[c] I have built
for your Name; 49then from heaven, your dwelling place, hear their prayer and
their plea, and uphold their cause. 50And forgive your people, who have sinned
against you; forgive all the offenses they have committed against you, and cause
their conquerors to show them mercy;[d] 51for they are your people and your inheritance,[e] whom you brought out of Egypt, out of that iron-smelting furnace.[f]

52"May your eyes be open to your servant's plea and to the plea of your people
Israel, and may you listen to them whenever they cry out to you. 53For you singled
them out from all the nations of the world to be your own inheritance,[g] just as you
declared through your servant Moses when you, O Sovereign LORD, brought our
fathers out of Egypt."

54When Solomon had finished all these prayers and supplications to the LORD, he rose
from before the altar of the LORD, where he had been kneeling with his hands spread out
toward heaven. 55He stood and blessed[h] the whole assembly of Israel in a loud voice, saying:

56"Praise be to the LORD, who has given rest[i] to his people Israel just as he
promised. Not one word has failed of all the good promises[j] he gave through his
servant Moses. 57May the LORD our God be with us as he was with our fathers; may
he never leave us nor forsake[k] us. 58May he turn our hearts[l] to him, to walk in all
his ways and to keep the commands, decrees and regulations he gave our fathers.
59And may these words of mine, which I have prayed before the LORD, be near to
the LORD our God day and night, that he may uphold the cause of his servant and
the cause of his people Israel according to each day's need, 60so that all the peoples[m] of the earth may know that the LORD is God and that there is no other.[n] 61But
your hearts must be fully committed[o] to the LORD our God, to live by his decrees
and obey his commands, as at this time."

The Dedication of the Temple

62Then the king and all Israel with him offered sacrifices before the LORD. 63Solomon
offered a sacrifice of fellowship offerings[a] to the LORD: twenty-two thousand cattle and
a hundred and twenty thousand sheep and goats. So the king and all the Israelites dedicated the temple of the LORD.

64On that same day the king consecrated the middle part of the courtyard in front of
the temple of the LORD, and there he offered burnt offerings, grain offerings and the fat

8:46 [x]Lev 26:33-39; Dt 28:64
8:47 [y]Lev 26:40; Ne 1:6 [z]Ps 106:6; Da 9:5
8:48 [a]Dt 4:29; Jer 29:12-14 [b]Da 6:10 [c]Jnh 2:4
8:50 [d]2Ch 30:9; Ps 106:46
8:51 [e]Dt 4:20; 9:29; Ne 1:10 [f]Jer 11:4
8:53 [g]Ex 19:5; Dt 9:26-29
8:55 [h]ver 14; 2Sa 6:18
8:56 [i]Dt 12:10 [j]Jos 21:45; 23:15
8:57 [k]Dt 31:6; Jos 1:5; Heb 13:5
8:58 [l]Ps 119:36
8:60 [m]Jos 4:24; 1Sa 17:46 [n]Dt 4:35; 1Ki 18:39; Jer 10:10-12
8:61 [o]1Ki 11:4; 15:3,14; 2Ki 20:3

[a] *63* Traditionally *peace offerings;* also in verse 64

8:46 the enemy, who takes them captive to his own land. Exile from the land was one of the most severe curses in the Sinaitic covenant (Lev 26:33–45; Dt 28:64–68; 30:1–5). Exile was also a curse in a number of ancient Near Eastern treaties. See note on verse 33.

8:47–48 See *WLC* 76.

8:50 forgive your people. Location outside the land of Israel did not mean that God's promises were no longer operative for his people (Ne 1:11; Ps 106:46). Solomon pleaded with God to forgive the repentant and to cause the exiles' captors to show mercy toward their captives. (This description fit well with the closing scene of 2Ki 25:27–29.)

8:51 Egypt . . . that iron-smelting furnace. The Israelite sojourn in Egypt was an exile from the land Abraham's family had settled in, an oppressive experience that tested and refined the people's character (Dt 4:20; Jer 11:4).

8:53 For you singled them out. Since God had specifically chosen the Israelites and liberated them from Egypt to become his own special inheritance (Ex 19:3–6; Dt 4:20; 9:26; 25:19), Solomon prayed that God would not forget this history of redemption when Israel was exiled.

■ **8:54–66** *Solomon's Closing Ceremonies and Speech.* Solomon brought the assembly to a close with a dedicatory speech and ceremony.

8:55–56 See *WLC* 129.

8:55 He stood and blessed the whole assembly. In verses 23–53, Solomon was praying to God before the altar on behalf of the assembly. Now facing the assembly, Solomon blessed the people on behalf of God and asked that God would heed his prayer (vv. 56–66).

8:56 the LORD, who has given rest to his people. After considerable upheaval during the period of desert wandering and the conquest of the land, Israel had experienced the fulfillment of the "good promises [God] gave through his servant Moses" (Ex 33:14; Dt 12:10)—the Lord's promised rest. See note on 5:4. In the New Testament, Christians are exhorted to make every effort to enter God's rest (Heb 4:11; cf. Rev 14:13).

8:60 there is no other. The other gods whom people worship are either fictitious or demonic; the only true God is the God of Israel (cf. Dt 4:35).

8:63 twenty-two thousand cattle. Over the course of 14 days of dedicatory festivities, Solomon and the great many people present in Jerusalem offered a multitude of sacrifices, more than at the comparatively modest later dedication of the second temple (Ezr 6:16–18). The sacrifices were so numerous that the normal temple procedures for slaughtering and offering sacrifices were insufficient. To handle the increased volume, Solomon dedicated additional space in the courtyard for the purpose of making the offerings (v. 64).

8:64 burnt offerings. For their significance, see note on "burnt

of the fellowship offerings, because the bronze altar[p] before the LORD was too small to
hold the burnt offerings, the grain offerings and the fat of the fellowship offerings.
65 So Solomon observed the festival[q] at that time, and all Israel with him—a vast assembly, people from Lebo[a] Hamath[r] to the Wadi of Egypt.[s] They celebrated it before the LORD
our God for seven days and seven days more, fourteen days in all. 66 On the following day he
sent the people away. They blessed the king and then went home, joyful and glad in heart
for all the good things the LORD had done for his servant David and his people Israel.

The LORD Appears to Solomon

9 When Solomon had finished[t] building the temple of the LORD and the royal palace,
and had achieved all he had desired to do, 2 the LORD appeared[u] to him a second
time, as he had appeared to him at Gibeon. 3 The LORD said to him:

"I have heard[v] the prayer and plea you have made before me; I have consecrated this temple, which you have built, by putting my Name there forever. My
eyes[w] and my heart will always be there.

4 "As for you, if you walk before me in integrity of heart[x] and uprightness, as
David[y] your father did, and do all I command and observe my decrees and laws,
5 I will establish[z] your royal throne over Israel forever, as I promised David your father when I said, 'You shall never fail[a] to have a man on the throne of Israel.'

6 "But if you[b] or your sons turn away[b] from me and do not observe the commands and decrees I have given you[b] and go off to serve other gods and worship
them, 7 then I will cut off Israel from the land[c] I have given them and will reject this
temple I have consecrated for my Name.[d] Israel will then become a byword[e] and
an object of ridicule[f] among all peoples. 8 And though this temple is now imposing, all who pass by will be appalled and will scoff and say, 'Why has the LORD done
such a thing to this land and to this temple?'[g] 9 People will answer, 'Because they
have forsaken the LORD their God, who brought their fathers out of Egypt, and
have embraced other gods, worshiping and serving them—that is why the LORD
brought all this disaster on them.' "

Solomon's Other Activities

10 At the end of twenty years, during which Solomon built these two buildings—the
temple of the LORD and the royal palace— 11 King Solomon gave twenty towns in Galilee
to Hiram king of Tyre, because Hiram had supplied him with all the cedar and pine and
gold[h] he wanted. 12 But when Hiram went from Tyre to see the towns that Solomon had
given him, he was not pleased with them. 13 "What kind of towns are these you have giv-
en me, my brother?" he asked. And he called them the Land of Cabul,[c][i] a name they have
to this day. 14 Now Hiram had sent to the king 120 talents[d] of gold.

8:64 [p]2Ch 4:1
8:65 [q]ver 2; Lev 23:34 [r]Nu 34:8; Jos 13:5; Jdg 3:3; 2Ki 14:25 [s]Ge 15:18
9:1 [t]1Ki 7:1; 2Ch 8:6
9:2 [u]1Ki 3:5
9:3 [v]2Ki 20:5; Ps 10:17 [w]Dt 11:12; 1Ki 8:29
9:4 [x]Ge 17:1 [y]1Ki 15:5
9:5 [z]1Ch 22:10 [a]2Sa 7:15; 1Ki 2:4
9:6 [b]2Sa 7:14
9:7 [c]2Ki 17:23; 25:21 [d]Jer 7:14 [e]Ps 44:14 [f]Dt 28:37
9:8 [g]Dt 29:24; Jer 22:8-9
9:11 [h]2Ch 8:2
9:13 [i]Jos 19:27

[a] *65* Or *from the entrance to* [b] *6* The Hebrew is plural. [c] *13* *Cabul* sounds like the Hebrew for *good for nothing.* [d] *14* That is, about 4 1/2 tons (about 4 metric tons)

offerings" at 3:4. **grain offerings.** That is, cereal offerings that often accompanied animal sacrifices (Lev 2; 7:11–14; 8:26; 9:4; 14:20; Nu 15:1–10) and indicated the worshiper's gratitude and praise. **fellowship offerings.** See Leviticus 3. **the bronze altar.** Located in front of the temple (vv. 22,54).

8:65 the festival. See note on "the festival" at verse 2. **Lebo Hamath.** See NIV text note. This site near the northern limit of the territory controlled by Israel was situated about 40 miles north of Kadesh on the Orontes River (Jos 13:5; 2Ki 14:25). **Wadi of Egypt.** Probably Wadi El-Arish in northeastern Sinai. Thus people from nearly the entire extent of Solomon's kingdom were present for these festivities (4:21).

8:66 all the good things the LORD had done for his servant David and his people Israel. God had graciously fulfilled his commitment to David that one of his offspring would build the temple David had wanted to build (2Sa 7:1–16). God had also graciously provided Israel with a centralized sanctuary (Dt 12) and with his promised rest (1Ki 5:4).

■ **9:1–9** *God's Response.* God responded to Solomon's prayer by promising blessing for obedience but also warning of disaster for disobedience. Both of these themes spoke directly to the original readers, who had suffered the consequences of Israel's flagrant violation of the covenant. They needed to keep their hopes focused on the faithfulness of their God, who had sanctified the temple by his presence.

9:3 have consecrated. God made the temple holy by his presence in it (8:10–13,29).

9:4 if you walk. The attention shifts to the conduct of Solomon and future kings. The dominion of David's descendants over Israel was contingent on their fidelity to the Torah (2:2–4; 8:25; see notes on 2:2–4). Yet, even if the sons of David were exiled, the dynasty of David would not be rejected (see notes on 2Sa 7:14–17).

9:7 cut off. The presence of the temple was not a guarantee against the consequences of prolonged covenant infidelity (see notes on 6:11–13 and on Jer 7:2–15); that is, the covenant curses would come into effect (Dt 28:37; Jer 19:8; 49:17).

9:9 forsaken. Other peoples would view the unusual spectacle of a people's own God destroying his temple and exiling his people (Dt 29:24–28).

■ **9:10–23** *Those Who Served Solomon After Construction.* In balance with 5:1–18, the writer returned to report on Hiram (vv. 10–14) and the conscripted laborers (vv. 15–23).

■ **9:10–14** *Hiram.* These verses report a remarkable event involving Hiram after he had helped build the temple.

9:10 At the end of twenty years. Given the earlier chronological notices (6:1,37–38; 7:1), this would be, at the earliest, around 946 B.C.

9:11 Solomon gave twenty towns. Although Solomon and Hiram had made an earlier agreement (5:1–12), it appears that Solomon was now in financial difficulty. In exchange for Hiram sending Solomon "120 talents" (4 1/2 tons) of gold (v. 14), Solomon provided Hiram with the use of 20 towns in Galilee (cf. 2Ch 8:1–2). Hiram later returned these towns (2Ch 8:2).

9:14 120 talents of gold. See NIV text note. This seems like an

9:15 [j]Jos 16:10; 1Ki 5:13 [k]ver 24; 2Sa 5:9 [l]Jos 19:36 [m]Jos 17:11
9:17 [n]Jos 16:3; 2Ch 8:5
9:18 [o]Jos 19:44
9:19 [p]ver 1 [q]1Ki 4:26
9:21 [r]Ge 9:25-26 [s]Jos 15:63; 17:12; Jdg 1:21,27,29 [t]Ezr 2:55,58
9:22 [u]Lev 25:39
9:23 [v]1Ki 5:16
9:24 [w]1Ki 3:1; 7:8 [x]2Sa 5:9; 1Ki 11:27; 2Ch 32:5
9:25 [y]Ex 23:14; 2Ch 8:12-13,16
9:26 [z]1Ki 22:48 [a]Nu 33:35; Dt 2:8
9:27 [b]1Ki 10:11; Eze 27:8
9:28 [c]1Ch 29:4

15 Here is the account of the forced labor King Solomon conscripted[j] to build the
LORD's temple, his own palace, the supporting terraces,[a][k] the wall of Jerusalem, and Hazor,[l] Megiddo and Gezer.[m] 16 (Pharaoh king of Egypt had attacked and captured Gezer.
He had set it on fire. He killed its Canaanite inhabitants and then gave it as a wedding
gift to his daughter, Solomon's wife. 17 And Solomon rebuilt Gezer.) He built up Lower
Beth Horon,[n] 18 Baalath,[o] and Tadmor[b] in the desert, within his land, 19 as well as all his
store cities[p] and the towns for his chariots[q] and for his horses[c]—whatever he desired to
build in Jerusalem, in Lebanon and throughout all the territory he ruled.

20 All the people left from the Amorites, Hittites, Perizzites, Hivites and Jebusites
(these peoples were not Israelites), 21 that is, their descendants[r] remaining in the land,
whom the Israelites could not exterminate[d][s]—these Solomon conscripted for his slave
labor force,[t] as it is to this day. 22 But Solomon did not make slaves[u] of any of the Israelites; they were his fighting men, his government officials, his officers, his captains,
and the commanders of his chariots and charioteers. 23 They were also the chief officials[v] in charge of Solomon's projects—550 officials supervising the men who did the
work.

24 After Pharaoh's daughter[w] had come up from the City of David to the palace Solomon had built for her, he constructed the supporting terraces.[x]

25 Three[y] times a year Solomon sacrificed burnt offerings and fellowship offerings[e] on
the altar he had built for the LORD, burning incense before the LORD along with them, and
so fulfilled the temple obligations.

26 King Solomon also built ships[z] at Ezion Geber,[a] which is near Elath in Edom, on the
shore of the Red Sea.[f] 27 And Hiram sent his men—sailors[b] who knew the sea—to serve
in the fleet with Solomon's men. 28 They sailed to Ophir[c] and brought back 420 talents[g]
of gold, which they delivered to King Solomon.

a *15* Or *the Millo;* also in verse 24 b *18* The Hebrew may also be read *Tamar.* c *19* Or *charioteers* d *21* The Hebrew term refers to the irrevocable giving over of things or persons to the LORD, often by totally destroying them. e *25* Traditionally *peace offerings* f *26* Hebrew *Yam Suph;* that is, Sea of Reeds g *28* That is, about 16 tons (about 14.5 metric tons)

---

astounding amount. But for comparison, Tiglath-Pileser III of Assyria claimed to have received 150 talents of gold from Tyre in 730 B.C.

■ **9:15–23** *Conscripted Laborers.* More is said about the laborers and what they accomplished after the construction of the temple.

9:15 supporting terraces. See NIV text note. As the city of Jerusalem expanded, it was necessary to build supporting earthworks to bolster its fortifications (cf. v. 24; 11:27; 2Sa 5:9; 2Ki 12:21; 2Ch 32:5). **Hazor, Megiddo and Gezer.** Strategically located towns along major trade routes. Hazor and Megiddo were in the north. Hazor was approximately 10 miles north of the Sea of Kinnereth (Galilee) and Megiddo approximately 23 miles west of the Jordan River and 13 miles east of the Mediterranean Sea. Gezer was approximately 20 miles northwest of Jerusalem. Archaeological excavations have revealed identical Solomonic gates at each of these sites. By fortifying these three sites, Solomon consolidated his control over trade and commerce within his kingdom.

9:16 Pharaoh . . . attacked and captured Gezer. Gezer had remained in Canaanite hands, despite the Israelite conquest (Jos 16:10; Jdg 1:29). The pharaoh captured Gezer, perhaps from the control of the Philistines. Since Egypt and Israel had a treaty (3:1), it was in the best commercial interest of both countries not to have Gezer in hostile hands.

9:17 Lower Beth Horon. About 11 miles northwest of Jerusalem (cf. Jos 10:10).

9:18 Baalath. About eight miles northeast of Ashdod near the Mediterranean coast (cf. Jos 15:24,29; 19:44). **Tadmor.** Or Tamar; see NIV text note. About 16 miles southwest of the Dead Sea (Jdg 1:16; Eze 47:19; 48:28).

9:20 the Amorites, Hittites, Perizzites, Hivites and Jebusites. When the Israelites entered the land of Canaan, they were commanded to exterminate (see NIV text note) these nations then living there (Dt 7:1; 20:17; Jos 3:10; 9:1; Jdg 3:5). Since the Israelites failed to do this in any systematic fashion (Jos 16:10; Jdg 1–2), Solomon's policy was to enslave the descendants of these peoples permanently (v. 21).

9:22 Solomon did not make slaves. Whereas Solomon permanently enslaved the various foreign peoples living in the land, he did not do so to those Israelite workers he conscripted (see notes on 5:13–15 and on 12:4,16).

■ **9:24–25** *Sacrificing After Temple Construction.* The writer returned to the motifs with which he had begun his record of the establishment of worship at the temple (3:1–3). He mentioned again the move of Pharaoh's daughter and the practice of sacrifices, but this time it appears that Solomon dedicated himself to sacrificing in the temple just as the generations to come were supposed to do.

9:24 After Pharaoh's daughter had come up. See 3:1 and 7:8.

9:25 and so fulfilled the temple obligations. Solomon sacrificed three times each year, probably at the three major festivals: the Feast of Unleavened Bread, the Feast of Weeks and the Feast of Tabernacles (cf. Ex 23:14–17; 34:18–24; Lev 23:1–44; Dt 16:1–17).

■ **9:26—11:13** *Solomon's Desecration of Worship.* Having reported how Solomon established the temple as the only acceptable location for the worship of God, the writer now turned to the period of the king's life during which he desecrated worship in Israel. Some hints of the circumstances leading to this defilement have already appeared (3:1–3; 7:8; 9:24–26), but the writer directly addressed Solomon's involvements with other nations (9:26—10:29), leading to his marriages to many foreign wives, who tragically turned Solomon to idolatry (11:1–13).

■ **9:26—10:29** *Solomon's International Involvements.* Solomon was deeply involved in international trading relationships. These alliances brought economic blessings to Israel and were thus of great value to the nation. Yet these positive events had negative repercussions. Solomon began to be adversely influenced by these relationships. Here the writer mentioned the visit of the queen of Sheba (9:26—10:13), followed by a general survey of Solomon's lucrative international trade ventures (10:14–29).

■ **9:26—10:13** *The Queen of Sheba.* Solomon's reach extended to the east, and his actions hurt Arabian caravan trade. The queen of Sheba may have come to visit Solomon in part to negotiate a trade agreement, but she ended up amazed at his abilities and accomplishments.

9:26 Ezion Geber. In order to avoid dependence on caravan trade from the east or the merchant navies and ports of other nations, Solomon built ships at Ezion Geber, his own (new) port. Because this represented a new venture, Solomon enlisted the help of his ally, Hiram of Tyre, who supplied sailors to accompany Solomon's own (v. 27). **Red Sea.** The Gulf of Aqaba (Jer 49:21).

9:28 Ophir. The location of Ophir is disputed (Job 28:16; Ps 45:9; Isa 13:12). Suggestions include western Arabia, the Horn of Africa, India and even Peru. **420 talents of gold.** (See NIV text note). Signifies that this joint maritime initiative proved lucrative.

The Queen of Sheba Visits Solomon

10 When the queen of Sheba[d] heard about the fame of Solomon and his relation
to the name of the LORD, she came to test him with hard questions.[e] 2 Arriving
at Jerusalem with a very great caravan—with camels carrying spices, large quantities of
gold, and precious stones—she came to Solomon and talked with him about all that she
had on her mind. 3 Solomon answered all her questions; nothing was too hard for the
king to explain to her. 4 When the queen of Sheba saw all the wisdom of Solomon and
the palace he had built, 5 the food on his table,[f] the seating of his officials, the attending
servants in their robes, his cupbearers, and the burnt offerings he made at[a] the temple
of the LORD, she was overwhelmed.

6 She said to the king, "The report I heard in my own country about your achievements
and your wisdom is true. 7 But I did not believe these things until I came and saw with
my own eyes. Indeed, not even half was told me; in wisdom and wealth[g] you have far exceeded the report I heard. 8 How happy your men must be! How happy your officials, who
continually stand before you and hear[h] your wisdom! 9 Praise[i] be to the LORD your God,
who has delighted in you and placed you on the throne of Israel. Because of the LORD's
eternal love for Israel, he has made you king, to maintain justice[j] and righteousness."

10 And she gave the king 120 talents[b] of gold,[k] large quantities of spices, and precious
stones. Never again were so many spices brought in as those the queen of Sheba gave
to King Solomon.

11 (Hiram's ships brought gold from Ophir;[l] and from there they brought great cargoes
of almugwood[c] and precious stones. 12 The king used the almugwood to make supports
for the temple of the LORD and for the royal palace, and to make harps and lyres for the
musicians. So much almugwood has never been imported or seen since that day.)

13 King Solomon gave the queen of Sheba all she desired and asked for, besides what
he had given her out of his royal bounty. Then she left and returned with her retinue to
her own country.

Solomon's Splendor

14 The weight of the gold[m] that Solomon received yearly was 666 talents,[d] 15 not including the revenues from merchants and traders and from all the Arabian kings and the
governors of the land.

16 King Solomon made two hundred large shields[n] of hammered gold; six hundred bekas[e] of gold went into each shield. 17 He also made three hundred small shields of hammered gold, with three minas[f] of gold in each shield. The king put them in the Palace of
the Forest of Lebanon.[o]

18 Then the king made a great throne inlaid with ivory and overlaid with fine gold.

10:1 [d]Ge 10:7,28; Mt 12:42; Lk 11:31 [e]Jdg 14:12
10:5 [f]1Ch 26:16
10:7 [g]1Ch 29:25
10:8 [h]Pr 8:34
10:9 [i]1Ki 5:7 [j]2Sa 8:15; Ps 33:5; 72:2
10:10 [k]ver 2
10:11 [l]Ge 10:29; 1Ki 9:27-28
10:14 [m]1Ki 9:28
10:16 [n]1Ki 14:26-28
10:17 [o]1Ki 7:2

[a] *5* Or *the ascent by which he went up to* [b] *10* That is, about 4 1/2 tons (about 4 metric tons) [c] *11* Probably a variant of *algumwood*; also in verse 12 [d] *14* That is, about 25 tons (about 23 metric tons) [e] *16* That is, about 7 1/2 pounds (about 3.5 kilograms) [f] *17* That is, about 3 3/4 pounds (about 1.7 kilograms)

10:1 Sheba. Two main suggestions for this location are southwest Arabia (modern Yemen) and northern Arabia, the land of the Sabeans (Job 1:15; 6:19; Ps 72:10). **his relation to the name of the LORD.** The queen of Sheba recognized a relationship between Solomon's renown and the hand of the Lord. **hard questions.** Wishing to discover whether Solomon's reputation was well deserved, the queen of Sheba tested him (cf. Jdg 14:12).
10:5 the food on his table. See notes on "eat at your table" at 2:7 and on 4:22. **his cupbearers.** The post of cupbearer was important in Oriental government (Ge 40:1–23; 41:9; Ne 1:11).
10:9 Praise be to the LORD your God. The queen of Sheba specifically mentioned the personal name of the God of Israel in her exclamation to Solomon (vv. 6–9). Jesus cited this queen in his indictment against the people of his own day (Mt 12:42; Lk 11:31).
10:11 Hiram's ships. In addition to helping Solomon build his fleet, Hiram of Tyre used some of his own ships to transport goods for Solomon (9:26–28; 10:22). **Ophir.** See note at 9:28. **almugwood.** See NIV text note. Suggestions as to the precise nature of this wood include red sandalwood and juniper.
10:12 harps and lyres for the musicians. Israelite royalty probably sponsored musicians to compose appropriate hymns and psalms for worship.
10:13 Solomon gave. The bestowal of presents was mutual, thus establishing an alliance between the two.
■ **10:14–29** *Solomon's Wealth From International Relations.* Solomon built a far-reaching international trade network. There were positive dimensions to these events (see v. 23), but the writer made it clear that Solomon committed serious violations of the Mosaic Law. He mentioned the large number of horses Solomon possessed (v. 26), as well as his many marriages that disregarded Deuteronomy 17:16. Moreover, Solomon's accumulation of gold and silver violated the law of Deuteronomy 17:17. As the writer would make clear in the next section (see 11:1), this prosperous trade entangled Solomon in political marriages that eventually led to his downfall.
10:14 Solomon received yearly. Annual, steady tribute was necessary to support all of Solomon's major projects and outlays.
10:15 the revenues from merchants and traders. Because Solomon controlled such a large geographical territory on the way north to Mesopotamia or south to Egypt, merchants had to pay duty. **governors of the land.** See 4:7–19.
10:16–17 large shields. These extremely heavy and valuable shields were crafted chiefly for ceremonial and aesthetic reasons. The use of such shields as a visible sign of a king's wealth and status is not unique to Solomon. In his campaign (c. 714 B.C.) against the city of Musasir in the region of Urartu (Biblical Ararat), King Sargon II claimed to have taken "six shields of gold" from the Musasir temple. **Palace.** Befitting their ornamental status, both the large and the small shields were kept in the Palace of the Forest of Lebanon (cf. 7:2).
10:18 a great throne inlaid with ivory. Solomon used the great influx of tribute to support an extravagant lifestyle (vv. 18–21,23–25). The frame of his throne was constructed of wood. This wooden core was overlaid with ivory and then plated with gold.

19 The throne had six steps, and its back had a rounded top. On both sides of the seat were
armrests, with a lion standing beside each of them. 20 Twelve lions stood on the six steps,
one at either end of each step. Nothing like it had ever been made for any other kingdom.
21 All King Solomon's goblets were gold, and all the household articles in the Palace of
the Forest of Lebanon were pure gold. Nothing was made of silver, because silver was
considered of little value in Solomon's days. 22 The king had a fleet of trading ships[a][p] at
sea along with the ships of Hiram. Once every three years it returned, carrying gold, silver and ivory, and apes and baboons.
23 King Solomon was greater in riches[q] and wisdom[r] than all the other kings of the
earth. 24 The whole world sought audience with Solomon to hear the wisdom[s] God had
put in his heart. 25 Year after year, everyone who came brought a gift—articles of silver
and gold, robes, weapons and spices, and horses and mules.
26 Solomon accumulated chariots and horses;[t] he had fourteen hundred chariots
and twelve thousand horses,[b] which he kept in the chariot cities and also with him in Jerusalem. 27 The king made silver as common[u] in Jerusalem as stones, and cedar as plentiful as sycamore-fig trees in the foothills. 28 Solomon's horses were imported from Egypt[c]
and from Kue[d]—the royal merchants purchased them from Kue. 29 They imported a chariot from Egypt for six hundred shekels[e] of silver, and a horse for a hundred and fifty.[f]
They also exported them to all the kings of the Hittites[v] and of the Arameans.

Solomon's Wives

11 King Solomon, however, loved many foreign women[w] besides Pharaoh's daughter—Moabites, Ammonites, Edomites, Sidonians and Hittites. 2 They were from
nations about which the LORD had told the Israelites, "You must not intermarry[x] with
them, because they will surely turn your hearts after their gods." Nevertheless, Solomon
held fast to them in love. 3 He had seven hundred wives of royal birth and three hundred
concubines, and his wives led him astray. 4 As Solomon grew old, his wives turned his
heart after other gods, and his heart was not fully devoted[y] to the LORD his God, as the
heart of David his father had been. 5 He followed Ashtoreth[z] the goddess of the Sidonians, and Molech[g][a] the detestable god of the Ammonites. 6 So Solomon did evil in the eyes
of the LORD; he did not follow the LORD completely, as David his father had done.
7 On a hill east[b] of Jerusalem, Solomon built a high place for Chemosh[c] the detestable

10:22 [p]1Ki 9:26
10:23 [q]1Ki 3:13 [r]1Ki 4:30
10:24 [s]1Ki 3:9,12,28
10:26 [t]Dt 17:16; 1Ki 4:26; 9:19; 2Ch 1:14; 9:25
10:27 [u]Dt 17:17
10:29 [v]2Ki 7:6-7
11:1 [w]Dt 17:17; Ne 13:26
11:2 [x]Ex 34:16; Dt 7:3-4
11:4 [y]1Ki 8:61; 9:4
11:5 [z]ver 33; Jdg 2:13; 2Ki 23:13 [a]ver 7
11:7 [b]2Ki 23:13 [c]Nu 21:29; Jdg 11:24

[a] *22* Hebrew *of ships of Tarshish* [b] *26* Or *charioteers* [c] *28* Or possibly *Muzur,* a region in Cilicia; also in verse 29 [d] *28* Probably *Cilicia* [e] *29* That is, about 15 pounds (about 7 kilograms) [f] *29* That is, about 3 3/4 pounds (about 1.7 kilograms) [g] *5* Hebrew *Milcom;* also in verse 33

Ivory carvings plated with gold have also been found in the Assyrian royal palaces at Nimrud (ancient Kalah). Solomon's penchant for the finest in furnishings and buildings weighed heavily on his subjects (12:4).

10:21 goblets were gold, and all the household articles . . . were pure gold. Beautiful golden vessels dating from ancient times have been found in Egypt (thirteenth century B.C.), Ugarit on the Mediterranean coast of modern Syria (thirteenth century B.C.) and Persia (sixth to fourth centuries B.C.).

10:22 a fleet of trading ships. These so-called "Tarshish ships" (see NIV text note) were built to make long ocean voyages.

10:23 Solomon was greater in riches and wisdom. Not only did Solomon become fabulously wealthy, thus fulfilling the promise of 3:13, but he also attracted visitors from all over the world, seeking "to hear the wisdom God put in his heart" (v. 24).

10:26 chariots and horses. The law of the king in Deuteronomy 17:16 forbade the monarch from accumulating great numbers of chariots and horses.

10:28 Egypt. See NIV text note and 2 Kings 7:6. **Kue.** Also known as Cilicia, located in southeastern Asia Minor.

10:29 They imported . . . They also exported. Not only did Solomon amass chariots and horses; he also initiated substantial trade in these commodities through his "royal merchants" (v. 28). In so doing Solomon exploited Israel's strategic geographic position. **the kings of the Hittites.** The Hittites were located in Anatolia and by this time were no longer unified as an empire. Rather, the Hittites were ruled by a number of minor kings, each of whom had his own domain. **the Arameans.** Syrians who lived northeast of Israel.

▪11:1–13 *Solomon's Idolatry in the Temple.* The international marriages that accompanied extensive foreign trade eventually led Solomon to worship other gods. Thus the one who had dedicated the temple as Israel's exclusive place for sacrifice to the Lord now erected altars to other gods (vv. 1–8) and endured God's harsh judgment in response (vv. 9–13).

▪11:1–8 *Solomon's Foreign Wives and Idolatry.* In a turn of events that must have seemed impossible for the wise king of Israel who had sponsored the construction of the temple, Solomon desecrated Jerusalem by worshiping other gods.

11:1 loved many foreign women. Whereas in the first part of Solomon's reign he "showed his love for the LORD by walking according to the statutes of his father David" (3:3), during the second period Solomon had alliances with many non-Israelite women. Although diplomatic marriages between dynasties in various kingdoms were common in the ancient Near East as a means of ratifying treaties, the multiplication of royal wives was forbidden in Deuteronomy 17:17. Moreover, there were strictures outlined in Exodus 34:16, Deuteronomy 7:1–3 and Joshua 23:12–13 against marrying foreign wives in the land Israel was to possess.

11:2 turn your hearts. The phrase is an allusion to the warning in Deuteronomy 7:4.

11:3 his wives led him astray. Solomon's enormous harem turned his heart away from God to the worship of idols (cf. v. 4 and note on v. 2).

11:4 as the heart of David his father had been. David, throughout the books of Kings, was presented as a model king (3:14; 9:4; 14:8; 15:3; 2Ki 8:18–19; 22:2). Solomon's father was not without his faults (2Sa 11–12; 24:1–15; 1Ki 15:5), but even when he sinned David's repentant response was exemplary (2Sa 12:16–17; 24:9–17). Never once does the author record that David worshiped any false god. His unwavering devotion to God was unparalleled. See *WCF* 24.3; *WLC* 151.

11:5 Ashtoreth. This Hebrew term was used for the Phoenician goddess Astarte (cf. Jdg 2:13; 1Ki 14:15; 2Ki 23:13). **Molech.** Or Milcom (see NIV text note), the national god of the Ammonites.

11:6 Solomon did evil. Solomon's many sins violated fundamental principles of Israelite religion: proliferation of wives (see notes on vv. 2,3), the worship of other gods (Ex 20:3,5) and the construction of sanctuaries for these foreign gods (vv. 7–8; Ex 20:4).

11:7 Chemosh. The national deity of the Moabites (cf. 2Ki 3:26–27).

god of Moab, and for Molech[d] the detestable god of the Ammonites. 8He did the same
for all his foreign wives, who burned incense and offered sacrifices to their gods.
9The LORD became angry with Solomon because his heart had turned away from the
LORD, the God of Israel, who had appeared[e] to him twice. 10Although he had forbidden
Solomon to follow other gods,[f] Solomon did not keep the LORD's command.[g] 11So the
LORD said to Solomon, "Since this is your attitude and you have not kept my covenant
and my decrees, which I commanded you, I will most certainly tear[h] the kingdom away
from you and give it to one of your subordinates. 12Nevertheless, for the sake of David
your father, I will not do it during your lifetime. I will tear it out of the hand of your son.
13Yet I will not tear the whole kingdom from him, but will give him one tribe[i] for the sake[j]
of David my servant and for the sake of Jerusalem, which I have chosen."[k]

Solomon's Adversaries

14Then the LORD raised up against Solomon an adversary, Hadad the Edomite, from
the royal line of Edom. 15Earlier when David was fighting with Edom, Joab the commander of the army, who had gone up to bury the dead, had struck down all the men in Edom.[l]
16Joab and all the Israelites stayed there for six months, until they had destroyed all the
men in Edom. 17But Hadad, still only a boy, fled to Egypt with some Edomite officials who
had served his father. 18They set out from Midian and went to Paran.[m] Then taking men
from Paran with them, they went to Egypt, to Pharaoh king of Egypt, who gave Hadad
a house and land and provided him with food.
19Pharaoh was so pleased with Hadad that he gave him a sister of his own wife, Queen
Tahpenes, in marriage. 20The sister of Tahpenes bore him a son named Genubath,
whom Tahpenes brought up in the royal palace. There Genubath lived with Pharaoh's
own children.
21While he was in Egypt, Hadad heard that David rested with his fathers and that Joab
the commander of the army was also dead. Then Hadad said to Pharaoh, "Let me go,
that I may return to my own country."
22"What have you lacked here that you want to go back to your own country?" Pharaoh asked.
"Nothing," Hadad replied, "but do let me go!"
23And God raised up against Solomon another adversary,[n] Rezon son of Eliada, who
had fled from his master, Hadadezer[o] king of Zobah. 24He gathered men around him and
became the leader of a band of rebels when David destroyed the forces[a] ⌞of Zobah⌟; the

11:7 [d]Lev 20:2-5; Ac 7:43
11:9 [e]ver 2-3; 1Ki 3:5; 9:2
11:10 [f]1Ki 9:6 [g]1Ki 6:12
11:11 [h]ver 31; 1Ki 12:15-16; 2Ki 17:21
11:13 [i]1Ki 12:20 [j]2Sa 7:15 [k]Dt 12:11
11:15 [l]Dt 20:13; 2Sa 8:14; 1Ch 18:12
11:18 [m]Nu 10:12
11:23 [n]ver 14 [o]2Sa 8:3

[a] 24 Hebrew *destroyed them*

■ **11:9–13** *God's Response of Judgment.* In contrast to the way in which God had responded to Solomon after his worship at the temple (9:1–9), the Lord here responded in severe judgment against the now wayward king and foretold the division of his king dom.

11:9–10 See *WLC* 151.

11:9 The LORD became angry with Solomon. The nature and scope of Solomon's transgressions were too severe to ignore. Despite God's paying him the unusual honor of appearing to him—twice (3:4–5; 9:1–9)—Solomon responded in an unexpected and disappointing way.

11:10 forbidden Solomon to follow other gods. See 3:14 and 9:6–9.

11:11 tear the kingdom away. See verses 29–39.

11:12 I will not do it during your lifetime. God's great love for David caused him to temper his judgment on Solomon in two respects. First, God postponed the tearing away of the kingdom until the reign of Solomon's son, and, second, God would not remove the entire kingdom from the Davidic dynasty (v. 13).

11:13 one tribe. This probably refers to Judah (12:20; 2Ki 17:18). However, since only ten tribes were to secede (vv. 29–39), at least two tribes were to be left in Davidic hands. This may indicate that Judah (the tribe of David) was presupposed to remain under Davidic control and that another would remain with it. If so, Benjamin may have been meant, since at least part of this tribe remained faithful (12:21; 2Ch 11:12), though it is also possible that these were simply counted as part of Judah by this time. Other Benjaminites apparently joined the northern tribes (see note on 12:29). The tribe of Levi may also be indicated, because it had no territory (Jos 21:1–42) and sided with Solomon's son Rehoboam (2Ch 11:13–14). Simeon may also have been intended, since its land lay within Judah's (Jos 19:1). **for the sake of Jerusalem.** God's chosen city, the site of Israel's central sanctuary anticipated in Deuteronomy 12 and constructed by Solomon. Jerusalem was a central symbol of God's love for his people and of the communion between God and his people throughout the Bible (Pss 68:29; 122:2–6; 135:21; 137:5–7; Isa 62:1; Da 9:25; Rev 3:12; 21:2,10).

■ **11:14–40** *Solomon's Curse of Rebellions.* In contrast with the earlier time period during which Solomon consolidated his power in Jerusalem and quieted rebellion (2:13 46), he now faced one rebellion after another because of his idolatry. These verses mention three such rebellions: Hadad's (vv. 14–22), Rezon's (vv. 23–25) and Jeroboam's (vv. 26–40).

■ **11:14–22** *Hadad's Rebellion.* David had subjugated Edom during his reign, but now Solomon's control over the region waned.

11:14 Hadad. The Lord raised up two enemies to chastise Solomon: Hadad of Edom and Rezon of Syria (vv. 23–25).

11:15 Earlier when David was fighting. See 2 Samuel 8:13–14. An earlier victory by Joab was reversed as Hadad returned from exile in Egypt and successfully rebelled against Solomon (v. 25).

11:18 from Midian. The Midianites then lived east of Moab and Edom. **Paran.** Situated in the Sinai peninsula southeast of Kadesh. **gave Hadad a house and land.** Given the power of David and Israel, Pharaoh had considered it in Egypt's interest to harbor David's foes in the hope that these enemies would one day curtail Israel's power (v. 21). Ancient treaties forbade providing asylum to political rebels.

11:22 do let me go! Following David's death, Hadad wished to return to his own land, despite Pharaoh's objections, probably because he wished to liberate it from Israelite domination (v. 25).

■ **11:23–25** *Rezon's Rebellion.* The writer mentioned a second rebellion against Solomon as a result of his idolatry.

11:23 another adversary. Earlier Solomon could boast that in his reign there was "no adversary or disaster" (5:4), but now God afflicted Solomon with a succession of adversaries. **Hadadezer king of Zobah.** On David's conquest of Hadadezer and Aram (or Syria), see 2 Samuel 8:3–6 and 10:15–19. See *BC* 13.

11:24 [p]2Sa 8:5; 10:8,18 rebels went to Damascus,[p] where they settled and took control. 25Rezon was Israel's adversary as long as Solomon lived, adding to the trouble caused by Hadad. So Rezon ruled
11:25 [q]2Sa 10:19 in Aram[q] and was hostile toward Israel.

Jeroboam Rebels Against Solomon

11:26 [r]2Sa 20:21; 1Ki 12:2; 2Ch 13:6 26Also, Jeroboam son of Nebat rebelled[r] against the king. He was one of Solomon's
officials, an Ephraimite from Zeredah, and his mother was a widow named Zeruah.
11:27 [s]1Ki 9:24 27Here is the account of how he rebelled against the king: Solomon had built the
supporting terraces[a][s] and had filled in the gap in the wall of the city of David his fa-
11:28 [t]Ru 2:1 [u]Pr 22:29 ther. 28Now Jeroboam was a man of standing,[t] and when Solomon saw how well[u] the
young man did his work, he put him in charge of the whole labor force of the house
of Joseph.
11:29 [v]1Ki 12:15; 14:2; 2Ch 9:29 29About that time Jeroboam was going out of Jerusalem, and Ahijah[v] the prophet of
Shiloh met him on the way, wearing a new cloak. The two of them were alone out in the
11:30 [w]1Sa 15:27 country, 30and Ahijah took hold of the new cloak he was wearing and tore[w] it into twelve
pieces. 31Then he said to Jeroboam, "Take ten pieces for yourself, for this is what the
11:31 [x]ver 11 LORD, the God of Israel, says: 'See, I am going to tear[x] the kingdom out of Solomon's hand
and give you ten tribes. 32But for the sake of my servant David and the city of Jerusalem,
which I have chosen out of all the tribes of Israel, he will have one tribe. 33I will do this
11:33 [y]ver 5-7 [z]1Ki 3:3 because they have[b] forsaken me and worshiped[y] Ashtoreth the goddess of the Sidonians, Chemosh the god of the Moabites, and Molech the god of the Ammonites, and have
not walked in my ways, nor done what is right in my eyes, nor kept my statutes[z] and laws
as David, Solomon's father, did.
34" 'But I will not take the whole kingdom out of Solomon's hand; I have made him
ruler all the days of his life for the sake of David my servant, whom I chose and who observed my commands and statutes. 35I will take the kingdom from his son's hands and
11:36 [a]ver 13; 1Ki 12:17 [b]1Ki 15:4; 2Ki 8:19 give you ten tribes. 36I will give one tribe[a] to his son so that David my servant may always
have a lamp[b] before me in Jerusalem, the city where I chose to put my Name. 37Howev-
11:37 [c]2Sa 3:21 er, as for you, I will take you, and you will rule over all that your heart desires;[c] you will
be king over Israel. 38If you do whatever I command you and walk in my ways and do
11:38 [d]Dt 17:19 [e]Jos 1:5; 2Sa 7:11,27 what is right in my eyes by keeping my statutes[d] and commands, as David my servant
did, I will be with you. I will build you a dynasty[e] as enduring as the one I built for Da-
vid and will give Israel to you. 39I will humble David's descendants because of this, but
11:40 [f]2Ch 12:2 not forever.' "
40Solomon tried to kill Jeroboam, but Jeroboam fled to Egypt, to Shishak[f] the king,
and stayed there until Solomon's death.

[a] *27* Or *the Millo* [b] *33* Hebrew; Septuagint, Vulgate and Syriac *because he has*

11:24 Damascus, where they settled and took control. From his base in Damascus, Rezon persistently caused trouble for Solomon.

■ **11:26–40** *Jeroboam's Rebellion.* Jeroboam rebelled against Solomon and escaped to Egypt until Solomon's death.

11:26 Also, Jeroboam son of Nebat rebelled. Whereas Hadad and Rezon were external enemies raised up by God, Jeroboam, an Ephraimite, was an internal foe, also raised up by God. **Zeredah.** Located about 21 miles east of Joppa in the tribal territory of Ephraim.

11:27 supporting terraces. See NIV text note and note on "supporting terraces" at 9:15.

11:28 the whole labor force of the house of Joseph. Jeroboam was in charge of the laborers Solomon had conscripted from the tribes of Ephraim and Manasseh (5:13–16) and thus was well aware of the resentment these tribes felt toward Solomon (12:4).

11:29 Shiloh. In Ephraim, about 12 miles east of Zeredah.

11:30 tore it into twelve pieces. Ahijah performed a symbolic action; i.e., he enacted a parable. Such colorful actions dramatized the reality of the spoken word and God's intervention in Israelite history (cf. 22:11; Isa 20; Jer 13:11). In this case, the torn pieces of Ahijah's robe vividly demonstrated the impending division of the kingdom.

11:31 Take ten pieces for yourself. On behalf of the Lord, Ahijah summoned Jeroboam to take 10 of the 12 pieces, symbolizing the ten northern tribes, over which Jeroboam would shortly become king. As with the earlier rebellions of Hadad and Rezon, Jeroboam's insurrection effected divine judgment against Solomon.

11:32 one tribe. See note on "one tribe" at verse 13.

11:33 they have forsaken me. See NIV text note. See *WLC* 109.

11:34 I have made him ruler. See notes on verses 12–13.

11:35 from his son's hands. That is, from Solomon's successor, Rehoboam (12:1–24).

11:36 so that David my servant may always have a lamp. The metaphor of a lamp signified the permanence of the Davidic dynasty in the city of Jerusalem (2Sa 21:17; 1Ki 15:4; 2Ki 8:19; 2Ch 21:7; Ps 132:17).

11:37 over all that your heart desires. A similar promise had been given to David (2Sa 3:21). **king over Israel.** That is, over the ten northern tribes. During the period of the divided kingdom, the term *Israel* most often designated these ten tribes. Conversely, the term *Judah* denoted the domain still ruled by David's descendants.

11:38 If you do whatever I command you. Jeroboam would be subject to the same covenantal stipulations that had been operative for Saul, David and Solomon (see notes on 2:2–4). **I will be with you.** These words assured God's presence and sustenance (Dt 31:8,23; Jdg 2:18; 6:12,16; 1Sa 3:19; 2Sa 5:10; 7:9). Ahijah hoped that Jeroboam would be more loyal to the covenant than Solomon had been.

11:39 I will humble David's descendants. Through the division, David's descendants would be punished and would be in a position to learn from their mistakes. **but not forever.** This phrase looked forward to a restoration of Davidic power. Such a restoration was attempted by Josiah of Judah (2Ki 22–23), but it failed (2Ki 23:29–30). The prophets also longed for a Messianic renewal of Davidic rule (Jer 30:9; Eze 34:23; 37:15–28; Hos 3:5; Am 9:11–12). These hopes were finally fulfilled in Jesus "the Christ," the Anointed One, or Messiah (Mt 1:1; Mk 1:1).

11:40 Shishak. A successor to the pharaoh of Egypt with whose daughter Solomon had arranged a marriage alliance (see notes on 3:1). Shishak was the first king over the twenty-second dynasty and ruled from 945–924 B.C. (14:25–26).

Solomon's Death

41 As for the other events of Solomon's reign—all he did and the wisdom he displayed—are they not written in the book of the annals of Solomon? 42 Solomon reigned
in Jerusalem over all Israel forty years. 43 Then he rested with his fathers and was buried
in the city of David his father. And Rehoboam[g] his son succeeded him as king. **11:43** [g]1Ki 14:21; Mt 1:7

Israel Rebels Against Rehoboam

12 Rehoboam went to Shechem, for all the Israelites had gone there to make him
king. 2 When Jeroboam son of Nebat heard this (he was still in Egypt, where he
had fled[h] from King Solomon), he returned from[a] Egypt. 3 So they sent for Jeroboam, and **12:2** [h]1Ki 11:40
he and the whole assembly of Israel went to Rehoboam and said to him: 4 "Your father
put a heavy yoke[i] on us, but now lighten the harsh labor and the heavy yoke he put on **12:4** [i]1Sa 8:11-18; 1Ki 4:20-28
us, and we will serve you."
5 Rehoboam answered, "Go away for three days and then come back to me." So the
people went away.
6 Then King Rehoboam consulted the elders[j] who had served his father Solomon dur- **12:6** [j]1Ki 4:2
ing his lifetime. "How would you advise me to answer these people?" he asked.
7 They replied, "If today you will be a servant to these people and serve them and give
them a favorable answer,[k] they will always be your servants." **12:7** [k]Pr 15:1
8 But Rehoboam rejected the advice the elders gave him and consulted the young men
who had grown up with him and were serving him. 9 He asked them, "What is your advice? How should we answer these people who say to me, 'Lighten the yoke your father
put on us'?"
10 The young men who had grown up with him replied, "Tell these people who have
said to you, 'Your father put a heavy yoke on us, but make our yoke lighter'—tell them,
'My little finger is thicker than my father's waist. 11 My father laid on you a heavy yoke;
I will make it even heavier. My father scourged you with whips; I will scourge you with
scorpions.' "
12 Three days later Jeroboam and all the people returned to Rehoboam, as the king
had said, "Come back to me in three days." 13 The king answered the people harshly. Rejecting the advice given him by the elders, 14 he followed the advice of the young men and
said, "My father made your yoke heavy; I will make it even heavier. My father scourged[l] **12:14** [l]Ex 1:14; 5:5-9, 16-18

[a] *2* Or *he remained in*

■ **11:41–43** *Solomon's Death and Burial.* The close of Solomon's reign counterbalances its opening (1:1—2:12).

11:41 the book of the annals of Solomon. One of the sources (no longer in existence) used by the writer to compose 1 and 2 Kings. Other official sources employed by the author of Kings include "the book of the annals of the kings of Israel" and "the book of the annals of the kings of Judah" (14:19,29). See "Introduction: Time and Place of Writing."

11:42 forty years. Approximately 970–930 B.C.

■ **12:1—2 Kings 17:41** *The Divided Monarchy.* These chapters treat the history of the kingdom from its division until the fall of Samaria, the capital of the northern tribes, called Israel. The writer alternated between events in the northern and southern kingdoms according to a consistent, chronological pattern. He described the reign of a given monarch of one kingdom until the end of the reign of the last king mentioned in the other kingdom. This pattern separates the reigns of the various kings into 15 sections (see "Introduction: Purposes and Distinctives"). The writer noted the sins of the kings as well as the continuing hope in God's promises to the house of David. By the end of the narrative in 1 Kings, however, the northern kingdom had been defeated and its population exiled by the Assyrians.

■ **12:1–24** *The Secession of the Northern Tribes.* The history of the divided period begins with a brief account of the initial break between the northern and southern kingdoms. The northern tribes felt mistreated by Solomon. Jeroboam appealed to Rehoboam for better treatment, but Rehoboam foolishly refused and sparked a division in the kingdom. The writer admitted to sin on both sides of this division, but he also acknowledged the legitimacy of the political separation of the north. He did not, however, condone the northern kingdom's separation from the temple in Jerusalem (see note at v. 24).

12:1 Shechem. A major Israelite center (Jos 8:30–35; 24:1–33) located in northern Ephraim, about 37 miles north of Jerusalem. **to make him king.** The citizens of the northern tribes did not immediately accept the rule of Solomon's son and successor, Rehoboam. They wanted assurances; hence, Rehoboam traveled to Shechem to meet with their leaders. For earlier precedents to this custom, see the acclamation of Saul in 1 Samuel 11:15 and the covenant the northern tribes made with David in 2 Samuel 5:1–3.

12:2 When Jeroboam . . . heard this. That is, heard of the death of Solomon (11:43). **returned from Egypt.** See NIV text note.

12:4 Your father put a heavy yoke. Throughout the Old Testament, the expression "heavy yoke" is characteristically used of the oppression of the Israelites by foreign rulers (Lev. 26:13; Dt 28:48; Isa 9:4; 10:27; 14:25; Jer 27:8,11; Eze 34:27). The use of the term here serves as an indictment against Solomon for imposing harsh labor on his own people (see notes on 5:13–16; 9:15–22; 11:28).

12:6 the elders. These older and more experienced advisors were well acquainted with the traditions of premonarchic Israel and understood how the monarchy affected the lives of ordinary Israelites.

12:7 If today you will be a servant. Though entrusted with great power, the Israelite king was supposed to establish justice and thus to serve both God and his people (Dt 17:14–20; Ps 72).

12:8 the young men who had grown up with him. These young advisors had, like Rehoboam, grown up in the royal court and were apparently willing to break with the historic Israelite traditions. They regarded as inalienable the privileges and rights of an oriental monarch.

12:10 My little finger is thicker than my father's waist. These foolishly boastful words signify how much more oppressive Rehoboam's yoke would be than his father's had been (v. 11). Neither the Hebrew text nor the Septuagint (the Greek translation of the OT) specify "finger." Rather, both read "my littleness." That Rehoboam omitted this phrase when speaking to Jeroboam and the northerners (v. 14) may indicate that it was impolite or even obscene, perhaps being a phallic allusion.

12:11 scorpions. Rehoboam was probably referring to spiked whips.

12:13–16 See *WLC* 130.

12:14 he followed the advice of the young men. Rehoboam foolishly rejected the judicious advice of the elders.

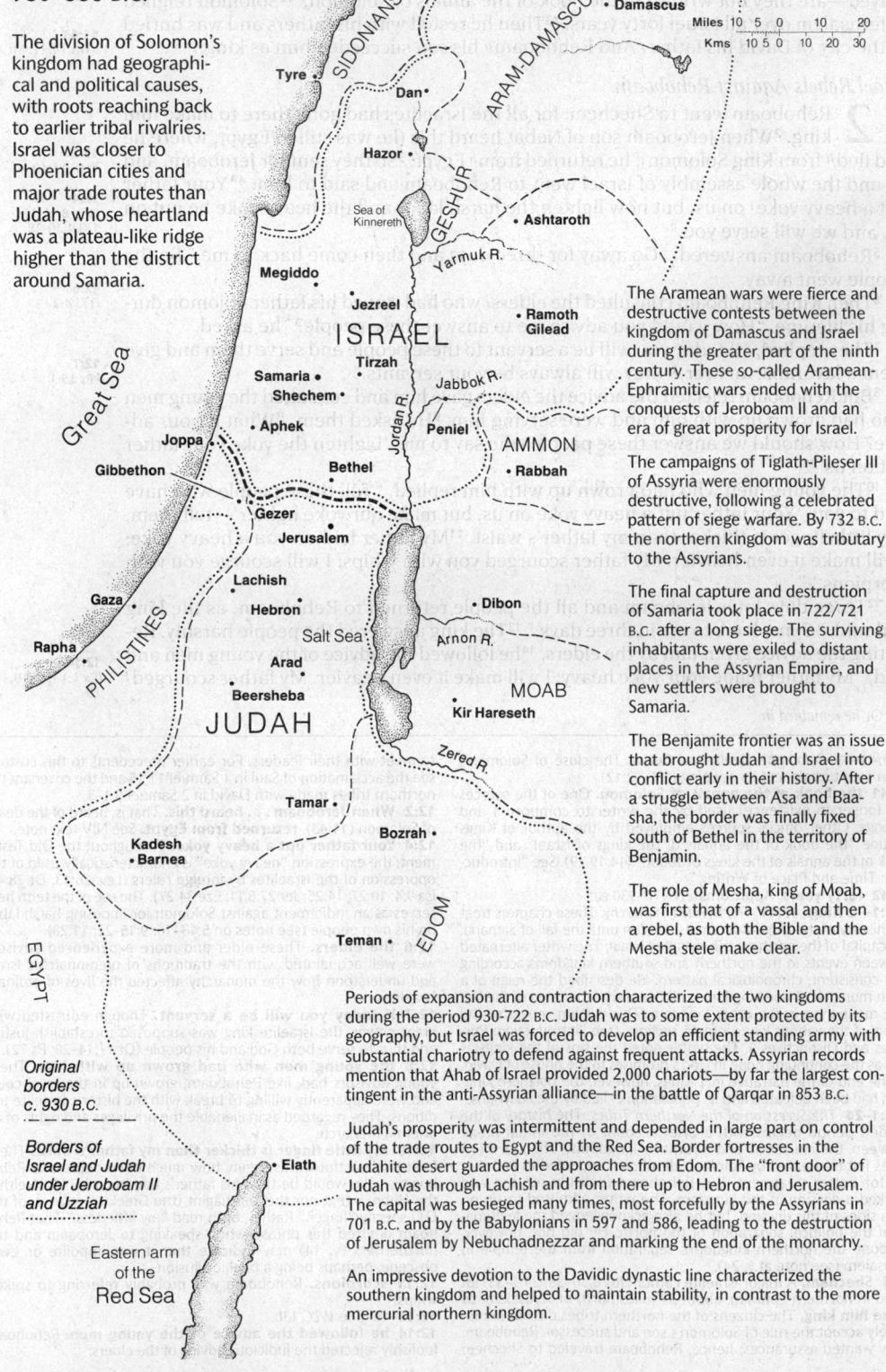

The Divided Kingdom

930–586 B.C.

The division of Solomon's kingdom had geographical and political causes, with roots reaching back to earlier tribal rivalries. Israel was closer to Phoenician cities and major trade routes than Judah, whose heartland was a plateau-like ridge higher than the district around Samaria.

The Aramean wars were fierce and destructive contests between the kingdom of Damascus and Israel during the greater part of the ninth century. These so-called Aramean-Ephraimitic wars ended with the conquests of Jeroboam II and an era of great prosperity for Israel.

The campaigns of Tiglath-Pileser III of Assyria were enormously destructive, following a celebrated pattern of siege warfare. By 732 B.C. the northern kingdom was tributary to the Assyrians.

The final capture and destruction of Samaria took place in 722/721 B.C. after a long siege. The surviving inhabitants were exiled to distant places in the Assyrian Empire, and new settlers were brought to Samaria.

The Benjamite frontier was an issue that brought Judah and Israel into conflict early in their history. After a struggle between Asa and Baasha, the border was finally fixed south of Bethel in the territory of Benjamin.

The role of Mesha, king of Moab, was first that of a vassal and then a rebel, as both the Bible and the Mesha stele make clear.

Periods of expansion and contraction characterized the two kingdoms during the period 930-722 B.C. Judah was to some extent protected by its geography, but Israel was forced to develop an efficient standing army with substantial chariotry to defend against frequent attacks. Assyrian records mention that Ahab of Israel provided 2,000 chariots—by far the largest contingent in the anti-Assyrian alliance—in the battle of Qarqar in 853 B.C.

Judah's prosperity was intermittent and depended in large part on control of the trade routes to Egypt and the Red Sea. Border fortresses in the Judahite desert guarded the approaches from Edom. The "front door" of Judah was through Lachish and from there up to Hebron and Jerusalem. The capital was besieged many times, most forcefully by the Assyrians in 701 B.C. and by the Babylonians in 597 and 586, leading to the destruction of Jerusalem by Nebuchadnezzar and marking the end of the monarchy.

An impressive devotion to the Davidic dynastic line characterized the southern kingdom and helped to maintain stability, in contrast to the more mercurial northern kingdom.

you with whips; I will scourge you with scorpions." 15So the king did not listen to the people, for this turn of events was from the LORD,[m] to fulfill the word the LORD had spoken
to Jeroboam son of Nebat through Ahijah[n] the Shilonite.
16When all Israel saw that the king refused to listen to them, they answered the king:

"What share do we have in David,
what part in Jesse's son?
To your tents, O Israel![o]
Look after your own house, O David!"

So the Israelites went home. 17But as for the Israelites who were living in the towns of
Judah,[p] Rehoboam still ruled over them.
18King Rehoboam sent out Adoniram,[a][q] who was in charge of forced labor, but all Israel stoned him to death. King Rehoboam, however, managed to get into his chariot and
escape to Jerusalem. 19So Israel has been in rebellion against the house of David[r] to this
day.
20When all the Israelites heard that Jeroboam had returned, they sent and called him
to the assembly and made him king over all Israel. Only the tribe of Judah remained loyal to the house of David.[s]
21When Rehoboam arrived in Jerusalem, he mustered the whole house of Judah and
the tribe of Benjamin—a hundred and eighty thousand fighting men—to make war[t]
against the house of Israel and to regain the kingdom for Rehoboam son of Solomon.
22But this word of God came to Shemaiah[u] the man of God: 23"Say to Rehoboam son
of Solomon king of Judah, to the whole house of Judah and Benjamin, and to the rest of
the people, 24'This is what the LORD says: Do not go up to fight against your brothers, the
Israelites. Go home, every one of you, for this is my doing.' " So they obeyed the word of
the LORD and went home again, as the LORD had ordered.

Golden Calves at Bethel and Dan

25Then Jeroboam fortified Shechem[v] in the hill country of Ephraim and lived there.
From there he went out and built up Peniel.[b][w]
26Jeroboam thought to himself, "The kingdom will now likely revert to the house of
David. 27If these people go up to offer sacrifices at the temple of the LORD in Jerusalem,[x]
they will again give their allegiance to their lord, Rehoboam king of Judah. They will kill
me and return to King Rehoboam."
28After seeking advice, the king made two golden calves.[y] He said to the people, "It
is too much for you to go up to Jerusalem. Here are your gods, O Israel, who brought you

12:15 [m]ver 24; Dt 2:30; Jdg 14:4; 2Ch 22:7; 25:20 [n]1Ki 11:29
12:16 [o]2Sa 20:1
12:17 [p]1Ki 11:13, 36
12:18 [q]2Sa 20:24; 1Ki 4:6; 5:14
12:19 [r]2Ki 17:21
12:20 [s]1Ki 11:13, 32
12:21 [t]2Ch 11:1
12:22 [u]2Ch 12:5-7
12:25 [v]Jdg 9:45 [w]Jdg 8:8, 17
12:27 [x]Dt 12:5-6
12:28 [y]Ex 32:4; 2Ki 10:29; 17:16

[a] *18* Some Septuagint manuscripts and Syriac (see also 1 Kings 4:6 and 5:14); Hebrew *Adoram*
[b] *25* Hebrew *Penuel,* a variant of *Peniel*

12:15 from the LORD. Rehoboam's foolishness was not excused by appeal to divine agency. Rather, God was acting to initiate a new state of affairs for his people through the course of human events. Rehoboam's misguided actions therefore constituted the instrument through which God fulfilled Ahijah's prophecy (11:29–39).
12:16 Look after your own house, O David! The northern tribes seceded from Judah and the authority of David's descendants. For an identical taunt against David himself, see 2 Samuel 20:1.
12:17 But as for the Israelites. The term "Israelites" here refers to members of the northern tribes who had settled in the south.
12:18 Adoniram. See NIV text note. Rehoboam unwisely sent out the chief of forced labor to quell the uprising. **all Israel.** That is, representatives of the northern tribes (v. 1).
12:19 to this day. This expression dates the writing of 1 Kings, or at least the source of this section, to a preexilic time (see note on "today" at 8:8).
12:20 to the assembly. Jeroboam did not seem to play an active role in the assembly at Shechem. Once he was made king, however, he took charge over Israelite affairs (vv. 25–33).
12:22 the man of God. This common expression designated a prophet (1Sa 2:27; 1Ki 13:1; 2Ki 4:7).
12:23 the rest of the people. This probably refers to the Israelites who had settled in Judah (v. 17).
12:24 Go home . . . for this is my doing. The prophet Shemaiah reaffirmed what the prophet Ahijah had earlier declared (11:29–39): The division of the kingdom conformed to the will of God. The existence of two realms had been ordained by God, and each now had the opportunity to prove its loyalty to his covenant

■ **12:25—14:20** *In Israel (930–909 B.C.): Jeroboam I of Israel.* The first segment of the divided kingdom concerns Jeroboam I, who led the northern tribes to break away from Judah (see 12:1–24). While this political division had been predicted and was now being carried out by God himself, Jeroboam created illegitimate worship centers in the north and violated one of the writer's chief theological principles: the exclusivity of the temple in Jerusalem (12:25–33). As a result, the record of Jeroboam's reign includes two prophetic condemnations (13:1–34; 14:1–18) before its close (14:19–20).
■ **12:25–33** *Jeroboam's False Worship Centers.* In an effort to solidify the people's loyalty, Jeroboam constructed golden calves at Bethel and Dan and instituted a system of worship to substitute for worship at the temple in Jerusalem. This passage warned the readers in exile against forsaking their hope of returning to the land and rebuilding the temple, the only acceptable place of worship.
12:25 Peniel. (Or "Penuel"; see NIV text note) Located along the River Jabbok in Transjordan. Jeroboam consolidated his rule by fortifying two critical cities, Shechem and Peniel.
12:27 If these people go up to offer sacrifices. Jeroboam feared that religious unity between north and south would lead to a return to political unity as well.
12:28 two golden calves. Canaanite art characteristically depicted pagan deities standing on bulls, calves or other animals. In contrast to these practices, Jeroboam may not have intended to construct images or representations of the Lord. Nevertheless, his worship innovation became a conduit of Canaanite religious practices into the northern kingdom. Under Jeroboam's direction, polytheism was reintroduced to Israel (see Ex 32:4).

up out of Egypt."[z] 29One he set up in Bethel,[a] and the other in Dan.[b] 30And this thing became a sin;[c] the people went even as far as Dan to worship the one there.
31Jeroboam built shrines[d] on high places and appointed priests[e] from all sorts of people, even though they were not Levites. 32He instituted a festival on the fifteenth day of
the eighth[f] month, like the festival held in Judah, and offered sacrifices on the altar. This
he did in Bethel, sacrificing to the calves he had made. And at Bethel he also installed
priests at the high places he had made. 33On the fifteenth day of the eighth month, a
month of his own choosing, he offered sacrifices on the altar he had built at Bethel.[g] So
he instituted the festival for the Israelites and went up to the altar to make offerings.

The Man of God From Judah

13 By the word of the LORD a man of God[h] came from Judah to Bethel,[i] as Jeroboam was standing by the altar to make an offering. 2He cried out against the altar by the word of the LORD: "O altar, altar! This is what the LORD says: 'A son named Josiah[j] will be born to the house of David. On you he will sacrifice the priests of the high
places who now make offerings here, and human bones will be burned on you.' " 3That
same day the man of God gave a sign:[k] "This is the sign the LORD has declared: The altar will be split apart and the ashes on it will be poured out."
4When King Jeroboam heard what the man of God cried out against the altar at Bethel, he stretched out his hand from the altar and said, "Seize him!" But the hand he
stretched out toward the man shriveled up, so that he could not pull it back. 5Also, the
altar was split apart and its ashes poured out according to the sign given by the man of
God by the word of the LORD.
6Then the king said to the man of God, "Intercede[l] with the LORD your God and pray
for me that my hand may be restored." So the man of God interceded with the LORD, and
the king's hand was restored and became as it was before.
7The king said to the man of God, "Come home with me and have something to eat,
and I will give you a gift."[m]
8But the man of God answered the king, "Even if you were to give me half your possessions,[n] I would not go with you, nor would I eat bread[o] or drink water here. 9For I was
commanded by the word of the LORD: 'You must not eat bread or drink water or return
by the way you came.' " 10So he took another road and did not return by the way he had
come to Bethel.
11Now there was a certain old prophet living in Bethel, whose sons came and told him

12:28 [z]Ex 32:8
12:29 [a]Ge 28:19 [b]Jdg 18:27-31
12:30 [c]1Ki 13:34; 2Ki 17:21
12:31 [d]1Ki 13:32 [e]Nu 3:10; 1Ki 13:33; 2Ki 17:32; 2Ch 11:14-15; 13:9
12:32 [f]Lev 23:33-34; Nu 29:12
12:33 [g]Nu 15:39; 1Ki 13:1; Am 7:13
13:1 [h]2Ki 23:17 [i]1Ki 12:32-33
13:2 [j]2Ki 23:15-16,20
13:3 [k]Jdg 6:17; Isa 7:14; Jn 2:11; 1Co 1:22
13:6 [l]Ex 8:8; 9:28; 10:17; Lk 6:27-28; Ac 8:24; Jas 5:16
13:7 [m]1Sa 9:7; 2Ki 5:15
13:8 [n]Nu 22:18; 24:13 [o]ver 16

12:29 Bethel . . . Dan. These sites represent, respectively, the southernmost and northernmost worship centers in Jeroboam's kingdom. While Bethel, situated in Benjamite territory, is just 12 miles north of Jerusalem, Dan is located 25 miles north of the Sea of Kinnereth, not far from Mount Hermon. Bethel, in particular, had been a historic Israelite worship center before the all-important centralization of worship during David's reign (Ge 12:8; 28:11–19; 35:6–7; Jdg 20:26–28; 1Sa 7:16).
12:30 this thing became a sin. The establishment of a rival system of worship to the one in Jerusalem is repeatedly referred to in Kings as the sin of Jeroboam (13:34; 14:16; 15:26,30; 16:2; 2Ki 3:3; 10:29; 13:2; 17:21). Unfortunately, every subsequent northern king followed the path first blazed by Jeroboam. No Israelite king attempted to institute a thorough reform. Hence, the sin of Israel's first king became characteristic of the northern kingdom and represented one of the chief reasons for its demise (2Ki 17:16,22–23).
12:31 shrines on high places. See note on 3:2. By promoting and facilitating worship at the high places, Jeroboam introduced further innovation into his cult. **priests from all sorts of people.** Jeroboam created his own priesthood, regardless of priestly qualifications, even allowing non-Levites to serve (Dt 18:1–8; Jdg 17:10–13).
12:32 He instituted a festival. Perhaps an imitation of the Feast of Tabernacles (Lev 23:34; 1Ki 8:4). Jeroboam gave rural sacred precincts the official approval and support of the state.
12:33 a month of his own choosing. That is, not one sanctioned by God. By instituting his own cult, festival and priesthood, Jeroboam deliberately disassociated himself and his people from the Jerusalem temple and the worship practiced there. This action clearly defies the intent of Jeroboam's commission as described in 11:11–13, 29–39 and 12:15, 21–24, which mandated a political, but not a religious, separation between Israel and Judah. Loyalty to the covenant (11:38) of necessity involved loyalty both to the temple established "to God's honor" and to the priests, festivals and system of sacrifices operative there (cf. 5:11; 6:1,23; 8:13,17–19; 11:7–8). See *WLC* 109.

■ **13:1–34** *A Confirmed Prophetic Condemnation.* A man of God from Judah denounced Israel's idolatry, was judged when he himself disobeyed God and was recognized by a prophet of Israel as a man of God. Yet Jeroboam was unmoved by the man's warnings and brought even worse judgment upon himself for continuing to designate ineligible priests for his worship centers. This passage not only taught the original readers that Israel's idolatry warranted the punishment of exile but also warned Judahites not to think of themselves as above obedience to divine directives.
13:1 man of God. See 12:22. **from Judah.** God sent a prophet from the southern kingdom to declaim Jeroboam's worship in the northern kingdom.
13:2 Josiah. This king of Judah ruled from 640 to 609 B.C., approximately three centuries after Jeroboam. **sacrifice the priests of the high places.** This prophecy was realized during Josiah's reign (2Ki 23:15–20). **human bones will be burned on you.** Josiah would desecrate the altar and make its location unfit for continued use as a sacred precinct (2Ki 23:16).
13:3 sign. The prophets sometimes gave a sign, an immediate proof, to corroborate a prophecy (2Ki 19:29; 20:8–9; Isa 38:22; Jer 44:29). **the ashes on it will be poured out.** The altar would thereby be profaned (Lev 6:10–13).
13:5 the altar was split apart. The fulfillment of the sign of verse 3 indicated not only the truth of the prophecy about Josiah (v. 2), but also, more immediately, that Jeroboam's cult was condemned by God.
13:6 the king's hand was restored. God, in generously healing Jeroboam's hand, reaffirmed the authority of his prophet.
13:8 eat bread or drink water. For the prophet to have engaged in such activity with Jeroboam would have implied a tacit acceptance of Jeroboam's policies.
13:9 You must not eat . . . or drink . . . or return. The prophet had explicit instructions from God regarding his own personal conduct, which he could disobey only at his own peril (v. 17).
13:11 living in Bethel. This elderly prophet, unlike the man of God from Judah, was a seer living in the northern kingdom.

all that the man of God had done there that day. They also told their father what he had
said to the king. 12Their father asked them, "Which way did he go?" And his sons
showed him which road the man of God from Judah had taken. 13So he said to his sons,
"Saddle the donkey for me." And when they had saddled the donkey for him, he mounted it 14and rode after the man of God. He found him sitting under an oak tree and asked,
"Are you the man of God who came from Judah?"
"I am," he replied.
15So the prophet said to him, "Come home with me and eat." 13:16
16The man of God said, "I cannot turn back and go with you, nor can I eat bread[p] or [p]ver 8
drink water with you in this place. 17I have been told by the word of the LORD: 'You must
not eat bread or drink water there or return by the way you came.' "
18The old prophet answered, "I too am a prophet, as you are. And an angel said to me
by the word of the LORD: 'Bring him back with you to your house so that he may eat bread
and drink water.' " (But he was lying[q] to him.) 19So the man of God returned with him 13:18
and ate and drank in his house. [q]Dt 13:3
20While they were sitting at the table, the word of the LORD came to the old prophet
who had brought him back. 21He cried out to the man of God who had come from Judah,
"This is what the LORD says: 'You have defied[r] the word of the LORD and have not kept 13:21
the command the LORD your God gave you. 22You came back and ate bread and drank [r]ver 26
water in the place where he told you not to eat or drink. Therefore your body will not be
buried in the tomb of your fathers.' "
23When the man of God had finished eating and drinking, the prophet who had 13:24
brought him back saddled his donkey for him. 24As he went on his way, a lion[s] met him [s]1Ki 20:36
on the road and killed him, and his body was thrown down on the road, with both the
donkey and the lion standing beside it. 25Some people who passed by saw the body
thrown down there, with the lion standing beside the body, and they went and reported it in the city where the old prophet lived.
26When the prophet who had brought him back from his journey heard of it, he said,
"It is the man of God who defied the word of the LORD. The LORD has given him over to
the lion, which has mauled him and killed him, as the word of the LORD had warned him."
27The prophet said to his sons, "Saddle the donkey for me," and they did so. 28Then
he went out and found the body thrown down on the road, with the donkey and the lion
standing beside it. The lion had neither eaten the body nor mauled the donkey. 29So the
prophet picked up the body of the man of God, laid it on the donkey, and brought it back
to his own city to mourn for him and bury him. 30Then he laid the body in his own tomb, 13:30
and they mourned over him and said, "Oh, my brother!"[t] [t]Jer 22:18
31After burying him, he said to his sons, "When I die, bury me in the grave where the 13:31
man of God is buried; lay my bones[u] beside his bones. 32For the message he declared by [u]2Ki 23:18
the word of the LORD against the altar in Bethel and against all the shrines on the high 13:32
places[v] in the towns of Samaria[w] will certainly come true."[x] [v]ver 2; Lev 26:30
33Even after this, Jeroboam did not change his evil ways, but once more appointed [w]1Ki 16:24,28 [x]2Ki 23:16
priests for the high places from all sorts[y] of people. Anyone who wanted to become a 13:33
priest he consecrated for the high places. 34This was the sin[z] of the house of Jeroboam [y]1Ki 12:31;
that led to its downfall and to its destruction[a] from the face of the earth. 2Ch 11:15; 13:9

Ahijah's Prophecy Against Jeroboam 13:34

14 At that time Abijah son of Jeroboam became ill, 2and Jeroboam said to his wife, [z]1Ki 12:30 [a]1Ki 14:10
"Go, disguise yourself, so you won't be recognized as the wife of Jeroboam. Then

13:18 he was lying to him. The narrator explained editorially to his readers that the prophet living in Bethel had lied. He had not received such instructions.
13:20 the word of the LORD came to the old prophet. Ironically, God now used the old, lying prophet to deliver a true prophecy (v. 18).
13:22 your body will not be buried in the tomb of your fathers. In Israelite tradition, it was considered important to be buried along with one's ancestors in the family burial plot (1:21; Ge 47:30; Jos 24:30; 2Sa 2:32; 17:23).
13:24 the donkey and the lion. Surprisingly, the lion did not attack the donkey, nor did these animals run away or touch the corpse. The miraculous nature of this incident was recognized by travelers, and the news eventually reached the old prophet, who immediately understood its significance.
13:30 Oh, my brother! This lament is appropriate for a peer and not for a superior (cf. Jer 22:18).
13:31 lay my bones beside his bones. The aged prophet recognized the truth of the prophecy uttered by the man of God from Judah (v. 32). He identified himself with him by commanding that his own body be buried next to the bones of the prophet from Judah. Later, when Josiah desecrated the Bethel altar, he respectfully declined to disturb the bones of the two prophets (2Ki 23:17–18).
13:34 the sin of the house of Jeroboam. See note on 12:30.
■ **14:1–18** *A Second Prophetic Condemnation.* The prophet Ahijah prophesied disaster on Jeroboam and his house. God had offered Jeroboam a great future, but his rank idolatry removed all hope for the northern kingdom.
14:1 Abijah son of Jeroboam became ill. People in Old Testament times sometimes looked to prophets to heal disease (2Ki 4:28; 5) or to predict the fate of someone who was ill (2Ki 1:2–4; 8:8).
14:2 disguise yourself. Although Jeroboam respected the power and authority of the prophet, he wanted to avoid a confrontation with him.

go to Shiloh. Ahijah[b] the prophet is there—the one who told me I would be king over this people. [3]Take ten loaves of bread[c] with you, some cakes and a jar of honey, and go to him. He will tell you what will happen to the boy." [4]So Jeroboam's wife did what he said and went to Ahijah's house in Shiloh.

Now Ahijah could not see; his sight was gone because of his age. [5]But the LORD had told Ahijah, "Jeroboam's wife is coming to ask you about her son, for he is ill, and you are to give her such and such an answer. When she arrives, she will pretend to be someone else."

[6]So when Ahijah heard the sound of her footsteps at the door, he said, "Come in, wife of Jeroboam. Why this pretense? I have been sent to you with bad news. [7]Go, tell Jeroboam that this is what the LORD, the God of Israel, says: 'I raised you up from among the people and made you a leader[d] over my people Israel. [8]I tore[e] the kingdom away from the house of David and gave it to you, but you have not been like my servant David, who kept my commands and followed me with all his heart, doing only what was right[f] in my eyes. [9]You have done more evil than all who lived before you. You have made for yourself other gods, idols[g] made of metal; you have provoked me to anger and thrust me behind your back.[h]

[10]" 'Because of this, I am going to bring disaster on the house of Jeroboam. I will cut off from Jeroboam every last male in Israel—slave or free.[i] I will burn up the house of Jeroboam as one burns dung, until it is all gone.[j] [11]Dogs[k] will eat those belonging to Jeroboam who die in the city, and the birds of the air will feed on those who die in the country. The LORD has spoken!'

[12]"As for you, go back home. When you set foot in your city, the boy will die. [13]All Israel will mourn for him and bury him. He is the only one belonging to Jeroboam who will be buried, because he is the only one in the house of Jeroboam in whom the LORD, the God of Israel, has found anything good.[l]

[14]"The LORD will raise up for himself a king over Israel who will cut off the family of Jeroboam. This is the day! What? Yes, even now.[a] [15]And the LORD will strike Israel, so that it will be like a reed swaying in the water. He will uproot[m] Israel from this good land that he gave to their forefathers and scatter them beyond the River,[b] because they provoked[n] the LORD to anger by making Asherah[o] poles.[c] [16]And he will give Israel up because of the sins[p] Jeroboam has committed and has caused Israel to commit."

[17]Then Jeroboam's wife got up and left and went to Tirzah.[q] As soon as she stepped over the threshold of the house, the boy died. [18]They buried him, and all Israel mourned for him, as the LORD had said through his servant the prophet Ahijah.

[19]The other events of Jeroboam's reign, his wars and how he ruled, are written in the book of the annals of the kings of Israel. [20]He reigned for twenty-two years and then rested with his fathers. And Nadab his son succeeded him as king.

Rehoboam King of Judah

[21]Rehoboam son of Solomon was king in Judah. He was forty-one years old when he

14:2 [b]1Sa 28:8; 2Sa 14:2; 1Ki 11:29
14:3 [c]1Sa 9:7
14:7 [d]2Sa 12:7-8; 1Ki 16:2
14:8 [e]1Ki 11:31,33,38 [f]1Ki 15:5
14:9 [g]Ex 34:17; 1Ki 12:28; 2Ch 11:15 [h]Ne 9:26; Ps 50:17; Eze 23:35
14:10 [i]Dt 32:36; 1Ki 21:21; 2Ki 9:8-9; 14:26 [j]1Ki 15:29
14:11 [k]1Ki 16:4; 21:24
14:13 [l]2Ch 12:12; 19:3
14:15 [m]Dt 29:28; 2Ki 15:29; 17:6; Ps 52:5 [n]Jos 23:15-16 [o]Ex 34:13; Dt 12:3
14:16 [p]1Ki 12:30; 13:34; 15:30,34; 16:2
14:17 [q]ver 12; 1Ki 15:33; 16:6-9

[a] *14* The meaning of the Hebrew for this sentence is uncertain. [b] *15* That is, the Euphrates
[c] *15* That is, symbols of the goddess Asherah; here and elsewhere in 1 Kings

14:3 Take ten loaves of bread. Jeroboam's wife was to take these gifts, which would be considered fit if from a commoner but not from royalty (1Sa 9:6–8; 2Ki 5:15; 8:8), to Ahijah in order to ingratiate herself to him.

14:11 Dogs will eat . . . the birds of the air. Language of the curses of the Sinaitic covenant and ancient Near Eastern treaties was applied to the demise of Jeroboam's house (Dt 28:26).

14:15 the LORD will strike Israel. Ahijah announced the eventual exile of the northern kingdom. **like a reed swaying in the water.** Ahijah used a curse formula, familiar from ancient Near Eastern treaties, to dramatize the ignominious fate of the northern kingdom. **He will uproot Israel from this good land.** This was not a new idea or threat. The possibility of exile for apostasy was raised in the Mosaic covenant (Dt 28:63–64; 29:28), in Joshua's farewell speech (Jos 23:15–16,) and in Solomon's temple prayer (8:33–34,46–53). **Asherah poles.** Asherah was worshiped as a Canaanite goddess who functioned, among other things, as a consort of Baal. Asherah poles (see NIV text note) were probably carved wooden images representing this deity (Ex 34:13; Dt 12:3).

14:16 sins Jeroboam has committed. See 12:26–33, 13:33–34, 15:26, 30 and 34, as well as 16:2, 13, 19 and 26.

14:17 Tirzah. Approximately seven miles north of Shechem, this site was first Jeroboam's place of residence (12:25) and later the capital of Israel (15:33), until the city of Samaria was constructed (16:24). **As soon as she stepped over the threshold.** The death of Jeroboam's son suggested that Ahijah's other prophecies would also come true (v. 18).

▪ **14:19–20** *Closing of Reign.* Having shown that Jeroboam was twice condemned by prophets for creating an alternative to worship at the temple in Jerusalem, the writer concluded Jeroboam's story.

14:19 The other events. The Biblical writer did not claim to have written an exhaustive account of Jeroboam's reign. Rather, he wrote what he considered important in order for his readers to learn from the past. **annals of the kings of Israel.** See note on 11:41 and "Introduction: Author and Time and Place of Writing."

14:20 twenty-two years. That is, from 930–909 B.C.

▪ **14:21—15:24** *In Judah (930–869 B.C.).* The writer shifted to events in Judah beginning with Rehoboam (14:21–31), continuing with Rehoboam's son Abijah (15:1–8) and concluding with Abijah's son Asa (15:9–24).

▪ **14:21–31** *Rehoboam of Judah (930–913 B.C.).* This record of Rehoboam's reign divides into four parts: the opening (v. 21), corruption of worship (vv. 22–24), invasion of Shishak (vv. 25–28) and the closing of the record (vv. 29–31). His reign was marked by increasing idolatry and immorality, loss of treasures to the king of Egypt and continual warfare with Jeroboam.

▪ **14:21** *Opening of the Reign.* The mention of Rehoboam's

became king, and he reigned seventeen years in Jerusalem, the city the LORD had chosen out of all the tribes of Israel in which to put his Name. His mother's name was Naamah; she was an Ammonite.[r]
[22]Judah[s] did evil in the eyes of the LORD. By the sins they committed they stirred up his
jealous anger[t] more than their fathers had done. [23]They also set up for themselves high
places, sacred stones[u] and Asherah poles on every high hill and under every spreading
tree.[v] [24]There were even male shrine prostitutes[w] in the land; the people engaged in all
the detestable practices of the nations the LORD had driven out before the Israelites.
[25]In the fifth year of King Rehoboam, Shishak king of Egypt attacked[x] Jerusalem. [26]He
carried off the treasures of the temple[y] of the LORD and the treasures of the royal palace.
He took everything, including all the gold shields[z] Solomon had made. [27]So King Rehoboam made bronze shields to replace them and assigned these to the commanders of the
guard on duty at the entrance to the royal palace. [28]Whenever the king went to the LORD's
temple, the guards bore the shields, and afterward they returned them to the guardroom.
[29]As for the other events of Rehoboam's reign, and all he did, are they not written in
the book of the annals of the kings of Judah? [30]There was continual warfare[a] between
Rehoboam and Jeroboam. [31]And Rehoboam rested with his fathers and was buried
with them in the City of David. His mother's name was Naamah; she was an Ammonite.[b]
And Abijah[a] his son succeeded him as king.

Abijah King of Judah

15 In the eighteenth year of the reign of Jeroboam son of Nebat, Abijah[b] became
king of Judah, [2]and he reigned in Jerusalem three years. His mother's name was
Maacah[c] daughter of Abishalom.[c]
[3]He committed all the sins his father had done before him; his heart was not fully devoted[d] to the LORD his God, as the heart of David his forefather had been. [4]Nevertheless,
for David's sake the LORD his God gave him a lamp[e] in Jerusalem by raising up a son to
succeed him and by making Jerusalem strong. [5]For David had done what was right in the
eyes of the LORD and had not failed to keep[f] any of the LORD's commands all the days of
his life—except in the case of Uriah[g] the Hittite.

14:21 [r]ver 31; 1Ki 11:1; 2Ch 12:13
14:22 [s]2Ch 12:1 [t]Dt 32:21; Ps 78:58; 1Co 10:22
14:23 [u]Dt 16:22; 2Ki 17:9-10; Eze 16:24-25 [v]Dt 12:2; Isa 57:5
14:24 [w]Dt 23:17; 1Ki 15:12; 2Ki 23:7
14:25 [x]1Ki 11:40; 2Ch 12:2
14:26 [y]1Ki 15:15,18 [z]1Ki 10:17
14:30 [a]1Ki 12:21; 15:6
14:31 [b]ver 21; 2Ch 12:16
15:2 [c]2Ch 11:20; 13:2
15:3 [d]1Ki 11:4; Ps 119:80
15:4 [e]2Sa 21:17; 1Ki 11:36; 2Ch 21:7
15:5 [f]1Ki 9:4; 14:8 [g]2Sa 11:2-27; 12:9

[a] *31* Some Hebrew manuscripts and Septuagint (see also 2 Chron. 12:16); most Hebrew manuscripts *Abijam* [b] *1* Some Hebrew manuscripts and Septuagint (see also 2 Chron. 12:16); most Hebrew manuscripts *Abijam*; also in verses 7 and 8 [c] *2* A variant of *Absalom*; also in verse 10

Ammonite mother is included both in the opening and closing sections of the account of his reign, emphasizing the influence of foreign idolatry to which he would succumb.
14:21 seventeen years. 930–913 B.C.
▪ **14:22–24** *Corruption of Worship.* Rehoboam violated the laws against idolatry, an important concern for the writer and the very sin that brought ruin to the northern kingdom.
14:22 Judah. The Septuagint (Greek translation of the OT) reads "he" in the singular, signifying Rehoboam (12:24; 2Ch 12:14).
14:23 high places. See note on 3:2. **sacred stones.** Pillars set erect in the ground. Many were intended to be religious in nature and were employed by the Canaanites in their worship. The use of sacred stones was forbidden in Israelite law (Ex 23:24; Lev 26:1; Dt 12:3; 16:21–22). **Asherah poles.** See note on "Asherah poles" at verse 15. **under every spreading tree.** Religious activities carried out near certain trees in Old Testament times were considered to be of special significance (Dt 12:2; 2Ki 17:10; Isa 57:5; Jer 2:20; Eze 6:13; Hos 4:13).
14:24 male shrine prostitutes. The Canaanites believed that ritual prostitution helped to ensure the fertility of land, flocks and people. The practice was forbidden in Israel (Dt 23:17–18; 1Ki 15:12; 22:47; 2Ki 23:7; Hos 4:14).
▪ **14:25–28** *Judgment of Shishak Invasion.* As God's discipline for Rehoboam's sin, the Egyptians invaded and set siege to Jerusalem.
14:25 Shishak. Founded the twenty-second dynasty and began to rule Egypt around 945 B.C. According to Egyptian sources, including a fragment of a stela (an inscribed stone slab or pillar used to commemorate events) from Shishak's campaign found at Megiddo, Shishak also invaded Israel, the northern kingdom, and inflicted widespread destruction.
14:26 He carried off the treasures of the temple. That is, treasures placed there by King Solomon (7:51). **gold shields.** See 10:16–17.
14:27 bronze shields. Judah was too small and too poor to replace Solomon's shields in kind. The replacement of gold shields with bronze demonstrated the lasting effects of God's judgment.
▪ **14:29–31** *Closure of the Reign.* The author left his audience with the impression of the curses that fell on Judah as a result of Rehoboam's idolatry, as well as with an implied reminder that his idolatry had been encouraged by his Ammonite mother.
14:29 book of the annals of the kings of Judah. See note on 11:41.
14:30 continual warfare. Minor skirmishes and full-fledged wars between Israel and Judah characterized the early history of the divided monarchy (12:24; 14:19; 15:6; 2Ch 13:1–20). These wars were also a mark of divine judgment against Rehoboam for his violations of God's law.
14:31 Naamah . . . an Ammonite. Rehoboam was the offspring of one of Solomon's marriages to a foreign woman (11:1).
▪ **15:1–8** *Abijah of Judah (913–910 B.C.).* These verses summarize the reign of Abijah in three simple steps: the opening (vv. 1–2); his sins, survival and struggle (vv. 3–6); and the closing (vv. 7–8). He continued in the evil ways of his father, Rehoboam.
15:1 In the eighteenth year of the reign of Jeroboam. For other instances of synchronism between the reigns of northern and southern kings, see verses 9, 25 and 33, as well as 16:8, 15 and 29 and note on 14:21. **Abijah.** See NIV text note.
15:2 he reigned in Jerusalem three years. From 913–910 B.C. **His mother's name was Maacah.** Probably due to the nature of his sources, the author lists the name of the king's mother only for monarchs of Judah. See "Introduction: Time and Place of Writing." **daughter of Abishalom.** See NIV text note. It is likely that the term "daughter" is used here to mean "granddaughter" (cf. 2Sa 3:3; 14:27; 2Ch 13:2). Similarly, verse 3 calls David Abijah's "father" (in Hebrew), meaning by this "forefather" (as translated by the NIV).
15:3 sins his father had done. See 14:22–24. **as the heart of David.** David was the model king (see note on 11:4). **forefather.** See note on "daughter of Abishalom" at verse 2.
15:4 a lamp. See note on 11:36. One of the prominent theological themes in Kings is the continuation of the promises to David, despite the exile. Here the writer noted that it was only because of God's promise to David that Abijah survived on the throne.
15:5 Uriah the Hittite. The husband of Bathsheba and one of David's "mighty men." David had murdered Uriah in an attempt to conceal his guilt. See 2 Samuel 11, as well as 23:8–39.

Rulers of the Divided Kingdom of Israel and Judah

DATA AND DATES IN ORDER OF SEQUENCE

	Scripture	Kings	Synchronism or Correlation	Length of Reign	Historical Data	Dates
1.	*1Ki 12:1-24*	***Rehoboam** (Judah)*		*17 years*		*930-913*
	1Ki 14:21-31					
2.	1Ki 12:25–14:20	**Jeroboam I** (Israel)		22 years		930-909
3.	*1Ki 15:1-8*	***Abijah** (Judah)*	*18th of Jeroboam*	*3 years*		*913-910*
4.	*1Ki 15:9-24*	***Asa** (Judah)*	*20th of Jeroboam*	*41 years*		*910-869*
5.	1Ki 15:25-31	**Nadab** (Israel)	2nd of Asa	2 years		909-908
6.	1Ki 15:32–16:7	**Baasha** (Israel)	3rd of Asa	24 years		908-886
7.	1Ki 16:8-14	**Elah** (Israel)	26th of Asa	2 years		886-885
8.	1Ki 16:15-20	**Zimri** (Israel)	27th of Asa	7days		885
9.	1Ki 16:21-22	**Tibni** (Israel)			Overlap with Omri	885-880
10.	1Ki 16:23-28	**Omri** (Israel)	27th of Asa		Made king by the people	885
					Overlap with Tibni	885-880
				12 years	Official reign = 11 actual years	885-874
			31st of Asa		Sole reign	880-874
11.	1Ki 16:29–22:40	**Ahab** (Israel)	38th of Asa	22 years	Official reign = 21 actual years	874-853
12.	*1Ki 22:41-50*	***Jehoshaphat** (Judah)*			*Coregency with Asa*	*872-869*
				25 years	*Official reign*	*872-848*
			4th of Ahab		*Sole reign*	*869-853*
					Has Jehoram as regent	*853-848*
13.	1Ki 22:51– 2Ki 1:18	**Ahaziah** (Israel)	17th of Jehoshaphat	2 years	Official reign = 1 yr. actual reign	853-852
14.	2Ki 1:17	**Joram** (Israel)	2nd of Jehoram			852
	2Ki 3:1–8:15		18th of Jehoshaphat	12 years	Official reign = 11 actual years	852-841
15.	*2Ki 8:16-24*	***Jehoram** (Judah)*	*5th of Joram*		*Coregency with Jehoshaphat*	*853-848*
					Sole reign	*848-841*
				8 years	*Official reign = 7 actual years*	*848-841*
16.	*2Ki 8:25-29*	***Ahaziah** (Judah)*	*12th of Joram*	*1 year*	*Nonaccession-year reckoning*	*841*
	2Ki 9:29		*11th of Joram*		*Accession-year reckoning*	*841*
17.	2Ki 9:30–10:36	**Jehu** (Israel)		28 years		841-814
18.	*2Ki 11*	***Athaliah** (Judah)*		*7 years*		*841-835*
19.	*2Ki 12*	***Joash** (Judah)*	*7th of Jehu*	*40 years*		*835-796*
20.	2Ki 13:1-9	**Jehoahaz** (Israel)	23rd of Joash	17 years		814-798
21.	2Ki 13:10-25	**Jehoash** (Israel)	37th of Joash	16 years		798-782

Scripture	Kings	Synchronism or Correlation	Length of Reign	Historical Data	Dates
22. *2Ki 14:1-22*	***Amaziah*** *(Judah)*	*2nd of Jehoash*	*29 years*		*796-767*
				Overlap with Azariah	*792-767*
23. 2Ki 14:23-29	**Jeroboam II** (Israel)			Coregency with Jehoash	793-782
			41 years	Total reign	793-753
		15th of Amaziah		Sole reign	782-753
24. *2Ki 15:1-7*	***Azariah*** *(Judah)*			*Overlap with Amaziah*	*792-767*
			52 years	*Total reign*	*792-740*
		27th of Jeroboam		*Sole reign*	*767-750*
25. 2Ki 15:8-12	**Zechariah** (Israel)	38th of Azariah	6 months		753
26. 2Ki 15:13-15	**Shallum** (Israel)	39th of Azariah	1 month		752
27. 2Ki 15:16-22	**Menahem** (Israel)	39th of Azariah	10 years	Ruled in Samaria	752-742
28. 2Ki 15:23-26	**Pekahiah** (Israel)	50th of Azariah	2 years		742-740
29. 2Ki 15:27-31	**Pekah** (Israel)			In Gilead; overlapping years	752-740
			20 years	Total reign	752-732
		52nd of Azariah		Sole reign	740-732
30. *2Ki 15:32-38*	***Jotham*** *(Judah)*	*2nd of Pekah*		*Coregency with Azariah*	*750-740*
2Ki 15:30			*16 years*	*Official reign*	*750-735*
				Reign to his 20th year	*750-732*
31. *2Ki 16*	***Ahaz*** *(Judah)*			*Total reign*	*735-715*
		17th of Pekah			*735*
			16 years	*From 20th of Jotham*	*732-715*
32. 2Ki 15:30	**Hoshea** (Israel)			20th of Jotham	732
2Ki 17		12th of Ahaz	9 years		732-722
33. *2Ki 18:1–20:21*	***Hezekiah*** *(Judah)*	*3rd of Hoshea*	*29 years*		*715-686*
				Coregency with Ahaz	*729-715*
34. *2Ki 21:1-18*	***Manasseh*** *(Judah)*			*Coregency with Hezekiah*	*697-686*
			55 years	*Total reign*	*697-642*
35. *2Ki 21:19-26*	***Amon*** *(Judah)*		*2 years*		*642-640*
36. *2Ki 22:1–23:30*	***Josiah*** *(Judah)*		*31 years*		*640-609*
37. *2Ki 23:31-33*	***Jehoahaz*** *(Judah)*		*3 months*		*609*
38. *2Ki 23:34–24:7*	***Jehoiakim*** *(Judah)*		*11 years*		*609-598*
39. *2Ki 24:8-17*	***Jehoiachin*** *(Judah)*		*3 months*		*598-597*
40. *2Ki 24:18–25:26*	***Zedekiah*** *(Judah)*		*11 years*		*597-586*

Italics denote kings of ***Judah.***
Non-italic type denotes kings of **Israel**

6 There was war[h] between Rehoboam[a] and Jeroboam throughout ⌞Abijah's⌟ lifetime.
7 As for the other events of Abijah's reign, and all he did, are they not written in the book
of the annals of the kings of Judah? There was war between Abijah and Jeroboam. 8 And
Abijah rested with his fathers and was buried in the City of David. And Asa his son succeeded him as king.

Asa King of Judah

9 In the twentieth year of Jeroboam king of Israel, Asa became king of Judah, 10 and he
reigned in Jerusalem forty-one years. His grandmother's name was Maacah[i] daughter
of Abishalom.
11 Asa did what was right in the eyes of the LORD, as his father David had done. 12 He
expelled the male shrine prostitutes[j] from the land and got rid of all the idols his fathers
had made. 13 He even deposed his grandmother Maacah from her position as queen
mother, because she had made a repulsive Asherah pole. Asa cut the pole down[k] and
burned it in the Kidron Valley. 14 Although he did not remove the high places, Asa's heart
was fully committed[l] to the LORD all his life. 15 He brought into the temple of the LORD the
silver and gold and the articles that he and his father had dedicated.[m]
16 There was war[n] between Asa and Baasha king of Israel throughout their reigns.
17 Baasha king of Israel went up against Judah and fortified Ramah[o] to prevent anyone
from leaving or entering the territory of Asa king of Judah.
18 Asa then took all the silver and gold that was left in the treasuries of the LORD's temple[p] and of his own palace. He entrusted it to his officials and sent[q] them to Ben-Hadad[r]
son of Tabrimmon, the son of Hezion, the king of Aram, who was ruling in Damascus.
19 "Let there be a treaty between me and you," he said, "as there was between my father
and your father. See, I am sending you a gift of silver and gold. Now break your treaty
with Baasha king of Israel so he will withdraw from me."
20 Ben-Hadad agreed with King Asa and sent the commanders of his forces against the
towns of Israel. He conquered[s] Ijon, Dan, Abel Beth Maacah and all Kinnereth in addition to Naphtali. 21 When Baasha heard this, he stopped building Ramah and withdrew
to Tirzah. 22 Then King Asa issued an order to all Judah—no one was exempt—and they
carried away from Ramah the stones and timber Baasha had been using there. With
them King Asa built up Geba[t] in Benjamin, and also Mizpah.
23 As for all the other events of Asa's reign, all his achievements, all he did and the cities he built, are they not written in the book of the annals of the kings of Judah? In his

15:6 [h]1Ki 14:30
15:10 [i]ver 2
15:12 [j]1Ki 14:24; 22:46
15:13 [k]Ex 32:20
15:14 [l]ver 3; 1Ki 8:61; 22:43
15:15 [m]1Ki 7:51
15:16 [n]ver 32
15:17 [o]Jos 18:25; 1Ki 12:27
15:18 [p]ver 15; 1Ki 14:26 [q]2Ki 12:18 [r]1Ki 11:23-24
15:20 [s]Jdg 18:29; 2Sa 20:14; 2Ki 15:29
15:22 [t]Jos 18:24; 21:17

[a] *6* Most Hebrew manuscripts; some Hebrew manuscripts and Syriac *Abijam* (that is, Abijah)

15:6 Rehoboam. See NIV text note.
15:7 the book of the annals of the kings of Judah. See note on 11:41 and "Introduction: Time and Place of Writing." **war between Abijah and Jeroboam.** See 2 Chronicles 13:1–20 and note on 1 Kings 14:30.
■ **15:9–24** *Asa of Judah (910–869 B.C.).* These verses summarize the long reign of Asa. They divide into the opening (vv. 9–10), his reforms of worship (vv. 11–15), his defilement of the temple (vv. 16–22) and the closure of his reign (vv. 23–24).
15:9 In the twentieth year of Jeroboam. The author correlates the histories of the two kingdoms. See note on verse 1.
15:10 he reigned . . . forty-one years. From 910–869 B.C. **Maacah daughter of Abishalom.** See notes on verse 2.
15:11 Asa did what was right. This was not a categorical commendation of Asa, as verses 16–22 demonstrate. Asa did well by expunging Canaanite religious symbols and by reforming the religious practices (vv. 12–14).
15:12 male shrine prostitutes. See note on 14:24. **the idols his fathers had made.** See notes on 14:23. See *WLC* 139. See *BC* 36.
15:13 queen mother. The queen mother could at times exercise considerable influence in the royal court (1:11–14,28–31; 2Ki 11:1–20). **Asherah pole.** See note at 14:23. **Kidron Valley.** Located east of Jerusalem.
15:14 high places. Such rural centers of worship could be devoted to the Lord, to one of the Canaanite deities or to some combination of both. See note on 3:2.
15:15 He brought into the temple. Asa tried to replace some of the treasures that had been lost during Shishak's invasion (14:25–26; 16:7–10).
15:16 war . . . throughout their reigns. This verse serves as a title for this entire section. The continuation of war between the northern and southern kingdoms demonstrated God's disapproval of what Asa had done. The reference is most likely not to a full-fledged war but to a continuous series of skirmishes and battles. See note on 14:30.
15:17 Ramah. A town in Benjamin, located only six miles north of Jerusalem. Since Ramah was strategically located, the king of Israel could effectively limit access to Jerusalem. Moreover, Israel was much larger than Judah; hence, the threat posed by Baasha's campaign and blockade was urgent.
15:18 all the silver and gold that was left. See note on verse 15. The "gift of silver and gold" (v. 19) constituted an inducement for Ben Hadad to break his treaty with Baasha. This would place great pressure on Israel because Aram, as a neighboring state of formidable strength, exercised considerable power in the region. **treasuries of the LORD's temple.** Asa violated the sanctity of the temple by giving the Lord's money to acquire a treaty with Baasha. This action violated the holiness of the temple and all that belonged there.
15:19 Let there be a treaty. If a treaty were ratified between Judah and Damascus, Damascus could come to Judah's aid in the event of an attack on Judah by Israel. It would therefore be incumbent upon Israel to withdraw.
15:20 Ben-Hadad agreed. The Aramean king gained booty from Judah and territory from Israel by betraying Baasha. **and all Kinnereth in addition to Naphtali.** Conquering these cities and areas to the north and west of the Sea of Kinnereth was a strategic victory, because control of this territory, and all the trade routes that traversed it, provided Ben-Hadad with direct access to the cities of Phoenicia on the Mediterranean coast.
15:21 Tirzah. See note on "Tirzah" at 14:17.
15:22 no one was exempt. Asa conscripted forced labor to build these sites (see notes on 5:13,15; 9:15–22). **Geba in Benjamin.** This site was just east of Ramah, while Mizpah was northwest of Ramah. By fortifying these sites, Asa discouraged another Israelite campaign against Judah (cf. 2Ch 14:5).
15:23 book of the annals of the kings of Judah. See note on 11:41. **his feet became diseased.** See 2 Chronicles 16:12.

old age, however, his feet became diseased. 24Then Asa rested with his fathers and was
buried with them in the city of his father David. And Jehoshaphat[u] his son succeeded him
as king.

Nadab King of Israel

25Nadab son of Jeroboam became king of Israel in the second year of Asa king of Judah, and he reigned over Israel two years. 26He did evil in the eyes of the LORD, walking
in the ways of his father[v] and in his sin, which he had caused Israel to commit.
27Baasha son of Ahijah of the house of Issachar plotted against him, and he struck
him down[w] at Gibbethon,[x] a Philistine town, while Nadab and all Israel were besieging
it. 28Baasha killed Nadab in the third year of Asa king of Judah and succeeded him as
king.
29As soon as he began to reign, he killed Jeroboam's whole family.[y] He did not leave
Jeroboam anyone that breathed, but destroyed them all, according to the word of the
LORD given through his servant Ahijah the Shilonite— 30because of the sins[z] Jeroboam
had committed and had caused Israel to commit, and because he provoked the LORD, the
God of Israel, to anger.
31As for the other events of Nadab's reign, and all he did, are they not written in the
book of the annals of the kings of Israel? 32There was war[a] between Asa and Baasha king
of Israel throughout their reigns.

Baasha King of Israel

33In the third year of Asa king of Judah, Baasha son of Ahijah became king of all Israel in Tirzah, and he reigned twenty-four years. 34He did evil[b] in the eyes of the LORD,
walking in the ways of Jeroboam and in his sin, which he had caused Israel to commit.

16 Then the word of the LORD came to Jehu[c] son of Hanani[d] against Baasha: 2"I
lifted you up from the dust[e] and made you leader[f] of my people Israel, but you
walked in the ways of Jeroboam and caused[g] my people Israel to sin and to provoke me
to anger by their sins. 3So I am about to consume Baasha and his house,[h] and I will
make your house like that of Jeroboam son of Nebat. 4Dogs[i] will eat those belonging to
Baasha who die in the city, and the birds of the air will feed on those who die in the
country."
5As for the other events of Baasha's reign, what he did and his achievements, are they
not written in the book of the annals[j] of the kings of Israel? 6Baasha rested with his fathers and was buried in Tirzah.[k] And Elah his son succeeded him as king.
7Moreover, the word of the LORD came[l] through the prophet Jehu[m] son of Hanani to
Baasha and his house, because of all the evil he had done in the eyes of the LORD, provoking him to anger by the things he did, and becoming like the house of Jeroboam—
and also because he destroyed it.

15:24 [u]Mt 1:8
15:26 [v]1Ki 12:30; 14:16
15:27 [w]1Ki 14:14 [x]Jos 19:44; 21:23
15:29 [y]1Ki 14:10,14
15:30 [z]1Ki 14:9,16
15:32 [a]ver 16
15:34 [b]ver 26; 1Ki 12:28-29; 13:33; 14:16
16:1 [c]ver 7; 2Ch 19:2; 20:34 [d]2Ch 16:7
16:2 [e]1Sa 2:8 [f]1Ki 14:7-9 [g]1Ki 15:34
16:3 [h]ver 11; 1Ki 14:10; 15:29; 21:22
16:4 [i]1Ki 14:11
16:5 [j]1Ki 14:19; 15:31
16:6 [k]1Ki 14:17; 15:33
16:7 [l]1Ki 15:27,29 [m]ver 1

15:24 Jehoshaphat. On his reign, see 22:41–50.
■ **15:25—22:40** *In Israel (909–853 B.C.).* The writer now returned to the account of events in the northern kingdom. See "Introduction: Purpose and Distinctives." This series of kings included Nadab (15:25–32), Baasha (15:33—16:7), Elah (16:8–14), Zimri (16:15–20), Omri (16:21–28) and Ahab (16:29—22:40).
■ **15:25–32** *Nadab of Israel (909–908 B.C.).* Verses 25–26 summarize the reign of Nadab and characterize him negatively. More attention is given to the subsequent actions of his assassin and successor, Baasha. As soon as Baasha became king, he killed Jeroboam's whole family (vv. 27–30). Verses 31–32 close Nadab's reign.
15:25 second year of Asa. See notes on 14:21 and 15:1. **two years.** From 909–908 B.C.
15:26 his sin, which he had caused Israel to commit. See notes on 12:30 and 14:16.
15:27–28 Nadab's reign was considered so evil that the only thing said about him was that he was assassinated.
15:27 Gibbethon. A Philistine site north of Ekron and three miles west of Gezer, where Baasha assassinated Nadab.
15:29–30 To consolidate his position, Baasha disposed of all potential claimants to the throne in Jeroboam's family. In so doing, he unwittingly fulfilled Ahijah's prophecy to Jeroboam (14:10–11).
15:29 he killed Jeroboam's whole family. The author of Kings did not commend Baasha's actions; on the contrary, he later condemned him for his wanton destruction (16:7).
15:30 because of the sins Jeroboam had committed. See note on 12:30.
15:31 book of the annals of the kings of Israel. See note on 11:41.
15:32 war between Asa and Baasha. See note on 14:30.
■ **15:33—16:7** *Baasha of Israel (908–886 B.C.).* This section recounts the reign of Baasha and characterizes him as evil. It opens his reign (15:33–34), reports Jehu's prophetic judgment (16:1–4), closes the reign (16:5–6) and adds an afterword about Jehu's prophecy (16:7–8).
15:33 In the third year. See notes on 14:21 and 15:1. **Tirzah.** The capital of Israel before Omri built Samaria (16:24). See note on "Tirzah" at 14:17.
15:34 the ways of Jeroboam. See note on 12:30; see also 14:16.
16:1–4 The prophet Jehu condemned Baasha to judgment because Baasha behaved like Jeroboam.
16:1 Jehu son of Hanani. See 2 Chronicles 16:7–10, 19:2 and 20:34.
16:2 I lifted you up from the dust. As with Ahijah's condemnation of Jeroboam (14:7–8), Jehu began his prophetic speech by rehearsing God's beneficence to Baasha. **the ways of Jeroboam.** See notes on 12:30 and 14:16.
16:3 Baasha and his house. Because Baasha followed the policies set by Jeroboam, Baasha and his house would suffer the same fate (15:29).
16:4 Dogs will eat . . . the birds of the air will feed. The same curses had been leveled against Jeroboam (14:11).
16:5 book of the annals of the kings of Israel. See note on 11:41.
16:7 Despite the fact that Baasha had fulfilled prophecy (see 15:29), he was responsible for his actions.

Elah King of Israel

8 In the twenty-sixth year of Asa king of Judah, Elah son of Baasha became king of Israel, and he reigned in Tirzah two years.
16:9 9 Zimri, one of his officials, who had command of half his chariots, plotted against him.
[n]2Ki 9:30-33 Elah was in Tirzah at the time, getting drunk[n] in the home of Arza, the man in charge[o]
[o]1Ki 18:3 of the palace at Tirzah. 10 Zimri came in, struck him down and killed him in the twenty-
seventh year of Asa king of Judah. Then he succeeded him as king.
16:11 11 As soon as he began to reign and was seated on the throne, he killed off Baasha's
[p]ver 3 whole family.[p] He did not spare a single male, whether relative or friend. 12 So Zimri destroyed the whole family of Baasha, in accordance with the word of the LORD spoken
against Baasha through the prophet Jehu— 13 because of all the sins Baasha and his son
16:13 Elah had committed and had caused Israel to commit, so that they provoked the LORD,
[q]Dt 32:21; 1Sa 12:21; Isa 41:29 the God of Israel, to anger by their worthless idols.[q]
14 As for the other events of Elah's reign, and all he did, are they not written in the
book of the annals of the kings of Israel?

Zimri King of Israel

16:15 15 In the twenty-seventh year of Asa king of Judah, Zimri reigned in Tirzah seven days.
[r]Jos 19:44; 1Ki 15:27 The army was encamped near Gibbethon,[r] a Philistine town. 16 When the Israelites in the
camp heard that Zimri had plotted against the king and murdered him, they proclaimed
Omri, the commander of the army, king over Israel that very day there in the camp.
17 Then Omri and all the Israelites with him withdrew from Gibbethon and laid siege to
Tirzah. 18 When Zimri saw that the city was taken, he went into the citadel of the royal
palace and set the palace on fire around him. So he died, 19 because of the sins he had
committed, doing evil in the eyes of the LORD and walking in the ways of Jeroboam and
in the sin he had committed and had caused Israel to commit.
20 As for the other events of Zimri's reign, and the rebellion he carried out, are they
not written in the book of the annals of the kings of Israel?

Omri King of Israel

21 Then the people of Israel were split into two factions; half supported Tibni son of
Ginath for king, and the other half supported Omri. 22 But Omri's followers proved stronger than those of Tibni son of Ginath. So Tibni died and Omri became king.
16:23 23 In the thirty-first year of Asa king of Judah, Omri became king of Israel, and he
[s]1Ki 15:21 reigned twelve years, six of them in Tirzah.[s] 24 He bought the hill of Samaria from She-
16:24 mer for two talents[a] of silver and built a city on the hill, calling it Samaria,[t] after Shemer,
[t]1Ki 13:32; Jn 4:4 the name of the former owner of the hill.

[a] *24* That is, about 150 pounds (about 70 kilograms)

■ **16:8–14** *Elah of Israel (886–885 B.C.).* Elah, son of Baasha, was assassinated by Zimri, who succeeded him as king and killed Baasha's whole family in accordance with the prophecy of Jehu (vv. 1–4,7). This section divides into the beginning of Elah's reign (v. 8), the assassination (vv. 9–10), the murders of Baasha's family (vv. 11–13) and the end of Elah's reign (v. 14).
16:8 twenty-sixth year of Asa. 886 B.C. **he reigned in Tirzah two years.** From 886–885 B.C.
16:10 Zimri . . . struck him down. Elah fell victim to a coup led by Zimri, one of his own officials. **twenty-seventh year of Asa.** 885 B.C.
16:11–13 Zimri murdered Baasha's family.
16:11 He did not spare a single male. This action fulfilled the prophecy of verses 3–4 (see note on 15:29).
16:13 because of all the sins Baasha and his son Elah. Zimri's actions fulfilled the judgment of God. **provoked . . . to anger by their worthless idols.** The writer reiterated his deep concern over idolatry and its consequences in Israel's history (see "Introduction: Purpose and Distinctives").
16:14 the book of the annals of the kings of Israel. See note on 11:41.
■ **16:15–20** *Zimri of Israel (885 B.C.).* These verses summarize the brief reign of Zimri, king of Israel. These comments open his reign, describe the rebellion against him and close his reign.
16:15 the twenty-seventh year. 885 B.C. **reigned in Tirzah seven days.** Zimri's tenure was extremely brief. The turnover in Israelite kings during this period was exceptionally high; in general, the northern monarchy was plagued by frequent coups and coup attempts. While Judah was ruled by 20 kings from 930–586 B.C., Israel saw a succession of 19 from just 930–722 B.C. The relative stability in Judah can be attributed, in part, to Judahite kingship remaining in the hands of one family, the Davidic dynasty. From the perspective of the Biblical writer, however, the instability in Israel was also due to the pervasive disregard for the covenant exhibited by northern kings. This consistent apostasy led the Lord to cast off entire royal dynasties and replace them with new ones. This pattern of upheaval was God's means of disciplining and renewing Israel's leadership (11:29–39; 14:7–18; 16:1–4; 21:19–22; 22:17; 2Ki 1:2–4). **Gibbethon.** See note on 15:27.
16:16 they proclaimed Omri. The Israelite soldiers refused to accept Zimri's kingship. **commander of the army.** Omri held a higher rank than Zimri (v. 9). The troops may have felt more obligation to follow Omri than Zimri.
16:19 because of the sins. In his usual fashion the writer explained that the king's reign was cut short because of his sins. **walking in the ways of Jeroboam.** See note on 12:30.
16:20 the book of the annals of the kings of Israel. See note on 11:41.
■ **16:21–28** *Omri of Israel (885–874 B.C.).* These verses summarize the reign of Omri, king of Israel. He acquired the site for and built the city of Samaria as capital of Israel, but he sinned "more than all those before him" (v. 25). These verses describe the opening of his reign (vv. 21–23), his sins (vv. 24–26) and the closure of his reign (vv. 27–28).
16:21 were split into two factions. Tibni contested Omri's succession to the vacant throne. **Tibni son of Ginath.** Little is known either about Tibni or his father.
16:22 Tibni died. It is unclear whether Tibni died of natural causes or was killed by Omri's followers.
16:23 in the thirty-first year of Asa. 880 B.C. The struggle for

25 But Omri did evil[u] in the eyes of the LORD and sinned more than all those before him.
26 He walked in all the ways of Jeroboam son of Nebat and in his sin, which he had
caused[v] Israel to commit, so that they provoked the LORD, the God of Israel, to anger by
their worthless idols.[w]
27 As for the other events of Omri's reign, what he did and the things he achieved, are
they not written in the book of the annals of the kings of Israel? 28 Omri rested with his
fathers and was buried in Samaria. And Ahab his son succeeded him as king.

Ahab Becomes King of Israel

29 In the thirty-eighth year of Asa king of Judah, Ahab son of Omri became king of Israel, and he reigned in Samaria over Israel twenty-two years. 30 Ahab son of Omri did
more[x] evil in the eyes of the LORD than any of those before him. 31 He not only considered
it trivial to commit the sins of Jeroboam son of Nebat, but he also married[y] Jezebel
daughter[z] of Ethbaal king of the Sidonians, and began to serve Baal[a] and worship him.
32 He set up an altar for Baal in the temple[b] of Baal that he built in Samaria. 33 Ahab also
made an Asherah pole[c] and did more[d] to provoke the LORD, the God of Israel, to anger
than did all the kings of Israel before him.
34 In Ahab's time, Hiel of Bethel rebuilt Jericho. He laid its foundations at the cost of
his firstborn son Abiram, and he set up its gates at the cost of his youngest son Segub,
in accordance with the word of the LORD spoken by Joshua son of Nun.[e]

Elijah Fed by Ravens

17 Now Elijah[f] the Tishbite, from Tishbe[a] in Gilead,[g] said to Ahab, "As the LORD,
the God of Israel, lives, whom I serve, there will be neither dew nor rain[h] in the
next few years except at my word."

[a] 1 Or *Tishbite, of the settlers*

16:25 [u]Dt 4:25; Mic 6:16
16:26 [v]ver 19 [w]Dt 32:21
16:30 [x]ver 25; 1Ki 14:9
16:31 [y]Dt 7:3; 1Ki 11:2 [z]Jdg 18:7; 2Ki 9:34 [a]2Ki 10:18; 17:16
16:32 [b]2Ki 10:21,27; 11:18
16:33 [c]2Ki 13:6 [d]ver 29, 30; 1Ki 14:9; 21:25
16:34 [e]Jos 6:26
17:1 [f]Mal 4:5; Jas 5:17 [g]Jdg 12:4 [h]Dt 10:8; 1Ki 18:1; 2Ki 3:14; Lk 4:25

control of Israel between Omri and Tibni lasted four years (v. 15). Since Tibni never dominated, these four years were credited to Omri's reign. **he reigned twelve years.** From 885–874 B.C.

16:24 Samaria. Omri, like David (2Sa 5:6–16), founded his own capital. Located approximately ten miles west of Tirzah, Samaria was easily defensible and therefore became Israel's permanent capital (20:1; 2Ki 6:25; 10:18; 13:6; 18:9–10). "Samaria" is sometimes used synonymously with "Israel" (2Ki 17:24; Isa 10:10; Am 3:10,15).

16:25 sinned more than all those before him. Omri sealed an alliance with Ethbaal of Tyre by arranging the marriage of his son Ahab to Ethbaal's daughter Jezebel (v. 31). In this manner Baal worship (essential to the religion of Tyre) was given official support in Israel. The spread of Canaanite religion had far-reaching consequences for Israel (vv. 31–33) and Judah as well (2Ki 11, especially v. 18).

16:26 the ways of Jeroboam. See note on 12:30.

16:27 the things he achieved. Politically and militarily Omri was quite successful. An inscription on the Moabite stone states that Omri subjugated Moab and took possession of Medeba (in Transjordan). The annals of a much later Assyrian king, Tiglath-Pileser III (c. 732 B.C.), still speak of Israel as the "house of Omri."

■ **16:29—22:40** *Ahab of Israel (874–853 B.C.).* The extended and evil reign of Ahab, Omri's son, over Israel divides into four parts: the opening (16:29–30), a summary of Ahab's sins (16:31–34), prophetic condemnation (17:1—22:38) and the closure of his reign (22:39–40). Ahab married Jezebel and introduced Baal worship into Israel. His blatant sin set the stage for confrontation with God's prophets, Elijah and Micaiah among them.

■ **16:29–30** *Opening of the Reign.* Ahab is introduced as the most evil king to this point in the history of the northern kingdom (v. 25 and 14:9).

16:29 the thirty-eighth year of Asa. 874 B.C. **twenty-two years.** From 874–853 B.C.

■ **16:31–34** *A Summary of Ahab's Sins.* The writer includes a brief summation of Ahab's sins, presumably in order to explain why Ahab became the object of extensive prophetic attention.

16:31 he . . . married Jezebel. See note on verse 25. **began to serve Baal and worship him.** The Biblical writer lambastes Ahab because this monarch not only permitted but also encouraged Baal worship (by his wife, among others). **Baal.** The term *Baal* means "lord" or "husband." Baal was worshiped as a storm god and was the dominant deity in Canaanite religion. As a god who controlled the weather, Baal was considered instrumental in bringing the life-giving rains and fertility that staved off death and sterility for land, livestock and people.

16:33 Asherah pole. See note at 14:23.

16:34 Hiel of Bethel rebuilt Jericho. After its earlier destruction (Jos 5:13—6:27), Jericho had been inhabited as a settlement (Jos 18:21; NIV text note on Jdg 3:13; 2Sa 10:5). Hiel's desire to turn the site of Jericho into a full-fledged city activated the curse in Joshua 6:26, which expressly prohibited the rebuilding of the city and outlined dire consequences for anyone attempting to do so.

■ **17:1—22:38** *Ahab and Prophetic Condemnation.* The apostasy of Ahab's day was so terrible that the writer of Kings devotes special attention to narratives that focus on the prophets Elijah, Micaiah and another, unnamed prophet, as they declared God's judgment against Ahab. These chapters divide into six main parts: Elijah's early ministry (17:1–24), his opposition to the prophets of Baal (18:1–46), his encounter with the Lord (19:1–21), Ahab's war with Aram (20:1–43), his dealings with Naboth's vineyard (21:1–29) and another war with Aram (22:1–38). Each of these episodes concludes with prophetic condemnation.

■ **17:1–24** *Elijah's Early Ministry.* Elijah delivered God's message of famine to Ahab (v. 1), hid in the desert, was fed by ravens (vv. 2–6) and performed miracles at the home of the widow in Zarephath (vv. 7–24), all within the first three years of his ministry (see 18:1).

17:1 Elijah. His name means "My God is Yah." "Yah" is a shortened form of the name "Yahweh," translated in the NIV as the LORD (cf. Ex 3:14–15). In many ways Elijah's name signifies the major theme of his ministry: My God is the Lord and there is no other. Elijah was the major defendant of and proponent for Yahweh at a time when Ahab and Jezebel were promoting Baal worship in Israel. **Tishbe.** See NIV text note. **Gilead.** This area was located in northern Transjordan, and Tishbe was probably located north of the Wadi Kerith in this region. The author of Kings concentrates his attention on the message and ministry of Elijah during this critical period in Israel's history. The New Testament explains that John the Baptist ministered in the spirit of Elijah (Mt 11:14; 17:12). John wore clothing reminiscent of Elijah's (2Ki 1:8; Mt 3:4); both endured the opposition of women as primary antagonists (1Ki 19:2; Mt 14:3,6); their successors were inaugurated at the Jordan with a vision of the Spirit's coming (2Ki 2:9–14; Mt 3:13–17); and these successors performed mighty miracles (2Ki 2:9; Mt 11:4–5). To carry the analogy still further, it is striking that Elisha and Jesus would perform similar miracles. **neither dew nor rain.** Baal (see note on "Baal" at 16:31) was the god of life and fertility, so this drought directly contested this idol's supposed ability to control the weather. Similar expressions about dew and rain also occur in the Ugaritic texts about Baal (in 1400 B.C.). **except at my word.** The drought and its eventual dramatic resolution would demonstrate to a wayward Israel that the Lord is the true and only God.

2Then the word of the LORD came to Elijah: 3"Leave here, turn eastward and hide in
17:4 [i]Ge 8:7 the Kerith Ravine, east of the Jordan. 4You will drink from the brook, and I have ordered
the ravens[i] to feed you there."
5So he did what the LORD had told him. He went to the Kerith Ravine, east of the Jor-
17:6 [j]Ex 16:8 dan, and stayed there. 6The ravens brought him bread and meat in the morning[j] and
bread and meat in the evening, and he drank from the brook.

The Widow at Zarephath

17:9 7Some time later the brook dried up because there had been no rain in the land.
[k]Ob 1:20 [l]Lk 4:26 8Then the word of the LORD came to him: 9"Go at once to Zarephath[k] of Sidon and stay
there. I have commanded a widow[l] in that place to supply you with food." 10So he went
to Zarephath. When he came to the town gate, a widow was there gathering sticks. He
17:10 called to her and asked, "Would you bring me a little water in a jar so I may have a
[m]Ge 24:17; Jn 4:7 drink?"[m] 11As she was going to get it, he called, "And bring me, please, a piece of
bread."
17:12 12"As surely as the LORD your God lives," she replied, "I don't have any bread—only
[n]ver 1; 2Ki 4:2 a handful of flour in a jar and a little oil[n] in a jug. I am gathering a few sticks to take home
and make a meal for myself and my son, that we may eat it—and die."
13Elijah said to her, "Don't be afraid. Go home and do as you have said. But first make
a small cake of bread for me from what you have and bring it to me, and then make
something for yourself and your son. 14For this is what the LORD, the God of Israel, says:
'The jar of flour will not be used up and the jug of oil will not run dry until the day the
LORD gives rain on the land.' "
15She went away and did as Elijah had told her. So there was food every day for Elijah and for the woman and her family. 16For the jar of flour was not used up and the jug
of oil did not run dry, in keeping with the word of the LORD spoken by Elijah.
17Some time later the son of the woman who owned the house became ill. He grew
17:18 worse and worse, and finally stopped breathing. 18She said to Elijah, "What do you have
[o]2Ki 3:13; Lk 5:8 against me, man of God? Did you come to remind me of my sin[o] and kill my son?"
19"Give me your son," Elijah replied. He took him from her arms, carried him to the
upper room where he was staying, and laid him on his bed. 20Then he cried out to the
17:21 LORD, "O LORD my God, have you brought tragedy also upon this widow I am staying with,
[p]2Ki 4:34; Ac 20:10 by causing her son to die?" 21Then he stretched[p] himself out on the boy three times and
cried to the LORD, "O LORD my God, let this boy's life return to him!"
22The LORD heard Elijah's cry, and the boy's life returned to him, and he lived. 23Eli-
jah picked up the child and carried him down from the room into the house. He gave him
17:24 to his mother and said, "Look, your son is alive!"
[q]Jn 3:2; 16:30 [r]Ps 119:43; Jn 17:17 24Then the woman said to Elijah, "Now I know[q] that you are a man of God and that
the word of the LORD from your mouth is the truth."[r]

Elijah and Obadiah

18:1 [s]1Ki 17:1; Lk 4:25; Jas 5:17 [t]Dt 28:12
18 After a long time, in the third[s] year, the word of the LORD came to Elijah: "Go and
18:3 [u]1Ki 16:9 [v]Ne 7:2 present yourself to Ahab, and I will send rain[t] on the land." 2So Elijah went to
present himself to Ahab.
18:4 [w]2Ki 9:7 Now the famine was severe in Samaria, 3and Ahab had summoned Obadiah, who was
in charge[u] of his palace. (Obadiah was a devout believer[v] in the LORD. 4While Jezebel[w] was

---

17:4 ravens to feed you. Despite Elijah's isolation in the wilderness, the Lord miraculously provided for him, much as he had done for the nation of Israel centuries earlier after the escape from Egypt (Ex 16:4–36; 17:17; Lev 11:1–35). Ironically, Israel was now residing in the promised land—but had forgotten who it was that sustained her.

17:9 Zarephath. A town on the Mediterranean coast about halfway between Tyre and Sidon. God commanded Elijah to travel away from Israel into the area in which Canaanite religion was supreme. **widow.** The word is often synonymous with poor, because in the ancient Near East widows had little protection under the law and were often the victims of exploitation (Dt 14:29; 16:11; 24:20; 26:12; Ps 94:6; Isa 47:8–9). This particular widow was not an Israelite.

17:12 As surely as the LORD your God lives. These words were an oath formula (see note on 1:17) taken in the name of Elijah's God. Either this was an act of deference to Elijah or the widow had a genuine faith in the God of Israel.

17:13 first make a small cake of bread for me. Elijah presented her with a test of faith that demanded complete commitment. Despite the scarcity of food, she was to feed God's prophet before she took care of herself and her son.

17:18 What do you have against me, man of God? The widow associated the visit of Elijah with her son's illness, because she believed Elijah's presence as a holy man called divine attention to her sin.

17:21 he stretched himself out on the boy three times. Elijah performed a symbolic action that dramatized the accompanying prophetic prayer (see note on 11:30). The warmth and life of the prophet, manifested through the thrice repeated physical contact with the boy's body, emphasized the need for warmth and life to be returned to the boy (cf. 2Ki 4:34; Ac 20:10). Hence, Elijah's prayer, "let this boy's life return to him," is consonant with the prophet's symbolic action.

■ **18:1–46** *Elijah's Confrontation With the Prophets of Baal.* Elijah's God defeated the prophets of Baal in a dramatic contest on Mount Carmel, resulting in the end of the drought and consequent famine.

18:3 in charge of his palace. An important position in the royal administration (4:6 note).

killing off the LORD's prophets, Obadiah had taken a hundred prophets and hidden[x] them
in two caves, fifty in each, and had supplied them with food and water.) 5Ahab had said to
Obadiah, "Go through the land to all the springs and valleys. Maybe we can find some grass
to keep the horses and mules alive so we will not have to kill any of our animals." 6So they
divided the land they were to cover, Ahab going in one direction and Obadiah in another.
7As Obadiah was walking along, Elijah met him. Obadiah recognized[y] him, bowed
down to the ground, and said, "Is it really you, my lord Elijah?"
8"Yes," he replied. "Go tell your master, 'Elijah is here.'"
9"What have I done wrong," asked Obadiah, "that you are handing your servant over
to Ahab to be put to death? 10As surely as the LORD your God lives, there is not a nation
or kingdom where my master has not sent someone to look[z] for you. And whenever a nation or kingdom claimed you were not there, he made them swear they could not find
you. 11But now you tell me to go to my master and say, 'Elijah is here.' 12I don't know
where the Spirit[a] of the LORD may carry you when I leave you. If I go and tell Ahab and
he doesn't find you, he will kill me. Yet I your servant have worshiped the LORD since my
youth. 13Haven't you heard, my lord, what I did while Jezebel was killing the prophets
of the LORD? I hid a hundred of the LORD's prophets in two caves, fifty in each, and supplied them with food and water. 14And now you tell me to go to my master and say, 'Elijah is here.' He will kill me!"
15Elijah said, "As the LORD Almighty lives, whom I serve, I will surely present[b] myself
to Ahab today."

Elijah on Mount Carmel

16So Obadiah went to meet Ahab and told him, and Ahab went to meet Elijah.
17When he saw Elijah, he said to him, "Is that you, you troubler[c] of Israel?"
18"I have not made trouble for Israel," Elijah replied. "But you[d] and your father's family have. You have abandoned[e] the LORD's commands and have followed the Baals.
19Now summon the people from all over Israel to meet me on Mount Carmel.[f] And bring
the four hundred and fifty prophets of Baal and the four hundred prophets of Asherah,
who eat at Jezebel's table."
20So Ahab sent word throughout all Israel and assembled the prophets on Mount Carmel. 21Elijah went before the people and said, "How long will you waver[g] between two
opinions? If the LORD is God, follow him; but if Baal is God, follow him."
But the people said nothing.
22Then Elijah said to them, "I am the only one of the LORD's prophets left,[h] but Baal
has four hundred and fifty prophets.[i] 23Get two bulls for us. Let them choose one for
themselves, and let them cut it into pieces and put it on the wood but not set fire to it. I
will prepare the other bull and put it on the wood but not set fire to it. 24Then you call
on the name of your god, and I will call on the name of the LORD. The god who answers
by fire[j]—he is God."
Then all the people said, "What you say is good."
25Elijah said to the prophets of Baal, "Choose one of the bulls and prepare it first,
since there are so many of you. Call on the name of your god, but do not light the fire."
26So they took the bull given them and prepared it.
Then they called on the name of Baal from morning till noon. "O Baal, answer us!"
they shouted. But there was no response;[k] no one answered. And they danced around
the altar they had made.
27At noon Elijah began to taunt them. "Shout louder!" he said. "Surely he is a god!

18:4 [x]ver 13; Isa 16:3
18:7 [y]2Ki 1:8
18:10 [z]1Ki 17:3
18:12 [a]2Ki 2:16; Eze 3:14; Ac 8:39
18:15 [b]1Ki 17:1
18:17 [c]Jos 7:25; 1Ki 21:20; Ac 16:20
18:18 [d]1Ki 16:31,33; 21:25 [e]2Ch 15:2
18:19 [f]Jos 19:26
18:21 [g]Jos 24:15; 2Ki 17:41; Mt 6:24
18:22 [h]1Ki 19:10 [i]ver 19
18:24 [j]ver 38; 1Ch 21:26
18:26 [k]Ps 115:4-5; Jer 10:5; 1Co 8:4; 12:2

18:4 Jezebel was killing off the LORD's prophets. Not content to promote her native religion, Jezebel persecuted followers of the Lord by having their prophets murdered. See *WLC* 135; *WSC* 68.
18:5 horses and mules. The drought jeopardized the viability of Ahab's government, because the military depended on these animals, for example, in its chariot forces. Ahab's reaction to the drought was purely practical (finding water) and did not get to the heart of the issue: Who is sovereign over nature and life itself?
18:12 where the Spirit of the LORD may carry you. Earlier Elijah had disappeared to Transjordan, only to reemerge in Zarephath.
18:17 you troubler of Israel. Ahab viewed Elijah as a troublemaker, a threat to the normal functioning of society. He failed to grasp the more fundamental issues at stake.
18:18–19 I have not made trouble . . . you and your father's family have. The source of trouble was neither Elijah nor the famine but the way Omri's dynasty had embraced the worship of Baal (16:31–32 note). **the Baals.** These were local manifestations of the god Baal. **Mount Carmel.** This mountain juts out along the northern Mediterranean coast about 15 miles north of Dor and six miles south of Akko. Because of its proximity to the Phoenician cities, the attraction of Baal religion was probably strong in this area. **Baal.** See note on "Baal" at 16:31. **Asherah.** See note on "Asherah poles" at 14:15. **who eat at Jezebel's table.** These prophets received state support for their livelihood (see note on "eat at your table" at 2:7).
18:24 The god who answers by fire. Since Baal's followers believed that Baal was the god of thunder, lightening and the storm, Elijah's challenge struck at the core of Baal's alleged power (16:31).
18:26 they danced around the altar. The Baal prophets engaged in a ritual dance to arouse the unresponsive Baal to action. See *WLC* 109.
18:27 Shout louder! Myths of Baal portray him traveling, fighting wars, visiting the underworld and even dying and coming back to

Perhaps he is deep in thought, or busy, or traveling. Maybe he is sleeping and must be
awakened."[l] 28 So they shouted louder and slashed[m] themselves with swords and spears,
as was their custom, until their blood flowed. 29 Midday passed, and they continued their
frantic prophesying until the time for the evening sacrifice.[n] But there was no response,
no one answered, no one paid attention.[o]
30 Then Elijah said to all the people, "Come here to me." They came to him, and he repaired the altar[p] of the LORD, which was in ruins. 31 Elijah took twelve stones, one for each
of the tribes descended from Jacob, to whom the word of the LORD had come, saying,
"Your name shall be Israel."[q] 32 With the stones he built an altar in the name[r] of the LORD,
and he dug a trench around it large enough to hold two seahs[a] of seed. 33 He arranged[s]
the wood, cut the bull into pieces and laid it on the wood. Then he said to them, "Fill four
large jars with water and pour it on the offering and on the wood."
34 "Do it again," he said, and they did it again.
"Do it a third time," he ordered, and they did it the third time. 35 The water ran down
around the altar and even filled the trench.
36 At the time of sacrifice, the prophet Elijah stepped forward and prayed: "O LORD,
God of Abraham,[t] Isaac and Israel, let it be known[u] today that you are God in Israel and
that I am your servant and have done all these things at your command.[v] 37 Answer me,
O LORD, answer me, so these people will know that you, O LORD, are God, and that you
are turning their hearts back again."
38 Then the fire[w] of the LORD fell and burned up the sacrifice, the wood, the stones and
the soil, and also licked up the water in the trench.
39 When all the people saw this, they fell prostrate and cried, "The LORD—he is God!
The LORD—he is God!"[x]
40 Then Elijah commanded them, "Seize the prophets of Baal. Don't let anyone get
away!" They seized them, and Elijah had them brought down to the Kishon Valley[y] and
slaughtered[z] there.
41 And Elijah said to Ahab, "Go, eat and drink, for there is the sound of a heavy rain."
42 So Ahab went off to eat and drink, but Elijah climbed to the top of Carmel, bent down
to the ground and put his face between his knees.[a]
43 "Go and look toward the sea," he told his servant. And he went up and looked.
"There is nothing there," he said.
Seven times Elijah said, "Go back."
44 The seventh time the servant reported, "A cloud[b] as small as a man's hand is rising from the sea."
So Elijah said, "Go and tell Ahab, 'Hitch up your chariot and go down before the rain
stops you.' "
45 Meanwhile, the sky grew black with clouds, the wind rose, a heavy rain came on
and Ahab rode off to Jezreel. 46 The power[c] of the LORD came upon Elijah and, tucking his
cloak into his belt,[d] he ran ahead of Ahab all the way to Jezreel.

Elijah Flees to Horeb

19 Now Ahab told Jezebel everything Elijah had done and how he had killed[e] all the
prophets with the sword. 2 So Jezebel sent a messenger to Elijah to say, "May the

[a] *32* That is, probably about 13 quarts (about 15 liters)

18:27 [l]Hab 2:19
18:28 [m]Lev 19:28; Dt 14:1
18:29 [n]Ex 29:41 [o]ver 26
18:30 [p]1Ki 19:10
18:31 [q]Ge 32:28; 35:10; 2Ki 17:34
18:32 [r]Col 3:17
18:33 [s]Ge 22:9; Lev 1:6-8
18:36 [t]Ex 3:6; Mt 22:32 [u]1Ki 8:43; 2Ki 19:19 [v]Nu 16:28
18:38 [w]Lev 9:24; Jdg 6:21; 1Ch 21:26; 2Ch 7:1; Job 1:16
18:39 [x]ver 24
18:40 [y]Jdg 4:7 [z]Dt 13:5; 18:20; 2Ki 10:24-25
18:42 [a]ver 19-20; Jas 5:18
18:44 [b]Lk 12:54
18:46 [c]2Ki 3:15 [d]2Ki 4:29; 9:1
19:1 [e]1Ki 18:40

life. Elijah knew these beliefs and taunted Baal's followers. **busy.** The word may be a euphemism for relieving oneself.
18:28 as was their custom. They abased themselves sacrificially to manipulate Baal into answering them. Such self-laceration was prohibited under Mosaic Law (Lev 19:28; Dt 14:1) but nevertheless was practiced by some (Hos 7:14; Jer 16:6; 41:5; 47:5). See *WLC* 109.
18:29 frantic prophesying. This description probably indicated an ecstatic state. **the time for the evening sacrifice.** Around 3 P.M. (Ex 29:38–41; Nu 28:3–8; 2Ki 16:15; Ac 3:1).
18:31 Elijah took twelve stones. Elijah emphasized the solidarity of the people, despite the division of the kingdom. In this manner Elijah also underscored that the contest at Mount Carmel was not merely significant for Israel but for Judah as well (Ex 20:25; 24:4; Jos 4:1–24). **Your name shall be Israel.** The words are a direct quotation of Genesis 35:10, in which God affirmed the special name he had earlier given Jacob.
18:33 pour it on the offering and on the wood. Elijah made it more difficult to produce fire and thereby obviated any accusation of deception.
18:36 At the time of the sacrifice. See note on verse 29. **prayed.** In contrast to the elaborate and frantic activities of the Baal prophets, Elijah's prayer was simple and direct.
18:37 you are turning their hearts back again. The human act of repentance is impossible without divine grace.
18:40 Kishon Valley. This valley runs northward in the plain below Mount Carmel. **slaughtered there.** Israel was a theocracy—a society founded by and constituted under God. Deuteronomy 13:1–5 mandated the death of false prophets. Deuteronomy 13:13–18 and 17:2–7 obligated Israelites to execute anyone embracing idolatry or inciting others to it. According to Deuteronomy 13:5, "you must purge the evil from among you."
18:41 eat and drink. Ahab could cease austerity measures, because the end of the famine was imminent. (Cf. Jas 5:17–18.)
18:44 before the rain stops you. The heavy rains would soon make the roads unfit for Ahab's chariot.
18:45 Ahab rode off to Jezreel. Ahab used the town of Jezreel (located near Mount Gilboa) as a second residence (in addition to Samaria; 16:24; 20:43; 21:1).
■ **19:1–21** *Elijah's Encounter With the Lord at Horeb.* Threatened by Jezebel, Elijah fled to Mount Horeb, where God revealed himself to

gods deal with me, be it ever so severely,[f] if by this time tomorrow I do not make your
life like that of one of them."
3 Elijah was afraid[a] and ran[g] for his life. When he came to Beersheba in Judah, he left
his servant there, 4 while he himself went a day's journey into the desert. He came to a
broom tree, sat down under it and prayed that he might die. "I have had enough, LORD,"
he said. "Take my life;[h] I am no better than my ancestors." 5 Then he lay down under the
tree and fell asleep.[i]
All at once an angel touched him and said, "Get up and eat." 6 He looked around, and
there by his head was a cake of bread baked over hot coals, and a jar of water. He ate
and drank and then lay down again.
7 The angel of the LORD came back a second time and touched him and said, "Get up
and eat, for the journey is too much for you." 8 So he got up and ate and drank. Strength-

19:2 [f] 1Ki 20:10; 2Ki 6:31; Ru 1:17
19:3 [g] Ge 31:21
19:4 [h] Nu 11:15; Jer 20:18; Jnh 4:8
19:5 [i] Ge 28:11

[a] 3 Or *Elijah saw*

the prophet. Elijah's successor, Elisha, is introduced in this chapter.
19:1 Ahab told Jezebel. Jezebel played a role of major importance in governing the affairs of Israel (see notes on 16:25 and 18:4). Together with Ahab, she attempted to prosecute Elijah for killing the Baal prophets (v. 2).
19:2 May the gods deal with me. Jezebel swore to exact vengeance on Elijah by calling down a curse on herself if within a day Elijah had not been killed. See note on 1:17.
19:3 Beersheba. Situated in the southern territory of Judah, 130 miles south of Jezreel. As in previous persecutions, Elijah fled outside the domain of the northern kingdom (17:3–6,9).
19:4 broom tree. This desert bush can grow to a height of nine feet. Elijah made use of its many branches and twigs for shade. **I have had enough.** Elijah, after a titanic struggle against the Baal prophets, was discouraged and depressed. Although the Lord had proved himself God over Baal, Elijah was a refugee from the would-be persecutions of Ahab and Jezebel. Because of the incongruity between the visible (the promoters of Baal who were still governing Israel) and the invisible (Yahweh's lordship), Elijah lamented and expressed a wish to die.
19:7 the journey is too much for you. Elijah had set his sights on traveling all the way to Mount Horeb (Mount Sinai), the original site of God's revelation to Moses. The exact location of Mount Horeb is unknown (Ex 3:1; 17:6; 33:6; Dt 1:2,6,19; 4:10,15).

Lives of Elijah and Elisha

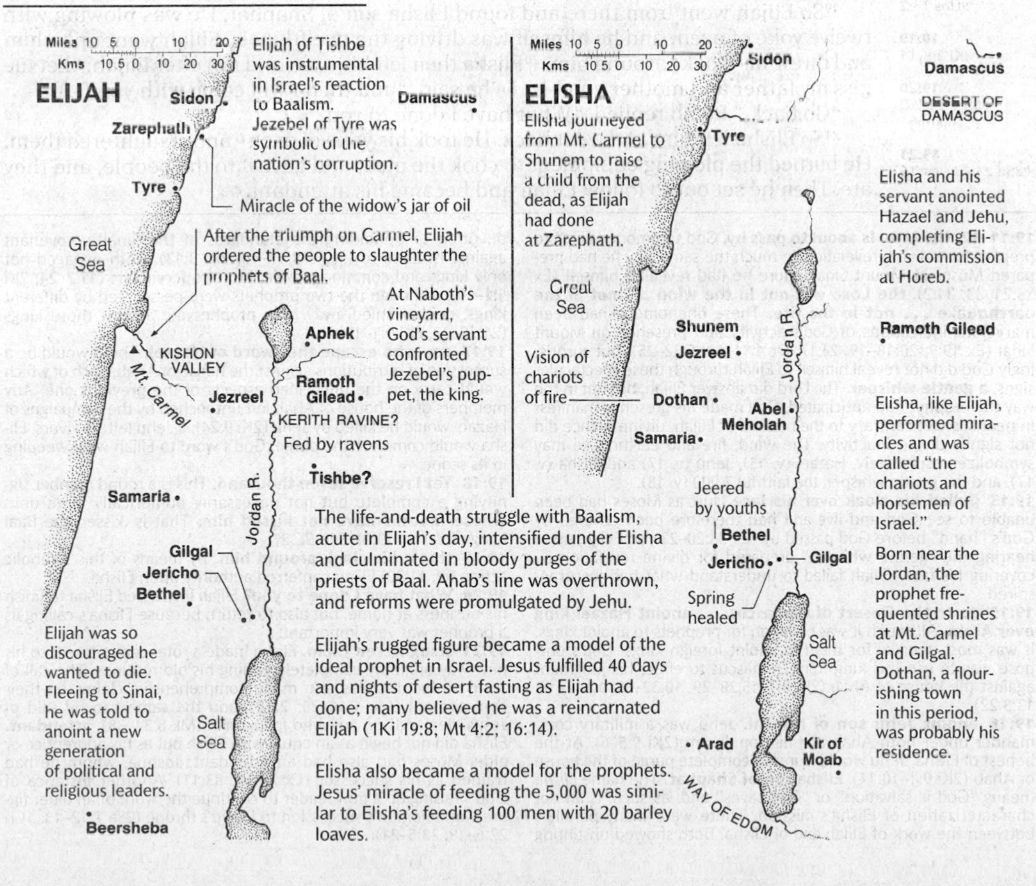
Miles 10 5 0 10 20
Kms 10 5 0 10 20 30
ELIJAH
Elijah of Tishbe was instrumental in Israel's reaction to Baalism. Jezebel of Tyre was symbolic of the nation's corruption.
Sidon
Damascus
Zarephath
Tyre
Miracle of the widow's jar of oil
Great Sea
After the triumph on Carmel, Elijah ordered the people to slaughter the prophets of Baal.
At Naboth's vineyard, God's servant confronted Jezebel's puppet, the king.
Aphek
KISHON VALLEY
Mt. Carmel
Ramoth Gilead
Jezreel
KERITH RAVINE?
Fed by ravens
Tishbe?
Samaria
Jordan R.
Gilgal
Jericho
Bethel
Elijah was so discouraged he wanted to die. Fleeing to Sinai, he was told to anoint a new generation of political and religious leaders.
Salt Sea
Beersheba
The life-and-death struggle with Baalism, acute in Elijah's day, intensified under Elisha and culminated in bloody purges of the priests of Baal. Ahab's line was overthrown, and reforms were promulgated by Jehu.
Elijah's rugged figure became a model of the ideal prophet in Israel. Jesus fulfilled 40 days and nights of desert fasting as Elijah had done; many believed he was a reincarnated Elijah (1Ki 19:8; Mt 4:2; 16:14).
Elisha also became a model for the prophets. Jesus' miracle of feeding the 5,000 was similar to Elisha's feeding 100 men with 20 barley loaves.
Miles 10 5 0 10 20
Kms 10 5 0 10 20 30
ELISHA
Sidon
Elisha journeyed from Mt. Carmel to Shunem to raise a child from the dead, as Elijah had done at Zarephath.
Tyre
Damascus
DESERT OF DAMASCUS
Elisha and his servant anointed Hazael and Jehu, completing Elijah's commission at Horeb.
Great Sea
Shunem
Jezreel
Vision of chariots of fire
Dothan
Abel Meholah
Jordan R.
Ramoth Gilead
Samaria
Elisha, like Elijah, performed miracles and was called "the chariots and horsemen of Israel."
Jeered by youths
Bethel
Jericho
Gilgal
Spring healed
Born near the Jordan, the prophet frequented shrines at Mt. Carmel and Gilgal. Dothan, a flourishing town in this period, was probably his residence.
Salt Sea
Arad
Kir of Moab
WAY OF EDOM

ened by that food, he traveled forty[j] days and forty nights until he reached Horeb,[k] the
mountain of God. 9There he went into a cave[l] and spent the night.

The LORD Appears to Elijah

And the word of the LORD came to him: "What are you doing here, Elijah?"
10He replied, "I have been very zealous[m] for the LORD God Almighty. The Israelites
have rejected your covenant, broken down your altars, and put your prophets to death
with the sword. I am the only one left,[n] and now they are trying to kill me too."
11The LORD said, "Go out and stand on the mountain[o] in the presence of the LORD, for
the LORD is about to pass by."
Then a great and powerful wind[p] tore the mountains apart and shattered the rocks
before the LORD, but the LORD was not in the wind. After the wind there was an earthquake, but the LORD was not in the earthquake. 12After the earthquake came a fire, but
the LORD was not in the fire. And after the fire came a gentle whisper.[q] 13When Elijah
heard it, he pulled his cloak over his face[r] and went out and stood at the mouth of the
cave.
Then a voice said to him, "What are you doing here, Elijah?"
14He replied, "I have been very zealous for the LORD God Almighty. The Israelites have
rejected your covenant, broken down your altars, and put your prophets to death with
the sword. I am the only one left,[s] and now they are trying to kill me too."
15The LORD said to him, "Go back the way you came, and go to the Desert of Damascus. When you get there, anoint Hazael[t] king over Aram. 16Also, anoint[u] Jehu son of Nimshi king over Israel, and anoint Elisha[v] son of Shaphat from Abel Meholah to succeed
you as prophet. 17Jehu will put to death any who escape the sword of Hazael,[w] and Elisha will put to death any who escape the sword of Jehu. 18Yet I reserve[x] seven thousand
in Israel—all whose knees have not bowed down to Baal and all whose mouths have not
kissed[y] him."

The Call of Elisha

19So Elijah went from there and found Elisha son of Shaphat. He was plowing with
twelve yoke of oxen, and he himself was driving the twelfth pair. Elijah went up to him
and threw his cloak[z] around him. 20Elisha then left his oxen and ran after Elijah. "Let me
kiss my father and mother good-by,"[a] he said, "and then I will come with you."
"Go back," Elijah replied. "What have I done to you?"
21So Elisha left him and went back. He took his yoke of oxen[b] and slaughtered them.
He burned the plowing equipment to cook the meat and gave it to the people, and they
ate. Then he set out to follow Elijah and became his attendant.[c]

19:8 [j]Ex 24:18; 34:28; Dt 9:9-11,18; Mt 4:2 [k]Ex 3:1
19:9 [l]Ex 33:22
19:10 [m]Nu 25:13 [n]1Ki 18:4,22; Ro 11:3*
19:11 [o]Ex 24:12 [p]Eze 1:4; 37:7
19:12 [q]Job 4:16; Zec 4:6
19:13 [r]ver 9; Ex 3:6
19:14 [s]ver 10
19:15 [t]2Ki 8:7-15
19:16 [u]2Ki 9:1-3,6 [v]ver 21; 2Ki 2:9,15
19:17 [w]2Ki 8:12,29; 9:14; 13:3,7,22
19:18 [x]Ro 11:4* [y]Hos 13:2
19:19 [z]2Ki 2:8,14
19:20 [a]Mt 8:21-22; Lk 9:61
19:21 [b]2Sa 24:22 [c]ver 16

19:11–12 the LORD is about to pass by. God summoned Elijah to prepare for a divine revelation, in much the same way he had prepared Moses at Mount Sinai before he had revealed himself (Ex 33:21–33; 34:2). **the LORD was not in the wind . . . not in the earthquake . . . not in the fire.** These phenomena had been marvelous indications of God's activity and presence on Mount Sinai (Ex 19:9; 20:18–19; 24:17; Dt 4:11–12; 5:22–25), but surprisingly God did not reveal himself to Elijah through these spectacular signs. **a gentle whisper.** The Lord did answer Elijah, but not in the way the prophet had anticipated. God made his presence manifest in near silence; contrary to the notions of Elijah, divine silence did not signify divine inactivity. The wind, fire and earthquake may symbolize, respectively, Hazael (v. 15), Jehu (v. 17) and Elisha (v. 17), and the gentle whisper, the faithful 7,000 (v. 18).
19:13 pulled his cloak over his face. Just as Moses had been unable to see God and live and had therefore been covered by God's "hand" before God passed by (Ex 33:20–23), so Elijah, upon hearing the "gentle whisper," prepared for divine revelation by covering his face. Elijah failed to understand what had just transpired.
19:15 go to the Desert of Damascus . . . anoint Hazael king over Aram. Although it was common for prophets to anoint kings, it was most unusual for them to anoint foreign kings. God's purpose was to use this king from Damascus to effect his judgment against the house of Ahab (2Ki 8:7–15,28–29; 10:32–33; 12:17–18; 13:3,22).
19:16 anoint Jehu son of Nimshi. Jehu was a military commander under both Ahab and his son Joram (2Ki 9:5–6). At the behest of Elisha, Jehu would launch a complete purge of the house of Ahab (2Ki 9:1–10:17). **Elisha son of Shaphat.** The name *Elisha* means "God is salvation" or "God saves" and, as such, is an apt characterization of Elisha's mission. There were many parallels between the work of Elijah and of Elisha. Both showed unstinting devotion to upholding the standards of the Sinaitic covenant against Israelite royalty (18:17–46; 2Ki 3:13). Both engaged not only kings and common people, but also foreigners (17:7–24; 2Ki 5:1–19). Although the two prophets were persecuted by different kings, neither shied away from prophesying against those kings (21:19–22; 2Ki 9:1–10).
19:17 any who escape the sword of Hazael. There would be a succession of retributions against the house of Ahab, each of which would carry on the unfinished aspects of the previous one. Any members of the house of Ahab left untouched by the campaigns of Hazael would be killed by Jehu (2Ki 9:24). If Jehu left survivors, Elisha would complete the purge. God's word to Elijah was sweeping in its scope.
19:18 Yet I reserve seven thousand. This is a round number signifying a complete but not necessarily numerically large unit. **whose mouths have not kissed him.** That is, kissed the Baal image (cf. Hos 13:2). See *BC* 27.
19:19 threw his cloak around him. By means of this symbolic action (cf. 11:30) Elijah conferred authority upon Elisha.
19:20 What have I done to you? Elijah instructed Elisha to finish his business at home, but also to return because Elisha's calling as a prophet was very important.
19:21 slaughtered them. Elisha made a total commitment to his new way of life by completely ending his old routines. The call of Jesus to his disciples also made comprehensive claims on their commitment (Mk 1:16–20; 2:14), and the same can be said of Jesus' demands on any who follow him (Mk 8:34–38). **attendant.** Elisha did not begin as an equal with Elijah but as his apprentice or aide. Moses had also had an attendant, Joshua, whom he had trained as his successor (Ex 24:13; 33:11). Another instance of God's raising up a new leader to continue the work of an older figure was Solomon's succession to David's throne (2Sa 7:12–13; 1Ch 22:6–19; 28:5–21).

Ben-Hadad Attacks Samaria

20 Now Ben-Hadad[d] king of Aram mustered his entire army. Accompanied by
thirty-two kings with their horses and chariots, he went up and besieged Samaria and attacked it. 2He sent messengers into the city to Ahab king of Israel, saying, "This
is what Ben-Hadad says: 3'Your silver and gold are mine, and the best of your wives and
children are mine.' "
4The king of Israel answered, "Just as you say, my lord the king. I and all I have are
yours."
5The messengers came again and said, "This is what Ben-Hadad says: 'I sent to demand your silver and gold, your wives and your children. 6But about this time tomorrow
I am going to send my officials to search your palace and the houses of your officials.
They will seize everything you value and carry it away.' "
7The king of Israel summoned all the elders of the land and said to them, "See how
this man is looking for trouble![e] When he sent for my wives and my children, my silver
and my gold, I did not refuse him."
8The elders and the people all answered, "Don't listen to him or agree to his demands."
9So he replied to Ben-Hadad's messengers, "Tell my lord the king, 'Your servant will
do all you demanded the first time, but this demand I cannot meet.' " They left and took
the answer back to Ben-Hadad.
10Then Ben-Hadad sent another message to Ahab: "May the gods deal with me, be it
ever so severely, if enough dust[f] remains in Samaria to give each of my men a handful."
11The king of Israel answered, "Tell him: 'One who puts on his armor should not
boast[g] like one who takes it off.' "
12Ben-Hadad heard this message while he and the kings were drinking[h] in their
tents,[a] and he ordered his men: "Prepare to attack." So they prepared to attack the city.

Ahab Defeats Ben-Hadad

13Meanwhile a prophet came to Ahab king of Israel and announced, "This is what the
LORD says: 'Do you see this vast army? I will give it into your hand today, and then you
will know[i] that I am the LORD.' "
14"But who will do this?" asked Ahab.
The prophet replied, "This is what the LORD says: 'The young officers of the provin-
cial commanders will do it.' "
"And who will start[j] the battle?" he asked.
The prophet answered, "You will."
15So Ahab summoned the young officers of the provincial commanders, 232 men.
Then he assembled the rest of the Israelites, 7,000 in all. 16They set out at noon while
Ben-Hadad and the 32 kings allied with him were in their tents getting drunk.[k] 17The
young officers of the provincial commanders went out first.
Now Ben-Hadad had dispatched scouts, who reported, "Men are advancing from Samaria."
18He said, "If they have come out for peace, take them alive; if they have come out for
war, take them alive."
19The young officers of the provincial commanders marched out of the city with the
army behind them 20and each one struck down his opponent. At that, the Arameans fled,

20:1 [d]1Ki 15:18; 22:31; 2Ki 6:24
20:7 [e]2Ki 5:7
20:10 [f]2Sa 22:43; 1Ki 19:2
20:11 [g]Pr 27:1; Jer 9:23
20:12 [h]ver 16; 1Ki 16:9
20:13 [i]ver 28; Ex 6:7
20:14 [j]Jdg 1:1
20:16 [k]ver 12; 1Ki 16:9

[a] 12 Or *in Succoth*; also in verse 16

■ **20:1–43** *Ahab's War With Aram and Prophetic Condemnation.* Ahab's release of Ben-Hadad, king of Aram, following victory over him in battle, brought a pronouncement of death to Ahab by an unnamed prophet of God.

20:1 Ben-Hadad king of Aram. Probably Ben-Hadad II, the grandson of the earlier Ben-Hadad (I) mentioned in 15:18–20 and 33. The early rulers of Aram commanded the city-state of Damascus, but not the entire region of Syria (or Aram), which was composed of many minor states. Ben-Hadad II managed to put together a coalition of 32 monarchs and petty rulers in this campaign against Ahab.

20:4 my lord the king. Ahab addressed Ben-Hadad as an inferior to a superior. **I and all I have are yours.** Ahab sent notice of his surrender to Ben-Hadad. Submission to Ben-Hadad would spare Ahab's life and protect the city from destruction and wholesale looting.

20:10 May the gods deal with me. Enraged, Ben-Hadad took an oath, cursing himself if his men would not completely destroy Samaria. See note on 1:17.

20:11 One who puts on his armor. Ahab responded with a proverb telling the Aramean king that a victory celebration was premature before the battle was even fought.

20:13 I will give it into your hand today. This assurance was common before wars in which the Lord was about to fight on Israel's side against an enemy (Jos 6:2,16; 8:1,18; Jdg 7:2; 18:10; 2Ch 13:16; 16:8; 18:5,11,14). In the Bible, God often defended the cause of his people against oppressors and enemies (Ex 15:1–21; Jdg 5:1–31; Hab 3:3–19; Rev 18:1–24). The prophet therefore made clear who was responsible for the impending victory.

20:15 So Ahab summoned. Ahab carefully obeyed the prophet's commands. **7,000 in all.** See notes on 19:18.

20:16 getting drunk. The 32 kings were either so confident of their victory or so callous about their responsibilities that they became intoxicated before the battle had even begun. See verses 10 and 12.

with the Israelites in pursuit. But Ben-Hadad king of Aram escaped on horseback with
some of his horsemen. 21 The king of Israel advanced and overpowered the horses and
20:22 chariots and inflicted heavy losses on the Arameans.
[l] ver 13 [m] ver 26; 22 Afterward, the prophet[l] came to the king of Israel and said, “Strengthen your po-
2Sa 11:1 sition and see what must be done, because next spring[m] the king of Aram will attack you
again.”
20:23 [n] 1Ki 14:23; 23 Meanwhile, the officials of the king of Aram advised him, “Their gods are gods[n] of
Ro 1:21-23 the hills. That is why they were too strong for us. But if we fight them on the plains, surely we will be stronger than they. 24 Do this: Remove all the kings from their commands
and replace them with other officers. 25 You must also raise an army like the one you
lost—horse for horse and chariot for chariot—so we can fight Israel on the plains. Then
20:26 surely we will be stronger than they.” He agreed with them and acted accordingly.
[o] ver 22 [p] 2Ki 13:17 26 The next spring[o] Ben-Hadad mustered the Arameans and went up to Aphek[p] to fight
against Israel. 27 When the Israelites were also mustered and given provisions, they
20:27 marched out to meet them. The Israelites camped opposite them like two small flocks of
[q] Jdg 6:6; 1Sa 13:6 goats, while the Arameans covered the countryside.[q]
20:28 28 The man of God came up and told the king of Israel, “This is what the LORD says: ‘Be-
[r] ver 23 [s] ver 13 cause the Arameans think the LORD is a god of the hills and not a god[r] of the valleys, I
will deliver this vast army into your hands, and you will know[s] that I am the LORD.’ ”
29 For seven days they camped opposite each other, and on the seventh day the battle
was joined. The Israelites inflicted a hundred thousand casualties on the Aramean foot
20:30 soldiers in one day. 30 The rest of them escaped to the city of Aphek,[t] where the wall col-
[t] ver 26 [u] 1Ki 22:25; lapsed on twenty-seven thousand of them. And Ben-Hadad fled to the city and hid[u] in an
2Ch 18:24 inner room.
31 His officials said to him, “Look, we have heard that the kings of the house of Isra-
20:31 [v] Ge 37:34 el are merciful. Let us go to the king of Israel with sackcloth[v] around our waists and
ropes around our heads. Perhaps he will spare your life.”
32 Wearing sackcloth around their waists and ropes around their heads, they went to
the king of Israel and said, “Your servant Ben-Hadad says: ‘Please let me live.’ ”
The king answered, “Is he still alive? He is my brother.”
33 The men took this as a good sign and were quick to pick up his word. “Yes, your
brother Ben-Hadad!” they said.
“Go and get him,” the king said. When Ben-Hadad came out, Ahab had him come up
20:34 into his chariot.
[w] 1Ki 15:20 [x] Jer 49:23-27 34 “I will return the cities[w] my father took from your father,” Ben-Hadad offered. “You
[y] Ex 23:32 may set up your own market areas in Damascus,[x] as my father did in Samaria.”
⌊Ahab said,⌋ “On the basis of a treaty[y] I will set you free.” So he made a treaty with
him, and let him go.

A Prophet Condemns Ahab

20:35 [z] 1Ki 13:21; 35 By the word of the LORD one of the sons of the prophets said to his companion,
2Ki 2:3-7 “Strike me with your weapon,” but the man refused.[z]
20:36 36 So the prophet said, “Because you have not obeyed the LORD, as soon as you leave
[a] 1Ki 13:24 me a lion[a] will kill you.” And after the man went away, a lion found him and killed him.

20:23 Their gods are gods of the hills. Both Samaria and Jerusalem are located in the central hill country, not on the coastal plain. The polytheistic Aramean advisors believed that there was an inherent relationship between Israel's God and Israel's land, such that their God was stronger in the hills of their homeland than in the plains. **fight them on the plains.** Since these peoples believed that wars were fought not only by armies but also by their gods, they wished to fight where their opponents' deities were weakest.
20:24 Remove all the kings from their commands. Whereas kings could be militarily inexperienced and irresponsible in battle (vv. 10,12,16), officers were seasoned fighters.
20:30 the wall collapsed. A calamity in addition to the battle defeat. **inner room.** See 22:25 and 2 Kings 9:2.
20:31 the kings of . . . Israel are merciful. Certain powers in the Near East, such as Assyria, were brutal toward the vanquished. **sackcloth . . . ropes.** The Aramean leaders wore sackcloth around their waists to symbolize their contrition. Prisoners of war were compelled to wear ropes around their heads as they were paraded away from a lost battle. By engaging in this behavior, the Aramean leaders were dramatizing their submission and servility to the Israelites.
20:32 Your servant. Earlier, Ahab had addressed Ben-Hadad as his superior; now the tables were turned. **He is my brother.** Ahab's surprising response depicted Ben-Hadad as an equal in a treaty relationship (9:13), a concession Ben-Hadad's officials were quick to seize (v. 33).
20:34 your own market areas. International trade could bring substantial income (10:23–29; Ne 13:16), and the guarantee of a market in another country would afford a distinct economic advantage for the merchants of Israel. **a treaty.** The two kings formalized their negotiations by ratifying a covenant or treaty.
20:35 sons. Not literally “male descendants” but figuratively members of an association. **sons of the prophets.** The prophetic guilds or associations (2Ki 2:3,5,7,15; 4:1,38; 5:22; 6:1; 9:1). Both Elijah and Elisha were likely spiritual leaders of such groups (18:29; 2Ki 2:3,5, 7,15; 4:1,38).
20:36 Because you have not obeyed the LORD. This highly unusual incident needs to be understood in the context of the previous account in which Ahab failed to obey the dictates of religious war. Aware of Ahab's treaty with Ben-Hadad II, the prophet dramatized the consequences of refusing to heed the word of God. The prophetic story therefore functions as a parable of what will happen to Ahab, who similarly refused to obey a command even though it too was given by the word of the Lord (v. 28; Dt 20). **a lion will kill you.** The old prophet from Bethel had uttered a similar decree of judgment against the man of God from Judah (13:20–25).

37The prophet found another man and said, "Strike me, please." So the man struck
him and wounded him. 38Then the prophet went and stood by the road waiting for the
king. He disguised himself with his headband down over his eyes. 39As the king passed
by, the prophet called out to him, "Your servant went into the thick of the battle, and
someone came to me with a captive and said, 'Guard this man. If he is missing, it will be
your life for his life,[b] or you must pay a talent[a] of silver.' 40While your servant was busy
here and there, the man disappeared."

"That is your sentence," the king of Israel said. "You have pronounced it yourself."

41Then the prophet quickly removed the headband from his eyes, and the king of Israel recognized him as one of the prophets. 42He said to the king, "This is what the LORD
says: 'You have set free a man I had determined should die.[b][c] Therefore it is your life for
his life,[d] your people for his people.' " 43Sullen and angry,[e] the king of Israel went to his
palace in Samaria.

Naboth's Vineyard

21 Some time later there was an incident involving a vineyard belonging to Naboth[f]
the Jezreelite. The vineyard was in Jezreel,[g] close to the palace of Ahab king of
Samaria. 2Ahab said to Naboth, "Let me have your vineyard to use for a vegetable garden, since it is close to my palace. In exchange I will give you a better vineyard or, if you
prefer, I will pay you whatever it is worth."

3But Naboth replied, "The LORD forbid that I should give you the inheritance[h] of my
fathers."

4So Ahab went home, sullen and angry[i] because Naboth the Jezreelite had said, "I will
not give you the inheritance of my fathers." He lay on his bed sulking and refused to eat.
5His wife Jezebel came in and asked him, "Why are you so sullen? Why won't you eat?"
6He answered her, "Because I said to Naboth the Jezreelite, 'Sell me your vineyard;
or if you prefer, I will give you another vineyard in its place.' But he said, 'I will not give
you my vineyard.' "

7Jezebel his wife said, "Is this how you act as king over Israel? Get up and eat! Cheer
up. I'll get you the vineyard[j] of Naboth the Jezreelite."
8So she wrote letters in Ahab's name, placed his seal[k] on them, and sent them to the
elders and nobles who lived in Naboth's city with him. 9In those letters she wrote:

> "Proclaim a day of fasting and seat Naboth in a prominent place among the
> people. 10But seat two scoundrels[l] opposite him and have them testify that he has
> cursed[m] both God and the king. Then take him out and stone him to death."

11So the elders and nobles who lived in Naboth's city did as Jezebel directed in the let-

20:39 [b]2Ki 10:24
20:42 [c]Jer 48:10 [d]ver 39; Jos 2:14; 1Ki 22:31-37
20:43 [e]1Ki 21:4
21:1 [f]2Ki 9:21 [g]1Ki 18:45-46
21:3 [h]Lev 25:23; Nu 36:7; Eze 46:18
21:4 [i]1Ki 20:43
21:7 [j]1Sa 8:14
21:8 [k]Ge 38:18; Est 3:12; 8:8,10
21:10 [l]Ac 6:11 [m]Ex 22:28; Lev 24:15-16

[a] *39* That is, about 75 pounds (about 34 kilograms) [b] *42* The Hebrew term refers to the irrevocable giving over of things or persons to the LORD, often by totally destroying them.

20:39 a talent of silver. Since this was an impossible quantity for a common soldier to afford (see NIV text note), the man's life was at stake.
20:40 That is your sentence. Ahab showed no mercy, thereby passing severe judgment upon himself (v. 42; 2Sa 12:7).
20:42 You have set free a man I had determined should die. See NIV text note, as well as Leviticus 27:28, Deuteronomy 7:2, 20:16, Joshua 6:17 and 7:1,20–26. The wars were campaigns fought and won by God himself, using the Israelites as his agents to secure victory. In such sacred wars, Israel was to conduct itself in a prescribed manner, observing stipulations of holy conduct. Ahab was perfectly willing to accept divine victory but not to abide by the standards by which such a war was conducted. He made a treaty with Ben-Hadad, violating the precepts of holy war that forbade the Israelites from yoking themselves to foreign powers (Dt 7:1–6; 20:16–18). **your life for his life, your people for his people.** Even though each person is responsible for good conduct before God, the actions of each inevitably affect the lives of others for good or ill.
■ **21:1–29** *Naboth's Vineyard and Prophetic Condemnation.* Elijah pronounced disaster on the house of Ahab for all his evil deeds, not the least of which was his murder of Naboth and the theft of his vineyard, as described in this chapter.
21:1 Jezreel. About 24 miles north of Samaria. Ahab maintained a palace there in addition to his palace in the capital (18:45).
21:2 Let me have your vineyard. In Canaanite nations, a king could seize property and personal belongings on a whim, because in theory all the property was owned by the royal family and entrusted to its subjects. In Israel, God was the King who owned the land (Ex 19:3–8; Lev 25:23) and entrusted it to the people as his stewards (Nu 14:8; 35:33; Dt 1:8; 8:7; 34:1). The powers of any Israelite monarch in real estate dealings were severely limited in contrast to those exercised by Canaanite kings (Dt 17:14–20; 1Sa 8:9–17; 10:25). Consequently, when Ahab desired his neighbor's vineyard, he attempted to negotiate a sale (cf. 16:24).
21:3 The LORD forbid. Naboth's reaction is one of shock, because this land was not merely a piece of property but a sacred inheritance from the Lord. When the Israelite tribes were apportioned land after they had entered Canaan (Jos 13:6—21:45), each family in every tribe received its own inheritance. The land, as a divine gift, was a trust. Since the vineyard represented Naboth's portion of his family's inheritance, to sell it would mean cutting off Naboth's descendants from their heritage (Lev 25:23; Nu 27:1–11; 36:1–12).
21:4 See *WLC* 148; *WSC* 81.
21:8 she wrote letters . . . to the elders and nobles who lived in Naboth's city. Jezebel systematically set out to subvert Jezreel's judicial system.
21:9–14 See *WLC* 113,145.
21:9 Proclaim a day of fasting. Jezebel, with Ahab's complicity, fostered apprehensiveness among the town's inhabitants, because fasting was a characteristic response to a crisis or major transgression (Jdg 20:26; 1Sa 7:5–6; 14:24; 2Ch 20:3; Jnh 3:5,7–9).
21:10 two scoundrels. Israelite law stipulated that two witnesses, not one, were required to convict someone of a capital offense (Nu 35:30; Dt 17:5–6; 19:15). **testify that he has cursed both God and the king.** The penalty for cursing God was death (Ex 22:28; Lev 24:10–16); hence, the "two scoundrels" successfully framed an unsuspecting Naboth.

21:12 [n]Isa 58:4
21:13 [o]2Ki 9:26
21:15 [p]1Sa 8:14
21:19 [q]2Ki 9:26; Ps 9:12; Isa 14:20 [r]1Ki 22:38
21:20 [s]1Ki 18:17 [t]ver 25; 2Ki 17:17; Ro 7:14
21:21 [u]1Ki 14:10; 2Ki 9:8
21:22 [v]1Ki 15:29; 16:3 [w]1Ki 12:30
21:23 [x]2Ki 9:10,34-36
21:24 [y]1Ki 14:11; 16:4
21:25 [z]ver 20; 1Ki 16:33
21:26 [a]Ge 15:16; Lev 18:25-30; 2Ki 21:11
21:27 [b]Ge 37:34; 2Sa 3:31; 2Ki 6:30
21:29 [c]2Ki 9:26
22:3 [d]Dt 4:43; Jos 21:38
22:4 [e]2Ki 3:7

ters she had written to them. 12They proclaimed a fast[n] and seated Naboth in a prominent place among the people. 13Then two scoundrels came and sat opposite him and
brought charges against Naboth before the people, saying, "Naboth has cursed both God
and the king." So they took him outside the city and stoned him to death.[o] 14Then they
sent word to Jezebel: "Naboth has been stoned and is dead."
15As soon as Jezebel heard that Naboth had been stoned to death, she said to Ahab,
"Get up and take possession of the vineyard[p] of Naboth the Jezreelite that he refused to
sell you. He is no longer alive, but dead." 16When Ahab heard that Naboth was dead, he
got up and went down to take possession of Naboth's vineyard.
17Then the word of the LORD came to Elijah the Tishbite: 18"Go down to meet Ahab
king of Israel, who rules in Samaria. He is now in Naboth's vineyard, where he has gone
to take possession of it. 19Say to him, 'This is what the LORD says: Have you not murdered
a man and seized his property?' Then say to him, 'This is what the LORD says: In the place
where dogs licked up Naboth's blood,[q] dogs[r] will lick up your blood—yes, yours!' "
20Ahab said to Elijah, "So you have found me, my enemy!"[s]
"I have found you," he answered, "because you have sold[t] yourself to do evil in the
eyes of the LORD. 21'I am going to bring disaster on you. I will consume your descendants
and cut off from Ahab every last male[u] in Israel—slave or free. 22I will make your house[v]
like that of Jeroboam son of Nebat and that of Baasha son of Ahijah, because you have
provoked me to anger and have caused Israel to sin.'[w]
23"And also concerning Jezebel the LORD says: 'Dogs[x] will devour Jezebel by the wall
of[a] Jezreel.'
24"Dogs[y] will eat those belonging to Ahab who die in the city, and the birds of the air
will feed on those who die in the country."
25(There was never[z] a man like Ahab, who sold himself to do evil in the eyes of the
LORD, urged on by Jezebel his wife. 26He behaved in the vilest manner by going after idols,
like the Amorites[a] the LORD drove out before Israel.)
27When Ahab heard these words, he tore his clothes, put on sackcloth[b] and fasted.
He lay in sackcloth and went around meekly.
28Then the word of the LORD came to Elijah the Tishbite: 29"Have you noticed how
Ahab has humbled himself before me? Because he has humbled himself, I will not bring
this disaster in his day, but I will bring it on his house in the days of his son."[c]

Micaiah Prophesies Against Ahab

22 For three years there was no war between Aram and Israel. 2But in the third year
Jehoshaphat king of Judah went down to see the king of Israel. 3The king of Israel had said to his officials, "Don't you know that Ramoth Gilead[d] belongs to us and yet
we are doing nothing to retake it from the king of Aram?"
4So he asked Jehoshaphat, "Will you go with me to fight[e] against Ramoth Gilead?"
Jehoshaphat replied to the king of Israel, "I am as you are, my people as your people,

[a] 23 Most Hebrew manuscripts; a few Hebrew manuscripts, Vulgate and Syriac (see also 2 Kings 9:26) *the plot of ground at*

21:13 outside the city. In accordance with the provisions of the Sinaitic covenant, they avoided ritual impurity (Lev 24:14; Nu 15:35–36). Second Kings 9:26 adds that Naboth's sons were also killed, thus eliminating any possible heirs.
21:22 I will make your house like that of Jeroboam. See 14:10, 15:29 and 2 Kings 9:26. **and that of Baasha.** See 16:1–4 and 11–13.
21:24 Dogs will eat . . . birds of the air will feed. See note on 14:11.
21:25 There was never a man like Ahab. See notes on 16:30–33.
21:26 Amorites. The word here refers to the pre-Israelite inhabitants of Canaan. See Genesis 15:16, Deuteronomy 1:7 and 2 Samuel 21:2.
21:27 tore his clothes, put on sackcloth. Marks of mourning and repentance (Ge 37:34; 2Sa 3:31; 2Ki 6:30; La 2:10; Joel 1:13; Mt 11:21). God's judgment, articulated through Elijah, changed Ahab's attitude. See *WCF* 16.7.
21:29 I will not bring this disaster in his day. God revised the punishment. The decree of the destruction of Ahab's dynasty was delayed a generation due to God's mercy. **his son.** Joram (2Ki 9:25–26). Ahab would not live to see the end of his dynasty; he and Jezebel would die ignominious deaths (22:37–38; 2 Kings 9:10,34–37). See *WCF* 16.7.
■ **22:1–38** *Ahab's War With Aram and Micaiah's Prophetic Condemnation.* Micaiah's prophecy of disaster for Ahab (vv. 1–28) was fulfilled when Ahab was killed in battle against the Arameans (vv. 29–40).
22:1 three years. Israel had peace for three years following the two-year war between Aram and Israel described in 20:1–26 and 34. During this three-year peace, Hadadeser (Ben-Hadad II) of Syria, Ahab of Israel and ten other kings formed a coalition to ward off an Assyrian invasion from the west led by Shalmaneser III. In the major battle of this campaign, fought at Qarqar on the Orontes River in 853 B.C., Ahab, according to Assyrian records, contributed 2,000 chariots and 10,000 soldiers, by far the largest contribution of any of the members of the coalition. Although the Assyrians claimed victory, the opposite result seems to have been more plausible. The Assyrians withdrew and did not try to invade again for four or five years. After having forged an alliance with Ben-Hadad II, Ahab now formed one with the king of Judah.
22:2 Jehoshaphat king of Judah. On his reign, see verses 41–50 and 2 Kings 3:7–27. Jehoshaphat traveled to Ahab for diplomatic reasons.
22:3 Ramoth Gilead. About 28 miles west of the Jordan River, near the Yarmuk River. It became Israel's possession during the conquest (Dt 4:43; Jos 20:8; 1Ki 4:13), and Ahab believed it was time to retrieve it from the Syrians (v. 4).
22:4 I am as you are. Diplomatic language signifying Jehoshaphat's ready assent to be a partner in the campaign against the Syrians. Jehoshaphat seemed to be a junior partner rather than a full

my horses as your horses." 5But Jehoshaphat also said to the king of Israel, "First seek
the counsel[f] of the LORD."
6So the king of Israel brought together the prophets—about four hundred men—and
asked them, "Shall I go to war against Ramoth Gilead, or shall I refrain?"
"Go,"[g] they answered, "for the Lord will give it into the king's hand."
7But Jehoshaphat asked, "Is there not a prophet[h] of the LORD here whom we can inquire of?"
8The king of Israel answered Jehoshaphat, "There is still one man through whom we
can inquire of the LORD, but I hate[i] him because he never prophesies anything good[j]
about me, but always bad. He is Micaiah son of Imlah."
"The king should not say that," Jehoshaphat replied.
9So the king of Israel called one of his officials and said, "Bring Micaiah son of Imlah
at once."
10Dressed in their royal robes, the king of Israel and Jehoshaphat king of Judah were
sitting on their thrones at the threshing floor[k] by the entrance of the gate of Samaria,
with all the prophets prophesying before them. 11Now Zedekiah son of Kenaanah had
made iron horns[l] and he declared, "This is what the LORD says: 'With these you will gore
the Arameans until they are destroyed.' "
12All the other prophets were prophesying the same thing. "Attack Ramoth Gilead
and be victorious," they said, "for the LORD will give it into the king's hand."
13The messenger who had gone to summon Micaiah said to him, "Look, as one man
the other prophets are predicting success for the king. Let your word agree with theirs,
and speak favorably."
14But Micaiah said, "As surely as the LORD lives, I can tell him only what the LORD
tells me."[m]
15When he arrived, the king asked him, "Micaiah, shall we go to war against Ramoth
Gilead, or shall I refrain?"
"Attack and be victorious," he answered, "for the LORD will give it into the king's
hand."
16The king said to him, "How many times must I make you swear to tell me nothing
but the truth in the name of the LORD?"
17Then Micaiah answered, "I saw all Israel scattered on the hills like sheep without
a shepherd,[n] and the LORD said, 'These people have no master. Let each one go home
in peace.' "
18The king of Israel said to Jehoshaphat, "Didn't I tell you that he never prophesies
anything good about me, but only bad?"
19Micaiah continued, "Therefore hear the word of the LORD: I saw the LORD sitting on
his throne[o] with all the host[p] of heaven standing around him on his right and on his left.
20And the LORD said, 'Who will entice Ahab into attacking Ramoth Gilead and going to
his death there?'
"One suggested this, and another that. 21Finally, a spirit came forward, stood before
the LORD and said, 'I will entice him.'
22" 'By what means?' the LORD asked.

22:5 [f]Ex 33:7; 2Ki 3:11
22:6 [g]1Ki 18:19
22:7 [h]2Ki 3:11
22:8 [i]Am 5:10 [j]Isa 5:20
22:10 [k]ver 6
22:11 [l]Dt 33:17; Zec 1:18-21
22:14 [m]Nu 22:18; 24:13; 1Ki 18:10, 15
22:17 [n]ver 34-36; Nu 27:17; Mt 9:36
22:19 [o]Isa 6:1; Eze 1:26; Da 7:9 [p]Job 1:6; 2:1; Ps 103:20-21; Mt 18:10; Heb 1:7, 14

---

equal to Ahab, because Ahab instructed Jehoshaphat on what a Judahite king was to do (vv. 15,18,30). Since Judah during the reign of Asa (15:7–23) was allied with the Syrians against the Israelites, this new arrangement marked a departure in the foreign policies of both Israel and Judah. At some point in Ahab's reign, he formalized his relationship with Judah by giving his daughter, Athaliah, in marriage to the son of the king of Judah (2Ki 8:18,26). Since Athaliah was an avid Baal worshiper, this diplomatic marriage introduced state-sponsored Baal worship in Judah, with negative consequences for the worship of Yahweh (2Ki 11:1–20).

22:5 First seek the counsel of the LORD. It was common practice to consult with God or his prophets before embarking on a major campaign (1Sa 23:1–4; 2Sa 2:1; 2Ki 3:11; 2Ch 20:3–17).

22:6 prophets—about four hundred men. The prophets whose words are recorded in the Scriptures comprise only a fraction of the total number of people who designated themselves as such during Old Testament times (18:19; 22:6; 2Ki 3:13; Jer 28). Prophets were also common in other societies of the ancient Near East. **"Go," they answered.** Most of the Israelite prophets were eager to please their benefactors, usually the crown, by uttering flattering and upbeat messages (Jer 28:1–4; Am 7:10–13).

22:7 Is there not a prophet of the LORD? Jehoshaphat was rightly skeptical of the prophets' credibility.

22:8 he never prophesies anything good. According to the prophet Jeremiah, one should be wary of prophets who prophesied too optimistically about the nation's future (Jer 29:8–9). **Micaiah son of Imlah.** The name *Micaiah* means "who is like Yah(weh)." He appears only in this chapter.

22:10 sitting on their thrones. Ahab and Jehoshaphat sat in the city at the customary place at which judicial and municipal decisions would be made (Dt 21:19; 25:7; Ru 4:1–12; Am 5:10–15).

22:11 Zedekiah. One of the prophets sought out by Ahab. **iron horns.** These symbolized the power with which the Israelites would "gore the Arameans" (Dt 33:17; Zec 1:18–21). On prophetic symbolic actions, see note on 11:30.

22:14 As surely as the LORD lives. An oath formula. See note on 1:17. **what the LORD tells me.** Even if Micaiah wanted to say something else, he was constrained to speak only the word of the Lord.

22:15 Attack and be victorious. Micaiah was sarcastic, and Ahab knew it.

22:17 I saw all Israel scattered. Micaiah depicted the defeated and leaderless armies of Israel in a state of anarchy. **without a shepherd.** The term *shepherd* can refer to a king (Zec 13:7). The prophecy stipulated that the armies of Israel would be leaderless, and Ahab's subsequent words (v. 18) show that he recognized that Micaiah prophesied against him.

22:22–23 See *WCF* 5.4.

22:22 [q]Jdg 9:23; 1Sa 16:14; 18:10; 19:9; Eze 14:9; 2Th 2:11
22:23 [r]Eze 14:9
22:24 [s]ver 11 [t]Ac 23:2
22:25 [u]1Ki 20:30
22:27 [v]2Ch 16:10
22:28 [w]Dt 18:22
22:30 [x]2Ch 35:32
22:31 [y]2Sa 17:2
22:34 [z]2Ch 35:23
22:36 [a]2Ki 14:12
22:38 [b]1Ki 21:19
22:39 [c]2Ch 9:17; Am 3:15
22:43 [d]2Ch 17:3

" 'I will go out and be a lying[q] spirit in the mouths of all his prophets,' he said.
" 'You will succeed in enticing him,' said the LORD. 'Go and do it.'
23 "So now the LORD has put a lying spirit in the mouths of all these prophets[r] of yours.
The LORD has decreed disaster for you."
24 Then Zedekiah[s] son of Kenaanah went up and slapped[t] Micaiah in the face. "Which
way did the spirit from[a] the LORD go when he went from me to speak to you?" he asked.
25 Micaiah replied, "You will find out on the day you go to hide[u] in an inner room."
26 The king of Israel then ordered, "Take Micaiah and send him back to Amon the ruler of the city and to Joash the king's son 27 and say, 'This is what the king says: Put this
fellow in prison[v] and give him nothing but bread and water until I return safely.' "
28 Micaiah declared, "If you ever return safely, the LORD has not spoken[w] through me."
Then he added, "Mark my words, all you people!"

Ahab Killed at Ramoth Gilead

29 So the king of Israel and Jehoshaphat king of Judah went up to Ramoth Gilead.
30 The king of Israel said to Jehoshaphat, "I will enter the battle in disguise,[x] but you wear
your royal robes." So the king of Israel disguised himself and went into battle.
31 Now the king of Aram had ordered his thirty-two chariot commanders, "Do not fight
with anyone, small or great, except the king[y] of Israel." 32 When the chariot commanders saw Jehoshaphat, they thought, "Surely this is the king of Israel." So they turned to
attack him, but when Jehoshaphat cried out, 33 the chariot commanders saw that he was
not the king of Israel and stopped pursuing him.
34 But someone drew his bow[z] at random and hit the king of Israel between the sections of his armor. The king told his chariot driver, "Wheel around and get me out of the
fighting. I've been wounded." 35 All day long the battle raged, and the king was propped
up in his chariot facing the Arameans. The blood from his wound ran onto the floor of
the chariot, and that evening he died. 36 As the sun was setting, a cry spread through the
army: "Every man to his town; everyone to his land!"[a]
37 So the king died and was brought to Samaria, and they buried him there. 38 They
washed the chariot at a pool in Samaria (where the prostitutes bathed),[b] and the dogs[b]
licked up his blood, as the word of the LORD had declared.
39 As for the other events of Ahab's reign, including all he did, the palace he built and
inlaid with ivory,[c] and the cities he fortified, are they not written in the book of the annals
of the kings of Israel? 40 Ahab rested with his fathers. And Ahaziah his son succeeded him
as king.

Jehoshaphat King of Judah

41 Jehoshaphat son of Asa became king of Judah in the fourth year of Ahab king of Israel. 42 Jehoshaphat was thirty-five years old when he became king, and he reigned in Jerusalem twenty-five years. His mother's name was Azubah daughter of Shilhi. 43 In everything
he walked in the ways of his father Asa[d] and did not stray from them; he did what was right

[a] *24* Or *Spirit of* [b] *38* Or *Samaria and cleaned the weapons*

22:22 I will go out and be a lying spirit. One of the celestial beings carried out God's wishes by using the four hundred prophets as a means of reinforcing Ahab's false sense of security. See 1 Samuel 16:14–16, Jeremiah 14:14–16, 23:16 and 26, Ezekiel 14:9, Job 1:12, 2:6 and Galatians 1:6–9.
22:25 hide in an inner room. When the outcome of the battle became known, Zedekiah would be disgraced and forced to seek refuge.
22:28 If you ever return. Regardless of Ahab's orders, the prophecy stood. See *WCF* 5.2.
22:30 disguise. Ahab's disguise indicated that he gave credence to Micaiah's words. **royal robes.** The cynical Ahab had Jehoshaphat dress in royal robes in the hope that, if a king were killed in battle (v. 17), that king would be Jehoshaphat.
22:31 Do not fight with anyone. Neutralizing the leader of an opposing army was critical, because that army might then disintegrate into a state of anarchy.
22:34 See *WCF* 5.2.
22:38 where the prostitutes bathed. The reference is possibly to sacred prostitutes from the temple of Baal, but see NIV text note. **the dogs licked up his blood.** This action is a partial realization of Elijah's prophecy in 21:19 (cf. 2Ki 9:25–26).
■ **22:39–40** *Closure of the Reign.* The writer indicated that Ahab was well known for his building programs, implying that his own record of Ahab, which focused on Ahab's idolatry and curse, was highly selective.
22:39 the palace he built and inlaid with ivory. Archaeological excavations at Samaria have discovered decorative inlays dating to this period. Although they were indicative of economic prosperity for the wealthy, the prophet Amos criticized such extravagance (Am 3:15). **cities he fortified.** Archaeological excavations reveal that Samaria and Megiddo were refortified during this period. **book of the annals of the kings of Israel.** See note on 11:41.
22:40 Ahaziah. On the reign of Ahaziah, see verses 51–53, as well as 2 Kings 1.
■ **22:41–50** *In Judah (869–848 B.C.)*: *Jehoshaphat of Judah.* The writer turned again to the southern kingdom (see "Introduction: Purpose and Distinctives"). These verses summarize the reign of Jehoshaphat. Like his father Asa, Jehoshaphat did "what was right in the eyes of the Lord" (v. 43). This material opens his reign (vv. 41–42), describes the mixture of success and failure under his leadership (vv. 43–49) and closes the account (v. 50).
22:41 in the fourth year. If Jehoshaphat were coregent with his father for three years, as some scholars believe, this year would be 869 B.C.
22:42 he reigned . . . twenty-five years. From 872–848 B.C.
22:43 he did what was right in the eyes of the LORD. Jehoshaphat was one of the southern kings depicted in a positive light by

in the eyes of the LORD. The high places,[e] however, were not removed, and the people continued to offer sacrifices and burn incense there. 44Jehoshaphat was also at peace with the
king of Israel.
45As for the other events of Jehoshaphat's reign, the things he achieved and his military exploits, are they not written in the book of the annals of the kings of Judah? 46He
rid the land of the rest of the male shrine prostitutes[f] who remained there even after the
reign of his father Asa. 47There was then no king[g] in Edom; a deputy ruled.
48Now Jehoshaphat built a fleet of trading ships[a h] to go to Ophir for gold, but they
never set sail—they were wrecked at Ezion Geber. 49At that time Ahaziah son of Ahab
said to Jehoshaphat, "Let my men sail with your men," but Jehoshaphat refused.
50Then Jehoshaphat rested with his fathers and was buried with them in the city of
David his father. And Jehoram his son succeeded him.

Ahaziah King of Israel

51Ahaziah son of Ahab became king of Israel in Samaria in the seventeenth year of Jehoshaphat king of Judah, and he reigned over Israel two years. 52He did evil[i] in the eyes
of the LORD, because he walked in the ways of his father and mother and in the ways of
Jeroboam son of Nebat, who caused Israel to sin. 53He served and worshiped Baal[j] and
provoked the LORD, the God of Israel, to anger, just as his father[k] had done.

22:43 [e]1Ki 3:2; 15:14; 2Ki 12:3
22:46 [f]Dt 23:17; 1Ki 14:24; 15:12
22:47 [g]2Sa 8:14; 2Ki 3:9; 8:20
22:48 [h]1Ki 9:26; 10:22
22:52 [i]1Ki 15:26; 21:25
22:53 [j]Jdg 2:11 [k]1Ki 16:30-32

a 48 Hebrew *of ships of Tarshish*

the author of Kings. **The high places, however, were not removed.** See note on 3:2.
22:44 Jehoshaphat was also at peace with the king of Israel. Whereas the early years of the divided kingdom were characterized by intermittent warfare, the treaty between Jehoshaphat and Ahab inaugurated a period of peaceful relations between Judah and Israel (cf. 2Ki 8:18,26).
22:45 military exploits. See 2 Kings 3:7–27, 2 Chronicles 17:11 and 2 Chronicles 20. **book of the annals of the kings of Judah.** See note on 11:41.
22:46 male shrine prostitutes. See note on 14:24.
22:47 a deputy ruled. There was no king in Edom, because in all likelihood Edom was at this time a vassal state of Judah. The king of Judah, therefore, had control over who governed Edom (2Ki 8:20–22).
22:48 built a fleet of trading ships. See NIV text note. Jehoshaphat, like Solomon, wished to establish his own maritime operations based at Ezion Geber (9:26–28; 10:22). Chronicles explains that this project failed because Jehoshaphat entered into an alliance with Israel (2Ch 20:35–37) **Ophir.** See note at 9:28.
22:49 Ahaziah son of Ahab. See 1 Kings 22:51—2 Kings 1:18. **Let my men sail with your men.** See 2 Chronicles 20:35–37.

■ **22:51—2 Kings 8:15** *In Israel (853–841 B.C.).* The reign of Jehoshaphat ended in 841 B.C., after the beginning of Ahaziah's reign in 853 B.C. For this reason, the writer now turned back to the history of the northern kingdom. See "Introduction: Purpose and Distinctives." This section divides into three parts: the reign of Ahaziah (22:51—2Ki 1:18), a transitional section on the transfer of power from Elijah to Elisha (2Ki 2:1–25) and the reign of Joram (3:1—8:15).
■ **22:51—2 Kings 1:18** *Ahaziah (853–852 B.C.).* Ahaziah was as evil as his father and mother had been (v. 52). The account of his reign opens (22:51–53), focuses on interactions with Elijah that explain his condemnation (2Ki 1:1–17a) and closes (2Ki 1:17b–18).
■ **22:51–53** *Opening of the Reign.* These ominous verses prepare the audience to expect great curses to fall on Ahaziah, just as they had fallen on Jeroboam, Ahab and Jezebel in punishment for evils and idolatries.
22:51 seventeenth year of Jehoshaphat. 853 B.C. **two years.** From 853–852 B.C.
22:52 in the ways of his father and mother. Ahab and Jezebel (16:29–34). **in the ways of Jeroboam.** See note on 12:30.
22:53 he served and worshiped Baal. Baal worship, introduced and supported by Ahab and Jezebel, was perpetuated by their son (see notes on 16:31).

2 KINGS

Introduction

See "Introduction to 1 Kings."

The LORD's Judgment on Ahaziah

1:1 [a]Ge 19:37; 2Sa 8:2; 2Ki 3:5

1:2 [b]ver 16 [c]Mk 3:22 [d]1Sa 6:2; Isa 2:6; 14:29; Mt 10:25 [e]Jdg 18:5; 2Ki 8:7-10

1 After Ahab's death, Moab[a] rebelled against Israel. 2 Now Ahaziah had fallen through
the lattice of his upper room in Samaria and injured himself. So he sent messengers,[b] saying to them, "Go and consult Baal-Zebub,[c] the god of Ekron,[d] to see if I will recover[e] from this injury."

1:3 [f]ver 15; Ge 16:7 [g]1Ki 17:1 [h]1Sa 28:8

1:4 [i]ver 6,16; Ps 41:8

3 But the angel[f] of the LORD said to Elijah[g] the Tishbite, "Go up and meet the messengers of the king of Samaria and ask them, 'Is it because there is no God in Israel[h] that
you are going off to consult Baal-Zebub, the god of Ekron?' 4 Therefore this is what the
LORD says: 'You will not leave[i] the bed you are lying on. You will certainly die!' " So Elijah went.

5 When the messengers returned to the king, he asked them, "Why have you come
back?"

6 "A man came to meet us," they replied. "And he said to us, 'Go back to the king who
sent you and tell him, "This is what the LORD says: Is it because there is no God in Israel that you are sending men to consult Baal-Zebub, the god of Ekron? Therefore you will
not leave the bed you are lying on. You will certainly die!" ' "

7 The king asked them, "What kind of man was it who came to meet you and told you
this?"

1:8 [j]1Ki 18:7; Zec 13:4; Mt 3:4; Mk 1:6

8 They replied, "He was a man with a garment of hair[j] and with a leather belt around
his waist."

The king said, "That was Elijah the Tishbite."

1:9 [k]2Ki 6:14 [l]Ex 18:25; Isa 3:3

9 Then he sent[k] to Elijah a captain[l] with his company of fifty men. The captain went
up to Elijah, who was sitting on the top of a hill, and said to him, "Man of God, the king
says, 'Come down!' "

1:10 [m]1Ki 18:38; Lk 9:54; Rev 11:5; 13:13

10 Elijah answered the captain, "If I am a man of God, may fire come down from heav-
en and consume you and your fifty men!" Then fire[m] fell from heaven and consumed the
captain and his men.

11 At this the king sent to Elijah another captain with his fifty men. The captain said
to him, "Man of God, this is what the king says, 'Come down at once!' "

12 "If I am a man of God," Elijah replied, "may fire come down from heaven and consume you and your fifty men!" Then the fire of God fell from heaven and consumed him
and his fifty men.

13 So the king sent a third captain with his fifty men. This third captain went up and

---

■ **1:1–17a** *Ahaziah's Prophetic Condemnation.* Ahaziah received harsh condemnation for his idolatry.

■ **1:1–2** *Ahaziah Seeks the Baal.* At a time when he was injured, Ahaziah showed himself unfaithful to the Lord by turning to Baal.

1:2 Baal-Zebub. "Lord of the Flies," an intentional change from its true name, Baal-Zabul, "the Lord is Prince," by Israelites wishing to mock this Baal.

■ **1:3–8** *Elijah Intervenes.* An angel called Elijah to stop Ahaziah's messengers and to condemn Ahaziah.

1:3 Elijah the Tishbite. See note on 1 Kings 17:1. **king of Samaria.** See note on 1 Kings 21:1.

1:8 garment of hair . . . a leather belt. The Hebrew for the phrase translated "a garment of hair" can also be translated "a hairy man." Elijah's garment was probably made from sheepskin or camel's hair (2:8,13; 1Ki 19:19; Zec 13:4), and his rough cloak was tied with a leather belt. The appearance, demeanor and lifestyle of John the Baptist resembled that of Elijah (Mt 3:4). Both prophets carried out ministries of judgment and repentance (Mt 3:1–12; Lk 3:2–18).

■ **1:9–17a** *Elijah Sends Fire From Heaven.* Ahaziah tried to have Elijah killed but failed—and died, just as Elijah had warned.

1:9 Man of God, the king says, "Come down!" For Ahaziah, Elijah's prophecy constituted interference in the affairs of state, and Elijah was therefore held accountable to the king for his actions. Ahaziah's response reveals a characteristically Canaanite understanding of the unbridled powers of kingship. See notes on Deuteronomy 17:14–20, 1 Samuel 8:11–17 and 1 Kings 21:2.

1:10 If I am a man of God. Powerful heads of state were as much subject to the covenant as were commoners (Dt 17:18–20; 1Sa 12:14–15; 1Ki 2:1–4).

fell on his knees before Elijah. "Man of God," he begged, "please have respect for my life[n]
and the lives of these fifty men, your servants! 14See, fire has fallen from heaven and consumed the first two captains and all their men. But now have respect for my life!"
15The angel[o] of the LORD said to Elijah, "Go down with him; do not be afraid[p] of him."
So Elijah got up and went down with him to the king.
16He told the king, "This is what the LORD says: Is it because there is no God in Israel
for you to consult that you have sent messengers[q] to consult Baal-Zebub, the god of Ekron? Because you have done this, you will never leave[r] the bed you are lying on. You will
certainly die!" 17So he died,[s] according to the word of the LORD that Elijah had spoken.
Because Ahaziah had no son, Joram[a] [t] succeeded him as king in the second year of Jehoram son of Jehoshaphat king of Judah. 18As for all the other events of Ahaziah's reign,
and what he did, are they not written in the book of the annals of the kings of Israel?

Elijah Taken Up to Heaven

2 When the LORD was about to take[u] Elijah up to heaven in a whirlwind,[v] Elijah and
Elisha[w] were on their way from Gilgal.[x] 2Elijah said to Elisha, "Stay here;[y] the LORD
has sent me to Bethel."
But Elisha said, "As surely as the LORD lives and as you live, I will not leave you."[z] So
they went down to Bethel.
3The company[a] of the prophets at Bethel came out to Elisha and asked, "Do you know
that the LORD is going to take your master from you today?"
"Yes, I know," Elisha replied, "but do not speak of it."
4Then Elijah said to him, "Stay here, Elisha; the LORD has sent me to Jericho.[b]"
And he replied, "As surely as the LORD lives and as you live, I will not leave you." So
they went to Jericho.
5The company[c] of the prophets at Jericho went up to Elisha and asked him, "Do you
know that the LORD is going to take your master from you today?"
"Yes, I know," he replied, "but do not speak of it."
6Then Elijah said to him, "Stay here;[d] the LORD has sent me to the Jordan."[e]
And he replied, "As surely as the LORD lives and as you live, I will not leave you."[f] So
the two of them walked on.
7Fifty men of the company of the prophets went and stood at a distance, facing the
place where Elijah and Elisha had stopped at the Jordan. 8Elijah took his cloak,[g] rolled
it up and struck[h] the water with it. The water divided[i] to the right and to the left, and
the two of them crossed over on dry[j] ground.
9When they had crossed, Elijah said to Elisha, "Tell me, what can I do for you before
I am taken from you?"
"Let me inherit a double[k] portion of your spirit,"[l] Elisha replied.
10"You have asked a difficult thing," Elijah said, "yet if you see me when I am taken
from you, it will be yours—otherwise not."
11As they were walking along and talking together, suddenly a chariot of fire[m] and
horses of fire appeared and separated the two of them, and Elijah went up to heaven[n]
in a whirlwind.[o] 12Elisha saw this and cried out, "My father! My father! The chariots[p] and

[a] 17 Hebrew *Jehoram*, a variant of *Joram*

1:13 [n]1Sa 26:21; Ps 72:14
1:15 [o]ver 3 [p]Isa 51:12; 57:11; Jer 1:17; Eze 2:6
1:16 [q]ver 2 [r]ver 4
1:17 [s]2Ki 8:15; Jer 20:6; 28:17 [t]2Ki 3:1; 8:16
2:1 [u]Ge 5:24; Heb 11:5 [v]ver 11; 1Ki 19:11; Isa 5:28; 66:15; Jer 4:13; Na 1:3 [w]1Ki 19:16,21 [x]Dt 11:30; 2Ki 4:38
2:2 [y]ver 6 [z]Ru 1:16; 1Sa 1:26; 2Ki 4:30
2:3 [a]1Sa 10:5; 2Ki 4:1, 38
2:4 [b]Jos 3:16; 6:26
2:5 [c]ver 3
2:6 [d]ver 2 [e]Jos 3:15 [f]Ru 1:16
2:8 [g]1Ki 19:19 [h]ver 14 [i]Ex 14:21 [j]Ex 14:22,29
2:9 [k]Dt 21:17 [l]Nu 11:17
2:11 [m]2Ki 6:17; Ps 68:17; 104:3,4; Isa 66:15; Hab 3:8; Zec 6:1 [n]Ge 5:24 [o]ver 1
2:12 [p]2Ki 6:17; 13:14

■ **1:17b–18** *Closure of the Reign.* Ahaziah died without an heir, so the kingdom passed to his brother.
1:17 Joram. See NIV text note. Joram, like Ahaziah, was a son of Ahab (3:1; 1Ki 22:51). This Joram should not be confused with Joram (or Jehoram), the son and successor to Jehoshaphat (see 8:16,18), who ruled in Judah at about the same time.
1:18 book of the annals of the kings of Israel. See note on 1 Kings 11:41.
■ **2:1–25** *The Transfer of Prophetic Ministry to Elisha.* In an addition to the account of Ahaziah, the writer describes how Elisha succeeded Elijah (vv. 1–18) and how Elisha's office was authenticated by miracles (vv. 19–25). These episodes demonstrated that Elijah and Elisha were authorized by God in their ministries.
■ **2:1–18** *Elijah Succeeded by Elisha.* Elijah was taken up to heaven in a whirlwind and was succeeded by Elisha.
2:1 up to heaven in a whirlwind. In the Bible only two individuals, Elijah and Enoch (Ge 5:24), were privileged to circumvent the death process by being taken up directly to heaven. The prophet Malachi declared that Elijah would reappear before the coming of the "day of the LORD" (Mal 4:5–6). Elijah would prepare the people for the Lord's ministry (see note on 1:8). **Elijah.** See note on 1 Kings 17:1. **Gilgal.** This site was located west of the Jordan near Jericho.
2:2 Bethel. A major Israelite city (see note on 1Ki 12:29).
2:8 struck the water. Elijah, like Moses and Joshua before him, witnessed the parting of the waters so that God's chosen might pass through safely on dry ground (Ex 14:13–31; Jos 3:1–17).
2:9 Let me inherit a double portion. In Israel the eldest son enjoyed a double portion of the family inheritance and with it the right of succession (Ge 25:31; Dt 21:17). Elisha's desire for "a double portion of your spirit" was therefore a bold request.
2:10 You have asked a difficult thing. It was not up to Elijah but to God to determine whether Elisha's daring request would be met.
2:11 a chariot of fire and horses of fire. God's heavenly attendants escorted Elijah "to heaven in a whirlwind." Fire appeared on a number of occasions in Elijah's ministry as a symbol of God's all-consuming power (1:10,12,14; 1Ki 18:38; cf. 1Ki 19:12).
2:12 My father! My father! A title of respect for a person of religious authority (Ge 45:8; Jdg 17:10; Mt 23:9); later used for Elisha (6:21; 13:14). See *WLC* 124.

horsemen of Israel!" And Elisha saw him no more. Then he took hold of his own clothes
and tore[q] them apart.
13 He picked up the cloak that had fallen from Elijah and went back and stood on the
bank of the Jordan. 14 Then he took the cloak[r] that had fallen from him and struck[s]
the water with it. "Where now is the LORD, the God of Elijah?" he asked. When he struck
the water, it divided to the right and to the left, and he crossed over.
15 The company[t] of the prophets from Jericho, who were watching, said, "The spirit[u]
of Elijah is resting on Elisha." And they went to meet him and bowed to the ground before him. 16 "Look," they said, "we your servants have fifty able men. Let them go and look
for your master. Perhaps the Spirit[v] of the LORD has picked him up[w] and set him down
on some mountain or in some valley."
"No," Elisha replied, "do not send them."
17 But they persisted until he was too ashamed[x] to refuse. So he said, "Send them."
And they sent fifty men, who searched for three days but did not find him. 18 When they
returned to Elisha, who was staying in Jericho, he said to them, "Didn't I tell you not
to go?"

Healing of the Water

19 The men of the city said to Elisha, "Look, our lord, this town is well situated, as you
can see, but the water is bad and the land is unproductive."
20 "Bring me a new bowl," he said, "and put salt in it." So they brought it to him.
21 Then he went out to the spring and threw[y] the salt into it, saying, "This is what the
LORD says: 'I have healed this water. Never again will it cause death or make the land unproductive.' " 22 And the water has remained wholesome[z] to this day, according to the
word Elisha had spoken.

Elisha Is Jeered

23 From there Elisha went up to Bethel. As he was walking along the road, some
youths came out of the town and jeered[a] at him. "Go on up, you baldhead!" they said.
"Go on up, you baldhead!" 24 He turned around, looked at them and called down a curse[b]
on them in the name[c] of the LORD. Then two bears came out of the woods and mauled
forty-two of the youths. 25 And he went on to Mount Carmel[d] and from there returned to
Samaria.

Moab Revolts

3 Joram[a][e] son of Ahab became king of Israel in Samaria in the eighteenth year of Jehoshaphat king of Judah, and he reigned twelve years. 2 He did evil[f] in the eyes of
the LORD, but not as his father[g] and mother had done. He got rid of the sacred stone[h] of

2:12 [q]Ge 37:29
2:14 [r]1Ki 19:19 [s]ver 8
2:15 [t]ver 7; 1Sa 10:5 [u]Nu 11:17
2:16 [v]1Ki 18:12 [w]Ac 8:39
2:17 [x]2Ki 8:11
2:21 [y]Ex 15:25; 2Ki 4:41; 6:6
2:22 [z]Ex 15:25
2:23 [a]Ex 22:28; 2Ch 36:16; Job 19:18; Ps 31:18
2:24 [b]Ge 4:11; Ne 13:25-27 [c]Dt 18:19
2:25 [d]1Ki 18:20; 2Ki 4:25
3:1 [e]2Ki 1:17
3:2 [f]1Ki 15:26 [g]1Ki 16:30-32 [h]Ex 23:24; 2Ki 10:18,26-28

[a] *1* Hebrew *Jehoram,* a variant of *Joram;* also in verse 6

2:13 He picked up the cloak. Earlier Elijah had cast his cloak on Elisha as a sign that Elisha would be his successor (1Ki 19:19). This prophecy had come to fruition.
2:14 it divided to the right and to the left, and he crossed over. God had authenticated the ministry of Joshua as the approved successor to Moses (Nu 27:12–23; Dt 31:1–8; 34:9; Jos 1:1–9) when Joshua led his people across the Jordan River into the promised land, much as Moses had led the people through the Red Sea (Ex 14–15; Jos 3). God publicly affirmed Elisha's ministry when Elisha miraculously passed over the Jordan, as Elijah with Elisha had passed over earlier (v. 8).
2:15 The company of the prophets . . . bowed to the ground before him. See note on 1 Kings 20:35. This incident verified Elisha's credentials as God's designated successor to Elijah.
▪ **2:19–25** *Elisha's First Miracles.* Elisha healed the water of Jericho (vv. 19–22) and, when jeered for being bald, called down a curse on those who were mocking him (vv. 23–25). These episodes demonstrated that he had in fact taken on Elijah's role as God's spokesperson.
2:19 The men of the city. Likely the leaders of the community. The city was evidently Jericho (v. 18).
2:20 new bowl. One that was ceremonially unpolluted by common use. **put salt in it.** Salt is a symbol for God's faithfulness in his promises and for the manner in which he maintains his people (Lev 2:13; Nu 18:19; 2Ch 13:5; Eze 43:24).
2:23 Bethel. See note on 1 Kings 12:29. **Go on up.** The verb translated "go up" was the same verb used to describe Elijah's entrance into heaven (v. 11); hence, the youths may have been taunting Elisha to ascend just as Elijah had. **baldhead.** In contrast to the hairy Elijah, Elisha was bald. The ideal in ancient Israel was a full head of hair (2Sa 14:25–26).
2:24 called down a curse. Elisha in his ministry was characteristically compassionate toward the repentant and stern with the unresponsive and obstinate. The mauling of the Bethel youths was another public manifestation of the power of God present in Elisha (vv. 14,21).
▪ **3:1–8:15** *Joram (852–841 B.C.).* Joram's reign provided the frame of reference for the rest of Elisha's activities. These materials divide into eight parts: the opening of Joram's reign (3:1–3), his war with Moab (3:4–27), Elisha helping the needy (4:1–44), Naaman of Syria (5:1–27), the prophets and the Syrian king (6:1–23), the Syrian siege of Samaria (6:24—7:20), the Shunammite woman (8:1–6) and Hazael of Syria (8:7–15).
▪ **3:1–3** *Opening of Reign.* Joram's reign in Israel was marked by minor reform, but also by a refusal to comply with proper worship in the temple at Jerusalem.
3:1 Joram. See NIV text note. **in the eighteenth year of Jehoshaphat.** Likely, given the information in 1:17, Jehoram of Judah and his father, Jehoshaphat, ruled as coregents for approximately five years (852–848 B.C.). Hence, "the second year of Jehoram" (1:17) was also "the eighteenth year of Jehoshaphat." See "Introduction to 1 Kings: Purpose and Distinctives: *Kings as History.*" **twelve years.** That is, from 852–841 B.C.
3:2 his father and mother. Ahab and Jezebel. **sacred stone of Baal.** This pillar represented the presence of Baal (see note on 1Ki 14:23). Joram initiated a minor reform, in which he attempted to undo some of the damage done by his parents.

Baal that his father had made. 3 Nevertheless he clung to the sins[i] of Jeroboam son of Nebat, which he had caused Israel to commit; he did not turn away from them.
4 Now Mesha king of Moab[j] raised sheep, and he had to supply the king of Israel with
a hundred thousand lambs[k] and with the wool of a hundred thousand rams. 5 But after
Ahab died, the king of Moab rebelled[l] against the king of Israel. 6 So at that time King Joram set out from Samaria and mobilized all Israel. 7 He also sent this message to Jehoshaphat king of Judah: "The king of Moab has rebelled against me. Will you go with me to
fight[m] against Moab?"
"I will go with you," he replied. "I am as you are, my people as your people, my horses as your horses."
8 "By what route shall we attack?" he asked.
"Through the Desert of Edom," he answered.
9 So the king of Israel set out with the king of Judah and the king of Edom.[n] After a
roundabout march of seven days, the army had no more water for themselves or for the
animals with them.
10 "What!" exclaimed the king of Israel. "Has the LORD called us three kings together
only to hand us over to Moab?"
11 But Jehoshaphat asked, "Is there no prophet of the LORD here, that we may inquire[o]
of the LORD through him?"
An officer of the king of Israel answered, "Elisha[p] son of Shaphat is here. He used to
pour water on the hands of Elijah.[a][q]"
12 Jehoshaphat said, "The word[r] of the LORD is with him." So the king of Israel and Jehoshaphat and the king of Edom went down to him.
13 Elisha said to the king of Israel, "What do we have to do with each other? Go to the
prophets of your father and the prophets of your mother."
"No," the king of Israel answered, "because it was the LORD who called us three kings
together to hand us over to Moab."
14 Elisha said, "As surely as the LORD Almighty lives, whom I serve, if I did not have respect for the presence of Jehoshaphat king of Judah, I would not look at you or even notice you. 15 But now bring me a harpist."[s]
While the harpist was playing, the hand[t] of the LORD came upon Elisha 16 and he said,
"This is what the LORD says: Make this valley full of ditches. 17 For this is what the LORD
says: You will see neither wind nor rain, yet this valley will be filled with water,[u] and you,
your cattle and your other animals will drink. 18 This is an easy[v] thing in the eyes of the
LORD; he will also hand Moab over to you. 19 You will overthrow every fortified city and
every major town. You will cut down every good tree, stop up all the springs, and ruin
every good field with stones."
20 The next morning, about the time[w] for offering the sacrifice, there it was—water
flowing from the direction of Edom! And the land was filled with water.[x]
21 Now all the Moabites had heard that the kings had come to fight against them; so
every man, young and old, who could bear arms was called up and stationed on the border. 22 When they got up early in the morning, the sun was shining on the water. To the
Moabites across the way, the water looked red—like blood. 23 "That's blood!" they said.
"Those kings must have fought and slaughtered each other. Now to the plunder, Moab!"

3:3 [i]1Ki 12:28-32; 14:9,16
3:4 [j]Ge 19:37; 2Ki 1:1 [k]Ezr 7:17; Isa 16:1
3:5 [l]2Ki 1:1
3:7 [m]1Ki 22:4
3:9 [n]1Ki 22:47
3:11 [o]Ge 25:22; 1Ki 22:7 [p]Ge 20:7 [q]1Ki 19:16
3:12 [r]Nu 11:17
3:15 [s]1Sa 16:23 [t]Jer 15:17; Eze 1:3
3:17 [u]Ps 107:35; Isa 32:2; 35:6; 41:18
3:18 [v]Ge 18:14; 2Ki 20:10; Isa 49:6; Jer 32:17, 27; Mk 10:27
3:20 [w]Ex 29:39,40 [x]Ex 17:6

[a] *11* That is, he was Elijah's personal servant.

3:3 sins of Jeroboam. See notes on 1 Kings 12:30–31. **he did not turn away from them.** Joram's reform was not thoroughgoing; he did not address the fundamental flaw of the worship in the northern kingdom.

■ **3:4–27** *Elisha's Service in Moabite War.* Elisha ministered during Joram's war with Moab.

3:4 Mesha king of Moab. According to the extrabiblical Moabite Stone, Mesha acknowledged that he had begun his reign as Israel's servant, having inherited vassalage to Israel from his predecessors. He also claimed to have freed his land from Israelite subjugation and boasted that "Israel has perished forever" (an obvious exaggeration). **he had to supply the king.** Part of Mesha's obligations to his suzerain, Israel, involved rendering regular tribute.

3:5 But after Ahab died, the king of Moab rebelled. See 1:1.

3:9 king of Edom. The ruler of Edom was likely a vassal of the king of Judah and therefore was compelled to assist his suzerain (cf. 8:20; 1Ki 22:47).

3:11 Is there no prophet of the LORD here . . . ? Jehoshaphat had asked the same question of Ahab (1Ki 22:7). **pour water on the hands of Elijah.** See NIV text note.

3:14 respect for the presence of Jehoshaphat. Elisha consented to prophesy for the coalition, but only for the sake of Jehoshaphat, whom the writer of Kings describes as doing "what was right in the eyes of the LORD" (1Ki 22:43).

3:15 bring me a harpist. The harpist provided a suitable context for the reception of divine revelation (cf. 1Sa 10:5–6). **the hand of the LORD.** The phrase expressed prophetic inspiration (Eze 1:3; 8:1; 13:9).

3:16 this valley. Usually identified with the Wadi Zered, which flowed into the southern portion of the Dead Sea (Dt 2:13).

3:19 You will cut down every good tree. Indicated that the armies did not have to follow the precepts of sacred war (Dt 20:19–20).

3:20 the time for offering the sacrifice. See Exodus 29:38–39 and Numbers 28:3–4. **water flowing from the direction of Edom.** The mountains of Edom were considerably higher than the Dead Sea (the lowest point on Earth); hence, the waters flowed from the south northward in the direction of the Dead Sea.

3:22 the water looked red—like blood. The water may have been colored by Edom's red sandstone (cf. Ge 25:30), or it may have looked red because of the reflected sunlight.

24 But when the Moabites came to the camp of Israel, the Israelites rose up and
fought them until they fled. And the Israelites invaded the land and slaughtered the Moabites. 25 They destroyed the towns, and each man threw a stone on every good field until it was covered. They stopped up all the springs and cut down every good tree. Only
Kir Hareseth[y] was left with its stones in place, but men armed with slings surrounded
it and attacked it as well.
26 When the king of Moab saw that the battle had gone against him, he took with him
seven hundred swordsmen to break through to the king of Edom, but they failed. 27 Then
he took his firstborn[z] son, who was to succeed him as king, and offered him as a sacrifice on the city wall. The fury against Israel was great; they withdrew and returned to
their own land.

The Widow's Oil

4 The wife of a man from the company[a] of the prophets cried out to Elisha, "Your servant my husband is dead, and you know that he revered the LORD. But now his creditor[b] is coming to take my two boys as his slaves."
2 Elisha replied to her, "How can I help you? Tell me, what do you have in your
house?"
"Your servant has nothing there at all," she said, "except a little oil."[c]
3 Elisha said, "Go around and ask all your neighbors for empty jars. Don't ask for just
a few. 4 Then go inside and shut the door behind you and your sons. Pour oil into all the
jars, and as each is filled, put it to one side."
5 She left him and afterward shut the door behind her and her sons. They brought the
jars to her and she kept pouring. 6 When all the jars were full, she said to her son, "Bring
me another one."
But he replied, "There is not a jar left." Then the oil stopped flowing.
7 She went and told the man of God,[d] and he said, "Go, sell the oil and pay your debts.
You and your sons can live on what is left."

The Shunammite's Son Restored to Life

8 One day Elisha went to Shunem.[e] And a well-to-do woman was there, who urged
him to stay for a meal. So whenever he came by, he stopped there to eat. 9 She said to her
husband, "I know that this man who often comes our way is a holy man of God. 10 Let's
make a small room on the roof and put in it a bed and a table, a chair and a lamp for him.
Then he can stay[f] there whenever he comes to us."
11 One day when Elisha came, he went up to his room and lay down there. 12 He said
to his servant Gehazi, "Call the Shunammite."[g] So he called her, and she stood before
him. 13 Elisha said to him, "Tell her, 'You have gone to all this trouble for us. Now what
can be done for you? Can we speak on your behalf to the king or the commander of the
army?' "
She replied, "I have a home among my own people."
14 "What can be done for her?" Elisha asked.
Gehazi said, "Well, she has no son and her husband is old."
15 Then Elisha said, "Call her." So he called her, and she stood in the doorway.
16 "About this time[h] next year," Elisha said, "you will hold a son in your arms."
"No, my lord," she objected. "Don't mislead your servant, O man of God!"
17 But the woman became pregnant, and the next year about that same time she gave
birth to a son, just as Elisha had told her.
18 The child grew, and one day he went out to his father, who was with the reapers.[i]
19 "My head! My head!" he said to his father.

3:25 [y]ver 19; Isa 15:1; 16:7; Jer 48:31,36
3:27 [z]Dt 12:31; 2Ki 16:3; 21:6; 2Ch 28:3; Ps 106:38; Jer 19:4-5; Am 2:1; Mic 6:7
4:1 [a]1Sa 10:5; 2Ki 2:3 [b]Ex 22:26; Lev 25:39-43; Ne 5:3-5; Job 22:6; 24:9
4:2 [c]1Ki 17:12
4:7 [d]1Ki 12:22
4:8 [e]Jos 19:18
4:10 [f]Mt 10:41; Ro 12:13
4:12 [g]2Ki 8:1
4:16 [h]Ge 18:10
4:18 [i]Ru 2:3

3:25 Kir Hareseth. Likely the capital of Moab (Isa 16:7,11; Jer 48:31,36), situated about 11 miles east of the Dead Sea and about 14 miles north of the Wadi Zered.

3:27 his firstborn son. This grisly act was performed to induce the god Chemosh to deliver the Moabites from certain defeat. Child sacrifice was expressly forbidden in Israel (Ex 34:20; Dt 18:10). Its practice by the king of Moab demonstrated his wickedness.

■ **4:1–44** *Elisha's Ministry to the Needy.* Elisha ministered to the needy by miraculous means: he multiplied a widow's oil (vv. 1–7), raised a Shunammite's dead son to life (vv. 8–37), restored a poisoned stew (vv. 38–41) and fed 100 people on 20 loaves of bread and some grain (vv. 42–44).

4:1 company of the prophets. See note on 1 Kings 20:35. **my two boys as his slaves.** The Torah allowed taking children as bond servants for a limited period of time in payment of a debt (Lev 25:39–46). Unfortunately, this allowance was often exploited (Ne 5:5–8; Jer 34:8–22; Am 2:6; 8:6).

4:8 Shunem. Located outside of Israel in northern Canaan (see note on 1Ki 1:3). **well-to-do woman.** See verse 22.

4:12 Gehazi. Elisha's personal attendant (5:19–27; 6:15).

4:14 she has no son and her husband is old. In the ancient Near East, an heir was of great importance because the family name and possessions were passed down to children. Lacking a son, the couple's home and goods would go to others. Moreover, the plight of widowhood (a real prospect for this woman) was difficult (see note on 1Ki 17:9).

4:17 she gave birth to a son. Throughout the Bible, God's grace to formerly barren women, such as Sarah (Ge 17:16–19), Rebekah (Ge 25:21–26), Rachel (Ge 29:31; 30:22–24), Hannah (1Sa 1) and Elizabeth (Lk 1:5–17), indicated his great love and compassion.

His father told a servant, "Carry him to his mother." 20After the servant had lifted him
up and carried him to his mother, the boy sat on her lap until noon, and then he died. 21She
went up and laid him on the bed[j] of the man of God, then shut the door and went out.
22She called her husband and said, "Please send me one of the servants and a donkey so I can go to the man of God quickly and return."
23"Why go to him today?" he asked. "It's not the New Moon[k] or the Sabbath."
"It's all right," she said.
24She saddled the donkey and said to her servant, "Lead on; don't slow down for me
unless I tell you." 25So she set out and came to the man of God at Mount Carmel.[l]
When he saw her in the distance, the man of God said to his servant Gehazi, "Look!
There's the Shunammite! 26Run to meet her and ask her, 'Are you all right? Is your husband all right? Is your child all right?' "
"Everything is all right," she said.
27When she reached the man of God at the mountain, she took hold of his feet. Gehazi came over to push her away, but the man of God said, "Leave her alone! She is in
bitter distress,[m] but the LORD has hidden it from me and has not told me why."
28"Did I ask you for a son, my lord?" she said. "Didn't I tell you, 'Don't raise my hopes'?"
29Elisha said to Gehazi, "Tuck your cloak into your belt,[n] take my staff[o] in your hand
and run. If you meet anyone, do not greet him, and if anyone greets you, do not answer.
Lay my staff on the boy's face."
30But the child's mother said, "As surely as the LORD lives and as you live, I will not
leave you." So he got up and followed her.
31Gehazi went on ahead and laid the staff on the boy's face, but there was no sound or
response. So Gehazi went back to meet Elisha and told him, "The boy has not awakened."
32When Elisha reached the house, there was the boy lying dead on his couch.[p] 33He
went in, shut the door on the two of them and prayed[q] to the LORD. 34Then he got on the
bed and lay upon the boy, mouth to mouth, eyes to eyes, hands to hands. As he
stretched[r] himself out upon him, the boy's body grew warm. 35Elisha turned away and
walked back and forth in the room and then got on the bed and stretched out upon him
once more. The boy sneezed seven times[s] and opened his eyes.[t]
36Elisha summoned Gehazi and said, "Call the Shunammite." And he did. When she
came, he said, "Take your son."[u] 37She came in, fell at his feet and bowed to the ground.
Then she took her son and went out.

Death in the Pot

38Elisha returned to Gilgal[v] and there was a famine[w] in that region. While the company of the prophets was meeting with him, he said to his servant, "Put on the large pot
and cook some stew for these men."
39One of them went out into the fields to gather herbs and found a wild vine. He gathered some of its gourds and filled the fold of his cloak. When he returned, he cut them
up into the pot of stew, though no one knew what they were. 40The stew was poured out
for the men, but as they began to eat it, they cried out, "O man of God, there is death in
the pot!" And they could not eat it.
41Elisha said, "Get some flour." He put it into the pot and said, "Serve it to the people to eat." And there was nothing harmful in the pot.[x]

Feeding of a Hundred

42A man came from Baal Shalishah,[y] bringing the man of God twenty loaves[z] of barley bread[a] baked from the first ripe grain, along with some heads of new grain. "Give it
to the people to eat," Elisha said.

4:21 [j]ver 32
4:23 [k]Nu 10:10; 1Ch 23:31; Ps 81:3
4:25 [l]1Ki 18:20; 2Ki 2:25
4:27 [m]1Sa 1:15
4:29 [n]1Ki 18:16; 2Ki 2:8, 14; 9:1 [o]Ex 4:2; 7:19; 14:16
4:32 [p]ver 21
4:33 [q]1Ki 17:20; Mt 6:6
4:34 [r]1Ki 17:21; Ac 20:10
4:35 [s]Jos 6:15 [t]2Ki 8:5
4:36 [u]Heb 11:35
4:38 [v]2Ki 2:1 [w]Lev 26:26; 2Ki 8:1
4:41 [x]Ex 15:25; 2Ki 2:21
4:42 [y]1Sa 9:4 [z]Mt 14:17; 15:36 [a]1Sa 9:7

4:21 laid him on the bed of the man of God. The woman refused to accept the death of her son and laid his body in Elisha's room, perhaps so that it wouldn't be discovered and the ritual of mourning could not begin (Ge 50:10; 2Ch 35:25; Job 2:12–13; Mk 5:38; Jn 11:33).
4:23 It's not the New Moon or the Sabbath. Ancient Israel operated under a lunar calendar, and a festival was celebrated at each New Moon (Nu 10:10; 28:11–15; Ezr 3:5; Ne 10:33; Isa 1:13–14; Am 8:5; Col 2:16). People were not supposed to work on the Sabbath or on the New Moon (Ex 16:23; 20:9–10; 1Sa 20:5–6).
4:25 Mount Carmel. About a 26-mile journey; the woman did not want to waste any time.
4:27 took hold of his feet. A sign both of desperation and of respect (Jn 11:32).
4:29 Tuck your cloak into your belt. To allow Gehazi to move much more quickly—his cloak wouldn't wrap around his legs as he ran. **Lay my staff on the boy's face.** Elisha seemed to expect that the staff, representing his own presence and the power of God, would revive the boy. God had previously revived a dead boy who was in Elijah's physical presence (1Ki 17:21).
4:38 Gilgal. See 2:1. **Put on the large pot.** In the midst of a famine, Elisha was not commanding his servant to do something easy.
4:39 wild vine. Looking far afield for stew ingredients, because of the famine, may have resulted in his gathering an unfamiliar plant. **gourds.** About the size of an orange, this fruit had a bitter taste.
4:41 nothing harmful in the pot. God miraculously rendered the stew edible.
4:42 Baal Shalishah. Situated on the Brook of Kanah in the hill country of Ephraim. **the first ripe grain.** Bread baked from the first milling of the season (Lev 23:20). The man brought the first-

43"How can I set this before a hundred men?" his servant asked.
But Elisha answered, "Give it to the people to eat.[b] For this is what the LORD says:
'They will eat and have some left over.[c]' " 44Then he set it before them, and they ate and
had some left over, according to the word of the LORD.

Naaman Healed of Leprosy

5 Now Naaman was commander of the army of the king of Aram.[d] He was a great
man in the sight of his master and highly regarded, because through him the LORD
had given victory to Aram. He was a valiant soldier, but he had leprosy.[a][e]
2Now bands[f] from Aram had gone out and had taken captive a young girl from Israel, and she served Naaman's wife. 3She said to her mistress, "If only my master would
see the prophet[g] who is in Samaria! He would cure him of his leprosy."
4Naaman went to his master and told him what the girl from Israel had said. 5"By all
means, go," the king of Aram replied. "I will send a letter to the king of Israel." So Naaman left, taking with him ten talents[b] of silver, six thousand shekels[c] of gold and ten sets
of clothing.[h] 6The letter that he took to the king of Israel read: "With this letter I am sending my servant Naaman to you so that you may cure him of his leprosy."
7As soon as the king of Israel read the letter,[i] he tore his robes and said, "Am I God?[j]
Can I kill and bring back to life?[k] Why does this fellow send someone to me to be cured
of his leprosy? See how he is trying to pick a quarrel[l] with me!"
8When Elisha the man of God heard that the king of Israel had torn his robes, he sent
him this message: "Why have you torn your robes? Have the man come to me and he will
know that there is a prophet[m] in Israel." 9So Naaman went with his horses and chariots and stopped at the door of Elisha's house. 10Elisha sent a messenger to say to him,
"Go, wash[n] yourself seven times[o] in the Jordan, and your flesh will be restored and you
will be cleansed."
11But Naaman went away angry and said, "I thought that he would surely come out
to me and stand and call on the name of the LORD his God, wave his hand[p] over the spot
and cure me of my leprosy. 12Are not Abana and Pharpar, the rivers of Damascus, better than any of the waters[q] of Israel? Couldn't I wash in them and be cleansed?" So he
turned and went off in a rage.[r]
13Naaman's servants went to him and said, "My father,[s] if the prophet had told you
to do some great thing, would you not have done it? How much more, then, when he tells
you, 'Wash and be cleansed'!" 14So he went down and dipped himself in the Jordan sev-
en times,[t] as the man of God had told him, and his flesh was restored[u] and became clean
like that of a young boy.[v]
15Then Naaman and all his attendants went back to the man of God[w]. He stood be-

4:43 [b]Lk 9:13 [c]Mt 14:20; Jn 6:12
5:1 [d]Ge 10:22; 2Sa 10:19 [e]Ex 4:6; Nu 12:10; Lk 4:27
5:2 [f]2Ki 6:23; 13:20; 24:2
5:3 [g]Ge 20:7
5:5 [h]ver 22; Ge 24:53; Jdg 14:12; 1Sa 9:7
5:7 [i]2Ki 19:14 [j]Ge 30:2 [k]Dt 32:39; 1Sa 2:6 [l]1Ki 20:7
5:8 [m]1Ki 22:7
5:10 [n]Jn 9:7 [o]Ge 33:3; Lev 14:7
5:11 [p]Ex 7:19
5:12 [q]Isa 8:6 [r]Pr 14:17, 29; 19:11; 29:11
5:13 [s]2Ki 6:21; 13:14
5:14 [t]Ge 33:3; Lev 14:7; Jos 6:15 [u]Ex 4:7 [v]Job 33:25; Lk 4:27
5:15 [w]Jos 2:11

[a] *1* The Hebrew word was used for various diseases affecting the skin—not necessarily leprosy; also in verses 3, 6, 7, 11 and 27. [b] *5* That is, about 750 pounds (about 340 kilograms) [c] *5* That is, about 150 pounds (about 70 kilograms)

---

fruits of the harvest to Elisha rather than taking them to the apostate priests at Bethel or Dan (Lev 2:14; 23:9–21; Dt 18:3–5).

▪ **5:1–27** *Elisha Cures Naaman of Syria.* Elisha cured Naaman, a prominent Gentile, of leprosy, after which Naaman converted to the worship of the Lord. When Elisha's servant, Gehazi, exacted payment from Naaman against Elisha's wishes, Elisha cursed him with the disease from which Naaman had suffered.

5:1 the king of Aram. Likely Ben-Hadad II (8:7; 1Ki 20:1).

5:2 bands from Aram. In keeping with a long history of tensions between Israel and Aram, skirmishes and raids often occurred along their mutual border.

5:5 a letter. It was common for kings in the ancient Near East to exchange diplomatic correspondence. In this case, the king of Aram sent an official letter introducing Naaman to the Israelite king and asking for a favor. The Aramean king mistakenly assumed that Elisha functioned at the behest of the Israelite king. **the king of Israel.** Probably Joram (1:17; 3:1; 9:24). **ten talents of silver, six thousand shekels of gold.** The amounts were substantial (see NIV text notes).

5:7 he tore his robes. A sign of great distress (see note on 1Ki 21:27). **kill and bring back to life.** These prerogatives belong only to God (Dt 32:39; 1Sa 2:6). Joram evidently did not consider asking Elisha to intercede with God on Naaman's behalf.

5:8 Why have you torn your robes? Elisha scolded the king for reacting to the Aramean request with such alarm; in fact, Naaman's coming to Israel could be perceived as a compliment. **he will know that there is a prophet in Israel.** See 3:11, 8:7–8, 1 Kings 17:24 and 18:36. Elisha responded affirmatively to the Aramean gesture.

5:10 Elisha sent a messenger. It was characteristic of both Elijah and Elisha to test the faith of the people to whom they ministered (1Ki 17:13; 2Ki 4:3–4). In this case, Elisha did not even meet with the notable Aramean directly but sent instructions through a messenger.

5:11 wave his hand over the spot. The precise reasons for Naaman's reaction are not explicit in the text. As a prominent man, he may have felt insulted at being assigned a petty task as opposed to one he would have perceived as more befitting his stature (v. 13). He may also have been angry that Elisha had not deigned to cure him immediately and personally. Perhaps not realizing the importance of divine freedom and the critical role of faith, Naaman may even have believed that Elisha was a magician who would cure the disease with at least a little fanfare.

5:12 Abana and Pharpar, the rivers of Damascus. The Abana flowed from the northeast toward Damascus, while the Pharpar flowed east from Mount Hermon to the marshlands east of Damascus. **better than . . . the waters of Israel.** The waters of the Jordan River in Israel were not particularly clear.

5:13 My father. See *WLC* 124–125.

5:15 there is no God in all the world except in Israel. Naaman claimed not merely that the Lord was more powerful than the Aramean gods but something more radical: that there was no God except the Lord. In making this strong confession, Naaman adopted the faith of Israel as his own (1Ki 18:39).

fore him and said, "Now I know[x] that there is no God in all the world except in Israel.
Please accept now a gift[y] from your servant."
16The prophet answered, "As surely as the LORD lives, whom I serve, I will not accept
a thing." And even though Naaman urged him, he refused.[z]
17"If you will not," said Naaman, "please let me, your servant, be given as much
earth[a] as a pair of mules can carry, for your servant will never again make burnt offerings and sacrifices to any other god but the LORD. 18But may the LORD forgive your servant for this one thing: When my master enters the temple of Rimmon to bow down and
he is leaning[b] on my arm and I bow there also—when I bow down in the temple of Rimmon, may the LORD forgive your servant for this."
19"Go in peace,"[c] Elisha said.
After Naaman had traveled some distance, 20Gehazi, the servant of Elisha the man of
God, said to himself, "My master was too easy on Naaman, this Aramean, by not accepting from him what he brought. As surely as the LORD[d] lives, I will run after him and get
something from him."
21So Gehazi hurried after Naaman. When Naaman saw him running toward him, he
got down from the chariot to meet him. "Is everything all right?" he asked.
22"Everything is all right," Gehazi answered. "My master sent me to say, 'Two young
men from the company of the prophets have just come to me from the hill country of
Ephraim. Please give them a talent[a] of silver and two sets of clothing.' "[e]
23"By all means, take two talents," said Naaman. He urged Gehazi to accept them,
and then tied up the two talents of silver in two bags, with two sets of clothing. He gave
them to two of his servants, and they carried them ahead of Gehazi. 24When Gehazi came
to the hill, he took the things from the servants and put them away in the house. He sent
the men away and they left. 25Then he went in and stood before his master Elisha.
"Where have you been, Gehazi?" Elisha asked.
"Your servant didn't go anywhere," Gehazi answered.
26But Elisha said to him, "Was not my spirit with you when the man got down from
his chariot to meet you? Is this the time[f] to take money, or to accept clothes, olive groves,
vineyards, flocks, herds, or menservants and maidservants?[g] 27Naaman's leprosy[h] will
cling to you and to your descendants forever." Then Gehazi[i] went from Elisha's presence
and he was leprous, as white as snow.[j]

An Axhead Floats

6 The company[k] of the prophets said to Elisha, "Look, the place where we meet with
you is too small for us. 2Let us go to the Jordan, where each of us can get a pole; and
let us build a place there for us to live."
And he said, "Go."
3Then one of them said, "Won't you please come with your servants?"
"I will," Elisha replied. 4And he went with them.
They went to the Jordan and began to cut down trees. 5As one of them was cutting
down a tree, the iron axhead fell into the water. "Oh, my lord," he cried out, "it was borrowed!"
6The man of God asked, "Where did it fall?" When he showed him the place, Elisha
cut a stick and threw[l] it there, and made the iron float. 7"Lift it out," he said. Then the
man reached out his hand and took it.

5:15 [x]Jos 4:24; 1Sa 17:46; Da 2:47 [y]1Sa 9:7; 25:27
5:16 [z]ver 20, 26; Ge 14:23; Da 5:17
5:17 [a]Ex 20:24
5:18 [b]2Ki 7:2
5:19 [c]1Sa 1:17; Ac 15:33
5:20 [d]Ex 20:7
5:22 [e]ver 5; Ge 45:22
5:26 [f]ver 16 [g]Jer 45:5
5:27 [h]Nu 12:10; 2Ki 15:5 [i]Col 3:5 [j]Ex 4:6
6:1 [k]1Sa 10:5; 2Ki 4:38
6:6 [l]Ex 15:25; 2Ki 2:21

[a] *22* That is, about 75 pounds (about 34 kilograms)

5:16 As surely as the LORD lives. The words constituted an oath (see note on 1Ki 1:17).
5:17 as much earth. Most non-Israelites believed that a deity could only be worshiped in its own territory.
5:18 Rimmon. *Rimmon* (Hebrew for "pomegranates") is a mocking wordplay on *Ramanu,* another name for Hadad, the storm god and chief deity of Aram (Zec 12:11).
5:22 company of the prophets. See note on 1 Kings 20:35. **hill country of Ephraim.** The central mountain range of Israel (Jos 17:15).
5:25 See *WLC* 145.
5:26 money. The word referred not to coinage (which was a later invention) but to gold or silver in varying weights. See *WLC* 151.
5:27 to you and to your descendants. Gehazi's sin had not only individual but also household ramifications (Ex 20:5).

■ **6:1–23** *Elisha, the Prophets and the Syrian King.* Elisha caused an iron axhead to float (vv. 1–7) and delivered blinded Arameans into the hands of the king of Israel (vv. 8–23). His counsel of mercy for the captured Arameans resulted in the end of Aramean raids on Israelite territory (vv. 22–23).
6:1 The company of the prophets. See note on 1 Kings 20:35.
6:2 build a place there for us to live. It is unclear whether the prophets were advocating a common living arrangement or larger meeting quarters because the Hebrew word translated "to live" can also be interpreted as "to sit."
6:5 iron axhead. An expensive and relatively rare tool. Because of this, and because the prophet had borrowed the axhead, its loss was a relatively serious matter.
6:6 See *WCF* 5.3.

Elisha Traps Blinded Arameans

[8]Now the king of Aram was at war with Israel. After conferring with his officers, he
said, "I will set up my camp in such and such a place."
[9]The man of God sent word to the king[m] of Israel: "Beware of passing that place, because the Arameans are going down there." [10]So the king of Israel checked on the place
indicated by the man of God. Time and again Elisha warned[n] the king, so that he was
on his guard in such places.

[11]This enraged the king of Aram. He summoned his officers and demanded of them,
"Will you not tell me which of us is on the side of the king of Israel?"

[12]"None of us, my lord the king[o]," said one of his officers, "but Elisha, the prophet
who is in Israel, tells the king of Israel the very words you speak in your bedroom."

[13]"Go, find out where he is," the king ordered, "so I can send men and capture him."
The report came back: "He is in Dothan."[p] [14]Then he sent[q] horses and chariots and a
strong force there. They went by night and surrounded the city.

[15]When the servant of the man of God got up and went out early the next morning,
an army with horses and chariots had surrounded the city. "Oh, my lord, what shall we
do?" the servant asked.

[16]"Don't be afraid,"[r] the prophet answered. "Those who are with us are more[s] than
those who are with them."

[17]And Elisha prayed, "O LORD, open his eyes so he may see." Then the LORD opened
the servant's eyes, and he looked and saw the hills full of horses and chariots[t] of fire all
around Elisha.

[18]As the enemy came down toward him, Elisha prayed to the LORD, "Strike these people with blindness."[u] So he struck them with blindness, as Elisha had asked.

[19]Elisha told them, "This is not the road and this is not the city. Follow me, and I will
lead you to the man you are looking for." And he led them to Samaria.

[20]After they entered the city, Elisha said, "LORD, open the eyes of these men so they
can see." Then the LORD opened their eyes and they looked, and there they were, inside
Samaria.

[21]When the king of Israel saw them, he asked Elisha, "Shall I kill them, my father?[v]
Shall I kill them?"

[22]"Do not kill them," he answered. "Would you kill men you have captured[w] with
your own sword or bow? Set food and water before them so that they may eat and drink
and then go back to their master." [23]So he prepared a great feast for them, and after they
had finished eating and drinking, he sent them away, and they returned to their master.
So the bands[x] from Aram stopped raiding Israel's territory.

Famine in Besieged Samaria

[24]Some time later, Ben-Hadad[y] king of Aram mobilized his entire army and marched
up and laid siege[z] to Samaria. [25]There was a great famine[a] in the city; the siege lasted
so long that a donkey's head sold for eighty shekels[a] of silver, and a quarter of a cab[b] of
seed pods[c][b] for five shekels.[d]

[26]As the king of Israel was passing by on the wall, a woman cried to him, "Help me,
my lord the king!"

[27]The king replied, "If the LORD does not help you, where can I get help for you? From
the threshing floor? From the winepress?" [28]Then he asked her, "What's the matter?"
She answered, "This woman said to me, 'Give up your son so we may eat him today,

6:9 [m]ver 12
6:10 [n]Jer 11:18
6:12 [o]ver 9
6:13 [p]Ge 37:17
6:14 [q]2Ki 1:9
6:16 [r]Ge 15:1 [s]2Ch 32:7; Ps 55:18; Ro 8:31; 1Jn 4:4
6:17 [t]2Ki 2:11,12; Ps 68:17; Zec 6:1-7
6:18 [u]Ge 19:11; Ac 13:11
6:21 [v]2Ki 5:13
6:22 [w]Dt 20:11; 2Ch 28:8-15; Ro 12:20
6:23 [x]2Ki 5:2
6:24 [y]1Ki 15:18; 20:1; 2Ki 8:7 [z]Dt 28:52
6:25 [a]Lev 26:26; Ru 1:1 [b]Isa 36:12

[a] *25* That is, about 2 pounds (about 1 kilogram) [b] *25* That is, probably about 1/2 pint (about 0.3 liter) [c] *25* Or *of doves' dung* [d] *25* That is, about 2 ounces (about 55 grams)

6:8 king of Aram. Most likely Ben-Hadad II (see note on 5:1; 8:7; 1Ki 20:1). **at war with Israel.** Despite a treaty between Israel and Aram (1Ki 20:34), the two nations continued hostilities, especially along their shared border (5:2; 1Ki 22:29–37).

6:9 the king of Israel. Probably Joram (1:17; 3:1; 9:24).

6:16 Those who are with us. Elisha referred to God's heavenly host (cf. Jos 5:13–15; 2Ch 32:7–8; Da 10:5–6,20; 12:1). The Israelites believed that the full might of God was on their side (Ex 15:1–12; Dt 20:1–4; 2Sa 22:7–16,31–51). See Matthew 26:53.

6:17 open his eyes. Elisha prayed that the servant would see something that did not appear to the naked eye: God's heavenly armies ready to do battle with the Arameans.

6:21 my father. This title of respect was consistently used by kings when addressing Elisha (see note on 2:12).

6:22 Would you kill men you have captured . . . ? Elisha's point was twofold. First, because God had captured the Arameans, the captives did not belong to the king. Second, it would have been unusual for a king to return home with enemy captives only to kill them (as opposed to using them for forced labor; cf. Dt 20:10). That God brought these captives to Samaria rather than killing them on the field indicated that he wanted them to live.

■ **6:24—7:20** *Elisha and the Aramean Siege of Samaria.* Elisha predicted God's intervention to end the Arameans' siege of Samaria.

6:24 Ben-Hadad. Most likely Ben-Hadad II (1Ki 20:1; 2Ki 8:7).

6:25 a donkey's head sold for eighty shekels of silver. See NIV text note. This unclean (Lev 11:2–7; Dt 14:4–8), undesirable part of an animal was selling for an enormous price.

6:28 Give up your son so we may eat him. The curses of the Sinaitic covenant envisioned exactly this grisly sort of cannibalism (Lev 26:29; Dt 28:52–57; cf. La 2:20; 4:10; Eze 5:10).

and tomorrow we'll eat my son.' [29]So we cooked my son and ate[c] him. The next day I said to her, 'Give up your son so we may eat him,' but she had hidden him."

[30]When the king heard the woman's words, he tore[d] his robes. As he went along the wall, the people looked, and there, underneath, he had sackcloth[e] on his body. [31]He said, "May God deal with me, be it ever so severely, if the head of Elisha son of Shaphat remains on his shoulders today!"

[32]Now Elisha was sitting in his house, and the elders[f] were sitting with him. The king sent a messenger ahead, but before he arrived, Elisha said to the elders, "Don't you see how this murderer[g] is sending someone to cut off my head?[h] Look, when the messenger comes, shut the door and hold it shut against him. Is not the sound of his master's footsteps behind him?"

[33]While he was still talking to them, the messenger came down to him. And ⌊the king⌋ said, "This disaster is from the LORD. Why should I wait[i] for the LORD any longer?"

7 Elisha said, "Hear the word of the LORD. This is what the LORD says: About this time tomorrow, a seah[a] of flour will sell for a shekel[b] and two seahs[c] of barley for a shekel[j] at the gate of Samaria."

[2]The officer on whose arm the king was leaning[k] said to the man of God, "Look, even if the LORD should open the floodgates[l] of the heavens, could this happen?"

"You will see it with your own eyes," answered Elisha, "but you will not eat[m] any of it!"

The Siege Lifted

[3]Now there were four men with leprosy[d][n] at the entrance of the city gate. They said to each other, "Why stay here until we die? [4]If we say, 'We'll go into the city'—the famine is there, and we will die. And if we stay here, we will die. So let's go over to the camp of the Arameans and surrender. If they spare us, we live; if they kill us, then we die."

[5]At dusk they got up and went to the camp of the Arameans. When they reached the edge of the camp, not a man was there, [6]for the Lord had caused the Arameans to hear the sound[o] of chariots and horses and a great army, so that they said to one another, "Look, the king of Israel has hired[p] the Hittite[q] and Egyptian kings to attack us!" [7]So they got up and fled[r] in the dusk and abandoned their tents and their horses and donkeys. They left the camp as it was and ran for their lives.

[8]The men who had leprosy[s] reached the edge of the camp and entered one of the tents. They ate and drank, and carried away silver, gold and clothes, and went off and hid them. They returned and entered another tent and took some things from it and hid them also.

[9]Then they said to each other, "We're not doing right. This is a day of good news and we are keeping it to ourselves. If we wait until daylight, punishment will overtake us. Let's go at once and report this to the royal palace."

[10]So they went and called out to the city gatekeepers and told them, "We went into the Aramean camp and not a man was there—not a sound of anyone—only tethered horses and donkeys, and the tents left just as they were." [11]The gatekeepers shouted the news, and it was reported within the palace.

[12]The king got up in the night and said to his officers, "I will tell you what the Arameans have done to us. They know we are starving; so they have left the camp to hide[t] in the countryside, thinking, 'They will surely come out, and then we will take them alive and get into the city.' "

[13]One of his officers answered, "Have some men take five of the horses that are left in the city. Their plight will be like that of all the Israelites left here—yes, they will only be like all these Israelites who are doomed. So let us send them to find out what happened."

6:29 [c]Lev 26:29; Dt 28:53-55
6:30 [d]2Ki 18:37; Isa 22:15 [e]Ge 37:34; 1Ki 21:27
6:32 [f]Eze 8:1; 14:1; 20:1 [g]1Ki 18:4 [h]ver 31
6:33 [i]Lev 24:11; Job 2:9; 14:14; Isa 40:31
7:1 [j]ver 16
7:2 [k]2Ki 5:18 [l]ver 19; Ge 7:11; Ps 78:23; Mal 3:10 [m]ver 17
7:3 [n]Lev 13:45-46; Nu 5:1-4
7:6 [o]Ex 14:24; 2Sa 5:24; Eze 1:24 [p]2Sa 10:6; Jer 46:21 [q]Nu 13:29
7:7 [r]Jdg 7:21; Ps 48:4-6; Pr 28:1; Isa 30:17
7:8 [s]Isa 33:23; 35:6
7:12 [t]Jos 8:4; 2Ki 6:25-29

[a] *1* That is, probably about 7 quarts (about 7.3 liters); also in verses 16 and 18 [b] *1* That is, about 2/5 ounce (about 11 grams); also in verses 16 and 18 [c] *1* That is, probably about 13 quarts (about 15 liters); also in verses 16 and 18 [d] *3* The Hebrew word is used for various diseases affecting the skin—not necessarily leprosy; also in verse 8.

6:30 tore his robes. A sign of distress (see note on 1Ki 21:27). **underneath, he had sackcloth on his body.** The king outwardly was trying to display bravado, but he actually was in a state of mourning (cf. Ge 37:34; 1Ki 21:27; Isa 22:12; Jnh 3:5–6).

6:32 the elders were sitting with him. The leaders of the city were conferring with Elisha, not with the king (see note on 1Ki 8:1).

7:1 a seah of flour will sell for a shekel. Elisha prophesied a sudden reversal of the city's disastrous conditions.

7:3 men with leprosy at the . . . city gate. The Torah prohibited people with skin diseases from living within the community (Lev 13:4–5,46; Nu 5:1–4; 12:10–15).

7:6 Hittite and Egyptian kings. The Hittites lived in Asia Minor. *Egypt* may not refer to the empire south of Judah but to a minor state with a similar name adjacent to the area in which the Hittites lived (see NIV text note on 1Ki 10:28).

7:16 [u]Isa 33:4,23 [v]ver 1
7:17 [w]ver 2; 2Ki 6:32

[14]So they selected two chariots with their horses, and the king sent them after the Aramean army. He commanded the drivers, "Go and find out what has happened." [15]They followed them as far as the Jordan, and they found the whole road strewn with the clothing and equipment the Arameans had thrown away in their headlong flight. So the messengers returned and reported to the king. [16]Then the people went out and plundered[u] the camp of the Arameans. So a seah of flour sold for a shekel, and two seahs of barley sold for a shekel,[v] as the LORD had said.

[17]Now the king had put the officer on whose arm he leaned in charge of the gate, and the people trampled him in the gateway, and he died,[w] just as the man of God had foretold when the king came down to his house. [18]It happened as the man of God had said to the king: "About this time tomorrow, a seah of flour will sell for a shekel and two seahs of barley for a shekel at the gate of Samaria."

7:19 [x]ver 2

[19]The officer had said to the man of God, "Look, even if the LORD should open the floodgates[x] of the heavens, could this happen?" The man of God had replied, "You will see it with your own eyes, but you will not eat any of it!" [20]And that is exactly what happened to him, for the people trampled him in the gateway, and he died.

The Shunammite's Land Restored

8:1 [y]2Ki 4:8-37 [z]Lev 26:26; Dt 28:22; Ru 1:1 [a]Ge 12:10; Ps 105:16; Hag 1:11

8 Now Elisha had said to the woman[y] whose son he had restored to life, "Go away with your family and stay for a while wherever you can, because the LORD has decreed a famine[z] in the land that will last seven years."[a] [2]The woman proceeded to do as the man of God said. She and her family went away and stayed in the land of the Philistines seven years.

8:5 [b]2Ki 4:35

[3]At the end of the seven years she came back from the land of the Philistines and went to the king to beg for her house and land. [4]The king was talking to Gehazi, the servant of the man of God, and had said, "Tell me about all the great things Elisha has done." [5]Just as Gehazi was telling the king how Elisha had restored[b] the dead to life, the woman whose son Elisha had brought back to life came to beg the king for her house and land.

Gehazi said, "This is the woman, my lord the king, and this is her son whom Elisha restored to life." [6]The king asked the woman about it, and she told him.

Then he assigned an official to her case and said to him, "Give back everything that belonged to her, including all the income from her land from the day she left the country until now."

Hazael Murders Ben-Hadad

8:7 [c]2Sa 8:5; 1Ki 11:24 [d]2Ki 6:24
8:8 [e]1Ki 19:15 [f]Ge 32:20; 1Sa 9:7; 2Ki 1:2 [g]Jdg 18:5

[7]Elisha went to Damascus,[c] and Ben-Hadad[d] king of Aram was ill. When the king was told, "The man of God has come all the way up here," [8]he said to Hazael,[e] "Take a gift[f] with you and go to meet the man of God. Consult[g] the LORD through him; ask him, 'Will I recover from this illness?' "

8:10 [h]Isa 38:1
8:11 [i]Jdg 3:25 [j]Lk 19:41

[9]Hazael went to meet Elisha, taking with him as a gift forty camel-loads of all the finest wares of Damascus. He went in and stood before him, and said, "Your son Ben-Hadad king of Aram has sent me to ask, 'Will I recover from this illness?' "

[10]Elisha answered, "Go and say to him, 'You will certainly recover';[h] but[a] the LORD has revealed to me that he will in fact die." [11]He stared at him with a fixed gaze until Hazael felt ashamed.[i] Then the man of God began to weep.[j]

[a] *10* The Hebrew may also be read *Go and say, 'You will certainly not recover,' for.*

7:16 a seah of flour sold for a shekel. The prophecy of Elisha (v. 1) was fulfilled.

7:17 trampled him in the gateway. Elisha's second prophecy (v. 2) was fulfilled.

■ **8:1–6** *Elisha and the Shunammite Woman.* The king of Israel restored the Shunammite woman's property because of her association with Elisha (see 4:8–37).

8:1 the woman whose son he had restored to life. See 4:8–37. **a famine.** The writer does not state how much time had elapsed between the famine of chapter 4 and this incident.

8:2 in the land of the Philistines. That is, on the southwestern plain, where rainfall was quite adequate for agriculture.

8:3 to beg for her house and land. As overseer of the nation's judicial system, the king heard special cases (see note on 1Ki 3:16). It was customary in Israel to restore property at the end of a seven-year period (Ex 21:2; Dt 15:1–8). Since her husband had apparently died (cf. 4:14), the woman had to establish her claim.

8:4 The king. Unnamed, but if this king is Joram (1:17; 3:13), it is surprising that he knew nothing of Elisha's activities. Either this incident took place soon after the events of 4:8–37 or the king referred to here is Jehu (9:1ff.). **Gehazi.** Elisha's personal attendant (see notes on 4:12; 5:27).

■ **8:7–15** *Elisha and Hazael of Syria.* Elisha predicted Hazael's rise to power in Aram and wept because of the harm Hazael would do to the Israelites in the future.

8:7 Elisha went to Damascus. The Lord's prophets normally dealt with the kings of Israel and Judah, and did not frequently visit the capitals of foreign countries. Elisha was on an unusual mission: to implement one of the three commands God had given Elijah on Mount Horeb (1Ki 19:15–16).**Ben-Hadad.** Probably Ben-Hadad II (see note on 1Ki 20:1).

8:8 Hazael. God had commanded Elijah to anoint Hazael as king of Aram to bring judgment against the house of Ahab (1Ki 19:15).

8:9 the finest wares of Damascus. Damascus had acquired an international reputation as a major trade center in the ancient Near East. **Your son Ben-Hadad.** This is a diplomatic formula indicating the high regard Ben-Hadad had for Elisha (1Sa 25:8; 2Ki 6:21; 13:14).

12 "Why is my lord weeping?" asked Hazael.
"Because I know the harm[k] you will do to the Israelites," he answered. "You will set
fire to their fortified places, kill their young men with the sword, dash[l] their little children[m] to the ground, and rip open[n] their pregnant women."
13 Hazael said, "How could your servant, a mere dog,[o] accomplish such a feat?"
"The LORD has shown me that you will become king[p] of Aram," answered Elisha.
14 Then Hazael left Elisha and returned to his master. When Ben-Hadad asked, "What
did Elisha say to you?" Hazael replied, "He told me that you would certainly recover."
15 But the next day he took a thick cloth, soaked it in water and spread it over the king's
face, so that he died.[q] Then Hazael succeeded him as king.

Jehoram King of Judah

16 In the fifth year of Joram[r] son of Ahab king of Israel, when Jehoshaphat was king
of Judah, Jehoram[s] son of Jehoshaphat began his reign as king of Judah. 17 He was thirty-two years old when he became king, and he reigned in Jerusalem eight years. 18 He
walked in the ways of the kings of Israel, as the house of Ahab had done, for he married
a daughter[t] of Ahab. He did evil in the eyes of the LORD. 19 Nevertheless, for the sake of
his servant David, the LORD was not willing to destroy[u] Judah. He had promised to
maintain a lamp[v] for David and his descendants forever.
20 In the time of Jehoram, Edom rebelled against Judah and set up its own king.[w] 21 So
Jehoram[a] went to Zair with all his chariots. The Edomites surrounded him and his chariot commanders, but he rose up and broke through by night; his army, however, fled
back home. 22 To this day Edom has been in rebellion[x] against Judah. Libnah[y] revolted
at the same time.
23 As for the other events of Jehoram's reign, and all he did, are they not written in the
book of the annals of the kings of Judah? 24 Jehoram rested with his fathers and was buried with them in the City of David. And Ahaziah his son succeeded him as king.

Ahaziah King of Judah

25 In the twelfth[z] year of Joram son of Ahab king of Israel, Ahaziah son of Jehoram king
of Judah began to reign. 26 Ahaziah was twenty-two years old when he became king, and
he reigned in Jerusalem one year. His mother's name was Athaliah,[a] a granddaughter
of Omri[b] king of Israel. 27 He walked in the ways of the house of Ahab[c] and did evil[d] in
the eyes of the LORD, as the house of Ahab had done, for he was related by marriage to
Ahab's family.

8:12 [k]1Ki 19:17; 2Ki 10:32; 12:17; 13:3,7 [l]Ps 137:9; Isa 13:16; Hos 13:16; Na 3:10; Lk 19:44 [m]Ge 34:29 [n]2Ki 15:16; Am 1:13
8:13 [o]1Sa 17:43; 2Sa 3:8 [p]1Ki 19:15
8:15 [q]2Ki 1:17
8:16 [r]2Ki 1:17; 3:1 [s]2Ch 21:1-4
8:18 [t]ver 26; 2Ki 11:1
8:19 [u]Ge 6:13 [v]2Sa 21:17; 7:13; 1Ki 11:36; Rev 21:23
8:20 [w]1Ki 22:47
8:22 [x]Ge 27:40 [y]Nu 33:20; Jos 21:13; 2Ki 19:8
8:25 [z]2Ki 9:29
8:26 [a]ver 18 [b]1Ki 16:23
8:27 [c]1Ki 16:30 [d]1Ki 15:26

[a] 21 Hebrew *Joram,* a variant of *Jehoram;* also in verses 23 and 24

8:12 set fire to their fortified places, kill their young men. These were typical occurrences in ancient wars (Ps 137:9; Isa 13:16; Hos 10:14; 13:16; Am 1:13; Na 3:10; Lk 19:44). Elisha did not approve of such actions; he mourned that his people would be subjected to the Lord's judgment executed by wicked men. The citizens of Damascus would not escape unscathed—the Lord would punish them for their abuse of his people (cf. Amos 1:3-5).
8:13 your servant, a mere dog. This expression of self-deprecation before a superior also occurred in a number of extrabiblical documents (the *Lachish Letters*) from early sixth-century B.C. Judah (see also a similar formula in 1Sa 17:43; 24:14; 2Sa 3:8). An ancient Assyrian inscription depicted Hazael as "the son of a nobody"; i.e., a commoner.
8:15 he took a thick cloth. Hazael took Elisha's prophecy as a license to commit murder, an indication of Hazael's ruthless nature. See *WCF* 5.6.
■ **8:16–29** *In Judah (848–841 B.C.).* Jehoram began to reign in Judah (848 B.C.) while Joram was still reigning in Israel (his reign ended in 841 B.C.). The writer therefore shifted focus again to the southern kingdom (see "Introduction to 1 Kings: Purpose and Distinctives: *Kings as History*"). This section, 8:16–29, includes the reigns of Jehoram (vv. 16–24) and Ahaziah (vv. 25–29).
■ **8:16–24** *Jehoram of Judah (848–841 B.C.).* Despite Jehoram's evil conduct, God spared Judah because of his promise to establish David's throne forever (2Sa 7:12–16). This record divides into the opening and general characterization (vv. 16–19), Jehoram's failure in war (vv. 20–22) and a closure (vv. 23–24).
8:16 fifth year of Joram . . . when Jehoshaphat was king of Judah. Jehoram was probably coregent with his father, Jehoshaphat, for five years before becoming the sole monarch of Judah (1:17; 1Ki 22:42).
8:17 reigned in Jerusalem eight years. That is, from 848–841 B.C. (see note on v. 16).
8:18 walked in the ways of the kings of Israel. Usually kings of Judah were evaluated with reference to their predecessors. Jehoram was purposely compared with the "house of Ahab" in Israel because he imitated its policies. Ahab introduced and sanctioned Baal worship in the northern kingdom, and Jehoram did the same in Judah. **a daughter of Ahab.** Although Athaliah was probably not a daughter of Jezebel (v. 26; 2Ch 21:6), the ruling dynasties of Israel and Judah were now linked both by ideology and by marriage. Athaliah, Jehoram's wife, promoted Baal worship much as Ahab's wife, Jezebel, had promoted it in the northern kingdom (1Ki 16:31; 18:4; 19:2).
8:19 for the sake of his servant David. Because of God's love for David, he was long-suffering in dealing with Judah (see notes on 2Sa 7:12–16; 1Ki 11:4). **maintain a lamp for David.** See note on 1 Kings 11:36.
8:20–22 Jehoram was preserved from utter defeat because of God's love for David and his dynasty, but he was unable to settle rebellion in Edom and Libnah.
8:22 To this day. See note on 1 Kings 8:8. **Libnah.** Located just outside the borders of Philistia, about 12 miles southeast of Ashdod.
8:23 book of the annals of the kings of Judah. See note on 1 Kings 11:41.
8:24 Ahaziah. Not to be confused with his uncle, King Ahaziah of Israel (1:2–18; 1Ki 22:40,51–53).
■ **8:25–29** *Ahaziah of Judah (841 B.C.).* Ahaziah succeeded Jehoram as king of Judah and, despite a brief reign, continued the evil ways of the family of his maternal grandfather, Ahab. Ahaziah's visit to Joram, king of Israel, during the latter's recuperation from wounds received in battle, set the stage for the disaster that befell both kings at the hands of Jehu in 9:1—10:36.
8:25 twelfth year of Joram son of Ahab. That is, 841 B.C.
8:26 Athaliah. Ahaziah's mother. See note on verse 18.
8:27 walked in the ways of the house of Ahab. Like his father, Jehoram, Ahaziah imitated Ahab's religious policies in sanctioning

28 Ahaziah went with Joram son of Ahab to war against Hazael king of Aram at Ramoth
Gilead.[e] The Arameans wounded Joram; 29 so King Joram returned to Jezreel[f] to recover
from the wounds the Arameans had inflicted on him at Ramoth[a] in his battle with Hazael[g] king of Aram.

Then Ahaziah son of Jehoram king of Judah went down to Jezreel to see Joram son of
Ahab, because he had been wounded.

Jehu Anointed King of Israel

9 The prophet Elisha summoned a man from the company[h] of the prophets and said
to him, "Tuck your cloak into your belt,[i] take this flask of oil[j] with you and go to Ramoth Gilead.[k] 2 When you get there, look for Jehu son of Jehoshaphat, the son of Nimshi. Go to him, get him away from his companions and take him into an inner room.
3 Then take the flask and pour the oil[l] on his head and declare, 'This is what the LORD
says: I anoint you king over Israel.' Then open the door and run; don't delay!"

4 So the young man, the prophet, went to Ramoth Gilead. 5 When he arrived, he
found the army officers sitting together. "I have a message for you, commander," he said.

"For which of us?" asked Jehu.

"For you, commander," he replied.

6 Jehu got up and went into the house. Then the prophet poured the oil[m] on Jehu's
head and declared, "This is what the LORD, the God of Israel, says: 'I anoint you king over
the LORD's people Israel. 7 You are to destroy the house of Ahab your master, and I will
avenge[n] the blood of my servants[o] the prophets and the blood of all the LORD's servants
shed by Jezebel.[p] 8 The whole house[q] of Ahab will perish. I will cut off from Ahab every
last male[r] in Israel—slave or free. 9 I will make the house of Ahab like the house of Jeroboam[s] son of Nebat and like the house of Baasha[t] son of Ahijah. 10 As for Jezebel, dogs[u]
will devour her on the plot of ground at Jezreel, and no one will bury her.' " Then he
opened the door and ran.

11 When Jehu went out to his fellow officers, one of them asked him, "Is everything all
right? Why did this madman[v] come to you?"

"You know the man and the sort of things he says," Jehu replied.

12 "That's not true!" they said. "Tell us."

Jehu said, "Here is what he told me: 'This is what the LORD says: I anoint you king over
Israel.' "

13 They hurried and took their cloaks and spread[w] them under him on the bare steps.
Then they blew the trumpet[x] and shouted, "Jehu is king!"

Jehu Kills Joram and Ahaziah

14 So Jehu son of Jehoshaphat, the son of Nimshi, conspired against Joram. (Now Joram and all Israel had been defending Ramoth Gilead[y] against Hazael king of Aram,
15 but King Joram[b] had returned to Jezreel to recover[z] from the wounds the Arameans had
inflicted on him in the battle with Hazael king of Aram.) Jehu said, "If this is the way you
feel, don't let anyone slip out of the city to go and tell the news in Jezreel." 16 Then he got

8:28 [e]Dt 4:43; 1Ki 22:3, 29
8:29 [f]2Ki 9:15 [g]1Ki 19:15, 17
9:1 [h]1Sa 10:5 [i]2Ki 4:29 [j]1Sa 10:1 [k]2Ki 8:28
9:3 [l]1Ki 19:16
9:6 [m]1Ki 19:16; 2Ch 22:7
9:7 [n]Ge 4:24; Rev 6:10 [o]Dt 32:43 [p]1Ki 18:4; 21:15
9:8 [q]2Ki 10:17 [r]Dt 32:36; 1Sa 25:22; 1Ki 21:21; 2Ki 14:26
9:9 [s]1Ki 14:10; 15:29; 16:3, 11 [t]1Ki 16:3
9:10 [u]ver 35-36; 1Ki 21:23
9:11 [v]Jer 29:26; Jn 10:20; Ac 26:24
9:13 [w]Mt 21:8; Lk 19:36 [x]2Sa 15:10; 1Ki 1:34, 39
9:14 [y]Dt 4:43; 2Ki 8:28
9:15 [z]2Ki 8:29

[a] *29* Hebrew *Ramah,* a variant of *Ramoth* [b] *15* Hebrew *Jehoram,* a variant of *Joram;* also in verses 17 and 21–24

the worship of the Canaanite god Baal in Judah (see notes on 1Ki 16:31).

8:28 Ahaziah went with Joram son of Ahab to war. Earlier King Jehoshaphat of Judah had allied himself with Ahab of Israel in a campaign against the Arameans at Ramoth Gilead (1Ki 22). This campaign, like that earlier one, ended in disaster.

8:29 King Joram returned to Jezreel. The kings of Israel maintained a residence at Jezreel (1Ki 18:45). Jezreel had also been the site of Ahab and Jezebel's horrendous crime against Naboth (1Ki 21). **Ramoth.** Short for Ramoth Gilead.

■ **9:1—10:36** *In Israel (841–814 B.C.): Jehu of Israel.* The end of Ahaziah's reign (841 B.C.) in Judah reaches the beginning of Jehu's reign in Israel, so the writer's focus shifts to the northern kingdom. The account of Jehu divides into several parts: Jehu was anointed king of Israel to execute divine judgment against the house of Ahab (9:1–13). He killed King Joram of Israel, King Ahaziah of Judah, Jezebel (9:14–37) and Ahab's whole family (10:1–17). Jehu also campaigned against Baal worship in Israel (10:18–33) before his reign ended (10:34–36).

■ **9:1–13** *Elisha Has Jehu Anointed.* At Elisha's direction, Jehu was anointed king of Israel and commissioned to execute divine judgment against the house of Ahab, in fulfillment of Elijah's prophecy (1Ki 21:21–24).

9:1 company of the prophets. See note on 1 Kings 20:35. **Tuck your cloak into your belt.** See note on 4:29.

9:3 pour the oil on his head. A ritual anointing to designate a (future) king (11:12; 23:30; 1Sa 9:16; 10:1; 2Sa 2:7).

9:8 slave or free. That is, without exception. Compare 1 Kings 14:10.

9:9 like the house of Jeroboam . . . like the house of Baasha. These were the two earlier dynasties of the northern kingdom that God had destroyed because of their unfaithfulness (1Ki 14:7–18; 16:1–4).

9:10 no one will bury her. A sign of disgrace (Jer 8:2; 16:4–6; 22:19; 25:33).

9:11 this madman. Exemplary of scornful viewpoint on the prophets by the military of the northern kingdom (cf. Jer 29:26; Hos 9:7).

9:13 they blew the trumpet. To draw public attention to the anointing of a new king (cf. 2Sa 15:10; 1Ki 1:34).

■ **9:14–37** *Jehu's Bloody Coup.* Jehu killed both Joram, king of Israel, and Ahaziah, king of Judah (vv. 14–29); then, in fulfillment of the words of Elijah, he commanded that Jezebel be killed (vv. 30–37).

into his chariot and rode to Jezreel, because Joram was resting there and Ahaziah[a] king
of Judah had gone down to see him.
17 When the lookout[b] standing on the tower in Jezreel saw Jehu's troops approaching,
he called out, "I see some troops coming."
"Get a horseman," Joram ordered. "Send him to meet them and ask, 'Do you come
in peace?[c]' "
18 The horseman rode off to meet Jehu and said, "This is what the king says: 'Do you
come in peace?' "
"What do you have to do with peace?" Jehu replied. "Fall in behind me."
The lookout reported, "The messenger has reached them, but he isn't coming back."
19 So the king sent out a second horseman. When he came to them he said, "This is
what the king says: 'Do you come in peace?' "
Jehu replied, "What do you have to do with peace? Fall in behind me."
20 The lookout reported, "He has reached them, but he isn't coming back either. The
driving is like[d] that of Jehu son of Nimshi—he drives like a madman."
21 "Hitch up my chariot," Joram ordered. And when it was hitched up, Joram king of
Israel and Ahaziah king of Judah rode out, each in his own chariot, to meet Jehu. They
met him at the plot of ground that had belonged to Naboth[e] the Jezreelite. 22 When Joram saw Jehu he asked, "Have you come in peace, Jehu?"
"How can there be peace," Jehu replied, "as long as all the idolatry and witchcraft of
your mother Jezebel[f] abound?"
23 Joram turned about and fled, calling out to Ahaziah, "Treachery,[g] Ahaziah!"
24 Then Jehu drew his bow[h] and shot Joram between the shoulders. The arrow pierced
his heart and he slumped down in his chariot. 25 Jehu said to Bidkar, his chariot officer,
"Pick him up and throw him on the field that belonged to Naboth the Jezreelite. Remember how you and I were riding together in chariots behind Ahab his father when the LORD
made this prophecy[i] about him: 26 'Yesterday I saw the blood of Naboth[j] and the blood
of his sons, declares the LORD, and I will surely make you pay for it on this plot of
ground, declares the LORD.'[a] Now then, pick him up and throw him on that plot, in accordance with the word of the LORD."[k]
27 When Ahaziah king of Judah saw what had happened, he fled up the road to Beth Hag-
gan.[b] Jehu chased him, shouting, "Kill him too!" They wounded him in his chariot on the
way up to Gur near Ibleam,[l] but he escaped to Megiddo[m] and died there. 28 His servants
took him by chariot[n] to Jerusalem and buried him with his fathers in his tomb in the City
of David. 29 (In the eleventh[o] year of Joram son of Ahab, Ahaziah had become king of Judah.)

Jezebel Killed

30 Then Jehu went to Jezreel. When Jezebel heard about it, she painted[p] her eyes, arranged her hair and looked out of a window. 31 As Jehu entered the gate, she asked,
"Have you come in peace, Zimri,[q] you murderer of your master?"[c]
32 He looked up at the window and called out, "Who is on my side? Who?" Two or
three eunuchs looked down at him. 33 "Throw her down!" Jehu said. So they threw her
down, and some of her blood spattered the wall and the horses as they trampled her underfoot.[r]
34 Jehu went in and ate and drank. "Take care of that cursed woman," he said, "and
bury her, for she was a king's daughter."[s] 35 But when they went out to bury her, they
found nothing except her skull, her feet and her hands. 36 They went back and told Jehu,

9:16 [a]2Ch 22:7
9:17 [b]Isa 21:6 [c]1Sa 16:4
9:20 [d]2Sa 18:27
9:21 [e]ver 26; 1Ki 21:1-7,15-19
9:22 [f]1Ki 16:30-33; 18:19; 2Ch 21:13; Rev 2:20
9:23 [g]2Ki 11:14
9:24 [h]1Ki 22:34
9:25 [i]1Ki 21:19-22,24-29
9:26 [j]1Ki 21:19 [k]1Ki 21:29
9:27 [l]Jdg 1:27 [m]2Ki 23:29
9:28 [n]2Ki 14:20; 23:30
9:29 [o]2Ki 8:25
9:30 [p]Jer 4:30; Eze 23:40
9:31 [q]1Ki 16:9-10
9:33 [r]Ps 7:5
9:34 [s]1Ki 16:31; 21:25

[a] *26* See 1 Kings 21:19. [b] *27* Or *fled by way of the garden house* [c] *31* Or *"Did Zimri have peace, who murdered his master?"*

9:21 Naboth the Jezreelite. Events came to a head at the very location at which Ahab and Jezebel had framed and killed Naboth (1Ki 21:1–26).
9:22 How can there be peace . . . ? Jehu's question addressed the heart of the issue. There could not be true peace (*shalom;* i.e., harmony among people and between people and God) when "idolatry and witchcraft" abounded. Compare 17:17, 21:6, Judges 2:17, 8:33 and 34, Jeremiah 2:1–13, Hosea 2:1–23 and Nahum 3:4.
9:25 when the LORD made this prophecy. See 1 Kings 21:21–24.
9:27 They wounded him. Jehu was not explicitly authorized to put to the sword the descendants of David who were related to the house of Ahab through Ahab's daughter Athaliah (cf. vv. 8–10). Jehu's zeal in carrying out his commission was excessive. Hosea, for instance, criticized him for "the massacre at Jezreel" (Hos 1:4).
9:29 In the eleventh year. This figure may not have included Ahaziah's accession year. Such an explanation brings the figures of 8:25 and this verse into line.
9:30 Jezreel. The scene of action ominously returned to the earlier site of Naboth's murder. **painted her eyes.** See *WLC* 139.
9:31 Zimri. Jezebel sarcastically alluded to Zimri's bloody purge almost half a century earlier (1Ki 16:8–15). Since Zimri had reigned only seven days, she may also have been implying that Jehu's actions would be unpopular and his reign short.
9:32 eunuchs. Commonly employed as guards and attendants of royal harems in the ancient Near East (20:18; Isa 39:7). The word may also refer to court officials (Da 1:3,7–18; see text note on Jer 38:7).
9:34 a king's daughter. Jehu did not dignify Jezebel with the title "queen of Israel" but referred to her as the daughter of Ethbaal, the Sidonian king (1Ki 16:31).

who said, "This is the word of the LORD that he spoke through his servant Elijah the Tishbite: On the plot of ground at Jezreel dogs[t] will devour Jezebel's flesh.[a u] [37]Jezebel's body
will be like refuse[v] on the ground in the plot at Jezreel, so that no one will be able to say,
'This is Jezebel.' "

Ahab's Family Killed

10 Now there were in Samaria[w] seventy sons[x] of the house of Ahab. So Jehu wrote
letters and sent them to Samaria: to the officials of Jezreel,[b y] to the elders and
to the guardians[z] of Ahab's children. He said, [2]"As soon as this letter reaches you, since
your master's sons are with you and you have chariots and horses, a fortified city and
weapons, [3]choose the best and most worthy of your master's sons and set him on his father's throne. Then fight for your master's house."

[4]But they were terrified and said, "If two kings could not resist him, how can we?"

[5]So the palace administrator, the city governor, the elders and the guardians sent this
message to Jehu: "We are your servants[a] and we will do anything you say. We will not
appoint anyone as king; you do whatever you think best."

[6]Then Jehu wrote them a second letter, saying, "If you are on my side and will obey
me, take the heads of your master's sons and come to me in Jezreel by this time tomorrow."

Now the royal princes, seventy of them, were with the leading men of the city, who
were rearing them. [7]When the letter arrived, these men took the princes and slaughtered all seventy[b] of them. They put their heads[c] in baskets and sent them to Jehu in
Jezreel. [8]When the messenger arrived, he told Jehu, "They have brought the heads of
the princes."

Then Jehu ordered, "Put them in two piles at the entrance of the city gate until morning."

[9]The next morning Jehu went out. He stood before all the people and said, "You are
innocent. It was I who conspired against my master and killed him, but who killed all
these? [10]Know then, that not a word the LORD has spoken against the house of Ahab will
fail. The LORD has done what he promised[d] through his servant Elijah."[e] [11]So Jehu[f] killed
everyone in Jezreel who remained of the house of Ahab, as well as all his chief men, his
close friends and his priests, leaving him no survivor.[g]

[12]Jehu then set out and went toward Samaria. At Beth Eked of the Shepherds, [13]he
met some relatives of Ahaziah king of Judah and asked, "Who are you?"

They said, "We are relatives of Ahaziah,[h] and we have come down to greet the families of the king and of the queen mother.[i]"

[14]"Take them alive!" he ordered. So they took them alive and slaughtered them by the
well of Beth Eked—forty-two men. He left no survivor.

[15]After he left there, he came upon Jehonadab[j] son of Recab,[k] who was on his way
to meet him. Jehu greeted him and said, "Are you in accord with me, as I am with you?"

"I am," Jehonadab answered.

"If so," said Jehu, "give me your hand."[l] So he did, and Jehu helped him up into the
chariot. [16]Jehu said, "Come with me and see my zeal[m] for the LORD." Then he had him
ride along in his chariot.

9:36 [t]Ps 68:23; Jer 15:3 [u]1Ki 21:23
9:37 [v]Ps 83:10; Isa 5:25; Jer 8:2; 9:22; 16:4; 25:33; Zep 1:17
10:1 [w]1Ki 13:32 [x]Jdg 8:30 [y]1Ki 21:1 [z]ver 5
10:5 [a]Jos 9:8; 1Ki 20:4, 32
10:7 [b]1Ki 21:21 [c]2Sa 4:8
10:10 [d]2Ki 9:7-10 [e]1Ki 21:29
10:11 [f]Hos 1:4 [g]ver 14; Job 18:19
10:13 [h]2Ki 8:24,29; 2Ch 22:8 [i]1Ki 2:19
10:15 [j]Jer 35:6,14-19 [k]1Ch 2:55; Jer 35:2 [l]Ezr 10:19; Eze 17:18
10:16 [m]Nu 25:13; 1Ki 19:10

[a] *36* See 1 Kings 21:23. [b] *1* Hebrew; some Septuagint manuscripts and Vulgate *of the city*

9:36 dogs will devour Jezebel's flesh. The judgment oracle Jezebel had so contemptuously scorned in her life was fulfilled in her death (1Ki 21:23). Dogs were also present at Ahab's death (1Ki 22:38).

■ 10:1–17 *Jehu Massacres Ahab's Family.* Jehu massacred Ahab's family in fulfillment of the word of the Lord spoken by Elijah (vv. 10–11,17; 1Ki 21:21–22).

10:1 seventy sons. This figure probably included grandsons. **elders.** See note on 1 Kings 8:1. **guardians.** Responsible for the upbringing of youths (cf. Ru 4:16,17; Est 2:7), who were young princes of the royal household in this case. Jehu addressed the various community leaders.

10:5 palace administrator. See note on 1 Kings 4:6. **city governor.** A position similar to that of the "ruler of the city" in 1 Kings 22:26. **elders and the guardians.** See notes on 10:1.

10:6 take the heads of your master's sons. Jehu's demand was ambiguous. The Hebrew word translated "head" can mean literally a person's head or "head" in the sense of "chief." It was therefore unclear whether Jehu was asking for the heads (skulls) of all of Ahab's male descendants or for the leaders among the royal princes.

10:7 slaughtered all seventy. The leaders of Samaria took no chances; they carried out Jehu's command literally. In this action, another component of Elijah's prophecy came to pass (1Ki 21:21–24).

10:8 Put them in two piles. Assyrian kings, such as Shalmaneser III, intimidated the populace by leaving heaps of heads by city gates as a warning of the vengeance that would follow any act of rebellion.

10:11 Jehu killed everyone. Jehu's actions went far beyond the mandate in Elijah's oracle (1Ki 21:21–24) and the oracle delivered personally to Jehu (2Ki 9:7–10).

10:12 Beth Eked of the Shepherds. Probably located a few miles northeast of Jenin.

10:13 families of the king and of the queen mother. That is, of Joram and Jezebel. These relatives did not realize that a coup had taken place.

10:15 Jehonadab son of Recab. Leader of a conservative Israelite group that advocated an austere lifestyle in the context of desert life. Based on a belief that this was the best way to worship the Lord, these people refused to grow crops or to drink wine (1Ch 2:55; Jer 35).

17When Jehu came to Samaria, he killed all who were left there of Ahab's family;[n] he
destroyed them, according to the word of the LORD spoken to Elijah.

Ministers of Baal Killed

18Then Jehu brought all the people together and said to them, "Ahab served[o] Baal a
little; Jehu will serve him much. 19Now summon[p] all the prophets of Baal, all his ministers and all his priests. See that no one is missing, because I am going to hold a great sacrifice for Baal. Anyone who fails to come will no longer live." But Jehu was acting deceptively in order to destroy the ministers of Baal.
20Jehu said, "Call an assembly[q] in honor of Baal." So they proclaimed it. 21Then he
sent word throughout Israel, and all the ministers of Baal came; not one stayed away.
They crowded into the temple of Baal until it was full from one end to the other. 22And
Jehu said to the keeper of the wardrobe, "Bring robes for all the ministers of Baal." So
he brought out robes for them.
23Then Jehu and Jehonadab son of Recab went into the temple of Baal. Jehu said to
the ministers of Baal, "Look around and see that no servants of the LORD are here with
you—only ministers of Baal." 24So they went in to make sacrifices and burnt offerings.
Now Jehu had posted eighty men outside with this warning: "If one of you lets any of the
men I am placing in your hands escape, it will be your life for his life."[r]
25As soon as Jehu had finished making the burnt offering, he ordered the guards and
officers: "Go in and kill[s] them; let no one escape."[t] So they cut them down with the
sword. The guards and officers threw the bodies out and then entered the inner shrine
of the temple of Baal. 26They brought the sacred stone[u] out of the temple of Baal and
burned it. 27They demolished the sacred stone of Baal and tore down the temple[v] of Baal,
and people have used it for a latrine to this day.
28So Jehu[w] destroyed Baal worship in Israel. 29However, he did not turn away from
the sins[x] of Jeroboam son of Nebat, which he had caused Israel to commit—the worship
of the golden calves[y] at Bethel[z] and Dan.
30The LORD said to Jehu, "Because you have done well in accomplishing what is right
in my eyes and have done to the house of Ahab all I had in mind to do, your descendants
will sit on the throne of Israel to the fourth generation."[a] 31Yet Jehu was not careful[b] to
keep the law of the LORD, the God of Israel, with all his heart. He did not turn away from
the sins[c] of Jeroboam, which he had caused Israel to commit.
32In those days the LORD began to reduce[d] the size of Israel. Hazael[e] overpowered the
Israelites throughout their territory 33east of the Jordan in all the land of Gilead (the region of Gad, Reuben and Manasseh), from Aroer[f] by the Arnon Gorge through Gilead to
Bashan.
34As for the other events of Jehu's reign, all he did, and all his achievements, are they
not written in the book of the annals[g] of the kings of Israel?
35Jehu rested with his fathers and was buried in Samaria. And Jehoahaz his son succeeded him as king. 36The time that Jehu reigned over Israel in Samaria was twenty-eight
years.

Athaliah and Joash

11 When Athaliah[h] the mother of Ahaziah saw that her son was dead, she proceeded to destroy the whole royal family. 2But Jehosheba, the daughter of King Je-

10:17 [n]2Ki 9:8
10:18 [o]Jdg 2:11; 1Ki 16:31-32
10:19 [p]1Ki 18:19; 22:6
10:20 [q]Ex 32:5; Joel 1:14
10:24 [r]1Ki 20:39
10:25 [s]Ex 22:20; 2Ki 11:18 [t]1Ki 18:40
10:26 [u]1Ki 14:23
10:27 [v]1Ki 16:32
10:28 [w]1Ki 19:17
10:29 [x]1Ki 12:30 [y]1Ki 12:28-29 [z]1Ki 12:32
10:30 [a]ver 35; 2Ki 15:12
10:31 [b]Pr 4:23 [c]1Ki 12:30
10:32 [d]2Ki 13:25 [e]1Ki 19:17; 2Ki 8:12
10:33 [f]Nu 32:34; Dt 2:36; Jdg 11:26; Isa 17:2
10:34 [g]1Ki 15:31
11:1 [h]2Ki 8:18

■ **10:18–33** *Jehu's Campaign Against Baal Worship.* Jehu campaigned against Baal worship in Israel by killing the priests of Baal and tearing down his temple. Despite God's offer to prolong his dynasty "to the fourth generation" (v. 30; through Zechariah, 2Ki 15:12), Jehu was "not careful to keep the law of the LORD, the God of Israel, with all his heart" (v. 31). The narrator adds the significant and ominous note that during the days of Jehu "the LORD began to reduce the size of Israel" (v. 32).

10:18 Ahab served Baal a little; Jehu will serve him much. Jehu enticed Baal supporters to reveal their allegiance publicly. Having destroyed the house of Ahab (v. 17), Jehu began his purge of Baal worship in Israel.

10:21 the temple of Baal. This was the structure Ahab had built in Samaria (1Ki 16:32).

10:26 sacred stone. See note on 1 Kings 14:23. **burned it.** A particularly effective way of destroying a standing stone was to heat it and then pour water over it.

10:27 demolished the sacred stone. This prevented its reuse. **used it for a latrine.** Not only did this desecrate the site, but it also dissuaded any future Baal worshipers from trying to rebuild the Baal temple.

10:30–31 you have done well . . . Yet. See *WCF* 16.7.

10:31 law of the LORD. On the importance of keeping the law, see notes on 1 Kings 2:3.

10:33 east of the Jordan. Hazael captured the Israelite territories in Transjordan, thus fulfilling Elisha's prophecy (8:12). **Aroer.** A few miles north of "the Arnon Gorge," east of the Dead Sea (Dt 2:36; Jos 12:2; 13:9,16).

■ **10:34–36** *Closure of Reign.* Jehu died and was succeeded by his son Jehoahaz.

10:34 other events of Jehu's reign. The Assyrian ruler Shalmaneser III claimed, in an inscription known as the Black Obelisk, that Jehu had paid him tribute shortly after Jehu had come to power. The author of Kings does not address this matter. **book of the annals of the kings of Israel.** See note on 1 Kings 11:41.

10:35 Jehoahaz. On his reign, see 13:1–9.

10:36 twenty-eight years. That is, from 841–814 B.C.

■ **11:1—12:21** *In Judah (841–796 B.C.).* After covering the reign of Jehu in Israel, which ended in 814 B.C., the writer returned to Judah to catch up on events that had taken place from the beginning of Ath-

horam[a] and sister of Ahaziah, took Joash[i] son of Ahaziah and stole him away from
among the royal princes, who were about to be murdered. She put him and his nurse in
a bedroom to hide him from Athaliah; so he was not killed.[j] **3**He remained hidden with
his nurse at the temple of the LORD for six years while Athaliah ruled the land.
4In the seventh year Jehoiada sent for the commanders of units of a hundred, the Carites[k] and the guards and had them brought to him at the temple of the LORD. He made
a covenant with them and put them under oath at the temple of the LORD. Then he
showed them the king's son. **5**He commanded them, saying, "This is what you are to do:
You who are in the three companies that are going on duty on the Sabbath[l]—a third of
you guarding the royal palace,[m] **6**a third at the Sur Gate, and a third at the gate behind
the guard, who take turns guarding the temple— **7**and you who are in the other two companies that normally go off Sabbath duty are all to guard the temple for the king. **8**Station yourselves around the king, each man with his weapon in his hand. Anyone who approaches your ranks[b] must be put to death. Stay close to the king wherever he goes."
9The commanders of units of a hundred did just as Jehoiada the priest ordered. Each
one took his men—those who were going on duty on the Sabbath and those who were going off duty—and came to Jehoiada the priest. **10**Then he gave the commanders the spears
and shields[n] that had belonged to King David and that were in the temple of the LORD.
11The guards, each with his weapon in his hand, stationed themselves around the king—
near the altar and the temple, from the south side to the north side of the temple.
12Jehoiada brought out the king's son and put the crown on him; he presented him
with a copy of the covenant[o] and proclaimed him king. They anointed[p] him, and the people clapped their hands[q] and shouted, "Long live the king!"[r]
13When Athaliah heard the noise made by the guards and the people, she went to the
people at the temple of the LORD. **14**She looked and there was the king, standing by the
pillar,[s] as the custom was. The officers and the trumpeters were beside the king, and all
the people of the land were rejoicing and blowing trumpets.[t] Then Athaliah tore[u] her
robes and called out, "Treason! Treason!"[v]
15Jehoiada the priest ordered the commanders of units of a hundred, who were in
charge of the troops: "Bring her out between the ranks[c] and put to the sword anyone
who follows her." For the priest had said, "She must not be put to death in the temple[w]
of the LORD." **16**So they seized her as she reached the place where the horses enter[x] the
palace grounds, and there she was put to death.[y]
17Jehoiada then made a covenant[z] between the LORD and the king and people that

11:2 [i]ver 21; 2Ki 12:1 [j]Jdg 9:5
11:4 [k]ver 19
11:5 [l]1Ch 9:25 [m]1Ki 14:27
11:10 [n]2Sa 8:7; 1Ch 18:7
11:12 [o]Ex 25:16; 2Ki 23:3 [p]1Sa 9:16; 1Ki 1:39 [q]Ps 47:1; 98:8; Isa 55:12 [r]1Sa 10:24
11:14 [s]1Ki 7:15; 2Ki 23:3; 2Ch 34:31 [t]1Ki 1:39 [u]Ge 37:29 [v]2Ki 9:23
11:15 [w]1Ki 2:30
11:16 [x]Ne 3:28; Jer 31:40 [y]Ge 4:14
11:17 [z]Ex 24:8; 2Sa 5:3; 2Ch 15:12; 23:3; 29:10; 34:31; Ezr 10:3

[a] 2 Hebrew *Joram,* a variant of *Jehoram* [b] 8 Or *approaches the precincts* [c] 15 Or *out from the precincts*

aliah's reign in 841 B.C. (see "Introduction to 1 Kings: Purpose and Distinctives: *Kings as History*"). These chapters divide into two parts: the coup against Athaliah (11:1–21) and the reign of Joash (12:1–21).

■ **11:1–21** *The Coup Against Athaliah of Judah (841–835 B.C.).* Jehoiada the priest led a coup against the usurper Athaliah, mother of Ahaziah, and installed young Joash, son of Ahaziah, as rightful king of Judah.

11:1 Athaliah. A daughter of Ahab, dedicated to seeing Baal worship flourish in Judah (8:18; 11:18). Her attempted purge of the royal family brought the Davidic dynasty to the brink of extinction.

11:2 Jehosheba. Likely not a daughter of Athaliah, and therefore a half sister of Ahaziah. In 2 Chronicles 22:11, she was identified as the wife of Jehoiada the priest (cf. vv. 4,9). **Joash.** A son of Ahaziah and Athaliah's own grandson. **in a bedroom.** Baby Joash, less than a year old (11:1–3,21) and not yet weaned, was providentially saved by Jehosheba from Athaliah's massacre.

11:3 at the temple of the LORD. While growing up at the temple, Joash was most likely instructed in God's law. **while Athaliah ruled the land.** The Biblical writer acknowledged that Athaliah ruled Judah, but because he regarded her reign as illegitimate, he did not dignify it with the usual formulaic introduction and conclusion (cf. vv. 1,20 with 11:21—12:3,19–21). Her years as Judah's head of state were counted as part of Joash's reign.

11:4 Jehoiada. The high priest at this time (see note on 1Ki 1:7). **commanders of units of a hundred.** Since these units each contained one hundred troops, Jehoiada was summoning many of the major military leaders. **the Carites.** The royal guard (cf. "Kerethites" at 20:23). The name is of uncertain origin, though some scholars depict the soldiers as mercenaries from Caria in southwest Asia Minor.

11:6 Sur Gate. Its location is unknown; 2 Chronicles 23:5 identifies it as the "Foundation Gate." **the gate behind the guard.** Probably in the southern wall separating the temple from the palace complex.

11:10 spears and shields that had belonged to King David. Perhaps part of the booty David had captured from King Hadadezer of Zobah (2Sa 8:3–11), which had been dedicated to the Lord, and subsequently placed in the temple (2Sa 8:7,11). Or possibly they were David's personal spears and shields.

11:12 copy of the covenant. A reference either to the Sinaitic covenant as a whole (Ex 25:16; 2Ki 23:3) or to a more limited document that specified the duties and limitations of kingship (v. 17; Dt 17:14–20).

11:14 standing by the pillar. The pillars named Jakin and Boaz stood before the entrance to the Holy Place (1Ki 7:15–22). When people gathered at the temple for major occasions, such as an address by the king, they stood in this large area at the temple, not in the temple itself. **all.** The large number of people may indicate that this event took place during a major festival (cf. Dt 16:16). **people of the land.** The precise meaning of this term is disputed by scholars. Here it apparently designated ordinary people who had remained faithful to the Lord. Its meaning likely changed during the course of Israelite history (cf. Ezr 9:1–2). **tore her robes.** See note on 1 Kings 21:27.

11:15 put to the sword anyone who follows her. This command was in accordance with the stipulations of Deuteronomy 13:12–18.

11:17 covenant between the Lord and the king and people. Jehoiada led the people and Joash in renewing their allegiance to the Mosaic covenant. Other covenant renewals had taken place in Israel's past (Dt 1:34–39; 29:1; Jos 8:30–35; 24:1–28). Chronicles mentions a number of covenant renewals during the course of the monarchy (2Ch 15:12; 23:3; 29:10; 34:31,32). Considering the promotion of Baal worship by Judah's recent rulers, it was appropriate for people to rededicate themselves to the Lord. **covenant between the king and the people.** Such an agreement delineated the responsibilities of both parties in the larger context of the Mosaic covenant (Dt 17:14–20; 2Sa 5:3).

they would be the LORD's people. He also made a covenant between the king and the people.[a] 18All the people of the land went to the temple[b] of Baal and tore it down. They
smashed[c] the altars and idols to pieces and killed Mattan the priest[d] of Baal in front of
the altars.
Then Jehoiada the priest posted guards at the temple of the LORD. 19He took with him
the commanders of hundreds, the Carites,[e] the guards and all the people of the land, and
together they brought the king down from the temple of the LORD and went into the palace, entering by way of the gate of the guards. The king then took his place on the royal throne, 20and all the people of the land rejoiced.[f] And the city was quiet, because Athaliah had been slain with the sword at the palace.
21Joash[a] was seven years old when he began to reign.

Joash Repairs the Temple

12 In the seventh year of Jehu, Joash[b][g] became king, and he reigned in Jerusalem
forty years. His mother's name was Zibiah; she was from Beersheba. 2Joash did
what was right in the eyes of the LORD all the years Jehoiada the priest instructed him.
3The high places,[h] however, were not removed; the people continued to offer sacrifices
and burn incense there.
4Joash said to the priests, "Collect[i] all the money that is brought as sacred offerings[j]
to the temple of the LORD—the money collected in the census,[k] the money received from
personal vows and the money brought voluntarily[l] to the temple. 5Let every priest receive
the money from one of the treasurers, and let it be used to repair whatever damage is
found in the temple."
6But by the twenty-third year of King Joash the priests still had not repaired the temple. 7Therefore King Joash summoned Jehoiada the priest and the other priests and
asked them, "Why aren't you repairing the damage done to the temple? Take no more
money from your treasurers, but hand it over for repairing the temple." 8The priests
agreed that they would not collect any more money from the people and that they
would not repair the temple themselves.
9Jehoiada the priest took a chest and bored a hole in its lid. He placed it beside the
altar, on the right side as one enters the temple of the LORD. The priests who guarded the
entrance[m] put into the chest all the money[n] that was brought to the temple of the LORD.
10Whenever they saw that there was a large amount of money in the chest, the royal secretary[o] and the high priest came, counted the money that had been brought into the
temple of the LORD and put it into bags. 11When the amount had been determined, they
gave the money to the men appointed to supervise the work on the temple. With it they
paid those who worked on the temple of the LORD—the carpenters and builders, 12the
masons and stonecutters.[p] They purchased timber and dressed stone for the repair of
the temple of the LORD, and met all the other expenses of restoring the temple.
13The money brought into the temple was not spent for making silver basins, wick trimmers, sprinkling bowls, trumpets or any other articles of gold[q] or silver for the temple of
the LORD; 14it was paid to the workmen, who used it to repair the temple. 15They did not
require an accounting from those to whom they gave the money to pay the workers, be-

11:17 [a]2Ki 23:3; Jer 34:8
11:18 [b]1Ki 16:32 [c]Dt 12:3 [d]1Ki 18:40; 2Ki 10:25; 23:20
11:19 [e]ver 4
11:20 [f]Pr 11:10; 28:12; 29:2
12:1 [g]2Ki 11:2
12:3 [h]1Ki 3:3; 2Ki 14:4; 15:35; 18:4
12:4 [i]2Ki 22:4 [j]Ex 35:5 [k]Ex 30:12 [l]Ex 35:29; 1Ch 29:3-9
12:9 [m]Jer 35:4 [n]2Ch 24:8; Mk 12:41; Lk 21:1
12:10 [o]2Sa 8:17
12:12 [p]2Ki 22:5-6
12:13 [q]1Ki 7:48-51; 2Ch 24:14

a *21* Hebrew *Jehoash,* a variant of *Joash* b *1* Hebrew *Jehoash,* a variant of *Joash;* also in verses 2, 4, 6, 7 and 18

11:18 people of the land. See note on verse 14. **temple of Baal.** Jehoiada led the people in a thorough reformation, which paralleled the earlier reformation led by Jehu in the north (10:18–29).
11:19 commanders of hundreds, the Carites. See notes on verse 4.
11:20 people of the land. See note on verse 14.
11:21 Joash was seven years old. Jehoiada was a major positive influence on Joash during the first part of the young king's reign (12:2; cf. 2Ch 24:22).
■**12:1–21** *Joash of Judah (835–796 B.C.).* This chapter summarizes the long reign of Joash, king of Judah, who did "what is right in the eyes of the LORD all the years Jehoida the priest instructed him" (v. 2). The passage divides into the opening of his reign (vv. 1–3), his restoration of the temple (vv. 4–16), his failure (vv. 17–18) and the end of his reign (vv. 19–21).
12:1 In the seventh year of Jehu. That is, in 835 B.C. **forty years.** That is, from 835–796 B.C.
12:2 did what was right. Joash was one of several kings of Judah who received positive evaluations (see "Introduction to 1 Kings: Purpose and Distinctives: *Kings as Theology*").
12:3 The high places. Joash's reign had its deficiencies. The people continued to worship at "the high places" (see note on 1Ki 3:2).
12:4–16 In line with the writer's emphasis on the temple, he described Joash's notable restoration of the structure.
12:4 sacred offerings to the temple. Joash proposed to use the revenue accrued to refurbish the temple (cf. Ne 10:32), which had suffered neglect during the reign of Athaliah (v. 5; 2Ch 24:7). **the census.** Israelite men at the age of twenty were obliged to enlist for a year of military service and to donate half a shekel for use in the sanctuary (Ex 30:11–16). **money brought voluntarily to the temple.** See Exodus 35:5 and 22, Numbers 31:50, Ezra 2:68–69 and 8:25–27.
12:9 The priests who guarded the entrance. The three priests who had the responsibility for blocking illegal temple entry (22:4; 23:4; 25:18; Jer 35:4; 52:24) were to deposit all offerings into the chest Jehoiada placed beside the altar at the entrance.
12:10 royal secretary. See 2 Samuel 8:17. **high priest.** That is, Jehoiada.
12:13 was not spent for making silver basins. See 1 Kings 7:50. Priority was given to repairing the physical structure of the temple. During Athaliah's regime, temple furnishings had been used for the worship of Baal (2Ch 24:7).

cause they acted with complete honesty.[r] 16 The money from the guilt offerings[s] and sin
offerings[t] was not brought into the temple of the LORD; it belonged[u] to the priests.
17 About this time Hazael[v] king of Aram went up and attacked Gath and captured it.
Then he turned to attack Jerusalem. 18 But Joash king of Judah took all the sacred objects
dedicated by his fathers—Jehoshaphat, Jehoram and Ahaziah, the kings of Judah—and
the gifts he himself had dedicated and all the gold found in the treasuries of the temple
of the LORD and of the royal palace, and he sent[w] them to Hazael king of Aram, who then
withdrew[x] from Jerusalem.
19 As for the other events of the reign of Joash, and all he did, are they not written in
the book of the annals of the kings of Judah? 20 His officials[y] conspired against him and
assassinated[z] him at Beth Millo,[a] on the road down to Silla. 21 The officials who murdered
him were Jozabad son of Shimeath and Jehozabad son of Shomer. He died and was buried with his fathers in the City of David. And Amaziah his son succeeded him as king.

Jehoahaz King of Israel

13 In the twenty-third year of Joash son of Ahaziah king of Judah, Jehoahaz son of
Jehu became king of Israel in Samaria, and he reigned seventeen years. 2 He did
evil[b] in the eyes of the LORD by following the sins of Jeroboam son of Nebat, which he had
caused Israel to commit, and he did not turn away from them. 3 So the LORD's anger[c]
burned against Israel, and for a long time he kept them under the power[d] of Hazael king
of Aram and Ben-Hadad[e] his son.
4 Then Jehoahaz sought[f] the LORD's favor, and the LORD listened to him, for he saw[g]
how severely the king of Aram was oppressing[h] Israel. 5 The LORD provided a deliverer[i]
for Israel, and they escaped from the power of Aram. So the Israelites lived in their own
homes as they had before. 6 But they did not turn away from the sins[j] of the house of Jeroboam, which he had caused Israel to commit; they continued in them. Also, the Asherah pole[a][k] remained standing in Samaria.
7 Nothing had been left[l] of the army of Jehoahaz except fifty horsemen, ten chariots
and ten thousand foot soldiers, for the king of Aram had destroyed the rest and made
them like the dust[m] at threshing time.
8 As for the other events of the reign of Jehoahaz, all he did and his achievements, are
they not written in the book of the annals of the kings of Israel? 9 Jehoahaz rested with
his fathers and was buried in Samaria. And Jehoash[b] his son succeeded him as king.

Jehoash King of Israel

10 In the thirty-seventh year of Joash king of Judah, Jehoash son of Jehoahaz became

12:15 [r]2Ki 22:7; 1Co 4:2
12:16 [s]Lev 5:14-19; Nu 18:9 [t]Lev 4:1-35 [u]Lev 7:7
12:17 [v]2Ki 8:12
12:18 [w]1Ki 15:18; 2Ch 21:16-17 [x]1Ki 15:21
12:20 [y]2Ki 14:5 [z]2Ch 24:25 [a]Jdg 9:6
13:2 [b]1Ki 12:26-33
13:3 [c]Dt 31:17; Jdg 2:14 [d]1Ki 8:12; 12:17; 19:17 [e]ver 24
13:4 [f]Dt 4:29; Ps 78:34 [g]Ex 3:7; Dt 26:7 [h]2Ki 14:26
13:5 [i]ver 25; 2Ki 14:25, 27
13:6 [j]1Ki 12:30 [k]1Ki 16:33
13:7 [l]2Ki 10:32-33 [m]2Sa 22:43

[a] 6 That is, a symbol of the goddess Asherah; here and elsewhere in 2 Kings [b] 9 Hebrew *Joash*, a variant of *Jehoash*; also in verses 12–14 and 25

12:16 guilt offerings. See, for example, the addition of a "fifth" at Leviticus 5:16, 6:5 and Numbers 5:7. **sin offerings.** Joash's restoration did not deprive priests of their income.
12:17 Gath. One of the five major Philistine cities, previously under the domain of Judah (1Ch 18:1; 2Ch 11:8,10).
12:18 all the sacred objects. Joash plundered his own palace and the temple as an inducement for Hazael to withdraw.
12:19 As for the other events. See 2 Chronicles 22:10—24:27. **book of the annals of the kings of Judah.** See note on 1 Kings 11:41.
12:20 officials. Joash's officials were sons of foreign women in the government's employ (14:5; 2Ch 24:26). The location of Joash's assassination is uncertain. **Beth Millo.** Means "house of the Millo" (the terrace built up by Solomon; 1Ki 11:27). This may have been a building constructed on the "Millo" in Jerusalem or on a site in Jerusalem northwest of the Ophel or City of David (cf. Jdg 9:6,20). **Silla.** The location of Silla is unknown.
12:21 Amaziah. On the reign of Amaziah, see 14:1–22.
■ **13:1–25** *In Israel (814–782 B.C.).* The reign of Joash extended to 796 B.C., so the writer returned to events that had taken place before this time in Israel (see "Introduction to 1 Kings: Purpose and Distinctives: *Kings as History*"). The account in chapter 13 includes the reigns of Jehoahaz (vv. 1–9) and Jehoash of Israel (vv. 10–25).
■ **13:1–9** *Jehoahaz of Israel (814–798 B.C.).* Jehoahaz succeeded his father, Jehu, as king of Israel. Jehoahaz returned to the idolatry introduced into Israel by Jeroboam I (1Ki 12:25–33). This record divides into three parts: the opening (vv. 1–3), a summation of his struggle with Aram (vv. 4–7) and the closure of his reign (vv. 8–9). Despite God's gracious deliverance from Aramean domination, the Israelites persisted in idolatry.
13:1 In the twenty-third year of Joash. That is, in 814 B.C. **reigned seventeen years.** That is, from 814–798 B.C. Jehoahaz probably began his reign as coregent with Jehu for three years (see v. 10).
13:2 the sins of Jeroboam. See notes on 1 Kings 12:31.
13:3 Ben-Hadad his son. That is, Ben-Hadad III. First and Second Kings mention two earlier Aramean monarchs by this name: Ben-Hadad I (1Ki 15:18–21) and Ben-Hadad II (1Ki 20:1; 2Ki 6:24; 8:7). Hazael reigned between Ben-Hadad II and Ben-Hadad III.
13:4–7 Jehoahaz suffered oppression from the Arameans, sought the Lord's help and was delivered. Yet the terrible results of Aram's oppression were still evident.
13:5 a deliverer for Israel. As in the time of the judges (Jdg 2:18–19), God provided temporary help from the Aramean onslaught. **deliverer.** This person is unnamed.
13:6 sins of the house of Jeroboam. See notes on 1 Kings 12:31. **Asherah pole.** The pole had been set up by Ahab (1Ki 16:33) and apparently had been left unscathed by Jehu's reforms (10:18–28). See NIV text note.
13:7 fifty horsemen, ten chariots and ten thousand foot soldiers. The king retained a sizable infantry but only limited cavalry and chariots. This crippled his ability to react quickly to a military crisis.
13:8 book of the annals of the kings of Israel. See note on 1 Kings 11:41.
■ **13:10–25** *Jehoash of Israel (798–782 B.C.).* These verses summarize the reign of Jehoash, king of Israel. They open with a summary of his reign (vv. 10–13) and then give attention to his conversation with Elisha and his recovery of Israelite towns (vv. 14–25).
13:10 the thirty-seventh year of Joash. That is, 798 B.C. **sixteen years.** That is, from 798–782 B.C.

king of Israel in Samaria, and he reigned sixteen years. 11 He did evil in the eyes of the LORD and did not turn away from any of the sins of Jeroboam son of Nebat, which he had caused Israel to commit; he continued in them.

12 As for the other events of the reign of Jehoash, all he did and his achievements, including his war against Amaziah[n] king of Judah, are they not written in the book of the annals[o] of the kings of Israel? 13 Jehoash rested with his fathers, and Jeroboam[p] succeeded him on the throne. Jehoash was buried in Samaria with the kings of Israel.

14 Now Elisha was suffering from the illness from which he died. Jehoash king of Israel went down to see him and wept over him. "My father! My father!" he cried. "The chariots[q] and horsemen of Israel!"

15 Elisha said, "Get a bow and some arrows,"[r] and he did so. 16 "Take the bow in your hands," he said to the king of Israel. When he had taken it, Elisha put his hands on the king's hands.

17 "Open the east window," he said, and he opened it. "Shoot!"[s] Elisha said, and he shot. "The LORD's arrow of victory, the arrow of victory over Aram!" Elisha declared. "You will completely destroy the Arameans at Aphek."[t]

18 Then he said, "Take the arrows," and the king took them. Elisha told him, "Strike the ground." He struck it three times and stopped. 19 The man of God was angry with him and said, "You should have struck the ground five or six times; then you would have defeated Aram and completely destroyed it. But now you will defeat it only three times."[u]

20 Elisha died and was buried.

Now Moabite raiders[v] used to enter the country every spring. 21 Once while some Israelites were burying a man, suddenly they saw a band of raiders; so they threw the man's body into Elisha's tomb. When the body touched Elisha's bones, the man came to life[w] and stood up on his feet.

22 Hazael king of Aram oppressed[x] Israel throughout the reign of Jehoahaz. 23 But the LORD was gracious to them and had compassion and showed concern for them because of his covenant[y] with Abraham, Isaac and Jacob. To this day he has been unwilling to destroy[z] them or banish them from his presence.[a]

24 Hazael king of Aram died, and Ben-Hadad[b] his son succeeded him as king. 25 Then Jehoash son of Jehoahaz recaptured from Ben-Hadad son of Hazael the towns he had taken in battle from his father Jehoahaz. Three times[c] Jehoash defeated him, and so he recovered[d] the Israelite towns.

Amaziah King of Judah

14 In the second year of Jehoash[a] son of Jehoahaz king of Israel, Amaziah son of Joash king of Judah began to reign. 2 He was twenty-five years old when he became king, and he reigned in Jerusalem twenty-nine years. His mother's name was Jehoaddin; she was from Jerusalem. 3 He did what was right in the eyes of the LORD, but not as his father David had done. In everything he followed the example of his father Joash. 4 The high places,[e] however, were not removed; the people continued to offer sacrifices and burn incense there.

13:12 [n]2Ki 14:15 [o]1Ki 15:31
13:13 [p]2Ki 14:23; Hos 1:1
13:14 [q]2Ki 2:12
13:15 [r]1Sa 20:20
13:17 [s]Jos 8:18 [t]1Ki 20:26
13:19 [u]ver 25
13:20 [v]2Ki 3:7; 24:2
13:21 [w]Mt 27:52
13:22 [x]1Ki 19:17; 2Ki 8:12
13:23 [y]Ge 13:16-17; Ex 2:24 [z]Dt 29:20 [a]Ex 33:15; 2Ki 14:27; 17:18; 24:3,20
13:24 [b]ver 3
13:25 [c]ver 18,19 [d]2Ki 10:32
14:4 [e]2Ki 12:3; 16:4

[a] *1* Hebrew *Joash*, a variant of *Jehoash*; also in verses 13, 23 and 27

13:11 the sins of Jeroboam. See notes on 1 Kings 12:31.
13:12 his war against Amaziah king of Judah. See 14:8–14 and 2 Chronicles 25:17–24. **book of the annals of the kings of Israel.** See note on 1 Kings 11:41.
13:13 Jeroboam. That is, Jeroboam II, who ruled from 793–753 B.C. See 14:23–29.
13:14–19 Jehoash . . . went down to see him. Elisha prophesied victory over Aram.
13:14 My father! Elisha had used this expression at the departure of Elijah; now Jehoash applied it to Elisha (see note on 2:12). See *WLC* 124.
13:17 east window. Toward Transjordan, which Aram controlled (10:32–33). **the arrow of victory over Aram!** Elisha began to explain the significance of the symbolic action in which Jehoash himself played a pivotal role.
13:20 Elisha died. From an illness (v. 14).
13:22–25 Jehoash endured oppression from Aram but defeated the Arameans three times, as Elisha had predicted.
13:23 because of his covenant. God's covenant commitment, unlike the vagaries of human dedication, was steadfast, constant and far-reaching (cf. 1Ki 18:36). **To this day.** The account was written from a preexilic perspective (see note on 1Ki 8:8; cf. Ex. 34:6, Nu. 14:18).
13:24 Ben-Hadad. That is, Ben-Hadad III (see note on v. 3).
13:25 Three times Jehoash defeated him. Fulfilling the last prophecy of Elisha (v. 19), the victories of Jehoash effectively curtailed Aramean expansion. Later, Jeroboam II also defeated the Arameans (14:25).
■ **14:1–22** *In Judah (796–767 B.C.): Amaziah of Judah.* The historian returned to Judah in 796 B.C., after reporting on the history in Israel up to 782 B.C. See "Introduction to 1 Kings: Purpose and Distinctives: *Kings as History.*" Following Joash's assassination by his own officials (12:20–21), Amaziah succeeded his father as king of Judah and followed Joash's godly example. His rash challenge to Jehoash, king of Israel, however, resulted in defeat for Judah in battle, as well as in the destruction of part of the wall of Jerusalem and looting of the temple and the royal treasuries. This chapter divides into the opening of his reign (vv. 1–5), his positive accomplishments (vv. 6–7), the battle with Israel (vv. 8–14) and the closure of this reign (vv. 15–22).
14:1 In the second year of Jehoash. That is, in 796 B.C.
14:2 twenty-nine years. That is, from 796–767 B.C.
14:3 did what was right in the eyes of the LORD. That is, he followed the prescriptions of the covenant (see notes on 1Ki 2:3). **but not as his father David had done.** See note on 1 Kings 11:4.
14:4 The high places . . . were not removed. Amaziah received qualified praise because he tolerated worship at hilltop shrines (see note on 1Ki 3:2).

14:5 [f]2Ki 21:24 [g]2Ki 12:20
14:6 [h]Dt 28:61 [i]Nu 26:11; Job 21:20; Jer 31:30; 44:3; Eze 18:4,20
14:7 [j]2Sa 8:13; 2Ch 25:11 [k]Jdg 1:36
14:9 [l]Jdg 9:8-15
14:10 [m]Dt 8:14; 2Ch 26:16; 32:25
14:11 [n]Jos 15:10
14:12 [o]2Sa 18:17
14:13 [p]1Ki 3:1; 2Ch 33:14; 36:19; Jer 39:2 [q]Ne 8:16; 12:39 [r]2Ch 25:23; Jer 31:38; Zec 14:10
14:15 [s]2Ki 13:12
14:19 [t]2Ki 12:20 [u]Jos 10:3; 2Ki 18:14,17
14:20 [v]2Ki 9:28
14:21 [w]2Ki 15:1; 2Ch 26:23
14:22 [x]1Ki 9:26; 2Ki 16:6
14:23 [y]2Ki 13:13

5After the kingdom was firmly in his grasp, he executed[f] the officials[g] who had murdered his father the king. **6**Yet he did not put the sons of the assassins to death, in accordance with what is written in the Book of the Law[h] of Moses where the LORD commanded: "Fathers shall not be put to death for their children, nor children put to death
for their fathers; each is to die for his own sins."[a] [i]
7He was the one who defeated ten thousand Edomites in the Valley of Salt[j] and captured Sela[k] in battle, calling it Joktheel, the name it has to this day.
8Then Amaziah sent messengers to Jehoash son of Jehoahaz, the son of Jehu, king of
Israel, with the challenge: "Come, meet me face to face."
9But Jehoash king of Israel replied to Amaziah king of Judah: "A thistle[l] in Lebanon
sent a message to a cedar in Lebanon, 'Give your daughter to my son in marriage.' Then
a wild beast in Lebanon came along and trampled the thistle underfoot. **10**You have indeed defeated Edom and now you are arrogant.[m] Glory in your victory, but stay at home!
Why ask for trouble and cause your own downfall and that of Judah also?"
11Amaziah, however, would not listen, so Jehoash king of Israel attacked. He and Amaziah king of Judah faced each other at Beth Shemesh[n] in Judah. **12**Judah was routed by
Israel, and every man fled to his home.[o] **13**Jehoash king of Israel captured Amaziah king
of Judah, the son of Joash, the son of Ahaziah, at Beth Shemesh. Then Jehoash went to
Jerusalem and broke down the wall[p] of Jerusalem from the Ephraim Gate[q] to the Corner Gate[r]—a section about six hundred feet long.[b] **14**He took all the gold and silver and
all the articles found in the temple of the LORD and in the treasuries of the royal palace.
He also took hostages and returned to Samaria.
15As for the other events of the reign of Jehoash, what he did and his achievements,
including his war[s] against Amaziah king of Judah, are they not written in the book of the
annals of the kings of Israel? **16**Jehoash rested with his fathers and was buried in Samaria with the kings of Israel. And Jeroboam his son succeeded him as king.
17Amaziah son of Joash king of Judah lived for fifteen years after the death of Jehoash
son of Jehoahaz king of Israel. **18**As for the other events of Amaziah's reign, are they not
written in the book of the annals of the kings of Judah?
19They conspired[t] against him in Jerusalem, and he fled to Lachish,[u] but they sent
men after him to Lachish and killed him there. **20**He was brought back by horse[v] and was
buried in Jerusalem with his fathers, in the City of David.
21Then all the people of Judah took Azariah,[c] [w] who was sixteen years old, and made
him king in place of his father Amaziah. **22**He was the one who rebuilt Elath[x] and restored
it to Judah after Amaziah rested with his fathers.

Jeroboam II King of Israel

23In the fifteenth year of Amaziah son of Joash king of Judah, Jeroboam[y] son of Jehoash king of Israel became king in Samaria, and he reigned forty-one years. **24**He did evil

[a] *6* Deut. 24:16 [b] *13* Hebrew *four hundred cubits* (about 180 meters) [c] *21* Also called *Uzziah*

14:5 executed the officials. See 12:20–21.
14:6 nor children put to death for their fathers. These words quoted Deuteronomy 24:16. See also Jeremiah 31:29–30 and Ezekiel 18:1–32.
14:7 defeated ten thousand Edomites. This major victory temporarily reversed earlier losses (cf. 8:20–22; 2Ch 25:5–13). **Valley of Salt.** Probably the salt flats south of the Dead Sea (cf. 2Sa 8:13; Ps 60). **Sela . . . Joktheel.** The Septuagint (Greek translation of the OT) identified *Sela* ("rock" in Hebrew) as *Petra* ("rock" in Greek), located along the north-south rift between the Red Sea and the Dead Sea. Some modern scholars place it five miles southwest of Tapla in Edomite territory (Nu 24:21; Jdg 1:36). **to this day.** Indicated a preexilic perspective (see note on 1Ki 8:8).
14:8–14 meet me face to face. Amaziah battled with Israel.
14:8 Jehoash. See 13:10–25.
14:9 A thistle. At this time Israel was more powerful than Judah (see note on 1Ki 15:17). Jehoash responded to Amaziah's challenge with a fable: A mere thistle (Amaziah) claimed parity with a Lebanon cedar (Jehoash), only to be trampled underfoot (cf. Jdg 9:8–15).
14:11 Beth Shemesh. Situated 15 miles west of Jerusalem (1Ki 4:9).
14:13 Jehoash . . . captured Amaziah. Jehoash probably took Amaziah back to Samaria (v. 14). Amaziah was forced to stay there until Jehoash's death, when he was finally released (v. 17). **Ephraim Gate.** A main gate located in the north wall. **Corner Gate.** Situated at the northwest angle of the wall (2Ch 26:9; Jer 31:38; Zec 14:10).
14:15 book of the annals of the kings of Israel. See note on 1 Kings 11:41.
14:16 Jeroboam. That is, Jeroboam II, who ruled from 793–753 B.C. (vv. 23–29).
14:17 Amaziah . . . lived for fifteen years. Likely Amaziah was in effect coregent with his son Azariah (15:1–7) for many years, because of Amaziah's capture by Jehoash.
14:18 book of the annals of the kings of Judah. See note on 1 Kings 11:41.
14:19 Lachish. A major city of Judah, located 15 miles west of Hebron.
14:21 sixteen years old. Probably Azariah was made king during his father's captivity in Samaria, so that the reigns of father and son overlapped for a number of years.
14:22 Elath. A seaport on the Gulf of Aqaba, first used by Solomon to foster sea trade with other nations (1Ki 9:26–28). Because Amaziah defeated Edom (v. 7), his son Azariah was able to rebuild Elath and use it once again as a Judahite port (cf. 1Ki 22:47–50; 2Ki 8:20–22; 16:6).
■ **14:23–29** *In Israel (793–753 B.C.): Jeroboam II of Israel.* These verses summarize briefly the long reign of Jeroboam II over Israel. Although he too did "evil in the eyes of the LORD" (v. 24), God nevertheless graciously used him to deliver Israel from the Arameans and to extend Israel's boundaries.
14:23 In the fifteenth year of Amaziah. That is, in 782 B.C. **Jeroboam.** That is, Jeroboam II. On the reign of Jeroboam I, see 1 Kings 11:26—14:20. **forty-one years.** That is, from 793–753 B.C.

in the eyes of the LORD and did not turn away from any of the sins of Jeroboam son of Nebat, which he had caused Israel to commit.[z] 25He was the one who restored the boundaries of Israel from Lebo[a] Hamath[a] to the Sea of the Arabah,[b][b] in accordance with the
word of the LORD, the God of Israel, spoken through his servant Jonah[c] son of Amittai,
the prophet from Gath Hepher.
26The LORD had seen how bitterly everyone in Israel, whether slave or free,[d] was suffering;[e] there was no one to help them.[f] 27And since the LORD had not said he would blot
out[g] the name of Israel from under heaven, he saved[h] them by the hand of Jeroboam son
of Jehoash.
28As for the other events of Jeroboam's reign, all he did, and his military achievements, including how he recovered for Israel both Damascus[i] and Hamath,[j] which had
belonged to Yaudi,[c] are they not written in the book of the annals[k] of the kings of Israel? 29Jeroboam rested with his fathers, the kings of Israel. And Zechariah his son succeeded him as king.

Azariah King of Judah

15 In the twenty-seventh year of Jeroboam king of Israel, Azariah[l] son of Amaziah
king of Judah began to reign. 2He was sixteen years old when he became king,
and he reigned in Jerusalem fifty-two years. His mother's name was Jecoliah; she was
from Jerusalem. 3He did what was right in the eyes of the LORD, just as his father Amaziah had done. 4The high places, however, were not removed; the people continued to
offer sacrifices and burn incense there.
5The LORD afflicted[m] the king with leprosy[d] until the day he died, and he lived in a separate house.[e][n] Jotham[o] the king's son had charge of the palace[p] and governed the people of the land.
6As for the other events of Azariah's reign, and all he did, are they not written in the
book of the annals of the kings of Judah? 7Azariah rested[q] with his fathers and was buried near them in the City of David. And Jotham[r] his son succeeded him as king.

Zechariah King of Israel

8In the thirty-eighth year of Azariah king of Judah, Zechariah son of Jeroboam became
king of Israel in Samaria, and he reigned six months. 9He did evil[s] in the eyes of the LORD,

14:24 [z]1Ki 15:30
14:25 [a]Nu 13:21; 1Ki 8:65 [b]Dt 3:17 [c]Jnh 1:1; Mt 12:39
14:26 [d]Dt 32:36 [e]2Ki 13:4 [f]Ps 18:41; 22:11; 72:12; 107:12; Isa 63:5; La 1:7
14:27 [g]2Ki 13:23 [h]Jdg 6:14
14:28 [i]2Sa 8:5; 1Ki 11:24 [j]2Ch 8:3 [k]1Ki 15:31
15:1 [l]ver 32; 2Ki 14:21
15:5 [m]Ge 12:17 [n]Lev 13:46 [o]2Ch 27:1 [p]Ge 41:40
15:7 [q]Isa 6:1; 14:28 [r]ver 5
15:9 [s]1Ki 15:26

[a] 25 Or *from the entrance to* [b] 25 That is, the Dead Sea [c] 28 Or *Judah* [d] 5 The Hebrew word was used for various diseases affecting the skin—not necessarily leprosy. [e] 5 Or *in a house where he was relieved of responsibility*

Probably Jeroboam II was coregent with his father, Jehoash, for 11 years at the beginning of his reign (see "Introduction to 1 Kings: Purpose and Distinctives: *Kings as History*").

14:24 the sins of Jeroboam. See notes on 1 Kings 12:31. Jeroboam II followed the ways of Jeroboam I. But politically and economically Jeroboam II was one of the most successful monarchs in the entire history of the northern kingdom (v. 25). During his reign he forced the Arameans to retreat beyond Damascus into central Aram. He also expanded Israelite territory toward the Dead Sea.

14:25 Lebo Hamath. In the northernmost part of Israelite land (Nu 13:21; 1Ki 8:65). **Sea of the Arabah.** That is, the Dead Sea (Jos 3:16; 12:3). Jeroboam expanded Israel's territory not only to the north, but also to the south on the eastern side of the Jordan (the lands of Ammon and Moab). Jeroboam II therefore controlled more land than had any previous northern king (cf. Am 6:13–14). **Jonah son of Amittai.** See "Introduction to Jonah." **Gath Hepher.** About 14 miles west of the southern part of the Sea of Kinnereth (Jos 19:13).

14:26 slave or free. Without exception. See 1 Kings 14:10.

14:27 blot out. In the ancient Near East it was customary to erase a name on an inscription before replacing it with another (Ex 32:32–33; Dt 9:14; 29:20). Similarly, one customarily washed the writing off a papyrus scroll before reusing it.

14:28 Damascus. The capital of Aram (Syria). **Hamath.** That is, Lebo Hamath. See note on verse 25. **Yaudi.** Mentioned in a few Assyrian inscriptions as a location in northern Syria. Or it may have been a variation of "Judah" (see NIV text note) and thus a reference to the control exercised by David and Solomon (who were both from Judah) over Damascus and Hamath (2Sa 8:6; 1Ki 8:65; 2Ch 8:3). **book of the annals of the kings of Israel.** See note on 1 Kings 11:41.

14:29 Zechariah. On the reign of Zechariah, see 15:8–12.

■ **15:1–7** *In Judah (792–740 B.C.): Azariah of Judah.* This section summarizes the long reign of Azariah, king of Judah, who followed the godly example of his father, Amaziah.

15:1 In the twenty-seventh year of Jeroboam. That is, in 767 B.C.

15:2 He was sixteen years old. Azariah, also called Uzziah (15:30,32,34; Isa 6:1), was likely coregent with his father for the first part of his reign (see note on 14:23). **fifty-two years.** That is, from 792–740 B.C. Azariah enjoyed a long reign, although he eventually became afflicted with a skin disease (v. 5).

15:3 did what was right in the eyes of the LORD. Azariah followed the dictates of the covenant (see notes on 1Ki 2:3).

15:4 The high places . . . were not removed. Praise for Azariah was qualified, as it had been for his father, Amaziah (14:4), because Azariah also failed to eliminate worship at hilltop shrines (see note on 1Ki 3:2).

15:5 leprosy. See NIV text note and 2 Chronicles 26:16–21. **lived in a separate house.** Because of his disease. **Jotham.** With his father isolated, Jotham took over the important administrative and judicial duties of the king. **charge of the palace.** This was the highest official post in the Judahite government (18:18; Isa 22:15–20). Hence, Jotham acted as regent in Azariah's later years and succeeded his father as king over Judah after Azariah's death (vv. 32–38).

15:6 book of the annals of the kings of Judah. See note on 1 Kings 11:41.

15:7 Jotham. See verses 32–38.

■ **15:8–31** *In Israel (753–732 B.C.).* The writer returned to events in Israel beginning in 753 B.C. (see "Introduction to 1 Kings: Purpose and Distinctives: *Kings as History*"). He briefly traced the reigns of Zechariah (vv. 8–12), Shallum (vv. 13–16), Menahem (vv. 17–22), Pekahiah (vv. 23–26) and Pekah (vv. 27–31).

■ **15:8–12** *Zechariah of Israel (753 B.C.).* These verses summarize the reign of Zechariah, King of Israel, the fourth and final of Jehu's descendants to rule Israel (v. 12; 10:30). Zechariah continued the evil conduct of his predecessors, and his brief reign ended with his assassination at the hands of Shallum.

15:8 In the thirty-eighth year of Azariah. That is, in 753 B.C.

Assyrian Campaigns Against Israel and Judah

The Assyrian invasions of the eighth century B.C. were the most traumatic political events in the entire history of Israel.

The brutal Assyrian style of warfare relied on massive armies, superbly equipped with the world's first great siege machines manipulated by an efficient corps of engineers.

Psychological terror, however, was Assyria's most effective weapon. It was ruthlessly applied, with corpses impaled on stakes, severed heads stacked in heaps, and captives skinned alive.

The shock of bloody military sieges on both Israel and Judah was profound. The prophets did not fail to scream out against their horror, while at the same time pleading with the people to see God's hand in history, to recognize spiritual causes in the present punishment.

1. CAMPAIGNS OF TIGLATH-PILESER III (738-732 B.C.)

King Tiglath-Pileser of Assyria (745-727 B.C.) proved to be a vigorous campaigner, first exacting tribute from Menahem and then annexing Hamath, Philistia, Galilee, Gilead and Aram-Damascus (738-732 B.C.) during the reign of Pekah.

The ferocious onslaught against the northern tribes left only central Israel and the capital city of Samaria intact.

By this time Israel was a tiny nation wracked by pro- and anti-Assyrian factions, multiple assassinations, hypocrisy, arrogance and fear.

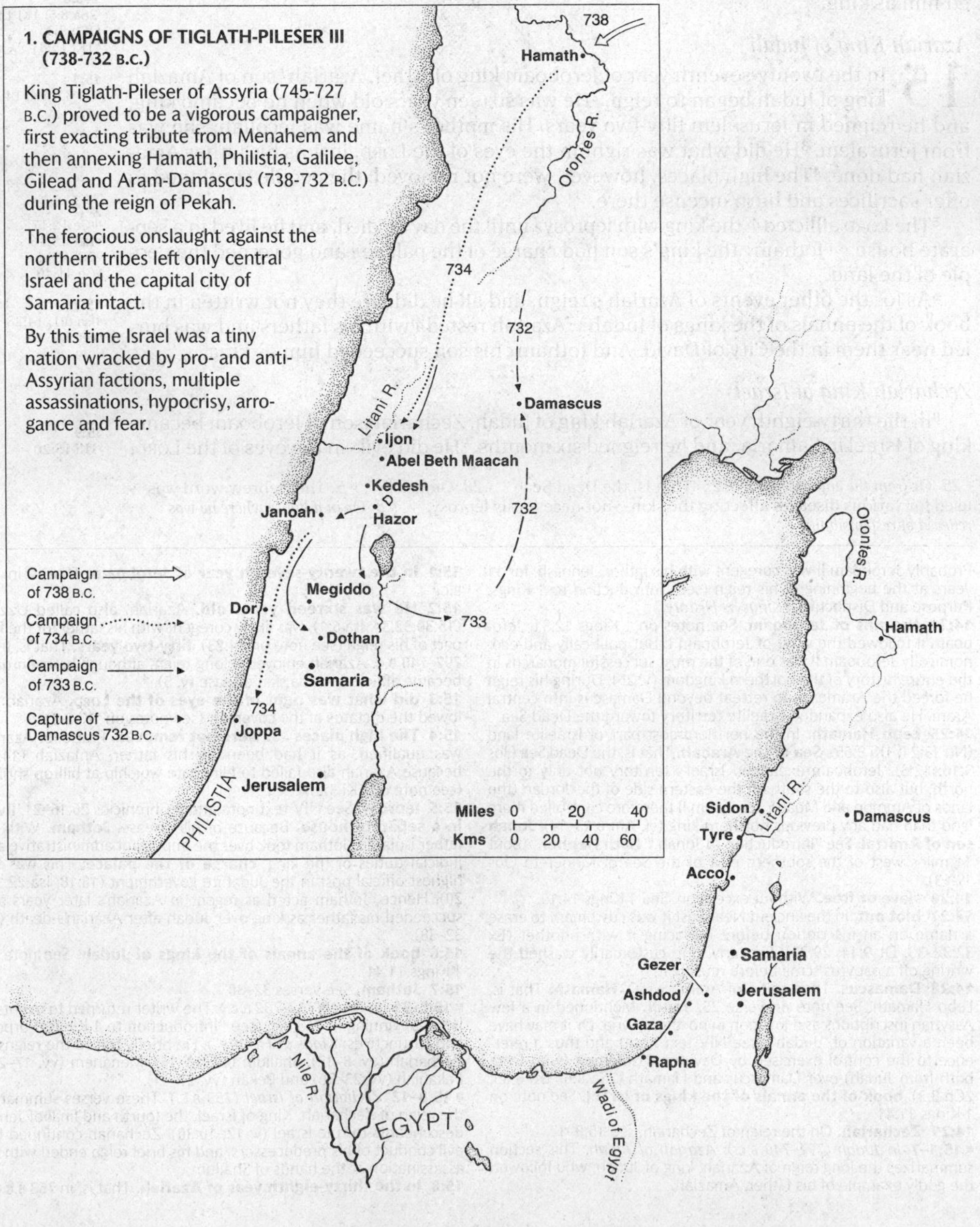

3. SENNACHERIB'S CAMPAIGN AGAINST JUDAH (701 B.C.)

In the 14th year of Hezekiah, the Assyrians finally attacked Judah. The Prism of Sennacherib calls Hezekiah "overbearing and proud," indicating that he was part of Philistia's and Egypt's effort to rebel against Assyria.

A battle in the plain of Eltekeh was won by Assyria; the Egyptian and Cushite charioteers fled. Lachish was besieged and taken. Sennacherib's annals note: "As for Hezekiah the Jew, he did not submit to my yoke. I laid siege to 46 of his strong cities, walled forts and the countless small villages in their vicinity, and conquered them by means of well-stamped earth ramps and battering-rams brought near to the walls combined with the attack by foot-soldiers, using mines, breaches and sapper work. I drove out 200,150 people, young and old, male and female, horses, mules, donkeys, camels, big and small cattle beyond counting, and considered them booty. Himself I made a prisoner in Jerusalem, his royal residence, like a bird in a cage."

Nowhere, however, does the boastful Assyrian king record the disaster mentioned in 2Ki 19:35-36; 2Ch 32:21; Isa 37:36-37.

2. CAMPAIGN OF SHALMANESER V (725-722 B.C.)

The last king of Israel, Hoshea, conspired with Egypt and withheld the annual tribute to the Assyrians.

A protracted three-year siege conducted by Shalmaneser and concluded by Sargon II saw the end of the Israelite kingdom in 722-721 B.C.

At that time, according to Assyrian annals, "I (Sargon) besieged and conquered Samaria, led away as booty 27,290 inhabitants. . . . I installed over (those remaining) an officer of mine and imposed upon them the tribute of the former king."

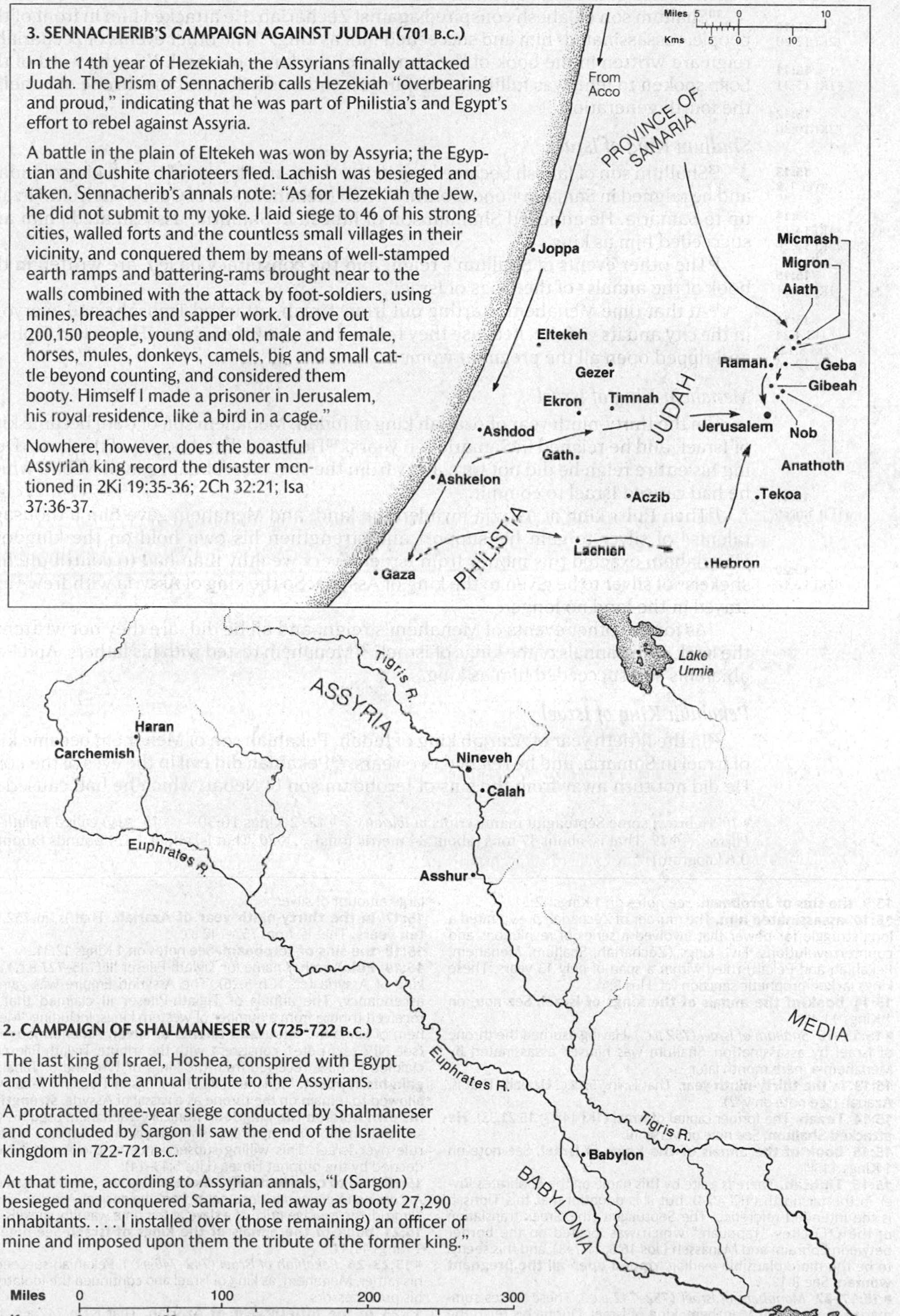

as his fathers had done. He did not turn away from the sins of Jeroboam son of Nebat,
which he had caused Israel to commit.
15:10 10 Shallum son of Jabesh conspired against Zechariah. He attacked him in front of the
[t]2Ki 12:20 people,[a] assassinated[t] him and succeeded him as king. 11 The other events of Zechariah's
15:11 reign are written in the book of the annals[u] of the kings of Israel. 12 So the word of the
[u]1Ki 15:31 LORD spoken to Jehu was fulfilled:[v] "Your descendants will sit on the throne of Israel to
15:12 the fourth generation."[b]
[v]2Ki 10:30

Shallum King of Israel

15:13 13 Shallum son of Jabesh became king in the thirty-ninth year of Uzziah king of Judah,
[w]ver 1,8 and he reigned in Samaria[w] one month. 14 Then Menahem son of Gadi went from Tirzah[x]
15:14 up to Samaria. He attacked Shallum son of Jabesh in Samaria, assassinated[y] him and
[x]1Ki 14:17 [y]2Ki 12:20 succeeded him as king.
15:15 15 The other events of Shallum's reign, and the conspiracy he led, are written in the
[z]1Ki 15:31 book of the annals[z] of the kings of Israel.
15:16 16 At that time Menahem, starting out from Tirzah, attacked Tiphsah[a] and everyone
[a]1Ki 4:24 in the city and its vicinity, because they refused to open[b] their gates. He sacked Tiphsah
[b]2Ki 8:12; Hos 13:16 and ripped open all the pregnant women.

Menahem King of Israel

17 In the thirty-ninth year of Azariah king of Judah, Menahem son of Gadi became king
of Israel, and he reigned in Samaria ten years. 18 He did evil in the eyes of the LORD. During his entire reign he did not turn away from the sins of Jeroboam son of Nebat, which
15:19 he had caused Israel to commit.
[c]1Ch 5:6,26 19 Then Pul[c][c] king of Assyria invaded the land, and Menahem gave him a thousand
talents[d] of silver to gain his support and strengthen his own hold on the kingdom.
15:20 20 Menahem exacted this money from Israel. Every wealthy man had to contribute fifty
[d]2Ki 12:18 shekels[e] of silver to be given to the king of Assyria. So the king of Assyria withdrew[d] and
stayed in the land no longer.
21 As for the other events of Menahem's reign, and all he did, are they not written in
the book of the annals of the kings of Israel? 22 Menahem rested with his fathers. And Pekahiah his son succeeded him as king.

Pekahiah King of Israel

23 In the fiftieth year of Azariah king of Judah, Pekahiah son of Menahem became king
of Israel in Samaria, and he reigned two years. 24 Pekahiah did evil in the eyes of the LORD.
He did not turn away from the sins of Jeroboam son of Nebat, which he had caused Is-

[a] *10* Hebrew; some Septuagint manuscripts *in Ibleam* [b] *12* 2 Kings 10:30 [c] *19* Also called *Tiglath-Pileser* [d] *19* That is, about 37 tons (about 34 metric tons) [e] *20* That is, about 1 1/4 pounds (about 0.6 kilogram)

15:9 the sins of Jeroboam. See notes on 1 Kings 12:31.
15:10 assassinated him. The murder of Zechariah precipitated a long struggle for power that involved a series of revolutions and counterrevolutions. Five kings (Zechariah, Shallum, Menahem, Pekahiah and Pekah) ruled within a span of only 13 years. These kings lacked prophetic sanction (cf. Hos 8:4).
15:11 book of the annals of the kings of Israel. See note on 1 Kings 11:41.
▪ 15:13–16 *Shallum of Israel (752 B.C.).* Having usurped the throne of Israel by assassination, Shallum was himself assassinated by Menahem a mere month later.
15:13 in the thirty-ninth year. That is, in 752 B.C. **Uzziah.** That is, Azariah (see note on v. 2).
15:14 Tirzah. The former capital of Israel (1Ki 14:17; 15:21,33). **He attacked Shallum.** See note on verse 10.
15:15 book of the annals of the kings of Israel. See note on 1 Kings 11:41.
15:16 Tiphsah. There is a site by this name on the Euphrates River in the far north (1Ki 4:24), but it is doubtful that this Tiphsah is the intended reference. The Septuagint (the Greek translation of the OT) cites "Tappuah," which was located on the border between Ephraim and Manasseh (Jos 16:8; 17:7–8), and this seems to be the more plausible reading. **ripped open all the pregnant women.** See 8:12.
▪ 15:17–22 *Menahem of Israel (752–742 B.C.).* These verses summarize the reign of Menahem, king of Israel. During his reign the Assyrians, to whom Israel would eventually fall, invaded the northern kingdom and withdrew only after having been paid a large amount of silver.
15:17 In the thirty-ninth year of Azariah. That is, in 752 B.C. **ten years.** That is, from 752–742 B.C.
15:18 the sins of Jeroboam. See notes on 1 Kings 12:31.
15:19 Pul. Another name for Tiglath-Pileser III (745–727 B.C.), the king of Assyria (cf. 1Ch 5:26). The Assyrian Empire was gaining ascendancy. The annals of Tiglath-Pileser III claimed that he received tribute from a number of western kings, including "Menahem of Samaria." **thousand talents of silver.** An enormous sum (see NIV text note), consistent with the tribute Tiglath-Pileser III claimed to have received from the kings of Tyre and of Tabal. **to gain his support.** Menahem, like the kings of Tyre and Tabal, was allowed to remain on the throne as a vassal of Assyria. **strengthen his own hold on the kingdom.** Ironically, Menahem used his vassal relationship with the dreaded Assyrians to consolidate his own rule over Israel. This willing subservience to the Assyrians was decried by the prophet Hosea (Hos 5:13–14).
15:20 had to contribute fifty shekels. This was a high assessment. According to economic documents from the ancient Assyrian city of Nimrud, the average price of a slave at this time was fifty shekels.
15:21 book of the annals of the kings of Israel. See note on 1 Kings 11:41.
▪ 15:23–26 *Pekahiah of Israel (742–740 B.C.).* Pekahiah succeeded his father, Menahem, as king of Israel and continued the idolatry of his predecessors.
15:23 In the fiftieth year of Azariah. That is, in 742 B.C. **two years.** That is, from 742–740 B.C.
15:24 the sins of Jeroboam. See notes on 1 Kings 12:31.

rael to commit. 25 One of his chief officers, Pekah[e] son of Remaliah, conspired against
him. Taking fifty men of Gilead with him, he assassinated[f] Pekahiah, along with Argob
and Arieh, in the citadel of the royal palace at Samaria. So Pekah killed Pekahiah and
succeeded him as king.
26 The other events of Pekahiah's reign, and all he did, are written in the book of the
annals of the kings of Israel.

Pekah King of Israel

27 In the fifty-second year of Azariah king of Judah, Pekah[g] son of Remaliah[h] became
king of Israel in Samaria, and he reigned twenty years. 28 He did evil in the eyes of the
LORD. He did not turn away from the sins of Jeroboam son of Nebat, which he had caused
Israel to commit.
29 In the time of Pekah king of Israel, Tiglath-Pileser[i] king of Assyria came and took
Ijon,[j] Abel Beth Maacah, Janoah, Kedesh and Hazor. He took Gilead and Galilee, including all the land of Naphtali,[k] and deported[l] the people to Assyria. 30 Then Hoshea[m] son
of Elah conspired against Pekah son of Remaliah. He attacked and assassinated[n] him,
and then succeeded him as king in the twentieth year of Jotham son of Uzziah.
31 As for the other events of Pekah's reign, and all he did, are they not written in the
book of the annals of the kings of Israel?

Jotham King of Judah

32 In the second year of Pekah son of Remaliah king of Israel, Jotham[o] son of Uzziah
king of Judah began to reign. 33 He was twenty-five years old when he became king, and
he reigned in Jerusalem sixteen years. His mother's name was Jerusha daughter of Zadok. 34 He did what was right[p] in the eyes of the LORD, just as his father Uzziah had done.
35 The high places,[q] however, were not removed; the people continued to offer sacrifices and burn incense there. Jotham rebuilt the Upper Gate[r] of the temple of the LORD.
36 As for the other events of Jotham's reign, and what he did, are they not written in
the book of the annals of the kings of Judah? 37 (In those days the LORD began to send Rezin[s] king of Aram and Pekah son of Remaliah against Judah.) 38 Jotham rested with his
fathers and was buried with them in the City of David, the city of his father. And Ahaz
his son succeeded him as king.

Ahaz King of Judah

16 In the seventeenth year of Pekah son of Remaliah, Ahaz[t] son of Jotham king of
Judah began to reign. 2 Ahaz was twenty years old when he became king, and he

15:25 [e]2Ch 28:6; Isa 7:1 [f]2Ki 12:20
15:27 [g]2Ch 28:6; Isa 7:1 [h]Isa 7:4
15:29 [i]2Ki 16:7; 17:6; 1Ch 5:26; 2Ch 28:20; Jer 50:17 [j]1Ki 15:20 [k]2Ki 16:9; 17:24; 2Ch 16:4; Isa 9:1 [l]2Ki 24:14-16; 1Ch 5:22; Isa 14:6, 17; 36:17; 45:13
15:30 [m]2Ki 17:1 [n]2Ki 12:20
15:32 [o]1Ch 5:17
15:34 [p]ver 3; 1Ki 14:8; 2Ch 26:4-5
15:35 [q]2Ki 12:3 [r]2Ch 23:20
15:37 [s]2Ki 16:5; Isa 7:1
16:1 [t]Isa 1:1; 14:28

15:25 Pekah son of Remaliah. A high-ranking officer in the northern kingdom, evidently part of an anti-Assyrian faction in Israel. Pekah pursued improved relations with the Arameans in an effort to counter Assyrian designs in the west (16:1–9; Isa 7:1–25). **fifty men of Gilead.** Pekah, like some of the rebels before him (vv. 10,14), may have been from Gilead. He may have reigned over Gilead before attempting to overthrow Pekahiah. **he assassinated Pekahiah.** See note on verse 10.
15:26 book of the annals of the kings of Israel. See note on 1 Kings 11:41.
■ **15:27–31** *Pekah of Israel (740–732 B.C.).* Having assassinated Pekahiah, Pekah succeeded him as king of Israel. The king of Assyria captured part of Israel's territory during Pekah's reign.
15:27 In the fifty-second year of Azariah. That is, in 740 B.C. **twenty years.** That is, from 752–732 B.C. The chronology of Pekah's rule is difficult to establish. He may have ruled in Transjordan concurrently with Menahem's and Pekahiah's reigns.
15:28 the sins of Jeroboam. See notes on 1 Kings 12:31.
15:29 Tiglath-Pileser. That is, Tiglath-Pileser III. All of the sites and areas listed belonged to the northern part of the Israelite kingdom. During this campaign of 733–732 B.C. Tiglath-Pileser also ravaged Aram and captured its capital, Damascus (16:9; see note on Isa 7:4). **deported the people to Assyria.** God was reducing Israel in terms of both land and population.
15:30 Hoshea. See 17:1–6. **in the twentieth year of Jotham.** That is, in 732 B.C.
15:31 book of the annals of the kings of Israel. See note on 1 Kings 11:41.
■ **15:32—16:20** *In Judah (750–715 B.C.).* After tracing events in Israel to 732 B.C., the writer returned to those in Judah in 750 B.C. (See "Introduction to 1 Kings: Purpose and Distinctives: *Kings as History*"). He described the reigns of Jotham (15:32–38) and Ahaz (16:1–20).
■ **15:32–38** *Jotham of Judah (750–735 B.C.).* These verses summarize the reign of Jotham, king of Judah, who did "what was right in the eyes of the LORD, just as his father Uzziah had done" (v. 34).
15:32 In the second year of Pekah. That is, in 750 B.C.
15:33 He was twenty-five years old. Jotham was likely coregent with his father, Azariah (or Uzziah), for the first ten years of his reign (see note on v. 2). **sixteen years.** That is, from 750–735 B.C.
15:34 did what was right in the eyes of the LORD. Jotham was loyal to the covenant (see notes on 1Ki 2:3).
15:35 The high places . . . were not removed. See note on 1 Kings 3:2. **Upper Gate of the temple of the LORD.** Also called the "Upper Gate of Benjamin at the LORD's temple" (Jer 20:2), this gate was located in the northern part of the temple complex, facing the territory of Benjamin.
15:36 book of the annals of the kings of Judah. See note on 1 Kings 11:41.
15:37 Rezin. The last king of Aram. **against Judah.** Aram and Israel forged an alliance to combat the Assyrians and were prepared to force the king of Judah to join them by invading Judah (see notes on v. 29 and 16:5).
■ **16:1–20** *Ahaz of Judah (735–715 B.C.).* This chapter summarizes the reign of Ahaz, king of Judah: the opening of his reign (vv. 1–4), his alliance with Assyria (vv. 5–9), his defilement of worship (vv. 10–18) and the closure of his reign (vv. 19–20). Unlike his father, Jotham, and his ancestor David, Ahaz perpetuated idolatry in Israel, even adding a pagan altar to the temple in Jerusalem.
■ **16:1–4** *Opening of Reign.* From the beginning, the reign of Ahaz was notoriously wicked.
16:1 In the seventeenth year of Pekah. That is, in 735 B.C. Scholars disagree over the precise chronology of Ahaz's reign in relation to those of the kings of Judah before and after him and to those of his contemporaries in the northern kingdom (cf. 15:33,37; 17:1; 18:1; see "Introduction to 1 Kings: Purpose and Distinctives: *Kings as History*").
16:2 Ahaz was twenty years old. Ahaz was likely coregent with

reigned in Jerusalem sixteen years. Unlike David his father, he did not do what was right[u]
in the eyes of the LORD his God. **3**He walked in the ways of the kings of Israel and even
sacrificed his son[v] in[a] the fire, following the detestable[w] ways of the nations the LORD had
driven out before the Israelites. **4**He offered sacrifices and burned incense at the high
places, on the hilltops and under every spreading tree.[x]
5Then Rezin[y] king of Aram and Pekah son of Remaliah king of Israel marched up to
fight against Jerusalem and besieged Ahaz, but they could not overpower him. **6**At that
time, Rezin[z] king of Aram recovered Elath[a] for Aram by driving out the men of Judah.
Edomites then moved into Elath and have lived there to this day.
7Ahaz sent messengers to say to Tiglath-Pileser[b] king of Assyria, "I am your servant
and vassal. Come up and save[c] me out of the hand of the king of Aram and of the king
of Israel, who are attacking me." **8**And Ahaz took the silver and gold found in the temple of the LORD and in the treasuries of the royal palace and sent it as a gift[d] to the king
of Assyria. **9**The king of Assyria complied by attacking Damascus[e] and capturing it. He
deported its inhabitants to Kir[f] and put Rezin to death.
10Then King Ahaz went to Damascus to meet Tiglath-Pileser king of Assyria. He saw
an altar in Damascus and sent to Uriah[g] the priest a sketch of the altar, with detailed
plans for its construction. **11**So Uriah the priest built an altar in accordance with all the
plans that King Ahaz had sent from Damascus and finished it before King Ahaz returned.
12When the king came back from Damascus and saw the altar, he approached it and presented offerings[b][h] on it. **13**He offered up his burnt offering[i] and grain offering, poured
out his drink offering, and sprinkled the blood of his fellowship offerings[c][j] on the altar.
14The bronze altar[k] that stood before the LORD he brought from the front of the temple—
from between the new altar and the temple of the LORD—and put it on the north side of
the new altar.
15King Ahaz then gave these orders to Uriah the priest: "On the large new altar, offer the morning[l] burnt offering and the evening grain offering, the king's burnt offering
and his grain offering, and the burnt offering of all the people of the land, and their grain
offering and their drink offering. Sprinkle on the altar all the blood of the burnt offerings
and sacrifices. But I will use the bronze altar for seeking guidance."[m] **16**And Uriah the
priest did just as King Ahaz had ordered.
17King Ahaz took away the side panels and removed the basins from the movable
stands. He removed the Sea from the bronze bulls that supported it and set it on a stone
base.[n] **18**He took away the Sabbath canopy[d] that had been built at the temple and removed the royal entryway outside the temple of the LORD, in deference to the king of Assyria.[o]

16:2 [u]1Ki 14:8
16:3 [v]Lev 18:21; 2Ki 21:6 [w]Lev 18:3; Dt 9:4; 12:31
16:4 [x]Dt 12:2; Eze 6:13
16:5 [y]2Ki 15:37; Isa 7:1,4
16:6 [z]Isa 9:12 [a]2Ki 14:22; 2Ch 26:2
16:7 [b]2Ki 15:29 [c]Isa 2:6; Jer 2:18; Eze 16:28; Hos 10:6
16:8 [d]2Ki 12:18
16:9 [e]2Ki 15:29 [f]Isa 22:6; Am 1:5; 9:7
16:10 [g]Isa 8:2
16:12 [h]2Ch 26:16
16:13 [i]Lev 6:8-13 [j]Lev 7:11-21
16:14 [k]2Ch 4:1
16:15 [l]Ex 29:38-41 [m]1Sa 9:9
16:17 [n]1Ki 7:27
16:18 [o]Eze 16:28

[a] 3 Or *even made his son pass through* [b] 12 Or *and went up* [c] 13 Traditionally *peace offerings*
[d] 18 Or *the dais of his throne* (see Septuagint)

his father for the first years of his reign (see note on 15:33). **sixteen years.** That is, from 732–715 B.C.

16:3 He walked in the ways of the kings of Israel. The sin of Jeroboam I (1Ki 12:26–33), perpetuated by all subsequent kings of Israel, was the construction of his own cult, with prescribed worship in Bethel and Dan instead of in Jerusalem. These northern worship sites became conduits for pagan religious practices and beliefs in the northern kingdom. Similarly, Ahaz introduced a foreign altar into Jerusalem, and Ahaz, like Jeroboam I, officiated over the inaugural sacrifices at this new altar (vv. 10–13; 1Ki 12:32–33). **sacrificed his son in the fire.** See NIV text note. The atrocity of child sacrifice was practiced by some of Judah's neighbors, but this heinous ritual was outlawed by the Torah (Lev 18:21; Dt 18:10; cf. 2Ki 3:27). Ahaz was not, however, the only king of Judah to sacrifice his own child (17:17; 21:6; 23:10; Jer 7:31; 32:35). **detestable ways of the nations.** Judah was becoming indistinguishable from Israel and from the nations that God had driven out so that his people could inhabit the land.

■ **16:5–9** *Ahaz's Alliance With Assyria.* Ahaz sought protection from Aram and Israel by forming an alliance with Assyria. The results of this coalition were devastating.

16:5 Rezin . . . and Pekah . . . marched up. To bring Judah forcibly under their control so that they could present a united front against Assyria (15:19,25,37). Into this crisis stepped the prophet Isaiah, who counseled the irresolute Ahaz to trust in the Lord (Isa 7:1–17).

16:6 Rezin . . . recovered Elath. This reversed Azariah's earlier victory (14:22). **Edomites then moved into Elath.** The Edomites exploited Judah's defeat for their own gain. **to this day.** See note on 1 Kings 8:8.

16:7 Tiglath-Pileser. See notes on 15:19 and 29.

16:8 Ahaz took the silver and gold. Ahaz, like a number of other kings before him, attempted to ensure Judah's security by means of a large gift (the Hebrew literally reads "bribe") to a foreign power (12:18; Ex 23:8; Dt 16:19; 1Ki 15:18; Isa 5:23; Eze 22:12). A list from Assyria of rulers who brought tribute to Tiglath-Pileser in 734 B.C. includes the name of "Jehoahaz" (Ahaz).

16:9 deported its inhabitants to Kir. The destruction of Aram fulfilled prophecies of both Isaiah (Isa 7:16) and Amos (Am 1:5). The exact location of Kir is unknown (Isa 22:6; Am 9:7).

■ **16:10–18** *Ahaz's Corruption of Worship.* Ahaz further violated the law of God by corrupting the worship of Judah.

16:13 burnt offering and grain offering. See notes on Leviticus 6:8–23. **fellowship offerings.** See Leviticus 7:11–21. Most of these sacrifices had also been offered at the dedication of Solomon's temple (1Ki 8:64). Ahaz therefore considered the construction of this foreign altar to be of great importance for his realm.

16:14 put it on the north side of the new altar. The bronze altar was moved from its place, thereby decreasing its centrality and restricting its everyday use.

16:15 morning burnt offering. See Exodus 29:38–39. **evening grain offering.** See note on 1 Kings 18:29. **king's burnt offering and his grain offering.** See Ezekiel 46:12. **use the bronze altar for seeking guidance.** Ironically, Ahaz bypassed normal use of the bronze altar and instead employed it for divination (a foreign practice of discovering the future by examining the entrails of sacrificial animals). Divination had been outlawed in Israel (Lev 19:26; Dt 18:10).

16:17 side panels and . . . basins. See 1 Kings 7:27–38. **Sea.** See 1 Kings 7:23–26. **bronze bulls.** Ahaz probably used the bronze to pay tribute to Assyria.

19 As for the other events of the reign of Ahaz, and what he did, are they not written
in the book of the annals of the kings of Judah? 20 Ahaz rested with his fathers and was
buried with them in the City of David. And Hezekiah his son succeeded him as king.

Hoshea Last King of Israel

17 In the twelfth year of Ahaz king of Judah, Hoshea[p] son of Elah became king of
Israel in Samaria, and he reigned nine years. 2 He did evil in the eyes of the LORD,
but not like the kings of Israel who preceded him.
3 Shalmaneser[q] king of Assyria came up to attack Hoshea, who had been Shalmaneser's vassal and had paid him tribute. 4 But the king of Assyria discovered that Hoshea
was a traitor, for he had sent envoys to So[a] king of Egypt, and he no longer paid tribute
to the king of Assyria, as he had done year by year. Therefore Shalmaneser seized him
and put him in prison. 5 The king of Assyria invaded the entire land, marched against Samaria and laid siege[r] to it for three years. 6 In the ninth year of Hoshea, the king of Assyria captured Samaria[s] and deported[t] the Israelites to Assyria. He settled them in Halah, in Gozan[u] on the Habor River and in the towns of the Medes.

Israel Exiled Because of Sin

7 All this took place because the Israelites had sinned[v] against the LORD their God, who
had brought them up out of Egypt[w] from under the power of Pharaoh king of Egypt. They
worshiped other gods 8 and followed the practices of the nations[x] the LORD had driven
out before them, as well as the practices that the kings of Israel had introduced. 9 The Israelites secretly did things against the LORD their God that were not right. From watchtower to fortified city[y] they built themselves high places in all their towns. 10 They set up
sacred stones and Asherah poles[z] on every high hill and under every spreading tree.[a]
11 At every high place they burned incense, as the nations whom the LORD had driven out
before them had done. They did wicked things that provoked the LORD to anger. 12 They
worshiped idols,[b] though the LORD had said, "You shall not do this."[b] 13 The LORD warned
Israel and Judah through all his prophets and seers:[c] "Turn from your evil ways.[d] Observe my commands and decrees, in accordance with the entire Law that I commanded
your fathers to obey and that I delivered to you through my servants the prophets."
14 But they would not listen and were as stiff-necked[e] as their fathers, who did not
trust in the LORD their God. 15 They rejected his decrees and the covenant[f] he had made
with their fathers and the warnings he had given them. They followed worthless idols[g]

17:1 [p]2Ki 15:30
17:3 [q]2Ki 18:9-12; Hos 10:14
17:5 [r]Hos 13:16
17:6 [s]Hos 13:16 [t]Dt 28:36,64; 2Ki 18:10-11 [u]1Ch 5:26
17:7 [v]Jos 23:16; Jdg 6:10 [w]Ex 14:15-31
17:8 [x]Lev 18:3; Dt 18:9; 2Ki 16:3
17:9 [y]2Ki 18:8
17:10 [z]Ex 34:13; Mic 5:14 [a]1Ki 14:23
17:12 [b]Ex 20:4
17:13 [c]1Sa 9:9 [d]Jer 18:11; 25:5; 35:15
17:14 [e]Ex 32:9; Dt 31:27; Ac 7:51
17:15 [f]Dt 29:25 [g]Dt 32:21; Ro 1:21-23

[a] *4* Or *to Sais, to the*; *So* is possibly an abbreviation for *Osorkon*. [b] *12* Exodus 20:4,5

■ **16:19–20** *Closure of Reign.* Ahaz died and was succeeded by his son Hezekiah.
16:19 book of the annals of the kings of Judah. See note on 1 Kings 11:41.
16:20 Hezekiah. On his reign, see 18:1—20:21.
■ **17:1–6** *In Israel (732–722 B.C.): Hoshea of Israel.* After describing events in Judah until 715 B.C. this section returns to the last king of Israel, who began to reign in 732 B.C. Because of Hoshea's refusal to continue paying tribute to Assyria, the king of Assyria invaded Israel, captured Hoshea and Samaria and deported the Israelites. The fall of Israel took place in 722 B.C.
17:1 In the twelfth year of Ahaz. That is, in 732 B.C. **reigned nine years.** That is, from 732–723 B.C.
17:3 Shalmaneser. Shalmaneser V, who succeeded Tiglath-Pileser III as king of Assyria, ruled from 727–722 B.C. Hoshea, unlike his predecessor, Pekah (see note on 15:27–31), was a vassal of Assyria.
17:4 So king of Egypt. See NIV text note. The "Sais" mentioned in that note is a site in Egypt. The name *So* may be a variation of Osorkon IV, king of Tanis and Bubastis in the eastern delta of Egypt. Switching his allegiance, Hoshea hoped that Egypt would protect him from any Assyrian reprisals. The prophet Hosea condemned this sort of diplomacy as "easily deceived and senseless" (Hos 7:11). **no longer paid tribute to the king of Assyria.** Withholding tribute due a suzerain overlord was tantamount to rebellion.
17:5 laid siege to it for three years. The Assyrian campaign followed the arrest of Hoshea in 724/23 B.C. During this long siege, Shalmaneser V died and was succeeded by Sargon II (Isa 20:1), who deported the inhabitants of Samaria (v. 6).
17:6 In the ninth year of Hoshea. That is, in 722/21 B.C. **the king of Assyria.** That is, Sargon II, who ruled Assyria from 722 to 705 B.C. **deported the Israelites.** Sargon II claimed, in his annals, to have deported 27,290 inhabitants of Israel to distant locations. The capture of Samaria marked the end of the northern kingdom (1Ch 5:25–26; see note on vv. 7–23). Archaeological evidence suggests that many fled Israel during the succession of Assyrian attacks and settled in Judah, where they stayed. This influx of refugees significantly increased the population of Jerusalem during the late eighth and early seventh centuries B.C. **Halah.** Located northeast of Nineveh. **Gozan.** An Assyrian provincial capital situated by a northern tributary (the Habor River) of the Euphrates River. **towns of the Medes.** Though not identified by name, they were likely located in the area northeast of the Tigris River and south of the Caspian Sea.
■ **17:7–41** *The Exile of Israel.* The writer of Kings reported and interpreted the deportation of the northern kingdom. He reflected on the event (vv. 7–23) and described the resettlement of the northern territories (vv. 24–41).
■ **17:7–23** *Reflection on the Exile of Israel.* The deportation of Israel requires explanation. The writer had time and again drawn attention to the sins of the kings of Israel, and he now summarized his view of the northern kingdom and explained why its king and people deserved to go into exile.
17:8 practices. Not only did Israel imitate the practices of its pagan neighbors (Ex 34:15; Dt 18:9; Jdg 2:13), but it also followed the cultic innovations of its wayward kings (1Ki 12:26–33; 16:30–34).
17:9 high places. See note on 1 Kings 3:2.
17:10 sacred stones. See note on 1 Kings 14:23. **Asherah poles.** See note on 1 Kings 14:15. **on every high hill and under every spreading tree.** See notes on 1 Kings 14:23, Deuteronomy 12:2, Jeremiah 2:20, 3:6 and 13 and 17:2.
17:12 idols. Any representation of a pagan deity or of the Lord was expressly forbidden (Ex 20:4; Dt 4:12,15–19,23–28).
17:13 the entire Law. That is, the Mosaic Law or stipulations of the covenant (see notes on 1Ki 2:3).
17:14 stiff-necked as their fathers. The Israelites during the period of the monarchy did not have a monopoly on stubbornness (cf. Ex 32:9; Dt 10:16).
17:15 worthless idols. See Deuteronomy 32:21, Jeremiah 2:5, 8:19, 14:22, 51:17 and 18, Hosea 11:2 and Romans 1:21–23.

17:15 ^{h}Dt 12:30-31
17:16 ^{i}1Ki 12:28 ^{j}1Ki 14:15,23 ^{k}2Ki 21:3 ^{l}1Ki 16:31
17:17 ^{m}Dt 18:10-12; 2Ki 16:3 ^{n}Lev 19:26 ^{o}1Ki 21:20

and themselves became worthless. They imitated the nations[h] around them although
the LORD had ordered them, "Do not do as they do," and they did the things the LORD had
forbidden them to do.
16 They forsook all the commands of the LORD their God and made for themselves two
idols cast in the shape of calves,[i] and an Asherah[j] pole. They bowed down to all the starry hosts,[k] and they worshiped Baal.[l]
17 They sacrificed[m] their sons and daughters in[a] the
fire. They practiced divination and sorcery[n] and sold[o] themselves to do evil in the eyes
of the LORD, provoking him to anger.

a 17 Or *They made their sons and daughters pass through*

17:16 two idols cast in the shape of calves. The cultic creations of Jeroboam I at Bethel and Dan (1Ki 12:26–33) were in part modeled on the construction of the golden calf by Aaron (Ex 32:4,8; Dt 9:12,16; Hos 13:2). **Asherah pole.** See note on 1 Kings 14:15. **starry hosts.** Worshiped by some of Israel's neighbors, a practice condemned in the Torah (Dt 4:19; 17:3). Nevertheless, some Israelites participated in such astral cults (21:5; 23:4–5; Am 5:26). **they worshiped Baal.** See 1 Kings 16:31–32.
17:17 sacrificed their sons and daughters. See notes on 3:27 and 16:3. **divination and sorcery.** See note on 16:15.

Exile of the Northern Kingdom

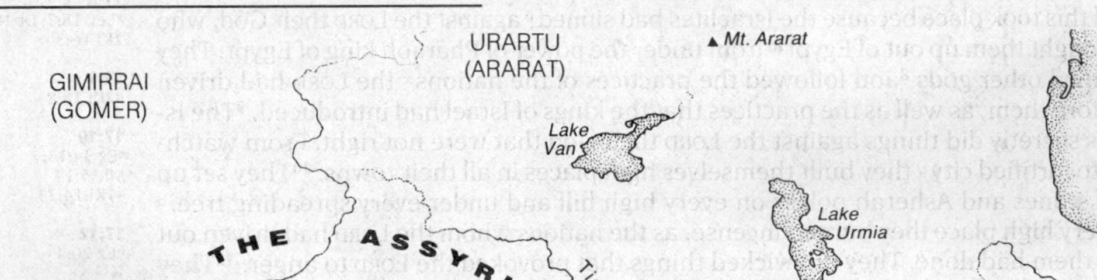

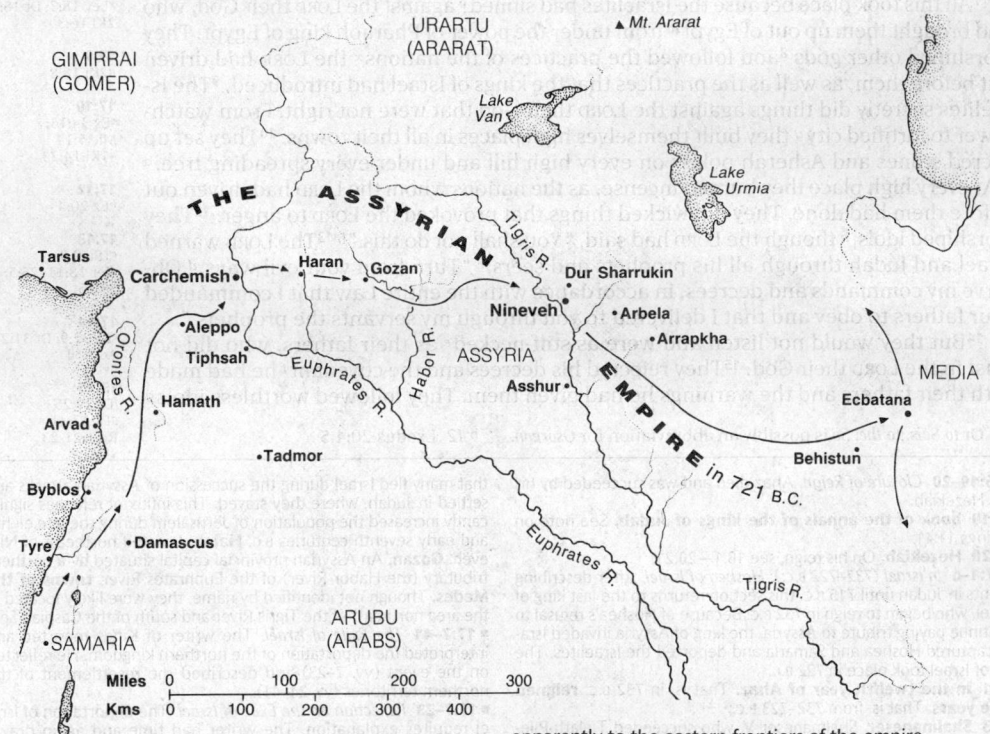

The mass deportation policy of the Assyrians was a companion piece to the brutal and calculated terror initiated by Ashurnasirpal and followed by all his successors. It was intended to forestall revolts but, like all Draconian measures, it merely spread misery and engendered hatred. In the end, it hastened the disintegration of the Assyrian Empire.

There is some evidence that Israel experienced its first deportations under Tiglath-Pileser III (745-727 B.C.), a cruelty repeated by Sargon II (721-705 B.C.) at the time of the fall of Samaria. The latter king's inscriptions boast of carrying away 27,290 inhabitants of the city "as booty." According to 2Ki 17:6, they were sent to Assyria, to Halah, to Gozan on the Habor River, and apparently to the eastern frontiers of the empire (to the towns of the Medes, most probably somewhere in the vicinity of Ecbatana, the modern Hamadan).

The sequel is provided by the inscriptions of Sargon: "The Arabs who live far away in the desert, who know neither overseers nor officials, and who had not yet brought their tribute to any king, I deported . . . and settled them in Samaria."

Much mythology has developed around the theme of the so-called ten lost tribes of Israel. A close examination of Assyrian records reveals that the deportations approximated only a limited percentage of the population, usually consisting of noble families. Agricultural workers, no doubt the majority, were deliberately left to care for the crops (cf. the Babylonian practice, 2Ki 24:14; 25:12).

18 So the LORD was very angry with Israel and removed them from his presence. Only the tribe of Judah was left, 19 and even Judah did not keep the commands of the LORD their God. They followed the practices Israel had introduced.[p] 20 Therefore the LORD rejected all the people of Israel; he afflicted them and gave them into the hands of plunderers,[q] until he thrust them from his presence.

21 When he tore[r] Israel away from the house of David, they made Jeroboam son of Nebat their king.[s] Jeroboam enticed Israel away from following the LORD and caused them to commit a great sin. 22 The Israelites persisted in all the sins of Jeroboam and did not turn away from them 23 until the LORD removed them from his presence, as he had warned through all his servants the prophets. So the people of Israel were taken from their homeland into exile in Assyria, and they are still there.

Samaria Resettled

24 The king of Assyria[t] brought people from Babylon, Cuthah, Avva, Hamath and Sepharvaim[u] and settled them in the towns of Samaria to replace the Israelites. They took over Samaria and lived in its towns. 25 When they first lived there, they did not worship the LORD; so he sent lions[v] among them and they killed some of the people. 26 It was reported to the king of Assyria: "The people you deported and resettled in the towns of Samaria do not know what the god of that country requires. He has sent lions among them, which are killing them off, because the people do not know what he requires."

27 Then the king of Assyria gave this order: "Have one of the priests you took captive from Samaria go back to live there and teach the people what the god of the land requires." 28 So one of the priests who had been exiled from Samaria came to live in Bethel and taught them how to worship the LORD.

29 Nevertheless, each national group made its own gods in the several towns[w] where they settled, and set them up in the shrines[x] the people of Samaria had made at the high places.[y] 30 The men from Babylon made Succoth Benoth, the men from Cuthah made Nergal, and the men from Hamath made Ashima; 31 the Avvites made Nibhaz and Tartak, and the Sepharvites burned their children in the fire as sacrifices to Adrammelech[z] and Anammelech, the gods of Sepharvaim.[a] 32 They worshiped the LORD, but they also appointed all sorts[b] of their own people to officiate for them as priests in the shrines at the high places. 33 They worshiped the LORD, but they also served their own gods in accordance with the customs of the nations from which they had been brought.

34 To this day they persist in their former practices. They neither worship the LORD nor adhere to the decrees and ordinances, the laws and commands that the LORD gave the descendants of Jacob, whom he named Israel.[c] 35 When the LORD made a covenant with the Israelites, he commanded them: "Do not worship[d] any other gods or bow down to them, serve them or sacrifice to them. 36 But the LORD, who brought you up out of Egypt with mighty power and outstretched arm,[e] is the one you must worship. To him you shall

17:19 [p] 1Ki 14:22-23; 2Ki 16:3
17:20 [q] 2Ki 15:29
17:21 [r] 1Ki 11:11 [s] 1Ki 12:20
17:24 [t] Ezr 4:2,10 [u] 2Ki 18:34
17:25 [v] Ge 37:20
17:29 [w] Jer 2:28 [x] 1Ki 12:31 [y] Mic 4:5
17:31 [z] 2Ki 19:37 [a] ver 24
17:32 [b] 1Ki 12:31
17:34 [c] Ge 32:28; 35:10; 1Ki 18:31
17:35 [d] Ex 20:5; Jdg 6:10
17:36 [e] Ex 3:20; 6:6; Ps 136:12

17:18 Only the tribe of Judah. Out of an original twelve-tribe confederation, only one tribe remained intact after the Assyrian deportation of the northern kingdom (but see note on 1Ki 11:13).
17:19 followed the practices Israel had introduced. See 8:18 and 11:1–21.
17:20 the LORD rejected all the people of Israel. God's rejection was signified by their deportation from the land he had given them (v. 6).
17:21 When he tore Israel away from the house of David. The creation of the northern kingdom had been a punishment against Solomon (1Ki 11:11–13), but it also had offered great blessings to the northern tribes (1Ki 11:29–39). **caused them to commit a great sin.** The reference is to Jeroboam's fashioning of two calves, one at Bethel and the other at Dan (see note on 1Ki 12:25–33).
17:22 persisted in all the sins of Jeroboam. See note on 1 Kings 12:30.
■ **17:24–41** *Resettlement by Assyrian Deportees.* The king of Assyria resettled Samaria and its surrounding towns with people deported from other countries.
17:24 king of Assyria. Most likely Sargon II. Along with deporting the upper classes of the Israelite kingdom, the Assyrians brought into Israel peoples from other lands. This policy was intended to ensure that defeated powers did not rise again. **Babylon.** At this time Babylon was under Assyrian control. **Cuthah.** Approximately eight miles northeast of Babylon. **Avva.** Or "Ivvah" (18:34; 19:13), probably located in Aram. **Hamath.** On the Orontes River (see note on 14:25), also under Assyrian dominion. **Sepharvaim.** Likely in Aram. Assyrian records attest that subsequent Assyrian monarchs sent more foreign immigrants to Samaria. **Samaria.** No longer called "Israel." (see note on 1Ki 16:24).
17:25 lions among them. Lions were sometimes used by God as instruments of judgment (1Ki 13:24; 20:36; cf. Am 3:12).
17:26 what the god of that country requires. The Assyrians, like many other peoples in the ancient Near East, believed that the customs and beliefs of local populations needed to be given some respect; otherwise, the deities of those lands would react negatively against the land's inhabitants.
17:29 each national group made its own gods. Bringing back an Israelite priest to serve at Bethel did not imply that the immigrants settling in Samaria had to follow the local religion. On the contrary, they continued to practice their native religious rituals by taking over local sanctuaries and worshiping their own gods in them. **the shrines . . . at the high places.** See 23:19 and 1 Kings 12:31 and 13:32. **the people of Samaria.** Or Samaritans. Although the Hebrew word this expression translates appears only here in the Old Testament, it occurred in extrabiblical documents as early as the eighth century B.C., referring to the residents of this region.
17:32 They worshiped the LORD, but. The religion was syncretistic—it combined elements of the worship of the Lord with the worship of many other deities.
17:34 To this day. See note on 1 Kings 8:8. **the descendants of Jacob, whom he named Israel.** Characteristic of the relationship between God and the people he had elected was the covenant ratified on Mount Sinai (v. 35; Ex 19–24) and renewed on the plains of Moab (Dt 1–34). To be an Israelite was not primarily an ethnic classification but a religious one: to be a follower of the Lord as revealed in the covenant.

17:37 [f]Dt 5:32
17:38 [g]Dt 4:23; 6:12
17:41 [h]ver 32-33; 1Ki 18:21; Mt 6:24
18:1 [i]Isa 1:1; 2Ch 28:27
18:2 [j]Isa 38:5
18:3 [k]Isa 38:5
18:4 [l]2Ch 31:1 [m]Ex 23:24 [n]Nu 21:9
18:5 [o]2Ki 19:10; 23:25
18:6 [p]Dt 10:20;; Jos 23:8
18:7 [q]Ge 39:3; 1Sa 18:14 [r]2Ki 16:7
18:8 [s]2Ki 17:9; Isa 14:29
18:9 [t]Isa 1:1
18:11 [u]Isa 37:12
18:12 [v]2Ki 17:15 [w]Da 9:6,10 [x]1Ki 9:6

bow down and to him offer sacrifices. 37You must always be careful[f] to keep the decrees
and ordinances, the laws and commands he wrote for you. Do not worship other gods.
38Do not forget[g] the covenant I have made with you, and do not worship other gods.
39Rather, worship the LORD your God; it is he who will deliver you from the hand of all
your enemies."
40They would not listen, however, but persisted in their former practices. 41Even while
these people were worshiping the LORD,[h] they were serving their idols. To this day their
children and grandchildren continue to do as their fathers did.

Hezekiah King of Judah

18 In the third year of Hoshea son of Elah king of Israel, Hezekiah[i] son of Ahaz king
of Judah began to reign. 2He was twenty-five years old when he became king,
and he reigned in Jerusalem twenty-nine years.[j] His mother's name was Abijah[a] daughter of Zechariah. 3He did what was right in the eyes of the LORD, just as his father David[k]
had done. 4He removed[l] the high places, smashed the sacred stones[m] and cut down the
Asherah poles. He broke into pieces the bronze snake[n] Moses had made, for up to that
time the Israelites had been burning incense to it. (It was called[b] Nehushtan.[c])
5Hezekiah trusted[o] in the LORD, the God of Israel. There was no one like him among
all the kings of Judah, either before him or after him. 6He held fast[p] to the LORD and did
not cease to follow him; he kept the commands the LORD had given Moses. 7And the LORD
was with him; he was successful[q] in whatever he undertook. He rebelled[r] against the
king of Assyria and did not serve him. 8From watchtower to fortified city,[s] he defeated
the Philistines, as far as Gaza and its territory.
9In King Hezekiah's fourth year,[t] which was the seventh year of Hoshea son of Elah
king of Israel, Shalmaneser king of Assyria marched against Samaria and laid siege to
it. 10At the end of three years the Assyrians took it. So Samaria was captured in Hezekiah's sixth year, which was the ninth year of Hoshea king of Israel. 11The king[u] of Assyria deported Israel to Assyria and settled them in Halah, in Gozan on the Habor River and
in towns of the Medes. 12This happened because they had not obeyed the LORD their God,
but had violated his covenant[v]—all that Moses the servant of the LORD commanded.[w]
They neither listened to the commands[x] nor carried them out.
13In the fourteenth year of King Hezekiah's reign, Sennacherib king of Assyria at-

[a] *2* Hebrew *Abi*, a variant of *Abijah* [b] *4* Or *He called it* [c] *4* *Nehushtan* sounds like the Hebrew for *bronze* and *snake* and *unclean thing.*

17:37 to keep the decrees and ordinances. See notes on verse 13 and on 1 Kings 2:3.
17:39 he who will deliver you. Just as God had delivered his people in the past, he could do so again in the future (Ex 20:1–2; 23:22; Dt 20:1–4; 23:14).
17:41 To this day. See note on 1 Kings 8:8. Although the deportation did not purify the inhabitants of the northern kingdom, centuries later descendants of the people of Samaria, called Samaritans, did embrace monotheism and the stipulations of the Sinaitic covenant.
■ **18:1—25:30** *Judah Alone (715–586 B.C.).* With most of the citizens of the northern kingdom deported, the writer returned to his account of Judah's kings, up to the time when the people of Judah and Jerusalem were themselves exiled. He recorded the reigns of Hezekiah (18:1—20:21), Manasseh (21:1–18), Amon (21:19–26), Josiah (22:1—23:30), Jehoahaz (23:31–35), Jehoiakim (23:36—24:7), Jehoiachin (24:8–17) and Zedekiah (24:18–20a).
■ **18:1—20:21** *Hezekiah (715–686 B.C.).* The importance of Hezekiah to the writer is evident in the quantity of material he devoted to this king. Hezekiah was outstanding in a number of ways, including his opposition to idolatry. He was especially noteworthy in the manner in which he trusted the Lord (18:5). This record of his reign divides into four parts: the opening of his reign (18:1–4), a summary of his tenure in office (18:5–8), the Assyrian invasions (18:9—20:19) and the closure of his reign (20:20–21).
■ **18:1–4** *Opening of the Reign.* Unlike his father, Ahaz, Hezekiah was loyal to the Lord.
18:1 In the third year of Hoshea. That is, in 729 B.C. Hezekiah may have begun his reign as coregent with his father, Ahaz (cf. 16:1; 17:1; see "Introduction to 1 Kings: Purpose and Distinctives: *Kings as History*").
18:2 twenty-nine years. Hezekiah's reign as sole king of Judah lasted from 715–686 B.C.
18:3 He did what was right in the eyes of the LORD. Hezekiah was one of the most highly praised kings in the entire history of Judah (see notes on vv. 4–8). **just as his father David had done.** On David's reign as the standard by which all other reigns were judged, see note on 1 Kings 11:4.
18:4 He removed the high places. Hezekiah, unlike earlier kings, reformed his people's worship by destroying local pagan shrines (see note on 1Ki 3:2). **sacred stones . . . Asherah poles.** See notes on "Asherah poles" at 1 Kings 14:15 and on "sacred stones" at verse 23. **the bronze snake.** Originally preserved to commemorate God's mercy to the Israelites when they were in the wilderness (Nu 21:6–9), it had by this time become an object of idolatrous worship. Compare Jn 3:14–15. See *WCF* 23.3; *HC* 97.
■ **18:5–8** *Summary of Hezekiah's Reign.* The writer furnished an overview of Hezekiah's character and accomplishments.
18:5 trusted . . . no one like him. Hezekiah was incomparable in the way in which he trusted the Lord. Other kings were considered unparalleled in other ways: Solomon for wisdom (1Ki 3:12) and Josiah for reform (2Ki 23:25).
18:7 He rebelled against the king of Assyria and did not serve him. Ahaz, Hezekiah's father, had been a vassal of Assyria and had modified temple arrangements to reflect this fact (16:7–9,18). Hezekiah's rebellion against the Assyrians probably involved withholding tribute from them.
18:8 he defeated the Philistines. During Ahaz's reign the Philistines had captured territory in Judah (2Ch 28:18). **Gaza and its territory.** Gaza was near the Mediterranean coast; hence, Hezekiah was able to penetrate far into Philistine territory.
■ **18:9—20:19** *Assyrian Invasions.* The writer described several important aspects of the Assyrian invasions of the promised land. His record divides into two main parts: the earlier destruction of Samaria (18:9–12) and Sennacherib's attack on Judah (18:13—20:19)
■ **18:9–12** *The Fall of Samaria.* The writer provided a summary of the fall of Samaria, an event that is narrated more fully in 17:1–6 and commented upon in 17:7–23. This summary serves as a prelude for the material to follow.
■ **18:13—20:19** *Sennacherib's Invasion of Judah.* The story of Sennacherib's campaign and siege was also recorded in Isaiah 36–39,

tacked all the fortified cities of Judah[y] and captured them. 14 So Hezekiah king of Judah
sent this message to the king of Assyria at Lachish: "I have done wrong.[z] Withdraw from
me, and I will pay whatever you demand of me." The king of Assyria exacted from Hezekiah king of Judah three hundred talents[a] of silver and thirty talents[b] of gold. 15 So Hezekiah gave[a] him all the silver that was found in the temple of the LORD and in the treasuries of the royal palace.
16 At this time Hezekiah king of Judah stripped off the gold with which he had covered
the doors and doorposts of the temple of the LORD, and gave it to the king of Assyria.

Sennacherib Threatens Jerusalem

17 The king of Assyria sent his supreme commander,[b] his chief officer and his field
commander with a large army, from Lachish to King Hezekiah at Jerusalem. They came
up to Jerusalem and stopped at the aqueduct of the Upper Pool,[c] on the road to the
Washerman's Field. 18 They called for the king; and Eliakim[d] son of Hilkiah the palace administrator, Shebna[e] the secretary, and Joah son of Asaph the recorder went out to them.
19 The field commander said to them, "Tell Hezekiah:

" 'This is what the great king, the king of Assyria, says: On what are you basing this confidence of yours? 20 You say you have strategy and military strength—
but you speak only empty words. On whom are you depending, that you rebel
against me? 21 Look now, you are depending on Egypt,[f] that splintered reed of a
staff,[g] which pierces a man's hand and wounds him if he leans on it! Such is Pharaoh king of Egypt to all who depend on him. 22 And if you say to me, "We are depending on the LORD our God"—isn't he the one whose high places and altars Hezekiah removed, saying to Judah and Jerusalem, "You must worship before this
altar in Jerusalem"?

23 " 'Come now, make a bargain with my master, the king of Assyria: I will give
you two thousand horses—if you can put riders on them! 24 How can you repulse
one officer[h] of the least of my master's officials, even though you are depending
on Egypt for chariots and horsemen[c]? 25 Furthermore, have I come to attack and
destroy this place without word from the LORD?[i] The LORD himself told me to
march against this country and destroy it.' "

26 Then Eliakim son of Hilkiah, and Shebna and Joah said to the field commander,
"Please speak to your servants in Aramaic,[j] since we understand it. Don't speak to us in
Hebrew in the hearing of the people on the wall."
27 But the commander replied, "Was it only to your master and you that my master
sent me to say these things, and not to the men sitting on the wall—who, like you, will
have to eat their own filth and drink their own urine?"
28 Then the commander stood and called out in Hebrew: "Hear the word of the great
king, the king of Assyria! 29 This is what the king says: Do not let Hezekiah deceive[k] you. He
cannot deliver you from my hand. 30 Do not let Hezekiah persuade you to trust in the LORD

18:13 [y]2Ch 32:1; Isa 1:7; Mic 1:9
18:14 [z]Isa 24:5
18:15 [a]1Ki 15:18; 2Ki 16:8
18:17 [b]Isa 20:1 [c]2Ki 20:20; 2Ch 32:4,30; Isa 7:3
18:18 [d]2Ki 19:2; Isa 22:20 [e]Isa 22:15
18:21 [f]Isa 20:5; Eze 29:6 [g]Isa 30:5,7
18:24 [h]Isa 10:8
18:25 [i]2Ki 19:6,22
18:26 [j]Ezr 4:7
18:29 [k]2Ki 19:10

[a] *14* That is, about 11 tons (about 10 metric tons) [b] *14* That is, about 1 ton (about 1 metric ton)
[c] *24* Or *charioteers*

with a few additions and omissions. The account here in 2 Kings divides into five main parts: the invasion of Judah (18:13–16), the attack on Jerusalem (18:17–37), divine deliverance (19:1–37), Hezekiah's healing (20:1–11) and the Babylonian envoys (20:12–19).

■ **18:13–16** *The Invasion of Judah.* Sennacherib invaded Judah and conquered most of its territory.

18:13 In the fourteenth year. In 701 B.C. **Sennacherib king of Assyria.** Sennacherib succeeded Sargon II in 705 B.C. **attacked all the fortified cities of Judah.** The annals of Sennacherib recorded his campaign against Phoenicia, Judah, the Philistine cities and Egypt. He claimed to have taken 46 cities and "countless small villages." He also boasted of shutting up Hezekiah in Jerusalem "like a bird in a cage." His annals, however, did not claim that Sennacherib captured Jerusalem (see notes on Mic 1:8–16).

18:14–16 Hezekiah attempted to convince Sennacherib to withdraw by paying a huge indemnity. In using temple and palace treasuries to influence the actions of a foreign king, Hezekiah failed to live according to the will of God. He followed the example of Asa (1Ki 15:18) and of his own father, Ahaz (2Ki 16:8–9). The annals of Sennacherib confirmed that Hezekiah sent tribute to the Assyrian king.

■ **18:17–37** *The Attack on Jerusalem.* Sennacherib laid siege to Jerusalem, and Hezekiah's doom seemed certain.

18:17 The king of Assyria sent. Some interpreters believe that this refers to a second campaign of Sennacherib against Hezekiah about 12 to 13 years after the first. While this view is possible, there is no solid evidence to support it and, in any event, it is an unnecessary assumption. Sennacherib's annals consistently reported that Sennacherib not only demanded tribute from kings who "did not bow in submission to [his] yoke," but also insisted on deposing such rebellious kings and replacing them with monarchs of his own choosing. Hezekiah only sent tribute; he did not abdicate (vv. 13–16). **Lachish.** A fortified city 28 miles southwest of Jerusalem (cf. Mic 1:13).

18:18 Eliakim . . . Shebna . . . Joah. Three Judahite officials, the palace administrator (cf. 1Ki 4:6), the secretary (cf. 2Sa 8:17) and the recorder (cf. 2Sa 8:16), conferred with the three Assyrian officials.

18:20 On whom are you depending . . . ? Trust is a central theme in verses 19–25.

18:23 two thousand horses. Judah's military was probably so decimated by earlier losses to the Assyrians (vv. 13–16) that this taunt had some truth in it. See Micah 5:1.

18:26 Please speak to your servants in Aramaic. Aramaic (the language of ancient Aram—Syria) had become by this time the international language of diplomacy.

18:30 Do not . . . trust in the LORD. The field commander blasphemed the power of God. See *WLC* 113.

when he says, ‘The LORD will surely deliver us; this city will not be given into the hand of
the king of Assyria.’
31 “Do not listen to Hezekiah. This is what the king of Assyria says: Make peace with
me and come out to me. Then every one of you will eat from his own vine and fig tree[l]
and drink water from his own cistern,[m] 32 until I come and take you to a land like your
own, a land of grain and new wine, a land of bread and vineyards, a land of olive trees
and honey. Choose life[n] and not death!
“Do not listen to Hezekiah, for he is misleading you when he says, ‘The LORD will deliver us.’ 33 Has the god[o] of any nation ever delivered his land from the hand of the king
of Assyria? 34 Where are the gods of Hamath[p] and Arpad?[q] Where are the gods of Sepharvaim, Hena and Ivvah? Have they rescued Samaria from my hand? 35 Who of all the
gods of these countries has been able to save his land from me? How then can the LORD
deliver Jerusalem from my hand?”[r]
36 But the people remained silent and said nothing in reply, because the king had commanded, “Do not answer him.”
37 Then Eliakim son of Hilkiah the palace administrator, Shebna the secretary and
Joah son of Asaph the recorder went to Hezekiah, with their clothes torn,[s] and told him
what the field commander had said.

Jerusalem's Deliverance Foretold

19 When King Hezekiah heard this, he tore[t] his clothes and put on sackcloth and
went into the temple of the LORD. 2 He sent Eliakim the palace administrator,
Shebna the secretary and the leading priests, all wearing sackcloth, to the prophet Isaiah[u] son of Amoz. 3 They told him, “This is what Hezekiah says: This day is a day of distress and rebuke and disgrace, as when children come to the point of birth and there is
no strength to deliver them. 4 It may be that the LORD your God will hear all the words of
the field commander, whom his master, the king of Assyria, has sent to ridicule[v] the living God, and that he will rebuke[w] him for the words the LORD your God has heard. Therefore pray for the remnant that still survives.”
5 When King Hezekiah's officials came to Isaiah, 6 Isaiah said to them, “Tell your
master, ‘This is what the LORD says: Do not be afraid of what you have heard—those
words with which the underlings of the king of Assyria have blasphemed[x] me. 7 Listen!
I am going to put such a spirit in him that when he hears a certain report, he will return
to his own country, and there I will have him cut down with the sword.[y]’ ”
8 When the field commander heard that the king of Assyria had left Lachish,[z] he withdrew and found the king fighting against Libnah.
9 Now Sennacherib received a report that Tirhakah, the Cushite[a] king ⌊of Egypt⌋, was
marching out to fight against him. So he again sent messengers to Hezekiah with this
word: 10 “Say to Hezekiah king of Judah: Do not let the god you depend[a] on deceive[b] you
when he says, ‘Jerusalem will not be handed over to the king of Assyria.’ 11 Surely you
have heard what the kings of Assyria have done to all the countries, destroying them

18:31 [l]Nu 13:23; 1Ki 4:25 [m]Jer 14:3; La 4:4
18:32 [n]Dt 8:7-9; 30:19
18:33 [o]2Ki 19:12; Isa 10:10-11
18:34 [p]2Ki 17:24; 19:13 [q]Isa 10:9
18:35 [r]Ps 2:1-2
18:37 [s]2Ki 6:30
19:1 [t]Ge 37:34; 1Ki 21:27; 2Ch 32:20-22
19:2 [u]Isa 1:1
19:4 [v]2Ki 18:35 [w]2Sa 16:12
19:6 [x]2Ki 18:25
19:7 [y]ver 37
19:8 [z]2Ki 18:14
19:10 [a]2Ki 18:5 [b]2Ki 18:29

[a] 9 That is, from the upper Nile region

18:31 vine and fig tree . . . cistern. A picture of a peaceful life (1Ki 4:25; Mic 4:4; Zec 3:10).
18:32 until I come and take you to a land like your own. These words parodied God's gift of the promised land to the Israelites. The Assyrian king thereby offered to replace the Lord's gifts with his own. Through the prophet Isaiah, the Lord called the field commander's claims blasphemous (19:1–6). **Choose life and not death!** The words were borrowed from Deuteronomy 30:15–20 but put to unholy use.
18:33 Has the god of any nation ever delivered . . . ? The Assyrian field commander saw no distinction—if the gods of other nations could not defeat Assyria, neither could the Lord.
18:34 Hamath . . . Sepharvaim . . . and Ivvah. See notes on 17:24. **Arpad.** Located near Hamath in Aram, Arpad was captured in 740 B.C.
18:35 See *WLC* 113.
18:36 the people remained silent. The Assyrian effort to rouse the populace against their king (vv. 29,31,32) proved to be an abject failure.
18:37 with their clothes torn. In mourning and distress. See note on 1 Kings 21:27.
■ **19:1–37** *Divine Deliverance.* Isaiah predicted God's deliverance of Jerusalem from the Assyrians, and his prophecy was fulfilled.
19:1 tore his clothes and put on sackcloth. See notes on 6:30 and on 1 Kings 21:27.
19:2 the palace administrator. See 1 Kings 4:6. **the secretary.** See 2 Samuel 8:17. **leading priests.** Probably the heads of the various priestly families in Jerusalem. **the prophet Isaiah.** Isaiah played a pivotal role in providing Hezekiah with sound counsel during this crisis. See also Isaiah 37.
19:4 the remnant that still survives. This group was comprised of the people left in Judah, whether from the tribe of Judah or from the northern tribes, after the Assyrian attacks and deportations (see note on 17:6).
19:8 Lachish. See 18:17. **Libnah.** A town located just outside the borders of Philistia, about 12 miles southeast of Ashdod. In his annals, Sennacherib boasted about how he had compelled Hezekiah to release the king of Ekron, whom Hezekiah was holding in Jerusalem, into his custody. Sennacherib was thus successful in reversing some of Hezekiah's earlier gains against the Philistines (18:8).
19:9 Tirhakah, the Cushite. See NIV text note. Tirhakah was the brother of the pharaoh Shebitku, who launched a campaign into the region much later known as Palestine in order to counter the Assyrian invasion by Sennacherib. **king.** Tirhakah did not become king until 690 or 688 B.C., but by the time of the composition of this passage, it was well known that he had ascended the throne. Hence it was natural to refer to him using this title.

completely. And will you be delivered? 12Did the gods of the nations that were destroyed
by my forefathers deliver[c] them: the gods of Gozan,[d] Haran,[e] Rezeph and the people of
Eden who were in Tel Assar? 13Where is the king of Hamath, the king of Arpad, the king
of the city of Sepharvaim, or of Hena or Ivvah?"[f]

Hezekiah's Prayer

14Hezekiah received the letter from the messengers and read it. Then he went up to
the temple of the LORD and spread it out before the LORD. 15And Hezekiah prayed to the
LORD: "O LORD, God of Israel, enthroned between the cherubim,[g] you alone are God over
all the kingdoms of the earth. You have made heaven and earth. 16Give ear,[h] O LORD, and
hear;[i] open your eyes,[j] O LORD, and see; listen to the words Sennacherib has sent to insult the living God.

17"It is true, O LORD, that the Assyrian kings have laid waste these nations and their
lands. 18They have thrown their gods into the fire and destroyed them, for they were not
gods[k] but only wood and stone, fashioned by men's hands.[l] 19Now, O LORD our God, deliver us from his hand, so that all kingdoms[m] on earth may know[n] that you alone,
O LORD, are God."

Isaiah Prophesies Sennacherib's Fall

20Then Isaiah son of Amoz sent a message to Hezekiah: "This is what the LORD, the
God of Israel, says: I have heard[o] your prayer concerning Sennacherib king of Assyria.
21This is the word that the LORD has spoken against him:

" 'The Virgin Daughter[p] of Zion
despises you and mocks[q] you.
The Daughter of Jerusalem
tosses her head[r] as you flee.
22Who is it you have insulted and blasphemed?
Against whom have you raised your voice
and lifted your eyes in pride?
Against the Holy One[s] of Israel!
23By your messengers
you have heaped insults on the Lord.
And you have said,[t]
"With my many chariots[u]
I have ascended the heights of the mountains,
the utmost heights of Lebanon.
I have cut down its tallest cedars,
the choicest of its pines.
I have reached its remotest parts,
the finest of its forests.
24I have dug wells in foreign lands
and drunk the water there.
With the soles of my feet
I have dried up all the streams of Egypt."

25" 'Have you not heard?[v]
Long ago I ordained it.
In days of old I planned[w] it;
now I have brought it to pass,
that you have turned fortified cities
into piles of stone.[x]
26Their people, drained of power,
are dismayed[y] and put to shame.

19:12 [c]2Ki 18:33 [d]2Ki 17:6 [e]Ge 11:31
19:13 [f]2Ki 18:34
19:15 [g]Ex 25:22
19:16 [h]Ps 31:2 [i]1Ki 8:29 [j]ver 4; 2Ch 6:40
19:18 [k]Isa 44:9-11; Jer 10:3-10 [l]Ps 115:4; Ac 17:29
19:19 [m]1Ki 8:43 [n]Ps 83:18
19:20 [o]2Ki 20:5
19:21 [p]Jer 14:17; La 2:13 [q]Ps 22:7-8 [r]Job 16:4; Ps 109:25
19:22 [s]Ps 71:22; Isa 5:24
19:23 [t]Isa 10:18 [u]Ps 20:7
19:25 [v]Isa 40:21,28 [w]Isa 10:5; 45:7 [x]Mic 1:6
19:26 [y]Ps 6:10

19:12 Gozan. See 17:6. **Haran.** See Genesis 11:31. **Rezeph.** Northeast of Hamath in Syria. **the people of Eden who were in Tel Assar.** Eden was a district south of Haran in Aram (Syria).
19:13 Hamath . . . Ivvah. See notes on 17:24 and 18:34. Sennacherib's litany of sites included cities where the Assyrians had settled Israelite deportees in order to impress on Hezekiah that Judah's fate would be similar to that of Israel.
19:15–16 Hezekiah prayed. See *WLC* 190.
19:18 they were not gods. The gods of the other nations the Assyrians defeated were human creations made of "wood and stone" (Dt 4:28,35; 32:17–21; Ps 115:3–8; Isa 40:13–24; 44:9–20).
19:20 Isaiah . . . sent a message. Unbeknownst to Hezekiah, God communicated his response to Isaiah.
19:21 Virgin Daughter of Zion. The phrase affectionately referred to Jerusalem (Isa 1:8). **tosses her head as you flee.** The words describe mocking sorrow as Assyria flees (Isa 37:22).
19:22 See *WLC* 113.
19:25 Have you not heard? The Assyrians mistakenly believed that their great victories stemmed from their own might. They failed to recognize that the Lord was responsible for their success (cf. Isa 10:12–19; 14:24–27).

19:26 [z]Isa 4:2 [a]Ps 129:6

They are like plants in the field,
like tender green shoots,[z]
like grass sprouting on the roof,
scorched[a] before it grows up.

19:27 [b]Ps 139:1-4

27 " 'But I know[b] where you stay
and when you come and go
and how you rage against me.
28 Because you rage against me
and your insolence has reached my ears,

19:28 [c]Eze 19:9; 29:4 [d]Isa 30:28 [e]ver 33

I will put my hook[c] in your nose
and my bit[d] in your mouth,
and I will make you return[e]
by the way you came.'

19:29 [f]2Ki 20:8-9; Lk 2:12 [g]Lev 25:5 [h]Ps 107:37

29 "This will be the sign[f] for you, O Hezekiah:

"This year you will eat what grows by itself,[g]
and the second year what springs from that.
But in the third year sow and reap,
plant vineyards[h] and eat their fruit.

19:30 [i]2Ch 32:22-23

30 Once more a remnant of the house of Judah
will take root[i] below and bear fruit above.
31 For out of Jerusalem will come a remnant,
and out of Mount Zion a band of survivors.

19:31 [j]Isa 9:7

The zeal[j] of the LORD Almighty will accomplish this.

32 "Therefore this is what the LORD says concerning the king of Assyria:

"He will not enter this city
or shoot an arrow here.
He will not come before it with shield
or build a siege ramp against it.

19:33 [k]ver 28

33 By the way that he came he will return;[k]
he will not enter this city,
declares the LORD.

19:34 [l]2Ki 20:6 [m]1Ki 11:12-13

34 I will defend[l] this city and save it,
for my sake and for the sake of David[m] my servant."

19:35 [n]Ex 12:23 [o]Job 24:24

35 That night the angel of the LORD[n] went out and put to death a hundred and eighty-five thousand men in the Assyrian camp. When the people got up the next morning—there were all the dead bodies![o] 36 So Sennacherib king of Assyria broke camp and withdrew. He returned to Nineveh[p] and stayed there.

19:36 [p]Ge 10:11; Jnh 1:2

19:37 [q]ver 7 [r]Ge 8:4 [s]Ezr 4:2

37 One day, while he was worshiping in the temple of his god Nisroch, his sons Adrammelech and Sharezer cut him down with the sword,[q] and they escaped to the land of Ararat.[r] And Esarhaddon[s] his son succeeded him as king.

Hezekiah's Illness

20 In those days Hezekiah became ill and was at the point of death. The prophet Isaiah son of Amoz went to him and said, "This is what the LORD says: Put your house in order, because you are going to die; you will not recover."

19:28 I will put my hook in your nose and my bit in your mouth. Reference to the Assyrian custom of treating captured enemies like animals in a caravan (2Ch 33:11; Eze 19:4,9). But God would turn the tables on Assyria. See *WCF* 5.4.
19:29 sign. That is, a verification of a future event (see notes on 1Ki 13:3; Isa 7:11).
19:30–31 Isaiah expanded on the meaning of verse 29. The Assyrians would not succeed in decimating the populace of Judah. **remnant.** See notes on verse 4 and on Isaiah 1:9. The remnant would not only survive but flourish.
19:34 I will defend this city. Isaiah returned to the theme with which he had begun: Jerusalem's survival would be due to the grace of God (v. 21). **for the sake of David my servant.** See note on 1 Kings 11:4.
19:35 angel of the LORD. For the angel as an instrument of destruction, see Genesis 19:15, Exodus 12:12 and 23 and 2 Samuel 24:16. The massive destruction of the Assyrian army fulfilled the prophecies of verses 21 and 32–34. See *WLC* 19.
19:36 Nineveh. The capital of the Assyrian Empire.
19:37 Nisroch. A god not mentioned in Assyrian records. **cut him down.** Assyrian documents state that in a struggle for the throne one of Sennacherib's sons murdered him in 681 B.C. Because the Biblical writer followed events to their conclusion, he telescoped Sennacherib's ignominious withdrawal (701 B.C.) and assassination (681 B.C.). **Ararat.** Another name for Urarutu, present-day Armenia (Ge 8:4). **Esarhaddon.** Ruled Assyria from 681–669 B.C.
■ **20:1–11** *Hezekiah's Healing.* In response to Hezekiah's prayer, God healed him of a fatal illness. See notes on 2 Ch 32:24–26 and Isa 38:1–8.
20:1 In those days. There is good reason to believe that this incident and the reception of the Babylonian envoys (vv. 12–19) refer to a time in Hezekiah's reign before the Assyrian invasion of Judah in 701 B.C. According to Babylonian documents, Merodach-Baladan died in 703 B.C. Since Hezekiah died in 686 B.C., the 15 years

2Hezekiah turned his face to the wall and prayed to the LORD, 3"Remember,[t] O LORD,
how I have walked before you faithfully[u] and with wholehearted devotion and have done
what is good in your eyes." And Hezekiah wept bitterly.
4Before Isaiah had left the middle court, the word of the LORD came to him: 5"Go back
and tell Hezekiah, the leader of my people, 'This is what the LORD, the God of your father
David, says: I have heard[v] your prayer and seen your tears;[w] I will heal you. On the third
day from now you will go up to the temple of the LORD. 6I will add fifteen years to your
life. And I will deliver you and this city from the hand of the king of Assyria. I will defend[x]
this city for my sake and for the sake of my servant David.' "
7Then Isaiah said, "Prepare a poultice of figs." They did so and applied it to the boil,[y]
and he recovered.
8Hezekiah had asked Isaiah, "What will be the sign that the LORD will heal me and
that I will go up to the temple of the LORD on the third day from now?"
9Isaiah answered, "This is the LORD's sign[z] to you that the LORD will do what he has
promised: Shall the shadow go forward ten steps, or shall it go back ten steps?"
10"It is a simple matter for the shadow to go forward ten steps," said Hezekiah.
"Rather, have it go back ten steps."
11Then the prophet Isaiah called upon the LORD, and the LORD made the shadow go
back[a] the ten steps it had gone down on the stairway of Ahaz.

Envoys From Babylon

12At that time Merodach-Baladan son of Baladan king of Babylon sent Hezekiah letters and a gift, because he had heard of Hezekiah's illness. 13Hezekiah received the messengers and showed them all that was in his storehouses—the silver, the gold, the spices and the fine oil—his armory and everything found among his treasures. There was
nothing in his palace or in all his kingdom that Hezekiah did not show them.
14Then Isaiah the prophet went to King Hezekiah and asked, "What did those men
say, and where did they come from?"
"From a distant land," Hezekiah replied. "They came from Babylon."
15The prophet asked, "What did they see in your palace?"
"They saw everything in my palace," Hezekiah said. "There is nothing among my treasures that I did not show them."
16Then Isaiah said to Hezekiah, "Hear the word of the LORD: 17The time will surely
come when everything in your palace, and all that your fathers have stored up until this
day, will be carried off to Babylon.[b] Nothing will be left, says the LORD. 18And some of
your descendants,[c] your own flesh and blood, that will be born to you, will be taken
away, and they will become eunuchs in the palace of the king of Babylon."
19"The word of the LORD you have spoken is good," Hezekiah replied. For he thought,
"Will there not be peace and security in my lifetime?"
20As for the other events of Hezekiah's reign, all his achievements and how he made
the pool[d] and the tunnel by which he brought water into the city, are they not written

20:3 [t]Ne 13:22 [u]2Ki 18:3-6
20:5 [v]1Sa 9:16; 1Ki 9:3; 2Ki 19:20 [w]Ps 39:12; 56:8
20:6 [x]2Ki 19:34
20:7 [y]Isa 38:21
20:9 [z]Dt 13:2; Jer 44:29
20:11 [a]Jos 10:13
20:17 [b]2Ki 24:13; 25:13; 2Ch 36:10; Jer 27:22; 52:17-23
20:18 [c]2Ki 24:15; 2Ch 33:11; Da 1:3
20:20 [d]Ne 3:16

God added to Hezekiah's life (v. 6) would place his sickness at least in the year 702 B.C., if not earlier. The order of the text here is thus topical rather than chronological. **Hezekiah became ill.** The cause and nature of Hezekiah's illness are not known, although we do know that one symptom was a boil (v. 7).

20:5 I have heard your prayer and seen your tears. God compassionately added 15 years (v. 6) to Hezekiah's life. Hezekiah's reforms (18:4–5), together with his abiding trust in God during the Assyrian invasion (18:7,22,30,32b,35; 19:4,10), revealed consistency of character. In this respect Hezekiah's conduct was exemplary. Not only does this passage underscore the importance of prayer, but it also emphasizes divine freedom, compassion and omnipotence (see also 1Ki 21:27–29).

20:6 I will deliver you and this city from the hand of the king of Assyria. See note on 1 Kings 11:13.

20:7 poultice. Divine agency in healing does not rule out the use of medicine (v. 5).

20:10 ten steps. On "the stairway of Ahaz" (v. 11; cf. 23:12; Jos 10:12–14; Isa 38:8).

■ **20:12–19** *The Babylonian Envoys.* Despite the blessings God had shown him, Hezekiah sought to secure himself against Assyria by forming an alliance with Babylon. Isaiah declared God's judgment against him for this action. See notes on Isaiah 39:1–8.

20:12 Merodach-Baladan. King over Babylon from 721 B.C. until forced by the Assyrian king Sargon II into a vassal relationship in 710 B.C. Shortly after Sargon's death (705 B.C.), Merodach-Baladan led his country to a short-lived independence in 704 B.C., before Sennacherib forced him out in 703 B.C. (see note on v. 1). **sent Hezekiah letters and a gift.** Assyria was the dominant world empire at that time, and it was likely that Merodach-Baladan, together with the king of Egypt, was seeking to encourage Hezekiah's independence against the Assyrians.

20:13 his armory and everything found among his treasures. This dates to a time before Hezekiah sent all of his treasures as tribute to the Assyrians (see notes on v. 1 and on 18:14–16). Hezekiah was attempting to impress his Babylonian visitors with all of his nation's wealth and military prowess. He therefore was receptive to the notion of allying himself with Egypt and Babylon. Just as Isaiah had opposed Ahaz's treaty with the foreign power of Assyria (Isa 7:1–17), he also opposed this attempt to forge a treaty with the foreign powers of Babylon and Egypt (Isa 30–31).

20:17 will be carried off to Babylon. Isaiah rebuked a naive Hezekiah. The same treasures that might induce a treaty might also eventually provoke an invasion. This happened in the Babylonian invasion of 598 B.C. and in the Babylonian exile of 587 B.C. Having sought refuge with the Babylonians, Hezekiah discovered that these people would in fact be Judah's ruin.

20:18 your own flesh and blood, that will be born to you, will be taken away. Hezekiah's son Manasseh was exiled by the Assyrians and held captive in Babylon (2Ch 33:11). Other descendants followed later (24:15; 25:7).

■ **20:20–21** *Closure of the Reign.* Hezekiah died and was succeeded by his son Manasseh.

20:20 the pool and the tunnel by which he brought water

in the book of the annals of the kings of Judah? 21 Hezekiah rested with his fathers. And Manasseh his son succeeded him as king.

Manasseh King of Judah

21 Manasseh was twelve years old when he became king, and he reigned in Jerusalem fifty-five years. His mother's name was Hephzibah.[e] 2 He did evil[f] in the eyes of the LORD, following the detestable practices[g] of the nations the LORD had driven out before the Israelites. 3 He rebuilt the high places[h] his father Hezekiah had destroyed; he also erected altars to Baal[i] and made an Asherah pole, as Ahab king of Israel had done. He bowed down to all the starry hosts[j] and worshiped them. 4 He built altars[k] in the temple of the LORD, of which the LORD had said, "In Jerusalem I will put my Name."[l] 5 In both courts[m] of the temple of the LORD, he built altars to all the starry hosts. 6 He sacrificed his own son[n] in[a] the fire, practiced sorcery and divination, and consulted mediums and spiritists.[o] He did much evil in the eyes of the LORD, provoking him to anger.

7 He took the carved Asherah pole[p] he had made and put it in the temple, of which the LORD had said to David and to his son Solomon, "In this temple and in Jerusalem, which I have chosen out of all the tribes of Israel, I will put my Name[q] forever. 8 I will not again[r] make the feet of the Israelites wander from the land I gave their forefathers, if only they will be careful to do everything I commanded them and will keep the whole Law that my servant Moses[s] gave them." 9 But the people did not listen. Manasseh led them astray, so that they did more evil[t] than the nations[u] the LORD had destroyed before the Israelites.

10 The LORD said through his servants the prophets: 11 "Manasseh king of Judah has committed these detestable sins. He has done more evil[v] than the Amorites[w] who preceded him and has led Judah into sin with his idols. 12 Therefore this is what the LORD, the God of Israel, says: I am going to bring such disaster[x] on Jerusalem and Judah that the ears of everyone who hears of it will tingle.[y] 13 I will stretch out over Jerusalem the measuring line used against Samaria and the plumb line[z] used against the house of Ahab. I will wipe[a] out Jerusalem as one wipes a dish, wiping it and turning it upside down. 14 I will forsake[b] the remnant[c] of my inheritance and hand them over to their enemies. They will be looted and plundered by all their foes, 15 because they have done evil[d] in my eyes and have provoked[e] me to anger from the day their forefathers came out of Egypt until this day."

[a] 6 Or *He made his own son pass through*

21:1 [e]Isa 62:4
21:2 [f]Jer 15:4 [g]2Ki 16:3
21:3 [h]2Ki 18:4 [i]Jdg 6:28; 1Ki 16:32 [j]Dt 17:3; 2Ki 17:16
21:4 [k]Jer 32:34 [l]2Sa 7:13; 1Ki 8:29
21:5 [m]1Ki 7:12; 2Ki 23:12
21:6 [n]Lev 18:21; Dt 18:10; 2Ki 16:3; 17:17 [o]Lev 19:31
21:7 [p]Dt 16:21; 2Ki 23:4 [q]2Sa 7:13; 1Ki 8:29; 9:3; 2Ki 23:27; Jer 32:34
21:8 [r]2Sa 7:10 [s]2Ki 18:12
21:9 [t]Pr 29:12 [u]Dt 9:4
21:11 [v]2Ki 24:3-4 [w]Ge 15:16; 1Ki 21:26
21:12 [x]2Ki 23:26; 24:3; Jer 15:4 [y]1Sa 3:11; Jer 19:3
21:13 [z]Isa 34:11; La 2:8; Am 7:7-9 [a]2Ki 23:27
21:14 [b]Ps 78:58-60 [c]2Ki 19:4; Mic 2:12
21:15 [d]Ex 32:22 [e]Jer 25:7

---

into the city. Hezekiah had made improvements to Jerusalem's water supply system in advance of the Assyrian invasion. An inscription in this tunnel (called the Siloam Tunnel) was found in 1880, and it celebrated the completion of this impressive engineering feat. The conduit ran from outside the city wall at the Gihon spring (cf. 1Ki 1:33) through 1,700 feet of solid rock to the Pool of Siloam inside the city. **book of the annals of the kings of Judah.** See note on 1 Kings 11:41.

■ **21:1–18** *Manasseh (686–642 B.C.).* These verses summarize the evil reign of Manasseh, king of Judah. Manasseh led Judah into sin by reintroducing idolatry; he also shed "much innocent blood" (v. 16). Manasseh's sin was so great that God pronounced disaster on Judah and Jerusalem. These verses divide into five parts: the opening (vv. 1–6), Manasseh's idolatry (vv. 7–9), prophetic condemnation (vv. 10–15), violence (v. 16) and the closure of the reign (vv. 17–18).

21:1 twelve years old. Manasseh most likely began his reign as coregent with his father, Hezekiah. **fifty-five years.** That is, from 697–642 B.C. Manasseh's reign was the longest of any king of Judah. Assyrian records attest that Manasseh was a vassal of both Esarhaddon (681–669 B.C.) and Ashurbanipal (669–627 B.C.).

21:2 He did evil. Manasseh presided over the worst period of infidelity in Judah's history. He reversed the reforms brought about by his father, Hezekiah. Manasseh also introduced pagan elements into Judah's worship that had been unprecedented during the entire prior period of the monarchy (see notes on vv. 3–7). **the detestable practices of the nations the LORD had driven out.** See Deuteronomy 4:25 and 26, 9:4, 18:9 and 1 Kings 14:24.

21:3 the high places his father Hezekiah had destroyed. See 18:4 and note on 1 Kings 3:2. **altars to Baal.** State-sanctioned Baal worship had been eradicated in the reforms led by the priest Jehoiada (11:18). **Asherah pole.** See note on 1 Kings 14:15. **as Ahab king of Israel had done.** Manasseh imitated the policies of the worst king of the northern kingdom (1Ki 16:30–33). **bowed down to all the starry hosts.** In nations such as Babylon, the sun, moon, and stars were personified as gods (17:16; 23:5,12). Astral worship was forbidden in Israel (Dt 4:19; 17:3).

21:4 altars in the temple. These altars were dedicated to "the starry hosts" (v. 5). **Jerusalem.** See note on 1 Kings 11:13.

21:6 sacrificed his own son. On the gruesome practice of child sacrifice, see Deuteronomy 12:29–31 and note on 2 Kings 16:3. **sorcery and divination.** See note on 16:15. **mediums and spiritists.** Both were forbidden in the law (Lev 19:31; 20:27; Dt 18:9–14).

21:7 Asherah pole. See note on 1 Kings 14:15. **to David and to . . . Solomon.** David had wished to build the temple himself (2Sa 7:1–3), but the Lord had instead promised that he would build David a dynasty and that his son Solomon would construct the temple (2Sa 7:8–16). That promise had been fulfilled during Solomon's reign, and God had blessed the temple as the divinely ordained place for sacrifice and prayer (1Ki 9:1–3; Dt 12:5).

21:8 if only they will be careful to do everything I commanded them. The land was a gift, but its possession depended on Israelite fidelity (Dt 1:8; 3:18; 4:1,26–28; 1Ki 9:4–9). **the whole Law that my servant Moses gave them.** See notes on 1 Kings 2:3.

21:11 Amorites. Used here as a general designation of the pre-Israelite inhabitants of Canaan (see note on 1Ki 21:26).

21:12 ears . . . will tingle. The magnitude of the threatened devastation would cause this metaphorical reaction (1Sa 3:11; Jer 19:3).

21:13 measuring line . . . plumb line. Walls that were not straight were commonly torn down to avoid accidental collapse. Both "Samaria" (17:5–6) and "the house of Ahab" were destroyed. The same standards would be used against Jerusalem.

21:14 I will forsake. The time for patience and forbearance was over. Jerusalem and Judah would not be defeated by a superior people or a superior god. On the contrary, Judah's own God was abandoning what was left of the original 12 tribes ("the remnant") to its enemies as punishment (Isa 1:1,5–8) of his own people. The Babylonian exile of 587 B.C. was in view (24:1–4).

21:15 from the day their forefathers came out of Egypt until this day. After liberating his people from slavery in Egypt, God had made a covenant with them at Mount Sinai (Ex 19:1—Nu 10:10). Although both God and Israel had made promises in that covenant, only God had remained faithful. Israel's history had been characterized by persistent rebellion.

16 Moreover, Manasseh also shed so much innocent blood[f] that he filled Jerusalem
from end to end—besides the sin that he had caused Judah to commit, so that they did
evil in the eyes of the LORD.
17 As for the other events of Manasseh's reign, and all he did, including the sin he committed, are they not written in the book of the annals of the kings of Judah? 18 Manasseh
rested with his fathers and was buried in his palace garden,[g] the garden of Uzza. And
Amon his son succeeded him as king.

Amon King of Judah

19 Amon was twenty-two years old when he became king, and he reigned in Jerusalem two years. His mother's name was Meshullemeth daughter of Haruz; she was from
Jotbah. 20 He did evil[h] in the eyes of the LORD, as his father Manasseh had done. 21 He
walked in all the ways of his father; he worshiped the idols his father had worshiped, and
bowed down to them. 22 He forsook the LORD, the God of his fathers, and did not walk[i]
in the way of the LORD.
23 Amon's officials conspired against him and assassinated[j] the king in his palace.
24 Then the people of the land killed[k] all who had plotted against King Amon, and they
made Josiah his son king in his place.
25 As for the other events of Amon's reign, and what he did, are they not written in the
book of the annals of the kings of Judah? 26 He was buried in his grave in the garden[l] of
Uzza. And Josiah his son succeeded him as king.

The Book of the Law Found

22 Josiah was eight years old when he became king, and he reigned in Jerusalem
thirty-one years. His mother's name was Jedidah daughter of Adaiah; she was
from Bozkath.[m] 2 He did what was right[n] in the eyes of the LORD and walked in all the
ways of his father David, not turning aside to the right[o] or to the left.
3 In the eighteenth year of his reign, King Josiah sent the secretary, Shaphan[p] son of
Azaliah, the son of Meshullam, to the temple of the LORD. He said: 4 "Go up to Hilkiah the
high priest and have him get ready the money that has been brought into the temple of
the LORD, which the doorkeepers have collected[q] from the people. 5 Have them entrust it
to the men appointed to supervise the work on the temple. And have these men pay the
workers who repair[r] the temple of the LORD— 6 the carpenters, the builders and the masons. Also have them purchase timber and dressed stone to repair the temple.[s] 7 But they
need not account for the money entrusted to them, because they are acting faithfully."[t]
8 Hilkiah the high priest said to Shaphan the secretary, "I have found the Book of the
Law[u] in the temple of the LORD." He gave it to Shaphan, who read it. 9 Then Shaphan the
secretary went to the king and reported to him: "Your officials have paid out the mon-

21:16 [f]2Ki 24:4
21:18 [g]ver 26
21:20 [h]ver 2-6
21:22 [i]1Ki 11:33
21:23 [j]2Ki 12:20; 2Ch 33:24-25
21:24 [k]2Ki 14:5
21:26 [l]ver 18
22:1 [m]Jos 15:39
22:2 [n]Dt 17:19 [o]Dt 5:32
22:3 [p]2Ch 34:20, Jer 39:14
22:4 [q]2Ki 12:4-5
22:5 [r]2Ki 12:5, 11-14
22:6 [s]2Ki 12:11-12
22:7 [t]2Ki 12:15
22:8 [u]Dt 31:24

21:16 shed so much innocent blood. This expression may either refer hyperbolically to the oppression and persecution of the poor and downtrodden (Jer 7:6; 22:3,17; Eze 22:6–31) or to actual deaths (cf. v. 6; 2Ch 32:6).
21:17 book of the annals of the kings of Judah. See note on 1 Kings 11:41.
▪ **21:19–26** *Amon (642–640 B.C.).* Amon succeeded Manasseh as king of Judah and continued his father's idolatrous practices.
21:19 he became king. It is probable that Amon, like Manasseh before him, was an Assyrian vassal. **two years.** That is, from 642–640 B.C. **Jotbah.** A town perhaps located in lower Galilee.
21:24 the people of the land. See note on 11:14. Desiring thorough reforms and not merely the demise of Amon, the people stepped forward and installed Amon's son as king, hoping that he would be loyal to the Davidic legacy.
21:25 book of the annals of the kings of Judah. See note on 1 Kings 11:41.
▪ **22:1—23:30** *Josiah (640–609 B.C.).* This section highlights the righteous reforms initiated by Josiah, king of Judah. Josiah ordered the repair of the temple and, in obedience to the Book of the Law found there, campaigned against idolatry in Judah and Samaria and reinstituted the celebration of the Passover. This material divides into five parts: the opening of Josiah's reign (22:1–2); repairing the temple (22:3–20); reforming Jerusalem, Judah and Samaria (23:1–20); the Passover (23:21–27); and the closure of his reign (23:28–30).
▪ **22:1–2** *Opening of the Reign.* Josiah's reign is introduced as exceptionally righteous.
22:1 thirty-one years. That is, from 640–609 B.C. **Bozkath.** A town about four miles southeast of Lachish in Judah.
22:2 walked in all the ways of his father David. The Biblical writer commends a number of Judahite kings: Asa (1Ki 15:11), Jehoshaphat (1Ki 22:41–43a), Joash (12:2), Amaziah (14:1,3), Azariah (15:1,3), Jotham (15:32,34) and Hezekiah (18:1,3), but he gives Josiah the highest praise (23:25). Josiah instituted the most thoroughgoing reforms of any king (23:1–24). The prophet Jeremiah also spoke highly of Josiah's reign (Jer 22:15–16). **not turning aside to the right or to the left.** Josiah's actions were wholly in accord with the mandate of the covenant (Dt 5:32; 17:11,20; 28:14; Jos 1:7; Pr 4:27).
▪ **22:3–20** *Repairing the Temple.* Josiah had the temple repaired, and during the course of this work the long-discarded Book of the Law was rediscovered. Because of Josiah's sorrow for his people's sin God's promised disaster on Judah and Jerusalem was delayed.
22:3 eighteenth year. That is, when Josiah was twenty-six years old. **the secretary.** The secretary would have been among the highest-ranking civil servants (12:10; 25:19). By the time of Josiah's reign the Assyrian Empire was in a state of decline. Josiah, unlike Manasseh, asserted Judah's independence from Assyria. Josiah exercised control over at least part of the former northern kingdom (23:4,15–20).
22:4 Hilkiah. Most likely not the father of Jeremiah (Jer 1:1), this Hilkiah was the grandfather of the high priest Seraiah, who was executed by Nebuchadnezzar at Riblah (25:18–21). **high priest.** See 1 Kings 1:7. **the doorkeepers have collected from the people.** King Joash had used the same technique for collecting funds to refurbish the temple (12:4–5). Josiah's first priority was to restore the temple after its neglect during the days of Manasseh and Amon.
22:8 the Book of the Law. Actually a scroll, probably containing the book of Deuteronomy (Dt 28:61; 31:24,26). The reforms that Josiah initiated (23:1–24) followed the dictates of Deuteronomy.

ey that was in the temple of the LORD and have entrusted it to the workers and supervisors at the temple." 10Then Shaphan the secretary informed the king, "Hilkiah the priest
has given me a book." And Shaphan read from it in the presence of the king.[v]
11When the king heard the words of the Book of the Law, he tore his robes. 12He gave
these orders to Hilkiah the priest, Ahikam[w] son of Shaphan, Acbor son of Micaiah, Shaphan the secretary and Asaiah the king's attendant: 13"Go and inquire of the LORD for me
and for the people and for all Judah about what is written in this book that has been
found. Great is the LORD's anger[x] that burns against us because our fathers have not
obeyed the words of this book; they have not acted in accordance with all that is written there concerning us."
14Hilkiah the priest, Ahikam, Acbor, Shaphan and Asaiah went to speak to the prophetess Huldah, who was the wife of Shallum son of Tikvah, the son of Harhas, keeper of
the wardrobe. She lived in Jerusalem, in the Second District.
15She said to them, "This is what the LORD, the God of Israel, says: Tell the man who
sent you to me, 16'This is what the LORD says: I am going to bring disaster[y] on this place
and its people, according to everything written in the book[z] the king of Judah has read.
17Because they have forsaken[a] me and burned incense to other gods and provoked me
to anger by all the idols their hands have made,[a] my anger will burn against this place
and will not be quenched.' 18Tell the king of Judah, who sent you to inquire[b] of the LORD,
'This is what the LORD, the God of Israel, says concerning the words you heard: 19Because
your heart was responsive and you humbled[c] yourself before the LORD when you heard
what I have spoken against this place and its people, that they would become accursed[d]
and laid waste,[e] and because you tore your robes and wept in my presence, I have heard
you, declares the LORD. 20Therefore I will gather you to your fathers, and you will be buried in peace.[f] Your eyes will not see all the disaster I am going to bring on this place.' "
So they took her answer back to the king.

Josiah Renews the Covenant

23 Then the king called together all the elders of Judah and Jerusalem. 2He went
up to the temple of the LORD with the men of Judah, the people of Jerusalem, the
priests and the prophets—all the people from the least to the greatest. He read[g] in their
hearing all the words of the Book of the Covenant, which had been found in the temple
of the LORD. 3The king stood by the pillar and renewed the covenant[h] in the presence of
the LORD—to follow[i] the LORD and keep his commands, regulations and decrees with all
his heart and all his soul, thus confirming the words of the covenant written in this book.
Then all the people pledged themselves to the covenant.
4The king ordered Hilkiah the high priest, the priests next in rank and the doorkeepers[j] to remove[k] from the temple of the LORD all the articles made for Baal and Asherah
and all the starry hosts. He burned them outside Jerusalem in the fields of the Kidron Valley and took the ashes to Bethel. 5He did away with the pagan priests appointed by the
kings of Judah to burn incense on the high places of the towns of Judah and on those

22:10 [v]Jer 36:21
22:12 [w]2Ki 25:22; Jer 26:24
22:13 [x]Dt 29:24-28; 31:17
22:16 [y]Dt 31:29; Jos 23:15 [z]Dt 29:27; Da 9:11
22:17 [a]Dt 29:25-27
22:18 [b]2Ch 34:26; Jer 21:2
22:19 [c]Ex 10:3; 1Ki 21:29; Ps 51:17; Isa 57:15; Mic 6:8 [d]Jer 26:6 [e]Lev 26:31
22:20 [f]Isa 57:1
23:2 [g]Dt 31:11; 2Ki 22:8
23:3 [h]2Ki 11:14,17 [i]Dt 13:4
23:4 [j]2Ki 25:18 [k]2Ki 21:7

[a] 17 Or *by everything they have done*

22:11 he tore his robes. See note on 1 Kings 21:27. Josiah was distraught because the stipulations of the Book of the Law were not being observed, and he recognized that the curses outlined in the covenant might soon occur (v. 13; Dt 6:10–19; 28:15–68).
22:12 Ahikam son of Shaphan. Ahikam was the father of Gedaliah, who was later appointed by Nebuchadnezzar to serve as governor of Judah after the Babylonian invasion of the region (25:22; Jer 26:24).
22:13 Go and inquire. Josiah, like a number of kings before him, consulted a prophet in a dire situation (19:2; 20:1–5; 1Ki 14:1–18; 20:13–14).
22:14 prophetess Huldah. Huldah resided in Jerusalem and was most likely a court prophetess consulted on important matters of state (cf. Dt 18:14–22). **the Second District.** Likely a recently developed quarter on the western hill of Jerusalem (cf. 2Ch 33:14; Zep 1:10).
22:20 See *WLC* 85; *BC* 13.
23:1–26 He read in their hearing. King Josiah led his people in following the Lord. See *WCF* 23.3.
■ **23:1–20** *Reforms in Jerusalem, Judah and Samaria.* Josiah publicly renewed the covenant (vv. 1–3) and removed idols in Jerusalem, Judah and the towns of Samaria (vv. 4–20).
23:1 elders. See note on 1 Kings 8:1.
23:2 Book of the Covenant. Scholars debate the precise contents of this book or scroll. Although Exodus 20–23 was called the "Book of the Covenant" (Ex 24:7), it is unlikely that merely those chapters in Exodus were in view. Judging by the kinds of reforms Josiah pursued (vv. 4–24), the term probably referred either to a version of Deuteronomy (see note on 22:8) or to a larger corpus of laws including Deuteronomy.
23:3–6 See *WCF* 20.4; *BC* 36.
23:3 by the pillar. This prominent location was in front of the temple (cf. 11:14 and 1Ki 7:15). **renewed the covenant.** Josiah, like Moses (Dt 29:1—30:20), Joshua (Jos 24:1–28) and Jehoiada (11:17) before him, led the people in renewing their commitment to God. During such a liturgy, the people would pledge themselves to "keep his commands, regulations and decrees." **with all his heart and all his soul.** See Deuteronomy 6:5 and Jesus' summary of the law in Matthew 22:36–40.
23:4 Baal. See note on 1 Kings 16:31. **Asherah.** See note on 1 Kings 14:15. **starry hosts.** See notes on 2 Kings 17:16 and 21:3. **ashes to Bethel.** Bethel was one of the two original sites at which Jeroboam I fashioned golden calves and instituted his own cult (1Ki 12:26–33). By depositing these ashes at Bethel, Josiah was desecrating the cult's worship center (cf. vv. 15–20).
23:5 pagan priests. See Hosea 10:5 and Zephaniah 1:4. **high places.** See note on 1 Kings 3:2. **Baal.** See note on 1 Kings 16:31. **starry hosts.** See notes on 2 Kings 17:16 and 21:3.

around Jerusalem—those who burned incense to Baal, to the sun and moon, to the constellations and to all the starry hosts.[l] 6He took the Asherah pole from the temple of the
LORD to the Kidron Valley outside Jerusalem and burned it there. He ground it to powder and scattered the dust over the graves of the common people.[m] 7He also tore down
the quarters of the male shrine prostitutes,[n] which were in the temple of the LORD and
where women did weaving for Asherah.

8Josiah brought all the priests from the towns of Judah and desecrated the high places, from Geba[o] to Beersheba, where the priests had burned incense. He broke down the
shrines[a] at the gates—at the entrance to the Gate of Joshua, the city governor, which is
on the left of the city gate. 9Although the priests of the high places did not serve[p] at the
altar of the LORD in Jerusalem, they ate unleavened bread with their fellow priests.

10He desecrated Topheth,[q] which was in the Valley of Ben Hinnom,[r] so no one could
use it to sacrifice his son[s] or daughter in[b] the fire to Molech. 11He removed from the entrance to the temple of the LORD the horses that the kings of Judah had dedicated to the
sun. They were in the court near the room of an official named Nathan-Melech. Josiah
then burned the chariots dedicated to the sun.[t]

12He pulled down the altars the kings of Judah had erected on the roof[u] near the upper room of Ahaz, and the altars Manasseh had built in the two courts[v] of the temple
of the LORD. He removed them from there, smashed them to pieces and threw the rubble into the Kidron Valley. 13The king also desecrated the high places that were east of
Jerusalem on the south of the Hill of Corruption—the ones Solomon[w] king of Israel had
built for Ashtoreth the vile goddess of the Sidonians, for Chemosh the vile god of
Moab, and for Molech[c] the detestable god of the people of Ammon. 14Josiah smashed[x]
the sacred stones and cut down the Asherah poles and covered the sites with human
bones.

15Even the altar[y] at Bethel, the high place made by Jeroboam[z] son of Nebat, who had
caused Israel to sin—even that altar and high place he demolished. He burned the high
place and ground it to powder, and burned the Asherah pole also. 16Then Josiah[a] looked
around, and when he saw the tombs that were there on the hillside, he had the bones
removed from them and burned on the altar to defile it, in accordance with the word of
the LORD proclaimed by the man of God who foretold these things.

17The king asked, "What is that tombstone I see?"

The men of the city said, "It marks the tomb of the man of God who came from Judah and pronounced against the altar of Bethel the very things you have done to it."

18"Leave it alone," he said. "Don't let anyone disturb his bones[b]." So they spared his
bones and those of the prophet who had come from Samaria.

19Just as he had done at Bethel, Josiah removed and defiled all the shrines at the high
places that the kings of Israel had built in the towns of Samaria that had provoked the

23:5 [l]2Ki 21:3; Jer 8:2
23:6 [m]Jer 26:23
23:7 [n]1Ki 14:24; 15:12; Eze 16:16
23:8 [o]1Ki 15:22
23:9 [p]Eze 44:10-14
23:10 [q]Isa 30:33; Jer 7:31,32; 19:6 [r]Jos 15:8 [s]Lev 18:21; Dt 18:10
23:11 [t]Dt 4:19
23:12 [u]Jer 19:13; Zep 1:5 [v]2Ki 21:5
23:13 [w]1Ki 11:7
23:14 [x]Ex 23:24; Dt 7:5, 25
23:15 [y]1Ki 13:1-3 [z]1Ki 12:33
23:16 [a]1Ki 13:2
23:18 [b]1Ki 13:31

[a] *8* Or *high places* [b] *10* Or *to make his son or daughter pass through* [c] *13* Hebrew *Milcom*

23:6 Asherah pole. See 21:7 and note on 1 Kings 14:15. **burned it there . . . ground it to powder and scattered the dust.** These actions were similar to those of Moses following the Israelites' worship of the golden calf (Ex 32:20; Dt 9:21). **over the graves of the common people.** Josiah did this to desecrate the Asherah pole, not to contaminate the graves (Nu 19:16; Jer 26:23).
23:7 male shrine prostitutes. See note on 1 Kings 14:24. See *WLC* 139.
23:8 all the priests from the towns of Judah. These priests, as opposed to the "pagan priests" (v. 5), were worshipers of the Lord. Hence, Josiah did not purge them but brought them into Jerusalem. **from Geba to Beersheba.** Geba was at the northern limits of the southern kingdom, while Beersheba was at the southern limits. Josiah centralized worship throughout the southern kingdom in accord with the prescriptions of Deuteronomy 12.
23:9 did not serve at the altar of the LORD. Deuteronomy 18:6–8 allowed local priests the option of joining the staff of the central sanctuary. However, the uncertain pedigrees of these priests may have rendered them unfit for this task (1Ki 12:31; 13:33), and so they could only aspire to secondary roles in the temple service. **ate unleavened bread.** The priests from the high places were allowed a portion of the priestly provisions (Lev 2:10; 6:16–18). See *WCF* 20.4.
23:10 Topheth. Child sacrifice had occurred at this location in the Valley of Ben Hinnom outside Jerusalem (16:3; 21:6; Isa 30:33; Jer 7:31–32; 19:5–6). **Molech.** See note on 1 Kings 11:5.
23:11 horses . . . dedicated to the sun. The sun was regarded as a deity by some of Israel's neighbors (17:16). Archaeologists have found miniature clay horses 300 feet south of the temple area of Jerusalem. On the horses' foreheads are dishes that some think represent the sun. In ancient Mesopotamia, horses played a number of religious roles. In Assyria, white horses were associated with the gods Ashur and Sin.
23:12 pulled down. By tearing down these altars used for astral worship, Josiah reversed the policies of Ahaz (16:2–4,10–16), Manasseh (21:1,3) and Amon (21:22–23).
23:13 the high places . . . Solomon king of Israel had built. Of all the kings of Judah, only Josiah was bold enough to tear down the high places that Solomon had built for the gods of his foreign wives (1Ki 11:1–8,33).
23:14 smashed . . . cut down. Josiah defiled sacred precincts dating to the time of Rehoboam, where "sacred stones" and "Asherah poles" stood (1Ki 14:21,23).
23:15 the altar at Bethel. See 1 Kings 12:31–33. It is unclear whether Josiah also defiled the cult center Jeroboam I had established at Dan (1Ki 12:28–30) or whether this cult center was even still in existence.
23:16 tombs. These tombs were those of the Bethel priests Jeroboam I had appointed (1Ki 12:31–32; 13:1,2). **in accordance with the word of the LORD.** See the prophecy of 1 Kings 13:2 and 32 and the story of which it is a part (1Ki 13:1–32).
23:18 Samaria. The name here probably designated the former northern kingdom (v. 19; 17:24,29; 1Ki 13:32) rather than the city of that name.
23:19 in the towns of Samaria. Although he began his northern reforms at Bethel, Josiah extended them throughout what had been the northern kingdom.

Nebuchadnezzar's Campaigns Against Judah

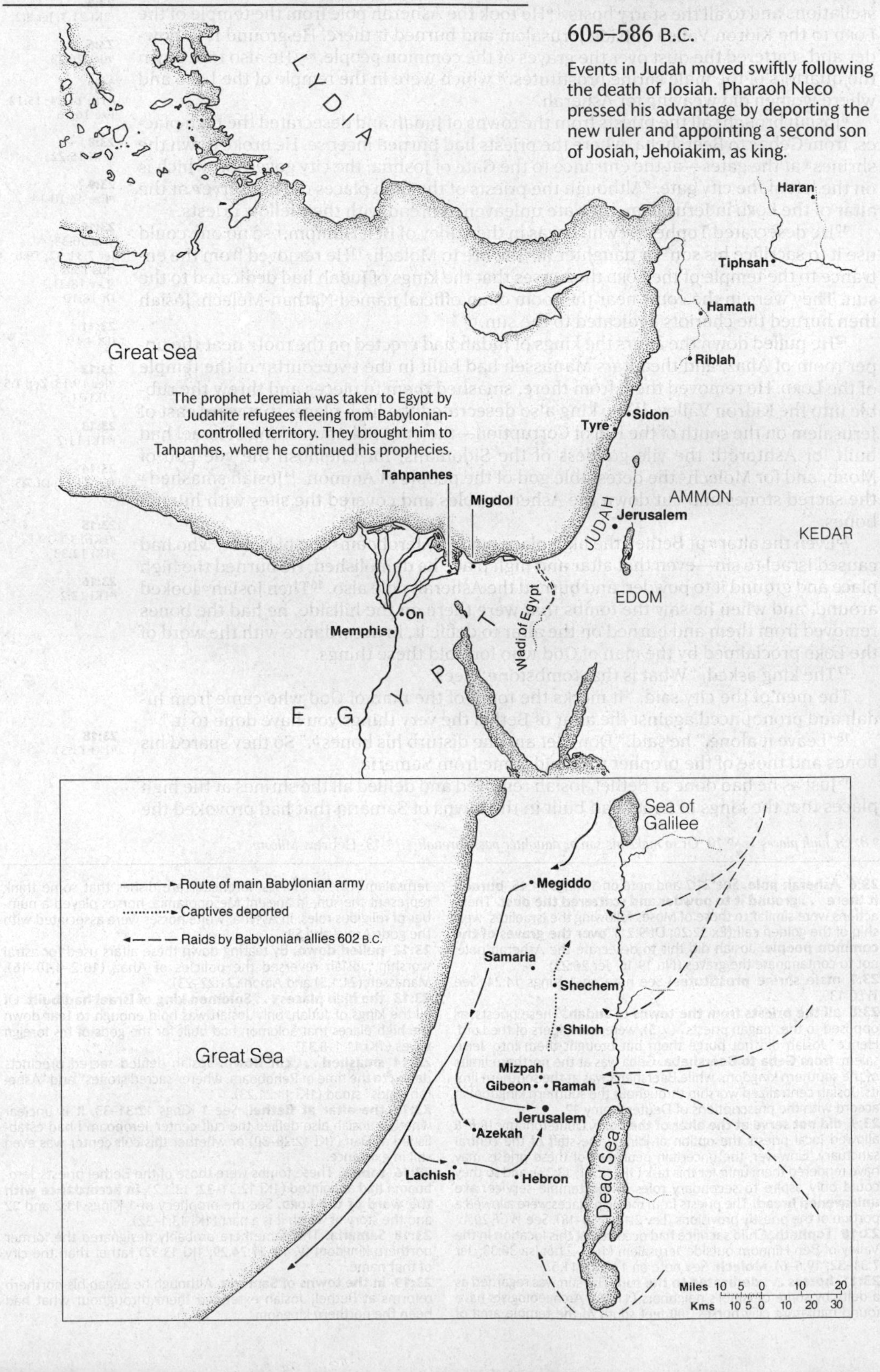

Soon a stronger power appeared in the north in the person of Nebuchadnezzar, king of the Chaldeans (Neo-Babylonians), who determined to follow the fierce policies of his Assyrian predecessors.

The tribute of Jehoiakim was paid at a distance when he heard of Nebuchadnezzar's approach. After three years as a Babylonian vassal, he rebelled, bringing a rapid response in the form of small-scale raids from Babylonians, Arameans, Moabites and Ammonites (c. 602 B.C.). Finally, Nebuchadnezzar's forces controlled all of the coastal territory north of the Wadi of Egypt.

When 18-year-old Jehoiachin had ruled just three months (597 B.C.), the main Babylonian army struck, capturing Jerusalem and exiling the king as a captive in Babylon. Ten thousand persons were deported.

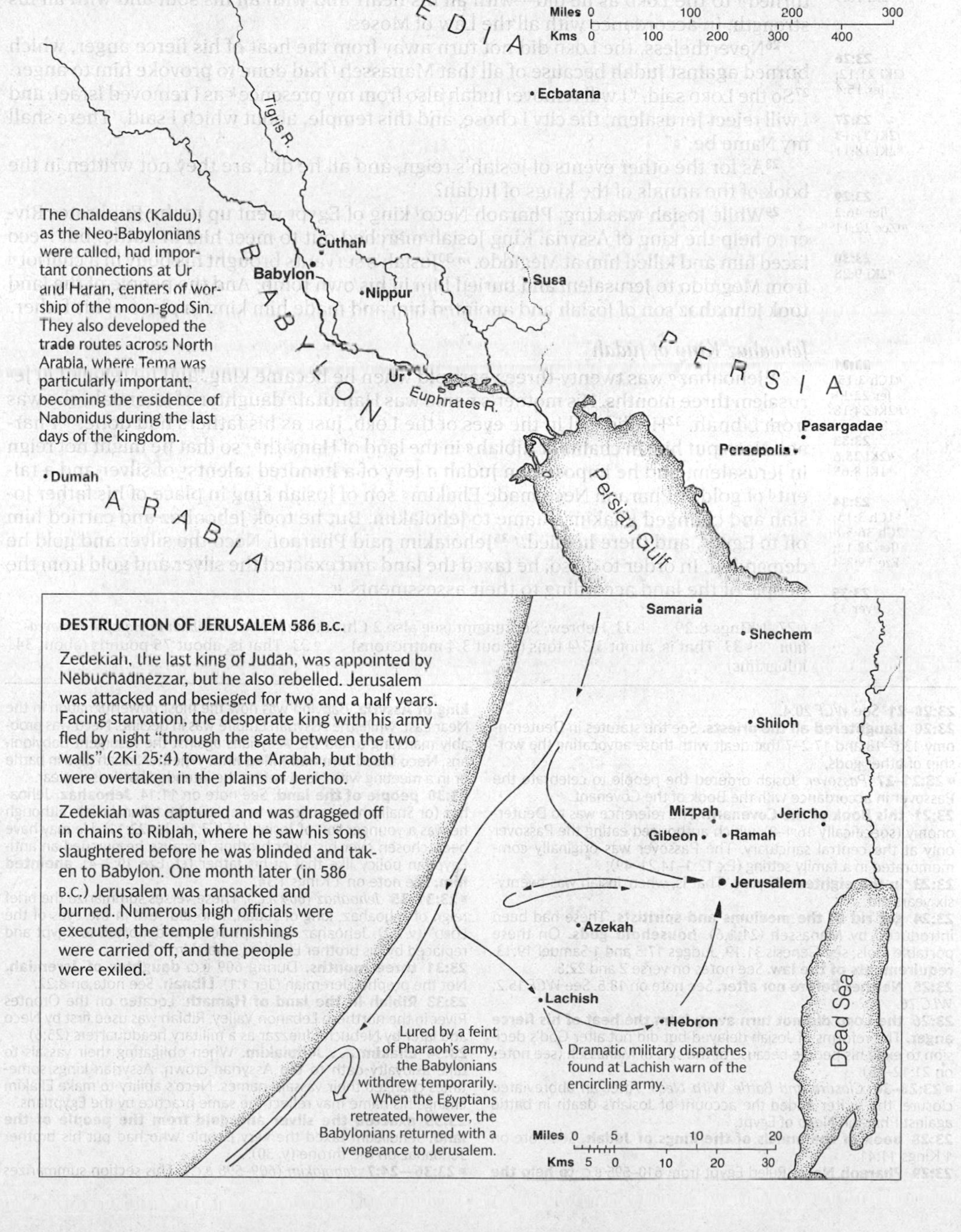

The Chaldeans (Kaldu), as the Neo-Babylonians were called, had important connections at Ur and Haran, centers of worship of the moon-god Sin. They also developed the trade routes across North Arabia, where Tema was particularly important, becoming the residence of Nabonidus during the last days of the kingdom.

DESTRUCTION OF JERUSALEM 586 B.C.

Zedekiah, the last king of Judah, was appointed by Nebuchadnezzar, but he also rebelled. Jerusalem was attacked and besieged for two and a half years. Facing starvation, the desperate king with his army fled by night "through the gate between the two walls" (2Ki 25:4) toward the Arabah, but both were overtaken in the plains of Jericho.

Zedekiah was captured and was dragged off in chains to Riblah, where he saw his sons slaughtered before he was blinded and taken to Babylon. One month later (in 586 B.C.) Jerusalem was ransacked and burned. Numerous high officials were executed, the temple furnishings were carried off, and the people were exiled.

Lured by a feint of Pharaoh's army, the Babylonians withdrew temporarily. When the Egyptians retreated, however, the Babylonians returned with a vengeance to Jerusalem.

Dramatic military dispatches found at Lachish warn of the encircling army.

LORD to anger. [20]Josiah slaughtered[c] all the priests of those high places on the altars and
burned human bones[d] on them. Then he went back to Jerusalem.
[21]The king gave this order to all the people: "Celebrate the Passover[e] to the LORD your
God, as it is written in this Book of the Covenant." [22]Not since the days of the judges who
led Israel, nor throughout the days of the kings of Israel and the kings of Judah, had any
such Passover been observed. [23]But in the eighteenth year of King Josiah, this Passover
was celebrated to the LORD in Jerusalem.
[24]Furthermore, Josiah got rid of the mediums and spiritists,[f] the household gods,[g] the
idols and all the other detestable things seen in Judah and Jerusalem. This he did to fulfill the requirements of the law written in the book that Hilkiah the priest had discovered
in the temple of the LORD. [25]Neither before nor after Josiah was there a king like him who
turned[h] to the LORD as he did—with all his heart and with all his soul and with all his
strength, in accordance with all the Law of Moses.
[26]Nevertheless, the LORD did not turn away from the heat of his fierce anger, which
burned against Judah because of all that Manasseh[i] had done to provoke him to anger.
[27]So the LORD said, "I will remove[j] Judah also from my presence[k] as I removed Israel, and
I will reject Jerusalem, the city I chose, and this temple, about which I said, 'There shall
my Name be.'[a]"
[28]As for the other events of Josiah's reign, and all he did, are they not written in the
book of the annals of the kings of Judah?
[29]While Josiah was king, Pharaoh Neco[l] king of Egypt went up to the Euphrates River to help the king of Assyria. King Josiah marched out to meet him in battle, but Neco
faced him and killed him at Megiddo.[m] [30]Josiah's servants brought his body in a chariot[n]
from Megiddo to Jerusalem and buried him in his own tomb. And the people of the land
took Jehoahaz son of Josiah and anointed him and made him king in place of his father.

Jehoahaz King of Judah

[31]Jehoahaz[o] was twenty-three years old when he became king, and he reigned in Jerusalem three months. His mother's name was Hamutal[p] daughter of Jeremiah; she was
from Libnah. [32]He did evil in the eyes of the LORD, just as his fathers had done. [33]Phar-
aoh Neco put him in chains at Riblah[q] in the land of Hamath[b][r] so that he might not reign
in Jerusalem, and he imposed on Judah a levy of a hundred talents[c] of silver and a talent[d] of gold. [34]Pharaoh Neco made Eliakim[s] son of Josiah king in place of his father Josiah and changed Eliakim's name to Jehoiakim. But he took Jehoahaz and carried him
off to Egypt, and there he died.[t] [35]Jehoiakim paid Pharaoh Neco the silver and gold he
demanded. In order to do so, he taxed the land and exacted the silver and gold from the
people of the land according to their assessments.[u]

23:20 [c]Ex 22:20; 2Ki 10:25; 11:18 [d]1Ki 13:2
23:21 [e]Ex 12:11; Nu 9:2; Dt 16:1-8
23:24 [f]Lev 19:31; Dt 18:11; 2Ki 21:6 [g]Ge 31:19
23:25 [h]2Ki 18:5
23:26 [i]2Ki 21:12; Jer 15:4
23:27 [j]2Ki 21:13 [k]2Ki 18:11
23:29 [l]Jer 46:2 [m]Zec 12:11
23:30 [n]2Ki 9:28
23:31 [o]1Ch 3:15; Jer 22:11 [p]2Ki 24:18
23:33 [q]2Ki 25:6 [r]1Ki 8:65
23:34 [s]1Ch 3:15; 2Ch 36:5-8 [t]Jer 22:12; Eze 19:3-4
23:35 [u]ver 33

[a] *27* 1 Kings 8:29 [b] *33* Hebrew; Septuagint (see also 2 Chron. 36:3) *Neco at Riblah in Hamath removed him* [c] *33* That is, about 3 3/4 tons (about 3.4 metric tons) [d] *33* That is, about 75 pounds (about 34 kilograms)

23:20–21 See *WCF* 20.4.
23:20 slaughtered all the priests. See the statutes in Deuteronomy 13:6–18 and 17:2–7 that dealt with those advocating the worship of other gods.
■ **23:21–27** *Passover.* Josiah ordered the people to celebrate the Passover in accordance with the Book of the Covenant.
23:21 this Book of the Covenant. The reference was to Deuteronomy (specifically 16:1–8), which authorized eating the Passover only at the central sanctuary. The Passover was originally commemorated in a family setting (Ex 12:1–14,21–49).
23:23 in the eighteenth year. That is, when Josiah was twenty-six years old.
23:24 got rid of the mediums and spiritists. These had been introduced by Manasseh (21:1,6). **household gods.** On these portable idols, see Genesis 31:19, Judges 17:5 and 1 Samuel 19:13. **requirements of the law.** See notes on verse 2 and 22:8.
23:25 Neither before nor after. See note on 18:5. See *WCF* 15.2; *WLC* 76.
23:26 the LORD did not turn away from the heat of his fierce anger. The reforms of Josiah delayed but did not alter God's decision to exile his people because of the sins of Manasseh (see notes on 21:12–15).
■ **23:28–30** *Closure and Battle With Neco.* After an abbreviated closure, the writer added the account of Josiah's death in battle against Pharaoh Neco of Egypt.
23:28 book of the annals of the kings of Judah. See note on 1 Kings 11:41.
23:29 Pharaoh Neco. Ruled Egypt from 610–595 B.C. **to help the king of Assyria.** Babylon was now the most powerful nation in the Near East, while the Assyrian Empire was in decline. Neco was probably marching to aid the Assyrians against the resurgent Babylonians. **Neco faced him and killed him.** Whether Josiah died in battle or in a meeting with Neco before the intended battle is unclear.
23:30 people of the land. See note on 11:14. **Jehoahaz.** Jehoahaz (or Shallum) was chosen to replace the fallen Josiah, although he was a younger son of Josiah (1Ch 3:15; Jer 22:11). He may have been chosen over his older brothers because he pursued an anti-Egyptian policy like that of his father (cf. Eze 19:3–4). **anointed him.** See note on 1 Kings 1:34.
■ **23:31–35** *Jehoahaz (609 B.C.).* These verses summarize the brief reign of Jehoahaz, king of Judah, who did "evil in the eyes of the LORD" (v. 32). Jehoahaz was captured and deported to Egypt and replaced by his brother Eliakim (Jehoiakim).
23:31 three months. During 609 B.C. **daughter of Jeremiah.** Not the prophet Jeremiah (Jer 1:1). **Libnah.** See note on 8:22.
23:33 Riblah in the land of Hamath. Located on the Orontes River in the northern Lebanon Valley, Riblah was used first by Neco and later by Nebuchadnezzar as a military headquarters (25:6).
23:34 Eliakim . . . Jehoiakim. When obligating their vassals to take a loyalty oath to the Assyrian crown, Assyrian kings sometimes changed their vassals' names. Neco's ability to make Eliakim change his name may reflect the same practice by the Egyptians.
23:35 exacted the silver and gold from the people of the land. Jehoiakim taxed the very people who had put his brother Jehoahaz on the throne (v. 30).
■ **23:36—24:7** *Jehoiakim (609–598 B.C.).* This section summarizes

Jehoiakim King of Judah

36Jehoiakim[v] was twenty-five years old when he became king, and he reigned in Jerusalem eleven years. His mother's name was Zebidah daughter of Pedaiah; she was
from Rumah. 37And he did evil in the eyes of the LORD, just as his fathers had done.
24 During Jehoiakim's reign, Nebuchadnezzar[w] king of Babylon invaded the land,
and Jehoiakim became his vassal for three years. But then he changed his mind
and rebelled against Nebuchadnezzar. 2The LORD sent Babylonian,[a] Aramean,[x] Moabite and Ammonite raiders against him. He sent them to destroy[y] Judah, in accordance
with the word of the LORD proclaimed by his servants the prophets. 3Surely these things
happened to Judah according to the LORD's command,[z] in order to remove them from his
presence because of the sins of Manasseh[a] and all he had done, 4including the shedding
of innocent blood.[b] For he had filled Jerusalem with innocent blood, and the LORD was
not willing to forgive.
5As for the other events of Jehoiakim's reign, and all he did, are they not written in
the book of the annals of the kings of Judah? 6Jehoiakim rested[c] with his fathers. And Jehoiachin his son succeeded him as king.
7The king of Egypt[d] did not march out from his own country again, because the king
of Babylon[e] had taken all his territory, from the Wadi of Egypt to the Euphrates River.

Jehoiachin King of Judah

8Jehoiachin[f] was eighteen years old when he became king, and he reigned in Jerusalem three months. His mother's name was Nehushta daughter of Elnathan; she was from
Jerusalem. 9He did evil in the eyes of the LORD, just as his father had done.
10At that time the officers of Nebuchadnezzar[g] king of Babylon advanced on Jerusalem and laid siege to it, 11and Nebuchadnezzar himself came up to the city while his officers were besieging it. 12Jehoiachin king of Judah, his mother, his attendants, his nobles and his officials all surrendered[h] to him.
In the eighth year of the reign of the king of Babylon, he took Jehoiachin prisoner. 13As
the LORD had declared,[i] Nebuchadnezzar removed all the treasures[j] from the temple of
the LORD and from the royal palace, and took away all the gold articles[k] that Solomon[l]
king of Israel had made for the temple of the LORD. 14He carried into exile[m] all Jerusalem: all the officers and fighting men, and all the craftsmen and artisans—a total of ten
thousand. Only the poorest[n] people of the land were left.
15Nebuchadnezzar took Jehoiachin captive to Babylon. He also took from Jerusalem
to Babylon the king's mother,[o] his wives, his officials and the leading men[p] of the land.
16The king of Babylon also deported to Babylon the entire force of seven thousand
fighting men, strong and fit for war, and a thousand craftsmen and artisans.[q] 17He made
Mattaniah, Jehoiachin's uncle, king in his place and changed his name to Zedekiah.[r]

[a] 2 Or *Chaldean*

23:36 [v]Jer 26:1
24:1 [w]Jer 25:1,9; Da 1:1
24:2 [x]Jer 35:11 [y]Jer 25:9
24:3 [z]2Ki 18:25 [a]2Ki 21:12; 23:26
24:4 [b]2Ki 21:16
24:6 [c]Jer 22:19
24:7 [d]Ge 15:18 [e]Jer 37:5-7; 46:2
24:8 [f]1Ch 3:16
24:10 [g]Da 1:1
24:12 [h]2Ki 25:27; Jer 22:24-30; 24:1; 25:1; 29:2; 52:28
24:13 [i]2Ki 20:17 [j]2Ki 25:15; Isa 39:6 [k]2Ki 25:14; Jer 20:5 [l]1Ki 7:51
24:14 [m]Jer 24:1; 52:28 [n]2Ki 25:12; Jer 40:7; 52:16
24:15 [o]Jer 22:24-28 [p]Est 2:6; Eze 17:12-14
24:16 [q]Jer 52:28
24:17 [r]1Ch 3:15; 2Ch 36:11; Jer 37:1

---

the reign of Jehoiakim, king of Judah, including his rebellion against the king of Babylon. The narrator made it clear that the disasters befalling Judah at the hands of foreign invaders were in fulfillment of God's word of judgment against Judah for Manasseh's sin (21:10–15; 24:2–4).

23:36 eleven years. That is, from 609–598 B.C. **Rumah.** A town about 14 miles west of the Sea of Kinnereth.

24:1 Nebuchadnezzar. Nebuchadnezzar II, king of Babylon from 605–562 B.C. Because Babylon defeated Neco of Egypt in a major battle at Carchemish (Jer 46:2), Judah was now under Babylonian, and not Egyptian, domination. **invaded the land.** According to Babylonian records, Nebuchadnezzar II subdued the "Hatti land," which included the "city of Judah." **three years.** That is, from 604–602 B.C. **he changed his mind and rebelled.** Ignoring Jeremiah's counsel (Jer 27:9–11), Jehoiakim may have been influenced by Egypt's successful defense of its territory against Nebuchadnezzar in 601 B.C.

24:2 The LORD sent Babylonian, Aramean, Moabite and Ammonite raiders. The reaction was swift against Judah's rebellion. The Arameans, Moabites and Ammonites were probably compelled, as vassals of Babylon, to assist in the invasion of Judah.

24:4 shedding of innocent blood. See note on 21:16. This breach of covenant was so reprehensible that the Lord was no longer "willing to forgive."

24:5 book of the annals of the kings of Judah. See note on 1 Kings 11:41.

24:6 Jehoiachin. Also called "Jeconiah" (see NIV text note on 1Ch 3:16) and "Coniah" (see NIV text note on Jer 22:24). **succeeded him as king.** Jehoiakim died (598 B.C.) before Jerusalem had surrendered to the Babylonians (vv. 8–12).

24:7 Wadi of Egypt. See 1 Kings 8:65.

■ **24:8–17** *Jehoiachin (598–597 B.C.).* Jehoiachin surrendered to the king of Babylon and, along with many others, was deported to Babylon.

24:8 three months. Since Babylonian records date the fall of Jerusalem to March 16, 597 B.C., the reign of Jehoiachin must have begun in December 598.

24:12 eighth year. That is, 597 B.C.

24:13 As the LORD had declared. See 20:17. **all the gold articles that Solomon . . . made for the temple.** See 1 Kings 7:51.

24:14 ten thousand. Jeremiah 52:28 stipulates 3,023 deportees, but that figure may not include women and children. **Only the poorest people of the land.** It was Babylonian policy to remove the upper classes and leadership from captured lands. In this manner, they crippled the economic structure of societies they defeated.

24:15 Nebuchadnezzar took Jehoiachin. Babylonian documents refer to Jehoiachin and five sons (cf. his seven sons in 1Ch 3:17).

24:16 seven thousand fighting men . . . a thousand craftsmen and artisans. The figure in verse 14 may presuppose these numbers.

24:17 Mattaniah. A brother of Jehoiakim (Jehoiachin's father) and a son of Josiah (1Ch 3:15; Jer 1:3). **Zedekiah.** Mattaniah's name was probably changed as an indication of his vassalage to Nebuchadnezzar (see note on 23:34).

Zedekiah King of Judah

18 Zedekiah[s] was twenty-one years old when he became king, and he reigned in Jerusalem eleven years. His mother's name was Hamutal[t] daughter of Jeremiah; she was
from Libnah. 19 He did evil in the eyes of the LORD, just as Jehoiakim had done. 20 It was
because of the LORD's anger that all this happened to Jerusalem and Judah, and in the
end he thrust[u] them from his presence.

The Fall of Jerusalem

Now Zedekiah rebelled against the king of Babylon.

25 So in the ninth year of Zedekiah's reign, on the tenth day of the tenth month,
Nebuchadnezzar[v] king of Babylon marched against Jerusalem with his whole
army. He encamped outside the city and built siege works[w] all around it. 2 The city was
kept under siege until the eleventh year of King Zedekiah. 3 By the ninth day of the
⌞fourth⌟[a] month the famine[x] in the city had become so severe that there was no food for
the people to eat. 4 Then the city wall was broken through,[y] and the whole army fled at
night through the gate between the two walls near the king's garden, though the Babylonians[b] were surrounding[z] the city. They fled toward the Arabah,[c] 5 but the Babylonian[d] army pursued the king and overtook him in the plains of Jericho. All his soldiers were
separated from him and scattered,[a] 6 and he was captured.[b] He was taken to the king of
Babylon at Riblah,[c] where sentence was pronounced on him. 7 They killed the sons of
Zedekiah before his eyes. Then they put out his eyes, bound him with bronze shackles
and took him to Babylon.[d]

8 On the seventh day of the fifth month, in the nineteenth year of Nebuchadnezzar
king of Babylon, Nebuzaradan commander of the imperial guard, an official of the king
of Babylon, came to Jerusalem. 9 He set fire[e] to the temple of the LORD, the royal palace
and all the houses of Jerusalem. Every important building he burned down.[f] 10 The
whole Babylonian army, under the commander of the imperial guard, broke down the
walls[g] around Jerusalem. 11 Nebuzaradan the commander of the guard carried into exile[h] the people who remained in the city, along with the rest of the populace and those
who had gone over to the king of Babylon.[i] 12 But the commander left behind some of the
poorest people[j] of the land to work the vineyards and fields.

13 The Babylonians broke up the bronze pillars, the movable stands and the bronze
Sea that were at the temple of the LORD and they carried the bronze to Babylon. 14 They
also took away the pots, shovels, wick trimmers, dishes and all the bronze articles[k] used

a 3 See Jer. 52:6. b 4 Or *Chaldeans*; also in verses 13, 25 and 26 c 4 Or *the Jordan Valley*
d 5 Or *Chaldean*; also in verses 10 and 24

24:18 [s]Jer 52:1 [t]2Ki 23:31
24:20 [u]Dt 4:26; 29:27
25:1 [v]Jer 34:1-7 [w]Eze 24:2
25:3 [x]Jer 14:18; La 4:9
25:4 [y]Eze 33:21 [z]Jer 4:17
25:5 [a]Eze 12:14
25:6 [b]Jer 34:21-22 [c]2Ki 23:33
25:7 [d]Jer 21:7; 32:4-5; Eze 12:11
25:9 [e]Isa 60:7 [f]Ps 74:3-8; Jer 2:15; Am 2:5; Mic 3:12
25:10 [g]Ne 1:3
25:11 [h]2Ki 24:14 [i]2Ki 24:1
25:12 [j]2Ki 24:14
25:14 [k]Ex 27:3; 1Ki 7:47-50

■ **24:18–20a** *Zedekiah (597–586 B.C.).* These verses summarize the reign of Zedekiah, the last king of Judah. The narrator again emphasized that the disasters befalling Judah and Jerusalem were divine judgments for sin (v. 20a). See Jeremiah 52:1–27.

24:18 eleven years. That is, from 597–586 B.C. **Jeremiah.** Not the prophet. **Libnah.** See note on 8:22.

24:19 just as Jehoiakim had done. See 23:36–37. The Biblical writer did not detail all of the evil that Zedekiah committed during his 11-year tenure. God's judgment had already been decreed, and Judah was quickly sliding into oblivion (20:17–18; 21:12–15; 22:16–17). Further information on Zedekiah's reign can be found in Jeremiah 21, 24, 27, 29, 32 and 37–39 and in Ezekiel 17:11–21.

■ **24:20b—25:30** *The Exile of Judah.* The writer described Jerusalem's destruction (24:20b—25:21), the assassination of Gedaliah (25:22–26) and the release of Jehoiachin (25:27–30). The severity of God's judgment was balanced by the hope stirred by Jehoiachin's release from prison in Babylon.

■ **24:20b—25:21** *Jerusalem's Destruction.* Zedekiah's rebellion against the king of Babylon provoked an attack by the Babylonians, which resulted in the destruction of Jerusalem (including the temple) and the deportation of Zedekiah and most of the people of Judah. The events narrated here took place in 586 B.C.

24:20b Zedekiah rebelled against the king of Babylon. In spite of being a vassal appointed by Nebuchadnezzar, Zedekiah plotted with Egypt and other nations against the Babylonians (Jer 27:3–8; Eze 17:11–21). Zedekiah's ill-fated decision to rebel against Babylon may have been encouraged by Pharaoh Hophra (Apries), who came to power in 589 B.C.

25:1 in the ninth year. That is, in January 588 B.C.

25:2 until the eleventh year. That is, July 586 B.C. (Jer 39:2; 52:5). Following a different dating system, some scholars place this event in 587 B.C.

25:3 famine. During the siege, Jerusalem experienced terrible privation (Jer 38:2a; La 4:10).

25:4 gate between the two walls. A gate located in the southwest wall of the City of David and perhaps identical to the Fountain Gate (Ne 2:14; 3:15; 12:37).

25:6 the king of Babylon at Riblah. See note on 23:33.

25:7 they put out his eyes. Blinding was a common punishment for rebellious slaves in the ancient Near East. **took him to Babylon.** Zedekiah had ignored the counsel of both Jeremiah (Jer 38:14–28) and Ezekiel (Eze 12:13). Jeremiah had urged the king to surrender to Babylon because the Lord's judgment was inevitable. Through a peaceful surrender Jerusalem would most likely have been spared destruction. Zedekiah's stubborn resistance brought about only horrific results for both his family and his people. Zedekiah died in Babylon (Jer 52:11).

25:8 On the seventh day. That is, during August 586 B.C.

25:9 Every important building. The massive carnage and destruction was deliberate. Nebuchadnezzar had no intention of reconstituting Judah around a Babylonian provincial center in Jerusalem. Nor did he, unlike the Assyrians in dealing with Israel (17:24–31; Ezr 4:2), import new settlers from other areas to replace the dead and exiled. Judah was depopulated.

25:10 broke down the walls. Walls were a city's defense against any potential enemy. By breaking down Jerusalem's walls, the Babylonians ensured that the city would not rebel again.

25:11 carried into exile. The Babylonians implemented a second deportation (24:10–17), leaving only the poorest to till the land (v. 12). **those who had gone over to the king of Babylon.** Apparently some Judahites threw their allegiance behind the Babylonians, even before the final siege. The Babylonians took these people with them to Babylon, either as a reward or for their own safety.

25:13 bronze pillars. See 1 Kings 7:15–22. **movable stands.** See 1 Kings 7:27–39. **bronze Sea.** See 1 Kings 7:23–26.

25:14 pots, shovels, wick trimmers. See 1 Kings 7:40, 45 and 50.

in the temple service. 15The commander of the imperial guard took away the censers and
sprinkling bowls—all that were made of pure gold or silver.
16The bronze from the two pillars, the Sea and the movable stands, which Solomon
had made for the temple of the LORD, was more than could be weighed. 17Each pillar[l] was
twenty-seven feet[a] high. The bronze capital on top of one pillar was four and a half feet[b]
high and was decorated with a network and pomegranates of bronze all around. The other pillar, with its network, was similar.
18The commander of the guard took as prisoners Seraiah[m] the chief priest, Zephaniah[n] the priest next in rank and the three doorkeepers. 19Of those still in the city, he took
the officer in charge of the fighting men and five royal advisers. He also took the secretary who was chief officer in charge of conscripting the people of the land and sixty of
his men who were found in the city. 20Nebuzaradan the commander took them all and
brought them to the king of Babylon at Riblah. 21There at Riblah, in the land of Hamath,
the king had them executed.
So Judah went into captivity, away from her land.[o]
22Nebuchadnezzar king of Babylon appointed Gedaliah[p] son of Ahikam, the son of
Shaphan, to be over the people he had left behind in Judah. 23When all the army officers

25:17 [l]1Ki 7:15-22

25:18 [m]1Ch 6:14; Ezr 7:1; Ne 11:11 [n]Jer 21:1; 29:25

25:21 [o]Ge 12:7; Dt 28:64; Jos 23:13; 2Ki 23:27

25:22 [p]Jer 39:14; 40:5,7

[a] 17 Hebrew *eighteen cubits* (about 8.1 meters) [b] 17 Hebrew *three cubits* (about 1.3 meters)

25:15 censers and sprinkling bowls. See 24:13, 1 Kings 7:50, Jeremiah 15:13, 20:5 and 27:16–22.
25:17 Each pillar. See 1 Kings 7:15–22.
25:18 Seraiah the chief priest. The grandson of Hilkiah (22:4,8; 1Ch 6:13–14) and the ancestor of Ezra (Ezr 7:1).
25:21 Riblah. See note on 23:33. **had them executed.** The Babylonian forces ruthlessly eliminated all of the remaining leaders of high rank, only some of whom were military personnel. **into captivity, away from her land.** Of all the covenant curses, exile was the most severe (Lev 26:33; Dt 28:36).
■ **25:22–26** *The Assassination of Gedaliah.* The king of Babylon appointed Gedaliah as governor in Judah, but Gedaliah was assassinated.
25:22 Gedaliah. Having abolished the monarchy, Nebuchadnezzar appointed Gedaliah as governor. Gedaliah's father, Ahikam, was a friend of Jeremiah (Jer 26:24). Nebuchadnezzar chose a

Exile of the Southern Kingdom

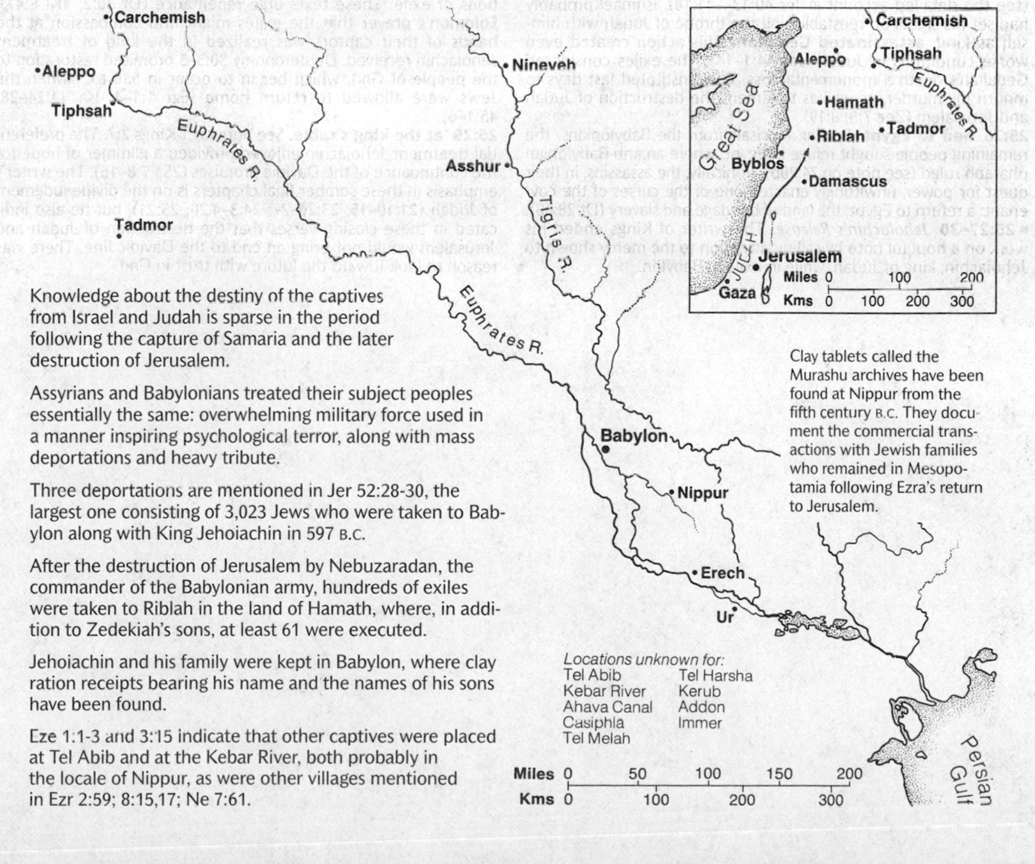

Knowledge about the destiny of the captives from Israel and Judah is sparse in the period following the capture of Samaria and the later destruction of Jerusalem.

Assyrians and Babylonians treated their subject peoples essentially the same: overwhelming military force used in a manner inspiring psychological terror, along with mass deportations and heavy tribute.

Three deportations are mentioned in Jer 52:28-30, the largest one consisting of 3,023 Jews who were taken to Babylon along with King Jehoiachin in 597 B.C.

After the destruction of Jerusalem by Nebuzaradan, the commander of the Babylonian army, hundreds of exiles were taken to Riblah in the land of Hamath, where, in addition to Zedekiah's sons, at least 61 were executed.

Jehoiachin and his family were kept in Babylon, where clay ration receipts bearing his name and the names of his sons have been found.

Eze 1:1-3 and 3:15 indicate that other captives were placed at Tel Abib and at the Kebar River, both probably in the locale of Nippur, as were other villages mentioned in Ezr 2:59; 8:15,17; Ne 7:61.

Clay tablets called the Murashu archives have been found at Nippur from the fifth century B.C. They document the commercial transactions with Jewish families who remained in Mesopotamia following Ezra's return to Jerusalem.

Locations unknown for:
Tel Abib, Kebar River, Ahava Canal, Casiphla, Tel Melah, Tel Harsha, Kerub, Addon, Immer

and their men heard that the king of Babylon had appointed Gedaliah as governor, they
came to Gedaliah at Mizpah—Ishmael son of Nethaniah, Johanan son of Kareah, Seraiah son of Tanhumeth the Netophathite, Jaazaniah the son of the Maacathite, and their
men. 24Gedaliah took an oath to reassure them and their men. "Do not be afraid of the
Babylonian officials," he said. "Settle down in the land and serve the king of Babylon,
and it will go well with you."

25In the seventh month, however, Ishmael son of Nethaniah, the son of Elishama,
who was of royal blood, came with ten men and assassinated Gedaliah and also the men
of Judah and the Babylonians who were with him at Mizpah. 26At this, all the people from
the least to the greatest, together with the army officers, fled to Egypt[q] for fear of the Babylonians.

25:26 [q]Isa 30:2; Jer 43:7
25:27 [r]2Ki 24:12; Jer 52:31-34
25:28 [s]Ezr 5:5; Ne 2:1; Da 2:48
25:29 [t]2Sa 9:7
25:30 [u]Est 2:9; Jer 28:4

Jehoiachin Released

27In the thirty-seventh year of the exile of Jehoiachin king of Judah, in the year Evil-
Merodach[a] became king of Babylon, he released Jehoiachin[r] from prison on the twenty-seventh day of the twelfth month. 28He spoke kindly to him and gave him a seat of
honor[s] higher than those of the other kings who were with him in Babylon. 29So Jehoiachin put aside his prison clothes and for the rest of his life ate regularly at the king's
table.[t] 30Day by day the king gave Jehoiachin a regular allowance as long as he lived.[u]

[a] *27* Also called *Amel-Marduk*

well-known native of Judah as governor in order to bring stability to the land (Jer 40:10–12). **Ahikam.** Gedaliah's father had been a close advisor to Josiah (22:12).

25:23 Mizpah. Located about eight miles north of Jerusalem, Mizpah became the base for Gedaliah's operations (Jer 40:1–6).

25:24 oath. See note on 1 Kings 1:17.

25:25 seventh month. That is, October 586 B.C. **Ishmael . . . who was of royal blood.** Ishmael's grandfather, Elishama, was royal secretary under Jehoiakim (Jer 36:12; 41:1). Ishmael was part of a faction in Judah that viewed Gedaliah as a collaborator with the enemy and favored continuing resistance to the Babylonians (see the detailed account in Jer 40:13—41:18). Ishmael probably had set his sights on reestablishing the throne of Judah with himself as king. **assassinated Gedaliah.** This action created even worse conditions in Judah (Jer 44:1–14). The exiles considered Gedaliah's death a monumental loss. They instituted fast days to mourn his murder, as well as to lament the destruction of Judah and Jerusalem (Zec 7:5; 8:19).

25:26 fled to Egypt. Fearing reprisals from the Babylonians, the remaining people sought refuge in Egypt, where an anti-Babylonian pharaoh ruled (see note on 24:20b). Ironically, the assassins, in their quest for power, unwittingly enacted one of the curses of the covenant: a return to Egypt, the land of bondage and slavery (Dt 28:68).

■ **25:27–30** *Jehoiachin's Release.* The writer of Kings ended his work on a hopeful note by calling attention to the mercy shown to Jehoiachin, king of Judah, while in exile in Babylon.

25:27 In the thirty-seventh year. That is, in March 561 B.C. **in the year Evil-Merodach became king.** Evil-Merodach was the son and successor of Nebuchadnezzar. Scholars disagree as to whether Evil-Merodach became king in 562 or 561 B.C. (see note on 24:1). **released Jehoiachin from prison.** Administrative texts from Babylonia mention payments of rations in oil and barley, to, among others, Yaukin (Jehoiachin), king of Iahudu (Judah), and five of his sons. Evil-Merodach may have initiated this act of mercy on the occasion of his accession.

25:28 a seat of honor. Deuteronomy 4:25–31, 30:1–10 and King Solomon's temple prayer in 1 Kings 8:46–53 all address the conditions of exile. These texts urge repentance (Dt 30:2; 1Ki 8:47). Solomon's prayer that the exiles might find compassion at the hands of their captors was realized in the kind of treatment Jehoiachin received. Deuteronomy 30:3–5 promised restoration to the people of God, which began to occur in 538 B.C., when the Jews were allowed to return home (Ezr 1:1–4; Isa 44:24–28; 45:1–6).

25:29 at the king's table. See note on 1 Kings 2:7. The preferential treatment Jehoiachin enjoyed provided a glimmer of hope for the continuance of the Davidic promises (2Sa 7:8–16). The writer's emphasis in these somber final chapters is on the divine judgment of Judah (21:10–15; 23:26–27; 24:3–4,20; 25:21), but he also indicated in these closing verses that the destruction of Judah and Jerusalem would not bring an end to the Davidic line. There was reason to look toward the future with trust in God.

1 CHRONICLES

Introduction

Overview

Author: Unknown

Purpose: To direct the restoration of the kingdom after the exile, with special emphases on the unity of Israel, the king, the temple and immediate blessings and curses

Date: c. 520–400 B.C.

Key Truths:

- The united kingdoms of David and Solomon provide models for God's people as they seek the blessings of God.
- The fate of each generation of Israel was determined by its adherence to God's ideals for kingship, the temple and the unity of God's people.
- Future generations of God's people must learn from Israel's history the priorities and patterns of faithfulness expected of them.

Author

Jewish tradition considered Ezra the primary author of the books of Chronicles (First and Second Chronicles are two halves of one book), Ezra and Nehemiah. At least two considerations suggest that he was the author of Chronicles: (1) The book was written during the postexilic period around the time of Ezra's ministry (see "Time and Place of Writing"). (2) Many passages in Chronicles reveal affinities with the priestly concerns that undergirded Ezra's work (see "Purposes and Distinctives").

Other considerations, however, cast doubt on this traditional view of authorship: (1) The date of composition for Chronicles cannot be limited to Ezra's lifetime (see "Time and Place of Writing"). (2) The Chronicler's focus on kingship (see "Purposes and Distinctives") is absent from Ezra's teaching. (3) Ezra's concern with apostasy due to intermarriage is not a prominent theme in Chronicles (2Ch 1:1—9:31 note).

The traditional viewpoint remains hypothetical. No doubt Ezra's ministry was in harmony with the teachings of Chronicles. He may even have contributed in some way to the composition of the book. Still, neither historical nor Scriptural evidences indicate conclusively that Ezra was the author of Chronicles. As a result, most modern interpreters simply refer to the author as "the Chronicler."

The Chronicler relied on many written sources as he composed his history. (1) He depended on a number of Biblical texts, drawing heavily from Samuel and Kings and following portions of the Pentateuch, Judges, Ruth, Psalms, Isaiah, Jeremiah and Zechariah. (2) He cited several otherwise unknown royal sources: "the book of the annals of King David" (27:24), "the book of the kings" (2Ch 24:27), "the book of the kings of Israel" (9:1; 2Ch 20:34), "the book of the kings of Judah and Israel" (2Ch 16:11; 25:26; 28:26; 32:32) and "the book of the kings of Israel and Judah" (2Ch 27:7; 35:27; 36:8). (3) He referred explicitly to a number of prophetic sources: the writings of Samuel (29:29), Nathan (2Ch 9:29), Gad (29:29), Ahijah (2Ch 9:29), Iddo (2Ch 9:29; 12:15; 13:22), Shemaiah (2Ch 12:15), Isaiah (2Ch 26:22) and anonymous "seers" (2Ch 33:19). (4) The style and content of many passages also suggest that the Chronicler used other, unspecified sources.

Time and Place of Writing

The final verses of 2 Chronicles (2Ch 36:21–23) indicate that the Chronicler wrote after the release of the exiles from Babylon (c. 538 B.C.). The lack of Hellenistic influences suggests that he composed his history before the Alexandrian period (c. 331 B.C.). Nevertheless, opinions vary over the precise date of composition.

Some interpreters have proposed that the Chronicler wrote as early as the reconstruction of the temple under Zerubbabel (c. 520–515 B.C.). At least three evidences support this view. (1) The Chronicler consistently presented the temple and its personnel in close partnership with the royal line of David (see "Purposes and Distinctives"). This emphasis suggests the possibility of composition near the days of Zerubbabel, when expectations of royal and priestly partnership were still high (e.g., Zec 4:1–14). (2) The Chronicler devoted much attention to the details of priestly and Levitical duties (see 6:1–53 note). This focus suggests a date of composition during the time when the new temple order was being established. (3) The Chronicler's omission of mention of Solomon's downfall due to intermarriage (1Ki 11:1–40) stands in striking contrast to Nehemiah's appeal to Solomon's difficulties (Ne 13:26). This omission suggests that the Chronicler may have written before intermarriage had become a major issue in the postexilic community.

The majority of interpreters have held that the Chronicler wrote during or after the ministries of Ezra and Nehemiah, in the latter half of the fifth century or the early decades of the fourth century B.C. The main evidence in favor of this view is the royal genealogy in 3:17–24, which some interpreters believe extends up to five generations after Zerubbabel—but see the note on 3:21.

A specific date of composition for Chronicles cannot be determined. It seems best to accept a range of possibilities from sometime near the days of Zerubbabel to sometime soon after the ministries of Ezra and Nehemiah (c. 515–400 B.C.). The major themes of the book fit well within these boundaries.

The Chronicler wrote for historical and theological reasons. His extensive use of historical documents (see "Author") and devotion to numerical and chronological details (e.g., 5:18; 2Ch 14:1,9; 16:1,12,13) indicate that he intended to give his readers an inerrant historical record. But he did not merely offer information about the past; he also wrote to convey a relevant theological message. Comparing the Chronicler's history with those of Samuel and Kings reveals that he shaped his account of Israel's past to address the needs of the postexilic community. He wrote to encourage and guide his readers as they sought the full restoration of the kingdom after the Babylonian exile.

The returnees from exile faced numerous difficulties. The restoration had not brought about the dramatic changes for which many had hoped. Instead, they endured discouraging economic hardship, foreign opposition and internal conflict. These difficulties raised many questions: Who may legitimately claim to be heirs to the promises God gave his people? What political and religious institutions should we embrace? Should we hope for a new Davidic king? What is the importance of the temple in our day? How may we find the blessings of security and prosperity for our restored community? The Chronicler addressed these and similar questions in his history.

Purposes and Distinctives

The book of Chronicles was originally untitled. Its traditional Hebrew name may be translated "the annals (events) of the days (time)." This expression appears often in the book of Kings with other qualifications (e.g., 1Ki 14:29). It also occurs elsewhere in this form without further qualification (Ne 12:23; Est 2:23; 6:1). Some Septuagint (Greek Translation of the OT) texts refer to Chronicles as "the things omitted"; i.e., a supplement to the history of Samuel and Kings. Jerome (and Luther following him) called the book "the chronicle of the entire sacred history." Our modern title stems from this tradition.

The Chronicler's theological message may be summarized in many ways, but three concerns were particularly prominent:

1. *The People of God.* Throughout his history the Chronicler identified the people who should be included among the heirs of God's covenant promises. The prominence of this theme appears in his frequent use of the expression "all Israel" (see notes on 11:1; 2Ch 10:1; 29:24). The Chronicler's concept of God's people was both narrow and broad. On the one hand, he looked on those who had been released from exile as the people of God. Representatives of Judah, Benjamin, Ephraim and Manasseh, who had returned to the land, were the chosen people (see note on 9:3). As such, they played a vital role in the restoration of the kingdom of Israel. On the other hand, however, the Chronicler identified God's people with all the tribes of Israel (see note on 2:3—9:1a). The restoration of Israel was incomplete so long as some of the tribes remained outside the land, separated from the Davidic king and the Jerusalem temple. As a result, the Chronicler went to great lengths to include both the northern and southern tribes in his genealogies (2:3—9:1a), to present an ideal of a united kingdom under David and Solomon extending to all the people (see note on 11:1) and to depict the reunification of the northern and southern kingdoms in the days of Hezekiah (see note on 2Ch 29:1—36:23). The returnees were the remnant of God's people, but they had to pray and hope for the restoration of all the people of God. As Hezekiah put it in his day, "If you return to the LORD, then your brothers and your children will be shown compassion by their captors and will come back to this land, for the LORD your God is gracious and compassionate" (2Ch 30:9).

2. *The King and Temple.* In the Chronicler's view, God had organized his people around two central institutions: the Davidic throne and the Jerusalem temple. These political and religious structures were fundamental to the life of Israel. In his genealogies, the Chronicler gave special attention to David's lineage (2:10–17; 3:1–24) and to the organization of the priests and Levites (6:1–81). He emphasized that God had chosen David's line as the permanent dynasty over the nation (ch. 17; 2Ch 13:5; 21:7; 23:3). The establishment of David's throne was a demonstration of divine love and blessing for Israel (14:2; 2Ch 2:11). The Chronicler also focused on the temple as the dwelling place of the Name (2Ch 7:12,16; 33:7). The joy and splendor of music in temple worship were chief concerns in the Chronicler's history. See notes on 6:31–47, 9:15–16 and 28–34, 15:16–24, 16:4–6, 25:1–31, 2 Chronicles 5:12–13, 7:6, 23:13 and 19, 29:25–30 and 34:12. The Chronicler drew a close connection between kingship and the temple in many other ways as well (e.g., 2Ch 13:4–12; 22:10—24:27). With this emphasis on king and temple, he instructed his postexilic readers not to lose sight of either institution. The full restoration of the kingdom could not take place apart from the Davidic king and the Jerusalem temple. As the Lord said to David, "I will raise up your offspring to succeed you, one of your own sons, and I will establish his kingdom. He is the one who will build a house for me, and I will establish his throne forever" (17:11–12).

3. *Divine Blessing and Judgment.* The Chronicler composed his history to show his readers how to receive God's blessings in their day. He accomplished this end by drawing close connections between fidelity and blessing, as well as infidelity and judgment (28:9; 2Ch 6:14; 7:11–22; 15:2; 16:7–9; 21:14–15; 24:20; 25:15–16; 28:9; 34:24–28). The king and the temple could not in themselves secure God's blessing for Israel. His blessings depended on obedience to the Mosaic Law (6:49; 15:13,15; 16:40; 22:12–13; 28:7; 29:19; 2Ch 6:16; 7:17–18; 12:1–2; 14:4; 15:12–14; 17:3–9; 19:8–10; 24:6,9; 25:4; 30:15–16; 31:3–21; 33:8; 34:19–33; 35:6–26) and to the prophetic/priestly instruction (2Ch 11:4; 12:5–8; 20:20; 21:12–19; 24:19–25; 25:7–10,15–20; 26:17–20). Blessings came to those who upheld the purity of temple worship (2Ch 15:1–19; 17:1–6; 24:1–16; 29:1—31:21; 34:1—35:19) and humbly relied on God instead of on human strength (5:20; 2Ch 13:18; 14:7; 16:7–8; 32:20). When the people of God and their kings turned to sin, the immediate retribution of illness and military defeat often followed (10:1–14; 2Ch 13:1–16; 16:12; 18:33–34; 21:15–19; 25:14–24; 26:19–20; 28:1–5; 33:1–11). Even so, when the people

came under God's judgment, they could be restored to blessing by humbly seeking God through repentance and prayer (21:1—22:1; 2Ch 7:13–15; 12:1–12; 33:10–13). By emphasizing these themes the Chronicler showed his postexilic readers the way to divine blessing in their day. The full restoration of God's people would come only as they lived in fidelity to the Lord. The prophet Azariah stated the matter succinctly to King Asa: "If you seek him, he will be found by you, but if you forsake him, he will forsake you" (2Ch 15:2).

As the book unfolds, prominent motifs appear a number of times, but certain themes are emphasized over others in each portion. The history divides into main parts: the genealogies of God's people (1:1—9:34), the united kingdom (9:35—2Ch 9:31), the divided kingdom (2Ch 10:1—28:27) and the reunited kingdom (2Ch 29:1—36:23). Each part contributes specific elements to the Chronicler's overall theological purpose.

The Genealogies of God's People (1:1—9:34). Genealogies in the ancient Near East followed a variety of forms and served many different functions. These variations appear in the Chronicler's use of genealogies in the first nine chapters of his history. Some passages follow the form of linear genealogies that trace a single family line through many generations (e.g., 2:34–41); others are segmented and sketch several family lines together (e.g., 6:1–3). The Chronicler's genealogies also skip generations without notice, emphasizing persons and events that were important to his concerns (e.g., 6:4–15). Beyond this, just as other ancient genealogies often included brief narratives highlighting significant events, the Chronicler paused on occasion to tell a story (4:9–10; 5:18–22).

In addition to different forms, the function of ancient genealogies varied. They occasionally sketched political, geographical and other social connections. In some such cases, the expressions "son of" and "father of" had a meaning other than immediate biological descent. In line with these ancient (yet ordinary for that time) functions of genealogies, the Chronicler provided an assortment of lists, including families (e.g., 3:17–24), political relations (e.g., 2:24,42,45,49–52) and trade guilds (e.g., 4:14,21–23).

The Chronicler included extensive genealogical records in his book to establish that his readers were the legitimate continuation of God's elect people. He accomplished this end by reporting the special election of Israel from all of humanity (1:2—2:2), the arrangement of the tribes of Israel (2:3—9:1a) and the representatives of the tribes who returned from Babylon (9:16–34).

By identifying the postexilic readers as the continuation of the chosen line, the Chronicler pointed to their opportunities and responsibilities. Since they were God's people, they were offered the opportunity of God's blessing in the promised land. They had a solid basis for hope in the full restoration of the kingdom. But their identity as God's elect people also entailed many responsibilities. The Chronicler's genealogies focused on the breadth and order of the tribes of Israel, emphasizing especially the importance of the Davidic and Levitical families (see note on 2:3—9:1a). If his readers were to receive the blessings of God, they had to observe these divinely ordained arrangements carefully.

The United Kingdom (9:35—2Ch 9:31). The Chronicler viewed the reigns of David and Solomon as Israel's period of glory. He focused on the positive qualities of these kings and chose not to reference many of their well-known shortcomings and troubles recorded in Samuel and Kings (see notes on 9:35—29:30 and 2Ch 1:1—9:31). David and Solomon ruled over all the tribes and territories of Israel (see note on 11:1), and they provided rich blessings through their political structures (14:2; 2Ch 2:11; 9:8) and the temple (22:1; 2Ch 7:11–22).

For this reason, the united kingdom laid the foundation of hope for the postexilic readers. God had chosen David's line and the temple in Jerusalem to be the instruments of blessing for his people through all generations.

But this hope of blessing was conditional. The Chronicler also presented David and Solomon as models to be imitated. The postexilic community had to devote itself to the ideals of the united kingdom. Humble and faithful reliance on God, commitment to Davidic rule and devotion to the temple were essential to receiving the blessing of God.

The Divided Kingdom (2Ch 10:1—28:27). The Chronicler's record of Israel's history from Rehoboam to Ahaz focuses on events in the southern kingdom, Judah. Although he relied on the book of Kings for much of his information, the Chronicler omitted large blocks of material dealing with the northern kingdom, Israel. In his view, the important historical events of this period took place in Judah, where the Davidic king and the temple resided.

In many respects, the Chronicler evaluated the kings of this period according to the ideal of the united kingdom. He applied several criteria to Judah's kings (see "Purposes and Distinctives: *Divine Blessing and Judgment*"). Was the king faithful to the Law of Moses? Did he support the temple order established by David and by Solomon? Did the king listen to prophetic and priestly instruction? Did he rely on foreign alliances, or seek God in humility and prayer? The writer evaluated some kings negatively (Jehoram [21:4–20]; Ahaziah [22:1–9]; Ahaz [28:1–27]) and others positively (Abijah [13:1—14:1]; Jotham [27:1–9]). For the most part, however, he distinguished between each king's years of fidelity and infidelity (Rehoboam [2Ch 10:1—12:16]; Asa [14:2—16:14]; Jehoshaphat [17:1—21:3]; Joash [22:10—24:27]; Amaziah [25:1–28]; Uzziah [26:1–23]).

The Chronicler reported these events to illustrate how the conditions of Israel depended on her fidelity to the ideals established in the united kingdom. With remarkable regularity, he demonstrated that God blessed his people when they proved faithful and chastised them when they turned away from him. Victory, security and prosperity came to those who sought the Lord, but defeat, trouble and illness to those who forgot him (see "Purposes and Distinctives: *Divine Blessing and Judgment*").

This portion of the Chronicler's history addressed the needs of the postexilic readers by explaining their situation and offering them guidance. Just as Judah's kings had experienced God's chastisement, the postexilic community suffered difficulties because of infidelity. God's promises of restoration had not failed; the people had failed. Similarly, just as the kings of Judah were blessed as they turned toward the Lord, the Chronicler's readers could hope for restoration, security and prosperity if they would do the same.

The Reunited Kingdom (2Ch 29:1—36:23). Beginning with Hezekiah, Israel entered a new phase of her history. The Chronicler presented Hezekiah as a new David/Solomon; Hezekiah reunited the faithful of Israel and Judah around the Davidic throne through worship and celebration at the temple (see notes on 29:1—36:23 and 29:24). This reunited people experienced several periods of failure: Manasseh's apostasy (33:1–10), Amon's entire reign (33:21–25) and the overall reigns of the kings of Judah just before the exile (36:2–14). But each of these failures was followed by God's gracious renewal of the people: Manasseh's restoration (33:11–17), Josiah's reforms (34:3—35:19) and the return from exile (36:22–23).

This portion of the Chronicler's history also offered hope and guidance to his readers. Despite the failures of the reunited kingdom, God continued to grant blessings to his repentant people. These events reminded the readers that God extended his mercy to them, offering them his blessing. At the same time, however, the events of this period demonstrated the requirements placed on those who longed for the full restoration of the kingdom during the postexilic period. The nation must turn to the Lord in humility and live faithfully before him.

Christ in Chronicles

Focusing on his concerns for the people of God, for the king and for the temple, as well as on divine blessing and judgment, the Chronicler wrote his history to bolster Israel's hope in the coming of the Messiah. His immediate focus was the restoration of the postexilic community, but the New Testament revealed that the Chronicler's ideal of the restored kingdom found fulfillment in Christ.

The Chronicler's hopes for the people of God became a reality in Christ. Those who follow Christ are the heirs of Israel's promises (Gal 3:14,29; 4:28; Eph 2:11–22; 3:6), as were the faithful of the postexilic community. Christ's church extends beyond Israel to include the Gentiles (Lk 2:32; Ac 9:15; 11:1,18). At the return of Christ all of God's elect will be united under the lordship of Christ (Eph 2:11–22).

The Chronicler's interest in the restoration of David's throne was also fulfilled in Christ. Christ was born the Son of David, the rightful heir to the Davidic throne (Lk 1:32; Ro 1:3; Rev 22:16). Jesus met all the conditions of obedience placed on David's line (Ro 5:19; Php 2:8; Heb 5:7–10). In the resurrection, Christ took his throne in heaven (Ac 2:33–35; Eph 1:20–23; Php 2:9; Rev 3:21). He leads his people into blessing and victory (Ro 8:37; Eph 4:7–13) and reigns until all his enemies are defeated (1Co 15:24–26).

The Chronicler's emphasis on the temple likewise finds fulfillment in Christ. Christ offered himself on the cross as the perfect atonement for sin (Heb 9:11–28; 1Pe 3:18a; 1Jn 2:2), and he intercedes in the heavenly palace of God on behalf of his people (Heb 3:1; 4:14–16; 6:20; 7:26; 8:1). On his return, Christ will bring all his people into the blessed presence of God (Jn 14:1–4; 1Th 4:16–17).

The Chronicler's focus on divine blessing and judgment also anticipated the work of Christ. Jesus warned his church of the necessity of fidelity to God (Mt 5:17–20). He suffered death on the cross so that his people might be delivered from judgment (Ro 3:21–26) and grants them new life so that they may be assured of the reward of eternal blessing (Jn 3:16; 2Pet 3:13; 1Jn 2:25).

The Chronicler wrote to encourage his postexilic readers to renew the kingdom in their day. But his history also pointed forward to the inauguration of the kingdom in the first coming of Christ and to the glorious consummation when he returns.

Outline

I. The Genealogies of God's People (1:1—9:34)
   A. Israel's Roots (1:1—2:2)
   B. The Breadth and Order of God's People (2:3—9:1a)
      1. Judah in First Place (2:3—4:23)
      2. Tribes Easily Forgotten (4:24—5:26)
      3. Levi in the Center (6:1–81)
      4. Other Tribes Easily Forgotten (7:1–40)
      5. Benjamin in Honor (8:1—9:1a)
   C. The Continuation of Israel (9:1b–34)

Israel's genealogies reveal the privileges and responsibilities of those who returned from exile.

II. The United Kingdom (9:35—2Ch 9:31)
   A. The Reign of David (9:35—29:30)
      1. David Becomes King (9:35—10:14)
         a. Divine Blessing on Saul (9:35–44)
         b. Divine Judgment Against Saul (10:1–14)
      2. David's Widespread Support (11:1—12:40)
         a. Anointing at Hebron and Establishment at Jerusalem (11:1–9)

The ideal reigns of David and Solomon illustrate the blessings that came to God's people when the king, the temple and all the people were united.

- b. Military Support at Hebron (11:10–47)
- c. Military Support at Ziklag (12:1–7)
- d. Military Support at the Desert Stronghold (12:8–19)
- e. More Military Support at Ziklag (12:20–22)
- f. More Military Support at Hebron (12:23–37)
- g. More on the Anointing at Hebron (12:38–40)

3. Preparations for the Temple (13:1—29:25)
   - a. David Brings the Ark to Jerusalem (13:1—16:43)
     - (1) David's Failed Transfer of the Ark (13:1–14)
     - (2) David's Distinguishing Blessings (14:1–17)
     - (3) David's Successful Transfer of the Ark (15:1—16:43)
       - (a) David Forms a New Plan (15:1–2)
       - (b) David Instructs Levites and Priests (15:3–24)
       - (c) David Moves the Ark (15:25—16:3)
       - (d) David Appoints Levites in Jerusalem (16:4–6)
       - (e) David's Psalm (16:7–36)
       - (f) David Appoints Levites and Priests in Jerusalem and Gibeon (16:37–42)
       - (g) David Accomplishes His Plan (16:43)
   - b. David Prepares for the Temple (17:1—29:25)
     - (1) David Accepts Commission to Prepare for Solomon (17:1–27)
     - (2) David Secures the Nation and Collects Temple Materials (18:1—20:8)
       - (a) David's Victories and Domestic Security (18:1–17)
       - (b) David's Victories Against Ammon and Aram (19:1—20:3)
       - (c) David's Victories Over the Philistines (20:4–8)
     - (3) David Discovers the Temple Site (21:1—22:1)
     - (4) David Commissions Temple Construction (22:2–19)
     - (5) David Transfers Power and Responsibility to Solomon (23:1—29:25)
       - (a) Those Whom David Gathered (23:1—27:34)
         - (i) Priests and Levites (23:1—26:32)
         - (ii) Military and Civilian Leaders (27:1–34)

- (b) David's Final Assembly (28:1—29:25)
  - (i) Introduction (28:1)
  - (ii) David's First Set of Speeches and Actions (28:2–19)
  - (iii) David's Second Set of Speeches and Actions (28:20—29:9)
  - (iv) David's Third Set of Speeches and Actions (29:10–25)

4. Closure of David's Reign (29:26–30)

B. The Reign of Solomon (2Ch 1:1—9:31)
1. Solomon's Great Wisdom and Wealth (1:1–17)
   - a. Solomon Receives Divine Promises (1:1–13)
   - b. Solomon Experiences Divine Promises (1:14–17)
2. Solomon's International Assistance (2:1–18)
3. Solomon's Temple-Building Project (3:1—5:1)
   - a. Solomon Begins Construction (3:1–2)
   - b. Solomon's Temple Building (3:3–17)
   - c. Solomon's Temple Furnishings (4:1–10)
   - d. Reiteration and Elaboration (4:11–22)
   - e. Solomon Completes Construction (5:1)
4. Solomon's Assembly to Dedicate the Temple (5:2—7:10)
   - a. Solomon's Assembly Gathers (5:2–3)
   - b. Solomon's Initial Celebration of the Temple (5:4—6:2)
   - c. Solomon's Praise for the Past (6:3–11)
   - d. Solomon's Prayer for the Future (6:12–42)
   - e. Solomon's Concluding Sacrifices and Celebration (7:1–7)
   - f. Solomon's Assembly Dismisses (7:8–10)
5. Solomon's Response From God (7:11–22)
6. More on Solomon's Building Projects (8:1–16)
7. More on Solomon's International Relations (8:17—9:21)
8. More on Solomon's Great Wisdom and Wealth (9:22–28)
9. Closure of Solomon's Reign (9:29–31)

III. The Divided Kingdom (10:1—28:27)

A. Judgments and Increasing Blessings in Judah (10:1—21:3)
1. Rehoboam's Reign (10:1—12:16)
   - a. Rehoboam's Early Sin, Prophetic Encounter and Blessing (10:1—11:23)
     - (1) Rehoboam's Sin and Israel's Rebellion (10:1–19)
     - (2) Rehoboam's Compliance and Blessing (11:1–23)

The reigns of the divided period illustrate how divine blessings and judgments came to the divided people of God.

(a) Rehoboam's Compliance With the Prophetic Word (11:1–4)
(b) Rehoboam's Blessings for Compliance (11:5–23)
b. Rehoboam's Later Sin, Prophetic Encounter and Blessing (12:1–12)
c. Closure of Rehoboam's Reign (12:13–16)
2. Abijah's Reign (13:1—14:1a)
a. Opening of Abijah's Reign (13:1–2a)
b. Abijah's Victory Over Jeroboam (13:2b–21)
c. Closure of Abijah's Reign (13:22—14:1a)
3. Asa's Reign (14:1b—16:14)
a. Opening of Asa's Reign (14:1b)
b. Asa Under Divine Blessing (14:2—15:19)
(1) Asa's Early Years of Reform and Blessings (14:2–7)
(2) Asa's Victory, Prophetic Approval and Obedience (14:8—15:19)
(a) Asa's Victory in Conflict (14:8–15)
(b) Asa's Prophetic Approval and Obedience (15:1–19)
c. Asa Under Divine Judgment (16:1–12)
(1) Asa's Failure, Prophetic Disapproval and Disobedience (16:1–10)
(2) Asa's Final Years of Judgment (16:11–12)
d. Closure of Asa's Reign (16:13–14)
4. Jehoshaphat's Reign (17:1—21:3)
a. Opening of Jehoshaphat's Reign (17:1–2)
b. Jehoshaphat's Earlier Years (17:3—19:3)
(1) Jehoshaphat's Earlier Fidelity (17:3–19)
(2) Jehoshaphat's Earlier Battle (18:1—19:3)
c. Jehoshaphat's Later Years (19:4—20:30)
(1) Jehoshaphat's Reforms (19:4–11)
(2) Jehoshaphat's Later Battle (20:1–30)
d. Closure of Jehoshaphat's Reign (20:31—21:3)
B. Northern Corruption in Judah (21:4—24:27)
1. Jehoram's Reign (21:4–20)
a. Opening of Jehoram's Reign (21:4–7)
b. Rebellion Against Jehoram (21:8–11)
c. Elijah's Condemnation of Jehoram (21:12–15)
d. More Rebellions Against Jehoram (21:16–17)
e. Closure of Jehoram's Reign (21:18–20)
2. Ahaziah's Reign (22:1–9)
3. Joash's Reign (22:10—24:27)
a. Joash's Rise Over Athaliah (22:10—23:21)

- b. Joash's Kingship (24:1–27)
  - (1) Opening of Joash's Reign (24:1–3)
  - (2) Joash's Early Years of Fidelity (24:4–14)
  - (3) Jehoiada's Death (24:15–16)
  - (4) Joash's Later Years of Infidelity (24:17–26)
  - (5) Closure of Joash's Reign (24:27)
- C. Deterioration Through Halfhearted Obedience (25:1—28:27)
  - 1. Amaziah's Reign (25:1–28)
    - a. Opening of Amaziah's Reign (25:1–2)
    - b. Amaziah's Halfhearted Fidelity (25:3–12)
    - c. Amaziah's Trouble From Israel (25:13)
    - d. Amaziah's Infidelity (25:14–24)
    - e. Closure of Amaziah's Reign (25:25–28)
  - 2. Uzziah's Reign (26:1–23)
    - a. Opening of Uzziah's Reign (26:1–5)
    - b. Uzziah's Fidelity and Blessing (26:6–15)
    - c. Uzziah's Infidelity and Curse (26:16–21)
    - d. Closure of Uzziah's Reign (26:22–23)
  - 3. Jotham's Reign (27:1–9)
  - 4. Ahaz's Reign (28:1–27)
    - a. Opening of Ahaz's Reign (28:1–5)
    - b. Northern Israel's Fidelity to God (28:6–15)
    - c. Ahaz's Infidelity to God (28:16–25)
    - d. Closure of Ahaz's Reign (28:26–27)

- IV. The Reunited Kingdom (29:1—36:23)
  - A. Hezekiah's Reign (29:1—32:33)
    - 1. Opening of Hezekiah's Reign (29:1–2)
    - 2. Hezekiah Reestablishes Temple Worship (29:3—31:21)
      - a. Hezekiah Initiates Temple Service (29:3–36)
      - b. Hezekiah Unites Israel in Passover Celebration (30:1—31:1)
      - c. Hezekiah's Enduring Provisions (31:2–21)
    - 3. Hezekiah's Inconsistencies During the Assyrian Invasion (32:1–31)
      - a. Hezekiah's Inconsistent Military Strategy (32:1–23)
      - b. Hezekiah's Inconsistent Pride (32:24–26)
      - c. Hezekiah's Inconsistent Alliance (32:27–31)
    - 4. Closure of Hezekiah's Reign (32:32–33)
  - B. Manasseh's Reign (33:1–20)
    - 1. Opening of Manasseh's Reign (33:1)
    - 2. Manasseh's Heinous Sins (33:2–9)
    - 3. Manasseh's Repentance and Return (33:10–13)
    - 4. Mansseh's Extensive Restorations (33:14–17)
    - 5. Closure of Manasseh's Reign (33:18–20)
  - C. Amon's Reign (33:21–25)

The reunited kingdom illustrates how God's blessings and judgments applied to the reunited people of God.

D. Josiah's Reign (34:1—35:27)
   1. Opening of Josiah's Reign (34:1–3a)
   2. Josiah's Fidelity in Worship Reforms (34:3b—35:19)
      a. Josiah's Earlier Reforms (34:3b–7)
      b. Josiah's Later Reforms (34:8—35:19)
         (1) Josiah Repairs the Temple (34:8–13)
         (2) Josiah Renews Covenant (34:14–33)
         (3) Josiah Observes Passover (35:1–19)
   3. Josiah's Infidelity in Deadly Battle (35:20–25)
   4. Closure of Josiah's Reign (35:26–27)
E. The Final Years (36:1–14)
F. Trouble, Exile and Hope (36:15–23)

Historical Records From Adam to Abraham

To Noah's Sons

1 Adam,[a] Seth, Enosh, 2 Kenan,[b] Mahalalel,[c] Jared,[d] 3 Enoch,[e] Methuselah,[f] Lamech,[g]
Noah.[h]

4 The sons of Noah:[a][i]
Shem, Ham and Japheth.[j]

The Japhethites

5 The sons[b] of Japheth:
Gomer, Magog, Madai, Javan, Tubal, Meshech and Tiras.
6 The sons of Gomer:
Ashkenaz, Riphath[c] and Togarmah.
7 The sons of Javan:
Elishah, Tarshish, the Kittim and the Rodanim.

The Hamites

8 The sons of Ham:
Cush, Mizraim,[d] Put and Canaan.
9 The sons of Cush:
Seba, Havilah, Sabta, Raamah and Sabteca.

1:1 [a]Ge 5:1-32; Lk 3:36-38
1:2 [b]Ge 5:9 [c]Ge 5:12 [d]Ge 5:15
1:3 [e]Ge 5:18; Jude 1:14 [f]Ge 5:21 [g]Ge 5:25 [h]Ge 5:29
1:4 [i]Ge 6:10; 10:1 [j]Ge 5:32

a *4* Septuagint; Hebrew does not have *The sons of Noah:* b *5* *Sons* may mean *descendants* or *successors* or *nations;* also in verses 6–10, 17 and 20. c *6* Many Hebrew manuscripts and Vulgate (see also Septuagint and Gen. 10:3); most Hebrew manuscripts *Diphath* d *8* That is, Egypt; also in verse 11

■ **1:1—9:34** *The Genealogies of God's People.* This extensive series of genealogies and lists explains the election and arrangement of the people of God throughout history. This material divides into three main sections: Israel's roots (1:1—2:2), the breadth and order of Israel (2:3—9:1a) and the continuation of Israel (9:1b–34). The Chronicler described God's sovereign choice of Israel from all the nations of the earth, the order God ordained for his people and the continuation of his elect people through those who had returned from exile. This material revealed the privileges and responsibilities of his postexilic readers who were the contemporary people of God (see "Introduction: Purposes and Distinctives").

■ **1:1—2:2** *Israel's Roots.* The Chronicler drew from Genesis to trace God's sovereign election of Israel from the nations of humanity. His record moves from Adam to Noah (1:1–3), through the descendants of Noah (1:4–27) and the offspring of Abraham (1:28—2:2).

1:1–3 Adam . . . Noah. The Chronicler drew on Genesis 5:1–32 and moved quickly through history before the flood. He mentioned only a few prominent representatives of the chosen line.

1:4–27 Shem . . . Abram. With his discussion of the sons of Noah, the Chronicler demonstrated how God had chosen some nations over others. The sons of Noah are treated individually: Japheth (vv. 5–7), Ham (vv. 8–16) and Shem (vv. 17–27). Relying selectively on Genesis 10:1–32 (see note on this passage), the Chronicler placed the chosen line last. From the descendants of Noah, the Shemites (Semitic people) alone were in special covenant relationship with God (see note on Ge 9:24–27).

1:5 sons of Japheth. The Chronicler mentioned seven descendants of Japheth but treated two of them, Gomer and Javan (vv. 6–7), in some detail. **sons.** See NIV text note. In ancient Near Eastern genealogies, the terms *sons* and *fathers* often described direct biological descent. But they also referred to familial relations in a broad sense, as well as to a variety of geographical and other social associations that had no element of kinship. Here "sons" points primarily to cultural and geographical relationships. Compare the geographical focus in 2:42–55, 4:1–23, 28 and 43, 6:54–81, 7:20–29, 9:2 and 11:10–47 (see "Introduction: Purposes and Distinctives: *Genealogies of God's People*").

1:8–16 sons of Ham. The Chronicler devoted more attention to the Hamites than to the Japhethites because Israel had more dealings with them. His list begins with all four sons of Ham but records only the descendants of Cush (vv. 9–10), Mizraim (vv. 11–12) and Canaan (vv. 13–16).

The sons of Raamah:
Sheba and Dedan.
10 Cush was the father[a] of
Nimrod, who grew to be a mighty warrior on earth.
11 Mizraim was the father of
the Ludites, Anamites, Lehabites, Naphtuhites, 12 Pathrusites, Casluhites (from whom the Philistines came) and Caphtorites.
13 Canaan was the father of
Sidon his firstborn,[b] and of the Hittites, 14 Jebusites, Amorites, Girgashites, 15 Hivites, Arkites, Sinites, 16 Arvadites, Zemarites and Hamathites.

The Semites

17 The sons of Shem:
Elam, Asshur, Arphaxad, Lud and Aram.
The sons of Aram[c]:
Uz, Hul, Gether and Meshech.
18 Arphaxad was the father of Shelah,
and Shelah the father of Eber.
19 Two sons were born to Eber:
One was named Peleg,[d] because in his time the earth was divided; his brother was named Joktan.
20 Joktan was the father of
Almodad, Sheleph, Hazarmaveth, Jerah, 21 Hadoram, Uzal, Diklah, 22 Obal,[e] Abimael, Sheba, 23 Ophir, Havilah and Jobab. All these were sons of Joktan.

1:24 [k]Ge 10:21-25; Lk 3:34-36

24 Shem,[k] Arphaxad,[f] Shelah,
25 Eber, Peleg, Reu,
26 Serug, Nahor, Terah
27 and Abram (that is, Abraham).

The Family of Abraham

28 The sons of Abraham:
Isaac and Ishmael.

Descendants of Hagar

29 These were their descendants:
Nebaioth the firstborn of Ishmael, Kedar, Adbeel, Mibsam, 30 Mishma, Dumah, Massa, Hadad, Tema, 31 Jetur, Naphish and Kedemah. These were the sons of Ishmael.

Descendants of Keturah

1:32 [l]Ge 22:24 [m]Ge 10:7

32 The sons born to Keturah, Abraham's concubine:[l]
Zimran, Jokshan, Medan, Midian, Ishbak and Shuah.
The sons of Jokshan:
Sheba and Dedan.[m]
33 The sons of Midian:
Ephah, Epher, Hanoch, Abida and Eldaah.
All these were descendants of Keturah.

[a] *10* *Father* may mean *ancestor* or *predecessor* or *founder*; also in verses 11, 13, 18 and 20. [b] *13* Or *of the Sidonians, the foremost* [c] *17* One Hebrew manuscript and some Septuagint manuscripts (see also Gen. 10:23); most Hebrew manuscripts do not have this line. [d] *19* *Peleg* means *division.* [e] *22* Some Hebrew manuscripts and Syriac (see also Gen. 10:28); most Hebrew manuscripts *Ebal* [f] *24* Hebrew; some Septuagint manuscripts *Arphaxad, Cainan* (see also note at Gen. 11:10)

1:17–27 sons of Shem. The Chronicler traced the narrowing of divine election among the Shemites to Abraham's family (vv. 17–23). He closely followed Genesis 10:21–31 and in 1:23–27 added a brief summary of Genesis 11:10–27a in order to extend the genealogy to Abraham.

1:24 Arphaxad, Shelah. See NIV text notes on verse 24 and Genesis 11:12,13.

1:28—2:2 Abraham. The Chronicler reported the plan of sovereign election from among the descendants of Abraham. As before, he dealt first with those not chosen (1:29–33) and then with the chosen line in Isaac (1:34—2:2).

1:29–31 Ishmael. The Chronicler followed Genesis in distinguishing Ishmael's descendants from the covenant line (see note on Ge 25:12–16). Ishmael was promised great blessings from God (Ge 16:11–12), but he was not the heir of the covenant of grace God had made with Abraham (Ge 17:18–21).

1:32–33 sons born to Keturah. See note on Genesis 25:1–4. Abraham's descendants through Keturah are also distinguished from the line of promise in Isaac.

Descendants of Sarah

34 Abraham[n] was the father of Isaac.[o]
The sons of Isaac:
Esau and Israel.[p]

Esau's Sons

35 The sons of Esau:[q]
Eliphaz, Reuel,[r] Jeush, Jalam and Korah.
36 The sons of Eliphaz:
Teman, Omar, Zepho,[a] Gatam and Kenaz;
by Timna: Amalek.[b][s]
37 The sons of Reuel:[t]
Nahath, Zerah, Shammah and Mizzah.

The People of Seir in Edom

38 The sons of Seir:
Lotan, Shobal, Zibeon, Anah, Dishon, Ezer and Dishan.
39 The sons of Lotan:
Hori and Homam. Timna was Lotan's sister.
40 The sons of Shobal:
Alvan,[c] Manahath, Ebal, Shepho and Onam.
The sons of Zibeon:
Aiah and Anah.[u]
41 The son of Anah:
Dishon.
The sons of Dishon:
Hemdan,[d] Eshban, Ithran and Keran.
42 The sons of Ezer:
Bilhan, Zaavan and Akan.[e]
The sons of Dishan[f]:
Uz and Aran.

The Rulers of Edom

43 These were the kings who reigned in Edom before any Israelite king reigned[g]:
Bela son of Beor, whose city was named Dinhabah.
44 When Bela died, Jobab son of Zerah from Bozrah succeeded him as king.
45 When Jobab died, Husham from the land of the Temanites[v] succeeded him as king.
46 When Husham died, Hadad son of Bedad, who defeated Midian in the country of Moab, succeeded him as king. His city was named Avith.
47 When Hadad died, Samlah from Masrekah succeeded him as king.
48 When Samlah died, Shaul from Rehoboth on the river[h] succeeded him as king.
49 When Shaul died, Baal-Hanan son of Acbor succeeded him as king.
50 When Baal-Hanan died, Hadad succeeded him as king. His city was named Pau,[i] and his wife's name was Mehetabel daughter of Matred, the daughter of Me-Zahab.
51 Hadad also died.

The chiefs of Edom were:
Timna, Alvah, Jetheth, 52 Oholibamah, Elah, Pinon, 53 Kenaz, Teman, Mibzar,
54 Magdiel and Iram. These were the chiefs of Edom.

1:34 [n] Lk 3:34 [o] Ge 21:2-3; Mt 1:2; Ac 7:8 [p] Ge 17:5; 25:25-26
1:35 [q] Ge 36:19 [r] Ge 36:4
1:36 [s] Ex 17:14
1:37 [t] Ge 36:17
1:40 [u] Ge 36:2
1:45 [v] Ge 36:11

[a] *36* Many Hebrew manuscripts, some Septuagint manuscripts and Syriac (see also Gen. 36:11); most Hebrew manuscripts *Zephi* [b] *36* Some Septuagint manuscripts (see also Gen. 36:12); Hebrew *Gatam, Kenaz, Timna and Amalek* [c] *40* Many Hebrew manuscripts and some Septuagint manuscripts (see also Gen. 36:23); most Hebrew manuscripts *Alian* [d] *41* Many Hebrew manuscripts and some Septuagint manuscripts (see also Gen. 36:26); most Hebrew manuscripts *Hamran* [e] *42* Many Hebrew and Septuagint manuscripts (see also Gen. 36:27); most Hebrew manuscripts *Zaavan, Jaakan* [f] *42* Hebrew *Dishon,* a variant of *Dishan* [g] *43* Or *before an Israelite king reigned over them* [h] *48* Possibly the Euphrates [i] *50* Many Hebrew manuscripts, some Septuagint manuscripts, Vulgate and Syriac (see also Gen. 36:39); most Hebrew manuscripts *Pai*

1:34—2:2 sons of Isaac: Esau and Israel. The chosen line of Isaac is divided between Esau (1:35–54) and Israel; i.e., Jacob (2:1–2). As the book of Genesis explained, Esau sold his birthright, and Jacob, the younger of the two, became heir of the promises (Ge 25:27–34; 27:1–40).

1:35–54 sons of Esau. The Chronicler drew selectively from Genesis 36:10–43 in his summary of Esau's descendants (vv. 35–37), the people of Seir (vv. 38–42) and Edomite rulers (vv. 43–54). Comparisons with Genesis reveal several textual difficulties in these lists (see NIV text notes on vv. 36,40,41,42,50).

Israel's Sons

2 These were the sons of Israel:
Reuben, Simeon, Levi, Judah, Issachar, Zebulun, 2 Dan, Joseph, Benjamin, Naphtali, Gad and Asher.

Judah

To Hezron's Sons

2:3 [w]Ge 29:35; 38:2-10 [x]Ge 38:5 [y]Ge 38:2 [z]Nu 26:19
2:4 [a]Ge 38:11-30 [b]Ge 11:31 [c]Ge 38:29

3 The sons of Judah:[w]
Er, Onan and Shelah.[x] These three were born to him by a Canaanite woman, the daughter of Shua.[y] Er, Judah's firstborn, was wicked in the LORD's sight; so the LORD put him to death.[z] 4 Tamar,[a] Judah's daughter-in-law,[b] bore him Perez[c] and Zerah. Judah had five sons in all.

2:5 [d]Ge 46:12 [e]Nu 26:21

5 The sons of Perez:[d]
Hezron[e] and Hamul.
6 The sons of Zerah:
Zimri, Ethan, Heman, Calcol and Darda[a]—five in all.

2:7 [f]Jos 7:1 [g]Jos 6:18

7 The son of Carmi:
Achar,[b][f] who brought trouble on Israel by violating the ban on taking devoted things.[c][g]
8 The son of Ethan:
Azariah.

2:9 [h]Nu 26:21

9 The sons born to Hezron[h] were:
Jerahmeel, Ram and Caleb.[d]

From Ram Son of Hezron

2:10 [i]Lk 3:32-33 [j]Ex 6:23 [k]Nu 1:7
2:12 [l]Ru 2:1 [m]Ru 4:17

10 Ram[i] was the father of
Amminadab[j], and Amminadab the father of Nahshon,[k] the leader of the people of Judah. 11 Nahshon was the father of Salmon,[e] Salmon the father of Boaz, 12 Boaz[l] the father of Obed and Obed the father of Jesse.[m]

2:13 [n]Ru 4:17 [o]1Sa 16:6
2:16 [p]1Sa 26:6 [q]2Sa 2:18 [r]2Sa 2:13
2:17 [s]2Sa 17:25

13 Jesse[n] was the father of
Eliab[o] his firstborn; the second son was Abinadab, the third Shimea, 14 the fourth Nethanel, the fifth Raddai, 15 the sixth Ozem and the seventh David. 16 Their sisters were Zeruiah[p] and Abigail. Zeruiah's[q] three sons were Abishai, Joab[r] and Asahel. 17 Abigail was the mother of Amasa,[s] whose father was Jether the Ishmaelite.

[a] 6 Many Hebrew manuscripts, some Septuagint manuscripts and Syriac (see also 1 Kings 4:31); most Hebrew manuscripts *Dara* [b] 7 *Achar* means *trouble; Achar* is called *Achan* in Joshua. [c] 7 The Hebrew term refers to the irrevocable giving over of things or persons to the LORD, often by totally destroying them. [d] 9 Hebrew *Kelubai,* a variant of *Caleb* [e] *11* Septuagint (see also Ruth 4:21); Hebrew *Salma*

2:1–2 sons of Israel. This list follows Genesis 35:23–26 except for the positioning of Dan. The Chronicler presented the 12 tribes of Israel as the goal of divine election during the primeval and patriarchal periods.

■ **2:3—9:1a** *The Breadth and Order of God's People.* This passage covers prominent figures in all the tribes except Dan and Zebulun. The writer offered a lengthy account of Judah (2:3—4:23), followed by relatively short reports on Simeon, Reuben, Gad and the half-tribe of Manasseh (4:24—5:26); he followed that with a lengthy account of Levi (6:1–81), succeeded by short reports on Issachar, Benjamin, Naphtali, Manasseh, Ephraim and Manasseh, and Asher (7:1–40) and concluded with a lengthy record on Benjamin (8:1—9:1a). These lists not only focus on the people of the tribes, but on many of their territorial possessions as well. This arrangement reveals the Chronicler's zeal for the eventual expansion of the postexilic community to include all the tribes and their territories (see note on 1:5).

■ **2:3—4:23** *Judah in First Place.* The Chronicler broke with the order of the tribes presented in 2:1–2 to place Judah first. Judah's priority reflected the importance of David's throne for the hope of blessing for the postexilic community. The Judahite material was arranged in a chiastic pattern (A B C D D' C' B' A'): (A) Judahite families (2:3–9), (B) descendants of Ram (2:10–17), (C) descendants of Caleb (2:18–24), (D) descendants of Jerahmeel (2:25–33); and correspondingly but in reverse order, (D') additional particulars on Jerahmeel's descendants (2:34–41), (C') supplementary information on Caleb's descendants (2:42–55), (B') further detail on Ram's descendants after David (3:1–24) and (A') added particulars on the Judahite families (4:1–23).

2:3–9 sons of Judah. These were Er, Onan and Shelah (by a Canaanite woman; Ge 38:2), as well as Perez and Zerah (by Tamar, Judah's daughter-in-law; Ge 38:11–30). The Chronicler showed primary interest in Perez and his son Hezron, who were ancestors of David. Zerah's lineage (vv. 6–8) interrupts the genealogy of Perez (vv. 5,9).

2:6 Ethan, Heman, Calcol and Darda. Traditional sages with whom Solomon is compared in 1 Kings 4:31. This Ethan and Heman probably were not David's musicians by the same names (1Ch 15:19; Pss 88–89).

2:7 Carmi. A son of "Zimri" who was mentioned in verse 6 (Jos 7:1).

2:10–17 Ram. The Chronicler broke with the order of Judah's sons as presented in verse 9 and placed Ram first in order to give prominence to the Davidic line (see note on 2:3—4:23). The Chronicler apparently depended on Ruth 4:18–22 for this genealogical information.

2:15 and the seventh David. According to 1 Samuel 17:12–14 David was Jesse's eighth son. The Chronicler omitted Elihu here, but mentioned him in 27:18. Perhaps Elihu was overlooked because he died without progeny and was thus unimportant to the Chronicler's purpose in these genealogies.

Caleb Son of Hezron

18 Caleb son of Hezron had children by his wife Azubah (and by Jerioth). These were
her sons: Jesher, Shobab and Ardon. 19 When Azubah died, Caleb[t] married Ephrath, who bore him Hur. 20 Hur was the father of Uri, and Uri the father of Bezalel.[u]
21 Later, Hezron lay with the daughter of Makir the father of Gilead[v] (he had married her when he was sixty years old), and she bore him Segub. 22 Segub was
the father of Jair, who controlled twenty-three towns in Gilead. 23 (But Geshur
and Aram captured Havvoth Jair,[a][w] as well as Kenath[x] with its surrounding
settlements—sixty towns.) All these were descendants of Makir the father of
Gilead.

24 After Hezron died in Caleb Ephrathah, Abijah the wife of Hezron bore him Ash-
hur[y] the father[b] of Tekoa.

Jerahmeel Son of Hezron

25 The sons of Jerahmeel the firstborn of Hezron:
Ram his firstborn, Bunah, Oren, Ozem and[c] Ahijah. 26 Jerahmeel had another
wife, whose name was Atarah; she was the mother of Onam.

27 The sons of Ram the firstborn of Jerahmeel:
Maaz, Jamin and Eker.
28 The sons of Onam:
Shammai and Jada.
The sons of Shammai:
Nadab and Abishur.
29 Abishur's wife was named Abihail, who bore him Ahban and Molid.
30 The sons of Nadab:
Seled and Appaim. Seled died without children.
31 The son of Appaim:
Ishi, who was the father of Sheshan.
Sheshan was the father of Ahlai.
32 The sons of Jada, Shammai's brother:
Jether and Jonathan. Jether died without children.
33 The sons of Jonathan:
Peleth and Zaza.
These were the descendants of Jerahmeel.
34 Sheshan had no sons—only daughters.
He had an Egyptian servant named Jarha. 35 Sheshan gave his daughter in marriage to his servant Jarha, and she bore him Attai.
36 Attai was the father of Nathan,
Nathan the father of Zabad,[z]
37 Zabad the father of Ephlal,
Ephlal the father of Obed,
38 Obed the father of Jehu,
Jehu the father of Azariah,
39 Azariah the father of Helez,
Helez the father of Eleasah,
40 Eleasah the father of Sismai,
Sismai the father of Shallum,
41 Shallum the father of Jekamiah,
and Jekamiah the father of Elishama.

2:19 [t]ver 42, 50
2:20 [u]Ex 31:2
2:21 [v]Nu 27:1
2:23 [w]Nu 32:41; Dt 3:14; Jos 13:30 [x]Nu 32:42
2:24 [y]1Ch 4:5
2:36 [z]1Ch 11:41

[a] *23* Or *captured the settlements of Jair* [b] *24* *Father* may mean *civic leader* or *military leader*; also in verses 42, 45, 49–52 and possibly elsewhere. [c] *25* Or *Oren and Ozem, by*

2:18–24 Caleb son of Hezron. The Chronicler proceeded to the line of Caleb. This Caleb was someone other than "Caleb son of Jephunneh" (Nu 13:6), whom the Chronicler mentioned in 4:15.
2:20 Bezalel. As the line of Ram recorded the background of David the monarch, the lineage of Caleb documented that of Bezalel, supervisor of the tabernacle construction in the days of Moses (Ex 31:1–5; 35:30—36:7). The proximity of the monarchial family (vv. 10–17) and the family of the tabernacle artisan reflects the Chronicler's joint concern for the throne of David and temple worship during the postexilic period (see note on 6:1–53).
2:25–33 Jerahmeel. The Chronicler provided the only genealogical information in the Bible on the Jerahmeelites, who lived in southern Judah (1Sa 27:10; 30:27–29).
2:34–41 Sheshan. This additional information on the Jerahmeelites (2:3—4:23 note) is separated from the preceding section by the closure "These were the descendants of Jerahmeel" (v. 33). This second list concentrates on the line from Sheshan (v. 31) to Elishama (v. 41). It is possible that Elishama was a contemporary of David (the twenty-third generation of Judah), but he may have been the scribe of King Jehoiakim (Jer 36:12,20). Apparently, Elishama's pedigree was important in the Chronicler's day. Perhaps the status of his descendants had been questioned by some in the postexilic community.

The Clans of Caleb

42 The sons of Caleb[a] the brother of Jerahmeel:
Mesha his firstborn, who was the father of Ziph, and his son Mareshah,[a] who
was the father of Hebron.
43 The sons of Hebron:
Korah, Tappuah, Rekem and Shema. 44 Shema was the father of Raham, and
Raham the father of Jorkeam. Rekem was the father of Shammai. 45 The son of
Shammai was Maon[b], and Maon was the father of Beth Zur.[c]
46 Caleb's concubine Ephah was the mother of Haran, Moza and Gazez. Haran was
the father of Gazez.
47 The sons of Jahdai:
Regem, Jotham, Geshan, Pelet, Ephah and Shaaph.
48 Caleb's concubine Maacah was the mother of Sheber and Tirhanah. 49 She also
gave birth to Shaaph the father of Madmannah[d] and to Sheva the father of
Macbenah and Gibea. Caleb's daughter was Acsah.[e] 50 These were the descendants of Caleb.

The sons of Hur[f] the firstborn of Ephrathah:
Shobal the father of Kiriath Jearim,[g] 51 Salma the father of Bethlehem, and Ha-
reph the father of Beth Gader.
52 The descendants of Shobal the father of Kiriath Jearim were:
Haroeh, half the Manahathites, 53 and the clans of Kiriath Jearim: the Ithrites,[h]
Puthites, Shumathites and Mishraites. From these descended the Zorathites
and Eshtaolites.
54 The descendants of Salma:
Bethlehem, the Netophathites,[i] Atroth Beth Joab, half the Manahathites, the
Zorites, 55 and the clans of scribes[b] who lived at Jabez: the Tirathites, Shimeath-
ites and Sucathites. These are the Kenites[j] who came from Hammath,[k] the father of the house of Recab.[c][l]

2:42 [a]ver 19
2:45 [b]Jos 15:55 [c]Jos 15:58
2:49 [d]Jos 15:31 [e]Jos 15:16
2:50 [f]1Ch 4:4 [g]ver 19
2:53 [h]2Sa 23:38
2:54 [i]Ezr 2:22; Ne 7:26; 12:28
2:55 [j]Ge 15:19; Jdg 1:16; Jdg 4:11 [k]Jos 19:35 [l]2Ki 10:15,23; Jer 35:2-19

The Sons of David

3 These were the sons of David[m] born to him in Hebron:
The firstborn was Amnon the son of Ahinoam of Jezreel;[n]
the second, Daniel the son of Abigail[o] of Carmel;
2 the third, Absalom the son of Maacah daughter of Talmai king of Geshur;
the fourth, Adonijah[p] the son of Haggith;
3 the fifth, Shephatiah the son of Abital;
and the sixth, Ithream, by his wife Eglah.
4 These six were born to David in Hebron,[q] where he reigned seven years and six
months.[r]
David reigned in Jerusalem thirty-three years, 5 and these were the children born to him
there:
Shammua,[d] Shobab, Nathan and Solomon. These four were by Bathsheba[e][s]
daughter of Ammiel. 6 There were also Ibhar, Elishua,[f] Eliphelet, 7 Nogah, Nepheg, Japhia, 8 Elishama, Eliada and Eliphelet—nine in all. 9 All these were the
sons of David, besides his sons by his concubines. And Tamar[t] was their sister.[u]

3:1 [m]1Ch 14:3; 28:5 [n]Jos 15:56 [o]1Sa 25:42
3:2 [p]1Ki 2:22
3:4 [q]2Sa 5:4; 1Ch 29:27 [r]2Sa 2:11; 5:5
3:5 [s]2Sa 11:3; 12:24
3:9 [t]2Sa 13:1 [u]1Ch 14:4

a *42* The meaning of the Hebrew for this phrase is uncertain. b *55* Or *of the Sopherites* c *55* Or *father of Beth Recab* d *5* Hebrew *Shimea,* a variant of *Shammua* e *5* One Hebrew manuscript and Vulgate (see also Septuagint and 2 Samuel 11:3); most Hebrew manuscripts *Bathshua* f *6* Two Hebrew manuscripts (see also 2 Samuel 5:15 and 1 Chron. 14:5); most Hebrew manuscripts *Elishama*

2:42–55 The sons of Caleb. See note on verses 18–24. This additional information on the Calebites (see note on 2:3—4:23) divides into two sections: Caleb (vv. 42–50a) and Hur (vv. 50b–55). This material includes many names that correspond to geographical sites (Ziph, Mareshah, Hebron, etc.). In these cases, "father of" means "founder or head of" (see note on "sons" at 1:5). The Chronicler pointed to settlements lying beyond the borders of the postexilic province to expand the geographical hopes of his postexilic audience to include all territories once occupied by the people of God (see note on 2:3—9:1a).
2:55 Kenites. These foreigners were related by marriage to Moses and adopted into Judah (Jdg 1:16; 4:11). The Chronicler included them as legitimate members of the people of God (2Ch 8:11 note).
3:1–24 the sons of David. The Chronicler added more material on the line of Ram, David's ancestor (see note on 2:3—4:23). Having delineated David's ancestry (2:10–17), he now turned to his descendants. His record divides into three sections: David's progeny born in Hebron and Jerusalem (vv. 1–9), Solomon's descendants (vv. 10–16) and the descendants of Jehoiachin (vv. 17–24). This material establishes the postexilic governor Zerubbabel (v. 19) as the legitimate heir of the Davidic line.
3:1–9 Hebron . . . Jerusalem. This list of David's sons in Hebron (vv.1–4a) and Jerusalem (vv. 4b–9) was likely derived from 2 Samuel 3:2–5, 5:13–16 and 13:1.

The Kings of Judah

10 Solomon's son was Rehoboam,[v]
Abijah his son,
Asa his son,
Jehoshaphat[w] his son,
11 Jehoram[a][x] his son,
Ahaziah[y] his son,
Joash[z] his son,
12 Amaziah[a] his son,
Azariah his son,
Jotham[b] his son,
13 Ahaz[c] his son,
Hezekiah[d] his son,
Manasseh[e] his son,
14 Amon[f] his son,
Josiah[g] his son.
15 The sons of Josiah:
Johanan the firstborn,
Jehoiakim[h] the second son,
Zedekiah[i] the third,
Shallum[j] the fourth.
16 The successors of Jehoiakim:
Jehoiachin[b][k] his son,
and Zedekiah.[l]

The Royal Line After the Exile

17 The descendants of Jehoiachin the captive:
Shealtiel[m] his son, 18 Malkiram, Pedaiah, Shenazzar,[n] Jekamiah, Hoshama and Nedabiah.[o]
19 The sons of Pedaiah:
Zerubbabel[p] and Shimei.
The sons of Zerubbabel:
Meshullam and Hananiah.
Shelomith was their sister.
20 There were also five others:
Hashubah, Ohel, Berekiah, Hasadiah and Jushab-Hesed.
21 The descendants of Hananiah:
Pelatiah and Jeshaiah, and the sons of Rephaiah, of Arnan, of Obadiah and of Shecaniah.
22 The descendants of Shecaniah:
Shemaiah and his sons:
Hattush,[q] Igal, Bariah, Neariah and Shaphat—six in all.

3:10 [v]1Ki 11:43; 14:21-31; 2Ch 12:16 [w]2Ch 17:1-21:3
3:11 [x]2Ki 8:16-24; 2Ch 21:1 [y]2Ch 22:1-10 [z]2Ki 11:1-12:21
3:12 [a]2Ki 14:1-22; 2Ch 25:1-28 [b]Isa 1:1; Hos 1:1; Mic 1:1
3:13 [c]2Ki 16:1-20; 2Ch 28:1; Isa 7:1 [d]2Ki 18:1-20:21; 2Ch 29:1; Jer 26:19 [e]2Ch 33:1
3:14 [f]2Ki 21:19-26; 2Ch 33:21; Zep 1:1 [g]2Ch 34:1; Jer 1:2; 3:6; 25:3
3:15 [h]2Ki 23:34 [i]Jer 37:1 [j]2Ki 23:31
3:16 [k]2Ki 24:6,8; Mt 1:11 [l]2Ki 24:18
3:17 [m]Ezr 3:2
3:18 [n]Ezr 1:8; 5:14 [o]Jer 22:30
3:19 [p]Ezr 2:2; 3:2; 5:2; Ne 7:7; 12:1; Hag 1:1; 2:2; Zec 4:6
3:22 [q]Ezr 8:2-3

a *11* Hebrew *Joram,* a variant of *Jehoram* b *16* Hebrew *Jeconiah,* a variant of *Jehoiachin;* also in verse 17

3:10–16 Solomon's. The Chronicler passed over David's other sons to focus on Solomon, the chosen descendant. In his portrait of Israel's history, the royal line moved unchallenged from David to Solomon (see note on 23:1). In this list the Chronicler referred to Azariah (v. 12). In later chapters the same king will be called Uzziah (see note on 2Ch 26:1).

3:15 sons of Josiah. Josiah's firstborn, Johanan (otherwise unknown), did not succeed him. Shallum (Jehoahaz) followed Josiah (2Ch 36:1,2; 2Ki 23:30–31). Pharaoh Neco removed Shallum from power and replaced him with his brother, Eliakim (Jehoiakim) (2Ch 36:3–4; 2Ki 23:32–34). Jehoiakim was succeeded by his son Jehoiachin (2Ch 36:9–10; 2Ki 24:8–16), but Nebuchadnezzar replaced Jehoiachin with Josiah's third son, Zedekiah (2Ch 36:10–14; 2Ki 24:18–20).

3:17–24 Jehoiachin. The Chronicler traced the continuation of the royal line through Jehoiachin. The prophet Jeremiah, whose life and words the Chronicler knew (2Ch 35:25; 36:12,21–22), announced God's rejection of Jehoiachin's family from the throne (see notes on Jer 22:28–30). In his mercy, however, God removed this curse and established Jehoiachin's line once again as the object of Israel's future royal hopes. Jehoiachin himself was released from prison in Babylon (2Ki 25:27–30). Sheshbazzar (spelled *Shenazzar* in v. 18) brought temple treasures back to Judah (Ezr 1:11; 5:14–16). Zerubbabel (v. 19), governor over the early postexilic community, rebuilt the temple (Ezr 3:1–13). God declared Zerubbabel his "signet ring" (Hag 2:23), reversing the curse on Jehoiachin (Jer 22:24). Zerubbabel never became king, but his line represented the royal hopes of the postexilic community. Both Matthew (Mt 1:12–13) and Luke (Lk 3:27) identify Jesus, the final Davidic King, with this lineage.

3:19 Pedaiah . . . Zerubbabel. Zerubbabel was called the son of Shealtiel (v. 17) elsewhere (Ezr 3:2,8; Ne 12:1; Hag 1:12,14; 2:2,23; Mt 1:12; Lk 3:27). Pedaiah may have become the head of the family at Shealtiel's death, adopting Zerubbabel as his own. Otherwise, Pedaiah may have married Shealtiel's widow through levirate marriage (Dt 25:5–6), making Zerubbabel the legal son of Shealtiel.

3:21 sons of Rephaiah . . . Shecaniah. Probably not further descendants of Zerubbabel but other Davidic families contemporary with Zerubbabel. If this is correct, the genealogy extends only two generations beyond Zerubbabel (see "Introduction: Time and Place of Writing").

3:22 six in all. This verse mentions only five sons of Shemaiah. One name may have been lost during the transmission of the text. It is also possible that "six" is intended to include Shemaiah and thus refers to the sum of Shecaniah's descendants.

[23]The sons of Neariah:
Elioenai, Hizkiah and Azrikam—three in all.
[24]The sons of Elioenai:
Hodaviah, Eliashib, Pelaiah, Akkub, Johanan, Delaiah and Anani—seven in all.

4:1 [r]Ge 29:35; 46:12; 1Ch 2:3 [s]Nu 26:21

Other Clans of Judah

4 The descendants of Judah:[r]
Perez, Hezron,[s] Carmi, Hur and Shobal.
[2]Reaiah son of Shobal was the father of Jahath, and Jahath the father of Ahumai and Lahad. These were the clans of the Zorathites.
[3]These were the sons[a] of Etam:
Jezreel, Ishma and Idbash. Their sister was named Hazzelelponi. [4]Penuel was the father of Gedor, and Ezer the father of Hushah.

4:4 [t]1Ch 2:50 [u]Ru 1:19

These were the descendants of Hur,[t] the firstborn of Ephrathah and father[b] of Bethlehem.[u]

4:5 [v]1Ch 2:24

[5]Ashhur[v] the father of Tekoa had two wives, Helah and Naarah.
[6]Naarah bore him Ahuzzam, Hepher, Temeni and Haahashtari. These were the descendants of Naarah.
[7]The sons of Helah:
Zereth, Zohar, Ethnan, [8]and Koz, who was the father of Anub and Hazzobebah and of the clans of Aharhel son of Harum.

[9]Jabez was more honorable than his brothers. His mother had named him Jabez,[c] saying, "I gave birth to him in pain." [10]Jabez cried out to the God of Israel, "Oh, that you
would bless me and enlarge my territory! Let your hand be with me, and keep me from
harm so that I will be free from pain." And God granted his request.

[11]Kelub, Shuhah's brother, was the father of Mehir, who was the father of Eshton.
[12]Eshton was the father of Beth Rapha, Paseah and Tehinnah the father of Ir Nahash.[d] These were the men of Recah.

4:13 [w]Jos 15:17

[13]The sons of Kenaz:
Othniel[w] and Seraiah.
The sons of Othniel:
Hathath and Meonothai.[e] [14]Meonothai was the father of Ophrah.
Seraiah was the father of Joab,
the father of Ge Harashim.[f] It was called this because its people were craftsmen.
[15]The sons of Caleb son of Jephunneh:
Iru, Elah and Naam.
The son of Elah:
Kenaz.
[16]The sons of Jehallelel:
Ziph, Ziphah, Tiria and Asarel.

4:17 [x]Ex 15:20

[17]The sons of Ezrah:
Jether, Mered, Epher and Jalon. One of Mered's wives gave birth to Miriam,[x] Shammai and Ishbah the father of Eshtemoa. [18](His Judean wife gave birth to Jered the father of Gedor, Heber the father of Soco, and Jekuthiel the father of Zanoah.[y]) These were the children of Pharaoh's daughter Bithiah, whom Mered had married.

4:18 [y]Jos 15:34

[a] 3 Some Septuagint manuscripts (see also Vulgate); Hebrew *father* [b] 4 *Father* may mean *civic leader* or *military leader*; also in verses 12, 14, 17, 18 and possibly elsewhere. [c] 9 *Jabez* sounds like the Hebrew for *pain.* [d] 12 Or *of the city of Nahash* [e] 13 Some Septuagint manuscripts and Vulgate; Hebrew does not have *and Meonothai.* [f] 14 *Ge Harashim* means *valley of craftsmen.*

4:1–23 Judah. The Chronicler returned to additional information on the Judahite clans (see note on 2:3—4:23). Personal and clan names are mixed with place names, some of which are outside the boundaries of the postexilic territory (see note on 2:42–55). This section pertains to Judah's sons Perez (vv. 1–20) and Shelah (vv. 21–23).
4:1 Carmi. May be a textual corruption of Caleb (2:9) or an alternative name for Caleb. If so, this verse represents a linear genealogy from Judah to Shobal (2:4,5,9,50).
4:9–10 Jabez was more honorable. The Chronicler inserted a brief example of extraordinary piety in the Judahite line. Blessing through prayerful reliance on God is a major theme in Chronicles (5:18–22; 17:16–27; 21:1—22:1; 2Ch 6:12–42; 7:11–16; 13:14; 14:11–13; 18:31; 20:5–30; 30:18–20; 32:20–24; 33:12–13). In line with the geographical references in this chapter, the focus here is on territorial expansion (4:10; see note on "sons" at 1:5), victory and safety through prayer (see note on 2Ch 6:34–35).
4:13 Othniel. Israel's first judge (Jos 15:17; Jdg 1:13; 3:9–11).
4:15 Caleb. See note on 2:18–24.
4:18 Pharaoh's daughter Bithiah. Mered's marriage to Pharaoh's daughter is otherwise unknown. It suggests a time when Israelites were prominent in Egypt, possibly during the days of Joseph.

19 The sons of Hodiah's wife, the sister of Naham:
the father of Keilah[z] the Garmite, and Eshtemoa the Maacathite.[a]
20 The sons of Shimon:
Amnon, Rinnah, Ben-Hanan and Tilon.
The descendants of Ishi:
Zoheth and Ben-Zoheth.
21 The sons of Shelah[b] son of Judah:
Er the father of Lecah, Laadah the father of Mareshah and the clans of the lin-
en workers at Beth Ashbea, 22 Jokim, the men of Cozeba, and Joash and Saraph,
who ruled in Moab and Jashubi Lehem. (These records are from ancient times.)
23 They were the potters who lived at Netaim and Gederah; they stayed there
and worked for the king.

Simeon

24 The descendants of Simeon:[c]
Nemuel, Jamin, Jarib,[d] Zerah and Shaul;
25 Shallum was Shaul's son, Mibsam his son and Mishma his son.
26 The descendants of Mishma:
Hammuel his son, Zaccur his son and Shimei his son.
27 Shimei had sixteen sons and six daughters, but his brothers did not have many children; so their entire clan did not become as numerous as the people of Judah. 28 They
lived in Beersheba,[e] Moladah,[f] Hazar Shual, 29 Bilhah, Ezem,[g] Tolad, 30 Bethuel, Hormah,[h] Ziklag, 31 Beth Marcaboth, Hazar Susim, Beth Biri and Shaaraim.[i] These were their
towns until the reign of David. 32 Their surrounding villages were Etam, Ain,[j] Rimmon,
Token and Ashan[k]—five towns— 33 and all the villages around these towns as far as Baalath.[a] These were their settlements. And they kept a genealogical record.

34 Meshobab, Jamlech, Joshah son of Amaziah, 35 Joel, Jehu son of Joshibiah, the son
of Seraiah, the son of Asiel, 36 also Elioenai, Jaakobah, Jeshohaiah, Asaiah, Adiel,
Jesimiel, Benaiah, 37 and Ziza son of Shiphi, the son of Allon, the son of Jedaiah,
the son of Shimri, the son of Shemaiah.

38 The men listed above by name were leaders of their clans. Their families increased
greatly, 39 and they went to the outskirts of Gedor[l] to the east of the valley in search of
pasture for their flocks. 40 They found rich, good pasture, and the land was spacious,
peaceful and quiet.[m] Some Hamites had lived there formerly.

41 The men whose names were listed came in the days of Hezekiah king of Judah. They
attacked the Hamites in their dwellings and also the Meunites[n] who were there and completely destroyed[b] them, as is evident to this day. Then they settled in their place, because
there was pasture for their flocks. 42 And five hundred of these Simeonites, led by Pelatiah, Neariah, Rephaiah and Uzziel, the sons of Ishi, invaded the hill country of Seir.[o] 43 They
killed the remaining Amalekites[p] who had escaped, and they have lived there to this day.

Reuben

5 The sons of Reuben[q] the firstborn of Israel (he was the firstborn, but when he defiled his father's marriage bed,[r] his rights as firstborn were given to the sons of Jo-

[a] *33* Some Septuagint manuscripts (see also Joshua 19:8); Hebrew *Baal* [b] *41* The Hebrew term refers to the irrevocable giving over of things or persons to the LORD, often by totally destroying them.

4:19 [z]Jos 15:44 [a]Dt 3:14
4:21 [b]Ge 38:5
4:24 [c]Ge 29:33 [d]Nu 26:12
4:28 [e]Ge 21:14 [f]Jos 15:26
4:29 [g]Jos 15:29
4:30 [h]Nu 14:45
4:31 [i]Jos 15:36
4:32 [j]Nu 34:11 [k]Jos 15:42
4:39 [l]Jos 15:58
4:40 [m]Jdg 18:7-10
4:41 [n]2Ch 20:1; 26:7
4:42 [o]Ge 14:6
4:43 [p]1Sa 15:8; 30:17; 2Sa 8:12; Est 3:1; 9:16
5:1 [q]Ge 29:32 [r]Ge 35:22; 49:4

4:21–23 Shelah. The Chronicler added a record of Judah's oldest surviving son, Shelah (2:3). The material includes personal names, place names and records of trade guilds (linen workers, potters and royal servants). See note on "sons" at 1:5.

■ **4:24—5:26** *Tribes Easily Forgotten.* Short reports on Simeon (4:24–43), Reuben (5:1–10) and Gad (5:11–17), as well as summaries of all Transjordanian tribes (5:18–22) and the half-tribe of Manasseh (5:23–26), follow the lengthy genealogies of Judah (see note on 2:3—9:1a).

4:24–43 Simeon. The tribe of Simeon was closely associated with the tribe of Judah (Ge 34:25–31; 49:5–12; Jos 19:1–9; Jdg 1:3). This material divides into three parts: the genealogy proper (vv. 24–27), geographical material (vv. 28–33) and historical notes on territorial expansion (vv. 34–43). See note on 1:5. For other genealogical records for the tribe of Simeon, see Genesis 46:10, Exodus 6:15 and Numbers 26:12–14.

4:28–33 lived in Beersheba. This list of Simeonite settlements was likely drawn from Joshua 19:2–8 (cf. Jos 15:26–32). The Chronicler pointed to the territorial background of preexilic times to instill hopes for geographical expansion in the postexilic community (see note on 2:42–55). Nehemiah 11:26–29 indicates that some of these cities (Moladah, Hazar, Shual, Beersheba, Ziklag, Ain and Rimmon—translated "En Rimmon" in Ne 11:29) were resettled after the exile.

4:34–43 Meshobab . . . The Chronicler listed some prominent Simeonite leaders (vv. 34–38) and then described how they expanded their territories in several directions (vv. 38–43). The Chronicler's interest in the extent of the land of promise for his readers is evident (see note on 2:42–55).

4:41,43 to this day. The expressions "today" and "this day" in Chronicles may refer to the Chronicler's own time as in these verses (5:26; 2Ch 20:26; 35:25). They may also refer to the earlier days of sources used by the Chronicler. At times, they may even indicate the days of the sources used by his sources (13:11; 2Ch 5:9; 8:8; 10:19; 21:10). It is also possible to understand the expression idiomatically for "from then on" or "in perpetuity."

5:1–26 The Chronicler reported on the Transjordanian tribes. This

seph[s] son of Israel;[t] so he could not be listed in the genealogical record in accordance
with his birthright,[u] 2and though Judah[v] was the strongest of his brothers and a ruler[w]
came from him, the rights of the firstborn[x] belonged to Joseph)— 3the sons of Reuben[y]
the firstborn of Israel:
Hanoch, Pallu,[z] Hezron and Carmi.
4 The descendants of Joel:
Shemaiah his son, Gog his son,
Shimei his son, 5Micah his son,
Reaiah his son, Baal his son,
6 and Beerah his son, whom Tiglath-Pileser[a][a] king of Assyria took into exile. Beerah was a leader of the Reubenites.
7 Their relatives by clans,[b] listed according to their genealogical records:
Jeiel the chief, Zechariah, 8and Bela son of Azaz, the son of Shema, the son of
Joel. They settled in the area from Aroer[c] to Nebo and Baal Meon. 9To the east
they occupied the land up to the edge of the desert that extends to the Euphrates River, because their livestock had increased in Gilead.[d]
10During Saul's reign they waged war against the Hagrites[e], who were defeated at their hands; they occupied the dwellings of the Hagrites throughout
the entire region east of Gilead.

Gad

11 The Gadites[f] lived next to them in Bashan, as far as Salecah:[g]
12 Joel was the chief, Shapham the second, then Janai and Shaphat, in Bashan.
13 Their relatives, by families, were:
Michael, Meshullam, Sheba, Jorai, Jacan, Zia and Eber—seven in all.
14 These were the sons of Abihail son of Huri, the son of Jaroah, the son of Gilead, the son of Michael, the son of Jeshishai, the son of Jahdo, the son of Buz.
15 Ahi son of Abdiel, the son of Guni, was head of their family.
16 The Gadites lived in Gilead, in Bashan and its outlying villages, and on all the pasturelands of Sharon as far as they extended.
17 All these were entered in the genealogical records during the reigns of Jotham[h] king
of Judah and Jeroboam[i] king of Israel.

18The Reubenites, the Gadites and the half-tribe of Manasseh had 44,760 men ready
for military service[j]—able-bodied men who could handle shield and sword, who could
use a bow, and who were trained for battle. 19They waged war against the Hagrites, Jetur,[k] Naphish and Nodab. 20They were helped[l] in fighting them, and God handed the
Hagrites and all their allies over to them, because they cried[m] out to him during the battle. He answered their prayers, because they trusted[n] in him. 21They seized the livestock
of the Hagrites—fifty thousand camels, two hundred fifty thousand sheep and two thousand donkeys. They also took one hundred thousand people captive, 22and many others
fell slain, because the battle[o] was God's. And they occupied the land until the exile.[p]

The Half-Tribe of Manasseh

23The people of the half-tribe of Manasseh were numerous; they settled in the land
from Bashan to Baal Hermon, that is, to Senir (Mount Hermon).[q]

5:1 [s]Ge 48:16,22; 49:26 [t]Ge 48:5 [u]1Ch 26:10
5:2 [v]Ge 49:10,12 [w]1Sa 9:16; 12:12; 2Sa 6:21; 1Ch 11:2; 2Ch 7:18; Ps 60:7; Mic 5:2; Mt 2:6 [x]Ge 25:31
5:3 [y]Ge 29:32; 46:9; Ex 6:14; Nu 26:5-11 [z]Nu 26:5
5:6 [a]ver 26; 2Ki 15:19; 16:10; 2Ch 28:20
5:7 [b]ver 17
5:8 [c]Nu 32:34
5:9 [d]Nu 32:26; Jos 22:9
5:10 [e]ver 18-21
5:11 [f]Jos 13:24-28 [g]Dt 3:10; Jos 13:11
5:17 [h]2Ki 15:32 [i]2Ki 14:16,28
5:18 [j]Nu 1:3
5:19 [k]ver 10; Ge 25:15; 1Ch 1:31
5:20 [l]Ps 37:40 [m]1Ki 8:44; 2Ch 13:14; 14:11; Ps 20:7-9; 22:5 [n]Ps 26:1; Da 6:23
5:22 [o]2Ch 32:8 [p]2Ki 15:29; 17:6
5:23 [q]Dt 3:8,9; SS 4:8

[a] 6 Hebrew *Tilgath-Pilneser,* a variant of *Tiglath-Pileser;* also in verse 26

---

material divides into four parts: Reuben (vv. 1–10), Gad (vv. 11–17), a brief narrative (vv. 18–22) and the half-tribe of Manasseh (vv. 23–26). The inclusion of these tribes among the people of God was no doubt part of the Chronicler's hope for repopulation and territorial possession during the postexilic times (see note on 2:42–55).

5:1–10 Reuben. The record of Reuben focuses on people (vv. 1–8a) and places (vv. 8b–10). **he was the firstborn, but . . .** The Chronicler explained why Reuben, the firstborn, was given so little prominence among the tribes. He had defiled his father's bed (Ge 35:22; 49:4) and lost his right as firstborn to the double portion of the inheritance (Dt 21:15–17). The Chronicler affirmed instead that Joseph received Reuben's double portion because his sons Ephraim and Manasseh were treated as separate tribes (Ge 48:1–22).

5:2 a ruler came from him. From Judah came David, and by implication Zerubbabel, his postexilic descendant (11:2; 17:7; 2Sa 5:2; 6:21; see note on 3:1–24).

5:6 Tiglath-Pileser. See NIV text note. The king of Assyria (745–727 B.C.), whose throne name was Pul (v. 26). He attacked Israel (2Ki 15:29) and required Ahaz to pay tribute (see note on 2Ch 28:21). See "Introduction[s]" to Amos, Isaiah, Hosea and Micah.

5:8 Aroer . . . Baal Meon. This geographical information might well have come from Numbers 32:38 and Joshua 13:15–23.

5:11–17 Gadites. This list of Gadites has no Biblical parallels and focuses on geography (vv. 11,16).

5:18–22 44,760 men . . . one hundred thousand. The Chronicler showed that the Transjordanian tribes overcame an army much larger than their own (see note on 19:6–7). **they cried out to him.** The Chronicler inserted a brief narrative concerning all three Transjordanian tribes (4:9–10). The story illustrates the importance of prayer and reliance on God in battle. This theme appears frequently in his history (see note on 2Ch 6:34–35). See also the contrasting account in verses 23–26.

5:22 until the exile. The deportation of the Transjordanian tribes by the Assyrians in 734 B.C. (vv. 6,26).

5:23–26 they were unfaithful. The reason the Transjordanian tribes suffered exile. The infidelity of the half-tribe of Manasseh led

24These were the heads of their families: Epher, Ishi, Eliel, Azriel, Jeremiah, Hodaviah and Jahdiel. They were brave warriors, famous men, and heads of their families. 25But
they were unfaithful[r] to the God of their fathers and prostituted[s] themselves to the gods
of the peoples of the land, whom God had destroyed before them. 26So the God of Israel stirred up the spirit of Pul[t] king of Assyria (that is, Tiglath-Pileser[u] king of Assyria),
who took the Reubenites, the Gadites and the half-tribe of Manasseh into exile. He took
them to Halah,[v] Habor, Hara and the river of Gozan, where they are to this day.

Levi

6 The sons of Levi:[w]
Gershon, Kohath and Merari.
2The sons of Kohath:
Amram, Izhar, Hebron and Uzziel.
3The children of Amram:
Aaron, Moses and Miriam.
The sons of Aaron:
Nadab, Abihu,[x] Eleazar and Ithamar.
4Eleazar was the father of Phinehas,
Phinehas the father of Abishua,
5Abishua the father of Bukki,
Bukki the father of Uzzi,
6Uzzi the father of Zerahiah,
Zerahiah the father of Meraioth,
7Meraioth the father of Amariah,
Amariah the father of Ahitub,
8Ahitub the father of Zadok,[y]
Zadok the father of Ahimaaz,
9Ahimaaz the father of Azariah,
Azariah the father of Johanan,
10Johanan the father of Azariah[z] (it was he who served as priest in the temple Solomon built in Jerusalem),
11Azariah the father of Amariah,
Amariah the father of Ahitub,
12Ahitub the father of Zadok,
Zadok the father of Shallum,
13Shallum the father of Hilkiah,[a]
Hilkiah the father of Azariah,
14Azariah the father of Seraiah,[b]
and Seraiah the father of Jehozadak.
15Jehozadak[c] was deported when the LORD sent Judah and Jerusalem into exile by
the hand of Nebuchadnezzar.

16The sons of Levi:[d]
Gershon,[a] Kohath and Merari.[e]

5:25 [r]Dt 32:15-18; 2Ki 17:7; 1Ch 9:1; 2Ch 26:16 [s]Ex 34:15
5:26 [t]2Ki 15:19 [u]2Ki 15:29 [v]2Ki 17:6; 18:11
6:1 [w]Ge 46:11; Ex 6:16; Nu 26:57; 1Ch 23:6
6:3 [x]Lev 10:1
6:8 [y]2Sa 8:17; 15:27; Ezr 7:2
6:10 [z]1Ki 4:2; 6:1; 2Ch 3:1; 26:17-18
6:13 [a]2Ki 22:1-20; 2Ch 34:9; 35:8
6:14 [b]2Ki 25:18; Ezr 2:2; Ne 11:11
6:15 [c]2Ki 25:18; Ne 12:1; Hag 1:1, 14; 2:2,4; Zec 6:11
6:16 [d]Ge 29:34; Ex 6:16; Nu 3:17-20 [e]Nu 26:57

a *16* Hebrew *Gershom,* a variant of *Gershon*; also in verses 17, 20, 43, 62 and 71

---

to divine retribution. These events stand in contrast to the preceding narrative of prayer and blessing (4:9–10).

5:25 prostituted themselves. See note on 2 Chronicles 21:11.

5:26 to this day. See note on 4:41 and 43.

■ 6:1–81 *Levi in the Center.* The Chronicler included a lengthy account of the tribe of Levi as a background to the arrangement of the temple personnel in the postexilic community. Royal hopes were connected with temple worship in the Chronicler's conception of the restored people. His record divides into two main parts: the arrangements of the families of Levi (vv. 1–53) and the territories allotted to the families (vv. 54–81). This twofold focus fits the pattern of the Chronicler's interest in the identity of the people of God and their territorial claims in postexilic times (see notes on 1:5 and 2:42–55).

6:1–53 The sons of Levi. A lengthy section on the families of Levi. This emphasis reveals the importance to the Chronicler of the temple and priesthood. If the returnees were to see God's blessing, then not only the royal family (Judah), but the temple personnel (Levi) must carry out their proper functions (see note on 29:22). This material divides into four sections: the priests descended from Aaron (vv. 1–15), a survey of all three clans of Levi (vv. 16–30), the temple musicians appointed by David (vv. 31–47) and the distinction between the duties of the sons of Aaron and those of other families (vv. 48–53). These materials provide a framework for the ordering of the tribe of Levi in the postexilic period. See notes on 15:1—16:43, 23:1—26:32, 2Ch 13:4–12 and 22:10—24:27.

6:1–15 The sons of Levi . . . The sons of Aaron. The list moves quickly from the three sons of Levi to the high priestly family of Aaron; from Aaron's sons to Eleazar (vv. 1–4a); then on to the descendants of Eleazar, who are traced to the exile (vv. 4b–15). See notes on verses 48–53 and on 23:28 and 32. A similar high priestly list occurs in Ezra 7:1–5.

6:8 Zadok. See note on 15:11.

6:10 Azariah. The Chronicler's interest in Solomon's temple arrangement as a model for the postexilic community caused him to comment on Azariah (1Ki 4:2; see "Introduction: Purposes and Distinctives").

6:14–15 Jehozadak. The Chronicler traced the high priestly line to Jehozadak, father of Jeshua (Joshua), who was high priest in the early postexilic period (Ezr 3:2; 5:2; 10:18; Hag 1:1; 2:2; Zec 3:1; 6:11).

6:16–30 The sons of Levi. A genealogy likely drawn from Exodus 6:16–19 and Numbers 3:17–20 and 26:57–61.

17 These are the names of the sons of Gershon:
Libni and Shimei.
18 The sons of Kohath:
Amram, Izhar, Hebron and Uzziel.

6:19 [f]Ge 46:11; 1Ch 23:21; 24:26

19 The sons of Merari:[f]
Mahli and Mushi.
These are the clans of the Levites listed according to their fathers:
20 Of Gershon:
Libni his son, Jehath his son,
Zimmah his son, 21 Joah his son,
Iddo his son, Zerah his son
and Jeatherai his son.

6:22 [g]Ex 6:24

22 The descendants of Kohath:
Amminadab his son, Korah[g] his son,
Assir his son, 23 Elkanah his son,
Ebiasaph his son, Assir his son,

6:24 [h]1Ch 15:5

24 Tahath his son, Uriel[h] his son,
Uzziah his son and Shaul his son.
25 The descendants of Elkanah:
Amasai, Ahimoth,
26 Elkanah his son,[a] Zophai his son,

6:27 [i]1Sa 1:1 [j]1Sa 1:20

Nahath his son, 27 Eliab his son,
Jeroham his son, Elkanah[i] his son
and Samuel[j] his son.[b]

6:28 [k]ver 33; 1Sa 8:2

28 The sons of Samuel:
Joel[c][k] the firstborn
and Abijah the second son.
29 The descendants of Merari:
Mahli, Libni his son,
Shimei his son, Uzzah his son,
30 Shimea his son, Haggiah his son
and Asaiah his son.

The Temple Musicians

6:31 [l]1Ch 25:1; 2Ch 29:25-26; Ne 12:45 [m]1Ch 9:33; 15:19; Ezr 3:10; Ps 68:25

31 These are the men[l] David put in charge of the music[m] in the house of the LORD after the ark came to rest there. 32 They ministered with music before the tabernacle, the
Tent of Meeting, until Solomon built the temple of the LORD in Jerusalem. They performed
their duties according to the regulations laid down for them.
33 Here are the men who served, together with their sons:

6:33 [n]1Ki 4:31; 1Ch 15:17; 25:1 [o]ver 28

From the Kohathites:
Heman,[n] the musician,
the son of Joel,[o] the son of Samuel,

6:34 [p]1Sa 1:1

34 the son of Elkanah,[p] the son of Jeroham,
the son of Eliel, the son of Toah,
35 the son of Zuph, the son of Elkanah,
the son of Mahath, the son of Amasai,
36 the son of Elkanah, the son of Joel,
the son of Azariah, the son of Zephaniah,
37 the son of Tahath, the son of Assir,

[a] *26* Some Hebrew manuscripts, Septuagint and Syriac; most Hebrew manuscripts *Ahimoth 26 and Elkanah. The sons of Elkanah:* [b] *27* Some Septuagint manuscripts (see also 1 Samuel 1:19,20 and 1 Chron. 6:33,34); Hebrew does not have *and Samuel his son.* [c] *28* Some Septuagint manuscripts and Syriac (see also 1 Samuel 8:2 and 1 Chron. 6:33); Hebrew does not have *Joel.*

6:16–19 Gershon, Kohath and Merari. The sons of Levi. The Chronicler listed the first generation following Levi's three sons (vv. 16–19). Then he covered each line in greater depth: Gershon (vv. 20–21), Kohath (vv. 22–28) and Merari (vv. 29–30).

6:22–23 Amminadab. Probably an alternate name for Izhar (vv. 2,37–38; Ex 6:18,21). **Assir . . . Elkanah . . . Ebiasaph.** These men were all sons of Korah (Ex 6:24).

6:26–27 Zophai . . . Nahath . . . Eliab. Probably alternate names for Zuph, Toah and Eliel (vv. 34–35). **Elkanah . . . Samuel.** 1 Samuel 1:1 identifies Elkanah as an Ephraimite. This designation may have indicated the location of his home, not his tribal lineage (see note on 1Sa 1:1).

6:31–47 David put in charge. David appointed groups from each of the three clans of Levi as musicians (15:16–26; 2Ch 35:3): the family of Heman from Kohath (vv. 33–38), the family of Asaph from Gershon (vv. 39–43) and the family of Ethan from Merari (vv. 44–47). The Chronicler frequently displayed his deep interest in the music of worship (see note on 15:16–24) and apparently presented this information to legitimize Levitical arrangements in the postexilic period.

the son of Ebiasaph, the son of Korah,[q]
38 the son of Izhar,[r] the son of Kohath,
the son of Levi, the son of Israel;
39 and Heman's associate Asaph,[s] who served at his right hand:
Asaph son of Berekiah, the son of Shimea,[t]
40 the son of Michael, the son of Baaseiah,[a]
the son of Malkijah, 41 the son of Ethni,
the son of Zerah, the son of Adaiah,
42 the son of Ethan, the son of Zimmah,
the son of Shimei, 43 the son of Jahath,
the son of Gershon, the son of Levi;
44 and from their associates, the Merarites, at his left hand:
Ethan son of Kishi, the son of Abdi,
the son of Malluch, 45 the son of Hashabiah,
the son of Amaziah, the son of Hilkiah,
46 the son of Amzi, the son of Bani,
the son of Shemer, 47 the son of Mahli,
the son of Mushi, the son of Merari,
the son of Levi.

48 Their fellow Levites[u] were assigned to all the other duties of the tabernacle, the
house of God. 49 But Aaron and his descendants were the ones who presented offerings
on the altar[v] of burnt offering and on the altar of incense[w] in connection with all that
was done in the Most Holy Place, making atonement for Israel, in accordance with all
that Moses the servant of God had commanded.

50 These were the descendants of Aaron:
Eleazar his son, Phinehas his son,
Abishua his son, 51 Bukki his son,
Uzzi his son, Zerahiah his son,
52 Meraioth his son, Amariah his son,
Ahitub his son, 53 Zadok[x] his son
and Ahimaaz his son.

54 These were the locations of their settlements[y] allotted as their territory (they were
assigned to the descendants of Aaron who were from the Kohathite clan, because the
first lot was for them):
55 They were given Hebron in Judah with its surrounding pasturelands. 56 But
the fields and villages around the city were given to Caleb son of Jephunneh.[z]
57 So the descendants of Aaron were given Hebron (a city of refuge), and Libnah,[b][a] Jattir,[b] Eshtemoa, 58 Hilen, Debir,[c] 59 Ashan,[d] Juttah[c] and Beth Shemesh, together with their pasturelands. 60 And from the tribe of Benjamin they were given
Gibeon,[d] Geba, Alemeth and Anathoth,[e] together with their pasturelands.
These towns, which were distributed among the Kohathite clans, were thirteen
in all.
61 The rest of Kohath's descendants were allotted ten towns from the clans of half the
tribe of Manasseh.
62 The descendants of Gershon, clan by clan, were allotted thirteen towns from the
tribes of Issachar, Asher and Naphtali, and from the part of the tribe of Manasseh that
is in Bashan.

6:37 [q]Ex 6:24
6:38 [r]Ex 6:21
6:39 [s]1Ch 25:1,9; 2Ch 29:13; Ne 11:17 [t]1Ch 15:17
6:48 [u]1Ch 23:32
6:49 [v]Ex 27:1-8 [w]Ex 30:1-7,10; 2Ch 26:18
6:53 [x]2Sa 8:17
6:54 [y]Nu 31:10
6:56 [z]Jos 14:13; 15:13
6:57 [a]Nu 33:20 [b]Jos 15:48
6:58 [c]Jos 10:3
6:59 [d]Jos 15:42
6:60 [e]Jer 1:1

[a] *40* Most Hebrew manuscripts; some Hebrew manuscripts, one Septuagint manuscript and Syriac *Maaseiah* [b] *57* See Joshua 21:13; Hebrew *given the cities of refuge: Hebron, Libnah.* [c] *59* Syriac (see also Septuagint and Joshua 21:16); Hebrew does not have *Juttah.* [d] *60* See Joshua 21:17; Hebrew does not have *Gibeon.*

6:48–53 Aaron and his descendants were the ones. The Chronicler highlighted the exclusive right of the Zadokites to offer sacrifices. This focus probably addressed a matter of controversy among the Levitical families during the postexilic period (see note on 15:11).
6:49 all that Moses . . . had commanded. See note on 16:40.
6:54–81 allotted as their territory. The Chronicler most likely drew from Joshua 21:5–39 and pointed to the wide-ranging properties to which Aaron's descendants had rightful claim. Most of these sites were outside the boundaries of the postexilic province and reflected the Chronicler's interest in the territorial expansion of the restored community (see note on 2:42–55). The Levitical possessions were traced in two parallel sets (A B C A' B' C'): (A) the Kohathites, especially the Aaronites (vv. 54–61); (B) the Gershonites (v. 62); and (C) the Merarites (v. 63); and correspondingly, (A') the Kohathites (vv. 66–70); (B') the Gershonites (vv. 71–76); and (C') the Merarites (vv. 77–81). Verses 66–81 repeatedly mention "pasturelands" (see note on 2:42–55).

63The descendants of Merari, clan by clan, were allotted twelve towns from the tribes
of Reuben, Gad and Zebulun.
64So the Israelites gave the Levites these towns[f] and their pasturelands. 65From the
tribes of Judah, Simeon and Benjamin they allotted the previously named towns.
66Some of the Kohathite clans were given as their territory towns from the tribe of
Ephraim.

67In the hill country of Ephraim they were given Shechem (a city of refuge), and
Gezer,[a][g] 68Jokmeam,[h] Beth Horon,[i] 69Aijalon[j] and Gath Rimmon,[k] together with
their pasturelands.

70And from half the tribe of Manasseh the Israelites gave Aner and Bileam, together with their pasturelands, to the rest of the Kohathite clans.

71The Gershonites[l] received the following:
From the clan of the half-tribe of Manasseh
they received Golan in Bashan[m] and also Ashtaroth, together with their pasturelands;
72from the tribe of Issachar
they received Kedesh, Daberath,[n] 73Ramoth and Anem, together with their
pasturelands;
74from the tribe of Asher
they received Mashal, Abdon,[o] 75Hukok[p] and Rehob,[q] together with their
pasturelands;
76and from the tribe of Naphtali
they received Kedesh in Galilee, Hammon[r] and Kiriathaim,[s] together with
their pasturelands.

77The Merarites (the rest of the Levites) received the following:
From the tribe of Zebulun
they received Jokneam, Kartah,[b] Rimmono and Tabor, together with their
pasturelands;
78from the tribe of Reuben across the Jordan east of Jericho
they received Bezer[t] in the desert, Jahzah, 79Kedemoth[u] and Mephaath, together with their pasturelands;
80and from the tribe of Gad
they received Ramoth in Gilead,[v] Mahanaim,[w] 81Heshbon and Jazer,[x] together with their pasturelands.[y]

Issachar

7 The sons of Issachar:[z]
Tola, Puah,[a] Jashub and Shimron—four in all.
2The sons of Tola:
Uzzi, Rephaiah, Jeriel, Jahmai, Ibsam and Samuel—heads of their families. During the reign of David, the descendants of Tola listed as fighting men in their genealogy numbered 22,600.
3The son of Uzzi:
Izrahiah.
The sons of Izrahiah:
Michael, Obadiah, Joel and Isshiah. All five of them were chiefs. 4According to
their family genealogy, they had 36,000 men ready for battle, for they had
many wives and children.
5The relatives who were fighting men belonging to all the clans of Issachar, as listed in their genealogy, were 87,000 in all.

Benjamin

6Three sons of Benjamin:[b]
Bela, Beker and Jediael.

6:64 [f]Nu 35:1-8; Jos 21:3,41-42
6:67 [g]Jos 10:33
6:68 [h]1Ki 4:12 [i]Jos 10:10
6:69 [j]Jos 10:12 [k]Jos 19:45
6:71 [l]1Ch 23:7 [m]Jos 20:8
6:72 [n]Jos 19:12
6:74 [o]Jos 19:28
6:75 [p]Jos 19:34 [q]Nu 13:21
6:76 [r]Jos 19:28 [s]Nu 32:37
6:78 [t]Jos 20:8
6:79 [u]Dt 2:26
6:80 [v]Jos 20:8 [w]Ge 32:2
6:81 [x]Nu 21:32 [y]2Ch 11:14
7:1 [z]Ge 30:18; Nu 26:23 [a]Ge 46:13
7:6 [b]Ge 46:21; Nu 26:38; 1Ch 8:1-40

[a] 67 See Joshua 21:21; Hebrew *given the cities of refuge: Shechem, Gezer.* [b] 77 See Septuagint and Joshua 21:34; Hebrew does not have *Jokneam, Kartah.*

■ **7:1–40** *Other Tribes Easily Forgotten.* Short reports are included on Issachar (vv. 1–5), Benjamin (vv. 6–12), Naphtali (v. 13), Manasseh (vv. 14–19), Ephraim and Manasseh (vv. 20–29), and Asher (vv. 30–40). See note on 2:3—9:1a.

7:1-5 Issachar. The record of Issachar was probably drawn from Genesis 46:13 and Numbers 1:28 and 26:23–25. Some portions of the material most likely stemmed from military lists (1Ch 7:2,4–5). For the numbers of fighting men, see note on 12:23–37.

7 The sons of Bela:
Ezbon, Uzzi, Uzziel, Jerimoth and Iri, heads of families—five in all. Their genealogical record listed 22,034 fighting men.
8 The sons of Beker:
Zemirah, Joash, Eliezer, Elioenai, Omri, Jeremoth, Abijah, Anathoth and Alemeth. All these were the sons of Beker. 9 Their genealogical record listed the heads of families and 20,200 fighting men.
10 The son of Jediael:
Bilhan.
The sons of Bilhan:
Jeush, Benjamin, Ehud, Kenaanah, Zethan, Tarshish and Ahishahar. 11 All these sons of Jediael were heads of families. There were 17,200 fighting men ready to go out to war.
12 The Shuppites and Huppites were the descendants of Ir, and the Hushites the descendants of Aher.

Naphtali

13 The sons of Naphtali:[c]
Jahziel, Guni, Jezer and Shillem[a]—the descendants of Bilhah.

Manasseh

14 The descendants of Manasseh:[d]
Asriel was his descendant through his Aramean concubine. She gave birth
to Makir the father of Gilead.[e] 15 Makir took a wife from among the Huppites and
Shuppites. His sister's name was Maacah.
Another descendant was named Zelophehad,[f] who had only daughters.
16 Makir's wife Maacah gave birth to a son and named him Peresh. His
brother was named Sheresh, and his sons were Ulam and Rakem.
17 The son of Ulam:
Bedan.
These were the sons of Gilead[g] son of Makir, the son of Manasseh. 18 His sister
Hammoleketh gave birth to Ishhod, Abiezer[h] and Mahlah.
19 The sons of Shemida were:
Ahian, Shechem, Likhi and Aniam.

Ephraim

20 The descendants of Ephraim:[i]
Shuthelah, Bered his son,
Tahath his son, Eleadah his son,
Tahath his son, 21 Zabad his son
and Shuthelah his son.
Ezer and Elead were killed by the native-born men of Gath, when they went
down to seize their livestock. 22 Their father Ephraim mourned for them many
days, and his relatives came to comfort him. 23 Then he lay with his wife again,
and she became pregnant and gave birth to a son. He named him Beriah,[b] because there had been misfortune in his family. 24 His daughter was Sheerah,
who built Lower and Upper Beth Horon[j] as well as Uzzen Sheerah.
25 Rephah was his son, Resheph his son,[c]
Telah his son, Tahan his son,
26 Ladan his son, Ammihud his son,
Elishama his son, 27 Nun his son
and Joshua his son.

7:13 [c]Ge 30:8; 46:24
7:14 [d]Ge 41:51; Jos 17:1; 1Ch 5:23 [e]Nu 26:30
7:15 [f]Nu 26:33; 36:1-12
7:17 [g]Nu 26:30; 1Sa 12:11
7:18 [h]Jos 17:2
7:20 [i]Ge 41:52; Nu 1:33; 26:35
7:24 [j]Jos 10:10; 16:3,5

[a] *13* Some Hebrew and Septuagint manuscripts (see also Gen. 46:24 and Num. 26:49); most Hebrew manuscripts *Shallum* [b] *23* *Beriah* sounds like the Hebrew for *misfortune.* [c] *25* Some Septuagint manuscripts; Hebrew does not have *his son.*

7:6–12 Benjamin. The Chronicler returned to the tribe of Benjamin again in 8:1–40 to trace the lineage of Saul. In the present chapter he drew on military lists (vv. 7,9,11). For the numbers of fighting men, see note on 12:23–37.

7:13 Naphtali. This list of the sons of Naphtali repeats information found in Genesis 46:24 and Numbers 26:48–50.

7:14–19 Manasseh. The tribe of Manasseh is mentioned a second time (see note on 5:23–26). Much of this material was likely taken from Numbers 26:29–34 and Joshua 17:1–18. The focus on women in this line probably stems from the importance of Zelophehad's daughters in Numbers 26:33.

7:20–29 Ephraim. The Chronicler's twofold interest in lineage and geography appears again (see note on 2:42–55). He traced the line of Ephraim to Joshua, son of Nun (vv. 20–27), information that may well have been largely drawn from Numbers 26:35. The

7:28 [k]Jos 10:33; 16:7
7:29 [l]Jos 17:11 [m]Jos 11:2

28 Their lands and settlements included Bethel and its surrounding villages, Naaran
to the east, Gezer[k] and its villages to the west, and Shechem and its villages all the way
to Ayyah and its villages. 29 Along the borders of Manasseh were Beth Shan,[l] Taanach,
Megiddo and Dor,[m] together with their villages. The descendants of Joseph son of Israel lived in these towns.

Asher

7:30 [n]Ge 46:17; Nu 1:40; 26:44

30 The sons of Asher:[n]
Imnah, Ishvah, Ishvi and Beriah. Their sister was Serah.
31 The sons of Beriah:
Heber and Malkiel, who was the father of Birzaith.
32 Heber was the father of Japhlet, Shomer and Hotham and of their sister Shua.
33 The sons of Japhlet:
Pasach, Bimhal and Ashvath.
These were Japhlet's sons.
34 The sons of Shomer:
Ahi, Rohgah,[a] Hubbah and Aram.
35 The sons of his brother Helem:
Zophah, Imna, Shelesh and Amal.
36 The sons of Zophah:
Suah, Harnepher, Shual, Beri, Imrah, 37 Bezer, Hod, Shamma, Shilshah, Ithran[b]
and Beera.
38 The sons of Jether:
Jephunneh, Pispah and Ara.
39 The sons of Ulla:
Arah, Hanniel and Rizia.
40 All these were descendants of Asher—heads of families, choice men, brave warriors
and outstanding leaders. The number of men ready for battle, as listed in their genealogy, was 26,000.

The Genealogy of Saul the Benjamite

8:1 [o]Ge 46:21; 1Ch 7:6

8 Benjamin[o] was the father of Bela his firstborn,
Ashbel the second son, Aharah the third,
2 Nohah the fourth and Rapha the fifth.
3 The sons of Bela were:

8:3 [p]Ge 46:21
8:4 [q]2Sa 23:9
8:6 [r]Jdg 3:12-30; 1Ch 2:52

Addar,[p] Gera, Abihud,[c] 4 Abishua, Naaman, Ahoah,[q] 5 Gera, Shephuphan and
Huram.
6 These were the descendants of Ehud,[r] who were heads of families of those living
in Geba and were deported to Manahath:
7 Naaman, Ahijah, and Gera, who deported them and who was the father of Uzza
and Ahihud.
8 Sons were born to Shaharaim in Moab after he had divorced his wives Hushim and
Baara. 9 By his wife Hodesh he had Jobab, Zibia, Mesha, Malcam, 10 Jeuz, Sakia
and Mirmah. These were his sons, heads of families. 11 By Hushim he had Abi-
tub and Elpaal.
12 The sons of Elpaal:

8:12 [s]Ezr 2:33; Ne 6:2; 7:37; 11:35
8:13 [t]Jos 10:12 [u]Jos 11:22

Eber, Misham, Shemed (who built Ono[s] and Lod with its surrounding villages), 13 and Beriah and Shema, who were heads of families of those living in Aijalon[t] and who drove out the inhabitants of Gath.[u]
14 Ahio, Shashak, Jeremoth, 15 Zebadiah, Arad, Eder, 16 Michael, Ishpah and Joha
were the sons of Beriah.

[a] 34 Or *of his brother Shomer: Rohgah* [b] 37 Possibly a variant of *Jether* [c] 3 Or *Gera the father of Ehud*

Chronicler then turned to a representative list (likely derived from Jos 16–17) of the territories of Ephraim (vv. 28–29).

7:30–40 Asher. The Chronicler may have depended on Genesis 46:17 and Numbers 26:44–46 as he traced the generations of Asher (vv. 30–39). For the numbers of fighting men, see note on 12:23–37.

■ **8:1—9:1a** *Benjamin in Honor.* The Chronicler closed his survey of the tribes of Israel with a second, more extensive treatment of the tribe of Benjamin (cf. 7:6–12). The genealogy of Benjamin compares in length to the treatment of Judah (2:3—4:23) and Levi (6:1–81). Benjamin was of special concern to the Chronicler because of its close association with Judah both before (1Ki 12:20–21) and after the exile (9:4–9). Moreover, Saul was the first king over Israel (1Sa 9:1—10:27; 1Ch 9:35–44). The material of chapter 8 is arranged according to geographical locations: Geba (vv. 1–7, especially v. 6), Moab (vv. 8–13, especially v. 8), Jerusalem (vv. 14–28, especially v. 28) and Gibeon (vv. 29–40, especially v. 29).

8:1–7 Benjamin was the father of. Compare the various lists in 7:6–12, Genesis 46:21–22 and Numbers 26:38–41.

8:8–13 Moab. For a listing of Israelites living in Moab (v. 8) see 1 Samuel 22:3–5 and Ruth 1:1–2.

17 Zebadiah, Meshullam, Hizki, Heber, 18 Ishmerai, Izliah and Jobab were the sons of
Elpaal.
19 Jakim, Zicri, Zabdi, 20 Elienai, Zillethai, Eliel, 21 Adaiah, Beraiah and Shimrath
were the sons of Shimei.
22 Ishpan, Eber, Eliel, 23 Abdon, Zicri, Hanan, 24 Hananiah, Elam, Anthothijah, 25 Iph-
deiah and Penuel were the sons of Shashak.
26 Shamsherai, Shehariah, Athaliah, 27 Jaareshiah, Elijah and Zicri were the sons of
Jeroham.
28 All these were heads of families, chiefs as listed in their genealogy, and they lived
in Jerusalem.

29 Jeiel[a] the father[b] of Gibeon lived in Gibeon.[v]
His wife's name was Maacah, 30 and his firstborn son was Abdon, followed by
Zur, Kish, Baal, Ner,[c] Nadab, 31 Gedor, Ahio, Zeker 32 and Mikloth, who was the
father of Shimeah. They too lived near their relatives in Jerusalem.
33 Ner[w] was the father of Kish,[x] Kish the father of Saul[y], and Saul the father of Jonathan, Malki-Shua, Abinadab and Esh-Baal.[d][z]
34 The son of Jonathan:[a]
Merib-Baal,[e][b] who was the father of Micah.
35 The sons of Micah:
Pithon, Melech, Tarea and Ahaz.
36 Ahaz was the father of Jehoaddah, Jehoaddah was the father of Alemeth, Azmaveth and Zimri, and Zimri was the father of Moza. 37 Moza was the father of
Binea; Raphah was his son, Eleasah his son and Azel his son.
38 Azel had six sons, and these were their names:
Azrikam, Bokeru, Ishmael, Sheariah, Obadiah and Hanan. All these were the
sons of Azel.
39 The sons of his brother Eshek:
Ulam his firstborn, Jeush the second son and Eliphelet the third. 40 The sons of
Ulam were brave warriors who could handle the bow. They had many sons and
grandsons—150 in all.
All these were the descendants of Benjamin.[c]

9 All Israel was listed in the genealogies recorded in the book of the kings of Israel.

The People in Jerusalem

The people of Judah were taken captive to Babylon because of their unfaithfulness.[d]
2 Now the first to resettle on their own property in their own towns[e] were some Israelites, priests, Levites and temple servants.[f]
3 Those from Judah, from Benjamin, and from Ephraim and Manasseh who lived in Jerusalem were:

8:29 [v]Jos 9:3
8:33 [w]1Sa 28:19 [x]1Sa 9:1 [y]1Sa 14:49 [z]2Sa 2:8
8:34 [a]2Sa 9:12 [b]2Sa 4:4
8:40 [c]Nu 26:38
9:1 [d]1Ch 5:25
9:2 [e]Jos 9:27; Ezr 2:70 [f]Ezr 2:43,58; 8:20; Ne 7:60

[a] *29* Some Septuagint manuscripts (see also 1 Chron. 9:35); Hebrew does not have *Jeiel.* [b] *29* *Father* may mean *civic leader* or *military leader.* [c] *30* Some Septuagint manuscripts (see also 1 Chron. 9:36); Hebrew does not have *Ner.* [d] *33* Also known as *Ish-Bosheth* [e] *34* Also known as *Mephibosheth*

8:28–40 heads of families. This genealogy traces the Benjamites in Gibeon to Saul (v. 33) and to many generations after him. See note on 9:35–44, where much of this list is repeated.
8:33 Esh-Baal. See NIV text note. Esh-Baal ("man of Baal") was probably his original name. He is also called Ishvi ("man of the LORD"; 1Sa 14:49) and Ish-Bosheth ("man of shame"; 2Sa 2:8).
8:34 Merib-Baal. The original name of Mephibosheth ("from the mouth of shame") was probably first spelled Meri-Baal (see note on 9:40; "hero of Baal" or "loved of Baal") and later changed to Merib-Baal (perhaps "opponent of Baal"). See NIV text note.
9:1a All Israel. The Chronicler summarizes his lists of the tribes of Israel as representative of the entire nation. This perspective stems from his desire to identify the historical people of God and their territories as a model for his postexilic readers. See notes on 11:1 and 2 Chronicles 10:1 and 29:24.
■ **9:1b–34** *The Continuation of Israel.* This passage contains a selective summary of Israelites who constituted the early postexilic community. Much of this material also appears in Nehemiah 11. The material divides into an introduction (vv. 2–3), followed by lists of Judahites (vv. 4–6), Benjamites (vv. 7–9), priests (vv. 10–13) and Levites (vv. 14–34).
9:1b–2 taken captive . . . resettle. The Chronicler downplayed the exile, mentioning it only briefly before moving to the initial stages of resettlement. This indicates his great interest in resettlement, and the importance he placed on the resettlement following the pattern established by prior possession in the promised land (as expounded in the genealogies of chapters 1–8).
9:2 their own property . . . towns. The returnees claimed land that was rightfully theirs. The writer's comment explains the geographical focus of the preceding lists (see note on 2:42–55). **Israelites, priests, Levites and temple servants.** The lists that follow (vv. 4–34) deal with each of these categories, with the exception of temple servants. These temple servants may have originally been foreigners who were incorporated into the ranks of the Levites (Jos 9:23; Ezr 8:20).
9:3 Judah . . . Benjamin . . . Ephraim . . . and Manasseh. From the Chronicler's perspective, the northern and southern kingdoms were reunited under Hezekiah (see note on 2Ch 29:1—36:23). People representing the entire nation went into exile and returned to the land. For this reason, the Chronicler was careful to mention Ephraim and Manasseh among the returnees. Nevertheless, he gave lengthy, separate treatment, as in preceding genealogies (see note on 2:3—9:1a), to Judahites (vv. 4–6) and Benjamites (vv. 7–9) because they represented the southern kingdom as the home of the line of David and of the temple. He did not give such specific attention to Ephraim and Manasseh.

4 Uthai son of Ammihud, the son of Omri, the son of Imri, the son of Bani, a descendant of Perez son of Judah.[g]
5 Of the Shilonites:
Asaiah the firstborn and his sons.
6 Of the Zerahites:
Jeuel.
The people from Judah numbered 690.
7 Of the Benjamites:
Sallu son of Meshullam, the son of Hodaviah, the son of Hassenuah;
8 Ibneiah son of Jeroham; Elah son of Uzzi, the son of Micri; and Meshullam son of Shephatiah, the son of Reuel, the son of Ibnijah.
9 The people from Benjamin, as listed in their genealogy, numbered 956. All these men were heads of their families.
10 Of the priests:
Jedaiah; Jehoiarib; Jakin;
11 Azariah son of Hilkiah, the son of Meshullam, the son of Zadok, the son of Meraioth, the son of Ahitub, the official in charge of the house of God;
12 Adaiah son of Jeroham, the son of Pashhur,[h] the son of Malkijah; and Maasai son of Adiel, the son of Jahzerah, the son of Meshullam, the son of Meshillemith, the son of Immer.
13 The priests, who were heads of families, numbered 1,760. They were able men, responsible for ministering in the house of God.
14 Of the Levites:
Shemaiah son of Hasshub, the son of Azrikam, the son of Hashabiah, a Merarite;
15 Bakbakkar, Heresh, Galal and Mattaniah[i] son of Mica, the son of Zicri, the son of Asaph;
16 Obadiah son of Shemaiah, the son of Galal, the son of Jeduthun; and Berekiah son of Asa, the son of Elkanah, who lived in the villages of the Netophathites.[j]
17 The gatekeepers:[k]
Shallum, Akkub, Talmon, Ahiman and their brothers, Shallum their chief
18 being stationed at the King's Gate[l] on the east, up to the present time. These
were the gatekeepers belonging to the camp of the Levites.
19 Shallum[m] son of
Kore, the son of Ebiasaph, the son of Korah, and his fellow gatekeepers from
his family (the Korahites) were responsible for guarding the thresholds of the
Tent[a] just as their fathers had been responsible for guarding the entrance to
the dwelling of the LORD.
20 In earlier times Phinehas[n] son of Eleazar was in
charge of the gatekeepers, and the LORD was with him.
21 Zechariah[o] son of Meshelemiah was the gatekeeper at the entrance to the Tent of Meeting.
22 Altogether, those chosen to be gatekeepers[p] at the thresholds numbered 212.
They were registered by genealogy in their villages. The gatekeepers had been assigned
to their positions of trust by David and Samuel the seer.[q]
23 They and their descendants
were in charge of guarding the gates of the house of the LORD—the house called the Tent.
24 The gatekeepers were on the four sides: east, west, north and south.
25 Their brothers
in their villages had to come from time to time and share their duties for seven-day[r] periods.
26 But the four principal gatekeepers, who were Levites, were entrusted with the
responsibility for the rooms and treasuries[s] in the house of God.
27 They would spend the
night stationed around the house of God,[t] because they had to guard it; and they had
charge of the key[u] for opening it each morning.
28 Some of them were in charge of the articles used in the temple service; they counted them when they were brought in and when they were taken out.
29 Others were assigned to take care of the furnishings and all the other articles of the sanctuary,[v] as well

9:4 [g]Ge 38:29; 46:12
9:12 [h]Ezr 2:38; 10:22; Ne 10:3; Jer 21:1; 38:1
9:15 [i]2Ch 20:14; Ne 11:22
9:16 [j]Ne 12:28
9:17 [k]ver 22; 1Ch 26:1; 2Ch 8:14; 31:14; Ezr 2:42; Ne 7:45
9:18 [l]1Ch 26:14; Eze 43:1; 46:1
9:19 [m]Jer 35:4
9:20 [n]Nu 25:7-13
9:21 [o]1Ch 26:2,14
9:22 [p]ver 17; 1Ch 26:1-2; 2Ch 31:15,18 [q]1Sa 9:9
9:25 [r]2Ki 11:5; 2Ch 23:8
9:26 [s]1Ch 26:22
9:27 [t]Nu 3:38; 1Ch 23:30-32 [u]Isa 22:22
9:29 [v]Nu 3:28; 1Ch 23:29

a *19* That is, the temple; also in verses 21 and 23

9:4–6 The Judahite returnees are traced to Judah's sons (see note on 2:3–9): Perez (v. 4), Shelah (v. 5—if Shilonites is emended to read "Shelanites"; cf. 2:3; 4:21–23 and Nu 26:20) and Zerah (v. 6).

9:11 Azariah . . . Ahitub. The high priestly line (cf. 6:12–15).

9:15–16 Asaph . . . Jeduthun. Levites in charge of music (6:39; 9:33). Their prominence in this list reflects the Chronicler's interest in worship music (see note on 15:16–24). **Netophathites.** Netophah was a town near Bethlehem (Ne 7:26; 12:28).

9:17–21 The gatekeepers. See also the list of gatekeepers in 26:1–19. This list extends back to the time of David (26:2–14).

9:22–27 guarding the gates. The Chronicler described the cycles of duty among the gatekeepers as a model for his postexilic readers to follow as they reestablished themselves in the promised land. David's tabernacle had required 24 guards for each of three daily shifts. Assignments and rotations were determined by lot (26:12–18).

9:28–34 in charge of the articles . . . the furnishings . . . the spices. The Chronicler specified a variety of functions in the temple performed by Levites. The returning exiles needed this information in order to restore these Levitical practices. Special exemption was made for the musicians (see note on 15:16–24).

as the flour and wine, and the oil, incense and spices. 30 But some[w] of the priests took
care of mixing the spices. 31 A Levite named Mattithiah, the firstborn son of Shallum the
Korahite, was entrusted with the responsibility for baking the offering bread. 32 Some of
their Kohathite brothers were in charge of preparing for every Sabbath the bread set out
on the table.[x]
33 Those who were musicians,[y] heads of Levite families, stayed in the rooms of the
temple and were exempt from other duties because they were responsible for the work
day and night.[z]
34 All these were heads of Levite families, chiefs as listed in their genealogy, and they
lived in Jerusalem.

The Genealogy of Saul

35 Jeiel[a] the father[a] of Gibeon lived in Gibeon.
His wife's name was Maacah, 36 and his firstborn son was Abdon, followed by
Zur, Kish, Baal, Ner, Nadab, 37 Gedor, Ahio, Zechariah and Mikloth. 38 Mikloth
was the father of Shimeam. They too lived near their relatives in Jerusalem.
39 Ner[b] was the father of Kish,[c] Kish the father of Saul, and Saul the father of Jonathan,[d] Malki-Shua, Abinadab and Esh-Baal.[b][e]
40 The son of Jonathan:
Merib-Baal,[c][f] who was the father of Micah.
41 The sons of Micah:
Pithon, Melech, Tahrea and Ahaz.[d]
42 Ahaz was the father of Jadah, Jadah[e] was the father of Alemeth, Azmaveth and
Zimri, and Zimri was the father of Moza. 43 Moza was the father of Binea; Rephaiah was his son, Eleasah his son and Azel his son.
44 Azel had six sons, and these were their names:
Azrikam, Bokeru, Ishmael, Sheariah, Obadiah and Hanan. These were the sons
of Azel.

Saul Takes His Life

10 Now the Philistines fought against Israel; the Israelites fled before them, and
many fell slain on Mount Gilboa. 2 The Philistines pressed hard after Saul and
his sons, and they killed his sons Jonathan, Abinadab and Malki-Shua. 3 The fighting
grew fierce around Saul, and when the archers overtook him, they wounded him.
4 Saul said to his armor-bearer, "Draw your sword and run me through, or these uncircumcised fellows will come and abuse me."
But his armor-bearer was terrified and would not do it; so Saul took his own sword
and fell on it. 5 When the armor-bearer saw that Saul was dead, he too fell on his sword
and died. 6 So Saul and his three sons died, and all his house died together.
7 When all the Israelites in the valley saw that the army had fled and that Saul and his
sons had died, they abandoned their towns and fled. And the Philistines came and occupied them.

9:30 [w]Ex 30:23-25
9:32 [x]Lev 24:5-8; 1Ch 23:29; 2Ch 13:11
9:33 [y]1Ch 6:31; 25:1-31 [z]Ps 134:1
9:35 [a]1Ch 8:29
9:39 [b]1Ch 8:33 [c]1Sa 9:1 [d]1Sa 13:22 [e]2Sa 2:8
9:40 [f]2Sa 4:4

[a] *35 Father* may mean *civic leader* or *military leader.* [b] *39* Also known as *Ish-Bosheth* [c] *40* Also known as *Mephibosheth* [d] *41* Vulgate and Syriac (see also Septuagint and 1 Chron. 8:35); Hebrew does not have *and Ahaz.* [e] *42* Some Hebrew manuscripts and Septuagint (see also 1 Chron. 8:36); most Hebrew manuscripts *Jarah, Jarah*

■ **9:35—2 Chronicles 9:31** *The United Kingdom.* After having established the identity, order and territories of the people of God in lists and genealogies, the Chronicler provided a portrait of the united kingdom. He briefly mentioned Saul (9:35—10:14) and then concentrated on David (11:1—29:30) and Solomon (2Ch 1:1—9:31). In the united kingdom, the Chronicler provided his postexilic readers with a portrait of the restoration of the kingdom in their day (see "Introduction: Purposes and Distinctives").

■ **9:35—29:30** *The Reign of David.* David's reign is idealized, attention being focused strongly on his successes to the exclusion of his failures. Particular emphasis is placed on his widespread support and on his interest in building the temple. This section proceeds in four main parts: (1) David becomes king (9:35—10:14); (2) David's widespread support (11:1—12:40); (3) his preparations for the temple (13:1—29:25); and (4) the closure of David's reign (29:26–30).

■ **9:35—10:14** *David Becomes King.* Unlike the lengthy record of Saul's rise and fall in Samuel, the Chronicler simply repeated Saul's genealogy (9:35–44) and reported the transfer of power from Saul to David (10:1–14).

■ **9:35–44** *Divine Blessing on Saul.* The Chronicler frequently mentioned numerous children as a sign of divine approval and blessing (14:3; 26:5; 2Ch 11:18–23; 13:20–21). Saul's genealogy demonstrates that he was greatly blessed by God. These blessings highlighted the severity of Saul's failure to be a faithful king.

9:40 Merib-Baal. The traditional (Masoretic) Hebrew text reads "Meri-Baal" (see note on 8:34).

■ **10:1–14** *Divine Judgment Against Saul.* The Chronicler appeared to have followed 1 Samuel 31:1–13 in his report of Saul's suicide (vv. 1–7), defilement (vv. 8–10) and burial (vv. 11–12). He delineated the reason for these tragic events in verses 13–14. See note on 8:29–40.

10:1 many fell slain. The soldiers (v. 1), Saul (vv. 4,6–8,12–14), Saul's sons (vv. 2,6–8,12) and the armor bearer (v. 5) all died, indicating that Saul was under severe divine judgment (v. 13).

10:4,13,14 See *WCF* 5.4.

10:6 all his house. Three of Saul's sons (v. 2) and his chief officers died, but not all his descendants; his son Ish-Bosheth survived (2Sa 2:8), as did his grandson Mephibosheth (8:33; 9:39; 2Sa 9:1–13). Saul's official house (dynasty) had come to an abrupt end, unlike David's, which God established permanently over Israel (see note on 17:1–15).

8 The next day, when the Philistines came to strip the dead, they found Saul and his
sons fallen on Mount Gilboa. 9 They stripped him and took his head and his armor, and
sent messengers throughout the land of the Philistines to proclaim the news among their
idols and their people. 10 They put his armor in the temple of their gods and hung up his
head in the temple of Dagon.[g]
11 When all the inhabitants of Jabesh Gilead[h] heard of everything the Philistines had
done to Saul, 12 all their valiant men went and took the bodies of Saul and his sons and
brought them to Jabesh. Then they buried their bones under the great tree in Jabesh, and
they fasted seven days.
13 Saul died[i] because he was unfaithful[j] to the LORD; he did not keep[k] the word of the
LORD and even consulted a medium[l] for guidance, 14 and did not inquire of the LORD. So
the LORD put him to death and turned[m] the kingdom[n] over to David son of Jesse.

David Becomes King Over Israel

11 All Israel[o] came together to David at Hebron[p] and said, "We are your own flesh
and blood. 2 In the past, even while Saul was king, you were the one who led Israel on their military campaigns.[q] And the LORD your God said to you, 'You will shepherd[r] my people Israel, and you will become their ruler.[s]' "
3 When all the elders of Israel had come to King David at Hebron, he made a compact
with them at Hebron before the LORD, and they anointed[t] David king over Israel, as the
LORD had promised through Samuel.

David Conquers Jerusalem

4 David and all the Israelites marched to Jerusalem (that is, Jebus). The Jebusites[u] who
lived there 5 said to David, "You will not get in here." Nevertheless, David captured the
fortress of Zion, the City of David.
6 David had said, "Whoever leads the attack on the Jebusites will become command-
er-in-chief." Joab[v] son of Zeruiah went up first, and so he received the command.
7 David then took up residence in the fortress, and so it was called the City of David.
8 He built up the city around it, from the supporting terraces[a][w] to the surrounding wall,
while Joab restored the rest of the city. 9 And David became more and more powerful,[x]
because the LORD Almighty was with him.

David's Mighty Men

10 These were the chiefs of David's mighty men—they, together with all Israel,[y] gave
his kingship strong support to extend it over the whole land, as the LORD had promised[z]— 11 this is the list of David's mighty men:[a]

10:10 [g]Jdg 16:23
10:11 [h]Jdg 21:8
10:13 [i]2Sa 1:1 [j]1Sa 15:23; 1Ch 5:25 [k]1Sa 13:13 [l]Lev 19:31; 20:6; Dt 18:9-14; 1Sa 28:7
10:14 [m]1Ch 12:23 [n]1Sa 13:14; 15:28
11:1 [o]1Ch 9:1 [p]Ge 13:18; 23:19
11:2 [q]1Sa 18:5,16 [r]Ps 78:71; Mt 2:6 [s]1Ch 5:2
11:3 [t]1Sa 16:1-13
11:4 [u]Ge 10:16; 15:18-21; Jos 3:10; 15:8; Jdg 1:21; 19:10
11:6 [v]2Sa 2:13; 8:16
11:8 [w]2Sa 5:9; 2Ch 32:5
11:9 [x]2Sa 3:1; Est 9:4
11:10 [y]ver 1 [z]ver 3; 1Ch 12:23
11:11 [a]2Sa 17:10

[a] *8* Or *the Millo*

10:9 took his head. Note the parallel with the narrative of David and Goliath (1Sa 17:54). The defilement of Saul's body by his enemies highlighted the dishonor of his defeat and death.

10:13–14 unfaithful . . . did not keep . . . inquire. The Chronicler added his explanation of the events of verses 1–12. Saul's demise was the result of divine judgment. God had put Saul to death because he had been "unfaithful to the LORD" by failing to "keep the word" and to "inquire of the LORD." The Chronicler characterized Saul as utterly unfaithful. In his view, Saul's consultation with the medium at Endor (strictly forbidden in Dt 18:9–14) was the climax of his failures (ch. 28). **inquire of the LORD.** See note on 2 Chronicles 7:14. See *WCF* 5.4; *WLC* 105.

■ **11:1—12:40** *David's Widespread Support.* Comparison with Samuel reveals that this section is arranged primarily by topic rather than chronology. The Chronicler focused on David's popular support from all Israel and his reign over the united kingdom as an encouragement and a model for his postexilic readers to unite in the hope of regaining the territory David had ruled (see "Introduction: Purposes and Distinctives"). The Chronicler ordered this material in an extensive chiasm (A B C D C' B' A'): (A) David's anointing at Hebron and establishment in Jerusalem (11:1–9); his military support at (B) Hebron (11:10–47), (C) Ziklag (12:1–7), (D) the desert stronghold (12:8–19) and again at (C') Ziklag (12:20–22) and (B') Hebron (12:23–37); and (A') David's anointing at Hebron (12:38–40).

■ **11:1–9** *Anointing at Hebron and Establishment at Jerusalem.* The Chronicler described David's anointing (vv. 1–3) and the establishment of Jerusalem as his capital (vv. 4–9). He omitted mention of David's struggle for control of the nation, reported in Samuel (2Sa 5:1–10). "All Israel" (v. 1) and "all the elders of Israel" (v. 3) recognized David as king.

11:1 All Israel. This and similar expressions depict the united nation as a whole under the reigns of David and Solomon (v. 10; 12:38; 14:8; 15:3,28; 18:14; 19:17; 21:5; 28:4,8; 2Ch 1:2; 7:8; 9:30). The repeated use of this expression reveals the Chronicler's hope for an inclusive, unified kingdom under a new Davidic king (see notes on 2Ch 10:1; 29:24; see also "Introduction: Purposes and Distinctives").

11:2 your God said. On several occasions in this section the Chronicler explained that the popular support David had received was the result of God's sovereign decree (vv. 3,9,10; 12:18,23). A legitimate king of Israel had to be chosen by God, not merely by popular sentiment (Dt 17:14–15). David met this qualification (2Ch 6:6).

11:4–9 the fortress of Zion. The Chronicler demonstrated David's success by reporting the establishment and fortification of his capital city. Successful building projects frequently displayed the blessing of God on a king. See 2 Chronicles 2:1—8:16 and notes on 2 Chronicles 11:5–12, 14:6–7, 17:12, 26:9, 27:3–6 and 32:27–29.

11:4 David and all the Israelites. Second Samuel 5:6 reads "the king and his men." The cooperation and support of all the tribes provided a model of harmonious reunification for the postexilic community (see note on 11:1).

■ **11:10–47** *Military Support at Hebron.* David found significant support at Hebron (12:23–37). Apart from an introduction (v. 10) and a final expansion (11:41–47), this list of chiefs and mighty men was in all likelihood largely derived from 2 Samuel 23:8–39. The Chronicler revealed his purpose in the opening verse (v. 10): The chiefs and mighty men supported David's kingship with "all Israel" over "the whole land, as the LORD had promised." The Chronicler's dual focus on people and territories is evident (see note on 2:42–55, as well as

Jashobeam,[a] a Hacmonite, was chief of the officers[b]; he raised his spear against three
hundred men, whom he killed in one encounter.
12 Next to him was Eleazar son of Dodai the Ahohite, one of the three mighty men.
13 He was with David at Pas Dammim when the Philistines gathered there for battle. At
a place where there was a field full of barley, the troops fled from the Philistines. 14 But
they took their stand in the middle of the field. They defended it and struck the Philistines down, and the LORD brought about a great victory.[b]
15 Three of the thirty chiefs came down to David to the rock at the cave of Adullam,
while a band of Philistines was encamped in the Valley[c] of Rephaim. 16 At that time David was in the stronghold,[d] and the Philistine garrison was at Bethlehem. 17 David longed
for water and said, "Oh, that someone would get me a drink of water from the well near
the gate of Bethlehem!" 18 So the Three broke through the Philistine lines, drew water
from the well near the gate of Bethlehem and carried it back to David. But he refused to
drink it; instead, he poured[e] it out before the LORD. 19 "God forbid that I should do this!"
he said. "Should I drink the blood of these men who went at the risk of their lives?" Because they risked their lives to bring it back, David would not drink it.
Such were the exploits of the three mighty men.
20 Abishai[f] the brother of Joab was chief of the Three. He raised his spear against three
hundred men, whom he killed, and so he became as famous as the Three. 21 He was doubly honored above the Three and became their commander, even though he was not included among them.
22 Benaiah son of Jehoiada was a valiant fighter from Kabzeel,[g] who performed great
exploits. He struck down two of Moab's best men. He also went down into a pit on a
snowy day and killed a lion.[h] 23 And he struck down an Egyptian who was seven and a
half feet[c] tall. Although the Egyptian had a spear like a weaver's rod[i] in his hand, Benaiah went against him with a club. He snatched the spear from the Egyptian's hand and
killed him with his own spear. 24 Such were the exploits of Benaiah son of Jehoiada; he
too was as famous as the three mighty men. 25 He was held in greater honor than any of
the Thirty, but he was not included among the Three. And David put him in charge of
his bodyguard.

26 The mighty men were:
Asahel[j] the brother of Joab,
Elhanan son of Dodo from Bethlehem,
27 Shammoth[k] the Harorite,
Helez the Pelonite,
28 Ira son of Ikkesh from Tekoa,
Abiezer[l] from Anathoth,
29 Sibbecai[m] the Hushathite,
Ilai the Ahohite,
30 Maharai the Netophathite,
Heled son of Baanah the Netophathite,
31 Ithai son of Ribai from Gibeah in Benjamin,
Benaiah[n] the Pirathonite,[o]
32 Hurai from the ravines of Gaash,
Abiel the Arbathite,
33 Azmaveth the Baharumite,
Eliahba the Shaalbonite,
34 the sons of Hashem the Gizonite,
Jonathan son of Shagee the Hararite,
35 Ahiam son of Sacar the Hararite,
Eliphal son of Ur,
36 Hepher the Mekerathite,
Ahijah the Pelonite,
37 Hezro the Carmelite,
Naarai son of Ezbai,

11:14 [b]Ex 14:30; 1Sa 11:13
11:15 [c]1Ch 14:9; Isa 17:5
11:16 [d]2Sa 5:17
11:18 [e]Dt 12:16
11:20 [f]1Sa 26:6
11:22 [g]Jos 15:21 [h]1Sa 17:36
11:23 [i]1Sa 17:7
11:26 [j]2Sa 2:18
11:27 [k]1Ch 27:8
11:28 [l]1Ch 27:12
11:29 [m]2Sa 21:18
11:31 [n]1Ch 27:14 [o]Jdg 12:13

[a] 11 Possibly a variant of *Jashob-Baal* [b] 11 Or *Thirty*; some Septuagint manuscripts *Three* (see also 2 Samuel 23:8) [c] 23 Hebrew *five cubits* (about 2.3 meters)

"Introduction: Purposes and Distinctives"). This record of mighty acts by David's men highlights their outstanding qualities, thus casting David in a positive light.
11:10 all Israel. See note on verse 1.

11:15–19 he poured it out. David's mighty men displayed skill and courage by fetching water for him from behind enemy lines. In response, David demonstrated humility by offering the water as a drink offering to the Lord (Ge 35:14; 2Ki 16:13; Jer 7:18).

38 Joel the brother of Nathan,
Mibhar son of Hagri,
39 Zelek the Ammonite,
Naharai the Berothite, the armor-bearer of Joab son of Zeruiah,
40 Ira the Ithrite,
Gareb the Ithrite,
41 Uriah[p] the Hittite,
Zabad[q] son of Ahlai,
42 Adina son of Shiza the Reubenite, who was chief of the Reubenites, and the thirty with him,
43 Hanan son of Maacah,
Joshaphat the Mithnite,
44 Uzzia the Ashterathite,[r]
Shama and Jeiel the sons of Hotham the Aroerite,
45 Jediael son of Shimri,
his brother Joha the Tizite,
46 Eliel the Mahavite,
Jeribai and Joshaviah the sons of Elnaam,
Ithmah the Moabite,
47 Eliel, Obed and Jaasiel the Mezobaite.

11:41 [p]2Sa 11:6 [q]1Ch 2:36
11:44 [r]Dt 1:4

Warriors Join David

12 These were the men who came to David at Ziklag,[s] while he was banished from
the presence of Saul son of Kish (they were among the warriors who helped him
in battle; 2 they were armed with bows and were able to shoot arrows or to sling stones
right-handed or left-handed;[t] they were kinsmen of Saul[u] from the tribe of Benjamin):

3 Ahiezer their chief and Joash the sons of Shemaah the Gibeathite; Jeziel and Pelet the sons of Azmaveth; Beracah, Jehu the Anathothite, 4 and Ishmaiah the Gibeonite, a mighty man among the Thirty, who was a leader of the Thirty; Jeremiah,
Jahaziel, Johanan, Jozabad the Gederathite,[v] 5 Eluzai, Jerimoth, Bealiah, Shemariah and Shephatiah the Haruphite; 6 Elkanah, Isshiah, Azarel, Joezer and Jashobeam the Korahites; 7 and Joelah and Zebadiah the sons of Jeroham from Gedor.[w]

8 Some Gadites[x] defected to David at his stronghold in the desert. They were brave
warriors, ready for battle and able to handle the shield and spear. Their faces were the
faces of lions,[y] and they were as swift as gazelles[z] in the mountains.
9 Ezer was the chief,
Obadiah the second in command, Eliab the third,
10 Mishmannah the fourth, Jeremiah the fifth,
11 Attai the sixth, Eliel the seventh,
12 Johanan the eighth, Elzabad the ninth,
13 Jeremiah the tenth and Macbannai the eleventh.
14 These Gadites were army commanders; the least was a match for a hundred,[a] and
the greatest for a thousand.[b] 15 It was they who crossed the Jordan in the first month
when it was overflowing all its banks,[c] and they put to flight everyone living in the valleys, to the east and to the west.
16 Other Benjamites[d] and some men from Judah also came to David in his stronghold.
17 David went out to meet them and said to them, "If you have come to me in peace, to help
me, I am ready to have you unite with me. But if you have come to betray me to my enemies
when my hands are free from violence, may the God of our fathers see it and judge you."
18 Then the Spirit[e] came upon Amasai,[f] chief of the Thirty, and he said:

12:1 [s]Jos 15:31; 1Sa 27:2-6
12:2 [t]Jdg 3:15; 20:16 [u]2Sa 3:19
12:4 [v]Jos 15:36
12:7 [w]Jos 15:58
12:8 [x]Ge 30:11 [y]2Sa 17:10 [z]2Sa 2:18
12:14 [a]Lev 26:8 [b]Dt 32:30
12:15 [c]Jos 3:15
12:16 [d]2Sa 3:19
12:18 [e]Jdg 3:10; 6:34; 1Ch 28:12; 2Ch 15:1; 20:14; 24:20 [f]2Sa 17:25

11:41b–47 Zabad . . . The Chronicler expanded the register of David's supporters beyond the "mighty men" listed in 2 Samuel 23:24–39. The repeated references to tribes and locations here illustrates the diverse and widespread support David received (see note on vv. 10–47).

■ **12:1–7** *Military Support at Ziklag.* David also received support at Ziklag (cf. vv. 20–22). When Saul banished David, a number of Saul's own relatives joined David at Ziklag. For other examples of Saul's family supporting David, see verses 16, 23 and 29.

■ **12:8–19** *Military Support at the Desert Stronghold.* At David's desert stronghold (1Sa 22:3–5; 23:14,29; 24:1), Israelites from various locations joined him: Gadites (vv. 8–15), more Benjamites and Judahites (vv. 16–18) and Manassehites (vv. 19). See note on 11:10–47.

12:8 faces of lions . . . swift as gazelles. Biblical writers commonly used animal metaphors for warriors and leaders. "Faces of lions" indicates the Gadites' ferocity. The best of the Gadite warriors supported David.

12:15 overflowing. In March and April northern melting snows frequently engorged the rivers of the region, and crossing the Jordan was particularly treacherous. The Chronicler focused on this detail apparently to emphasize the superior courage of David's supporters among the Gadites (v. 14).

12:18 the Spirit. By mentioning the Holy Spirit, the Chronicler demonstrated that the defection of Benjamites to David was not misguided.

"We are yours, O David!
We are with you, O son of Jesse!
Success,[g] success to you,
and success to those who help you,
for your God will help you."

So David received them and made them leaders of his raiding bands.
19 Some of the men of Manasseh defected to David when he went with the Philistines to fight against Saul. (He and his men did not help the Philistines because, after
consultation, their rulers sent him away. They said, "It will cost us our heads if he deserts to his master Saul.")[h] 20 When David went to Ziklag,[i] these were the men of Manasseh who defected to him: Adnah, Jozabad, Jediael, Michael, Jozabad, Elihu and Zillethai, leaders of units of a thousand in Manasseh. 21 They helped David against
raiding bands, for all of them were brave warriors, and they were commanders in his
army. 22 Day after day men came to help David, until he had a great army, like the army
of God.[a]

Others Join David at Hebron

23 These are the numbers of the men armed for battle who came to David at Hebron[j]
to turn[k] Saul's kingdom over to him, as the LORD had said:[l]
24 men of Judah, carrying shield and spear—6,800 armed for battle;
25 men of Simeon, warriors ready for battle—7,100;
26 men of Levi—4,600, 27 including Jehoiada, leader of the family of Aaron, with
3,700 men, 28 and Zadok,[m] a brave young warrior, with 22 officers from his family;
29 men of Benjamin,[n] Saul's kinsmen—3,000, most[o] of whom had remained loyal to Saul's house until then;
30 men of Ephraim, brave warriors, famous in their own clans—20,800;
31 men of half the tribe of Manasseh, designated by name to come and make David king—18,000;
32 men of Issachar, who understood the times and knew what Israel should do[p]—200 chiefs, with all their relatives under their command;
33 men of Zebulun, experienced soldiers prepared for battle with every type of weapon, to help David with undivided loyalty—50,000;
34 men of Naphtali—1,000 officers, together with 37,000 men carrying shields and spears;
35 men of Dan, ready for battle—28,600;
36 men of Asher, experienced soldiers prepared for battle—40,000;
37 and from east of the Jordan, men of Reuben, Gad and the half-tribe of Manasseh, armed with every type of weapon—120,000.

38 All these were fighting men who volunteered to serve in the ranks. They came to Hebron fully determined to make David king over all Israel.[q] All the rest of the Israelites
were also of one mind to make David king. 39 The men spent three days there with David, eating and drinking,[r] for their families had supplied provisions for them. 40 Also, their
neighbors from as far away as Issachar, Zebulun and Naphtali came bringing food on
donkeys, camels, mules and oxen. There were plentiful supplies[s] of flour, fig cakes, raisin[t] cakes, wine, oil, cattle and sheep, for there was joy[u] in Israel.

[a] 22 Or *a great and mighty army*

12:18 [g] 1Sa 25:5-6
12:19 [h] 1Sa 29:2-11
12:20 [i] 1Sa 27:6
12:23 [j] 2Sa 2:3-4 [k] 1Ch 10:14 [l] 1Sa 16:1; 1Ch 11:10
12:28 [m] 2Sa 8:17; 1Ch 6:8; 15:11; 16:39; 27:17
12:29 [n] 2Sa 3:19 [o] 2Sa 2:8-9
12:32 [p] Est 1:13
12:38 [q] 2Sa 5:1-3; 1Ch 9:1
12:39 [r] 2Sa 3:20; Isa 25:6-8
12:40 [s] 2Sa 16:1; 17:29 [t] 1Sa 25:18 [u] 1Ch 29:22

12:19 He . . . did not help the Philistines. The Chronicler protected David's reputation by reporting that David did not fight against other Israelites. See 1 Samuel 29 for a fuller account of this period.

■ **12:20–22** *More Military Support at Ziklag.* David received further support at Ziklag (see note on vv. 1–7).

12:22 like the army of God. Hyperbole was used to idealize and glorify David's army.

■ **12:23–37** *More Military Support at Hebron.* David found other supporters at Hebron (see note on 11:10–47). The Chronicler recorded a listing of representatives from each of the tribes. Three explanations of these large numbers are possible: (1) The Hebrew word translated "thousand" may be a technical term referring to units of considerably less than a thousand. In this case, verse 24 would read "men of Judah, carrying shield and spear—six units with eight hundred armed for battle." (2) The Hebrew word translated "thousand" may be emended to read "chiefs." Thus, verse 24 would read "six chiefs with eight hundred armed for battle." (3) The possibility of hyperbole cannot be entirely ruled out (see note on v. 22).

■ **12:38–40** *More on the Anointing at Hebron.* The Chronicler returned to the narrative of the ceremonies that began this section (11:1–3). He closed his report of David's widespread support with the observation that the people at Hebron and the rest of the nation were "of one mind" (v. 38) to make David king. David's countless supporters celebrated their new king with joy and feasting. The Chronicler offered this event as an expression of his hope for joyful celebration in the postexilic community.

12:38 all Israel. See note on 11:1.

Bringing Back the Ark

13 David conferred with each of his officers, the commanders of thousands and commanders of hundreds. [2]He then said to the whole assembly of Israel, "If it seems good to you and if it is the will of the LORD our God, let us send word far and wide to the rest of our brothers throughout the territories of Israel, and also to the priests and Levites who are with them in their towns and pasturelands, to come and join us. [3]Let us bring the ark of our God back to us,[v] for we did not inquire[w] of[a] it[b] during the reign of Saul." [4]The whole assembly agreed to do this, because it seemed right to all the people.

[5]So David assembled all the Israelites,[x] from the Shihor River[y] in Egypt to Lebo[c] Hamath,[z] to bring the ark of God from Kiriath Jearim.[a] [6]David and all the Israelites with him went to Baalah[b] of Judah (Kiriath Jearim) to bring up from there the ark of God the LORD, who is enthroned between the cherubim[c]—the ark that is called by the Name.

[7]They moved the ark of God from Abinadab's[d] house on a new cart, with Uzzah and Ahio guiding it. [8]David and all the Israelites were celebrating with all their might before God, with songs and with harps, lyres, tambourines, cymbals and trumpets.[e]

[9]When they came to the threshing floor of Kidon, Uzzah reached out his hand to steady the ark, because the oxen stumbled. [10]The LORD's anger[f] burned against Uzzah, and he struck him down[g] because he had put his hand on the ark. So he died there before God.

[11]Then David was angry because the LORD's wrath had broken out against Uzzah, and to this day that place is called Perez Uzzah.[d][h]

[12]David was afraid of God that day and asked, "How can I ever bring the ark of God to me?" [13]He did not take the ark to be with him in the City of David. Instead, he took it aside to the house of Obed-Edom[i] the Gittite. [14]The ark of God remained with the family of Obed-Edom in his house for three months, and the LORD blessed his household[j] and everything he had.

David's House and Family

14 Now Hiram king of Tyre sent messengers to David, along with cedar logs,[k] stonemasons and carpenters to build a palace for him. [2]And David knew that the LORD had established him as king over Israel and that his kingdom had been highly exalted[l] for the sake of his people Israel.

[3]In Jerusalem David took more wives and became the father of more sons[m] and daugh-

13:3 [v]1Sa 7:1-2 [w]2Ch 1:5
13:5 [x]1Ch 11:1; 15:3 [y]Jos 13:3 [z]Nu 13:21 [a]1Sa 6:21; 7:2
13:6 [b]Jos 15:9; 2Sa 6:2 [c]Ex 25:22; 2Ki 19:15
13:7 [d]Nu 4:15; 1Sa 7:1
13:8 [e]2Sa 6:5; 1Ch 15:16,19,24; 2Ch 5:12; Ps 92:3
13:10 [f]1Ch 15:13,15 [g]Lev 10:2
13:11 [h]1Ch 15:13; Ps 7:11
13:13 [i]1Ch 15:18,24; 16:38; 26:4-5,15
13:14 [j]2Sa 6:11; 1Ch 26:4-5
14:1 [k]2Ch 2:3; Ezr 3:7
14:2 [l]Nu 24:7; Dt 26:19
14:3 [m]1Ch 3:1

[a] 3 Or *we neglected* [b] 3 Or *him* [c] 5 Or *to the entrance to* [d] 11 *Perez Uzzah* means *outbreak against Uzzah.*

▪ **13:1—29:25** *Preparations for the Temple.* The Chronicler reported the second essential ingredient in David's model kingdom, his enthusiastic preparations for the temple. This account divides into two main parts: centralization of worship in Jerusalem (13:1—16:43) and temple preparations (17:1—29:25).

▪ **13:1—16:43** *David Brings the Ark to Jerusalem.* The Chronicler recounted David's successful centralization of worship in Jerusalem. Comparison with 2 Samuel 5–6 indicates that the materials in Samuel and Chronicles are arranged topically and not in strict chronological order. The Chronicler's account divides into three main sections: the failed attempt to transfer the ark to Jerusalem (13:1–14), David's blessings (14:1–17) and the successful retrieval of the ark and ensuing celebration (15:1—16:43).

▪ **13:1–14** *David's Failed Transfer of the Ark.* David's first attempt to bring the ark to Jerusalem failed miserably because he mishandled the ark.

13:1–9 See *WCF* 23.3.

13:1–4 These verses reflect the Chronicler's special focus on "the whole assembly" (v. 4) as supportive of Jerusalem worship (vv. 4,5,6,8; see note on 11:1). The verses have no parallel in the account of this event in 2 Samuel 5–6.

13:2 good to you . . . will of the LORD. The Chronicler depicted cooperation between David and the people as they sought the will of God as a model for cooperation among his postexilic readers (v. 4; 2Ch 30:4–5).

13:3 we did not inquire of it. The Chronicler contrasted David with Saul (cf. 11:2). David's concern for the ark highlights Saul's blatant neglect. See note on 2 Chronicles 7:14.

13:4 whole assembly agreed. See note on verse 2.

13:6 enthroned between the cherubim. The ark of the covenant represented the presence of God among his people in a variety of ways. Here it stood as God's moveable throne. **called by the Name.** The "Name" of God refers to his nearness, to the divine power dwelling in the temple and accessible through prayer and sacrifice (16:2,8,10,29,35,41; 17:24; 21:19; 22:7–8,10,19; 23:13; 28:3; 29:13,16; 2Ch 2:1,4; 6:5–10,20,24,26,32–34,38; 7:14,16,20; 12:13; 14:11; 18:15; 20:8–9; 33:4,7,18). This concept is reflected in the New Testament injunction to pray in the name of Jesus (see Jn 12:28; 14:13,14; 16:24).

13:7 on a new cart. The Israelites neglected the divinely ordained manner of transporting the ark with poles on the priests' shoulders (Ex 25:12–15). They handled it with disregard for the holiness and commandment of God.

13:8 celebrating with . . . songs. See note on 15:16–24.

13:10 he struck him down. Uzzah demonstrated utter disregard for the sanctity of worship by touching the ark (Nu 4:15). Far from a minor offense, Uzzah's violation was a flagrant expression of disdain for the holiness of God and for worship regulations (see note on v. 7).

13:11 to this day. See note on 4:41 and 43.

13:13 Obed-Edom. A Levite (15:18,21,24) who was blessed with many sons (26:4–5), presumably because he cared properly for the ark. The Chronicler frequently mentioned numerous children as a sign of divine approval and blessing (14:3; 26:5; 2Ch 11:18–23; 13:20–21).

▪ **14:1–17** *David's Distinguishing Blessings.* The Chronicler inserted this material into his account to illustrate that despite David's failure (13:1–14) God established and blessed him. Three items appear: palace preparations (vv. 1–2), David's children in Jerusalem (v. 3) and David's victory over the Philistines (vv. 8–17).

14:1 Hiram king of Tyre sent messengers. The Chronicler introduces the motif of David's international recognition, summarized in verse 17 (see its note).

14:2 the LORD had established . . . exalted for the sake of his people. David recognized that the establishment of his kingdom was a blessing for the people. With these remarks the Chronicler encouraged his postexilic readers to hope for the benefits of a Davidic king in their own day (see note on 2Ch 2:11).

14:3 more sons and daughters. The increase in David's progeny indicated God's favor toward him and his Jerusalem capital (3:4–9; see note on 13:13).

ters. 4These are the names of the children born to him there:[n] Shammua, Shobab, Nathan, Solomon, 5Ibhar, Elishua, Elpelet, 6Nogah, Nepheg, Japhia, 7Elishama, Beeliada[a]
and Eliphelet.

David Defeats the Philistines

8When the Philistines heard that David had been anointed king over all Israel,[o] they
went up in full force to search for him, but David heard about it and went out to meet
them. 9Now the Philistines had come and raided the Valley[p] of Rephaim; 10so David inquired of God: "Shall I go and attack the Philistines? Will you hand them over to me?"
The LORD answered him, "Go, I will hand them over to you."
11So David and his men went up to Baal Perazim,[q] and there he defeated them. He
said, "As waters break out, God has broken out against my enemies by my hand." So that
place was called Baal Perazim.[b] 12The Philistines had abandoned their gods there, and
David gave orders to burn[r] them in the fire.[s]
13Once more the Philistines raided the valley;[t] 14so David inquired of God again, and
God answered him, "Do not go straight up, but circle around them and attack them in
front of the balsam trees. 15As soon as you hear the sound of marching in the tops of the
balsam trees, move out to battle, because that will mean God has gone out in front of you
to strike the Philistine army." 16So David did as God commanded him, and they struck
down the Philistine army, all the way from Gibeon[u] to Gezer.[v]
17So David's fame[w] spread throughout every land, and the LORD made all the nations
fear[x] him.

The Ark Brought to Jerusalem

15 After David had constructed buildings for himself in the City of David, he prepared[y] a place for the ark of God and pitched[z] a tent for it. 2Then David said,
"No one but the Levites[a] may carry[b] the ark of God, because the LORD chose them to carry the ark of the LORD and to minister[c] before him forever."
3David assembled all Israel[d] in Jerusalem to bring up the ark of the LORD to the place
he had prepared for it. 4He called together the descendants of Aaron and the Levites:
5From the descendants of Kohath,
Uriel the leader and 120 relatives;
6from the descendants of Merari,
Asaiah the leader and 220 relatives;
7from the descendants of Gershon,[c]
Joel the leader and 130 relatives;
8from the descendants of Elizaphan,[e]
Shemaiah the leader and 200 relatives;
9from the descendants of Hebron,[f]
Eliel the leader and 80 relatives;
10from the descendants of Uzziel,
Amminadab the leader and 112 relatives.
11Then David summoned Zadok[g] and Abiathar[h] the priests, and Uriel, Asaiah, Joel,

14:4 [n]1Ch 3:9
14:8 [o]1Ch 11:1
14:9 [p]ver 13; Jos 15:8; 1Ch 11:15
14:11 [q]Isa 28:21
14:12 [r]Ex 32:20 [s]Jos 7:15
14:13 [t]ver 9
14:16 [u]Jos 9:3 [v]Jos 10:33
14:17 [w]Jos 6:27; 2Ch 26:8 [x]Ex 15:14-16; Dt 2:25
15:1 [y]Ps 132:1-18 [z]1Ch 16:1; 17:1
15:2 [a]Nu 4:15; Dt 10:8; 2Ch 5:5 [b]Dt 31:9 [c]1Ch 23:13
15:3 [d]1Ki 8:1; 1Ch 13:5
15:8 [e]Ex 6:22
15:9 [f]Ex 6:18
15:11 [g]1Ch 12:28 [h]1Sa 22:20

[a] 7 A variant of *Eliada* [b] 11 *Baal Perazim* means *the lord who breaks out.* [c] 7 Hebrew *Gershom,* a variant of *Gershon*

14:8–12 he defeated them. David's victory over the Philistines contrasted with Saul's defeat (10:1–7). David inquired of the Lord (vv. 10,14), while Saul inquired of the medium (10:13). This event also contrasted with David's failed attempt to retrieve the ark (13:1–14). While God had "broken out" against Uzzah (13:11), David now declared that "God has broken out" against the Philistines (v. 11).
14:8 all Israel. See note on 11:1.
14:12 gave orders to burn them. This expression is not found in the traditional Hebrew (Masoretic) text of 2 Samuel 5:21. It occurs in some other texts and probably appeared in the Chronicler's version of Samuel. David followed Mosaic regulations in burning these idols (Dt 7:5,25).
14:17 all the nations fear him. This verse was added to the 2 Samuel 5 account by the Chronicler to highlight David's international fame (see note on v. 1). David stood strong against his enemies. Other nations saw the power of God in the king's victory and were afraid (Jos 2:11; 2Ch 17:10; 20:29). See also Solomon's prayer that foreigners may fear the Lord (2Ch 6:32–33). The Chronicler encouraged his readers to hope for a new David to provide international security in their day (cf. Hag 2:6–7,20–23; Zec 9:1–13).

■ **15:1—16:43** *David's Successful Transfer of the Ark.* In this account of successful retrieval and celebration, the Chronicler followed material from 2 Samuel 6:12–19 in 15:25—16:3 and added 15:1–24 and 16:4–43. This section describes David's plan (15:1–2), his instructions for the Levites and priests (15:3–24), the ark's move to Jerusalem (15:25—16:3), David's appointment of Levites in Jerusalem and his arrangements for worship (16:4–6), David's psalm (16:7–36), David's appointment of Levites and priests in Jerusalem and Gibeon (16:37–42) and the people's return to their homes (16:43). See note on 6:1–53.
■ **15:1–2** *David Forms a New Plan.* The Chronicler went to great lengths in verses 2 and 13–15 to show that David transferred the ark in compliance with Mosaic legislation (Ex 25:12–15; Dt 10:8; 18:5).
15:1 pitched a tent. The tabernacle was still in Gibeon (16:39), so David constructed a new tabernacle for the ark.
■ **15:3–24** *David Instructs Levites and Priests.* All three divisions of the tribe of Levi (Kohathites, Merarites and Gershonites) were included in David's worship organization. These events reveal the Chronicler's interest in David's Levitical orders for the postexilic period (see note on 6:1–53).
15:3 all Israel. See note on 11:1.

Shemaiah, Eliel and Amminadab the Levites. 12He said to them, "You are the heads of
the Levitical families; you and your fellow Levites are to consecrate[i] yourselves and bring
up the ark of the LORD, the God of Israel, to the place I have prepared for it. 13It was because you, the Levites,[j] did not bring it up the first time that the LORD our God broke out
in anger against us.[k] We did not inquire of him about how to do it in the prescribed way."
14So the priests and Levites consecrated themselves in order to bring up the ark of the
LORD, the God of Israel. 15And the Levites carried the ark of God with the poles on their
shoulders, as Moses had commanded[l] in accordance with the word of the LORD.
16David told the leaders of the Levites to appoint their brothers as singers[m] to sing
joyful songs, accompanied by musical instruments: lyres, harps and cymbals.[n]
17So the Levites appointed Heman[o] son of Joel; from his brothers, Asaph[p] son of Berekiah; and from their brothers the Merarites,[q] Ethan son of Kushaiah; 18and with them
their brothers next in rank: Zechariah,[a] Jaaziel, Shemiramoth, Jehiel, Unni, Eliab, Benaiah, Maaseiah, Mattithiah, Eliphelehu, Mikneiah, Obed-Edom[r] and Jeiel,[b] the gatekeepers.
19The musicians Heman,[s] Asaph and Ethan were to sound the bronze cymbals;
20Zechariah, Aziel, Shemiramoth, Jehiel, Unni, Eliab, Maaseiah and Benaiah were to play
the lyres according to *alamoth*,[c] 21and Mattithiah, Eliphelehu, Mikneiah, Obed-Edom, Jeiel and Azaziah were to play the harps, directing according to *sheminith*.[c] 22Kenaniah the
head Levite was in charge of the singing; that was his responsibility because he was skillful at it.
23Berekiah and Elkanah were to be doorkeepers for the ark. 24Shebaniah, Joshaphat,
Nethanel, Amasai, Zechariah, Benaiah and Eliezer the priests were to blow trumpets[t] before the ark of God. Obed-Edom and Jehiah were also to be doorkeepers for the ark.
25So David and the elders of Israel and the commanders of units of a thousand went
to bring up the ark[u] of the covenant of the LORD from the house of Obed-Edom, with rejoicing. 26Because God had helped the Levites who were carrying the ark of the covenant
of the LORD, seven bulls and seven rams[v] were sacrificed. 27Now David was clothed in a
robe of fine linen, as were all the Levites who were carrying the ark, and as were the singers, and Kenaniah, who was in charge of the singing of the choirs. David also wore a lin-
en ephod. 28So all Israel brought up the ark of the covenant of the LORD with shouts, with
the sounding of rams' horns[w] and trumpets, and of cymbals, and the playing of lyres and
harps.
29As the ark of the covenant of the LORD was entering the City of David, Michal
daughter of Saul watched from a window. And when she saw King David dancing and
celebrating, she despised him in her heart.
16 They brought the ark of God and set it inside the tent that David had pitched[x]
for it, and they presented burnt offerings and fellowship offerings[d] before God.
2After David had finished sacrificing the burnt offerings and fellowship offerings, he
blessed[y] the people in the name of the LORD. 3Then he gave a loaf of bread, a cake of
dates and a cake of raisins to each Israelite man and woman.
4He appointed some of the Levites to minister[z] before the ark of the LORD, to make

15:12 [i]Ex 19:14-15; Lev 11:44; 2Ch 35:6
15:13 [j]1Ki 8:4 [k]2Sa 6:3; 1Ch 13:7-10
15:15 [l]Ex 25:14; Nu 4:5, 15
15:16 [m]Ps 68:25 [n]1Ch 13:8; 25:1; Ne 12:27,36
15:17 [o]1Ch 6:33 [p]1Ch 6:39 [q]1Ch 6:44
15:18 [r]1Ch 26:4-5
15:19 [s]1Ch 25:6
15:24 [t]ver 28; 1Ch 16:6; 2Ch 7:6
15:25 [u]1Ch 13:13; 2Ch 1:4
15:26 [v]Nu 23:1-4,29
15:28 [w]1Ch 13:8
16:1 [x]1Ch 15:1
16:2 [y]Ex 39:43
16:4 [z]1Ch 15:2

[a] *18* Three Hebrew manuscripts and most Septuagint manuscripts (see also verse 20 and 1 Chron. 16:5); most Hebrew manuscripts *Zechariah son and* or *Zechariah, Ben and* [b] *18* Hebrew; Septuagint (see also verse 21) *Jeiel and Azaziah* [c] *20,21* Probably a musical term [d] *1* Traditionally *peace offerings*; also in verse 2

15:11 Zadok and Abiathar. The two high priests during David's reign. Zadok served at the Mosaic tabernacle in Gibeon, and Abiathar served in Jerusalem (18:16; 27:34). Solomon later excluded Abiathar because Abiathar supported Adonijah (1Ki 1:7; 2:26–27). Zadok and his descendants represented the high priestly family for the Chronicler and his postexilic audience (see notes on 6:1–53; 6:1–15; 6:48–53).
15:12–14 See *WLC* 175.
15:13 inquire of him. See note on 2 Chronicles 7:14.
15:15 as Moses had commanded. See note on 16:40.
15:16–24 singers . . . musical instruments. The Chronicler added details concerning the music performed during the event. He frequently displayed a keen interest in the music of worship (6:31–47; 9:15–16,33; 13:8; 15:28; 16:4–6; 23:5; 25:1–7; 2Ch 5:12–13; 7:6; 23:13; 29:25–30; 34:12). His concern for the restoration of proper worship during the postexilic period lay behind this emphasis (see note on 6:1–53).
■ **15:25—16:3** *David Moves the Ark.* In contrast with his first attempt, David cautiously moved the ark toward Jerusalem.
15:27 a robe of fine linen, as were all the Levites. David, along with all the Levites, wore priestly garb. The robe of fine linen, as well as the linen ephod, was typical priestly attire (1Sa 2:18; 22:18). By this dress David showed himself to be a king-priest. The popular misconception that David was only partially clad (based on Michal's comments in 2Sa 6:20) is ruled out by the Chronicler's description. In light of this description, if Michal's criticism had any basis in fact, it may have meant that David had put off his royal robes in exchange for the clothing of a priest. See also note on verse 29.
15:28 all Israel. See note on 11:1. **rams' horns . . . harps.** See note on verses 16–24.
15:29 Michal daughter of Saul. The Chronicler called attention to the hardened heart of Saul's daughter. In contrast to the people, the Levites and David, Michal was repulsed by David's enthusiastic expression of worship. Her sarcastic rebuke is omitted in 2 Samuel 6:20, perhaps to avoid casting any doubt on the purity of David's worship.
16:2 in the name. See note on 13:6.
■ **16:4–6** *David Appoints Levites in Jerusalem.* The Chronicler drew attention to the Davidic arrangement of the Levites (see note on 6:1–53).

petition, to give thanks, and to praise the LORD, the God of Israel: 5 Asaph was the chief,
Zechariah second, then Jeiel, Shemiramoth, Jehiel, Mattithiah, Eliab, Benaiah, Obed-
Edom and Jeiel. They were to play the lyres and harps, Asaph was to sound the cymbals,
6 and Benaiah and Jahaziel the priests were to blow the trumpets regularly before the ark
of the covenant of God.

David's Psalm of Thanks

7 That day David first committed to Asaph and his associates this psalm[a] of thanks to
the LORD:

8 Give thanks[b] to the LORD, call on his name;
make known among the nations[c] what he has done.
9 Sing to him, sing praise[d] to him;
tell of all his wonderful acts.
10 Glory in his holy name;
let the hearts of those who seek the LORD rejoice.
11 Look to the LORD and his strength;
seek[e] his face always.
12 Remember[f] the wonders he has done,
his miracles,[g] and the judgments he pronounced,
13 O descendants of Israel his servant,
O sons of Jacob, his chosen ones.

14 He is the LORD our God;
his judgments[h] are in all the earth.
15 He remembers[a] his covenant forever,
the word he commanded, for a thousand generations,
16 the covenant[i] he made with Abraham,
the oath he swore to Isaac.
17 He confirmed it to Jacob[j] as a decree,
to Israel as an everlasting covenant:
18 "To you I will give the land of Canaan[k]
as the portion you will inherit."
19 When they were but few in number,[l]
few indeed, and strangers in it,
20 they[b] wandered from nation to nation,
from one kingdom to another.
21 He allowed no man to oppress them;
for their sake he rebuked kings:[m]
22 "Do not touch my anointed ones;
do my prophets[n] no harm."

23 Sing to the LORD, all the earth;
proclaim his salvation day after day.
24 Declare his glory among the nations,
his marvelous deeds among all peoples.
25 For great is the LORD and most worthy of praise;[o]
he is to be feared[p] above all gods.[q]
26 For all the gods of the nations are idols,
but the LORD made the heavens.[r]

16:7 [a]2Sa 23:1
16:8 [b]ver 34; Ps 136:1 [c]2Ki 19:19
16:9 [d]Ex 15:1
16:11 [e]1Ch 28:9; 2Ch 7:14; Ps 24:6; 119:2, 58
16:12 [f]Ps 77:11 [g]Ps 78:43
16:14 [h]Isa 26:9
16:16 [i]Ge 12:7; 15:18; 17:2; 22:16-18; 26:3; 28:13; 35:11
16:17 [j]Ge 35:9-12
16:18 [k]Ge 13:14-17
16:19 [l]Ge 34:30; Dt 7:7
16:21 [m]Ge 12:17; 20:3; Ex 7:15-18
16:22 [n]Ge 20:7
16:25 [o]Ps 48:1 [p]Ps 76:7; 89:7 [q]Dt 32:39
16:26 [r]Lev 19:4; Ps 102:25

a *15* Some Septuagint manuscripts (see also Psalm 105:8); Hebrew *Remember* b *18–20* One Hebrew manuscript, Septuagint and Vulgate (see also Psalm 105:12); most Hebrew manuscripts *inherit, / 19though you are but few in number, / few indeed, and strangers in it." / 20They*

16:4 to make petition, to give thanks, and to praise. These are the three principal kinds of psalms.
16:5–6 play the lyres . . . trumpets. See note on 15:16–24.
■ **16:7–36** *David's Psalm.* The Chronicler added a psalm of celebration not found in Samuel. The passage is similar to portions of several psalms (cf. vv. 8–22 with Ps 105:1–15; vv. 23–33 with Ps 96; and vv. 34–36 with Ps 106:1,47–48). David celebrated the entry of the ark into Jerusalem as a mighty act of God, but his words also spoke to the Chronicler's postexilic readers. He called for the praise of God (vv. 8–13) and recalled the promise of the land and divine protection in the wanderings of the past (vv. 15–22). The Chronicler's readers had experienced similar blessings in their return to the land. David enjoined his readers to praise once again (vv. 23–34) and invited the people to cry out for further protection and deliverance (v. 35). The Chronicler's postexilic audience needed the same help from God. Finally, the people responded with praise and joy at the blessings of God (v. 36), just as the Chronicler's audience was to praise God in their day.

16:8,10,29,35 [his holy] name. See note on 13:6.

16:10,11 seek. See note on 2 Chronicles 7:14.

16:26 See *HC* 95.

27 Splendor and majesty are before him;
strength and joy in his dwelling place.
28 Ascribe to the LORD, O families of nations,
ascribe to the LORD glory and strength,[s]
29 ascribe to the LORD the glory due his name.
Bring an offering and come before him;
worship the LORD in the splendor of his[a] holiness.[t]
30 Tremble[u] before him, all the earth!
The world is firmly established; it cannot be moved.
31 Let the heavens rejoice, let the earth be glad;[v]
let them say among the nations, "The LORD reigns![w]"
32 Let the sea resound, and all that is in it;[x]
let the fields be jubilant, and everything in them!
33 Then the trees[y] of the forest will sing,
they will sing for joy before the LORD,
for he comes to judge[z] the earth.
34 Give thanks[a] to the LORD, for he is good;[b]
his love endures forever.[c]
35 Cry out, "Save us, O God our Savior;[d]
gather us and deliver us from the nations,
that we may give thanks to your holy name,
that we may glory in your praise."
36 Praise be to the LORD, the God of Israel,[e]
from everlasting to everlasting.

Then all the people said "Amen" and "Praise the LORD."

37 David left Asaph and his associates before the ark of the covenant of the LORD to
minister there regularly, according to each day's requirements.[f] 38 He also left Obed-
Edom[g] and his sixty-eight associates to minister with them. Obed-Edom son of Jeduthun,
and also Hosah,[h] were gatekeepers.
39 David left Zadok[i] the priest and his fellow priests before the tabernacle of the LORD
at the high place in Gibeon[j] 40 to present burnt offerings to the LORD on the altar of burnt
offering regularly, morning and evening, in accordance with everything written in the
Law[k] of the LORD, which he had given Israel. 41 With them were Heman[l] and Jeduthun
and the rest of those chosen and designated by name to give thanks to the LORD, "for his
love endures forever." 42 Heman and Jeduthun were responsible for the sounding of the
trumpets and cymbals and for the playing of the other instruments for sacred song.[m] The
sons of Jeduthun were stationed at the gate.
43 Then all the people left, each for his own home, and David returned home to bless
his family.

God's Promise to David

17 After David was settled in his palace, he said to Nathan the prophet, "Here I am, living in a palace of cedar, while the ark of the covenant of the LORD is under a tent.[n]"

2 Nathan replied to David, "Whatever you have in mind,[o] do it, for God is with you."

16:28 [s]Ps 29:1-2
16:29 [t]Ps 29:1-2
16:30 [u]Ps 114:7
16:31 [v]Isa 44:23; 49:13 [w]Ps 93:1
16:32 [x]Ps 98:7
16:33 [y]Isa 55:12 [z]Ps 96:10; 98:9
16:34 [a]ver 8 [b]Na 1:7 [c]2Ch 5:13; 7:3; Ezr 3:11; Ps 136:1-26; Jer 33:11
16:35 [d]Mic 7:7
16:36 [e]Dt 27:15; 1Ki 8:15; Ps 72:18-19
16:37 [f]2Ch 8:14
16:38 [g]1Ch 13:13 [h]1Ch 26:10
16:39 [i]2Sa 8:17; 1Ch 15:11 [j]1Ki 3:4; 2Ch 1:3
16:40 [k]Ex 29:38; Nu 28:1-8
16:41 [l]1Ch 6:33; 25:1-6; 2Ch 5:13
16:42 [m]2Ch 7:6
17:1 [n]1Ch 15:1
17:2 [o]2Ch 6:7

[a] 29 Or *LORD with the splendor of*

■ **16:37–42** *David Appoints Levites and Priests in Jerusalem and Gibeon.* David's effort to centralize worship through the transfer of the ark concluded with his arrangement of the Levites (see note on vv. 4–6).

16:40 everything written in the Law of the LORD. The Chronicler highlighted David's commitment to observing the Mosaic Law as a model for the reorganization of the postexilic community (6:49; 15:13,15; 22:12–13; 28:7; 29:19; 2Ch 6:16; 7:17–18; 12:1–2; 14:4; 15:12–14; 17:3–9; 19:8–10; 24:6,9; 25:4; 30:15–16; 31:3–21; 33:8; 34:19–33; 35:6–26). See "Introduction: Purposes and Distinctives."

■ **16:43** *David Accomplishes His Plan.* David's plan (15:1–2) was brought to completion.

■ **17:1—29:25** *David Prepares for the Temple.* The Chronicler turned to one of David's most important contributions to Israel's history: his preparations for the temple. This portion divides into five major sections: divine commission (17:1–27), military preparations (18:1—20:8), discovering the temple site (21:1—22:1), commissioning the builders (22:2–19) and arranging personnel and transferring power and responsibility to Solomon (23:1—29:25).

■ **17:1–27** *David Accepts Commission to Prepare for Solomon.* God's commission for David to prepare for the temple presented political problems for David, but he readily accepted his role. The Chronicler closely followed 2 Samuel 7:1–29.

17:1–15 palace . . . house . . . house. One Hebrew word (usually translated "house") lies at the heart of this passage. The same term refers to David's "palace" (v. 1), the Lord's "house" (the temple; vv. 4–6) and David's "house" (dynasty; v. 10). David saw his own house ("palace") and desired to build a "house" (temple) for God. But God declared that he would build a "house" (dynasty) for David. David's son would build a "house" (temple) for the Lord.

17:1 settled in his palace. The Chronicler omitted the reference to David's rest from enemies found in 2 Samuel 7:1. He viewed David primarily as a warrior (but see v. 8; 22:18) and thus unqualified to build the temple (see note on 22:6–10).

3 That night the word of God came to Nathan, saying:

4 "Go and tell my servant David, 'This is what the LORD says: You[p] are not the one to build me a house to dwell in. 5 I have not dwelt in a house from the day I brought Israel up out of Egypt to this day. I have moved from one tent site to another, from one dwelling place to another. 6 Wherever I have moved with all the Israelites, did I ever say to any of their leaders[a] whom I commanded to shepherd my people, "Why have you not built me a house of cedar?" '

7 "Now then, tell my servant David, 'This is what the LORD Almighty says: I took you from the pasture and from following the flock, to be ruler[q] over my people Israel. 8 I have been with you wherever you have gone, and I have cut off all your enemies from before you. Now I will make your name like the names of the greatest men of the earth. 9 And I will provide a place for my people Israel and will plant them so that they can have a home of their own and no longer be disturbed. Wicked people will not oppress them anymore, as they did at the beginning 10 and have done ever since the time I appointed leaders[r] over my people Israel. I will also subdue all your enemies.

" 'I declare to you that the LORD will build a house for you: 11 When your days are over and you go to be with your fathers, I will raise up your offspring to succeed you, one of your own sons, and I will establish his kingdom. 12 He is the one who will build[s] a house for me, and I will establish his throne forever.[t] 13 I will be his father,[u] and he will be my son.[v] I will never take my love away from him, as I took it away from your predecessor. 14 I will set him over my house and my kingdom forever; his throne[w] will be established forever.[x]' "

15 Nathan reported to David all the words of this entire revelation.

David's Prayer

16 Then King David went in and sat before the LORD, and he said:

"Who am I, O LORD God, and what is my family, that you have brought me this far? 17 And as if this were not enough in your sight, O God, you have spoken about the future of the house of your servant. You have looked on me as though I were the most exalted of men, O LORD God.

18 "What more can David say to you for honoring your servant? For you know your servant, 19 O LORD. For the sake[y] of your servant and according to your will, you have done this great thing and made known all these great promises.[z]

20 "There is no one like you, O LORD, and there is no God but you,[a] as we have heard with our own ears. 21 And who is like your people Israel—the one nation on earth whose God went out to redeem[b] a people for himself, and to make a name for yourself, and to perform great and awesome wonders by driving out nations from before your people, whom you redeemed from Egypt? 22 You made your people Israel your very own forever,[c] and you, O LORD, have become their God.

23 "And now, LORD, let the promise[d] you have made concerning your servant and his house be established forever. Do as you promised, 24 so that it will be established and that your name will be great forever. Then men will say, 'The LORD

17:4 [p]1Ch 28:3
17:7 [q]2Sa 6:21
17:10 [r]Jdg 2:16
17:12 [s]1Ki 5:5 [t]2Ch 7:18
17:13 [u]2Co 6:18 [v]Lk 1:32, Heb 1:5*
17:14 [w]1Ki 2:12; 1Ch 28:5 [x]Ps 132:11; Jer 33:17
17:19 [y]2Sa 7:16-17; 2Ki 20:6; Isa 9:7; 37:35; 55:3 [z]2Sa 7:25
17:20 [a]Ex 8:10; 9:14; 15:11; Isa 44:6; 46:9
17:21 [b]Ex 6:6
17:22 [c]Ex 19:5-6
17:23 [d]1Ki 8:25

[a] 6 Traditionally *judges*; also in verse 10

17:7–14 Nathan reported God's dynastic promises to David associated with the Davidic covenant. The covenant with David was also celebrated in Psalms 89 and 132. God promised that David's seed would be the permanent dynasty over Israel. Individual Davidic kings were subject to severe chastisement (2Sa 7:14; 2Ch 6:16; Pss 89:30–32; 132:11,12), but the line of David would never be permanently rejected from the throne (2Sa 7:15–16; 2Ch 6:16; Ps 89:33–37). The Chronicler depended on this covenant as the basis of hope for the restoration of Israel (see "Introduction: Purposes and Distinctives"). The New Testament revealed that the promises to David were fulfilled in Christ. Jesus kept the conditions of the covenant perfectly (Heb 4:15) and served as the mediator of the covenant of grace (Ac 2:25–36; Heb 1:5).

17:13–14 The Chronicler did not provide a parallel for 2Sa 7:14b, which threatened chastisement for Solomon and his descendants when they sinned. His omission of this statement presents Solomon as an ideal for the postexilic readers (see note on 2Ch 1:1—9:31). **his father . . . my son.** This familial language indicates the special adoption of the chosen king, not a belief in the divinity of the king as in other ancient Near Eastern cultures (see Ps 89:27 and notes on Ps 2:7 and Ps 45:6). New Testament writers treated these words about Solomon as a foreshadowing of Christ, the final Davidic King (Mk 1:11; Lk 1:32–33; Heb 1:5). Christ's sonship was more complex: He was the Son of God because he was the heir to David's throne, but he was also conceived by the Holy Spirit (Lk 1:35) and is the second person of the Godhead (Jn 1:1–18; 17:1). **never take my love away . . . his throne will be established forever.** The Chronicler omitted the material found in 2 Samuel 7:14b, which threatened chastisement for Solomon and his descendants when they sinned, in order to present Solomon as an ideal for the postexilic readers (see note on 2Ch 1:1—9:31). God designated David's line as the permanent dynasty over his people. This promise was the basis of royal hopes in the Chronicler's postexilic community and was fulfilled in Jesus, who reigns on the throne of David forever (see note on vv. 7–14; 2Ch 21:7).

17:16 Who am I . . . ? David's extraordinary humility fit well with the Chronicler's idealized portrait. See notes on 29:14–16 and on 2 Chronicles 2:6.

17:24 your name will be great. See note on 13:6.

Almighty, the God over Israel, is Israel's God!' And the house of your servant David will be established before you.
25 "You, my God, have revealed to your servant that you will build a house for
him. So your servant has found courage to pray to you. 26 O LORD, you are God! You
have promised these good things to your servant. 27 Now you have been pleased
to bless the house of your servant, that it may continue forever in your sight;[e] for
you, O LORD, have blessed it, and it will be blessed forever."

David's Victories

18 In the course of time, David defeated the Philistines and subdued them, and he
took Gath and its surrounding villages from the control of the Philistines.
2 David also defeated the Moabites,[f] and they became subject to him and brought tribute.
3 Moreover, David fought Hadadezer king of Zobah,[g] as far as Hamath, when he went
to establish his control along the Euphrates River.[h] 4 David captured a thousand of his
chariots, seven thousand charioteers and twenty thousand foot soldiers. He hamstrung[i]
all but a hundred of the chariot horses.
5 When the Arameans of Damascus[j] came to help Hadadezer king of Zobah, David
struck down twenty-two thousand of them. 6 He put garrisons in the Aramean kingdom
of Damascus, and the Arameans became subject to him and brought tribute. The LORD
gave David victory everywhere he went.
7 David took the gold shields carried by the officers of Hadadezer and brought them
to Jerusalem. 8 From Tebah[a] and Cun, towns that belonged to Hadadezer, David took a
great quantity of bronze, which Solomon used to make the bronze Sea,[k] the pillars and
various bronze articles.
9 When Tou king of Hamath heard that David had defeated the entire army of Hadadezer king of Zobah, 10 he sent his son Hadoram to King David to greet him and congratulate him on his victory in battle over Hadadezer, who had been at war with Tou. Hadoram brought all kinds of articles of gold and silver and bronze.
11 King David dedicated these articles to the LORD, as he had done with the silver and
gold he had taken from all these nations: Edom[l] and Moab, the Ammonites and the Philistines, and Amalek.[m]
12 Abishai son of Zeruiah struck down eighteen thousand Edomites[n] in the Valley of
Salt. 13 He put garrisons in Edom, and all the Edomites became subject to David. The LORD
gave David victory everywhere he went.

David's Officials

14 David reigned[o] over all Israel,[p] doing what was just and right for all his people.
15 Joab[q] son of Zeruiah was over the army; Jehoshaphat son of Ahilud was recorder; 16 Zadok[r] son of Ahitub and Ahimelech[b][s] son of Abiathar were priests; Shavsha was secretary; 17 Benaiah son of Jehoiada was over the Kerethites and Pelethites;[t] and David's sons
were chief officials at the king's side.

17:27 [e]Ps 16:11; 21:6
18:2 [f]Nu 21:29
18:3 [g]1Ch 19:6 [h]Ge 2:14
18:4 [i]Ge 49:6
18:5 [j]2Ki 16:9; 1Ch 19:6
18:8 [k]1Ki 7:23; 2Ch 4:12,15-16
18:11 [l]Nu 24:18 [m]Nu 24:20
18:12 [n]1Ki 11:15
18:14 [o]1Ch 29:26 [p]1Ch 11:1
18:15 [q]2Sa 5:6-8; 1Ch 11:6
18:16 [r]2Sa 8:17; 1Ch 6:8 [s]1Ch 24:6
18:17 [t]1Sa 30:14; 2Sa 8:18; 15:18

[a] *8* Hebrew *Tibhath,* a variant of *Tebah* [b] *16* Some Hebrew manuscripts, Vulgate and Syriac (see also 2 Samuel 8:17); most Hebrew manuscripts *Abimelech*

■ **18:1—20:8** *David Secures the Nation and Collects Temple Materials.* This section concerns David's military and political accomplishments. Apparently taken selectively from 2 Samuel 8, 10–11 and 21, it divides it into three main parts: victories and domestic security (18:1–17), victories against Ammon and Aram (19:1—20:3) and victories over Philistines (20:4–8). This material has at least four principal purposes. (1) It demonstrates how David established the political security necessary for temple construction in Solomon's day (see notes on 18:11b–13 and 22:17–19). (2) It offers the background for David's enormous contributions to the temple construction (see note on 18:8,11). (3) It anticipates David's disqualification from temple building because of his involvement in warfare (see notes on 22:6–10). (4) David's victories inspired the postexilic readers to hope for victory over the enemies of their day (see note on 19:1—20:3). The omission of David's adultery with Bathsheba (2Sa 11:1—21:14) resulted from the Chronicler's presentation of David as a model for his postexilic readers (see note on 9:35—29:30). David's acceptance of Mephibosheth into his court (2Sa 9:1–13), while generous, was also omitted, probably because it may have encouraged some Benjamites to hope that the family of Saul would take the throne again (see 2Sa 16:1–3; 20:1–2).

■ **18:1–17** *David's Victories and Domestic Security.* See 2 Samuel 8:1–14 and its notes. The only noteworthy omission is David's severe treatment of the Moabites (2Sa 8:2). The reason for this omission is unclear.

18:4 seven thousand. See NIV text note on 2 Samuel 8:4.

18:8,11 Solomon used . . . David dedicated. The Chronicler indicated one way in which David's victories prepared the way for Solomon to build the temple. David devoted the spoils of warfare to temple construction. **Edom . . . Amalek.** The list of enemies in verse 11 covers the majority of armies mentioned in 18:1—20:8.

18:11b–13 The LORD gave David victory. The extent of David's victories provided a secure political environment in which Solomon could concentrate on building (see 19:1—20:3 note).

18:14 David reigned. See 2 Samuel 8:15–18 and notes. David's domestic arrangements also provided the necessary political stability for the building projects of his son (see note on 18:1—20:8). **all Israel.** The Chronicler apparently carried this expression over from 2 Samuel 8:15, but it fits well with his theological outlook (see note on 11:1).

18:16 Zadok . . . Ahimelech son of Abiathar. See notes on 15:11.

18:17 Kerethites and Pelethites. Foreign mercenaries from among the king's guards (2Sa 8:18; 20:23). **chief officials.** The

The Battle Against the Ammonites

19 In the course of time, Nahash king of the Ammonites[u] died, and his son succeeded him as king. [2]David thought, "I will show kindness to Hanun son of Nahash, because his father showed kindness to me." So David sent a delegation to express
his sympathy to Hanun concerning his father.

When David's men came to Hanun in the land of the Ammonites to express sympathy to him, [3]the Ammonite nobles said to Hanun, "Do you think David is honoring your
father by sending men to you to express sympathy? Haven't his men come to you to explore and spy out[v] the country and overthrow it?" [4]So Hanun seized David's men,
shaved them, cut off their garments in the middle at the buttocks, and sent them away.
[5]When someone came and told David about the men, he sent messengers to meet
them, for they were greatly humiliated. The king said, "Stay at Jericho till your beards
have grown, and then come back."

[6]When the Ammonites realized that they had become a stench[w] in David's nostrils,
Hanun and the Ammonites sent a thousand talents[a] of silver to hire chariots and charioteers from Aram Naharaim,[b] Aram Maacah and Zobah.[x] [7]They hired thirty-two thousand chariots and charioteers, as well as the king of Maacah with his troops, who came
and camped near Medeba,[y] while the Ammonites were mustered from their towns and
moved out for battle.

[8]On hearing this, David sent Joab out with the entire army of fighting men. [9]The Ammonites came out and drew up in battle formation at the entrance to their city, while the
kings who had come were by themselves in the open country.

[10]Joab saw that there were battle lines in front of him and behind him; so he selected some of the best troops in Israel and deployed them against the Arameans. [11]He put
the rest of the men under the command of Abishai[z] his brother, and they were deployed
against the Ammonites. [12]Joab said, "If the Arameans are too strong for me, then you are
to rescue me; but if the Ammonites are too strong for you, then I will rescue you. [13]Be
strong and let us fight bravely for our people and the cities of our God. The LORD will do
what is good in his sight."

[14]Then Joab and the troops with him advanced to fight the Arameans, and they fled
before him. [15]When the Ammonites saw that the Arameans were fleeing, they too fled
before his brother Abishai and went inside the city. So Joab went back to Jerusalem.

[16]After the Arameans saw that they had been routed by Israel, they sent messengers
and had Arameans brought from beyond the River,[c] with Shophach the commander of
Hadadezer's army leading them.

[17]When David was told of this, he gathered all Israel[a] and crossed the Jordan; he advanced against them and formed his battle lines opposite them. David formed his lines
to meet the Arameans in battle, and they fought against him. [18]But they fled before Israel, and David killed seven thousand of their charioteers and forty thousand of their foot
soldiers. He also killed Shophach the commander of their army.

[19]When the vassals of Hadadezer saw that they had been defeated by Israel, they
made peace with David and became subject to him.

So the Arameans were not willing to help the Ammonites anymore.

The Capture of Rabbah

20 In the spring, at the time when kings go off to war, Joab led out the armed forces. He laid waste the land of the Ammonites and went to Rabbah[b] and besieged
it, but David remained in Jerusalem. Joab attacked Rabbah and left it in ruins.[c] [2]David

19:1 [u]Ge 19:38; Jdg 10:17-11:33; 2Ch 20:1-2; Zep 2:8-11
19:3 [v]Nu 21:32
19:6 [w]Ge 34:30 [x]1Ch 18:3,5,9
19:7 [y]Nu 21:30; Jos 13:9,16
19:11 [z]1Sa 26:6
19:17 [a]1Ch 9:1
20:1 [b]Dt 3:11; 2Sa 12:26 [c]Am 1:13-15

[a] *6* That is, about 37 tons (about 34 metric tons) [b] *6* That is, Northwest Mesopotamia [c] *16* That is, the Euphrates

Chronicler replaced the Hebrew term used in 2 Samuel 8:18 (often translated "priests" but rendered "royal advisors" in the NIV; see note on 2Sa 8:18). Thus he clarified that David and his sons were not considered priests. His concern for the proper ordering of the royal and priestly families underlies this variation (see note on 6:1–53).
■ **19:1—20:3** *David's Victories Against Ammon and Aram.* Compare 2 Samuel 10:1–19, 11:1, 12:29–31 and their notes. For the omission of an account of David's sin with Bathsheba and the ensuing troubles in the Davidic house (2Sa 11:1—21:14), see notes on 9:35—29:30 and 18:1—20:8.
19:1 Ammonites. The Ammonites were longstanding enemies of Israel (Jdg 10:7–9; 10:17—11:40; 1Sa 11:1–11; 14:47), who also troubled the postexilic community (Ne 2:19; 4:3,7).
19:6–7 Aram Naharaim. The Chronicler replaced the less familiar name Beth Rehob in the 2 Samuel account with Aram Naharaim (Mesopotamia) and omitted "men from Tob" (see note on 2Sa 10:6). **thirty-two thousand.** He highlighted Israel's victory by reporting the numbers of the opposing army (5:18–22; 19:7; 2Ch 12:2–4; 13:3; 14:9; 20:2).
19:17 all Israel. See note on 11:1.
19:18 seven thousand. Second Samuel 10:18 reads "seven hundred." Possibly the higher number in Chronicles is due to an error in the transmission of the text.
20:1 In the spring. Armies typically advanced after the first spring harvest, when food was more abundant (2Sa 11:1 and 1Ki 20:22,26).

took the crown from the head of their king[a]—its weight was found to be a talent[b] of gold,
and it was set with precious stones—and it was placed on David's head. He took a great
20:3 [d]Dt 29:11
quantity of plunder from the city [3]and brought out the people who were there, consigning them to labor with saws and with iron picks and axes.[d] David did this to all the Ammonite towns. Then David and his entire army returned to Jerusalem.

War With the Philistines

20:4 [e]Jos 10:33 [f]Ge 14:5
[4]In the course of time, war broke out with the Philistines, at Gezer.[e] At that time Sibbecai the Hushathite killed Sippai, one of the descendants of the Rephaites,[f] and the Philistines were subjugated.
[5]In another battle with the Philistines, Elhanan son of Jair killed Lahmi the brother
20:5 [g]1Sa 17:7
of Goliath the Gittite, who had a spear with a shaft like a weaver's rod.[g]
[6]In still another battle, which took place at Gath, there was a huge man with six fingers
on each hand and six toes on each foot—twenty-four in all. He also was descended from
Rapha. [7]When he taunted Israel, Jonathan son of Shimea, David's brother, killed him.
[8]These were descendants of Rapha in Gath, and they fell at the hands of David and
his men.

David Numbers the Fighting Men

21:1 [h]2Ch 18:21; Ps 109:6 [i]2Ch 14:8; 25:5
21 Satan[h] rose up against Israel and incited David to take a census[i] of Israel. [2]So
David said to Joab and the commanders of the troops, "Go and count[j] the Isra-
21:2 [j]1Ch 27:23-24
elites from Beersheba to Dan. Then report back to me so that I may know how many
there are."
21:3 [k]Dt 1:11
[3]But Joab replied, "May the LORD multiply his troops a hundred times over.[k] My lord
the king, are they not all my lord's subjects? Why does my lord want to do this? Why
should he bring guilt on Israel?"
[4]The king's word, however, overruled Joab; so Joab left and went throughout Israel
21:5 [l]1Ch 9:1
and then came back to Jerusalem. [5]Joab reported the number of the fighting men to David: In all Israel[l] there were one million one hundred thousand men who could handle
a sword, including four hundred and seventy thousand in Judah.
[6]But Joab did not include Levi and Benjamin in the numbering, because the king's
command was repulsive to him. [7]This command was also evil in the sight of God; so he
punished Israel.
[8]Then David said to God, "I have sinned greatly by doing this. Now, I beg you, take
21:9 [m]1Sa 22:5 [n]1Sa 9:9
away the guilt of your servant. I have done a very foolish thing."
[9]The LORD said to Gad,[m] David's seer,[n] [10]"Go and tell David, 'This is what the LORD
says: I am giving you three options. Choose one of them for me to carry out against you.' "
[11]So Gad went to David and said to him, "This is what the LORD says: 'Take your

[a] *2* Or *of Milcom,* that is, Molech [b] *2* That is, about 75 pounds (about 34 kilograms)

20:2 great quantity of plunder. See note on "Solomon used . . . David dedicated" at 18:8 and 11.

■ **20:4–8** *David's Victories Over the Philistines.* The Chronicler returned to the topic he had addressed in 18:1—David's warfare with the Philistines (see note on 18:1—20:8)—setting off 18:1—20:8 as a unified story.

20:4 were subjugated. This comment summarizing the battle with the Philistines is not found in the parallel account in 2 Samuel 21:18. The Chronicler evidently added it to indicate that the promise of 17:10 had been fulfilled (2Ch 13:18; contrast 2Ch 28:19).

20:8 Rapha. Perhaps vicious warriors of large size or tremendous reputation (Ge 15:19–20; Dt 2:10–11).

■ **21:1—22:1** *David Discovers the Temple Site.* The Chronicler moved to David's discovery of the temple site (see note on 17:1—29:25). The theme of military victory (19:1—20:8) led to an account of David's military census. With two major exceptions, the Chronicler appears to have closely followed 2 Samuel 24 (see notes on 21:1 and 21:28—22:1). In Samuel, the narrative reports how David brought trouble on the nation but successfully interceded on its behalf. The Chronicler apparently adapted this account to show how God had led David to discover the site for the temple.

21:1–4 See *WLC* 195.

21:1 Satan rose up. Second Samuel 24:1 reads "he [the LORD] incited David." The Chronicler clarified this matter by pointing to Satan as the instrument leading David to sin. God himself tempts no one (Jas 1:13), but in his anger he allowed Satan to lead David astray so that the people might fall under judgment. (see note on 2Ch 10:15; see also 11:4; 25:20; Ex 4:21; 7:3; 9:12; 10:1,20,27; 11:10; 14:4; Jos 11:20; 1Ki 22:22–23; Job 1:12; 2:10; Eze 3:20; 14:9; Mt 6:13; Ac 4:27–28). **Satan.** Without the definite article, "Satan" probably functioned as a proper name. See NIV text notes on Job 1:6 and Zechariah 3:1. See *WCF* 5.4; *WLC* 195.

21:3 bring guilt on Israel. Census taking was not prohibited under Old Testament law, although there were specific regulations for it (Ex 30:12; Nu 1:2; 26:2). David may have wanted a count of his military personnel in order to bolster his sense of reliance on human might rather than on divine power (see notes on 2Ch 13:18 and on "Introduction" at Ps 30). In the light of Joab's response (v. 6; 27:23–24), David may have insisted that the Levites be counted for military service as well (see note on v. 6).

21:5 all Israel. Second Samuel 24:9 reads simply "Israel." See note on 11:1. **one million one hundred thousand men . . . including four hundred and seventy thousand in Judah.** The differences between this account and the one in 2 Samuel are problematic. Second Samuel 24:9 reads "eight hundred thousand" in Israel and "five hundred thousand" in Judah. The NIV attempts to solve this problem by translating verse 5 "including four hundred . . ." instead of "and four hundred . . ." (as it may be translated). The Chronicler may have excluded some unknown elements from his count (see notes on v. 6), and it is also possible that both numbers represent loose approximations. Beyond this, one or both texts may suffer from errors in transmission.

21:6 Joab did not include. Joab did not carry through completely with the census David had ordered (see note on v. 3). **Levi and Benjamin.** These tribes were not included in the census. The tribe of Levi was excluded according to Mosaic Law (Nu 1:49; 2:33), and Benjamin may have been excluded because the tabernacle was in Gibeon at the time (v. 29).

choice: **12**three years of famine,[o] three months of being swept away[a] before your enemies, with their swords overtaking you, or three days of the sword[p] of the LORD[q]—days
of plague in the land, with the angel of the LORD ravaging every part of Israel.' Now then,
decide how I should answer the one who sent me."
13David said to Gad, "I am in deep distress. Let me fall into the hands of the LORD, for
his mercy[r] is very great; but do not let me fall into the hands of men."
14So the LORD sent a plague on Israel, and seventy thousand men of Israel fell dead.[s]
15And God sent an angel[t] to destroy Jerusalem.[u] But as the angel was doing so, the LORD
saw it and was grieved[v] because of the calamity and said to the angel who was destroying[w] the people, "Enough! Withdraw your hand." The angel of the LORD was then standing at the threshing floor of Araunah[b] the Jebusite.
16David looked up and saw the angel of the LORD standing between heaven and
earth, with a drawn sword in his hand extended over Jerusalem. Then David and the elders, clothed in sackcloth, fell facedown.[x]
17David said to God, "Was it not I who ordered the fighting men to be counted? I am
the one who has sinned and done wrong. These are but sheep.[y] What have they done?
O LORD my God, let your hand fall upon me and my family,[z] but do not let this plague remain on your people."
18Then the angel of the LORD ordered Gad to tell David to go up and build an altar to
the LORD on the threshing floor[a] of Araunah the Jebusite. **19**So David went up in obedience to the word that Gad had spoken in the name of the LORD.
20While Araunah was threshing wheat,[b] he turned and saw the angel; his four sons
who were with him hid themselves. **21**Then David approached, and when Araunah
looked and saw him, he left the threshing floor and bowed down before David with his
face to the ground.
22David said to him, "Let me have the site of your threshing floor so I can build an altar to the LORD, that the plague on the people may be stopped. Sell it to me at the full
price."
23Araunah said to David, "Take it! Let my lord the king do whatever pleases him.
Look, I will give the oxen for the burnt offerings, the threshing sledges for the wood, and
the wheat for the grain offering. I will give all this."
24But King David replied to Araunah, "No, I insist on paying the full price. I will not
take for the LORD what is yours, or sacrifice a burnt offering that costs me nothing."
25So David paid Araunah six hundred shekels[c] of gold for the site. **26**David built an altar to the LORD there and sacrificed burnt offerings and fellowship offerings.[d] He called on
the LORD, and the LORD answered him with fire[c] from heaven on the altar of burnt offering.
27Then the LORD spoke to the angel, and he put his sword back into its sheath. **28**At
that time, when David saw that the LORD had answered him on the threshing floor of
Araunah the Jebusite, he offered sacrifices there. **29**The tabernacle of the LORD, which Moses had made in the desert, and the altar of burnt offering were at that time on the high
place at Gibeon.[d] **30**But David could not go before it to inquire of God, because he was
afraid of the sword of the angel of the LORD.

21:12 [o]Dt 32:24 [p]Eze 30:25 [q]Ge 19:13
21:13 [r]Ps 6:4; 86:15; 130:4,7
21:14 [s]1Ch 27:24
21:15 [t]Ge 32:1 [u]Ps 125:2 [v]Ge 6:6; Ex 32:14 [w]Ge 19:13
21:16 [x]Nu 14:5; Jos 7:6
21:17 [y]2Sa 7:8; Ps 74:1 [z]Jnh 1:12
21:18 [a]2Ch 3:1
21:20 [b]Jdg 6:11
21:26 [c]Lev 9:24; Jdg 6:21
21:29 [d]1Ki 3:4; 1Ch 16:39

[a] *12* Hebrew; Septuagint and Vulgate (see also 2 Samuel 24:13) *of fleeing* [b] *15* Hebrew *Ornan,* a variant of *Araunah*; also in verses 18–28 [c] *25* That is, about 15 pounds (about 7 kilograms)
[d] *26* Traditionally *peace offerings*

21:13 his mercy is very great. Despite the severity of divine chastisement, David trusted the abundant mercy of God. Undoubtedly, God's promises to David in 17:1–14 supply a background to David's confident trust in God's mercy.
21:16 David . . . saw the angel of the LORD. This verse is not found in the traditional (Masoretic) Hebrew text of 2 Samuel 24. Recently discovered texts of Samuel (Qumran) and other witnesses suggest that the verse was probably original to Samuel and appeared in the version used as a source by the Chronicler.
21:19 in the name. See note on 13:6.
21:20–21 Araunah was threshing. The report of Araunah threshing does not appear in the traditional (Masoretic) Hebrew text of 2 Samuel 24:20. Recently discovered texts of Samuel (Qumran) and other witnesses suggest that the information was original to Samuel and was in the version used as a source by the Chronicler.
21:22–25 paying the full price. An allusion to Abraham's purchase of the burial site for Sarah (Ge 23:1–20). David purchased Araunah's site at full price. As a result, the temple site (see note on 21:28—22:1) was a royal possession devoted to the temple.
21:25 six hundred shekels of gold for the site. Second Samuel 24:24 reads "David bought the threshing floor and the oxen and paid fifty shekels of silver for them." Samuel focuses on "the threshing floor," while the Chronicler calculated the purchase for the whole site, not just the threshing floor and the oxen.
21:26 answered him with fire. A rare occurrence, indicating God's particular approval of David's actions (Lev 9:24; 1Ki 18:37–38). This event anticipated Solomon's temple dedication later at this site (see note on 2Ch 7:1).
21:28—22:1 he offered sacrifices there. These verses are not found in 2 Samuel 24. They reflect the Chronicler's interest in sacrifice (21:28) and explain David's neglect of the tabernacle (21:29–30). Most importantly, they report that David recognized the threshing floor of Araunah as the site for the future temple (22:1). This remarkable ending reveals why the Chronicler included this moral blemish in his record of David's life. It establishes the place where the Chronicler's postexilic readers must turn for sacrifice, forgiveness and answered prayer (see notes on 2Ch 3:1; 6:12–42).
21:30 inquire of God. See note on 2 Chronicles 7:14.

22 Then David said, "The house of the LORD God[e] is to be here, and also the altar
of burnt offering for Israel."

Preparations for the Temple

2 So David gave orders to assemble the aliens[f] living in Israel, and from among them
he appointed stonecutters[g] to prepare dressed stone for building the house of God. 3 He
provided a large amount of iron to make nails for the doors of the gateways and for the
fittings, and more bronze than could be weighed.[h] 4 He also provided more cedar logs[i]
than could be counted, for the Sidonians and Tyrians had brought large numbers of
them to David.

5 David said, "My son Solomon is young[j] and inexperienced, and the house to be built
for the LORD should be of great magnificence and fame and splendor in the sight of all
the nations. Therefore I will make preparations for it." So David made extensive preparations before his death.

6 Then he called for his son Solomon and charged him to build[k] a house for the LORD,
the God of Israel. 7 David said to Solomon: "My son, I had it in my heart[l] to build[m] a house
for the Name[n] of the LORD my God. 8 But this word of the LORD came to me: 'You have shed
much blood and have fought many wars.[o] You are not to build a house for my Name,[p] because you have shed much blood on the earth in my sight. 9 But you will have a son who
will be a man of peace[q] and rest, and I will give him rest from all his enemies on every side.
His name will be Solomon,[a][r] and I will grant Israel peace and quiet[s] during his reign. 10 He
is the one who will build a house for my Name.[t] He will be my son,[u] and I will be his father. And I will establish the throne of his kingdom over Israel forever.'[v]

11 "Now, my son, the LORD be with[w] you, and may you have success and build the
house of the LORD your God, as he said you would. 12 May the LORD give you discretion and
understanding[x] when he puts you in command over Israel, so that you may keep the law
of the LORD your God. 13 Then you will have success if you are careful to observe the decrees and laws[y] that the LORD gave Moses for Israel. Be strong and courageous.[z] Do not
be afraid or discouraged.

14 "I have taken great pains to provide for the temple of the LORD a hundred thousand
talents[b] of gold, a million talents[c] of silver, quantities of bronze and iron too great to be
weighed, and wood and stone. And you may add to them.[a] 15 You have many workmen:
stonecutters, masons and carpenters, as well as men skilled in every kind of work 16 in
gold and silver, bronze and iron—craftsmen[b] beyond number. Now begin the work, and
the LORD be with you."

17 Then David ordered[c] all the leaders of Israel to help his son Solomon. 18 He said to
them, "Is not the LORD your God with you? And has he not granted you rest[d] on every
side?[e] For he has handed the inhabitants of the land over to me, and the land is subject
to the LORD and to his people. 19 Now devote your heart and soul to seeking the LORD your
God.[f] Begin to build the sanctuary of the LORD God, so that you may bring the ark of the

22:1 [e]Ge 28:17; 1Ch 21:18-29; 2Ch 3:1
22:2 [f]1Ki 9:21; Isa 56:6 [g]1Ki 5:17-18
22:3 [h]ver 14; 1Ki 7:47; 1Ch 29:2-5
22:4 [i]1Ki 5:6
22:5 [j]1Ki 3:7; 1Ch 29:1
22:6 [k]Ac 7:47
22:7 [l]1Ch 17:2 [m]2Sa 7:2; 1Ki 8:17 [n]Dt 12:5, 11
22:8 [o]1Ki 5:3 [p]1Ch 28:3
22:9 [q]1Ki 5:4 [r]2Sa 12:24 [s]1Ki 4:20
22:10 [t]1Ch 17:12 [u]2Sa 7:13 [v]2Sa 7:14; 2Ch 6:15
22:11 [w]ver 16
22:12 [x]1Ki 3:9-12; 2Ch 1:10
22:13 [y]1Ch 28:7 [z]Dt 31:6; Jos 1:6-9; 1Ch 28:20
22:14 [a]ver 3; 1Ch 29:2-5, 19
22:16 [b]ver 11; 2Ch 2:7
22:17 [c]1Ch 28:1-6
22:18 [d]ver 9; 1Ch 23:25 [e]2Sa 7:1
22:19 [f]ver 7; 1Ki 8:6; 1Ch 28:9; 2Ch 5:7; 7:14

a *9 Solomon* sounds like and may be derived from the Hebrew for *peace.* b *14* That is, about 3,750 tons (about 3,450 metric tons) c *14* That is, about 37,500 tons (about 34,500 metric tons)

22:2—29:20 David gave orders . . . This is the longest section added by the Chronicler to the account of David's life as found in Samuel, and it deals with David's finalization of temple preparations. The Chronicler framed the material by royal assemblies (22:2–19; 28:1—29:25). The two assemblies shared topics and language at several points (cf. 22:8 with 28:3; 22:13 with 28:20; and 22:17 with 28:21).

■ **22:2–19** *David Commissions Temple Construction.* The report of the first assembly, in which David commissioned foreign laborers (vv. 2–4), Solomon (vv. 5–16) and the Israelite leaders (vv. 17–19).

22:2 aliens. David and Solomon used conscripted labor made up primarily of foreigners (2Sa 20:24; 1Ki 5:13–18; 9:15–23; 11:28; 2Ch 2:2,17–18; 8:7–10). The Chronicler's mention of aliens participating in the construction of the first temple anticipated the expectation that foreigners would contribute to the reconstruction efforts during the postexilic period (Isa 60:10–12).

22:3 iron. Presumably taken from the Philistines whom David had conquered (1Sa 13:19–22). **bronze.** Taken from the spoils of war (see note on 18:8,11).

22:5 young and inexperienced. David considered Solomon too inexperienced to handle the responsibility of preparing for the temple (cf. 29:1 and 2Ch 13:7). **extensive preparations.** The central theme of this section. In the Chronicler's view David virtually provided everything for Solomon's temple: plans, materials, workers, personnel assignments, political stability and popular support. In effect, the Chronicler viewed the temple as the joint project of David and Solomon (see notes on 22:2—29:20; 2Ch 2:3–10; 7:10). See "Introduction: Purposes and Distinctives."

22:6–10 These verses constitute the Chronicler's explanation as to why David could not build the temple himself. First Kings 5:3–5 states that David was preoccupied with warfare, but the Chronicler explained more specifically that David was ritually defiled by bloodshed, so that he could not be directly involved in the building project (2Ch 6:9).

22:7–8,10,19 Name. See note on 13:6.

22:9 peace and rest . . . peace and quiet. On several occasions the Chronicler presented peace and rest from warfare as God's reward for his faithful people (v. 18; 2Ch 14:1,5–7; 15:13,15; 20:30; 23:21). This blessing was extended to his postexilic readers for their troubled days.

22:12–13 keep the law of the LORD . . . observe the decrees and laws. See note on 16:40.

22:13 Be strong and courageous. David's commission of Solomon (vv. 12–13) alluded to Joshua's commission (cf. 28:20 and Jos 1:6–9).

22:17–19 has he not granted you rest . . . ? The Chronicler explained that David's success in war provided the political stability necessary for temple construction (see note on 18:1—20:8).

22:18 rest. See note on verse 9.

22:19 seeking the LORD. See note on 2 Chronicles 7:14.

covenant of the LORD and the sacred articles belonging to God into the temple that will
be built for the Name of the LORD."

The Levites

23 When David was old and full of years, he made his son Solomon[g] king over Israel.[h]
2He also gathered together all the leaders of Israel, as well as the priests and Levites.
3The Levites thirty years old or more[i] were counted, and the total number of men was
thirty-eight thousand.[j] 4David said, "Of these, twenty-four thousand are to supervise[k] the
work of the temple of the LORD and six thousand are to be officials and judges.[l] 5Four
thousand are to be gatekeepers and four thousand are to praise the LORD with the musical instruments[m] I have provided for that purpose."[n]
6David divided[o] the Levites into groups corresponding to the sons of Levi: Gershon,
Kohath and Merari.

Gershonites

7Belonging to the Gershonites:
Ladan and Shimei.
8The sons of Ladan:
Jehiel the first, Zetham and Joel—three in all.
9The sons of Shimei:
Shelomoth, Haziel and Haran—three in all.
These were the heads of the families of Ladan.
10And the sons of Shimei:
Jahath, Ziza,[a] Jeush and Beriah.
These were the sons of Shimei—four in all.
11Jahath was the first and Ziza the second, but Jeush and Beriah did not have
many sons; so they were counted as one family with one assignment.

Kohathites

12The sons of Kohath:[p]
Amram, Izhar, Hebron and Uzziel—four in all.
13The sons of Amram:[q]
Aaron and Moses.
Aaron was set apart,[r] he and his descendants forever, to consecrate the most
holy things, to offer sacrifices before the LORD, to minister before him and to
pronounce blessings[s] in his name forever. 14The sons of Moses the man[t] of God
were counted as part of the tribe of Levi.
15The sons of Moses:
Gershom and Eliezer.[u]
16The descendants of Gershom:[v]
Shubael was the first.
17The descendants of Eliezer:
Rehabiah was the first.
Eliezer had no other sons, but the sons of Rehabiah were very numerous.
18The sons of Izhar:
Shelomith was the first.
19The sons of Hebron:[w]

23:1 [g]1Ki 1:33-39; 1Ch 28:5 [h]1Ki 1:30; 1Ch 29:28
23:3 [i]ver 24; Nu 8:24 [j]Nu 4:3-49
23:4 [k]Ezr 3:8 [l]1Ch 26:29; 2Ch 19:8
23:5 [m]1Ch 15:16 [n]Ne 12:45
23:6 [o]2Ch 8:14; 29:25
23:12 [p]Ex 6:18
23:13 [q]Ex 6:20; 28:1 [r]Ex 30:7-10; Dt 21:5 [s]Nu 6:23
23:14 [t]Dt 33:1
23:15 [u]Ex 18:4
23:16 [v]1Ch 26:24-28
23:19 [w]1Ch 24:23

a *10* One Hebrew manuscript, Septuagint and Vulgate (see also verse 11); most Hebrew manuscripts *Zina*

▪**23:1—29:25** *David Transfers Power and Responsibility to Solomon.* The opening verse (23:1) serves as a topical heading for 23:1—29:25.
▪**23:1—27:34** *Those Whom David Gathered.* David's organization of religious (23:1—26:32) and civil (27:1–34) personnel not only established arrangements for Solomon's administration but also provided a model for the reorganization of the people in the postexilic community.
▪**23:1—26:32** *Priests and Levites.* David established religious leaders for Solomon's administration. The Chronicler used this example to show the postexilic community that it needed to gather leaders of the same ancestry for its reconstruction program.
23:1 he made his son Solomon king over Israel. Just as the Chronicler omitted the checkered history of David's rise to power (see notes on 9:35—29:30 and 11:1–9), so he also opted not to mention Solomon's struggle for kingship (1Ki 1–2). In his idealized portrait, the Chronicler presented a smooth transition of power from David to Solomon. The same perspective underlies 28:1— 29:25 (see note on 3:10–16 and "Introduction: Purposes and Distinctives").
23:2–32 Levites. Between introductory (vv. 1–6) and concluding remarks (vv. 24–32), the Chronicler listed the divisions of Levites from the Gershonites (vv. 7–11), Kohathites (vv. 12–20) and Merarites (vv. 21–23). See note on 6:1–81.
23:3 thirty years old. Apparently the age at which Levites began service could be adjusted according to need: 30 years (Nu 4:1–3), 25 years (Nu 8:23–24) and 20 years (1Ch 23:24,27). A period of apprenticeship was possibly in view in some passages.
23:5 musical instruments. See note on 15:16–24.
23:6–23 the sons of Levi. Compare similar lists in 6:16–30 and 24:20–30.
23:13 in his name. See note on 13:6.

Jeriah the first, Amariah the second, Jahaziel the third and Jekameam the fourth.

20 The sons of Uzziel:

Micah the first and Isshiah the second.

Merarites

21 The sons of Merari:[x]

Mahli and Mushi.

The sons of Mahli:

Eleazar and Kish.

22 Eleazar died without having sons: he had only daughters. Their cousins, the sons of Kish, married them.

23 The sons of Mushi:

Mahli, Eder and Jerimoth—three in all.

24 These were the descendants of Levi by their families—the heads of families as they were registered under their names and counted individually, that is, the workers twenty years old or more[y] who served in the temple of the LORD. 25 For David had said, "Since the LORD, the God of Israel, has granted rest[z] to his people and has come to dwell in Jerusalem forever, 26 the Levites no longer need to carry the tabernacle or any of the articles used in its service."[a] 27 According to the last instructions of David, the Levites were counted from those twenty years old or more.

28 The duty of the Levites was to help Aaron's descendants in the service of the temple of the LORD: to be in charge of the courtyards, the side rooms, the purification[b] of all sacred things and the performance of other duties at the house of God. 29 They were in charge of the bread set out on the table,[c] the flour for the grain offerings,[d] the unleavened wafers, the baking and the mixing, and all measurements of quantity and size.[e] 30 They were also to stand every morning to thank and praise the LORD. They were to do the same in the evening[f] 31 and whenever burnt offerings were presented to the LORD on Sabbaths and at New Moon[g] festivals and at appointed feasts.[h] They were to serve before the LORD regularly in the proper number and in the way prescribed for them.

32 And so the Levites[i] carried out their responsibilities for the Tent of Meeting,[j] for the Holy Place and, under their brothers the descendants of Aaron, for the service of the temple of the LORD.[k]

The Divisions of Priests

24 These were the divisions[l] of the sons of Aaron:[m]

The sons of Aaron were Nadab, Abihu, Eleazar and Ithamar.[n] 2 But Nadab and Abihu died before their father did,[o] and they had no sons; so Eleazar and Ithamar served as the priests. 3 With the help of Zadok[p] a descendant of Eleazar and Ahimelech a descendant of Ithamar, David separated them into divisions for their appointed order of ministering. 4 A larger number of leaders were found among Eleazar's descendants than among Ithamar's, and they were divided accordingly: sixteen heads of families from Eleazar's descendants and eight heads of families from Ithamar's descendants. 5 They divided them impartially by drawing lots,[q] for there were officials of the sanctuary and officials of God among the descendants of both Eleazar and Ithamar.

6 The scribe Shemaiah son of Nethanel, a Levite, recorded their names in the presence of the king and of the officials: Zadok the priest, Ahimelech[r] son of Abiathar and the heads of families of the priests and of the Levites—one family being taken from Eleazar and then one from Ithamar.

7 The first lot fell to Jehoiarib,

the second to Jedaiah,[s]

23:21 [x]1Ch 24:26
23:24 [y]Nu 4:3; 10:17,21
23:25 [z]1Ch 22:9
23:26 [a]Nu 4:5,15; 7:9; Dt 10:8
23:28 [b]2Ch 29:15; Ne 13:9; Mal 3:3
23:29 [c]Ex 25:30 [d]Lev 2:4-7; 6:20-23 [e]Lev 19:35-36; 1Ch 9:29,32
23:30 [f]1Ch 9:33; Ps 134:1
23:31 [g]2Ki 4:23 [h]Lev 23:4; Nu 28:9-29:39; Isa 1:13-14; Col 2:16
23:32 [i]Nu 1:53; 1Ch 6:48 [j]Nu 3:6-8,38 [k]2Ch 23:18; 31:2; Eze 44:14
24:1 [l]1Ch 23:6; 28:13; 2Ch 5:11; 8:14; 23:8; 31:2; 35:4,5; Ezr 6:18 [m]Nu 3:2-4 [n]Ex 6:23
24:2 [o]Lev 10:1-2; Nu 3:4
24:3 [p]2Sa 8:17
24:5 [q]ver 31; 1Ch 25:8
24:6 [r]1Ch 18:16
24:7 [s]Ezr 2:36; Ne 12:6

23:24,27 twenty years old. See note on verse 3.

23:28,32 duty of the Levites. The Levites were under the authority of the Aaronic priests (see notes on 6:1–15 and 48–53).

24:1–2 the divisions of the sons of Aaron. The traditional division of the sons of Aaron (cf. 6:3; Ex 6:23; Nu 3:2–4). The descendants of Eleazar and Ithamar alone served as priests (see note on 6:1–81; Nu 3:4; Lev 10:1–3).

24:3 Zadok. See note on 15:11.

24:5 impartially by drawing lots. The practice of casting lots after careful adherence to revealed standards was designed to ensure that decisions were made according to divine direction rather than human prejudices (Pr 16:33; Lk 1:8–9; Ac 1:26). See note on verse 31.

24:7–18 The first lot . . . the twenty-fourth. Twenty-four divisions were established to provide for regular rotation of duty among the priestly families. Note the similar practice in New Testament times (Lk 1:8–9).

24:7 Jehoiarib. The father of the Maccabees (Mattathias) was in the division of Jehoiarib; compare 1 Maccabees 2:1 (an Apocryphal book that is not a part of the Protestant canon).

8 the third to Harim,[t]
the fourth to Seorim,
9 the fifth to Malkijah,
the sixth to Mijamin,
10 the seventh to Hakkoz,
the eighth to Abijah,[u]
11 the ninth to Jeshua,
the tenth to Shecaniah,
12 the eleventh to Eliashib,
the twelfth to Jakim,
13 the thirteenth to Huppah,
the fourteenth to Jeshebeab,
14 the fifteenth to Bilgah,
the sixteenth to Immer,[v]
15 the seventeenth to Hezir,[w]
the eighteenth to Happizzez,
16 the nineteenth to Pethahiah,
the twentieth to Jehezkel,
17 the twenty-first to Jakin,
the twenty-second to Gamul,
18 the twenty-third to Delaiah
and the twenty-fourth to Maaziah.

19 This was their appointed order of ministering when they entered the temple of the
LORD, according to the regulations prescribed for them by their forefather Aaron, as the
LORD, the God of Israel, had commanded him.

The Rest of the Levites

20 As for the rest of the descendants of Levi:[x]
from the sons of Amram: Shubael;
from the sons of Shubael: Jehdeiah.
21 As for Rehabiah,[y] from his sons:
Isshiah was the first.
22 From the Izharites: Shelomoth;
from the sons of Shelomoth: Jahath.
23 The sons of Hebron:[z] Jeriah the first,[a] Amariah the second, Jahaziel the third and
Jekameam the fourth.
24 The son of Uzziel: Micah;
from the sons of Micah: Shamir.
25 The brother of Micah: Isshiah;
from the sons of Isshiah: Zechariah.
26 The sons of Merari:[a] Mahli and Mushi.
The son of Jaaziah: Beno.
27 The sons of Merari:
from Jaaziah: Beno, Shoham, Zaccur and Ibri.
28 From Mahli: Eleazar, who had no sons.
29 From Kish: the son of Kish:
Jerahmeel.
30 And the sons of Mushi: Mahli, Eder and Jerimoth.

These were the Levites, according to their families. 31 They also cast lots,[b] just as their
brothers the descendants of Aaron did, in the presence of King David and of Zadok,
Ahimelech, and the heads of families of the priests and of the Levites. The families of the
oldest brother were treated the same as those of the youngest.

24:8 [t]Ezr 2:39; Ne 10:5
24:10 [u]Ne 12:4, 17; Lk 1:5
24:14 [v]Jer 20:1
24:15 [w]Ne 10:20
24:20 [x]1Ch 23:6
24:21 [y]1Ch 23:17
24:23 [z]1Ch 23:19
24:26 [a]1Ch 6:19; 23:21
24:31 [b]ver 5

[a] *23* Two Hebrew manuscripts and some Septuagint manuscripts (see also 1 Chron. 23:19); most Hebrew manuscripts *The sons of Jeriah:*

24:10 Abijah. The father of John the Baptist (Zechariah) was part of the division of Abijah (Lk 1:5).
24:31 families of the oldest brother were treated the same. Apparently the Chronicler was addressing a priestly controversy of his own day. The equal treatment of all the families was a model to be followed by the postexilic readers (see note on verse 5).

25:1 [c]1Ch 6:39 [d]1Ch 6:33 [e]1Ch 16:41,42; Ne 11:17 [f]1Sa 10:5; 2Ki 3:15 [g]1Ch 15:16 [h]1Ch 6:31 [i]2Ch 5:12; 8:14; 34:12; 35:15; Ezr 3:10
25:3 [j]1Ch 16:41-42 [k]Ge 4:21; Ps 33:2
25:6 [l]1Ch 15:16 [m]1Ch 15:19 [n]2Ch 23:18; 29:25
25:8 [o]1Ch 26:13
25:9 [p]1Ch 6:39

The Singers

25 David, together with the commanders of the army, set apart some of the sons of Asaph,[c] Heman[d] and Jeduthun[e] for the ministry of prophesying,[f] accompanied by harps, lyres and cymbals.[g] Here is the list of the men[h] who performed this service:[i]

2From the sons of Asaph:
Zaccur, Joseph, Nethaniah and Asarelah. The sons of Asaph were under the supervision of Asaph, who prophesied under the king's supervision.
3As for Jeduthun, from his sons:[j]
Gedaliah, Zeri, Jeshaiah, Shimei,[a] Hashabiah and Mattithiah, six in all, under the supervision of their father Jeduthun, who prophesied, using the harp[k] in thanking and praising the LORD.
4As for Heman, from his sons:
Bukkiah, Mattaniah, Uzziel, Shubael and Jerimoth; Hananiah, Hanani, Eliathah, Giddalti and Romamti-Ezer; Joshbekashah, Mallothi, Hothir and Mahazioth.
5All these were sons of Heman the king's seer. They were given him through the promises of God to exalt him.[b] God gave Heman fourteen sons and three daughters.

6All these men were under the supervision of their fathers[l] for the music of the temple of the LORD, with cymbals, lyres and harps, for the ministry at the house of God. Asaph, Jeduthun and Heman[m] were under the supervision of the king.[n]
7Along with their relatives—all of them trained and skilled in music for the LORD—they numbered 288.
8Young and old alike, teacher as well as student, cast lots[o] for their duties.

9The first lot, which was for Asaph,[p] fell to Joseph,
his sons and relatives,[c] 12[d]
the second to Gedaliah,
he and his relatives and sons, 12
10the third to Zaccur,
his sons and relatives, 12
11the fourth to Izri,[e]
his sons and relatives, 12
12the fifth to Nethaniah,
his sons and relatives, 12
13the sixth to Bukkiah,
his sons and relatives, 12
14the seventh to Jesarelah,[f]
his sons and relatives, 12
15the eighth to Jeshaiah,
his sons and relatives, 12
16the ninth to Mattaniah,
his sons and relatives, 12
17the tenth to Shimei,
his sons and relatives, 12
18the eleventh to Azarel,[g]
his sons and relatives, 12
19the twelfth to Hashabiah,
his sons and relatives, 12
20the thirteenth to Shubael,
his sons and relatives, 12
21the fourteenth to Mattithiah,
his sons and relatives, 12

a *3* One Hebrew manuscript and some Septuagint manuscripts (see also verse 17); most Hebrew manuscripts do not have *Shimei.* b *5* Hebrew *exalt the horn* c *9* See Septuagint; Hebrew does not have *his sons and relatives.* d *9* See the total in verse 7; Hebrew does not have *twelve.* e *11* A variant of *Zeri* f *14* A variant of *Asarelah* g *18* A variant of *Uzziel*

25:1–31 harps, lyres and cymbals. The Chronicler's interest in the music of worship appears numerous times (see note on 15:16–24).
25:1 commanders of the army. The mention of David's military advisors was likely intended to highlight his assignments (11:10; 12:32) as a model for the organization of the postexilic community. **prophesying.** The Chronicler on several occasions presented temple personnel in prophetic roles (2Ch 20:14–17; 24:19–22; 29:30; 35:15; cf. 2Ki 23:2; 2Ch 34:30). This motif reflects his interest in the role of priests as guides for the restoration of the postexilic community (Zec 6:9–15).
25:8 cast lots for their duties. See notes on 24:5 and 31.
25:9–31 first . . . twenty-fourth. See note on 24:7–18.

22 the fifteenth to Jerimoth,	
his sons and relatives,	12
23 the sixteenth to Hananiah,	
his sons and relatives,	12
24 the seventeenth to Joshbekashah,	
his sons and relatives,	12
25 the eighteenth to Hanani,	
his sons and relatives,	12
26 the nineteenth to Mallothi,	
his sons and relatives,	12
27 the twentieth to Eliathah,	
his sons and relatives,	12
28 the twenty-first to Hothir,	
his sons and relatives,	12
29 the twenty-second to Giddalti,	
his sons and relatives,	12
30 the twenty-third to Mahazioth,	
his sons and relatives,	12
31 the twenty-fourth to Romamti-Ezer,	
his sons and relatives,	12[q]

The Gatekeepers

26 The divisions of the gatekeepers:[r]

From the Korahites: Meshelemiah son of Kore, one of the sons of Asaph.
2 Meshelemiah had sons:
Zechariah[s] the firstborn,
Jediael the second,
Zebadiah the third,
Jathniel the fourth,
3 Elam the fifth,
Jehohanan the sixth
and Eliehoenai the seventh.
4 Obed-Edom also had sons:
Shemaiah the firstborn,
Jehozabad the second,
Joah the third,
Sacar the fourth,
Nethanel the fifth,
5 Ammiel the sixth,
Issachar the seventh
and Peullethai the eighth.
(For God had blessed Obed-Edom.[t])

6 His son Shemaiah also had sons, who were leaders in their father's family because
they were very capable men. 7 The sons of Shemaiah: Othni, Rephael, Obed and
Elzabad; his relatives Elihu and Semakiah were also able men. 8 All these were descendants of Obed-Edom; they and their sons and their relatives were capable
men with the strength to do the work—descendants of Obed-Edom, 62 in all.
9 Meshelemiah had sons and relatives, who were able men—18 in all.
10 Hosah the Merarite had sons: Shimri the first (although he was not the firstborn,
his father had appointed him the first),[u] 11 Hilkiah the second, Tabaliah the
third and Zechariah the fourth. The sons and relatives of Hosah were 13 in all.
12 These divisions of the gatekeepers, through their chief men, had duties for ministering[v] in the temple of the LORD, just as their relatives had. 13 Lots[w] were cast for each
gate, according to their families, young and old alike.
14 The lot for the East Gate[x] fell to Shelemiah.[a] Then lots were cast for his son Zech-

25:31 [q]1Ch 9:33
26:1 [r]1Ch 9:17
26:2 [s]1Ch 9:21
26:5 [t]2Sa 6:10; 1Ch 13:13; 16:38
26:10 [u]Dt 21:16; 1Ch 5:1
26:12 [v]1Ch 9:22
26:13 [w]1Ch 24:5,31; 25:8
26:14 [x]1Ch 9:18

[a] 14 A variant of *Meshelemiah*

26:1–19 gatekeepers. The specific duties of gatekeepers is described in 9:22–29.
26:4 Obed-Edom. See note on 13:13.
26:5 For God had blessed Obed-Edom. The Chronicler mentioned having numerous children as a sign of divine blessing (see note on 13:13).
26:13–16 Lots . . . lot. See note on 24:5.

ariah,[y] a wise counselor, and the lot for the North Gate fell to him. 15 The lot for the South
Gate fell to Obed-Edom,[z] and the lot for the storehouse fell to his sons. 16 The lots for the
West Gate and the Shalleketh Gate on the upper road fell to Shuppim and Hosah.
Guard was alongside of guard: 17 There were six Levites a day on the east, four a day
on the north, four a day on the south and two at a time at the storehouse. 18 As for the
court to the west, there were four at the road and two at the court itself.
19 These were the divisions of the gatekeepers who were descendants of Korah and
Merari.[a]

The Treasurers and Other Officials

20 Their fellow Levites[b] were[a] in charge of the treasuries of the house of God and the
treasuries for the dedicated things.[c]
21 The descendants of Ladan, who were Gershonites through Ladan and who were
heads of families belonging to Ladan the Gershonite,[d] were Jehieli, 22 the sons of Jehieli, Zetham and his brother Joel. They were in charge of the treasuries[e] of the temple of the LORD.
23 From the Amramites, the Izharites, the Hebronites and the Uzzielites:[f]

24 Shubael,[g] a descendant of Gershom son of Moses, was the officer in charge of the
treasuries. 25 His relatives through Eliezer: Rehabiah his son, Jeshaiah his son,
Joram his son, Zicri his son and Shelomith[h] his son. 26 Shelomith and his relatives were in charge of all the treasuries for the things dedicated[i] by King David, by the heads of families who were the commanders of thousands and commanders of hundreds, and by the other army commanders. 27 Some of the
plunder taken in battle they dedicated for the repair of the temple of the LORD.
28 And everything dedicated by Samuel the seer[j] and by Saul son of Kish, Abner son of Ner and Joab son of Zeruiah, and all the other dedicated things were
in the care of Shelomith and his relatives.

29 From the Izharites: Kenaniah and his sons were assigned duties away from the
temple, as officials and judges[k] over Israel.

30 From the Hebronites: Hashabiah[l] and his relatives—seventeen hundred able
men—were responsible in Israel west of the Jordan for all the work of the LORD
and for the king's service. 31 As for the Hebronites,[m] Jeriah was their chief according to the genealogical records of their families. In the fortieth[n] year of David's reign a search was made in the records, and capable men among the Hebronites were found at Jazer in Gilead. 32 Jeriah had twenty-seven hundred
relatives, who were able men and heads of families, and King David put them
in charge of the Reubenites, the Gadites and the half-tribe of Manasseh for every matter pertaining to God and for the affairs of the king.

Army Divisions

27 This is the list of the Israelites—heads of families, commanders of thousands
and commanders of hundreds, and their officers, who served the king in all that
concerned the army divisions that were on duty month by month throughout the year.
Each division consisted of 24,000 men.

2 In charge of the first division, for the first month, was Jashobeam[o] son of Zabdiel. There
were 24,000 men in his division. 3 He was a descendant of Perez and chief of all
the army officers for the first month.

4 In charge of the division for the second month was Dodai[p] the Ahohite; Mikloth was
the leader of his division. There were 24,000 men in his division.

5 The third army commander, for the third month, was Benaiah[q] son of Jehoiada the

26:14 [y]1Ch 9:21
26:15 [z]1Ch 13:13; 2Ch 25:24
26:19 [a]2Ch 35:15; Ne 7:1; Eze 44:11
26:20 [b]2Ch 24:5 [c]1Ch 28:12
26:21 [d]1Ch 23:7; 29:8
26:22 [e]1Ch 9:26
26:23 [f]Nu 3:27
26:24 [g]1Ch 23:16
26:25 [h]1Ch 23:18
26:26 [i]2Sa 8:11
26:28 [j]1Sa 9:9
26:29 [k]Dt 17:8-13; 1Ch 23:4; Ne 11:16
26:30 [l]1Ch 27:17
26:31 [m]1Ch 23:19 [n]2Sa 5:4
27:2 [o]2Sa 23:8; 1Ch 11:11
27:4 [p]2Sa 23:9
27:5 [q]2Sa 23:20

[a] 20 Septuagint; Hebrew *As for the Levites, Ahijah was*

26:14 East Gate. The main entrance to the temple, patrolled by six guards (v. 17).
26:15 South Gate fell to Obed-Edom. The South Gate was the main entrance for the king. Obed-Edom was highly honored by this assignment (vv. 4–5).
26:20–32 fellow Levites. The Levites were given responsibilities both in the temple (vv. 20–28) and away from Jerusalem (vv. 29–32).
26:20–28 treasuries. The temple was a place of great wealth (29:6–9; 2Ch 4:1–22; 34:9–11; 36:7,10,18–19). The Levites were in charge of collecting and managing these extensive resources.
26:26–28 David . . . Samuel . . . Saul . . . Abner . . . Joab. Apparently special attention was given to temple donations received from important figures.
26:29–32 as officials and judges. Legal and administrative functions for Levites were established in Mosaic legislation (Dt 17:8–13). See notes on 2 Chronicles 17:7–8 and 19:4–11.

▪ **27:1–34** *Military and Civilian Leaders.* The Chronicler turned to the subjects of military order (vv. 1–15), tribal heads (vv. 16–24), royal overseers (vv. 25–31) and royal counselors (vv. 32–34). David's extensive organization of his kingdom laid the groundwork for Solomon's temple project (see note on 22:5).

27:1 month by month. The duties in the military organization rotated much like priestly responsibilities (see note on 24:7–18).

27:2–15 24,000 men. See note on 12:23–37. Many officers listed here also appear in a similar list in 11:11–47 (cf. 2Sa 23:8–39).

priest. He was chief and there were 24,000 men in his division. 6This was the Benaiah who was a mighty man among the Thirty and was over the Thirty. His son
Ammizabad was in charge of his division.

7The fourth, for the fourth month, was Asahel[r] the brother of Joab; his son Zebadiah was his successor. There were 24,000 men in his division.

8The fifth, for the fifth month, was the commander Shamhuth[s] the Izrahite. There were 24,000 men in his division.

9The sixth, for the sixth month, was Ira[t] the son of Ikkesh the Tekoite. There were 24,000 men in his division.

10The seventh, for the seventh month, was Helez[u] the Pelonite, an Ephraimite. There were 24,000 men in his division.

11The eighth, for the eighth month, was Sibbecai[v] the Hushathite, a Zerahite. There were 24,000 men in his division.

12The ninth, for the ninth month, was Abiezer[w] the Anathothite, a Benjamite. There were 24,000 men in his division.

13The tenth, for the tenth month, was Maharai[x] the Netophathite, a Zerahite. There were 24,000 men in his division.

14The eleventh, for the eleventh month, was Benaiah[y] the Pirathonite, an Ephraimite. There were 24,000 men in his division.

15The twelfth, for the twelfth month, was Heldai[z] the Netophathite, from the family of Othniel.[a] There were 24,000 men in his division.

Officers of the Tribes

16The officers over the tribes of Israel:

over the Reubenites: Eliezer son of Zicri;
over the Simeonites: Shephatiah son of Maacah;
17over Levi: Hashabiah[b] son of Kemuel;
over Aaron: Zadok;[c]
18over Judah: Elihu, a brother of David;
over Issachar: Omri son of Michael;
19over Zebulun: Ishmaiah son of Obadiah;
over Naphtali: Jerimoth son of Azriel;
20over the Ephraimites: Hoshea son of Azaziah;
over half the tribe of Manasseh: Joel son of Pedaiah;
21over the half-tribe of Manasseh in Gilead: Iddo son of Zechariah;
over Benjamin: Jaasiel son of Abner;
22over Dan: Azarel son of Jeroham.
These were the officers over the tribes of Israel.

23David did not take the number of the men twenty years old or less,[d] because the
LORD had promised to make Israel as numerous as the stars[e] in the sky. 24Joab son of Zeruiah began to count the men but did not finish. Wrath came on Israel on account of this
numbering,[f] and the number was not entered in the book[a] of the annals of King David.

The King's Overseers

25Azmaveth son of Adiel was in charge of the royal storehouses.

Jonathan son of Uzziah was in charge of the storehouses in the outlying districts, in the towns, the villages and the watchtowers.

26Ezri son of Kelub was in charge of the field workers who farmed the land.

27Shimei the Ramathite was in charge of the vineyards.

Zabdi the Shiphmite was in charge of the produce of the vineyards for the wine vats.

28Baal-Hanan the Gederite was in charge of the olive and sycamore-fig[g] trees in the western foothills.

Joash was in charge of the supplies of olive oil.

29Shitrai the Sharonite was in charge of the herds grazing in Sharon.

Shaphat son of Adlai was in charge of the herds in the valleys.

27:7 [r]2Sa 2:18; 1Ch 11:26
27:8 [s]1Ch 11:27
27:9 [t]2Sa 23:26; 1Ch 11:28
27:10 [u]2Sa 23:26; 1Ch 11:27
27:11 [v]2Sa 21:18
27:12 [w]2Sa 23:27; 1Ch 11:28
27:13 [x]2Sa 23:28; 1Ch 11:30
27:14 [y]1Ch 11:31
27:15 [z]2Sa 23:29 [a]Jos 15:17
27:17 [b]1Ch 26:30 [c]2Sa 8:17; 1Ch 12:28
27:23 [d]1Ch 21:2-5 [e]Ge 15:5
27:24 [f]2Sa 24:15; 1Ch 21:7
27:28 [g]1Ki 10:27; 2Ch 1:15

a 24 Septuagint; Hebrew *number*

27:16,22 tribes of Israel. The Chronicler omitted mention of Gad and Asher for no apparent reason.

27:23–24 the number was not entered. These verses refer to David's census in 21:1—22:1 (2Sa 24). Because of God's negative reaction to the census, the count never became part of the official court record.

27:25–31 royal storehouses. A partial list indicating how much property and wealth David had acquired in preparation for Solomon (see note on 22:5).

30 Obil the Ishmaelite was in charge of the camels.
Jehdeiah the Meronothite was in charge of the donkeys.
31 Jaziz the Hagrite[h] was in charge of the flocks.
All these were the officials in charge of King David's property.

32 Jonathan, David's uncle, was a counselor, a man of insight and a scribe. Jehiel son
of Hacmoni took care of the king's sons.
33 Ahithophel[i] was the king's counselor.
Hushai[j] the Arkite was the king's friend. 34 Ahithophel was succeeded by Jehoiada son
of Benaiah and by Abiathar.[k]
Joab[l] was the commander of the royal army.

David's Plans for the Temple

28 David summoned all the officials[m] of Israel to assemble at Jerusalem: the officers over the tribes, the commanders of the divisions in the service of the king,
the commanders of thousands and commanders of hundreds, and the officials in charge
of all the property and livestock belonging to the king and his sons, together with the palace officials, the mighty men and all the brave warriors.
2 King David rose to his feet and said: "Listen to me, my brothers and my people. I had
it in my heart[n] to build a house as a place of rest for the ark of the covenant of the LORD,
for the footstool[o] of our God, and I made plans to build it. 3 But God said to me,[p] 'You are
not to build a house for my Name,[q] because you are a warrior and have shed blood.'[r]
4 "Yet the LORD, the God of Israel, chose me[s] from my whole family[t] to be king over
Israel forever. He chose Judah[u] as leader, and from the house of Judah he chose my family, and from my father's sons he was pleased to make me king over all Israel. 5 Of all my
sons—and the LORD has given me many[v]—he has chosen my son Solomon[w] to sit on the
throne of the kingdom of the LORD over Israel. 6 He said to me: 'Solomon your son is the
one who will build my house and my courts, for I have chosen him to be my son,[x] and I
will be his father. 7 I will establish his kingdom forever if he is unswerving in carrying out
my commands and laws,[y] as is being done at this time.'
8 "So now I charge you in the sight of all Israel and of the assembly of the LORD, and
in the hearing of our God: Be careful to follow all the commands[z] of the LORD your God,
that you may possess this good land and pass it on as an inheritance to your descendants
forever.[a]
9 "And you, my son Solomon, acknowledge the God of your father, and serve him with
wholehearted devotion[b] and with a willing mind, for the LORD searches every heart[c] and
understands every motive behind the thoughts. If you seek him,[d] he will be found by you;
but if you forsake[e] him, he will reject[f] you forever. 10 Consider now, for the LORD has chosen you to build a temple as a sanctuary. Be strong and do the work."
11 Then David gave his son Solomon the plans[g] for the portico of the temple, its
buildings, its storerooms, its upper parts, its inner rooms and the place of atonement.
12 He gave him the plans of all that the Spirit[h] had put in his mind for the courts of the
temple of the LORD and all the surrounding rooms, for the treasuries of the temple of God
and for the treasuries for the dedicated things.[i] 13 He gave him instructions for the divisions[j] of the priests and Levites, and for all the work of serving in the temple of the LORD,
as well as for all the articles to be used in its service. 14 He designated the weight of gold
for all the gold articles to be used in various kinds of service, and the weight of silver for
all the silver articles to be used in various kinds of service: 15 the weight of gold for the
gold lampstands[k] and their lamps, with the weight for each lampstand and its lamps;

27:31 [h]1Ch 5:10
27:33 [i]2Sa 15:12 [j]2Sa 15:37
27:34 [k]1Ki 1:7 [l]1Ch 11:6
28:1 [m]1Ch 11:10; 27:1-31
28:2 [n]1Ch 17:2 [o]Ps 99:5; 132:7
28:3 [p]2Sa 7:5 [q]1Ch 22:8 [r]1Ki 5:3; 1Ch 17:4
28:4 [s]1Ch 17:23,27; 2Ch 6:6 [t]1Sa 16:1-13 [u]Ge 49:10; 1Ch 5:2
28:5 [v]1Ch 3:1 [w]1Ch 22:9; 23:1
28:6 [x]2Sa 7:13; 1Ch 22:9-10
28:7 [y]1Ch 22:13
28:8 [z]Dt 6:1 [a]Dt 4:1
28:9 [b]1Ch 29:19 [c]1Sa 16:7; Ps 7:9 [d]Ps 40:16; Jer 29:13 [e]Jos 24:20; 2Ch 15:2 [f]Ps 44:23
28:11 [g]Ex 25:9
28:12 [h]1Ch 12:18 [i]1Ch 26:20
28:13 [j]1Ch 24:1
28:15 [k]Ex 25:31

27:32–34 Jonathan . . . Joab. David's closest advisors (18:14–17), highlighting the organization of David's government.

■ **28:1—29:25** *David's Final Assembly.* The Chronicler introduced David's final assembly (28:1) and described three sets of speeches and actions: 28:2–19, 28:20—29:9 and 29:10–25. See note on 22:2—29:20.

■ **28:1** *Introduction.* The Chronicler recalled the personnel listed in 27:1–34. These officials represented the entire nation (see note on 11:1).

■ **28:2–19** *David's First Set of Speeches and Actions.* David charged Solomon to build the temple and instructed the people to support Solomon. He warned that only obedience to God would lead to success in this endeavor. David also turned over to Solomon the materials and plans for the temple.

28:3 my Name. See note on 13:6.

28:4,8 all Israel. See note on 11:1.

28:5 he has chosen. Solomon was designated as David's successor because of divine election, not on the basis of human maneuvering. This was an essential requirement for a legitimate Israelite king (Dt 17:15).

28:6 my son. See note on 17:13–14.

28:7 carrying out my commands and laws. See note on 16:40.

28:9 If you seek him . . . but if you forsake him. Basic covenantal conditions applied to the promises given to David and his line. Although the Davidic dynasty itself would not be rejected, individual kings and the nation could suffer severely under God's judgment for flagrant apostasy. For similar expressions of this principle see 2 Chronicles 6:14 and 16, 7:17–22, 15:2, 16:7–9, 19:2–3, 21:14–19, 24:20, 25:16, 28:9–11 and 34:23–28 (also see "Introduction: Purposes and Distinctives"). See *WLC* 104,106; *WSC* 46.

28:12 the Spirit had put in his mind. David actively planned for the temple, and his efforts were directed by the Holy Spirit. The Chronicler highlighted the need for the postexilic community to follow the pattern that David and Solomon had arranged for the temple (see "Introduction: Purpose and Distinctives").

and the weight of silver for each silver lampstand and its lamps, according to the use of
each lampstand; 16 the weight of gold for each table[l] for consecrated bread; the weight
of silver for the silver tables; 17 the weight of pure gold for the forks, sprinkling bowls[m]
and pitchers; the weight of gold for each gold dish; the weight of silver for each silver
dish; 18 and the weight of the refined gold for the altar of incense.[n] He also gave him the
plan for the chariot,[o] that is, the cherubim of gold that spread their wings and shelter[p]
the ark of the covenant of the LORD.

19 "All this," David said, "I have in writing from the hand of the LORD upon me, and he
gave me understanding in all the details[q] of the plan.[r]"

20 David also said to Solomon his son, "Be strong and courageous,[s] and do the work.
Do not be afraid or discouraged, for the LORD God, my God, is with you. He will not fail
you or forsake[t] you until all the work for the service of the temple of the LORD is finished.[u]
21 The divisions of the priests and Levites are ready for all the work on the temple of God,
and every willing man skilled[v] in any craft will help you in all the work. The officials and
all the people will obey your every command."

Gifts for Building the Temple

29 Then King David said to the whole assembly: "My son Solomon, the one whom
God has chosen, is young and inexperienced.[w] The task is great, because this
palatial structure is not for man but for the LORD God. 2 With all my resources I have provided for the temple of my God—gold[x] for the gold work, silver for the silver, bronze for
the bronze, iron for the iron and wood for the wood, as well as onyx for the settings, turquoise,[a][y] stones of various colors, and all kinds of fine stone and marble—all of these
in large quantities.[z] 3 Besides, in my devotion to the temple of my God I now give my personal treasures of gold and silver for the temple of my God, over and above everything
I have provided[a] for this holy temple: 4 three thousand talents[b] of gold (gold of Ophir)[b]
and seven thousand talents[c] of refined silver,[c] for the overlaying of the walls of the buildings, 5 for the gold work and the silver work, and for all the work to be done by the craftsmen. Now, who is willing to consecrate himself today to the LORD?"

6 Then the leaders of families, the officers of the tribes of Israel, the commanders of
thousands and commanders of hundreds, and the officials[d] in charge of the king's work
gave willingly.[e] 7 They[f] gave toward the work on the temple of God five thousand talents[d]
and ten thousand darics[e] of gold, ten thousand talents[f] of silver, eighteen thousand talents[g] of bronze and a hundred thousand talents[h] of iron. 8 Any who had precious stones[g]
gave them to the treasury of the temple of the LORD in the custody of Jehiel the Gershonite.[h] 9 The people rejoiced at the willing response of their leaders, for they had given freely and wholeheartedly[i] to the LORD. David the king also rejoiced greatly.

David's Prayer

10 David praised the LORD in the presence of the whole assembly, saying,

"Praise be to you, O LORD,
God of our father Israel,
from everlasting to everlasting.

28:16 [l]Ex 25:23
28:17 [m]Ex 27:3
28:18 [n]Ex 30:1-10 [o]Ex 25:18-22 [p]Ex 25:20
28:19 [q]1Ki 6:38 [r]Ex 25:9
28:20 [s]Dt 31:6; 1Ch 22:13; 2Ch 19:11; Hag 2:4 [t]Dt 4:31; Jos 24:20 [u]1Ki 6:14; 2Ch 7:11
28:21 [v]Ex 35:25-36:5
29:1 [w]1Ki 3:7; 1Ch 22:5; 2Ch 13:7
29:2 [x]ver 7,14,16; Ezr 1:4; 6:5; Hag 2:8 [y]Isa 54:11 [z]1Ch 22:2-5
29:3 [a]2Ch 24:10; 31:3; 35:8
29:4 [b]Ge 10:29 [c]1Ch 22:14
29:6 [d]1Ch 27:1; 28:1 [e]ver 9; Ex 25:1-8; 35:20-29; 36:2; 2Ch 24:10; Ezr 7:15
29:7 [f]Ex 25:2; Ne 7:70-71
29:8 [g]Ex 35:27 [h]1Ch 26:21
29:9 [i]1Ki 8:61; 2Co 9:7

[a] *2* The meaning of the Hebrew for this word is uncertain. [b] *4* That is, about 110 tons (about 100 metric tons) [c] *4* That is, about 260 tons (about 240 metric tons) [d] *7* That is, about 190 tons (about 170 metric tons) [e] *7* That is, about 185 pounds (about 84 kilograms) [f] *7* That is, about 375 tons (about 345 metric tons) [g] *7* That is, about 675 tons (about 610 metric tons) [h] *7* That is, about 3,750 tons (about 3,450 metric tons)

■ **28:20—29:9** *David's Second Set of Speeches and Actions.* David encouraged Solomon and instructed the people to follow Solomon's directions. He donated generously of his own wealth for the building project, inspiring many others to do the same.
28:20 Be strong and courageous. An allusion again to the commissioning of Joshua (see note on 22:13).
28:21 will help you . . . will obey your every command. David organized the priests, Levites and artisans for the building of the temple (see note on "extensive preparations" at 22:5).
29:1–9 who is willing to consecrate himself. David followed Moses' example in asking for contributions to the temple project (Ex 25:1–8; 35:4–9,20–29). The Chronicler anticipated the situation of his postexilic readers, who would easily forget the importance of continued contribution to the new temple (Hag 1:2–11; Mal 3:8–10). See notes on 2 Chronicles 24:10–12 and 29:31.
29:1 young and inexperienced. See note at 22:5.
29:2–5 With all my resources. David declared all his provision for Solomon's temple (see notes on 22:5 and 27:1–34). **I now give my personal treasures.** David donated his own wealth in addition to the spoils of war (see notes on 18:8,11 and 2Ch 30:24; cf. 35:7–8). David served as an example to the postexilic community of generous contribution to the temple (see note on 29:18).
29:7 darics. The daric was Persian currency used in the Chronicler's day. He updated the terminology for the sake of his readers (see "Introduction: Author").
■ **29:10–25** *David's Third Set of Speeches and Actions.* David praised God for what had been accomplished (vv. 10–13), asked for continued empowerment for the people and for Solomon (vv. 14–19) and followed up with specific actions (vv. 21–25).
29:10–13 Yours, O LORD . . . splendor. Probably the source for the traditional expansion of the Lord's prayer (see NIV text note on Mt 6:13). **your glorious name.** See note on 13:6. See *WLC* 196; *WSC* 107.

11 Yours, O LORD, is the greatness and the power[j]
and the glory and the majesty and the splendor,
for everything in heaven and earth is yours.[k]
Yours, O LORD, is the kingdom;
you are exalted as head over all.[l]
12 Wealth and honor[m] come from you;
you are the ruler[n] of all things.
In your hands are strength and power
to exalt and give strength to all.
13 Now, our God, we give you thanks,
and praise your glorious name.

14 "But who am I, and who are my people, that we should be able to give as generously as this? Everything comes from you, and we have given you only what comes from your hand. 15 We are aliens and strangers[o] in your sight, as were all our forefathers. Our days on earth are like a shadow,[p] without hope. 16 O LORD our God, as for all this abundance that we have provided for building you a temple for your Holy Name, it comes from your hand, and all of it belongs to you. 17 I know, my God, that you test the heart[q] and are pleased with integrity. All these things have I given willingly and with honest intent. And now I have seen with joy how willingly your people who are here have given to you.[r] 18 O LORD, God of our fathers Abraham, Isaac and Israel, keep this desire in the hearts of your people forever, and keep their hearts loyal to you. 19 And give my son Solomon the wholehearted devotion[s] to keep your commands, requirements and decrees[t] and to do everything to build the palatial structure for which I have provided."[u]

20 Then David said to the whole assembly, "Praise the LORD your God." So they all praised the LORD, the God of their fathers; they bowed low and fell prostrate before the LORD and the king.

Solomon Acknowledged as King

21 The next day they made sacrifices to the LORD and presented burnt offerings to him:[v] a thousand bulls, a thousand rams and a thousand male lambs, together with their drink offerings, and other sacrifices in abundance for all Israel. 22 They ate and drank with great joy[w] in the presence of the LORD that day.

Then they acknowledged Solomon son of David as king a second time, anointing him before the LORD to be ruler and Zadok[x] to be priest. 23 So Solomon sat on the throne[y] of the LORD as king in place of his father David. He prospered and all Israel obeyed him. 24 All the officers and mighty men, as well as all of King David's sons, pledged their submission to King Solomon.

25 The LORD highly exalted Solomon in the sight of all Israel and bestowed on him royal splendor[z] such as no king over Israel ever had before.[a]

The Death of David

26 David son of Jesse was king[b] over all Israel. 27 He ruled over Israel forty years—seven in Hebron and thirty-three in Jerusalem.[c] 28 He died[d] at a good old age, having enjoyed long life, wealth and honor. His son Solomon succeeded him as king.[e]

29 As for the events of King David's reign, from beginning to end, they are written in the records of Samuel the seer,[f] the records of Nathan[g] the prophet and the records of Gad[h] the seer, 30 together with the details of his reign and power, and the circumstances that surrounded him and Israel and the kingdoms of all the other lands.

29:11 [j]Ps 24:8; 59:17; 62:11 [k]Ps 89:11 [l]Rev 5:12-13
29:12 [m]2Ch 1:12 [n]2Ch 20:6; Ro 11:36
29:15 [o]Ps 39:12; Heb 11:13 [p]Job 14:2
29:17 [q]Ps 139:23; Pr 15:11; 17:3; Jer 11:20; 17:10 [r]1Ch 28:9; Ps 15:1-5
29:19 [s]1Ch 28:9 [t]Ps 72:1 [u]1Ch 22:14
29:21 [v]1Ki 8:62
29:22 [w]1Ch 23:1 [x]1Ki 1:33-39
29:23 [y]1Ki 2:12
29:25 [z]2Ch 1:1,12 [a]1Ki 3:13; Ecc 2:9
29:26 [b]1Ch 18:14
29:27 [c]2Sa 5:4-5; 1Ki 2:11; 1Ch 3:4
29:28 [d]Ge 15:15; Ac 13:36 [e]1Ch 23:1
29:29 [f]1Sa 9:9 [g]2Sa 7:2 [h]1Sa 22:5

29:14–16 who am I . . . ? David perceived of himself as powerless and hopeless apart from God's blessing (2Ch 1:9; 20:6,12). See notes on 17:16 and on 2 Chronicles 2:6. **Everything comes from you.** Although David worked hard to prepare for Solomon's temple, he acknowledged that all his accomplishments actually came from the sovereign hand of God. **your Holy Name.** See note on 13:6.
29:18 keep this desire . . . forever. The people contributed enthusiastically to God for the building of the temple (v. 17) because of their desire to glorify him and to be blessed by him. David's words spoke directly to the Chronicler's readers, who needed to continue to give freely to temple worship. See *WLC* 175.
29:19 keep your commands. See note on 16:40.
29:21–22 with great joy. The Chronicler reported the transfer of power to Solomon, closing in a grand celebration of sacrifice (v. 21), feasting (v. 22) and national harmony (vv. 22b–25). See note on 23:1. **Solomon . . . to be ruler and Zadok to be priest.** The close association of the Davidic king and the priestly line of Zadok was characteristic of the Chronicler's outlook on the postexilic period (see note on 6:1–53). **a second time.** This expression is absent from some Septuagint (Greek translation of the OT) texts and the Peshitta (Syriac translation of the OT); it may be a late addition. Perhaps, however, the Chronicler has in mind 1 Kings 1:32–36, which he omitted, as the scene of the first anointing. Both Saul (1Sa 10:1; 11:14–15) and David (1Sa 16:13; 2Sa 2:4; 5:3) received multiple anointings.
29:24 pledged their submission. Apparently, initial loyalty was given to Solomon, but some of these men rebelled with Adonijah (see note on 23:1; 1Ki 1:9,19,25; 2Ch 1:1—9:31).
29:25 as no king over Israel ever had before. In the Chronicler's view Solomon's reign transcended that of David, due, in part, to the fact that Solomon built the temple.
■ **29:26–30** *Closure of David's Reign.* The Chronicler referred to many other sources for David's reign besides the books of Samuel and Kings (see "Introduction: Author").

2 CHRONICLES

Introduction

Introduction: see "Introduction to 1 Chronicles"

Solomon Asks for Wisdom

1 Solomon son of David established[a] himself firmly over his kingdom, for the LORD his
God was with[b] him and made him exceedingly great.[c]
[2]Then Solomon spoke to all Israel[d]—to the commanders of thousands and commanders of hundreds, to the judges and to all the leaders in Israel, the heads of families—[3]and
Solomon and the whole assembly went to the high place at Gibeon, for God's Tent of
Meeting[e] was there, which Moses[f] the LORD's servant had made in the desert. [4]Now David had brought up the ark[g] of God from Kiriath Jearim to the place he had prepared for
it, because he had pitched a tent[h] for it in Jerusalem. [5]But the bronze altar[i] that Bezalel[j] son of Uri, the son of Hur, had made was in Gibeon in front of the tabernacle of the
LORD; so Solomon and the assembly inquired[k] of him there. [6]Solomon went up to the
bronze altar before the LORD in the Tent of Meeting and offered a thousand burnt offerings on it.
[7]That night God appeared[l] to Solomon and said to him, "Ask for whatever you want
me to give you."
[8]Solomon answered God, "You have shown great kindness to David my father and
have made me[m] king in his place. [9]Now, LORD God, let your promise[n] to my father David be confirmed, for you have made me king over a people who are as numerous as the
dust of the earth.[o] [10]Give me wisdom and knowledge, that I may lead[p] this people, for
who is able to govern this great people of yours?"
[11]God said to Solomon, "Since this is your heart's desire and you have not asked for
wealth,[q] riches or honor, nor for the death of your enemies, and since you have not

1:1 [a]1Ki 2:12,26; 2Ch 12:1 [b]Ge 21:22; 39:2; Nu 14:43 [c]1Ch 29:25
1:2 [d]1Ch 9:1; 28:1
1:3 [e]Ex 36:8 [f]Ex 40:18
1:4 [g]2Sa 6:2; 1Ch 15:25 [h]2Sa 6:17; 1Ch 15:1
1:5 [i]Ex 38:2 [j]Ex 31:2 [k]1Ch 13:3
1:7 [l]2Ch 7:12
1:8 [m]1Ch 23:1; 28:5
1:9 [n]2Sa 7:25; 1Ki 8:25 [o]Ge 12:2
1:10 [p]Nu 27:17; 2Sa 5:2; Pr 8:15-16
1:11 [q]Dt 17:17

■ **1:1—9:31** *The Reign of Solomon.* The Chronicler depicted Solomon as the ideal successor to David. He omitted Solomon's struggle for power (see note on 1Ch 23:1), describing the extent of Solomon's kingdom as "all Israel" (see note on 1Ch 11:1). He also passed over Solomon's downfall due to intermarriage (1Ki 11:1–40), depicting him as fully committed to building the temple (2:1—8:16). See "Introduction to 1 Chronicles: Purpose and Distinctives." The record of Solomon's reign forms a large-scale chiasm (A B C D D' C' B' A')—a literary arrangement that parallels statements beginning from the outside and working in, as shown in the matched pairs of letters [e.g., A and A', as above]. The pattern of Solomon's reign is: (A) Solomon's great wisdom and wealth (1:1–17), (B) international assistance (2:1–18), (C) temple building and furnishings (3:1—5:1), (D) dedication of the temple (5:2—7:10), (D') divine response to the dedication (7:11–22), (C') conclusion of temple building (8:1–16), (B') international recognition (8:17—9:21) and (A') great wisdom and wealth (9:22–28). The Chronicler concludes with a brief account of Solomon's death (9:29–31).

■ **1:1–17** *Solomon's Great Wisdom and Wealth.* Solomon asked for wisdom, God promised to answer (vv. 1–13) and God fulfilled his promise (vv. 14–17). This section balances with its chiastic parallel on Solomon's wisdom and wealth (9:13–28). See note on 1:1—9:31.

■ **1:1–13** *Solomon Receives Divine Promises.* In response to Solomon's humble prayer, God promised to give him wisdom and wealth.

1:1 established himself. The Chronicler frequently used this and similar expressions to indicate success after difficulty (12:13; 13:21; 17:1; 21:4; 25:11; 27:6). He acknowledged that Solomon's rise to power was tumultuous, but he omitted details (1Ki 2) in order to idealize Solomon (see notes on 1:1—9:31; 1Ch 23:1). God was with the king, and Solomon's rise was the result of God's sovereign blessing in fulfillment of David's hopes (1Ch 22:11,16; 28:20).

1:2–13 This passage roughly follows 1 Kings 3:4–15, but the Chronicler expanded the account in verses 2–6 to emphasize the theme of Solomon's reign over all Israel (v. 2) and to explain why Solomon went to Gibeon to sacrifice (vv. 3–6).

1:2 all Israel. See note on 1 Chronicles 11:1.

1:5 Bezalel. Bezalel was the chief artisan in the tabernacle construction narrative. Solomon emerged as Bezalel's counterpart during the building of the temple. See notes on 1 Chronicles 2:20. See also Exodus 31:1–11 and 35:5–9. **inquired of him.** See notes on 2 Chronicles 7:14.

1:7 appeared . . . said. The Chronicler followed Kings and reported that God spoke directly to Solomon in dreams (7:12). He exalted Solomon to the position of David as an instrument of revelation for Israel (1Ch 22:8; 28:6,19).

1:9 let your promise to my father David be confirmed. The Chronicler included this request to tie Solomon's reign to David (see notes on 1Ch 17:1–15; 22:5). Solomon depended fully on God for the ability to carry out his role as king (see note on 1Ch 29:14–16). **numerous as the dust.** Solomon recognized the multiplication of Israel as fulfillment of God's promise to Abraham (Ge 13:16; 22:17). This reminder to the postexilic readers instilled within them hope for massive repopulation of the promised land in their day (Ne 1:8–9; Zec 8:7–8).

1:10 wisdom. The Chronicler exalted the ideal order established by Solomon as being the result of Solomon's divinely bestowed wisdom. In his wisdom, Solomon foreshadowed Christ, the divine son of David who possesses God's wisdom in full measure (Isa 11:1–2; Col 2:3).

asked for a long life but for wisdom and knowledge to govern my people over whom I
have made you king, [12]therefore wisdom and knowledge will be given you. And I will also
give you wealth, riches and honor,[r] such as no king who was before you ever had and
none after you will have.[s]"
[13]Then Solomon went to Jerusalem from the high place at Gibeon, from before the
Tent of Meeting. And he reigned over Israel.
[14]Solomon accumulated chariots[t] and horses; he had fourteen hundred chariots
and twelve thousand horses,[a] which he kept in the chariot cities and also with him in Jerusalem. [15]The king made silver and gold[u] as common in Jerusalem as stones, and cedar as plentiful as sycamore-fig trees in the foothills. [16]Solomon's horses were imported from Egypt[b] and from Kue[c]—the royal merchants purchased them from Kue. [17]They
imported a chariot[v] from Egypt for six hundred shekels[d] of silver, and a horse for a hundred and fifty.[e] They also exported them to all the kings of the Hittites and of the Arameans.

Preparations for Building the Temple

2 Solomon gave orders to build a temple[w] for the Name of the LORD and a royal palace for himself.[x] [2]He conscripted seventy thousand men as carriers and eighty thousand as stonecutters in the hills and thirty-six hundred as foremen over them.[y]
[3]Solomon sent this message to Hiram[f][z] king of Tyre:
"Send me cedar logs[a] as you did for my father David when you sent him cedar
to build a palace to live in. [4]Now I am about to build a temple[b] for the Name of the
LORD my God and to dedicate it to him for burning fragrant incense[c] before him,
for setting out the consecrated bread[d] regularly, and for making burnt offerings[e]
every morning and evening and on Sabbaths[f] and New Moons and at the appointed feasts of the LORD our God. This is a lasting ordinance for Israel.
[5]"The temple I am going to build will be great,[g] because our God is greater
than all other gods.[h] [6]But who is able to build a temple for him, since the heavens, even the highest heavens, cannot contain him?[i] Who then am I[j] to build a
temple for him, except as a place to burn sacrifices before him?
[7]"Send me, therefore, a man skilled to work in gold and silver, bronze and iron,
and in purple, crimson and blue yarn, and experienced in the art of engraving, to
work in Judah and Jerusalem with my skilled craftsmen,[k] whom my father David provided.
[8]"Send me also cedar, pine and algum[g] logs from Lebanon, for I know that your
men are skilled in cutting timber there. My men will work with yours [9]to provide
me with plenty of lumber, because the temple I build must be large and magnificent. [10]I will give your servants, the woodsmen who cut the timber, twenty thousand cors[h] of ground wheat, twenty thousand cors of barley, twenty thousand
baths[i] of wine and twenty thousand baths of olive oil.[l]"

1:12 [r]1Ch 29:12 [s]1Ch 29:25; 2Ch 9:22; Ne 13:26
1:14 [t]1Sa 8:11; 1Ki 4:26; 9:19
1:15 [u]1Ki 9:28; Isa 60:5
1:17 [v]SS 1:9
2:1 [w]Dt 12:5 [x]Ecc 2:4
2:2 [y]ver 18; 2Ch 10:4
2:3 [z]2Sa 5:11 [a]1Ch 14:1
2:4 [b]ver 1; Dt 12:5 [c]Ex 30:7 [d]Ex 25:30 [e]Ex 29:42; 2Ch 13:11 [f]Nu 28:9-10
2:5 [g]1Ch 22:5; Ps 135:5 [h]1Ch 16:25
2:6 [i]1Ki 8:27; 2Ch 6:18; Jer 23:24 [j]Ex 3:11
2:7 [k]ver 13-14; Ex 35:31; 1Ch 22:16
2:10 [l]Ezr 3:7

[a] *14* Or *charioteers* [b] *16* Or possibly *Muzur,* a region in Cilicia; also in verse 17 [c] *16* Probably Cilicia
[d] *17* That is, about 15 pounds (about 7 kilograms) [e] *17* That is, about 3 3/4 pounds (about 1.7 kilograms) [f] *3* Hebrew *Huram,* a variant of *Hiram;* also in verses 11 and 12 [g] *8* Probably a variant of *almug;* possibly juniper [h] *10* That is, probably about 125,000 bushels (about 4,400 kiloliters)
[i] *10* That is, probably about 115,000 gallons (about 440 kiloliters)

1:13 Solomon went to Jerusalem. The account in Kings ends with Solomon showing wisdom by sacrificing in Jerusalem (1Ki 3:15). The Chronicler omitted this passage and the following legal case of the two prostitutes (1Ki 3:16–28) in order to focus on Solomon's temple construction as the major demonstration of his wisdom.

■ **1:14–17** *Solomon Experiences Divine Promises.* The Chronicler immediately indicated that God kept his promise to make Solomon wealthy (v. 12). He connected this passage with its parallel (9:13–28) in the large-scale chiasm (see note on 1:1—9:31) by repeating the topic of horse trade (cf. vv. 14,16–17 with 9:25–28) and the words "silver and gold as common . . . as stones . . . sycamore-fig trees in the foothills" (cf. v. 15 with 9:27).

■ **2:1–18** *Solomon's International Assistance.* The central concern of the Chronicler's portrait of Solomon is the building of the temple. The mention of the temple and palace (v. 1) and of Hiram (v. 3) connects this passage with its chiastic parallel in 8:1–16 (see note on 1:1—9:31). Remarks on Solomon's workers (vv. 1–2,17–18) enclose Solomon's letter to Hiram (vv. 3–10) and Hiram's reply (vv. 11–16).

2:1 Name. See note on 1 Chronicles 13:6. **palace for himself.** The Chronicler mentions Solomon's palace on several occasions (v. 12; 7:11; 8:1; 9:3,11), but he omits the description of lengthy palace construction in 1 Kings 7:1–12 to focus attention on the temple. For the author, the construction of the temple took precedence over all other efforts. This priority instructed the postexilic readers about their own responsibilities (cf. Hag 1:1–15).

2:2 conscripted seventy thousand men. See note on 1 Chronicles 22:2.

2:3–10 Send me cedar logs. In verses 3–7 the Chronicler reported a different portion of the correspondence between Solomon and Hiram than is recorded in 1 Kings 5:3–5, possibly to connect Solomon's building effort more directly with David's preparations. See note on 1 Chronicles 22:5.

2:4 Name. See note on 1 Chronicles 13:6. **a lasting ordinance for Israel.** The Chronicler reminded his readers that Solomon's temple services were to be observed in their day.

2:6 cannot contain him. Solomon recognized that his temple was incapable of containing the omnipresent Creator (6:18). Nevertheless, the splendor of the temple must reflect the greatness of God. **Who then am I . . . ?** Solomon recognized that he was unworthy of God's blessing, just as his father had been before him (see note on 1Ch 17:16).

11Hiram king of Tyre replied by letter to Solomon:

"Because the LORD loves[m] his people, he has made you their king."

12And Hiram added:

"Praise be to the LORD, the God of Israel, who made heaven and earth![n] He has given King David a wise son, endowed with intelligence and discernment, who will build a temple for the LORD and a palace for himself.

13"I am sending you Huram-Abi,[o] a man of great skill, 14whose mother was from Dan[p] and whose father was from Tyre. He is trained[q] to work in gold and silver, bronze and iron, stone and wood, and with purple and blue[r] and crimson yarn and fine linen. He is experienced in all kinds of engraving and can execute any design given to him. He will work with your craftsmen and with those of my lord, David your father.

15"Now let my lord send his servants the wheat and barley and the olive oil[s] and wine he promised, 16and we will cut all the logs from Lebanon that you need and will float them in rafts by sea down to Joppa.[t] You can then take them up to Jerusalem."

17Solomon took a census of all the aliens[u] who were in Israel, after the census[v] his father David had taken; and they were found to be 153,600. 18He assigned[w] 70,000 of them to be carriers and 80,000 to be stonecutters in the hills, with 3,600 foremen over them to keep the people working.

Solomon Builds the Temple

3 Then Solomon began to build[x] the temple of the LORD[y] in Jerusalem on Mount Moriah, where the LORD had appeared to his father David. It was on the threshing floor of Araunah[a][z] the Jebusite, the place provided by David. 2He began building on the second day of the second month in the fourth year of his reign.[a]

3The foundation Solomon laid for building the temple of God was sixty cubits long and twenty cubits wide[b][b] (using the cubit of the old standard). 4The portico at the front of the temple was twenty cubits[c] long across the width of the building and twenty cubits[d] high.

He overlaid the inside with pure gold. 5He paneled the main hall with pine and covered it with fine gold and decorated it with palm tree[c] and chain designs. 6He adorned the temple with precious stones. And the gold he used was gold of Parvaim. 7He overlaid the ceiling beams, doorframes, walls and doors of the temple with gold, and he carved cherubim[d] on the walls.

8He built the Most Holy Place,[e] its length corresponding to the width of the temple—twenty cubits long and twenty cubits wide. He overlaid the inside with six hundred talents[e] of fine gold. 9The gold nails[f] weighed fifty shekels.[f] He also overlaid the upper parts with gold.

2:11 [m]1Ki 10:9; 2Ch 9:8
2:12 [n]Ne 9:6; Ps 8:3; 33:6; 102:25
2:13 [o]1Ki 7:13
2:14 [p]Ex 31:6 [q]Ex 35:31 [r]Ex 35:35
2:15 [s]ver 10; Ezr 3:7
2:16 [t]Jos 19:46; Jnh 1:3
2:17 [u]1Ch 22:2 [v]2Sa 24:2
2:18 [w]ver 2; 1Ch 22:2; 2Ch 8:8
3:1 [x]Ac 7:47 [y]Ge 28:17 [z]2Sa 24:18; 1Ch 21:18
3:2 [a]Ezr 5:11
3:3 [b]Eze 41:2
3:5 [c]Eze 40:16
3:7 [d]Ge 3:24; 1Ki 6:29-35; Eze 41:18
3:8 [e]Ex 26:33
3:9 [f]Ex 26:32

[a] *1* Hebrew *Ornan,* a variant of *Araunah* [b] *3* That is, about 90 feet (about 27 meters) long and 30 feet (about 9 meters) wide [c] *4* That is, about 30 feet (about 9 meters); also in verses 8, 11 and 13 [d] *4* Some Septuagint and Syriac manuscripts; Hebrew *and a hundred and twenty* [e] *8* That is, about 23 tons (about 21 metric tons) [f] *9* That is, about 1 1/4 pounds (about 0.6 kilogram)

2:11 Because the LORD loves his people. Through the words of Hiram, the Chronicler told his readers that the establishment of the Davidic line was an act of divine love toward Israel (see note on 1Ch 14:2).
2:12 wise son. The focus in this section becomes clear; Hiram connected Solomon's wisdom with temple building (see note on 1:13).
2:13–14 I am sending you Huram-Abi. As Solomon and Bezalel were counterparts in the temple and tabernacle accounts, so were Huram-Abi and Oholiab (see note on 1Ch 2:20).
2:13 Huram-Abi . . . from Dan. First Kings 7:14 reports that Huram-Abi's mother was from Naphtali. His mother may have been a Danite living in the territory of Naphtali.
2:17–18 aliens . . . carriers . . . stonecutters . . . foremen . . . keep the people working. See note on 1 Chronicles 22:2.
■ **3:1—5:1** *Solomon's Temple-Building Project.* Solomon began to build after arranging the materials and workforce. This section divides into the initiation of construction (3:1–2), the temple structure itself (3:3–17), the furnishings of the temple (4:1–22) and a notice of the completion of building (5:1). This material balances with that of 8:1–16 (see note on 1:1—9:31).
■ **3:1–2** *Solomon Begins Construction.* Having finished the preparations, Solomon initiated the building process on the holy site.
3:1 Mount Moriah . . . the threshing floor of Araunah. This information does not appear in Kings. The location of Solomon's temple is identified with the mount of Abraham's testing (Ge 22:2,14) and the site David purchased after his census (1Ch 21:1—22:1). The Chronicler pointed to the holiness of the site and tied Solomon's building directly to David's preparation (see note on 1Ch 22:5).
3:2 second day . . . second month . . . fourth year. The report of the date of building is based on 1 Kings 6:1.
■ **3:3–17** *Solomon's Temple Building.* The Chronicler significantly abbreviated the account of temple construction found in 1 Kings 6:4–20 and devoted more attention to the details of ornamentation (vv. 4–9). He mentioned dimensions (vv. 3–4a), as well as the decorations of the main hall (vv. 4b–7), the Most Holy Place (vv. 8–14) and the portico (vv. 15–17).
3:4 portico. The vestibule of the temple brought the length of the entire structure to 80 cubits (about 120 feet, or 36 meters).
3:5 main hall. That is, the Holy Place.

10 In the Most Holy Place he made a pair[g] of sculptured cherubim and overlaid them with gold. 11 The total wingspan of the cherubim was twenty cubits. One wing of the first cherub was five cubits[a] long and touched the temple wall, while its other wing, also five cubits long, touched the wing of the other cherub. 12 Similarly one wing of the second cherub was five cubits long and touched the other temple wall, and its other wing, also five cubits long, touched the wing of the first cherub. 13 The wings of these cherubim[h] extended twenty cubits. They stood on their feet, facing the main hall.[b]

14 He made the curtain[i] of blue, purple and crimson yarn and fine linen, with cherubim[j] worked into it.

15 In the front of the temple he made two pillars,[k] which ⌊together⌋ were thirty-five cubits[c] long, each with a capital[l] on top measuring five cubits. 16 He made interwoven chains[d][m] and put them on top of the pillars. He also made a hundred pomegranates[n] and attached them to the chains. 17 He erected the pillars in the front of the temple, one to the south and one to the north. The one to the south he named Jakin[e] and the one to the north Boaz.[f]

The Temple's Furnishings

4 He made a bronze altar[o] twenty cubits long, twenty cubits wide and ten cubits high.[g] 2 He made the Sea[p] of cast metal, circular in shape, measuring ten cubits from rim to rim and five cubits[a] high. It took a line of thirty cubits[h] to measure around it. 3 Below the rim, figures of bulls encircled it—ten to a cubit.[i] The bulls were cast in two rows in one piece with the Sea.

4 The Sea stood on twelve bulls, three facing north, three facing west, three facing south and three facing east.[q] The Sea rested on top of them, and their hindquarters were toward the center. 5 It was a handbreadth[j] in thickness, and its rim was like the rim of a cup, like a lily blossom. It held three thousand baths.[k]

6 He then made ten basins[r] for washing and placed five on the south side and five on the north. In them the things to be used for the burnt offerings[s] were rinsed, but the Sea was to be used by the priests for washing.

7 He made ten gold lampstands[t] according to the specifications[u] for them and placed them in the temple, five on the south side and five on the north.

8 He made ten tables[v] and placed them in the temple, five on the south side and five on the north. He also made a hundred gold sprinkling bowls.[w]

9 He made the courtyard[x] of the priests, and the large court and the doors for the court, and overlaid the doors with bronze. 10 He placed the Sea on the south side, at the southeast corner.

11 He also made the pots and shovels and sprinkling bowls.

So Huram finished[y] the work he had undertaken for King Solomon in the temple of God:

3:10 [g]Ex 25:18
3:13 [h]Ex 25:18
3:14 [i]Ex 26:31, 33; Heb 9:3 [j]Ge 3:24
3:15 [k]1Ki 7:15; Rev 3:12 [l]1Ki 7:22
3:16 [m]1Ki 7:17 [n]1Ki 7:20
4:1 [o]Ex 20:24; 27:1-2; 40:6; 1Ki 8:64; 2Ki 16:14
4:2 [p]Rev 4:6; 15:2
4:4 [q]Nu 2:3-25; Eze 48:30-34; Rev 21:13
4:6 [r]Ex 30:18 [s]Ne 13:5,9; Eze 40:38
4:7 [t]Ex 25:31 [u]Ex 25:40
4:8 [v]Ex 25:23 [w]Nu 4:14
4:9 [x]1Ki 6:36; 2Ki 21:5; 2Ch 33:5
4:11 [y]1Ki 7:14

[a] *11* That is, about 7 1/2 feet (about 2.3 meters); also in verse 15 [b] *13* Or *facing inward* [c] *15* That is, about 52 feet (about 16 meters) [d] *16* Or possibly *made chains in the inner sanctuary*; the meaning of the Hebrew for this phrase is uncertain. [e] *17* *Jakin* probably means *he establishes.* [f] *17* *Boaz* probably means *in him is strength.* [g] *1* That is, about 30 feet (about 9 meters) long and wide, and about 15 feet (about 4.5 meters) high [h] *2* That is, about 45 feet (about 13.5 meters) [i] *3* That is, about 1 1/2 feet (about 0.5 meter) [j] *5* That is, about 3 inches (about 8 centimeters) [k] *5* That is, about 17,500 gallons (about 66 kiloliters)

3:10 cherubim. Decorations on the walls, not to be confused with the cherubim on the ark of the covenant (Ex 25:18–20).
3:14 curtain. Solomon's temple followed the pattern of Moses' tabernacle (Ex 26:31–35). A curtain separated the Most Holy Place from the Holy Place (NIV "main hall"). The curtain prohibited visual and physical access to the Most Holy Place. This restriction was done away with in the New Testament era (see notes on Mt 27:51; Heb 9:1–15; 10:11–22).
3:15 together were thirty-five cubits long. First Kings 7:15 reads "eighteen cubits" (each). Here the NIV translators have inserted "together" to harmonize these differences. Yet the possibility exists of error in transmission of the text.
■ **4:1–10** *Solomon's Temple Furnishings.* The splendor of the temple was also displayed in the elaborate furnishings Solomon provided.
4:1 bronze altar. Mentioned also in 1 Kings 8:64 and 2 Kings 16:14. The bronze altar was the main altar in Solomon's temple. The large measurements are the dimensions of the base, from which steps led up to the altar (Eze 43:13–17).
4:2 Sea of cast metal. Solomon's replacement for the "bronze basin" of Moses' tabernacle (Ex 30:18). The water of this Sea was used for priestly ritual cleansing (v. 6). See notes on 1 Kings 7:27 and 38.
4:3 bulls. First Kings 7:24 reads "gourds." The expression may be literally translated, "that looked like bulls." The text describes the appearance of the gourds.
4:4 twelve bulls. See note on 1 Kings 7:25. The arrangement of the 12 bulls was oriented to the four points of the compass. This may represent the pattern of Israel's encampment around the tabernacle (Nu 2).
4:5 three thousand baths. First Kings 7:26 reads "two thousand baths." The Hebrew numbers "two thousand" and "three thousand" could easily have been confused in transmission.
4:9 courtyard of the priests, and the large court. Both courtyards are mentioned in Kings (1Ki 6:36; 7:12). The large court was for the laity (see Eze 40–48 and its notes).
■ **4:11–22** *Reiteration and Elaboration.* The text follows 1 Kings 7:40–50 in the description of Huram-Abi's work, which elaborates on what had been described in the previous sections.
4:11 Huram. That is, Huram-abi, the artisan sent by Hiram of Tyre (2:13; 4:16).

12 the two pillars;
the two bowl-shaped capitals on top of the pillars;
the two sets of network decorating the two bowl-shaped capitals on top of the pillars;
13 the four hundred pomegranates for the two sets of network (two rows of pomegranates for each network, decorating the bowl-shaped capitals on top of the pillars);
14 the stands[z] with their basins;
15 the Sea and the twelve bulls under it;
16 the pots, shovels, meat forks and all related articles.

All the objects that Huram-Abi[a] made for King Solomon for the temple of the LORD
were of polished bronze. 17 The king had them cast in clay molds in the plain of the Jordan between Succoth[b] and Zarethan.[a] 18 All these things that Solomon made amounted
to so much that the weight of the bronze[c] was not determined.

19 Solomon also made all the furnishings that were in God's temple:

the golden altar;
the tables[d] on which was the bread of the Presence;
20 the lampstands[e] of pure gold with their lamps, to burn in front of the inner sanctuary as prescribed;
21 the gold floral work and lamps and tongs (they were solid gold);
22 the pure gold wick trimmers, sprinkling bowls, dishes[f] and censers;[g] and the gold doors of the temple: the inner doors to the Most Holy Place and the doors of the main hall.

5 When all the work Solomon had done for the temple of the LORD was finished,[h] he
brought in the things his father David had dedicated[i]—the silver and gold and all
the furnishings—and he placed them in the treasuries of God's temple.

The Ark Brought to the Temple

2 Then Solomon summoned to Jerusalem the elders of Israel, all the heads of the tribes
and the chiefs of the Israelite families, to bring up the ark[j] of the LORD's covenant from
Zion, the City of David. 3 And all the men of Israel[k] came together to the king at the time
of the festival in the seventh month.

4 When all the elders of Israel had arrived, the Levites took up the ark, 5 and they
brought up the ark and the Tent of Meeting and all the sacred furnishings in it. The
priests, who were Levites,[l] carried them up; 6 and King Solomon and the entire assembly of Israel that had gathered about him were before the ark, sacrificing so many sheep
and cattle that they could not be recorded or counted.

7 The priests then brought the ark[m] of the LORD's covenant to its place in the inner
sanctuary of the temple, the Most Holy Place, and put it beneath the wings of the cherubim. 8 The cherubim[n] spread their wings over the place of the ark and covered the ark
and its carrying poles. 9 These poles were so long that their ends, extending from the ark,
could be seen from in front of the inner sanctuary, but not from outside the Holy Place;
and they are still there today. 10 There was nothing in the ark except[o] the two tablets[p]
that Moses had placed in it at Horeb, where the LORD made a covenant with the Israelites after they came out of Egypt.

4:14 [z]1Ki 7:27-30
4:16 [a]1Ki 7:13
4:17 [b]Ge 33:17
4:18 [c]1Ki 7:23
4:19 [d]Ex 25:23, 30
4:20 [e]Ex 25:31
4:22 [f]Nu 7:14 [g]Lev 10:1
5:1 [h]1Ki 6:14 [i]2Sa 8:11
5:2 [j]Nu 3:31; 2Sa 6:12; 1Ch 15:25
5:3 [k]1Ch 9:1; 2Ch 7:8-10
5:5 [l]Nu 3:31; 1Ch 15:2
5:7 [m]Rev 11:19
5:8 [n]Ge 3:24
5:10 [o]Heb 9:4 [p]Ex 16:34; Dt 10:2

[a] 17 Hebrew *Zeredatha,* a variant of *Zarethan*

■ **5:1** *Solomon Completes Construction.* In balance with 3:1–2 (see note on 1:1—9:31), the end of Solomon's building activities is reported.
5:1 David had dedicated. The Chronicler tied Solomon's temple directly to David's preparations (see notes on 1Ch 18:8,11 and 22:5).
■ **5:2—7:10** *Solomon's Assembly to Dedicate the Temple.* The text closely follows the account of temple dedication in 1 Kings 8:1–66. The report divides into six balanced parts: the assembly gathered (5:2–3), initial celebration (5:4—6:2), praise for the past (6:3–11), prayer for the future (6:12–42), concluding celebration (7:1–7) and the assembly dismissed (7:8–10).
5:2—6:2 summoned . . . to bring up the ark. See 1 Kings 8:1–11, which the Chronicler followed closely.
■ **5:2–3** *Solomon's Assembly Gathers.* The whole nation joined with Solomon at a holy assembly, a model for the postexilic readers of Chronicles.
5:3 all the men of Israel. While this expression appears in 1 Kings 8:2, it fits well with the Chronicler's desire to show that Solomon received widespread support from Israel (see note on 1Ch 11:1). **seventh month.** The month of Tishri ("Ethanim"; 1Ki 8:2), the time ordained for the Feast of Tabernacles. The temple was completed in the eighth month of Solomon's eleventh year (1Ki 6:38). Apparently, this dedication event occurred 11 months after the completion of construction.
■ **5:4—6:2** *Solomon's Initial Celebration of the Temple.* The assembly opened with representatives of all the tribes and with a special role for the priests and Levites.
5:4–14 Levites . . . priests. The repeated references to priests and Levites demonstrate how Solomon carefully observed tabernacle/temple regulations (see note on 1Ch 6:1–81).
5:9 there today. See note on 1 Chronicles 4:41 and 43.
5:10 nothing . . . except the two tablets. In contrast with Moses' tabernacle, where the ark also contained Aaron's staff (Nu 17:10–11) and the jar of manna (Ex 16:32–34).

11The priests then withdrew from the Holy Place. All the priests who were there had
consecrated themselves, regardless of their divisions.[q] 12All the Levites who were musicians[r]—Asaph, Heman, Jeduthun and their sons and relatives—stood on the east side
of the altar, dressed in fine linen and playing cymbals, harps and lyres. They were accompanied by 120 priests sounding trumpets.[s] 13The trumpeters and singers joined in unison, as with one voice, to give praise and thanks to the LORD. Accompanied by trumpets,
cymbals and other instruments, they raised their voices in praise to the LORD and sang:

"He is good;
his love endures forever."[t]

Then the temple of the LORD was filled with a cloud, 14and the priests could not perform[u] their service because of the cloud,[v] for the glory[w] of the LORD filled the temple of
God.

6 Then Solomon said, "The LORD has said that he would dwell in a dark cloud;[x] 2I have
built a magnificent temple for you, a place for you to dwell forever.[y]"
3While the whole assembly of Israel was standing there, the king turned around and
blessed them. 4Then he said:

"Praise be to the LORD, the God of Israel, who with his hands has fulfilled what
he promised with his mouth to my father David. For he said, 5'Since the day I
brought my people out of Egypt, I have not chosen a city in any tribe of Israel to
have a temple built for my Name to be there, nor have I chosen anyone to be the
leader over my people Israel. 6But now I have chosen Jerusalem[z] for my Name[a]
to be there, and I have chosen David[b] to rule my people Israel.'
7"My father David had it in his heart[c] to build a temple for the Name of the
LORD, the God of Israel. 8But the LORD said to my father David, 'Because it was in
your heart to build a temple for my Name, you did well to have this in your heart.
9Nevertheless, you are not the one to build the temple, but your son, who is your
own flesh and blood—he is the one who will build the temple for my Name.'
10"The LORD has kept the promise he made. I have succeeded David my father
and now I sit on the throne of Israel, just as the LORD promised, and I have built the
temple for the Name of the LORD, the God of Israel. 11There I have placed the ark,
in which is the covenant[d] of the LORD that he made with the people of Israel."

Solomon's Prayer of Dedication

12Then Solomon stood before the altar of the LORD in front of the whole assembly of
Israel and spread out his hands. 13Now he had made a bronze platform,[e] five cubits[a]
long, five cubits wide and three cubits[b] high, and had placed it in the center of the outer court. He stood on the platform and then knelt down[f] before the whole assembly of
Israel and spread out his hands toward heaven. 14He said:

"O LORD, God of Israel, there is no God like you[g] in heaven or on earth—you
who keep your covenant of love[h] with your servants who continue wholehearted-

5:11 [q]1Ch 24:1
5:12 [r]1Ki 10:12; 1Ch 25:1; Ps 68:25 [s]1Ch 13:8; 15:24
5:13 [t]1Ch 16:34,41; 2Ch 7:3; 20:21; Ezr 3:11; Ps 100:5; 136:1; Jer 33:11
5:14 [u]Ex 40:35; Rev 15:8 [v]Ex 19:16 [w]Ex 29:43; 2Ch 7:2
6:1 [x]Ex 19:9; 1Ki 8:12-50
6:2 [y]Ezr 6:12; 7:15; Ps 135:21
6:6 [z]Dt 12:5; Isa 14:1 [a]Ex 20:24; 2Ch 12:13 [b]1Ch 28:4
6:7 [c]1Sa 10:7; 1Ch 17:2; 28:2; Ac 7:46
6:11 [d]Dt 10:2; 2Ch 5:10; Ps 25:10; 50:5
6:13 [e]Ne 8:4 [f]Ps 95:6
6:14 [g]Ex 8:10; 15:11 [h]Dt 7:9

[a] *13* That is, about 7 1/2 feet (about 2.3 meters) [b] *13* That is, about 4 1/2 feet (about 1.3 meters)

5:12–13 musicians . . . playing cymbals, harps and lyres . . . trumpeters and singers joined. The Chronicler added many details here (cf. 1Ki 8:10–11), in line with his interest in the music of worship (see note on 1Ch 15:16–24).
5:13–14 cloud . . . glory. God blessed Solomon's temple with his presence as he had earlier blessed Moses' tabernacle (Ex 40:34–38). Old Testament prophets hoped for the return of God's glory to the temple after the exile (Eze 43:1–5; Hag 2:7–9; Zec 2:10; 8:3).
5:13 He is good . . . forever. A familiar line of descriptive praise honoring God for his enduring goodness and mercy (7:3,6; Pss 106; 107; 136).
6:1–2 a place for you to dwell forever. Solomon's hope for the permanence of God's presence in the temple, a keen concern for the postexilic audience (see note on 5:13–14).
■ **6:3–11** *Solomon's Praise for the Past.* On this momentous day, Solomon's heart was drawn toward the many blessings God had lavished on his people in the past, and especially on his promises to David.
6:3–11 the whole assembly of Israel was standing there. See notes on 1 Kings 8:14–21.
6:5–10,20,24,26,32–34,38 Name. See note on 1 Chronicles 13:6.
6:9 you are not the one. See 1 Chronicles 22:6–10 and its note.
6:10 the promise he made. See note on 1 Chronicles 17:1–15.
6:11 with the people of Israel. First Kings 8:21 reads "with our fathers, when he brought them out of Egypt." The reference to the exodus was well known to the original readers. It was most likely omitted here to emphasize the Davidic (v. 10) instead of the Mosaic administration of the covenant. The Davidic administration of the covenant was particularly central to the royal hopes of the postexilic community (see notes on vv. 40–42; 1Ch 17:1–27).
■ **6:12–42** *Solomon's Prayer for the Future.* The Chronicler closely followed 1 Kings 8:22–53 in his account of Solomon's prayer. The main difference appears at the end of the prayer—compare verses 41–42 with 1 Kings 8:51–53. Solomon's dedicatory prayer focused on the temple as a center for prayer. The prayer divides into four parts: the setting (vv. 12–13), a doxology (vv. 14–15), petition for the Davidic dynasty (vv. 16–17) and petitions for the temple (vv. 18–42).
6:13 outer court. See note on 4:9. **spread out his hands.** This verse is missing from the traditional Hebrew (Masoretic) text of 1 Kings 8. It is likely, however, that it was lost from Kings at some stage of transmission. The repetition of "spread out his hands" (vv. 12–13) may have caused a scribe to skip the intervening material as he copied Kings.
6:14 keep your covenant . . . your servants who continue . . . in your way. Solomon's words of praise touched on both sides of the covenant relationship between God and his people. God keeps

ly in your way. 15 You have kept your promise to your servant David my father; with
your mouth you have promised[i] and with your hand you have fulfilled it—as it is
today.
16 "Now LORD, God of Israel, keep for your servant David my father the promises you made to him when you said, 'You shall never fail[j] to have a man to sit before me on the throne of Israel, if only your sons are careful in all they do to walk
before me according to my law,[k] as you have done.' 17 And now, O LORD, God of Israel, let your word that you promised your servant David come true.
18 "But will God really dwell[l] on earth with men? The heavens,[m] even the highest heavens, cannot contain you. How much less this temple I have built! 19 Yet give
attention to your servant's prayer and his plea for mercy, O LORD my God. Hear the
cry and the prayer that your servant is praying in your presence. 20 May your
eyes[n] be open toward this temple day and night, this place of which you said you
would put your Name[o] there. May you hear[p] the prayer your servant prays toward
this place. 21 Hear the supplications of your servant and of your people Israel
when they pray toward this place. Hear from heaven, your dwelling place; and
when you hear, forgive.[q]
22 "When a man wrongs his neighbor and is required to take an oath[r] and he
comes and swears the oath before your altar in this temple, 23 then hear from heav-
en and act. Judge between your servants, repaying[s] the guilty by bringing down
on his own head what he has done. Declare the innocent not guilty and so establish his innocence.
24 "When your people Israel have been defeated[t] by an enemy because they
have sinned against you and when they turn back and confess your name, praying and making supplication before you in this temple, 25 then hear from heaven
and forgive the sin of your people Israel and bring them back to the land you gave
to them and their fathers.
26 "When the heavens are shut up and there is no rain[u] because your people
have sinned against you, and when they pray toward this place and confess your
name and turn from their sin because you have afflicted them, 27 then hear from
heaven and forgive[v] the sin of your servants, your people Israel. Teach them the
right way to live, and send rain on the land you gave your people for an inheritance.
28 "When famine[w] or plague comes to the land, or blight or mildew, locusts or
grasshoppers, or when enemies besiege them in any of their cities, whatever disaster or disease may come, 29 and when a prayer or plea is made by any of your
people Israel—each one aware of his afflictions and pains, and spreading out his
hands toward this temple— 30 then hear from heaven, your dwelling place. Forgive,[x] and deal with each man according to all he does, since you know his heart
(for you alone know the hearts of men),[y] 31 so that they will fear you[z] and walk in
your ways all the time they live in the land you gave our fathers.
32 "As for the foreigner who does not belong to your people Israel but has

6:15 [i]1Ch 22:10
6:16 [j]2Sa 7:13,15; 1Ki 2:4; 2Ch 7:18; 23:3 [k]Ps 132:12
6:18 [l]Rev 21:3 [m]2Ch 2:6; Ps 11:4; Isa 40:22; 66:1; Ac 7:49
6:20 [n]Ex 3:16; Ps 34:15 [o]Dt 12:11 [p]2Ch 7:14; 30:20
6:21 [q]Ps 51:1; Isa 33:24; 40:2; 43:25; 44:22; 55:7; Mic 7:18
6:22 [r]Ex 22:11
6:23 [s]Isa 3:11; 65:6; Mt 16:27
6:24 [t]Lev 26:17
6:26 [u]Lev 26:19; Dt 11:17; 28:24; 2Sa 1:21; 1Ki 17:1
6:27 [v]ver 30,39; 2Ch 7:14
6:28 [w]2Ch 20:9
6:30 [x]ver 27 [y]1Sa 16:7; 1Ch 28:9; Ps 7:9; 44:21; Pr 16:2; 17:3
6:31 [z]Ps 103:11,13; Pr 8:13

his covenant, but his people must persevere in fidelity. Flagrant violation of the covenant would result in divine retribution (Dt 7:9–12; 30:15–19). This covenantal structure was central to the Chronicler's theological outlook (see note on 1Ch 28:9).

6:16 if only your sons are careful. Solomon emphasized the responsibility to persevere. These words come from 1 Kings 8:25, but they fit well with the Chronicler's desire to motivate his postexilic readers to fidelity (see notes on v. 14; 1Ch 17:7–14). **walk . . . according to my law.** See note on 1 Chronicles 16:40.

6:17 let your word . . . come true. Solomon prayed for the monarchy by referring to the promise, conveyed through Nathan, of a permanent dynasty (see note on 1Ch 17:7–14).

6:18–39 May your eyes be open toward this temple. Solomon turned to the heart of his concerns, prayers for the future of the temple (cf. 1Ki 8:27–46). He prayed that the temple would be the national center for effective prayer. He began with a general request for God to listen to prayers offered (vv. 18–21) and listed seven specific situations in which prayers might be given in or toward the temple (vv. 22–39). The author likely included this material in his history to impress on his postexilic readers their need to regard the restored temple as the center of prayer in their day.

6:18 the highest heavens, cannot contain you. See note on 2:6.

6:19–21 prayer . . . pray. See note on 7:14.

6:21 Hear from heaven, your dwelling place. Solomon used this expression four times in his prayer (vv. 21,30,33,39). The temple was the earthly place that provided access to the heavenly court through the Name dwelling there (see note on 1Ch 13:6).

6:22–39 in this temple. While these situations for prayer are relevant to God's people in all ages, several scenarios were particularly applicable to the postexilic audience: military defeat (vv. 24–25), drought (vv. 26–27), famine and plague (vv. 28–31), foreigners (vv. 32–33), war (vv. 34–35) and exile (vv. 36–39).

6:22–23 required to take an oath. For the sorts of legal procedures in mind here, see Exodus 22:10–11 and Leviticus 6:1–7. See *WCF* 22.1.

6:24–25 defeated . . . because they have sinned. Military defeat is often listed as a curse for flagrant covenant violators (Lev 26:17; Dt 28:25–26,36–37,47–57).

6:24,26,32,34,38 praying . . . pray. See note on 7:14.

6:24,26,38 turn. See note on 7:14.

6:26–27 no rain . . . rain. Rain and drought were covenant blessings and curses, respectively (see note on 7:13–15; see Lev 26:3–4; Dt 11:13–14; 28:22; Jer 3:3; Joel 2:23–27; Hag 1:10–14).

6:28–31 famine or plague . . . locusts. Famines and plagues of various sorts were covenant curses (Lev 26:16,20,25–26; Dt 28:20–22,27–28,35,42). See note on 7:13–15.

6:32–33 foreigner. Solomon hoped that foreigners would also receive answers to prayer at the temple. Old Testament prophets anticipated the inclusion of Gentiles among the people of God in record numbers after the exile (Isa 56:6–8; Joel 2:28; Zec 8:20–23;

6:32 [a]2Ch 9:6; Jn 12:20; Ac 8:27 [b]Ex 3:19, 20
6:33 [c]2Ch 7:14
6:34 [d]Dt 28:7 [e]1Ch 5:20
6:36 [f]Job 15:14; Ps 143:2; Ecc 7:20; Jer 17:9; Jas 3:1; 1Jn 1:8-10 [g]Lev 26:44
6:37 [h]2Ch 7:14; 33:12, 19,23; Jer 29:13
6:40 [i]2Ch 7:15; Ne 1:6, 11; Ps 17:1,6
6:41 [j]Isa 33:10 [k]1Ch 28:2 [l]Ps 132:16 [m]Ps 116:12
6:42 [n]Ps 89:24,28; Isa 55:3
7:1 [o]Lev 9:24; 1Ki 18:38 [p]Ex 16:10 [q]Ps 26:8
7:2 [r]1Ki 8:11 [s]Ex 29:43; 40:35; 2Ch 5:14
7:3 [t]1Ch 16:34; 2Ch 5:13; 20:21
7:6 [u]1Ch 15:16 [v]2Ch 5:12

come[a] from a distant land because of your great name and your mighty hand[b] and
your outstretched arm—when he comes and prays toward this temple, 33then hear
from heaven, your dwelling place, and do whatever the foreigner[c] asks of you, so
that all the peoples of the earth may know your name and fear you, as do your own
people Israel, and may know that this house I have built bears your Name.
34"When your people go to war against their enemies,[d] wherever you send
them, and when they pray[e] to you toward this city you have chosen and the temple I have built for your Name, 35then hear from heaven their prayer and their plea,
and uphold their cause.
36"When they sin against you—for there is no one who does not sin[f]—and you
become angry with them and give them over to the enemy, who takes them captive[g] to a land far away or near; 37and if they have a change of heart[h] in the land
where they are held captive, and repent and plead with you in the land of their
captivity and say, 'We have sinned, we have done wrong and acted wickedly';
38and if they turn back to you with all their heart and soul in the land of their captivity where they were taken, and pray toward the land you gave their fathers, toward the city you have chosen and toward the temple I have built for your Name;
39then from heaven, your dwelling place, hear their prayer and their pleas, and uphold their cause. And forgive your people, who have sinned against you.
40"Now, my God, may your eyes be open and your ears attentive[i] to the prayers
offered in this place.

41 "Now arise,[j] O LORD God, and come to your resting place,[k]
you and the ark of your might.
May your priests,[l] O LORD God, be clothed with salvation,
may your saints rejoice in your goodness.[m]
42 O LORD God, do not reject your anointed one.
Remember the great love[n] promised to David your
servant."

The Dedication of the Temple

7 When Solomon finished praying, fire[o] came down from heaven and consumed the
burnt offering and the sacrifices, and the glory of the LORD filled[p] the temple.[q] 2The
priests could not enter[r] the temple of the LORD because the glory[s] of the LORD filled it.
3When all the Israelites saw the fire coming down and the glory of the LORD above the
temple, they knelt on the pavement with their faces to the ground, and they worshiped
and gave thanks to the LORD, saying,

"He is good;
his love endures forever."[t]

4Then the king and all the people offered sacrifices before the LORD. 5And King Solomon
offered a sacrifice of twenty-two thousand head of cattle and a hundred and twenty thousand sheep and goats. So the king and all the people dedicated the temple of God. 6The
priests took their positions, as did the Levites[u] with the LORD's musical instruments,[v]

14:16–21; cf. Ps 87). This petition is probably included to point out the centrality of the temple in the expansion of the kingdom to other nations. The massive inclusion of Gentiles in the kingdom was fulfilled through Christ (Ro 3:29; Gal 3:14).
6:34–35 go to war. The Chronicler frequently reported on how God answers prayer offered in battle (see notes on 12:6–7,12; 13:14; 14:11; 18:31; 20:12,15; 32:20; 1Ch 5:18–22).
6:36–39 takes them captive . . . uphold their cause. Exile and captivity were curses for flagrant covenant violators (Dt 28:36–37, 64). Solomon's request was realized twice in the history given in 2 Chronicles. Both Manasseh (33:10–13) and the entire remnant of Israel (36:21–23) went into exile in Babylon but were restored to the promised land.
6:37 repent. See note on 7:14.
6:38 toward the land . . . city . . . temple. Note the practice of both Daniel (Da 6:10) and Jonah (Jnh 2:4).
6:40–42 come to your resting place . . . do not reject your anointed one. Solomon's petitions closed with a twofold concern, for the temple and for the throne. The Chronicler omits 1 Kings 8:50b–51 and includes a rendition of Psalm 132:8–10. The ending of the prayer as recorded in Kings focuses on the Mosaic covenant, but the attention is shifted here toward the Davidic covenant (6:42; cf. 6:11). Solomon called on God to be present in the temple (v. 41a), to bring joy and celebration to the priests and to the people (v. 41b) and to remember his promise of love to David (v. 42). This additional material spoke directly to the hopes of the postexilic audience for the full restoration of glorious worship in Jerusalem (see note on 5:13–14).
■ **7:1–7** *Solomon's Concluding Sacrifices and Celebration.* The Chronicler closed the dedication ceremony on a note of joy and celebration that paralleled its opening (see note on 3:1—5:1). He included verses 1–3 and omitted material from 1 Kings 8:54b–61. He then roughly followed 1 Kings 8:62–66.
7:1 fire came down. See note on 1 Chronicles 21:26.
7:2–3 the glory of the LORD filled it. The repetition of elements in 5:13b–14 balances the initial celebration (5:2—6:2) with the closing celebration (7:1–10; see note on 1:1—9:31). See especially the descriptive praise for God's enduring mercy (cf. 7:3,6 with 6:13). See note on 5:13.
7:3 fire coming down. See note on 1 Chronicles 21:26.
7:6–8 all the Israelites . . . all Israel. The Chronicler referred to the involvement of the whole nation (see note on 1Ch 11:1).
7:6 with the LORD's musical instruments. The Chronicler included this material, in line with his interest in the music of worship, to depict the splendor of the celebration (see note on 1Ch 15:16–24).

which King David had made for praising the LORD and which were used when he gave thanks, saying, "His love endures forever." Opposite the Levites, the priests blew their trumpets, and all the Israelites were standing.

7Solomon consecrated the middle part of the courtyard in front of the temple of the LORD, and there he offered burnt offerings and the fat of the fellowship offerings,[a] because the bronze altar he had made could not hold the burnt offerings, the grain offerings and the fat portions.

8So Solomon observed the festival[w] at that time for seven days, and all Israel with

7:8 [w]2Ch 30:26

[a] 7 Traditionally *peace offerings*

■ **7:8–10** *Solomon's Assembly Dismisses.* In balance with the opening of this section (5:2–3), the assembly ended.

7:8 festival. The Feast of Tabernacles (see note on 5:3).

Prayer: Why Should We Pray?

REFORMED theology has consistently insisted on the importance and effectiveness of prayer. God made us and redeemed us in order that we might have fellowship with him, and that is what prayer is: fellowship with God. God speaks to us through revelation, both the special revelation of Scripture and the general revelation of creation. He also speaks to us as the Holy Spirit enables us to understand this revelation, convicts us of our sin and works in us, empowering us to obey and to rejoice in the revelation we have received. In response, we engage in prayer to speak to God about himself, ourselves, our relationship with him and everything that exists and takes place in his creation.

There is no tension or inconsistency between the reality that God is sovereign over all things and the fact that prayer is effective. Just as God has ordained eating as a means by which hunger may be satisfied, so he has ordained prayer as a means by which events may come to pass. God has even ordained our prayers themselves, so they are fully in accord with his eternal council. Divine sovereignty does not contradict but affirms our responsibility to pray.

Although God has commanded us to pray, this is not the only reason we do so. We pray because we are entirely dependent upon God, needing him and his fellowship. We pray because God sovereignly controls all things and can therefore do whatever he pleases, and we pray so that he will choose to do good things for ourselves and others. Of all the human means that God uses to carry out his eternal plan, prayer is certainly one of the most powerful and effective because prayer calls on the all-powerful God to act on our behalf and on behalf of others for whom we intercede. As James expressed it, "The prayer of a righteous man is powerful and effective" (Jas 5:16).

Prayer takes different forms and emphases in different situations, and there are many legitimate ways to summarize the Bible's teaching on the subject. One helpful way to think of prayer is as a fourfold activity to be performed by God's people individually and collectively, both privately (Mt 6:5–8) and with each other (Ac 1:14; 4:24). We are to: (1) express adoration and praise; (2) offer contrite confession of sin and seek forgiveness; (3) thank the Lord for benefits received; and (4) petition and supplicate on behalf of ourselves and others. The Lord's Prayer (Mt 6:9–13; Lk 11:2–4) embodies adoration, petition and confession; the Psalter models all four elements of prayer.

Petition is our humble acknowledgment that we both need and trust God, that we depend on his sovereign wisdom and goodness. This is perhaps the most prominent dimension of prayer as expressed throughout the Bible (e.g., Ge 18:16–33; Ex 32:31—33:17; Ezr 9:5–15; Ne 1:5–11; 4:4–5,9; 6:9,14; Da 9:4–19; Mt 7:7–11; Jn 16:24; 17:1–26; Eph 6:18–20; Jas 5:16–18; 1Jn 5:14–16). Petition, along with the other modes of prayer, should ordinarily be directed to the Father, as the Lord's Prayer demonstrates, but we may also direct our requests to Christ (Jn 14:14), especially those for salvation and healing (Ac 7:59; Ro 10:8–13; 2Co 12:7–9). And we may petition the Holy Spirit for grace and peace (Rev 1:4). It cannot be wrong to present petitions to God as triune or to request a spiritual blessing from any one of the three persons of the Trinity, but there is wisdom in following the New Testament pattern.

Jesus teaches that petition to the Father is to be made in Christ's name (Jn 14:13–14; 15:16; 16:23–24). This means invoking Jesus' merit as the basis for our access to the Father and looking to Jesus, as our intercessor in the Father's presence, for support. We can only do so, however, when what we ask accords with God's revealed will (1Jn 5:14) and stems from proper motives (Jas 4:3).

Jesus teaches that we may press God with fervent persistence when we bring needs to him (Lk 11:5–13; 18:1–8) and that he will answer such prayer in positive terms. But we must remember that God, who knows what is best in a way that we cannot, may deny our specific requests as to how these needs should be met. When God doesn't give us what we request, it is often because he has something better for us, as when the Lord declined to heal the "thorn" in Paul's flesh (2Co 12:7–9).

Christians who pray to God sincerely, reverently, humbly and penitently, with a sense of privilege and with a purified heart, will find that the Holy Spirit prompts them to pray even more and to trust in their heavenly Father implicitly (Ro 8:15; Gal 4:6). They will find themselves compelled to pray even though they may not know what thoughts or desires to express (Ro 8:26–27). The mysterious reality of the Holy Spirit's help in prayer becomes known only to those who actively engage in this indispensable spiritual exercise.

7:8 [x]Ge 15:18
7:9 [y]Lev 23:36
7:12 [z]Dt 12:5
7:13 [a]2Ch 6:26-28; Am 4:7
7:14 [b]Lev 26:41; 2Ch 6:37; Jas 4:10 [c]1Ch 16:11 [d]Isa 55:7; Zec 1:4 [e]2Ch 6:27 [f]2Ch 30:20; Isa 30:26; 57:18
7:15 [g]2Ch 6:40
7:16 [h]ver 12; 2Ch 6:6
7:17 [i]1Ki 9:4
7:18 [j]2Ch 6:16 [k]2Sa 7:13; 2Ch 13:5
7:19 [l]Dt 28:15 [m]Lev 26:14, 33
7:20 [n]Dt 29:28 [o]1Ki 14:15 [p]Dt 28:37
7:21 [q]Dt 29:24

him—a vast assembly, people from Lebo[a] Hamath to the Wadi of Egypt.[x] 9 On the eighth
day they held an assembly, for they had celebrated the dedication of the altar for seven
days and the festival[y] for seven days more. 10 On the twenty-third day of the seventh
month he sent the people to their homes, joyful and glad in heart for the good things the
LORD had done for David and Solomon and for his people Israel.

The LORD Appears to Solomon

11 When Solomon had finished the temple of the LORD and the royal palace, and had
succeeded in carrying out all he had in mind to do in the temple of the LORD and in his
own palace, 12 the LORD appeared to him at night and said:

"I have heard your prayer and have chosen this place for myself[z] as a temple
for sacrifices.
13 "When I shut up the heavens so that there is no rain,[a] or command locusts
to devour the land or send a plague among my people, 14 if my people, who are
called by my name, will humble[b] themselves and pray and seek my face[c] and
turn[d] from their wicked ways, then will I hear from heaven and will forgive[e] their
sin and will heal[f] their land. 15 Now my eyes will be open and my ears attentive to
the prayers offered in this place.[g] 16 I have chosen[h] and consecrated this temple
so that my Name may be there forever. My eyes and my heart will always be there.
17 "As for you, if you walk before me[i] as David your father did, and do all I command, and observe my decrees and laws, 18 I will establish your royal throne, as I
covenanted with David your father when I said, 'You shall never fail to have a man[j]
to rule over Israel.'[k]
19 "But if you[b] turn away[l] and forsake[m] the decrees and commands I have giv-
en you[b] and go off to serve other gods and worship them, 20 then I will uproot[n] Israel from my land,[o] which I have given them, and will reject this temple I have consecrated for my Name. I will make it a byword and an object of ridicule[p] among
all peoples. 21 And though this temple is now so imposing, all who pass by will be
appalled and say,[q] 'Why has the LORD done such a thing to this land and to this
temple?' 22 People will answer, 'Because they have forsaken the LORD, the God of
their fathers, who brought them out of Egypt, and have embraced other gods, worshiping and serving them—that is why he brought all this disaster on them.' "

Solomon's Other Activities

8 At the end of twenty years, during which Solomon built the temple of the LORD and
his own palace, 2 Solomon rebuilt the villages that Hiram[c] had given him, and set-

[a] 8 Or *from the entrance to* [b] 19 The Hebrew is plural. [c] 2 Hebrew *Huram,* a variant of *Hiram;* also in verse 18

7:10 for David and Solomon. First Kings 8:66 reads simply "David." The Chronicler viewed the temple construction as a joint effort of David and Solomon (see note on 1Ch 22:5).

■ **7:11–22** *Solomon's Response From God.* Despite the literary proximity of this passage to the preceding material, God responded to Solomon's dedicatory prayer 13 years later, after Solomon had completed his palace (1Ki 7:1; 9:10). The Chronicler followed 1 Kings 9:1–9, but his account differs from that of Kings in ways that were especially relevant to his postexilic audience. This section balances with 5:2—7:10 (see note on 1:1—9:31).

7:12 the LORD appeared to him. The Chronicler omitted the reference to Solomon's dream at Gibeon (1Ki 9:2). By doing so, he connected God's response more directly with the completion of the temple (see note on 7:11–22).

7:13–15 These verses do not appear in Kings. They report God's response to several requests mentioned in Solomon's prayer (6:14–42) that were of particular significance to the Chronicler's postexilic audience. See "Introduction to 1 Chronicles: Time and Place of Writing."

7:13 rain . . . locusts . . . plague. A specific reference to 6:26–31.

7:14,16,20 name . . . Name. See note on 1 Chronicles 13:6.

7:14 if my people. God promised that the nation would receive relief from hardship caused by sin if the people would turn to him in humility and prayer. Within this general parameter, God retained the prerogative to bless when and how he saw fit. This divine pledge applied directly to the postexilic situation. Relief from the privations faced by the restored community would come only if the returnees were to meet these conditions. A number of events in the divided and reunited kingdoms recall the principles of this passage (see note on 12:6–7,12; also see notes on 13:14; 14:8–15; 18:31; 20:12,15; 30:18–20; 32:20; 33:12–13). Numerous times in Chronicles the concepts in this passage appear as the decisive factor for divine blessing and curses. **humble.** An attitude of contrition and dependence on God (12:6–7,12; 30:11; 33:12,19,23; 34:27; 36:12). **pray.** To call on God for help in times of need (6:19,21,24,26,32,34,38; 30:18; 32:20,24; 33:13). **seek.** To worship and pursue God faithfully and earnestly (11:16; 15:4,15; 20:4; 1Ch 16:10–11). Also, see the related concept (although a different Hebrew word, often translated "consult" or "inquire") in 12:14, 14:4,7, 15:12, 16:12, 17:4, 18:4,7, 19:3, 20:3, 22:9, 25:15,20, 26:5, 30:19, 31:21, 34:3,21,26, 1 Chronicles 10:13–14, 13:3, 15:13, 16:11, 21:30, 22:19 and 28:9. **turn.** To turn from sin and toward obedience (6:24,26,37–38; 15:4; 24:19; 30:6,9; 36:13). See *HC* 117.

7:17–22 I will establish your royal throne. The promise of a permanent dynasty for David was the basis of the postexilic readers' hope for the restoration of the Davidic throne in their day. While the promise to David's line was irrevocable, the nation always faced the threat of punishment and exile (see notes on 1Ch 17:7–14; 28:9).

7:17 observe my decrees and laws. See note on 1 Chronicles 16:40.

■ **8:1–16** *More on Solomon's Building Projects.* The Chronicler reported on an assortment of Solomon's building projects and temple arrangements, the content of which balances with that of 3:1—5:1 (see note on 1:1—9:31). He roughly followed 1 Kings 9:10–28.

8:2 villages that Hiram had given him. Solomon first presented these cities to Hiram, who later returned them (1Ki 9:10–14). The author omitted this detail to focus on Solomon's improvements of the sites.

tled Israelites in them. [3]Solomon then went to Hamath Zobah and captured it. [4]He also built up Tadmor in the desert and all the store cities he had built in Hamath. [5]He rebuilt Upper Beth Horon[r] and Lower Beth Horon as fortified cities, with walls and with gates and bars, [6]as well as Baalath and all his store cities, and all the cities for his chariots and for his horses[a]—whatever he desired to build in Jerusalem, in Lebanon and throughout all the territory he ruled.

[7]All the people left from the Hittites, Amorites, Perizzites, Hivites and Jebusites[s] (these peoples were not Israelites), [8]that is, their descendants remaining in the land, whom the Israelites had not destroyed—these Solomon conscripted[t] for his slave labor force, as it is to this day. [9]But Solomon did not make slaves of the Israelites for his work; they were his fighting men, commanders of his captains, and commanders of his chariots and charioteers. [10]They were also King Solomon's chief officials—two hundred and fifty officials supervising the men.

[11]Solomon brought Pharaoh's daughter[u] up from the City of David to the palace he had built for her, for he said, "My wife must not live in the palace of David king of Israel, because the places the ark of the LORD has entered are holy."

[12]On the altar[v] of the LORD that he had built in front of the portico, Solomon sacrificed burnt offerings to the LORD, [13]according to the daily requirement[w] for offerings commanded by Moses for Sabbaths,[x] New Moons and the three[y] annual feasts—the Feast of Unleavened Bread, the Feast of Weeks[z] and the Feast of Tabernacles. [14]In keeping with the ordinance of his father David, he appointed the divisions[a] of the priests for their duties, and the Levites[b] to lead the praise and to assist the priests according to each day's requirement. He also appointed the gatekeepers[c] by divisions for the various gates, because this was what David the man of God[d] had ordered.[e] [15]They did not deviate from the king's commands to the priests or to the Levites in any matter, including that of the treasuries.

[16]All Solomon's work was carried out, from the day the foundation of the temple of the LORD was laid until its completion. So the temple of the LORD was finished.

[17]Then Solomon went to Ezion Geber and Elath on the coast of Edom. [18]And Hiram sent him ships commanded by his own officers, men who knew the sea. These, with Solomon's men, sailed to Ophir and brought back four hundred and fifty talents[b] of gold,[f] which they delivered to King Solomon.

The Queen of Sheba Visits Solomon

9 When the queen of Sheba[g] heard of Solomon's fame, she came to Jerusalem to test him with hard questions. Arriving with a very great caravan—with camels carrying spices, large quantities of gold, and precious stones—she came to Solomon and talked with him about all she had on her mind. [2]Solomon answered all her questions; nothing was too hard for him to explain to her. [3]When the queen of Sheba saw the wisdom of Solomon,[h] as well as the palace he had built, [4]the food on his table, the seating of his officials, the attending servants in their robes, the cupbearers in their robes and the burnt offerings he made at[c] the temple of the LORD, she was overwhelmed.

[5]She said to the king, "The report I heard in my own country about your achievements and your wisdom is true. [6]But I did not believe what they said until I came[i] and saw with my own eyes. Indeed, not even half the greatness of your wisdom was told me; you have far exceeded the report I heard. [7]How happy your men must be! How happy your officials, who continually stand before you and hear your wisdom! [8]Praise be to the LORD your God, who has delighted in you and placed you on his throne[j] as king to rule for the LORD your God. Because of the love of your God for Israel and his desire to uphold them forever, he has made you king[k] over them, to maintain justice and righteousness."

8:5 [r]1Ch 7:24; 2Ch 14:7
8:7 [s]Ge 10:16
8:8 [t]1Ki 4:6; 9:21
8:11 [u]1Ki 3:1; 7:8
8:12 [v]1Ki 8:64; 2Ch 4:1; 15:8
8:13 [w]Ex 29:38; Nu 28:3 [x]Nu 28:9 [y]Ex 23:14; Dt 16:16 [z]Ex 23:16
8:14 [a]1Ch 24:1 [b]1Ch 25:1 [c]1Ch 9:17; 26:1 [d]Ne 12:24,36 [e]1Ch 23:6; Ne 12:45
8:18 [f]2Ch 9:9
9:1 [g]Ge 10:7; Eze 23:42; Mt 12:42; Lk 11:31
9:3 [h]1Ki 5:12
9:6 [i]2Ch 6:32
9:8 [j]1Ki 2:12; 1Ch 17:14; 28:5; 29:23; 2Ch 13:8 [k]2Ch 2:11

[a] *6* Or *charioteers* [b] *18* That is, about 17 tons (about 16 metric tons) [c] *4* Or *the ascent by which he went up to*

8:8 Solomon conscripted. See note on 1 Chronicles 22:2. **to this day.** See note on 1 Chronicles 4:41 and 43.
8:11 the places . . . are holy. Kings also reports that Solomon moved his Egyptian wife (1Ki 9:24). The Chronicler added detail concerning his motivation. Solomon moved his Gentile wife out of regard for the holiness of the ark and the temple-palace complex. Unlike the authors of the books of Kings (1Ki 11:1–13) and Nehemiah (Ne 13:26–27), the Chronicler did not comment negatively on Solomon's international marriages (see note on 2Ch 1:1—9:31).
8:12–15 Solomon sacrificed . . . appointed the divisions of the priests . . . In line with his interest in the temple, the Chronicler provided details regarding worship, as well as about Levites and priests, beyond the material included in his source in Kings (cf. 1Ki 9:25; see note on 1Ch 6:1–81).
■ **8:17—9:21** *More on Solomon's International Relations.* The text follows 1 Kings 9:26—10:13, with some variations. It turns to the theme of Solomon's international recognition (see notes on 1:1—9:31; 2:1–18). The passage focuses on Hiram (8:17–18) and the queen of Sheba (9:1–12).
9:1–12 See 1 Kings 10:1–22, which the Chronicler followed closely.
9:8 to uphold them forever. The queen of Sheba recognized Solomon's wise rule as God's provision for the well-being of Israel. This motif fits well the Chronicler's attempt to motivate his postexilic readers to reach for a renewal of Solomon's kingdom in their day.

[9]Then she gave the king 120 talents[a] of gold,[l] large quantities of spices, and precious stones. There had never been such spices as those the queen of Sheba gave to King Solomon.

[10](The men of Hiram and the men of Solomon brought gold from Ophir;[m] they also brought algumwood[b] and precious stones. [11]The king used the algumwood to make steps for the temple of the LORD and for the royal palace, and to make harps and lyres for the musicians. Nothing like them had ever been seen in Judah.)

[12]King Solomon gave the queen of Sheba all she desired and asked for; he gave her more than she had brought to him. Then she left and returned with her retinue to her own country.

Solomon's Splendor

[13]The weight of the gold that Solomon received yearly was 666 talents,[c] [14]not including the revenues brought in by merchants and traders. Also all the kings of Arabia[n] and the governors of the land brought gold and silver to Solomon.

[15]King Solomon made two hundred large shields of hammered gold; six hundred bekas[d] of hammered gold went into each shield. [16]He also made three hundred small shields[o] of hammered gold, with three hundred bekas[e] of gold in each shield. The king put them in the Palace of the Forest of Lebanon.[p]

[17]Then the king made a great throne inlaid with ivory[q] and overlaid with pure gold. [18]The throne had six steps, and a footstool of gold was attached to it. On both sides of the seat were armrests, with a lion standing beside each of them. [19]Twelve lions stood on the six steps, one at either end of each step. Nothing like it had ever been made for any other kingdom. [20]All King Solomon's goblets were gold, and all the household articles in the Palace of the Forest of Lebanon were pure gold. Nothing was made of silver, because silver was considered of little value in Solomon's day. [21]The king had a fleet of trading ships[f] manned by Hiram's[g] men. Once every three years it returned, carrying gold, silver and ivory, and apes and baboons.

[22]King Solomon was greater in riches and wisdom than all the other kings of the earth.[r] [23]All the kings[s] of the earth sought audience with Solomon to hear the wisdom God had put in his heart. [24]Year after year, everyone who came brought a gift[t]—articles of silver and gold, and robes, weapons and spices, and horses and mules.

[25]Solomon had four thousand stalls for horses and chariots,[u] and twelve thousand horses,[h] which he kept in the chariot cities and also with him in Jerusalem. [26]He ruled[v] over all the kings from the River[i][w] to the land of the Philistines, as far as the border of Egypt.[x] [27]The king made silver as common in Jerusalem as stones, and cedar as plentiful as sycamore-fig trees in the foothills. [28]Solomon's horses were imported from Egypt[j] and from all other countries.

Solomon's Death

[29]As for the other events of Solomon's reign, from beginning to end, are they not written in the records of Nathan[y] the prophet, in the prophecy of Ahijah[z] the Shilonite and in the visions of Iddo the seer concerning Jeroboam[a] son of Nebat? [30]Solomon reigned in Jerusalem over all Israel forty years. [31]Then he rested with his fathers and was buried in the city of David[b] his father. And Rehoboam his son succeeded him as king.

Israel Rebels Against Rehoboam

10 Rehoboam went to Shechem, for all the Israelites had gone there to make him king. [2]When Jeroboam[c] son of Nebat heard this (he was in Egypt, where he had

9:9 [l]2Ch 8:18
9:10 [m]2Ch 8:18
9:14 [n]2Ch 17:11; Isa 21:13; Jer 25:24; Eze 27:21; 30:5
9:16 [o]2Ch 12:9 [p]1Ki 7:2
9:17 [q]1Ki 22:39
9:22 [r]1Ki 3:13; 2Ch 1:12
9:23 [s]1Ki 4:34
9:24 [t]2Ch 32:23; Ps 45:12; 68:29; 72:10; Isa 18:7
9:25 [u]1Sa 8:11; 1Ki 4:26
9:26 [v]1Ki 4:21 [w]Ps 72:8-9 [x]Ge 15:18-21
9:29 [y]2Sa 7:2; 1Ch 29:29 [z]1Ki 11:29 [a]2Ch 10:2
9:31 [b]1Ki 2:10
10:2 [c]2Ch 9:29

[a] *9* That is, about 4 1/2 tons (about 4 metric tons) [b] *10* Probably a variant of *almugwood* [c] *13* That is, about 25 tons (about 23 metric tons) [d] *15* That is, about 7 1/2 pounds (about 3.5 kilograms) [e] *16* That is, about 3 3/4 pounds (about 1.7 kilograms) [f] *21* Hebrew *of ships that could go to Tarshish* [g] *21* Hebrew *Huram,* a variant of *Hiram* [h] *25* Or *charioteers* [i] *26* That is, the Euphrates [j] *28* Or possibly *Muzur,* a region in Cilicia

▪ **9:22–28** *More on Solomon's Great Wisdom and Wealth.* In balance with 1:1–17 (see note on 1:1—9:31), the Chronicler reported an assortment of Solomon's accomplishments from 1 Kings 10:23–29 in order to demonstrate Solomon's wealth and wisdom.
9:23 All the kings of the earth. Solomon's international recognition foreshadowed Israel's hope for prosperity and international recognition during the postexilic period.
9:27–28 silver . . . trees . . . horses. See note on 1:14–17.
▪ **9:29–31** *Closure of Solomon's Reign.* The desire to present Solomon as a model for the postexilic community led the author to omit mention of the trouble caused by the king's foreign wives (1Ki 11:1–40). He moved directly from the king's glory to the end of his reign, much as he had omitted discussion of David's sin with Bathsheba and the ensuing troubles in his kingdom (see notes on 1:1—9:31; 1Ch 9:35—29:30).
9:29 written in the records of. See "Introduction to 1 Chronicles: Author."
▪ **10:1—28:27** *The Divided Kingdom.* The Chronicler drew selectively from 1 Kings 12:1—2 Kings 17:41. His record of the divided period avoids much of the harsh condemnation of the north that is

fled[d] from King Solomon), he returned from Egypt. 3So they sent for Jeroboam, and he
and all Israel[e] went to Rehoboam and said to him: 4"Your father put a heavy yoke on
us,[f] but now lighten the harsh labor and the heavy yoke he put on us, and we will serve
you."
5Rehoboam answered, "Come back to me in three days." So the people went away.
6Then King Rehoboam consulted the elders[g] who had served his father Solomon during his lifetime. "How would you advise me to answer these people?" he asked.
7They replied, "If you will be kind to these people and please them and give them a
favorable answer,[h] they will always be your servants."
8But Rehoboam rejected[i] the advice the elders[j] gave him and consulted the young
men who had grown up with him and were serving him. 9He asked them, "What is your
advice? How should we answer these people who say to me, 'Lighten the yoke your father put on us'?"
10The young men who had grown up with him replied, "Tell the people who have said
to you, 'Your father put a heavy yoke on us, but make our yoke lighter'—tell them, 'My
little finger is thicker than my father's waist. 11My father laid on you a heavy yoke; I will
make it even heavier. My father scourged you with whips; I will scourge you with scorpions.'"
12Three days later Jeroboam and all the people returned to Rehoboam, as the king
had said, "Come back to me in three days." 13The king answered them harshly. Rejecting the advice of the elders, 14he followed the advice of the young men and said, "My father made your yoke heavy; I will make it even heavier. My father scourged you with
whips; I will scourge you with scorpions." 15So the king did not listen to the people, for
this turn of events was from God,[k] to fulfill the word the LORD had spoken to Jeroboam
son of Nebat through Ahijah the Shilonite.[l]
16When all Israel[m] saw that the king refused to listen to them, they answered the king:

"What share do we have in David,[n]
what part in Jesse's son?
To your tents, O Israel!
Look after your own house, O David!"

So all the Israelites went home. 17But as for the Israelites who were living in the towns
of Judah, Rehoboam still ruled over them.
18King Rehoboam sent out Adoniram,[a][o] who was in charge of forced labor, but the
Israelites stoned him to death. King Rehoboam, however, managed to get into his chariot and escape to Jerusalem. 19So Israel has been in rebellion against the house of David to this day.

[a] 18 Hebrew *Hadoram*, a variant of *Adoniram*

10:2 [d]1Ki 11:40
10:3 [e]1Ch 9:1
10:4 [f]2Ch 2:2
10:6 [g]Job 8:8-9; 12:12; 15:10; 32:7
10:7 [h]Pr 15:1
10:8 [i]2Sa 17:14 [j]Pr 13:20
10:15 [k]2Ch 11:4; 25:16-20 [l]1Ki 11:29
10:16 [m]1Ch 9:1 [n]ver 19; 2Sa 20:1
10:18 [o]1Ki 5:14

found in Kings and focuses on events in Judah, where the temple was located and the king resided. Throughout this section he reported on how the nation's level of fidelity to God determined conditions in the kingdom. This lengthy portion of his history divides into three main sections: the early reigns of judgment and increasing blessings (10:1—21:3), northern corruption in Judah (21:4—24:27) and halfhearted obedience in Judah (25:1—28:27). As the postexilic readers considered these events, they saw more clearly the choices that would result in blessing and cursing in their own day. (See "Introduction to 1 Chronicles: Purpose and Distinctives.")

■ **10:1—21:3** *Judgments and Increasing Blessings in Judah.* This first phase of the divided kingdom included the reigns of Rehoboam (10:1—12:16), Abijah (13:1—14:1a), Asa (14:1b—16:14) and Jehoshaphat (17:1—21:3). The unifying themes in these reigns were their focus on separation from the northern kingdom, battle narratives and reactions to the word of God.

■ **10:1—12:16** *Rehoboam's Reign.* The account of Rehoboam's reign incorporates much from Kings (cf. 10:1—11:4 with 1Ki 12:1–24; 12:9–16 with 1Ki 14:21,25–31), and expands and arranges this material with theological emphases. Rehoboam's reign divides into two parallel sections (10:1—11:23 and 12:1–12); each part consists of a problematic situation, a prophetic encounter and a divine blessing. To these accounts the Chronicler added a regnal summary and a notice of death (12:13–16). By this arrangement, he showed his postexilic readers an example of God's curse against pride and infidelity and pointed out the benefits of living in humility and obedience to the prophetic word (see note on 20:20).

■ **10:1—11:23** *Rehoboam's Early Sin, Prophetic Encounter and Blessing.* These chapters deal with the earlier years of the king's reign by reporting how his sins led to Israel's rebellion (10:1–19) and his compliance with the prophetic word to blessings (11:1–23).

■ **10:1–19** *Rehoboam's Sin and Israel's Rebellion.* The first section on Rehoboam's reign focuses on his first three years as king (11:17), a period during which there was conflict between Judah and Israel. It divides into three parts: Rehoboam's foolish mistreatment of the north (vv. 1–17), his failure to subjugate the north (v. 18) and an authorial comment (v. 19).

10:1 Rehoboam. Reigned from 930–913 B.C. **all the Israelites.** For the period of the divided monarchy, the Chronicler used this and similar expressions variously to denote: the southern kingdom alone (11:3; 12:1; 28:23), the northern kingdom alone (v. 16; 11:13; 13:4,15) or the north and south together (18:16; 24:5; see notes on 29:24; 1Ch 11:1).

10:3 all Israel. First Kings 12:3 reads "the whole assembly of Israel." The Chronicler replaced this with his characteristic expression (see note on v. 1).

10:15 from God, to fulfill the word the LORD had spoken. The text follows Kings here and explains that Rehoboam's reaction must be seen in the light of God's sovereign purposes. Ahijah's prophecy to Jeroboam (1Ki 11:29–39) was fulfilled by this turn of events. Divine sovereignty extends beyond the sinful actions of human beings (see note on 1Ch 21:1).

10:16 all Israel. See note on 10:1.

10:19 to this day. See note on 1 Chronicles 4:41 and 43.

11:1 [p]1Ki 12:21
11:2 [q]2Ch 12:5-7,15
11:4 [r]2Ch 28:8-11
11:14 [s]Nu 35:2-5 [t]2Ch 13:9
11:15 [u]1Ki 13:33 [v]1Ki 12:31 [w]Lev 17:7 [x]1Ki 12:28; 2Ch 13:8
11:16 [y]2Ch 15:9
11:17 [z]2Ch 12:1
11:20 [a]1Ki 15:2 [b]2Ch 13:2
11:21 [c]Dt 17:17
11:22 [d]Dt 21:15-17
12:1 [e]ver 13 [f]2Ch 11:17

11 When Rehoboam arrived in Jerusalem,[p] he mustered the house of Judah and Benjamin—a hundred and eighty thousand fighting men—to make war against Israel and to regain the kingdom for Rehoboam.

2 But this word of the LORD came to Shemaiah[q] the man of God: 3 "Say to Rehoboam son of Solomon king of Judah and to all the Israelites in Judah and Benjamin, 4 'This is what the LORD says: Do not go up to fight against your brothers.[r] Go home, every one of you, for this is my doing.' " So they obeyed the words of the LORD and turned back from marching against Jeroboam.

Rehoboam Fortifies Judah

5 Rehoboam lived in Jerusalem and built up towns for defense in Judah: 6 Bethlehem, Etam, Tekoa, 7 Beth Zur, Soco, Adullam, 8 Gath, Mareshah, Ziph, 9 Adoraim, Lachish, Azekah, 10 Zorah, Aijalon and Hebron. These were fortified cities in Judah and Benjamin. 11 He strengthened their defenses and put commanders in them, with supplies of food, olive oil and wine. 12 He put shields and spears in all the cities, and made them very strong. So Judah and Benjamin were his.

13 The priests and Levites from all their districts throughout Israel sided with him. 14 The Levites[s] even abandoned their pasturelands and property,[t] and came to Judah and Jerusalem because Jeroboam and his sons had rejected them as priests of the LORD. 15 And he appointed[u] his own priests[v] for the high places and for the goat[w] and calf[x] idols he had made. 16 Those from every tribe of Israel[y] who set their hearts on seeking the LORD, the God of Israel, followed the Levites to Jerusalem to offer sacrifices to the LORD, the God of their fathers. 17 They strengthened[z] the kingdom of Judah and supported Rehoboam son of Solomon three years, walking in the ways of David and Solomon during this time.

Rehoboam's Family

18 Rehoboam married Mahalath, who was the daughter of David's son Jerimoth and of Abihail, the daughter of Jesse's son Eliab. 19 She bore him sons: Jeush, Shemariah and Zaham. 20 Then he married Maacah[a] daughter of Absalom, who bore him Abijah,[b] Attai, Ziza and Shelomith. 21 Rehoboam loved Maacah daughter of Absalom more than any of his other wives and concubines. In all, he had eighteen wives[c] and sixty concubines, twenty-eight sons and sixty daughters.

22 Rehoboam appointed Abijah[d] son of Maacah to be the chief prince among his brothers, in order to make him king. 23 He acted wisely, dispersing some of his sons throughout the districts of Judah and Benjamin, and to all the fortified cities. He gave them abundant provisions and took many wives for them.

Shishak Attacks Jerusalem

12 After Rehoboam's position as king was established[e] and he had become strong,[f] he and all Israel[a] with him abandoned the law of the LORD. 2 Because they had

[a] *1* That is, Judah, as frequently in 2 Chronicles

■ **11:1–23** *Rehoboam's Compliance and Blessing.* The Chronicler closely followed Kings in most of this material (cf. 2Ch 10:18—11:4 with 1Ki 12:18–24). Rehoboam prepared to attack Israel but relented at the prophetic warning (vv. 1–4). The author delineated a series of blessings Rehoboam received for his obedience after these events (vv. 5–23).

■ **11:1–4** *Rehoboam's Compliance With the Prophetic Word.* Although Rehoboam was intent on making war with the rebellious northern tribes in order to regain his kingdom, the prophet Shemaiah forbade him to do so, and he obeyed.

11:2 Shemaiah. This prophet appeared twice in the account of Rehoboam's reign (cf. 12:5–8). To Rehoboam's credit and benefit, he gave heed to Shemaiah's word both times.

11:3 all the Israelites. See note on 10:1.

11:4 this is my doing. See note on 10:15.

■ **11:5–23** *Rehoboam's Blessings for Compliance.* To demonstrate the results of Rehoboam's response to the prophetic warning (see note on 20:20), this section mentions fortifications and military strength in Judah and Benjamin (vv. 5–12), the defection of Levites from the north (vv. 13–17) and the increase of Rehoboam's family (vv. 18–23).

11:5–12 built up towns. See note on 1 Chronicles 11:4–9.

11:13 all . . . Israel. See note on 10:1.

11:14 Jeroboam . . . had rejected them. The Chronicler omitted the account of Jeroboam establishing syncretistic worship centers at Dan and Bethel (1Ki 12:25—14:20), but that event lies behind his remark. Jeroboam rejected the priests and Levites who refused to abandon Jerusalem as the proper site for worship. As a result, they defected to Rehoboam. The theme of the faithful from the north coming to Judah appears several times in the accounts of the divided and reunited periods (13:8–11; 15:9; 30:10–12) and provides a model for the postexilic incorporation of the faithful of the northern tribes into the restored kingdom (see note on 1Ch 9:3; see "Introduction: Purposes and Distinctives: *The Divided Kingdom*").

11:16 seeking. See note on 7:14.

11:17 three years, walking in the ways of David and Solomon. Rehoboam received God's blessing because he imitated the fidelity of the ideal monarchs, David and Solomon, for the first three years of his reign.

11:18–23 She bore him sons. The Chronicler frequently mentioned increases in family size to demonstrate God's blessing (see note on 1Ch 13:13).

11:20 Maacah. See 13:2.

■ **12:1–12** *Rehoboam's Later Sin, Prophetic Encounter and Blessing.* For the second major portion of Rehoboam's reign (see note on 10:1—12:16), the Chronicler expanded the account of 1 Kings 14:25–28. He reported Rehoboam's disobedience during his fourth year and the divine retribution of Shishak's invasion in the fifth year (12:2).

12:1–2 abandoned the law . . . unfaithful to the LORD. See 1 Kings 14:22–24 for more details on this apostasy. See note on 1 Chronicles 16:40.

been unfaithful[g] to the LORD, Shishak[h] king of Egypt attacked Jerusalem in the fifth year
of King Rehoboam. 3With twelve hundred chariots and sixty thousand horsemen and the
innumerable troops of Libyans, Sukkites and Cushites[a] [i] that came with him from Egypt,
4he captured the fortified cities[j] of Judah and came as far as Jerusalem.
5Then the prophet Shemaiah[k] came to Rehoboam and to the leaders of Judah who
had assembled in Jerusalem for fear of Shishak, and he said to them, "This is what the
LORD says, 'You have abandoned me; therefore, I now abandon[l] you to Shishak.' "
6The leaders of Israel and the king humbled themselves and said, "The LORD is just."[m]
7When the LORD saw that they humbled themselves, this word of the LORD came to
Shemaiah: "Since they have humbled themselves, I will not destroy them but will soon
give them deliverance.[n] My wrath will not be poured out on Jerusalem through Shishak.
8They will, however, become subject[o] to him, so that they may learn the difference between serving me and serving the kings of other lands."
9When Shishak king of Egypt attacked Jerusalem, he carried off the treasures of the
temple of the LORD and the treasures of the royal palace. He took everything, including
the gold shields[p] Solomon had made. 10So King Rehoboam made bronze shields to replace them and assigned these to the commanders of the guard on duty at the entrance
to the royal palace. 11Whenever the king went to the LORD's temple, the guards went with
him, bearing the shields, and afterward they returned them to the guardroom.
12Because Rehoboam humbled himself, the LORD's anger turned from him, and he
was not totally destroyed. Indeed, there was some good[q] in Judah.
13King Rehoboam established himself firmly in Jerusalem and continued as king. He
was forty-one years old when he became king, and he reigned seventeen years in Jerusalem, the city the LORD had chosen out of all the tribes of Israel in which to put his
Name.[r] His mother's name was Naamah; she was an Ammonite. 14He did evil because
he had not set his heart on seeking the LORD.
15As for the events of Rehoboam's reign, from beginning to end, are they not written
in the records of Shemaiah[s] the prophet and of Iddo the seer that deal with genealogies?
There was continual warfare between Rehoboam and Jeroboam. 16Rehoboam rested with
his fathers and was buried in the City of David. And Abijah[t] his son succeeded him as king.

Abijah King of Judah

13 In the eighteenth year of the reign of Jeroboam, Abijah became king of Judah,
2and he reigned in Jerusalem three years. His mother's name was Maacah,[b] a
daughter[c] of Uriel of Gibeah.
There was war between Abijah[u] and Jeroboam.[v] 3Abijah went into battle with a force
of four hundred thousand able fighting men, and Jeroboam drew up a battle line against
him with eight hundred thousand able troops.

12:2 [g]1Ki 14:22-24 [h]1Ki 11:40
12:3 [i]2Ch 16:8; Na 3:9
12:4 [j]2Ch 11:10
12:5 [k]2Ch 11:2 [l]Dt 28:15; 2Ch 15:2
12:6 [m]Ex 9:27; Da 9:14
12:7 [n]1Ki 21:29; Ps 78:38
12:8 [o]Dt 28:48
12:9 [p]2Ch 9:16
12:12 [q]1Ki 14:13; 2Ch 19:3
12:13 [r]Dt 12:5; 2Ch 6:6
12:15 [s]2Ch 9:29; 11:2
12:16 [t]2Ch 11:20
13:2 [u]2Ch 11:20 [v]1Ki 15:6

[a] 3 That is, people from the upper Nile region [b] 2 Most Septuagint manuscripts and Syriac (see also 2 Chron. 11:20 and 1 Kings 15:2); Hebrew *Micaiah* [c] 2 Or *granddaughter*

12:1 all Israel. See note on 10:1.
12:2 Shishak. Founder of the twenty-second dynasty of Egypt (c. 945–924 B.C.). His military campaign extended to the plains of Jezreel and Megiddo.
12:3–9 the prophet Shemaiah. These verses parallel with Rehoboam's previous encounter with Shemaiah (cf. 11:2–4; see note on 10:1—11:23).
12:3 twelve hundred . . . sixty thousand . . . innumerable. See note on 1 Chronicles 19:6–7.
12:6–7,12 humbled themselves. The reader is reminded that this event illustrates God's response to Solomon's prayer (see note on 7:14).
12:7–8 Since they have humbled themselves. Although Shemaiah modified his first warning, God's sovereign plan was not overturned. Prophetic warnings were designed to stir repentance. When the proper response occurred the threat of judgment was often removed, postponed or mollified (Jer 18:1–12; Joel 2:12–14; Jnh 3:1–10; see theological article "Providence" at Jer 18).
12:12 some good in Judah. While Rehoboam continued to suffer personally for his sins, God graciously established his kingdom and blessed the nation.
■ **12:13–16** *Closure of Rehoboam's Reign.* The Chronicler expanded the summary of Rehoboam's reign in 1 Kings 14:29–31 to add his own emphases.
12:13 Name. See note on 1 Chronicles 13:6.
12:14 He did evil. Probably a reference to the sins of Rehoboam's fourth year (see note on vv. 1–2). **seeking the LORD.** See note on 7:14.
12:15 written in the records. See "Introduction to 1 Chronicles: Author."
■ **13:1—14:1a** *Abijah's Reign.* The Chronicler closely followed the accounts in Kings of Abijah's early reign (cf. 13:1–2a with 1Ki 15:1–2), as well as of the close of his reign (cf. 2Ch 13:22—14:1a with 1Ki 15:7–8). The middle portion of his record (13:2b–21) differs considerably from that in Kings (1Ki 15:3–5). The Chronicler emphasized the positive side of Abijah's reign, while the writer of Kings focused on the negative (1Ki 15:3). The record divides into three parts: the opening of Abijah's reign (13:1–2a), his victory over Jeroboam (13:2b–21) and the closure of his reign (13:22—14:1a). The Chronicler focused especially on Abijah's speech against the northern kingdom (13:4–12) and his prayerful reliance on God in battle (13:14).
■ **13:1–2a** *Opening of Abijah's Reign.* He reigned from 913–910 B.C., while Jeroboam I ruled the northern kingdom (930–909 B.C.).
13:2a Maacah. See NIV text note. Also see 11:20.
■ **13:2b–21** *Abijah's Victory Over Jeroboam.* First Kings 15:7 mentions war between Abijah and Jeroboam, but the Chronicler added details. His report includes the drawing of battle lines (vv. 2b–3), Abijah's speech (vv. 4–12), the battle (vv. 13–18) and the outcome for each king (vv. 19–21).
13:3 four hundred thousand . . . eight hundred thousand. The Chronicler indicated that Judah was greatly outnumbered and highlighted the power of God at work on behalf of faithful Judah (see notes on 1Ch 12:23–37 and 19:6–7).

4 Abijah stood on Mount Zemaraim,[w] in the hill country of Ephraim, and said, "Jeroboam and all Israel,[x] listen to me! 5 Don't you know that the LORD, the God of Israel, has
given the kingship of Israel to David and his descendants forever[y] by a covenant of salt?[z]
6 Yet Jeroboam son of Nebat, an official of Solomon son of David, rebelled[a] against his
master. 7 Some worthless scoundrels[b] gathered around him and opposed Rehoboam son
of Solomon when he was young and indecisive and not strong enough to resist them.

8 "And now you plan to resist the kingdom of the LORD, which is in the hands of David's descendants. You are indeed a vast army and have with you the golden calves[c] that
Jeroboam made to be your gods. 9 But didn't you drive out the priests of the LORD,[d] the
sons of Aaron, and the Levites, and make priests of your own as the peoples of other
lands do? Whoever comes to consecrate himself with a young bull[e] and seven rams may
become a priest of what are not gods.[f]

10 "As for us, the LORD is our God, and we have not forsaken him. The priests who serve
the LORD are sons of Aaron, and the Levites assist them. 11 Every morning and evening[g]
they present burnt offerings and fragrant incense to the LORD. They set out the bread on
the ceremonially clean table[h] and light the lamps on the gold lampstand every evening.
We are observing the requirements of the LORD our God. But you have forsaken him.
12 God is with us; he is our leader. His priests with their trumpets will sound the battle
cry against you.[i] Men of Israel, do not fight against the LORD,[j] the God of your fathers,
for you will not succeed."

13 Now Jeroboam had sent troops around to the rear, so that while he was in front of
Judah the ambush[k] was behind them. 14 Judah turned and saw that they were being attacked at both front and rear. Then they cried out[l] to the LORD. The priests blew their
trumpets 15 and the men of Judah raised the battle cry. At the sound of their battle cry,
God routed Jeroboam and all Israel[m] before Abijah and Judah. 16 The Israelites fled before Judah, and God delivered[n] them into their hands. 17 Abijah and his men inflicted
heavy losses on them, so that there were five hundred thousand casualties among Israel's able men. 18 The men of Israel were subdued on that occasion, and the men of Judah
were victorious because they relied[o] on the LORD, the God of their fathers.

19 Abijah pursued Jeroboam and took from him the towns of Bethel, Jeshanah and
Ephron, with their surrounding villages. 20 Jeroboam did not regain power during the
time of Abijah. And the LORD struck him down and he died.

21 But Abijah grew in strength. He married fourteen wives and had twenty-two sons
and sixteen daughters.

22 The other events of Abijah's reign, what he did and what he said, are written in the
annotations of the prophet Iddo.

14 And Abijah rested with his fathers and was buried in the City of David. Asa his
son succeeded him as king, and in his days the country was at peace for ten
years.

13:4 [w]Jos 18:22 [x]1Ch 11:1
13:5 [y]2Sa 7:13 [z]Lev 2:13; Nu 18:19
13:6 [a]1Ki 11:26
13:7 [b]Jdg 9:4
13:8 [c]1Ki 12:28; 2Ch 11:15
13:9 [d]2Ch 11:14-15 [e]Ex 29:35-36 [f]Jer 2:11
13:11 [g]Ex 29:39; 2Ch 2:4 [h]Lev 24:5-9
13:12 [i]Nu 10:8-9 [j]Ac 5:39
13:13 [k]Jos 8:9
13:14 [l]2Ch 14:11
13:15 [m]2Ch 14:12
13:16 [n]2Ch 16:8
13:18 [o]1Ch 5:20; 2Ch 14:11; Ps 22:5

13:4–12 the kingship of Israel to David . . . the priests . . . are sons of Aaron. The addition of Abijah's speech against Israel reflects two main concerns: God's approval of David's dynasty (vv. 5–8a) and the exclusive legitimacy of the Jerusalem temple (vv. 8b–12). Abijah's words called on the postexilic readers to avoid syncretism (combining worship of the Lord with worship of other gods) and to remain faithful to the institutions of the Davidic throne and the Jerusalem temple (see note on 1Ch 6:1–53).
13:4 Mount Zemaraim. Its precise location is unknown, but it was in the territory of Benjamin (Jos 18:22). **all Israel.** See note on 10:1.
13:6 Jeroboam . . . rebelled. Abijah appealed to the northern army by blaming the rebellion against Rehoboam directly on Jeroboam.
13:7 young and indecisive and not strong enough. Abijah explained that Rehoboam's offense against the northern tribes (10:1–17) was the result of his youth and inexperience (cf. 1Ch 22:5; 29:1).
13:8 kingdom of the LORD. Despite Rehoboam's offense, resisting David's dynasty was tantamount to resisting God himself.
13:9 drive out the priests . . . and the Levites. The Chronicler had already mentioned the defection of these Levites as an indication of God's blessing toward Rehoboam (see note on 11:14).
13:10 we have not forsaken. In contrast with the northern kingdom, Judah had remained fundamentally loyal to the temple, priests and Levites, but see 12:1–2. This assessment of Judah's condition was reversed later, in Hezekiah's day (see notes on 29:4–11; 30:6–9).
13:11–12 We are observing the requirements. Abijah's speech presented the Chronicler's outlook on the proper observance of worship, a vital message for his postexilic readers (see note on 1Ch 6:1–53).
13:12 God is with us. See note on Isaiah 7:14. See also Numbers 14:9, Psalm 46:7 and Matthew 1:23. The presence of God with the army of Judah secured victory. Abijah asserted that God would side with Judah against the northern kingdom of God's people.
13:14 cried out to the LORD. This event recalls Solomon's dedicatory prayer (see note on 6:34–35). The Chronicler presented prayer as the decisive factor in the battle (see note on 1Ch 4:9–10).
13:15 all Israel. See note on 10:1.
13:18 were subdued. See note on 1 Chronicles 20:4. **because they relied on the LORD.** The Chronicler explained Abijah's victory in terms of Judah's dependance on God. Reliance on the power of the Lord instead of on human strength is a dominant theme in the author's message to his postexilic readers (see note on 16:2).
13:20–21 Jeroboam did not again regain power. The Chronicler contrasted the outcomes for Jeroboam and Abijah, respectively, to indicate God's disapproval and approval. Jeroboam never recovered from his defeat. Abijah, however, grew stronger and had many children (see note on 1Ch 13:13).
▪ **13:22—14:1a** *Closure of Abijah's Reign.* Abijah died and was succeeded by his son Asa.
13:22 annotations of the prophet Iddo. See "Introduction to 1 Chronicles: Author."
▪ **14:1b—16:14** *Asa's Reign.* The account of Asa's reign is considerably more extensive than that found in 1 Kings 15:9–24. It closely follows the positive account of Kings at several points (cf. 1Ki

Asa King of Judah

2Asa did what was good and right in the eyes of the LORD his God. 3He removed the
foreign altars and the high places, smashed the sacred stones and cut down the Asherah poles.[a][p] 4He commanded Judah to seek the LORD, the God of their fathers, and to
obey his laws and commands. 5He removed the high places and incense altars[q] in every
town in Judah, and the kingdom was at peace under him. 6He built up the fortified cities of Judah, since the land was at peace. No one was at war with him during those years,
for the LORD gave him rest.[r]
7"Let us build up these towns," he said to Judah, "and put walls around them, with
towers, gates and bars. The land is still ours, because we have sought the LORD our God;
we sought him and he has given us rest on every side." So they built and prospered.
8Asa had an army of three hundred thousand men from Judah, equipped with large
shields and with spears, and two hundred and eighty thousand from Benjamin, armed
with small shields and with bows. All these were brave fighting men.
9Zerah the Cushite[s] marched out against them with a vast army[b] and three hundred
chariots, and came as far as Mareshah.[t] 10Asa went out to meet him, and they took up
battle positions in the Valley of Zephathah near Mareshah.
11Then Asa called[u] to the LORD his God and said, "LORD, there is no one like you to
help the powerless against the mighty. Help us, O LORD our God, for we rely[v] on you, and
in your name[w] we have come against this vast army. O LORD, you are our God; do not let
man prevail[x] against you."
12The LORD struck down[y] the Cushites before Asa and Judah. The Cushites fled, 13and
Asa and his army pursued them as far as Gerar.[z] Such a great number of Cushites fell that
they could not recover; they were crushed before the LORD and his forces. The men of Judah carried off a large amount of plunder. 14They destroyed all the villages around Gerar,
for the terror[a] of the LORD had fallen upon them. They plundered all these villages, since
there was much booty there. 15They also attacked the camps of the herdsmen and carried
off droves of sheep and goats and camels. Then they returned to Jerusalem.

Asa's Reform

15 The Spirit of God came upon[b] Azariah son of Oded. 2He went out to meet Asa
and said to him, "Listen to me, Asa and all Judah and Benjamin. The LORD is with

14:3 [p]Ex 34:13; Dt 7:5; 1Ki 15:12-14
14:5 [q]2Ch 34:4,7
14:6 [r]1Ch 22:9; 2Ch 15:15
14:9 [s]2Ch 12:3; 16:8 [t]2Ch 11:8
14:11 [u]2Ch 13:14 [v]2Ch 13:18 [w]1Sa 17:45 [x]1Sa 14:6; Ps 9:19
14:12 [y]2Ch 13:15
14:13 [z]Ge 10:19
14:14 [a]Ge 35:5; 2Ch 17:10
15:1 [b]Nu 11:25,26; 24:2; 2Ch 20:14; 24:20

[a] *3* That is, symbols of the goddess Asherah; here and elsewhere in 2 Chronicles [b] *9* Hebrew *with an army of a thousand thousands* or *with an army of thousands upon thousands*

15:11–12 with 2Ch 14:2–3; 1Ki 15:13–16 with 2Ch 15:16–19; 1Ki 15:17–22 with 2Ch 16:1–6; 1Ki 15:23–24 with 2Ch 16:11—17:1). It also expands and shapes the narrative to present Asa's reign in four parts: the opening (14:1b), the years of fidelity and blessing (14:2—15:19), the later years of infidelity and curse (16:1–12) and the closure (16:13–14). The text focuses on Asa's response to prophetic instruction (15:8–19; 16:10–14), as the account of Rehoboam's reign had previously done (see note on 20:20), and it contrasts the results of relying on God with those of depending on human power in battle (see note on 16:2).

■ **14:1b** *Opening of Asa's Reign.* Asa's reign began positively.

14:1b peace. See note on 1 Chronicles 22:9. **for ten years.** The Chronicler made several explicit chronological notations on Asa's reign: ten years of peace (v. 1), covenant renewal in the fifteenth year (15:10), enjoyment of peace until the thirty-fifth year (15:19), invasion in the thirty-sixth year (16:1), illness in the thirty-ninth year (16:12) and death in the forty-first year of his reign (16:13).

■ **14:2—15:19** *Asa Under Divine Blessing.* These chapters concern the period during which Asa was faithful to God, received blessings (14:2–7) and was rewarded with victory for responding appropriately to God's prophet (14:8—15:19).

■ **14:2–7** *Asa's Early Years of Reform and Blessings.* The Chronicler arranged and expanded the material from 1 Kings 15:11–12 to present a glorious portrait of Asa's early years.

14:2 Asa. Reigned from 911/10–870/69 B.C.

14:3 removed . . . the high places. Asa is reported to have removed pagan high places also in verse 5, but 15:17 (1Ki 15:14) indicates that later in his life he failed to follow through on these initial efforts. A similar explanation holds for the descriptions of Jehoshaphat's removal of high places (cf. 17:6; 20:33). **Asherah poles.** See NIV text note.

14:4 seek the LORD. See note on 7:14. **obey his laws and commands.** See note on 1 Chronicles 16:40.

14:6–7 He built up . . . Let us build up. Divine blessing is also illustrated by Asa's successful building projects (see note on 1Ch 11:4–9).

14:6 No one was at war. Apparently the Chronicler meant that there were no major wars during this period. Later he did acknowledge that Asa had captured some towns in Ephraim during this time (15:8). **peace . . . rest.** The Chronicler presented peace during Asa's reign as a blessing for devotion and obedience to God (see note on 14:1b—16:14). The theme of peace was vital to the postexilic readers who lived under the constant threat of conflict (see note on 1Ch 22:9).

14:7 because we have sought the LORD. Asa explicitly attributed his success to his having sought the Lord (see note on 7:14).

■ **14:8—15:19** *Asa's Victory, Prophetic Approval and Obedience.* During battle with Zerah, Asa proved faithful and was granted great victory and blessing.

■ **14:8–15** *Asa's Victory in Conflict.* When Zerah attacked, Asa sought the Lord and gained victory. This battle directly contrasts with Asa's later battle against Baasha (16:1–6; see note on 14:1b—16:14) and presents an example of God answering Solomon's dedicatory prayer (see note on 6:34–35).

14:8 men from Judah . . . from Benjamin. Asa's army is said to have totaled 580,000, while the attacking army is reported as having been nearly twice as large. See NIV text note on verse 9. For possible explanations of these inordinately large numbers, see note on 1 Chronicles 12:23–37.

14:9 Zerah the Cushite. Probably a general of Pharaoh Osorkon I, second ruler of the twenty-second dynasty of Egypt. **vast army and three hundred chariots.** See note on 1 Chronicles 19:6–7.

14:11 powerless. Asa expressed his utter inadequacy for battle against Zerah (see note on 20:12). **we rely on you.** Reliance on the Lord's power was the key to Asa's victory (see note on 16:2). **name.** See note on 1 Chronicles 13:6. See *WLC* 196.

■ **15:1–19** *Asa's Prophetic Approval and Obedience.* This chapter divides into Azariah's prophetic encouragement (vv. 5:1–7) and Asa's response of further reforms (vv. 8–19). These passages stand in sharp contrast to Hanani's prophetic rebuke (16:7–9) and Asa's rebellious response (16:10). See note on 14:1b—16:14.

15:1–7 Azariah expressed the principle of retribution so characteristic of the Chronicler's portrait of the divided kingdom. Fidelity

you[c] when you are with him.[d] If you seek[e] him, he will be found by you, but if you forsake him, he will forsake you.[f] 3For a long time Israel was without the true God, without a priest to teach[g] and without the law.[h] 4But in their distress they turned to the LORD,
the God of Israel, and sought him,[i] and he was found by them. 5In those days it was not
safe to travel about,[j] for all the inhabitants of the lands were in great turmoil. 6One nation was being crushed by another and one city by another,[k] because God was troubling
them with every kind of distress. 7But as for you, be strong[l] and do not give up, for your
work will be rewarded."[m]

8When Asa heard these words and the prophecy of Azariah son of[a] Oded the prophet, he took courage. He removed the detestable idols from the whole land of Judah and
Benjamin and from the towns he had captured[n] in the hills of Ephraim. He repaired the
altar[o] of the LORD that was in front of the portico of the LORD's temple.

9Then he assembled all Judah and Benjamin and the people from Ephraim, Manasseh and Simeon who had settled among them, for large numbers[p] had come over to him
from Israel when they saw that the LORD his God was with him.

10They assembled at Jerusalem in the third month of the fifteenth year of Asa's reign.
11At that time they sacrificed to the LORD seven hundred head of cattle and seven thousand sheep and goats from the plunder[q] they had brought back. 12They entered into a
covenant[r] to seek the LORD,[s] the God of their fathers, with all their heart and soul. 13All
who would not seek the LORD, the God of Israel, were to be put to death,[t] whether small
or great, man or woman. 14They took an oath to the LORD with loud acclamation, with
shouting and with trumpets and horns. 15All Judah rejoiced about the oath because they
had sworn it wholeheartedly. They sought God[u] eagerly, and he was found by them. So
the LORD gave them rest[v] on every side.

16King Asa also deposed his grandmother Maacah from her position as queen mother, because she had made a repulsive Asherah pole.[w] Asa cut the pole down, broke it up
and burned it in the Kidron Valley. 17Although he did not remove the high places from
Israel, Asa's heart was fully committed ⌊to the LORD⌋ all his life. 18He brought into the temple of God the silver and gold and the articles that he and his father had dedicated.

19There was no more war until the thirty-fifth year of Asa's reign.

Asa's Last Years

16 In the thirty-sixth year of Asa's reign Baasha[x] king of Israel went up against Judah and fortified Ramah to prevent anyone from leaving or entering the territory of Asa king of Judah.

2Asa then took the silver and gold out of the treasuries of the LORD's temple and of
his own palace and sent it to Ben-Hadad king of Aram, who was ruling in Damascus.

15:2 [c]ver 4,15; 2Ch 20:17 [d]Jas 4:8 [e]Jer 29:13 [f]1Ch 28:9; 2Ch 24:20
15:3 [g]Lev 10:11 [h]2Ch 17:9; La 2:9
15:4 [i]Dt 4:29
15:5 [j]Jdg 5:6
15:6 [k]Mt 24:7
15:7 [l]Jos 1:7,9 [m]Ps 58:11
15:8 [n]2Ch 13:19 [o]2Ch 8:12
15:9 [p]2Ch 11:16-17
15:11 [q]2Ch 14:13
15:12 [r]2Ki 11:17; 2Ch 23:16; 34:31 [s]1Ch 16:11
15:13 [t]Ex 22:20; Dt 13:9-16
15:15 [u]Dt 4:29 [v]1Ch 22:9; 2Ch 14:7
15:16 [w]Ex 34:13; 2Ch 14:2-5
16:1 [x]Jer 41:9

[a] *8* Vulgate and Syriac (see also Septuagint and verse 1); Hebrew does not have *Azariah son of.*

---

to God will result in blessing, disloyalty in chastisement (see "Introduction to 1 Chronicles: Purposes and Distinctives").

15:2 If you seek him. See notes on 7:14 and on 1 Chronicles 28:9.

15:4,15 sought. See note on 7:14.

15:4 turned to the LORD. See note on 7:14.

15:8–19 removed the detestable idols. Asa responded with further reforms (v. 8) and an assembly of covenant renewal (vv. 9–15); he even deposed his own grandmother because of her religious apostasy (vv. 16–19).

15:9 had come over to him. The Chronicler mentioned the defection and cooperation of many from Israel (see note on 11:14), in line with his interest in the centrality of Jerusalem and the reunification of Israel during the postexilic period.

15:12–13 See *WCF* 20.4; 23.3.

15:12 entered into a covenant. Covenant renewal indicated the continuity of God's relationship with his people in all generations. The Chronicler presented Asa (v. 12), Jehoiada (23:16), Hezekiah (29:10) and Josiah (34:30–32) as leading the nation in covenant renewals. He emphasized these renewals to call his own readers to covenant renewal (cf. Ezr 10:1–17) as the way to receiving God's blessing. **seek the LORD.** See notes on 7:14 and on 1 Chronicles 16:40.

15:13 put to death. Capital punishment was required in the Mosaic Law for all who sought other gods (Dt 13:6–16).

15:15 rest on every side. See note on 1 Chronicles 22:9.

15:16 deposed his grandmother. See *WCF* 20.4.

15:17 all his life. See note on 14:3.

15:19—16:1 thirty-fifth year . . . thirty-sixth year. Kings reports that Elah succeeded Baasha in Asa's twenty-sixth year (1Ki 15:33; 16:8), Zimri in Asa's twenty-seventh year (1Ki 16:10,15) and Omri in Asa's thirty-first year (1Ki 16:23). Consequently, this battle could not have taken place during Asa's thirty-sixth year (16:1). Two explanations seem feasible. First, the Chronicler may have been calculating from the division of the kingdom (930 B.C.), actually making these dates the fifteenth and sixteenth years of Asa's reign. This would be unusual but not impossible. Second, thirty-fifth (15:19) and thirty-sixth (16:1) may be corruptions of original twenty-fifth and twenty-sixth; this seems the more likely explanation.

15:19 no more war. See note on 14:6.

■ **16:1–12** *Asa Under Divine Judgment.* In contrast with the preceding chapters, here Asa failed in conflict, was rebuked by a prophet and refused to obey (vv. 1–10). Therefore, his final years were under God's judgment (vv. 11–12).

■ **16:1–10** *Asa's Failure, Prophetic Disapproval and Disobedience.* Asa's battle with Baasha of Israel began his downfall. Asa sought the assistance of Ben-Hadad of Syria. These events sharply contrast with Asa's battle against Zerah, during which Asa had relied on the Lord (see note on 14:1b—16:14).

16:2 treasuries of the LORD's temple . . . to Ben-Hadad. Asa's actions were wrong on two counts. He took from the temple treasuries, showing disregard for the temple and its worship (cf. 28:21). Beyond this, he allied himself with a foreign power, demonstrating his failure to rely on the Lord. The Chronicler demonstrated repeatedly the benefits of dependence on God (13:18; 14:11–15; 16:7–8; 32:10; 1Ch 5:20) and also deplored foreign alliances, pointing to their dire consequences (2Ch 16:7–10; 18:1; 19:1–3; 20:35–37; 22:3–9; 25:7; 28:16–21; see note on 35:21). The author emphasized avoiding foreign alliances to guide his postexilic audience toward reliance on God instead of on other nations (see "Introduction to 1 Chronicles: Purposes and Distinctives").

3 "Let there be a treaty[y] between me and you," he said, "as there was between my father
and your father. See, I am sending you silver and gold. Now break your treaty with Baasha king of Israel so he will withdraw from me."
4 Ben-Hadad agreed with King Asa and sent the commanders of his forces against the
towns of Israel. They conquered Ijon, Dan, Abel Maim[a] and all the store cities of Naphtali. 5 When Baasha heard this, he stopped building Ramah and abandoned his work.
6 Then King Asa brought all the men of Judah, and they carried away from Ramah the
stones and timber Baasha had been using. With them he built up Geba and Mizpah.
7 At that time Hanani[z] the seer came to Asa king of Judah and said to him: "Because
you relied on the king of Aram and not on the LORD your God, the army of the king of
Aram has escaped from your hand. 8 Were not the Cushites[b][a] and Libyans a mighty army
with great numbers of chariots and horsemen[c]? Yet when you relied on the LORD, he delivered[b] them into your hand. 9 For the eyes[c] of the LORD range throughout the earth to
strengthen those whose hearts are fully committed to him. You have done a foolish[d]
thing, and from now on you will be at war."
10 Asa was angry with the seer because of this; he was so enraged that he put him in
prison. At the same time Asa brutally oppressed some of the people.
11 The events of Asa's reign, from beginning to end, are written in the book of the kings
of Judah and Israel. 12 In the thirty-ninth year of his reign Asa was afflicted with a disease
in his feet. Though his disease was severe, even in his illness he did not seek help from
the LORD,[e] but only from the physicians. 13 Then in the forty-first year of his reign Asa died
and rested with his fathers. 14 They buried him in the tomb that he had cut out for himself in the City of David. They laid him on a bier covered with spices and various blended perfumes,[f] and they made a huge fire[g] in his honor.

Jehoshaphat King of Judah

17 Jehoshaphat his son succeeded him as king and strengthened himself against
Israel. 2 He stationed troops in all the fortified cities of Judah and put garrisons
in Judah and in the towns of Ephraim that his father Asa had captured.[h]
3 The LORD was with Jehoshaphat because in his early years he walked in the ways his
father David[i] had followed. He did not consult the Baals 4 but sought[j] the God of his father and followed his commands rather than the practices of Israel. 5 The LORD estab
lished the kingdom under his control; and all Judah brought gifts[k] to Jehoshaphat, so
that he had great wealth and honor.[l] 6 His heart was devoted[m] to the ways of the LORD;
furthermore, he removed the high places[n] and the Asherah poles[o] from Judah.[p]
7 In the third year of his reign he sent his officials Ben-Hail, Obadiah, Zechariah, Ne-

16:3 [y]2Ch 20:35
16:7 [z]1Ki 16:1
16:8 [a]2Ch 12:3; 14:9 [b]2Ch 13:16
16:9 [c]Pr 15:3; Jer 16:17; Zec 4:10 [d]1Sa 13:13
16:12 [e]Jer 17:5-6
16:14 [f]Ge 50:2; Jn 19:39-40 [g]2Ch 21:19; Jer 34:5
17:2 [h]2Ch 15:8
17:3 [i]1Ki 22:43
17:4 [j]1Ki 12:28; 2Ch 22:9
17:5 [k]1Sa 10:27 [l]2Ch 18:1
17:6 [m]1Ki 8:61; 2Ch 15:17 [n]1Ki 15:11; 2Ch 19:3; 20:33 [o]Ex 34:13 [p]2Ch 21:12

a 4 Also known as *Abel Beth Maacah* b 8 That is, people from the upper Nile region c 8 Or *charioteers*

16:7–10 put him in prison. In contrast to the earlier episode of Azariah's encouragement and Asa's reforms (15:1–19), Hanani rebuked the king, and Asa reacted negatively (see note on 14:1b—16:14). See *WLC* 195.
16:7–8 relied . . . relied. See note on verse 2.
16:7 escaped from your hand. Baasha deserted his position before Asa and Ben-Hadad arrived, cutting short Asa's victory (v. 5).
16:8 Were not the Cushites . . . ? Hanani referred directly to the contrast with Asa's victory over Zerah (14:8–15).
16:9 from now on you will be at war. Hanani threatened divine judgment because of Asa's infidelity (see notes on 14:6; 1Ch 28:9).
16:10 some of the people. Likely those who supported Hanani's outlook.
■ **16:11–12** *Asa's Final Years of Judgment.* Asa's rejection of the prophetic word led to his disease and death (see note on 14:1b—16:14).
16:12 disease. See note on 26:20. **did not seek help from the LORD, but only from the physicians.** Asa continued to turn away from the Lord and to rely on human strength. The physicians mentioned here may have invoked magical powers forbidden by God (see note on "seek" at 7:14). The Old Testament demonstrates no hesitancy to prescribe medical treatment for physical maladies (cf. 2Ki 20:5–8 and the use of balsam in Jer 8:22; 46:11; 51:8), but it never divorces "natural" means from seeking divine assistance (Dt 32:39).
■ **16:13–14** *Closure of Asa's Reign.* Despite Asa's failures later in life, he received an honorable burial befitting a son of David.
16:14 made a huge fire in his honor. Contrast with the response to Jehoram's death (21:19).
■ **17:1—21:3** *Jehoshaphat's Reign.* The account of Jehoshaphat's reign incorporates most of the record found in Kings (cf. 1Ki 22:1–35 with 2Ch 18:2–34; 1Ki 22:41–46,49 with 2Ch 20:31–36) but adds new material. After the opening of his reign (17:1–2), which parallels the closure (20:31—21:3), these chapters form an alternating pattern (A B A' B') between his earlier (17:3—19:3) and later years (19:4—20:30). (A) Jehoshaphat was faithful (17:3–19) and (B) faced battle (18:1—19:3). (A') He was faithful again (19:4–11) and (B') again faced battle (20:1–30). Here the Chronicler focused on the dangers of foreign alliances (18:1—19:3), the necessity of proper response to the prophetic/priestly word (18:4–27; 20:14–21) and the power of effective prayer (18:31; 20:5–17).
■ **17:1–2** *Opening of Jehoshaphat's Reign.* Jehoshaphat succeeded his father, Asa, as king of Judah and built up military defenses against Israel.
17:1 Jehoshaphat. He reigned from 872–848 B.C. Jehoshaphat was probably coregent with Asa for three years (872–869 B.C.) because of Asa's illness (16:11–14).
17:2 towns of Ephraim. See note on 14:6.
■ **17:3—19:3** *Jehoshaphat's Earlier Years.* The Chronicler introduced Jehoshaphat with a positive summary of his early years of fidelity. He was faithful (17:3–19) and entered battle (18:1—19:3).
■ **17:3–19** *Jehoshaphat's Earlier Fidelity.* The king was strong because he was faithful.
17:3 in his early years. The Chronicler explicitly limited these positive comments to the early period of Jehoshaphat's reign.
17:4–9 followed his commands . . . taking . . . the Book of the Law. See note on 1 Chronicles 16:40.
17:4 sought. See note on 7:14.
17:5 wealth and honor. See note on 17:3–19.
17:6 high places and the Asherah poles. See notes on 14:3.
17:7–8 officials . . . Levites. The royal officials were accompanied by Levites, as Moses had ordained, to teach the people (see notes on 19:4–11; 1Ch 26:29–32).

thanel and Micaiah to teach[q] in the towns of Judah. 8With them were certain Levites[r]—Shemaiah, Nethaniah, Zebadiah, Asahel, Shemiramoth, Jehonathan, Adonijah, Tobijah and Tob-Adonijah—and the priests Elishama and Jehoram. 9They taught throughout Judah, taking with them the Book of the Law[s] of the LORD; they went around to all the towns of Judah and taught the people.

10The fear[t] of the LORD fell on all the kingdoms of the lands surrounding Judah, so that they did not make war with Jehoshaphat. 11Some Philistines brought Jehoshaphat gifts and silver as tribute, and the Arabs[u] brought him flocks:[v] seven thousand seven hundred rams and seven thousand seven hundred goats.

12Jehoshaphat became more and more powerful; he built forts and store cities in Judah 13and had large supplies in the towns of Judah. He also kept experienced fighting men in Jerusalem. 14Their enrollment[w] by families was as follows:

From Judah, commanders of units of 1,000:
Adnah the commander, with 300,000 fighting men;
15next, Jehohanan the commander, with 280,000;
16next, Amasiah son of Zicri, who volunteered[x] himself for the service of the LORD, with 200,000.
17From Benjamin:[y]
Eliada, a valiant soldier, with 200,000 men armed with bows and shields;
18next, Jehozabad, with 180,000 men armed for battle.

19These were the men who served the king, besides those he stationed in the fortified cities[z] throughout Judah.[a]

Micaiah Prophesies Against Ahab

18 Now Jehoshaphat had great wealth and honor,[b] and he allied[c] himself with Ahab[d] by marriage. 2Some years later he went down to visit Ahab in Samaria. Ahab slaughtered many sheep and cattle for him and the people with him and urged him to attack Ramoth Gilead. 3Ahab king of Israel asked Jehoshaphat king of Judah, "Will you go with me against Ramoth Gilead?"

Jehoshaphat replied, "I am as you are, and my people as your people; we will join you in the war." 4But Jehoshaphat also said to the king of Israel, "First seek the counsel of the LORD."

5So the king of Israel brought together the prophets—four hundred men—and asked them, "Shall we go to war against Ramoth Gilead, or shall I refrain?"

"Go," they answered, "for God will give it into the king's hand."

6But Jehoshaphat asked, "Is there not a prophet of the LORD here whom we can inquire of?"

7The king of Israel answered Jehoshaphat, "There is still one man through whom we can inquire of the LORD, but I hate him because he never prophesies anything good about me, but always bad. He is Micaiah son of Imlah."

"The king should not say that," Jehoshaphat replied.

8So the king of Israel called one of his officials and said, "Bring Micaiah son of Imlah at once."

9Dressed in their royal robes, the king of Israel and Jehoshaphat king of Judah were sitting on their thrones at the threshing floor by the entrance to the gate of Samaria, with

17:7 [q]Lev 10:11; Dt 6:4-9; 2Ch 15:3; 35:3
17:8 [r]2Ch 19:8; Ne 8:7-8
17:9 [s]Dt 6:4-9; 28:61
17:10 [t]Ge 35:5; Dt 2:25; 2Ch 14:14
17:11 [u]2Ch 9:14; 26:8 [v]2Ch 21:16
17:14 [w]2Sa 24:2
17:16 [x]Jdg 5:9; 1Ch 29:9
17:17 [y]Nu 1:36
17:19 [z]2Ch 11:10 [a]2Ch 25:5
18:1 [b]2Ch 17:5 [c]2Ch 19:1-3; 22:3 [d]2Ch 21:6

17:7 In the third year. This teaching mission probably took place after Asa's death (see note on v. 1).
17:9 the Book of the Law of the LORD. The identity of this book is uncertain. It may have included the entire Pentateuch, but in light of Jehoshaphat's reforms (19:4–11) it may have consisted solely of the book of Deuteronomy.
17:10 fear of the LORD. Other nations were afraid of the power that the Lord displayed in strengthening Jehoshaphat militarily, so they refrained from making war with Judah (see note on 1Ch 14:17).
17:11 Philistines . . . Arabs. The wealth of other nations coming to Israel was a vital aspect of the Chronicler's hope for his postexilic situation (Isa 60:13; Mic 4:13).
17:12 he built forts and store cities. See note on 1 Chronicles 11:4–9.
17:14–19 300,000 . . . 280,000. Concerning these large numbers, see note on 1 Chronicles 12:23–37.
■ **18:1—19:3** *Jehoshaphat's Earlier Battle.* The Chronicler followed 1 Kings 22:1–28 (see notes). He added a new beginning (18:1–2) and ending (19:1–3) and omitted the elaboration on Ahab's death (1Ki 22:36–40). In contrast with Jehoshaphat's early years (17:3), the king later came under God's curse because he ignored the prophetic warning and made an alliance with the northern kingdom (see notes on 16:2; 20:20). This section divides into the deliberations (18:1–27) and the battle (18:28—19:3).
18:1–2 he allied himself with Ahab. The Chronicler added these verses to highlight the blessings given to Jehoshaphat and to contrast him with Ahab of Israel.
18:1 wealth and honor. See 17:5. **allied himself . . . by marriage.** The Chronicler referred to the marriage of Jehoshaphat's son, Jehoram, to Athaliah, daughter of Ahab (21:6; 22:2). In Kings, Ahab represented the nadir of apostasy in the northern kingdom (1Ki 16:30). Compare 19:1–3 and see note on 16:2.
18:2 urged him. The Hebrew expression can have the connotation of enticing into apostasy (Dt 13:6; 1Ch 21:1). **Ramoth Gilead.** A city in Transjordan. It had belonged to Israel since the time of Moses (Dt 4:43; Jos 20:8). Ben-Hadad failed to return the city to Israel as he had agreed (1Ki 20:34).
18:3 See *WLC* 195.
18:4 seek the counsel of the LORD. See note on 7:14.
18:7 inquire of the LORD. See note on 7:14.

all the prophets prophesying before them. 10Now Zedekiah son of Kenaanah had made
iron horns, and he declared, "This is what the LORD says: 'With these you will gore the
Arameans until they are destroyed.' "
11All the other prophets were prophesying the same thing. "Attack Ramoth Gilead[e]
and be victorious," they said, "for the LORD will give it into the king's hand."
12The messenger who had gone to summon Micaiah said to him, "Look, as one man
the other prophets are predicting success for the king. Let your word agree with theirs,
and speak favorably."
13But Micaiah said, "As surely as the LORD lives, I can tell him only what my God says."[f]
14When he arrived, the king asked him, "Micaiah, shall we go to war against Ramoth
Gilead, or shall I refrain?"
"Attack and be victorious," he answered, "for they will be given into your hand."
15The king said to him, "How many times must I make you swear to tell me nothing
but the truth in the name of the LORD?"
16Then Micaiah answered, "I saw all Israel[g] scattered on the hills like sheep without
a shepherd,[h] and the LORD said, 'These people have no master. Let each one go home
in peace.' "
17The king of Israel said to Jehoshaphat, "Didn't I tell you that he never prophesies
anything good about me, but only bad?"
18Micaiah continued, "Therefore hear the word of the LORD: I saw the LORD sitting on
his throne[i] with all the host of heaven standing on his right and on his left. 19And the
LORD said, 'Who will entice Ahab king of Israel into attacking Ramoth Gilead and going
to his death there?'
"One suggested this, and another that. 20Finally, a spirit came forward, stood before
the LORD and said, 'I will entice him.'
" 'By what means?' the LORD asked.
21" 'I will go and be a lying spirit[j] in the mouths of all his prophets,' he said.
" 'You will succeed in enticing him,' said the LORD. 'Go and do it.'
22"So now the LORD has put a lying spirit in the mouths of these prophets of yours.[k]
The LORD has decreed disaster for you."
23Then Zedekiah son of Kenaanah went up and slapped[l] Micaiah in the face. "Which
way did the spirit from[a] the LORD go when he went from me to speak to you?" he asked.
24Micaiah replied, "You will find out on the day you go to hide in an inner room."
25The king of Israel then ordered, "Take Micaiah and send him back to Amon the ruler of the city and to Joash the king's son, 26and say, 'This is what the king says: Put this
fellow in prison[m] and give him nothing but bread and water until I return safely.' "
27Micaiah declared, "If you ever return safely, the LORD has not spoken through me."
Then he added, "Mark my words, all you people!"

Ahab Killed at Ramoth Gilead

28So the king of Israel and Jehoshaphat king of Judah went up to Ramoth Gilead.
29The king of Israel said to Jehoshaphat, "I will enter the battle in disguise, but you wear
your royal robes." So the king of Israel disguised[n] himself and went into battle.
30Now the king of Aram had ordered his chariot commanders, "Do not fight with anyone, small or great, except the king of Israel." 31When the chariot commanders saw Jehoshaphat, they thought, "This is the king of Israel." So they turned to attack him, but Jehoshaphat cried out,[o] and the LORD helped him. God drew them away from him, 32for when the
chariot commanders saw that he was not the king of Israel, they stopped pursuing him.
33But someone drew his bow at random and hit the king of Israel between the sections
of his armor. The king told the chariot driver, "Wheel around and get me out of the fighting. I've been wounded." 34All day long the battle raged, and the king of Israel propped
himself up in his chariot facing the Arameans until evening. Then at sunset he died.[p]

18:11 [e]2Ch 22:5
18:13 [f]Nu 22:18, 20, 35
18:16 [g]1Ch 9:1 [h]Nu 27:17; Eze 34:5-8
18:18 [i]Da 7:9
18:21 [j]1Ch 21:1; Job 1:6; Zec 3:1; Jn 8:44
18:22 [k]Job 12:16; Isa 19:14; Eze 14:9
18:23 [l]Jer 20:2; Mk 14:65; Ac 23:2
18:26 [m]2Ch 16:10; Heb 11:36
18:29 [n]1Sa 28:8
18:31 [o]2Ch 13:14
18:34 [p]2Ch 22:5

[a] 23 Or *Spirit of*

18:15 name. See note on 1 Chronicles 13:6.
18:16 all Israel. See note on 10:1.
18:19–22 I will entice him. Micaiah's vision of heavenly deliberations (cf. Job 1:6–12; Isa 6:1–8; Zec 3:1–10) demonstrated that the sovereignty of God extends over evil (see note on 1Ch 21:1).
18:28 Jehoshaphat . . . went up to Ramoth Gilead. In contrast with Rehoboam (11:4) and Asa in his first battle (15:1–8), Jehoshaphat paid no attention to the prophet's warning. As a result, he barely escaped with his life (v. 31). See note on 20:20.
18:31 Jehoshaphat cried out, and the LORD helped him. God drew them away from him. The traditional (Masoretic) Hebrew text of 1 Kings 22:32 reads simply that "Jehoshaphat cried out." Some Septuagint (Greek translation of the OT) manuscripts of Kings read "and the Lord helped him." These words reflect an important aspect of the Chronicler's outlook. Although Jehoshaphat had turned away from the Lord, when he cried out in prayer God mercifully delivered. This event recalls Solomon's dedicatory prayer (see notes on 6:34–35; 7:14).

19 When Jehoshaphat king of Judah returned safely to his palace in Jerusalem, 2Jehu[q] the seer, the son of Hanani, went out to meet him and said to the king, "Should you help the wicked[r] and love[a] those who hate the LORD?[s] Because of this, the wrath[t] of the LORD is upon you. 3There is, however, some good[u] in you, for you have rid the land of the Asherah poles[v] and have set your heart on seeking God.[w]"

Jehoshaphat Appoints Judges

4Jehoshaphat lived in Jerusalem, and he went out again among the people from Beersheba to the hill country of Ephraim and turned them back to the LORD, the God of their fathers. 5He appointed judges[x] in the land, in each of the fortified cities of Judah. 6He told them, "Consider carefully what you do,[y] because you are not judging for man[z] but for the LORD, who is with you whenever you give a verdict. 7Now let the fear of the LORD be upon you. Judge carefully, for with the LORD our God there is no injustice[a] or partiality[b] or bribery."

8In Jerusalem also, Jehoshaphat appointed some of the Levites, priests and heads of Israelite families to administer[c] the law of the LORD and to settle disputes. And they lived in Jerusalem. 9He gave them these orders: "You must serve faithfully and wholeheartedly in the fear of the LORD. 10In every case that comes before you from your fellow countrymen who live in the cities—whether bloodshed or other concerns of the law, commands, decrees or ordinances—you are to warn them not to sin against the LORD;[d] otherwise his wrath will come on you and your brothers. Do this, and you will not sin.

11"Amariah the chief priest will be over you in any matter concerning the LORD, and Zebadiah son of Ishmael, the leader of the tribe of Judah, will be over you in any matter concerning the king, and the Levites will serve as officials before you. Act with courage,[e] and may the LORD be with those who do well."

Jehoshaphat Defeats Moab and Ammon

20 After this, the Moabites and Ammonites with some of the Meunites[b][f] came to make war on Jehoshaphat.

2Some men came and told Jehoshaphat, "A vast army is coming against you from Edom,[c] from the other side of the Sea.[d] It is already in Hazazon Tamar[g]" (that is, En Gedi). 3Alarmed, Jehoshaphat resolved to inquire of the LORD, and he proclaimed a fast[h] for all Judah. 4The people of Judah came together to seek help from the LORD; indeed, they came from every town in Judah to seek him.

5Then Jehoshaphat stood up in the assembly of Judah and Jerusalem at the temple of the LORD in the front of the new courtyard 6and said:

"O LORD, God of our fathers,[i] are you not the God who is in heaven?[j] You rule over all the kingdoms[k] of the nations. Power and might are in your hand, and no one can withstand you. 7O our God, did you not drive out the inhabitants of this land before your people Israel and give it forever to the descendants of Abraham

19:2 [q]1Ki 16:1 [r]2Ch 16:2-9 [s]Ps 139:21-22 [t]2Ch 24:18; 32:25; Ps 7:11
19:3 [u]1Ki 14:13; 2Ch 12:12 [v]2Ch 17:6 [w]2Ch 18:1; 20:35; 25:7; Ezr 7:10
19:5 [x]Ge 47:6; Ex 18:26
19:6 [y]Lev 19:15 [z]Dt 1:17; 16:18-20; 17:8-13
19:7 [a]Ge 18:25; Dt 32:4 [b]Dt 10:17; Job 34:19; Ro 2:11; Col 3:25
19:8 [c]2Ch 17:8-9
19:10 [d]Dt 17:8-13
19:11 [e]1Ch 28:20
20:1 [f]1Ch 4:41
20:2 [g]Ge 14:7
20:3 [h]1Sa 7:6; 2Ch 19:3; Ezr 8:21; Jer 36:9; Jnh 3:5,7
20:6 [i]Mt 6:9 [j]Dt 4:39 [k]1Ch 29:11-12

[a] 2 Or *and make alliances with* [b] 1 Some Septuagint manuscripts; Hebrew *Ammonites* [c] 2 One Hebrew manuscript; most Hebrew manuscripts, Septuagint and Vulgate *Aram* [d] 2 That is, the Dead Sea

19:1–3 The Chronicler added these verses to report that Jehoshaphat had escaped death because he had cried to the Lord (18:31). Even so, Jehu rebuked him for his sin. The author emphasized that God had chastised Jehoshaphat for his dependence on a foreign alliance, as he had done through Hanani's prophecy against Asa (see notes on 1Ch 28:9; 16:7–10). See *WLC* 195.
19:3 some good in you. Although Jehoshaphat had been inconsistent (18:1–34), he was assured of continued blessings from God. **Asherah.** See note and NIV text note on 14:3. **seeking God.** See note on 7:14.
■ **19:4—20:30** *Jehoshaphat's Later Years.* The second major section on Jehoshaphat's reign (see note on 17:1—21:3) reports his reforms (19:4–11) and a second battle in which Jehoshaphat gained victory because he relied fully on the Lord (20:1–30).
■ **19:4–11** *Jehoshaphat's Reforms.* Jehoshaphat established a system of courts throughout Judah to enforce Mosaic Law (1Ch 26:20–32). The analogy with his teaching endeavor (17:7–9) is evident.
19:6 with you whenever. Not in the sense of approving each judgment but of watching the judges to ensure that they practiced justice (vv. 7,10) and of protecting them when they handed down an unpopular verdict.
19:8–11 See *WCF* 23.3; 31.2; *WLC* 144.
19:8 administer the law of the LORD. See note on 1 Chronicles 16:40.
■ **20:1–30** *Jehoshaphat's Later Battle.* The Chronicler included a battle account not found in Kings. Jehoshaphat responded to a serious military threat with exemplary reliance on the Lord (see the contrasting report of the battle in 18:1—19:3). The Chronicler undoubtedly reported this event as a model for his postexilic readers to follow as they faced an uncertain and threatening international environment.
20:1 Moabites and Ammonites. The Chronicler almost certainly specified these particular enemies because his postexilic audience was troubled by the descendants of these same hostile nations (Ne 2:19; 4:1–3; 6:1–4; 13:1–27). **Meunites.** A tribe from the southwest near Mount Seir in Edom (26:7; 1Ch 4:41).
20:2 A vast army . . . against you. See note on 1 Chronicles 19:6–7. **Edom.** See NIV text note.
20:3–4 proclaimed a fast . . . to seek help from the LORD. Jehoshaphat responded immediately by calling Judah to fast and seek the Lord. His actions recalled Solomon's dedicatory prayer (see notes on 6:34–35 and 7:14).
20:5–19 Jehoshaphat's assembly followed the liturgical pattern often associated with prayers of lament: Corporate prayer was offered (vv. 5–13), an oracle of deliverance was given (vv. 14–17) and the supplicants responded with praise (vv. 18–19).
20:6–12 Jehoshaphat offered praise (vv. 6–9), complaints (vv. 10–11) and petitions (v. 12). See note on verses 5–19.
20:6 See *WLC* 190,196.
20:8–9 Name. See note 1 Chronicles 13:6.

your friend?[l] 8They have lived in it and have built in it a sanctuary[m] for your Name,
saying, 9'If calamity comes upon us, whether the sword of judgment, or plague or
famine,[n] we will stand in your presence before this temple that bears your Name
and will cry out to you in our distress, and you will hear us and save us.'
10"But now here are men from Ammon, Moab and Mount Seir, whose territory you would not allow Israel to invade when they came from Egypt;[o] so they
turned away from them and did not destroy them. 11See how they are repaying us
by coming to drive us out of the possession[p] you gave us as an inheritance.
12O our God, will you not judge them?[q] For we have no power to face this vast
army that is attacking us. We do not know what to do, but our eyes are upon
you.[r]"
13All the men of Judah, with their wives and children and little ones, stood there before the LORD.
14Then the Spirit[s] of the LORD came upon Jahaziel son of Zechariah, the son of Benaiah, the son of Jeiel, the son of Mattaniah, a Levite and descendant of Asaph, as he stood
in the assembly.
15He said: "Listen, King Jehoshaphat and all who live in Judah and Jerusalem! This is
what the LORD says to you: 'Do not be afraid or discouraged[t] because of this vast army.
For the battle[u] is not yours, but God's. 16Tomorrow march down against them. They will
be climbing up by the Pass of Ziz, and you will find them at the end of the gorge in the
Desert of Jeruel. 17You will not have to fight this battle. Take up your positions; stand firm
and see[v] the deliverance the LORD will give you, O Judah and Jerusalem. Do not be afraid;
do not be discouraged. Go out to face them tomorrow, and the LORD will be with you.' "
18Jehoshaphat bowed[w] with his face to the ground, and all the people of Judah and
Jerusalem fell down in worship before the LORD. 19Then some Levites from the Kohathites and Korahites stood up and praised the LORD, the God of Israel, with very loud voice.
20Early in the morning they left for the Desert of Tekoa. As they set out, Jehoshaphat
stood and said, "Listen to me, Judah and people of Jerusalem! Have faith[x] in the LORD your
God and you will be upheld; have faith in his prophets and you will be successful.[y]" 21Af-
ter consulting the people, Jehoshaphat appointed men to sing to the LORD and to praise
him for the splendor of his[a] holiness[z] as they went out at the head of the army, saying:

"Give thanks to the LORD,
for his love endures forever."[a]

22As they began to sing and praise, the LORD set ambushes[b] against the men of Ammon and Moab and Mount Seir who were invading Judah, and they were defeated. 23The
men of Ammon[c] and Moab rose up against the men from Mount Seir[d] to destroy and annihilate them. After they finished slaughtering the men from Seir, they helped to destroy
one another.[e]
24When the men of Judah came to the place that overlooks the desert and looked toward the vast army, they saw only dead bodies lying on the ground; no one had escaped.
25So Jehoshaphat and his men went to carry off their plunder, and they found among
them a great amount of equipment and clothing[b] and also articles of value—more than
they could take away. There was so much plunder that it took three days to collect it.
26On the fourth day they assembled in the Valley of Beracah, where they praised the
LORD. This is why it is called the Valley of Beracah[c] to this day.

20:7 [l]Isa 41:8; Jas 2:23
20:8 [m]2Ch 6:20
20:9 [n]2Ch 6:28
20:10 [o]Nu 20:14-21; Dt 2:4-6,9,18-19
20:11 [p]Ps 83:1-12
20:12 [q]Jdg 11:27 [r]Ps 25:15; 121:1-2
20:14 [s]2Ch 15:1
20:15 [t]2Ch 32:7 [u]Ex 14:13-14; 1Sa 17:47
20:17 [v]Ex 14:13; 2Ch 15:2
20:18 [w]Ex 4:31
20:20 [x]Isa 7:9 [y]Ge 39:3; Pr 16:3
20:21 [z]1Ch 16:29; Ps 29:2 [a]2Ch 5:13; Ps 136:1
20:22 [b]Jdg 7:22; 2Ch 13:13
20:23 [c]Ge 19:38 [d]2Ch 21:8 [e]Jdg 7:22; 1Sa 14:20; Eze 38:21

a *21* Or *him with the splendor of corpses* b *25* Some Hebrew manuscripts and Vulgate; most Hebrew manuscripts *corpses* c *26* *Beracah* means *praise.*

20:9 you will hear us and save us. Jehoshaphat explicitly applied Solomon's dedicatory prayer to his own situation (see notes on 6:14–42).
20:10–12 O. See *WLC* 190,196.
20:12 we have no power. The themes of human impotence, humility and reliance on divine power also appear in Asa's prayer (see note on 14:11).
20:15 not yours, but God's. Human effort in Israel's warfare was overshadowed by divine power. The Judahites would not even have to fight in the battle, for the Lord would defeat their enemies by turning them against one another (vv. 22–23). The prophet reminded Jehoshaphat that God is completely capable of protecting his people whether or not they contribute anything to their own defense. This emphasis was particularly vital to the postexilic audience, who were obliged to rely on divine power against their foes (cf. Ne 4:1–23; Hag 2:20–23; Zec 9:1–8).
20:20–30 Jehoshaphat appointed men to sing to the LORD and to praise him. The strategy and outcome of this battle form a striking contrast with those of Jehoshaphat's previous battle (see notes on 18:28,31).
20:20 have faith in his prophets and you will be successful. The Chronicler frequently emphasized the importance of trusting and obeying the prophetic word. Those who follow the prophets are blessed, while those who reject them are cursed (see notes on 10:1—12:16; 14:1b—16:14; 18:1—19:3; 24:19; 25:15–16; 28:9–15; 36:15). Jehoshaphat's instruction here contrasts with his earlier rejection of Micaiah (18:1–32). If the postexilic readers were to receive God's blessing, they too had to give heed to the prophetic word (cf. Ne 9:30; Hag 1:12; Zec 1:2–6; 7:11; see "Introduction to 1 Chronicles: Purposes and Distinctives").
20:21 his love endures forever. See note on 5:13.
20:26 to this day. See note on 1 Chronicles 4:41 and 43.

27 Then, led by Jehoshaphat, all the men of Judah and Jerusalem returned joyfully to
Jerusalem, for the LORD had given them cause to rejoice over their enemies. 28 They entered Jerusalem and went to the temple of the LORD with harps and lutes and trumpets.
29 The fear[f] of God came upon all the kingdoms of the countries when they heard how
the LORD had fought[g] against the enemies of Israel. 30 And the kingdom of Jehoshaphat
was at peace, for his God had given him rest[h] on every side.

The End of Jehoshaphat's Reign

31 So Jehoshaphat reigned over Judah. He was thirty-five years old when he became
king of Judah, and he reigned in Jerusalem twenty-five years. His mother's name was
Azubah daughter of Shilhi. 32 He walked in the ways of his father Asa and did not stray
from them; he did what was right in the eyes of the LORD. 33 The high places,[i] however,
were not removed, and the people still had not set their hearts on the God of their fathers.
34 The other events of Jehoshaphat's reign, from beginning to end, are written in the
annals of Jehu[j] son of Hanani, which are recorded in the book of the kings of Israel.
35 Later, Jehoshaphat king of Judah made an alliance[k] with Ahaziah king of Israel, who
was guilty of wickedness.[l] 36 He agreed with him to construct a fleet of trading ships.[a] After these were built at Ezion Geber, 37 Eliezer son of Dodavahu of Mareshah prophesied
against Jehoshaphat, saying, "Because you have made an alliance with Ahaziah, the
LORD will destroy what you have made." The ships[m] were wrecked and were not able to
set sail to trade.[b]

21 Then Jehoshaphat rested with his fathers and was buried with them in the City
of David. And Jehoram[n] his son succeeded him as king. 2 Jehoram's brothers, the
sons of Jehoshaphat, were Azariah, Jehiel, Zechariah, Azariahu, Michael and Shephatiah. All these were sons of Jehoshaphat king of Israel.[c] 3 Their father had given them many
gifts[o] of silver and gold and articles of value, as well as fortified cities[p] in Judah, but he
had given the kingdom to Jehoram because he was his firstborn son.

Jehoram King of Judah

4 When Jehoram established[q] himself firmly over his father's kingdom, he put all his
brothers[r] to the sword along with some of the princes of Israel. 5 Jehoram was thirty-two
years old when he became king, and he reigned in Jerusalem eight years. 6 He walked in
the ways of the kings of Israel,[s] as the house of Ahab had done, for he married a daughter of Ahab.[t] He did evil in the eyes of the LORD. 7 Nevertheless, because of the covenant
the LORD had made with David,[u] the LORD was not willing to destroy the house of David.[v]
He had promised to maintain a lamp[w] for him and his descendants forever.
8 In the time of Jehoram, Edom[x] rebelled against Judah and set up its own king. 9 So

20:29 [f]Ge 35:5; Dt 2:25; 2Ch 14:14; 17:10 [g]Ex 14:14
20:30 [h]1Ch 22:9; 2Ch 14:6-7; 15:15
20:33 [i]2Ch 17:6; 19:3
20:34 [j]1Ki 16:1
20:35 [k]2Ch 16:3 [l]2Ch 19:1-3
20:37 [m]1Ki 9:26; 2Ch 9:21
21:1 [n]1Ch 3:11
21:3 [o]2Ch 11:23 [p]2Ch 11:10
21:4 [q]1Ki 2:12 [r]Jdg 9:5
21:6 [s]1Ki 12:28-30 [t]2Ch 18:1; 22:3
21:7 [u]2Sa 7:13 [v]2Sa 7:15; 2Ch 23:3 [w]2Sa 21:17; 1Ki 11:36
21:8 [x]2Ch 20:22-23

[a] *36* Hebrew *of ships that could go to Tarshish* [b] *37* Hebrew *sail for Tarshish* [c] *2* That is, Judah, as frequently in 2 Chronicles

---

20:29 fear of God. See note on 17:10.
20:30 peace . . . rest. See note on 1 Chronicles 22:9.
■ **20:31—21:3** *Closure of Jehoshaphat's Reign.* The Chronicler followed 1 Kings 22:41–50. He summarized Jehoshaphat's reign, added an account of the king's disastrous maritime alliance and recorded his death and burial.
20:31 twenty-five years. Second Kings 3:1 and 8:16 bring Jehoshaphat's reign to 22 years. The Chronicler included the three years during which Jehoshaphat was coregent with Asa (see note on 17:1).
20:33 high places. See note on 14:3.
20:34 written in the annals. See "Introduction to 1 Chronicles: Author."
20:35–37 the LORD will destroy what you have made. A brief reminder of another time Jehoshaphat had received a prophetic rebuke for entering into an alliance with the northern kingdom (see note on 16:2).
20:37 Eliezer . . . prophesied. See note on verse 20.
21:1 Jehoram. Jehoram reigned as coregent with Jehoshaphat from 853–848 B.C. (2Ki 1:17; 3:1). He reigned exclusively from 848–841 B.C.
■ **21:4—24:27** *Northern Corruption in Judah.* The reigns of Jehoram (21:4–20), Ahaziah (22:1–9) and Joash (22:10—24:27) are unified by the theme of the influence of the northern kingdom on Judah.
■ **21:4–20** *Jehoram's Reign.* The Chronicler expanded the record of Jehoram's reign in Kings (2Ki 8:16–24). As in Kings, his presentation is entirely negative. Jehoram murdered his brothers (vv. 4–7); Edom and Libnah rebelled against him (vv. 8–11); Elijah prophesied judgment (vv. 12–15); more rebellions ensued (vv. 16–17); and his reign closed (vv. 18–20). The Chronicler depicted Jehoram in this way ostensibly to warn his postexilic readers against infidelity and to assure them that despite the sins of individual kings, God's grace remained with the Davidic line (see notes on 1Ch 17:13–14).
■ **21:4–7** *Opening of Jehoram's Reign.* Jehoram's reign was marked by unmitigated wickedness. Only God's faithfulness to his covenant with David restrained him from obliterating Jehoram and all his house.
21:4 Israel. See note on 10:1.
21:5 eight years. As sole monarch (see note on v. 1).
21:6 in the ways of the kings of Israel . . . a daughter of Ahab. The Chronicler followed Kings as he referred to the marriage alliance between Jehoshaphat and Ahab (see note on 18:1), and he characterized Jehoram by comparing him with the apostate kings of Israel (cf. 2Ki 8:18).
21:7 not willing to destroy the house of David. The house of David was on the brink of annihilation. Jehoram deserved to die, but God preserved his life to fulfill his promise to David of a permanent dynasty. Despite the sins of individual descendants of David, the Davidic line would never be entirely rejected (see note on 1Ch 17:7–14).
■ **21:8–11** *Rebellion Against Jehoram.* God's displeasure toward Jehoram became evident when two nations subject to Judah successfully rebelled against him.
21:8 Edom. Jehoshaphat had subjugated Edom because of righteous dependence on God (20:1–30). Jehoram, on the other hand, failed in his attempt.

Jehoram went there with his officers and all his chariots. The Edomites surrounded him
and his chariot commanders, but he rose up and broke through by night. 10 To this day
Edom has been in rebellion against Judah.

Libnah[y] revolted at the same time, because Jehoram had forsaken the LORD, the God
of his fathers. 11 He had also built high places on the hills of Judah and had caused the
people of Jerusalem to prostitute themselves and had led Judah astray.

12 Jehoram received a letter from Elijah[z] the prophet, which said:

> "This is what the LORD, the God of your father[a] David, says: 'You have not walked
> in the ways of your father Jehoshaphat or of Asa[b] king of Judah. 13 But you have
> walked in the ways of the kings of Israel, and you have led Judah and the people
> of Jerusalem to prostitute themselves, just as the house of Ahab did.[c] You have
> also murdered your own brothers, members of your father's house, men who were
> better[d] than you. 14 So now the LORD is about to strike your people, your sons, your
> wives and everything that is yours, with a heavy blow. 15 You yourself will be very
> ill with a lingering disease[e] of the bowels, until the disease causes your bowels to
> come out.' "

16 The LORD aroused against Jehoram the hostility of the Philistines and of the Arabs[f]
who lived near the Cushites. 17 They attacked Judah, invaded it and carried off all the
goods found in the king's palace, together with his sons and wives. Not a son was left to
him except Ahaziah,[a] the youngest.[g]

18 After all this, the LORD afflicted Jehoram with an incurable disease of the bowels. 19 In
the course of time, at the end of the second year, his bowels came out because of the disease, and he died in great pain. His people made no fire in his honor,[h] as they had for
his fathers.

20 Jehoram was thirty-two years old when he became king, and he reigned in Jerusalem eight years. He passed away, to no one's regret, and was buried[i] in the City of David, but not in the tombs of the kings.

Ahaziah King of Judah

22 The people[j] of Jerusalem[k] made Ahaziah, Jehoram's youngest son, king in his
place, since the raiders,[l] who came with the Arabs into the camp, had killed all
the older sons. So Ahaziah son of Jehoram king of Judah began to reign.

2 Ahaziah was twenty-two[b] years old when he became king, and he reigned in Jerusalem one year. His mother's name was Athaliah, a granddaughter of Omri.

3 He too walked[m] in the ways of the house of Ahab,[n] for his mother encouraged him
in doing wrong. 4 He did evil in the eyes of the LORD, as the house of Ahab had done, for
after his father's death they became his advisers, to his undoing. 5 He also followed their
counsel when he went with Joram[c] son of Ahab king of Israel to war against Hazael king
of Aram at Ramoth Gilead.[o] The Arameans wounded Joram; 6 so he returned to Jezreel

21:10 [y]Nu 33:20
21:12 [z]2Ki 1:16-17 [a]2Ch 17:3-6 [b]2Ch 14:2
21:13 [c]ver 6,11; 1Ki 16:29-33 [d]ver 4; 1Ki 2:32
21:15 [e]ver 18-19; Nu 12:10
21:16 [f]2Ch 17:10-11; 22:1; 26:7
21:17 [g]2Ki 12:18; 2Ch 22:1; 25:23; Joel 3:5
21:19 [h]2Ch 16:14
21:20 [i]2Ch 24:25; 28:27; 33:20; Jer 22:18, 28
22:1 [j]2Ch 33:25; 36:1 [k]2Ch 23:20-21; 26:1 [l]2Ch 21:16-17
22:3 [m]2Ch 18:1 [n]2Ch 21:6
22:5 [o]2Ch 18:11,34

a 17 Hebrew *Jehoahaz,* a variant of *Ahaziah* b 2 Some Septuagint manuscripts and Syriac (see also 2 Kings 8:26); Hebrew *forty-two* c 5 Hebrew *Jehoram,* a variant of *Joram;* also in verses 6 and 7

21:10 To this day. See note on 1 Chronicles 4:41 and 43. **Libnah.** An area situated between Judah and Philistia. **because Jehoram had forsaken the LORD.** These words were evidently added to explain that rebellion in Jehoram's kingdom was the result of his infidelity (see note on vv. 4–20).

21:11 built high places. While Asa and Jehoshaphat merely failed to rid the land of all pagan high places (see note on 14:3), Jehoram actively constructed more (cf. 28:25). **prostitute themselves.** Perhaps literally by involvement with prostitution in pagan worship rituals or metaphorically by spiritual infidelity (1Ch 5:25).

■ **21:12–15** *Elijah's Condemnation of Jehoram.* The Chronicler adds an account of Elijah's prophetic letter (cf. v. 20 with 2Ki 8:23–24).

21:12 Elijah. The only mention of the prophet in Chronicles. Compare the lengthy account in 1 Kings 17:1—2 Kings 2:12.

■ **21:16–17** *More Rebellions Against Jehoram.* The theme of rebellion as a sign of God's displeasure continues.

■ **21:18–20** *Closure of Jehoram's Reign.* God ended Jehoram's reign by inflicting him with a fatal disease. He died in dishonor.

21:18–19 disease. See note on 26:20.

21:19 made no fire. Contrast with the response to Asa's death (16:14). Jehoram (v. 20), Joash (24:25), Ahaz (28:27) and Manasseh (33:20) died in ignominy. Uzziah was buried near the kings but not with them because of his leprosy (cf. 26:23), and Amon was disgracefully assassinated (cf. 33:85).

21:20 He passed away, to no one's regret. The Chronicler expanded the record of Jehoram's death and burial as recorded in Kings with details that reveal Jehoram's utter disgrace (cf. 2Ki 8:24). **eight years.** See note on verse 5.

■ **22:1–9** *Ahaziah's Reign.* The Chronicler's account of Ahaziah's reign is shorter than the record in Kings (2Ki 8:25—9:29). He loosely followed portions of Kings, but his record ties Ahaziah closely to Jehoram (21:4–20). Both kings were deeply influenced by Athaliah (21:6; 22:3–4), and in both reigns the Davidic dynasty barely escaped annihilation (21:16–17; 22:7–9). Both kings were evaluated negatively (21:6; 22:3–4). Ahaziah's reign divides into his rise to power (v. 2), his downfall through an alliance with Joram of the northern kingdom (vv. 3–6a) and the closure of his reign (vv. 6b–9).

22:1 killed . . . sons. See 21:16–17.

22:2 Ahaziah. Reigned in 841 B.C. **twenty-two.** See NIV text note. The traditional (Masoretic) Hebrew text reads "forty-two." This would make Ahaziah older than his father (21:5,20). Second Kings 8:26 reads "twenty-two" and represents the original reading. "Forty-two" apparently resulted from an error in transmission.

22:3–6a He too walked in the ways of the house of Ahab. The Chronicler presented Ahaziah's rapid downfall as divine chastisement for his alliance with the northern kingdom (see note on 16:2).

22:5 Hazael. See 1 Kings 19:15 and 2 Kings 8:7–15.

22:6 [p]1Ki 19:15; 2Ki 8:13-15; 9:15
22:7 [q]2Ki 9:16; 2Ch 10:15
22:8 [r]2Ki 10:13
22:9 [s]Jdg 9:5 [t]2Ch 17:4
23:2 [u]Nu 35:2-5
23:3 [v]2Ki 11:17 [w]2Sa 7:12; 1Ki 2:4; 2Ch 6:16; 7:18; 21:7
23:6 [x]1Ch 23:28-29; Zec 3:7
23:8 [y]2Ki 11:9 [z]1Ch 24:1

to recover from the wounds they had inflicted on him at Ramoth[a] in his battle with Hazael[p] king of Aram.
Then Ahaziah[b] son of Jehoram king of Judah went down to Jezreel to see Joram son
of Ahab because he had been wounded.
7 Through Ahaziah's[q] visit to Joram, God brought about Ahaziah's downfall. When Ahaziah arrived, he went out with Joram to meet Jehu son of Nimshi, whom the LORD had anointed to destroy the house of Ahab. 8 While Jehu was executing judgment on the house of Ahab,[r]
he found the princes of Judah and the sons of Ahaziah's relatives, who had been attending
Ahaziah, and he killed them. 9 He then went in search of Ahaziah, and his men captured him
while he was hiding[s] in Samaria. He was brought to Jehu and put to death. They buried him,
for they said, "He was a son of Jehoshaphat, who sought[t] the LORD with all his heart." So
there was no one in the house of Ahaziah powerful enough to retain the kingdom.

Athaliah and Joash

10 When Athaliah the mother of Ahaziah saw that her son was dead, she proceeded
to destroy the whole royal family of the house of Judah. 11 But Jehosheba,[c] the daughter
of King Jehoram, took Joash son of Ahaziah and stole him away from among the royal
princes who were about to be murdered and put him and his nurse in a bedroom. Because Jehosheba,[c] the daughter of King Jehoram and wife of the priest Jehoiada, was
Ahaziah's sister, she hid the child from Athaliah so she could not kill him. 12 He remained
hidden with them at the temple of God for six years while Athaliah ruled the land.

23 In the seventh year Jehoiada showed his strength. He made a covenant with the
commanders of units of a hundred: Azariah son of Jeroham, Ishmael son of Jehohanan, Azariah son of Obed, Maaseiah son of Adaiah, and Elishaphat son of Zicri.
2 They went throughout Judah and gathered the Levites[u] and the heads of Israelite families from all the towns. When they came to Jerusalem, 3 the whole assembly made a covenant[v] with the king at the temple of God.
Jehoiada said to them, "The king's son shall reign, as the LORD promised concerning
the descendants of David.[w] 4 Now this is what you are to do: A third of you priests and Levites who are going on duty on the Sabbath are to keep watch at the doors, 5 a third of you
at the royal palace and a third at the Foundation Gate, and all the other men are to be in
the courtyards of the temple of the LORD. 6 No one is to enter the temple of the LORD except the priests and Levites on duty; they may enter because they are consecrated, but all
the other men are to guard[x] what the LORD has assigned to them.[d] 7 The Levites are to station themselves around the king, each man with his weapons in his hand. Anyone who
enters the temple must be put to death. Stay close to the king wherever he goes."
8 The Levites and all the men of Judah did just as Jehoiada the priest ordered.[y] Each
one took his men—those who were going on duty on the Sabbath and those who were
going off duty—for Jehoiada the priest had not released any of the divisions.[z] 9 Then he
gave the commanders of units of a hundred the spears and the large and small shields
that had belonged to King David and that were in the temple of God. 10 He stationed all
the men, each with his weapon in his hand, around the king—near the altar and the temple, from the south side to the north side of the temple.

[a] 6 Hebrew *Ramah,* a variant of *Ramoth* [b] 6 Some Hebrew manuscripts, Septuagint, Vulgate and Syriac (see also 2 Kings 8:29); most Hebrew manuscripts *Azariah* [c] 11 Hebrew *Jehoshabeath,* a variant of *Jehosheba* [d] 6 Or *to observe the LORD's command ⌊not to enter⌋*

22:8 Jehu was executing judgment. Kings reports that Elisha anointed Jehu to destroy the house of Omri (2Ki 9:1—10:31).
22:9 He . . . went in search of Ahaziah. The reign of Ahaziah ended in tragedy. His death was part of God's judgment on the house of Omri. **They buried him, for they said, "He was a son of Jehoshaphat."** Ahaziah received an honorable burial not because of his own character but because of his grandfather Jehoshaphat. **sought the LORD.** See note on 7:14.
■ **22:10—24:27** *Joash's Reign.* The Chronicler relied heavily on 2 Kings 11:1—12:21 for his record of Joash's reign, but he reworked much of the material and added his own viewpoints. The account divides into two main parts: Joash's opposition to Athaliah (22:10—23:21) and Joash's reign (24:1–27). This portion of Chronicles illustrates the close association between king and priest. The Davidic line was preserved by the priest Jehoiada (22:10—23:21), the Davidic king served faithfully under the influence of the priest (24:1–16) and the king failed when he rejected priestly instruction (24:17–27). The cooperation between king and priest was essential to the Chronicler's vision for the postexilic community (see note on 1Ch 6:1–53).
■ **22:10—23:21** *Joash's Rise Over Athaliah.* This material largely follows 2 Kings 11:1–21. Jehoshaphat's marriage alliance (see note on 18:1) finally yielded its worst result. Athaliah nearly destroyed the Davidic line to establish herself as queen.
22:11 Joash. Reigned from 835–796 B.C.
22:12 Athaliah ruled the land. Athaliah was the only queen to rule in Judah (841–835 B.C.).
23:1–11 Jehoiada showed his strength. The priest Jehoiada resisted Queen Athaliah and gained the military support necessary for temple and political reform. The Chronicler likely reported this material to emphasize the connection between the priests and kings (see note on 22:10—23:21). The support of this Zadokite priest for the Davidic king reflected the postexilic expectation of royal and priestly leadership (Zec 3:1—4:14; 6:9–15).
23:2 throughout Judah . . . all the towns. This verse was added to depict Joash's widespread support throughout Judah (see notes on 1:1—9:31; 1Ch 11:1—12:40).
23:3 as the LORD promised. See note on 1 Chronicles 17:13–14.

11 Jehoiada and his sons brought out the king's son and put the crown on him; they
presented him with a copy[a] of the covenant and proclaimed him king. They anointed him
and shouted, "Long live the king!"
12 When Athaliah heard the noise of the people running and cheering the king, she
went to them at the temple of the LORD. 13 She looked, and there was the king,[b] standing by his pillar[c] at the entrance. The officers and the trumpeters were beside the king,
and all the people of the land were rejoicing and blowing trumpets, and singers with musical instruments were leading the praises. Then Athaliah tore her robes and shouted,
"Treason! Treason!"
14 Jehoiada the priest sent out the commanders of units of a hundred, who were in
charge of the troops, and said to them: "Bring her out between the ranks[a] and put to the
sword anyone who follows her." For the priest had said, "Do not put her to death at the
temple of the LORD." 15 So they seized her as she reached the entrance of the Horse Gate[d]
on the palace grounds, and there they put her to death.
16 Jehoiada then made a covenant[e] that he and the people and the king[b] would be the
LORD's people. 17 All the people went to the temple of Baal and tore it down. They
smashed the altars and idols and killed[f] Mattan the priest of Baal in front of the altars.
18 Then Jehoiada placed the oversight of the temple of the LORD in the hands of the
priests, who were Levites,[g] to whom David had made assignments in the temple,[h] to present the burnt offerings of the LORD as written in the Law of Moses, with rejoicing and
singing, as David had ordered. 19 He also stationed doorkeepers[i] at the gates of the LORD's
temple so that no one who was in any way unclean might enter.
20 He took with him the commanders of hundreds, the nobles, the rulers of the people and all the people of the land and brought the king down from the temple of the LORD.
They went into the palace through the Upper Gate[j] and seated the king on the royal
throne, 21 and all the people of the land rejoiced. And the city was quiet, because Athaliah had been slain with the sword.[k]

Joash Repairs the Temple

24 Joash was seven years old when he became king, and he reigned in Jerusalem
forty years. His mother's name was Zibiah; she was from Beersheba. 2 Joash did
what was right in the eyes of the LORD[l] all the years of Jehoiada the priest. 3 Jehoiada
chose two wives for him, and he had sons and daughters.
4 Some time later Joash decided to restore the temple of the LORD. 5 He called together the priests and Levites and said to them, "Go to the towns of Judah and collect the
money[m] due annually from all Israel,[n] to repair the temple of your God. Do it now." But
the Levites[o] did not act at once.
6 Therefore the king summoned Jehoiada the chief priest and said to him, "Why
haven't you required the Levites to bring in from Judah and Jerusalem the tax imposed
by Moses the servant of the LORD and by the assembly of Israel for the Tent of the Testimony?"[p]
7 Now the sons of that wicked woman Athaliah had broken into the temple of God and
had used even its sacred objects for the Baals.
8 At the king's command, a chest was made and placed outside, at the gate of the tem-

23:11 [a]Ex 25:16; Dt 17:18; 1Sa 10:24
23:13 [b]1Ki 1:41 [c]1Ki 7:15
23:15 [d]Ne 3:28; Jer 31:40
23:16 [e]2Ch 29:10; 34:31; Ne 9:38
23:17 [f]Dt 13:6-9
23:18 [g]1Ch 23:28-32; 2Ch 5:5 [h]1Ch 23:6; 25:6
23:19 [i]1Ch 9:22
23:20 [j]2Ki 15:35
23:21 [k]2Ch 22:1
24:2 [l]2Ch 25:2; 26:5
24:5 [m]Ex 30:16; Ne 10:32-33; Mt 17:24 [n]1Ch 11:1 [o]1Ch 26:20
24:6 [p]Ex 30:12-16; Nu 1:50

a 14 Or *out from the precincts* b 16 Or *covenant between* ⌞*the LORD*⌟ *and the people and the king that they* (see 2 Kings 11:17)

23:11 copy of the covenant. Either the covenant made in verse 3 or the book of Deuteronomy (Dt 17:18–20).
23:13 trumpets . . . singers . . . musical instruments. The Chronicler added these musical details in line with his interest in temple music (see note on 1Ch 15:16–24).
23:16 made a covenant. See note on 15:12.
23:17 temple of Baal. Probably a shrine to Baal erected for Athaliah (1Ki 11:1–8).
23:18–19 The Chronicler expanded his account beyond that of 2 Kings 11:18 to indicate that the new temple order under Jehoiada and Joash was according to Mosaic and Davidic design. This emphasis reminded the postexilic readers of the standards they were to follow in their day.
23:18 rejoicing and singing, as David had ordered. The Chronicler's interest in music is once again in evidence (see note on 1Ch 15:16–24).
23:21 quiet. See note on 1 Chronicles 22:9.
▪ **24:1–27** *Joash's Kingship.* The Chronicler significantly reshaped the account of Joash's renovation of the temple in 2 Kings 12:1–21. His largest addition was in verses 15–22. Joash's kingship divides into the opening of his reign (vv. 1–3), his years of fidelity (vv. 4–14), Jehoiada's death (vv. 15–16), Joash's later years of infidelity (vv. 17–26) and the closure of his reign (v. 27).
▪ **24:1–3** *Opening of Joash's Reign.* Joash's reign began by his exhibiting faithfulness to the Lord.
24:2 all the years of Jehoiada. Joash's positive accomplishments were attributed to the influence of Jehoiada (v. 14). After Jehoiada's death, Joash turned away from the Lord (vv. 17–19; cf. 26:5). The Chronicler once again illustrated the importance of mutual support between king and priest (see note on 22:10—24:27).
▪ **24:4–14** *Joash's Early Years of Fidelity.* Joash served the Lord faithfully under the supervision of Jehoiada.
24:5 priests and Levites. The text, beyond the account of Kings (2Ki 12:1–3), emphasizes the need for proper Levitical order. **money due annually.** See verse 9. This was the half-shekel tax of Exodus 30:11–16 and 38:24–26.
24:6,9 imposed by Moses . . . Moses . . . had required. See note on 1 Chronicles 16:40.

ple of the LORD. [9]A proclamation was then issued in Judah and Jerusalem that they should
bring to the LORD the tax that Moses the servant of God had required of Israel in the desert. [10]All the officials and all the people brought their contributions gladly,[q] dropping
them into the chest until it was full. [11]Whenever the chest was brought in by the Levites
to the king's officials and they saw that there was a large amount of money, the royal secretary and the officer of the chief priest would come and empty the chest and carry it
back to its place. They did this regularly and collected a great amount of money. [12]The
king and Jehoiada gave it to the men who carried out the work required for the temple
of the LORD. They hired[r] masons and carpenters to restore the LORD's temple, and also
workers in iron and bronze to repair the temple.
[13]The men in charge of the work were diligent, and the repairs progressed under
them. They rebuilt the temple of God according to its original design and reinforced it.
[14]When they had finished, they brought the rest of the money to the king and Jehoiada,
and with it were made articles for the LORD's temple: articles for the service and for the
burnt offerings, and also dishes and other objects of gold and silver. As long as Jehoiada lived, burnt offerings were presented continually in the temple of the LORD.
[15]Now Jehoiada was old and full of years, and he died at the age of a hundred and thirty. [16]He was buried with the kings in the City of David, because of the good he had done
in Israel for God and his temple.

The Wickedness of Joash

[17]After the death of Jehoiada, the officials of Judah came and paid homage to the king,
and he listened to them. [18]They abandoned[s] the temple of the LORD, the God of their fathers, and worshiped Asherah poles and idols.[t] Because of their guilt, God's anger[u] came
upon Judah and Jerusalem. [19]Although the LORD sent prophets to the people to bring
them back to him, and though they testified against them, they would not listen.[v]
[20]Then the Spirit[w] of God came upon Zechariah[x] son of Jehoiada the priest. He stood before the people and said, "This is what God says: 'Why do you disobey the LORD's commands?
You will not prosper.[y] Because you have forsaken the LORD, he has forsaken[z] you.' "
[21]But they plotted against him, and by order of the king they stoned[a] him to death[b]
in the courtyard of the LORD's temple.[c] [22]King Joash did not remember the kindness Zechariah's father Jehoiada had shown him but killed his son, who said as he lay dying, "May
the LORD see this and call you to account."[d]
[23]At the turn of the year,[a] the army of Aram marched against Joash; it invaded Judah
and Jerusalem and killed all the leaders of the people.[e] They sent all the plunder to their
king in Damascus. [24]Although the Aramean army had come with only a few men,[f] the
LORD delivered into their hands a much larger army.[g] Because Judah had forsaken the
LORD, the God of their fathers, judgment was executed on Joash. [25]When the Arameans
withdrew, they left Joash severely wounded. His officials conspired against him for murdering the son of Jehoiada the priest, and they killed him in his bed. So he died and was
buried[h] in the City of David, but not in the tombs of the kings.
[26]Those who conspired against him were Zabad,[b] son of Shimeath an Ammonite woman, and Jehozabad, son of Shimrith[c] [i] a Moabite woman.[j] [27]The account of his sons, the many
prophecies about him, and the record of the restoration of the temple of God are written in
the annotations on the book of the kings. And Amaziah his son succeeded him as king.

24:10 [q]Ex 25:2; 1Ch 29:3,6,9
24:12 [r]2Ch 34:11
24:18 [s]ver 4; Jos 24:20; 2Ch 7:19 [t]Ex 34:13; 1Ki 14:23; 2Ch 33:3; Jer 17:2 [u]Jos 22:20; 2Ch 19:2
24:19 [v]Nu 11:29; Jer 7:25; Zec 1:4
24:20 [w]Jdg 3:10; 1Ch 12:18; 2Ch 20:14 [x]Mt 23:35; Lk 11:51 [y]Nu 14:41 [z]Dt 31:17; 2Ch 15:2
24:21 [a]Jos 7:25; Ac 7:58-59 [b]Ne 9:26; Jer 26:21 [c]Jer 20:2; Mt 23:35
24:22 [d]Ge 9:5
24:23 [e]2Ki 12:17-18
24:24 [f]2Ch 14:9; 16:8; 20:2,12 [g]Lev 26:23-25; Dt 28:25
24:25 [h]2Ch 21:20
24:26 [i]2Ki 12:21 [j]Ru 1:4

[a] *23* Probably in the spring [b] *26* A variant of *Jozabad* [c] *26* A variant of *Shomer*

24:10–12 brought their contributions gladly. The generous and joyful giving of the officials and people was exemplary for the postexilic audience who needed to contribute freely to the new temple (see note on 1Ch 29:1–9).
24:15–22 The Chronicler added this material to depict the serious consequences of Joash's infidelity after Jehoiada's death.
■ **24:15–16** *Jehoiada's Death.* The loss of Jehoiada proved to be Joash's downfall.
■ **24:17–26** *Joash's Later Years of Infidelity.* With Jehoiada gone Joash resisted the prophetic word and suffered God's wrath.
24:17 the officials of Judah . . . he listened to them. Compare the priestly instruction given to kings in verse 20 and in 26:17–18.
24:18 Asherah poles. See NIV text note on 14:3.
24:19 prophets . . . they would not listen. As he had done frequently, the author tied apostasy to the rejection of God's prophets (see note on 20:20).
24:20–22 Zechariah son of Jehoiada the priest. The extent of Joash's apostasy is illustrated by his refusal to listen to priestly instruction and by his plot to murder Jehoiada's son Zechariah (see note on 26:17).
24:20 you have forsaken the LORD, he has forsaken you. See note on 1 Chronicles 28:9.
24:23–24 the army of Aram . . . invaded Judah. The Chronicler frequently mentioned military defeat as the judgment of God against sin (1Ch 10:1–14; 2Ch 13:1–16; 18:33–34; 21:16–17; 25:14–24; 28:1–5; 33:1–11).
24:24 Aramean army had come with only a few men. The tables were turned against Judah as had been threatened in the covenant (see note on 1Ch 19:6–7).
24:25 not in the tombs of the kings. His burial contrasted with that of Jehoiada (v. 16). See note on 21:19.
24:26 Ammonite . . . Moabite. This incident contrasts with Jehoshaphat's earlier defeat of their peoples (see note on 20:1–30).
■ **24:27** *Closure of Joash's Reign.* Joash died and was succeeded by his son Amaziah.
24:27 annotations on the book of the kings. See "Introduction to 1 Chronicles: Author."

Amaziah King of Judah

25 Amaziah was twenty-five years old when he became king, and he reigned in Jerusalem twenty-nine years. His mother's name was Jehoaddin[a]; she was from
Jerusalem. 2 He did what was right in the eyes of the LORD, but not wholeheartedly.[k] 3 After the kingdom was firmly in his control, he executed the officials who had murdered
his father the king. 4 Yet he did not put their sons to death, but acted in accordance with
what is written in the Law, in the Book of Moses,[l] where the LORD commanded: "Fathers
shall not be put to death for their children, nor children put to death for their fathers;
each is to die for his own sins."[b][m]
5 Amaziah called the people of Judah together and assigned them according to their families to commanders of thousands and commanders of hundreds for all Judah and Benjamin. He then mustered[n] those twenty years old[o] or more and found that there were three
hundred thousand men ready for military service,[p] able to handle the spear and shield. 6 He
also hired a hundred thousand fighting men from Israel for a hundred talents[c] of silver.
7 But a man of God came to him and said, "O king, these troops from Israel[q] must not
march with you, for the LORD is not with Israel—not with any of the people of Ephraim.
8 Even if you go and fight courageously in battle, God will overthrow you before the enemy, for God has the power to help or to overthrow."[r]
9 Amaziah asked the man of God, "But what about the hundred talents I paid for these
Israelite troops?"
The man of God replied, "The LORD can give you much more than that."[s]
10 So Amaziah dismissed the troops who had come to him from Ephraim and sent
them home. They were furious with Judah and left for home in a great rage.[t]
11 Amaziah then marshaled his strength and led his army to the Valley of Salt, where he
killed ten thousand men of Seir. 12 The army of Judah also captured ten thousand men alive,
took them to the top of a cliff and threw them down so that all were dashed to pieces.[u]
13 Meanwhile the troops that Amaziah had sent back and had not allowed to take part
in the war raided Judean towns from Samaria to Beth Horon. They killed three thousand
people and carried off great quantities of plunder.
14 When Amaziah returned from slaughtering the Edomites, he brought back the
gods of the people of Seir. He set them up as his own gods,[v] bowed down to them and
burned sacrifices to them. 15 The anger of the LORD burned against Amaziah, and he sent
a prophet to him, who said, "Why do you consult this people's gods, which could not
save[w] their own people from your hand?"
16 While he was still speaking, the king said to him, "Have we appointed you an adviser to the king? Stop! Why be struck down?"

25:2 [k]ver 14; 1Ki 8:61; 2Ch 24:2
25:4 [l]Dt 28:61 [m]Nu 26:11; Dt 24:16
25:5 [n]2Sa 24:2 [o]Ex 30:14 [p]Nu 1:3; 1Ch 21:1; 2Ch 17:14-19
25:7 [q]2Ch 16:2-9; 19:1-3
25:8 [r]2Ch 14:11; 20:6
25:9 [s]Dt 8:18; Pr 10:22
25:10 [t]ver 13
25:12 [u]Ps 141:6; Ob 1:3
25:14 [v]Ex 20:3; 2Ch 28:23; Isa 44:15
25:15 [w]Ps 96:5; Isa 36:20

[a] *1* Hebrew *Jehoaddan,* a variant of *Jehoaddin* [b] *4* Deut. 24:16 [c] *6* That is, about 3 3/4 tons (about 3.4 metric tons); also in verse 9

■ **25:1—28:27** *Deterioration Through Halfhearted Obedience.* The final phase of the divided kingdom includes the reigns of Amaziah (25:1–28), Uzziah (26:1–23), Jotham (27:1–9) and Ahaz (28:1–27). Many themes appear in these chapters, but the material is unified by the observation that Amaziah did not serve God wholeheartedly (see 25:2), by the alignment of the following kings with him (26:4; 27:2) and by the defeat of Ahaz by Israel (cf. 25:14–24; 28:6:15).

■ **25:1–28** *Amaziah's Reign.* The account of Amaziah's reign opens and closes with material taken from Kings (cf. 2Ki 14:1–6 with vv. 1–4; 2Ki 14:8–20 with vv. 17–28). The middle portion of the account (vv. 5–16) was added by the Chronicler from other source document(s) no longer available. Amaziah's reign is divided into five parts: its opening (vv. 1–2), Amaziah's halfhearted obedience and victory (vv. 3–12), trouble from Israel (v. 13), Amaziah's disobedience and defeat (vv. 14–24), a summary of his reign and an account of his death (vv. 25–28). The Chronicler focused on how foreign alliances, response to prophetic instruction and syncretism affected Israel's military security. His account divides between fidelity and infidelity, much like his records of the reigns of Joash and Uzziah (see note on 22:10—24:27).

■ **25:1–2** *Opening of Amaziah's Reign.* Amaziah's reign was marked by some obedience to God, but not by love for him.

25:1 Amaziah. Reigned from 796–767 B.C.

25:2 did what was right . . . but not wholeheartedly. The Chronicler omitted some of the harsh condemnation of Amaziah found in 2 Kings 14:3–4, but he admitted that Amaziah had significant flaws.

■ **25:3–12** *Amaziah's Halfhearted Fidelity.* Amaziah failed to be wholeheartedly devoted to the Lord, but he did respond appropriately to the prophetic warning (see note on 20:20).

25:4 Book of Moses. See 1 Chronicles 16:40.

25:5–12 The text expands 2 Kings 14:7 to report Amaziah's dramatic victory over Edom.

25:5–6 three hundred thousand . . . a hundred thousand. For these large numbers, see note on 1 Chronicles 12:23–37.

25:7 troops from Israel must not march. The Chronicler again condemned an alliance with the northern kingdom (see note on 16:2). **the LORD is not with Israel . . . Ephraim.** Abijah had voiced a similar opinion concerning the northern kingdom (see note on 13:12).

25:8 God has the power. In typical fashion, the author proclaimed the need to rely solely upon divine power in battle (see note on 16:2).

25:10 furious with Judah . . . rage. Although Amaziah obeyed the prophetic word, the northern mercenaries were angry. Their anger probably stemmed from the loss of booty (v. 13).

25:12 all were dashed to pieces. Amaziah followed Mosaic instructions for holy war (Dt 20:13–18).

■ **25:13** *Amaziah's Trouble From Israel.* This section is comprised of a brief note forming a transition between the two periods of Amaziah's reign.

■ **25:14–24** *Amaziah's Infidelity.* The Chronicler here contrasted Amaziah's early victory with his later defeat due to syncretism (combining worship of the Lord with the worship of other gods).

25:14 brought back the gods. In contrast with Amaziah's earlier obedience (v. 12), the Chronicler reported that Amaziah disobeyed Mosaic instructions (Ex 20:3; Dt 7:25) and David's example (1Ch 14:12) by bringing the Edomite gods to Jerusalem. He eventually worshiped these gods.

25:15–16 "Stop! Why be struck down?" In contrast with his earlier repentance at the prophetic word (vv. 7–10), Amaziah now

So the prophet stopped but said, "I know that God has determined to destroy you, because you have done this and have not listened to my counsel."
17 After Amaziah king of Judah consulted his advisers, he sent this challenge to Jehoash[a] son of Jehoahaz, the son of Jehu, king of Israel: "Come, meet me face to face."
18 But Jehoash king of Israel replied to Amaziah king of Judah: "A thistle[x] in Lebanon
sent a message to a cedar in Lebanon, 'Give your daughter to my son in marriage.' Then
a wild beast in Lebanon came along and trampled the thistle underfoot. 19 You say to
yourself that you have defeated Edom, and now you are arrogant and proud. But stay at
home! Why ask for trouble and cause your own downfall and that of Judah also?"
20 Amaziah, however, would not listen, for God so worked that he might hand them
over to ⌊Jehoash⌋, because they sought the gods of Edom.[y] 21 So Jehoash king of Israel attacked. He and Amaziah king of Judah faced each other at Beth Shemesh in Judah. 22 Judah was routed by Israel, and every man fled to his home. 23 Jehoash king of Israel captured Amaziah king of Judah, the son of Joash, the son of Ahaziah,[b] at Beth Shemesh.
Then Jehoash brought him to Jerusalem and broke down the wall of Jerusalem from the
Ephraim Gate[z] to the Corner Gate[a]—a section about six hundred feet[c] long. 24 He took
all the gold and silver and all the articles found in the temple of God that had been in the
care of Obed-Edom,[b] together with the palace treasures and the hostages, and returned
to Samaria.
25 Amaziah son of Joash king of Judah lived for fifteen years after the death of Jehoash
son of Jehoahaz king of Israel. 26 As for the other events of Amaziah's reign, from beginning to end, are they not written in the book of the kings of Judah and Israel? 27 From the
time that Amaziah turned away from following the LORD, they conspired against him in
Jerusalem and he fled to Lachish[c], but they sent men after him to Lachish and killed him
there. 28 He was brought back by horse and was buried with his fathers in the City of Judah.

Uzziah King of Judah

26 Then all the people of Judah[d] took Uzziah,[d] who was sixteen years old, and
made him king in place of his father Amaziah. 2 He was the one who rebuilt Elath
and restored it to Judah after Amaziah rested with his fathers.
3 Uzziah was sixteen years old when he became king, and he reigned in Jerusalem fifty-two years. His mother's name was Jecoliah; she was from Jerusalem. 4 He did what was
right in the eyes of the LORD, just as his father Amaziah had done. 5 He sought God during the days of Zechariah, who instructed him in the fear[e] of God.[e] As long as he sought
the LORD, God gave him success.[f]
6 He went to war against the Philistines[g] and broke down the walls of Gath, Jabneh
and Ashdod.[h] He then rebuilt towns near Ashdod and elsewhere among the Philistines.
7 God helped him against the Philistines and against the Arabs[i] who lived in Gur Baal and
against the Meunites.[j] 8 The Ammonites[k] brought tribute to Uzziah, and his fame spread
as far as the border of Egypt, because he had become very powerful.

25:18 [x]Jdg 9:8-15
25:20 [y]1Ki 12:15; 2Ch 10:15; 22:7
25:23 [z]2Ki 14:13; Ne 8:16; 12:39 [a]2Ch 26:9; Jer 31:38
25:24 [b]1Ch 26:15
25:27 [c]Jos 10:3
26:1 [d]2Ch 22:1
26:5 [e]2Ch 15:2; 24:2; Da 1:17 [f]2Ch 27:6
26:6 [g]Isa 2:6; 11:14; 14:29; Jer 25:20 [h]Am 1:8; 3:9
26:7 [i]2Ch 21:16 [j]2Ch 20:1
26:8 [k]Ge 19:38; 2Ch 17:11

[a] *17* Hebrew *Joash,* a variant of *Jehoash;* also in verses 18, 21, 23 and 25 [b] *23* Hebrew *Jehoahaz,* a variant of *Ahaziah* [c] *23* Hebrew *four hundred cubits* (about 180 meters) [d] *1* Also called *Azariah*
[e] *5* Many Hebrew manuscripts, Septuagint and Syriac; other Hebrew manuscripts *vision*

rebuffed the prophet and received in response a stern warning (see note on 20:20).

25:15 consult this people's gods. See note on 7:14.

25:16 God has determined to destroy you. See note on 1 Chronicles 28:9.

25:20 Amaziah . . . would not listen, for God so worked. The sovereignty of God extends to hardening the hearts of sinners so that they will not respond to warnings (see note on 1Ch 21:1). **sought the gods.** See note on 7:14.

25:22–24 Judah was routed by Israel. The defeat of Amaziah contrasts with his earlier victory (vv. 11–13).

■ **25:25–28** *Closure of Amaziah's Reign.* Because Amaziah had turned away from God, God allowed him to be hunted down and killed by conspirators.

25:26 book of the kings. See "Introduction to 1 Chronicles: Author."

■ **26:1–23** *Uzziah's Reign.* The Chronicler expanded the brief notices given to Uzziah in Kings. He incorporated some material from Kings (cf. vv. 1–4 with 2Ki 14:21–22 and 15:1–3; vv. 21–23 with 2Ki 15:5–7) and added a middle section (vv. 5–20) based on other sources no longer available. He presented Uzziah's reign in four segments: Uzziah's rise to power (vv. 1–5), obedience and blessing (vv. 6–15), disobedience and a curse (vv. 16–21) and a summary of his reign and death (vv. 22–23). The account of Uzziah's reign is patterned after those of his father and grandfather (see notes on 22:10—24:27; 25:1–28).

■ **26:1–5** *Opening of Uzziah's Reign.* Uzziah's reign began well because he was faithful to the Lord.

26:1 Uzziah. Reigned from 792/91–740/39 B.C. The book of Kings frequently (though not always) uses the name *Azariah* for the same king. Uzziah may have been his throne name and Azariah his personal name. See NIV text note and note on 1 Chronicles 3:10–16.

26:4 as his father Amaziah. The Chronicler explicitly compared Uzziah with his father, whose reign he also presented as divided between blessing and curse (see note on vv. 1–23).

26:5 sought God . . . sought the LORD. See note on 7:14. **during the days of Zechariah.** An unknown royal advisor. He may have been associated with Isaiah (Isa 8:2), but this identification is uncertain. As Joash was obedient so long as Jehoiada lived, so Uzziah did well under Zechariah's tutelage (see note on 24:2).

■ **26:6–15** *Uzziah's Fidelity and Blessing.* The Chronicler illustrated Uzziah's blessings in international conflict (vv. 6–8), domestic affairs (vv. 9–10) and military strength (vv. 11–15).

26:7 Meunites. See note on 20:1. Uzziah's blessing recalls Jehoshaphat's victory (20:1–30).

26:8 Ammonites. See note on 1 Chronicles 19:1.

9 Uzziah built towers in Jerusalem at the Corner Gate,[l] at the Valley Gate[m] and at the
angle of the wall, and he fortified them. 10 He also built towers in the desert and dug many
cisterns, because he had much livestock in the foothills and in the plain. He had people
working his fields and vineyards in the hills and in the fertile lands, for he loved the soil.
11 Uzziah had a well-trained army, ready to go out by divisions according to their numbers as mustered by Jeiel the secretary and Maaseiah the officer under the direction of
Hananiah, one of the royal officials. 12 The total number of family leaders over the fighting men was 2,600. 13 Under their command was an army of 307,500 men trained for
war, a powerful force to support the king against his enemies. 14 Uzziah provided shields,
spears, helmets, coats of armor, bows and slingstones for the entire army.[n] 15 In Jerusalem he made machines designed by skillful men for use on the towers and on the corner defenses to shoot arrows and hurl large stones. His fame spread far and wide, for he
was greatly helped until he became powerful.
16 But after Uzziah became powerful, his pride[o] led to his downfall.[p] He was unfaithful[q] to the LORD his God, and entered the temple of the LORD to burn incense[r] on the altar of incense. 17 Azariah[s] the priest with eighty other courageous priests of the LORD followed him in. 18 They confronted him and said, "It is not right for you, Uzziah, to burn
incense to the LORD. That is for the priests,[t] the descendants[u] of Aaron,[v] who have been
consecrated to burn incense.[w] Leave the sanctuary, for you have been unfaithful; and
you will not be honored by the LORD God."
19 Uzziah, who had a censer in his hand ready to burn incense, became angry. While
he was raging at the priests in their presence before the incense altar in the LORD's temple, leprosy[a][x] broke out on his forehead. 20 When Azariah the chief priest and all the other priests looked at him, they saw that he had leprosy on his forehead, so they hurried
him out. Indeed, he himself was eager to leave, because the LORD had afflicted him.
21 King Uzziah had leprosy until the day he died. He lived in a separate house[b][y]—leprous, and excluded from the temple of the LORD. Jotham his son had charge of the palace and governed the people of the land.
22 The other events of Uzziah's reign, from beginning to end, are recorded by the
prophet Isaiah[z] son of Amoz. 23 Uzziah[a] rested with his fathers and was buried near them
in a field for burial that belonged to the kings, for people said, "He had leprosy." And Jotham his son succeeded him as king.[b]

Jotham King of Judah

27 Jotham[c] was twenty-five years old when he became king, and he reigned in Jerusalem sixteen years. His mother's name was Jerusha daughter of Zadok. 2 He
did what was right in the eyes of the LORD, just as his father Uzziah had done, but unlike
him he did not enter the temple of the LORD. The people, however, continued their cor-

26:9 [l]2Ki 14:13; 2Ch 25:23 [m]Ne 2:13; 3:13
26:14 [n]Jer 46:4
26:16 [o]2Ki 14:10 [p]Dt 32:15; 2Ch 25:19 [q]1Ch 5:25 [r]2Ki 16:12
26:17 [s]1Ki 4:2; 1Ch 6:10
26:18 [t]Nu 16:39 [u]Nu 18:1-7 [v]Ex 30:7 [w]1Ch 6:49
26:19 [x]Nu 12:10; 2Ki 5:25-27
26:21 [y]Ex 1:6; Lev 13:46; 14:8; Nu 5:2; 19:12
26:22 [z]2Ki 15:1; Isa 1:1; 6:1
26:23 [a]Isa 1:1; 6:1 [b]2Ki 14:21; 15:7; Am 1:1
27:1 [c]2Ki 15:5, 32; 1Ch 3:12

[a] *19* The Hebrew word was used for various diseases affecting the skin—not necessarily leprosy; also in verses 20, 21 and 23. [b] *21* *Or in a house where he was relieved of responsibilities*

26:9 Uzziah built. A reversal of the destruction in Amaziah's defeat (25:23). See note on 1 Chronicles 11:4–9.
26:13 307,500 men. For a possible explanation of the large number see note on 1 Chronicles 12:23–37.
26:15 machines. Probably defensive structures on the city towers.
▪ **26:16–21** *Uzziah's Infidelity and Curse.* The Chronicler turned to an event that illustrated God's judgment against Uzziah's pride. As with Rehoboam (12:1), initial success led to disregard for God and his law. The Chronicler expanded the brief notice of Uzziah's leprosy in 2 Kings 15:5.
26:16 pride. Moses had earlier warned the Israelites to take heed lest their success lead to the pride of relying on self rather than on God (Dt 8:10–18).
26:17 Azariah. An otherwise unknown priest. He and 80 other courageous priests delivered God's judgment to Uzziah. Compare the courage of Zechariah (24:20–22). The Chronicler for a third time highlighted the role of priests as instructors of royalty (cf. 24:17,20).
26:18 That is for the priests. In Mosaic legislation burning incense was restricted to the priests (Ex 30:7–9; Nu 16:39–40). The Chronicler revealed his concern for proper observance of temple regulations (see note on 1Ch 6:1–81). See *WCF* 23.3.
26:20 leprosy. Uzziah's disease is depicted as punishment for his sin (16:12; 21:15,18–19; also Dt 28:58–61).
26:21 excluded from the temple. Uzziah was quarantined and restricted from entering the temple, in accord with Mosaic legislation (Lev 13:46; Nu 5:1–4).
▪ **26:22–23** *Closure of Uzziah's Reign.* Uzziah died and was succeeded by his son Jotham.
26:22 recorded by the prophet Isaiah. See "Introduction to 1 Chronicles: Author."
26:23 in a field. Uzziah was buried away from the royal family because of his leprosy.
▪ **27:1–9** *Jotham's Reign.* The Chronicler followed the brief account of Jotham's reign in Kings (2Ki 15:33–38) but added the material in verses 3b–6 and omitted that in 2 Kings 15:37. Unlike the record from Joash to Uzziah, where each reign was balanced between obedience and disobedience (see note on 22:10—24:27), the Chronicler made a fully positive evaluation of Jotham. This positive portrait stands in contrast with the fully negative treatment of Ahaz that follows (28:1–27). The Chronicler focused on fidelity to God as the way to success in construction projects and military conflict. The material divides into three parts: Jotham's rise (vv. 1–2), his positive accomplishments (vv. 3–6) and a summary of his reign and death (vv. 7–9).
27:1 Jotham . . . sixteen years. Reigned from 750–732/31 B.C. Jotham's reign overlapped with those of Uzziah (750–740 B.C.) and Ahaz (735–732/31 B.C.). The 16 years may be calculated inclusively from the time of his accession to the time of Ahaz's accession.
27:2 did not enter the temple. Jotham did not violate priestly regulations as Uzziah had done (see note on 26:17). **The people, however, continued.** The Chronicler explained that culpability for continuing corruption rested with the people and not with Jotham (cf. 2Ki 15:35).

rupt practices. 3Jotham rebuilt the Upper Gate of the temple of the LORD and did extensive work on the wall at the hill of Ophel.[d] 4He built towns in the Judean hills and forts
and towers in the wooded areas.
5Jotham made war on the king of the Ammonites[e] and conquered them. That year the
Ammonites paid him a hundred talents[a] of silver, ten thousand cors[b] of wheat and ten
thousand cors of barley. The Ammonites brought him the same amount also in the second and third years.
6Jotham grew powerful[f] because he walked steadfastly before the LORD his God.
7The other events in Jotham's reign, including all his wars and the other things he did,
are written in the book of the kings of Israel and Judah. 8He was twenty-five years old
when he became king, and he reigned in Jerusalem sixteen years. 9Jotham rested with
his fathers and was buried in the City of David. And Ahaz his son succeeded him as king.

Ahaz King of Judah

28 Ahaz[g] was twenty years old when he became king, and he reigned in Jerusalem
sixteen years. Unlike David his father, he did not do what was right in the eyes
of the LORD. 2He walked in the ways of the kings of Israel and also made cast idols[h] for
worshiping the Baals. 3He burned sacrifices in the Valley of Ben Hinnom[i] and sacrificed
his sons[j] in the fire, following the detestable[k] ways of the nations the LORD had driven
out before the Israelites. 4He offered sacrifices and burned incense at the high places,
on the hilltops and under every spreading tree.
5Therefore the LORD his God handed him over to the king of Aram.[l] The Arameans defeated him and took many of his people as prisoners and brought them to Damascus.
He was also given into the hands of the king of Israel, who inflicted heavy casualties
on him. 6In one day Pekah[m] son of Remaliah killed a hundred and twenty thousand soldiers in Judah[n]—because Judah had forsaken the LORD, the God of their fathers. 7Zicri,
an Ephraimite warrior, killed Maaseiah the king's son, Azrikam the officer in charge of
the palace, and Elkanah, second to the king. 8The Israelites took captive from their kinsmen[o] two hundred thousand wives, sons and daughters. They also took a great deal of
plunder, which they carried back to Samaria.[p]
9But a prophet of the LORD named Oded was there, and he went out to meet the army
when it returned to Samaria. He said to them, "Because the LORD, the God of your fathers, was angry[q] with Judah, he gave them into your hand. But you have slaughtered
them in a rage that reaches to heaven.[r] 10And now you intend to make the men and
women of Judah and Jerusalem your slaves.[s] But aren't you also guilty of sins against the
LORD your God? 11Now listen to me! Send back your fellow countrymen you have taken
as prisoners, for the LORD's fierce anger rests on you.[t]"
12Then some of the leaders in Ephraim—Azariah son of Jehohanan, Berekiah son of
Meshillemoth, Jehizkiah son of Shallum, and Amasa son of Hadlai—confronted those
who were arriving from the war. 13"You must not bring those prisoners here," they said,
"or we will be guilty before the LORD. Do you intend to add to our sin and guilt? For our
guilt is already great, and his fierce anger rests on Israel."

27:3 [d]2Ch 33:14; Ne 3:26
27:5 [e]Ge 19:38
27:6 [f]2Ch 26:5
28:1 [g]1Ch 3:13; Isa 1:1
28:2 [h]Ex 34:17; 2Ch 22:3
28:3 [i]Jos 15:8; 2Ki 23:10 [j]Lev 18:21; 2Ki 3:27; 2Ch 33:6; Eze 20:26 [k]Dt 18:9; 2Ch 33:2
28:5 [l]Isa 7:1
28:6 [m]2Ki 15:25,27 [n]ver 8; Isa 9:21; 11:13
28:8 [o]Dt 28:25-41; 2Ch 11:4 [p]2Ch 29:9
28:9 [q]2Ch 25:15; Isa 10:6; 47:6; Zec 1:15 [r]Ezr 9:6; Rev 18:5
28:10 [s]Lev 25:39-46
28:11 [t]2Ch 11:4; Jas 2:13

[a] 5 That is, about 3 3/4 tons (about 3.4 metric tons) [b] 5 That is, probably about 62,000 bushels (about 2,200 kiloliters)

27:3–6 Jotham rebuilt . . . He built . . . made war. The Chronicler apparently added these verses to demonstrate divine approval of Jotham in his successful building projects (see note on 1Ch 11:4–9) and victory in war.
27:7 in the book of the kings. See "Introduction to 1 Chronicles: Author."
■ **28:1–27** *Ahaz's Reign.* The Chronicler loosely followed the record of Ahaz in Kings at the beginning (cf. vv. 1–4 with 2Ki 16:2–4) and end (cf. vv. 22–27 with 2Ki 16:10–11,19–20) of his account. He added much new material in the middle portion (vv. 5–21) from other sources no longer available. He reported Ahaz's rise (vv. 1–5), the contrasting fidelity of the northern kingdom (vv. 6–15), Ahaz's infidelity (vv. 16–25) and his death (vv. 26–27). Ahaz's reign contrasted sharply with his father's (see note on 27:1–9), and the account focuses on how infidelity led to military defeat.
■ **28:1–5** *Opening of Ahaz's Reign.* From the very beginning, Ahaz was unfaithful to the Lord.
28:1 Ahaz . . . sixteen years. Ahaz reigned from 735–716/15 B.C. He was coregent with Jotham from 735–732 B.C. and sole monarch of Judah from 732–716/15 B.C.
28:3 sacrificed his sons. Ahaz's apostasy was so severe that he practiced human sacrifice (cf. Lev 18:21; Dt 12:31; 18:10; 2Ki 16:3; 17:17; 21:6; 23:10; 2Ch 33:6; Ps 106:37–38; Isa 57:5; Jer 7:30–31; 19:5; 32:35; Eze 16:20–21; Mic 6:7). The traditional (Masoretic) Hebrew text of 2 Kings 16:3 reads "son," but some Septuagint (Greek translation of the OT) manuscripts read "sons," as does Chronicles.
28:5 king of Aram . . . king of Israel. Rezin (king of Aram) and Pekah (king of Israel) joined forces against Ahaz (2Ki 16:5–6; Isa 7:1–14). The author dealt with these kings separately, evidently to highlight the reaction of the northern kingdom to the prophet's word (vv. 9–15).
■ **28:6–15** *Northern Israel's Fidelity to God.* The Chronicler contrasts the northern kingdom with Ahaz, who was defeated in battle because of divine judgment for his flagrant apostasy (vv. 5–6).
28:9–15 The Chronicler broke from his usual pattern of focusing on the southern kingdom to report that some citizens of the northern kingdom gave heed to the prophetic rebuke. The actions of these Israelites contrasted with the apostasy at that time in Judah. These events set the stage for Hezekiah's later evaluation of the north and south (see notes on 20:20 and 29:4–11).
28:11 the LORD's fierce anger rests on you. See note on 1 Chronicles 28:9.

14 So the soldiers gave up the prisoners and plunder in the presence of the officials and
all the assembly. 15 The men designated by name took the prisoners, and from the plunder they clothed all who were naked. They provided them with clothes and sandals, food
and drink,[u] and healing balm. All those who were weak they put on donkeys. So they
took them back to their fellow countrymen at Jericho, the City of Palms,[v] and returned
to Samaria.
16 At that time King Ahaz sent to the king[a] of Assyria[w] for help. 17 The Edomites[x] had
again come and attacked Judah and carried away prisoners,[y] 18 while the Philistines[z] had
raided towns in the foothills and in the Negev of Judah. They captured and occupied Beth
Shemesh, Aijalon[a] and Gederoth, as well as Soco, Timnah and Gimzo, with their surrounding villages. 19 The LORD had humbled Judah because of Ahaz king of Israel,[b] for he
had promoted wickedness in Judah and had been most unfaithful[b] to the LORD. 20 Tiglath-
Pileser[c][c] king of Assyria came to him, but he gave him trouble instead of help.[d] 21 Ahaz
took some of the things from the temple of the LORD and from the royal palace and from
the princes and presented them to the king of Assyria, but that did not help him.
22 In his time of trouble King Ahaz became even more unfaithful[e] to the LORD. 23 He offered sacrifices to the gods[f] of Damascus, who had defeated him; for he thought, "Since
the gods of the kings of Aram have helped them, I will sacrifice to them so they will help
me."[g] But they were his downfall and the downfall of all Israel.
24 Ahaz gathered together the furnishings from the temple of God[h] and took them
away.[d] He shut the doors[i] of the LORD's temple and set up altars[j] at every street corner
in Jerusalem. 25 In every town in Judah he built high places to burn sacrifices to other gods
and provoked the LORD, the God of his fathers, to anger.
26 The other events of his reign and all his ways, from beginning to end, are written
in the book of the kings of Judah and Israel. 27 Ahaz rested[k] with his fathers and was buried[l] in the city of Jerusalem, but he was not placed in the tombs of the kings of Israel. And
Hezekiah his son succeeded him as king.

Hezekiah Purifies the Temple

29 Hezekiah[m] was twenty-five years old when he became king, and he reigned in
Jerusalem twenty-nine years. His mother's name was Abijah daughter of Zechariah. 2 He did what was right in the eyes of the LORD, just as his father David[n] had done.
3 In the first month of the first year of his reign, he opened the doors of the temple of
the LORD and repaired[o] them. 4 He brought in the priests and the Levites, assembled them

28:15 [u]2Ki 6:22; Pr 25:21-22 [v]Dt 34:3; Jdg 1:16
28:16 [w]2Ki 16:7
28:17 [x]Ps 137:7; Isa 34:5 [y]2Ch 29:9
28:18 [z]Eze 16:27,57 [a]Jos 10:12
28:19 [b]2Ch 21:2
28:20 [c]2Ki 15:29; 1Ch 5:6 [d]2Ki 16:7
28:22 [e]Jer 5:3
28:23 [f]2Ch 25:14 [g]Jer 44:17-18
28:24 [h]2Ki 16:18 [i]2Ch 29:7 [j]2Ch 30:14
28:27 [k]Isa 14:28-32 [l]2Ch 21:20; 24:25
29:1 [m]1Ch 3:13
29:2 [n]2Ch 28:1; 34:2
29:3 [o]2Ch 28:24

a *16* One Hebrew manuscript, Septuagint and Vulgate (see also 2 Kings 16:7); most Hebrew manuscripts *kings* b *19* That is, Judah, as frequently in 2 Chronicles c *20* Hebrew *Tilgath-Pilneser,* a variant of *Tiglath-Pileser* d *24* Or *and cut them up*

■ **28:16–25** *Ahaz's Infidelity to God.* Ahaz revealed his lack of trust in God by turning to Assyria (vv. 16–21) and to the gods of Aram (Syria) (vv. 22–25).

28:16–21 sent to the king of Assyria for help. The Chronicler continued to recount Ahaz's failures by reporting his reliance on Tiglath-Pileser of Assyria (745–727 B.C.). See note on 16:2.

28:19 humbled Judah. Or "subdued Judah." See the contrasts with 13:18 and 1 Chronicles 20:4.

28:21 took . . . from the temple of the LORD. See note on 16:2. **did not help him.** Tiglath-Pileser of Assyria gave some temporary relief from the threats of Aram and Israel (2Ki 16:7–9), but Judah became subservient to Assyria.

28:22–25 He offered sacrifices to the gods of Damascus. Ahaz turned to the gods of Aram and of other nations for help; they were, of course, unable to rescue him.

28:24–25 shut the doors of the LORD's temple. The Chronicler expanded the account in Kings (2Ki 16:17–18) to show that Ahaz had completely closed the temple in Jerusalem (see note on 29:3).

28:25 built high places. See note on 21:11.

■ **28:26–27** *Closure of Ahaz's Reign.* Ahaz died and was succeeded by his son Hezekiah.

28:26 the book of the kings of Judah and Israel. See "Introduction to 1 Chronicles: Author."

28:27 not . . . tombs. See 21:19.

■ **29:1—36:23** *The Reunited Kingdom.* In the Chronicler's outlook, the reign of Hezekiah began a new era in the history of Israel. The northern kingdom had been destroyed by the Assyrians, and only Judah remained. Hezekiah evaluated the north and south equally and joined representatives from both kingdoms to form a reunited kingdom with one king and one temple in Jerusalem. From this time forward, the experiences of blessings and trials, exile and deliverance, were the joint experiences of a reunited people. This portion of the history stresses the importance of unity among the people of God, both then and now. See "Introduction to 1 Chronicles: Purpose and Distinctives."

■ **29:1—32:33** *Hezekiah's Reign.* The Chronicler devoted more attention to Hezekiah than to any other king, with the exceptions of David and Solomon. He incorporated material from 2 Kings 18:1—20:21 but deviated from the Kings commentary more than usual, especially in his extensive account of Hezekiah's temple reforms and Passover celebration (29:3—31:1). He presented Hezekiah's reign as a return to the glory of Solomon's kingdom. Hezekiah reunited the people (30:25) and restored the temple and its ceremonies (29:3—31:1). The record divides into four main parts: the opening (29:1–2), the reestablishment of worship (29:3—31:21), Hezekiah's inconsistencies (32:1–31) and the closure of his reign (32:32–33).

29:1–36 See *WCF* 23.3; 31.2.

■ **29:1–2** *Opening of Hezekiah's Reign.* Hezekiah was so obedient to the Lord that he was compared to David.

29:1 Hezekiah . . . twenty-nine years. He reigned from 716/15–687/86 B.C.

■ **29:3—31:21** *Hezekiah Reestablishes Temple Worship.* The account of Hezekiah's temple renovation includes the initiation of temple services (29:3–36), the Passover celebration (30:1—31:1) and the provisions for the temple (31:2–21).

■ **29:3–36** *Hezekiah Initiates Temple Service.* The restoration of the temple involved many activities, including opening the building, restoring the priesthood and instituting sacrifices.

29:3–11 brought in the priests and the Levites. The Chronicler added this material in line with his interest in the Levites (see note on 1Ch 6:1–81).

29:3 opened the doors . . . and repaired them. Hezekiah overturned the actions of his father, Ahaz (see note on 28:24–25), and

in the square on the east side 5and said: "Listen to me, Levites! Consecrate[p] yourselves
now and consecrate the temple of the LORD, the God of your fathers. Remove all defilement from the sanctuary. 6Our fathers[q] were unfaithful;[r] they did evil in the eyes of the
LORD our God and forsook him. They turned their faces away from the LORD's dwelling
place and turned their backs on him. 7They also shut the doors of the portico and put out
the lamps. They did not burn incense or present any burnt offerings at the sanctuary to
the God of Israel. 8Therefore, the anger of the LORD has fallen on Judah and Jerusalem;
he has made them an object of dread and horror[s] and scorn,[t] as you can see with your
own eyes. 9This is why our fathers have fallen by the sword and why our sons and daughters and our wives are in captivity.[u] 10Now I intend to make a covenant[v] with the LORD,
the God of Israel, so that his fierce anger will turn away from us. 11My sons, do not be
negligent now, for the LORD has chosen you to stand before him and serve him,[w] to minister[x] before him and to burn incense."
12Then these Levites[y] set to work:

from the Kohathites,
  Mahath son of Amasai and Joel son of Azariah;
from the Merarites,
  Kish son of Abdi and Azariah son of Jehallelel;
from the Gershonites,
  Joah son of Zimmah and Eden[z] son of Joah;
13from the descendants of Elizaphan,
  Shimri and Jeiel;
from the descendants of Asaph,[a]
  Zechariah and Mattaniah;
14from the descendants of Heman,
  Jehiel and Shimei;
from the descendants of Jeduthun,
  Shemaiah and Uzziel.

15When they had assembled their brothers and consecrated themselves, they went in
to purify[b] the temple of the LORD, as the king had ordered, following the word of the LORD.
16The priests went into the sanctuary of the LORD to purify it. They brought out to the
courtyard of the LORD's temple everything unclean that they found in the temple of the
LORD. The Levites took it and carried it out to the Kidron Valley.[c] 17They began the consecration on the first day of the first month, and by the eighth day of the month they
reached the portico of the LORD. For eight more days they consecrated the temple of the
LORD itself, finishing on the sixteenth day of the first month.
18Then they went in to King Hezekiah and reported: "We have purified the entire temple of the LORD, the altar of burnt offering with all its utensils, and the table for setting
out the consecrated bread, with all its articles. 19We have prepared and consecrated all
the articles[d] that King Ahaz removed in his unfaithfulness while he was king. They are
now in front of the LORD's altar."
20Early the next morning King Hezekiah gathered the city officials together and went
up to the temple of the LORD. 21They brought seven bulls, seven rams, seven male lambs
and seven male goats as a sin offering[e] for the kingdom, for the sanctuary and for Judah.

29:5 [p]2Ch 35:6
29:6 [q]Ps 106:6-47; Jer 2:27 [r]1Ch 5:25; Eze 8:16
29:8 [s]Dt 28:25; 2Ch 24:18 [t]Jer 18:16; 19:8; 25:9, 18
29:9 [u]2Ch 28:5-8, 17
29:10 [v]2Ch 15:12; 23:16
29:11 [w]Nu 3:6; 8:6, 14 [x]1Ch 15:2
29:12 [y]Nu 3:17-20 [z]2Ch 31:15
29:13 [a]1Ch 6:39
29:15 [b]ver 5; 1Ch 23:28; 2Ch 30:12
29:16 [c]2Sa 15:23
29:19 [d]2Ch 28:24
29:21 [e]Lev 4:13-14

restored the gold ornamentation that had been stripped from the temple doors (2Ki 16:8–10).
29:4–11 Listen to me, Levites! Hezekiah's speech stands in contrast with Abijah's earlier assessments (13:4–12 notes). Judah was no longer different from the north; both had forsaken God. Judah must repent as well (see note on 28:9–15).
29:6,9 Our fathers. Hezekiah may have had in mind all the failures during the period of the divided kingdom, but he referred especially to events in the preceding generation (21:4—28:27).
29:8 on Judah and Jerusalem. Hezekiah asserted that even Judah and Jerusalem were under the curse of God because of their neglect of the temple. This focus no doubt suited the Chronicler's desire to motivate his postexilic readers to faithful support of the temple in their own day.
29:9 in captivity. During the days of Ahaz many Judahites were taken into exile by the Arameans (28:5–8) and Edomites (28:17). These events foreshadowed the Babylonian captivity to come (36:15–23) and portrayed the reign of Hezekiah as a model for restoration after exile.
29:10 make a covenant. See note on 15:12. **anger will turn away from us.** The resolution for the divine curse was repentance and recommitment to the temple. Hezekiah built on the perspectives offered in God's response to Solomon's dedicatory prayer (see note on 7:13–15).
29:12–14 Kohathites . . . Merarites . . . Gershonites. The three divisions of the tribe of Levi. **Elizaphan . . . Asaph . . . Heman . . . Jeduthun.** The four families of Levite singers. The Chronicler apparently mentioned representatives from these groups to depict Hezekiah's reforms as having been widely supported by the Levites and in accordance with Davidic and Solomonic order (see notes on 1Ch 6:1–81).
29:13 Elizaphan. A prominent leader of the Kohathites (Nu 3:30).
29:16 priests . . . sanctuary . . . Levites. The Chronicler offered these details to demonstrate that Hezekiah's renovation strictly accorded with Mosaic legislation. **Kidron Valley.** Compare 15:16, 30:14 and 2 Kings 23:4, 6 and 12.
29:20–36 Hezekiah . . . went up to the temple. Hezekiah's dedication of the temple is reported in three parts: sacrifices brought by the leaders (vv. 20–24), arrangement of music (vv. 25–30) and sacrifices brought by the people (vv. 31–36).
29:21 sin offering. See Leviticus 4:1—5:13. **for the kingdom, for the sanctuary and for Judah.** Sacrifices were made on behalf of the royal family, the priests and Levites and the people. All three groups were involved in apostasy under Ahaz (2Ki 16:1–20).

The king commanded the priests, the descendants of Aaron, to offer these on the altar
of the LORD. 22So they slaughtered the bulls, and the priests took the blood and sprinkled
it on the altar; next they slaughtered the rams and sprinkled their blood on the altar;
then they slaughtered the lambs and sprinkled their blood[f] on the altar. 23The goats for
the sin offering were brought before the king and the assembly, and they laid their
hands[g] on them. 24The priests then slaughtered the goats and presented their blood on
the altar for a sin offering to atone[h] for all Israel, because the king had ordered the burnt
offering and the sin offering for all Israel.
25He stationed the Levites in the temple of the LORD with cymbals, harps and lyres in
the way prescribed by David[i] and Gad[j] the king's seer and Nathan the prophet; this was
commanded by the LORD through his prophets. 26So the Levites stood ready with David's
instruments,[k] and the priests with their trumpets.[l]
27Hezekiah gave the order to sacrifice the burnt offering on the altar. As the offering
began, singing to the LORD began also, accompanied by trumpets and the instruments[m]
of David king of Israel. 28The whole assembly bowed in worship, while the singers sang
and the trumpeters played. All this continued until the sacrifice of the burnt offering was
completed.
29When the offerings were finished, the king and everyone present with him knelt
down and worshiped.[n] 30King Hezekiah and his officials ordered the Levites to praise the
LORD with the words of David and of Asaph the seer. So they sang praises with gladness
and bowed their heads and worshiped.
31Then Hezekiah said, "You have now dedicated yourselves to the LORD. Come and
bring sacrifices[o] and thank offerings to the temple of the LORD." So the assembly brought
sacrifices and thank offerings, and all whose hearts were willing[p] brought burnt offerings.
32The number of burnt offerings the assembly brought was seventy bulls, a hundred
rams and two hundred male lambs—all of them for burnt offerings to the LORD. 33The animals consecrated as sacrifices amounted to six hundred bulls and three thousand
sheep and goats. 34The priests, however, were too few to skin all the burnt offerings;[q] so
their kinsmen the Levites helped them until the task was finished and until other priests
had been consecrated,[r] for the Levites had been more conscientious in consecrating
themselves than the priests had been. 35There were burnt offerings in abundance, together with the fat[s] of the fellowship offerings[a][t] and the drink offerings[u] that accompanied the burnt offerings.
So the service of the temple of the LORD was reestablished. 36Hezekiah and all the people rejoiced at what God had brought about for his people, because it was done so quickly.

Hezekiah Celebrates the Passover

30 Hezekiah sent word to all Israel and Judah and also wrote letters to Ephraim and
Manasseh,[v] inviting them to come to the temple of the LORD in Jerusalem and
celebrate the Passover[w] to the LORD, the God of Israel. 2The king and his officials and the
whole assembly in Jerusalem decided to celebrate[x] the Passover in the second month.
3They had not been able to celebrate it at the regular time because not enough priests
had consecrated[y] themselves and the people had not assembled in Jerusalem. 4The plan

a *35* Traditionally *peace offerings*

29:22 [f]Lev 4:18
29:23 [g]Lev 4:15
29:24 [h]Ex 29:36; Lev 4:26
29:25 [i]1Ch 25:6; 2Ch 8:14 [j]1Sa 22:5; 2Sa 24:11
29:26 [k]1Ch 15:16 [l]1Ch 15:24; 23:5; 2Ch 5:12
29:27 [m]2Ch 23:18
29:29 [n]2Ch 20:18
29:31 [o]Heb 13:15-16 [p]Ex 25:2; 35:22
29:34 [q]2Ch 35:11 [r]2Ch 30:3,15
29:35 [s]Ex 29:13; Lev 3:16 [t]Lev 7:11-21 [u]Nu 15:5-10
30:1 [v]Ge 41:52 [w]Ex 12:11; Nu 28:16
30:2 [x]Nu 9:10
30:3 [y]2Ch 29:34

29:24 all Israel . . . all Israel. In the reunited kingdom (29:1—36:23), the expression "all Israel" (30:1; 31:1; 35:3) refers to the people of the northern and southern kingdoms together (see notes on 10:1 and on 1Ch 11:1). Hezekiah ordered that sacrifices be made not simply for Judah (v. 21), but for "all Israel." Hezekiah's concern for both north and south connected him with the reigns of David and Solomon and anticipated his desire for all the tribes to join in the Passover (30:1–6).

29:25–30 singing to the LORD. See note on 1 Chronicles 15:16–24.

29:31 whose hearts were willing. The enthusiasm of the people in Hezekiah's day exemplified the kind of willingness expected from the Chronicler's readers (see note on 1Ch 29:1–9).

29:32–35 six hundred bulls and three thousand sheep and goats. The numerous sacrifices were reminiscent of Solomon's dedication of the temple (7:4–6).

29:36 done so quickly. The restoration of the temple took less than three weeks (vv. 3,17,20), a dramatic display of divine power and a cause for celebration.

■ **30:1—31:1** *Hezekiah Unites Israel in Passover Celebration.* The Chronicler included an extensive record of Hezekiah's Passover celebration. The writer of Kings emphasized the Passover under Josiah (2Ki 23:21–23; 2Ch 35:1–19) and did not deal with this event. The Chronicler exalted this celebration because Hezekiah succeeded in reuniting the people of both Israel and Judah in temple worship. This event had striking relevance for the reunification of God's people in the Chronicler's day (see "Introduction to 1 Chronicles: Purposes and Distinctives"). The passage divides into three parts: preparations (30:1–12), celebration (30:13–22) and extended celebration (30:23—31:1).

30:1–27 See *WCF* 23.3; 31.2.

30:1 all Israel and Judah . . . Ephraim and Manasseh. In this heading to the entire account, the Chronicler emphasized that Hezekiah reached out to people of both the north and the south. The same theme appears throughout this chapter (vv. 5–6, 10–11,18,21,25).

30:2 king . . . officials . . . whole assembly. Hezekiah followed the example of David (see note on 1Ch 13:1–4). **the second month.** Normally, the Feasts of Unleavened Bread and of Passover were to be observed in the first month (Ex 12:2,6; Dt 16:1–8; cf. 2Ch 35:1). However, exceptions were made for those who were traveling or temporarily "unclean" (Nu 9:9–13). Hezekiah applied this exception corporately to the entire nation (v. 3).

seemed right both to the king and to the whole assembly. 5They decided to send a proclamation throughout Israel, from Beersheba to Dan,[z] calling the people to come to Jerusalem and celebrate the Passover to the LORD, the God of Israel. It had not been celebrated in large numbers according to what was written.
6At the king's command, couriers went throughout Israel and Judah with letters from
the king and from his officials, which read:

"People of Israel, return to the LORD, the God of Abraham, Isaac and Israel, that
he may return to you who are left, who have escaped from the hand of the kings
of Assyria. 7Do not be like your fathers[a] and brothers, who were unfaithful to the
LORD, the God of their fathers, so that he made them an object of horror,[b] as you
see. 8Do not be stiff-necked,[c] as your fathers were; submit to the LORD. Come to
the sanctuary, which he has consecrated forever. Serve the LORD your God, so that
his fierce anger[d] will turn away from you. 9If you return[e] to the LORD, then your
brothers and your children will be shown compassion[f] by their captors and will
come back to this land, for the LORD your God is gracious and compassionate.[g] He
will not turn his face from you if you return to him."

10The couriers went from town to town in Ephraim and Manasseh, as far as Zebulun,
but the people scorned and ridiculed[h] them. 11Nevertheless, some men of Asher, Manasseh and Zebulun humbled themselves and went to Jerusalem.[i] 12Also in Judah the hand
of God was on the people to give them unity[j] of mind to carry out what the king and his
officials had ordered, following the word of the LORD.
13A very large crowd of people assembled in Jerusalem to celebrate the Feast of Unleavened Bread[k] in the second month. 14They removed the altars[l] in Jerusalem and
cleared away the incense altars and threw them into the Kidron Valley.[m]
15They slaughtered the Passover lamb on the fourteenth day of the second month.
The priests and the Levites were ashamed and consecrated[n] themselves and brought
burnt offerings to the temple of the LORD. 16Then they took up their regular positions[o]
as prescribed in the Law of Moses the man of God. The priests sprinkled the blood handed to them by the Levites. 17Since many in the crowd had not consecrated themselves,
the Levites had to kill[p] the Passover lambs for all those who were not ceremonially clean
and could not consecrate ⌊their lambs⌋ to the LORD. 18Although most of the many people
who came from Ephraim, Manasseh, Issachar and Zebulun had not purified themselves,[q] yet they ate the Passover, contrary to what was written. But Hezekiah prayed for
them, saying, "May the LORD, who is good, pardon everyone 19who sets his heart on seeking God—the LORD, the God of his fathers—even if he is not clean according to the rules
of the sanctuary." 20And the LORD heard[r] Hezekiah and healed[s] the people.[t]
21The Israelites who were present in Jerusalem celebrated the Feast of Unleavened
Bread[u] for seven days with great rejoicing, while the Levites and priests sang to the LORD
every day, accompanied by the LORD's instruments of praise.[a]
22Hezekiah spoke encouragingly to all the Levites, who showed good understanding
of the service of the LORD. For the seven days they ate their assigned portion and offered
fellowship offerings[b] and praised the LORD, the God of their fathers.
23The whole assembly then agreed to celebrate[v] the festival seven more days; so for

30:5 [z]Jdg 20:1
30:7 [a]Ps 78:8, 57; 106:6; Eze 20:18 [b]2Ch 29:8
30:8 [c]Ex 32:9 [d]Nu 25:4; 2Ch 29:10
30:9 [e]Dt 30:2-5; Isa 1:16; 55:7 [f]1Ki 8:50; Ps 106:46 [g]Ex 34:6-7; Dt 4:31; Mic 7:18
30:10 [h]2Ch 36:16
30:11 [i]ver 25
30:12 [j]Jer 32:39; Eze 11:19; Php 2:13
30:13 [k]Nu 28:16
30:14 [l]2Ch 28:24 [m]2Sa 15:23
30:15 [n]2Ch 29:34
30:16 [o]2Ch 35:10
30:17 [p]2Ch 29:34
30:18 [q]Ex 12:43-49; Nu 9:6-10
30:20 [r]2Ch 6:20 [s]2Ch 7:14; Mal 4:2 [t]Jas 5:16
30:21 [u]Ex 12:15, 17; 13:6
30:23 [v]1Ki 8:65; 2Ch 7:9

[a] *21* Or *priests praised the LORD every day with resounding instruments belonging to the LORD*
[b] *22* Traditionally *peace offerings*

30:4 to the king and to the whole assembly. See note on 1 Chronicles 13:2.
30:5 in large numbers. Originally Passover was a family celebration (Ex 12). In Mosaic legislation it was ordained as an annual pilgrimage for the nation (Nu 28:16–25). The last full-scale observance had been held during the time of Solomon (v. 26).
30:6–9 couriers went throughout Israel and Judah. Hezekiah's outlook on the people of Israel was similar to his perspective on the Judahites (see note on 29:4–11). The identical letter went to both Israel and to Judah (v. 6). His letter contrasts with Abijah's speech to the people of the northern kingdom (13:3–12). By Hezekiah's day Judah and Israel were both in need of repentance and renewal.
30:6 return to the LORD. See note on 7:14. **you who are left, who have escaped.** The Hebrew expression may be translated "the remnant of you who have escaped." The Chronicler used this terminology in the technical sense of those who had been spared by God to represent the continuation of the nation (see note on 36:20).
30:9 return to the LORD . . . return to him. See note on 7:14. **shown compassion by their captors and will come back to this land.** Hezekiah recalled Solomon's dedicatory prayer (6:36–39). His concern for the return of those who had been deported reflected the Chronicler's desire for the repopulation of the land during the postexilic period (Zec 8:1–8).
30:11 Nevertheless, some men . . . went to Jerusalem. The presence of people of the northern kingdom at Hezekiah's Passover celebration was crucial to the Chronicler's outlook (see note on 30:1—31:1; 11:14). **humbled themselves.** See note on 7:14.
30:16 Law of Moses. See note on 1 Chronicles 16:40.
30:18–20 had not purified themselves, yet they ate. The failure of some to be ritually cleansed caused illness to break out among the participants. Hezekiah interceded, and God healed the people. Hezekiah's effective prayer made the reunification of the nation possible (see note on 7:13–15). See *WLC* 171,175.
30:18 prayed. See note on 7:14.
30:19 seeking God. See note on 7:14.
30:21–23 See *WLC* 174,175.
30:21–27 celebrated . . . with great rejoicing. As Solomon's temple celebration had been extended, so Hezekiah's feast continued for another week (7:8–9).

another seven days they celebrated joyfully. 24 Hezekiah king of Judah provided[w] a thousand bulls and seven thousand sheep and goats for the assembly, and the officials provided them with a thousand bulls and ten thousand sheep and goats. A great number of priests consecrated themselves. 25 The entire assembly of Judah rejoiced, along with the priests and Levites and all who had assembled from Israel[x], including the aliens who had come from Israel and those who lived in Judah. 26 There was great joy in Jerusalem, for since the days of Solomon[y] son of David king of Israel there had been nothing like this in Jerusalem. 27 The priests and the Levites stood to bless[z] the people, and God heard them, for their prayer reached heaven, his holy dwelling place.

31 When all this had ended, the Israelites who were there went out to the towns of Judah, smashed the sacred stones and cut down[a] the Asherah poles. They destroyed the high places and the altars throughout Judah and Benjamin and in Ephraim and Manasseh. After they had destroyed all of them, the Israelites returned to their own towns and to their own property.

Contributions for Worship

2 Hezekiah[b] assigned the priests and Levites to divisions[c]—each of them according to their duties as priests or Levites—to offer burnt offerings and fellowship offerings,[a] to minister,[d] to give thanks and to sing praises[e] at the gates of the LORD's dwelling.[f] 3 The king contributed[g] from his own possessions for the morning and evening burnt offerings and for the burnt offerings on the Sabbaths, New Moons and appointed feasts as written in the Law of the LORD.[h] 4 He ordered the people living in Jerusalem to give the portion[i] due the priests and Levites so they could devote themselves to the Law of the LORD. 5 As soon as the order went out, the Israelites generously gave the firstfruits[j] of their grain, new wine,[k] oil and honey and all that the fields produced. They brought a great amount, a tithe of everything. 6 The men of Israel and Judah who lived in the towns of Judah also brought a tithe[l] of their herds and flocks and a tithe of the holy things dedicated to the LORD their God, and they piled them in heaps.[m] 7 They began doing this in the third month and finished in the seventh month.[n] 8 When Hezekiah and his officials came and saw the heaps, they praised the LORD and blessed[o] his people Israel.

9 Hezekiah asked the priests and Levites about the heaps; 10 and Azariah the chief priest, from the family of Zadok,[p] answered, "Since the people began to bring their contributions to the temple of the LORD, we have had enough to eat and plenty to spare, because the LORD has blessed his people, and this great amount is left over."[q]

11 Hezekiah gave orders to prepare storerooms in the temple of the LORD, and this was done. 12 Then they faithfully brought in the contributions, tithes and dedicated gifts. Conaniah,[r] a Levite, was in charge of these things, and his brother Shimei was next in rank. 13 Jehiel, Azaziah, Nahath, Asahel, Jerimoth, Jozabad,[s] Eliel, Ismakiah, Mahath and Benaiah were supervisors under Conaniah and Shimei his brother, by appointment of King Hezekiah and Azariah the official in charge of the temple of God.

14 Kore son of Imnah the Levite, keeper of the East Gate, was in charge of the freewill offerings given to God, distributing the contributions made to the LORD and also the consecrated gifts. 15 Eden,[t] Miniamin, Jeshua, Shemaiah, Amariah and Shecaniah assisted him faithfully in the towns[u] of the priests, distributing to their fellow priests according to their divisions, old and young alike.

16 In addition, they distributed to the males three years old or more whose names were in the genealogical records[v]—all who would enter the temple of the LORD to perform the

a 2 Traditionally *peace offerings*

30:24 [w]1Ki 8:5; 2Ch 29:34; 35:7; Ezr 6:17; 8:35
30:25 [x]ver 11
30:26 [y]2Ch 7:8
30:27 [z]Ex 39:43; Nu 6:23; Dt 26:15; 2Ch 23:18; Ps 68:5
31:1 [a]2Ki 18:4; 2Ch 32:12; Isa 36:7
31:2 [b]2Ch 29:9 [c]1Ch 24:1 [d]1Ch 15:2 [e]Ps 7:17; 9:2; 47:6; 71:22 [f]1Ch 23:28-32
31:3 [g]1Ch 29:3; 2Ch 35:7; Eze 45:17 [h]Nu 28:1-29:40
31:4 [i]Nu 18:8; Dt 18:8; Ne 13:10; Mal 2:7
31:5 [j]Nu 18:12,24; Ne 13:12; Eze 44:30 [k]Dt 12:17
31:6 [l]Lev 27:30; Ne 13:10-12 [m]Dt 14:28; Ru 3:7
31:7 [n]Ex 23:16
31:8 [o]Ps 144:13-15
31:10 [p]2Sa 8:17 [q]Ex 36:5; Eze 44:30; Mal 3:10-12
31:12 [r]2Ch 35:9
31:13 [s]2Ch 35:9
31:15 [t]2Ch 29:12 [u]Jos 21:9-19
31:16 [v]1Ch 23:3; Ezr 3:4

30:24 Hezekiah . . . provided. Hezekiah followed the example of David in supporting the temple at his own expense (see notes on 35:7–8).
30:25–26 See *WLC* 175.
30:27 heaven, his holy dwelling place. Compare the similar language in Solomon's prayer (6:21,30,33,39).
31:1 smashed . . . cut down . . . destroyed. The Chronicler cited the end of Hezekiah's Passover as the circumstance of many of the events reported in 2 Kings 18:4. **Israelites . . . Israelites.** Literally, "all Israel . . . all Israel" (see note on 29:24). **Asherah poles.** See NIV text note on 14:3.
■ **31:2–21** *Hezekiah's Enduring Provisions.* The Chronicler turned attention to Hezekiah's provisions for the continuation of temple services. Apart from verses 20–21 (cf. 2Ki 18:5–7) this material was added and reflects interest in temple services. The Chronicler evidently presented Hezekiah's enthusiasm as inspiration to his postexilic readers to offer proper support for the temple.
31:2 assigned the priests and Levites to divisions. Hezekiah returned to the order of Solomon (8:14), who in turn had followed David's design (see note on 1Ch 6:1–81).
31:3–4 from his own possessions . . . He ordered the people. As David had done, Hezekiah donated from his own treasury before appealing to the people for support (see note on 1Ch 29:2–5). **the Law of the LORD.** See note on 1 Chronicles 16:40.
31:5–8 generously gave the firstfruits. The reaction of the people in Hezekiah's day served as a model for the postexilic community (Ne 10:35–39; 12:47; 13:10–13; Mal 3:8–10).
31:16 three years old. Perhaps a reference to the inclusion of the weaned children of the Levites in the distribution of food (see also v. 18). However, "three" could be an error in transmission for "thirty," the age of active service in the temple (see note on 1Ch 23:3).

daily duties of their various tasks, according to their responsibilities and their divisions. 17 And they distributed to the priests enrolled by their families in the genealogical records and likewise to the Levites twenty years old or more, according to their responsibilities and their divisions. 18 They included all the little ones, the wives, and the sons and daughters of the whole community listed in these genealogical records. For they were faithful in consecrating themselves.

19 As for the priests, the descendants of Aaron, who lived on the farm lands around their towns or in any other towns,[w] men were designated by name to distribute portions to every male among them and to all who were recorded in the genealogies of the Levites.

20 This is what Hezekiah did throughout Judah, doing what was good and right and faithful[x] before the LORD his God. 21 In everything that he undertook in the service of God's temple and in obedience to the law and the commands, he sought his God and worked wholeheartedly. And so he prospered.[y]

Sennacherib Threatens Jerusalem

32 After all that Hezekiah had so faithfully done, Sennacherib[z] king of Assyria came and invaded Judah. He laid siege to the fortified cities, thinking to conquer them for himself. 2 When Hezekiah saw that Sennacherib had come and that he intended to make war on Jerusalem,[a] 3 he consulted with his officials and military staff about blocking off the water from the springs outside the city, and they helped him. 4 A large force of men assembled, and they blocked all the springs[b] and the stream that flowed through the land. "Why should the kings[a] of Assyria come and find plenty of water?" they said. 5 Then he worked hard repairing all the broken sections of the wall[c] and building towers on it. He built another wall outside that one and reinforced the supporting terraces[b][d] of the City of David. He also made large numbers of weapons[e] and shields.

6 He appointed military officers over the people and assembled them before him in the square at the city gate and encouraged them with these words: 7 "Be strong and courageous.[f] Do not be afraid or discouraged[g] because of the king of Assyria and the vast army with him, for there is a greater power with us than with him.[h] 8 With him is only the arm of flesh,[i] but with us[j] is the LORD our God to help us and to fight our battles."[k] And the people gained confidence from what Hezekiah the king of Judah said.

9 Later, when Sennacherib king of Assyria and all his forces were laying siege to Lachish,[l] he sent his officers to Jerusalem with this message for Hezekiah king of Judah and for all the people of Judah who were there:

> 10 "This is what Sennacherib king of Assyria says: On what are you basing your confidence,[m] that you remain in Jerusalem under siege? 11 When Hezekiah says, 'The LORD our God will save us from the hand of the king of Assyria,' he is misleading[n] you, to let you die of hunger and thirst. 12 Did not Hezekiah himself remove this god's high places and altars, saying to Judah and Jerusalem, 'You must worship before one altar[o] and burn sacrifices on it'?
>
> 13 "Do you not know what I and my fathers have done to all the peoples of the other lands? Were the gods of those nations ever able to deliver their land from my hand?[p] 14 Who of all the gods of these nations that my fathers destroyed has been able to save his people from me? How then can your god deliver you from my hand? 15 Now do not let Hezekiah deceive[q] you and mislead you like this. Do not believe him, for no god of any nation or kingdom has been able to deliver[r] his peo-

31:19 [w]ver 12-15; Lev 25:34; Nu 35:2-5
31:20 [x]2Ki 20:3; 22:2
31:21 [y]Dt 29:9
32:1 [z]2Ki 18:13-19; Isa 36:1; 37:9,17, 37
32:2 [a]Isa 22:7; Jer 1:15
32:4 [b]2Ki 18:17; 20:20; Isa 22:9,11; Na 3:14
32:5 [c]2Ch 25:23; Isa 22:10 [d]1Ki 9:24; 1Ch 11:8 [e]Isa 22:8
32:7 [f]Dt 31:6; 1Ch 22:13 [g]2Ch 20:15 [h]Nu 14:9; 2Ki 6:16
32:8 [i]Job 40:9; Isa 52:10; Jer 17:5; 32:21 [j]Dt 3:22; 1Sa 17:45; 2Ch 13:12 [k]1Ch 5:22; 2Ch 20:17; Ps 20:7; Isa 28:6
32:9 [l]Jos 10:3,31
32:10 [m]Eze 29:16
32:11 [n]Isa 37:10
32:12 [o]2Ch 31:1
32:13 [p]ver 15
32:15 [q]Isa 37:10 [r]Da 3:15

a 4 Hebrew; Septuagint and Syriac *king* b 5 Or *the Millo*

31:20–21 And so he prospered. The author presented Hezekiah's prosperity as a reward for his fidelity and obedience.
31:21 sought his God. See note on 7:14.
■ **32:1–31** *Hezekiah's Inconsistencies During the Assyrian Invasion.* The Chronicler illustrated God's blessing and reward to Hezekiah in delivering him from invasion (vv. 1–23), healing his illness and forgiving his pride (vv. 24–26) and granting him wealth (vv. 27–31). These verses reveal Hezekiah's inconsistencies.
■ **32:1–23** *Hezekiah's Inconsistent Military Strategy.* In Kings the account of Sennacherib's invasion is the most prominent episode mentioned with regard to Hezekiah's reign (2Ki 18:17—19:37). The Chronicler shortened the account and used it as an illustration of inconsistency and divine blessing granted because of fidelity, trust and prayer.
32:2–8 consulted with his officials and military staff. The Chronicler likely included this material to highlight Hezekiah's failure to turn first to God. As becomes evident in verse 25, Hezekiah was guilty of pride even as he remained faithful to worshiping the Lord.
32:7–8 greater power with us than with him. Hezekiah's speech demonstrated reliance on divine power to overcome his powerful enemy. Dependence on sovereign intervention in battle was a major concern of the Chronicler (see note on 16:2). Yet manifesting the pride for which he was later rebuked (see v. 25), he did not turn to God immediately but worked first to strengthen his human power.
32:9 sent his officers. The Chronicler omitted portions of the account in 2 Kings 18 (vv. 14–16,17b–18,20–21, 23–27; see Isa 37:14–20), most likely because these details were commonly known to his readers.
32:10 your confidence. See note on 16:2.

ple from my hand or the hand of my fathers.[s] How much less will your god deliver you from my hand!"

16Sennacherib's officers spoke further against the LORD God and against his servant
Hezekiah. 17The king also wrote letters[t] insulting[u] the LORD, the God of Israel, and saying this against him: "Just as the gods[v] of the peoples of the other lands did not rescue
their people from my hand, so the god of Hezekiah will not rescue his people from my
hand." 18Then they called out in Hebrew to the people of Jerusalem who were on the
wall, to terrify them and make them afraid in order to capture the city. 19They spoke
about the God of Jerusalem as they did about the gods of the other peoples of the
world—the work of men's hands.[w]

20King Hezekiah and the prophet Isaiah son of Amoz cried out in prayer to heaven
about this. 21And the LORD sent an angel,[x] who annihilated all the fighting men and the
leaders and officers in the camp of the Assyrian king. So he withdrew to his own land in
disgrace. And when he went into the temple of his god, some of his sons cut him down
with the sword.[y]

22So the LORD saved Hezekiah and the people of Jerusalem from the hand of Sennacherib king of Assyria and from the hand of all others. He took care of them[a] on every side.
23Many brought offerings to Jerusalem for the LORD and valuable gifts[z] for Hezekiah king
of Judah. From then on he was highly regarded by all the nations.

Hezekiah's Pride, Success and Death

24In those days Hezekiah became ill and was at the point of death. He prayed to the
LORD, who answered him and gave him a miraculous sign. 25But Hezekiah's heart was
proud[a] and he did not respond to the kindness shown him; therefore the LORD's wrath[b]
was on him and on Judah and Jerusalem. 26Then Hezekiah repented[c] of the pride of his
heart, as did the people of Jerusalem; therefore the LORD's wrath did not come upon them
during the days of Hezekiah.[d]

27Hezekiah had very great riches and honor,[e] and he made treasuries for his silver
and gold and for his precious stones, spices, shields and all kinds of valuables. 28He also
made buildings to store the harvest of grain, new wine and oil; and he made stalls for
various kinds of cattle, and pens for the flocks. 29He built villages and acquired great
numbers of flocks and herds, for God had given him very great riches.[f]

30It was Hezekiah who blocked[g] the upper outlet of the Gihon[h] spring and channeled
the water down to the west side of the City of David. He succeeded in everything he undertook. 31But when envoys were sent by the rulers of Babylon[i] to ask him about the
miraculous sign[j] that had occurred in the land, God left him to test[k] him and to know
everything that was in his heart.

32The other events of Hezekiah's reign and his acts of devotion are written in the vision of the prophet Isaiah son of Amoz in the book of the kings of Judah and Israel. 33Hez-
ekiah rested with his fathers and was buried on the hill where the tombs of David's
descendants are. All Judah and the people of Jerusalem honored him when he died. And
Manasseh his son succeeded him as king.

32:15 [s]Ex 5:2
32:17 [t]Isa 37:14 [u]Ps 74:22; Isa 37:4,17 [v]2Ki 19:12
32:19 [w]2Ki 19:18; Ps 115:4-8; Isa 2:8; 17:8
32:21 [x]Ge 19:13 [y]2Ki 19:7
32:23 [z]2Ch 9:24; 17:5; Isa 45:14; Zec 14:16-17
32:25 [a]2Ki 14:10; 2Ch 26:16 [b]2Ch 19:2; 24:18
32:26 [c]Jer 26:18-19 [d]2Ch 34:27,28; Isa 39:8
32:27 [e]1Ch 29:12
32:29 [f]1Ch 29:12
32:30 [g]2Ki 18:17 [h]1Ki 1:33
32:31 [i]Isa 39:1 [j]ver 24; Isa 38:7 [k]Ge 22:1; Dt 8:16

[a] *22* Hebrew; Septuagint and Vulgate *He gave them rest*

32:20 Hezekiah and . . . Isaiah . . . cried out in prayer. At this point Hezekiah turned to the Lord. The Chronicler abbreviated the more detailed account of these events in Kings (2Ki 19:1–34). The value of prayer in battle is illustrated repeatedly in the Old Testament (see note on 6:34–35). This episode illustrates God's mercy to those who turn to him, even after they have tried to control their own situation without his help.

■ **32:24–26** *Hezekiah's Inconsistent Pride.* The Chronicler abbreviated the account of illness and prayer recorded in Kings (2Ki 20:1–11; see also note on 32:20) and used the event to reveal not only that Hezekiah had sinned in attempting to strengthen his forces without the Lord's help (vv. 2–8) but also that he received forgiveness for this pride (vv. 25–26).

32:24 prayed. See note on 7:14.

32:25–26 Hezekiah's heart was proud. See note on 26:16. See *WCF* 5.5.

■ **32:27–31** *Hezekiah's Inconsistent Alliance.* Even after seeing God deliver him from the Assyrians, Hezekiah turned to the Babylonians to secure his future. This act brought the judgment of God against Judah.

32:27–29 very great riches. Hezekiah's wealth reflected that of Solomon's kingdom (1:1–17; 9:13–28). **buildings . . . He built.** See note on 1 Chronicles 11:4–9.

32:31 envoys . . . of Babylon. The Babylonian envoys came to investigate reports of Hezekiah's miracle (v. 24). Apparently they desired a military alliance with Hezekiah against Assyria. The Chronicler abbreviated the record of 2 Kings 20:12–19 (cf. Isa 39:1–8), in which Isaiah warned Hezekiah that his treasures would be taken captive to Babylon. The author ostensibly assumed that his readers knew the account in Kings and thereby omitted Isaiah's harsh rebuke. **to test him.** The Chronicler acknowledged that Hezekiah was tested to see whether he would form an alliance with Babylon against Assyria. As the book of Kings reports, Hezekiah failed the test (2Ki 20:12–19). See *WCF* 5.5; *WLC* 195.

■ **32:32–33** *Closure of Hezekiah's Reign.* Hezekiah was honored in death and was succeeded by his son Manasseh.

32:32 written in the vision of the prophet Isaiah . . . the book of the kings. The Chronicler may be referring to the canonical book of Isaiah ("vision"; Isa 1:1). See "Introduction to 1 Chronicles: Author."

32:33 All Judah . . . honored him. The text expands the parallel account in Kings (2Ki 20:20–21) to give a final approval of Hezekiah's reign (see note on 21:19).

Manasseh King of Judah

33 Manasseh[l] was twelve years old when he became king, and he reigned in Jerusalem fifty-five years. **2**He did evil in the eyes of the LORD,[m] following the detestable[n] practices of the nations the LORD had driven out before the Israelites. **3**He rebuilt
the high places his father Hezekiah had demolished; he also erected altars to the Baals
and made Asherah poles.[o] He bowed down[p] to all the starry hosts and worshiped them.
4He built altars in the temple of the LORD, of which the LORD had said, "My Name[q] will
remain in Jerusalem forever." **5**In both courts of the temple of the LORD,[r] he built altars
to all the starry hosts. **6**He sacrificed his sons[s] in[a] the fire in the Valley of Ben Hinnom,
practiced sorcery, divination and witchcraft, and consulted mediums[t] and spiritists.[u] He
did much evil in the eyes of the LORD, provoking him to anger.
7He took the carved image he had made and put it in God's temple,[v] of which God
had said to David and to his son Solomon, "In this temple and in Jerusalem, which I have
chosen out of all the tribes of Israel, I will put my Name forever. **8**I will not again make
the feet of the Israelites leave the land[w] I assigned to your forefathers, if only they will
be careful to do everything I commanded them concerning all the laws, decrees and ordinances given through Moses." **9**But Manasseh led Judah and the people of Jerusalem
astray, so that they did more evil than the nations the LORD had destroyed before the Israelites.[x]
10The LORD spoke to Manasseh and his people, but they paid no attention. **11**So the
LORD brought against them the army commanders of the king of Assyria, who took Manasseh prisoner,[y] put a hook in his nose, bound him with bronze shackles[z] and took him
to Babylon. **12**In his distress he sought the favor of the LORD his God and humbled[a] himself greatly before the God of his fathers. **13**And when he prayed to him, the LORD was
moved by his entreaty and listened to his plea; so he brought him back to Jerusalem and
to his kingdom. Then Manasseh knew that the LORD is God.
14Afterward he rebuilt the outer wall of the City of David, west of the Gihon[b] spring
in the valley, as far as the entrance of the Fish Gate[c] and encircling the hill of Ophel;[d]
he also made it much higher. He stationed military commanders in all the fortified cities in Judah.
15He got rid of the foreign gods and removed[e] the image from the temple of the LORD,
as well as all the altars he had built on the temple hill and in Jerusalem; and he threw
them out of the city. **16**Then he restored the altar of the LORD and sacrificed fellowship
offerings[b] and thank offerings[f] on it, and told Judah to serve the LORD, the God of Israel. **17**The people, however, continued to sacrifice at the high places, but only to the LORD
their God.

33:1 [l]1Ch 3:13
33:2 [m]Jer 15:4 [n]Dt 18:9; 2Ch 28:3
33:3 [o]Dt 16:21-22 [p]Dt 17:3; 2Ch 31:1
33:4 [q]2Ch 7:16
33:5 [r]2Ch 4:9
33:6 [s]Lev 18:21; Dt 18:10; 2Ch 28:3 [t]Lev 19:31 [u]1Sa 28:13
33:7 [v]2Ch 7:16
33:8 [w]2Sa 7:10
33:9 [x]Jer 15:4
33:11 [y]Dt 28:36 [z]Ps 149:8
33:12 [a]2Ch 6:37; 32:26; 1Pe 5:6
33:14 [b]1Ki 1:33 [c]Ne 3:3; 12:39; Zep 1:10 [d]2Ch 27:3; Ne 3:26
33:15 [e]ver 3-7; 2Ki 23:12
33:16 [f]Lev 7:11-18

[a] 6 Or *He made his sons pass through* [b] 16 Traditionally *peace offerings*

■ **33:1–20** *Manasseh's Reign.* The Chronicler's portrait of Manasseh forms a striking contrast to the record in 2 Kings 21:1–18. The Chronicler followed Kings with few changes at the beginning and end of his account (cf. vv. 1–10 with 2Ki 21:1–9; vv. 18–20 with 2Ki 21:17–18) but replaced the harsh condemnation of Manasseh (2Ki 21:10–16) with an account of his exile, repentance, return and reforms (vv. 11–17). The record divides into five parts: the opening (v. 1), Manasseh's sins (vv. 2–9), his punishment and forgiveness (vv. 10–13), his reforms (vv. 14–17) and a summary of his reign and death (vv. 18–20). The writer of Kings blamed Manasseh for the downfall of Jerusalem (2Ki 21:10–16), while the Chronicler encouraged his readers by demonstrating that even the worst of sinners can be forgiven and restored through repentance, humility and prayer.

■ **33:1** *Opening of Manasseh's Reign.* Manasseh reigned from 697/96–643/42 B.C., the longest term of any king in Judah.

■ **33:2–9** *Manasseh's Heinous Sins.* The account follows 2 Kings 21:1–9, with some omissions and expansions.

33:2 practices of the nations . . . driven out. Note the repetition of this theme in verse 9, and see the similar evaluation of Ahaz (28:3). Manasseh's sins were so great that he deserved ruin as much as the Canaanites whom God had destroyed during the conquest of the promised land.

33:3 Asherah poles. See NIV text note on 14:3.

33:4 My Name. See verse 7 and note on 1 Chronicles 13:6.

33:6 sacrificed his sons. Another similarity between Manasseh and Ahaz (see notes on 28:3 and 33:2).

33:7,18 Name . . . name. See note on 1 Chronicles 13:6.

33:8 if only. The covenant conditions applicable to the Davidic dynasty continued in force during Manasseh's day (see note on 1Ch 17:13–14). **Moses.** See note on 1 Chronicles 16:40.

■ **33:10–13** *Manasseh's Repentance and Return.* The text adds a report of Manasseh's exile, repentance and return.

33:10 The LORD spoke. The Chronicler abbreviated but did not contradict the fuller description in 2 Kings 21:10–15.

33:11 the king of Assyria. Either Esarhaddon (681–669 B.C.) or Ashurbanipal (669–627 B.C.). **to Babylon.** It is possible that Manasseh was involved in the rebellion (652–648 B.C.) of Shamash-Shum-Ukin of Babylon against the Assyrian king Ashurbanipal. That Manasseh went to Babylon and returned to the promised land reminded the readers of their own Babylonian exile and restoration.

33:12–13 he sought the favor of the LORD. Manasseh's prayer and restoration were in line with Solomon's temple dedication (6:36–39) and God's response to it (see note on 7:13–15).

33:12 humbled himself. See verses 19 and 23, as well as note on 7:14.

33:13 prayed. See note on 7:14.

■ **33:14–17** *Manasseh's Extensive Restorations.* On his return, Manasseh restored the kingdom. His actions stood as a model for the Chronicler's readers as they faced their own need for kingdom restoration.

33:14–16 For similar reforms see 17:1–6.

33:14 rebuilt the outer wall. The Chronicler noted Manasseh's building projects as a sign of God's blessing (see note on 1Ch 11:4–9). Manasseh's rebuilding after exile also served as a model for the postexilic audience in their restoration efforts.

33:15 all the altars. The Chronicler emphasized the results of Manasseh's reforms, but the writer of Kings noted that Josiah had to destroy altars to foreign gods that Manasseh had erected (2Ki 23:12). Apparently Manasseh's reforms did not continue throughout the remainder of his life.

33:17 The people, however. See note on 20:33.

18 The other events of Manasseh's reign, including his prayer to his God and the words
the seers spoke to him in the name of the LORD, the God of Israel, are written in the annals of the kings of Israel.[a] 19 His prayer and how God was moved by his entreaty, as well
as all his sins and unfaithfulness, and the sites where he built high places and set up
Asherah poles and idols before he humbled[g] himself—all are written in the records of
the seers.[b][h] 20 Manasseh rested with his fathers and was buried[i] in his palace. And
Amon his son succeeded him as king.

Amon King of Judah

21 Amon[j] was twenty-two years old when he became king, and he reigned in Jerusalem two years. 22 He did evil in the eyes of the LORD, as his father Manasseh had done.
Amon worshiped and offered sacrifices to all the idols Manasseh had made. 23 But unlike
his father Manasseh, he did not humble[k] himself before the LORD; Amon increased his
guilt.

24 Amon's officials conspired against him and assassinated him in his palace. 25 Then
the people[l] of the land killed all who had plotted against King Amon, and they made Josiah his son king in his place.

Josiah's Reforms

34 Josiah[m] was eight years old when he became king,[n] and he reigned in Jerusalem thirty-one years. 2 He did what was right in the eyes of the LORD and walked
in the ways of his father David,[o] not turning aside to the right or to the left.

3 In the eighth year of his reign, while he was still young, he began to seek the God[p]
of his father David. In his twelfth year he began to purge Judah and Jerusalem of high
places, Asherah poles, carved idols and cast images. 4 Under his direction the altars of
the Baals were torn down; he cut to pieces the incense altars that were above them, and
smashed the Asherah poles,[q] the idols and the images. These he broke to pieces and
scattered over the graves of those who had sacrificed to them.[r] 5 He burned[s] the bones
of the priests on their altars, and so he purged Judah and Jerusalem. 6 In the towns of Manasseh, Ephraim and Simeon, as far as Naphtali, and in the ruins around them, 7 he tore
down the altars and the Asherah poles and crushed the idols to powder[t] and cut to pieces all the incense altars throughout Israel. Then he went back to Jerusalem.

8 In the eighteenth year of Josiah's reign, to purify the land and the temple, he sent
Shaphan son of Azaliah and Maaseiah the ruler of the city, with Joah son of Joahaz, the
recorder, to repair the temple of the LORD his God.

9 They went to Hilkiah[u] the high priest and gave him the money that had been

33:19 [g]2Ch 6:37 [h]2Ki 21:17
33:20 [i]2Ki 21:18; 2Ch 21:20
33:21 [j]1Ch 3:14
33:23 [k]ver 12; Ex 10:3; 2Ch 7:14; Ps 18:27; 147:6; Pr 3:34
33:25 [l]2Ch 22:1
34:1 [m]1Ch 3:14 [n]Zep 1:1
34:2 [o]2Ch 29:2
34:3 [p]1Ki 13:2; 1Ch 16:11; 2Ch 15:2; 33:17, 22
34:4 [q]Ex 34:13 [r]Ex 32:20; Lev 26:30; 2Ki 23:11; Mic 1:5
34:5 [s]1Ki 13:2
34:7 [t]Ex 32:20; 2Ch 31:1
34:9 [u]1Ch 6:13; 2Ch 35:8

[a] *18* That is, Judah, as frequently in 2 Chronicles [b] *19* One Hebrew manuscript and Septuagint; most Hebrew manuscripts *of Hozai*

■ **33:18–20** *Closure of Manasseh's Reign.* The Chronicler expanded 2 Kings 21:17–18 to remind his readers of the important elements in his portrait of Manasseh's reign.
33:18–19 the annals of the kings of Israel . . . records of the seers. See "Introduction to 1 Chronicles: Author."
33:19 Asherah poles. See NIV text note on 14:3.
33:20 rested with his fathers. See note on 21:19.
■ **33:21–25** *Amon's Reign.* The record of Amon's reign follows 2 Kings 21:19–26 with only minor changes. It reports Amon's rise (v. 21), his sins (vv. 22–23) and his death and burial (vv. 24–25). Amon is presented as an example of utter infidelity.
33:21 **Amon . . . two years.** Reigned from 643/42–641/40 B.C.
33:23 he did not humble himself. Added by the Chronicler in contrast to his record of Manasseh's repentance (vv. 11–13). As far as this record is concerned, Amon did nothing worthwhile.
33:24–25 assassinated him. The final notice of Amon's death (2Ki 21:25–26) may have been purposefully omitted to indicate this king's disgrace.
■ **34:1—35:27** *Josiah's Reign.* The record of Josiah's reign depends heavily on Kings (2Ki 22:1—23:30), but significant variations do occur. The account divides into four parts: Josiah's rise (34:1–3a), his early reforms (34:3b—35:19), his infidelity in battle (35:20–25) and his death (35:26–27).
■ **34:1–3a** *Opening of Josiah's Reign.* This account is derived with only slight changes from 2 Kings 22:1–2.
34:1 Josiah . . . thirty-one years. Reigned from 640–609 B.C.
34:3a while he was still young. At an early age, Josiah began to reverse the policies of Amon. **seek the God of his father.** See note on 7:14.
■ **34:3b—35:19** *Josiah's Fidelity in Worship Reforms.* The Chronicler based his account of Josiah's reforms on 2 Kings 22:3—23:23, but the order of events differs. Broadly speaking, Kings summarizes the reforms geographically: discovering the book in the temple (2Ki 22:1—23:3), reforming the city and nation (2Ki 23:4–20) and the Passover celebration at the temple (2Ki 23:21–23). The Chronicler, on the other hand, ordered the events chronologically: reforming the city and nation (34:3b–7), discovering the book in the temple (34:8–33) and the Passover celebration (35:1–19). The chronological references to the 8th and 12th years (34:3) and to the 18th year (34:8; 35:19) make it clear that the reforms (34:3–7) began before the discovery of the book (34:8–33).
■ **34:3b–7** *Josiah's Earlier Reforms.* In these verses, the Chronicler abbreviated material from 2 Kings 23:4–20 in order to draw attention to Josiah's temple renovation (vv. 8–33) and Passover celebration (35:1–19).
34:3b Asherah poles. See NIV text note on 14:3.
34:6 Manasseh, Ephraim . . . as far as Naphtali. The writer of Kings mentioned Josiah's efforts in the north (2Ki 23:15–20), but the Chronicler listed several tribes to emphasize the extent of Josiah's reforms. These actions remind the readers of the need in the postexilic period for all of Israel to be reformed (see note on 29:1—36:23).
■ **34:8—35:19** *Josiah's Later Reforms.* The Chronicler moved to reforms that occurred during Josiah's 18th year (marked off as a unit by the references in 34:8 and 35:19 to the eighteenth year of Josiah's reign). The events include repairs to the temple (34:8–13), renewal of the covenant (34:14–33) and the Passover celebration (35:1–19).
■ **34:8–13** *Josiah Repairs the Temple.* The Chronicler largely followed the account in 2 Kings 22:3–20.

brought into the temple of God, which the Levites who were the doorkeepers had collected from the people of Manasseh, Ephraim and the entire remnant of Israel and from all the people of Judah and Benjamin and the inhabitants of Jerusalem. 10 Then they entrusted it to the men appointed to supervise the work on the LORD's temple. These men paid the workers who repaired and restored the temple. 11 They also gave money[v] to the carpenters and builders to purchase dressed stone, and timber for joists and beams for the buildings that the kings of Judah had allowed to fall into ruin.[w]

12 The men did the work faithfully.[x] Over them to direct them were Jahath and Obadiah, Levites descended from Merari, and Zechariah and Meshullam, descended from Kohath. The Levites—all who were skilled in playing musical instruments—[y] 13 had charge of the laborers[z] and supervised all the workers from job to job. Some of the Levites were secretaries, scribes and doorkeepers.

The Book of the Law Found

14 While they were bringing out the money that had been taken into the temple of the LORD, Hilkiah the priest found the Book of the Law of the LORD that had been given through Moses. 15 Hilkiah said to Shaphan the secretary, "I have found the Book of the Law[a] in the temple of the LORD." He gave it to Shaphan.

16 Then Shaphan took the book to the king and reported to him: "Your officials are doing everything that has been committed to them. 17 They have paid out the money that was in the temple of the LORD and have entrusted it to the supervisors and workers." 18 Then Shaphan the secretary informed the king, "Hilkiah the priest has given me a book." And Shaphan read from it in the presence of the king.

19 When the king heard the words of the Law,[b] he tore[c] his robes. 20 He gave these orders to Hilkiah, Ahikam son of Shaphan[d], Abdon son of Micah,[a] Shaphan the secretary and Asaiah the king's attendant: 21 "Go and inquire of the LORD for me and for the remnant in Israel and Judah about what is written in this book that has been found. Great is the LORD's anger that is poured out[e] on us because our fathers have not kept the word of the LORD; they have not acted in accordance with all that is written in this book."

22 Hilkiah and those the king had sent with him[b] went to speak to the prophetess[f] Huldah, who was the wife of Shallum son of Tokhath,[c] the son of Hasrah,[d] keeper of the wardrobe. She lived in Jerusalem, in the Second District.

23 She said to them, "This is what the LORD, the God of Israel, says: Tell the man who sent you to me, 24 'This is what the LORD says: I am going to bring disaster[g] on this place and its people[h]—all the curses[i] written in the book that has been read in the presence of the king of Judah. 25 Because they have forsaken me[j] and burned incense to other gods and provoked me to anger by all that their hands have made,[e] my anger will be poured out on this place and will not be quenched.' 26 Tell the king of Judah, who sent you to inquire of the LORD, 'This is what the LORD, the God of Israel, says concerning the words you heard: 27 Because your heart was responsive[k] and you humbled[l] yourself before God when you heard what he spoke against this place and its people, and because you humbled yourself before me and tore your robes and wept in my presence, I have heard you, declares the LORD. 28 Now I will gather you to your fathers,[m] and you will be buried in peace. Your eyes will not see all the disaster I am going to bring on this place and on those who live here.' "[n]

So they took her answer back to the king.

29 Then the king called together all the elders of Judah and Jerusalem. 30 He went up to the temple of the LORD[o] with the men of Judah, the people of Jerusalem, the priests and the Levites—all the people from the least to the greatest. He read in their hearing all the words of the Book of the Covenant, which had been found in the temple of the

34:11 [v]2Ch 24:12 [w]2Ch 33:4-7
34:12 [x]2Ki 12:15 [y]1Ch 25:1
34:13 [z]1Ch 23:4
34:15 [a]2Ki 22:8; Ezr 7:6; Ne 8:1
34:19 [b]Dt 28:3-68 [c]Jos 7:6; Isa 36:22; 37:1
34:20 [d]2Ki 22:3
34:21 [e]2Ch 29:8; La 2:4; 4:11; Eze 36:18
34:22 [f]Ex 15:20; Ne 6:14
34:24 [g]Pr 16:4; Isa 3:9; Jer 40:2; 42:10; 44:2,11 [h]2Ch 36:14-20 [i]Dt 28:15-68
34:25 [j]2Ch 33:3-6; Jer 22:9
34:27 [k]2Ch 12:7; 32:26 [l]Ex 10:3; 2Ch 6:37
34:28 [m]2Ch 35:20-25 [n]2Ch 32:26
34:30 [o]2Ki 23:2; Ne 8:1-3

[a] *20* Also called *Acbor son of Micaiah* [b] *22* One Hebrew manuscript, Vulgate and Syriac; most Hebrew manuscripts do not have *had sent with him.* [c] *22* Also called *Tikvah* [d] *22* Also called *Harhas* [e] *25* Or *by everything they have done*

34:12–13 The Levites . . . doorkeepers. The Chronicler added this description of the elaborate involvement of the Levites to show that Josiah's reforms were patterned after David's (1Ch 6:1–81), Solomon's (2Ch 7:6; 8:14) and Hezekiah's (29:1–19).
34:12 playing musical instruments. The Chronicler added this detail in accordance with his emphasis on music. See note on 1 Chronicles 15:16–24.
■ **34:14–33** *Josiah Renews Covenant.* These verses tie the discovery of the book to Josiah's continuing reforms and covenant renewal.
34:15 the Book of the Law . . . of the LORD. Probably Deuteronomy (see note on 2Ki 22:8). The Chronicler included the record of this discovery to indicate the importance of reform according to the law in the postexilic period (cf. Ezr 7:6–10; Ne 8:1—9:38).
34:18–19 he tore his robes. See *WLC* 155.
34:19 words of the Law. See note on 1 Chronicles 16:40.
34:21,26 inquire of the LORD. See note on 7:14. See *WLC* 157.
34:23–28 disaster on this place. The prophet announced divine judgment because of the violation of God's law. Yet Josiah's humility postponed the disaster (see note on 1Ch 28:9).
34:26–28 See *WLC* 155.
34:27 humbled yourself. See note on 7:14. See *WLC* 157.

LORD. 31The king stood by his pillar[p] and renewed the covenant[q] in the presence of the
LORD—to follow[r] the LORD and keep his commands, regulations and decrees with all his
heart and all his soul, and to obey the words of the covenant written in this book.
32Then he had everyone in Jerusalem and Benjamin pledge themselves to it; the people of Jerusalem did this in accordance with the covenant of God, the God of their fathers.
33Josiah removed all the detestable[s] idols from all the territory belonging to the Israelites, and he had all who were present in Israel serve the LORD their God. As long as he
lived, they did not fail to follow the LORD, the God of their fathers.

Josiah Celebrates the Passover

35 Josiah celebrated the Passover[t] to the LORD in Jerusalem, and the Passover lamb
was slaughtered on the fourteenth day of the first month. 2He appointed the
priests to their duties and encouraged them in the service of the LORD's temple. 3He said
to the Levites, who instructed[u] all Israel and who had been consecrated to the LORD: "Put
the sacred ark in the temple that Solomon son of David king of Israel built. It is not to
be carried about on your shoulders. Now serve the LORD your God and his people Israel. 4Prepare yourselves by families in your divisions,[v] according to the directions written by David king of Israel and by his son Solomon.
5"Stand in the holy place with a group of Levites for each subdivision of the families
of your fellow countrymen, the lay people. 6Slaughter the Passover lambs, consecrate
yourselves[w] and prepare ⌞the lambs⌟ for your fellow countrymen, doing what the LORD
commanded through Moses."
7Josiah provided for all the lay people who were there a total of thirty thousand sheep
and goats for the Passover offerings,[x] and also three thousand cattle—all from the
king's own possessions.[y]
8His officials also contributed[z] voluntarily to the people and the priests and Levites.
Hilkiah,[a] Zechariah and Jehiel, the administrators of God's temple, gave the priests
twenty-six hundred Passover offerings and three hundred cattle. 9Also Conaniah[b] along
with Shemaiah and Nethanel, his brothers, and Hashabiah, Jeiel and Jozabad,[c] the
leaders of the Levites, provided five thousand Passover offerings and five hundred head
of cattle for the Levites.
10The service was arranged and the priests stood in their places with the Levites in
their divisions[d] as the king had ordered.[e] 11The Passover lambs were slaughtered,[f] and
the priests sprinkled the blood handed to them, while the Levites skinned the animals.
12They set aside the burnt offerings to give them to the subdivisions of the families of the
people to offer to the LORD, as is written in the Book of Moses. They did the same with
the cattle. 13They roasted the Passover animals over the fire as prescribed,[g] and boiled
the holy offerings in pots, caldrons and pans and served them quickly to all the people.
14After this, they made preparations for themselves and for the priests, because the
priests, the descendants of Aaron, were sacrificing the burnt offerings and the fat portions[h] until nightfall. So the Levites made preparations for themselves and for the Aaronic priests.
15The musicians,[i] the descendants of Asaph, were in the places prescribed by David,
Asaph, Heman and Jeduthun the king's seer. The gatekeepers at each gate did not need
to leave their posts, because their fellow Levites made the preparations for them.
16So at that time the entire service of the LORD was carried out for the celebration of
the Passover and the offering of burnt offerings on the altar of the LORD, as King Josiah
had ordered. 17The Israelites who were present celebrated the Passover at that time and
observed the Feast of Unleavened Bread for seven days. 18The Passover had not been observed like this in Israel since the days of the prophet Samuel; and none of the kings of

34:31 [p]1Ki 7:15; 2Ki 11:14 [q]2Ki 11:17; 2Ch 23:16; 29:10 [r]Dt 13:4
34:33 [s]ver 3-7; Dt 18:9
35:1 [t]Ex 12:1-30; Nu 9:3; 28:16
35:3 [u]Dt 33:10; 1Ch 23:26; 2Ch 5:7; 17:7
35:4 [v]ver 10; 1Ch 9:10-13; 24:1; 2Ch 8:14; Ezr 6:18
35:6 [w]Lev 11:44; 2Ch 29:5, 15
35:7 [x]2Ch 30:24 [y]2Ch 31:3
35:8 [z]1Ch 29:3; 2Ch 29:31-36 [a]1Ch 6:13
35:9 [b]2Ch 31:12 [c]2Ch 31:13
35:10 [d]ver 4; Ezr 6:18 [e]2Ch 30:16
35:11 [f]2Ch 29:22, 34; 30:17
35:13 [g]Ex 12:2-11; Lev 6:25; 1Sa 2:13-15
35:14 [h]Ex 29:13
35:15 [i]1Ch 25:1; 26:12-19; 2Ch 29:30; Ne 12:46; Ps 68:25

34:31 renewed the covenant. See note on 15:12.
34:33 from all the territory belonging to the Israelites. Most likely added to emphasize that Josiah's reforms reached to the remnant of the northern tribes (see note on v. 6). See *WCF* 20.4; 23.3.
■ **35:1–19** *Josiah Observes Passover.* The Chronicler expanded the brief notice in 2 Kings 23:21–23 into a major focus of his record. He evidently developed this portion of Josiah's reforms to inspire his post-exilic readers to participate fully in the ceremonies of the restored temple. Like Hezekiah (30:1—31:1), Josiah enthusiastically observed the national Passover celebration at the temple (cf. Ezr 6:13–22).
35:1 first month. See note on 30:2.
35:3 all Israel. The Chronicler mentioned the entire nation, presumably to highlight the inclusion of the northern tribes in the celebration. From his perspective, the north and south were reunited during this period (see note on 29:1—36:23).
35:4 directions written by David . . . and . . . Solomon. The Chronicler highlighted Josiah's exemplary celebration by pointing to the standards of David and Solomon.
35:6 what the Lord commanded through Moses. See note on 1 Chronicles 16:40.
35:6,12 Moses . . . Moses. Josiah's celebration is highlighted further by its compliance with Mosaic standards (see note on 34:15).
35:7–8 Josiah provided . . . thirty thousand sheep and goats . . . Josiah followed a pattern similar to David's (see notes on 1Ch 29:2–5) and Hezekiah's (see note on 30:24). Josiah's contributions were followed by enthusiastic donations from others.
35:18 none of the kings of Israel had ever celebrated such a Passover. The Chronicler made a similar remark concerning Hezekiah's Passover (30:26). The number of celebrants and offerings exceeded those in Hezekiah's day (30:25).

Israel had ever celebrated such a Passover as did Josiah, with the priests, the Levites and
all Judah and Israel who were there with the people of Jerusalem. 19This Passover was
celebrated in the eighteenth year of Josiah's reign.

The Death of Josiah

20After all this, when Josiah had set the temple in order, Neco king of Egypt went up to
fight at Carchemish[j] on the Euphrates,[k] and Josiah marched out to meet him in battle. 21But
Neco sent messengers to him, saying, "What quarrel is there between you and me, O king
of Judah? It is not you I am attacking at this time, but the house with which I am at war. God
has told[l] me to hurry; so stop opposing God, who is with me, or he will destroy you."
22Josiah, however, would not turn away from him, but disguised[m] himself to engage
him in battle. He would not listen to what Neco had said at God's command but went to
fight him on the plain of Megiddo.
23Archers[n] shot King Josiah, and he told his officers, "Take me away; I am badly
wounded." 24So they took him out of his chariot, put him in the other chariot he had and
brought him to Jerusalem, where he died. He was buried in the tombs of his fathers, and
all Judah and Jerusalem mourned for him.
25Jeremiah composed laments for Josiah, and to this day all the men and women singers commemorate Josiah in the laments.[o] These became a tradition in Israel and are written in the Laments.
26The other events of Josiah's reign and his acts of devotion, according to what is written in the Law of the LORD— 27all the events, from beginning to end, are written in the
36 book of the kings of Israel and Judah. 1And the people of the land took Jehoahaz son of Josiah and made him king in Jerusalem in place of his father.

Jehoahaz King of Judah

2Jehoahaz[a] was twenty-three years old when he became king, and he reigned in Jerusalem three months. 3The king of Egypt dethroned him in Jerusalem and imposed on
Judah a levy of a hundred talents[b] of silver and a talent[c] of gold. 4The king of Egypt made
Eliakim, a brother of Jehoahaz, king over Judah and Jerusalem and changed Eliakim's name
to Jehoiakim. But Neco[p] took Eliakim's brother Jehoahaz and carried him off to Egypt.

Jehoiakim King of Judah

5Jehoiakim[q] was twenty-five years old when he became king, and he reigned in Jerusalem eleven years. He did evil in the eyes of the LORD his God. 6Nebuchadnezzar[r] king
of Babylon attacked him and bound him with bronze shackles to take him to Babylon.[s]
7Nebuchadnezzar also took to Babylon articles from the temple of the LORD and put them
in his temple[d] there.[t]
8The other events of Jehoiakim's reign, the detestable things he did and all that was
found against him, are written in the book of the kings of Israel and Judah. And Jehoiachin his son succeeded him as king.

35:20 [j]Isa 10:9; Jer 46:2 [k]Ge 2:14
35:21 [l]1Ki 13:18; 2Ki 18:25
35:22 [m]Jdg 5:19; 1Sa 28:8; 2Ch 18:29
35:23 [n]1Ki 22:34
35:25 [o]Jer 22:10, 15-16
36:4 [p]Jer 22:10-12
36:5 [q]Jer 22:18; 26:1; 35:1
36:6 [r]Jer 25:9; 27:6; Eze 29:18 [s]2Ch 33:11; Eze 19:9; Da 1:1
36:7 [t]2Ki 24:13; Ezr 1:7; Da 1:2

[a] *2* Hebrew *Joahaz,* a variant of *Jehoahaz;* also in verse 4 [b] *3* That is, about 3 3/4 tons (about 3.4 metric tons) [c] *3* That is, about 75 pounds (about 34 kilograms) [d] *7* Or *palace*

■ **35:20–25** *Josiah's Infidelity in Deadly Battle.* The brief notice of 2 Kings 23:28–30 is expanded by the Chronicler to demonstrate that even a king who had set the temple in order (v. 20) would suffer divine retribution if he were to ignore the Word of God (v. 22).
35:21–22 Added in all likelihood to explain why Josiah fell prey to death in battle. He refused to obey the divinely directed words of Pharaoh Neco.
35:21 house with which I am at war. Probably a reference to Babylon. The Chronicler depicted Josiah in alliance with the Babylonians. Josiah violated the principle of nonalignment, as noted so frequently by the Chronicler of the kings of Judah (see note on 16:2).
35:22 what Neco had said at God's command. Much as the sovereign God had once spoken through a donkey (Nu 22:26–30), he now spoke through a pagan king. That Josiah's actions placed him in alignment with Babylon should have indicated to him that the pharaoh's words agreed with God's law in this matter.
35:24b–25 all Judah and Jerusalem mourned. May have been added to indicate that despite his failure, Josiah was still an honorable king of Judah.
35:25 Jeremiah composed laments. Traditionally, this passage has been used to support Jeremiah's authorship of the book of Lamentations, but this conclusion is unsubstantiated (see "Introduction to Lamentations: Author"). **to this day.** See note on 1 Chronicles 4:41 and 43.
■ **35:26–27** *Closure of Josiah's Reign.* The Chronicler closed his account of Josiah's reign by referring his readers to other sources for more details.
35:27 the book of the kings. See "Introduction to 1 Chronicles: Author."
■ **36:1–14** *The Final Years.* The Chronicler quickly traced the reigns of Josiah's three sons (Jehoahaz, Jehoiakim and Zedekiah) and his grandson (Jehoiachin). In several places he abbreviated the record found in Kings (2Ki 23:31—24:20), and he identified failure and disobedience as causes leading to exile in Babylon (see notes on 1Ch 3:15; 3:17–24).
36:2–4 Jehoahaz . . . became king. Reigned in 609 B.C. See 2 Kings 23:31–34.
36:3 king of Egypt. After Josiah's defeat by Neco (609 B.C.), Egypt dominated Judah.
36:4 changed Eliakim's name. To change another king's name demonstrated full political dominance over that king.
36:5–8 Jehoiakim. Reigned from 609–598 B.C. See 2 Kings 23:36—24:7.
36:6 Nebuchadnezzar king of Babylon. After the Babylonians had defeated the Egyptians at Carchemish (605 B.C.), Judah became subject to Babylon (see Jer 25–26; 36).
36:9–10 Jehoiachin . . . became king. Reigned during 597 B.C. The Chronicler radically abbreviated the account in 2 Kings

Jehoiachin King of Judah

9Jehoiachin[u] was eighteen[a] years old when he became king, and he reigned in Jerusalem three months and ten days. He did evil in the eyes of the LORD. **10**In the spring, King
Nebuchadnezzar sent for him and brought him to Babylon,[v] together with articles of value from the temple of the LORD, and he made Jehoiachin's uncle,[b] Zedekiah, king over
Judah and Jerusalem.

Zedekiah King of Judah

11Zedekiah[w] was twenty-one years old when he became king, and he reigned in Jerusalem eleven years. **12**He did evil in the eyes of the LORD[x] his God and did not humble[y]
himself before Jeremiah the prophet, who spoke the word of the LORD. **13**He also rebelled
against King Nebuchadnezzar, who had made him take an oath[z] in God's name. He became stiff-necked[a] and hardened his heart and would not turn to the LORD, the God of
Israel. **14**Furthermore, all the leaders of the priests and the people became more and
more unfaithful,[b] following all the detestable practices of the nations and defiling the
temple of the LORD, which he had consecrated in Jerusalem.

The Fall of Jerusalem

15The LORD, the God of their fathers, sent word to them through his messengers[c]
again and again,[d] because he had pity on his people and on his dwelling place. **16**But they
mocked God's messengers, despised his words and scoffed[e] at his prophets until the
wrath[f] of the LORD was aroused against his people and there was no remedy.[g] **17**He
brought up against them the king of the Babylonians,[c] who killed their young men with
the sword in the sanctuary, and spared neither young man[h] nor young woman, old man
or aged. God handed all of them over to Nebuchadnezzar.[i] **18**He carried to Babylon all
the articles[j] from the temple of God, both large and small, and the treasures of the LORD's
temple and the treasures of the king and his officials. **19**They set fire[k] to God's temple[l]
and broke down the wall[m] of Jerusalem; they burned all the palaces and destroyed[n] everything of value there.[o]
20He carried into exile[p] to Babylon the remnant, who escaped from the sword, and
they became servants[q] to him and his sons until the kingdom of Persia came to power.
21The land enjoyed its sabbath rests;[r] all the time of its desolation it rested,[s] until the seventy years[t] were completed in fulfillment of the word of the LORD spoken by Jeremiah.
22In the first year of Cyrus[u] king of Persia, in order to fulfill the word of the LORD spoken by Jeremiah, the LORD moved the heart of Cyrus king of Persia to make a proclamation throughout his realm and to put it in writing:

23"This is what Cyrus king of Persia says:

" 'The LORD, the God of heaven, has given me all the kingdoms of the earth and
he has appointed[v] me to build a temple for him at Jerusalem in Judah. Anyone of
his people among you—may the LORD his God be with him, and let him go up.' "

a *9* One Hebrew manuscript, some Septuagint manuscripts and Syriac (see also 2 Kings 24:8); most Hebrew manuscripts *eight* b *10* Hebrew *brother,* that is, relative (see 2 Kings 24:17) c *17* Or *Chaldeans*

36:9 [u]Jer 22:24-28; 52:31
36:10 [v]ver 18; 2Ki 20:17; Ezr 1:7; Jer 22:25; 24:1; 29:1; 37:1; Eze 17:12
36:11 [w]2Ki 24:17; Jer 27:1; 28:1
36:12 [x]Jer 37:1-39:18 [y]Dt 8:3; 2Ch 7:14; 2Ch 33:23; Jer 21:3-7
36:13 [z]Eze 17:13 [a]2Ki 17:14; 2Ch 30:8
36:14 [b]1Ch 5:25
36:15 [c]Isa 5:4; 44:26; Jer 7:25; Hag 1:13; Zec 1:4; Mal 2:7; 3:1 [d]Jer 7:13,25; 25:3-4; 35:14,15; 44:4-6
36:16 [e]2Ki 2:23; Pr 1:25; Jer 5:13 [f]Ezr 5:12; Pr 1:30-31 [g]2Ch 30:10; Pr 29:1; Zec 1:2
36:17 [h]Jer 6:11 [i]Ezr 5:12; Jer 32:28
36:18 [j]ver 7,10
36:19 [k]Jer 11:16; 17:27; 21:10,14; 22:7; 32:29; 39:8; La 4:11; Eze 20:47; Am 2:5; Zec 11:1 [l]1Ki 9:8-9 [m]2Ki 14:13 [n]La 2:6 [o]Ps 79:1-3
36:20 [p]Lev 26:44; 2Ki 24:14; Ezr 2:1; Ne 7:6 [q]Jer 27:7
36:21 [r]Lev 25:4; 26:34 [s]1Ch 22:9 [t]Jer 1:1; 25:11; 27:22; 29:10; 40:1; Da 9:2; Zec 1:12; 7:5
36:22 [u]Isa 44:28; 45:1, 13; Jer 25:12; 29:10; Da 1:21; 6:28; 10:1
36:23 [v]Jdg 4:10

24:8–17. The writer of Kings closed his history with the release of Jehoiachin from prison, evidently to give his readers hope for future restoration. The Chronicler omitted this event and moved toward the Cyrus edict (vv. 22–23).

36:11–21 Zedekiah . . . became king. Reigned from 597–586 B.C. The Chronicler opened this section with material from 2 Kings 24:18–19 and Jeremiah 52:1–3 but added material from other sources no longer available (vv. 13b–23). Zedekiah sought help from Egypt, but to no avail. The Babylonians laid siege to Jerusalem for two years and finally took the city in 586 B.C.

36:12 did not humble himself. See note on 7:14.

36:13–14 became more and more unfaithful. This comment indicates that the priests and the people, as well as the king, deserved to fall under the covenant curse of exile.

36:13 turn to the LORD. See note on 7:14.

■ **36:15–23** *Trouble, Exile and Hope.* The Chronicler summarized his message by stating that God's people had continually rejected the Lord's rebukes and warnings and eventually had provoked their own exile. Nevertheless, after the appointed period of their punishment had ended, God offered hope of restoration to the promised land through the policy of the Persian king Cyrus.

36:15 his messengers. Throughout his record, the Chronicler emphasized the warnings of prophets (see note on 20:20). Jeremiah was particularly prominent at the time of Zedekiah (Jer 1:3,21; 34; 37; 38; 52).

36:16 no remedy. Compare Hebrews 6:4–6.

36:20 the remnant. From the Chronicler's point of view, those taken to Babylon constituted the remnant of Israel: They comprised the group out of whom the restored nation would come (see notes on 30:6; 1Ch 9:1b–34).

36:21 land enjoyed its sabbath rests. The Chronicler demonstrated that God had a benevolent purpose in the exile (Lev 26:40–45). **seventy years . . . spoken by Jeremiah.** See Jeremiah 25:1–14 and Daniel 9. The author assigned the end of the 70 years (v. 21) to the first year of Cyrus (538 B.C.). Perhaps he calculated from the first deportation (605/4 B.C.) under Jehoiachin (but see also Zec 1:12–17).

36:22–23 Cyrus king of Persia. This passage is repeated with some variation in Ezra 1:1–4. Cyrus exercised a liberal policy toward many peoples deported by the Babylonians. Israel's release recalled Solomon's prayer of dedication (see note on 6:36–39).

36:23 appointed me to build a temple for him at Jerusalem. The Chronicler closed his history with a report that Cyrus released the remnant of Israel, under God's direction, specifically to rebuild the temple. The Chronicler urged his postexilic readers to renew their commitment to the new temple in their day.

EZRA

Introduction

Overview

Author: Unknown
Purpose: To encourage those who returned to the promised land to continue the work that Zerubbabel, Ezra and Nehemiah had begun
Date: c. 430–400 B.C.
Key Truths:

- God endorsed and blessed Zerubbabel, Ezra and Nehemiah as they furthered the restoration after exile.
- Ezra and Nehemiah provided faithful leadership as the restoration of Israel faltered.
- The temple and Jerusalem played a central role in bringing God's blessing to his people.
- The people of God must be led to repentance and holiness in order to receive God's blessing.

Author

The same author composed Ezra and Nehemiah. Although modern translations of Ezra and Nehemiah treat them as two separate books, they were originally one work. The Hebrew Bible, the Talmud, the writings of Josephus (c. A.D. 37–100) and the oldest manuscripts of the Septuagint (the Greek translation of the OT) all treat them as one book. Origen (A.D. 185–253) was among the first to separate Ezra and Nehemiah into two books. Jerome did likewise in the translation of the Latin Vulgate (A.D. 390–405), as have modern translations.

Ezra has traditionally been considered the essential author of Ezra-Nehemiah, as well as of 1 and 2 Chronicles. Yet differences between Chronicles and Ezra-Nehemiah strongly suggest that different people wrote them (see "Introduction to 1 Chronicles"). Given Ezra's important role in Israel and his literary skills (see note on 7:6), it is likely that he was at least significantly involved in the writing of this book. Ezra no doubt wrote his memoirs (7:27—9:15) as Nehemiah wrote his (Ne 1:1—7:5; 12:27–43; 13:4–31). Ezra and Nehemiah were probably completed around 430–400 B.C.

Time and Place of Writing

In recent interpretation, questions have been raised as to the interconnections between the ministries of Ezra and Nehemiah. It has traditionally been held that Ezra came to Jerusalem in 458 B.C., "the seventh year" (7:8) of Artaxerxes I, and that Nehemiah followed him in "the twentieth year" (445 B.C.; Ne 2:1). Some interpreters have argued that Ezra 7:8 actually refers to Artaxerxes II, thus placing Ezra's arrival in 398 B.C. (after Nehemiah's in 445 B.C.). Other interpreters have amended "seventh" in Ezra 7:8 to "twenty-seventh" or "thirty-seventh," thus placing Ezra's arrival after Nehemiah's. Nevertheless, the content of the book favors the more traditional view, in which Ezra arrived before Nehemiah and their ministries overlapped. They appeared together at the reading of the law (Ne 8:9) and at the dedication of the city wall (Ne 12:26,36).

Following the traditional view, Ezra-Nehemiah was finalized between 430 and 400 B.C. Ezra most likely wrote while he worked on the restoration in and near Jerusalem.

Original Audience

Ezra-Nehemiah was written to the community of Jews in and around Jerusalem during the restoration attempt. Since the initial move toward restoration had begun a century earlier, many in the original audience must have descended from families that had lived in the area for several generations. Because the restoration continued for an extended period of time under Zerubbabel, Ezra and Nehemiah and drew a continuing influx of Jews to the area, others in the original audience were more recent transplants to the Jerusalem locale. While Ezra wrote mainly to encourage and direct those who had returned to participate in the restoration, it is likely that he also intended his work to persuade those still living in Babylon to join the restoration efforts.

Purpose and Distinctives

Ezra-Nehemiah is a historical narrative that presents the work of Zerubbabel, Ezra and Nehemiah in a very positive light. By showing only the positive side of their leadership, the book encouraged those who had returned from exile to continue the work these leaders had begun.

At least three other closely related concerns appear time and again in the book. These vital themes appear in the opening record of the decree of Cyrus (1:2–4): (1) divine authorization of the restoration program, (2) the importance of rebuilding the house of God and (3) the essential role of all the people of God in the project.

The record of the Cyrus edict twice mentions the divine authorization of the restoration program. First, Cyrus issued his all-important decree because "the LORD moved the heart of Cyrus" (1:1). Second, Cyrus himself acknowledged that his decree came from God (1:2). As the book continues, the Lord legitimated the actions of the returnees time and again. For example, those who returned did so because the Lord had moved their hearts (1:5), Ezra succeeded because the gracious hand of God was upon him (7:9) and Artaxerxes supported the rebuilding enterprise because the Lord put it in his heart (7:27).

Cyrus commissioned the return from exile for the express purposes of rebuilding "a temple . . . at Jerusalem in Judah" (1:2) and of bringing offerings "for the temple of God in Jerusalem" (1:4). The reconstruction of the temple and the city of Jerusalem was a central feature of the restoration (see "Introduction to 1 Chronicles"). The book therefore concentrates on how the temple was completed (6:13–18) and how the wall surrounding the city was built and dedicated (Ne 12:27–47). The readers who lived after these initial construction projects had ended were encouraged to perpetuate the orientation of the people of God toward the city and its temple.

Cyrus's commission was directed toward all the people of God, not merely toward this or that leader. Cyrus stressed that "anyone of [God's] people" (1:3) and "the people of any place" (1:4) could return to the land. The long lists of otherwise unknown individuals also underscore the fact that the people of God as a whole were deeply involved in the restoration of the nation (2:3–70; repeated in Ne 7:8–73). The reforms that Ezra and Nehemiah led were not limited to a select few but were designed to transform the entire community of returnees (ch. 10; Ne 13). The book stresses that all of God's people needed to be sanctified for the restoration of the nation to God's blessings.

Ezra-Nehemiah is a compilation of a number of separate documents that were masterfully woven together to form a beautiful and powerful whole. Lists play a significant role. Included are records of (1) the temple articles (1:9–11); (2) those who initially returned from exile (2:3–70; repeated in Ne 7:8–73); (3) the leaders who returned with Ezra (8:2–14); (4) those involved in mixed marriages (10:18–43); (5) those who rebuilt the wall (Ne 3); (6) those who sealed the covenant (Ne 10:1–27); (7) new residents in Jerusalem and in the surrounding towns (Ne 11); and (8) the priests and Levites who returned with Zerubbabel (Ne 12:1–26).

A good deal of official correspondence has also been included. These letters were not even translated, but were kept in their original Aramaic, the language of international diplomacy at that time and place. They include (1) the letter of Rehum to Artaxerxes (4:11–16); (2) the reply of Artaxerxes (4:17–22); (3) the letter of Tattenai to Darius (5:7–17); (4) the memorandum regarding the decree of Cyrus (6:2–5); (5) the reply of Darius to Tattenai (6:6–12); and (6) the letter of Artaxerxes on behalf of Ezra (7:12–26). Beyond this, the decree of Cyrus (1:2–4), the memoirs of Ezra (7:27—9:15) and the memoirs of Nehemiah (Ne 1:1—7:5; 12:27–43; 13:4–31) have been included.

Christ in Ezra-Nehemiah

The revelation of Christ is an important distinctive in the book of Ezra-Nehemiah. The book reveals Christ in at least five ways.

1. The work of Ezra and Nehemiah was based on the efforts of Zerubbabel, the descendant of David who represented the royal family at the beginning of the final restoration of God's people to blessing (Hag 1–2; Zec 1–8). Zerubbabel's efforts fell short of expectations, but Jesus would later descend from the line of Zerubbabel (Mt 1:12–16) and receive the promises given the house of David after exile.

2. The idealistic portrayals of Zerubbabel, Ezra and Nehemiah as leaders anticipate the work of Christ. As they devoted their lives to leading God's people toward the blessings of God, Christ leads his own toward ultimate and eternal blessings. Like Christ (Mt 23:1–39), Ezra and Nehemiah confronted and corrected sin within Israel (9:1–15; 10:10–14; Ne 1:6–7; 9:1–3,26–38; 13:15–27). Also like Christ (Jn 17:6–26),

Return From Exile

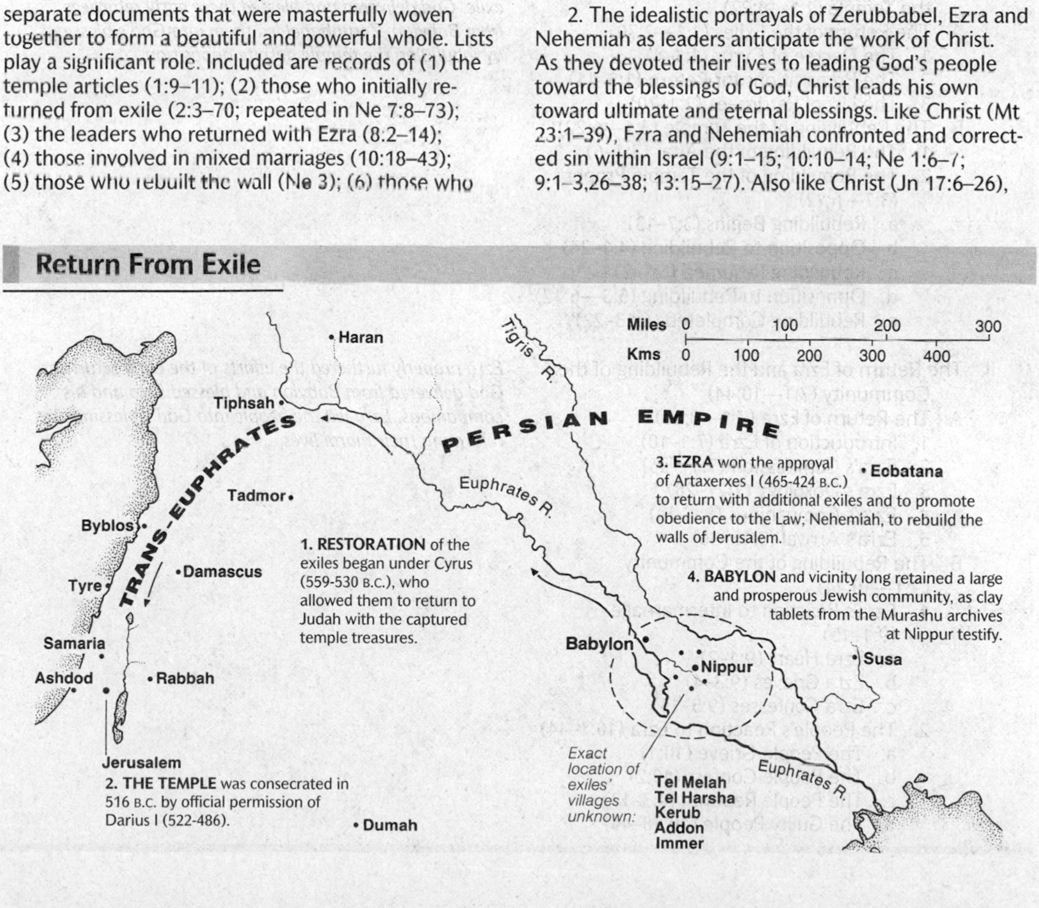
Miles 0 100 200 300
Kms 0 100 200 300 400
Haran
Tigris R.
Tiphsah
PERSIAN EMPIRE
TRANS-EUPHRATES
Tadmor
Euphrates R.
Byblos
Tyre
Damascus
Samaria
Ashdod
Rabbah
Jerusalem
Dumah
Babylon
Nippur
Susa
Ecbatana
Euphrates R.
Exact location of exiles' villages unknown:
Tel Melah
Tel Harsha
Kerub
Addon
Immer
1. RESTORATION of the exiles began under Cyrus (559-530 B.C.), who allowed them to return to Judah with the captured temple treasures.
2. THE TEMPLE was consecrated in 516 B.C. by official permission of Darius I (522-486).
3. EZRA won the approval of Artaxerxes I (465-424 B.C.) to return with additional exiles and to promote obedience to the Law; Nehemiah, to rebuild the walls of Jerusalem.
4. BABYLON and vicinity long retained a large and prosperous Jewish community, as clay tablets from the Murashu archives at Nippur testify.

they identified themselves with God's sinful people and prayed for them (9:6–15; Ne 1:4–11).

3. The focus on reconstructing and properly operating the temple in Jerusalem anticipates Christ. The temple is central in the Christian faith. Christ not only cleansed the temple (Mt 21:12–13; Jn 2:13–17); he also *became* the temple (Jn 2:19–22). He established the church as the temple of God (1Co 3:16–17; 2Co 6:16) and now ministers in the heavenly temple (Heb 9:11–12,24). When he returns, Christ will bring the new Jerusalem from heaven to the earth to make the new heavens and the new earth the holy city of God, with himself and the Father as its temple (Rev 21:22). The themes of holiness, sacrifices, prayers, forgiveness, the priesthood and the presence of God, associated with the temple in Ezra-Nehemiah, are all fulfilled in Christ.

4. The moral reforms that Ezra and Nehemiah brought to the nation also find ultimate fulfillment in Christ. Christ also called God's covenant people to return to the Lord and his law (Mt 5:17–19). In fact, through his death, his resurrection and the empowerment of his Spirit, he cleanses those who believe in him from unrighteousness and leads them into faithful living (1Jn 1:7–9), so they may inherit the blessings of God (Mt 25:34–40; Ro 6:1–23; 1Pe 3:9–12).

5. During Ezra's brief stay in Jerusalem he reconstituted Israel and gave its faith a form in which it could survive through the centuries. Ezra organized the Jewish community around the law, the Torah. From this time on, the distinguishing mark of a Jew would not be geographical or national, but adherence to the law. The law opened a way to overcome the ethnic and geographical limitations of former days. This change in Jewish faith laid the groundwork for many of the characteristics of the Christian faith. Christian worship, church organization, community life, missionary efforts and the like depended heavily on the changes that grew out of Ezra's ministry.

Outline

I. The Return of the Exiles and the Rebuilding of the Temple (1:1—6:22)

The early returnees properly began the restoration after exile. God delivered and blessed these early returnees from Babylon. Zerubbabel led them into God's blessings by rebuilding the temple despite opposition.

- A. The Return of the Exiles (1:1—2:70)
  - 1. The Decree of Cyrus (1:1–4)
  - 2. The Preparations for Return (1:5–11)
  - 3. The List of Returnees (2:1–70)
- B. The Rebuilding of the Temple (3:1—6:22)
  - 1. The Rebuilding of the Altar (3:1–6)
  - 2. The Rebuilding of the Temple Proper (3:7—6:22)
    - a. Rebuilding Begins (3:7–13)
    - b. Opposition to Rebuilding (4:1–24)
    - c. Rebuilding Resumed (5:1–2)
    - d. Opposition to Rebuilding (5:3—6:12)
    - e. Rebuilding Completed (6:13–22)

II. The Return of Ezra and the Rebuilding of the Community (7:1—10:44)

Ezra properly furthered the efforts of the early returnees. God delivered from Babylon and blessed Ezra and his companions. Ezra led the people into God's blessings by reforming their moral lives.

- A. The Return of Ezra (7:1—8:36)
  - 1. Introduction of Ezra (7:1–10)
  - 2. Ezra's Commission (7:11–26)
  - 3. Ezra's Doxology (7:27–28)
  - 4. Ezra's Companions (8:1–14)
  - 5. Ezra's Arrival (8:15–36)
- B. The Rebuilding of the Community (9:1—10:44)
  - 1. Ezra's Reaction to Intermarriage (9:1–15)
    - a. Ezra Hears (9:1–2)
    - b. Ezra Grieves (9:3–4)
    - c. Ezra Confesses (9:5–15)
  - 2. The People's Reaction to Ezra (10:1–44)
    - a. The People Grieve (10:1)
    - b. The People Confess (10:2)
    - c. The People Repent (10:3–17)
    - d. The Guilty People (10:18–44)

Cyrus Helps the Exiles to Return

1 In the first year of Cyrus king of Persia, in order to fulfill the word of the LORD spoken by Jeremiah,[a] the LORD moved the heart[b] of Cyrus king of Persia to make a proclamation throughout his realm and to put it in writing:

2 "This is what Cyrus king of Persia says:
" 'The LORD, the God of heaven, has given me all the kingdoms of the earth and
he has appointed[c] me to build[d] a temple for him at Jerusalem in Judah. 3 Anyone
of his people among you—may his God be with him, and let him go up to Jerusalem in Judah and build the temple of the LORD, the God of Israel, the God who is
in Jerusalem. 4 And the people of any place where survivors[e] may now be living are
to provide him with silver and gold, with goods and livestock, and with freewill offerings[f] for the temple of God in Jerusalem.' "[g]

5 Then the family heads of Judah and Benjamin,[h] and the priests and Levites—everyone whose heart God had moved[i]—prepared to go up and build the house[j] of the LORD
in Jerusalem. 6 All their neighbors assisted them with articles of silver and gold, with
goods and livestock, and with valuable gifts, in addition to all the freewill offerings.
7 Moreover, King Cyrus brought out the articles belonging to the temple of the LORD,
which Nebuchadnezzar had carried away from Jerusalem and had placed in the temple
of his god.[a][k] 8 Cyrus king of Persia had them brought by Mithredath the treasurer, who
counted them out to Sheshbazzar[l] the prince of Judah.
9 This was the inventory:

gold dishes	30
silver dishes	1,000
silver pans[b]	29

1:1 [a]Jer 25:11-12; 29:10-14 [b]2Ch 36:22,23
1:2 [c]Isa 44:28; 45:13 [d]Ezr 5:13
1:4 [e]Isa 10:20-22 [f]Nu 15:3; Ps 50:14; 54:6; 116:17 [g]Ezr 1:3; 5:13; 6:3, 14
1:5 [h]Ezr 4:1; Ne 11:4 [i]ver 1; Ex 35:20-22; 2Ch 36:22; Hag 1:14; Php 2:13 [j]Ps 127:1
1:7 [k]2Ki 24:13; 2Ch 36:7, 10; Ezr 5:14; 6:5
1:8 [l]Ezr 5:14

[a] 7 Or *gods* [b] 9 The meaning of the Hebrew for this word is uncertain.

▪ **1:1—6:22** *The Return of the Exiles and the Rebuilding of the Temple.* The book begins with an account of the early returnees under the leadership of Zerubbabel. These chapters divide into two main parts: the return from exile (1:1—2:70) and the reconstruction of the temple (3:1—6:22).

▪ **1:1—2:70** *The Return of the Exiles.* After the exile, Zerubbabel led some of God's people back to the land. Their return is described in three parts: the Cyrus edict (1:1–4), the preparations for their return (1:5–11) and a list of returnees (2:1–70).

▪ **1:1–4** *The Decree of Cyrus.* Cyrus, the Persian emperor, issued a decree that gave direction to the early returnees.

1:1–3 In the first . . . let him go up. The same words, with minor differences, close 2 Chronicles.

1:1 the first year. Refers to the year 538 B.C., the first year Cyrus king of Persia reigned over Babylon, which he conquered in October, 539 B.C. He reigned over Persia from 559 to 530 B.C. **to fulfill the word of the LORD.** Jeremiah had prophesied a 70-year captivity in Babylon (Jer 25:11–12; 29:10). Seventy years was a standard ancient Near Eastern way of describing a period of divine judgment. It was roughly equivalent to a lifetime (Ps 90:10) or to the lifetime of the king under which the judgment would take place (Isa 23:15), but it could be lengthened or abbreviated (see notes on Isa 23:15,17; Da 9:2; Zec 1:12). From 605 B.C. (when the first captives were deported) to 538 B.C. (when the decree to return was issued) covers a span of 67 years. Other prophecies may also be in view (see Jer 16:14–15; 27:22). The Lord brought to pass the word he had spoken over half a century earlier. **the LORD moved the heart.** God had a special role for Cyrus (see Isa 44:28; 45:1). God's work in Cyrus's heart expresses a major theme of the book: God's approval of this program of restoration (see "Introduction: Purpose and Distinctives").

1:2 the God of heaven. Cyrus used a common postexilic name for God—a title that identifies the Lord as the supreme authority and power—found primarily in Ezra, Nehemiah and Daniel. **has given me . . . has appointed me.** Cyrus testified to God's endorsement of his policy. It is doubtful that he actually understood and believed his own testimony because similar statements are made about Marduk on the Cyrus Cylinder (see note on 1:3).

1:3 Cyrus treated his other subject peoples in the same way he treated Israel. His purpose was to enlist the gods of these peoples in his own service (note the motivation of Darius in 6:10 and of Artaxerxes in 7:23). The Lord's controlling purpose, however, was to continue the progress of his redemptive purposes. **Anyone of his people.** Cyrus's commission was directed to the common people, not the leaders, expressing a major theme of the book (see "Introduction: Purpose and Distinctives"). The people of God as a whole are vital to the accomplishment of God's redemptive plan. **let him go up.** This phrase alludes to the return from exile as a new exodus. The verb translated "go up" is the same as that used to describe how the Lord brought Israel up from Egypt (Ex 32:1,4,7,8,23). The God who brought Israel from Egypt was at work to bring salvation to his people (Isa 11:11; Jer 16:14–15). **the temple . . . in Jerusalem.** Literally, "a house of the LORD . . . in Jerusalem." This "house" refers in the first place to the temple, but the reconstruction effort also included the city of God. The rebuilding of the house of God is another dominant theme in Ezra-Nehemiah (see "Introduction: Purpose and Distinctives").

1:4 people of any place. Jews had been scattered throughout the territories that were now controlled by Cyrus. **survivors.** Those who had escaped death at the hand of the Babylonians (2Ch 36:20, Ne 1:2). **to provide.** Another echo of the exodus, when the Egyptians sent the Israelites out with gifts (Ex 12:35–36).

▪ **1:5–11** *The Preparations for Return.* Following the pattern of the original exodus from Egypt, the people of God prepared to return by receiving gifts and supplies from their captors.

1:5 family heads. The patriarchs of extended families. The reference would include all those under their authority, including servants. **Judah and Benjamin.** The two tribes exiled by the Babylonians. **priests and Levites.** They played an important role among the returnees because the restoration of the temple required their services (8:15–17). **had moved.** The same Hebrew verb is used in verse 1. God's sovereign power generated both the decree and the response (see "Introduction: Purpose and Distinctives").

1:7 Nebuchadnezzar had carried away. In 597 B.C. (2Ch 36:7). It was usual for victorious armies to carry away the religious accoutrements from the temples of their enemies.

1:8 Mithredath. A Persian official. **Sheshbazzar.** Opinions have varied throughout ancient and modern history regarding his identification. This name may simply be a Persian name for Zerubbabel. It is also possible that Sheshbazzar was the official leader (perhaps Persian) whom Cyrus designated, and that Zerubbabel was the popular Jewish leader.

1:9–11 The sum of the numbers in verses 9–10 is 2,499—not the 5,400 of verse 11. For some reason, not all of the articles are included in the count at this point. There is no evident solution, and the problem is compounded by not knowing exactly what the "dishes" and "bowls" were (vv. 9–10). The emergence of the articles must have encouraged the hearts of God's people, as the articles testified to the truthfulness of his word and to his covenant faithfulness (Jer 27:22).

10 gold bowls	30
matching silver bowls	410
other articles	1,000

11 In all, there were 5,400 articles of gold and of silver. Sheshbazzar brought all these along when the exiles came up from Babylon to Jerusalem.

The List of the Exiles Who Returned

2:1 [m]2Ch 36:20; Ne 7:6 [n]2Ki 24:16; 25:12 [o]Ne 7:73
2:2 [p]1Ch 3:19 [q]Ezr 3:2 [r]Ne 10:2

2 Now these are the people of the province who came up from the captivity of the exiles,[m] whom Nebuchadnezzar king of Babylon[n] had taken captive to Babylon (they returned to Jerusalem and Judah, each to his own town,[o] 2 in company with Zerubbabel,[p] Jeshua,[q] Nehemiah, Seraiah,[r] Reelaiah, Mordecai, Bilshan, Mispar, Bigvai, Rehum and Baanah):

The list of the men of the people of Israel:

2:3 [s]Ezr 8:3
2:13 [t]Ezr 8:13
2:21 [u]Mic 5:2
2:26 [v]Jos 18:25
2:28 [w]Ge 12:8
2:34 [x]1Ki 16:34; 2Ch 28:15

3 the descendants of Parosh[s]	2,172
4 of Shephatiah	372
5 of Arah	775
6 of Pahath-Moab (through the line of Jeshua and Joab)	2,812
7 of Elam	1,254
8 of Zattu	945
9 of Zaccai	760
10 of Bani	642
11 of Bebai	623
12 of Azgad	1,222
13 of Adonikam[t]	666
14 of Bigvai	2,056
15 of Adin	454
16 of Ater (through Hezekiah)	98
17 of Bezai	323
18 of Jorah	112
19 of Hashum	223
20 of Gibbar	95
21 the men of Bethlehem[u]	123
22 of Netophah	56
23 of Anathoth	128
24 of Azmaveth	42
25 of Kiriath Jearim,[a] Kephirah and Beeroth	743
26 of Ramah[v] and Geba	621
27 of Micmash	122
28 of Bethel and Ai[w]	223
29 of Nebo	52
30 of Magbish	156
31 of the other Elam	1,254
32 of Harim	320
33 of Lod, Hadid and Ono	725
34 of Jericho[x]	345
35 of Senaah	3,630

36 The priests:

2:36 [y]1Ch 24:7

the descendants of Jedaiah[y] (through the family of Jeshua)	973

[a] *25* See Septuagint (see also Neh. 7:29); Hebrew *Kiriath Arim*.

1:11 The exiles returned to Jerusalem with the articles for the temple, according to the decree of Cyrus. The Lord kept his promise that after chastening his people for breaking the covenant, he would bring them back to the promised land (Dt 30:1–5).

■ **2:1–70** *The List of Returnees.* This list is repeated with some variations in Nehemiah 7:6–73 (see also a non-canonical book, 1 Esdras 5:4–46). Many numerical differences can be explained as errors in transmission. This list illustrates the fact that, as in every age, common people are vital to the accomplishment of God's redemptive plan (see "Introduction: Purpose and Distinctives"). In fact, "the rest of the people" (Ne 7:72) contributed more to the rebuilding than did "the heads of the families" and the governor (Ne 7:70).

2:2 Zerubbabel. He was a descendant of David, a grandson of King Jehoiachin and the leader responsible for the laying of the temple's foundation (3:8–10). **Jeshua.** The Aramaic form of the Hebrew "Joshua" and the Greek "Jesus." **Nehemiah.** Not the Nehemiah of the book of Nehemiah. **Mordecai.** Not the Mordecai of the book of Esther.

2:3–35 The first group listed is the laity. The list is divided into two parts: Part one (vv. 3–20) provides the family names of the returnees, and part two (vv. 21–35) lists the towns from which they came. That the laity is mentioned ahead of the clergy is in keeping with the emphasis in Ezra and Nehemiah on the significance of the common people in rebuilding the kingdom (see note on vv. 1–70).

Chronology: Ezra-Nehemiah

Dates below are given according to a Nisan-to-Nisan Jewish calendar (see chart, p. 115).
Roman numerals represent months;
Arabic numerals represent days.

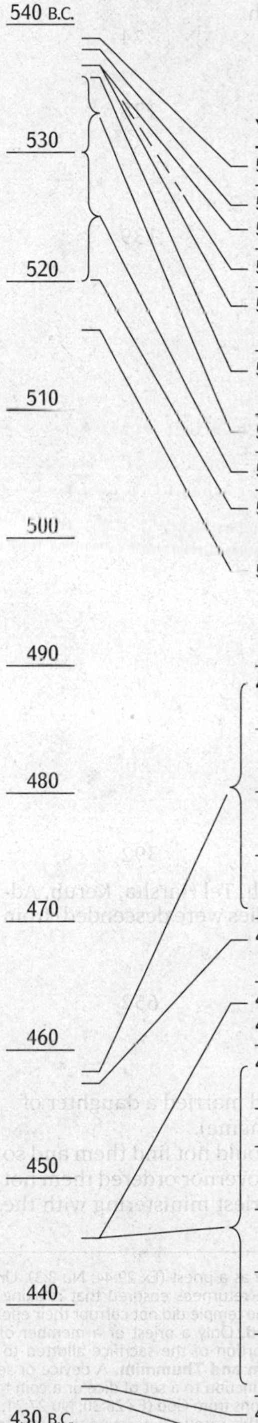

Year	Month	Day	Event	Reference
539 B.C.	Oct.	12	Capture of Babylon	Da 5:30
538 **537**	Mar. to Mar.	24 11	Cyrus's first year	Ezr 1:1-4
537(?)			Return under Sheshbazzar	Ezr 1:11
537	VII		Building of altar	Ezr 3:1
536	II		Work on temple begun	Ezr 3:8
536-530			Opposition during Cyrus's reign	Ezr 4:1-5
530-520			Work on temple ceased	Ezr 4:24
520	VI =Sept.	24 21	Work on temple renewed under Darius	Ezr 5:2; Hag 1:14
516	XII =Mar.	3 12	Temple completed	Ezr 6:15
458	I =Apr.	1 8	Ezra departs from Babylon	Ezr 7:6-9
	V =Aug.	1 4	Ezra arrives in Jerusalem	Ezr 7:8-9
	IX =Dec.	20 19	People assemble	Ezr 10:9
	X =Dec.	1 29	Committee begins investigation	Ezr 10:16
457	I =Mar.	1 27	Committee ends investigation	Ezr 10:17
445 **444**	Apr to Apr.	13 2	20th year of Artaxerxes I	Ne 1:1
444	I =Mar.–Apr.		Nehemiah approaches the king	Ne 2:1
	Aug.(?)		Nehemiah arrives in Jerusalem	Ne 2:11
	VI =Oct.	25 2	Completion of wall	Ne 6:15
	VII=Oct. to Nov.	8 5	Public assembly	Ne 7:73—8:1
	VII =Oct.	15-22 22-28	Feast of Tabernacles	Ne 8:14
	VII =Oct.	24 30	Fast	Ne 9:1
433 **432**	Apr. to Apr.	1 19	32nd year of Artaxerxes; Nehemiah's recall and return	Ne 5:14; 13:6

2:37 [z]1Ch 24:14
2:38 [a]1Ch 9:12
2:39 [b]1Ch 24:8
2:40 [c]Ge 29:34; Nu 3:9; Dt 18:6-7; 1Ch 16:4; Ezr 7:7; 8:15; Ne 12:24 [d]Ezr 3:9
2:41 [e]1Ch 15:16
2:42 [f]1Sa 3:15; 1Ch 9:17
2:43 [g]1Ch 9:2; Ne 11:21
2:58 [h]1Ki 9:21; 1Ch 9:2
2:59 [i]Nu 1:18
2:61 [j]2Sa 17:27
2:62 [k]Nu 3:10; 16:39-40
2:63 [l]Lev 2:3, 10 [m]Ex 28:30; Nu 27:21

37 of Immer[z] 1,052
38 of Pashhur[a] 1,247
39 of Harim[b] 1,017

40 The Levites:[c]

the descendants of Jeshua[d] and Kadmiel (through the line of Hodaviah) 74

41 The singers:[e]

the descendants of Asaph 128

42 The gatekeepers[f] of the temple:

the descendants of
Shallum, Ater, Talmon,
Akkub, Hatita and Shobai 139

43 The temple servants:[g]

the descendants of
Ziha, Hasupha, Tabbaoth,
44 Keros, Siaha, Padon,
45 Lebanah, Hagabah, Akkub,
46 Hagab, Shalmai, Hanan,
47 Giddel, Gahar, Reaiah,
48 Rezin, Nekoda, Gazzam,
49 Uzza, Paseah, Besai,
50 Asnah, Meunim, Nephussim,
51 Bakbuk, Hakupha, Harhur,
52 Bazluth, Mehida, Harsha,
53 Barkos, Sisera, Temah,
54 Neziah and Hatipha

55 The descendants of the servants of Solomon:

the descendants of
Sotai, Hassophereth, Peruda,
56 Jaala, Darkon, Giddel,
57 Shephatiah, Hattil,
Pokereth-Hazzebaim and Ami

58 The temple servants[h] and the descendants of the servants of Solomon 392

59 The following came up from the towns of Tel Melah, Tel Harsha, Kerub, Addon and Immer, but they could not show that their families were descended[i] from Israel:

60 The descendants of
Delaiah, Tobiah and Nekoda 652

61 And from among the priests:

The descendants of
Hobaiah, Hakkoz and Barzillai (a man who had married a daughter of Barzillai the Gileadite[j] and was called by that name).

62 These searched for their family records, but they could not find them and so were excluded from the priesthood[k] as unclean. 63 The governor ordered them not to eat any of the most sacred food[l] until there was a priest ministering with the Urim and Thummim.[m]

2:36–58 The next groups were officially associated with the temple service: the priests (vv. 36–39), the Levites (v. 40), the singers (v. 41), the gatekeepers (v. 42), the temple servants (vv. 43–54) and the servants of Solomon (vv. 55–57). That the servants of Solomon served in the temple seems clear enough, since they are counted together with the temple servants in verse 58.
2:59–63 The final group of returnees was made up of those who could not prove their ancestry. The laity is again listed first (v. 60), followed by the priests (v. 61).
2:62 excluded . . . as unclean. A man needed to prove his descent from Aaron in order to serve as a priest (Ex 29:44; Nu 3:3). Under Zerubbabel's leadership the returnees ensured that relaxing the requirements for service in the temple did not corrupt their efforts.
2:63 the most sacred food. Only a priest or a member of his household could eat the portion of the sacrifice allotted to the priests (Lev 22:10). **the Urim and Thummim.** A device or set of devices, possibly similar in function to a set of dice or a coin to be tossed, used to obtain decisions from God (Ex 28:30; Nu 27:21; 1Sa 28:6). They were needed in this case to determine the ancestry of these priests.

64The whole company numbered 42,360, 65besides their 7,337 menservants
and maidservants; and they also had 200 men and women singers.[n] 66They had
736 horses,[o] 245 mules, 67435 camels and 6,720 donkeys.

68When they arrived at the house of the LORD in Jerusalem, some of the heads of the
families[p] gave freewill offerings toward the rebuilding of the house of God on its site.
69According to their ability they gave to the treasury for this work 61,000 drachmas[a] of
gold, 5,000 minas[b] of silver and 100 priestly garments.

70The priests, the Levites, the singers, the gatekeepers and the temple servants settled in their own towns, along with some of the other people, and the rest of the Israelites settled in their towns.[q]

Rebuilding the Altar

3 When the seventh month came and the Israelites had settled in their towns,[r] the people assembled[s] as one man in Jerusalem. 2Then Jeshua[t] son of Jozadak[u] and his fellow priests and Zerubbabel son of Shealtiel[v] and his associates began to build the altar of
the God of Israel to sacrifice burnt offerings on it, in accordance with what is written in the
Law of Moses[w] the man of God. 3Despite their fear[x] of the peoples around them, they built
the altar on its foundation and sacrificed burnt offerings on it to the LORD, both the morning and evening sacrifices.[y] 4Then in accordance with what is written, they celebrated the
Feast of Tabernacles[z] with the required number of burnt offerings prescribed for each day.
5After that, they presented the regular burnt offerings, the New Moon[a] sacrifices and the
sacrifices for all the appointed sacred feasts of the LORD,[b] as well as those brought as freewill offerings to the LORD. 6On the first day of the seventh month they began to offer burnt
offerings to the LORD, though the foundation of the LORD's temple had not yet been laid.

Rebuilding the Temple

7Then they gave money to the masons and carpenters, and gave food and drink and
oil to the people of Sidon and Tyre, so that they would bring cedar logs[c] by sea from Lebanon[d] to Joppa, as authorized by Cyrus[e] king of Persia.

8In the second month of the second year after their arrival at the house of God in Jerusalem, Zerubbabel[f] son of Shealtiel, Jeshua son of Jozadak and the rest of their brothers (the priests and the Levites and all who had returned from the captivity to Jerusalem)
began the work, appointing Levites twenty[g] years of age and older to supervise the build-

2:65 [n]2Sa 19:35
2:66 [o]Isa 66:20
2:68 [p]Ex 25:2
2:70 [q]ver 1; 1Ch 9:2; Ne 11:3-4
3:1 [r]Ne 7:73; 8:1 [s]Lev 23:24
3:2 [t]Ezr 2:2; Ne 12:1, 8; Hag 2:2 [u]Hag 1:1; Zec 6:11 [v]1Ch 3:17 [w]Ex 20:24; Dt 12:5-6
3:3 [x]Ezr 4:4; Da 9:25 [y]Ex 29:39; Nu 28:1-8
3:4 [z]Ex 23:16; Nu 29:12-38; Ne 8:14-18; Zec 14:16-19
3:5 [a]Nu 28:3, 11, 14; Col 2:16 [b]Lev 23:1-44; Nu 29:39
3:7 [c]1Ch 14:1 [d]Isa 35:2 [e]Ezr 1:2-4; 6:3
3:8 [f]Zec 4:9 [g]1Ch 23:24

[a] *69* That is, about 1,100 pounds (about 500 kilograms) [b] *69* That is, about 3 tons (about 2.9 metric tons)

2:64 42,360. The same total is given in Nehemiah 7:66. However, the sum of the figures in the list in Ezra is only 29,818, while the sum of the list in Nehemiah 7 is 31,089. Either certain groups were counted but not listed or the numbers in the text have suffered corruption at some stage(s) of transmission (see note on 1:9–11).
2:68–69 freewill offerings . . . According to their ability. The first temple was also built with enthusiastic freewill offerings (1Ch 29:1–9), not with the tithe. The principle of giving beyond the tithe and according to one's ability is still at work in the new covenant in building the kingdom (2Co 8:11).
2:70 This final verse balances verse 1. In verse 1 they "came up" and "returned"; in verse 70 they "settled." The Lord had returned the people of promise to the land of promise. **in their own towns . . . in their towns.** An important element of the early restoration program was that the returnees reoccupy their ancient family inheritances (see notes on 1Ch 6:66–80).
■ **3:1—6:22** *The Rebuilding of the Temple.* The returnees rebuilt the temple in several stages. Their efforts received the Lord's endorsement and promoted the importance of the temple for the restored community. These chapters divide into two main sections: rebuilding the altar (vv. 1–6) and rebuilding the temple proper (3:7—6:22).
■ **3:1–6** *The Rebuilding of the Altar.* Zerubbabel first gave attention to restoring the altar area of the temple so that sacrifices could be presented to God.
3:1 the seventh month. Tishri (September–October) is the month of the greatest feast of the Old Testament: the Feast of Tabernacles (Lev 23:33). The desire to celebrate this feast (3:4) no doubt provided the stimulation needed to rebuild the altar.
3:2 burnt offerings. Burnt offerings were stressed (v. 6) because they were the primary offerings made (Lev 1), but others were also in view (v. 5). The burnt offering was the basis upon which a sinful people could live in the presence of a holy God (Ex 29:42); the sacrifice of Christ is the final sacrifice that brings forgiven sinners into the presence of God (Heb 10:19–20). **in accordance with what is written.** The exile resulted from the failure of God's people to keep the covenant by living according to the law. The returnees expressed concern to keep the covenant mediated through Moses (see also v. 4). Despite their commitments and accomplishments, they were unable to keep the law perfectly. Christ, who did keep the law flawlessly, became the basis of justification (Ro 5:12–21).
3:3 Despite their fear. They had the courage to build the altar and to lay the foundation of the temple. But their courage would soon be tested (4:4–5) and the work would stop (4:24).
3:4–6 Not only was the Feast of Tabernacles celebrated, but the entire sacrificial system was also set in motion from the start because sacrifices were essential for maintaining Israel's covenant with God (Heb 9:22).
■ **3:7—6:22** *The Rebuilding of the Temple Proper.* No sooner had the first sacrifices been offered than provisions were made to begin rebuilding the temple. Nevertheless, the construction of the temple was opposed, and the project required perseverance. These chapters alternate between building (3:7–13; 5:1–2; 6:13–22) and opposition to the building (4:1–24; 5:3—6:12).
■ **3:7–13** *Rebuilding Begins.* The temple was so important to the restoration of Israel that Zerubbabel and his company immediately began to rebuild it. Despite the differences between Zerubbabel's temple and that of Solomon, the verbal and thematic parallels between these verses and a variety of passages in 1 Chronicles (e.g., chs. 22–23; 28–29), as well as the mention of David's instructions (v. 10), indicate that the rebuilt temple was the genuine continuation of Solomon's temple.
3:7 Although resumption of sacrifices had a certain priority over the rebuilding of the temple, no sooner had the first sacrifices been offered than provisions were made to begin rebuilding the temple. The language of verse 7 recalls the way materials were provided for Solomon's temple (1Ch 22:2–4; 2Ch 2:8–16).
3:8 the second month. Iyyar (April–May), the same month in which Solomon began building the original temple (2Ch 3:2). **the second year.** 536 B.C. **to supervise the building of the house of**

3:9 [h]Ezr 2:40
3:10 [i]Ezr 5:16 [j]Nu 10:2; 1Ch 16:6 [k]1Ch 25:1 [l]1Ch 6:31 [m]Zec 6:12
3:11 [n]1Ch 16:34,41; 2Ch 7:3; Ps 107:1; 118:1 [o]Ne 12:24
3:12 [p]Hag 2:3,9
3:13 [q]Job 8:21; Ps 27:6; Isa 16:9

ing of the house of the LORD. 9Jeshua[h] and his sons and brothers and Kadmiel and his
sons (descendants of Hodaviah[a]) and the sons of Henadad and their sons and brothers—
all Levites—joined together in supervising those working on the house of God.
10When the builders laid[i] the foundation of the temple of the LORD, the priests in their
vestments and with trumpets,[j] and the Levites (the sons of Asaph) with cymbals, took
their places to praise[k] the LORD, as prescribed by David[l] king of Israel.[m] 11With praise
and thanksgiving they sang to the LORD:

"He is good;
his love to Israel endures forever."[n]

And all the people gave a great shout[o] of praise to the LORD, because the foundation of
the house of the LORD was laid. 12But many of the older priests and Levites and family
heads, who had seen the former temple,[p] wept aloud when they saw the foundation of
this temple being laid, while many others shouted for joy. 13No one could distinguish the
sound of the shouts of joy[q] from the sound of weeping, because the people made so
much noise. And the sound was heard far away.

[a] 9 Hebrew *Yehudah,* probably a variant of *Hodaviah*

the LORD. Virtually identical to the language used with regard to the Solomonic temple (1Ch 23:4).
3:10–11 When the builders laid the foundation. The text is less concerned with the physical structure than with the response of the people, an important theme in Ezra-Nehemiah (see "Introduction: Purpose and Distinctives").
3:12–13 But many of the older . . . who had seen the former temple. The continuity between the original temple and the newly rising temple is underscored by the presence of those who had actually seen the former temple. Moses had promised that the returnees would be blessed beyond previous generations (Dt 30:5). The older members of the community were not weeping tears of joy but tears of disappointment at the contrast between this small beginning (Zec 4:10) and the splendor of Solomon's temple. Similar disappointment would later need to be rebuked (Hag 2:1–5), but for the moment the joy of the Lord was the strength of many.

Zerubbabel's Temple

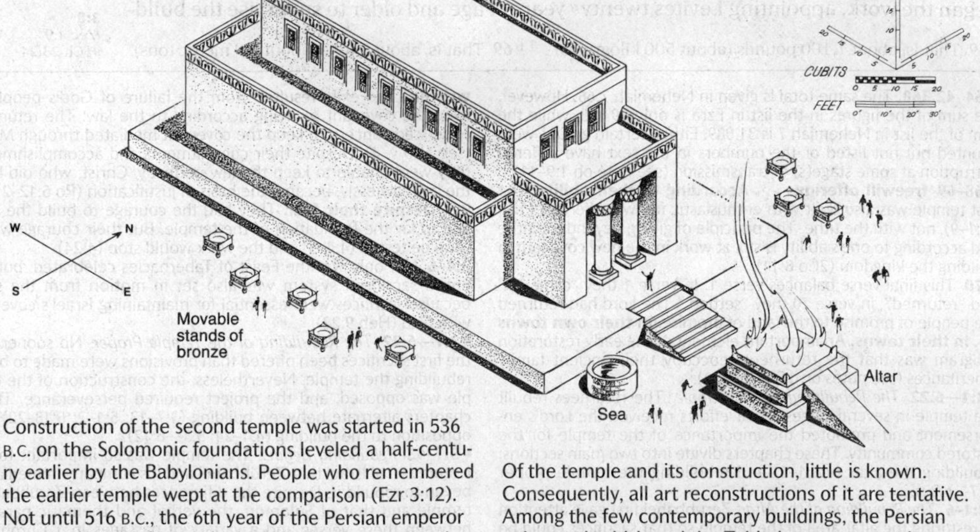

Construction of the second temple was started in 536 B.C. on the Solomonic foundations leveled a half-century earlier by the Babylonians. People who remembered the earlier temple wept at the comparison (Ezr 3:12). Not until 516 B.C., the 6th year of the Persian emperor Darius I (522-486), was the temple finally completed at the urging of Haggai and Zechariah (Ezr 6:13-15).

Archaeological evidence confirms that the Persian period in the Holy Land was a comparatively impoverished one in terms of material culture. Later Aramaic documents from Elephantine in Upper Egypt illustrate the official process of gaining permission to construct a Jewish place of worship and the opposition engendered by such a project.

Of the temple and its construction, little is known. Consequently, all art reconstructions of it are tentative. Among the few contemporary buildings, the Persian palace at Lachish and the Tobiad monument at Iraq el-Amir may be compared in terms of technique.

Unlike the more famous structures razed in 586 B.C. and A.D. 70, the temple begun by Zerubbabel suffered no major hostile destruction, but was gradually repaired and reconstructed over a long period. Eventually it was replaced entirely by Herod's magnificent edifice.

Opposition to the Rebuilding

4 When the enemies of Judah and Benjamin heard that the exiles were building a temple for the LORD, the God of Israel, 2they came to Zerubbabel and to the heads of the
families and said, "Let us help you build because, like you, we seek your God and have been
sacrificing to him since the time of Esarhaddon[r] king of Assyria, who brought us here."[s]
3But Zerubbabel, Jeshua and the rest of the heads of the families of Israel answered,
"You have no part with us in building a temple to our God. We alone will build it for the
LORD, the God of Israel, as King Cyrus, the king of Persia, commanded us."[t]
4Then the peoples around them set out to discourage the people of Judah and make
them afraid to go on building.[a][u] 5They hired counselors to work against them and frustrate their plans during the entire reign of Cyrus king of Persia and down to the reign of
Darius king of Persia.

Later Opposition Under Xerxes and Artaxerxes

6At the beginning of the reign of Xerxes,[b][v] they lodged an accusation against the people of Judah and Jerusalem.[w]
7And in the days of Artaxerxes[x] king of Persia, Bishlam, Mithredath, Tabeel and the
rest of his associates wrote a letter to Artaxerxes. The letter was written in Aramaic script
and in the Aramaic[y] language.[c,d]
8Rehum the commanding officer and Shimshai the secretary wrote a letter against Jerusalem to Artaxerxes the king as follows:
9Rehum the commanding officer and Shimshai the secretary, together with the
rest of their associates[z]—the judges and officials over the men from Tripolis, Persia,[e] Erech and Babylon, the Elamites of Susa, 10and the other people whom the
great and honorable Ashurbanipal[f] deported and settled in the city of Samaria and
elsewhere in Trans-Euphrates.[a]
11(This is a copy of the letter they sent him.)

4:2 [r]2Ki 17:24; 19:37 [s]2Ki 17:41
4:3 [t]Ezr 1:1-4; Ne 2:20
4:4 [u]Ezr 3:3
4:6 [v]Est 1:1; Da 9:1 [w]Est 3:13; 9:5
4:7 [x]Ezr 7:1; Ne 2:1 [y]2Ki 18:26; Isa 36:11; Da 2:4
4:9 [z]Ezr 5:6; 6:6,13
4:10 [a]Ver 17; Ne 4:2

[a] 4 Or *and troubled them as they built* [b] 6 Hebrew *Ahasuerus,* a variant of Xerxes' Persian name [c] 7 Or *written in Aramaic and translated* [d] 7 The text of Ezra 4:8—6:18 is in Aramaic. [e] 9 Or *officials, magistrates and governors over the men from* [f] 10 Aramaic *Osnappar,* a variant of *Ashurbanipal*

■**4:1–24** *Opposition to Rebuilding.* The disappointment of some of the people was compounded by rising opposition. The writer chronologically summarized a number of attempts to stop the reconstruction effort: those during the reigns of Cyrus in 559–530 B.C. (vv. 1–5), Xerxes in 486–465 B.C. (v. 6) and Artaxerxes I in 465–424 B.C. (vv. 7–23). He then reverted to the time of Darius I in 522–486 B.C. (v. 24).

4:1–5 This passage continues the narrative begun at 3:1 by describing the origin of the initial opposition experienced by the returnees.

4:1–2 the enemies. Though on the surface they came with good intentions ("Let us help you build"), it is clear from the initial reference to them as enemies and from the following events that they had an agenda to undermine the work of restoring the true worship of God. Although the conflict had a political manifestation, it was also a religious dispute. The enemies were the Samaritans, a group of people from various places who had been transplanted into Samaria, the area north of Judah, after the destruction of the northern kingdom of Israel in 722 B.C. (see note on 4:9–10). They worshiped many gods and incorporated the Lord into their polytheism (2Ki 17:24–41). The animosity between the Jews and the Samaritans forms an important part of the background of the New Testament (Jn 4:1–42).

4:3 We alone will build it. The motivation was neither racial nor political, but religious. From the early days of living in the promised land (Jdg 3:6) and throughout the history of the Israelites (2Ki 17:7–17), alliances with non-Israelites led to idolatry and ultimately to being exiled from the land (2Ki 17:18–23). The failure to separate would again be encountered (Ezr 9–10). This same principle of religious separation is still operative in the new covenant (2Co 6:14—7:1). When non-Israelites converted to Israel's worship, they were welcomed into the community (e.g., Ru 1:16; 4:13–22).

4:4 the peoples around them. The enemies of verse 1.

4:5 hired counselors. Perhaps referring to the bribing of a Persian official. In Moses' day Balak, king of Moab, had hired Balaam to curse Israel (Nu 22:1–20). In Nehemiah's day Sanballat hired a prophet to make Nehemiah afraid to continue building the wall. Whereas the hiring failed to stop Nehemiah, Ezra and the returnees were stalled at this point for about 17 years (4:24).

4:6–23 In verses 1–5 we read the first account of opposition experienced by the returnees in the days of Cyrus (559–530 B.C.), but we are not told the result of that opposition. In verse 24 the result is recorded: The work stopped until the second year of the reign of Darius (522–486 B.C.). The intervening verses (vv. 6–23) are a parenthesis describing opposition to rebuilding the wall after the reign of Darius and during the reigns of Xerxes (486–465 B.C.) and Artaxerxes I (464–424 B.C.). The parenthesis serves three purposes. (1) It justifies the reference to the Samaritans in verse 1 as "enemies." (2) It shows that the opposition was not a brief and passing problem but a foretaste of the prolonged opposition to be endured by the people of God in rebuilding the kingdom. (3) It links the rebuilding of the temple and the rebuilding of the wall as one construction project.

4:6 Xerxes. Successor to Darius and king of Persia from 486 to 465 B.C. **they lodged an accusation.** The subject of the verb is not specified, but the context indicates the troublemakers to have been a later generation of the "enemies" of verse 1. We are given no information about the nature of the accusation.

4:7 Artaxerxes. Artaxerxes I, successor to Xerxes and king of Persia from 464 to 424 B.C. **wrote a letter.** We are given no information about the content of this letter. However, given the context (it follows the accusation in verse 6 and precedes the letter of complaint in verses 11–16), it is clear that the letter was written in opposition to the work of rebuilding the wall. **Aramaic.** The language of international diplomacy in the ancient Near East at the time.

4:8—6:18 This section is written not in Hebrew but in Aramaic, the language in which the recorded documents were originally composed.

4:8 secretary. A high official, analogous to the modern secretary of state of the United States. **wrote a letter.** A third record of opposition to the work of rebuilding the wall. The content is provided in verses 11–16.

4:9–10 the rest of their associates. The opposition did not come from a few but was broadly based. **Ashurbanipal.** The last successful king of Assyria (668–627 B.C.). He may be the unnamed king of 2 Kings 17:24. He transplanted various peoples into Samaria after its destruction in 722 B.C. **Trans-Euphrates.** The area west of the Euphrates, including Aram, Phoenicia and the area only much later known as Palestine.

To King Artaxerxes,

From your servants, the men of Trans-Euphrates:

12The king should know that the Jews who came up to us from you have gone
to Jerusalem and are rebuilding that rebellious and wicked city. They are restoring the walls and repairing the foundations.[b]
13Furthermore, the king should know that if this city is built and its walls are
restored, no more taxes, tribute or duty[c] will be paid, and the royal revenues will
suffer. 14Now since we are under obligation to the palace and it is not proper for
us to see the king dishonored, we are sending this message to inform the king, 15so
that a search may be made in the archives[d] of your predecessors. In these records
you will find that this city is a rebellious city, troublesome to kings and provinces, a place of rebellion from ancient times. That is why this city was destroyed.[e]
16We inform the king that if this city is built and its walls are restored, you will be
left with nothing in Trans-Euphrates.

17The king sent this reply:

To Rehum the commanding officer, Shimshai the secretary and the rest of their
associates living in Samaria and elsewhere in Trans-Euphrates:[f]

Greetings.

18The letter you sent us has been read and translated in my presence. 19I issued
an order and a search was made, and it was found that this city has a long history of revolt[g] against kings and has been a place of rebellion and sedition. 20Jeru-
salem has had powerful kings ruling over the whole of Trans-Euphrates,[h] and taxes, tribute and duty were paid to them. 21Now issue an order to these men to stop
work, so that this city will not be rebuilt until I so order. 22Be careful not to neglect
this matter. Why let this threat grow, to the detriment of the royal interests?[i]

23As soon as the copy of the letter of King Artaxerxes was read to Rehum and Shimshai the secretary and their associates,[j] they went immediately to the Jews in Jerusalem
and compelled them by force to stop.

24Thus the work on the house of God in Jerusalem came to a standstill until the second year of the reign of Darius[k] king of Persia.

Tattenai's Letter to Darius

5 Now Haggai[l] the prophet and Zechariah[m] the prophet, a descendant of Iddo,
prophesied[n] to the Jews in Judah and Jerusalem in the name of the God of Israel,
who was over them. 2Then Zerubbabel[o] son of Shealtiel and Jeshua[p] son of Jozadak set
to work[q] to rebuild the house of God in Jerusalem. And the prophets of God were with
them, helping them.
3At that time Tattenai,[r] governor of Trans-Euphrates, and Shethar-Bozenai[s] and
their associates went to them and asked, "Who authorized you to rebuild this temple

4:12 [b]Ezr 5:3,9
4:13 [c]Ezr 7:24; Ne 5:4
4:15 [d]Ezr 5:17; 6:1 [e]Est 3:8
4:17 [f]ver 10
4:19 [g]2Ki 18:7
4:20 [h]Ge 15:18-21; Ex 23:31; Jos 1:4; 1Ki 4:21; 1Ch 18:3; Ps 72:8-11
4:22 [i]Da 6:2
4:23 [j]ver 9
4:24 [k]Ne 2:1-8; Da 9:25; Hag 1:1,15; Zec 1:1
5:1 [l]Ezr 6:14; Hag 1:1, 3, 12; 2:1,10,20 [m]Zec 1:1; 7:1 [n]Hag 1:14-2:9; Zec 4:9-10; 8:9
5:2 [o]1Ch 3:19; Hag 1:14; 2:21; Zec 4:6-10 [p]Ezr 2:2; 3:2 [q]ver 8; Hag 2:2-5
5:3 [r]Ezr 6:6 [s]Ezr 6:6

4:12–13 See *WLC* 145.
4:12 restoring the walls. The opposition of verses 6–23 was not a response to the rebuilding of the temple mentioned in verses 1–5 and 24 but to the rebuilding of the walls of the city that occurred at a later time (see note on verses 6–23).
4:13 Although the argumentation is in economic terms, the root of the conflict was religious, as verses 1–3 indicate.
4:14 we are under obligation to the palace. Literally, "we have salted with the salt of the palace." Probably refers to the covenantal obligation of a vassal to his overlord (Lev 2:13; Nu 18:19; 2Ch 13:5).
4:15 the archives. The various Aramaic documents used in writing this section of Ezra would have been kept in a similar archive. **a rebellious city . . . was destroyed.** The charge contains more truth than its composers realized. Although the composer of the charge was referring to rebellion against political overlords (2Ki 18:7; 24:1), the residents of Jerusalem had rebelled against their covenant Lord and acted wickedly, which resulted in the destruction of Jerusalem in 586 B.C. (2Ki 23:26–27; 24:18–20; Jer 1:14–16).
4:16 left with nothing. An obvious exaggeration that was intended to sway the king.
4:17–22 A copy of Artaxerxes' reply.
4:18 read and translated. Literally, "having been separated and was read." The king was not given a summary, but the letter was read to him word for word.
4:19–23 In the land of promise, God's people were subject to the rule of the ungodly (see 9:9 and its note) to the extent that work on the wall was halted by a decree of Artaxerxes.
4:24 After the parenthesis dealing with the later opposition to the rebuilding of the wall (vv. 6–23), the author returned to the topic of verses 1–5: the rebuilding of the temple. Whereas verses 4–5 state that the work was hindered, here we realize that it was actually stopped until the second year of Darius (about 17 years).
■ **5:1–2** *Rebuilding Resumed.* These verses continue the narrative of 4:24. The year in which Haggai and Zechariah began to prophecy was the same year referred to in 4:24, the second year of Darius (Hag 1:1; Zec 1:1). The work resumed not because of a decree by Darius but because of the preaching of God's prophets and the obedient response of God's people (Hag 1:14–15).
5:1 over them. Refers back to "the name." Both the people (Dt 28:10) and the prophets (Jer 15:16) had God's name pronounced "over them," indicating that they belonged to him.
5:2 helping them. Through courageous preaching and constant encouragement (see the books of Haggai and Zechariah).
■ **5:3—6:12** *Opposition to Rebuilding.* As soon as the work on the temple resumed, opposition came from the Persian officials of the area.

and restore this structure?"[t] 4 They also asked, "What are the names of the men constructing this building?"[a] 5 But the eye of their God[u] was watching over the elders of the Jews, and they were not stopped until a report could go to Darius and his written reply be received.

6 This is a copy of the letter that Tattenai, governor of Trans-Euphrates, and Shethar-Bozenai and their associates, the officials of Trans-Euphrates, sent to King Darius. 7 The report they sent him read as follows:

To King Darius:

Cordial greetings.

8 The king should know that we went to the district of Judah, to the temple of the great God. The people are building it with large stones and placing the timbers in the walls. The work[v] is being carried on with diligence and is making rapid progress under their direction.

9 We questioned the elders and asked them, "Who authorized you to rebuild this temple and restore this structure?"[w] 10 We also asked them their names, so that we could write down the names of their leaders for your information.

11 This is the answer they gave us:

"We are the servants of the God of heaven and earth, and we are rebuilding the temple[x] that was built many years ago, one that a great king of Israel built and finished. 12 But because our fathers angered[y] the God of heaven, he handed them over to Nebuchadnezzar the Chaldean, king of Babylon, who destroyed this temple and deported the people to Babylon.[z]

13 "However, in the first year of Cyrus king of Babylon, King Cyrus issued a decree[a] to rebuild this house of God. 14 He even removed from the temple[b] of Babylon the gold and silver articles of the house of God, which Nebuchadnezzar had taken from the temple in Jerusalem and brought to the temple[b] in Babylon.[b]

"Then King Cyrus gave them to a man named Sheshbazzar,[c] whom he had appointed governor, 15 and he told him, 'Take these articles and go and deposit them in the temple in Jerusalem. And rebuild the house of God on its site.' 16 So this Sheshbazzar came and laid the foundations of the house of God[d] in Jerusalem. From that day to the present it has been under construction but is not yet finished."

17 Now if it pleases the king, let a search be made in the royal archives[e] of Babylon to see if King Cyrus did in fact issue a decree to rebuild this house of God in Jerusalem. Then let the king send us his decision in this matter.

The Decree of Darius

6 King Darius then issued an order, and they searched in the archives[f] stored in the treasury at Babylon. 2 A scroll was found in the citadel of Ecbatana in the province of Media, and this was written on it:

5:3 [t]ver 9; Ezr 1:3; 4:12
5:5 [u]2Ki 25:28; Ezr 7:6,9,28; 8:18,22,31; Ne 2:8,18; Ps 33:18; Isa 66:14
5:8 [v]ver 2
5:9 [w]Ezr 4:12
5:11 [x]1Ki 6:1; 2Ch 3:1-2
5:12 [y]2Ch 36:16 [z]Dt 21:10; 28:36; 2Ki 24:1; 25:8,9,11; Jer 1:3
5:13 [a]Ezr 1:1
5:14 [b]Ezr 1:7; 6:5; Da 5:2 [c]1Ch 3:18
5:16 [d]Ezr 3:10; 6:15
5:17 [e]Ezr 4:15; 6:1,2
6:1 [f]Ezr 4:15; 5:17

a 4 See Septuagint; Aramaic *4We told them the names of the men constructing this building.* b 14 Or *palace*

5:5 This time God chose to intervene, and the officials permitted the work to continue until they should hear from Darius. Here, as throughout Ezra-Nehemiah, God intervened through the actions of humans.
5:7–17 A copy of the letter to Darius.
5:8 district of Judah. At this time Judah was a province in the Persian Empire, not an independent political state. **rapid progress.** Owing to the watchful supervision of God (v. 5), the preaching of the prophets (vv. 1–2) and the leadership of Zerubbabel and Jeshua (v. 2).
5:9 Who authorized you . . . ? Underscores Judah's lack of independence.
5:11–16 The reply of the Jewish leaders to the questions of the Persian officials (vv. 3–4) is included in the letter to Darius.
5:11 God of heaven and earth. A fuller form of the more frequent title "God of heaven" (see note on 1:2). **a great king of Israel.** Solomon built the original temple in the years 966 to 959 B.C. (1Ki 6:1,38).
5:12 Nebuchadnezzar destroyed the temple and deported the people, but he did so only as the human agent of the sovereign God. **handed them over.** Literally, "gave them into the hand of." God, in anger, gave the Israelites into the hand of Nebuchadnezzar to punish them for breaking the covenant and to provide a preview of the eternal destruction that awaits all those who do not trust in Christ. Those who do put their faith in Jesus have no fear of such punishment (1Jn 4:17–18). **Chaldean.** The Chaldeans inhabited southern Mesopotamia and established the Neo-Babylonian Empire by overthrowing the Assyrians in 612 B.C. The Chaldeans/Neo-Babylonians reigned until the Persians overthrew them in 539 B.C.
5:13 issued a decree. Here is the answer on the human level to the question posed in verse 3.
5:14 Sheshbazzar. See note on 1:8.
5:16 From that day . . . it has been under construction. Not continuously, for there was a break in the work of about 17 years (see note on 4:24).
5:17 let a search be made. The first search (4:15) resulted in a stoppage of the building of the wall. This second would result in the completion of the temple.
6:1–2 Darius responded to Tattenai's request. The search began in the treasury at Babylon, but the decree was found in Ecbatana, a city almost 300 miles to the northeast of Babylon and probably the location from which Cyrus issued the decree.

Memorandum:
3In the first year of King Cyrus, the king issued a decree concerning the temple of God in Jerusalem:

Let the temple be rebuilt as a place to present sacrifices, and let its foundations
be laid.[g] It is to be ninety feet[a] high and ninety feet wide, 4with three courses[h] of
large stones and one of timbers. The costs are to be paid by the royal treasury.[i]
5Also, the gold[j] and silver articles of the house of God, which Nebuchadnezzar
took from the temple in Jerusalem and brought to Babylon, are to be returned to
their places in the temple in Jerusalem; they are to be deposited in the house of
God.[k]

6Now then, Tattenai,[l] governor of Trans-Euphrates, and Shethar-Bozenai[m]
and you, their fellow officials of that province, stay away from there. 7Do not interfere with the work on this temple of God. Let the governor of the Jews and the
Jewish elders rebuild this house of God on its site.
8Moreover, I hereby decree what you are to do for these elders of the Jews in
the construction of this house of God:
The expenses of these men are to be fully paid out of the royal treasury,[n] from
the revenues[o] of Trans-Euphrates, so that the work will not stop. 9Whatever is
needed—young bulls, rams, male lambs for burnt offerings[p] to the God of heav-
en, and wheat, salt, wine and oil, as requested by the priests in Jerusalem—must
be given them daily without fail, 10so that they may offer sacrifices pleasing to the
God of heaven and pray for the well-being of the king and his sons.[q]
11Furthermore, I decree that if anyone changes this edict, a beam is to be pulled
from his house and he is to be lifted up and impaled[r] on it. And for this crime his
house is to be made a pile of rubble.[s] 12May God, who has caused his Name to
dwell there,[t] overthrow any king or people who lifts a hand to change this decree
or to destroy this temple in Jerusalem.
I Darius[u] have decreed it. Let it be carried out with diligence.

Completion and Dedication of the Temple

13Then, because of the decree King Darius had sent, Tattenai, governor of Trans-Euphrates, and Shethar-Bozenai and their associates[v] carried it out with diligence. 14So the
elders of the Jews continued to build and prosper under the preaching[w] of Haggai the
prophet and Zechariah, a descendant of Iddo. They finished building the temple according to the command of the God of Israel and the decrees of Cyrus,[x] Darius[y] and Artaxerxes,[z] kings of Persia. 15The temple was completed on the third day of the month Adar,
in the sixth year of the reign of King Darius.[a]
16Then the people of Israel—the priests, the Levites and the rest of the exiles—celebrated the dedication[b] of the house of God with joy. 17For the dedication of this house
of God they offered[c] a hundred bulls, two hundred rams, four hundred male lambs and,

6:3 [g]Ezr 3:10; Hag 2:3
6:4 [h]1Ki 6:36 [i]ver 8; Ezr 7:20
6:5 [j]1Ch 29:2 [k]Ezr 1:7; 5:14
6:6 [l]Ezr 5:3 [m]Ezr 5:3
6:8 [n]ver 4 [o]1Sa 9:20
6:9 [p]Lev 1:3,10
6:10 [q]Ezr 7:23; 1Ti 2:1-2
6:11 [r]Dt 21:22-23; Est 2:23; 5:14; 9:14 [s]Ezr 7:26; Da 2:5; 3:29
6:12 [t]Ex 20:24; Dt 12:5; 1Ki 9:3; 2Ch 6:2 [u]ver 14
6:13 [v]Ezr 4:9
6:14 [w]Ezr 5:1 [x]Ezr 1:1-4 [y]ver 12 [z]Ezr 7:1; Ne 2:1
6:15 [a]Zec 1:1; 4:9
6:16 [b]1Ki 8:63; 2Ch 7:5
6:17 [c]2Sa 6:13; 2Ch 29:21; 30:24; Ezr 8:35

[a] 3 Aramaic *sixty cubits* (about 27 meters)

6:3–5 This copy of the decree differs somewhat from that recorded in 1:2–4 (e.g., there is no reference to the Lord here). The copy in 1:2–4 is that of the heralds who proclaimed the decree to the Jews. The copy in verses 3–5 is the official record.
6:3 ninety feet high and ninety feet wide. These dimensions are larger than those of Solomon's temple (1Ki 6:2). They probably do not specify the size of the actual temple but may set an outer limit on the size of a temple Cyrus was willing to subsidize.
6:6–12 Having found the original decree, Darius issued a second that reinforced Cyrus's.
6:6–7 stay away . . . Do not interfere. As a result of the opposition, God's people could rebuild the temple under the protection of the Persian government.
6:8 expenses . . . paid out. Also as a result of the opposition, additional financial support was granted to God's people for rebuilding the temple.
6:9 Whatever is needed. Provision was made for the continuing operation of the temple service.
6:10 pray for the well-being of the king. See note on 1:3.
6:11 if anyone changes this edict. To pronounce curses on any who would change an official document was customary (Rev 22:18–19). As a result of the opposition, God's people were granted irrevocable support to rebuild the temple.
6:12 or to destroy this temple. Again as a result of the opposition, provision was made for the preservation of the temple once it had been rebuilt.
■ **6:13–22** *Rebuilding Completed.* Having faced and overcome serious opposition, the returnees finally completed the temple.
6:14 the preaching of Haggai . . . and Zechariah. The preaching of the prophets moved the people to resume the work (5:1–2) and complete it. **They finished . . . Persia.** The reference to Artaxerxes may seem out of place since the temple proper had been completed before he became king. However, "the temple" is not explicitly mentioned in the Aramaic text of verse 14, so the reference could be a preview to the completion of the rebuilding of the entire "house of God," including the community and the wall, which were reconstructed under the authority of Artaxerxes (Ezr 7:11–26; Ne 2:1,8).
6:15 The temple was completed. On March 12, 515 B.C., four years after the work had been renewed (Hag 1:15), 20 years after the project had been begun (3:8) and almost exactly 70 years after the Solomonic temple had been destroyed in 586 B.C.
6:16 the dedication of the house of God. With the dedication of the temple, a major milestone was reached. The parenthesis at 4:6–23 has already given a preview of trouble to come. The dedication of the wall (Ne 12:27) and the final reforms (Ne 13) would complete the rebuilding first mentioned in 1:2–4.
6:17 they offered. The number of offerings is small in comparison to those of Solomon (1Ki 8:62–63). The reference to the sin

as a sin offering for all Israel, twelve male goats, one for each of the tribes of Israel. 18 And
they installed the priests in their divisions[d] and the Levites in their groups[e] for the service of God at Jerusalem, according to what is written in the Book of Moses.[f]

The Passover

19 On the fourteenth day of the first month, the exiles celebrated the Passover.[g] 20 The
priests and Levites had purified themselves and were all ceremonially clean. The Levites
slaughtered[h] the Passover lamb for all the exiles, for their brothers the priests and for
themselves. 21 So the Israelites who had returned from the exile ate it, together with all
who had separated themselves[i] from the unclean practices[j] of their Gentile neighbors
in order to seek the LORD,[k] the God of Israel. 22 For seven days they celebrated with joy
the Feast of Unleavened Bread,[l] because the LORD had filled them with joy by changing
the attitude[m] of the king of Assyria, so that he assisted them in the work on the house
of God, the God of Israel.

Ezra Comes to Jerusalem

7 After these things, during the reign of Artaxerxes[n] king of Persia, Ezra son of Seraiah, the son of Azariah, the son of Hilkiah,[o] 2 the son of Shallum, the son of Zadok,[p]
the son of Ahitub,[q] 3 the son of Amariah, the son of Azariah, the son of Meraioth, 4 the son
of Zerahiah, the son of Uzzi, the son of Bukki, 5 the son of Abishua, the son of Phinehas,
the son of Eleazar, the son of Aaron the chief priest— 6 this Ezra[r] came up from Babylon.
He was a teacher well versed in the Law of Moses, which the LORD, the God of Israel, had
given. The king had granted him everything he asked, for the hand of the LORD his God
was on him.[s] 7 Some of the Israelites, including priests, Levites, singers, gatekeepers and
temple servants, also came up to Jerusalem in the seventh year of King Artaxerxes.[t]
8 Ezra arrived in Jerusalem in the fifth month of the seventh year of the king. 9 He had
begun his journey from Babylon on the first day of the first month, and he arrived in Jerusalem on the first day of the fifth month, for the gracious hand of his God was on him.[u]
10 For Ezra had devoted himself to the study and observance of the Law of the LORD, and
to teaching[v] its decrees and laws in Israel.

King Artaxerxes' Letter to Ezra

11 This is a copy of the letter King Artaxerxes had given to Ezra the priest and teacher, a man learned in matters concerning the commands and decrees of the LORD for Israel:

6:18 [d]1Ch 23:6; 2Ch 35:4; Lk 1:5 [e]1Ch 24:1 [f]Nu 3:6-9; 8:9-11; 18:1-32
6:19 [g]Ex 12:11; Nu 28:16
6:20 [h]2Ch 30:15,17; 35:11
6:21 [i]Ezr 9:1; Ne 9:2 [j]Dt 18:9; Ezr 9:11; Eze 36:25 [k]1Ch 22:19; Ps 14:2
6:22 [l]Ex 12:17 [m]Ezr 1:1
7:1 [n]Ezr 4:7; 6:14; Ne 2:1 [o]2Ki 22:4
7:2 [p]1Ki 1:8; 1Ch 6:8 [q]Ne 11:11
7:6 [r]Ne 12:36 [s]Ezr 5:5; Isa 41:20
7:7 [t]Ezr 8:1
7:9 [u]ver 6
7:10 [v]ver 25; Dt 33:10; Ne 8:1-8

---

offering shows the people's awareness of sin and faith in God, who keeps his covenant of love (Dt 7:9).
6:18 written in the Book of Moses. The phrase refers to the entire service of dedication in general, not specifically to the "divisions" instituted by David (1Ch 24:1–19), even though they were in keeping with the foundational precepts given through Moses. Here ends the first Aramaic section of Ezra.
■ **7:1—10:44** *The Return of Ezra and the Rebuilding of the Community.* Attention shifts from the initial reconstruction effort under Zerubbabel to the work of Ezra. About 60 years passed between the events at the end of chapter 6 and those at the beginning of chapter 7. The lack of intervening material portrays Ezra's work as the legitimate continuation of Zerubbabel's. These chapters divide into two main parts: Ezra's return (7:1—8:36) and his rebuilding of the community (9:1—10:44).
■ **7:1—8:36** *The Return of Ezra.* Ezra arrived in the promised land at a later time and began his own restoration program. This record of his return divides into five parts: introduction of Ezra (7:1–10), his commission (7:11–26), his doxology for God's care (7:27–28), a record of his companions (8:1–14) and his actual arrival (8:15–36).
■ **7:1–10** *Introduction of Ezra.* Ezra is introduced by a summary of his background and his arrival in Jerusalem.
7:1 After these things. The only information we have on the period between Zerubbabel and Ezra from the book of Ezra-Nehemiah concerns the opposition in the days of Xerxes (4:6). The events in the book of Esther occurred during that time (Est 1:1). **Artaxerxes.** Most likely Artaxerxes I, king of Persia from 464 to 424 B.C. **Ezra son of.** The first information given about Ezra is his ancestry. The genealogy is full, but not complete; "son of" is often used for "descendant." Enough information is given to trace Ezra's ancestry back to Aaron, establishing his priestly authority for his subsequent actions.
7:6 came up from Babylon. Not all of the believing exiles had returned with Sheshbazzar (Zerubbabel; see 1:8) in 538 B.C. Ezra's family had not. Ezra had probably not been born at the time of the first return. He grew up in Babylon, where most of the exiles lived. **a teacher well versed in the Law of Moses.** This information indicates Ezra's role in the rest of the narrative. "Teacher" translates the word traditionally rendered "scribe." In the Old Testament a scribe was a government official who carried out one or more administrative functions (e.g., wielding the staff of authority [Jdg 5:14], being an army officer in charge of conscripting people [2Ki 25:19] or being in charge of the palace [Isa 22:15]) and/or of literary functions (e.g., taking dictation [Jer 36:32]). As used in reference to Ezra, "scribe" would include governmental authority (v. 25), but the focus is on his role as a teacher of God's law (vv. 10–11,14; Ne 8:1,4,9). **which the LORD . . . had given.** The Law of Moses is divine in origin (2Ti 3:16) and may refer to the first five books of the Bible. **The king had granted him everything he asked, for the hand of the LORD . . . was on him.** God himself authorized Ezra and thus legitimized his ministry (see v. 9; see also "Introduction: Purpose and Distinctives").
7:7 Some . . . came up. Ezra did not return alone; he led a second group of returnees. **the seventh year.** 458 B.C.
7:9 He had begun . . . he arrived. The trip took place in the spring, when there would have been ample water along the way, and required about four months. **for the gracious hand of his God.** The Lord's support again authorized Ezra's ministry (see note on v. 6; see also "Introduction: Purpose and Distinctives").
7:10 For. Ezra's goal in going to Jerusalem was to teach others so that they, too, might hear and do.
■ **7:11–26** *Ezra's Commission.* Artaxerxes authorized Ezra's work via a letter.
7:11 letter. The letter (vv. 12–26), written in Aramaic, the language of international diplomacy in the ancient Near East, gave Ezra the authority he would need to carry out the reforms recorded in the following chapters. The letter may have been written by Ezra and then signed by Artaxerxes, or Artaxerxes may have had Jewish advisors help compose the letter, as some of the details seem to indicate.

12[a] Artaxerxes, king of kings,[w]

To Ezra the priest, a teacher of the Law of the God of heaven:

Greetings.

13Now I decree that any of the Israelites in my kingdom, including priests and
Levites, who wish to go to Jerusalem with you, may go. 14You are sent by the king
and his seven advisers[x] to inquire about Judah and Jerusalem with regard to the
Law of your God, which is in your hand. 15Moreover, you are to take with you the
silver and gold that the king and his advisers have freely given[y] to the God of Israel, whose dwelling[z] is in Jerusalem, 16together with all the silver and gold[a] you may
obtain from the province of Babylon, as well as the freewill offerings of the people
and priests for the temple of their God in Jerusalem.[b] 17With this money be sure to
buy bulls, rams and male lambs,[c] together with their grain offerings and drink offerings,[d] and sacrifice[e] them on the altar of the temple of your God in Jerusalem.
18You and your brother Jews may then do whatever seems best with the rest of
the silver and gold, in accordance with the will of your God. 19Deliver[f] to the God
of Jerusalem all the articles entrusted to you for worship in the temple of your God.
20And anything else needed for the temple of your God that you may have occasion to supply, you may provide from the royal treasury.[g]
21Now I, King Artaxerxes, order all the treasurers of Trans-Euphrates to provide with diligence whatever Ezra the priest, a teacher of the Law of the God of
heaven, may ask of you— 22up to a hundred talents[b] of silver, a hundred cors[c] of
wheat, a hundred baths[d] of wine, a hundred baths[d] of olive oil, and salt without
limit. 23Whatever the God of heaven has prescribed, let it be done with diligence
for the temple of the God of heaven. Why should there be wrath against the
realm of the king and of his sons?[h] 24You are also to know that you have no authority to impose taxes, tribute or duty[i] on any of the priests, Levites, singers, gatekeepers, temple servants or other workers at this house of God.[j]
25And you, Ezra, in accordance with the wisdom of your God, which you possess, appoint[k] magistrates and judges to administer justice to all the people of
Trans-Euphrates—all who know the laws of your God. And you are to teach[l] any
who do not know them. 26Whoever does not obey the law of your God and the law
of the king must surely be punished by death, banishment, confiscation of property, or imprisonment.[m]

27Praise be to the LORD, the God of our fathers, who has put it into the king's heart[n]
to bring honor[o] to the house of the LORD in Jerusalem in this way 28and who has extended his good favor[p] to me before the king and his advisers and all the king's powerful officials. Because the hand of the LORD my God was on me,[q] I took courage and gathered
leading men from Israel to go up with me.

7:12 [w]Eze 26:7; Da 2:37
7:14 [x]Est 1:14
7:15 [y]1Ch 29:6 [z]1Ch 29:6,9; 2Ch 6:2
7:16 [a]Ezr 8:25 [b]Zec 6:10
7:17 [c]2Ki 3:4 [d]Nu 15:5-12 [e]Dt 12:5-11
7:19 [f]Ezr 5:14; Jer 27:22
7:20 [g]Ezr 6:4
7:23 [h]Ezr 6:10
7:24 [i]Ezr 4:13 [j]Ezr 8:36
7:25 [k]Ex 18:21,26; Dt 16:18 [l]ver 10; Lev 10:11
7:26 [m]Ezr 6:11
7:27 [n]Ezr 1:1; 6:22 [o]1Ch 29:12
7:28 [p]2Ki 25:28 [q]Ezr 5:5; 9:9

[a] *12* The text of Ezra 7:12–26 is in Aramaic. [b] *22* That is, about 3 3/4 tons (about 3.4 metric tons) [c] *22* That is, probably about 600 bushels (about 22 kiloliters) [d] *22* That is, probably about 600 gallons (about 2.2 kiloliters)

7:12 king of kings. A typical title used by Persian monarchs to indicate their supremacy over all subject kings. That God is the true King of kings is implicit in the book of Ezra (see note on 1:1) and explicit elsewhere in Scripture (1Ti 6:15; Rev 17:14; 19:16). **teacher.** See note on 7:6.
7:13 This permission to return extended to all who were willing to go, as did the original permission by Cyrus in 1:3. Thus Ezra's ministry stressed the importance of participation by all of God's people (see "Introduction: Purpose and Distinctives").
7:14 to inquire. Whereas Cyrus commissioned the first returnees "to build" a temple (1:2), Artaxerxes commissioned Ezra "to inquire" about the spiritual condition of the people. The theme of 7:1—10:44 is therefore that of rebuilding the community, an essential element if the restored community was to continue after the days of Ezra.
7:15–17 Artaxerxes' knowledge of the details of Israelite worship strongly suggests that Ezra or Jewish advisors either wrote the letter or helped Artaxerxes in composing it (see note on v. 1).
7:18 the will of your God. Conformity to God's will is a major theme in the rest of the book: God authorized all that was done in this restoration program (see "Introduction: Purpose and Distinctives").
7:20 anything else needed. The generosity of Artaxerxes was like that of Darius (6:9).
7:23,25–28 See *WCF* 20.4; 23.3.
7:25 Ezra's role was twofold: He was to exercise governmental authority and teach the law of God (see note on v. 6). **to all the people of Trans-Euphrates.** This phrase must be interpreted in light of verse 14. It was therefore not absolute but referred to the repatriated Jews in Judah and Jerusalem.
7:26 Whoever does not obey . . . must surely be punished. Ezra himself was not explicitly given the authority to punish; the "officials and elders" (10:8) exercised this authority. Here ends the second Aramaic section of Ezra.
■ **7:27–28** *Ezra's Doxology.* Ezra offered thanks to God for his kindness and was encouraged.
7:27 put it into the king's heart. The actions of Artaxerxes are traced back to the sovereign action of God. Thus his command was legitimated.
7:28 extended his good favor. "Good favor" translates the Hebrew word *hesed,* which is used to refer to God's covenant loyalty. This exact idiom occurs in 9:9, where it is used in terms of God not deserting his people. Artaxerxes' favor toward Ezra was owing to God's covenant loyalty to his people. **Because the hand of the LORD.** Ezra's awareness of God's providential control was a source of encouragement for the tasks that lay ahead. **on me.** The first reference to Ezra in the first person and the beginning of the Ezra memoirs (see "Introduction: Author").

List of the Family Heads Returning With Ezra

8 These are the family heads and those registered with them who came up with me
from Babylon during the reign of King Artaxerxes:[r]
2 of the descendants of Phinehas, Gershom;
of the descendants of Ithamar, Daniel;
of the descendants of David, Hattush 3 of the descendants of Shecaniah;[s]
of the descendants of Parosh,[t] Zechariah, and with him were registered 150
men;
4 of the descendants of Pahath-Moab,[u] Eliehoenai son of Zerahiah, and with him
200 men;
5 of the descendants of Zattu,[a] Shecaniah son of Jahaziel, and with him 300 men;
6 of the descendants of Adin,[v] Ebed son of Jonathan, and with him 50 men;
7 of the descendants of Elam, Jeshaiah son of Athaliah, and with him 70 men;
8 of the descendants of Shephatiah, Zebadiah son of Michael, and with him 80 men;
9 of the descendants of Joab, Obadiah son of Jehiel, and with him 218 men;
10 of the descendants of Bani,[b] Shelomith son of Josiphiah, and with him 160 men;
11 of the descendants of Bebai, Zechariah son of Bebai, and with him 28 men;
12 of the descendants of Azgad, Johanan son of Hakkatan, and with him 110 men;
13 of the descendants of Adonikam,[w] the last ones, whose names were Eliphelet, Jeuel and Shemaiah, and with them 60 men;
14 of the descendants of Bigvai, Uthai and Zaccur, and with them 70 men.

The Return to Jerusalem

15 I assembled them at the canal that flows toward Ahava,[x] and we camped there
three days. When I checked among the people and the priests, I found no Levites[y] there.
16 So I summoned Eliezer, Ariel, Shemaiah, Elnathan, Jarib, Elnathan, Nathan, Zechariah and Meshullam, who were leaders, and Joiarib and Elnathan, who were men of
learning, 17 and I sent them to Iddo, the leader in Casiphia. I told them what to say to Iddo
and his kinsmen, the temple servants[z] in Casiphia, so that they might bring attendants
to us for the house of our God. 18 Because the gracious hand of our God was on us,[a] they
brought us Sherebiah, a capable man, from the descendants of Mahli son of Levi, the son
of Israel, and Sherebiah's sons and brothers, 18 men; 19 and Hashabiah, together with
Jeshaiah from the descendants of Merari, and his brothers and nephews, 20 men. 20 They
also brought 220 of the temple servants[b]—a body that David and the officials had established to assist the Levites. All were registered by name.
21 There, by the Ahava Canal,[c] I proclaimed a fast, so that we might humble ourselves
before our God and ask him for a safe journey[d] for us and our children, with all our possessions. 22 I was ashamed to ask the king for soldiers[e] and horsemen to protect us from
enemies on the road, because we had told the king, "The gracious hand of our God is on
everyone[f] who looks to him, but his great anger is against all who forsake him.[g]" 23 So
we fasted[h] and petitioned our God about this, and he answered our prayer.
24 Then I set apart twelve of the leading priests, together with Sherebiah,[i] Hashabiah and ten of their brothers, 25 and I weighed out[j] to them the offering of silver and gold
and the articles that the king, his advisers, his officials and all Israel present there had

8:1 [r]Ezr 7:7
8:3 [s]1Ch 3:22 [t]Ezr 2:3
8:4 [u]Ezr 2:6
8:6 [v]Ezr 2:15; Ne 7:20; 10:16
8:13 [w]Ezr 2:13
8:15 [x]ver 21,31 [y]Ezr 2:40; 7:7
8:17 [z]Ezr 2:43
8:18 [a]Ezr 5:5
8:20 [b]1Ch 9:2; Ezr 2:43
8:21 [c]ver 15; 2Ch 20:3 [d]Ps 5:8; 107:7
8:22 [e]Ne 2:9; Ezr 7:6,9, 28 [f]Ezr 5:5 [g]Dt 31:17; 2Ch 15:2
8:23 [h]2Ch 20:3; 33:13
8:24 [i]ver 18
8:25 [j]ver 33; Ezr 7:15, 16

[a] *5* Some Septuagint manuscripts (also 1 Esdras 8:32); Hebrew does not have *Zattu.* [b] *10* Some Septuagint manuscripts (also 1 Esdras 8:36); Hebrew does not have *Bani.*

■ **8:1–14** *Ezra's Companions.* Not all the exiles returned in response to the decree of Cyrus in 538 B.C. A second but significantly smaller group returned with Ezra about 80 years after the first return.
■ **8:15–36** *Ezra's Arrival.* Ezra recalls his preparations, travel and arrival in Jerusalem.
8:15 the canal that flows toward Ahava. The location is not known. **no Levites.** Ezra wanted more Levites for service in the temple, for general service (v. 17) and perhaps for the particular service of helping with the sacrifices (v. 35). But perhaps he also wanted Levites to be part of the caravan to the promised land, as they had been at the time of the exodus from Egypt and the first return from Babylon (see note on 1:2).
8:16–17 So I summoned. Ezra selected a group of influential men to persuade some Levites to return with him. **the leader in Casiphia.** The location is uncertain, but it may be Ctesiphon on the Tigris River, north of Babylon (literally, "Casiphia the place"). Since "the place" (Dt 12:5; see Jer 7:2–3) referred to a holy place, it seems that Casiphia was the site of a sanctuary.
8:18–20 the gracious hand of our God. Ezra did not weary of ascribing his success to God's providential control (see note on 7:6). God's gracious support legitimated Ezra's actions. Thirty-eight Levites, three key Levitical leaders and 220 temple servants were persuaded to return. Just as the Lord had stirred the hearts of Cyrus (1:1), the first returnees (1:5) and Artaxerxes (7:27), so his gracious hand moved these Levites to accept Ezra's call.
8:21 a fast. Fasting is here connected with the humbling of oneself for the purpose of making a request of God (2Ch 20:3). **safe journey.** Safety from bandits, among other dangers, is in view (v. 31).
8:22 we had told the king. Ezra had been so confident of God's approval and providential care that he would have felt hypocritical in requesting a military escort. (For a contrast between Ezra and Nehemiah in this regard, see notes on Ne 2:7,9.)
8:23 he answered our prayer. Not then and there with words, but throughout the journey with actions (vv. 31–32).
8:24 twelve. Twelve priests and twelve Levites (v. 35).
8:25 the king . . . had donated. The total contribution listed in

donated for the house of our God. 26 I weighed out to them 650 talents[a] of silver, silver articles weighing 100 talents,[b] 100 talents[b] of gold, 27 20 bowls of gold valued at 1,000 darics,[c] and two fine articles of polished bronze, as precious as gold.

28 I said to them, "You as well as these articles are consecrated to the LORD.[k] The silver and gold are a freewill offering to the LORD, the God of your fathers. 29 Guard them carefully until you weigh them out in the chambers of the house of the LORD in Jerusalem before the leading priests and the Levites and the family heads of Israel." 30 Then the priests and Levites received the silver and gold and sacred articles that had been weighed out to be taken to the house of our God in Jerusalem.

31 On the twelfth day of the first month we set out from the Ahava Canal[l] to go to Jerusalem. The hand of our God was on us, and he protected us from enemies and bandits along the way. 32 So we arrived in Jerusalem, where we rested three days.[m]

33 On the fourth day, in the house of our God, we weighed out the silver and gold and the sacred articles into the hands of Meremoth[n] son of Uriah, the priest. Eleazar son of Phinehas was with him, and so were the Levites Jozabad son of Jeshua and Noadiah son of Binnui.[o] 34 Everything was accounted for by number and weight, and the entire weight was recorded at that time.

35 Then the exiles who had returned from captivity sacrificed burnt offerings to the God of Israel: twelve bulls for all Israel, ninety-six rams, seventy-seven male lambs and, as a sin offering, twelve male goats.[p] All this was a burnt offering to the LORD. 36 They also delivered the king's orders[q] to the royal satraps and to the governors of Trans-Euphrates, who then gave assistance to the people and to the house of God.[r]

Ezra's Prayer About Intermarriage

9 After these things had been done, the leaders came to me and said, "The people of Israel, including the priests and the Levites, have not kept themselves separate[s] from the neighboring peoples with their detestable practices, like those of the Canaanites, Hittites, Perizzites, Jebusites, Ammonites,[t] Moabites, Egyptians and Amorites.[u] 2 They have taken some of their daughters[v] as wives for themselves and their sons, and have mingled the holy race[w] with the peoples around them. And the leaders and officials have led the way in this unfaithfulness."[x]

3 When I heard this, I tore my tunic and cloak, pulled hair from my head and beard and sat down appalled. 4 Then everyone who trembled[y] at the words of the God of Isra-

8:28 [k]Lev 21:6; 22:2-3
8:31 [l]ver 15
8:32 [m]Ge 40:13; Ne 2:11
8:33 [n]Ne 3:4,21 [o]Ne 3:24
8:35 [p]2Ch 29:21; Ezr 6:17
8:36 [q]Ezr 7:21-24 [r]Est 9:3
9:1 [s]Ezr 6:21; Ne 9:2 [t]Ge 19:38 [u]Ex 13:5
9:2 [v]Ex 34:16 [w]Ex 22:31 [x]Ezr 10:2
9:4 [y]Ezr 10:3

[a] *26* That is, about 25 tons (about 22 metric tons) [b] *26* That is, about 3 3/4 tons (about 3.4 metric tons) [c] *27* That is, about 19 pounds (about 8.5 kilograms)

---

verse 26 is enormous, so much so that some interpreters have doubted the authenticity of the list. The Persian kings were, however, known for their great wealth and generosity toward the religions of subject peoples; there were also wealthy Jewish families in Babylon by this time.
8:28–29 consecrated to the LORD . . . Guard them carefully. Literally, "holy to the Lord." Holiness is an attribute of the Lord (Lev 19:2) and, by extension, of anyone or anything devoted to him, especially priests (Lev 21:6), Levites (Nu 3:11–13; the NIV rendering "set apart" is literally "made holy") and temple articles (Ex 30:22–29). Ezra's strict command arose from the fact that contact between the holy and the profane results in disastrous consequences.
8:31–32 twelfth day. Ezra 7:9 says that the departure took place on the first day. The difference is to be explained by the delay experienced in order to find the needed Levites. **The hand of our God . . . So we arrived.** Ezra again attributed his success to God's support and approval. **rested three days.** Compare the similar rest of Nehemiah (Ne 2:11; see also Jos 3:2).
8:33–34 we weighed out . . . Everything was accounted for. Prayer and fasting are effective: God granted the request for a safe journey for the articles (v. 21).
8:35 sacrificed. Just as provisions had been received (7:17), so the sacrifices were offered. A picture of complete success is portrayed.
■ **9:1—10:44** *The Rebuilding of the Community.* Having set the temple into fuller operation, Ezra turned to the purification of the returnees. These chapters divide into two sections: Ezra's response to widespread intermarriage (9:1–15) and the people's reaction (10:1–44).
■ **9:1–15** *Ezra's Reaction to Intermarriage.* Ezra was told that the vast majority of returnees had married women from outside Israel and adopted their religious practices. Ezra reacted strongly to this corruption of the community. These verses divide into three parts: Ezra heard the news (vv. 1–2), grieved (vv. 3–4) and confessed before the Lord (vv. 5–15).
■ **9:1–2** *Ezra Hears.* Ezra was told of the widespread intermarriage.
9:1 After these things. Four and one-half months after the arrival (cf. 8:31 and 10:9). **the leaders came to me and said.** Ezra had come to teach the law (see note on 7:10), and perhaps in response to this teaching the leaders made him aware of sin that had been tolerated for some time. **have not kept themselves separate.** The issue was not racial but religious separation, as the following verses indicate (see vv. 10–12 and note on 4:3) and the New Testament confirms (1Co 7:39). **the neighboring peoples.** Of the list that follows, only the Ammonites, Moabites and Egyptians existed in the days of Ezra. The others were in the land during the conquest, and the mention of them may have brought to mind the original prohibitions against intermarriage (Ex 34:10–16; Dt 7:1–4).
9:2 mingled the holy race. The issue was not the mixing of racial groups but the mixing of those set apart as holy to the Lord with those still in the uncleanness of sin (see note on 8:28–29). **the leaders . . . have led the way.** The word for "leaders" here is the same one as in verse 1. Apparently not all the leaders led the way in sin; some led the way in reform.
■ **9:3–4** *Ezra Grieves.* Ezra's first reaction to the sins of the people was to grieve and mourn on their behalf.
9:3 I tore my tunic and cloak. A typical way of expressing grief (2Sa 13:19). **pulled hair from my head and beard.** An unusual way of expressing grief that appears only here in the Scriptures. Some years later Nehemiah would encounter the same sin, but rather than pulling out his own hair, he would pull out the hair of the offenders (Ne 13:25).
9:4 everyone who trembled. There was a group that had not intermarried; they had feared the Lord and kept his law (Isa 66:2). **the evening sacrifice.** About 3:00 P.M., a time of prayer as well as of sacrifice (Ps 141:2).

el gathered around me because of this unfaithfulness of the exiles. And I sat there appalled until the evening sacrifice.
5Then, at the evening sacrifice,[z] I rose from my self-abasement, with my tunic and
cloak torn, and fell on my knees with my hands spread out to the LORD my God 6and
prayed:

"O my God, I am too ashamed and disgraced to lift up my face to you, my God,
because our sins are higher than our heads and our guilt has reached to the heavens.[a] 7From the days of our forefathers[b] until now, our guilt has been great. Because
of our sins, we and our kings and our priests have been subjected to the sword[c] and
captivity,[d] to pillage and humiliation[e] at the hand of foreign kings, as it is today.
8"But now, for a brief moment, the LORD our God has been gracious[f] in leaving
us a remnant[g] and giving us a firm place[h] in his sanctuary, and so our God gives
light to our eyes[i] and a little relief in our bondage. 9Though we are slaves,[j] our God
has not deserted us in our bondage. He has shown us kindness[k] in the sight of the
kings of Persia: He has granted us new life to rebuild the house of our God and repair its ruins,[l] and he has given us a wall of protection in Judah and Jerusalem.
10"But now, O our God, what can we say after this? For we have disregarded
the commands[m] 11you gave through your servants the prophets when you said:
'The land you are entering to possess is a land polluted[n] by the corruption of its
peoples. By their detestable practices[o] they have filled it with their impurity from
one end to the other. 12Therefore, do not give your daughters in marriage to their
sons or take their daughters for your sons. Do not seek a treaty of friendship with
them[p] at any time, that you may be strong and eat the good things of the land and
leave it to your children as an everlasting inheritance.'
13"What has happened to us is a result of our evil deeds and our great guilt, and
yet, our God, you have punished us less than our sins have deserved[q] and have giv-
en us a remnant like this. 14Shall we again break your commands and intermarry[r]
with the peoples who commit such detestable practices? Would you not be angry
enough with us to destroy us,[s] leaving us no remnant[t] or survivor? 15O LORD, God
of Israel, you are righteous![u] We are left this day as a remnant. Here we are before
you in our guilt, though because of it not one of us can stand[v] in your presence.[w]"

9:5 [z]Ex 29:41
9:6 [a]2Ch 28:9; Job 42:6; Ps 38:4; Rev 18:5
9:7 [b]2Ch 29:6 [c]Eze 21:1-32 [d]Dt 28:64 [e]Dt 28:37
9:8 [f]Ps 25:16; Isa 33:2 [g]Ge 45:7 [h]Ecc 12:11; Isa 22:23 [i]Ps 13:3
9:9 [j]Ex 1:14; Ne 9:36 [k]Ezr 7:28 [l]Ps 69:35; Isa 43:1; Jer 32:44
9:10 [m]Dt 11:8; Isa 1:19-20
9:11 [n]Lev 18:25-28 [o]Dt 9:4
9:12 [p]Ex 34:15; Dt 7:3; 23:6
9:13 [q]Job 11:6; Ps 103:10
9:14 [r]Ne 13:27 [s]Dt 9:8 [t]Dt 9:14
9:15 [u]Ge 18:25; Ps 51:4; Jer 12:1; Da 9:7 [v]Ne 9:33; Ps 130:3; Mal 3:2 [w]1Ki 8:47

■ **9:5–15** *Ezra Confesses.* Ezra's initial grief turned into a prayer for forgiveness.
9:5 fell on my knees with my hands spread out. Kneeling expresses humility before the majestic Lord (Ps 95:6), and the spreading of the hands often accompanies petitioning the Lord (Ps 28:2). Elsewhere (1Ki 8:54), as here, they occur together.
9:6 ashamed and disgraced. Ezra had previously been ashamed to ask Artaxerxes for protection on the return trip (8:22). Now his shame was of a different kind—a shame joined with the guilt that results from sin. **our sins . . . our guilt.** Note the progressions from "sins" (the breaking of the law) to "guilt" (the resultant status and feeling) and from "higher than our heads" to "has reached to the heavens." Ezra was acutely aware of the people's guilt before God. Note also the sudden shift from "I" to "our." Though Ezra was not personally guilty of the particular sin in view, he identified himself with the people in their sin, as did Nehemiah concerning usury (Ne 5:1–13) and the coming suffering servant (Isa 53:12; 2Co 5:21).
9:7 From the days of our forefathers . . . our guilt . . . our sins. Solidarity throughout the generations produced a sense of corporate responsibility that spanned those generations.
9:8 a brief moment. The status of the returnees as the recipients of God's favor was in jeopardy. **God has been gracious . . . a remnant.** Justice demanded the absolute end of the people of God, but grace preserved a remnant. Through this remnant the Messiah would come and redemption would be accomplished (see notes on Isa 1:9; 10:20–22). **firm place.** Literally, "a peg." A peg was used to secure a tent (Isa 54:2) or to hang things on (Isa 22:23). The temple, where God's presence was manifest, was the place of dependence and security for God's people. As it was earlier destroyed because of covenant breech, so it could again be destroyed because of similar covenant failure. **light to our eyes.** An idiom for increased vigor (1Sa 14:25–30; Ps 13:3).
9:9 we are slaves. Though restored to their land, the people of God were not politically independent, as they had been during the monarchy (see 4:19–23 and its note). **God has not deserted us.** The word translated "deserted" is the same rendered "disregarded" in verse 10 and "forsook" elsewhere (e.g., 2Ch 29:6). God's promise not to desert the nation was, like all the typological blessings of the Mosaic covenant, conditional (see note on 10:5). If Israel forsook God and the covenant by disregarding the law, she would forfeit the blessings and experience the curses (Dt 28:20; 29:24–25; 31:16–17). God finally deserted the nation to execute his justice on Israel and to foreshadow what will happen on the day of judgment to all who stand before God on the basis of their own keeping of the law. **shown us kindness.** See 7:28, where this same idiom is translated "extended his good favor." **the kings of Persia.** Specifically Cyrus (559–530 B.C.), who issued the decree to return; Darius (522–486 B.C.), who confirmed the decree; and Artaxerxes (465–424 B.C.), who commissioned Ezra to teach the people. **a wall of protection.** Not referring to the wall built later by Nehemiah, but a figure for the protection afforded the returnees. (Note the other figurative language in v. 8 and the fact that the wall of Nehemiah was not built around Judah.)
9:10–12 See *WLC* 151.
9:10 disregarded the commands. The nation had so flagrantly departed from God's commands that covenant curses could fall upon the people at any time (see note on "deserted us" at v. 9).
9:11–12 The citation is not a quotation of a single text but a summary of the theology of separation culled from numerous texts (e.g., Lev 18:25; Dt 4:5; 7:3; 18:9; 27:23; 2Ki 21:16). It is clear that the separation was religiously, not racially, motivated. Intermarriage would result in abandoning the true worship of the living God. **the prophets.** Moses was the prophet who initially gave the command (Dt 7:1–3), but other prophets had reissued it in their preaching (Mal 2:11–12).
9:13–14 See *WCF* 19.6; *WLC* 151.
9:13 result of our evil. The exile was an execution of justice (see note on "deserted us" at v. 9). **less than our sins have deserved . . . a remnant.** The restoration was on the basis of grace and the promise of the Abrahamic covenant (Dt 4:25–31), as was the initial entrance into the land (Dt 9:5).
9:14 angry . . . leaving us no remnant. Ezra feared that the current breach of the covenant might result in ultimate judgment. Although judgment would later come upon the nation (Lk 20:9–19; Heb 8:13), even then there would be a remnant chosen by grace (Ro 11:1–5).
9:15 Ezra expressed no hope. He did not ask for forgiveness or restoration, believing that justice would prevail. Yet "where sin increased, grace increased all the more" (Ro 5:20).

The People's Confession of Sin

10 While Ezra was praying and confessing,[x] weeping and throwing himself down
before the house of God, a large crowd of Israelites—men, women and children—gathered around him. They too wept bitterly. 2Then Shecaniah son of Jehiel, one
of the descendants of Elam, said to Ezra, "We have been unfaithful[y] to our God by marrying foreign women from the peoples around us. But in spite of this, there is still hope
for Israel.[z] 3Now let us make a covenant[a] before our God to send away[b] all these wom-
en and their children, in accordance with the counsel of my lord and of those who fear
the commands of our God. Let it be done according to the Law. 4Rise up; this matter is
in your hands. We will support you, so take courage and do it."
5So Ezra rose up and put the leading priests and Levites and all Israel under oath[c] to
do what had been suggested. And they took the oath. 6Then Ezra withdrew from before
the house of God and went to the room of Jehohanan son of Eliashib. While he was there,
he ate no food and drank no water,[d] because he continued to mourn over the unfaithfulness of the exiles.
7A proclamation was then issued throughout Judah and Jerusalem for all the exiles
to assemble in Jerusalem. 8Anyone who failed to appear within three days would forfeit
all his property, in accordance with the decision of the officials and elders, and would
himself be expelled from the assembly of the exiles.
9Within the three days, all the men of Judah and Benjamin[e] had gathered in Jerusalem. And on the twentieth day of the ninth month, all the people were sitting in the
square before the house of God, greatly distressed by the occasion and because of the
rain. 10Then Ezra the priest stood up and said to them, "You have been unfaithful; you
have married foreign women, adding to Israel's guilt. 11Now make confession to the
LORD, the God of your fathers, and do his will. Separate yourselves from the peoples
around you and from your foreign wives."[f]
12The whole assembly responded with a loud voice:[g] "You are right! We must do as
you say. 13But there are many people here and it is the rainy season; so we cannot stand
outside. Besides, this matter cannot be taken care of in a day or two, because we have
sinned greatly in this thing. 14Let our officials act for the whole assembly. Then let everyone in our towns who has married a foreign woman come at a set time, along with

10:1 [x]2Ch 20:9; Da 9:20
10:2 [y]Ezr 9:2; Ne 13:27 [z]Dt 30:8-10
10:3 [a]2Ch 34:31 [b]Ex 34:16; Dt 7:2-3; Ezr 9:4
10:5 [c]Ne 5:12; 13:25
10:6 [d]Ex 34:28; Dt 9:18
10:9 [e]Ezr 1:5
10:11 [f]ver 3; Dt 24:1; Ne 9:2; Mal 2:10-16
10:12 [g]Jos 6:5

■ **10:1–44** *The People's Reaction to Ezra.* The people responded positively to Ezra's reaction to their intermarriages. These verses divide into four parts: grief (v. 1), confession (v. 2), repentance (vv. 3–17) and a list of the guilty people (vv. 18–44).
■ **10:1** *The People Grieve.* Taking their cue from Ezra's grief, the people began to weep as well.
10:1 Ezra . . . weeping . . . They too wept. The leaders had previously set the pace for sin (9:2). Here Ezra set the pace for repentance, not by exhorting the people to mourn, but by mourning himself.
■ **10:2** *The People Confess.* Ezra's confession in 9:14 became the confession of the people through one of their leaders, Shecaniah.
10:2 there is still hope. Whereas Ezra seemed to have despaired (see note on 9:15), Shecaniah encouraged him that all was not lost.
■ **10:3–17** *The People Repent.* Grief and confession led to full repentance among the people.
10:3 make a covenant. Not the making of an entirely new covenant, but the renewal of the Mosaic covenant in terms of an oath (v. 5) to keep the stipulation regarding intermarriage (see Dt 7:3; see also Jer 34:8–22 for a similar covenant renewal). **to send away.** The Hebrew word used here is not the one normally used for divorce; it is used only in this text for putting away a wife. Moreover, the Hebrew word used in verse 2 for "marrying" is not that normally used for marriage; it is used in the same way only in Nehemiah 13 (an analogous situation). Also, the Hebrew word for "foreign women" (v. 2) is used in Proverbs to refer to harlots. The author's choice of language seems to indicate that he did not regard the unions as legitimate marriages nor the sending away as actual divorces. **according to the Law.** The law does not contain a prescription for this exact situation. The phrase may refer to sending a woman away with her children and some provisions (Ge 21:14) and with certain legal rights (Dt 21:10–14). Paul instructs Christians not to marry unbelievers (1Co 7:39), but not to seek divorce from unbelieving spouses, though they are to allow the unbelieving spouse to depart if he or she wishes. In the New Testament, the unbeliever is sanctified, in a sense, through the believer, making their children holy (1Co 7:14). In Ezra's situation, however, unbelievers had so defiled the nation that extreme measures had to be taken.
10:4 Rise up . . . take courage. Ezra's despair was evident to Shecaniah.
10:5 Ezra rose up. Ezra responded to the encouragement of Shecaniah and put his advice into practice. **put . . . under oath.** The covenant was conditional, as the swearing of the oath by the Israelites (and not by the Lord) indicates. See note on 9:9. See also Jeremiah 34:8–22; *WCF* 22.2.
10:6 the room. Located in the temple. **ate no food and drank no water.** A total fast was rare (Dt 9:18). This one indicates that Ezra did not perceive the exiles to be safe from the covenant curses on the basis of their oath alone. The oath had to be confirmed by this act of contrition.
10:8 within three days. A span of time sufficient for any who wished to travel to Jerusalem, owing to the reduced territory of Judah. **forfeit . . . be expelled.** Failure to comply would result in the loss of property and in excommunication (7:26).
10:9 all the men. The people as a whole responded to the proclamation. **Judah and Benjamin.** See note on 1:5. **the twentieth day of the ninth month.** December, one of the months of the heaviest rainfall (v. 13). **greatly distressed by the occasion.** Ezra's distress had spread throughout the populace (see note on v. 1). **and because of the rain.** The use of the plural probably indicates heavy rains, which would not have been unusual for that time of year (see above entry at this note). It was highly unusual to be distressed by the rains, which were usually regarded as a blessing (Dt 11:13–15; 28:12). Torrential rains were considered, however, a sign of God's wrath (Eze 13:10–13).
10:11 make confession. Literally, "give thanks/praise to." When one confesses sin and trusts in God for mercy, praise is thereby given to God. (See Ps 103, where the psalmist praises God by confessing who God is and what he has done.) **do his will.** Confession must lead to repentance (see note on v. 6). **Separate yourselves.** See note on 9:11–12.
10:12 The whole assembly responded. Not only did all the men assemble and express their distress (v. 9), but they also agreed with Ezra as to their sin and guilt.
10:13 But. This was not an attempt to escape the responsibility to repent but an expression of genuine concern that the repentance be carried out well.
10:14 fierce anger. Perhaps perceived in the heavy rains (see note on v. 9).

the elders and judges[h] of each town, until the fierce anger[i] of our God in this matter is
turned away from us." 15Only Jonathan son of Asahel and Jahzeiah son of Tikvah, supported by Meshullam and Shabbethai[j] the Levite, opposed this.
16So the exiles did as was proposed. Ezra the priest selected men who were family
heads, one from each family division, and all of them designated by name. On the first
day of the tenth month they sat down to investigate the cases, 17and by the first day of
the first month they finished dealing with all the men who had married foreign women.

Those Guilty of Intermarriage

18 Among the descendants of the priests, the following had married foreign women:[k]

From the descendants of Jeshua[l] son of Jozadak, and his brothers: Maaseiah, Eliezer, Jarib and Gedaliah. 19(They all gave their hands[m] in pledge to put away
their wives, and for their guilt they each presented a ram from the flock as a
guilt offering.)[n]

20 From the descendants of Immer:[o]
Hanani and Zebadiah.
21 From the descendants of Harim:[p]
Maaseiah, Elijah, Shemaiah, Jehiel and Uzziah.
22 From the descendants of Pashhur:[q]
Elioenai, Maaseiah, Ishmael, Nethanel, Jozabad and Elasah.

23 Among the Levites:[r]
Jozabad, Shimei, Kelaiah (that is, Kelita), Pethahiah, Judah and Eliezer.
24 From the singers:
Eliashib.[s]
From the gatekeepers:
Shallum, Telem and Uri.

25 And among the other Israelites:

From the descendants of Parosh:[t]
Ramiah, Izziah, Malkijah, Mijamin, Eleazar, Malkijah and Benaiah.
26 From the descendants of Elam:[u]
Mattaniah, Zechariah, Jehiel, Abdi, Jeremoth and Elijah.
27 From the descendants of Zattu:
Elioenai, Eliashib, Mattaniah, Jeremoth, Zabad and Aziza.
28 From the descendants of Bebai:
Jehohanan, Hananiah, Zabbai and Athlai.
29 From the descendants of Bani:
Meshullam, Malluch, Adaiah, Jashub, Sheal and Jeremoth.
30 From the descendants of Pahath-Moab:
Adna, Kelal, Benaiah, Maaseiah, Mattaniah, Bezalel, Binnui and Manasseh.
31 From the descendants of Harim:
Eliezer, Ishijah, Malkijah, Shemaiah, Shimeon, 32Benjamin, Malluch and
Shemariah.
33 From the descendants of Hashum:
Mattenai, Mattattah, Zabad, Eliphelet, Jeremai, Manasseh and Shimei.
34 From the descendants of Bani:
Maadai, Amram, Uel, 35Benaiah, Bedeiah, Keluhi, 36Vaniah, Meremoth, Eliashib, 37Mattaniah, Mattenai and Jaasu.
38 From the descendants of Binnui:[a]
Shimei, 39Shelemiah, Nathan, Adaiah, 40Macnadebai, Shashai, Sharai, 41Aza-
rel, Shelemiah, Shemariah, 42Shallum, Amariah and Joseph.
43 From the descendants of Nebo:
Jeiel, Mattithiah, Zabad, Zebina, Jaddai, Joel and Benaiah.

44All these had married foreign women, and some of them had children by these wives.[b]

10:14 [h]Dt 16:18 [i]Nu 25:4; 2Ch 29:10; 30:8
10:15 [j]Ne 11:16
10:18 [k]Jdg 3:6 [l]Ezr 2:2
10:19 [m]2Ki 10:15 [n]Lev 5:15; 6:6
10:20 [o]1Ch 24:14
10:21 [p]1Ch 24:8
10:22 [q]1Ch 9:12
10:23 [r]Ne 8:7; 9:4
10:24 [s]Ne 3:1; 12:10; 13:7,28
10:25 [t]Ezr 2:3
10:26 [u]ver 2

[a] *37,38* See Septuagint (also 1 Esdras 9:34); Hebrew *Jaasu* [38]*and Bani and Binnui,* [b] *44* Or *and they sent them away with their children*

10:15 opposed this. They probably opposed the delay, although they may have opposed the sending away of the foreign women.

10:16–17 So the exiles did as was proposed. The distress and confession led to repentance.

■ **10:18–44** *The Guilty People.* From this list of those guilty of intermarriage it is evident that the individual who sins cannot find sanctuary within the larger community (Dt 29:19–21). But for those who avail themselves of the sacrifice provided by God, there is always forgiveness (see v. 19).

NEHEMIAH

Introduction

See "Introduction to Ezra"

Outline
(See also "Introduction to Ezra: Outline")

Outline

Nehemiah returned to Jerusalem with the approval of God and the king. Nehemiah's return was motivated by holy desires for Jerusalem and the people. With God's help Nehemiah proved faithful and successful in building the city wall despite much opposition.

I. The Return of Nehemiah and the Rebuilding of the Wall (1:1—7:3)
  A. The Return of Nehemiah (1:1—2:10)
    1. The Preparations for the Return (1:1—2:8)
      a. The Report From Judah (1:1–3)
      b. The Response of Nehemiah (1:4–11)
      c. The Request Before the King (2:1–8)
    2. Nehemiah's Return (2:9–10)
  B. The Rebuilding of the Wall (2:11—7:3)
    1. The Rebuilding Proposed (2:11–18)
    2. External Opposition (2:19–20)
    3. The Rebuilding Begun (3:1–32)
    4. Further External Opposition (4:1–14)
    5. The Rebuilding Continued (4:15–23)
    6. Internal Opposition (5:1–19)
    7. The Final Opposition (6:1–14)
    8. The Rebuilding Completed (6:15—7:3)

Nehemiah's program of restoration included bringing more people to Jerusalem and sanctifying the nation. The repopulation of Jerusalem was a central feature of Nehemiah's restoration program. Nehemiah led the people in covenant renewal, in devotion to the city, and in moral and social reforms.

II. The Return of the Exiles and the Rebuilding of the Community (7:4—13:31)
  A. The Return of the Exiles (7:4–73a)
    1. The Need to Repopulate Jerusalem (7:4–5)
    2. The Record of Returnees (7:5–73a)
  B. The Rebuilding of the Community (7:73b—13:31)
    1. The Renewal of the Covenant (7:73b–10:39)
      a. The Reading of the Law (7:73b—8:18)
      b. The Confessing of Sin (9:1–37)
      c. The Ratifying of the Oath (9:38—10:39)
    2. The Dedication of the Wall (11:1—12:47)
      a. The Preparations for the Dedication (11:1—12:26)
      b. The Dedication Proper (12:27–43)
      c. The Provisions for Clergy (12:44–47)
    3. The Reformation of the People (13:1–31)
      a. Foreigners (13:1–3)
      b. The Temple (13:4–14)
      c. The Sabbath (13:15–22)
      d. Intermarriage (13:23–31)

Nehemiah's Prayer

1 The words of Nehemiah son of Hacaliah:
In the month of Kislev[a] in the twentieth year, while I was in the citadel of Susa, 2Ha-
nani,[b] one of my brothers, came from Judah with some other men, and I questioned
them about the Jewish remnant[c] that survived the exile, and also about Jerusalem.
3They said to me, "Those who survived the exile and are back in the province are in
great trouble and disgrace. The wall of Jerusalem is broken down, and its gates have
been burned with fire.[d]"
4When I heard these things, I sat down and wept.[e] For some days I mourned and fasted[f] and prayed before the God of heaven. 5Then I said:

"O LORD, God of heaven, the great and awesome God,[g] who keeps his covenant
of love[h] with those who love him and obey his commands, 6let your ear be attentive and your eyes open to hear[i] the prayer[j] your servant is praying before you day
and night for your servants, the people of Israel. I confess the sins we Israelites,
including myself and my father's house, have committed against you. 7We have
acted very wickedly[k] toward you. We have not obeyed the commands, decrees and
laws you gave your servant Moses.
8"Remember[l] the instruction you gave your servant Moses, saying, 'If you are
unfaithful, I will scatter[m] you among the nations, 9but if you return to me and obey
my commands, then even if your exiled people are at the farthest horizon, I will
gather[n] them from there and bring them to the place I have chosen as a dwelling
for my Name.'[o]
10"They are your servants and your people, whom you redeemed by your great
strength and your mighty hand.[p] 11O Lord, let your ear be attentive[q] to the prayer
of this your servant and to the prayer of your servants who delight in revering your
name. Give your servant success today by granting him favor in the presence of
this man."

I was cupbearer[r] to the king.

1:1 [a]Ne 10:1; Zec 7:1
1:2 [b]Ne 7:2 [c]Jer 52:28
1:3 [d]2Ki 25:10; Ne 2:3, 13,17
1:4 [e]Ps 137:1 [f]Ezr 9:4
1:5 [g]Dt 7:21; Ne 4:14 [h]Ex 20:6; Da 9:4
1:6 [i]1Ki 8:29 [j]Da 9:17
1:7 [k]Dt 28:14-15; Ps 106:6
1:8 [l]2Ki 20:3 [m]Lev 26:33
1:9 [n]Dt 30:4 [o]1Ki 8:48; Jer 29:14
1:10 [p]Ex 32:11; Dt 9:29
1:11 [q]ver 6 [r]Ge 40:1

▪ **1:1—7:3** *The Return of Nehemiah and the Rebuilding of the Wall.* Nehemiah returned to the promised land and furthered the reconstruction effort begun by Zerubbabel and originally moved forward by Ezra. These chapters divide into two main parts: Nehemiah's return (1:1—2:10) and the reconstruction of Jerusalem's wall (2:11—7:3).

▪ **1:1—2:10** *The Return of Nehemiah.* After hearing about conditions in Jerusalem, Nehemiah was determined to return. These verses consist of two main components: his preparations (1:1—2:8) and his return (2:9–10).

▪ **1:1—2:8** *The Preparations for the Return.* Nehemiah recounted the way he determined to join the returnees. He received a report (1:1–3), responded to it (1:4–11) and asked for permission to go (2:1–8).

▪ **1:1–3** *The Report From Judah.* Nehemiah was properly motivated to join the returnees. A report of the difficult conditions in Judea inspired him to go.

1:1 The words of . . . Hacaliah. The book of Nehemiah was originally a continuation of the book of Ezra. **Nehemiah.** Means "The LORD has comforted." **Kislev . . . twentieth year.** November-December, 446 B.C., the twentieth year of Artaxerxes I (2:1; Ezr 7:1). **I.** The use of the first person indicates that these materials are from Nehemiah's own memoirs (see "Introduction to Ezra: Author"). **Susa.** A winter residence of the Persian kings (Est 1:2,5; 2:3; 3:15; 9:11ff.; Da 8:2).

1:2 Hanani. A shortened form of Hananiah, which means "The LORD is gracious." A certain Hananiah who was head of Jewish affairs is mentioned in the Elephantine papyri, Aramaic texts discovered in a sixth-century Jewish settlement in Egypt. He is believed by some to have been the brother of Nehemiah (7:2). **remnant.** See notes at Ezra 1:4, Isaiah 1:9, Micah 2:12 and 4:7.

1:3 The wall . . . burned with fire. Perhaps the result of the events recorded in Ezra 4:7–23, but the reference to "gates" makes the destruction by Nebuchadnezzar in 586 B.C. the more likely cause (see Isa 58:12; 61:4; 64:10 and their notes).

▪ **1:4–11** *The Response of Nehemiah.* Nehemiah revealed his holy motives for returning to the land.

1:4–6 See *WLC* 189.

1:4 fasted. Fasting is here connected with mourning (see also 1Sa 31:13) as well as with making a request of God (see note on Ezr 8:21; see also Isa 58:3 and its note). **prayed.** Nehemiah is characterized in this book as a man of prayer, an indication of why God blessed his efforts so richly (2:4; 4:4,9; 5:19; 6:9,14; 13:14,22,29,31). **the God of heaven.** See notes on Ezra 1:2 and Daniel 4:27 and 37.

1:5 In this address Nehemiah acknowledged both the transcendence and the immanence of Israel's God. The true God is not only far above his people as the "God of heaven" (see note on v. 4), but also near his people as the God of the covenant. **love.** See Ezra 7:28.

1:6 day and night. An idiom for "continually" (Jos 1:8; Ps 1:2). The reference is to the prayer of one particular day (v. 11), following four months of prayer and fasting (see 1:4; see also note on 2:1). **I confess . . . we Israelites.** See note on Ezra 9:6.

1:7 We have not obeyed. The covenant relationship between God and his people made blessings and curses dependent on the people's fidelity. The Lord would keep his promises if Israel would obey his commands (v. 5), but Israel had failed to obey, and the result was exile (see note on Ezr 9:9).

1:8 Remember. A common petition in Scripture (Dt 9:27; Ps 132:1; Jer 14:21) and particularly in Nehemiah (5:19; 6:14; 13:14,22,29,31). It does not imply that God can forget information, for he is omniscient (see theological article "Divine Omniscience" at Ps 139). It means to act upon or enact covenant blessings and judgments.

1:9 I will gather them. The Mosaic covenant promised restoration after exile (Dt 30:1–5) on the basis of the covenant made with Abraham (e.g., Ge 15:18–21). God had not revealed to Moses the specific individuals who would return or the specific time when the restoration would take place. The offer of restoration was open to all generations based upon the condition of repentance (Lev 26:40–45; Dt 4:25–31). **dwelling for my Name.** The name of God in this context is a substitution for God himself, for his near, evocable presence as he acts on behalf of his people. The place of his name is the place where he can be met and worshiped (Dt 12:5; 1Ki 8:27–30).

1:10 redeemed. The reference is to the exodus from Egypt (Ex 32:11; Mic 6:4).

1:11 who delight in revering. "Revering" translates the Hebrew word often rendered "fearing." The fear of the Lord is the proper covenantal response to God's self-revelation. To fear God is to know him (Pr 9:10), to trust him (Pss 5:7; 34:11,22) and to obey him (Pr 8:13). **this man.** Artaxerxes I. **cupbearer.** A member of the royal court whose responsibility it was to select wine (2:1) and safeguard it from poison; his access to the king entailed prestige and influence at court.

Artaxerxes Sends Nehemiah to Jerusalem

2:1 [s]Ezr 7:1

2 In the month of Nisan in the twentieth year of King Artaxerxes,[s] when wine was
brought for him, I took the wine and gave it to the king. I had not been sad in his
presence before; 2so the king asked me, "Why does your face look so sad when you are
not ill? This can be nothing but sadness of heart."

2:3 [t]1Ki 1:31; Da 2:4; 5:10; 6:6,21 [u]Ps 137:6 [v]Ne 1:3

I was very much afraid, 3but I said to the king, "May the king live forever![t] Why should
my face not look sad when the city[u] where my fathers are buried lies in ruins, and its
gates have been destroyed by fire?[v]"
4The king said to me, "What is it you want?"
Then I prayed to the God of heaven, 5and I answered the king, "If it pleases the king
and if your servant has found favor in his sight, let him send me to the city in Judah where
my fathers are buried so that I can rebuild it."

2:6 [w]Ne 5:14; 13:6

6Then the king[w], with the queen sitting beside him, asked me, "How long will your
journey take, and when will you get back?" It pleased the king to send me; so I set a time.
7I also said to him, "If it pleases the king, may I have letters to the governors of Trans-

2:7 [x]Ezr 8:36

Euphrates,[x] so that they will provide me safe-conduct until I arrive in Judah? 8And may

2:8 [y]Ne 7:2 [z]ver 18; Ezr 5:5; 7:6

I have a letter to Asaph, keeper of the king's forest, so he will give me timber to make
beams for the gates of the citadel[y] by the temple and for the city wall and for the residence I will occupy?" And because the gracious hand of my God was upon me,[z] the king
granted my requests. 9So I went to the governors of Trans-Euphrates and gave them the

2:9 [a]Ezr 8:22

king's letters. The king had also sent army officers and cavalry[a] with me.

2:10 [b]ver 19; Ne 4:1,7 [c]Ne 4:3; 13:4-7 [d]Est 10:3

10When Sanballat[b] the Horonite and Tobiah[c] the Ammonite official heard about this,
they were very much disturbed that someone had come to promote the welfare of the Israelites.[d]

Nehemiah Inspects Jerusalem's Walls

2:11 [e]Ge 40:13

11I went to Jerusalem, and after staying there three days[e] 12I set out during the night
with a few men. I had not told anyone what my God had put in my heart to do for Jerusalem. There were no mounts with me except the one I was riding on.

2:13 [f]2Ch 26:9 [g]Ne 3:13 [h]Ne 1:3

13By night I went out through the Valley Gate[f] toward the Jackal[a] Well and the Dung
Gate,[g] examining the walls[h] of Jerusalem, which had been broken down, and its gates,

2:14 [i]Ne 3:15 [j]2Ki 18:17

which had been destroyed by fire. 14Then I moved on toward the Fountain Gate[i] and the
King's Pool,[j] but there was not enough room for my mount to get through; 15so I went
up the valley by night, examining the wall. Finally, I turned back and reentered through
the Valley Gate. 16The officials did not know where I had gone or what I was doing, be-

[a] 13 Or *Serpent* or *Fig*

■ **2:1–8** *The Request Before the King.* God's authorization of Nehemiah's return was affirmed by the king's unexpected response.

2:1 Nisan . . . twentieth year. March–April of 445 B.C., four months after Nehemiah had received the report about Jerusalem. It was the Persian New Year, a time of celebration, perhaps alluded to by the reference to wine (see note on 1:11). **King Artaxerxes.** See note on Ezra 4:7.

2:2 much afraid. Perhaps Nehemiah feared the king's wrath (see Pr 16:14), either because Nehemiah was sad on a festive occasion or because he was about to ask the king to reverse a previous decision (Ezr 4:21). Or perhaps Nehemiah feared that he would fail in his mission to gain permission to rebuild Jerusalem.

2:5 so that I can rebuild it. Rebuilding the city was one aspect of rebuilding the "house of God," a major theme in Ezra-Nehemiah (see "Introduction to Ezra: Purpose and Distinctives") and the focus of Nehemiah 1:1—7:3.

2:6 How long . . . I set a time. It may seem doubtful that Nehemiah requested the 12-year absence presumed in 5:14, but his request to rebuild the gates of a residence (v. 8) seems to indicate that more than a brief leave was in view from the beginning.

2:7–8 I also said . . . my requests. Nehemiah made several specific requests. **letters.** The two references to letters in verses 7–8 are part of a major theme in Ezra-Nehemiah. **timber . . . for the gates.** Here the scope of the building project becomes clear: fortress, walls, governor's palace. **the gracious hand of my God.** Nehemiah's success was owed to God's sovereign good pleasure (Ezr 7:6), and it indicated God's approval of Nehemiah's role in the restoration program (see "Introduction to Ezra: Purpose and Distinctives").

■ **2:9–10** *Nehemiah's Return.* Nehemiah left for the promised land, but his return stirred up trouble.

2:10 When Sanballat . . . heard. References to the enemies having "heard" punctuate the rest of Nehemiah 1:1—7:3 like a refrain (2:19; 4:1,5,15; 6:1,16). At each step the conflict escalated until it was resolved (6:16). **Sanballat.** A Babylonian name, meaning "Sin [the moon god] gives life." He was the governor of Samaria, the area north of Judah. That he worshiped Yahweh, the God of Israel, in some fashion (2Ki 17:24–41) is suggested by the names of his sons, Deliah and Shelemiah, both of which contain a shortened form of "Yahweh." **Tobiah.** Probably the governor of Ammon, the area east of Judah. The name means "The LORD is good," which indicates that his parents probably worshiped the God of Israel and suggests that perhaps he did too (6:17–18; 13:4). **very much disturbed.** The opposition had a political aspect but was religious at its root (see v. 20; see also note on Ezr 4:3–4). The resistance experienced here encourages the readers of this book to persevere against opponents in their own day. See *WLC* 148.

■ **2:11—7:3** *The Rebuilding of the Wall.* Nehemiah devoted himself to erecting the walls of Jerusalem not only to bring political stability but also to create a holy city for the temple of God. These chapters alternate between Nehemiah's efforts to rebuild (2:11–18; 3:1–32; 4:15–23; 6:15—7:3) and opposition that he overcame (2:19–20; 4:1–15; 5:1–19; 6:1–14).

■ **2:11–18** *The Rebuilding Proposed.* Nehemiah arrived in Jerusalem, surveyed the situation and proposed the reconstruction of the city walls.

2:11 three days. His decision was carefully considered. Nehemiah's three-day wait after arriving in Jerusalem compares with Ezra and his three-day wait (Ezr 8:32). Ezra acted publicly; Nehemiah, secretly (note the emphasis on "had not told anyone" in v. 12; see also v. 16).

2:13 Valley Gate. A gate from the Persian period has been uncovered by archaeologists and identified as this gate.

cause as yet I had said nothing to the Jews or the priests or nobles or officials or any others who would be doing the work.
[17]Then I said to them, "You see the trouble we are in: Jerusalem lies in ruins, and its
gates have been burned with fire.[k] Come, let us rebuild the wall[l] of Jerusalem, and we
will no longer be in disgrace.[m]" [18]I also told them about the gracious hand of my God
upon me[n] and what the king had said to me.
They replied, "Let us start rebuilding." So they began this good work.
[19]But when Sanballat the Horonite, Tobiah the Ammonite official and Geshem[o] the
Arab heard about it, they mocked and ridiculed us.[p] "What is this you are doing?" they
asked. "Are you rebelling against the king?"
[20]I answered them by saying, "The God of heaven will give us success. We his servants
will start rebuilding, but as for you, you have no share[q] in Jerusalem or any claim or historic right to it."

Builders of the Wall

3 Eliashib[r] the high priest and his fellow priests went to work and rebuilt[s] the Sheep
Gate.[t] They dedicated it and set its doors in place, building as far as the Tower of
the Hundred, which they dedicated, and as far as the Tower of Hananel.[u] [2]The men of
Jericho[v] built the adjoining section, and Zaccur son of Imri built next to them.
[3]The Fish Gate[w] was rebuilt by the sons of Hassenaah. They laid its beams and put

2:17 [k]Ne 1:3 [l]Ps 102:16; Isa 30:13; 58:12 [m]Eze 5:14
2:18 [n]2Sa 2:7
2:19 [o]Ne 6:1,2,6 [p]Ps 44:13-16
2:20 [q]Ezr 4:3
3:1 [r]Ezr 10:24 [s]Isa 58:12 [t]ver 32; Ne 12:39 [u]Ne 12:39; Jer 31:38; Zec 14:10
3:2 [v]Ne 7:36
3:3 [w]2Ch 33:14; Ne 12:39

2:17 ruins. The city had lain in ruins for almost 150 years (see note on 1:3). An earlier attempt to rebuild the wall had been stopped (Ezr 4:7–23). **rebuild the wall.** See note on verse 5.
2:18 God . . . the king. Nehemiah's acknowledgment of God's sovereignty as the ultimate source of his plan undergirded the actions of the human king. **Let us start.** Nehemiah's initiative met with wholehearted support on the part of the leaders of Judah. The response of the leaders led to success and to God's blessing (see note on Ezr 1:5).
■ **2:19–20** *External Opposition.* Upon hearing of Nehemiah's work, nations surrounding Judah opposed him, but Nehemiah expressed his confidence in God.
2:19 Sanballat . . . Tobiah. See verse 10 and its note. **Geshem the Arab.** A third opponent of Nehemiah, along with Sanballat and Tobiah (v. 10). He was probably an Arab chief controlling the area to the south of Judah. Nehemiah is pictured as virtually surrounded by opponents: Sanballat to the north, Tobiah to the east and Geshem to the south (see note on 4:7–8).
2:20 God of heaven. See note on 1:5. **success.** Nehemiah had previously requested success from God (1:11). Here he expressed confidence that the sovereign God of heaven would grant success to the people. **you have no share.** On this religious exclusivity, see note on Ezra 4:3.
■ **3:1–32** *The Rebuilding Begun.* The record of the reconstruction of the wall proceeds with a list of various people responsible for different portions of it. The entire perimeter of the city is covered, and the involvement of all the people of God is underscored, as the book stresses in a number of places (see "Introduction to Ezra: Purpose and Distinctives").
3:1 Eliashib. The grandson of Jeshua, the high priest during the days of Zerubbabel (see note on Ezr 2:2). **Sheep Gate.** Located at the northeast corner of the city (Jn 5:2). The description in the following verses moves counterclockwise, returning to the Sheep Gate in verse 32. **Tower . . . Tower.** Their locations are not precisely known, but they would have been on the northern flank of the wall, the section of the city with the least natural defense.
3:3 Fish Gate. A main gate on the north side (2Ch 33:14; Zep 1:10), probably the gate through which the merchants would have entered (13:16).

Jerusalem of the Returning Exiles

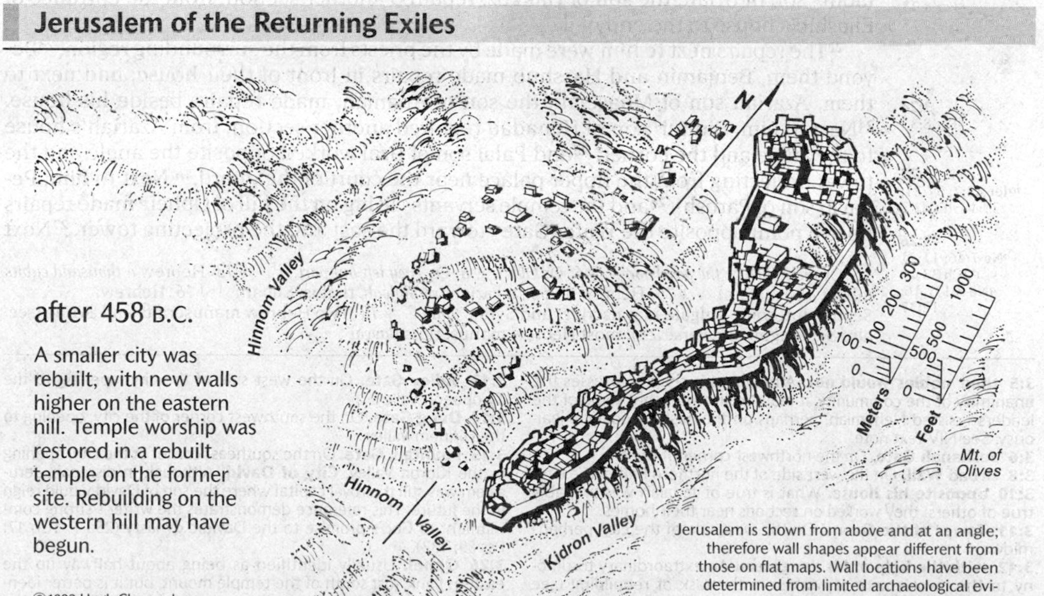

after 458 B.C.

A smaller city was rebuilt, with new walls higher on the eastern hill. Temple worship was restored in a rebuilt temple on the former site. Rebuilding on the western hill may have begun.

Jerusalem is shown from above and at an angle; therefore wall shapes appear different from those on flat maps. Wall locations have been determined from limited archaeological evidence; houses are artist's concept.

its doors and bolts and bars in place. **4**Meremoth son of Uriah, the son of Hakkoz, repaired the next section. Next to him Meshullam son of Berekiah, the son of Meshezabel,
made repairs, and next to him Zadok son of Baana also made repairs. **5**The next section
3:5 [x]2Sa 14:2 was repaired by the men of Tekoa,[x] but their nobles would not put their shoulders to the
work under their supervisors.[a]

3:6 [y]Ne 12:39 **6**The Jeshanah[b] Gate[y] was repaired by Joiada son of Paseah and Meshullam son of
Besodeiah. They laid its beams and put its doors and bolts and bars in place. **7**Next to
3:7 [z]Jos 9:3; Ne 2:7 them, repairs were made by men from Gibeon[z] and Mizpah—Melatiah of Gibeon and Ja-
don of Meronoth—places under the authority of the governor of Trans-Euphrates. **8**Uzziel son of Harhaiah, one of the goldsmiths, repaired the next section; and Hananiah, one
of the perfume-makers, made repairs next to that. They restored[c] Jerusalem as far as the
3:8 [a]Ne 12:38 Broad Wall.[a] **9**Rephaiah son of Hur, ruler of a half-district of Jerusalem, repaired the next
section. **10**Adjoining this, Jedaiah son of Harumaph made repairs opposite his house, and
Hattush son of Hashabneiah made repairs next to him. **11**Malkijah son of Harim and Has-
3:11 [b]Ne 12:38 shub son of Pahath-Moab repaired another section and the Tower of the Ovens.[b] **12**Shallum son of Hallohesh, ruler of a half-district of Jerusalem, repaired the next section with
the help of his daughters.

3:13 [c]2Ch 26:9 [d]Jos 15:34 **13**The Valley Gate[c] was repaired by Hanun and the residents of Zanoah.[d] They rebuilt
[e]Ne 2:13 it and put its doors and bolts and bars in place. They also repaired five hundred yards[d]
of the wall as far as the Dung Gate.[e]

3:14 **14**The Dung Gate was repaired by Malkijah son of Recab, ruler of the district of Beth
[f]Jer 6:1 Hakkerem.[f] He rebuilt it and put its doors and bolts and bars in place.

15The Fountain Gate was repaired by Shallun son of Col-Hozeh, ruler of the district
3:15 of Mizpah. He rebuilt it, roofing it over and putting its doors and bolts and bars in place.
[g]Isa 8:6; Jn 9:7 He also repaired the wall of the Pool of Siloam,[e][g] by the King's Garden, as far as the steps
going down from the City of David. **16**Beyond him, Nehemiah son of Azbuk, ruler of a half-
3:16 [h]Jos 15:58 [i]Ac 2:29 district of Beth Zur,[h] made repairs up to a point opposite the tombs[f][i] of David, as far as
the artificial pool and the House of the Heroes.
3:17 **17**Next to him, the repairs were made by the Levites under Rehum son of Bani. Beside
[j]Jos 15:44 him, Hashabiah, ruler of half the district of Keilah,[j] carried out repairs for his district.
18Next to him, the repairs were made by their countrymen under Binnui[g] son of Henadad, ruler of the other half-district of Keilah. **19**Next to him, Ezer son of Jeshua, ruler of
Mizpah, repaired another section, from a point facing the ascent to the armory as far as
the angle. **20**Next to him, Baruch son of Zabbai zealously repaired another section, from
the angle to the entrance of the house of Eliashib the high priest. **21**Next to him, Mere-
3:21 [k]Ezr 8:33 moth[k] son of Uriah, the son of Hakkoz, repaired another section, from the entrance of
Eliashib's house to the end of it.

22The repairs next to him were made by the priests from the surrounding region. **23**Beyond them, Benjamin and Hasshub made repairs in front of their house; and next to
3:24 them, Azariah son of Maaseiah, the son of Ananiah, made repairs beside his house.
[l]Ezr 8:33 **24**Next to him, Binnui[l] son of Henadad repaired another section, from Azariah's house
to the angle and the corner, **25**and Palal son of Uzai worked opposite the angle and the
3:25 [m]Jer 32:2; 37:21; tower projecting from the upper palace near the court of the guard.[m] Next to him, Pe-
39:14 [n]Ezr 2:3 daiah son of Parosh[n] **26**and the temple servants[o] living on the hill of Ophel[p] made repairs
up to a point opposite the Water Gate[q] toward the east and the projecting tower. **27**Next

3:26 [o]Ne 7:46; 11:21 [p]2Ch 33:14 [q]Ne 8:1,3,16; 12:37

[a] *5* Or *their Lord* or *the governor* [b] *6* Or *Old* [c] *8* Or *They left out part of* [d] *13* Hebrew *a thousand cubits* (about 450 meters) [e] *15* Hebrew *Shelah,* a variant of *Shiloah,* that is, Siloam [f] *16* Hebrew; Septuagint, some Vulgate manuscripts and Syriac *tomb* [g] *18* Two Hebrew manuscripts and Syriac (see also Septuagint and verse 24); most Hebrew manuscripts *Bavvai*

3:5 their nobles would not. Although this chapter stresses the unanimity of the community, it realistically notes that some of the leaders resisted Nehemiah, perhaps on the basis of political jealousy. See NIV text note.
3:6 Jeshanah Gate. On the northwest corner of the city.
3:8 Broad Wall. On the west side of the northern half of the city.
3:10 opposite his house. What is true of Jedaiah was probably true of others: they worked on sections near their homes.
3:11 Tower of the Ovens. On the west side of the city, perhaps midway.
3:12 with the help of his daughters. An extraordinary testimony to the involvement of women in the task of rebuilding (see notes on 5:1; 12:43).
3:13 Valley Gate. On the west side of the city, opening to the Tyropoeon Valley.
3:14 Dung Gate. On the southwest corner of the city, opening to the Hinnom Valley.
3:15 Fountain Gate. On the southeast corner of the city, opening to the Kidron Valley. **City of David.** Although in disrepair, Jerusalem was still the royal capital where the son of David would reign in the future. This reference demonstrates the writer's strong commitment to God's promise to the Davidic dynasty (2Sa 7; 1Ch 17; Pss 89; 132).
3:26 Ophel. Usually identified as being about halfway up the eastern flank, just south of the temple mount, but it is better identified as also including the southern portion of the city below the

to them, the men of Tekoa[r] repaired another section, from the great projecting tower[s]
to the wall of Ophel.

28Above the Horse Gate,[t] the priests made repairs, each in front of his own house.
29Next to them, Zadok son of Immer made repairs opposite his house. Next to him, Shemaiah son of Shecaniah, the guard at the East Gate, made repairs. 30Next to him, Hananiah son of Shelemiah, and Hanun, the sixth son of Zalaph, repaired another section.
Next to them, Meshullam son of Berekiah made repairs opposite his living quarters.
31Next to him, Malkijah, one of the goldsmiths, made repairs as far as the house of the
temple servants and the merchants, opposite the Inspection Gate, and as far as the room
above the corner; 32and between the room above the corner and the Sheep Gate[u] the
goldsmiths and merchants made repairs.

Opposition to the Rebuilding

4 When Sanballat[v] heard that we were rebuilding the wall, he became angry and was
greatly incensed. He ridiculed the Jews, 2and in the presence of his associates[w] and
the army of Samaria, he said, "What are those feeble Jews doing? Will they restore their
wall? Will they offer sacrifices? Will they finish in a day? Can they bring the stones back
to life from those heaps of rubble[x]—burned as they are?"
3Tobiah[y] the Ammonite, who was at his side, said, "What they are building—if even
a fox climbed up on it, he would break down their wall of stones!"[z]

4Hear us, O our God, for we are despised.[a] Turn their insults back on their own heads.
Give them over as plunder in a land of captivity. 5Do not cover up their guilt[b] or blot out
their sins from your sight,[c] for they have thrown insults in the face of[a] the builders.

6So we rebuilt the wall till all of it reached half its height, for the people worked with
all their heart.
7But when Sanballat, Tobiah,[d] the Arabs, the Ammonites and the men of Ashdod
heard that the repairs to Jerusalem's walls had gone ahead and that the gaps were being closed, they were very angry. 8They all plotted together[e] to come and fight against
Jerusalem and stir up trouble against it. 9But we prayed to our God and posted a guard
day and night to meet this threat.
10Meanwhile, the people in Judah said, "The strength of the laborers[f] is giving out,
and there is so much rubble that we cannot rebuild the wall."
11Also our enemies said, "Before they know it or see us, we will be right there among
them and will kill them and put an end to the work."
12Then the Jews who lived near them came and told us ten times over, "Wherever you
turn, they will attack us."
13Therefore I stationed some of the people behind the lowest points of the wall at the
exposed places, posting them by families, with their swords, spears and bows. 14After I
looked things over, I stood up and said to the nobles, the officials and the rest of the people, "Don't be afraid[g] of them. Remember[h] the Lord, who is great and awesome,[i] and
fight[j] for your brothers, your sons and your daughters, your wives and your homes."
15When our enemies heard that we were aware of their plot and that God had frustrated it,[k] we all returned to the wall, each to his own work.

[a] 5 Or *have provoked you to anger before*

3:27 [r]ver 5 [s]Ps 48:12
3:28 [t]2Ki 11:16; 2Ch 23:15; Jer 31:40
3:32 [u]ver 1; Jn 5:2
4:1 [v]Ne 2:10
4:2 [w]Ezr 4:9-10 [x]Ps 79:1; Jer 26:18
4:3 [y]Ne 2:10 [z]Job 13:12; 15:3
4:4 [a]Ps 44:13; 79:12; 123:3-4; Jer 33:24
4:5 [b]Isa 2:9; La 1:22 [c]2Ki 14:27; Ps 51:1; 69:27-28; 109:14; Jer 18:23
4:7 [d]Ne 2:10
4:8 [e]Ps 2:2; 83:1-18
4:10 [f]1Ch 23:4
4:14 [g]Ge 28:15; Nu 14:9; Dt 1:29 [h]Ne 1:8 [i]Ne 1:5 [j]2Sa 10:12
4:15 [k]2Sa 17:14; Job 5:12

Water Gate. **Water Gate.** About midway up the east side of the city, opening to the Kidron Valley and the Gihon Spring, the main water source.
3:28 Horse Gate. On the northeast side of the city.
3:29 East Gate. Just north of the Horse Gate.
3:31 Inspection Gate. Just north of the East Gate and just south of the Sheep Gate.
3:32 Sheep Gate. The description has come full circle (see note on v. 1).
■**4:1–14** *Further External Opposition.* The opposition from outside the Jewish community escalated.
4:1–3 When Sanballat heard. See note on 2:10.
4:4–5 This is the first of three such imprecatory prayers that called down just curses on the enemies of God (6:14; 13:29). Such prayers were offered in the extreme circumstances of Israel's holy conflicts with aggressive enemies (Pss 79:12; 94:1–3; 137:7–9). This kind of prayer must be understood within the framework of Old Testament holy war and must be balanced with the principle of mercy and kindness toward others (Mt 5:43–45; Ro 12:14–21). Even as the people of God sacrificially serve others who oppose them, they pray for Christ's victory, which will one day involve eternal judgment for his enemies.
4:7–8 when Sanballat . . . heard. One more group is added to the list of enemies: the men of Ashdod. Nehemiah was now completely encircled by opponents, as Ashdod lay to the west (see note on 2:19).
4:10 the people in Judah. Literally, "Judah." A collective term is used, emphasizing the widespread nature of the discouragement. **The strength . . . the wall.** A poetic couplet that was perhaps being sung by the people. The discouragement arose, in part, simply from the difficult nature of the work.
4:11–12 Also our enemies said. The intimidation by the enemies was finally having an effect. **ten times over.** The threat of violence was growing in the minds of the people.
4:13 stationed. Nehemiah stationed additional guards at the most vulnerable points. The tension continued to rise as the people of Judah took up arms for the first time after the exile.
■**4:15–23** *The Rebuilding Continued.* Nehemiah led the people to continue to build the wall despite opposition.
4:15 God had frustrated it. In Ezra 4:5 and 24 the enemy had

16 From that day on, half of my men did the work, while the other half were equipped with spears, shields, bows and armor. The officers posted themselves behind all the people of Judah 17 who were building the wall. Those who carried materials did their work with one hand and held a weapon[l] in the other, 18 and each of the builders wore his sword at his side as he worked. But the man who sounded the trumpet[m] stayed with me.

19 Then I said to the nobles, the officials and the rest of the people, "The work is extensive and spread out, and we are widely separated from each other along the wall. 20 Wherever you hear the sound of the trumpet,[n] join us there. Our God will fight[o] for us!"

21 So we continued the work with half the men holding spears, from the first light of dawn till the stars came out. 22 At that time I also said to the people, "Have every man and his helper stay inside Jerusalem at night, so they can serve us as guards by night and workmen by day." 23 Neither I nor my brothers nor my men nor the guards with me took off our clothes; each had his weapon, even when he went for water.[a]

Nehemiah Helps the Poor

5 Now the men and their wives raised a great outcry against their Jewish brothers. 2 Some were saying, "We and our sons and daughters are numerous; in order for us to eat and stay alive, we must get grain."

3 Others were saying, "We are mortgaging our fields,[p] our vineyards and our homes to get grain during the famine."[q]

4 Still others were saying, "We have had to borrow money to pay the king's tax[r] on our fields and vineyards. 5 Although we are of the same flesh and blood[s] as our countrymen and though our sons are as good as theirs, yet we have to subject our sons and daughters to slavery.[t] Some of our daughters have already been enslaved, but we are powerless, because our fields and our vineyards belong to others."[u]

6 When I heard their outcry and these charges, I was very angry. 7 I pondered them in my mind and then accused the nobles and officials. I told them, "You are exacting usury[v] from your own countrymen!" So I called together a large meeting to deal with them 8 and said: "As far as possible, we have bought[w] back our Jewish brothers who were sold to the Gentiles. Now you are selling your brothers, only for them to be sold back to us!" They kept quiet, because they could find nothing to say.[x]

9 So I continued, "What you are doing is not right. Shouldn't you walk in the fear of our God to avoid the reproach[y] of our Gentile enemies? 10 I and my brothers and my men are also lending the people money and grain. But let the exacting of usury stop![z] 11 Give

4:17 [l]Ps 149:6
4:18 [m]Nu 10:2
4:20 [n]Eze 33:3 [o]Ex 14:14; Dt 1:30; 20:4; Jos 10:14
5:3 [p]Ps 109:11 [q]Ge 47:23
5:4 [r]Ezr 4:13
5:5 [s]Ge 29:14 [t]Lev 25:39-43,47; 2Ki 4:1; Isa 50:1 [u]Dt 15:7-11; 2Ki 4:1
5:7 [v]Ex 22:25-27; Lev 25:35-37; Dt 23:19-20; 24:10-13
5:8 [w]Lev 25:47 [x]Jer 34:8
5:9 [y]Isa 52:5
5:10 [z]Ex 22:25

a *23* The meaning of the Hebrew for this clause is uncertain.

---

frustrated the plan to build the temple; now God responded in kind to frustrate the plan to stop the work on the wall. **we all returned to the wall.** Nehemiah's twofold action to stem the tide of discouragement—adding guards and exhorting the people—met with success.

4:16 spears . . . armor. The arms first mentioned in verse 13 are supplemented here with shield and armor (a chest guard of metal).

4:17 Those who carried . . . held a weapon. The carriers had a hand free to hold a "weapon," which may have been no more than a stone for throwing.

4:18 the builders wore his sword. The builders needed two hands to work, so they wore swords at their sides. **the trumpet.** The trumpet, or shofar, had numerous functions in the Old Testament. In this context it would have been used for rallying the troops (v. 20), as in Judges 3:27.

4:21 till the stars came out. Indicates how strong the resolve to complete the work had become, because work usually ended at sundown.

4:23 he went for water. See NIV text note.

■ **5:1–19** *Internal Opposition.* This section contains a digression from the main topic of antagonism from outsiders to draw attention to related internal problems. There were economic problems for at least four reasons: (1) Judah was cut off commercially from the neighboring peoples; (2) the effort to build the wall resulted in a decrease in grain production, since the farmers were staying in Jerusalem (4:22); (3) climatic factors contributed to the famine (v. 3); and (4) the previous administrators had placed heavy burdens on the people (v. 15). As a result, some had no money to buy grain (v. 2), some had to mortgage their property to buy it (v. 3) and others had to borrow money to pay taxes to the Persian king (v. 4). The lending of money at perhaps excessive interest rates made the situation intolerable. When some of the borrowers were unable to pay off their debts, their children were taken into slavery (v. 5). The economic and social fabric was in danger of unraveling.

5:1 and their wives. Since women play a minor role in Ezra-Nehemiah, their mention here emphasizes the severe nature of the crisis (see notes on 3:12; 12:43). **against their Jewish brothers.** The problem in this context came from within the community, not from without.

5:2 Some . . . we must get grain. This group was probably landless; their work on the wall without pay would have meant that they had insufficient money to buy food for their often large families.

5:3 Others . . . to get grain. This group was comprised of landowners whose fields had probably been neglected, owing, among other reasons, to their work on the wall. They therefore turned to others for grain but did not have the money needed to pay for it. As a result they had mortgaged their properties to buy the needed grain. **famine.** Famines were often signs of God's judgment (Dt 11:16–17; 1Ch 21:12; Hag 1:7–11). Perhaps this famine was God's judgment upon the leaders' failure to do what was right.

5:4 Still others . . . to pay the king's tax. This group was comprised of landowners whose lack of income resulted in an inability to pay the taxes owed to the Persian king. As a result they had borrowed money to pay the taxes.

5:5 This verse probably applies to all three previously mentioned groups. **slavery.** According to Leviticus 25:39–43 a man who became poor could sell himself, along with his family, to a fellow Israelite in order to get back on his feet financially. He was to be treated as a hired worker, not as a slave. The error in Nehemiah's day seems to have been twofold: (1) Only the children were being sold, resulting in the breakup of family units; and (2) the children were being treated as slaves, not as hired workers.

5:7 accused the nobles. A bold step on Nehemiah's part. **usury.** See Exodus 22:25–27, Leviticus 25:36 and Deuteronomy 23:20.

5:10 I and my brothers. Apparently Nehemiah had contributed to the problem by making interest-bearing loans, perhaps simply

back to them immediately their fields, vineyards, olive groves and houses, and also the
usury[a] you are charging them—the hundredth part of the money, grain, new wine and
oil."
12“We will give it back,” they said. “And we will not demand anything more from
them. We will do as you say.”
Then I summoned the priests and made the nobles and officials take an oath[b] to do
what they had promised. 13I also shook[c] out the folds of my robe and said, “In this way
may God shake out of his house and possessions every man who does not keep this
promise. So may such a man be shaken out and emptied!”
At this the whole assembly said, “Amen,”[d] and praised the LORD. And the people did
as they had promised.
14Moreover, from the twentieth year of King Artaxerxes,[e] when I was appointed to be
their governor[f] in the land of Judah, until his thirty-second year—twelve years—neither
I nor my brothers ate the food allotted to the governor. 15But the earlier governors—those
preceding me—placed a heavy burden on the people and took forty shekels[a] of silver from
them in addition to food and wine. Their assistants also lorded it over the people. But out
of reverence for God[g] I did not act like that. 16Instead,[h] I devoted myself to the work on
this wall. All my men were assembled there for the work; we[b] did not acquire any land.
17Furthermore, a hundred and fifty Jews and officials ate at my table, as well as those
who came to us from the surrounding nations. 18Each day one ox, six choice sheep and
some poultry[i] were prepared for me, and every ten days an abundant supply of wine of
all kinds. In spite of all this, I never demanded the food allotted to the governor, because
the demands were heavy on these people.
19Remember[j] me with favor, O my God, for all I have done for these people.

Further Opposition to the Rebuilding

6 When word came to Sanballat, Tobiah,[k] Geshem[l] the Arab and the rest of our en-
emies that I had rebuilt the wall and not a gap was left in it—though up to that time
I had not set the doors in the gates— 2Sanballat and Geshem sent me this message:
“Come, let us meet together in one of the villages[c] on the plain of Ono.[m]”
But they were scheming to harm me; 3so I sent messengers to them with this reply:
“I am carrying on a great project and cannot go down. Why should the work stop while
I leave it and go down to you?” 4Four times they sent me the same message, and each
time I gave them the same answer.
5Then, the fifth time, Sanballat[n] sent his aide to me with the same message, and in
his hand was an unsealed letter 6in which was written:

5:11 [a]Isa 58:6
5:12 [b]Ezr 10:5
5:13 [c]Mt 10:14; Ac 18:6 [d]Dt 27:15-26
5:14 [e]Ne 2:6; 13:6 [f]Ge 42:6; Ezr 6:7; Jer 40:7; Hag 1:1
5:15 [g]Ge 20:11
5:16 [h]2Th 3:7-10
5:18 [i]1Ki 4:23
5:19 [j]Ge 8:1; 2Ki 20:3; Ne 1:8; 13:14,22,31
6:1 [k]Ne 2:10 [l]Ne 2:19
6:2 [m]1Ch 8:12
6:5 [n]Ne 2:10

[a] *15* That is, about 1 pound (about 0.5 kilogram) [b] *16* Most Hebrew manuscripts; some Hebrew manuscripts, Septuagint, Vulgate and Syriac *I* [c] *2* Or *in Kephirim*

by neglect (1:6–7). **let the exacting of usury stop!** Literally, “Let us absolve this loan.” In the Hebrew text the repentance called for seems to include Nehemiah.
5:11 grain, new wine and oil. This triad is always found in this order, which reflects the agricultural cycle: first the grain harvest, then the grape (wine) harvest and finally the olive (oil) harvest.
5:12 take an oath. A renewal of the stipulations of the Mosaic covenant pertaining to lending and debt-slavery. See *WCF* 22.3.
5:13 shook out the folds. Covenant renewal often involved a dramatization of the curses that would ensue for noncompliance with the oath (Ge 15:9–19; Jer 34:8–22). **Amen.** The people submitted themselves to the oath. That which was promised was put into action. Nehemiah was used by God to stave off another attack against the building project.
5:14 twentieth year . . . thirty-second year. 445 to 433 B.C. This twelve-year period covered Nehemiah’s first term as governor. He was recalled to the Persian court after 12 years (13:6–7). After that time he returned to Jerusalem for a second term of unknown length. **food allotted.** A governor had the right to collect taxes for his personal support. Nehemiah waived this right for the benefit of the people (see v. 18; see also 1Co 9:4,12; 2Th 3:8–9).
5:15 earlier governors . . . heavy burden. Sheshbazzar (see note Ezr 1:8 about possible identity with Zerubbabel, and see Ezra 5:14) and Zerubbabel (Hag 1:1) were earlier governors, but they were probably not those in view here, since their terms as governor had occurred some 100 years earlier. The governors in view were Nehemiah’s more immediate predecessors, whose policies had contributed to the economic problems of the day (see note on vv. 1–19). **reverence for God.** See 1:11 and its note.
5:16 Nehemiah’s reason for being governor was service rather than personal advancement, which corresponded to his reason for going to Judah in the first place (2:5).
5:17 ate at my table. According to Persian custom, Nehemiah, as governor, had to entertain the officials under his authority as well as visiting dignitaries from other countries.
5:18 Each day. Nehemiah was clearly a man of considerable wealth and a sacrificing spirit, for the food listed would have fed approximately 700 people.
5:19 Remember me. The second use of “remember” in a prayer (see note on 1:8) and the first of four prayers in the form “remember me” (13:14,22,31).
■ **6:1–14** *The Final Opposition.* Nehemiah now turned to the final stage of opposition he faced.
6:1 word came to Sanballat. This phrase continues the series of similar phrases (see note on 2:10) and brings the reader back to the main topic of Nehemiah 1:1—7:3, from which 5:1–19 is a digression (see note on 5:1–13). The conflict that had been steadily escalating here reached its climax, as the wall was virtually complete. This final attempt to stop the work had a threefold goal: (1) to harm (vv. 2–4), (2) to frighten (vv. 5–9) and (3) to discredit (vv. 10–13).
6:2 to harm me. A vague phrase perhaps referring to murder (v. 10). Or perhaps they intended to frame Nehemiah by later saying that his trip to Ono was made in an attempt to enlist others in his revolt against Persia.
6:3 Why should the work stop . . . ? Nehemiah perceived the ultimate plot to be that of stopping the work on the wall.
6:4 Four times. There was great persistence on both sides as the conflict reached its climax.
6:5 unsealed letter. The usual custom was for letters to be sealed. Sanballat wanted the content of the letter to be known, to ensure that the work would stop.

6:6 [o]Ne 2:19 "It is reported among the nations—and Geshem[a][o] says it is true—that you and
the Jews are plotting to revolt, and therefore you are building the wall. Moreover,
according to these reports you are about to become their king 7and have even appointed prophets to make this proclamation about you in Jerusalem: 'There is a
king in Judah!' Now this report will get back to the king; so come, let us confer together."

8I sent him this reply: "Nothing like what you are saying is happening; you are just
making it up out of your head."

9They were all trying to frighten us, thinking, "Their hands will get too weak for the
work, and it will not be completed."

⌊But I prayed,⌋ "Now strengthen my hands."

10One day I went to the house of Shemaiah son of Delaiah, the son of Mehetabel, who
6:10 [p]Nu 18:7 was shut in at his home. He said, "Let us meet in the house of God, inside the temple[p],
and let us close the temple doors, because men are coming to kill you—by night they are
coming to kill you."

11But I said, "Should a man like me run away? Or should one like me go into the temple to save his life? I will not go!" 12I realized that God had not sent him, but that he had
6:12 [q]Eze 13:22-23 prophesied against me[q] because Tobiah and Sanballat[r] had hired him. 13He had been
[r]Ne 2:10 hired to intimidate me so that I would commit a sin by doing this, and then they would
6:13 give me a bad name to discredit me.[s]
[s]Jer 20:10

6:14 14Remember[t] Tobiah and Sanballat,[u] O my God, because of what they have done; re-
[t]Ne 1:8 [u]Ne 2:10 member also the prophetess[v] Noadiah and the rest of the prophets[w] who have been try-
[v]Ex 15:20; ing to intimidate me.
Eze 13:17-23;
Ac 21:9; Rev 2:20
[w]Ne 13:29;
Jer 23:9-40;
Zec 13:2-3

The Completion of the Wall

15So the wall was completed on the twenty-fifth of Elul, in fifty-two days. 16When all
our enemies heard about this, all the surrounding nations were afraid and lost their self-
confidence, because they realized that this work had been done with the help of our God.

17Also, in those days the nobles of Judah were sending many letters to Tobiah, and
replies from Tobiah kept coming to them. 18For many in Judah were under oath to him,
since he was son-in-law to Shecaniah son of Arah, and his son Jehohanan had married
the daughter of Meshullam son of Berekiah. 19Moreover, they kept reporting to me his
7:1 good deeds and then telling him what I said. And Tobiah sent letters to intimidate me.

[x]1Ch 9:27; 26:12-19; Ne 6:1,15 **7** After the wall had been rebuilt and I had set the doors in place, the gatekeepers[x]
[y]Ps 68:25 [z]Ne 8:9 and the singers[y] and the Levites[z] were appointed. 2I put in charge of Jerusalem my
7:2 brother Hanani,[a] along with[b] Hananiah[b] the commander of the citadel,[c] because he was
[a]Ne 1:2 [b]Ne 10:23 a man of integrity and feared[d] God more than most men do. 3I said to them, "The gates
[c]Ne 2:8 [d]1Ki 18:3 of Jerusalem are not to be opened until the sun is hot. While the gatekeepers are still on
duty, have them shut the doors and bar them. Also appoint residents of Jerusalem as
guards, some at their posts and some near their own houses."

[a] *6* Hebrew *Gashmu,* a variant of *Geshem*   [b] *2* Or *Hanani, that is,*

6:6–8 See *WLC* 145.
6:6–7 The accusation was plausible because (1) the wall was being rebuilt, (2) Judah had a history of rebelling against her overlords and (3) Nehemiah was a leader of great skill with a passion for his homeland.
6:9 to frighten us . . . not be completed. The purpose of the letter was, on the surface, to frighten the people, but ultimately it was to stop the completion of the wall. **But I prayed.** These words are not in the Hebrew but make explicit what is implicit in the Hebrew text. **Now strengthen my hands.** Another of the brief prayers so characteristic of Nehemiah (see note on 1:4).
6:10 Shemaiah. He may have been both a prophet (v. 12) and a priest, providing him access to the temple. **Let us meet in the house of God.** The final ploy of verses 10–13 now unfolds. While finding asylum at the altar in the courtyard may have been a legitimate option for Nehemiah (Ex 21:12–14), entering the temple proper was not, since Nehemiah was not a priest (Nu 18:7). The rationale for this ploy is exposed in verse 13.
6:11 Nehemiah's courage again shines through (see note on 5:7).
6:12 I realized. Since Shemaiah's council was to break the law, Nehemiah perceived him to be a false prophet (Dt 13:1–5).
6:13 to intimidate . . . to discredit. The final ploy was to frighten Nehemiah into taking a sinful course of action so that his reputation would be ruined, resulting ultimately in the wall not being completed.
6:14 Remember. The third use of "remember" in a prayer (see note on 5:19) and the second imprecatory prayer (see note on 4:4–5), as the remembering here is unto judgment.
■ **6:15—7:3** *The Rebuilding Completed.* The wall around Jerusalem was completed successfully despite strong opposition.
6:15 So the wall was completed. This verse actually forms the conclusion to the previous section that began in verse 1, with verse 16 opening the final episode of 1:1—7:3. The last of six attempts to stop the work had failed. **Elul.** August–September of 445 B.C.
6:16 When all our enemies heard. The phrase produces the expectation of further conflict, but instead, the resolution is reported: The enemies halted their attempts to stop the work.
6:17–19 Meshullam. See 3:4 and 30 and 13:4.
7:1–3 Although the completion of the wall could no longer be hindered by the enemy, other forms of opposition might have arisen, so appropriate measures were taken to secure the city.
7:1 set the doors in place. This step indicated that the wall was complete (6:1).
7:2 put in charge. Leaders were appointed to oversee the security of the city. **feared God.** See note on 1:11.
7:3 Guards were appointed to secure the gates at night. **until the sun is hot.** The gates were usually opened at dawn; the delay provided further security for the city.

The List of the Exiles Who Returned

4 Now the city was large and spacious, but there were few people in it,[e] and the houses had not yet been rebuilt. 5 So my God put it into my heart to assemble the nobles, the
officials and the common people for registration by families. I found the genealogical record of those who had been the first to return. This is what I found written there:

6 These are the people of the province who came up from the captivity of the exiles[f] whom Nebuchadnezzar king of Babylon had taken captive (they returned to
Jerusalem and Judah, each to his own town, 7 in company with Zerubbabel,[g] Jeshua, Nehemiah, Azariah, Raamiah, Nahamani, Mordecai, Bilshan, Mispereth, Bigvai, Nehum and Baanah):

The list of the men of Israel:

8 the descendants of Parosh 2,172
9 of Shephatiah 372
10 of Arah 652
11 of Pahath-Moab (through the line of Jeshua and Joab) 2,818
12 of Elam 1,254
13 of Zattu 845
14 of Zaccai 760
15 of Binnui 648
16 of Bebai 628
17 of Azgad 2,322
18 of Adonikam 667
19 of Bigvai 2,067
20 of Adin[h] 655
21 of Ater (through Hezekiah) 98
22 of Hashum 328
23 of Bezai 324
24 of Hariph 112
25 of Gibeon 95

26 the men of Bethlehem and Netophah[i] 188
27 of Anathoth[j] 128
28 of Beth Azmaveth 42
29 of Kiriath Jearim, Kephirah[k] and Beeroth[l] 743
30 of Ramah and Geba 621
31 of Micmash 122
32 of Bethel and Ai[m] 123
33 of the other Nebo 52
34 of the other Elam 1,254
35 of Harim 320
36 of Jericho[n] 345
37 of Lod, Hadid and Ono[o] 721
38 of Senaah 3,930

39 The priests:
the descendants of Jedaiah (through the family of Jeshua) 973
40 of Immer 1,052

7:4 [e]Ne 11:1
7:6 [f]2Ch 36:20; Ezr 2:1-70; Ne 1:2
7:7 [g]1Ch 3:19; Ezr 2:2
7:20 [h]Ezr 8:6
7:26 [i]2Sa 23:28; 1Ch 2:54
7:27 [j]Jos 21:18
7:29 [k]Jos 18:26 [l]Jos 18:25
7:32 [m]Ge 12:8
7:36 [n]Ne 3:2
7:37 [o]1Ch 8:12

■ **7:4—13:31** *The Return of the Exiles and the Rebuilding of the Community.* The final major section of Ezra-Nehemiah focuses on the rebuilding of the community as one aspect of rebuilding the "house of God," as did Ezra 7–10 (see "Introduction to Ezra: Purpose and Distinctives"). These chapters divide into two main parts: More exiles return to the land (7:4–73a), and Nehemiah rebuilds the community (7:73b—13:31).

■ **7:4–73a** *The Return of the Exiles.* Nehemiah faced the difficulty of encouraging more exiles to return to the land. These verses form two sections: the need for more people to return (vv. 4–5) and the list of those who did return at this time (vv. 5–73a).

■ **7:4–5** *The Need to Repopulate Jerusalem.* Although a number of people had returned to the land by this time, Jerusalem was still relatively unpopulated, perhaps because it was the center of international tensions. The prophetic expectation was that Jerusalem would be overflowing with people (Zec 8:4–8). Nehemiah therefore pressed for more returnees to come to the city.

■ **7:5–73a** *The Record of Returnees.* For some of the theological significance of this list, see note on Ezra 2:1–70. As this list stands near the beginning of the first major division of Ezra-Nehemiah (Ezr 1–7), so it appears at the beginning of the last major division (Ne 7:4—13:31). The repetition not only marks the beginning of the first and last divisions, but also underscores the continuity of this later generation of the people of God with the first returnees.

7:5 God put it into my heart. Once again, divine authorization of this restoration program is made clear (see "Introduction to Ezra: Purpose and Distinctives"). **for registration by families.** For the purpose of repopulating Jerusalem, as will become clear when this topic is revisited in 11:1–2.

7:6–73a See notes on Ezra 2:1–70.

7:6,8 See *WLC* 157.

41 of Pashhur 1,247
42 of Harim 1,017

43 The Levites:

the descendants of Jeshua (through Kadmiel through the line of Hodaviah) 74

7:44 pNe 11:23
44 The singers:[p]

the descendants of Asaph 148

7:45 q1Ch 9:17
45 The gatekeepers:[q]

the descendants of
Shallum, Ater, Talmon, Akkub, Hatita and Shobai 138

7:46 rNe 3:26
46 The temple servants:[r]

the descendants of
Ziha, Hasupha, Tabbaoth,
47 Keros, Sia, Padon,
48 Lebana, Hagaba, Shalmai,
49 Hanan, Giddel, Gahar,
50 Reaiah, Rezin, Nekoda,
51 Gazzam, Uzza, Paseah,
52 Besai, Meunim, Nephussim,
53 Bakbuk, Hakupha, Harhur,
54 Bazluth, Mehida, Harsha,
55 Barkos, Sisera, Temah,
56 Neziah and Hatipha

57 The descendants of the servants of Solomon:

the descendants of
Sotai, Sophereth, Perida,
58 Jaala, Darkon, Giddel,
59 Shephatiah, Hattil,
Pokereth-Hazzebaim and Amon

7:60 s1Ch 9:2
60 The temple servants and the descendants of the servants of Solomon[s] 392

61 The following came up from the towns of Tel Melah, Tel Harsha, Kerub, Addon and Immer, but they could not show that their families were descended from Israel:

62 the descendants of
Delaiah, Tobiah and Nekoda 642

63 And from among the priests:

the descendants of
Hobaiah, Hakkoz and Barzillai (a man who had married a daughter of Barzillai the Gileadite and was called by that name).

64 These searched for their family records, but they could not find them and so
were excluded from the priesthood as unclean. 65 The governor, therefore, ordered
them not to eat any of the most sacred food until there should be a priest minis-
7:65 tEx 28:30; Ne 8:9
tering with the Urim and Thummim.[t]

66 The whole company numbered 42,360, 67 besides their 7,337 menservants
and maidservants; and they also had 245 men and women singers. 68 There were
736 horses, 245 mules,[a] 69 435 camels and 6,720 donkeys.

70 Some of the heads of the families contributed to the work. The governor gave
to the treasury 1,000 drachmas[b] of gold, 50 bowls and 530 garments for priests.
7:71 u1Ch 29:7
71 Some of the heads of the families[u] gave to the treasury for the work 20,000 drachmas[c] of gold and 2,200 minas[d] of silver. 72 The total given by the rest of the people
7:72 vEx 25:2
was 20,000 drachmas of gold, 2,000 minas[e] of silver and 67 garments for priests.[v]

a 68 Some Hebrew manuscripts (see also Ezra 2:66); most Hebrew manuscripts do not have this verse.
b 70 That is, about 19 pounds (about 8.5 kilograms) c 71 That is, about 375 pounds (about 170 kilograms); also in verse 72 d 71 That is, about 1 1/3 tons (about 1.2 metric tons) e 72 That is, about 1 1/4 tons (about 1.1 metric tons)

73 The priests, the Levites, the gatekeepers, the singers and the temple servants,[w] along with certain of the people and the rest of the Israelites, settled in
their own towns.[x]

Ezra Reads the Law

When the seventh month came and the Israelites had settled in their towns,[y]
8 1 all the people assembled as one man in the square before the Water Gate.[z] They
told Ezra the scribe to bring out the Book of the Law of Moses,[a] which the LORD had
commanded for Israel.
2 So on the first day of the seventh month[b] Ezra the priest brought the Law[c] before the
assembly, which was made up of men and women and all who were able to understand.
3 He read it aloud from daybreak till noon as he faced the square before the Water
Gate[d] in the presence of the men, women and others who could understand. And all the
people listened attentively to the Book of the Law.
4 Ezra the scribe stood on a high wooden platform[e] built for the occasion. Beside him
on his right stood Mattithiah, Shema, Anaiah, Uriah, Hilkiah and Maaseiah; and on his
left were Pedaiah, Mishael, Malkijah, Hashum, Hashbaddanah, Zechariah and Meshullam.
5 Ezra opened the book. All the people could see him because he was standing[f] above
them; and as he opened it, the people all stood up. 6 Ezra praised the LORD, the great God;
and all the people lifted their hands[g] and responded, "Amen! Amen!" Then they bowed
down and worshiped the LORD with their faces to the ground.
7 The Levites[h]—Jeshua, Bani, Sherebiah, Jamin, Akkub, Shabbethai, Hodiah, Maaseiah, Kelita, Azariah, Jozabad, Hanan and Pelaiah—instructed[i] the people in the Law while
the people were standing there. 8 They read from the Book of the Law of God, making it
clear[a] and giving the meaning so that the people could understand what was being read.
9 Then Nehemiah the governor, Ezra the priest and scribe, and the Levites[j] who were instructing the people said to them all, "This day is sacred to the LORD your God. Do not mourn
or weep."[k] For all the people had been weeping as they listened to the words of the Law.
10 Nehemiah said, "Go and enjoy choice food and sweet drinks, and send some to
those who have nothing[l] prepared. This day is sacred to our Lord. Do not grieve, for the
joy[m] of the LORD is your strength."
11 The Levites calmed all the people, saying, "Be still, for this is a sacred day. Do not
grieve."
12 Then all the people went away to eat and drink, to send portions of food and to celebrate with great joy,[n] because they now understood the words that had been made
known to them.
13 On the second day of the month, the heads of all the families, along with the
priests and the Levites, gathered around Ezra the scribe to give attention to the words

7:73 [w]Ne 1:10; Ps 34:22; 103:21; 113:1; 135:1 [x]Ezr 3:1; Ne 11:1 [y]Ezr 3:1
8:1 [z]Ne 3:26 [a]Dt 28:61; 2Ch 34:15; Ezr 7:6
8:2 [b]Lev 23:23-25; Nu 29:1-6 [c]Dt 31:11
8:3 [d]Ne 3:26
8:4 [e]2Ch 6:13
8:5 [f]Jdg 3:20
8:6 [g]Ex 4:31; Ezr 9:5; 1Ti 2:8
8:7 [h]Ezr 10:23 [i]Lev 10:11; 2Ch 17:7
8:9 [j]Ne 7:1,65,70 [k]Dt 12:7,12; 16:14-15
8:10 [l]1Sa 25:8; Lk 14:12-14 [m]Lev 23:40; Dt 12:18; 16:11, 14-15
8:12 [n]Est 9:22

a 8 Or *God, translating it*

■ **7:73b—13:31** *The Rebuilding of the Community.* Simply having Jerusalem fortified was not enough to secure God's blessings. The people needed to be rebuilt into a holy community as well. This aspect of the restoration program divides into three main parts: the renewal of covenant commitments (7:73b—10:39), the dedication of the wall (11:1—12:47) and the reform of the people (13:1–31).

■ **7:73b—10:39** *The Renewal of the Covenant.* True to the directions of Moses' Law, Nehemiah led the people to renew their covenant commitments. Three steps were taken: The law was read (7:73b—8:18), sins were confessed (9:1–37) and an oath was sworn (9:38—10:39).

■ **7:73b—8:18** *The Reading of the Law.* Relevant portions of the law were read and explained to the people.

8:2–10 See *WLC* 156,157.

8:2 first day of the seventh month. The time for celebrating the Feast of Trumpets (Nu 29:1–6). On this occasion the Feast of Trumpets and the Feast of Tabernacles flowed into one another. **men and women and all who were able to understand.** These participants (repeated in v. 3) are in keeping with those required to be present at the reading of the law prescribed for the Feast of Tabernacles (Dt 31:10–13).

8:3 He read it aloud. For the public reading of the law in the context of covenant ratification or renewal, see Exodus 24:7 (see also Dt 11:29; Jos 8:30–35; 2Ki 23:1–3).

8:5 book. A scroll. **all stood up.** Reverence for the law was expressed bodily (v. 6).

8:6 lifted their hands. Praise for God is elsewhere expressed by lifting the hands (Ps 63:4). **Amen! Amen!** "Amen" here indicates that the people concurred in the praise offered by Ezra. The repetition expresses the superlative degree of concurrence. **bowed down and worshiped.** The first verb refers to dropping to one's knees; the second to lowering one's face to the ground.

8:7–8 The law was not simply read, it was also explained to ensure that the people grasped its meaning. The doctrine of the clarity of the Scriptures does not preclude the necessity of their faithful exposition by those trained in them (Ezr 7:6–10). See *WLC* 155; *WSC* 89.

8:9 Nehemiah . . . Ezra . . . Levites. There was unity among all the leaders on this occasion. **This day is sacred . . . Do not mourn.** The rationale for declining to mourn (repeated in vv. 10–11) is not that holiness and mourning are mutually exclusive (Lev 23:26–32; Isa 6:3–5) but that the Feast of Tabernacles as one particular holy day was to be a time of joy (Lev 23:40; Dt 16:13–15). **For all . . . had been weeping.** Probably because they had understood the role of the law in convicting people of sin, but did not understand how the law leads us to seek God's provision for forgiveness. See theological article "The Three Uses of the Law" at Psalm 119.

8:10 those who have nothing. Those who were materially secure were to share with those who had nothing, as in Psalm 22:26. Here lies the background for understanding the sin in 1 Corinthians 11:17–34.

8:12 great joy, because they now understood. How the law directs us toward faith in God's redemption. (see note on v. 9).

of the Law. 14They found written in the Law, which the LORD had commanded through Moses, that the Israelites were to live in booths during the feast of the seventh month 15and that they should proclaim this word and spread it throughout their towns and in Jerusalem: "Go out into the hill country and bring back branches from olive and wild olive trees, and from myrtles, palms and shade trees, to make booths"—as it is written.[a]

16So the people went out and brought back branches and built themselves booths on their own roofs, in their courtyards, in the courts of the house of God and in the square by the Water Gate and the one by the Gate of Ephraim.[o] 17The whole company that had returned from exile built booths and lived in them. From the days of Joshua son of Nun until that day, the Israelites had not celebrated[p] it like this. And their joy was very great.

18Day after day, from the first day to the last, Ezra read[q] from the Book of the Law of God. They celebrated the feast for seven days, and on the eighth day, in accordance with the regulation,[r] there was an assembly.

The Israelites Confess Their Sins

9 On the twenty-fourth day of the same month, the Israelites gathered together, fasting and wearing sackcloth and having dust on their heads.[s] 2Those of Israelite descent had separated themselves from all foreigners.[t] They stood in their places and confessed their sins and the wickedness of their fathers.[u] 3They stood where they were and read from the Book of the Law of the LORD their God for a quarter of the day, and spent another quarter in confession and in worshiping the LORD their God. 4Standing on the stairs were the Levites[v]—Jeshua, Bani, Kadmiel, Shebaniah, Bunni, Sherebiah, Bani and Kenani—who called with loud voices to the LORD their God. 5And the Levites—Jeshua, Kadmiel, Bani, Hashabneiah, Sherebiah, Hodiah, Shebaniah and Pethahiah—said: "Stand up and praise the LORD your God,[w] who is from everlasting to everlasting.[b]"

"Blessed be your glorious name, and may it be exalted above all blessing and praise. 6You alone are the LORD.[x] You made the heavens,[y] even the highest heavens, and all their starry host, the earth[z] and all that is on it, the seas[a] and all that is in them.[b] You give life to everything, and the multitudes of heaven worship you.

7"You are the LORD God, who chose Abram and brought him out of Ur of the Chaldeans[c] and named him Abraham.[d] 8You found his heart faithful to you, and you made a covenant with him to give to his descendants the land of the Canaanites, Hittites, Amorites, Perizzites, Jebusites and Girgashites.[e] You have kept your promise[f] because you are righteous.[g]

9"You saw the suffering of our forefathers in Egypt;[h] you heard their cry at the Red Sea.[c][i] 10You sent miraculous signs[j] and wonders against Pharaoh, against all his officials and all the people of his land, for you knew how arrogantly the Egyptians treated them. You made a name[k] for yourself, which remains to this day. 11You divided the sea before them,[l] so that they passed through it on dry ground, but you hurled their pursuers into the depths, like a stone into mighty waters.[m] 12By day you led[n] them with a pillar of cloud,[o] and by night with a pillar of fire to give them light on the way they were to take.

13"You came down on Mount Sinai;[p] you spoke[q] to them from heaven. You gave them regulations and laws that are just[r] and right, and decrees and com-

8:16 [o]2Ki 14:13; Ne 12:39
8:17 [p]2Ch 7:8; 8:13; 30:21
8:18 [q]Dt 31:11 [r]Lev 23:36,40; Nu 29:35
9:1 [s]Jos 7:6; 1Sa 4:12
9:2 [t]Ne 13:3,30 [u]Ezr 10:11; Ps 106:6
9:4 [v]Ezr 10:23
9:5 [w]Ps 78:4
9:6 [x]Dt 6:4 [y]2Ki 19:15 [z]Ge 1:1; Isa 37:16 [a]Ps 95:5 [b]Dt 10:14
9:7 [c]Ge 11:31 [d]Ge 17:5
9:8 [e]Ge 15:18-21 [f]Jos 21:45 [g]Ge 15:6; Ezr 9:15
9:9 [h]Ex 3:7 [i]Ex 14:10-30
9:10 [j]Ex 10:1 [k]Jer 32:20; Da 9:15
9:11 [l]Ex 14:21; Ps 78:13 [m]Ex 15:4-5,10; Heb 11:29
9:12 [n]Ex 15:13 [o]Ex 13:21
9:13 [p]Ex 19:11 [q]Ex 19:19 [r]Ps 119:137

[a] *15* See Lev. 23:37-40. [b] *5* Or *God for ever and ever* [c] *9* Hebrew *Yam Suph*; that is, Sea of Reeds

8:14 the feast of the seventh month. The Feast of Tabernacles (Lev 23:37–40).
8:15 to make booths. A reminder of life in the wilderness after the redemption from Egypt but before entrance into the promised land (Lev 23:42–43).
■**9:1–37** *The Confessing of Sin.* When the law was understood, the people realized and confessed their failures.
9:1 gathered together. In 8:1 the people gathered to hear the law. Here they gathered to confess their sins in response to the law (v. 3).
9:2 their sins . . . their fathers. See note on Ezra 9:7.
9:3–5 See *WLC* 156.
9:3 Law of the LORD. See 8:1 and its note. The law calls for at least two responses: confession and worship.
9:7–8 The praise of God continued with the recollection of Abraham's election and the subsequent covenant of promise (Ge 12–17).
9:8 made a covenant. This covenant with Abraham (Ge 15) was to be the basis upon which God's grace would continue to be extended time and again to his unfaithful people (as expressed in the remainder of the song). **You have kept your promise.** Receiving the promised blessings was conditioned upon Abraham and his descendants' faithfulness to God ("faithful to you"; cf. Ge 17:1–2,14). Because Abraham had been counted faithful to the covenant (Ge 15:6), God's pledge to bless Abraham by giving his descendants the promised land stood fast. Nevertheless, because subsequent generations had been unfaithful, they had not received the promised blessings (vv. 16–32). Nehemiah recognized that the restoration opportunity in his own day resulted from God's promise to Abraham and that the blessing of restoration that was taking shape might come to fruition if the people repented of their sin and kept the terms of the covenant (vv. 32–38). See "Major Covenants in the Bible" on page 25.
9:9–12 The praise of God continued with the recollection of the redemption of Israel from Egypt (Ex 1–19). That redemption and offer of blessing in the promised land paralleled in many ways the offer of blessing and restoration to the promised land in Nehemiah's day.
9:13–21 The praise of God continued with the recollection of the giving of the law at Mount Sinai and of God's gracious provisions in the wilderness.
9:13 regulations . . . that are good. The law was perceived to be

mands that are good.[s] 14You made known to them your holy Sabbath[t] and gave
them commands, decrees and laws through your servant Moses. 15In their hunger you gave them bread from heaven[u] and in their thirst you brought them water from the rock;[v] you told them to go in and take possession of the land you had
sworn with uplifted hand to give them.[w]
16"But they, our forefathers, became arrogant and stiff-necked, and did not
obey your commands.[x] 17They refused to listen and failed to remember[y] the miracles you performed among them. They became stiff-necked and in their rebellion
appointed a leader in order to return to their slavery.[z] But you are a forgiving God,
gracious and compassionate, slow to anger[a] and abounding in love.[b] Therefore
you did not desert them,[c] 18even when they cast for themselves an image of a calf[d]
and said, 'This is your god, who brought you up out of Egypt,' or when they committed awful blasphemies.
19"Because of your great compassion you did not abandon them in the desert. By
day the pillar of cloud did not cease to guide them on their path, nor the pillar of fire
by night to shine on the way they were to take. 20You gave your good Spirit[e] to instruct them. You did not withhold your manna[f] from their mouths, and you gave
them water[g] for their thirst. 21For forty years you sustained them in the desert; they
lacked nothing,[h] their clothes did not wear out nor did their feet become swollen.[i]
22"You gave them kingdoms and nations, allotting to them even the remotest
frontiers. They took over the country of Sihon[a][j] king of Heshbon and the country
of Og king of Bashan.[k] 23You made their sons as numerous as the stars in the sky,
and you brought them into the land that you told their fathers to enter and possess. 24Their sons went in and took possession of the land.[l] You subdued before
them the Canaanites, who lived in the land; you handed the Canaanites over to
them, along with their kings and the peoples of the land, to deal with them as they
pleased. 25They captured fortified cities and fertile land; they took possession of
houses filled with all kinds of good things, wells already dug, vineyards, olive
groves and fruit trees in abundance. They ate to the full and were well-nour-
ished;[m] they reveled in your great goodness.[n]
26"But they were disobedient and rebelled against you; they put your law behind
their backs.[o] They killed your prophets,[p] who had admonished them in order to
turn them back to you; they committed awful blasphemies.[q] 27So you handed
them over to their enemies,[r] who oppressed them. But when they were oppressed
they cried out to you. From heaven you heard them, and in your great compassion[s]
you gave them deliverers, who rescued them from the hand of their enemies.
28"But as soon as they were at rest, they again did what was evil in your sight.
Then you abandoned them to the hand of their enemies so that they ruled over
them. And when they cried out to you again, you heard from heaven, and in your
compassion you delivered them[t] time after time.
29"You warned them to return to your law, but they became arrogant[u] and disobeyed your commands. They sinned against your ordinances, by which a man
will live if he obeys them.[v] Stubbornly they turned their backs on you, became
stiff-necked and refused to listen.[w] 30For many years you were patient with them.
By your Spirit you admonished them through your prophets.[x] Yet they paid no attention, so you handed them over to the neighboring peoples. 31But in your great

9:13 [s]Ex 20:1
9:14 [t]Ge 2:3; Ex 20:8-11
9:15 [u]Ex 16:4; Jn 6:31 [v]Ex 17:6; Nu 20:7-13 [w]Dt 1:8,21
9:16 [x]Dt 1:26-33; 31:29
9:17 [y]Ps 78:42 [z]Nu 14:1-4 [a]Ex 34:6 [b]Nu 14:17-19 [c]Ps 78:11
9:18 [d]Ex 32:4
9:20 [e]Nu 11:17; Isa 63:11,14 [f]Ex 16:15 [g]Ex 17:6
9:21 [h]Dt 2:7 [i]Dt 8:4
9:22 [j]Nu 21:21 [k]Nu 21:33
9:24 [l]Jos 11:23
9:25 [m]Dt 6:10-12 [n]Nu 13:27; Dt 32:12-15
9:26 [o]1Ki 14:9 [p]Mt 21:35-36 [q]Jdg 2:12-13
9:27 [r]Jdg 2:14 [s]Ps 106:45
9:28 [t]Ps 106:43
9:29 [u]Ps 5:5; Isa 2:11; Jer 43:2 [v]Dt 30:16 [w]Zec 7:11-12
9:30 [x]2Ki 17:13-18; 2Ch 36:16

a *22* One Hebrew manuscript and Septuagint; most Hebrew manuscripts *Sihon, that is, the country of the*

a delight rather than a burden. See theological article "The Three Uses of the Law" at Psalm 119.

9:14 Sabbath. In many respects, the Sabbath stood as the apex of the law (Isa 56:2,4,6; Eze 20–23, especially the refrain in 20:13, 16,21,24; 22:8; 23:38). See *WLC* 121.

9:15 sworn with uplifted hand. The reference is to God's oath to Abraham (Ex 6:8).

9:16–17a The first confession of sin.

9:17b appointed a leader. See Numbers 14:1–4. In contrast to the unfaithfulness of Israel is the faithfulness of God to his oath to Abraham (vv. 8,15; see note on Ezr 9:13).

9:18 even when. God's grace shines all the more brightly when juxtaposed against Israel's sin (Ro 9:22–24). **cast . . . an image.** See Exodus 32.

9:19–21 God's continual care in the wilderness was not owing to Israel's obedience but to his own compassion, stemming from his promise to Abraham (vv. 7–8).

9:22–28 The praise of God continued with the recollection of his grace and patience during the period of the conquest and the judges.

9:22–25 God granted the Israelites the conquest of the land of Canaan in keeping with his promise to Abraham (vv. 7–8).

9:23 numerous as the stars. In fulfillment of the promise made to Abraham (Ge 15:4–5).

9:26–28 Israel had responded to God's faithfulness with rebellion during the days of the judges. For the pattern of rebellion, oppression, petition and salvation, see Judges 2:10–19.

9:29–31 The praise of God continued with recollection of his patience during the monarchy.

9:29 live if he obeys. Like all Biblical covenants the Mosaic covenant required human loyalty. See "Major Covenants in the Bible" on page 25 (see also Lev 18:5; Ro 7:10; 10:5). Israel's failure to merit life in the land testifies to the universal need for a substitute through whom the righteous requirements of the law might be fully met by those unable to meet them on their own (Ro 8:3–4).

9:31 [y]Isa 48:9; Jer 4:27
9:32 [z]Ps 24:8 [a]Dt 7:9
9:33 [b]Ge 18:25 [c]Jer 44:3; Da 9:7-8, 14
9:34 [d]2Ki 23:11 [e]Jer 44:17
9:35 [f]Isa 63:7 [g]Dt 28:45-48
9:36 [h]Dt 28:48; Ezr 9:9
9:37 [i]Dt 28:33; La 5:5
9:38 [j]2Ch 23:16 [k]Isa 44:5

mercy you did not put an end[y] to them or abandon them, for you are a gracious
and merciful God.
32"Now therefore, O our God, the great, mighty[z] and awesome God, who
keeps his covenant of love,[a] do not let all this hardship seem trifling in your eyes—
the hardship that has come upon us, upon our kings and leaders, upon our
priests and prophets, upon our fathers and all your people, from the days of the
kings of Assyria until today. 33In all that has happened to us, you have been just;[b]
you have acted faithfully, while we did wrong.[c] 34Our kings,[d] our leaders, our
priests and our fathers[e] did not follow your law; they did not pay attention to your
commands or the warnings you gave them. 35Even while they were in their kingdom, enjoying your great goodness[f] to them in the spacious and fertile land you
gave them, they did not serve you[g] or turn from their evil ways.
36"But see, we are slaves[h] today, slaves in the land you gave our forefathers so
they could eat its fruit and the other good things it produces. 37Because of our sins,
its abundant harvest goes to the kings you have placed over us. They rule over our
bodies and our cattle as they please. We are in great distress.[i]

The Agreement of the People

38"In view of all this, we are making a binding agreement,[j] putting it in writing,[k] and
our leaders, our Levites and our priests are affixing their seals to it."

10:2 [l]Ezr 2:2
10:3 [m]1Ch 9:12
10:5 [n]1Ch 24:8
10:9 [o]Ne 12:1
10:16 [p]Ezr 8:6
10:20 [q]1Ch 24:15

10 Those who sealed it were:

Nehemiah the governor, the son of Hacaliah.
Zedekiah, 2Seraiah,[l] Azariah, Jeremiah,
3Pashhur,[m] Amariah, Malkijah,
4Hattush, Shebaniah, Malluch,
5Harim,[n] Meremoth, Obadiah,
6Daniel, Ginnethon, Baruch,
7Meshullam, Abijah, Mijamin,
8Maaziah, Bilgai and Shemaiah.
These were the priests.

9The Levites:[o]

Jeshua son of Azaniah, Binnui of the sons of Henadad, Kadmiel,
10and their associates: Shebaniah,
Hodiah, Kelita, Pelaiah, Hanan,
11Mica, Rehob, Hashabiah,
12Zaccur, Sherebiah, Shebaniah,
13Hodiah, Bani and Beninu.

14The leaders of the people:

Parosh, Pahath-Moab, Elam, Zattu, Bani,
15Bunni, Azgad, Bebai,
16Adonijah, Bigvai, Adin,[p]
17Ater, Hezekiah, Azzur,
18Hodiah, Hashum, Bezai,
19Hariph, Anathoth, Nebai,
20Magpiash, Meshullam, Hezir,[q]

9:32–33 See *WCF* 2.1.
9:32 covenant of love. All divine covenants express God's love for his people, but here the covenant with Abraham is particularly in view (Dt 7:7–9). **hardship seem trifling.** The petition is that God would do now what he had done in the past; i.e., see the distress of his people and come to their aid. **kings of Assyria.** The Neo-Assyrian kings from the late tenth century B.C. They were succeeded by the Neo-Babylonian kings in the late seventh century, who were in turn succeeded by the Persian kings in the mid sixth century.
9:33 you have been just. The execution of the covenant curses throughout Israel's history was in perfect harmony with the principle of divine justice (see note on Ezr 9:9).
9:34–35 The leaders were singled out as particularly responsible.
9:36 we are slaves. See note on Ezra 9:9.
9:37 We are in great distress. Implicit in this statement is a request for aid (see note on v. 32).
■**9:38—10:39** *The Ratifying of the Oath.* The people not only prayed for help, but also renewed their commitment to keep the stipulations of the covenant. From the beginning the covenant was renewed after periods of covenant violation (Ex 34; 1Sa 12; 2Ki 23).
9:38 binding agreement. A synonym for *covenant.*
10:1–27 Lists the leaders who renewed the covenant. Strikingly, Ezra, who played a significant role in Nehemiah 8, has quietly disappeared from the scene. His job was successfully completed; therefore, by 9:3 the people themselves were reading from the law and understanding it on their own.
10:1 Those who sealed it. This list of people, who for the most part are unknown, reinforces one of the major themes of Ezra-Nehemiah: The people of God as a whole, not just the great leaders, are vital for the accomplishing of God's redemptive plan (see "Introduction to Ezra: Purpose and Distinctives").

21 Meshezabel, Zadok, Jaddua,
22 Pelatiah, Hanan, Anaiah,
23 Hoshea, Hananiah,[r] Hasshub,
24 Hallohesh, Pilha, Shobek,
25 Rehum, Hashabnah, Maaseiah,
26 Ahiah, Hanan, Anan,
27 Malluch, Harim and Baanah.

28 "The rest of the people—priests, Levites, gatekeepers, singers, temple servants[s] and all who separated themselves from the neighboring peoples[t] for the
sake of the Law of God, together with their wives and all their sons and daughters
who are able to understand— 29 all these now join their brothers the nobles, and
bind themselves with a curse and an oath[u] to follow the Law of God given through
Moses the servant of God and to obey carefully all the commands, regulations and
decrees of the LORD our Lord.

30 "We promise not to give our daughters in marriage to the peoples around us
or take their daughters for our sons.[v]

31 "When the neighboring peoples bring merchandise or grain to sell on the
Sabbath,[w] we will not buy from them on the Sabbath or on any holy day. Every
seventh year we will forgo working the land[x] and will cancel all debts.[y]

32 "We assume the responsibility for carrying out the commands to give a third
of a shekel[a] each year for the service of the house of our God: 33 for the bread set
out on the table;[z] for the regular grain offerings and burnt offerings; for the offerings on the Sabbaths, New Moon[a] festivals and appointed feasts; for the holy offerings; for sin offerings to make atonement for Israel; and for all the duties of the
house of our God.[b]

34 "We—the priests, the Levites and the people—have cast lots[c] to determine
when each of our families is to bring to the house of our God at set times each year
a contribution of wood[d] to burn on the altar of the LORD our God, as it is written
in the Law.

35 "We also assume responsibility for bringing to the house of the LORD each
year the firstfruits[e] of our crops and of every fruit tree.[f]

36 "As it is also written in the Law, we will bring the firstborn[g] of our sons and
of our cattle, of our herds and of our flocks to the house of our God, to the priests
ministering there.[h]

37 "Moreover, we will bring to the storerooms of the house of our God, to the
priests, the first of our ground meal, of our ⌞grain⌟ offerings, of the fruit of all our
trees and of our new wine and oil.[i] And we will bring a tithe[j] of our crops to the
Levites,[k] for it is the Levites who collect the tithes in all the towns where we work.[l]
38 A priest descended from Aaron is to accompany the Levites when they receive
the tithes, and the Levites are to bring a tenth of the tithes[m] up to the house of our
God, to the storerooms of the treasury. 39 The people of Israel, including the Levites, are to bring their contributions of grain, new wine and oil to the storerooms
where the articles for the sanctuary are kept and where the ministering priests,
the gatekeepers and the singers stay.

"We will not neglect the house of our God."[n]

The New Residents of Jerusalem

11 Now the leaders of the people settled in Jerusalem, and the rest of the people
cast lots to bring one out of every ten to live in Jerusalem,[o] the holy city,[p] while

10:23 [r]Ne 7:2
10:28 [s]Ps 135:1 [t]2Ch 6:26; Ne 9:2
10:29 [u]Nu 5:21; Ps 119:106
10:30 [v]Ex 34:16; Dt 7:3; Ne 13:23
10:31 [w]Ne 13:16,18; Jer 17:27; Eze 23:38; Am 8:5 [x]Ex 23:11; Lev 25:1-7 [y]Dt 15:1
10:33 [z]Lev 24:6 [a]Nu 10:10; Ps 81:3; Isa 1:14 [b]2Ch 24:5
10:34 [c]Lev 16:8 [d]Ne 13:31
10:35 [e]Ex 22:29; 23:19; Nu 18:12 [f]Dt 26:1-11
10:36 [g]Ex 13:2; Nu 18:14-16 [h]Ne 13:31
10:37 [i]Lev 23:17; Nu 18:12 [j]Lev 27:30; Nu 18:21 [k]Dt 14:22-29 [l]Eze 44:30
10:38 [m]Nu 18:26
10:39 [n]Dt 12:6; Ne 13:11,12
11:1 [o]Ne 7:4 [p]ver 18; Isa 48:2; 52:1; 64:10; Zec 14:20-21

[a] *32* That is, about 1/8 ounce (about 4 grams)

10:28–29 The rest of the people who renewed the covenant and swore the general oath of obedience to its stipulations.
10:29 bind themselves. The swearing of the oath by the people indicates their ratification of the covenant renewal. See *WCF* 21.5.
10:30–39 The particular pledges to obedience.
10:30 marriage. See Exodus 34:15–16 and Deuteronomy 7:3–4. This was a recurring, significant problem throughout the history of Israel (see note on Ezr 4:3).
10:31 Sabbath. See Exodus 20:8–11 and Deuteronomy 5:12–15. See also note on 9:14. **Every seventh year.** See Exodus 23:10–11 and Leviticus 25:1–7.
10:32 third of a shekel. Exodus 30:13–14 prescribes half a shekel as the yearly contribution. Perhaps the difference here is owing to a different monetary system under the Persians.
10:33 the bread. See Leviticus 24:5–6. **offerings.** See Leviticus 1–7.
10:34–36 Particular pledges by the priests and Levites.
10:35 firstfruits. See Deuteronomy 26:1–11.
10:36 firstborn. See Exodus 22:29–30.
10:37–39 Final pledges by all the people.
10:37 tithe. See Leviticus 27:30–33.
10:39 not neglect the house of our God. Rebuilding the house of God is a major theme in Ezra-Nehemiah (see "Introduction to Ezra: Purpose and Distinctives").
■ **11:1—12:47** *The Dedication of the Wall.* The dedication of the wall of Jerusalem was closely tied to the reordering of the commu-

11:1 [q]Ne 7:73
11:3 [r]1Ch 9:2-3; Ezr 2:1
11:4 [s]Ezr 1:5 [t]Ezr 2:70

the remaining nine were to stay in their own towns.[q] 2The people commended all the
men who volunteered to live in Jerusalem.

3These are the provincial leaders who settled in Jerusalem (now some Israelites,
priests, Levites, temple servants and descendants of Solomon's servants lived in the
towns of Judah, each on his own property in the various towns,[r] 4while other people from
both Judah and Benjamin[s] lived in Jerusalem):[t]

From the descendants of Judah:

Athaiah son of Uzziah, the son of Zechariah, the son of Amariah, the son of
Shephatiah, the son of Mahalalel, a descendant of Perez; 5and Maaseiah son of
Baruch, the son of Col-Hozeh, the son of Hazaiah, the son of Adaiah, the son of Joiarib, the son of Zechariah, a descendant of Shelah. 6The descendants of Perez who
lived in Jerusalem totaled 468 able men.

7From the descendants of Benjamin:

Sallu son of Meshullam, the son of Joed, the son of Pedaiah, the son of Kolaiah,
the son of Maaseiah, the son of Ithiel, the son of Jeshaiah, 8and his followers, Gab-
bai and Sallai—928 men. 9Joel son of Zicri was their chief officer, and Judah son
of Hassenuah was over the Second District of the city.

10From the priests:

11:11 [u]2Ki 25:18; Ezr 2:2 [v]Ezr 7:2

Jedaiah; the son of Joiarib; Jakin; 11Seraiah[u] son of Hilkiah, the son of Meshullam,
the son of Zadok, the son of Meraioth, the son of Ahitub,[v] supervisor in the house
of God, 12and their associates, who carried on work for the temple—822 men;
Adaiah son of Jeroham, the son of Pelaliah, the son of Amzi, the son of Zechariah, the son of Pashhur, the son of Malkijah, 13and his associates, who were heads
of families—242 men; Amashsai son of Azarel, the son of Ahzai, the son of Meshillemoth, the son of Immer, 14and his[a] associates, who were able men—128. Their
chief officer was Zabdiel son of Haggedolim.

15From the Levites:

11:16 [w]Ezr 10:15 [x]Ezr 8:33
11:17 [y]1Ch 9:15; Ne 12:8 [z]2Ch 5:12 [a]1Ch 25:1
11:18 [b]Rev 21:2

Shemaiah son of Hasshub, the son of Azrikam, the son of Hashabiah, the son of
Bunni; 16Shabbethai[w] and Jozabad,[x] two of the heads of the Levites, who had
charge of the outside work of the house of God; 17Mattaniah[y] son of Mica, the son
of Zabdi, the son of Asaph,[z] the director who led in thanksgiving and prayer; Bakbukiah, second among his associates; and Abda son of Shammua, the son of Galal, the son of Jeduthun.[a] 18The Levites in the holy city[b] totaled 284.

19The gatekeepers:

Akkub, Talmon and their associates, who kept watch at the gates—172 men.

20The rest of the Israelites, with the priests and Levites, were in all the towns of Judah, each on his ancestral property.

11:21 [c]Ezr 2:43; Ne 3:26

21The temple servants[c] lived on the hill of Ophel, and Ziha and Gishpa were in
charge of them.

11:22 [d]1Ch 9:15
11:23 [e]Ne 7:44

22The chief officer of the Levites in Jerusalem was Uzzi son of Bani, the son of Hashabiah, the son of Mattaniah,[d] the son of Mica. Uzzi was one of Asaph's descendants, who
were the singers responsible for the service of the house of God. 23The singers[e] were under the king's orders, which regulated their daily activity.

a *14* Most Septuagint manuscripts; Hebrew *their*

---

nity. These chapters divide into three parts: preparations (11:1—12:26), the dedication itself (12:27–43) and provisions made for the clergy (12:44–47).

■ **11:1—12:26** *The Preparations for the Dedication.* The city was prepared for the dedication of the wall through its repopulation. This section divides into two main lists: (1) the common people who repopulated Jerusalem and the surrounding area (11:1–36) and (2) the priests and Levites who repopulated Jerusalem (12:1–26).

11:1–36 Those who lived in and near Jerusalem are listed.

11:1 cast lots. Ties this list to the pledges in 10:30–39 (see 10:34) and shows the quick implementation of those pledges. **one out of every ten.** Further ties this list to that of the pledges in 10:30–39, as the tithe is mentioned in 10:37–38. Populating the city by means of a tithe of the people was the first step taken against neglecting the house of God, as pledged in 10:39. **the holy city.** A rare phrase used only here and in verse 18, Isaiah 48:2 and Isaiah 52:1. Holiness had expanded from holy vessels (8:28; Ezr 1:7) to holy priests (Ezr 8:28) to holy people (Ezr 9:2) to the holy place/sanctuary (Ezr 9:8) to holy gates (3:1) to holy Sabbaths (9:14) to the point that the entire city was now holy. The city with all that was in it had become holy, the "house of God" that the Lord had purposed to build in Ezra 1:2 (see note on Ezr 1:3; see also "Introduction to Ezra: Purpose and Distinctives"). Now that the "house of God" was complete, the final dedication could take place (see 12:27–43).

11:2 volunteered. Probably refers not to a second group in addition to these chosen by lot but to the willing spirit of those who were so chosen.

11:4–9 Judah . . . Benjamin. See Ezra 1:5 and its note.

11:23 under the king's orders. The reference may be to David (12:24; 1Ch 25) or to King Artaxerxes (Ezr 7:21–24).

24 Pethahiah son of Meshezabel, one of the descendants of Zerah[f] son of Judah, was
the king's agent in all affairs relating to the people.
25 As for the villages with their fields, some of the people of Judah lived in Kiriath Arba[g]
and its surrounding settlements, in Dibon[h] and its settlements, in Jekabzeel and its villages, 26 in Jeshua, in Moladah, in Beth Pelet,[i] 27 in Hazar Shual, in Beersheba[j] and its settlements, 28 in Ziklag,[k] in Meconah and its settlements, 29 in En Rimmon, in Zorah,[l] in Jarmuth,[m] 30 Zanoah, Adullam[n] and their villages, in Lachish[o] and its fields, and in Azekah[p]
and its settlements. So they were living all the way from Beersheba[q] to the Valley of Hinnom.
31 The descendants of the Benjamites from Geba[r] lived in Micmash,[s] Aija, Bethel and
its settlements, 32 in Anathoth,[t] Nob[u] and Ananiah, 33 in Hazor,[v] Ramah and Gittaim,[w]
34 in Hadid, Zeboim[x] and Neballat, 35 in Lod and Ono,[y] and in the Valley of the Craftsmen.
36 Some of the divisions of the Levites of Judah settled in Benjamin.

Priests and Levites

12 These were the priests[z] and Levites who returned with Zerubbabel[a] son of
Shealtiel and with Jeshua:[b]
Seraiah,[c] Jeremiah, Ezra,
2 Amariah, Malluch, Hattush,
3 Shecaniah, Rehum, Meremoth,
4 Iddo,[d] Ginnethon,[a] Abijah,[e]
5 Mijamin,[b] Moadiah, Bilgah,
6 Shemaiah, Joiarib, Jedaiah,[f]
7 Sallu, Amok, Hilkiah and Jedaiah.
These were the leaders of the priests and their associates in the days of Jeshua.
8 The Levites were Jeshua, Binnui, Kadmiel, Sherebiah, Judah, and also Mattaniah,[g]
who, together with his associates, was in charge of the songs of thanksgiving. 9 Bakbukiah and Unni, their associates, stood opposite them in the services.
10 Jeshua was the father of Joiakim, Joiakim the father of Eliashib,[h] Eliashib the father
of Joiada, 11 Joiada the father of Jonathan, and Jonathan the father of Jaddua.
12 In the days of Joiakim, these were the heads of the priestly families:
of Seraiah's family, Meraiah;
of Jeremiah's, Hananiah;
13 of Ezra's, Meshullam;
of Amariah's, Jehohanan;
14 of Malluch's, Jonathan;
of Shecaniah's,[c] Joseph;
15 of Harim's, Adna;
of Meremoth's,[d] Helkai;
16 of Iddo's,[i] Zechariah;
of Ginnethon's, Meshullam;
17 of Abijah's, Zicri;
of Miniamin's and of Moadiah's, Piltai;
18 of Bilgah's, Shammua;
of Shemaiah's, Jehonathan;
19 of Joiarib's, Mattenai;
of Jedaiah's, Uzzi;
20 of Sallu's, Kallai;
of Amok's, Eber;
21 of Hilkiah's, Hashabiah;
of Jedaiah's, Nethanel.

11:24 [f]Ge 38:30
11:25 [g]Ge 35:27; Jos 14:15 [h]Nu 21:30
11:26 [i]Jos 15:27
11:27 [j]Ge 21:14
11:28 [k]1Sa 27:6
11:29 [l]Jos 15:33 [m]Jos 10:3
11:30 [n]Jos 15:35 [o]Jos 10:3 [p]Jos 10:10 [q]Jos 15:28
11:31 [r]Jos 21:17; Isa 10:29 [s]1Sa 13:2
11:32 [t]Jos 21:18; Isa 10:30 [u]1Sa 21:1
11:33 [v]Jos 11:1 [w]2Sa 4:3
11:34 [x]1Sa 13:18
11:35 [y]1Ch 8:12
12:1 [z]Ne 10:1-8 [a]1Ch 3:19 [b]Ezr 2:2 [c]Ezr 2:2
12:4 [d]Zec 1:1 [e]Lk 1:5
12:6 [f]1Ch 24:7
12:8 [g]Ne 11:17
12:10 [h]Ezr 10:24
12:16 [i]ver 4

a *4* Many Hebrew manuscripts and Vulgate (see also Neh. 12:16); most Hebrew manuscripts *Ginnethoi*
b *5* A variant of *Miniamin*
c *14* Very many Hebrew manuscripts, some Septuagint manuscripts and Syriac (see also Neh. 12:3); most Hebrew manuscripts *Shebaniah's*
d *15* Some Septuagint manuscripts (see also Neh. 12:3); Hebrew *Meraioth's*

11:25–36 The list of those who resettled the surrounding area. This list links with Ezra 2:21–35, thus binding Ezra-Nehemiah into a united whole.
12:1–26 The lists of various priests and Levites conclude the section discussing final preparation for the dedication of the wall, which follows in verses 27–43.
12:1–10 The list of priests and Levites who returned under Zerubbabel binds the end of Nehemiah to the beginning of Ezra, thus uniting the work of Zerubbabel, Ezra and Nehemiah.
12:1 Zerubbabel . . . Jeshua. See Ezra 2:2 and its note. **Ezra.** Not the main character of the book, as he returned 80 years after Zerubbabel (see Ezr 7:6 and its note).
12:9 opposite them. For antiphonal singing (v. 24).
12:12–21 The list of priests and Levites in the days of Joiakim, son of Jeshua the high priest of the first return, repeated from verses 1–7 with the deletion of Hattush (v. 2) and the variations in the following names: Rehum (v. 3) = Harim (v. 15); Mijamin (v. 5) = Miniamin (v. 17).

22 The family heads of the Levites in the days of Eliashib, Joiada, Johanan and Jaddua, as well as those of the priests, were recorded in the reign of Darius the Persian. 23 The family heads among the descendants of Levi up to the time of Johanan son of Eliashib were recorded in the book of the annals. 24 And the leaders of the Levites[j] were Hashabiah, Sherebiah, Jeshua son of Kadmiel, and their associates, who stood opposite them to give praise and thanksgiving, one section responding to the other, as prescribed by David the man of God.

25 Mattaniah, Bakbukiah, Obadiah, Meshullam, Talmon and Akkub were gatekeepers who guarded the storerooms at the gates. 26 They served in the days of Joiakim son of Jeshua, the son of Jozadak, and in the days of Nehemiah the governor and of Ezra the priest and scribe.

Dedication of the Wall of Jerusalem

27 At the dedication[k] of the wall of Jerusalem, the Levites were sought out from where they lived and were brought to Jerusalem to celebrate joyfully the dedication with songs of thanksgiving and with the music of cymbals,[l] harps and lyres.[m] 28 The singers also were brought together from the region around Jerusalem—from the villages of the Netophathites,[n] 29 from Beth Gilgal, and from the area of Geba and Azmaveth, for the singers had built villages for themselves around Jerusalem. 30 When the priests and Levites had purified themselves ceremonially, they purified the people,[o] the gates and the wall.

31 I had the leaders of Judah go up on top[a] of the wall. I also assigned two large choirs to give thanks. One was to proceed on top[b] of the wall to the right, toward the Dung Gate.[p] 32 Hoshaiah and half the leaders of Judah followed them, 33 along with Azariah, Ezra, Meshullam, 34 Judah, Benjamin,[q] Shemaiah, Jeremiah, 35 as well as some priests with trumpets,[r] and also Zechariah son of Jonathan, the son of Shemaiah, the son of Mattaniah, the son of Micaiah, the son of Zaccur, the son of Asaph, 36 and his associates—Shemaiah, Azarel, Milalai, Gilalai, Maai, Nethanel, Judah and Hanani—with musical instruments[s] ⌞prescribed by⌟ David the man of God.[t] Ezra[u] the scribe led the procession. 37 At the Fountain Gate[v] they continued directly up the steps of the City of David on the ascent to the wall and passed above the house of David to the Water Gate[w] on the east.

38 The second choir proceeded in the opposite direction. I followed them on top[c] of the wall, together with half the people—past the Tower of the Ovens[x] to the Broad Wall,[y] 39 over the Gate of Ephraim,[z] the Jeshanah[d] Gate,[a] the Fish Gate,[b] the Tower of Hananel[c] and the Tower of the Hundred,[d] as far as the Sheep Gate.[e] At the Gate of the Guard they stopped.

40 The two choirs that gave thanks then took their places in the house of God; so did I, together with half the officials, 41 as well as the priests—Eliakim, Maaseiah, Miniamin, Micaiah, Elioenai, Zechariah and Hananiah with their trumpets— 42 and also Maaseiah, Shemaiah, Eleazar, Uzzi, Jehohanan, Malkijah, Elam and Ezer. The choirs sang under the direction of Jezrahiah. 43 And on that day they offered great sacrifices, rejoicing because God had given them great joy. The women and children also rejoiced. The sound of rejoicing in Jerusalem could be heard far away.

44 At that time men were appointed to be in charge of the storerooms[f] for the contributions, firstfruits and tithes.[g] From the fields around the towns they were to bring into the storerooms the portions required by the Law for the priests and the Levites, for Judah

12:24 [j]Ezr 2:40
12:27 [k]Dt 20:5 [l]2Sa 6:5 [m]1Ch 15:16,28; 25:6; Ps 92:3
12:28 [n]1Ch 2:54; 9:16
12:30 [o]Ex 19:10; Job 1:5
12:31 [p]Ne 2:13
12:34 [q]Ezr 1:5
12:35 [r]Ezr 3:10
12:36 [s]1Ch 15:16 [t]2Ch 8:14 [u]Ezr 7:6
12:37 [v]Ne 2:14; 3:15 [w]Ne 3:26
12:38 [x]Ne 3:11 [y]Ne 3:8
12:39 [z]2Ki 14:13; Ne 8:16 [a]Ne 3:6 [b]2Ch 33:14; Ne 3:3 [c]Ne 3:1 [d]Ne 3:1 [e]Ne 3:1
12:44 [f]Ne 13:4,13 [g]Lev 27:30

[a] *31* Or *go alongside* [b] *31* Or *proceed alongside* [c] *38* Or *them alongside* [d] *39* Or *Old*

12:22–26 The list of the heads of Levitical families.
12:22 Darius the Persian. Either Darius II Nothus (423–404 B.C.) or Darius III Codomannus (336–331 B.C.).
■ **12:27–43** *The Dedication Proper.* The dedication ceremony was for the wall in the first place, but it was also, by extension, for the whole "house of God" (temple, community, city), which was now complete (see "Introduction to Ezra: Purpose and Distinctives"; see also note on Ezr 6:14). This material was probably part of the Nehemiah memoirs, as Nehemiah spoke in the first person.
12:27 Levites were sought. The dedication could not have taken place without the aid of the Levites; hence the lists that precede in verses 1–26.
12:28–29 singers also were brought. Hence the list in 11:22–23.
12:30 purified. Ceremonial purity was a means of teaching moral purity (Lev 16:30).
12:31–39 A grand procession took place, which apparently began at the Valley Gate (2:13,15; 3:13). Part of the procession (vv. 31–37), led by Ezra (v. 36), moved counterclockwise (v. 31), passing the Dung Gate (v. 31), the Fountain Gate (v. 37) and the Water Gate (v. 37) before proceeding to the temple. The other part of the procession (vv. 38–39), accompanied by Nehemiah (v. 38), moved clockwise (v. 38), passing the gates on the northwest and north sides of the city before proceeding to the temple. For the location of these sites, see chapter 3 and its notes.
12:40–43 The procession reached the temple (v. 40), where the ceremony culminated in singing (v. 42), sacrificing (v. 43) and rejoicing (v. 43).
12:43 God had given them great joy. The people rejoiced, but only because their sovereign God had enabled them, thus reinforcing the books' primary theme (see "Introduction to Ezra: Purpose and Distinctives"). **women and children.** This reference serves to underscore the magnitude of the celebration (see notes on 3:12; 5:1).
■ **12:44–47** *The Provisions for Clergy.* The implementation of the pledges that had been made in 10:30–39 was begun in 11:1 (see note) and was still being carried out in 12:44–47. These verses show that the people did not neglect the house of God, as was pledged in 10:39.
12:44 contributions, firstfruits and tithes. As were pledged in 10:34–37.

was pleased with the ministering priests and Levites.[h] 45They performed the service of
their God and the service of purification, as did also the singers and gatekeepers, according to the commands of David[i] and his son Solomon.[j] 46For long ago, in the days of David and Asaph,[k] there had been directors for the singers and for the songs of praise[l] and
thanksgiving to God. 47So in the days of Zerubbabel and of Nehemiah, all Israel contributed the daily portions for the singers and gatekeepers. They also set aside the portion for
the other Levites, and the Levites set aside the portion for the descendants of Aaron.[m]

Nehemiah's Final Reforms

13 On that day the Book of Moses was read aloud in the hearing of the people and
there it was found written that no Ammonite or Moabite should ever be admitted into the assembly of God,[n] 2because they had not met the Israelites with food and
water but had hired Balaam[o] to call a curse down on them.[p] (Our God, however, turned
the curse into a blessing.)[q] 3When the people heard this law, they excluded from Israel
all who were of foreign descent.[r]

4Before this, Eliashib the priest had been put in charge of the storerooms[s] of the
house of our God. He was closely associated with Tobiah,[t] 5and he had provided him
with a large room formerly used to store the grain offerings and incense and temple articles, and also the tithes[u] of grain, new wine and oil prescribed for the Levites, singers
and gatekeepers, as well as the contributions for the priests.

6But while all this was going on, I was not in Jerusalem, for in the thirty-second year
of Artaxerxes[v] king of Babylon I had returned to the king. Some time later I asked his permission 7and came back to Jerusalem. Here I learned about the evil thing Eliashib[w] had
done in providing Tobiah a room in the courts of the house of God. 8I was greatly displeased and threw all Tobiah's household goods out of the room.[x] 9I gave orders to purify the rooms,[y] and then I put back into them the equipment of the house of God, with
the grain offerings and the incense.

10I also learned that the portions assigned to the Levites had not been given to
them,[z] and that all the Levites and singers responsible for the service had gone back to
their own fields. 11So I rebuked the officials and asked them, "Why is the house of God
neglected?"[a] Then I called them together and stationed them at their posts.

12All Judah brought the tithes[b] of grain, new wine and oil into the storerooms.[c] 13I put
Shelemiah the priest, Zadok the scribe, and a Levite named Pedaiah in charge of the
storerooms and made Hanan son of Zaccur, the son of Mattaniah, their assistant, because these men were considered trustworthy. They were made responsible for distributing the supplies to their brothers.[d]

14Remember[e] me for this, O my God, and do not blot out what I have so faithfully
done for the house of my God and its services.

15In those days I saw men in Judah treading winepresses on the Sabbath and bring-

12:44 [h]Dt 18:8
12:45 [i]1Ch 25:1; 2Ch 8:14 [j]1Ch 6:31; 23:5
12:46 [k]2Ch 35:15 [l]2Ch 29:27; Ps 137:4
12:47 [m]Nu 18:21; Dt 18:8
13:1 [n]ver 23; Dt 23:3
13:2 [o]Nu 22:3-11 [p]Nu 23:7; Dt 23:3 [q]Nu 23:11; Dt 23:4-5
13:3 [r]ver 23; Ne 9:2
13:4 [s]Ne 12:44 [t]Ne 2:10
13:5 [u]Lev 27:30; Nu 18:21
13:6 [v]Ne 2:6; 5:14
13:7 [w]Ezr 10:24
13:8 [x]Mt 21:12-13; Jn 2:13-16
13:9 [y]1Ch 23:28; 2Ch 29:5
13:10 [z]Dt 12:19
13:11 [a]Ne 10:37-39; Hag 1:1-9
13:12 [b]2Ch 31:6 [c]1Ki 7:51; Ne 10:37-39; Mal 3:10
13:13 [d]Ne 12:44; Ac 6:1-5
13:14 [e]Ge 8:1

12:45 commands of David . . . Solomon. See 1 Chronicles 25 and 2 Chronicles 8:14.
12:47 all Israel contributed. Reinforces the theme that the people of God as a whole, not just the great leaders, are vital for the accomplishing of God's redemptive plan (see "Introduction to Ezra: Purpose and Distinctives").
■ **13:1–31** *The Reformation of the People.* Nehemiah's final act in this book was to bring reform to the community. This sanctification of the people took place by excluding foreigners (vv. 1–3), attending to the temple (vv. 4–14), observing the Sabbath (vv. 15–22) and divorcing foreign wives (vv. 23–31).
■ **13:1–3** *Foreigners.* The potential for the corruption of the restoration program required the exclusion of foreigners. The pledge to general obedience to the law of God (10:28–29) entailed separation from neighboring peoples for the sake of avoiding religious corruption and idolatry (10:28). The people had reneged on this aspect of the pledge.
13:1 On that day. Although a general reference, this clearly occurred during Nehemiah's second term as governor, as indicated by the following sequences in verses 4 and 6. **Book of Moses.** Links 13:1–3 with the pledge in 10:28–29. The text in view is Deuteronomy 23:3–6 (see note on 7:73b—8:1).
13:3 heard this law. Although Ezra was not on the scene, his labor was still bearing fruit (see note on 10:1–27). **excluded.** In keeping with the former pledge in 10:28–29. This exclusion was religious, not racial or political (see note on Ezr 4:3).
■ **13:4–14** *The Temple.* The final pledge not to neglect the house of God (10:39) had been violated (v. 11), as had the pledges regarding the storerooms and the tithes (10:37–39; 13:12). Reform was needed.
13:4 Eliashib. Perhaps the high priest (3:1), but more likely a priest with the same name, for it is not likely that the high priest would have been put in charge of the storerooms. **storerooms.** Links this section with the pledge in 10:37–39. **Tobiah.** See 2:10.
13:5 formerly used to store. The house of God was being neglected, contrary to the pledge in 10:39.
13:6–7 I was not in Jerusalem. See note on 5:14. **king of Babylon.** The Persian kings bore this title after the conquest of the Babylonian Empire (Ezr 5:13).
13:8 threw. See Matthew 21:12–13.
13:10 portions . . . Levites. Links this section to the pledge in 13:37. The Levites possessed no land (Nu 18:20–24; Dt 14:29; 18:1), although some may have had private income (Dt 18:8). The dependence of the Levites on the support of the people may explain the reluctance of many Levites to leave Babylonia (Ezr 8:15–20). For the justification of this reluctance, see Malachi 2:17 and 3:13–15.
13:11 I rebuked. See 5:7 and its note. **neglected.** The pledge not to neglect the house of God (10:39) had been violated.
13:12 brought the tithes. In keeping with the pledge in 10:37.
13:13 trustworthy. See Acts 6:1–5 and 2 Corinthians 8:16–21.
13:14 Remember me. The fourth use of "remember" in a prayer (see note on 6:14) and the second of four such prayers by Nehemiah (see note on 5:19).
13:15–23 See *WCF* 21.8; *WLC* 121; *WSC* 60.
■ **13:15–22** *The Sabbath.* The pledge to keep the Sabbath in 10:31

ing in grain and loading it on donkeys, together with wine, grapes, figs and all other
kinds of loads. And they were bringing all this into Jerusalem on the Sabbath.[f] Therefore
I warned them against selling food on that day. 16 Men from Tyre who lived in Jerusalem
were bringing in fish and all kinds of merchandise and selling them in Jerusalem on the
Sabbath[g] to the people of Judah. 17 I rebuked the nobles of Judah and said to them, "What
is this wicked thing you are doing—desecrating the Sabbath day? 18 Didn't your forefathers do the same things, so that our God brought all this calamity upon us and upon this
city? Now you are stirring up more wrath against Israel by desecrating the Sabbath."[h]

19 When evening shadows fell on the gates of Jerusalem before the Sabbath,[i] I ordered
the doors to be shut and not opened until the Sabbath was over. I stationed some of my
own men at the gates so that no load could be brought in on the Sabbath day. 20 Once
or twice the merchants and sellers of all kinds of goods spent the night outside Jerusalem. 21 But I warned them and said, "Why do you spend the night by the wall? If you do
this again, I will lay hands on you." From that time on they no longer came on the Sabbath. 22 Then I commanded the Levites to purify themselves and go and guard the gates
in order to keep the Sabbath day holy.

Remember[j] me for this also, O my God, and show mercy to me according to your
great love.

23 Moreover, in those days I saw men of Judah who had married[k] women from Ashdod, Ammon and Moab.[l] 24 Half of their children spoke the language of Ashdod or the
language of one of the other peoples, and did not know how to speak the language of
Judah. 25 I rebuked them and called curses down on them. I beat some of the men and
pulled out their hair. I made them take an oath[m] in God's name and said: "You are not
to give your daughters in marriage to their sons, nor are you to take their daughters in
marriage for your sons or for yourselves. 26 Was it not because of marriages like these that
Solomon king of Israel sinned? Among the many nations there was no king like him.[n]
He was loved by his God,[o] and God made him king over all Israel, but even he was led
into sin by foreign women.[p] 27 Must we hear now that you too are doing all this terrible
wickedness and are being unfaithful to our God by marrying[q] foreign women?"

28 One of the sons of Joiada son of Eliashib[r] the high priest was son-in-law to Sanballat[s] the Horonite. And I drove him away from me.

29 Remember[t] them, O my God, because they defiled the priestly office and the covenant of the priesthood and of the Levites.

30 So I purified the priests and the Levites of everything foreign,[u] and assigned them
duties, each to his own task. 31 I also made provision for contributions of wood[v] at designated times, and for the firstfruits.

Remember[w] me with favor, O my God.

13:15 [f]Ex 20:8-11; 34:21; Dt 5:12-15; Ne 10:31
13:16 [g]Ne 10:31
13:18 [h]Ne 10:31; Jer 17:21-23
13:19 [i]Lev 23:32
13:22 [j]Ge 8:1; Ne 12:30
13:23 [k]Ezr 9:1-2; Mal 2:11 [l]ver 1; Ne 10:30
13:25 [m]Ezr 10:5
13:26 [n]1Ki 3:13; 2Ch 1:12 [o]2Sa 12:25 [p]1Ki 11:3
13:27 [q]Ezr 9:14; 10:2
13:28 [r]Ezr 10:24 [s]Ne 2:10
13:29 [t]Ne 6:14
13:30 [u]Ne 10:30
13:31 [v]Ne 10:34 [w]ver 14, 22; Ge 8:1

---

had been violated. Reform was needed (see 9:14 and its note). See *WLC* 117.
13:15 Sabbath . . . bringing . . . selling. Three links with the pledge in 10:31 that had been violated. See *WLC* 118.
13:16 Men from Tyre. One of the "neighboring peoples" in view in 10:31.
13:17 I rebuked. See 10:11. See also *WCF* 20.4; *WLC* 118.
13:19 evening. The Israelites at times reckoned the day from sunset to sunset, as indicated by the phrases "night and day" (Dt 28:66) and "evenings and mornings" (Da 8:14), while at other times they reckoned it from morning to morning, as indicated by the phrase "day and night" (Lev 8:35). Here the Sabbath began at sunset. See *WLC* 117,121.
13:21–22 See *WCF* 20.4; 21.8; *WSC* 60.
13:21 lay hands on you. No idle threat (v. 25).
13:22 Remember me. The fifth use of "remember" in a prayer (see note on 1:8) and the third of four such prayers by Nehemiah (see note on v. 14). See *WCF* 16.4.
■ **13:23–31** *Intermarriage.* The pledge in 10:30 had been violated. Nehemiah understood that reformation that begins in the heart bears fruit in the home. The New Testament makes it clear that God's people remain barred from marrying those outside the covenant community (1Co 7:39).
13:23 married. Links this section with the pledge in 10:30. Ezra had dealt with the same issue some 25 years earlier (see note on Ezr 9:1). This was a perennial problem throughout Israel's history (see note on Ezr 4:3). **Ashdod.** See 4:7 and its note. **Ammon and Moab.** See Genesis 19:36–38 and its note.
13:25–27 See *WCF* 24.3.
13:25 I rebuked them. See verse 17 and its note. **pulled out their hair.** Nehemiah's action can be contrasted with Ezra's in Ezra 9:3 (see Isa 50:6). **not to give.** Ezra dissolved the illegitimate unions (see note on Ezr 10:3), whereas Nehemiah only attempted to prevent such unions in the future. See *WCF* 20.4; 22.2.
13:26 even he. The argument was from major to minor: If Solomon, great as he was, was not spared when he married foreign women, how much less would they be spared?
13:28 son-in-law. This marriage was doubly grievous: First, a high priest in particular was not to marry a foreigner (Lev 21:14), and second, Sanballat was an enemy (2:19; 4:1; 6:1).
13:29 Remember them. The sixth use of "remember" in a prayer (see note on 1:8) and the third imprecatory prayer (see note on 4:4–5).
13:30 See *WCF* 20.4.
13:31 wood. In keeping with the pledge in 10:34. **Remember me.** The seventh use of "remember" in a prayer (see note on 1:8) and the fourth such prayer by Nehemiah (see note on v. 22). It is significant that Ezra-Nehemiah did not end on the high note of Nehemiah 12:27–47, but on the note of failure to carry out the pledges of 10:30–39 and the subsequent reform. This final chapter delineating needed reform demonstrates that the "house of God" envisioned in Ezra 1:2 was not yet complete. Ezra-Nehemiah is open-ended, looking to the future time when the shadowy "house of God" would give way to the reality (Eph 4:1–16).

ESTHER

Introduction

Overview

Author: Unknown

Purpose: To establish the feast of Purim as a remembrance of God's deliverance of his people and as a reminder to remain faithful to him even when living under oppression

Date: c. 460–350 B.C.

Key Truths:

- The people of God will suffer severely at times at the hands of God's enemies.
- God will preserve his people in their times of oppression.
- The Lord will reverse the fortunes of those who oppress his people and will exalt his people from their humble state.
- The people of God must seek help from God and remain faithful to him despite the trials of suffering.
- The people of God should regularly commemorate the wonders of God's deliverances in the past for courage in their present trials.

Author

Although the author of the book of Esther is unknown, his interest in the origin and observance of the festival of Purim, his intense nationalism and his intimate knowledge of the Persian court, customs and geography suggest that he was a Persian Jew living in Susa.

Time and Place of Writing

The earliest possible date for the book's composition is sometime after the events described in the book, during the fifth century B.C. (cf. the writer's perspective in 9:19), and the latest possible date is the first century B.C. A late-fifth-century or early-fourth-century date is generally preferred by scholars, who point to linguistic evidence as well as to such factors as the author's favorable attitude toward the Persian king and to Gentiles in general as evidence for an early date. Some scholars believe that the lack of influence from the Greek language strongly suggests a date before 331 B.C., when the Persian Empire fell to Alexander the Great.

Purpose and Distinctives

The writer of Esther clearly intended the book to explain the origin of the celebration of Purim, to institutionalize it as a commemoration of the great deliverance of the Jews during the Persian period (see note on 9:20–32).

The book of Esther is renowned for its literary artistry, which functions as the principal vehicle for the book's religious meaning. It is a tightly woven and detailed narrative that focuses on the actions and roles of its characters. The author created narrative tensions by recording reversals or sharp contrasts in fortunes, as well as frequently ironic expectations and roles. Notice particularly:

The descriptions of the banquets of Xerxes and of Vashti, the first in such detail and the second so terse (cf. 1:1–8 with 1:9).

The striking contrast between the initial portrait of the king as a pompous and mighty potentate (1:1–8) and the subsequent revelation of his incompetence and lack of power (see note on 1:13–14).

The contrast between the king's response to Vashti's failure to appear and to Esther's unbidden appearance (1:11–21; 5:1–3).

The intensely ironic reversal in the anticipated and actual fortunes of Haman (6:4–12).

The pathetic scene in which Haman pleads for Esther's mercy—only to be accused of attempted rape (7:7–9).

The specific reversals that take place between Haman's (3:12—4:3) and Mordecai's decrees (8:9–17).

The poetic justice in Haman hanging on the very gallows he had gleefully prepared for Mordecai (7:9–10; 8:1–2; 9:25).

Such reversals are clearly beyond coincidence and reveal that this story is about God's hand in the salvation history of his people (see 1Sa 2:1–10).

The writer also used the compositional technique of repetition or duplication to weave together the various parts of the story. Notice:

The symmetrical positioning of the three references in the book to annals (2:23; 6:1; 10:2).

The three sets of paired banquets marking the beginning (by Xerxes; 1:3–4; 5–8), middle (by Esther; 5:4–8; 7:1–10) and end (the two celebrations of Purim; 9:18–32) of the book. See more of the banquet motif in 1:9, 2:18, 3:15, 8:17 and 9:17.

The threefold mention of the size of Xerxes' empire (1:1; 8:9; 9:30).

The repeated promise to Esther of "even up to half the kingdom" (5:3,6; 7:2; cf. 9:12).

The repeated insistence that the Hebrews did not plunder their enemies (9:10,15,16).

The two accounts of Esther's hidden identity (2:10,20).

The two times the virgins were assembled (2:8,19).

Haman's two interchanges with his wife and friends (5:10–14; 6:13–14).

The two coverings of Haman's head (6:12; 7:8).

The conflicting edicts regarding the fate of the Jews (3:12–14; 8:9–14; cf. 1:22).

The two references to the subsiding of Xerxes' anger (2:1; 7:10).

The double reminder of the permanency of the laws of the Medes and Persians (1:19; 8:8).

The recurrence of the number seven (1:5,10,14; 2:9,16).

Esther's repeated desire for and receiving of favor (2:9,15,17; 5:2, 8; 7:3; 8:9).

The rehearsal of the entire story in 9:24–25.

The literary technique of foreshadowing is also employed in the book of Esther. Most striking is the prediction by Haman's wife that he would "surely come to ruin" because Mordecai was a Jew (6:13). The author was a master of suspense and paced the narrative well (e.g., Esther's postponement of her request [5:4ff.], which heightened the tension). The continual references to time not only present the events as history (1:1–2) and underscore the theme of God's providential working in history, but also keep the story moving (e.g., "later" [2:1]; "when" [2:15]; "now" [2:17]; "when" [2:19]; "during" [2:21]; and "after" [3:1]).

The writer of Esther creatively connected the names of two of the main characters, Haman and Mordecai, to emphasize the conflict between them and those they represented (see notes on 2:5–6; 3:1), specifically the Amalekites and the Jews, respectively. Similarities in phraseology, setting, plot and emphases also suggest that the Joseph story provided an important model for the author as he structured this account (note, e.g., the similarities between 2:2–4 and Ge 41:34–37; 3:10 and Ge 41:42; and 8:6 and Ge 44:34).

A number of important themes are interlaced throughout the book:

Feasting or banqueting sets the scene for each primary action in the narrative, leading up to the ultimate celebration of Purim and contrasting with the theme of fasting (4:3,16; 9:31).

Conflicting loyalties and the themes of obedience versus disobedience run through the book. The initial disobedience of Vashti in chapter 1 sets the stage for the challenges set before Esther with regard to obeying Mordecai (2:10,20; 4:8–16) and standing up against the law (4:11,16; 5:1–2); for Mordecai's noncompliance with Haman's command, which was construed as disobedience on the part of all Jews (3:2–8); and for Mordecai's willingness to carry out Esther's instructions (4:17) to serve both the Persian king and the best interests of the Jews.

The inviolability of the Jews, most explicitly stated in 4:14, is both foundational to the narrative and a reason for the book's continuing significance among the community of faith. Related to this theme is that of the rest and relief from enemies that the feast of Purim commemorates (9:16,22, cf. Dt 25:19).

Christ in Esther

The subtle theological style of Esther does not diminish the importance for Christians of seeing the events narrated in this book in the light of Christ and salvation in him. The people of God were in exile, separated from the seat of their faith, Jerusalem, with its temple and king. Even so, the Lord cared for them, bringing safety and deliverance that have been commemorated through the feast of Purim from that time forward.

These features of the narrative point in the first place to the life of Christ himself. In his state of humiliation, he too suffered under the rule of God's enemies. His faithful service, even to the point of death, brought salvation for all who follow him (Ac 2:36).

Beyond this, the narrative reminds Christian readers that during the present time, when they are separated from their King and temple, Jesus (Jn 16:7; Ac 1:7–9), they should expect to suffer for their identification with Christ (Ac 14:22; Ro 8:35; 1Pe 4:16). Even so, while followers of Christ endure pain innocently as they wait for the new Jerusalem to descend from heaven, they are not alone. Jesus promised his presence, through the indwelling of the Holy Spirit, to be with the church until the end of the church age (Mt 28:20; Eph 1:13–14). Christians today should not wage spiritual or religious conflict with political might or with instruments of physical death. They are to rely instead on spiritual armor for protection as they take the gospel into a hostile world (Eph 6:10–20). The courage and faith of Esther, Mordecai and the Jews reveal for believers today how they are to follow Christ until he returns in glory.

Outline

I. Opening and Setting (1:1–22)	*God arranged Persian royal history to provide an opportunity for the salvation and blessing of his people.*
II. The King's First Decree Results in Mortal Danger for Israel (2:1—3:15) A. The Rise of Queen Esther (2:1–18) B. A Conspiracy Discovered (2:19–23) C. Haman's Promotion and Plot (3:1–15)	*God raised Mordecai and Esther to prominence in the Persian court, but they were endangered by Haman's edict of genocide against the Jews.*
III. Conflict Between Haman and Mordecai (4:1—5:14) A. Mordecai's Counterplan (4:1–17) B. Esther's Unsummoned Audience (5:1–8) C. Haman's Plan to Hang Mordecai (5:9–14)	*God protected Mordecai and Esther as they worked within the Persian system to counteract Haman's edict.*

IV. Mordecai's Triumph Over Haman (6:1—7:10) A. Haman's Humiliation and Mordecai's Reward (6:1–13) B. Haman's Demise (6:14—7:10)	*The plans of the proud enemy of God's people were reversed.*
V. The King's Second Decree Results in Salvation for Israel (8:1—9:32) A. The Plan for Deliverance (8:1–17) B. Victory for the Jews (9:1–19) C. The Establishment of the Feast of Purim (9:20–32)	*The people of God were protected because of courage and faithfulness.*
VI. Epilogue (10:1–3)	*The people of God were honored even outside of their land.*

Queen Vashti Deposed

1 This is what happened during the time of Xerxes,[a] [a] the Xerxes who ruled over 127 provinces[b] stretching from India to Cush[b]:[c] 2At that time King Xerxes reigned from his royal throne in the citadel of Susa,[d] 3and in the third year of his reign he gave a banquet[e] for all his nobles and officials. The military leaders of Persia and Media, the princes, and the nobles of the provinces were present.

4For a full 180 days he displayed the vast wealth of his kingdom and the splendor and glory of his majesty. 5When these days were over, the king gave a banquet, lasting seven days,[f] in the enclosed garden[g] of the king's palace, for all the people from the least to the greatest, who were in the citadel of Susa. 6The garden had hangings of white and blue linen, fastened with cords of white linen and purple material to silver rings on marble pillars. There were couches[h] of gold and silver on a mosaic pavement of porphyry, marble, mother-of-pearl and other costly stones. 7Wine was served in goblets of gold, each one different from the other, and the royal wine was abundant, in keeping with the king's liberality.[i] 8By the king's command each guest was allowed to drink in his own way, for the king instructed all the wine stewards to serve each man what he wished.

9Queen Vashti also gave a banquet[j] for the women in the royal palace of King Xerxes.

10On the seventh day, when King Xerxes was in high spirits[k] from wine,[l] he commanded the seven eunuchs who served him—Mehuman, Biztha, Harbona,[m] Bigtha, Abagtha, Zethar and Carcas— 11to bring[n] before him Queen Vashti, wearing her royal crown, in order to display her beauty[o] to the people and nobles, for she was lovely to look at. 12But when the attendants delivered the king's command, Queen Vashti refused to come. Then the king became furious and burned with anger.[p]

13Since it was customary for the king to consult experts in matters of law and justice,

1:1 [a]Ezr 4:6; Da 9:1 [b]Est 9:30; Da 3:2; 6:1 [c]Est 8:9
1:2 [d]Ezr 1:9; Ne 1:1; Est 2:8
1:3 [e]1Ki 3:15; Est 2:18
1:5 [f]Jdg 14:17 [g]2Ki 21:18; Est 7:7-8
1:6 [h]Est 7:8; Eze 23:41; Am 3:12; 6:4
1:7 [i]Est 2:18; Da 5:2
1:9 [j]1Ki 3:15
1:10 [k]Jdg 16:25; Ru 3:7 [l]Ge 14:18; Est 3:15; 5:6; 7:2; Pr 31:4-7; Da 5:1-4 [m]Est 7:9
1:11 [n]SS 2:4 [o]Ps 45:11; Eze 16:14
1:12 [p]Ge 39:19; Est 2:21; 7:7; Pr 19:12

a *1* Hebrew *Ahasuerus,* a variant of Xerxes' Persian name; here and throughout Esther b *1* That is, the upper Nile region

---

■ **1:1–22** *Opening and Setting.* The book begins with a description of the background of the main events of the narrative. Queen Vashti was deposed, opening the way for Esther to become queen. Although God is not mentioned, these remarkable events would be understood by the faithful as the result of divine providence, ultimately leading to the rescue of the Jews from annihilation.

1:1 Xerxes. Also known as Ahasuerus (485/6–465 B.C.), Xerxes was the Persian king mentioned in Ezra 4:6, renowned for consolidating his father Darius's empire, for his successful building projects and for his wars against the Greeks from 480–470 B.C. **127 provinces.** This large number of divisions in the 20 larger administrative districts, or satrapies, in the Persian Empire illustrates the grandeur of the empire. **Cush.** A country south of Egypt, situated in the northern part of today's Republic of Sudan, as well as in Ethiopia.

1:2 citadel of Susa. The acropolis, the fortified palace that stood 120 feet above the surrounding city of Susa, was one of three Persian capitals and the royal winter residence. It is distinguished from the rest of Susa in 3:12, 8:9 and 9:3. The citadel has been excavated several times since 1851.

1:3 in the third year. That is, from 483–482 B.C.

1:4–7 For a full 180 days he displayed the vast wealth. The reason for this celebration is not explicitly stated. Some interpreters suggest that it was staged for the planning of Persia's campaigns against the Greeks (482–479 B.C.)—which ultimately failed. **the king gave a banquet.** The extravagant, seven-day outdoor feast culminated the celebrations. The elaborate details about the drinking vessels and the abundance of the wine highlight the king's lavish generosity.

1:9 Vashti. The name, possibly related to the Persian word meaning "the beloved" or "the best," is not found elsewhere. Extra-biblical sources name Xerxes' queen as Amestris, though he may have had multiple queens.

1:12 Queen Vashti refused to come. Reasons for Vashti's disobedience are not delineated in the Hebrew text, though early Jewish interpreters speculated that she was either commanded to appear naked, wearing only her crown, or that she had some disfigurement. She was deposed for this insubordination (about 484–483 B.C.).

1:13–14 the times. This expression usually refers to astrology, though in this context it probably means "the proper course to follow" (see 1Ch 12:32). The satirical flavor of the narrative is obvious as the writer noted that the king who had just displayed all the potency and glory of his magnificent kingdom had to consult experts on matters of law and justice—as well as seven nobles (Ezra 7:14)—for advice on dealing with his wife's behavior.

he spoke with the wise men who understood the times[q] 14 and were closest to the king—Carshena, Shethar, Admatha, Tarshish, Meres, Marsena and Memucan, the seven nobles[r] of Persia and Media who had special access to the king and were highest in the kingdom.

15 "According to law, what must be done to Queen Vashti?" he asked. "She has not obeyed the command of King Xerxes that the eunuchs have taken to her."

16 Then Memucan replied in the presence of the king and the nobles, "Queen Vashti has done wrong, not only against the king but also against all the nobles and the peoples of all the provinces of King Xerxes. 17 For the queen's conduct will become known to all the women, and so they will despise their husbands and say, 'King Xerxes commanded Queen Vashti to be brought before him, but she would not come.' 18 This very day the Persian and Median women of the nobility who have heard about the queen's conduct will respond to all the king's nobles in the same way. There will be no end of disrespect and discord.[s]

19 "Therefore, if it pleases the king,[t] let him issue a royal decree and let it be written in the laws of Persia and Media, which cannot be repealed,[u] that Vashti is never again to enter the presence of King Xerxes. Also let the king give her royal position to someone else who is better than she. 20 Then when the king's edict is proclaimed throughout all his vast realm, all the women will respect their husbands, from the least to the greatest."

21 The king and his nobles were pleased with this advice, so the king did as Memucan proposed. 22 He sent dispatches to all parts of the kingdom, to each province in its own script and to each people in its own language,[v] proclaiming in each people's tongue that every man should be ruler over his own household.

Esther Made Queen

2 Later when the anger of King Xerxes had subsided,[w] he remembered Vashti and what she had done and what he had decreed about her. 2 Then the king's personal attendants proposed, "Let a search be made for beautiful young virgins for the king. 3 Let the king appoint commissioners in every province of his realm to bring all these beautiful girls into the harem at the citadel of Susa. Let them be placed under the care of Hegai, the king's eunuch, who is in charge of the women; and let beauty treatments be given to them. 4 Then let the girl who pleases the king be queen instead of Vashti." This advice appealed to the king, and he followed it.

5 Now there was in the citadel of Susa a Jew of the tribe of Benjamin, named Mordecai son of Jair, the son of Shimei, the son of Kish,[x] 6 who had been carried into exile from Jerusalem by Nebuchadnezzar king of Babylon, among those taken captive with Jehoiachin[a][y] king of Judah.[z] 7 Mordecai had a cousin named Hadassah, whom he had brought

1:13 [q]1Ch 12:32; Jer 10:7; Da 2:12
1:14 [r]2Ki 25:19; Ezr 7:14
1:18 [s]Pr 19:13; 27:15
1:19 [t]Ecc 8:4 [u]Est 8:8; Da 6:8, 12
1:22 [v]Ne 13:24; Est 8:9; Eph 5:22-24; 1Ti 2:12
2:1 [w]Est 1:19-20; 7:10
2:5 [x]1Sa 9:1; Est 3:2
2:6 [y]2Ki 24:6, 15; 2Ch 36:10, 20 [z]Da 1:1-5; 5:13

[a] 6 Hebrew *Jeconiah,* a variant of *Jehoiachin*

1:16–18 all the women. Memucan, a nobleman close to Xerxes (v. 14), exaggerated the king's problem and suggested that because of Vashti's disobedience the wives of the men present (the Persian and Median noblewomen; v. 18) would despise their husbands, bringing disrespect and discord into their families.
1:19 written in the laws of Persia and Media, which cannot be repealed. The incontrovertible nature of royal law is an important feature in the plot of the story (4:11; 8:8; see also Da 6:8). The decree to banish Vashti and to transfer her position to someone better (either in the sense of being more beautiful or more obedient) was irrevocable.
1:20 all the women will respect their husbands. Memucan's strategy was that Vashti's crime and punishment would intimidate all the other women in the empire into submission to their husbands.
1:21–22 dispatches to all parts of the kingdom. The Persian postal system, renowned for its efficiency, was used to announce the unalterable royal edict throughout the kingdom (3:12–14; 8:9–10; cf. 9:20,30).
■ **2:1—3:15** *The King's First Decree Results in Mortal Danger for Israel.* These chapters recall the events leading up to Xerxes' decree of genocide against the Jews. They divide into three main parts: the rise of Queen Esther (2:1–18), Mordecai's exposure of a conspiracy against the king (2:19–23) and Haman's promotion and plot against the Jews (3:1–15).
■ **2:1–18** *The Rise of Queen Esther.* Esther became the queen by the king's decree.
2:1 Later. According to verse 16, Esther became queen in 479 B.C., after Xerxes' wars with the Greeks (see note on 1:4–7). **subsided.** The use of the same rare verb in 7:10 suggests a parallel between the dismissal of Vashti and the hanging of Haman. **remembered Vashti.** The king may have regretted banishing her, but it was too late; the legislation had made his action irretrievable.
2:3–4 Let the king appoint commissioners. In the story of Joseph, Pharaoh is similarly advised to appoint commissioners (see Ge 41:34–37). See also "Introduction: Purpose and Distinctives."
2:5–6 Mordecai. A name derived from Marduk, the Babylonian city-god, although like Esther Mordecai may have had a Jewish name as well. The discovery of the Babylonian personal name *Mardukaya* in texts, including one dated about 485 B.C., and the discovery of an archive of texts in Nippur (about a hundred miles south of present-day Baghdad) containing the names of Jews from the time of Artaxerxes I and Darius II, point to the authenticity of Mordecai's name and more generally to the historicity of the events in the story. Mordecai was a Jew living in the citadel of Susa, which suggests that he was an official of the Persian government. The names in his genealogy probably refer to his remote rather than immediate ancestors, Shimei (2Sa 16:5–14) and Kish (1Sa 9:1–2; 1Ch 8:33). The reference to being "carried into exile . . . by Nebuchadnezzar . . . with Jehoiachin" (v. 6) in 597 B.C. (2Ki 24:6–17; 25:27–30) is not to Mordecai but to his ancestors, and this may imply that his family was among the Judean nobility (2Ki 24:10–16). Mordecai's connection with Saul, who was also a Benjamite, takes on significance when we learn that Haman, Mordecai's enemy, may have been a distant relative of Agag the Amalekite, Saul's enemy (see notes on 3:1 and "Introduction: Purpose and Distinctives").
2:6 Jehoiachin. See notes on 2 Kings 24:8–17 and 2 Chronicles 36:9–10.

up because she had neither father nor mother. This girl, who was also known as Esther,[a]
was lovely[b] in form and features, and Mordecai had taken her as his own daughter when
her father and mother died.
8When the king's order and edict had been proclaimed, many girls were brought to
the citadel of Susa[c] and put under the care of Hegai. Esther also was taken to the king's
palace and entrusted to Hegai, who had charge of the harem. 9The girl pleased him and
won his favor.[d] Immediately he provided her with her beauty treatments and special
food.[e] He assigned to her seven maids selected from the king's palace and moved her and
her maids into the best place in the harem.
10Esther had not revealed her nationality and family background, because Mordecai
had forbidden her to do so.[f] 11Every day he walked back and forth near the courtyard of
the harem to find out how Esther was and what was happening to her.
12Before a girl's turn came to go in to King Xerxes, she had to complete twelve
months of beauty treatments prescribed for the women, six months with oil of myrrh and
six with perfumes[g] and cosmetics. 13And this is how she would go to the king: Anything
she wanted was given her to take with her from the harem to the king's palace. 14In the
evening she would go there and in the morning return to another part of the harem to
the care of Shaashgaz, the king's eunuch who was in charge of the concubines.[h] She
would not return to the king unless he was pleased with her and summoned her by
name.[i]
15When the turn came for Esther (the girl Mordecai had adopted, the daughter of his
uncle Abihail[j]) to go to the king,[k] she asked for nothing other than what Hegai, the
king's eunuch who was in charge of the harem, suggested. And Esther won the favor[l] of
everyone who saw her. 16She was taken to King Xerxes in the royal residence in the tenth
month, the month of Tebeth, in the seventh year of his reign.
17Now the king was attracted to Esther more than to any of the other women, and she
won his favor and approval more than any of the other virgins. So he set a royal crown
on her head and made her queen[m] instead of Vashti. 18And the king gave a great banquet,[n] Esther's banquet, for all his nobles and officials.[o] He proclaimed a holiday
throughout the provinces and distributed gifts with royal liberality.[p]

Mordecai Uncovers a Conspiracy

19When the virgins were assembled a second time, Mordecai was sitting at the king's
gate.[q] 20But Esther had kept secret her family background and nationality just as Mordecai had told her to do, for she continued to follow Mordecai's instructions as she had
done when he was bringing her up.[r]
21During the time Mordecai was sitting at the king's gate, Bigthana[a] and Teresh, two
of the king's officers[s] who guarded the doorway, became angry[t] and conspired to assassinate King Xerxes. 22But Mordecai found out about the plot and told Queen Esther, who
in turn reported it to the king, giving credit to Mordecai. 23And when the report was investigated and found to be true, the two officials were hanged[u] on a gallows.[b] All this
was recorded in the book of the annals[v] in the presence of the king.

2:7 [a]Ge 41:45 [b]Ge 39:6
2:8 [c]ver 3,15; Ne 1:1; Est 1:2; Da 8:2
2:9 [d]Ge 39:21 [e]ver 3, 12; Ge 37:3; 1Sa 9:22-24; 2Ki 25:30; Eze 16:9-13; Da 1:5
2:10 [f]ver 20
2:12 [g]Pr 27:9; SS 1:3; Isa 3:24
2:14 [h]1Ki 11:3; SS 6:8; Da 5:2 [i]Est 4:11
2:15 [j]Est 9:29 [k]Ps 45:14 [l]Ge 18:3; 30:27; Est 5:8
2:17 [m]Est 1:11; Eze 16:9-13
2:18 [n]1Ki 3:15; Est 1:3 [o]Ge 10:20 [p]Est 1:7
2:19 [q]ver 21; Est 3:2; 4:2; 5:13
2:20 [r]ver 10
2:21 [s]Ge 40:2; Est 6:2 [t]Est 1:12; 3:5; 5:9; 7:7
2:23 [u]Ge 40:19; Ps 7:14-16; Pr 26:27 [v]Est 6:1; 10:2

a *21* Hebrew *Bigthan,* a variant of *Bigthana* b *23* Or *were hung* (or *impaled*) *on poles;* similarly elsewhere in Esther

---

2:7 Hadassah. Esther's Hebrew name, meaning "myrtle." **Esther.** Perhaps derived from the Persian "star," though it could be from Ishtar, a Babylonian deity.
2:9 pleased. Literally, "was good" (1:21; 2:4—twice). Compare the adjective "good," which is translated "high" (1:10), "lovely" (1:11; 2:7), "better" (1:19), "beautiful" (2:2,3) and "best" (2:9). **won his favor.** Pleasing and gaining favor were necessary for survival in Xerxes' court. Esther possessed these qualities as the result of God's providence (cf. v. 17; 5:2; see a more explicit reference to God's providence in Da 1:9).
2:12 twelve months of beauty treatments. The elaborate preparations for going in to the king were in keeping with the other excesses of the court (cf. 1:4–8).
2:18 Esther's banquet. The celebration of Esther's coronation contrasts with Vashti's banquet in 1:9. Vashti administered her own banquet with only women in attendance, whereas the king hosted Esther's banquet and invited all his nobles and officials. **a holiday.** Literally, a "rest"; a celebration that may have included a remission of taxes or debt, release of slaves or cancellation of military service, as well as gifts. These celebrations foreshadow the great banquet and rest for the Jews in 9:16, 17, 18 and 22. See "Introduction: Purpose and Distinctives."
■ **2:19–23** *A Conspiracy Discovered.* Mordecai, with Esther's help, foiled a plot to assassinate the king.
2:19 at the king's gate. This expression (cf. v. 21; 3:2; 5:9,13; 6:10,12) may imply that Mordecai was a palace official, in a position that enabled him to find out about the conspiracy to assassinate the king (v. 21). Mordecai's status may have incited Haman's jealousy (5:13).
2:23 hanged. Hanging a body was normally a method used to exhibit the corpse after execution by impalement or some other means. **on a gallows.** Literally, "on a tree"; may refer to impalement on wooden stakes (see NIV text note). To the Jews this signified that the two officials were under God's curse (Dt 21:22–23), confirming the appropriateness of Mordecai's loyalty to the pagan king. **recorded in the book of the annals.** The mention of the annals foreshadowed the important part they would play later in the story. Though Mordecai's deed was recorded, he was not duly rewarded at that time. The narrative turned instead to Haman's promotion (3:1).

Haman's Plot to Destroy the Jews

3 After these events, King Xerxes honored Haman son of Hammedatha, the Agagite,[w]
elevating him and giving him a seat of honor higher than that of all the other nobles. 2All the royal officials at the king's gate knelt down and paid honor to Haman, for
the king had commanded this concerning him. But Mordecai would not kneel down or
pay him honor.
3Then the royal officials at the king's gate asked Mordecai, "Why do you disobey the
king's command?"[x] 4Day after day they spoke to him but he refused to comply.[y] Therefore they told Haman about it to see whether Mordecai's behavior would be tolerated,
for he had told them he was a Jew.
5When Haman saw that Mordecai would not kneel down or pay him honor, he was
enraged.[z] 6Yet having learned who Mordecai's people were, he scorned the idea of killing only Mordecai. Instead Haman looked for a way[a] to destroy[b] all Mordecai's people,
the Jews,[c] throughout the whole kingdom of Xerxes.
7In the twelfth year of King Xerxes, in the first month, the month of Nisan, they cast
the *pur*[d] (that is, the lot[e]) in the presence of Haman to select a day and month. And the
lot fell on[a] the twelfth month, the month of Adar.[f]
8Then Haman said to King Xerxes, "There is a certain people dispersed and scattered
among the peoples in all the provinces of your kingdom whose customs[g] are different
from those of all other people and who do not obey[h] the king's laws; it is not in the king's
best interest to tolerate them.[i] 9If it pleases the king, let a decree be issued to destroy
them, and I will put ten thousand talents[b] of silver into the royal treasury for the men
who carry out this business."[j]
10So the king took his signet ring[k] from his finger and gave it to Haman son of Hammedatha, the Agagite, the enemy of the Jews. 11"Keep the money," the king said to Haman, "and do with the people as you please."
12Then on the thirteenth day of the first month the royal secretaries were summoned. They wrote out in the script of each province and in the language[l] of each people all Haman's orders to the king's satraps, the governors of the various provinces and
the nobles of the various peoples. These were written in the name of King Xerxes himself and sealed[m] with his own ring. 13Dispatches were sent by couriers to all the king's
provinces with the order to destroy, kill and annihilate all the Jews[n]—young and old,
women and little children—on a single day, the thirteenth day of the twelfth month, the
month of Adar,[o] and to plunder[p] their goods. 14A copy of the text of the edict was to be
issued as law in every province and made known to the people of every nationality so
they would be ready for that day.[q]
15Spurred on by the king's command, the couriers went out, and the edict was issued
in the citadel of Susa.[r] The king and Haman sat down to drink,[s] but the city of Susa was
bewildered.[t]

3:1 [w]ver 10; Ex 17:8-16; Nu 24:7; Dt 25:17-19; 1Sa 14:48; Est 5:11
3:3 [x]Est 5:9; Da 3:12
3:4 [y]Ge 39:10
3:5 [z]Est 2:21; 5:9
3:6 [a]Pr 16:25 [b]Ps 74:8; 83:4 [c]Est 9:24
3:7 [d]Est 9:24,26 [e]Lev 16:8; 1Sa 10:21 [f]ver 13; Ezr 6:15; Est 9:19
3:8 [g]Ac 16:20-21 [h]Jer 29:7; Da 6:13 [i]Ezr 4:15
3:9 [j]Est 7:4
3:10 [k]Ge 41:42; Est 7:6; 8:2
3:12 [l]Ne 13:24 [m]Ge 38:18; 1Ki 21:8; Est 8:8-10
3:13 [n]1Sa 15:3; Ezr 4:6; Est 8:10-14 [o]ver 7 [p]Est 8:11; 9:10
3:14 [q]Est 8:8; 9:1
3:15 [r]Est 8:14 [s]Est 1:10 [t]Est 8:15

[a] 7 Septuagint; Hebrew does not have *And the lot fell on.* [b] 9 That is, about 375 tons (about 345 metric tons)

■ **3:1–15** *Haman's Promotion and Plot.* Mordecai insulted Haman by refusing to bow to him, as a direct result of which Haman convinced the king to decree the annihilation of the Jews.

3:1 Haman son of Hammedatha, the Agagite. Haman's genealogy is debated. Although the names *Haman* and *Hammedatha* may be Persian, the identification of Haman as "the Agagite" suggests an important association of Haman with Agag, the king of the Amalekites, archenemies of Israel, who had been opposed by Saul (Ex 17:8–16; Dt 25:17–19; 1Sa 14:47–48; 15). Haman's promotion without apparent cause contrasts with Mordecai's lack of promotion after his heroic action (2:21–23).

3:2–6 Mordecai would not kneel. The reasons for Mordecai's refusal to do obeisance to Haman are unclear since Jews did not regard the practice of bowing down before kings (1Sa 24:8; 2Sa 18:28) and other persons (Ge 23:7; 33:3; 2Ki 2:15) to be a violation of the first and second commandments (Ex 20:3–6). However, if Haman and Mordecai are viewed as representative of the ancient hostility between the Amalekites and the Israelites, (the Benjamite-Agagite enmity; 1Sa 15:7–9), then Mordecai's refusal to bow down to his hereditary enemy (v. 4) because "he was a Jew" is understandable and even laudable—to bow might have been interpreted as tacit approval of the crimes of the Agagites. Similarly, Haman's seemingly excessive passion to avenge the entire Jewish nation for Mordecai's insolence is explained (v. 6).

3:7 ***pur*** **(that is, the lot).** Haman used the ancient practice of casting lots (1Sa 14:41ff.; Pr 16:33) to determine the most propitious time to set in motion his plans to destroy the Jews. The plural form of *pur, purim,* is the name of the celebration that commemorates the demise of Haman, "the enemy of all the Jews" (9:23–32). See "Introduction: Purpose and Distinctives." See *WLC* 113.

3:9 ten thousand talents of silver. An enormous bribe, calculated to be about two-thirds the annual revenue of the Persian Empire under King Darius (*Herodotus*, 3.95).

3:10 signet ring. Another of the king's impulsive responses authorized Haman to issue royal edicts (cf. Ge 41:42). **the enemy of the Jews.** The repetition of Haman's full name together with the added phrase, "the enemy of the Jews," underlines the terrible predicament of the Jews at this point.

3:13 destroy, kill and annihilate all the Jews. The piling up of nearly synonymous verbs in the edict conveys its full horror. The allusion to Samuel's condemnation of the Amalekites is evident in the similarity of expressions (see 1Sa 15:3). **to plunder their goods.** Compare the Jews' refusal to plunder (9:10,15ff.).

Mordecai Persuades Esther to Help

4 When Mordecai learned of all that had been done, he tore his clothes,[u] put on sackcloth and ashes,[v] and went out into the city, wailing[w] loudly and bitterly. 2But he
went only as far as the king's gate,[x] because no one clothed in sackcloth was allowed
to enter it. 3In every province to which the edict and order of the king came, there was
great mourning among the Jews, with fasting, weeping and wailing. Many lay in sackcloth and ashes.
4When Esther's maids and eunuchs came and told her about Mordecai, she was in
great distress. She sent clothes for him to put on instead of his sackcloth, but he would
not accept them. 5Then Esther summoned Hathach, one of the king's eunuchs assigned
to attend her, and ordered him to find out what was troubling Mordecai and why.
6So Hathach went out to Mordecai in the open square of the city in front of the king's
gate. 7Mordecai told him everything that had happened to him, including the exact amount
of money Haman had promised to pay into the royal treasury for the destruction of the
Jews.[y] 8He also gave him a copy of the text of the edict for their annihilation, which had
been published in Susa, to show to Esther and explain it to her, and he told him to urge
her to go into the king's presence to beg for mercy and plead with him for her people.
9Hathach went back and reported to Esther what Mordecai had said. 10Then she instructed him to say to Mordecai, 11"All the king's officials and the people of the royal
provinces know that for any man or woman who approaches the king in the inner court
without being summoned[z] the king has but one law:[a] that he be put to death. The only
exception to this is for the king to extend the gold scepter[b] to him and spare his life. But
thirty days have passed since I was called to go to the king."
12When Esther's words were reported to Mordecai, 13he sent back this answer: "Do
not think that because you are in the king's house you alone of all the Jews will escape.
14For if you remain silent[c] at this time, relief[d] and deliverance[e] for the Jews will arise from
another place, but you and your father's family will perish. And who knows but that you
have come to royal position for such a time as this?"[f]
15Then Esther sent this reply to Mordecai: 16"Go, gather together all the Jews who are
in Susa, and fast[g] for me. Do not eat or drink for three days, night or day. I and my maids
will fast as you do. When this is done, I will go to the king, even though it is against the
law. And if I perish, I perish."[h]
17So Mordecai went away and carried out all of Esther's instructions.

Esther's Request to the King

5 On the third day Esther put on her royal robes[i] and stood in the inner court of the
palace, in front of the king's[j] hall. The king was sitting on his royal throne in the

4:1 [u]Nu 14:6 [v]2Sa 13:19; Eze 27:30-31; Jnh 3:5-6 [w]Ex 11:6; Ps 30:11
4:2 [x]Est 2:19
4:7 [y]Est 3:9; 7:4
4:11 [z]Est 2:14 [a]Da 2:9 [b]Est 5:1,2; 8:4
4:14 [c]Ecc 3:7; Isa 62:1; Am 5:13 [d]Est 9:16, 22 [e]Ge 45:7; Dt 28:29 [f]Ge 50:20
4:16 [g]2Ch 20:3; Est 9:31 [h]Ge 43:14
5:1 [i]Est 4:16; Eze 16:13 [j]Est 6:4; Pr 21:1

■ **4:1—5:14** *Conflict Between Haman and Mordecai.* Mordecai rose against Haman to prevent the outworking of the genocide plan that Haman had set into motion. These chapters divide into three main parts: Mordecai's counterplan (4:1–17), Esther's approach to the king (5:1–8) and Haman's intention to hang Mordecai (5:9–14).
■ **4:1–17** *Mordecai's Counterplan.* Mordecai learned of Haman's plot against the Jews and enlisted Esther's help to deliver the Jews from annihilation.
4:1 tore his clothes . . . sackcloth and ashes . . . wailing loudly and bitterly. The responses of Mordecai (vv. 1–2) and of Jews in every province (v. 3) signified the intensity of grief and horror they felt when they heard Haman's edict (cf. Ge 37:29,34; Da 9:3; Jnh 3:6).
4:3 fasting, weeping and wailing . . . sackcloth and ashes. Although calling on the Lord is not mentioned explicitly in this passage, the actions taken by the Jews were often associated with prayer for forgiveness and for help (e.g., Joel 2:12; Jnh 3:8). Likely these responses conveyed that the Jews reacted with cries to the Lord for his help (see note on "Go, gather . . . fast for me" at 4:16).
4:4 maids and eunuchs came and told her. Although Esther's attendants did not know that she and Mordecai were cousins, they correctly presumed that she would want to know that he was in mourning. **sent clothes.** Esther may have wanted Mordecai to be properly attired so that she could speak with him in person (v. 2).
4:5 Hathach. His name may mean "the good one" or perhaps "courier." He mediated communication between Esther and Mordecai, probably because Mordecai was inappropriately attired as he participated with other Jews in mourning.
4:8 edict. Mordecai saw to it that Esther not only received a copy of the edict but had it explained to her (perhaps translated) before he charged her to entreat the king for mercy for her people. Here Mordecai reversed his previous charge that Esther conceal her Jewish identity (2:10).
4:12–14 you and your father's family will perish. Mordecai may have meant that Esther's identity would somehow be exposed when her relationship to him was revealed, or he may have been suggesting that her silence in the face of her people's great need would constitute sufficient reason for God to curse her. See theological article "The Will of God" at Ezekiel 18. **you have come to royal position for such a time as this.** Mordecai implied his belief that God had providentially ordered the events of Esther's life to put her in position to act on behalf of the Jews. He challenged Esther to act in courage and faith so that God would bless her.
4:16 Go, gather . . . fast for me. With a combination of conviction, faith and trepidation, Esther directed that a fast (and prayer, which always accompanied religious fasting; see Dt 9:9; Jdg 20:26–27; 2Sa 12:16; Ezr 8:21–23; Da 9:3) be undertaken on her behalf. That God honored the faith of the Jews at this time is demonstrated in the saving events that followed. **three days, night or day.** Fasts generally were prescribed for only one day. This unusually long fast points to the seriousness of the situation and effectively contrasts with the feasts that stand at the beginning and end of the book (1:3,5,9; 2:18; 9:17f.). **against the law.** Appearing unbidden before the king was potentially a capital offense (4:11). Esther's quandary reintroduces the theme of obedience since compliance with Mordecai's request entailed disobeying the law. **if I perish, I perish.** If the king did not choose to receive Esther when she appeared unbidden before him, she could be executed. Courage rather than passive resignation is reflected here. This expression may be an allusion to the story of Joseph ("if I am bereaved, I am bereaved"; Ge 43:14). See *WCF* 21.5.
■ **5:1–8** *Esther's Unsummoned Audience.* Esther placed her life at risk by appearing before her husband to plead on behalf of the Jews.

hall, facing the entrance. 2When he saw Queen Esther standing in the court, he was pleased with her and held out to her the gold scepter that was in his hand. So Esther approached and touched the tip of the scepter.[k]

3Then the king asked, "What is it, Queen Esther? What is your request? Even up to half the kingdom,[l] it will be given you."

4"If it pleases the king," replied Esther, "let the king, together with Haman, come today to a banquet I have prepared for him."

5"Bring Haman at once," the king said, "so that we may do what Esther asks."

So the king and Haman went to the banquet Esther had prepared. 6As they were drinking wine,[m] the king again asked Esther, "Now what is your petition? It will be given you. And what is your request? Even up to half the kingdom,[n] it will be granted."[o]

7Esther replied, "My petition and my request is this: 8If the king regards me with favor[p] and if it pleases the king to grant my petition and fulfill my request, let the king and Haman come tomorrow to the banquet[q] I will prepare for them. Then I will answer the king's question."

Haman's Rage Against Mordecai

9Haman went out that day happy and in high spirits. But when he saw Mordecai at the king's gate and observed that he neither rose nor showed fear in his presence, he was filled with rage[r] against Mordecai.[s] 10Nevertheless, Haman restrained himself and went home.

Calling together his friends and Zeresh,[t] his wife, 11Haman boasted[u] to them about his vast wealth, his many sons,[v] and all the ways the king had honored him and how he had elevated him above the other nobles and officials. 12"And that's not all," Haman added. "I'm the only person[w] Queen Esther invited to accompany the king to the banquet she gave. And she has invited me along with the king tomorrow. 13But all this gives me no satisfaction as long as I see that Jew Mordecai sitting at the king's gate.[x]"

14His wife Zeresh and all his friends said to him, "Have a gallows built, seventy-five feet[a] high,[y] and ask the king in the morning to have Mordecai hanged[z] on it. Then go with the king to the dinner and be happy." This suggestion delighted Haman, and he had the gallows built.

Mordecai Honored

6 That night the king could not sleep;[a] so he ordered the book of the chronicles,[b] the record of his reign, to be brought in and read to him. 2It was found recorded there that Mordecai had exposed Bigthana and Teresh, two of the king's officers who guarded the doorway, who had conspired to assassinate King Xerxes.

3"What honor and recognition has Mordecai received for this?" the king asked.

"Nothing has been done for him,"[c] his attendants answered.

4The king said, "Who is in the court?" Now Haman had just entered the outer court of the palace to speak to the king about hanging Mordecai on the gallows he had erected for him.

5His attendants answered, "Haman is standing in the court."

"Bring him in," the king ordered.

6When Haman entered, the king asked him, "What should be done for the man the king delights to honor?"

[a] 14 Hebrew *fifty cubits* (about 23 meters)

5:2 [k]Est 4:11; 8:4; Pr 21:1
5:3 [l]Est 7:2; Da 5:16; Mk 6:23
5:6 [m]Est 1:10 [n]Mk 6:23 [o]Est 7:2; 9:12
5:8 [p]Est 2:15; 7:3; 8:5 [q]1Ki 3:15; Est 6:14
5:9 [r]Est 2:21; Pr 14:17 [s]Est 3:3,5
5:10 [t]Est 6:13
5:11 [u]Pr 13:16 [v]Est 9:7-10,13
5:12 [w]Job 22:29; Pr 16:18; 29:23
5:13 [x]Est 2:19
5:14 [y]Est 7:9 [z]Ezr 6:11; Est 6:4
6:1 [a]Da 2:1; 6:18 [b]Est 2:23; 10:2
6:3 [c]Ecc 9:13-16

5:1–2 Esther put on her royal robes. Wearing royal robes that undoubtedly enhanced her beauty and announced her position (in contrast to mourning attire that she probably wore in 4:15–16; see note on 4:3), Esther approached the king. By holding out his gold scepter, he spared her life, a gesture to which Esther responded by touching its tip (see 4:11).

5:3–8 half the kingdom. This generous offer reflected a courtly convention and was not to be taken literally (v. 6; cf. Mk 6:23). Esther's initial request was that the king and Haman attend a banquet (v. 4). Her second response (v. 8) effectively obliged the king to grant her new petition. But it was only after other events unfolded that Esther finally answered the king's question (7:3–4). Esther's delaying tactics not only demonstrated her wisdom and self-control, but also augment the suspense in the story.

■ **5:9–14** *Haman's Plan to Hang Mordecai.* On the counsel of Haman's wife and friends, Haman determined to have Mordecai executed.

5:13 See *WLC* 148; *WSC* 81.

5:14 seventy-five feet high. This description may be hyperbole, or the gallows may have been built atop another structure. **hanged.** See notes on 2:23.

■ **6:1—7:10** *Mordecai's Triumph Over Haman.* In an ironic reversal of what Haman had planned, Mordecai was honored and Haman executed. These chapters divide into two parts: Haman's humiliation and Mordecai's reward (6:1–13), and Haman's demise (6:14—7:10).

■ **6:1–13** *Haman's Humiliation and Mordecai's Reward.* Xerxes recalled Mordecai's earlier service (2:19–23) and belatedly honored him.

6:1 could not sleep. Although the text does not directly mention God, this circumstance was understood as an act of God on behalf of his people. This event marks the literary center of the story and the beginning of reversals that the book will describe.

6:2–3 See *WLC* 127,129.

6:6–9 What should be done for the man the king delights to honor? The identity of the one to be honored was concealed, just

Now Haman thought to himself, “Who is there that the king would rather honor than
me?” 7So he answered the king, “For the man the king delights to honor, 8have them
bring a royal robe[d] the king has worn and a horse[e] the king has ridden, one with a royal crest placed on its head. 9Then let the robe and horse be entrusted to one of the king’s
most noble princes. Let them robe the man the king delights to honor, and lead him on
the horse through the city streets, proclaiming before him, ‘This is what is done for the
man the king delights to honor![f]’ ”

10“Go at once,” the king commanded Haman. “Get the robe and the horse and do just
as you have suggested for Mordecai the Jew, who sits at the king’s gate. Do not neglect
anything you have recommended.”

11So Haman got[g] the robe and the horse. He robed Mordecai, and led him on horseback through the city streets, proclaiming before him, “This is what is done for the man
the king delights to honor!”

12Afterward Mordecai returned to the king’s gate. But Haman rushed home, with his
head covered[h] in grief, 13and told Zeresh[i] his wife and all his friends everything that had
happened to him.

His advisers and his wife Zeresh said to him, “Since Mordecai, before whom your
downfall[j] has started, is of Jewish origin, you cannot stand against him—you will surely come to ruin!” 14While they were still talking with him, the king’s eunuchs arrived and
hurried Haman away to the banquet[k] Esther had prepared.

Haman Hanged

7 So the king and Haman went to dine[l] with Queen Esther, 2and as they were drinking
wine[m] on that second day, the king again asked, “Queen Esther, what is your petition?
It will be given you. What is your request? Even up to half the kingdom,[n] it will be granted.[o]”

3Then Queen Esther answered, “If I have found favor[p] with you, O king, and if it pleases your majesty, grant me my life—this is my petition. And spare my people—this is my
request. 4For I and my people have been sold for destruction and slaughter and annihilation.[q] If we had merely been sold as male and female slaves, I would have kept quiet,
because no such distress would justify disturbing the king.[a]”

5King Xerxes asked Queen Esther, “Who is he? Where is the man who has dared to
do such a thing?”

6Esther said, “The adversary and enemy is this vile Haman.”

Then Haman was terrified before the king and queen. 7The king got up in a rage,[r] left
his wine and went out into the palace garden.[s] But Haman, realizing that the king had
already decided his fate,[t] stayed behind to beg Queen Esther for his life.

8Just as the king returned from the palace garden to the banquet hall, Haman was
falling on the couch[u] where Esther was reclining.[v]

The king exclaimed, “Will he even molest the queen while she is with me in the
house?”[w]

As soon as the word left the king’s mouth, they covered Haman’s face.[x] 9Then Harbona,[y] one of the eunuchs attending the king, said, “A gallows seventy-five feet[b] high[z]
stands by Haman’s house. He had it made for Mordecai, who spoke up to help the king.”

The king said, “Hang him on it!”[a] 10So they hanged Haman[b] on the gallows[c] he had
prepared for Mordecai.[d] Then the king’s fury subsided.[e]

6:8 [d]Ge 41:42; Isa 52:1 [e]1Ki 1:33
6:9 [f]Ge 41:43
6:11 [g]Ge 41:42
6:12 [h]2Sa 15:30; Jer 14:3,4; Mic 3:7
6:13 [i]Est 5:10 [j]Ps 57:6; Pr 26:27; 28:18
6:14 [k]1Ki 3:15; Est 5:8
7:1 [l]Ge 40:20-22; Mt 22:1-14
7:2 [m]Est 1:10 [n]Est 5:3 [o]Est 9:12
7:3 [p]Est 2:15
7:4 [q]Est 3:9
7:7 [r]Ge 34:7; Est 1:12; Pr 19:12; 20:1-2 [s]2Ki 21:18 [t]Est 6:13
7:8 [u]Est 1:6 [v]Ge 39:14 [w]Ge 34:7 [x]Est 6:12
7:9 [y]Est 1:10 [z]Est 5:14 [a]Ps 7:14-16; 9:16; Pr 11:5-6; 26:27; Mt 7:2
7:10 [b]Pr 10:28 [c]Est 9:25 [d]Da 6:24 [e]Est 2:1

a *4* Or *quiet, but the compensation our adversary offers cannot be compared with the loss the king would suffer*
b *9* Hebrew *fifty cubits* (about 23 meters)

as Haman had intentionally veiled the identity of the people to be destroyed (3:8). Haman, assuming that he himself was the man, unveiled his personal dream list, which focused not on material gain or position but on public acclaim and adulation (cf. Ge 41:42–43).

6:12–13 See *WLC* 132.

6:13 you cannot stand against him. Haman’s wife and advisors voiced the belief that the Jewish people were indomitable and perhaps even the intuition that the Jewish God was the living God (see the predictions about the fall of Amalek before Israel; Ex 17:16; Nu 24:20; Dt 25:17–19; 1Sa 15; 2Sa 1:8–16; cf. Jos 2:11; 9:29; Eze 38:23; Da 6:26–27).

■**6:14–7:10** *Haman’s Demise.* In a reversal highly satisfying to the reader, Haman was executed on the gallows he had prepared for Mordecai.

6:14 hurried Haman away. It was oriental custom for servants to escort guests to special functions.

7:3 Then Queen Esther answered. After so long a delay, the dramatic tension is high when Esther voices her petition for her own life and the lives of her people.

7:4 sold. Esther undoubtedly referred to Haman’s initial bribe (3:9; 4:7). **for destruction and slaughter and annihilation.** The Hebrew verbs are precisely those used in the initial decree (3:13). **I would have kept quiet.** See NIV text note. Esther’s meaning is not altogether clear. In any case, she demonstrated humility before the king and won his favor.

7:8 falling on the couch. Haman’s pride and terror were revealed in his violation of protocol toward Esther. This impulsive and ill-considered action sealed his fate. **covered Haman’s face.** The court attendants, understanding that Haman was now under a death sentence, covered his face. This may have entailed blindfolding and gagging.

7:9–10 Hang him on it! The order to hang Haman on the gallows intended for Mordecai marks one of the most notable reversals in the story.

The King's Edict in Behalf of the Jews

8 That same day King Xerxes gave Queen Esther the estate of Haman,[f] the enemy of
the Jews. And Mordecai came into the presence of the king, for Esther had told how
he was related to her. 2The king took off his signet ring,[g] which he had reclaimed from
Haman, and presented it to Mordecai. And Esther appointed him over Haman's estate.[h]
3Esther again pleaded with the king, falling at his feet and weeping. She begged him to
put an end to the evil plan of Haman the Agagite, which he had devised against the Jews.
4Then the king extended the gold scepter[i] to Esther and she arose and stood before him.
5"If it pleases the king," she said, "and if he regards me with favor and thinks it the
right thing to do, and if he is pleased with me, let an order be written overruling the dispatches that Haman son of Hammedatha, the Agagite, devised and wrote to destroy the
Jews in all the king's provinces. 6For how can I bear to see disaster fall on my people?
How can I bear to see the destruction of my family?"[j]
7King Xerxes replied to Queen Esther and to Mordecai the Jew, "Because Haman attacked the Jews, I have given his estate to Esther, and they have hanged him on the gallows. 8Now write another decree[k] in the king's name in behalf of the Jews as seems best
to you, and seal it with the king's signet ring[l]—for no document written in the king's
name and sealed with his ring can be revoked."[m]
9At once the royal secretaries were summoned—on the twenty-third day of the third
month, the month of Sivan. They wrote out all Mordecai's orders to the Jews, and to the
satraps, governors and nobles of the 127 provinces stretching from India to Cush.[a][n]
These orders were written in the script of each province and the language of each people and also to the Jews in their own script and language.[o] 10Mordecai wrote in the name
of King Xerxes, sealed the dispatches with the king's signet ring, and sent them by
mounted couriers, who rode fast horses especially bred for the king.
11The king's edict granted the Jews in every city the right to assemble and protect
themselves; to destroy, kill and annihilate any armed force of any nationality or province
that might attack them and their women and children; and to plunder[p] the property of
their enemies. 12The day appointed for the Jews to do this in all the provinces of King Xerxes was the thirteenth day of the twelfth month, the month of Adar.[q] 13A copy of the text
of the edict was to be issued as law in every province and made known to the people of
every nationality so that the Jews would be ready on that day[r] to avenge themselves on
their enemies.
14The couriers, riding the royal horses, raced out, spurred on by the king's command.
And the edict was also issued in the citadel of Susa.
15Mordecai[s] left the king's presence wearing royal garments of blue and white, a large
crown of gold and a purple robe of fine linen.[t] And the city of Susa held a joyous celebration.[u] 16For the Jews it was a time of happiness and joy,[v] gladness and honor.[w] 17In
every province and in every city, wherever the edict of the king went, there was joy[x] and
gladness among the Jews, with feasting and celebrating. And many people of other nationalities became Jews because fear[y] of the Jews had seized them.[z]

Triumph of the Jews

9 On the thirteenth day of the twelfth month, the month of Adar,[a] the edict commanded by the king was to be carried out. On this day the enemies of the Jews had

8:1 [f]Est 2:7; 7:6; Pr 22:22-23
8:2 [g]Ge 41:42; Est 3:10 [h]Pr 13:22; Da 2:48
8:4 [i]Est 4:11; 5:2
8:6 [j]Est 7:4; 9:1
8:8 [k]Est 3:12-14 [l]Ge 41:42 [m]Est 1:19; Da 6:15
8:9 [n]Est 1:1 [o]Est 1:22
8:11 [p]Est 9:10,15,16
8:12 [q]Est 3:13; 9:1
8:13 [r]Est 3:14
8:15 [s]Est 9:4 [t]Ge 41:42 [u]Est 3:15
8:16 [v]Ps 97:10-12 [w]Ps 112:4
8:17 [x]Est 9:19,27; Ps 35:27; Pr 11:10 [y]Ex 15:14,16; Dt 11:25 [z]Est 9:3
9:1 [a]Est 8:12

[a] *9* That is, the upper Nile region

■ **8:1—9:32** *The King's Second Decree Results in Salvation for Israel.* In contrast with the first royal decree against the Jews, these chapters explain how Esther influenced the king to decree their deliverance. These verses divide into three parts: the plan for deliverance (8:1–17), victory for the Jews (9:1–19) and the commemoration of the Feast of Purim (9:20–32).

■ **8:1–17** *The Plan for Deliverance.* The king, Esther and Mordecai formed a plan to deliver the Jews from destruction. Much of the language of this section alludes to expressions in 3:1—4:3.

8:1–2 gave Queen Esther the estate of Haman. According to Persian custom, the property of a traitor was confiscated by the crown. **Mordecai came into the presence of the king.** Mordecai was granted official status (1:14) and given Haman's former official and personal position.

8:7–8 write another decree . . . as seems best to you. Although the king could not revoke the earlier decree (1:19), he authorized Esther and Mordecai to issue another decree that would essentially nullify the first edict.

8:9–14 granted the Jews . . . the right to . . . protect themselves. The new decree, issued two months and ten days after the first (3:12), was worded almost identically to Haman's initial edict (3:12–15). Note however the significant differences between 8:11 and 3:13. In 3:13, all the Jews, young and old, including women and children, are objects of the order to destroy. But in 8:11 there is some ambiguity. The edict might be interpreted as giving the Jews the right to destroy not only any armed force that might attack them, but also the women and children belonging to members of that armed force. Alternatively, the edict might be interpreted as giving the Jews the right to destroy any armed force that attacked any of the Jews, including Jewish women or children.

8:14–17 spurred on by the king's command. Compare the similar expressions in 3:15—4:3.

8:17 many people . . . became Jews. The conversion of those from other nations who feared the Jews is a wonderful result of God's salvation of the Jews (cf. Ex 15:14–16; Jos 2:9; Ps 105:38).

■ **9:1–19** *Victory for the Jews.* Instead of suffering genocide, the Jews rose triumphant over all who sought their destruction.

hoped to overpower them, but now the tables were turned and the Jews got the upper
hand[b] over those who hated them.[c] 2 The Jews assembled in their cities[d] in all the provinces of King Xerxes to attack those seeking their destruction. No one could stand
against them,[e] because the people of all the other nationalities were afraid of them. 3 And
all the nobles of the provinces, the satraps, the governors and the king's administrators
helped the Jews,[f] because fear of Mordecai had seized them. 4 Mordecai was prominent[g]
in the palace; his reputation spread throughout the provinces, and he became more and
more powerful.[h]
5 The Jews struck down all their enemies with the sword, killing and destroying
them,[i] and they did what they pleased to those who hated them. 6 In the citadel of Susa,
the Jews killed and destroyed five hundred men. 7 They also killed Parshandatha, Dal-
phon, Aspatha, 8 Poratha, Adalia, Aridatha, 9 Parmashta, Arisai, Aridai and Vaizatha,
10 the ten sons[j] of Haman son of Hammedatha, the enemy of the Jews. But they did not
lay their hands on the plunder.[k]
11 The number of those slain in the citadel of Susa was reported to the king that same
day. 12 The king said to Queen Esther, "The Jews have killed and destroyed five hundred
men and the ten sons of Haman in the citadel of Susa. What have they done in the rest
of the king's provinces? Now what is your petition? It will be given you. What is your request? It will also be granted."[l]
13 "If it pleases the king," Esther answered, "give the Jews in Susa permission to carry out this day's edict tomorrow also, and let Haman's ten sons[m] be hanged[n] on gallows."
14 So the king commanded that this be done. An edict was issued in Susa, and they
hanged[o] the ten sons of Haman. 15 The Jews in Susa came together on the fourteenth day
of the month of Adar, and they put to death in Susa three hundred men, but they did not
lay their hands on the plunder.[p]
16 Meanwhile, the remainder of the Jews who were in the king's provinces also assembled to protect themselves and get relief[q] from their enemies.[r] They killed seventy-five
thousand of them[s] but did not lay their hands on the plunder. 17 This happened on the
thirteenth day of the month of Adar, and on the fourteenth they rested and made it a day
of feasting[t] and joy.

Purim Celebrated

18 The Jews in Susa, however, had assembled on the thirteenth and fourteenth, and
then on the fifteenth they rested and made it a day of feasting and joy.
19 That is why rural Jews—those living in villages—observe the fourteenth of the
month of Adar[u] as a day of joy and feasting, a day for giving presents to each other.[v]
20 Mordecai recorded these events, and he sent letters to all the Jews throughout the
provinces of King Xerxes, near and far, 21 to have them celebrate annually the fourteenth
and fifteenth days of the month of Adar 22 as the time when the Jews got relief[w] from their
enemies, and as the month when their sorrow was turned into joy and their mourning

9:1 [b]Jer 29:4-7 [c]Est 3:12-14; Pr 22:22-23
9:2 [d]ver 15-18 [e]Est 8:11,17; Ps 71:13,24
9:3 [f]Ezr 8:36
9:4 [g]Ex 11:3 [h]2Sa 3:1; 1Ch 11:9
9:5 [i]Ezr 4:6
9:10 [j]Est 5:11 [k]Ge 14:23; 1Sa 14:32; Est 3:13; 8:11
9:12 [l]Est 5:6; 7:2
9:13 [m]Est 5:11 [n]Dt 21:22-23
9:14 [o]Ezr 6:11
9:15 [p]Ge 14:23; Est 8:11
9:16 [q]Est 4:14 [r]Dt 25:19 [s]1Ch 4:43
9:17 [t]1Ki 3:15
9:19 [u]Est 3:7 [v]ver 22; Dt 16:11,14; Ne 8:10,12; Est 2:9; Rev 11:10
9:22 [w]Est 4:14

9:1 the edict commanded by the king was to be carried out. This is a reference to the second edict authorizing the Jews to take vengeance on their enemies (8:13). No further reference is made in the story to the first edict. **tables were turned.** The theme of reversals is again stressed. See "Introduction: Purpose and Distinctives."

9:2–3 the people . . . were afraid of them . . . fear of Mordecai. Fear of the God of the Jews stood behind the pervasive fear of the Jews (see Ex 15:15ff.). The reversal (see notes on v. 1) was so complete that all the officials who were to have enforced the extermination of the Jews in fact aided them (v. 3).

9:5–11 they did what they pleased. This expression signifies sovereign favor (1:8). The extent of the killing is underlined (vv. 6–11), as is the fact that the Jews did not plunder their enemies (v. 10; contrast the plundering of the Amalekites, which led to Saul's demise in 1Sa 15:17–19). This moral restraint regarding pillaging, which would have been legal according to the edict in 8:11, suggests the proper nature of the Jews' conduct in this final encounter with the "Amalekites," despite the extent of the killing.

9:12–15 carry out this day's edict tomorrow also. Esther's requests for further vengeance (v. 13), which may have been due to the intense degree of hatred against the Jews in that city, led to a second day of bloodshed in Susa (v. 15). Notably, the emphasis in the narrative is on killing "enemies" (e.g., v. 5) and not simply on winning a victory. The second day of bloodshed also led to traditional differences as to the date on which Purim was to be observed annually (vv. 17–19). Purim is presently celebrated by Jews on the 14th day of Adar, except in Jerusalem, where it is celebrated on the 15th. **they hanged the ten sons.** The bodies of the dead sons (v. 12) were displayed as a warning and a sign of dishonor.

9:13 hanged. See note at 2:23.

9:16–17 relief from their enemies. The rest granted to the Jews at this time became the basis for the annual celebration of Purim (see v. 22). **killed seventy-five thousand.** The slaughter of a further 75,000 enemies did not create a moral problem for the narrator. Rather it emphasized the extent of the antagonism toward the Jews throughout the empire and served to justify the celebrations that followed.

9:19 giving presents to each other. The exchange of gifts, usually food (v. 22), enabled even the poorest Jew to join in the celebrations (cf. Dt 16:11,14; Ne 8:10,12) and is a further instance of providential care for the oppressed within the Jewish community.

■ **9:20–32** *The Establishment of the Feast of Purim.* Mordecai established Purim as a permanent celebration in Israel. These verses clarify that one of the main purposes of the book was to institutionalize Purim as a festival to be commemorated by each new generation of Jews and to set standards for how it was to be celebrated.

9:20–22 Mordecai recorded these events. He dispatched letters of instruction about the celebration of Purim as a day of joy and feasting, celebrating relief from the Jews' enemies.

9:22 See *WCF* 21.5.

into a day of celebration.[x] He wrote them to observe the days as days of feasting and joy
and giving presents of food[y] to one another and gifts to the poor.
23 So the Jews agreed to continue the celebration they had begun, doing what Mordecai had written to them. 24 For Haman son of Hammedatha, the Agagite,[z] the enemy
of all the Jews, had plotted against the Jews to destroy them and had cast the *pur*[a] (that
is, the lot[b]) for their ruin and destruction. 25 But when the plot came to the king's attention,[a] he issued written orders that the evil scheme Haman had devised against the Jews
should come back onto his own head,[c] and that he and his sons should be hanged[d] on
the gallows.[e] 26 (Therefore these days were called Purim, from the word *pur*.[f]) Because
of everything written in this letter and because of what they had seen and what had happened to them, 27 the Jews took it upon themselves to establish the custom that they and
their descendants and all who join them should without fail observe these two days every year, in the way prescribed and at the time appointed. 28 These days should be remembered and observed in every generation by every family, and in every province and
in every city. And these days of Purim should never cease to be celebrated by the Jews,
nor should the memory of them die out among their descendants.
29 So Queen Esther, daughter of Abihail,[g] along with Mordecai the Jew, wrote with full
authority to confirm this second letter concerning Purim. 30 And Mordecai sent letters to
all the Jews in the 127 provinces[h] of the kingdom of Xerxes—words of goodwill and assurance— 31 to establish these days of Purim at their designated times, as Mordecai the
Jew and Queen Esther had decreed for them, and as they had established for themselves
and their descendants in regard to their times of fasting[i] and lamentation.[j] 32 Esther's decree confirmed these regulations about Purim, and it was written down in the records.

The Greatness of Mordecai

10 King Xerxes imposed tribute throughout the empire, to its distant shores.[k]
2 And all his acts of power and might, together with a full account of the greatness of Mordecai[l] to which the king had raised him,[m] are they not written in the book
of the annals[n] of the kings of Media and Persia? 3 Mordecai the Jew was second[o] in rank[p]
to King Xerxes,[q] preeminent among the Jews, and held in high esteem by his many fellow Jews, because he worked for the good of his people and spoke up for the welfare of
all the Jews.[r]

a *25* Or *when Esther came before the king*

9:22 [x]Ne 8:12; Ps 30:11-12 [y]2Ki 25:30
9:24 [z]Ex 17:8-16 [a]Est 3:7 [b]Lev 16:8
9:25 [c]Ps 7:16 [d]Dt 21:22-23 [e]Est 7:10
9:26 [f]ver 20; Est 3:7
9:29 [g]Est 2:15
9:30 [h]Est 1:1
9:31 [i]Est 4:16 [j]Est 4:1-3
10:1 [k]Ps 72:10; 97:1; Isa 24:15
10:2 [l]Est 8:15; 9:4 [m]Ge 41:44 [n]Est 2:23
10:3 [o]Da 5:7 [p]Ge 41:43 [q]Ge 41:40 [r]Ne 2:10; Jer 29:4-7; Da 6:3

9:24–25 Haman son of Hammedatha, the Agagite, the enemy of all the Jews. This brief summary of the events of the preceding chapters focuses not on Esther and Mordecai but rather on the king and Haman. It presents Haman as the archetypal adversary of all Jews, past and present (see 3:10; cf. 8:1; 9:10). ***pur.*** See note on 3:7. See "Introduction: Purpose and Distinctives." See *WLC* 113.

9:29–32 to establish these days of Purim. Esther and Mordecai distributed a final, official letter regarding Purim, setting the feast in the context of the more established Israelite practices of fasting and lamentation (v. 31). Purim was institutionalized as an official religious celebration, a task the writer seemed to view as important because of the non-Mosaic origin of the festival.

■ **10:1–3** *Epilogue.* This postscript to the book focuses attention on King Xerxes and Mordecai and directs the reader to "the book of the annals of the kings of Media and Persia" (v. 2) for further information (cf. 1 Ki 14:19,29). Esther's absence from the postscript is noticeable but unexplained.

10:2 are they not written . . . ? The royal annals are mentioned also in 2:23.

10:3 second in rank to King Xerxes. Mordecai was esteemed as an ideal Jewish official, his rank paralleling that of Joseph in Egypt (Ge 41:39–44). His importance as a model for the Jews and in establishing the feast of Purim was acknowledged in the Apocryphal book of Maccabees, where Purim is called "the Day of Mordecai" (2 Maccabees 15:36). See *WLC* 147.

Introduction to the Poetic and Wisdom Books

Old Testament Poetry

The Hebrew Bible regards only Job, Psalms and Proverbs as poetic books. In the English Bible the poetic books also include Ecclesiastes and Song of Songs. Neither arrangement is entirely satisfactory. For one thing, Song of Songs is written in poetry and excluded from the Hebrew arrangement. On the other hand, Ecclesiastes is a mixture of prose and poetry but included in the English arrangement. All five books have in common only that they are not historical or prophetic in a strict sense. Since, however, four of them are composed entirely in poetry, and one partially, it has become customary to speak of them all as the poetic books. Poetry is extremely common throughout the Old Testament, and the ideas discussed below apply to it wherever it is found.

Biblical poetry can be distinguished from prose in at least four important ways: regular rhythmic structures, frequent use of figures of speech, heavy reliance on imagery and intense emotional expression. Terseness of phrasing is also quite common. Prose exhibits all of these features to some degree, but they appear more frequently and noticeably in poetry.

Rhythmic Structure: In addition to features such as assonance and consonance, the formal rhythmic structure of Hebrew poetry is most clearly seen in parallelism, which is the close coordination or affiliation of one line of poetry with another. Parallel lines consist of at least two "versets" making up a verse. The second verset adds to, stresses or constrasts some dimension or dimensions of the first verset. The basic idea is "A, and what's more, B" (or "A, but on the other hand, B").

The significance of this feature of poetry in the Old Testament may be illustrated by comparing the two records of Jael's treatment of Sisera in Judges. In the prose account of Judges 4:19 we read: " 'I'm thirsty,' he said. 'Please give me some water.' She opened a skin of milk, gave him a drink, and covered him up." In the poetic account of Judges 5:25, however, we read:

> A verset: "He asked for water, she gave him milk;"
> B verset: "in a bowl fit for nobles she brought him curdled milk."

In the poetic account the rhythm of parallelism between the versets is evident. The second verset, stereophonically enriches "she gave him" with "in a bowl fit for nobles she brought him" and "milk" with "curdled milk." It draws attention to the curdled milk and to the aristocratic goblet in which Jael served the delicacy. By this means, the audience could see and feel Jael's cunning. She treated her battle-weary guest as royalty in order to put him at ease and so render him vulnerable. In this sense, the prose account focuses more on the straightforward facts, and the parallelism of the poem creates a fuller impression.

Figures of Speech: Poetry also relies on figures of speech much more than does prose. A figure may be defined simply as an indirect way of saying something, or saying one thing while meaning another, according to conventions shared by the writer and reader. Poets often use figures of speech such as hyperbole or exaggeration; they employ symbolism, metaphors, similes, metonyms, synechdoches, sarcasm, irony and a number of other well-known techniques of indirect communication.

For example, Psalm 1:3 employs the simile of a fruitful tree to describe the positive condition of those who meditate on the law of God:

> "He is like a tree planted by streams of water,
> which yields its fruit in season."

Ps 34:10 uses a hyperbole of claiming to have no physical needs in order to convey David's satisfaction in God's answer to his prayers:

> "The lions may grow weak and hungry,
> but those who seek the LORD lack no good thing."

Readers of poetry must be alert to the frequency of figures of speech and to how they work. Interpretations can be misleading if poetical texts are read in a woodenly literal fashion.

Imagery: Imagery may be defined as the expression of thoughts in ways that evokes mental experiences of the senses. To be sure, prose relies on imagination to communicate a writer's thoughts, but poetry relies much more on the imaginative power of language. Rather than speaking plainly about a matter, Biblical poets often lead their readers into imaginative, sensory experiences of their topics.

For instance, Psalm 42:7 depicts the troubles of the psalmist in powerful language calling to mind the sound and feel of being overcome by a rushing waterfall:

> "Deep calls to deep
> in the roar of your waterfalls;
> all your waves and breakers
> have swept over me."

Psalm 23:2 portrays the protection of God in a picturesque expression of refreshment, comfort, color and quiet:

> "He makes me lie down in green pastures;
> He leads me beside quiet waters."

Interpreters of Biblical poetry must always be aware of the frequent use of imagery. The poetic devices often afford readers opportunities for meaningful, life-changing reflection.

Emotional Expression: Biblical poetry is also especially effective at expressing and stirring up the full range of emotions appropriate for the faithful. It touches on joy and pain, praise and lament, love and hatred; hardly any emotion is omitted.

For example, in Psalm 130:1–2 we find desperate lament:

"Out of the depths I cry to you, O LORD;
O Lord, hear my voice.
Let your ear be attentive
to my cry for mercy."

At the same time, in Psalm 57:7–8 we discover ecstatic praise:

"My heart is steadfast, O God,
my heart is steadfast;
I will sing and make music.
Awake my soul!
Awake, harp and lyre!
I will awaken the dawn."

The emotional focus of Biblical poetry calls upon interpreters to give careful attention to their own emotional reactions to these Scriptures. As we encounter the intense feelings expressed in these texts, we are challenged to bring our deepest passions into submission to the Scriptures.

Old Testament Wisdom

Three of the five poetic books comprise the Old Testament books of wisdom: Job, Proverbs and Ecclesiastes. Wisdom passages appear occasionally in other books but only in limited fashion. Large portions of the wisdom books are poetry and exhibit the qualities we have mentioned above. Yet wisdom books can be distinguished from other poetic books in a number of ways.

Characteristics of Wisdom: The books of wisdom have at least three distinguishing characteristics. First, the word "wisdom" and its synonyms, such as "understanding," appear more frequently in these books than in others. Second, they share a common mode of revelation in that they rely more on observations of life than on supernatural visions. Third, because their inspiration is drawn mostly from contemporary observations of creation and human experiences, they do not focus much on the history of salvation. Little direct reflection is made on the grand redemptive events that took place in Israel's history.

Definition of Wisdom: Wisdom may be defined on two levels. On a more superficial level wisdom is significant skillfulness; i.e., the possession of survival skills (Pr 30:24–28), technical skills (Ex 28:3; 36:1) and administrative-judicial skills (Dt 1:15–18; 1Ki 3:1–28). On a deeper level, however, wisdom is rooted in the created order. The Scriptures explain that God brought wisdom into existence before the rest of creation. Thus wisdom stands behind all natural and social relationships (Pr 3:19–20; 8:22–31). Insight into this created order makes one wise in the fuller sense of the term. The sages of Scripture expound this cosmic wisdom under the inspiration of God's Spirit (Pr 25:2; Ecc 12:9–12).

As central as ordinary observation is to the process of gaining wisdom, it was not divorced from religious commitments. The sages who contributed to and compiled the wisdom books regularly depended on the teachings of Moses and David to guide their interpretations of experience. For example, the opening superscription of Proverbs informs its readers: "The proverbs of Solomon son of David, king of Israel" (Pr 1:1). Solomon spoke as Israel's covenant king; he brought to the task not only eyes opened wide toward the world and social behavior, but also a heart of faith from his godly heritage that led him to depend on previous revelation. Even Agur, the proselyte sage from Massa, informed his readers that he found wisdom possible only within Israel's faith. Citing first David (Ps 18:30) and then Moses (Dt 4:2), he stated:

"Every word of God is flawless;
he is a shield to those who take refuge in him.
Do not add to his words,
or he will rebuke you and prove you a liar"
(Pr 30:5–6).

Didactic and Reflective Wisdom: Two main types of wisdom appear in the Old Testament. In the first place, *didactic* or proverbial wisdom is represented primarily in the book of Proverbs. Didactic wisdom was wisdom taught usually within a family context (Pr 1:8,10). It consisted primarily of easily memorized and often provocative wise sayings, riddles and parables (Pr 1:6) that were designed to teach practical wisdom. By learning proverbs, the young of Israel were trained to discern direction for living on a plethora of subjects.

The practical value of proverbial wisdom results not only from its direct insights, but also from recognition that it is not always easy to coordinate proverbial wisdom with experience in our fallen world.

For example, Proverbs 22:29 reads,

"Do you see a man skilled in his work?
He will serve before kings;
he will not serve before obscure men."

It does not take much familiarity with life to know that a measure of dissonance exists between this proverb and much of our experience. We know that this maxim does not describe an inevitable series of events because skilled people do not always serve before kings. Instead, observations of life teach us that this proverb was intended to encourage the development of skills by instilling a hope of recognition. It did not promise that everyone who is skilled will gain such recognition. Similar qualifications apply to many proverbs because sin has caused the world to fall short of the ideal patterns often described in didactic wisdom. Much of proverbial wisdom points to approximations of the ideal order that are experienced from time to time, and it directs the faithful to hope in a future beyond this world (Pr 12:28; 14:32; 23:17–18; 24:19–20) after all has been made right by the final judgment. Then

Introduction to the Poetic and Wisdom Books

every dissonance between proverbial wisdom and experience will be eliminated.

In the second place, *reflective* wisdom appears in Job and Ecclesiastes. This style of writing explores the proper uses of proverbial wisdom by drawing attention to the enigmas of this life. These books help interpreters to avoid over-reading or expecting too much from proverbial wisdom. The book of Job tests the usefulness of proverbial wisdom for those who endure suffering. Where is God's justice when the righteous suffer and the wicked use proverbial wisdom to accuse them falsely? How much of God's wisdom in such circumstances can human beings understand? Similarly, Ecclesiastes marks the limits of proverbial wisdom in the pursuit of contentment and significance. Why is there so little joy in the fruit of hard work? What value is pursuing knowledge or acquiring wealth when from all appearances the righteous and wicked lose all they have accomplished in death? Both books warn against simplistic interpretations of didactic wisdom that raise expectations for immediate justice and enduring blessings.

Both Job and Ecclesiastes endorse the value of proverbial wisdom but also open the way for fuller insight. First, they stress that human beings are severely limited in their ability to discern the wisdom of God, especially with respect to the perplexing anomalies of life. It is the height of folly to presume that we can actually master the wisdom required to understand all of God's ways (Job 28; 40–42). Second, they remind readers that acquiring even limited awareness of wisdom requires a constant, reverential fear of the Lord (Pr 1:7). Job 28:28 concludes, "The fear of the Lord—that is wisdom, and to shun evil is understanding." In much the same vein, Ecclesiastes 12:13 reads, "Now all has been heard; here is the conclusion of the matter: Fear God and keep his commandments, for this is the whole duty of man." Reflective wisdom stresses that recognizing human limitations and the need for submission to the Lord enables us to live as wise people.

JOB

Introduction

Overview

Author: Unknown

Purpose: To explore the limits and proper uses of traditional proverbial wisdom in the case of a righteous individual's suffering

Date: c. 970–586 B.C.

Key Truths:

- God has purposes behind all suffering, but these are largely hidden from us.
- Conventional proverbial wisdom applies easily to some situations—but not to the suffering of the righteous.
- Righteous sufferers must humbly join their laments to affirmations of God's goodness and justice.
- Human grasp of wisdom is limited and always begins with the fear of God and obedience to his commands.

Author

Although the book contains many speeches by Job, it includes no indication that he is the author. An unknown poet of Israel, a sage who probably used earlier source material (oral and written) from the patriarchal times, was most likely the author of this book. We learn that the author was an Israelite by observing that he called God by his covenant name, *Yahweh* (LORD).

Time and Place of Writing

We do not know exactly when the author of Job lived and wrote. Although the prologue places the events of the book during the patriarchal times, its final form probably took shape during or soon following the era of Solomon (c. 970–586) in the region that later came to be known as Palestine. The discovery of fragments from Job among the Dead Sea Scrolls has ruled out attempts to date the writing of Job in the postexilic period or later.

Purpose and Distinctives

Among the wisdom writings of the Old Testament (Job, Proverbs, Ecclesiastes) the book of Job stands with Ecclesiastes as an exploration of the limits and proper uses of conventional, proverbial wisdom. Such wisdom describes the ideals of life and gives guidance for navigating through the normal course of human experience. Yet it is possible to misunderstand and to wrongly appropriate proverbial wisdom as though the ideal and the ordinary were always applicable. Many circumstances arise that call for deeper reflection and struggle beyond the guidance of proverbial wisdom. This is especially true of the suffering of the righteous. The book of Job counters a naïve reliance on proverbial wisdom by wrestling with questions raised about the goodness and justice of God as he allows his faithful people to suffer.

The book of Job presents at least three possible explanations for the suffering of the righteous. First, God is not just and good. The faithful endure hardship because God is at least partly evil. The book rejects this possibility, forcefully affirming God's goodness in both the prologue and the epilogue. The prologue depicts Job's affirmation of God's goodness in the midst of suffering (1:1—2:13), and in the epilogue (42:7–17) God honors Job's trust in his goodness and justice by restoring him.

Second, the righteous suffer because God is not sovereign, and suffering is beyond his control. Yet the book of Job also dismisses this possibility, attesting that God is omnipotent and all-powerful and that he sovereignly controls all things (37:14–24; 42:2).

Third, God is both good and sovereign, but mere creatures cannot always understand the outworkings of his sovereign goodness. His ways are so far beyond human analysis that they cannot be fully fathomed (ch. 28). In Job's case, the opening chapter gives readers a minuscule glimpse into God's reasons for Job's suffering. God and Satan were engaged in a challenge that involved the testing of Job's faith. Yet, as in most cases, Job suffered without a hint of what was going on in heaven. Although God welcomes the laments and cries of his people (36:14–15), the righteous understand themselves and God aright when they balance their honest complaints with humility and reverence for God (see note at 28:28).

This perspective on suffering develops slowly as the book unfolds. The prologue provides a heavenly viewpoint (1:1—2:13). God chose Job to be one of his suffering servants, an instrument through whom he would accomplish a spiritual triumph: "Have you considered my servant Job?" (1:8; 2:3). The accuser (Satan) falsely accused Job of serving God only on account of the material blessings he enjoyed (1:9–11). So Job was granted the dubious honor of being tested to see whether he would remain true to God even when all was taken away and only horrible suffering became his daily lot in life.

While the prologue gives us a heavenly perspective, the dialogues present an earthly outlook (3:1—27:23). Like most people who suffer, Job knew nothing about what took place in the divine council. He struggled with his friends' misuse of conventional proverbial wisdom as they alleged that all suffering is a direct result of human sin (compare Jn 9:2). Job's counselors believed that Job's affliction was in proportion to his sin. But as the book explains, they were wrong. They commonly misunderstood and misapplied Scripture—even Job himself fell into this trap. As a result, neither Job nor his friends are trustworthy as independent sources of Old Testament or Christian theology. When Job or the counselors are in agreement with normative theology, their statements can be accepted. But when their theology runs counter to that of the rest of Scripture, it must be rejected as erroneous.

As Job confronted his heartless friends, he said some things for which he later had to repent (42:5–6). He believed deeply that the counselors were wrong but could offer no alternative explanation as to why a righteous person should suffer so much while the godless around him enjoyed health and material blessings (12:6).

Like the psalmists, Job habitually complained to God in the language of a legal dispute. Job wrestled with God and shared openly with him his every doubt and fear. His relationship with God was vibrant, while his friends reduced their faith to platitudes. They were insensitive and theologically presumptuous (13:4–5; 16:2; 19:21). Job was not presumptuous, as some may suppose, when he called for vindication. Even as he imagined God as angry with him, he clung to the resolution that God is just and would provide a Vindicator, a Champion, a Redeemer (16:19–21; 19:23–27).

This hope became a reality when God appeared in the storm (38:1—41:34). Job was not rebuked as one suffering for his sins but was humbled before the Lord as one who struggled too much for his own vindication and not enough for God's vindication (38:2; 42:2–3). Job never found out precisely why he was suffering, only that his pain was within the scope of God's sovereign will and that God expected his trust and loyalty. After his eyes had seen the Lord and he had repented in dust and ashes, Job came to understand the good news that God sits sovereignly on his throne and that he does finally reward those who hold fast to him through periods of distress.

Christ in Job

The book of Job anticipates the person and work of Christ in a number of ways. The most direct connection between Christ and this book lies in the fact that Christ is "the wisdom of God" (1Co 1:24) and that in him "are hidden all the treasures of wisdom and knowledge" (Col 2:3). This identification of Christ with wisdom stems both from the fact that he is the eternal Logos through "whom all things were made "(Jn 1:3) and that as the incarnate Messiah he is the One on whom rests "the Spirit of wisdom and of understanding, the Spirit of counsel and of power, the Spirit of knowledge and of the fear of the LORD" (Isa 11:2). That for which Job and his friends yearned, namely understanding and wisdom, is found in Christ. When we look for wisdom apart from him, we are doomed to find only worldly foolishness (1Co 3:19). When men and women are united with Christ, he grants them wisdom. The grace given to those who believe is poured out "with all wisdom and understanding" (Eph 1:8). That is to say, wisdom begins with faith in Christ and derives from the grace that is found in following and trusting him. Any believer who "lacks wisdom . . . should ask God, who gives generously to all" (Jas 1:5). Even so, unlike the contentious spirit that Job and his friends exhibited as they dialogued, "wisdom that comes from heaven is first of all pure; then peace-loving, considerate, submissive, full of mercy and good fruit, impartial and sincere" (Jas 3:17).

Second, the book of Job insists that the human ability to understand wisdom is so limited that for us wisdom may be summarized in two elements: fearing God and obeying his commands (see note at 28:28). This theme is fulfilled in Christ in that wisdom from God amounts to submitting to Christ in reverence and obedience.

Third, on a number of occasions the book of Job acknowledges the desperate need that humans have for a mediator between themselves and God (see 5:1; 9:33; 16:20; 19:25; 33:23). The predicament of fallen humanity is so horrendous that we need someone with access to the throne of God to plead our case. We are helpless in ourselves. Christ fulfills that need as the only Mediator between humanity and God (1Ti 5:2).

Fourth, as a righteous man whose loyalty to God was tested through suffering, Job anticipated the fulfillment of testing in Christ. Christ far exceeded Job's righteousness in that he was entirely without sin. Yet he suffered temptation in the wilderness and throughout his entire humiliation only to endure all without fault (Heb 4:15). For this reason, when the faithful fail to be perfect in their sufferings, they may rest assured that Christ has suffered on their behalf and that his righteousness and reward are imputed to them through the grace of God.

Outline

I. The Prologue (1:1—2:13)
   A. Job Blessed and Pious (1:1–5)
   B. Job Tested (1:6—2:13)
      1. Satan's Accusation (1:6–12)
      2. Trouble and Job's Reaction (1:13–22)
      3. Satan's Second Accusation (2:1–6)
      4. Trouble and Job's Reaction (2:7–10)
      5. The Arrival of Job's Friends (2:11–13)

Readers are given insight into the heavenly contest that lay behind Job's suffering.

II. Dialogues Between Job and His Friends (3:1—27:23)
  A. Job's Opening Lament (3:1–26)
  B. The First Cycle of Speeches (4:1—14:22)
    1. Eliphaz (4:1—5:27)
      a. Complements and Challenges (4:1–11)
      b. Claim of Revelation (4:12–21)
      c. Profile of a Fool (5:1–7)
      d. Praise for God's Goodness (5:8–16)
      e. Praise for Divine Discipline (5:17–27)
    2. Job's Reply to Eliphaz (6:1—7:21)
      a. Rejection of Eliphaz (6:1–30)
      b. Lament to God (7:1–21)
    3. Bildad (8:1–22)
      a. Rebuke for Job (8:1–10)
      b. Appeal to Proverbial Wisdom (8:11–22)
    4. Job's Reply to Bildad (9:1—10:22)
      a. Affirmation of God's Power and Wisdom (9:1–13)
      b. Questions About God's Justice (9:14–29)
      c. Questions to God Himself (9:30—10:22)
    5. Zophar (11:1–20)
      a. Rebuke for Idle Talk (11:1–6)
      b. Praise for God's Wisdom and Power (11:7–12)
      c. Call to Repentance (11:13–20)
    6. Job's Reply to Zophar (12:1—14:22)
      a. Sarcastic Rebuke (12:1—13:19)
      b. Cries to God (13:20–27)
      c. Lament Over Humanity's Condition (13:28—14:22)
  C. The Second Cycle of Speeches (15:1—21:34)
    1. Eliphaz (15:1–35)
      a. Questions and Accusations (15:1–16)
      b. Affirmation of Proverbial Wisdom (15:17–35)
    2. Job's Reply to Eliphaz (16:1—17:16)
      a. Cynical Rebuke (16:1–6)
      b. Lament to God (16:7—17:16)
    3. Bildad (18:1–21)
      a. Unsympathetic Rebuke (18:1–4)
      b. Affirmation of Proverbial Wisdom (18:5–21)
    4. Job's Reply to Bildad (19:1–29)
      a. Appeal for Sympathy (19:1–6)
      b. Laments to God (19:7–20)
      c. Appeal and Warnings (19:21–29)
    5. Zophar (20:1–29)
      a. Personal Offense (20:1–3)
      b. Affirmation of Proverbial Wisdom (20:4–29)
    6. Job's Reply to Zophar (21:1–34)
      a. An Appeal to Be Heard (21:1–3)
      b. Rejection of Zophar's Views (21:4–34)

Job and his friends struggled to understand how Job's suffering fit with the justice, goodness and sovereignty of God. In their dialogues they explored the limits of traditional, proverbial wisdom in this situation.

- D. The Third Cycle of Speeches (22:1—26:14)
  - 1. Eliphaz (22:1–30)
    - a. Divine Indifference (22:1–5)
    - b. Accusations Against Job (22:6–11)
    - c. Correction of Job (22:12–14)
    - d. Affirmation of Proverbial Wisdom (22:15–20)
    - e. Call to Repentance (22:21–30)
  - 2. Job's Reply to Eliphaz (23:1—24:25)
    - a. God's Absence (23:1–9)
    - b. God's Control (23:10–17)
    - c. Injustices in the World (24:1–12)
    - d. Justice for the Wicked (24:13–25)
  - 3. Bildad: God's Glory and Humanity's Insignificance (25:1–6)
  - 4. Job's Reply to Bildad (26:1–14)
    - a. Sarcastic Rejection (26:1–4)
    - b. Affirmation of God's Supremacy (26:5–14)
- E. Job's Closing Discourse (27:1–23)
  - 1. Protest of Innocence (27:1–12)
  - 2. The Fate of the Wicked (27:13–23)

III. Interlude on Wisdom (28:1–28)
- A. Human Abilities (28:1–11)
- B. Human Limitations (28:12–19)
- C. Divine Prerogatives (28:20–28)

Despite the many accomplishments of humanity, only God fully grasps wisdom. In the end, people must humbly revere God and obey him.

IV. The Monologues (29:1—42:6)
- A. Job's Final Oration (29:1—31:40)
  - 1. Job's Past Experience (29:1–25)
  - 2. Job's Present Experience (30:1–31)
  - 3. Job's Protest of Innocence (31:1–40)
- B. Elihu's Speeches (32:1—37:24)
  - 1. Introductory Explanation (32:1–5)
  - 2. Elihu's First Speech (32:6—33:33)
    - a. Defense of Elihu (32:6–14)
    - b. Soliloquy (32:15–22)
    - c. Words for Job (33:1–33)
  - 3. Elihu's Second Speech (34:1–37)
    - a. Call to the Wise (34:1–4)
    - b. Job's Erroneous Words (34:5–9)
    - c. Divine Justice (34:10–30)
    - d. Call for Repentance (34:31–37)
  - 4. Elihu's Third Speech: Job's Inconsistencies (35:1–16)
  - 5. Elihu's Fourth Speech (36:1—37:24)
    - a. Apology (36:1–4)
    - b. Job's Erroneous Words (36:5–15)
    - c. Call for Repentance (36:16–21)
    - d. Divine Purposes (36:22—37:13)
    - e. Call for Repentance (37:14–24)
- C. God's Responses (38:1—42:6)
  - 1. God's First Discourse (38:1—40:2)
  - 2. Job's Humility (40:3–5)
  - 3. God's Second Discourse (40:6—41:34)
  - 4. Job's Repentance (42:1–6)

Both Elihu and God himself corrected Job. Through these encounters Job realized his errors and repented.

V. The Epilogue (42:7–17)
- A. Rebuke for Job's Friends (42:7–9)
- B. Blessings for Job (42:10–17)

God rebuked Job's friends for their arrogance but blessed Job with more than he had enjoyed before because Job humbly repented and honored God.

Prologue

1 In the land of Uz[a] there lived a man whose name was Job.[b] This man was blameless[c] and upright; he feared God[d] and shunned evil. 2He had seven sons and three
daughters,[e] 3and he owned seven thousand sheep, three thousand camels, five hundred
yoke of oxen and five hundred donkeys, and had a large number of servants. He was the
greatest man[f] among all the people of the East.
4His sons used to take turns holding feasts in their homes, and they would invite their
three sisters to eat and drink with them. 5When a period of feasting had run its course,
Job would send and have them purified. Early in the morning he would sacrifice a burnt
offering[g] for each of them, thinking, "Perhaps my children have sinned[h] and cursed God[i]
in their hearts." This was Job's regular custom.

Job's First Test

6One day the angels[a][j] came to present themselves before the LORD, and Satan[b] also
came with them.[k] 7The LORD said to Satan, "Where have you come from?"
Satan answered the LORD, "From roaming through the earth and going back and forth
in it."[l]
8Then the LORD said to Satan, "Have you considered my servant Job?[m] There is no one
on earth like him; he is blameless and upright, a man who fears God and shuns evil."[n]
9"Does Job fear God for nothing?"[o] Satan replied. 10"Have you not put a hedge
around him and his household and everything he has?[p] You have blessed the work of his
hands, so that his flocks and herds are spread throughout the land.[q] 11But stretch out
your hand and strike everything he has,[r] and he will surely curse you to your face."[s]
12The LORD said to Satan, "Very well, then, everything he has is in your hands, but on
the man himself do not lay a finger."
Then Satan went out from the presence of the LORD.
13One day when Job's sons and daughters were feasting and drinking wine at the oldest brother's house, 14a messenger came to Job and said, "The oxen were plowing and
the donkeys were grazing nearby, 15and the Sabeans[t] attacked and carried them off.
They put the servants to the sword, and I am the only one who has escaped to tell you!"
16While he was still speaking, another messenger came and said, "The fire of God fell
from the sky[u] and burned up the sheep and the servants,[v] and I am the only one who
has escaped to tell you!"
17While he was still speaking, another messenger came and said, "The Chaldeans[w]
formed three raiding parties and swept down on your camels and carried them off. They
put the servants to the sword, and I am the only one who has escaped to tell you!"
18While he was still speaking, yet another messenger came and said, "Your sons and
daughters were feasting and drinking wine at the oldest brother's house, 19when suddenly a mighty wind[x] swept in from the desert and struck the four corners of the house.

1:1 [a]Jer 25:20 [b]Eze 14:14,20; Jas 5:11 [c]Ge 6:9; 17:1 [d]Ge 22:12; Ex 18:21
1:2 [e]Job 42:13
1:3 [f]Job 29:25
1:5 [g]Ge 8:20; Job 42:8 [h]Job 8:4 [i]1Ki 21:10,13
1:6 [j]Job 38:7 [k]Job 2:1
1:7 [l]1Pe 5:8
1:8 [m]Jos 1:7; Job 42:7-8 [n]ver 1
1:9 [o]1Ti 6:5
1:10 [p]Ps 34:7 [q]ver 3; Job 29:6; 31:25; Ps 128:1-2
1:11 [r]Job 19:21 [s]Job 2:5
1:15 [t]Ge 10:7; Job 6:19
1:16 [u]Ge 19:24 [v]Lev 10:2; Nu 11:1-3
1:17 [w]Ge 11:28,31
1:19 [x]Jer 4:11; 13:24

[a] 6 Hebrew *the sons of God* [b] 6 *Satan* means *accuser.*

■ **1:1—2:13** *The Prologue.* In this opening prose section of the book, the writer made the reader privy to a heavenly perspective on all the events that follow. These chapters divide into two main parts: an introduction to faithful Job (1:1–5) and an explanation of the tests of his faithfulness (1:6—2:13).

■ **1:1–5** *Job Blessed and Pious.* Job was richly blessed by, and fully devoted to, God.

1:1 Uz. An extended region east of Judah, perhaps on the edge of the desert, but conducive to raising crops (v. 14) and cattle (v. 3). Job was not a nomad but an elder in a major town (29:7). **blameless and upright.** The thought is not that Job was sinless but that he was morally and spiritually "mature" and "straight."

1:3 sheep . . . camels . . . oxen . . . donkeys. Patriarchal wealth was measured in livestock (cf. Ge 30:43).

1:5 have them purified. Job was rightly concerned for the spiritual welfare of his children. **he would sacrifice a burnt offering.** The patriarch Job, like Abraham (Ge 15:9–10), filled the role of priest for the family. He consecrated his children to the Lord by offering sacrifices on their behalf and hoped that God would forgive them. **cursed God in their hearts.** The Hebrew reads literally "blessed God," but that is a euphemism. Cursing God was a sin about which Job himself would be tested (v. 11). See *WCF* 21.6; *WLC* 129.

■ **1:6—2:13** *Job Tested.* The writer revealed the developments in heaven that led to Job's misery on Earth. These chapters divide into five sections: Satan's accusation about Job (1:6–12), Job's initial, faithful reaction to tragedy (1:13–22), Satan's second accusation (2:1–6), Job's continuing faith (2:7–10) and the arrival of Job's friends (2:11–13).

■ **1:6–12** *Satan's Accusation.* This is the first of two scenes in heaven depicting the divine council and focusing on the encounter between the Lord and Satan. *Satan* literally means "the accuser." He is not the Lord's prosecutor-general but opposes the will of God, in keeping with the role of the serpent in Genesis 3. In verse 9 he questioned Job's religious motivations. The use of "the LORD" (*Yahweh*), Israel's covenant name for God, throughout chapters 1 and 2 (also in 38:1; 40:1; ch. 42), reveals that the author was an Israelite.

1:6 Satan. See theological article "Satan" on page 753.

1:8 Have you considered my servant Job? God honored Job by approving of him as a true and faithful servant. It was God, not Satan, who singled out Job for the honor of being tested.

1:11 curse you to your face. Job was sensitive to the possibility of his children cursing God; Satan claimed that Job would entirely reverse his attitude toward God if God were to remove his blessings.

1:12 do not lay a finger. The accuser was allowed to test Job, but at this point, only with regard to his possessions and family. Satan's power was restricted to what was permitted by the Lord. All testings of the faithful are fully under God's control and are used for his purpose (see note on Mt 6:13). See *WLC* 19; *HC* 28.

■ **1:13–22** *Trouble and Job's Reaction.* Despite Satan's divinely permitted (and divinely limited) assaults on his possessions, servants and children, Job remained steadfast in his belief that God is good.

It collapsed on them and they are dead, and I am the only one who has escaped to tell you!"

20At this, Job got up and tore his robe[y] and shaved his head. Then he fell to the ground in worship[z] 21and said:

> "Naked I came from my mother's womb,
> and naked I will depart.[a][a]

[a] 21 Or *will return there*

1:20 [y]Ge 37:29 [z]1Pe 5:6

1:21 [a]Ecc 5:15; 1Ti 6:7

1:20–22 Job uttered a wise saying about submission to the secret will of God. Everything belongs to the Creator who gave it. God's people must praise him for whatever he does with what is his. The word "praised" (or "blessed"; see v. 21) is the same used in verse 11 for "cursed." By using it here, the author is stressing how Job has frustrated Satan's predictions in verse 11. Instead of cursing God, Job praised him. In verse 22 the author announced that Job had passed the test. See *WLC* 105,192; *WSC* 103; *BC* 13,23; *HC* 28.

Satan: Did the Devil Make Me Do It?

BELIEVING in God and his Word leads us also to believe that Satan is real. Like the rest of the fallen angels, their leader Satan comes into full view only in the New Testament. In Hebrew his name means "adversary" (opponent of God and of his people) in the sense of a legal accuser in the court of heaven, and the Old Testament introduces him in this role (1Ch 21:1; Job 1–2; Zec 3:1–2). It is worth noting that Satan does not fill a legitimate role in heaven's court—he is an interloper who brings false charges. In Job, Satan enters the heavenly court in order to "present himself" (Job 2:1; cf. 1:6), not to serve the court; in Zechariah 3:2, the Lord rebukes Satan's false accusations; in 1 Chronicles 21:1, Satan opposes the Lord's chosen people and incites their king to sin. The New Testament gives him revealing titles: The devil (*diabolos*) means "one who brings false accusations" or "adversary" (i.e., of God's people; Rev 12:9–10); Apollyon (Rev 9:11) means "destroyer"; tempter (Mt 4:3; 1Th 3:5) and evil one (1Jn 5:18-19) mean exactly what they say; and "prince of this world" and "god of this age" point to Satan as presiding over humanity's sinful lifestyles (Jn 12:31; 14:30; 16:11 "prince of this world"; 2Co 4:4 "god of this age"; cf. Eph 2:2 "ruler of the kingdom of the air"). Jesus stated that Satan has always been a murderer and that he is the father of lies—Satan is both the original liar and the sponsor of all subsequent falsehood and deceit (Jn 8:44). Finally, he is identified with the serpent who duped Eve in Eden (Rev 12:9; 20:2). The picture is one of unimaginable malice, fury and cruelty directed against God, against God's truth and against those to whom God has extended his saving love.

The elaborate scenario of Satan's celestial rebellion and fall that is familiar to most Christians today stems more from literary imagination than from the Scriptures. Paul implied that Satan fell because of pride (1Ti 3:6), but he did not elaborate. The identity of the "morning star," which some translations render "Lucifer" (cf. 2Pe 1:19) in Isaiah 14:12, is stated explicitly as "the king of Babylon" (Isa 14:4, see notes there; cf. the similar description of the king of Tyre in Eze 28). Although it is conceivable that Isaiah 14:12 assumes Satan to be the "prince" of the Babylonian kingdom (see notes on Da 10:13,20) or alludes to a prior tradition regarding Satan's primeval fall, these are purely speculative ideas that find no actual support in the Bible and no confirmation in external sources. In the end, God's Word tells us very little about Satan's origins.

Despite the fact that we do not know a great deal about Satan, the Scriptures caution us to take his opposition seriously, to note his strategies and to keep in mind that we are at war with him (2Co 2:11; Eph 6:16). We know that Satan is deceptive and cunning. He comes in the guise of an angel of light, disguising evil as good (2Co 11:14). His destructive ferocity comes out in the descriptions of him as a roaring, devouring lion (1Pe 5:8) and as a dragon (Rev 12:9). As he was Christ's sworn foe (Mt 4:1–11; 16:23; Lk 4:13; Jn 14:30; cf. Lk 22:3, 53), so now he is the Christian's, always probing for weaknesses; misdirecting strengths; and undermining faith, hope and character (Lk 22:31,32; 2Co 2:11; 11:3–15; Eph 6:16). He should be taken seriously, for malice and cunning render him fearsome.

Even so, there is no reason for followers of Christ to fear Satan. Satan is a creature, superior to humans for the time being but not divine; he has much knowledge and power, but he is not omniscient, omnipotent or omnipresent. He can be defeated—in fact, Christ has already decisively defeated him. During the inauguration of the kingdom of God in his earthly ministry, Jesus dealt with Satan face-to-face. Not only did Jesus effectively resist Satan's temptations (Mt 4:1–11; Lk 4:1–13), but he also empowered his disciples to drive out Satan's demons (Lk 9:1; see theological article "Demons" at 1Co 10), so that Jesus confessed that he saw "Satan fall from heaven like lightning" (Lk 10:18). As a result of Jesus' life, death and resurrection, Satan, "the strong man," was bound (Mt 12:25–29) and rendered relatively impotent (Heb 2:14). He once ruled over the Gentile nations (Mt 4:8–9) but is no longer able to deceive "the nations" (Rev 20:1–3). As a result, as the kingdom of God continues throughout church history, the gospel goes forth into the world with much success. Christians will triumph over Satan in their personal lives too, if they resist him with the resources that Christ supplies (Eph 6:10–18; Jas 4:7; 1Pe 5:8–10): "The one who is in you is greater than the one who is in the world" (1Jn 4:4). When Jesus returns he will bring the kingdom to its consummation. At that time, Satan and his armies will be cast forever into the lake of fire (Rev 20:10). His condemnation is sure.

1:21 [b]1Sa 2:7 [c]Job 2:10; Eph 5:20; 1Th 5:18

The LORD gave and the LORD has taken away;[b]
may the name of the LORD be praised."[c]

1:22 [d]Job 2:10

22In all this, Job did not sin by charging God with wrongdoing.[d]

Job's Second Test

2:1 [e]Job 1:6

2 On another day the angels[a] came to present themselves before the LORD, and Satan also came with them[e] to present himself before him. 2And the LORD said to
Satan, "Where have you come from?"
Satan answered the LORD, "From roaming through the earth and going back and forth
in it."

2:3 [f]Job 1:1,8 [g]Job 27:6 [h]Job 9:17

3Then the LORD said to Satan, "Have you considered my servant Job? There is no one
on earth like him; he is blameless and upright, a man who fears God and shuns evil.[f] And
he still maintains his integrity,[g] though you incited me against him to ruin him without
any reason."[h]

2:5 [i]Job 19:20 [j]Job 1:11

4"Skin for skin!" Satan replied. "A man will give all he has for his own life. 5But stretch
out your hand and strike his flesh and bones,[i] and he will surely curse you to your face."[j]

2:6 [k]Job 1:12

6The LORD said to Satan, "Very well, then, he is in your hands; but you must spare his
life."[k]

2:7 [l]Dt 28:35; Job 7:5

2:8 [m]Job 42:6; Jer 6:26; Eze 27:30; Mt 11:21

7So Satan went out from the presence of the LORD and afflicted Job with painful sores
from the soles of his feet to the top of his head.[l] 8Then Job took a piece of broken pottery and scraped himself with it as he sat among the ashes.[m]
9His wife said to him, "Are you still holding on to your integrity? Curse God and die!"
10He replied, "You are talking like a foolish[b] woman. Shall we accept good from God,
and not trouble?"[n]
In all this, Job did not sin in what he said.[o]

2:10 [n]Job 1:21 [o]Job 1:22; Ps 39:1; Jas 1:12; 5:11

Job's Three Friends

2:11 [p]Ge 36:11; Jer 49:7 [q]Ge 25:2 [r]Job 42:11; Ro 12:15

2:12 [s]Jos 7:6; Ne 9:1; La 2:10; Eze 27:30

2:13 [t]Ge 50:10; Eze 3:15

11When Job's three friends, Eliphaz the Temanite,[p] Bildad the Shuhite[q] and Zophar
the Naamathite, heard about all the troubles that had come upon him, they set out from
their homes and met together by agreement to go and sympathize with him and comfort him.[r] 12When they saw him from a distance, they could hardly recognize him; they
began to weep aloud, and they tore their robes and sprinkled dust on their heads.[s]
13Then they sat on the ground with him for seven days and seven nights.[t] No one said a
word to him, because they saw how great his suffering was.

Job Speaks

3 After this, Job opened his mouth and cursed the day of his birth. 2He said:

3:3 [u]Job 10:18-19; Jer 20:14-18

3"May the day of my birth perish,
and the night it was said, 'A boy is born!'[u]

a *1* Hebrew *the sons of God* b *10* The Hebrew word rendered *foolish* denotes moral deficiency.

■ **2:1–6** *Satan's Second Accusation.* Further developments in heaven—another round of accusations from Satan—preceded more suffering for Job on Earth.

2:3 maintains his integrity . . . without any reason. The accuser, who had lost the first round, was humiliated by the Lord through a bit of irony. The same word Satan had used to accuse Job in 1:9 ("for nothing") is translated here "without any reason" (2:3). God turned Satan's words back on him.

2:4 "Skin for skin!" Satan suggested that even Job's statement of faith in 1:21 was nothing but a ploy. He would sacrifice anything for his own skin. If God would only stretch out his hand and strike Job's body, then he would curse God to his face.

2:6 you must spare his life. God permitted the accuser to be his instrument to strike Job. Satan, however, as a creature, was reined in. He was allowed to go only as far as God permitted. The word translated "spare" can be rendered "safeguard"; it appears that Satan was held responsible for Job's life. See *HC* 28.

■ **2:7–10** *Trouble and Job's Reaction.* Despite Satan's divinely permitted (and divinely limited) attacks on his body, Job held firmly to his conviction that God is praiseworthy.

2:7 painful sores. We have no way of knowing the exact nature of Job's disease. This description may have been only one stage of the malady.

2:8 sat among the ashes. A way of expressing lament and mourning over tragic circumstances (see 42:6; Est 4:1–3).

2:9 Curse God and die! Again, the theme of cursing/blessing God appears (see notes at 1:20–22). Job's wife was unaware of God's guarantee that Job's life would not be taken.

2:10 foolish. The Hebrew word translated "foolish" indicates faithlessness and religious apostasy (see Pss 14:1; 53:1). It is more an ethical judgment than an intellectual one. As in all wisdom literature in Scripture, true insight means moral understanding. **Job did not sin in what he said.** This stress on the purity of Job's speech anticipates the contrast that will come in the dialogue, where Job's words will be less pure.

■ **2:11–13** *The Arrival of Job's Friends.* Job's friends arrived to comfort him in the midst of his terrible suffering.

2:12 dust on their heads. See note at 2:8.

2:13 they sat on the ground with him for seven days and seven nights. No one said a word to him. This behavior, tied to the number of completeness (seven), expressed the most intense form of grief they could display (see Eze 3:15). Near Eastern customs demanded that Job should be the first to speak. For the practice of mourning seven days over the dead, see Genesis 50:10.

■ **3:1—27:23** *Dialogues Between Job and His Friends.* Job and his friends debated his situation. At the heart of their dialogues was the value and applicability of conventional, proverbial wisdom to Job's circumstance. His friends insisted that standard wisdom sayings applied directly and mechanically to Job, but Job insisted that they did not. Their discussions reveal that none of them had complete insight into Job's situation. They struggled, as all humans do, to understand suffering by testing the limits of conventional wis-

[4] That day—may it turn to darkness;
may God above not care about it;
may no light shine upon it.
[5] May darkness and deep shadow[a][v] claim it once more;
may a cloud settle over it;
may blackness overwhelm its light.
[6] That night—may thick darkness[w] seize it;
may it not be included among the days of the year
nor be entered in any of the months.
[7] May that night be barren;
may no shout of joy be heard in it.
[8] May those who curse days[b] curse that day,
those who are ready to rouse Leviathan.[x]
[9] May its morning stars become dark;
may it wait for daylight in vain
and not see the first rays of dawn,[y]
[10] for it did not shut the doors of the womb on me
to hide trouble from my eyes.

[11] "Why did I not perish at birth,
and die as I came from the womb?[z]
[12] Why were there knees to receive me[a]
and breasts that I might be nursed?
[13] For now I would be lying down[b] in peace;
I would be asleep and at rest[c]
[14] with kings and counselors of the earth,[d]
who built for themselves places now lying in ruins,[e]
[15] with rulers[f] who had gold,
who filled their houses with silver.[g]
[16] Or why was I not hidden in the ground like a stillborn child,[h]
like an infant who never saw the light of day?
[17] There the wicked cease from turmoil,
and there the weary are at rest.[i]
[18] Captives also enjoy their ease;
they no longer hear the slave driver's shout.[j]
[19] The small and the great are there,
and the slave is freed from his master.

[20] "Why is light given to those in misery,
and life to the bitter of soul,[k]
[21] to those who long for death that does not come,[l]
who search for it more than for hidden treasure,[m]
[22] who are filled with gladness
and rejoice when they reach the grave?
[23] Why is life given to a man
whose way is hidden,
whom God has hedged in?[n]
[24] For sighing comes to me instead of food;[o]
my groans pour out like water.[p]
[25] What I feared has come upon me;
what I dreaded[q] has happened to me.
[26] I have no peace, no quietness;
I have no rest,[r] but only turmoil."

3:5 [v]Job 10:21,22; Ps 23:4; Jer 2:6; 13:16
3:6 [w]Job 23:17
3:8 [x]Job 41:1,8,10,25
3:9 [y]Job 41:18
3:11 [z]Job 10:18
3:12 [a]Ge 30:3; Isa 66:12
3:13 [b]Job 17:13 [c]Job 7:8-10,21; 10:22; 14:10-12; 19:27; 21:13,23
3:14 [d]Job 12:17 [e]Job 15:28
3:15 [f]Job 12:21 [g]Job 27:17
3:16 [h]Ps 58:8; Ecc 6:3
3:17 [i]Job 17:16
3:18 [j]Job 39:7
3:20 [k]1Sa 1:10; Jer 20:18; Eze 27:30 31
3:21 [l]Rev 9:6 [m]Pr 2:4
3:23 [n]Job 19:6,8,12; Ps 88:8; La 3:7
3:24 [o]Job 6:7; 33:20 [p]Ps 42:3,4
3:25 [q]Job 30:15
3:26 [r]Job 7:4,14

[a] 5 Or *and the shadow of death* [b] 8 Or *the sea*

dom. These chapters divide into five main sections: an introduction of Job's lament (3:1–26); a first (4:1—14:22), a second (15:1—21:34) and a third (22:1—26:14) cycle of speeches; and Job's closing reflections (27:1–23).

■ **3:1–26** *Job's Opening Lament.* Job broke the silence with a fiercely emotional lamentation. He expressed the same kind of depression that overtook the psalmist (Ps 88) and also Jeremiah (Jer 20:14–15), whose bitter lament echoes Job's. His circumstances were so unbearable that he cursed the day he was born.

3:3–10 May the day of my birth perish. Job cursed his birth. He did not challenge God directly, but came dangerously close to questioning God's wisdom in creating him. The progression of his thought moved from birth (vv. 3–10) to the desirability of being stillborn (vv. 11–16) to premature death (vv. 20,23).

3:11–26 Why did I not perish at birth? Verses 3–10 were set in the form of curses, but these next verses took the form of rhetorical questions. Job vented his frustration, asking the agonizing question of why he had not been stillborn (vv. 11–12,16). He went on to ask a similar question about premature death (vv. 20,23).

Eliphaz

4 Then Eliphaz the Temanite replied:

2 "If someone ventures a word with you, will you be
impatient?
But who can keep from speaking?[s]
3 Think how you have instructed many,
how you have strengthened feeble hands.[t]
4 Your words have supported those who stumbled;
you have strengthened faltering knees.[u]
5 But now trouble comes to you, and you are discouraged;
it strikes[v] you, and you are dismayed.[w]
6 Should not your piety be your confidence[x]
and your blameless[y] ways your hope?

7 "Consider now: Who, being innocent, has ever perished?[z]
Where were the upright ever destroyed?[a]
8 As I have observed, those who plow evil[b]
and those who sow trouble reap it.[c]
9 At the breath of God[d] they are destroyed;
at the blast of his anger they perish.[e]
10 The lions may roar and growl,
yet the teeth of the great lions are broken.[f]
11 The lion perishes for lack of prey,[g]
and the cubs of the lioness are scattered.

12 "A word was secretly brought to me,
my ears caught a whisper[h] of it.[i]
13 Amid disquieting dreams in the night,
when deep sleep falls on men,[j]
14 fear and trembling seized me
and made all my bones shake.[k]
15 A spirit glided past my face,
and the hair on my body stood on end.
16 It stopped,
but I could not tell what it was.
A form stood before my eyes,
and I heard a hushed voice:
17 'Can a mortal be more righteous than God?[l]
Can a man be more pure than his Maker?[m]
18 If God places no trust in his servants,
if he charges his angels with error,[n]
19 how much more those who live in houses of clay,[o]
whose foundations[p] are in the dust,[q]
who are crushed more readily than a moth!
20 Between dawn and dusk they are broken to pieces;
unnoticed, they perish forever.[r]

4:2 [s]Job 32:20
4:3 [t]Isa 35:3; Heb 12:12
4:4 [u]Isa 35:3; Heb 12:12
4:5 [v]Job 19:21 [w]Job 6:14
4:6 [x]Pr 3:26 [y]Job 1:1
4:7 [z]Job 36:7 [a]Job 8:20; Ps 37:25
4:8 [b]Job 15:35 [c]Pr 22:8; Hos 10:13; Gal 6:7-8
4:9 [d]Job 15:30; Isa 30:33; 2Th 2:8 [e]Job 40:13
4:10 [f]Job 5:15; Ps 58:6
4:11 [g]Job 27:14; Ps 34:10
4:12 [h]Job 26:14 [i]Job 33:14
4:13 [j]Job 33:15
4:14 [k]Jer 23:9; Hab 3:16
4:17 [l]Job 9:2 [m]Job 35:10
4:18 [n]Job 15:15
4:19 [o]Job 10:9 [p]Job 22:16 [q]Ge 2:7
4:20 [r]Job 14:2,20; 20:7; Ps 90:5-6

■ **4:1—14:22** *The First Cycle of Speeches.* The first cycle of speeches consists of declarations by Job's three friends and his penetrating replies to them. The speeches touched on many different perspectives and possible explanations, but all of them fell short. These chapters fall into six segments: Eliphaz's speech (4:1—5:27), Job's reply to Eliphaz (6:1—7:21), Bildad's speech (8:1–22), Job's reply to Bildad (9:1—10:22), Zophar's declarations (11:1–20) and Job's reply to Zophar (12:1—14:22).

■ **4:1—5:27** *Eliphaz.* Eliphaz presented his perspective on Job's circumstances. He complimented and challenged Job (4:1–11); claimed that his own insights had come from revelation (4:12–21); and recited a poem about a fool (5:1–7), a hymn of praise (5:8–16) and a celebration of God's discipline (5:17–27).

■ **4:1–11** *Compliments and Challenges.* Eliphaz was the least caustic of Job's three friends, at least in his first speech. His opening words, which assumed Job's innocence (v. 7), should be compared with 22:1–11, where he was fully convinced that Job was getting what he deserved. Eliphaz complimented Job for being a wisdom teacher (vv. 3–4), but in verse 5 he warned Job lest he fail to apply to himself what he had taught others.

4:6 your piety. Literally, "your fear"; i.e., the fear you have of God, which refers to true reverence and worship of God. See *WLC* 145.

4:8 those who sow trouble reap it. This proverbial wisdom is true to a degree, but Eliphaz applied it as though it were an absolute rule.

■ **4:12–21** *Claim of Revelation.* Eliphaz described a mystical experience by which he claimed to have received divine revelation.

4:16 A form . . . a hushed voice. Eliphaz was uncertain who or what it was, but he was convinced it was a supernatural revelation.

4:17 Can a mortal be more righteous than God? Another way to render this phrase is, "Can a mortal be righteous before God?" The question was not whether humans can be more righteous than God, which was unthinkable, but whether they can be righteous at all in his sight. According to Eliphaz, even the angels are not pure in God's sight (v. 18). It is possible that only verse 17 was the oracle that came from the Spirit, and that verses 18–21 were a comment by Eliphaz on this revelation. The closing quotation mark, then, would come after verse 17 instead of after verse 21.

[21] Are not the cords of their tent pulled up,[s]
so that they die without wisdom?'[a][t]

5

"Call if you will, but who will answer you?
To which of the holy ones[u] will you turn?
[2] Resentment kills a fool,
and envy slays the simple.[v]
[3] I myself have seen a fool taking root,[w]
but suddenly his house was cursed.[x]
[4] His children are far from safety,[y]
crushed in court[z] without a defender.
[5] The hungry consume his harvest,[a]
taking it even from among thorns,
and the thirsty pant after his wealth.
[6] For hardship does not spring from the soil,
nor does trouble sprout from the ground.
[7] Yet man is born to trouble[b]
as surely as sparks fly upward.

[8] "But if it were I, I would appeal to God;
I would lay my cause before him.[c]
[9] He performs wonders that cannot be fathomed,[d]
miracles that cannot be counted.
[10] He bestows rain on the earth;
he sends water upon the countryside.[e]
[11] The lowly he sets on high,[f]
and those who mourn are lifted to safety.
[12] He thwarts the plans[g] of the crafty,
so that their hands achieve no success.
[13] He catches the wise in their craftiness,[h]
and the schemes of the wily are swept away.
[14] Darkness[i] comes upon them in the daytime;
at noon they grope as in the night.[j]
[15] He saves the needy[k] from the sword in their mouth;
he saves them from the clutches of the powerful.[l]
[16] So the poor have hope,
and injustice shuts its mouth.[m]

[17] "Blessed is the man whom God corrects;[n]
so do not despise the discipline[o] of the Almighty.[b][p]
[18] For he wounds, but he also binds up;[q]
he injures, but his hands also heal.[r]
[19] From six calamities he will rescue you;
in seven no harm will befall you.[s]
[20] In famine[t] he will ransom you from death,
and in battle from the stroke of the sword.[u]
[21] You will be protected from the lash of the tongue,[v]

4:21 [s]Job 8:22 [t]Job 18:21; 36:12
5:1 [u]Job 15:15
5:2 [v]Pr 12:16
5:3 [w]Ps 37:35; Jer 12:2 [x]Job 24:18
5:4 [y]Job 4:11 [z]Am 5:12
5:5 [a]Job 18:8-10
5:7 [b]Job 14:1
5:8 [c]Ps 35:23; 50:15
5:9 [d]Job 42:3; Ps 40:5
5:10 [e]Job 36:28
5:11 [f]Ps 113:7-8
5:12 [g]Ne 4:15; Ps 33:10
5:13 [h]1Co 3:19*
5:14 [i]Job 12:25 [j]Dt 28:29
5:15 [k]Ps 35:10 [l]Job 4:10
5:16 [m]Ps 107:42
5:17 [n]Jas 1:12 [o]Ps 94:12; Pr 3:11 [p]Heb 12:5-11
5:18 [q]Isa 30:26 [r]1Sa 2:6
5:19 [s]Ps 34:19; 91:10
5:20 [t]Ps 33:19 [u]Ps 144:10
5:21 [v]Ps 31:20

[a] *21* Some interpreters end the quotation after verse 17. [b] *17* Hebrew *Shaddai*; here and throughout Job

4:21 die without wisdom. That is, their death was without any purpose and therefore was meaningless. They perish forever (v. 20), without ever having had a purpose to their lives.

■ **5:1–7** *Profile of a Fool.* This poem on the fool is typical of the discursive style often used by Job and his counselors. Eliphaz had Job in mind, but did not explicitly say so.

5:1 To which of the holy ones will you turn? None of the "sons of God" (i.e., the holy angels) would dare plead Job's cause. This verse is the first in the book to mention the concept of a mediator who might arbitrate between God and human beings.

5:7 man is born to trouble. Trouble is not like a weed that springs up; it is sown by those who will reap it (see v. 6). The verb "is born" might be better read "engenders" or "assists in causing (something or someone) to be born." The verb was typically used of a midwife. **as sparks fly upward.** Literally, "the sons of Resheph fly upward." Resheph was the pagan god of pestilence, lightning and destruction. A similar idiom is found in Song of Songs 8:6, where love is described as "Reshephs of fire." In other Biblical references the idiom is used for bolts of lightning (Ps 78:48) and for pestilence (Dt 32:24; Hab 3:5).

■ **5:8–16** *Praise for God's Goodness.* This section is a hymn of praise and confidence adapted to the dialogues with Job.

5:13 He catches the wise in their craftiness. This is the only verse in the book of Job that is quoted in the New Testament (1Co 3:19). There Paul highlighted the foolishness of worldly wisdom, quoting from this hymn on God's justice and goodness (vv. 8–16).

■ **5:17–27** *Praise for Divine Discipline.* Eliphaz rejoiced over the manner in which God blesses those whom he chastises. This reference to the disciplinary nature of human suffering is the only instance in the speeches of the three counselors in which the subject of divine discipline is even broached. Eliphaz believed this discipline to be only temporary for the godly (v. 18).

5:19 From six . . . in seven. Neither number should be stressed. This is a poetic idiom meaning "many" (see, for instance, Am 1:3, 6,9,11,13; 2:1).

and need not fear[w] when destruction comes.
22 You will laugh at destruction and famine,
and need not fear the beasts of the earth.[x]
23 For you will have a covenant with the stones[y] of the field,
and the wild animals will be at peace with you.[z]
24 You will know that your tent is secure;
you will take stock of your property and find nothing missing.[a]
25 You will know that your children will be many,[b]
and your descendants like the grass of the earth.[c]
26 You will come to the grave in full vigor,[d]
like sheaves gathered in season.

27 "We have examined this, and it is true.
So hear it and apply it to yourself."

Job

6 Then Job replied:

2 "If only my anguish could be weighed
and all my misery be placed on the scales![e]
3 It would surely outweigh the sand[f] of the seas—
no wonder my words have been impetuous.[g]
4 The arrows[h] of the Almighty are in me,[i]
my spirit drinks[j] in their poison;
God's terrors[k] are marshaled against me.[l]
5 Does a wild donkey bray when it has grass,
or an ox bellow when it has fodder?
6 Is tasteless food eaten without salt,
or is there flavor in the white of an egg[a]?
7 I refuse to touch it;
such food makes me ill.[m]

8 "Oh, that I might have my request,
that God would grant what I hope for,[n]
9 that God would be willing to crush me,
to let loose his hand and cut me off![o]
10 Then I would still have this consolation—
my joy in unrelenting pain—
that I had not denied the words[p] of the Holy One.[q]
11 "What strength do I have, that I should still hope?
What prospects, that I should be patient?[r]
12 Do I have the strength of stone?
Is my flesh bronze?

5:21 [w]Ps 91:5
5:22 [x]Ps 91:13; Eze 34:25
5:23 [y]Ps 91:12 [z]Isa 11:6-9
5:24 [a]Job 8:6
5:25 [b]Ps 112:2 [c]Ps 72:16; Isa 44:3-4
5:26 [d]Ge 15:15
6:2 [e]Job 31:6
6:3 [f]Pr 27:3 [g]Job 23:2
6:4 [h]Ps 38:2 [i]Job 16:12,13 [j]Job 21:20 [k]Job 30:15 [l]Ps 88:15-18
6:7 [m]Job 3:24
6:8 [n]Job 14:13
6:9 [o]Nu 11:15; 1Ki 19:4
6:10 [p]Job 22:22; 23:12 [q]Lev 19:2; Isa 57:15
6:11 [r]Job 21:4

[a] 6 The meaning of the Hebrew for this phrase is uncertain.

5:23 a covenant with the stones of the field. Some interpreters explain such a covenant as figurative language meaning that the stones will not inhibit raising crops. Others read "offspring" in place of "stones," interpreting this phrase as another mention of "wild animals" (cf. "beasts of the earth" in v. 22), such that the phrase "a covenant with the stones of the field" is synonymous with "the wild animals will be at peace with you." Both readings may potentially be supported by poetic parallelism (see "Introduction to the Poetical Books") even if "stones" is the proper reading. If a parallel is seen between both halves of verse 23, "stones" may be a symbol for "wild animals." If a parallel is seen instead between verses 22 and 23, "covenant with the stones" means something similar to "laugh at destruction and famine," such that the stones do not cause these things by ruining or inhibiting crops.
5:25 your children will be many. Considering that Job had recently lost all of his children, this statement appears both unnecessary and cruel.
5:26 to the grave in full vigor. At this point, neither Job nor Eliphaz could have imagined that this statement would come true for Job.
5:27 We have examined this, and it is true. This final verbal volley shows that Eliphaz was in error. He thought he understood what was happening to Job, but he was wrong. Such an assertion reveals the spiritual arrogance that characterized all of Job's friends.
■ **6:1—7:21** *Job's Reply to Eliphaz.* Job upbraided Eliphaz for uttering presumptuous, insensitive, not to mention false, words about him (6:1–30). Then he addressed his complaint to God (7:1–21).
■ **6:1–30** *Rejection of Eliphaz.* In no uncertain terms Job rejected what Eliphaz had said as in applicable to his suffering.
6:3–4 my words have been impetuous. The arrows of the Almighty are in me. Job excused his raging by fantasizing that God had become his enemy.
6:6–7 tasteless food . . . I refuse. Eliphaz had offered him no real food (v. 5); i.e., words of comfort. What was supposed to be good food (words) made Job sick.
6:8–10 grant what I hope for. Ostensibly for Job, the only comfort left was the release from pain that death would bring. He strongly affirmed continued faith in the Lord. Note that this passage reflects Job's belief in a blissful afterlife.
6:11 that I should be patient? James 5:11 has been translated to speak of the "patience" of Job, but the NIV has corrected this to refer to his "perseverance." Here Job admitted that he was not patient—at least not in a passive, quiet sense. See also 4:2 and 21:4.

13 Do I have any power to help myself,[s]
now that success has been driven from me?

14 "A despairing man[t] should have the devotion[u] of his friends,
even though he forsakes the fear of the Almighty.
15 But my brothers are as undependable as intermittent streams,[v]
as the streams that overflow
16 when darkened by thawing ice
and swollen with melting snow,
17 but that cease to flow in the dry season,
and in the heat[w] vanish from their channels.
18 Caravans turn aside from their routes;
they go up into the wasteland and perish.
19 The caravans of Tema[x] look for water,
the traveling merchants of Sheba look in hope.
20 They are distressed, because they had been confident;
they arrive there, only to be disappointed.[y]
21 Now you too have proved to be of no help;
you see something dreadful and are afraid.[z]
22 Have I ever said, 'Give something on my behalf,
pay a ransom for me from your wealth,
23 deliver me from the hand of the enemy,
ransom me from the clutches of the ruthless'?

24 "Teach me, and I will be quiet;[a]
show me where I have been wrong.
25 How painful are honest words![b]
But what do your arguments prove?
26 Do you mean to correct what I say,
and treat the words of a despairing man as wind?[c]
27 You would even cast lots[d] for the fatherless
and barter away your friend.

28 "But now be so kind as to look at me.
Would I lie to your face?[e]
29 Relent, do not be unjust;
reconsider, for my integrity is at stake.[a][f]
30 Is there any wickedness on my lips?[g]
Can my mouth not discern[h] malice?

7 "Does not man have hard service[i] on earth?[j]
Are not his days like those of a hired man?[k]
2 Like a slave longing for the evening shadows,
or a hired man waiting eagerly for his wages,[l]
3 so I have been allotted months of futility,
and nights of misery have been assigned to me.[m]
4 When I lie down I think, 'How long before I get up?'[n]
The night drags on, and I toss till dawn.
5 My body is clothed with worms[o] and scabs,
my skin is broken and festering.

6 "My days are swifter than a weaver's shuttle,[p]
and they come to an end without hope.[q]

6:13 [s]Job 26:2
6:14 [t]Job 4:5 [u]Job 15:4
6:15 [v]Ps 38:11; Jer 15:18
6:17 [w]Job 24:19
6:19 [x]Ge 25:15; Isa 21:14
6:20 [y]Jer 14:3
6:21 [z]Ps 38:11
6:24 [a]Ps 39:1
6:25 [b]Ecc 12:11
6:26 [c]Job 8:2; 15:3
6:27 [d]Joel 3:3; Na 3:10; 2Pe 2:3
6:28 [e]Job 27:4; 33:1,3; 36:3,4
6:29 [f]Job 23:7,10; 34:5,36; 42:6
6:30 [g]Job 27:4 [h]Job 12:11
7:1 [i]Job 14:14; Isa 40:2 [j]Job 5:7 [k]Job 14:6
7:2 [l]Lev 19:13
7:3 [m]Job 16:7; Ps 6:6
7:4 [n]Dt 28:67
7:5 [o]Job 17:14; Isa 14:11
7:6 [p]Job 9:25 [q]Job 13:15; 17:11,15

[a] *29* Or *my righteousness still stands*

6:14 devotion of his friends. Job asked only for love and sympathy, which would cost them nothing (v. 22–23).
6:25 How painful are honest words! The difference between Job and his friends is summed up here. As we read the speeches of the friends we note that they mouthed platitudes that are often correct in the abstract but did not necessarily apply to Job. Indeed, they falsely accused Job of having lived a sinful life for which he was being punished. Job insisted on speaking honest words about his life. He had not forsaken God or lived in a profligate way.
6:27 cast lots for the fatherless. Later, Job would speak of his own loving care for the fatherless (31:16–22).
6:29 is at stake. Literally, "is in it." The "it" was their insistence that Job was suffering for his sins. Either he or they must be wrong.
6:30 my mouth. Literally, "my palate." In verses 6–7 Job had already spoken of their words as bad food. Here he pleaded that they change what they were feeding him.
■ **7:1–21** *Lament to God.* Job now directed his words toward God. This is a prayer in the form of a complaint, a method the psalmists often employed (cf. Ps 22; 88).
7:1 hard service. The terminology often refers to military service, but compare Isaiah 40:2.
7:5 My body. Job's malady may have been a combination of diseases. Repugnant symptoms, however, appeared all over his skin.

7:7 [r]Ps 78:39; Jas 4:14 [s]Job 9:25
7:8 [t]Job 20:7,9,21
7:9 [u]Job 11:8 [v]2Sa 12:23; Job 30:15
7:10 [w]Job 27:21,23 [x]Job 8:18
7:11 [y]Ps 40:9 [z]1Sa 1:10
7:12 [a]Eze 32:2-3
7:13 [b]Job 9:27
7:14 [c]Job 9:34
7:15 [d]1Ki 19:4
7:16 [e]Job 9:21; 10:1
7:17 [f]Ps 8:4; 144:3; Heb 2:6
7:18 [g]Job 14:3
7:19 [h]Job 9:18
7:20 [i]Job 35:6 [j]Job 16:12
7:21 [k]Job 10:14 [l]Job 10:9; Ps 104:29
8:2 [m]Job 6:26

7 Remember, O God, that my life is but a breath;[r]
my eyes will never see happiness again.[s]
8 The eye that now sees me will see me no longer;
you will look for me, but I will be no more.[t]
9 As a cloud vanishes and is gone,
so he who goes down to the grave[a] [u] does not return.[v]
10 He will never come to his house again;
his place[w] will know him no more.[x]

11 "Therefore I will not keep silent;[y]
I will speak out in the anguish of my spirit,
I will complain in the bitterness of my soul.[z]
12 Am I the sea, or the monster of the deep,[a]
that you put me under guard?
13 When I think my bed will comfort me
and my couch will ease my complaint,[b]
14 even then you frighten me with dreams
and terrify[c] me with visions,
15 so that I prefer strangling and death,[d]
rather than this body of mine.
16 I despise my life;[e] I would not live forever.
Let me alone; my days have no meaning.

17 "What is man that you make so much of him,
that you give him so much attention,[f]
18 that you examine him every morning
and test him every moment?[g]
19 Will you never look away from me,
or let me alone even for an instant?[h]
20 If I have sinned, what have I done to you,[i]
O watcher of men?
Why have you made me your target?[j]
Have I become a burden to you?[b]
21 Why do you not pardon my offenses
and forgive my sins?[k]
For I will soon lie down in the dust;[l]
you will search for me, but I will be no more."

Bildad

8 Then Bildad the Shuhite replied:

2 "How long will you say such things?
Your words are a blustering wind.[m]

a 9 Hebrew *Sheol* b 20 A few manuscripts of the Masoretic Text, an ancient Hebrew scribal tradition and Septuagint; most manuscripts of the Masoretic Text *I have become a burden to myself.*

7:7 never see happiness again. Worse than the pain was Job's loss of hope for a return to health.
7:9 does not return. This is phenomenal (as it appears) language. Job was not developing a doctrine but merely stating what all can easily observe. Later, Job would express his belief in the possibility of resurrection (14:12–15; 19:26–27).
7:11 will not keep silent. Like the psalmist, Job insisted on complaining out of his bitterness of soul; but note that he complained to God here, not to other people.
7:12 Am I the sea. The Hebrew uses "sea" as a proper name here without the definite article. This is poetic language for the boisterous Canaanite deity Yam (Sea). Job did not worship Yam, but he knew the story about him.
7:14 you frighten me. Job imagined that God was actually doing all this. The reader knows from the prologue that God in fact permitted Satan to afflict God's servant.
7:15 I prefer . . . death. Job envisioned death as the way out, but Satan was not permitted to go that far, nor would death have served Satan's purpose of getting Job to curse God to his face.
7:16 Let me alone. Again Job imagined that God was the one who tormented him. We know from the prologue, however, that God had a high and holy purpose in permitting Satan to touch Job.
7:17 What is man that you make so much of him . . . ? Compare Psalms 8:4 and 144:3. The psalmist was not suffering, so his thoughts on this subject were positive. He marveled that God cared so much for the creature he had made to reflect his own image. But Job, in his distress, wished that God would leave him alone.
7:19 for an instant. Literally, "long enough to swallow my spittle."
7:20 O watcher of men. Job felt that God was too scrupulous. For what sin was God punishing him so severely? **a burden to you.** Some Hebrew scribes thought this language went too far, so they emended the text to read, "a burden to myself." But the stronger language is the more accurate.
7:21 Why do you not . . . forgive my sins? Although Job stressed his integrity (i.e., his honest commitment to godliness and righteousness), he never denied that he was a sinner.
■ **8:1–22** *Bildad.* Bildad's reply presents the man as blunt and unfeeling. He had failed to hear Job's cry for compassion (6:13–14,26), and his message was forthright: Job and his family had gotten what they deserved. If Job would only repent of the shameless deeds that had perpetrated these disasters, he could be restored to even greater prosperity and happiness than that which he had earlier enjoyed. After rebuking Job (vv. 1–10) Bildad recited a poem of proverbial wisdom (vv. 11–22).

3 Does God pervert justice?[n]
Does the Almighty pervert what is right?[o]
4 When your children sinned against him,
he gave them over to the penalty of their sin.[p]
5 But if you will look to God
and plead[q] with the Almighty,
6 if you are pure and upright,
even now he will rouse himself on your behalf[r]
and restore you to your rightful place.[s]
7 Your beginnings will seem humble,
so prosperous[t] will your future be.

8 "Ask the former generations[u]
and find out what their fathers learned,
9 for we were born only yesterday and know nothing,[v]
and our days on earth are but a shadow.[w]
10 Will they not instruct you and tell you?
Will they not bring forth words from their understanding?
11 Can papyrus grow tall where there is no marsh?
Can reeds thrive without water?
12 While still growing and uncut,
they wither more quickly than grass.[x]
13 Such is the destiny of all who forget God;[y]
so perishes the hope of the godless.[z]
14 What he trusts in is fragile[a];
what he relies on is a spider's web.[a]
15 He leans on his web,[b] but it gives way;
he clings to it, but it does not hold.[c]
16 He is like a well-watered plant in the sunshine,
spreading its shoots[d] over the garden;[e]
17 it entwines its roots around a pile of rocks
and looks for a place among the stones.
18 But when it is torn from its spot,
that place disowns it and says, 'I never saw you.'[f]
19 Surely its life withers[g] away,
and[b] from the soil other plants grow.[h]
20 "Surely God does not reject a blameless[i] man
or strengthen the hands of evildoers.[j]
21 He will yet fill your mouth with laughter[k]
and your lips with shouts of joy.[l]
22 Your enemies will be clothed in shame,[m]
and the tents of the wicked will be no more."[n]

Job

9 Then Job replied:

2 "Indeed, I know that this is true.
But how can a mortal be righteous before God?[o]

8:3 [n]Dt 32:4; 2Ch 19:7; Ro 3:5 [o]Ge 18:25
8:4 [p]Job 1:19
8:5 [q]Job 11:13
8:6 [r]Ps 7:6 [s]Job 5:24
8:7 [t]Job 42:12
8:8 [u]Dt 4:32; 32:7; Job 15:18
8:9 [v]Ge 47:9 [w]1Ch 29:15; Job 7:6
8:12 [x]Ps 129:6; Jer 17:6
8:13 [y]Ps 9:17 [z]Job 11:20; 13:16; 15:34; Pr 10:28
8:14 [a]Isa 59:5
8:15 [b]Job 27:18 [c]Ps 49:11
8:16 [d]Ps 80:11 [e]Ps 37:35; Jer 11:16
8:18 [f]Job 7:8; Ps 37:36
8:19 [g]Job 20:5 [h]Ecc 1:4
8:20 [i]Job 1:1 [j]Job 21:30
8:21 [k]Job 5:22 [l]Ps 126:2; 132:16
8:22 [m]Ps 35:26; 109:29; 132:18 [n]Job 18:6, 14,21
9:2 [o]Job 4:17; Ps 143:2; Ro 3:20

a 14 The meaning of the Hebrew for this word is uncertain. b 19 Or *Surely all the joy it has / is that*

■ **8:1–10** *Rebuke for Job.* In scathing language, Bildad confronted Job and accused him of not being righteous enough to receive God's blessing.
8:2 Your words are a blustering wind. This was a cutting accusation; Bildad's tone was unlike that of Eliphaz, who had attempted a soft approach at first (4:2).
8:6 if you are pure and upright. In Bildad's mind, God had mercy only when human beings deserved it. True mercy, however, cannot ever be deserved. If it is deserved, it is justice rather than mercy.
8:8 Ask the former generations. Eliphaz had appealed to revelation as his authority, even though that revelation was somewhat enigmatic (4:12–17). Bildad appealed to human tradition.
■ **8:11–22** *Appeal to Proverbial Wisdom.* In the tradition of the sages, Bildad recited a poem that drew on analogies and patterns in nature to support his point of view.
8:13–14 See *WCF* 18.1.
8:13 the godless. Bildad drew on several illustrations from nature to describe the hopelessness of those whom he called "the godless." The Hebrew word refers to someone who is defiled by sin or estranged from God. As Bildad saw it, Job was a case in point.
8:20 Surely God does not reject a blameless man. This verse contains the heart of Bildad's theology of suffering. As standard wisdom it was not wrong. Psalm 1:6 does teach that the Lord cares about the way of the righteous but that the way of the wicked shall perish. Bildad's error consisted in assuming that because Job was suffering he had to be a godless person.
■ **9:1—10:22** *Job's Reply to Bildad.* Job's reply to Bildad in chapters 9–10 started with a discourse on God's power and wisdom (9:1–13) but shifted to questioning God's justice (9:14–29). Job then began to direct his words to God (9:30—10:22).

3 Though one wished to dispute with him,
he could not answer him one time out of a thousand.[p]
4 His wisdom[q] is profound, his power is vast.[r]
Who has resisted him and come out unscathed?[s]
5 He moves mountains without their knowing it
and overturns them in his anger.[t]
6 He shakes the earth[u] from its place
and makes its pillars tremble.[v]
7 He speaks to the sun and it does not shine;
he seals off the light of the stars.[w]
8 He alone stretches out the heavens[x]
and treads on the waves of the sea.[y]
9 He is the Maker of the Bear and Orion,
the Pleiades and the constellations of the south.[z]
10 He performs wonders[a] that cannot be fathomed,
miracles that cannot be counted.[b]
11 When he passes me, I cannot see him;
when he goes by, I cannot perceive him.[c]
12 If he snatches away, who can stop him?[d]
Who can say to him, 'What are you doing?'[e]
13 God does not restrain his anger;
even the cohorts of Rahab[f] cowered at his feet.

14 "How then can I dispute with him?
How can I find words to argue with him?
15 Though I were innocent, I could not answer him;[g]
I could only plead[h] with my Judge for mercy.
16 Even if I summoned him and he responded,
I do not believe he would give me a hearing.
17 He would crush me[i] with a storm[j]
and multiply[k] my wounds for no reason.[l]
18 He would not let me regain my breath
but would overwhelm me with misery.[m]
19 If it is a matter of strength, he is mighty!
And if it is a matter of justice, who will summon him[a]?
20 Even if I were innocent, my mouth would condemn me;
if I were blameless, it would pronounce me guilty.

21 "Although I am blameless,[n]
I have no concern for myself;
I despise my own life.[o]
22 It is all the same; that is why I say,
'He destroys both the blameless and the wicked.'[p]
23 When a scourge[q] brings sudden death,
he mocks the despair of the innocent.[r]
24 When a land falls into the hands of the wicked,[s]

9:3 [p]Job 10:2; 40:2
9:4 [q]Job 11:6 [r]Job 36:5 [s]2Ch 13:12
9:5 [t]Mic 1:4
9:6 [u]Isa 2:21; Hag 2:6; Heb 12:26 [v]Job 26:11
9:7 [w]Isa 13:10; Eze 32:8
9:8 [x]Ge 1:6; Ps 104:2-3 [y]Job 38:16; Ps 77:19
9:9 [z]Ge 1:16; Job 38:31; Am 5:8
9:10 [a]Ps 71:15 [b]Job 5:9
9:11 [c]Job 23:8-9; 35:14
9:12 [d]Job 11:10 [e]Isa 45:9; Ro 9:20
9:13 [f]Job 26:12; Ps 89:10; Isa 30:7; 51:9
9:15 [g]Job 10:15 [h]Job 8:5
9:17 [i]Job 16:12 [j]Job 30:22 [k]Job 16:14 [l]Job 2:3
9:18 [m]Job 7:19; 27:2
9:21 [n]Job 1:1 [o]Job 7:16
9:22 [p]Job 10:8; Ecc 9:2, 3; Eze 21:3
9:23 [q]Heb 11:36 [r]Job 24:1, 12
9:24 [s]Job 10:3; 16:11

[a] *19* See Septuagint; Hebrew *me.*

■ **9:1–13** *Affirmation of God's Power and Wisdom.* Job had not lost his belief in the awesome sovereignty and knowledge of God. He acknowledged his humble state before God and his inability to protest effectively.
9:2–3 See *WCF* 16.4.
9:2 But how can a mortal be righteous before God? Job agreed with Bildad that God punishes the wicked and cares for the righteous (Ps 1:6), but is there anybody who is wholly righteous?
9:4–13 His wisdom is profound. These verses constitute a poem on the omnipotence and justice of God.
9:5 without their knowing it. The pronoun "their" is indefinite. The phrase means "without anyone knowing it."
9:6 its pillars. That is, the mountains.
9:7 sun . . . does not shine. A reference to an eclipse of the sun. **seals off the light of the stars.** A reference to the disappearance of certain stars over the seasons.
9:8 stretches out the heavens and treads on the waves. Poetic figures referring to God's creation and control over the forces of nature.
9:11 I cannot perceive him. Job desired an audience with God to confirm his innocence but was afraid that his cause might be hopeless (vv. 14–20,32–35).
9:13 Rahab. The Semitic sea monster. Compare 26:12. In Isaiah 30:7 the same monster symbolized Egypt.
■ **9:14–29** *Questions About God's Justice.* Job reflected on whether or not God is truly just in his ways.
9:15 plead . . . for mercy. Even during this desperate fantasizing Job understood that God is merciful. This is a point that his counselors never fully appreciated.
9:17 for no reason. Job was beginning to question the justice of God. But it should be noted that even at this low point he had not really given up on this issue, as verses 19–20 prove.
9:20 See *WCF* 16.6.
9:21–24 It is all the same. These verses represent the lowest point of Job's speeches. As tends to happen to anyone who suffers greatly over a long time, Job teetered toward apathetic fatalism, blowing both hot and cold, vacillating between hope and doubt (cf. v. 22).

he blindfolds its judges.[t]
If it is not he, then who is it?

25 "My days are swifter than a runner;[u]
they fly away without a glimpse of joy.
26 They skim past like boats of papyrus,[v]
like eagles swooping down on their prey.[w]
27 If I say, 'I will forget my complaint,[x]
I will change my expression, and smile,'
28 I still dread[y] all my sufferings,
for I know you will not hold me innocent.[z]
29 Since I am already found guilty,
why should I struggle in vain?[a]
30 Even if I washed myself with soap[a]
and my hands[b] with washing soda,[c]
31 you would plunge me into a slime pit
so that even my clothes would detest me.

32 "He is not a man like me that I might answer him,[d]
that we might confront each other in court.[e]
33 If only there were someone to arbitrate between us,[f]
to lay his hand upon us both,
34 someone to remove God's rod from me,[g]
so that his terror would frighten me no more.
35 Then I would speak up without fear of him,
but as it now stands with me, I cannot.[h]

10 "I loathe my very life;[i]
therefore I will give free rein to my complaint
and speak out in the bitterness of my soul.[j]
2 I will say to God: Do not condemn me,
but tell me what charges[k] you have against me.
3 Does it please you to oppress me,[l]
to spurn the work of your hands,[m]
while you smile on the schemes of the wicked?[n]
4 Do you have eyes of flesh?
Do you see as a mortal sees?[o]
5 Are your days like those of a mortal
or your years like those of a man,[p]
6 that you must search out my faults
and probe after my sin[q]—
7 though you know that I am not guilty
and that no one can rescue me from your hand?

8 "Your hands shaped[r] me and made me.
Will you now turn and destroy me?
9 Remember that you molded me like clay.[s]

9:24 [t]Job 12:6
9:25 [u]Job 7:6
9:26 [v]Isa 18:2 [w]Hab 1:8
9:27 [x]Job 7:11
9:28 [y]Job 3:25; Ps 119:120 [z]Job 7:21
9:29 [a]Ps 37:33
9:30 [b]Job 31:7 [c]Jer 2:22
9:32 [d]Ro 9:20 [e]Ps 143:2; Ecc 6:10
9:33 [f]1Sa 2:25
9:34 [g]Job 13:21; Ps 39:10
9:35 [h]Job 13:21
10:1 [i]1Ki 19:4 [j]Job 7:11
10:2 [k]Job 9:29
10:3 [l]Job 9:22 [m]Job 14:15; Ps 138:8; Isa 64:8 [n]Job 21:16; 22:18
10:4 [o]1Sa 16:7
10:5 [p]Ps 90:2,4; 2Pe 3:8
10:6 [q]Job 14:16
10:8 [r]Ps 119:73
10:9 [s]Isa 64:8

[a] *30* Or *snow*

9:24 If it is not he, then who is it? These sad but profound words reflected Job's belief in the absolute sovereignty of God. He would not have felt this perplexity had he viewed God as limited.
9:25–29 Since I am already found guilty, why should I struggle in vain? Job saw himself caught in an impossible dilemma. He believed he was innocent, but knew there was truth in the traditional view of suffering. He saw the logic in interpreting his experience as evidence that God had found him guilty and realized that he could not vindicate himself if that were true.
■ **9:30—10:22** *Questions to God Himself.* Job turned directly toward God to express his burning questions about God's goodness toward him.
9:32–33 See *WCF* 7.1.
9:33 If only there were someone. Eliphaz had tormented Job with the thought that no heavenly being would think of defending him (5:1). Here Job touched upon a profound truth, that sinful humans need an arbiter who can lay a hand on both God and themselves. Although not a direct prediction, this verse expressed the need for "one mediator between God and men" (1Ti 2:5).
10:1 I loathe. Compare 7:16 and 9:21. Job did not truly want to die but saw death as his only means of escape (6:8–9). Nothing worse could happen, so he felt no reticence about complaining freely.
10:2 tell me what charges. Job spoke from the assumption that the traditional view of suffering held by his counselors was correct.
10:3 Does it please you . . . ? Literally, "Is it good?" It can also be translated "Is it right?" **you smile on the schemes of the wicked.** No wonder the Lord would later accuse Job of discrediting his justice! (40:8).
10:4–7 you know that I am not guilty and that no one can rescue me from your hand. Job's perceived dilemma is full of irony: He acknowledged that God is omniscient and that he does not have to search out sins like a human prosecutor. The only possible explanation was that the Lord knew Job was innocent but chose to make him his helpless victim.
10:8–12 Your hands shaped me. Like the author of Psalm 139:13–16, Job understood that God had fashioned him in the womb, given him life and blessed him. Now he could not comprehend how the same good God could treat him so callously.

10:9 [t]Ge 2:7
10:11 [u]Ps 139:13,15
10:12 [v]Job 33:4
10:13 [w]Job 23:13
10:14 [x]Job 7:21
10:15 [y]Job 9:13; Isa 3:11 [z]Job 9:15
10:16 [a]Isa 38:13; La 3:10 [b]Job 5:9
10:17 [c]Job 16:8 [d]Ru 1:21
10:18 [e]Job 3:11
10:20 [f]Job 14:1 [g]Job 7:19 [h]Job 7:16
10:21 [i]2Sa 12:23; Job 3:13; 16:22 [j]Ps 23:4; 88:12
11:2 [k]Job 8:2
11:3 [l]Job 17:2; 21:3
11:4 [m]Job 6:10 [n]Job 10:7
11:6 [o]Job 9:4

Will you now turn me to dust again?[t]
10 Did you not pour me out like milk
and curdle me like cheese,
11 clothe me with skin and flesh
and knit me together[u] with bones and sinews?
12 You gave me life[v] and showed me kindness,
and in your providence watched over my spirit.

13 "But this is what you concealed in your heart,
and I know that this was in your mind:[w]
14 If I sinned, you would be watching me
and would not let my offense go unpunished.[x]
15 If I am guilty—woe to me![y]
Even if I am innocent, I cannot lift my head,[z]
for I am full of shame
and drowned in[a] my affliction.
16 If I hold my head high, you stalk me like a lion[a]
and again display your awesome power against me.[b]
17 You bring new witnesses against me[c]
and increase your anger toward me;[d]
your forces come against me wave upon wave.

18 "Why then did you bring me out of the womb?[e]
I wish I had died before any eye saw me.
19 If only I had never come into being,
or had been carried straight from the womb to the grave!
20 Are not my few days[f] almost over?[g]
Turn away from me[h] so I can have a moment's joy
21 before I go to the place of no return,[i]
to the land of gloom and deep shadow,[b][j]
22 to the land of deepest night,
of deep shadow and disorder,
where even the light is like darkness."

Zophar

11

Then Zophar the Naamathite replied:

2 "Are all these words to go unanswered?[k]
Is this talker to be vindicated?
3 Will your idle talk reduce men to silence?
Will no one rebuke you when you mock?[l]
4 You say to God, 'My beliefs are flawless[m]
and I am pure[n] in your sight.'
5 Oh, how I wish that God would speak,
that he would open his lips against you
6 and disclose to you the secrets of wisdom,[o]

[a] *15* Or *and aware of* [b] *21* Or *and the shadow of death*; also in verse 22

10:13 But this is what. To what does the pronoun "this" refer? Job conceived of a divine plan from the beginning of his life to keep him under surveillance and punish him for any misdeed. He did not comprehend that although God did have a plan in his suffering, punishment was not involved in it.
10:14–15 If I sinned. All of this was predicated on the mistaken assumption that his torment was the result of God's punitive wrath.
10:18–19 I wish I had died. Job reverted to the same despondent theme he had voiced in 3:11.
10:20–22 Turn away from me. Here he repeated his sentiments from 7:17–19.
10:21 the place of no return. Notice Job's description of that place as a land of darkness, while earlier in 3:13–19 he had looked on it as a place of peace and rest. Job's emotional raging must not be used as a basis for constructing normative Old Testament or Christian theology (see "Introduction: Purpose and Distinctives").
■ **11:1–20** *Zophar.* This man was the most severe of Job's counselors and spoke his mind ruthlessly on Job's plight, in the process misapplying some truths about God. He confronted Job for his idle talk (vv. 1–6), praised the power and wisdom of God (vv. 7–12) and called Job to repentance (vv. 13–20).
■ **11:1–6** *Rebuke for Idle Talk.* Zophar expressed frustration that no one was confronting Job and correcting his foolish assessments of God and of his situation.
11:4 I am pure in your sight. This was not a precise quotation of Job, who did not deny that he was a sinner. Job claimed to be "blameless" (9:21), an assertion that God himself had made on Job's behalf in 1:8 and 2:3. Job knew he was a sinner (7:21; 9:2; 13:26); he simply claimed that he was not guilty of the kind of sinful life that should result in such severe affliction.
11:6 true wisdom has two sides. It is unclear what Zophar meant by the two sides of true wisdom. Perhaps he was referring to the human and divine perspectives, for he went on to emphasize the mysteries that lie with God alone. **forgotten some of your sin.** The words reflect Zophar's supposition of the enormity of Job's offenses.

for true wisdom has two sides.
Know this: God has even forgotten some of your sin.[p]

7 "Can you fathom[q] the mysteries of God?
Can you probe the limits of the Almighty?
8 They are higher than the heavens[r]—what can you do?
They are deeper than the depths of the grave[a]—what can you know?
9 Their measure is longer than the earth
and wider than the sea.

10 "If he comes along and confines you in prison
and convenes a court, who can oppose him?[s]
11 Surely he recognizes deceitful men;
and when he sees evil, does he not take note?[t]
12 But a witless man can no more become wise
than a wild donkey's colt can be born a man.[b]

13 "Yet if you devote your heart[u] to him
and stretch out your hands to him,[v]
14 if you put away the sin that is in your hand
and allow no evil[w] to dwell in your tent,[x]
15 then you will lift up your face[y] without shame;
you will stand firm and without fear.
16 You will surely forget your trouble,[z]
recalling it only as waters gone by.[a]
17 Life will be brighter than noonday,[b]
and darkness will become like morning.
18 You will be secure, because there is hope;
you will look about you and take your rest[c] in safety.[d]
19 You will lie down, with no one to make you afraid,[e]
and many will court your favor.[f]
20 But the eyes of the wicked will fail,[g]
and escape will elude them;[h]
their hope will become a dying gasp."[i]

Job 12

Then Job replied:

2 "Doubtless you are the people,
and wisdom will die with you![j]
3 But I have a mind as well as you;
I am not inferior to you.
Who does not know all these things?[k]

4 "I have become a laughingstock[l] to my friends,
though I called upon God and he answered[m]—
a mere laughingstock, though righteous and blameless![n]
5 Men at ease have contempt for misfortune
as the fate of those whose feet are slipping.
6 The tents of marauders are undisturbed,[o]

11:6 [p]Ezr 9:13; Job 15:5
11:7 [q]Ecc 3:11; Ro 11:33
11:8 [r]Job 22:12
11:10 [s]Job 9:12; Rev 3:7
11:11 [t]Job 34:21-25; Ps 10:14
11:13 [u]1Sa 7:3; Ps 78:8 [v]Ps 88:9
11:14 [w]Ps 101:4 [x]Job 22:23
11:15 [y]Job 22:26; 1Jn 3:21
11:16 [z]Isa 65:16 [a]Job 22:11
11:17 [b]Job 22:28; Ps 37:6; Isa 58:8, 10
11:18 [c]Ps 3:5 [d]Lev 26:6; Pr 3:24
11:19 [e]Lev 26:6 [f]Isa 45:14
11:20 [g]Dt 28:65; Job 17:5 [h]Job 27:22; 34:22 [i]Job 8:13
12:2 [j]Job 17:10
12:3 [k]Job 13:2
12:4 [l]Job 21:3 [m]Ps 91:15 [n]Job 6:29
12:6 [o]Job 22:18

[a] 8 Hebrew *than Sheol* [b] 12 Or *wild donkey can be born tame*

■ **11:7–12** *Praise for God's Wisdom and Power.* These words are an eloquent expression of the transcendence of God in contrast to the humble state of humans.
11:7–9 See *WCF* 2.1; *WLC* 7; *WSC* 4.
11:12 can be born a man. Note the alternate translation in the NIV text note: "wild donkey can be born tame." The word *witless* contrasts with *wise* as *wild* does with *tame.*
■ **11:13–20** *Call to Repentance.* While this was good advice for a profligate sinner, it did not properly apply to Job. Like Bildad, Zophar made no allowance for mercy: Job in his opinion had to become righteous before God would accept him.
11:14–15 if you . . . then you. It was arrogance on Zophar's part to think that he knew why Job was suffering. We understand from the prologue that it was not because Job had sinned. Job was called by God to join that grand company of innocent sufferers for the glory of the Lord.
■ **12:1—14:22** *Job's Reply to Zophar.* Job's response in this long speech started with a blast of sarcasm against his counselors (12:1—13:19). Job then cried out to God, creating a major break in the speech (13:20–27). This inclination of Job to talk to God (pray) contrasts to the style of the counselors, who never said a word to God but only spoke about him. In 13:28—14:22 Job lamented the condition of humanity.
■ **12:1—13:19** *Sarcastic Rebuke.* Job disdained his counselors' attempts to advise him.
12:2 Doubtless you are the people. Job's sarcasm reveals his frustration with their simplistic application of proverbial wisdom to his life.
12:4–6 I have become a laughingstock. Job agonized that he had become an object of ridicule, even to his friends, while evildo-

and those who provoke God are secure[p]—
those who carry their god in their hands.[a]

7 "But ask the animals, and they will teach you,
or the birds of the air, and they will tell you;
8 or speak to the earth, and it will teach you,
or let the fish of the sea inform you.
9 Which of all these does not know
that the hand of the LORD has done this?[q]
10 In his hand is the life of every creature
and the breath of all mankind.[r]
11 Does not the ear test words
as the tongue tastes food?[s]
12 Is not wisdom found among the aged?[t]
Does not long life bring understanding?[u]

13 "To God belong wisdom[v] and power;[w]
counsel and understanding are his.[x]
14 What he tears down[y] cannot be rebuilt;[z]
the man he imprisons cannot be released.
15 If he holds back the waters,[a] there is drought;[b]
if he lets them loose, they devastate the land.[c]
16 To him belong strength and victory;
both deceived and deceiver are his.[d]
17 He leads counselors away stripped[e]
and makes fools of judges.[f]
18 He takes off the shackles[g] put on by kings
and ties a loincloth[b] around their waist.
19 He leads priests away stripped
and overthrows men long established.[h]
20 He silences the lips of trusted advisers
and takes away the discernment of elders.[i]
21 He pours contempt on nobles
and disarms the mighty.
22 He reveals the deep things of darkness[j]
and brings deep shadows[k] into the light.[l]
23 He makes nations great, and destroys them;[m]
he enlarges nations,[n] and disperses them.
24 He deprives the leaders of the earth of their reason;
he sends them wandering through a trackless waste.[o]
25 They grope in darkness with no light;[p]
he makes them stagger like drunkards.[q]

13 "My eyes have seen all this,
my ears have heard and understood it.
2 What you know, I also know;
I am not inferior to you.[r]
3 But I desire to speak to the Almighty
and to argue my case with God.[s]

12:6 [p]Job 9:24; 21:9
12:9 [q]Isa 41:20
12:10 [r]Job 27:3; 33:4; Ac 17:28
12:11 [s]Job 34:3
12:12 [t]Job 15:10 [u]Job 32:7,9
12:13 [v]Job 11:6 [w]Job 9:4 [x]Job 32:8; 38:36
12:14 [y]Job 19:10 [z]Job 37:7; Isa 25:2
12:15 [a]1Ki 8:35 [b]1Ki 17:1 [c]Ge 7:11
12:16 [d]Job 13:7,9
12:17 [e]Job 19:9 [f]Job 3:14
12:18 [g]Ps 116:16
12:19 [h]Job 24:12,22; 34:20,28; 35:9
12:20 [i]Job 32:9
12:22 [j]1Co 4:5 [k]Job 3:5 [l]Da 2:22
12:23 [m]Jer 25:9 [n]Ps 107:38; Isa 9:3; 26:15
12:24 [o]Ps 107:40
12:25 [p]Job 5:14 [q]Ps 107:27; Isa 24:20
13:2 [r]Job 12:3
13:3 [s]Job 23:3-4

[a] 6 Or *secure / in what God's hand brings them* [b] 18 Or *shackles of kings / and ties a belt*

ers and idolators tended to live in ease and security. **who carry their god in their hands.** Job referred to a small plaque, bearing the image of a god, that was in widespread use among the Canaanites.

12:7–8 ask the animals . . . speak to the earth. Like Eliphaz who had called upon revelation and Bildad who had appealed to tradition to support their arguments, Job summoned every creature in the universe to bear witness to his argument that the wicked do prosper and the righteous do suffer.

12:12 Is not wisdom . . . ? An alternate translation of this verse might be, "Should not wisdom be found among the aged? Should not long life bring understanding?" Even as it stands in the NIV, the verse should be understood as irony directed at the counselors, who were aged but foolish, in anticipation of the better counsel of the youngest adviser, Elihu (32:6).

12:13–25 To God belong wisdom and power. A unit of poetry in which Job expounded on God's sovereign freedom. Some have maintained that these words reflect a tongue-in-cheek attitude and that Job was subtly criticizing God for mismanaging the universe. People who hold such a view perceive in the book a limited God whom we humans have to "forgive." But throughout, even when Job raged over his suffering and expressed doubts about God's justice, he predicated all on the assumptions that God is sovereign and that humans can effectively plead with him to alter what he does. Job wrestled with a great mystery, too deep and profound for these shallow advisers to understand. This part of the speech may have been provoked by Zophar's question in 11:7, "Can you fathom the mysteries of God?" The poem may also be a response to Eliphaz's creedal hymn in 5:18–26, in which he stated that only good things happen to good people—which is hardly the case in this stanza.

13:3 to argue my case with God. In the latter part of this chap-

[4] You, however, smear me with lies;[t]
you are worthless physicians, all of you!
[5] If only you would be altogether silent!
For you, that would be wisdom.[u]
[6] Hear now my argument;
listen to the plea of my lips.
[7] Will you speak wickedly on God's behalf?
Will you speak deceitfully for him?[v]
[8] Will you show him partiality?[w]
Will you argue the case for God?
[9] Would it turn out well if he examined you?
Could you deceive him as you might deceive men?[x]
[10] He would surely rebuke you
if you secretly showed partiality.
[11] Would not his splendor[y] terrify you?
Would not the dread of him fall on you?
[12] Your maxims are proverbs of ashes;
your defenses are defenses of clay.

[13] "Keep silent and let me speak;
then let come to me what may.
[14] Why do I put myself in jeopardy
and take my life in my hands?
[15] Though he slay me, yet will I hope[z] in him;[a]
I will surely[a] defend my ways to his face.[b]
[16] Indeed, this will turn out for my deliverance,[c]
for no godless man would dare come before him!
[17] Listen carefully to my words;[d]
let your ears take in what I say.
[18] Now that I have prepared my case,[e]
I know I will be vindicated.
[19] Can anyone bring charges against me?[f]
If so, I will be silent and die.[g]

[20] "Only grant me these two things, O God,
and then I will not hide from you:
[21] Withdraw your hand[h] far from me,
and stop frightening me with your terrors.
[22] Then summon me and I will answer,[i]
or let me speak, and you reply.[j]
[23] How many wrongs and sins have I committed?[k]
Show me my offense and my sin.
[24] Why do you hide your face[l]
and consider me your enemy?[m]
[25] Will you torment a windblown leaf?[n]
Will you chase after dry chaff?[o]
[26] For you write down bitter things against me
and make me inherit the sins of my youth.[p]

13:4 [t]Ps 119:69; Jer 23:32
13:5 [u]Pr 17:28
13:7 [v]Job 36:4
13:8 [w]Lev 19:15
13:9 [x]Job 12:16; Gal 6:7
13:11 [y]Job 31:23
13:15 [z]Job 7:6 [a]Ps 23:4; Pr 14:32 [b]Job 27:5
13:16 [c]Isa 12:1
13:17 [d]Job 21:2
13:18 [e]Job 23:4
13:19 [f]Job 40:4; Isa 50:8 [g]Job 10:8
13:21 [h]Ps 39:10
13:22 [i]Job 14:15 [j]Job 9:16
13:23 [k]1Sa 26:18
13:24 [l]Dt 32:20; Ps 13:1; Isa 8:17 [m]Job 19:11; La 2:5
13:25 [n]Lev 26:36 [o]Job 21:18; Isa 42:3
13:26 [p]Ps 25:7

a *15* Or *He will surely slay me; I have no hope — / yet I will*

ter Job would return to this subject, but first he wanted to set the record straight with the counselors.
13:4–12 You . . . smear me with lies. Job fiercely rebuked his detractors, accusing them not only of being miserable counselors but of speaking, ostensibly on God's behalf, from a wrong motive—thinking inwardly that God was blameworthy but trying to cover this presumption by false accusations against Job. **Would it turn out well if he examined you?** Job believed that they might be able to mislead people about their motivation but that they could not deceive God as to whether or not they were honoring him (vv. 7–11).
13:7–8 See *WLC* 99.
13:14 take my life in my hands. Job intended to defend himself even if God were to slay him as impudent.
13:15 Though he slay me, yet will I hope in him. This is often quoted as the supreme expression of trust in the Lord, but a variant reading renders it, "Behold he will slay me; I have no hope" (also see NIV text note). Others translate the second clause "I will not quaver" or "I will not wait." See *WCF* 18.4; *WLC* 81.
13:18 I will be vindicated. Job expressed confidence that he would be acquitted of the charges the counselors had levied against him.
■ **13:20–27** *Cries to God.* Job implored God to help him but found no relief.
13:23 How many wrongs and sins have I committed? This was no claim of sinless perfection, as verse 26 verifies. It was merely Job's assertion that he was not and never had been guilty of the kind of unbridled wickedness believed to lead to the degree of suffering he was enduring. See notes on 11:4 and 29:11–17.
13:24 Why do you . . . consider me your enemy? This was the delusive fantasy with which Job struggled. God had never considered Job his enemy.

13:27 [q]Job 33:11

13:28 [r]Isa 50:9; Jas 5:2

14:1 [s]Job 5:7; Ecc 2:23

14:2 [t]Jas 1:10 [u]Ps 90:5-6 [v]Job 8:9

14:3 [w]Ps 8:4; 144:3 [x]Ps 143:2

14:4 [y]Ps 51:10 [z]Eph 2:1-3 [a]Jn 3:6; Ro 5:12

14:5 [b]Job 21:21

14:6 [c]Job 7:19 [d]Job 7:1, 2; Ps 39:13

14:10 [e]Job 13:19

14:11 [f]Isa 19:5

14:12 [g]Rev 20:11; 21:1 [h]Ac 3:21

14:13 [i]Isa 26:20

14:15 [j]Job 13:22

14:16 [k]Ps 139:1-3; Pr 5:21; Jer 32:19 [l]Job 10:6

14:17 [m]Dt 32:34 [n]Hos 13:12

27 You fasten my feet in shackles;[q]
you keep close watch on all my paths
by putting marks on the soles of my feet.

28 "So man wastes away like something rotten,
like a garment eaten by moths.[r]

14

"Man born of woman
is of few days and full of trouble.[s]
2 He springs up like a flower[t] and withers away;[u]
like a fleeting shadow,[v] he does not endure.
3 Do you fix your eye on such a one?[w]
Will you bring him[a] before you for judgment?[x]
4 Who can bring what is pure[y] from the impure?[z]
No one![a]
5 Man's days are determined;
you have decreed the number of his months[b]
and have set limits he cannot exceed.
6 So look away from him and let him alone,[c]
till he has put in his time like a hired man.[d]

7 "At least there is hope for a tree:
If it is cut down, it will sprout again,
and its new shoots will not fail.
8 Its roots may grow old in the ground
and its stump die in the soil,
9 yet at the scent of water it will bud
and put forth shoots like a plant.
10 But man dies and is laid low;
he breathes his last and is no more.[e]
11 As water disappears from the sea
or a riverbed becomes parched and dry,[f]
12 so man lies down and does not rise;
till the heavens are no more,[g] men will not awake
or be roused from their sleep.[h]

13 "If only you would hide me in the grave[b]
and conceal me till your anger has passed![i]
If only you would set me a time
and then remember me!
14 If a man dies, will he live again?
All the days of my hard service
I will wait for my renewal[c] to come.
15 You will call and I will answer you;[j]
you will long for the creature your hands have made.
16 Surely then you will count my steps[k]
but not keep track of my sin.[l]
17 My offenses will be sealed up in a bag;[m]
you will cover over my sin.[n]

18 "But as a mountain erodes and crumbles
and as a rock is moved from its place,

[a] 3 Septuagint, Vulgate and Syriac; Hebrew *me* [b] 13 Hebrew *Sheol* [c] 14 Or *release*

13:27 marks on the soles of my feet. Job envisioned himself a prisoner with his feet branded so that his path could easily be traced.

■ **13:28—14:22** *Lament Over Humanity's Condition.* In this poem Job bewailed the sad estate of human beings. He was feeling sorry for himself and for all of humanity. He imagined that God was constantly punishing human beings for their misdeeds.

14:4 See *WCF* 6.3; *WLC* 26; *BC* 15; *HC* 8.

14:7–22 If a man dies, will he live again? Job suggested that God allow him to die and then raise him up again after his (God's) anger had cooled down (v. 13). The reader, however, knows that God was never angry to begin with. This chapter does not clearly teach a doctrine of resurrection, as Job asserted that this raising up would not happen (v. 20), but it does indicate that the idea of a resurrection was already in view.

14:7 a tree . . . will sprout again. The Hebrew for "sprout" has the same root as the word for Job's "renewal" in verse 14.

14:13 If only you would hide me in the grave. Job doubted that God would inflict temporary death and finally concluded that he would not. But Job still believed in God's ability to do it.

14:14 I will wait. Here, and in succeeding verses, some translate "will" as "would" (e.g., "I would wait" and "you would call" [v. 15]).

14:18–22 Job concluded that God actually destroys human hope (v. 19).

[19] as water wears away stones
and torrents wash away the soil,
so you destroy man's hope.[o]
[20] You overpower him once for all, and he is gone;
you change his countenance and send him away.
[21] If his sons are honored, he does not know it;
if they are brought low, he does not see it.[p]
[22] He feels but the pain of his own body
and mourns only for himself."

Eliphaz

15 Then Eliphaz the Temanite replied:

[2] "Would a wise man answer with empty notions
or fill his belly with the hot east wind?[q]
[3] Would he argue with useless words,
with speeches that have no value?
[4] But you even undermine piety
and hinder devotion to God.
[5] Your sin prompts your mouth;
you adopt the tongue of the crafty.[r]
[6] Your own mouth condemns you, not mine;
your own lips testify against you.[s]

[7] "Are you the first man ever born?[t]
Were you brought forth before the hills?[u]
[8] Do you listen in on God's council?[v]
Do you limit wisdom to yourself?
[9] What do you know that we do not know?
What insights do you have that we do not have?[w]
[10] The gray-haired and the aged[x] are on our side,
men even older than your father.
[11] Are God's consolations[y] not enough for you,
words[z] spoken gently to you?[a]
[12] Why has your heart[b] carried you away,
and why do your eyes flash,
[13] so that you vent your rage against God
and pour out such words from your mouth?

[14] "What is man, that he could be pure,
or one born of woman,[c] that he could be righteous?[d]
[15] If God places no trust in his holy ones,
if even the heavens are not pure in his eyes,[e]
[16] how much less man, who is vile and corrupt,[f]
who drinks up evil like water![g]

[17] "Listen to me and I will explain to you;
let me tell you what I have seen,
[18] what wise men have declared,
hiding nothing received from their fathers[h]

14:19 [o]Job 7:6
14:21 [p]Ecc 9:5; Isa 63:16
15:2 [q]Job 6:26
15:5 [r]Job 5:13
15:6 [s]Lk 19:22
15:7 [t]Job 38:21 [u]Ps 90:2; Pr 8:25
15:8 [v]Ro 11:34; 1Co 2:11
15:9 [w]Job 13:2
15:10 [x]Job 32:6-7
15:11 [y]2Co 1:3-4 [z]Zec 1:13 [a]Job 36:16
15:12 [b]Job 11:13
15:14 [c]Job 14:4; 25:4 [d]Pr 20:9; Ecc 7:20
15:15 [e]Job 4:18; 25:5
15:16 [f]Ps 14:1 [g]Job 34:7; Pr 19:28
15:18 [h]Job 8:8

14:20–22 you change his countenance. A description of a corpse.

■ **15:1—21:34** *The Second Cycle of Speeches.* Job and his friends exchanged words again. The order is the same here as in the first cycle: Eliphaz (15:1–35), Job (16:1—17:16), Bildad (18:1–21), Job (19:1–29), Zophar (20:1–29) and Job (21:1–34).

■ **15:1–35** *Eliphaz.* This friend began the second cycle of speeches (15:1—21:34), moving away from the tactful approach he had exhibited earlier (chs. 4–5). He began with a series of questions and accusations (vv. 1–16), once again drawing on traditional wisdom (vv. 17–35).

■ **15:1–16** *Questions and Accusations.* In a series of rapid-fire questions and accusations, Eliphaz tried to expose with sarcasm what he considered to be Job's arrogance.

15:8 Do you limit wisdom to yourself? Eliphaz returned to Job the very sarcasm Job had used against him in 12:2.

15:9 What do you know that we do not know? Eliphaz continued to throw Job's own words back at him. Compare 12:3 and 13:2.

15:10 the aged are on our side. Job's irony in 12:12 (see note) was not lost on Eliphaz. He expressed certainty that all the elders were on the friends' side, not Job's.

15:12–13 According to Eliphaz, Job expressed himself with eyes flashing, venting rage.

15:14–15 What is man, that he could be pure . . . ? Eliphaz again brought up the oracle he had received. Compare verses 15–16 with 4:18–19. See *WCF* 6.3; *WLC* 26.

■ **15:17–35** *Affirmation of Proverbial Wisdom.* Eliphaz called for Job to remember what the sages of the past had said. After an introduction (vv. 17–19) he recited a poem on the fate of a wicked person. He used numerous metaphors to convey the idea that the wicked, not the righteous, are the ones who suffer at God's hands; therefore, Job must be a wicked man.

15:18 wise men have declared. Eliphaz drew on the teachings of sages in order to instruct Job.

19 (to whom alone the land was given
when no alien passed among them):
20 All his days the wicked man suffers torment,
the ruthless through all the years stored up for him.[i]
21 Terrifying sounds fill his ears;[j]
when all seems well, marauders attack him.[k]
22 He despairs of escaping the darkness;
he is marked for the sword.[l]
23 He wanders about[m]—food for vultures[a];
he knows the day of darkness is at hand.[n]
24 Distress and anguish fill him with terror;
they overwhelm him, like a king poised to attack,
25 because he shakes his fist at God
and vaunts himself against the Almighty,[o]
26 defiantly charging against him
with a thick, strong shield.

27 "Though his face is covered with fat
and his waist bulges with flesh,[p]
28 he will inhabit ruined towns
and houses where no one lives,[q]
houses crumbling to rubble.[r]
29 He will no longer be rich and his wealth will not endure,[s]
nor will his possessions spread over the land.
30 He will not escape the darkness;[t]
a flame[u] will wither his shoots,
and the breath of God's mouth[v] will carry him away.
31 Let him not deceive himself by trusting what is worthless,[w]
for he will get nothing in return.
32 Before his time[x] he will be paid in full,[y]
and his branches will not flourish.[z]
33 He will be like a vine stripped of its unripe grapes,[a]
like an olive tree shedding its blossoms.
34 For the company of the godless will be barren,
and fire will consume the tents of those who love
bribes.[b]
35 They conceive trouble and give birth to evil;[c]
their womb fashions deceit."

Job 16

Then Job replied:

2 "I have heard many things like these;
miserable comforters are you all![d]
3 Will your long-winded speeches never end?
What ails you that you keep on arguing?[e]
4 I also could speak like you,
if you were in my place;
I could make fine speeches against you
and shake my head[f] at you.
5 But my mouth would encourage you;
comfort from my lips would bring you relief.

15:20 [i]Job 24:1; 27:13-23
15:21 [j]Job 18:11; 20:25 [k]Job 27:20; 1Th 5:3
15:22 [l]Job 19:29; 27:14
15:23 [m]Ps 59:15; 109:10 [n]Job 18:12
15:25 [o]Job 36:9
15:27 [p]Ps 17:10
15:28 [q]Isa 5:9 [r]Job 3:14
15:29 [s]Job 27:16-17
15:30 [t]Job 5:14 [u]Job 22:20 [v]Job 4:9
15:31 [w]Isa 59:4
15:32 [x]Ecc 7:17 [y]Job 22:16; Ps 55:23 [z]Job 18:16
15:33 [a]Hab 3:17
15:34 [b]Job 8:22
15:35 [c]Ps 7:14; Isa 59:4; Hos 10:13
16:2 [d]Job 13:4
16:3 [e]Job 6:26
16:4 [f]Ps 22:7; 109:25; La 2:15; Zep 2:15; Mt 27:39

[a] 23 Or *about, looking for food*

15:25 shakes his fist at God. Eliphaz indirectly accused Job of defiance against God in challenging God's supremacy with his questions and protests.
15:34 See *WLC* 142.
15:35 They conceive trouble and give birth to evil. Repeated in Isaiah 59:4.
■ **16:1—17:16** *Job's Reply to Eliphaz.* Job dismissed Eliphaz's harangue as a sickening repetition of a defective outlook on suffering. He addressed his friends (16:1–6) and turned to God with a lament (16:7—17:16).

■ **16:1–6** *Cynical Rebuke.* Job fired back at Eliphaz with cynicism for applying traditional proverbs to his situation.

16:2 I have heard. Job was already aware of the traditional perspectives that Eliphaz recited—and was duly unimpressed. **miserable comforters.** Literally "comforters of trouble" or "mischief." That is, comforters who cause trouble.

16:3 long-winded . . . arguing. Job has grown weary not only of the length of their speeches, but of their emptiness of any helpful content.

6 "Yet if I speak, my pain is not relieved;
and if I refrain, it does not go away.
7 Surely, O God, you have worn me out;[g]
you have devastated my entire household.
8 You have bound me—and it has become a witness;
my gauntness[h] rises up and testifies against me.[i]
9 God assails me and tears[j] me in his anger
and gnashes his teeth at me;[k]
my opponent fastens on me his piercing eyes.[l]
10 Men open their mouths[m] to jeer at me;
they strike my cheek[n] in scorn
and unite together against me.[o]
11 God has turned me over to evil men
and thrown me into the clutches of the wicked.[p]
12 All was well with me, but he shattered me;
he seized me by the neck and crushed me.[q]
He has made me his target;[r]
13 his archers surround me.
Without pity, he pierces[s] my kidneys
and spills my gall on the ground.
14 Again and again[t] he bursts upon me;
he rushes at me like a warrior.[u]

15 "I have sewed sackcloth[v] over my skin
and buried my brow in the dust.
16 My face is red with weeping,
deep shadows ring my eyes;
17 yet my hands have been free of violence[w]
and my prayer is pure.

18 "O earth, do not cover my blood;[x]
may my cry never be laid to rest![y]
19 Even now my witness[z] is in heaven;
my advocate is on high.
20 My intercessor is my friend[a]
as my eyes pour out[a] tears to God;
21 on behalf of a man he pleads[b] with God
as a man pleads for his friend.

22 "Only a few years will pass
before I go on the journey of no return.[c]

17

1 My spirit is broken,
my days are cut short,
the grave awaits me.[d]
2 Surely mockers[e] surround me;
my eyes must dwell on their hostility.

3 "Give me, O God, the pledge you demand.[f]
Who else will put up security[g] for me?[h]
4 You have closed their minds to understanding;
therefore you will not let them triumph.

16:7 [g]Job 7:3
16:8 [h]Job 19:20 [i]Job 10:17
16:9 [j]Hos 6:1 [k]Ps 35:16; La 2:16; Ac 7:54 [l]Job 13:24
16:10 [m]Ps 22:13 [n]Isa 50:6; La 3:30; Mic 5:1; Ac 23:2 [o]Ps 35:15
16:11 [p]Job 1:15,17
16:12 [q]Job 9:17 [r]La 3:12
16:13 [s]Job 20:24
16:14 [t]Job 9:17 [u]Joel 2:7
16:15 [v]Ge 37:34
16:17 [w]Isa 59:6; Jnh 3:8
16:18 [x]Isa 26:21 [y]Ps 66:18-19
16:19 [z]Ge 31:50; Ro 1:9; 1Th 2:5
16:20 [a]La 2:19
16:21 [b]Ps 9:4
16:22 [c]Ecc 12:5
17:1 [d]Ps 88:3-4
17:2 [e]1Sa 1:6-7
17:3 [f]Ps 119:122 [g]Pr 6:1 [h]Isa 38:14

[a] *20* Or *My friends treat me with scorn*

■ **16:7—17:16** *Lament to God.* Again Job turned to God and poured out his heart. In verse 9 the figure is that of a lion. Some think it should be translated "He sniffs and tears." In verses 12–14 a graphic warrior figure is employed.

16:18 do not cover my blood. The earth, personified, was called as a witness to Job's murder.

16:19 my witness . . . my advocate. Job believed he had a witness in heaven, a notion that had been summarily dismissed by Eliphaz (5:1). But the thought gave Job a ray of hope that all might be well someday. Many interpreters see here a glimmer of faith in a Christ figure, an advocate for the righteous in the heavenly court. Job certainly hoped that someone in the heavenly realms would speak for him; the clarity of his understanding remains uncertain.

16:20 intercessor. This word may be translated in various ways, depending on how the Hebrew text is understood. The NIV has good support for translating it "mediator" in 33:23 and "spokesman" in Isaiah 43:27. The translation chosen here, "intercessor," fits the context (v. 19, "witness," "advocate").

16:22 Only a few years. Job anticipated a lingering death. The NIV leaves a space after verse 21 to reflect that verse 22 fits best with the beginning of chapter 17. Chapter divisions are not inspired.

17:3 Give me . . . the pledge you demand. Job asked God to vouch for his innocence and to prove it to the counselors.

17:4 their minds. That is, the minds of the counselors.

17:5 [i]Job 11:20
17:6 [j]Job 30:9
17:7 [k]Job 16:8
17:8 [l]Job 22:19
17:9 [m]Pr 4:18 [n]Job 22:30
17:10 [o]Job 12:2
17:11 [p]Job 7:6
17:13 [q]Job 3:13
17:14 [r]Job 13:28; 30:28, 30; Ps 16:10 [s]Job 21:26
17:15 [t]Job 7:6
17:16 [u]Job 3:17-19; Jnh 2:6
18:3 [v]Ps 73:22
18:4 [w]Job 13:14
18:5 [x]Job 21:17; Pr 13:9; 20:20; 24:20
18:7 [y]Pr 4:12 [z]Job 5:13 [a]Job 15:6
18:8 [b]Job 22:10; Ps 9:15; 35:7
18:11 [c]Job 15:21; Jer 6:25; 20:3 [d]Job 20:8

5 If a man denounces his friends for reward,
the eyes of his children will fail.[i]

6 "God has made me a byword[j] to everyone,
a man in whose face people spit.
7 My eyes have grown dim with grief;[k]
my whole frame is but a shadow.
8 Upright men are appalled at this;
the innocent are aroused[l] against the ungodly.
9 Nevertheless, the righteous[m] will hold to their ways,
and those with clean hands[n] will grow stronger.

10 "But come on, all of you, try again!
I will not find a wise man among you.[o]
11 My days have passed, my plans are shattered,
and so are the desires of my heart.[p]
12 These men turn night into day;
in the face of darkness they say, 'Light is near.'
13 If the only home I hope for is the grave,[a][q]
if I spread out my bed in darkness,
14 if I say to corruption,[r] 'You are my father,'
and to the worm,[s] 'My mother' or 'My sister,'
15 where then is my hope?[t]
Who can see any hope for me?
16 Will it go down to the gates of death[a]?[u]
Will we descend together into the dust?"

Bildad

18 Then Bildad the Shuhite replied:

2 "When will you end these speeches?
Be sensible, and then we can talk.
3 Why are we regarded as cattle
and considered stupid in your sight?[v]
4 You who tear yourself[w] to pieces in your anger,
is the earth to be abandoned for your sake?
Or must the rocks be moved from their place?

5 "The lamp of the wicked is snuffed out;[x]
the flame of his fire stops burning.
6 The light in his tent becomes dark;
the lamp beside him goes out.
7 The vigor of his step is weakened;[y]
his own schemes[z] throw him down.[a]
8 His feet thrust him into a net[b]
and he wanders into its mesh.
9 A trap seizes him by the heel;
a snare holds him fast.
10 A noose is hidden for him on the ground;
a trap lies in his path.
11 Terrors startle him on every side[c]
and dog[d] his every step.

[a] 13,16 Hebrew *Sheol*

17:6 God has made me . . . a man in whose face people spit. Since God had not vindicated him, Job imagined that God was responsible for his awful condition. Compare 30:10.

17:7 eyes have grown dim . . . frame is but a shadow. The symptoms of his disease evidently included boils and sores (2:7), worms and scabs (7:5) and nightmares (7:14). Here and in 19:20 are added loss of weight, bad breath (19:17), black skin and fever (30:30) and unremitting pain (30:17).

17:12 These men turn night into day. Zophar had admonished Job that if he would turn from his wickedness, God would make his life brighter than noonday (11:17). Here Job ridiculed Zophar's words.

■ **18:1–21** *Bildad.* Job was accused by Bildad for a second time. Bildad rebuked Job (vv. 1–4) and repeated his earlier exposition on the destiny of the wicked (vv. 5–21; see 8:8–19).

■ **18:1–4** *Unsympathetic Rebuke.* Bildad opened his speech with a heartless rebuke of one who was suffering greatly.

■ **18:5–21** *Affirmation of Proverbial Wisdom.* Bildad had not moved from his position as expressed in his earlier speech (ch. 8).

[12] Calamity is hungry[e] for him;
disaster is ready for him when he falls.
[13] It eats away parts of his skin;
death's firstborn devours his limbs.[f]
[14] He is torn from the security of his tent[g]
and marched off to the king of terrors.
[15] Fire resides[a] in his tent;
burning sulfur[h] is scattered over his dwelling.
[16] His roots dry up below[i]
and his branches wither above.[j]
[17] The memory of him perishes from the earth;
he has no name in the land.[k]
[18] He is driven from light into darkness[l]
and is banished from the world.
[19] He has no offspring[m] or descendants[n] among his people,
no survivor where once he lived.[o]
[20] Men of the west are appalled at his fate;[p]
men of the east are seized with horror.
[21] Surely such is the dwelling[q] of an evil man;
such is the place of one who knows not God."[r]

Job

19

Then Job replied:

[2] "How long will you torment me
and crush me with words?
[3] Ten times now you have reproached me;
shamelessly you attack me.
[4] If it is true that I have gone astray,
my error[s] remains my concern alone.
[5] If indeed you would exalt *your*selves above me[t]
and use my humiliation against me,
[6] then know that God has wronged me[u]
and drawn his net[v] around me.

[7] "Though I cry, 'I've been wronged!' I get no response;[w]
though I call for help, there is no justice.[x]
[8] He has blocked my way so I cannot pass;[y]
he has shrouded my paths in darkness.[z]
[9] He has stripped[a] me of my honor
and removed the crown from my head.[b]
[10] He tears me down[c] on every side till I am gone;
he uproots my hope[d] like a tree.[e]
[11] His anger[f] burns against me;
he counts me among his enemies.[g]
[12] His troops advance in force;[h]
they build a siege ramp[i] against me
and encamp around my tent.

[a] *15* Or *Nothing he had remains*

18:12 [e]Isa 8:21
18:13 [f]Zec 14:12
18:14 [g]Job 8:22
18:15 [h]Ps 11:6
18:16 [i]Isa 5:24; Hos 9:1-16; Am 2:9 [j]Job 15:30; Mal 4:1
18:17 [k]Ps 34:16; Pr 2:22; 10:7
18:18 [l]Job 5:14
18:19 [m]Jer 22:30 [n]Isa 14:22 [o]Job 27:14-15
18:20 [p]Ps 37:13; Jer 50:27,31
18:21 [q]Job 21:28 [r]Jer 9:3; 1Th 4:5
19:4 [s]Job 6:24
19:5 [t]Ps 35:26; 38:16; 55:12
19:6 [u]Job 27:2 [v]Job 18:8
19:7 [w]Job 30:20 [x]Job 9:24; Hab 1:2-4
19:8 [y]Job 3:23; La 3:7 [z]Job 30:26
19:9 [a]Job 12:17 [b]Ps 89:39,44; La 5:16
19:10 [c]Job 12:14 [d]Job 7:6 [e]Job 24:20
19:11 [f]Job 16:9 [g]Job 13:24
19:12 [h]Job 16:13 [i]Job 30:12

18:14 the king of terrors. A personification of death. The Canaanites understood death as a god with one lip touching the earth and the other the heavens, so that he swallowed up everything. According to Bildad, "death's firstborn," following in the footsteps of his father, eats away the skin and devours the limbs of the wicked (like Job). Isaiah reversed the figure and envisioned the Lord swallowing up death forever (Isa 25:8; cf. 1Co 15:54).

■ **19:1–29** *Job's Reply to Bildad.* Job responded angrily to his friends, challenging them to acknowledge what God had done to him (vv. 1–6). He commenced a lengthy list of laments about his mistreatment (vv. 7–20) and then appealed to his friends and warned them (vv. 21–29).

■ **19:1–6** *Appeal for Sympathy.* Job called for his advisers to end their attacks by reassessing what God was doing to him.

19:6 God has wronged me. Job examined his life and concluded not that he was perfectly innocent but that he did not deserve what he had received from God. Bildad simplistically asserted that God does not violate justice (8:3) and contended that every element of suffering represents justified divine judgment. Job insisted that in his case God had not been just.

■ **19:7–20** *Laments to God.* Job wrestled with God over the apparent meaninglessness of his suffering, which was actually the work of the accuser but ordained by the Lord to accomplish a higher purpose. Job could not understand why God had allowed such extreme torment to come to him. God was not listening to his plea for justice (vv. 7–8) but was stripping him of honor and attacking him (vv. 9–12) to the point that he felt ashamed before others (vv. 13–20).

19:13 [j]Ps 69:8 [k]Job 16:7; Ps 88:8

13 "He has alienated my brothers[j] from me;
my acquaintances are completely estranged from me.[k]
14 My kinsmen have gone away;
my friends have forgotten me.
15 My guests and my maidservants count me a stranger;
they look upon me as an alien.
16 I summon my servant, but he does not answer,
though I beg him with my own mouth.
17 My breath is offensive to my wife;
I am loathsome to my own brothers.

19:18 [l]2Ki 2:23

18 Even the little boys[l] scorn me;
when I appear, they ridicule me.

19:19 [m]Ps 55:12-13 [n]Ps 38:11

19 All my intimate friends[m] detest me;[n]
those I love have turned against me.

19:20 [o]Job 33:21; Ps 102:5

20 I am nothing but skin and bones;[o]
I have escaped with only the skin of my teeth.[a]

21 "Have pity on me, my friends, have pity,
for the hand of God has struck me.

19:22 [p]Job 13:25; 16:11 [q]Ps 69:26

22 Why do you pursue[p] me as God does?
Will you never get enough of my flesh?[q]

19:23 [r]Isa 30:8

23 "Oh, that my words were recorded,
that they were written on a scroll,[r]
24 that they were inscribed with an iron tool on[b] lead,
or engraved in rock forever!

19:25 [s]Ps 78:35; Pr 23:11; Isa 43:14; Jer 50:34 [t]Job 16:19

25 I know that my Redeemer[c][s] lives,[t]
and that in the end he will stand upon the earth.[d]

19:26 [u]Ps 17:15; Mt 5:8; 1Co 13:12; 1Jn 3:2

26 And after my skin has been destroyed,
yet[e] in[f] my flesh I will see God;[u]
27 I myself will see him
with my own eyes—I, and not another.

19:27 [v]Ps 73:26

How my heart yearns[v] within me!

28 "If you say, 'How we will hound him,
since the root of the trouble lies in him,[g]'

19:29 [w]Job 15:22 [x]Job 22:4; Ps 1:5; 9:7

29 you should fear the sword yourselves;
for wrath will bring punishment by the sword,[w]
and then you will know that there is judgment.[h]"[x]

[a] 20 Or *only my gums* [b] 24 Or *and* [c] 25 Or *defender* [d] 25 Or *upon my grave* [e] 26 Or *And after I awake, / though this ⌊body⌋ has been destroyed, / then* [f] 26 Or */ apart from* [g] 28 Many Hebrew manuscripts, Septuagint and Vulgate; most Hebrew manuscripts *me* [h] 29 Or */ that you may come to know the Almighty*

■ **19:21–29** *Appeal and Warnings.* The counselors had reduced God and his actions to an impersonal formula. They were incapable of understanding the agony of Job's predicament or of showing him any mercy. Job appealed to them by reaffirming his abiding faith, and he warned them of the consequences of their actions.

19:21 Have pity. Compare 6:14. Job needed heartfelt friendship, but nothing of the sort was possible from his "friends," who only added to his misery.

19:23–24 engraved in rock forever. Job had an important message that he wanted permanently inscribed for posterity (see Hab 2:2). Even through all of his suffering he had not entirely lost his hope. His faith in a future vindication remained strong.

19:25 I know that my Redeemer lives. The word *Redeemer* can be rendered "Champion," "Avenger," "Guarantor," "Vindicator" or "Kinsman-Redeemer." Who was this person? If God were Job's enemy, as he imagined, then he certainly needed a mediator, a vindicator, a champion. Although the readers know from the prologue that God was not Job's enemy and that in the end God did become his vindicator (42:7), Job hoped for a heavenly third party to represent his case (see 9:33–34; 16:18–21). The fuller revelation of the New Testament shows that this advocate is none other than Jesus Christ (1Ti 2:5). **the end.** Not necessarily "the end time"; the whole phrase could be rendered "afterward," indicating that Job was simply thinking of the end of his life, or that he did not know when his defense would come—only that it would be later. **he will stand.** That is, he will defend Job.

19:26–27 after my skin has been destroyed. Literally, "after my skin they have struck off—this." It may be that "this" referred to the ravages of his disease. The precise meaning of these words is somewhat uncertain, though the NIV gives the general sense. **in my flesh.** The meaning of the preposition translated *in* can be either "in" (my flesh), as in the NIV, or "apart from." Since the book of Job does touch in chapter 14 on the idea of resurrection, it seems likely that, if Job was speaking of his death in the first part of this verse, then resurrection was in mind here and the translation of the preposition should be "in." It is certain that Job believed he had a Kinsman-Redeemer who loved him and for whom his heart yearned. The whole passage is strongly evocative of every sinner's need of a divine-human mediator. See *WCF* 32.2; *WLC* 86; *WSC* 37.

19:28 root of the trouble. Job's friends were wrong. His statement of faith in the midst of suffering (vv. 23–27) proved that he was not the problem.

19:29 sword . . . punishment . . . judgment. The insensitive and false accusations of Job's friends had to stop or the friends would be subject to divine justice (see 42:7–9).

Zophar

20

Then Zophar the Naamathite replied:

2 "My troubled thoughts prompt me to answer
because I am greatly disturbed.
3 I hear a rebuke[y] that dishonors me,
and my understanding inspires me to reply.

4 "Surely you know how it has been from of old,
ever since man[a] was placed on the earth,
5 that the mirth of the wicked is brief,
the joy of the godless lasts but a moment.[z]
6 Though his pride reaches to the heavens
and his head touches the clouds,[a]
7 he will perish forever,[b] like his own dung;
those who have seen him will say, 'Where is he?'[c]
8 Like a dream[d] he flies away,[e] no more to be found,
banished[f] like a vision of the night.[g]
9 The eye that saw him will not see him again;
his place will look on him no more.[h]
10 His children[i] must make amends to the poor;
his own hands must give back his wealth.[j]
11 The youthful vigor[k] that fills his bones
will lie with him in the dust.[l]

12 "Though evil is sweet in his mouth
and he hides it under his tongue,
13 though he cannot bear to let it go
and keeps it in his mouth,[m]
14 yet his food will turn sour in his stomach;
it will become the venom of serpents within him.
15 He will spit out the riches he swallowed;
God will make his stomach vomit them up.
16 He will suck the poison[n] of serpents;
the fangs of an adder will kill him.[o]
17 He will not enjoy the streams,
the rivers flowing with honey[p] and cream.[q]
18 What he toiled for he must give back uneaten;
he will not enjoy the profit from his trading.
19 For he has oppressed the poor and left them destitute;[r]
he has seized houses he did not build.

20 "Surely he will have no respite from his craving;[s]
he cannot save himself by his treasure.
21 Nothing is left for him to devour;
his prosperity will not endure.[t]
22 In the midst of his plenty, distress will overtake him;
the full force of misery will come upon him.
23 When he has filled his belly,
God will vent his burning anger against him
and rain down his blows upon him.[u]
24 Though he flees[v] from an iron weapon,
a bronze-tipped arrow pierces him.
25 He pulls it out of his back,
the gleaming point out of his liver.

20:3 [y]Job 19:3
20:5 [z]Job 8:12; Ps 37:35-36; 73:19
20:6 [a]Isa 14:13-14; Ob 1:3-4
20:7 [b]Job 4:20 [c]Job 7:10; 8:18
20:8 [d]Ps 73:20 [e]Job 27:21-23 [f]Job 18:18 [g]Ps 90:5
20:9 [h]Job 7:8
20:10 [i]Job 5:4 [j]Job 27:16-17
20:11 [k]Job 13:26 [l]Job 21:26
20:13 [m]Nu 11:18-20
20:16 [n]Dt 32:32 [o]Dt 32:24
20:17 [p]Dt 32:13 [q]Job 29:6
20:19 [r]Job 24:4, 14; 35:9
20:20 [s]Ecc 5:12-14
20:21 [t]Job 15:29
20:23 [u]Ps 78:30-31
20:24 [v]Isa 24:18; Am 5:19

[a] 4 Or *Adam*

■ **20:1–29** *Zophar.* Chapter 20 is another eloquent statement of the fate of the wicked. In it, Zophar expressed the truth of the moral governance of the world by God, but he failed to apply it correctly in Job's case. He expressed personal offense (vv. 1–3) and again affirmed proverbial wisdom (vv. 4–29).

■ **20:1–3** *Personal Offense.* Zophar began by admitting that Job had personally offended him with his responses.

20:2 I am greatly disturbed. Job's closing words in 19:28–29 were not lost on Zophar.

■ **20:4–29** *Affirmation of Proverbial Wisdom.* Zophar explained the ways of the righteous and the wicked from traditional proverbial wisdom: The two groups follow distinct ways with distinct results.

20:19 See *WLC* 142.

Terrors[w] will come over him;[x]
26 total darkness[y] lies in wait for his treasures.
A fire unfanned will consume him[z]
and devour what is left in his tent.
27 The heavens will expose his guilt;
the earth will rise up against him.[a]
28 A flood will carry off his house,[b]
rushing waters[a] on the day of God's wrath.[c]
29 Such is the fate God allots the wicked,
the heritage appointed for them by God."[d]

Job 21

Then Job replied:

2 "Listen carefully to my words;
let this be the consolation you give me.
3 Bear with me while I speak,
and after I have spoken, mock on.[e]

4 "Is my complaint directed to man?
Why should I not be impatient?[f]
5 Look at me and be astonished;
clap your hand over your mouth.[g]
6 When I think about this, I am terrified;
trembling seizes my body.
7 Why do the wicked live on,
growing old and increasing in power?[h]
8 They see their children established around them,
their offspring before their eyes.[i]
9 Their homes are safe and free from fear;[j]
the rod of God is not upon them.
10 Their bulls never fail to breed;
their cows calve and do not miscarry.[k]
11 They send forth their children as a flock;
their little ones dance about.
12 They sing to the music of tambourine and harp;
they make merry to the sound of the flute.[l]
13 They spend their years in prosperity[m]
and go down to the grave[b] in peace.[c]
14 Yet they say to God, 'Leave us alone![n]
We have no desire to know your ways.[o]
15 Who is the Almighty, that we should serve him?
What would we gain by praying to him?'[p]
16 But their prosperity is not in their own hands,
so I stand aloof from the counsel of the wicked.

17 "Yet how often is the lamp of the wicked snuffed out?[q]
How often does calamity come upon them,
the fate God allots in his anger?

20:25 [w]Job 18:11 [x]Job 16:13
20:26 [y]Job 18:18 [z]Ps 21:9
20:27 [a]Dt 31:28
20:28 [b]Dt 28:31 [c]Job 21:17, 20, 30
20:29 [d]Job 27:13
21:3 [e]Job 16:10
21:4 [f]Job 6:11
21:5 [g]Jdg 18:19; Job 29:9; 40:4
21:7 [h]Job 12:6; Ps 73:3; Jer 12:1; Hab 1:13
21:8 [i]Ps 17:14
21:9 [j]Ps 73:5
21:10 [k]Ex 23:26
21:12 [l]Ps 81:2
21:13 [m]Job 36:11
21:14 [n]Job 22:17 [o]Pr 1:29
21:15 [p]Ex 5:2; Job 34:9; Mal 3:14
21:17 [q]Job 18:5

[a] *28* Or *The possessions in his house will be carried off, / washed away* [b] *13* Hebrew *Sheol* [c] *13* Or *in an instant*

20:29 Such is the fate God allots the wicked. What Zophar taught will happen in the future, but he expressed no awareness of the anomalies of human experience here and now. He simplistically insisted that people suffer because they deserve it and receive God's blessing only by earning it.

■ **21:1–34** *Job's Reply to Zophar.* Job closed this second cycle with a firm rejection of the friends' arguments that the wicked always suffer, alluding to their very words (cf. 20:11 with 21:7; 8:19 with 21:8; 18:5 with 21:17; 5:4 and 20:10 with 21:19; 20:5–7 with 21:28–30).

■ **21:1–3** *An Appeal to Be Heard.* The consolation Job desired was simply a momentary audience.

■ **21:4–34** *Rejection of Zophar's Views.* Job knew that Zophar's description of the righteous and wicked was inadequate (see 20:4–29).

21:5 Look at me and be astonished; clap your hand over your mouth. He wanted them to observe his condition and allow its awfulness to silence their attacks. Job wanted them to exhibit compassion by simply listening to him.

21:7–15 spend their years in prosperity and go down to the grave in peace. Bildad had claimed that the wicked have no descendants to remember them. But Job contended that those who flatly reject God (v. 14) often have happy and joyous lives characterized by domestic tranquility.

21:7 Why do the wicked live on . . . ? Job admitted that he was nonplussed. The counselors, on the other hand, believed that they saw the truth with clarity.

21:14–15 See *WCF* 16.7; *WLC* 192.

18 How often are they like straw before the wind,
like chaff[r] swept away by a gale?
19 ⌊It is said,⌋ 'God stores up a man's punishment for his sons.'[s]
Let him repay the man himself, so that he will know it!
20 Let his own eyes see his destruction;
let him drink[t] of the wrath of the Almighty.[a u]
21 For what does he care about the family he leaves behind
when his allotted months[v] come to an end?

22 "Can anyone teach knowledge to God,[w]
since he judges even the highest?[x]
23 One man dies in full vigor,
completely secure and at ease,
24 his body[b] well nourished,
his bones rich with marrow.[y]
25 Another man dies in bitterness of soul,
never having enjoyed anything good.
26 Side by side they lie in the dust,
and worms cover them both.[z]

27 "I know full well what you are thinking,
the schemes by which you would wrong me.
28 You say, 'Where now is the great man's[a] house,
the tents where wicked men lived?'[b]
29 Have you never questioned those who travel?
Have you paid no regard to their accounts—
30 that the evil man is spared from the day of calamity,[c]
that he is delivered from[c] the day of wrath?[d]
31 Who denounces his conduct to his face?
Who repays him for what he has done?
32 He is carried to the grave,
and watch is kept over his tomb.
33 The soil in the valley is sweet to him;[e]
all men follow after him,
and a countless throng goes[d] before him.[f]

34 "So how can you console me[g] with your nonsense?
Nothing is left of your answers but falsehood!"

Eliphaz

22

Then Eliphaz the Temanite replied:

2 "Can a man be of benefit to God?[h]
Can even a wise man benefit him?
3 What pleasure would it give the Almighty if you were righteous?
What would he gain if your ways were blameless?

4 "Is it for your piety that he rebukes you
and brings charges against you?[i]
5 Is not your wickedness great?
Are not your sins[j] endless?

21:18 [r]Job 13:25; Ps 1:4
21:19 [s]Ex 20:5; Jer 31:29; Eze 18:2
21:20 [t]Ps 75:8; Isa 51:17 [u]Jer 25:15; Rev 14:10
21:21 [v]Job 14:5
21:22 [w]Job 35:11; 36:22; Isa 40:13-14; Ro 11:34 [x]Ps 82:1
21:24 [y]Pr 3:8
21:26 [z]Job 24:20; Ecc 9:2-3; Isa 14:11
21:28 [a]Job 1:3; 12:21; 31:37 [b]Job 8:22
21:30 [c]Pr 16:4 [d]Job 20:22,28; 2Pe 2:9
21:33 [e]Job 3:22; 17:16; 24:21 [f]Job 3:19
21:34 [g]Job 16:2
22:2 [h]Lk 17:10
22:4 [i]Job 14:3; 19:29; Ps 143:2
22:5 [j]Job 11:6; 15:5

a *17–20* Verses 17 and 18 may be taken as exclamations and 19 and 20 as declarations.
b *24* The meaning of the Hebrew for this word is uncertain. c *30* Or *man is reserved for the day of calamity, / that he is brought forth to* d *33* Or */ as a countless throng went*

21:22 Can anyone teach knowledge to God . . . ? Job's high view of God only made his problem more perplexing.

■ **22:1—26:14** *The Third Cycle of Speeches.* The third cycle of dialogue between Job and his counselors brings the discussions to a close. Perhaps to indicate that Job has confounded his friends, this portion omits a third speech by Zophar (cf. 11:1–20; 20:1–29) but presents the words of Eliphaz (22:1–30) and Bildad (25:1–6), as well as Job's responses to them (23:1—24:25; 26:1–14).

■ **22:1–30** *Eliphaz.* The third cycle of speeches includes a reaction to Job's belief in God's indifference (vv. 1–5), a list of Job's sins (vv. 6–11), corrections for Job (vv. 12–14), an affirmation of proverbial wisdom (vv. 15–20) and a call for him to repent (vv. 21–30).

■ **22:1–5** *Divine Indifference.* Eliphaz reacted to Job's statement that God allows wickedness to go unpunished, but he went to the opposite extreme, suggesting that nothing humans do has any effect on God.

22:2–3 See *WCF* 2.2; 7.1; 16.5.

22:3 What pleasure would it give the Almighty if you were righteous? An alternate translation might be, "Would it please the Almighty if you were vindicated?"

22:5 Are not your sins endless? Eliphaz reached the same conclusion that Zophar and Bildad had already expressed—that Job's sins were never-ending.

6 You demanded security[k] from your brothers for no reason;
you stripped men of their clothing, leaving them naked.
7 You gave no water to the weary
and you withheld food from the hungry,[l]
8 though you were a powerful man, owning land—
an honored man,[m] living on it.
9 And you sent widows away empty-handed[n]
and broke the strength of the fatherless.
10 That is why snares are all around you,
why sudden peril terrifies you,
11 why it is so dark[o] you cannot see,
and why a flood of water covers you.[p]

12 "Is not God in the heights of heaven?[q]
And see how lofty are the highest stars!
13 Yet you say, 'What does God know?[r]
Does he judge through such darkness?[s]
14 Thick clouds[t] veil him, so he does not see us
as he goes about in the vaulted heavens.'
15 Will you keep to the old path
that evil men have trod?
16 They were carried off before their time,[u]
their foundations washed away by a flood.[v]
17 They said to God, 'Leave us alone!
What can the Almighty do to us?'[w]
18 Yet it was he who filled their houses with good things,[x]
so I stand aloof from the counsel of the wicked.[y]

19 "The righteous see their ruin and rejoice;[z]
the innocent mock[a] them, saying,
20 'Surely our foes are destroyed,
and fire[b] devours their wealth.'

21 "Submit to God and be at peace with him;
in this way prosperity will come to you.[c]
22 Accept instruction from his mouth
and lay up his words in your heart.
23 If you return[d] to the Almighty, you will be restored:[e]
If you remove wickedness far from your tent[f]
24 and assign your nuggets to the dust,
your gold of Ophir to the rocks in the ravines,[g]
25 then the Almighty will be your gold,
the choicest silver for you.[h]
26 Surely then you will find delight in the Almighty[i]
and will lift up your face to God.
27 You will pray to him,[j] and he will hear you,
and you will fulfill your vows.
28 What you decide on will be done,
and light will shine on your ways.
29 When men are brought low and you say, 'Lift them up!'
then he will save the downcast.[k]
30 He will deliver even one who is not innocent,
who will be delivered through the cleanness of your hands."[l]

22:6 [k]Ex 22:26; Dt 24:6, 17; Eze 18:12, 16
22:7 [l]Job 31:17, 21, 31
22:8 [m]Isa 3:3; 9:15
22:9 [n]Job 24:3, 21
22:11 [o]Job 5:14 [p]Ps 69:1-2; 124:4-5; La 3:54
22:12 [q]Job 11:8
22:13 [r]Ps 10:11; Isa 29:15 [s]Eze 8:12
22:14 [t]Job 26:9
22:16 [u]Job 15:32 [v]Job 14:19; Mt 7:26-27
22:17 [w]Job 21:15
22:18 [x]Job 12:6 [y]Job 21:16
22:19 [z]Ps 58:10; 107:42 [a]Ps 52:6
22:20 [b]Job 15:30
22:21 [c]Ps 34:8-10
22:23 [d]Job 8:5; Isa 31:6; Zec 1:3 [e]Isa 19:22; Ac 20:32 [f]Job 11:14
22:24 [g]Job 31:25
22:25 [h]Isa 33:6
22:26 [i]Job 27:10; Isa 58:14
22:27 [j]Job 33:26; 34:28; Isa 58:9
22:29 [k]Mt 23:12; 1Pe 5:5
22:30 [l]Job 42:7-8

■ **22:6–11** *Accusations Against Job.* This was a direct personal attack on Job for specific sins, especially social abuses against the poor and widows. Later Job would emphasize his social righteousness (chs. 29; 31).

■ **22:12–14** *Correction of Job.* Eliphaz refuted Job's complaint that God was absent (cf. 9:18; 13:24). In his suffering-induced state of emotional instability, Job complained that God was either too observant—too present and unwilling to leave him alone (7:17–19; 10:8; 16:9)—or altogether absent.

■ **22:15–20** *Affirmation of Proverbial Wisdom.* Eliphaz contrasted the ways in which the wicked and the righteous respond to God.

■ **22:21–30** *Call to Repentance.* As the counselors had done so often before, Eliphaz called on Job to repent of behaving like the wicked. Job, he stressed, should call out to God, and God would deliver him. Eliphaz spoke proverbial truth about the ways of God toward those who repent, but once again he demonstrated a complete lack of insight into Job's particular circumstances.

Job

23

Then Job replied:

2 "Even today my complaint[m] is bitter;[n]
his hand[a] is heavy in spite of[b] my groaning.
3 If only I knew where to find him;
if only I could go to his dwelling!
4 I would state my case[o] before him
and fill my mouth with arguments.
5 I would find out what he would answer me,
and consider what he would say.
6 Would he oppose me with great power?[p]
No, he would not press charges against me.
7 There an upright man could present his case before him,[q]
and I would be delivered forever from my judge.

8 "But if I go to the east, he is not there;
if I go to the west, I do not find him.
9 When he is at work in the north, I do not see him;
when he turns to the south, I catch no glimpse of him.[r]
10 But he knows the way that I take;
when he has tested me,[s] I will come forth as gold.[t]
11 My feet have closely followed his steps;[u]
I have kept to his way without turning aside.[v]
12 I have not departed from the commands of his lips;[w]
I have treasured the words of his mouth more than my daily
bread.[x]

13 "But he stands alone, and who can oppose him?
He does whatever he pleases.[y]
14 He carries out his decree against me,
and many such plans he still has in store.[z]
15 That is why I am terrified before him;
when I think of all this, I fear him.
16 God has made my heart faint;[a]
the Almighty[b] has terrified me.
17 Yet I am not silenced by the darkness,[c]
by the thick darkness that covers my face.

24

"Why does the Almighty not set times for judgment?[d]
Why must those who know him look in vain for such days?[e]
2 Men move boundary stones;[f]
they pasture flocks they have stolen.
3 They drive away the orphan's donkey
and take the widow's ox in pledge.[g]
4 They thrust the needy from the path
and force all the poor[h] of the land into hiding.[i]
5 Like wild donkeys in the desert,
the poor go about their labor[j] of foraging food;
the wasteland provides food for their children.

23:2 [m]Job 7:11 [n]Job 6:3
23:4 [o]Job 13:18
23:6 [p]Job 9:4
23:7 [q]Job 13:3
23:9 [r]Job 9:11
23:10 [s]Ps 66:10; 139:1-3 [t]1Pe 1:7
23:11 [u]Ps 17:5 [v]Ps 44:18
23:12 [w]Job 6:10 [x]Jn 4:32, 34
23:13 [y]Ps 115:3
23:14 [z]1Th 3:3
23:16 [a]Dt 20:3; Ps 22:14; Jer 51:46 [b]Job 27:2
23:17 [c]Job 19:8
24:1 [d]Jer 46:10 [e]Ac 1:7
24:2 [f]Dt 19:14; 27:17; Pr 23:10
24:3 [g]Dt 24:6, 10, 12, 17; Job 22:6
24:4 [h]Job 29:12; 30:25; Ps 41:1 [i]Pr 28:28
24:5 [j]Ps 104:23

[a] 2 Septuagint and Syriac; Hebrew / *the hand on me* [b] 2 Or *heavy on me in*

■ **23:1—24:25** *Job's Reply to Eliphaz.* Job protested that if God were to hear his case, God would not condemn him. His response touched on the themes of his inability to find God (23:1–9), God's control over all (23:10–17), injustices (24:1–12) and justice for the wicked (24:13–25).

■ **23:1–9** *God's Absence.* Job declared that he had futilely searched for God in order that he might speak with him.

23:7 I would be delivered. Job remained convinced that if he had the opportunity to be heard in heaven, God would not condemn him. Yet he apparently could not reach heaven or find a way to confer directly with God about his case.

23:8 I catch no glimpse of him. Job's God is invisible but has an all-seeing eye (v. 10).

■ **23:10–17** *God's Control.* Job affirmed that God is sovereign over the world.

23:13 He does whatever he pleases. Job never questioned the sovereign freedom of God. His acknowledgement of God's sovereignty over his creation was the root of his dilemma (9:21–24). Verse 13 is a strong affirmation of monotheism.

■ **24:1–12** *Injustices in the World.* These verses point out the cruelties people inflict on each other while God ostensibly does nothing. The descriptions here are of some of the most devastating tragedies people experience.

24:1 not set times for judgment. In effect, Job wondered why God does not regularly intervene in the world to right its wrongs and injustices. He recognized that the meting out of justice against the wicked does not operate mechanically in this world, but according to God's prerogative.

6 They gather fodder in the fields
and glean in the vineyards of the wicked.
7 Lacking clothes, they spend the night naked;
they have nothing to cover themselves in the cold.[k]
8 They are drenched by mountain rains
and hug[l] the rocks for lack of shelter.
9 The fatherless[m] child is snatched from the breast;
the infant of the poor is seized for a debt.
10 Lacking clothes, they go about naked;
they carry the sheaves, but still go hungry.
11 They crush olives among the terraces[a];
they tread the winepresses, yet suffer thirst.
12 The groans of the dying rise from the city,
and the souls of the wounded cry out for help.[n]
But God charges no one with wrongdoing.[o]

13 "There are those who rebel against the light,[p]
who do not know its ways
or stay in its paths.[q]
14 When daylight is gone, the murderer rises up
and kills the poor and needy;
in the night he steals forth like a thief.[r]
15 The eye of the adulterer watches for dusk;[s]
he thinks, 'No eye will see me,'[t]
and he keeps his face concealed.
16 In the dark, men break into houses,[u]
but by day they shut themselves in;
they want nothing to do with the light.[v]
17 For all of them, deep darkness is their morning[b];
they make friends with the terrors of darkness.[c]

18 "Yet they are foam[w] on the surface of the water;[x]
their portion of the land is cursed,
so that no one goes to the vineyards.
19 As heat and drought snatch away the melted snow,[y]
so the grave[d][z] snatches away those who have sinned.
20 The womb forgets them,
the worm feasts on them;
evil men are no longer remembered[a]
but are broken like a tree.[b]
21 They prey on the barren and childless woman,
and to the widow show no kindness.[c]
22 But God drags away the mighty by his power;
though they become established, they have no assurance of
life.[d]
23 He may let them rest in a feeling of security,[e]
but his eyes are on their ways.[f]
24 For a little while they are exalted, and then they are gone;[g]
they are brought low and gathered up like all others;
they are cut off like heads of grain.[h]

25 "If this is not so, who can prove me false
and reduce my words to nothing?"[i]

24:7 [k]Ex 22:27; Job 22:6
24:8 [l]La 4:5
24:9 [m]Dt 24:17
24:12 [n]Eze 26:15 [o]Job 9:23
24:13 [p]Jn 3:19-20 [q]Isa 5:20
24:14 [r]Ps 10:9
24:15 [s]Pr 7:8-9 [t]Ps 10:11
24:16 [u]Ex 22:2; Mt 6:19 [v]Jn 3:20
24:18 [w]Job 9:26 [x]Job 22:16
24:19 [y]Job 6:17 [z]Job 21:13
24:20 [a]Job 18:17; Pr 10:7 [b]Ps 31:12; Da 4:14
24:21 [c]Job 22:9
24:22 [d]Dt 28:66
24:23 [e]Job 12:6 [f]Job 11:11
24:24 [g]Job 14:21; Ps 37:10 [h]Isa 17:5
24:25 [i]Job 6:28; 27:4

a *11* Or *olives between the millstones*; the meaning of the Hebrew for this word is uncertain. b *17* Or *them, their morning is like the shadow of death* c *17* Or *of the shadow of death* d *19* Hebrew *Sheol*

■ **24:13–25** *Justice for the Wicked.* Job agreed with his friends about what ought to happen to the wicked; his problem was that often circumstances didn't follow this pattern. He insisted that it is careless to judge a person's righteousness or unrighteousness simply on the basis of his or her level of prosperity.

24:13–17 While no one doubts that the wicked should be punished, they frequently appear to escape justice.

24:18–25 Despite the temporary prosperity of the wicked, God will eventually bring them to ruin, even if only after death. It is also legitimate to translate these verses as Job's call for redress against evildoers (e.g., "May their portion of the land be cursed . . . may the grave snatch away").

24:23–25 He may let them rest . . . but his eyes are on their ways. These verses must be connected with verse 1 in order to understand the point of the chapter. Job was trying to show that the wicked are indeed punished but that the process takes place little by little (vv. 23–24)—a frustration for the righteous, who want to see justice meted out completely and summarily.

Bildad

25 Then Bildad the Shuhite replied:

2 "Dominion and awe belong to God;[j]
he establishes order in the heights of heaven.
3 Can his forces be numbered?
Upon whom does his light not rise?[k]
4 How then can a man be righteous before God?
How can one born of woman be pure?[l]
5 If even the moon[m] is not bright
and the stars are not pure in his eyes,[n]
6 how much less man, who is but a maggot—
a son of man,[o] who is only a worm!"[p]

Job

26 Then Job replied:

2 "How you have helped the powerless![q]
How you have saved the arm that is feeble![r]
3 What advice you have offered to one without wisdom!
And what great insight you have displayed!
4 Who has helped you utter these words?
And whose spirit spoke from your mouth?

5 "The dead are in deep anguish,[s]
those beneath the waters and all that live in them.
6 Death[a][t] is naked before God;
Destruction[b] lies uncovered.[u]
7 He spreads out the northern ⌊skies⌋[v] over empty space;
he suspends the earth over nothing.
8 He wraps up the waters[w] in his clouds,[x]
yet the clouds do not burst under their weight.
9 He covers the face of the full moon,
spreading his clouds[y] over it.
10 He marks out the horizon on the face of the waters[z]
for a boundary between light and darkness.[a]
11 The pillars of the heavens quake,
aghast at his rebuke.
12 By his power he churned up the sea;[b]

25:2 [j]Job 9:4; Rev 1:6
25:3 [k]Jas 1:17
25:4 [l]Job 4:17; 14:4
25:5 [m]Job 31:26 [n]Job 15:15
25:6 [o]Job 7:17 [p]Ps 22:6
26:2 [q]Job 6:12 [r]Ps 71:9
26:5 [s]Ps 88:10
26:6 [t]Ps 139:8 [u]Job 41:11; Pr 15:11; Heb 4:13
26:7 [v]Job 9:8
26:8 [w]Pr 30:4 [x]Job 37:11
26:9 [y]Job 22:14; Ps 97:2
26:10 [z]Pr 8:27,29 [a]Job 38:8-11
26:12 [b]Ex 14:21; Isa 51:15; Jer 31:35

[a] 6 Hebrew *Sheol* [b] 6 Hebrew *Abaddon*

■ **25:1–6** *Bildad: God's Glory and Humanity's Insignificance.* Bildad attempted to answer Job. Job argued that God neglects justice for both the great and small of humanity. Bildad responded with an inadequate assessment of God's view of humanity.

25:2 Dominion and awe. Bildad told part of the truth when he affirmed that God is supreme and sovereign, but his concept of humanity was twisted.

25:4 can a man be righteous before God? If God is so far above the human race, how can any sinful person be considered righteous? Bildad failed to account for divine mercy and grace toward the human race.

25:6 man, who is but a maggot . . . only a worm! Bildad overstated the depth of human worthlessness. This was his way of dealing with the problem of evil. God cannot be questioned in what he does because humans are so worthless. Although experience might sometimes incline us to accept this view of humanity, it is not what Scripture teaches. Even in its sin humanity retains the image of God, which affords dignity and value to each individual (see Ge 1:26–29). Bildad's view stands in contrast to that of Psalm 8:4, which admits that humans are infinitesimal compared to the heavenly bodies but goes on to assert that God has nonetheless crowned humanity with great glory and honor (vv. 5–9). Because human beings are not maggots in God's eyes, injustices in the world still raise impenetrable questions about God's justice.

■ **26:1–14** *Job's Reply to Bildad.* Job affirmed the supremacy of God in response to Bildad's implicit objection that Job did not acknowledge God's power (ch. 25). There are two distinct parts of chapter 26: Job's sarcastic rejection of Bildad's counsel (vv. 1–4) and Job's affirmation of God's supremacy (vv. 5–14). The rhetorical questions of verses 1–4 end with Job's suggestion that his counselors were inspired by an outside source. The prologue implies that the accuser played a role in writing their material (2:6).

■ **26:1–4** *Sarcastic Rejection.* In a series of rhetorical questions, Job sarcastically rejected Bildad's assessment of the human predicament. Bildad's outlook helped no one.

■ **26:5–14** *Affirmation of God's Supremacy.* Job celebrated God's preeminence to counter Bildad's objection (ch. 25). Job's words are reminiscent of those he had spoken in 9:5–10, so they should not be assigned to one of the counselors. Job's objections did not imply a denial of divine sovereignty over creation.

26:5–6 Death is naked. Unlike the Canaanite gods, each of whom had a domain of power, the true God is the Lord even of Sheol (cf. Pr 15:11), the supposed domain of Mot, the god of death. See 28:22.

26:7–8 he suspends the earth over nothing. Job spoke poetically from the perspective of an earthly observer. His purpose was not to teach scientific cosmography or meteorology but to express his amazement at the mystery of what he saw in nature as the work of God.

26:9 the full moon. An alternate translation is "his throne" (cf. Ps 104:3–13; Am 9:6).

26:10 a boundary. The horizon.

26:11 The pillars. The mountains, which often extend into the clouds, appearing to support the heavens.

26:12 churned up the sea. God's limitless power and dominion

26:12 [c]Job 12:13
26:13 [d]Isa 27:1
26:14 [e]Job 36:29
27:1 [f]Job 29:1
27:2 [g]Job 34:5 [h]Job 9:18
27:3 [i]Job 32:8; 33:4
27:4 [j]Job 6:28
27:5 [k]Job 2:9; 13:15
27:6 [l]Job 2:3
27:8 [m]Job 8:13 [n]Job 11:20; Lk 12:20
27:9 [o]Job 35:12; Pr 1:28; Isa 1:15; Jer 14:12; Mic 3:4
27:10 [p]Job 22:26
27:13 [q]Job 15:20; 20:29
27:14 [r]Dt 28:41; Job 15:22; Hos 9:13 [s]Job 20:10
27:15 [t]Ps 78:64
27:16 [u]Zec 9:3
27:17 [v]Pr 28:8; Ecc 2:26
27:18 [w]Job 8:14 [x]Isa 1:8
27:19 [y]Job 7:8
27:20 [z]Job 15:21 [a]Job 20:8

by his wisdom[c] he cut Rahab to pieces.
13 By his breath the skies became fair;
his hand pierced the gliding serpent.[d]
14 And these are but the outer fringe of his works;
how faint the whisper we hear of him!
Who then can understand the thunder of his power?"[e]

27 And Job continued his discourse:[f]

2 "As surely as God lives, who has denied me justice,[g]
the Almighty, who has made me taste bitterness of soul,[h]
3 as long as I have life within me,
the breath of God[i] in my nostrils,
4 my lips will not speak wickedness,
and my tongue will utter no deceit.[j]
5 I will never admit you are in the right;
till I die, I will not deny my integrity.[k]
6 I will maintain my righteousness and never let go of it;
my conscience will not reproach me as long as I live.[l]

7 "May my enemies be like the wicked,
my adversaries like the unjust!
8 For what hope has the godless[m] when he is cut off,
when God takes away his life?[n]
9 Does God listen to his cry
when distress comes upon him?[o]
10 Will he find delight in the Almighty?[p]
Will he call upon God at all times?

11 "I will teach you about the power of God;
the ways of the Almighty I will not conceal.
12 You have all seen this yourselves.
Why then this meaningless talk?

13 "Here is the fate God allots to the wicked,
the heritage a ruthless man receives from the Almighty:[q]
14 However many his children, their fate is the sword;[r]
his offspring will never have enough to eat.[s]
15 The plague will bury those who survive him,
and their widows will not weep for them.[t]
16 Though he heaps up silver like dust
and clothes like piles of clay,[u]
17 what he lays up the righteous will wear,[v]
and the innocent will divide his silver.
18 The house he builds is like a moth's cocoon,[w]
like a hut[x] made by a watchman.
19 He lies down wealthy, but will do so no more;[y]
when he opens his eyes, all is gone.
20 Terrors overtake him like a flood;[z]
a tempest snatches him away in the night.[a]

over the domain of Yam, the Canaanite sea god. **Rahab.** A Canaanite monster of the deep, like Leviathan (see 3:8; 41:1). This poetic imagery enriches the concept of God's great power over the boisterous sea. God demonstrated his power over these demonic powers and the spheres of their supposed influence at creation (Ge 1:1–2), when he delivered Israel from Egypt through the sea (see Ps 89:9–10; Isa 51:9) and when Jesus calmed the sea (Mt 8:23–27). He has also pledged to do so again when he recreates the earth without any seas (Rev 21:1).
26:13–14 *WCF* 2.1; 4.1.
■ **27:1–23** *Job's Closing Discourse.* The opening words of verse 1 are different from those used at the beginning of each preceding speech, implying that this was Job's concluding comment, which structurally corresponds to his opening lament (3:1–26). This discourse divides into two parts: Job's protest of his innocence (vv. 1–12) and his affirmation of the fate of the wicked (vv. 13–23).
■ **27:1–12** *Protest of Innocence.* These words were directed at the counselors. With an oath founded on God's existence, Job denied their false accusations while at the same time asserting his integrity. Job could not have done this unless he really believed that God was just, despite his serious questioning into this matter (9:14–31; 16:7–14; 19:7–12).
27:5–6 See *WLC* 145.
27:7–10 May my enemies be like the wicked . . . Imprecations like these were used by the psalmists (Pss 109:6–15; 139:19–22). They are an honorable rhetorical device are still used in the Semitic world. This one served the purpose of condemning the wicked with strong language in order to stand unequivocally on God's side against evil.
■ **27:13–23** *The Fate of the Wicked.* Job turned to discuss the fate of the wicked, a topic overworked by the counselors. His comments show that he understood the issues as well as they did. However, at this point the counselors, not Job, were the implied objects of the destiny described.

[21] The east wind carries him off, and he is gone;
it sweeps him out of his place.[b]
[22] It hurls itself against him without mercy[c]
as he flees headlong from its power.[d]
[23] It claps its hands in derision
and hisses him out of his place.[e]

28

"There is a mine for silver
and a place where gold is refined.
[2] Iron is taken from the earth,
and copper is smelted from ore.[f]
[3] Man puts an end to the darkness;[g]
he searches the farthest recesses
for ore in the blackest darkness.
[4] Far from where people dwell he cuts a shaft,
in places forgotten by the foot of man;
far from men he dangles and sways.
[5] The earth, from which food comes,[h]
is transformed below as by fire;
[6] sapphires[a] come from its rocks,
and its dust contains nuggets of gold.
[7] No bird of prey knows that hidden path,
no falcon's eye has seen it.
[8] Proud beasts do not set foot on it,
and no lion prowls there.
[9] Man's hand assaults the flinty rock
and lays bare the roots of the mountains.
[10] He tunnels through the rock;
his eyes see all its treasures.
[11] He searches[b] the sources of the rivers
and brings hidden things to light.

[12] "But where can wisdom be found?[i]
Where does understanding dwell?
[13] Man does not comprehend its worth;[j]
it cannot be found in the land of the living.
[14] The deep says, 'It is not in me';
the sea says, 'It is not with me.'
[15] It cannot be bought with the finest gold,
nor can its price be weighed in silver.[k]
[16] It cannot be bought with the gold of Ophir,
with precious onyx or sapphires.
[17] Neither gold nor crystal can compare with it,
nor can it be had for jewels of gold.[l]
[18] Coral and jasper are not worthy of mention;
the price of wisdom is beyond rubies.[m]

27:21 [b]Job 7:10; 21:18
27:22 [c]Jer 13:14; Eze 5:11; 24:14 [d]Job 11:20
27:23 [e]Job 18:18
28:2 [f]Dt 8:9
28:3 [g]Ecc 1:13
28:5 [h]Ps 104:14
28:12 [i]Ecc 7:24
28:13 [j]Pr 3:15; Mt 13:44-46
28:15 [k]Pr 3:13-14; 8:10-11; 16:16
28:17 [l]Pr 16:16
28:18 [m]Pr 3:15

[a] *6* Or *lapis lazuli;* also in verse 16 [b] *11* Septuagint, Aquila and Vulgate; Hebrew *He dams up*

■ **28:1–28** *Interlude on Wisdom.* At this point, a different type of wisdom literature is introduced. Rather than dialogue, a wisdom poem appears, asking where true wisdom can be found. Job and his friends had searched in vain to understand Job's situation. His self-appointed advisers had relied on conventional wisdom with no allowance for the particularities of Job's experience, and Job had rejected their views with little else to offer except affirmations of basic truths about God and frustration with his circumstances. At this point, either Job or the writer of the book paused to reflect on the dialogues. This chapter divides into three parts: human abilities (vv. 1–11); human inability to discover divine wisdom (vv. 12–19); and God's exclusive possession of ultimate, comprehensive wisdom (vv. 20–28).

■ **28:1–11** *Human Abilities.* The poet expressed amazement at the human ability to unearth treasure by describing ancient mining techniques. He admitted that much had been accomplished.

28:3 end to the darkness. Miners brought light to the depths of the earth.

28:4 Far from where people dwell. Some of the greatest mines of the ancient Near East were in remote regions of deserts and mountain ranges. The poet was astounded that discoveries were made and mining developed in such out-of-the-way places.

28:7–8 No bird . . . no lion. Unlike human discoveries such as sources of water and salt deposits that animals find even before humans do, only people identify places to mine the treasures of the earth.

■ **28:12–19** *Human Limitations.* As impressive as human exploration and discovery may be, people cannot begin to fathom divine wisdom. The greatest human minds cannot discover or mine it. Just as Job and his friends had tried so diligently but unsuccessfully to verify God's wise understanding of Job's situation, so ultimate wisdom always remains elusive, beyond human grasp.

28:12 where can wisdom be found? This is the heart of this poem. Where is wisdom able to be discovered? See verse 20.

28:13–19 it cannot be found . . . it cannot be bought. Humans cannot attain full divine insight or wisdom, no matter where they go (vv. 13–14) or what amounts they are willing to pay (vv. 15–19).

28:19 [n]Pr 8:19
28:20 [o]ver 23,28
28:22 [p]Job 26:6
28:23 [q]Pr 8:22-31
28:24 [r]Ps 33:13-14 [s]Pr 15:3
28:25 [t]Job 12:15; Ps 135:7
28:26 [u]Job 37:3,8,11; 38:25,27
28:28 [v]Dt 4:6; Ps 111:10; Pr 1:7; 9:10
29:1 [w]Job 13:12; 27:1
29:2 [x]Jer 31:28
29:3 [y]Job 11:17
29:4 [z]Ps 25:14; Pr 3:32
29:6 [a]Job 20:17 [b]Ps 81:16 [c]Dt 32:13
29:7 [d]Job 31:21
29:9 [e]Job 21:5

19 The topaz of Cush cannot compare with it;
it cannot be bought with pure gold.[n]

20 "Where then does wisdom come from?
Where does understanding dwell?[o]
21 It is hidden from the eyes of every living thing,
concealed even from the birds of the air.
22 Destruction[a] [p] and Death say,
'Only a rumor of it has reached our ears.'
23 God understands the way to it
and he alone knows where it dwells,[q]
24 for he views the ends of the earth[r]
and sees everything under the heavens.[s]
25 When he established the force of the wind
and measured out the waters,[t]
26 when he made a decree for the rain
and a path for the thunderstorm,[u]
27 then he looked at wisdom and appraised it;
he confirmed it and tested it.
28 And he said to man,
'The fear of the Lord—that is wisdom,
and to shun evil is understanding.[v]' "

29

Job continued his discourse:[w]

2 "How I long for the months gone by,
for the days when God watched over me,[x]
3 when his lamp shone upon my head
and by his light I walked through darkness![y]
4 Oh, for the days when I was in my prime,
when God's intimate friendship blessed my house,[z]
5 when the Almighty was still with me
and my children were around me,
6 when my path was drenched with cream[a]
and the rock[b] poured out for me streams of olive oil.[c]

7 "When I went to the gate[d] of the city
and took my seat in the public square,
8 the young men saw me and stepped aside
and the old men rose to their feet;
9 the chief men refrained from speaking
and covered their mouths with their hands;[e]
10 the voices of the nobles were hushed,

a *22* Hebrew *Abaddon*

■ **28:20–28** *Divine Prerogatives.* Although no one knows how to discover wisdom, God epitomizes and personifies it (Pr 3:19–20). Through his revelation in Christ (Col 2:3) and through his word (Ps 111:10), God imparts some measure of wisdom to those who fear him, but he never reveals all (Dt 29:29; Jas 1:5).

28:21 birds of the air. From the perspective of ancient peoples, birds could see more than any other creature as they flew in the sky and looked down on the earth. Yet they could not perceive wisdom.

28:22 Destruction and Death. Here the mysterious world beyond human experience is personified, but "only a rumor" of wisdom's habitation is heard there. Surely it is far beyond human grasp. See 26:6.

28:26 a path for the thunderstorm. As in other cultures of the ancient world, divine wisdom was closely connected to the complex order of nature.

28:28 The fear of the Lord—that is wisdom. This cryptic statement constitutes the application of this poem. Human beings will always fall short of grasping the full extent of God's wisdom. Yet people can learn wisdom to the degree that they fear God and obey his commands (Dt 4:5–6; Pr 8:4–9; 9:10). Although ultimate answers to God's ways with his creation lie beyond human reach, the all-knowing God reveals how people should live. To hold fast to this revelation in fear and obedience is true human wisdom. Compare Psalm 111:10, Proverbs 9:10 and Ecclesiastes 12:13. See *WCF* 19.1.

■ **29:1—42:6** *The Monologues.* The dialogues of 3:1—27:23 are balanced by monologues that lead directly to the conclusion of the book. Three monologues—Job's (29:1—31:40), Elihu's (32:1—37:24) and God's (38:1—42:6)—speak to issues raised by the earlier dialogues.

■ **29:1—31:40** *Job's Final Oration.* Job's final, lengthy speech was his last appeal for resolution to his suffering. He began with nostalgic reflections on the past (29:1–25), contrasted his current difficulties (30:1–31) and closed with a protest of innocence (31:1–40).

■ **29:1–25** *Job's Past Experience.* Job looked back at the days before his suffering had begun and wished to return to them. He remembered how God had blessed him (vv. 2–6), how he had received honor (vv. 7–10), extended great kindness to others (vv. 11–17), expected to receive more blessings (vv. 18–20) and found honor from others around him (vv. 21–25).

29:1–6 How I long . . . for the days when God watched over me. Job bemoaned the loss of God's favor on himself and his family.

29:7–10 the old men rose to their feet. Job recalled how everyone in the public square had honored him.

29:11–17 I rescued the poor. Job recalled the noble reputation he had built as one who demonstrated kindness and mercy to those in need. See *WLC* 129.

and their tongues stuck to the roof of their mouths.[f]
11 Whoever heard me spoke well of me,
and those who saw me commended me,
12 because I rescued the poor[g] who cried for help,
and the fatherless[h] who had none to assist him.[i]
13 The man who was dying blessed me;[j]
I made the widow's[k] heart sing.
14 I put on righteousness[l] as my clothing;
justice was my robe and my turban.
15 I was eyes[m] to the blind
and feet to the lame.
16 I was a father to the needy;[n]
I took up the case of the stranger.
17 I broke the fangs of the wicked
and snatched the victims from their teeth.[o]

18 "I thought, 'I will die in my own house,
my days as numerous as the grains of sand.[p]
19 My roots will reach to the water,[q]
and the dew will lie all night on my branches.
20 My glory will remain fresh in me,
the bow[r] ever new in my hand.'[s]

21 "Men listened to me expectantly,
waiting in silence for my counsel.
22 After I had spoken, they spoke no more;
my words fell gently on their ears.[t]
23 They waited for me as for showers
and drank in my words as the spring rain.
24 When I smiled at them, they scarcely believed it;
the light of my face was precious to them.[a]
25 I chose the way for them and sat as their chief;
I dwelt as a king[u] among his troops;
I was like one who comforts mourners.[v]

30 "But now they mock me,[w]
men younger than I,
whose fathers I would have disdained
to put with my sheep dogs.
2 Of what use was the strength of their hands to me,
since their vigor had gone from them?
3 Haggard from want and hunger,
they roamed[b] the parched land
in desolate wastelands at night.
4 In the brush they gathered salt herbs,
and their food[c] was the root of the broom tree.
5 They were banished from their fellow men,
shouted at as if they were thieves.
6 They were forced to live in the dry stream beds,
among the rocks and in holes in the ground.
7 They brayed among the bushes
and huddled in the undergrowth.
8 A base and nameless brood,
they were driven out of the land.

29:10 [f]Ps 137:6
29:12 [g]Job 24:4 [h]Job 31:17,21 [i]Ps 72:12; Pr 21:13
29:13 [j]Job 31:20 [k]Job 22:9
29:14 [l]Job 27:6; Ps 132:9; Isa 59:17; 61:10; Eph 6:14
29:15 [m]Nu 10:31
29:16 [n]Job 24:4; Pr 29:7
29:17 [o]Ps 3:7
29:18 [p]Ps 30:6
29:19 [q]Job 18:16; Jer 17:8
29:20 [r]Ps 18:34 [s]Ge 49:24
29:22 [t]Dt 32:2
29:25 [u]Job 1:3; 31:37 [v]Job 4:4
30:1 [w]Job 12:4

[a] *24* The meaning of the Hebrew for this clause is uncertain. [b] *3* Or *gnawed* [c] *4* Or *fuel*

29:14 justice was my robe and my turban. This is an emphatic assertion of Job's way of life in the past. The opening of the book indicates that Job was not boasting falsely (see 1:1).
29:18–20 My glory will remain fresh. In light of his past deeds, Job had expected to be vigorous into the later years of his life.
29:21–25 I chose the way . . . and sat as their chief. Job had been held in great dignity and honor.
■ **30:1–31** *Job's Present Experience.* Here, point for point, Job lamented how the blessings he had enjoyed had been snatched from him.
30:1–15 now they mock me. Job bewailed his dishonor from the sons of those who were once the lowest of society (compare 29:7–10,21–25).
30:1 whose fathers I would have disdained. Job was not boasting of his arrogance in the past, but admitted it to contrast dramatically with the sons who mocked him now (vv. 3–9).

9 "And now their sons mock me[x] in song;[y]
I have become a byword[z] among them.
10 They detest me and keep their distance;
they do not hesitate to spit in my face.[a]
11 Now that God has unstrung my bow and afflicted me,[b]
they throw off restraint[c] in my presence.
12 On my right the tribe[a] attacks;
they lay snares for my feet,[d]
they build their siege ramps against me.[e]
13 They break up my road;[f]
they succeed in destroying me—
without anyone's helping them.[b]
14 They advance as through a gaping breach;
amid the ruins they come rolling in.
15 Terrors overwhelm me;[g]
my dignity is driven away as by the wind,
my safety vanishes like a cloud.[h]

16 "And now my life ebbs away;[i]
days of suffering grip me.
17 Night pierces my bones;
my gnawing pains never rest.
18 In his great power ⌊God⌋ becomes like clothing to me[c];
he binds me like the neck of my garment.
19 He throws me into the mud,[j]
and I am reduced to dust and ashes.

20 "I cry out to you, O God, but you do not answer;[k]
I stand up, but you merely look at me.
21 You turn on me ruthlessly;[l]
with the might of your hand[m] you attack me.[n]
22 You snatch me up and drive me before the wind;[o]
you toss me about in the storm.[p]
23 I know you will bring me down to death,[q]
to the place appointed for all the living.[r]

24 "Surely no one lays a hand on a broken man
when he cries for help in his distress.[s]
25 Have I not wept for those in trouble?
Has not my soul grieved for the poor?[t]
26 Yet when I hoped for good, evil came;
when I looked for light, then came darkness.[u]
27 The churning inside me never stops;[v]
days of suffering confront me.
28 I go about blackened,[w] but not by the sun;
I stand up in the assembly and cry for help.[x]
29 I have become a brother of jackals,[y]
a companion of owls.[z]
30 My skin grows black and peels;[a]
my body burns with fever.[b]
31 My harp is tuned to mourning,[c]
and my flute to the sound of wailing.

30:9 [x]Ps 69:11 [y]Job 12:4; La 3:14, 63 [z]Job 17:6
30:10 [a]Nu 12:14; Dt 25:9; Isa 50:6; Mt 26:67
30:11 [b]Ru 1:21 [c]Ps 32:9
30:12 [d]Ps 140:4-5 [e]Job 19:12
30:13 [f]Isa 3:12
30:15 [g]Job 31:23; Ps 55:4-5 [h]Job 3:25; Hos 13:3
30:16 [i]Job 3:24; Ps 22:14; 42:4
30:19 [j]Ps 69:2,14
30:20 [k]Job 19:7
30:21 [l]Job 19:6,22 [m]Job 16:9,14 [n]Job 10:3
30:22 [o]Job 27:21 [p]Job 9:17
30:23 [q]Job 9:22; 10:8 [r]Job 3:19
30:24 [s]Job 19:7
30:25 [t]Job 24:4; Ps 35:13-14; Ro 12:15
30:26 [u]Job 3:25-26; 19:8; Jer 8:15
30:27 [v]La 2:11
30:28 [w]Ps 38:6; 42:9; 43:2 [x]Job 19:7
30:29 [y]Ps 44:19 [z]Ps 102:6; Mic 1:8
30:30 [a]La 4:8 [b]Ps 102:3
30:31 [c]Isa 24:8

a *12* The meaning of the Hebrew for this word is uncertain. b *13* Or *me.* / *'No one can help him,'* ⌊*they say*⌋.
c *18* Hebrew; Septuagint ⌊*God*⌋ *grasps my clothing*

30:11 unstrung my bow. Directly the opposite of his previous years (29:20).
30:15 my dignity is driven away as by the wind. See note at 25:6 and compare Psalm 1:4.
30:16–23 He throws me into the mud. Job felt that he no longer had the blessing of God (compare 29:2–6,18–20).
30:18 becomes like clothing. There is some textual evidence for the reading "grasps my clothing" (see NIV text note). Job felt as though God were strangling him.
30:23 I know. Job was convinced that the end of his suffering would be death.
30:24–31 when I hoped for good, evil came. Job received no compassion from his friends: They forgot his earlier kindness and offered none in return (compare 29:11–17).
30:29 jackals . . . owls. Perhaps a reference to his cries of distress (compare Mic 1:8). Alternatively, with verse 28 it may indicate that he had been rejected by the community of God's people and had been counted as an unclean animal.

31

"I made a covenant with my eyes
not to look lustfully at a girl.[d]
2 For what is man's lot from God above,
his heritage from the Almighty on high?[e]
3 Is it not ruin[f] for the wicked,
disaster for those who do wrong?[g]
4 Does he not see my ways[h]
and count my every step?[i]
5 "If I have walked in falsehood
or my foot has hurried after deceit[j]—
6 let God weigh me in honest scales[k]
and he will know that I am blameless—
7 if my steps have turned from the path,[l]
if my heart has been led by my eyes,
or if my hands[m] have been defiled,
8 then may others eat what I have sown,[n]
and may my crops be uprooted.[o]
9 "If my heart has been enticed[p] by a woman,
or if I have lurked at my neighbor's door,
10 then may my wife grind another man's grain,
and may other men sleep with her.[q]
11 For that would have been shameful,
a sin to be judged.[r]
12 It is a fire[s] that burns to Destruction[a];[t]
it would have uprooted my harvest.[u]
13 "If I have denied justice to my menservants and
maidservants
when they had a grievance against me,[v]
14 what will I do when God confronts me?
What will I answer when called to account?
15 Did not he who made me in the womb make them?
Did not the same one form us both within our mothers?[w]
16 "If I have denied the desires of the poor[x]
or let the eyes of the widow[y] grow weary,
17 if I have kept my bread to myself,
not sharing it with the fatherless[z]—
18 but from my youth I reared him as would a father,
and from my birth I guided the widow—
19 if I have seen anyone perishing for lack of clothing,[a]
or a needy[b] man without a garment,
20 and his heart did not bless me
for warming him with the fleece from my sheep,
21 if I have raised my hand against the fatherless,[c]
knowing that I had influence in court,
22 then let my arm fall from the shoulder,
let it be broken off at the joint.[d]
23 For I dreaded destruction from God,
and for fear of his splendor[e] I could not do such things.

31:1 [d]Mt 5:28
31:2 [e]Job 20:29
31:3 [f]Job 21:30 [g]Job 34:22
31:4 [h]2Ch 16:9 [i]Pr 5:21
31:5 [j]Mic 2:11
31:6 [k]Job 6:2; 27:5-6
31:7 [l]Job 23:11 [m]Job 9:30
31:8 [n]Lev 26:16; Job 20:18 [o]Mic 6:15
31:9 [p]Job 24:15
31:10 [q]Dt 28:30; Jer 8:10
31:11 [r]Ge 38:24; Lev 20:10; Dt 22:22-24
31:12 [s]Job 15:30 [t]Job 26:6 [u]Job 20:28
31:13 [v]Dt 24:14-15
31:15 [w]Job 10:3
31:16 [x]Job 5:16; 20:19 [y]Job 22:9
31:17 [z]Job 22:7; 29:12
31:19 [a]Job 22:6 [b]Job 24:4
31:21 [c]Job 22:9
31:22 [d]Job 38:15
31:23 [e]Job 13:11

[a] 12 Hebrew *Abaddon*

■ **31:1–40** *Job's Protest of Innocence.* Job argued against the false accusation that he was simply a wicked man getting what he deserved. This chapter is based on a practice in the jurisprudence of Job's day. He defended himself by signing a written statement declaring his innocence and appealing to God with an oath in the divine name and with a call for divine sanctions if he were lying. Job did not proclaim his innocence of all sins but only of more grievous ones that would be likely to result in the suffering he had endured. He was not caught up in an attitude of self-righteousness. Rather, like the psalmists (see Pss 18:23; 31:1), Job was the victim of false accusation and was passionate to defend himself against those charges.

31:1–4 Job began with denials that he had sinned with his eyes. He may not have spoken of ordinary lust but of something far worse—the worship of a fertility goddess. The word translated "girl" (v. 1) was used of a goddess of fertility, the maiden Anat, in the Canaanite literature from Ugarit. See *WLC* 138.

31:5–8 Job denied having acted in avarice.

31:9–12 Job had not committed adultery.

31:13–15 Job had not performed injustice. See *WLC* 145.

31:16–23 Job had not neglected the needy or abused the helpless. See *WLC* 135.

31:24 [f]Job 22:25 [g]Mt 6:24; Mk 10:24
31:25 [h]Ps 62:10
31:26 [i]Eze 8:16
31:28 [j]Dt 17:2-7
31:29 [k]Ob 1:12 [l]Pr 17:5; 24:17-18
31:31 [m]Job 22:7
31:32 [n]Ge 19:2-3; Ro 12:13
31:33 [o]Pr 28:13 [p]Ge 3:8
31:34 [q]Ex 23:2
31:35 [r]Job 19:7; 30:28 [s]Job 27:7; 35:14
31:37 [t]Job 1:3; 29:25
31:38 [u]Ge 4:10
31:39 [v]1Ki 21:19 [w]Lev 19:13; Jas 5:4
31:40 [x]Ge 3:18
32:1 [y]Job 10:7; 33:9
32:2 [z]Ge 22:21

24 "If I have put my trust in gold[f]
or said to pure gold, 'You are my security,'[g]
25 if I have rejoiced over my great wealth,[h]
the fortune my hands had gained,
26 if I have regarded the sun[i] in its radiance
or the moon moving in splendor,
27 so that my heart was secretly enticed
and my hand offered them a kiss of homage,
28 then these also would be sins to be judged,[j]
for I would have been unfaithful to God on high.

29 "If I have rejoiced at my enemy's misfortune[k]
or gloated over the trouble that came to him[l]—
30 I have not allowed my mouth to sin
by invoking a curse against his life—
31 if the men of my household have never said,
'Who has not had his fill of Job's meat?'[m]—
32 but no stranger had to spend the night in the street,
for my door was always open to the traveler[n]—
33 if I have concealed[o] my sin as men do,[a]
by hiding[p] my guilt in my heart
34 because I so feared the crowd[q]
and so dreaded the contempt of the clans
that I kept silent and would not go outside

35 ("Oh, that I had someone to hear me![r]
I sign now my defense—let the Almighty answer me;
let my accuser[s] put his indictment in writing.
36 Surely I would wear it on my shoulder,
I would put it on like a crown.
37 I would give him an account of my every step;
like a prince[t] I would approach him.)—

38 "if my land cries out against me[u]
and all its furrows are wet with tears,
39 if I have devoured its yield without payment[v]
or broken the spirit of its tenants,[w]
40 then let briers[x] come up instead of wheat
and weeds instead of barley."

The words of Job are ended.

Elihu

32 So these three men stopped answering Job, because he was righteous in his own
eyes.[y] 2 But Elihu son of Barakel the Buzite,[z] of the family of Ram, became very

[a] 33 Or *as Adam did*

31:24–27 Job had not engaged in idolatry with regard to gold or to foreign gods.
31:29–34 Job cleared himself of hatred, selfishness and hypocrisy. See *WLC* 147; *WSC* 80.
31:35 I sign. Job attached his binding signature and made a challenge for a specific list of indictments. **my accuser.** This was not necessarily a reference to God but might be an allusion to any accuser. Up to this point Job's accusers had been his counselors.
31:37 I would give him an account. Job had already expressed confidence that he would be vindicated if given an opportunity to present his case (13:14–16). As already noted, this certitude rested on his firm belief in God's justice.
31:38–40a Job took a final oath, this time attesting to his social justice.
31:40b The words of Job are ended. Job officially rested his case. The outcome was up to the Judge.
■ **32:1—37:24** *Elihu's Speeches.* These chapters present the second monologue, that of the young man Elihu. Unlike the rest of the characters, he bore a name that was common among the Jews of his day. He is not mentioned in the epilogue (ch. 42) along with Job's other friends because he was not guilty of the same errors as the other three. Elihu centered his sharp critique on Job's words uttered during the dispute. He often quoted Job but did not accuse him of suffering for living a wicked life. Although his was just another human voice, he stressed an issue neglected by the counselors: the disciplinary and redemptive role of suffering. Eliphaz had touched on the former subject (5:17), but it was never mentioned again. This section contains an explanation (32:1–5) followed by four speeches (32:6—33:33; 34:1–37; 35:1–16; 36:1—37:24).
■ **32:1–5** *Introductory Explanation.* A brief section of prose introduces the setting of Elihu's speeches. These verses provide an interpretive framework for his speeches, which follow.
32:2–3 very angry with Job . . . also angry with the three friends. Although he had heard what was said, Elihu had taken neither side of the earlier dialogues (3:1—27:23). In fact, he was irritated with both stances of the debate. **for justifying himself rather than God.** Job was incorrect at some points in his responses because he was more concerned about proving his own innocence than he was in maintaining belief in the righteousness of God. This was not to say that everything Job had said was wrong, only that he had gone too far at times. **found no way to refute . . . yet had condemned him.** An ancient scribal tradition reads, "and so had condemned God." If this latter reading is correct, there are at least two ways in which they may be thought to have condemned God:

angry with Job for justifying himself rather than God.[a] 3He was also angry with the three
friends, because they had found no way to refute Job, and yet had condemned him.[a]
4Now Elihu had waited before speaking to Job because they were older than he. 5But
when he saw that the three men had nothing more to say, his anger was aroused.

6So Elihu son of Barakel the Buzite said:

"I am young in years,
and you are old;[b]
that is why I was fearful,
not daring to tell you what I know.
7 I thought, 'Age should speak;
advanced years should teach wisdom.'
8 But it is the spirit[b] in a man,
the breath of the Almighty,[c] that gives him understanding.[d]
9 It is not only the old[c] who are wise,[e]
not only the aged who understand what is right.

10 "Therefore I say: Listen to me;
I too will tell you what I know.
11 I waited while you spoke,
I listened to your reasoning;
while you were searching for words,
12 I gave you my full attention.
But not one of you has proved Job wrong;
none of you has answered his arguments.
13 Do not say, 'We have found wisdom;[f]
let God refute him, not man.'
14 But Job has not marshaled his words against me,
and I will not answer him with your arguments.

15 "They are dismayed and have no more to say;
words have failed them.
16 Must I wait, now that they are silent,
now that they stand there with no reply?
17 I too will have my say;
I too will tell what I know.
18 For I am full of words,
and the spirit within me compels me;
19 inside I am like bottled-up wine,
like new wineskins ready to burst.
20 I must speak and find relief;
I must open my lips and reply.
21 I will show partiality[g] to no one,[h]
nor will I flatter any man;
22 for if I were skilled in flattery,
my Maker would soon take me away.

33

"But now, Job, listen to my words;
pay attention to everything I say.[i]

32:2 [a]Job 27:5; 30:21
32:6 [b]Job 15:10
32:8 [c]Job 27:3; 33:4 [d]Pr 2:6
32:9 [e]1Co 1:26
32:13 [f]Jer 9:23
32:21 [g]Lev 19:15; Job 13:10 [h]Mt 22:16
33:1 [i]Job 13:6

a 3 Masoretic Text; an ancient Hebrew scribal tradition *Job, and so had condemned God* b 8 Or *Spirit*; also in verse 18 c 9 Or *many*; or *great*

(1) They argued that God only punishes the unrighteous while they had conceded that Job was righteous. (2) They failed to refute Job's doubts that God was treating him justly (see note on 34:10). If the reading that they had condemned Job is correct, their fault was in having condemned Job without sufficient evidence.

■ **32:6—33:33** *Elihu's First Speech.* It took Elihu this entire section just to make his introduction and give his reason for speaking. It appears that he possessed more self-awareness and humility, in combination with strong convictions, than did Job's other friends. He alone called Job by his name (33:1,31). He offered a defense of his own fitness to address the situation (32:6–14), a soliloquy (32:15–22) and words of advice to Job (33:1–33).

■ **32:6–14** *Defense of Elihu.* Elihu provided an apology for injecting himself into the debate.

32:6 what I know. In this speech, Elihu stated three times that he would tell what he knew (see vv. 10,17). The repetition of this expression indicated his own certainty and prepares the reader for the confidence that Job, should have in Elihu's words.

32:7,9 See *WLC* 151.

32:14 with your arguments. Elihu distanced himself from Job's other friends; he did not concede to Job, but did not take the friends' side either.

■ **32:15–22** *A Soliloquy.* Elihu reflected on how much he wanted to speak and on his commitment to voice truth and not flattery.

32:15–18 words have failed them . . . I am full of words. Elihu claimed to have something to say that would be different from the opinions of the others.

■ **33:1–33** *Words for Job.* At this point Elihu spoke directly to Job, referring to Job's own words to show him that he was more concerned with justifying himself than he was with justifying God (see 32:2).

2 I am about to open my mouth;
my words are on the tip of my tongue.
3 My words come from an upright heart;
my lips sincerely speak what I know.[j]
4 The Spirit of God has made me;[k]
the breath of the Almighty[l] gives me life.
5 Answer me[m] then, if you can;
prepare[n] yourself and confront me.
6 I am just like you before God;
I too have been taken from clay.[o]
7 No fear of me should alarm you,
nor should my hand be heavy upon you.[p]

8 "But you have said in my hearing—
I heard the very words—
9 'I am pure[q] and without sin;[r]
I am clean and free from guilt.
10 Yet God has found fault with me;
he considers me his enemy.[s]
11 He fastens my feet in shackles;[t]
he keeps close watch on all my paths.'[u]

12 "But I tell you, in this you are not right,
for God is greater than man.[v]
13 Why do you complain to him[w]
that he answers none of man's words[a]?
14 For God does speak[x]—now one way, now another—
though man may not perceive it.
15 In a dream,[y] in a vision of the night,
when deep sleep falls on men
as they slumber in their beds,
16 he may speak[z] in their ears
and terrify them with warnings,
17 to turn man from wrongdoing
and keep him from pride,
18 to preserve his soul from the pit,[b][a]
his life from perishing by the sword.[c][b]
19 Or a man may be chastened on a bed of pain
with constant distress in his bones,[c]
20 so that his very being finds food[d] repulsive
and his soul loathes the choicest meal.[e]
21 His flesh wastes away to nothing,
and his bones, once hidden, now stick out.[f]
22 His soul draws near to the pit,[d]
and his life to the messengers of death.[e][g]

23 "Yet if there is an angel on his side
as a mediator, one out of a thousand,
to tell a man what is right for him,[h]
24 to be gracious to him and say,
'Spare him from going down to the pit[f];[i]
I have found a ransom for him'—

33:3 [j]Job 6:28; 27:4; 36:4
33:4 [k]Ge 2:7; Job 10:3 [l]Job 27:3
33:5 [m]ver 32 [n]Job 13:18
33:6 [o]Job 4:19
33:7 [p]Job 9:34; 13:21; 2Co 2:4
33:9 [q]Job 10:7 [r]Job 13:23; 16:17
33:10 [s]Job 13:24
33:11 [t]Job 13:27 [u]Job 14:16
33:12 [v]Ecc 7:20
33:13 [w]Job 40:2; Isa 45:9
33:14 [x]Ps 62:11
33:15 [y]Job 4:13
33:16 [z]Job 36:10,15
33:18 [a]ver 22,24,28,30 [b]Job 15:22
33:19 [c]Job 30:17
33:20 [d]Ps 107:18 [e]Job 3:24; 6:6
33:21 [f]Job 16:8; 19:20
33:22 [g]Ps 88:3
33:23 [h]Mic 6:8
33:24 [i]Isa 38:17

a 13 Or *that he does not answer for any of his actions* b 18 Or *preserve him from the grave* c 18 Or *from crossing the River* d 22 Or *He draws near to the grave* e 22 Or *to the dead* f 24 Or *grave*

33:4 See *WCF* 4.1.
33:8 the very words. Literally, "the sound of the words." Elihu used Job's own speeches against him (cf. 33:10b–11 with 13:24b and 27a), but, as was the custom, he did not quote Job verbatim.
33:12–22 For God does speak. Elihu's appeal to God's transcendence repeated what the counselors had already said, but he handled the theme differently. His purpose was to show that, despite God's transcendence, he does speak to people: through revelation (vv. 14–18) and through the experience of finding humility and gratitude for God's mercy through suffering (vv. 19–30).
33:23–30 I sinned . . . did not get what I deserved. Unlike the counselors who saw no place for grace or mediation (5:1), Elihu understood that God provides both.
33:23 an angel . . . as a mediator. Elihu understood that God provides a mediator to represent the righteous who suffer, just as Job had desired (see "Introduction: Christ in Job"). His understanding anticipated what Christians know to be true of Christ (1Ti 2:5).
■ **34:1–37** *Elihu's Second Speech.* In his second speech, Elihu took up one of Job's claims—his assertion of innocence. The speech

25 then his flesh is renewed like a child's;
it is restored as in the days of his youth.[i]
26 He prays to God and finds favor with him,[k]
he sees God's face and shouts for joy;[l]
he is restored by God to his righteous state.[m]
27 Then he comes to men and says,
'I sinned,[n] and perverted what was right,[o]
but I did not get what I deserved.[p]
28 He redeemed my soul from going down to the pit,[a]
and I will live to enjoy the light.'[q]

29 "God does all these things to a man[r]—
twice, even three times—
30 to turn back his soul from the pit,[b]
that the light of life[s] may shine on him.

31 "Pay attention, Job, and listen to me;
be silent, and I will speak.
32 If you have anything to say, answer me;
speak up, for I want you to be cleared.
33 But if not, then listen to me;
be silent, and I will teach you wisdom.[t]"

34

Then Elihu said:

2 "Hear my words, you wise men;
listen to me, you men of learning.
3 For the ear tests words
as the tongue tastes food.[u]
4 Let us discern for ourselves what is right;
let us learn together what is good.[v]

5 "Job says, 'I am innocent,[w]
but God denies me justice.[x]
6 Although I am right,
I am considered a liar;
although I am guiltless,
his arrow inflicts an incurable wound.'[y]
7 What man is like Job,
who drinks scorn like water?[z]
8 He keeps company with evildoers;
he associates with wicked men.[a]
9 For he says, 'It profits a man nothing
when he tries to please God.'[b]

10 "So listen to me, you men of understanding.
Far be it from God to do evil,[c]
from the Almighty to do wrong.[d]
11 He repays a man for what he has done;[e]
he brings upon him what his conduct deserves.[f]
12 It is unthinkable that God would do wrong,
that the Almighty would pervert justice.[g]

33:25 [i]2Ki 5:14
33:26 [k]Job 34:28 [l]Job 22:26 [m]Ps 50:15; 51:12
33:27 [n]2Sa 12:13 [o]Lk 15:21 [p]Ro 6:21
33:28 [q]Job 22:28
33:29 [r]1Co 12:6; Eph 1:11; Php 2:13
33:30 [s]Ps 56:13
33:33 [t]Ps 34:11
34:3 [u]Job 12:11
34:4 [v]1Th 5:21
34:5 [w]Job 33:9 [x]Job 27:2
34:6 [y]Job 6:4
34:7 [z]Job 15:16
34:8 [a]Job 22:15; Ps 50:18
34:9 [b]Job 21:15; 35:3
34:10 [c]Ge 18:25 [d]Dt 32:4; Job 8:3; Ro 9:14
34:11 [e]Ps 62:12; Mt 16:27; Ro 2:6; 2Co 5:10 [f]Jer 32:19; Eze 33:20
34:12 [g]Job 8:3

[a] *28* Or *redeemed me from going down to the grave* [b] *30* Or *turn him back from the grave*

divides into four parts: a call for the wise to listen (vv. 1–4), a recollection of Job's words (vv. 5–9), a defense of God's justice (vv. 10–30) and a call for Job to repent (vv. 31–37).

■ **34:1–4** *Call to the Wise.* With boldness Elihu called for the wise to listen to what he had to say about Job's situation.

34:4 learn together what is good. Elihu recognized that the search for wisdom must be carried out in association with other wise people. Wisdom remains elusive and impossible to grasp fully (ch. 28).

■ **34:5–9** *Job's Erroneous Words.* Elihu quoted words of Job that were easy to refute (12:4; 13:18; 27:2,6).

34:5 I am innocent. Job had never claimed to be entirely without sin (see note at 13:23). He simply did not think himself deserving of the degree of suffering he had endured.

34:6 I am considered a liar. The counselors had accused Job of lying (15:5), and Job in turn had pointed his finger at them (13:4).

■ **34:10–30** *Divine Justice.* True to his anger toward Job (32:2), Elihu defended the goodness and justice of God. No matter what Job's circumstances were, to conclude that God was unjust was an inappropriate response.

34:10 Far be it from God to do evil. For the next 21 verses of the text, Elihu expounded on this theme. In moments of extreme emotional stress Job had expressed doubts on this subject (10:3; 12:4–6; 21:7,8; 24:1–12). Elihu urged that Job had gone too far in this but not far enough in self-reflection.

13 Who appointed him over the earth?
Who put him in charge of the whole world?[h]
14 If it were his intention
and he withdrew his spirit[a] and breath,[i]
15 all mankind would perish together
and man would return to the dust.[j]

16 "If you have understanding, hear this;
listen to what I say.
17 Can he who hates justice govern?[k]
Will you condemn the just and mighty One?[l]
18 Is he not the One who says to kings, 'You are worthless,'
and to nobles, 'You are wicked,'[m]
19 who shows no partiality[n] to princes
and does not favor the rich over the poor,[o]
for they are all the work of his hands?[p]
20 They die in an instant, in the middle of the night;[q]
the people are shaken and they pass away;
the mighty are removed without human hand.[r]

21 "His eyes are on the ways of men;
he sees their every step.[s]
22 There is no dark place,[t] no deep shadow,[u]
where evildoers can hide.
23 God has no need to examine men further,
that they should come before him for judgment.[v]
24 Without inquiry he shatters the mighty[w]
and sets up others in their place.[x]
25 Because he takes note of their deeds,
he overthrows them in the night and they are crushed.
26 He punishes them for their wickedness
where everyone can see them,
27 because they turned from following him[y]
and had no regard for any of his ways.[z]
28 They caused the cry of the poor to come before him,
so that he heard the cry of the needy.[a]
29 But if he remains silent, who can condemn him?
If he hides his face, who can see him?
Yet he is over man and nation alike,
30 to keep a godless man from ruling,
from laying snares for the people.[b]

31 "Suppose a man says to God,
'I am guilty but will offend no more.
32 Teach me what I cannot see;[c]
if I have done wrong, I will not do so again.'[d]
33 Should God then reward you on your terms,
when you refuse to repent?[e]
You must decide, not I;
so tell me what you know.

34 "Men of understanding declare,
wise men who hear me say to me,
35 'Job speaks without knowledge;[f]

34:13 [h]Job 38:4,6
34:14 [i]Ps 104:29
34:15 [j]Ge 3:19; Job 9:22
34:17 [k]2Sa 23:3-4 [l]Job 40:8
34:18 [m]Ex 22:28
34:19 [n]Dt 10:17; Ac 10:34 [o]Lev 19:15 [p]Job 10:3
34:20 [q]Ex 12:29 [r]Job 12:19
34:21 [s]Job 31:4; Pr 15:3
34:22 [t]Ps 139:12 [u]Am 9:2-3
34:23 [v]Job 11:11
34:24 [w]Job 12:19 [x]Da 2:21
34:27 [y]Ps 28:5; Isa 5:12 [z]1Sa 15:11
34:28 [a]Ex 22:23; Job 35:9; Jas 5:4
34:30 [b]Pr 29:2-12
34:32 [c]Job 35:11; Ps 25:4 [d]Job 33:27
34:33 [e]Job 41:11
34:35 [f]Job 35:16; 38:2

[a] *14* Or *Spirit*

34:14–15 If . . . he withdrew his . . . breath. God's continual common grace is necessary for any of his creatures to continue their existence.
34:16–22 he sees their every step. Job had asked why God does not set judgment times for the wicked (24:1). Elihu answered that God is judging them all the time, although his involvement is not always evident. See *WCF* 5.3.
34:23–28 has no need to examine men further. Elihu argued that nothing is hidden from God. His omniscience guarantees that he will never make a mistake. His ways are always just and true, even if limited humans cannot comprehend how this is so.
34:29 But if he remains silent, who can condemn him? Silence is God's sovereign prerogative, since humans do not understand what God knows.
■ **34:31–37** *Call for Repentance.* Elihu called on Job to adjust his outlook. Job, he maintained, had not held fast to the truth that God is just. The Hebrew text contains some difficulties in verses 31–33. In general, the admonition is that God is never subject to humans.

his words lack insight.'
36 Oh, that Job might be tested to the utmost
for answering like a wicked man![g]
37 To his sin he adds rebellion;
scornfully he claps his hands[h] among us
and multiplies his words against God."[i]

34:36 [g]Job 22:15
34:37 [h]Job 27:23 [i]Job 23:2

35

Then Elihu said:

2 "Do you think this is just?
You say, 'I will be cleared by God.[a]'
3 Yet you ask him, 'What profit is it to me,[b]
and what do I gain by not sinning?'[j]

4 "I would like to reply to you
and to your friends with you.
5 Look up at the heavens[k] and see;
gaze at the clouds so high above you.[l]
6 If you sin, how does that affect him?
If your sins are many, what does that do to him?[m]
7 If you are righteous, what do you give to him,[n]
or what does he receive[o] from your hand?[p]
8 Your wickedness affects only a man like yourself,
and your righteousness only the sons of men.

9 "Men cry out[q] under a load of oppression;
they plead for relief from the arm of the powerful.[r]
10 But no one says, 'Where is God my Maker,[s]
who gives songs in the night,[t]
11 who teaches[u] more to us than to[c] the beasts of the earth
and makes us wiser than[d] the birds of the air?'
12 He does not answer[v] when men cry out
because of the arrogance of the wicked.
13 Indeed, God does not listen to their empty plea;
the Almighty pays no attention to it.[w]
14 How much less, then, will he listen
when you say that you do not see him,[x]
that your case[y] is before him
and you must wait for him,
15 and further, that his anger never punishes
and he does not take the least notice of wickedness.[e]
16 So Job opens his mouth with empty talk;
without knowledge he multiplies words."[z]

35:3 [j]Job 9:29-31; 34:9
35:5 [k]Ge 15:5 [l]Job 22:12
35:6 [m]Pr 8:36
35:7 [n]Ro 11:35 [o]Pr 9:12 [p]Job 22:2-3; Lk 17:10
35:9 [q]Ex 2:23 [r]Job 12:19
35:10 [s]Job 27:10; Isa 51:13 [t]Ps 42:8; 149:5; Ac 16:25
35:11 [u]Ps 94:12
35:12 [v]Pr 1:28
35:13 [w]Job 27:9; Pr 15:29; Isa 1:15; Jer 11:11
35:14 [x]Job 9:11 [y]Ps 37:6
35:16 [z]Job 34:35, 37

36

Elihu continued:

2 "Bear with me a little longer and I will show you
that there is more to be said in God's behalf.
3 I get my knowledge from afar;
I will ascribe justice to my Maker.[a]

36:3 [a]Job 8:3; 37:23

[a] *2* Or *My righteousness is more than God's* [b] *3* Or *you* [c] *11* Or *teaches us by* [d] *11* Or *us wise by*
[e] *15* Symmachus, Theodotion and Vulgate; the meaning of the Hebrew for this word is uncertain.

■ **35:1–16** *Elihu's Third Speech: Job's Inconsistencies.* Job struggled with the justice of God. He expected vindication and was impatient about coming into God's presence, but he also doubted that God was just. Elihu warned against going too far. Honest lament must be balanced by a commitment to "wait for [God]" (v. 14).
35:3 what do I gain by not sinning? Compare 13.13–19 and 35:3. This question is closer to Eliphaz's words in 22:3 but may have been extrapolated from Job's own reflections in 9:14–31.
35:7–8 See *WCF* 7.1; 16.5.
35:9–13 who gives songs . . . teaches more to us . . . makes us wiser. Job had complained in chapter 23 that God was indifferent to his condition. Elihu countered with sound advice: Even in times of affliction, the righteous must not forget the wondrous gifts God has given to human beings. See *WLC* 17.
35:14–16 with empty talk. Elihu accused Job of sharing this meaninglessness as he complained against God. Job had become so overwhelmed by his awareness of suffering that he had denied truths that must always be believed and affirmed.
■ **36:1—37:24** *Elihu's Fourth Speech.* At this point, Elihu focused on Job's suffering from the perspective of God's perfect righteousness and absolute power. He began with an apology (36:1–4), recalled Job's erroneous words (36:5–15), called for repentance (36:16–21), explained how God's purposes are incomprehensible (36:22—37:13) and called again for repentance (37:14–24).
■ **36:1–4** *Apology.* Elihu opened this speech with an apology in which he reasserted his credentials (cf. 32:6–14).

4 Be assured that my words are not false;[b]
one perfect in knowledge[c] is with you.

5 "God is mighty, but does not despise men;[d]
he is mighty, and firm in his purpose.[e]
6 He does not keep the wicked alive[f]
but gives the afflicted their rights.[g]
7 He does not take his eyes off the righteous;[h]
he enthrones them with kings[i]
and exalts them forever.
8 But if men are bound in chains,[j]
held fast by cords of affliction,
9 he tells them what they have done—
that they have sinned arrogantly.[k]
10 He makes them listen[l] to correction
and commands them to repent of their evil.[m]
11 If they obey and serve him,[n]
they will spend the rest of their days in prosperity
and their years in contentment.
12 But if they do not listen,
they will perish by the sword[a][o]
and die without knowledge.[p]

13 "The godless in heart[q] harbor resentment;
even when he fetters them, they do not cry for help.
14 They die in their youth,
among male prostitutes of the shrines.[r]
15 But those who suffer he delivers in their suffering;
he speaks to them in their affliction.

16 "He is wooing[s] you from the jaws of distress
to a spacious place free from restriction,
to the comfort of your table[t] laden with choice food.
17 But now you are laden with the judgment due the
wicked;
judgment and justice have taken hold of you.[u]
18 Be careful that no one entices you by riches;
do not let a large bribe turn you aside.[v]
19 Would your wealth
or even all your mighty efforts
sustain you so you would not be in distress?
20 Do not long for the night,[w]
to drag people away from their homes.[b]
21 Beware of turning to evil,[x]
which you seem to prefer to affliction.[y]

22 "God is exalted in his power.
Who is a teacher like him?[z]
23 Who has prescribed his ways for him,[a]
or said to him, 'You have done wrong'?[b]
24 Remember to extol his work,[c]
which men have praised in song.[d]

36:4 [b]Job 33:3 [c]Job 37:5,16,23
36:5 [d]Ps 22:24 [e]Job 12:13
36:6 [f]Job 8:22 [g]Job 5:15
36:7 [h]Ps 33:18 [i]Ps 113:8
36:8 [j]Ps 107:10,14
36:9 [k]Job 15:25
36:10 [l]Job 33:16 [m]2Ki 17:13
36:11 [n]Isa 1:19
36:12 [o]Job 15:22 [p]Job 4:21
36:13 [q]Ro 2:5
36:14 [r]Dt 23:17
36:16 [s]Hos 2:14 [t]Ps 23:5
36:17 [u]Job 22:11
36:18 [v]Job 34:33
36:20 [w]Job 34:20,25
36:21 [x]Ps 66:18 [y]Heb 11:25
36:22 [z]Isa 40:13; 1Co 2:16
36:23 [a]Job 34:13 [b]Job 8:3
36:24 [c]Ps 92:5; 138:5 [d]Ps 59:16; Rev 15:3

a *12* Or *will cross the River* b *20* The meaning of the Hebrew for verses 18–20 is uncertain.

■ **36:5–15** *Job's Erroneous Words.* Elihu struggled with Job's complaint about the wicked prospering and the righteous experiencing distress (v. 6). With that in mind he dwelled on God's power (v. 5), goodness (v. 6), justice (vv. 5,8–9) and mercy (vv. 10,15).

36:13–15 godless in heart . . . those who suffer. Elihu distinguished two reactions to suffering. When the godless suffer they "harbor resentment . . . [and] do not cry for help" (v. 13). Their end is death (v. 14). The righteous sufferers, however, will eventually be delivered; God "speaks to them in their affliction" (v. 15). Job had come dangerously close to the behavior of the godless.

■ **36:16–21** *Call for Repentance.* Elihu assured Job of God's good purpose in his pain and sternly admonished him to hold fast to the hope of deliverance from distress.

36:16 He is wooing you. Elihu explained that God was using Job's suffering to draw Job into a life of blessing. This is a process of testing and refinement that requires enduring commitment and patience (see 1Pe 4:19).

36:21 See *WLC* 99.

■ **36:22—37:13** *Divine Purposes.* Elihu now returned to his opening thesis (v. 5) concerning the sovereignty of God: God's ways are beyond human comprehension, and Job was admonished to set his grief and confusion alongside a recognition of God's supremacy.

36:24 See *WLC* 112; *WSC* 54.

25 All mankind has seen it;
men gaze on it from afar.
26 How great is God—beyond our understanding![e]
The number of his years is past finding out.[f]
27 "He draws up the drops of water,
which distill as rain to the streams[a];[g]
28 the clouds pour down their moisture
and abundant showers fall on mankind.[h]
29 Who can understand how he spreads out the clouds,
how he thunders from his pavilion?[i]
30 See how he scatters his lightning about him,
bathing the depths of the sea.
31 This is the way he governs[b] the nations[j]
and provides food in abundance.[k]
32 He fills his hands with lightning
and commands it to strike its mark.[l]
33 His thunder announces the coming storm;
even the cattle make known its approach.[c]

37 "At this my heart pounds
and leaps from its place.
2 Listen! Listen to the roar of his voice,
to the rumbling that comes from his mouth.[m]
3 He unleashes his lightning beneath the whole heaven
and sends it to the ends of the earth.
4 After that comes the sound of his roar;
he thunders with his majestic voice.
When his voice resounds,
he holds nothing back.
5 God's voice thunders in marvelous ways;
he does great things beyond our understanding.[n]
6 He says to the snow,[o] 'Fall on the earth,'
and to the rain shower, 'Be a mighty downpour.'[p]
7 So that all men he has made may know his work,
he stops every man from his labor.[d][q]
8 The animals take cover;
they remain in their dens.[r]
9 The tempest comes out from its chamber,
the cold from the driving winds.
10 The breath of God produces ice,
and the broad waters become frozen.[s]
11 He loads the clouds with moisture;
he scatters his lightning through them.[t]
12 At his direction they swirl around
over the face of the whole earth
to do whatever he commands them.[u]
13 He brings the clouds to punish men,[v]
or to water his earth[e] and show his love.[w]

14 "Listen to this, Job;
stop and consider God's wonders.
15 Do you know how God controls the clouds
and makes his lightning flash?
16 Do you know how the clouds hang poised,
those wonders of him who is perfect in knowledge?[x]
17 You who swelter in your clothes
when the land lies hushed under the south wind,

36:26 [e]1Co 13:12 [f]Job 10:5; Ps 90:2; 102:24; Heb 1:12
36:27 [g]Job 38:28; Ps 147:8
36:28 [h]Job 5:10
36:29 [i]Job 26:14; 37:16
36:31 [j]Job 37:13 [k]Ps 136:25; Ac 14:17
36:32 [l]Job 37:12,15
37:2 [m]Ps 29:3-9
37:5 [n]Job 5:9
37:6 [o]Job 38:22 [p]Job 36:27
37:7 [q]Job 12:14
37:8 [r]Job 38:40; Ps 104:22
37:10 [s]Job 38:29-30; Ps 147:17
37:11 [t]Job 36:27,29
37:12 [u]Ps 148:8
37:13 [v]1Sa 12:17 [w]Ex 9:18; 1Ki 18:45; Job 38:27
37:16 [x]Job 36:4

[a] *27 Or distill from the mist as rain* [b] *31 Or nourishes* [c] *33 Or announces his coming— / the One zealous against evil* [d] *7 Or / he fills all men with fear by his power* [e] *13 Or to favor them*

■ **37:14–24** *Call for Repentance.* Here the link with the divine speeches (chs. 38–41) becomes more pronounced. Elihu did not attempt to explain Job's suffering. He recognized that God's justice does not operate as a shallow understanding of proverbial wisdom may suggest, but he also knew that God is just. His resolution was that Job had to acknowledge how little he understood of God's ways.

18 can you join him in spreading out the skies,[y]
hard as a mirror of cast bronze?

19 "Tell us what we should say to him;
we cannot draw up our case because of our darkness.
20 Should he be told that I want to speak?
Would any man ask to be swallowed up?
21 Now no one can look at the sun,
bright as it is in the skies
after the wind has swept them clean.
22 Out of the north he comes in golden splendor;
God comes in awesome majesty.
23 The Almighty is beyond our reach and exalted in power;[z]
in his justice[a] and great righteousness, he does not oppress.[b]
24 Therefore, men revere him,[c]
for does he not have regard for all the wise[d] in heart?[a]"

The LORD Speaks

38

Then the LORD answered Job out of the storm.[e] He said:

2 "Who is this that darkens my counsel
with words without knowledge?[f]
3 Brace yourself like a man;
I will question you,
and you shall answer me.[g]

4 "Where were you when I laid the earth's foundation?[h]
Tell me, if you understand.
5 Who marked off its dimensions?[i] Surely you know!
Who stretched a measuring line across it?
6 On what were its footings set,
or who laid its cornerstone[j]—
7 while the morning stars sang together
and all the angels[b] shouted for joy?

8 "Who shut up the sea behind doors[k]
when it burst forth from the womb,[l]
9 when I made the clouds its garment
and wrapped it in thick darkness,
10 when I fixed limits for it[m]
and set its doors and bars in place,[n]
11 when I said, 'This far you may come and no farther;
here is where your proud waves halt'?[o]

12 "Have you ever given orders to the morning,
or shown the dawn its place,
13 that it might take the earth by the edges

37:18 [y]Job 9:8; Ps 104:2; Isa 44:24
37:23 [z]Job 9:4; 36:4; 1Ti 6:16 [a]Job 8:3 [b]Isa 63:9; Eze 18:23,32
37:24 [c]Mt 10:28 [d]Mt 11:25
38:1 [e]Job 40:6
38:2 [f]Job 35:16; 42:3; 1Ti 1:7
38:3 [g]Job 40:7
38:4 [h]Ps 104:5; Pr 8:29
38:5 [i]Pr 8:29; Isa 40:12
38:6 [j]Job 26:7
38:8 [k]Jer 5:22 [l]Ge 1:9-10
38:10 [m]Ps 33:7; 104:9 [n]Job 26:10
38:11 [o]Ps 89:9

a *24* Or *for he does not have regard for any who think they are wise.* b *7* Hebrew *the sons of God*

37:24 revere him. Elihu closed with his final analysis of the matter. When an understanding of God's ways is unattainable, the way of wisdom is not to defy God or to accuse him of injustice. Rather, the wise will fear or reverence him all the more. This response was required of Job (see note on 28:28).

■ **38:1—42:6** *God's Responses.* Until this time, God had remained silent. Although the readers have known all along that God had high purposes for Job's suffering, Job had not been privy to this information. Now God spoke to Job, correcting him and invoking him to faithful service. God did not even mention Job's torment, much less provide an answer to the question the counselors and Job had considered so important—the reason for his suffering. Job learned that he had to leave his case, including his burning desire for vindication, in the hands of a sovereign and good God whose ways cannot be fathomed but who must nonetheless be feared and trusted. These chapters divide into four parts: God's first discourse (38:1—40:2), Job's humility (40:3–5), God's second discourse (40:6—41:34) and Job's repentance (42:1–6).

38:1—41:34 See *WCF* 5.1.

■ **38:1—40:2** *God's First Discourse.* By exposing Job's weakness and foolishness, the Lord called upon his servant to withdraw his accusations against him.

38:1 the LORD. The divine covenant name (*Yahweh*) is used again, as in the prologue, probably because the Israelite author was the one through whom this divine revelation was mediated.

38:2 my counsel. Perhaps a reference to the activities of God's heavenly court, which the reader already knows from the prologue, or simply to God's purpose in Job's suffering as expressed there.

38:4—39:30 Tell me, if you understand. In this cross-examination of Job the Lord revealed his sovereignty over the natural world: (1) as Creator (38:4–14) of the earth (38:4–7), of the sea (38:8–11) and of day and night (38:12–15) and (2) as Lord of inanimate (38:16–38) as well as (3) of animate nature (38:39—39:30).

38:5 Surely you know! The irony here and in verses 18 and 21 is not sarcasm but a loving reminder that God is the Creator.

38:7 morning stars sang. For the personification of natural forces as God's angels, see Psalm 104:4 and Hebrews 1:7.

and shake the wicked[p] out of it?
14 The earth takes shape like clay under a seal;
its features stand out like those of a garment.
15 The wicked are denied their light,[q]
and their upraised arm is broken.[r]

16 "Have you journeyed to the springs of the sea
or walked in the recesses of the deep?[s]
17 Have the gates of death[t] been shown to you?
Have you seen the gates of the shadow of death[a]?
18 Have you comprehended the vast expanses of the earth?[u]
Tell me, if you know all this.

19 "What is the way to the abode of light?
And where does darkness reside?
20 Can you take them to their places?
Do you know the paths[v] to their dwellings?
21 Surely you know, for you were already born![w]
You have lived so many years!

22 "Have you entered the storehouses of the snow[x]
or seen the storehouses of the hail,
23 which I reserve for times of trouble,[y]
for days of war and battle?[z]
24 What is the way to the place where the lightning is dispersed,
or the place where the east winds are scattered over the earth?
25 Who cuts a channel for the torrents of rain,
and a path for the thunderstorm,[a]
26 to water[b] a land where no man lives,
a desert with no one in it,
27 to satisfy a desolate wasteland
and make it sprout with grass?[c]
28 Does the rain have a father?[d]
Who fathers the drops of dew?
29 From whose womb comes the ice?
Who gives birth to the frost from the heavens[e]
30 when the waters become hard as stone,
when the surface of the deep is frozen?[f]

31 "Can you bind the beautiful[b] Pleiades?
Can you loose the cords of Orion?[g]
32 Can you bring forth the constellations in their seasons[c]
or lead out the Bear[d] with its cubs?
33 Do you know the laws[h] of the heavens?
Can you set up ⌊God's[e]⌋ dominion over the earth?

34 "Can you raise your voice to the clouds
and cover yourself with a flood of water?[i]
35 Do you send the lightning bolts on their way?[j]
Do they report to you, 'Here we are'?
36 Who endowed the heart[f] with wisdom[k]
or gave understanding[l] to the mind[f]?

38:13 [p]Ps 104:35
38:15 [q]Job 18:5 [r]Ps 10:15
38:16 [s]Ps 77:19
38:17 [t]Ps 9:13
38:18 [u]Job 28:24
38:20 [v]Job 26:10
38:21 [w]Job 15:7
38:22 [x]Job 37:6
38:23 [y]Isa 30:30; Eze 13:11 [z]Ex 9:18; Jos 10:11; Rev 16:21
38:25 [a]Job 28:26
38:26 [b]Job 36:27
38:27 [c]Ps 104:14; 107:35
38:28 [d]Ps 147:8; Jer 14:22
38:29 [e]Ps 147:16-17
38:30 [f]Job 37:10
38:31 [g]Job 9:9; Am 5:8
38:33 [h]Ps 148:6; Jer 31:36
38:34 [i]Job 22:11; 36:27-28
38:35 [j]Job 36:32; 37:3
38:36 [k]Job 9:4 [l]Job 32:8; Ps 51:6; Ecc 2:26

a *17* Or *gates of deep shadows* b *31* Or *the twinkling*; or *the chains of the* c *32* Or *the morning star in its season*
d *32* Or *out Leo* e *33* Or *his*; or *their* f *36* The meaning of the Hebrew for this word is uncertain.

38:15 wicked . . . denied their light. The light of the wicked is darkness. Compare Isaiah 5:20 and Luke 11:35.
38:17 the gates of death. The "gates" stand for dominion (cf. Mt 16:18). The Lord is even sovereign over this invisible realm that no living person has ever seen (17:16). According to the pagan religions of Canaan, the god Mot was sovereign over the realm of death, but Job knew otherwise (cf. 26:6).
38:23 for days of war. Compare Joshua 10:11 and Isaiah 28:2.
38:26 to water . . . a desert. In an environment in which rainwater was precious, God expressed his sovereign freedom to act in a manner that perplexes human beings.
38:31 bind . . . Pleiades? . . . loose the cords of Orion? A literary borrowing of the imaginary figures seen in the constellations. God alone has cosmic dominion over the "fetters" that hold together the cluster of stars called Pleiades and those that make up the belt of the hunter Orion.
38:33 God's dominion. These words are literally "his inscription." Perhaps "his signature" is closer to its meaning here: "Can you put his signature on the earth?"
38:36 the heart . . . mind. The precise meanings of the Hebrew words here have been lost. Some think that the first refers to the ibis bird and the second to the rooster, the habits of which were sometimes thought to foretell the flooding of the Nile and the coming of rain. "Inner parts" in Psalm 51:6 is another translation of

37 Who has the wisdom to count the clouds?
Who can tip over the water jars of the heavens
38 when the dust becomes hard
and the clods of earth stick together?

39 "Do you hunt the prey for the lioness
and satisfy the hunger of the lions[m]
40 when they crouch in their dens[n]
or lie in wait in a thicket?
41 Who provides food for the raven[o]
when its young cry out to God
and wander about for lack of food?[p]

39

"Do you know when the mountain goats[q] give birth?
Do you watch when the doe bears her fawn?
2 Do you count the months till they bear?
Do you know the time they give birth?
3 They crouch down and bring forth their young;
their labor pains are ended.
4 Their young thrive and grow strong in the wilds;
they leave and do not return.

5 "Who let the wild donkey[r] go free?
Who untied his ropes?
6 I gave him the wasteland[s] as his home,
the salt flats as his habitat.[t]
7 He laughs at the commotion in the town;
he does not hear a driver's shout.[u]
8 He ranges the hills for his pasture
and searches for any green thing.

9 "Will the wild ox[v] consent to serve you?
Will he stay by your manger at night?
10 Can you hold him to the furrow with a harness?
Will he till the valleys behind you?
11 Will you rely on him for his great strength?
Will you leave your heavy work to him?
12 Can you trust him to bring in your grain
and gather it to your threshing floor?

13 "The wings of the ostrich flap joyfully,
but they cannot compare with the pinions and feathers of the stork.
14 She lays her eggs on the ground
and lets them warm in the sand,
15 unmindful that a foot may crush them,
that some wild animal may trample them.
16 She treats her young harshly,[w] as if they were not hers;
she cares not that her labor was in vain,
17 for God did not endow her with wisdom
or give her a share of good sense.[x]
18 Yet when she spreads her feathers to run,
she laughs at horse and rider.

19 "Do you give the horse his strength
or clothe his neck with a flowing mane?

38:39 [m]Ps 104:21
38:40 [n]Job 37:8
38:41 [o]Lk 12:24 [p]Ps 147:9; Mt 6:26
39:1 [q]Dt 14:5
39:5 [r]Job 6:5; 11:12; 24:5
39:6 [s]Job 24:5; Ps 107:34; Jer 2:24 [t]Hos 8:9
39:7 [u]Job 3:18
39:9 [v]Nu 23:22; Dt 33:17
39:16 [w]La 4:3
39:17 [x]Job 35:11

the word rendered "heart" here and accounts for the NIV translation. The word rendered "mind" appears only here in Scripture.
38:39 Do you hunt the prey . . . ? The questions shift from inanimate to animate creation: a sampling of God's creatures great and small.
39:1–2 Do you know . . . ? Do you watch . . . ? Do you count . . . ? God spoke of his creative, wise and sustaining work in the barren hills where people could scarcely live.
39:5 Who let the wild donkey go free? This undomesticated creature was greatly admired for its freedom and ability to survive in "the salt flats" (v. 6). Ishmael was complimented when called "a wild donkey of a man" (Ge 16:12).
39:9 Will the wild ox consent to serve you? This animal was already rare in Job's day. It was subsequently hunted to extinction by the Egyptians and Assyrians.
39:13–18 she laughs at horse and rider. The question put to Job about the ostrich is implicit rather than explicit. Could Job have devised a creature more baffling—a bird with joyful but useless wings, lacking the sense even to protect its young—yet one that runs faster than a horse? Job complained of paradoxes in his life

[20] Do you make him leap like a locust,[y]
striking terror with his proud snorting?[z]
[21] He paws fiercely, rejoicing in his strength,
and charges into the fray.[a]
[22] He laughs at fear, afraid of nothing;
he does not shy away from the sword.
[23] The quiver rattles against his side,
along with the flashing spear and lance.
[24] In frenzied excitement he eats up the ground;
he cannot stand still when the trumpet sounds.[b]
[25] At the blast of the trumpet[c] he snorts, 'Aha!'
He catches the scent of battle from afar,
the shout of commanders and the battle cry.[d]

[26] "Does the hawk take flight by your wisdom
and spread his wings toward the south?
[27] Does the eagle soar at your command
and build his nest on high?[e]
[28] He dwells on a cliff and stays there at night;
a rocky crag is his stronghold.
[29] From there he seeks out his food;[f]
his eyes detect it from afar.
[30] His young ones feast on blood,
and where the slain are, there is he."[g]

40 The LORD said to Job:[h]

[2] "Will the one who contends with the Almighty correct him?
Let him who accuses God answer him!"

[3]Then Job answered the LORD:

[4] "I am unworthy[i]—how can I reply to you?
I put my hand over my mouth.[j]
[5] I spoke once, but I have no answer[k]—
twice, but I will say no more."[l]

[6]Then the LORD spoke to Job out of the storm:[m]

[7] "Brace yourself like a man;
I will question you,
and you shall answer me.[n]

[8] "Would you discredit my justice?[o]
Would you condemn me to justify yourself?
[9] Do you have an arm like God's,[p]
and can your voice thunder like his?[q]
[10] Then adorn yourself with glory and splendor,
and clothe yourself in honor and majesty.[r]
[11] Unleash the fury of your wrath,[s]
look at every proud man and bring him low,[t]
[12] look at every proud man and humble him,[u]
crush[v] the wicked where they stand.

39:20 [y]Joel 2:4-5 [z]Jer 8:16
39:21 [a]Jer 8:6
39:24 [b]Jer 4:5,19; Eze 7:14; Am 3:6
39:25 [c]Jos 6:5 [d]Am 1:14; 2:2
39:27 [e]Jer 49:16; Ob 1:4
39:29 [f]Job 9:26
39:30 [g]Mt 24:28; Lk 17:37
40:1 [h]Job 10:2; 13:3; 23:4; 31:35; 33:13
40:4 [i]Job 42:6 [j]Job 29:9
40:5 [k]Job 9:3 [l]Job 9:15
40:6 [m]Job 38:1
40:7 [n]Job 38:3; 42:4
40:8 [o]Job 27:2; Ro 3:3
40:9 [p]2Ch 32:8 [q]Job 37:5; Ps 29:3-4
40:10 [r]Ps 93:1; 104:1
40:11 [s]Isa 42:25; Na 1:6 [t]Isa 2:11,12,17; Da 4:37
40:12 [u]1Sa 2:7 [v]Isa 13:11; 63:2-3,6

---

and was shown natural paradoxes that can be resolved only in God.
39:19 Do you give the horse his strength . . . ? The horse is the only animal in the list that is not wild (horses were imported to Job's homeland). It was considered the strongest and smartest animal.
39:29 his eyes detect it from afar. In addition to the mysterious migratory instinct of birds (v. 26), these words speak of the phenomenal eyesight of eagles.
40:1–2 Let him who accuses God answer him! This conclusion of God's first speech should be compared with its opening in 38:2. Both are directed toward Job's unfortunate utterances during his moments of doubt. Though Job was not crushed, he was humbled.
■ **40:3–5** *Job's Humility.* Job forgot his obsession with being vindicated. It was his turn to speak, but he had nothing to say. He was brought low in awe of God.
■ **40:6—41:34** *God's Second Discourse.* This speech opened in the same way as the first discourse (cf. 40:6–7 with 38:1–3). Nevertheless, a new line of reasoning addressed Job's problem with God's justice in judging the wicked. In the first speech God revealed himself as Lord of nature; here he is Lord of the moral realm.
40:8–14 Do you have an arm like God's . . . ? In the first speech Job was called upon to see God as Creator. Here he was to view him as Savior. These verses are a prologue to the descriptions of the fearsome monsters, behemoth and leviathan, that highlight God's power over the mighty forces of evil. One must conclude that these monsters represent those forces.
40:11–12 every proud man. The Hebrew does not include here the word for "man." The translation "every proud one" would include the accuser of the prologue.

40:14 [w]Ps 20:6; 60:5; 108:6
40:19 [x]Job 41:33
40:20 [y]Ps 104:14 [z]Ps 104:26
40:22 [a]Isa 44:4
40:24 [b]Job 41:2,7,26
41:1 [c]Job 3:8; Ps 104:26; Isa 27:1
41:2 [d]Isa 37:29
41:4 [e]Ex 21:6
41:10 [f]Job 3:8 [g]Jer 50:44
41:11 [h]Ro 11:35 [i]Ex 19:5; Dt 10:14; Ps 24:1; 50:12; 1Co 10:26

13 Bury them all in the dust together;
shroud their faces in the grave.
14 Then I myself will admit to you
that your own right hand can save you.[w]

15 "Look at the behemoth,[a]
which I made along with you
and which feeds on grass like an ox.
16 What strength he has in his loins,
what power in the muscles of his belly!
17 His tail[b] sways like a cedar;
the sinews of his thighs are close-knit.
18 His bones are tubes of bronze,
his limbs like rods of iron.
19 He ranks first among the works of God,[x]
yet his Maker can approach him with his sword.
20 The hills bring him their produce,[y]
and all the wild animals play[z] nearby.
21 Under the lotus plants he lies,
hidden among the reeds in the marsh.
22 The lotuses conceal him in their shadow;
the poplars by the stream[a] surround him.
23 When the river rages, he is not alarmed;
he is secure, though the Jordan should surge against his mouth.
24 Can anyone capture him by the eyes,[c]
or trap him and pierce his nose?[b]

41

"Can you pull in the leviathan[d][c] with a fishhook
or tie down his tongue with a rope?
2 Can you put a cord through his nose
or pierce his jaw with a hook?[d]
3 Will he keep begging you for mercy?
Will he speak to you with gentle words?
4 Will he make an agreement with you
for you to take him as your slave for life?[e]
5 Can you make a pet of him like a bird
or put him on a leash for your girls?
6 Will traders barter for him?
Will they divide him up among the merchants?
7 Can you fill his hide with harpoons
or his head with fishing spears?
8 If you lay a hand on him,
you will remember the struggle and never do it again!
9 Any hope of subduing him is false;
the mere sight of him is overpowering.
10 No one is fierce enough to rouse him.[f]
Who then is able to stand against me?[g]
11 Who has a claim against me that I must pay?[h]
Everything under heaven belongs to me.[i]

12 "I will not fail to speak of his limbs,
his strength and his graceful form.
13 Who can strip off his outer coat?

[a] *15* Possibly the hippopotamus or the elephant [b] *17* Possibly trunk [c] *24* Or *by a water hole*
[d] *1* Possibly the crocodile

40:15 behemoth. Although the Hebrew root is used of bovine creatures (e.g., bulls), the Hebrew form here implies the meaning "the beast beyond comparison." This and other parts of the description (especially v. 19) must be hyperbole if this is only a hippopotamus or the like.

41:1 leviathan. On the surface, this appears to be something like a crocodile. Its description, along with that of the behemoth (40:15), forms a poetic repetition. Both the behemoth and the leviathan epitomize wickedness. In the Bible these are not considered mythological creatures, but, like Leviathan in Psalm 74:14 and Isaiah 27:1, they represent evil forces of both heavenly and earthly realms (cf. Rev 12–13).

41:10 able to stand against me. Humans shudder before the forces of evil, but God is far superior to the greatest evil and should be revered all the more on this account.

Who would approach him with a bridle?
14 Who dares open the doors of his mouth,
ringed about with his fearsome teeth?
15 His back has[a] rows of shields
tightly sealed together;
16 each is so close to the next
that no air can pass between.
17 They are joined fast to one another;
they cling together and cannot be parted.
18 His snorting throws out flashes of light;
his eyes are like the rays of dawn.[j]
19 Firebrands stream from his mouth;
sparks of fire shoot out.
20 Smoke pours from his nostrils
as from a boiling pot over a fire of reeds.
21 His breath[k] sets coals ablaze,
and flames dart from his mouth.[l]
22 Strength resides in his neck;
dismay goes before him.
23 The folds of his flesh are tightly joined;
they are firm and immovable.
24 His chest is hard as rock,
hard as a lower millstone.
25 When he rises up, the mighty are terrified;
they retreat before his thrashing.
26 The sword that reaches him has no effect,
nor does the spear or the dart or the javelin.
27 Iron he treats like straw
and bronze like rotten wood.
28 Arrows do not make him flee;
slingstones are like chaff to him.
29 A club seems to him but a piece of straw;
he laughs at the rattling of the lance.
30 His undersides are jagged potsherds,
leaving a trail in the mud like a threshing sledge.[m]
31 He makes the depths churn like a boiling caldron
and stirs up the sea like a pot of ointment.
32 Behind him he leaves a glistening wake;
one would think the deep had white hair.
33 Nothing on earth is his equal[n]—
a creature without fear.
34 He looks down on all that are haughty;
he is king over all that are proud.[o]"

Job

42 Then Job replied to the LORD:

2 "I know that you can do all things;[p]
no plan of yours can be thwarted.[q]
3 ⌞You asked,⌟ 'Who is this that obscures my counsel without knowledge?'[r]
Surely I spoke of things I did not understand,
things too wonderful for me to know.[s]

4 ⌞"You said,⌟ 'Listen now, and I will speak;

41:18 [j]Job 3:9
41:21 [k]Isa 40:7 [l]Ps 18:8
41:30 [m]Isa 41:15
41:33 [n]Job 40:19
41:34 [o]Job 28:8
42:2 [p]Ge 18:14; Mt 19:26 [q]2Ch 20:6
42:3 [r]Job 38:2 [s]Ps 40:5; 131:1; 139:6

[a] *15* Or *His pride is his*

41:18–21 flashes of light . . . sparks of fire. Some interpret this as an extremely hyperbolic description of an ordinary creature, such as a crocodile or a whale. More likely, these verses are poetic representations of evil drawn from the ancient Near Eastern world.
41:33–34 Nothing on earth is his equal . . . he is king over all that are proud. This description fits 40:11–12 of the poem's prologue perfectly.
■ **42:1–6** *Job's Repentance.* Appropriately, Job was more than humbled; he was repentant, not of an evil life for which he was suffering (as his counselors thought), but of the times when his cries of suffering had questioned the goodness of God.

42:4
[t]Job 38:3; 40:7

42:5
[u]Job 26:14; Ro 10:17
[v]Jdg 13:22; Isa 6:5; Eph 1:17-18

42:6
[w]Job 40:4 [x]Ezr 9:6

42:7
[y]Job 32:3

42:8
[z]Nu 23:1,29
[a]Job 1:5
[b]Ge 20:17; Jas 5:15-16; 1Jn 5:16
[c]Job 22:30

42:10
[d]Dt 30:3; Ps 14:7
[e]Job 1:3; Ps 85:1-3; 126:5-6

42:11
[f]Job 19:13

42:17
[g]Ge 15:15; 25:8

I will question you,
and you shall answer me.'[t]
5 My ears had heard of you[u]
but now my eyes have seen you.[v]
6 Therefore I despise myself[w]
and repent in dust and ashes."[x]

Epilogue

7 After the LORD had said these things to Job, he said to Eliphaz the Temanite, "I am
angry with you and your two friends,[y] because you have not spoken of me what is right,
as my servant Job has. 8 So now take seven bulls and seven rams[z] and go to my servant
Job and sacrifice a burnt offering[a] for yourselves. My servant Job will pray for you, and
I will accept his prayer[b] and not deal with you according to your folly.[c] You have not spoken of me what is right, as my servant Job has." 9 So Eliphaz the Temanite, Bildad the
Shuhite and Zophar the Naamathite did what the LORD told them; and the LORD accepted Job's prayer.

10 After Job had prayed for his friends, the LORD made him prosperous again[d] and gave
him twice as much as he had before.[e] 11 All his brothers and sisters and everyone who had
known him before[f] came and ate with him in his house. They comforted and consoled
him over all the trouble the LORD had brought upon him, and each one gave him a piece
of silver[a] and a gold ring.

12 The LORD blessed the latter part of Job's life more than the first. He had fourteen
thousand sheep, six thousand camels, a thousand yoke of oxen and a thousand donkeys.
13 And he also had seven sons and three daughters. 14 The first daughter he named Jemi-
mah, the second Keziah and the third Keren-Happuch. 15 Nowhere in all the land were
there found women as beautiful as Job's daughters, and their father granted them an inheritance along with their brothers.

16 After this, Job lived a hundred and forty years; he saw his children and their children to the fourth generation. 17 And so he died, old and full of years.[g]

a *11* Hebrew *him a kesitah*; a kesitah was a unit of money of unknown weight and value.

42:5 but now my eyes have seen you. Job's physical eyes could not have penetrated through the storm out of which God spoke (38:1; 40:6), so he must have been expressing a deeper meaning. He had known God at a verbal, rational level, but he now experienced God's living presence in his innermost being and had come to know him as Savior and Friend—and, above all, as God.

■ **42:7–17** *The Epilogue.* The drama introduced in the prose prologue (1:1—2:13) comes full circle in this closing section of prose. The close divides into two sections: the rebuke of Job's friends (vv. 7–9) and Job's restoration to blessing (vv. 10–17).

■ **42:7–9** *Rebuke for Job's Friends.* God rebuked Job's counselors but accepted Job's prayers on their behalf.

42:7 what is right. The counselors had failed miserably, since they did not know why Job was suffering and had spoken presumptuously and arrogantly and had wrongly accused Job of unbridled wickedness. See notes on 32:2–3.

42:8 will pray for you. The roles of Job and his friends were reversed. They had come to stand between Job and God (2:11–13), but now Job mediated for them. They had treated Job as though they were his superiors, but now they had to humble themselves before him as their intercessor.

■ **42:10–17** *Blessings for Job.* God restored Job, doubling the blessings he had lost at the hand of Satan.

42:12 The LORD blessed. Job was restored, and those who had refused to be near him in his darkest hour (19:13–20) were forgiven and brought him gifts. God had allowed Satan (the accuser) to strike Job in order to prove that God's faithful servant would remain true. Although Job never did understand why he had suffered, the reader perceives that Satan has been proved a liar and that God has been glorified. So it was God's sovereign good pleasure to reward his faithful servant. Although this outcome for Job does not guarantee that all righteous sufferers will find restoration to blessing in this life, God does guarantee that those who remain faithful through the trials of this life will be rewarded in the new world to come (Ro 8:18–39).

PSALMS

Introduction

Overview

Authors: Moses, David, Solomon, the sons of Korah, the sons of Asaph, Ethan the Ezrahite and various unknown authors

Date: c. 1440–400 B.C.

Purpose: To provide Israel with a collection of songs for worship appropriate for a variety of situations

Key Truths:

- God deserves praise.
- God protects and rescues the righteous when they are in need.
- God will bless the obedient and judge the disobedient.
- God's revelation should be the foundation for worship.
- Genuine worship entails a broad range of emotions that stem from experiences of life.

Authorship and Titles

Title of the Book

The title found in English versions of the book, Psalms, derives from the early Greek translation of the Old Testament. It is also the name found in the New Testament (Lk 20:42; 24:44; Ac 1:20). This Greek title may be rendered "Songs" and corresponds to the Hebrew term *mizmor* (translated "psalm" in the NIV, from a verbal root "to sing" or "to pluck an instrument"), which occurs frequently in individual psalm titles.

The Hebrew title is "Book of Praises," which is striking since psalms using the literary form of lament significantly outnumber those using the literary form of hymn. However, almost all the laments express confidence in the Lord at the end, while in the book as a whole there is a movement away from the lament form and toward an increasing number of hymns of praise.

Individual Psalm Titles

Many, though not all, of the psalms begin with titles. Most English versions, including the NIV, do not assign a verse number to the titles, giving the impression that these titles are not part of the Hebrew text. In truth, however, the titles are usually the first verse of the psalm in the standard Hebrew text, and they also appear as such in the Septuagint (the Greek translation of the OT). The titles, therefore, are either part of the inspired text or at least stem from early tradition.

The titles may be divided into five basic types: authorship, historical, musical notations, genre and worship instructions. Interestingly, Habakkuk 3 presents an isolated psalm that contains titles both before and after the text of the poem. The titles of authorship and genre appear before the psalm (Hab 3:1), but the instructions regarding the one who is to make use of the psalm ("the director of music"; Hab 3:19) and instrumentation ("On my stringed instruments"; Hab 3:19) appear at the end. This is an indication that similar titles in the psalms may belong at the end of the psalm preceding the one for which they are listed.

Authorship Titles

A majority of the titles link the psalm with a particular individual or group, using a single Hebrew preposition that may denote dedication ("to David") or subject matter ("concerning David") or authorship ("of David"). However, in one of the few psalm titles that provides an expanded context (that of Ps 18) there is no doubt that the title intends to identify the composer of the psalm. David is by far the most frequently cited author, most of his psalms being found in the first two books (see "Structure"), though there is also a small collection of Davidic psalms at the very end (Pss 138–145). The tradition that associates David with singing and psalm composition is so strong that, in principle, there is little room for argument over his authorship of the psalms that bear his name in the titles (see, for instance, 1Sa 16:14–23; 2Sa 1:17–27; cf. 2Sa 22 with Ps 18; 2Sa 23:1; 2Ch 6:31; 15:16; 16:7; Am 6:5).

Authors other than David appear in psalm titles: Moses (Ps 90), Solomon (72), the sons of Korah (42–49; 84–85; 87–88), the sons of Asaph (50; 73–83) and Ethan the Ezrahite (89). A fair number of psalms have no authorship designation (e.g., 1); these are often referred to as "orphan" psalms.

Historical Titles

Far fewer psalms have historical titles than have authorship titles (see 3; 7; 18; 30; 34; 51; 52; 54; 56; 57; 59; 60; 63; 142). The authenticity of the historical titles has also been debated. There is no textual evidence that they were added later. However, some believe that the apparent disharmony between psalm and title (as in 30) or between title and historical books (Ps 56 compared with 1Sa 21:10–15) indicates that their origin is late and artificial. Others argue that, if the historical titles were add-ons, it is likely that the later editors who supplied them would assure a close connection between title and psalm. Why, for instance, would a later editor connect Psalm 30 with the dedication of the temple since there is no mention of the temple in the psalm?

History and Psalm Composition

The historical titles may give us an indication of the origins of the psalms, but they generally provide little help in interpretation. That is, while a psalm may have been written in relation to a particular historical event, the composer was usually careful not to be too specific in the body of the poem. Thus, though the title of Psalm 3 includes "When he fled from his son Absalom," the psalm itself begins "O LORD, how many are my foes!" rather than "O LORD, Absalom rises up against me!" One reason for this is that psalmists wrote their poetry for use during formal and public worship. They made certain to express thoughts and emotions that others could share.

Nevertheless, the historical titles do give us a glimpse into psalm composition. They also provide historical illustrations of the messages of the psalms, since, after all, the events mentioned in the titles were the original motivations for composition (e.g., Ps 51 and David's sin with Bathsheba). However, it is not necessary for interpreters to reconstruct the historical background of every psalm (a practice of many earlier psalm commentators) in order to make practical application and use of it.

Genre Titles
A number of the terms in the titles classify the psalms into different literary types. It is difficult for us to gain a precise understanding of many of these terms. Some are quite general and appear often: *mizmor* ("psalm"; see 139) and *shir* ("song"). Others occur rarely and with uncertain meaning: *shiggaion* (see 7). Two such terms may occur in a single psalm title (see 30). While this ancient classification is interesting, and we wish we had a clearer understanding of the terms, present-day genre distinctions are drawn from the mood and content of the psalms.

Musical Notations
Some of the genre terms are also musical notations, most notably *mizmor* ("psalm," from a verbal root "to sing") and *shir* ("song"). There are others as well, often uncertain in terms of meaning. A common term appears to dedicate the psalm to the musical ministry of the formal worship establishment ("For the director of music"; see 140). Others appear rarely and are probably names of tunes (NIV makes this explicit; e.g., 60: "To the tune of 'The Lily of the Covenant.'")

Another apparently musical term that occurs frequently outside the title is the word *Selah*. Again, no one today is certain of its meaning or function.

Worship Instructions
Occasionally the title indicates how the psalm functioned in the formal worship of Israel. The best known of these are the "songs of ascent" (see 120–134; see "Introduction" to Ps 120) and the psalm "For the Sabbath day" (92).

Structure
During the time of the Old Testament, from Moses (90) to the postexilic period (126), new psalms were added to the book of praise. The resulting structure of the book is difficult to discern. There is no overarching principle of order that is explicit throughout the book. Nonetheless, a few striking features are noteworthy.

Early tradition divides the Psalter into five books, paralleling the five books of Moses. Each closes with a doxology and has other characteristics that separate it from the others (see "Outline"). There are also mini-groups of psalms bound together either by common authorship (e.g., 73–83, by the sons of Asaph), common usage (e.g., 120–134, songs of ascent) or common theme (e.g., 93; 96–100). It also appears that Psalms 1–2 were intentionally placed at the beginning of the Psalter to serve as a kind of entryway into the sanctuary of the Psalms, much as Psalms 146–150 serve at the end as a magnificent doxology, a veritable fireworks of praise.

Genres
There are 150 separate poetic compositions in the Psalter, each one containing unique beauty and power. However, there are also some similarities among the songs that allow them to be grouped together in various ways. These notes will sometimes refer to the following genre classifications:

1. *Hymns of Praise.* Hymns are easily recognized by their exuberant praise of the Lord. God is praised for who he is and for his actions of power and mercy. Hymns of praise commonly include the following elements: a call to praise, a reason for praise, and a demonstration of faith. For examples, see 8, 24, 29, 33, 47 and 48.

2. *Laments (Complaints or Petitions).* Laments are at the opposite end of the emotional spectrum from hymns. In a lament, the psalmist honestly unveiled to God the innermost confidences of his heart—a heart often filled with anguish, fear, bitterness and/or anger. Common petitions in laments include requests for God to save or offer refuge and for him to exact vengeance on enemies. In Hebrew poetry laments typically include the following elements: an address to God, an expression of the author's emotional complaint, an expression of confidence in the Lord, a petition for God's help, and an expression of praise to the Lord. When appropriate they often included a confession of guilt as well. Given these fairly standard elements, it should not be surprising when laments include groups of verses that sound like hymns of praise. For examples, see 25, 39, 51, 86, 102 and 120.

3. *Thanksgiving Psalms.* These were sung, appropriately, after the Lord had answered the psalmist's earlier lament. Indeed, the first three psalm types form a kind of triad. The psalmist sang hymns when he felt right with the Lord, laments when he was out of harmony with him and then gave thanks when the relationship was restored. For examples, see 18, 66, 107, 118 and 138.

4. *Songs of Confidence (or Trust or Mercy).* While many hymns and even laments express trust in God, some psalms are dominated by this theme. They are often brief and contain a striking metaphor depicting the psalmist's trusting attitude. For examples, see 23, 121 and 131.

5. *Kingship Psalms.* Since God, the King of the universe, is the subject of the psalms and since David, the human king, was both writer and subject of many psalms, kingship is an important institution and concept in the Psalter. However, a few psalms so intensely focus on either God's kingship (24; 47; 95) or on the human king (20; 21; 45) that they stand out from the others.

6. *Wisdom Psalms.* In thinking of Biblical wisdom, we normally consider books like Proverbs, Job and Ecclesiastes. Some of the themes in the wisdom books are also prominent in the wisdom psalms. For instance, the strong contrast between the righteous and the wicked that we find in the book of Proverbs is also prominent in Psalm 1. For other examples, see Psalms 37 and 49. For a treatment of interpretive issues peculiar to Wisdom Literature, see "Introduction to the Poetic and Wisdom Books" on page 745.

Poetic Style and Devices

Poetry is a form of written communication that pays particular attention to how its message is communicated to the reader. The poets enjoyed using language in a way that stretches not only the mind but also the imagination and emotions. To read "The LORD is my shepherd" (23:1) does more than inform; it evokes a picture and touches emotions in a way that surpasses nonfigurative language. For a treatment of interpretive issues peculiar to poetry, see "Introduction to the Poetic and Wisdom Books" on page 745.

Parallelism. This literary device is by far the most prevalent in all Hebrew poetry. It is used to connect words or phrases to one another in order to nuance meaning. see "Introduction to the Poetic and Wisdom Books" on page 745 for a detailed explanation and examples.

Acrostics. Another literary device that appears occasionally in the psalms bears specific mentioning here: *acrostic.* An acrostic is a relationship between the first letters of different lines of verse. For example, in an acrostic based on the alphabet, each line would begin with a successive letter of the alphabet. Acrostics may also be used to form words, or even to demonstrate unity by beginning each line with the same letter. A good example of an acrostic is Psalm 119, in which the stanzas are arranged according to the Hebrew alphabet, with each line in any given stanza beginning with the letter of the stanza.

Theology of the Psalms

Just as the formation of the Psalter took place during the Old Testament period as a whole, so the theology of the Psalter is as extensive as that of the entire Old Testament. Martin Luther called the Psalms "a little Bible, and the summary of the Old Testament."

Theological truths, however, are not presented systematically or abstractly in Psalms; the realities conveyed here were related to life and spoken in the context of a covenant faith.

Christ in Psalms

Christian readers of the Psalms rightly see Christ revealed throughout the Psalter. The entire Old Testament, including the Psalter, looked forward to Jesus' person and work, including not only those associated with his first advent but also those that the New Testament assigns to his return. Jesus himself and the New Testament writers took psalm after psalm upon their lips to express such issues as Jesus' suffering (e.g., Mt 27:46) and glorification (e.g., Mt 22:41–46). In addition, for the Christian Jesus becomes the object of the worship of the Psalter. The song-prayers of the Psalms are directed to God. Jesus Christ, as the second person of the Trinity, is also the proper object of the hymns and laments of the Psalms. Jesus is at once singer (Heb 2:12) and subject of the songs. Believers in Christ can sing to him their praise (hymns), turn to him with their complaints and petitions (laments) and thank him when he answers their prayers (thanksgivings). Furthermore, they remember what he accomplished for them on the cross (psalms of remembrance) and extol him as their king (kingship psalms). He is the source of their trust (psalms of confidence) and the embodiment of God's wisdom (wisdom psalms).

Even the psalms that include imprecations, or cursing, find fulfillment in Christ. These psalms cry out for the vindication of the righteous and for God's judgment on the wicked (e.g., Ps 69:22–29). Such prayers reflected the calling of the Israelites to holy war as God's instruments of judgment. With the coming of Christ to bear God's judgment, the nature of the warfare of God's people has changed. It is now more intense, but directed first and foremost against the "spiritual forces of evil in the heavenly realms" (Eph 6:12). When Christ returns in glory, the time of mercy will be ended and the imprecations (curses) of the psalms will be fulfilled against all the enemies of God.

Outline

I. Book One (1–41)

II. Book Two (42–72)

III. Book Three (73–89)

IV. Book Four (90–106)

V. Book Five (107–150)

BOOK I

Psalms 1–41

Psalm 1

1 Blessed is the man
who does not walk[a] in the counsel of the wicked
or stand in the way of sinners
or sit[b] in the seat of mockers.
2 But his delight[c] is in the law of the LORD,[d]
and on his law he meditates[e] day and night.
3 He is like a tree[f] planted by streams of water,[g]
which yields its fruit[h] in season
and whose leaf does not wither.
Whatever he does prospers.[i]

4 Not so the wicked!
They are like chaff[j]
that the wind blows away.
5 Therefore the wicked will not stand[k] in the judgment,[l]
nor sinners in the assembly of the righteous.

6 For the LORD watches over[m] the way of the righteous,
but the way of the wicked will perish.[n]

1:1 [a]Pr 4:14 [b]Ps 26:4; Jer 15:17
1:2 [c]Ps 119:16,35 [d]Ps 119:1 [e]Jos 1:8
1:3 [f]Ps 128:3 [g]Jer 17:8 [h]Eze 47:12 [i]Ge 39:3
1:4 [j]Job 21:18; Isa 17:13
1:5 [k]Ps 5:5 [l]Ps 9:7-8,16
1:6 [m]Ps 37:18; 2Ti 2:19 [n]Ps 9:6

Psalm 2

1 Why do the nations conspire[a]
and the peoples plot[o] in vain?
2 The kings[p] of the earth take their stand
and the rulers gather together
against the LORD
and against his Anointed[q] One.[b][r]
3 "Let us break their chains," they say,
"and throw off their fetters."[s]

4 The One enthroned in heaven laughs;[t]
the Lord scoffs at them.
5 Then he rebukes them in his anger
and terrifies them in his wrath,[u] saying,

2:1 [o]Ps 21:11
2:2 [p]Ps 48:4 [q]Jn 1:41 [r]Ps 74:18,23; Ac 4:25-26*
2:3 [s]Jer 5:5
2:4 [t]Ps 37:13; 59:8; Pr 1:26
2:5 [u]Ps 21:9; 78:49-50

[a] *1* Hebrew; Septuagint *rage* [b] *2* Or *anointed one*

Psalm 1 *Introduction.* Psalm 1 stands at the beginning of the Psalter as a gateway to a sanctuary. It is a wisdom psalm exhorting worshipers to have the right attitude toward the law of God before entering into intimate conversation with him. Quite simply, the righteous love God's law and desire to saturate themselves in it, while the wicked hate and ignore it. The righteous may also be identified as those who keep covenant with, love and obey God, thus demonstrating that they are his. The wicked break covenant with God.
1:1–2 See *HC* 114.
1:1 Blessed. A stronger word than *happy*, though it often includes happiness. One who is blessed is the object of God's special favor and grace. **not walk . . . or stand . . . or sit.** The righteous are described here by what they avoid. The verbs progress from lesser to greater commitment: The righteous neither walk nor stand nor sit in the seat of wickedness. **counsel . . . way . . . seat.** The righteous do not follow the advice of the wicked or adopt their behavior or views. See *WLC* 113.
1:2 his delight. The righteous love God's law, and God's law expresses his will. Therefore, the righteous desire to do what God requires of them. **law.** Can refer to a specific command, but here it probably indicates the whole of Scripture that was available at the time. The righteous are formed by their obedient response to the Scriptures, which embody the will of God. **he meditates.** The righteous memorize, repeat and reflect on the law. God's word shapes and informs meditation. See *WLC* 157.
1:3 like a tree. As Joseph prospered in Egypt, so the righteous will tend to flourish, like a tree that continually blooms because life-giving water is near. Such a tree is vital, deep rooted and productive.
1:4 Not so the wicked! The contrast is strong. The wicked, like the righteous, are described as a plant, but one that is dead and rootless. The slightest puff of wind will carry it away.
1:5 not stand. Though the wicked will be present at God's judgment, they will fall under condemnation.
1:6 the LORD watches over. The two ways of life determine the destinies of those who follow them. **the way of the righteous.** Jesus Christ fulfilled the ideal righteous life.
Psalm 2 *Introduction.* The theme of kingship permeates Psalms. Most other kingship psalms focus on either divine or human kingship. Psalm 2 masterfully integrates the two, while contrasting the divine King and his human counterpart with the hostile kings "of the earth." The psalm does not have a title, but both Peter and John ascribed it to David (Ac 4:25). The New Testament frequently quoted and alluded to this psalm (Mt 3:17; 17:5; Ac 4:25–27; 13:33; Ro 1:4; Heb 1:5; 5:5). Jesus Christ is at once the son of David and the Son of God. The promises given to David are and will be fulfilled in Christ.
2:1 the nations. The Gentiles.
2:2 kings. The nations were organized by their political leaders. **gather together.** An ungodly coalition of the kings of the earth direct their hostility toward God and the human king he has delegated. **Anointed One.** Some take this as a reference to Jesus exclusively (note capitalization in the NIV), but in its Old Testament context the general office of Davidic king was intended. This king reflected the glory of the Messiah because he foreshadowed Christ.
2:3 break their chains. A metaphor for rebellion. See *BC* 29.

6 “I have installed my King[a]
on Zion, my holy hill.”

7 I will proclaim the decree of the LORD:

He said to me, “You are my Son[b];
today I have become your Father.[c v]
8 Ask of me,
and I will make the nations your inheritance,
the ends of the earth[w] your possession.
9 You will rule them with an iron scepter[d; x]
you will dash them to pieces[y] like pottery.[z]”

10 Therefore, you kings, be wise;
be warned, you rulers of the earth.
11 Serve the LORD with fear
and rejoice[a] with trembling.[b]
12 Kiss the Son,[c] lest he be angry
and you be destroyed in your way,
for his wrath[d] can flare up in a moment.
Blessed are all who take refuge[e] in him.

Psalm 3

A psalm of David. When he fled from his son Absalom.[f]

1 O LORD, how many are my foes!
How many rise up against me!
2 Many are saying of me,
“God will not deliver him.[g]” *Selah*[e]

3 But you are a shield[h] around me, O LORD;
you bestow glory on me and lift[f] up my head.[i]
4 To the LORD I cry aloud,
and he answers me from his holy hill.[j] *Selah*

5 I lie down and sleep;[k]
I wake again, because the LORD sustains me.
6 I will not fear[l] the tens of thousands
drawn up against me on every side.

7 Arise,[m] O LORD!

2:7 [v]Ac 13:33*; Heb 1:5*
2:8 [w]Ps 22:27
2:9 [x]Rev 12:5 [y]Ps 89:23 [z]Rev 2:27*
2:11 [a]Heb 12:28 [b]Ps 119:119-120
2:12 [c]Jn 5:23 [d]Rev 6:16 [e]Ps 34:8; Ro 9:33
3:1 [f]2Sa 15:14
3:2 [g]Ps 71:11
3:3 [h]Ge 15:1; Ps 28:7 [i]Ps 27:6
3:4 [j]Ps 2:6
3:5 [k]Lev 26:6; Pr 3:24
3:6 [l]Ps 27:3
3:7 [m]Ps 7:6

[a] 6 Or *king* [b] 7 Or *son*; also in verse 12 [c] 7 Or *have begotten you* [d] 9 Or *will break them with a rod of iron* [e] 2 A word of uncertain meaning, occurring frequently in the Psalms; possibly a musical term [f] 3 Or *LORD, / my Glorious One, who lifts*

2:6 my King. The Lord counters the plotting of the kings by pointing to his earthly representative, established by God in Jerusalem. The passage anticipates Christ, but the reference is to the king of Israel, who was a type of Christ. **on Zion.** Zion was a hill north of Jerusalem. Its importance had nothing to do with its size, but rather with the temple located there; it was the place God chose to make his presence known to his people. The name Zion is sometimes used as a synonym for Jerusalem. Zion was the physical symbol of the dwelling of God in heaven, and much of the symbolism of the temple pointed to heaven. See *WCF* 8.1; *WLC* 42; *WSC* 23.
2:7 He said to me, “You are my Son.” David reflected on God’s promise in 2 Samuel 7:14. In the Davidic covenant God had promised this intimate relationship with those obedient descendants of David who would rule from Jerusalem. Davidic kingship is fulfilled in the kingship of Jesus Christ (Ac 13:33–34; Ro 1:4; Heb 1:5; 5:5). **today.** This reference marks the poem as a coronation psalm, celebrating the day on which the monarch took control. See *BC* 10; *HC* 35.
2:8–11 See *WCF* 25.2; *WLC* 45,62; *WSC* 23; *BC* 10; *HC* 117.
2:10–12 be warned, you rulers of the earth. An admonition to the hostile kings. See *WCF* 23.2.
2:11 Serve the LORD with fear. See 34:8–14 and 103:13 and 17–18. See also note on 34:7, as well as “Introduction to Proverbs: Purpose and Distinctives.”
2:12 Kiss. An act of submission (cf. 1Sa 10;1). The hostile kings of the nations must submit themselves not only to God, but also to the king of Israel, his human representative. Otherwise, God will grant his people military victory over them. **the Son.** The Davidic king. The word used for “Son” is not the common Hebrew word, *ben,* but an Aramaic term, *bar.* The NIV capitalizes “Son” and rightly points us to the Messianic fulfillment of the verse (see notes on v. 7 and “Introduction” to this psalm).
Psalm 3 *Introduction.* Psalm 3 contains elements both of lament and of confidence (see “Introduction: Structure: *Genres*”). Although surrounded by trouble, David not only cried out to the Lord in distress but also expressed deep trust in God. The title relates the writing of the psalm to David’s flight from and battle against Absalom (2Sa 15:1—18:18). The military terminology throughout the psalm suggests that it continued to be used in situations of warfare.
3:1 how many are my foes! The number and nature of the foes indicates the royal origin of the psalm. The foes of the nation were also the king’s foes.
3:3 lift up my head. An image of encouragement.
3:4 holy hill. Zion, the site of the Jerusalem temple, chosen and prepared during David’s lifetime. See note on “on Zion” at verse 6.
3:5 I lie down and sleep. The psalmist slept in the war camp even though the enemy was near. He was confident that God, the Divine Warrior, protected him. See Psalm 91.
3:7 Arise. This expression is typical in psalms that were sung in situations of holy war. **Deliver.** God fights for his people against their flesh-and-blood enemies.

3:7 [n]Ps 6:4 [o]Job 16:10 [p]Ps 58:6
3:8 [q]Isa 43:3,11
4:1 [r]Ps 25:16 [s]Ps 17:6
4:2 [t]Ps 31:6
4:3 [u]Ps 31:23 [v]Ps 6:8
4:4 [w]Eph 4:26* [x]Ps 77:6
4:5 [y]Dt 33:19; Ps 37:3
4:6 [z]Nu 6:25
4:7 [a]Ac 14:17 [b]Isa 9:3
4:8 [c]Ps 3:5 [d]Lev 25:18
5:2 [e]Ps 3:4 [f]Ps 84:3
5:3 [g]Ps 88:13

Deliver me,[n] O my God!
Strike[o] all my enemies on the jaw;
break the teeth[p] of the wicked.

8 From the LORD comes deliverance.[q]
May your blessing be on your people. *Selah*

Psalm 4

For the director of music. With stringed instruments.
A psalm of David.

1 Answer me when I call to you,
O my righteous God.
Give me relief from my distress;
be merciful[r] to me and hear my prayer.[s]

2 How long, O men, will you turn my glory into shame[a]?
How long will you love delusions and seek false gods[b]?[t] *Selah*
3 Know that the LORD has set apart the godly[u] for himself;
the LORD will hear[v] when I call to him.

4 In your anger do not sin;[w]
when you are on your beds,[x]
search your hearts and be silent. *Selah*
5 Offer right sacrifices
and trust in the LORD.[y]

6 Many are asking, "Who can show us any good?"
Let the light of your face shine upon us,[z] O LORD.
7 You have filled my heart[a] with greater joy[b]
than when their grain and new wine abound.
8 I will lie down and sleep[c] in peace,
for you alone, O LORD,
make me dwell in safety.[d]

Psalm 5

For the director of music. For flutes. A psalm of David.

1 Give ear to my words, O LORD,
consider my sighing.
2 Listen to my cry for help,[e]
my King and my God,[f]
for to you I pray.
3 In the morning,[g] O LORD, you hear my voice;
in the morning I lay my requests before you
and wait in expectation.

[a] 2 Or *you dishonor my Glorious One* [b] 2 Or *seek lies*

Psalm 4 *Introduction.* Psalm 4 shares some traits with Psalm 3. Both relate to distressing circumstances, and in both David exhibited his profound reliance upon God. Also like Psalm 3, this psalm meditates on faith in the night (vv. 4,8). Because of his covenant relationship with God, David had confidence that God would hear his prayers and answer him.
4:1 my righteous God. Here, as often in the Old Testament, God's righteousness is his covenant fidelity. David fearlessly called on God to keep the terms of the covenant by delivering him from distress.
4:2 turn my glory into shame. This phrase is difficult to interpret (see NIV text note). It may be best understood as an expression of anger at people who turn away from the true God to worship and serve the false gods of the nations. **delusions.** Literally, "empty things." **seek false gods.** Literally, "seek lies." Idols are equated with "lies" in the sense that they are not real gods.
4:3 godly. Hebrew *hasid,* usually rendered in the NIV as "the godly" or "saints." The term refers to all those who are in covenant with God.
4:5 right sacrifices. Sacrifices offered not only in accordance with priestly regulations (Lev 1–7), but also from a fitting attitude of heart (see 40:6–8; 51:17). See *WCF* 18.3.
4:6 good. The unbelieving lamented that nothing was good. The psalmist responded to their doubts with an appeal to God to reveal himself. **light of your face.** The phrase reflects the blessing that God instructed the priests to invoke on behalf of the people (see Nu 6:25–26).
4:8 sleep in peace. God's intimate presence allowed the psalmist to sleep serenely and with full confidence. His heart was spilling over with spiritual blessing.
Psalm 5 *Introduction.* This psalm, a lament, petitioned the Lord from the midst of distress. David's distress was caused by people whose wickedness was particularly manifest in their speech. Sharp contrast is drawn between the psalmist's words and those of his wicked adversaries.
5:1 sighing. The Hebrew word implies a kind of muttering or under-the-breath speech.
5:2 my . . . my. The psalmist enjoyed an intimate relationship with God. **King.** David, Israel's king, addressed God as his own King. Speaking of God's kingship was a way to express God's sovereignty and power.

4 You are not a God who takes pleasure in evil;
with you the wicked[h] cannot dwell.
5 The arrogant[i] cannot stand[j] in your presence;
you hate[k] all who do wrong.
6 You destroy those who tell lies;[l]
bloodthirsty and deceitful men
the LORD abhors.

7 But I, by your great mercy,
will come into your house;
in reverence will I bow down[m]
toward your holy temple.
8 Lead me, O LORD, in your righteousness[n]
because of my enemies—
make straight your way[o] before me.

9 Not a word from their mouth can be trusted;
their heart is filled with destruction.
Their throat is an open grave;[p]
with their tongue they speak deceit.[q]
10 Declare them guilty, O God!
Let their intrigues be their downfall.
Banish them for their many sins,[r]
for they have rebelled[s] against you.

11 But let all who take refuge in you be glad;
let them ever sing for joy.[t]
Spread your protection over them,
that those who love your name[u] may rejoice in you.[v]
12 For surely, O LORD, you bless the righteous;
you surround them[w] with your favor as with a shield.

Psalm 6

For the director of music. With stringed instruments.
According to *sheminith*.[a] A psalm of David.

1 O LORD, do not rebuke me in your anger[x]
or discipline me in your wrath.
2 Be merciful to me, LORD, for I am faint;
O LORD, heal me,[y] for my bones are in agony.[z]
3 My soul is in anguish.[a]
How long,[b] O LORD, how long?

4 Turn, O LORD, and deliver me;

5:4 [h]Ps 11:5; 92:15
5:5 [i]Ps 73:3 [j]Ps 1:5 [k]Ps 11:5
5:6 [l]Ps 55:23; Rev 21:8
5:7 [m]Ps 138:2
5:8 [n]Ps 31:1 [o]Ps 27:11
5:9 [p]Lk 11:44 [q]Ro 3:13*
5:10 [r]Ps 9:16 [s]Ps 107:11
5:11 [t]Ps 2:12 [u]Ps 69:36 [v]Isa 65:13
5:12 [w]Ps 32:7
6:1 [x]Ps 38:1
6:2 [y]Hos 6:1 [z]Ps 22:14; 31:10
6:3 [a]Jn 12:27 [b]Ps 90:13

[a] Title: Probably a musical term

5:4–6 See *WCF* 2.1; *HC* 10,11.
5:4 You are not a God who takes pleasure in evil. This is poetic understatement. God hates sin. **the wicked cannot dwell.** God is holy; he is completely without sin and separate from all evil. Therefore, sinful people may not come into his presence without a substitutionary sacrifice. See *BC* 13.
5:7 I . . . will come into your house. The psalmist protested his innocence by expressing his desire to worship the Lord. When David composed this psalm, "your house" and "your holy temple" generally referred either to the tent of meeting (see 1Sa 1:7) or to the future temple. After the temple was built, the terms were identified almost exclusively with the temple. **by your great mercy.** The psalmist knew that he was different from the wicked only because of God's grace. His own sin would destroy him if God did not show compassion as he approached the divine presence. See *WLC* 174.
5:8 your righteousness. God's righteousness would be revealed in defending his king and vindicating him against his unjust enemies. See note on 4:1. **your way.** The path of safety God opens is the path of obedience to his will.
5:9 destruction . . . open grave. Note how evil speech is directly equated with a sentence of death.
5:10 Let their intrigues be their downfall. The psalmist called for punishment for the wicked. They are guilty, so God should declare them and treat them as such. Sin often produces its own dire consequences. See "Introduction: Christ in Psalms."
5:11 take refuge. Whereas the deceitful rebel against God (v. 6), his people seek his protection. He is a fortress to those who trust him, and divine protection results in joy.
5:12 as with a shield. Emphasizes God's protection for his people.
Psalm 6 *Introduction.* The psalm is a personal lament. As with many laments, the psalmist expressed his trust in the Lord at the end of the psalm. The original motivation for the psalm may have been a severe illness (vv. 2,5). This psalm is one of seven "penitential" psalms (along with 32; 38; 51; 102; 130; 143).
6:1 rebuke . . . discipline. The psalmist begged the Lord to refrain from verbally and physically punishing him in anger, imploring God instead to demonstrate mercy (v. 2). See Hebrews 12:1–13.
6:2 I am faint . . . my bones are in agony. The psalmist experienced physical suffering, most probably from a serious illness. However, some commentators interpret the language figuratively, indicating a spiritual rather than a physical crisis. **heal me.** David called upon the Lord to intervene and save him.
6:3 My soul. This term may also be rendered "my life." The poetic conjunction of this phrase with "my bones" (v. 2) denotes the entire person. See theological article "Body and Soul in the Bible" at Genesis 2. **How long . . . ?** An expression of anguish meaning "How long will you permit this suffering to continue?"

save me because of your unfailing love.[c]
5 No one remembers you when he is dead.
Who praises you from the grave[a]?[d]

6 I am worn out[e] from groaning;
all night long I flood my bed with weeping
and drench my couch with tears.[f]
7 My eyes grow weak[g] with sorrow;
they fail because of all my foes.

8 Away from me,[h] all you who do evil,[i]
for the LORD has heard my weeping.
9 The LORD has heard my cry for mercy;[j]
the LORD accepts my prayer.
10 All my enemies will be ashamed and dismayed;
they will turn back in sudden disgrace.[k]

Psalm 7

A *shiggaion*[b] of David, which he sang to the LORD concerning Cush, a Benjamite.

1 O LORD my God, I take refuge in you;
save and deliver me from all who pursue me,[l]
2 or they will tear me like a lion[m]
and rip me to pieces with no one to rescue[n] me.

3 O LORD my God, if I have done this
and there is guilt on my hands[o]—
4 if I have done evil to him who is at peace with me
or without cause have robbed my foe—
5 then let my enemy pursue and overtake me;
let him trample my life to the ground
and make me sleep in the dust. *Selah*

6 Arise,[p] O LORD, in your anger;
rise up against the rage of my enemies.[q]
Awake,[r] my God; decree justice.
7 Let the assembled peoples gather around you.
Rule over them from on high;
8 let the LORD judge the peoples.
Judge me, O LORD, according to my righteousness,[s]
according to my integrity, O Most High.
9 O righteous God,[t]
who searches minds and hearts,[u]
bring to an end the violence of the wicked
and make the righteous secure.[v]

10 My shield[c] is God Most High,
who saves the upright in heart.[w]

6:4 [c]Ps 17:13
6:5 [d]Ps 30:9; 88:10-12; Ecc 9:10; Isa 38:18
6:6 [e]Ps 69:3 [f]Ps 42:3
6:7 [g]Ps 31:9
6:8 [h]Ps 119:115 [i]Mt 7:23; Lk 13:27
6:9 [j]Ps 116:1
6:10 [k]Ps 71:24; 73:19
7:1 [l]Ps 31:15
7:2 [m]Isa 38:13 [n]Ps 50:22
7:3 [o]1Sa 24:11; Isa 59:3
7:6 [p]Ps 94:2 [q]Ps 138:7 [r]Ps 44:23
7:8 [s]Ps 18:20; 96:13
7:9 [t]Jer 11:20 [u]1Ch 28:9; Ps 26:2; Rev 2:23 [v]Ps 37:23
7:10 [w]Ps 125:4

[a] *5* Hebrew *Sheol* [b] Title: Probably a literary or musical term [c] *10* Or *sovereign*

6:4 Turn, O LORD. The metaphor implies that God had turned away from the psalmist, that David did not feel his divine presence. **unfailing love.** The Hebrew word thus translated summarizes all the devotion by which God bound himself to Israel and to David through his covenant (89:4,24,28,33; 2Sa 7:15; Isa 55:3).
6:5 No one remembers. See a similar expression in 30:9. David may have meant that the dead do not praise God among the living, or he may have been referring to death from the perspective of the body. See theological article "Body and Soul in the Bible" at Genesis 2. **grave.** Often transliterated *Sheol,* a word appearing most often in poetic contexts. Both the righteous and the wicked go there after death (Job 3:17).
6:8 all you who do evil. This reference, along with the allusion to foes in the preceding verse, is abrupt. Possibly the foes were those who, like the "friends" of Job, blamed David's illness on his sin.
Psalm 7 *Introduction.* Psalm 7 is a lament by an individual who was beset by enemies but innocent of the charges levied against him. David appealed his case to God's court of justice. His claim of innocence refers to the specific charges—it is not an assertion of sinlessness. See Psalms 11, 17, 26, 27, 31 and 71. The reference in the title to "Cush, a Benjamite" may link the psalm to David's persecution by Saul, who was also a Benjamite.
7:2 like a lion. Though not found there today, lions were plentiful in ancient Israel and the broader Near East. The lion often symbolized power, cruelty and ruthlessness (e.g., Isa 5:29; Na 2:11,12).
7:3–5 if . . . then. The psalmist swore an oath to his innocence, calling down curses on himself should he be lying (see note on Job 31:1–40).
7:6 Arise, O LORD. The psalmist petitioned God to intervene in the situation. This language is frequently found in laments, particularly in contexts which call upon God to wage war on behalf of the psalmist. See note on 3:7.
7:8 Judge me, O LORD. The passage reflects a judicial tone. David asked God to judge the case between himself and his opponents.

11 God is a righteous judge,[x]
a God who expresses his wrath every day.
12 If he does not relent,
he[a] will sharpen his sword;[y]
he will bend and string his bow.
13 He has prepared his deadly weapons;
he makes ready his flaming arrows.

14 He who is pregnant with evil
and conceives trouble gives birth[z] to disillusionment.
15 He who digs a hole and scoops it out
falls into the pit he has made.[a]
16 The trouble he causes recoils on himself;
his violence comes down on his own head.

17 I will give thanks to the LORD because of his righteousness[b]
and will sing praise[c] to the name of the LORD Most High.

Psalm 8

For the director of music. According to *gittith.*[b]
A psalm of David.

1 O LORD, our Lord,
how majestic is your name in all the earth!

You have set your glory
above the heavens.[d]
2 From the lips of children and infants
you have ordained praise[c][e]
because of your enemies,
to silence the foe[f] and the avenger.

3 When I consider your heavens,[g]
the work of your fingers,
the moon and the stars,[h]
which you have set in place,
4 what is man that you are mindful of him,
the son of man that you care for him?[i]
5 You made him a little lower than the heavenly beings[d]
and crowned him with glory and honor.[j]

6 You made him ruler[k] over the works of your hands;
you put everything under his feet:[l][m]
7 all flocks and herds,

7:11 [x]Ps 50:6
7:12 [y]Dt 32:41
7:14 [z]Job 15:35; Isa 59:4; Jas 1:15
7:15 [a]Job 4:8
7:17 [b]Ps 71:15-16 [c]Ps 9:2
8:1 [d]Ps 57:5; 113:4; 148:13
8:2 [e]Mt 21:16* [f]Ps 44:16; 1Co 1:27
8:3 [g]Ps 89:11 [h]Ps 136:9
8:4 [i]Job 7:17; Ps 144:3; Heb 2:6
8:5 [j]Ps 21:5; 103:4
8:6 [k]Ge 1:28 [l]Heb 2:6-8* [m]1Co 15:25, 27*; Eph 1:22

[a] 12 Or *If a man does not repent, / God* than God [b] Title: Probably a musical term [c] 2 Or *strength* [d] 5 Or

7:14–16 pregnant with evil . . . digs a hole. Sin brings its own retribution.
7:17 give thanks. The psalm concludes on a positive note. Though David was in the midst of distress, he could still praise the Lord because he knew that the omnipotent God was his just judge.
Psalm 8 *Introduction.* A hymn in praise of the Creator. Since created order was a major theme of the sages of Israel, the psalm may also be categorized as a wisdom poem. It exhibits a reflective and reverential tone toward God and his universe and focuses on God's privileged treatment of humanity, in conferring upon people dominance over the rest of creation. See *WLC* 112,190; *HC* 6.
8:1 LORD. The personal, or covenantal, name of God that he revealed to Moses at the burning bush (cf. Ex 3). **our Lord.** A title that can also be translated "governor" or "master." David could call God "our" Lord because of the covenant the Lord had established with Israel (cf. Ge 17:7; Ex 20:2; Lev 26:1). **how majestic is your name.** God's name signifies his character or reputation. The repetition of this opening line at the end of the psalm imparts a reverential air to the entire composition. **set your glory above.** The expression "set . . . above" elsewhere means "set . . . upon." God has robed himself with the glory of the heavens.
8:2 children . . . enemies. Note the contrast between the weak and the strong. Because of the God whose praise they sing, the weak silence the powerful. See Matthew 21:16.
8:3 the work of your fingers. The almost limitless universe is described as the work of God's fingers. This anthropomorphic line impresses us with the power of God. The verse reflects on Genesis 1.
8:4–6. everything under his feet. A reference to man's dominion over creation (see note on v. 8; cf. Ge 1:26–28). Applied to Jesus in Hebrews 2:6–8. Christ was both a perfect human and God incarnate. Jesus is the model of redeemed humanity and restored human dominion over creation. See also 1 Corinthians 15:27 and Ephesians 1:22.
8:4 what is man . . . ? Compare 144:3, Job 7:17 and 25:6. In light of the vastness of the universe and the immensity of God's power, humanity pales into seeming insignificance.
8:5 heavenly beings. Hebrew *'elohim,* usually translated "God" (see NIV text note). The Septuagint (the Greek translation of the OT), renders it "angels" (as quoted in Heb 2:7). "Angels" is an appropriate translation, because the Hebrew word can mean "supernatural beings" or even "rulers" (see note on Da 10:3).
8:6 You made him ruler. Describes humanity's God-given significance and recalls the cultural mandate given to Adam in the garden (Ge 1:28). Humanity was given dominance over all other creatures on the earth (v. 7), in the air or in the seas (v. 8).

and the beasts of the field,
8 the birds of the air,
and the fish of the sea,
all that swim the paths of the seas.

9 O LORD, our Lord,
how majestic is your name in all the earth![n]

8:9 [n]ver 1

Psalm 9[a]

For the director of music. To ⌊the tune of⌋ "The Death of the Son." A psalm of David.

1 I will praise you, O LORD, with all my heart;[o]
I will tell of all your wonders.[p]
2 I will be glad and rejoice[q] in you;
I will sing praise to your name,[r] O Most High.

3 My enemies turn back;
they stumble and perish before you.
4 For you have upheld my right and my cause;[s]
you have sat on your throne, judging righteously.[t]
5 You have rebuked the nations and destroyed the wicked;
you have blotted out their name[u] for ever and ever.
6 Endless ruin has overtaken the enemy,
you have uprooted their cities;
even the memory of them[v] has perished.

7 The LORD reigns forever;
he has established his throne[w] for judgment.
8 He will judge the world in righteousness;[x]
he will govern the peoples with justice.
9 The LORD is a refuge for the oppressed,
a stronghold in times of trouble.[y]
10 Those who know your name[z] will trust in you,
for you, LORD, have never forsaken[a] those who seek you.

11 Sing praises to the LORD, enthroned in Zion;[b]
proclaim among the nations[c] what he has done.[d]
12 For he who avenges blood[e] remembers;
he does not ignore the cry of the afflicted.

13 O LORD, see how my enemies[f] persecute me!
Have mercy and lift me up from the gates of death,
14 that I may declare your praises[g]
in the gates of the Daughter of Zion
and there rejoice in your salvation.[h]

9:1 [o]Ps 86:12 [p]Ps 26:7
9:2 [q]Ps 5:11 [r]Ps 92:1; 83:18
9:4 [s]Ps 140:12 [t]1Pe 2:23
9:5 [u]Pr 10:7
9:6 [v]Ps 34:16
9:7 [w]Ps 89:14
9:8 [x]Ps 96:13
9:9 [y]Ps 32:7
9:10 [z]Ps 91:14 [a]Ps 37:28
9:11 [b]Ps 76:2 [c]Ps 107:22 [d]Ps 105:1
9:12 [e]Ge 9:5
9:13 [f]Ps 38:19
9:14 [g]Ps 106:2 [h]Ps 13:5; 51:12

[a] Psalms 9 and 10 may have been originally a single acrostic poem, the stanzas of which begin with the successive letters of the Hebrew alphabet. In the Septuagint they constitute one psalm.

Psalm 9 *Introduction.* The petitions of verses 13 and 19–20 suggest that this psalm is a lament. However, the psalm begins like a hymn of praise and thanksgiving. In verse 13 and following the psalmist turned to the Lord with new petitions, and the psalm concludes on this note. The wicked still oppressed David, and he called once again on God to deliver him. Psalms 9 and 10 are closely related—originally they were probably a single psalm (see NIV text note on 10:1). The Septuagint (Greek translation of the OT) treated them as a unified psalm.
9:1 praise you. The psalm begins like a hymn of thanksgiving. **wonders.** The great acts of God and his intervention in human affairs, sometimes involving miracles, as, for example, in the exodus from Egypt.
9:2 your name. David praised God not only for his acts but also for revealing his nature. Compare 8:1.
9:3 My enemies turn back. The Hebrew may imply an element of time: "*When* my enemies turn back." Interpreted this way, this is a statement of future hope rather than of past reality.
9:4 throne, judging righteously. David was confident not in himself but in the nature of God as a righteous judge. See note on 4:1.
9:5 blotted out. To be remembered no more, as if "erased" from a papyrus scroll (see Nu 5:23; Dt 9:14; 25:19; 29:20; 2Ki 14:27). **their name.** Contrasted with God's name (v. 2), which will be praised forever.
9:7 reigns . . . established his throne for judgment. As royal judge from heaven (see 11:4).
9:8 in righteousness. He is a righteous judge; only the wicked need fear him. Compare 98:9. See note on 4:1.
9:9 refuge for the oppressed. While the wicked should fear him, the Lord gives the oppressed hope. The oppressed were those who, like the psalmist, were being coerced by outside evil forces (the enemy).
9:11 enthroned in Zion. Refers specifically to the ark of the covenant that symbolized God's presence on the site of the temple in Jerusalem. The afflicted should know that God is present with them in the world.
9:12 avenges blood. Literally, "seeks blood." God does not allow wickedness to go unrequited (Ge 9:6; Na 1:2–6).
9:13 gates of death. Similar to the modern expression "the brink of death." This verse is the first hint of the psalmist's present distress.

15 The nations have fallen into the pit they have dug;[i]
their feet are caught in the net they have hidden.[j]
16 The LORD is known by his justice;
the wicked are ensnared by the work of their hands.
Higgaion.[a] *Selah*
17 The wicked return to the grave,[b][k]
all the nations that forget God.[l]
18 But the needy will not always be forgotten,
nor the hope[m] of the afflicted[n] ever perish.

19 Arise, O LORD, let not man triumph;
let the nations be judged in your presence.
20 Strike them with terror, O LORD;
let the nations know they are but men.[o] *Selah*

Psalm 10[c]

1 Why, O LORD, do you stand far off?[p]
Why do you hide yourself[q] in times of trouble?
2 In his arrogance the wicked man hunts down the weak,
who are caught in the schemes he devises.
3 He boasts[r] of the cravings of his heart;
he blesses the greedy and reviles the LORD.
4 In his pride the wicked does not seek him;
in all his thoughts there is no room for God.[s]
5 His ways are always prosperous;
he is haughty and your laws are far from him;
he sneers at all his enemies.
6 He says to himself, "Nothing will shake me;
I'll always be happy[t] and never have trouble."
7 His mouth is full of curses[u] and lies and threats;[v]
trouble and evil are under his tongue.[w]
8 He lies in wait near the villages;
from ambush he murders the innocent,[x]
watching in secret for his victims.
9 He lies in wait like a lion in cover;
he lies in wait to catch the helpless;[y]
he catches the helpless and drags them off in his net.
10 His victims are crushed, they collapse;
they fall under his strength.
11 He says to himself, "God has forgotten;[z]
he covers his face and never sees."

9:15 [i]Ps 7:15-16 [j]Ps 35:8; 57:6
9:17 [k]Ps 49:14 [l]Job 8:13; Ps 50:22
9:18 [m]Ps 71:5; Pr 23:18 [n]Ps 12:5
9:20 [o]Ps 62:9; Isa 31:3
10:1 [p]Ps 22:1,11 [q]Ps 13:1
10:3 [r]Ps 94:4
10:4 [s]Ps 14:1; 36:1
10:6 [t]Rev 18:7
10:7 [u]Ro 3:14* [v]Ps 73:8 [w]Ps 140:3
10:8 [x]Ps 94:6
10:9 [y]Ps 17:12; 59:3; 140:5
10:11 [z]Job 22:13

[a] *16* Or *Meditation*; possibly a musical notation [b] *17* Hebrew *Sheol* [c] Psalms 9 and 10 may have been originally a single acrostic poem, the stanzas of which begin with the successive letters of the Hebrew alphabet. In the Septuagint they constitute one psalm.

9:14 the gates of the Daughter of Zion. Contrasted with "gates of death" in the previous verse. David prayed that he might praise God in the most public of places for answered prayer. **Daughter of Zion.** That is, Jerusalem.
9:15 have fallen into the pit they have dug. Compare 7:14–16. The wickedness of the psalmist's adversaries would come back to haunt them.
9:17 The wicked. They are "all the nations that forget God." **grave.** Hebrew *Sheol.* See notes on 6:5.
9:18 the needy. Like the psalmist, someone afflicted unjustly. **will not always be forgotten.** The wicked nations forget God, but God does not forget the afflicted.
9:19 Arise, O LORD. See note on 7:6.
Psalm 10 *Introduction.* Most likely in its original form this was a single psalm, along with Psalm 9. See "Introduction" to Psalm 9. Taken separately, however, Psalm 10 is an individual's lament. It bemoans the wicked who have victimized the righteous and calls on God to restore justice.
Title. This is an "orphan" psalm; that is, there is no title. This absence supports the original unity of Psalms 9 and 10.
10:1 Why . . . do you stand far off? The psalmist was more troubled by God's apparent absence than by the affliction of his enemies. It was in the lack of justice that he experienced the absence of God.
10:3 blesses the greedy and reviles the LORD. The wicked person makes topsy-turvy ethical judgments.
10:5 always prosperous. From the limited perspective of the oppressed, it appears that the wicked have not a care in the world (cf. 73:12). **sneers at all his enemies.** The wicked disdain not only God but also any who oppose them on the human plane.
10:6 He says to himself, "Nothing will shake me." An expression of prideful confidence based upon human ability and supposed invincibility rather than upon God. See 30:6.
10:7 mouth . . . tongue. A reference to sins of speech. The apostle Paul alluded to this verse in Romans 3:14.
10:8–9 near the villages. The best place for murderers to waylay the unwary is where the victims cannot escape and where no aid can reach them. The image may suggest the boldness of these wicked individuals or the political power they wielded that allowed them to ambush their victims near inhabited villages.
10:9 like a lion. Known for their stealth and for their propensity to prey on the weak, lions also stalk their prey. **in his net.** The wicked, as a hunter, schemes to deceive the weak and vulnerable (see v. 2).

10:12
[a]Ps 17:7; Mic 5:9
[b]Ps 9:12

10:14
[c]Ps 22:11 [d]Ps 37:5
[e]Ps 68:5

10:15
[f]Ps 37:17

10:16
[g]Ps 29:10 [h]Dt 8:20

10:17
[i]1Ch 29:18; Ps 34:15

10:18
[j]Ps 82:3 [k]Ps 9:9

12 Arise, LORD! Lift up your hand,[a] O God.
Do not forget the helpless.[b]
13 Why does the wicked man revile God?
Why does he say to himself,
"He won't call me to account"?
14 But you, O God, do see trouble[c] and grief;
you consider it to take it in hand.
The victim commits himself to you;[d]
you are the helper[e] of the fatherless.
15 Break the arm of the wicked and evil man;[f]
call him to account for his wickedness
that would not be found out.

16 The LORD is King for ever and ever;[g]
the nations[h] will perish from his land.
17 You hear, O LORD, the desire of the afflicted;[i]
you encourage them, and you listen to their cry,
18 defending the fatherless[j] and the oppressed,[k]
in order that man, who is of the earth, may terrify no more.

Psalm 11

For the director of music. Of David.

11:1
[l]Ps 56:11

11:2
[m]Ps 7:13
[n]Ps 64:3-4

11:3
[o]Ps 82:5

11:4
[p]Ps 18:6
[q]Ps 103:19
[r]Ps 33:13
[s]Ps 34:15-16

11:5
[t]Ge 22:1; Jas 1:12
[u]Ps 5:5

11:6
[v]Eze 38:22
[w]Jer 4:11-12

1 In the LORD I take refuge.[l]
How then can you say to me:
"Flee like a bird to your mountain.
2 For look, the wicked bend their bows;
they set their arrows[m] against the strings
to shoot from the shadows
at the upright in heart.[n]
3 When the foundations[o] are being destroyed,
what can the righteous do[a]?"

4 The LORD is in his holy temple;[p]
the LORD is on his heavenly throne.[q]
He observes the sons of men;[r]
his eyes examine[s] them.
5 The LORD examines the righteous,[t]
but the wicked[b] and those who love violence
his soul hates.[u]
6 On the wicked he will rain
fiery coals and burning sulfur;[v]
a scorching wind[w] will be their lot.

[a] 3 Or *what is the Righteous One doing* [b] 5 Or *The LORD, the Righteous One, examines the wicked, /*

10:11 He says to himself, "God has forgotten." Lack of apparent justice signified God's absence to the wicked, thus encouraging them to even more malicious behavior on the premise that God would not call them to account (v. 13).
10:12 Arise, LORD! See note on 7:6. **Lift up your hand.** A metaphor calling for God's active intervention on behalf of the persecuted.
10:14 helper of the fatherless. The fatherless and the widow were extreme examples of helplessness, since they lacked the regular sources of protection a family provided.
10:16 The LORD is King. God is the covenant Lord. **nations.** The Gentiles; in this context, those who worship other gods and who persecute God's people.
10:17–18 you encourage them. The lament concludes with a strong statement of trust in a God who delivers the weak from oppression. God gave the psalmist security; foes may terrify, but God overrules human wickedness. See *WLC* 172,182.
Psalm 11 *Introduction.* Threatened by his enemies, the psalmist confidently sought refuge in God.
11:1 Flee like a bird. David was being advised to save himself rather than to trust in God to protect him.
11:2 bows . . . arrows. Imagery familiar to a warrior like David. While it would find an appropriate use during periods of holy war, the psalm could relate to other types of affliction as well.
11:3 foundations are being destroyed. The reference is to the foundations of the kingdom as a political entity: economy, military, etc. **what can the righteous do?** Or "what is the Righteous One doing?" See NIV text note. This does fit the context, as the next verses describe God's actions. See note on 4:1.
11:4 on his heavenly throne. As King of the universe, God controls it. Nothing escapes his notice—certainly not the actions of the wicked.
11:5 The LORD examines the righteous. That is, he tests them.
11:6 burning sulfur. Reminiscent of the judgment on Sodom and Gomorrah, recorded in Genesis 19:24. The evil will be completely burned up. **their lot.** Literally, "the portion of their cup." The psalms refer to the cup of God's blessing (Ps 23:5) as well as of his wrath, which the wicked will drink to its dregs (75:8) to their own destruction.
11:7 will see his face. An expression denoting access to God, especially in his court via the temple.
Psalm 12 *Introduction.* The psalmist complained to the Lord about enemies who oppressed verbally. He spoke both for himself and for the community of the afflicted: This psalm is a communal

7 For the LORD is righteous,[x]
he loves justice;[y]
upright men will see his face.[z]

11:7 [x]Ps 7:9,11; 45:7 [y]Ps 33:5 [z]Ps 17:15

Psalm 12

For the director of music. According to *sheminith.*[a]
A psalm of David.

1 Help, LORD, for the godly are no more;[a]
the faithful have vanished from among men.
2 Everyone lies to his neighbor;
their flattering lips speak with deception.[b]
3 May the LORD cut off all flattering lips
and every boastful tongue[c]
4 that says, "We will triumph with our tongues;
we own our lips[b] —who is our master?"
5 "Because of the oppression of the weak
and the groaning of the needy,
I will now arise," says the LORD.
"I will protect them[d] from those who malign them."
6 And the words of the LORD are flawless,[e]
like silver refined in a furnace of clay,
purified seven times.
7 O LORD, you will keep us safe
and protect us from such people forever.[f]
8 The wicked freely strut[g] about
when what is vile is honored among men.

12:1 [a]Isa 57:1
12:2 [b]Ps 10:7; 41:6; 55:21; Ro 16:18
12:3 [c]Da 7:8; Rev 13:5
12:5 [d]Ps 10:18; 34:6
12:6 [e]2Sa 22:31; Ps 18:30; Pr 30:5
12:7 [f]Ps 37:28
12:8 [g]Ps 55:10-11

Psalm 13

For the director of music. A psalm of David.

1 How long, O LORD? Will you forget me forever?
How long will you hide your face[h] from me?
2 How long must I wrestle with my thoughts[i]
and every day have sorrow in my heart?
How long will my enemy triumph over me?[j]
3 Look on me and answer,[k] O LORD my God.
Give light to my eyes,[l] or I will sleep in death;[m]
4 my enemy will say, "I have overcome him,[n]"
and my foes will rejoice when I fall.
5 But I trust in your unfailing love;[o]
my heart rejoices in your salvation.[p]
6 I will sing[q] to the LORD,
for he has been good to me.

13:1 [h]Job 13:24; Ps 44:24
13:2 [i]Ps 42:4 [j]Ps 42:9
13:3 [k]Ps 5:1 [l]Ezr 9:8 [m]Jer 51:39
13:4 [n]Ps 25:2
13:5 [o]Ps 52:8 [p]Ps 9:14
13:6 [q]Ps 116:7

[a] Title: Probably a musical term [b] *4* Or */ our lips are our plowshares*

lament. Notice how the words of the Lord are contrasted with those of flatterers and boasters (vv. 5–7).
12:1 the godly. See note on 4:3. **are no more.** Like Elijah (1Ki 19:14), the psalmist felt alone in his devotion to the Lord.
12:2 Everyone lies. Literally, "they speak lies." The noun "lies" is more accurately "emptiness," a term that not only embraces outright falsehood but also insincerity and irresponsibility. See *WLC* 145.
12:3–4 May the LORD cut off all flattering lips. An imprecation (curse) that God would punish insincere and proud speech, not a reference to physical mutilation. To be cut off usually means to be excluded from the community, sometimes by death (to be "cut off" from the living). See "Introduction: Christ in Psalms."
12:5 I will now arise. See note on 7:6.
12:6 purified seven times. That is, completely refined. The words of the Lord are contrasted with those of flatterers (vv. 3–4). See *WLC* 4; *BC* 7.

Psalm 13 *Introduction.* A lament from the perspective of an individual. The situation of distress is not clearly defined. If the language ("enemy") is taken literally, then a situation of warfare is in view. Verse 3, however, may indicate that David was ill and near death. In either case, it is clear that he had not abandoned hope but continued to put his trust in the Lord.

13:1 How long . . . ? See note on 6:3. The fourfold repetition emphasized David's anguish. **hide your face.** Since the psalmist experienced distress with no relief, he inferred that his covenant God did not look upon him favorably.

13:5 unfailing love. See note on 6:4. A covenant term that could also be translated "the gracious devotion," the type of love by which God binds himself to his people. **rejoices.** Contrast with verse 4. His enemy would rejoice if David were to fall (die), but David would rejoice if God were to deliver him.

Psalm 14

For the director of music. Of David.

14:1 [r]Ps 10:4

1 The fool[a] says in his heart,
"There is no God."[r]
They are corrupt, their deeds are vile;
there is no one who does good.

14:2 [s]Ps 33:13 [t]Ps 92:6

2 The LORD looks down from heaven[s]
on the sons of men
to see if there are any who understand,[t]
any who seek God.

14:3 [u]Ps 58:3 [v]Ps 143:2 [w]Ro 3:10-12*

3 All have turned aside,
they have together become corrupt;[u]
there is no one who does good,[v]
not even one.[w]

14:4 [x]Ps 82:5 [y]Ps 27:2 [z]Ps 79:6; Isa 64:7

4 Will evildoers never learn—[x]
those who devour my people[y] as men eat bread
and who do not call on the LORD?[z]
5 There they are, overwhelmed with dread,
for God is present in the company of the righteous.

14:6 [a]Ps 9:9; 40:17

6 You evildoers frustrate the plans of the poor,
but the LORD is their refuge.[a]

14:7 [b]Ps 53:6

7 Oh, that salvation for Israel would come out of Zion!
When the LORD restores the fortunes[b] of his people,
let Jacob rejoice and Israel be glad!

Psalm 15

A psalm of David.

15:1 [c]Ps 27:5-6 [d]Ps 24:3-5

1 LORD, who may dwell in your sanctuary?[c]
Who may live on your holy hill?[d]

15:2 [e]Ps 24:4; Zec 8:3, 16; Eph 4:25

15:3 [f]Ex 23:1

2 He whose walk is blameless
and who does what is righteous,
who speaks the truth[e] from his heart
3 and has no slander[f] on his tongue,
who does his neighbor no wrong
and casts no slur on his fellowman,

a *1* The Hebrew words rendered *fool* in Psalms denote one who is morally deficient.

Psalm 14 *Introduction.* This psalm may be referred to as a wisdom lament. It conveys an attitude of quiet meditation, while focusing on human evil. Note that Psalm 53 is extremely similar to Psalm 14. Psalm 14 uses God's covenant name, Yahweh, while Psalm 53 substitutes the generic word "God." There is also a difference between verses 5 and 6 of the two psalms.

14:1 The fool. The opposite of the wise, who knows how to get along in God's world. The fool may be highly intelligent by the world's standards but is oblivious to the true nature of reality (Ecc 2:14). To call someone a fool is to make a moral judgment. **says . . . "There is no God."** The fool denies that God's existence is relevant to life. This is "practical atheism." God is considered to be unconcerned about the affairs of the world and especially about those of the individual. **corrupt.** Note the use of this psalm by Paul in Romans 3:10–18. In this context foolishness points to lack of morality rather than to lack of intelligence. See *WLC* 105; *WSC* 47.

14:2 any who seek God. Fallen humanity does not actively seek God.

14:3 All have turned aside. From God and his law.

14:4 devour my people as men eat bread. "Devour" and "eat" translate the same Hebrew root, which is the normal word for "eat." The wicked exploit their fellow human beings frequently and shamelessly. Such mistreatment is as natural to them as eating bread, the staple of life. **do not call on the LORD?** A sign of unbelieving independence. See *WCF* 16.7.

14:5 overwhelmed with dread. The wicked experience dread because God is absent from them in terms of his special love and concern (see theological article "The Presence of God" at 1Ki 8). He is, however, present with the righteous.

14:6 their refuge. God can overrule the wicked plans of the evildoers for the good of the afflicted. This principle is illustrated in the Joseph narrative (Ge 50:20) and is applied to the crucifixion in Acts 2:22–24.

14:7 Zion. The place where God most personally and directly revealed his presence to the Israelites. See note on 9:11.

Psalm 15 *Introduction.* Psalm 15 focuses on the requirements to approach God's holy presence at the sanctuary. This meditation on holiness, with its connection to law and obedience, reminds the reader of Psalm 1. Its closest analogue in the Psalter is Psalm 24:3–6. These two passages (cf. also Isa 33:14–16) have been called "entrance liturgies," since they answer the question "Who can enter the holy place of God?" See *HC* 112.

15:1 who may dwell in your sanctuary? Literally, tent. Before the temple was built, God's dwelling place with his people was a tent. Ten requirements for entrance follow in verses 2–5. Note that these are moral, not ritualistic, in nature. See *WLC* 99. **holy hill.** Mount Zion, where the temple was located.

15:2 whose walk is blameless . . . does what is righteous . . . speaks the truth. The first three requirements are positive. Both positive action and speech are demanded. See *WLC* 141,144.

15:3 has no slander . . . does his neighbor no wrong . . . casts no slur. The next three requirements are negative in that they describe actions to be avoided. Sins of the tongue are emphasized here. See *WLC* 144,145; *WSC* 78.

4 who despises a vile man
but honors[g] those who fear the LORD,
who keeps his oath[h]
even when it hurts,
5 who lends his money without usury[i]
and does not accept a bribe[j] against the innocent.

He who does these things
will never be shaken.[k]

Psalm 16

A *miktam*[a] of David.

1 Keep me safe,[l] O God,
for in you I take refuge.[m]

2 I said to the LORD, "You are my Lord;
apart from you I have no good thing."[n]
3 As for the saints who are in the land,[o]
they are the glorious ones in whom is all my delight.[b]
4 The sorrows[p] of those will increase
who run after other gods.[q]
I will not pour out their libations of blood
or take up their names[r] on my lips.

5 LORD, you have assigned me my portion[s] and my cup;[t]
you have made my lot secure.
6 The boundary lines have fallen for me in pleasant places;
surely I have a delightful inheritance.[u]
7 I will praise the LORD, who counsels me;[v]
even at night[w] my heart instructs me.
8 I have set the LORD always before me.
Because he is at my right hand,[x]
I will not be shaken.

9 Therefore my heart is glad[y] and my tongue rejoices;
my body also will rest secure,[z]
10 because you will not abandon me to the grave,[c]
nor will you let your Holy One[d] see decay.[a]
11 You have made[e] known to me the path of life;[b]
you will fill me with joy in your presence,[c]
with eternal pleasures[d] at your right hand.

15:4 [g]Ac 28:10 [h]Jdg 11:35
15:5 [i]Ex 22:25 [j]Ex 23:8; Dt 16:19 [k]2Pe 1:10
16:1 [l]Ps 17:8 [m]Ps 7:1
16:2 [n]Ps 73:25
16:3 [o]Ps 101:6
16:4 [p]Ps 32:10 [q]Ps 106:37-38 [r]Ex 23:13
16:5 [s]Ps 73:26 [t]Ps 23:5
16:6 [u]Ps 78:55; Jer 3:19
16:7 [v]Ps 73:24 [w]Ps 77:6
16:8 [x]Ps 73:23
16:9 [y]Ps 4:7; 30:11 [z]Ps 4:8
16:10 [a]Ac 13:35*
16:11 [b]Mt 7:14 [c]Ac 2:25-28* [d]Ps 36:7-8

[a] Title: Probably a literary or musical term [b] *3* Or *As for the pagan priests who are in the land / and the nobles in whom all delight, I said:* [c] *10* Hebrew *Sheol* [d] *10* Or *your faithful one* [e] *11* Or *You will make*

15:4–5 See *WLC* 99.
15:4 who despises . . . but honors. Two positive requirements. **even when it hurts.** More accurately, "and does not falter." The point is the same, however. When they promise, the righteous fulfill their word. See *WCF* 22.4; *WLC* 141,144.
15:5 lends . . . without usury . . . does not accept a bribe. Again, a pair of requirements, this time negative (cf. v. 4). See Deuteronomy 23:19–20. A foreigner, but not a fellow Israelite, could be charged interest. Unlike today, loans were only taken in periods of extreme need, so to require interest was a form of severe exploitation. See *WLC* 142; *HC* 110.
Psalm 16 *Introduction.* Psalm 16 expresses confidence in the Lord, though it is difficult to determine whether the crisis was past or present to the psalmist. Verse 10 suggests that death threatened him.
16:1 Keep me safe, O God. An invocation of the Lord and a plea for help. This line suggests that the crisis was still present.
16:2–4 apart from you I have no good thing. A meditation on the blessings of the people of God and on the ultimate distress of idolaters. See *WCF* 16.5.
16:3 saints. Literally, "those who are set apart," God's elect people. See note on 4:3.
16:4 other gods. The temptation to worship gods besides or in addition to the Lord was always present in Israel (cf. 1Ki 18). The psalms frequently address this issue either by direct warning (as here) or by attributing the powers of the pagan gods to Yahweh (as in Ps 29). **their libations of blood . . . their names.** Two examples of ways that the religions of the surrounding nations sought to manipulate their gods. See *WLC* 108.
16:5 portion . . . cup . . . lot. Three metaphors describing life as a gift from God.
16:6 boundary lines. Probably metaphoric for the psalmist's quality of life. Not only was the life that God had given David "secure" (v. 5); it was also "delightful."
16:7 heart. Literally, "kidneys," but like *heart* it stands for the very core of a person's being.
16:9. See *WLC* 86.
16:10 you will not abandon me to the grave. The immediate application of this psalm was to David and then to the Old Testament saints who meditated on it (see note on 6:5). It can refer to deliverance from the immediate threat of death, but it goes beyond this in pointing prophetically to the son of David, whom the historical David anticipated. Both Peter and Paul recognized the fulfillment of this verse in Jesus (Ac 2:25–28; 13:35). See *WLC* 50.
16:11 path of life. A common metaphor found particularly in Proverbs 1–9. The psalm depicts life as a process. **joy in your presence . . . eternal pleasures.** The psalmist pointed beyond the death he had spoken of in verse 10. See *WLC* 54,90.

Psalm 17

A prayer of David.

1 Hear, O LORD, my righteous plea;
listen to my cry.[e]
Give ear to my prayer—
it does not rise from deceitful lips.[f]
2 May my vindication come from you;
may your eyes see what is right.

3 Though you probe my heart and examine me at night,
though you test me,[g] you will find nothing;[h]
I have resolved that my mouth will not sin.[i]
4 As for the deeds of men—
by the word of your lips
I have kept myself
from the ways of the violent.
5 My steps have held to your paths;[j]
my feet have not slipped.[k]

6 I call on you, O God, for you will answer me;[l]
give ear to me[m] and hear my prayer.[n]
7 Show the wonder of your great love,[o]
you who save by your right hand[p]
those who take refuge in you from their foes.
8 Keep me as the apple of your eye;[q]
hide me in the shadow of your wings
9 from the wicked who assail me,
from my mortal enemies who surround me.[r]

10 They close up their callous hearts,[s]
and their mouths speak with arrogance.[t]
11 They have tracked me down, they now surround me,[u]
with eyes alert, to throw me to the ground.
12 They are like a lion[v] hungry for prey,
like a great lion crouching in cover.

13 Rise up, O LORD, confront them, bring them down;[w]
rescue me from the wicked by your sword.
14 O LORD, by your hand save me from such men,
from men of this world[x] whose reward is in this life.

You still the hunger of those you cherish;
their sons have plenty,
and they store up wealth[y] for their children.
15 And I—in righteousness I will see your face;
when I awake, I will be satisfied with seeing your likeness.[z]

17:1 [e]Ps 61:1 [f]Isa 29:13
17:3 [g]Ps 26:2; 66:10 [h]Job 23:10; Jer 50:20 [i]Ps 39:1
17:5 [j]Ps 44:18; 119:133 [k]Ps 18:36
17:6 [l]Ps 86:7 [m]Ps 116:2 [n]Ps 88:2
17:7 [o]Ps 31:21 [p]Ps 20:6
17:8 [q]Dt 32:10
17:9 [r]Ps 31:20; 109:3
17:10 [s]Ps 73:7 [t]1Sa 2:3
17:11 [u]Ps 37:14; 88:17
17:12 [v]Ps 7:2; 10:9
17:13 [w]Ps 7:12; 22:20; 73:18
17:14 [x]Lk 16:8 [y]Ps 73:3-7
17:15 [z]Nu 12:8; Ps 4:6-7; 16:11; 1Jn 3:2

Psalm 17 *Introduction.* This is another psalm of lament seeking refuge in the Lord. David, falsely accused and assaulted by his enemies, protested his innocence of their charges and committed his case to the Lord.

Title. **A prayer of David.** The psalms are not only a book of songs for worship; they are also a prayer book that can teach us much about how to pray.

17:1 righteous plea. As elsewhere in the psalm, David strongly asserted his innocence. He did not deny that he was a sinner; his words addressed the specific charges leveled against him. See *WLC* 185.

17:2 vindication. Literally, "judgment." David appealed his case to God.

17:3 you probe my heart. *Heart* was considered the very core of a person's being, the center of emotions, thoughts and motivations. God in his omniscience is able to read the heart. The psalmist was confident that he would be acquitted of the charges against him.

17:4 word of your lips. God's will, disclosed in the law of God.

17:5 your paths. As spelled out in God's Word, in contrast to the "ways of the violent" in the previous verse.

17:7 great love. The Hebrew word denotes God's covenant devotion. See note on "unfailing love" at 6:4. **you who save.** David knew God as Savior. He could look back over the history of Israel and identify the many times God had rescued his distressed people. The exodus, prefiguring the atonement of Christ, was the prime example of God's saving activity up to that time.

17:8 apple of your eye. The pupil, one of the most delicate parts of the body, needing constant protection (see Dt 32:10; Pr 7:2; Zec 2:8).

17:10 their callous hearts. One alternate translation of "their fat," which could be a caricature of the physical appearance of these wicked people.

17:11 tracked me down. The enemy took the initiative to destroy David.

17:12 lion hungry for prey. The lion was known for its power and for stalking and ambushing its prey (cf. Pss 7:2; 10:9; 22:13).

17:13 Rise up. See note on 7:6.

17:14 You still the hunger of those you cherish. A difficult phrase to translate, it expressed the general principle that the righteous will not lack.

17:15 will see your face. The psalmist will know God's presence (see his likeness) and feel his vindication. See note on 11:7.

Psalm 18

For the director of music. Of David the servant of the LORD. He sang to the LORD the words of this song when the LORD delivered him from the hand of all his enemies and from the hand of Saul. He said:

1 I love you, O LORD, my strength.

2 The LORD is my rock,[a] my fortress and my deliverer;
my God is my rock, in whom I take refuge.
He is my shield[b] and the horn[a] of my salvation,[c] my stronghold.
3 I call to the LORD, who is worthy of praise,[d]
and I am saved from my enemies.

4 The cords of death[e] entangled me;
the torrents[f] of destruction overwhelmed me.
5 The cords of the grave[b] coiled around me;
the snares of death[g] confronted me.
6 In my distress I called to the LORD;
I cried to my God for help.
From his temple he heard my voice;[h]
my cry came before him, into his ears.

7 The earth trembled and quaked,[i]
and the foundations of the mountains shook;
they trembled because he was angry.[j]
8 Smoke rose from his nostrils;
consuming fire[k] came from his mouth,
burning coals blazed out of it.
9 He parted the heavens and came down;[l]
dark clouds were under his feet.
10 He mounted the cherubim[m] and flew;
he soared on the wings of the wind.[n]
11 He made darkness his covering,[o] his canopy around him—
the dark rain clouds of the sky.
12 Out of the brightness of his presence[p] clouds advanced,
with hailstones and bolts of lightning.[q]
13 The LORD thundered[r] from heaven;
the voice of the Most High resounded.[c]
14 He shot his arrows and scattered ⌊the enemies⌋,

18:2 [a]Ps 19:14 [b]Ps 59:11 [c]Ps 75:10
18:3 [d]Ps 48:1
18:4 [e]Ps 116:3 [f]Ps 124:4
18:5 [g]Ps 116:3
18:6 [h]Ps 34:15
18:7 [i]Jdg 5:4 [j]Ps 68:7-8
18:8 [k]Ps 50:3
18:9 [l]Ps 144:5
18:10 [m]Ps 80:1 [n]Ps 104:3
18:11 [o]Dt 4:11; Ps 97:2
18:12 [p]Ps 104:2 [q]Ps 97:3
18:13 [r]Ps 29:3; 104:7

a *2 Horn* here symbolizes strength. b *5* Hebrew *Sheol* c *13* Some Hebrew manuscripts and Septuagint (see also 2 Samuel 22:14); most Hebrew manuscripts *resounded, / amid hailstones and bolts of lightning*

Psalm 18 *Introduction.* A psalm of thanksgiving to the Lord for a mighty deliverance. Specifically, it extols God for appearing as a warrior (vv. 7–15) and for saving the king (v. 50) in the context of battle. The same psalm appears in 2 Samuel 22 with only minor changes.

Title. See "Introduction: Authorship and Titles: *Musical Notations.*" **He said.** The title unambiguously attributes this psalm to David. The historical title refers to the period before David assumed the throne, when he was fleeing from Saul.

18:1 I love you. Not the usual Hebrew word for love, this one carries nuances of intensity and intimacy. This verse was added to the psalm as it appears in 2 Samuel 22. It expressed David's personal devotion.

18:2 my rock, my fortress and my deliverer. A series of metaphors that emphasize God's protection. **rock . . . rock.** Two different Hebrew words. The image connotes protection; God was David's unfailing refuge and rescuer. When David fled from Saul, he frequently sought asylum in the caves and cliffs of the wadis. **horn.** A figure of speech that substitutes the part for the whole—the horn for the ox (see note on 1Sa 2:1).

18:3 See *WCF* 21.1.

18:4 cords of death. Death's tentacles came up from Sheol and began to drag David down. **torrents of destruction.** The powers of evil and death were frequently likened to an overwhelming flood (see notes on 46:2; 69:1–2; also see Isa 28:15,17–18; Mt 16:18).

18:6 From his temple. The place of God's special presence on Earth, and the place where his heavenly court intersected with the earthly realm. Solomon indicated that a prayer directed toward the temple was the proper response to trouble (1Ki 8).

18:7 The earth trembled. When God reveals himself as a warrior, nature goes into paroxysms (Isa 24:4ff.; Na 1:5). **the mountains.** A symbol of all that is firm and established in the world.

18:8 nostrils . . . mouth. These metaphors describe God in human terms. Smoke and fire (perhaps volcano imagery) frequently accompanied God's appearance in the Old Testament (Ge 15:17; Ex 19:18; Na 1:6).

18:9 dark clouds were under his feet. God was pictured as riding a storm cloud chariot into battle. The image appears frequently in the Old Testament (68:4; 104:3; Na 1:3; Da 7:13), and the New Testament predicted that Jesus Christ would ride the cloud chariot (Mk 13:26; Rev 1:7).

18:10 cherubim. Angelic beings first mentioned in Genesis 3:24. Their role in Genesis 3, as well as the fact they are symbolically represented at key places in the tabernacle (Ex 26:1;31), indicates that they are guardians of God's holiness. They also served as the means of locomotion for God's war chariot (Eze 1 and 10).

18:11 dark rain clouds. The cloud chariot was specifically a storm cloud.

18:13 thundered . . . voice. Thunder; compare 29:3–9 and Job 37:2–5.

18:14 his arrows. Lightning. See 77:17, 144:6 and Habukkuk 3:11.

great bolts of lightning and routed them.[s]
15 The valleys of the sea were exposed
and the foundations of the earth laid bare
at your rebuke,[t] O LORD,
at the blast of breath from your nostrils.

16 He reached down from on high and took hold of me;
he drew me out of deep waters.[u]
17 He rescued me from my powerful enemy,
from my foes, who were too strong for me.[v]
18 They confronted me in the day of my disaster,
but the LORD was my support.[w]
19 He brought me out into a spacious place;[x]
he rescued me because he delighted in me.[y]

20 The LORD has dealt with me according to my righteousness;
according to the cleanness of my hands[z] he has rewarded me.
21 For I have kept the ways of the LORD;[a]
I have not done evil by turning[b] from my God.
22 All his laws are before me;[c]
I have not turned away from his decrees.
23 I have been blameless before him
and have kept myself from sin.
24 The LORD has rewarded me according to my righteousness,[d]
according to the cleanness of my hands in his sight.

25 To the faithful[e] you show yourself faithful,
to the blameless you show yourself blameless,
26 to the pure you show yourself pure,
but to the crooked you show yourself shrewd.[f]
27 You save the humble
but bring low those whose eyes are haughty.[g]
28 You, O LORD, keep my lamp burning;
my God turns my darkness into light.[h]
29 With your help[i] I can advance against a troop[a];
with my God I can scale a wall.

30 As for God, his way is perfect;[j]
the word of the LORD is flawless.[k]
He is a shield
for all who take refuge[l] in him.
31 For who is God besides the LORD?[m]
And who is the Rock[n] except our God?
32 It is God who arms me with strength[o]
and makes my way perfect.
33 He makes my feet like the feet of a deer;[p]
he enables me to stand on the heights.[q]

18:14 [s]Ps 144:6
18:15 [t]Ps 76:6; 106:9
18:16 [u]Ps 144:7
18:17 [v]Ps 35:10
18:18 [w]Ps 59:16
18:19 [x]Ps 31:8 [y]Ps 118:5
18:20 [z]Ps 24:4
18:21 [a]2Ch 34:33 [b]Ps 119:102
18:22 [c]Ps 119:30
18:24 [d]1Sa 26:23
18:25 [e]1Ki 8:32; Ps 62:12; Mt 5:7
18:26 [f]Pr 3:34
18:27 [g]Pr 6:17
18:28 [h]Job 18:6; 29:3
18:29 [i]Heb 11:34
18:30 [j]Dt 32:4; Rev 15:3 [k]Ps 12:6 [l]Ps 17:7
18:31 [m]Dt 32:39; 86:8; Isa 45:5,6,14,18,21 [n]Dt 32:31; 1Sa 2:2
18:32 [o]Isa 45:5
18:33 [p]Hab 3:19 [q]Dt 32:13

[a] *29* Or *can run through a barricade*

18:15 were exposed . . . laid bare. When God appears as a warrior, the waters (which represent chaos and evil) shrink back (cf. 77:16–19—reflecting on the exodus; Na 1:4; Rev 21:1). **at your rebuke.** God controls the chaotic waters of the sea (106:9). Jesus showed himself to be God when he controlled the turbulent waters by his rebuke (Lk 8:22–25).
18:16 deep waters. Symbol of trouble and distress; compare 60:2.
18:19 spacious place. This may be an allusion to the exodus and/or to the conquest. God delivered the Israelites from deep waters (the Red Sea) and brought them to a spacious place (the promised land). The spacious place contrasts with a tight spot from which it would be difficult or impossible to escape from the enemy.
18:21 the ways of the LORD. That is, God's covenant law.
18:25–29 These verses describe God's justice as related generally to the righteous and the wicked. Verses 25–27 teach this truth by means of opposed parallels, emphasizing the contrast between the righteous and the wicked. Verses 28–29 apply this issue to the psalmist's personal experience.
18:25 faithful . . . show yourself faithful. The noun and the verb come from the same root in Hebrew that in other contexts is translated "covenant loving-kindness."
18:27 You save the humble. A repeated teaching of the Old Testament in general and the Psalms in particular, most notably Psalm 113:7–9. See *BC* 23.
18:30 the word of the LORD. His revelation to his people. Since this is a psalm of David written in a warfare setting, perhaps the reference is more specifically to 2 Samuel 7, which delineates the Davidic covenant in which God promised to be David's Father-God.
18:31 who is God besides the LORD? A rhetorical question. Such questions, whose answers are obvious, are used for emphasis: There is no god or place of refuge like the Lord. Compare Exodus 15:11.
18:32 makes my way perfect. Compare verse 30. Only God can make someone's way perfect, but in this life the Lord's work remains unfinished.
18:33 like the feet of a deer. A deer is surefooted.

34 He trains my hands for battle;[r]
my arms can bend a bow of bronze.
35 You give me your shield of victory,
and your right hand sustains[s] me;
you stoop down to make me great.
36 You broaden the path beneath me,
so that my ankles do not turn.

37 I pursued my enemies[t] and overtook them;
I did not turn back till they were destroyed.
38 I crushed them so that they could not rise;[u]
they fell beneath my feet.[v]
39 You armed me with strength for battle;
you made my adversaries bow at my feet.
40 You made my enemies turn their backs[w] in flight,
and I destroyed[x] my foes.
41 They cried for help, but there was no one to save them[y]—
to the LORD, but he did not answer.[z]
42 I beat them as fine as dust borne on the wind;
I poured them out like mud in the streets.

43 You have delivered me from the attacks of the people;
you have made me the head of nations;[a]
people I did not know[b] are subject to me.
44 As soon as they hear me, they obey me;
foreigners[c] cringe before me.
45 They all lose heart;
they come trembling from their strongholds.[d]

46 The LORD lives! Praise be to my Rock!
Exalted be God my Savior![e]
47 He is the God who avenges me,
who subdues nations[f] under me,
48 who saves[g] me from my enemies.
You exalted me above my foes;
from violent men you rescued me.
49 Therefore I will praise you among the nations, O LORD;
I will sing[h] praises to your name.[i]
50 He gives his king great victories;
he shows unfailing kindness to his anointed,
to David[j] and his descendants forever.[k]

Psalm 19

For the director of music. A psalm of David.

1 The heavens[l] declare[m] the glory of God;
the skies proclaim the work of his hands.

18:34 [r]Ps 144:1
18:35 [s]Ps 119:116
18:37 [t]Ps 37:20; 44:5
18:38 [u]Ps 36:12 [v]Ps 47:3
18:40 [w]Ps 21:12 [x]Ps 94:23
18:41 [y]Ps 50:22 [z]Job 27:9; Pr 1:28
18:43 [a]2Sa 8:1-14 [b]Isa 52:15; 55:5
18:44 [c]Ps 66:3
18:45 [d]Mic 7:17
18:46 [e]Ps 51:14
18:47 [f]Ps 47:3
18:48 [g]Ps 59:1
18:49 [h]Ps 108:1 [i]Ro 15:9*
18:50 [j]Ps 144:10 [k]Ps 89:4
19:1 [l]Isa 40:22 [m]Ps 50:6; Ro 1:19

18:34 bow of bronze. In ancient Israel bows were constructed primarily of wood, though at times they were reinforced with metal. The "bow of bronze" was such a composite bow or a poetic reference to God-given strength.
18:35 stoop down. David acknowledged the mercy of the incomparably great God who was willing to condescend to care for him.
18:36 my ankles do not turn. Small rocks are innumerable and paths narrow in Israel. God's protection against sprained ankles was a significant blessing to the warrior-psalmist.
18:38–39 beneath my feet . . . bow at my feet. Ancient Near Eastern tablets and stone memorials depict enemies under the feet of their conquerors and prisoners of war bowing before their captors.
18:41 They cried for help . . . to the LORD. David was battling other Israelites.
18:43 delivered me . . . made me the head . . . subject to me. David's strong personal imprint. God had granted him victories over neighboring nations that were subsequently brought under his rule (2Sa 8:1–14).
18:49 among the nations. Quoted by Paul in Romans 15:9 as having been fulfilled by Christ, who summoned the Gentiles to join in his praise of God the Father.

18:50 his anointed. David, God's chosen king. At his coronation, a king was anointed with oil by the priest, signifying that God had set him apart as holy. Jesus the Messiah ("anointed one") ultimately fulfills the role of anointed Davidic king.

Psalm 19 *Introduction.* This psalm praises the Lord for two of his great gifts to humankind: the creation and the law. Using theological terminology, it speaks of God's general revelation in nature and his special revelation in the Scriptures. At the conclusion David turned to his private life, praying that God would keep him on the true and right path.

19:1–6 The heavens declare the glory of God. The Bible clearly teaches that God is revealed by his creation. It is equally clear in asserting that men and women suppress that knowledge (Ro 1:19–20). See *WCF* 1.1; *WLC* 2.

19:1 skies. The psalmist uses creation language here; see Genesis 1:1–6, where this word is translated "expanse" or, in some other versions, "firmament." See *BC* 2.

2 Day after day they pour forth speech;
night after night they display knowledge.[n]
3 There is no speech or language
where their voice is not heard.[a]
4 Their voice[b] goes out into all the earth,
their words to the ends of the world.[o]

In the heavens he has pitched a tent[p] for the sun,
5 which is like a bridegroom coming forth from his pavilion,
like a champion rejoicing to run his course.
6 It rises at one end of the heavens
and makes its circuit to the other;[q]
nothing is hidden from its heat.

7 The law of the LORD is perfect,
reviving the soul.[r]
The statutes of the LORD are trustworthy,[s]
making wise the simple.[t]
8 The precepts of the LORD are right,[u]
giving joy to the heart.
The commands of the LORD are radiant,
giving light to the eyes.
9 The fear of the LORD is pure,
enduring forever.
The ordinances of the LORD are sure
and altogether righteous.[v]
10 They are more precious than gold,[w]
than much pure gold;
they are sweeter than honey,
than honey from the comb.
11 By them is your servant warned;
in keeping them there is great reward.

12 Who can discern his errors?
Forgive my hidden faults.[x]
13 Keep your servant also from willful sins;
may they not rule over me.
Then will I be blameless,
innocent of great transgression.

14 May the words of my mouth and the meditation of my heart
be pleasing[y] in your sight,
O LORD, my Rock[z] and my Redeemer.[a]

19:2 [n]Ps 74:16
19:4 [o]Ro 10:18* [p]Ps 104:2
19:6 [q]Ps 113:3; Ecc 1:5
19:7 [r]Ps 23:3 [s]Ps 93:5; 111:7 [t]Ps 119:98-100
19:8 [u]Ps 12:6; 119:128
19:9 [v]Ps 119:138,142
19:10 [w]Pr 8:10
19:12 [x]Ps 51:2; 90:8; 139:6
19:14 [y]Ps 104:34 [z]Ps 18:2 [a]Isa 47:4

[a] *3* Or *They have no speech, there are no words; / no sound is heard from them* [b] *4* Septuagint, Jerome and Syriac; Hebrew *line*

19:2 pour forth speech. This metaphor claims that the creation, specifically the heavens, constantly attest to God's power and goodness.
19:3 There is no speech. See NIV text note. Its rendering is preferred to maintain the poetic paradox of wordless speech.
19:4 all the earth. As opposed to God's special revelation, which is limited in scope, his revelation in creation is manifest to all. Paul applied this verse to gospel proclamation that is also to be manifested to all (Ro 10:18). **pitched a tent.** The sky—the heavens—is the sun's tent, pitched for it by God. The sun is personified throughout this section (though not deified as in other ancient Near Eastern religions). The context indicates that the tent is probably where the sun goes during the night when it is absent from the sky.
19:5 like a bridegroom. Resplendent, bursting with energy. **like a champion.** Robust and strong as it courses across the sky. The sun is God's creation and the supreme metaphor in the created realm for the glory of God, making its presence known to every creature on Earth. How much more glorious and powerful is the God who created it?
19:6 nothing is hidden. As nothing escapes the heat of the sun, so the presence of its Creator is felt by all.
19:7–14 See *WCF* 15.5; 19.6; *WLC* 4,95,105,155,157,190,195; *WSC* 89; *BC* 7; *HC* 113.
19:7–11 The law of the LORD is perfect. The law, God's special revelation, reflects the character of its author. Different names are used for the law, but they are nearly synonymous and point to the whole of God's special revelation to humankind.
19:7 the law. Torah, the most general term for the law. **reviving the soul.** Instilling energy and hope in those who follow it. **making wise.** Wisdom is not superior intellectual knowledge. God's Word implants within the hearer the fear of God, providing knowledge of him and of how to live rightly before him. See *WLC* 99; *BC* 2.
19:12–13 hidden faults . . . willful sins. The psalmist was aware that he sinned both consciously and unconsciously (in ignorance of God's requirements or simply in oblivion). He prayed that God would protect him from both. **will I be blameless.** Only by God's grace.

Psalm 20

For the director of music. A psalm of David.

1 May the LORD answer you when you are in distress;
may the name of the God of Jacob[b] protect you.[c]
2 May he send you help from the sanctuary[d]
and grant you support from Zion.
3 May he remember[e] all your sacrifices
and accept your burnt offerings.[f] *Selah*
4 May he give you the desire of your heart[g]
and make all your plans succeed.
5 We will shout for joy when you are victorious
and will lift up our banners[h] in the name of our God.
May the LORD grant all your requests.[i]

6 Now I know that the LORD saves his anointed;[j]
he answers him from his holy heaven
with the saving power of his right hand.
7 Some trust in chariots and some in horses,[k]
but we trust in the name of the LORD our God.[l]
8 They are brought to their knees and fall,
but we rise up[m] and stand firm.[n]

9 O LORD, save the king!
Answer[a] us[o] when we call!

Psalm 21

For the director of music. A psalm of David.

1 O LORD, the king rejoices in your strength.
How great is his joy in the victories you give![p]
2 You have granted him the desire of his heart[q]
and have not withheld the request of his lips. *Selah*
3 You welcomed him with rich blessings
and placed a crown of pure gold[r] on his head.
4 He asked you for life, and you gave it to him—
length of days, for ever and ever.[s]
5 Through the victories[t] you gave, his glory is great;
you have bestowed on him splendor and majesty.
6 Surely you have granted him eternal blessings
and made him glad with the joy[u] of your presence.[v]
7 For the king trusts in the LORD;
through the unfailing love of the Most High
he will not be shaken.

8 Your hand will lay hold[w] on all your enemies;
your right hand will seize your foes.

20:1 [b]Ps 46:7,11 [c]Ps 91:14
20:2 [d]Ps 3:4
20:3 [e]Ac 10:4 [f]Ps 51:19
20:4 [g]Ps 21:2; 145:16, 19
20:5 [h]Ps 9:14; 60:4 [i]1Sa 1:17
20:6 [j]Ps 28:8; 41:11; Isa 58:9
20:7 [k]Ps 33:17; Isa 31:1 [l]2Ch 32:8
20:8 [m]Mic 7:8 [n]Ps 37:23
20:9 [o]Ps 3:7; 17:6
21:1 [p]Ps 59:16-17
21:2 [q]Ps 37:4
21:3 [r]2Sa 12:30
21:4 [s]Ps 61:5-6; 91:16; 133:3
21:5 [t]Ps 18:50
21:6 [u]Ps 43:4 [v]1Ch 17:27
21:8 [w]Isa 10:10

[a] 9 Or *save! / O King, answer*

Psalm 20 *Introduction.* Perhaps "of David" as subject, not author. The opening benediction (vv. 1–5) infuses the psalm with a liturgical mood. It is a prayer for God's blessing on the king as he sets out for battle—a confident prayer that expresses Israel's faith that God is the One who provides victory.
20:2 from the sanctuary. Compare 1 Kings 8:44–45.
20:4 desire of your heart. Victory in battle.
20:5 when you are victorious. The psalms contain hymns of praise that were sung to God after victory. Two examples are Psalms 24 and 98.
20:6 I know. Either the king speaks here or the corporate "I" stands for the entire congregation. Israel will win the battle because of the Lord's presence. The nation's trust is rooted in God's promise to protect his people in warfare when they are obedient to his commands (Dt 7; 20). **anointed.** The Davidic king, anticipating the son of David, Jesus Christ, who will sit on the throne forever.
20:7 we trust in the name of the LORD. The essence of holy war in the Old Testament.
20:8 They . . . fall . . . but we rise up. Because of God's grace.

Psalm 21 *Introduction.* This psalm celebrates God's victory over the king's enemies and, on that basis, looks forward to the future with confidence even though threats will continue. The first part of Psalm 21 sounds like the answer to the prayer in Psalm 20. Like Psalm 20, Psalm 21 may be "of David" as subject rather than as author.
21:2 the desire of his heart. Compare Psalm 20:4. Similar language is used, though it is uncertain whether the same occasion inspired both psalms.
21:3 placed a crown . . . on his head. While some think this verse indicates the psalm's setting during the coronation, it more likely refers to David's transition from a war leader (a position in which he would not have worn his crown) to a king sitting on his throne.
21:4 asked you for life. The king prayed that his life would be spared during battle. **for ever and ever.** See 1 Kings 1:31, a common blessing on the king. It is not certain that the psalmist had more in mind than a blessing of long life or the continuance of the Davidic line. Only Jesus ultimately fulfills these words.

[9] At the time of your appearing
you will make them like a fiery furnace.
In his wrath the LORD will swallow them up,
and his fire will consume them.[x]
[10] You will destroy their descendants from the earth,
their posterity from mankind.[y]
[11] Though they plot evil[z] against you
and devise wicked schemes,[a] they cannot succeed;
[12] for you will make them turn their backs[b]
when you aim at them with drawn bow.

[13] Be exalted, O LORD, in your strength;
we will sing and praise your might.

21:9 [x]Ps 50:3; La 2:2; Mal 4:1
21:10 [y]Dt 28:18; Ps 37:28
21:11 [z]Ps 2:1 [a]Ps 10:2
21:12 [b]Ps 7:12-13; 18:40

Psalm 22

For the director of music. To ⌊the tune of⌋ "The Doe of the Morning." A psalm of David.

[1] My God, my God, why have you forsaken me?[c]
Why are you so far[d] from saving me,
so far from the words of my groaning?
[2] O my God, I cry out by day, but you do not answer,
by night,[e] and am not silent.

[3] Yet you are enthroned as the Holy One;[f]
you are the praise[g] of Israel.[a]
[4] In you our fathers put their trust;
they trusted and you delivered them.
[5] They cried to you and were saved;
in you they trusted and were not disappointed.[h]

[6] But I am a worm[i] and not a man,
scorned by men[j] and despised[k] by the people.
[7] All who see me mock me;
they hurl insults,[l] shaking their heads:[m]
[8] "He trusts in the LORD;
let the LORD rescue him.[n]
Let him deliver him,
since he delights[o] in him."

[9] Yet you brought me out of the womb;[p]
you made me trust in you
even at my mother's breast.
[10] From birth[q] I was cast upon you;
from my mother's womb you have been my God.
[11] Do not be far from me,
for trouble is near
and there is no one to help.[r]

22:1 [c]Mt 27:46*; Mk 15:34* [d]Ps 10:1
22:2 [e]Ps 42:3
22:3 [f]Ps 99:9 [g]Dt 10:21
22:5 [h]Isa 49:23
22:6 [i]Job 25:6; Isa 41:14 [j]Ps 31:11 [k]Isa 49:7; 53:3
22:7 [l]Mt 27:39,44 [m]Mk 15:29
22:8 [n]Ps 91:14 [o]Mt 27:43
22:9 [p]Ps 71:6
22:10 [q]Isa 46:3
22:11 [r]Ps 72:12

[a] 3 Or *Yet you are holy, / enthroned on the praises of Israel*

21:9 your appearing. The presence of God instills great joy in those who are in covenant with him (v. 6) but brings judgment to those who are his enemies.

Psalm 22 *Introduction.* The psalm begins as a personal lament in which David expressed the ferocity with which his enemies were attacking him. To make matters worse, they were doing so without cause. The psalm is well known for its many citations and allusions in the New Testament (Mt 27:35,39,43; Jn 19:23–24,28; Heb 2:12). It has many thematic similarities with Psalm 69.

22:1 why have you forsaken me? The lament begins with a cry of abandonment. The psalmist bemoaned in anguish the "why?" of the righteous sufferer. Where was the presence God has promised? (Jos 1:5). The same cry was taken up by Jesus, who, though sinless, endured a total abandonment of which David had experienced only a shadow. In the place of David and all the people of God, Jesus bore the curse that sin deserves. See *WCF* 18.4; *WLC* 81.

22:3 Yet you are enthroned. A confession of trust in the God of the fathers follows the opening lament. The Hebrew accents suggest that the verse be translated "Yet you are holy, enthroned on the praises of Israel" (see NIV text note). While God's kingship does not depend on human response for its reality, it becomes manifest to men and women through their praise. Israel's praises were to be directed toward the temple in which God was enthroned in the Most Holy Place.

22:4–5 our fathers. David may have been thinking back to the incidents in which Abraham was delivered from the five kings (Ge 14), Joseph from the Egyptian jail (Ge 41) or, perhaps most significantly, Moses and the Israelites from the hand of the Egyptians (Ex 1–15).

22:6 scorned . . . despised. The lament resumes, describing the scorn and mockery flung on the sufferer. See *WLC* 48.

22:7 hurl insults. David's enemies ridiculed his trust in God. This verse is alluded to in Matthew 27:41–44, where Christ, the truly righteous Sufferer, endured the ridicule of hypocritical priests and of criminals.

22:9 out of the womb. The psalmist affirmed his longstanding trust in God's ability to save him from distress. The psalm continues

12 Many bulls[s] surround me;
strong bulls of Bashan[t] encircle me.
13 Roaring lions[u] tearing their prey
open their mouths wide[v] against me.
14 I am poured out like water,
and all my bones are out of joint.[w]
My heart has turned to wax;
it has melted away[x] within me.
15 My strength is dried up like a potsherd,
and my tongue sticks to the roof of my mouth;[y]
you lay me[a] in the dust[z] of death.
16 Dogs[a] have surrounded me;
a band of evil men has encircled me,
they have pierced[b][b] my hands and my feet.
17 I can count all my bones;
people stare[c] and gloat over me.[d]
18 They divide my garments among them
and cast lots[e] for my clothing.

19 But you, O LORD, be not far off;
O my Strength, come quickly[f] to help me.
20 Deliver my life from the sword,
my precious life[g] from the power of the dogs.
21 Rescue me from the mouth of the lions;
save[c] me from the horns of the wild oxen

22 I will declare your name to my brothers;
in the congregation I will praise you.[h]
23 You who fear the LORD, praise him![i]
All you descendants of Jacob, honor him!
Revere him,[j] all you descendants of Israel!
24 For he has not despised or disdained
the suffering of the afflicted one;
he has not hidden his face[k] from him
but has listened to his cry for help.[l]

25 From you comes the theme of my praise in the great assembly;[m]
before those who fear you[d] will I fulfill my vows.[n]
26 The poor will eat[o] and be satisfied;
they who seek the LORD will praise him—[p]

22:12 [s]Ps 68:30 [t]Dt 32:14
22:13 [u]Ps 17:12 [v]Ps 35:21
22:14 [w]Ps 31:10 [x]Job 30:16; Da 5:6
22:15 [y]Ps 38:10; Jn 19:28 [z]Ps 104:29
22:16 [a]Ps 59:6 [b]Isa 53:5; Zec 12:10; Jn 19:34
22:17 [c]Lk 23:35 [d]Lk 23:27
22:18 [e]Mt 27:35*; Lk 23:34; Jn 19:24*
22:19 [f]Ps 70:5
22:20 [g]Ps 35:17
22:22 [h]Heb 2:12*
22:23 [i]Ps 86:12; 135:19 [j]Ps 33:8
22:24 [k]Ps 69:17 [l]Heb 5:7
22:25 [m]Ps 35:18 [n]Ecc 5:4
22:26 [o]Ps 107:9 [p]Ps 40:16

a *15* Or / *I am laid* b *16* Some Hebrew manuscripts, Septuagint and Syriac; most Hebrew manuscripts / *like the lion,* c *21* Or / *you have heard* d *25* Hebrew *him*

to alternate between lament and confession of trust. David had put his confidence in God as far back as he could remember.

22:11 no one to help. The sufferer is forsaken by all other human beings; God is his only hope and help.

22:12 bulls of Bashan. These bulls were noted for their power and great size (cf. Am 4:1). The lament resumes—in vivid images describing the encircling enemies (vv. 12–18).

22:13 Roaring lions. Here lions represented power, ferocity and ruthlessness (Na 2:14; Zep 3:3).

22:14 my bones . . . My heart. Outward attack is matched by inward agony. The images reflect David's inward turmoil, induced by the encompassing threat of his enemies. As fulfilled in Christ, the prophetic words foreshadow the agony of one crucified.

22:16 Dogs have surrounded me. Another metaphor for enemies, stressing their threat and ferocity and depravity. **pierced.** The Hebrew here is difficult. Literally, "like the lion," best emended to "pierced" on the evidence of the ancient Greek version and others. See *BC* 21.

22:17 people stare. David was wasting away in his distress. As his enemies observed his emaciated frame, they rejoiced. In a similar manner Jesus' battered body was exposed on the cross.

22:18 They divide my garments. In remarkable foreshadowing, David spoke metaphorically of his own situation in terms that applied quite literally to Jesus, whose enemies, as though he were already dead, divided up his garments during his crucifixion. See *WLC* 113.

22:19–21 O my Strength, come quickly to help me. After the laments and confessions of trust came the climax: a plea to the Lord for help.

22:20 sword . . . dogs . . . lions . . . oxen. Notice that the order of the enemies is reversed from that of verses 12–16.

22:21 save me. The reading in the NIV text note ("you have heard" me) is to be preferred. The assurance of being heard is present in other psalms of lament (3:4; 28:6; cf. 27:13; 34:4,6; 38:15; 118:5,21).

22:22 I will declare. In assurance of being heard, the suffering David pledged his vow of praise. His admiration would be offered in the midst of the worshiping congregation in payment of his vow. Reference to the vow is common in the psalms of personal lament (13:6; 27:6; 35:18; 54:6; 69:30,31; cf. 51:16; 116:13,14). The reference is to the vow of a sufferer to bring a thank offering to the temple after God had granted his prayer for deliverance (Lev 7:16; 22:23; Dt 12:6–7). The writer of Hebrews applied this verse to Christ (2:12), the triumphant son of David, "Israel's singer of songs" (2Sa. 23:1), who led the great congregation in praise. See *BC* 28. **your name.** See notes on 1 Samuel 1:3, 17:45 and 1 Chronicles 13:6.

22:24 he has not hidden his face. The reason for the shift from lament to praise. David's enemies despised him, but God did not.

22:25 From you comes the theme. Literally, "From you comes my praise." The vow of praise leads to doxology. This, too, is prophetic, anticipating the praises of Christ in glory. **great assembly.** The corporate and public worship of the Lord. **fulfill my vows.** See note on 22:22.

22:26 will eat and be satisfied. Likely a reference to the sacrifi-

22:27 [q]Ps 2:8 [r]Ps 86:9
22:28 [s]Ps 47:7-8
22:29 [t]Ps 45:12 [u]Isa 26:19
22:30 [v]Ps 102:28
22:31 [w]Ps 78:6
23:1 [x]Isa 40:11; Jn 10:11; 1Pe 2:25 [y]Php 4:19
23:2 [z]Eze 34:14; Rev 7:17
23:3 [a]Ps 19:7 [b]Ps 5:8; 85:13
23:4 [c]Job 10:21-22 [d]Ps 3:6; 27:1 [e]Isa 43:2
23:5 [f]Ps 92:10 [g]Ps 16:5

may your hearts live forever!
27 All the ends of the earth[q]
will remember and turn to the LORD,
and all the families of the nations
will bow down before him,[r]
28 for dominion belongs to the LORD[s]
and he rules over the nations.

29 All the rich[t] of the earth will feast and worship;
all who go down to the dust[u] will kneel before him—
those who cannot keep themselves alive.
30 Posterity[v] will serve him;
future generations will be told about the Lord.
31 They will proclaim his righteousness
to a people yet unborn[w]—
for he has done it.

Psalm 23

A psalm of David.

1 The LORD is my shepherd,[x] I shall not be in want.[y]
2 He makes me lie down in green pastures,
he leads me beside quiet waters,[z]
3 he restores my soul.[a]
He guides me in paths of righteousness[b]
for his name's sake.
4 Even though I walk
through the valley of the shadow of death,[a][c]
I will fear no evil,[d]
for you are with me;[e]
your rod and your staff,
they comfort me.

5 You prepare a table before me
in the presence of my enemies.
You anoint my head with oil;[f]
my cup[g] overflows.
6 Surely goodness and love will follow me
all the days of my life,
and I will dwell in the house of the LORD
forever.

[a] *4* Or *through the darkest valley*

cial meal of the "peace offering" in which the vow is discharged and the worshipers join in. See *WLC* 174.
22:27–31 See *WLC* 62.
22:27 All the ends of the earth. The scope of praise expanded in prophetic reference to Christ.
22:28 he rules over the nations. The Lord is more than the God of Israel; he is the God of the Gentiles as well.
22:29 All the rich. Not only the poor (v. 26) but also the rich will worship God. **those who cannot keep themselves alive.** Another possible reading is "The victor himself restores to life."
22:30 See *WCF* 8.1.
22:31 he has done it. The final victory of salvation is accomplished by God.
Psalm 23 *Introduction.* This song of confidence represents a literary unity but presents two separate metaphors (vv. 1–4; 5–6), both of which communicate God's care and goodness. Its original purpose was to comfort God's people in any distress.
23:1 The LORD is my shepherd. Sheep depend totally on their shepherd for food, water and protection from wild animals. In the ancient Near East and in Israel, kings were often seen to fulfill similar roles for their people, and were thus often referred to as shepherds. David, the shepherd turned king, saw God as his own King and Shepherd (vv. 1–4), the One who cared for him at all times, even when death seemed imminent. The New Testament would later present Jesus as the Shepherd-Leader of his people (Jn 10:11,14), fulfilling the prophecy that God himself would come to shepherd his people (Eze. 34:7–16,23).
23:2–3 makes me lie down . . . leads me . . . restores . . . guides me. These verses expand the metaphor of the shepherd's care for the sheep. The Lord lovingly attends his people. **for his name's sake.** The last phrase breaks the pattern, being not an action taken by God but God's motivation, and is thus the climax.
23:4 shadow of death. This phrase translates a single and difficult Hebrew word. The NIV text note provides the legitimate alternate reading "darkest valley." See Job 10:21–22. **rod . . . staff.** Both were used by shepherds, the former to fight off wild animals and the latter to direct the flock.
23:5 You prepare a table. The image shifts to that of a banquet in a victory celebration. **You anoint my head.** Kings were anointed upon coronation (and often beforehand), but guests were also anointed at feasts (Ps 104:15; Lk 7:46). **my cup overflows.** In spite of David's distressed situation, God's blessings overflowed to him (see Jer 33:3).
23:6 goodness and love. "Love" refers to God's covenant devotion. In devotion and grace, God bound himself to Israel and to David. **I will dwell.** David may have been alluding to his plans to return to worship in Jerusalem, where the ark resided.

Psalm 24

Of David. A psalm.

1 The earth is the LORD's,[h] and everything in it,
the world, and all who live in it;[i]
2 for he founded it upon the seas
and established it upon the waters.

3 Who may ascend the hill[j] of the LORD?
Who may stand in his holy place?[k]
4 He who has clean hands[l] and a pure heart,[m]
who does not lift up his soul to an idol
or swear by what is false.[a]
5 He will receive blessing from the LORD
and vindication from God his Savior.
6 Such is the generation of those who seek him,
who seek your face,[n] O God of Jacob.[b] *Selah*

7 Lift up your heads, O you gates;[o]
be lifted up, you ancient doors,
that the King of glory[p] may come in.
8 Who is this King of glory?
The LORD strong and mighty,
the LORD mighty in battle.[q]
9 Lift up your heads, O you gates;
lift them up, you ancient doors,
that the King of glory may come in.
10 Who is he, this King of glory?
The LORD Almighty—
he is the King of glory. *Selah*

Psalm 25[c]

Of David.

1 To you, O LORD, I lift up my soul;[r]
2 in you I trust,[s] O my God.
Do not let me be put to shame,
nor let my enemies triumph over me.
3 No one whose hope is in you
will ever be put to shame,[t]
but they will be put to shame
who are treacherous without excuse.

4 Show me your ways, O LORD,

24:1 [h]Ex 9:29; Job 41:11; Ps 89:11 [i]1Co 10:26*
24:3 [j]Ps 2:6 [k]Ps 15:1; 65:4
24:4 [l]Job 17:9 [m]Mt 5:8
24:6 [n]Ps 27:8
24:7 [o]Isa 26:2 [p]Ps 97:6; 1Co 2:8
24:8 [q]Ps 76:3-6
25:1 [r]Ps 86:4
25:2 [s]Ps 41:11
25:3 [t]Isa 49:23

[a] 4 Or *swear falsely* [b] 6 Two Hebrew manuscripts and Syriac (see also Septuagint); most Hebrew manuscripts *face, Jacob* [c] This psalm is an acrostic poem, the verses of which begin with the successive letters of the Hebrew alphabet.

Psalm 24 *Introduction.* In this hymn the army extols God's victory over the enemy as it returns to Jerusalem. First God is proclaimed as Lord of the universe (vv. 1–2); then, as the procession approaches the holy city and its sacred precincts, the singers inquire concerning the requirements for admission into God's presence (vv. 3–6). The end of the psalm personifies the gates and doors as they are asked to open to welcome and celebrate the Lord's return and victory (vv. 7–10). The psalm may be sung by Christians to celebrate their divine warrior, Jesus Christ, who has entered the ultimate Holy Place, heaven. Jesus alone is qualified to ascend to heaven (vv. 3–4), and he is the victorious Lord, for whom the gates of glory open (vv. 7–10).
24:1 The earth is the LORD's. God created and sustains the whole earth; it belongs to him.
24:2 he founded it upon the seas. This section reflects the creation account in Genesis 1. However, in the ancient Hebrew worldview, the seas were also the abode of monsters (cf. 74:13; 89:9–10; Job 7:12; 41:1; Isa 27:1) and were a poetic image for evil. Throughout the Psalms and the Prophets, God is pictured as victorious over the seas (29:10; 77:16 20; 104:5–9; Da 7; Na 1:4).
24:3 hill of the LORD. See note on "on Zion" at 2:6.
24:4–5 See *WLC* 99.
24:4 clean hands. Righteous action. **pure heart.** Righteous thoughts and motives. **lift up his soul.** In worship. **what is false.** By the names of false gods. See *WCF* 22.4; *WLC* 113.
24:7,9 Lift up your heads. The gates to either the city or the temple are personified. **may come in.** The return of the King of glory implies that he has gone out to battle and now returns victoriously.
24:10 LORD Almighty. Literally, LORD of Hosts, referring to God's role as divine warrior. See note on 1 Samuel 1:3.
Psalm 25 *Introduction.* Psalm 25 is primarily the lament of an individual (vv. 16–21), but the last verse applies it to the community. David looked to the Lord both to remove his sins and to protect him from his enemies. Compared to many other laments (e.g., Ps 22), however, this one expresses quiet confidence despite distress. Covenantal (v. 10) and wisdom (vv. 4–5) language permeate the poem. It is also an acrostic (see "Introduction: Structure: *Poetic Style and Devices*").
25:1 lift up my soul. In prayer.
25:3 will ever be put to shame. The psalmist's initial concern about his enemy was put to rest when he realized that God protects his faithful people.

teach me your paths;[u]
5 guide me in your truth and teach me,
for you are God my Savior,
and my hope is in you all day long.
6 Remember, O LORD, your great mercy and love,[v]
for they are from of old.
7 Remember not the sins of my youth[w]
and my rebellious ways;
according to your love[x] remember me,
for you are good, O LORD.

8 Good and upright[y] is the LORD;
therefore he instructs[z] sinners in his ways.
9 He guides[a] the humble in what is right
and teaches them[b] his way.
10 All the ways of the LORD are loving and faithful[c]
for those who keep the demands of his covenant.[d]
11 For the sake of your name,[e] O LORD,
forgive my iniquity, though it is great.
12 Who, then, is the man that fears the LORD?
He will instruct him in the way[f] chosen for him.
13 He will spend his days in prosperity,[g]
and his descendants will inherit the land.[h]
14 The LORD confides[i] in those who fear him;
he makes his covenant known[j] to them.
15 My eyes are ever on the LORD,[k]
for only he will release my feet from the snare.

16 Turn to me[l] and be gracious to me,
for I am lonely and afflicted.
17 The troubles of my heart have multiplied;
free me from my anguish.[m]
18 Look upon my affliction and my distress[n]
and take away all my sins.
19 See how my enemies[o] have increased
and how fiercely they hate me!
20 Guard my life[p] and rescue me;
let me not be put to shame,
for I take refuge in you.
21 May integrity[q] and uprightness protect me,
because my hope is in you.

22 Redeem Israel,[r] O God,
from all their troubles!

25:4 [u]Ex 33:13
25:6 [v]Ps 103:17; Isa 63:7,15
25:7 [w]Job 13:26; Jer 3:25 [x]Ps 51:1
25:8 [y]Ps 92:15 [z]Ps 32:8
25:9 [a]Ps 23:3 [b]Ps 27:11
25:10 [c]Ps 40:11 [d]Ps 103:18
25:11 [e]Ps 31:3; 79:9
25:12 [f]Ps 37:23
25:13 [g]Pr 19:23 [h]Ps 37:11
25:14 [i]Pr 3:32 [j]Jn 7:17
25:15 [k]Ps 141:8
25:16 [l]Ps 69:16
25:17 [m]Ps 107:6
25:18 [n]2Sa 16:12
25:19 [o]Ps 3:1
25:20 [p]Ps 86:2
25:21 [q]Ps 41:12
25:22 [r]Ps 130:8

Psalm 26

Of David.

1 Vindicate me, O LORD,
for I have led a blameless life;[s]

26:1 [s]Ps 7:8; Pr 20:7

25:6–7 Remember . . . mercy and love . . . Remember not. These words are all closely connected with God's covenant, which is the basis of the psalmist's trust.

25:9 the humble. Compare the Beatitudes of Jesus (Mt 5:3–10). The psalmist recognized that the way of humility and lowliness is also the way of truth.

25:10 those who keep. The Bible teaches that salvation is by grace alone. However, the psalmist (along with Dt 27–28 and the book of Pr) warned against a presumptuous, dead faith. God blesses those who obey him from the heart. **demands of his covenant.** God's expressed will for our lives; that is, his law.

25:12 fears the LORD. Compare Proverbs 1:7 and Ecclesiastes 12:13. The fear of the Lord is a proper reverential awe toward God—not life-disrupting anxiety. See notes on 2:11 and 111:10.

25:13 prosperity. Literally, "goodness." **inherit the land.** The blessings and curses of Deuteronomy 27 and 28 made it clear that the Israelites would retain the land given them by God if they were to remain faithful to the demands of the covenant (cf. v. 10).

25:18–19 my sins . . . my enemies. David recognized that his troubles were caused both by his own sins and by the attacks of outside forces ("my enemies").

Psalm 26 *Introduction.* David strongly asserted that he was innocent of transgression. He did this in the context of a lament, fearing that God would treat him like one of the ungodly (v. 9). The setting of the psalm is difficult to ascertain. It may be a prayer for admission into the sanctuary, perhaps for refuge. If so, David pled that he was innocent of the crimes of which he was being accused. He did not claim to be free from all sin but fully recognized his need for God's mercy and grace.

26:1 blameless life. This was not a claim of perfection but one of innocence of the charges against him. It is best understood as a hyperbolic statement that sought to identify David in his motives and actions with the "righteous" rather than with the wicked.

I have trusted[t] in the LORD
without wavering.[u]
2 Test me,[v] O LORD, and try me,
examine my heart and my mind;[w]
3 for your love is ever before me,
and I walk continually[x] in your truth.
4 I do not sit[y] with deceitful men,
nor do I consort with hypocrites;
5 I abhor[z] the assembly of evildoers
and refuse to sit with the wicked.
6 I wash my hands in innocence,[a]
and go about your altar, O LORD,
7 proclaiming aloud your praise
and telling of all your wonderful deeds.[b]
8 I love[c] the house where you live, O LORD,
the place where your glory dwells.

9 Do not take away my soul along with sinners,
my life with bloodthirsty men,[d]
10 in whose hands are wicked schemes,
whose right hands are full of bribes.[e]
11 But I lead a blameless life;
redeem me[f] and be merciful to me.

12 My feet stand on level ground;[g]
in the great assembly[h] I will praise the LORD.

Psalm 27

Of David.

1 The LORD is my light[i] and my salvation[j]—
whom shall I fear?
The LORD is the stronghold of my life—
of whom shall I be afraid?[k]
2 When evil men advance against me
to devour my flesh,[a]
when my enemies and my foes attack me,
they will stumble and fall.[l]
3 Though an army besiege me,
my heart will not fear;[m]
though war break out against me,
even then will I be confident.[n]

4 One thing[o] I ask of the LORD,
this is what I seek:
that I may dwell in the house of the LORD
all the days of my life,[p]
to gaze upon the beauty of the LORD
and to seek him in his temple.
5 For in the day of trouble
he will keep me safe in his dwelling;

26:1 [t]Ps 28:7 [u]2Ki 20:3; Heb 10:23
26:2 [v]Ps 17:3 [w]Ps 7:9
26:3 [x]2Ki 20:3
26:4 [y]Ps 1:1
26:5 [z]Ps 31:6; 139:21
26:6 [a]Ps 73:13
26:7 [b]Ps 9:1
26:8 [c]Ps 27:4
26:9 [d]Ps 28:3
26:10 [e]1Sa 8:3
26:11 [f]Ps 69:18
26:12 [g]Ps 27:11; 40:2 [h]Ps 22:22
27:1 [i]Isa 60:19 [j]Ex 15:2 [k]Ps 118:6
27:2 [l]Ps 9:3; 14:4
27:3 [m]Ps 3:6 [n]Job 4:6
27:4 [o]Ps 90:17 [p]Ps 23:6; 26:8

[a] 2 Or *to slander me*

26:4 I do not sit . . . nor do I consort. Compare Psalm 1:1.
26:6 wash my hands . . . go about your altar. The language befits a prayer for admission into the sanctuary. See *WLC* 171.
26:9 Do not take away my soul along with sinners. David wanted to distance himself from the wicked, who would be quickly destroyed if they were to enter the sanctuary precincts (see vv. 6–8).
26:12 on level ground. A metaphor for personal stability and right relationship with the Lord.
Psalm 27 *Introduction.* This psalm begins with a note of quiet confidence in God (vv. 1–6), while the second half presents the petitions of a lament (vv 7–12). Like Psalm 25, it is a calm expression of the psalmist's desire that God continue to protect him. The psalmist's quiet spirit is the result of his deep trust in the Lord (vv. 13–14).

27:1 The LORD is my light. God grants clarity of mind, order, understanding and well-being, as opposed to darkness, which is viewed as evil and chaotic. See Nahum 1:8, where the defeat of the enemy is expressed by their pursuit into darkness.

27:2 devour my flesh. The immediate context argues for this translation. The enemy sought to harm David physically. The expression, however, also carries an idiomatic meaning "slander me" (see NIV text note).

27:4 house of the LORD. The temple was the place God chose to make his presence known.

27:5 [q]Ps 17:8; 31:20 [r]Ps 40:2
27:6 [s]Ps 3:3 [t]Ps 107:22
27:7 [u]Ps 13:3
27:9 [v]Ps 69:17
27:11 [w]Ps 5:8; 25:4; 86:11
27:12 [x]Mt 26:60; Ac 9:1
27:13 [y]Ps 31:19 [z]Jer 11:19; Eze 26:20
27:14 [a]Ps 40:1
28:1 [b]Ps 83:1 [c]Ps 88:4
28:2 [d]Ps 138:2; 140:6 [e]Ps 5:7
28:3 [f]Ps 12:2; Ps 26:9; Jer 9:8

he will hide me[q] in the shelter of his tabernacle
and set me high upon a rock.[r]
6 Then my head will be exalted[s]
above the enemies who surround me;
at his tabernacle will I sacrifice[t] with shouts of joy;
I will sing and make music to the LORD.

7 Hear my voice when I call, O LORD;
be merciful to me and answer me.[u]
8 My heart says of you, "Seek his[a] face!"
Your face, LORD, I will seek.
9 Do not hide your face[v] from me,
do not turn your servant away in anger;
you have been my helper.
Do not reject me or forsake me,
O God my Savior.
10 Though my father and mother forsake me,
the LORD will receive me.
11 Teach me your way, O LORD;
lead me in a straight path[w]
because of my oppressors.
12 Do not turn me over to the desire of my foes,
for false witnesses[x] rise up against me,
breathing out violence.

13 I am still confident of this:
I will see the goodness of the LORD[y]
in the land of the living.[z]
14 Wait[a] for the LORD;
be strong and take heart
and wait for the LORD.

Psalm 28

Of David.

1 To you I call, O LORD my Rock;
do not turn a deaf ear to me.
For if you remain silent,[b]
I will be like those who have gone down to the pit.[c]
2 Hear my cry for mercy[d]
as I call to you for help,
as I lift up my hands
toward your Most Holy Place.[e]

3 Do not drag me away with the wicked,
with those who do evil,
who speak cordially with their neighbors
but harbor malice in their hearts.[f]
4 Repay them for their deeds

[a] *8* Or *To you, O my heart, he has said, "Seek my*

27:5 high upon a rock. Above all trouble.
27:6 shouts of joy. Thank offerings for the victory that the Lord would grant David would be rendered with loud rejoicing and praise.
27:8 heart. The core of his being. **Seek his face.** To seek God's face is to seek intimate fellowship with him (see theological article "The Presence of God" at 1Ki 8).
27:9 Do not hide your face. David recognized that, no matter how strong his desire, he could see God's face only if God were to reveal himself. God does participate in intimate fellowship with those he loves.
27:12 false witnesses. This may be an allusion to the specific occasion that motivated the writing of the psalm.
27:13 I will see the goodness of the LORD. David was confident that he would experience God's vindication while he was still alive.
27:14 Wait for the LORD. In the midst of present trouble, David counseled, don't give up, but allow God time to answer.

Psalm 28 *Introduction.* Psalm 28 opens with the petitions of a lament. David's enemies pressed him, so he called for God's justice. As with most laments, the psalmist turned to God in confidence and ended the psalm on a note of praise.

28:1 my Rock. The psalmist recognized God as his protection and strength (see 78:35; Dt 32:4,18,31). **turn a deaf ear.** Represents God's absence and judgment, his refusal to hear and to act on behalf of the petitioner. **gone down to the pit.** Died. The pit is a metaphor for the grave/Sheol (see note on 6:5; cf. 30:1; 40:2).

28:2 Most Holy Place. The innermost room in the tabernacle, in which the ark of the covenant resided.

28:3 speak cordially. Literally, "speak peace." The psalmist recognized the hypocrisy of his enemies.

28:4 Repay them. An imprecation (or curse). The psalmist entreated the Lord to judge his adversaries for their deeds.

and for their evil work;
repay them for what their hands have done[g]
and bring back upon them what they deserve.[h]
5 Since they show no regard for the works of the LORD
and what his hands have done,[i]
he will tear them down
and never build them up again.

6 Praise be to the LORD,
for he has heard my cry for mercy.
7 The LORD is my strength[j] and my shield;
my heart trusts[k] in him, and I am helped.
My heart leaps for joy
and I will give thanks to him in song.[l]

8 The LORD is the strength of his people,
a fortress of salvation for his anointed one.[m]
9 Save your people and bless your inheritance;[n]
be their shepherd[o] and carry them[p] forever.

Psalm 29

A psalm of David.

1 Ascribe to the LORD,[q] O mighty ones,
ascribe to the LORD glory[r] and strength.
2 Ascribe to the LORD the glory due his name;
worship the LORD in the splendor of his[a] holiness.[s]

3 The voice[t] of the LORD is over the waters;
the God of glory thunders,[u]
the LORD thunders over the mighty waters.
4 The voice of the LORD is powerful;[v]
the voice of the LORD is majestic.
5 The voice of the LORD breaks the cedars;
the LORD breaks in pieces the cedars of Lebanon.[w]
6 He makes Lebanon skip[x] like a calf,
Sirion[b][y] like a young wild ox.
7 The voice of the LORD strikes
with flashes of lightning.
8 The voice of the LORD shakes the desert;
the LORD shakes the Desert of Kadesh.[z]
9 The voice of the LORD twists the oaks[c]
and strips the forests bare.
And in his temple all cry, "Glory!"[a]

10 The LORD sits[d] enthroned over the flood;[b]

28:4 [g]2Ti 4:14; Rev 22:12 [h]Rev 18:6
28:5 [i]Isa 5:12
28:7 [j]Ps 18:1 [k]Ps 13:5 [l]Ps 40:3; 69:30
28:8 [m]Ps 20:6
28:9 [n]Dt 9:29; Ezr 1:4 [o]Isa 40:11 [p]Dt 1:31; 32:11
29:1 [q]1Ch 16:28 [r]Ps 96:7-9
29:2 [s]2Ch 20:21
29:3 [t]Job 37:5 [u]Ps 18:13
29:4 [v]Ps 68:33
29:5 [w]Jdg 9:15
29:6 [x]Ps 114:4 [y]Dt 3:9
29:8 [z]Nu 13:26
29:9 [a]Ps 26:8
29:10 [b]Ge 6:17

[a] *2* Or *LORD with the splendor of* [b] *6* That is, Mount Hermon [c] *9* Or *LORD makes the deer give birth*
[d] *10* Or *sat*

28:5 he will tear them down. In the previous verse David had appealed for judgment; in this one he pronounced it. Or it may be that these words were spoken by the priest to David to assure him that his request had been heard. This would explain the positive turn in the next verse.
28:7 my shield. God protected the psalmist from the vicious attacks of his enemies. Assurance of being heard leads to praise. See notes on 22:22 and the verses following. See *WLC* 175.
28:8 the strength of his people. David broadened his appeal to the Lord to include the whole nation. See *BC* 14.
28:9 their shepherd. See note on 23:1. See *WLC* 183.
Psalm 29 *Introduction.* A song of praise to God the King. The psalm employs themes current in the religions of the surrounding nations: God as the force behind the storm (vv. 3–9) and the victor over the floodwaters (vv. 10–11). The psalmist attacked the religions of the Canaanites and Mesopotamians by crediting the Lord with these powers, which they ascribed to their false gods (see note on v. 3). The picture of God as king, enthroned over the vanquished floodwaters, is one of many indications that the psalm was used to celebrate a divinely orchestrated victory in battle.
29:1 O mighty ones. Literally, "sons of god(s)." The phrase occurs in the religious texts of the Canaanites and refers to their gods collectively. For its use in the Old Testament, see note on Genesis 6:2.
29:2 his name. God's reputation, achieved through his acts in history. See *WLC* 104,112; *WSC* 46.
29:3 voice of the LORD. Thunder. Powerful storms reveal God's power. The Canaanites believed that Baal provided rain and fertility and that his power was revealed in the storm. He was called "cloud rider" in their religious texts. But the psalmist knew that the Lord, not Baal, controls nature (cf. 1 Kings 18). **waters . . . mighty waters.** An allusion to the religions of the Near East, in which the waters represented the forces of chaos and evil. See Psalms 18:4, 47:1–2 and 69:1–2.
29:6 Lebanon . . . Sirion. Mountain regions. The otherwise immovable mountains shake before the power of God. See Psalm 46:2.
29:8 Desert of Kadesh. Perhaps best translated "holy desert." If "Desert of Kadesh" is correct, its location is uncertain.
29:10 enthroned over the flood. See verse 3. The theme of God as victor and ruler over the chaos of waters appears frequently in the Psalms and Prophets (see also Ge 6:17).

the LORD is enthroned as King forever.[c]
11 The LORD gives strength to his people;[d]
the LORD blesses his people with peace.[e]

Psalm 30

A psalm. A song. For the dedication of the temple.[a] Of David.

1 I will exalt you, O LORD,
for you lifted me out of the depths
and did not let my enemies gloat over me.[f]
2 O LORD my God, I called to you for help[g]
and you healed me.[h]
3 O LORD, you brought me up from the grave[b];
you spared me from going down into the pit.[i]

4 Sing to the LORD, you saints[j] of his;
praise his holy name.[k]
5 For his anger[l] lasts only a moment,
but his favor lasts a lifetime;
weeping may remain for a night,
but rejoicing comes in the morning.[m]

6 When I felt secure, I said,
"I will never be shaken."
7 O LORD, when you favored me,
you made my mountain[c] stand firm;
but when you hid your face,[n]
I was dismayed.

8 To you, O LORD, I called;
to the Lord I cried for mercy:
9 "What gain is there in my destruction,[d]
in my going down into the pit?
Will the dust praise you?
Will it proclaim your faithfulness?[o]
10 Hear, O LORD, and be merciful to me;
O LORD, be my help."

11 You turned my wailing into dancing;
you removed my sackcloth and clothed me with
joy,[p]
12 that my heart may sing to you and not be silent.
O LORD my God, I will give you thanks[q] forever.[r]

29:10 [c]Ps 10:16
29:11 [d]Ps 28:8 [e]Ps 37:11
30:1 [f]Ps 25:2; 28:9
30:2 [g]Ps 88:13 [h]Ps 6:2
30:3 [i]Ps 28:1; 86:13
30:4 [j]Ps 149:1 [k]Ps 97:12
30:5 [l]Ps 103:9 [m]2Co 4:17
30:7 [n]Dt 31:17; Ps 104:29
30:9 [o]Ps 6:5
30:11 [p]Ps 4:7; Jer 31:4, 13
30:12 [q]Ps 16:9 [r]Ps 44:8

[a] Title: Or *palace* [b] 3 Hebrew *Sheol* [c] 7 Or *hill country* [d] 9 Or *there if I am silenced*

Psalm 30 *Introduction.* David thanked the Lord for hearing his prayers for healing from sickness. He admitted that, in his pride (vv. 6–7), he had forgotten God. When his life was threatened (vv. 8–10), he learned to call on God again for salvation.

Title.: The historical title indicates that the psalm was written for the dedication of the temple. The NIV text note gives the alternate rendering "palace"—in David's time the temple had not yet been built. However, in favor of the "temple" rendering, David could have prepared the psalm in anticipation of the temple's dedication, just as he anticipated its building by gathering materials (1Ch 22). A greater difficulty is the lack of any clear connection with either palace or temple in the body of the psalm (see "Introduction: Authorship and Titles: *Historical Titles*"). Attempts to link the psalm with the plague recorded in 1 Chronicles 21:1—22:1 fail to take into account that David himself was not afflicted.

30:1 lifted me out. The Hebrew verb is used of drawing a bucket out of a well. It is an appropriate image of saving someone from Sheol, which is often pictured as a wet and muddy pit.

30:2 you healed me. Indicates that the psalm is one of thanksgiving in response to physical healing.

30:4 you saints of his. The word translated *saint* is related to the noun that means "covenant loving-kindness" and specifies those men and women who are part of God's covenant.

30:5 anger lasts only a moment. God's mercy is certain and overwhelming. See Romans 8:18 and 2 Corinthians 4:17. **remain for a night.** Literally, "come in at evening to lodge." The figure is that of a guest enjoying accommodations for only one night. **rejoicing comes in the morning.** See 90:14.

30:7 my mountain. Mountains, as opposed to the sea, are the height of stability and often represent God and his presence (see Pss 29:6; 46:2). David admitted that he had become filled with pride when God had prospered him. "My mountain" may originally have referred to the grandeur of David's palace (built on a hill), which was an impetus for David to arrogance.

30:9 What gain is there? In the sense of profit. **in my destruction.** One approach to this difficult passage assumes that David had little knowledge of the afterlife as he spoke these words. He thus bargained with God for his life (see Ge 18) by pointing out that God would regain a voice of praise if he were to heal him. Others argue that the afterlife is not the issue here: The dead do not praise God among the living. See note on 6:5.

Psalm 31

For the director of music. A psalm of David.

1 In you, O LORD, I have taken refuge;
let me never be put to shame;
deliver me in your righteousness.
2 Turn your ear to me,
come quickly to my rescue;
be my rock of refuge,[s]
a strong fortress to save me.
3 Since you are my rock and my fortress,[t]
for the sake of your name[u] lead and guide me.
4 Free me from the trap that is set for me,
for you are my refuge.[v]
5 Into your hands I commit my spirit;[w]
redeem me, O LORD, the God of truth.

6 I hate those who cling to worthless idols;
I trust in the LORD.[x]
7 I will be glad and rejoice in your love,
for you saw my affliction[y]
and knew the anguish[z] of my soul.
8 You have not handed me over[a] to the enemy
but have set my feet in a spacious place.

9 Be merciful to me, O LORD, for I am in distress;
my eyes grow weak with sorrow,[b]
my soul and my body with grief.
10 My life is consumed by anguish
and my years by groaning;[c]
my strength fails because of my affliction,[a]
and my bones grow weak.[d]
11 Because of all my enemies,
I am the utter contempt of my neighbors;[e]
I am a dread to my friends—
those who see me on the street flee from me.
12 I am forgotten by them as though I were dead;[f]
I have become like broken pottery.
13 For I hear the slander of many;
there is terror on every side;[g]
they conspire against me
and plot to take my life.[h]

14 But I trust[i] in you, O LORD;
I say, "You are my God."
15 My times[j] are in your hands;
deliver me from my enemies
and from those who pursue me.

31:2 [s]Ps 18:2
31:3 [t]Ps 18:2 [u]Ps 23:3
31:4 [v]Ps 25:15
31:5 [w]Lk 23:46; Ac 7:59
31:6 [x]Jnh 2:8
31:7 [y]Ps 90:14 [z]Ps 10:14; Jn 10:27
31:8 [a]Dt 32:30
31:9 [b]Ps 6:7
31:10 [c]Ps 13:2 [d]Ps 38:3; 39:11
31:11 [e]Job 19:13; Ps 38:11; 64:8; Isa 53:4
31:12 [f]Ps 88:4
31:13 [g]Jer 20:3,10; La 2:22 [h]Mt 27:1
31:14 [i]Ps 140:6
31:15 [j]Job 24:1; Ps 143:9

[a] *10* Or *guilt*

Psalm 31 *Introduction.* Psalm 31 is one of refuge. The accusations against David are not specified. The psalm could have been recited by different worshipers under diverse circumstances. David occasionally appeared desperate (vv. 9–13), but trust (vv. 7–8,19–20) and praise (vv. 21–25) are the final notes of his prayer.
31:1 in your righteousness. The psalmist appealed to the Lord's righteousness because his distress was caused by the wickedness of the enemy. God's righteousness means that God is committed to saving those who are in covenant relationship with him. See note on 4:1.
31:5 I commit my spirit. David entrusted his very life into the hands of God. Jesus, who quoted these words from the cross (Lk 23:46), often found that the desperate cries of the lament psalms expressed his own anguish as he faced the rejection of the world (e.g., 22; 69). Jesus went further than David's expression here, entrusting himself to the Father in his certain death.
31:6 worthless idols. Idols are useless because they cannot act in any way to help those who worship them. David, on the other hand, trusted the Lord, the "God of truth" (v. 5).
31:7 I will . . . rejoice in your love. Specifically in God's love for David as his covenant partner, which motivated God's response to David's distress.
31:10 affliction. The NIV text note offers "guilt" as an alternate translation, following the Masoretic text. However, on contextual grounds "affliction," which is found in a prominent Greek text, is preferred. David's present distress was attributable to outside forces, not to his own guilt.
31:12 broken pottery. A metaphor for serious illness, even death (Ecc 12:6).
31:14 I say, "You are my God." A simple and foundational confession of an individual in covenant with God.
31:15 My times. David knew that God controls history in general and controlled his life in particular. This assurance comforted him in his distress.

31:16 [k]Nu 6:25; Ps 4:6
31:17 [l]Ps 25:2-3 [m]Ps 115:17
31:18 [n]Ps 120:2 [o]Ps 94:4
31:19 [p]Ro 11:22 [q]Isa 64:4
31:20 [r]Ps 27:5 [s]Job 5:21
31:21 [t]Ps 17:7 [u]1Sa 23:7
31:22 [v]Ps 116:11 [w]La 3:54
31:23 [x]Ps 34:9 [y]Ps 145:20 [z]Ps 94:2
31:24 [a]Ps 27:14
32:1 [b]Ps 85:2
32:2 [c]Ro 4:7-8*; 2Co 5:19 [d]Jn 1:47
32:3 [e]Ps 31:10
32:4 [f]Job 33:7

16 Let your face shine[k] on your servant;
save me in your unfailing love.
17 Let me not be put to shame,[l] O LORD,
for I have cried out to you;
but let the wicked be put to shame
and lie silent[m] in the grave.[a]
18 Let their lying lips[n] be silenced,
for with pride and contempt
they speak arrogantly[o] against the righteous.

19 How great is your goodness,[p]
which you have stored up for those who fear you,
which you bestow in the sight of men[q]
on those who take refuge in you.
20 In the shelter of your presence you hide[r] them
from the intrigues of men;[s]
in your dwelling you keep them safe
from accusing tongues.

21 Praise be to the LORD,
for he showed his wonderful love[t] to me
when I was in a besieged city.[u]
22 In my alarm[v] I said,
"I am cut off from your sight!"
Yet you heard my cry[w] for mercy
when I called to you for help.

23 Love the LORD, all his saints![x]
The LORD preserves the faithful,[y]
but the proud he pays back[z] in full.
24 Be strong and take heart,[a]
all you who hope in the LORD.

Psalm 32

Of David. A *maskil.*[b]

1 Blessed is he
whose transgressions are forgiven,
whose sins are covered.[b]
2 Blessed is the man
whose sin the LORD does not count against him[c]
and in whose spirit is no deceit.[d]

3 When I kept silent,
my bones wasted away[e]
through my groaning all day long.
4 For day and night
your hand was heavy[f] upon me;
my strength was sapped

[a] *17* Hebrew *Sheol* [b] Title: Probably a literary or musical term

31:16 Let your face shine. Compare the priestly blessing in Numbers 6:25. God's face is a metaphor for his loving presence. When God's face shines, blessing and deliverance come. **unfailing love.** God's covenant loving-kindness.
31:19 those who fear you. Those in covenant relationship with God exhibit a reverential awe toward him.
31:21 in a besieged city. A difficult phrase. Some suggest a simple textual emendation so that it can be translated "in a difficult time," which fits the context well. However, David could be remembering an earlier act of divine deliverance, or this could be a metaphor for the threat he had experienced.
31:22 cut off from your sight. See notes on verse 16 and on 13:1. See *WCF* 18.4; *WLC* 81,172.
31:23 his saints. See note on 4:3. See *WCF* 21.1.
Psalm 32 *Introduction.* In Psalm 32 David expressed the blessedness of forgiveness after sincere and unreserved repentance and confession of sin. He delighted in a renewed sense of God's protection and of joy. The song has traditionally been numbered among the penitential psalms (see Ps 6) because of its strong expression of repentance (v. 5). It also includes thankfulness for answered prayer and some distinctive wisdom language (vv. 1–2,8–10).
32:1–2 Blessed . . . Blessed. See note on 1:1. **sins . . . sin.** The Hebrew word translated "sin" in verse 2 is different from the word rendered as "sins" in verse 1. Perhaps a better translation of the more specific term in verse 2 would be "iniquity." Three different Hebrew words for sin are used in the first two verses in order to emphasize different perspectives on human rebellion against God. Paul cited these two verses in Romans 4:6–8 to describe the grace of God's forgiveness. See *WCF* 7.6; *BC* 22,23.
32:3–4 my bones wasted away. In David's case, sin had physical consequences. This language should neither be dismissed as "merely poetic" nor taken as teaching a general principle that sin always has physical consequences. **my strength was sapped.** Guilt had immobilized and enervated David. See *WCF* 17.3.

as in the heat of summer. *Selah*
5 Then I acknowledged my sin to you
and did not cover up my iniquity.
I said, "I will confess[g]
my transgressions[h] to the LORD"—
and you forgave
the guilt of my sin.[i] *Selah*

6 Therefore let everyone who is godly pray to you
while you may be found;[j]
surely when the mighty waters rise,
they will not reach him.[k]
7 You are my hiding place;
you will protect me from trouble[l]
and surround me with songs of deliverance.[m] *Selah*

8 I will instruct[n] you and teach you in the way you should go;
I will counsel you and watch over[o] you.
9 Do not be like the horse or the mule,
which have no understanding
but must be controlled by bit and bridle[p]
or they will not come to you.
10 Many are the woes of the wicked,[q]
but the LORD's unfailing love
surrounds the man who trusts[r] in him.

11 Rejoice in the LORD[s] and be glad, you righteous;
sing, all you who are upright in heart!

Psalm 33

1 Sing joyfully to the LORD, you righteous;
it is fitting[t] for the upright[u] to praise him.
2 Praise the LORD with the harp;
make music to him on the ten-stringed lyre.[v]
3 Sing to him a new song;[w]
play skillfully, and shout for joy.

4 For the word of the LORD is right[x] and true;
he is faithful in all he does.
5 The LORD loves righteousness and justice;[y]
the earth is full of his unfailing love.[z]

6 By the word[a] of the LORD were the heavens made,
their starry host by the breath of his mouth.
7 He gathers the waters of the sea into jars[a];

32:5 [g]Pr 28:13 [h]Ps 103:12 [i]Lev 26:40
32:6 [j]Ps 69:13; Isa 55:6 [k]Isa 43:2
32:7 [l]Ps 9:9 [m]Ex 15:1
32:8 [n]Ps 25:8 [o]Ps 33:18
32:9 [p]Pr 26:3
32:10 [q]Ro 2:9 [r]Pr 16:20
32:11 [s]Ps 64:10
33:1 [t]Ps 147:1 [u]Ps 32:11
33:2 [v]Ps 92:3
33:3 [w]Ps 96:1
33:4 [x]Ps 19:8
33:5 [y]Ps 11:7 [z]Ps 119:64
33:6 [a]Heb 11:3

a 7 Or *sea as into a heap*

32:5–6 See *WCF* 15.6; *WLC* 178; *WSC* 98.
32:5 I acknowledged my sin to you. David recalled his confession of sin and God's consequent forgiveness. This psalm is a witness to God's willingness and authority to forgive. See *WCF* 11.5; *HC* 115.
32:6 godly. The same word elsewhere translated "saints"; see note on 4:3. **mighty waters.** Elsewhere translated "deep waters." See notes on 18:16, 29:3 and 10, 46:2 and 4, 69:1–2 and 144:7.
32:8 I will instruct you. God's response to David's prayer. Using the language found in wisdom sections of the Old Testament (e.g., Ps 1 and Pr 1–9), God promised to direct the psalmist in the way of the covenant and of righteousness.
32:9 Do not be like the horse or the mule. In other words, add obedience to trust. The horse and the mule do the will of their master only under compulsion. Compare Proverbs 26:3. The righteous obey out of love and gratitude to their God.
32:10 unfailing love. God's covenant loving-kindness.
32:11 See *WLC* 104.
Psalm 33 *Introduction.* The psalmist joyfully praised God for his righteous character (vv. 1–5), for his creation of the world (vv. 6–11) and for entering history to save his people (vv. 16–19). The occasion for the psalm is not obvious. It would, however, be an appropriate model prayer in a war situation as the people of God waited on God for deliverance (vv. 20–21). The length of the psalm, 22 poetic lines (also verses), probably reflects the 22 letters of the Hebrew alphabet, though the psalm is not an acrostic.
33:3 new song. Frequently these "new" compositions are found in contexts of victorious holy war and can properly be viewed as victory shouts. Compare Psalms 96, 98, 144, 149, Isaiah 42:10 and Revelation 5:9 and 14:3.
33:4 the word of the LORD is right and true. God's words exhibit his character. He leads his people into truth. The Bible, as God's written Word, reflects these characteristics of truthfulness.
33:5–6 See *WCF* 4.1.
33:5 unfailing love. God's covenant loving-kindness.
33:6 By the word of the LORD. Begins a meditation on Genesis 1 and on God's creation of the universe by means of his word alone. This reflection underscores the rightness and truth of God's word and his faithfulness in carrying it out (v. 4). **starry host.** Literally, "hosts"; may refer not merely to the innumerable stars of heaven but also to the heavenly armies. See *BC* 11; *HC* 26.
33:7 the waters of the sea. God's creation is pictured poetically here as his control of the chaos waters. See notes on 18:16 and

he puts the deep into storehouses.
8 Let all the earth fear the LORD;
let all the people of the world revere him.[b]
9 For he spoke, and it came to be;
he commanded,[c] and it stood firm.
10 The LORD foils the plans of the nations;[d]
he thwarts the purposes of the peoples.
11 But the plans of the LORD stand firm forever,
the purposes[e] of his heart through all generations.

12 Blessed is the nation whose God is the LORD,[f]
the people he chose[g] for his inheritance.
13 From heaven the LORD looks down
and sees all mankind;[h]
14 from his dwelling place[i] he watches
all who live on earth—
15 he who forms[j] the hearts of all,
who considers everything they do.[k]
16 No king is saved by the size of his army;[l]
no warrior escapes by his great strength.
17 A horse[m] is a vain hope for deliverance;
despite all its great strength it cannot save.
18 But the eyes[n] of the LORD are on those who fear him,
on those whose hope is in his unfailing love,[o]
19 to deliver them from death
and keep them alive in famine.[p]
20 We wait[q] in hope for the LORD;
he is our help and our shield.
21 In him our hearts rejoice,[r]
for we trust in his holy name.
22 May your unfailing love rest upon us, O LORD,
even as we put our hope in you.

Psalm 34[a]

Of David. When he pretended to be insane before Abimelech, who drove him away, and he left.

1 I will extol the LORD at all times;[s]
his praise will always be on my lips.
2 My soul will boast[t] in the LORD;
let the afflicted hear and rejoice.[u]
3 Glorify the LORD with me;
let us exalt[v] his name together.

4 I sought the LORD,[w] and he answered me;
he delivered me from all my fears.
5 Those who look to him are radiant;[x]

33:8 [b]Ps 67:7; 96:9
33:9 [c]Ge 1:3; Ps 148:5
33:10 [d]Isa 8:10
33:11 [e]Job 23:13
33:12 [f]Ps 144:15 [g]Ex 19:5; Dt 7:6
33:13 [h]Job 28:24; Ps 11:4
33:14 [i]1Ki 8:39
33:15 [j]Job 10:8 [k]Jer 32:19
33:16 [l]Ps 44:6
33:17 [m]Ps 20:7; Pr 21:31
33:18 [n]Job 36:7; Ps 34:15 [o]Ps 147:11
33:19 [p]Job 5:20
33:20 [q]Ps 130:6
33:21 [r]Zec 10:7; Jn 16:22
34:1 [s]Ps 71:6; Eph 5:20
34:2 [t]Jer 9:24; 1Co 1:31 [u]Ps 119:74
34:3 [v]Lk 1:46
34:4 [w]Mt 7:7
34:5 [x]Ps 36:9

[a] This psalm is an acrostic poem, the verses of which begin with the successive letters of the Hebrew alphabet.

29:3; also see "Introduction" to Psalm 29. There may also be a poetical reflection of the Song of the Sea (Ex 15).
33:8 fear the Lord . . . revere him. That is, have a properly reverential attitude of love toward him.
33:10–11 foils the plans of the nations. Gentile nations that seek their own will and not God's. **the plans of the LORD stand firm.** In contrast to the plans of the nations. God is in control of world events. See *WCF* 5.1; *WLC* 12.
33:12 the people he chose. Israel is the nation that he chose. Notice that God is the One who initiated the relationship (Dt 7:7–11).
Psalm 34 *Introduction.* The psalm thanks the Lord for answering prayer. While the original occasion for the prayer is not found in the psalm itself, the title connects it with David and specifically with the time period before he was crowned king. The psalm's content, however, lacks historical specificity, most likely so that it could be applied to different people in varying situations. There is a strong didactic tone in the psalm, relating it to Biblical wisdom literature (vv. 8–22). Instruction follows praise. The psalm, with two irregularities, is an acrostic, each line beginning with successive letters of the Hebrew alphabet (see "Introduction: Structure: *Poetic Style and Devices*").
Title. See 1 Samuel 21:10–15 for the historical situation alluded to in the title. **Abimelech.** Probably a royal title for the king of the Philistines, not the proper name of the king (which in 1Sa is Achish).
34:2 boast in the LORD. While boasting in one's self is the height of arrogance and godlessness (Ro 1:30), it is right to boast in God (Jer 9:24; 2Co 10:17).
34:3 his name. His reputation: the Lord as he reveals himself. Exhortation to witness to his great acts in history and in our lives.
34:5–6 See *BC* 26.
34:5 are radiant. They reflect the Lord's shining upon them (see notes on 13:1 and 31:16). A radiant demeanor reflects the joy of God's presence. God's absence brings the darkness of shame.

their faces are never covered with shame.[y]
6 This poor man called, and the LORD heard him;
he saved him out of all his troubles.
7 The angel of the LORD[z] encamps around those who fear him,
and he delivers them.

8 Taste and see that the LORD is good;[a]
blessed is the man who takes refuge[b] in him.
9 Fear the LORD, you his saints,
for those who fear him lack nothing.[c]
10 The lions may grow weak and hungry,
but those who seek the LORD lack no good thing.[d]

11 Come, my children, listen to me;
I will teach you[e] the fear of the LORD.
12 Whoever of you loves life[f]
and desires to see many good days,
13 keep your tongue from evil
and your lips from speaking lies.[g]
14 Turn from evil and do good;[h]
seek peace[i] and pursue it.

15 The eyes of the LORD[j] are on the righteous[k]
and his ears are attentive to their cry;
16 the face of the LORD is against[l] those who do evil,[m]
to cut off the memory[n] of them from the earth.

17 The righteous cry out, and the LORD hears[o] them;
he delivers them from all their troubles.
18 The LORD is close[p] to the brokenhearted[q]
and saves those who are crushed in spirit.

19 A righteous man may have many troubles,[r]
but the LORD delivers him from them all;[s]
20 he protects all his bones,
not one of them will be broken.[t]

21 Evil will slay the wicked;[u]
the foes of the righteous will be condemned.
22 The LORD redeems[v] his servants;
no one will be condemned who takes refuge in him.

Psalm 35

Of David.

1 Contend, O LORD, with those who contend with me;
fight[w] against those who fight against me.
2 Take up shield and buckler;
arise[x] and come to my aid.

34:5 [y]Ps 25:3
34:7 [z]2Ki 6:17; Da 6:22
34:8 [a]1Pe 2:3 [b]Ps 2:12
34:9 [c]Ps 23:1
34:10 [d]Ps 84:11
34:11 [e]Ps 32:8
34:12 [f]1Pe 3:10
34:13 [g]1Pe 2:22
34:14 [h]Ps 37:27 [i]Heb 12:14
34:15 [j]Ps 33:18 [k]Job 36:7
34:16 [l]Lev 17:10; Jer 44:11 [m]1Pe 3:10-12* [n]Pr 10:7
34:17 [o]Ps 145:19
34:18 [p]Ps 145:18 [q]Isa 57:15
34:19 [r]ver 17 [s]ver 4,6; Pr 24:16
34:20 [t]Jn 19:36*
34:21 [u]Ps 94:23
34:22 [v]1Ki 1:29; Ps 71:23
35:1 [w]Ps 43:1
35:2 [x]Ps 62:2

34:6 This poor man. David himself, a fugitive among the Philistines, living more by his wits than by his assets. The Hebrew word translated "poor" implies oppression and affliction.
34:7 The angel of the LORD. See note on Exodus 3:2. **encamps around.** Elisha's servant learned the truth of this statement when Elisha prayed for the servant's eyes to be opened and the man witnessed the army of the Lord protecting them from the Arameans (2Ki 6:8–23). This does not propagate a doctrine of individual guardian angels. **those who fear him.** Those in a right relationship with him. See note on 2:11.
34:8 Taste. The psalmist described his personal experience of God's goodness. After experiencing God's goodness in Christ, Peter alluded to this passage (1Pe 2:3). Verses 8–14 provide instruction in the fear of the Lord, namely through trust and obedience.
34:10 The lions may grow weak. The statement may be metaphoric, meaning that while those who are strong and ruthless don't always get what they want, God's people, depicted in the psalm as poor and afflicted, lack nothing that God defines as good for them. But it also may contrast the value God places on his people with that of the animal life he has created. While the Lord might allow wild beasts to go hungry, he will provide for his covenant people.
34:11 my children. This may be a reference to biological children, or perhaps to those whom the psalmist would instruct.
34:12–16 See *WCF* 19.6.
34:15 the righteous. Those who are in a covenant relationship with the Lord and are obedient to his law.
34:16 those who do evil. The rebellious who neglect God's law.
34:19 See *HC* 117.
34:20 not one of them will be broken. John (19:36) applied this verse to Jesus Christ, the only perfectly righteous man.
Psalm 35 *Introduction.* David wrote this lament as an appeal to the Lord for protection. It concerns a time when his life was threatened. The psalm contains the language of warfare (vv. 1–3) as well as legal language (vv. 11,23–24). It may relate to enemies accusing the Israelite king of treaty violations as they wage war against him. Twice the psalm comes to a climax with the figure of the offering of a vow in praise (vv. 19,28).
35:1 Contend. The word is a technical legal term that means "bring a case against someone." Legal language runs throughout the psalm (vv. 11–16,23–24), as David commits his case to God.
35:2 arise. See note on 3:7.

3 Brandish spear and javelin[a]
against those who pursue me.
Say to my soul,
"I am your salvation."

4 May those who seek my life
be disgraced[y] and put to shame;
may those who plot my ruin
be turned back in dismay.
5 May they be like chaff[z] before the wind,
with the angel of the LORD driving them away;
6 may their path be dark and slippery,
with the angel of the LORD pursuing them.
7 Since they hid their net for me without cause
and without cause dug a pit for me,
8 may ruin overtake them by surprise—[a]
may the net they hid entangle them,
may they fall into the pit,[b] to their ruin.
9 Then my soul will rejoice[c] in the LORD
and delight in his salvation.[d]
10 My whole being will exclaim,
"Who is like you,[e] O LORD?
You rescue the poor from those too strong[f] for them,
the poor and needy[g] from those who rob them."
11 Ruthless witnesses[h] come forward;
they question me on things I know nothing about.
12 They repay me evil for good[i]
and leave my soul forlorn.
13 Yet when they were ill, I put on sackcloth
and humbled myself with fasting.[j]
When my prayers returned to me unanswered,
14 I went about mourning
as though for my friend or brother.
I bowed my head in grief
as though weeping for my mother.
15 But when I stumbled, they gathered in glee;
attackers gathered against me when I was unaware.
They slandered[k] me without ceasing.
16 Like the ungodly they maliciously mocked[b];
they gnashed their teeth[l] at me.
17 O Lord, how long[m] will you look on?
Rescue my life from their ravages,
my precious life[n] from these lions.
18 I will give you thanks in the great assembly;[o]
among throngs of people I will praise you.[p]

19 Let not those gloat over me
who are my enemies without cause;

35:4 [y]Ps 70:2
35:5 [z]Job 21:18; Ps 1:4; Isa 29:5
35:8 [a]1Th 5:3 [b]Ps 9:15
35:9 [c]Lk 1:47 [d]Isa 61:10
35:10 [e]Ex 15:11 [f]Ps 18:17 [g]Ps 37:14
35:11 [h]Ps 27:12
35:12 [i]Jn 10:32
35:13 [j]Job 30:25; Ps 69:10
35:15 [k]Job 30:1,8
35:16 [l]Job 16:9; La 2:16
35:17 [m]Hab 1:13 [n]Ps 22:20
35:18 [o]Ps 22:25 [p]Ps 22:22

a *3* Or *and block the way* b *16* Septuagint; Hebrew may mean *ungodly circle of mockers.*

35:3 your salvation. In the Old Testament, this phrase connoted victory in battle.
35:5 like chaff. Chaff is lightweight, worthless matter that is disposed of when grain is harvested. David prayed that his enemies might be carried away, never becoming established or rooted, that they might forever flee so that they could do no harm. See 1:4, where the image is also applied to the wicked and contrasted with the righteous, who are like deeply-rooted trees.
35:6 path. A frequent Biblical image for one's life course. The psalmist is calling for divine judgment on evildoers.
35:8 may ruin overtake them. David asked that, in justice, the traps they had set for him close on them instead—that their judgment match their evil intent. Their evil becomes their own judgment, a frequent theme in the Prophets. See Psalms 7:14–16 and 34:21.
35:10 Who is like you, O LORD? A rhetorical question, to which the answer is readily apparent—No one is like God. Compare Exodus 15:11 within its context as another divine warrior psalm.
35:11 Ruthless witnesses. Note the law in Exodus 23:1 that prohibits this kind of witness. The adjective indicates witnesses who are seeking violence against the defendant.
35:12 evil for good. The height of injustice; compare Genesis 44:4, 1 Samuel 25:21, Psalms 38:20 and 109:5 and Proverbs 17:13.
35:13–14 I put on sackcloth. The psalmist did no evil to those who attacked him; rather, he actively and sacrificially pursued their welfare.
35:15–16 See *WLC* 145.
35:17 how long will you look on? Without acting to save the psalmist. See note on 6:3. **lions.** A common Biblical metaphor for those who are ruthless and violent. See note on 7:2.
35:18 will give you thanks. With assurance of deliverance, David promised to discharge his vow of praise (see Ps 22:22).
35:19 wink the eye. Taunt.

let not those who hate me without reason[q]
maliciously wink the eye.[r]
20 They do not speak peaceably,
but devise false accusations
against those who live quietly in the land.
21 They gape[s] at me and say, "Aha! Aha![t]
With our own eyes we have seen it."

22 O LORD, you have seen[u] this; be not silent.
Do not be far[v] from me, O Lord.
23 Awake,[w] and rise to my defense!
Contend for me, my God and Lord.
24 Vindicate me in your righteousness, O LORD my God;
do not let them gloat over me.
25 Do not let them think, "Aha, just what we wanted!"
or say, "We have swallowed him up."[x]

26 May all who gloat over my distress
be put to shame[y] and confusion;
may all who exalt themselves over me[z]
be clothed with shame and disgrace.
27 May those who delight in my vindication[a]
shout for joy[b] and gladness;
may they always say, "The LORD be exalted,
who delights[c] in the well-being of his servant."
28 My tongue will speak of your righteousness[d]
and of your praises all day long.

Psalm 36

For the director of music. Of David the servant of the LORD.

1 An oracle is within my heart
concerning the sinfulness of the wicked:[a]
There is no fear of God
before his eyes.[e]
2 For in his own eyes he flatters himself
too much to detect or hate his sin.
3 The words of his mouth[f] are wicked and deceitful;
he has ceased to be wise[g] and to do good.[h]
4 Even on his bed he plots evil;[i]
he commits himself to a sinful course[j]
and does not reject what is wrong.[k]

5 Your love, O LORD, reaches to the heavens,
your faithfulness to the skies.
6 Your righteousness is like the mighty mountains,
your justice like the great deep.[l]
O LORD, you preserve both man and beast.
7 How priceless is your unfailing love!

35:19 [q]Ps 38:19; 69:4; Jn 15:25* [r]Ps 13:4; Pr 6:13
35:21 [s]Ps 22:13 [t]Ps 40:15
35:22 [u]Ex 3:7 [v]Ps 10:1; 28:1
35:23 [w]Ps 44:23
35:25 [x]La 2:16
35:26 [y]Ps 40:14; 109:29 [z]Ps 38:16
35:27 [a]Ps 9:4 [b]Ps 32:11 [c]Ps 40:16; 147:11
35:28 [d]Ps 51:14
36:1 [e]Ro 3:18*
36:3 [f]Ps 10:7 [g]Ps 94:8 [h]Jer 4:22
36:4 [i]Pr 4:16; Mic 2:1 [j]Isa 65:2 [k]Ps 52:3; Ro 12:9
36:6 [l]Job 11:8; Ps 77:19; Ro 11:33

a *1* Or *heart: / Sin proceeds from the wicked.*

35:20 peaceably. A technical term in ancient treaties. The enemies were breaking covenant with the psalmist's people.
35:21 See *WLC* 145.
35:28 My tongue will speak. Praise was pledged, although the deliverance had not yet come.
Psalm 36 *Introduction.* Psalm 36 is a meditation on the sinfulness of the wicked. Over against human evil, the psalmist contrasted God's covenant love and mercy.
36:1 An oracle. Usually in the formula "oracle of the Lord." The term identifies what follows as divinely inspired. **no fear of God.** The psalmist identified a fundamental source of human evil. Proverbs 1:7 cites the fear of God as the beginning of all knowledge. The fear of God is an objective revelation, resulting in a reverential awe that recognizes one's total dependence upon the Lord. The opposite is a self-reliant pride, which leads to a different type of fear of the Lord—dread. See note on 2:11.
36:2 flatters himself. Not merely in self-righteousness but based on the smug, conceited notion that he is accountable to no one but himself.
36:3 wicked . . . wise. Notice the ethical side to wisdom: To be wise is to do good. See *WCF* 16.7.
36:4 on his bed he plots evil. Wickedness is a full-time occupation. Even at night when people should be praying before sleep, the wicked plot and scheme. See *WLC* 151.
36:5 love. A special word for the devotion by which God binds himself to his covenant people. It might be translated "covenant loving-kindness."
36:6 mighty mountains. See notes on 29:6, 30:7 and 46:2. **great deep.** Often (though not here) contrasted with the mountains (Ps 46). Here the image denotes profundity and abundance.

Both high and low among men
find[a] refuge in the shadow of your wings.[m]
8 They feast on the abundance of your house;[n]
you give them drink from your river[o] of delights.
9 For with you is the fountain of life;[p]
in your light[q] we see light.

10 Continue your love to those who know you,
your righteousness to the upright in heart.
11 May the foot of the proud not come against me,
nor the hand of the wicked drive me away.
12 See how the evildoers lie fallen—
thrown down, not able to rise![r]

36:7 [m]Ru 2:12; Ps 17:8
36:8 [n]Ps 65:4 [o]Job 20:17; Rev 22:1
36:9 [p]Jer 2:13 [q]1Pe 2:9
36:12 [r]Ps 140:10

Psalm 37[b]

Of David.

1 Do not fret because of evil men
or be envious[s] of those who do wrong;[t]
2 for like the grass they will soon wither,
like green plants they will soon die away.[u]

3 Trust in the LORD and do good;
dwell in the land[v] and enjoy safe pasture.[w]
4 Delight[x] yourself in the LORD
and he will give you the desires of your heart.

5 Commit your way to the LORD;
trust in him[y] and he will do this:
6 He will make your righteousness[z] shine like the dawn,[a]
the justice of your cause like the noonday sun.

7 Be still[b] before the LORD and wait patiently[c] for him;
do not fret when men succeed in their ways,
when they carry out their wicked schemes.

8 Refrain from anger[d] and turn from wrath;
do not fret—it leads only to evil.
9 For evil men will be cut off,
but those who hope in the LORD will inherit the land.[e]

10 A little while, and the wicked will be no more;[f]
though you look for them, they will not be found.
11 But the meek will inherit the land[g]
and enjoy great peace.

12 The wicked plot against the righteous
and gnash their teeth[h] at them;

37:1 [s]Pr 23:17-18 [t]Ps 73:3
37:2 [u]Ps 90:6
37:3 [v]Dt 30:20 [w]Isa 40:11; Jn 10:9
37:4 [x]Isa 58:14
37:5 [y]Ps 4:5; Ps 55:22; Pr 16:3; 1Pe 5:7
37:6 [z]Mic 7:9 [a]Job 11:17
37:7 [b]Ps 62:5; La 3:26 [c]Ps 40:1
37:8 [d]Eph 4:31; Col 3:8
37:9 [e]Isa 57:13; 60:21
37:10 [f]Job 7:10; 24:24
37:11 [g]Mt 5:5
37:12 [h]Ps 35:16

[a] 7 Or *love, O God! / Men find*; or *love! / Both heavenly beings and men / find* [b] This psalm is an acrostic poem, the stanzas of which begin with the successive letters of the Hebrew alphabet.

36:7 unfailing love. See note on verse 5. **high and low among men.** The Hebrew is difficult here (see NIV text note). However, the verse definitely teaches that those who take refuge in God are safe in his care. **shadow of your wings.** God is portrayed as a mother bird that shelters and protects her young.
36:8 They feast. The psalmist pictures God as a rich and generous host.
36:9 fountain of life. God is the source and provider of all life. **light.** All knowledge and insight originate with God.
36:10 See *WLC* 175.
Psalm 37 *Introduction.* In this wisdom meditation (see "Introduction: Structure: *Genre*"), David reflects on whether the wicked or the righteous will enjoy the blessings of the promised land. He concludes that the prosperity of the wicked will be short-lived, while God's people will have a lasting blessing from the Lord. Structurally, this is an alphabetic acrostic in which two verses are devoted to each letter of the Hebrew alphabet, though there are some irregularities to the pattern. See "Introduction: Structure: *Poetic Style and Devices*."
37:1 See *WLC* 142.
37:2 grass. The metaphor is apt. In Israel the grass comes up and appears healthy in the winter, but in the summertime the relentless sun withers it.
37:4 See *WLC* 104.
37:7 wait patiently for him. The prosperity of the wicked is only temporary. Eventually God will bring judgment against them and blessings to the righteous. See *WLC* 142.
37:8–11 See *WLC* 135.
37:9 cut off. A term often meaning that a person will be excommunicated from his people (exiled) or even assigned the death penalty (that is, "cut off from the living"). See Genesis 17:1 and Leviticus 17:14.
37:11 the meek will inherit the land. Those who hope in the Lord, who trustingly look to him to bestow life and its associated blessings, will inherit the land, as opposed to those who live apart from God and by evil means try to take possession of the land and its wealth. The land was viewed as the basis for life, so that the height of physical blessing for an Israelite was a share in the promised land. See Matthew 5:5. See *WCF* 19.6.

13 but the Lord laughs at the wicked,
for he knows their day is coming.[i]

14 The wicked draw the sword
and bend the bow[j]
to bring down the poor and needy,[k]
to slay those whose ways are upright.
15 But their swords will pierce their own hearts,[l]
and their bows will be broken.

16 Better the little that the righteous have
than the wealth[m] of many wicked;
17 for the power of the wicked will be broken,[n]
but the LORD upholds the righteous.

18 The days of the blameless are known to the LORD,[o]
and their inheritance will endure forever.
19 In times of disaster they will not wither;
in days of famine they will enjoy plenty.

20 But the wicked will perish:
The LORD's enemies will be like the beauty of the fields,
they will vanish—vanish like smoke.[p]

21 The wicked borrow and do not repay,
but the righteous give generously;[q]
22 those the LORD blesses will inherit the land,
but those he curses[r] will be cut off.

23 If the LORD delights[s] in a man's way,
he makes his steps firm;[t]
24 though he stumble, he will not fall,[u]
for the LORD upholds[v] him with his hand.

25 I was young and now I am old,
yet I have never seen the righteous forsaken[w]
or their children begging bread.
26 They are always generous and lend freely;
their children will be blessed.[x]

27 Turn from evil and do good;[y]
then you will dwell in the land forever.
28 For the LORD loves the just
and will not forsake his faithful ones.

They will be protected forever,
but the offspring of the wicked will be cut off;[z]
29 the righteous will inherit the land[a]
and dwell in it forever.

30 The mouth of the righteous man utters wisdom,
and his tongue speaks what is just.
31 The law of his God is in his heart;[b]
his feet do not slip.[c]

37:13 [i]1Sa 26:10; Ps 2:4
37:14 [j]Ps 11:2 [k]Ps 35:10
37:15 [l]Ps 9:16
37:16 [m]Pr 15:16
37:17 [n]Job 38:15; Ps 10:15
37:18 [o]Ps 1:6
37:20 [p]Ps 102:3
37:21 [q]Ps 112:5
37:22 [r]Job 5:3; Pr 3:33
37:23 [s]Ps 147:11 [t]1Sa 2:9
37:24 [u]Pr 24:16 [v]Ps 145:14; 147:6
37:25 [w]Heb 13:5
37:26 [x]Ps 147:13
37:27 [y]Ps 34:14
37:28 [z]Ps 21:10; Isa 14:20
37:29 [a]ver 9; Pr 2:21
37:31 [b]Dt 6:6; Ps 40:8; Isa 51:7 [c]ver 23

37:13 the Lord laughs at the wicked. See Psalm 2:4. Vivid language that describes the folly of rebelling against the Almighty. David predicted that their schemes and manipulations would fail in the end and that God's will would be accomplished.
37:15 their swords will pierce their own hearts. The punishments for sin are often sin's natural consequences. See 7:14–16, 34:21 and 35:8.
37:16 See *HC* 125.
37:18 blameless. The righteous, the wise—not the sinless, but those possessing moral integrity (see 1Ki 9:4).
37:20 like the beauty of the fields. Such beauty is transitory. See verse 2. The wicked will wither like grass under the scorching summer sun.
37:21 The wicked borrow and do not repay. They break the eighth commandment by neglecting to repay their debts. **the righteous give generously.** In contrast to the wicked who grasp their money, the righteous not only pay their debts but also give generously. Those willing to hold onto their blessings loosely and freely donate their resources will prosper in the end. See *WLC* 142.
37:24 stumble, he will not fall. A common metaphor in wisdom writings: Life is a path. The wise may sin or encounter difficulties, but God will unfailingly protect them and restrain them from abandoning their faith.
37:25–26 never seen the righteous forsaken. David, based on long experience, could offer his personal observation that over the long run the righteous are blessed by the Lord. Psalm 73 and the book of Job provide a complementary perspective and reminder that this verse may not be turned into a kind of "health and wealth" theology.
37:30–31 law of his God is in his heart. The source of righteousness is love for God's law.

32 The wicked lie in wait[d] for the righteous,
seeking their very lives;
33 but the LORD will not leave them in their power
or let them be condemned when brought to trial.[e]

34 Wait for the LORD[f]
and keep his way.
He will exalt you to inherit the land;
when the wicked are cut off, you will see[g] it.

35 I have seen a wicked and ruthless man
flourishing[h] like a green tree in its native soil,
36 but he soon passed away and was no more;
though I looked for him, he could not be found.[i]

37 Consider the blameless, observe the upright;
there is a future[a] for the man of peace.[j]
38 But all sinners will be destroyed;
the future[b] of the wicked will be cut off.[k]

39 The salvation[l] of the righteous comes from the LORD;
he is their stronghold in time of trouble.[m]
40 The LORD helps[n] them and delivers[o] them;
he delivers them from the wicked and saves them,
because they take refuge in him.

Psalm 38

A psalm of David. A petition.

1 O LORD, do not rebuke me in your anger
or discipline me in your wrath.[p]
2 For your arrows[q] have pierced me,
and your hand has come down upon me.
3 Because of your wrath there is no health in my body;
my bones[r] have no soundness because of my sin.
4 My guilt has overwhelmed me
like a burden too heavy to bear.[s]

5 My wounds fester and are loathsome
because of my sinful folly.[t]
6 I am bowed down and brought very low;
all day long I go about mourning.[u]
7 My back is filled with searing pain;[v]
there is no health in my body.
8 I am feeble and utterly crushed;
I groan[w] in anguish of heart.

9 All my longings lie open before you, O Lord;
my sighing[x] is not hidden from you.

37:32 [d]Ps 10:8
37:33 [e]Ps 109:31; 2Pe 2:9
37:34 [f]Ps 27:14 [g]Ps 52:6
37:35 [h]Job 5:3
37:36 [i]Job 20:5
37:37 [j]Isa 57:1-2
37:38 [k]Ps 1:4
37:39 [l]Ps 3:8 [m]Ps 9:9
37:40 [n]1Ch 5:20 [o]Isa 31:5
38:1 [p]Ps 6:1
38:2 [q]Job 6:4; Ps 32:4
38:3 [r]Ps 6:2; Isa 1:6
38:4 [s]Ezr 9:6
38:5 [t]Ps 69:5
38:6 [u]Job 30:28; Ps 35:14; 42:9
38:7 [v]Ps 102:3
38:8 [w]Ps 22:1
38:9 [x]Job 3:24; Ps 6:6; 10:17

[a] *37* Or *there will be posterity* [b] *38* Or *posterity*

37:31 heart. The core of a person's being, including the mind. When God's law is in the heart, the tongue speaks wisely.
37:35 like a green tree. Compare 1:3. David admitted that he had seen the wicked prosper as only the righteous justly should. Nevertheless, he knew that their prosperity was ephemeral.
37:37–38 future . . . future. The contrasting prospects of the upright and the sinner: One has a future, while the other does not. It is unclear whether the individual's later life or his children are meant here.
Psalm 38 *Introduction.* This lament has traditionally been grouped with the penitential psalms (see introduction to Ps 6). David was suffering from an illness, the cause for which he attributed to sin and guilt. He called upon the Lord for help in the midst of his intense pain.
38:2 your arrows. A vivid metaphor for God's blows (see Job 6:4; 34:6; La 3:12; Eze 5:16). Always before God had fought on David's behalf against the enemy in judgment (18:14). Here, however, David used the metaphor of war to describe the discipline God leveled against him. Although the outward elements of discipline may be indistinguishable from judgment, God's motives and the ultimate outcome are very different. God disciplines in love (Pr 3:11–12), with the result that the sinner is sanctified.
38:3 Because of your wrath . . . because of my sin. These two phrases are parallel to one another and show a dual (divine and human) reason for David's illness. **no health.** Some, but not all, illness falls upon believers as part of God's discipline in response to their sin (see "Introduction to Job: Purpose and Distinctives"; John 9:1–12).
38:5 My wounds fester. The mention of wounds seems to imply some kind of physical abuse by others, perhaps as a result of battle. It is impossible to relate all the symptoms to a particular disease or physical malady, and it has been suggested that they are actually a catalogue of physical distress experienced by the psalmist over a period of time.

10 My heart pounds, my strength fails[y] me;
even the light has gone from my eyes.[z]
11 My friends and companions avoid me because of my wounds;[a]
my neighbors stay far away.
12 Those who seek my life set their traps,[b]
those who would harm me talk of my ruin;[c]
all day long they plot deception.[d]

13 I am like a deaf man, who cannot hear,
like a mute, who cannot open his mouth;
14 I have become like a man who does not hear,
whose mouth can offer no reply.
15 I wait[e] for you, O LORD;
you will answer,[f] O Lord my God.
16 For I said, "Do not let them gloat[g]
or exalt themselves over me when my foot slips."[h]

17 For I am about to fall,
and my pain is ever with me.
18 I confess my iniquity;[i]
I am troubled by my sin.
19 Many are those who are my vigorous enemies;[j]
those who hate me without reason[k] are numerous.
20 Those who repay my good with evil[l]
slander me when I pursue what is good.

21 O LORD, do not forsake me;
be not far[m] from me, O my God.
22 Come quickly to help me,[n]
O Lord my Savior.[o]

38:10 [y]Ps 31:10 [z]Ps 6:7
38:11 [a]Ps 31:11
38:12 [b]Ps 140:5 [c]Ps 35:4; 54:3 [d]Ps 35:20
38:15 [e]Ps 39:7 [f]Ps 17:6
38:16 [g]Ps 35:26 [h]Ps 13:4
38:18 [i]Ps 32:5
38:19 [j]Ps 18:17 [k]Ps 35:19
38:20 [l]Ps 35:12; 1Jn 3:12
38:21 [m]Ps 35:22
38:22 [n]Ps 40:13 [o]Ps 27:1

Psalm 39

For the director of music. For Jeduthun. A psalm of David.

1 I said, "I will watch my ways[p]
and keep my tongue from sin;[q]
I will put a muzzle on my mouth
as long as the wicked are in my presence."
2 But when I was silent[r] and still,
not even saying anything good,
my anguish increased.
3 My heart grew hot within me,
and as I meditated, the fire burned;
then I spoke with my tongue:

4 "Show me, O LORD, my life's end
and the number of my days;[s]
let me know how fleeting is my life.[t]
5 You have made my days[u] a mere handbreadth;

39:1 [p]1Ki 2:4 [q]Job 2:10; Jas 3:2
39:2 [r]Ps 38:13
39:4 [s]Ps 90:12 [t]Ps 103:14
39:5 [u]Ps 89:45

38:11 My friends . . . avoid me. Friends were at this juncture of no help to David. They may have been offended by his sins or repulsed by the intensity of his suffering or wounds. Here and elsewhere in the psalm we are reminded of the book of Job.
38:13 deaf man . . . mute. It is unclear whether David refused to reply to his enemies, waiting instead for the Lord to act on his behalf (vv. 15–16), or if this description pertained because in his infirmity his senses were so dulled and his body so weakened.
38:15 I wait for you. The most positive note of confidence in the psalm. David was waiting for God's help and was confident that he would receive it.
38:16 Do not let them gloat. David appealed to God in part because of the shame that would accompany the enemies' rejoicing at his downfall. This sentiment is frequently expressed in the psalms and linked with God's shame as the enemy gloats over the fall of one of his chosen (42:10; 79:10; 115:2).
Psalm 39 *Introduction.* Psalm 39 is a lament by David regarding an illness (vv. 10–11). His concern with the brevity of life (vv. 4–6,13) may suggest that he wrote it in his later life. He vowed to avoid sin and desired to be close with God. The psalm is more personal and autobiographical than most laments and shows a connection to the canonical wisdom books: Some lines are reminiscent of the book of Ecclesiastes, and the emotion expressed is not unlike Job's (cf. v. 13 with Job 7:17–10; 10:20–21; 14:6). See *WLC* 113.
39:1 keep my tongue from sin. David resolved not to speak in a sinful manner, likely referring to the avoidance of rebellious words prompted by his suffering, in the presence of wicked people. He was determined to accept the discipline God was meting out to him (v. 9). **muzzle.** A metaphor for a determination not to speak.
39:2 not even saying anything good. Apparently fearing that his speech might get away from him if he spoke, David refrained even from saying good things. **my anguish.** Silence didn't alleviate his suffering—repressing his speech actually increased it. The inner tension ultimately erupted into speech (v. 3).
39:4 fleeting. The faithful often question God's wisdom and justice as they think about their sometimes short and/or difficult lives.
39:5 handbreadth. One of the smallest measures in the Hebrew

39:5 [v]Ps 62:9
39:6 [w]1Pe 1:24 [x]Ps 127:2 [y]Lk 12:20
39:7 [z]Ps 38:15
39:8 [a]Ps 51:9 [b]Ps 44:13
39:9 [c]Job 2:10
39:10 [d]Job 9:34; Ps 32:4
39:11 [e]2Pe 2:16 [f]Job 13:28
39:12 [g]1Pe 2:11 [h]Heb 11:13
39:13 [i]Job 10:21; 14:10
40:1 [j]Ps 27:14 [k]Ps 34:15
40:2 [l]Ps 69:14 [m]Ps 27:5
40:3 [n]Ps 33:3
40:4 [o]Ps 34:8 [p]Ps 84:12
40:5 [q]Ps 136:4

the span of my years is as nothing before you.
Each man's life is but a breath.[v] *Selah*
6 Man is a mere phantom[w] as he goes to and fro:
He bustles about, but only in vain;[x]
he heaps up wealth, not knowing who will get it.[y]

7 "But now, Lord, what do I look for?
My hope is in you.[z]
8 Save me[a] from all my transgressions;[b]
do not make me the scorn of fools.
9 I was silent; I would not open my mouth,[c]
for you are the one who has done this.
10 Remove your scourge from me;
I am overcome by the blow of your hand.[d]
11 You rebuke[e] and discipline men for their sin;
you consume their wealth like a moth[f]—
each man is but a breath. *Selah*

12 "Hear my prayer, O LORD,
listen to my cry for help;
be not deaf to my weeping.
For I dwell with you as an alien,[g]
a stranger,[h] as all my fathers were.
13 Look away from me, that I may rejoice again
before I depart and am no more."[i]

Psalm 40

For the director of music. Of David. A psalm.

1 I waited patiently[j] for the LORD;
he turned to me and heard my cry.[k]
2 He lifted me out of the slimy pit,
out of the mud and mire;[l]
he set my feet on a rock[m]
and gave me a firm place to stand.
3 He put a new song[n] in my mouth,
a hymn of praise to our God.
Many will see and fear
and put their trust in the LORD.

4 Blessed is the man[o]
who makes the LORD his trust,[p]
who does not look to the proud,
to those who turn aside to false gods.[a]
5 Many, O LORD my God,
are the wonders[q] you have done.
The things you planned for us

[a] 4 Or *to falsehood*

system. **breath.** The same word occurs frequently in the book of Ecclesiastes, translated there as "meaningless."
39:6 in vain. From the same word translated as "breath" in the previous verse. This word, along with the comment about wealth, expresses a sentiment similar to that found in the book of Ecclesiastes (see Ecc 5:8–20).
39:10 your scourge . . . blow of your hand. Could be a reference to sickness but may refer to other setbacks in life and/or depression.
39:12 an alien, a stranger. David's lack of means and consequent reliance on God's mercy was extreme. God's delay in acting on David's behalf was so excruciating that David broke into tears.
39:13 Look away from me. Compare Job 7:17–10, 10:20–21 and 14:6.
Psalm 40 *Introduction.* This psalm does not fit neatly into any single genre category. It opens with thanksgiving but in verse 11 shifts to lament, asking the Lord to save from distress. Some suggest that there are two psalms mis-united in Psalm 40, but the composition is best read as thanksgiving for past blessings, despite present distress. Verses 9–10 provide an appropriate transition between the two sections. The psalmist's petitions had been graciously answered in the past, and he looked to God again in a new crisis. Verses 13–17 of Psalm 40 are virtually the same as Psalm 70; see notes there.
40:2 slimy pit . . . rock. The metaphor contrasts a muddy pit with the sure footing provided by a rock. It is also significant that Sheol, or the grave, is quite often pictured as a pit (30:3). Perhaps the psalmist was gravely ill or faced the threat of death in battle.
40:3 new song. See note on 33:3 and compare 98:1 and its note. In most contexts "new song" refers to a victory song and may indicate that the threat was of a military nature.
40:4 Blessed. See note on 1:1. **the proud.** A rare word, used of Egypt in 87:4 and there simply translated Rahab. Here it probably refers to the false idols of the surrounding nations.
40:5 the wonders you have done. God's past acts were frequently recounted in the psalms and provided the basis for present trust. Because he has saved in the past, he can be counted on to rescue in the present and future.

no one can recount[r] to you;
were I to speak and tell of them,
they would be too many to declare.

6 Sacrifice and offering you did not desire,[s]
but my ears you have pierced[a,b];
burnt offerings[t] and sin offerings
you did not require.
7 Then I said, "Here I am, I have come—
it is written about me in the scroll.[c]
8 I desire to do your will,[u] O my God;
your law is within my heart."[v]

9 I proclaim righteousness in the great assembly;[w]
I do not seal my lips,
as you know,[x] O LORD.
10 I do not hide your righteousness in my heart;
I speak of your faithfulness[y] and salvation.
I do not conceal your love and your truth
from the great assembly.[z]

11 Do not withhold your mercy from me, O LORD;
may your love[a] and your truth[b] always protect me.
12 For troubles[c] without number surround me;
my sins have overtaken me, and I cannot see.[d]
They are more than the hairs of my head,[e]
and my heart fails[f] within me.

13 Be pleased, O LORD, to save me;
O LORD, come quickly to help me.[g]
14 May all who seek to take my life
be put to shame and confusion;
may all who desire my ruin[h]
be turned back in disgrace.
15 May those who say to me, "Aha! Aha!"
be appalled at their own shame.
16 But may all who seek you
rejoice and be glad in you;
may those who love your salvation always say,
"The LORD be exalted!"[i]

17 Yet I am poor and needy;
may the Lord think of me.
You are my help and my deliverer;
O my God, do not delay.[j]

Psalm 41

For the director of music. A psalm of David.

1 Blessed is he who has regard for the weak;[k]
the LORD delivers him in times of trouble.

40:5 [r]Ps 139:18; Isa 55:8
40:6 [s]1Sa 15:22; Am 5:22 [t]Isa 1:11
40:8 [u]Jn 4:34 [v]Ps 37:31
40:9 [w]Ps 22:25 [x]Jos 22:22; Ps 119:13
40:10 [y]Ps 89:1 [z]Ac 20:20
40:11 [a]Pr 20:28 [b]Ps 43:3
40:12 [c]Ps 116:3 [d]Ps 38:4 [e]Ps 69:4 [f]Ps 73:26
40:13 [g]Ps 70:1
40:14 [h]Ps 35:4
40:16 [i]Ps 35:27
40:17 [j]Ps 70:5
41:1 [k]Ps 82:3-4; Pr 14:21

[a] *6* Hebrew; Septuagint *but a body you have prepared for me* (see also Symmachus and Theodotion)
[b] *6* Or *opened* [c] *7* Or *come / with the scroll written for me*

40:6 you did not desire. This phrase is an obvious example of hyperbole. God certainly desired his people to keep his law, which required sacrifices. But more important to God than the sacrifices was the devoted heart of the worshiper. **my ears you have pierced.** Or "opened" (see NIV text note), though the Hebrew is actually closer to "dug," perhaps meaning "you have created me with two ears." God has revealed to the psalmist that he desires not sacrifices but listening ears and submissive obedience (see 1Sa 15:22). The clause is cited in Hebrews 10:5–7, from the Septuagint (early Greek translation of the OT), translated "a body you have prepared for me." The meaning there is quite similar to that suggested here.
40:7–8 See *WCF* 8.4.
40:7 it is written about me in the scroll. See NIV text note. The law of the king (Dt 17:14–20) required David to write a copy of the law on a scroll for himself. By either reading, David may be presenting himself to God as his servant, with the scroll of the law in hand, indicating willing obedience and expectation according to its words.
40:8 I desire to do your will. This verse gets to the heart of the matter. The psalmist offered what God requires—heartfelt obedience, not mere ritual.
40:9–10 See *HC* 103.
40:9 I proclaim. The frequent pledge of praise by one who is assured of deliverance. (See Ps 22:22). **great assembly.** Either the assembled worshipers or the whole nation.
40:11 love. Specifically, God's covenant loving-kindness.
40:12 troubles . . . sins. The psalmist identified the source of his troubles as both external (enemies seeking to thwart him) and internal (his own sin).

41:2 [l]Ps 37:22 [m]Ps 27:12
41:4 [n]Ps 6:2 [o]Ps 51:4
41:5 [p]Ps 38:12
41:6 [q]Ps 12:2 [r]Pr 26:24
41:7 [s]Ps 56:5; 71:10-11
41:9 [t]2Sa 15:12; Ps 55:12 [u]Job 19:19; Ps 55:20; Mt 26:23; Jn 13:18*
41:10 [v]Ps 3:3
41:11 [w]Ps 147:11 [x]Ps 25:2
41:12 [y]Ps 37:17 [z]Job 36:7
41:13 [a]Ps 72:18 [b]Ps 89:52; 106:48

2 The LORD will protect him and preserve his life;
he will bless him in the land[l]
and not surrender him to the desire of his foes.[m]
3 The LORD will sustain him on his sickbed
and restore him from his bed of illness.

4 I said, "O LORD, have mercy[n] on me;
heal me, for I have sinned[o] against you."
5 My enemies say of me in malice,
"When will he die and his name perish?[p]"
6 Whenever one comes to see me,
he speaks falsely,[q] while his heart gathers slander;[r]
then he goes out and spreads it abroad.

7 All my enemies whisper together[s] against me;
they imagine the worst for me, saying,
8 "A vile disease has beset him;
he will never get up from the place where he lies."
9 Even my close friend,[t] whom I trusted,
he who shared my bread,
has lifted up his heel against me.[u]

10 But you, O LORD, have mercy on me;
raise me up,[v] that I may repay them.
11 I know that you are pleased with me,[w]
for my enemy does not triumph over me.[x]
12 In my integrity you uphold me[y]
and set me in your presence forever.[z]

13 Praise be to the LORD, the God of Israel,[a]
from everlasting to everlasting.
Amen and Amen.[b]

BOOK II

Psalms 42–72

Psalm 42[a]

For the director of music. A *maskil*[b] of the Sons of Korah.

42:1 [c]Ps 119:131

1 As the deer pants for streams of water,
so my soul pants[c] for you, O God.

[a] In many Hebrew manuscripts Psalms 42 and 43 constitute one psalm. [b] Title: Probably a literary or musical term

Psalm 41 *Introduction.* Psalm 41 closes the first book of the Psalter (see "Introduction: Outline"), concluding it with a doxology (v. 13). The psalm begins with a beatitude—a blessing—for the person who shows regard for the weak. This introduction provides the aura of a wisdom psalm. However, the mood shifts in verse 4 with David's appeal to the Lord for help in distress. His lament was motivated by a life-threatening illness.
41:1 Blessed. See note on 1:1. **has regard for the weak.** That is, understands or empathizes. The paradigm for leadership in Israel was not despotism but shepherd-kingship (see note on 23:1; see also 1Ch 11:2). **the LORD delivers him.** In his own weakness (vv. 4,10), David was in need of healing and deliverance. Given this setting, verses 1–3 may reflect the words of another, perhaps a priest, to David in his time of suffering, or they may simply be a hopeful affirmation by David in anticipation of his own healing.
41:2 in the land. In Israel, the promised land. Not only would the Lord preserve the life of his shepherd-king; he would also prosper him in the land.
41:3 will sustain him on his sickbed. See note on verse 1.
41:4 I have sinned. The psalmist perceived his illness as divine chastisement. He confessed his sin in order to motivate God to heal him.
41:5 enemies. David had enemies both within and outside the kingdom. They wanted him to die so that they might destroy his rule.
41:6 he speaks falsely. Some of David's enemies visited him while he was ill, speaking words of feigned comfort but afterward spreading malicious lies about the king.
41:9 lifted up his heel. The idiom is difficult to interpret, but help comes from Genesis 25:26 and Jeremiah 9:4 (see NIV text notes on both verses), where the noun *heel* is associated with the verb *to deceive.* David's close friend had betrayed him. Jesus quoted this verse in reference to Judas Iscariot (Jn 13:18).
41:11–12 my enemy does not triumph over me . . . you uphold me. That he still lived and that his enemy remained frustrated were signs of hope to David, and on this note he concluded his prayer.
41:13 Praise be. Doxology ends Book I of the Psalter (See Introduction: Structure).
Psalm 42 *Introduction.* Psalms 42 and 43 appear originally to have been a single psalm. Not only do a number of early Hebrew manuscripts place them together, but a common refrain unites them (42:5,11; 43:5). The absence of a title before Psalm 43 is also significant in this portion of the Psalter, where almost every psalm is titled. The two psalms unite to form a single lament that may be divided into three parts (vv. 1–5,6–11; Ps 43), each concluding with a common refrain. The psalmist lamented God's absence. It appears that he was forced to be away from Jerusalem, the place God had chosen for his dwelling. The psalmist's distance from the Lord, compounded with the presence of his enemies, caused him to cry out to God for help.
42:1–2 See *WLC* 172.

2 My soul thirsts[d] for God, for the living God.[e]
When can I go[f] and meet with God?
3 My tears[g] have been my food
day and night,
while men say to me all day long,
"Where is your God?"[h]
4 These things I remember
as I pour out my soul:
how I used to go with the multitude,
leading the procession to the house of God,[i]
with shouts of joy and thanksgiving[j]
among the festive throng.

5 Why are you downcast,[k] O my soul?
Why so disturbed within me?
Put your hope in God,[l]
for I will yet praise him,
my Savior[m] and 6 my God.

My[a] soul is downcast within me;
therefore I will remember you
from the land of the Jordan,
the heights of Hermon—from Mount Mizar.
7 Deep calls to deep
in the roar of your waterfalls;
all your waves and breakers
have swept over me.[n]

8 By day the LORD directs his love,[o]
at night[p] his song[q] is with me—
a prayer to the God of my life.

9 I say to God my Rock,
"Why have you forgotten me?
Why must I go about mourning,[r]
oppressed by the enemy?"
10 My bones suffer mortal agony
as my foes taunt me,
saying to me all day long,
"Where is your God?"

11 Why are you downcast, O my soul?
Why so disturbed within me?
Put your hope in God,
for I will yet praise him,
my Savior and my God.[s]

42:2 [d]Ps 63:1 [e]Jer 10:10 [f]Ps 43:4
42:3 [g]Ps 80:5 [h]Ps 79:10
42:4 [i]Isa 30:29 [j]Ps 100:4
42:5 [k]Ps 38:6; 77:3 [l]La 3:24 [m]Ps 44:3
42:7 [n]Ps 88:7; Jnh 2:3
42:8 [o]Ps 57:3 [p]Job 35:10 [q]Ps 63:6; 149:5
42:9 [r]Ps 38:6
42:11 [s]Ps 43:5

[a] 5,6 A few Hebrew manuscripts, Septuagint and Syriac; most Hebrew manuscripts *praise him for his saving help. / 6O my God, my*

42:1 As the deer pants for streams of water. A powerful image of the psalmist's deep desire for God's presence. He was like a thirsty deer that could find no water. He required the Lord's presence for survival in his distress.
42:2 meet with God. Because the psalmist was at a distance from Jerusalem, where the ark of God resided, he desired to return there, to God's life-giving presence. Due to Jesus' redemptive work on the cross, the Christian has access to the Lord in prayer at all times and in all places. Though believing people in the Old Testament also possessed and used that privilege, God's presence was particularly experienced at the designated worship site, later the temple, in Jerusalem (see 2Sa 7:18; 2Ki 19:14–15).
42:3 My tears have been my food. If the psalmist spoke of literal food, his distress may have suppressed his appetite, or he may have had no food. He also may have been fasting in order to move God to answer his prayer. If he spoke figuratively (cf. "pants," v. 1, and "thirsts," v. 2), he may have meant that he hungered and thirsted after God but had to resign himself to tears in God's absence. His condition was exacerbated by the taunts of his enemies.
42:4 These things I remember. The psalmist recalled past enjoyment of God's presence in the worship processions in Jerusalem. (The songs of ascent, Pss 120–134, were sung at these celebrations.)
42:5 Why are you downcast, O my soul? This refrain occurs twice more (v. 11; 43:5). In dialogue with himself, the psalmist took a fresh hold on God. See *WLC* 172,175.
42:6 I will remember you. The psalmist sought through memory to reestablish his closeness with God (cf. Ps 77). **Hermon . . . Mount Mizar.** Hermon is the mountain range at the far north of Israel's boundaries. It is located near the source of the Jordan River. Mizar is of uncertain location.
42:7 have swept over me. The overwhelming waters of chaos constitute a well-known image of despair and trouble in the Bible. Compare Psalms 18:4, 32:6, 46:2–3, 69:1–2 and 114:3.
42:8 his love. Specifically, God's covenant loving-kindness. See *WLC* 175.
42:11 Why are you downcast . . . ? See note on 42:5 and compare 43:5. See *WLC* 172.

Psalm 43[a]

43:1 [t] 1Sa 24:15; Ps 26:1; 35:1 [u] Ps 5:6

1 Vindicate me, O God,
and plead my cause[t] against an ungodly nation;
rescue me from deceitful and wicked men.[u]

43:2 [v] Ps 44:9 [w] Ps 42:9

2 You are God my stronghold.
Why have you rejected[v] me?
Why must I go about mourning,
oppressed by the enemy?[w]

43:3 [x] Ps 36:9 [y] Ps 42:4 [z] Ps 84:1

3 Send forth your light[x] and your truth,
let them guide me;
let them bring me to your holy mountain,[y]
to the place where you dwell.[z]

43:4 [a] Ps 26:6 [b] Ps 33:2

4 Then will I go to the altar[a] of God,
to God, my joy and my delight.
I will praise you with the harp,[b]
O God, my God.

43:5 [c] Ps 42:6

5 Why are you downcast, O my soul?
Why so disturbed within me?
Put your hope in God,
for I will yet praise him,
my Savior and my God.[c]

Psalm 44

For the director of music. Of the Sons of Korah. A *maskil*.[b]

44:1 [d] Ex 12:26; Ps 78:3

1 We have heard with our ears, O God;
our fathers have told us[d]
what you did in their days,
in days long ago.

44:2 [e] Ps 78:55 [f] Ex 15:17 [g] Ps 80:9

2 With your hand you drove out[e] the nations
and planted[f] our fathers;
you crushed the peoples
and made our fathers flourish.[g]

44:3 [h] Dt 8:17; Jos 24:12 [i] Ps 77:15 [j] Dt 4:37; 7:7-8

3 It was not by their sword[h] that they won the land,
nor did their arm bring them victory;
it was your right hand, your arm,[i]
and the light of your face, for you loved[j] them.

44:4 [k] Ps 74:12

4 You are my King[k] and my God,
who decrees[c] victories for Jacob.

44:5 [l] Ps 108:13

5 Through you we push back our enemies;
through your name we trample[l] our foes.

44:6 [m] Ps 33:16

6 I do not trust in my bow,[m]
my sword does not bring me victory;

44:7 [n] Ps 136:24

7 but you give us victory[n] over our enemies,

a In many Hebrew manuscripts Psalms 42 and 43 constitute one psalm. b Title: Probably a literary or musical term c 4 Septuagint, Aquila and Syriac; Hebrew *King, O God; / command*

Psalm 43 *Introduction.* See the introduction to Psalm 42.
43:1 Vindicate me . . . plead my cause. Technical, legal terms that give the psalm a judicial setting. **ungodly.** A negation of a word formed from the same root as "covenant loving-kindness." Thus, the phrase refers to nations that do not enjoy a covenant relationship with God.
43:3–5 See *WLC* 175.
43:3 your holy mountain. Mount Zion, in Jerusalem, where the temple was located. God's stable mountain (cf. 42:6) contrasted with the turbulent waters of chaos (42:7).
43:5 Why are you downcast . . . ? See note on 42:5 and compare 42:11.
Psalm 44 *Introduction.* The psalmist pleaded with the Lord on behalf of the nation following a military defeat. The alternation between the first-person singular and plural suggests that the psalmist spoke from the perspective of Israel's king. After recalling God's past deliverance (vv. 1–8) and asserting the nation's covenant fidelity (vv. 17–22), the psalmist pleaded with the Lord to reverse Israel's miserable fortunes (vv. 23–26).
44:1 what you did in their days. Memory plays a key role in the psalms (see Ps 77). In present distress, remembering God's gracious acts of the past bolsters faith. In Psalm 44, however, God's past deliverances raise a question: Why doesn't God rescue us in the present as he did our fathers in the past?
44:2 planted our fathers. In the conquest and settlement of the land, as recorded in the book of Joshua.
44:3 it was your right hand. The accounts of the conquest make clear that the Israelites did not take possession of the land by their own might or strategy but through God's power. He revealed himself as a warrior in their midst (see Jos 6). Compare also Deuteronomy 7.
44:4 Jacob. Another name for the nation of Israel, just as it was for Israel the patriarch (Ge 32:28).
44:6 my sword does not bring me victory. At the heart of holy war in the Old Testament was the fact that God won victories for his people. These victories were not based on the strength of their army or military arsenal.

you put our adversaries to shame.[o]
8 In God we make our boast[p] all day long,
and we will praise your name forever.[q] *Selah*

9 But now you have rejected[r] and humbled us;
you no longer go out with our armies.[s]
10 You made us retreat[t] before the enemy,
and our adversaries have plundered us.
11 You gave us up to be devoured like sheep[u]
and have scattered us among the nations.[v]
12 You sold your people for a pittance,[w]
gaining nothing from their sale.

13 You have made us a reproach to our neighbors,[x]
the scorn[y] and derision of those around us.
14 You have made us a byword among the nations;
the peoples shake their heads[z] at us.
15 My disgrace is before me all day long,
and my face is covered with shame
16 at the taunts of those who reproach and revile[a] me,
because of the enemy, who is bent on revenge.

17 All this happened to us,
though we had not forgotten[b] you
or been false to your covenant.
18 Our hearts had not turned[c] back;
our feet had not strayed from your path.
19 But you crushed[d] us and made us a haunt for jackals
and covered us over with deep darkness.[e]

20 If we had forgotten[f] the name of our God
or spread out our hands to a foreign god,[g]
21 would not God have discovered it,
since he knows the secrets of the heart?[h]
22 Yet for your sake we face death all day long;
we are considered as sheep to be slaughtered.[i]

23 Awake,[j] O Lord! Why do you sleep?[k]
Rouse yourself! Do not reject us forever.[l]
24 Why do you hide your face[m]
and forget our misery and oppression?[n]

25 We are brought down to the dust;[o]
our bodies cling to the ground.
26 Rise up[p] and help us;
redeem[q] us because of your unfailing love.

Psalm 45

For the director of music. To ˪the tune of˩ "Lilies." Of the Sons of Korah. A *maskil*.[a] A wedding song.

1 My heart is stirred by a noble theme
as I recite my verses for the king;
my tongue is the pen of a skillful writer.

44:7 [o]Ps 53:5
44:8 [p]Ps 34:2 [q]Ps 30:12
44:9 [r]Ps 74:1 [s]Ps 60:1, 10
44:10 [t]Lev 26:17; Jos 7:8; Ps 89:41
44:11 [u]Ro 8:36 [v]Dt 4:27; 28:64; Ps 106:27
44:12 [w]Isa 52:3; Jer 15:13; 52:3; Jer 15:13
44:13 [x]Ps 79:4; 80:6 [y]Dt 28:37
44:14 [z]Ps 109:25; Jer 24:9
44:16 [a]Ps 74:10
44:17 [b]Ps 78:7, 57; Da 9:13
44:18 [c]Job 23:11
44:19 [d]Ps 51:8 [e]Job 3:5
44:20 [f]Ps 78:11 [g]Dt 6:14; Ps 81:9
44:21 [h]Ps 139:1-2; Jer 17:10
44:22 [i]Isa 53:7; Ro 8:36*
44:23 [j]Ps 7:6 [k]Ps 78:65 [l]Ps 77:7
44:24 [m]Job 13:24 [n]Ps 42:9
44:25 [o]Ps 119:25
44:26 [p]Ps 35:2 [q]Ps 25:22

[a] Title: Probably a literary or musical term

44:9 you have rejected and humbled us. The psalmist observed a present quite different from the past: God had been with the Israelite army at Jericho, but he no longer led them into battle or empowered them for victory. As a result, they were easily defeated.
44:12 You sold your people for a pittance. Bold words to God, an example of the brutal honesty of the psalmist in prayer.
44:17 though we had not forgotten you. The psalmist was confused. God had promised to deliver his people from foreign oppression if they were obedient to the covenant. The promise was that the nations would fear Israel (Dt 28:10), but here these enemies humiliated the Israelites.
44:19 deep darkness. Reserved for God's enemies (Na 1:8).
44:20–21 See *WLC* 106; *WSC* 48; *BC* 26.
44:22 for your sake. A reference to the fact that the Israelites had remained faithful to God (vv. 20–21). Despite their fidelity, the world seemed utterly turned around for the psalmist. He and his people still suffered and continued to be defeated.
44:23 Awake, O Lord! The psalmist called on the Lord to fight on behalf of Israel. Sleep as a metaphor for God's inaction implies that he is unaware of Israel's plight (cf. 7:6; 35:23; 1Ki 18:27). This image demonstrated the psalmist's frustration—the usual call to God before a battle was to "arise" (see note on 3:7).

45:2 [r]Lk 4:22
45:3 [s]Heb 4:12; Rev 1:16 [t]Isa 9:6
45:4 [u]Rev 6:2
45:6 [v]Ps 93:2; 98:9
45:7 [w]Ps 33:5 [x]Isa 61:1 [y]Ps 21:6; Heb 1:8-9*
45:8 [z]SS 1:3
45:9 [a]SS 6:8 [b]1Ki 2:19
45:10 [c]Dt 21:13
45:11 [d]Ps 95:6 [e]Isa 54:5
45:12 [f]Ps 22:29; Isa 49:23
45:13 [g]Isa 61:10
45:14 [h]SS 1:4
45:17 [i]Mal 1:11 [j]Ps 138:4

2 You are the most excellent of men
and your lips have been anointed with grace,[r]
since God has blessed you forever.
3 Gird your sword[s] upon your side, O mighty one;[t]
clothe yourself with splendor and majesty.
4 In your majesty ride forth victoriously[u]
in behalf of truth, humility and righteousness;
let your right hand display awesome deeds.
5 Let your sharp arrows pierce the hearts of the king's enemies;
let the nations fall beneath your feet.
6 Your throne, O God, will last for ever and ever;[v]
a scepter of justice will be the scepter of your kingdom.
7 You love righteousness[w] and hate wickedness;
therefore God, your God, has set you above your companions
by anointing[x] you with the oil of joy.[y]
8 All your robes are fragrant[z] with myrrh and aloes and cassia;
from palaces adorned with ivory
the music of the strings makes you glad.
9 Daughters of kings[a] are among your honored women;
at your right hand[b] is the royal bride in gold of Ophir.

10 Listen, O daughter, consider and give ear:
Forget your people[c] and your father's house.
11 The king is enthralled by your beauty;
honor[d] him, for he is your lord.[e]
12 The Daughter of Tyre will come with a gift,[a][f]
men of wealth will seek your favor.

13 All glorious[g] is the princess within ⌞her chamber⌟;
her gown is interwoven with gold.
14 In embroidered garments she is led to the king;[h]
her virgin companions follow her
and are brought to you.
15 They are led in with joy and gladness;
they enter the palace of the king.

16 Your sons will take the place of your fathers;
you will make them princes throughout the land.
17 I will perpetuate your memory through all generations;[i]
therefore the nations will praise you[j] for ever and ever.

[a] 12 Or *A Tyrian robe is among the gifts*

44:26 your unfailing love. Specifically, God's covenant lovingkindness. The psalmist appealed again to the covenant as he urged God to intervene on behalf of the nation.

Psalm 45 *Introduction.* Psalm 45 is a rare example of a wedding song. The closest Biblical parallels are the love poems found in the Song of Songs. This wedding song is royal, but it is impossible to identify the specific wedding that inspired the initial composition. It was probably used in many royal weddings throughout the history of Israel. Since the Davidic kingship reflected God's ultimate kingship and anticipated Jesus Christ as King, the psalm also connects us to Christ, the King-Groom, and to his bride, the church (Eph 5:25–32). Thus, Psalm 45 was applied to Jesus Christ in Hebrews 1:8–9.

45:1 noble theme. The wedding of the king. The king was the center of Israelite society. His wedding was an important ceremony, especially in light of the dynastic principle of succession that continued the line of David in Judah. **tongue.** Suggests that this psalm (as well as many others) was first composed orally and later written down.

45:2 most excellent. A better translation would be "most beautiful," referring to the king's physical appearance. Here the poet took the bride's part in extolling the beauty of her lover. **blessed you forever.** Reflects the promises of the Davidic covenant, the terms of which are outlined in Psalms 89 and 132 and in 2 Samuel 7. The fulfillment of this promise is in Jesus Christ, the son of David, who rules as King from heaven.

45:3 Gird your sword upon your side. The Davidic king, the head of the military forces of Israel, was ordained by the Lord to fight to protect God's people. In this too the king reflected God's greater glory, since the Lord fought as a warrior on behalf of Israel. In the New Testament Jesus Christ is presented as the divine Warrior who leads the church against demonic forces (Eph 6:10–20) and who will return again to destroy all evil (Rev 19:11–16).

45:6 Your throne, O God. The Davidic king is symbolically addressed as God because he is God's representative and vice-regent and because he sits on the throne of Israel, which is ultimately God's throne (cf. 2Ch 9:8).

45:7 anointing you. Davidic kings were anointed at their inauguration (2Sa 2:4; 5:3; 1Ki 1:34,39; 1Ch 29:22). See *WCF* 8.3; 26.3; *WLC* 42; *HC* 31.

45:8 myrrh and aloes and cassia. The spices with which the king was anointed for his wedding, reminiscent of another love song, Song of Songs 5:10–16.

45:10 Forget your people. It appears that the bride was the daughter of a foreign king. Many royal marriages of the ancient Near East were the result of such interdynastic arrangements entered into as a means of sealing international relationships. Arrangements of this kind often led Israel astray (Dt 17:17; 1Ki 11:1–8; 16:31).

45:11 See *WLC* 110; *WSC* 52.

45:12 will seek your favor. The new queen would command respect from other powerful figures in the world.

45:16 Your sons. The descendants of the king. The psalmist's praise turned from the queen back to the king.

45:17 your memory. Literally, "your name." The praise of the nations will be given to God's anointed. See *WLC* 62.

Psalm 46

For the director of music. Of the Sons of Korah. According to *alamoth*.[a] A song.

1 God is our refuge[k] and strength,
an ever-present[l] help in trouble.
2 Therefore we will not fear,[m] though the earth give way[n]
and the mountains fall[o] into the heart of the sea,
3 though its waters roar[p] and foam
and the mountains quake with their surging. *Selah*

4 There is a river whose streams make glad the city of God,[q]
the holy place where the Most High dwells.
5 God is within her,[r] she will not fall;
God will help[s] her at break of day.
6 Nations[t] are in uproar, kingdoms[u] fall;
he lifts his voice, the earth melts.[v]

7 The LORD Almighty is with us;[w]
the God of Jacob is our fortress.[x] *Selah*

8 Come and see the works of the LORD,[y]
the desolations[z] he has brought on the earth.
9 He makes wars[a] cease to the ends of the earth;
he breaks the bow[b] and shatters the spear,
he burns the shields[b] with fire.[c]
10 "Be still, and know that I am God;[d]
I will be exalted[e] among the nations,
I will be exalted in the earth."

11 The LORD Almighty is with us;
the God of Jacob is our fortress. *Selah*

Psalm 47

For the director of music. Of the Sons of Korah. A psalm.

1 Clap your hands,[f] all you nations;
shout to God with cries of joy.[g]

46:1 [k]Ps 9:9; 14:6 [l]Dt 4:7
46:2 [m]Ps 23:4 [n]Ps 82:5 [o]Ps 18:7
46:3 [p]Ps 93:3
46:4 [q]Ps 48:1,8; Isa 60:14
46:5 [r]Isa 12:6; Eze 43:7 [s]Ps 37:40
46:6 [t]Ps 2:1 [u]Ps 68:32 [v]Mic 1:4
46:7 [w]2Ch 13:12 [x]Ps 9:9
46:8 [y]Ps 66:5 [z]Isa 61:4
46:9 [a]Isa 2:4 [b]Ps 76:3 [c]Eze 39:9
46:10 [d]Ps 100:3 [e]Isa 2:11
47:1 [f]Ps 98:8; Isa 55:12 [g]Ps 106:47

[a] Title: Probably a musical term [b] 9 Or *chariots*

Psalm 46 *Introduction.* This psalm is a moving affirmation of trust in the Lord in the midst of extreme adversity. The source of the psalmist's confidence was that God was with his people. The Lord in his temple would protect them. To assert that "God is with us" is at the heart of the covenant. There are some affinities here with Psalms 48, 76, 84 and 87, which are called "Zion Songs." Though Zion is not specifically mentioned in Psalm 46, it is alluded to in verses 4 and 5. Martin Luther was moved by this psalm to write "A Mighty Fortress Is Our God." As the Israelites could look at the temple in faith and know that God was with them, so Christians can look to Jesus Christ as their Immanuel, "God with us."
46:2 the mountains fall into the heart of the sea. This imagery on one level described a violent earthquake. However, the language is clearly hyperbolic and must be understood as an allusion to ancient Near Eastern religious concepts that are found elsewhere in the Bible. The sea represents chaos and evil (see note on 24:2; cf. 18:4; 29:3; 69:1–2). God battles the sea to accomplish his purposes (18; 74; 77; Na 1). The mountains are the opposite, representing stability. God dwelt on a mountain (Zion). Psalm 46, therefore, describes a situation of the utmost crisis: The stable mountains have fallen into the heart of the chaotic sea.
46:4 a river. Jerusalem has no river. This figurative reference most likely draws upon the common equation of Jerusalem in the promised land with the Garden of Eden, which had a prominent river (Ge 2:10). Both Eden and Jerusalem served as loci of God's special presence on Earth (see note on Ge 2:8). Ezekiel's vision also included a river flowing from God's temple throughout the land (Eze 47). Note also the river of life flowing from God's presence in Revelation. 22:1–2 and Jesus' teaching about the living water that flows from those who believe in him (Jn 4:14; 7:38). **the city of God, the holy place where the Most High dwells.** Jerusalem. As the Israelites looked at the temple, they felt secure in this symbol of God's protecting presence. Later on in Israel's history the people presumed on God's presence and viewed the temple as an inviolable sanctuary that necessarily ensured their safety from the Babylonians (Jer 7:4). Psalm 46 describes the faithful, devoted and obedient looking to the temple for security.
46:5 she will not fall. This assurance, like all God's blessings, was conditioned upon obedience to the covenant (cf. Lev 26; Dt 28). When Jerusalem did fall to the Babylonians in 586 B.C., God had already abandoned the city because of the people's sin (Eze 9–11). **break of day.** When the battle would break out once again. See *BC* 27.
46:6 the earth melts. This verse emphasizes God's power. The nations were locked in mortal conflict, and confusion reigned. God needed only to utter a word, and all the nations would be consumed.
46:7 with us. The refrain (also in v. 11) is an affirmation of trust in God as Israel's warrior and a remembrance of his covenant promise that "I will walk among you and be your God, and you will be my people" (Lev 26:12).
46:8 Come and see. The psalmist invited the reader to review and survey the magnificent acts of power that God has accomplished on Earth, both natural (like earthquakes) and military (like victories in warfare).
46:10 Be still. Submission is the proper response to such a powerful God. The contrast is with the nations in verse 6. This command is for these nations to be in reverential silence.
Psalm 47 *Introduction.* This is a kingship psalm (see "Introduction: Structure: *Genres: 5. Kingship Psalms.*") The image of God's enthronement is at its heart. The occasion is a great military victory over the enemy. Notice that God is King not just of Israel but of

47:2 [h]Dt 7:21 [i]Mal 1:14
47:3 [j]Ps 18:39,47
47:4 [k]1Pe 1:4
47:5 [l]Ps 68:33; 98:6
47:6 [m]Ps 68:4; 89:18
47:7 [n]Zec 14:9 [o]Col 3:16
47:8 [p]1Ch 16:31
47:9 [q]Ps 72:11; 89:18 [r]Ps 97:9
48:1 [s]Ps 96:4 [t]Ps 46:4 [u]Isa 2:2-3; Mic 4:1; Zec 8:3
48:2 [v]Ps 50:2; La 2:15 [w]Mt 5:35
48:3 [x]Ps 46:7
48:4 [y]2Sa 10:1-19
48:5 [z]Ex 15:16

2 How awesome[h] is the LORD Most High,
the great King[i] over all the earth!
3 He subdued[j] nations under us,
peoples under our feet.
4 He chose our inheritance[k] for us,
the pride of Jacob, whom he loved. *Selah*

5 God has ascended amid shouts of joy,
the LORD amid the sounding of trumpets.[l]
6 Sing praises[m] to God, sing praises;
sing praises to our King, sing praises.

7 For God is the King of all the earth;[n]
sing to him a psalm[a][o] of praise.
8 God reigns[p] over the nations;
God is seated on his holy throne.
9 The nobles of the nations assemble
as the people of the God of Abraham,
for the kings[b] of the earth belong to God;[q]
he is greatly exalted.[r]

Psalm 48

A song. A psalm of the Sons of Korah.

1 Great is the LORD,[s] and most worthy of praise,
in the city of our God,[t] his holy mountain.[u]
2 It is beautiful[v] in its loftiness,
the joy of the whole earth.
Like the utmost heights of Zaphon[c] is Mount Zion,
the[d] city of the Great King.[w]
3 God is in her citadels;
he has shown himself to be her fortress.[x]

4 When the kings joined forces,
when they advanced together,[y]
5 they saw ⌊her⌋ and were astounded;
they fled in terror.[z]
6 Trembling seized them there,
pain like that of a woman in labor.

[a] 7 Or *a maskil* (probably a literary or musical term) [b] 9 Or *shields* [c] 2 *Zaphon* can refer to a sacred mountain or the direction north. [d] 2 Or *earth, / Mount Zion, on the northern side / of the*

the entire universe. The Christian may use this prayer to celebrate the ascension and rule of Jesus Christ, who is both King and Warrior (Lk 19:38; 23:38; Jn 1:49).
47:1 all you nations. Since God is King over all the earth and not just of Israel, all the nations are called to join in the praise.
47:2 awesome. Instilling reverential fear.
47:3 He subdued nations. God as divine warrior won innumerable military victories for the Israelites throughout their history, beginning with the great victory at the Red Sea (Ex 15).
47:4 our inheritance. Refers to the conquest and allotment of the promised land. In Deuteronomy 7:7–11, Moses explained that it was only through God's grace that the Israelites would conquer and possess the promised land.
47:5 has ascended. The picture is that of an enthronement, but it was not of God becoming King of Israel for the first time. God was King from all eternity (Ps 93:2). However, after victory, his kingship was celebrated anew.
47:7 sing to him. The proper response to God's kingship is to extol him with songs of praise. See *WCF* 21.3.
47:9 The nobles of the nations assemble. This should take place in the present, but it will definitely occur in the future when Christ returns. **the God of Abraham.** God promised Abraham that he would make him a blessing to all the nations (Ge 12:1–3). He accomplished this definitively through his Son, Jesus Christ.
Psalm 48 *Introduction.* Psalm 48 is a hymn of praise with a number of similarities to Psalm 46. Both praise God for his presence in his temple and conclude with an invitation to the reader to acknowledge God. Psalm 48 extols Zion as the center of God's protective presence (see theological article "The Presence of God" at 1Ki 8). Also compare this psalm with Psalms 76, 84, 87 and 122.
48:1 the city of our God. Jerusalem, where the temple was located. **his holy mountain.** Mount Zion, the specific location in Jerusalem at which the temple was located.
48:2 joy of the whole earth. Even though the nations do not acknowledge him, God is the King of the universe, not just of Israel. A day would come when the Gentile nations, too, would come to Zion (Mic 4:1–5). Jesus Christ began to bring this to pass when he broke down the wall of partition between Jew and Gentile (Eph 2:11–22). When he returns, he will finish his work, and all nations will worship the Lord in the new earth (Isa 66:22; Rev 21:1—22:5). **Zaphon.** The supposed dwelling place of the false god Baal, according to religious texts of the Canaanites. It is not unusual for Yahweh to be described in terms that parallel or, more usually, exceed, that of the neighboring false religions. This was done to show that Yahweh is the only true God, who did everything that the false gods were supposed to do.
48:3 God is in her citadels. God's presence assured the security of Jerusalem. Compare the notes on 46:4.
48:4 the kings joined forces. The language is similar to that of Psalm 2:1–3. Even in their combined might the nations are helpless against God.
48:5 in terror. Their fear was due to God's power, concentrated in Jerusalem (see theological article "The Presence of God" at 1Ki 8), because he had chosen that city as his dwelling place. God is a mighty warrior who vanquishes the foe (Ex 15).

7 You destroyed them like ships of Tarshish
shattered by an east wind.[a]

8 As we have heard,
so have we seen
in the city of the LORD Almighty,
in the city of our God:
God makes her secure forever.[b] *Selah*

9 Within your temple, O God,
we meditate on your unfailing love.[c]
10 Like your name,[d] O God,
your praise reaches to the ends of the earth;[e]
your right hand is filled with righteousness.
11 Mount Zion rejoices,
the villages of Judah are glad
because of your judgments.[f]

12 Walk about Zion, go around her,
count her towers,
13 consider well her ramparts,
view her citadels,[g]
that you may tell of them to the next generation.[h]
14 For this God is our God for ever and ever;
he will be our guide[i] even to the end.

Psalm 49

For the director of music. Of the Sons of Korah. A psalm.

1 Hear this, all you peoples;[j]
listen, all who live in this world,[k]
2 both low and high,
rich and poor alike:
3 My mouth will speak words of wisdom;[l]
the utterance from my heart will give understanding.[m]
4 I will turn my ear to a proverb;[n]
with the harp I will expound my riddle:[o]

5 Why should I fear[p] when evil days come,
when wicked deceivers surround me—
6 those who trust in their wealth[q]
and boast of their great riches?
7 No man can redeem the life of another
or give to God a ransom for him—
8 the ransom for a life is costly,
no payment is ever enough—[r]
9 that he should live on[s] forever
and not see decay.

48:7 [a]Jer 18:17; Eze 27:26
48:8 [b]Ps 87:5
48:9 [c]Ps 26:3
48:10 [d]Dt 28:58; Jos 7:9 [e]Isa 41:10
48:11 [f]Ps 97:8
48:13 [g]ver 3; Ps 122:7 [h]Ps 78:6
48:14 [i]Ps 23:4
49:1 [j]Ps 78:1 [k]Ps 33:8
49:3 [l]Ps 37:30 [m]Ps 119:130
49:4 [n]Ps 78:2 [o]Nu 12:8
49:5 [p]Ps 23:4
49:6 [q]Job 31:24
49:8 [r]Mt 16:26
49:9 [s]Ps 22:29; 89:48

48:7 ships of Tarshish. Ocean-going vessels.
48:8 LORD Almighty. Literally, God of hosts, a military title. See note on 1 Samuel 1:3. It identified God as the divine warrior who led his heavenly army into battle for the protection of his people.
48:9 unfailing love. Specifically, God's covenant devotion.
48:14 our guide. The psalmist recognized that Israel's fate was not a matter of chance or of human striving. God was in control, and the Israelites would follow him as sheep follow their shepherd (23:1; 77:20).
Psalm 49 *Introduction.* Psalm 49 was written in the wisdom tradition (see "Introduction: Structure: *Genres: 6. Wisdom Psalms*") and deals with issues found elsewhere in wisdom books. The psalmist wrestled with two problems: the prosperity of the rich and the reality of death. He wrote to comfort the righteous who suffer at the hands of the wicked rich. This psalm is one of only a few Old Testament texts that explicitly expresses confidence in the resurrection of the dead. God will triumph over the grave and bring justice to the righteous poor. The New Testament Christian has a clearer view of the resurrection because Jesus has led the way, inspiring even greater confidence in the Lord and in his justice.
49:1 all you peoples. Addressed not just to Israel but to the Gentiles as well.
49:2 rich and poor. These two basic social classes were specifically addressed because the psalmist was burdened by the complacency of the rich.
49:3 words of wisdom. The psalmist identified himself with the sages of Israel. This psalm would provide practical insight into the problem at hand.
49:4 proverb . . . riddle. Two words that position the psalm and the psalmist in the wisdom tradition.
49:5 evil days. The days when one's death approaches. Compare Ecclesiastes 12:1.
49:6 trust in their wealth. The rich are tempted to find security in worldly possessions rather than in God.
49:7–9 See *HC* 14.
49:7 No man can redeem the life of another. Even great wealth cannot ward off death. If someone is kidnapped, payment may be made to restore that person to his family. Money, though, cannot delay death by even a moment. See *HC* 42.

49:10 [t]Ecc 2:16 [u]Ecc 2:18,21

10 For all can see that wise men die;[t]
the foolish and the senseless alike perish
and leave their wealth to others.[u]
11 Their tombs will remain their houses[a] forever,
their dwellings for endless generations,
though they had[b] named[v] lands after themselves.

49:11 [v]Ge 4:17; Dt 3:14

12 But man, despite his riches, does not endure;
he is[c] like the beasts that perish.

49:13 [w]Lk 12:20

13 This is the fate of those who trust in themselves,[w]
and of their followers, who approve their sayings. *Selah*

49:14 [x]Job 24:19; Ps 9:17 [y]Da 7:18; Mal 4:3; 1Co 6:2; Rev 2:26

14 Like sheep they are destined for the grave,[d][x]
and death will feed on them.
The upright will rule[y] over them in the morning;
their forms will decay in the grave,[d]
far from their princely mansions.

49:15 [z]Ps 56:13; Hos 13:14 [a]Ps 73:24

15 But God will redeem my life[e] from the grave;[z]
he will surely take me to himself.[a] *Selah*

16 Do not be overawed when a man grows rich,
when the splendor of his house increases;

49:17 [b]Ps 17:14; 1Ti 6:7

17 for he will take nothing with him when he dies,
his splendor will not descend with him.[b]

49:18 [c]Dt 29:19; Lk 12:19

18 Though while he lived he counted himself blessed—[c]
and men praise you when you prosper—

49:19 [d]Ge 15:15 [e]Job 33:30

19 he will join the generation of his fathers,[d]
who will never see the light[e] ⌊of life⌋.

49:20 [f]Ecc 3:19

20 A man who has riches without understanding
is like the beasts that perish.[f]

Psalm 50

A psalm of Asaph.

50:1 [g]Jos 22:22 [h]Ps 113:3

1 The Mighty One, God, the LORD,[g]
speaks and summons the earth
from the rising of the sun to the place where it sets.[h]

50:2 [i]Ps 48:2 [j]Dt 33:2; Ps 80:1

2 From Zion, perfect in beauty,[i]
God shines forth.[j]

50:3 [k]Ps 96:13 [l]Ps 97:3; Da 7:10

3 Our God comes[k] and will not be silent;
a fire devours before him,[l]

[a] *11* Septuagint and Syriac; Hebrew *In their thoughts their houses will remain* [b] *11* Or / *for they have* [c] *12* Hebrew; Septuagint and Syriac read verse 12 the same as verse 20. [d] *14* Hebrew *Sheol*; also in verse 15 [e] *15* Or *soul*

49:10 wise men die. This thought is reminiscent of the words of the Teacher in Ecclesiastes 2:12–16. Both the wise and the foolish die. The psalmist obviously would classify the rich oppressor in the latter category.
49:11 Their tombs will remain their houses forever. Many wealthy people spend much of their lifetimes constructing, furnishing and entertaining in expansive earthly homes. However, in the context of eternity, most of their time will be spent beneath the ground.
49:12 he is like the beasts that perish. In drawing a comparison between humans and animals in death, the psalmist once again paralleled the thought of the Teacher in Ecclesiastes (Ecc 3:18–21).
49:14 Like sheep. A simile that emphasizes that they are unaware of danger. **death will feed on them.** Those who trust in themselves will die and rot in the grave.
49:15 But God will redeem my life from the grave. In contrast to his treatment of those who trust in themselves (v. 14), God will not ultimately abandon the righteous to their graves. While God does not accept a ransom for death (v. 7), he provided it in the case of the righteous psalmist. Here we catch a hint of the Old Testament awareness of redemption from death. Key to this understanding is the unbreakable nature of fellowship with God: "He will surely take me to himself."
49:16–20 he will take nothing with him when he dies. Conclusion: From the perspective of eternity, the rich have no advantage over the poor and the afflicted. See *BC* 14.
Psalm 50 *Introduction.* Psalm 50 has a kind of prophetic cast since a large part of it is composed of two oracles of the Lord, one directed toward the righteous (who still need instruction) and the other against the wicked. God places special focus on his demand that he receive thanksgiving offerings (see vv. 14–15,22–23).
Title. See "Introduction: Authorship and Titles."
50:1 The Mighty One, God, the LORD. The psalmist described God appearing to his people from Zion to deliver an oracle. The psalm opens by stacking three names for God, giving it a solemn tone. The list of three culminates with God's covenant name, Yahweh. See notes on Exodus 3:13–15 and on 1 Samuel 1:3. **the earth.** God addressed all people, in blessing or in judgment, rather than just the Israelites. In verse 4 this summons was expanded to include the heavens. **from the rising of the sun to the place where it sets.** From east to west; that is, the whole earth.
50:2 Zion. The location of the temple, the place God chose to make his presence known. See 2:6. **shines forth.** The language is that of a theophany, an appearance of God. God's presence is manifest from his temple in Jerusalem. See Deuteronomy 33:2.
50:3 a fire devours before him. God's theophanies were often accompanied by powerful and dangerous forces, especially when he spoke in judgment (Ex 19; Isa 24; Na 1).

and around him a tempest rages.
4 He summons the heavens above,
and the earth,[m] that he may judge his people:
5 "Gather to me my consecrated ones,[n]
who made a covenant[o] with me by sacrifice."
6 And the heavens proclaim[p] his righteousness,
for God himself is judge.[q] *Selah*
7 "Hear, O my people, and I will speak,
O Israel, and I will testify[r] against you:
I am God, your God.[s]
8 I do not rebuke you for your sacrifices
or your burnt offerings,[t] which are ever before me.
9 I have no need of a bull[u] from your stall
or of goats from your pens,
10 for every animal of the forest is mine,
and the cattle on a thousand hills.[v]
11 I know every bird in the mountains,
and the creatures of the field are mine.
12 If I were hungry I would not tell you,
for the world[w] is mine, and all that is in it.
13 Do I eat the flesh of bulls
or drink the blood of goats?
14 Sacrifice thank offerings[x] to God,
fulfill your vows[y] to the Most High,
15 and call[z] upon me in the day of trouble;
I will deliver you, and you will honor[a] me."

16 But to the wicked, God says:

"What right have you to recite my laws
or take my covenant on your lips?[b]
17 You hate my instruction
and cast my words behind[c] you.
18 When you see a thief, you join[d] with him;
you throw in your lot with adulterers.
19 You use your mouth for evil
and harness your tongue to deceit.[e]
20 You speak continually against your brother[f]
and slander your own mother's son.
21 These things you have done and I kept silent;[g]

50:4 [m]Dt 4:26; Isa 1:2
50:5 [n]Ps 30:4 [o]Ex 24:7
50:6 [p]Ps 89:5 [q]Ps 75:7
50:7 [r]Ps 81:8 [s]Ex 20:2
50:8 [t]Ps 40:6; Hos 6:6
50:9 [u]Ps 69:31
50:10 [v]Ps 104:24
50:12 [w]Ex 19:5
50:14 [x]Heb 13:15 [y]Dt 23:21
50:15 [z]Ps 81:7 [a]Ps 22:23
50:16 [b]Isa 29:13
50:17 [c]Ne 9:26; Ro 2:21-22
50:18 [d]Ro 1:32; 1Ti 5:22
50:19 [e]Ps 10:7; 52:2
50:20 [f]Mt 10:21
50:21 [g]Ecc 8:11; Isa 42:14

50:4–5 his people. The first oracle is addressed to the nation of Israel. **consecrated ones.** The word is formed from the same root as for "covenant loving-kindness." It refers to those who are participants in a covenant relationship with God. **a covenant with me by sacrifice.** Here the term "covenant," as in most places in Scripture, signifies the bond between God and his people. Since people are sinful, that relationship must be accompanied by sacrifice, which in the Old Testament was one means by which God applied forgiveness to believers. To enter into the presence of a holy God, men and women had to seek atonement for their own sins through sacrifice. See *WLC* 174.

50:6 heavens. In the judicial setting of this verse, "heavens" is probably a poetic reference to the members of God's heavenly court, the angels.

50:7 testify. The covenant was a legal instrument, taking the form of a treaty between nations. When there was some disruption in the people's faithfulness, they were frequently "put on trial" by the Lord or by one of his prophets (Mic 6:1–8).

50:8 I do not rebuke you for your sacrifices. The people's problem was not connected to their observance of the sacrificial rites. They were faithful to perform them but apparently misunderstood their significance.

50:9 no need. The people felt that God required their sacrifices in order to meet his own needs. The surrounding nations believed that their gods ate the sacrifices and grew hungry when deprived. For example, in the "Flood Narrative" of the ancient Babylonian *Gilgamish Epic,* Ishtar bemoaned the lack of sacrifices that resulted in her god-sized hunger.

50:10–12 mine . . . mine. God owned and ruled over all the creatures of the world. Even those sacrificed to him were taken from among his own possessions—the nation of Israel merely administrated what already belonged to God. If he had needed animals for food or for any other reason, he would not have required the assistance of human beings to procure them.

50:13 Do I eat the flesh of bulls . . . ? This rhetorical question made it clear that the Lord did not literally eat the meat of the sacrifices.

50:14–17 See *WLC* 113,179; *HC* 82,99,116.

50:14 thank offerings. God desired these offerings as a sign that the people recognized that their deliverance from trouble was an act of God (Lev 7:12–15). **fulfill your vows.** Though God didn't need sacrifices, the people needed to offer them. God desired sacrifices not for sustenance but for the people's atonement and as demonstration of their attitude of giving to the Lord (Lev 1–7). See *WCF* 22.6; *WLC* 175; *HC* 103.

50:16 wicked. Most likely a reference to the wicked within the covenant community, since they know God's law. This implies that they were hypocrites as well as wicked. **What right have you . . .?** A rhetorical question expressing judgment against hypocrites. **recite my laws.** Perhaps in a covenant renewal ceremony in which the members of the community recited the law together and reaffirmed their intention to keep it (Dt 31:9–11).

50:17 hate my instruction. An unmistakable sign of a fool (Pr 1:7)

50:18–19 you see a thief, you join with him. The psalmist cited the seventh, eighth and ninth commandments. See *WLC* 142.

50:20 See *WLC* 145.

50:21 I kept silent. God's silence was frequently taken by the wicked as a sign that he didn't care whether or not they sinned.

you thought I was altogether[a] like you.
But I will rebuke you
and accuse[h] you to your face.

22 "Consider this, you who forget God,[i]
or I will tear you to pieces, with none to rescue:[j]
23 He who sacrifices thank offerings honors me,
and he prepares the way[k]
so that I may show him[b] the salvation of God.[l]"

Psalm 51

For the director of music. A psalm of David. When the prophet Nathan came to him after David had committed adultery with Bathsheba.

1 Have mercy on me, O God,
according to your unfailing love;
according to your great compassion
blot out[m] my transgressions.[n]
2 Wash away[o] all my iniquity
and cleanse[p] me from my sin.

3 For I know my transgressions,
and my sin is always before me.[q]
4 Against you, you only, have I sinned
and done what is evil in your sight,[r]
so that you are proved right when you speak
and justified when you judge.[s]
5 Surely I was sinful[t] at birth,
sinful from the time my mother conceived me.
6 Surely you desire truth in the inner parts[c];
you teach[d] me wisdom[u] in the inmost place.[v]

7 Cleanse me with hyssop,[w] and I will be clean;
wash me, and I will be whiter than snow.[x]
8 Let me hear joy and gladness;[y]
let the bones you have crushed rejoice.
9 Hide your face from my sins[z]
and blot out all my iniquity.

50:21 [h]Ps 90:8
50:22 [i]Job 8:13; Ps 9:17 [j]Ps 7:2
50:23 [k]Ps 85:13 [l]Ps 91:16
51:1 [m]Ac 3:19 [n]Isa 43:25; Col 2:14
51:2 [o]1Jn 1:9 [p]Heb 9:14
51:3 [q]Isa 59:12
51:4 [r]Ge 20:6; Lk 15:21 [s]Ro 3:4*
51:5 [t]Job 14:4
51:6 [u]Pr 2:6 [v]Ps 15:2
51:7 [w]Lev 14:4; Heb 9:19 [x]Isa 1:18
51:8 [y]Isa 35:10
51:9 [z]Jer 16:17

[a] 21 Or *thought the 'I AM' was* [b] 23 Or *and to him who considers his way / I will show* [c] 6 The meaning of the Hebrew for this phrase is uncertain. [d] 6 Or *you desired . . . ; / you taught*

They should have realized that his patience, signified by the silence, would soon wear thin and turn to judgment. See *WCF* 5.4; *WLC* 105.

50:22 I will tear you to pieces. God insists on obedience from the wicked hypocrites; otherwise, they will meet a fearsome end.

50:23 he prepares the way. The psalmist reminded the first group (the righteous) that their sacrifices, though not necessary in order to sustain God, were essential to their own salvation because they were means through which God applied to them the blessings of salvation.

Psalm 51 *Introduction.* Psalm 51 is one of the most powerful statements of the depths of sin and of repentance to be found anywhere in the Bible. It is the most striking of the so-called "prayers of penitence" (see notes on Ps 6) that are a subset of the individual lament. The last two verses give the psalm a national impact. The psalm points out to Christians the depth of their sin and turns them toward God in heartfelt repentance. Repentance comes about as we approach God with a "broken spirit" and a "contrite heart" (v. 17). See *WCF* 15.6.

Title. See *WCF* 17.3.

51:1–7 See *WCF* 15.6; *WSC* 105; *HC* 89,126.

51:1 according to your unfailing love. David was guilty of great sin against the bond of God's covenant. Uriah, the husband of Bathsheba, had shown covenant devotion to King David (2Sa 11:11; 23:39), but David had dreadfully exploited his loyalty. Yet a penitent David now pleaded based on God's gracious devotion to his people and to himself in particular. **great compassion.** God's forgiving David was the result of his long-suffering mercy. David deserved death, but God granted life (cf. 2Sa 12:13). **blot out.** The metaphor signifies blotting out words of a scroll (cf. 2 Kings 14:27). Here the meaning is "forget."

51:2 Wash. A specific reference to washing clothes. David compared his iniquity to filthy garments in need of laundering.

51:4 you only. This affirmation is striking in the light of the historical title. David committed adultery with Bathsheba and had Uriah murdered. In what sense could David claim that he had sinned *only* against God? David understated his culpability toward Uriah and Bathsheba in order to emphasize his accountability before God, whose character, as expressed in the law, David had violated. **proved right . . . justified.** David recognized that God's judgment against him was just in the light of his sin. See *WCF* 15.2; *WLC* 151.

51:5 I was sinful at birth. Children are sinners; no one is born innocent. Even children, then, need God's salvation. See *WCF* 6.3; *WLC* 26; *BC* 15; *HC* 7.

51:6 inner parts . . . inmost place. This may be a reference to the mother's womb but probably refers to the core of one's being. See *BC* 22.

51:7–12 See *WCF* 11.5; 15.6; 17.3; 18.4; *WLC* 81,194; *WSC* 105; *HC* 90.

51:7 with hyssop. The allusion is to Leviticus 14:6 and following, in which the cleansing of a leper was described. **I will be clean.** David was certain that, though his sin was grave, God could and would forgive and restore him. See *WCF* 15.6; *WSC* 105. **wash me.** Perhaps an allusion to Numbers 19:19, where the command was given for ritual washing after contact with a dead person.

10 Create in me a pure heart,[a] O God,
and renew a steadfast spirit within me.[b]
11 Do not cast me from your presence
or take your Holy Spirit[c] from me.
12 Restore to me the joy of your salvation[d]
and grant me a willing spirit, to sustain me.

13 Then I will teach transgressors your ways,[e]
and sinners will turn back to you.[f]
14 Save me from bloodguilt,[g] O God,
the God who saves me,[h]
and my tongue will sing of your righteousness.[i]

51:10 [a]Ps 78:37; Ac 15:9 [b]Eze 18:31
51:11 [c]Eph 4:30
51:12 [d]Ps 13:5
51:13 [e]Ac 9:21-22 [f]Ps 22:27
51:14 [g]2Sa 12:9 [h]Ps 25:5 [i]Ps 35:28

51:10 Create. The word is the same used for the creation of the world in Genesis 1. David knew that only God could bring about such a reorientation of his desires and thoughts. See *WCF* 17.3; *WLC* 195.
51:11 Holy Spirit. David spoke here of the anointing and gifting of the Holy Spirit that he had received as king of Israel, not of the Spirit's indwelling presence. He asked God not to take the kingdom away from him as he had taken it from Saul and not to remove the special gifting David had received and that enabled him to lead effectively.
51:12 joy of your salvation. David may have implied that spiritual dullness had prompted his heinous immorality. To prevent such dullness from affecting him similarly in the future, he prayed for joy. Alternatively, he simply may have been asking for the joy that would naturally flow from a restored relationship with God. See *WCF* 17.3; 18.4; *WLC* 81,194,195; *HC* 90.
51:13 I will teach transgressors your ways. If forgiven and restored to joy, the psalmist promised to help other sinners find forgiveness as well.
51:14 bloodguilt. David prayed for forgiveness from God, and perhaps also for the suspension of any civil sanctions that might be brought against him, such as retribution at the hands of Uriah's family (Nu 35:16–21; Dt 19:11–13) or death as punishment for adultery (Lev 20:10). **sing of your righteousness.** See note on 4:1. In the legal setting of this psalm (v. 4), righteousness includes justice. How could David praise God for his *justice* in remitting his blood guilt? Here we move beyond the concept that God is just in defending an innocent member of his covenant to the reality of God's justice in

Repentance: How Sorry Do I Have To Be?

IN the first of his "95 Theses" Martin Luther proclaimed, "Our Lord and Master Jesus Christ, when He said 'repent,' willed that the whole life of believers should be one of repentance." This recovery of Biblical truth has inspired generations since to a reformation of thought and heart concerning the nature of the Christian life.

The call to repent was a fundamental summons in the preaching of John the Baptist (Mt 3:2), Jesus (Mt 4:17), the Twelve (Mk 6:12), Peter at Pentecost (Ac 2:38), Paul to the Gentiles (Ac 17:30; 26:20) and the glorified Christ to five of the seven churches in Asia Minor (Rev 2:5,16,21–22; 3:3,19). It was part of Jesus' summary of the gospel that was to be taken to all the world (Lk 24:47), and it corresponds to the Old Testament prophets' constant insistence that the Israelites return to the God from whom they had strayed (e.g., Isa 30:15; 59:20; Jer 23:22; 25:4,5; Eze 14:6; Hos 11:5; Zec 1:3–6). Repentance is continually set forth as a work of faith by which God applies forgiveness of sins to his people and restores them to his favor; impenitence, on the other hand, is the road to ruin (Lk 13:1–5).

Faith and repentance are mutual conditions for salvation (Mt 21:32; Mk 1:15; Ac 20:21; cf. Ac 2:38; 3:19; 16:31; Ro 10:9–10). Both are gifts of God that result from regeneration (Ac 11:18; Php 1:29; see theological article "Regeneration and New Birth" at Jn 3)—the heart set free from sin gratefully conforms to the command to repent and believe the gospel. Repentance, whether a firstfruit of God's work of regeneration (Ac 11:18; *WLC* 76) or a mature response to sin (2Sa 12:13; 2Ch 32:26; Job 42:6), is a gift of God accompanying both saving faith (Ro 10:9–10) and the ongoing faith flowing from the Holy Spirit (Gal 5:22—6:1). One cannot turn to God in faith without first turning from sin in repentance.

Theologians often distinguish between two kinds of repentance. The first is *attrition,* which is the mere affirmation that sinners deserve to be punished, lacking both a corresponding intention to cease from sinning and an appeal in faith to God for forgiveness. Attrition is not heartfelt sorrow in agreement with God, but a selfishly motivated response to actual or threatened punishment or loss. This is the kind of repentance Esau demonstrated (Ge 27:30–46). As the author of Hebrews commented, Esau was not sorry for his sin but merely regretted having lost his birthright (see note on Heb 12:17).

On the other hand, *contrition* is true (though always imperfect) repentance. It involves remorse for having offended God and, when appropriate, for having offended another person or persons as well (Ps 51:4; Lk 15:21–24). There is a general sense of contrition that should be acknowledged due to the fallen human condition (Ps. 51:3–5), but specific repentance ought to take place whenever particular sins are recognized (e.g., 2Sa 12:13; 24:10; Lk 15:18,21. This proper acknowledgement of sin is not merely a turning away from disobedience but a move toward positive behavior, including the willingness to make restitution where appropriate (Ex 22:3–14; Lev 24:18–21; 1Sa 12:3; Mt 3:8; Lk 19:8). This was the repentance manifested by David as he prayed, "Create in me a pure heart, O God, and renew a steadfast spirit within me . . . The sacrifices of God are a broken spirit; a broken and contrite heart, O God, you will not despise" (Ps 51:10,17). When repentance is offered in this spirit, God promises to forgive us and to restore us to full fellowship with him. As John wrote, "If we confess our sins, he is faithful and just and will forgive us our sins and purify us from all unrighteousness" (1Jn 1:9). See *WCF* 15; *WLC* 75–78.

15 O Lord, open my lips,[j]
 and my mouth will declare your praise.
16 You do not delight in sacrifice,[k] or I would bring it;
 you do not take pleasure in burnt offerings.
17 The sacrifices of God are[a] a broken spirit;
 a broken and contrite heart,[l]
 O God, you will not despise.

18 In your good pleasure make Zion[m] prosper;
 build up the walls of Jerusalem.
19 Then there will be righteous sacrifices,[n]
 whole burnt offerings[o] to delight you;
 then bulls[p] will be offered on your altar.

Psalm 52

For the director of music. A maskil[b] *of David. When Doeg the Edomite*[q] *had gone to Saul and told him: "David has gone to the house of Ahimelech."*

1 Why do you boast of evil, you mighty man?
 Why do you boast[r] all day long,
 you who are a disgrace in the eyes of God?
2 Your tongue plots destruction;
 it is like a sharpened razor,[s]
 you who practice deceit.[t]
3 You love evil rather than good,
 falsehood[u] rather than speaking the truth. *Selah*
4 You love every harmful word,
 O you deceitful tongue![v]

5 Surely God will bring you down to everlasting ruin:
 He will snatch you up and tear[w] you from your tent;
 he will uproot[x] you from the land of the living.[y] *Selah*
6 The righteous will see and fear;
 they will laugh[z] at him, saying,
7 "Here now is the man
 who did not make God his stronghold
 but trusted in his great wealth[a]
 and grew strong by destroying others!"

8 But I am like an olive tree[b]
 flourishing in the house of God;
 I trust[c] in God's unfailing love
 for ever and ever.
9 I will praise you forever[d] for what you have done;

51:15 [j]Ps 9:14
51:16 [k]1Sa 15:22; Ps 40:6
51:17 [l]Ps 34:18
51:18 [m]Ps 102:16; Isa 51:3
51:19 [n]Ps 4:5 [o]Ps 66:13 [p]Ps 66:15
52:1 [q]1Sa 22:9 [r]Ps 94:4
52:2 [s]Ps 57:4 [t]Ps 50:19
52:3 [u]Jer 9:5
52:4 [v]Ps 120:2,3
52:5 [w]Isa 22:19 [x]Pr 2:22 [y]Ps 27:13
52:6 [z]Job 22:19; Ps 37:34; 40:3
52:7 [a]Ps 49:6
52:8 [b]Jer 11:16 [c]Ps 13:5
52:9 [d]Ps 30:12

[a] 17 Or *My sacrifice, O God, is* [b] Title: Probably a literary or musical term

forgiving sin through imputed righteousness (see theological article "Justification and Merit" at Ro 3). See *WCF* 15.6; 17.3; 18.4.
51:15 See *WLC* 190.
51:16 You do not delight in sacrifice. Biblical authors placed heartfelt obedience over outward religious conformity in terms of importance to God (e.g., see 40:6–8; Mic 6:6–8). Psalm 51 does not condemn the sacrificial system (see v. 19) or deny that it was an effective means of grace, but David expressed the truth that God wanted more than ritual conformity—he desired wholehearted commitment.
51:17 See *WLC* 185; *HC* 89; *CD* 3–4.IV.
51:18–19 Zion . . . Jerusalem. The restoration of the king would lead to blessing for Zion. See *WLC* 184.
Psalm 52 *Introduction.* The psalmist stood amazed as he pondered the arrogance of the wicked. He recognized that, even though the wicked boasted, they were on the brink of divine judgment. He contrasted his own fate (vv. 8–9) with that of the wicked. This psalm is difficult to classify. It expresses confidence in the Lord like a psalm of trust, pronounces judgment on the wicked like a lament and uses wisdom language.
Title. The historical title cites the event recorded in 1 Samuel 22:6–23. In effect, the title identifies Doeg with the boastful, wicked man and David with the righteous psalmist. However, the psalm itself is historically nonspecific.
52:1–4 The violent wickedness of evil men. See *WLC* 145.
52:1 mighty man. A technical term for a warrior. See *WLC* 151.
52:4 harmful. More exactly, "confused." The Wisdom Literature consistently taught that confusion was on the side of the wicked and order on the side of righteousness. Order was attuned to the manner in which God had created the world.
52:6 will see and fear; they will laugh. The verb *fear* may seem a strange word choice in association with laughter. The meaning, however, is not terror but rather reverence and awe. The righteous observe the justice of God's judgment against the wicked.
52:7 who did not make God his stronghold. The evil individual depicted in this psalm was the antithesis of everything the Psalms stand for. The Psalms urge God's people to make the Lord their stronghold and to put no trust in themselves. Behind this imagery is the idea of God as Divine Warrior, the power behind his people in all of their military victories.
52:8 olive tree. Reminiscent of Psalm 1. Olive trees live for a very long time. **flourishing.** Full of sap.

in your name I will hope, for your name is good.[e]
I will praise you in the presence of your saints.

Psalm 53

For the director of music. According to *mahalath*.[a]
A *maskil*[b] of David.

1 The fool[f] says in his heart,
"There is no God."[g]
They are corrupt, and their ways are vile;
there is no one who does good.

2 God looks down from heaven[h]
on the sons of men
to see if there are any who understand,
any who seek God.[i]
3 Everyone has turned away,
they have together become corrupt;
there is no one who does good,
not even one.[j]

4 Will the evildoers never learn—
those who devour my people as men eat bread
and who do not call on God?
5 There they were, overwhelmed with dread,
where there was nothing to dread.[k]
God scattered the bones[l] of those who attacked you;
you put them to shame, for God despised them.

6 Oh, that salvation for Israel would come out of Zion!
When God restores the fortunes of his people,
let Jacob rejoice and Israel be glad!

Psalm 54

For the director of music. With stringed instruments.
A *maskil*[b] of David. When the Ziphites had gone to Saul
and said, "Is not David hiding among us?"

1 Save me, O God, by your name;[m]
vindicate me by your might.[n]
2 Hear my prayer, O God;[o]
listen to the words of my mouth.

3 Strangers are attacking me;[p]
ruthless men seek my life[q]—
men without regard for God.[r] *Selah*

4 Surely God is my help;[s]
the Lord is the one who sustains me.[t]

5 Let evil recoil[u] on those who slander me;
in your faithfulness[v] destroy them.

52:9 [e]Ps 54:6
53:1 [f]Ps 14:1-7; Ro 3:10 [g]Ps 10:4
53:2 [h]Ps 33:13 [i]2Ch 15:2
53:3 [j]Ro 3:10-12*
53:5 [k]Lev 26:17 [l]Eze 6:5
54:1 [m]Ps 20:1 [n]2Ch 20:6
54:2 [o]Ps 5:1; 55:1
54:3 [p]Ps 86:14 [q]Ps 40:14 [r]Ps 36:1
54:4 [s]Ps 118:7 [t]Ps 41:12
54:5 [u]Ps 94:23 [v]Ps 89:49; 143:12

[a] Title: Probably a musical term [b] Title: Probably a literary or musical term

52:9 in the presence of your saints. In public worship. See note on 4:3.
Psalm 53 *Introduction.* A meditation on the wickedness of the fool. Compare Psalm 14. God will destroy the fool and restore Israel's fortunes. Psalm 53, in contrast to Psalm 14, uses *Elohim* ("God") rather than *Yahweh* ("the LORD"). This usage is characteristic of the entire collection of psalms in Book II of the Psalter. Psalms 14 and 53 express an attitude of quiet meditation, while focusing on the evil of the wicked.
53:1–4 The fool says. See notes on 14:1–4.
53:5 There they were, overwhelmed with dread. The first line of this verse parallels Psalm 14:5. After this, there is a departure in wording. **scattered the bones.** Showed disdain for them by disregarding their fallen corpses, treating them as refuse (Isa 14:18–20; Jer 8:1–2).
53:6 Oh, that salvation for Israel would come. An expression of hope for the deliverance from evil. Compare notes on 14:7.
Psalm 54 *Introduction.* Psalm 54 is a lament in which David appeals to God for help and promises to return thanks for God's deliverance if God should save him.
Title. The historical title locates the inspiration of the psalm in David's premonarchical days. He wrote the psalm after having been betrayed by the Ziphites; compare 1 Samuel 23:19 and 26:11.
54:1 vindicate. Identifies his complaint as a judicial one. David had been unjustly betrayed by the Ziphites, fellow members of the tribe of Judah.
54:3 Strangers are attacking me. Even though the Ziphites were of his own tribe, Judah, David did not personally know them and could see no cause for them to betray him to Saul.

6 I will sacrifice a freewill offering[w] to you;
I will praise your name, O LORD,
for it is good.[x]
7 For he has delivered me[y] from all my troubles,
and my eyes have looked in triumph on my foes.[z]

Psalm 55

For the director of music. With stringed instruments.
A *maskil*[a] of David.

1 Listen to my prayer, O God,
do not ignore my plea;[a]
2 hear me and answer me.[b]
My thoughts trouble me and I am distraught[c]
3 at the voice of the enemy,
at the stares of the wicked;
for they bring down suffering upon me[d]
and revile me in their anger.[e]

4 My heart is in anguish within me;
the terrors[f] of death assail me.
5 Fear and trembling[g] have beset me;
horror has overwhelmed me.
6 I said, "Oh, that I had the wings of a dove!
I would fly away and be at rest—
7 I would flee far away
and stay in the desert; *Selah*
8 I would hurry to my place of shelter,
far from the tempest and storm.[h]"

9 Confuse the wicked, O Lord, confound their speech,
for I see violence and strife[i] in the city.
10 Day and night they prowl about on its walls;
malice and abuse are within it.
11 Destructive forces[j] are at work in the city;
threats and lies[k] never leave its streets.

12 If an enemy were insulting me,
I could endure it;
if a foe were raising himself against me,
I could hide from him.
13 But it is you, a man like myself,
my companion, my close friend,[l]
14 with whom I once enjoyed sweet fellowship
as we walked with the throng at the house of God.[m]

15 Let death take my enemies by surprise;[n]
let them go down alive to the grave,[b][o]
for evil finds lodging among them.

54:6 [w]Ps 50:14 [x]Ps 52:9
54:7 [y]Ps 34:6 [z]Ps 59:10
55:1 [a]Ps 27:9; 61:1
55:2 [b]Ps 66:19 [c]Ps 77:3; Isa 38:14
55:3 [d]2Sa 16:6-8; Ps 17:9 [e]Ps 71:11
55:4 [f]Ps 116:3
55:5 [g]Job 21:6; Ps 119:120
55:8 [h]Isa 4:6
55:9 [i]Jer 6:7
55:11 [j]Ps 5:9 [k]Ps 10:7
55:13 [l]2Sa 15:12; Ps 41:9
55:14 [m]Ps 42:4
55:15 [n]Ps 64:7 [o]Nu 16:30, 33

[a] Title: Probably a literary or musical term [b] *15* Hebrew *Sheol*

54:6–7 I will sacrifice. A vow to sacrifice to the Lord if David should be delivered from trouble. See note on 22:22. **freewill offering.** This differs from the thanksgiving offering in that David was not giving thanks for a specific act of deliverance.

Psalm 55 *Introduction.* As with so many laments, Psalm 55 bemoaned an enemy attack. Atypical, however, is the fact that it is a lament over betrayal by a friend who had participated with David in worshiping the Lord. The psalm, while descending into the pits of despair, turns at the end toward the Lord with hope. It anticipated the sufferings of Christ, who would be betrayed by a disciple from within his inner circle (Mt 26:47–56).

55:3 enemy. As in many psalms the enemy remained faceless. Because the psalm was composed for corporate worship, David spoke of his adversaries and the circumstances only in general terms.

55:6 I would fly away. David knew how to deal with enemies, but being betrayed by his friend was almost too much to bear. He felt the urge to escape the source of his distress but found himself unable to do so.

55:9 confound their speech. An allusion to the judgment the Lord had brought upon the wicked generation who had constructed the tower of Babel (Ge 11:1–9). David was asking the Lord to thwart the plans of his enemies.

55:10 prowl about on its walls. The lawless were at large and active on the walls, which constituted the city's primary security. The implication is that the city was defenseless against them.

55:12–15 See *WLC* 151.

55:12 If an enemy. While it is unpleasant to be treated poorly by an enemy, it is understandable. David knew that his adversaries were after his blood.

55:13 a man like myself, my companion, my close friend. Notice the progression. The terms become increasingly intimate.

55:14 enjoyed sweet fellowship. The most stinging reality was that this former close friend had been a fellow worshiper with Da-

[16] But I call to God,
and the LORD saves me.
[17] Evening,[p] morning[q] and noon
I cry out in distress,
and he hears my voice.
[18] He ransoms me unharmed
from the battle waged against me,
even though many oppose me.
[19] God, who is enthroned forever,[r]
will hear[s] them and afflict them— *Selah*
men who never change their ways
and have no fear of God.

[20] My companion attacks his friends;[t]
he violates his covenant.[u]
[21] His speech is smooth as butter,
yet war is in his heart;
his words are more soothing than oil,[v]
yet they are drawn swords.[w]

[22] Cast your cares on the LORD
and he will sustain you;[x]
he will never let the righteous fall.[y]
[23] But you, O God, will bring down the wicked
into the pit[z] of corruption;
bloodthirsty and deceitful men[a]
will not live out half their days.[b]

But as for me, I trust in you.[c]

Psalm 56

For the director of music. To ˪the tune of˩ "A Dove on Distant Oaks." Of David. A *miktam*.[a] When the Philistines had seized him in Gath.

[1] Be merciful to me, O God, for men hotly pursue me;[d]
all day long they press their attack.
[2] My slanderers pursue me all day long;[e]
many are attacking me in their pride.[f]

[3] When I am afraid,[g]
I will trust in you.
[4] In God, whose word I praise,
in God I trust; I will not be afraid.
What can mortal man do to me?[h]

[5] All day long they twist my words;[i]

55:17 [p]Ps 141:2; Ac 3:1 [q]Ps 5:3
55:19 [r]Dt 33:27 [s]Ps 78:59
55:20 [t]Ps 7:4 [u]Ps 89:34
55:21 [v]Pr 5:3 [w]Ps 28:3; Ps 57:4, 59:7
55:22 [x]Ps 37:5; Mt 6:25-34; 1Pe 5:7 [y]Ps 37:24
55:23 [z]Ps 73:18 [a]Ps 5:6 [b]Job 15:32; Pr 10:27 [c]Ps 25:2
56:1 [d]Ps 57:1-3
56:2 [e]Ps 57:3 [f]Ps 35:1
56:3 [g]Ps 55:4-5
56:4 [h]Ps 118:6; Heb 13:6
56:5 [i]Ps 41:7

[a] Title: Probably a literary or musical term

vid. Betrayal can take place even within the house of God. This perfidy by a close friend hurt more than that of a known enemy.
55:15 alive to the grave. David's anger was intense. He went so far as to express a wish that his enemies be buried alive.
55:16 I call to God. David was confident that the Lord would hear and answer his prayer.
55:18 the battle. Most likely a metaphor for the struggles the psalmist experienced with the enemies and even with the friends who surrounded him.
55:19 enthroned forever. Because God could never be unseated from his heavenly throne, and because David was God's vice-regent on Earth, David felt confident that he himself would not be dethroned. God would hear David's prayers from his heavenly throne room and would come to David's aid.
55:20 his covenant. In ancient times there were covenants between people as well as between God and his people (Ge 21:27). The psalmist described the willful breaking of a formal agreement between friends.
55:21 smooth as butter . . . more soothing than oil. Descriptions of hypocrisy and deceit.
55:22 he will never let the righteous fall. The righteous will not always be happy and prosperous, but God will not leave them in a fallen position forever. He will vindicate them in the end. See *HC* 26,28,125.
55:23 the pit of corruption. The grave.
Psalm 56 *Introduction.* Psalm 56 is a lament by David regarding a situation during which he was in distress and pressed by his enemies. Throughout the psalm he made known his underlying confidence in God's ability to save him.

Title. It is difficult to fit this title into David's life as it is known from the historical books. The closest parallel is the time when David feigned madness in order to escape the king of Gath (1Sa 21:10–15).
56:1 hotly pursue me. The verb may also be translated "pant after me," "snap at me" or even "hound me." The image is of the enemies as ruthless animals who hunted David.
56:4 mortal man. Literally, "flesh." David knew that God, the all-powerful, was on his side. The enemy, though he appeared strong, could do nothing in comparison with God.
56:5 See *WLC* 145.

they are always plotting to harm me.

56:6 [j]Ps 59:3 [k]Ps 71:10

6 They conspire,[j] they lurk,
they watch my steps,
eager to take my life.[k]

56:7 [l]Ps 36:12; 55:23

7 On no account let them escape;
in your anger, O God, bring down the nations.[l]

56:8 [m]Mal 3:16

8 Record my lament;
list my tears on your scroll[a]—
are they not in your record?[m]

56:9 [n]Ps 9:3 [o]Ps 102:2 [p]Ro 8:31

9 Then my enemies will turn back[n]
when I call for help.[o]
By this I will know that God is for me.[p]
10 In God, whose word I praise,
in the LORD, whose word I praise—
11 in God I trust; I will not be afraid.
What can man do to me?

56:12 [q]Ps 50:14

12 I am under vows[q] to you, O God;
I will present my thank offerings to you.

56:13 [r]Ps 116:8 [s]Job 33:30

13 For you have delivered me[b] from death[r]
and my feet from stumbling,
that I may walk before God
in the light of life.[c][s]

Psalm 57

For the director of music. ⌊To the tune of⌋ "Do Not Destroy."
Of David. A *miktam.*[d] When he had fled from Saul into the cave.

57:1 [t]Ps 2:12 [u]Ps 17:8 [v]Isa 26:20

1 Have mercy on me, O God, have mercy on me,
for in you my soul takes refuge.[t]
I will take refuge in the shadow of your wings[u]
until the disaster has passed.[v]

57:2 [w]Ps 138:8

2 I cry out to God Most High,
to God, who fulfills ⌊his purpose⌋ for me.[w]

57:3 [x]Ps 18:9,16 [y]Ps 56:1 [z]Ps 40:11

3 He sends from heaven and saves me,[x]
rebuking those who hotly pursue me;[y] *Selah*
God sends his love and his faithfulness.[z]

57:4 [a]Ps 35:17 [b]Ps 55:21; Pr 30:14

4 I am in the midst of lions;[a]
I lie among ravenous beasts—
men whose teeth are spears and arrows,
whose tongues are sharp swords.[b]

57:5 [c]Ps 108:5

5 Be exalted, O God, above the heavens;
let your glory be over all the earth.[c]

[a] *8* Or / *put my tears in your wineskin* [b] *13* Or *my soul* [c] *13* Or *the land of the living* [d] Title: Probably a literary or musical term

56:7 bring down the nations. The enemies were apparently the foreign nations that surrounded Israel. The king's adversaries included the enemies of the nation.
56:8 Record. An appeal for God to hear, remember and respond. **my lament.** That is, this psalm.
56:9 God is for me. David reflected on God's covenant promises. Deuteronomy 28:7 is an example of a promise that God would scatter the enemies of his people.
56:12 thank offerings. David promised that after his prayer had been answered he would return to give thanks by offering sacrifices and singing thanksgiving songs (similar to 34). See note on 22:22.
56:13 you have delivered me from death. By saving him from the enemies so eager to destroy him.
Psalm 57 *Introduction.* Psalm 57 is a lament sung at a time when David was being pressed by vicious enemies and in which he called on the Lord for deliverance. The psalm ends with a particularly intense statement of confidence in the Lord. This concluding statement is similar in wording to the first five verses of Psalm 108.

Title. The historical title places the psalm's composition during the period after David had been anointed king but before he assumed the throne, specifically when he was hiding from Saul in a cave. Many scholars relate this psalm to the event recorded in 1 Samuel 24, but a closer parallel may be found in 1 Samuel 22:1–5, when David fled to the cave of Adullam.
57:1 in the shadow of your wings. God was David's only refuge in danger. The image of God as a mother bird protecting her young communicates God's compassion for his people. See note on 131:2.
57:2 who fulfills his purpose for me. A Hebrew phrase better rendered "who avenges me"; refers to God judging his people's enemies.
57:4 lions. Lions were numerous in the ancient Near East. This animal symbolized, among other traits, power and ruthlessness.
57:5 above the heavens. God is so great that not even the heavens can hold him (1Ki 8:27).

6 They spread a net for my feet—
I was bowed down[d] in distress.
They dug a pit[e] in my path—
but they have fallen into it themselves.[f] *Selah*

7 My heart is steadfast, O God,
my heart is steadfast;[g]
I will sing and make music.
8 Awake, my soul!
Awake, harp and lyre![h]
I will awaken the dawn.

9 I will praise you, O Lord, among the nations;
I will sing of you among the peoples.
10 For great is your love, reaching to the heavens;
your faithfulness reaches to the skies.[i]

11 Be exalted, O God, above the heavens;
let your glory be over all the earth.[j]

57:6 [d]Ps 145:14 [e]Ps 35:7 [f]Ps 7:15; Pr 28:10
57:7 [g]Ps 108:1
57:8 [h]Ps 16:9; 30:12; 150:3
57:10 [i]Ps 36:5; 103:11
57:11 [j]ver 5

Psalm 58

For the director of music. ⌊To the tune of⌋ "Do Not Destroy."
Of David. A *miktam*.[a]

1 Do you rulers indeed speak justly?[k]
Do you judge uprightly among men?
2 No, in your heart you devise injustice,
and your hands mete out violence on the earth.[l]
3 Even from birth the wicked go astray;
from the womb they are wayward and speak lies.
4 Their venom is like the venom of a snake,[m]
like that of a cobra that has stopped its ears,
5 that will not heed the tune of the charmer,
however skillful the enchanter may be.

6 Break the teeth in their mouths, O God;[n]
tear out, O LORD, the fangs of the lions![o]
7 Let them vanish like water that flows away;[p]
when they draw the bow, let their arrows be blunted.[q]
8 Like a slug melting away as it moves along,
like a stillborn child,[r] may they not see the sun.

9 Before your pots can feel ⌊the heat of⌋ the thorns[s]—
whether they be green or dry—the wicked will be swept away.[b][t]

58:1 [k]Ps 82:2
58:2 [l]Ps 94:20; Mal 3:15
58:4 [m]Ps 140:3; Ecc 10:11
58:6 [n]Ps 3:7 [o]Job 4:10
58:7 [p]Jos 7:5; Ps 112:10 [q]Ps 64:3
58:8 [r]Job 3:16
58:9 [s]Ps 118:12 [t]Pr 10:25

[a] Title: Probably a literary or musical term [b] 9 The meaning of the Hebrew for this verse is uncertain.

57:6 a net . . . a pit. The image is that of the enemy as a hunter who had set snares and traps for David. **have fallen into it themselves.** The principle that evil people find themselves caught by their own wicked schemes is a theme that runs throughout the Psalms and the Prophets. See 7:14–16, 34:21, 35:8 and 37:15.
57:7 My heart is steadfast. That is, David was so firmly set on praising the Lord that nothing could divert him from offering up his hymn of adoration.
57:8 I will awaken the dawn. That is, he would praise the Lord through the night with his songs, and as dawn arose, he would awaken it (rather than the dawn awakening him).
57:9 among the nations. David realized that the Lord is more than just the God of Israel. He is the King of the Gentile nations, too, so David would witness to his great deeds throughout the world.
57:10 your love. Specifically the love God has for his covenant people.
Psalm 58 *Introduction.* Psalms of lament often contain sections of imprecations—curses—directed against the evil and the unjust. The curse against the enemy dominates this short lament. The objects of David's scorn in this instance were unjust judges. Early Christian tradition associated this psalm with the actions of the high priest and the Sanhedrin as they condemned Jesus (Mt 26:57–68).
Title. Identical to Psalm 57 with respect to the historical title.
58:1 rulers. The word in Hebrew is difficult; it is generally used to mean "gods." In this case, though, it referred to human judges who acted as though they thought themselves "gods," especially by their life and death decisions (cf. Ps 82). As in Psalm 82, the problem was corrupt judges. Just judges are to judge uprightly, "acquitting the innocent and condemning the guilty" (Dt 25:1).
58:3 from birth the wicked go astray. David knew that, in some sense, this was also true of himself (51:5), just as it is true of all people. Men and women are born in sin with a desire to rebel against God. This truth is often expressed under the heading of the doctrine of original sin. However, David meant more than this here. These judges were particularly evil, and he spoke of them as committing atrocious sins in their infancy that, in reality, only depraved adults could conceive.
58:4–5 venom of a snake. David likened the wicked rulers to snakes. The serpent's role in the story of the fall (Ge 3) nuances the image. The words of these immoral judges destroyed like the venom of the snake, and they turned a deaf ear to righteous argument and against divine judgments addressed to them.
58:6 Break the teeth. David invoked a series of curses against the wicked rulers, asking the Lord to bring their evil schemes to a violent end.
58:7 let their arrows be blunted. Thwart their evil schemes.
58:9 the wicked will be swept away. As the NIV text note men-

10 The righteous will be glad when they are avenged,[u]
when they bathe their feet in the blood of the wicked.[v]
11 Then men will say,
"Surely the righteous still are rewarded;
surely there is a God who judges the earth."[w]

Psalm 59

For the director of music. ⌊To the tune of⌋ "Do Not Destroy."
Of David. A *miktam*.[a] When Saul had sent men to watch
David's house in order to kill him.

1 Deliver me from my enemies, O God;[x]
protect me from those who rise up against me.
2 Deliver me from evildoers
and save me from bloodthirsty men.[y]

3 See how they lie in wait for me!
Fierce men conspire[z] against me
for no offense or sin of mine, O LORD.
4 I have done no wrong, yet they are ready to attack me.[a]
Arise to help me; look on my plight!
5 O LORD God Almighty, the God of Israel,
rouse yourself to punish all the nations;
show no mercy to wicked traitors.[b] *Selah*

6 They return at evening,
snarling like dogs,[c]
and prowl about the city.
7 See what they spew from their mouths—
they spew out swords[d] from their lips,
and they say, "Who can hear us?"[e]
8 But you, O LORD, laugh at them;[f]
you scoff at all those nations.[g]

9 O my Strength, I watch for you;
you, O God, are my fortress,[h] 10 my loving God.

God will go before me
and will let me gloat over those who slander me.
11 But do not kill them, O Lord our shield,[b][i]
or my people will forget.[j]
In your might make them wander about,
and bring them down.[k]

58:10 [u]Ps 64:10; 91:8 [v]Ps 68:23
58:11 [w]Ps 9:8; 18:20
59:1 [x]Ps 143:9
59:2 [y]Ps 139:19
59:3 [z]Ps 56:6
59:4 [a]Ps 35:19,23
59:5 [b]Jer 18:23
59:6 [c]ver 14
59:7 [d]Ps 57:4 [e]Ps 10:11
59:8 [f]Ps 37:13; Pr 1:26 [g]Ps 2:4
59:9 [h]Ps 9:9; 62:2
59:11 [i]Ps 84:9 [j]Dt 4:9 [k]Ps 106:27

[a] Title: Probably a literary or musical term [b] *11* Or *sovereign*

tions, the exact wording of this verse is difficult, but the basic meaning is clear: God will suddenly judge the wicked.

58:10 The righteous will be glad. The destruction of the enemies of God's righteous people is a covenant blessing (Lev 26:7–8). As such, it is to be received from God with joy. Believers do feel a tension between this fact and the call to love our enemies (Mt 5:44; Lk 6:27,35). Nevertheless, believers rightly rejoice in the security and peace they receive when their enemies are destroyed, and they are gladdened that justice is served and God's holiness honored.

58:11 the righteous still are rewarded. When the wicked prosper and/or the righteous suffer (see Job), the faith of the righteous is sometimes shaken because the covenant promises provide for curses on the wicked and blessings for the righteous (e.g. Lev 26; Dt 28). When the wicked fall under judgment, this confirms the covenant and vindicates God's justice.

Psalm 59 *Introduction.* In this lament an individual called on God to rescue him from the enemies who sought to harm him. He called down imprecations (curses) against them and their plots.

Title. The historical title relates the psalm to David's life, specifically to the period before he had assumed the throne. Saul sent men to David's house to kill him, but David's wife Michal, who was also Saul's daughter, lowered her husband from a window and he escaped (1Sa 19:11–17).

59:3 for no offense or sin of mine. David was not claiming to be without sin but asserting that his enemy, Saul, had no cause to seek his life. David had done nothing to antagonize Saul. See Psalm 26.

59:4 Arise. See note on 3:7. This plea is common in the Psalter in situations in which the psalmist wanted the Lord to come as a warrior to protect him.

59:5 LORD God Almighty. Literally, "God of Hosts." See note on 1 Samuel 1:3. God is a warrior with heavenly armies at his command. **nations . . . wicked traitors.** The enemies were both from the nations outside of Israel and from within Israel's borders.

59:6 like dogs. The enemies were like a pack of dogs that roamed the streets seeking violence against its inhabitants. Dogs were not held in high esteem in Israel.

59:7 "Who can hear us?" The enemy didn't take God seriously.

59:9 I watch for you. David's eyes were on the Lord, not on the enemy. Knowing God as he did, he fully expected him to act on his behalf.

59:10 God will go before me. God would lead the way in the fight against the enemy, as in the time of the conquest when the ark of the covenant, symbolic of God's mighty presence, had led Israel into the promised land. **will let me gloat.** Right now the enemy gloated over David, but David rightly expected a reversal.

59:11 do not kill them. David was not motivated by compassion—his enemies were more useful to him alive. As they suffered, they would become an example to the rest of Israel that evil doesn't pay.

[12] For the sins of their mouths,[l]
for the words of their lips,[m]
let them be caught in their pride.[n]
For the curses and lies they utter,
[13] consume them in wrath,
consume them till they are no more.[o]
Then it will be known to the ends of the earth
that God rules over Jacob.[p] *Selah*

[14] They return at evening,
snarling like dogs,
and prowl about the city.
[15] They wander about for food[q]
and howl if not satisfied.
[16] But I will sing of your strength,[r]
in the morning[s] I will sing of your love;[t]
for you are my fortress,
my refuge in times of trouble.[u]

[17] O my Strength, I sing praise to you;
you, O God, are my fortress, my loving God.

59:12 [l]Ps 10:7 [m]Pr 12:13 [n]Zep 3:11
59:13 [o]Ps 104:35 [p]Ps 83:18
59:15 [q]Job 15:23
59:16 [r]Ps 21:13 [s]Ps 88:13 [t]Ps 101:1 [u]Ps 46:1

Psalm 60

For the director of music. To ⌞the tune of⌟ "The Lily of the Covenant." A *miktam*[a] of David. For teaching. When he fought Aram Naharaim[b] and Aram Zobah,[c] and when Joab returned and struck down twelve thousand Edomites in the Valley of Salt.

[1] You have rejected us,[v] O God, and burst forth upon us;
you have been angry[w]—now restore us![x]
[2] You have shaken the land[y] and torn it open;
mend its fractures,[z] for it is quaking.
[3] You have shown your people desperate times;[a]
you have given us wine that makes us stagger.[b]
[4] But for those who fear you, you have raised a banner
to be unfurled against the bow. *Selah*
[5] Save us and help us with your right hand,[c]
that those you love[d] may be delivered.
[6] God has spoken from his sanctuary:
"In triumph I will parcel out Shechem[e]
and measure off the Valley of Succoth.

60:1 [v]2Sa 5:20; Ps 44:9 [w]Ps 79:5 [x]Ps 80:3
60:2 [y]Ps 18:7 [z]2Ch 7:14
60:3 [a]Ps 71:20 [b]Isa 51:17; Jer 25:16
60:5 [c]Ps 17:7; 108:6 [d]Ps 127:2
60:6 [e]Ge 12:6

[a] Title: Probably a literary or musical term [b] Title: That is, Arameans of Northwest Mesopotamia
[c] Title: That is, Arameans of central Syria

59:12 sins of their mouths. Words are powerful; they may either bring great blessing or tremendous harm to another. When they result in the latter, the speaker deserves a comparable punishment.
59:13 it will be known. The object of the curse against the enemy was that the glory of God's justice would be seen.
Psalm 60 *Introduction.* Psalm 60 marked the occasion of a military defeat. The psalmist lamented the situation and asked God why he had rejected his people. For the most part, the community voice dominates, and the psalm addresses God in the first-person plural. However, at the end of the psalm (v. 9) an individual voice is heard, presumably that of the king who represented the people.

Title. Psalm 60 bears the longest title of any psalm in the Psalter. The historical title reflects the events recorded in 2 Samuel 8 and 1 Chronicles 18. The historical books, however, reveal only the conclusion of the battles—victory. The title and the psalm itself suggest that David encountered some setbacks along the way to this positive outcome. There is also a discrepancy between the historical renditions and the psalm in terms of the number of Edomites killed in the Valley of Salt. The most likely explanation is a textual error. Also note that while the title associates Joab with this victory, 2 Samuel 8:13 cites David and 1 Chronicles 18:12 Abishai. David was the king and Joab and Abishai high commanders in his army, so all three could be credited with the victory.

60:1 You have rejected us. When God rejected his people, he abandoned them to the power of their enemies. It was only in the light of God's presence that the people of Israel had any reason for confidence.
60:2 mend its fractures. The Israelites had been defeated because God had abandoned them to the enemy in battle. Military victory could only be achieved with God's help, so David appealed to him for military aid.
60:3 wine that makes us stagger. This image was employed frequently in the prophets. The cup that made a nation stagger was the cup of judgment (cf. Jer 25:15–38; Na 3:11). Jesus drank the cup of God's wrath to the dregs (bottom) on behalf of his people (cf. Mt 26:39 and parallels).
60:4 you have raised a banner. This verse is difficult to translate but appears to be a token of hope for the faithful. The sense is that God has given his people protection from the weapons of the enemy.
60:6–7 God has spoken from his sanctuary. The divine oracle was probably spoken through a prophet associated with one of Israel's holy sites (e.g. the tabernacle, the tent David pitched to house the ark, the temple that was soon to be built). The gist of his message was that victory would be forthcoming—an oracle borne out by the report in 2 Samuel 8. **I will parcel out.** These two

60:7 [f]Jos 13:31 [g]Dt 33:17 [h]Ge 49:10
60:8 [i]2Sa 8:1
60:10 [j]Jos 7:12; Ps 44:9; 108:11
60:11 [k]Ps 146:3
60:12 [l]Nu 24:18; Ps 44:5
61:1 [m]Ps 64:1 [n]Ps 86:6
61:2 [o]Ps 77:3 [p]Ps 18:2
61:3 [q]Ps 62:7 [r]Pr 18:10
61:4 [s]Ps 23:6 [t]Ps 91:4
61:5 [u]Ps 56:12 [v]Ps 86:11
61:6 [w]Ps 21:4
61:7 [x]Ps 41:12 [y]Ps 40:11
61:8 [z]Ps 65:1; 71:22

7 Gilead[f] is mine, and Manasseh is mine;
Ephraim is my helmet,
Judah[g] my scepter.[h]
8 Moab is my washbasin,
upon Edom I toss my sandal;
over Philistia I shout in triumph.[i]"

9 Who will bring me to the fortified city?
Who will lead me to Edom?
10 Is it not you, O God, you who have rejected us
and no longer go out with our armies?[j]
11 Give us aid against the enemy,
for the help of man is worthless.[k]
12 With God we will gain the victory,
and he will trample down our enemies.[l]

Psalm 61

For the director of music. With stringed instruments.
Of David.

1 Hear my cry, O God;[m]
listen to my prayer.[n]

2 From the ends of the earth I call to you,
I call as my heart grows faint;[o]
lead me to the rock[p] that is higher than I.
3 For you have been my refuge,[q]
a strong tower against the foe.[r]

4 I long to dwell[s] in your tent forever
and take refuge in the shelter of your wings.[t] *Selah*
5 For you have heard my vows,[u] O God;
you have given me the heritage of those who fear your
name.[v]
6 Increase the days of the king's life,
his years for many generations.[w]
7 May he be enthroned in God's presence forever;[x]
appoint your love and faithfulness to protect him.[y]

8 Then will I ever sing praise to your name[z]
and fulfill my vows day after day.

---

verses exult in the inheritance of the promised land. **Shechem . . . Succoth.** These names are associated with the Jacob account in Genesis 33:17–20 as the first two places Jacob stopped after returning from his reconciliation to Esau. They were, respectively, on the eastern and western sides of the Jordan. **Gilead . . . Manasseh.** Both these areas were located at least in part in the region of Transjordan. **Ephraim . . . Judah.** The two most powerful tribes in Israel. They were frequently rivals, but here they were united in God's army. **scepter.** See Genesis 49:10.

60:8 Moab . . . Edom . . . Philistia. David turned to the small, non-Israelite states that surrounded God's people. Throughout much of Old Testament history these nations vexed God's people, but here God exulted in his power and authority over them. **I toss my sandal.** A gesture of contempt.

60:9 me. Most likely the king, speaking on behalf of the nation.

60:12 we will gain the victory. David confessed that it was only through God's power that Israel would triumph. This attitude was proper, for it was at the heart of the concept of holy war in the Old Testament.

Psalm 61 *Introduction.* This brief lament petitions God for protection.

Title. See "Introduction: Authorship and Titles: *Musical Notations.*"

61:1 Hear my cry. David began with a typical call on the Lord to attend to his prayer.

61:2 From the ends of the earth. At a distance from the sanctuary in Jerusalem. David knew that even though he was far from God's holy place, the Lord could hear his prayer. **rock.** He had come to the critical recognition that he did not have the strength to rescue himself; he could only turn to God in trust.

61:3 you have been my refuge. God had protected David in the past against his enemies. **against the foe.** This phrase implies that David was not only physically distant from the sanctuary but engaged in a military action for which he needed God's help.

61:4 your tent. Perhaps originally a reference to the tabernacle. **in the shelter of your wings.** A metaphor of a mother bird that protects her children. Feminine imagery is often used to convey God's compassion; see note on Psalm 131:2.

61:5 my vows. In the process of petitioning the Lord, David made promises of obedience to God. Sometimes those vows were in the form of promised sacrifices. See note on 22:22; see 1 Samuel 1:11. **heritage.** As a member of God's community, David received the promises of the covenant. Among other things, these included the land of Israel and the pledge that God would protect him.

61:6 the king's life. The king was the center of the Israelite community. A long life for the king implied stability for the whole society. More importantly, the royal office had theological implications (see theological article "Human Kingship" at 1Sa 8). The human king reflected the glory of the divine King and anticipated Jesus Christ, the son of David, who sits enthroned forever.

61:7 enthroned . . . forever. Jesus Christ, David's greater son, fulfilled this verse beyond the expectation of the psalmist. **love.** More specifically, covenant loving-kindness.

61:8 See *WCF* 22.5.

Psalm 62

For the director of music. For Jeduthun. A psalm of David.

1 My soul finds rest[a] in God alone; — 62:1 [a]Ps 33:20
my salvation comes from him.
2 He alone is my rock[b] and my salvation; — 62:2 [b]Ps 89:26
he is my fortress, I will never be shaken.

3 How long will you assault a man?
Would all of you throw him down—
this leaning wall,[c] this tottering fence? — 62:3 [c]Isa 30:13
4 They fully intend to topple him
from his lofty place;
they take delight in lies.
With their mouths they bless,
but in their hearts they curse.[d] *Selah* — 62:4 [d]Ps 28:3

5 Find rest, O my soul, in God alone;
my hope comes from him.
6 He alone is my rock and my salvation;
he is my fortress, I will not be shaken.
7 My salvation and my honor depend on God[a];
he is my mighty rock, my refuge.[e] — 62:7 [e]Ps 46:1; 85:9; Jer 3:23
8 Trust in him at all times, O people;
pour out your hearts to him,[f] — 62:8 [f]1Sa 1:15; Ps 42:4; La 2:19
for God is our refuge. *Selah*

9 Lowborn men are but a breath,[g] — 62:9 [g]Ps 39:5,11
the highborn are but a lie; — [h]Isa 40:15
if weighed on a balance,[h] they are nothing;
together they are only a breath.
10 Do not trust in extortion — 62:10 [i]Isa 61:8
or take pride in stolen goods;[i] — [j]Job 31:25; 1Ti 6:6-10
though your riches increase,
do not set your heart on them.[j]

11 One thing God has spoken,
two things have I heard:
that you, O God, are strong,
12 and that you, O Lord, are loving.
Surely you will reward each person — 62:12 [k]Job 34:11; Mt 16:27
according to what he has done.[k]

Psalm 63

A psalm of David. When he was in the Desert of Judah.

1 O God, you are my God,
earnestly I seek you;

[a] 7 Or / *God Most High is my salvation and my honor*

Psalm 62 *Introduction.* Psalm 62 speaks calmly of trust in God, contrasting the confidence one can have in God with human unreliability. While God protects the needy, malevolent people seek their destruction. David composed this psalm from the perspective of one under attack (vv. 3–4). See *HC* 125.

62:1 finds rest. Literally, "is silent." David knew that true contentment can be found only in a relationship with God.

62:2 my rock . . . my fortress. Images of God's protection from the dangers of life.

62:3 this leaning wall, this tottering fence. The modern idiom is that of kicking a man when he's down. Evil men and women take advantage of the hurting and needy of the world.

62:4 they bless. The wicked added hypocrisy to violence.

62:5 my hope. For relief from the enemy and for salvation.

62:8 O people. The psalmist addressed the faithful in the congregation and encouraged them to put their trust in God alone. See *WCF* 21.1; *WLC* 178; *WSC* 98; *HC* 117.

62:9 breath . . . breath. The word may be variously translated. It is the most characteristic word in the Teacher's speech in Ecclesiastes, where it is often translated "meaningless." David's point was that men and women are insignificant in and of themselves. He took comfort in this; his persecutors in reality were unimportant. See *BC* 7.

62:10 though your riches increase. Other psalms grapple with the problem of wicked people prospering through evil means (e.g., Ps 73). In this psalm David depicted such riches as transitory. The wicked may grow wealthy, but their ill-gotten gain will do them no good in the end. See *WLC* 142.

62:11 you, O God, are strong. God is mighty in his ability to accomplish his desired ends both in the world and in human lives. He was fully able to save David from his enemies.

62:12 you, O Lord, are loving. The particular Hebrew word for "love" connects God's affection with his covenant. Thus, God was not only able to save David but desired to do so. **reward.** The psalmist spoke from a long-range perspective, since in the setting of the psalm he was suffering at the hands of the wicked. The New

my soul thirsts for you,[l]
my body longs for you,
in a dry and weary land
where there is no water.

[2] I have seen you in the sanctuary[m]
and beheld your power and your glory.
[3] Because your love is better than life,[n]
my lips will glorify you.
[4] I will praise you as long as I live,[o]
and in your name I will lift up my hands.[p]
[5] My soul will be satisfied as with the richest of foods;[q]
with singing lips my mouth will praise you.

[6] On my bed I remember you;
I think of you through the watches of the night.[r]
[7] Because you are my help,[s]
I sing in the shadow of your wings.
[8] My soul clings to you;
your right hand upholds me.[t]

[9] They who seek my life will be destroyed;[u]
they will go down to the depths of the earth.[v]
[10] They will be given over to the sword
and become food for jackals.

[11] But the king will rejoice in God;
all who swear by God's name will praise him,[w]
while the mouths of liars will be silenced.

Psalm 64

For the director of music. A psalm of David.

[1] Hear me, O God, as I voice my complaint;[x]
protect my life from the threat of the enemy.[y]
[2] Hide me from the conspiracy of the wicked,[z]
from that noisy crowd of evildoers.

[3] They sharpen their tongues like swords
and aim their words like deadly arrows.[a]
[4] They shoot from ambush at the innocent man;[b]
they shoot at him suddenly, without fear.[c]

63:1 [l]Ps 42:2; 84:2
63:2 [m]Ps 27:4
63:3 [n]Ps 69:16
63:4 [o]Ps 104:33 [p]Ps 28:2
63:5 [q]Ps 36:8
63:6 [r]Ps 42:8
63:7 [s]Ps 27:9
63:8 [t]Ps 18:35
63:9 [u]Ps 40:14 [v]Ps 55:15
63:11 [w]Dt 6:13; Ps 21:1; Isa 45:23
64:1 [x]Ps 55:2 [y]Ps 140:1
64:2 [z]Ps 56:6; 59:2
64:3 [a]Ps 58:7
64:4 [b]Ps 11:2 [c]Ps 55:19

Testament viewpoint is that many injustices in the present life will not be redressed until Jesus Christ returns.

Psalm 63 *Introduction.* Psalm 63 beautifully expresses quiet confidence in God's ability to protect the psalmist. While David was in distress, he praised God, knowing that he was safe in God's hand.

Title. The historical title locates the setting of the psalm in the desert of Judah.

63:1 thirsts for you. Compare Psalm 42:1. **my body.** The Psalms permit no false spiritualization. The whole person, not just some nonphysical aspect of the individual, yearned for God (see theological article "Body and Soul in the Bible" at Ge 2). **dry and weary land.** As the title indicates, the reference may originally be to the actual setting of the poem. However, it also extends the image of spiritual desire as physical thirst.

63:2 I have seen you. David recalled his former visits to the sanctuary in Jerusalem, the place God chose to bless with His special presence (see theological article "The Presence of God" at 1Ki 8).

63:3 your love. Specifically, covenant loving-kindness, the love God shows his people in the context of the covenant.

63:4–5 See *WLC* 174.

63:4 I will lift up my hands. Toward heaven in prayer.

63:5 will be satisfied. Only in praise to God, in intimate communion with him, will David feel spiritually contented.

63:6 On my bed. As David meditated on the Lord in wakeful hours of the night, he began to feel close to him, even though he was so far from the sanctuary. **watches of the night.** Those times when David was most vulnerable to anxiety and attack. See *WLC* 104.

63:7 shadow of your wings. God is envisioned as a mother bird that protects her young, an apt metaphor for a psalm of confidence. See note on 57:1.

63:8 My soul clings to you. Though far removed from the sanctuary, the place where he had experienced God's presence, David still experienced intimate communion with his Lord. His clinging to the Lord rested in his confidence that God would continue to uphold him. Clinging to God means finding in him one's only hope (cf. Dt 10:20; 11:22).

63:9 seek my life. His life was in danger—the first explicit indication in the poem of distress.

63:11 all who swear by God's name will praise him. God's justice will win out. Those who love God will continue to praise him, while the wicked will be stifled.

Psalm 64 *Introduction.* This lament begins by speaking about the hostility and injustice of the enemy's attacks. However, God reversed the situation by shooting his "arrows" (v. 7) at the wicked. Accordingly, the psalm ends on notes of confidence and praise.

64:1 the threat of the enemy. The psalmist turned to the Lord in prayer because of the attacks of an enemy. The enemy was unnamed; no specific historical situation has been identified with the writing of Psalm 61.

64:2 conspiracy of the wicked. His enemies secretly plotted together against the psalmist.

64:3 like swords . . . like deadly arrows. The Bible consistently teaches that words are powerful and can be used for either good (Pr 25:15) or evil (Pr 12:18; 25:18).

5 They encourage each other in evil plans,
they talk about hiding their snares;
they say, "Who will see them[a]?"[d]
6 They plot injustice and say,
"We have devised a perfect plan!"
Surely the mind and heart of man are cunning.

7 But God will shoot them with arrows;
suddenly they will be struck down.
8 He will turn their own tongues against them[e]
and bring them to ruin;
all who see them will shake their heads[f] in scorn.

9 All mankind will fear;
they will proclaim the works of God
and ponder what he has done.[g]
10 Let the righteous rejoice in the LORD
and take refuge in him;[h]
let all the upright in heart praise him![i]

64:5 [d]Ps 10:11
64:8 [e]Ps 9:3; Pr 18:7 [f]Ps 22:7
64:9 [g]Jer 51:10
64:10 [h]Ps 25:20 [i]Ps 32:11

Psalm 65

For the director of music. A psalm of David. A song.

1 Praise awaits[b] you, O God, in Zion;
to you our vows will be fulfilled.[j]
2 O you who hear prayer,
to you all men will come.[k]
3 When we were overwhelmed by sins,[l]
you forgave[c] our transgressions.[m]
4 Blessed are those you choose[n]
and bring near to live in your courts!
We are filled with the good things of your house,[o]
of your holy temple.

5 You answer us with awesome deeds of righteousness,
O God our Savior,[p]
the hope of all the ends of the earth
and of the farthest seas,[q]
6 who formed the mountains by your power,
having armed yourself with strength,[r]
7 who stilled the roaring of the seas,[s]

65:1 [j]Ps 116:18
65:2 [k]Isa 66:23
65:3 [l]Ps 38:4 [m]Heb 9:14
65:4 [n]Ps 4:3; 33:12 [o]Ps 36:8
65:5 [p]Ps 85:4 [q]Ps 107:23
65:6 [r]Ps 93:1
65:7 [s]Mt 8:26

[a] 5 Or *us* [b] 1 Or *befits*; the meaning of the Hebrew for this word is uncertain. [c] 3 Or *made atonement for*

64:5 "Who will see them?" They did not fear the psalmist or other people, and by their question they demonstrated that they did not fear God either. They wrongly believed that their acts went unnoticed, forgetting that there is a just God in heaven who watched their every move (Ps 2).
64:6 a perfect plan! To their other crimes, these evildoers added the sin of pride.
64:7 shoot them with arrows. Contrast with verse 4. Some of the same words are used to highlight the reversal. The wicked who tried to shoot the righteous were themselves struck by the arrows of God.
64:8 their own tongues. Contrast with verse 3. God reversed the effects of their slanderous and biting words. They spoke against the psalmist but ended up incriminating themselves.
64:9 All . . . will fear. The judgment of the wicked would startle the world, forcing people to reconsider their own acts in the light of God's dealings with these impious individuals. People would be more hesitant to sin once they realized that they were subject to the outcomes of their own wicked deeds.
Psalm 65 *Introduction.* Israel's agricultural economy depended on its variable rainfall. Psalm 65 celebrates God's provision of rain in answer to prayer. It is a hymn of thanksgiving to God, who cares for the physical well-being of his people.
65:1 in Zion. The location of the temple, the place God chose as his dwelling. Accordingly, it was the place toward which praise was to be directed. See notes on 2:6 and 50:2. **our vows.** When the Israelites brought petitions before the Lord, they frequently promised to offer sacrifices in response to answered prayer. Here the Lord obviously had answered their prayers (vv. 9–13), so they affirmed their willingness to carry through with their vows (see note on 22:22).
65:2 See *WCF* 21.3; *WLC* 179.
65:3 you forgave our transgressions. From the perspective of the sinners, there was no hope. God in his grace, however, forgave them, and this was a source of great joy to the psalmist.
65:4 Blessed. See Psalm 1:1. **those you choose.** God's free grace is the source of his blessing—in this case the highest blessing of all, the privilege of being near him.
65:5 awesome deeds. God is not a distant deity who has nothing to do with his creation. He answers prayer by intervening in history and specifically in the lives of his people. **ends of the earth.** In the theologies of the surrounding lands, it was thought that there were different gods for different localities (e.g., Marduk of Babylon and Baal of Ugarit). The psalmist knew that the Lord is not another god among many; in the entire universe, he is the only true God, the only One in whom people may appropriately place their hope. See *BC* 16.
65:6 the mountains. A symbol of stability and strength. That God had created them demonstrates his power and greatness. See note on 46:2. **having armed.** God was a warrior who conquered the enemies of Israel (Ex 15; Jos 5:13–15; Jdg 5).
65:7 the roaring of the seas. As mountains symbolize stability and power (see v. 6), so the seas represent chaos and evil (see notes

65:7 [t]Isa 17:12-13

the roaring of their waves,
and the turmoil of the nations.[t]
8 Those living far away fear your wonders;
where morning dawns and evening fades
you call forth songs of joy.

65:9 [u]Ps 68:9-10 [v]Ps 46:4; 104:14

9 You care for the land and water it;[u]
you enrich it abundantly.
The streams of God are filled with water
to provide the people with grain,[v]
for so you have ordained it.[a]
10 You drench its furrows
and level its ridges;
you soften it with showers
and bless its crops.
11 You crown the year with your bounty,
and your carts overflow with abundance.

65:12 [w]Job 28:26

12 The grasslands of the desert overflow;[w]
the hills are clothed with gladness.

65:13 [x]Ps 144:13 [y]Ps 72:16 [z]Ps 98:8; Isa 55:12

13 The meadows are covered with flocks[x]
and the valleys are mantled with grain;[y]
they shout for joy and sing.[z]

Psalm 66

For the director of music. A song. A psalm.

66:1 [a]Ps 100:1
66:2 [b]Ps 79:9
66:3 [c]Ps 65:5 [d]Ps 18:44
66:4 [e]Ps 22:27 [f]Ps 67:3

1 Shout with joy to God, all the earth![a]
2 Sing the glory of his name;[b]
make his praise glorious!
3 Say to God, "How awesome are your deeds![c]
So great is your power
that your enemies cringe[d] before you.
4 All the earth bows down[e] to you;
they sing praise[f] to you,
they sing praise to your name." *Selah*

66:5 [g]Ps 106:22
66:6 [h]Ex 14:22
66:7 [i]Ps 145:13 [j]Ps 11:4 [k]Ps 140:8

5 Come and see what God has done,
how awesome his works[g] in man's behalf!
6 He turned the sea into dry land,[h]
they passed through the waters on foot—
come, let us rejoice in him.
7 He rules forever[i] by his power,
his eyes watch[j] the nations—
let not the rebellious[k] rise up against him. *Selah*

66:8 [l]Ps 98:4
66:9 [m]Ps 121:3

8 Praise[l] our God, O peoples,
let the sound of his praise be heard;
9 he has preserved our lives
and kept our feet from slipping.[m]

[a] 9 Or *for that is how you prepare the land*

on 77:16,19; cf. 18:4; 29:3; 47:1–2; 69:1–2), particularly that characteristic of the surrounding nations that preyed on Israel (Da 7:1ff.).

65:8 Those living far away. A statement indicating the universal nature of God's domain. As far to the west or to the east as the psalmist could imagine, God's acts were known and praised. This verse takes on a deeper meaning now that Jesus Christ has come and broken down the dividing wall between Jews and Gentiles (Eph 2:11–14).

65:9 water it. God provided the rain that brought fertility to the land. He blessed his people with an abundant crop. To understand what a great blessing this was, compare 1 Kings 17–19, which took place during the time of Elijah, when God cursed his rebellious people by withholding rain.

Psalm 66 *Introduction.* Psalm 66 offers thanksgiving and adoration to the Lord. The first part of the psalm (vv. 1–12) praises God for his great acts on behalf of the nation, while the conclusion (vv. 13–20) offers an individual's thanks.

66:1 all the earth! The psalmist confessed that the Lord was God of all the universe, not just of Israel. His audience, however, was composed of the faithful in Israel.

66:3 awesome. Great and fearful. **cringe.** When God appeared as a warrior, the enemy rightly feared destruction (Jos 2:11).

66:5 Come and see. Compare 46:8. The psalmist invited the hearers to remember God's great acts in history.

66:6 sea . . . waters. There is a double reference in this verse. In the first phrase, the psalmist recalled the crossing of the Red Sea (Ex 14–15), and in the second he referred to the crossing of the Jordan 40 years later (Jos 3). These great acts demonstrated God's power not only to his people but also to all who had heard of those miracles.

66:9 preserved our lives. The psalmist's reference is unspecified. This may be another allusion to the exodus, but the testing that Israel had endured was probably a more recent event.

10 For you, O God, tested us;
you refined us like silver.[n]
11 You brought us into prison
and laid burdens[o] on our backs.
12 You let men ride over our heads;[p]
we went through fire and water,
but you brought us to a place of abundance.[q]

13 I will come to your temple with burnt offerings
and fulfill my vows[r] to you—
14 vows my lips promised and my mouth spoke
when I was in trouble.
15 I will sacrifice fat animals to you
and an offering of rams;
I will offer bulls and goats.[s] *Selah*

16 Come and listen,[t] all you who fear God;
let me tell[u] you what he has done for me.
17 I cried out to him with my mouth;
his praise was on my tongue.
18 If I had cherished sin in my heart,
the Lord would not have listened;[v]
19 but God has surely listened
and heard my voice[w] in prayer.
20 Praise be to God,
who has not rejected[x] my prayer
or withheld his love from me!

Psalm 67

For the director of music. With stringed instruments.
A psalm. A song.

1 May God be gracious to us and bless us
and make his face shine upon us,[y] *Selah*
2 that your ways may be known on earth,
your salvation[z] among all nations.[a]

3 May the peoples praise you, O God;
may all the peoples praise you.
4 May the nations be glad and sing for joy,
for you rule the peoples justly[b]
and guide the nations of the earth. *Selah*
5 May the peoples praise you, O God;
may all the peoples praise you.

6 Then the land will yield its harvest,[c]
and God, our God, will bless us.

66:10 [n]Ps 17:3; Isa 48:10; Zec 13:9; 1Pe 1:6-7
66:11 [o]La 1:13
66:12 [p]Isa 51:23 [q]Isa 43:2
66:13 [r]Ecc 5:4
66:15 [s]Nu 6:14; Ps 51:19
66:16 [t]Ps 34:11 [u]Ps 71:15, 24
66:18 [v]Job 36:21; Isa 1:15; Jas 4:3
66:19 [w]Ps 116:1-2
66:20 [x]Ps 22:24; 68:35
67:1 [y]Nu 6:24-26; Ps 4:6
67:2 [z]Isa 52:10 [a]Tit 2:11
67:4 [b]Ps 96:10-13
67:6 [c]Lev 26:4; Ps 85:12; Eze 34:27

66:10 tested us. God occasionally laid difficult decisions before his people to test whether they would obey him in spite of their suffering (Ex 15:25). **like silver.** When silver is refined it is purified; the dross (surface scum) is removed. When God had tested his people, the disobedient had been taken away, but the faithful remained.
66:11 into prison. The Lord had brought both the psalmist and the faithful through a period of affliction (the exact reference is unknown).
66:12 a place of abundance. A reference to a recent deliverance from distress, which may allude to the conquest.
66:13–14 See *WCF* 22.5,6.
66:13 fulfill my vows. The psalmist turned from corporate thanks to individual thanks. Apparently God had recently rescued him from some distress. While suffering, he had promised to worship God with sacrifices if God were to hear his prayer (see note on 22:22).
66:16 Come and listen. Fulfilling the vow often led to public praise, a visible witness to God's salvation.
66:18–20 See *WLC* 172.
Psalm 67 *Introduction.* This hymn calls down God's blessing on Israel and even on the whole world. The universal scope of Psalm 67 is striking, even in the book of Psalms where such far-reaching vision is not rare. The climax of the psalm is on the fertility of the land, although this is just a manifestation of the real blessing: God's presence. See *WLC* 191; *WSC* 103.
67:1–4 See *WLC* 190; *WSC* 101.
67:1 make his face shine upon us. The psalmist picked up the common priestly blessing found in Numbers 6:25, a summons to God to continue to be present with his people. The poet knew that he would be happy and prosperous only if God were to remain accessible.
67:2 all nations. The psalmist called on the Lord to bless not only Israel but the entire earth. Unlike the false gods of the surrounding nations, the Lord is God of all, not just of a particular country. His blessing would extend to the nations, however, only if they were to worship him (see v. 7).
67:3 all the peoples. The psalmist's desire to see peoples from many different nations praise the Lord began to be realized especially after the crucifixion and resurrection, when the "the dividing wall of hostility" had been removed (Eph 2:11–14).
67:4 you rule. God is King in heaven, and history proceeds by his powerful decrees. Even the nations that do not acknowledge him are under his almighty sway.
67:6 its harvest. This psalm was probably sung at one of the major agricultural festivals, most possibly the Feast of Ingathering (Ex

67:7 [d]Ps 33:8

[7] God will bless us,
and all the ends of the earth will fear him.[d]

Psalm 68

For the director of music. Of David. A psalm. A song.

68:1 [e]Nu 10:35; Isa 33:3
68:2 [f]Hos 13:3 [g]Isa 9:18; Mic 1:4
68:3 [h]Ps 32:11
68:4 [i]Ps 66:2 [j]Dt 33:26 [k]Ex 6:3; Ps 83:18
68:5 [l]Ps 10:14 [m]Dt 10:18 [n]Dt 26:15
68:6 [o]Ps 113:9 [p]Ac 12:6 [q]Ps 107:34
68:7 [r]Ex 13:21; Jdg 4:14
68:8 [s]Jdg 5:4 [t]Ex 19:16, 18
68:9 [u]Dt 11:11
68:10 [v]Ps 74:19

[1] May God arise, may his enemies be scattered;
may his foes flee[e] before him.
[2] As smoke[f] is blown away by the wind,
may you blow them away;
as wax melts[g] before the fire,
may the wicked perish before God.
[3] But may the righteous be glad
and rejoice[h] before God;
may they be happy and joyful.

[4] Sing to God, sing praise to his name,[i]
extol him who rides on the clouds[a][j]—
his name is the LORD[k]—
and rejoice before him.
[5] A father to the fatherless,[l] a defender of widows,[m]
is God in his holy dwelling.[n]
[6] God sets the lonely in families,[b][o]
he leads forth the prisoners[p] with singing;
but the rebellious live in a sun-scorched land.[q]

[7] When you went out[r] before your people, O God,
when you marched through the wasteland, *Selah*
[8] the earth shook,
the heavens poured down rain,[s]
before God, the One of Sinai,[t]
before God, the God of Israel.
[9] You gave abundant showers,[u] O God;
you refreshed your weary inheritance.
[10] Your people settled in it,
and from your bounty, O God, you provided[v] for the poor.

[11] The Lord announced the word,
and great was the company of those who proclaimed it:

[a] 4 Or / *prepare the way for him who rides through the deserts* [b] 6 Or *the desolate in a homeland*

23:14–17). The harvest, so crucial to life, was a powerful sign of God's presence with Israel.

67:7 all the ends of the earth will fear him. As Israel was blessed, the nations would observe God's power and change their attitude toward him to one of worship.

Psalm 68 *Introduction.* Psalm 68 is perhaps the most enigmatic in the second book. Its thoughts appear to be so disconnected that some have thought it a collection of first lines from other poems not found in the Psalter. While it is impossible to locate the historical setting of the narrative, there are clearly common themes and attitudes. Psalm 68 expresses a hymnlike mood of joy with frequent allusions to community worship. Also, the appearance of God as a warrior is at its center. God's victory over his enemies depicted in this psalm foreshadowed Jesus' victory over the forces of Satan at the time of his ascension (Eph 4:7–13).

68:1 May God arise. The psalm opens with a quotation of Numbers 10:35. This verse recalls the first words Moses spoke during the wilderness period each day Israel prepared to march. As he spoke, the ark of the covenant was raised in preparation for its role in leading the procession. The ark symbolized God's presence, specifically his attendance as a warrior who would vanquish Israel's enemies. See *WLC* 191; *WSC* 102.

68:2 smoke . . . wax. These two images called on God to deal with the enemy quickly and effortlessly.

68:3 rejoice. The destruction of the wicked brings joy to the oppressed righteous (see note on 58:10).

68:4 who rides on the clouds. God's riding astride the clouds is a recurring description in the Scriptures (Pss 18:7–15; 104:3; Da 7:13; Na 1:3). The clouds depict a war chariot that God rides into battle on behalf of the righteous. These passages provide background for our understanding of Jesus' ascending and descending on clouds (Mk 13:26; Rev 1:7). See *WLC* 112; *WSC* 54.

68:5 fatherless . . . widows. In the family-oriented society of ancient Israel, the widow and orphan were particularly vulnerable because they lacked the protection, provision and legal representation a patriarch would have afforded. God's law commanded the Israelites to care for such individuals (Ex 22:22; Dt 10:18). See also the book of Ruth. By attending to the needs of the orphan and the widow, God demonstrated his own concern for the helpless.

68:6 the lonely. Since the family was central to Israelite society, those outside its structure were alone and frequently needy. God sets these individuals within a family structure for their blessing. **prisoners.** The image is of captives rather than criminals. God aids the oppressed.

68:7 through the wasteland. The reference is to the 40 years of desert wandering. God went out before Israel, represented by the ark of the covenant (Nu 10:35).

68:8 the earth shook. A metaphoric representation of the military and political impact God has when he appears as a warrior for his people (Isa 24). **the One of Sinai.** The God before whom the earth shook at Sinai (Ex 19:18–19).

68:9 abundant showers. A particularly appreciated blessing in a land not known for its rainfall. Prolonged droughts inevitably had devastating effects (1Ki 17–19).

68:10 provided for the poor. God accomplished this in many ways. He had provided for the needy and oppressed Israelites coming out of Egypt, leading them to the land of Canaan. God's law and grace had also provided for the poor in later generations (Lev 25:25–28).

68:11 company. Or "host"; a military term for an army.

[12] "Kings and armies flee[w] in haste;
in the camps men divide the plunder.
[13] Even while you sleep among the campfires,[a][x]
the wings of ⌊my⌋ dove are sheathed with silver,
its feathers with shining gold."
[14] When the Almighty[b] scattered[y] the kings in the land,
it was like snow fallen on Zalmon.

[15] The mountains of Bashan are majestic mountains;
rugged are the mountains of Bashan.
[16] Why gaze in envy, O rugged mountains,
at the mountain where God chooses[z] to reign,
where the LORD himself will dwell forever?
[17] The chariots of God are tens of thousands
and thousands of thousands;[a]
the Lord ⌊has come⌋ from Sinai into his sanctuary.
[18] When you ascended on high,
you led captives[b] in your train;
you received gifts from men,[c]
even from[c] the rebellious—
that you,[d] O LORD God, might dwell there.
[19] Praise be to the Lord, to God our Savior,[d]
who daily bears our burdens.[e] *Selah*
[20] Our God is a God who saves;
from the Sovereign LORD comes escape from death.[f]
[21] Surely God will crush the heads[g] of his enemies,
the hairy crowns of those who go on in their sins.
[22] The Lord says, "I will bring them from Bashan;
I will bring them from the depths of the sea,[h]
[23] that you may plunge your feet in the blood of your foes,[i]
while the tongues of your dogs[j] have their share."

[24] Your procession has come into view, O God,
the procession of my God and King into the sanctuary.[k]
[25] In front are the singers, after them the musicians;
with them are the maidens playing tambourines.[l]
[26] Praise God in the great congregation;
praise the LORD in the assembly of Israel.[m]
[27] There is the little tribe[n] of Benjamin, leading them,
there the great throng of Judah's princes,
and there the princes of Zebulun and of Naphtali.

[28] Summon your power, O God[e];
show us your strength, O God, as you have done before.
[29] Because of your temple at Jerusalem

68:12 [w]Jos 10:16
68:13 [x]Ge 49:14
68:14 [y]Jos 10:10
68:16 [z]Dt 12:5
68:17 [a]Dt 33:2; Da 7:10
68:18 [b]Jdg 5:12 [c]Eph 4:8*
68:19 [d]Ps 65:5 [e]Ps 55:22
68:20 [f]Ps 56:13
68:21 [g]Ps 110:5; Hab 3:13
68:22 [h]Nu 21:33
68:23 [i]Ps 58:10 [j]1Ki 21:19
68:24 [k]Ps 63:2
68:25 [l]Jdg 11:34; 1Ch 13:8
68:26 [m]Ps 26:12; Isa 48:1
68:27 [n]1Sa 9:21

[a] *13* Or *saddlebags* [b] *14* Hebrew *Shaddai* [c] *18* Or *gifts for men, / even* [d] *18* Or *they* [e] *28* Many Hebrew manuscripts, Septuagint and Syriac; most Hebrew manuscripts *Your God has summoned power for you*

68:12 flee in haste. See Judges 5:30.

68:15–16 the mountain where God chooses to reign. Though the Bashan mountains were physically majestic, far more imposing than Zion, their spiritual significance paled in comparison with that of the mountain of God's dwelling.

68:17 chariots of God. God accompanied his heavenly army to battle (cf. 1Ki 6:8–23).

68:18 you led captives. God defeated his enemies and led them in the victory parade (cf. Eph 4:7–13). **received gifts.** In his quotation of this verse in Ephesians 4:7, Paul rendered this as "gave gifts." In a triumphant procession, the victor would both receive and distribute gifts. See *WLC* 53,191; *WSC* 102.

68:19 who daily bears our burdens. God cares for his people and is constantly in touch with their needs. This passage may be contrasted with Isaiah 26:1–4, in which the prophet decried the inability of the idols to care for their adherents.

68:20 a God who saves. The Lord commonly saved his obedient people from illness and death in battle. In Jesus Christ he also delivers them from death by granting eternal life.

68:22 from Bashan. Most likely a reference to the defeat of Og, king of Bashan, during the period before the Israelite conquest of the promised land (Dt 3). **from the depths of the sea.** God had delivered Israel from death at the Red Sea (Ex 14).

68:23 in the blood of your foes. See note on 58:10.

68:24 Your procession. After a victory that God had orchestrated, the triumphant army would return to the city of Jerusalem. The ark, symbolizing God's presence, would be at its head (see Ps 24). The troops would return it to the temple amid worshiping crowds.

68:26 See *HC* 103.

68:28 as you have done before. In the midst of a present crisis, the psalmist invoked the great acts of deliverance that God had performed in the past.

68:29 Because of your temple. Jerusalem's prestige had a single, spiritual cause. God had chosen it as the place of his dwelling (Dt 12; 2Sa 7).

68:29 [o]Ps 72:10
68:30 [p]Ps 22:12 [q]Ps 89:10
68:31 [r]Isa 19:19; 45:14
68:33 [s]Ps 18:10 [t]Ps 29:4
68:34 [u]Ps 29:1
68:35 [v]Ps 29:11 [w]Ps 66:20

kings will bring you gifts.[o]
30 Rebuke the beast among the reeds,
the herd of bulls[p] among the calves of the nations.
Humbled, may it bring bars of silver.
Scatter the nations[q] who delight in war.
31 Envoys will come from Egypt;[r]
Cush[a] will submit herself to God.

32 Sing to God, O kingdoms of the earth,
sing praise to the Lord, *Selah*
33 to him who rides[s] the ancient skies above,
who thunders with mighty voice.[t]
34 Proclaim the power[u] of God,
whose majesty is over Israel,
whose power is in the skies.
35 You are awesome, O God, in your sanctuary;
the God of Israel gives power and strength to his people.[v]

Praise be to God![w]

Psalm 69

For the director of music. To ⌊the tune of⌋ "Lilies." Of David.

69:1 [x]Jnh 2:5
69:2 [y]Ps 40:2
69:3 [z]Ps 6:6 [a]Ps 119:82; Isa 38:14
69:4 [b]Jn 15:25* [c]Ps 35:19; 38:19
69:5 [d]Ps 38:5 [e]Ps 44:21

1 Save me, O God,
for the waters have come up to my neck.[x]
2 I sink in the miry depths,[y]
where there is no foothold.
I have come into the deep waters;
the floods engulf me.
3 I am worn out calling for help;[z]
my throat is parched.
My eyes fail,[a]
looking for my God.
4 Those who hate me without reason[b]
outnumber the hairs of my head;
many are my enemies without cause,[c]
those who seek to destroy me.
I am forced to restore
what I did not steal.

5 You know my folly,[d] O God;
my guilt is not hidden from you.[e]

6 May those who hope in you
not be disgraced because of me,
O Lord, the LORD Almighty;
may those who seek you

[a] *31* That is, the upper Nile region

68:30 Rebuke. More than a verbal assault—a euphemism for "destroy." **the beast among the reeds.** Either the crocodile or the hippopotamus, both symbols of Egypt.
68:31 Cush. A traditional ally of Egypt (cf. Na 3:8; see note on Est 1:1).
68:33 rides the ancient skies. Once again (see v. 4), the psalmist alluded to the divine war chariot.
Psalm 69 *Introduction.* In Psalm 69 David lamented his circumstances as his enemies sought to destroy him. He called on God to reverse the situation and destroy the adversary, closing on a note of praise because of his confidence that the Lord would hear and answer his prayer. This psalm is well known because of New Testament citations. Its words aptly expressed the anguish of Jesus, God's righteous Servant, as he sought his father's will during his earthly ministry.
69:1 the waters. A slow sinking down into water is a picture of acute distress. The raging waters are a frequent Biblical image for social and, as here, personal chaos. See 18:4 and 46:2–3.
69:2 the floods engulf me. A poetic image that may stem from the ancient Near Eastern practice of the water ordeal, in which someone suspected of a crime was cast into a river. The river was expected to overwhelm and carry away the guilty but to spare the innocent.
69:3 I am worn out. An appeal to the Lord for help and a complaint that God had not yet revealed himself. God's seeming absence deeply distressed the psalmist.
69:4 without reason . . . without cause. The law (see Ex 22:1ff.) required that a thief restore what he had stolen. Figuratively or actually, the psalmist had been falsely charged and convicted of theft See *BC* 21.
69:5 my guilt. David, though innocent of the charge, realized that he was not completely without sin in his life. He quickly followed his denial of the false charge with a confession of guilt that was extraneous to the charges.
69:6 those who hope in you. An expression of concern not only for himself but for the other faithful souls in Israel. Often sins, especially those of a prominent person, reflect on the whole community of God.

not be put to shame because of me,
O God of Israel.
7 For I endure scorn for your sake,[f]
and shame covers my face.[g]
8 I am a stranger to my brothers,
an alien to my own mother's sons;[h]
9 for zeal for your house consumes me,[i]
and the insults of those who insult you fall on me.[j]
10 When I weep and fast,[k]
I must endure scorn;
11 when I put on sackcloth,[l]
people make sport of me.
12 Those who sit at the gate mock me,
and I am the song of the drunkards.[m]

13 But I pray to you, O LORD,
in the time of your favor;[n]
in your great love,[o] O God,
answer me with your sure salvation.
14 Rescue me from the mire,
do not let me sink;
deliver me from those who hate me,
from the deep waters.[p]
15 Do not let the floodwaters[q] engulf me
or the depths swallow me up[r]
or the pit close its mouth over me.
16 Answer me, O LORD, out of the goodness of your love;[s]
in your great mercy turn to me.
17 Do not hide your face[t] from your servant;
answer me quickly, for I am in trouble.[u]
18 Come near and rescue me;
redeem[v] me because of my foes.

19 You know how I am scorned,[w] disgraced and shamed;
all my enemies are before you.
20 Scorn has broken my heart
and has left me helpless;
I looked for sympathy, but there was none,
for comforters,[x] but I found none.[y]
21 They put gall in my food
and gave me vinegar for my thirst.[z]

22 May the table set before them become a snare;
may it become retribution and[a] a trap.
23 May their eyes be darkened so they cannot see,
and their backs be bent forever.[a]
24 Pour out your wrath[b] on them;
let your fierce anger overtake them.
25 May their place be deserted;[c]
let there be no one to dwell in their tents.[d]

69:7 [f]Jer 15:15 [g]Ps 44:15
69:8 [h]Ps 31:11; Isa 53:3
69:9 [i]Jn 2:17* [j]Ps 89:50-51; Ro 15:3*
69:10 [k]Ps 35:13
69:11 [l]Ps 35:13
69:12 [m]Job 30:9
69:13 [n]Isa 49:8; 2Co 6:2 [o]Ps 51:1
69:14 [p]ver 2; Ps 144:7
69:15 [q]Ps 124:4-5 [r]Nu 16:33
69:16 [s]Ps 63:3
69:17 [t]Ps 27:9 [u]Ps 66:14
69:18 [v]Ps 49:15
69:19 [w]Ps 22:6
69:20 [x]Job 16:2 [y]Isa 63:5
69:21 [z]Mt 27:34; Mk 15:23; Jn 19:28-30
69:23 [a]Isa 6:9-10; Ro 11:9-10*
69:24 [b]Ps 79:6
69:25 [c]Mt 23:38 [d]Ac 1:20*

a 22 Or *snare / and their fellowship become*

69:8 a stranger to my brothers. David had experienced abandonment by his own family.
69:9 for your house. The psalmist's love for God had attracted the hatred of his enemy. Paul quoted the second half of the verse in Romans 15:3, because it described Jesus' selfless life as he sought his Father's will.
69:11 I put on sackcloth. The psalmist was ridiculed when he performed religious acts such as fasting. See *WLC* 145.
69:12 Those who sit at the gate. Men of influence; e.g., elders of the city.
69:13 love. Specifically the love reserved for those in covenant with God.
69:14 mire . . . deep waters. The language of the first section, describing the psalmist's plight, used in appeal to the Lord for help.
69:15 the pit. A reference to Sheol (see notes on 6:5; 30:1; 40:2). The psalmist feared death and asked God to intervene.
69:20–21 Scorn has broken my heart. His friends have become his enemies. **gall . . . vinegar.** Gall is bitter and vinegar sour. Both increase rather than slake thirst. Note that when the psalmist was served in such a manner by his friends (v. 20) he responded with a curse (vv. 22–29). The metaphor became reality when Jesus Christ was offered gall (Mt 27:34) and vinegar (Mt 27:48) at the crucifixion. Our Savior, however, demonstrated forbearance and forgiveness toward his tormentors (Lk 23:34).
69:22 table. The image of prosperity. The psalmist was upset because the wicked prospered while he, though righteous, suffered. He petitioned the Lord for their just destruction.
69:25 May their place be deserted. David importuned God for

69:26 [e]Isa 53:4; Zec 1:15
69:27 [f]Ne 4:5 [g]Ps 109:14; Isa 26:10
69:28 [h]Ex 32:32-33; Lk 10:20; Php 4:3 [i]Eze 13:9
69:29 [j]Ps 59:1; 70:5
69:30 [k]Ps 28:7 [l]Ps 34:3
69:31 [m]Ps 50:9-13
69:32 [n]Ps 34:2 [o]Ps 22:26
69:33 [p]Ps 12:5; 68:6
69:34 [q]Ps 96:11; 148:1; Isa 44:23; 49:13; 55:12
69:35 [r]Ob 1:17 [s]Ps 51:18; Isa 44:26
69:36 [t]Ps 37:29; 102:28
70:1 [u]Ps 40:13
70:2 [v]Ps 35:4 [w]Ps 35:26
70:5 [x]Ps 40:17 [y]Ps 141:1
71:1 [z]Ps 25:2-3; 31:1

26 For they persecute those you wound
and talk about the pain of those you hurt.[e]
27 Charge them with crime upon crime;[f]
do not let them share in your salvation.[g]
28 May they be blotted out of the book of life[h]
and not be listed with the righteous.[i]

29 I am in pain and distress;
may your salvation, O God, protect me.[j]

30 I will praise God's name in song[k]
and glorify him[l] with thanksgiving.
31 This will please the LORD more than an ox,
more than a bull with its horns and hoofs.[m]
32 The poor will see and be glad[n]—
you who seek God, may your hearts live![o]
33 The LORD hears the needy[p]
and does not despise his captive people.

34 Let heaven and earth praise him,
the seas and all that move in them,[q]
35 for God will save Zion[r]
and rebuild the cities of Judah.[s]
Then people will settle there and possess it;
36 the children of his servants will inherit it,
and those who love his name will dwell there.[t]

Psalm 70

For the director of music. Of David. A petition.

1 Hasten, O God, to save me;
O LORD, come quickly to help me.[u]
2 May those who seek my life[v]
be put to shame and confusion;
may all who desire my ruin
be turned back in disgrace.[w]
3 May those who say to me, "Aha! Aha!"
turn back because of their shame.
4 But may all who seek you
rejoice and be glad in you;
may those who love your salvation always say,
"Let God be exalted!"

5 Yet I am poor and needy;[x]
come quickly to me,[y] O God.
You are my help and my deliverer;
O LORD, do not delay.

Psalm 71

1 In you, O LORD, I have taken refuge;
let me never be put to shame.[z]

---

the death of the wicked. Peter connected these words to Judas, citing them concerning Judas's death and the void left among the disciples (Ac 1:20).
69:26 they persecute those you wound. The enemy increased the pain of the afflicted. God may chastise, but he does not permit others to exacerbate the hurt.
69:28 blotted out of the book of life. A call for the enemies' death. See note on Revelation 3:5.
69:30 I will praise. An abrupt transition from a statement of pain and a call for judgment to praise. The psalms sometimes compressed time, reflecting on understanding that had developed from the agony of suffering into the joy of assurance.
69:31 more than an ox. More than the most expensive sacrifice. The point of the verse is that God loves true devotion.
69:32 The poor . . . glad. The psalmist's deliverance would instill hope in the poor.
69:35–36 rebuild the cities of Judah. These last few verses were probably added much later than the lifetime of David, either during the period of the exile or soon thereafter.
Psalm 70 *Introduction.* This short psalm, in which the author begged God to come and save him quickly, is identical (with a few minor changes) to the last few verses of Psalm 40 (vv. 13–17).
Title. **A petition.** In the Psalms, this term is used elsewhere only in 38:1.
70:1 Hasten . . . to save me. The psalmist boldly invoked the Lord to rescue him from his desperate plight.
70:2 be turned back in disgrace. Enemies sought both the psalmist's ruin and his life; he appealed to God to ruin them instead.
70:5 poor and needy. In this context not necessarily an economic description. It may be that, but the words described David's spiritual condition as well.

2 Rescue me and deliver me in your righteousness;
turn your ear[a] to me and save me.
3 Be my rock of refuge,
to which I can always go;
give the command to save me,
for you are my rock and my fortress.[b]
4 Deliver me, O my God, from the hand of the wicked,[c]
from the grasp of evil and cruel men.

5 For you have been my hope, O Sovereign LORD,
my confidence[d] since my youth.
6 From birth[e] I have relied on you;
you brought me forth from my mother's womb.[f]
I will ever praise[g] you.
7 I have become like a portent[h] to many,
but you are my strong refuge.[i]
8 My mouth[j] is filled with your praise,
declaring your splendor[k] all day long.

9 Do not cast[l] me away when I am old;[m]
do not forsake me when my strength is gone.
10 For my enemies speak against me;
those who wait to kill[n] me conspire[o] together.
11 They say, "God has forsaken him;
pursue him and seize him,
for no one will rescue[p] him."
12 Be not far[q] from me, O God;
come quickly, O my God, to help[r] me.
13 May my accusers perish in shame;
may those who want to harm me
be covered with scorn and disgrace.[s]

14 But as for me, I will always have hope;[t]
I will praise you more and more.
15 My mouth will tell[u] of your righteousness,
of your salvation all day long,
though I know not its measure.
16 I will come and proclaim your mighty acts,[v] O Sovereign LORD;
I will proclaim your righteousness, yours alone.
17 Since my youth, O God, you have taught[w] me,
and to this day I declare your marvelous deeds.[x]
18 Even when I am old and gray,[y]
do not forsake me, O God,
till I declare your power to the next generation,
your might to all who are to come.[z]

19 Your righteousness reaches to the skies,[a] O God,
you who have done great things.[b]
Who, O God, is like you?[c]

71:2 [a]Ps 17:6
71:3 [b]Ps 18:2; 31:2-3; 44:4
71:4 [c]Ps 140:4
71:5 [d]Job 4:6; Jer 17:7
71:6 [e]Ps 22:10 [f]Ps 22:9; Isa 46:3 [g]Ps 9:1; 34:1; 52:9; 119:164; 145:2
71:7 [h]Isa 8:18; 1Co 4:9 [i]2Sa 22:3; Ps 61:3
71:8 [j]Ps 51:15; 63:5 [k]Ps 35:28; 96:6; 104:1
71:9 [l]Ps 51:11 [m]ver 18; Ps 92:14; Isa 46:4
71:10 [n]Ps 10:8; 59:3; Pr 1:18 [o]Ps 31:13; 56:6; Mt 12:14
71:11 [p]Ps 7:2
71:12 [q]Ps 35:22; 38:21 [r]Ps 38:22; 70:1
71:13 [s]ver 24
71:14 [t]Ps 130:7
71:15 [u]Ps 35:28; 40:5
71:16 [v]Ps 106:2
71:17 [w]Dt 4:5 [x]Ps 26:7
71:18 [y]ver 9 [z]Ps 22:30, 31; 78:4
71:19 [a]Ps 36:5; 57:10 [b]Ps 126:2; Lk 1:49 [c]Ps 35:10

Psalm 71 *Introduction.* Psalm 71 is the lament of an older man (v. 9) who is still persecuted by his enemies. He has experienced God's grace (vv. 14–18) in the past and so can end on a note of confidence.

Title. This is one of the few untitled psalms in the first two books of the Psalter.

71:2 in your righteousness. See note on 31:1.

71:3 my rock and my fortress. God was the psalmist's only source of protection. See note on 61:2.

71:5 since my youth. This phrase betrays the fact that David was older, which enabled him to look back over his life and ponder his relationship with God.

71:6 from my mother's womb. A hyperbole indicating that the psalmist could remember no time at which he had not had saving faith in the Lord.

71:7 This verse could also be translated, "I have been a marvel to many; you are my strong refuge." If the psalmist was or appeared to be under judgment, he may have meant that others took his example as a warning. On the other hand, he may have intended to convey that heretofore his life had been a marvelous reflection that God protects those who trust him.

71:11 God has forsaken him. The psalmist's enemies, like Job's friends, came to the wrong conclusion about his suffering.

71:12 Be not far from me. The psalmist, while confident that God was his refuge, did harbor some fears that God would abandon him; through prayer he pleaded with God to remain close by.

71:13 perish in shame. David called upon God to turn the tables on the enemy. His adversaries wanted him to die in shame; he called on God to inflict the same consequence on them.

71:14 I will always have hope. David could look back over his long life and cite how God had saved him in the past. His memory strengthened his devotion.

71:15 though I know not its measure. Even uninterrupted praise cannot adequately express God's mercy; the salvation he proffers is beyond comprehension.

71:16 I will come. To the sanctuary.

71:18 I declare your power to the next generation. It was the duty of the older members of God's community to teach the younger ones what God had done in their lives.

71:20
[d]Ps 60:3 [e]Hos 6:2

71:21
[f]Ps 18:35 [g]Ps 23:4; 86:17; Isa 12:1; 49:13

71:22
[h]Ps 33:2 [i]Ps 92:3; 144:9 [j]2Ki 19:22

71:23
[k]Ps 103:4

71:24
[l]Ps 35:28 [m]ver 13

72:2
[n]Isa 9:7; 11:4-5; 32:1

72:4
[o]Isa 11:4

72:6
[p]Dt 32:2; Hos 6:3

72:7
[q]Ps 92:12; Isa 2:4

72:8
[r]Ex 23:31
[s]Zec 9:10

20 Though you have made me see troubles,[d] many and bitter,
you will restore[e] my life again;
from the depths of the earth
you will again bring me up.
21 You will increase my honor[f]
and comfort[g] me once again.

22 I will praise you with the harp[h]
for your faithfulness, O my God;
I will sing praise to you with the lyre,[i]
O Holy One of Israel.[j]
23 My lips will shout for joy
when I sing praise to you—
I, whom you have redeemed.[k]
24 My tongue will tell of your righteous acts
all day long,[l]
for those who wanted to harm me[m]
have been put to shame and confusion.

Psalm 72

Of Solomon.

1 Endow the king with your justice, O God,
the royal son with your righteousness.
2 He will[a] judge your people in righteousness,[n]
your afflicted ones with justice.
3 The mountains will bring prosperity to the people,
the hills the fruit of righteousness.
4 He will defend the afflicted among the people
and save the children of the needy;[o]
he will crush the oppressor.

5 He will endure[b] as long as the sun,
as long as the moon, through all generations.
6 He will be like rain[p] falling on a mown field,
like showers watering the earth.
7 In his days the righteous will flourish;[q]
prosperity will abound till the moon is no more.

8 He will rule from sea to sea
and from the River[c][r] to the ends of the earth.[d][s]

[a] *2* Or *May he;* similarly in verses 3–11 and 17 [b] *5* Septuagint; Hebrew *You will be feared* [c] *8* That is, the Euphrates [d] *8* Or *the end of the land*

71:19 reaches to the skies. God's righteousness is so limitless that it cannot be contained. **Who . . . is like you?** The implied answer to this rhetorical question is "No one." See *WLC* 104.
71:20 you have made me see troubles. The psalmist was not under any illusions. He knew that life can be difficult and that God had not sheltered him from all trouble. Nonetheless, he had confidence that God would ultimately deliver him.
71:21 comfort me once again. Job is an example of the type of suffering that David endured. Following Job's intense affliction, God did reinstate his servant's blessings of family, health and wealth. The palmist looked for similar restoration. All the faithful have the same hope, but sometimes God's reward for the innocent sufferer does not come in this life. Some blessings come first in heaven; others, such as bodily restoration, come only in the resurrection of believers.
Psalm 72 *Introduction.* This concluding psalm in the second book of the Psalter is a royal or kingship psalm, petitioning God for a blessing of prosperity on the just king. As the king succeeds, so will the nation flourish. Some of the language is hyperbolic as applied to the human king and anticipates the Messiah.
Title. See "Introduction: Authorship and Titles." Some find it hard to believe that Solomon wrote this psalm, with its petition for blessing on the king, though such an appeal would not have been improper. The Septuagint (early Greek translation of the OT) took the title's reference to Solomon as identifying the psalm's subject matter rather than its authorship.
72:1 your justice . . . your righteousness. The psalmist rightly recognized God, the divine King, as the source of all justice and righteousness. The human king could only reflect these qualities if God had first endowed him with them.
72:2 He will judge. The human king was a reflection and extension of the divine King. His divinely appointed rule over God's people included the obligation to judge them.
72:3 prosperity. The Hebrew word signifies peace or wholeness.
72:4 afflicted . . . needy. The king had a particular responsibility to the vulnerable in society, just as God has a special concern and love for the poor.
72:5 as long as the sun. As applied to the human king, this was, of course, hyperbole, similar to the cry "O king, live forever!" (Da 2:4). But the language anticipated the true and ultimate King who does indeed live forever (Heb 7:24), whose reign on the throne of David has no end (2Sa 7:13).
72:6 like rain. Crop fertility was an important issue in ancient Israel because the limited rainfall made life precarious in many areas. The king's presence was valued as highly as the much-needed rainfall because his righteous rule would bring great blessings on the nation, including God's blessings on crops, but also extending to many other benefits. This verse, as others, reflects the close connection between the king and the land.
72:7 righteous will flourish. The ideal king would assure that God's people, not the wicked enemy, would prosper. Some psalms specifically addressed the problem of the wicked flourishing and the righteous withering away (Pss 71 and 73).

[9]The desert tribes will bow before him
and his enemies will lick the dust.
[10]The kings of Tarshish and of distant shores
will bring tribute to him;
the kings of Sheba[t] and Seba
will present him gifts.[u]
[11]All kings will bow down to him
and all nations will serve him.

[12]For he will deliver the needy who cry out,
the afflicted who have no one to help.
[13]He will take pity on the weak and the needy
and save the needy from death.
[14]He will rescue[v] them from oppression and violence,
for precious[w] is their blood in his sight.

[15]Long may he live!
May gold from Sheba[x] be given him.
May people ever pray for him
and bless him all day long.
[16]Let grain abound throughout the land;
on the tops of the hills may it sway.
Let its fruit flourish like Lebanon;[y]
let it thrive like the grass of the field.
[17]May his name endure forever;[z]
may it continue as long as the sun.[a]

All nations will be blessed through him,
and they will call him blessed.[b]

[18]Praise be to the LORD God, the God of Israel,[c]
who alone does marvelous deeds.[d]
[19]Praise be to his glorious name forever;
may the whole earth be filled with his glory.[e]
Amen and Amen.[f]

[20]This concludes the prayers of David son of Jesse.

BOOK III

Psalms 73–89

Psalm 73

A psalm of Asaph.

[1]Surely God is good to Israel,
to those who are pure in heart.[g]

72:10 [t]Ge 10:7 [u]2Ch 9:24
72:14 [v]Ps 69:18 [w]1Sa 26:21; Ps 116:15
72:15 [x]Isa 60:6
72:16 [y]Ps 104:16
72:17 [z]Ex 3:15 [a]Ps 89:36 [b]Ge 12:3; Lk 1:48
72:18 [c]1Ch 29:10; Ps 41:13; 106:48 [d]Job 5:9
72:19 [e]Nu 14:21; Ne 9:5 [f]Ps 41:13
73:1 [g]Mt 5:8

72:8 from sea to sea. An allusion to the promised boundaries of Exodus 23:31, but the declaration far exceeded even that land, encompassing the entire earth. As God rules the whole world, so will his representative on Earth. Once again the language anticipated the Messiah.
72:9 desert tribes. The ideal king would subdue the difficult-to-control tribes of the desert.
72:10 Tarshish . . . Sheba . . . Seba. Locations all quite distant, from an early Old Testament Israelite perspective. Tarshish is usually associated with Tartessus in Spain, while Sheba and probably Seba may have been located in southern Arabia.
72:15 ever pray for him. Even the righteous king was sustained only by prayer.
72:17 May his name endure forever. This verse reflects the blessing to Abraham in Genesis 12:2. The king, as the focal point of the society of God's people, represented the people and was the heir of promises. It is in Jesus Christ that these promises come to ultimate fulfillment. See *WCF* 25.5.
72:18–19 Praise be to his glorious name. A doxology concludes the second book of the Psalter. Each of the five books ends with a doxology praising the name of the Lord.
72:20 the prayers of David. At one point in the development of the Psalter (see "Introduction: Structure") all of the Davidic psalms were grouped together in the first two books. This unity was not preserved as the book continued to expand. Thus this note is now appended to the end of a Solomonic psalm.
Psalm 73 *Introduction.* Psalm 73 begins with the assertion of God's goodness. However, the psalmist had come to this belief only after a long struggle with what he observed in the world. The issue that confused him was the prosperity of the wicked. The psalm thus shares an important theme with the book of Job. There are also thematic similarities with Psalms 37 and 49. Verses 1–14 voice the psalmist's problem: How can God be just when the wicked prosper and the righteous struggle? The second half of the psalm (vv. 15–28) expresses the psalmist's resolution of the problem, the result of an encounter with God (v. 17). The New Testament teaches Christians that suffering is unavoidable in this present evil world (Ro 8:17; 2Ti 3:12), that God uses our suffering for his purposes (Ro 5:3–5; Php 1:29; Col 1:24; 1Pe 4:12–16) and that our attitude toward it should emulate that of Jesus Christ (1Pe 3:14–4:1). For Christians, present affliction will bring future joy (Ro 8:17). See *WCF* 5.5.
73:1 God is good. This psalm was clearly composed after the

[2] But as for me, my feet had almost slipped;
I had nearly lost my foothold.
[3] For I envied[h] the arrogant
when I saw the prosperity of the wicked.[i]

[4] They have no struggles;
their bodies are healthy and strong.[a]
[5] They are free[j] from the burdens common to man;
they are not plagued by human ills.
[6] Therefore pride is their necklace;[k]
they clothe themselves with violence.[l]
[7] From their callous hearts[m] comes iniquity[b];
the evil conceits of their minds know no limits.
[8] They scoff, and speak with malice;
in their arrogance[n] they threaten oppression.
[9] Their mouths lay claim to heaven,
and their tongues take possession of the earth.
[10] Therefore their people turn to them
and drink up waters in abundance.[c]
[11] They say, "How can God know?
Does the Most High have knowledge?"

[12] This is what the wicked are like—
always carefree, they increase in wealth.[o]

[13] Surely in vain[p] have I kept my heart pure;
in vain have I washed my hands in innocence.[q]
[14] All day long I have been plagued;
I have been punished every morning.

[15] If I had said, "I will speak thus,"
I would have betrayed your children.
[16] When I tried to understand[r] all this,
it was oppressive to me
[17] till I entered the sanctuary[s] of God;
then I understood their final destiny.[t]

[18] Surely you place them on slippery ground;[u]
you cast them down to ruin.
[19] How suddenly[v] are they destroyed,
completely swept away by terrors!
[20] As a dream[w] when one awakes,[x]
so when you arise, O Lord,
you will despise them as fantasies.

[21] When my heart was grieved

73:3 [h]Ps 37:1; Pr 23:17 [i]Job 21:7; Jer 12:1
73:5 [j]Job 21:9
73:6 [k]Ge 41:42 [l]Ps 109:18
73:7 [m]Ps 17:10
73:8 [n]Ps 17:10; Jude 16
73:12 [o]Ps 49:6
73:13 [p]Job 21:15; 34:9 [q]Ps 26:6
73:16 [r]Ecc 8:17
73:17 [s]Ps 77:13 [t]Ps 37:38
73:18 [u]Ps 35:6
73:19 [v]Isa 47:11
73:20 [w]Job 20:8 [x]Ps 78:65

[a] *4* With a different word division of the Hebrew; Masoretic Text *struggles at their death; / their bodies are healthy* [b] *7* Syriac (see also Septuagint); Hebrew *Their eyes bulge with fat* [c] *10* The meaning of the Hebrew for this verse is uncertain.

psalmist had resolved the issue that had clouded his heart and his relationship with the Lord. He had been unable to reconcile the goodness of God with the prosperity of the wicked.
73:2–3 See *WLC* 105.
73:2 lost my foothold. The righteous life was often pictured as a walk along a straight path (see especially Pr 1–9). The psalmist described his doubt and skepticism as falling off that path.
73:3 the prosperity of the wicked. The psalmist's personal experience could leave no doubt: As a general rule, the wicked prosper! Didn't God promise that the righteous would be blessed and the wicked cursed? What about the covenant? (Dt 28; 29).
73:4 They have no struggles. In his doubt the psalmist overstated and overgeneralized his complaint. Surely not every wicked person was thriving. Yet, if even one such person flourished while one righteous individual faltered, the problem continued to exist. Why did God allow such injustice? See *WLC* 142.
73:6 pride . . . violence. The prosperity of the wicked led to even deeper sins: pride and violence.
73:9 lay claim to heaven. The pride of the wicked took an extreme form. The psalmist accused them of claiming total autonomy from God and total ownership of all things, even of the abode to God.
73:10 drink up waters. This verse probably indicated that people listened eagerly and approvingly to what the wicked had to say.
73:12 always carefree. Summarizes the preceding verses in describing the wicked as being free from anxiety or angst.
73:13–15 See *WLC* 105,113.
73:13 in vain have I kept my heart pure. A description of Asaph's attitude before he resolved the issue that troubled him. See *WLC* 172.
73:15 will speak thus. That is, if he had voiced his doubts and complaints. **betrayed your children.** He would have instilled doubt in the community of God, thereby turning its members against God. See *WCF* 18.4; *WLC* 81.
73:17 entered the sanctuary. The psalmist's attitudinal turnaround had come when he had entered the presence of God. His present peace issued from a deeper knowledge of God. **their final destiny.** Asaph had come to understand that, though the ungodly appeared to enjoy success, their final lot is destruction.
73:20 As a dream. When God destroys the wicked in judgment, their former prosperity will be revealed as fleeting and empty.

and my spirit embittered,
22 I was senseless[y] and ignorant;
I was a brute beast[z] before you.
23 Yet I am always with you;
you hold me by my right hand.
24 You guide[a] me with your counsel,[b]
and afterward you will take me into glory.
25 Whom have I in heaven but you?
And earth has nothing I desire besides you.[c]
26 My flesh and my heart[d] may fail,[e]
but God is the strength of my heart
and my portion forever.

27 Those who are far from you will perish;[f]
you destroy all who are unfaithful to you.
28 But as for me, it is good to be near God.[g]
I have made the Sovereign LORD my refuge;
I will tell of all your deeds.[h]

73:22 [y]Ps 49:10; 92:6 [z]Ecc 3:18
73:24 [a]Ps 48:14 [b]Ps 32:8
73:25 [c]Php 3:8
73:26 [d]Ps 84:2 [e]Ps 40:12
73:27 [f]Ps 119:155
73:28 [g]Heb 10:22; Jas 4:8 [h]Ps 40:5

Psalm 74

A *maskil*[a] of Asaph.

1 Why have you rejected us forever,[i] O God?
Why does your anger smolder against the sheep of your pasture?[j]
2 Remember the people you purchased[k] of old,[l]
the tribe of your inheritance, whom you redeemed[m]—
Mount Zion, where you dwelt.[n]
3 Turn your steps toward these everlasting ruins,
all this destruction the enemy has brought on the sanctuary.

4 Your foes roared[o] in the place where you met with us;
they set up their standards[p] as signs.
5 They behaved like men wielding axes
to cut through a thicket of trees.[q]
6 They smashed all the carved[r] paneling
with their axes and hatchets.
7 They burned your sanctuary to the ground;
they defiled the dwelling place of your Name.
8 They said in their hearts, "We will crush[s] them completely!"
They burned every place where God was worshiped in the land.
9 We are given no miraculous signs;
no prophets[t] are left,
and none of us knows how long this will be.

74:1 [i]Dt 29:20; Ps 44:23 [j]Ps 79:13; 95:7; 100:3
74:2 [k]Ex 15:16 [l]Dt 32:7 [m]Ex 15:13 [n]Ps 68:16
74:4 [o]La 2:7 [p]Nu 2:2
74:5 [q]Jer 46:22
74:6 [r]1Ki 6:18
74:8 [s]Ps 83:4
74:9 [t]1Sa 3:1

[a] Title: Probably a literary or musical term

73:21 When my heart was grieved. The psalmist reflected back on his earlier position.
73:22–23 See *WLC* 172.
73:22 senseless and ignorant. Negative emotions had blocked his ability to reflect clearly about God and his ways. See *WLC* 105.
73:23 you hold me by my right hand. An ancient Near Eastern expression that indicated a close relationship between the deity and the worshiper. It also indicates that God was the psalmist's guide. See *WLC* 81.
73:24–28 See *WLC* 1,104; *WSC* 105.
73:24 will take me into glory. The exact reference is ambiguous. Some take this phrase as referring to the climax of God's temporal blessing: earthly renown and reputation. In the context of the psalmist's perspective of "final destiny" (v. 17), however, it is more likely a reference to eternal glory. Nothing could interrupt the intimate fellowship between God and the psalmist.
Psalm 74 *Introduction.* Psalm 74 laments the destruction of the temple in 587 B.C. It is comparable in tone and subject to the mournful book of Lamentations. While the present was bleak, in God there was cause for hope—the impetus for the transition in verses 12–17.
74:1 rejected us. Israel's defeat at the hands of the Babylonians indicated that God had abandoned his chosen people and would protect them no longer (cf. Lev 26; Dt 28). The prophets (see Eze 9–11) described the divine abandonment of God's temple, implicating Israel's sin and unbelief. See note on Psalm 22:1. **the sheep.** In his plea for restoration the psalmist appealed to the intimate relationship between God and his people. See Psalm 23:1.
74:2 Remember. The word implies more than mental recall; the psalmist desired God to act on his memory by saving his people. **Mount Zion.** The location of the temple and thus the place at which God made his presence known in a special way (see theological article "The Presence of God" at 1Ki 8). See 2:6, 50:2, 128:5 and 129:5.
74:3 Turn your steps. The psalmist invited the Lord to survey the destruction of the holy temple, in the hope that God would respond through saving acts. **sanctuary.** When Nebuchadnezzar took Jerusalem in 587 B.C. he ordered the demolition of the temple.
74:9 no miraculous signs; no prophets. God was completely silent in the face of the destruction. It is likely that this psalm was written soon after the devastation, since a number of prophets were active during the period of restoration.

74:10 [u]Ps 44:16
74:11 [v]La 2:3
74:12 [w]Ps 44:4
74:13 [x]Ex 14:21 [y]Isa 51:9; Eze 29:3
74:15 [z]Ex 17:6; Nu 20:11 [a]Jos 2:10; 3:13
74:16 [b]Ge 1:16; Ps 136:7-9
74:17 [c]Dt 32:8; Ac 17:26 [d]Ge 8:22
74:18 [e]Dt 32:6; Ps 39:8
74:19 [f]Ps 9:18
74:20 [g]Ge 17:7; Ps 106:45
74:21 [h]Ps 103:6 [i]Ps 35:10
74:22 [j]Ps 53:1
74:23 [k]Ps 65:7

10 How long will the enemy mock you, O God?
Will the foe revile[u] your name forever?
11 Why do you hold back your hand, your right hand?[v]
Take it from the folds of your garment and destroy them!

12 But you, O God, are my king[w] from of old;
you bring salvation upon the earth.
13 It was you who split open the sea[x] by your power;
you broke the heads of the monster[y] in the waters.
14 It was you who crushed the heads of Leviathan
and gave him as food to the creatures of the desert.
15 It was you who opened up springs[z] and streams;
you dried up[a] the ever flowing rivers.
16 The day is yours, and yours also the night;
you established the sun and moon.[b]
17 It was you who set all the boundaries[c] of the earth;
you made both summer and winter.[d]

18 Remember how the enemy has mocked you, O LORD,
how foolish people[e] have reviled your name.
19 Do not hand over the life of your dove to wild beasts;
do not forget the lives of your afflicted[f] people forever.
20 Have regard for your covenant,[g]
because haunts of violence fill the dark places of the land.
21 Do not let the oppressed[h] retreat in disgrace;
may the poor and needy[i] praise your name.
22 Rise up, O God, and defend your cause;
remember how fools[j] mock you all day long.
23 Do not ignore the clamor of your adversaries,[k]
the uproar of your enemies, which rises continually.

Psalm 75

For the director of music. ⌊To the tune of⌋ "Do Not Destroy."
A psalm of Asaph. A song.

75:1 [l]Ps 145:18 [m]Ps 44:1; 71:16
75:3 [n]Isa 24:19 [o]1Sa 2:8

1 We give thanks to you, O God,
we give thanks, for your Name is near;[l]
men tell of your wonderful deeds.[m]

2 You say, "I choose the appointed time;
it is I who judge uprightly.
3 When the earth and all its people quake,[n]
it is I who hold its pillars[o] firm. *Selah*

74:10 revile your name. An appeal to the divine reputation. The psalmist was perplexed and angry with God's apparent inactivity.
74:11 your right hand. The hand with which God could destroy his enemies (Ex 15:6).
74:12 my king. God is in charge of everything; he rules over all because he created all. **salvation.** In this context, salvation primarily meant deliverance from the enemy and restoration from destruction.
74:13 the sea. An allusion to the Near Eastern concept of creation. In Mesopotamia and Canaan it was believed that Marduk or Baal defeated the Sea (personified in the stories) and out of the Sea's body created the universe. Creation came about by splitting the Sea's body in two and creating the heavens from one half and the earth from the other. The psalmist's use of these mythological images in a poetic context does not demonstrate that he believed them. On the contrary, by applying these images to the Lord, he indicated that the God of Israel was the Creator of all; the gods of the Near East were not true gods. At least some were actually demons (106:37; Dt 32:17; 1Co 10:20–21), while others were no doubt purely imaginary. See notes on 18:4, 29:3 and 69:1–2.
74:14 heads of Leviathan. Leviathan (Lotan) was one of the sea monsters whom Baal defeated, according to the texts discovered at Ugarit. The texts describe Leviathan as seven-headed (see Rev 13).
74:15–17 It was you. God created the world. These verses are reminiscent not only of the creation account in Genesis 1 but also of God's promises to Noah after God's judgment against the wicked in the flood (Ge 8:22).
74:18 the enemy has mocked you. God had used the Babylonians and other foreign nations as the instruments of his righteous judgment against the chosen people. These nations did not acknowledge God but sought their own glory. The psalmist appealed to God to remember their presumption and to reverse their situation. See *WLC* 190.
74:20 your covenant. God's covenant with Israel. Because the Israelites had been chronically disobedient, the Lord had judged them and handed them over to the Babylonians. The psalmist, however, expected an eventual restoration for the remnant in light of the covenant promises and prophetic statements and types (e.g., Jer 29:10; Da 9:24–25).
74:22–23 See *WLC* 190.
74:22 Rise up . . . remember. See note on 7:6.
Psalm 75 *Introduction.* Psalm 75 bears a similarity of general theme with Hannah's song in 1 Samuel 2 and with Mary's Magnificat in Luke 1. The author thanked the Lord for casting down the wicked and lifting up the righteous.
75:1 We. This psalm begins as a communal thanksgiving, though at the end an individual speaks for the community. **Name.** See note on 8:1. **your wonderful deeds.** God's great acts in the arena of history. His greatest deed in the Old Testament was commonly portrayed as the exodus.

[4] To the arrogant I say, 'Boast no more,'
and to the wicked, 'Do not lift up your horns.[p]
[5] Do not lift your horns against heaven;
do not speak with outstretched neck.' "

[6] No one from the east or the west
or from the desert can exalt a man.
[7] But it is God who judges:[q]
He brings one down, he exalts another.[r]
[8] In the hand of the LORD is a cup
full of foaming wine mixed[s] with spices;
he pours it out, and all the wicked of the earth
drink it down to its very dregs.[t]

[9] As for me, I will declare[u] this forever;
I will sing praise to the God of Jacob.
[10] I will cut off the horns of all the wicked,
but the horns of the righteous will be lifted up.[v]

Psalm 76

For the director of music. With stringed instruments. A psalm of Asaph. A song.

[1] In Judah God is known;
his name is great in Israel.
[2] His tent is in Salem,[w]
his dwelling place in Zion.
[3] There he broke the flashing arrows,
the shields and the swords, the weapons of war.[x] *Selah*

[4] You are resplendent with light,
more majestic than mountains rich with game.
[5] Valiant men lie plundered,
they sleep their last sleep;[y]
not one of the warriors
can lift his hands.
[6] At your rebuke, O God of Jacob,
both horse and chariot[z] lie still.
[7] You alone are to be feared.[a]
Who can stand[b] before you when you are angry?[c]
[8] From heaven you pronounced judgment,
and the land feared[d] and was quiet—
[9] when you, O God, rose up to judge,[e]
to save all the afflicted of the land. *Selah*
[10] Surely your wrath against men brings you praise,[f]
and the survivors of your wrath are restrained.[a]

75:4 [p]Zec 1:21
75:7 [q]Ps 50:6 [r]1Sa 2:7; Ps 147:6; Da 2:21
75:8 [s]Pr 23:30 [t]Job 21:20; Jer 25:15
75:9 [u]Ps 40:10
75:10 [v]Ps 89:17; 92:10; 148:14
76:2 [w]Ge 14:18
76:3 [x]Ps 46:9
76:5 [y]Ps 13:3
76:6 [z]Ex 15:1
76:7 [a]1Ch 16:25 [b]Ezr 9:15; Rev 6:17 [c]Ps 2:5; Na 1:6
76:8 [d]1Ch 16:30; 2Ch 20:29-30
76:9 [e]Ps 9:8
76:10 [f]Ex 9:16; Ro 9:17

[a] *10* Or *Surely the wrath of men brings you praise, / and with the remainder of wrath you arm yourself*

75:3 I who hold its pillars firm. Figurative language used to denote that God provides the underlying stability to the created order and to social and political relationships. Evil people attempt to wreak chaos and to damage the stability God has established, but God restrains them from causing harm beyond what he has ordained to use as means of judgment and discipline (v. 2). There is a hint here of the doctrine of common grace, which states that God mercifully provides a measure of good things even to the reprobate (Mt 5:45).
75:4 your horns. A common image used both in the Bible and elsewhere in the ancient Near East. The picture was of a powerful horned beast (e.g., an ox or bull) that proudly raised its head, shaking its horns in defiance and anger. God warned the wicked not to act presumptuously against him.
75:6–7 No one . . . can exalt a man . . . it is God who judges. God rules over all people, rendering righteous, incontrovertible judgments regarding both blessing and condemnation. Some of these judgments directly control human social and political structures.
75:8 a cup. See note on 11:6.

Psalm 76 *Introduction.* Psalm 76 celebrated a great victory over Israel's enemies. God had provided the victory and was at the center of Israel's praise. Christians too can sing this song, praising God for his victory on the cross and looking forward to the great final victory over evil at the end of the ages (Rev 19:11–21).
76:2 His tent is in Salem. *Salem* was the ancient name for Jerusalem. God's "tent" was his sanctuary. The tabernacle was actually in the form of a tent, but the temple was a permanent structure that could still be referred to poetically as a tent. **Zion.** The mountain on which the temple was situated; see 2:6.
76:3 he broke. God defeated the enemy in Jerusalem. We cannot be specific as to which battle this originally referred to, but a good example would be the siege by Sennacherib by 701 B.C. (2Ki 18–19; Isa 37).
76:4 resplendent with light. See John 1:4 and 7:8–9.
76:5 Valiant men lie plundered. God had destroyed powerful soldiers; they were no match for him.
76:6 your rebuke. God's rebuke is the word of this powerful judgment. When he speaks his rebuke, the forces of chaos and evil flee before him and peace reigns (Na 1:4; Mt 8:23–27; 17:18).

76:11 [g]Ps 50:14; Ecc 5:4-5 [h]2Ch 32:23; Ps 68:29

11 Make vows to the LORD your God and fulfill them;[g]
let all the neighboring lands
bring gifts[h] to the One to be feared.
12 He breaks the spirit of rulers;
he is feared by the kings of the earth.

Psalm 77

For the director of music. For Jeduthun. Of Asaph. A psalm.

77:1 [i]Ps 3:4
77:2 [j]Ps 50:15; Isa 26:9, 16 [k]Job 11:13 [l]Ge 37:35
77:3 [m]Ps 143:4
77:5 [n]Dt 32:7; Ps 44:1; 143:5; Isa 51:9

1 I cried out to God[i] for help;
I cried out to God to hear me.
2 When I was in distress,[j] I sought the Lord;
at night I stretched out untiring hands[k]
and my soul refused to be comforted.[l]

3 I remembered you, O God, and I groaned;
I mused, and my spirit grew faint.[m] *Selah*
4 You kept my eyes from closing;
I was too troubled to speak.
5 I thought about the former days,[n]
the years of long ago;
6 I remembered my songs in the night.
My heart mused and my spirit inquired:

77:7 [o]Ps 85:1
77:8 [p]2Pe 3:9
77:9 [q]Ps 25:6; 40:11; 51:1 [r]Isa 49:15

7 "Will the Lord reject forever?
Will he never show his favor[o] again?
8 Has his unfailing love vanished forever?
Has his promise[p] failed for all time?
9 Has God forgotten to be merciful?[q]
Has he in anger withheld his compassion?[r]" *Selah*

77:10 [s]Ps 31:22
77:11 [t]Ps 143:5

10 Then I thought, "To this I will appeal:
the years of the right hand[s] of the Most High."
11 I will remember the deeds of the LORD;
yes, I will remember your miracles[t] of long ago.
12 I will meditate on all your works
and consider all your mighty deeds.

77:13 [u]Ex 15:11; Ps 71:19; 86:8
77:15 [v]Ex 6:6; Dt 9:29

13 Your ways, O God, are holy.
What god is so great as our God?[u]
14 You are the God who performs miracles;
you display your power among the peoples.
15 With your mighty arm you redeemed your people,[v]
the descendants of Jacob and Joseph. *Selah*

76:10 your wrath . . . brings you praise. God's wrath brought praise because it was directed against the wicked and unjust who afflicted the poor and vulnerable. His wrath restrained wickedness because fear of it kept the wicked from fully working out their schemes. See *WCF* 5.4.
76:11 vows. See Leviticus 27. See *WCF* 22.6; *WLC* 108.
76:12 he is feared by the kings of the earth. Kings feared him because they saw the great victory he had won and knew that they could not endure before him (v. 7). See note on 2:11.
Psalm 77 *Introduction.* In Psalm 77 an individual spoke on behalf of the community (vv. 7–9). He bemoaned God's abandoning his people in anger. In his anguish, though, the psalmist remembered God's great acts of the past, recalling particularly the exodus (vv. 16–20).
77:1–12 See *WCF* 5.5; 18.3; 18.4; *WLC* 81,172.
77:2 stretched out untiring hands. One of the physical stances used in prayer during the Old Testament period was raising one's hands to heaven. The psalmist's hands may have been untiring because of his intense distress. Alternatively, he may have spoken figuratively about the fact that his hands did not falter, regardless of whether or not they were actually tired.
77:5 the former days. The days when God was near and acted to save Israel from distress.
77:7 Will the Lord reject forever? The Lord's promise to attend his people in blessing required their obedience (Lev 26; Dt 28). Though God was longsuffering, at times his patience would run out. He would then abandon his people in judgment. See 1 Samuel 4 and Ezekiel 9–11, as well as the book of Lamentations.
77:8 unfailing love. That is, the love God shows his covenant people. The people of God appealed to the Lord to return in order to be with them (see theological article "The Presence of God" at 1Ki 8).
77:9 Has God forgotten to be merciful? The psalmist knew that God is merciful and compassionate (Ex 34:4–7); with these words he urged God to make his presence known again.
77:10 I thought, "To this I will appeal." A transition in the psalm. By remembering God's great acts in the past, the psalmist built confidence in the present and for the future. **years of the right hand.** God's right hand is symbolic of the power by which he vanquished enemies (Ex 15:6).
77:13 holy . . . great. As the psalmist recalled God's great acts in the past, he remembered two of God's attributes: his holiness and his unique power. God is set apart from sin and is able to accomplish great things.
77:14 among the peoples. God is transcendent over all his creation—even over those nations that worship false gods (cf. v. 3). However, he has chosen to be intimately involved in human affairs, particularly those of his people. In protecting and providing for them, he demonstrated his power in ways that surrounding nations could observe.
77:15 redeemed your people. The psalmist referred to the liberation of Israel from Egypt.

16 The waters[w] saw you, O God,
the waters saw you and writhed;[x]
the very depths were convulsed.
17 The clouds poured down water,[y]
the skies resounded with thunder;
your arrows flashed back and forth.
18 Your thunder was heard in the whirlwind,
your lightning lit up the world;
the earth trembled and quaked.[z]
19 Your path led through the sea,[a]
your way through the mighty waters,
though your footprints were not seen.

20 You led your people[b] like a flock[c]
by the hand of Moses and Aaron.

Psalm 78

A *maskil*[a] of Asaph.

1 O my people, hear my teaching;[d]
listen to the words of my mouth.
2 I will open my mouth in parables,[e]
I will utter hidden things, things from of old—
3 what we have heard and known,
what our fathers have told us.[f]
4 We will not hide them from their children;[g]
we will tell the next generation
the praiseworthy deeds[h] of the LORD,
his power, and the wonders he has done.
5 He decreed statutes[i] for Jacob[j]
and established the law in Israel,
which he commanded our forefathers
to teach their children,
6 so the next generation would know them,
even the children yet to be born,[k]
and they in turn would tell their children.
7 Then they would put their trust in God
and would not forget[l] his deeds
but would keep his commands.[m]
8 They would not be like their forefathers[n]—
a stubborn[o] and rebellious[p] generation,

77:16 [w]Ex 14:21,28; Hab 3:8 [x]Ps 114:4; Hab 3:10
77:17 [y]Jdg 5:4
77:18 [z]Jdg 5:4
77:19 [a]Hab 3:15
77:20 [b]Ex 13:21 [c]Ps 78:52; Isa 63:11
78:1 [d]Isa 51:4; 55:3
78:2 [e]Ps 49:4; Mt 13:35*
78:3 [f]Ps 44:1
78:4 [g]Dt 11:19 [h]Ps 26:7; 71:17
78:5 [i]Ps 19:7; 81:5 [j]Ps 147:19
78:6 [k]Ps 22:31; 102:18
78:7 [l]Dt 6:12 [m]Dt 5:29
78:8 [n]2Ch 30:7 [o]Ex 32:9 [p]ver 37; Isa 30:9

[a] Title: Probably a literary or musical term

77:16 the waters saw you. In this poetic recollection of the exodus, the waters of the Red Sea were personified. The crossing of the Red Sea was depicted as a battle against the waters of chaos (see notes on 18:4; 29:3; 46:2; 69:1–2 and 114:3).
77:19 mighty waters. This image describes the crossing of the Red Sea as a violent conflict between God and the waters of chaos (see note on v 16). **your footprints were not seen.** God's invisible presence.
77:20 You led your people like a flock. In contrast to verses 16 through 19, the mood is calm as the shepherd God of Israel leads Moses and Aaron by the hand through the danger, shielding them from the violence of the ordeal.
Psalm 78 *Introduction.* Psalm 78, one of the longest, recounts God's great acts in Israel's past. It emphasizes God's grace to Israel as that nation continued to sin against him. His judgments renewed their repentance. The historical retrospect extends back to the Red Sea, the desert wanderings and the early monarchy, under Saul. It concludes on a positive note: God's choice of David as king and Jerusalem as the site of the temple.
78:2 parables. This term does not imply that the events are not historical. Rather it emphasizes the theme of the preamble; past events were recounted as examples from which present instruction was drawn.
78:3 told us. Most instruction during the Old Testament period was disseminated through oral teaching. Writing materials were scarce, and literacy was not high. Parents would teach their children about God's relationship with his people. See Deuteronomy 6:4–9 and 32:7.
78:4 praiseworthy deeds of the LORD. God entered human history to save his people and to judge his foes. This psalm recounted a few of the significant acts of God in the history of Israel, his chosen people.
78:5–7 See *WLC* 156.
78:5 statutes . . . law. God established a relationship with his people based on grace alone. In the context of grace, he gave them laws by which they should live and demonstrate their gratefulness to him (Jos 24:1–15; 51:12–13; 119:146). These laws were summarized in the Ten Commandments (Ex 20; Dt 5) and specifically applied to Israel in the Book of the Covenant (Ex 21–23), as well as in Leviticus, Numbers and Deuteronomy.
78:6 they . . . would tell their children. See note on verse 3.
78:7 keep his commands. The object of the history lesson was not the study of antiquities, but a deepening of the faith and obedience of God's people.
78:8 were not faithful to him. Time and again the Israelites rebelled against the Lord. The earliest and most likely date for the composition of this psalm is during David's reign when they could look back over generations of relationship with God, a relationship frequently marred by Israel's stubbornness. The psalmist would recount some of these instances in the verses to follow.

whose hearts were not loyal to God,
whose spirits were not faithful to him.

9 The men of Ephraim, though armed with bows,[q]
turned back on the day of battle;[r]
10 they did not keep God's covenant[s]
and refused to live by his law.
11 They forgot what he had done,[t]
the wonders he had shown them.
12 He did miracles[u] in the sight of their fathers
in the land of Egypt,[v] in the region of Zoan.[w]
13 He divided the sea[x] and led them through;
he made the water stand firm like a wall.[y]
14 He guided them with the cloud by day
and with light from the fire all night.[z]
15 He split the rocks[a] in the desert
and gave them water as abundant as the seas;
16 he brought streams out of a rocky crag
and made water flow down like rivers.

17 But they continued to sin[b] against him,
rebelling in the desert against the Most High.
18 They willfully put God to the test[c]
by demanding the food they craved.[d]
19 They spoke against God,[e] saying,
"Can God spread a table in the desert?
20 When he struck the rock, water gushed out,[f]
and streams flowed abundantly.
But can he also give us food?
Can he supply meat[g] for his people?"
21 When the LORD heard them, he was very angry;
his fire broke out[h] against Jacob,
and his wrath rose against Israel,
22 for they did not believe in God
or trust[i] in his deliverance.
23 Yet he gave a command to the skies above
and opened the doors of the heavens;[j]
24 he rained down manna[k] for the people to eat,
he gave them the grain of heaven.
25 Men ate the bread of angels;
he sent them all the food they could eat.
26 He let loose the east wind[l] from the heavens
and led forth the south wind by his power.
27 He rained meat down on them like dust,
flying birds like sand on the seashore.
28 He made them come down inside their camp,
all around their tents.
29 They ate till they had more than enough,[m]
for he had given them what they craved.
30 But before they turned from the food they craved,

78:9 [q]ver 57; 1Ch 12:2 [r]Jdg 20:39
78:10 [s]2Ki 17:15
78:11 [t]Ps 106:13
78:12 [u]Ps 106:22 [v]Ex 7-12 [w]Nu 13:22
78:13 [x]Ex 14:21; Ps 136:13 [y]Ex 15:8
78:14 [z]Ex 13:21; Ps 105:39
78:15 [a]Nu 20:11; 1Co 10:4
78:17 [b]Dt 9:22; Isa 63:10; Heb 3:16
78:18 [c]1Co 10:9 [d]Ex 16:2; Nu 11:4
78:19 [e]Nu 21:5
78:20 [f]Nu 20:11 [g]Nu 11:18
78:21 [h]Nu 11:1
78:22 [i]Dt 1:32; Heb 3:19
78:23 [j]Ge 7:11; Mal 3:10
78:24 [k]Ex 16:4; Jn 6:31*
78:26 [l]Nu 11:31
78:29 [m]Nu 11:20

78:9 men of Ephraim. This verse should be compared to verses 67–68, where the choice of David of Judah is coupled with the rejection of Ephraim. There is also a connection with the rejection of Saul, whom David replaced. Saul was best associated with the northern tribes even though he descended from the southern tribe of Benjamin, and Ephraim was the most powerful tribe of the north.
78:10 God's covenant. God had pledged to destroy his people if they were disobedient (Dt 27:9—28:68).
78:13 He divided the sea. Chief among the remarkable acts of God was the deliverance from Egypt by which God had rescued his people from bondage and brought them into their own land. The Red Sea crossing constituted the greatest demonstration of God's power in the past and, accordingly, was often called to memory by psalmists and prophets.
78:14 He guided them. God had guided his people through the desert by means of a pillar of cloud by day and of fire by might (Ex 40:36–38).
78:15 He split the rocks. He had also provided for their physical needs in the desert through miraculous means (Nu 20:1–13).
78:17 See *WLC* 150; *WSC* 83.
78:18 put God to the test. The Israelites frequently grumbled about the lack of food and water in the desert, and God repeatedly provided for their needs (95:8; Ex 16:2; 17:2).
78:20 can he also give us food? God's provision of water in the desert (Ex 17:6; Nu 20:8–11) should have led to faith and trust. Instead the Israelites tested the Lord with regard to food. Compare John 6:25–58.
78:21 he was very angry. Rebellion against the Lord had led to judgment (Nu 11:1–3), but he had afterward returned with his grace (Ps 78:23–39), to which the Israelites had responded with further rebellion (vv. 30–31).
78:22 See *WLC* 105.
78:26–31 The story is found in Numbers 11.

even while it was still in their mouths,[n]
31 God's anger rose against them;
he put to death the sturdiest[o] among them,
cutting down the young men of Israel.

32 In spite of all this, they kept on sinning;
in spite of his wonders,[p] they did not believe.[q]
33 So he ended their days in futility[r]
and their years in terror.
34 Whenever God slew them, they would seek[s] him;
they eagerly turned to him again.
35 They remembered that God was their Rock,[t]
that God Most High was their Redeemer.[u]
36 But then they would flatter him with their mouths,[v]
lying to him with their tongues;
37 their hearts were not loyal[w] to him,
they were not faithful to his covenant.
38 Yet he was merciful;[x]
he forgave[y] their iniquities[z]
and did not destroy them.
Time after time he restrained his anger
and did not stir up his full wrath.
39 He remembered that they were but flesh,[a]
a passing breeze[b] that does not return.

40 How often they rebelled[c] against him in the desert[d]
and grieved him[e] in the wasteland!
41 Again and again they put God to the test;[f]
they vexed the Holy One of Israel.[g]
42 They did not remember his power—
the day he redeemed them from the oppressor,
43 the day he displayed his miraculous signs in Egypt,
his wonders in the region of Zoan.
44 He turned their rivers to blood;[h]
they could not drink from their streams.
45 He sent swarms of flies[i] that devoured them,
and frogs[j] that devastated them.
46 He gave their crops to the grasshopper,
their produce to the locust.[k]
47 He destroyed their vines with hail[l]
and their sycamore-figs with sleet.
48 He gave over their cattle to the hail,
their livestock[m] to bolts of lightning.
49 He unleashed against them his hot anger,[n]
his wrath, indignation and hostility—
a band of destroying angels.
50 He prepared a path for his anger;
he did not spare them from death
but gave them over to the plague.
51 He struck down all the firstborn of Egypt,[o]
the firstfruits of manhood in the tents of Ham.[p]

78:30 [n]Nu 11:33
78:31 [o]Isa 10:16
78:32 [p]ver 11 [q]ver 22
78:33 [r]Nu 14:29,35
78:34 [s]Hos 5:15
78:35 [t]Dt 32:4 [u]Dt 9:26
78:36 [v]Eze 33:31
78:37 [w]ver 8; Ac 8:21
78:38 [x]Ex 34:6 [y]Isa 48:10 [z]Nu 14:18,20
78:39 [a]Ge 6:3; Ps 103:14 [b]Job 7:7; Jas 4:14
78:40 [c]Heb 3:16 [d]Ps 95:8; 106:14 [e]Eph 4:30
78:41 [f]Nu 14:22 [g]2Ki 19:22; Ps 89:18
78:44 [h]Ex 7:20-21; Ps 105:29
78:45 [i]Ex 8:24; Ps 105:31 [j]Ex 8:2,6
78:46 [k]Ex 10:13
78:47 [l]Ex 9:23; Ps 105:32
78:48 [m]Ex 9:25
78:49 [n]Ex 15:7
78:51 [o]Ex 12:29; Ps 135:8 [p]Ps 105:23; 106:22

78:32 all this. All God's wonderful acts of salvation and judgment. This pattern was repeated throughout the Old Testament, perhaps best represented by the book of Judges. See *WLC* 150; *WSC* 83.
78:33 in futility. The meaning is identical to that favorite adjective of the Teacher in the book of Ecclesiastes, "meaningless" (see note on 62:9; see Ecc 1:2). The term describes the world apart from God, under the curse of the fall. Apart from God, the human race has nothing to which to cling; people's lives lack purpose and significance, and they live in fear of death.
78:34–37 See *WLC* 151.
78:34 they would seek him. When the Israelites sinned, God judged them. Their habitual pattern was then to return to him. Proverbs 3:12 and 13:25 teach that God regularly disciplines those whom he loves. This applies not only on an individual basis, but also on a corporate level. By afflicting his covenant people in the desert, he strongly prompted them to obey him.
78:36 lying to him. Despite their repentance, the Israelites soon fell into sin again. The cycle repeated itself throughout the desert journey (e.g., Nu 11; 14; 16); and continued in the promised land (See Jdg 2:6–23).
78:37 not faithful to his covenant. See verse 10. God initiated a relationship with Israel through his grace and expressed his will to his people through his law, which was backed by the curses and blessings of the covenant. The Israelites, however, through their disobedience called down God's judgment upon themselves.
78:40 often they rebelled. See Numbers 11, 14 and 16 for examples.
78:42–51 The psalmist listed six of the plagues on Egypt. The plagues had graphically displayed God's power to judge; yet Israel, as well as Pharaoh, had remained hard of heart.

78:52 [q]Ps 77:20
78:53 [r]Ex 14:28 [s]Ps 106:10
78:54 [t]Ex 15:17; Ps 44:3
78:55 [u]Ps 44:2 [v]Jos 13:7
78:57 [w]Eze 20:27 [x]Hos 7:16
78:58 [y]Jdg 2:12 [z]Lev 26:30 [a]Ex 20:4; Dt 32:21
78:59 [b]Dt 32:19
78:60 [c]Jos 18:1
78:61 [d]Ps 132:8 [e]1Sa 4:17
78:63 [f]Nu 11:1 [g]Jer 7:34; 16:9
78:64 [h]1Sa 4:17; 22:18
78:65 [i]Ps 44:23
78:66 [j]1Sa 5:6
78:68 [k]Ps 87:2
78:70 [l]1Sa 16:1
78:71 [m]2Sa 5:2; Ps 28:9
78:72 [n]1Ki 9:4

52 But he brought his people out like a flock;[q]
he led them like sheep through the desert.
53 He guided them safely, so they were unafraid;
but the sea engulfed[r] their enemies.[s]
54 Thus he brought them to the border of his holy land,
to the hill country his right hand[t] had taken.
55 He drove out nations[u] before them
and allotted their lands to them as an inheritance;[v]
he settled the tribes of Israel in their homes.

56 But they put God to the test
and rebelled against the Most High;
they did not keep his statutes.
57 Like their fathers[w] they were disloyal and faithless,
as unreliable as a faulty bow.[x]
58 They angered him[y] with their high places;[z]
they aroused his jealousy with their idols.[a]
59 When God heard them, he was very angry;
he rejected Israel[b] completely.
60 He abandoned the tabernacle of Shiloh,[c]
the tent he had set up among men.
61 He sent ⌊the ark of⌋ his might[d] into captivity,[e]
his splendor into the hands of the enemy.
62 He gave his people over to the sword;
he was very angry with his inheritance.
63 Fire consumed[f] their young men,
and their maidens had no wedding songs;[g]
64 their priests were put to the sword,[h]
and their widows could not weep.

65 Then the Lord awoke as from sleep,[i]
as a man wakes from the stupor of wine.
66 He beat back his enemies;
he put them to everlasting shame.[j]
67 Then he rejected the tents of Joseph,
he did not choose the tribe of Ephraim;
68 but he chose the tribe of Judah,
Mount Zion,[k] which he loved.
69 He built his sanctuary like the heights,
like the earth that he established forever.
70 He chose David[l] his servant
and took him from the sheep pens;
71 from tending the sheep he brought him
to be the shepherd[m] of his people Jacob,
of Israel his inheritance.
72 And David shepherded them with integrity of heart;[n]
with skillful hands he led them.

78:52 like a flock. See 77:20.
78:54–64 Like their fathers. God had blessed his people by making them at home in the promised land, but they had once again quickly forgotten him.
78:55 He drove out nations. Israel had fought, but the faithful knew that it was God, the Divine Warrior, who had won the victories against their enemies. The defeat of Jericho demonstrated that reliance on God would be necessary in all the battles of the conquest (Jos 5:13—6:27).
78:56 they put God to the test. The Israelites had failed to comply with God's law in the desert, neither had they kept it in the promised land. See Judges 2:10–15. See *WLC* 150; *WSC* 83.
78:58 with their idols. The height of their rebellion was their idolatry.
78:60 the tabernacle of Shiloh. In the promised land the tabernacle was set up at Shiloh (Jos 18:1), where it housed the ark during Eli's judgeship. Shiloh was approximately 20 miles northeast of Jerusalem, in the tribal territory of Ephraim.
78:61 the ark . . . into captivity. During Samuel's youth, God had judged Israel and its leaders, particularly Eli's sons, by abandoning Israel in battle and allowing the Philistines to capture the ark (1Sa 4:1—5:12).
78:65 as from sleep. God had abandoned the Israelites in judgment and refused to listen to their cries for justice. It was as though he were in a deep sleep, from which he could not be aroused. At last, like a warrior awakening, he came to their rescue. See note on 44:23.
78:67 he rejected . . . Ephraim. Refers to God's abandonment of the Shiloh sanctuary and perhaps also to the rejection of Saul's monarchy.
78:68 he chose the tribe of Judah. Jerusalem succeeded Shiloh as the location of God's special presence (see theological article "The Presence of God" at 1Ki 8). Though not belonging to the tribe of Judah, it became David's capital; since it bordered Judah, it came to be considered a part of it. When the north and the south broke apart under Rehoboam, Jerusalem, as the seat of the monarchy, remained in the control of David's dynasty. **Mount Zion.** See note on 2:6.
78:70 sheep pens. An image recalling David's humble origins (1Sa 16:11–13).

Psalm 79

A psalm of Asaph.

[1] O God, the nations have invaded your inheritance;[o]
they have defiled your holy temple,
they have reduced Jerusalem to rubble.[p]
[2] They have given the dead bodies of your servants
as food to the birds of the air,
the flesh of your saints to the beasts of the earth.[q]
[3] They have poured out blood like water
all around Jerusalem,
and there is no one to bury the dead.[r]
[4] We are objects of reproach to our neighbors,
of scorn and derision to those around us.[s]

[5] How long,[t] O LORD? Will you be angry[u] forever?
How long will your jealousy burn like fire?[v]
[6] Pour out your wrath[w] on the nations
that do not acknowledge[x] you,
on the kingdoms
that do not call on your name;[y]
[7] for they have devoured Jacob
and destroyed his homeland.
[8] Do not hold against us the sins of the fathers;[z]
may your mercy come quickly to meet us,
for we are in desperate need.[a]

[9] Help us,[b] O God our Savior,
for the glory of your name;
deliver us and forgive our sins
for your name's sake.[c]
[10] Why should the nations say,
"Where is their God?"[d]
Before our eyes, make known among the nations
that you avenge[e] the outpoured blood of your servants.
[11] May the groans of the prisoners come before you;
by the strength of your arm
preserve those condemned to die.

[12] Pay back into the laps[f] of our neighbors seven times[g]
the reproach they have hurled at you, O Lord.
[13] Then we your people, the sheep of your pasture,[h]
will praise you forever;[i]
from generation to generation
we will recount your praise.

79:1 [o]Ps 74:2 [p]2Ki 25:9
79:2 [q]Dt 28:26; Jer 7:33
79:3 [r]Jer 16:4
79:4 [s]Ps 44:13; 80:6
79:5 [t]Ps 74:10 [u]Ps 74:1; 85:5 [v]Dt 29:20; Ps 89:46; Zep 3:8
79:6 [w]Ps 69:24; Rev 16:1 [x]Jer 10:25; 2Th 1:8 [y]Ps 14:4
79:8 [z]Isa 64:9 [a]Ps 116:6; 142:6
79:9 [b]2Ch 14:11 [c]Ps 25:11; 31:3; Jer 14:7
79:10 [d]Ps 42:10 [e]Ps 94:1
79:12 [f]Isa 65:6; Jer 32:18 [g]Ge 4:15
79:13 [h]Ps 74:1; 95:7 [i]Ps 44:8

78:72 David . . . with integrity of heart. A positive conclusion: A faithful king was established in Jerusalem, the place of God's special presence.

Psalm 79 *Introduction.* Psalm 79 is a lament in which the psalmist spoke on behalf of the community of the faithful as they mourned the destruction of Jerusalem and its temple. The reference to the destruction of the temple (v. 1) dates this psalm during the period following the Babylonian defeat of Jerusalem in 587 B.C.

79:1 the nations have invaded your inheritance. God had established the Israelites as his chosen people in Canaan. They were to become a blessing to the nations around them (Ge 12:1–3; 22:18), and God would prosper them in the land. However, as they disobeyed the covenant, God carried out the covenant curses he had threatened (Dt 28:15–68) by sending a foreign nation (in this case the Babylonians) against them. Both city and temple were destroyed in 587 B.C. (1Ki 25; 1Ch 36:15–23; La 1–5).

79:2 your servants . . . your saints. Though the destruction of Jerusalem was the direct result of Judah's general rejection of the Lord, those who remained faithful also suffered at the hands of the Babylonians. The psalmist specified the death of the faithful as he appealed to God for restoration.

79:5 How long . . . ? The psalmist's endurance was at an end. See note on 6:3. **your jealousy.** The psalmist did not deny the appropriateness of the punishment but begged the Lord to bring it to a conclusion. See note on Exodus 20:5.

79:6 Pour out your wrath on the nations. The psalmist called for a reversal. He desired the Lord to turn his wrath away from Israel toward the nations God was using to punish his people. The Lord ultimately answered the psalmist's prayer, restoring Israel (Ezr; Ne; Hag; Zec) while devastating Babylonia (Da 5).

79:8 sins of the fathers. This psalm may have been written a long time after the destruction of Jerusalem. The sins of the fathers, chief of which was idolatry, are recounted, particularly in 1 and 2 Kings.

79:10 "Where is their God?" To the surrounding nations, Israel's defeat would have implied either that God had been defeated by the Babylonian god Marduk or that God had abandoned Israel in favor of the Babylonians. While God had enabled the Babylonians in order to bring judgment against Israel, he did not favor or support them as a people. Rather, he rejected them as idolaters; the Babylonians, who were polytheists, believed that the God of Israel was subordinate to Marduk. The psalmist appealed to the Lord to save Israel in order to protect his own reputation by dispelling the Babylonians' false notion (v. 9).

79:11 the prisoners. The psalmist appealed to God's special concern for the oppressed and vulnerable, portraying his people as suffering prisoners rather than emphasizing the sin for which they had been justly sent into exile.

Psalm 80

For the director of music. To ⌊the tune of⌋ "The Lilies of the Covenant." Of Asaph. A psalm.

80:1 jPs 77:20 kEx 25:22
80:2 lNu 2:18-24 mPs 35:23
80:3 nPs 85:4; La 5:21 oNu 6:25
80:5 pPs 42:3; Isa 30:20
80:6 qPs 79:4
80:8 rIsa 5:1-2; Jer 2:21 sJos 13:6; Ac 7:45
80:11 tPs 72:8
80:12 uPs 89:40; Isa 5:5
80:13 vJer 5:6
80:14 wIsa 63:15

1 Hear us, O Shepherd of Israel,
you who lead Joseph like a flock;[j]
you who sit enthroned between the cherubim,[k] shine forth
2 before Ephraim, Benjamin and Manasseh.[l]
Awaken[m] your might;
come and save us.

3 Restore[n] us,[o] O God;
make your face shine upon us,
that we may be saved.

4 O LORD God Almighty,
how long will your anger smolder
against the prayers of your people?
5 You have fed them with the bread of tears;
you have made them drink tears by the bowlful.[p]
6 You have made us a source of contention to our neighbors,
and our enemies mock us.[q]

7 Restore us, O God Almighty;
make your face shine upon us,
that we may be saved.

8 You brought a vine[r] out of Egypt;
you drove out[s] the nations and planted it.
9 You cleared the ground for it,
and it took root and filled the land.
10 The mountains were covered with its shade,
the mighty cedars with its branches.
11 It sent out its boughs to the Sea,[a]
its shoots as far as the River.[b] [t]

12 Why have you broken down its walls[u]
so that all who pass by pick its grapes?
13 Boars from the forest ravage[v] it
and the creatures of the field feed on it.
14 Return to us, O God Almighty!
Look down from heaven and see![w]
Watch over this vine,
15 the root your right hand has planted,
the son[c] you have raised up for yourself.

[a] *11* Probably the Mediterranean [b] *11* That is, the Euphrates [c] *15* Or *branch*

Psalm 80 *Introduction.* Psalm 80 laments God's anger against the community and pleads with him repeatedly (vv. 3,7,19) to return his blessing to it. The mention of the tribes of Ephraim, Manasseh and Benjamin in verse 2 suggests that the psalm was written during the last days of the northern kingdom (2Ki 17).
80:1 O Shepherd. God was called Israel's shepherd (see Ps 23) because he guided the nation and provided for the people's needs. In the ancient Near East this epithet was often conferred upon kings. Thus, the title as applied to God implies that he is a king who cares for his people. Compare 77:20, 78:53, 71–72 and 79:13. **between the cherubim.** Above the ark of the covenant (God's footstool) in the Most Holy Place of the temple. The wings of the cherubim flanked the invisible throne (Ex 25:22; Nu 7:89). **shine forth.** Note the parallel with the priestly benediction in Numbers 6:24–26. The psalmist invoked the Lord to reveal his gracious presence to his people.
80:2 Ephraim, Benjamin and Manasseh. The chief tribes of the northern kingdom (see introduction to this psalm).
80:5 bread of tears. The people's mourning was as frequent as their meals.
80:8 vine. Israel was the vine that God had transplanted from bondage in Egypt to the fruitful soil of Canaan. The psalmist appealed to God's ownership of Israel and to his noteworthy acts of the past. Isaiah 5:1–7 also develops the image of Israel as a vine. Both these passages provide background for the symbolism of Jesus' description of himself as the "true vine" (Jn 15:1). See Genesis 49:22 for the possible backdrop to the psalm.
80:10 covered with its shade. The lowly vine (Israel) had become so great through the blessings of God that even the mountains and gigantic cedars were protected by its shade, meaning that it had greatly expanded its territory.
80:11 the Sea. The Mediterranean. **the River.** The Euphrates. This language is reminiscent of the promise to Abraham of a vast land (Ge 15:18) and of Moses' description of the promised land (Dt 1:6–8).
80:12 Why have you broken . . . ? The psalmist recognized that, no matter which human army were to defeat Israel, God, the One who controlled all the nations, would have to allow it. The answer to the psalmist's question is the theme of the book of Kings, which described the apostasy of the northern kingdom in graphic terms (see especially 1Ki 17:7–23).
80:15 the son. It is unnecessary to emend this word to "branch." Israel, the vine, is also God's son; Jesus the true vine is the true and unique Son, through whom the relation of sonship is restored.

[16] Your vine is cut down, it is burned with fire;
at your rebuke[x] your people perish.
[17] Let your hand rest on the man at your right hand,
the son of man you have raised up for yourself.
[18] Then we will not turn away from you;
revive us, and we will call on your name.

[19] Restore us, O LORD God Almighty;
make your face shine upon us,
that we may be saved.

Psalm 81

For the director of music. According to *gittith*.[a] Of Asaph.

[1] Sing for joy to God our strength;
shout aloud to the God of Jacob![y]
[2] Begin the music, strike the tambourine,[z]
play the melodious harp[a] and lyre.

[3] Sound the ram's horn at the New Moon,
and when the moon is full, on the day of our Feast;
[4] this is a decree for Israel,
an ordinance of the God of Jacob.
[5] He established it as a statute for Joseph
when he went out against Egypt,[b]
where we heard a language we did not understand.[bc]

[6] He says, "I removed the burden from their shoulders;[d]
their hands were set free from the basket.
[7] In your distress you called[e] and I rescued you,
I answered[f] you out of a thundercloud;
I tested you at the waters of Meribah.[g] *Selah*

[8] "Hear, O my people,[h] and I will warn you—
if you would but listen to me, O Israel!
[9] You shall have no foreign god[i] among you;
you shall not bow down to an alien god.
[10] I am the LORD your God,
who brought you up out of Egypt.[j]
Open wide your mouth and I will fill[k] it.

[11] "But my people would not listen to me;
Israel would not submit to me.[l]

80:16 [x]Ps 39:11; 76:6
81:1 [y]Ps 66:1
81:2 [z]Ex 15:20 [a]Ps 92:3
81:5 [b]Ex 11:4 [c]Ps 114:1
81:6 [d]Isa 9:4
81:7 [e]Ex 2:23; Ps 50:15 [f]Ex 19:19 [g]Ex 17:7
81:8 [h]Ps 50:7
81:9 [i]Ex 20:3; Dt 32:12; Isa 43:12
81:10 [j]Ex 20:2 [k]Ps 107:9
81:11 [l]Ex 32:1-6

[a] Title: Probably a musical term [b] 5 Or / *and we heard a voice we had not known*

80:17 the son of man. Though the reference might be to Israel, it is more likely to the Davidic king and is therefore Messianic in nature.

Psalm 81 *Introduction.* It is difficult to fit this psalm into one of the basic genres outlined in the Introduction. It begins like a hymn, but the bulk of the psalm contains a divine pronouncement in which God reminded Israel of the exodus and of the nation's subsequent apostasy. God called upon the Israelites to return to him, promising to subdue their enemies and provide for their needs. The original setting of the psalm was most likely the Feast of Tabernacles. (see v. 3).

81:2 Begin the music. The psalms teach exuberant worship, and the hymns in particular enthusiastically praise God's name.

81:3 New Moon. Although we lack a systematic description of this event, the Bible occasionally mentions a special celebration that took place at the time of the new moon. See 1 Samuel 20:5 and 18, 2 Kings 4:23, Isaiah 66:23, Ezekiel 46:1 and 6 and Amos 8:5. In Colossians 2:16 Paul called the commemoration "a shadow of the things that were to come."

81:4 this. That is, the celebration of the New Moon.

81:5 a language we did not understand. There are at least two possible interpretations of this phrase. The first is as a reference to Egyptian, the language of Israel's pre-exodus oppressors. The second translates the whole clause "and we heard a voice we had not known" (see NIV text note) and understands it to be an introduction to the divine oracle that follows.

81:6 I removed the burden. God reminded the Israelites of how he had delivered them from slavery in Egypt.

81:7 out of a thundercloud. God often appeared accompanied by thunder and lightening, but perhaps this reference is specifically to his manifestation at Mount Sinai (Exodus 19:16–25). **Meribah.** See Exodus 17:1–7 and Numbers 20:1–13.

81:9 you shall not bow down to an alien god. God reminded Israel of the first and foundational commandment: to worship the Lord only (Ex 20:3). The warning implied that his people were not observing this commandment faithfully.

81:10–12 See *WCF* 5.6; *WLC* 68,195; *WSC* 47.

81:10 I am the LORD your God. Reminiscent of the words that precede the Ten Commandments (Ex 20:1). This declaration established the basic relationship—of grace—between Israel and God. **I will fill it.** Much of Israel's history, as recorded in the books of Joshua through Chronicles, is the story of God's people seeking satisfaction apart from God. If they were anxious about a lack of rain, they turned to Baal (1Ki 18). If they were apprehensive about enemies, they sought a strong king (1Sa 8). The Israelites habitually forgot that they had a God who both could and would fulfill all their needs.

81:11 Israel would not submit to me. A summary statement of the sad truth that characterized Israel's history: God's chosen people continually bypassed the true God and sought after idols. See *WLC* 105.

81:12 [m]Ac 7:42; Ro 1:24
81:13 [n]Dt 5:29; Isa 48:18
81:14 [o]Ps 47:3 [p]Am 1:8
81:16 [q]Dt 32:14

12 So I gave them over[m] to their stubborn hearts
to follow their own devices.

13 "If my people would but listen to me,[n]
if Israel would follow my ways,
14 how quickly would I subdue[o] their enemies
and turn my hand against[p] their foes!
15 Those who hate the LORD would cringe before him,
and their punishment would last forever.
16 But you would be fed with the finest of wheat;[q]
with honey from the rock I would satisfy you."

Psalm 82

A psalm of Asaph.

82:1 [r]Ps 58:11; Isa 3:13
82:2 [s]Dt 1:17 [t]Ps 58:1-2; Pr 18:5
82:3 [u]Dt 24:17 [v]Jer 22:16
82:5 [w]Ps 14:4; Mic 3:1 [x]Isa 59:9 [y]Ps 11:3
82:6 [z]Jn 10:34*
82:7 [a]Ps 49:12; Eze 31:14
82:8 [b]Ps 12:5 [c]Ps 2:8; Rev 11:15

1 God presides in the great assembly;
he gives judgment[r] among the "gods":

2 "How long will you[a] defend the unjust
and show partiality[s] to the wicked?[t] *Selah*
3 Defend the cause of the weak and fatherless;[u]
maintain the rights of the poor[v] and oppressed.
4 Rescue the weak and needy;
deliver them from the hand of the wicked.

5 "They know nothing, they understand nothing.[w]
They walk about in darkness;[x]
all the foundations[y] of the earth are shaken.

6 "I said, 'You are "gods";[z]
you are all sons of the Most High.'
7 But you will die[a] like mere men;
you will fall like every other ruler."

8 Rise up,[b] O God, judge the earth,
for all the nations are your inheritance.[c]

Psalm 83

A song. A psalm of Asaph.

83:1 [d]Ps 28:1; 35:22

1 O God, do not keep silent;[d]
be not quiet, O God, be not still.

[a] *2* The Hebrew is plural.

81:13 If my people would but listen to me. The yearning and pathos of God's compassion for Israel are clearly demonstrated in this statement. Though his own people continued to reject and ignore him, God expressed his profound desire for an intimate relationship with them.
81:14 subdue their enemies. The tragedy of the Israelites' apostasy was that, though they sought other saviors, God was the only One who could save them from their enemies.
Psalm 82 *Introduction.* Psalm 82, though brief, presents some challenges. Chief among them is the interpretation of the "gods" mentioned in verses 1 and 6. The psalm is difficult to categorize by genre. As is the case with Psalm 81, much of it is a divine oracle. However, the psalm ends like a lament, with the author entreating the Lord to "rise up," a typical petition in psalms sung in the context of holy war.
82:1 the great assembly. The exact scope of the assembly is unclear. Either God made judgments in the context of the heavenly assembly (which included only the spiritual powers) or in the context of the assembly of all his creatures. The object of his judgment is earthly. **gods.** The meaning of the Hebrew term *elohim,* here translated "gods," is somewhat flexible. In most of its Old Testament uses it denotes God himself and is translated "God." Less often it is plural in meaning, referring to the false "gods." In this use, the word identifies supernatural, created beings who wield authority in heaven or over the nations. Although the most common reference is to false gods (therefore associated with demons rather than with angels), at least some angelic powers could easily be categorized as "gods" by virtue of their nature and authority. In a related use, it sometimes refers to human rulers. In Psalm 82 a number of scholars take *elohim* as a reference to the angelic powers that comprise God's heavenly council. A second interpretation, typically held by more liberal scholars, interprets "gods" as pagan deities subordinate to Yahweh. Possibly the best interpretation understands the "gods" as human judges. This approach is supported by precedent in the use of "god" for human judges in Exodus 21:6, as well as in 22:8 and following. The human nature of these "gods" is indicated by verses 6–7, of which a rough interpretative paraphrase might be, "you are like God as judges, but you are like everyone else, since you are mortal." Compare 138:1.
82:3–6 See *WCF* 23.2; *WLC* 135; *BC* 36.
82:3 Defend . . . the weak and needy. An important responsibility of the king was to care for the vulnerable in society, preeminently the widows and the fatherless who lacked a familial support system.
8:6 gods. See note on verse 1.
82:8 judge the earth. Since the human judges were failing to reflect his justice, God himself would have to undertake this task.
Psalm 83 *Introduction.* Psalm 83 is a poem of lament on behalf of the people of God. The psalmist specifically requested that the Lord aid the nation of Israel against the foreign enemies who wanted to destroy it. The psalmist called on the Lord to rise up as the divine warrior to curtail Israel's attackers. Though a number of specific nations and tribes are mentioned (vv. 5–8), the psalm cannot with certainty be dated (see note on v. 5). It comprises a model prayer for the Christian's spiritual warfare—Christians invoke the

[2]See how your enemies are astir,[e]
how your foes rear their heads.[f]
[3]With cunning they conspire[g] against your people;
they plot against those you cherish.
[4]"Come," they say, "let us destroy[h] them as a nation,
that the name of Israel be remembered[i] no more."

[5]With one mind they plot together;[j]
they form an alliance against you—
[6]the tents of Edom[k] and the Ishmaelites,
of Moab[l] and the Hagrites,[m]
[7]Gebal,[a n] Ammon and Amalek,
Philistia, with the people of Tyre.[o]
[8]Even Assyria has joined them
to lend strength to the descendants of Lot.[p] *Selah*

[9]Do to them as you did to Midian,[q]
as you did to Sisera and Jabin at the river Kishon,[r]
[10]who perished at Endor
and became like refuse[s] on the ground.
[11]Make their nobles like Oreb and Zeeb,[t]
all their princes like Zebah and Zalmunna,[u]
[12]who said, "Let us take possession[v]
of the pasturelands of God."

[13]Make them like tumbleweed, O my God,
like chaff[w] before the wind.
[14]As fire consumes the forest
or a flame sets the mountains ablaze,[x]
[15]so pursue them with your tempest
and terrify them with your storm.[y]
[16]Cover their faces with shame[z]
so that men will seek your name, O LORD.

[17]May they ever be ashamed and dismayed;
may they perish in disgrace.[a]
[18]Let them know that you, whose name is the LORD—
that you alone are the Most High over all the earth.[b]

83:2 [e]Ps 2:1; Isa 17:12 [f]Jdg 8:28; Ps 81:15
83:3 [g]Ps 31:13
83:4 [h]Est 3:6 [i]Jer 11:19
83:5 [j]Ps 2:2
83:6 [k]Ps 137:7 [l]2Ch 20:1 [m]Ge 25:16
83:7 [n]Jos 13:5 [o]Eze 27:3
83:8 [p]Dt 2:9
83:9 [q]Jdg 7:1-23 [r]Jdg 4:23-24
83:10 [s]Zep 1:17
83:11 [t]Jdg 7:25 [u]Jdg 8:12,21
83:12 [v]2Ch 20:11
83:13 [w]Ps 35:5; Isa 17:13
83:14 [x]Dt 32:22; Isa 9:18
83:15 [y]Job 9:17
83:16 [z]Ps 109:29; 132:18
83:17 [a]Ps 35:4
83:18 [b]Ps 59:13

[a] 7 That is, Byblos

Lord to vanquish the spiritual forces of evil (see "Introduction: Christ in Psalms"). See *WLC* 190; *WSC* 101.
83:1 do not keep silent . . . be not still. At the heart of the covenant was God's promise to be present with his people. From the psalmist's perspective, though, God was absent from them as they confronted the enemy. As his presence in warfare led to victory, so his absence resulted in defeat. Accordingly, the psalmist began his lament with a call for God to make his warlike presence known. See theological article "The Presence of God" at 1 Kings 8.
83:2 your enemies are astir. In contrast with the apparent inactivity of God, the enemy was in motion to destroy Israel.
83:3 they conspire. Israel's enemies were bound by a common cause: They banded together to plot the downfall of God's people (cf. 2:1–3; 48:4).
83:5 they. The nations involved in the plot against Israel, listed in verses 6–8. Attempts have been made to pinpoint the historical situation behind the psalm, but no period can be identified during which all of these enemies were actively hostile toward Israel at the same time. The closest scenario was Jehoshaphat's war, recorded in 1 Chronicles 20, but no mention is made there of Assyria.
83:8 descendants of Lot. That is, Moab and Ammon; compare Genesis 19:30–38.
83:9 Midian. Through his supremacy as divine warrior, God had empowered Gideon to destroy the Midianites (Jdg 7). **Sisera and Jabin.** Early on in the period of the Judges, Jabin was a Canaanite king and Sisera his general. They had oppressed Israel, but God had delivered the Israelites by destroying these adversaries through the military strategizing of Deborah (Jdg 4–5).
83:11 Oreb and Zeeb. Two leaders destroyed by Ephraimites during Gideon's battle against the Midianites (Jdg 7:25—8:3). **Zebah and Zalmunna.** The Midianite kings who had been captured and executed by Gideon; see Judges 8:4–21.
83:12 the pasturelands of God. A description of the promised land in which God, the Shepherd, had settled his sheep, the Israelites. The quote was ascribed to Israel's enemies to highlight the blasphemous nature of their plots. They justly deserved the punishment that would be meted out to them.
83:13 like tumbleweed . . . like chaff. As opposed to the righteous, who are identified elsewhere in the Psalter (Ps 1) as deep-rooted trees, the wicked are likened to the tumbleweed and chaff that are blown away by the least gust of wind and serve no productive function whatsoever.
83:15 your tempest . . . your storm. God's wrath was often compared to a violent storm; compare 18:7–15 and Nahum 1:3.
83:16 seek your name. A redemptive reason behind the judgment: As God wrathfully judged the wickedness of the attackers, they would recognize their folly and turn to him.
83:18 Most High. The Hebrew sounds similar to the most common epithet given to the Canaanite god Baal. The psalmist asked the Lord to judge the nations so they would see that Yahweh himself, not Baal, was the only God of all the world. See *WLC* 190.

Psalm 84

For the director of music. According to *gittith*.[a] Of the Sons of Korah. A psalm.

84:1 cPs 27:4; 43:3; 132:5
84:2 dPs 42:1-2
84:3 ePs 43:4 fPs 5:2
84:5 gPs 81:1 hJer 31:6
84:6 iJoel 2:23
84:7 jPr 4:18 kDt 16:16
84:9 lPs 59:11 m1Sa 16:6; Ps 2:2; 132:17
84:10 n1Ch 23:5
84:11 oIsa 60:19; Rev 21:23 pGe 15:1

1 How lovely is your dwelling place,[c]
O LORD Almighty!
2 My soul yearns,[d] even faints,
for the courts of the LORD;
my heart and my flesh cry out
for the living God.

3 Even the sparrow has found a home,
and the swallow a nest for herself,
where she may have her young—
a place near your altar,[e]
O LORD Almighty, my King and my God.[f]
4 Blessed are those who dwell in your house;
they are ever praising you. *Selah*

5 Blessed are those whose strength[g] is in you,
who have set their hearts on pilgrimage.[h]
6 As they pass through the Valley of Baca,
they make it a place of springs;
the autumn[i] rains also cover it with pools.[b]
7 They go from strength to strength,[j]
till each appears[k] before God in Zion.

8 Hear my prayer, O LORD God Almighty;
listen to me, O God of Jacob. *Selah*
9 Look upon our shield,[c] [l] O God;
look with favor on your anointed one.[m]

10 Better is one day in your courts
than a thousand elsewhere;
I would rather be a doorkeeper[n] in the house of my God
than dwell in the tents of the wicked.
11 For the LORD God is a sun[o] and shield;[p]
the LORD bestows favor and honor;

a Title: Probably a musical term b 6 Or *blessings* c 9 Or *sovereign*

Psalm 84 *Introduction.* In Psalm 84 the author expressed a deep longing for the presence of God. The opening of the psalm sounds similar to the better known Psalm 42 and indicates that the psalmist was far from the temple, the place where God chose to reveal his presence. While Christians do not have to travel to a special location to enjoy God's presence (Jn 4:21–24), the psalm nonetheless gives voice to the yearning and blessedness experienced in Christ's nearness.

84:1 your dwelling place. The temple, the place where God chose to reveal himself to his people (1Ki 8). **LORD Almighty.** Also translated "LORD of Hosts." The title was often connected with God's activity as a warrior who protected his people. See note on 1 Samuel 1:3.

84:2 living God. The true object of the psalmist's devotion was not the sanctuary but the God who revealed himself there. It was tempting for Israel to forget God and rely on the external trappings of religion (Jer 7).

84:3 sparrow . . . swallow. Note the playful envy expressed by the psalmist, who stated that he was jealous of the birds that were able to nest near God's altar. Through this imagery he conveyed his deep longings to be as close as possible to God.

84:4 Blessed. See note on 1:1. **your house.** The place where God dwelled on Earth was heaven on Earth. Christians can regard this verse as a glimpse of the current happiness of heaven, where God's people bask continually in his presence, ever praising his name, and of the future happiness of the new earth (Rev 21:1—22:5).

84:5 Blessed. See note on 1:1. **whose strength is in you.** That is, those whose vitality is found in God's power, not in their own. **pilgrimage.** A special trip made during festival time in which a person from outside Jerusalem journeyed to the temple in order to enjoy God's presence in worship. The songs of ascents (Pss 120–134) were most likely set during these trips (see "Introduction" to Ps 120).

84:6 Valley of Baca. The location of this valley is unknown. Some commentators relate the name to a similar-sounding Hebrew verb (*bakah*) that means "to weep." Some identify the noun (*baka'*) with a kind of tree that flourishes in dry locales: balsam or aspen. The context indicates that the valley, though arid, was transformed by the presence of the joyful pilgrims as they made their way toward Jerusalem. **pools.** The NIV text note indicates that the word could also be rendered as "blessings." The "pools" were a specific type of blessing.

84:7 in Zion. The location of the temple and the goal and destination of the pilgrimage. See notes on 2:6, 50:2, 74:2 and 137:1.

84:9 our shield . . . your anointed one. In the midst of his prayer of longing for God's presence, the psalmist interceded for the king. The king was not only the political leader of Israel but also the reflection of God's kingship on Earth. He represented God before the people and the people before God.

84:10 in your courts. The psalmist expressed the intensity of his desire to be in God's presence by stating that he would rather accept the lowest of functions in the sanctuary for a short time than to dwell permanently (and presumably enjoy a higher status) anywhere else.

84:11 the LORD God is a sun. The radiant sun provides life-giving warmth and light; the glorious God gives life through his favor. The powerful, burning rays of the sun in the semiarid region of which the psalmist wrote would suggest use of the sun as an apt image for God's power. **no good thing does he withhold.** See Romans 8:28–39, especially verse 32.

no good thing does he withhold[q]
from those whose walk is blameless.

12 O LORD Almighty,
blessed[r] is the man who trusts in you.

Psalm 85

For the director of music. Of the Sons of Korah. A psalm.

1 You showed favor to your land, O LORD;
you restored the fortunes[s] of Jacob.
2 You forgave[t] the iniquity[u] of your people
and covered all their sins. *Selah*
3 You set aside all your wrath[v]
and turned from your fierce anger.[w]

4 Restore[x] us again, O God our Savior,
and put away your displeasure toward us.
5 Will you be angry with us forever?[y]
Will you prolong your anger through all generations?
6 Will you not revive[z] us again,
that your people may rejoice in you?
7 Show us your unfailing love, O LORD,
and grant us your salvation.

8 I will listen to what God the LORD will say;
he promises peace[a] to his people, his saints—
but let them not return to folly.
9 Surely his salvation[b] is near those who fear him,
that his glory[c] may dwell in our land.

10 Love and faithfulness[d] meet together;
righteousness[e] and peace kiss each other.
11 Faithfulness springs forth from the earth,
and righteousness[f] looks down from heaven.
12 The LORD will indeed give what is good,[g]
and our land will yield[h] its harvest.
13 Righteousness goes before him
and prepares the way for his steps.

Psalm 86

A prayer of David.

1 Hear, O LORD, and answer[i] me,
for I am poor and needy.

84:11 [q]Ps 34:10
84:12 [r]Ps 2:12
85:1 [s]Ps 14:7; Jer 30:18; Eze 39:25
85:2 [t]Nu 14:19 [u]Ps 78:38
85:3 [v]Ps 106:23 [w]Ex 32:12; Dt 13:17; Ps 78:38; Jnh 3:9
85:4 [x]Ps 80:3, 7
85:5 [y]Ps 79:5
85:6 [z]Ps 80:18; Hab 3:2
85:8 [a]Zec 9:10
85:9 [b]Isa 46:13 [c]Zec 2:5
85:10 [d]Ps 89:14; Pr 3:3 [e]Ps 72:2-3; Isa 32:17
85:11 [f]Isa 45:8
85:12 [g]Ps 84:11; Jas 1:17 [h]Lev 26:4; Ps 67:6; Zec 8:12
86:1 [i]Ps 17:6

Psalm 85 *Introduction.* Psalm 85 reflects back on the past with thanksgiving for salvation and looks ahead to the future with confidence, all the while dealing with God's wrath in the present. The psalm is a lament that calls for revival.
85:1 restored the fortunes. The psalmist recalled an earlier time when Israel had been languishing but when God had intervened to restore prosperity and happiness. No single event is specified by the psalmist, but a number of scenarios in Biblical history are illustrative: Perhaps most appropriate (though the psalm may have been composed years earlier) was the return from Babylonian captivity.
85:2 forgave the iniquity. The ill fortune of the Israelites was directly connected to their sin. Forgiveness of sins was requisite for the removal of God's wrath. Though repentance was necessary for forgiveness, all was based on the grace of God. See theological article "Repentance" at Psalm 51.
85:4 Restore us again. The past mercies of God were a reminder to both God and Israel that God could change the nation's fortunes. Past redemptive history provided present hope.
85:7 your unfailing love. That is, the love God has for those who are in covenant with him.
85:8 I will listen. The community had to this point been speaking ("us"), but here an individual stepped forward. Whoever he was (priest or prophet), he spoke on behalf of God, who gave the people assurance of future blessings. **he promises peace.** The word "peace" here indicates health and wholeness and, like "unfailing love," is associated with the covenant. God promised the restoration of intimate relationship with his people. **his saints.** This word is formed from the same root as that of "unfailing love" (v. 7) and refers to those who are in covenant with God. See *WLC* 175.
85:10 meet together . . . kiss each other. The blissful harmony of life in covenant with God is here described as consisting of life, love, friendship, faithfulness, righteousness and peace.
85:11 from the earth . . . from heaven. The future restored relationship with God would join God's blessing from heaven with the faithfulness of his people on Earth.
85:12 yield its harvest. The fertility of the land was a significant indicator of God's care and love for his covenant people. In semiarid Canaan, the harvest was often precarious. The Israelites knew that God was responsible for their harvest.
85:13 Righteousness goes before him. God's righteousness is here personified as his herald, announcing his arrival to his people (see Ps 23:6). See note on 4:1.
Psalm 86 *Introduction.* In Psalm 86 the psalmist unpretentiously called upon God to help him deal with his arrogant enemies.
Title. **A prayer.** For commentary on "prayer," see "Introduction: *Title*" to Psalm 17."
86:1 I am poor and needy. Aware of his own weakness and limitations, the psalmist laid his struggles before the Lord in prayer.

2 Guard my life, for I am devoted to you.
You are my God; save your servant
who trusts in you.[j]
3 Have mercy[k] on me, O Lord,
for I call[l] to you all day long.
4 Bring joy to your servant,
for to you, O Lord,
I lift[m] up my soul.

5 You are forgiving and good, O Lord,
abounding in love[n] to all who call to you.
6 Hear my prayer, O LORD;
listen to my cry for mercy.
7 In the day of my trouble[o] I will call to you,
for you will answer me.

8 Among the gods there is none like you,[p] O Lord;
no deeds can compare with yours.
9 All the nations you have made
will come and worship[q] before you, O Lord;
they will bring glory[r] to your name.
10 For you are great and do marvelous deeds;[s]
you alone[t] are God.

11 Teach me your way,[u] O LORD,
and I will walk in your truth;
give me an undivided[v] heart,
that I may fear your name.
12 I will praise you, O Lord my God, with all my heart;
I will glorify your name forever.
13 For great is your love toward me;
you have delivered me from the depths of the grave.[a]

14 The arrogant are attacking me, O God;
a band of ruthless men seeks my life—
men without regard for you.[w]
15 But you, O Lord, are a compassionate and gracious[x] God,
slow to anger, abounding in love and faithfulness.[y]
16 Turn to me and have mercy on me;
grant your strength to your servant
and save the son of your maidservant.[b][z]
17 Give me a sign of your goodness,
that my enemies may see it and be put to shame,
for you, O LORD, have helped me and comforted me.

Psalm 87

Of the Sons of Korah. A psalm. A song.

1 He has set his foundation on the holy mountain;
2 the LORD loves the gates of Zion[a]

86:2 [j]Ps 25:2; 31:14
86:3 [k]Ps 4:1; 57:1 [l]Ps 88:9
86:4 [m]Ps 25:1; 143:8
86:5 [n]Ex 34:6; Ne 9:17; Ps 103:8; 145:8; Joel 2:13; Jnh 4:2
86:7 [o]Ps 50:15
86:8 [p]Ex 15:11; Dt 3:24; Ps 89:6
86:9 [q]Ps 66:4; Rev 15:4 [r]Isa 43:7
86:10 [s]Ps 72:18 [t]Dt 6:4; Mk 12:29; 1Co 8:4
86:11 [u]Ps 25:5 [v]Jer 32:39
86:14 [w]Ps 54:3
86:15 [x]Ps 103:8 [y]Ex 34:6; Ne 9:17; Joel 2:13
86:16 [z]Ps 116:16
87:2 [a]Ps 78:68

[a] *13* Hebrew *Sheol* [b] *16* Or *save your faithful son*

86:2 who trusts in you. David recognized not only his own inability but also the source of true strength.
86:3 Have mercy on me. The psalmist knew that God's answer to his prayer was a manifestation of pure grace. God owed him nothing.
86:5 abounding in love. The special love God has for those in covenant with him. **to all who call to you.** God does not forgive indiscriminately; he forgives those who turn to him in repentance.
86:8 there is none like you. None of the gods of the surrounding nations measured up to the Lord in nature or deed. This confession of the uniqueness of God neither affirms nor denies the existence of other gods (see v. 10). The psalmist was simply comparing the foreign conception of the gods with the reality of Yahweh.
86:9 All the nations you have made. God is sovereign over all nations, whether or not they recognize him as such. No nation can exist unless God allows it.
86:10–13 See *WLC* 190.
86:11 undivided heart. A heart totally set on God.
86:13 your love. Covenant loving-kindness. **you have delivered.** The context is uncertain, but the reference was likely to a redemptive act in the past that the psalmist recalled in the present to instill future hope within himself and his audience.
86:15 slow to anger. A description of God's compassionate nature. Compare Exodus 34:6. See *WLC* 190.
Psalm 87 *Introduction.* The object of Psalm 87 was to glorify Zion, the seat of God's special presence. As the location of the temple, the house of God, Zion was the focal point of worship during much of the Old Testament period. It was the worldwide center of the worship of God. As a song of Zion, this psalm shares characteristics with Psalms 46, 48 and 76. The unique contribution of Psalm 87, however, is its glimpse of the global character of the worship of God. Indeed,

more than all the dwellings of Jacob.
3 Glorious things are said of you,
O city of God:[b] *Selah*
4 "I will record Rahab[a][c] and Babylon
among those who acknowledge me—
Philistia too, and Tyre[d], along with Cush[b]—
and will say, 'This[c] one was born in Zion.[e]' "

5 Indeed, of Zion it will be said,
"This one and that one were born in her,
and the Most High himself will establish her."
6 The LORD will write in the register[f] of the peoples:
"This one was born in Zion." *Selah*
7 As they make music[g] they will sing,
"All my fountains[h] are in you."

87:3
[b]Ps 46:4; Isa 60:1
87:4
[c]Job 9:13
[d]Ps 45:12
[e]Isa 19:25
87:6
[f]Ps 69:28; Isa 4:3; Eze 13:9
87:7
[g]Ps 149:3 [h]Ps 36:9

Psalm 88

A song. A psalm of the Sons of Korah. For the director of music. According to *mahalath leannoth.*[d] A *maskil*[e] of Heman the Ezrahite.

1 O LORD, the God who saves me,[i]
day and night I cry out[j] before you.
2 May my prayer come before you;
turn your ear to my cry.

3 For my soul is full of trouble
and my life draws near the grave.[f][k]
4 I am counted among those who go down to the pit;[l]
I am like a man without strength.
5 I am set apart with the dead,
like the slain who lie in the grave,
whom you remember no more,
who are cut off[m] from your care.

88:1
[i]Ps 51:14 [j]Ps 22:2; 27:9, Lk 18:7
88:3
[k]Ps 107:18,26
88:4
[l]Ps 28:1
88:5
[m]Ps 31:22; Isa 53:8

[a] *4* A poetic name for Egypt [b] *4* That is, the upper Nile region [c] *4* Or *"O Rahab and Babylon, / Philistia, Tyre and Cush, / I will record concerning those who acknowledge me: / 'This* [d] Title: Possibly a tune, "The Suffering of Affliction" [e] Title: Probably a literary or musical term [f] *3* Hebrew *Sheol*

the psalm's universalistic language foreshadowed the day when the Gentiles would become "heirs together with Israel" (Eph 3:6).
87:1 his foundation. The reference is to the building of the temple on Mount Zion. This mountain was located north of the city of David and overlooked it. **holy mountain.** Zion was set apart from all other mountains, not because of its physical characteristics but because it was the place at which God had chosen to reveal his presence to his people. See theological article "The Presence of God" at 1 Kings 8. See note on 2:6.
87:2 gates of Zion. The Lord's love for Zion encompassed the whole city of Jerusalem, which at times, as here, was simply called Zion. **loves . . . more than.** The point is not that God hated the other parts of Israel but that he blessed Jerusalem with his special presence. As a result, the people living in other parts of the promised land traveled to Jerusalem if they wanted the most intimate possible communion with God.
87:3 Glorious things are said of you. In the divine pronouncement in the following verses.
87:4 I will record. This formal introduction to the divine pronouncement described God as keeping written records similar to those in the "book of life" (see Ex 32:32; Pss 69:28; 139:16; Isa 4:3). See note on Revelation 3:5. **Rahab and Babylon.** Rahab was a name for Egypt (Isa 30:7). Egypt and Babylon were two of the superpowers that repeatedly squeezed the life out of Israel. **those who acknowledge me.** There were occasional foreigners who worshiped the Lord during the Old Testament period (e.g., Rahab of Jericho [Jos 6] and Ruth) However, this verse amazingly looks forward to entire Gentile nations bowing before the Lord. **Philistia.** A nation located within the boundaries of the promised land (to the west), whose inhabitants beset and at times dominated Israel until after David's reign. **Tyre.** The affluent maritime power located north of Israel's traditional boundaries. **Cush.** A traditional ally of Egypt (cf. Na 3:8; see note on Est 1:1). As the NIV text note points out, Cush was located in the upper Nile region, including areas that are now in northern Sudan and Ethiopia.
87:5 were born in her. Given the listing of Gentile nations gathered to worship the Lord (v. 4), this verse must refer to a metaphoric birth in Zion. Zion was symbolically the mother of those who shared Israel's faith.
87:6 register. A written record. See note on verse 4.
87:7 they make music. The worshipers responded to the divine pronouncement with music and song. **my fountains.** The nations will desire spiritual blessings (cf. 42:1–2) that flow from God (cf. 36:8–9; Eze 47:1–12; Rev 22:1–2), who resides in Jerusalem.
Psalm 88 *Introduction.* Psalm 88 is perhaps the blackest of all the laments in the Psalter. The composer's agonizing cry reverberates from beginning to end because his pain has lasted from his youth (v. 15) on. Most laments turn to confidence and praise at the end, but not this one. The only glimmer of hope that emanates from it is the fact that the psalmist prayed at all and that he referred to God as the One "who saves me" (v. 1). Christians are not exempt from the suffering of this world. Indeed, the Christian's lot is often one of affliction and pain. Our hope is not in the avoidance of suffering but in the meaning that suffuses our suffering because of the anguish experienced by our Lord Jesus Christ. See *WCF* 18.3; 18.4; *WLC* 81,172.
88:1 the God who saves me. In this desolate cry the psalmist still acknowledged the Lord as the only One who could relieve his pain. **day and night.** Without ceasing.
88:3 near the grave. Language appropriate to someone who believed that death was imminent.
88:5 I am set apart with the dead. The psalmist presented himself as so feeble that he was treated as though he were already dead. **who are cut off from your care.** The psalmist spoke truth from a physical perspective: Dead bodies don't receive certain of God's gifts, such as breath, food, health or energy. See theological article "Body and Soul in the Bible" at Genesis 2.

88:6 [n]Ps 69:15; La 3:55
88:7 [o]Ps 42:7
88:8 [p]Job 19:13; Ps 31:11 [q]Jer 32:2
88:9 [r]Ps 38:10 [s]Ps 86:3 [t]Job 11:13; Ps 143:6
88:10 [u]Ps 6:5
88:11 [v]Ps 30:9
88:13 [w]Ps 30:2 [x]Ps 5:3 [y]Ps 119:147
88:14 [z]Ps 43:2 [a]Job 13:24; Ps 13:1
88:15 [b]Job 6:4
88:17 [c]Ps 22:16; 124:4
88:18 [d]ver 8; Job 19:13; Ps 38:11
89:1 [e]Ps 59:16; Ps 101:1 [f]Ps 36:5; 40:10

6 You have put me in the lowest pit,
in the darkest depths.[n]
7 Your wrath lies heavily upon me;
you have overwhelmed me with all your waves.[o] *Selah*
8 You have taken from me my closest friends[p]
and have made me repulsive to them.
I am confined[q] and cannot escape;
9 my eyes[r] are dim with grief.

I call[s] to you, O LORD, every day;
I spread out my hands[t] to you.
10 Do you show your wonders to the dead?
Do those who are dead rise up and praise you?[u] *Selah*
11 Is your love declared in the grave,
your faithfulness[v] in Destruction[a]?
12 Are your wonders known in the place of darkness,
or your righteous deeds in the land of oblivion?

13 But I cry to you for help,[w] O LORD;
in the morning[x] my prayer comes before you.[y]
14 Why, O LORD, do you reject[z] me
and hide your face[a] from me?

15 From my youth I have been afflicted and close to death;
I have suffered your terrors[b] and am in despair.
16 Your wrath has swept over me;
your terrors have destroyed me.
17 All day long they surround me like a flood;[c]
they have completely engulfed me.
18 You have taken my companions[d] and loved ones from me;
the darkness is my closest friend.

Psalm 89

A *maskil*[b] of Ethan the Ezrahite.

1 I will sing[e] of the LORD's great love forever;
with my mouth I will make your faithfulness known[f] through
all generations.

[a] *11* Hebrew *Abaddon* [b] Title: Probably a literary or musical term

88:7 Your wrath. The psalmist attributed his dire straits to God's wrath against him. Nowhere did he suggest why God was angry. However, throughout the pages of the Old Testament we are told that God's anger against his people's sin led to suffering and judgment. Consider, for example, Achan (Jos 7), Saul (1Sa 15), David (2Sa 12–21) and the entire nation of Judah at the time of the Babylonian exile. While not all suffering is God's direct judgment or discipline in response to sin (Job), it is undeniably true that sin often leads to suffering. It is also true that at many times God responds to sin by causing suffering. Nevertheless, Scripture teaches that even if the wicked appear to prosper in the present God will set things right in the end (Ps 37:35–36).
88:8 repulsive. The psalmist's condition was reminiscent of the suffering of Job.
88:9 spread out my hands. An attitude of prayer. Even though (or perhaps because) God was afflicting him, the psalmist recognized that he had only one place to turn for relief: God.
88:10 show your wonders to the dead. The same sentiment is expressed in 30:9 (see its note).
88:14 Why . . . do you reject me . . . ? Affliction and unanswered prayers are often signs of God's absence and rejection. Heman knew that in his own case these signs indicated that he was under God's discipline.
88:17 flood. The waters of chaos. A common Near Eastern literary image and a reference to the so-called water ordeal (see notes on 18:4; 29:3; 46:2; 69:1–2). There are allusions to waters also in verses 7 and 16.
88:18 the darkness is my closest friend. Heman's closest friends and loved ones were gone (v. 8), leaving him alone with the darkness. This psalm, uniquely in the Psalter, both begins and ends on this downcast note (see "Introduction" to this psalm).

Psalm 89 *Introduction.* Though Psalm 89 opens with the joyful strains of a hymn, it is in the final analysis a lament. At its heart is the Davidic covenant. In 1 Samuel 7:4–17 God had established an intimate father-son relationship with David, later extending that relationship to David's obedient sons. God's language was bold; the covenant was to last "forever" (2Sa 7:13). This promise was ringing in the ears of the psalmist as he faced his present, stark reality, a situation in which God's wrath burned like fire (v. 46). The psalm called on God to reverse the broken condition of his people (vv. 38–51).

The history of Israel, despite its judgment cycles, resoundingly teaches God's perfect faithfulness and incredible compassion. The promise to establish David's dynasty "forever" was conditional. God warned each inheritor of the covenant promises that "when he does wrong, I will punish him with the rod of men, with floggings inflicted by men" (see vv. 31–32). Indeed, David's son Solomon had already begun the downward slide into national apostasy by his acceptance of the religious beliefs and practices of his foreign wives (1Ki 11). God in his great compassion had allowed the Davidic dynasty to continue for hundreds of years in spite of the repeated failures of David's progeny. Finally, however, the Lord's pent-up wrath broke out against them and their people, and he exiled the nation—effectively ending, it would seem, the Davidic dynasty. The exile was not the end of the story, however. The failure of the Davidic kings only highlighted the New Testament renewal of the Davidic covenant, which is and will continue to be fulfilled in Christ. Jesus Christ, the son of David (Ro 1:3), rules forever at the right hand of the Father as our covenant King. This ultimately triumphant psalm brings the third book of the Psalter to a close (see "Introduction: Structure"). Verse 52 functions as a doxology for all of Book III.
89:1 great love. A celebration of the wonder of God's devotion to his people as reflected in his covenant love. **faithfulness.** God is

2 I will declare that your love stands firm forever,
that you established your faithfulness in heaven itself.[g]

3 You said, "I have made a covenant with my chosen one,
I have sworn to David my servant,
4 'I will establish your line forever
and make your throne firm through all generations.' "[h] *Selah*

5 The heavens[i] praise your wonders, O LORD,
your faithfulness too, in the assembly of the holy ones.
6 For who in the skies above can compare with the LORD?
Who is like the LORD among the heavenly beings?[j]
7 In the council of the holy ones God is greatly feared;
he is more awesome than all who surround him.[k]
8 O LORD God Almighty, who is like you?[l]
You are mighty, O LORD, and your faithfulness surrounds you.

9 You rule over the surging sea;
when its waves mount up, you still them.[m]
10 You crushed Rahab[n] like one of the slain;
with your strong arm you scattered[o] your enemies.
11 The heavens are yours, and yours also the earth;[p]
you founded the world and all that is in it.[q]
12 You created the north and the south;
Tabor[r] and Hermon[s] sing for joy[t] at your name.
13 Your arm is endued with power;
your hand is strong, your right hand exalted.

14 Righteousness and justice are the foundation of your throne;[u]
love and faithfulness go before you.
15 Blessed are those who have learned to acclaim you,
who walk in the light[v] of your presence, O LORD.
16 They rejoice in your name[w] all day long;
they exult in your righteousness.
17 For you are their glory and strength,
and by your favor you exalt our horn.[a][x]
18 Indeed, our shield[b] belongs to the LORD,
our king[y] to the Holy One of Israel.

19 Once you spoke in a vision,
to your faithful people you said:
"I have bestowed strength on a warrior;
I have exalted a young man from among the people.

89:2 [g]Ps 36:5
89:4 [h]2Sa 7:12-16; 1Ki 8:16; Ps 132:11-12; Isa 9:7; Lk 1:33
89:5 [i]Ps 19:1
89:6 [j]Ps 113:5
89:7 [k]Ps 47:2
89:8 [l]Ps 71:19
89:9 [m]Ps 65:7
89:10 [n]Ps 87:4 [o]Ps 68:1
89:11 [p]1Ch 29:11; Ps 24:1 [q]Ge 1:1
89:12 [r]Jos 19:22 [s]Dt 3:8; Jos 12:1 [t]Ps 98:8
89:14 [u]Ps 97:2
89:15 [v]Ps 44:3
89:16 [w]Ps 105:3
89:17 [x]Ps 75:10; 92:10; 148:14
89:18 [y]Ps 47:9

[a] *17 Horn* here symbolizes strong one. [b] *18* Or *sovereign*

not fickle or capricious. When he makes a promise, he keeps it. The experience of the covenant curses and the hope of future covenant blessings based on God's promise to David motivated the lament at the end of the psalm (vv. 38–51).
89:3 covenant with . . . David. See 2 Samuel 7 and 1 Chronicles 17.
89:4 establish . . . forever. The issue: the promised permanence of David's dynasty, in light of God's wrathful rejection of his anointed (v. 38 ff.). See "Introduction" to this psalm.
89:5 heavens. The heavens are personified, with "heaven" standing for its inhabitants, including angels and, more specifically, cherubim. Even these powerful spiritual beings praise God for his mighty acts and for his faithfulness. **assembly.** God is not alone in heaven. He is surrounded by angelic beings, the divine assembly through which he works his perfect will.
89:6 in the skies above. The psalmist pointed out God's uniqueness as compared to other heavenly beings. They, like human beings, are creatures of God. The writings of the Canaanites and Mesopotamians also mention an "assembly of the holy ones"—in this case an assembly of gods wielding varying degrees of power. The psalmist distanced himself from these pagan ideas by affirming God's unique divinity.
89:9 surging sea. For the sea as a potent image of the forces of evil and chaos, see notes on 18:4, 29:3, 46:2, 69:1–2 and 114:3. God manifested his power by subduing the sea. In this way the Lord revealed himself as the divine warrior, able to save from all the power of evil.
89:10 Rahab. A mythological sea monster (like Leviathan), standing for the forces of evil and chaos (Job 9:13). Not infrequently the name Rahab is applied to Egypt (see note on 87:4).
89:11 you founded the world. Unlike the heathen gods, the Lord is the Creator of the world. This provided grounds for the psalmist's unequivocal praise.
89:12 Tabor and Hermon. Two distinctive mountains within the promised land. Hermon, in the far north, was the highest peak, while Tabor, located in the Megiddo plain, had a distinctive shape, providing a landmark for the boundaries of three tribes.
89:14 Righteousness and justice. As King, God was responsible for the administration of law in the land. He did not arbitrarily punish anyone but punished only in accordance with his laws. See note on 4:1. **go before you.** See Psalm 85:13.
89:15 Blessed. See note on 1:1.
89:17 our horn. The king. The horn was associated with the bull, which stood for strength. God endowed the human king with power. This thought is specified in verse 18.
89:19 in a vision. Though the details of this revelation are not recorded elsewhere in Scripture, the allusion is probably to the prophetic insight given to Nathan in 2 Samuel 7 or to the initial divine word concerning David's kingship granted to Samuel in 1 Samuel 16.

20 I have found David[z] my servant;[a]
with my sacred oil I have anointed[b] him.
21 My hand will sustain him;
surely my arm will strengthen him.[c]
22 No enemy will subject him to tribute;
no wicked man will oppress[d] him.
23 I will crush his foes before him[e]
and strike down his adversaries.[f]
24 My faithful love will be with him,[g]
and through my name his horn[a] will be exalted.
25 I will set his hand over the sea,
his right hand over the rivers.[h]
26 He will call out to me, 'You are my Father,[i]
my God, the Rock my Savior.'[j]
27 I will also appoint him my firstborn,[k]
the most exalted[l] of the kings[m] of the earth.
28 I will maintain my love to him forever,
and my covenant with him will never fail.[n]
29 I will establish his line forever,
his throne as long as the heavens endure.[o]

30 "If his sons forsake my law
and do not follow my statutes,
31 if they violate my decrees
and fail to keep my commands,
32 I will punish their sin with the rod,
their iniquity with flogging;[p]
33 but I will not take my love from him,[q]
nor will I ever betray my faithfulness.
34 I will not violate my covenant
or alter what my lips have uttered.[r]
35 Once for all, I have sworn by my holiness—
and I will not lie to David—
36 that his line will continue forever
and his throne endure before me like the sun;
37 it will be established forever like the moon,
the faithful witness in the sky." *Selah*

38 But you have rejected,[s] you have spurned,
you have been very angry with your anointed one.

89:20 [z]Ac 13:22 [a]Ps 78:70 [b]1Sa 16:1,12
89:21 [c]Ps 18:35
89:22 [d]2Sa 7:10
89:23 [e]Ps 18:40 [f]2Sa 7:9
89:24 [g]2Sa 7:15
89:25 [h]Ps 72:8
89:26 [i]2Sa 7:14 [j]2Sa 22:47
89:27 [k]Col 1:18 [l]Nu 24:7 [m]Rev 1:5; 19:16
89:28 [n]ver 33-34; Isa 55:3
89:29 [o]ver 4,36; Dt 11:21; Jer 33:17
89:32 [p]2Sa 7:14
89:33 [q]2Sa 7:15
89:34 [r]Nu 23:19
89:38 [s]Dt 32:19; 1Ch 28:9; Ps 44:9

[a] *24 Horn* here symbolizes strength.

89:21 My hand will sustain him. The king had daunting responsibilities, both politically and religiously. God promised to provide David with the strength needed to carry out his divinely appointed tasks.
89:23 I will crush his foes. God promised, as divine warrior, to protect his son, the king.
89:24 My faithful love. Literally, "my faithfulness and my love." These two key words reverberate throughout the psalm, beginning already in verse 1 (see its note).
89:26 You are my Father. A reference to the intimate relationship established between God and David in 2 Samuel 7:14. The king played an important role as mediator of the covenant between God and his people. This function made the apostasy of later kings especially heinous, as it not only involved idolatry on the part of the king but also limited the people's access to God's mercies.
89:27 my firstborn. The firstborn son in a family was the most honored and received the greatest inheritance. David's relationship with God foreshadowed that between God and David's greatest son, Jesus Christ.
89:29 forever. David's earthly, political dynasty lasted a long time, but not forever. The persistent disobedience of his descendants led to their removal and to the deterioration and destruction of the nation of Israel as an independent political entity. First the kingdom was divided into northern and southern states, leaving the Davidic kings in control only of the southern tribes. Then, after Assyria had captured the northern kingdom (Israel), Babylon overran the southern kingdom (Judah). However, the demise of the political shadow anticipated the greater spiritual reality of Jesus Christ, son of David, as King.
89:30–34 See *WCF* 11.5; 17.3; 19.6.
89:31 my commands. God's will as summarized in the Torah. Deuteronomy 17:19 commanded the king to be well versed in and obedient to God's law.
89:32 I will punish their sin. The warning that accompanied God's covenant with David (2Sa 7:14). God frequently punished the kings of Israel by raising up opponents either from within (like Jeroboam; 1Ki 11:9–40) or outside the kingdom (Egyptians, Assyrians, Babylonians).
89:34 I will not violate. God's covenant stands forever. Receiving the blessings or curses of the Davidic covenant was conditional; obedience would result in blessing, while disobedience would result in curses. Nevertheless, the covenant itself would remain in force forever, always leaving an opportunity for an obedient son of David to obtain its blessings.
89:36 his line will continue forever. God intended eventually to send a son of David who would keep the terms of the covenant perfectly and who would inherit all the covenant blessings. See *BC* 27.
89:38 you have rejected . . . spurned . . . been very angry. To this point the psalm has celebrated the special covenant relationship between God and the king. But at verse 38 the focus shifts to the terrible rift in that fellowship. The psalmist specified that God had rejected the king in anger, presumably over the king's sin. This rejection was experienced as God's absence. See theological article "The Presence of God" at 1 Kings 8. **your anointed one.** An unnamed Davidic king.

39 You have renounced the covenant with your servant
and have defiled his crown in the dust.[t]
40 You have broken through all his walls[u]
and reduced his strongholds[v] to ruins.
41 All who pass by have plundered him;
he has become the scorn of his neighbors.[w]
42 You have exalted the right hand of his foes;
you have made all his enemies rejoice.[x]
43 You have turned back the edge of his sword
and have not supported him in battle.[y]
44 You have put an end to his splendor
and cast his throne to the ground.
45 You have cut short the days of his youth;
you have covered him with a mantle of shame.[z] *Selah*

46 How long, O LORD? Will you hide yourself forever?
How long will your wrath burn like fire?[a]
47 Remember how fleeting is my life.[b]
For what futility you have created all men!
48 What man can live and not see death,
or save himself from the power of the grave[a]?[c] *Selah*
49 O Lord, where is your former great love,
which in your faithfulness you swore to David?
50 Remember, Lord, how your servant has[b] been mocked,[d]
how I bear in my heart the taunts of all the nations,
51 the taunts with which your enemies have mocked, O LORD,
with which they have mocked every step of your anointed one.[e]

52 Praise be to the LORD forever!
Amen and Amen.[f]

89:39 [t]La 5:16
89:40 [u]Ps 80:12 [v]La 2:2
89:41 [w]Ps 44:13
89:42 [x]Ps 13:2; 80:6
89:43 [y]Ps 44:10
89:45 [z]Ps 44:15; 109:29
89:46 [a]Ps 79:5
89:47 [b]Job 7:7; Ps 39:5
89:48 [c]Ps 22:29; 49:9
89:50 [d]Ps 69:19
89:51 [e]Ps 74:10
89:52 [f]Ps 41:13; 72:19

BOOK IV

Psalms 90–106

Psalm 90

A prayer of Moses the man of God.

1 Lord, you have been our dwelling place[g]
throughout all generations.
2 Before the mountains were born[h]
or you brought forth the earth and the world,
from everlasting to everlasting you are God.[i]
3 You turn men back to dust,
saying, "Return to dust, O sons of men."[j]

90:1 [g]Dt 33:27; Eze 11:16
90:2 [h]Job 15:7; Pr 8:25 [i]Ps 102:24-27
90:3 [j]Ge 3:19; Job 34:15

[a] *48* Hebrew *Sheol* [b] *50* Or *your servants have*

89:39 renounced the covenant. Strong language befitting strong emotion. The psalmist spoke in no uncertain terms in order to prompt God to break the divine silence and answer him.
89:41 have plundered him. God's absence is experienced through the victory of the nation's enemies. He no longer protects his own as their divine warrior.
89:49 where is your former great love . . . ? The word for *love* is closely connected with the covenant. It is that fidelity by which God binds himself to his people in covenant devotion. This love is no longer restraining God from laying the covenant curses on the psalmist and his people.
89:51 they have mocked . . . your anointed one. By mocking God's anointed king, the nations mocked God himself. God could preserve his reputation and honor by rescuing the king and the nation.
89:52 Praise be to the LORD forever! A doxology to conclude Book III of the Psalter (see "Introduction: Structure").
Psalm 90 *Introduction.* Psalm 90 is the only one ascribed to Moses. In it a contrast is drawn between God's eternality and human mortality. It presents the moving prayer of Moses for God's blessing on the members of a generation doomed to wander in the wilderness, as well as on their children.

Title. The ascription to Moses makes Psalm 90 the oldest datable poem in the collection. **prayer.** See "Introduction: *Title*" to Psalm 17.

90:2 from everlasting to everlasting you are God. Moses affirmed the eternal existence of God. While the creation (Ge 1) brought the whole of the universe into existence, God was always there. See *WCF* 2.1; *WLC* 7; *WSC* 4.

90:3 back to dust. The creation account informs us that humankind was made from the dust of the ground and the breath of God (Ge 2:7). God's judgment returns people to the dust in death (Ge 3:19). This judgment was symbolically repeated when God doomed faithless Israel to return to the dusty wilderness and to death (Nu 13–14).

4 For a thousand years in your sight
are like a day that has just gone by,
or like a watch in the night.[k]
5 You sweep men away[l] in the sleep of death;
they are like the new grass of the morning—
6 though in the morning it springs up new,
by evening it is dry and withered.[m]

7 We are consumed by your anger
and terrified by your indignation.
8 You have set our iniquities before you,
our secret sins[n] in the light of your presence.
9 All our days pass away under your wrath;
we finish our years with a moan.[o]
10 The length of our days is seventy years—
or eighty, if we have the strength;
yet their span[a] is but trouble and sorrow,
for they quickly pass, and we fly away.[p]

11 Who knows the power of your anger?
For your wrath is as great as the fear that is due you.[q]
12 Teach us to number our days[r] aright,
that we may gain a heart of wisdom.[s]

13 Relent, O LORD! How long[t] will it be?
Have compassion on your servants.[u]
14 Satisfy[v] us in the morning with your unfailing love,
that we may sing for joy[w] and be glad all our days.[x]

90:4 [k]2Pe 3:8
90:5 [l]Ps 73:20; Isa 40:6
90:6 [m]Mt 6:30; Jas 1:10
90:8 [n]Ps 19:12
90:9 [o]Ps 78:33
90:10 [p]Job 20:8
90:11 [q]Ps 76:7
90:12 [r]Ps 39:4 [s]Dt 32:29
90:13 [t]Ps 6:3 [u]Dt 32:36; Ps 135:14
90:14 [v]Ps 103:5 [w]Ps 85:6 [x]Ps 31:7

a 10 Or *yet the best of them*

90:4 like a day. God is not bound by time as men and women are. An incredibly long period of time from the perspective of humankind is but a moment to the One who always exists.
90:5 like the new grass. A simile for the brevity of human life.
90:7 consumed by your anger. Human life is brief because it is subject to God's judgment against sin.
90:8 our secret sins. People commit sins that they presume to hide in their hearts, such as envy, hatred and lust. But we stand before God transparent and exposed.
90:10 seventy years. When one is young, 70 years appears to be a long time. However, in the light of God's eternality, such a time period is brief indeed. Life on Earth is difficult under God's curse (Ge 3:16–19) and judgment against sin.
90:11 Who knows the power of your anger? Only Jesus Christ, who drank the full cup of God's wrath for sinners, understands its full power.
90:12 a heart of wisdom. A heart that understands not only that life is fleeting, but why it is so—a heart that will flee to God, our eternal dwelling place, for forgiveness and blessing.
90:13 Relent. Literally, "return." God in judgment doomed humankind to return to the dust (v. 3). Now Moses pleaded for God to return, not in judgment, but in compassion and mercy. **How long . . . ?** See note at 6:3.
90:14 your unfailing love. God's loving mercy is the only hope for a morning of blessing and for days of joy to equal in number the days of grief (v. 15).

The Self-existence of God: Who Made God?

CHILDREN sometimes ask, "Who made God?" The clearest answer is that God never needed to be made, because he was always there. He exists in a different way from ourselves: We, his creatures, exist in a dependent, derived, finite, fragile way, but our Maker exists in an eternal, self-sustaining, necessary way. It is part of God's nature that he cannot cease to exist, just as it is part of our nature that we cannot live forever in this fallen world (Ro 5:12–14). We necessarily age and die, because it is our present nature to do that; God necessarily continues forever unchanged, because it is his eternal nature to do that (Ps 90:2). This is one of many contrasts between creature and Creator.

God's self-existence is a basic truth. At the outset of his presentation of the unknown God to the Athenian idolaters, Paul explained that this God, the world's Creator, "is not served by human hands, as if he needed anything, because he himself gives all men life and breath and everything else" (Ac 17:25). Sacrifices offered to idols, in today's tribal religions, as in ancient Athens, are thought of as somehow sustaining the gods' "physical" needs for such things as food, but the Creator needs no such support system (Ps 50:9–13). God has life in himself and draws his unending energy from himself (Pss 90:1–4; 102:25–27; Isa 40:28–31; Jn 5:26; Rev 4:10), a fact that theologians often refer to as his "aseity" (*a se* in Latin means "from himself").

In theology, life and faith, endless mistakes result from supposing that the conditions, bounds and limits of our own finite existence apply to God—we impoverish ourselves by embracing an idea of God that is too limited and small. The doctrine of God's self-existence stands as a bulwark against such mistakes. It is vital for spiritual health to believe in the God in all his greatness (cf. Ps 95:1–7), and grasping the truth of his aseity is an early step on the road to doing this.

15 Make us glad for as many days as you have afflicted us,
for as many years as we have seen trouble.
16 May your deeds be shown to your servants,
your splendor to their children.[y]

17 May the favor[a] of the Lord our God rest upon us;
establish the work of our hands for us—
yes, establish the work of our hands.[z]

Psalm 91

1 He who dwells in the shelter[a] of the Most High
will rest in the shadow[b] of the Almighty.[b]
2 I will say[c] of the LORD, "He is my refuge[c] and my fortress,
my God, in whom I trust."

3 Surely he will save you from the fowler's snare[d]
and from the deadly pestilence.[e]
4 He will cover you with his feathers,
and under his wings you will find refuge;[f]
his faithfulness will be your shield[g] and rampart.
5 You will not fear[h] the terror of night,
nor the arrow that flies by day,
6 nor the pestilence that stalks in the darkness,
nor the plague that destroys at midday.
7 A thousand may fall at your side,
ten thousand at your right hand,
but it will not come near you.
8 You will only observe with your eyes
and see the punishment of the wicked.[i]

9 If you make the Most High your dwelling—
even the LORD, who is my refuge—
10 then no harm[j] will befall you,
no disaster will come near your tent.
11 For he will command his angels[k] concerning you
to guard you in all your ways;[l]
12 they will lift you up in their hands,
so that you will not strike your foot against a stone.[m]
13 You will tread upon the lion and the cobra;
you will trample the great lion and the serpent.[n]

14 "Because he loves me," says the LORD, "I will rescue him;
I will protect him, for he acknowledges my name.
15 He will call upon me, and I will answer him;
I will be with him in trouble,

90:16 [y]Ps 44:1; Hab 3:2
90:17 [z]Isa 26:12
91:1 [a]Ps 31:20 [b]Ps 17:8
91:2 [c]Ps 142:5
91:3 [d]Ps 124:7; Pr 6:5 [e]1Ki 8:37
91:4 [f]Ps 17:8 [g]Ps 35:2
91:5 [h]Job 5:21
91:8 [i]Ps 37:34; 58:10; Mal 1:5
91:10 [j]Pr 12:21
91:11 [k]Heb 1:14 [l]Ps 34:7
91:12 [m]Mt 4:6*; Lk 4:10-11*
91:13 [n]Da 6:22; Lk 10:19

a *17* Or *beauty* b *1* Hebrew *Shaddai* c *2* Or *He says*

90:16 your deeds. God's blessings and redemptive acts. **splendor to their children.** Moses composed this psalm before Israel had entered Canaan (Dt 34:4–5). He prayed that God would greatly bless the generations that would dwell in the promised land.
90:17 the favor of the Lord our God. Or the "beauty of the Lord." In the midst of life in the wilderness, only the blessing of God's own presence could instill meaning and joy. **establish the work of our hands.** Wanderers in the desert may leave no monuments, but God can give eternal significance to the deeds of hands that serve him.
Psalm 91 *Introduction.* Psalm 91 expresses trust in God in spite of adversity. The original setting of the poem appears to be warfare with its attendant threats of battle and plague in the war camp (vv. 3–8). In contrast to the harsh realities of war, God is depicted as a solicitous mother bird protecting its young (v. 4). The psalmist could express such confidence in God's protection because he knew God as his refuge. How much more can the Christian express trust in God in light of Christ's death on the cross (Ro 8:31–39)?
91:1 He who dwells . . . will rest. The theme of the psalm. Those who draw close to God can find inner peace even in difficult circumstances (Php 4:6–7). This rest is the result of God's greatness and his mercy extended to his own. **Most High.** See note on 92:1.
91:4 with his feathers. Psalms of confidence, like this one (see also Ps 23), usually have at their core a metaphor of God's compassion. The psalmist depicted God as a mother bird sheltering her young. **his faithfulness.** God's steadfast love and the certainty that he will hold to his covenant promises.
91:5 the terror of night. Perhaps a reference to a highly communicable disease that could sweep through a war camp (v. 6). A nighttime attack may also be in view (cf. Ge 14:15; Jer 6:5). **arrow.** A reference to battle. The original context of the psalm was probably holy war.
91:11–12 his angels. God often works his will through his spiritual aids, his angels. Angels are invisible, created beings endowed with substantial power.
91:12 they will lift you up. Satan cited this verse out of context when tempting Jesus. See note on Matthew 4:6.
91:14 Because he loves me. God's pledge to protect the psalmist is not an open promise applicable to everyone. It is restricted to those who have faith in the Lord and is in this way similar to the frequently cited New Testament passage that "God works for the good of those who love him" (Ro 8:28).

I will deliver him and honor him.[o]
16 With long life[p] will I satisfy him
and show him my salvation.[q]"

Psalm 92

A psalm. A song. For the Sabbath day.

1 It is good to praise the LORD
and make music to your name,[r] O Most High,[s]
2 to proclaim your love in the morning[t]
and your faithfulness at night,
3 to the music of the ten-stringed lyre
and the melody of the harp.[u]

4 For you make me glad by your deeds, O LORD;
I sing for joy at the works of your hands.[v]
5 How great are your works,[w] O LORD,
how profound your thoughts![x]
6 The senseless man[y] does not know,
fools do not understand,
7 that though the wicked spring up like grass
and all evildoers flourish,
they will be forever destroyed.

8 But you, O LORD, are exalted forever.

9 For surely your enemies, O LORD,
surely your enemies will perish;
all evildoers will be scattered.[z]
10 You have exalted my horn[a][a] like that of a wild ox;
fine oils[b] have been poured upon me.
11 My eyes have seen the defeat of my adversaries;
my ears have heard the rout of my wicked foes.[c]

12 The righteous will flourish like a palm tree,
they will grow like a cedar of Lebanon;[d]
13 planted in the house of the LORD,
they will flourish in the courts of our God.[e]
14 They will still bear fruit[f] in old age,
they will stay fresh and green,
15 proclaiming, "The LORD is upright;
he is my Rock, and there is no wickedness in him.[g]"

Psalm 93

1 The LORD reigns,[h] he is robed in majesty;[i]
the LORD is robed in majesty
and is armed with strength.[j]

91:15 [o]1Sa 2:30; Ps 50:15; Jn 12:26
91:16 [p]Dt 6:2; Ps 21:4 [q]Ps 50:23
92:1 [r]Ps 147:1 [s]Ps 135:3
92:2 [t]Ps 89:1
92:3 [u]1Sa 10:5; Ne 12:27; Ps 33:2
92:4 [v]Ps 8:6; 143:5
92:5 [w]Rev 15:3 [x]Ps 40:5; 139:17; Isa 28:29; Ro 11:33
92:6 [y]Ps 73:22
92:9 [z]Ps 68:1; 89:10
92:10 [a]Ps 89:17 [b]Ps 23:5
92:11 [c]Ps 54:7; 91:8
92:12 [d]Ps 1:3; 52:8; Jer 17:8; Hos 14:6
92:13 [e]Ps 100:4
92:14 [f]Jn 15:2
92:15 [g]Job 34:10
93:1 [h]Ps 97:1 [i]Ps 104:1 [j]Ps 65:6

a *10 Horn* here symbolizes strength.

Psalm 92 *Introduction.* This exuberant hymn praises God for his mighty deeds (v. 4). Specifically, the psalmist extolled the Lord for routing the enemy (vv. 9–10). A strong contrast is drawn between the prosperity of the righteous (vv. 12–15) and the defeat of the wicked (v. 7).

Title. See *WLC* 117,121; *WSC* 60.

92:1 Most High. God is exalted above all others, and all power and authority derive from him. This title is similar to one commonly given to Baal in Canaanite religious texts. Its application to Yahweh was likely a direct jibe at those who were tempted to worship Baal. See 83:18.

92:2 your love . . . your faithfulness. These traits are linked closely with God's covenant with his chosen people. His people could have confidence that God would honor his promises.

92:4 your deeds . . . the works of your hands. The psalmist did not dwell on praising the intangible nature of God, concentrating instead on God's great acts in time and space. God is in touch with his created reality.

92:5 How great . . . how profound. God's acts and thoughts overwhelm us as we contemplate them. They draw us in reverent fascination and humble devotion but always surpass our feeble grasp.

92:7 the wicked spring up like grass. In many parts of Canaan, grass springs up quickly but soon withers and dies under the blazing sun. Contrast verse 12.

92:9 your enemies will perish. They cannot stand in the face of God's greatness and justice.

92:10 You have exalted my horn. The horn of an animal was a symbol of power. The wild ox lifted its horns with pride and confidence. See notes on 75:4 and 89:17.

92:12 The righteous. See note at 1:5. **like a palm tree . . . like a cedar.** A strong contrast between the flourishing of the righteous and the destruction of the wicked (v. 7). The wicked were likened to fragile grass, whereas the righteous were stalwart, vital, productive trees. See a similar contrast in Psalm 1.

92:13–14 See *WLC* 121.

92:13 planted in the house of the LORD. The source of the vitality of the righteous is God.

Psalm 93 *Introduction.* Psalm 93 is a short poem that stands at the

The world is firmly established;
it cannot be moved.[k]
2 Your throne was established long ago;
you are from all eternity.[l]

3 The seas[m] have lifted up, O LORD,
the seas have lifted up their voice;
the seas have lifted up their pounding waves.
4 Mightier than the thunder[n] of the great waters,
mightier than the breakers of the sea—
the LORD on high is mighty.

5 Your statutes stand firm;
holiness[o] adorns your house
for endless days, O LORD.

Psalm 94

1 O LORD, the God who avenges,[p]
O God who avenges, shine forth.[q]
2 Rise up, O Judge[r] of the earth;
pay back[s] to the proud what they deserve.
3 How long will the wicked, O LORD,
how long will the wicked be jubilant?

4 They pour out arrogant[t] words;
all the evildoers are full of boasting.[u]
5 They crush your people,[v] O LORD;
they oppress your inheritance.
6 They slay the widow and the alien;
they murder the fatherless.
7 They say, "The LORD does not see;[w]
the God of Jacob pays no heed."

8 Take heed, you senseless ones[x] among the people;
you fools, when will you become wise?
9 Does he who implanted the ear not hear?
Does he who formed the eye not see?[y]
10 Does he who disciplines nations not punish?
Does he who teaches[z] man lack knowledge?
11 The LORD knows the thoughts of man;
he knows that they are futile.[a]

93:1 [k]Ps 96:10
93:2 [l]Ps 45:6
93:3 [m]Ps 96:11
93:4 [n]Ps 65:7
93:5 [o]Ps 29:2
94:1 [p]Na 1:2; Ro 12:19 [q]Ps 80:1
94:2 [r]Ge 18:25 [s]Ps 31:23
94:4 [t]Ps 31:18 [u]Ps 52:1
94:5 [v]Isa 3:15
94:7 [w]Job 22:14; Ps 10:11
94:8 [x]Ps 92:6
94:9 [y]Ex 4:11; Pr 20:12
94:10 [z]Job 35:11; Isa 28:26
94:11 [a]1Co 3:20*

---

head of a group of psalms that praise God as King (93–100—except 94). Comparison may also be made to Psalms 24 and 47. Most of these psalms, including Psalm 93, emphasize God's universal kingdom.
93:1 The LORD reigns. A phrase found, with slight variation, throughout this section of the Psalter (cf. 96:10; 97:1; 99:1). The verb translated "reigns" is formed from the same root as the noun "king." The phrase proclaims that God is King, a powerful metaphor for his omnipotence and his sovereign control over the world. The royal metaphor is closely associated with God's covenant: God is the great King who rules over those who are in covenant with him. **The world is firmly established.** Assurance based on the fact that the King created and maintains the earth, so that the forces of evil, disorder and chaos (see vv. 3–4) cannot overwhelm it. Compare God's assurance to Noah in Genesis 8:21–22 in the context of the Noahic covenant.
93:2 you are from all eternity. As a non-created being, God has no beginning. He always was and always will be in control. This concept of God as eternal King stood in stark contrast to the theologies of Mesopotamia and Canaan, in which the kingship of the gods changed from time to time due to fluctuations in the roles of various gods in the upper echelon of the pantheon. Change in leadership among the gods were thought to correspond to political changes.
93:3 the seas. An ancient symbol of the forces of chaos and evil. See notes on 18:4, 29:3, 46:2 and 69:1–2. **lifted up their voice.** The power of disorder is subordinate to Yahweh; indeed, it praises God.
93:5 Your statutes. The psalmist's theme was the stability and order in place because of the eternal kingship of God. Here God's law establishes and maintains order.
Psalm 94 *Introduction.* In Psalm 94 the psalmist called on the Lord as Judge to bring justice to the arrogant evildoers who paid no attention to him. The mention of a "corrupt throne" indicates that the king was at the root of the problem (vv. 20–23).
94:1 the God who avenges. The psalmist knew that the Lord hated evil, punished those who practised it and would liberate the oppressed.
94:2 Rise up. See note on 3:7.
94:3 How long . . . ? See note on 6:3.
94:4 full of boasting. They should be ashamed and silent. Instead they shout their evil accomplishments from the rooftops.
94:6 widow . . . alien . . . fatherless. These three classes of people were particularly vulnerable in ancient Near Eastern society. They did not have the support of family to help them, nor did they have adequate legal representation. Biblical law emphasized the responsibility of king and of society to protect and help such people.
94:7 The LORD does not see. The wicked reasoned from the vantage point of their prosperity that God was unconcerned about their activities.
94:8–11 See *WCF* 5.1.
94:8 become wise. The wicked would become wise only when they shed their illusions that God did not know about their evil schemes and/or was unable to do anything about them.
94:11 knows the thoughts of man. The Lord is omniscient. He knows all things, even the secret thoughts hidden away in the heart (Ps 90:8). See *BC* 14.

12 Blessed is the man you discipline,[b] O LORD,
the man you teach[c] from your law;
13 you grant him relief from days of trouble,
till a pit[d] is dug for the wicked.
14 For the LORD will not reject his people;[e]
he will never forsake his inheritance.
15 Judgment will again be founded on righteousness,[f]
and all the upright in heart will follow it.

16 Who will rise up[g] for me against the wicked?
Who will take a stand for me against evildoers?[h]
17 Unless the LORD had given me help,[i]
I would soon have dwelt in the silence of death.
18 When I said, "My foot is slipping,[j]"
your love, O LORD, supported me.
19 When anxiety was great within me,
your consolation brought joy to my soul.

20 Can a corrupt throne be allied with you—
one that brings on misery by its decrees?[k]
21 They band together[l] against the righteous
and condemn the innocent[m] to death.
22 But the LORD has become my fortress,
and my God the rock in whom I take refuge.[n]
23 He will repay[o] them for their sins
and destroy them for their wickedness;
the LORD our God will destroy them.

Psalm 95

1 Come, let us sing for joy to the LORD;
let us shout aloud[p] to the Rock[q] of our salvation.
2 Let us come before him[r] with thanksgiving
and extol him with music[s] and song.

3 For the LORD is the great God,[t]
the great King above all gods.[u]
4 In his hand are the depths of the earth,
and the mountain peaks belong to him.
5 The sea is his, for he made it,
and his hands formed the dry land.[v]

6 Come, let us bow down[w] in worship,
let us kneel[x] before the LORD our Maker;[y]
7 for he is our God
and we are the people of his pasture,[z]
the flock under his care.

Today, if you hear his voice,

94:12 [b]Job 5:17; Heb 12:5 [c]Dt 8:3
94:13 [d]Ps 55:23
94:14 [e]1Sa 12:22; Ps 37:28; Ro 11:2
94:15 [f]Ps 97:2
94:16 [g]Nu 10:35; Ps 17:13 [h]Ps 59:2
94:17 [i]Ps 124:2
94:18 [j]Ps 38:16
94:20 [k]Ps 58:2
94:21 [l]Ps 56:6 [m]Ps 106:38; Pr 17:15,26
94:22 [n]Ps 18:2; 59:9
94:23 [o]Ps 7:16
95:1 [p]Ps 81:1 [q]2Sa 22:47
95:2 [r]Mic 6:6 [s]Ps 81:2; Eph 5:19
95:3 [t]Ps 48:1; 145:3 [u]Ps 96:4; 97:9
95:5 [v]Ge 1:9; Ps 146:6
95:6 [w]Php 2:10 [x]2Ch 6:13 [y]Ps 100:3; 149:2; Isa 17:7; Da 6:10-11; Hos 8:14
95:7 [z]Ps 74:1; 79:13

94:12 discipline. The righteous love God's discipline because they recognize that it is for their own good (Heb 12:1–13).
94:13 till a pit is dug. The psalmist recognized that there is often a delay between a wicked deed and its punishment. However, he had no doubt that the wicked will pay for their crimes.
94:14 will not reject his people. The psalmist believed that God will never abandon the righteous, although he might discipline them (v. 12) to bring them into conformity with his will.
94:15 will again. In contrast to the perverse justice handed down by the corrupt throne (v. 20), God will make things right again.
94:16 for me. A personal note. The author desired, and received, God's deliverance from evildoers (v. 17).
94:18 your love. Specifically, God's covenant love.
94:20 corrupt throne. A king who perverted justice rather than reflecting the kingship of God, particularly in justice and compassion. There were numerous examples of corrupt kings throughout the history of Israel and Judah.
94:22 my God the rock. Wicked kings drove the faithful back to God and made them look forward to the day when God would reinstate justice.

Psalm 95 *Introduction.* Psalm 95 opens as an exuberant hymn of praise to God, the King. The psalmist called on the congregation to bow in worship. However, a word from God breaks in at the end with a warning to listen to his voice and obey him.
95:1 let us. The worship leader, probably a priest, summoned the congregation to worship the Lord together with himself.
95:2–3 See *WSC* 52.
95:3 the great King above all gods. The supreme Being of the universe, sovereign over all. The reference to other gods does affirm pagan religious views (see note on 74:13).
95:4–5 depths . . . mountain peaks . . . sea . . . dry land. God controls the whole earth, from every extreme to all that lies between (cf. Ps 139).
95:6–7 See *WLC* 104.
95:6 our Maker. We owe him our submission and worship because he is our Creator. See *WSC* 52; *BC* 28.
95:7 the people of his pasture. Once again God is depicted as a shepherd and his people as his sheep (see Pss 23; 100). **Today.** This is an ever-present today; it is every day.

8 do not harden your hearts as you did at Meribah,[a] [a]
as you did that day at Massah[b] in the desert,
9 where your fathers tested[b] and tried me,
though they had seen what I did.
10 For forty years[c] I was angry with that generation;
I said, "They are a people whose hearts go astray,
and they have not known my ways."
11 So I declared on oath[d] in my anger,
"They shall never enter my rest."[e]

95:8 [a]Ex 17:7
95:9 [b]Nu 14:22; Ps 78:18; 1Co 10:9
95:10 [c]Ac 7:36; Heb 3:17
95:11 [d]Nu 14:23 [e]Dt 1:35; Heb 4:3*

Psalm 96

1 Sing to the LORD[f] a new song;
sing to the LORD, all the earth.
2 Sing to the LORD, praise his name;
proclaim his salvation[g] day after day.
3 Declare his glory among the nations,
his marvelous deeds among all peoples.

4 For great is the LORD and most worthy of praise;[h]
he is to be feared[i] above all gods.[j]
5 For all the gods of the nations are idols,
but the LORD made the heavens.[k]
6 Splendor and majesty are before him;
strength and glory[l] are in his sanctuary.

7 Ascribe to the LORD,[m] O families of nations,[n]
ascribe to the LORD glory and strength.
8 Ascribe to the LORD the glory due his name;
bring an offering[o] and come into his courts.
9 Worship the LORD in the splendor of his[c] holiness;[p]
tremble[q] before him, all the earth.[r]
10 Say among the nations, "The LORD reigns."[s]
The world is firmly established, it cannot be moved;[t]
he will judge the peoples with equity.[u]
11 Let the heavens rejoice, let the earth be glad;[v]
let the sea resound, and all that is in it;
12 let the fields be jubilant, and everything in them.
Then all the trees of the forest[w] will sing for joy;[x]
13 they will sing before the LORD, for he comes,
he comes to judge[y] the earth.
He will judge the world in righteousness
and the peoples in his truth.

96:1 [f]1Ch 16:23
96:2 [g]Ps 71:15
96:4 [h]Ps 18:3; 145:3 [i]Ps 89:7 [j]Ps 95:3
96:5 [k]Ps 115:15
96:6 [l]Ps 29:1
96:7 [m]Ps 29:1 [n]Ps 22:27
96:8 [o]Ps 45:12; 72:10
96:9 [p]Ps 29:2 [q]Ps 114:7 [r]Ps 33:8
96:10 [s]Ps 97:1 [t]Ps 93:1 [u]Ps 67:4
96:11 [v]Ps 97:1; 98:7; Isa 49:13
96:12 [w]Isa 44:23 [x]Ps 65:13
96:13 [y]Rev 19:11

Psalm 97

1 The LORD reigns,[z] let the earth be glad;[a]
let the distant shores rejoice.

97:1 [z]Ps 96:10 [a]Ps 96:11

[a] 8 *Meribah* means *quarreling.* [b] 8 *Massah* means *testing.* [c] 9 Or *LORD with the splendor of*

95:8 at Meribah . . . at Massah. Respectively, references to "quarreling" and "testing." The statement aptly summed up Israel's attitude toward God during the 40 years of the desert sojourn. See Exodus 17:1–7 (and notes) and Numbers 20:1–13.
95:11 "They shall never enter my rest." Those who rebelled against the Lord in the wilderness never entered the promised land. The writer of Hebrews applied the passage to the Christian's life (3:7–19). Professing Christians must remain faithful if they are to enter his eternal rest.
Psalm 96 *Introduction.* The psalmist called on all the nations of the world to proclaim God as their king. In the process he contrasted God to the lifeless idols the other nations worshiped (vv. 4–6). With its theme of God's universal kingship, Psalm 96 is similar to Psalms 47, 93, 97, 99 and particularly 98. Part of David's thanksgiving song when he brought the ark to Jerusalem was a variation of Psalm 96 (see 1Ch 16:23–33).
96:1 a new song. See note on 33:3. **all the earth.** The theme of the psalm is the kingship of God. Since God is King of the whole earth and not just of Israel, the psalmist called on all God's subjects to praise him. Not until Jesus Christ had come did significant numbers of the Gentiles join the universal chorus of praise.
96:2 his salvation. In the context of a kingship psalm, a military deliverance was probably in view.
96:3 his marvelous deeds. God's mighty acts gave his people more than ample reason to praise him.
96:5 the gods of the nations are idols. The psalmist highlighted the superiority of the Lord over the gods of the nations. Many were lifeless idols, pieces of wood and metal, whereas the Lord is alive and active in the world; others were demons (see note on 74:13). **made the heavens.** To make his point, the psalmist cited one of God's greatest acts, the creation of the universe.
96:8 an offering. See Leviticus 2. The word was also used for the tribute due a king (2Ki. 17:4).
96:10 "The LORD reigns." See note on 93:1. **it cannot be moved.** Since God created the world, he holds the forces of chaos in check (see note on Ge 1:2). **judge . . . with equity.** God does not rule ac-

97:2
*b*Ex 19:9; Ps 18:11
*c*Ps 89:14

97:3
*d*Da 7:10 *e*Hab 3:5
*f*Ps 18:8

97:4
*g*Ps 104:32

97:5
*h*Ps 46:2,6; Mic 1:4
*i*Jos 3:11

97:6
*j*Ps 50:6 *k*Ps 19:1

97:7
*l*Lev 26:1
*m*Jer 10:14
*n*Heb 1:6

2 Clouds and thick darkness[b] surround him;
righteousness and justice are the foundation of his throne.[c]
3 Fire[d] goes before[e] him
and consumes[f] his foes on every side.
4 His lightning lights up the world;
the earth sees and trembles.[g]
5 The mountains melt[h] like wax before the LORD,
before the Lord of all the earth.[i]
6 The heavens proclaim his righteousness,[j]
and all the peoples see his glory.[k]

7 All who worship images[l] are put to shame,[m]
those who boast in idols—
worship him,[n] all you gods!

8 Zion hears and rejoices
and the villages of Judah are glad

---

cording to whim but on the basis of justice and righteousness. As there is stability in creation, so there is solidity in justice.
Psalm 97 *Introduction.* Psalm 97 calls on all the earth to celebrate God's kingship (cf. Pss. 47; 93; 96; 98; 99). It opens with a description of God's appearance as a warrior-judge (vv. 1–6) and closes with a word to the righteous.
97:1 The LORD reigns. See note on 93:1. **the earth.** The psalmist called on all the earth to praise the Lord, though the world did not yet acknowledge his power.
97:2 Clouds and thick darkness. See Psalms 18 and 29. The coming of God was often likened to a storm. The storm imagery expressed God's power. **righteousness and justice.** God is not arbitrary and is always true to his own nature. He can be counted upon because his promises are inviolable.
97:3 Fire goes before him. The fire metaphor is related to the storm imagery and likely refers to lightning. Compare 18:7–15.
97:5 mountains. See notes on 46:2 and 4.
97:7 those who boast in idols. See note on 96:5. See *WLC* 190.

Divine Sovereignty: Is God Sovereign or Am I Free?

ABSOLUTE sovereignty is based on the Biblical truth that God is the King over all. Unlike human kings, however, there is no limit to God's sovereignty—the entire universe utterly depends on him. Reformed theology has stressed God's sovereignty in at least three ways: creation, providence and grace.

In the first place, God is the sovereign Creator of all things. As the great King he simply commanded the universe into existence out of nothing (Ge 1:1–3). All things came into existence only through complete dependence on his creative power. God also demonstrated his sovereignty in creation by shaping and ordering the universe as he wished until it pleased him (Ge 1:4,10,12,18,21,25,31).

In the second place, God continues to rule over all things and does with them as he pleases in his providential control of history. The vision of God on the throne appears throughout the Scriptures (1Ki 22:19; Isa 6:1; Eze 1:26; Da 7:9; Rev 4:2; cf. Pss 11:4; 45:6; 47:8–9; Heb 12:2; Rev 3:21), and we are continually told in explicit terms that the LORD (Yahweh) reigns as king, exercising dominion over great and tiny things alike (Ex 15:18; Pss 47; 93; 96:10; 97; 99:1–5; 146:10; Pr 16:33; 21:1; Isa 24:23; 52:7; Da 4:34–35; 5:21–28; 6:26; Mt 10:29–31). God's dominion over history is total; he carries out all that he decrees, and none can stay his hand or thwart his eternal plan.

Third, God is sovereign in salvation as well. Many Christian traditions affirm God's general sovereignty over nature but hold that salvation is somehow not entirely a divine prerogative on which we utterly depend. The Scriptures teach, however, that God freely grants salvation to those he loves at his own discretion (Ex 33:19; Ro 9:15). In this way human beings are without exception completely dependent on God for salvation. From beginning to end, salvation is a gift rising out of God's grace (Dt 7:7ff; Eph 2:8–9). We cannot come to Christ initially unless the ability is given to us (Jn 6:44,65), nor can we continue in the faith by our own human effort (Gal 3:3–6). Moreover, we have no power to rise up and receive salvation on the day of judgment; God's power raises us up in Christ (Eph 2:4–7). To be sure, the grace of God in our lives has the effect of holiness and obedience. Yet, we do not contribute in any way to our salvation (Php 2:12–13). This is the wonder of sovereign grace.

That God is sovereign in all these ways does not deny the reality of human dignity and choice. The Scriptures are clear that we are moral beings, answerable to God for what we do and fail to do (Dt 7:9–10). We are free agents (see theological article "The Freedom and Bondage of the Will" at Jos 24), whose choices have significant effects on history.

Needless to say, to believe both that God is absolutely sovereign and that humans are responsible, free agents stretches our mental capacities. Normally we link moral responsibility to the ability to act independently of control, but in the Biblical perspective we are both under God's control and morally responsible. It is a wondrous mystery that our sovereign God created us not as puppets but as moral creatures, but this is often a difficult concept for Christians to accept. Paul himself anticipated an objection to the teaching of God's sovereign grace that is still popular today: "Then why does God still blame us? For who resists his will?" (Ro 9:19). Nevertheless, it is important to remember that it is precisely because God is utterly sovereign that he can determine the responsibilities we bear. It is because he is in control that he can be our judge.

because of your judgments,[o] O LORD.
9 For you, O LORD, are the Most High over all the earth;[p]
you are exalted[q] far above all gods.

10 Let those who love the LORD hate evil,[r]
for he guards the lives of his faithful ones[s]
and delivers[t] them from the hand of the wicked.[u]
11 Light is shed[v] upon the righteous
and joy on the upright in heart.
12 Rejoice in the LORD, you who are righteous,
and praise his holy name.[w]

Psalm 98

A psalm.

1 Sing to the LORD a new song,[x]
for he has done marvelous things;[y]
his right hand[z] and his holy arm[a]
have worked salvation for him.
2 The LORD has made his salvation known[b]
and revealed his righteousness to the nations.
3 He has remembered[c] his love
and his faithfulness to the house of Israel;
all the ends of the earth have seen
the salvation of our God.

4 Shout for joy[d] to the LORD, all the earth,
burst into jubilant song with music;
5 make music to the LORD with the harp,[e]
with the harp and the sound of singing,[f]
6 with trumpets[g] and the blast of the ram's horn—
shout for joy before the LORD, the King.[h]

7 Let the sea resound, and everything in it,
the world, and all who live in it.[i]
8 Let the rivers clap their hands,
let the mountains[j] sing together for joy;
9 let them sing before the LORD,
for he comes to judge the earth.
He will judge the world in righteousness
and the peoples with equity.[k]

Psalm 99

1 The LORD reigns,[l]
let the nations tremble;
he sits enthroned between the cherubim,[m]
let the earth shake.

97:8 [o]Ps 48:11
97:9 [p]Ps 83:18; 95:3 [q]Ex 18:11
97:10 [r]Ps 34:14; Am 5:15; Ro 12:9 [s]Pr 2:8 [t]Da 3:28 [u]Ps 37:40; Jer 15:21
97:11 [v]Job 22:28
97:12 [w]Ps 30:4
98:1 [x]Ps 96:1 [y]Ps 96:3 [z]Ex 15:6 [a]Isa 52:10
98:2 [b]Isa 52:10
98:3 [c]Lk 1:54
98:4 [d]Isa 44:23
98:5 [e]Ps 92:3 [f]Isa 51:3
98:6 [g]Nu 10:10 [h]Ps 47:7
98:7 [i]Ps 24:1
98:8 [j]Isa 55:12
98:9 [k]Ps 96:10
99:1 [l]Ps 97:1 [m]Ex 25:22

97:8 because of your judgments. The people of God rejoiced in God's judgments as fair and just. They recognized that these righteous judgments resulted in the removal of the wicked and thus in their own liberation.
Psalm 98 *Introduction.* Psalm 98 is a hymn praising the Lord for his past deliverance (vv. 1–3), his present kingship (vv. 4–6) and his future role as judge (vv. 7–9). Its emphasis on God's kingship relates it to Psalms 47, 93, 96 and 99, and its unifying theme is God as the victorious warrior who saves Israel and is celebrated as the nation's King. The psalm is appropriately sung to Jesus by Christians; Christ has saved them in the past, is their present King and will come back one day to judge the world.
98:1 marvelous things. Same word as "wonders" in 9:1 (see its note). **worked salvation.** The reference was to a military victory, a deliverance from enemies.
98:2 to the nations. By winning a great victory for Israel over the nation's enemies, the Lord demonstrated to the surrounding peoples that he was just and true to his covenant.
98:3 has remembered. More than an intellectual act, remembrance entails action. In this case God acted to save the Israelites from their enemies by giving them victory.
98:4 Shout for joy. A call to the people to demonstrate deep love for the Lord through enthusiastic worship. The style of this worship was to be active and noisy.
98:6 the King. See 5:2.
98:7 the sea. Nature is here personified as praising the Lord as the Creator of all, both animate and inanimate (95:5).
98:8 the rivers . . . the mountains. See notes on v. 7 and on 46:4.
98:9 judge . . . in righteousness. See notes on 4:1 and on 96:10.
Psalm 99 *Introduction.* The theme of Psalm 99 is once again divine kingship, placing this psalm closely alongside Psalms 47, 93, 96, 97 and 98. Psalm 99 reflects a quiet, reverential air as it contemplates God's sovereignty and justice. The psalmist stood in awe as he spoke of God's forgiveness of Israel. The psalm may be divided into three uneven stanzas based on a refrain repeated three times with some variation (vv. 3,5,9).
99:1–5 See *HC* 99.
99:1 The LORD reigns. See notes on 5:2 and especially on 93:1. **between the cherubim.** See note on 80:1. Cherubim are a class of

99:2 [n]Ps 48:1 [o]Ps 97:9; 113:4

2 Great is the LORD[n] in Zion;
he is exalted[o] over all the nations.

99:3 [p]Ps 76:1

3 Let them praise your great and awesome name[p]—
he is holy.

99:4 [q]Ps 11:7 [r]Ps 98:9

4 The King is mighty, he loves justice[q]—
you have established equity;[r]
in Jacob you have done
what is just and right.

99:5 [s]Ps 132:7

5 Exalt[s] the LORD our God
and worship at his footstool;
he is holy.

99:6 [t]Ex 24:6 [u]Jer 15:1 [v]1Sa 7:9

6 Moses[t] and Aaron were among his priests,
Samuel[u] was among those who called on his name;
they called on the LORD
and he answered[v] them.

99:7 [w]Ex 33:9

7 He spoke to them from the pillar of cloud;[w]
they kept his statutes and the decrees he gave them.

99:8 [x]Nu 14:20

8 O LORD our God,
you answered them;
you were to Israel[a] a forgiving God,[x]
though you punished their misdeeds.[b]
9 Exalt the LORD our God
and worship at his holy mountain,
for the LORD our God is holy.

Psalm 100

A psalm. For giving thanks.

100:1 [y]Ps 98:4

1 Shout for joy[y] to the LORD, all the earth.

100:2 [z]Ps 95:2

2 Worship the LORD with gladness;
come before him[z] with joyful songs.

100:3 [a]Ps 46:10 [b]Job 10:3 [c]Ps 74:1; Eze 34:31

3 Know that the LORD is God.[a]
It is he who made us,[b] and we are his[c];
we are his people, the sheep of his pasture.[c]

100:4 [d]Ps 116:17

4 Enter his gates with thanksgiving
and his courts with praise;
give thanks to him and praise his name.[d]

[a] 8 Hebrew *them* [b] 8 Or / *an avenger of the wrongs done to them* [c] 3 Or *and not we ourselves*

---

angels, spiritual beings who dwelt in heaven with God. They are guardians of God's holiness, as evidenced by their role in protecting the garden after the fall (Ge 3:24). Cherubim were symbolically represented in the tabernacle, both on the innermost curtain (Ex 35:36) and in the Most Holy Place (37:1–9). **the earth shake.** God's appearance sent reverberations throughout the whole earth. This imagery was inspired once again by the world of nature, in this case denoting earthquakes.

99:2 in Zion. The location of the temple. See note on 3:4.

99:3 name. See note on 8:1. **he is holy.** God is completely set apart from all his creatures and is in fact a totally separate and unique class of being. This is true by virtue of his uncreated nature, his power and his moral perfection. See theological article "Divine and Human Holiness" at Isaiah 6.

99:4 he loves justice. See note on 96:10.

99:5 he is holy. The refrain (see note on v. 3; cf. v. 9).

99:6 Moses . . . Aaron . . . Samuel. Three of the most prominent leaders of Israel before the monarchy, all of whom served as mediators between God and his people. **his priests.** The emphasis of this section of the psalm is on the amazing fact that God condescends to speak to his people when they turn to him for help in prayer. The priests were allowed closer access to God's presence than were the rest of the Israelites (see theological article "The Presence of God" at 1Ki 8).

99:7 from the pillar of cloud. The pillar was the visible sign God gave Israel during the period of the desert journey and before the construction of the tabernacle. When the people saw the cloud, they knew that God was present with them. After the construction of the tabernacle, God continued to appear in the form of a cloud, guiding the people during their travels (e.g., Nu 10:12) and dwelling in the tabernacle when they camped (Ex 40:34–38).

99:8 a forgiving God. God is gracious and compassionate toward his repentant people. **you punished their misdeeds.** For their correction and the preservation of his holiness, God punished his people for the sins that they committed, often by turning them over to foreign enemies.

99:9 God is holy. See note on verse 3; compare verse 5.

Psalm 100 *Introduction.* Psalm 100 is a summons from a worship leader, possibly a priest, to a congregation to join him in thanking the Lord. The psalm provides a fitting conclusion to the kingship psalms (93–100, except 94). Verse 4 suggests that it was sung during a festive entry into the temple precincts.

100:1 all the earth. As in the preceding kingship psalms, the call went out beyond the chosen people to all the peoples of the earth. God was their King too, whether or not they were aware of it or willing to acknowledge him. God spoke to the nations through his faithfulness to Israel.

100:2–3 See *WCF* 7.1.

100:2 with gladness. God was no despot who forced his people to serve him. He desired their loving service, rendered in grateful response to his grace. See *WLC* 192.

100:3 the sheep of his pasture. See 23:1 for a note on the royal overtones of the shepherd image. See *BC* 100.3.

100:4 his gates . . . his courts. Those of the temple.

[5]For the LORD is good[e] and his love endures forever;[f]
his faithfulness[g] continues through all generations.

100:5
[e]1Ch 16:34; Ps 25:8 [f]Ezr 3:11; Ps 106:1
[g]Ps 119:90

Psalm 101

Of David. A psalm.

[1]I will sing of your love[h] and justice;
to you, O LORD, I will sing praise.
[2]I will be careful to lead a blameless life—
when will you come to me?

I will walk in my house
with blameless heart.
[3]I will set before my eyes
no vile thing.[i]

The deeds of faithless men I hate;[j]
they will not cling to me.
[4]Men of perverse heart[k] shall be far from me;
I will have nothing to do with evil.

[5]Whoever slanders his neighbor[l] in secret,
him will I put to silence;
whoever has haughty eyes[m] and a proud heart,
him will I not endure.

[6]My eyes will be on the faithful in the land,
that they may dwell with me;
he whose walk is blameless[n]
will minister to me.

[7]No one who practices deceit
will dwell in my house;
no one who speaks falsely
will stand in my presence.

[8]Every morning[o] I will put to silence
all the wicked[p] in the land;
I will cut off every evildoer[q]
from the city of the LORD.[r]

101:1
[h]Ps 51:14; 89:1; 145:7

101:3
[i]Dt 15:9 [j]Ps 40:4

101:4
[k]Pr 11:20

101:5
[l]Ps 50:20
[m]Ps 10:5; Pr 6:17

101:6
[n]Ps 119:1

101:8
[o]Jer 21:12
[p]Ps 75:10
[q]Ps 118:10-12
[r]Ps 46:4

Psalm 102

A prayer of an afflicted man. When he is faint and pours out his lament before the LORD.

[1]Hear my prayer, O LORD;
let my cry for help[s] come to you.

102:1
[s]Ex 2:23

100:5 his love. That is, his covenant loving-kindness.

Psalm 101 *Introduction.* In Psalm 101 King David affirmed his loyalty to the Lord and pledged to live in obedience. He would practice holiness in his own life and seek to root out evil from his kingdom. Although David did not live up to his own ideals (e.g. 2Sa 11–13; 1Ch 21), he lived a life of repentance, and God forgave his sins. Many believe that this psalm was used as a coronation psalm, beginning with Solomon. Solomon too demonstrated that high ideals could degenerate into disobedience and even into rank idolatry. It was not until Jesus Christ came that people witnessed perfect obedience.

101:1 love. God's covenant loving-kindness. **justice.** God's judgments. David praised the Lord because they were righteous and never arbitrary.

101:2 a blameless life. As defined by the law of God. See Micah 6:8 for a description of the individual who was considered blameless before God. **when will you come to me?** The question may hint at deeper problems in David's life. It appears to presuppose that God was not present with David at the moment and may indicate that the psalm is a lament, bemoaning the fact that all is not right with him.

101:3 I hate. David strongly repudiated wicked deeds, pledging not to tolerate them in his company. In this he sought to emulate his holy God.

101:5 will I put to silence . . . will I not endure. David pledged an active stance against evil within his sphere of authority. **haughty eyes . . . proud heart.** The expression of the eyes reveals one's character, while the heart is the foundation of one's being or personality. See Psalm 131:1. See *WLC* 144.

101:6 will minister to me. One has only to think of Nathan (2Sa 12) for an example of what David had in mind. However, one needs only to think of Joab (2Sa 3) to observe David's own failure to meet this ideal.

101:8 See *BC* 36.

Psalm 102 *Introduction.* Psalm 102 is the powerful lament of an individual whose personal fate was tied up with a calamity that struck the people of God. He spoke on his own behalf (vv. 1–11; 23–27) and on behalf of the covenant people (vv. 12–22; 28). Traditionally the psalm has been included with the penitential psalms (see "Introduction to Psalm 6"), but complaint, not repentance, was the psalmist's predominant expression.

Title. See "Introduction: Authorship and Titles." The title is unusual in that it specifies the appropriate type of situation for the psalm's use. **prayer.** See "Introduction to Psalm 17: Title."

102:2 [t]Ps 69:17
102:3 [u]Jas 4:14
102:4 [v]Ps 37:2
102:6 [w]Job 30:29; Isa 34:11
102:7 [x]Ps 77:4 [y]Ps 38:11
102:9 [z]Ps 42:3
102:10 [a]Ps 38:3
102:11 [b]Job 14:2
102:12 [c]Ps 9:7 [d]Ps 135:13
102:13 [e]Isa 60:10
102:15 [f]1Ki 8:43 [g]Ps 138:4
102:16 [h]Isa 60:1-2
102:17 [i]Ne 1:6
102:18 [j]Ro 15:4 [k]Ps 22:31
102:19 [l]Dt 26:15
102:20 [m]Ps 79:11
102:21 [n]Ps 22:22

2 Do not hide your face[t] from me
  when I am in distress.
Turn your ear to me;
  when I call, answer me quickly.

3 For my days vanish like smoke;[u]
  my bones burn like glowing embers.
4 My heart is blighted and withered like grass;[v]
  I forget to eat my food.
5 Because of my loud groaning
  I am reduced to skin and bones.
6 I am like a desert owl,[w]
  like an owl among the ruins.
7 I lie awake;[x] I have become
  like a bird alone[y] on a roof.
8 All day long my enemies taunt me;
  those who rail against me use my name as a
    curse.
9 For I eat ashes as my food
  and mingle my drink with tears[z]
10 because of your great wrath,[a]
  for you have taken me up and thrown me aside.
11 My days are like the evening shadow;[b]
  I wither away like grass.

12 But you, O LORD, sit enthroned forever;[c]
  your renown endures[d] through all generations.
13 You will arise and have compassion[e] on Zion,
  for it is time to show favor to her;
  the appointed time has come.
14 For her stones are dear to your servants;
  her very dust moves them to pity.
15 The nations will fear[f] the name of the LORD,
  all the kings[g] of the earth will revere your glory.
16 For the LORD will rebuild Zion
  and appear in his glory.[h]
17 He will respond to the prayer[i] of the destitute;
  he will not despise their plea.

18 Let this be written[j] for a future generation,
  that a people not yet created[k] may praise the LORD:
19 "The LORD looked down[l] from his sanctuary on high,
  from heaven he viewed the earth,
20 to hear the groans of the prisoners[m]
  and release those condemned to death."
21 So the name of the LORD will be declared[n] in Zion
  and his praise in Jerusalem

102:2 Do not hide your face. The psalmist wondered at God's absence, which he viewed as a sign of God's wrath (v. 10).
102:3 vanish like smoke. A simile depicting the brevity and fragility of life. **like glowing embers.** Points to the pain and suffering of life and, more specifically, to a raging fever.
102:5 skin and bones. The psalmist's suffering was physical, as well as spiritual and psychological.
102:6 like a desert owl. He was silent and alone in his affliction., with neither friends nor supporters to aid him.
102:8 my enemies. As is typical in a lament, one significant source of the psalmist's distress was his unnamed enemies. Because they are anonymous, the psalm may be applied directly to the circumstances of many people.
102:10 your great wrath. Although the enemy increased his pain, the psalmist recognized the root cause of his suffering: God's anger. In his anger, God had abandoned the psalmist (and probably the nation), so that defeat and suffering were inevitable. The psalmist never disputed the justice of that anger but turned to God to beg its cessation.
102:11 evening shadow . . . grass. Figures of speech stressing the brevity and fragility of life (see v. 3).
102:12 sit enthroned. Mention of God's kingship (see note on 93:1) indicated the psalmist's awareness that God remained in control, a realization that infused him with hope in the midst of his suffering. **forever.** Over against the fragility of the psalmist's life stood the constancy of the eternal Lord.
102:13 You will arise. In typical laments, the psalmist appealed to the Lord to arise to save (see note on 3:7); here the composer already possessed assurance that he would. **on Zion.** See 2:6 and 3:3. The references to the destruction of Zion lead many commentators to date the psalm just after the Babylonian captivity. While it may have been composed at that time, earlier military defeats could equally have prompted the author. See *BC* 27.
102:15 The nations will fear. As a devastated Jerusalem rises out of the dust, all who witness the restoration will be led to praise the Lord who caused it to happen.
102:18 See *WLC* 112; *BC* 3.
102:20 to hear . . . and release. Even though God remains above all in heaven (v. 19), he has nonetheless entered the world and is available to help the afflicted.

22 when the peoples and the kingdoms
assemble to worship the LORD.

23 In the course of my life[a] he broke my strength;
he cut short my days.
24 So I said:
"Do not take me away, O my God, in the midst of my days;
your years go on[o] through all generations.
25 In the beginning[p] you laid the foundations of the earth,
and the heavens are the work of your hands.
26 They will perish,[q] but you remain;
they will all wear out like a garment.
Like clothing you will change them
and they will be discarded.
27 But you remain the same,[r]
and your years will never end.
28 The children of your servants[s] will live in your presence;
their descendants[t] will be established before you."

Psalm 103

Of David.

1 Praise the LORD, O my soul;[u]
all my inmost being, praise his holy name.
2 Praise the LORD, O my soul,
and forget not all his benefits—
3 who forgives all your sins[v]
and heals[w] all your diseases,
4 who redeems your life from the pit
and crowns you with love and compassion,
5 who satisfies your desires with good things
so that your youth is renewed like the eagle's.[x]

6 The LORD works righteousness
and justice for all the oppressed.

7 He made known[y] his ways[z] to Moses,
his deeds[a] to the people of Israel:
8 The LORD is compassionate and gracious,[b]
slow to anger, abounding in love.
9 He will not always accuse,
nor will he harbor his anger forever;[c]
10 he does not treat us as our sins deserve[d]

102:24 [o]Ps 90:2; Isa 38:10
102:25 [p]Ge 1:1; Heb 1:10-12*
102:26 [q]Isa 34:4; Mt 24:35; 2Pe 3:7-10; Rev 20:11
102:27 [r]Mal 3:6; Heb 13:8; Jas 1:17
102:28 [s]Ps 69:36 [t]Ps 89:4
103:1 [u]Ps 104:1
103:3 [v]Ps 130:8 [w]Ex 15:26
103:5 [x]Isa 40:31
103:7 [y]Ps 99:7; 147:19 [z]Ex 33:13 [a]Ps 106:22
103:8 [b]Ex 34:6; Ps 86:15; Jas 5:11
103:9 [c]Ps 30:5; Isa 57:16; Jer 3:5,12; Mic 7:18
103:10 [d]Ezr 9:13

[a] 23 Or *By his power*

102:23 cut short my days. Through the sickness that now threatens the psalmist's life.
102:24 your years go on through all generations. God is eternal, having neither beginning nor end of existence. Generations of humans come and go, but the Lord is constant, both in terms of his being and of his character.
102:25 In the beginning. A different Hebrew phrase from the one in Genesis 1:1. God existed before his creation. The author of Hebrews applied this and the next two verses to Jesus Christ (1:10–12) to support his assertion that Jesus was vastly superior to the angels, who were created, not eternal, beings. Jesus, the second person of the Trinity, preexisted.
102:27 your years will never end. As God's existence stretches back to the unimaginable past, so it stretches forward forever—his future is never-ending.
102:28 The children of your servants. The psalmist's hope lay with future generations. Though he suffered in the present, he foresaw a brighter future. See *WCF* 25.5.
Psalm 103 *Introduction.* Psalm 103 voiced thanks to the Lord for all the good things he had done for the author and for his people. Gratitude and hymnic praise mingle in this psalm to evoke a joyful response from the reader. It both opens and closes with an exhortation to praise God.
103:1 O my soul. The psalmist carried on a public dialogue with himself. By so encouraging himself to praise, he also motivated others who observed his example. See *WLC* 190.
103:3–4 See *HC* 56.
103:3 forgives all your sins. The first benefit of grace is the forgiveness of sins. God was and is compassionate toward his repentant people.
103:4 from the pit. A continuation of the final phrase of the preceding verse. The pit is *sheol,* the grave. Thus the psalmist claimed that God had saved him from death. **love.** Specifically, the love of God's gracious covenant devotion.
103:5 with good things. God provided gifts for his people, meeting both their needs and their desires. Sometimes God's people want things that are not good for them. God responds to such desires either by withholding them for our own good or by giving them to teach us to desire better things. But ultimately everything God gives us is constructive and wholesome for our spiritual growth.
103:6 for all the oppressed. A common theme throughout the Bible (cf. Mt 5:3–10).
103:7 to Moses. The psalmist looked away from the benefits God had personally given him and alluded to God's great acts in redemptive history. By referring to Moses, the psalmist called to mind all of God's blessings associated with the exodus, desert journey and even the conquest.
103:8–10 See *HC* 11,56.

or repay us according to our iniquities.
11 For as high as the heavens are above the earth,
so great is his love[e] for those who fear him;
12 as far as the east is from the west,
so far has he removed our transgressions[f] from us.
13 As a father has compassion[g] on his children,
so the LORD has compassion on those who fear him;
14 for he knows how we are formed,[h]
he remembers that we are dust.
15 As for man, his days are like grass,[i]
he flourishes like a flower[j] of the field;
16 the wind blows[k] over it and it is gone,
and its place[l] remembers it no more.
17 But from everlasting to everlasting
the LORD's love is with those who fear him,
and his righteousness with their children's children—
18 with those who keep his covenant
and remember to obey his precepts.[m]

19 The LORD has established his throne in heaven,
and his kingdom rules[n] over all.

20 Praise the LORD, you his angels,[o]
you mighty ones[p] who do his bidding,
who obey his word.
21 Praise the LORD, all his heavenly hosts,[q]
you his servants who do his will.
22 Praise the LORD, all his works[r]
everywhere in his dominion.

Praise the LORD, O my soul.

Psalm 104

1 Praise the LORD, O my soul.[s]

O LORD my God, you are very great;
you are clothed with splendor and majesty.
2 He wraps[t] himself in light as with a garment;
he stretches out the heavens[u] like a tent
3 and lays the beams[v] of his upper chambers on their waters.
He makes the clouds[w] his chariot
and rides on the wings of the wind.[x]

103:11 [e]Ps 57:10
103:12 [f]2Sa 12:13
103:13 [g]Mal 3:17
103:14 [h]Isa 29:16
103:15 [i]Ps 90:5 [j]Job 14:2; Jas 1:10; 1Pe 1:24
103:16 [k]Isa 40:7 [l]Job 7:10
103:18 [m]Dt 7:9
103:19 [n]Ps 47:2
103:20 [o]Ps 148:2; Heb 1:14 [p]Ps 29:1
103:21 [q]1Ki 22:19
103:22 [r]Ps 145:10
104:1 [s]Ps 103:22
104:2 [t]Da 7:9 [u]Isa 40:22
104:3 [v]Am 9:6 [w]Isa 19:1 [x]Ps 18:10

103:11 as high as the heavens. God's love knows no bounds. The word for love here is the same as in verse 4 (see its note).
103:12 as far as the east is from the west. When God forgives sins, he completely removes them. The height and breadth of his mercy are infinite. See *HC* 56.
103:13 As a father. Paul developed the picture of God as a compassionate and loving father in Romans 8:12–17. See Exodus 4:22 and following, as well as Hosea 11:8–9. See *WCF* 12; *WLC* 74.
103:14–16 See *HC* 127.
103:14 for he knows. God, our Creator, knows us infinitely better than we know ourselves. **we are dust.** God used the dust of the ground and the breath of his nostrils to form Adam (Ge 2:7). Because they are animated by God's breath, humans have special ties to him. Because they were formed from the dust, people also are connected to the other creatures on Earth (Ge 2:19). As dust, human beings are frail creatures.
103:15 like grass. Grass comes up quickly, flourishes but soon withers under the scorching sun. Human life is similarly vulnerable and fleeting.
103:17 the LORD's love is with those who fear him. There was and is a reciprocal relationship between the divine initiative and the human response. God first loved the Israelites but required reciprocal love and obedience from them. In the same way God loved and chose Christians, but still requires their devoted obedience.
103:18 who keep his covenant. The obedience of those who kept God's covenant served as the occasion for God to express his infinite mercy and love.
103:19 his throne . . . his kingdom. The psalmist brought his praise to a dramatic conclusion by asserting God's dominion over all. See note on 93:1. See *WLC* 18; *WSC* 11.
103:20–21 See *WLC* 16,192; *WSC* 103; *HC* 124.
103:21 his heavenly hosts. The divine army, composed of angels and other heavenly creatures. See *BC* 12.
Psalm 104 *Introduction.* Psalm 104 begins and ends (vv. 1,35), like the preceding one, with a self-exhortation to praise the Lord. It is an individual hymn focused on God's great act of creation and as such reflects the teaching and vocabulary of Genesis 1, but it applies this teaching to reflections on God's providence, his continuing work in the world he has made. Parallels may also be observed between the psalm and the Egyptian hymn of Amenhotep IV (Akhenaton) to the sun disk. One purpose of the psalm was to demonstrate that the Creator and not an aspect of the creation (like the sun) should be worshiped. See *HC* 26.
104:1–4 The Lord—the Creator and Master.
104:1 you are clothed. A metaphor of various aspects of the creation as God's garments. The psalm emphasizes the distinction between the Creator and his creation and thus implicitly ridicules those who would worship an aspect of the creation, such as the sun (see Ro 1:22).
104:2 in light. A reference to the first day of creation (Ge 1:3). **the heavens.** An allusion to the second day of creation (Ge 1:6–8).
104:3 the clouds . . . on the wings of the wind. God is not only the Creator of all nature, but nature is his servant. The image of God riding his chariot on the clouds is brought to mind (see note on 18:9).

4 He makes winds his messengers,[a] [y]
flames of fire[z] his servants.

5 He set the earth[a] on its foundations;
it can never be moved.
6 You covered it[b] with the deep[c] as with a garment;
the waters stood above the mountains.
7 But at your rebuke[d] the waters fled,
at the sound of your thunder they took to flight;
8 they flowed over the mountains,
they went down into the valleys,
to the place you assigned[e] for them.
9 You set a boundary they cannot cross;
never again will they cover the earth.

10 He makes springs[f] pour water into the ravines;
it flows between the mountains.
11 They give water to all the beasts of the field;
the wild donkeys quench their thirst.

104:4 [y]Ps 148:8; Heb 1:7* [z]2Ki 2:11
104:5 [a]Job 26:7; Ps 24:1-2
104:6 [b]Ge 7:19 [c]Ge 1:2
104:7 [d]Ps 18:15
104:8 [e]Ps 33:7
104:10 [f]Ps 107:33; Isa 41:18

[a] *4* Or *angels*

104:4 flames of fire. Even God's heavenly servants have an awesome appearance. How much more powerful must God, their Master, be? A polemic against Canaanite Baal worship is implicit in this reference, since the servants of El (the progenitor of the Canaanite pantheon) are described as flames of fire in the mythological texts. See *WLC* 16,19.
104:5 it can never be moved. The world is stable and ordered, not chaotic. God created it so, and his continuing control is comforting to those who recognize it.
104:7 the waters. God created the waters and then ordered them to their rightful position in lakes, rivers, seas and oceans. In the polytheistic religions of the nations surrounding Israel, the sea was deified as a chaotic entity and set over against the gods of order. The psalmist picked up this imagery but placed it within the context of Israel's monotheism. (Pss 18:4; 46:2,3; 74:13, Na 1).
104:9 never again. A reference to the promise God made to Noah after the flood (Ge 9:11).
104:11 They . . . quench their thirst. God was not only able to

God, the Creator of Heaven and Earth: What's the Relationship Between God and Creation?

THE Scriptures begin with one of the most important tenets of the Christian faith: God created the heavens and the earth (Ge 1:1). He created all by his command, without any preexisting material. He resolved that things should exist (e.g., "Let there be . . ."; Ge 1:3,6,14), calling them into being and forming them and imbuing them with an existence that depended on him but was distinct from him. Father, Son and Holy Spirit were involved together in this creative act (Ge 1:2; Pss 33:6,9; 148:5; Jn 1:1–3; Col 1:15–16; Heb 1:2; 11:3).

Reformed theology has traditionally highlighted several truths about God's relationship to creation, including:

God is transcendent over his creation. Space and time are dimensions of the created order; God is neither "in" nor bound by either. God created *ex nihilo,* "out of nothing," for his own glory (Isa 43:7), and he now resides enthroned above the earth (Isa 40:22), entirely independent of his creation. Contrary to those who believe that God is dependent on his creation, God is self-contained (see theological article "The Self-existence of God" at Ps 90). He is able to accomplish all his will (see theological article "Divine Sovereignty" at Ps 97) and knows every detail of the future because he designs and controls it (Ps 115:3; Isa 46:10; see theological articles "Divine Omniscience" at Ps 139 and "Providence" at Jer 18).

The world in which we live is no more self-sustaining than it was self-created. The creation is not part of God, and God is not part of the creation. Nevertheless, the ongoing stability of the universe depends on God constantly sustaining every dimension of creation (Col 1:17; Heb 1:3). Without the preserving power of God every created thing, animate and inanimate alike, would cease to exist. As Paul told the Athenians, "He himself gives all men life and breath and everything else . . . In him we live and move and have our being" (Ac 17:25,28; see note on Ac 17:25).

God providentially interacts with and governs the universe. The utter dependence of the creation on the Creator explains how God is free to work through or apart from creaturely, second causes. Although he normally uses secondary causes to accomplish his will, at times he reaches his purposes without them, above what he has enabled them to do and even against the normal workings of the universe (*BC* 13; *HC* 27; *WCF* 5; *WLC* 18; see theological article "Providence" at Jer 18).

Knowing that God is our Creator is the foundation for faithful, fruitful living. God is to be praised for the marvelous order, variety and beauty of his works (see Ps 104). He is also to be trusted as the sovereign Lord who has both an eternal plan, covering all events and destinies without exception, and the power to redeem, re-create and renew. Realizing our constant dependence on God the Creator requires us to offer him our gratitude and loyalty in every area of life.

104:12 [g]Mt 8:20
104:13 [h]Ps 147:8; Jer 10:13
104:14 [i]Job 38:27; Ps 147:8 [j]Ge 1:30; Job 28:5
104:15 [k]Jdg 9:13 [l]Ps 23:5; 92:10; Lk 7:46
104:17 [m]ver 12
104:18 [n]Pr 30:26
104:19 [o]Ge 1:14 [p]Ps 19:6
104:20 [q]Isa 45:7 [r]Ps 74:16 [s]Ps 50:10
104:21 [t]Job 38:39; Ps 145:15; Joel 1:20
104:22 [u]Job 37:8
104:23 [v]Ge 3:19
104:24 [w]Ps 40:5 [x]Pr 3:19
104:25 [y]Ps 69:34
104:26 [z]Ps 107:23; Eze 27:9 [a]Job 41:1
104:27 [b]Job 36:31; Ps 136:25; 145:15; 147:9
104:28 [c]Ps 145:16
104:29 [d]Dt 31:17 [e]Job 34:14; Ecc 12:7

12 The birds of the air[g] nest by the waters;
they sing among the branches.
13 He waters the mountains[h] from his upper chambers;
the earth is satisfied by the fruit of his work.
14 He makes grass grow[i] for the cattle,
and plants for man to cultivate—
bringing forth food[j] from the earth:
15 wine[k] that gladdens the heart of man,
oil[l] to make his face shine,
and bread that sustains his heart.
16 The trees of the LORD are well watered,
the cedars of Lebanon that he planted.
17 There the birds[m] make their nests;
the stork has its home in the pine trees.
18 The high mountains belong to the wild goats;
the crags are a refuge for the coneys.[a n]
19 The moon marks off the seasons,[o]
and the sun[p] knows when to go down.
20 You bring darkness,[q] it becomes night,[r]
and all the beasts of the forest[s] prowl.
21 The lions roar for their prey
and seek their food from God.[t]
22 The sun rises, and they steal away;
they return and lie down in their dens.[u]
23 Then man goes out to his work,[v]
to his labor until evening.
24 How many are your works,[w] O LORD!
In wisdom you made[x] them all;
the earth is full of your creatures.
25 There is the sea,[y] vast and spacious,
teeming with creatures beyond number—
living things both large and small.
26 There the ships[z] go to and fro,
and the leviathan,[a] which you formed to frolic there.
27 These all look to you
to give them their food[b] at the proper time.
28 When you give it to them,
they gather it up;
when you open your hand,
they are satisfied[c] with good things.
29 When you hide your face,[d]
they are terrified;
when you take away their breath,
they die and return to the dust.[e]

[a] *18* That is, the hyrax or rock badger

subdue the waters of chaos but used those waters to sustain the life of his creation (Ge 1:9–13).
104:14 He makes grass grow. A reference to the third day of creation (Ge 1:9–13).
104:15 wine that gladdens the heart. God not only provided sustenance for survival but instilled joy in the hearts of his people with a drink that does more than satisfy physical thirst.
104:19 The moon . . . the sun. An allusion to the fourth day of creation; God created the sun and moon to separate day from night (Ge 1:14–19).
104:21 from God. That which appears to be an act of nature, lions seeking prey, is actually an act of providence. The psalmist rightly saw the hand of God behind natural cycles, events and phenomena.
104:23 Then man goes out. God endowed his creation with a wonderfully ordered rhythm. The dark/light cycle provided an appointed time for nocturnal animals to prowl about in search of sustenance, as well as for men and women to go about their daily labors.
104:24 In wisdom. See notes on Proverbs 8:22–31. The divine response to Job (Job 38–41) contained many allusions to God's wisdom in his acts of creation. See *WCF* 4.1; 5.1; *WLC* 18; *WSC* 11.
104:25 the sea . . . teeming with creatures. A reference to the fifth day of creation. (Ge 1:20–23).
104:26 the ships . . . the leviathan. The psalmist's imagination was caught by God's mysterious sea. On its surface ships glide to and from distant ports, while underneath lurks the sea monster leviathan, a symbol both of power and of God's creative ability (see Job 41).
104:27–30 See *HC* 94,125.
104:27 These all look to you. God not only created all things but provides for their needs as well.
104:29 hide your face. A metaphor describing God's withdrawal or withholding of covenant blessings, usually in anger (see theological article "the Presence of God" at 1Ki 8). Although the psalmist was particularly concerned about God's covenant people, the broad language pertaining to creation may imply that he was also thinking of God's covenant with all the creatures on the earth (Ge 9:9–10) as the backdrop for this imagery.

30 When you send your Spirit,
they are created,
and you renew the face of the earth.

31 May the glory of the LORD endure forever;
may the LORD rejoice in his works[f]—
32 he who looks at the earth, and it trembles,[g]
who touches the mountains,[h] and they smoke.[i]

33 I will sing[j] to the LORD all my life;
I will sing praise to my God as long as I live.
34 May my meditation be pleasing to him,
as I rejoice[k] in the LORD.
35 But may sinners vanish[l] from the earth
and the wicked be no more.

Praise the LORD, O my soul.

Praise the LORD.[a][m]

Psalm 105

1 Give thanks to the LORD,[n] call on his name;[o]
make known among the nations what he has done.
2 Sing to him,[p] sing praise to him;
tell of all his wonderful acts.
3 Glory in his holy name;
let the hearts of those who seek the LORD rejoice.
4 Look to the LORD and his strength;
seek his face[q] always.

5 Remember the wonders[r] he has done,
his miracles, and the judgments he pronounced,[s]
6 O descendants of Abraham his servant,[t]
O sons of Jacob, his chosen[u] ones.
7 He is the LORD our God;
his judgments are in all the earth.

8 He remembers his covenant[v] forever,
the word he commanded, for a thousand generations,
9 the covenant he made with Abraham,[w]
the oath he swore to Isaac.
10 He confirmed it[x] to Jacob as a decree,
to Israel as an everlasting covenant:
11 "To you I will give the land of Canaan[y]
as the portion you will inherit."

12 When they were but few in number,[z]

104:31 [f]Ge 1:31
104:32 [g]Ps 97:4 [h]Ex 19:18 [i]Ps 144:5
104:33 [j]Ps 63:4
104:34 [k]Ps 9:2
104:35 [l]Ps 37:38 [m]Ps 105:45; 106:48
105:1 [n]1Ch 16:34 [o]Ps 99:6
105:2 [p]Ps 96:1
105:4 [q]Ps 27:8
105:5 [r]Ps 40:5 [s]Ps 77:11
105:6 [t]ver 42 [u]Ps 106:5
105:8 [v]Ps 106:45; Lk 1:72
105:9 [w]Ge 12:7; 17:2; 22:16-18; Gal 3:15-18
105:10 [x]Ge 28:13-15
105:11 [y]Ge 13:15; 15:18
105:12 [z]Ge 34:30; Dt 7:7

a *35* Hebrew *Hallelu Yah*; in the Septuagint this line stands at the beginning of Psalm 105.

104:30 your Spirit. Refers to the sixth day of creation, alluding to Genesis 2:4–8, which recounts the creation of humankind. See *BC* 11.
104:32 the mountains . . . smoke. Mountains symbolize stability and strength (see 46:2–3). God's mere touch sets them aflame.
104:35 may sinners vanish from the earth. See "Introduction: Christ in Psalms."
Psalm 105 *Introduction.* Psalm 105 focuses on God's great acts in history from the time of the patriarchs and the Abrahamic covenant to the entry into the promised land. The psalmist directed the people to praise the Lord and assured them that God would be faithful to his covenant promises. While Psalm 104 praises God's acts in creating the world, this psalm meditates on his actions in the world's continuing history. The following psalm (106) also recounts the history of redemption but highlights human failings. The first 15 verses of Psalm 105 are quoted (along with Ps 96 and part of 106) in 1 Chronicles 16, perhaps indicating a liturgical use of the psalm.
105:1 among the nations. Israel was not to hide its light in a jar. The people of God were called upon to bear witness to God's grace to the entire world.
105:2 his wonderful acts. Those acts of grace and judgment that God performs in space and time. That God enters into history and acts on behalf of his people is a manifestation of pure grace. See *WLC* 112.
105:4 seek his face. That is, always dwell in his presence. The psalmists often witnessed to the horror associated with the absence of God (cf. 22:4; 28:1).
105:5 Remember. The act of remembrance in the Old Testament was more than a mere intellectual activity but involved an attitude of faith and obedience. Apostasy was linked to a failure to remember. See *WLC* 112.
105:6 O descendants of Abraham. The addressees of the psalm.
105:8 He remembers. Once again (see v. 5) remembrance involves action as well as intellect. In this case, God acted in the present based on his promises earlier given to Abraham. **his covenant.** See "Introduction: Theology of the Psalms." The covenant in view was the Abrahamic covenant (see v. 9).
105:9 with Abraham. See Genesis 12:1–3, 15 and 17. **to Isaac.** God reaffirmed his covenant relationship with each of the descendants of Abraham. See Genesis 26:3.
105:11 I will give the land of Canaan. See Genesis 15:17–20.

105:12 [a]Ge 23:4; Heb 11:9
105:14 [b]Ge 35:5 [c]Ge 12:17-20
105:15 [d]Ge 26:11
105:16 [e]Ge 41:54; Lev 26:26; Isa 3:1; Eze 4:16
105:17 [f]Ge 37:28; 45:5; Ac 7:9
105:18 [g]Ge 40:15
105:19 [h]Ge 40:20-22
105:20 [i]Ge 41:14
105:22 [j]Ge 41:43-44
105:23 [k]Ge 46:6; Ac 13:17
105:24 [l]Ex 1:7,9
105:25 [m]Ex 4:21 [n]Ex 1:6-10; Ac 7:19
105:26 [o]Ex 3:10 [p]Nu 16:5; 17:5-8
105:27 [q]Ex 7:8-12:51
105:28 [r]Ex 10:22
105:29 [s]Ps 78:44 [t]Ex 7:21
105:30 [u]Ex 8:2,6
105:31 [v]Ex 8:21-24 [w]Ex 8:16-18
105:32 [x]Ex 9:22-25
105:33 [y]Ps 78:47
105:34 [z]Ex 10:4,12-15
105:36 [a]Ex 12:29

few indeed, and strangers in it,[a]
13 they wandered from nation to nation,
from one kingdom to another.
14 He allowed no one to oppress[b] them;
for their sake he rebuked kings:[c]
15 "Do not touch[d] my anointed ones;
do my prophets no harm."

16 He called down famine[e] on the land
and destroyed all their supplies of food;
17 and he sent a man before them—
Joseph, sold as a slave.[f]
18 They bruised his feet with shackles,[g]
his neck was put in irons,
19 till what he foretold[h] came to pass,
till the word of the LORD proved him true.
20 The king sent and released him,
the ruler of peoples set him free.[i]
21 He made him master of his household,
ruler over all he possessed,
22 to instruct his princes[j] as he pleased
and teach his elders wisdom.

23 Then Israel entered Egypt;[k]
Jacob lived as an alien in the land of Ham.
24 The LORD made his people very fruitful;
he made them too numerous[l] for their foes,
25 whose hearts he turned[m] to hate his people,
to conspire[n] against his servants.
26 He sent Moses[o] his servant,
and Aaron, whom he had chosen.[p]
27 They performed[q] his miraculous signs among them,
his wonders in the land of Ham.
28 He sent darkness[r] and made the land dark—
for had they not rebelled against his words?
29 He turned their waters into blood,[s]
causing their fish to die.[t]
30 Their land teemed with frogs,[u]
which went up into the bedrooms of their rulers.
31 He spoke, and there came swarms of flies,[v]
and gnats[w] throughout their country.
32 He turned their rain into hail,[x]
with lightning throughout their land;
33 he struck down their vines[y] and fig trees
and shattered the trees of their country.
34 He spoke, and the locusts came,[z]
grasshoppers without number;
35 they ate up every green thing in their land,
ate up the produce of their soil.
36 Then he struck down all the firstborn[a] in their land,
the firstfruits of all their manhood.

105:12 strangers. Abraham, Isaac and Jacob lived in the promised land, but as resident aliens. They moved from place to place within Canaan.
105:14 he rebuked kings. See Genesis 12:10–20, as well as Genesis 26.
105:15 my prophets. Abraham was referred to in Genesis 20:7 as a prophet.
105:16–22 a man before them—Joseph. God had promoted Joseph to a position of power in Egypt.
105:16 He called down famine. Reference is made to the Joseph narrative (Ge 38–50), specifically to the famine about which God had warned Egypt through Joseph (Ge 41). God directed the course of events so that Joseph rose to power and was in a position to "save many lives" (see Ge 50:20).
105:23 Israel entered Egypt. See Genesis 46. **the land of Ham.** Ham was the son of Noah and the Father of Mizraim, who was also known as Egypt (cf. 78:51; Ge 10:6; 1Ch 1:8).
105:25 See *BC* 13.
105:28 He sent darkness. The psalmist emphasized the ninth plague on Egypt by naming it first.
105:29 into blood. The first plague.
105:30 with frogs. The second plague.
105:31 flies, and gnats. The fourth and the third plagues, respectively, but the psalmist consolidated them.
105:32 hail. The seventh plague. The psalmist omitted mention of the fifth and sixth plagues.
105:34 locusts. The eighth plague.
105:36 the firstborn. The tenth and final plague, after which Egypt allowed Israel to leave Goshen.

37 He brought out Israel, laden with silver and gold,[b]
and from among their tribes no one faltered.
38 Egypt was glad when they left,
because dread of Israel[c] had fallen on them.
39 He spread out a cloud[d] as a covering,
and a fire to give light at night.[e]
40 They asked,[f] and he brought them quail[g]
and satisfied them with the bread of heaven.[h]
41 He opened the rock,[i] and water gushed out;
like a river it flowed in the desert.

42 For he remembered his holy promise[j]
given to his servant Abraham.
43 He brought out his people with rejoicing,[k]
his chosen ones with shouts of joy;
44 he gave them the lands of the nations,[l]
and they fell heir to what others had toiled for—
45 that they might keep his precepts
and observe his laws.[m]

Praise the LORD.[a]

Psalm 106

1 Praise the LORD.[b]

Give thanks to the LORD, for he is good;[n]
his love endures forever.
2 Who can proclaim the mighty acts[o] of the LORD
or fully declare his praise?
3 Blessed are they who maintain justice,
who constantly do what is right.[p]
4 Remember me,[q] O LORD, when you show favor to your people,
come to my aid when you save them,
5 that I may enjoy the prosperity[r] of your chosen ones,
that I may share in the joy[s] of your nation
and join your inheritance in giving praise.

6 We have sinned,[t] even as our fathers did;
we have done wrong and acted wickedly.
7 When our fathers were in Egypt,
they gave no thought to your miracles;
they did not remember[u] your many kindnesses,
and they rebelled by the sea,[v] the Red Sea.[c]

105:37 [b]Ex 12:35
105:38 [c]Ex 12:33; 15:16
105:39 [d]Ex 13:21 [e]Ne 9:12; Ps 78:14
105:40 [f]Ps 78:18,24 [g]Ex 16:13 [h]Jn 6:31
105:41 [i]Ex 17:6; Nu 20:11; Ps 78:15-16; 1Co 10:4
105:42 [j]Ge 15:13-16
105:43 [k]Ex 15:1-18; Ps 106:12
105:44 [l]Jos 13:6-7
105:45 [m]Dt 4:40; 6:21-24
106:1 [n]Ps 100:5; 105:1
106:2 [o]Ps 145:4,12
106:3 [p]Ps 15:2
106:4 [q]Ps 119:132
106:5 [r]Ps 1:3 [s]Ps 118:15
106:6 [t]Da 9:5
106:7 [u]Ps 78:11,42 [v]Ex 14:11-12

[a] *45* Hebrew *Hallelu Yah* [b] *1* Hebrew *Hallelu Yah*; also in verse 48 [c] *7* Hebrew *Yam Suph*; that is, Sea of Reeds; also in verses 9 and 22

105:37 laden with . . . gold. God's great mercy and generosity are evident here. As members of a slave nation within Egypt, the Israelites possessed little of their own. Through the plagues, however, God so struck fear into the hearts of the Egyptians that they not only allowed God's people to leave but handed over their valuables to expedite their departure (see Ex 12:33–36).
105:40 the bread of heaven. Manna. God's mercy went beyond bringing his people out of Egypt; he provided food and drink for them throughout their grueling desert sojourn.
105:42 his holy promise. The Abrahamic covenant, which included the promises that God would free his people from Egypt and give them the Egyptians' possessions (v. 37; Ge 15:14), as well as that they would receive the lands of other nations (v. 44; Ge 15:18–21).
105:44 the lands of the nations. A reference to the conquest.
105:45 observe his laws. The covenant relationship between God and his people was established by God alone as an act of grace. However, the Israelites were responsible to respond with thanks by keeping his commandments.
Psalm 106 *Introduction.* Like Psalm 105, Psalm 106 recounts redemptive history. However, while the previous psalm was primarily concerned with God's great redemptive acts, this psalm focuses on human sin. Despite his people's sin, the psalmist recounted, God showed mercy. Psalm 106 contains characteristics of both the hymn (in reference to God) and the lament (in reference to human sin). The concluding cry of the psalm, however, in verse 47 (v. 48 is a doxology that serves the whole of Book IV), invoked God to help his people in their distress. Note that verses 1 and 47–48 are paralleled in 1 Chronicles 16:34–36.
106:1 Praise the LORD. In Hebrew, *Hallelu Yah.* This phrase both opens and closes (v. 48) the psalm. **for he is good.** Though the psalmist was concerned about the Israelites' suffering, he recognized that the source of their affliction was the people's sin and not some flaw in God's character. **his love.** Specifically, God's covenant devotion.
106:3 Blessed. See note on 1:1. **what is right.** As the psalmist confessed, the Israelites were continually engaging in sin. This explained their lack of blessing.
106:4 Remember. See note on 105:5. **me.** The psalmist had no doubt that God would aid his chosen people, but he did not assume that he personally would enjoy God's blessing. He did seek this blessing in prayer.
106:6 We have sinned. An introductory statement of the theme for the body of the psalm to verse 39. Israel had deliberately and continuously rebelled against the Lord.
106:7 they rebelled by the sea. The psalmist stood amazed at the hard-heartedness and bullheadedness of his people. He recalled

8 Yet he saved them for his name's sake,[w]
to make his mighty power known.
9 He rebuked[x] the Red Sea, and it dried up;[y]
he led them through[z] the depths as through a desert.
10 He saved them[a] from the hand of the foe;
from the hand of the enemy he redeemed them.[b]
11 The waters covered[c] their adversaries;
not one of them survived.
12 Then they believed his promises
and sang his praise.[d]

13 But they soon forgot[e] what he had done
and did not wait for his counsel.
14 In the desert they gave in to their craving;
in the wasteland they put God to the test.[f]
15 So he gave them[g] what they asked for,
but sent a wasting disease[h] upon them.

16 In the camp they grew envious[i] of Moses
and of Aaron, who was consecrated to the LORD.
17 The earth opened[j] up and swallowed Dathan;
it buried the company of Abiram.
18 Fire blazed[k] among their followers;
a flame consumed the wicked.

19 At Horeb they made a calf[l]
and worshiped an idol cast from metal.
20 They exchanged their Glory[m]
for an image of a bull, which eats grass.
21 They forgot the God[n] who saved them,
who had done great things[o] in Egypt,
22 miracles in the land of Ham[p]
and awesome deeds by the Red Sea.
23 So he said he would destroy[q] them—
had not Moses, his chosen one,
stood in the breach[r] before him
to keep his wrath from destroying them.

24 Then they despised the pleasant land;[s]
they did not believe[t] his promise.
25 They grumbled[u] in their tents
and did not obey the LORD.
26 So he swore[v] to them with uplifted hand
that he would make them fall in the desert,[w]
27 make their descendants fall among the nations
and scatter[x] them throughout the lands.

28 They yoked themselves to the Baal of Peor[y]
and ate sacrifices offered to lifeless gods;

106:8 [w]Ex 9:16
106:9 [x]Ps 18:15 [y]Ex 14:21; Na 1:4 [z]Isa 63:11-14
106:10 [a]Ex 14:30 [b]Ps 107:2
106:11 [c]Ex 14:28; 15:5
106:12 [d]Ex 15:1-21
106:13 [e]Ex 15:24
106:14 [f]1Co 10:9
106:15 [g]Nu 11:31 [h]Isa 10:16
106:16 [i]Nu 16:1-3
106:17 [j]Dt 11:6
106:18 [k]Nu 16:35
106:19 [l]Ex 32:4
106:20 [m]Jer 2:11; Ro 1:23
106:21 [n]Ps 78:11 [o]Dt 10:21
106:22 [p]Ps 105:27
106:23 [q]Ex 32:10 [r]Ex 32:11-14
106:24 [s]Dt 8:7; Eze 20:6 [t]Heb 3:18-19
106:25 [u]Nu 14:2
106:26 [v]Eze 20:15; Heb 3:11 [w]Nu 14:28-35
106:27 [x]Lev 26:33; Ps 44:11
106:28 [y]Nu 25:2-3; Hos 9:10

how a previous generation had doubted God's power even though the people had just witnessed the ten plagues against Egypt.
106:9 He rebuked the Red Sea. By personifying the Red Sea, the psalmist placed its division in the context of God's war against the powers of chaos. **he led them through.** In spite of the Israelites' sin, God saved them. His overwhelming mercy in the face of their rejection is a major theme in this psalm, and indeed of the Bible.
106:10 saved . . . redeemed. God is Savior of his people. These verbs usually referred to the political-military deliverances of the Old Testament Israelites.
106:13 they soon forgot. The people's faith and thanks were short-lived. As remembrance (see note on 105:5) included obedience, so forgetting led to disobedience and sin.
106:17 Dathan . . . Abiram. See Numbers 16.
106:19 a calf. See Exodus 32.
106:20 They exchanged their Glory. That is, they placed an idol composed of metal in the place of God and worshiped it. As Paul later pointed out, the essence of idolatry is worshiping a piece of creation as though it were God (Ro 1:21–23).
106:22 miracles in the land of Ham. For Ham as another name for Egypt, see note on 105:23. The miracles in view were predominantly the ten plagues.
106:23 Moses . . . stood in the breach. See Exodus 32:11–14. Moses interceded on behalf of his people and saved them from the wrath of God. In this he foreshadowed the greater work of Jesus Christ, who not only prayed but died to save his own.
106:24 they despised the pleasant land. The land was Canaan, which God had promised his people as their inheritance. They despised the land by failing to exercise faith that God could indeed give it to them (Nu 13–14).
106:26 with uplifted hand. The gesture that accompanied a formal oath. It demonstrated God's determination to bring judgment on that generation of Israelites.
106:28 yoked themselves. A derogatory metaphor. Worshiping this foreign idol was likened to becoming beasts of burden. **Baal of Peor.** Baal was the god of the eastern Mediterranean nations at the time Israel was entering the land. Slightly different characteristics were attributed to this idol at the various local worship sites,

29 they provoked the LORD to anger by their wicked deeds,
and a plague broke out among them.
30 But Phinehas stood up and intervened,
and the plague was checked.[z]
31 This was credited to him[a] as righteousness
for endless generations to come.

32 By the waters of Meribah[b] they angered the LORD,
and trouble came to Moses because of them;
33 for they rebelled against the Spirit of God,
and rash words came from Moses' lips.[a][c]

34 They did not destroy[d] the peoples
as the LORD had commanded[e] them,
35 but they mingled[f] with the nations
and adopted their customs.
36 They worshiped their idols,[g]
which became a snare to them.
37 They sacrificed their sons[h]
and their daughters to demons.
38 They shed innocent blood,
the blood of their sons[i] and daughters,
whom they sacrificed to the idols of Canaan,
and the land was desecrated by their blood.
39 They defiled themselves[j] by what they did;
by their deeds they prostituted[k] themselves.

40 Therefore the LORD was angry[l] with his people
and abhorred his inheritance.[m]
41 He handed them over[n] to the nations,
and their foes ruled over them.
42 Their enemies oppressed them
and subjected them to their power.
43 Many times he delivered them,
but they were bent on rebellion[o]
and they wasted away in their sin.
44 But he took note of their distress
when he heard their cry;[p]
45 for their sake he remembered his covenant[q]
and out of his great love[r] he relented.
46 He caused them to be pitied[s]
by all who held them captive.

47 Save us, O LORD our God,
and gather us[t] from the nations,
that we may give thanks to your holy name
and glory in your praise.

106:30 [z]Nu 25:8
106:31 [a]Nu 25:11-13
106:32 [b]Nu 20:2-13; Ps 81:7
106:33 [c]Nu 20:8-12
106:34 [d]Jdg 1:21 [e]Dt 7:16
106:35 [f]Jdg 3:5-6
106:36 [g]Jdg 2:12
106:37 [h]2Ki 16:3; 17:17
106:38 [i]Nu 35:33
106:39 [j]Eze 20:18 [k]Lev 17:7; Nu 15:39
106:40 [l]Jdg 2:14; Ps 78:59 [m]Dt 9:29
106:41 [n]Jdg 2:14; Ne 9:27
106:43 [o]Jdg 2:16-19
106:44 [p]Jdg 3:9; 10:10
106:45 [q]Lev 26:42; Ps 105:8 [r]Jdg 2:18
106:46 [s]Ezr 9:9; Jer 42:12
106:47 [t]Ps 147:2

a *33* Or *against his spirit, / and rash words came from his lips*

---

and so Baal was often identified by region. **lifeless gods.** Literally, "sacrifices of the dead." The reference could be to the rituals accompanying funerals in Canaan. These ceremonial customs involved heavy drinking, feasting and lovemaking. The incident summarized in verses 28–31 was initiated by Balaam and reported in Numbers 25.

106:31 credited to him as righteousness. When Israel took the fateful step toward idolatry and God's condemnation, Phinehas, a priest, took violent steps to halt the trend and to set Israel back on a path toward God. As a result of his righteous action, God entered into a covenant relationship with Phinehas's family members, to ensure that they would remain priests in future generations. Similar language was used in connection with the covenant promises given to Abraham (Ge 15:6). The New Testament drew a connection between Abraham's faith and our own (Ro. 4:3).

106:32 Meribah. See Numbers 20:1–13.

106:33 they rebelled. By failing to trust God to provide for their survival in the wilderness.

106:34 They did not destroy. God commanded the Israelites to eradicate the inhabitants of the promised land (Dt 7:1–6). Israel was called to be the tool of God's judgment against the Canaanites' excessive wickedness. God's people failed, and the surviving Canaanites became instruments of God's judgment against them.

106:37 to demons. The poet perceived the spiritual reality behind many fabricated, lifeless idols (see note on 74:13).

106:39 they prostituted themselves. By joining themselves to false gods, the Israelites committed spiritual adultery. See *WLC* 109.

106:43 they were bent on rebellion. The book of Judges clearly reflects the cycle of sin-repentance-deliverance that repeated itself seemingly ad infinitum throughout the history of God's Old Testament people.

106:45 he remembered his covenant. It was on the basis of God's covenant with his people that he kept listening to them after they had turned their backs on him. For a discussion of remembrance, see Psalm 105:5. For comments on the covenant, see "Introduction: Theology of the Psalms."

106:48
[u]Ps 41:13

48 Praise be to the LORD, the God of Israel,
from everlasting to everlasting.
Let all the people say, "Amen!"[u]

Praise the LORD.

BOOK V

Psalms 107–150

Psalm 107

107:1 [v]Ps 106:1
107:2 [w]Ps 106:10
107:3 [x]Ps 106:47; Isa 43:5-6
107:4 [y]Nu 14:33; 32:13
107:6 [z]Ps 50:15
107:7 [a]Ezr 8:21
107:9 [b]Ps 22:26; Lk 1:53 [c]Ps 34:10
107:10 [d]Lk 1:79 [e]Job 36:8
107:11 [f]Ps 106:7; La 3:42 [g]2Ch 36:16
107:12 [h]Ps 22:11
107:14 [i]Ps 116:16; Lk 13:16; Ac 12:7
107:17 [j]Isa 65:6-7; La 3:39

1 Give thanks to the LORD,[v] for he is good;
his love endures forever.
2 Let the redeemed[w] of the LORD say this—
those he redeemed from the hand of the foe,
3 those he gathered[x] from the lands,
from east and west, from north and south.[a]

4 Some wandered in desert[y] wastelands,
finding no way to a city where they could settle.
5 They were hungry and thirsty,
and their lives ebbed away.
6 Then they cried out[z] to the LORD in their trouble,
and he delivered them from their distress.
7 He led them by a straight way[a]
to a city where they could settle.
8 Let them give thanks to the LORD for his unfailing love
and his wonderful deeds for men,
9 for he satisfies[b] the thirsty
and fills the hungry with good things.[c]

10 Some sat in darkness[d] and the deepest gloom,
prisoners suffering in iron chains,[e]
11 for they had rebelled[f] against the words of God
and despised the counsel[g] of the Most High.
12 So he subjected them to bitter labor;
they stumbled, and there was no one to help.[h]
13 Then they cried to the LORD in their trouble,
and he saved them from their distress.
14 He brought them out of darkness and the deepest gloom
and broke away their chains.[i]
15 Let them give thanks to the LORD for his unfailing love
and his wonderful deeds for men,
16 for he breaks down gates of bronze
and cuts through bars of iron.

17 Some became fools through their rebellious ways
and suffered affliction[j] because of their iniquities.

[a] 3 Hebrew *north and the sea*

Psalm 107 *Introduction.* This psalm is an expression of thanksgiving that accompanied the offering of sacrifices on the part of the community (v. 22). The circumstances of original composition are uncertain, but the return from the exile may be in view. The main body of the psalm is presented in the first four stanzas (vv. 4–9,10–16,17–22,23–32), which extol God's great deliverance from distress. These stanzas each follow a similar pattern: suffering as a result of sin, calling on the Lord and deliverance. By recounting these situations the psalmist led Israel to praise and obedience. The last two stanzas (vv. 33–38,39–42), respectively, deal with God's sovereignty over fertility and infertility and with the judgment and blessing of God's people. The final verse concludes the psalm with an exhortation to wisdom. See *WCF* 21.5.

107:1 he is good. This introduction sets the tone for the psalm, which recounts God's goodness to his people. He had saved them when they had called for help in their distress. **his love.** God's covenant devotion, by which he binds himself to his people. The same Hebrew word is also used in verses 8, 15, 21, 31 and 43.

107:3 those he gathered. Suggests the situation after the Babylonian exile.

107:4–9 Some wandered in desert wastelands. God had guided those wandering in the desert to a city. This stanza is the first of four that illustrate God's willingness and ability to answer the prayers of his people with salvation, as evidence of "the great love of the LORD" (v. 43).

107:6 they cried out . . . he delivered them. Their prayers were effective.

107:8 his unfailing love. See note on verse 1.

107:10–16 Some sat in darkness . . . prisoners. The second of the four illustrations (see note on vv. 4–9). God had liberated his imprisoned people.

107:12 he subjected them. God had chastised his wayward people in order to purify them. See Hebrews 12:1–13.

107:13 they cried to the LORD . . . he saved them. See note on verse 6.

107:15 his unfailing love. See note on verse 1.

18 They loathed all food[k]
and drew near the gates of death.[l]
19 Then they cried to the LORD in their trouble,
and he saved them from their distress.
20 He sent forth his word[m] and healed them;[n]
he rescued[o] them from the grave.[p]
21 Let them give thanks to the LORD for his unfailing love
and his wonderful deeds for men.
22 Let them sacrifice thank offerings[q]
and tell of his works[r] with songs of joy.

23 Others went out on the sea in ships;
they were merchants on the mighty waters.
24 They saw the works of the LORD,
his wonderful deeds in the deep.
25 For he spoke[s] and stirred up a tempest[t]
that lifted high the waves.[u]
26 They mounted up to the heavens and went down to the depths;
in their peril their courage melted[v] away.
27 They reeled and staggered like drunken men;
they were at their wits' end.
28 Then they cried out to the LORD in their trouble,
and he brought them out of their distress.
29 He stilled the storm[w] to a whisper;
the waves[x] of the sea were hushed.
30 They were glad when it grew calm,
and he guided them to their desired haven.
31 Let them give thanks to the LORD for his unfailing love
and his wonderful deeds for men.
32 Let them exalt him in the assembly[y] of the people
and praise him in the council of the elders.

33 He turned rivers into a desert,[z]
flowing springs into thirsty ground,
34 and fruitful land into a salt waste,[a]
because of the wickedness of those who lived there.
35 He turned the desert into pools of water[b]
and the parched ground into flowing springs;
36 there he brought the hungry to live,
and they founded a city where they could settle.
37 They sowed fields and planted vineyards[c]
that yielded a fruitful harvest;
38 he blessed them, and their numbers greatly increased,[d]
and he did not let their herds diminish.

39 Then their numbers decreased,[e] and they were humbled

107:18 [k]Job 33:20 [l]Job 33:22; Ps 9:13; 88:3
107:20 [m]Mt 8:8 [n]Ps 103:3 [o]Job 33:28 [p]Ps 30:3; 49:15
107:22 [q]Lev 7:12; Ps 50:14; 116:17 [r]Ps 9:11; 73:28; 118:17
107:25 [s]Ps 105:31 [t]Jnh 1:4 [u]Ps 93:3
107:26 [v]Ps 22:14
107:29 [w]Mt 8:26 [x]Ps 89:9
107:32 [y]Ps 22:22,25; 35:18
107:33 [z]1Ki 17:1; Ps 74:15
107:34 [a]Ge 13:10; 14:3; 19:25
107:35 [b]Ps 114:8; Isa 41:18
107:37 [c]Isa 65:21
107:38 [d]Ge 12:2; 17:16, 20; Ex 1:7
107:39 [e]2Ki 10:32; Eze 5:12

107:17–22 Some became fools. The third of the four illustrations (see note on vv. 4–9). God had saved even foolish rebels when they had called on him.
107:17 fools. Not because they were devoid of intelligence but because they wickedly refused to face the reality that the Lord is God. In Old Testament thought foolishness was an ethical and spiritual category, not an intellectual one.
107:18 They loathed . . . food. Symptomatic of a physical affliction or illness—God's discipline resulting from their sin (v. 17).
107:19 they cried to the LORD . . . he saved them. See note on verse 6.
107:20 sent forth his word and healed. As early as the creation account, God's word was shown to accomplish his will.
107:21 his unfailing love. See note on verse 1.
107:22 thank offerings . . . songs of joy. Suggest the psalm's liturgical use in the temple.
107:23–32 Others went out on the seas. The final of the four illustrations (see note on vv. 4–9). God had rescued those in peril on the seas.
107:24 the works of the LORD. These sailing merchants had witnessed the mystery, power and beauty of the sea and its teeming inhabitants. God must be powerful indeed to have created such wonders! See Genesis 1:9–10 and 21.
107:26 They mounted up . . . and went down. A picture of a ship rising and falling on monstrous waves.
107:28 they cried out to the LORD . . . he brought them out. See note on verse 6.
107:29 He stilled the storm. God had revealed his divine power and might by controlling the chaotic sea. See notes on 18:4, 29:3, 46:2 and 69:1–2. Similarly, Jesus Christ demonstrated his divine power when he stilled the wind and the waters (Mk 4:35–41).
107:31 unfailing love. See note on verse 1.
107:33–38 turned rivers into a desert. God, who controls all things, had turned fertility into waste (vv. 33–34) and waste into fertility (vv. 35–38).
107:34 because of the wickedness. God did not arbitrarily bring destruction on people. Here the reason was identified as their sin. A historical example may be found in 1 Kings 17, a situation in which God withheld rain and even dew from Israel because Ahab and Jezebel had turned the nation to Baal worship.
107:36 they founded a city. The reference was to the conquest, in which God had turned the land of Canaan over to Israel. The Israelites had passed from the arduous conditions of the desert journey to the pleasant land of Canaan.

by oppression, calamity and sorrow;
40 he who pours contempt on nobles[f]
made them wander in a trackless waste.[g]
41 But he lifted the needy[h] out of their affliction
and increased their families like flocks.
42 The upright see and rejoice,[i]
but all the wicked shut their mouths.[j]

43 Whoever is wise,[k] let him heed these things
and consider the great love[l] of the LORD.

107:40 [f]Job 12:21 [g]Job 12:24
107:41 [h]1Sa 2:8; Ps 113:7-9
107:42 [i]Job 22:19 [j]Job 5:16; Ps 63:11; Ro 3:19
107:43 [k]Jer 9:12; Hos 14:9 [l]Ps 64:9

Psalm 108

A song. A psalm of David.

1 My heart is steadfast, O God;
I will sing and make music with all my soul.
2 Awake, harp and lyre!
I will awaken the dawn.
3 I will praise you, O LORD, among the nations;
I will sing of you among the peoples.
4 For great is your love, higher than the heavens;
your faithfulness reaches to the skies.
5 Be exalted, O God, above the heavens,
and let your glory be over all the earth.[m]

6 Save us and help us with your right hand,
that those you love may be delivered.
7 God has spoken from his sanctuary:
"In triumph I will parcel out Shechem
and measure off the Valley of Succoth.
8 Gilead is mine, Manasseh is mine;
Ephraim is my helmet,
Judah[n] my scepter.
9 Moab is my washbasin,
upon Edom I toss my sandal;
over Philistia I shout in triumph."

10 Who will bring me to the fortified city?
Who will lead me to Edom?
11 Is it not you, O God, you who have rejected us
and no longer go out with our armies?[o]
12 Give us aid against the enemy,
for the help of man is worthless.
13 With God we will gain the victory,
and he will trample down our enemies.

108:5 [m]Ps 57:5
108:8 [n]Ge 49:10
108:11 [o]Ps 44:9

Psalm 109

For the director of music. Of David. A psalm.

1 O God, whom I praise,
do not remain silent,[p]

109:1 [p]Ps 83:1

107:39–42 contempt on nobles . . . lifted the needy. God both punished and blessed his people according to their obedience or disobedience to his covenant.
107:40 in a trackless waste. Perhaps a reference to the Babylonian exile.
107:43 the great love. See note on verse 1.
Psalm 108 *Introduction.* This psalm consists of portions of two earlier psalms: Verses 1–5 parallel 57:7–11 (see notes there) and verses 6–13 parallel 60:5–12 (see notes there). Though the changes of wording are minor, the overall effect is quite different. Psalm 57 begins as an individual complaint but ends with a strong expression of trust. Psalm 60 opens with a corporate complaint and, again, closes with assurance. The union of the sections of confidence in Psalm 108 produces a particularly powerful message of conviction in the midst of conflict.
108:1 steadfast. See note on 57:7.
108:2 I will awaken the dawn. See note on 57:8.
108:3 among the nations. See note on 57:9.
108:4 your love. See note on 57:10.
108:5 above the heavens. God is so great that not even the heavens can contain him (1Ki 8:27). He is transcendent but also immanent; in compassion he dwells with his people.
108:7–8 God has spoken from his sanctuary. See notes on 60:6–7.
108:9 Moab . . . Edom . . . Philistia. See notes on 60:8.
108:10 me. See note on 60:9.
108:13 With God. See note on 60:12.
Psalm 109 *Introduction.* The psalmist was accused of a crime for which he stood trial. He was innocent, but he faced a corrupt court. In distress, he turned to God for help, asking him to reverse

2 for wicked and deceitful men
have opened their mouths against me;
they have spoken against me with lying tongues.[q]
3 With words of hatred[r] they surround me;
they attack me without cause.[s]
4 In return for my friendship they accuse me,
but I am a man of prayer.[t]
5 They repay me evil for good,[u]
and hatred for my friendship.

6 Appoint[a] an evil man[b] to oppose him;
let an accuser[c][v] stand at his right hand.
7 When he is tried, let him be found guilty,
and may his prayers condemn[w] him.
8 May his days be few;
may another take his place[x] of leadership.
9 May his children be fatherless
and his wife a widow.[y]
10 May his children be wandering beggars;
may they be driven[d] from their ruined homes.
11 May a creditor seize all he has;
may strangers plunder the fruits of his labor.[z]
12 May no one extend kindness to him
or take pity[a] on his fatherless children.
13 May his descendants be cut off,[b]
their names blotted out[c] from the next generation.
14 May the iniquity of his fathers[d] be remembered before the LORD;
may the sin of his mother never be blotted out.
15 May their sins always remain before the LORD,
that he may cut off the memory[e] of them from the earth.

16 For he never thought of doing a kindness,
but hounded to death the poor
and the needy[f] and the brokenhearted.[g]
17 He loved to pronounce a curse—
may it[e] come on him;[h]
he found no pleasure in blessing—
may it be[f] far from him.
18 He wore cursing[i] as his garment;
it entered into his body like water,[j]
into his bones like oil.
19 May it be like a cloak wrapped about him,
like a belt tied forever around him.
20 May this be the LORD's payment[k] to my accusers,
to those who speak evil[l] of me.

21 But you, O Sovereign LORD,

109:2 [q]Ps 52:4; 120:2
109:3 [r]Ps 69:4 [s]Ps 35:7; Jn 15:25
109:4 [t]Ps 69:13
109:5 [u]Ps 35:12; 38:20
109:6 [v]Zec 3:1
109:7 [w]Pr 28:9
109:8 [x]Ac 1:20*
109:9 [y]Ex 22:24
109:11 [z]Job 5:5
109:12 [a]Isa 9:17
109:13 [b]Job 18:19; Ps 37:28 [c]Pr 10:7
109:14 [d]Ex 20:5; Ne 4:5; Jer 18:23
109:15 [e]Job 18:17; Ps 34:16
109:16 [f]Ps 37:14,32 [g]Ps 34:18
109:17 [h]Pr 14:14; Eze 35:6
109:18 [i]Ps 73:6 [j]Nu 5:22
109:20 [k]Ps 94:23; 2Ti 4:14 [l]Ps 71:10

[a] *6* Or ⌊*They say:*⌋ *"Appoint* (with quotation marks at the end of verse 19) [b] *6* Or *the Evil One* [c] *6* Or *let Satan* [d] *10* Septuagint; Hebrew *sought* [e] *17* Or *curse, / and it has* [f] *17* Or *blessing, / and it is*

roles: to allow him to escape punishment and judge the unjust court, particularly one individual (either the judge or the accuser). The psalmist was brutally honest with God and did not water down his strong feelings of hatred for his enemies (see "Introduction: Christ in Psalms").
109:1 do not remain silent. See note on 83:1.
109:4 they accuse me. The legal language here and elsewhere in the psalm reflects a courtroom setting.
109:5 evil for good. See note on 35:12. **for my friendship.** David's accusers were his former friends, who had turned treacherously against him, returning hatred for his love. David's experience of betrayal, though common to human experience, evokes for Christians the thought of Judas and Jesus (see v. 8).
109:6 an evil man . . . an accuser. David appealed for judicial redress, as well as for God to reverse the situation and match his false accuser's penalty with his malicious intent against David. Under Old Testament law, someone who had falsely accused another was to receive the penalty the accused would have received if convicted (Dt 19:16–21).
109:8 may another take his place of leadership. David desired that the same circumstance befall his accuser as the accuser had attempted to inflict upon him. Peter applied this verse to the process of seeking a replacement for Judas among the disciples (Ac 1:20).
109:9 fatherless . . . widow. A hard-hitting curse in a culture based on kinship, calling for punishment not only on the accuser but on his family as well.
109:13 their names blotted out. Most of these curses focus on eradicating the accuser's family line. To anticipate descendents stretching into the distant future was one of God's greatest covenant blessings (Ge 1:28; 8:17; 9:1,7; 17:2,6; 22:17; 26:4; 28:14; 35:11; 48:4). See Leviticus 26:9, 21–22, as well as Deuteronomy 28:4, 11, 18, 32 and 41.
109:17 may it come on him. See note on verse 6.

deal well with me for your name's sake;[m]
out of the goodness of your love,[n] deliver me.
22 For I am poor and needy,
and my heart is wounded within me.
23 I fade away like an evening shadow;[o]
I am shaken off like a locust.
24 My knees give[p] way from fasting;
my body is thin and gaunt.
25 I am an object of scorn[q] to my accusers;
when they see me, they shake their heads.[r]

26 Help me,[s] O LORD my God;
save me in accordance with your love.
27 Let them know[t] that it is your hand,
that you, O LORD, have done it.
28 They may curse,[u] but you will bless;
when they attack they will be put to shame,
but your servant will rejoice.[v]
29 My accusers will be clothed with disgrace
and wrapped in shame[w] as in a cloak.

30 With my mouth I will greatly extol the LORD;
in the great throng[x] I will praise him.
31 For he stands at the right hand[y] of the needy one,
to save his life from those who condemn him.

Psalm 110

Of David. A psalm.

1 The LORD says[z] to my Lord:
"Sit at my right hand
until I make your enemies
a footstool for your feet."[a]

2 The LORD will extend your mighty scepter[b] from
Zion;
you will rule in the midst of your enemies.
3 Your troops will be willing
on your day of battle.
Arrayed in holy majesty,[c]

109:21 [m]Ps 79:9 [n]Ps 69:16
109:23 [o]Ps 102:11
109:24 [p]Heb 12:12
109:25 [q]Ps 22:6 [r]Mt 27:39; Mk 15:29
109:26 [s]Ps 119:86
109:27 [t]Job 37:7
109:28 [u]2Sa 16:12 [v]Isa 65:14
109:29 [w]Ps 35:26; 132:18
109:30 [x]Ps 35:18; 111:1
109:31 [y]Ps 16:8; 73:23; 121:5
110:1 [z]Mt 22:44*; Mk 12:36*; Lk 20:42*; Ac 2:34* [a]1Co 15:25
110:2 [b]Ps 45:6
110:3 [c]Jdg 5:2; Ps 96:9

109:21 for your name's sake. David appealed to the Lord's reputation (see 8:1). Should David die at the hands of the wicked, it would appear as though evil were stronger than God.
109:25 shake their heads. In disgust.
109:26 in accordance with your love. The Hebrew word here translated "love" connects the psalmist's salvation with God's covenant faithfulness.
109:31 stands at the right hand. God was David's support and the source of his strength.
Psalm 110 *Introduction.* A prophetic-Messianic interpretation of Psalm 110 was well known among Jewish interpreters, and the New Testament leaves no doubt that the psalm looked forward to Jesus Christ. Jesus cited it to demonstrate David's realization that its fulfillment would come in someone greater than David (Mk 12:35–37). Psalm 110 was likely composed as a coronation song, possibly after David had conquered Jebus (Jerusalem). It celebrated his victory and enthronement there. This timing would explain the reference to the kingship-priesthood of Melchizedek (v. 4).
The psalm focuses on two divine oracles. The first (v. 1) shows the close but subordinate relationship of the human to the divine King. Jesus, who, though "being in very nature God, did not consider equality with God something to be grasped" (Php. 2:6). However, after Jesus' resurrection, God exalted his Son to a place at his right hand. The New Testament writers cited this oracle to demonstrate Jesus' postresurrection, glory and to point to the cosmic struggle between God and the spiritual powers of evil (Ac 2:34,35; 1Co 15:25; Eph 1:20; Col 3:1; Heb 1:13; 1Pe 3:22). The second oracle appointed the king as a special type of priest. As opposed to the hereditary Aaronic priesthood, this priesthood descended from Melchizedek (Ge 14:18–23), who foreshadowed Jesus Christ, the great high priest (Heb 5:6; 7:17; 8:1; 10:12ff.). See *WLC* 45,54.
Title. This psalm is one of the few in which the reliability of the authorship in the title is foundational to its New Testament interpretation and application (Mk 12:35–37).
110:1–2 See *HC* 51.
110:1 LORD. The divine name, referring to God. **Lord.** A title of respect, though not necessarily a divine title, roughly equivalent to "master" or even "sir" (as in Ge 23:6; 43:20; Jdg 6:13). However, the New Testament made clear that David, Israel's king, called his own future heir his "lord," indicating that the promised Messiah would be greater than David (Mk 12:35–37). **at my right hand.** A place designated for the king's favorite, the seat of highest honor next to that of the king. After the resurrection Jesus was exalted to the place of honor at God's right hand in heaven (see Mk 12:35–37). **your enemies.** Originally denoting hostile people and nations. Applied to Jesus, however, the application is extended to spiritual warfare as well (cf. 1Co 15:24–26). **footstool.** An image of disgrace, symbolizing subjugation. After a victory, Near Eastern war leaders often humiliated their conquered foes by placing their own feet on the heads or necks of the defeated (Jos 10:25–26). See *WCF* 8.8.
110:2 will extend. God would enlarge the king's authority. **scepter.** A symbol of royal power and authority. **from Zion.** See note at 2:6.
110:3 the dew of your youth. A difficult phrase in the Hebrew, but if translated as in the NIV text note, "your young men will come to you like the dew," the image would compare the morning dew that seems to appear out of nowhere with the mysterious appearance of the king's troops. See *WCF* 10.1; *WLC* 45.

from the womb of the dawn
you will receive the dew of your youth.[a]

4 The LORD has sworn
and will not change his mind:[d]
"You are a priest forever,[e]
in the order of Melchizedek."[f]

5 The Lord is at your right hand;[g]
he will crush kings[h] on the day of his wrath.[i]
6 He will judge the nations,[j] heaping up the dead[k]
and crushing the rulers[l] of the whole earth.
7 He will drink from a brook beside the way[b];
therefore he will lift up his head.[m]

Psalm 111[c]

1 Praise the LORD.[d]

I will extol the LORD with all my heart
in the council of the upright and in the assembly.

2 Great are the works[n] of the LORD;
they are pondered by all who delight in them.
3 Glorious and majestic are his deeds,
and his righteousness endures forever.
4 He has caused his wonders to be remembered;
the LORD is gracious and compassionate.[o]
5 He provides food[p] for those who fear him;
he remembers his covenant forever.
6 He has shown his people the power of his works,
giving them the lands of other nations.
7 The works of his hands are faithful and just;
all his precepts are trustworthy.[q]
8 They are steadfast for ever[r] and ever,
done in faithfulness and uprightness.
9 He provided redemption[s] for his people;
he ordained his covenant forever—
holy and awesome[t] is his name.

110:4 [d]Nu 23:19 [e]Heb 5:6*; 7:21* [f]Heb 7:15-17*
110:5 [g]Ps 16:8 [h]Ps 2:12 [i]Ps 2:5; Ro 2:5
110:6 [j]Isa 2:4 [k]Isa 66:24 [l]Ps 68:21
110:7 [m]Ps 27:6
111:2 [n]Ps 92:5; 143:5
111:4 [o]Ps 103:8
111:5 [p]Mt 6:26, 31-33
111:7 [q]Ps 19:7; Rev 15:3
111:8 [r]Isa 40:8; Mt 5:18
111:9 [s]Lk 1:68 [t]Ps 99:3; Lk 1:49

[a] 3 Or / *your young men will come to you like the dew* [b] 7 Or / *The One who grants succession will set him in authority* [c] This psalm is an acrostic poem, the lines of which begin with the successive letters of the Hebrew alphabet. [d] 1 Hebrew *Hallelu Yah*

110:4 the order of Melchizedek. The regular priesthood of Israel was Aaronic and limited to the duties assigned by Levitical law. Melchizedek, however, was both king and priest (Ge 14:18–20). Thus his priesthood could aptly be applied to David. It was even more appropriate to Jesus Christ, who is a Priest-King not descended from Aaron (see Heb 5–7). See *BC* 21,27; *HC* 31.
110:5 Lord. See note on verse 1. **your right hand.** See note on verse 1.
110:6 judge the nations. God frequently used the human king to bring judgment against nations in the form of warfare. As applied to Jesus, this verse anticipated the judgment that will take place at the end of time.
110:7 He will drink. A difficult verse in Hebrew (see the less likely alternate translation in the NIV text note). The king would find refreshment during the battle to enable him to carry on the Lord's work of judgment.
Psalm 111 *Introduction.* Psalm 111 is a hymn of praise that begins with a resounding *Hallelujah*—"praise the LORD"—as do the next two psalms, 112 and 113. The focus of praise in 111 is God's wonderful acts in history, specifically the exodus, the desert journey and the conquest of Canaan. Beyond the hymnic elements in the psalm are wisdom elements. Psalm 111 is an acrostic, each half-line beginning with a succeeding letter of the Hebrew alphabet (see "Introduction: Structure: *Poetic Style and Devices*"). This acrostic design is common among the wisdom poems and binds this psalm closely to 112. Secondly, Psalm 111 ends on a note that calls to mind key thematic verses in the book of Proverbs (e.g., Pr 1:7; 9:10; 15:33; see v. 10).
111:1 Praise the LORD. In Hebrew, *Hallelu* (praise) *Yah* (a short form of God's covenant name *Yahweh*). **in the assembly.** The congregation gathered to praise the Lord in the sanctuary.
111:2 the works of the LORD. The great acts of redemption that God had performed in Israel's past, such as the exodus, in which God intervened to save his people from death at the hands of the Egyptians.
111:3 his righteousness. God's acts conform to his character, to his covenantal promises and to his law. Through his great historical acts, people can recognize his righteousness.
111:4 to be remembered. Remembrance involved more than an act of the memory; it also entailed devotion and obedience. See note on 44:1. **gracious and compassionate.** Israel, due to sin, did not deserve God's salvation; the psalmist realized that God chose to save because of his love for his people. See Exodus 34:6.
111:5 provides food. Since there is a reference in the next line to the conquest, this likely alluded to the desert journey, which preceded the conquest and during which God had miraculously provided food for Israel (see, e.g., Numbers 11). **remembers his covenant.** See "Major Covenants in the Bible" on page 25. When God acted to save his people, he did so on the basis of the relationship he had already established with them. **forever.** God is never fickle. His people may depend on him and on his promises.
111:6 giving them the lands. An allusion to the conquest. God gave his people land already occupied by a number of wicked, idolatrous nations (see Dt 7:1–6).
111:7 all his precepts. Not only did his acts in history reflect God's righteous nature; so did his laws. See 19:7–11.
111:9 holy and awesome is his name. This verse brings the sec-

111:10
[u]Pr 9:10
[v]Ecc 12:13
[w]Ps 145:2

10 The fear of the LORD is the beginning of wisdom;[u]
all who follow his precepts have good understanding.[v]
To him belongs eternal praise.[w]

Psalm 112[a]

112:1
[x]Ps 128:1
[y]Ps 119:14,16,47,92

112:4
[z]Job 11:17
[a]Ps 97:11

112:5
[b]Ps 37:21,26

112:6
[c]Pr 10:7

112:7
[d]Ps 57:7; Pr 1:33

112:8
[e]Ps 59:10

112:9
[f]2Co 9:9*
[g]Ps 75:10

112:10
[h]Ps 86:17
[i]Ps 37:12 [j]Ps 58:7-8 [k]Pr 11:7

1 Praise the LORD.[b]

Blessed is the man who fears the LORD,[x]
who finds great delight[y] in his commands.

2 His children will be mighty in the land;
the generation of the upright will be blessed.
3 Wealth and riches are in his house,
and his righteousness endures forever.
4 Even in darkness light dawns[z] for the upright,
for the gracious and compassionate and righteous[a] man.[c]
5 Good will come to him who is generous and lends freely,[b]
who conducts his affairs with justice.
6 Surely he will never be shaken;
a righteous man will be remembered[c] forever.
7 He will have no fear of bad news;
his heart is steadfast,[d] trusting in the LORD.
8 His heart is secure, he will have no fear;
in the end he will look in triumph on his foes.[e]
9 He has scattered abroad his gifts to the poor,[f]
his righteousness endures forever;
his horn[d] will be lifted[g] high in honor.
10 The wicked man will see[h] and be vexed,
he will gnash his teeth[i] and waste away;[j]
the longings of the wicked will come to nothing.[k]

Psalm 113

113:1
[l]Ps 135:1

1 Praise the LORD.[e]

Praise, O servants of the LORD,[l]

[a] This psalm is an acrostic poem, the lines of which begin with the successive letters of the Hebrew alphabet. [b] *1* Hebrew *Hallelu Yah* [c] *4* Or / *for* ⌊*the* LORD⌋ *is gracious and compassionate and righteous* [d] *9* *Horn* here symbolizes dignity. [e] *1* Hebrew *Hallelu Yah*; also in verse 9

---

tion to a climactic close. Because of God's redeeming acts and covenant with Israel, his name was set above all other names, and he was reverentially feared.

111:10 fear of the LORD. A common Old Testament phrase delineating the right way to approach the Lord. One appropriately reverences God's name and trembles before his presence, even when rejoicing (cf. 2:11), recognizing that God is worthy of our full and unadulterated devotion. See notes on 2:11, 34:7, 36:1, 128:1 and 130:4. **beginning of wisdom.** A right relationship with God is the only proper foundation for knowledge and wisdom.

Psalm 112 *Introduction.* Psalm 112 is the central psalm of three that begin with the expression *Hallelujah* ("Praise the LORD"). It forms an especially close pair with Psalm 111. Not only are they both acrostics (see "Introduction: Structure: *Poetic Style and Devices*"), but they complement one another in content. While Psalm 111 focuses on God and his deeds, Psalm 112 describes the blessedness of the person who "fears" him. Furthermore, Psalm 112 is similar to 1. As wisdom psalms, both describe the delights of righteousness, contrasting them with the sufferings of the wicked.

112:1 Praise the LORD. See note on 111:1. **Blessed.** See 1:1. **fears the LORD.** See 111:10. **in his commands.** The righteous do not find keeping God's law a burden. Since it has come from God, its requirements are a joy, observed out of gratitude for his great salvation. The happiness of the person who loves and obeys God is also the theme of Psalms 1 and 119.

112:4 Even in darkness. A metaphor for troubled times. While he focused on God's tremendous blessings to the righteous, the psalmist acknowledged that these people also endured inevitable hard times. He recognized, however, a long-term reality later voiced by the apostle Paul: "In all things God works for the good of those who love him" (Ro 8:28). **gracious and compassionate.** The godly reflect the attributes of their Lord. Compare Psalm 111:4.

112:7 no fear of bad news. The righteous are not to worry about trouble or distress because they know that God is able to bring them though it.

112:8 he will have no fear. As long as the righteous hold the Lord in reverential awe (v. 1), they do not need to be afraid of anything or anyone else. **in the end.** The righteous will experience trouble and distress, but their confidence is in God's ability and willingness to redeem them from their trouble.

112:9–10 See *WLC* 148.

112:9 scattered abroad his gifts. The psalmist encouraged generosity as a characteristic of the righteous who had been blessed (see v. 5). Paul quoted verse 9 in 2 Corinthians 9:9 to encourage liberal giving to the poor. God bestows upon his people wonderful gifts, and they in turn reflect his character by their openhandedness to others.

112:10 will see. The wicked will observe the vindication and prosperity of the righteous.

Psalm 113 *Introduction.* In Psalm 113 the psalmist celebrated the Lord's incomparable greatness (transcendence; vv. 4–6), while standing in awe of his compassionate intervention in the lives of the needy (immanence; vv. 7–9). This hymn of praise begins and ends with the command to "Praise the LORD" (*Hallelu Yah*), an opening that unites 111–113. Psalm 113 begins the so-called Egyptian Hallel (113–118), which probably drew its traditional moniker from its association with Passover and the exodus from Egypt. The Egyptian Hallel was used to celebrate the three great annual festivals of Israel: Passover, Weeks and Tabernacles, as well as the New Moon and the dedication of the temple. Psalms 113–118 were traditionally sung during the celebration of the Passover, so it is likely that Jesus and his disciples sang them during their last evening to-

praise the name of the LORD.
2 Let the name of the LORD be praised,
both now and forevermore.[m]
3 From the rising of the sun[n] to the place where it sets,
the name of the LORD is to be praised.

4 The LORD is exalted[o] over all the nations,
his glory above the heavens.[p]
5 Who is like the LORD our God,[q]
the One who sits enthroned[r] on high,
6 who stoops down to look[s]
on the heavens and the earth?

7 He raises the poor[t] from the dust
and lifts the needy[u] from the ash heap;
8 he seats them[v] with princes,
with the princes of their people.
9 He settles the barren[w] woman in her home
as a happy mother of children.

Praise the LORD.

113:2 [m]Da 2:20
113:3 [n]Isa 59:19; Mal 1:11
113:4 [o]Ps 99:2 [p]Ps 8:1; 97:9
113:5 [q]Ps 89:6 [r]Ps 103:19
113:6 [s]Ps 11:4; 138:6; Isa 57:15
113:7 [t]1Sa 2:8 [u]Ps 107:41
113:8 [v]Job 36:7
113:9 [w]1Sa 2:5; Ps 68:6; Isa 54:1

Psalm 114

1 When Israel came out of Egypt,[x]
the house of Jacob from a people of foreign tongue,
2 Judah became God's sanctuary,
Israel his dominion.

3 The sea looked and fled,[y]
the Jordan turned back;[z]
4 the mountains skipped like rams,
the hills like lambs.

5 Why was it, O sea, that you fled,
O Jordan, that you turned back,
6 you mountains, that you skipped like rams,
you hills, like lambs?

114:1 [x]Ex 13:3
114:3 [y]Ex 14:21; Ps 77:16 [z]Jos 3:16

gether (Mt 26:26,30; Mk 14:22,26). It is interesting to note the similarities between Psalm 113, Hannah's song of praise in 1 Samuel 2 (see especially vv. 5,8) and Mary's Magnificat (Lk 1:46–55).

113:1 Praise the LORD. See note on 111:1. **O servants of the LORD.** The faithful among the congregation. **the name of the LORD.** See 8:1.

113:3 From the rising of the sun to the place where it sets. That is, in every place.

113:4 exalted over all the nations. In the ancient Near East each nation believed that its own gods ruled in its own territory. Most nations acknowledged the power of their neighbors' gods within their supposed spheres of influence. Only the God of Israel made the seemingly brazen claim that he was the God of all the nations, indeed of the entire creation.

113:5–6 See *WCF* 7.1.

113:5 Who is like . . . ? A rhetorical question. The implied answer is "no one."

113:6 stoops down. Despite God's overwhelming greatness, he still condescends in his limitless love to act in its history. **on the heavens.** Often the heavens were spoken of as the abode of God, but here God's transcendence is expressed as being so great that the heavens are unable to contain him (see 1Ki 8:27).

113:7 poor . . . needy. God's compassion extends to those who lack standing and means in the world (see Mt 5:3–10).

113:9 as a happy mother. The Lord ultimately controls barrenness and fertility, granting children as a blessing that brings happiness.

Psalm 114 *Introduction.* Psalm 114 continues the Egyptian Hallel begun in 113 (see "Introduction" to Ps 113). Later Jewish tradition assigned 114 to the eighth day of Passover. Though it is impossible to determine how far back that tradition goes, the psalm is clearly appropriate to the theme of the Passover, which commenced the exodus. The poet subtly described the tremendous power of God's appearance (theophany) at the time of Israel's salvation from Egypt and entry into Canaan.

114:1 came out of Egypt. The exodus was frequently regarded as the most tremendous display of God's redemptive power during the Old Testament period. It was continually remembered and served as a source of encouragement for later generations. Since God had saved the exodus generation against such tremendous odds, he could rescue later generations of his people as well.

114:2 God's sanctuary. A sanctuary is a dwelling place of God. Wherever God chose to be present became holy ground (see theological article "The Presence of God" at 1Ki 8). Having chosen Canaan for the location of his dwelling on Earth, God led Israel in its conquest. First the tabernacle and then the temple were located there. In this sense Judah/Israel became the special dwelling place of God.

114:3 The sea. The poet personified the Red Sea and recounted with wonder the miracle of its crossing by the descendants of Israel (Exodus 14–15). He implicitly described the crossing as a conflict between the Lord and the sea, thus relating this passage to others in which the sea represented the forces of evil and chaos (see notes on 18:4; 29:3; 46:2; 69:1–2). **the Jordan.** The second half of the parallel carried the history to the time God confirmed the continuity of his power and love toward the Israelites by drying up the Jordan River to allow them to cross into the promised land (Jos 3).

114:4 the mountains. The mountains were a symbol of power, stability and endurance (see Ps 46). God's appearance, though, caused these otherwise immobile landforms to move as agilely as bounding rams, thus demonstrating the earth-shaking power of his presence. Moving mountains are characteristic of earthquakes, but it was also common to speak of God's military actions in similar terms (cf. Jdg 5:4–5; see notes on Mic 1:3–7).

114:5 Why was it . . . ? The psalmist addressed the personified sea and mountains in order to interview them concerning their actions. This device allowed him to make explicit what was implicit in the first two stanzas of the poem: The presence of the Lord (v. 7) had been causal.

114:7 [a]Ps 96:9
114:8 [b]Ex 17:6; Nu 20:11; Ps 107:35
115:1 [c]Ps 96:8; Isa 48:11; Eze 36:32
115:2 [d]Ps 42:3; 79:10
115:3 [e]Ps 103:19 [f]Ps 135:6; Da 4:35
115:4 [g]Dt 4:28; Jer 10:3-5
115:5 [h]Jer 10:5
115:10 [i]Ps 118:3
115:13 [j]Ps 128:1,4
115:14 [k]Dt 1:11

7 Tremble, O earth,[a] at the presence of the Lord,
at the presence of the God of Jacob,
8 who turned the rock into a pool,
the hard rock into springs of water.[b]

Psalm 115

1 Not to us, O LORD, not to us
but to your name be the glory,[c]
because of your love and faithfulness.

2 Why do the nations say,
"Where is their God?"[d]
3 Our God is in heaven;[e]
he does whatever pleases him.[f]
4 But their idols are silver and gold,
made by the hands of men.[g]
5 They have mouths, but cannot speak,[h]
eyes, but they cannot see;
6 they have ears, but cannot hear,
noses, but they cannot smell;
7 they have hands, but cannot feel,
feet, but they cannot walk;
nor can they utter a sound with their throats.
8 Those who make them will be like them,
and so will all who trust in them.

9 O house of Israel, trust in the LORD—
he is their help and shield.
10 O house of Aaron,[i] trust in the LORD—
he is their help and shield.
11 You who fear him, trust in the LORD—
he is their help and shield.

12 The LORD remembers us and will bless us:
He will bless the house of Israel,
he will bless the house of Aaron,
13 he will bless those who fear[j] the LORD—
small and great alike.

14 May the LORD make you increase,[k]
both you and your children.

114:7 Tremble. When God comes in judgment and with power, the earth should fear because its inhabitants may be the objects of his wrath. Nothing can stand in his way.
114:8 turned the rock into a pool. God's wonderful acts at Horeb (Ex 17:6) and Kadesh (Nu 20:1–13) demonstrated his power and compassion.
Psalm 115 *Introduction.* Israel often abandoned the Lord and worshiped the false gods of the surrounding nations. Psalm 115 was a liturgy enacted in public worship, reasserting Israel's faith in the Lord against the worthless idols of the nations. The worship was led by a priest who sometimes spoke with the congregation (vv. 1–8,12–13,16–18) and at other times addressed the worshipers (vv. 9–11,14–15). For commentary on the use of this psalm during the celebration of Passover, see the "Introduction" to Psalm 113. See *WLC* 63.
115:1–2 See *WLC* 63.
115:1 your name. See 8:1. **your love.** God's covenantal affection toward his people. See *BC* 22,26; *HC* 122,128.
115:2 the nations. The nations that surrounded Israel at different time periods, such as Babylon, Assyria, Persia, Egypt and the various nations within Canaan. **"Where is their God?"** This taunt may have arisen because of the low estate of the people of God at the time of the psalm's composition. As the nations observed Israel struggling, they would deduce that Israel's God was either impotent or unwilling to help his people.
115:3 in heaven. The psalmist did not deny God's nearness but emphasized his transcendence—his majesty—as something that the other nations' gods clearly lacked. **whatever pleases him.** Not an expression of divine arbitrariness but rather of God's sovereignty. God acts according to his own character, not in conformity to human will. See *WCF* 2.1; *BC* 13.
115:4 their idols. The psalmist drew a sharp contrast between the living God of Israel and the deities of the surrounding Near Eastern peoples. See note on 74:13. Paul would later capture the essence and folly of idolatry in Romans 1:21–23. See also Isaiah's biting satire in Isaiah 44:6–23.
115:8 will be like them. On the one hand, people adopt the values and perspectives of the gods they create and/or worship. In the case of Israel's neighbors, this often resulted in horrifying cruelty and immorality (e.g., Lev 18:21). On the other hand, idolaters become impotent and worthless in the eyes of the true God, just as their gods already are (vv. 5–7). They will ultimately be destroyed, along with their gods, under the Lord's judgment. See 2 Kings 17:15.
115:9 house of Israel. A reference to all the people of God. **trust in the LORD.** A call for faith in God as the One able to deliver his people from their troubles and distresses. See *WLC* 63.
115:10 house of Aaron. A reference to the priests of Israel.
115:11 You who fear him. See note on 111:10. Either the faithful in Israel or, in accordance with later usage, proselytes (see note on Ac 10:2).
115:12–13 See *WCF* 16.2.
115:12 remembers. See 44:1. **will bless us.** See 1:1. **house of Israel.** See verse 9. **house of Aaron.** See verse 10.
115:13 those who fear the LORD. See note on verse 11.

[15] May you be blessed by the LORD,
the Maker of heaven[l] and earth.

[16] The highest heavens belong to the LORD,[m]
but the earth he has given[n] to man.
[17] It is not the dead[o] who praise the LORD,
those who go down to silence;
[18] it is we who extol the LORD,
both now and forevermore.[p]

Praise the LORD.[a]

Psalm 116

[1] I love the LORD,[q] for he heard my voice;
he heard my cry[r] for mercy.
[2] Because he turned his ear[s] to me,
I will call on him as long as I live.

[3] The cords of death[t] entangled me,
the anguish of the grave[b] came upon me;
I was overcome by trouble and sorrow.
[4] Then I called on the name[u] of the LORD:
"O LORD, save me![v]"
[5] The LORD is gracious and righteous;[w]
our God is full of compassion.
[6] The LORD protects the simplehearted;
when I was in great need,[x] he saved me.

[7] Be at rest[y] once more, O my soul,
for the LORD has been good[z] to you.

[8] For you, O LORD, have delivered my soul[a] from death,
my eyes from tears,
my feet from stumbling,
[9] that I may walk before the LORD
in the land of the living.[b]
[10] I believed;[c] therefore[c] I said,
"I am greatly afflicted."
[11] And in my dismay I said,
"All men are liars."[d]

[12] How can I repay the LORD
for all his goodness to me?
[13] I will lift up the cup of salvation
and call on the name[e] of the LORD.

115:15 [l]Ge 1:1; 14:19; Ps 96:5
115:16 [m]Ps 89:11 [n]Ps 8:6-8
115:17 [o]Ps 6:5; 88:10-12; Isa 38:18
115:18 [p]Ps 113:2; Da 2:20
116:1 [q]Ps 18:1 [r]Ps 66:19
116:2 [s]Ps 40:1
116:3 [t]Ps 18:4-5
116:4 [u]Ps 118:5 [v]Ps 22:20
116:5 [w]Ezr 9:15; Ne 9:8; Ps 103:8; 145:17
116:6 [x]Ps 19:7; 79:8
116:7 [y]Jer 6:16; Mt 11:29 [z]Ps 13:6
116:8 [a]Ps 56:13
116:9 [b]Ps 27:13
116:10 [c]2Co 4:13*
116:11 [d]Ro 3:4
116:13 [e]Ps 16:5; 80:18

[a] *18* Hebrew *Hallelu Yah* [b] *3* Hebrew *Sheol* [c] *10* Or *believed even when*

115:15 the Maker of heaven and earth. God's role as Creator was emphasized to assert his ability to provide for his people the material blessings they needed.
115:16 the earth he has given to man. God created the earth, and it is his. In his generosity he gave it to the human race as a place on which to live and grow. Along with this gift came the responsibility of faithful stewardship.
115:17 It is not the dead. See note on 88:5.
115:18 Praise the LORD. See 11:1.
Psalm 116 *Introduction.* Psalm 116 is an exuberant expression of thanksgiving to the Lord for delivering the psalmist from death. It is impossible to be precise about the threat that hung over the psalmist—possibly sickness—but he looked back to his cry of distress to the Lord and proclaimed with gladness that God had heard him. Therefore he determined to offer sacrifices to the Lord. For the use of this psalm in the context of a festival, see "Introduction" to Psalm 113.
116:1 I love the LORD. The psalmist expressed his deep affection for the Lord, which he based on God's acts of love toward him. God had first shown his love toward the psalmist by hearing and acting on his prayer. **my cry for mercy.** The psalmist's earlier prayer, a lament expressing a fear that he was dying.
116:2 I will call on him. The Lord had given the psalmist clear evidence that he hears and answers the prayers of his people. Therefore the psalmist would keep praying to him.
116:3 The cords of death. The psalmist felt as though ropes had emerged from a grave and had started pulling him into the ground. **the anguish of the grave.** As he felt threatened by death, his anxiety level rose dramatically.
116:4 "O LORD, save me!" A quote from his earlier prayer of lament.
116:5 gracious . . . righteous . . . full of compassion. God revealed his nature through his answer to the psalmist's request. He did not stand at a distance as his people suffered. This description of God reflects God's exposition of the meaning of his name *Yahweh* (Ex 34:5–7). See note on 4:1.
116:6 he saved me. In answer to his earlier prayer (v. 4).
116:10 therefore I said. The psalmist's faith had led him to lay his petitions before God in the first place.
116:11 "All men are liars." Another quotation from his earlier lament (cf. v. 4). The psalmist had apparently been the object of someone's false accusation.
116:12–19 See *HC* 116.
116:13 the cup of salvation. May refer to the drink offering of

116:14 [f]Ps 22:25; Jnh 2:9
116:15 [g]Ps 72:14
116:16 [h]Ps 119:125; 143:12 [i]Ps 86:16
116:17 [j]Lev 7:12; Ps 50:14
116:19 [k]Ps 96:8; 135:2

14 I will fulfill my vows[f] to the LORD
in the presence of all his people.

15 Precious in the sight[g] of the LORD
is the death of his saints.
16 O LORD, truly I am your servant;[h]
I am your servant, the son of your maidservant[a];[i]
you have freed me from my chains.

17 I will sacrifice a thank offering[j] to you
and call on the name of the LORD.
18 I will fulfill my vows to the LORD
in the presence of all his people,
19 in the courts[k] of the house of the LORD—
in your midst, O Jerusalem.

Praise the LORD.[b]

Psalm 117

117:1 [l]Ro 15:11*
117:2 [m]Ps 100:5

1 Praise the LORD, all you nations;[l]
extol him, all you peoples.
2 For great is his love toward us,
and the faithfulness of the LORD[m] endures forever.

Praise the LORD.[b]

Psalm 118

118:1 [n]1Ch 16:8 [o]Ps 106:1; 136:1
118:2 [p]Ps 115:9
118:5 [q]Ps 120:1 [r]Ps 18:19
118:6 [s]Heb 13:6*

1 Give thanks to the LORD,[n] for he is good;
his love endures forever.[o]

2 Let Israel say:[p]
"His love endures forever."
3 Let the house of Aaron say:
"His love endures forever."
4 Let those who fear the LORD say:
"His love endures forever."

5 In my anguish[q] I cried to the LORD,
and he answered[r] by setting me free.
6 The LORD is with me;[s] I will not be afraid.

[a] *16* Or *servant, your faithful son* [b] *19,2* Hebrew *Hallelu Yah*

Numbers 15:10 or be a metaphor contrasting with the more frequently occurring "cup of God's wrath" (see 75:8).
116:14 in the presence of all his people. The psalmist vowed to provide a public witness to God's great acts. (See note on 22:22.)
116:15 Precious. In the sense of "costly." That is, God is grieved by the death of his faithful people.
116:16 your servant. Some see royal language here, with the king of God's people as the servant to the superior King, who is the Lord (see note on Ex 20:1–17). It is probably better to understand the psalmist as simply expressing his deep devotion to the Lord.
116:19 the house of the LORD. The temple in Jerusalem. **Praise the LORD.** See 111:1.
Psalm 117 *Introduction.* Psalm 117 is the shortest psalm in the Psalter and, indeed, the shortest chapter in the Bible. However, within its brief compass it expresses an exuberant call to praise to all nations. Paul brought out its amazing implications by citing it in his argument that the Gentiles share in the covenant promises (Ro 15:7–13). Because of its brevity, many have thought that Psalm 117 was originally connected with another psalm, but there is no firm evidence for this. It is appropriately set in the context of a number of other psalms beginning with the Hebrew *Hallelujah* (see "Introduction" to Ps 111 and note on 111:1).
117:1 all you nations. The call to praise goes beyond the borders of Israel to all the surrounding nations. Paul quoted this verse in Romans 15:11. See "Introduction" to Psalm 117.
117:2 his love. Specifically the love connected with his covenant relationships. This verse, though using different vocabulary, may be seen as a meditation on the truths about God so eloquently expressed in Exodus 34:6. It celebrates God's covenant relationship with his people.
Psalm 118 *Introduction.* Psalm 118 concludes the Egyptian Hallel (113–118; see "Introduction" to Ps 113), sung in the celebration of Passover. As the last song of that group, it may have been the final psalm in the mind of our Lord as he celebrated Passover with his disciples (Mk 14:26). In any case, the psalm anticipated the suffering and glorification of the Messiah. Jesus quoted verses 22–23 concerning himself (Mk 12:10–11; see Mt 23:29; Lk 13:35; cf. Ac 4:11), and the people greeted him at his triumphal entry into Jerusalem with shouts of joy quoted from this psalm (Mk 11:9–10; Lk 19:38; Jn 12:13). Psalm 118 was a favorite of New Testament writers (see following notes). It is an expression of gratitude for life and military victory. The main speaker was an individual, most likely the king (vv. 5–21), but the psalm is a liturgy including other speakers (vv. 21–27). The references to altar, temple and procession (vv. 19–20,27) reflect its use in corporate worship.
118:1 Give thanks. The worship leader called on the congregation to praise God for his character and his wonderful acts. The rest of the psalm principally celebrated victory in battle. Note the similar introduction to Psalm 136. **his love endures forever.** A refrain both in this psalm and throughout 136.
118:6 The LORD is with me. This is the heart of the covenant: God with his representative, the king. The king recognized the implication of this truth: He had nothing to fear from any person because God was in control. This reality was at the heart of holy war. Victory was not the result of larger numbers of troops or more advanced weaponry; it was a gift from God.

What can man do to me?[t]
7 The LORD is with me; he is my helper.[u]
I will look in triumph on my enemies.[v]

8 It is better to take refuge in the LORD[w]
than to trust in man.[x]
9 It is better to take refuge in the LORD
than to trust in princes.[y]

10 All the nations surrounded me,
but in the name of the LORD I cut them off.[z]
11 They surrounded me[a] on every side,[b]
but in the name of the LORD I cut them off.
12 They swarmed around me like bees,[c]
but they died out as quickly as burning thorns;[d]
in the name of the LORD I cut them off.

13 I was pushed back and about to fall,
but the LORD helped me.[e]
14 The LORD is my strength[f] and my song;
he has become my salvation.[g]

15 Shouts of joy[h] and victory
resound in the tents of the righteous:
"The LORD's right hand[i] has done mighty things!
16 The LORD's right hand is lifted high;
the LORD's right hand has done mighty things!"

17 I will not die[j] but live,
and will proclaim[k] what the LORD has done.
18 The LORD has chastened me severely,
but he has not given me over to death.[l]

19 Open for me the gates[m] of righteousness;
I will enter and give thanks to the LORD.
20 This is the gate of the LORD
through which the righteous may enter.[n]
21 I will give you thanks, for you answered me;[o]
you have become my salvation.

22 The stone the builders rejected
has become the capstone;[p]
23 the LORD has done this,
and it is marvelous in our eyes.
24 This is the day the LORD has made;
let us rejoice and be glad in it.

25 O LORD, save us;
O LORD, grant us success.

118:6 [t]Ps 27:1; 56:4
118:7 [u]Ps 54:4 [v]Ps 59:10
118:8 [w]Ps 40:4 [x]Jer 17:5
118:9 [y]Ps 146:3
118:10 [z]Ps 18:40
118:11 [a]Ps 88:17 [b]Ps 3:6
118:12 [c]Dt 1:44 [d]Ps 58:9
118:13 [e]Ps 86:17; 140:4
118:14 [f]Ex 15:2 [g]Isa 12:2
118:15 [h]Ps 68:3 [i]Ps 89:13
118:17 [j]Ps 6:5; Hab 1:12 [k]Ex 15:6; Ps 73:28
118:18 [l]2Co 6:9
118:19 [m]Isa 26:2
118:20 [n]Ps 24:7; Isa 35:8; Rev 22:14
118:21 [o]Ps 116:1
118:22 [p]Mt 21:42; Mk 12:10; Lk 20:17*; Ac 4:11*; 1Pe 2:7*

118:9 than to trust in princes. The Israelites lost sight of this truth when they requested a king who could lead them in battle (1Sa 8).
118:10 in the name of the LORD. Through God's power the king and his army were able to thwart Israel's enemies. See 8:1. God, the divine warrior, secured victory.
118:12 as burning thorns. The image has two connotations. Thorns prick, and so are apt images for the enemy. They also burn quickly when lighted, a property exploited by the psalmist to indicate swift downfall.
118:14 my salvation. The victory God had given the king and the nation over their enemies.
118:15–16 Shouts of joy. Israel's proper response to God's deliverance was to sing victory songs that rejoiced in God's salvation. **The LORD's right hand.** A metaphor for God's strength, likening God's power to a soldier's battle arm with which he wielded the sword in holy war (Ex 15:6,12).
118:19 the gates of righteousness. The entrance to the sanctuary, through which the king could approach the Lord and offer thanks for safety in battle. The gates were called righteous because both the One who dwelt behind them and those permitted access were righteous (see Pss 15; 24). See note 4:1.
118:21 my salvation. See note on verse 14.
118:22 The stone. The figure of the stone likely referred to the king, who represented his people. **rejected.** Defeated in battle. **the capstone.** The most important stone in a structure. (The term may refer to the cornerstone as the chief stone.) This is an image of the lowly, after having been rejected, being exalted to the chief place. Jesus applied this passage to himself (Mt 21:42; Mk 12:10; Lk 20:17, see also Ac 4:11; 1Pe 2:7). Jesus is the cornerstone (Eph 2:20), the One cast away by the earthly rulers of his day but ultimately exalted to the right hand of the Father. He caused some to stumble (see Isa 8:14, which is explicitly cited in 1Pe 2:7 but seems to be in Luke's mind as well; see Lk 20:18). See *WLC* 121.
118:24 the day the LORD has made. Through his victory God had made this particular day a day of life rather than of death for the psalmist and his people. Therefore they would devote the day to worship of the Lord. See *WLC* 121.
118:25 save us. A call for continued help against enemies.

118:26 qMt 21:9*; Mk 11:9*; Lk 13:35*; 19:38*; Jn 12:13*
118:27 r1Pe 2:9
118:28 sIsa 25:1 tEx 15:2

26 Blessed is he who comes[q] in the name of the LORD.
From the house of the LORD we bless you.[a]
27 The LORD is God,
and he has made his light shine[r] upon us.
With boughs in hand, join in the festal procession
up[b] to the horns of the altar.

28 You are my God, and I will give you thanks;
you are my God,[s] and I will exalt[t] you.

29 Give thanks to the LORD, for he is good;
his love endures forever.

Psalm 119[c]

א Aleph

119:1 uPs 128:1
119:2 vDt 6:5
119:3 w1Jn 3:9; 5:18

1 Blessed are they whose ways are blameless,
who walk[u] according to the law of the LORD.
2 Blessed are they who keep his statutes
and seek him with all their heart.[v]
3 They do nothing wrong;[w]
they walk in his ways.
4 You have laid down precepts
that are to be fully obeyed.
5 Oh, that my ways were steadfast
in obeying your decrees!
6 Then I would not be put to shame
when I consider all your commands.
7 I will praise you with an upright heart
as I learn your righteous laws.

a *26* The Hebrew is plural. b *27* Or *Bind the festal sacrifice with ropes / and take it* c This psalm is an acrostic poem; the verses of each stanza begin with the same letter of the Hebrew alphabet.

118:26 Blessed is he who comes in the name of the LORD. A reference to the king, who led the armies in battle against the enemy. In the New Testament, the crowds welcomed Jesus into Jerusalem with this cry, thinking him to be the new divine warrior. He would win the ultimate battle against Satan (Mt 21:9), but the people would fail to understand or acknowledge it.
118:27 the festal procession. The celebration in public worship of the Lord in the temple precincts.
118:29 Give thanks to the LORD. The psalm ends as it began (see note on v. 1).
Psalm 119 *Introduction.* Psalm 119, with its 176 verses, is by far the longest in the Psalter. Its length is attributable both to its author's remarkable devotion to the law of God and to its formidable poetic structure—the most extensive acrostic (see "Introduction: Structure: *Poetic Styles and Devices*") found in the Bible (the closest rival is Lamentations). It is a wisdom psalm composed of 22 eight-line stanzas, one stanza for each successive letter of the Hebrew alphabet, with all the lines in each stanza starting with that particular Hebrew letter.

The number of lines in each stanza may relate to the eight words that recur throughout the poem and reveal its main theme: "law," "testimonies," "precepts," "statutes," "commandments," "judgments," "word" and "promise." The theme is Scripture, specifically obedience to the law, with all eight words being used in a loosely synonymously way. Although these words sometimes carry different nuances, their meanings all significantly overlap. Moreover, given that Psalm 119 is poetry and that a typical poetic device is to use the name of a part to symbolize the whole (e.g., "law" to mean "Scripture"), all eight words are relatively interchangeable in this context. Psalm 119 is an incredible poetic achievement. Modern readers may find it too artificial for their tastes, but it was a great aesthetic delight to many in antiquity. It reflects beauty within the constraints of a particularly exacting form of expression.

While the psalmist expressed his love for the law and his desire to obey it (cf. other wisdom psalms, 1 and 19), he also recognized his failures. Elements of lament and petition are intertwined with expressions of confidence and pleas of innocence.

Christians may tend to ignore or set aside God's law. To be sure, it does condemn us because we cannot keep it perfectly, yet it expresses the will and character of our holy God. If we cannot love his law, how can we love him? We may legitimately praise God because he has sent his perfect Son to keep the law for us. It no longer condemns us, but it still serves to guide us in pleasing him. See theological articles "The Three Uses of the Law" at Psalm 119 and "The Law of God" at Exodus 20.
119:1–8 ***Aleph.*** The psalmist wished to be among the blessed ones who kept God's law.
119:1 Blessed. See Psalm 1:1. **who walk.** A metaphor for one's daily life activities. **the law of the LORD.** The law, or Torah, may refer either to the first five books of the Bible as a whole or to the legal sections in those books. The context indicates that the latter was meant. The psalmist was encouraging conformity to God's will as expressed through the Ten Commandments and the other laws of the Pentateuch. See *WLC* 192.
119:2 with all their heart. Not mere external, hypocritical adherence to the law. The psalmist called for obedience stemming from deep-seated faith in the Lord.
119:3 They do nothing wrong. The psalmist looked in amazement at the happiness of those who obeyed God's law. In this life, we cannot obey God's law perfectly. But insofar as we do, we do no wrong.
119:4–6 See *WCF* 19.6; *WLC* 192.
119:4 You have laid down precepts. In the Torah God entered into a covenant relationship with his people out of free grace, and within the context of that relationship he communicated his law, including the general command that they obey it in all its aspects. This was not a call to works righteousness; God required the thankful obedience of those in covenant with himself. See theological articles "Justification and Merit" at Romans 3 and "The Three Uses of the Law" at Psalm 119.
119:5 that my ways were steadfast. From one perspective, the psalmist did not consider himself to be as obedient (v. 4) as the blessed (v. 2), but see verses 101–104. See *HC* 123.
119:6 shame. The psalmist recognized his guilt and felt contrition. His aversion to shame reflected his desire to refrain from sin, not a wish to avoid proper repentance. See *WCF* 15.2; *WLC* 76.
119:7 as I learn. There is a relationship between worship and obedience. Obedience is a learning process.

8 I will obey your decrees;
do not utterly forsake me.

ב Beth

9 How can a young man keep his way pure?
By living according to your word.[x]
10 I seek you with all my heart;[y]
do not let me stray from your commands.[z]
11 I have hidden your word in my heart[a]
that I might not sin against you.
12 Praise be to you, O LORD;
teach me your decrees.[b]
13 With my lips I recount
all the laws that come from your mouth.[c]
14 I rejoice in following your statutes
as one rejoices in great riches.
15 I meditate on your precepts[d]
and consider your ways.
16 I delight[e] in your decrees;
I will not neglect your word.

ג Gimel

17 Do good to your servant,[f] and I will live;
I will obey your word.
18 Open my eyes that I may see
wonderful things in your law.
19 I am a stranger on earth;[g]
do not hide your commands from me.
20 My soul is consumed[h] with longing
for your laws[i] at all times.
21 You rebuke the arrogant, who are cursed
and who stray[j] from your commands.
22 Remove from me scorn[k] and contempt,
for I keep your statutes.
23 Though rulers sit together and slander me,
your servant will meditate on your decrees.
24 Your statutes are my delight;
they are my counselors.

ד Daleth

25 I am laid low in the dust;[l]
preserve my life[m] according to your word.
26 I recounted my ways and you answered me;
teach me your decrees.[n]

119:9 [x]2Ch 6:16
119:10 [y]2Ch 15:15 [z]ver 21,118
119:11 [a]Ps 37:31; Lk 2:19, 51
119:12 [b]ver 26
119:13 [c]Ps 40:9
119:15 [d]Ps 1:2
119:16 [e]Ps 1:2
119:17 [f]Ps 13:6; 116:7
119:19 [g]1Ch 29:15; Ps 39:12; 2Co 5:6; Heb 11:13
119:20 [h]Ps 42:2; 84:2 [i]Ps 63:1
119:21 [j]ver 10
119:22 [k]Ps 39:8
119:25 [l]Ps 44:25 [m]Ps 143:11
119:26 [n]Ps 25:4; 27:11; 86:11

119:8 I will obey. The psalmist was determined to follow God's law. See *WLC* 192.
119:9–16 ***Beth.*** The psalmist sought to keep his behavior pure by meditating on God's law.
119:9 according to your word. God has not left us in the dark as to what pleases him. He has stated it clearly throughout his Word.
119:10 I seek . . . do not let me stray. Those who strive after moral perfection often come to realize the truth that no one can refrain from sin apart from God's power (see notes on Mt 5:48; 1Co 10:13; see theological article "Justification and Merit" at Ro 3).
119:11 I have hidden your word. The psalmist sheltered God's law like a treasure in his memory. See *WLC* 160; *WSC* 90.
119:14 as one rejoices in great riches. The law was not a tremendous external burden (Dt 30:11–14; see note on Ro 7:9)—its stipulations could be kept outwardly. The great difficulty was obeying from the heart, but for the faithful even this was possible. For the obedient faithful, God's law produced many blessings (see 1:1). As the Wisdom Literature pointed out (e.g., Pr 3:13–18), God's rules for living were far more precious than wealth.
119:15 I meditate. Relating to God's law requires more than surface reading or rote memorization; it demands careful reflection and deep soul searching.
119:17–24 ***Gimel.*** The psalmist requested mercy and grace to enable him to obey the law.
119:17 and I will live. The psalmist's very life depended on the grace God would show him.
119:18 Open my eyes. The psalmist asked God to illumine his word. **wonderful things.** That is, things bordering on and including the miraculous. See *WLC* 4,157,160; *WSC* 90.
119:19 stranger. See Hebrews 11:13. The psalmist's true home was not on this earth but with God.
119:22 Remove from me. The psalmist went beyond praise of the law to petition for God's grace in distress.
119:23 rulers . . . slander me. May indicate the psalmist's royal status.
119:25–32 ***Daleth.*** The psalmist asked that God use his word to keep his faithful ones from shame and sorrow.
119:25 preserve my life. The author realized that the Lord and his word were the only sources of hope for him when he was despondent.

119:27 oPs 145:5
119:28 pPs 107:26 qPs 20:2; 1Pe 5:10
119:31 rDt 11:22
119:33 sver 12
119:36 t1Ki 8:58 uEze 33:31; Mk 7:21-22; Lk 12:15; Heb 13:5
119:37 vPs 71:20; Isa 33:15
119:38 w2Sa 7:25
119:40 xver 20
119:42 yPr 27:11
119:46 zMt 10:18; Ac 26:1-2

27 Let me understand the teaching of your precepts;
then I will meditate on your wonders.[o]
28 My soul is weary with sorrow;[p]
strengthen me[q] according to your word.
29 Keep me from deceitful ways;
be gracious to me through your law.
30 I have chosen the way of truth;
I have set my heart on your laws.
31 I hold fast[r] to your statutes, O LORD;
do not let me be put to shame.
32 I run in the path of your commands,
for you have set my heart free.

ה He

33 Teach me,[s] O LORD, to follow your decrees;
then I will keep them to the end.
34 Give me understanding, and I will keep your law
and obey it with all my heart.
35 Direct me in the path of your commands,
for there I find delight.
36 Turn my heart[t] toward your statutes
and not toward selfish gain.[u]
37 Turn my eyes away from worthless things;
preserve my life[v] according to your word.[a]
38 Fulfill your promise[w] to your servant,
so that you may be feared.
39 Take away the disgrace I dread,
for your laws are good.
40 How I long[x] for your precepts!
Preserve my life in your righteousness.

ו Waw

41 May your unfailing love come to me, O LORD,
your salvation according to your promise;
42 then I will answer[y] the one who taunts me,
for I trust in your word.
43 Do not snatch the word of truth from my mouth,
for I have put my hope in your laws.
44 I will always obey your law,
for ever and ever.
45 I will walk about in freedom,
for I have sought out your precepts.
46 I will speak of your statutes before kings[z]
and will not be put to shame,
47 for I delight in your commands
because I love them.

[a] *37* Two manuscripts of the Masoretic Text and Dead Sea Scrolls; most manuscripts of the Masoretic Text *life in your way*

119:29 Keep me from deceitful ways. The psalmist recognized that, if left to himself, he would inevitably disobey God's law.
119:30 I have chosen. The writer was enabled to follow God only because of God's grace (v. 29), and he committed himself to God as a conscious choice.
119:32 you have set my heart free. From bondage to sin and death. See *WCF* 18.3.
119:33–40 *He.* The psalmist entreated the Lord for instruction in his law.
119:34 with all my heart. That is, with his whole mind, strength and will (cf. Mt 22:37). The psalmist expressed deep devotion to the Lord: He loved God and wanted to obey. Jesus told his disciples, "If you love me, you will obey what I command" (Jn 14:15). See *BC* 18.
119:35–36 See *WLC* 192.
119:35 delight. The psalmist obeyed the Lord out of joyful gratitude, not as though he were compelled to do so or under a heavy burden.
119:36 Turn my heart. He realized that the source of his love for God was God himself. See *WSC* 103.
119:37 Turn my eyes away. Matching his longing to move closer to God's law was a corresponding desire to move away from those worthless things that were not of God. **worthless things.** Predominantly idols (see note on 31:6).
119:38 your promise. Most likely God's covenant promise of blessing.
119:41–48 *Waw.* The psalmist would obey and witness to the blessings of God's law.
119:41 your unfailing love. God's devotion to those in covenant with himself.
119:45 in freedom. By keeping God's laws the psalmist would be liberated from slavery to his sin.

[48] I lift up my hands to[a] your commands, which I love,
and I meditate on your decrees.

ז Zayin

[49] Remember your word to your servant,
for you have given me hope.
[50] My comfort in my suffering is this:
Your promise preserves my life.[a]

119:50
[a]Ro 15:4

[a] *48* Or *for*

119:49–56 ***Zayin.*** The author would obey God's laws as his source of hope.

119:49 Remember. See 44:1.

The Three Uses of the Law: What Good Is the Law?

THROUGHOUT the history of the church there has been widespread confusion over the role of the Old Testament law in the Christian life. Many theologians have utterly rejected the law as irrelevant to New Testament believers. Although there have been varied opinions concerning specific issues, traditional Reformed theology has summarized this matter in terms of three valid uses of the law. Some theological writers present these in the order given below; others reverse the first two, so there is some discontinuity within the Reformed tradition as to what are the "first" and the "second" uses of the law.

What we shall call the first function of the law is the *pedagogical* use. The law reveals both the perfect righteousness of God and our own shortcomings that drive us to Christ for salvation. The law gives knowledge of sin (Ro 3:20; 4:15; 5:13), and our sinful nature takes this knowledge as opportunity for even further rebellion (Ro 7:7–11), thus condemning us to judgment. By revealing to us our need of pardon the law leads us to Christ in repentance and faith (Gal 3:19–24). In this sense, believers are *not* under the law. The apostle Paul identified this use of the law with the ways of the age of sin and death prior to the coming of Christ (see theological article "The Plan of the Ages" at Heb 7). The law came so that sin would increase (e.g., to the point that Israel was condemned to exile), but where sin increased grace increased all the more when Christ came (Ro 5:20–21). Those who are united with Christ are set free from the judgment of the law when they pass from this age to the age to come. We are not "under law, but under grace" (Ro 6:14) in the sense that we are not under the *condemnation* of the law but under the grace of God in Christ (Ro 8:1–4). Nevertheless, believers continue to need the law's pedagogy to remind us that we still sin and need God's forgiveness (1Jn 1:8–9) and Christ's intercession (Ro 8:34; Heb 7:25). The law forces us to return to the cross of Jesus, to see that we have no hope in ourselves and that Jesus' atonement alone can take away our sin and its consequences. This function of the law also continues to apply to unbelievers even today, showing them their need for repentance, forgiveness and conversion.

The second function of the law is its *civil* use. The moral standards of the Old Testament law restrain evil through threats of punishment. Though the law cannot change the heart, it can inhibit lawlessness by its threats of judgment, especially when backed by a civil code that administers punishment for proven offenses (Dt 13:6–11; 19:16–21; Ro 13:3–4). Thus it secures some civil order and protects the weak from the unjust. Although the Scriptures never use the expression "under the law" to refer to this civil function, it is apparent that at times even Christians are restrained by the threat of punishment. Although obedience out of love for God is the ideal for which we are to strive (1Jn 4:18), we can benefit from the restraint this use of the law provides. This restraining function of the law was clearly in view during the Old Testament period (Ex 21–23). Yet it was also affirmed for the New Testament time when Paul wrote that the law is not for the righteous but for sinners (1Ti 1:8–11).

The third function of the law is the *normative* or *moral* use. The moral standards of the law provide guidance for believers as we seek to live in humble gratitude for the grace God has shown us. As the prologue to the Ten Commandments makes clear (Ex 20:2), obedience to God's commands rightly flows from a heart thankful for the redemption that has been received as a free gift of grace from God. It is often helpful for us, as believers living after the first coming of Christ, to distinguish between the moral, ceremonial and civil dimensions of the law. Reformed theologians have historically expressed general agreement that God gave certain ceremonial and civil expressions of the law for specific situations in history, rather than for all believers at all times (e.g., OT dietary laws; see note on Ac 10:15). Even these, however, continue to instruct us about the principles of God's wisdom and justice. Because the whole law expresses and reflects God's unchanging character, its moral dimension remains normative for all time (Mt 5:17–19; Ro 3:31; 13:8–9; Eph 6:2; Jas 2:10–11; 1Jn 2:3–7; cf. *BC* 25; *HC* 91; *WCF* 19). Calvin considered the moral guidance of the law its principle use in the sense that the other uses occur only because of sin's presence in the world, whereas its moral use derives directly from God's character. Paul spoke of this third use of the law when he wrote, "I am not free from God's law but am under Christ's law" (1Co 9:21), "Christ's law" being the law as interpreted and applied by Christ.

51 The arrogant mock me[b] without restraint,
but I do not turn[c] from your law.
52 I remember[d] your ancient laws, O LORD,
and I find comfort in them.
53 Indignation grips me[e] because of the wicked,
who have forsaken your law.[f]
54 Your decrees are the theme of my song
wherever I lodge.
55 In the night I remember[g] your name, O LORD,
and I will keep your law.
56 This has been my practice:
I obey your precepts.

ח Heth

57 You are my portion,[h] O LORD;
I have promised to obey your words.
58 I have sought your face with all my heart;
be gracious to me[i] according to your promise.[j]
59 I have considered my ways[k]
and have turned my steps to your statutes.
60 I will hasten and not delay
to obey your commands.
61 Though the wicked bind me with ropes,
I will not forget[l] your law.
62 At midnight[m] I rise to give you thanks
for your righteous laws.
63 I am a friend to all who fear you,[n]
to all who follow your precepts.
64 The earth is filled with your love,[o] O LORD;
teach me your decrees.

ט Teth

65 Do good to your servant
according to your word, O LORD.
66 Teach me knowledge and good judgment,
for I believe in your commands.
67 Before I was afflicted I went astray,[p]
but now I obey your word.
68 You are good,[q] and what you do is good;
teach me your decrees.[r]
69 Though the arrogant have smeared me with lies,[s]
I keep your precepts with all my heart.
70 Their hearts are callous[t] and unfeeling,
but I delight in your law.
71 It was good for me to be afflicted
so that I might learn your decrees.
72 The law from your mouth is more precious to me
than thousands of pieces of silver and gold.[u]

119:51 [b]Jer 20:7 [c]ver 157; Job 23:11; Ps 44:18
119:52 [d]Ps 103:18
119:53 [e]Ezr 9:3 [f]Ps 89:30
119:55 [g]Ps 63:6
119:57 [h]Ps 16:5; La 3:24
119:58 [i]1Ki 13:6 [j]ver 41
119:59 [k]Lk 15:17-18
119:61 [l]Ps 140:5
119:62 [m]Ac 16:25
119:63 [n]Ps 101:6-7
119:64 [o]Ps 33:5
119:67 [p]Jer 31:18-19; Heb 12:11
119:68 [q]Ps 106:1; 107:1; Mt 19:17 [r]ver 12
119:69 [s]Job 13:4; Ps 109:2
119:70 [t]Ps 17:10; Isa 6:10; Ac 28:27
119:72 [u]Ps 19:10; Pr 8:10-11,19

119:52 your ancient laws. Given through Moses and contained in the books of the Pentateuch.
119:54 the theme of my song. The law was not simply a matter of obedience to the psalmist but also a motivation for praise and worship.
119:55 name. See 8:1.
119:57–64 *Heth.* The psalmist was fully devoted to the Lord and to his law.
119:57 my portion. The portion referred to by the psalmist was not his inheritance in the land but the Lord himself (see Nu 18:20).
119:58 I have sought your face. The writer yearned to be in God's presence. In the Old Testament this desire could best be satisfied by dwelling in the sanctuary (see note on 114:2).
119:59 See *WCF* 15.2; *WLC* 76.
119:63 a friend. The psalmist supported and aided others who obeyed the Lord. **who fear you.** See 34:7.
119:64 your love. God's covenant loving-kindness.
119:65–72 *Teth.* The psalmist's affliction brought him back from his wandering away from God.
119:65 according to your word. A petition that God remain faithful to his promised covenant blessings.
119:67 I went astray. God had apparently used distress and suffering in the psalmist's life to bring him back to himself (see note on v. 71; see also Ps 31; Heb 12:1–13).
119:68–69 See *WCF* 2.2; 21.1; *WLC* 145.
119:70 callous and unfeeling. Compare 1 Timothy 4:2.
119:71 It was good for me to be afflicted. In retrospect, the psalmist thanked the Lord for his suffering because it had led to a deeper level of intimacy with the Lord. See *WCF* 20.1.

י Yodh

73 Your hands made me[v] and formed me;
give me understanding to learn your commands.
74 May those who fear you rejoice[w] when they see me,
for I have put my hope in your word.
75 I know, O LORD, that your laws are righteous,
and in faithfulness[x] you have afflicted me.
76 May your unfailing love be my comfort,
according to your promise to your servant.
77 Let your compassion[y] come to me that I may live,
for your law is my delight.
78 May the arrogant[z] be put to shame for wronging me without cause;[a]
but I will meditate on your precepts.
79 May those who fear you turn to me,
those who understand your statutes.
80 May my heart be blameless toward your decrees,
that I may not be put to shame.

כ Kaph

81 My soul faints[b] with longing for your salvation,
but I have put my hope in your word.
82 My eyes fail,[c] looking for your promise;
I say, "When will you comfort me?"
83 Though I am like a wineskin in the smoke,
I do not forget your decrees.
84 How long[d] must your servant wait?
When will you punish my persecutors?
85 The arrogant dig pitfalls[e] for me,
contrary to your law.
86 All your commands are trustworthy;[f]
help me,[g] for men persecute me without cause.[h]
87 They almost wiped me from the earth,
but I have not forsaken[i] your precepts.
88 Preserve my life according to your love,
and I will obey the statutes of your mouth.

ל Lamedh

89 Your word, O LORD, is eternal;[j]
it stands firm in the heavens.
90 Your faithfulness[k] continues through all generations;
you established the earth, and it endures.[l]
91 Your laws endure[m] to this day,
for all things serve you.
92 If your law had not been my delight,
I would have perished in my affliction.
93 I will never forget your precepts,
for by them you have preserved my life.

119:73 [v]Job 10:8; Ps 100:3; 138:8; 139:13-16
119:74 [w]Ps 34:2
119:75 [x]Heb 12:5-11
119:77 [y]ver 41
119:78 [z]Jer 50:32 [a]ver 86, 161
119:81 [b]Ps 84:2
119:82 [c]Ps 69:3; La 2:11
119:84 [d]Ps 39:4; Rev 6:10
119:85 [e]Ps 35:7; Jer 18:20, 22
119:86 [f]Ps 35:19 [g]Ps 109:26 [h]ver 78
119:87 [i]Isa 58:2
119:89 [j]Mt 24:34-35; 1Pe 1:25
119:90 [k]Ps 36:5 [l]Ps 148:6; Ecc 1:4
119:91 [m]Jer 33:25

119:73–80 ***Yodh.*** The psalmist requested that God use his law to increase the intimacy between the Lord and his worshipers.
119:74 those who fear you. Compare note on 34:7. **when they see me.** As others who shared the psalmist's deep commitment to the Lord perceived his evident prosperity and happiness, they would rejoice with him and be encouraged to continue in their own faithfulness (cf. note on 81–88).
119:75 you have afflicted me. See verses 67 and 71.
119:79 those who fear you. See verse 74.
119:80 See *WLC* 192.
119:81–88 ***Kaph.*** The psalmist expressed his understanding that the obedient sometimes suffer rather than prosper. Nevertheless, he was resolved to remain obedient to the Lord and to trust him for salvation and refuge.
119:81 for your salvation. The psalmist was referring to deliverance from his persecutors (v. 84).
119:82 My eyes fail. Because he had been gazing in expectation for so long.
119:83 a wineskin in the smoke. Smoke damaged wineskins; this is paralleled by the harm the psalmist experienced from his enemies.
119:84 When will you punish my persecutors? The psalmist expected God to come to his aid by judging those who were persecuting him unjustly.
119:86 without cause. See note on 35:19.
119:87 but I have not forsaken your precepts. The poet's obedience did not depend on his circumstances. He expected that eventually God would reward his patience, but for now he would obey even while he suffered.
119:89–96 ***Lamedh.*** God's word is eternal, perfect and life saving.
119:89 eternal. As God exists forever, so does his word. Because God's word reflects his character, it is always valid and speaks to all people at all times.
119:93 forget. To forget in this context means to disobey.

94 Save me, for I am yours;
I have sought out your precepts.
95 The wicked are waiting to destroy me,
but I will ponder your statutes.
96 To all perfection I see a limit;
but your commands are boundless.

מ Mem

119:97 [n]Ps 1:2

97 Oh, how I love your law!
I meditate[n] on it all day long.

119:98 [o]Dt 4:6

98 Your commands make me wiser[o] than my enemies,
for they are ever with me.
99 I have more insight than all my teachers,
for I meditate on your statutes.

119:100 [p]Job 32:7-9

100 I have more understanding than the elders,
for I obey your precepts.[p]

119:101 [q]Pr 1:15

101 I have kept my feet[q] from every evil path
so that I might obey your word.
102 I have not departed from your laws,
for you yourself have taught me.

119:103 [r]Ps 19:10; Pr 8:11 [s]Pr 24:13-14

103 How sweet are your words to my taste,
sweeter than honey[r] to my mouth![s]

119:104 [t]ver 128

104 I gain understanding from your precepts;
therefore I hate every wrong path.[t]

נ Nun

119:105 [u]Pr 6:23

105 Your word is a lamp to my feet
and a light[u] for my path.

119:106 [v]Ne 10:29

106 I have taken an oath[v] and confirmed it,
that I will follow your righteous laws.
107 I have suffered much;
preserve my life, O LORD, according to your word.

119:108 [w]Hos 14:2; Heb 13:15

108 Accept, O LORD, the willing praise of my mouth,[w]
and teach me your laws.

119:109 [x]Jdg 12:3; Job 13:14

109 Though I constantly take my life in my hands,[x]
I will not forget your law.

119:110 [y]Ps 140:5; 141:9 [z]ver 10

110 The wicked have set a snare[y] for me,
but I have not strayed[z] from your precepts.
111 Your statutes are my heritage forever;
they are the joy of my heart.

119:112 [a]ver 33

112 My heart is set on keeping your decrees
to the very end.[a]

ס Samekh

119:113 [b]Jas 1:8

113 I hate double-minded men,[b]
but I love your law.

119:96 your commands are boundless. That is, they are infinitely perfect.

119:97–104 ***Mem.*** The psalmist rejoiced in the wisdom God gave him through the law.

119:97 I love your law! The psalmist cherished God's law because it was an expression of the character of his God and Savior. By extolling the law, he articulated his love for God. The law was God's guidebook for appropriate living in the world. See *WLC* 157.

119:98 wiser than my enemies. The enemies rebelled against God and rejected his law. They lived apart from the insight that God, their Creator, could give them.

119:99 more insight than all my teachers. An emphatic statement of the poet's devotion to God's law. His insight did not result from diligent meditation; his meditation was the means through which God graciously bestowed the psalmist's increased understanding (see note on v. 102).

119:101 every evil path. Teachers in the wisdom tradition frequently likened life to walking along a path. See Proverbs 1:22, 2:20 and 4:10–19. See *WCF* 19.6.

119:102 you yourself have taught me. The psalmist did not claim superior intelligence or even superior determination in study; he attributed all his knowledge and insight to God.

119:104 every wrong path. See note on verse 101. See *WCF* 19.6.

119:105–112 ***Nun.*** Though the enemy continued to pursue the psalmist, he nonetheless clung to the Lord in faith and obedience.

119:105 a lamp to my feet . . . a light for my path. God's revelation provided the insight to guide the righteous. Consequently they would not trip in the darkness. See *WCF* 1.7; *HC* 123.

119:106 See *WCF* 15.2.

119:109 I constantly take my life in my hands. The psalmist's obedience was not risk-free—obedience to the Lord often brings persecution (cf. 2Ti 3:12; Heb 11:35–38). He could have wished to be free of the danger but was more concerned about living a godly life in spite of it.

119:112 See *WLC* 192.

119:113–120 ***Samekh.*** The psalmist proclaimed his love for the Lord, his hope in his word and his disdain for the wicked who rejected God.

119:113 double-minded men. The psalmist was single-minded, unequivocally loving God and his law. This brought him stability (as opposed to the volatility of the double-minded, cf. Jas 1:8).

114 You are my refuge and my shield;[c]
I have put my hope[d] in your word.
115 Away from me,[e] you evildoers,
that I may keep the commands of my God!
116 Sustain me[f] according to your promise, and I will live;
do not let my hopes be dashed.[g]
117 Uphold me, and I will be delivered;
I will always have regard for your decrees.
118 You reject all who stray from your decrees,
for their deceitfulness is in vain.
119 All the wicked of the earth you discard like dross;[h]
therefore I love your statutes.
120 My flesh trembles[i] in fear of you;
I stand in awe of your laws.

ע Ayin

121 I have done what is righteous and just;
do not leave me to my oppressors.
122 Ensure your servant's well-being;[j]
let not the arrogant oppress me.
123 My eyes fail, looking for your salvation,
looking for your righteous promise.[k]
124 Deal with your servant according to your love
and teach me your decrees.[l]
125 I am your servant;[m] give me discernment
that I may understand your statutes.
126 It is time for you to act, O LORD;
your law is being broken.
127 Because I love your commands
more than gold,[n] more than pure gold,
128 and because I consider all your precepts right,
I hate every wrong path.[o]

פ Pe

129 Your statutes are wonderful;
therefore I obey them.
130 The unfolding of your words gives light;[p]
it gives understanding to the simple.[q]
131 I open my mouth and pant,[r]
longing for your commands.[s]
132 Turn to me and have mercy[t] on me,
as you always do to those who love your name.
133 Direct my footsteps according to your word;[u]
let no sin rule[v] over me.
134 Redeem me from the oppression of men,[w]
that I may obey your precepts.
135 Make your face shine[x] upon your servant
and teach me your decrees.

119:114 [c]Ps 32:7; 91:1 [d]ver 74
119:115 [e]Ps 6:8; 139:19; Mt 7:23
119:116 [f]Ps 54:4 [g]Ps 25:2; Ro 5:5; 9:33
119:119 [h]Eze 22:18,19
119:120 [i]Hab 3:16
119:122 [j]Job 17:3
119:123 [k]ver 82
119:124 [l]ver 12
119:125 [m]Ps 116:16
119:127 [n]Ps 19:10
119:128 [o]ver 104,163
119:130 [p]Pr 6:23 [q]Ps 19:7
119:131 [r]Ps 42:1 [s]ver 20
119:132 [t]Ps 25:16; 106:4
119:133 [u]Ps 17:5 [v]Ps 19:13; Ro 6:12
119:134 [w]Ps 142:6; Lk 1:74
119:135 [x]Nu 6:25; Ps 4:6

119:119 dross. The waste that results when metal is smelted. When the wicked are poured off, the righteous remain as refined silver. Compare Proverbs 25:3–5 and Isaiah 1:22 and 25.
119:120 in fear of you. See 36:1 and 40:3.
119:121–128 ***Ayin.*** The psalmist petitioned the Lord to save his people by bringing swift judgment against his enemies.
119:123 My eyes fail. See note at verse 82.
119:124 according to your love. That is, the devotion God shows to his covenant children, demonstrating his mercy and compassion.
119:126 It is time for you to act. The psalmist, with characteristic honesty, informed God that, at least in his opinion, he has delayed his judgment long enough. The wicked deserved the punishment they were about to receive.
119:128 every wrong path. See verses 101 and 104. See *WCF* 15.2; 19.6; *WLC* 76
119:129–136 ***Pe.*** The psalmist loved the law of God and mourned over those who ignored it.
119:129 See *WLC* 4.
119:130 The unfolding of your words. Literally, "the opening of your word." It is unclear whether the psalmist referred to the initial act of revelation, the process of interpretation of God's word or the application of the law to his heart. Perhaps the expression included all three as a single process that brought light, hope and understanding to his dark soul. See *WCF* 1.7.
119:131 pant. See note on 42:1. The concept is the same as that in Psalm 42, although the Hebrew word is different.
119:132 to those who love your name. Compare Romans 8:28.
119:133 Direct my footsteps. The psalmist wanted the Lord to guide him through life and recognized that this would entail obeying God's word. But he also knew that obedience was impossible for him unless God gave him the power to obey (see note on v. 10). See *WLC* 195.
119:135 Make your face shine upon your servant. The psalmist asked God to come and be with him. He wanted to live in God's presence (see theological article "The Presence of God" at 1Ki 8). Compare the priestly blessing in Numbers 6:22–27.

119:136 [y]Jer 9:1,18 [z]Eze 9:4
119:137 [a]Ezr 9:15; Jer 12:1 [b]Ne 9:13
119:138 [c]Ps 19:7
119:139 [d]Ps 69:9; Jn 2:17
119:140 [e]Ps 12:6
119:141 [f]Ps 22:6
119:142 [g]Ps 19:7
119:144 [h]Ps 19:9
119:147 [i]Ps 5:3; 57:8; 108:2
119:148 [j]Ps 63:6
119:151 [k]Ps 34:18; 145:18 [l]ver 142
119:152 [m]Lk 21:33
119:153 [n]La 5:1 [o]Pr 3:1
119:154 [p]Mic 7:9 [q]1Sa 24:15
119:155 [r]Job 5:4
119:156 [s]2Sa 24:14

136 Streams of tears[y] flow from my eyes,
for your law is not obeyed.[z]

צ Tsadhe

137 Righteous are you,[a] O LORD,
and your laws are right.[b]
138 The statutes you have laid down are righteous;[c]
they are fully trustworthy.
139 My zeal wears me out,[d]
for my enemies ignore your words.
140 Your promises have been thoroughly tested,[e]
and your servant loves them.
141 Though I am lowly and despised,[f]
I do not forget your precepts.
142 Your righteousness is everlasting
and your law is true.[g]
143 Trouble and distress have come upon me,
but your commands are my delight.
144 Your statutes are forever right;
give me understanding[h] that I may live.

ק Qoph

145 I call with all my heart; answer me, O LORD,
and I will obey your decrees.
146 I call out to you; save me
and I will keep your statutes.
147 I rise before dawn[i] and cry for help;
I have put my hope in your word.
148 My eyes stay open through the watches of the night,[j]
that I may meditate on your promises.
149 Hear my voice in accordance with your love;
preserve my life, O LORD, according to your laws.
150 Those who devise wicked schemes are near,
but they are far from your law.
151 Yet you are near,[k] O LORD,
and all your commands are true.[l]
152 Long ago I learned from your statutes
that you established them to last forever.[m]

ר Resh

153 Look upon my suffering[n] and deliver me,
for I have not forgotten[o] your law.
154 Defend my cause[p] and redeem me;[q]
preserve my life according to your promise.
155 Salvation is far from the wicked,
for they do not seek out[r] your decrees.
156 Your compassion is great, O LORD;
preserve my life[s] according to your laws.

119:136 See *WLC* 104.
119:137–144 ***Tsadhe.*** The Lord is righteous and, accordingly, so is his word.
119:137 **Righteous are you.** Implied is that God acts according to his nature, which is never arbitrary or inconsistent. See note on 4:1. **your laws are right.** God's laws express his nature as well; like God's character, they are neither capricious nor inconsistent, but unfailingly fair.
119:140 **have been thoroughly tested.** The psalmist could look back over history and trace how God had fulfilled his promises. One example was the promise of the land to Abraham, which came to fulfillment many centuries later during the conquest. See *WLC* 4.
119:145–152 ***Qoph.*** The psalmist fervently prayed to the Lord for help in distress.
119:145 **with all my heart.** The psalmist was a model of ardent and honest prayer to the Lord.
119:147 **I rise before dawn.** The psalmist's first thought as he awakened was of the Lord. His prayers were frequent and impassioned.
119:149 **in accordance with your love . . . according to your laws.** God's loving devotion for his people was fully compatible with his law.
119:151 **Yet you are near, O LORD.** God's presence nullified that of the enemy (v. 150).
119:153–160 ***Resh.*** Though the psalmist suffered and complained, he acknowledged the wonder and truth of God's word.
119:153 **for I have not forgotten your law.** The psalmist expected that God would bless him because of his obedience. Such an expectation could become presumptuous (a sin the book of Job sought to guard against), but it could also arise from faith.
119:154 **Defend my cause.** Courtroom terminology. The psalmist asked the Lord to intercede as his advocate against his enemies.
119:156 **Your compassion is great.** See Lamentations 3:23.

157 Many are the foes who persecute me,[t]
but I have not turned from your statutes.
158 I look on the faithless with loathing,[u]
for they do not obey your word.
159 See how I love your precepts;
preserve my life, O LORD, according to your love.
160 All your words are true;
all your righteous laws are eternal.

ש Sin and Shin

161 Rulers persecute me[v] without cause,
but my heart trembles at your word.
162 I rejoice in your promise
like one who finds great spoil.[w]
163 I hate and abhor falsehood
but I love your law.
164 Seven times a day I praise you
for your righteous laws.
165 Great peace[x] have they who love your law,
and nothing can make them stumble.
166 I wait for your salvation,[y] O LORD,
and I follow your commands.
167 I obey your statutes,
for I love them greatly.
168 I obey your precepts and your statutes,
for all my ways are known[z] to you.

ת Taw

169 May my cry come[a] before you, O LORD;
give me understanding according to your word.
170 May my supplication come[b] before you;
deliver me[c] according to your promise.
171 May my lips overflow with praise,[d]
for you teach me[e] your decrees.
172 May my tongue sing of your word,
for all your commands are righteous.
173 May your hand be ready to help[f] me,
for I have chosen[g] your precepts.
174 I long for your salvation,[h] O LORD,
and your law is my delight.
175 Let me live[i] that I may praise you,
and may your laws sustain me.
176 I have strayed like a lost sheep.[j]
Seek your servant,
for I have not forgotten your commands.

Psalm 120

A song of ascents.

1 I call on the LORD in my distress,[k]
and he answers me.

119:157 [t]Ps 7:1
119:158 [u]Ps 139:21
119:161 [v]1Sa 24:11
119:162 [w]1Sa 30:16
119:165 [x]Pr 3:2; Isa 26:3, 12; 32:17
119:166 [y]Ge 49:18
119:168 [z]Pr 5:21
119:169 [a]Ps 18:6
119:170 [b]Ps 28:2 [c]Ps 31:2
119:171 [d]Ps 51:15 [e]Ps 94:12
119:173 [f]Ps 37:24 [g]Jos 24:22
119:174 [h]ver 166
119:175 [i]Isa 55:3
119:176 [j]Isa 53:6
120:1 [k]Ps 102:2; Jnh 2:2

119:158 with loathing. See "Introduction: Christ in Psalms."
119:161–168 *Sin* and *Shin*. The psalmist expressed his devotion to the Lord and to his law.
119:161 Rulers persecute me. The fact that the psalmist provoked the ire of rulers indicates that he too was a powerful person, perhaps the king of Israel. **without cause.** See 38:19. **my heart trembles.** With awe and excitement (see v. 162).
119:164 Seven times a day. A poetic way of saying "throughout the entire day."
119:167 for I love them greatly. Obedience was not onerous to the psalmist; he followed God's law because he wanted to.
119:169–176 *Taw*. The psalmist prayed for understanding and for deliverance.
119:169 give me understanding. Expresses one of the major themes of the psalm: the desire for insight into God's will so that the psalmist might be better equipped to obey.
119:170 deliver me. This line climaxes another (see v. 169) major theme of the psalm: the psalmist's need for deliverance.
119:175 Let me live. Indicates that the psalmist wrote from the perspective of a time when he was in trouble.
119:176 Seek your servant. The psalmist concluded by invoking God as his Shepherd (see Ps 23; Eze 34; Jn 10); he begged him to bring him back into the flock.
Psalm 120 *Introduction.* Psalm 120 is the first of 15 songs of ascent (120–134). It appears from tradition and content that these were written to be sung by travelers as they journeyed on a pilgrimage to

120:2 [l]Pr 12:22 [m]Ps 52:4

2 Save me, O LORD, from lying lips[l]
and from deceitful tongues.[m]

3 What will he do to you,
and what more besides, O deceitful tongue?

120:4 [n]Ps 45:5

4 He will punish you with a warrior's sharp arrows,[n]
with burning coals of the broom tree.

120:5 [o]Ge 25:13; Jer 49:28

5 Woe to me that I dwell in Meshech,
that I live among the tents of Kedar![o]
6 Too long have I lived
among those who hate peace.
7 I am a man of peace;
but when I speak, they are for war.

Psalm 121

A song of ascents.

1 I lift up my eyes to the hills—
where does my help come from?

121:2 [p]Ps 115:15; 124:8

2 My help comes from the LORD,
the Maker of heaven and earth.[p]

3 He will not let your foot slip—
he who watches over you will not slumber;
4 indeed, he who watches over Israel
will neither slumber nor sleep.

121:5 [q]Isa 25:4

5 The LORD watches over[q] you—
the LORD is your shade at your right hand;

121:6 [r]Ps 91:5; Isa 49:10; Rev 7:16

6 the sun[r] will not harm you by day,
nor the moon by night.

121:7 [s]Ps 41:2; 91:10-12

7 The LORD will keep you from all harm[s]—
he will watch over your life;

121:8 [t]Dt 28:6

8 the LORD will watch over your coming and going
both now and forevermore.[t]

Psalm 122

A song of ascents. Of David.

1 I rejoiced with those who said to me,
"Let us go to the house of the LORD."

---

the mountain of God (Zion) to worship. Psalm 120 opens the collection appropriately since it is the song of a faithful worshiper far away from the temple among pagan people (see note on v. 5). The psalmist was particularly provoked by their slanderous attacks.

Title. **A song of ascents.** See "Introduction: Authorship and Titles: *Worship Instructions.*"

120:1 and he answers me. As the psalmist called on the Lord in his distress, he also registered certainty that his prayer would be heard.

120:2 lying lips . . . deceitful tongues. The psalmist's enemies slandered him unmercifully.

120:3 he. The Lord in his wrath. **to you.** The enemy who was besetting the psalmist.

120:4 with a warrior's sharp arrows. The Lord would appear as the divine warrior to bring judgment against the enemy.

120:5 Meshech . . . Kedar! The psalmist lamented that he dwelt in a foreign land. If the language is figurative, he compared the treatment he received from God's covenant people to what he might have expected to receive among the ungodly. If literal places were intended, he was far from the land. Since Meshech was in Asia Minor (Ge 10:2; Eze 38:2) and Kedar in Arabia (Isa 21:16; Eze 21:17), these references could have cited two opposite geographical directions in order to signify remote regions in general.

Psalm 121 *Introduction.* The first verse suggests why Psalm 121 was included among the songs of ascent (see "Introduction" to Ps 120). The psalmist's vision was set firmly on his goal, Jerusalem, and on the hill of God, Zion. Since his eyes were on the Lord, he expressed profound trust in him (cf. 91; 131). The pronoun shift (compare, e.g., vv. 1–2 with 3–8) indicates that either the psalmist was carrying on an internal dialogue (along the lines of Psalms 42–43 or Psalm 103) or, more likely, that the psalmist-pilgrim began the psalm and a priest responded with words of assurance.

Title. **A song of ascents.** See "Introduction" to Psalm 120.

121:1 to the hills. Jerusalem was located in the hill country and was surrounded by hills. One of these, Zion, was of special importance to the psalmist because God had made his presence known in a special way there. See note on 2:6.

121:3 He will not let your foot slip. A particularly apt image for God's careful protection; Israel was notorious for rocky and slippery terrain.

121:4 watches over Israel. God not only cared for the individual psalmist but for all of his people. **will neither slumber nor sleep.** God needs no sleep, so there was no danger that the psalmist would be forgotten or overlooked. Elijah ridiculed the prophets of Baal by accusing their god of falling asleep when they needed him (1Ki 18:27).

121:5 your shade. As a person's shadow (shade) is always present when the sun is shining, so God, our Sun, is perpetually with his people. The image comes from ancient treaty language and has covenantal overtones.

Psalm 122 *Introduction.* Psalm 122 conforms to the purpose of the songs of ascent (see "Introduction" to Ps 120). The first two verses record the psalmist's decision to accompany a group to visit the temple of God in Jerusalem. The next stanza (vv. 3–5) describes the glories of Jerusalem, where God dwelt and David's dynasty ruled (cf. 2Sa 7). The last part (vv. 6–9) is a petition asking

2 Our feet are standing
in your gates, O Jerusalem.

3 Jerusalem is built like a city
that is closely compacted together.
4 That is where the tribes go up,
the tribes of the LORD,
to praise the name of the LORD
according to the statute given to Israel.
5 There the thrones for judgment stand,
the thrones of the house of David.

6 Pray for the peace of Jerusalem:
"May those who love[u] you be secure.
7 May there be peace within your walls
and security within your citadels."
8 For the sake of my brothers and friends,
I will say, "Peace be within you."
9 For the sake of the house of the LORD our God,
I will seek your prosperity.[v]

122:6 [u]Ps 51:18
122:9 [v]Ne 2:10

Psalm 123

A song of ascents.

1 I lift up my eyes to you,
to you whose throne[w] is in heaven.
2 As the eyes of slaves look to the hand of their master,
as the eyes of a maid look to the hand of her mistress,
so our eyes look to the LORD[x] our God,
till he shows us his mercy.

3 Have mercy on us, O LORD, have mercy on us,
for we have endured much contempt.
4 We have endured much ridicule from the proud,
much contempt from the arrogant.

123:1 [w]Ps 11:4; 121:1; 141:8
123:2 [x]Ps 25:15

God to protect Jerusalem and its inhabitants. Psalm 122 is similar, therefore, to the so-called Zion songs (46; 48; 76) that extol the city of Jerusalem. Jerusalem was prized above all other cities because God had chosen to reveal himself there to his people. Since Jesus has now come, God no longer restricts the special manifestation of his presence to Jerusalem (see theological article "The Presence of God" at 1Ki 8), and no longer requires that worship be centralized in Jerusalem. Believers can meet God in Christ anywhere (Jn 4:21–24). The name "Jerusalem" still symbolizes the City of God, composed of all believers, both in the past and in the present (Gal 4:26). It also typifies the coming New Jerusalem (Rev 21:9–27).

Title. **A song of ascents.** See "Introduction" to Psalm 120. **Of David.** See "Introduction: Authorship and Titles: *Worship Instructions*."

122:1 I. According to the title, the reference was in the first place to David, although we cannot reconstruct the historical situation in which he composed the psalm. In later usage, however, the first-person speaker—the pilgrim—was one who made a trip to Jerusalem, probably to worship at one of the major festivals (Ex 23:14–19). **those who said to me.** The pilgrims who accompanied the poet.

122:3 closely compacted together. The psalmist marveled at the construction and planning of the city of God.

122:4 where the tribes go up. In worship, especially during the three great festivals (see note on v. 1). **according to the statute given to Israel.** Perhaps a reference to the law centralizing Israel's worship in Deuteronomy 12 or to laws connected with the annual festivals (see note on v. 1).

122:5 thrones for judgment. The king was the chief judge in the land and Jerusalem the political as well as religious capital of Israel.

122:6 peace. The well-known Hebrew term *shalom,* which denotes wholeness and health. The prayer was for the absence of war and for prosperity and growth.

122:6–9 See *WLC* 147,184; *HC* 123.

122:8 For the sake of my brothers and friends. The psalm promoted a sense of community among the people of God. The name "Jerusalem" connoted not chiefly buildings and other structures but people in relationship with one another and with God.

122:9 the house of the LORD our God. The temple, but not a reference to the building per se. The building represented the presence of God in the midst of his people. See *WCF* 23.3.

Psalm 123 *Introduction.* The last two verses of Psalm 123 reflect that this prayer arose from a situation of great distress and persecution. The people of God had suffered much and for a prolonged period of time. The psalmist opened his poetic composition by leading the people to the throne of God's grace ("mercy," v. 2). Compare Psalm 121:1. Though the poet's physical gaze rested on Mount Zion, where the temple stood, he understood through eyes of faith that the building symbolized heavenly realities (1Ki 8).

Title. **A song of ascents.** See "Introduction" to Psalm 120.

123:1–2 See *WLC* 175.

123:1 I lift up my eyes. See 121:1. **whose throne is in heaven.** The Most Holy Place served as God's earthly throne room, but the psalmist, like Solomon, recognized that "the heavens, even the highest heaven, cannot contain [God]" (1Ki 8:27). See *WLC* 189.

123:2 so our eyes look to the LORD our God. The psalmist drew a parallel between the attitude of a slave toward his or her master and that of God's faithful people toward the Lord. The servant observed the master's hand motions and gestures for a variety of reasons: (1) to recognize nonverbal commands; (2) to watch out for unexpected punishment, or (3) for gestures of kindness and provision. All three could be in mind here, since the psalmist taught that God's people depended on him for their overall well-being.

123:3 for we have endured much contempt. The people of God had been subject to trouble and derision for some time. This statement leads many to believe that the psalm was written during the exilic or postexilic period.

Psalm 124

A song of ascents. Of David.

124:1 [y]Ps 129:1

1 If the LORD had not been on our side—
let Israel say[y]—
2 if the LORD had not been on our side
when men attacked us,
3 when their anger flared against us,
they would have swallowed us alive;
4 the flood would have engulfed us,
the torrent would have swept over us,
5 the raging waters
would have swept us away.

6 Praise be to the LORD,
who has not let us be torn by their teeth.
7 We have escaped like a bird
out of the fowler's snare;[z]
the snare has been broken,
and we have escaped.
8 Our help is in the name of the LORD,
the Maker of heaven[a] and earth.

124:7 [z]Ps 91:3; Pr 6:5

124:8 [a]Ge 1:1; Ps 121:2; 134:3

Psalm 125

A song of ascents.

1 Those who trust in the LORD are like Mount Zion,
which cannot be shaken[b] but endures forever.
2 As the mountains surround Jerusalem,
so the LORD surrounds[c] his people
both now and forevermore.

3 The scepter of the wicked will not remain[d]
over the land allotted to the righteous,
for then the righteous might use
their hands to do evil.[e]

4 Do good, O LORD,[f] to those who are good,
to those who are upright in heart.[g]
5 But those who turn[h] to crooked ways[i]
the LORD will banish with the evildoers.

Peace be upon Israel.[j]

125:1 [b]Ps 46:5

125:2 [c]Ps 121:8; Zec 2:4-5

125:3 [d]Ps 89:22; Pr 22:8; Isa 14:5 [e]1Sa 24:10; Ps 55:20

125:4 [f]Ps 119:68 [g]Ps 7:10; 36:10; 94:15

125:5 [h]Job 23:11 [i]Pr 2:15; Isa 59:8 [j]Ps 128:6

Psalm 124 *Introduction.* Psalm 124 is a rare expression of communal thanksgiving. The people together praised the Lord for delivering them from a dangerous confrontation with their enemies. The situation during David's reign that inspired the psalm is unknown. In any case, the song entered the temple collection of hymns and laments and was used in response to a variety of situations. Indeed, according to its inclusion in the songs of ascent, it was sung during festal pilgrimages; thus the liberation envisioned was not necessarily a recent occurrence but might well have been a great deliverance of the nation's past (e.g., the exodus). The psalm serves today as a song of thanks and trust in the Lord as the One who is able to protect his church from such threats as the attacks of the powers and authorities of the spiritual realm (see Eph 6:10–20).

Title. **A song of ascents.** See "Introduction" to Psalm 120. **Of David.** See "Introduction: Authorship and Titles: *Worship Instructions.*"

124:1 had not been on our side. God promised in covenant to protect his obedient people from the attack of their enemies (Dt 28:7). However, they could not faithlessly presume on his presence (1Sa 4–5; book of La); essential to holy war was God's promise to be with his holy people to deliver them (Dt 7; 20). **let Israel say.** These words were pronounced by the priest who led the congregation in corporate thanksgiving to the Lord.

124:3 they would have swallowed us alive. That is, the enemies would have killed them. There may be an allusion here to Sheol (see 28:1) as the place of the dead.

124:4–5 the flood . . . the raging waters. See notes on 18:4, 29:3, 32:6, 42:7, 46:2, 69:1–2 and 114:3.

124:6 by their teeth. The psalmist personified the enemy as a vicious animal, most likely a lion (34:10; 58:6) or a wild dog (59:6,14).

124:8 Maker of heaven and earth. Israel had nothing to fear as long as God, the Divine Warrior, fought on its side.

Psalm 125 *Introduction.* The sixth of the songs of ascents (see "Introduction" to Ps 120) begins like a hymn of confidence such as a Zion song (cf. 46; 48; 76). The Lord provided protection for his people that was especially felt from his temple on Mount Zion. They needed his help because their enemies were in possession of parts of the promised land. The concern of verse 3, that the heathen in the land might corrupt Israel, existed during the time of Joshua and again under Persian domination after the exile.

Title. **A song of ascents.** See "Introduction" to Psalm 120.

125:1 like Mount Zion. Mount Zion was the site on which the temple was built (see 2:6). As the dwelling place of God, it represented stability, order and permanence. These traits were transferred to those who trusted God. They could remain firm and resolute in the face of trouble (Jas 1:2–8).

125:2 As the mountains surround Jerusalem. An apt description of Jerusalem, nestled within a mountainous region. These surrounding mountains were important to the defense of the city and depict God's protective presence. See 2 Kings 6:17.

125:3 The scepter of the wicked. The scepter is a symbol of political-military rule and in this case points to the oppression of the people of God by a wicked, perhaps foreign, force. **the righteous might use their hands to do evil.** Especially by way of imitation (v. 5).

125:4 Do good . . . to those who are good. The psalmist called

Psalm 126

A song of ascents.

1 When the LORD brought back[k] the captives to[a] Zion,
we were like men who dreamed.[b]
2 Our mouths were filled with laughter,
our tongues with songs of joy.[l]
Then it was said among the nations,
"The LORD has done great things[m] for them."
3 The LORD has done great things for us,
and we are filled with joy.[n]

4 Restore our fortunes,[c] O LORD,
like streams in the Negev.[o]
5 Those who sow in tears
will reap with songs of joy.[p]
6 He who goes out weeping,
carrying seed to sow,
will return with songs of joy,
carrying sheaves with him.

126:1 [k]Ps 85:1; Hos 6:11
126:2 [l]Job 8:21; Ps 51:14 [m]Ps 71:19
126:3 [n]Isa 25:9
126:4 [o]Isa 35:6; 43:19
126:5 [p]Isa 35:10

Psalm 127

A song of ascents. Of Solomon.

1 Unless the LORD builds[q] the house,
its builders labor in vain.
Unless the LORD watches[r] over the city,
the watchmen stand guard in vain.
2 In vain you rise early
and stay up late,
toiling for food[s] to eat—
for he grants sleep[t] to[d] those he loves.

3 Sons are a heritage from the LORD,
children a reward[u] from him.

127:1 [q]Ps 78:69 [r]Ps 121:4
127:2 [s]Ge 3:17 [t]Job 11:18
127:3 [u]Ge 33:5

[a] *1* Or *LORD restored the fortunes of* [b] *1* Or *men restored to health* [c] *4* Or *Bring back our captives*
[d] *2* Or *eat— / for while they sleep he provides for*

on God to fulfill his covenant promise to bless those who had faith in God and obeyed his law (Dt 28:1–14). See *WLC* 184.

125:5 those who turn to crooked ways. Those Israelites who gave in to the wicked example referred to in verse 3.

Psalm 126 *Introduction.* Psalm 126 begins with an exclamation of praise for God's deliverance (vv. 1–3). On this basis the psalmist, who spoke for the community, petitioned the Lord to restore his people's fortunes (vv. 4–6). The psalm is a communal lament, but note the strong confidence with which the people's petition was presented to the Lord. He had saved them in the past and could be active as well in their present and future. The language of the first verse seems to identify the return from exile that began under the Persian ruler Cyrus. It was with great joy that the remnant returned, but the settlers' struggles were far from over.

Title. **A song of ascents.** See "Introduction" to Psalm 120.

126:1 When the LORD brought back the captives to Zion. Most likely an allusion to the return from the exile to the promised land (see the books of Ezr and Ne). The psalmist recognized that Cyrus's decision to allow the people to return was not merely adherence to political policy but the result of God's intervention.

126:4 Restore our fortunes. Restoration from captivity entailed much more than a return to the land. God's help would be sorely needed. **like streams in the Negev.** The Negev, in the south of Israel, is arid. When there is the occasional rainstorm, dry wadis (riverbeds) are suddenly filled with rushing water.

126:5 will reap with songs of joy. God would reverse the fortunes of his people, overriding evil with good and replacing suffering with blessing (cf. 30:11–12; Jn 16:20).

Psalm 127 *Introduction.* This wise prayer falls into two separate yet related parts. In the first stanza (vv. 1–2) the psalmist expressed his belief that human effort is vain apart from the Lord (paralleling the message of Ecc), using three areas of endeavor as illustrations: building a house (v. 1); defending a city (v. 1) and earning a living (v. 2). As a song of ascent (see "Introduction" to Psalm 120) and a Solomonic psalm, its references to house and city would naturally make the pilgrims think of the temple and of Jerusalem. The second stanza (vv. 3–5) focuses on another meaning of house building; e.g., raising children. Children were considered gifts from God and covenant blessings. Sons in particular could support their elderly parents (but see Ru 4:15). Children also were a fulfillment of the Abrahamic covenant promise that the chosen people would become a great and numerous nation (Ge 15:5; 17:2)—a promise that would eventually lead to Jesus Christ.

Title. **A song of ascents.** See "Introduction" to Psalm 120. **Of Solomon.** See "Introduction: Authorship and Titles: *Worship Instructions*" and "Introduction" to Psalm 127.

127:1–2 See *HC* 125.

127:1 builds the house. The primary reference was to the actual construction of a residence, but since this is a song of ascent written by Solomon, it is natural for us to think of the temple (commonly referred to in the Old Testament by the Hebrew word "house"). Furthermore, in the light of the second half of the psalm, the house may refer to the family members as well as to the structure itself. See note on 1 Chronicles 17:1–15. **watches over the city.** The psalmist believed that a city was never secure simply on the basis of its defenses but only in the protection of the Lord. In the context of a song of ascent the psalmist may have had Jerusalem specifically in mind. If so, this psalm reminded the pilgrims that Jerusalem was not an enchanted place of automatic protection and security. All depended on the Lord's favor (cf. Jer 7:3–8).

127:2 he grants sleep to those he loves. The contrast is between working long hours and sleeping little, on the one hand, and working normal hours and getting a full night's sleep on the other. Since the Lord increases the harvest of those he loves (85:12; Lev 26:3–5; Dt 11:10–17), as well as grants them children to help work the land (v. 3), it is more beneficial to depend on God than to seek security in one's own abilities and efforts. See *WLC* 135.

127:3–5 See *WLC* 127.

[4]Like arrows in the hands of a warrior
are sons born in one's youth.
[5]Blessed is the man
whose quiver is full of them.
They will not be put to shame
when they contend with their enemies[v] in the gate.

127:5 [v]Pr 27:11

Psalm 128

A song of ascents.

[1]Blessed are all who fear the LORD,[w]
who walk in his ways.[x]
[2]You will eat the fruit of your labor;[y]
blessings and prosperity[z] will be yours.
[3]Your wife will be like a fruitful vine[a]
within your house;
your sons will be like olive shoots[b]
around your table.
[4]Thus is the man blessed
who fears the LORD.

[5]May the LORD bless you from Zion[c]
all the days of your life;
may you see the prosperity of Jerusalem,
[6] and may you live to see your children's children.[d]

Peace be upon Israel.[e]

128:1 [w]Ps 112:1 [x]Ps 119:1-3
128:2 [y]Isa 3:10 [z]Ecc 8:12
128:3 [a]Eze 19:10 [b]Ps 52:8; 144:12
128:5 [c]Ps 20:2; 134:3
128:6 [d]Ge 50:23; Job 42:16 [e]Ps 125:5

Psalm 129

A song of ascents.

[1]They have greatly oppressed me from my youth[f]—
let Israel say[g]—
[2]they have greatly oppressed me from my youth,
but they have not gained the victory[h] over me.
[3]Plowmen have plowed my back
and made their furrows long.
[4]But the LORD is righteous;[i]
he has cut me free from the cords of the wicked.

129:1 [f]Ps 88:15; Hos 2:15 [g]Ps 124:1
129:2 [h]Mt 16:18
129:4 [i]Ps 119:137

127:3 children. Literally, "the fruit of the womb." The psalmist concentrated on sons, since in his culture sons could provide for their parents' needs and ensure their just treatment in old age. Nevertheless, in the second part of the verse he expanded "sons" to "children."
127:4 Like arrows. Sons were like weapons who could come to a father's aid.
127:5 in the gate. Perhaps a reference to formal court proceedings.
Psalm 128 *Introduction.* In Psalm 128 the psalmist pronounced a blessing of success, fertility and abundance on the godly, extending this blessing to Jerusalem and Israel as well. The psalm moves from a description of the nature of God's blessing (vv. 1–4) to the blessing itself (vv. 5–6) and from the godly person and his family to the whole of Israel. The mention of Zion, Jerusalem and Israel in the last couple of verses makes the psalm a song of ascent (see "Introduction" to Ps 120). The psalm shares with Psalm 127 the theme of a fertile and strong family.
Title. **A song of ascents.** See "Introduction" to Psalm 120.
128:1 Blessed. See note on 1:1. **fear the LORD.** See notes on 34:7, 36:1 and 119:63. **his ways.** God's will as manifested in his law.
128:2 You will eat the fruit of your labor. One result of the fall was that people would have to work hard to secure their daily sustenance (Ge 3:17–19). The Teacher in the book of Ecclesiastes was driven to despair by the fact that some people labored while others, less deserving, sat back and reaped the benefits of those labors (Ecc 5:8—6:12). The psalmist envisioned the righteous prospering from their own labor—a just situation.
128:3 a fruitful vine. A symbol of fertility, confirmed by the mention of sons in the same verse. **olive shoots.** The olive tree was a staple of Israelite agriculture. The gift of children, particularly of sons, was prized in Israel (see 127:3–5).
128:5 bless you. See verse 1. **from Zion.** That is, from the temple (see 2:6; 50:2).
128:6 your children's children. Long life and large families signified blessing in ancient Israel, particularly in light of the Abrahamic covenant (Ge 15:5; 17:2). **Peace.** Hebrew *shalom.* A word with rich connotations, it implies not only the absence of war but the presence of prosperity and fertility.
Psalm 129 *Introduction.* Psalm 129 cursed Israel's enemies (vv. 5–8). The psalmist in his introduction (vv. 1–4) confidently asserted that in the past the Lord had frequently overturned evil plans against his people. They had suffered at the hands of their enemies but had never been completely destroyed.
Title. **A song of ascents.** See "Introduction" to Psalm 120.
129:1 oppressed me. The nation of Israel is personified as an individual speaking in the first person. Israel's history had included much suffering and oppression, beginning with the Egyptian bondage and continuing to the end of the Old Testament period and beyond. **from my youth.** That is, from Israel's inception as a nation.
129:2 they have not gained the victory. Throughout the Old Testament period Israel's enemies never completely destroyed or eliminated God's people. The Egyptian bondage led to the exodus, the Babylonian exile to the restoration.
129:3 have plowed my back. A metaphor describing Israel's suffering.
129:4 he has cut me free. It was as though the wicked had held Israel as a prisoner bound by strong ropes, but the Lord had freed the nation.

5 May all who hate Zion[j]
be turned back in shame.[k]
6 May they be like grass on the roof,
which withers[l] before it can grow;
7 with it the reaper cannot fill his hands,
nor the one who gathers fill his arms.
8 May those who pass by not say,
"The blessing of the LORD be upon you;
we bless you[m] in the name of the LORD."

Psalm 130

A song of ascents.

1 Out of the depths[n] I cry to you, O LORD;
2 O Lord, hear my voice.[o]
Let your ears be attentive[p]
to my cry for mercy.

3 If you, O LORD, kept a record of sins,
O Lord, who could stand?[q]
4 But with you there is forgiveness;[r]
therefore you are feared.[s]

5 I wait for the LORD,[t] my soul waits,
and in his word[u] I put my hope.
6 My soul waits for the Lord
more than watchmen[v] wait for the morning,
more than watchmen wait for the morning.[w]

7 O Israel, put your hope[x] in the LORD,
for with the LORD is unfailing love
and with him is full redemption.
8 He himself will redeem[y] Israel
from all their sins.

Psalm 131

A song of ascents. Of David.

1 My heart is not proud,[z] O LORD,
my eyes are not haughty;
I do not concern myself with great matters
or things too wonderful for me.
2 But I have stilled and quieted my soul;

129:5 [j]Mic 4:11 [k]Ps 71:13
129:6 [l]Ps 37:2
129:8 [m]Ru 2:4; Ps 118:26
130:1 [n]Ps 42:7; 69:2; La 3:55
130:2 [o]Ps 28:2 [p]2Ch 6:40; Ps 64:1
130:3 [q]Ps 76:7; 143:2
130:4 [r]Ex 34:7; Isa 55:7; Jer 33:8 [s]1Ki 8:40
130:5 [t]Ps 27:14; 33:20; Isa 8:17 [u]Ps 119:81
130:6 [v]Ps 63:6 [w]Ps 119:147
130:7 [x]Ps 131:3
130:8 [y]Lk 1:68
131:1 [z]Ps 101:5; Ro 12:16

129:5 Zion. See notes on 2:6, 50:2 and 128:5.
129:6 grass on the roof. Grass is used figuratively in the Psalter as a symbol for the brevity and fragility of human life (37:2; 90:5–6; 92:7). The image is here intensified: Grass on a roof could not root or find shelter from the burning sun.
129:7 cannot fill his hands. There is so little of it.
129:8 May those who pass by not say. There would be no blessing given to those who worked against the Lord. See Ruth 2:4.
Psalm 130 *Introduction.* As is clear from the first two verses, Psalm 130 is a complaint in which the psalmist cried out to God in his distress. However, it is a complaint of a special kind, since the author did not call for the destruction of an enemy but turned meekly to God for forgiveness for his own sins. This song has long been grouped with the penitential psalms (see "Introduction" to Ps 6). In his closing two verses the psalmist moved beyond his personal experience to exhort the entire community to put their hope in God, their covenant Lord.
Title. **A song of ascents.** See "Introduction" to Psalm 120.
130:1 Out of the depths. An allusion to the deep waters of chaos that overwhelmed the psalmist. The same word is found in 69:2. See also the closely related expressions in 18:4, 29:3 and 10, 32:6, 42:7, 46:2 and 4 and 114:3.
130:3–4 See *WLC* 194.
130:3 who could stand? This was a rhetorical question; the psalmist was well aware that no one was without sin (53:1–3; Ro 3:9–20). See *WCF* 16.5; *HC* 14.
130:4 there is forgiveness. The Old Testament is replete with accounts of the Lord saving his repentant people (see 1Ki 8:46–51). **you are feared.** See 36:1, 34:7 and 128:1. See also *WCF* 18.3.
130:5 I wait for the LORD. Although he was in deep trouble (vv. 1–2), the poet could wait with patience on the Lord to save him because he trusted in God's forgiveness (see v. 4).
130:6 more than watchmen wait for the morning. An expression of intense yearning and certain hope.
130:7 O Israel. The psalmist invoked the whole nation to share his penitence and hope. See *WLC* 104.
Psalm 131 *Introduction.* David expressed his deep-seated confidence in the Lord with this simple yet profound prayer. Psalm 131 voices the trust that is appropriate to an intimate personal relationship with the Lord; it rightly was included among the songs of ascent (see "Introduction" to Ps 120). There were many periods in David's life during which he displayed this kind of trust. While fleeing from Saul he waited for God's timing and declined to vindicate himself. However, David could not have prayed this prayer during the period of his sin with Bathsheba (2Sa 12). Jesus alone could enjoy this deep trust in God at all times and in the face of the worst danger and adversity (Mt 26:36–46).
Title. **A song of ascents.** See "Introduction" to Psalm 120. **Of David.** See "Introduction: Authorship and Titles: *Worship Instructions.*"
131:1 My heart . . . eyes . . . great matters. The first verse expresses a threefold denial of pride: in the heart, in perception (eyes) and in actions (great matters).

131:2 [a]Mt 18:3; 1Co 14:20
131:3 [b]Ps 130:7

like a weaned child with its mother,
like a weaned child is my soul[a] within me.

3 O Israel, put your hope[b] in the LORD
both now and forevermore.

Psalm 132

A song of ascents.

132:2 [c]Ge 49:24
132:5 [d]Ac 7:46
132:6 [e]1Sa 17:12 [f]1Sa 7:2
132:7 [g]Ps 5:7 [h]Ps 99:5
132:8 [i]Nu 10:35; Ps 78:61
132:9 [j]Job 29:14; Isa 61:3, 10
132:11 [k]Ps 89:3-4, 35 [l]2Sa 7:12

1 O LORD, remember David
and all the hardships he endured.

2 He swore an oath to the LORD
and made a vow to the Mighty One of Jacob:[c]
3 "I will not enter my house
or go to my bed—
4 I will allow no sleep to my eyes,
no slumber to my eyelids,
5 till I find a place[d] for the LORD,
a dwelling for the Mighty One of Jacob."

6 We heard it in Ephrathah,[e]
we came upon it in the fields of Jaar[a]:[b][f]
7 "Let us go to his dwelling place;[g]
let us worship at his footstool[h]—
8 arise, O LORD,[i] and come to your resting place,
you and the ark of your might.
9 May your priests be clothed with righteousness;[j]
may your saints sing for joy."

10 For the sake of David your servant,
do not reject your anointed one.

11 The LORD swore an oath to David,[k]
a sure oath that he will not revoke:
"One of your own descendants[l]
I will place on your throne—
12 if your sons keep my covenant
and the statutes I teach them,

[a] *6* That is, Kiriath Jearim [b] *6* Or *heard of it in Ephrathah, / we found it in the fields of Jaar.* (And no quotes around verses 7–9)

131:2 like a weaned child. The psalmist drew a beautiful picture of the confidence he enjoyed in the Lord. He pictured himself as a weaned child in order to convey quietness and calmness before God. An unweaned child is hardly calm in demanding milk from its mother. The picture is one of implicit trust and contentment.
131:3 O Israel. As in Psalm 130 this intensely personal prayer becomes corporate at the end.
Psalm 132 *Introduction.* Psalm 132 is a lament calling on the Lord to rise and save the king (vv. 1,6–9). The rest of the psalm grounds the petition in God's covenant with David (vv. 10–12; cf. 2Sa 7; Ps 89) and choice of Zion as his divine dwelling place (see 46; 48; 76). The psalm must have originated after David's lifetime since it looks back on that period (v. 10). Since verses 8–10 are quoted in 2 Chronicles 6:41–42, Solomon's prayer of temple dedication, it is likely that this was the period of its composition. After the dissolution of the monarchy the psalm's anticipation of the Messiah became increasingly evident to God's people.
Title. **A song of ascents.** See "Introduction" to Psalm 120.
132:1 remember. More than an appeal to bring David to mind. Remembrance in the Old Testament involved action based on previous commitment. **the hardships.** The historical books record numerous troubles that David endured as he sought to serve the Lord faithfully. He spent much of his young adulthood fleeing Saul and much of his maturity dealing with troubles in his realm (e.g., Absalom's revolt; 2Sa 15:1—18:18). The many laments in the Psalter that bear his name as author testify to his struggles (69:8–12).
132:2–5 See *WCF* 22.6.
132:2 an oath. This oath illustrated David's devotion to the Lord. In his order of priority God's interests were above his own comfort. The reference to the fulfillment of the oath (vv. 6–9) suggests that the psalm may have referred to the time David ordered the ark to be brought up from Kiriath-Jearim to Jerusalem (2Sa 6).
132:3 I will not enter my house. Similar to the sentiment recorded in 2 Samuel 7; David felt that it was not fitting for him to live in a comfortable house while the ark of the covenant, the primary symbol of God's presence, was still housed in a tent.
132:6 Ephrathah. That is, Bethlehem. **the fields of Jaar.** Kiriath-Jearim (1Sa 6:21—7:2).
132:7 dwelling place. The ark was returned to its proper place. **at his footstool.** A common way to refer to the ark of the covenant. The Lord was pictured as enthroned over the ark with his feet resting on it.
132:8 arise, O LORD. See note on 3:7.
132:10 For the sake of David your servant. The psalmist climaxed the psalm with an appeal to the Lord to bless the descendant of David ruling on David's throne. God had promised David that his descendants would rule after him (2Sa 7:11–16). Even after the kingdom was divided a son of David ruled in Jerusalem for centuries, "so that David my servant may always have a lamp before me in Jerusalem" (1Ki 11:36). Eventually, however, the sins of the kings of Judah led to their removal. God's promises, though, were not thwarted. Jesus, David's greater son, fulfilled and will fulfill the Davidic covenant. Not surprisingly, the psalm was regarded as Messianic by the early church (Ac 2:30).
132:11 swore an oath. See verse 2. **I will place on your throne.** See 2 Samuel 7:11–16. See *BC* 18; *HC* 35.
132:12 if your sons keep my covenant. The conditional ele-

then their sons will sit
on your throne[m] for ever and ever."

13 For the LORD has chosen Zion,[n]
he has desired it for his dwelling:
14 "This is my resting place for ever and ever;[o]
here I will sit enthroned, for I have desired it—
15 I will bless her with abundant provisions;
her poor will I satisfy with food.[p]
16 I will clothe her priests[q] with salvation,
and her saints will ever sing for joy.

17 "Here I will make a horn[a] grow[r] for David
and set up a lamp[s] for my anointed one.
18 I will clothe his enemies with shame,[t]
but the crown on his head will be resplendent."

Psalm 133

A song of ascents. Of David.

1 How good and pleasant it is
when brothers live together[u] in unity!
2 It is like precious oil poured on the head,[v]
running down on the beard,
running down on Aaron's beard,
down upon the collar of his robes.
3 It is as if the dew of Hermon[w]
were falling on Mount Zion.
For there the LORD bestows his blessing,[x]
even life forevermore.[y]

Psalm 134

A song of ascents.

1 Praise the LORD, all you servants[z] of the LORD
who minister by night[a] in the house of the LORD.
2 Lift up your hands[b] in the sanctuary
and praise the LORD.

132:12 [m]Lk 1:32; Ac 2:30
132:13 [n]Ps 48:1-2
132:14 [o]Ps 68:16
132:15 [p]Ps 107:9; 147:14
132:16 [q]2Ch 6:41
132:17 [r]Eze 29:21; Lk 1:69 [s]1Ki 11:36; 2Ch 21:7
132:18 [t]Ps 35:26; 109:29
133:1 [u]Ge 13:8; Heb 13:1
133:2 [v]Ex 30.25
133:3 [w]Dt 4:48 [x]Lev 25:21; Dt 28:8 [y]Ps 42:8
134:1 [z]Ps 135:1-2 [a]1Ch 9:33
134:2 [b]Ps 28:2; 1Ti 2:8

[a] *17 Horn* here symbolizes strong one, that is, king.

ment in the Davidic covenant. David's descendants would rule only if they obeyed the covenant stipulations.

132:13 Zion. See notes on 2:6 and 50:2. Compare Psalms 46, 48 and 72.

132:14 I will sit enthroned. God chose Zion and arranged to have his temple built there both as the earthly reflection of his heavenly residence and as his palace from which he ruled the world.

132:15 I will bless her. Although the text speaks specifically of Jerusalem, the holy city belonged to all Israel as its center of worship and represented the entire nation, just as the Lord reigned over all Israel from his palace in Jerusalem (v. 14). As a generous king, the Lord would tend his holy nation with a particular eye on the destitute. Note the delineation of the blessings of the covenant in Deuteronomy 28:1–14.

132:17 horn. A common Biblical and Near Eastern symbol for strength—in particular, political strength. **a lamp.** See 1 Kings 11:36.

Psalm 133 *Introduction.* A meditation on the blessings of unity among the people of God. In this song of ascent (see "Introduction" to Ps 120) "brothers" referred to the relationship among fellow Israelites as they worshiped the Lord together at Mount Zion. The psalm may be read from a Christian perspective as a blessing on unity in Christ with other believers, both in the local body and in the universal church.

Title. **A song of ascents.** See "Introduction" to Psalm 120 and "Introduction: Authorship and Titles: *Worship Instructions.*" Psalm 133 was illustrated negatively in the lives of David's sons. These half-brothers—Absalom against Amnon, Adonijah against Solomon—lived in disunity.

133:1 brothers. Could refer to biological siblings, but in a song of ascent the term likely refers to tribal and national families united to worship the Lord God.

133:2 like precious oil. The first simile likens the unity of God's people to the special and exclusive blending of oil (Ex 30:22-33) used to anoint Aaron as high priest. The rich and fragrant oil was poured out extravagantly, so that it ran down Aaron's beard to the collar of his sacred robes. In the same way the unity of the people of God was a rich perfume making their worship acceptable to God (cf. Col 3:14–16).

133:3 the dew of Hermon . . . on Mount Zion. Hermon, the majestic mountain on the northern boundary of Israel, was known for its heavy dewfall. Unity also is likened to dew that refreshes and delights. In both images (see v. 2) the liquid is so abundant that it flows downward, indicating rich blessings. God gives the blessing of unity—through the gift of the Holy Spirit (Eph 4:3). **there.** Mount Zion, the place of unity among the families of Israel.

Psalm 134 *Introduction.* Psalm 134, the brief conclusion of the songs of ascent, is composed of a call to worship (vv. 1–2) followed by a blessing (v. 3). The dynamics of the psalm are difficult to perceive because the references are somewhat obscure. Many interpret the first two verses as an exhortation to praise on the part of the departing worshipers to the priests who tended the temple precincts at night. In this scenario the priests in turn blessed the congregation. The psalm is a reminder that God's praise is a continual activity, not limited to a step in a daily routine (1Th 5:17) or to a formal worship setting.

Title. See "Introduction" to Psalm 120.

134:1 servants of the LORD. Can be interpreted, as above, as priests and Levites who tended the temple at night. **house of the LORD.** The temple. See 2:6.

134:2 Lift up your hands. A common stance for those in prayer.

134:3 [c]Ps 124:8 [d]Ps 128:5

[3] May the LORD, the Maker of heaven[c] and earth,
bless you from Zion.[d]

Psalm 135

135:1 [e]Ps 113:1; 134:1
135:2 [f]Lk 2:37 [g]Ps 116:19
135:3 [h]Ps 119:68 [i]Ps 147:1
135:4 [j]Dt 10:15; 1Pe 2:9 [k]Ex 19:5; Dt 7:6
135:5 [l]Ps 48:1 [m]Ps 97:9
135:6 [n]Ps 115:3
135:7 [o]Jer 10:13; Zec 10:1 [p]Job 28:25 [q]Job 38:22
135:8 [r]Ex 12:12; Ps 78:51
135:9 [s]Dt 6:22 [t]Ps 136:10-15
135:10 [u]Nu 21:21-25; Ps 136:17-21
135:11 [v]Nu 21:21 [w]Jos 12:7-24
135:12 [x]Ps 78:55
135:13 [y]Ex 3:15 [z]Ps 102:12
135:14 [a]Dt 32:36

[1] Praise the LORD.[a]

Praise the name of the LORD;
praise him, you servants[e] of the LORD,
[2] you who minister in the house[f] of the LORD,
in the courts[g] of the house of our God.

[3] Praise the LORD, for the LORD is good;[h]
sing praise to his name, for that is pleasant.[i]
[4] For the LORD has chosen Jacob[j] to be his own,
Israel to be his treasured possession.[k]

[5] I know that the LORD is great,[l]
that our Lord is greater than all gods.[m]
[6] The LORD does whatever pleases him,[n]
in the heavens and on the earth,
in the seas and all their depths.
[7] He makes clouds rise from the ends of the earth;
he sends lightning with the rain[o]
and brings out the wind[p] from his storehouses.[q]

[8] He struck down the firstborn[r] of Egypt,
the firstborn of men and animals.
[9] He sent his signs[s] and wonders into your midst, O Egypt,
against Pharaoh and all his servants.[t]
[10] He struck down many[u] nations
and killed mighty kings—
[11] Sihon[v] king of the Amorites,
Og king of Bashan
and all the kings of Canaan[w]—
[12] and he gave their land as an inheritance,[x]
an inheritance to his people Israel.

[13] Your name, O LORD, endures forever,[y]
your renown,[z] O LORD, through all generations.
[14] For the LORD will vindicate his people
and have compassion on his servants.[a]

[15] The idols of the nations are silver and gold,
made by the hands of men.

[a] *1* Hebrew *Hallelu Yah*; also in verses 3 and 21

134:3 the Maker of heaven and earth. This epithet supported the blessing by pointing to God's power. **from Zion.** The temple, the place from which God chose to reveal himself to Israel (see v. 1).

Psalm 135 *Introduction.* Psalm 135 is both a call to praise (vv. 1–2,19–21) and a hymn of praise. The praises focus on the Lord's control over nature (vv. 5–7) and history (vv. 8–12), his choice of Israel as his special people (v. 4) and his superiority over lifeless idols (vv. 15–18). The psalm, with its own distinctive power, echoes the language of many other passages, from both the Psalms and other portions of Scripture.

135:1 Praise the LORD. In Hebrew, *Hallelu Yah* (see "Introduction" to Ps 111 and note on 111:1). This exhortation and exclamation of praise opens and closes (v. 21) the psalm. **name.** See Psalm 8:1. **servants.** A probable reference to the priests and Levites who served in the temple. Some scholars claim that *servants* was not used in such a restricted manner, but the next two phrases (see v. 2) specify the temple personnel.

135:2 minister. Literally, "stand." **the house of our God.** The temple.

135:3 his name. See verse 1.

135:4 chosen . . . to be his own. The Lord had handpicked Israel as the object of his grace and unconditional love, but not because of any quality of the people (see Dt 7:7–11). **treasured possession.** God lifted the lowly and made them great in his eyes. This was one of the greatest blessings of God's covenant (Ex 19:5–6).

135:5 greater than all gods. The other nations could not conceive of a God like the Lord.

135:6 in the heavens and on the earth. The foreign gods (see v. 5) were pictured at best as having limited spheres of influence and power. The Lord, the only true God, controls all realms and all things, including the gods of other nations. **in the seas.** Special reference was made to the seas since they represent the forces of chaos. God controls even the frightening and dangerous waters (see 18:4; 29:3,10; 46:2,4). See *WCF* 5.1.

135:7 lightning with the rain. God's control over storms may have had special reference to Canaanite theology (adopted by many apostate Israelites), which attributed power over the storm to its chief god, Baal (see Ps 29).

135:8 the firstborn of Egypt. The culmination of the ten plagues God had used to effect liberation for his people (Ex 11).

135:11 Sihon . . . Og. Kings of Transjordan at the time when Moses led the people through the desert toward the promised land (Nu 21:21–35).

135:12 gave their land as an inheritance. Canaan, at the time of the conquest.

135:13 name. See 8:1.

135:15 The idols of the nations. Other nations worshiped gods

[16] They have mouths, but cannot speak,
eyes, but they cannot see;
[17] they have ears, but cannot hear,
nor is there breath in their mouths.
[18] Those who make them will be like them,
and so will all who trust in them.

[19] O house of Israel, praise the LORD;
O house of Aaron, praise the LORD;
[20] O house of Levi, praise the LORD;
you who fear him, praise the LORD.
[21] Praise be to the LORD from Zion,[b]
to him who dwells in Jerusalem.

Praise the LORD.

135:21 [b]Ps 134:3

Psalm 136

[1] Give thanks to the LORD, for he is good.[c]
His love endures forever.[d]
[2] Give thanks to the God of gods.[e]
His love endures forever.
[3] Give thanks to the Lord of lords:
His love endures forever.

[4] to him who alone does great wonders,[f]
His love endures forever.
[5] who by his understanding[g] made the heavens,[h]
His love endures forever.
[6] who spread out the earth[i] upon the waters,[j]
His love endures forever.
[7] who made the great lights[k]—
His love endures forever.
[8] the sun to govern[l] the day,
His love endures forever.
[9] the moon and stars to govern the night;
His love endures forever.

[10] to him who struck down the firstborn[m] of Egypt
His love endures forever.
[11] and brought Israel out[n] from among them
His love endures forever.
[12] with a mighty hand and outstretched arm;[o]
His love endures forever.

[13] to him who divided the Red Sea[a][p] asunder
His love endures forever.
[14] and brought Israel through[q] the midst of it,
His love endures forever.

136:1 [c]Ps 106:1 [d]1Ch 16:34; 2Ch 20:21
136:2 [e]Dt 10:17
136:4 [f]Ps 72:18
136:5 [g]Pr 3:19; Jer 51:15 [h]Ge 1:1
136:6 [i]Ge 1:9; Jer 10:12 [j]Ps 24:2
136:7 [k]Ge 1:14,16
136:8 [l]Ge 1:16
136:10 [m]Ex 12:29; Ps 135:8
136:11 [n]Ex 6:6; 12:51
136:12 [o]Dt 4:34; Ps 44:3
136:13 [p]Ex 14:21; Ps 78:13
136:14 [q]Ex 14:22

[a] 13 Hebrew *Yam Suph*; that is, Sea of Reeds; also in verse 15

in the form of statues constructed from wood and precious metals. The psalmist, like Isaiah (see Isa 44), ridiculed this practice. Such people manipulated the creation and exalted it above the Creator (Ro 1:21–23).
135:18 will be like them. God created humanity in his image, while pagan theology created gods in a human image. Those who fashioned lifeless idols would become like them. See note on 115:8. See Isaiah 44:9–20 and Romans 1:22–24.
135:19 house of Israel. All of Israel. **house of Aaron.** The priests. See 115:9–11 for a similar sequence.
135:20 house of Levi . . . you who fear him. See 115:9–11.
135:21 from Zion. The location of the temple (see 2:6; 50:2; 128:5; 129:5).
Psalm 136 *Introduction.* Psalm 136 is well known for its recurrent refrain "his love endures forever." The psalm is an antiphonal liturgy of praise to the Lord. A priest or soloist chanted the first part of each verse, and the congregation responded with the refrain. The performance of this liturgy must have been powerfully moving as the priest led the congregation in extolling God's goodness (vv. 1–3), his power in creation (vv. 4–9), his mighty acts in history (vv. 10–22) and, as a final crescendo, his present salvation and providential care (vv. 23–26). The Christian can extend this song to include the climax of God's redemptive acts in Jesus Christ.
136:1 Give thanks to the LORD, for he is good. The rest of the psalm expands and specifies this first line. The psalmist focused on the Lord's great acts. ***His love endures forever.*** The refrain sung by the congregation in response to the priestly liturgy. God's love referred to his devotion to his people, to whom he had bound himself in covenant by his own pledge. His grace, lasting and certain, called for continuing praise.
136:5 by his understanding. God's wisdom was frequently associated with the creation (cf. Pr 8).
136:7 the great lights. The sun and the moon (vv. 5,9).
136:10 the firstborn of Egypt. A reference to the tenth and climactic plague preceding the exodus (Ex 11).
136:13 who divided the Red Sea asunder. See Exodus 14–15.

136:15 [r]Ex 14:27; Ps 135:9
136:16 [s]Ex 13:18
136:17 [t]Ps 135:9-12
136:18 [u]Dt 29:7
136:19 [v]Nu 21:21-25
136:21 [w]Jos 12:1
136:23 [x]Ps 113:7
136:24 [y]Ps 107:2
136:25 [z]Ps 104:27; 145:15

15 but swept Pharaoh and his army into the Red Sea;[r]
His love endures forever.

16 to him who led his people through the desert,[s]
His love endures forever.

17 who struck down great kings,[t]
His love endures forever.

18 and killed mighty kings[u]—
His love endures forever.

19 Sihon king of the Amorites[v]
His love endures forever.

20 and Og king of Bashan—
His love endures forever.

21 and gave their land[w] as an inheritance,
His love endures forever.

22 an inheritance to his servant Israel;
His love endures forever.

23 to the One who remembered us[x] in our low estate
His love endures forever.

24 and freed us from our enemies,[y]
His love endures forever.

25 and who gives food[z] to every creature.
His love endures forever.

26 Give thanks to the God of heaven.
His love endures forever.

Psalm 137

137:1 [a]Eze 1:1,3 [b]Ne 1:4
137:3 [c]Ps 80:6
137:6 [d]Eze 3:26

1 By the rivers of Babylon[a] we sat and wept[b]
when we remembered Zion.
2 There on the poplars
we hung our harps,
3 for there our captors asked us for songs,
our tormentors demanded[c] songs of joy;
they said, "Sing us one of the songs of Zion!"

4 How can we sing the songs of the LORD
while in a foreign land?
5 If I forget you, O Jerusalem,
may my right hand forget ⌊its skill⌋.
6 May my tongue cling to the roof[d] of my mouth
if I do not remember you,
if I do not consider Jerusalem
my highest joy.

136:19 Sihon. See Numbers 21:21–35.
136:20 Og. See Numbers 21:21–35.
136:21–22 an inheritance. A reference to the conquest under Joshua (Jos 11:23).
136:23 remembered us. The psalmist used a personal pronoun to apply God's salvation to his contemporary situation. God continued to work as he had worked in the past to save his people from their enemies.
136:24 from our enemies. The enemies were unspecified, allowing subsequent generations to apply the reference anew to their particular situations.
Psalm 137 *Introduction.* Psalm 137 is a prayer connected with the exile of Judah to Babylon. There is conflicting evidence as to whether it was composed and sung during the exile or immediately afterward (see note on v. 1). The despair of that heart-wrenching event is eloquently expressed both in grief and in anger directed toward the heartless enemy (vv. 7–9). The psalm may also be contrasted with the songs of Zion (cf. 46; 48). Instead of a victory and a resplendent Jerusalem as in the songs of Zion, there is defeat and a deserted Jerusalem. The mourning of the psalmist was due to his separation from the place of God's revelation (cf. Ps 42–43).
137:1 the rivers of Babylon. The Tigris and Euphrates and perhaps their numerous canals. The psalmist was likely highlighting the great distance between God's people and Zion. **we sat and wept.** Expressing their deep despair because of the captivity (v. 4). This might either be a recounting of a contemporary experience or a recollection of the past. **Zion.** See 2:6, 50:2, 65:1, 74:2, 128:5 and 129:5.
137:2 harps. Instruments of joy. Following victory in holy war, Israel responded with song (Ex 15; Jdg 5). After defeat, however, silence ensued (Isa 24:8–9).
137:3 our captors. The Babylonians. **one of the songs of Zion.** Songs like Psalms 46 and 48, praising the greatness of Jerusalem and of Zion, the location of the temple. The Babylonians themselves had destroyed Jerusalem and the temple (2Ch 36:17–19), so their request for a song was meant to ridicule their captives.
137:5 my right hand forget. How to play the harp. He could play one of the songs of Zion (v. 3) only if he forgot the trouble that had befallen Jerusalem.
137:6 my highest joy. Jerusalem was venerated as the place where God chose to dwell (see theological article "The Presence of God" at 1Ki 8). Since Jesus Christ has come there are no special holy places for centralized worship, but during the period of the psalms there was just one—Zion. Jerusalem symbolized all believers and typified the new heavens and the new earth (Rev 21).

[7] Remember, O LORD, what the Edomites[e] did
on the day Jerusalem fell.[f]
"Tear it down," they cried,
"tear it down to its foundations!"

[8] O Daughter of Babylon, doomed to destruction,[g]
happy is he who repays you
for what you have done to us—
[9] he who seizes your infants
and dashes them[h] against the rocks.

Psalm 138

Of David.

[1] I will praise you, O LORD, with all my heart;
before the "gods"[i] I will sing your praise.
[2] I will bow down toward your holy temple[j]
and will praise your name
for your love and your faithfulness,
for you have exalted above all things
your name and your word.[k]
[3] When I called, you answered me;
you made me bold and stouthearted.[l]

[4] May all the kings of the earth[m] praise you, O LORD,
when they hear the words of your mouth.
[5] May they sing of the ways of the LORD,
for the glory of the LORD is great.

[6] Though the LORD is on high, he looks upon the lowly,[n]
but the proud[o] he knows from afar.
[7] Though I walk[p] in the midst of trouble,
you preserve my life;
you stretch out your hand against the anger of my foes,[q]
with your right hand[r] you save me.[s]
[8] The LORD will fulfill ⌊his purpose⌋[t] for me;
your love, O LORD, endures forever—
do not abandon the works of your hands.[u]

137:7 [e]Jer 49:7; La 4:21-22; Eze 25:12 [f]Ob 1:11
137:8 [g]Isa 13:1,19; Jer 25:12,26; Jer 50:15; Rev 18:6
137:9 [h]2Ki 8:12; Isa 13:16
138:1 [i]Ps 95:3; 96:4
138:2 [j]1Ki 8:29; Ps 5:7; 28:2 [k]Isa 42:21
138:3 [l]Ps 28:7
138:4 [m]Ps 102:15
138:6 [n]Ps 113:6; Isa 57:15 [o]Pr 3:34; Jas 4:6
138:7 [p]Ps 23:4 [q]Jer 51:25 [r]Ps 20:6 [s]Ps 71:20
138:8 [t]Ps 57:2; Php 1:6 [u]Job 10:3,8; 14:15

137:7 what the Edomites did. The book of Obadiah (particularly vv. 8–14) bears witness to the callousness and active hostility of the Edomites at the time Jerusalem fell to the Babylonians. **"Tear it down."** The psalmist called on the Lord to destroy Edom in retaliation for its actions against Judah (see "Introduction: Christ in Psalms").
137:8 Daughter of Babylon. Babylon personified.
137:9 dashes them against the rocks. Because children left alive could grow up to challenge the authority of the conquerors, intentional destruction of children was part of ancient warfare. God himself commanded Israel to adopt this practice in the context of holy war (Dt 20:16). The psalmist prayed God's blessing on those who would carry out this aspect of his vengeance against Babylon. From his perspective, the deaths of the Babylonian children were appropriate retribution for the enormous tragedy the Babylonians had inflicted on Israel (doubtless including the killing of Israelite children). See Isaiah 13:16, Hosea 13:16 and Nahum 3:10. See also "Introduction: Christ in Psalms" for commentary on cries for retributive justice.
Psalm 138 *Introduction.* David's hand again is seen in the Psalter. Psalm 138 and the next seven psalms bear titles attesting to his authorship. In this song David thanked the Lord for having heard his prayer (v. 3) and called on all the kings of the earth to join him in praise of the Lord (vv. 4–5). David was not specific about the nature of his earlier lament (described in general terms in vv. 6–8), but it involved a matter of life and death (v. 7). Even after the Lord had answered his earlier prayer David continued to depend on him for his life (v. 8).
138:1–3 See *WLC* 190; *WSC* 54.
138:1 before the "gods." See "Introduction" to Psalm 82.
138:2 toward your holy temple. See notes on 2:6 and 15:1. **your name.** See 8:1. **your love.** Specifically, God's covenant loving-kindness. See *WLC* 112.
138:3 I called, you answered me. David's motivation in writing this psalm.
138:4 all the kings of the earth. David recognized that his individual praise was inadequate to the greatness of God. He envisioned all the rulers of the world calling on the Lord. Of course, this never happened during the Old Testament period. The rulers of Gentile nations opposed God (Pss 2; 48). When Jesus Christ came, however, the gospel began to be received by many Gentile nations. When Jesus returns, all nations and their rulers will, at last, join in the choir and praise. All the kings of the earth will bring their glory into the new Jerusalem (Rev 21:24). See theological article "The Kingdom of God" at Matthew 4.
138:6 the LORD is on high. The psalmist acknowledged that God was indeed exalted above the creation and transcendent in his majesty. **he looks upon the lowly.** God's transcendence does not separate him from his creation: He cares personally for the lowly and meets their intimate needs.
138:7 in the midst of trouble. The general language permitted later worshipers to apply the psalm in their own adverse circumstances. **your right hand.** See notes on 74:11 and 118:15–16.
138:8 your love. See note on verse 2.

Psalm 139

For the director of music. Of David. A psalm.

139:1 [v]Ps 17:3 [w]Jer 12:3
139:2 [x]2Ki 19:27 [y]Mt 9:4; Jn 2:24
139:3 [z]Job 31:4
139:4 [a]Heb 4:13
139:5 [b]Ps 34:7
139:6 [c]Job 42:3; Ro 11:33
139:7 [d]Jer 23:24; Jnh 1:3
139:8 [e]Am 9:2-3 [f]Pr 15:11
139:10 [g]Ps 23:3
139:12 [h]Job 34:22; Da 2:22
139:13 [i]Ps 119:73 [j]Job 10:11
139:14 [k]Ps 40:5
139:15 [l]Job 10:11 [m]Ps 63:9

1 O LORD, you have searched me[v]
and you know[w] me.
2 You know when I sit and when I rise;[x]
you perceive my thoughts[y] from afar.
3 You discern my going out and my lying down;
you are familiar with all my ways.[z]
4 Before a word is on my tongue
you know it completely,[a] O LORD.

5 You hem me in[b]—behind and before;
you have laid your hand upon me.
6 Such knowledge is too wonderful for me,
too lofty[c] for me to attain.

7 Where can I go from your Spirit?
Where can I flee[d] from your presence?
8 If I go up to the heavens,[e] you are there;
if I make my bed[f] in the depths,[a] you are there.
9 If I rise on the wings of the dawn,
if I settle on the far side of the sea,
10 even there your hand will guide me,[g]
your right hand will hold me fast.

11 If I say, "Surely the darkness will hide me
and the light become night around me,"
12 even the darkness will not be dark[h] to you;
the night will shine like the day,
for darkness is as light to you.

13 For you created my inmost being;[i]
you knit me together[j] in my mother's womb.
14 I praise you because I am fearfully and wonderfully made;
your works are wonderful,[k]
I know that full well.
15 My frame was not hidden from you
when I was made in the secret place.
When I was woven together[l] in the depths of the earth,[m]

[a] 8 Hebrew *Sheol*

Psalm 139 *Introduction.* A discussion of Psalm 139, best known for its first 18 verses, must take into account its last 6 verses (vv. 19–24). In them the psalmist invoked the Lord to crush his enemies and to proclaim his innocence. The psalm is the complaint of an individual who has called on God to vindicate him of invalid charges. It is with this purpose in mind that he meditated on the character of God. He explored God's deep wisdom (his omniscience and incomprehensibility), his pervasive personal presence (omnipresence) and his creation of the psalmist himself. This powerful expression of God's sovereignty clearly revealed God's personal and intimate relation to the psalmist.

139:1–7 See *WLC* 7.

139:1 you have searched me . . . you know me. Compare the appeal in verses 23–24. The all-knowing God had intimate understanding of the psalmist and of all of his creation.

139:2 you perceive my thoughts. An expression of God's omniscience. People tend to perceive their thoughts as private, but even these cannot be hidden from the Lord.

139:4 Before a word is on my tongue. God knew the psalmist's thoughts before he could express them. This is one reason that we can pray to God silently, even to the point of meditating without being able to articulate our thoughts and feelings (cf. Ro 8:26).

139:5 You hem me in. The Lord set limits to the psalmist's actions. **laid your hand.** To restrain and guide him in life.

139:7 your Spirit . . . your presence. Acknowledgment of God's personal presence throughout his creation. The force of these twin rhetorical questions is that there was nowhere the psalmist could have gone that would have been outside God's purview.

139:8 to the heavens . . . in the depths. The psalmist expressed God's omnipresence through a series of contrasts. The first pairing is spatial. God in heaven is not surprising; his presence "in the depths" startles us. "Depths" is a translation of the Hebrew *Sheol,* the grave. Not even the realm of death escapes God's presence (see theological article "Hell" at Rev 19). The hope of life beyond the grave shines through this expression. (See v. 10)

139:9 the wings of the dawn . . . the far side of the sea. As far east or west as one could go. The implication is that God is present and active everywhere on Earth.

139:10 will guide me. God would not merely be aware of the psalmist wherever he was but would be at his side to help him. **your right hand.** See 73:23–26, 74:11 and 138:7.

139:11–12 the darkness . . . as light to you. Another contrasting pair (see v. 8). Darkness could not hide the psalmist's actions from God.

139:13 you created my inmost being. God's intimate knowledge of the psalmist went back to the time of his conception, when the Lord had given him life. **knit.** More precisely, "wove." God took an active, personal role in forming the psalmist's unborn body and person.

139:14 your works are wonderful. That includes the work of creating the psalmist (and by inference all human beings). The wonder of the developing child in the womb has become even more evident to modern people and should motivate us to praise the Creator even more passionately for the wonder of life.

139:15 in the secret place. That is, in his mother's womb. **in the depths of the earth.** A metaphor for his mother's womb. The word here translated "depths" is different from that in verse 8.

16 your eyes saw my unformed body.
All the days ordained for me
were written in your book
before one of them came to be.

17 How precious to[a] me are your thoughts, O God![n]
How vast is the sum of them!
18 Were I to count them,
they would outnumber the grains of sand.
When I awake,
I am still with you.

19 If only you would slay the wicked,[o] O God!
Away from me,[p] you bloodthirsty men!
20 They speak of you with evil intent;
your adversaries misuse your name.[q]
21 Do I not hate those[r] who hate you, O LORD,
and abhor those who rise up against you?
22 I have nothing but hatred for them;
I count them my enemies.
23 Search me,[s] O God, and know my heart;[t]
test me and know my anxious thoughts.

139:17 [n]Ps 40:5
139:19 [o]Isa 11:4 [p]Ps 119:115
139:20 [q]Jude 15
139:21 [r]2Ch 19:2; Ps 31:6; 119:113; Ps 119:158
139:23 [s]Job 31:6; Ps 26:2 [t]Jer 11:20

[a] 17 Or *concerning*

139:16 All the days ordained for me. The psalmist rejoiced in God's predestination of all the events of his life, knowing that every blessing he received was ultimately a gift of God's grace.
139:17 precious to me. God's incomprehensibly great knowledge both overwhelmed and comforted the psalmist, especially in his present distress (see vv. 19–24).
139:19 slay the wicked. See "Introduction: Christ in Psalms." **Away from me.** The psalmist may have wanted to distance himself from the wicked for a number of reasons, such as: (1) God's judgment was going to come on them, and he did not want to be caught in the crossfire; (2) he did not want to be a victim of their "bloodthirsty" crimes; and (3) their wickedness angered or sickened him.
139:20 See *WLC* 113.
139:22 I count them my enemies. That is, the psalmist was of one mind with the Lord. God's enemies were his enemies.
139:23–24 See *HC* 113.

Divine Omniscience: Does God Know Everything?

OMNISCIENT means "all-knowing." Scripture declares that God's eyes run everywhere (Job 24:23; Pss 33:13–15, 139:13–16; Pr 15:3; Jer 16:17; Heb 4:13). He searches all hearts and observes everyone's ways (1Sa 16:7; 1Ki 8:39; 1Ch 28:9; Ps 139:1–6,23; Jer 17:10; Lk 16:15; Ro 8:27; Rev 2:23). In other words, he knows everything all of the time. He knows the future no less than the past and the present, and possible events that never happen no less than the actual events that do (1Sa 23:9–13; 2Ki 13:19; Ps 81:14–15; Isa 48:18-19). He does not have to acquire information; all his knowledge is immediately and directly before his mind. The authors of the Bible stood in awe of the capacity of God's mind (Pss 139:1–6; 147:5; Isa 40:13–14,28; cf. Ro 11:33– 36).

As God interacted with human beings in Scripture, he often referred to his own knowledge in ways that made it possible for his creatures to understand him and react to him. He asked questions (e.g., "Where are you?" [Ge 3:8–9]; "Where is your brother?" [Ge 4:9]), remembered (Ge 9:16), tested the faith of his people (Ge 22:1; Dt 8:2) and expressed regret over the outcomes of events (Ge 6:6). In these situations God already knew all things, even before they took place. Yet, as God related to human beings in their weakness and humility, he often stooped low and spoke of himself in human terms. He taught, led and congratulated human beings by referring to his own involvement in history in ways they could understand. Never once, however, was God actually ignorant of even the smallest detail.

Some theologians have denied God's omniscience on the basis that Jesus Christ, who was both God and man, claimed not to know certain things. As a man, Jesus increased in wisdom (Lk 2:52) and even expressed ignorance on one occasion (Mt 24:36; Mk 13:32). But he also possessed supernatural knowledge (Mt 9:4; 12:25; Lk 5:22; 6:8; 11:17; Jn 16:30; 21:17). In his divine nature Jesus is omniscient, but in his human nature he knows only what he has learned (see notes on Mt 24:36 and Mk 13:32 and theological article "Jesus Christ, God and Man" at Jn 1).

God's knowledge is linked with his sovereignty: He knows each fact, thought and possibility, each individual, animal, plant and inanimate object, both in itself and in relation to all others, because he created them, sustains them and makes them function every moment according to his plan (Eph 1:11; see theological article "Providence" at Jer 18). For believers God's omniscience brings the assurance that God will not forget us but will work out good results for us according to his promises (Isa 40:27–31, Ro 8:28). To unbelievers, however, the truth of God's universal knowledge must bring dread, for it comes as a reminder that they cannot hide from his impending judgment (Pss 94:1–11; 139:7–12; Jn 1:1–12).

139:24 [u]Ps 5:8; 143:10; Pr 15:9

24 See if there is any offensive way in me,
and lead me[u] in the way everlasting.

Psalm 140

For the director of music. A psalm of David.

140:1 [v]Ps 17:13 [w]Ps 18:48
140:2 [x]Ps 36:4; 56:6
140:3 [y]Ps 57:4 [z]Ps 58:4; Jas 3:8

1 Rescue me,[v] O LORD, from evil men;
protect me from men of violence,[w]
2 who devise evil plans[x] in their hearts
and stir up war every day.
3 They make their tongues as sharp as[y] a serpent's;
the poison of vipers[z] is on their lips. *Selah*

140:4 [a]Ps 141:9 [b]Ps 71:4
140:5 [c]Ps 31:4; 35:7

4 Keep me,[a] O LORD, from the hands of the wicked;[b]
protect me from men of violence
who plan to trip my feet.
5 Proud men have hidden a snare for me;
they have spread out the cords of their net
and have set traps[c] for me along my path. *Selah*

140:6 [d]Ps 16:2 [e]Ps 116:1; 143:1
140:7 [f]Ps 28:8
140:8 [g]Ps 10:2-3

6 O LORD, I say to you, "You are my God."[d]
Hear, O LORD, my cry for mercy.[e]
7 O Sovereign LORD,[f] my strong deliverer,
who shields my head in the day of battle—
8 do not grant the wicked[g] their desires, O LORD;
do not let their plans succeed,
or they will become proud. *Selah*

140:9 [h]Ps 7:16
140:10 [i]Ps 11:6; 21:9
140:11 [j]Ps 34:21

9 Let the heads of those who surround me
be covered with the trouble their lips have caused.[h]
10 Let burning coals fall upon them;
may they be thrown into the fire,[i]
into miry pits, never to rise.
11 Let slanderers not be established in the land;
may disaster hunt down men of violence.[j]

140:12 [k]Ps 9:4 [l]Ps 35:10
140:13 [m]Ps 97:12 [n]Ps 11:7

12 I know that the LORD secures justice for the poor
and upholds the cause[k] of the needy.[l]
13 Surely the righteous will praise your name[m]
and the upright will live[n] before you.

Psalm 141

A psalm of David.

141:1 [o]Ps 22:19; 70:5 [p]Ps 143:1
141:2 [q]Rev 5:8; 8:3 [r]1Ti 2:8 [s]Ex 29:39, 41

1 O LORD, I call to you; come quickly[o] to me.
Hear my voice[p] when I call to you.
2 May my prayer be set before you like incense;[q]
may the lifting up of my hands[r] be like the evening sacrifice.[s]

139:23 Search . . . know . . . test. The psalmist was so convinced of his innocence that he invited God to probe his thoughts and feelings and to attest to his blamelessness (compare v. 1). At the same time he invited God's correction and direction. He did not claim to be innocent of all sin but only of the charges that had been brought against him.

Psalm 140 *Introduction.* The purpose of Psalm 140 is clear from the imperatives throughout its opening verses. David called on the Lord to deliver him from his ruthless and slanderous enemies. The psalm is a complaint, which, like many others in the same genre, turns to the Lord at the end with confidence (vv. 12–13). The enemies may have been actual adversaries in battle (vv. 2,7), but the battle language could also be metaphoric (notice the parallels with hunting in vv. 4–5). David's description of his enemies includes attributes typically associated with wickedness in general, as confirmed by Paul's application of verse 3 to all sinners (Ro 3:13).

140:2 stir up war. If literal, the setting of the psalm was holy war. In the context of this psalm, however, the language might instead be metaphorical, analogous to the hunting motif of verse 5.

140:3 the poison of vipers. The enemy, through gossip and slander, had carefully orchestrated David's destruction.

140:4 See *WLC* 190.

140:7 who shields my head in the day of battle. David appealed to God for protection from his enemies, whether military or otherwise (see the "Introduction" to Ps 140).

140:8 See *WLC* 190.

140:9 with the trouble their lips have caused. David asked the Lord to bring upon his persecutors the evil they had perpetrated against him. See notes on 7:14–15.

140:10 may they be thrown into the fire. See "Introduction: Christ in Psalms."

140:12 upholds the cause of the needy. God shows himself powerful, particularly with respect to those elements in society who are unable to care for themselves: widows, orphans, prisoners, the poor and (as here) the oppressed.

Psalm 141 *Introduction.* In Psalm 141 David once again called upon the Lord for help against enemies who sought to destroy him (vv. 1,8–10). In this complaint he voiced particular concern that he might be drawn into personal involvement in the evil against which he protested (vv. 3–5), and he requested that God annihilate his enemies (vv. 6–7). The images in verse 2 suggest that the prayer was offered in a formal worship setting.

3 Set a guard over my mouth, O LORD;
keep watch over the door of my lips.
4 Let not my heart be drawn to what is evil,
to take part in wicked deeds
with men who are evildoers;
let me not eat of their delicacies.[t]

5 Let a righteous man[a] strike me—it is a kindness;
let him rebuke me[u]—it is oil on my head.[v]
My head will not refuse it.

Yet my prayer is ever against the deeds of evildoers;
6 their rulers will be thrown down from the cliffs,
and the wicked will learn that my words were well spoken.
7 ⌊They will say,⌋ "As one plows and breaks up the earth,
so our bones have been scattered at the mouth[w] of the grave.[b]"

8 But my eyes are fixed[x] on you, O Sovereign LORD;
in you I take refuge[y]—do not give me over to death.
9 Keep me[z] from the snares they have laid for me,
from the traps set[a] by evildoers.
10 Let the wicked fall[b] into their own nets,
while I pass by in safety.

141:4 [t]Pr 23:6
141:5 [u]Pr 9:8 [v]Ps 23:5
141:7 [w]Ps 53:5
141:8 [x]Ps 25:15 [y]Ps 2:12
141:9 [z]Ps 140:4 [a]Ps 38:12
141:10 [b]Ps 35:8

Psalm 142

A *maskil*[c] of David. When he was in the cave. A prayer.

1 I cry aloud to the LORD;
I lift up my voice to the LORD for mercy.[c]
2 I pour out my complaint[d] before him;
before him I tell my trouble.

3 When my spirit grows faint[e] within me,
it is you who know my way.
In the path where I walk
men have hidden a snare for me.
4 Look to my right and see;
no one is concerned for me.
I have no refuge;
no one cares[f] for my life.

5 I cry to you, O LORD;
I say, "You are my refuge,[g]
my portion[h] in the land of the living."[i]
6 Listen to my cry,[j]
for I am in desperate need;[k]

142:1 [c]Ps 30:8
142:2 [d]Isa 26:16
142:3 [e]Ps 140:5; 143:4,7
142:4 [f]Ps 31:11; Jer 30:17
142:5 [g]Ps 46:1 [h]Ps 16:5 [i]Ps 27:13
142:6 [j]Ps 17:1 [k]Ps 79:8; 116:6

a 5 Or *Let the Righteous One* b 7 Hebrew *Sheol* c Title: Probably a literary or musical term

141:2 like incense . . . like the evening sacrifice. This image proceeds from the sacrificial worship of Israel and suggests that the psalm was set in such a context. As the incense was holy and precious (Ex 30:34–38) to the Lord, so the psalmist hoped his prayers would be received favorably by God. Similarly, in Revelation 8:3–5 the prayers of the saints were said to be brought with incense to the throne of God by an angel.
141:3 Set a guard over my mouth. It is unclear whether the psalmist had already sinned in his anger or was tempted to do so. However, he knew where to turn for help in controlling his tongue.
141:4 to take part in wicked deeds. The psalmist asked the Lord to prevent him from compromising his integrity.
141:5 let him rebuke me. The wise rejoice in God's correction, knowing that those who refuse it will be destroyed (Pr 29:1). Compare Hebrews 12:1–13.
141:9 the snares. A hunting image; see note on 140:2.
141:10 fall into their own nets. See notes on 7:14–16.
Psalm 142 *Introduction.* Psalm 142 is the complaint of someone at the end of his resources. The psalmist was weak (v. 2), beset by enemies (v. 3), with no one to help him (v. 4). His only hope was the Lord.

Title. **When he was in the cave.** This historical title is the last to appear in the book and is the only one outside the first two books of the Psalter. Compare the title to Psalm 57. **prayer.** See "Introduction" to Psalm 17.

142:3 my spirit grows faint. The psalmist was worn down from the pressure of unremitting persecution by his enemies. **a snare.** Compare 140:5 and 141:9.

142:4 to my right. The direction from which the psalmist pictured help coming, the side associated with strength (16:8; 110:5; and 121:5). **I have no refuge.** The psalmist was beset by unmitigated troubles. Compare verse 5.

142:5 You are my refuge. A petition for the Lord to shelter him from his troubles.

142:6 they are too strong for me. The psalmist turned to the Lord because he was broken; he knew that he lacked the strength in himself to meet his adversity.

142:7
[l]Ps 146:7 [m]Ps 13:6

rescue me from those who pursue me,
for they are too strong for me.
7 Set me free from my prison,[l]
that I may praise your name.

Then the righteous will gather about me
because of your goodness to me.[m]

Psalm 143

A psalm of David.

143:1
[n]Ps 140:6
[o]Ps 89:1-2
[p]Ps 71:2

1 O LORD, hear my prayer,
listen to my cry for mercy;[n]
in your faithfulness[o] and righteousness[p]
come to my relief.

143:2
[q]Ps 14:3; Ecc 7:20; Ro 3:20

2 Do not bring your servant into judgment,
for no one living is righteous[q] before you.

3 The enemy pursues me,
he crushes me to the ground;
he makes me dwell in darkness
like those long dead.

143:4
[r]Ps 142:3

4 So my spirit grows faint within me;
my heart within me is dismayed.[r]

143:5
[s]Ps 77:6

5 I remember[s] the days of long ago;
I meditate on all your works
and consider what your hands have done.

143:6
[t]Ps 63:1; 88:9

6 I spread out my hands[t] to you;
my soul thirsts for you like a parched land. *Selah*

143:7
[u]Ps 69:17
[v]Ps 27:9; 28:1

7 Answer me quickly,[u] O LORD;
my spirit fails.
Do not hide your face[v] from me
or I will be like those who go down to the pit.

143:8
[w]Ps 46:5; 90:14
[x]Ps 27:11
[y]Ps 25:1-2

8 Let the morning bring me word of your unfailing love,[w]
for I have put my trust in you.
Show me the way[x] I should go,
for to you I lift up my soul.[y]

143:9
[z]Ps 31:15

9 Rescue me from my enemies,[z] O LORD,
for I hide myself in you.

143:10
[a]Ne 9:20; Ps 23:3; 25:4-5

10 Teach me to do your will,
for you are my God;
may your good Spirit
lead[a] me on level ground.

143:11
[b]Ps 119:25
[c]Ps 31:1

11 For your name's sake, O LORD, preserve my life;[b]
in your righteousness,[c] bring me out of trouble.

142:7 from my prison. In light of the psalm title, the original reference was to the cave. **the righteous will gather about me.** Either to join him in thanksgiving for salvation from his troubles, or as human refuge put in place by God as an answer to his petition (cf. v. 4).
Psalm 143 *Introduction.* Psalm 143 is the last of the so-called penitential psalms (see "Introduction" to Ps 6). These compositions highlight human sinfulness, the need for repentance and the reality of God's grace. The reason for this psalm's inclusion in the group is crystallized in verse 2, which may be Paul's point of reference in such significant contexts as Romans 3:20 and Galatians 2:16. Psalm 143 has many similarities to 142. Both appeal to God for help in persecution and trouble at a time when the psalmist realized that he had exhausted his own resources. In both instances he turned to the Lord and rested in his covenant faithfulness and love (143:1,11–12).
143:1 in your faithfulness and righteousness. The psalmist appealed to God for help because of what he knew about God's nature and on the basis of the quality of his relationship with him. God promised to care for his people, and the psalmist invoked him to fulfill that promise in his particular case. See *HC* 123.
143:2 no one living is righteous before you. The psalmist knew his own heart and, by inference, the hearts of all sinners. No one can plead perfection at the bar of God's judgment, and the suppliant accordingly called on the Lord for mercy. Paul alluded to this clause in Romans 3:20 and in Galatians 2:16. See *WCF* 16.5; 16.6; *BC* 23; *HC* 126.
143:4 my spirit grows faint within me. See note on 142:3.
143:5 I remember. See 63:6 and 77:3–11; contrast 78:42.
143:6 spread out my hands. In prayer. **my soul thirsts.** Compare 42:1–2.
143:7 hide your face. The psalmist feared God's absence while he was in trouble. Compare 22:1, 28:1 and 74:1. **who go down to the pit.** Who die. See note 28:1; compare 30:1 and 40:2.
143:8 the morning. The psalmist uttered his prayer either at night or in the very early morning, hoping that a divine oracle would greet him at dawn. **unfailing love.** The love of God's covenant devotion. **Show me.** The psalmist not only desired deliverance; he wanted God's guidance. He knew that it was only as he walked in the way of the Lord that he would live safely.
143:11 your name's sake. See 8:1.

12 In your unfailing love, silence my enemies;
destroy all my foes,[d]
for I am your servant.[e]

143:12 [d]Ps 52:5; 54:5 [e]Ps 116:16

Psalm 144

Of David.

1 Praise be to the LORD my Rock,[f]
who trains my hands for war,
my fingers for battle.
2 He is my loving God and my fortress,[g]
my stronghold and my deliverer,
my shield,[h] in whom I take refuge,
who subdues peoples[a] under me.

3 O LORD, what is man[i] that you care for him,
the son of man that you think of him?
4 Man is like a breath;
his days are like a fleeting shadow.[j]

5 Part your heavens,[k] O LORD, and come down;
touch the mountains, so that they smoke.[l]
6 Send forth lightning and scatter ⌊the enemies⌋;
shoot your arrows[m] and rout them.
7 Reach down your hand from on high;
deliver me and rescue me
from the mighty waters,[n]
from the hands of foreigners[o]
8 whose mouths are full of lies,[p]
whose right hands are deceitful.

9 I will sing a new song to you, O God;
on the ten-stringed lyre[q] I will make music to you,
10 to the One who gives victory to kings,
who delivers his servant David[r] from the deadly sword.

11 Deliver me and rescue me
from the hands of foreigners
whose mouths are full of lies,
whose right hands are deceitful.[s]

12 Then our sons in their youth
will be like well-nurtured plants,[t]

144:1 [f]Ps 18:2,34
144:2 [g]Ps 59:9; 91:2 [h]Ps 84:9
144:3 [i]Ps 8:4; Heb 2:6
144:4 [j]Ps 39:11; 102:11
144:5 [k]Ps 18:9; Isa 64:1 [l]Ps 104:32
144:6 [m]Ps 7:12-13; 18:14
144:7 [n]Ps 69:2 [o]Ps 18:44
144:8 [p]Ps 12:2
144:9 [q]Ps 33:2-3
144:10 [r]Ps 18:50
144:11 [s]Ps 12:2; Isa 44:20
144:12 [t]Ps 128:3

[a] *2* Many manuscripts of the Masoretic Text, Dead Sea Scrolls, Aquila, Jerome and Syriac; most manuscripts of the Masoretic Text *subdues my people*

143:12 unfailing love. See notes on verse 8.
Psalm 144 *Introduction.* Psalm 144 is set in a situation of conflict (v. 11), but the speaker did not panic as he called on the Lord to appear (vv. 5–8) as the divine warrior to save him from his enemies. The language of God's appearance is similar to that of another Davidic psalm, 18. Psalm 144 ends with a beautiful picture of peace and prosperity that would arise in the aftermath of victorious holy war (vv. 12–14).
144:1 my Rock. See notes on 28:7, 62:2, Ex 17:6 and Dt 32:18. **who trains my hands for war.** The association of God with warfare is difficult for some Christians to understand and may be an obstacle to their appreciation of the Old Testament. However, there is in reality no conflict between the Old and New Testaments on this issue. Because the church is not a nation, it does not wage war against literal human military forces. Nevertheless, the New Testament does affirm the right of nations to engage in just wars (Ro 13:1–7), as the Old Testaments saints did (2Ki 6:15–17). Christians are embroiled in spiritual war against Satan and his forces (Eph 6:10–20), as well as against worldly thinking (2Co 10:3–5). God trained the Israelites in warfare to enable them to protect themselves but also so that they might be used as an instrument of his wrath in judgment. See notes on Psalm 20 and Deuteronomy 7 and 20.
144:2 loving . . . fortress. The Bible sees no conflict between God's love and his warfare. God often demonstrated his love for his people by defeating their enemies in battle. **under me.** That is, David and later on any faithful Davidic kings.
144:3 what is man . . . ? Compare 8:4.
144:4 like a breath. That is, ephemeral and short-lived. In light of man's brief existence, the psalmist was amazed at the measure and quality of the Lord's care.
144:5 Part your heavens. Compare 18:9. In Psalm 18 David looked back on God's deliverance and described it in these terms. In Psalm 144 he used the same image in an appeal to the Lord to come and save him. **so that they smoke.** God's appearance as the divine warrior was often accompanied by fire and smoke (see Ex 19:16–19; 2Sa 22:9; Mic 1:4). Language describing other disruptions of the natural order was also common (Isa 24:4ff.; Na 1:5).
144:7 the mighty waters. The psalmist's enemies are compared to the cosmic waters of chaos (see 18:4; 29:3,10; 46:2,4; 69:1–2; 114:3).
144:9 a new song. See note on 33:3.
144:11 Deliver me. A renewed appeal. **from the hands of foreigners.** The threat in this instance is from outside of Israel.
144:12 our sons . . . our daughters. The psalmist looked to the next generation. After the oppressive foreigners (see v. 11) had been ousted, the next generation could flourish.

and our daughters will be like pillars
carved to adorn a palace.
13 Our barns will be filled
with every kind of provision.
Our sheep will increase by thousands,
by tens of thousands in our fields;
14 our oxen will draw heavy loads.[a]
There will be no breaching of walls,
no going into captivity,
no cry of distress in our streets.

15 Blessed are the people[u] of whom this is true;
blessed are the people whose God is the LORD.

Psalm 145[b]

A psalm of praise. Of David.

1 I will exalt you,[v] my God the King;[w]
I will praise your name for ever and ever.
2 Every day I will praise[x] you
and extol your name for ever and ever.

3 Great is the LORD and most worthy of praise;
his greatness no one can fathom.[y]
4 One generation[z] will commend your works to another;
they will tell of your mighty acts.
5 They will speak of the glorious splendor of your majesty,
and I will meditate on your wonderful works.[c][a]
6 They will tell of the power of your awesome works,[b]
and I will proclaim[c] your great deeds.
7 They will celebrate your abundant goodness[d]
and joyfully sing of your righteousness.[e]
8 The LORD is gracious and compassionate,[f]
slow to anger and rich in love.[g]
9 The LORD is good[h] to all;
he has compassion on all he has made.
10 All you have made will praise you,[i] O LORD;
your saints will extol you.[j]
11 They will tell of the glory of your kingdom
and speak of your might,
12 so that all men may know of your mighty acts[k]
and the glorious splendor of your kingdom.

144:15 [u]Ps 33:12
145:1 [v]Ps 30:1; 34:1 [w]Ps 5:2
145:2 [x]Ps 71:6
145:3 [y]Job 5:9; Ps 147:5; Ro 11:33
145:4 [z]Isa 38:19
145:5 [a]Ps 119:27
145:6 [b]Ps 66:3 [c]Dt 32:3
145:7 [d]Isa 63:7 [e]Ps 51:14
145:8 [f]Ps 86:15 [g]Ex 34:6; Nu 14:18
145:9 [h]Ps 100:5
145:10 [i]Ps 19:1 [j]Ps 68:26
145:12 [k]Ps 105:1

[a] *14* Or *our chieftains will be firmly established* [b] This psalm is an acrostic poem, the verses of which (including verse 13b) begin with the successive letters of the Hebrew alphabet. [c] *5* Dead Sea Scrolls and Syriac (see also Septuagint); Masoretic Text *On the glorious splendor of your majesty / and on your wonderful works I will meditate*

144:13 Our barns. God would make the land fertile.
144:14 no breaching of walls. The psalmist envisioned complete security from outside military intervention.
144:15 Blessed. See note on 1:1.
Psalm 145 *Introduction.* Psalm 145 is the first of six hymns that close the Psalter with a fireworks display of praise. This group of psalms functions as a concluding doxology. The focus of the psalmist's praise in Psalm 145 was on God's kingship (v. 1), which is glorious and everlasting (vv. 11–13), as well as on God himself, who is mighty, majestic and merciful. Psalm 145 is an acrostic, with each parallel line beginning with a consecutive letter of the Hebrew alphabet (see "Introduction: Structure: *Poetic Style and Devices*"). *Nun* is the only missing letter, and the evidence of the ancient versions is that this is due to a scribal, rather than a compositional, omission. See *WLC* 190; *HC* 122.
145:1 my God the King. See note on 93:1.
145:2 your name. See notes on 8:1.
145:3 Great is the LORD. Compare 48:1. **no one can fathom.** God's power and might are so great that finite human minds cannot begin to grasp their reality. This verse indicates that in many respects God is far beyond comprehension. Human beings may truly know things that God has shown in creation and taught in Scripture, but never with the depth of knowledge and wisdom that God possesses, and never seeing the full interrelatedness between the various truths God has revealed. Some human limitations are due to the fact that God has not revealed everything; others are intrinsic to the fact that God is infinite, while human beings are finite. See *WCF* 2.1; *BC* 1.
145:4 One generation . . . to another. See 78:4. It was, and still is, the duty of the father to instruct his children in the ways of the Lord (see Dt 6:20–25).
145:5 your majesty . . . your wonderful works. The psalmist considered how great God is in his nature and his deeds.
145:7 See *WCF* 5.1.
145:8 The LORD is gracious. This wording occurs a number of times throughout the Scripture, first at Exodus 34:6 (see its notes). **compassionate.** That God allows people to live in spite of their deep-seated sin is a sign of his mercy. **rich in love.** The love of God's covenant devotion.
145:11 your kingdom. Verses 11–13 focus on God's kingdom. That God is pictured as a King who rules a kingdom emphasizes his sovereign power and control over his creation.

13 Your kingdom is an everlasting kingdom,[l]
and your dominion endures through all generations.

The LORD is faithful to all his promises
and loving toward all he has made.[a]
14 The LORD upholds[m] all those who fall
and lifts up all[n] who are bowed down.
15 The eyes of all look to you,
and you give them their food[o] at the proper time.
16 You open your hand
and satisfy the desires[p] of every living thing.

17 The LORD is righteous in all his ways
and loving toward all he has made.
18 The LORD is near[q] to all who call on him,[r]
to all who call on him in truth.
19 He fulfills the desires[s] of those who fear him;
he hears their cry[t] and saves them.
20 The LORD watches over all who love him,[u]
but all the wicked he will destroy.[v]

21 My mouth will speak[w] in praise of the LORD.
Let every creature[x] praise his holy name
for ever and ever.

Psalm 146

1 Praise the LORD.[b]

Praise the LORD,[y] O my soul.
2 I will praise the LORD all my life;[z]
I will sing praise to my God as long as I live.

3 Do not put your trust in princes,[a]
in mortal men,[b] who cannot save.
4 When their spirit departs, they return to the ground;[c]
on that very day their plans come to nothing.[d]
5 Blessed is he[e] whose help[f] is the God of Jacob,
whose hope is in the LORD his God,
6 the Maker of heaven[g] and earth,
the sea, and everything in them—
the LORD, who remains faithful[h] forever.
7 He upholds the cause of the oppressed[i]
and gives food to the hungry.[j]

145:13 [l]1Ti 1:17; 2Pe 1:11
145:14 [m]Ps 37:24 [n]Ps 146:8
145:15 [o]Ps 104:27; 136:25
145:16 [p]Ps 104:28
145:18 [q]Dt 4:7 [r]Jn 4:24
145:19 [s]Ps 37:4 [t]Pr 15:29
145:20 [u]Ps 31:23; 97:10 [v]Ps 9:5
145:21 [w]Ps 71:8 [x]Ps 65:2
146:1 [y]Ps 103:1
146:2 [z]Ps 104:33
146:3 [a]Ps 118:9 [b]Isa 2:22
146:4 [c]Ps 104:29; Ecc 12:7 [d]Ps 33:10; 1Co 2:6
146:5 [e]Ps 144:15; Jer 17:7 [f]Ps 71:5
146:6 [g]Ps 115:15; Ac 14:15; Rev 14:7 [h]Ps 117:2
146:7 [i]Ps 103:6 [j]Ps 107:9

a *13* One manuscript of the Masoretic Text, Dead Sea Scrolls and Syriac (see also Septuagint); most manuscripts of the Masoretic Text do not have the last two lines of verse 13. b *1* Hebrew *Hallelu Yah*; also in verse 10

145:13 an everlasting kingdom. God is eternal, and therefore his kingdom will never be destroyed. Compare Nebuchadnezzar's confession in Daniel 4:34 (see theological article "The Kingdom of God" at Mt 4). **faithful to all his promises.** The Scriptures record how God fulfilled his promises to his people. He promised offspring and land to Abraham and gave the promised land to Isaac and, centuries later, to their descendants. He promised David a dynasty (2Sa 7); David's descendants ruled for the next four and a half centuries—and Christ, David's descendant, will rule forever. The ultimate fulfillment of all the promises of God is found in Jesus Christ (2Co 1:20).
145:14 upholds all those who fall. God shows particular compassion toward the weak and also restores the erring.
145:15–16 See *HC* 125.
145:16 of every living thing. God gives gifts to all his creatures, both human and nonhuman, his saints and his enemies alike.
145:17–20 See *WCF* 2.2; 5.1; *WLC* 18,179; *WSC* 11; *HC* 117.
145:18 to all who call on him. While God is kind to all his creatures, the psalm goes on to specify his particular kindness toward those who love him and turn to him.
145:19 those who fear him. See notes on 2:11, 34:7 and 36:1.
Psalm 146 *Introduction.* Psalm 146 continues the hymnic mood begun in Psalm 145 and opens a new, final grouping. The last five psalms are not only hymnic but characterized by their opening and closing cries of *Hallelujah!* (see "Introduction" to Ps 111 and note on 111:1). The call of Psalm 146 is to put hope and trust in God, not in any human power. God is powerful as Creator (v. 6) and as King (v. 10). He is also compassionate toward the weak and oppressed (vv. 7–9). See *HC* 125.
146:1 Praise the LORD. Characterizes the mood of the entire psalm and brackets the whole (v. 10). **O my soul.** See 103:1.
146:3 in princes. Some commentators believe that the reference was to postexilic foreign rulers over the promised land. If the psalm was written after the exile, this could be correct, but there were earlier times when the children of Israel misguidedly trusted in rulers from among their own people (1Sa 8).
146:5 Blessed. See Psalm 1:1. **whose help.** God is the only sufficient help for those in distress—the theme of the psalm. The verses that follow describe God's power and compassion.
146:6 the Maker. God's role as Creator is highlighted to emphasize his power. **the sea.** Compare 24:2.
146:7 the oppressed . . . the hungry. God's power exercised for the needy, demonstrating his compassion, goodness and mercy.

146:7 [k]Ps 68:6
146:8 [l]Mt 9:30
146:9 [m]Ex 22:22; Dt 10:18; Ps 68:5
146:10 [n]Ex 15:18; Ps 10:16

The LORD sets prisoners free,[k]
8 the LORD gives sight to the blind,[l]
the LORD lifts up those who are bowed down,
the LORD loves the righteous.
9 The LORD watches over the alien
and sustains the fatherless and the widow,[m]
but he frustrates the ways of the wicked.

10 The LORD reigns[n] forever,
your God, O Zion, for all generations.

Praise the LORD.

Psalm 147

147:1 [o]Ps 135:3 [p]Ps 33:1
147:2 [q]Ps 102:16 [r]Dt 30:3
147:4 [s]Isa 40:26
147:5 [t]Ps 48:1 [u]Isa 40:28
147:6 [v]Ps 146:8-9
147:7 [w]Ps 33:3
147:8 [x]Job 38:26 [y]Ps 104:14
147:9 [z]Ps 104:27-28; Mt 6:26 [a]Job 38:41
147:10 [b]1Sa 16:7 [c]Ps 33:16-17

1 Praise the LORD.[a]

How good it is to sing praises to our God,
how pleasant[o] and fitting to praise him![p]

2 The LORD builds up Jerusalem;[q]
he gathers the exiles[r] of Israel.
3 He heals the brokenhearted
and binds up their wounds.
4 He determines the number of the stars[s]
and calls them each by name.
5 Great is our Lord[t] and mighty in power;
his understanding has no limit.[u]
6 The LORD sustains the humble[v]
but casts the wicked to the ground.

7 Sing to the LORD[w] with thanksgiving;
make music to our God on the harp.
8 He covers the sky with clouds;
he supplies the earth with rain[x]
and makes grass grow[y] on the hills.
9 He provides food[z] for the cattle
and for the young ravens[a] when they call.

10 His pleasure is not in the strength[b] of the horse,[c]
nor his delight in the legs of a man;
11 the LORD delights in those who fear him,
who put their hope in his unfailing love.

12 Extol the LORD, O Jerusalem;
praise your God, O Zion,
13 for he strengthens the bars of your gates
and blesses your people within you.

a *1* Hebrew *Hallelu Yah*; also in verse 20

146:9 he frustrates the ways of the wicked. God promotes the cause of the weak and thwarts the proud, the powerful and the abusive.
146:10 reigns forever. See 93:1. **O Zion.** See note on 2:6; compare 50:2, 74:2, 84:7, 128:5, 129:5 and 137:6. **Praise the LORD.** See verse 1.
Psalm 147 *Introduction.* In its present location in the Scripture canon Psalm 147 is part of the great doxology that concludes the Psalter (see "Introduction" to Ps 145 and "Introduction" to Ps 146). It praises the Lord for rebuilding Jerusalem (vv. 2,13) and was probably composed during the period of restoration (cf. Ne 12:27–47). As in Psalm 146 God's power and might (vv. 7–9,16–18) are radically contrasted with human might (vv. 10–11). Though the Septuagint (Greek translation of the OT) divided this psalm into two parts (vv. 1–11 and vv. 12–20), its unity is apparent.
147:1 Praise the LORD. See note on 146:1. **How good.** Not simply a pronouncement of truth, but an exhortation to the congregation to praise the Lord.
147:2 gathers the exiles. See "Introduction" to Psalm 147. Likely referred to the return of Judahites to the promised land after Cyrus's decree (2Ch 36:22–23).
147:4 the number of the stars. From a human perspective, the number of stars seems infinite (cf. the force of the metaphor in Ge 15:5).
147:5 his understanding has no limit. God is so far beyond human intelligence as to be unfathomable to his finite image-bearers. See *WCF* 2.2; *WLC* 7; *WSC* 4.
147:6 the humble . . . the wicked. Two classes of people: God favors those confident in him but judges those confident in themselves.
147:8–9 clouds . . . rain . . . grass . . . food. God administers all the processes that provide food for his creatures.
147:10 the legs of a man. Goes does not judge people on the basis of physical appearance or fitness but on the degree of their fear of and hope in him (v. 11; 1Sa 16:10).
147:11 who fear him. See 34:7 and 36:1. **unfailing love.** God's special covenant love.
147:12 Zion. See note on 2:6.
147:13 the bars of your gates. See the "Introduction" to Psalm

14 He grants peace[d] to your borders
and satisfies you[e] with the finest of wheat.

15 He sends his command[f] to the earth;
his word runs swiftly.
16 He spreads the snow[g] like wool
and scatters the frost[h] like ashes.
17 He hurls down his hail like pebbles.
Who can withstand his icy blast?
18 He sends his word[i] and melts them;
he stirs up his breezes, and the waters flow.

19 He has revealed his word to Jacob,
his laws and decrees[j] to Israel.
20 He has done this for no other nation;[k]
they do not know his laws.

Praise the LORD.

Psalm 148

1 Praise the LORD.[a]

Praise the LORD from the heavens,
praise him in the heights above.
2 Praise him, all his angels,[l]
praise him, all his heavenly hosts.
3 Praise him, sun and moon,
praise him, all you shining stars.
4 Praise him, you highest heavens
and you waters above the skies.[m]
5 Let them praise the name of the LORD,
for he commanded[n] and they were created.
6 He set them in place for ever and ever;
he gave a decree[o] that will never pass away.

7 Praise the LORD from the earth,
you great sea creatures[p] and all ocean depths,
8 lightning and hail, snow and clouds,
stormy winds that do his bidding,[q]
9 you mountains and all hills,[r]
fruit trees and all cedars,
10 wild animals and all cattle,
small creatures and flying birds,
11 kings of the earth and all nations,
you princes and all rulers on earth,
12 young men and maidens,
old men and children.

147:14 [d]Isa 60:17-18 [e]Ps 132:15
147:15 [f]Job 37:12
147:16 [g]Job 37:6 [h]Job 38:29
147:18 [i]Ps 33:9
147:19 [j]Dt 33:4; Mal 4:4
147:20 [k]Dt 4:7-8,32-34
148:2 [l]Ps 103:20
148:4 [m]Ge 1:7; 1Ki 8:27
148:5 [n]Ge 1:1,6; Ps 33:6,9
148:6 [o]Job 38:33; Ps 89:37; Jer 33:25
148:7 [p]Ps 74:13-14
148:8 [q]Ps 147:15-18
148:9 [r]Isa 44:23; 49:13; 55:12

[a] *1* Hebrew *Hallelu Yah*; also in verse 14

147 concerning the opinion that it was composed during the period of restoration. The gate bars represent the security of the city. (Note what happens when they are weak, in Na 3:13.) God provides security, in this case using human means.
147:14 the finest of wheat. A symbol of fertility and provision.
147:15 his word runs swiftly. It accomplishes its purpose quickly.
147:19–20 See *WLC* 63,190; *CD* 3–4.V.
147:19 revealed . . . his laws and decrees. By so doing, he guided Israel's corporate behavior.
147:20 Praise the LORD. See 146:1.
Psalm 148 *Introduction.* Psalm 148 continues and heightens the call to praise that concludes the Psalter (see "Introduction" to Ps 145 and "Introduction" to Ps 146). Indeed, in this psalm the summons to praise takes precedence over the reasons for praise. The initial exhortation is directed toward the heavenly creatures (vv. 1–6), the second to the earth (vv. 7–12) and the closing to the chosen people (vv. 13–14).
148:1 Praise the LORD. See note on 146:1. The psalm begins and ends with this phrase (see v. 14). **the heavens.** The heavens were visualized as including different levels, though this paradigm was never spelled out in detail in the Bible (cf. 2Co 12:2). The fact that the highest heavens cannot contain God (1 Ki 8:27) and must praise him emphasizes God's transcendence. The theme of God's praise in the heavens is expanded upon in the following verses.
148:4 waters above the skies. See Genesis 1:7.
148:7 from the earth. God's praise from the earth is elaborated in the following verses as different aspects of the earthly realm are exhorted to praise God. **sea creatures.** The sea was a source of special fascination and fear for the Israelites. Typically the sea represented everything opposed to God and his creation order (see 18:4; 29:3,10; 46:2,4). In this verse, though, God's greatness is demonstrated by the fact that he requires praise from the sea and its creatures.
148:11 all rulers on earth. The universal praise due to the Lord even from the Gentiles. It was not until Jesus Christ came that such praise started to take place on a broad scale, and it will not be declared to its full potential until Jesus returns (see theological article "The Kingdom of God" at Mt 4).

148:13 [s]Isa 12:4 [t]Ps 8:1; 113:4
148:14 [u]Ps 75:10

13 Let them praise the name of the LORD,[s]
for his name alone is exalted;
his splendor is above the earth and the heavens.[t]
14 He has raised up for his people a horn,[a u]
the praise of all his saints,
of Israel, the people close to his heart.

Praise the LORD.

Psalm 149

149:1 [v]Ps 33:2 [w]Ps 35:18
149:2 [x]Ps 95:6 [y]Ps 47:6; Zec 9:9
149:3 [z]Ps 81:2; 150:4
149:4 [a]Ps 35:27 [b]Ps 132:16
149:5 [c]Ps 132:16 [d]Job 35:10
149:6 [e]Ps 66:17 [f]Heb 4:12; Rev 1:16
149:9 [g]Dt 7:1; Eze 28:26 [h]Ps 148:14

1 Praise the LORD.[b v]

Sing to the LORD a new song,
his praise in the assembly[w] of the saints.
2 Let Israel rejoice in their Maker;[x]
let the people of Zion be glad in their King.[y]
3 Let them praise his name with dancing
and make music to him with tambourine and harp.[z]
4 For the LORD takes delight[a] in his people;
he crowns the humble with salvation.[b]
5 Let the saints rejoice[c] in this honor
and sing for joy on their beds.[d]

6 May the praise of God be in their mouths[e]
and a double-edged[f] sword in their hands,
7 to inflict vengeance on the nations
and punishment on the peoples,
8 to bind their kings with fetters,
their nobles with shackles of iron,
9 to carry out the sentence written against them.[g]
This is the glory of all his saints.[h]

Praise the LORD.

Psalm 150

150:1 [i]Ps 102:19 [j]Ps 19:1
150:2 [k]Dt 3:24 [l]Ps 145:5-6
150:3 [m]Ps 149:3
150:4 [n]Ex 15:20

1 Praise the LORD.[c]

Praise God in his sanctuary;[i]
praise him in his mighty heavens.[j]
2 Praise him for his acts of power;[k]
praise him for his surpassing greatness.[l]
3 Praise him with the sounding of the trumpet,
praise him with the harp and lyre,[m]
4 praise him with tambourine and dancing,[n]

a *14* *Horn* here symbolizes strong one, that is, king. b *1* Hebrew *Hallelu Yah*; also in verse 9
c *1* Hebrew *Hallelu Yah*; also in verse 6

148:13 the name of the LORD. See 8:1.
148:14 a horn. The image comes from that of a powerful beast, symbolizing strength and vigor. It could refer either to the nation or to the king. **the people close to his heart.** See Deuteronomy 7:7–12. **Praise the LORD.** See 146:1.
Psalm 149 *Introduction.* Psalm 149 continues the doxology begun in Psalm 145. It begins and ends with *Hallelujah*, as do all the psalms from 146 through 150. The focus of praise is God as King and Warrior. The reference to a "new song" (see v. 1) and the warfare language of verses 6–9 suggest that the song was sung in celebration of a victory in battle. While the psalm's martial tone seems removed from much modern Christian experience, the church is engaged in strenuous warfare with the realm of Satan (Eph 6:10–20) and anticipates the ultimate struggle at the return of Christ (Rev 19:11–21).
149:1 Praise the LORD. See note on 146:1. The psalm beings and ends with this phrase (see v. 9). **new song.** See note on 33:3.
149:2 their Maker . . . their King. God created Israel as a holy, sovereign nation at the time of the exodus, and at Sinai he ruled over his people. These were ample reasons for joyous worship. **people of Zion.** See note on 2:6.
149:3 with dancing . . . with tambourine and harp. The psalmist called upon Israel to celebrate the Lord actively, enthusiastically and joyfully.
149:5 on their beds. The people were to worship God at all times—both in private and in public.
149:7 to inflict vengeance on the nations. God used his people to judge the nations. One of the most notable examples from Biblical history is the judgment inflicted on the Canaanites at the time of Joshua.
149:9 Praise the LORD. See 146:1.
Psalm 150 *Introduction.* The climactic song of the Psalter, Psalm 150, also concludes the final series of praise songs (146–150; see "Introduction" to Ps 146). It is composed of a series of exhortations to worship God.
150:1 Praise the LORD. See 146:1. The psalm beings and ends with this phrase (see v. 6). **in his sanctuary . . . in his mighty heavens.** Locations toward which worship was to be directed.
150:2 for his acts of power . . . for his surpassing greatness. God's character and power as demonstrated in such events as miracles and military victories should motivate his people to thankful praise.

praise him with the strings[o] and flute,
5 praise him with the clash of cymbals,[p]
praise him with resounding cymbals.

6 Let everything[q] that has breath praise the Lord.

Praise the Lord.

150:4 [o]Isa 38:20
150:5 [p]1Ch 13:8; 15:16
150:6 [q]Ps 145:21

150:3–5 trumpet . . . harp and lyre . . . tambourine and dancing . . . strings and flute . . . cymbals. The psalmist encouraged the use of musical instrumentation and dancing in worship.
150:6 Praise the Lord. See 146:1.

PROVERBS

Introduction

Overview

Author: Various, including Solomon, Hezekiah, Agur, Lemuel and others

Purpose: To provide a resource for teaching wisdom to young people, primarily for the royal family and secondarily for all other families in Israel

Date: 960–686 B.C.

Key Truths:

- God is the source of all wisdom, and he has revealed wisdom for humans to learn.
- Human wisdom can be gained only in the context of reverence for God.
- Young people need instruction from older and wiser fathers and mothers.
- The leaders of God's people especially must be schooled in the ways of wisdom.

Author

Several authors are mentioned in the book of Proverbs: Solomon (1:1; 10:1; 25:1), Hezekiah (25:1), Agur (30:1) and Lemuel (31:1). Some interpreters, however, have argued that the sections attributed to Solomon were actually written by others under his name. Yet the case for accepting the Solomonic authorship of Proverbs 1–24 is strong in at least five ways.

(1) In addition to the claims of the book, the Scriptures testify that Solomon wrote many proverbs (1Ki 4:29–34). Further, Old Testament references to Solomon's unsurpassed wisdom are numerous (1Ki 3:5–14; 4:29–34; 5:7,12; 10:1–9,23–24; 11:41; 2Ch 1:7–12; 9:1–8,22–23), and writing and compiling various proverbs is entirely consistent with that characterization.

(2) Proverbs is strikingly similar in structure and content to comparable Wisdom Literature from Egypt, Mesopotamia and the Levant that dates from before the time of Solomon. For example, Egyptian wisdom instruction exists in two types. One type includes a title and maxims (cf. 24:23–35); the other includes a long title (1:1), preamble/prologue (1:2—9:18), short title (10:1) and maxims (10:2—22:16). These similarities suggest a date for Proverbs during Israel's monarchy. The greatest similarities in form and content exist between Proverbs 22:16—24:22 and the Egyptian "Wisdom of Amenemope," which is roughly contemporary with the time of Solomon.

(3) It is reasonable to assume that the literature of various nations was known in Israel during the time of Solomon's extensive international trade. Egyptian archives (c. 1350 B.C.) contain cuneiform literary texts from Babylon that scribes used when preparing for foreign diplomatic service. We may assume that foreign literary works also reached Israel for similar reasons. It would have been fitting for the brilliant Solomon to familiarize himself with Egyptian instruction in this way.

(4) The attributions to Solomon (1:1; 10:1; 25:1)—as well as to King Hezekiah (25:1) and to King Lemuel (31:1)—are entirely consistent with the practices of royalty in the ancient Near East, where kings sponsored wisdom and wisdom supported kings. Many proverbs speak not only *about* kings and courtiers but also *to* and *for* them. In sum, Wisdom Literature of the sort found in Proverbs was typically at home in the royal court. No better candidate than Solomon fits this setting.

(5) Stylistic features also favor acceptance of Solomon as the author of chapters 1–24 and of the proverbs in chapters 25–29. Binary (two-line) parallelism is clearly attested both in Wisdom Literature and in other genres from the third millennium B.C. to well into the first millennium B.C. After 500 B.C., the popularity of binary parallelism began to wane in wisdom texts, both in Egyptian and in Aramaic literature.

Time and Place of Writing

King Solomon (see "Introduction: Author") began to reign in approximately 970 B.C., earlier if he held a coregency with David (see note on 1Ki 2:11). Assuming that Solomon reigned some years before the Lord granted him wisdom (cf. 1Ki 2–3), and allowing at least some time for his study and compilation of his proverbs, an early date for the portions of the book attributed to Solomon can be set at around 960 B.C. Hezekiah, in turn, reigned until 687/86 B.C., setting the latest date for the portions of the book compiled under his rule. Lemuel is otherwise unknown (see note on 31:1), so reference to him does not help establish the date of composition.

The setting of the royal court for the writing of Proverbs should be distinguished from the settings of its dissemination. Unlike some other ancient Near Eastern wisdom literature, Proverbs names no explicit addressee or class in its title. Presumably, the author intended for the book to be used by everyone, anticipating that its maxims would be taught in godly homes. Solomon intended to transmit his wisdom to Israel's youths by putting his proverbs into the mouths of godly parents (1:8), even as Moses had advocated dissemination of the law in the home (Dt 6:7–9). The references to the father and his son(s) in the book's prologue are best taken literally. Egyptian wisdom books are addressed to the author's sons, never to unrelated students. References to the mother as a teacher of both the Mosaic Law (cf. Dt 6:7–9) and Solomon's proverbs also establish a home setting (see Ex 20:12; Lev 19:3; Dt 5:16; 6:6–9; 21:18–21; Pr 4:3; 6:20; 10:1; 15:20; 23:22,24–25; 29:15; 31:1,26–28; Lk 2:51; 2Ti 1:5; 3:14). The use of Proverbs in home education finds further corroboration in 4:1–9, where the godly family—including grandfather, father, mother and son—is figuratively represented as transmitting the family's spiritual inheritance.

Purpose and Distinctives

Whereas the historical books trace the development of the kingdom of God through covenants with Israel, Biblical Wisdom Literature never explicitly mentions Israel's election or covenants and contains little acknowledgment of the historical details of Israel's faith. Nevertheless, it can be easily integrated with Israel's historical faith by their common appeal to the "fear of the LORD" (cf. Dt 6:5; Jos 24:14; Pr 1:7). "The LORD" is God's name that expresses his personal commitment to Israel (Ge 12:8; Ex 3:15; 6:2–8). To "fear" him means to submit to his revealed will, whether voiced by Moses or Solomon, because one trusts him to keep his promises of life for the faithful and his threats of death for the unfaithful. Moses, Solomon and the prophets each sought to establish God's rule. Although the theology of Proverbs complements the unified historical orientation of other parts of the Old Testament, Proverbs focuses more on everyday life than on history, more on the usual than on the unique, more on the individual (although not outside the context of social relationships) than on the nation, more on personal experience than on sacred tradition.

Unfortunately, Proverbs is often misunderstood to promise success, health, happiness and wealth to those who follow its teaching (see 3:1–10 and "Introduction to the Poetic and Wisdom Books: Old Testament Wisdom"). While it does describe prosperity as a blessing of wisdom, many of the benefits mentioned are little more than observations of the normal course of events. The sober person rather than the drunkard (see 23:29–35), the cool-tempered individual rather than the hotheaded one (15:18; 19:19; 22:24; 29:22) and the diligent rather than the indolent typically experience health and wealth.

Second, various proverbs qualify each other. Although many proverbs speak of positive benefits for the righteous and judgment for the wicked, many others assert or imply that the wicked prosper while the innocent suffer. For example, Proverbs 10:2 teaches that the wicked person has treasures gained by wickedness (i.e., at the expense of the righteous), but the very next proverb (10:3) states that the wicked person's craving will be frustrated.

Taken in their entirety, the proverbs teach that the wicked prosper for a season (10:2a) but that in the end their riches will not deliver them from death (10:2b). In contrast, the righteous, who at present are afflicted by the wicked, will finally be delivered from death (10:2b) and be fully satisfied (10:3a). Similarly, the several "better than" proverbs (e.g., "Better a little with righteousness than much gain with injustice"; 16:8) assume the reality that for the moment the wicked, rather than the righteous, enjoy material blessings (cf. 16:19; 17:1; 19:1,22; 21:9,19; 22:1; 25:24; 28:6; Ps 37:16; Ecc 4:6). To understand what a single proverb means or how it is true, one must read it within the context of the whole book, not in isolation.

Third, as a primer on morality to encourage young people to righteous living, Proverbs appropriately focuses on the rise of the righteous rather than on the difficulties the righteous face. For instance, the maxim "Though a righteous man falls seven times, he rises again, but the wicked are brought down by calamity" (24:16) downplays the harsh reality that the righteous may at times be destroyed in favor of the more positive hope that they will rise. By contrast, Job and Ecclesiastes focus on the sufferings of the righteous before they rise in the end.

Fourth, some texts explicitly teach that the righteous enjoy a blessed future that outlasts death (cf. 12:28; 14:32; 23:17). The "tree of life" in Proverbs figuratively represents perpetual healing that ensures eternal life (3:18; 11:30; 13:12; 15:4; cf. Ge 2:9; 3:24). The book's concept of justice demands such a hope. The opening situation depicted in the father's first lecture resembles the first recorded situation of fallen humanity outside of the Garden of Eden. Even as Cain murdered the righteous Abel, sending him to a premature death in contrast to his own natural life span, so a traveler's innocent "blood" (1:11) is dispatched to a premature death by venal sinners (1:10–19). For justice to be accomplished, as Proverbs assures the reader it will be (e.g., 3:31–35; 16:4–5), it must be executed in some realm beyond present human experience.

Christ in Proverbs

Proverbs, like the Law of Moses, bears witness to Christ by portraying his person and work. In the law we see the righteous and holy person and the work of that son of Abraham who would inherit God's covenant blessings and mediate them to all nations. In Proverbs (and in the Wisdom Literature as a whole) we see the discernment and work of the wise disciple. Only the Lord Jesus completely fulfills this vision. Proverbs, in conjunction with all the Wisdom Literature, also reveals that likeness into which all true Israel will be conformed by grace through faith: the likeness of Jesus, the Wisdom of God incarnate (1Co 1:24,30; Col 2:2–3).

Outline

The lessons of the father to his son provide many insights into wisdom that are founded on reverence for God.

- I. A Father's Wisdom (1:1—9:18)
  - A. Prologue: The Purpose of Studying Proverbs (1:1–7)
  - B. The Father's Lessons (1:8—9:18)
    1. Lesson One: Rival Invitations (1:8–19)
       - a. Introduction (1:8–9)
       - b. Sinners' Invitation (1:10–19)
    2. First Interlude: Wisdom's Rebuke of the Gullible (1:20–33)
       - a. Introduction (1:20–21)
       - b. Rebuke (1:22–27)
       - c. Future Outcomes (1:28–33)
    3. Lesson Two: The Moral Benefits of Wisdom (2:1–22)
       - a. The Son's Development (2:1–11)
       - b. The Son's Deliverance (2:12–22)
    4. Lesson Three: The Material Benefits of Wisdom (3:1–12)
       - a. Introduction (3:1–2)
       - b. Call to Piety and Blessings (3:3–10)
       - c. Conclusion (3:11–12)
    5. Lesson Four: The Value of Wisdom (3:13–35)
       - a. Exhortation to Seek Wisdom for Its Value (3:13–26)
       - b. A Neighbor Needing Help (3:27–35)
    6. Lesson Five: Get Wisdom (4:1–9)
       - a. Introduction (4:1–2)
       - b. The Grandfather's Lesson (4:3–9)
    7. Lesson Six: Stay Off the Wrong Way (4:10–19)
       - a. The Way of Wisdom (4:10–13)
       - b. The Way of the Wicked (4:14–17)
       - c. Summation (4:18–19)
    8. Lesson Seven: Don't Turn Off the Right Way (4:20–27)
       - a. Introduction (4:20–22)
       - b. Devotion to the Right Path (4:23–27)
    9. Lesson Eight: The Folly of Adultery and the Wisdom of Marriage (5:1–23)
       - a. Introduction (5:1–6)
       - b. Sexual Folly and Wisdom (5:7–20)
       - c. Conclusion (5:21–23)
    10. Lesson Nine: Three Inferior Types of People (6:1–19)
        - a. One Responsible for Another's Debt (6:1–5)
        - b. The Sluggard (6:6–11)
        - c. The Troublemaker (6:12–19)
    11. Lesson Ten: The High Price of an Adulteress (6:20–35)
        - a. Introduction (6:20–24)
        - b. Paying for the Adulteress (6:25–35)
    12. Lesson Eleven: The Seductive Tactics of the Adulteress (7:1–27)
        - a. Introduction (7:1–5)
        - b. Seduction by an Adulteress (7:6–23)
        - c. Conclusion (7:24–27)
    13. Second Interlude: Wisdom's Self-Praise to the Gullible (8:1–36)
        - a. Introduction (8:1–11)

b. Wisdom in Historical and Primordial Times (8:12–31)
c. Final Invitation and Warning (8:32–36)
14. Lesson Twelve: The Rival Banquets of Wisdom and Folly (9:1–18)
a. Woman Wisdom (9:1–6)
b. The Father's Instructions (9:7–12)
c. Woman Folly (9:13–18)

II. Proverbs of Solomon (10:1—22:16)

Solomon's proverbs describe many dimensions of the connection between righteousness and wisdom. They also provide insight into the relationship between wisdom and divine and human rule.

A. Righteousness and Wisdom (10:1—15:29)
1. Wealth (10:1–5)
2. Effects of Speech (10:6–14)
3. Wealth and Security (10:15–16)
4. Deeds and Destinies (10:17—11:31)
a. Introduction (10:17)
b. Speech and Expectations (10:18–32)
c. Security Through Honesty and Righteousness (11:1–8)
d. Words in Community (11:9–15)
e. Benevolence and Community (11:16–22)
f. Desires and Paradoxical Fulfillment (11:23–27)
g. Certain Gain or Loss (11:28–31)
5. Speech and Deeds (12:1–28)
a. One Look at Speech and Deeds (12:1–14)
(1) Introduction (12:1–3)
(2) Two Kinds of Speech (12:4–7)
(3) Two Kinds of Deeds (12:8–12)
(4) Conclusion (12:13–14)
b. Another Look at Speech and Deeds (12:15–28)
(1) Introduction (12:15–16)
(2) Two Kinds of Speech (12:17–23)
(3) Two Kinds of Deeds (12:24–27)
(4) Conclusion (12:28)
6. Good Teaching and Ethical Living (13:1–25)
a. Introduction (13:1)
b. Speech (13:2–6)
c. Wealth and Ethics (13:7–11)
d. Longings Satisfied (13:12–19)
e. Eternal Destinies (13:20–25)
7. Living in Wisdom (14:1–32)
a. Walking in Wisdom (14:1–7)
b. Not Living by Appearances (14:8–15)
c. Contrasting Behaviors and Consequences (14:16–32)
8. Upholding Righteousness With a Gentle Tongue (14:33—15:4)
9. The Importance of Instruction (15:5–19)
a. The Consequences of Accepting or Rejecting Instruction (15:5–12)
b. The Triumph of the Heart Over Circumstances (15:13–19)
10. The Consequences of Righteousness and Wickedness (15:20–29)
B. Wisdom and Ruling (15:30—22:16)
1. The Relationship Between the People, the Lord and the King (15:30—16:15)
a. Introduction (15:30–33)

- b. The Lord's Rule (16:1–9)
- c. The King's Rule (16:10–15)
2. Wise and Foolish Speech (16:16–30)
   - a. Introduction (16:16–19)
   - b. Winsome Speech (16:20–24)
   - c. Destructive Speech (16:25–30)
3. Old Age Through Righteousness (16:31—17:6)
4. Fools (17:7–28)
5. Foolish and Wise Speech (18:1–21)
   - a. Speech of Fools (18:1–11)
   - b. Speech of the Wise (18:12–21)
6. Wealth and Wisdom in the Court and in the Home (18:22—19:22)
   - a. Wealth and Friends (18:22—19:7)
     - (1) Rich, Poor and Friends (18:22–24)
     - (2) Wealth and Ethics (19:1–3)
     - (3) Wealth and Friends in Court (19:4–7)
   - b. Wisdom, Wealth and Friends in Court and at Home (19:8–15)
   - c. Wisdom and Instruction (19:16–22)
7. Kings and Fools (19:23—20:11)
   - a. Catalog of Fools (19:23—20:1)
   - b. Cleansing the Realm of Fools (20:2–11)
8. Speech and Commerce (20:12–19)
9. Trusting the Lord (20:20–28)
10. Doing Righteousness and Justice (20:29—21:31)
    - a. Introduction (20:29—21:2)
    - b. The Righteous Over the Wicked (21:3–29)
      - (1) Introduction (21:3)
      - (2) Defeat for the Wicked (21:4–8)
      - (3) The Righteous Triumph Over the Wicked (21:9–18)
      - (4) Endurance and Death (21:19–29)
    - c. Conclusion (21:30–31)
11. Wealth and Moral Instruction (22:1–16)
    - a. The Lord's Sovereignty Over Wealth (22:1–9)
    - b. Moral Instruction About Wealth (22:10–16)

III. Anonymous Sayings (22:17—24:34)

Anonymous proverbs teach wisdom on a variety of issues.

- A. Thirty Sayings of the Wise (22:17—24:22)
  1. Prologue (22:17–21)
  2. A Decalogue of Sayings (22:22—23:11)
  3. An Obedient Son (23:12—24:2)
  4. Wisdom, Strategy and Strength (24:3–12)
  5. Prohibitions Against Involvement With the Wicked (24:13–22)
- B. Further Sayings of the Wise (24:23–34)

IV. Hezekiah's Collection of Solomon's Proverbs (25:1—29:27)

Hezekiah's collection of Solomon's proverbs gives wisdom, especially for living in the royal court.

- A. God and the King, the Righteous and Wicked (25:1–27)
  1. Title (25:1)
  2. God and the King (25:2–3)
  3. The Righteous and Wicked (25:4–5)

4. Etiquette in the Royal Court (25:6–15) 5. Conflict Outside and Inside the Court (25:16–27) B. Seven Moral Inferiors (25:28—26:28) C. Friends and Friendship (27:1–22) D. Sustaining Blessings for the Future (27:23–27) E. God and Kings, Instruction and Righteousness (28:1—29:27)	
V. Oracle of Agur (30:1–33)	*The proverbs of Agur focus on greed, pride and the moral order.*
VI. The Sayings of Lemuel (31:1–31) A. Superscription (31:1) B. The Noble King (31:2–9) C. The Noble Wife (31:10–31)	*The proverbs of Lemuel provide guidance in the areas of nobility and marriage.*

Prologue: Purpose and Theme

1 The proverbs of Solomon[a] son of David, king of Israel:[b]

2 for attaining wisdom and discipline;
for understanding words of insight;
3 for acquiring a disciplined and prudent life,
doing what is right and just and fair;
4 for giving prudence to the simple,[c]
knowledge and discretion[d] to the young—
5 let the wise listen and add to their learning,[e]

1:1 [a]1Ki 4:29-34 [b]Pr 10:1; 25:1; Ecc 1:1
1:4 [c]Pr 8:5 [d]Pr 2:10-11; 8:12
1:5 [e]Pr 9:9

■ **1:1—9:18** *A Father's Wisdom.* This first section comes from Solomon and sets forth the central message of the entire book. It divides into two main parts: the reasons for studying the proverbs (vv. 1–7) and a father's call to his son to embrace wisdom and reject folly (1:8—9:18).
■ **1:1–7** *Prologue: The Purpose of Studying Proverbs.* The wisdom in this book will benefit those who meditate on it. The explicit reference to this collection's purpose (vv. 2–6) suggests that it was intended to be used in formal education (see "Introduction: Time and Place of Writing").
1:1 proverbs. Comparisons or analogies modeling general truth and directed to a select group—in this case, those who fear the Lord (see v. 7). Wisdom restricts the acceptance of her words "to the discerning," "to those who have knowledge" (8:9). A proverb calls for readers to exercise imagination in the fear of God to forge some sort of connection between what is said and their own unique situations. **Solomon.** See "Introduction: Author."
1:2 wisdom. "Wisdom" generally means "masterful understanding," "skill" or "expertise." In Biblical texts outside of Proverbs, the term is used of technical and artistic skills (Ex 28:3; 31:6), of the arts of magic (Ex 7:11; Isa 3:3), of government (Ecc 4:13; Jer 50:35), of diplomacy (1Ki 5:7) and of war (Isa 10:13). Some have the wisdom (or skill) to judge (1Ki 3:28; Isa 11:1–6) and to separate the guilty from the community and so to rule a nation (20:26). Wisdom also endows rulers with the ability to handle situations masterfully (2Sa 14:20; Job 39:17). Solomon's wisdom also included botanical and biological knowledge (1Ki 4:33). The possession of wisdom enables a person to cope with adversity and so to promote the life of the individual and community (21:22; cf. 24:5; Ecc 7:19; 9:13–16). **discipline.** That is, "instruction," a necessary means to wisdom. The disciple must humbly submit (15:33) to an authority (e.g., his father or mother) in order to quell his innate waywardness (cf. 22:15). Character shaping instruction is acquired primarily through verbal lessons, but also through reflection on human experience and nature (19:25; 24:32; cf. Dt 11:2; Eze 5:15). The disciple must listen to instruction (v. 8), accept it (v. 3; 19:20; 23:23), love it (12:1), prize it more highly than money (4:7; 23:23) and refuse to let go of it (4:13). **words.** The plural refers to the adages themselves, not to the individual words that make up a saying. Both the eye (cf. 3:21) and the ear (cf. 1:8) were involved in perceiving proverbs, which were both written and read aloud. **insight.** The faculty of intellectual discernment and interpretation. The term also refers to reason and intelligence applied to the content of Solomon's teaching (e.g., v. 2; 3:5).
1:3 prudent life. "Prudent" denotes wise behavior and good sense (cf. 10:5,19; 14:35; 15:24; 17:2; 19:14; 21:16) and designates the ability to make beneficial decisions in a variety of situations. David's "success" (from the same Hebrew root) against the Philistines is a textbook example of this virtue (see 1Sa 18:5,14–15,30). **right.** Or "righteousness." The metaphor "I put on righteousness as my clothing" (Job 29:14) reflects that "righteousness" is a pattern of life, not merely a set of specific acts. **Just.** That which is just ("justice") occurs when the righteous order is restored after having been disturbed. The Hebrew root may also refer to an obligation (see Ex 26:30; Jdg 13:2; Job 32:9).
1:4 prudence. That is, "cunning," "shrewdness," the talent for devising and using adroit tactics to attain one's goals. Cunning must be used to meet legitimate moral requirements (see v. 3; 8:12). **simple.** That is, "gullible." The related Hebrew verb denotes being easily taken in, seduced or tempted (e.g., "entice" in v. 10). Although intellectually flawed, gullible people are the most innocuous of the negative characters in this book because they possess the potential to improve (v. 4; 8:5; 19:25; 21:11), retaining hope of joining the company of the wise (cf. v. 22; 9:4). Wisdom and Folly compete for their allegiance (ch. 9) because they are capable of being either led (9:1–6) or misled (9:13–18). **discretion.** Often refers to thoughts that pertain to planning. Such thoughts may be hostile and full of intrigue (24:8) and so condemned by God (12:2) and the community (14:17), or, as here, informed by the sage (v. 4; 2:11; 3:21; 5:2) and so inseparable from wisdom (8:12). This power protects from temptations. **young.** The Hebrew term may be applied to an infant (Ex 2:6; 1Sa 1:22,24; 4:21), a 17-year-old youth (Ge 37:2) or even a 30-year-old man (Ge 41:12; cf. 41:46). Presumably the description applied to any age prior to the time one was reckoned an elder (see 17:6; 20:29). The distinction pertains as well to inexperience versus experience (cf. 2Sa 14:21; 18:5; Jer 1:6). A youth was held fully accountable when 20 years old (cf. Nu 1:3,18; 14:29; 26:2,4). The "youth" addressed in Proverbs was on the threshold of maturity, and an intentional decision to join the wise was imperative in order for him to obtain the sage's knowledge.
1:5 wise. The wise one is the second addressee of the book. Solomon subtly placed his son among the wise rather than the gullible by combining "Let the wise listen" (v. 5) with "Listen, my son" (v. 8). The heart of a wise person loves the Lord, the sage and his teaching (see 15:30–33). Instead of being self-assured (26:5,11–12,16) the wise person is teachable, seeking the knowledge needed by the "simple" (see 18:15) and storing it up (10:14). The wise listen to in-

and let the discerning get guidance—
6 for understanding proverbs and parables,[f]
the sayings and riddles[g] of the wise.

7 The fear of the LORD[h] is the beginning of knowledge,
but fools[a] despise wisdom and discipline.

Exhortations to Embrace Wisdom

Warning Against Enticement

8 Listen, my son,[i] to your father's instruction
and do not forsake your mother's teaching.[j]
9 They will be a garland to grace your head
and a chain to adorn your neck.[k]

10 My son, if sinners entice[l] you,
do not give in[m] to them.[n]
11 If they say, "Come along with us;
let's lie in wait[o] for someone's blood,
let's waylay some harmless soul;
12 let's swallow them alive, like the grave,[b]
and whole, like those who go down to the pit;[p]
13 we will get all sorts of valuable things
and fill our houses with plunder;
14 throw in your lot with us,
and we will share a common purse"—
15 my son, do not go along with them,
do not set foot[q] on their paths;[r]
16 for their feet rush into sin,
they are swift to shed blood.[s]
17 How useless to spread a net
in full view of all the birds!
18 These men lie in wait for their own blood;
they waylay only themselves!
19 Such is the end of all who go after ill-gotten gain;
it takes away the lives of those who get it.[t]

1:6 [f]Ps 49:4; 78:2 [g]Nu 12:8
1:7 [h]Job 28:28; Ps 111:10; Pr 9:10; 15:33; Ecc 12:13
1:8 [i]Pr 4:1 [j]Pr 6:20
1:9 [k]Pr 4:1-9
1:10 [l]Ge 39:7 [m]Dt 13:8 [n]Pr 16:29; Eph 5:11
1:11 [o]Ps 10:8
1:12 [p]Ps 28:1
1:15 [q]Ps 119:101 [r]Ps 1:1; Pr 4:14
1:16 [s]Pr 6:18; Isa 59:7
1:19 [t]Pr 15:27

[a] 7 The Hebrew words rendered *fool* in Proverbs, and often elsewhere in the Old Testament, denote one who is morally deficient. [b] *12* Hebrew *Sheol*

struction (13:1) and counsel (12:5), accept commands (10:8) and even love reproof (9:8). A wise person walks with the wise (13:20) and is continuously increasing in wisdom (v. 5; 29:9; cf. 4:18). Such a person has control over his or her emotions (29:11) and rules over fools (11:29). Wise individuals bring joy to their parents (15:20; 23:24) and healing to others (12:18). The wise spread knowledge (15:7) and become fountains of life for those around them (13:14). All of these characteristics flow from fearing the Lord and departing from evil (3:7) because all wisdom comes from God (2:6; cf. Job 9:4; Isa 31:2). The wise person needs no instruction (Isa 40:12–14). Wisdom issues forth from his or her own being (8:22–31); only the wise know wisdom's place and the way to it (30:2–5; Job 28:23). **discerning.** Or "insightful." Wisdom provides the intellectual ability to distinguish between right and wrong, good and bad—to identify and espouse the moral order God ordains and maintains (see v. 2; 9:10). **guidance.** Perhaps a nautical term for ropes used to steer a ship. If so, the word connotes that the book's guidance enables the insightful to lead themselves and others through life much as a well-steered ship navigates a difficult waterway.

1:6 proverbs and parables . . . riddles. The same words are used synonymously in Habakkuk 2:6. Many proverbs are enigmatic in the sense that they must be applied differently in different situations. Thus their intended meaning is not always immediately apparent, and they require careful reflection.

1:7 The fear of the LORD. See "Introduction: Purpose and Distinctives." The fear of God is a wholesome and appropriate reaction to God's supremacy and holiness. **beginning.** Here means the foundation (see also 9:10). The reference is to the first rung of a ladder. A personal commitment of reverence for God is the basis of true knowledge. **fools.** Unlike the simple or the gullible, the fool is a "blockhead." Fools are reprehensibly ignorant, undiscerning and unteachable. Hebrew has two derogatory words normally translated "fool," both of which refer to such people as morally deficient characters who act in irrational ways.

■ **1:8—9:18** *The Father's Lessons.* A series of lessons given by a wise father to his son.

■ **1:8–19** *Lesson One: Rival Invitations.* The father's first lesson immediately sets before his son the fact that two conflicting ways of life vie for his acceptance: his family's tradition of wisdom and the world's devotion to folly. The introduction refers to the son's allegiance to the family's inherited worldview (vv. 8–9), which the lesson clearly reveals as different from that of the people who are seeking to draw him into corruption (vv. 10–19).

■ **1:8–9** *Introduction.* The typical introduction to a lesson consists of an address and an exhortation to listen (v. 8), including a motivation for doing so (v. 9).

1:8 father's . . . mother's. See "Introduction: Time and Place of Writing." See *HC* 104.

1:9 a garland . . . a chain. These metaphors portray the victory of the wise son over his enemies, including death.

■ **1:10–19** *Sinners' Invitation.* The main section of this lesson contains three parts: the introduction, which includes a summary of the invitation and an exhortation (v. 10); the body, which reveals the sinner's temptation (vv. 11–14) and reports the father's warning (vv. 15–18); and the conclusion (v. 19).

1:10–11 See *WLC* 135.

1:12 grave. The Hebrew is *Sheol,* a poetic term for the grave. It symbolizes separation from life on Earth, not a place of torment.

1:15–16 See *WLC* 135.

1:15 my son. The address is repeated to reinforce the command to avoid evil men.

1:17 spread. Setting the trap within sight of the intended victim defeats its purpose.

1:19 The conclusion universalizes the father's scenario regarding

Warning Against Rejecting Wisdom

20 Wisdom calls aloud[u] in the street,
she raises her voice in the public squares;
21 at the head of the noisy streets[a] she cries out,
in the gateways of the city she makes her speech:

22 "How long will you simple ones[b][v] love your simple ways?
How long will mockers delight in mockery
and fools hate knowledge?
23 If you had responded to my rebuke,
I would have poured out my heart to you
and made my thoughts known to you.
24 But since you rejected me when I called[w]
and no one gave heed when I stretched out my hand,
25 since you ignored all my advice
and would not accept my rebuke,
26 I in turn will laugh[x] at your disaster;
I will mock when calamity overtakes you[y]—
27 when calamity overtakes you like a storm,
when disaster sweeps over you like a whirlwind,
when distress and trouble overwhelm you.

28 "Then they will call to me but I will not answer;[z]
they will look for me but will not find me.[a]
29 Since they hated knowledge
and did not choose to fear the LORD,[b]
30 since they would not accept my advice
and spurned my rebuke,[c]
31 they will eat the fruit of their ways
and be filled with the fruit of their schemes.[d]
32 For the waywardness of the simple will kill them,
and the complacency of fools will destroy them;[e]

1:20 [u]Pr 8:1; 9:1-3,13-15
1:22 [v]Pr 8:5; 9:4,16
1:24 [w]Isa 65:12; 66:4; Jer 7:13; Zec 7:11
1:26 [x]Ps 2:4 [y]Pr 6:15; 10.24
1:28 [z]1Sa 8:18; Isa 1:15; Jer 11:11; Mic 3:4 [a]Job 27:9; Pr 8:17; Eze 8:18; Zec 7:13
1:29 [b]Job 21:14
1:30 [c]ver 25; Ps 81:11
1:31 [d]Job 4:8; Pr 14:14; Isa 3:11; Jer 6:19
1:32 [e]Jer 2:19

[a] *21* Hebrew; Septuagint / *on the tops of the walls* [b] *22* The Hebrew word rendered *simple* in Proverbs generally denotes one without moral direction and inclined to evil.

this gang of villains. The father makes an analogous assertion signified by "such." The retribution is based on the conviction that God himself governs the world, not on a belief in an impersonal moral world order (5:21; 10:3,29; cf. Mt 26:52; Gal 6:7). See *WLC* 99.

■ **1:20–33** *First Interlude: Wisdom's Rebuke of the Gullible.* There is a momentary pause in the father's straightforward lecturing (see also 8:1–36) to allow for the compelling address by Wisdom (personified as a woman). Whereas the father's lectures are addressed to the son (singular) in the home, Wisdom's two discourses in 1:20–33 and 8:1–36 are addressed to the gullible (plural) in the gate. Were a proper use of proverbs the normal practice of the masses, Wisdom would not have to stand at the gate of the city pleading for a hearing (vv. 20–21; 8:1–4). Wisdom echoes the same themes taught by the father (cf. 6:23–24 and 7:4; 4:20–22 and 8:32–36; 1:33 and 3:23). In 8:32–36 the line between Wisdom and Solomon becomes so attenuated that one is uncertain of who is speaking in 9:6—and it does not matter. The present material divides into an introduction (vv. 20–21); a rebuke of the unresponsive, gullible youth (vv. 22–27); and reflections on the ensuing outcomes (vv. 28–33).

■ **1:20–21** *Introduction.* Wisdom is presented as calling in the streets. See *WCF* 21.6.

1:20 Wisdom calls aloud. The Hebrew noun for wisdom is feminine, and accordingly Wisdom is personified as a woman, just as "Folly" is elsewhere (9:13). Wisdom, wearing the mantle of a prophet, carrying the scrolls of wise men and wearing a goddesslike diadem, addresses the gullible at the city gate. She rubs shoulders with the masses and invites unresponsive youths to repent at her rebuke before eternal death overtakes them. Elsewhere the woman Wisdom is personified as a guide (6:22), a beloved sister (or bride; 7:4) and a hostess (9:1–6). In these and many other ways, the personification of Wisdom foreshadows Christ, the Wisdom of God.

1:21 gateways. Before the gullible enter the city they must choose Wisdom. The town gate was the public forum for counsel and judgment (Dt 22:15; 25:7; Ru 4:1,11; 2Sa 19:8).

■ **1:22–27** *Rebuke.* The simple ones and mockers were rebuked for rejecting Wisdom's offer of salvation.

1:22 simple ones. The gullible (see v. 4). **mockers.** The most hardened apostates. Mockers are the antithesis of the discerning (14:6; 19:25) and the wise (9:12; 13:1; 20:1; 21:4), whom apostates hate (9:7–8; 15:12). They are lumped together with fools (3:34–35; 14:7–8; 19:29; see note on 1:7), the gullible (see note on v. 4), and the proud and haughty (21:24). Their spiritual problem is rooted in their pride (21:24), which blocks them from Wisdom (14:6). They have a genius for denigrating others that impresses the gullible (19:25; 21:11). They unleash the tensions and strains within a community (22:20; 29:8) and destroy it (21:24; 22:10; 29:8). If order is to be restored mockers must be driven out of the community by force (22:10). God himself ultimately scoffs at them, and they, too, will disappear (Isa 29:20). **fools.** See note on verse 7. **knowledge.** See note on 1:2.

1:23 my heart. That is, "my thoughts." See *WLC* 32.

1:24 See *WCF* 21.6.

1:25 advice. Or "plan," "counsel." The same term is used for Jethro's advice to Moses (Ex 18:19) and for God's immutable plans and purposes (19:21; Ps 33:10ff.; Eph 1:11), which are not open to debate (2:6; 8:14).

1:26 laugh at your disaster. Wisdom expresses the inward joy and disdain that a mighty conqueror feels toward the defeat of his enemies (cf. Pss 2:4; 37:13; 59:8). Her shock tactics aim to persuade the young to turn to her.

■ **1:28–33** *Future Outcomes.* In another attempt to persuade the gullible to repent, Wisdom speaks of the futures of those who listen and of those who do not.

1:28 I will not answer. As with the rejection of the grace of God in salvation, there comes a point of no return for those who continually reject Wisdom. This reinforces the urgency of the message.

1:29 fear the LORD. See note on verse 7.

1:31 fruit. That is, the normal consequences of the act.

1:32 complacency of fools. The ignorant self-satisfaction of those who perceive no need to learn anything from anyone.

33 but whoever listens to me will live in safety[f]
and be at ease, without fear of harm."[g]

Moral Benefits of Wisdom

2 My son, if you accept my words
and store up my commands within you,
2 turning your ear to wisdom
and applying your heart to understanding,[h]
3 and if you call out for insight
and cry aloud for understanding,
4 and if you look for it as for silver
and search for it as for hidden treasure,[i]
5 then you will understand the fear of the LORD
and find the knowledge of God.[j]
6 For the LORD gives wisdom,[k]
and from his mouth come knowledge and understanding.
7 He holds victory in store for the upright,
he is a shield[l] to those whose walk is blameless,[m]
8 for he guards the course of the just
and protects the way of his faithful ones.[n]

9 Then you will understand what is right and just
and fair—every good path.
10 For wisdom will enter your heart,[o]
and knowledge will be pleasant to your soul.
11 Discretion will protect you,
and understanding will guard you.[p]

12 Wisdom will save you from the ways of wicked men,
from men whose words are perverse,
13 who leave the straight paths
to walk in dark ways,[q]
14 who delight in doing wrong
and rejoice in the perverseness of evil,[r]

1:33 [f]Ps 25:12; Pr 3:23 [g]Ps 112:8
2:2 [h]Pr 22:17
2:4 [i]Job 3:21; Pr 3:14; Mt 13:44
2:5 [j]Pr 1:7
2:6 [k]1Ki 3:9,12; Jas 1:5
2:7 [l]Pr 30:5-6 [m]Ps 84:11
2:8 [n]1Sa 2:9; Ps 66:9
2:10 [o]Pr 14:33
2:11 [p]Pr 4:6; 6:22
2:13 [q]Pr 4:19; Jn 3:19
2:14 [r]Pr 10:23; Jer 11:15

■ **2:1–22** *Lesson Two: The Moral Benefits of Wisdom.* This poem is a single sentence consisting of 22 verses, corresponding to the number of letters in the Hebrew alphabet, perhaps to convey completeness. Although it is one lengthy, complex sentence in Hebrew, its parts are clearly indicated as it advances along a single line of thought. It divides into two parts: the development of the son's character (vv. 1–11) and the son's subsequent deliverance (vv. 12–22).
■ **2:1–11** *The Son's Development.* The son is to mature in character. By internalizing his parents' teaching (vv. 1–4) he receives a valuable religious (vv. 5–8) and ethical education (vv. 9–11).
2:1–6 See *WLC* 153,157; *WSC* 85.
2:1 accept. Lays the foundation for all the subsequent conditions (vv. 1–4) and promises (vv. 5–22; cf. Lk 8:15). The condition entails commitment. **store up . . . within you.** That is, "to hide or conceal as a treasure" (see v. 4; 10:14; Job 15:20; 21:19; Ps 119:11; Hos 13:12). The son is to memorize and love his father's teachings. See *WLC* 160.
2:2 heart. "Heart" is the most important anthropological term in the Old Testament (see 4:20–27, especially v. 23), but the English language has no equivalent word that combines the interplay of intellect, sensibility and will that the Hebrew term denotes. In Biblical anthropology the heart controls the body (14:13), including its facial expressions (15:13), the tongue (12:23; 15:28) and all its other members (4:23–27; 6:18). The Scriptures also attribute to the heart control over psychological functions (see 17:3; 24:12) and mention it as the seat of emotional experience (see 12:25; 14:10,30; 15:15; 17:3; 24:12). The heart thinks, reflects and ponders (24:2). When a person lacks insight or judgment the Hebrew attributes the deficit to a lack of heart (10:13). The heart plans (6:14,18; 16:9) and functions as the inner forum where decisions are made. The heart also accepts and trusts in the religious sphere (3:5). Closely related to its pious function is its ethical activity (see 6:25; 15:14; 23:17; 2Sa 24:10). Thus the condition of the heart is all-important. The heart can be wise (14:33) and pure (20:9) or perverse (6:14,18; 12:23; 15:7; 17:16,20; 19:3; 24:2; 26:23–25). This direction or bent of the heart determines its decisions and, in turn, the person's actions (cf. Ex 14:5; 35:21; Nu 32:9; 1Ki 12:27; 18:37). Since the heart is the source of an individual's emotional, intellectual, religious and moral activity, it must be safeguarded above all things (4:23). Paradoxically, although the eyes and ears are gates to the heart (4:21–23), the heart decides what they will hear and see (4:23–26).
2:5 you will understand . . . LORD. Verses 1–4 explain the spiritual processes of attaining the fear of the Lord and of knowing God, the foundation of wisdom.
2:6 the LORD gives wisdom . . . from his mouth. That is, he reveals wisdom and inspires his sages.
2:7 victory. Or "success."
2:8 faithful ones. That is, those who are in covenant with God and practice unfeigned love for him in all circumstances (see 1:17).
2:9 every good path. The vast array of life's choices cannot be comprehensively addressed in the Scriptures. Just as Solomon found that he needed wisdom in addition to the Mosaic Law (1Ki 2:3–4; 3:4–14; 4:29–34), so the son requires wisdom to apply the principles taught in the Scriptures to all areas of life.
2:10 soul. In the Old Testament "soul" refers to the passionate drives and appetites of *all* animate creatures, including their hunger for food and sex (6:30; 10:3; 12:10; 16:26; 19:15; 23:2; 25:25; 27:7; 28:25; see Dt 23:24–25; Ps 78:18; Isa 5:14; Jer 2:24). The human craving for God, however, distinguishes human "soul" from animal "soul" (Pss 42:1–3; 84:2–3; 119:20,81). The Hebrew word may also be translated in a variety of ways, including: "hunger" (6:30), "self" (e.g., "themselves" in 1:18; "yourself" in 22:25) and "life" (1:19; 19:16).
■ **2:12–22** *The Son's Deliverance.* If the son develops wisdom in his life, he will be delivered from "wicked men" (see vv. 12–15) and the "adulteress" (see vv. 16–19); in this way he will experience life, not death (vv. 20–22).
2:12–15 The promised protection is first defined as deliverance from wicked men who have opted for dark and crooked paths instead of the father's well-lit and straight ways (see 1:10–19). These verses are bound together by the repetition of "ways" (vv. 12–13), "paths" (vv. 13,15), "wicked" (v. 12) and "evil" (v. 14) and "perverse" (v. 12) and "perverseness" (v. 14). Verses 12–13 define wicked men, and verses 14–15 elaborate upon their religious affections (v. 14) and depraved ways (v. 15). See *WLC* 151.

15 whose paths are crooked[s]
and who are devious in their ways.[t]

16 It will save you also from the adulteress,[u]
from the wayward wife with her seductive words,
17 who has left the partner of her youth
and ignored the covenant she made before God.[a v]
18 For her house leads down to death
and her paths to the spirits of the dead.[w]
19 None who go to her return
or attain the paths of life.[x]

20 Thus you will walk in the ways of good men
and keep to the paths of the righteous.
21 For the upright will live in the land,[y]
and the blameless will remain in it;
22 but the wicked will be cut off from the land,[z]
and the unfaithful will be torn from it.[a]

Further Benefits of Wisdom

3 My son, do not forget my teaching,[b]
but keep my commands in your heart,
2 for they will prolong your life many years[c]
and bring you prosperity.

3 Let love and faithfulness never leave you;
bind them around your neck,
write them on the tablet of your heart.[d]
4 Then you will win favor and a good name
in the sight of God and man.[e]

2:15 [s]Ps 125:5 [t]Pr 21:8
2:16 [u]Pr 5:1-6; 6:20-29; 7:5-27
2:17 [v]Mal 2:14
2:18 [w]Pr 7:27
2:19 [x]Ecc 7:26
2:21 [y]Ps 37:29
2:22 [z]Job 18:17; Ps 37:38 [a]Dt 28:63; Pr 10:30
3:1 [b]Pr 4:5
3:2 [c]Pr 4:10
3:3 [d]Ex 13:9; Pr 6:21; 7:3; 2Co 3:3
3:4 [e]1Sa 2:26; Lk 2:52

[a] 17 *Or covenant of her God*

2:16–20 See *WLC* 138.
2:16–19 Proper sexual conduct and deliverance from the enticements of the deadly woman are also offered the son. Her profile is expanded in 5:1–23, 6:20–35, 7:1–27, 22:14 and 23:27.
2:16 adulteress . . . wayward wife. She has betrayed her faithful husband (v. 16; 5:20; 6:24; 7:5). **Seductive words.** She prostitutes herself (6:26) and lustfully stalks the streets to seduce young men (7:10–21).
2:17 partner. That is, her husband as her teacher. **covenant she made before God.** The Hebrew literally reads "covenant of her God," suggesting that she is apostate, and perhaps that her illicit affairs have resulted in her marrying outside of the covenant community (cf. 6:29; 7:19). These conclusions are strengthened if her current religious obligations involve sexual activity, even allowing fornication (see note on 7:14). See *WCF* 24.1; *WLC* 151.
2:18 death. Not merely ceasing to live in the physical sense, but an irreversible descent into the disorder of moral perversity (see 5:23, where to die is to be "led astray"). Solomon never described the wicked as being in the realm of light and life, despite the fact that they were physically alive. Rather, they already exist in a region of darkness and death because they have no saving relationship with the living God. The texts predicting death represent that present state as terminating in a tragic, final end, although not necessarily a premature death. Sinners regret their incorrigibility only after the flesh and body are spent (5:11). The pursuit of wisdom and the practice of righteousness rescue the wise from the realm and destiny of death, but, in the final analysis, nothing can resuscitate the wicked (10:2; 11:4,19; 13:14; 14:27; 15:24). Death is their final end, whereas life is the destination of the righteous (see Mt 25:46).
2:19 life. Sometimes "life" refers to mere physical existence (see 27:27; 31:12). Most often, however, the term implies an abundance of health, prosperity and social esteem (3:21–22; 4:13; 8:35; 16:15; 21:21; 22:4) that is added to physical animation. In this sense, life is wisdom's reward, never to be tarnished by death (4:22; 6:23; 10:17; 11:19; 12:28; 13:14; 15:31; 19:23; 22:4; see also 4:4; 7:2; 9:6; 15:27). See "Introduction: Purpose and Distinctives."
2:20–22 As in the first lesson (see 1:19), the father caps off the second with a generalization on deliverance from death based on the specific deliverance from the wicked man and woman.
2:22 land. The Hebrew word can refer, among other things, to arable ground in general or to Israel in particular. Biblical Wisdom Literature often treats humanity apart from Israel's historic covenants, so it is likely that "land" refers primarily to the ground in general, with its fatness (Ge 27:28), increase (Lev 26:4,20) and fruit (Nu 13:20). As such, the term "land" represents life itself. The good earth contrasts with the grave (vv. 18–19). Nevertheless, the language alludes to the covenant land promises to Israel: Both are the Lord's climactic gift to his people; both make living in the land dependent on keeping God's commandments (Dt 4:1; cf. Ex 20:12; Dt 5:16; 25:15); both cement his blessings to those who are loyal to him (Dt 28:1–14); and both threaten that the disloyal will be torn from the land (Dt 28:15–68).
■ **3:1–12** *Lesson Three: The Material Benefits of Wisdom.* Lesson 3 consists of six sections that alternate between admonitions (vv. 1,3,5,6a,7,9,11) and motivations (vv. 2,4,6b,8,10,12). The father begins the lesson with his typical introduction, including a motivating reason to listen to his teaching (vv. 1–2). He then issues commands for piety supported by further motivators (vv. 3–10). He concludes with an admonition not to reject the Lord's fatherly discipline, including a final motivation (vv. 11–12).
■ **3:1–2** *Introduction.* Anchoring his teachings ever more strongly in the Lord (cf. 2:6), the father begins his admonitions with a call to preserve his teaching (v. 1) for a reasonably expected outcome of long life and peace (v. 2).
3:2 prolong your life. See "Introduction: Purpose and Distinctives." The expectation is that wisdom normally leads to a long, prosperous life (Ex 20:12). **prosperity.** The Hebrew word *shalom* means "peace and prosperity." Its presence meets every need, freeing one from hostility and lack and filling one with God's gifts of inner contentment, delight, joy and pleasure. In reality, endless years without peace are a curse.
■ **3:3–10** *Call to Piety and Blessings.* The father issues a call to ethical behavior (v. 3), trust (v. 5), humility (v. 7), worship (v. 9) and submissiveness (v. 11). The results achieved from fulfilling these commands are favor with God and people (v. 4), a straight path (v. 6), total healing (v. 8) and abundant harvests (v. 10).
3:3 love and faithfulness. This covenantal language indicates that wisdom is seen as part of Israel's covenant life. **bind . . . neck.** The teachings are implicitly likened to a necklace that symbolizes protection, guidance, eternal life and social exaltation (see 1:9). **write . . . heart.** The sense is the same as that in verse 1 (i.e., make them a part of you by committing them to memory and then conforming your will to them (cf 7:3; Dt 6:6).
3:4 win favor. Or "win grace" (see Ge 6:8), meaning "find accept-

[5] Trust in the LORD[f] with all your heart
and lean not on your own understanding;
[6] in all your ways acknowledge him,
and he will make your paths[g] straight.[a h]

[7] Do not be wise in your own eyes;[i]
fear the LORD and shun evil.[j]
[8] This will bring health to your body[k]
and nourishment to your bones.[l]

[9] Honor the LORD with your wealth,
with the firstfruits[m] of all your crops;
[10] then your barns will be filled[n] to overflowing,
and your vats will brim over with new wine.[o]

[11] My son, do not despise the LORD's discipline[p]
and do not resent his rebuke,
[12] because the LORD disciplines those he loves,[q]
as a father[b] the son he delights in.[r]

[13] Blessed is the man who finds wisdom,
the man who gains understanding,
[14] for she is more profitable than silver
and yields better returns than gold.[s]
[15] She is more precious than rubies;[t]
nothing you desire can compare with her.[u]
[16] Long life is in her right hand;
in her left hand are riches and honor.[v]
[17] Her ways are pleasant ways,
and all her paths are peace.[w]
[18] She is a tree of life[x] to those who embrace her;
those who lay hold of her will be blessed.

[19] By wisdom the LORD laid the earth's foundations,[y]
by understanding he set the heavens[z] in place;
[20] by his knowledge the deeps were divided,
and the clouds let drop the dew.

3:5 [f]Ps 37:3,5
3:6 [g]1Ch 28:9 [h]Pr 16:3; Isa 45:13
3:7 [i]Ro 12:16 [j]Job 1:1; Pr 16:6
3:8 [k]Pr 4:22 [l]Job 21:24
3:9 [m]Ex 22:29; 23:19; Dt 26:1-15
3:10 [n]Dt 28:8 [o]Joel 2:24
3:11 [p]Job 5:17
3:12 [q]Pr 13:24; Rev 3:19 [r]Dt 8:5; Heb 12:5-6*
3:14 [s]Job 28:15; Pr 8:19; 16:16
3:15 [t]Job 28:18 [u]Pr 8:11
3:16 [v]Pr 8:18
3:17 [w]Pr 16:7; Mt 11:28-30
3:18 [x]Ge 2:9; Pr 11:30; Rev 2:7
3:19 [y]Ps 104:24 [z]Pr 8:27-29

[a] *6* Or *will direct your paths* [b] *12* Hebrew; Septuagint / *and he punishes*

ance." In the context of the covenant, the word refers to the free, unmerited gift of God. Here it almost certainly refers to God's covenant love (v. 3). **good name.** Literally, "good success."

3:5 Trust in the LORD. The trust in view is based on a sense of security, usually in the face of danger. Since the teaching has no value unless God backs it up, the disciple must trust in the Lord (see 16:3,20; 22:19; 28:25; 29:25). Confiding in God's promises and renouncing self-reliance (cf. 18:10–11; 28:11,26) are unnatural to fallen humanity (see theological article "Effectual Calling and Conversion" at Ac 16); such an attitude must come as a gift of God, mediated in part through the admonitions and promises (see 2:6; cf. Ro 9:14–17; Eph 2:8–9). **lean . . . understanding.** The contrast is between a perception of reality that takes God's revealed word as the authority for all truth and one that assumes that human conjecture is the last word. See *WLC* 157.

3:6 acknowledge him. Literally, "know him" (i.e., take him into consideration). Personal knowledge of God flows from obeying God's specific teachings in full reliance upon him to keep his associated promises.

3:7 wise . . . eyes. A state worse than being a fool (26:12; cf. Ro 12:16). The phrase summarizes the humanistic assumption that our intellect and reason are capable of reaching truth apart from the mercy of God. "Mockers" fall into this category (see note on 1:22).

3:9 Honor the LORD. That is, confer upon God social esteem by offering him the best of your material benefits. **firstfruits.** Symbolic of the best (cf. Nu 18:12f.; Eze 48:14; Am 6:6).

■ **3:11–12** *Conclusion.* The father appeals to the heavenly Father, whose instruction and discipline are not to be resisted.

3:11 discipline. See note on 1:2. As the loving Father God desires the son to experience blessings, but there is a condition to realizing this goal: satisfying obligations. God disciplines the son to cause him to meet these obligations so that he may receive blessings.

3:12 Not surprisingly the passage concludes with the metaphor of God as a father reproving his son. Only the Lord can grant the rewards of long life, peace (v. 2) and a heavenly Father's love.

■ **3:13–35** *Lesson Four: The Value of Wisdom.* This lecture emphatically repeats and expands the father's admonitions to guard his teaching (vv. 1–12). The terms in verses 1–12 that referred to parental instruction (v. 1) and piety (vv. 3,5,7,9) are replaced by the words "wisdom," "understanding" (vv. 13,19; cf. 1:2), "knowledge" (v. 20; cf. 1:2), "sound judgment" and "discernment" (v. 21; cf. 1:4; 2:11). The lecture consists of four formerly independent poems (vv. 13–18,19–20,21–26,27–35). Verses 13–26 motivate the son to obtain and adhere to the father's teaching in order to benefit himself, while verses 27–35 focus on helping needy neighbors.

■ **3:13–26** *Exhortation to Seek Wisdom for Its Value.* This passage divides into three stanzas: the value of wisdom to people (vv. 13–18), to the Lord as Creator (vv. 19–20) and to the son (vv. 21–26).

3:13–18 Wisdom has value for all people because it brings numerous blessings.

3:13 Blessed. Refers to the ideal future, intended by the Creator, resulting from a present relationship with God (cf. Mt 5:3–12).

3:18 tree of life. "See Introduction: Purpose and Distinctives." Compare 13:12.

3:19–20 By wisdom . . . understanding . . . his knowledge. The immensity and complexity of creation are impossible for humans to fathom. Yet these are the marks of divine wisdom, for God alone can measure the wind and the sea. One can understand what is wise only when one comprehends the whole, as Solomon (8:22–31), Agur (see 30:1–6) and the audience of the book of Job well knew (see Job 28). Human wisdom finds its basis within the wisdom of God, who knows all (cf. Ps 104:24; Jer 10:12), but human beings can only know wisdom to the degree that God reveals it (Dt 29:29).

3:20 were divided. In conjunction with "founded" and "established," this refers to the time of creation (see Ge 1:9,10; Job

[21] My son, preserve sound judgment and discernment,
do not let them out of your sight;[a]
[22] they will be life for you,
an ornament to grace your neck.[b]
[23] Then you will go on your way in safety,
and your foot will not stumble;[c]
[24] when you lie down,[d] you will not be afraid;
when you lie down, your sleep[e] will be sweet.
[25] Have no fear of sudden disaster
or of the ruin that overtakes the wicked,
[26] for the LORD will be your confidence
and will keep your foot[f] from being snared.

[27] Do not withhold good from those who deserve it,
when it is in your power to act.
[28] Do not say to your neighbor,
"Come back later; I'll give it tomorrow"—
when you now have it with you.[g]
[29] Do not plot harm against your neighbor,
who lives trustfully near you.
[30] Do not accuse a man for no reason—
when he has done you no harm.
[31] Do not envy[h] a violent man
or choose any of his ways,
[32] for the LORD detests a perverse man[i]
but takes the upright into his confidence.[j]
[33] The LORD's curse[k] is on the house of the wicked,[l]
but he blesses the home of the righteous.[m]
[34] He mocks proud mockers
but gives grace to the humble.[n]
[35] The wise inherit honor,
but fools he holds up to shame.

3:21 [a]Pr 4:20-22
3:22 [b]Pr 1:8-9
3:23 [c]Ps 37:24; Pr 4:12
3:24 [d]Lev 26:6; Ps 3:5 [e]Job 11:18
3:26 [f]1Sa 2:9
3:28 [g]Lev 19:13; Dt 24:15
3:31 [h]Ps 37:1; Pr 24:1-2
3:32 [i]Pr 11:20 [j]Job 29:4; Ps 25:14
3:33 [k]Dt 11:28; Mal 2:2 [l]Zec 5:4 [m]Ps 1:3
3:34 [n]Jas 4:6*; 1Pe 5:5*

Wisdom Is Supreme

4 Listen, my sons,[o] to a father's instruction;
pay attention and gain understanding.
[2] I give you sound learning,
so do not forsake my teaching.
[3] When I was a boy in my father's house,
still tender, and an only child of my mother,

4:1 [o]Pr 1:8

38:8–12; Ps 104:8–13). The phrase has a hostile sense, probably retaining the imagery, but not the theology, of ancient battle myths of creation. In these myths a creator deity splits open what Genesis 1:2 calls "the deep" (see note on Ps 74:13) to release the essential forces for life (land, sky and life-giving water; cf. Isa 27:1; 51:9).
3:21–26 Wisdom is of value not only to people in general and to God, but to the son as well. These verses explain that value. A play on the concept of "preserve" or "keep" (see vv. 21,26) forms a frame around the stanza: If the son will "preserve" the Lord's wisdom (v. 21), the Lord will "keep" him from "being snared" (v. 26). The stanza consists of an admonition to heed the teaching (vv. 21–22), the argumentation that the teaching leads to security (vv. 23–24) and the invitation not to fear disaster because the Lord gives security (vv. 25–26).
■ **3:27–35** *A Neighbor Needing Help.* The tension between the promise of blessing (vv. 13–26) and the reality of needing assistance (vv. 27–35) represents two faces of truth: The Lord protects his covenant people from the doom of the wicked, but until the end the good person may be in need (vv. 3,24). The first section teaches the son not to "withhold good" (i.e., help) from a good neighbor (vv. 27–28) and not to harm such a neighbor in any way (vv. 29–30). The frame of reference widens with regard to neighbors. It moves from a petitioner (vv. 27–28) to a trusting neighbor (vv. 28–29) to people in general (v. 30). The stanza's admonitions also move from withholding help from a neighbor (vv. 27–28) to plotting evil against him (vv. 29–30) to becoming in any way a violent neighbor (v. 31).
3:29–30 See *WLC* 142.
■ **4:1–9** *Lesson Five: Get Wisdom.* The father's fifth lecture expands again the admonitions in 2:1–4 and consists of two parts: the typical introduction (vv. 1–2) and the lesson (vv. 3–9). This lesson is in fact the grandfather's lecture to the father. By quoting his father and setting himself up as an example, the father gives credibility to wisdom by implying the antiquity of the teaching and by his own sympathetic experience within the tradition.
■ **4:1–2** *Introduction.* The father includes addresses and admonitions to listen.
4:1 sons. Son, grandson and great-grandson. See *HC* 104.
■ **4:3–9** *The Grandfather's Lesson.* This lesson is one that was passed from the grandfather to the father and in turn from the father to the son. In autobiographical style the father introduces himself as the addressee (vv. 3–4a) and then quotes the content of the lecture (vv. 4b–9). This teaching also includes the typical introduction (v. 4b) and lesson (vv. 5–9), which is brought to a climactic conclusion with the promise that wisdom will give the son the victor's crown (1:9).
4:3–4 See *WLC* 127.
4:3 boy. Or "son." A true son to his father reproduces the father's spiritual nature (cf. 14:26; Ge 1:11–12; 3:15). In Hebrew thought sonship was understood not merely as a matter of biology but also as an issue of conformity to the father's will. A rebellious child could be disowned (cf. Dt 21:18–21; 32:19–20; Hos 1:9; Lk 15:18–19; Heb 12:8; cf. Mk 3:31–33). **tender.** His body and character were weak and sensitive because they were undeveloped and inexperienced (cf. 1Ch 22:5; 29:1), as easily shaped as a tender

4 he taught me and said,
“Lay hold of my words with all your heart;
keep my commands and you will live.[p]
5 Get wisdom,[q] get understanding;
do not forget my words or swerve from them.
6 Do not forsake wisdom, and she will protect you;[r]
love her, and she will watch over you.
7 Wisdom is supreme; therefore get wisdom.
Though it cost all[s] you have,[a] get understanding.[t]
8 Esteem her, and she will exalt you;
embrace her, and she will honor you.[u]
9 She will set a garland of grace on your head
and present you with a crown of splendor.[v]”

10 Listen, my son, accept what I say,
and the years of your life will be many.[w]
11 I guide[x] you in the way of wisdom
and lead you along straight paths.
12 When you walk, your steps will not be hampered;
when you run, you will not stumble.[y]
13 Hold on to instruction, do not let it go;
guard it well, for it is your life.[z]
14 Do not set foot on the path of the wicked
or walk in the way of evil men.[a]
15 Avoid it, do not travel on it;
turn from it and go on your way.
16 For they cannot sleep till they do evil;[b]
they are robbed of slumber till they make someone fall.
17 They eat the bread of wickedness
and drink the wine of violence.

18 The path of the righteous[c] is like the first gleam of dawn,
shining ever brighter till the full light of day.[d]
19 But the way of the wicked is like deep darkness;[e]
they do not know what makes them stumble.

20 My son, pay attention to what I say;
listen closely to my words.[f]
21 Do not let them out of your sight,[g]
keep them within your heart;
22 for they are life to those who find them

4:4 [p]Pr 7:2
4:5 [q]Pr 16:16
4:6 [r]2Th 2:10
4:7 [s]Mt 13:44-46 [t]Pr 23:23
4:8 [u]1Sa 2:30; Pr 3:18
4:9 [v]Pr 1:8-9
4:10 [w]Pr 3:2
4:11 [x]1Sa 12:23
4:12 [y]Job 18:7; Pr 3:23
4:13 [z]Pr 3:22
4:14 [a]Ps 1:1; Pr 1:15
4:16 [b]Ps 36:4; Mic 2:1
4:18 [c]Isa 26:7 [d]2Sa 23:4; Da 12:3; Mt 5:14; Php 2:15
4:19 [e]Job 18:5; Pr 2:13; Isa 59:9-10; Jn 12:35
4:20 [f]Pr 5:1
4:21 [g]Pr 3:21; 7:1-2

a 7 Or *Whatever else you get*

twig (Eze 17:22). **only child.** His mother cherished him (i.e., regarded him as “the only one”). The adjective highlights his unique and beloved status with her. By way of comparison, although Abraham had other sons, Isaac is referred to as Abraham’s “only son” (Ge 22:2,12,16) to emphasize the special status of Sarah’s offspring. The Septuagint (the Greek translation of the OT) renders it “beloved.”
4:5–9 The grandfather’s lecture is repeated to command the son to get wisdom (vv. 5,7) and to motivate this pursuit by informing him that wisdom will both protect (v. 6) and honor (vv. 8–9) her lover.
4:5 Get. Literally, “buy.”
4:7 Though it cost all. Even if it costs all your possessions, gain insight. Jesus used a similar saying with regard to the pearl of great price (Mt 13:45–46).
4:8 Esteeming wisdom and holding to it yields ample returns.
4:9 See note on 1:9.
■ **4:10–19** *Lesson Six: Stay Off the Wrong Way.* The boundary between verses 1–9 and verses 10–19 is marked by the typical introductory address and command—“Listen, my son” (v. 10; cf. 1:8; 4:1)—and by the thematic shift from acquiring wisdom to moving in wisdom’s way. The paths we take depend not only on what we have inherited, but also on our individual choices. The father’s lecture divides into equal halves: an admonition to embrace his teaching and move in the way of wisdom (vv. 10–13) and a warning not to stray near the path of the wicked (vv. 14–17). The lesson ends with a summation (vv. 18–19).
■ **4:10–13** *The Way of Wisdom.* The son is encouraged to follow the path of wisdom because of the blessings that are there.
■ **4:14–17** *The Way of the Wicked.* These verses contrast the direction of life taken by wicked people with the way of wisdom.
4:16 cannot sleep. A distinctive contribution of this lecture is its description of the wicked as fully devoted to evil. The wicked are so addicted to sin that it has become their sedative by night and their food and drink by day. The father hopes that his son will recoil in horror from this gruesome picture of their cravings.
■ **4:18–19** *Summation.* This summarizing conclusion contrasts light in the path of wisdom with darkness in the way of the wicked.
4:18 See *WSC* 36.
■ **4:20–27** *Lesson Seven: Don’t Turn Off the Right Way.* The previous lecture warned the son against entering the path of the wicked (vv. 10–19). This lesson admonishes the son to walk straight ahead on the track without swerving. It directs him to use his eyes and tongue as a means of finding truth and direction, not as a means of perversity (see 6:12–19; Pss 115:5–7; 135:16–17). This lecture begins with the typical introduction (vv. 20–22), which includes an address (v. 20), admonitions to heed the teaching (vv. 20–21) and substantiating motivational reasons to do so (v. 22); it continues with instruction for the son to dedicate himself to the straight way (vv. 23–27). Verse 23 functions as a transition, uniquely containing within one verse both admonition (v. 23a) and argument (v. 23b).
■ **4:20–22** *Introduction.* The introduction summons the son to listen and cites the motivation of great benefit.

and health to a man's whole body.[h]
23 Above all else, guard your heart,
for it is the wellspring of life.[i]
24 Put away perversity from your mouth;
keep corrupt talk far from your lips.
25 Let your eyes look straight ahead,
fix your gaze directly before you.
26 Make level[a] paths for your feet[j]
and take only ways that are firm.
27 Do not swerve to the right or the left;[k]
keep your foot from evil.

Warning Against Adultery

5 My son, pay attention to my wisdom,
listen well to my words[l] of insight,
2 that you may maintain discretion
and your lips may preserve knowledge.
3 For the lips of an adulteress drip honey,
and her speech is smoother than oil;[m]
4 but in the end she is bitter as gall,[n]
sharp as a double-edged sword.
5 Her feet go down to death;
her steps lead straight to the grave.[b][o]
6 She gives no thought to the way of life;
her paths are crooked, but she knows it not.[p]

7 Now then, my sons, listen[q] to me;
do not turn aside from what I say.
8 Keep to a path far from her,[r]
do not go near the door of her house,
9 lest you give your best strength to others
and your years to one who is cruel,
10 lest strangers feast on your wealth
and your toil enrich another man's house.
11 At the end of your life you will groan,

4:22 [h]Pr 3:8; 12:18
4:23 [i]Mt 12:34; Lk 6:45
4:26 [j]Heb 12:13*
4:27 [k]Dt 5:32; 28:14
5:1 [l]Pr 4:20; 22:17
5:3 [m]Ps 55:21; Pr 2:16; 7:5
5:4 [n]Ecc 7:26
5:5 [o]Pr 7:26-27
5:6 [p]Pr 30:20
5:7 [q]Pr 7:24
5:8 [r]Pr 7:1-27

[a] 26 Or *Consider the* [b] 5 Hebrew *Sheol*

▪ 4:23–27 *Devotion to the Right Path.* The way of wisdom is portrayed as a path that is worthy of the son's full devotion.
4:23 it is the wellspring of life. That is, "Everything you do flows from it" (see note on 2:2; cf. Mt 12:35; Mk 7:21; Ro 2:29; Jas 3:13–18).
4:24 Put away . . . mouth. That is, "Keep your mouth free of perversity."
4:26 Make . . . paths. Or "Give careful thought to the paths." **take only ways that are firm.** Or "Be steadfast in all your ways."
▪ 5:1–23 *Lesson Eight: The Folly of Adultery and the Wisdom of Marriage.* The eighth lecture includes an introduction (vv. 1–6), the lesson itself (vv. 7–20) and the conclusion (vv. 21–23). The lecture concludes with a sober prediction of the fatal consequences of sinning against God and spurning the father's instruction (vv. 21–23). In addition to the main themes—namely, advocating distance from another's wayward wife (v. 8) and devotion to and intimacy with one's own wife (v. 15)—the theme of accepting the father's teaching punctuates the whole. Note the explicit commands (vv. 1,7), the foolish son's belated regret that he has rejected the teaching (vv. 12–13) and the concluding summary, stressing that a sinner dies for lack of instruction and for his intractable insolence against wisdom (v. 23). This subtheme is necessary because the father is countering the honeyed speech of the loose woman.
▪ 5:1–6 *Introduction.* This robust warning against adultery begins with an address and a call for attentiveness (vv. 1–2), followed by motivating reasons for doing so (vv. 3–6). These verses describe the seducing adulteress as being sweetness and light on the surface, but underneath the stench of death.
5:1 My son. The son was old enough to experience sexual temptation and pleasure. He was either married or on the verge of marriage. Marriage often occurred at an early age in the ancient Near East. For example, Josiah and Amon married at age 14, Jehoiachin at age 16. The marriageable age in Egypt for girls was 12 years and for boys 15 years.
5:3 lips . . . drip honey. Her seductive speech draws her victim irresistibly toward mystery, excitement and delight. Her dripping lips and smooth palate probably carry sexual connotations (see SS 4:11). **lips.** The son's lips must speak the truth (e.g., Ge 39:8–9) to fend off speech from the lips of the wayward wife (see 2:16–19). Sexuality is associated with speech: courting speech, seductive speech, love songs, whispered sweet nothings, etc. In contrast to verse 2, the process of seduction begins with deceptive words that are full of charm. Compare the sweetness of true love in Song of Songs 4:11.
5:4 gall. Or wormwood, a plant that is particularly bitter to the taste. It is used as a metaphor for the experience of affliction (Dt 29:18). **double-edged sword.** The promise of a relationship (v. 3) is empty, and the liaison leads only to injury.
▪ 5:7–20 *Sexual Folly and Wisdom.* The body of this section sets forth the folly of adultery (vv. 7–14) and the wisdom of lovemaking within marriage (vv. 15–20).
5:7–14 The first stanza presents the father introducing the body of the lesson with another urgent call to attentiveness (v. 7; cf. 7:24; 8:32) to the command to avoid adultery (v. 8). In the following three balanced verses, the father paints the economic and social downside of becoming involved with the adulteress (vv. 9–14), first by objectively stating the facts (vv. 9–11) and then by presenting the fool's deprecating self-speech (vv. 12–14). The son's economic ruin pertains to strangers (vv. 9–10), while his social ruin pertains to his own people (vv. 12–13) and to the congregation (v. 14). Verse 11 is a transition that looks back to verses 9–10. The potential economic and social ruin that the adulteress brings, not to mention the Lord's death sentence (vv. 21–23), provide sufficient reason to obey. See *WLC* 138,139,145,151.
5:9 you give. Unlike the innocent one whom thugs plotted to plunder (1:10–19), the son who turns to the adulteress volunteers his life for destruction. **one who is cruel.** A figure of the outraged husband (6:34–35).

when your flesh and body are spent.
12 You will say, "How I hated discipline!
How my heart spurned correction![s]
13 I would not obey my teachers
or listen to my instructors.
14 I have come to the brink of utter ruin
in the midst of the whole assembly."

15 Drink water from your own cistern,
running water from your own well.
16 Should your springs overflow in the streets,
your streams of water in the public squares?
17 Let them be yours alone,
never to be shared with strangers.
18 May your fountain[t] be blessed,
and may you rejoice in the wife of your youth.[u]
19 A loving doe, a graceful deer[v]—
may her breasts satisfy you always,
may you ever be captivated by her love.
20 Why be captivated, my son, by an adulteress?
Why embrace the bosom of another man's wife?

21 For a man's ways are in full view[w] of the LORD,
and he examines all his paths.[x]
22 The evil deeds of a wicked man ensnare him;[y]
the cords of his sin hold him fast.[z]
23 He will die for lack of discipline,[a]
led astray by his own great folly.

Warnings Against Folly

6 My son, if you have put up security for your neighbor,[b]
if you have struck hands in pledge[c] for another,

5:12 [s]Pr 1:29; 12:1
5:18 [t]SS 4:12-15 [u]Ecc 9:9; Mal 2:14
5:19 [v]SS 2:9; 4:5
5:21 [w]Ps 119:168; Hos 7:2 [x]Job 14:16; Job 31:4; 34:21; Pr 15:3; Jer 16:17; 32:19; Heb 4:13
5:22 [y]Ps 9:16 [z]Nu 32:23; Ps 7:15-16; Pr 1:31-32
5:23 [a]Job 4:21; 36:12
6:1 [b]Pr 17:18 [c]Pr 11:15; 22:26-27

5:12 say. His confession suggests that physical chastisement led to his salvation. It takes humility to make this type of confession, which entails repentance and acceptance of rebuke. Chastisement is a positive educational force, a way to wisdom (see 12:1; 15:5, 31–32), life (6:23; 10:17; 15:31) and honor (13:18).
5:14 assembly. Refers to a number of persons gathered together for a particular purpose. Here it is used for the legal assembly at a public court hearing (see 26:26; cf. Sirach 7:7 [an Apocryphal book]). A vivid picture of the convening of such an assembly, including the leaders of the people sitting in the gate of the city, is given in the trial of Jeremiah at the temple (Jer 26:9–10). The convened congregation also seems to have been called "the entire assembly of people" (Jer 26:17).
5:15–20 The second stanza of the father's lesson shifts to the wisdom of sexual satisfaction with one's own wife. He uses an allegory (vv. 15–17) to teach that conjugal fidelity can be the fulfillment of youthful sexual urges (vv. 18–19; cf. 1Co 7:9). The life-quickening enjoyment of making love with one's own wife provides a concrete protection against the adulteress (v. 20). Enjoyment of sex, not procreation, is its theme.
5:15 Drink water. The allegory almost exhausts the vocabulary for sources of water: "cistern," "well," "springs" (v. 16) "streams of water" (v. 16). The key to its interpretation, mediated through "fountain" in verse 18a, is given in the parallel in verse 18b: "Rejoice in the wife of your youth." "Water" (v. 15; cf. SS 4:15) stands for quenching one's sexual thirst. Satisfying the sexual drive is likened to solid food in 30:20 and to water and food in 9:17. **your own cistern . . . your own well.** That is, your own wife.
5:16 springs overflow in the streets. The whole allegory rests on the matter of private property versus common property: one's own cistern (v. 15) as opposed to the springs and channels of water in the streets (v. 16); the water that belongs to you alone (v. 17) in contrast to water in the open places that is the property of foreigners (v. 17). The cistern, which usually was privately owned in Old Testament times (2Ki 18:31; Isa 36:16), gives point to this metaphor. Over and against this privately owned possession (v. 15) appear the "streams of water in the public squares" (v. 16), a symbol of common property to which everyone has access. The street and the open places are the harlot's places (cf. 7:12).
5:17 Let . . . alone. This phrase continues the admonition to find sexual pleasure in the privacy of marriage, not from the "springs" among the common rabble. The privacy of conjugal love is underscored by "yours alone."
5:18 May . . . be blessed. In order to quench his thirst, the son's well must be a constant source of sweet water. So the father prays that his son will have a wife who can quench his thirst at all times and in the most satisfying way. **wife of your youth.** The phrase could be translated "your youthful [wife]," but the similar constructions in 2:17 and Malachi 2:14 validate the given translation. The expression anticipates sons marrying at an early age (see 2:17).
5:19–20 See *WLC* 138.
5:19 The erotic language of this verse is similar to that of the Song of Songs. The imagery of a graceful animal of rare beauty emphasizes physical pleasures as integral to wholesome sexual relations (see SS 1:2–3; 4:1–7).
■ **5:21–23** *Conclusion.* In conclusion the father grounds his teaching in the reality of the Lord's omniscience (v. 21) and justice (vv. 22–23). The combination entails perfect justice for all. Verse 21 refers to God's omniscience and verses 22–23 to his justice in consigning the sinner to his death.
■ **6:1–19** *Lesson Nine: Three Inferior Types of People.* These verses lack the father's typical introductory imperatives to listen; they thereby form an appendix to the father's eighth lesson (5:1–23). They draw attention to three types of people: the one who takes the debt of another (vv. 1–5), the sluggard (vv. 6–11) and the troublemaker (vv. 12–19). Although the first of these lessons was addressed to the son, the second was directed to the sluggard and the third lacked any addressee; neither the sluggard nor the troublemaker was reckoned as a son (see 4:3).
6:1–6 See *WLC* 141.
■ **6:1–5** *One Responsible for Another's Debt.* These verses consist of an introduction, which includes an address expressing the foolishness of taking responsibility for another's debt (vv. 1–2); the main body, which includes the admonition to escape the situation immediately (vv. 3–4); and a summary, which includes the admonition to deliver oneself immediately from the trap (v. 5). The main body consists of six short, urgent admonitions. The key admonition to deliver oneself (vv. 3,5) is qualified by the others, which explain how to go to one's neighbor, swallow one's pride, plead with one's neighbor (v. 3b) and do so immediately, denying oneself untimely sleep and indolent slumber (v. 4).
6:1 struck hands in pledge. Striking hands, similar to a hand-

[2] if you have been trapped by what you said,
ensnared by the words of your mouth,
[3] then do this, my son, to free yourself,
since you have fallen into your neighbor's hands:
Go and humble yourself;
press your plea with your neighbor!
[4] Allow no sleep to your eyes,
no slumber to your eyelids.[d]
[5] Free yourself, like a gazelle from the hand of the hunter,
like a bird from the snare of the fowler.[e]

[6] Go to the ant, you sluggard;[f]
consider its ways and be wise!
[7] It has no commander,
no overseer or ruler,
[8] yet it stores its provisions in summer
and gathers its food at harvest.[g]

[9] How long will you lie there, you sluggard?[h]
When will you get up from your sleep?
[10] A little sleep, a little slumber,
a little folding of the hands to rest[i]—
[11] and poverty[j] will come on you like a bandit
and scarcity like an armed man.[a]

[12] A scoundrel and villain,
who goes about with a corrupt mouth,
[13] who winks with his eye,[k]
signals with his feet
and motions with his fingers,
[14] who plots evil[l] with deceit in his heart—
he always stirs up dissension.[m]
[15] Therefore disaster will overtake him in an instant;
he will suddenly be destroyed—without remedy.[n]

[16] There are six things the LORD hates,
seven that are detestable to him:
[17] haughty eyes,
a lying tongue,[o]
hands that shed innocent blood,[p]
[18] a heart that devises wicked schemes,

6:4 [d]Ps 132:4
6:5 [e]Ps 91:3
6:6 [f]Pr 20:4
6:8 [g]Pr 10:4
6:9 [h]Pr 24:30-34
6:10 [i]Pr 24:33
6:11 [j]Pr 24:30-34
6:13 [k]Ps 35:19
6:14 [l]Mic 2:1 [m]ver 16-19
6:15 [n]2Ch 36:16
6:17 [o]Ps 120:2; Pr 12:22 [p]Dt 19:10; Isa 1:15; 59:7

a *11* Or *like a vagrant / and scarcity like a beggar*

shake, sealed the matter (see 11:15; 17:18; 22:26). **another.** Or "stranger."

6:3 neighbor's hands. By accepting responsibility for another's debts you have allowed another to take control of your life. **humble yourself.** Or "exhaust yourself."

■ **6:6–11** *The Sluggard.* The theme of self-inflicted economic impoverishment continues in this warning to the sluggard (lazy person). Whereas the agent of the financial affliction heretofore was the debtor (vv. 1–5), here it is the created order itself that brings trouble. The sluggard challenges this order. The reverse side of the warning against laziness is an admonition toward diligence (cf. 10:4ff.; 13:4; 15:19). The poem consists of two parts (vv. 6–8,9–11), both of which are introduced by "you sluggard" (vv. 6,9). The first part admonishes the indolent person to consider the ant (cf. 1Ki 4:33); the second condemns him for his folly and sloth. The sluggard was a good-for-nothing who stood far below the animal in terms of worth. Although satirizing the idle person, Solomon did not destroy him but offered constructive criticism to make him wise, assuming that he possessed the ability to reform himself.

6:7 no commander . . . ruler. Rather than having leaders who both organize the work with regard to its nature and timing and ensure that it is carried through to completion, the ant possesses a God-given instinct to work and, just as significantly, to order the work wisely.

6:10–11 See 24:33–34.

6:10 hands. That is, "arms." This gesture epitomizes the sluggard's refusal to work (Ecc 4:5).

6:11 poverty. There are warnings in Proverbs against the kinds of life-denying behavior that produce poverty. Indolence is one such behavior (10:4–5; 19:15; 20:13), but it must be pointed out that not all poverty is the result of folly (14:31; 17:5; 19:1,17,22; 21:12; 22:22; 28:3,11).

■ **6:12–19** *The Troublemaker.* This lesson against the troublemaker, or insurrectionist, probably consists of two originally independent sections that Solomon combined: a naming of the troublemaker and a list of some of his reprehensible behaviors (vv. 12–15) that escalates into a catalog of seven things the Lord abhors about him (vv. 16–19). The two parts are forged together by cataloging the troublemaker's unhealthy body members: lying mouth/tongue (vv. 12,17), eyes and fingers/hands (vv. 13,17), feet (vv. 13,18), and especially his heart (vv. 14,18).

6:12 scoundrel. This term refers to a revolutionary, an insurrectionist, a troublemaker, one who creates social and moral disorder.

6:13 winks. He winks in the sense of "winks maliciously."

6:16–19 The description of the troublemaker falls into three parts: an introduction of the things the Lord abhors (v. 16), a catalog of misused body parts (vv. 17–18) and antisocial actions (v. 19). Each one causes the ruin of his victims but destroys himself as well. See *WLC* 145.

6:16 six . . . seven. In such pairings, the true number is the second one ("seven"). Hebrew poetry moves from a lower number to a higher in parallel lines to assert the idea of "how much more" in the second line. See *WLC* 145.

6:18 [q]Ge 6:5
6:19 [r]Ps 27:12 [s]ver 12-15

feet that are quick to rush into evil,[q]
19 a false witness[r] who pours out lies
and a man who stirs up dissension among brothers.[s]

Warning Against Adultery

6:20 [t]Pr 1:8
6:21 [u]Pr 3:3; 7:1-3
6:23 [v]Ps 19:8; 119:105
6:24 [w]Pr 2:16; 7:5
6:26 [x]Pr 7:22-23; 29:3
6:29 [y]Ex 20:14 [z]Pr 2:16-19; 5:8
6:31 [a]Ex 22:1-14
6:32 [b]Ex 20:14 [c]Pr 7:7; 9:4,16
6:33 [d]Pr 5:9-14
6:34 [e]Nu 5:14 [f]Ge 34:7
6:35 [g]Job 31:9-11; SS 8:7

20 My son, keep your father's commands
and do not forsake your mother's teaching.[t]
21 Bind them upon your heart forever;
fasten them around your neck.[u]
22 When you walk, they will guide you;
when you sleep, they will watch over you;
when you awake, they will speak to you.
23 For these commands are a lamp,
this teaching is a light,[v]
and the corrections of discipline
are the way to life,
24 keeping you from the immoral woman,
from the smooth tongue of the wayward wife.[w]
25 Do not lust in your heart after her beauty
or let her captivate you with her eyes,
26 for the prostitute reduces you to a loaf of bread,
and the adulteress preys upon your very life.[x]
27 Can a man scoop fire into his lap
without his clothes being burned?
28 Can a man walk on hot coals
without his feet being scorched?
29 So is he who sleeps[y] with another man's wife;[z]
no one who touches her will go unpunished.

30 Men do not despise a thief if he steals
to satisfy his hunger when he is starving.
31 Yet if he is caught, he must pay sevenfold,[a]
though it costs him all the wealth of his house.
32 But a man who commits adultery[b] lacks judgment;[c]
whoever does so destroys himself.
33 Blows and disgrace are his lot,
and his shame will never[d] be wiped away;
34 for jealousy[e] arouses a husband's fury,[f]
and he will show no mercy when he takes revenge.
35 He will not accept any compensation;
he will refuse the bribe, however great it is.[g]

■ **6:20–35** *Lesson Ten: The High Price of an Adulteress.* This lecture focuses again on the adulteress (cf. 2:16–19; chs. 5,7). It consists of the typical introduction in second person address (vv. 20–24) and the lesson, which is given in third person address (vv. 25–35).

■ **6:20–24** *Introduction.* The introduction consists of an admonition to the son to preserve the parental teaching (vv. 20–21) and an argument that this teaching should guide and protect the faithful (vv. 22–23). Specifically, it is given to protect one from the "wayward wife" (v. 24). This elaboration forms the transition to the main body. A play on a synonymous Hebrew word pair—"keep [the teaching]" (v. 20) and "[the teaching] keeping you" (v. 24) frames the introduction (see 2:8; 4:4,6).

6:20 commands. Or "command." Here and in verse 23 this word is a reference to this lesson.

6:24 immoral woman. Or "your neighbor's wife."

■ **6:25–35** *Paying for the Adulteress.* This lesson consists of an admonition not to desire the adulteress (v. 25) and its supporting arguments (vv. 26,34). The son is warned not to lust for her because the price of adultery is severe, inevitable and unending (vv. 26–31) and because a jealous, betrayed husband will never accept any compensation for the wrong done him short of the total destruction of the adulterer (vv. 32–35).

6:25 Do not lust in your heart. The command assumes the son can govern his heart (4:23) by binding the parental teaching to it (cf. 6:21). The parallel between "Do not lust in your heart after her beauty" and "or let her captivate you with her eyes" suggests that the source of coveting and folly begins with eye contact (cf. Mt 5:28; Jas 1:14–15).

6:26 prostitute reduces you to. Or "prostitute can be had for." The axiom contrasts the price of a prostitute, who offers sex for hire, with that of this adulteress. A cheap prostitute can be had for a meal. By contrast, the unfaithful wife (2:16–19; 5:1–23; 6:20—7:27) demands no payment (7:14–20). This verse does not condone hiring harlots, but simply stresses the greater harm done by the adulteress. Those who engage in prostitution will incur God's wrath (1Co 6:13–20; Gal 5:19–21; Eph 5:5; 1Th 4:1–8). Adultery, however, is worse, because it involves breaking the marriage vow (2:17), wronging a spouse, destroying a home and incurring an immeasurable debt.

6:29 touches. Literally, "to touch [with the hands]," a figure of speech meaning to engage in sexual relations (see Ge 20:6; cf. 1Co 7:1).

6:30–35 See *WLC* 151.

6:31 sevenfold. The satisfactions for damages from stealing vary according to the circumstances, ranging from double to fivefold (Ex 22:1,6–9; cf. Lk 19:8), but never sevenfold. "Seven times" is figurative for full compensation (cf. Ge 4:15; Lev 26:28; cf. Mt 18:21–22).

6:33 Blows. The same Hebrew word for "touches" in verse 29. See *WLC* 145.

Warning Against the Adulteress

7 My son, [h] keep my words
and store up my commands within you.
2 Keep my commands and you will live; [i]
guard my teachings as the apple of your eye.
3 Bind them on your fingers;
write them on the tablet of your heart. [j]
4 Say to wisdom, "You are my sister,"
and call understanding your kinsman;
5 they will keep you from the adulteress,
from the wayward wife with her seductive words. [k]

6 At the window of my house
I looked out through the lattice.
7 I saw among the simple,
I noticed among the young men,
a youth who lacked judgment. [l]
8 He was going down the street near her corner,
walking along in the direction of her house
9 at twilight, [m] as the day was fading,
as the dark of night set in.

10 Then out came a woman to meet him,
dressed like a prostitute and with crafty intent.
11 (She is loud [n] and defiant,
her feet never stay at home;
12 now in the street, now in the squares,
at every corner she lurks.) [o]
13 She took hold of him [p] and kissed him
and with a brazen face she said: [q]

14 "I have fellowship offerings [a] [r] at home;
today I fulfilled my vows.

7:1 [h]Pr 1:8; 2:1
7:2 [i]Pr 4:4
7:3 [j]Dt 6:8; Pr 3:3
7:5 [k]ver 21; Job 31:9; Pr 2:16; 6:24
7:7 [l]Pr 1:22; 6:32
7:9 [m]Job 24:15
7:11 [n]Pr 9:13; 1Ti 5:13
7:12 [o]Pr [illegible]; 23:26-28
7:13 [p]Ge 39:12 [q]Pr 1:20
7:14 [r]Lev 7:11-18

a *14* Traditionally *peace offerings*

■ **7:1–27** *Lesson Eleven: The Seductive Tactics of the Adulteress.* In this lecture the father graphically portrays the dangers of the adulteress in a gripping autobiographical narrative of her seduction. His narrative is an artistically embellished autobiography, but his detailed eyewitness report of her brash and lewd seduction is so engaging and plausible that it seems authentic. He counters her enticing images of dining on savory meats, of smelling rare spices and of lovemaking on a lush bed with just as memorable images of an ox and stag going to the slaughter and of a bird darting into a trap. At the end of the lecture he exposes the woman as being in league with death. The lecture's structure suggests the father's sense of urgency to protect his son. The father's characterizations of the unfaithful wife both open (vv. 1–5) and close (vv. 24–27) his calls to listen. The adulteress embodies all that is against true faith (vv. 6–23).
■ **7:1–5** *Introduction.* The father once again calls on his son to pay close attention to him, including a motivational reason for doing so (v. 5).
7:3 Bind them on your fingers. The metaphor may refer to putting on prayer bands or phylacteries (see Mt 23:5; see also Josephus, *Antiquities,* 4,8,13), although it is uncertain how old this practice is (see Dt 6:8, 11:18). The phylactery was also strapped around the middle finger. Since one could not bind verbal commands to the fingers, the practice possibly functioned as a metaphor for memorizing the commands and constantly recalling them. Since the hands are always visible, the admonishing metaphor (cf. 3:3; 6:21) may also signify keeping the father's teaching visible for others to see and as a constant reminder to oneself. There also may be a related play on the sexual language of "touch" in 6:29—objects tied to the son's fingers would not only be visible during an act of adultery, but might physically hinder sexual activity. **write . . . heart.** Another metaphor for memorization and permanent retention of the father's commands and teaching (cf. Isa 30:8). The figure connotes their indelible impression upon one's character. Assimilating the commands as a way of life changes and develops a person's character so that one keeps the commands from inner motivation (2:2; 4:23; cf. Jer 31:31–34).
7:4 sister. This terminology expresses at the least an acceptance of wisdom as one's dear family. It probably is also the language of love to designate the groom's commitment to his bride (SS 4:9–10,12; 5:1–2; cf. Job 17:14; Sirach 15:2 [an Apocryphal book]), for whom he left his father and mother (Ge 2:23–24; cf. Tobit 7:16 [an Apocyphal book]).
7:5 See *WLC* 139.
■ **7:6–23** *Seduction by an Adulteress.* This lesson has three main parts: the encounter as observed by the father (vv. 6–13), the woman's smooth talk (vv. 14–20) and the father's concluding statement about its deadly effectiveness as the gullible one submits to her (vv. 21–23).
7:7 young men. Or "sons." "Among the young men" connotes the intimate relationship the sons should have had with their fathers (cf. 1:8; 4:3) and the transition that should have occurred (but did not) from one generation to the next.
7:8 In the direction of. Although it requires powerful persuasion to entice him into bed with the adulteress, the gullible young man nonetheless lacks a firm commitment to the right way (cf. vv. 1–4) and the sense to avoid the woman and thereby moral jeopardy, so he strays into her path (see v. 25).
7:10 dressed. To the insightful her shameless outfit betrays her hidden intentions, but to the morally ignorant it is a camouflage. She aims only to indulge her sensual lusts. She feigns fidelity to her wealthy husband when he is at home but flatters her lover as her only beloved while her husband is away. In truth she uses both and loves neither. This steely wife knows full well that her husband will take from her victim everything he owns should they be caught and that society will strip her victim of all dignity and respect (cf. 5:7–14; 6:33–35). She has no fear for herself, however. See *WLC* 139.
7:11 loud. Or "unruly." See 9:13.
7:13 See *WLC* 139,151.
7:14–20 Her seduction takes place in two escalating phases. First she spreads a veil of serious intention over her lustful restlessness and rebelliousness (vv. 14–17) and then propositions the gullible, arguing that they have nothing to fear (vv. 18–20). She hides her intentions by appearing to be in need of a sexual partner for religious reasons (v. 14), by idolizing the brainless youth (v. 15) and by lav-

[15] So I came out to meet you;
I looked for you and have found you!
[16] I have covered my bed
with colored linens from Egypt.
[17] I have perfumed my bed[s]
with myrrh,[t] aloes and cinnamon.
[18] Come, let's drink deep of love till morning;
let's enjoy ourselves with love![u]
[19] My husband is not at home;
he has gone on a long journey.
[20] He took his purse filled with money
and will not be home till full moon."

[21] With persuasive words she led him astray;
she seduced him with her smooth talk.[v]
[22] All at once he followed her
like an ox going to the slaughter,
like a deer[a] stepping into a noose[b][w]
[23] till an arrow pierces[x] his liver,
like a bird darting into a snare,
little knowing it will cost him his life.[y]

[24] Now then, my sons, listen[z] to me;
pay attention to what I say.
[25] Do not let your heart turn to her ways
or stray into her paths.[a]
[26] Many are the victims she has brought down;
her slain are a mighty throng.
[27] Her house is a highway to the grave,[c]
leading down to the chambers of death.[b]

Wisdom's Call

8

Does not wisdom call out?[c]
Does not understanding raise her voice?

7:17 [s]Est 1:6; Isa 57:7; Eze 23:41; Am 6:4 [t]Ge 37:25
7:18 [u]Ge 39:7
7:21 [v]Pr 5:3
7:22 [w]Job 18:10
7:23 [x]Job 15:22; 16:13 [y]Pr 6:26; Ecc 7:26; 9:12
7:24 [z]Pr 1:8-9; 5:7; 8:32
7:25 [a]Pr 5:7-8
7:27 [b]Pr 2:18; 5:5; 9:18; Rev 22:15
8:1 [c]Pr 1:20; 9:3

[a] *22* Syriac (see also Septuagint); Hebrew *fool* [b] *22* The meaning of the Hebrew for this line is uncertain. [c] *27* Hebrew *Sheol*

ishly preparing for him her erotic boudoir for a night of lovemaking (vv. 16–17).
7:14–15 See *WLC* 151.
7:14 have fellowship offerings at home. Or "have food from my fellowship offering." In Canaanite worship, after the deity had devoured the fat and intestines and certain pieces were presented to the priests, the worshiper and invited guests ate the remainder of the offering at home. According to the Mosaic Law and, presumably, Canaanite religious practices, the meal that fulfilled the vow had to be eaten on the day the sacrifice took place or on the following day, since whatever remained following that time became defiled and could not be eaten (Lev 7:16–18). Presuming her connection with Canaanite fertility worship, the communal meal would also have involved her need for a male partner for sexual intercourse (Ex 32:1–6; Nu 25:1f.). The invitation to have sex with her was also an invitation to participate in fertility rites. But was she telling the truth? The phrase "brazen face" (v. 13) probably means "told a boldface lie." Her speech is so full of falsehoods and double entendres that it cannot be taken at face value. The father characterizes the sly vixen's speech as "seductive" (v. 5) and identifies her dress as part of her cunning camouflage. He also characterizes her as rebellious rather than religious. She lies about how she has come to meet the young man (vv. 11–13,15), and probably about her husband, for the gullible youth is ultimately caught (vv. 19–23).
7:17 myrrh, aloes and cinnamon. These perfumes were purchased from merchants who traveled great distances, and they were prized and displayed as part of a king's treasury (2Ki 20:13). Only kings and the very wealthy could afford to use them lavishly (Ps 45:7–8; SS 3:6–7). The merchant's wife was willing to spend all this to gratify her sexual passion. Her deceived lover could not afford to ignore such an opportunity, she implicitly argued.
7:18 love. Or "lovemaking." The temptress promises sexual love without erotic restraint, but she denies the fundamental commitment of herself, which is required of true love. Her sort of eroticism leads to complications, even death, and must be rejected. To give oneself physically while holding back emotionally and spiritually on the basis of covenanted commitment is to live a lie—a split that is ultimately stressful and destructive.
7:19 long journey. This is a lie, to judge from the dire consequences that her victim suffers (v. 22; cf. 5:9–10).
7:20 till. She freely acknowledges that her husband will be back in two weeks, implying that she intends to remain married, though unfaithful, leaving the ignorant young man without moral excuse for his adultery. He cannot hope to avoid the jealous rage referred to in 6:33–35. **full moon.** Fellowship sacrifices were offered at the New Moon (v. 14), when the moonless dusk is particularly dark and obscure (v. 9).
7:21–22 See *WLC* 139.
7:21 The seductive power of words is a constant theme (see 2:16; 5:3; 6:24; 9:16). Contrast the healing power of the words of wisdom (e.g., 2:1–6; 3:1–2; 5:1–2; 7:24–25).
7:22–23 ox . . . deer . . . bird. The ox simile compares the simple to the king of domesticated animals and connotes that by following his animal instincts the youth deprives himself of all his opportunities and strength, and even of his life. The stag simile intensifies the fatal reality and adds the deer's grace to the bull's strength. "Stepping into a noose" adds the notion of entrapment (v. 22). The bird simile adds to the notion of entrapment the speed with which the apostate comes to his fatal destiny.
■ **7:24–27** *Conclusion.* This section closes with another call to listen carefully to the instructions given because of the devastating results of succumbing to the adulteress. See *WLC* 139.
7:26 slain. Her bedroom is not a boudoir but a battlefield with corpses lying about. It is the place from which many are sent to the grave (2:18ff.; 5:5; 9:18), even to the most inner chambers of the fortress of death that are destined for the most disrespected among the dead (Eze 32:23,27; Isa 14:15–20).
■ **8:1–36** *Second Interlude: Wisdom's Self-Praise to the Gullible.* This chapter balances with the previous interlude on wisdom (1:20–33). More importantly, it stands in contrast with the descrip-

2 On the heights along the way,
where the paths meet, she takes her stand;
3 beside the gates leading into the city,
at the entrances, she cries aloud:[d]
4 "To you, O men, I call out;
I raise my voice to all mankind.
5 You who are simple,[e] gain prudence;[f]
you who are foolish, gain understanding.
6 Listen, for I have worthy things to say;
I open my lips to speak what is right.
7 My mouth speaks what is true,[g]
for my lips detest wickedness.
8 All the words of my mouth are just;
none of them is crooked or perverse.
9 To the discerning all of them are right;
they are faultless to those who have knowledge.
10 Choose my instruction instead of silver,
knowledge rather than choice gold,[h]
11 for wisdom is more precious[i] than rubies,
and nothing you desire can compare with her.[j]

12 "I, wisdom, dwell together with prudence;
I possess knowledge and discretion.[k]
13 To fear the LORD is to hate evil;[l]
I hate[m] pride and arrogance,
evil behavior and perverse speech.
14 Counsel and sound judgment are mine;
I have understanding and power.[n]
15 By me kings reign
and rulers[o] make laws that are just;
16 by me princes govern,
and all nobles who rule on earth.[a]
17 I love those who love me,[p]
and those who seek me find me.[q]
18 With me are riches and honor,[r]
enduring wealth and prosperity.[s]

8:3 [d]Job 29:7
8:5 [e]Pr 1:22 [f]Pr 1:4
8:7 [g]Ps 37:30; Jn 8:14
8:10 [h]Pr 3:14-15
8:11 [i]Job 28:17-19 [j]Pr 3:13-15
8:12 [k]Pr 1:4
8:13 [l]Pr 16:6 [m]Jer 44:4
8:14 [n]Pr 21:22; Ecc 7:19
8:15 [o]Da 2:21; Ro 13:1
8:17 [p]1Sa 2:30; Ps 91:14; Jn 14:21-24 [q]Pr 1:28; Jas 1:5
8:18 [r]Pr 3:16 [s]Dt 8:18; Mt 6:33

[a] *16* Many Hebrew manuscripts and Septuagint; most Hebrew manuscripts *and nobles—all righteous rulers*

---

tions of the adulteress in chapter 7. The adulteress moves covertly at dusk and speaks falsely; Wisdom moves publicly and speaks direct and authoritative truth. Unlike the deceptive, twisted speech of the woman, Wisdom says only what is straight, right and true. The foreign wife leads her victims into slavery, impoverishment and death; Wisdom leads her followers into kingship, wealth and life. The foreign wife inhabits the earthly and mundane; Wisdom soars in heaven, above space and time. Both rub shoulders in the city and appeal for the love of the uncommitted, gullible youth—the adulteress does so erotically, Wisdom spiritually. The house of the unfaithful wife is a deathtrap; the mansion of Wisdom is the abundant life. This material divides into three main parts: an introduction (vv. 1–11), which exhorts the son to listen; the body of the lesson, which touches on Wisdom's historical and primordial qualities (vv. 12–31); and the final invitation and warning (vv. 32–36).

■ **8:1–11** *Introduction.* This introduction provides a setting for Wisdom's speech and an exhortation to listen because of Wisdom's value.

8:4–11 Wisdom names the addressees (vv. 4–5) in connection with the call to attentiveness (v. 6), which is followed by motivations for giving heed (vv. 6–9). She frames this stanza (vv. 6–11) with imperatives from listening to her words to accepting her chastening lesson. She deserves an audience because her words are flawless (vv. 7–9) and priceless (v. 10). She must emphasize the value of her words, for she has some hard things to say about self-discipline.

8:7 true. That is, "reliable."

8:9 To the discerning. That which is known is deeply influenced by the character of the knower. Thus knowing operates within the framework of spiritual commitments (see 2:5; Jn 8:31–32). Those unwilling to make a fundamental commitment to Wisdom will distort even her plain and truthful speech.

8:10 silver. When wealth is the reward of Wisdom, it edifies (see vv. 17–21); but when made the aim of one's life, wealth corrupts (1Ti 6:9–10). One either loves Wisdom or riches; there is no third way (Mt 6:24). Wisdom will withdraw herself, leaving the person, at best, a rich fool headed for eternal death. Wisdom, however, does not disparage wealth its rightful place (3:14–15; 8:17–21).

■ **8:12–31** *Wisdom in Historical and Primordial Times.* Wisdom divides her perspectives into two sections of ten verses each. The first pertains to historical time (vv. 12–21) and the second to primordial time (vv. 22–31). The first section features Wisdom's communicable attributes of counsel, understanding and strength that enable kings to rule and that bestow wealth and honor on her lovers. The second section pertains to her existence before creation and to her competence and authority (vv. 22–31), which enable her to bestow authority and order upon rulers in historical time (vv. 12–21). The wise ruler's ability to decree social order conforms to Wisdom's delight in God's decrees that ordered the cosmos (vv. 22–31).

8:13 To fear the LORD. See 1:7.

8:14 power. For counsel to be worthwhile, one must have not only a strategy for success but also the strength to carry it out in the face of opposition.

8:15–16 The proper function of human rulers is defined by the wisdom that ordered God's creation (Ge 1:26–28). Rulers should not depart from Wisdom (Dt 17:16–17; 1Sa 8:11–18; 1Ki 11:1–8; 15:33–34). For this reason the Messiah will rule by perfect wisdom (Isa 11:1–3). See *WCF* 23.2; *BC* 36.

8:17 I love those who love me. This statement contrasts with Wisdom being hidden from fools (1:28–29; see note on 1:7). Wisdom cares for her own (4:6,8–9). **those who seek me find me.** This statement suggests a relationship between Wisdom and the grace of God (cf. Isa 55:6). Jesus embodies divine wisdom and thus applied this saying to himself (Mt 7:7). See 2:4–5; 3:13–15.

8:18 riches and honor. Solomon's early reign was an example of

19 My fruit is better than fine gold;
what I yield surpasses choice silver.[t]
20 I walk in the way of righteousness,
along the paths of justice,
21 bestowing wealth on those who love me
and making their treasuries full.[u]

22 "The LORD brought me forth as the first of his works,[a,b]
before his deeds of old;
23 I was appointed[c] from eternity,
from the beginning, before the world began.
24 When there were no oceans, I was given birth,
when there were no springs abounding with water;[v]
25 before the mountains were settled in place,
before the hills, I was given birth,[w]
26 before he made the earth or its fields
or any of the dust of the world.[x]
27 I was there when he set the heavens in place,[y]
when he marked out the horizon on the face of the deep,
28 when he established the clouds above
and fixed securely the fountains of the deep,
29 when he gave the sea its boundary[z]
so the waters would not overstep his command,[a]
and when he marked out the foundations of the earth.[b]
30 Then I was the craftsman at his side.[c]
I was filled with delight day after day,
rejoicing always in his presence,
31 rejoicing in his whole world
and delighting in mankind.[d]

32 "Now then, my sons, listen to me;
blessed are[e] those who keep my ways.[f]
33 Listen to my instruction and be wise;
do not ignore it.
34 Blessed is the man who listens[g] to me,
watching daily at my doors,
waiting at my doorway.
35 For whoever finds me[h] finds life
and receives favor from the LORD.[i]

8:19 [t]Pr 3:13-14; 10:20
8:21 [u]Pr 24:4
8:24 [v]Ge 7:11
8:25 [w]Job 15:7
8:26 [x]Ps 90:2
8:27 [y]Pr 3:19
8:29 [z]Ge 1:9; Job 38:10; Ps 16:6 [a]Ps 104:9 [b]Job 38:5
8:30 [c]Jn 1:1-3
8:31 [d]Ps 16:3; 104:1-30
8:32 [e]Lk 11:28 [f]Ps 119:1-2
8:34 [g]Pr 3:13,18
8:35 [h]Pr 3:13-18 [i]Pr 12:2

[a] *22* Or *way;* or *dominion* [b] *22* Or *The LORD possessed me at the beginning of his work;* or *The LORD brought me forth at the beginning of his work* [c] *23* Or *fashioned*

the material and social benefits of Wisdom (1Ki 10:1–9). See 3:2 and 16. **prosperity.** Literally, "righteousness," which includes not only obedience to God's law but also proper order and right relationships among God, people and creation.
8:19 See note on verses 10–11.
8:20 righteousness. See note on verse 18. **justice.** An approximate synonym for righteousness (see note on 1:3).
8:22–31 These verses depict Wisdom's celebration of herself in her primordial glory. The passage breaks into two equal stanzas. The first pertains to her existence before creation (vv. 22–26) and the second to her presence during the creation (vv. 27–31). These halves are linked by corresponding themes: Wisdom's origins (vv. 22–23), a negative presentation of the creation (vv. 24–26), a positive presentation of the creation (vv. 27–29) and Wisdom's celebration of humanity's origins (vv. 30–31). This highly imaginative and figurative poem functions in three ways. First, it invests Solomon's wisdom with a patent nobility by tracing its antiquity before creation (vv. 22–26). Second, it makes clear that Wisdom possesses full knowledge, qualifying her to counsel. Only one who has observed creation from its beginning knows the whole story and so has the knowledge to counsel others (cf. Job 38:1–4). This knowledge makes Wisdom competent to speak dogmatically. Third, the verbal link (both translate the same Hebrew root) between "make laws" (v. 15) and "marked out" (vv. 27,29) illuminates the fact that Wisdom delighted in and celebrated God's creative decrees that gave enduring structure to the cosmos (vv. 27–31), and that she in turn enables rulers to issue decrees that confer enduring structure upon society. Their civil order reflects in miniature the divine cosmic order. Wisdom's revelation comports with the Lord's inviolable creation decrees (vv. 27–31).
8:22 brought me forth. Solomon's teachings derived from God's own character. See *BC* 8. **the first of his works.** Wisdom is the purpose of God's will (Eph 1:11), the eternal decree that establishes all things in their right relationships and determines the course of history. Wisdom is commended as the means by which we are put in touch with reality. **before his deeds of old.** Wisdom is prior to God's self-revelation in his covenant and saving acts.
8:23 appointed . . . began. Or "formed long ages ago"; i.e., at the very beginning, when the world came to be.
8:24 I was given birth. Since Wisdom was already present before the existence of the depths and the springs, before the formation of the mountains and the hills (vv. 24–31), she ranks above the creation and is close to God.
8:27–31 Wisdom was present when the Lord securely structured the universe that houses humanity (vv. 27–29). She was in constant delight, especially when God created humankind (vv. 30–31).
■ **8:32–36** *Final Invitation and Warning.* This conclusion is marked off by an address to the sons (v. 32), imperatives to "listen" (vv. 32–34) and argumentation or motivation (v. 35). Wisdom replaces her guise as one at the city gate addressing the masses (vv. 1–21) and as a primordial figure beside the Creator (vv. 22–31) with that of the owner of a house addressing the sons and inviting them to find her. Finding her is a matter of life and death.
8:33–36 See *WCF* 21.6; *WLC* 153,160; *WSC* 85,90.

36 But whoever fails to find me harms himself;[j]
all who hate me love death."

8:36
[j]Pr 15:32

Invitations of Wisdom and of Folly

9 Wisdom has built[k] her house;
she has hewn out its seven pillars.
2 She has prepared her meat and mixed her wine;
she has also set her table.[l]
3 She has sent out her maids, and she calls[m]
from the highest point of the city.[n]
4 "Let all who are simple come in here!"
she says to those who lack judgment.[o]
5 "Come, eat my food
and drink the wine I have mixed.[p]
6 Leave your simple ways and you will live;[q]
walk in the way of understanding.

7 "Whoever corrects a mocker invites insult;
whoever rebukes a wicked man incurs abuse.[r]
8 Do not rebuke a mocker[s] or he will hate you;
rebuke a wise man and he will love you.[t]
9 Instruct a wise man and he will be wiser still;
teach a righteous man and he will add to his learning.[u]
10 "The fear of the LORD[v] is the beginning of wisdom,
and knowledge of the Holy One is understanding.
11 For through me your days will be many,
and years will be added to your life.[w]
12 If you are wise, your wisdom will reward you;
if you are a mocker, you alone will suffer."

13 The woman Folly is loud;[x]
she is undisciplined and without knowledge.[y]
14 She sits at the door of her house,
on a seat at the highest point of the city,[z]
15 calling out to those who pass by,

9:1 [k]Eph 2:20-22; 1Pe 2:5
9:2 [l]Lk 14:16-23
9:3 [m]Pr 8:1-3 [n]ver 14
9:4 [o]Pr 6:32
9:5 [p]Isa 55:1
9:6 [q]Pr 8:35
9:7 [r]Pr 23:9
9:8 [s]Pr 15:12 [t]Ps 141:5
9:9 [u]Pr 1:5,7
9:10 [v]Job 28:28; Pr 1:7
9:11 [w]Pr 3:16; 10:27
9:13 [x]Pr 7:11 [y]Pr 5:6
9:14 [z]ver 3

■ **9:1–18** *Lesson Twelve: The Rival Banquets of Wisdom and Folly.* In this epilogue Wisdom is depicted as a noble patroness (vv. 1–6); Folly as a pretentious hostess (vv. 13–18). Both invite the gullible to their respective houses for a feast. Wisdom, out of true love, competes for the hearts of the uncommitted; Folly, out of erotic lust, competes for their bodies. Those who accept Wisdom's invitation will live, while apostates will die. The wise son eagerly anticipates Wisdom's urging to enter, whereas the gullible must be coaxed in. The invitations of the two women to the gullible are almost identical frames (vv. 1–6,13–18) for the chapter. Between these two invitations is the father's instruction (vv. 7–12).
■ **9:1–6** *Woman Wisdom.* These verses describe how the woman Wisdom invites young men to come to her and receive life. Her invitation stands in sharp contrast with that of her rival, Folly (vv. 13–18).
9:1 hewn out. Or "erected." **seven pillars.** Considering the space restrictions in ancient Israelite cities, seven supporting pillars points to an exceptionally large, grand and stately structure able to accommodate numerous guests. "Seven" in this literary fiction also symbolizes perfection (cf. 6:16; 24:16; 26:16,25); her perfect house has plenty of room to entertain everyone.
9:2 mixed her wine. Probably with honey and/or herbs to make the wine more spicy, potent and enjoyable (see SS 8:2; cf. Ps 75:8; Isa 5:22). **set her table.** The table's food and bowls signify that Solomon's proverbs are arranged for the enjoyment of those that study them. The lectures of the prologue have prepared the son for the collections that follow (chs. 10–31).
9:3 her maids. They represent the sages, such as the father and mother, who teach Solomon's wisdom (see Mt 22:1–14; Lk 14:15–24) and coax the gullible to eat and drink their wisdom. Their wise sons need no such coaxing (see 1:5; 8:34). **from the highest point.** Wisdom is open to all and pertains to the life of the city (see 1:20–21; 8:1–4; cf. Isa 52:7). The repetition of this setting in the exposition of Folly shows her vying with Wisdom to win over the gullible (v. 14).
9:4 come. Literally, "let him turn aside" (see 3:7; 5:7). The gullible is to humble himself, repenting of having been uncommitted and publicly confessing his commitment to the sage's wisdom. In this way he becomes wise and a guest worthy to sit at Wisdom's table, which is ultimately fulfilled in the heavenly banquet of the redeemed (Mt 22:1–13; 26:29; Rev 19).
9:6 Leave your simple ways. See 1:4 and 22. **and you will live.** See 2:19, 3:2 and 18, 8:35 and their notes.
■ **9:7–12** *The Father's Instructions.* This instructional interlude is divided into three parts: Verses 7–9 contrast the responses of the mocker, which result in rejection and shame, with those of the wise, which result in acceptance and love. Verse 10 looks back to verses 7–9, stating that the essential foundation of being wise is "the fear of the LORD" and identifying the resulting insight as the foundation for Wisdom's benefits. Verses 11–12 contrast the personal gain of being wise with the great loss of being a mocker.
9:10 See *HC* 94.
■ **9:13–18** *Woman Folly.* Instead of building a house, preparing a banquet and sending maidservants in preparation for her banquet, the personified Folly pompously sits on an elevated throne at the opening of her house (vv. 13–15). From this posturing and prominent position she seduces the gullible (v. 16). Tragically, the gullible are unaware that her house is a deathtrap (v. 17; 2:18; 7:27).
9:13 The woman Folly. Very similar to the adulteress. Both Folly and the adulteress are turbulent and unruly (7:11), ignorant (5:6), interested in the gullible one's body rather than his mind (v. 17; 7:13). Both Folly and the adulteress proposition him (vv. 15–16; 7:7,18), are already married (v. 17; 7:19) and are deadly (2:18–19; 5:23; 7:27). **loud.** Unruly or aggressive.
9:14 sits . . . seat. Or "sits . . . throne [or chair]," the posture of an authoritative teacher (cf. Mt 5:1; 23:2; Lk 4:20). In Proverbs the chair or throne often symbolizes a seat of honor (cf. 16:12; 20:8,28; 25:5; 29:14). The pretentious imposter presents herself as an empress who rules a city, and the gullible bow to her authority.
9:15 calling out. Folly sits as the city's queen, having prepared no meat, having mixed and decanted no wine, having set no table and having sent no messengers. Because her lifestyle so titillates and she demands no moral rectitude, she needs no discipline, industry

who go straight on their way.
16 "Let all who are simple come in here!"
she says to those who lack judgment.
17 "Stolen water is sweet;
food eaten in secret is delicious![a]"
18 But little do they know that the dead are there,
that her guests are in the depths of the grave.[a] [b]

Proverbs of Solomon

10

The proverbs of Solomon:[c]

A wise son brings joy to his father,[d]
but a foolish son grief to his mother.

2 Ill-gotten treasures are of no value,[e]
but righteousness delivers from death.[f]

3 The LORD does not let the righteous go hungry[g]
but he thwarts the craving of the wicked.

4 Lazy hands make a man poor,[h]
but diligent hands bring wealth.[i]

5 He who gathers crops in summer is a wise son,
but he who sleeps during harvest is a disgraceful son.

6 Blessings crown the head of the righteous,
but violence overwhelms the mouth of the wicked.[b] [j]

7 The memory of the righteous[k] will be a blessing,
but the name of the wicked[l] will rot.[m]

8 The wise in heart accept commands,
but a chattering fool comes to ruin.[n]

9 The man of integrity[o] walks securely,[p]
but he who takes crooked paths will be found out.[q]

10 He who winks maliciously[r] causes grief,
and a chattering fool comes to ruin.

9:17 [a]Pr 20:17
9:18 [b]Pr 2:18; 7:26-27
10:1 [c]Pr 1:1 [d]Pr 15:20; 29:3
10:2 [e]Pr 21:6 [f]Pr 11:4, 19
10:3 [g]Mt 6:25-34
10:4 [h]Pr 19:15 [i]Pr 12:24; 13:4; 21:5
10:6 [j]ver 8, 11, 14
10:7 [k]Ps 112:6 [l]Ps 109:13 [m]Ps 9:6
10:8 [n]Mt 7:24-27
10:9 [o]Isa 33:15 [p]Ps 23:4 [q]Pr 28:18
10:10 [r]Ps 35:19

a *18* Hebrew *Sheol*   b *6* *Or but the mouth of the wicked conceals violence*; also in verse 11

---

or investment to attract the senseless. Her crude invitation is sufficient to allure the masses to her fatal meal. Her zeal to make converts (1:11–14) compares to Wisdom's (v. 4). **who go straight.** The art of seduction consists in dissuading in a skillful manner someone from his preconceived way. The gullible do not aim to go outside the bounds of moral conduct (see 3:6; 15:21). Lacking a firm resolve, they are vulnerable prey to those who have a clear purpose (see 7:10–22).

9:17 Stolen water. That is, illicit sex (see chs. 5,7). **food eaten in secret.** It is so eaten because it is stolen or forbidden.

■ **10:1—22:16** *Proverbs of Solomon.* The superscription "Proverbs of Solomon" and a significant change in style separate this collection of Solomon's proverbs (10:1—22:16) from the preceding section (1:1—9:18) and from that which follows (22:17—24:22). These chapters divide into one section of largely antithetical (contrasting) parallel lines that shows that the morally righteous person is wise (10:1—15:29) and a second section with fewer antithetical parallels that contrasts the righteous and the wicked, especially within the royal court (15:30—22:16).

■ **10:1—15:29** *Righteousness and Wisdom.* By means of a series of proverbs, most of which are antithetical (contrasting) parallels, moral rectitude or righteousness is connected with Wisdom. These chapters divide into relatively independent sections that touch on various subjects: wealth (10:1–5), effects of speech (10:6–14), wealth and security (10:15–16), deeds and destinies (10:17—11:31), speech and deeds (12:1–28), good teaching and ethical living (13:1–25), living in wisdom (14:1–32), the gentle tongue (14:33—15:4), the importance of instruction (15:5–19) and the consequences of righteousness and wickedness (15:20–29).

■ **10:1–5** *Wealth.* The contrast between wise and foolish sons is fleshed out in two sections (vv. 2–3,4–5).

10:1 The proverbs of Solomon. See "Introduction: Author." **wise.** See 1:2.

10:2–3 The gain of the wicked does not profit them and their craving is frustrated, but the righteous are delivered from death and do not go hungry. Both verses address the relationships of the wicked and righteous to material possessions. Verse 2 pertains to the security of their lives and verse 3 to the gratification of their appetites.

10:2 Ill-gotten treasures. Literally, "treasures gained by wickedness." **are of no value.** Or "have no lasting value." **righteousness.** See 1:3.

10:3 does not let the righteous go hungry. The frustration of the wicked and the satisfaction of the righteous occur in the indefinite future, not necessarily in the present. Until the time of justice the righteous may suffer (see Lk 4:21; 6:21; 1Co 4:11; 2Co 11:27). See "Introduction: Purpose and Distinctives." **thwarts the craving of the wicked.** God does not ultimately reward labor that is motivated by self-ambition (cf. v. 22; 20:21; 28:22; Ps 127:1; 1Ti 6:9,10; Jas 3:1–16).

10:4 See *WLC* 141.

■ **10:6–14** *Effects of Speech.* This unit falls into equal halves containing four antithetical proverbs (vv. 6–9,11–14) around a pivot (v. 10). It concerns the effects of good and bad communication on oneself (vv. 6–9) and others (vv. 11–14).

10:6 Blessings. The plural denotes not only large amounts but also many kinds of blessings (e.g., victory, childbearing and the increase of herds and crops). God is always understood as the Giver of blessing, even when he is not explicitly mentioned. The Creator may mediate his blessings through a sacred person such as a patriarch (Ge 27:7), a priest (Lev 9:23), a king (2Sa 6:18), a dying man (Job 29:13) or the sacred congregation (11:26; 1Ki 8:66).

10:7 The memory . . . blessing. Or "The name of the righteous is invoked in blessings."

11 The mouth of the righteous is a fountain of life,[s]
but violence overwhelms the mouth of the wicked.[t]

12 Hatred stirs up dissension,
but love covers over all wrongs.[u]

13 Wisdom is found on the lips of the discerning,[v]
but a rod is for the back of him who lacks judgment.[w]

14 Wise men store up knowledge,
but the mouth of a fool invites ruin.[x]

15 The wealth of the rich is their fortified city,[y]
but poverty is the ruin of the poor.[z]

16 The wages of the righteous bring them life,
but the income of the wicked brings them punishment.[a]

17 He who heeds discipline shows the way to life,[b]
but whoever ignores correction leads others astray.

18 He who conceals his hatred has lying lips,
and whoever spreads slander is a fool.

19 When words are many, sin is not absent,
but he who holds his tongue is wise.[c]

20 The tongue of the righteous is choice silver,
but the heart of the wicked is of little value.

21 The lips of the righteous nourish many,
but fools die for lack of judgment.[d]

22 The blessing of the LORD brings wealth,[e]
and he adds no trouble to it.

10:11 [s]Ps 37:30; Pr 13:12,14,19 [t]ver 6
10:12 [u]Pr 17:9; 1Co 13:4-7; 1Pe 4:8
10:13 [v]ver 31 [w]Pr 26:3
10:14 [x]Pr 18:6,7
10:15 [y]Pr 18:11 [z]Pr 19:7
10:16 [a]Pr 11:18-19
10:17 [b]Pr 6:23
10:19 [c]Pr 17:28; Ecc 5:3; Jas 1:19; 3:2-12
10:21 [d]Pr 5:22-23; Hos 4:1,6,14
10:22 [e]Ge 24:35; Ps 37:22

10:11 fountain of life. The open, benevolent speech of the righteous is just as necessary for a community as a fountain of water, offering all abundant life—physical, intellectual, moral and spiritual. The right word, spoken at the right time (15:23) and in the right way (15:1; 17:27) supports or corrects a community (v. 10).
10:12 love. Love cherishes the wrongdoer as a friend to be won, not as an enemy with whom to get even (1:22). **covers.** The lover draws the curtain down in order to conceal all transgressions, however many or however bad (Jas 5:20; 1Pe 4:8). Instead of placing the transgressor on stage, withdrawing the veil to expose his faults (see 17:9; 25:21f.) and so exacting revenge, love endures his wrongs to save him from death (cf. 25:21ff.; 1Co 13:4–7; Jas 5:20) and to preserve the peace (cf. 19:11). Love withdraws the burning wood of gossip (cf. 17:9; 26:20ff.), but the quarrelsome and hot-tempered fuel the conflict into disastrous proportions, producing still further transgressions (26:21ff.). This truth must be held in tension with the fact that a spiritual friend also corrects the sinful offender (cf. Lev 19:17; Gal 6:1).
10:13 rod. Denotes a part of a tree from which a staff or weapon could be made. Persons in authority—such as God (Job 21:9; 37:13), a father (13:23ff.; 22:15; 29:15) or even the Messiah (Ps 2:9)—used it to inflict remedial punishment on a slave (Ex 21:20) and a fool (26:3). Most frequently, the rod is the symbol of a father's authority over his children (13:24; 22:15; 23:13–14; 29:15; cf. 2Sa 7:14; Isa 10:15).
10:14 store up knowledge. Wise people "store up" (2:1) this book's knowledge to defuse the fool's words that at any moment can explode and rock the community.
▪ **10:15–16** *Wealth and Security.* The words "rich" and "poor" (v. 15) pertain to economic status, while "wages" and "income" (v. 16) pertain to money's use. Lest one value money's security too highly, it is juxtaposed with moral security: Righteousness bestows eternal life, while wickedness yields sin and death.
10:15 the rich. Wealth is good in the hands of the wise because they earn it through honest work and use it to help others. Yet "the rich" in this book are consistently viewed as evil because they acquire wealth at the expense of others and/or use it selfishly. The book of Proverbs warns against the dangers of ill-gotten wealth. Such gain deceives the rich into thinking that it provides real security (18:11), seduces them into becoming wise in their own eyes (28:11; see 26:12; note on 1:7), and leads them to lord it over the poor (see 22:7; cf. 2Sa 12:1ff.) and reject their pleas for mercy (18:23). One impoverishes oneself by giving gifts to the rich (22:16), whose ways are perverse (28:6). Other references to the "rich" should also be read as negative assessments (14:20; 22:2,7). Riches are fleeting (23:4ff.). Too much wealth seduces a person to deny God (30:8). Whoever trusts in riches will fall (11:28), but whoever trusts in the Lord is secure (3:5; 18:10; 22:19). The rich may find temporary life and pleasure, but when death strikes their moral insufficiency will ruin them (Ps 49; Lk 12:13–21). **ruin.** Or "terror," a reference to the constant suspense, fear and worry of the poor due to the threat of imminent death, starvation and injustice. The temptation to steal also hounds every step of the destitute.
▪ **10:17—11:31** *Deeds and Destinies.* These verses, arranged in seven subunits (not counting the transition in 11:9), establish a number of connections between actions and their consequences: the introduction (10:17), speech and expectations (10:18–32), security through honesty and righteousness (11:1–8), words in community (11:9–15), benevolence and community (11:16–22), desires and paradoxical fulfillment (11:23–27) and certain gain or loss (11:28–31).
▪ **10:17** *Introduction.* The introductory educational proverb of verse 1 asserts the effects of child rearing on parents; this one speaks of its effects on society.
▪ **10:18–32** *Speech and Expectations.* This first subunit of 10:17—11:31 is framed by attention to organs of speech, their effects on others (vv. 18–22) and their endurance (vv. 31–32). Its core pertains to expectations with regard to pain and pleasure (vv. 23–26) and security (vv. 27–30).
10:19 When . . . absent. Many warnings appear against effusive and flattering speech and against placing unwarranted confidence in another person's words (see 13:5; 14:15,23; 18:8,13; 22:12; 26:22; 29:12,19; 30:8; cf. 23:8; Ecc 5:1–7; 6:11; 7:8,21; 10:12–14,20).
10:20–21 These verses promote the good use of speech by the righteous in contrast to the preceding focus on the need to restrain the bad speech of fools.
10:20 choice silver. Good speech has the highest value because it is free from evil intentions and effects (see v. 21). **heart.** Here the word is parallel with tongue. The mind, will and inner character of the wicked are the source of his futile words (Mt 15:18–19).
10:21 nourish. Literally, "shepherd." In the ancient Near East, ideal kings were said to shepherd their people. Ezekiel 34:23–24 and Psalm 23 exploit this figure. Kings provided for, led, revived and defended their wards (Mic 5:4). Here this royal image serves as an example for anyone who is in a position to lead someone else. Whereas a multitude of words does no good (v. 19), the few choice words of one righteous person give life to many (see 7:26).

23 A fool finds pleasure in evil conduct,[f]
but a man of understanding delights in wisdom.

24 What the wicked dreads[g] will overtake him;
what the righteous desire will be granted.[h]

25 When the storm has swept by, the wicked are gone,
but the righteous stand firm[i] forever.[j]

26 As vinegar to the teeth and smoke to the eyes,
so is a sluggard to those who send him.[k]

27 The fear of the LORD adds length to life,[l]
but the years of the wicked are cut short.[m]

28 The prospect of the righteous is joy,
but the hopes of the wicked come to nothing.[n]

29 The way of the LORD is a refuge for the righteous,
but it is the ruin of those who do evil.[o]

30 The righteous will never be uprooted,
but the wicked will not remain in the land.[p]

31 The mouth of the righteous brings forth wisdom,[q]
but a perverse tongue will be cut out.

32 The lips of the righteous know what is fitting,[r]
but the mouth of the wicked only what is perverse.

11

The LORD abhors dishonest scales,[s]
but accurate weights are his delight.[t]

2 When pride comes, then comes disgrace,[u]
but with humility comes wisdom.[v]

3 The integrity of the upright guides them,
but the unfaithful are destroyed by their duplicity.[w]

4 Wealth is worthless in the day of wrath,[x]
but righteousness delivers from death.[y]

5 The righteousness of the blameless makes a straight way for them,
but the wicked are brought down by their own wickedness.[z]

6 The righteousness of the upright delivers them,
but the unfaithful are trapped by evil desires.

7 When a wicked man dies, his hope perishes;
all he expected from his power comes to nothing.[a]

8 The righteous man is rescued from trouble,
and it comes on the wicked instead.[b]

10:23 [f]Pr 2:14; 15:21
10:24 [g]Isa 66:4 [h]Ps 145:17-19; Mt 5:6; 1Jn 5:14-15
10:25 [i]Ps 15:5 [j]Pr 12:3,7; Mt 7:24-27
10:26 [k]Pr 26:6
10:27 [l]Pr 9:10-11 [m]Job 15:32
10:28 [n]Job 8:13; Pr 11:7
10:29 [o]Pr 21:15
10:30 [p]Ps 37:9,28-29; Pr 2:20-22
10:31 [q]Ps 37:30
10:32 [r]Ecc 10:12
11:1 [s]Lev 19:36; Dt 25:13-16; Pr 20:10,23 [t]Pr 16:11
11:2 [u]Pr 16:18 [v]Pr 18:12; 29:23
11:3 [w]Pr 13:6
11:4 [x]Eze 7:19; Zep 1:18 [y]Ge 7:1; Pr 10:2
11:5 [z]Pr 5:21-23
11:7 [a]Pr 10:28
11:8 [b]Pr 21:18

10:22–32 These verses focus on pain and pleasure (vv. 22–30), as well as on security (vv. 31–32).
10:22 trouble. Or "painful work."
10:26 teeth. Syriac, "broken teeth." One may assume that without modern dental hygiene and medicine, many adults in the ancient Near East had poor teeth. **who send him.** Royal messengers in the ancient Near East held very high, even courtly, social status. Often they were entrusted with a high degree of authority that transcended the mere transmission of instructions (13:17). The information gathered and communicated by the messenger was diligently sought out and communicated to assure its accuracy and therefore the expeditious and successful conclusion of a matter. If the messenger turned out to be a sluggard (lazy person), the effect would have been unexpectedly bitter.
10:25 See Matthew 7:24–27.
10:27 The fear of the LORD. See 1:7, 9:10 and their notes.
10:29 righteous. Meaning "blameless."
10:31–32 These verses pertain to the permanence and impermanence of righteous and wicked mouths. The topic returns to the organs of speech (see vv. 17–21) to focus on their destiny (see vv. 22–30).
■ **11:1–8** *Security Through Honesty and Righteousness.* This subunit of 10:17—11:31 develops the theme of security through honesty (vv. 1–2) and righteousness (vv. 3–8).
11:1–2 The explicit mention of the Lord's moral reaction in verse 1 underscores that he is the agent determining the destinies of the righteous and the wicked. Otherwise, apart from verse 20, God's role is mostly kept in the background.
11:1 are his delight. See *WLC* 142; *HC* 110.
11:2 humility . . . wisdom. Modest people judge their limits well, accept them calmly and confidently comport themselves according to their honest assessment. Modesty is the opposite of pride, an exaggerated opinion that exceeds limits. Thus wisdom ends in honor (3:35), while disgrace is the result of folly (16:18).
11:3–8 Verses 3–8 develop the theme of security through righteousness and stress the certainty that death constitutes God's final judgment for the wicked. The subunit consists of two proverb pairs (vv. 3–4,5–6) that emphasize the saving power of integrity. The upright make their way straight, and God delivers them from death. By contrast, the perversity of the unfaithful devastates them in final ruin. The conclusion (vv. 7–8) indicates that no mortal can save another; when the Lord saves the righteous from their present adversity, he puts the wicked in their place.
11:8 The neat system of justice that seems to be described in the

9 With his mouth the godless destroys his neighbor,
but through knowledge the righteous escape.

10 When the righteous prosper, the city rejoices;[c]
when the wicked perish, there are shouts of joy.

11 Through the blessing of the upright a city is exalted,
but by the mouth of the wicked it is destroyed.[d]

12 A man who lacks judgment derides his neighbor,[e]
but a man of understanding holds his tongue.

13 A gossip betrays a confidence,[f]
but a trustworthy man keeps a secret.

14 For lack of guidance a nation falls,[g]
but many advisers make victory sure.[h]

15 He who puts up security[i] for another will surely suffer,
but whoever refuses to strike hands in pledge is safe.

16 A kindhearted woman gains respect,[j]
but ruthless men gain only wealth.

17 A kind man benefits himself,
but a cruel man brings trouble on himself.

18 The wicked man earns deceptive wages,
but he who sows righteousness reaps a sure reward.[k]

19 The truly righteous man attains life,
but he who pursues evil goes to his death.

20 The LORD detests men of perverse heart
but he delights in those whose ways are blameless.[l]

21 Be sure of this: The wicked will not go unpunished,
but those who are righteous will go free.[m]

22 Like a gold ring in a pig's snout
is a beautiful woman who shows no discretion.

23 The desire of the righteous ends only in good,
but the hope of the wicked only in wrath.

24 One man gives freely, yet gains even more;
another withholds unduly, but comes to poverty.

25 A generous man will prosper;
he who refreshes others will himself be refreshed.[n]

11:10 [c]Pr 28:12
11:11 [d]Pr 29:8
11:12 [e]Pr 14:21
11:13 [f]Lev 19:16; Pr 20:19; 1Ti 5:13
11:14 [g]Pr 20:18 [h]Pr 15:22; 24:6
11:15 [i]Pr 6:1
11:16 [j]Pr 31:31
11:18 [k]Hos 10:12-13
11:20 [l]1Ch 29:17; Ps 119:1; Pr 12:2, 22
11:21 [m]Pr 16:5
11:25 [n]Mt 5:7; 2Co 9:6-9

earlier chapters must be seen in the light of eternity. The wicked eventually become the permanent inheritors of trouble, but the righteous experience trouble only temporarily (see 3:1–12; 10:28). Until the final judgment, justice does not manifest itself perfectly. See "Introduction: Purpose and Distinctives."

■ **11:9–15** *Words in Community.* This subunit of 10:17—11:31 reaffirms the power of words to revive or to destroy community (see 10:6–14). Verse 15 pertains to words because one takes responsibility for another's debt by verbal agreement and because one must use words to free oneself of this debt (6:1–5). Verses 9–13 pertain to good and bad speech, and verses 14–15 advise that the wise must be careful to discern when to speak and when not to speak.

11:10–11 The just fates of the righteous and wicked cause the community to rejoice (v. 10) because its well-being depends on justice. The righteous prosper with the community's full approval (cf. 10:8; 28:12,28; 29:2,16), but the wicked perish in disgrace.

11:11 blessing of the upright. The phrase refers to God's bestowal of blessing on them and/or to the blessing the upright confer on the city through their beneficent presence and prayers.

11:12–13 These verses teach self-restraint in speech and point out the destructive effects on the community of derogatory comments by individuals. The gossips and slanderers stand in sharp contrast to the wise, who are silent in the face of insults.

11:14–15 Verse 14 balances the teaching of prudent silence (vv. 12–13) with a call for prudent speech. Verses 14–15 juxtapose imprudent action that brings disaster with prudent action that offers security. Verse 14 pertains to civic matters and verse 15 to personal business. See *WCF* 31.2; *WLC* 141.

■ **11:16–22** *Benevolence and Community.* The frame of this subunit of 10:17—11:31 contrasts a gracious woman who gains true honor (v. 16) with the indiscreet beauty who has no honor (v. 22). Benevolence is contrasted with selfishness (vv. 16–17); these characteristics bring life and death, respectively (vv. 18–19), as guaranteed by the Lord's judgment (vv. 20–21).

11:16 A gracious woman gains glory and wealth, while powerful men accrue merely temporary riches. Kindness, not brute strength, yields truly valuable rewards.

11:17 Kind people benefit themselves as well as others, but selfish people hurt both themselves and those with whom they come in contact.

11:20–21 God's attitude toward individuals in verse 20 corresponds to the outcome of their lives in verse 21.

■ **11:23–27** *Desires and Paradoxical Fulfillment.* Verses 23 and 27 form a frame around this subunit of 10:17—11:31 on deeds and destinies. Verses 23–25 flesh out the paradox that the giver gains and the victimizer victimizes himself (vv. 17–21).

11:24 gives freely. Literally, "scatters," which in this context means to distribute widely, generously, paying little attention to where the beneficence ends up. **poverty.** Literally, "only to poverty."

26 People curse the man who hoards grain,
but blessing crowns him who is willing to sell.

27 He who seeks good finds goodwill,
but evil comes to him who searches for it.[o]

28 Whoever trusts in his riches will fall,[p]
but the righteous will thrive like a green leaf.[q]

29 He who brings trouble on his family will inherit only wind,
and the fool will be servant to the wise.[r]

30 The fruit of the righteous is a tree of life,[s]
and he who wins souls is wise.

31 If the righteous receive their due[t] on earth,
how much more the ungodly and the sinner!

11:27 [o]Est 7:10; Ps 7:15-16
11:28 [p]Job 31:24-28; Ps 49:6; 52:7; Mk 10:25; 1Ti 6:17 [q]Ps 1:3; 92:12-14; Jer 17:8
11:29 [r]Pr 14:19
11:30 [s]Jas 5:20
11:31 [t]Pr 13:21; Jer 25:29; 1Pe 4:18

12

Whoever loves discipline loves knowledge,
but he who hates correction is stupid.[u]

2 A good man obtains favor from the LORD,
but the LORD condemns a crafty man.

3 A man cannot be established through wickedness,
but the righteous cannot be uprooted.[v]

4 A wife of noble character is her husband's crown,
but a disgraceful wife is like decay in his bones.[w]

12:1 [u]Pr 9:7-9; 15:5,10,12,32
12:3 [v]Pr 10:25
12:4 [w]Pr 14:30

11:26 People . . . grain. Literally, "As for him who hoards grain, people curse him." See *WLC* 142.
11:27 seeks good. In this context "evil" refers to harming others and "good" to providing for their well-being (v. 23; 3:27).
■ **11:28–31** *Certain Gain or Loss.* These verses continue the theme of gain or loss as the final subunit of 10:17—11:31, but the emphasis is more on their certainty than on the activity of serving others or self (cf. vv. 16–22). These verses are constructed similarly to verses 24–26. Verse 29 elaborates the house image in verse 28 (assuming that "fall" refers to a building), and verse 30 elaborates the tree image in verse 28.
11:29–30 Verses 29–30 elaborate further upon the two images of verse 28. A foolish man ruins his household and ends up a slave to the wise (v. 29). In contrast, the righteous, who are truly wise, produce abundant life for others and save them from death (v. 30).
11:29 trouble. Or "ruin." **inherit only wind.** "Inherit" denotes the passing on of ancient property (both land and houses; cf. Lev 25) that provided the family with its sustenance and shelter, and "wind" is a metaphor for being left with nothing (Job 15:2; 16:3; Ecc 1:14; Isa 26:18; Jer 5:13). **and the fool.** By losing his property the fool foregoes his freedom, so that his property may be used positively by another for society's benefit (14:19; 17:2). The fool's miserliness leads to his misery. Instead of passing on the inherited property (cf. 19:14) and building it up by wisdom (14:1; 24:3–4,27), he reduces the family's heritage to nothing and himself becomes a slave. The family's property is turned over to one who knows and values God's eternal social order of serving others (vv. 23–27).
11:30 This verse compares the flourishing of the righteous to a fruit-bearing tree (cf. v. 28). The righteous rescues people from death as they turn aside to eat of his attractive, healing, life-giving fruit. **is a tree of life.** Or "is the fruit of a tree of life." **wins souls.** Better, "saves lives." Literally, "takes lives." Since elsewhere "takes lives" refers to killing, it is best understood here as an intentional irony.
11:31 This section is drawn to a conclusion with a climactic assertion that crime does not pay. This is the first time the form of climax ("how much more") occurs. The premise assumes that the righteousness of even the best is woefully inadequate (cf. Job 4:17–19; 25:4–6; Ecc 7:20; Ps 143:2). **the righteous receive their due.** Not even the righteous can escape the scrutiny of judgment. They receive what they deserve. The Septuagint (the Greek translation of the OT) accurately paraphrases the principle thus: "If a righteous man is barely saved" (see 1Pe 4:18). **on earth.** This verse implies a distinction between the present remedial punishment of the righteous "on earth" and the future penal punishment of the wicked, the theme of this section. The preceding proverbs leave no doubt that their eternal death is in view.
■ **12:1–28** *Speech and Deeds.* Chapter 12 consists of two subunits that are of equal length and deal with speech and deeds (vv. 1–14,15–28). Each half begins with an educational aphorism contrasting the teachable wise person with the incorrigible fool (vv. 1,15), in order to encourage the son to accept the teachings in the verses that follow. Each half concludes by promising the righteous life, both now and forevermore (vv. 14,28).
■ **12:1–14** *One Look at Speech and Deeds.* The first look at this topic divides into the introduction, which lays down foundational truths about wisdom (vv. 1–3); the body, which focuses on speech (vv. 4–7) and deeds (vv. 8–12); and the conclusion (vv. 13–14), which joins the themes of speech and deeds.
■ **12:1–3** *Introduction.* The introduction sets forth the fundamental elements of the unit: a characterization of the wise and foolish as open or closed to shaping (v. 1), the Lord as the agent who upholds the moral order (v. 2), and the eternal destinies of the wicked and righteous (v. 3). Like 10:1–3, this introduction also continues the educational proverb with an ethical (v. 2) and a theological statement (v. 3) with reference to contrasting eternal destinies (cf. vv. 21–22).
12:1 discipline. Or "instruction." **stupid.** The Hebrew word means "as brutish as an animal" (see Ps 73:22).
12:2 good. In this context a good person is one who contributes to the community's well-being out of unfailing kindness (cf. 3:3). **condemns.** The Lord pronounces the impious and unethical person guilty of violating the norms of wisdom and so hands him over to death (cf. Mal 3:5; Jn 3:19–20).
■ **12:4–7** *Two Kinds of Speech.* These verses contrast two kinds of wives (v. 4) and, assuming that the noble and competent wife is righteous and the shameful wife is wicked, conclude with contrasting the impermanence and stability of their respective households (v. 7). This frame relates one's speech and destiny to the well-being of one's whole household (v. 7). This striking reference to the wife sets off the body (vv. 4–12) from the introduction (vv. 1–3).
12:4 husband's. The Hebrew expression means broadly "lord" or, in this context, "lord of his household." Peter holds up Sarah as an ideal wife because in her self-talk she called Abraham her "master" (1Pe 3:6; cf. Ge 18:12). This proverb assumes that the husband reciprocates with his own service to his wife because he is pious and prayerful (18:22; 19:14), wise and righteous, kind and generous, sacrificing himself for her good rather than acting in a self-serving manner (cf. 1Pe 3:7). **crown.** A crown, the symbol of honor and authority, is elevated, outward and highly visible, while decay in the bones is deep, inward and invisible. The shameful wife robs her husband of social standing, whereas the noble and capable wife strengthens his very being by conferring upon him social honor and empowering him to rule in the community (cf. 31:23). **disgraceful.** The Hebrew word connotes that the husband risked himself in marriage to gain dignity and the full measure of his stature but instead experienced the opposite (see 10:5). She undermined him by being unfaithful (2:17) and contentious (19:13; 21:9,19) and/or impious and incompetent (cf. 31:10–31).

5 The plans of the righteous are just,
but the advice of the wicked is deceitful.

6 The words of the wicked lie in wait for blood,
but the speech of the upright rescues them.[x]

7 Wicked men are overthrown and are no more,[y]
but the house of the righteous stands firm.[z]

8 A man is praised according to his wisdom,
but men with warped minds are despised.

9 Better to be a nobody and yet have a servant
than pretend to be somebody and have no food.

10 A righteous man cares for the needs of his animal,
but the kindest acts of the wicked are cruel.

11 He who works his land will have abundant food,
but he who chases fantasies lacks judgment.[a]

12 The wicked desire the plunder of evil men,
but the root of the righteous flourishes.

13 An evil man is trapped by his sinful talk,[b]
but a righteous man escapes trouble.[c]

14 From the fruit of his lips a man is filled with good things[d]
as surely as the work of his hands rewards him.[e]

15 The way of a fool seems right to him,[f]
but a wise man listens to advice.

16 A fool shows his annoyance at once,
but a prudent man overlooks an insult.[g]

17 A truthful witness gives honest testimony,
but a false witness tells lies.[h]

12:6 [x]Pr 14:3
12:7 [y]Ps 37:36 [z]Pr 10:25
12:11 [a]Pr 28:19
12:13 [b]Pr 18:7 [c]Pr 21:23; 2Pe 2:9
12:14 [d]Pr 13:2; 15:23; 18:20 [e]Isa 3:10-11
12:15 [f]Pr 14:12; 16:2,25; Lk 18:11
12:16 [g]Pr 29:11
12:17 [h]Pr 14:5,25

■ **12:8–12** *Two Kinds of Deeds.* These verses pertain to deeds and how they affect property. They begin by contrasting generally the characters of those having and lacking good sense (v. 8) and conclude with an aphorism contrasting their permanence versus impermanence (v. 12; cf. vv. 3,7). All three proverbs are rooted in the agricultural life.

12:9 servant. Elsewhere rendered "slave" (cf. 19:10). In view is a person who voluntarily sold himself into slavery in order to repay his debt (Lev 25:39–43). A slave did the hard field work to supply his owner with food. The antithetical parallel, having "no food" (i.e., lacking the basics to sustain life), suggests that having a slave was judged as a necessity for life (cf. 30:8–9). In early Israel the value of a slave was 30 shekels (Ex 21:32; cf. also 2 Maccabees 8:11 [an Apocryphal book]; Mt 27:3), which placed ownership of a slave within reach of those in modest circumstances.

12:10 animal. See Exodus 20:12 and 23:11 (see also Lev 25:7; Dt 11:15; Ne 12:14; Pss 36:7; 104:14,17; Isa 30:6; 46:1; Jnh 4:11). Providing for the needs of the working ox functioned in the law as a symbol for taking care of one's workers (Dt 25:4; 1Co 9:9–10). There may be a connection between owning a slave (v. 9) and caring for him by anticipating his needs (v. 10). By contrast, if the wicked are cruel to animals (lesser creatures) in their care, they certainly cannot be trusted to care for human beings (greater creatures) under their authority. Compare Matthew 25:23.

12:11 fantasies. Ventures or gambles that do not involve hard work and/or do not contribute to the common wealth. The abstraction is broad enough to include any get-rich-quick scheme (21:5–6) or the inaction of waiting for "one's ship to come in." The book of Proverbs balances the truth that poor behavior sometimes brings poverty with the reality that poverty may also be due to poor environment and poor government (13:23; cf. 1Sa 8:11–17).

12:12 plunder. Or "stronghold."

■ **12:13–14** *Conclusion.* These verses are united by references to organs of speech: "talk" (lit., "lips"; v. 13) and "lips" (lit., "mouth"; v. 14). The corrupt speech of a sinner leads to his death (v. 13), while the upright speech of the righteous sates him with good things (v. 14). The verses conclude verses 1–14 by combining the topics of words (cf. vv. 4–7,14) and work (cf. vv. 8–12,14).

■ **12:15–28** *Another Look at Speech and Deeds.* An educational aphorism (vv. 15–16) is followed by the main body, comprised of a collection of proverbs on words (vv. 17–23) and works (vv. 24–27). As in verses 1–14, the wisdom vocabulary of the introductory child-rearing proverb (i.e., "fool" and "wise man" [v. 15]) gives way to the ethical terms "wicked" (v. 21) and "righteous" (v. 26), and the passage begins with a generalization that is followed by specifics. The entire unit is framed by a focus on "the way" (vv. 15,28).

■ **12:15–16** *Introduction.* The conceited fool thinks himself upstanding and without need of correction (v. 15), but his lack of uprightness becomes known by public evaluation when he fails to exhibit self-control (v. 16).

■ **12:17–23** *Two Kinds of Speech.* Although these verses do not pertain directly to speech, they are foundational to it. If "a wise man listens to advice" (v. 15), then "the tongue of the wise brings healing" (v. 18).

12:17–19 Verse 17 pertains to speech that either intentionally pursues righteousness or misleads away from righteousness, while verse 18 pertains to speech that unintentionally damages others (cf. Lev 5:1). Verse 17 promotes truthful speech in the courtroom and verse 19 more generally, although in the Septuagint (the Greek translation of the OT) it also carries courtroom connotations ("a hasty witness has an unjust tongue"). Verse 17 pertains to the positive effect of the trustworthy witness's words on the verdict and the meting out of justice, while verse 19 elaborates on his character and underscores his endurance. See *WLC* 136.

12:17 witness. A person who possesses personal knowledge of an event or one who can testify on the basis of a firsthand report that he has heard (cf. Lev 5:1). Such a person is under obligation to testify truthfully (cf. 6:18; 29:24); the very life of the accused depends on the testimony of a reliable witness (14:25). Since ancient society lacked modern, sophisticated scientific methods of establishing forensic evidence, an eyewitness report was crucial for determining truth (cf. 14:5,25; 18:21; 19:5,9,28; 21:28; 24:28; 25:18; 29:24; Ex 23:1–3). Accordingly, a false witness was to suffer the same punishment he had intended for his victim (Dt 19:16–19). See *WLC* 145.

12:18 [i]Ps 57:4 [j]Pr 15:4

18 Reckless words pierce like a sword,[i]
but the tongue of the wise brings healing.[j]

19 Truthful lips endure forever,
but a lying tongue lasts only a moment.

20 There is deceit in the hearts of those who plot evil,
but joy for those who promote peace.

12:21 [k]Ps 91:10

21 No harm befalls the righteous,[k]
but the wicked have their fill of trouble.

12:22 [l]Pr 6:17; Rev 22:15 [m]Pr 11:20

22 The LORD detests lying lips,[l]
but he delights in men who are truthful.[m]

12:23 [n]Pr 10:14; 13:16

23 A prudent man keeps his knowledge to himself,[n]
but the heart of fools blurts out folly.

12:24 [o]Pr 10:4

24 Diligent hands will rule,
but laziness ends in slave labor.[o]

12:25 [p]Pr 15:13; Isa 50:4

25 An anxious heart weighs a man down,[p]
but a kind word cheers him up.

26 A righteous man is cautious in friendship,[a]
but the way of the wicked leads them astray.

27 The lazy man does not roast[b] his game,
but the diligent man prizes his possessions.

12:28 [q]Dt 30:15

28 In the way of righteousness there is life;[q]
along that path is immortality.

13:1 [r]Pr 10:1

13

A wise son heeds his father's instruction,
but a mocker does not listen to rebuke.[r]

13:2 [s]Pr 12:14

2 From the fruit of his lips a man enjoys good things,[s]
but the unfaithful have a craving for violence.

13:3 [t]Jas 3:2 [u]Pr 21:23 [v]Pr 18:7,20-21

3 He who guards his lips[t] guards his life,[u]
but he who speaks rashly will come to ruin.[v]

4 The sluggard craves and gets nothing,
but the desires of the diligent are fully satisfied.

[a] *26* Or *man is a guide to his neighbor* [b] *27* The meaning of the Hebrew for this word is uncertain.

12:20–23 These verses on the "heart" (vv. 20,23; see note on 2:2) move from the deceit the heart plans to the folly it proclaims. Verses 20–22 resemble both the introduction (vv. 1–3) and verses 15–19. They first characterize people's inner dispositions (v. 20) and then contrast their destinies (v. 21). They then point to the Lord as the agent (v. 22). The wicked are deceitful (v. 20) and full of "harm" (v. 21), while the righteous are full of joy (v. 20), and no evil befalls them (v. 21). The wise seek the good of others and obtain the same for themselves. See *HC* 110,112.
12:23 keeps . . . to himself. The fool cannot hide his moral insolence—he is quick to speak foolish words. The prudent, however, speaks only when it is wise to do so.
■ **12:24–27** *Two Kinds of Deeds.* This final set of verses reintroduces the topic of work, bringing to a conclusion the unit's link between discreet speech and prudent work as twin essentials of wisdom (e.g., vv. 4–14; 10:1–15).
12:24 slave labor. Or "forced labor."
12:25 The pairing of this verse with verse 24 presumes a close relationship between social subjugation (v. 24) and psychological depression. Depression can be cured through healing words (cf. v. 18).
12:26 is cautious in friendship. Or "chooses his intimate friend carefully." A good word comes from a good person, and it can keep another from straying into sin, which leads to death (cf. 5:23; 10:17).
12:27 his. Or "any." **prizes his possessions.** Or "feeds on the riches of the hunt." The sluggard (lazy individual) does not bother to secure available food to sustain his life. As the incorrigible starve spiritually in the midst of abundant teaching (10:21), the lazy starve physically in the midst of ample food. By contrast, the diligent take advantage of God's benevolence and "roast" the game that they have hunted.
■ **12:28** *Conclusion.* The righteous retain a relationship with God forever, from which even physical death cannot separate them (see "Introduction: Purpose and Distinctives").
■ **13:1–25** *Good Teaching and Ethical Living.* Verse 2 trumpets the chapter's theme: Through morally good teaching and behavior one will eat what is materially good. These verses escalate from the implicit admonition to the son to listen to his parents (v. 1) to an implicit admonition to parents to discipline their sons (v. 24). This chapter consists of an introduction (v. 1) followed by four subunits that pertain to speech (vv. 2–6), wealth and ethics (vv. 7–11), satisfied longings (vv. 12–19) and eternal destinies (vv. 20–25).
■ **13:1** *Introduction.* The introduction to verses 1–25 recalls the vocabulary of the prologue (1:1–9), which calls upon the son to listen to the parents' instructions. Like its parallels in 10:1 and 16 and 12:1 and 15, this verse stands at the head of a unit and implicitly admonishes the covenant youth to listen to the instructions to follow (cf. 1:5).
■ **13:2–6** *Speech.* This subunit pertains to speech, a dominant topic of chapters 10–15. These verses refer to the positive values of productive speech (v. 2) and restraint in speech (v. 3) as they relate to both the righteous and the wicked (vv. 5–6).
13:2 craving. Or "appetite." See note on 2:10, where the same word is translated "soul." **violence.** The Hebrew word denotes infringement upon others' rights. In this case it is primarily through the use of speech that victims are plundered of their "good things" (see 4:17; cf. 10:11; 11:9).
13:3 guards his lips. The wise have open ears (v. 1) and closed mouths, whereas the foolish have closed ears (v. 1) and open mouths.

[5] The righteous hate what is false,
but the wicked bring shame and disgrace.

[6] Righteousness guards the man of integrity,
but wickedness overthrows the sinner.[w]

[7] One man pretends to be rich, yet has nothing;
another pretends to be poor, yet has great wealth.[x]

[8] A man's riches may ransom his life,
but a poor man hears no threat.

[9] The light of the righteous shines brightly,
but the lamp of the wicked is snuffed out.[y]

[10] Pride only breeds quarrels,
but wisdom is found in those who take advice.

[11] Dishonest money dwindles away,[z]
but he who gathers money little by little makes it grow.

[12] Hope deferred makes the heart sick,
but a longing fulfilled is a tree of life.

[13] He who scorns instruction will pay for it,[a]
but he who respects a command is rewarded.

[14] The teaching of the wise is a fountain of life,[b]
turning a man from the snares of death.[c]

[15] Good understanding wins favor,
but the way of the unfaithful is hard.[a]

[16] Every prudent man acts out of knowledge,
but a fool exposes his folly.[d]

[17] A wicked messenger falls into trouble,
but a trustworthy envoy brings healing.[e]

[18] He who ignores discipline comes to poverty and shame,
but whoever heeds correction is honored.[f]

13:6 [w]Pr 11:3,5
13:7 [x]2Co 6:10
13:9 [y]Job 18:5; Pr 4:18-19; 24:20
13:11 [z]Pr 10:2
13:13 [a]Nu 15:31; 2Ch 36:16
13:14 [b]Pr 10:11 [c]Pr 14:27
13:16 [d]Pr 12:23
13:17 [e]Pr 25:13
13:18 [f]Pr 15:5,31-32

a 15 Or *unfaithful does not endure*

13:5 See *HC* 112.
■ **13:7–11** *Wealth and Ethics.* This second subunit of verses 1–25 contains a play on "great wealth" (v. 7) and "makes it [wealth] grow" (v. 11), which forms a frame around this subunit on wealth and ethics.
13:7 In contrast to real wealth attained through industry (v. 4) and in comparison to false speech (vv. 2–3) and wickedness (vv. 5–6), verse 7 speaks of feigned wealth belying actual poverty.
13:8 may ransom his life, but a poor man hears no threat. The word "threat" implies judgment against serious sin. Wealth is both a motivation and means to ransom the lives of wealthy sinners and to make reparations for their sin. Conversely, the threat of judgment has little force against the poor, who have nothing to lose. All three incorrigibles—the mocker (v. 1), the disadvantaged sinner (v. 8) and the wicked (v. 9)—are doomed.
13:9 light . . . lamp. "Light" is a shortened version of the common phrase "light of the lamp" (Jer 25:10; cf. Job 18:5–6; Pr 6:23), so that "light" and "lamp" are synonymous in this instance. The light of a lamp symbolizes a person's success and well-being, not merely his physical life (cf. 24:20; 2Sa 21:17; Job 18:5–6; 21:17; 22:28; La 3:2; Am 5:18,20). God blesses the righteous with prosperity but curses the wicked (cf. Ps 1).
13:10 Pride. An exaggerated opinion of one's importance and a refusal to accept one's place within the social structures under God.
13:11 Dishonest. The Hebrew word translated "dishonest" means "puff of air/vapor" and is often used metaphorically for that which lacks permanence. The metaphor of obtaining money from a vapor suggests what English speakers refer to as "easy money," calling to mind riches accrued through tyranny, injustice, extortion, lies and windfalls at the expense of others. Instead of these methods, the book prescribes gaining wealth through patience, diligence, prudence, generosity and faith—virtues that have stood the test of time. **little by little.** Literally, "upon the hand." A slow, steady accumulation of wealth by the handful, not by a "windfall."
■ **13:12–19** *Longings Satisfied.* This third subunit to verses 1–25 is framed by the words "longing fulfilled" (vv. 12,19), which indicate the topic of this subunit: fulfillment through wisdom in contrast with frustration through folly.
13:12 This proverb contrasts the unfulfilled expectations of the godless with the satisfied desires of the godly (cf. v. 11). Although this proverb lacks ethical terms, it balances with verse 19 and implies that the wise and righteous eat of the tree of life, whereas the godless and foolish do not. Although they experience trials, the righteous are never ultimately disappointed (cf. Ge 15:3; 21:3–6; Pss 126; 137; Hag 2:7; Lk 2:25–30; see Mt 13:16–17; Lk 24:41; Ac 12:12–16). This proverb contrasts lives that are heading toward despair in death with those moving toward fulfillment of every desire in the everlasting presence of the Lord (Ro 8:19,23–25; 1Co 15:51–54; 2Co 5:1–4; Heb 10:37–38; Rev 22:7,12,20). **tree of life.** See "Introduction: Purpose and Distinctives." Compare 3:18.
13:13 instruction. Literally, "word," which in this context refers to God's Word, the Scriptures (cf. 16:20). **will pay for it.** The incorrigible, who thumb their noses at God's Word, are guilty and will repay their debt at the time of judgment, when the Lord fulfills the moral order that evil deeds yield bitter and irrevocable consequences (Ex 5:2; 14:28; Jer 36:23–32; Heb 12:25; 1Pe 3:20; 2Pe 2:5). See *WLC* 105.
13:17 Messengers were professionally trained according to relatively high standards and were expected to have some facility in both writing and foreign languages in order to fulfill their roles as diplomats, soldiers, royal agents, military governors, intelligence agents, postmen and chaperones. Professional couriers had to be courageous and bold, and their training probably included the study of military strategy and tactics. Their special status entitled them to privileged treatment. Although authorized to speak in the "I" style of the one whom they represented, they were required to

19 A longing fulfilled is sweet to the soul,
but fools detest turning from evil.

13:20 [g]Pr 15:31
20 He who walks with the wise grows wise,
but a companion of fools suffers harm.[g]

13:21 [h]Ps 32:10
21 Misfortune pursues the sinner,
but prosperity is the reward of the righteous.[h]

13:22 [i]Job 27:17; Ecc 2:26
22 A good man leaves an inheritance for his children's children,
but a sinner's wealth is stored up for the righteous.[i]

23 A poor man's field may produce abundant food,
but injustice sweeps it away.

13:24 [j]Pr 19:18; 22:15; 23:13-14; 29:15, 17; Heb 12:7
24 He who spares the rod hates his son,
but he who loves him is careful to discipline him.[j]

13:25 [k]Ps 34:10; Pr 10:3
25 The righteous eat to their hearts' content,
but the stomach of the wicked goes hungry.[k]

14:1 [l]Pr 24:3
14 The wise woman builds her house,[l]
but with her own hands the foolish one tears hers down.

2 He whose walk is upright fears the LORD,
but he whose ways are devious despises him.

14:3 [m]Pr 12:6
3 A fool's talk brings a rod to his back,
but the lips of the wise protect them.[m]

4 Where there are no oxen, the manger is empty,
but from the strength of an ox comes an abundant harvest.

14:5 [n]Pr 6:19; 12:17
5 A truthful witness does not deceive,
but a false witness pours out lies.[n]

6 The mocker seeks wisdom and finds none,
but knowledge comes easily to the discerning.

7 Stay away from a foolish man,
for you will not find knowledge on his lips.

14:8 [o]ver 24
8 The wisdom of the prudent is to give thought to their ways,
but the folly of fools is deception.[o]

---

be precise and yet flexible within the terms and parameters of the negotiations (see 10:26).

■ **13:20–25** *Eternal Destinies.* This final subunit of verses 1–25 elaborates on the topic of the results of good and evil. It begins with an introductory verse that calls upon the son to join the company of the wise (v. 20). Verse 21 asserts that evil hounds the sinner to a final death but that goodness rewards the righteous in the end. In the interim good people as a general rule pass on their wealth as an inheritance from generation to generation, but sinners ultimately lose the whole (v. 22). In an alternating pattern, verse 23 qualifies verse 21 by noting that tyranny reduces the abundance of food available to all, and verse 24 qualifies verse 22 by noting that success requires firm discipline. Verse 25 rounds out the unit with the renewed assurance that, in spite of present difficulties, the righteous will finally have their every appetite gratified, while the wicked will starve to death (see 10:2–3).

13:20 He who walks with the wise grows wise. Or "Walk with the wise and become wise."

13:23–24 These two proverbs qualify verses 21 and 22, respectively. Outside the family, tyranny prevents righteous retribution from being consistently realized prior to God's judgment. Within the family, discipline based on love between the generations provides for the successful transmission of wealth.

13:23 A poor man's field. The Hebrew word for "field" generally indicates ground that is lying fallow. This probably implies that the poor in view worked hard to collect food during the Sabbath year, either by gleaning in the fields of others (cf. Ex 23:11) or by collecting crops from their own meager landholdings. The concept may be that the poor were to store up food that would supply them well beyond that time (cf. Ge 41:35ff.). **injustice.** This proverb rejects a simplistic understanding of the principles asserted in the preceding proverbs. Because injustice presently exists, perfect retribution must come in a future that lies beyond clinical death.

■ **14:1–32** *Living in Wisdom.* The reference in verse 1 to a wise woman building her house resonates with 9:1, suggesting that verse 1 also functions as an introduction to a new unit. This unit consists thematically of three subunits: walking in wisdom (vv. 1–7), not living by sight (vv. 8–15) and the characterizations and consequences of proper and improper social deportment (vv. 15–32).

■ **14:1–7** *Walking in Wisdom.* The first subunit of verses 1–32 follows a balanced pattern. It begins and ends with implicit admonitions to embrace a wise wife and fear the Lord (vv. 1–2) and to avoid mockers and fools (vv. 6–7). The body of this section speaks of foolish and wise speech affecting the future (v. 3), balanced by a discussion of character-determining speech (v. 5). Verse 4 is pivotal, pointing out that wealth increases through initiative and industry. Like other units presented thus far in this collection (10:1—22:16), discreet speech and industry are coupled as the joint benchmarks of wisdom.

14:1 Proverbs 31:10–31 exemplifies how a wise woman builds her house and also connects her wisdom with the fear of the Lord (see v. 2; 31:30). **tears hers down.** Without a wise wife a godly home is scarcely possible. Ruth 4:11 speaks of building the family through childbearing, but childbearing should not be separated from child rearing (see 1:8; 31:26).

14:3 A fool's talk brings a rod to his back. The fool finds a rod (i.e., tongue) in his mouth, and with it he lashes himself. He is his own worst enemy.

14:5 See *WLC* 144; *WSC* 11,77.

■ **14:8–15** *Not Living by Appearances.* This second subunit of verses 1–32 warns the wise not to live as fools do—by appearances—and so destroy their own houses (cf. vv. 1,12). This section consists of balancing proverbs: Verse 8 speaks of the prudent and the foolish. Verse 15 contrasts the gullible and the prudent. Verse 9

9 Fools mock at making amends for sin,
but goodwill is found among the upright.

10 Each heart knows its own bitterness,
and no one else can share its joy.

11 The house of the wicked will be destroyed,
but the tent of the upright will flourish.[p]

12 There is a way that seems right to a man,[q]
but in the end it leads to death.[r]

13 Even in laughter[s] the heart may ache,
and joy may end in grief.

14 The faithless will be fully repaid for their ways,[t]
and the good man rewarded for his.[u]

15 A simple man believes anything,
but a prudent man gives thought to his steps.

16 A wise man fears the LORD and shuns evil,[v]
but a fool is hotheaded and reckless.

17 A quick-tempered man does foolish things,[w]
and a crafty man is hated.

18 The simple inherit folly,
but the prudent are crowned with knowledge.

19 Evil men will bow down in the presence of the good,
and the wicked at the gates of the righteous.[x]

20 The poor are shunned even by their neighbors,
but the rich have many friends.[y]

21 He who despises his neighbor sins,[z]
but blessed is he who is kind to the needy.[a]

22 Do not those who plot evil go astray?
But those who plan what is good find[a] love and faithfulness.

23 All hard work brings a profit,
but mere talk leads only to poverty.

24 The wealth of the wise is their crown,
but the folly of fools yields folly.

14:11 [p]Pr 3:33; 12:7
14:12 [q]Pr 12:15 [r]Pr 16:25
14:13 [s]Ecc 2:2
14:14 [t]Pr 1:31 [u]Pr 12:14
14:16 [v]Pr 22:3
14:17 [w]ver 29
14:19 [x]Pr 11:29
14:20 [y]Pr 19:4,7
14:21 [z]Pr 11:12 [a]Ps 41:1; Pr 19:17

[a] 22 Or *show*

touches on making amends for sin. Verse 14 speaks of being repaid in kind for sin. Verses 10 and 13 address the secrets of the heart, while verses 11–12 speak of the way to destruction and death.

14:8 deception. The parallelism suggests that, in addition to the normal meaning of deceiving others, self-deception may also be in view.

■ **14:16–32** *Contrasting Behaviors and Consequences.* This third subunit of verses 1–32 consists of three parts. The first encourages the youth, through characterizations, to join the ranks of the wise (vv. 16–18). The second promotes wise ethical behavior to this group by reviewing the respective consequences of good and bad social behavior (vv. 19–24). The third combines the notions of characterizations and consequences, concluding climactically that the wicked will be thrown down in final destruction but that even in his death the righteous will find refuge in God (vv. 25–32).

14:19–22 This cluster of proverbs admonishes youth to lay hold of good ethical comportment and to reject evil, because providence will reward the righteous and punish the wicked. These statements address relations among people who differ morally or socioeconomically.

14:20 This verse is a necessary qualification to verse 19, conceding that evil people may enjoy wealth for a time. Due to human depravity the affluent person who possesses material sufficiency but moral deficiency is not wanting for friends, while the poor man who is materially deficient but morally sufficient may lack companionship. The poor man may be despised by all, but his well-to-do counterpart is "loved" and wooed by the wrong kinds of people.

14:21 Verse 21 counteracts the possibility of misinterpreting verse 20 as a rationalization for shunning a needy neighbor. The proverb cautions against being the kind of person who steels himself against his poor or oppressed neighbor on the basis of hardhearted arrogance. Only the person who shows kindness to his disadvantaged neighbor is in a position to enjoy a right relationship with the Lord, as well as future happiness. And only the Lord, who controls the future, is able to fulfill the threats and promises of this proverb (see 3:1–10).

14:22 Verse 22 explains God's favor (v. 21) in terms of his gracious kindness and faithfulness.

14:23–24 Through their hard, honest toil, those who work toward morally good goals are rewarded with gains that exceed their expenditures (see 10:4–5; Isa 49:4; Heb 6:10; see Jn 6:27).

14:25–32 With the exception of verse 28, this cluster of proverbs combines five characterizations of the wise and the foolish, along with their respective consequences. The first characterization is that of the honest versus the false witness (v. 25). The second is that of being a God-fearer (vv. 26–27). The third characterization (v. 28) stands apart as the first of many royal maxims in the collection. Fourth is the characterization of the patient versus the impatient individual, with a description of their respective fortune and misfortune (vv. 29–30). The fifth pertains to piety and social behavior and their eternal consequences (vv. 31–32). Climactically, the final pair of proverbs points to the Lord, both explicitly (v. 31) and implicitly (v. 32), as the upholder of the moral order.

25 A truthful witness saves lives,
but a false witness is deceitful.[b]

26 He who fears the LORD has a secure fortress,[c]
and for his children it will be a refuge.

27 The fear of the LORD is a fountain of life,
turning a man from the snares of death.[d]

28 A large population is a king's glory,
but without subjects a prince is ruined.

29 A patient man has great understanding,
but a quick-tempered man displays folly.[e]

30 A heart at peace gives life to the body,
but envy rots the bones.[f]

31 He who oppresses the poor shows contempt for their Maker,[g]
but whoever is kind to the needy honors God.

32 When calamity comes, the wicked are brought down,[h]
but even in death the righteous have a refuge.[i]

33 Wisdom reposes in the heart of the discerning[j]
and even among fools she lets herself be known.[a]

34 Righteousness exalts a nation,[k]
but sin is a disgrace to any people.

35 A king delights in a wise servant,
but a shameful servant incurs his wrath.[l]

15

A gentle answer turns away wrath,[m]
but a harsh word stirs up anger.

2 The tongue of the wise commends knowledge,
but the mouth of the fool gushes folly.[n]

3 The eyes[o] of the LORD are everywhere,[p]
keeping watch on the wicked and the good.[q]

4 The tongue that brings healing is a tree of life,
but a deceitful tongue crushes the spirit.

5 A fool spurns his father's discipline,
but whoever heeds correction shows prudence.[r]

14:25 [b]ver 5
14:26 [c]Pr 18:10; 19:23; Isa 33:6
14:27 [d]Pr 13:14
14:29 [e]Ecc 7:8-9; Jas 1:19
14:30 [f]Pr 12:4
14:31 [g]Pr 17:5
14:32 [h]Pr 6:15 [i]Job 13:15; 2Ti 4:18
14:33 [j]Pr 2:6-10
14:34 [k]Pr 11:11
14:35 [l]Mt 24:45-51; 25:14-30
15:1 [m]Pr 25:15
15:2 [n]Pr 12:23
15:3 [o]2Ch 16:9 [p]Job 31:4; Heb 4:13 [q]Job 34:21; Jer 16:17
15:5 [r]Pr 13:1

[a] *33* Hebrew; Septuagint and Syriac / *but in the heart of fools she is not known*

14:25 This verse prevents a possible misinterpretation of verse 23. Although mere talk does not produce wealth, testimony in court can mean the difference between the life and death of the defendant. See *WLC* 144; *WSC* 77.
14:26–27 The phrases "fears the LORD" (v. 26) and "fear of the LORD" (v. 27) link the pair. God-fearers gain security for themselves, their families and the lives of others. See *WCF* 12; *WLC* 74.
14:28 Like several other royal sayings, this verse stands in close proximity to proverbs about the Lord (cf. 16:1–15; 20:26–28; 21:1–14; 22:11–12; 25:2–7; 29:12–14). This juxtaposition stresses that obedience to the Lord is particularly imperative for kings, in whose hands rest the lives of their subjects.
14:29 patient. Literally, "to relax the face." The patient person is unperturbed when wronged and controls his emotions so that he may think and act according to piety and ethics. He is not ruffled or goaded into overreacting in order to avenge himself or to seek revenge rather than trusting the Lord.
14:30 The physical response of patience is complemented by an inner tranquility. Serenity will preserve one's life, but the stress of irritation can result in death. See *WLC* 136; *HC* 106.
14:31 Inflamed passions caused by rivalry with a neighbor can spill over into oppressing or slandering the defenseless poor, actions which impugn God's name.
14:32 have a refuge. The righteous find a refuge beyond death.
■ **14:33—15:4** *Upholding Righteousness With a Gentle Tongue.* Following an introductory proverb (14:33), a proverb pair connects wisdom with the king's responsibility to reward and punish officials (14:34–35). A sequel on speech (15:1–4) addresses painful words that stir up anger versus gentle words that mend damage.
14:33 This educational proverb admonishes youth to move beyond the sage's revelation of wisdom to internalizing wisdom, giving it a final resting place in their hearts.
14:34 exalts. Describes people politically and territorially. Serving others, not self, provides political and moral leadership and derives from its prestige the benefits of power, peace and prosperity. **is a disgrace.** Or "condemns."
14:35 incurs his wrath. The moral posture of a nation depends to a large extent on the morality of its officials.
15:1–2 Gentle answers do not compromise truth (v. 1)—they adorn it (v. 2). Harsh responses (v. 1), however, promote folly rather than knowledge (v. 2). Verse 1 is a sequel to 14:35, instructing the servant to turn away the king's wrath through a gentle answer and warning the king against using stinging words in his fury against incompetence, in order that destructive anger may be avoided (cf. 16:14). See *WLC* 135,136.
15:3 The Lord's treatment of those who do good versus evil matches the king's response to prudent and shameful servants, respectively. The principles of reward and punishment connect the Lord in heaven with his representatives on Earth (cf. 14:27–28).
15:4 tree of life. A gentle tongue can heal the fracture inflicted by perverse speech. See "Introduction: Purpose and Distinctives."
■ **15:5–19** *The Importance of Instruction.* This unit consists of two subunits: the consequences of accepting or rejecting instruction

6 The house of the righteous contains great treasure,[s]
but the income of the wicked brings them trouble.

7 The lips of the wise spread knowledge;
not so the hearts of fools.

8 The LORD detests the sacrifice of the wicked,[t]
but the prayer of the upright pleases him.[u]

9 The LORD detests the way of the wicked
but he loves those who pursue righteousness.[v]

10 Stern discipline awaits him who leaves the path;
he who hates correction will die.[w]

11 Death and Destruction[a] lie open before the LORD[x]—
how much more the hearts of men![y]

12 A mocker resents correction;[z]
he will not consult the wise.

13 A happy heart makes the face cheerful,
but heartache crushes the spirit.[a]

14 The discerning heart seeks knowledge,[b]
but the mouth of a fool feeds on folly.

15 All the days of the oppressed are wretched,
but the cheerful heart has a continual feast.[c]

16 Better a little with the fear of the LORD
than great wealth with turmoil.[d]

17 Better a meal of vegetables where there is love
than a fattened calf with hatred.[e]

18 A hot-tempered man stirs up dissension,[f]
but a patient man calms a quarrel.[g]

19 The way of the sluggard is blocked with thorns,[h]
but the path of the upright is a highway.

15:6 [s]Pr 8:21
15:8 [t]Pr 21:27; Isa 1:11; Jer 6:20 [u]ver 29
15:9 [v]Pr 21:21; 1Ti 6:11
15:10 [w]Pr 1:31-32; 5:12
15:11 [x]Job 26:6; Ps 139:8 [y]2Ch 6:30; Ps 44:21
15:12 [z]Am 5:10
15:13 [a]Pr 12:25; 17:22; 18:14
15:14 [b]Pr 18:15
15:15 [c]ver 13
15:16 [d]Ps 37:16-17; Pr 16:8; 1Ti 6:6
15:17 [e]Pr 17:1
15:18 [f]Pr 26:21 [g]Ge 13:8
15:19 [h]Pr 22:5

[a] *11* Hebrew *Sheol and Abaddon*

(vv. 5–12) and the triumph of the heart over the tyranny of circumstances (vv. 13–19).

▪ **15:5–12** *The Consequences of Accepting or Rejecting Instruction.* Verses 5 and 12 form a frame around this section: The incorrigible fool who refuses discipline (v. 5) escalates into the mocker who hates wisdom (v. 12). Three proverb pairs develop the argument within the frame: (1) The righteous are rewarded with riches, but the wicked are brought to ruin (vv. 6–7); (2) the Lord is involved in the process (vv. 8–9); and (3) the escalation to certain death for incorrigible apostates is informed by divine omniscience (vv. 10–11).

15:6–7 The house of the righteous accumulates great wealth that also profits others, much as the heart of the wise accumulates and stores knowledge (2:1; 9:8–9; 10:14; 13:1) to dispense broadly and generously to others.

15:7 spread. Or "scatter." The Hebrew word connotes a situation in which something is thrown or spread about loosely and widely.

15:8–9 This proverb pair, linked by the catchword "detests," returns to the topic of the righteous and the wicked. Verse 9 provides the theological rationale for verse 8. The treasures of the righteous are rooted in their favor with the Lord, while the ruin of the wicked is grounded in the Lord's rejection of them.

15:8 sacrifice . . . prayer. A broken phrase referring to the two essential acts of worship: slaying a costly animal and the accompanying prayer for favor (cf. v. 29; 21:3,27; 28:9,13; Dt 26:1–15; 1Ki 8:22–63; 2Ch 29:27–31; Ps 4:5).

15:9 The criterion for God's favor is not the scrupulous performance of ritual but the ardent pursuit of serving others, accompanied by proper ritual.

15:11 Death. Hebrew *Sheol* (see note on 1:12). **Destruction.** The Hebrew (*Abaddon*) intensifies the symbolism of the grave (*Sheol*) as the place of destruction.

15:12 Verse 12 (by its connection with vv. 5,10–11) draws the subunit to its conclusion. The spurning fool of verse 5 is now the obstinate mocker. The apostate, who abandons the way of life (v. 10), finds a complement in the mocker, who refuses to go to the wise.

▪ **15:13–19** *The Triumph of the Heart Over Circumstances.* The first partial unit presents the ability of the heart to overcome (vv. 13–17). The concluding proverb pair points to the peaceful person in contrast to the angry one and the upright person in contrast to the sluggard (lazy individual) as concrete examples of spiritual dispositions that either triumph over circumstances or are defeated by them (vv. 18–19).

15:13 cheerful. Better translation "attractive" (same word rendered "commends" in v. 2).

15:14 The second part of the proverb pair traces back the heart's joy or trouble to whether or not it seeks knowledge. The heart of the discerning can be distinguished from that of the fool by observing their opposing appetites and manners of speech. **feeds on.** Or "is bent on."

15:15 This transitional proverb continues the topic of the heart's spiritual condition but shifts from its manifestations to its importance relative to the lesser significance of material well-being (vv. 16–17). The afflicted in health and/or wealth may possess a cheerful heart that enables them to endure and to overcome their adverse circumstances (cf. 2Co 4:8; 6:9–10; Heb 10:34).

15:16–17 The cheerful heart is based on "the fear of the LORD" (v. 16) and "love" (v. 17).

15:18–19 This pair presents two kinds of people: those who overcome and those who succumb to their circumstances. The first half of the pair contrasts the loving person, whose reward is peace, to the hothead; the second compares the upright person, whose reward is a clear path, to the indolent, who struggle to forge a trail through prickly underbrush.

15:20 [i]Pr 10:1
15:21 [j]Pr 10:23
15:22 [k]Pr 11:14
15:23 [l]Pr 12:14 [m]Pr 25:11
15:25 [n]Pr 12:7 [o]Dt 19:14; Ps 68:5-6; Pr 23:10-11
15:26 [p]Pr 6:16
15:27 [q]Ex 23:8; Isa 33:15
15:28 [r]1Pe 3:15
15:29 [s]Ps 145:18-19
15:31 [t]ver 5
15:32 [u]Pr 1:7
15:33 [v]Pr 1:7 [w]Pr 18:12

20 A wise son brings joy to his father,[i]
but a foolish man despises his mother.

21 Folly delights a man who lacks judgment,[j]
but a man of understanding keeps a straight course.

22 Plans fail for lack of counsel,
but with many advisers they succeed.[k]

23 A man finds joy in giving an apt reply[l]—
and how good is a timely word![m]

24 The path of life leads upward for the wise
to keep him from going down to the grave.[a]

25 The LORD tears down the proud man's house[n]
but he keeps the widow's boundaries intact.[o]

26 The LORD detests the thoughts of the wicked,[p]
but those of the pure are pleasing to him.

27 A greedy man brings trouble to his family,
but he who hates bribes will live.[q]

28 The heart of the righteous weighs its answers,[r]
but the mouth of the wicked gushes evil.

29 The LORD is far from the wicked
but he hears the prayer of the righteous.[s]

30 A cheerful look brings joy to the heart,
and good news gives health to the bones.

31 He who listens to a life-giving rebuke
will be at home among the wise.[t]

32 He who ignores discipline despises himself,[u]
but whoever heeds correction gains understanding.

33 The fear of the LORD[v] teaches a man wisdom,[b]
and humility comes before honor.[w]

a *24* Hebrew *Sheol*   b *33* Or *Wisdom teaches the fear of the LORD*

▪ **15:20–29** *The Consequences of Righteousness and Wickedness.* This last unit of 10:1—15:29 begins with an introduction (v. 20) that recalls that of its first unit (10:1; cf. 12:1; 13:1) and thereby forms a frame around the entire section. Once again the mother is mentioned (v. 20; cf. 1:8; 10:1). This final unit returns to the collection's dominant theme of contrasting the righteous and the wicked. Its first subunit pertains to joy in the educational process (vv. 20–23), a smooth transition from the preceding unit's theme of the importance of instruction (vv. 5–19).

15:20–23 The key word "joy" frames these verses and enables the disciple to follow the connection between the joy of parents having a teachable son and the grown son's joy in giving wise counsel after he has grown to manhood. The essential goal of the educational venture (v. 20) that is bounded by ethics (v. 21) and promoted by counsel and humility (v. 22) is right conduct and right speaking (v. 23).

15:22 In adulthood, counselors replace parents.

15:23 Parents experience joy when their children receive and employ their good counsel (v. 20), and wise adults find joy in accepting ethical counsel (v. 22) and in voicing apt words at the right time (v. 23).

15:24 The terms "understanding" (v. 21) and "wise" (v. 24) and the metaphor of travel link this transitional verse with the preceding subunit. The words "life" (v. 24) and "live" (v. 27) form a frame around this cluster (vv. 24–27).

15:25–29 The references to "the LORD" (vv. 25,29) frame this climax. The Lord secures those who are on the path of life and draws near to them to hear their prayers.

15:25 Verse 25 qualifies verse 24 by implying that oppressors who take advantage of the weak will finally be punished by the Lord (cf. Isa 1:10–17; 5:8; Am 2:6–8; Mic 2:1–11), who is like a consuming fire that devours the wicked without consuming his own people (cf. Ex 3:1–15)—even though his judgment occurs in the midst of his visible, covenant community. **widow's boundaries.** The wicked move the boundary stone an imperceptible half-inch at a time.

15:27 brings trouble. Or "brings ruin." This verse is bound to verse 25 by the words "house" (v. 25) and "family" (v. 27) and mentions bribery as a concrete example of how the proud (v. 25) and the wicked (v. 26) bring their houses to ruin.

▪ **15:30—22:16** *Wisdom and Ruling.* This second section of Solomon's proverbs (10:1—22:16) concerns issues gathered around the theme of ruling with wisdom. It divides into 11 main sections: the relationship between the people, the Lord and the king (15:30—16:15); wise and foolish speech (16:16–30); reaching old age through righteousness (16:31—17:6); fools (17:7–28); foolish and wise speech (18:1–21); wealth and wisdom in the court and in the home (18:22—19:22); kings and fools (19:23—20:11); speech and commerce (20:12–19); trusting the Lord (20:20–28); righteousness and justice (20:29—21:31); and wealth and moral instruction (22:1–16).

▪ **15:30—16:15** *The Relationship Between the People, the Lord and the King.* This introduction to the second section of Solomon's proverbs (see note on 10:1—22:16) consists of its own introduction (15:30–33) and a body pertaining to the Lord's sovereign rule (16:1–9) and to the king's subsidiary role (16:10–15).

▪ **15:30–33** *Introduction.* These verses, which introduce 15:30—16:15, comprise a pair of educational proverbs that function as an introduction to the following unit (15:30—16:15) and possibly to the entire next section (15:30—22:16).

15:30 cheerful look. Literally, "light in the eyes." This metaphor connotes the manifestation of the inward vitality and joy of the one bringing good news, as the parallel clause suggests, and is associated with righteousness (13:9) and life (see 4:18; 6:23; 13:9; 16:15; Job 3:16; 33:28). Proverbs associates light and life exclusively with the wise, suggesting that illuminated eyes belong to the wise (v. 13).

15:31 The focus shifts from the illuminated sage and his disciple's revived heart to the disciple's receptive ear (2:2) that hears the sage's life-giving correction.

15:32 Accepting or rejecting correction is a matter of survival or suicide.

16

To man belong the plans of the heart,
but from the LORD comes the reply of the tongue.[x]

16:1 [x]Pr 19:21

2 All a man's ways seem innocent to him,
but motives are weighed by the LORD.[y]

16:2 [y]Pr 21:2

3 Commit to the LORD whatever you do,
and your plans will succeed.[z]

16:3 [z]Ps 37:5-6; Pr 3:5-6

4 The LORD works out everything for his own ends[a]—
even the wicked for a day of disaster.[b]

16:4 [a]Isa 43:7 [b]Ro 9:22

5 The LORD detests all the proud of heart.[c]
Be sure of this: They will not go unpunished.[d]

16:5 [c]Pr 6:16 [d]Pr 11:20-21

6 Through love and faithfulness sin is atoned for;
through the fear of the LORD a man avoids evil.[e]

16:6 [e]Pr 14:16

7 When a man's ways are pleasing to the LORD,
he makes even his enemies live at peace with him.

8 Better a little with righteousness
than much gain[f] with injustice.

16:8 [f]Ps 37:16

9 In his heart a man plans his course,
but the LORD determines his steps.[g]

16:9 [g]Jer 10:23

10 The lips of a king speak as an oracle,
and his mouth should not betray justice.

11 Honest scales and balances are from the LORD;
all the weights in the bag are of his making.[h]

16:11 [h]Pr 11:1

12 Kings detest wrongdoing,
for a throne is established through righteousness.[i]

16:12 [i]Pr 25:5

13 Kings take pleasure in honest lips;
they value a man who speaks the truth.[j]

16:13 [j]Pr 14:35

14 A king's wrath is a messenger of death,[k]
but a wise man will appease it.

16:14 [k]Pr 19:12

15:33 The concluding verse of the introduction grounds the instruction in "the fear of the LORD" and adds the motivation of achieving social honor. The vocabulary of this verse recalls the book's motto (1:7) and is repeated, in part, in 18:12.

▪ **16:1–9** *The Lord's Rule.* Wisdom cannot be attained apart from the recognition that God is in control of all things and holds humans responsible for their actions.

16:1 God does not author an evil and/or ineffective answer. Humans plan what they will say and do, but the Lord decrees what will endure and become part of his eternal purposes (see Eph 1:11). See *BC* 13.

16:2 seem innocent. Or "may be pure."

16:3 your plans will succeed. Or "he will establish your plans." Since the Lord assumes ownership of the disciple's initiatives (v. 1) and evaluates the disciple's motives (v. 2), the disciple should conform his plans according to the Lord's revealed will and rely on God as his strength in accomplishing them. This will lead to results that outlast the temporary triumphs of the wicked (v. 3; cf. Ps 127:1).

16:4 for his own ends. In contrast to the righteous, whose plans and deeds are confirmed, the wicked and their deeds will be destroyed. See *WCF* 2.1; 3.3; *WLC* 15.

16:5–7 Verses 5 and 7 pertain to the Lord's moral sensibilities, which ensure that the wicked will be punished (v. 5) and the righteous triumph over them (v. 7). **love and faithfulness.** Refers, in this context, to human kindness to the needy. The proverb points to the human virtues that accompanied the sacrificial system that made provision for atonement (see Lev 1:4; 4:4; 16:21). The point is not that beneficent works are the basis on which, or even the means by which, the Lord grants forgiveness. Rather, it is that the sacrificial system is of no avail to a person not characterized by genuine love for others (15:8; 1Sa 15:22). This is because saving faith always produces love for others (cf. Jas 2; see theological articles "Justification and Merit" at Ro 3. **through the fear of the LORD.** "The fear of the LORD," which entails expressing "love and faithfulness" to others, is God's gift, received by faith; it is not generated by independent human effort (see 2:1–5).

16:8 In its context, this "better than" proverb, like 15:16–17, qualifies the assertions in verses 5–7 of divine punishment on the arrogant and blessings on the virtuous (see "Introduction: Purpose and Distinctives").

▪ **16:10–15** *The King's Rule.* The Lord mediated his justice on Earth through his wise and just king. The king of Israel, who foreshadowed the perfect King, the Messiah, stood in the place of God. These six verses fall into three segments: the king's authority to give just verdicts (vv. 10–11), his moral sensibilities toward justice (vv. 12–13) and, climactically, his ability to effect life and death (vv. 14–15).

16:10 oracle. Or "inspired verdict." The Lord enacted divine justice (cf. v. 1) by inspiring his wise king to hand down verdicts that did not betray justice. Solomon prayed for a discerning heart to distinguish between right and wrong so that he might rightly govern God's people (1Ki 3:9). The law by itself did not suffice (cf. 1Ki 2:1–4)—wisdom was needed to understand and apply it rightly.

16:11 are from. Or "belong to." The Lord established justice by the honest weights and measures that he ordained for the marketplace and that the king was to uphold. The king was not free to manufacture arbitrary balances and scales to suit his convenience.

16:12–13 The just verdicts of the ideal king (vv. 10–11) and the execution of the corresponding sentences (vv. 14–15) were to be informed by his moral sensibilities toward work (v. 12) and words (v. 13).

16:14–15 The king's just verdicts were to be coupled with the will and power to effect them.

16:14 a messenger of death. Alludes to an ancient Near Eastern myth in which Mot, the god of death, sent messengers to prophesy of coming deaths. In the same way the king's wrath presaged death (cf. 19:12; 20:2).

16:15 [l]Job 29:24

15 When a king's face brightens, it means life;[l]
his favor is like a rain cloud in spring.

16:16 [m]Pr 8:10,19

16 How much better to get wisdom than gold,
to choose understanding rather than silver![m]

17 The highway of the upright avoids evil;
he who guards his way guards his life.

16:18 [n]Pr 11:2; 18:12

18 Pride goes before destruction,
a haughty spirit before a fall.[n]

19 Better to be lowly in spirit and among the oppressed
than to share plunder with the proud.

16:20 [o]Ps 2:12; 34:8; Pr 19:8; Jer 17:7

20 Whoever gives heed to instruction prospers,
and blessed is he who trusts in the LORD.[o]

16:21 [p]ver 23

21 The wise in heart are called discerning,
and pleasant words promote instruction.[a][p]

16:22 [q]Pr 13:14

22 Understanding is a fountain of life to those who have it,[q]
but folly brings punishment to fools.

23 A wise man's heart guides his mouth,
and his lips promote instruction.[b]

16:24 [r]Pr 24:13-14

24 Pleasant words are a honeycomb,
sweet to the soul and healing to the bones.[r]

16:25 [s]Pr 12:15 [t]Pr 14:12

25 There is a way that seems right to a man,[s]
but in the end it leads to death.[t]

26 The laborer's appetite works for him;
his hunger drives him on.

16:27 [u]Jas 3:6

27 A scoundrel plots evil,
and his speech is like a scorching fire.[u]

16:28 [v]Pr 15:18 [w]Pr 17:9

28 A perverse man stirs up dissension,[v]
and a gossip separates close friends.[w]

16:29 [x]Pr 1:10; 12:26

29 A violent man entices his neighbor
and leads him down a path that is not good.[x]

30 He who winks with his eye is plotting perversity;
he who purses his lips is bent on evil.

16:31 [y]Pr 20:29

31 Gray hair is a crown of splendor;[y]
it is attained by a righteous life.

[a] *21* Or *words make a man persuasive* [b] *23* Or *mouth / and makes his lips persuasive*

16:15 When a king's face brightens. Literally, "in the light of the king's face," an expression connoting the ruler's beneficent favor.

■ **16:16–30** *Wise and Foolish Speech.* This unit consists of an introduction (vv. 16–19) and a body that considers the winsome speech of the wise (vv. 20–24) and the destructive speech of the malevolent (vv. 25–30).

■ **16:16–19** *Introduction.* The introduction speaks of security in wisdom and recalls the vocabulary of the book's prologue (cf. 3:13–14; 4:5,7; 8:10–11,19). Verses 16–17 link the acquisition of wisdom with uprightness. Verse 18 states that pride precedes a fall, but verse 19 qualifies that statement by implying that for a time the arrogant may plunder the humble and afflicted.

16:18–19 The focus shifts from outward ethical behavior to inner spiritual attitudes. The imagery depends on the contrast between *high* in the sense of pride and *low* in the sense of abasement. Instead of looking where they are going, in defiance of the first principle of wisdom (see 15:33), the arrogant raise their eyes above God and humanity (cf. 30:13) and stumble to their perdition (see 18:12).

16:19 spirit and among. Or "spirit along with." Before the proud stumble and fall (v. 18) they may trample the oppressed underfoot (cf. v. 8; 15:16).

■ **16:20–24** *Winsome Speech.* Having laid the foundations of wisdom, this second subunit of verses 16–30 explains how prudent speech benefits others. Variant words for "speech" occur in every verse apart from the central one (v. 22).

16:24 This verse draws the subunit on wise speech to its climactic conclusion. It compares healing and aesthetically pleasing words to overflowing honey.

■ **16:25–30** *Destructive Speech.* These verses explicitly warn against going one's own way and implicitly caution against accepting the teaching of evil speakers, including the "scoundrel" (lit., "insurrectionist man"; v. 27), the "perverse" (v. 28), the "gossip" (v. 28) and the "violent" (v. 29). In verse 26 the mouth functions as an organ to gratify the appetite, not as an organ of speech. Verse 30 may be included here to safeguard the disciple against the fundamental urge to gratify drives and appetites through the kind of speaking that exploits others. The catalog of four malevolent speakers reaches its climax in verse 29, both in its depiction of the speaker as violent and in its description of its deadly effect. Verse 30 brings the unit to a close, moving from evil communication to the crime itself.

16:26 See *WLC* 135.

■ **16:31—17:6** *Old Age Through Righteousness.* "Crown of splendor" (16:31) and "crown to the aged" (17:6) frame this unit and refer to its main theme: Youth are to win the crown of age. Instead of viewing old age as a time of physical weakness and decline, when virility and fertility have ceased (Ge 18:11ff.; 2Ki 4:14), this unit views

32 Better a patient man than a warrior,
a man who controls his temper than one who takes a city.

33 The lot is cast into the lap,
but its every decision is from the LORD.[z]

16:33 [z]Pr 18:18; 29:26

17

1 Better a dry crust with peace and quiet
than a house full of feasting,[a] with strife.[a]

17:1 [a]Pr 15:16,17

2 A wise servant will rule over a disgraceful son,
and will share the inheritance as one of the brothers.

3 The crucible for silver and the furnace for gold,[b]
but the LORD tests the heart.[c]

17:3 [b]Pr 27:21 [c]1Ch 29:17; Ps 26:2; Jer 17:10

4 A wicked man listens to evil lips;
a liar pays attention to a malicious tongue.

5 He who mocks the poor shows contempt for their Maker;[d]
whoever gloats over disaster[e] will not go unpunished.[f]

17:5 [d]Pr 14:31 [e]Job 31:29 [f]Ob 1:12

6 Children's children[g] are a crown to the aged,
and parents are the pride of their children.

17:6 [g]Pr 13:22

7 Arrogant[b] lips are unsuited to a fool—
how much worse lying lips to a ruler!

8 A bribe is a charm to the one who gives it;
wherever he turns, he succeeds.

9 He who covers over an offense promotes love,[h]
but whoever repeats the matter separates close friends.[i]

17:9 [h]Pr 10:12 [i]Pr 16:28

10 A rebuke impresses a man of discernment
more than a hundred lashes a fool.

11 An evil man is bent only on rebellion;
a merciless official will be sent against him.

12 Better to meet a bear robbed of her cubs
than a fool in his folly.

[a] *1* Hebrew *sacrifices* [b] *7* Or *Eloquent*

this stage of life as a period of authority, status and dignity, symbolized by a crown (16:31). If gray hair in and of itself constitutes a crown that displays a person's righteous life (cf. 20:29; Ps 92:15), how much more of a crown are his children to whom he has passed on his wisdom? This unit lays the foundations of righteousness in righteous living (16:32—17:3; e.g., self-control) and concludes with two unrighteous speakers under God's judgment—the liar and the mocker of the poor (17:4–5)—followed by a reflection on the glorious splendor God confers upon the aging righteous (17:6).

16:32 a man who controls his temper. Or "a man with self-control," referring not only to temper but to the whole person.

16:33 The lot. The lot (see 1:14) was a small stone used to reveal God's selection of someone or something out of several possibilities in cases in which a clear choice was not otherwise evident. Verse 33 adds a necessary caveat to verse 32: Ultimately, the Lord rules over history. See *WCF* 3.1; *HC* 27.

17:3 This verse bases the truth of verse 2 on God's competence to test character and to reward virtue. By the images of a crucible to test the purity of silver and a small melting oven to determine the genuineness of gold (cf. 27:21), this verse teaches that God knows the human heart (15:3,11; 16:2; 21:2) and separates appearances and pretense from reality.

17:4–5 Like the preceding unit, which concluded with four malevolent speakers, so also this unit concludes with two wicked communicators: the liar (v. 4), whose speech unleashes misery upon the community; and the mocker of the poor (v. 5), who blasphemes God. Both will be punished by the Lord (v. 5) and, presumably, shunned by those who are crowned with old age.

■ **17:7–28** *Fools.* This subunit of 15:30—22:16 is a collection of proverbs on fools that picks up where the preceding subunit left off. It elaborates and expands the catalog of malevolent communicators (vv. 4–5), mentioning the liar (v. 7), the briber (v. 8) and the gossip (v. 9). Like an overture to a symphony, this introduction sounds themes that will be picked up in the remainder of the chapter: corrupt officials and justice (vv. 7,15,26), bribery (vv. 8,21) and reserved speech and friendship (vv. 9,17,19,27–28). Various Hebrew words are translated "fool" and "foolish" throughout these verses, all of which are fairly synonymous in this context.

17:7 Arrogant. Or "eloquent."

17:8 A bribe . . . succeeds. The proverb moves beyond cautioning the noble against lying (v. 7) to warning against bribery (cf. v. 23; 15:27). The law forbade bribery because it opposed God's character; God shows no partiality and accepts no bribe (Dt 10:17; cf. Ex 23:8). In contrast, the Christian even invites to his table those who cannot repay him (Lk 14:12–14). **to the one who.** Literally, "in the eyes of," a phrase that denotes a fool's state of self-delusion and reliance upon his own opinion (see 12:15; 16:2; 21:2; 26:5,12, 16; 28:11; 30:12).

17:9 The final evil communicator is the gossip (v. 9), who destroys a community already threatened by transgression. This verse also forms a transition to the next subunit on proper responses to fools, laying the foundation in love. The disciple restores a community threatened by wrongdoing by drawing a veil over another's sin in order to win his friendship. See *WLC* 144.

17:10–15 Verse 10 qualifies the admonition to cover over transgression (v. 9) with an implicit admonition to rebuke the discerning person and flog the mocker, while cautioning that flogging a fool will do little good by comparison (v. 10). God's messenger of death will ultimately punish him (v. 11). The second pair warns against the danger of encountering a bestial, unbridled fool (v. 12) and calls attention to the fool seeking to repay good with evil and to his punishment (v. 13). The third pair shifts from a caution against an encounter with a raging fool to a forewarning not to provoke his anger in the first place (v. 14) and a caution against perverting justice by acquitting him when he is in fact guilty (v. 15). See *WLC* 145.

17:11 merciless official. Or "messenger of death."

17:13 [j]Ps 109:4-5; Jer 18:20

13 If a man pays back evil[j] for good,
evil will never leave his house.

17:14 [k]Pr 20:3

14 Starting a quarrel is like breaching a dam;
so drop the matter before a dispute breaks out.[k]

17:15 [l]Pr 18:5 [m]Ex 23:6-7; Isa 5:23

15 Acquitting the guilty and condemning the innocent[l]—
the LORD detests them both.[m]

17:16 [n]Pr 23:23

16 Of what use is money in the hand of a fool,
since he has no desire to get wisdom?[n]

17 A friend loves at all times,
and a brother is born for adversity.

17:18 [o]Pr 6:1-5; 11:15; 22:26-27

18 A man lacking in judgment strikes hands in pledge
and puts up security for his neighbor.[o]

19 He who loves a quarrel loves sin;
he who builds a high gate invites destruction.

20 A man of perverse heart does not prosper;
he whose tongue is deceitful falls into trouble.

17:21 [p]Pr 10:1

21 To have a fool for a son brings grief;
there is no joy for the father of a fool.[p]

17:22 [q]Ps 22:15; Pr 15:13

22 A cheerful heart is good medicine,
but a crushed spirit dries up the bones.[q]

17:23 [r]Ex 23:8

23 A wicked man accepts a bribe[r] in secret
to pervert the course of justice.

17:24 [s]Ecc 2:14

24 A discerning man keeps wisdom in view,
but a fool's eyes[s] wander to the ends of the earth.

17:25 [t]Pr 10:1

25 A foolish son brings grief to his father
and bitterness to the one who bore him.[t]

17:26 [u]Pr 18:5

26 It is not good to punish an innocent man,[u]
or to flog officials for their integrity.

17:27 [v]Pr 14:29; Jas 1:19

27 A man of knowledge uses words with restraint,
and a man of understanding is even-tempered.[v]

17:28 [w]Job 13:5

28 Even a fool is thought wise if he keeps silent,
and discerning if he holds his tongue.[w]

18

An unfriendly man pursues selfish ends;
he defies all sound judgment.

18:2 [x]Pr 12:23

2 A fool finds no pleasure in understanding
but delights in airing his own opinions.[x]

17:12 Verses 11–12 are connected by the association of bears, known for the dangerous threat they posed (cf. 2Sa 17:18; 2 Ki 2:23ff.; Am 5:19), with a cruel messenger of death. Verse 12 implicitly cautions the disciple to avoid an encounter with a raging fool, a situation comparable to confronting a ferocious bear.
17:16–20 These verses contrast the loving friend with one who loves causing strife. Each of these adages is part of a proverb pair in which the second saying qualifies the first.
17:16 Of what use . . . wisdom? The introductory proverb calls upon the disciple to accept correction in order to attain the moral capacity to comprehend the sage's teaching. The scenario depicts a fool approaching the sage with money in hand to buy his wisdom. The sage does not wait for an answer to his rhetorical question but expresses his exasperation at the absurd situation.
17:17 Unlike a "fair-weather" friend, a true friend or brother will stick by you even in times of trouble.
17:18 See 6:1–3.
17:19 a high gate. The gate of the fool's house symbolizes his pride.
17:21–28 These verses about fools focus on injustice and the reserved speech of the wise. They divide into two groups (vv. 21–25 and 26–28). Verses 21 and 25 concern the failed rearing of a fool. The second batch picks up on the theme of injustice (vv. 26–28). Verse 26 escalates the theme of injustice from bribing officials to punishing righteous officials. Verses 27–28 counsel the wise to respond to the fool's vexations with forbearance, returning to the need for self-control (see 16:32).
17:22 Verse 22 asserts the psychosomatic effects of verse 21 (cf. 14:30; 15:13,30; 16:24; 18:14). Grief and joy can be matters, respectively, of death and life. See *WLC* 135.
17:24 ends of the earth. These words establish a metaphor for wrong and unobtainable goals. To the Israelite the phrase connoted places far removed from the place of residence of the covenant people (cf. Dt 13:8; 28:49,64; Ps 135:7). David, as an exiled king, called to God in anguish of heart "from the ends of the earth" (Ps 61:2). The fool fails because he orients himself to distant, godless and unobtainable goals instead of to attainable Wisdom that stands ready to serve him well (see 8:9; 14:6; Dt 30:11–13). His quest for godless profit in this verse may be related to his accepting bribes in the preceding; either will come to nothing.
17:26 flog officials. The tyrant is a highly visible magistrate, in a position to flog subordinate nobles in the government's hierarchical structure.
17:27–28 These verses caution the disciple to respond to provocation with restrained speech (v. 27) or total silence (v. 28; cf. Ecc 5:7; Isa 53:7).
■ **18:1–21** *Foolish and Wise Speech.* This unit juxtaposes the anti-

3 When wickedness comes, so does contempt,
and with shame comes disgrace.

4 The words of a man's mouth are deep waters,
but the fountain of wisdom is a bubbling brook.

5 It is not good to be partial to the wicked[y]
or to deprive the innocent of justice.[z]

6 A fool's lips bring him strife,
and his mouth invites a beating.

7 A fool's mouth is his undoing,
and his lips are a snare[a] to his soul.[b]

8 The words of a gossip are like choice morsels;
they go down to a man's inmost parts.[c]

9 One who is slack in his work
is brother to one who destroys.[d]

10 The name of the LORD is a strong tower;[e]
the righteous run to it and are safe.

11 The wealth of the rich is their fortified city;[f]
they imagine it an unscalable wall.

12 Before his downfall a man's heart is proud,
but humility comes before honor.[g]

13 He who answers before listening—
that is his folly and his shame.[h]

14 A man's spirit sustains him in sickness,
but a crushed spirit who can bear?[i]

15 The heart of the discerning acquires knowledge;[j]
the ears of the wise seek it out.

16 A gift[k] opens the way for the giver
and ushers him into the presence of the great.

17 The first to present his case seems right,
till another comes forward and questions him.

18 Casting the lot settles disputes[l]
and keeps strong opponents apart.

18:5 [y]Lev 19:15; Pr 24:23-25; 28:21 [z]Ps 82:2; Pr 17:15
18:7 [a]Ps 140:9 [b]Ps 64:8; Pr 10:14; 12:13; 13:3; Ecc 10:12
18:8 [c]Pr 26:22
18:9 [d]Pr 28:24
18:10 [e]2Sa 22:3; Ps 61:3
18:11 [f]Pr 10:15
18:12 [g]Pr 11:2; 15:33; 16:18
18:13 [h]Pr 20:25; Jn 7:51
18:14 [i]Pr 15:13; 17:22
18:15 [j]Pr 15:14
18:16 [k]Ge 32:20
18:18 [l]Pr 16:33

---

social speech of fools (vv. 1–11) against the reconciling speech of the wise (vv. 12–21).

■ **18:1–11** *Speech of Fools.* These verses include descriptions of the fool's antisocial nature and activities and of their consequences (vv. 1–9), as well as the defense of the righteous against him (vv. 10–11).

18:1–9 This first partial unit consists of an introduction (vv. 1–3), body (vv. 4–8) and conclusion (v. 9). Verse 9 draws the matter to its conclusion by arguing that if laziness is closely connected to destruction (v. 9), malicious gossip is even more so (v. 8).

18:1–3 Verses 1–3 introduce the fool and his social disgrace. He is labeled a self-serving loner (v. 1), an incorrigible fool (v. 2) and wicked (v. 3). The fool speaks boldly of his moral bankruptcy in contrast to the sage, who councils restrained speech for the wise and silence for fools (17:27–28).

18:4–9 The abstract descriptions of the wicked are here narrowed down to specific instances of his foolish speech. The passage escalates from the concealing speech by an ordinary person (v. 4) to perverse courtroom sentences (vv. 5–7) to slander that pits one person against another (v. 8). The perversion of justice, which picks up on a major theme of the preceding unit (cf. 17:8,23,26), stands at its center, between obscure speech and slander.

18:4 deep. In poetry the term "deep" describes physical depth, always with the negative connotations of inaccessibility and/or foreboding danger. The term "deep waters" here and in 20:5 connotes that the ordinary person's words and plans are unfathomable, inaccessible and possibly even potentially dangerous (cf. Ps 64:6). If they were intended to benefit others, they would be accessible and comprehensible. **bubbling brook.** Or "rushing stream." Combined with "fountain" the metaphors connote a constant, accessible, inexhaustible supply of living water.

18:7 to his soul. Or "to his very life," escalating the fool's punishment to death. See *WLC* 142.

18:10–11 This proverb pair contrasts the true security of the righteous in the Lord (v. 10) with the false security of the rich in their wealth (v. 11).

■ **18:12–21** *Speech of the Wise.* These verses teach that an instructed person upholds justice, resolves conflicts and speaks powerfully. The introduction stresses the importance of being teachable (vv. 12–15), and the body moves to settling disputes in the courtroom (vv. 16–19) and to the power of speech (vv. 20–21). The effect of speech is especially noticeable in the courtroom, where the tongue has the power of life and death (v. 21).

18:12–15 The introduction has an alternating structure: future destruction and honor, depending on a person's heart (v. 12); the non-listening fool (v. 13); present triumph and depression, depending on a person's spirit (v. 14); and the listening wise (v. 15).

18:16–19 Verses 16–17 imply the need for an impartial judicial system by exposing the bribe. Verses 18–19 present resolutions in light of the limitations of the best of courts.

18:16 gift. A more appropriate translation in this context would be "bribe."

18:17 The first . . . him. Or "In a lawsuit the first to speak seems right, until someone comes forward to cross-examine." For justice to be served, the litigant must be cross-examined to sift out the truth.

18:18–19 This proverb pair pertains to conflict resolution beyond what can be achieved in court.

19 An offended brother is more unyielding than a fortified city,
and disputes are like the barred gates of a citadel.

20 From the fruit of his mouth a man's stomach is filled;
with the harvest from his lips he is satisfied.[m]

21 The tongue has the power of life and death,
and those who love it will eat its fruit.[n]

22 He who finds a wife finds what is good[o]
and receives favor from the LORD.[p]

23 A poor man pleads for mercy,
but a rich man answers harshly.

24 A man of many companions may come to ruin,
but there is a friend who sticks closer than a brother.[q]

19

Better a poor man whose walk is blameless
than a fool whose lips are perverse.[r]

2 It is not good to have zeal without knowledge,
nor to be hasty and miss the way.[s]

3 A man's own folly ruins his life,
yet his heart rages against the LORD.

4 Wealth brings many friends,
but a poor man's friend deserts him.[t]

5 A false witness[u] will not go unpunished,
and he who pours out lies will not go free.[v]

6 Many curry favor with a ruler,[w]
and everyone is the friend of a man who gives gifts.[x]

7 A poor man is shunned by all his relatives—
how much more do his friends avoid him!
Though he pursues them with pleading,
they are nowhere to be found.[a][y]

8 He who gets wisdom loves his own soul;
he who cherishes understanding prospers.[z]

9 A false witness will not go unpunished,
and he who pours out lies will perish.[a]

10 It is not fitting for a fool[b] to live in luxury—
how much worse for a slave to rule over princes![c]

11 A man's wisdom gives him patience;[d]
it is to his glory to overlook an offense.

12 A king's rage is like the roar of a lion,
but his favor is like dew[e] on the grass.[f]

[a] 7 The meaning of the Hebrew for this sentence is uncertain.

18:20 [m]Pr 12:14
18:21 [n]Pr 13:2-3; Mt 12:37
18:22 [o]Pr 12:4 [p]Pr 19:14; 31:10
18:24 [q]Pr 17:17; Jn 15:13-15
19:1 [r]Pr 28:6
19:2 [s]Pr 29:20
19:4 [t]Pr 14:20
19:5 [u]Ex 23:1 [v]Dt 19:19; Pr 21:28
19:6 [w]Pr 29:26 [x]Pr 17:8; 18:16
19:7 [y]ver 4; Ps 38:11
19:8 [z]Pr 16:20
19:9 [a]ver 5
19:10 [b]Pr 26:1 [c]Pr 30:21-23; Ecc 10:5-7
19:11 [d]Pr 16:32
19:12 [e]Ps 133:3 [f]Pr 16:14-15

18:20–21 This unit's concluding pair is bound together by the notion of the certain effects of either good or bad speech. Good speech produces results that benefit the speaker; evil speech produces results that harm the speaker.

■ **18:22—19:22** *Wealth and Wisdom in the Court and in the Home.* This unit explores how wisdom leads to wealth in both legal and domestic settings. It divides into three parts (18:22—19:7; 19:8–15; 19:16–22).

■ **18:22—19:7** *Wealth and Friends.* After an introductory proverb about the closest of human relationships, that of a husband and wife (18:22), these verses take up the topics of friends and of wealth's moral ambiguities. These verses again divide into three parts: wealth and friends (18:23–24), wealth and ethics (19:1–3) and wealth and companions in court (19:4–7).

■ **18:22–24** *Rich, Poor and Friends.* The rich tend to have many friends, while the poor often have few, but a true friend is one who is closer than a brother. The connection of these partial subunits suggests that the companions in view are not wise but that they can be bought (v. 23; 19:1–3,4–7); it is folly to depend upon them (v. 24).

■ **19:1–3** *Wealth and Ethics.* The temptation of the poor is to neglect morality in order to pursue wealth. The Lord will punish such folly.

■ **19:4–7** *Wealth and Friends in Court.* Wealth adds companions in court (vv. 4,6), and the poor person tends to lose them (vv. 4,7), but perjurers are no one's friends and will not escape punishment.

19:5 See *WLC* 145; *HC* 112.

■ **19:8–15** *Wisdom, Wealth and Friends in Court and at Home.* These verses explore the complex interconnections of obtaining wisdom and properly assessing the place of wealth and companionship both in the courts and at home.

19:8 **soul.** Or "life." **prospers.** Or "will soon prosper."

19:13 **dripping.** Or "dripping of a leaky roof," which is not only annoying but also destructive.

13 A foolish son is his father's ruin,[g]
and a quarrelsome wife is like a constant dripping.[h]

14 Houses and wealth are inherited from parents,[i]
but a prudent wife is from the LORD.[j]

15 Laziness brings on deep sleep,
and the shiftless man goes hungry.[k]

16 He who obeys instructions guards his life,
but he who is contemptuous of his ways will die.[l]

17 He who is kind to the poor lends to the LORD,
and he will reward him for what he has done.[m]

18 Discipline your son, for in that there is hope;
do not be a willing party to his death.[n]

19 A hot-tempered man must pay the penalty;
if you rescue him, you will have to do it again.

20 Listen to advice and accept instruction,[o]
and in the end you will be wise.[p]

21 Many are the plans in a man's heart,
but it is the LORD's purpose that prevails.[q]

22 What a man desires is unfailing love[a];
better to be poor than a liar.

23 The fear of the LORD leads to life:
Then one rests content, untouched by trouble.[r]

24 The sluggard buries his hand in the dish;
he will not even bring it back to his mouth![s]

25 Flog a mocker, and the simple will learn prudence;
rebuke a discerning man, and he will gain knowledge.[t]

26 He who robs his father and drives out his mother[u]
is a son who brings shame and disgrace.

27 Stop listening to instruction, my son,
and you will stray from the words of knowledge.

28 A corrupt witness mocks at justice,
and the mouth of the wicked gulps down evil.[v]

29 Penalties are prepared for mockers,
and beatings for the backs of fools.[w]

20

Wine is a mocker and beer a brawler;
whoever is led astray by them is not wise.[x]

2 A king's wrath is like the roar of a lion;[y]
he who angers him forfeits his life.[z]

19:13 [g]Pr 10:1 [h]Pr 21:9
19:14 [i]2Co 12:14 [j]Pr 18:22
19:15 [k]Pr 6:9; 10:4
19:16 [l]Pr 16:17; Lk 10:28
19:17 [m]Mt 10:42; 2Co 9:6-8
19:18 [n]Pr 13:24; 23:13-14
19:20 [o]Pr 4:1 [p]Pr 12:15
19:21 [q]Ps 33:11; Pr 16:9; Isa 14:24,27
19:23 [r]Ps 25:13; Pr 12:21; 1Ti 4:8
19:24 [s]Pr 26:15
19:25 [t]Pr 9:9; 21:11
19:26 [u]Pr 28:24
19:28 [v]Job 15:16
19:29 [w]Pr 26:3
20:1 [x]Pr 31:4
20:2 [y]Pr 19:12 [z]Pr 8:36

[a] 22 Or *A man's greed is his shame*

■ **19:16–22** *Wisdom and Instruction.* An educational proverb begins this unit (vv. 16–17). The remainder (vv. 18–22) consists of child-rearing proverbs. The first, in a rare direct address in this collection, admonishes the father to discipline his son but not to aspire either to kill him (v. 18) or to ease the penalty incurred by a hothead (v. 19). The remaining verses call on the son to consider the importance of wisdom by contrasting a person's natural desires with the way of wisdom (vv. 20–22).
■ **19:23—20:11** *Kings and Fools.* After a child-rearing proverb (19:23), the unit consists of two subunits: a catalog of fools (19:24—20:1) and advice to cleanse the realm of their existence (20:2–11).
■ **19:23—20:1** *Catalog of Fools.* This seven-verse subunit follows an alternating pattern of failed child-rearing types and the appropriate punishment for fools. The catalog of fools escalates from the sluggard (lazy person), who damages and punishes himself (19:24); to the shameful son, who destroys the family (19:26); to corrupt witnesses, who destroy social order (19:28); to the brawling drunkard, who endangers everyone around him (20:1; 26:9). The punishment of fools begins with the flogging of the mocker in order that the gullible will learn (19:25) and ends with the divine punishments and physical beatings of the mocking revolutionary.
19:26 See *WLC* 128.
■ **20:2–11** *Cleansing the Realm of Fools.* This ten-verse subunit of 19:23—20:11 pertains to the righteous king cleansing his kingdom of all fools. It begins with the monarch's powerful roar as he threatens judgment on the wicked (v. 2) and ends with his divinely conferred authority as he cleanses his realm of evil (v. 8). Power without justice is tyranny, and justice without power is weak. Sandwiched between this frame is a second catalog of fools: the quarreling fool (v. 3), the deluded sluggard (indolent person) (v. 4), the conniver (v. 5) and the hypocritical masses (v. 6). The second

20:3 [a]Pr 17:14
20:6 [b]Ps 12:1
20:7 [c]Ps 37:25-26; 112:2
20:8 [d]ver 26; Pr 25:4-5
20:9 [e]1Ki 8:46; Ecc 7:20; 1Jn 1:8
20:10 [f]ver 23; Pr 11:1
20:11 [g]Mt 7:16
20:12 [h]Ps 94:9
20:13 [i]Pr 6:11; 19:15
20:16 [j]Ex 22:26 [k]Pr 27:13
20:17 [l]Pr 9:17
20:18 [m]Pr 11:14; 24:6
20:19 [n]Pr 11:13
20:20 [o]Pr 30:11 [p]Ex 21:17; Job 18:5

3 It is to a man's honor to avoid strife,
but every fool is quick to quarrel.[a]

4 A sluggard does not plow in season;
so at harvest time he looks but finds nothing.

5 The purposes of a man's heart are deep waters,
but a man of understanding draws them out.

6 Many a man claims to have unfailing love,
but a faithful man who can find?[b]

7 The righteous man leads a blameless life;
blessed are his children after him.[c]

8 When a king sits on his throne to judge,
he winnows out all evil with his eyes.[d]

9 Who can say, "I have kept my heart pure;
I am clean and without sin"?[e]

10 Differing weights and differing measures—
the LORD detests them both.[f]

11 Even a child is known by his actions,
by whether his conduct is pure[g] and right.

12 Ears that hear and eyes that see—
the LORD has made them both.[h]

13 Do not love sleep or you will grow poor;[i]
stay awake and you will have food to spare.

14 "It's no good, it's no good!" says the buyer;
then off he goes and boasts about his purchase.

15 Gold there is, and rubies in abundance,
but lips that speak knowledge are a rare jewel.

16 Take the garment of one who puts up security for a stranger;
hold it in pledge[j] if he does it for a wayward woman.[k]

17 Food gained by fraud tastes sweet to a man,[l]
but he ends up with a mouth full of gravel.

18 Make plans by seeking advice;
if you wage war, obtain guidance.[m]

19 A gossip betrays a confidence;[n]
so avoid a man who talks too much.

20 If a man curses his father or mother,[o]
his lamp will be snuffed out in pitch darkness.[p]

---

partial unit tempers punishment and universal justice with the reality of universal human depravity (vv. 9–11).
20:2 See 16:14.
20:3 See 15:18 and 17:14.
20:4 The wisdom theme of the right time is expounded in Ecclesiastes 3:1–8 (see Pr 6:6–11).
20:5 deep waters. See 18:4 and its note. **draws them out.** The metaphor represents the competent person's ability to uncover the conniver's dangerous counsel from beneath its verbal camouflage.
20:9–11 Verses 8 and 10 reflect that God stood behind his king's judgment, for the Lord detests deceit (see 16:1–15). The omniscient God sees all evil, and his anointed king's eyes searched it out (vv. 5,8). In spite of human cleverness, none of the wicked will escape in the end. See *WCF* 6.5; *WLC* 142.
■ **20:12–19** *Speech and Commerce.* This unit consists of four proverb pairs. The first pair (vv. 12–13) introduces the passage by insisting on human responsibility. We are to use the eyes and ears God has given instead of sleeping our way through life. The body (vv. 14–18) focuses on business practices that easily escalate into folly. The first portion of the body contrasts the common practice of boasting about having lied in order to haggle down a price (v. 14) with the rarity of knowledgeable lips that do not lie or boast (v. 15). The second section of the body begins with rash, imprudent speech in the marketplace that results in taking responsibility for another's debt (v. 16, see 6:1–5) and escalates to false speech (v. 17). The last pair (vv. 18–19) forms the conclusion and admonishes one to seek counsel, but not with a gossip.
20:16 wayward woman. There is a textual difficulty in this verse. Some manuscripts suggest the reading "outsider," which agrees more closely in meaning with "stranger" in the first half of the verse.
■ **20:20–28** *Trusting the LORD.* This unit consists of an introduction (vv. 20–21), body (vv. 22–25) and conclusion (vv. 26–28). The introductory pair of proverbs, linked by the antonyms "curses" (v. 20) and "blessed" (v. 21), warns the son not to curse his parents or to seize his inheritance, implying his responsibility to honor and obey his mother and father (cf. 30:17). The law (Lev 20:9) regarded cursing parents as tantamount to blasphemy because parents represent God's authority to a child. The body consists of an admonition not to seek revenge but to trust the Lord (v. 22), who is just (v. 23) and sovereign (v. 24). It is imprudent to make a rash vow to consecrate something to God because the future, which is outside human control, may make it difficult or impossible to fulfill the vow (v. 25). Verses 26–28 conclude the unit with the reward-punishment motif. God's surrogate king was unfailingly to punish the wicked (v.

[21] An inheritance quickly gained at the beginning
will not be blessed at the end.

[22] Do not say, "I'll pay you back for this wrong!"[q]
Wait for the LORD, and he will deliver you.[r]

[23] The LORD detests differing weights,
and dishonest scales do not please him.[s]

[24] A man's steps are directed by the LORD.
How then can anyone understand his own way?[t]

[25] It is a trap for a man to dedicate something rashly
and only later to consider his vows.[u]

[26] A wise king winnows out the wicked;
he drives the threshing wheel over them.[v]

[27] The lamp of the LORD searches the spirit of a man[a];
it searches out his inmost being.

[28] Love and faithfulness keep a king safe;
through love his throne is made secure.[w]

[29] The glory of young men is their strength,
gray hair the splendor of the old.[x]

[30] Blows and wounds cleanse[y] away evil,
and beatings purge the inmost being.

21 The king's heart is in the hand of the LORD;
he directs it like a watercourse wherever he pleases.

[2] All a man's ways seem right to him,
but the LORD weighs the heart.[z]

[3] To do what is right and just
is more acceptable to the LORD than sacrifice.[a]

[4] Haughty eyes[b] and a proud heart,
the lamp of the wicked, are sin!

[5] The plans of the diligent lead to profit[c]
as surely as haste leads to poverty.

20:22 [q]Pr 24:29 [r]Ro 12:19
20:23 [s]ver 10
20:24 [t]Jer 10:23
20:25 [u]Ecc 5:2,4-5
20:26 [v]ver 8
20:28 [w]Pr 29:14
20:29 [x]Pr 16:31
20:30 [y]Pr 22:15
21:2 [z]Pr 16:2; 24:12; Lk 16:15
21:3 [a]1Sa 15:22; Pr 15:8; Isa 1:11; Hos 6:6; Mic 6:6-8
21:4 [b]Pr 6:17
21:5 [c]Pr 10:4; 28:22

[a] 27 Or *The spirit of man is the LORD's lamp*

26) and show kindness to the needy (v. 28). Sandwiched between these royal proverbs pertaining to the king's execution of justice, verse 27 assures perfect justice by asserting the close connection between the Lord and every human being. "Lamp," a metaphor for human life in the introduction (v. 20), escalates to human discernment in the conclusion (v. 27) and frames this unit.

20:20 See *HC* 104.

20:25 See *WLC* 151.

■ **20:29—21:31** *Doing Righteousness and Justice.* The preceding conclusion—that the king was to protect the needy against wrong (20:20–28)—is now qualified by a focus on actively performing righteousness and justice. This unit is framed by attention to the Lord and his king and consists of an introduction (20:29—21:2), body (21:3–29) and conclusion (21:30–31).

■ **20:29—21:2** *Introduction.* The introduction consists of two proverb pairs. The first pair (vv. 29–30) focuses on the pedagogical relationship between the older generation (i.e., the wise) and the younger. This passage features physical blows rather than verbal rebukes because the body pertains primarily to nearly incorrigible young people who will not respond to words and need stronger action to save them from final death. Proverbs 20:29 presents the mutual dependence of the generations on each other by featuring their splendors: the strength of youth and the wisdom of age. Proverbs 20:30 teaches that youths who misdirect their physical strength (cf. v. 29) can be corrected by corporal punishment. The second pair of proverbs sets teaching within the thematic frame of the Lord's sovereignty exercised through his king (21:1–2). Here the Lord worked salvation through his king, not through parents, as elsewhere in Proverbs.

21:1 See *BC* 13; *HC* 28.

21:2 See *HC* 110.

■ **21:3–29** *The Righteous Over the Wicked.* This section begins with an introduction that explores human behavior with reference to righteousness and justice (v. 3). The refrain about the "quarrelsome wife" (vv. 9,19; cf. 19:13–14) divides the body into three subunits (vv. 4–8,10–18,20–29). Once again a reference to women functions as an organizing principle in the collection (cf. 11:16,22; 12:4; 18:22; 19:13). These startling and unexpected transitional verses about the dangers of the quarrelsome wife (vv. 9,19) make clear the importance of having a wise wife. Verses 4–8 focus on the defeat of the wicked; verses 9–18 concern the triumph of the righteous over them; and verses 19–29 speak of the lasting gratification of the righteous and the demise of the wicked.

■ **21:3** *Introduction.* The introduction to verses 3–29 conveys the main theme: exploring human behavior with reference to righteousness and justice.

■ **21:4–8** *Defeat for the Wicked.* Verse 8 sums up this passage by contrasting the devious behavior of the guilty with the straightforward conduct of the pure. In verses 4–7 the wicked are categorized into several self-serving types by the motif of their body parts: "haughty eyes" (v. 4), a "proud heart" (v. 4) and a "lying tongue" (v. 6). The arrogance of the wicked derives from their unrestrained heart (v. 4), lack of discipline (v. 4) and "haste [to make money]" (v. 5). Their haste is expanded to acquiring "fortune . . . by a lying tongue" (v. 6) and escalates to "violence" (v. 7) and a refusal to "do what is right" (v. 7).

21:4 heart, the lamp of the wicked, are sin! Or "heart—the unplowed field of the wicked—produce sin."

21:6 [d]2Pe 2:3

6 A fortune made by a lying tongue
is a fleeting vapor and a deadly snare.[a][d]

7 The violence of the wicked will drag them away,
for they refuse to do what is right.

21:8 [e]Pr 2:15

8 The way of the guilty is devious,[e]
but the conduct of the innocent is upright.

21:9 [f]Pr 25:24

9 Better to live on a corner of the roof
than share a house with a quarrelsome wife.[f]

10 The wicked man craves evil;
his neighbor gets no mercy from him.

21:11 [g]Pr 19:25

11 When a mocker is punished, the simple gain wisdom;
when a wise man is instructed, he gets knowledge.[g]

21:12 [h]Pr 14:11

12 The Righteous One[b] takes note of the house of the wicked
and brings the wicked to ruin.[h]

21:13 [i]Mt 18:30-34; Jas 2:13

13 If a man shuts his ears to the cry of the poor,
he too will cry out and not be answered.[i]

21:14 [j]Pr 18:16; 19:6

14 A gift given in secret soothes anger,
and a bribe concealed in the cloak pacifies great wrath.[j]

21:15 [k]Pr 10:29

15 When justice is done, it brings joy to the righteous
but terror to evildoers.[k]

21:16 [l]Ps 49:14

16 A man who strays from the path of understanding
comes to rest in the company of the dead.[l]

21:17 [m]Pr 23:20-21,29-35

17 He who loves pleasure will become poor;
whoever loves wine and oil will never be rich.[m]

21:18 [n]Pr 11:8; Isa 43:3

18 The wicked become a ransom[n] for the righteous,
and the unfaithful for the upright.

21:19 [o]ver 9

19 Better to live in a desert
than with a quarrelsome and ill-tempered wife.[o]

20 In the house of the wise are stores of choice food and oil,
but a foolish man devours all he has.

21:21 [p]Mt 5:6

21 He who pursues righteousness and love
finds life, prosperity[c] and honor.[p]

21:22 [q]Ecc 9:15-16

22 A wise man attacks the city of the mighty[q]
and pulls down the stronghold in which they trust.

21:23 [r]Jas 3:2 [s]Pr 12:13; 13:3

23 He who guards his mouth[r] and his tongue
keeps himself from calamity.[s]

[a] 6 Some Hebrew manuscripts, Septuagint and Vulgate; most Hebrew manuscripts *vapor for those who seek death* [b] *12* Or *The righteous man* [c] *21* Or *righteousness*

21:6 See *WLC* 142.
■ **21:9–18** *The Righteous Triumph Over the Wicked.* Verses 10–18 continue the theme of doing justice, but they pertain more specifically to the triumph of the righteous over the greedy and the merciless wicked. References to the "wicked" frame this partial unit (vv. 10,18). In verses 4–8 the righteous are not mentioned, but here the wicked are contrasted with the "righteous" (vv. 15,18), who are wise. In the Hebrew text "righteous" is the second word in every third verse between verses 10–21 (vv. 12,15,18, cf. v. 21). Accordingly, this partial unit consists of three clusters: verses 10–12, 13–15 and 16–18. The theme of the triumph of the righteous over the wicked commences with the Righteous One overthrowing the wicked (vv. 10–12). It is developed by noting that justice (v. 15; cf. v. 3) causes sheer joy in the righteous but fills the wicked with terror (vv. 13–15). The clusters come to a climax by promising that the wicked will die the death they intended for the righteous (vv. 16–18).
21:9 This verse shifts dramatically from wicked men to the wicked wife to point to the need for a wise wife.
21:17 See *WLC* 142; *WSC* 75.
21:18 ransom. Compensation to pay a penalty to free a wrongly imprisoned victim and save his life (cf. 13:8; Ex 21:29ff.; Isa 43:3). The wicked are expendable, given over to imprisonment in order that the righteous might go free.
■ **21:19–29** *Endurance and Death.* This passage contrasts the eternal endurance of the righteous with the death of the wicked. It consists of two smaller clusters (vv. 20–23 and 24–29).
21:20–23 These four proverbs feature the righteous wise. They find a supply of grain and oil (v. 20); life, prosperity and honor (v. 21); victory over evil and the wicked (v. 22); and security (v. 23). The cluster assumes that the Lord supplies these blessings. See *WLC* 141.
21:22 The proverb escalates the material gain of the wise (v. 20) to a climactic assertion: Nothing and no one can stop the ultimate triumph of the wise over evil and wicked men. Though the wise man may have begun his life's journey poor and despised (cf. Ecc 9:16), he is now likened to a warrior and described as stronger than a multitude who lack his spiritual virtue (cf. Pss 18:29–30; 144:1).
21:23 Verses 22 and 23 are linked by military motifs, moving from

[24] The proud and arrogant[t] man—"Mocker" is his name;
he behaves with overweening pride.

21:24 [t]Ps 1:1; Pr 1:22; Isa 16:6; Jer 48:29

[25] The sluggard's craving will be the death of him,[u]
because his hands refuse to work.

21:25 [u]Pr 13:4

[26] All day long he craves for more,
but the righteous give without sparing.[v]

21:26 [v]Ps 37:26; Mt 5:42; Eph 4:28

[27] The sacrifice of the wicked is detestable[w]—
how much more so when brought with evil intent![x]

21:27 [w]Isa 66:3; Jer 6:20; Am 5:22 [x]Pr 15:8

[28] A false witness will perish,[y]
and whoever listens to him will be destroyed forever.[a]

21:28 [y]Pr 19:5

[29] A wicked man puts up a bold front,
but an upright man gives thought to his ways.

[30] There is no wisdom,[z] no insight, no plan
that can succeed against the LORD.[a]

21:30 [z]Jer 9:23 [a]Isa 8:10; Ac 5:39

[31] The horse is made ready for the day of battle,
but victory rests with the LORD.[b]

21:31 [b]Ps 3:8; 33:12-19; Isa 31:1

22

A good name is more desirable than great riches;
to be esteemed is better than silver or gold.[c]

22:1 [c]Ecc 7:1

[2] Rich and poor have this in common:
The LORD is the Maker of them all.[d]

22:2 [d]Job 31:15

[3] A prudent man sees danger and takes refuge,[e]
but the simple keep going and suffer for it.[f]

22:3 [e]Pr 14:16 [f]Pr 27:12

[4] Humility and the fear of the LORD
bring wealth and honor and life.

[5] In the paths of the wicked lie thorns and snares,[g]
but he who guards his soul stays far from them.

22:5 [g]Pr 15:19

[6] Train[b] a child in the way he should go,[h]
and when he is old he will not turn from it.

22:6 [h]Eph 6:4

[a] *28* Or / *but the words of an obedient man will live on* [b] *6* Or *Start*

the offense of the wise man against evil to his defense against it by wise speech.

21:24–29 The topic shifts dramatically from the wise man (vv. 20–23) to his antagonist, the mocker, who heads a list of wicked types. This list matches that in verses 4–8: the proud (vv. 4,24), the sluggard or lazy person (vv. 5,25–26), the liar (vv. 6,28) and, climactically, the brazenly wicked man (v. 29). The four wicked types (vv. 24–25,28–29) encircle the hypocritical worshiper (v. 27).

21:24–26 Both the mocker and the sluggard destroy the community by their aggressive, destructive acts ("behaves"; see note on v. 24) and refusal to work.

21:24 overweening pride. Or "insolent fury."

▪ **21:30–31** *Conclusion.* This conclusion to 20:29—21:31, along with the introduction (21:1–2), form a frame around the unit. The frame affirms the Lord's sovereignty over humanity in general (vv. 2,30) and over kings and their armies in particular (vv. 1,31). Behind the victory of the righteous/wise over the wicked/fool stands the invincible Lord.

▪ **22:1–16** *Wealth and Moral Instruction.* These verses focus on the need to conjoin wealth and moral instruction. They divide into two parts: the Lord's sovereignty over wealth (vv. 1–9) and the need for moral instruction about wealth (vv. 10–16).

▪ **22:1–9** *The Lord's Sovereignty Over Wealth.* Apart from verse 6 every verse in this section contains terms pertaining to wealth. Israel's God is mentioned explicitly in verses 2 and 4 and implicitly ("blessed") in verse 9. This passage consists of an introduction, which asserts the priority of a good name over wealth (v. 1), followed by a coupling of the Lord's sovereignty with human accountability (vv. 2–4), the need for education in such matters (vv. 5–6) and the Lord's retribution (vv. 7–9). The passage asserts the equality of rich and poor before the Lord in heaven (vv. 2–4), despite their inequality on Earth (vv. 7–9). Thus this unit sobers the rich, consoles the poor, warns the oppressor and comforts the oppressed. A disciple must stay away from the contagion of greed, and a child must be initiated in the way of generosity (v. 6).

22:1 The introduction gives a proper orientation to the value of wealth by comparing it unfavorably with a good name or unsullied reputation. See *WLC* 144.

22:2–4 While material possessions distinguish people, rich and poor meet on common ground before the Lord. He created both, thereby reminding both social classes of their human equality (v. 2; cf. 19:17). Verses 3–4 prevent this saying from being interpreted in a fatalistic fashion. By prudence, as opposed to gullibility, one can avoid "danger" (v. 3), and the "fear of the LORD" brings wealth, honor and life (v. 4). See *HC* 27.

22:5–6 These verses focus on the need for educating youth in the way that leads to true riches. The concept of paying attention to one's way (vv. 3–4) and the need to orient youth to the right way (vv. 5–6) link the pair.

22:6 Train. This term may be better translated "dedicate," with the connotation of starting the youth off with a strong, even religious, commitment to a certain course of action. **child.** The other six uses of this Hebrew term characterize his way as foolish. He is gullible (1:4), lacks sense (7:7), dissembles (20:11), has folly in his heart (22:15) and so is in need of correction (23:13). Left to himself he will disgrace his mother (29:15). The youth must be redirected from the beginning to counteract his inherent folly. **not turn.** The proverb must not be pushed to mean that the parent or educator is ultimately responsible for the youth's entire moral orientation. Rather, it expresses a single component of a complex truth that must be fit together with other elements in order to approximate the more complex patterns of real life. Young people have freedom to choose sin and to apostatize by taking up with villains (2:11–15) and whores (2:16–19; 5:11–14). Even Solomon eventually stopped listening to instruction and strayed from knowledge (19:27). The proverb promises that the educator's early, moral initiative has a permanent effect on a person for good, but that does not exhaust the whole truth about religious education. The book is addressed

7 The rich rule over the poor,
and the borrower is servant to the lender.

22:8 [i]Job 4:8 [j]Ps 125:3

8 He who sows wickedness reaps trouble,[i]
and the rod of his fury will be destroyed.[j]

22:9 [k]2Co 9:6 [l]Pr 19:17

9 A generous man will himself be blessed,[k]
for he shares his food with the poor.[l]

22:10 [m]Pr 18:6; 26:20

10 Drive out the mocker, and out goes strife;
quarrels and insults are ended.[m]

22:11 [n]Pr 16:13; Mt 5:8

11 He who loves a pure heart and whose speech is gracious
will have the king for his friend.[n]

12 The eyes of the LORD keep watch over knowledge,
but he frustrates the words of the unfaithful.

22:13 [o]Pr 26:13

13 The sluggard says, "There is a lion outside!"[o]
or, "I will be murdered in the streets!"

22:14 [p]Pr 2:16; 5:3-5; 7:5; 23:27 [q]Ecc 7:26

14 The mouth of an adulteress is a deep pit;[p]
he who is under the LORD's wrath will fall into it.[q]

22:15 [r]Pr 13:24; 23:14

15 Folly is bound up in the heart of a child,
but the rod of discipline will drive it far from him.[r]

16 He who oppresses the poor to increase his wealth
and he who gives gifts to the rich—both come to poverty.

Sayings of the Wise

22:17 [s]Pr 5:1

17 Pay attention and listen to the sayings of the wise;[s]
apply your heart to what I teach,
18 for it is pleasing when you keep them in your heart
and have all of them ready on your lips.
19 So that your trust may be in the LORD,
I teach you today, even you.
20 Have I not written thirty[a] sayings for you,
sayings of counsel and knowledge,

22:21 [t]Lk 1:3-4; 1Pe 3:15

21 teaching you true and reliable words,[t]
so that you can give sound answers
to him who sent you?

22:22 [u]Zec 7:10 [v]Ex 23:6; Mal 3:5

22 Do not exploit the poor[u] because they are poor
and do not crush the needy in court,[v]

[a] *20* Or *not formerly written*; or *not written excellent*

to youths, not parents (1:4). Were parents ultimately responsible for their children's moral choices, there would be no point in addressing youths.

22:7–9 These verses warn the poor to be on their guard against tyranny (v. 7) and commend benevolence shown to them (v. 9). The tyrant will be punished (v. 8) and the generous rewarded (v. 9).

▪ **22:10–16** *Moral Instruction About Wealth.* These verses consist of three proverb pairs. The first indirectly motivates the youth to accept parental teaching by contrasting the fate of the mocker (v. 10) with that of the pure and gracious individual (v. 11). After the transition (v. 12) the second pair warns against the deceptive speech of the sluggard or lazy person (v. 13) and of the wiles of the unfaithful wife (v. 14). Verse 12 links the king with the Lord (cf. 14:27–28), who supports truth and subverts the unfaithful. The treacherous words of the sluggard (lazy person) and the adulteress threaten the family's economic future (cf. 5:1–23; 10:1–5). In the third pair verse 15 focuses on the use of the rod to keep youth on the right path, and verse 16 reiterates the unit's theme of the Lord's sovereign control over rich and poor.

▪ **22:17—24:34** *Anonymous Sayings.* The proverbs in this section lack attribution to a collector or author but follow the prior materials by Solomon without being distinguished as coming from another source. This strongly suggests that Solomon adopted and adapted these sayings for Israel. This section consists of a main collection of sayings (22:17—24:22) and an appendix (24:23–24).

▪ **22:17—24:22** *Thirty Sayings of the Wise.* This collection of "thirty sayings" consists of a prologue (22:17–21) and four sections delimited by their introductory educational axioms (22:22; 23:12; 23:26; 24:13) and by their distinctive structures and themes. Commands to "trust . . . in the LORD" (22:19) and to "fear the LORD" (24:21) frame the collection. Its prologue and first section, a set of ten commands (22:22—23:11), reveal a close connection with Egyptian sayings of Amenemope (c. 1100 B.C.).

▪ **22:17–21** *Prologue.* The prologue consists of two units (vv. 17–18,20–21) positioned around a central verse (v. 19). The first unit (vv. 17–18) contains the typical admonition to the son to accept wholeheartedly the statements of the wise (v. 17), including proper motivation to do so (v. 18). The second unit (vv. 20–21), which pertains to the father, defines Solomon's (see note on 22:17—24:34) proverbs (v. 20) and his purpose in writing (v. 21). Verse 19 focuses on the son and the father and points to the need for both to trust in the Lord. A complex pattern of Hebrew catchwords holds these stanzas together as a unified literary unit.

22:17–18 The learning process progresses from the outward ear, which receives or acquires the proverbs; to the interior heart, which applies them (v. 17); to the belly (represented as housing the heart), which preserves them; to the outward lips, which represent them to others (v. 18; see 4:20–27).

22:17 **apply your heart.** Or "turn your ear."

22:19–21 See *WCF* 1.1.

22:19 The sayings facilitate a dynamic, trusting relationship with Israel's covenant-keeping God.

22:21 **teaching . . . you?** The aphorisms also make the son reliable to those who commission him.

[23] for the LORD will take up their case[w]
and will plunder those who plunder them.[x]

[24] Do not make friends with a hot-tempered man,
do not associate with one easily angered,
[25] or you may learn his ways
and get yourself ensnared.[y]

[26] Do not be a man who strikes hands in pledge[z]
or puts up security for debts;
[27] if you lack the means to pay,
your very bed will be snatched from under you.[a]

[28] Do not move an ancient boundary stone[b]
set up by your forefathers.

[29] Do you see a man skilled in his work?
He will serve[c] before kings;
he will not serve before obscure men.

23

When you sit to dine with a ruler,
note well what[a] is before you,
[2] and put a knife to your throat
if you are given to gluttony.
[3] Do not crave his delicacies,[d]
for that food is deceptive.

[4] Do not wear yourself out to get rich;
have the wisdom to show restraint.
[5] Cast but a glance at riches, and they are gone,
for they will surely sprout wings
and fly off to the sky like an eagle.[e]

[6] Do not eat the food of a stingy man,
do not crave his delicacies;[f]
[7] for he is the kind of man
who is always thinking about the cost.[b]
"Eat and drink," he says to you,
but his heart is not with you.
[8] You will vomit up the little you have eaten
and will have wasted your compliments.

[9] Do not speak to a fool,
for he will scorn the wisdom of your words.[g]

[10] Do not move an ancient boundary stone[h]
or encroach on the fields of the fatherless,
[11] for their Defender[i] is strong;
he will take up their case against you.[j]

22:23 [w]Ps 12:5 [x]1Sa 25:39; Pr 23:10-11
22:25 [y]1Co 15:33
22:26 [z]Pr 11:15
22:27 [a]Pr 17:18
22:28 [b]Dt 19:14; Pr 23:10
22:29 [c]Ge 41:46
23:3 [d]ver 6-8
23:5 [e]Pr 27:24
23:6 [f]Ps 141:4
23:9 [g]Pr 1:7; 9:7; Mt 7:6
23:10 [h]Dt 19:14; Pr 22:28
23:11 [i]Job 19:25 [j]Pr 22:22-23

a *1* Or *who* b *7* *Or for as he thinks within himself, / so he is; or for as he puts on a feast, / so he is*

■ **22:22—23:11** *A Decalogue of Sayings.* Proscriptions against taking advantage of the poor (22:22) and the fatherless (23:10), along with threats that the Lord will plead their cause (22:23; 23:11), frame this decalogue of proverbs and sound its dominant theme. These verses divide into ten units, all but one of which begin with "do not" (22:22–23; 22:24–25; 22:26–27; 22:28; 22:29—23:3; 23:4–5; 23:6–7; 23:8; 23:9; 23:10–11). Apart from the ninth saying (23:9) all of them pertain to wealth. The first four proverbs prohibit illegitimate forms of money making, while sayings six through eight escalate these prohibitions to proscriptions against greed.

22:22–28 The decalogue's first four proverbs forbid enriching oneself through injustice. Prohibitions forbidding the exploitation of the weak (the poor and the widow) frame them (vv. 22–23,28). Job 24:2 combines in a single verse these two commands. The two middle sayings of this unit prohibit associating with the antisocial hothead (vv. 24–25) and assuming responsibility for another's debts (vv. 26–27). The outer two axioms address gaining property through folly (vv. 22–23,28), and the middle two (vv. 24–27) touch on preventing its loss, again through folly.

22:26–27 The decalogue's theme of wise stewardship continues with a caution against taking responsibility for a stranger's debts (see 6:1–5; 11:15; 17:18; 20:16; 27:13).

22:29—23:8 These maxims focus on greed. All three warn that things are not as they appear. The superior's offering of food is not a sign of friendship, and wealth is not a sign of security. Those things that appear to be desirable for advancing the potential of a fuller life actually veil harsh realities that hinder its full enjoyment.

22:29 He will serve before kings. Far from a guarantee of success, these words are an indirect exhortation to excellence, which, in the Egyptian schools of the wise, was the way of promotion in an elite civil service (see note on 22:17—24:22).

23:5 See *WLC* 142.

23:6–8 This warning cautions the son against attempting to advance himself by pushing himself as an uninvited guest on an unwilling host.

23:6 stingy man. Or "a begrudging host."

23:10 See *WLC* 142.

12 Apply your heart to instruction
and your ears to words of knowledge.

13 Do not withhold discipline from a child;
if you punish him with the rod, he will not die.
14 Punish him with the rod
and save his soul from death.[a]

15 My son, if your heart is wise,
then my heart will be glad;
16 my inmost being will rejoice
when your lips speak what is right.[k]

17 Do not let your heart envy[l] sinners,
but always be zealous for the fear of the LORD.
18 There is surely a future hope for you,
and your hope will not be cut off.[m]

19 Listen, my son, and be wise,
and keep your heart on the right path.
20 Do not join those who drink too much wine[n]
or gorge themselves on meat,
21 for drunkards and gluttons become poor,[o]
and drowsiness clothes them in rags.

22 Listen to your father, who gave you life,
and do not despise your mother when she is old.[p]
23 Buy the truth and do not sell it;
get wisdom, discipline and understanding.[q]
24 The father of a righteous man has great joy;
he who has a wise son delights in him.[r]
25 May your father and mother be glad;
may she who gave you birth rejoice!

26 My son,[s] give me your heart
and let your eyes keep to my ways,[t]
27 for a prostitute is a deep pit[u]
and a wayward wife is a narrow well.
28 Like a bandit she lies in wait,[v]
and multiplies the unfaithful among men.

29 Who has woe? Who has sorrow?
Who has strife? Who has complaints?
Who has needless bruises? Who has bloodshot eyes?
30 Those who linger over wine,[w]

23:16 [k]ver 24; Pr 27:11
23:17 [l]Ps 37:1; Pr 28:14
23:18 [m]Ps 9:18; Pr 24:14,19-20
23:20 [n]Isa 5:11,22; Ro 13:13; Eph 5:18
23:21 [o]Pr 21:17
23:22 [p]Lev 19:32; Pr 1:8; 30:17; Eph 6:1-2
23:23 [q]Pr 4:7
23:24 [r]ver 15-16; Pr 10:1; 15:20
23:26 [s]Pr 3:1; 5:1-6 [t]Ps 18:21; Pr 4:4
23:27 [u]Pr 22:14
23:28 [v]Pr 7:11-12; Ecc 7:26
23:30 [w]Ps 75:8; Isa 5:11; Eph 5:18

[a] *14* Hebrew *Sheol*

■ **23:12—24:2** *An Obedient Son.* An educational proverb reminiscent of the prologues (1:8—9:18; 22:17–21) marks off the next set of aphorisms on the obedient son (23:12,13–14,15–16,17–18,19–21, 22–25,26–28,29–35; 24:1–2). These admonitions have a strong personal reference. "My son" occurs three times (23:15,19,26); "I" or "father" or a reference to the father occurs five times (23:15,22,24, 25,26), and "mother" occurs twice (23:22,25). The sayings also advance chronologically, spanning one's entire lifetime, from youth (23:13–14) to a mother grown old (23:22). The son's loyalty to his parents is matched by his radical separation from sinners. He must neither envy sinners (23:17–18) nor join drunkards (23:19–21) nor barter away parental wisdom for an alternative view of life (23:22–25).

23:13–14 An admonition to the son not to withhold discipline from a youth follows the preceding call to apply his heart to instruction (v. 12). An apprentice in moral education must practice obedience himself before he becomes a disciplinarian (cf. Dt 6:5–9).

23:15–16 This proverb also escalates from being wise to becoming a wisdom teacher and delineates the father's glad response to both situations.

23:17–18 A prohibition not to envy sinners now complements the admonition to embrace the parent's wisdom (vv. 15–16; cf. 1:8–9,10–19).

23:18 future hope . . . cut off. This passage refers to the end result of continuously fearing the Lord. "Your hope" (see also 10:28) refers to a future time when God will reverse the present situation by punishing the wicked with loss of everything and rewarding the righteous with prosperity. The metaphor "will not be cut off" (cf. Nu 13:23–24; 1Sa 24:5) signifies that the hoped for abundant life will not be annihilated. God will fulfill the hope of the righteous for an abundant life (cf. 24:20; Ps 73:17; Jer 29:11ff.; Jn 13:7; Jas 5:11; Rev 13:10).

23:20–22 See *WLC* 124,127,142; *WSC* 75; *HC* 104,105,107,110.

23:25 See *WLC* 124.

23:26–28 The first part of this proverb contains two direct admonitions to the son to apply his whole being to his father's direction (v. 26). Heretofore the receptive organs—heart and ear—played the dominating role, but now the eyes are brought into play because they first perceive the seductive woman (see 6:25). The second part of this dictum validates the admonitions. The son's only adequate resistance to seduction is a prior commitment of his heart and eyes to God (represented by the father).

23:27 prostitute. Or "an adulterous woman."

23:29–35 The sayings turn to the folly of those who linger over wine (v. 30). A listing of the terrible consequences of overindulgence confronts the young man. After a series of humiliating experiences the passage ends with the drunkard starting the whole process over again (v. 35). See *WLC* 136,139,151.

who go to sample bowls of mixed wine.
31 Do not gaze at wine when it is red,
when it sparkles in the cup,
when it goes down smoothly!
32 In the end it bites like a snake
and poisons like a viper.
33 Your eyes will see strange sights
and your mind imagine confusing things.
34 You will be like one sleeping on the high seas,
lying on top of the rigging.
35 "They hit me," you will say, "but I'm not hurt!
They beat me, but I don't feel it!
When will I wake up
so I can find another drink?"

24

Do not envy[x] wicked men,
do not desire their company;
2 for their hearts plot violence,
and their lips talk about making trouble.[y]

3 By wisdom a house is built,[z]
and through understanding it is established;
4 through knowledge its rooms are filled
with rare and beautiful treasures.[a]

5 A wise man has great power,
and a man of knowledge increases strength;
6 for waging war you need guidance,
and for victory many advisers.[b]
7 Wisdom is too high for a fool;
in the assembly at the gate he has nothing to say.

8 He who plots evil
will be known as a schemer.
9 The schemes of folly are sin,
and men detest a mocker.

10 If you falter in times of trouble,
how small is your strength![c]

11 Rescue those being led away to death;
hold back those staggering toward slaughter.[d]
12 If you say, "But we knew nothing about this,"
does not he who weighs[e] the heart perceive it?
Does not he who guards your life know it?
Will he not repay each person according to what he has done?[f]

13 Eat honey, my son, for it is good;
honey from the comb is sweet to your taste.

24:1 [x]Ps 37:1; 73:3; Pr 3:31-32; 23:17-18
24:2 [y]Ps 10:7
24:3 [z]Pr 14:1
24:4 [a]Pr 8:21
24:6 [b]Pr 11:14; 20:18; Lk 14:31
24:10 [c]Job 4:5; Jer 51:46; Heb 12:3
24:11 [d]Ps 82:4; Isa 58:6-7
24:12 [e]Pr 21:2 [f]Job 34:11; Ps 62:12; Ro 2:6*

■ **24:3–12** *Wisdom, Strategy and Strength.* This third section of the "thirty sayings" motivates the son to lay hold of the wisdom that will provide him strength and strategy in conflict. After the typical introductory educational axiom (vv. 3–4), the next sounds the theme (vv. 5–6) by inferentially calling for wisdom in order to equip one with both strength (v. 5) and strategy (v. 6). Both are necessary virtues for any undertaking, but they are especially necessary in the case of war. The section's third and fourth sayings motivate the son to lay hold of these virtues by assessing the fool's incompetence to strategize wisely (v. 7) and by labeling the fool a social pariah. The section's fifth and final saying induces the son to lay hold of wisdom's strength by shaming him if he should falter (v. 10) and by threatening him with divine judgment (vv. 11–12).
24:5 strength. See note on vv. 10–12.
24:7 This dictum is connected to the preceding two by the words "wisdom" and "wise" (vv. 3,5,7). It functions as a foil to the second maxim by noting the incompetence of incorrigible fools to speak in the gate, where public policy was formulated.
24:8–9 This aphorism also functions as a foil to the second by contrasting the accredited and competent counsel of the wise with the public's condemnation of the self-serving plans of fools. The sage's evaluation that the fool must be silenced (v. 7) escalates to public censor.
24:10–12 The need for wise and competent counsel for success in war (v. 6)—in contrast to the silence demanded of fools by the sage (v. 7) and by society (vv. 8–9)—is now expanded to include wisdom as strength in times of distress (cf. v. 5). "Strength," the last word of verses 5 and 10, binds together the two sayings. If fortified strength is a sign of a person's wisdom (v. 5), then meager strength in crisis signifies an individual's lack or loss of wisdom (vv. 10–12). The phrase "times of trouble" (v. 10) finds concrete expression in people being led away to their slaughter (v. 11). The final proverb in this section is connected with the preceding two (vv. 7,8–9), which pertain to fools and their antisocial behavior, by warning the son against passive complicity with them. See *WLC* 135.
■ **24:13–22** *Prohibitions Against Involvement With the Wicked.* These verses mark off the final section of the "thirty sayings." The five dictums are all proverb pairs consisting of double admonitions (vv. 13–14,15,17,19,21) with validations (vv. 14,16,18,20,22). The endearing term "my son" (vv. 13,21) frames the whole. The section

24:14 [g]Ps 119:103; Pr 16:24 [h]Pr 23:18
24:16 [i]Job 5:19; Ps 34:19; Mic 7:8
24:17 [j]Ob 1:12 [k]Job 31:29
24:19 [l]Ps 37:1
24:20 [m]Job 18:5; Pr 13:9; 23:17-18
24:21 [n]Ro 13:1-5; 1Pe 2:17
24:23 [o]Pr 1:6 [p]Lev 19:15 [q]Pr 28:21
24:24 [r]Pr 17:15
24:28 [s]Ps 7:4; Pr 25:18; Eph 4:25
24:29 [t]Pr 20:22; Mt 5:38-41; Ro 12:17
24:30 [u]Pr 6:6-11; 26:13-16

14 Know also that wisdom is sweet to your soul;
if you find it, there is a future hope for you,
and your hope will not be cut off.[g h]

15 Do not lie in wait like an outlaw against a righteous man's house,
do not raid his dwelling place;
16 for though a righteous man falls seven times, he rises again,
but the wicked are brought down by calamity.[i]

17 Do not gloat[j] when your enemy falls;
when he stumbles, do not let your heart rejoice,[k]
18 or the LORD will see and disapprove
and turn his wrath away from him.

19 Do not fret[l] because of evil men
or be envious of the wicked,
20 for the evil man has no future hope,
and the lamp of the wicked will be snuffed out.[m]

21 Fear the LORD and the king,[n] my son,
and do not join with the rebellious,
22 for those two will send sudden destruction upon them,
and who knows what calamities they can bring?

Further Sayings of the Wise

23 These also are sayings of the wise:[o]

To show partiality[p] in judging is not good:[q]
24 Whoever says to the guilty, "You are innocent"[r]—
peoples will curse him and nations denounce him.
25 But it will go well with those who convict the guilty,
and rich blessing will come upon them.

26 An honest answer
is like a kiss on the lips.

27 Finish your outdoor work
and get your fields ready;
after that, build your house.

28 Do not testify against your neighbor without cause,[s]
or use your lips to deceive.
29 Do not say, "I'll do to him as he has done to me;
I'll pay that man back for what he did."[t]

30 I went past the field of the sluggard,[u]
past the vineyard of the man who lacks judgment;
31 thorns had come up everywhere,
the ground was covered with weeds,
and the stone wall was in ruins.
32 I applied my heart to what I observed
and learned a lesson from what I saw:

---

begins with the promise of eternal life for the wise (vv. 14a,16a) and moves to the certainty of eternal death for the wicked (vv. 16b,20,22).

24:14 sweet to your soul. Or "like honey for you."

24:19–20 This saying protects the preceding one (vv. 17–18) from the misconception that the wicked will enjoy a blessed future because the Lord will turn away his wrath from them. Their bottom line is still zero; they will be destroyed. The Lord's stay of execution is only long enough to deprive gloaters of their malignant joy. That truth leads to the admonition not to burn with envy at their temporary prosperity.

24:21–22 The last axiom builds on the preceding one, pointing to the Lord and his righteous king as the agents who uphold the principle of retribution. Both God and the king will inflict disaster so certain, sudden and extensive that no one knows its limits (see 14:35; 16:10–15; 19:12; 20:2,8; 22:11; 25:2–5).

■ **24:23–34** *Further Sayings of the Wise.* The title of this section (see v. 23) indicates the beginning of a fifth collection of sayings (see note on 22:17—24:34). "Also" (v. 23) indicates that a collector appended these five proverbs to the "thirty sayings" of the wise (see note on 22:17—24:22). Since Solomon adopted and adapted those sayings for Israel (see note on 22:17—24:34), it is plausible to think that these verses also came from his hand. They alternate among three situations that are repeated: court (vv. 23–25,28), speaking and thinking (vv. 26,29) and behavior at work (vv. 27, 30–34).

24:30–34 The vineyard of the sleeping sluggard (lazy individual) becomes an analogy for an inheritance lost through negligence. Weeds of all sorts have grown up and supplanted fields arduously planted by an earlier generation (vv. 30–31). The centerline (v. 32) is a transition between the beginning and ending. "I observed" carries on the narrative begun in verse 30, and "learned a lesson" introduces the second proverb pair (vv. 33–34), which is driven home using the second person. The analogy closes with laziness allowing poverty to infiltrate as a parasitic vagrant and a violent bandit to snatch away the entire inheritance (vv. 33–34).

33 A little sleep, a little slumber,
a little folding of the hands to rest[v]—
34 and poverty will come on you like a bandit
and scarcity like an armed man.[a][w]

More Proverbs of Solomon

25 These are more proverbs[x] of Solomon, copied by the men of Hezekiah king of Judah:[y]

2 It is the glory of God to conceal a matter;
to search out a matter is the glory of kings.[z]

3 As the heavens are high and the earth is deep,
so the hearts of kings are unsearchable.

4 Remove the dross from the silver,
and out comes material for[b] the silversmith;
5 remove the wicked from the king's presence,[a]
and his throne will be established[b] through righteousness.[c]

6 Do not exalt yourself in the king's presence,
and do not claim a place among great men;
7 it is better for him to say to you, "Come up here,"[d]
than for him to humiliate you before a nobleman.

What you have seen with your eyes
8 do not bring[c] hastily to court,
for what will you do in the end
if your neighbor puts you to shame?[e]

9 If you argue your case with a neighbor,
do not betray another man's confidence,
10 or he who hears it may shame you
and you will never lose your bad reputation.

24:33 [v]Pr 6:10
24:34 [w]Pr 10:4; Ecc 10:18
25:1 [x]1Ki 4:32 [y]Pr 1:1
25:2 [z]Pr 16:10-15
25:5 [a]Pr 20:8 [b]2Sa 7:13 [c]Pr 16:12; 29:14
25:7 [d]Lk 14:7-10
25:8 [e]Mt 5:25-26

[a] *34* *Or like a vagrant / and scarcity like a beggar* [b] *4* *Or comes a vessel from* [c] *7,8* *Or nobleman / on whom you had set your eyes. / 8Do not go*

■ **25:1—29:27** *Hezekiah's Collection of Solomon's Proverbs.* During the reign of Hezekiah (715–686 B.C.) Judah underwent a period of significant reform (see 2Ki 18–20). It is not surprising that Hezekiah would have called upon his court personnel to pull together the proverbs of Solomon (25:1).
■ **25:1–27** *God and the King, the Righteous and Wicked.* After a title (v. 1) this collection's introduction (vv. 2–5) presents the unit's two themes that set the parameters of meaning within which all its saying are to be interpreted. Verses 2–3 establish the God-king-subject hierarchy, while verses 4–5 posit the fundamental conflict between the righteous and the wicked that permeates every area of human life. The first half of the body (vv. 6–15) pertains to the opening theme and the second (vv. 16–27) to the closing.
■ **25:1** *Title.* The title indicates that Solomon authored or adapted for use in Israel the proverbs contained in this collection and that they were subsequently accumulated and edited by Hezekiah's wise men.
25:1 copied. Or "compiled." **Hezekiah.** See "Introduction: Author."
■ **25:2–3** *God and the King.* The repetitions of "kings" and "search" link verses 2–3. God increases glory by being unfathomable and inscrutable, as did his king within his own realm (vv. 2–3). None of the king's subjects could comprehend the king's vast knowledge or penetrate his motives, which set him high above them. God, in turn, was inscrutable even to the king, demonstrating that the Lord was set high above even the king (cf. Dt 29:29; Job 26:14; Ro 11:33–36). In sum, verses 2–3 set up a hierarchy of wisdom, authority and power: the king above his subjects and God above the king and the king's subjects. God's appointed king was awesome and not to be toyed with; to a far greater extent this was also the case with God himself.
■ **25:4–5** *The Righteous and Wicked.* The next proverb pair is linked with the preceding one by repeating the word "kings" (vv. 2,3,5) and by advancing the activity of the wise king from his investigation of matters of state to his elimination of wicked officials. As a silversmith can produce a precious vessel only with silver that has been purified of dross (v. 4), so a king's throne (i.e., his dynasty) could endure only when wicked officials had been removed from his presence (cf. 20:8,26; Isa 1:21–26; Eze 22:18–22; Mal 3:2). The refiner's pure vessel illustrated the king's uncontaminated, valuable and enduring throne. Removing unscrupulous officials and replacing them with nobles ready to help the poor and needy were standard tasks for all conscientious kings, both within and outside Israel (cf. 14:34; Ps 101:4–8; Mal 3:3,17–18; Mt 13:40–43).
25:4 material. Or "vessel."
25:5 wicked. Or "wicked official."
■ **25:6–15** *Etiquette in the Royal Court.* This batch of proverbs pertaining to court behavior formally falls into two equal halves: admonitions (vv. 6–10) and sayings (vv. 11–15). Both forms contributed to the courtier's education, teaching him humility (vv. 6–7a), thorough preparation (vv. 7b–8), confidentiality (vv. 9–10), appropriate speech and willingness to accept reproof (vv. 11–12), reliability (vv. 13–14) and tactful gentleness (v. 15).
25:6–10 Verses 6–7a concern the jockeying for power, position and glory among the king's men, and verses 7b–10 concern legal disputes among peers in which one is ultimately declared to be in the right and the other in the wrong.
25:6–7a Do not cross over on your own initiative into the higher social rank of the king and his nobles, counsels the proverb. It is better that superiors elevate you because your aptitude and record warrant the promotion than that you overreach your limits and risk a reprimand or loss of face that will damage your prospects (Lk 14:8–11).
25:7b–10 The first pair of these closely related proverbs dissuades the courtier from impetuous litigation. The second urges him to plead a well-prepared case without breaching a confidence. Conflicts are to be resolved in an appropriate manner: through investigation (vv. 7b–8) without gossip (vv. 9–10). These verses counsel the audience not to jump to a conclusion merely on the basis of what they have seen or to breach a confidence in any quarrel.
25:8,9 neighbor. Or "peer."
25:9–10 See *WLC* 145.

25:11 [f]ver 12; Pr 15:23
25:12 [g]ver 11; Ps 141:5; Pr 13:18; 15:31
25:13 [h]Pr 10:26; 13:17
25:15 [i]Ecc 10:4 [j]Pr 15:1
25:16 [k]ver 27
25:18 [l]Ps 57:4; Pr 12:18
25:22 [m]Ps 18:8 [n]2Sa 16:12; 2Ch 28:15; Mt 5:44; Ro 12:20*

11 A word aptly spoken
is like apples of gold in settings of silver.[f]

12 Like an earring of gold or an ornament of fine gold
is a wise man's rebuke to a listening ear.[g]

13 Like the coolness of snow at harvest time
is a trustworthy messenger to those who send him;
he refreshes the spirit of his masters.[h]

14 Like clouds and wind without rain
is a man who boasts of gifts he does not give.

15 Through patience a ruler can be persuaded,[i]
and a gentle tongue can break a bone.[j]

16 If you find honey, eat just enough—
too much of it, and you will vomit.[k]
17 Seldom set foot in your neighbor's house—
too much of you, and he will hate you.

18 Like a club or a sword or a sharp arrow
is the man who gives false testimony against his
neighbor.[l]

19 Like a bad tooth or a lame foot
is reliance on the unfaithful in times of trouble.

20 Like one who takes away a garment on a cold day,
or like vinegar poured on soda,
is one who sings songs to a heavy heart.

21 If your enemy is hungry, give him food to eat;
if he is thirsty, give him water to drink.
22 In doing this, you will heap burning coals[m] on his head,
and the LORD will reward you.[n]

23 As a north wind brings rain,
so a sly tongue brings angry looks.

25:11–12 The harmony between a decision and its circumstance bestows beauty and value upon finely crafted mediation (v. 11), and the harmony between the reproving decision and its acceptance enhances its beauty and value (v. 12).
25:12 man's. Perhaps "judge's."
25:13–14 The final proverb pair is linked by weather imagery involving unexpected contradictions (snow in harvest; clouds and wind without rain). Their topic pertains to faithfulness, both positively (v. 13) and negatively (v. 14). The reliable envoy, who held a high position in ancient Near Eastern politics, refreshed his superior, giving him joy (v. 13), while the unreliable windbag promised a gift but defrauded the rightful beneficiary.
25:13 snow at harvest time. During the hot summers laborers brought snow and ice down from the high mountains and stored them in snow houses or snow caves.
25:15 This single verse brings the preceding seven proverb pairs to closure. This proverb adds inward patience and outward gentleness to the other virtues for court etiquette.
■ **25:16–27** *Conflict Outside and Inside the Court.* The words "eat" and "honey" (vv. 16,27) form a frame around the second subunit. Whereas the first subunit (vv. 2–15) concerned matters of the royal court, these admonitions and sayings explore human conflict in general, although verse 18 returns to the court in a strict sense.
25:16–22 Verses 16–20 present human conflict negatively and without resolution, while verses 21–22 present a resolution.
25:16–17 Admonitions for moderation and restraint warn that even something as delightful and desirable as honey, or as neighborliness, can become loathsome through excess. See *WLC* 135.
25:18–20 The theme is developed by descending from the perjurer (v. 18) to the undependable (v. 19) to the tactless (v. 20)—all of whom should be avoided.
25:20 soda. Or "wound." The lethal talker and silent traitor give way to the insensitive and inept speaker. Singing joyful songs to a sullen heart inflicts pain with no therapeutic value, comparable to putting off a warm garment on a frosty day or pouring stinging vinegar on a wound (cf. Ps 137:3–4).
25:21–22 The concluding proverb pair of verses 16–22 instructs the son to resolve the conflicts he has created with his neighbor by noting and relieving the neighbor's point of need.
25:22 you will heap burning coals on his head. Many interpreters think this verse refers to a form of punishment or vengeance, but the parallel, "the LORD will reward you," raises questions about this interpretation. The book of Proverbs elsewhere rejects any form of personal revenge (17:13; 20:22; 24:17–18). Both the Old and New Testaments instruct members of the covenant community to love, not hate, their enemies (Lev 19:17–18; Ps 35:13; Mt 5:43). The "burning coals" may then be viewed as morally good deeds that are pleasing to the Lord. The Septuagint (the Greek translation of the OT) adds "the LORD will reward you for your good" (see Ro 12:17–21). The alternative interpretation that "burning coals" refers to pangs of shame that a man feels when good is returned for evil is supported by an Egyptian penitential ritual involving carrying a basin of fiery coals on the head to signify regret and shame. On the other hand, the same ritual might be seen to support the idea that heaping coals on a person's head is a good thing because it signifies the repentance of the offender.
25:23–26 This subunit consists of two proverb pairs using weather and water imagery, respectively. The first pair pertains to unexpected conflicts due to sly or quarrelsome speech; the second contrasts restoration with ruin, again advocating doing good to restore a conflicted situation (cf. 25:21–22,25).
25:23–24 In the promised land the cold north wind normally clears the sky and brings good visibility, unlike the northwest wind that brings rain. Hidden slander, like rain from a north wind, inflicts unexpected damage, as does a nagging wife (v. 24). Both the backbiting tongue and the niggling wife precipitate unexpected conflicts. Verse 23 pictures bad weather, while verse 24 portrays a man exposed to inclement weather, which is still to be preferred over exposure to the storms of a tempestuous wife.
25:23 As . . . looks. Better, "Like a north wind that brings rain, so a sly tongue brings a look as though struck by a curse." See *WLC* 144.

24 Better to live on a corner of the roof
than share a house with a quarrelsome wife.[o]

25 Like cold water to a weary soul
is good news from a distant land.[p]

26 Like a muddied spring or a polluted well
is a righteous man who gives way to the wicked.

27 It is not good to eat too much honey,[q]
nor is it honorable to seek one's own honor.[r]

28 Like a city whose walls are broken down
is a man who lacks self-control.

26 Like snow in summer or rain[s] in harvest,
honor is not fitting for a fool.[t]

2 Like a fluttering sparrow or a darting swallow,
an undeserved curse does not come to rest.[u]

3 A whip for the horse, a halter for the donkey,[v]
and a rod for the backs of fools![w]

4 Do not answer a fool according to his folly,
or you will be like him yourself.[x]

5 Answer a fool according to his folly,
or he will be wise in his own eyes.[y]

6 Like cutting off one's feet or drinking violence
is the sending of a message by the hand of a fool.[z]

7 Like a lame man's legs that hang limp
is a proverb in the mouth of a fool.[a]

8 Like tying a stone in a sling
is the giving of honor to a fool.[b]

9 Like a thornbush in a drunkard's hand
is a proverb in the mouth of a fool.[c]

10 Like an archer who wounds at random
is he who hires a fool or any passer-by.

25:24 [o]Pr 21:9
25:25 [p]Pr 15:30
25:27 [q]ver 16 [r]Pr 27:2; Mt 23:12
26:1 [s]1Sa 12:17 [t]ver 8; Pr 19:10
26:2 [u]Nu 23:8; Dt 23:5
26:3 [v]Ps 32:9 [w]Pr 10:13
26:4 [x]ver 5; Isa 36:21
26:5 [y]ver 4; Pr 3:7
26:6 [z]Pr 10:26
26:7 [a]ver 9
26:8 [b]ver 1
26:9 [c]ver 7

25:25–26 The last proverb pair is linked by the image of precious drinking water that revitalizes life: The first saying is positive, the second negative. The pair pertains to perseverance, contrasting the restoration of a weary person by a good word with the ruin of a righteous person by equivocation. The unexpected word of encouragement stands in marked contrast to the backbiting or nagging word.
25:25 soul. Better, "person."
25:26 muddied spring. To befoul a water hole on a track across the desert is an unforgivable sin among the Bedouin. Such a spring threatens life, which depends on good water. **righteous man.** See 13:16 and 21:12.
25:27 to seek one's own honor. This proverb compares the intellectual person who seeks honor to an individual who eats too much honey (cf. v. 16; Jer 17:10). See *WLC* 135.
■ **25:28—26:28** *Seven Moral Inferiors.* The second unit of chapters 25–29 warns against seven types of people whose lifestyles are to be avoided: the undisciplined (25:28), the fool (26:1–12), the sluggard or lazy individual (26:13–16), the busybody (26:17), the mischief maker (26:18–19), the slanderer (26:20–22) and the son's personal enemy (26:23–28). The number seven symbolizes completeness.
25:28 The fool is characterized by a lack of self-control (cf. 12:16).
26:1–12 The key word "fool/fools" occurs in every verse of this section except verse 2. Formally, this passage consists of ten axioms (vv. 1–3,6–12) and two admonitions (vv. 4–5). Apart from the concluding verse these ten sayings have essentially the same structure. The theme of this material is that it is inappropriate and dangerous to honor a fool by educating him with proverbs and entrusting him with responsible service, but it is fitting to punish and rebuke him. The introduction sounds the caution not to give fools honor (vv. 1–3), the body develops both the positive and negative aspects of that theme (vv. 4–10), and the conclusion features its positive aspect (vv. 11–12).
26:1–3 Verse 1 summarizes the negative aspect of the theme: "Honor is not fitting for a fool" because bestowing social standing on a fool will cause great damage. Verse 2 functions as a comparison and contrast, identifying the utterance of a curse against an innocent person as unfitting. Verse 3, however, points to the deserved recompense for a fool.
26:4–10 The seven-verse body consists of two partial units: two admonitions that prescribe correction as fitting for the fool (vv. 4–5) and five aphorisms that proscribe and define honor as unbefitting a fool (vv. 6–10).
26:4–5 Two admonitions develop the theme of what is fitting for a fool. In addition to physical caning to control such a person, the wise disciple needs to give the fool a verbal answer (vv. 4–5). The apparent contradiction between "Do not answer a fool" (v. 4) and "Answer a fool" (v. 5) is resolved by clarifying the ambiguous preposition "according to" in light of the negative consequence to be avoided. The son's answer must distinguish between what is unsuitable (v. 4) and what is appropriate (v. 5). It is improper to meet the fool's insult with insult (2Pe 3:9). If the disciple replies vindictively, harshly and/or with lies—in the manner of the fool—he will also come under the fool's condemnation. Rather, without lowering himself to the fool's level in a debate, but by overcoming evil with good (25:21ff.), the wise person shows the fool's folly for what it is. The judicious individual is not silently to accept or tolerate the fool's folly, for to do so affirms the fool. One must answer a fool in order to destabilize him—without becoming like him.
26:6–10 The following five adages return to the introduction's form, using negative images from the created order to expand on the theme of honor and why it is "not fitting for a fool" (v. 1). The similes escalate from impersonal weather images (v. 1) to animal images (vv. 2–3) to striking and ludicrous human images (vv. 6–10).
26:7 As a lame person has legs but cannot use them for locomotion, so a noble proverb in the mouth of a fool gets him nowhere.

11 As a dog returns to its vomit,[d]
so a fool repeats his folly.[e]

12 Do you see a man wise in his own eyes?[f]
There is more hope for a fool than for him.[g]

13 The sluggard says,[h] "There is a lion in the road,
a fierce lion roaming the streets!"[i]

14 As a door turns on its hinges,
so a sluggard turns on his bed.[j]

15 The sluggard buries his hand in the dish;
he is too lazy to bring it back to his mouth.[k]

16 The sluggard is wiser in his own eyes
than seven men who answer discreetly.

17 Like one who seizes a dog by the ears
is a passer-by who meddles in a quarrel not his own.

18 Like a madman shooting
firebrands or deadly arrows
19 is a man who deceives his neighbor
and says, "I was only joking!"

20 Without wood a fire goes out;
without gossip a quarrel dies down.[l]

21 As charcoal to embers and as wood to fire,
so is a quarrelsome man for kindling strife.[m]

22 The words of a gossip are like choice morsels;
they go down to a man's inmost parts.[n]

23 Like a coating of glaze[a] over earthenware
are fervent lips with an evil heart.

24 A malicious man disguises himself with his lips,[o]
but in his heart he harbors deceit.[p]
25 Though his speech is charming,[q] do not believe him,
for seven abominations fill his heart.[r]
26 His malice may be concealed by deception,
but his wickedness will be exposed in the assembly.
27 If a man digs a pit,[s] he will fall into it;[t]
if a man rolls a stone, it will roll back on him.[u]
28 A lying tongue hates those it hurts,
and a flattering mouth[v] works ruin.

27

1 Do not boast[w] about tomorrow,
for you do not know what a day may bring forth.[x]

26:11 [d]2Pe 2:22* [e]Ex 8:15; Ps 85:8
26:12 [f]Pr 3:7 [g]Pr 29:20
26:13 [h]Pr 6:6-11; 24:30-34 [i]Pr 22:13
26:14 [j]Pr 6:9
26:15 [k]Pr 19:24
26:20 [l]Pr 22:10
26:21 [m]Pr 14:17; 15:18
26:22 [n]Pr 18:8
26:24 [o]Ps 31:18 [p]Ps 41:6; Pr 10:18; 12:20
26:25 [q]Ps 28:3 [r]Jer 9:4-8
26:27 [s]Ps 7:15 [t]Est 6:13 [u]Est 2:23; 7:9; Ps 35:8; 141:10; Pr 28:10; 29:6; Isa 50:11
26:28 [v]Ps 12:3; Pr 29:5
27:1 [w]1Ki 20:11 [x]Mt 6:34; Lk 12:19-20; Jas 4:13-16

a *23* With a different word division of the Hebrew; Masoretic Text *of silver dross*

26:11–12 These verses inferentially elaborate the positive theme that discipline befits a fool. Verse 11 pillories the fool as incapable of saving himself, but verse 12 speaks of hope for his salvation.
26:13–16 The sluggard or indolent individual again moves into view, appearing in every verse. The movement of thought narrows: He does not leave his house (v. 13), does not make it off his couch (v. 14), does not even get his hand from the dish to his mouth (v. 15). Although the portrayal of the sluggard is somewhat comical, the poem climactically represents him as under the illusion that he is wiser than the wisest (v. 16). In reality, though, laziness thwarts talent, position, wealth and power.
26:17–28 Hezekiah's compilers now focus on four malevolent, antisocial types who cause dissension, mostly by their speech (see 6:12–15,16–19; 16:27–30), escalating from the busybody, who hurts himself (v. 17), to the mischief maker (vv. 18–19) to the slanderer (vv. 20–22) to the son's hateful enemy (vv. 23–28).
26:18–19 deceives. The jester intends to harm his neighbor; he is not merely a prankster or practical joker. He condemns himself by his mean and cynical question. The cruel buffoon cannot discern the difference between a joke and heartlessness.
26:20–22 The slanderer sustains the strife (v. 20), inflames it (v. 21) and transforms society into his own image (v. 22).
26:23–28 Finally, the compilers narrow down the antisocial types to the son's hateful enemy. The imperative "Do not believe him" (v. 25) reflects the aim of these verses: Do not accept him or anything he has to say, no matter how attractive it may seem. The first triplet of sayings depicts the enemy's deception (vv. 23–25) and the second, his destruction (vv. 26–28). See *WLC* 144.
■ **27:1–22** *Friends and Friendship.* This unit brings together a loose collection of proverbs that primarily pertain to friendship. The key synonyms "friend" and "neighbor" occur in verses 6, 9, 10 and 14. Other proverbs are paired with these and indirectly pertain to the topic. The unit falls into two balanced halves (vv. 1–10 and 11–22). These two sections parallel each other: introductory admonitions

2 Let another praise you, and not your own mouth;
someone else, and not your own lips.[y]

3 Stone is heavy and sand[z] a burden,
but provocation by a fool is heavier than both.

4 Anger is cruel and fury overwhelming,
but who can stand before jealousy?[a]

5 Better is open rebuke
than hidden love.

6 Wounds from a friend can be trusted,
but an enemy multiplies kisses.[b]

7 He who is full loathes honey,
but to the hungry even what is bitter tastes sweet.

8 Like a bird that strays from its nest[c]
is a man who strays from his home.

9 Perfume[d] and incense bring joy to the heart,
and the pleasantness of one's friend springs from his earnest counsel.

10 Do not forsake your friend and the friend of your father,
and do not go to your brother's house when disaster[e] strikes you—
better a neighbor nearby than a brother far away.

11 Be wise, my son, and bring joy to my heart;[f]
then I can answer anyone who treats me with contempt.[g]

12 The prudent see danger and take refuge,
but the simple keep going and suffer for it.[h]

13 Take the garment of one who puts up security for a stranger;
hold it in pledge if he does it for a wayward woman.[i]

14 If a man loudly blesses his neighbor early in the morning,
it will be taken as a curse.

15 A quarrelsome wife is like
a constant dripping[j] on a rainy day;
16 restraining her is like restraining the wind
or grasping oil with the hand.

17 As iron sharpens iron,
so one man sharpens another.

27:2 [y]Pr 25:27
27:3 [z]Job 6:3
27:4 [a]Nu 5:14
27:6 [b]Ps 141:5; Pr 28:23
27:8 [c]Isa 16:2
27:9 [d]Est 2:12; Ps 45:8
27:10 [e]Pr 17:17; 18:24
27:11 [f]Pr 10:1; 23:15-16 [g]Ge 24:60
27:12 [h]Pr 22:3
27:13 [i]Pr 20:16
27:15 [j]Est 1:18; Pr 19:13

---

regarding relationships (vv. 1–2,11–12), negative teachings about folly in relationships (vv. 3–4,13–16) and positive teachings about the nature and value of friendship (vv. 5–10,17–22).

27:1–2 Both proverbs caution that self-praise is unsuitable because a mortal does not control his own destiny (v. 1). Together they espouse an attitude of humility before the sovereignty of God and the judgment of the community.

27:3–4 The next proverb pair pertains to irrational and destructive emotional stimulations; namely "provocation" (v. 3), "anger" (v. 4) and "jealousy" (v. 4). A person who exhibits such emotions is the opposite of a friend and is to be avoided.

27:5–6 Friendship with a fool is impossible (vv. 3–4), but wrongdoing by a friend must be resolved.

27:7–8 These verses pertain to gratifying one's appetites in the right way and to the loss of the most intimate of friendships, that of a husband and a wife.

27:9–10 Verses 9–10 are united by the key word "friend" and by the theme of the importance of friends to provide counsel and support in time of need.

27:11–21 These verses look at actions and relationships to be avoided; namely, putting up security for a stranger (v. 13); the hypocritical friend (v. 14); and the shrewish wife, who should be closer than the closest friend (v. 15–16). Verses 17–21 pertain to true friendship. Such a relationship sharpens one (v. 17) and enables the other to attain an accurate self-evaluation (vv. 19,21). Verse 18 indicates the importance of preventing the fracturing of relationships by protecting one's master (v. 18) and by restraining one's appetite (v. 20). Both imply being a reliable friend, being loyal to a master and refusing to covet a neighbor's property.

27:14–16 Both the overzealous blesser and the shrew prove false and threaten ruin. The victim expects good from both but receives bad.

27:14 Real friendship is expressed in deed and in truth (1Jn 3:18), not in pious but unusual pronouncements, such as loud speech in the early morning hours.

27:15 a constant . . . day. Or "a leaky roof in a cloudburst." The man takes shelter under the roof of his home, expecting to find protection from the storm. Instead he discovers that his leaky roof provides him no shelter from the torrential downpour. Likewise, he marries with the expectation of finding good, but the wife from whom he expects protection from the discourtesy of the world harshly attacks him at home. Both render his home situation intolerable. Like a bird that takes flight from its nest, he flees his home, seeking shelter elsewhere (cf. 19:13).

27:16 The topic shifts from false back to true friendship (vv. 5–10,14). This proverb likens the sharpening of an iron sword or tool by a whetting iron to the sharpening of a man's wit through a relationship with an authentic friend.

27:18 [k]1Co 9:7 [l]Lk 19:12-27

18 He who tends a fig tree will eat its fruit,[k]
and he who looks after his master will be honored.[l]

19 As water reflects a face,
so a man's heart reflects the man.

27:20 [m]Pr 30:15-16; Hab 2:5 [n]Ecc 1:8; 6:7

20 Death and Destruction[a] are never satisfied,[m]
and neither are the eyes of man.[n]

27:21 [o]Pr 17:3

21 The crucible for silver and the furnace for gold,[o]
but man is tested by the praise he receives.

22 Though you grind a fool in a mortar,
grinding him like grain with a pestle,
you will not remove his folly from him.

27:23 [p]Pr 12:10

23 Be sure you know the condition of your flocks,[p]
give careful attention to your herds;

27:24 [q]Pr 23:5

24 for riches do not endure forever,[q]
and a crown is not secure for all generations.
25 When the hay is removed and new growth appears
and the grass from the hills is gathered in,
26 the lambs will provide you with clothing,
and the goats with the price of a field.
27 You will have plenty of goats' milk
to feed you and your family
and to nourish your servant girls.

28:1 [r]2Ki 7:7 [s]Lev 26:17; Ps 53:5 [t]Ps 138:3

28

The wicked man flees[r] though no one pursues,[s]
but the righteous are as bold as a lion.[t]

2 When a country is rebellious, it has many rulers,
but a man of understanding and knowledge maintains order.

3 A ruler[b] who oppresses the poor
is like a driving rain that leaves no crops.

4 Those who forsake the law praise the wicked,
but those who keep the law resist them.

5 Evil men do not understand justice,
but those who seek the LORD understand it fully.

28:6 [u]Pr 19:1

6 Better a poor man whose walk is blameless
than a rich man whose ways are perverse.[u]

28:7 [v]Pr 23:19-21

7 He who keeps the law is a discerning son,
but a companion of gluttons disgraces his father.[v]

28:8 [w]Ex 18:21 [x]Job 27:17; Pr 13:22 [y]Ps 112:9; Pr 14:31; Lk 14:12-14

8 He who increases his wealth by exorbitant interest[w]
amasses it for another,[x] who will be kind to the poor.[y]

28:9 [z]Ps 66:18; 109:7; Pr 15:8; Isa 1:13

9 If anyone turns a deaf ear to the law,
even his prayers are detestable.[z]

a *20* Hebrew *Sheol and Abaddon* b *3* Or *A poor man*

27:22 See *WLC* 151.
■ **27:23-27** *Sustaining Blessings for the Future.* The previous section is summarized by analogies to the care given to sustain flocks and herds over time. Initial success in following the outlooks of the chapter will not be sustained unless careful attention is given.
27:23–27 See *WLC* 141.
27:24 do not endure. Good relationships and conditions in life do not automatically endure.
27:25 hay is removed . . . gathered in. The arduous work of gathering grass from the field indicates that the wise person makes appropriate efforts to ensure the continuation of blessings.
27:26-27 will provide . . . have plenty. Paying attention to sustaining blessings results in satisfaction and joy in life.
■ **28:1—29:27** *God and Kings, Instruction and Righteousness.* The men of Hezekiah (25:1) organized this section by strategic placement of proverbs employing the Hebrew words "righteous" and "wicked." The section both begins (28:1) and ends (29:27) with these words, and four proverbs within the collection employ these terms (28:12,18 ["blameless" and "perverse"]; 29:2,16). These verses, each from a particular primary emphasis, shed light on the structure of connections between a relationship with God, instruction, righteousness and rulership.
28:1–11 The receiving of instruction is a measure for ruling, especially of the rich over the poor (vv. 2–11). The introductory framing proverb contrasts the psychological insecurity of the wicked with the psychological confidence of the righteous (v. 1). The rest of the unit centers on submission to inspired "instruction" in administering justice, with particular reference to wealth. The application of justice to wealth brings prosperity to all, whereas its abuse brings disaster. These verses touch on various aspects of discernment: the importance of being a judicious person in government (vv. 2,7), lack of sensitivity as expressed through oppression of the poor (vv.

10 He who leads the upright along an evil path
will fall into his own trap,[a]
but the blameless will receive a good inheritance.

11 A rich man may be wise in his own eyes,
but a poor man who has discernment sees through him.

12 When the righteous triumph, there is great elation;[b]
but when the wicked rise to power, men go into hiding.[c]

13 He who conceals his sins[d] does not prosper,
but whoever confesses and renounces them finds mercy.[e]

14 Blessed is the man who always fears the LORD,
but he who hardens his heart falls into trouble.

15 Like a roaring lion or a charging bear
is a wicked man ruling over a helpless people.

16 A tyrannical ruler lacks judgment,
but he who hates ill-gotten gain will enjoy a long life.

17 A man tormented by the guilt of murder
will be a fugitive[f] till death;
let no one support him.

18 He whose walk is blameless is kept safe,
but he whose ways are perverse will suddenly fall.[g]

19 He who works his land will have abundant food,
but the one who chases fantasies will have his fill of poverty.[h]

20 A faithful man will be richly blessed,
but one eager to get rich will not go unpunished.[i]

21 To show partiality is not good[j]—
yet a man will do wrong for a piece of bread.[k]

22 A stingy man is eager to get rich
and is unaware that poverty awaits him.[l]

23 He who rebukes a man will in the end gain more favor
than he who has a flattering tongue.[m]

24 He who robs his father or mother[n]
and says, "It's not wrong"—
he is partner to him who destroys.[o]

25 A greedy man stirs up dissension,
but he who trusts in the LORD[p] will prosper.

26 He who trusts in himself is a fool,[q]
but he who walks in wisdom is kept safe.

27 He who gives to the poor will lack nothing,[r]
but he who closes his eyes to them receives many curses.

28 When the wicked rise to power, people go into hiding;[s]
but when the wicked perish, the righteous thrive.

29 A man who remains stiff-necked after many rebukes
will suddenly be destroyed—without remedy.[t]

28:10 [a]Pr 26:27
28:12 [b]2Ki 11:20 [c]Pr 11:10; 29:2
28:13 [d]Job 31:33 [e]Ps 32:1-5; 1Jn 1:9
28:17 [f]Ge 9:6
28:18 [g]Pr 10:9
28:19 [h]Pr 12:11
28:20 [i]ver 22; Pr 10:6; 1Ti 6:9
28:21 [j]Pr 18:5 [k]Eze 13:19
28:22 [l]ver 20; Pr 23:6
28:23 [m]Pr 27:5-6
28:24 [n]Pr 19:26 [o]Pr 18:9
28:25 [p]Pr 29:25
28:26 [q]Ps 4:5; Pr 3:5
28:27 [r]Dt 15:7; 24:19; Pr 19:17; 22:9
28:28 [s]ver 12
29:1 [t]2Ch 36:16; Pr 6:15

3,8), instruction and social relationships as the basis of discernment (vv. 4,9), insight regarding evil people and others (vv. 5,10) and the benefits of acuity (e.g., advantage of being poor and discerning as opposed to rich and indiscriminate [vv. 6,11]).

28:12–28 This unit is set off by verses 12 and 28, which contrast the righteous and the wicked. Verses 13–27 specify various types of wicked people, including the hypocrite, the hard-hearted, the tyrant, the murderer, the perverse, the chaser after fantasies, the opportunist, the biased, the stingy, the flatterer, the robber of parents, the self-confident and the callous. The body of the unit consists of three subunits: God and the ruler (vv. 13–18), hard work and easy money (vv. 19–24) and generosity versus stinginess (vv. 25–27). See *WCF* 15.6; *WLC* 142,145; *WSC* 75.

29:1 The compilers (see 25:1) highlight the importance of heeding correction by positioning this verse at the center of this unit (chs. 28–29). As the centerpiece this proverb colors the entire section with the danger of resisting the sage's corrective observations (cf. 2Ti 3:16). See *WLC* 151.

29:2–16 Within the frame of the section (vv. 2,16) the unit's inner frame (vv. 3,15) pertains to rearing the son. Verses 3 and 15 are tightly linked by "his father" (v. 3) and "his mother" (v. 15; see 1:8; 10:1). A second inner frame positively comments on the "king"

29:2 [u]Est 8:15 [v]Pr 28:12

2 When the righteous thrive, the people rejoice;[u]
when the wicked rule, the people groan.[v]

29:3 [w]Pr 10:1 [x]Pr 5:8-10; Lk 15:11-32

3 A man who loves wisdom brings joy to his father,[w]
but a companion of prostitutes squanders his wealth.[x]

29:4 [y]Pr 8:15-16

4 By justice a king gives a country stability,[y]
but one who is greedy for bribes tears it down.

5 Whoever flatters his neighbor
is spreading a net for his feet.

29:6 [z]Ecc 9:12

6 An evil man is snared by his own sin,[z]
but a righteous one can sing and be glad.

29:7 [a]Job 29:16; Ps 41:1; Pr 31:8-9

7 The righteous care about justice for the poor,[a]
but the wicked have no such concern.

29:8 [b]Pr 11:11; 16:14

8 Mockers stir up a city,
but wise men turn away anger.[b]

9 If a wise man goes to court with a fool,
the fool rages and scoffs, and there is no peace.

29:10 [c]1Jn 3:12

10 Bloodthirsty men hate a man of integrity
and seek to kill the upright.[c]

29:11 [d]Pr 12:16; 19:11

11 A fool gives full vent to his anger,
but a wise man keeps himself under control.[d]

12 If a ruler listens to lies,
all his officials become wicked.

29:13 [e]Pr 22:2; Mt 5:45

13 The poor man and the oppressor have this in common:
The LORD gives sight to the eyes of both.[e]

29:14 [f]Ps 72:1-5; Pr 16:12

14 If a king judges the poor with fairness,
his throne will always be secure.[f]

29:15 [g]Pr 10:1; 13:24; 17:21,25

15 The rod of correction imparts wisdom,
but a child left to himself disgraces his mother.[g]

29:16 [h]Ps 37:35-36; 58:10; 91:8; 92:11

16 When the wicked thrive, so does sin,
but the righteous will see their downfall.[h]

29:17 [i]ver 15; Pr 10:1

17 Discipline your son, and he will give you peace;
he will bring delight to your soul.[i]

29:18 [j]Ps 1:1-2; 119:1-2; Jn 13:17

18 Where there is no revelation, the people cast off restraint;
but blessed is he who keeps the law.[j]

(v. 4), who through "justice" (v. 4) establishes his "country" (v. 4) or "throne" (v. 14). Verses 3–4 and 14–15 suggest that responsible child rearing and righteous rule belong together. The body of this unit falls into two subunits: verses 3–6 and 8–15. Verse 7 associates them by mentioning the "righteous" (cf. v. 6) and the "poor" (cf. v. 14). This unit, like 28:1–11 and 28:12–27, has a strong court coloring. Reference is made to the "king" (v. 4), the "ruler" (v. 12), the "officials" (v. 12) and effecting justice (vv. 4,7,9,14). The other proverbs, mostly about the wise and the fool, probably alert the king to wise court procedures in protecting the poor.

29:3–6 These verses present three different ways that wealth can be squandered due to the hostility of others. The prostitute enriches herself through illicit sex (v. 3); the officials through corrupt courts (v. 4); and the neighbor through flattering scams (v. 5). Both the prostitute and the deceitful neighbor use cunning words to disarm their victims (5:3) and then proceed to plunder them while their defenses are down. Verse 6, however, gives the righteous the last word.

29:8–15 The catchwords "wise" and "wisdom" (vv. 8–9,15) frame this unit, which pertains to restoring peace and security through righteous courts. See *WLC* 145.

29:8–11 Verses 8–10 represent three morally inferior kinds of people: mockers, who set a community at loggerheads (v. 8); the fool, who refuses to listen to reason (v. 9); and murderers, who seek to kill upright people (v. 10). Verse 11 returns to the fool.

29:12–15 Royal proverbs again come to the fore, giving more specific direction about judicious court procedures (cf. v. 4). At their center stands the truth that all human lives depend upon the Lord (v. 13; cf. 22:2), suggesting that God stands behind the just court (cf. 16:11; 28:25). Verse 15, a child-rearing proverb, completes the frame that began with verse 3 (see note on vv. 2–16).

29:15 The rod of correction. Or "rod and rebuke." See *WLC* 129.

29:16–27 Within the framing proverbs (vv. 16,27), the fourth unit consists of a decalogue comprised of two equal halves (vv. 17–21 and 22–26). The first alternates between the household and the public to instruct the son on the necessity of discipline both in his household and in the nation. In Biblical thought, relations in marriage and family, between masters and servants and in the body politic were generally conceived as parallel hierarchical structures (cf. Ro 13:1–7; Tit 2:1–3,8; 1Pe 3:13–22). The second half warns the son against reprobates: the angry (v. 22), the proud (v. 23) and the accomplice of a thief (v. 24). A concluding proverb pair instructs him to trust the Lord (vv. 25–26), implicitly warning him against the cowardly (v. 25) and those who seek royal favors (v. 26). Once again the unit is drawn to its conclusion by sayings about the Lord, calling for reverence for and trust in him (vv. 13,25–26; cf. 28:25). See *HC* 99.

29:18 law. A better translation here would be "instruction." The proverb shifts from people who have no means to attain the sage's true wisdom to the critical issue of the members of the community who do possess such means.

19 A servant cannot be corrected by mere words;
though he understands, he will not respond.

20 Do you see a man who speaks in haste?
There is more hope for a fool than for him.[k]

21 If a man pampers his servant from youth,
he will bring grief[a] in the end.

22 An angry man stirs up dissension,
and a hot-tempered one commits many sins.[l]

23 A man's pride brings him low,
but a man of lowly spirit gains honor.[m]

24 The accomplice of a thief is his own enemy;
he is put under oath and dare not testify.[n]

25 Fear of man will prove to be a snare,
but whoever trusts in the LORD[o] is kept safe.

26 Many seek an audience with a ruler,[p]
but it is from the LORD that man gets justice.

27 The righteous detest the dishonest;
the wicked detest the upright.[q]

Sayings of Agur

30 The sayings of Agur son of Jakeh—an oracle[b]:

This man declared to Ithiel,
to Ithiel and to Ucal:[c]

2 "I am the most ignorant of men;
I do not have a man's understanding.
3 I have not learned wisdom,
nor have I knowledge of the Holy One.[r]
4 Who has gone up[s] to heaven and come down?
Who has gathered up the wind in the hollow[t] of his hands?
Who has wrapped up the waters[u] in his cloak?[v]
Who has established all the ends of the earth?
What is his name,[w] and the name of his son?
Tell me if you know!

5 "Every word of God is flawless;[x]
he is a shield[y] to those who take refuge in him.
6 Do not add[z] to his words,
or he will rebuke you and prove you a liar.

29:20 [k]Pr 26:12; Jas 1:19
29:22 [l]Pr 14:17; 15:18; 26:21
29:23 [m]Pr 11:2; 15:33; 16:18; Isa 66:2; Mt 23:12
29:24 [n]Lev 5:1
29:25 [o]Pr 28:25
29:26 [p]Pr 19:6
29:27 [q]ver 10
30:3 [r]Pr 9:10
30:4 [s]Ps 24:1-2; Jn 3:13; Eph 4:7-10 [t]Ps 104:3; Isa 40:12 [u]Job 26:8; 38:8-9 [v]Ge 1:2 [w]Rev 19:12
30:5 [x]Ps 12:6; 18:30 [y]Ge 15:1; Ps 84:11
30:6 [z]Dt 4:2; 12:32; Rev 22:18

[a] *21* The meaning of the Hebrew for this word is uncertain. [b] *1* Or *Jakeh of Massa* [c] *1* Masoretic Text; with a different word division of the Hebrew *declared, "I am weary, O God; / I am weary, O God, and faint.*

■ **30:1–33** *Oracle of Agur.* This passage is an integrated, four-part argument: (1) superscription (v. 1); (2) Agur's autobiographical confession (vv. 2–9), which divides into his claim of inspiration (vv. 2–6) and his prayer for truthfulness and modesty (vv. 7–9); (3) seven numerical sayings (vv. 10–31) that consist of a first collection of proverbs (without titles) focusing on greed (vv. 10–16) and a second (with titles), on pride (vv. 11–31); and (4) a conclusion, which warns sons not to upset the moral order (vv. 32–33).

30:1 Agur son of Jakeh. His identity is otherwise unknown, but this sage claims inspiration by referring to his sayings as an "oracle." **to Ithiel . . . Ucal.** These words could be translated "Ithiel. I am weary, God, but I can prevail," which would comprise a summary of his argument in verses 2–6 that humanity can overcome some limitations by divine inspiration.

30:2–6 Agur's thematic movement from human ignorance of wisdom to the possession of it follows the same logic as that of Baruch 3:29—4:1 (an Apocryphal book) and Job 28:12–28. All three sages move from confessions that they, on their own, could not find wisdom (vv. 2–3) to assertions through rhetorical questions that God alone possesses wisdom and has a "son" whom he teaches (v. 4).

30:2 I am the most ignorant of men. The meaning of the Hebrew is more accurately translated, "Surely I am too stupid to be considered a man." This is hyperbole, like David's "But I am a worm and not a man" (Ps 22:6; cf. Job 25:4–6; Ps 73:21–22). Agur implies that to be truly human one must know God.

30:3 As a human being Agur did not possess the requisite wisdom to fathom the depths of the enigma with which the Creator confronts the human being (cf. Job 28:12–22). Without that ability to interpret the human situation he could not reach certainty about living skillfully.

30:4 Agur's two sets of rhetorical questions challenge his audience to breach the "unbridgeable" gulf between the Lord's knowledge of wisdom and human helplessness. This verse points to a personal relationship with the wise Sovereign as the means to overcoming the human predicament of ignorance and death.

30:5–6 This theological assessment of God's Word suggests that Agur, a proselyte to Israel's faith, was now reasoning within the framework of Israel's law and prophetic writings. Verse 5 quotes Psalm 18:30, and verse 6 echoes Deuteronomy 4:2, showing that

7 "Two things I ask of you, O LORD;
do not refuse me before I die:
8 Keep falsehood and lies far from me;
give me neither poverty nor riches,
but give me only my daily bread.[a]
9 Otherwise, I may have too much and disown[b] you
and say, 'Who is the LORD?'[c]
Or I may become poor and steal,
and so dishonor the name of my God.[d]

10 "Do not slander a servant to his master,
or he will curse you, and you will pay for it.

11 "There are those who curse their fathers
and do not bless their mothers;[e]
12 those who are pure in their own eyes[f]
and yet are not cleansed of their filth;[g]
13 those whose eyes are ever so haughty,[h]
whose glances are so disdainful;
14 those whose teeth[i] are swords
and whose jaws are set with knives[j]
to devour[k] the poor[l] from the earth,
the needy from among mankind.[m]

15 "The leech has two daughters.
'Give! Give!' they cry.

"There are three things that are never satisfied,[n]
four that never say, 'Enough!':
16 the grave,[a][o] the barren womb,
land, which is never satisfied with water,
and fire, which never says, 'Enough!'

17 "The eye that mocks[p] a father,
that scorns obedience to a mother,
will be pecked out by the ravens of the valley,
will be eaten by the vultures.[q]

18 "There are three things that are too amazing for me,
four that I do not understand:
19 the way of an eagle in the sky,

30:8 [a]Mt 6:11
30:9 [b]Jos 24:27; Isa 1:4; 59:13 [c]Dt 6:12; 8:10-14; Hos 13:6 [d]Dt 8:12
30:11 [e]Pr 20:20
30:12 [f]Pr 16:2; Lk 18:11 [g]Jer 2:23,35
30:13 [h]2Sa 22:28; Job 41:34; Ps 131:1; Pr 6:17
30:14 [i]Job 4:11; 29:17; Ps 3:7 [j]Ps 57:4 [k]Job 24:9; Ps 14:4 [l]Am 8:4; Mic 2:2 [m]Job 19:22
30:15 [n]Pr 27:20
30:16 [o]Pr 27:20; Isa 5:14; 14:9,11; Hab 2:5
30:17 [p]Dt 21:18-21; Pr 23:22 [q]Job 15:23

a *16* Hebrew *Sheol*

---

knowledge of God comes only through revelation and is received by faith (see note on 1:7). See *BC* 7.

30:7–9 Agur's petition to keep him from lies (v. 8) looks back to his assertion that anyone who adds to God's Word will be proved a liar (v. 7) and implies that his words are truthful and God-inspired. His petition for modesty points to God, not human effort, as the means of overcoming human greed (vv. 10–16), breaking down boundaries (vv. 17–31) and quelling insubordination (vv. 32–33). In sum, Agur overcame his human inability to acquire wisdom by depending upon God and a desire for God's renown. See *WLC* 113,193; *WSC* 104.

30:10–31 Agur's numerical sayings contain seven—the number of completion—carefully structured proverbs (vv. 11–14,15a,15b–16, 18–20,21–23,24–28,29–31) that are introduced and divided into two units by single-line introductions (vv. 10,17). Verse 10 condemns slander; verse 17 the haughty eye. The two notions are placed in parallel position also in Psalm 101:5. Slander and haughty eyes both have to do with arrogance, an attitude God will not tolerate (6:17; 2Sa 22:8; Ps 18:27). Verse 10 is followed by three untitled numerical sayings (vv. 11–14,15a,15b–16) and verse 17 by four titled numerical sayings (vv. 18–20,21–23,24–28,29–31). These seven numerical sayings essentially aim to preserve social order by implicitly calling Ithiel to renounce pride and greed.

30:10 The first introduction warns the ruler that if he slanders a subject badly enough, the Lord's curse will overthrow him as ruler.

30:11–16 The three numerical sayings without titles escalate from a voracious leech (v. 14) to two insatiable leeches (v. 15) to four unappeasable types: "the grave," "the barren womb," arid "land" and "fire" (v. 16). The three sayings pertain to pride and greed, the climactic vices of the evil generation; the proverbial leeches; and the four insatiable things, which "never [say], 'Enough!' " (v. 16). See *WLC* 128.

30:16 The four insatiable things, which juxtapose life and death and good and evil, engage in an eternal battle as long as the earth endures. Until God separates the wheat from the chaff (see 2:20–22), greedy tyrants (cf. vv. 11–14,15) will never be satisfied (cf. 27:20), and the righteous will ever strive to produce life.

30:17 The second introduction, which occurs exactly at the midpoint of Agur's sayings, threatens the arrogant child with a humiliating death from carrion birds in the sky, probably symbolizing the Lord's heavenly visitation. See *WLC* 99,128,151.

30:18–31 The first proverb pertains to the four behaviors within the created order that amaze Agur, climaxing in human, erotic love (vv. 18–19). Second, his awe of human eros with a virgin stands in contrast to the attitude of the adulteress, who sees no more wrong in demeaning her sexuality with several partners than in eating a meal (v. 20). Her breach of marital fidelity forms a transition to four incongruous things in the social order (vv. 21–23). The third saying names four extraordinarily wise beasts, climaxing in the lizard living in a king's palace (vv. 24–28). This reference to the king forms a transition to the fourth saying, which pertains to animals with regal treads and climaxes in the stride of the king whom no one dares resist (vv. 29–31). The fourth saying refers to the queen mother in the climax (see note on v. 23). In sum, the titled numerical sayings move from order within the home to order within society to order within the state.

the way of a snake on a rock,
the way of a ship on the high seas,
and the way of a man with a maiden.

20 "This is the way of an adulteress:
She eats and wipes her mouth
and says, 'I've done nothing wrong.'[r]

21 "Under three things the earth trembles,
under four it cannot bear up:
22 a servant who becomes king,[s]
a fool who is full of food,
23 an unloved woman who is married,
and a maidservant who displaces her mistress.

24 "Four things on earth are small,
yet they are extremely wise:
25 Ants are creatures of little strength,
yet they store up their food in the summer;[t]
26 coneys[a] [u] are creatures of little power,
yet they make their home in the crags;
27 locusts[v] have no king,
yet they advance together in ranks;
28 a lizard can be caught with the hand,
yet it is found in kings' palaces.

29 "There are three things that are stately in their stride,
four that move with stately bearing:
30 a lion, mighty among beasts,
who retreats before nothing;
31 a strutting rooster, a he-goat,
and a king with his army around him.[b]

32 "If you have played the fool and exalted yourself,
or if you have planned evil,
clap your hand over your mouth![w]
33 For as churning the milk produces butter,
and as twisting the nose produces blood,
so stirring up anger produces strife."

Sayings of King Lemuel

31 The sayings[x] of King Lemuel—an oracle[c] his mother taught him:

2 "O my son, O son of my womb,
O son of my vows,[d] [y]
3 do not spend your strength on women,
your vigor on those who ruin kings.[z]

30:20 [r]Pr 5:6
30:22 [s]Pr 19:10; 29:2
30:25 [t]Pr 6:6-8
30:26 [u]Ps 104:18
30:27 [v]Ex 10:4
30:32 [w]Job 21:5; 29:9
31:1 [x]Pr 22:17
31:2 [y]Jdg 11:30; Isa 49:15
31:3 [z]Dt 17:17; 1Ki 11:3; Ne 13:26; Pr 5:1-14

[a] *26* That is, the hyrax or rock badger [b] *31* Or *king secure against revolt* [c] *1* Or *of Lemuel king of Massa, which* [d] *2* Or */ the answer to my prayers*

30:20 See *WLC* 145.
30:23 mistress. Sometimes a queen's title.
30:32–33 Agur closed his material with an exhortation to his son not to usurp his superior's authority.
30:32 have played . . . exalted . . . have planned. It is better to read these verbs as descriptive of current activity ("play . . . exalt . . . plan") and the associated exhortation ("clap your hand over your mouth!") as an instruction by which to cease from these sins.
■ **31:1–31** *The Sayings of Lemuel.* After a typical title this collection consists of two sections: one on the noble king (vv. 2–9) and one on the noble wife (vv. 10–31).
■ **31:1** *Superscription.* The historical setting may well indicate that Lemuel's mother gave him these instructions when he assumed the throne, which would have been a time when he was most open to counsel.
31:1 King Lemuel. Probably an otherwise unattested long form of Lael (Nu 3:24), which means "belonging to God" or "dedicated to God" (cf. "son of my vows"; v. 2). Since a king by this name is unknown in Israel's literature, he was probably a proselyte to Israel's faith. His sayings (especially vv. 4,8–9) resemble the Egyptian and Babylonian wisdom literature that also aimed to equip rulers to discharge their duties as wise and just kings. **an oracle.** See note on 30:1.
■ **31:2–9** *The Noble King.* These admonitions divide into three main parts: a call to hear (v. 2), appeals to show restraint (vv. 3–7) that focus on women (v. 3) and intoxicants (vv. 4–7) and a request to issue new edicts regarding the poor (vv. 8–9). The queen's admonitions primarily urged her royal son to preserve the current statutes that protected the poor (vv. 4–5) and to enact new laws to safeguard them further (vv. 8–9).
31:2 O my son, O son . . . O son. Or "Listen, my son! Listen, son of my womb! Listen, son of my vows!" **son of my vows.** See 7:14 and 20:25. To mirror their close relationship, Lemuel's mother traced his close connection to herself, beginning with the present and moving backward in time to her vows before pregnancy (cf. 1Sa 1:11; Ps 116:16; Eph 6:4; 2Ti 1:5; 3:15). Lemuel immortalized his mother's life and teachings by passing them on to others.
31:3 women . . . who ruin kings. She first cautioned Lemuel

4 “It is not for kings, O Lemuel—
not for kings to drink wine,[a]
not for rulers to crave beer,
5 lest they drink[b] and forget what the law decrees,[c]
and deprive all the oppressed of their rights.
6 Give beer to those who are perishing,
wine[d] to those who are in anguish;
7 let them drink[e] and forget their poverty
and remember their misery no more.

8 “Speak[f] up for those who cannot speak for themselves,
for the rights of all who are destitute.
9 Speak up and judge fairly;
defend the rights of the poor and needy.”[g]

Epilogue: The Wife of Noble Character

10 [a] A wife of noble character[h] who can find?[i]
She is worth far more than rubies.
11 Her husband[j] has full confidence in her
and lacks nothing of value.[k]
12 She brings him good, not harm,
all the days of her life.
13 She selects wool and flax
and works with eager hands.[l]
14 She is like the merchant ships,
bringing her food from afar.
15 She gets up while it is still dark;
she provides food for her family
and portions for her servant girls.
16 She considers a field and buys it;
out of her earnings she plants a vineyard.
17 She sets about her work vigorously;
her arms are strong for her tasks.
18 She sees that her trading is profitable,
and her lamp does not go out at night.
19 In her hand she holds the distaff
and grasps the spindle with her fingers.
20 She opens her arms to the poor
and extends her hands to the needy.[m]

31:4 [a]Pr 20:1; Ecc 10:16-17; Isa 5:22
31:5 [b]1Ki 16:9 [c]Pr 16:12; Hos 4:11
31:6 [d]Ge 14:18
31:7 [e]Est 1:10
31:8 [f]1Sa 19:4; Job 29:12-17
31:9 [g]Lev 19:15; Dt 1:16; Pr 24:23; 29:7; Isa 1:17; Jer 22:16
31:10 [h]Ru 3:11; Pr 12:4; 18:22 [i]Pr 8:35; 19:14
31:11 [j]Ge 2:18 [k]Pr 12:4
31:13 [l]1Ti 2:9-10
31:20 [m]Dt 15:11; Eph 4:28; Heb 13:16

a *10* Verses 10–31 are an acrostic, each verse beginning with a successive letter of the Hebrew alphabet.

against unrestrained sexual gratification, which was also part of Agur's burden. She referred either to women who were willing to provide sexual favors outside of marriage (2:16–19) and/or to a large harem of concubines (cf. 1Ki 11:11; Est 2:10–14). Obsession with such women corrupted the king's sovereign power and wasted his money. Gratification of lust distracted his attention from serving the people, blunted his wit, undermined his good judgment, exposed him to palace intrigues and squandered the national wealth (see 13:22).

31:4–5 not for kings to drink wine. Not a warning to avoid all alcohol, but advice not to succumb to drunkenness (v. 4) because it distorts justice (v. 5; cf. 20:1; 21:17; 23:20,29–35).

31:6–7 Give beer . . . wine. The command to supply intoxicants to all those dying of hunger in order to anesthetize them is probably intended as sarcasm. The perishing and miserable in verse 6 are further defined in verse 7 as those suffering from grinding poverty. Drowning one's sorrows in drink solves nothing; its anesthetic effects merely deepen the drinker's inability to face his problems (see 20:1; 23:29ff.). Instead, the following proverb pair specifically commands the king to deliver the poor from their miserable poverty.

31:8–9 These verses positively command the king to enact righteous decrees to protect the poor. See *WLC* 135,144.

■ **31:10–31** *The Noble Wife.* This well-known passage is structured as an acrostic (each verse beginning with the successive letters of the Hebrew alphabet) and draws the book to its conclusion (cf. Sirach 51:13–20). This description of the competent wife divides into three main parts: the introduction (vv. 10–12), which describes her general worth (inferred from her rarity [v. 10]) and her worth to her husband (vv. 11–12); the body of the passage, which describes her activities (vv. 13–27) in industry (vv. 13–19), as well as her social achievements (vv. 20–27); and a conclusion, which notes the praise she receives (vv. 28–31) from her family (vv. 28–29) and others (vv. 30–31).

31:10 noble. The Hebrew concept, particularly as expounded in the proverbs of this chapter, is better rendered “noble and competent.”

31:11 has full confidence. Or “trusts.” Aside from this text and Judges 20:36, Scripture condemns trust in anyone or anything other than God (cf. Dt 8:52; 2Ki 18:21; Ps 118:8–9; Isa 36:5; Jer 5:17; 12:52; 18:10; 48:7; Eze 33:13; Mic 7:5). See *WLC* 138.

31:13–18 Her industry provides the economic basis for her trading to enrich the household.

31:13–15 Positive emotions drive her work in manufacturing thread from the raw materials of animals (“wool” [v. 13]) and vegetation (“flax” [v. 13], for linen thread). In ancient societies women who acquired skills in spinning and weaving were greatly admired and desired.

31:15 gets up. Better, “arises like a lioness,” which makes clear that her arising at night belongs to the preying imagery and should not be interpreted literally.

31:17 strong. Sarah (Ge 18:6–8), Rebekah (Ge 24:18–20) and Rachel (Ge 29:9–10) all demonstrate that women of high social rank and wealth were not above manual, and even menial, labor (cf. Ex 2:16; 2Sa 13:5–9).

31:18 lamp does not go out. A sign of her enduring prosperity. In a well-ordered household the lamp burned all night as a sign of life; its extinction marked calamity (Job 18:6; Jer 25:10).

21 When it snows, she has no fear for her household;
for all of them are clothed in scarlet.
22 She makes coverings for her bed;
she is clothed in fine linen and purple.
23 Her husband is respected at the city gate,
where he takes his seat among the elders[n] of the land.
24 She makes linen garments and sells them,
and supplies the merchants with sashes.
25 She is clothed with strength and dignity;
she can laugh at the days to come.
26 She speaks with wisdom,
and faithful instruction is on her tongue.[o]
27 She watches over the affairs of her household
and does not eat the bread of idleness.
28 Her children arise and call her blessed;
her husband also, and he praises her:
29 "Many women do noble things,
but you surpass them all."
30 Charm is deceptive, and beauty is fleeting;
but a woman who fears the LORD is to be praised.
31 Give her the reward she has earned,
and let her works bring her praise[p] at the city gate.

31:23 [n]Ex 3:16; Ru 4:1, 11; Pr 12:4
31:26 [o]Pr 10:31
31:31 [p]Pr 11:16

31:20–28 The second half of the poem's body (vv. 20–27) itemizes this woman's mostly tangible contributions to the household and community. The noble wife's accomplishments empower her husband to lead the nation in righteousness and justice. See *WLC* 127,138.
31:20 Pride of place is given to her ministry to the afflicted and destitute in the community (cf. Job 29:12–17; Ac 9:39). As the noble king was to open his mouth to defend their interest in court (vv. 8–9), the noble woman was to be openhanded to meet their palpable needs.
31:28–31 The poet concluded his description of the noble wife by rewarding her with praise, first by citing her household's admiration (vv. 28–29) and then by calling upon the community to commend her (vv. 30–31; cf. 27:2).
31:28 **arise.** A sign of highest respect (cf. Job 29:8; Isa 49:7). See *WLC* 127.
31:29 The husband's praise is based on years of experience, as indicated by the maturity of their children. **women.** Literally, "daughters," a more delicate name for women that completes a parallelism with "children" (lit., "sons") and implies that those virtuous women had embraced their parents' wisdom while they were still in the home (see 1:8). **surpass.** This idealized wife surpasses other women who do noble things, the very quality that the poet cited as most rare among women (v. 10).
31:30 **deceptive.** Charm and beauty deceive because they pass away, and with them passes the hope of happiness based on them.
31:31 **Give . . . earned.** A call to extol her for what her hands have produced.

ECCLESIASTES

Introduction

Overview

Author: Solomon or an unknown sage in the royal court

Purpose: To demonstrate that life viewed merely from a realistic human perspective must result in pessimism, and to offer hope through humble obedience and faithfulness to God until the final judgment

Date: 930–586 B.C.

Key Truths:

- When we are left to mere human outlooks and efforts, life seems hopeless and meaningless.
- Human beings cannot begin to fathom the divine wisdom that undergirds and controls all things.
- Once human limitations are recognized, the faithful will gain a godly vision of life by renewing their reverence for God and loyalty to his commands.
- In the final judgment God will eliminate the perplexing anomalies of life by judging everything good or evil.

Author

It has traditionally been argued that this book was the work of Solomon. The Teacher, who is identified in 1:1 as the one who reflects on his experiences in the book, is strongly associated with Solomon because of his lineage (1:1), Jerusalem kingship (1:12), unsurpassed wisdom (1:16) and unrivaled wealth (2:4–9). This identification has led some to place the book during the period of Solomon's apostasy, when he may have dwelt on the kinds of thoughts expressed in this book (see 1Ki 11), or sometime afterward, when he may have reflected on those earlier, despondent times.

Although it seems clear that Solomon's wise sayings deeply influenced this book, it is not indisputable that Solomon actually authored it. Unlike the book of Proverbs, which freely attributes much of its material to Solomon, Ecclesiastes nowhere explicitly identifies Solomon by name. Even the expression "son of David" (1:1) may be translated "descendant of David," or possibly "an official in David's court." In fact, the writer appears intentionally to distance himself from Solomon. It would have been odd for Solomon to say that he "was king" (1:12), using the past tense, for there was never a time when he ceased being king prior to his death. The statement that others had ruled in Jerusalem before him (1:16) also appears an unlikely—although not impossible (see note on 1:16)—statement for Solomon to make. The book reflects on hardship (1:2–8), death (3:1–15), injustice (4:1–3), pagan tyranny (5:7,9–19) and suffering at the hands of rulers (8:9). None of these descriptions fit well with Solomon. It is possible therefore that sometime after Solomon's reign an unknown sage compiled, edited, shaped and framed reflections that may have come in part from Solomon and added introductory and summary perspectives (1:1; 12:9–14). However, it should be remembered that, like all wise men in Jerusalem's royal court, this writer drew heavily upon Solomon's wisdom in all that he wrote (cf. Hezekiah's wise men in Pr 25:1).

Time and Place of Writing

The association of Ecclesiastes with the Davidic court makes Jerusalem the likely place of composition, but the date of Ecclesiastes is uncertain. If Solomon was the author of the book, it must be dated to the tenth century. The reference to the "son of David" (1:1) strongly suggests that the book was written after the end of the monarchy in Jerusalem (586 B.C.). Thus the range of possible dates extends from 930 to 586 B.C.

Purpose and Distinctives

The title "Ecclesiastes" derives from the Vulgate (the Latin translation of the Bible) and the Septuagint (the Greek translation of the OT) translations of the Hebrew *qoheleth,* which is translated in the NIV as "Teacher," possibly meaning "leader of the assembly"(see NIV text note on 1:1).

Ecclesiastes focuses on how God's people should live on Earth in the face of life's difficulties and enigmas. Ecclesiastes is thus not an apologetic to those who are ignorant of God or rebellious against him; it is wise counsel to those cognizant of, but perplexed by, God's ways. In this respect, Ecclesiastes is like the book of Job. While Job's dialogues and monologues search for understanding of God's wisdom within the circumstance of an innocent man's suffering, Ecclesiastes is more philosophical in its approach and speaks of the condition of all humans. Ecclesiastes also probes the limits of conventional proverbial wisdom (see 12:9) by balancing expectations of justice and prosperity often raised by proverbial wisdom with the harsh realities of living in a fallen world controlled by the inscrutable wisdom of God. It also encourages fidelity to God in the perplexing difficulties so many people face.

In the end, however, the conclusion of Ecclesiastes is very similar to that of Job. Despite our inability to understand fully the good wisdom of God, our appropriate and wise human response is to "fear God and keep his commandments" (12:13; see note on Job 28:28). That is, we are to submit to God and demonstrate our awareness of his supreme wisdom by obeying his law, trusting that he is full of wisdom and goodness in spite of the enigmas life presents even to those who know him.

The Teacher's words are arranged in three cycles (1:3—3:8; 3:9—6:7; 6:8—12:7), each of which begins with a similar phrase: "What does man gain?" (1:3), "What does the worker gain?" (3:9) and "What advantage has a wise man?" (6:8). Each cycle contains an introduction (1:3–11; 3:9–21; 6:8–12), followed by variously arranged sections. Words are positioned to build textual units and are used in multiple senses to provoke meditation on the book's ideas. While repetition of topics and words builds concentric structural units, there is progression of thought in Ecclesiastes. The writer pairs the themes of work and wisdom. His first cycle contains three pairs of sections (1:12–15 and 1:16–18; 2:1–11 and 2:12–17; 2:18–26 and 3:1–8) presenting the conclusion that although the employment of human labor and understanding provides the satisfaction of accomplishment, the profit achieved for a human being is canceled by death.

The paired themes of work and wisdom are subsequently elaborated in the book's second and third cycles, respectively. The second cycle (3:9—6:7) develops the theme of human labor, contrasting it with God's perfect, enduring works and counseling enjoyment of the simple blessings God provides in this life, even in the face of human oppression. The third cycle (6:8—12:7) elaborates the theme of human wisdom, contrasting it with the inscrutability of God's ways. This cycle advises the audience to enjoy life and to work diligently, even though effort and righteousness may not be appropriately rewarded in this life.

The author's conclusion that death renders all labor and efforts to acquire superhuman wisdom vain (1:14,17; 2:11,17) does not imply, as some ancients thought, that people should abandon society and cultural efforts. On the contrary, the writer instructed God's people to enjoy life—despite its apparent futility, harsh realities and uncertainties—and to work with full vigor (9:7–10). This realistic approach views life as a gift from God (3:13; 5:19) for those who fear him and keep his commands (5:1–7; 12:13–14).

Ecclesiastes grapples with the question of how people should live in fidelity to God (6:12) in a world in which the good Creator (3:11,14) and just Judge (3:17) sovereignly ordains that "bad" things happen to the righteous (7:13–14) as well as to the wicked, rather than that each individual will receive his or her deserved recompense in this life (8:14; 9:1). Faith in God's wisdom despite human inability fully to discern it is to be exercised not only in the face of human oppression (3:22—4:3) but also in the context of the futility brought by the prospect of death (9:7–10).

Christ in Ecclesiastes

This book relates to Christ and the New Testament in a number of ways. First, in his initial coming Christ, who embodies the wisdom of God (1Co 1:24,30), revealed wisdom to those who followed him (Co 1:9; 2:23; 3:16). Through faith in Christ we have access to God's wisdom (Jas 1:5) beyond the understanding of Old Testament believers. As Ecclesiastes calls for fear and obedience (12:13), the New Testament echoes these themes (Ac 6:7; 9:31; 2Co 5:11; 9:13; 10:5; 2Th 1:8; 1Pe 1:2; 2:17; Rev 14:7; 15:4; 19:5) in its call to embrace the gospel of Christ as the very wisdom of God (1Co 1:21-24; Col 1:9–12,28; Jas 3:13–17). Second, even though Christ has come, Ecclesiastes reminds us that God's elect still live as aliens in this world (1Pe 1.1). Although we have been forgiven of our sins and made alive in Christ, we still live amid profound frustrations and tensions until Christ brings an end to this present evil age. Until then, the enigmas of life are often so great that we do not even know how to pray, but we can gain confidence in our struggles through our knowledge that the Spirit of Christ, who knows the mind of God, prays for us (Ro 8:18–23). Third, the New Testament assures us that the final judgment mentioned in this book (12:14) will come when Christ returns in glory (Rev 19). At that time the good wisdom of God, so often hidden from human sight now, will be clearly revealed.

Outline

I. Prologue (1:1–2)
   A. Introduction (1:1)
   B. Main Theme (1:2)

The Teacher is introduced, along with his main themes.

II. Limitations of Work and Wisdom (1:3—3:8)
   A. Cycles in Creation (1:3–11)
   B. Futility of Work and Wisdom (1:12–18)
   C. Ephemeral Rewards of Work and Wisdom (2:1–17)
   D. Enigmas of Work and Wisdom (2:18—3:8)

Although the employment of human labor and understanding provides some satisfaction, from a human point of view the profit achieved is canceled by death.

III. Work in Fear Before God, Whose Work Endures (3:9—6:7)
   A. God As Creator and Judge (3:9–21)
   B. Contentment or Envy (3:22—4:16)
   C. Sincere Commitment to God (5:1–7)
   D. (Dis)satisfaction in Work (5:8—6:7)

Human labor contrasts with God's enduring works, so we must enjoy the simple blessings God provides in this life, even in the face of troubles.

IV. Humility Before God, Whose Wisdom Is Unfathomable (6:8—12:7) A. The Futility of Contending With God (6:8–12) B. What Is Good for Humans (7:1–18) C. Wisdom's Power (7:19—8:8) D. Unfulfilled Judgment (8:9—9:10) E. Folly's Power (9:11—10:7) F. Advice for Wise Living (10:8—12:7)	*Human wisdom contrasts with the inscrutability of God's ways, so we should work diligently and enjoy life, even though righteousness may not be appropriately rewarded in this life.*
V. Epilogue (12:8–14) A. Main Theme (12:8) B. Conclusion (12:9–14)	*Human beings should be humble before God and demonstrate faithfulness to him because he will one day eliminate all the anomalies of the fallen world in his final judgment.*

Everything Is Meaningless

1:1 [a]ver 12; Ecc 7:27; 12:10 [b]Pr 1:1

1 The words of the Teacher,[a] [a] son of David, king in Jerusalem:[b]

2 "Meaningless! Meaningless!"
says the Teacher.
"Utterly meaningless!
Everything is meaningless."[c]

1:2 [c]Ps 39:5-6; 62:9; 144:4; Ecc 12:8; Ro 8:20-21

3 What does man gain from all his labor
at which he toils under the sun?[d]

1:3 [d]Ecc 2:11,22; 3:9; 5:15-16

4 Generations come and generations go,
but the earth remains forever.[e]

1:4 [e]Ps 104:5; 119:90

5 The sun rises and the sun sets,
and hurries back to where it rises.[f]

1:5 [f]Ps 19:5-6

6 The wind blows to the south
and turns to the north;
round and round it goes,
ever returning on its course.
7 All streams flow into the sea,
yet the sea is never full.
To the place the streams come from,
there they return again.[g]

1:7 [g]Job 36:28

8 All things are wearisome,
more than one can say.
The eye never has enough of seeing,[h]
nor the ear its fill of hearing.

1:8 [h]Pr 27:20

[a] *1* Or *leader of the assembly*; also in verses 2 and 12

■ **1:1–2** *Prologue.* These verses introduce the Teacher and the message of this book.
■ **1:1** *Introduction.* The Teacher presented himself as one of high standing and authority.
1:1 Teacher. The Hebrew literally means a convener of the assembly of Israel. The words of this book were directed to God's people, not to unbelievers. **son of David.** May be translated "descendant of David" or "official in David's court." See "Introduction: Author."
■ **1:2** *Main Theme.* In this verse the motif that dominates this entire book is revealed: the apparent meaninglessness of life when viewed from a purely human perspective.
1:2 Meaningless! Concretely the word here refers to "breath, vapor, mist," while abstractly it means "insubstantial, ephemeral, futile." **Everything.** This noun is not used absolutely but is qualified by the phrase "under the sun" (v. 3). The word therefore refers to everything people experience in this fallen world as understood from a merely human vantage point (v. 8).
■ **1:3—3:8** *Limitations of Work and Wisdom.* This first of three cycles in Ecclesiastes focuses the reader's attention on the futility of pursuing labor and wisdom. Although some satisfaction comes to us by significant accomplishments, from a human perspective death renders them meaningless. These chapters divide into four parts: the cycles of creation (1:3–11), the futility of work and wisdom (1:12–18), the ephemeral rewards of work and wisdom (2:1–17) and the enigmas of work and wisdom (2:18—3:8).
■ **1:3–11** *Cycles in Creation.* The Teacher initially explained his outlooks by pointing to the apparently endlessly repeating cycles that characterize creation.
1:3–8 Humanity continuously replicates cultural endeavors and is never completely satisfied with its results.
1:3 What does man gain . . . ? This expression marks the beginning of the first cycle (cf. 3:9–21; 6:8–12). The rhetorical question implies the answer "nothing"—made explicit in 2:11. Jesus alluded to this passage in Mark 8:36–38 and announced that there is gain only if we live by faith and devote our attention to the life to come. **under the sun?** This phrase is synonymous in Ecclesiastes with "under heaven" and "on earth."
1:4 come . . . go. These verbs are reversed in the Hebrew, emphasizing that human beings are constantly starting over, while, by contrast, the earth (to which people return) abides. **earth remains forever.** The physical world appears secure and permanent compared with human life.
1:6 round and round. Central to the poem (vv. 4–8), this is an image for the recurring refrain "a chasing after the wind" and a model for Ecclesiastes' cyclic literary structure.
1:7 come from. Verses 7–8 are paired: Human efforts never satisfy.

[9] What has been will be again,
what has been done will be done again;[i]
there is nothing new under the sun.
[10] Is there anything of which one can say,
"Look! This is something new"?
It was here already, long ago;
it was here before our time.
[11] There is no remembrance of men of old,
and even those who are yet to come
will not be remembered
by those who follow.[j]

Wisdom Is Meaningless

[12] I, the Teacher,[k] was king over Israel in Jerusalem. [13] I devoted myself to study and
to explore by wisdom all that is done under heaven. What a heavy burden God has laid
on men![l] [14] I have seen all the things that are done under the sun; all of them are meaningless, a chasing after the wind.[m]

[15] What is twisted cannot be straightened;[n]
what is lacking cannot be counted.

[16] I thought to myself, "Look, I have grown and increased in wisdom more than anyone who has ruled over Jerusalem before me;[o] I have experienced much of wisdom and
knowledge." [17] Then I applied myself to the understanding of wisdom,[p] and also of madness and folly,[q] but I learned that this, too, is a chasing after the wind.

[18] For with much wisdom comes much sorrow;
the more knowledge, the more grief.[r]

Pleasures Are Meaningless

2 I thought in my heart, "Come now, I will test you with pleasure[s] to find out what is
good." But that also proved to be meaningless. [2] "Laughter,"[t] I said, "is foolish. And
what does pleasure accomplish?" [3] I tried cheering myself with wine,[u] and embracing folly[v]—my mind still guiding me with wisdom. I wanted to see what was worthwhile for
men to do under heaven during the few days of their lives.
[4] I undertook great projects: I built houses for myself[w] and planted vineyards.[x] [5] I

1:9 [i]Ecc 2:12; 3:15
1:11 [j]Ecc 2:16
1:12 [k]ver 1
1:13 [l]Ge 3:17; Ecc 3:10
1:14 [m]Ecc 2:11,17
1:15 [n]Ecc 7:13
1:16 [o]1Ki 3:12; 4:30; Ecc 2:9
1:17 [p]Ecc 7:23 [q]Ecc 2:3, 12; 7:25
1:18 [r]Ecc 2:23; 12:12
2:1 [s]Ecc 7:4; 8:15; Lk 12:19
2:2 [t]Pr 14:13; Ecc 7:6
2:3 [u]ver 24-25; Ecc 3:12-13 [v]Ecc 1:17
2:4 [w]1Ki 7:1-12 [x]SS 8:11

1:9–11 From the perspective of the Teacher, there is nothing new in this world to alter the processes of nature or of people reproducing the achievements of their predecessors, dying and then being forgotten.

▪ **1:12–18** *Futility of Work and Wisdom.* The benefits for the individual of legitimate work (vv. 12–15) and wisdom's insights (vv. 16–18) are overshadowed by the fact that they pass away with the person in death.

1:12–15 The Teacher's personal investigation concluded that human culture is misdirected and futile.

1:12 I, the Teacher. In the previous chapter the Teacher had spoken in the third person. From this verse until the epilogue (12:8–14) he reverted to the first person (except 7:27). These variations may indicate that the book was constructed upon autobiographical reflections that were compiled and interpreted by another writer or by the same writer at a later time. **was king . . . in Jerusalem.** See "Introduction: Author."

1:13–14 under heaven . . . under the sun. These are synonymous terms. The Teacher experienced the ineffectuality of cultural efforts, in the sense that they do not contribute to building anything eternal. In contrast, the work of the Lord is not in vain (Jn 6:27–29; 1Co 15:58).

1:13 by wisdom. It is godly to view as fruitless and frustrating the endeavors of this world apart from faith in the Lord and his often inscrutable eternal purposes. **heavy burden.** Human existence entails divinely imposed burdens (cf. v. 15; 7:13; Ge 3:16–18; Ro 8:22–23), which Jesus makes bearable (Mt 11:28–30). **God.** The generic term, rather than the personal covenant name *Yahweh* (NIV, the "LORD"), is used for deity in Ecclesiastes, highlighting the broader international character of the Biblical Wisdom Literature (see "Introduction to Proverbs").

1:14 I have seen all. The Teacher had an informed outlook because of God's gift (2:26; 1Ki 3; Jas 1:5) and, implicitly, because of his meditation on God's revealed Word (v. 13). **chasing after the wind.** These words appear nine times in the first six chapters (see also v. 17; 2:11,17,26; 4:4,6,16; 6:9) and provide a powerful image for human attempts to capture meaningfulness and wisdom.

1:15 twisted . . . lacking. That is, the result not only of human evil, but also of the divine curse (7:13; Ge 3:16–18). The realities of life are so unalterable as to frustrate every attempt to overcome the cycles of life by mere human effort. Although believers are to give themselves to work in service to God, that service will remain futile apart from the approval of God's final judgment. In this sense even the pursuit of ultimate or final wisdom by human effort is fruitless. Only in service to the Lord is human effort not in vain (12:13–14; 1Co 15:58).

1:16–18 Ironically, an increase in true wisdom heightens one's sensitivity to creation's pollution and to the frustrating human condition. Increased mental pain, rather than expected satisfaction, results.

1:16 wisdom. Refers to godly, as opposed to pagan or humanistic wisdom. The Teacher pondered the weight of God's curse on humans (Ge 3:16–19). See "Introduction: Purpose and Distinctives." **anyone who has ruled over Jerusalem before me.** This reference to rulers does not necessarily exclude the idea that Solomon himself was the Teacher (see "Introduction: Author"); it could be to ancient, non-Israelite kings (e.g., Ge 14:18; Jos 10:1).

▪ **2:1–17** *Ephemeral Rewards of Work and Wisdom.* The benefits and insight that can be gained by an individual from hard work are at best fleeting.

2:1–11 Mere human accomplishments are ultimately unsatisfying, even for those who can boast extraordinary achievements (1Ki 4–11). Nor can pleasure provide significance or satisfy human longings.

2:1 in my heart. See verse 15. This phrase is appropriately translated "to myself" in 1:16. **pleasure.** A reference to the satisfaction of productive labor, as well as to entertainment.

2:3 my mind still guiding me with wisdom. See verse 9. To determine what was good for human beings to do, the Teacher investigated life not as a hedonist but through the pursuit of godly wisdom.

2:4–9 great . . . greater. The world's wealth flowed into Jerusalem for Solomon's disposition (see 1Ki 4–11).

made gardens and parks and planted all kinds of fruit trees in them. 6 I made reservoirs
to water groves of flourishing trees. 7 I bought male and female slaves and had other
slaves who were born in my house. I also owned more herds and flocks than anyone in
Jerusalem before me. 8 I amassed silver and gold[y] for myself, and the treasure of kings
and provinces. I acquired men and women singers,[z] and a harem[a] as well—the delights
of the heart of man. 9 I became greater by far than anyone in Jerusalem before me.[a] In
all this my wisdom stayed with me.

2:8 [y]1Ki 9:28; 10:10, 14,21 [z]2Sa 19:35
2:9 [a]1Ch 29:25; Ecc 1:16

10 I denied myself nothing my eyes desired;
  I refused my heart no pleasure.
My heart took delight in all my work,
  and this was the reward for all my labor.
11 Yet when I surveyed all that my hands had done
  and what I had toiled to achieve,
everything was meaningless, a chasing after the wind;[b]
  nothing was gained under the sun.[c]

2:11 [b]Ecc 1:14 [c]Ecc 1:3

Wisdom and Folly Are Meaningless

12 Then I turned my thoughts to consider wisdom,
  and also madness and folly.[d]
What more can the king's successor do
  than what has already been done?[e]
13 I saw that wisdom[f] is better than folly,[g]
  just as light is better than darkness.
14 The wise man has eyes in his head,
  while the fool walks in the darkness;
but I came to realize
  that the same fate overtakes them both.[h]

2:12 [d]Ecc 1:17 [e]Ecc 1:9; 7:25
2:13 [f]Ecc 7:19; 9:18 [g]Ecc 7:11-12
2:14 [h]Ps 49:10; Pr 17:24; Ecc 3:19; 6:6; 7:2; 9:3,11-12

15 Then I thought in my heart,

"The fate of the fool will overtake me also.
  What then do I gain by being wise?"[i]
I said in my heart,
  "This too is meaningless."
16 For the wise man, like the fool, will not be long remembered;
  in days to come both will be forgotten.[j]
Like the fool, the wise man too must die!

2:15 [i]Ecc 6:8
2:16 [j]Ecc 1:11; 9:5

Toil Is Meaningless

17 So I hated life, because the work that is done under the sun was grievous to me. All of
it is meaningless, a chasing after the wind.[k] 18 I hated all the things I had toiled for under the
sun, because I must leave them to the one who comes after me.[l] 19 And who knows whether he will be a wise man or a fool? Yet he will have control over all the work into which I have
poured my effort and skill under the sun. This too is meaningless. 20 So my heart began to
despair over all my toilsome labor under the sun. 21 For a man may do his work with wisdom,
knowledge and skill, and then he must leave all he owns to someone who has not worked

2:17 [k]Ecc 4:2
2:18 [l]Ps 39:6; 49:10

[a] 8 The meaning of the Hebrew for this phrase is uncertain.

2:8 harem. Solomon had 700 wives and 300 concubines (1Ki 11:3), many of whom were unconverted foreigners. This was a blatant violation of Moses' directives (see Dt 17:17). His multiplicity of wives proved to be his downfall rather than investing his life with significance.

2:10–11 delight . . . reward . . . nothing was gained under the sun. The Teacher experienced joy in performing work but failed to achieve the satisfaction of producing anything that proved to be of immediate or direct eternal worth. His efforts alone, viewed apart from God's redeeming work in the background, failed to rise above the temporary. By God's mercy even the weakest of human efforts can be turned into eternal reward (1Co 15:58), but when viewed in a vacuum, human work is indeed meaningless.

2:12–17 Wisdom is better than folly, but from a purely human perspective that advantage is nearly nullified by death.

2:13 wisdom . . . folly . . . light . . . darkness. Even at a human level wisdom is profitable, in much the same way as light is superior to darkness; both wisdom and light provide guidance for avoiding some pitfalls in this life. Yet at the end of this life the wise and foolish meet the same fate (v. 14).

2:15 gain. Wisdom's profit is, in the view of the Teacher, canceled by its inability to give the wise person an obvious advantage at death. Mere human judgment indicates that the wise and foolish end up in the same condition.

2:17 hated. The curse of death, from the perspective of one lacking knowledge of salvation or eternal reward, erases the profits of labor and of seeking understanding.

■ **2:18—3:8** *Enigmas of Work and Wisdom.* Understanding work and deriving wisdom from observing work are complicated by mysteries that mere human insight cannot penetrate.

2:18–23 I hated all things. The Teacher reflected on the frustrations associated with the fact that a person works hard to gain worldly possessions only to lose them at death. This situation is exacerbated by the fact that an individual's assets may be passed down to a fool (vv. 18–19) or to an unappreciative heir (vv. 20–21). See *WLC* 136.

for it. This too is meaningless and a great misfortune. 22 What does a man get for all the toil
and anxious striving with which he labors under the sun?[m] 23 All his days his work is pain
and grief;[n] even at night his mind does not rest. This too is meaningless.
24 A man can do nothing better than to eat and drink[o] and find satisfaction in his
work.[p] This too, I see, is from the hand of God,[q] 25 for without him, who can eat or find
enjoyment? 26 To the man who pleases him, God gives wisdom, knowledge and happiness, but to the sinner he gives the task of gathering and storing up wealth[r] to hand it
over to the one who pleases God.[s] This too is meaningless, a chasing after the wind.

A Time for Everything

3 There is a time[t] for everything,
and a season for every activity under heaven:

2 a time to be born and a time to die,
a time to plant and a time to uproot,
3 a time to kill and a time to heal,
a time to tear down and a time to build,
4 a time to weep and a time to laugh,
a time to mourn and a time to dance,
5 a time to scatter stones and a time to gather them,
a time to embrace and a time to refrain,
6 a time to search and a time to give up,
a time to keep and a time to throw away,
7 a time to tear and a time to mend,
a time to be silent[u] and a time to speak,
8 a time to love and a time to hate,
a time for war and a time for peace.

9 What does the worker gain from his toil?[v] 10 I have seen the burden God has laid on
men.[w] 11 He has made everything beautiful in its time.[x] He has also set eternity in the
hearts of men; yet they cannot fathom[y] what God has done from beginning to end.[z] 12 I
know that there is nothing better for men than to be happy and do good while they live.
13 That everyone may eat and drink,[a] and find satisfaction[b] in all his toil—this is the gift
of God.[c] 14 I know that everything God does will endure forever; nothing can be added
to it and nothing taken from it. God does it so that men will revere him.[d]

15 Whatever is has already been,[e]
and what will be has been before;[f]
and God will call the past to account.[a]

[a] *15* Or *God calls back the past*

2:22 [m]Ecc 1:3; 3:9
2:23 [n]Job 5:7; 14:1; Ecc 1:18
2:24 [o]Ecc 8:15; 1Co 15:32 [p]Ecc 3:22 [q]Ecc 3:12-13; 5:17-19; 9:7-10
2:26 [r]Job 27:17 [s]Pr 13:22
3:1 [t]ver 11,17; Ecc 8:6
3:7 [u]Am 5:13
3:9 [v]Ecc 1:3
3:10 [w]Ecc 1:13
3:11 [x]ver 1 [y]Job 11:7; Ecc 8:17 [z]Job 28:23; Ro 11:33
3:13 [a]Ecc 2:3 [b]Ps 34:12 [c]Dt 12:7,18; Ecc 2:24; 5:19
3:14 [d]Job 23:15; Ecc 5:7; 7:18; 8:12-13; Jas 1:17
3:15 [e]Ecc 6:10 [f]Ecc 1:9

2:23 not rest. A person's certain, ever-present and painful burden of living in the world in its fallen condition undermines even the ephemeral pleasure associated with toil (v. 10) and can deprive the laborer of the blessing of restful sleep.
2:24 nothing better. Similar expressions appear elsewhere in this book (2:12–13,22; 5:18–20; 8:15; 9:7). Upon reflection the Teacher recognized that it is appropriate simply to enjoy the good gifts that God bestows. Constantly striving to move beyond the limitations set for human insight will rob a person of the joys of life. Trust in God's inscrutable but superior wisdom will give us the freedom to accept and appreciate the temporary joys he gives us. See *WLC* 141.
2:26 To the man who pleases him . . . sinner. Contemplating the curse of death elicits consideration of the contrast between the righteous and the wicked, a distinction that will be made clear at the final judgment (3:17; 12:14). **meaningless.** See note on 1:2. The term applies here to the uselessness of passing along the fruit of one's labor to another—a further illustration of the point made in verses 20–21.
3:1–8 The Teacher found a measure of resolve by taking into account the various seasons or passages that God has ordained for the lives of people.
3:1 time . . . for every activity. No single activity or emotion is appropriate at all times. As the conditions of life shift a wise person will do whatever is suitable for a particular time or season. Under certain circumstances one response is desirable, while in other situations the very opposite is appropriate. One way to avoid despair is to pursue life's tasks according to divine timing.
3:4 See *WLC* 135.
■ **3:9—6:7** *Work in Fear Before God, Whose Work Endures.* This second cycle (see notes on 1:3—3:8; 6:8—12:7) is concerned with contrasting temporal, human toil with God's enduring work. Human beings are encouraged to enjoy the simple blessings God provides and to leave the things of eternity in God's hands. See "Introduction: Purpose and Distinctives."
■ **3:9–21** *God As Creator and Judge.* The Teacher reflected on the human situation in light of God's creative power and righteous judgment. God in his infinite wisdom has eternal purposes for whatever happens on Earth.
3:9–14 God the Creator is in view. His perfect, enduring, unfathomable work should elicit reverence from his people. See *WLC* 141.
3:9 What does the worker gain . . . ? This expression marks the beginning of the second cycle (cf. 1:3; 6:8).
3:11 eternity. This is the Hebrew term translated "forever" in verse 14 and explained in verse 11 as "from beginning to end." Short-lived human beings who lack the benefit of an eternal perspective know that history is long lasting, but they cannot discern its pattern of events. See *WLC* 135.
3:12 nothing better. The author's major application is his repeated advice (v. 22; 2:24–26; 5:18–20; 8:15) and command (9:7–10) to find a measure of contentment in what God has ordained for one's life.
3:13 gift of God. A contented trust in God's control does not originate from people; it is a God-given spiritual fruit (Ac 2:38; 8:14–20; 10:45; 11:17; Php 4:11–13).
3:14 revere. The term refers to acknowledging and worshiping God as Sovereign Lord. God created and controls his world with the goal that human beings will be astounded and worship him.
3:15–21 God the Judge comes into view.

16 And I saw something else under the sun:

In the place of judgment—wickedness was there,
 in the place of justice—wickedness was there.

17 I thought in my heart,

"God will bring to judgment[g]
 both the righteous and the wicked,
for there will be a time for every activity,
 a time for every deed."[h]

18 I also thought, "As for men, God tests them so that they may see that they are like
the animals.[i] 19 Man's fate[j] is like that of the animals; the same fate awaits them both:
As one dies, so dies the other. All have the same breath[a]; man has no advantage over the
animal. Everything is meaningless. 20 All go to the same place; all come from dust, and
to dust all return.[k] 21 Who knows if the spirit of man rises upward[l] and if the spirit of the
animal[b] goes down into the earth?"
22 So I saw that there is nothing better for a man than to enjoy his work,[m] because that
is his lot.[n] For who can bring him to see what will happen after him?

Oppression, Toil, Friendlessness

4 Again I looked and saw all the oppression[o] that was taking place under the sun:

I saw the tears of the oppressed—
 and they have no comforter;
power was on the side of their oppressors—
 and they have no comforter.[p]
2 And I declared that the dead,[q]
 who had already died,
are happier than the living,
 who are still alive.[r]
3 But better than both
 is he who has not yet been,[s]
who has not seen the evil
 that is done under the sun.[t]

4 And I saw that all labor and all achievement spring from man's envy of his neighbor.
This too is meaningless, a chasing after the wind.[u]

5 The fool folds his hands[v]
 and ruins himself.
6 Better one handful with tranquillity
 than two handfuls with toil[w]
 and chasing after the wind.

7 Again I saw something meaningless under the sun:

8 There was a man all alone;
 he had neither son nor brother.
There was no end to his toil,
 yet his eyes were not content[x] with his wealth.

3:17 [g]Job 19:29; Ecc 11:9; Mt 16:27; Ro 2:6-8; 2Th 1:6-7 [h]ver 1
3:18 [i]Ps 73:22
3:19 [j]Ecc 2:14
3:20 [k]Ge 2:7; 3:19; Job 34:15
3:21 [l]Ecc 12:7
3:22 [m]Ecc 2:24; 5:18 [n]Job 31:2
4:1 [o]Ps 12:5; Ecc 3:16 [p]La 1:16
4:2 [q]Jer 20:17-18; 22:10 [r]Job 3:17; 10:18
4:3 [s]Job 3:16; Ecc 6:3 [t]Job 3:22
4:4 [u]Ecc 1:14
4:5 [v]Pr 6:10
4:6 [w]Pr 15:16-17; 16:8
4:8 [x]Pr 27:20

[a] *19* Or *spirit* [b] *21* Or *Who knows the spirit of man, which rises upward, or the spirit of the animal, which*

3:17 the righteous and the wicked. As punishment for sin human beings, like animals (vv. 18–20), die (Ge 3:19). The distinction between the righteous and the wicked is not made clear at death from a human vantage point. Even so, that difference will be revealed at God's judgment. **time.** God ordains whatever occurs on the earth (vv. 1–8), but he has also appointed a day for judgment.
3:21 Who knows if the spirit of man . . . ? See 2:19. An alternative rendering of the Hebrew is "Who knows the spirit of man which . . . ?" The material, tangible body returns to dust, but a person's spirit returns to God (12:7), who will judge all of humanity (11:9).
■ **3:22—4:16** *Contentment or Envy.* The Teacher explored an individual's options to go through life either with contentment or with destructive envy.
3:22 nothing better. See notes on 2:24–26, 3:12, 5:18–20 and 8:15.
4:1 oppression . . . oppressed. As was appropriate for wise royalty, the Teacher was concerned about political oppression (see 3:16; Pr 31:8–9). **comforter.** Earthly power is too often perverted to oppress rather than to liberate. In Christ there is comfort in the midst of suffering (2Co 1:3–7).
4:3 evil. The evil of this present age is the catalyst for this assessment of earthly existence.
4:4–16 Envy and lack of contentment fuel humanity's futile drive for earthly satisfaction.
4:5–6 tranquillity. Sufficiency with contentment is better than need resulting from laziness (v. 5) or excess accompanied by restless toil (v. 8).
4:8 all alone. Even before the fall into sin, it was not good for a human to be alone (Ge 2:18). After the fall rendered human existence painful and frustrating, this need for companionship became even more pressing. See *WLC* 142.

"For whom am I toiling," he asked,
"and why am I depriving myself of enjoyment?"
This too is meaningless—
a miserable business!

9 Two are better than one,
because they have a good return for their work:
10 If one falls down,
his friend can help him up.
But pity the man who falls
and has no one to help him up!
11 Also, if two lie down together, they will keep warm.
But how can one keep warm alone?
12 Though one may be overpowered,
two can defend themselves.
A cord of three strands is not quickly broken.

Advancement Is Meaningless

13 Better a poor but wise youth than an old but foolish king who no longer knows how
to take warning. 14 The youth may have come from prison to the kingship, or he may have
been born in poverty within his kingdom. 15 I saw that all who lived and walked under
the sun followed the youth, the king's successor. 16 There was no end to all the people
who were before them. But those who came later were not pleased with the successor.
This too is meaningless, a chasing after the wind.

Stand in Awe of God

5 Guard your steps when you go to the house of God. Go near to listen rather than to offer the sacrifice of fools, who do not know that they do wrong.

2 Do not be quick with your mouth,
do not be hasty in your heart
to utter anything before God.[y]
God is in heaven
and you are on earth,
so let your words be few.[z]
3 As a dream[a] comes when there are many cares,
so the speech of a fool when there are many words.[b]

4 When you make a vow to God, do not delay in fulfilling it.[c] He has no pleasure in
fools; fulfill your vow.[d] 5 It is better not to vow than to make a vow and not fulfill it.[e] 6 Do
not let your mouth lead you into sin. And do not protest to the ⌊temple⌋ messenger, "My
vow was a mistake." Why should God be angry at what you say and destroy the work of
your hands? 7 Much dreaming and many words are meaningless. Therefore stand in awe
of God.[f]

Riches Are Meaningless

8 If you see the poor oppressed[g] in a district, and justice and rights denied, do not be
surprised at such things; for one official is eyed by a higher one, and over them both are

5:2 [y]Jdg 11:35 [z]Job 6:24; Pr 10:19; 20:25
5:3 [a]Job 20:8 [b]Ecc 10:14
5:4 [c]Dt 23:21; Jdg 11:35; Ps 119:60 [d]Nu 30:2; Ps 66:13-14; 76:11
5:5 [e]Nu 30:2-4; Pr 20:25; Jnh 2:9; Ac 5:4
5:7 [f]Ecc 3:14; 12:13
5:8 [g]Ps 12:5; Ecc 4:1

4:9–12 Two . . . two . . . two. Cooperation, rather than strife rooted in envy, produces success and provides protection from the covetous.
4:13–16 Humanity's characteristic discontent blinds it to the difference between wise and foolish leaders. Although it is preferable to be ruled by someone good-hearted and humble, any individual's leadership is temporary and will bring no permanent resolution—in this sense it is pointless. See *WLC* 151.
▪ **5:1–7** *Sincere Commitment to God.* As with other Biblical Wisdom Literature, the only hope held out for more than bare survival through the trials of life is sincere reverence for God (Job 28:28; Pr 1:9). These verses comprise the structural center of Ecclesiastes; the concluding summary (12:13) repeats the exhortation to fear God (v. 7).
5:1–6 See *WCF* 21.3; 22.5; *WLC* 112,151,175.
5:1 Guard your steps. That is, "Watch your ways [in worship]." Worship should focus on God ("listen"). See *WLC* 112,185.
5:2 quick with your mouth. An admonition not to offer rash vows. The thoughts of the heart are expressed in the words of the mouth, and God will judge them (Mt 12:34–37). See *WLC* 112.
5:3 The temptation must be avoided to make numerous and even rash promises in times of trouble.
5:4–5 vow. A sincere vow is evidence of voluntary, conscious commitment to God (Dt 23:21–23). Vows must be fulfilled quickly to lessen the likelihood that they will be broken. See *WCF* 21.5.
5:6 mouth. See note on verse 2. **messenger.** This word can be rendered "angel" and refers to either the divine angel of the Lord or to his priestly representative (Mal 2:7). **a mistake.** That is, "in error."
5:7 stand in awe of. The same word is translated "revere" in 3:14 and "fear" in 12:13.
▪ **5:8—6:7** *(Dis)satisfaction in Work.* Once again labor comes into focus as the Teacher examined the reasons for job-related satisfaction and dissatisfaction.
5:8–17 Human greed is responsible for many of the detrimental aspects of wealth.
5:8 do not be surprised. Oppression and injustice will inevitably occur in a fallen world (4:1–3); envy's eye greedily gazes down (v. 9) as well as up (4:4–16).

others higher still. 9The increase from the land is taken by all; the king himself profits
from the fields.

10 Whoever loves money never has money enough;
whoever loves wealth is never satisfied with his income.
This too is meaningless.

11 As goods increase,
so do those who consume them.
And what benefit are they to the owner
except to feast his eyes on them?

12 The sleep of a laborer is sweet,
whether he eats little or much,
but the abundance of a rich man
permits him no sleep.[h]

5:12 [h]Job 20:20

13I have seen a grievous evil under the sun:[i]

5:13 [i]Ecc 6:1-2

wealth hoarded to the harm of its owner,
14 or wealth lost through some misfortune,
so that when he has a son
there is nothing left for him.
15 Naked a man comes from his mother's womb,
and as he comes, so he departs.[j]
He takes nothing from his labor[k]
that he can carry in his hand.[l]

5:15 [j]Job 1:21 [k]Ps 49:17; 1Ti 6:7 [l]Ecc 1:3

16This too is a grievous evil:

As a man comes, so he departs,
and what does he gain,
since he toils for the wind?[m]
17 All his days he eats in darkness,
with great frustration, affliction and anger.

5:16 [m]Pr 11:29; Ecc 1:3

18Then I realized that it is good and proper for a man to eat and drink,[n] and to find
satisfaction in his toilsome labor[o] under the sun during the few days of life God has giv-
en him—for this is his lot. 19Moreover, when God gives any man wealth and possessions,[p] and enables him to enjoy them,[q] to accept his lot[r] and be happy in his work—
this is a gift of God.[s] 20He seldom reflects on the days of his life, because God keeps him
occupied with gladness of heart.[t]

5:18 [n]Ecc 2:3 [o]Ecc 2:10, 24
5:19 [p]1Ch 29:12; 2Ch 1:12 [q]Ecc 6:2 [r]Job 31:2 [s]Ecc 2:24; 3:13
5:20 [t]Dt 12:7, 18

6 I have seen another evil under the sun, and it weighs heavily on men: 2God gives a
man wealth, possessions and honor, so that he lacks nothing his heart desires, but
God does not enable him to enjoy them,[u] and a stranger enjoys them instead. This is
meaningless, a grievous evil.[v]
3A man may have a hundred children and live many years; yet no matter how long
he lives, if he cannot enjoy his prosperity and does not receive proper burial, I say that
a stillborn[w] child is better off than he.[x] 4It comes without meaning, it departs in darkness, and in darkness its name is shrouded. 5Though it never saw the sun or knew anything, it has more rest than does that man— 6even if he lives a thousand years twice over
but fails to enjoy his prosperity. Do not all go to the same place?

6:2 [u]Ps 17:14; Ecc 5:19 [v]Ecc 5:13
6:3 [w]Job 3:16; Ecc 4:3 [x]Job 3:3

7 All man's efforts are for his mouth,
yet his appetite is never satisfied.[y]

6:7 [y]Pr 16:26; 27:20

5:10–12 loves money. Greed is insatiable and robs one of sleep; contentment, on the other hand, enables revitalizing rest (see 1Ti 6:6–10). See *WLC* 135,142.
5:13–17 The Teacher pondered the tragedies of unused and lost wealth. The latter condition applies to all individuals at death; because of this investing too much of oneself in wealth and labor is ill-advised.
5:18—6:7 God sovereignly distributes wealth, but his ways and reasons are often inscrutable.
5:18 good. Recognizing the futility of a person's labor, his or her responsibility is to take a measure of satisfaction and joy in the blessings God gives in this life (see notes on 2:24–26; 3:12,22; 8:15).
5:19 gift of God. Even though it will not ultimately satisfy, the ability to affirm and enjoy earthly labor is a blessing from God that is granted to rich (v. 9) and poor (v. 12) alike.
6:1–2 See *WLC* 136.
6:2 God. God grants riches to some, but the futility of placing too much significance on wealth is demonstrated by the fact that these possessions often end up being enjoyed by strangers. See *WLC* 142.
6:3 he cannot enjoy his prosperity. Literally, "his soul is not satisfied with the goodness." Circumstances of life such as adversity, sickness or simple dissatisfaction often keep those who possess much from enjoying their blessings. Their condition is more pitiable than that of a stillborn child who never possesses anything this world has to offer.
6:6 to the same place? That is, to the decomposed elements of dust, having no eternal destiny.
6:7 appetite . . . satisfied. Literally, "soul . . . filled." Rather than

8 What advantage has a wise man
over a fool?[z]
What does a poor man gain
by knowing how to conduct himself before others?
9 Better what the eye sees
than the roving of the appetite.
This too is meaningless,
a chasing after the wind.[a]

10 Whatever exists has already been named,
and what man is has been known;
no man can contend
with one who is stronger than he.
11 The more the words,
the less the meaning,
and how does that profit anyone?

12 For who knows what is good for a man in life, during the few and meaningless days[b]
he passes through like a shadow?[c] Who can tell him what will happen under the sun after he is gone?

Wisdom

7

A good name is better than fine perfume,[d]
and the day of death better than the day of birth.
2 It is better to go to a house of mourning
than to go to a house of feasting,
for death[e] is the destiny[f] of every man;
the living should take this to heart.
3 Sorrow is better than laughter,[g]
because a sad face is good for the heart.
4 The heart of the wise is in the house of mourning,
but the heart of fools is in the house of pleasure.[h]
5 It is better to heed a wise man's rebuke[i]
than to listen to the song of fools.
6 Like the crackling of thorns[j] under the pot,
so is the laughter[k] of fools.
This too is meaningless.

7 Extortion turns a wise man into a fool,
and a bribe[l] corrupts the heart.

8 The end of a matter is better than its beginning,
and patience[m] is better than pride.
9 Do not be quickly provoked[n] in your spirit,
for anger resides in the lap of fools.

10 Do not say, "Why were the old days better than these?"
For it is not wise to ask such questions.

6:8 [z]Ecc 2:15
6:9 [a]Ecc 1:14
6:12 [b]Job 10:20 [c]Job 14:2; Ps 39:6; Jas 4:14
7:1 [d]Pr 22:1; SS 1:3
7:2 [e]Pr 11:19 [f]Ps 90:12
7:3 [g]Pr 14:13
7:4 [h]Ecc 2:1; Jer 16:8
7:5 [i]Ps 141:5; Pr 13:18; 15:31-32
7:6 [j]Ps 58:9; 118:12 [k]Ecc 2:2
7:7 [l]Ex 18:21; 23:8; Dt 16:19
7:8 [m]Pr 14:29; Gal 5:22; Eph 4:2
7:9 [n]Mt 5:22; Pr 14:17; Jas 1:19

---

maintaining that no one is satisfied with labor's provisions (contrast 5:12–13; 18–20) the Teacher concludes that earthly toil cannot fully satisfy the strivings of a person's soul (1:8).

■ **6:8—12:7** *Humility Before God, Whose Wisdom Is Unfathomable.* In this third cycle the theme of wisdom is elaborated by contrasting mortal wisdom with the eternal wisdom of God (see "Introduction: Purpose and Distinctives"). These chapters divide into six main parts: the futility of contending with God (6:8–12), human good (7:1–18), wisdom's power (7:19—8:8), unfulfilled judgment (8:9—9:10), folly's power (9:11—10:7) and advice for wise living (10:8—12:7).

■ **6:8–12** *The Futility of Contending With God.* The Teacher wrestled with the reality that irreverently contending with God produces no advantage or blessing.

6:8 What advantage . . . ? This expression begins the third cycle (cf. 1:3–11; 3:9–21).

6:9 Better. Repeats the theme that contentment is preferable to dissatisfaction.

6:10 named . . . known. God characterizes people as sinners (7:20). **contend.** Humans have no legal defense before God, the Judge. **one who is stronger.** That is, God.

6:12 what. Here are the two thematic questions taken up in the remainder of the book. The previous answer (2:24–26) to the first question will be practically elaborated. The negative answer to the second question raises the issue of life's uncertainties, the context for considering how people should live.

■ **7:1–18** *What Is Good for Humans.* These verses set forth at least seven good things in response to the first question of 6:12.

7:1 day of death better. Although death is a curse on humanity (Ge 2:17) and remains our final enemy (1Co 15:26), it is better than birth in the sense that it constitutes release from the futility of this fallen world and takes believers one step closer to resurrection and eventual life in the new heavens and the new earth (2Co 5:8; Php 1:21–23).

7:2,4 house of mourning. A funeral provides perspective on the destination of our earthly journey. See *HC* 114.

7:7 Extortion. The Hebrew word here is the same as that translated "oppression" in 4:1. The characteristic harshness of unredeemed humanity is a threat to spiritual life.

7:9 anger resides. If unquenched, anger, ignited by life's difficulties, kills spiritual life.

7:11 [o]Pr 8:10-11; Ecc 2:13 [p]Ecc 11:7

11 Wisdom, like an inheritance, is a good thing[o]
and benefits those who see the sun.[p]
12 Wisdom is a shelter
as money is a shelter,
but the advantage of knowledge is this:
that wisdom preserves the life of its possessor.

7:13 [q]Ecc 2:24 [r]Ecc 1:15

13 Consider what God has done:[q]

Who can straighten
what he has made crooked?[r]
14 When times are good, be happy;
but when times are bad, consider:
God has made the one
as well as the other.
Therefore, a man cannot discover
anything about his future.

7:15 [s]Job 7:7 [t]Ecc 8:12-14; Jer 12:1

15 In this meaningless life[s] of mine I have seen both of these:

a righteous man perishing in his righteousness,
and a wicked man living long in his wickedness.[t]
16 Do not be overrighteous,
neither be overwise—
why destroy yourself?
17 Do not be overwicked,
and do not be a fool—
why die before your time?[u]
18 It is good to grasp the one
and not let go of the other.
The man who fears God[v] will avoid all ⌞extremes⌟.[a]

7:17 [u]Job 15:32; Ps 55:23
7:18 [v]Ecc 3:14
7:19 [w]Ecc 2:13 [x]Ecc 9:13-18

19 Wisdom[w] makes one wise man more powerful[x]
than ten rulers in a city.

7:20 [y]Ps 14:3 [z]1Ki 8:46; 2Ch 6:36; Pr 20:9; Ro 3:23

20 There is not a righteous man[y] on earth
who does what is right and never sins.[z]

7:21 [a]Pr 30:10

21 Do not pay attention to every word people say,
or you[a] may hear your servant cursing you—
22 for you know in your heart
that many times you yourself have cursed others.

7:23 [b]Ecc 1:17; Ro 1:22

23 All this I tested by wisdom and I said,

"I am determined to be wise"[b]—
but this was beyond me.
24 Whatever wisdom may be,
it is far off and most profound—
who can discover it?[c]

7:24 [c]Job 28:12

[a] *18* Or *will follow them both*

7:11–12 Wisdom . . . preserves the life. Acknowledgement of the limitations of human ability to acquire divine wisdom benefits those who possess it in countless ways. The relentless pursuit of human wisdom beyond these limits leads to futility and frustration (1:16-18). See verses 13–14.
7:13 Who can straighten . . . ? God is almighty, able to do what humans cannot; even the curse of Genesis 3 will be reversed at the consummation of Christ's return. Purely human efforts to find the wisdom that will bring resolution to the problems of this fallen world are doomed to fail (1:15).
7:14 times are good . . . bad. God has ordained not only good but also bad times. We must accept this reality and trust in him to bring these experiences to resolution (Ge 50:20; Ro 8:28). **man cannot discover.** Human beings will always remain limited in their comprehension, uncertain about what will happen in the future and unable to alter life's course.
7:15 righteous . . . wicked. The frequent lack of an immediate and discernible divine response to individual human behavior contributes to people's uncertainty of God's ways.
7:16–17 Do not be overrighteous . . . overwicked. Righteousness and wickedness do not always result in immediate judgment (v.15). Thus the extremes of legalism on the one hand and libertinism on the other are equally ineffective.
7:18 the one . . . the other. The wise avoid becoming overly involved in the self-centered and fanatical pursuit of purity, which leads to self-righteous hypocrisy as well as wickedness, in an attempt to secure their future. Instead, they pursue the fear of God and expend themselves in faithful service to him (12:13–14).
■ **7:19—8:8** *Wisdom's Power.* The Teacher considered both the profundity of wisdom and the depth of sin.
7:19 wise man. Those who understand that true wisdom is not tantamount to perfection (vv. 17–18) find strength and power in their lives.
7:20 not a righteous man. All people are guilty before God (Pss 14:3; 53:3). To scrutinize others too closely is folly (v. 21). See *WCF* 6.5; *WLC* 149; *WSC* 82.
7:22 many times. All people are multiple offenders in God's sight.
7:24 who can discover it? No one can encompass God's under-

25 So I turned my mind to understand,
to investigate and to search out wisdom and the scheme of things[d]
and to understand the stupidity of wickedness
and the madness of folly.[e]
26 I find more bitter than death
the woman who is a snare,[f]
whose heart is a trap
and whose hands are chains.
The man who pleases God will escape her,
but the sinner she will ensnare.[g]

27 "Look," says the Teacher,[a h] "this is what I have discovered:

"Adding one thing to another to discover the scheme of things—
28 while I was still searching
but not finding—
I found one ⌊upright⌋ man among a thousand,
but not one ⌊upright⌋ woman[i] among them all.
29 This only have I found:
God made mankind upright,
but men have gone in search of many schemes."

8 Who is like the wise man?
Who knows the explanation of things?
Wisdom brightens a man's face
and changes its hard appearance.

Obey the King

2 Obey the king's command, I say, because you took an oath before God. 3 Do not be
in a hurry to leave the king's presence.[j] Do not stand up for a bad cause, for he will do
whatever he pleases. 4 Since a king's word is supreme, who can say to him, "What are you
doing?[k]"

5 Whoever obeys his command will come to no harm,
and the wise heart will know the proper time and procedure.
6 For there is a proper time and procedure for every matter,[l]
though a man's misery weighs heavily upon him.

7 Since no man knows the future,
who can tell him what is to come?
8 No man has power over the wind to contain it[b];
so no one has power over the day of his death.
As no one is discharged in time of war,
so wickedness will not release those who practice it.

9 All this I saw, as I applied my mind to everything done under the sun. There is a time
when a man lords it over others to his own[c] hurt. 10 Then too, I saw the wicked buried[m]—

7:25 [d]Job 28:3 [e]Ecc 1:17
7:26 [f]Ex 10:7; Jdg 14:15 [g]Pr 2:16-19; 5:3-5; 7:23; 22:14
7:27 [h]Ecc 1:1
7:28 [i]1Ki 11:3
8:3 [j]Ecc 10:4
8:4 [k]Job 9:12; Est 1:19; Da 4:35
8:6 [l]Ecc 3:1
8:10 [m]Ecc 1:11

a 27 Or *leader of the assembly* b 8 Or *over his spirit to retain it* c 9 Or *to their*

standing; it is qualitatively beyond the capacity of human knowledge or insight (cf. 8:16–17; 1Co 2:11).
7:27,29 scheme . . . schemes. In verse 27 "scheme" refers to the "sum total" or "plan [of human history]." In verse 29 the same Hebrew word is rendered "ingenious [war] machines" (cf. 1Ch 26:15).
7:27 Adding one thing to another. The Teacher reflected on what he had accomplished in his life. He observed life, inductively gathering information. Here he searched for righteous human beings.
7:28 one upright man . . . not one upright woman. This report should not be taken as a reflection on the relative righteousness of the genders. The Teacher merely reported what he saw. His conclusion was that only a few who appeared to be upright (not perfect) could actually be characterized as such. This led him rightly to understand that the human race is captive to the tyranny of sin.
7:29 made mankind upright. God created humanity morally good (Ge 1:31), but subsequent to the fall all people participate in sin (Ro 3:23; 5:12). See *WCF* 4.2; 6.2; 9.2; 19.1; *WLC* 17,21; *WSC* 13; *BC* 14.
8:1 wise man? See note on 7:19.
8:2 oath before God. That is, an oath of loyalty to a king (cf. Ro 13:1–5; 1Pe 2:13–17).
8:4 What are you doing? It was improper for an inferior to challenge a king, who had legitimate authority to do whatever he discerned to be the appropriate course of action. Paul drew upon this principle when he noted that human beings have no right to challenge the divine King regarding what he does with his creatures (see Ro 9:20).
8:5,6 proper time and procedure. In verse 5 these words refer to behavior before the king (vv. 2–4); in verse 6 to God ordaining all things (cf. vv. 7–8; 3:1–8).
8:8 power. Only God can control the future, the wind, death or evil. Relying on human wisdom alone is utter folly.
■ **8:9—9:10** *Unfulfilled Judgment.* The Teacher struggled with God's apparent failure to mete out judgment against the wicked in this life.

those who used to come and go from the holy place and receive praise[a] in the city where
they did this. This too is meaningless.
11 When the sentence for a crime is not quickly carried out, the hearts of the people
are filled with schemes to do wrong. 12 Although a wicked man commits a hundred
crimes and still lives a long time, I know that it will go better[n] with God-fearing men,[o]
who are reverent before God.[p] 13 Yet because the wicked do not fear God,[q] it will not go
well with them, and their days[r] will not lengthen like a shadow.
14 There is something else meaningless that occurs on earth: righteous men who get
what the wicked deserve, and wicked men who get what the righteous deserve.[s] This too,
I say, is meaningless.[t] 15 So I commend the enjoyment of life[u], because nothing is better
for a man under the sun than to eat and drink[v] and be glad.[w] Then joy will accompany
him in his work all the days of the life God has given him under the sun.
16 When I applied my mind to know wisdom[x] and to observe man's labor on earth[y]—
his eyes not seeing sleep day or night— 17 then I saw all that God has done.[z] No one can
comprehend what goes on under the sun. Despite all his efforts to search it out, man cannot discover its meaning. Even if a wise man claims he knows, he cannot really comprehend it.[a]

A Common Destiny for All

9 So I reflected on all this and concluded that the righteous and the wise and what
they do are in God's hands, but no man knows whether love or hate awaits him.[b]
2 All share a common destiny—the righteous and the wicked, the good and the bad,[b] the
clean and the unclean, those who offer sacrifices and those who do not.

As it is with the good man,
so with the sinner;
as it is with those who take oaths,
so with those who are afraid to take them.[c]

3 This is the evil in everything that happens under the sun: The same destiny overtakes
all.[d] The hearts of men, moreover, are full of evil and there is madness in their hearts
while they live,[e] and afterward they join the dead.[f] 4 Anyone who is among the living has
hope[c]—even a live dog is better off than a dead lion!

5 For the living know that they will die,
but the dead know nothing;[g]
they have no further reward,
and even the memory of them[h] is forgotten.[i]
6 Their love, their hate
and their jealousy have long since vanished;
never again will they have a part
in anything that happens under the sun.[j]

8:12 [n]Dt 12:28; Ps 37:11,18-19; Pr 1:32-33; Isa 3:10-11 [o]Ex 1:20 [p]Ecc 3:14
8:13 [q]Ecc 3:14; Isa 3:11 [r]Dt 4:40; Job 5:26; Ps 34:12; Isa 65:20
8:14 [s]Job 21:7; Ps 73:14; Mal 3:15 [t]Ecc 7:15
8:15 [u]Ps 42:8 [v]Ex 32:6; Ecc 2:3 [w]Ecc 2:24; 3:12-13; 5:18; 9:7
8:16 [x]Ecc 1:17 [y]Ecc 1:13
8:17 [z]Job 28:3 [a]Job 5:9; 28:23; Ecc 3:11; Ro 11:33
9:1 [b]Dt 33:3; Job 12:10; Ecc 10:14
9:2 [c]Job 9:22; Ecc 2:14; 6:6; 7:2
9:3 [d]Job 9:22; Ecc 2:14 [e]Jer 11:8; 13:10; 16:12; 17:9 [f]Job 21:26
9:5 [g]Job 14:21 [h]Ps 9:6 [i]Ecc 1:11; 2:16; Isa 26:14
9:6 [j]Job 21:21

a *10* Some Hebrew manuscripts and Septuagint (Aquila); most Hebrew manuscripts *and are forgotten*
b *2* Septuagint (Aquila), Vulgate and Syriac; Hebrew does not have *and the bad.* c *4* Or *What then is to be chosen? With all who live, there is hope*

8:9–15 The Teacher combined instruction on the theme of injustice with a recommendation to be content in life and to enjoy and appreciate the good in one's circumstances (cf. 4:1–3). See *WLC* 113.
8:9 to his own. See NIV text note. The Teacher pointed to rulers who irresponsibly execute their God-given authority (cf. Ro 13:3–4).
8:10 buried . . . praise. Religious hypocrites, perhaps the leaders in verse 9, receive honor that is not rightly due to them.
8:11 filled with schemes. In this fallen world the lack of justice against criminals only encourages more crime. See *WLC* 113.
8:12–13 I know. The sage expressed his belief about the ultimate end of the wicked and the righteous, even though his conclusion contrasted with his observations of life (vv.9–11). **go better . . . not go well.** God can distinguish genuine from hypocritical worshipers and will at the judgment reward the righteous and condemn the wicked.
8:14 on earth. In this life the righteous and the wicked do not necessarily receive their just deserts.
8:15 commend. In the face of present inequality and with the hope of future justice, the Teacher commended a positive and thankful attitude and intentional, purposeful enjoyment of life. **nothing is better.** See notes on 2:24–26, 3:12,22 and 5:18–20. **eat . . . drink . . . be glad.** These and similar words can be stated (as here) in humility and sincere gratitude for God's kindness (5:19; 9:7; Dt 8) or in pride and defiance (Lk 12:19–20; 1Co 15:32).
8:17 all that God has done. See 7:13 and 11:5. In this verse we find the focus of the third cycle in Ecclesiastes (see note on 6:8—12:7). See "Introduction: Purpose and Distinctives." **cannot really comprehend.** Even the wise man is unable to fathom God's work; much more is kept secret by God than he has chosen to reveal (Dt 29:29; Pr 25:2).
9:1–10 The Teacher commended enjoyment of life, despite the common curse of death.
9:1 in God's hands, but no man knows. God sovereignly controls the affairs of all, but humans comprehend only the very surface, especially in terms of the concealed future. **love or hate.** Until Christ returns in glory (Mt 5:44–45; Lk 13:1–5), both "good" and "bad" things happen to righteous and wicked alike, according to God's inscrutable design.
9:2–3 common destiny. In terms of earthly existence both the righteous, wise individual and the wicked fool die (2:14–15). **full of evil . . . madness in their hearts.** Sin corrupts the inner person and turns every individual away from the path of true wisdom and righteousness. See *WLC* 113.
9:4 hope. The Teacher's point might be summed up in the adage "Where there's life there's hope." But hope based on humanistic, earthly factors is tragically misguided.

7 Go, eat your food with gladness, and drink your wine[k] with a joyful heart,[l] for it is
now that God favors what you do. 8 Always be clothed in white,[m] and always anoint your
head with oil. 9 Enjoy life with your wife,[n] whom you love, all the days of this meaningless life that God has given you under the sun—all your meaningless days. For this is your
lot[o] in life and in your toilsome labor under the sun. 10 Whatever[p] your hand finds to do,
do it with all your might,[q] for in the grave,[a][r] where you are going, there is neither working nor planning nor knowledge nor wisdom.[s]

11 I have seen something else under the sun:

The race is not to the swift
  or the battle to the strong,[t]
nor does food come to the wise[u]
  or wealth to the brilliant
  or favor to the learned;
but time and chance[v] happen to them all.[w]

12 Moreover, no man knows when his hour will come:

As fish are caught in a cruel net,
  or birds are taken in a snare,
so men are trapped by evil times[x]
  that fall unexpectedly upon them.[y]

Wisdom Better Than Folly

13 I also saw under the sun this example of wisdom[z] that greatly impressed me:
14 There was once a small city with only a few people in it. And a powerful king came
against it, surrounded it and built huge siegeworks against it. 15 Now there lived in that
city a man poor but wise, and he saved the city by his wisdom. But nobody remembered
that poor man.[a] 16 So I said, "Wisdom is better than strength." But the poor man's wisdom is despised, and his words are no longer heeded.[b]

17 The quiet words of the wise are more to be heeded
  than the shouts of a ruler of fools.
18 Wisdom[c] is better than weapons of war,
  but one sinner destroys much good.

10

As dead flies give perfume a bad smell,
  so a little folly[d] outweighs wisdom and honor.
2 The heart of the wise inclines to the right,
  but the heart of the fool to the left.
3 Even as he walks along the road,
  the fool lacks sense
  and shows everyone[e] how stupid he is.
4 If a ruler's anger rises against you,
  do not leave your post;[f]
  calmness can lay great errors to rest.[g]

5 There is an evil I have seen under the sun,
  the sort of error that arises from a ruler:

9:7 [k]Nu 6:20 [l]Ecc 2:24; 8:15
9:8 [m]Ps 23:5; Rev 3:4
9:9 [n]Pr 5:18 [o]Job 31:2
9:10 [p]1Sa 10:7 [q]Ecc 11:6; Ro 12:11; Col 3:23 [r]Nu 16:33 [s]Ecc 2:24
9:11 [t]Am 2:14-15 [u]Job 32:13; Isa 47:10; Jer 9:23 [v]Ecc 2:14 [w]Dt 8:18
9:12 [x]Pr 29:6 [y]Ps 73:22; Ecc 2:14; 8:7
9:13 [z]2Sa 20:22
9:15 [a]Ge 40:14; Ecc 1:11; 2:16; 4:13
9:16 [b]Pr 21:22; Ecc 7:19
9:18 [c]ver 16
10:1 [d]Pr 13:16; 18:2
10:3 [e]Pr 13:16; 18:2
10:4 [f]Ecc 8:3 [g]Pr 16:14; 25:15

a *10* Hebrew *Sheol*

9:7–9 This passage closely parallels a section from the Babylonian text *The Epic of Gilgamesh.* This indicates the international quality of Israel's wisdom traditions.
9:7 Go, eat . . . drink. In the face of earthly injustice and inevitable death, the reader is counseled to enjoy life as fully as possible (see note on 8:15).
9:10 with all your might. The Teacher called for energetic labor during life because from mere human observation there is nothing to do in death.
■**9:11—10:7** *Folly's Power.* Human evil and folly may appear to be more rewarding than wisdom, but in the end wisdom will prove more valuable.
9:11–12 The Teacher considered the uncertainties of life that call into question the value of living according to wisdom.
9:11 chance. No mere statistical probability is in view here, but a potentially ominous, personal encounter, an event that cannot be predicted by a person but has been planned by God. Human beings simply do not have control of their lives. **happen.** Skills do not guarantee success. God frequently orders events in unexpected ways.
9:12 hour. A time of misfortune or death. **unexpectedly.** Human beings cannot forecast calamities.
9:13–16 The Teacher recounted a story of a city saved from certain defeat by the words of a poor but wise man. The defeat of the enemy based on wisdom demonstrated that wisdom is superior to strength; ironically, the folly of people was revealed by the fact that the wise man's counsel was all too soon despised.
9:16 Wisdom . . . strength. This comparison reflects back on the second cycle (see note on 3:9—6:7), which dealt with labor (cf. vv. 9–10). **despised.** Although wisdom can overcome might, it often goes unacknowledged and unappreciated.
9:18—10:7 Human folly predominates over wisdom in this sinful world.
10:2 right . . . left. Associated with good and bad or with blessing and cursing, respectively.

10:6 [h]Pr 29:2

6 Fools are put in many high positions,[h]
while the rich occupy the low ones.

10:7 [i]Pr 19:10

7 I have seen slaves on horseback,
while princes go on foot like slaves.[i]

10:8 [j]Ps 7:15; 57:6; Pr 26:27 [k]Est 2:23; Ps 9:16; Am 5:19

8 Whoever digs a pit may fall into it;[j]
whoever breaks through a wall may be bitten by a snake.[k]

10:9 [l]Pr 26:27

9 Whoever quarries stones may be injured by them;
whoever splits logs may be endangered by them.[l]

10 If the ax is dull
and its edge unsharpened,
more strength is needed
but skill will bring success.

10:11 [m]Ps 58:5; Isa 3:3

11 If a snake bites before it is charmed,
there is no profit for the charmer.[m]

10:12 [n]Pr 10:32 [o]Pr 10:14; 14:3; 15:2; 18:7

12 Words from a wise man's mouth are gracious,[n]
but a fool is consumed by his own lips.[o]

10:14 [p]Pr 15:2; Ecc 5:3; 6:12; 8:7 [q]Ecc 9:1

13 At the beginning his words are folly;
at the end they are wicked madness—
14 and the fool multiplies words.[p]

No one knows what is coming—
who can tell him what will happen after him?[q]

15 A fool's work wearies him;
he does not know the way to town.

10:16 [r]Isa 3:4-5, 12

16 Woe to you, O land whose king was a servant[a] [r]
and whose princes feast in the morning.

10:17 [s]Dt 14:26; 1Sa 25:36; Pr 31:4

17 Blessed are you, O land whose king is of noble birth
and whose princes eat at a proper time—
for strength and not for drunkenness.[s]

10:18 [t]Pr 20:4; 24:30-34

18 If a man is lazy, the rafters sag;
if his hands are idle, the house leaks.[t]

10:19 [u]Ge 14:18; Jdg 9:13

19 A feast is made for laughter,
and wine[u] makes life merry,
but money is the answer for everything.

10:20 [v]Ex 22:28

20 Do not revile the king[v] even in your thoughts,
or curse the rich in your bedroom,
because a bird of the air may carry your words,
and a bird on the wing may report what you say.

Bread Upon the Waters

11:1 [w]ver 6; Isa 32:20; Hos 10:12 [x]Dt 24:19; Pr 19:17; Mt 10:42

11

Cast[w] your bread upon the waters,
for after many days you will find it again.[x]

[a] *16* Or *king is a child*

10:5 error. Rulers who are expected and even considered to be wise often govern inappropriately and unjustly.
10:6–7 The dominance of foolishness over wisdom is illustrated by fools ruling over the rich and slaves being honored over princes. The rich and princes, as opposed to the fools and slaves, are presumed to have had the privilege of training in wisdom.
■ **10:8—12:7** *Advice for Wise Living.* The Teacher pointed out some practical ways to minimize the trials of life and sustain hope for the future.
10:8—11:6 The Teacher reflected on laziness in a variety of ways, all of which illustrate the necessity of devoting wisdom and energy to work.
10:8–9 digs . . . breaks . . . quarries . . . splits. Potential dangers associated with labor can be used as excuses for indolence.
10:10–11 ax . . . snake. These images counsel the reader to take a proactive approach to such dangers and obstacles: A properly prepared worker can gain the advantage over labor's impediments.
10:12–14a Words. Words, superficial though they may at times seem, still reveal the deep-seated thoughts and values of a person's heart (Mt 12:34–37). James made a similar connection between speech and wisdom (Jas 3:1–18).
10:14b what is coming. That is, "what will be." Despite human attempts to secure one's status, the fact remains that the future is always indefinite.
10:15 not know the way to town. The fool lacks common sense.
10:19 everything. This can mean either "both" (i.e., money is needed for feasting and wine) or "all" (i.e., money provides for life's needs; cf. 7:12). It is not likely a sarcastic comment so much as a directive against laziness.
10:20 bird. That is, an informant.
11:1 bread upon the waters. That is, grain to be traded by sea. Here the Teacher advised against being overly cautious. These words may allude to Solomon's vast sea trade as an example of wisdom at work.

[2] Give portions to seven, yes to eight,
for you do not know what disaster may come upon the land.

[3] If clouds are full of water,
they pour rain upon the earth.
Whether a tree falls to the south or to the north,
in the place where it falls, there will it lie.
[4] Whoever watches the wind will not plant;
whoever looks at the clouds will not reap.

[5] As you do not know the path of the wind,[y]
or how the body is formed[a] in a mother's womb,[z]
so you cannot understand the work of God,
the Maker of all things.

[6] Sow your seed in the morning,
and at evening let not your hands be idle,[a]
for you do not know which will succeed,
whether this or that,
or whether both will do equally well.

Remember Your Creator While Young

[7] Light is sweet,
and it pleases the eyes to see the sun.[b]
[8] However many years a man may live,
let him enjoy them all.
But let him remember[c] the days of darkness,
for they will be many.
Everything to come is meaningless.

[9] Be happy, young man, while you are young,
and let your heart give you joy in the days of your youth.
Follow the ways of your heart
and whatever your eyes see,
but know that for all these things
God will bring you to judgment.[d]
[10] So then, banish anxiety[e] from your heart
and cast off the troubles of your body,
for youth and vigor are meaningless.[f]

12 Remember[g] your Creator
in the days of your youth,
before the days of trouble[h] come
and the years approach when you will say,
"I find no pleasure in them"—
[2] before the sun and the light
and the moon and the stars grow dark,
and the clouds return after the rain;
[3] when the keepers of the house tremble,
and the strong men stoop,
when the grinders cease because they are few,

11:5 [y]Jn 3:8-10 [z]Ps 139:14-16
11:6 [a]Ecc 9:10
11:7 [b]Ecc 7:11
11:8 [c]Ecc 12:1
11:9 [d]Job 19:29; Ecc 2:24; 3:17; 12:14; Ro 14:10
11:10 [e]Ps 94:19 [f]Ecc 2:24
12:1 [g]Ecc 11:8 [h]2Sa 19:35

[a] 5 Or *know how life* (or *the spirit*) / *enters the body being formed*

11:2 seven . . . eight. The Teacher may mean either "spread the risks you take" (cf. v. 6) or "generosity will be recycled." **not know.** Uncertainty is the motivation for diversity in estate management. See verse 6.
11:3,4 clouds. A caution not to use uncertainty about the outcome of an endeavor as an excuse for inaction.
11:5 work of God. People lack the ability to get their arms around the uncertainties of life; all circumstances are controlled by God.
11:6 not know. See note on verse 2.
11:7—12:7 The Teacher advocates that the student enjoy life, remembering that God is both the good Creator and the righteous Judge.
11:8 enjoy . . . remember. Again, enjoyment is recommended even in the context of difficulties.
11:9 judgment. Indiscriminate pursuit of joy must be tempered by responsibility for actions.
12:1 days of trouble. If pleasure is unrestrained in youth, both pleasure and the Creator will be unknown in later years. See *WLC* 104.
12:2–7 The Teacher commented on aging and death, using the extended metaphor of a house in the process of dilapidation. Note the manner in which he contrasted the house's deterioration with nature's permanence throughout these verses. It is best to treat the symbolism here for its overall effect rather than to speculate on the meaning of each individual image. As the following notes indicate, some associations are clearer than others.
12:3 keepers of the house. The phrases here probably refer to body parts in terms of members of a household.

and those looking through the windows grow dim;
4 when the doors to the street are closed
and the sound of grinding fades;
when men rise up at the sound of birds,
but all their songs grow faint;[i]
5 when men are afraid of heights
and of dangers in the streets;
when the almond tree blossoms
and the grasshopper drags himself along
and desire no longer is stirred.
Then man goes to his eternal home[j]
and mourners[k] go about the streets.

6 Remember him—before the silver cord is severed,
or the golden bowl is broken;
before the pitcher is shattered at the spring,
or the wheel broken at the well,
7 and the dust returns[l] to the ground it came from,
and the spirit returns to God[m] who gave it.[n]

8 "Meaningless! Meaningless!" says the Teacher.[a]
"Everything is meaningless![o]"

The Conclusion of the Matter

9 Not only was the Teacher wise, but also he imparted knowledge to the people. He
pondered and searched out and set in order many proverbs.[p] 10 The Teacher searched
to find just the right words, and what he wrote was upright and true.[q]
11 The words of the wise are like goads, their collected sayings like firmly embedded
nails[r]—given by one Shepherd. 12 Be warned, my son, of anything in addition to them.
Of making many books there is no end, and much study wearies the body.[s]

13 Now all has been heard;
here is the conclusion of the matter:
Fear God and keep his commandments,[t]
for this is the whole ⌞duty⌟ of man.[u]
14 For God will bring every deed into judgment,[v]
including every hidden thing,[w]
whether it is good or evil.

12:4 [i]Jer 25:10
12:5 [j]Job 17:13; 10:21 [k]Jer 9:17; Am 5:16
12:7 [l]Ge 3:19; Job 34:15; Ps 146:4 [m]Ecc 3:21 [n]Job 20:8; Zec 12:1
12:8 [o]Ecc 1:2
12:9 [p]1Ki 4:32
12:10 [q]Pr 22:20-21
12:11 [r]Ezr 9:8
12:12 [s]Ecc 1:18
12:13 [t]Dt 4:2; 10:12 [u]Mic 6:8
12:14 [v]Ecc 3:17 [w]Mt 10:26; 1Co 4:5

[a] 8 Or *the leader of the assembly*; also in verses 9 and 10

12:5 the almond tree blossoms. The blossoms' white color is associated with the hoary head of the aged. **eternal home.** The words refer not just to the grave but also to the presence of one's Creator-Judge (v. 7).
12:6 golden bowl. These words describe a lamp crushed in a fall caused by a broken link in a silver chain. Broken vessels and severed cords suggest the frailty that comes with aging.
12:7 spirit returns. An affirmation that human beings continue to exist beyond physical death. See *WCF* 4.2; 32.1; *WLC* 17; *BC* 14.
■ **12:8–14** *Epilogue.* The book closes with a final reiteration of the main theme and a tribute to the Teacher's success and reliability.
■ **12:8** *Main Theme.* This verse reiterates the Teacher's theme. From the perspective just given on the deterioration of a human being, all is meaningless apart from a divine intervention of redemption and restoration.
■ **12:9–14** *Conclusion.* The book concludes with an epilogue regarding the Teacher's method and provides a final analysis of the message he advocated in this book.
12:10 right . . . upright. The Teacher used extensive effort and wisdom to construct an aesthetically pleasing communication of truth.
12:11 given by one Shepherd. The words of Ecclesiastes, like those of every other Biblical book, are God-breathed (2Ti 3:16).
12:12 See *WLC* 136.
12:13 conclusion. Loyal submission to the rule of God is the central and summary admonition of the Bible's Wisdom Literature (5:7; Job 28:28; Pr 1:7; 9:10). Human beings cannot fathom much of what God knows to be true, nor can they understand the ways of his world, which are controlled by his infinite wisdom. The wisest course of action, therefore, is to submit to his commands in honorable reverence.
12:14 judgment. God's judgment of humanity's deeds has been emphasized at structural centers throughout the book because this reality was central to the Teacher's hope for resolution to the dilemmas he and his readers faced (3:17; 8:12–13; 11:9; cf. 2Co 5:10). At the final judgment all the perplexing anomalies of life in this fallen world will be resolved because everything and everyone will be judged and shown to be either good or evil. See *WCF* 33.1.

SONG OF SONGS

Introduction

Overview

Author: Unknown

Purpose: To celebrate the blessing of romantic love between husbands and wives

Date: Probably 960–931 B.C.

Key Truths:

- God gave romantic love between a husband and wife as a wondrous gift.
- Men and women in the bonds of marriage should delight in each other emotionally and physically.

Author

The traditional view among both Jews and Christians has been that Solomon wrote this entire book (see 1Ki 4:32). The evidence of the book places it in or near Solomon's reign, but it is impossible to know for certain who actually wrote it. Each evidence in favor of Solomon as author is open to other interpretations. First, the opening verse begins "Solomon's Song of Songs" (1:1), but the Hebrew could also indicate that the Song of Songs was "for" (i.e., dedicated to) Solomon. Second, it is possible that the superscription of 1:1 refers not to the entire book, but just to the first portion, as is the case in Proverbs 1:1 (see "Introduction to Proverbs"). Third, Solomon is mentioned a number of times (1:1,5; 3:7,9,11; 8:11–12), but some of these passages seem to treat him from a distance. Ironically, 3:6–11 praises him, while 8:10–12 raises a questionable policy. Fourth, the reference to Tirzah (the first capital of northern Israel during the reign of Jeroboam I [930–909 B.C.]) in parallel with Jerusalem (capital of Judah) in 6:4 has been taken to indicate that the book could not have been written until after the division of the kingdom. Yet the positive comparison between the cities may actually indicate the time of Solomon, before hostility between north and south led to division. Fifth, attempts to place the book at a much later time on the basis of linguistic evidence have proven unconvincing.

Time and Place of Writing

In view of the preponderance of evidence, it seems most likely that the book was written in Judah or Jerusalem in the tenth century B.C. during or slightly after Solomon's reign. The subject matter of the book focuses on romantic love in terms appropriate especially for royalty, but it was easily used outside royal circles as well.

Purpose and Distinctives

The word "Song" in the title (1:1) is the common Hebrew term for any happy melody. It has no special religious connotation. The expression "Song of Songs" means "the greatest of all songs" (cf. the expression "King of kings" in Rev 17:14). It prepares us for a single song of outstanding quality.

Apart from the title, the Song is written entirely in verse. It is love poetry (see "Introduction to the Poetic and Wisdom Books"). The lines are short and rhythmic, and the language is rich in imagery and highly sensual. It deals more with feelings than with objective facts. For example, the song is not concerned with whether or not the woman addressed in 6:9 was really "perfect" and "unique" in any demonstrable way. The words were an expression of the young man's deep affection for her—no more and no less. The Song is a rhapsody of love, an outpouring of the words and feelings of people experiencing human love with its concomitant pains, pleasures and sexual impulses. It is a book for those who want to know or remember how God has honored the love between a husband and a wife.

There appear to be two leading characters: a country girl (called "the Shulammite" in 6:13) and a male shepherd (see 1:7; 6:3). Solomon is mentioned apart from the title (1:5; 3:7,9,11; 8:11–12), and there are a host of minor figures: mother, brothers, watchmen and women of Jerusalem.

The presence of such characters has led many commentators to conclude that the book is about a relationship between the girl and a shepherd, with Solomon as an intruder. Other commentators, however, find it difficult to see how Solomon could be featured so unfavorably in a book that was either written by him or dedicated to him. Also, many find it difficult to identify a clear story line and to decide which words to assign to Solomon and which to the shepherd-lover.

If the correct reading is that Solomon is an intruder, he likely wrote the book about a woman who had declined his marriage proposal. Given that he ultimately had 700 wives and 300 concubines (1Ki 11:3), such rejection was probably rare for Solomon. If he wrote later in his life, after increasing his harem so dramatically, the woman's rejection of Solomon in favor of her true love might well have inspired Solomon to write the Song as a reflection on the type of love that he longed for but no longer knew. If Solomon is not an intruder, then it is most likely that he presented himself both as the shepherd and as the king.

Because of problems like these some interpreters in recent years have suggested that the book is an anthology of love poems with common themes, rather than a tightly knit single drama. But such a division of the book into separate poems is unnecessary and unhelpful. Apart from the title, there are clear indications within the text itself that it is indeed a single work. A refrain occurs in almost identical form at three points in the Song (2:7; 3:5; 8:4). It is addressed to the women of Jerusalem, and its essence is this: "Don't try to force love. Let it take its natural course. The consummation will come at its proper time." This refrain creates movement and suspense. The couple experienced separation, hostility and interference, but the refrain anticipates that their relationship was nevertheless moving steadily toward consummation. At the end of the book there is indeed a sense of fulfillment as the couple, at last united and at ease together in public, walked arm in arm to the home of the parents, the place where their relationship had begun (8:5). Following this, some general, summarizing remarks are given about the nature of love (8:6–7). This is the climax of the Song, but not quite the end. After the climax a postscript appears (8:8–14) that quietly reviews some of the key elements of the work and draws it to a close.

Between the expressions of longing at the beginning and the consummation at the end there is a dream sequence (3:1; 5:2) in chapters 3–6. This central section records the girl's dreams about her wedding and the lovemaking that would follow. There is everything that we might expect here: erotic reveries, nightmares, fears of loss and deeply romantic experiences.

In many respects, the book is realistic about love. The author knew how hard it can be to wait for marriage. He knew about erotic dreams, meddling relatives and the struggle that occurs when a couple attempts to establish a relationship in the face of separation and hostility. He understood that humans no longer live in the Garden of Eden, but in a fallen world where love, too, has its pain.

But there is also idealism here. The overwhelming impression the book leaves with the reader is that love is a beautiful thing in which one may find deep satisfaction and contentment. The shepherd is portrayed as the archetypal lover, and the Song shows us a world in which he and a country girl may be as happy and fulfilled as the king upon his throne (8:11–12). In so doing the Song puts wealth and power in their place.

Concerns over the unconcealed sensuality of the Song have led many interpreters to regard it merely as an allegory of God's love for Israel or for the church (see "Introduction: Christ in Song of Songs"). The mention of Solomon in the title (1:1), however, links the book with Biblical Wisdom Literature, which focuses much on the common spheres of everyday human relationships. The book of Proverbs, in fact, uses language similar to that of the Song of Songs in talking about marital love (e.g., Pr 5:15–18). The beauty and worth of the sexual love that this book celebrates are rooted in the ordinances established when God created human beings, male and female, in his image (Ge 1:27; cf. 2:19–25). Sexual love is at the heart of God's ideal order for the world and for the human race.

Christ in Song of Songs

There has been a long tradition of relating this book to Christ by drawing analogies between the experiences of the two lovers and the experience of Christ and his church. In fact, the image of God as the husband and of his covenant people as his wife is also found in the Old Testament (e.g., Jer 2:2; Hos 2:14–20). Because Christ claims the church as his bride (cf. Eph 5:22–33), one legitimate application of Song of Songs is to realize that the love described in the book is in many ways similar to the love that Jesus has for the church (e.g., this is the predominant use of the Song of Songs in the Westminster Standards). At least three central dimensions instruct modern readers about the nature of this love: self-giving, desire and commitment. Jesus delights in us and gives himself to us in love. He desires us wholly for himself, and he feels deeply both the pain and pleasure of his relationship with us. Christ gave his very life for the church and even now devotes himself to her good as a loving husband. The church looks to Christ for protection and affection; she honors him for his wondrous care and seeks his glory every day. Both Christ and the church long for the day of their final union, the day of the great wedding feast at Christ's return (Rev 19:7,9).

Outline

I. Title (1:1)

The Song was associated with Solomon.

II. Mutual Praise and Longing (1:2—2:17)
- A. The Young Woman (1:2–4a)
- B. The Friends (1:4b)
- C. The Young Woman (1:4c–7)
- D. The Friends (1:8)
- E. The Young Man (1:9–10)
- F. The Friends (1:11)
- G. The Young Woman (1:12–14)
- H. The Young Man (1:15)
- I. The Young Woman (1:16)
- J. The Young Man (1:17)
- K. The Young Woman (2:1)
- L. The Young Man (2:2)
- M. The Young Woman (2:3–13)
- N. The Young Man (2:14–15)
- O. The Young Woman (2:16–17)

The woman and the man experienced the wonder of romantic love and expressed their feelings in praise of, and their longing for, each other.

III. The Bride's Dream (3:1—6:13) A. The Young Woman (3:1–11) B. The Young Man (4:1–15) C. The Young Woman (4:16) D. The Young Man (5:1a–b) E. The Friends (5:1c) F. The Young Woman (5:2–8) G. The Friends (5:9) H. The Young Woman (5:10–16) I. The Friends (6:1) J. The Young Woman (6:2–3) K. The Young Man (6:4–9) L. The Friends (6:10) M. The Young Man (6:11–12) N. The Friends (6:13a) O. The Young Man (6:13b)	*The woman dreamed of her young man and endured scenes of disappointment and pain, as well as the splendor of consummating her relationship with the one she loved.*
IV. More Mutual Praise and Longing (7:1—8:4) A. The Young Man (7:1–9a) B. The Young Woman (7:9b—8:4)	*The man and woman again expressed praise and longing for each other.*
V. Reminiscences to the Wedding (8:5–14) A. The Friends (8:5a) B. The Young Man (8:5b–7) C. The Friends (8:8–9) D. The Young Woman (8:10–12) E. The Young Man (8:13) F. The Young Woman (8:14)	*The man and woman expressed their joy and desire as events led up to their wedding.*

1 Solomon's Song of Songs.[a]

1:1 [a]1Ki 4:32

Beloved[a]

[2] Let him kiss me with the kisses of his mouth—
for your love[b] is more delightful than wine.
[3] Pleasing is the fragrance of your perfumes;[c]
your name[d] is like perfume poured out.
No wonder the maidens[e] love you!
[4] Take me away with you—let us hurry!
Let the king bring me into his chambers.[f]

1:2 [b]SS 4:10
1:3 [c]SS 4:10 [d]Ecc 7:1 [e]Ps 45:14
1:4 [f]Ps 45:15

Friends

We rejoice and delight in you[b];
we will praise your love more than wine.

a Primarily on the basis of the gender of the Hebrew pronouns used, male and female speakers are indicated in the margins by the captions *Lover* and *Beloved* respectively. The words of others are marked *Friends*. In some instances the divisions and their captions are debatable. b *4* The Hebrew is masculine singular.

■ **1:1** *Title.* The book begins with a title that provides an orientation to the time and setting within which it was written.

1:1 Solomon's. This expression can also be translated "for Solomon" (i.e., dedicated to Solomon). See "Introduction: Author."

■ **1:2—2:17** *Mutual Praise and Longing.* In this opening section of the book, the young man and woman expressed their love and longing for each other through mutual, lavish praise.

■ **1:2–4a** *The Young Woman.* The woman fantasized about the kisses of the man she loved. Third person expressions in verses 2 and 4 ("Let him kiss me . . . Let the king bring me") open and close the paragraph, which is otherwise in the second person ("your love . . . your name"). The girl oscillated between thinking about the absent young man and addressing him as though he were present.

1:4a Let the king bring me. Or "the king has brought me." This is the first of five locations in which the word "king" occurs (see also v. 12; 3:9,11; 7:5). Either the king was Solomon, who had tried unsuccessfully to win the girl's affections, or he was her young man, whom she romantically fantasized as her king. The paragraph ends as it began, with the girl referring to the absent young man in the third person (see note on vv. 2–4a). See *WCF* 10.1.

■ **1:4b** *The Friends.* The speakers were the "daughters of Jerusalem" (v. 5), who were apparently friends of the young woman. Here they agreed with her that the love of her young man was better than wine (v. 2).

■ **1:4c–7** *The Young Woman.* The girl in turn concurred with her friends but immediately expressed feelings of inadequacy.

Beloved

How right they are to adore you!

1:5
[g]SS 2:14; 4:3
[h]SS 2:7; 5:8; 5:16

5 Dark am I, yet lovely,[g]
O daughters of Jerusalem,[h]
dark like the tents of Kedar,
like the tent curtains of Solomon.[a]
6 Do not stare at me because I am dark,
because I am darkened by the sun.
My mother's sons were angry with me
and made me take care of the vineyards;[i]
my own vineyard I have neglected.

1:6
[i]Ps 69:8; SS 8:12

7 Tell me, you whom I love, where you graze your flock
and where you rest your sheep[j] at midday.
Why should I be like a veiled woman
beside the flocks of your friends?

1:7
[j]SS 3:1-4; Isa 13:20

Friends

1:8
[k]SS 5:9; 6:1

8 If you do not know, most beautiful of women,[k]
follow the tracks of the sheep
and graze your young goats
by the tents of the shepherds.

Lover

1:9
[l]2Ch 1:17

9 I liken you, my darling, to a mare
harnessed to one of the chariots[l] of Pharaoh.

1:10
[m]SS 5:13
[n]Isa 61:10

10 Your cheeks[m] are beautiful with earrings,
your neck with strings of jewels.[n]
11 We will make you earrings of gold,
studded with silver.

Beloved

1:12
[o]SS 4:11-14

12 While the king was at his table,
my perfume spread its fragrance.[o]
13 My lover is to me a sachet of myrrh
resting between my breasts.

1:14
[p]SS 4:13
[q]1Sa 23:29

14 My lover is to me a cluster of henna[p] blossoms
from the vineyards of En Gedi.[q]

[a] 5 Or *Salma*

1:5–6 The young woman, though beautiful, was concerned about her complexion: "Dark am I" (v. 5). She was deeply bronzed by the sun because her brothers compelled her to work in the vineyards. As a result, she had not, in her opinion, cared well for her "own vineyard" (v. 6); that is, her body.

1:5 tents of Kedar. Kedar is a general term for the Bedouin tribes that inhabited the desert fringe to the east of Israel. The woman compared herself with their tents because they were made of dark goat's hair.

1:7 where you graze your flock. The young man is portrayed as a shepherd. The girl could not endure being apart from him and wanted to know where he was so that she could go directly to him. **veiled woman.** The girl did not want to be mistaken for a prostitute.

■ **1:8** *The Friends.* The daughters of Jerusalem encouraged their friend to go out as a shepherdess and to find her young man for whom she so desperately longed.

1:8 most beautiful of women. Just as the man was portrayed as handsome (v. 16), the girl was described as supremely beautiful. The two were idealized as a striking couple.

■ **1:9–10** *The Young Man.* The young man assured the young woman that he considered her beautiful. Despite the hard work imposed on her, she had no reason for apprehension with regard to her appearance (see vv. 5,6).

1:9 a mare harnessed to one of the chariots of Pharaoh. Solomon began his reign by cementing a marriage alliance with Pharaoh's household (1Ki 3:1), and he traded in horses from Egypt (1Ki 10:28). We can assume that Pharaoh's chariots, with their twin stallions, were well known and much admired in Israel. But what is envisaged here would have been exceptional: a bejeweled mare among the stallions—a cause for wonder and excitement.

■ **1:11** *The Friends.* Contrary to the NIV, this verse should probably be designated for the daughters of Jerusalem, whose role was similar to that of the chorus in a classical Greek drama.

1:11 We. See verse 4. The friends, echoing the maiden's praise of her young man, responded similarly to his praise of her. It is also possible, although less likely, that the young man spoke these words, as he had those of the previous two verses, using courtly language.

■ **1:12–14** *The Young Woman.* The scene changed to that of the couple spending time alone in the woods.

1:12 the king. The royal language is continued. See the previous three lines and the note on verse 4a. **at his table.** The Hebrew here is an unusual expression, meaning literally, "in his surroundings." If the king was again the young man, the environs in view highlighted the splendors of nature, the grass and trees (vv. 15–17). **my perfume.** The girl was overwhelmed by the aromas of her fantasy. She spoke of the perfume of the young man as being "between [her] breasts" (v. 13).

1:14 henna blossoms. A small shrub with aromatic blossoms. The young woman was captivated by the thought of the young man's distinctive scent, which she considered an adornment. **En Gedi.** A lush oasis halfway down the slope of the western shore of the Dead Sea.

Lover

15 How beautiful[r] you are, my darling!
Oh, how beautiful!
Your eyes are doves.[s]

Beloved

16 How handsome you are, my lover!
Oh, how charming!
And our bed is verdant.

Lover

17 The beams of our house are cedars;[t]
our rafters are firs.

Beloved[a]

2

I am a rose[b][u] of Sharon,[v]
a lily[w] of the valleys.

Lover

2 Like a lily among thorns
is my darling among the maidens.

Beloved

3 Like an apple tree among the trees of the forest
is my lover[x] among the young men.
I delight[y] to sit in his shade,
and his fruit is sweet to my taste.[z]
4 He has taken me to the banquet hall,[a]
and his banner[b] over me is love.
5 Strengthen me with raisins,
refresh me with apples,[c]
for I am faint with love.[d]
6 His left arm is under my head,
and his right arm embraces me.[e]
7 Daughters of Jerusalem, I charge you[f]
by the gazelles and by the does of the field:
Do not arouse or awaken love
until it so desires.[g]

a *1* Or *Lover* b *1* Possibly a member of the crocus family

1:15 [r]SS 4:7 [s]SS 2:14; 4:1; 5:2, 12; 6:9
1:17 [t]1Ki 6:9
2:1 [u]Isa 35:1 [v]S 1Ch 27:29 [w]SS 5:13; Hos 14:5
2:3 [x]SS 1:14 [y]SS 1:4 [z]SS 4:16
2:4 [a]Est 1:11 [b]Nu 1:52
2:5 [c]SS 7:8 [d]SS 5:8
2:6 [e]SS 8:3
2:7 [f]SS 5:8 [g]SS 3:5; 8:4

■ **1:15** *The Young Man.* The young man responded with wonder at his beloved's eyes. With the rest of the face probably concealed, this was the feature that drew and held his admiring gaze.
1:15 Your eyes are doves. The point of the comparison is unclear. Perhaps the reference was to the gentleness of her look. The girl indirectly returned this compliment in 5:12.
■ **1:16** *The Young Woman.* The girl complimented the young man for his charm and beauty, but her attention expanded to the larger picture of the scene surrounding them as well.
1:16 our bed. The image is of their marriage bed. **verdant.** Grassy and green. Developing the shepherd image even further, the young woman fantasized lying with the young man on soft and lush green grass. See *WCF* 24.
■ **1:17** *The Young Man.* In light of the alternation between the woman and the man in this section, it may be best to take this verse as the young man's expansion of the woman's description of their bedroom.
1:17 beams . . . are cedars . . . rafters are firs. The cedars and firs of the forests surrounding the grazing lands formed the beams and rafters of the shepherd's grand villa.
■ **2:1** *The Young Woman.* The woman described herself in terms of lush flora, an indication of her beauty and delicacy.
2:1 rose. The Hebrew indicates a plant of the bulb family (see NIV text note)—perhaps the white narcissus, which is plentiful in season in the region of Sharon. **Sharon.** The plain extending south from Mount Carmel along the Mediterranean coastline. The girl modestly compared herself to some familiar wildflowers.
■ **2:2** *The Young Man.* In contrast to all other maidens, the young woman stood out in his estimation as a lovely flower among thorns. His love for her eliminated any fascination with other women.
■ **2:3–13** *The Young Woman.* The maiden launched into an extended and elaborate depiction. First she likened herself to delicate flowers (v. 3), as he had in verse 2; then she compared him to trees whose shade and fruit she relished.
2:4 banquet hall. The actual setting for this exchange between the couple was outdoors (see note on 1:12). Their "house" to this point had been the forest (1:16–17). Now they moved to a different "house"—the young man's vineyard, his "house" of wine. The expression continues the royal imagery of 1:4 and 12 and the comparison between love and wine in 1:2. **his banner.** Banners commonly adorned royal banquet halls, but this banquet hall had only one banner, love. Love was also the only "wine" that would be imbibed at the banquet.
2:5 raisins . . . apples. Raisins or "raisin cakes" are associated elsewhere in the Old Testament with religious rites, sometimes even in a pagan context (2Sa 6:19; Isa 16:7; Hos 3:1). This has led some commentators to conjecture that the Song of Songs may have originated as the script of a pagan fertility rite involving ritual sex (cf. Hos 4:11–14). But the lovemaking in the Song has no clear religious dimension. The raisins spoken of here, like the apples, were aphrodisiacs. The girl called for these fruits as a flirtation in her fantasized lovemaking.

8 Listen! My lover!
Look! Here he comes,
leaping across the mountains,
bounding over the hills.[h]

2:8 [h]ver 17; SS 8:14

9 My lover is like a gazelle[i] or a young stag.[j]
Look! There he stands behind our wall,
gazing through the windows,
peering through the lattice.

2:9 [i]2Sa 2:18 [j]ver 17; SS 8:14

10 My lover spoke and said to me,
"Arise, my darling,
my beautiful one, and come with me.
11 See! The winter is past;
the rains are over and gone.
12 Flowers appear on the earth;
the season of singing has come,
the cooing of doves
is heard in our land.
13 The fig tree forms its early fruit;[k]
the blossoming[l] vines spread their fragrance.
Arise, come, my darling;
my beautiful one, come with me."

2:13 [k]Isa 28:4; Jer 24:2; Hos 9:10; Mic 7:1; Na 3:12 [l]SS 7:12

Lover

14 My dove[m] in the clefts of the rock,
in the hiding places on the mountainside,
show me your face,
let me hear your voice;
for your voice is sweet,
and your face is lovely.[n]
15 Catch for us the foxes,[o]
the little foxes
that ruin the vineyards,[p]
our vineyards that are in bloom.[q]

2:14 [m]Ge 8:8; SS 1:15 [n]SS 1:5; 8:13

2:15 [o]Jdg 15:4 [p]SS 1:6 [q]SS 7:12

Beloved

16 My lover is mine and I am his;[r]
he browses among the lilies.[s]
17 Until the day breaks
and the shadows flee,[t]
turn, my lover,[u]
and be like a gazelle
or like a young stag[v]
on the rugged hills.[a][w]

2:16 [r]SS 7:10 [s]SS 4:5; 6:3

2:17 [t]SS 4:6 [u]SS 1:14 [v]ver 9 [w]ver 8

[a] 17 Or *the hills of Bether*

2:8–9 The shepherd is pictured as a gazelle or a young stag on the hills (vv. 8–9,17). In all likelihood this image refers not only to the beauty of the animals, but to their potency and agility as well. After her brief address to the daughters of Jerusalem (v. 7), the girl returned to her musings.

■ **2:14–15** *The Young Man.* Continuing the images of lovely natural settings, the man expressed his desire metaphorically to see the woman's face and to hear her voice.

2:15 the little foxes that ruin the vineyards. The foxes are the one negative element in the otherwise idyllic spring setting of verses 10–15. The young woman had already used the vineyard as a metaphor for her body (1:6), and the vineyard imagery may also suggest that their bodies were ready for lovemaking. It is possible for the Hebrew to be translated, "May the foxes be caught . . ." If this is correct, then the whole verse was a wish by the couple that nothing be allowed to inerfere with or spoil their lovemaking.

■ **2:16–17** *The Young Woman.* The maiden described metaphorically how her young man would enjoy physically expressing his love for her.

2:16 he browses among the lilies. In view of the context, this is most likely a metaphor for lovemaking (see v. 15; 6:2), though at this point in the narrative it is still merely a fantasy.

2:17 Until the day breaks and the shadows flee. Traditionally this has been coupled with what follows, but it may make better sense if it is read with verse 16. The woman or the couple fantasized that the virile young man made love the entire night, all the while realizing that when day broke the couple would have to part. The young man's return to the hills marks the end of the unit that opened in verse 8. See note on 2:8–17. **like a gazelle . . . young stag on . . . hills.** When he was with the woman, the young man was like these animals as they ambled about the varied terrain of the mountainside with both strength and grace.

■ **3:1—6:13** *The Bride's Dream.* In this central section the woman reported her dreams about her wedding and the lovemaking that would follow. A more explicit indication of her dream state is given in 5:2–3. It is unclear where this dream sequence begins and ends, but it likely includes all of chapters 3–6.

3 All night long on my bed
I looked[x] for the one my heart loves;
I looked for him but did not find him.
2 I will get up now and go about the city,
through its streets and squares;
I will search for the one my heart loves.
So I looked for him but did not find him.
3 The watchmen found me
as they made their rounds in the city.[y]
"Have you seen the one my heart loves?"
4 Scarcely had I passed them
when I found the one my heart loves.
I held him and would not let him go
till I had brought him to my mother's house,[z]
to the room of the one who conceived me.[a]
5 Daughters of Jerusalem, I charge you[b]
by the gazelles and by the does of the field:
Do not arouse or awaken love
until it so desires.[c]

6 Who is this coming up from the desert[d]
like a column of smoke,
perfumed with myrrh[e] and incense
made from all the spices[f] of the merchant?
7 Look! It is Solomon's carriage,
escorted by sixty warriors,[g]
the noblest of Israel,
8 all of them wearing the sword,
all experienced in battle,
each with his sword at his side,
prepared for the terrors of the night.[h]
9 King Solomon made for himself the carriage;
he made it of wood from Lebanon.
10 Its posts he made of silver,
its base of gold.
Its seat was upholstered with purple,
its interior lovingly inlaid
by[a] the daughters of Jerusalem.
11 Come out, you daughters of Zion,[i]
and look at King Solomon wearing the crown,
the crown with which his mother crowned him
on the day of his wedding,
the day his heart rejoiced.[j]

a *10* *Or its inlaid interior a gift of love / from*

3:1 [x]SS 5:6; Isa 26:9
3:3 [y]SS 5:7
3:4 [z]SS 8:2 [a]SS 6:9
3:5 [b]SS 2:7 [c]SS 8:4
3:6 [d]SS 8:5 [e]SS 1:13; 4:6,14 [f]Ex 30:34
3:7 [g]1Sa 8:11
3:8 [h]Job 15:22; Ps 91:5
3:11 [i]Isa 4:4 [j]Isa 62:5

■**3:1–11** *The Young Woman.* The dream sequence begins with the woman recalling her dreams.
3:1 All night long on my bed. The girl was not yet with the young man but was alone on her bed, envisioning various encounters with him.
3:2–4 This search either followed the girl's night of dreaming or was itself one of her dreams. The presence of the watchmen patrolling the city streets suggests that it was nighttime and, therefore, that she was actually asleep. The parallel in 5:2–8 is certainly a dream, as indicated by 5:2. Both have a nightmarish quality, the one in chapter 5 more obviously than this one.
3:4 my mother's house. This was presumably where the unmarried girl lay sleeping (v. 1). In her dream she had brought the young man home. See *WLC* 175.
3:5 This second occurrence of the refrain confirms that the lovemaking at this stage was imaginary. The consummation remained future (see note on 2:7).
3:6–11 Placed as it is between the two indications that the girl was at home in bed (3:1; 5:2), this wedding scene may be part of her dream. If the shepherd is here idealized as Solomon, then her nightmare gave way to idyllic fantasy. She envisaged her own wedding day, but in her fancy it was transformed into a grand, royal occasion, and her shepherd became a monarch—even Solomon himself (cf. 1:4,12; 2:4)!
3:8 prepared for the terrors of the night. Probably this refers to protection against marauders who might attempt to interfere with the wedding procession, since weddings were normally celebrated at nightfall. **of the night.** Or literally, "by the night." The same expression is echoed in 3:1: "All night long on my bed" or literally, "upon my bed by night." This splendid vision banished the girl's own "terrors of the night," at least temporarily (see note on vv. 2–4).
3:11 Zion. An alternative name for Jerusalem (e.g., Isa 40:9). **the crown.** At his coronation an Israelite king was crowned by the high priest as God's representative (2Ki 11:9–12). The crown in view here is probably a celebratory one (cf. Job 19:9). **his mother.** The family structure reflected in the Song appears to be matriarchal (1:6; 3:4; 6:9; 8:1–2,5). There is no reference to a father, and within the relationship between the couple there appears to be mutuality. **the day of his wedding.** The real Solomon in fact had many weddings (1Ki 11:3; cf. 6:8). Either the day in view here is a romantic ideal (see note on vv. 6–11) or the portrayal is of the current wedding.

Lover

4

How beautiful you are, my darling!
Oh, how beautiful!
Your eyes behind your veil are doves.[k]
Your hair is like a flock of goats
descending from Mount Gilead.[l]
2 Your teeth are like a flock of sheep just shorn,
coming up from the washing.
Each has its twin;
not one of them is alone.[m]
3 Your lips are like a scarlet ribbon;
your mouth[n] is lovely.
Your temples behind your veil
are like the halves of a pomegranate.[o]
4 Your neck is like the tower[p] of David,
built with elegance[a];
on it hang a thousand shields,[q]
all of them shields of warriors.
5 Your two breasts[r] are like two fawns,
like twin fawns of a gazelle[s]
that browse among the lilies.[t]
6 Until the day breaks
and the shadows flee,[u]
I will go to the mountain of myrrh[v]
and to the hill of incense.
7 All beautiful[w] you are, my darling;
there is no flaw in you.

8 Come with me from Lebanon, my bride,[x]
come with me from Lebanon.
Descend from the crest of Amana,
from the top of Senir,[y] the summit of Hermon,[z]
from the lions' dens
and the mountain haunts of the leopards.
9 You have stolen my heart, my sister, my bride;
you have stolen my heart
with one glance of your eyes,
with one jewel of your necklace.[a]
10 How delightful[b] is your love[c], my sister, my bride!
How much more pleasing is your love than wine,
and the fragrance of your perfume than any spice!
11 Your lips drop sweetness as the honeycomb, my bride;
milk and honey are under your tongue.[d]
The fragrance of your garments is like that of Lebanon.[e]
12 You are a garden locked up, my sister, my bride;
you are a spring enclosed, a sealed fountain.[f]
13 Your plants are an orchard of pomegranates[g]
with choice fruits,

4:1 [k]SS 1:15; 5:12 [l]SS 6:5; Mic 7:14
4:2 [m]SS 6:6
4:3 [n]SS 5:16 [o]SS 6:7
4:4 [p]SS 7:4 [q]Eze 27:10
4:5 [r]SS 7:3 [s]Pr 5:19 [t]SS 2:16; 6:2-3
4:6 [u]SS 2:17 [v]ver 14
4:7 [w]SS 1:15
4:8 [x]SS 5:1 [y]Dt 3:9 [z]1Ch 5:23
4:9 [a]Ge 41:42
4:10 [b]SS 7:6 [c]SS 1:2
4:11 [d]Ps 19:10; SS 5:1 [e]Hos 14:6
4:12 [f]Pr 5:15-18
4:13 [g]SS 6:11; 7:12

[a] *4* The meaning of the Hebrew for this word is uncertain.

■ **4:1–15** *The Young Man.* In this unit the young man praised his beloved (vv. 1–15). She responded with an invitation (v. 16), which he accepted (5:1).
4:1 Mount Gilead. The high plateau to the east of the Jordan River.
4:4 the tower of David. The identity of this tower is unknown. It does not refer to the present-day tower by that name that is just inside the Jaffa Gate in Jerusalem, for it dates from no earlier than the time of Herod the Great. The girl's neck was adorned with jewelry, much as the famous tower was adorned with shields.
4:6 Until the day breaks. Again, the time was approaching when the couple must part (see note on 2:17). **the mountain of myrrh . . . the hill of incense.** Incense (or "frankincense"), like myrrh, was an imported aromatic spice (cf. Mt 2:11). If a particular hill was intended, its location is unknown. Despite the exotic language, the reference was probably to the local hill country, which was fragrant with spring blossoms (cf. 1:13,17).
4:8 Lebanon . . . Amana . . . Senir . . . Hermon. These are all sites in the remote north of Canaan. It is doubtful whether one should think of the woman as actually living on the summit of Mount Hermon. Rather, the place-names are probably symbols of the inaccessibility that the wooing was meant to overcome. **my bride.** That is, "my bride-to-be."
4:9 my sister. In literature from the ancient Near East, "sister" was commonly used as a term of endearment for wives. Here, however, the sister was a bride-to-be who had not yet entered into a sexual relationship with the young man (see v. 12 and its note).
4:10 more pleasing . . . than wine. The compliment of 1:2 was returned. See *WLC* 168,169.
4:12 a garden locked . . . a spring enclosed. These are images of virginity. **spring . . . fountain.** The young man yearned for her sexually as a thirsty traveler longs for refreshing water (Pr 5:15–20).

with henna[h] and nard,
14 nard and saffron,
calamus and cinnamon,[i]
with every kind of incense tree,
with myrrh[j] and aloes
and all the finest spices.[k]
15 You are[a] a garden fountain,
a well of flowing water
streaming down from Lebanon.

Beloved

16 Awake, north wind,
and come, south wind!
Blow on my garden,
that its fragrance may spread abroad.
Let my lover come into his garden
and taste its choice fruits.[l]

Lover

5

I have come into my garden, my sister, my bride;[m]
I have gathered my myrrh with my spice.
I have eaten my honeycomb and my honey;
I have drunk my wine and my milk.[n]

Friends

Eat, O friends, and drink;
drink your fill, O lovers.

Beloved

2 I slept but my heart was awake.
Listen! My lover is knocking:
"Open to me, my sister, my darling,
my dove, my flawless[o] one.[p]
My head is drenched with dew,
my hair with the dampness of the night."
3 I have taken off my robe—
must I put it on again?
I have washed my feet—
must I soil them again?
4 My lover thrust his hand through the latch-opening;
my heart began to pound for him.
5 I arose to open for my lover,
and my hands dripped with myrrh,[q]
my fingers with flowing myrrh,

4:13 [h]SS 1:14
4:14 [i]Ex 30:23 [j]SS 3:6 [k]SS 1:12
4:16 [l]SS 2:3; 5:1
5:1 [m]SS 4:8 [n]SS 4:11; Isa 55:1
5:2 [o]SS 4:7 [p]SS 6:9
5:5 [q]ver 13

[a] *15* Or *I am* (spoken by the *Beloved*)

4:13–14 Your plants. The image of the locked garden is further developed (see note on 4:12). "Plants" alludes to the anticipated delights of her lovemaking.
4:15 flowing water streaming down. The young man desired that his beloved "no longer [be] a sealed fountain" (see v. 12 and its note). This is an implicit invitation to sexual surrender.
■ **4:16** *The Young Woman.* The woman expressed intense yearning for the man she was to marry.
4:16 Let my lover come into his garden. The young woman unlocked the "garden" of her virginity and invited him to enter (see note on v. 12).
5:1–6 See *WLC* 175.
■ **5:1a–b** *The Young Man.* The man delighted to accept the young woman's invitation.
5:1a–b I have come into my garden. The young man indicated his acceptance of his beloved's invitation. **my sister, my bride.** See notes on 4:8 and 9.
■ **5:1c** *The Friends.* The friends of the woman join with the couple in extolling the delights of their union.
5:1c Eat . . . drink . . . O lovers. The speakers are not specified, but they echoed the language used by the young man himself in the previous two lines ("I have eaten . . . I have drunk"). Eating and drinking are images of lovemaking. The girl dreamed of the time when her relationship with her beloved would not only be consummated, but also approved by family and friends.
■ **5:2–8** *The Young Woman.* The woman's dream took a turn toward a horrible scenario. Her man disappeared, and she searched frantically for him in the city's night streets.
5:2–4 See *WCF* 17.3; 18.4; *WLC* 81.
5:2 slept . . . awake. See notes on 3:1 and 2–4.
5:5 flowing myrrh. This is myrrh in its virgin, liquid state, exactly as it flows from the tree, and therefore a rare and precious substance (cf. Ex 30:23). It is unclear from the Hebrew whether the girl had applied the myrrh liberally to herself before going to the door or whether the disappointed young man had left it on the door latch as a token of his love. The repetition of the exact expression in verse 13 marginally favors the latter.

on the handles of the lock.
6 I opened for my lover,[r]
but my lover had left; he was gone.[s]
My heart sank at his departure.[a]
I looked[t] for him but did not find him.
I called him but he did not answer.
7 The watchmen found me
as they made their rounds in the city.[u]
They beat me, they bruised me;
they took away my cloak,
those watchmen of the walls!
8 O daughters of Jerusalem, I charge you[v]—
if you find my lover,
what will you tell him?
Tell him I am faint with love.[w]

Friends

9 How is your beloved better than others,
most beautiful of women?[x]
How is your beloved better than others,
that you charge us so?

Beloved

10 My lover is radiant and ruddy,
outstanding among ten thousand.[y]
11 His head is purest gold;
his hair is wavy
and black as a raven.
12 His eyes are like doves[z]
by the water streams,
washed in milk,[a]
mounted like jewels.
13 His cheeks[b] are like beds of spice[c]
yielding perfume.
His lips are like lilies[d]
dripping with myrrh.
14 His arms are rods of gold
set with chrysolite.
His body is like polished ivory
decorated with sapphires.[b][e]
15 His legs are pillars of marble
set on bases of pure gold.
His appearance is like Lebanon,[f]
choice as its cedars.
16 His mouth[g] is sweetness itself;
he is altogether lovely.
This is my lover,[h] this my friend,
O daughters of Jerusalem.[i]

5:6 [r]SS 6:1 [s]SS 6:2 [t]SS 3:1
5:7 [u]SS 3:3
5:8 [v]SS 2:7; 3:5 [w]SS 2:5
5:9 [x]SS 1:8; 6:1
5:10 [y]Ps 45:2
5:12 [z]SS 1:15; 4:1 [a]Ge 49:12
5:13 [b]SS 1:10 [c]SS 6:2 [d]SS 2:1
5:14 [e]Job 28:6
5:15 [f]1Ki 4:33; SS 7:4
5:16 [g]SS 4:3 [h]SS 7:9 [i]SS 1:5

[a] *6* Or *heart had gone out to him when he spoke* [b] *14* Or *lapis lazuli*

5:6 my lover had left. At this point the dream degenerated into a nightmare as the girl's fears mounted up to confront her. Her first fear was that of losing him. **at his departure.** The context favors this translation rather than the alternative in the NIV text note, although the latter reflects the more common usage of the Hebrew verb involved. See *WCF* 17.3; 18.4; *WLC* 81.

5:7 beat me . . . bruised me . . . took away my cloak. The nightmare escalated as the girl envisioned herself being assaulted, perhaps raped (see note on v. 6).

5:8 Tell him. The woman called for her friends to go after the man and tell him that she longed for him.

■ **5:9** *The Friends.* The friends wondered what was so special about this man, and the woman answered with remarkable praise of him.

■ **5:10–16** *The Young Woman.* The girl responded to the implied devaluation of the young man in the previous verse by praising him in elaborate terms.

5:12 His eyes are like doves. The compliment of 1:15 and 4:1 was returned (see note on 1:15). The contrast with "hair . . . black as a raven" in the previous line is striking. Her description suggests that he was characterized by both strength and gentleness. **washed in milk.** This probably refers to the whites of the eyes.

5:13 dripping with myrrh. Literally, "dripping with flowing myrrh." See note on verse 5.

5:14 chrysolite. The precise type of precious stone referred to by the Hebrew word is unknown, but the association with gold here recalls Exodus 28:20, where the same type of stone was set in gold on the breastpiece worn by the high priest.

5:16 my lover . . . my friend. The male-female relationship en-

Friends

6

Where has your lover[j] gone,
most beautiful of women?[k]
Which way did your lover turn,
that we may look for him with you?

Beloved

2 My lover has gone[l] down to his garden,[m]
to the beds of spices,[n]
to browse in the gardens
and to gather lilies.
3 I am my lover's and my lover is mine;[o]
he browses among the lilies.[p]

Lover

4 You are beautiful, my darling, as Tirzah,[q]
lovely as Jerusalem,[r]
majestic as troops with banners.[s]
5 Turn your eyes from me;
they overwhelm me.
Your hair is like a flock of goats
descending from Gilead.[t]
6 Your teeth are like a flock of sheep
coming up from the washing.
Each has its twin,
not one of them is alone.[u]
7 Your temples behind your veil[v]
are like the halves of a pomegranate.[w]
8 Sixty queens[x] there may be,
and eighty concubines,[y]
and virgins beyond number;
9 but my dove,[z] my perfect one,[a] is unique,
the only daughter of her mother,
the favorite of the one who bore her.[b]
The maidens saw her and called her blessed;
the queens and concubines praised her.

Friends

10 Who is this that appears like the dawn,
fair as the moon, bright as the sun,
majestic as the stars in procession?

6:1 [j]SS 5:6 [k]SS 1:8
6:2 [l]SS 5:6 [m]SS 4:12 [n]SS 5:13
6:3 [o]SS 7:10 [p]SS 2:16
6:4 [q]Jos 12:24 [r]Ps 48:2; 50:2 [s]ver 10
6:5 [t]SS 4:1
6:6 [u]SS 4:2
6:7 [v]Ge 24:65 [w]SS 4:3
6:8 [x]Ps 45:9 [y]Ge 22:24
6:9 [z]SS 1:15 [a]SS 5:2 [b]SS 3:4

---

visaged in the Song is broader than lovemaking, although lovemaking is central to it. It involves companionship as well.

■ **6:1** *The Friends.* The friends were inspired by the woman's praise of the young man and asked her to tell them where they should look for him (cf. 5:9). In light of the young woman's reaction (see vv. 2–3) it is possible that they wanted to search for him for themselves, rather than for her.

■ **6:2–3** *The Young Woman.* The language of these two verses is borrowed from two earlier passages dealing with imagined encounters (2:16; 5:1). Most likely because she suspected their motives (see note on v. 1), the girl in effect rejected the offer of the women of Jerusalem to help her search for her young man, and she returned to musing about her times of intimacy with him.

■ **6:4–9** *The Young Man.* The young man broke into his own picturesque praise of his bride-to-be.

6:4 Tirzah. This city was about six miles northeast of Shechem, situated in an area of great natural beauty. It was the capital of the breakaway northern kingdom for approximately 50 years following Solomon's death and continued to be a place of political intrigue until its destruction in the seventh century B.C. (1Ki 14:17; 15:21; 16:8–18; 2Ki 15:14–16). The positive reference to Tirzah here, particularly in parallel with Jerusalem, lends support to the traditional view that the Song originated during the time of Solomon, before the division of the northern and southern kingdoms. See "Introduction: Author."

6:5 Gilead. See note on 4:1.

6:8 This clearly opens a section that is concluded (in v. 9) by the second reference to queens and concubines. In the man's eyes, the girl was more beautiful than all the women of Solomon's harem (see 8:11–12 and their notes). **Sixty . . . eighty.** At its height, Solomon's harem included many more wives and concubines than this (1Ki 11:13). There is a suggestion of its potential for future growth in the expression "virgins beyond number." **concubines.** In Old Testament times, a concubine was not an illicit or casual partner; she was a wife, albeit of secondary status (Ge 25:6; 36:12; Jdg 20:4).

6:9 my dove, my perfect one. These words are an exact repetition in the Hebrew of "my dove, my flawless one" (5:2). In her dreams the girl returned again and again to her beloved's terms of endearment. **the only daughter of her mother.** The close relationship between the daughter and her mother is apparent throughout the book (see note on 3:11), but there is no sign of possessiveness on the mother's part.

■ **6:10** *The Friends.* The young woman was being praised here. These may be the "queens" and "concubines" mentioned in verse 9.

6:10 dawn . . . moon . . . sun. The young woman was described here as a virtual goddess, a "Queen of Heaven" (Jer 7:18). **majestic as the stars in procession?** The meaning of the Hebrew is uncertain, but this is an exact repetition of the last line of verse 4. The praise echoes that of her young man and rounds off the unit (vv. 4–10).

Lover

6:11 [c]SS 7:12

[11]I went down to the grove of nut trees
to look at the new growth in the valley,
to see if the vines had budded
or the pomegranates were in bloom.[c]
[12]Before I realized it,
my desire set me among the royal chariots of my people.[a]

Friends

[13]Come back, come back, O Shulammite;
come back, come back, that we may gaze on you!

Lover

6:13 [d]Ex 15:20
7:1 [e]Ps 45:13

Why would you gaze on the Shulammite
as on the dance[d] of Mahanaim?

7

How beautiful your sandaled feet,
O prince's[e] daughter!
Your graceful legs are like jewels,
the work of a craftsman's hands.
[2]Your navel is a rounded goblet
that never lacks blended wine.
Your waist is a mound of wheat
encircled by lilies.

7:3 [f]SS 4:5
7:4 [g]Ps 144:12; SS 4:4 [h]Nu 21:26 [i]SS 5:15
7:5 [j]Isa 35:2
7:6 [k]SS 1:15 [l]SS 4:10
7:7 [m]SS 4:5

[3]Your breasts[f] are like two fawns,
twins of a gazelle.
[4]Your neck is like an ivory tower.[g]
Your eyes are the pools of Heshbon[h]
by the gate of Bath Rabbim.
Your nose is like the tower of Lebanon[i]
looking toward Damascus.
[5]Your head crowns you like Mount Carmel.[j]
Your hair is like royal tapestry;
the king is held captive by its tresses.
[6]How beautiful[k] you are and how pleasing,
O love, with your delights![l]
[7]Your stature is like that of the palm,
and your breasts[m] like clusters of fruit.
[8]I said, "I will climb the palm tree;
I will take hold of its fruit."

[a] *12* Or *among the chariots of Amminadab*; or *among the chariots of the people of the prince*

■ **6:11–12** *The Young Man.* As the NIV text note indicates (v. 12), the Hebrew is obscure. At the very least the verse indicates that the girl was still fantasizing (whether awake or asleep) that she was a princess and that he was a prince or a king. See note on 3:6–11.

■ **6:13a** *The Friends.* These unnamed speakers were male, as indicated by the response of the young man in verse 13b: "Why would you [masculine plural] gaze . . . ?" They were possibly the watchmen of 5:7 from whom she had presumably fled. This would explain the suggestions of lust in their call. If the watchmen are in view here, the young woman was still dreaming. The nightmarish quality of her dream returned just before it was dispelled by the timely appearance of the young man.

■ **6:13b** *The Young Man.* In effect, the young man rebuked the men for lusting after his bride-to-be.

6:13b Shulammite. This probably refers to the girl's hometown: Shulam (or Shulem). Its location is unknown. **Mahanaim?** Literally, "two camps." This is the name of a town east of the Jordan River (Ge 32:2). The nature of the "dance of Mahanaim" is unknown, but the repetition of the word "gaze" suggests that the girl's honor would have been compromised had she performed it and that this is why the young man intervened as he did.

■ **7:1—8:4** *More Mutual Praise and Longing.* With the dream sequence ended, the man and woman praised and longed for each other again.

■ **7:1–9a** *The Young Man.* The man praised the young woman first.

7:1 prince's daughter! "Prince's" here is the same word that the NIV renders adverbially as "royal" in 6:12. There the girl imagined herself to be a princess; here the young man addressed her as such. She was in fact a country maiden (1:5–6).

7:4 Heshbon. A city east of the Jordan River, opposite Jerusalem, that had been captured by the Israelites in the time of Moses (Nu 21:25–26). Excavations have revealed large reservoirs near the city, perhaps the pools mentioned here. **gate of Bath Rabbim.** Or "the gate, Bath Rabbim." The Hebrew suggests that Bath Rabbim ("daughter of many") is the name of the gate, possibly one of the gates of Heshbon. **tower of Lebanon.** The identity of this tower is unknown. The great height suggested by looking toward or over Damascus has led some to take it as referring to the Lebanon mountain range (v. 5).

7:5 like Mount Carmel. Literally, "like Carmel." There are two places with this name in the Old Testament. One is a location in the relatively arid south, in the hills west of the Dead Sea (1Sa 15:12). The other, located in the lush north, is the famous mountain upon which Elijah confronted the prophets of Baal (1Ki 18). The connotations of beauty imply that the latter is in view here. It is located on the Mediterranean coast, west of the Sea of Galilee. **the king.** The Hebrew lacks the article and may be read as indefinite; i.e., "a king." The young man was probably fancying himself as a king, entranced by the beauty of his princess (v. 1; cf. 1:4,12; 6:12).

May your breasts be like the clusters of the vine,
the fragrance of your breath like apples,[n]
9 and your mouth like the best wine.

Beloved

May the wine go straight to my lover,[o]
flowing gently over lips and teeth.[a]
10 I belong to my lover,
and his desire[p] is for me.[q]
11 Come, my lover, let us go to the countryside,
let us spend the night in the villages.[b]
12 Let us go early to the vineyards[r]
to see if the vines have budded,[s]
if their blossoms[t] have opened,
and if the pomegranates[u] are in bloom[v]—
there I will give you my love.
13 The mandrakes[w] send out their fragrance,
and at our door is every delicacy,
both new and old,
that I have stored up for you, my lover.[x]

8 If only you were to me like a brother,
who was nursed at my mother's breasts!
Then, if I found you outside,
I would kiss you,
and no one would despise me.
2 I would lead you
and bring you to my mother's house[y]—
she who has taught me.
I would give you spiced wine to drink,
the nectar of my pomegranates.
3 His left arm is under my head
and his right arm embraces me.[z]
4 Daughters of Jerusalem, I charge you:
Do not arouse or awaken love
until it so desires.[a]

Friends

5 Who is this coming up from the desert[b]
leaning on her lover?

7:8 [n]SS 2:5
7:9 [o]SS 5:16
7:10 [p]Ps 45:11 [q]SS 2:16; 6:3
7:12 [r]SS 1:6 [s]SS 2:15 [t]SS 2:13 [u]SS 4:13 [v]SS 6:11
7:13 [w]Ge 30:14 [x]SS 4:16
8:2 [y]SS 3:4
8:3 [z]SS 2:6
8:4 [a]SS 2:7; 3:5
8:5 [b]SS 3:6

a 9 Septuagint, Aquila, Vulgate and Syriac; Hebrew *lips of sleepers* b 11 Or *henna bushes*

7:8 I will climb . . . take hold. These are images of lovemaking (v. 7; cf. 5:1). **fragrance . . . best wine.** Once again the tastes and smells of lovemaking captivated the speaker.
■ **7:9b—8:4** *The Young Woman.* The woman responded in kind to the young man's praise.
7:9b–13 Here, as in 4:16—5:1, the girl responded to the young man's wooing with glad surrender.
7:13 mandrakes. This plant, with its purple flowers and orange, tomato-like fruit, was believed to be an aphrodisiac (Ge 30:14–16). **at our door.** Simply means "ready at hand." Note the figurative use of "house" in 1:17. The location for the couple's meeting was in fact outdoors (v. 12).
8:1 like a brother. The key word here is "like." The beloved did not, of course, wish that her young man were actually her brother but only that she had the freedom to kiss him in public (v. 2).
8:2 mother's house. See 3:4 and its note. **she who has taught me.** The Hebrew can also mean "you [the young man] would teach me." The context seems to require this latter meaning. The young man would then be the girl's teacher in the art of lovemaking.
8:3 This verse is identical to 2:6. In both cases the girl was dreaming of being in her young man's embrace.
8:4 For the last time, this refrain points to the consummation that was yet to occur (2:7; 3:5; see "Introduction: Purpose and Distinctives").
■ **8:5–14** *Reminiscences to the Wedding.* As the song ends, the long-awaited wedding comes into view.
■ **8:5a** *The Friends.* The dream gave way to reality. The happy couple no longer had to conceal their relationship. They could walk out in public together as lovers, arm in arm. Contrast verse 1 (see also note on v. 1).
8:5a Who is this coming up from the desert . . . ? This is an exact repetition of 3:6a, where the wedding segment of the girl's dream was introduced (see note on 3:6–11). **leaning on her lover?** This simple image captures the gracious leadership exercised by the man and the joyful acceptance of it by the woman (see Eph 5:21–25; see also "Introduction: Time and Place of Writing").
■ **8:5b–7** *The Young Man.* The man reviewed the process by which he had wooed his bride. The text is unclear as to whether the young man or woman was speaking here and in the next three lines. The received tradition makes the girl the speaker (as does the NIV). The content of the lines, however, has suggested that it may, in fact, have been the man who was speaking (at least to the end of v. 5). Compare especially the words "there your mother conceived you" (v. 5) with the way the girl herself had spoken about her mother in verse 2 and in 3:4. Whoever the speaker was, the essential nature of the passage is the same; the couple was reminiscing about how it had all begun.

Beloved

8:5 [c]SS 3:4

Under the apple tree I roused you;
there your mother conceived[c] you,
there she who was in labor gave you birth.

8:6 [d]SS 1:2 [e]Nu 5:14

6 Place me like a seal over your heart,
like a seal on your arm;
for love[d] is as strong as death,
its jealousy[a][e] unyielding as the grave.[b]
It burns like blazing fire,
like a mighty flame.[c]

8:7 [f]Pr 6:35

7 Many waters cannot quench love;
rivers cannot wash it away.
If one were to give
all the wealth of his house for love,
it[d] would be utterly scorned.[f]

Friends

8 We have a young sister,
and her breasts are not yet grown.
What shall we do for our sister
for the day she is spoken for?
9 If she is a wall,
we will build towers of silver on her.
If she is a door,
we will enclose her with panels of cedar.

Beloved

8:11 [g]Ecc 2:4 [h]Isa 7:23

8:12 [i]SS 1:6

10 I am a wall,
and my breasts are like towers.
Thus I have become in his eyes
like one bringing contentment.
11 Solomon had a vineyard[g] in Baal Hamon;
he let out his vineyard to tenants.
Each was to bring for its fruit
a thousand shekels[e][h] of silver.
12 But my own vineyard[i] is mine to give;
the thousand shekels are for you, O Solomon,
and two hundred[f] are for those who tend its fruit.

[a] *6* Or *ardor* [b] *6* Hebrew *Sheol* [c] *6* Or / *like the very flame of the LORD* [d] *7* Or *he* [e] *11* That is, about 25 pounds (about 11.5 kilograms); also in verse 12 [f] *12* That is, about 5 pounds (about 2.3 kilograms)

8:5b I roused you. That is, "began to woo you." **there.** Presumably this does not refer to "apple tree" but to her parent's home, which the two were now approaching. The girl had dreamed about bringing him home (3:4; 8:2); now she was doing so.

8:6 seal. This was a signet made of metal or stone that was worn around the neck (and therefore over the heart) or on an armband (Ge 38:18). **strong as death.** Love is as strong as the most powerful negative human experience. This is the beginning of a short "hymn to love" that was spoken by the bride. **jealousy.** In parallel with "love" here, jealousy is a positive trait; for example, the possessiveness of God himself (Ex 20:5). Like God's love, the love being celebrated here was not casual, but committed—a bond tolerating no rivals. **a mighty flame.** The implicit comparison is further confirmed by this expression. It means, literally, "the flame of Yah," where "Yah" is a shortened form of the divine name *Yahweh* (NIV, "the LORD").

■ **8:8–9** *The Friends.* In this unit, which continued the reminiscence, unnamed associates, perhaps the young woman's biological brothers (v. 8), were protective of her before she reached a marriageable age (1:6).

8:8 We have a young sister. The term "sister" may be used in both narrower and broader ways. It can mean a female sibling, a cousin or even a beloved fellow Israelite woman. **spoken for?** That is, "asked for as a prospective bride."

8:9 If she is a wall. That is, "if she is firm in refusing the marriage proposal." The brothers' response in this situation would be to "build towers of silver on her"; that is, to confirm her refusal and honor her for it. **If she is a door.** That is, "if she accepts the proposal." In this case the brothers would "enclose her with panels of cedar"; i.e., refuse to give their permission for her to marry. See note on 8:12.

■ **8:10–12** *The Young Woman.* The young woman delighted in the man's attraction toward her.

8:10 I am a wall and my breasts are like towers. The girl affirmed not only her strong moral integrity but also her sexual maturity (cf. v. 8a). **contentment.** That is, "Shalom" or "complete well-being." By implication, the Song points to the marriage relationship as the sphere within which such fulfillment is to be found.

8:11 a vineyard in Baal Hamon. Some have regarded this as a metaphor for Solomon's harem, but the designation of a specific place suggests otherwise. The location of Baal Hamon is unknown. **for its fruit.** That is, as income from the sale of the fruit.

8:12 The Hebrew does not make clear who was speaking in this verse, but the expression "my own vineyard" suggests that it was the girl. Compare the similar language of 1:8. Here, as there, a metaphorical use of "vineyard" follows its literal use. The girl's

Lover

13 You who dwell in the gardens
with friends in attendance,
let me hear your voice!

Beloved

14 Come away, my lover,
and be like a gazelle[j]
or like a young stag[k]
on the spice-laden mountains.[l]

8:14
[j]Pr 5:19 [k]SS 2:9
[l]SS 2:8, 17

"vineyard" was her body, with its natural, rustic beauty. With that treasure to share, she was content. If Solomon is seen as an intruder (see "Introduction: Purpose and Distinctives"), the silver may represent a bride-price. The woman's refusal to accept the silver would then be a rejection of Solomon's marriage proposal in favor of remaining with her shepherd. **mine to give.** Although the woman's brothers planned to prevent her marriage (see note on 8:9), she was determined to oppose them and to prevail.

■ **8:13** *The Young Man.* The last word of the man to his bride-to-be expressed his sincere desire to be with her. The reminiscences reached to the actual ceremony.

8:13 friends in attendance. Probably refers to the wedding guests. **let me hear your voice!** The bridegroom was eager to hear his bride speak to him.

■ **8:14** *The Young Woman.* The woman agreed to separate from all others and to go to her husband.

8:14 Come away, my lover. The desire was mutual. In language reminiscent of the lovemaking of her dreams (2:8–9; 4:6), she invited him to come in with her.

Introduction to the Prophetic Books

Arrangement of Books

THE books of Isaiah through Malachi (with the exceptions of Lamentations and Daniel) correspond to the section of the Hebrew canon known as "the latter prophets." These prophetic books divide into two smaller groups: "major prophets" (Isaiah, Jeremiah, Ezekiel) and "minor prophets" (Hosea through Malachi). Within these two broad categories the prophets are arranged in roughly chronological order.

Historical Backgrounds

Most prophetic books have superscriptions designed to provide an orientation to the settings within which the prophets ministered. Joel, Obadiah, Jonah, Nahum, Habakkuk and Malachi have no such information, so their historical setting must be inferred from their contents. To whatever degree we may ascertain the original settings of prophetic ministries and writings, the information contributes significantly to responsible interpretation.

In very general terms we may speak of three sets of historical circumstances that occupied the center stage of the prophets' ministries.

(1) *Assyrian Judgment.* During the eighth century B.C. Assyria became the dominant empire in the ancient Near East and thus of great concern to the prophets. In response to Israel's prolonged, flagrant sin, God determined to use the armies of Assyria to bring judgment against his people. This aggression took place in three major stages. First, in c. 734 B.C. the northern kingdom of Israel joined forces with Syria to resist Assyrian dominance, but this coalition led to Syria's defeat and Israel's harsh subjugation to Assyria (2Ki 15:20–29). Second, in 722 B.C. the Assyrians reacted to further rebellion by destroying Samaria, the capital of northern Israel, and exiling many citizens of the nation. Third, in 701 B.C. the Assyrian king Sennacherib waged a successful war against Judah and even laid siege to Jerusalem, but the Lord turned him back at the last moment (2Ki 17–19). The prophets who ministered in this period spoke frequently about these and related events.

(2) *Babylonian Judgment.* In 612 B.C. the Babylonians conquered Nineveh, the capital of Assyria, and became the dominant empire in the region. With the northern kingdom of Israel already defeated and exiled by the Assyrians, God used the Babylonians to bring judgment against the southern kingdom of Judah through major incursions and deportations in 605, 597 and 586 B.C. The first incursion resulted in subjugation and the deportation of some of Judah's elite, such as Daniel and his friends (Da 1:3–6). The second offensive brought more hardship and the deportation of more Judahites, such as Ezekiel (Eze 33:21; 2Ki 24:14). The third assault resulted in the destruction of Jerusalem and full-scale exile (2Ki 25:1–21). Many prophets predicted these events, interpreted them as they happened and reflected on them once they had occurred.

(3) *Restoration.* In 539–538 B.C. the Persian emperor Cyrus defeated Babylon and released the Jews to return to Jerusalem. A small number of Jews returned to the land under the leadership of Zerubbabel, a descendant of David, and Joshua the high priest. After a delay of some time, the temple was rebuilt in 520–515 B.C. Despite this relatively positive beginning for the restored community, by the time of Ezra and Nehemiah and the decades that followed them (c. 450–400 B.C.) false religion had so taken root among the returnees that all hope for the kingdom of God to reach its glorious end was cast into the distant future, which we now know as the New Testament period. Many prophets concerned themselves with these events as well.

The following chart summarizes the major periods, approximate dates, Biblical references and audiences of each writing prophet:

Period	Prophet	Date	Biblical Reference	Audience
Assyrian Judgment	Amos	793–740	2Ki 14:21—15:7	Israel
	Jonah	786–746	2Ki 14:23–29	Assyria
	Hosea	753–722	2Ki 15–18	Israel
	Micah	742–686	2Ki 14:23—20:21	Israel/Judah
	Isaiah	740–686	2Ki 15:1—20:21	Israel/Judah
Babylonian Judgment	Nahum	663–627	2Ki 21:1—23:35	Assyria
	Zephaniah	640–609	2Ki 22:1—23:35	Judah
	Jeremiah	626–586	2Ki 22–25	Judah
	Habakkuk	605	2Ki 23:36—25:21	Judah
	Ezekiel	592–572	2Ki 24–25	Judah in exile
	Obadiah	585	(cf. Jer 49:7–22)	Edom
Restoration	Haggai	520	Ezr 5–6	Judah
	Zechariah	520	Ezr 5–6	Judah
	Malachi	458–433	(cf. Ne 13)	Judah
?	Joel	uncertain		Judah

True prophecy ceased in Israel at about the time of Malachi. Three times the author of the Apocalyptic book of 1 Maccabees (4:46; 9:27; 14:41), which is on the whole a sober history of events during the Jewish revolt against Antiochus Epiphanes (c. 165 B.C.), clearly stated that there was no prophet in Israel, implying that this had been true for a considerable length of time.

This intertestamental period of silence ended with the voice of John the Baptist, who announced that God was about to establish his kingdom (Mt 3:12; Mk 1:3–8; Lk 3:2–17). Malachi ended Old Testament prophecy with a prediction that God would send a messenger, a new "Elijah," to prepare the way for the future coming of God to his people (Mal 3:1; 4:5). The evangelists and Jesus identified John the Baptist as the Elijah foretold in Malachi (Mt 17:12–13). Thus John opened a new day of prophecy — the day of the kingdom of God in Christ.

The Role of Prophets

A prophet was God's "mouth" or spokesperson. The Lord told Moses that Aaron would be "a mouth for you, and you shall be to him as God" (Ex 4:16) and later summarized this role in this way: "Aaron your brother shall be your prophet" (Ex 7:1). To be a prophet was to speak authoritatively on behalf of God.

This basic role of prophets comes to clear expression in three accounts of God's prophetic call that closely resemble God's call to Moses in Exodus 3:1–12 (Isa 6:1–13; Jer 1:1–10; Eze 1:1—3:11). In each case God directly confronted the prophet with an introductory word and commission: at the burning bush (Ex 3:1–10), in the temple (Isa 6:1–10), in an unspecified place (Jer 1:4–5), and in the calm of a storm (Eze 1:1—2:5). After the prophet objected (Ex 3:11; Isa 6:11; Jer 1:6; implied in Eze 2:6,8) the Lord reassured him, sometimes with a sign (Ex 3:12; Isa 6:11–13; Jer 1:7–10; Eze 2:6—3:11). These divine vocations not only assured the prophets themselves of God's call but also authorized the prophets in the eyes of others as those who would speak not with their own authority but with the authority of God.

Prior to the rise of human kingship in Israel prophets spoke for God in a number of diverse ways. When human kingship was instituted, prophets became increasingly associated with Israel's royal statecraft. Israel's prophets served as emissaries between God, the great King, and his human king and nation, Israel. On analogy with international political practices in the ancient world, the divine King of Israel sent prophetic emissaries to give direction, commend loyalty and prosecute violations of the covenants he had established with his vassal people (see chart, "Major Covenants in the Bible," on p. 25).

This emissarial role was central to the ministry of all writing prophets in the Old Testament. They threatened curses and offered blessings according to the covenant established between God and Israel (see Lev 26; Dt 28–30; cf. Isa 1:2; Jer 2:9; Hos 4:1; Mic 1:2; 6:2). In compliance with the terms of the covenant the prophets announced a number of lesser curses, as well as the greatest curse of total destruction and exile from the land. They also proclaimed many lesser blessings, as well as the greatest blessing of restoration after exile. All of these prophetic concerns revealed their role as emissaries of Israel's divine, covenant King.

True Prophets and Their Predictions

In light of the fact that prophets spoke as God's covenant emissaries, it was vitally important for God's people to distinguish between true and false prophets. The test of a true prophet was threefold: He had to be an Israelite (Dt 18:15); he had to be loyal to the covenant mediated by Moses (Dt 13:1–5); and his predictions had to come to pass (Dt 18:21–22). In Israel's history many who claimed to be God's prophets failed these tests, but the writing prophets of the Bible satisfied them all.

The third criterion requiring that all predictions come to pass must be understood carefully. On the one hand, it is beyond question that God's eternal decrees include "whatsoever comes to pass" and that these decrees are immutable; God accomplishes all that he decreed without fail (*WCF* 3.2; *BC* 13). Therefore, when prophets disclosed eternal decrees in their predictions, their prophecies would indeed without fail come to pass. But we make a serious mistake if we believe that every prophecy reveals God's eternal, immutable decree. More often than not, prophets spoke of future events that were not immutably decreed by God (see paragraph to follow). Their primary task was to be vehicles of God's providence (see theological article "Providence" at Jer 18).

Jeremiah 18:1–11 plainly teaches that not everything true prophets said about the future would necessarily take place. On the contrary, prophets often spoke to motivate rather than to prognosticate. They frequently announced future judgments as threats, not as inescapable condemnations, and spoke of future blessings as offers, not sure promises. In fact, the prophets revealed that God had different levels of determination to carry through with prophetic predictions. At times the conditional nature of a prophecy was explicit (e.g., Jer 22:4–5) but at other times implicit (e.g., Jer 7:5–7; Isa 7:9). Sometimes God offered words or signs to confirm his high level of determination to carry out a prophecy (Isa 38:7; Jer 44:29). Occasionally prophets reported that God was so determined to carry through with a prophecy that he swore to do it (Isa 45:23; Jer 22:4–5; 49:13). In this last category the divine oath demonstrated the inevitability of a prediction's fulfillment; it raised the prophetic word to the level of the immutable because God cannot break his own solemn vows (Nu 23:19). Even so, details such as how, when, where, to what degree and for/against whom the fulfillment would come usually remained unspecified and hidden until the sworn prophecy was fulfilled.

As a result, to one degree or another all prophetic predictions could be affected by human reactions to a prophecy. The Scriptures are replete with examples in which repentance, prayer, recalcitrance and indifference moved God to cancel, postpone, extend, shorten, hasten, mollify or intensify the fulfillments of prophetic predictions (Ex 32:12; 2Sa 12:14–22; Jn 3:4–9).

For this reason, when we apply the criterion of fulfilled predictions to true prophets, we must always ask how the prophets *intended* their predictions to be taken. What level of divine determination did the prophet's words indicate? Did the prophet mean for his prediction to be taken as conditional or inevitable? We must not be satisfied with a mechanical understanding of the prophetic word divorced from such prophetic intentions.

Even so, Biblical prophecies are so comprehensive and specific that they put pagan prophets to shame (see notes on Isa 41:21–29). All times and all peoples, especially in the ancient Near East, have known diviners, seers or sorcerers who claim to announce the future (Dt 18:9–13; 1Ki 18:19,25,40). In all of the ancient Near Eastern literature, however, there is nothing to rival the prophecies collected in Scripture. Their remarkable specificity and record of fulfillment, as well as their magnificent, comprehensive grasp of history, are unparalleled in any other literature. Often their prophesies of doom were given at the very moment a nation was at the apogee of its power, and their prophecies of victory came when situations looked most hopeless.

The Forms of Prophetic Literature

The prophets employed three main forms of literature in their books: (1) narratives—both biographical (Da 1–3), and autobiographical (Isa 6; Jer 1); (2) addresses to God—laments (Jer 9:10; Lam; Eze 2:3–10), petitions (Jer 42:2; Da 9:17) and praise (Isa 12:1–6); and (3) addresses to people—such as taunt songs (Isa 14), wisdom sayings (Isa 28:23–29) and disputations (Isa 1:18; 43:26), to name a few.

Oracles addressed to people dominate the prophetic books. These addresses may be categorized by their tendency to focus more on covenant curses or covenant blessings. Although the prophets addressed people with many different forms of speech, a number of basic patterns appear so frequently that it is helpful to identify and describe them.

On one side several forms of speech primarily announced curses, ranging from lesser covenant curses to the greatest threat, namely exile:

1. **Lawsuits.** As emissaries of Israel's heavenly King, prophets heard and sometimes participated in the court of heaven. They then reported what they had seen and heard in the formal language of that courtroom. God brought his people to trial for having flagrantly broken covenant and sentenced them to severe curses (Isa 3:13; Mic 6:1–2).
2. **Oracles of Judgment.** Prophets also delivered messages of doom with language that did not so closely reflect the formalities of the heavenly court. These oracles usually consisted of an address followed by one or more accusations and sentences (Eze 7:7–10; Zec 9:1–8).
3. **Woe Oracles.** When judgment from God was particularly dire, prophets expressed woes. These speeches were usually very similar to judgment oracles (address, accusations, sentences) with the addition of a cry of "woe." They warned of how terrible things would be when the curses finally fell (Isa 3:9–11; 5:8–22; Eze 13:3–18; Hos 7:13; Nah 3:1).

On the other side, prophets also announced blessings, ranging from relatively small and personal advantages to the grand blessing of restoration from exile. These prophecies normally took one of two forms:

1. **Oracles of Salvation.** The prophets comforted Israel with oracles of salvation or deliverance. These oracles took a number of different shapes but usually included some kind of announcement of blessing followed by elaborations on the wonder of the blessing. The most prominent focus of oracles of salvation was the restoration of God's people from exile. In fact, whole sections of the Major Prophets reflected this concern (Isa 40–55; Jer 30–33; Eze 34–40). These consoling prophecies were based on God's covenant promises to the patriarchs (Ge 15:1–21 notes; 17:1–22 notes; 22:15–18 notes), which Moses later confirmed as he described the time after a future exile as one of unprecedented mercy and blessing for God's people (Dt 30:1–10).

Restoration promises found a measure of fulfillment in the return from exile in 539–538 B.C. (see 2Ch 36:22–23; Zec 1:8–17), but the New Testament reveals that their complete fulfillment is in Christ. In this sense restoration prophecies were inspired by the Spirit of Christ for his church (1Pe 1:10–12; 2Pe 1:19–20). Some prophecies pertain more directly to Christ's earthly ministry, while other predictions relate more to his ministry and rule from heaven and to the ongoing work of the church. All restoration prophecies will find their ultimate completion in the realities of the new heavens and the new earth when Christ returns.

2. **Oracles Against the Nations.** Another way in which prophets brought a message of hope and salvation to the people of God was through pronouncing judgments against other nations that had rebelled against God. Although in a formal sense these prophecies were judgments, they served as positive assurances of salvation for the faithful people of God because they were leveled against the enemies of God's people. Nahum and Obadiah, in their entirety, describe holy war against Gentiles. Within the larger books, major sections consist of oracles against the nations (Isa 13–24; Jer 46–51; Eze 25–32).

Oracles against the nations divide into two main types. On the one hand a number of prophecies announced that God would judge specific nations through the aggressions of other nations (e.g., Am 1:2—2:3; Zep 1:18–21). On the other hand a number of prophets proclaimed that a final worldwide judgment against the nations would take place after God's people had been restored from exile (Eze 38:17–23; Am 9:12; Hag 2:20–23).

Introduction to the Prophetic Books *(continued)*

Christ in the Prophets

Old Testament prophets pointed to Christ and his work in a variety of ways. In all cases Christ fulfilled dimensions of these prophetic expectations in his first coming, continues to fulfill them in his ministry to the church today, and will ultimately fulfill them in the consummation of all things at his second coming (see theological article "The Kingdom of God" at Mt 4).

In most cases the prophets anticipated Christ quite indirectly. This was especially true when they spoke of lesser judgments and blessings whose fulfillments characteristically took place during Old Testament times. These acts of divine justice and mercy had already taken place, but they also foreshadowed the greater judgments and blessings that Christ would bring.

Prophets predicted Christ and his work more directly when they focused on the great judgment of exile and the blessing of restoration from exile (with the associated judgment against the nations at the restoration). The destruction and exile of Israel and Judah were mere preludes to the eternal judgment that will come against the covenant people who rebel against God. Similarly, the restoration of God's faithful people to the promised land and the blessings they received, as well as the judgment against the nations predicted for the days of restoration, anticipated the final reward and judgment that Christ would bring.

The most direct predictions of Christ appear when the prophets spoke of specific royal, priestly and prophetic activities that would take place in association with the restoration after exile ("I will restore David's fallen tent" [Am 9:11]; "my signet ring" [Hag 2:23]). It is in this context that specifically royal, Messianic prophecies appear. As the prophets spoke of the days of God's kingdom after the exile, they made references to the ways in which the great son of David would bring judgment against God's enemies and grant eternal blessings to his people. These predictions were fulfilled, are being fulfilled and will be fulfilled in none other than Jesus Christ.

ISAIAH

Introduction

Overview

Author: The prophet Isaiah

Purpose: To encourage the prophet's contemporaries to be loyal to the Lord and to exhort future readers in exile to repent of sin and trust the Lord to bring the faithful remnant of Israel and other nations to unprecedented blessings after the exile

Date: c. 686–650 B.C.

Key Truths:

- God called Isaiah to warn his people of the judgment of exile and to assure them of future restoration to tremendous blessing after the exile.
- Isaiah's reliability was demonstrated by the fulfillment of many of his earlier prophecies by the time of the writing of the book.
- Isaiah's astounding predictions about the end of the Babylonian exile and the restoration were sure to take place, but only the repentant in Israel and the nations would enjoy these future blessings.

Author

Jewish and Christian traditions have followed the book's own identification of Isaiah as its author (1:1). Little is known about the personal life of Isaiah. He lived in Judah, was married at least once and had at least two sons (see notes on 7:13–14): Shear-Jashub (7:3) and Maher-Shalal-Hash-Baz (8:3). During his lifetime Isaiah not only composed this book but also wrote a history of the reign of Uzziah (2Ch 26:22). Several ancient traditions suggest that the prophet suffered martyrdom during the reign of Manasseh (697–642 B.C.).

In recent history an increasing number of interpreters have disputed the unity of the book. Although older Jewish and Christian traditions affirmed Isaiah's authorship of the entire work, many recent interpreters have argued that the book resulted from a much more complex history of composition. In general terms they have divided Isaiah into several books: They ascribe most of chapters 1–39, called Proto-Isaiah ("First Isaiah"), to Isaiah himself. Chapters 40–55, called Deutero-Isaiah ("Second Isaiah"), are attributed to a late exilic or early postexilic prophet writing in the tradition of Isaiah. Chapters 56–66, called Trito-Isaiah ("Third Isaiah"), have been ascribed to a postexilic prophet living in Judea.

At least three major objections may be raised against the proposal of multiple authors of this book.

1. For the most part, these theories were developed by interpreters who assumed that Israel's prophets concentrated almost exclusively on events that were taking place in their own day. Chapters 1–39 primarily concern the Assyrian judgment (c. 740–700 B.C.) and chapters 40–66 the Babylonian exile and return (c. 586–500 B.C.). On this basis, many modern critics have argued that more than one prophet must have written the book of Isaiah. However, this outlook cannot be sustained in light of the fact that Biblical prophets characteristically spoke about events that would come to pass after their lifetimes.

2. These same interpreters often assumed that miraculous prophecy, such as the identification of Cyrus by name more than a century before he had arrived on the scene (45:1), did not occur in Israel. Yet the book of Isaiah itself reproved naturalistic outlooks on prophecy. In Isaiah 40–55 the Lord's call to Israel directly pointed to the supernatural quality of the prophetic word (41:21–29; 44:24—45:8). Under divine inspiration Isaiah predicted some events with meticulous specificity.

3. Variations in language and style among the alleged sections of the book have also been used to support the argument for multiple authors. The differences that do exist, however, may be due to differences in subject matter, changed perspectives or the maturation of the prophet.

More positively, at least three important considerations offer strong support for maintaining that the prophet Isaiah was the real and fundamental author of the entire book.

1. The book itself explicitly references Isaiah as the source of its prophecies in a number of superscriptions (2:1; 7:3; 13:1; 20:2; 37:2,6,21; 38:1,4,21; 39:3,5,8). Other books of the Old Testament that have multiple authors, such as Psalms and Proverbs, use superscriptions to identify their various authors, but nothing of this sort occurs in the book of Isaiah.

2. The repetition of themes, literary images, vocabulary and metaphors throughout the book (e.g., "glory," "the Holy One of Israel," "Zion," "city") strongly supports a single author. Note also the satirical scorn of idolatry found in all sections of the book (see 2:8 note).

3. The New Testament witness validates this outlook on the book. A number of passages identify various portions of the book of Isaiah as coming from the prophet (e.g., Mt 12:17–21 [Isa 42:1–4]; Ro 10:16,20 [Isa 53:1; 65:1]). Most importantly, the apostle John attributed prophecies from Isaiah 6:10 and 53:10 (from allegedly "First Isaiah" and "Deutero-Isaiah," respectively) simply to Isaiah (Jn 12:38–41).

Time and Place of Writing

Isaiah's public ministry took place during the reigns of Uzziah (792–740 B.C.), Jotham (750–731 B.C.), Ahaz

(735–715 B.C.) and Hezekiah (715–686 B.C.), "kings of Judah" (1:1). He ministered in Judah during the time when God brought judgment against his people through Assyrian aggression (740–686 B.C.). Isaiah also prophesied about the Babylonian judgment (612–538 B.C.), which took place after his lifetime. The latest event mentioned in the book as a past occurrence is the succession of Esarhaddon to the throne of Assyria (37:38), which occurred in 681 B.C. The book of Isaiah could not have been completed until after that event.

Isaiah's ministry divides into five major segments:

1. *Early Assyrian Judgment (c. 740–734 B.C.).* During the middle decades of the eighth century B.C., Assyria became a dominant power in the ancient Near East. During this time Isaiah began to minister (6:1). He railed against hypocritical (1:10–15), greedy (5:18), self-indulgent (5:11) and cynical leaders (5:19) who had led the people of God into moral ruin and warned that God was preparing to judge his people in both the northern and southern kingdoms through the armies of Assyria.

2. *The Syrian-Israelite Coalition (734–732 B.C.).* When Syria and Israel formed a coalition to resist Assyrian dominance (see notes on chs. 7–8), King Pekah of Israel and King Rezin of Syria confronted King Ahaz of Judah to force him to join their alliance. Isaiah offered Ahaz God's protection from all of his foes, but Ahaz responded with fear and unbelief. Instead of trusting God for deliverance, he turned to the Assyrians for help. As a result, God not only incited Assyria to attack Syria and Israel, but Judah became subservient to the Assyrian Empire as well.

3. *Destruction of Samaria (722 B.C.).* The northern kingdom suffered severe hardship and rebelled against the Assyrian Empire. This rebellion led to the fulfillment of Isaiah's prophecy that Assyria would invade the northern kingdom, destroy Samaria (the capital of the northern kingdom) and exile many citizens of Israel.

4. *Invasion of Judah and Jerusalem's Siege (705–701 B.C.).* Despite the demise of the northern kingdom, Judah continued in sinful rebellion against God and resisted Assyrian dominance in its region as well. As a result, God also moved the Assyrians against Judah. King Sennacherib of Assyria (705–681 B.C.) attacked Hezekiah's kingdom, destroyed much of Judah and laid siege to Jerusalem (36:1—37:38). Isaiah warned against seeking help from other nations and called on Hezekiah to trust the Lord to deliver him from the Assyrians. Unlike Ahaz, Hezekiah finally trusted in the Lord (37:14–35), and God drove the Assyrians away before they could destroy Jerusalem (36:1—37:37).

5. *Babylonian Judgment and Restoration (586–539 B.C.).* Despite God's mercy toward him, Hezekiah immediately sought to secure his position against future troubles by forming an alliance with the Babylonians (39:1–2). In response to this lack of faith, Isaiah announced that Judah's royal treasures would one day be taken to Babylon (39:6–7). Thus he predicted that Jerusalem would fall to the Babylonians and that Judah's citizens would be exiled, as their northern counterparts had been in previous decades. Much of this book explains these future events and offers hope to those who would one day be exiled to Babylon. Isaiah predicted the fall of Babylon and a grand restoration of Israel and Judah (chs. 40–66).

Purpose and Distinctives

As God's prophet Isaiah applied both the blessings and judgments of God's covenants with Israel (See "Introduction to the Prophetic Books"). On the one hand Isaiah's ministry consisted largely of bringing charges, condemnations and judgments as he declared covenant curses on Israel and Judah for their flagrant violations of their covenant obligations (1:2–31; 13:1—23:18; 56:9—57:13; 65:1–16). The prophet spoke of many different curses that would come, the most serious of which would be destruction and exile. In fact, both Israel and Judah had fallen so far from the ideals of the covenant that God commanded Isaiah to prophesy in order to harden the people's hearts so that the judgment of exile might not be averted (6:1–13).

On the other hand Isaiah balanced his message of judgment with words of hope. He spoke of many different kinds of blessings, but for the most part his positive words focused on the principal blessing of restoration after exile (chs. 40–66). As a result, Isaiah called the godly to persevere in seeking the Lord, in cultivating hope for God's kingdom, in experiencing God's peace within themselves during times of trouble and in responding to God's new acts of redemption in faith (2:5; 8:13–17; 26:20–21; 33:14–16; 40:28–31; 48:20–21; 55:1–12; 60:1–3; 61:10–11; 63:7—64:12; 66:5–6). Isaiah promised that a remnant would survive the exile, return to the land and enjoy the unprecedented blessings of God.

Christ in Isaiah

The prophecies of Isaiah anticipate Christ in at least three ways. First, Isaiah warned of judgments to come against God's rebellious people and the nations who resisted him (1:20; 3:13–15; 11:4; 34:2; 51:5). Ultimately the judgments of God that Isaiah threatened were fulfilled in the ministry of Christ (53:4–6,12; 2Co 1:15; Heb 9:26).

Second, Isaiah assured God's faithful people that they would enjoy a glorious restoration after exile—a restoration he called "the new heavens and the new earth" (66:22; see also 65:17). Jesus inaugurated this new creation by an earthly ministry that separated anew light and darkness (Jn 1.1–9). He continues this new creation throughout the history of the church (2Co 4:6; 5:17; Gal 6:15; Jas 1:18) and will bring it to its fullness when he returns (Rev 21:1–3). See theological article "The Kingdom of God" at Matthew 4.

Third, the New Testament refers to Isaiah more than to any other Old Testament book to indicate how Jesus fulfilled the Old Testament expectations of the Messiah. The most important way in which Jesus fulfilled Isaiah's prophecies was with respect to Isaiah's prevalent servant motif (see note on 42:1). Isaiah predicted that the "servant" to come would bring justice to the nations (42:1–4), reestablish Israel's covenant with the Lord (42:5–7), become a light to the Gentiles (49:1–7), take away the sins of the elect and be raised from the dead (52:13—53:12). The New Testament identifies this Servant-Savior as Jesus, the incarnate Lord (Mt 8:17; 16:21; 27:26,29,31,38,57–60; Mk 14:49,61; 15:27,43–46; Lk 2:14; 18:31–33; 23:32; Jn 1:10–11,29; 3:17; 12:38; 19:1,7,18,38–41; Ac 2:23; 3:13; 7:32–33; 8:32–33; 10:43; Ro 4:25; 8:34; 10:15–16; 15:21; 1Co 15:3; Eph 3:4–5; Php 2:9; Heb 5:8; 9:28; 1Pe 2:22–25; 1Jn 3:5; Rev 14:5).

Outline

I. Superscription (1:1)

Isaiah identified himself and the times of his ministry.

II. Isaiah's Message of Judgment and Restoration (1:2—6:13)

Isaiah proclaimed words of judgment against Israel and Judah but also extended the hope of restoration after exile.

- A. Judgment and Restoration to Righteousness and Justice (1:2—2:5)
  1. Lawsuit Against Unrighteousness and Injustice (1:2–31)
  2. Zion's Future Righteousness and Justice (2:1–5)
- B. Judgment and Restoration on That Day (2:6—4:6)
  1. Pride and Syncretism on That Day (2:6–22)
  2. Jerusalem's Leaders on That Day (3:1–15)
  3. Haughty Women on That Day (3:16—4:1)
  4. The Royal Branch on That Day (4:2–6)
- C. Judgment Leading to Restoration (5:1—6:13)
  1. The Song of the Vineyard (5:1–7)
  2. Woes Over God's People (5:8–30)
  3. Isaiah's Mission of Judgment and Restoration (6:1–13)

III. Isaiah's Response to the Assyrian Judgment (7:1—39:8)

Isaiah's response to the Assyrian judgment included threats of judgment and the hope of restoration, which later generations needed to apply to themselves. Isaiah's reliability as a prophet is demonstrated in these chapters.

- A. The Syrian-Israelite Coalition (7:1—12:6)
  1. The Assyrian Judgment and Isaiah's Sons (7:1—8:18)
  2. The Assyrian Judgment and Israel (8:19—10:4)
     - a. The Call to Inquire of God (8:19–22)
     - b. Israel's Hope in David's Throne (9:1–7)
     - c. The Condemnation of Israel's Pride (9:8—10:4)
  3. The Assyrian Judgment and Judah (10:5—12:6)
     - a. Woe to Assyria (10:5–19)
     - b. Judah's Remnant (10:20–34)
     - c. Judah's Hope in David's Throne (11:1–16)
     - d. A Song of Praise in Zion (12:1–6)
- B. International Upheaval During the Assyrian Judgment (13:1—27:13)
  1. Oracles Concerning Specific Nations (13:1—23:18)
     - a. Babylon (Assyria) (13:1—14:27)
     - b. Philistia (14:28–32)
     - c. Moab (15:1—16:14)
     - d. Damascus (17:1–14)
     - e. Cush and Egypt (18:1—20:6)
     - f. Babylon (21:1–10)
     - g. Edom (21:11–12)
     - h. Arabia (21:13–17)
     - i. Jerusalem (22:1–25)
     - j. Tyre (23:1–18)
  2. The Goal of International Upheaval (24:1—27:13)
     - a. Judgment Leading to Joy (24:1–23)
     - b. Praise for God's Faithfulness (25:1–8)
     - c. Praise in the Future (25:9—26:8)
     - d. Waiting for the Future (26:9—27:13)

- C. Sennacherib's Invasion (28:1—39:8)
  - 1. Oracles Relating to the Invasion (28:1—35:10)
    - a. Samaria and Jerusalem (28:1—29:24)
      - (1) Woe Against Samaria (28:1–13)
      - (2) A Lesson for Jerusalem (28:14–29)
      - (3) Woe Against Jerusalem (29:1–16)
      - (4) Hope for the Future (29:17–24)
    - b. The Problem of Egypt (30:1—32:20)
      - (1) Woe Against the Obstinate (30:1–7)
      - (2) Accusations Against Judah (30:8–14)
      - (3) Call to Repentance (30:15–18)
      - (4) Restoration of Blessing and Joy (30:19–26)
      - (5) Assyria's Certain End (30:27–33)
      - (6) Woe Against Reliance on Egypt (31:1–3)
      - (7) God's Salvation and Judgment (31:4–9)
      - (8) The Coming Righteous Rulers (32:1–8)
      - (9) Call Away From False Confidence (32:9–20)
    - c. The Future of Assyria and Jerusalem (33:1—35:10)
      - (1) Assyria's Judgment and Zion's Salvation (33:1–12)
      - (2) The Future People and King of Zion (33:13–24)
      - (3) The Future Day of Vengeance (34:1–17)
      - (4) The Wonder of Returning to Zion (35:1–10)
  - 2. The Account of Sennacherib's Invasion (36:1—39:8)
    - a. The First Encounter (36:1—37:8)
      - (1) Assyria's Military Success (36:1–3)
      - (2) The Field Commander's Challenge (36:4–20)
      - (3) Response to the Assyrian Challenge (36:21—37:7)
      - (4) Withdrawal of Assyrian Army (37:8)
    - b. The Second Encounter (37:9–38)
      - (1) Sennacherib's Challenge (37:9–13)
      - (2) Response to Sennacherib's Challenge (37:14–35)
        - (a) Hezekiah's Prayer (37:14–20)
        - (b) Isaiah's Prophecy (37:21–35)
      - (3) The Assyrian Defeat (37:36–38)
    - c. Hezekiah's Blessing and Curse (38:1—39:8)
      - (1) Hezekiah's Healing (38:1–22)
      - (2) Hezekiah's Failure and Judgment (39:1–8)

- IV. Isaiah and the Babylonian Judgment (40:1—66:24)
  - A. Isaiah's Call to Proclaim Restoration (40:1–11)
    - 1. The Call to Comfort (40:1–2)
    - 2. The Message of Comfort (40:3–5)

Isaiah's response to the Babylonian judgment was to bring comfort to the future exiles by assuring them of God's ability to restore them, specifying the instruments God was going to use and explaining how they could participate in the salvation to come.

3. The Prophet's Reluctance (40:6–8)
4. The Call to Proclaim (40:9–11)

B. God's Power to Restore His People (40:12—44:23)
   1. Disputation Over God's Power (40:12–31)
   2. Courtroom Speech Against the Nations (41:1–7)
   3. Salvation for Israel (41:8–20)
   4. Courtroom Speech Against Idols (41:21–29)
   5. Salvation for Israel Through God's Servant (42:1–17)
   6. Disputation Over God's Sight and Hearing (42:18–25)
   7. Salvation for Israel (43:1–7)
   8. Courtroom Speech Against Nations and Their Idols (43:8–13)
   9. Salvation for Israel (43:14–21)
   10. Disputation Over God's Requirements (43:22–28)
   11. Salvation for Israel (44:1–5)
   12. Courtroom Speech Against Nations and Idols (44:6–20)
   13. Salvation for Israel (44:21–23)

C. God's Instruments of His Sure Salvation (44:24—55:13)
   1. God's Plan for Cyrus (44:24—48:22)
      a. The Lord's Hymn of Self-Glorification (44:24–28)
      b. Royal Oracle Concerning Cyrus (45:1–8)
      c. Woe to Disputers (45:9–14)
      d. Acceptance of God's Plan (45:15–17)
      e. The Lord Is Able (45:18–25)
      f. Babylon's Certain Fate (46:1–13)
      g. Judgment Against Babylon (47:1–15)
      h. The Call to Listen and Leave (48:1–22)
   2. God's Plan for His Servant (49:1—55:13)
      a. Royal Oracle About the Servant (49:1–13)
      b. Disputations Against Israel's Unbelief (49:14—50:3)
      c. The Servant's Psalm of Confidence (50:4–11)
      d. Disputation Over God's Compassion and Righteousness (51:1–8)
      e. Lament and Responses (51:9—52:12)
      f. The Suffering and Exalted Servant (52:13—53:12)
      g. Call for Jerusalem to Praise (54:1–17)
      h. The Invitation to Come (55:1–13)

D. Israel's Sin, Repentance and Restoration (56:1—66:24)
   1. The Importance of the Sabbath of Justice (56:1—58:14)
      a. The Decisive Importance of Sabbath Keeping (56:1–8)
      b. The Righteous and Wicked in Israel (56:9—57:21)
      c. Observing Sabbath and Justice (58:1–14)

2. Repentance and Restoration (59:1—66:24)
   a. Repentance and Response (59:1—63:6)
      (1) Call to Repentance (59:1–13)
      (2) God's Response of Salvation (59:14—63:6)
         (a) Evil Will Be Overcome (59:14—60:22)
         (b) The Year of the Lord's Favor Proclaimed (61:1–11)
         (c) Glorious Jerusalem to Come (62:1–12)
         (d) Judgment on the Nations (63:1–6)
   b. Repentance and Response (63:7—66:24)
      (1) Lament and Repentance (63:7—64:12)
      (2) God's Response of Judgment and Salvation (65:1—66:24)
         (a) Judgment and Salvation to Come (65:1—66:17)
         (b) The Glorious New World (66:18–24)

1 The vision[a] concerning Judah and Jerusalem[b] that Isaiah son of Amoz saw[c] during the reigns of Uzziah,[d] Jotham, Ahaz[e] and Hezekiah, kings of Judah.

A Rebellious Nation

2 Hear, O heavens! Listen, O earth!
  For the LORD has spoken:[f]
"I reared children and brought them up,
  but they have rebelled[g] against me.
3 The ox knows his master,
  the donkey his owner's manger,
but Israel does not know,[h]
  my people do not understand."

4 Ah, sinful nation,
  a people loaded with guilt,
a brood of evildoers,[i]
  children given to corruption!
They have forsaken the LORD;

1:1 [a]Nu 12:6 [b]Isa 40:9 [c]Isa 2:1 [d]2Ch 26:22 [e]2Ki 16:1
1:2 [f]Mic 1:2 [g]Isa 30:1, 9; 65:2
1:3 [h]Jer 8:7; 9:3,6
1:4 [i]Isa 14:20

■ **1:1** *Superscription.* The book begins with an identification of the prophet and the extent of his ministry. Other superscriptions occur in 2:1, 13:1, 14:28, 15:1, 17:1, 19:1, 21:1,11 and13, 22:1 and 23:1, but all attribute the material of this book to Isaiah. The book is a collection of revelations from God that came to Isaiah during the reigns of Uzziah (792–740 B.C.), Jotham (750–731 B.C.), Ahaz (735–715 B.C.) and Hezekiah (729–686 B.C.). Isaiah's name means "The LORD saves" (see 8:18).

■ **1:2—6:13** *Isaiah's Message of Judgment and Restoration.* These chapters provide a summary of Isaiah's prophecies. Severe judgment was coming against God's rebellious people through destruction and exile, but this judgment would eventually result in the cleansing and grand restoration of the people of God. These materials divide into three cycles that begin with declarations of judgment but give way to reflections on the blessings of future restoration (1:2—2:5; 2:6—4:6; 5:1—6:13).

■ **1:2—2:5** *Judgment and Restoration to Righteousness and Justice.* In these verses Isaiah announced God's lawsuit against his people (1:2–31) and followed it with a declaration of Zion's future exaltation (2:1–5). The repeated concern of these verses is judgment against the lack of righteousness and justice in Jerusalem and the restoration of such to the city following judgment.

■ **1:2–31** *Lawsuit Against Unrighteousness and Injustice.* Isaiah began his prophetic book with a dramatic look into the court of heaven, where God declared his case against Judah and pronounced his sentence of judgment.

1:2 Hear. God called his court into session by ordering witnesses to hear his case. Later (1:10) he would also call on the defendant (Judah) to hear him as well. **heavens . . . earth.** Following the legal pattern of the covenant established through Moses (Dt 30:19; 32:1), God invoked the whole of creation to bear witness against Israel. **children.** In typical fashion for a lawsuit, God declared his kindness toward his people. The Israelites were God's precious children; he had tenderly cared for them as he had brought them from Egypt (see 45:11; 49:7; 64:8; Dt 32:6,18; Mal 2:10). **rebelled.** Despite his kindness the Israelites had willfully transgressed the Lord's gracious rule (1:28; 43:27; 46:8; 48:8; 53:12; 59:13; 66:24).

1:3 ox . . . donkey . . . Israel . . . my people. God highlighted the sinfulness of his people by drawing a comparison between them and animals known for their stupidity. See *WLC* 151.

1:4–5 See *WLC* 105.

1:4 forsaken. The flagrantly apostate turned from God and his

1:4 [j]Isa 5:19,24

they have spurned the Holy One[j] of Israel
and turned their backs on him.

1:5 [k]Isa 31:6 [l]Isa 33:6, 24

5 Why should you be beaten anymore?
Why do you persist in rebellion?[k]
Your whole head is injured,
your whole heart afflicted.[l]

1:6 [m]Ps 38:3 [n]Isa 30:26; Jer 8:22 [o]Lk 10:34

6 From the sole of your foot to the top of your head
there is no soundness[m]—
only wounds and welts
and open sores,
not cleansed or bandaged[n]
or soothed with oil.[o]

1:7 [p]Lev 26:34

7 Your country is desolate,[p]
your cities burned with fire;
your fields are being stripped by foreigners
right before you,
laid waste as when overthrown by strangers.
8 The Daughter of Zion is left
like a shelter in a vineyard,

1:8 [q]Job 27:18

like a hut[q] in a field of melons,
like a city under siege.

1:9 [r]Isa 10:20-22; 37:4,31-32 [s]Ge 19:24; Ro 9:29*

9 Unless the LORD Almighty
had left us some survivors,[r]
we would have become like Sodom,
we would have been like Gomorrah.[s]

1:10 [t]Isa 28:14 [u]Isa 3:9; Eze 16:49; Ro 9:29; Rev 11:8 [v]Isa 8:20

10 Hear the word of the LORD,[t]
you rulers of Sodom;[u]
listen to the law[v] of our God,
you people of Gomorrah!
11 "The multitude of your sacrifices—
what are they to me?" says the LORD.

1:11 [w]Ps 50:8 [x]Jer 6:20 [y]1Sa 15:22; Mal 1:10

"I have more than enough of burnt offerings,
of rams and the fat of fattened animals;[w]
I have no pleasure
in the blood of bulls[x] and lambs and goats.[y]

1:12 [z]Ex 23:17

12 When you come to appear before me,
who has asked this of you,[z]
this trampling of my courts?

1:13 [a]Isa 66:3 [b]Jer 7:9 [c]1Ch 23:31

13 Stop bringing meaningless offerings![a]
Your incense[b] is detestable to me.
New Moons, Sabbaths and convocations[c]—
I cannot bear your evil assemblies.

---

covenant. **the Holy One of Israel.** Isaiah's special designation for the Lord that calls attention to his uniqueness and awe-inspiring splendor. The term occurs 26 times in Isaiah (e.g., 5:19,24; 12:6; 30:11–12,15; 41:14,16,20; 45:11; 48:17; 55:5; 60:9,14). See also "the Holy One of Jacob" (29:23), "Holy One" (10:17; 40:25) and "your Holy One" (43:15).

1:5–6 beaten . . . sores. By the time of this prophecy Judah had been attacked by Syria, northern Israel, Edom and Philistia (2Ch 28:5–18), as well as possibly by Assyria in 701 B.C. (36:1–2). These attacks should have brought sincere repentance, but they had little lasting effect.

1:8 Daughter of Zion. An endearing personification of Jerusalem. Here Zion signifies the people of Judah who experienced God's judgment. **shelter.** A temporary structure used by watchmen during the harvest. See note on 4:6. **hut.** A temporary structure used by the night guard (24:20).

1:9 LORD Almighty. Literally, "LORD of armies," a designation for God as the divine warrior (5:26; 9:6; 13:4; 24:14–16; 30:27; 40:10–11; 42:13,25; 59:17; 66:15–16), the commander over his troops, whether in heaven or on Earth. His battles and wars always end in victory for him. Israel's ultimate survival was due not to the enemy's weakness but to God's sovereign power. **survivors.** The attacks against Judah would be so severe that some of its citizens would survive only due to God's faithfulness to his promises (Ro 9:29). Isaiah taught that God would preserve a righteous remnant; the prophet encouraged the people to belong to that remnant and held out hope for great blessings to this group. **Sodom . . . Gomorrah.** God's people had become like the wicked inhabitants of these Canaanite cities, which had been utterly destroyed (1:10; see Ge 18:20–21; 19:24–25). Sodom and Gomorrah symbolize the kingdoms of this world on whom God's impending judgment rests (3:9; 13:19; Lk 17:28–29; Ro 9:29; 2Pe 2:6–10; Jude 7; Rev 11:8). See *BC* 27.

1:10 Hear . . . rulers of Sodom . . . people of Gomorrah! Having likened Judah to Sodom and Gomorrah (see 3:9), God called on the defendants to listen to the legal reasoning of the court (cf. 1:2). See *WLC* 81,129,172.

1:11–17 See *WCF* 15.4; *WLC* 175; *WSC* 87; *HC* 82.

1:11–15 burnt offerings. See Leviticus 1:3–17 and 6:8–13. God desires obedience from the heart rather than animal sacrifices offered from habit or tradition (1Sa 15:22–23; Mic 6:6–8; Mt 23:23). **no pleasure . . . not listen.** God was intolerant of the hypocritical religious practices of his faithless, disobedient people (see Ps 51:16). **hide.** See note on 8:17. See *WCF* 16.7; *BC* 7.

14 Your New Moon festivals and your appointed
feasts[d]
my soul hates.
They have become a burden to me;
I am weary[e] of bearing them.
15 When you spread out your hands in prayer,
I will hide[f] my eyes from you;
even if you offer many prayers,
I will not listen.
Your hands are full of blood;[g]
16 wash and make yourselves clean.
Take your evil deeds
out of my sight![h]
Stop doing wrong,[i]
17 learn to do right!
Seek justice,[j]
encourage the oppressed.[a]
Defend the cause of the fatherless,[k]
plead the case of the widow.

18 "Come now, let us reason together,"[l]
says the LORD.
"Though your sins are like scarlet,
they shall be as white as snow;[m]
though they are red as crimson,
they shall be like wool.
19 If you are willing and obedient,
you will eat the best from the land;[n]
20 but if you resist and rebel,
you will be devoured by the sword."[o]
For the mouth of the LORD has spoken.[p]

21 See how the faithful city
has become a harlot![q]
She once was full of justice;
righteousness used to dwell in her—
but now murderers!
22 Your silver has become dross,
your choice wine is diluted with water.
23 Your rulers are rebels,
companions of thieves;
they all love bribes[r]
and chase after gifts.
They do not defend the cause of the fatherless;
the widow's case does not come before them.[s]
24 Therefore the Lord, the LORD Almighty,
the Mighty One of Israel, declares:
"Ah, I will get relief from my foes

1:14 [d]Lev 23:1-44; Nu 28:11-29:39; Isa 29:1 [e]Isa 7:13; 43:22,24
1:15 [f]Isa 8:17; 59:2; Mic 3:4 [g]Isa 59:3
1:16 [h]Isa 52:11 [i]Isa 55:7; Jer 25:5
1:17 [j]Zep 2:3 [k]Ps 82:3
1:18 [l]Isa 41:1; 43:9,26 [m]Ps 51:7; Rev 7:14
1:19 [n]Dt 30:15-16; Isa 55:2
1:20 [o]Isa 3:25; 65:12 [p]Isa 34:16; 40:5; 58:14; Mic 4:4
1:21 [q]Isa 57:3-9; Jer 2:20
1:23 [r]Ex 23:8 [s]Isa 10:2; Jer 5:28; Eze 22:6-7; Zec 7:10

[a] 17 Or / *rebuke the oppressor*

1:17 right . . . justice. Here the prophet revealed the heart of God's case against Judah: the corruption of Jerusalem's legal system and its social injustice. See 1:17, 21 and 26–27. **oppressed . . . widow.** Although concern for the needy should never be confused with saving faith, it is a primary demonstration of true godliness (cf. v. 23; see 58:7; Jer 22:16; Jas 1:27). See *WLC* 129.
1:18 scarlet. The color depicts the people's hands as being "full of blood" (v. 15). **white as snow.** Despite Judah's terrible condition, repentance would bring forgiveness to individuals and communities, thus averting the wrath of God at least in some measure (see Jer 18:1–18). See *WCF* 15.4; *WLC* 175.
1:20 be devoured. Repentance would lead to eating the bounty of the land; rebellion to being devoured by enemies.
1:21–31 Isaiah closed the courtroom scene with a declaration of the guilt of Zion and the punishment that would lead to the removal of evil.
1:21 faithful city . . . harlot! Perhaps carrying further the personification of Jerusalem in verse 8. The city had been faithful after it had been founded by David, but it had more recently become overwhelmingly perfidious. Note the theme of harlotry in Hosea 1–3. In this case Jerusalem's profligacy was primarily associated with the influence of false religions on the courts. **justice . . . righteousness.** See note on 1:17. Notice the restoration of this character for the city in verse 26.
1:23 bribes. The practice of bribery is strongly condemned in God's law, for it fosters injustice (Ex 23:8; Dt 10:17; 16:19; 27:25; see also Isa 5:23; 33:15; 45:13). **fatherless . . . widow's case.** Orphans and widows were particularly vulnerable to inequity and were therefore of particular concern to God (e.g., Dt 10:18; 17:19; 24:17–19; 26:12–13; Ps 146:9).
1:24 my foes . . . my enemies. The Judahites had so violated their covenant with God that they had become his enemies and were thus subject to his holy wrath delivered through Assyrian—and later Babylonian—aggression.

and avenge[t] myself on my enemies.
25 I will turn my hand against you;
I will thoroughly purge away your dross
and remove all your impurities.[u]
26 I will restore your judges as in days of old,[v]
your counselors as at the beginning.
Afterward you will be called
the City of Righteousness,[w]
the Faithful City.[x]"

27 Zion will be redeemed with justice,
her penitent ones with righteousness.[y]
28 But rebels and sinners will both be broken,
and those who forsake the LORD will perish.[z]

29 "You will be ashamed because of the sacred oaks[a]
in which you have delighted;
you will be disgraced because of the gardens[b]
that you have chosen.
30 You will be like an oak with fading leaves,
like a garden without water.
31 The mighty man will become tinder
and his work a spark;
both will burn together,
with no one to quench the fire.[c]"

The Mountain of the LORD

2 This is what Isaiah son of Amoz saw concerning Judah and Jerusalem:[d]

2 In the last days

the mountain[e] of the LORD's temple will be established
as chief among the mountains;
it will be raised above the hills,
and all nations will stream to it.

3 Many peoples will come and say,

"Come, let us go up to the mountain of the LORD,
to the house of the God of Jacob.
He will teach us his ways,
so that we may walk in his paths."
The law[f] will go out from Zion,
the word of the LORD from Jerusalem.[g]

1:24 [t]Isa 35:4; 59:17; 61:2; 63:4
1:25 [u]Eze 22:22; Mal 3:3
1:26 [v]Jer 33:7,11 [w]Isa 33:5; 62:1; Zec 8:3 [x]Isa 60:14; 62:2
1:27 [y]Isa 35:10; 62:12; 63:4
1:28 [z]Ps 9:5; Isa 24:20; 66:24; 2Th 1:8-9
1:29 [a]Isa 57:5 [b]Isa 65:3; 66:17
1:31 [c]Isa 5:24; 9:18-19; 26:11; 33:14; 66:15-16,24
2:1 [d]Isa 1:1
2:2 [e]Isa 27:13; 56:7; 66:20; Mic 4:7
2:3 [f]Isa 51:4,7 [g]Lk 24:47

1:25 purge . . . dross . . . remove . . . impurities. Jerusalem's judgment was intended to purify it of corruption.
1:26 I will restore. The cleansing of judgment would eventually lead to the restoration of the city, not to its final destruction. In view here is the reinstatement of "judges" and "counselors" who would bring justice to the city after the exile. **days of old . . . the beginning.** Restored Jerusalem would be similar to what it had been in the beginning—only better. Both leaders and people would live in harmony with God's will (24:23; 32:1). The city would be filled with godly men and women who would practice righteousness and demonstrate faithful service to God and to other people (see note on v. 21).
1:27–28 A sharp contrast is drawn between the "penitent ones" (v. 27) and "those who forsake the LORD" (v. 28). The former would be "redeemed" (v. 27), while the latter would "perish" (v. 28). The Assyrian and Babylonian judgments against Judah accomplished this to some degree, but ultimate judgment and redemption will be fulfilled by Christ at his return.
1:29 ashamed . . . disgraced. The sinners of Judah would perceive how wrong they had been when they came to ruin (26:11; 29:22; 44:9,11; 65:13; 66:5). **sacred oaks . . . gardens.** The locations of the fertility rituals that had corrupted Judah (see notes on 65:3; 66:17). The corruption of the courts of Jerusalem evidently resulted, either directly or indirectly, from their adopting unjust practices (v. 27) promoted by false religions. **delighted.** Judgment exposes lust.
1:30–31 without water . . . fire. Drought (v. 30) and fire (v. 31) signify God's judgment. Moreover, in Isaiah the image of water signifies free, gracious and bountiful salvation (11:9; 32:2; 41:18; 48:21; 55:1; 58:11), while its absence portends futility and separation from God's blessings (3:1; 7:19; 41:17; 50:2).
■ **2:1–5** *Zion's Future Righteousness and Justice.* To balance his lawsuit against unrighteousness and injustice, Isaiah added an assurance of Zion's glorious future, when righteousness and justice would not only be present in the city but also overflow to the nations.
2:2 last days. See note on Hosea 3:5 and theological article "The Plan of the Ages" at Hebrews 7. **mountain.** The prophet spoke of the temple mount because it was the centerpiece of the capital of the Lord's kingdom that would one day be exalted above all other kingdoms (cf. 11:9; 65:11,25; 66:20). Mount Zion replicated the heavenly realms and foreshadowed heavenly Jerusalem, which will descend to the earth when history reaches its consummation in Christ. God's people now come directly to that heavenly reality through the priesthood of the ascended Lord Jesus (see Heb 9:23–24; 12:22–24). When Christ returns the new Jerusalem will descend from heaven and be the center of the new heavens and the new earth (Rev 21:1–4). **chief.** Pagans also worshiped their gods at mountain shrines. By describing Zion in this way, Isaiah indicated that Israel's God, who is worshiped on Mount Zion, would establish himself in the eyes of all races and nations as the only true and living God. In Christ many Gentiles already worship the Lord, and he will be universally acknowledged when Christ returns.
2:3 let us go. Peoples from the Gentile nations would encourage each other to worship God from regenerate hearts. **law . . . from Zion.** The law of God would be observed by his people in the

4 He will judge between the nations
and will settle disputes for many peoples.
They will beat their swords into plowshares
and their spears into pruning hooks.[h]
Nation will not take up sword against nation,[i]
nor will they train for war anymore.

5 Come, O house of Jacob,[j]
let us walk in the light[k] of the LORD.

The Day of the LORD

6 You have abandoned[l] your people,
the house of Jacob.
They are full of superstitions from the East;
they practice divination like the Philistines[m]
and clasp hands[n] with pagans.[o]
7 Their land is full of silver and gold;
there is no end to their treasures.
Their land is full of horses;[p]
there is no end to their chariots.[q]
8 Their land is full of idols;[r]
they bow down to the work of their hands,
to what their fingers[s] have made.
9 So man will be brought low[t]
and mankind humbled[u]—
do not forgive them.[a][v]

10 Go into the rocks,
hide in the ground
from dread of the LORD
and the splendor of his majesty![w]
11 The eyes of the arrogant man will be humbled
and the pride[x] of men brought low;
the LORD alone will be exalted in that day.

2:4 [h]Joel 3:10 [i]Ps 46:9; Isa 9:5; 11:6-9; 32:18; Hos 2:18; Zec 9:10
2:5 [j]Isa 58:1 [k]Isa 60:1, 19-20; 1Jn 1:5,7
2:6 [l]Dt 31:17 [m]2Ki 1:2 [n]Pr 6:1 [o]2Ki 16:7
2:7 [p]Dt 17:16 [q]Isa 31:1; Mic 5:10
2:8 [r]Isa 10:9-11 [s]Isa 17:8
2:9 [t]Ps 62:9 [u]Isa 5:15 [v]Ne 4:5
2:10 [w]2Th 1:9; Rev 6:15-16
2:11 [x]Isa 5:15; 37:23

[a] 9 Or *not raise them up*

restoration, and justice would thus be established. Moreover, in the time of restoration Jews and Gentiles from all nations who had escaped the judgment of God would observe this law together (see 11:9–12; 27:13; 56:3,6–8; 65:25; 66:19–24). This prophecy began to be fulfilled in the spread of God's kingdom to Gentile nations through the gospel of Christ in the New Testament period, and it will come to final fruition in the universal dominion of the kingdom at Christ's return (see theological article "The Kingdom of God" at Mt 4). See *WCF* 26.2.

2:4 judge. The Lord will rule over the nations. His kingdom will extend to the whole earth and will effect peace among the nations. To this end our Lord Jesus came (Lk 2:14). **swords into plowshares.** Instead of agricultural implements being forged into weapons of war (Joel 3:10), the Lord's rule will eventually end all warfare forever.

2:5 light. Here light stands for God's blessings, presence and revelation (9:2; 30:26; 42:6,16; 58:8,10; 60:1,3). The Lord is the light in blessing and in judgment (10:17; 45:7; 60:19–20; cf. Jn 1:4; 8:12). People who exchange God's light for the darkness of their corrupt minds (5:20; 8:20) will experience his judgment and live in the darkness of separation from God (5:30; 13:10; 50:11; 59:9; cf. Jn 3:19–20).

■ **2:6—4:6** *Judgment and Restoration on That Day.* This portion of the summary of Isaiah's message (see note on 1:2—6:13) consists of oracles drawn together by the theme of "that day" (2:11,17,20; 3:7,18; 4:1–2); i.e., the "day of the LORD" (13:6,9). That day would be a time of severe judgment (2:6—4:1), but it would also bring immeasurable blessings for God's people (4:2–6).

■ **2:6–22** *Pride and Syncretism on That Day.* Isaiah introduced the judgment of the day of the Lord by declaring that God would deal harshly with widespread syncretism and pride in the land. Isaiah first acknowledged God's sentence against Judah (v. 6a), listed a number of accusations (vv. 6b–8), announced the sentence once again (v. 9) and connected it with an elaborate description of the day of the Lord (vv. 10–22).

2:6–8 Syncretism and pride led to the sentencing of verses 6 and 9.

2:6 You. Isaiah acknowledged to God that he understood the reality of the judgment to come. **abandoned.** God abandoned his people to suffer harm from other nations because they had first abandoned him (cf. 2Ch 12:5). **East . . . Philistines.** References to the pagan cultures to the east and to the west of Judah. The Lord had commanded Israel to avoid all forms of pagan influence (Lev 19:26; Dt 18:10–11). **clasp hands.** This may refer to military alliances with Gentiles or to adoption of their religious practices.

2:7 silver and gold. Wealth had turned Judah away from faithful service to God. **horses . . . chariots.** The people relied on their own strength (30:16; 31:1,3) rather than on the Lord (see Pss 20:7; 37:17; 147:10).

2:8 Isaiah ridiculed the impotence of idols (2:18,20; 17:7–8; 30:22; 31:7; 37:19; 40:19–20; 41:7,22–24,28–29; 42:17; 44:9–20; 45:16,20; 46:1–2,6–7; 48:5,14; 57:13) and affirmed the power of the Lord (42:8–9; 44:6–8; 45:5–6,14–15,22; 46:9–10).

2:9 man . . . mankind. Not only would Judah be humbled because of syncretism (simultaneous allegiance to various gods), but the idolatrous nations surrounding her would also be brought low (see chs. 13–27).

2:10–22 God would deal with the pride and syncretism mentioned in 2:6–9 by means of severe judgment on the day of the Lord. The repetition of this refrain in verses 10, 19 and 21 both divides this material into sections and draws it into one coherent unit. God would be exalted through his judgment as supreme, and sinners would be appropriately humbled for their syncretism and pride.

2:10 rocks. At God's judgment people may seek shelter, but no one can successfully hide from him.

2:11 in that day. Although different aspects are emphasized in particular passages, the day of the Lord describes any day in which God dramatically intervenes to destroy his enemies (among the Gentiles and within Israel) and to bless his faithful people (within Israel and among the Gentiles). See "Introduction to Zephaniah." God may act directly or through instruments such as Assyria and

12 The LORD Almighty has a day in store
for all the proud and lofty,
for all that is exalted[y]
(and they will be humbled),[z]
13 for all the cedars of Lebanon, tall and lofty,
and all the oaks of Bashan,[a]
14 for all the towering mountains
and all the high hills,[b]
15 for every lofty tower
and every fortified wall,[c]
16 for every trading ship[a][d]
and every stately vessel.
17 The arrogance of man will be brought low
and the pride of men humbled;
the LORD alone will be exalted in that day,[e]
18 and the idols will totally disappear.[f]

19 Men will flee to caves in the rocks
and to holes in the ground
from dread of the LORD
and the splendor of his majesty,
when he rises to shake the earth.[g]
20 In that day men will throw away
to the rodents and bats[h]
their idols of silver and idols of gold,
which they made to worship.
21 They will flee to caverns in the rocks
and to the overhanging crags
from dread of the LORD
and the splendor of his majesty,
when he rises to shake the earth.[i]

22 Stop trusting in man,[j]
who has but a breath in his nostrils.
Of what account is he?[k]

Judgment on Jerusalem and Judah

3 See now, the Lord,
the LORD Almighty,
is about to take from Jerusalem and Judah
both supply and support:
all supplies of food[l] and all supplies of water,[m]
2 the hero and warrior,[n]
the judge and prophet,
the soothsayer and elder,[o]
3 the captain of fifty and man of rank,
the counselor, skilled craftsman and clever enchanter.
4 I will make boys their officials;
mere children will govern them.[p]
5 People will oppress each other—
man against man, neighbor against neighbor.[q]

2:12 [y]Isa 24:4,21; Mal 4:1 [z]Job 40:11
2:13 [a]Zec 11:2
2:14 [b]Isa 30:25; 40:4
2:15 [c]Isa 25:2,12
2:16 [d]1Ki 10:22
2:17 [e]ver 11
2:18 [f]Isa 21:9
2:19 [g]Heb 12:26
2:20 [h]Lev 11:19
2:21 [i]ver 19
2:22 [j]Ps 146:3; Jer 17:5 [k]Ps 8:4; 144:3; Isa 40:15; Jas 4:14
3:1 [l]Lev 26:26 [m]Isa 5:13; Eze 4:16
3:2 [n]Eze 17:13 [o]2Ki 24:14; Isa 9:14-15
3:4 [p]Ecc 10:16 *fn*
3:5 [q]Isa 9:19; Jer 9:8; Mic 7:2,6

a *16* Hebrew *every ship of Tarshish*

Babylon (3:7,17; 7:18,20–21,23; 11:10–11; 20:6; 24:21; 27:1–2, 12–13; 52:6; see also notes on Joel 2:31; Zep 1:7; 2:13–18).
2:12–16 LORD Almighty. See note on 1:9. **proud . . . stately vessel.** The prophet listed a number of things in which people took pride.
2:17 in that day. See note on 2:11.
2:20 In that day. See note on 2:11. Idols would be helpless. For commentary on Isaiah's polemic against idolatry, see 2:8.
2:22 man . . . breath. The breath of life is derived from God, not from dependent, finite human beings.
■ **3:1–15** *Jerusalem's Leaders on That Day.* Isaiah confronted the failures of Jerusalem's leaders first by reporting judgments coming against them on the day of the Lord (v. 7), mixed with some accusations (vv. 1–12), and then by closing with a heavenly courtroom scene in which serious accusations were made (vv. 13–15).
3:1–3 food . . . water. The chaotic conditions of coming judgment would result in lack of food and water. See note on 1:30. **hero . . . enchanter.** The Lord would enter into judgment against various corrupt leaders on whom the people had depended. See note on 11:2.
3:4 boys . . . children. The traditional leadership by elders would be so destroyed that young men without experience would be compelled to take the lead.
3:5 Judah's collapse would come in the form of social chaos: rich

The young will rise up against the old,
the base against the honorable.

6 A man will seize one of his brothers
at his father's home, and say,
"You have a cloak, you be our leader;
take charge of this heap of ruins!"
7 But in that day he will cry out,
"I have no remedy.[r]
I have no food or clothing in my house;
do not make me the leader of the people."

8 Jerusalem staggers,
Judah is falling;[s]
their words[t] and deeds are against the LORD,
defying[u] his glorious presence.
9 The look on their faces testifies against them;
they parade their sin like Sodom;[v]
they do not hide it.
Woe to them!
They have brought disaster[w] upon themselves.

10 Tell the righteous it will be well[x] with them,
for they will enjoy the fruit of their deeds.[y]
11 Woe to the wicked! Disaster[z] is upon them!
They will be paid back for what their hands have done.

12 Youths[a] oppress my people,
women rule over them.
O my people, your guides lead you astray;[b]
they turn you from the path.
13 The LORD takes his place in court;
he rises to judge[c] the people.
14 The LORD enters into judgment[d]
against the elders and leaders of his people:
"It is you who have ruined my vineyard;
the plunder[e] from the poor is in your houses.
15 What do you mean by crushing my people[f]
and grinding the faces of the poor?"
declares the Lord, the LORD Almighty.

16 The LORD says,
"The women of Zion[g] are haughty,
walking along with outstretched necks,
flirting with their eyes,
tripping along with mincing steps,
with ornaments jingling on their ankles.
17 Therefore the Lord will bring sores on the heads of the women
of Zion;
the LORD will make their scalps bald."

3:7 [r]Eze 34:4; Hos 5:13
3:8 [s]Isa 1:7 [t]Isa 9:15, 17 [u]Ps 73:9, 11
3:9 [v]Ge 13:13 [w]Pr 8:36; Ro 6:23
3:10 [x]Dt 28:1-14 [y]Ps 128:2
3:11 [z]Dt 28:15-68
3:12 [a]ver 4 [b]Isa 9:16
3:13 [c]Mic 6:2
3:14 [d]Job 22:4 [e]Job 24:9; Jas 2:6
3:15 [f]Ps 94:5
3:16 [g]SS 3:11

against poor, young against old, base against honorable. See *WLC* 128,151.
3:6–7 In poignant hyperbole, the prophet described the coming judgment as so dire that leaders would be chosen simply because they had a cloak to wear—but those leaders themselves would recognize how little help they had to offer.
3:7 in that day. See note on 2:11.
3:8 against the LORD, defying his glorious presence. Judah had been blessed with the special presence of God in the temple, but this blessing increased the severity of God's judgment against the people's rebellion (cf. Am 3:2). **glorious.** See note on 4:2.
3:9 look on their faces. A reference to defiance and pride. The Judahites had no more shame than the inhabitants of Sodom. See 1:9–10. **Woe.** Introduces a dire threat (v. 11; 6:5; 24:16).
3:10 righteous. Those who had not strayed into flagrant violations of the covenant. They would not fail forever to see the fruit of their faithfulness.
3:12 Youths . . . women. Under good conditions older men of wisdom and age would normally rule in Israel, but rebellion against God would oblige the nation to accept the leadership of foolish youth and haughty women (see 3:16).
3:13–15 his place in court. Isaiah explicitly described the heavenly courtroom scene in which he had received the preceding judgments and accusations. Here he dramatically conveyed the accusations of the court. **the people . . . elders and leaders.** The divine judge brought accusations against the leaders of Israel for leading the people astray. **the poor . . . my people.** The abuses of Judah's leaders were especially visible in their mistreatment of the poor. **LORD Almighty.** See note on 1:9.
■ **3:16—4:1** *Haughty Women on That Day.* The mention of women in 3:12, as well as the repeated focus on the day of the Lord (3:18; 4:1), led to this oracle against proud and wealthy women in Judah (cf. Am 4:1–3). They shared the guilt of living to the fullest at the expense of others. Their outward adornments reflected an inner attitude of pride (1Pe 3:3–4).
3:16 Zion. See note on 1:8. See *WLC* 139.

18 In that day the Lord will snatch away their finery: the bangles and headbands and crescent necklaces,[h] 19 the earrings and bracelets and veils, 20 the headdresses[i] and ankle chains and sashes, the perfume bottles and charms, 21 the signet rings and nose rings, 22 the fine robes and the capes and cloaks, the purses 23 and mirrors, and the linen garments and tiaras and shawls.

24 Instead of fragrance[j] there will be a stench;
instead of a sash,[k] a rope;
instead of well-dressed hair, baldness;[l]
instead of fine clothing, sackcloth;[m]
instead of beauty,[n] branding.
25 Your men will fall by the sword,[o]
your warriors in battle.
26 The gates of Zion will lament and mourn;[p]
destitute, she will sit on the ground.[q]

4 In that day seven women
will take hold of one man[r]
and say, "We will eat our own food[s]
and provide our own clothes;
only let us be called by your name.
Take away our disgrace!"[t]

The Branch of the Lord

2 In that day the Branch of the Lord[u] will be beautiful and glorious, and the fruit[v] of the land will be the pride and glory of the survivors in Israel. 3 Those who are left in Zion, who remain[w] in Jerusalem, will be called holy,[x] all who are recorded[y] among the living in Jerusalem. 4 The Lord will wash away the filth[z] of the women of Zion; he will cleanse the bloodstains[a] from Jerusalem by a spirit[a] of judgment[b] and a spirit[a] of fire.[c] 5 Then the Lord will create over all of Mount Zion and over those who assemble there a cloud of smoke by day and a glow of flaming fire by night;[d] over all the glory[e] will be a canopy. 6 It will be a shelter[f] and shade from the heat of the day, and a refuge[g] and hiding place from the storm and rain.

The Song of the Vineyard

5 I will sing for the one I love
a song about his vineyard:[h]

a 4 Or *the Spirit*

3:18 [h]Jdg 8:21
3:20 [i]Ex 39:28
3:24 [j]Est 2:12 [k]Pr 31:24 [l]Isa 22:12 [m]La 2:10; Eze 27:30-31 [n]1Pe 3:3
3:25 [o]Isa 1:20
3:26 [p]Jer 14:2 [q]La 2:10
4:1 [r]Isa 13:12 [s]2Th 3:12 [t]Ge 30:23
4:2 [u]Isa 11:1-5; 53:2; Jer 23:5-6; Zec 3:8; 6:12 [v]Ps 72:16
4:3 [w]Ro 11:5 [x]Isa 52:1; 60:21 [y]Lk 10:20
4:4 [z]Isa 3:24 [a]Isa 1:15 [b]Isa 28:6 [c]Isa 1:31; Mt 3:11
4:5 [d]Ex 13:21 [e]Isa 60:1
4:6 [f]Ps 27:5 [g]Isa 25:4
5:1 [h]Ps 80:8-9

3:17 sores . . . scalps. The Lord would disgrace these women (v. 24). **Zion.** See note on 1:8.
3:18 In that day. See note on 2:11. The Lord would remove all false securities. **finery.** See note on 4:2.
3:24 stench . . . branding. The women would be destitute and subject to horrors on the day of the Lord.
3:26 gates. The gates of Jerusalem are personified as joining in the lament over the impending judgment (cf. Ps 24:7). **Zion.** See note on 1:8.
4:1 in that day. See note on 2:11.
■ **4:2–6** *The Royal Branch on That Day.* The prophet balanced his words of judgment (2:6—4:1) with the way salvation would come to God's people on the day of the Lord through the Branch, the great son of David.
4:2 In that day. See note on 2:11. **Branch.** A metaphorical title for the son of David, the Messiah, who would bring about the restoration of God's people from exile (see 11:1–5; 53:2). The New Testament explains that Jesus is this son of David who brings eternal salvation to those who have faith in him (see Jer 23:5; Zec 3:8; Jn 15:1–8). **glorious.** The glory of God is the display of his brilliance and wonder in his general providence and in redemption. The Messiah would be the premiere display of his glory (3:8; 4:5; 6:3; 11:10; 40:5; 42:8,12; 43:7; 48:11; 58:8; 59:19; 66:18,19). **survivors.** See note on 1:8.
4:3 left . . . remain. The godly remnant (see note on 1:8) would survive exile and return to the land. **Zion.** See note on 1:8. **holy.** The returnees would be consecrated to God, the Holy One of Israel (see note on 1:4; see 62:12), who would establish his holy residence among his people (57:15) on the new earth (11:9; 27:13; 65:25; 66:20). **recorded.** The names of those who enter this new world were written in the book of life, never to be removed (Ex 32:32–33; Ps 69:28; Da 12:1; Mal 3:16; Rev 20:12).
4:4 Zion. See note on 1:8. **spirit . . . spirit.** Possibly the Holy Spirit. **fire.** Literally, "burning." A metaphor for judgment (1:31; 10:17; 30:27; 42:25) that consumes the rebellious and purifies the faithful. Compare John the Baptist's expectations of Jesus' baptism with the Holy Spirit (Lk 3:16).
4:5–6 See *WLC* 63.
4:5 create. The future redemption is a re-creation in which everything in heaven and on Earth (40:26; 42:5; 45:12,18; 57:16) is renewed. The process of re-creative redemption began with the restoration from exile but reaches its final stages in the work of Christ (see notes on Jn 1:1–3; 2Co 4:6; 5:17)—especially in the new heavens and the new earth in which all the redeemed will one day gather to the new Jerusalem (Rev 3:12; 21:1–3). **cloud of smoke . . . glow of flaming fire.** Symbols of God's protective presence with his elect, as at the Red Sea (Ex 13:20–22), in the tabernacle (Ex 40:34–38) and in the wilderness (Nu 9:15–23). Here it symbolizes God's protective covering over restored and sanctified Mount Zion (see note on 2:2). **fire.** Used here as an expression of God's judgment (1:7,31; 5:24; 26:11; 33:11,14; 47:14; 64:2; 65:5; 66:15–16, 24) in contrast to the symbol of his blessed presence (v. 5; 43:2; cf. Ex 24:17; Dt 4:24; 9:3; 2Sa 22:9; Ps 18:8; Heb 12:29). **glory.** See note on 4:2.
4:6 shelter. A permanent protection, in contrast to a temporary shelter (1:8; cf. Ps 31:20). **shade.** See note on 30:2. **refuge.** In contrast to human deceptions (28:15,17) the Lord will provide lasting shelter from all harm for his people. Although Christ has already brought refuge to his people in part, this enduring safety will come in its fullness when he returns in glory (25:4; cf. Pss 14:6; 46:1; 62:7; 94:22).
■ **5:1—6:13** *Judgment Leading to Restoration.* In these verses this

My loved one had a vineyard
  on a fertile hillside.
2 He dug it up and cleared it of stones
  and planted it with the choicest vines.[i]
He built a watchtower in it
  and cut out a winepress as well.
Then he looked for a crop of good grapes,
  but it yielded only bad fruit.[j]

3 "Now you dwellers in Jerusalem and men of Judah,
  judge between me and my vineyard.[k]
4 What more could have been done for my vineyard
  than I have done for it?[l]
When I looked for good grapes,
  why did it yield only bad?
5 Now I will tell you
  what I am going to do to my vineyard:
I will take away its hedge,
  and it will be destroyed;
I will break down its wall,[m]
  and it will be trampled.[n]
6 I will make it a wasteland,
  neither pruned nor cultivated,
  and briers and thorns[o] will grow there.
I will command the clouds
  not to rain on it."

7 The vineyard[p] of the LORD Almighty
  is the house of Israel,
and the men of Judah
  are the garden of his delight.
And he looked for justice,[q] but saw bloodshed;
  for righteousness, but heard cries of distress.

Woes and Judgments

8 Woe[r] to you who add house to house
  and join field to field[s]
till no space is left
  and you live alone in the land.

9 The LORD Almighty has declared in my hearing:[t]

"Surely the great houses will become desolate,[u]
  the fine mansions left without occupants.
10 A ten-acre[a] vineyard will produce only a bath[b] of wine,
  a homer[c] of seed only an ephah[d] of grain."[v]

5:2 [i]Jer 2:21 [j]Mt 21:19; Mk 11:13; Lk 13:6
5:3 [k]Mt 21:40
5:4 [l]2Ch 36:15; Jer 2:5-7; Mic 6:3-4; Mt 23:37
5:5 [m]Ps 80:12 [n]Isa 28:3,18; La 1:15; Lk 21:24
5:6 [o]Isa 7:23,24; Heb 6:8
5:7 [p]Ps 80:8 [q]Isa 59:15
5:8 [r]Jer 22:13 [s]Mic 2:2; Hab 2:9-12
5:9 [t]Isa 22:14 [u]Isa 6:11-12; Mt 23:38
5:10 [v]Lev 26:26

[a] *10* Hebrew *ten-yoke,* that is, the land plowed by 10 yoke of oxen in one day [b] *10* That is, probably about 6 gallons (about 22 liters) [c] *10* That is, probably about 6 bushels (about 220 liters) [d] *10* That is, probably about 3/5 bushel (about 22 liters)

---

opening summary of Isaiah's message of doom and hope (see note on 1:2—6:13) focuses on how the judgment of God had to be carried out (5:1–30) until the predicted destruction took place (6:1–13). These materials divide into a parable of a vineyard (5:1–7), a series of woes (5:8–30) and the call of Isaiah to his prophetic mission (6:1–13).

■ **5:1–7** *The Song of the Vineyard.* Isaiah sang about the ways Judah had rebelled against God, using the images of a vineyard and a gardener (see Mt 21:33–44; Jn 15:1–6).

5:1 the one I love. God. **vineyard.** God's people, who are Israel and Judah (see v. 7).

5:2 dug . . . planted. God had carefully prepared and established his people for generations to come. **watchtower . . . good grapes.** These images reinforce the expectation that the redemption of God's people from Egypt would result in an abundant harvest. **bad fruit.** Literally, "stinking things."

5:3 my vineyard. The prophet quoted the gardener (God) as he spoke of his vineyard. God revealed how graciously he had dealt with his people in order to draw attention to the severity of their ingratitude and rebellion.

5:4 See *WLC* 113.

5:6 briers and thorns. These weeds represent God's curse (7:23–25; 9:18; 10:17; 27:4; 32:13). After exile God would replace the briers and thorns with the bounty of pine trees and myrtles (55:13).

5:7 house of Israel . . . men of Judah. The prophet explained the parable of the vineyard.

■ **5:8–30** *Woes Over God's People.* The prophet declared six oracles of woe to express the dire circumstances God's people would encounter when they suffered his judgment.

5:8–10 The first woe condemned greed.

5:8 Woe. Introduces a dire threat. The land belonged to God (Lev 25:23), had been allotted by him (Nu 33:54) and was the basis for every family's livelihood. Deprived of land, Israel's middle class citizens would become day laborers or slaves. See *WLC* 142.

5:9 LORD Almighty. See note on 1:9. God's judgment targeted the opulent and self-indulgent lifestyle of many in Israel. Their mansions provided no protection.

5:10 bath. A liquid measure of about six gallons. **homer.** A dry

11 Woe to those who rise early in the morning
to run after their drinks,
who stay up late at night
till they are inflamed with wine.[w]
12 They have harps and lyres at their banquets,
tambourines and flutes and wine,
but they have no regard[x] for the deeds of the LORD,
no respect for the work of his hands.[y]
13 Therefore my people will go into exile[z]
for lack of understanding;[a]
their men of rank will die of hunger
and their masses will be parched with thirst.
14 Therefore the grave[a][b] enlarges its appetite
and opens its mouth[c] without limit;
into it will descend their nobles and masses
with all their brawlers and revelers.
15 So man will be brought low[d]
and mankind humbled,[e]
the eyes of the arrogant[f] humbled.
16 But the LORD Almighty will be exalted by his justice,[g]
and the holy God will show himself holy[h] by his righteousness.
17 Then sheep will graze as in their own pasture;[i]
lambs will feed[b] among the ruins of the rich.

18 Woe to those who draw sin along with cords of deceit,
and wickedness[j] as with cart ropes,
19 to those who say, "Let God hurry,
let him hasten his work
so we may see it.
Let it approach,
let the plan of the Holy One of Israel come,
so we may know it."[k]

20 Woe to those who call evil good
and good evil,
who put darkness for light
and light for darkness,[l]
who put bitter for sweet
and sweet for bitter.[m]

21 Woe to those who are wise in their own eyes[n]
and clever in their own sight.

22 Woe to those who are heroes at drinking wine[o]
and champions at mixing drinks,
23 who acquit the guilty for a bribe,[p]
but deny justice[q] to the innocent.[r]
24 Therefore, as tongues of fire lick up straw
and as dry grass sinks down in the flames,

5:11 [w]Pr 23:29-30
5:12 [x]Job 34:27 [y]Ps 28:5; Am 6:5-6
5:13 [z]Hos 4:6 [a]Isa 1:3; Hos 4:6
5:14 [b]Pr 30:16 [c]Nu 16:30
5:15 [d]Isa 10:33 [e]Isa 2:9 [f]Isa 2:11
5:16 [g]Isa 28:17; 30:18; 33:5; 61:8 [h]Isa 29:23
5:17 [i]Isa 7:25; Zep 2:6, 14
5:18 [j]Isa 59:4-8; Jer 23:14
5:19 [k]Jer 17:15; Eze 12:22; 2Pe 3:4
5:20 [l]Mt 6:22-23; Lk 11:34-35 [m]Am 5:7
5:21 [n]Pr 3:7; Ro 12:16; 1Co 3:18-20
5:22 [o]Pr 23:20
5:23 [p]Ex 23:8 [q]Isa 10:2 [r]Ps 94:21; Jas 5:6

[a] *14* Hebrew *Sheol* [b] *17* Septuagint; Hebrew / *strangers will eat*

measure of about six bushels. **ephah.** A dry measure of about 3/5 of a bushel. A sizeable vineyard (ten acres) would produce only a little.
5:11–17 The second woe condemned social corruption.
5:11 Woe. Introduces a dire threat. **wine.** See note on 24:11. Over-indulgence in intoxicating drink often characterizes social corruption and moral laxity (see chs. 22,28; Am 4:1–3; 6:6–7).
5:12 See *WLC* 113,136.
5:13–16 Therefore. The sentencing followed the indictments of the preceding verses. **my people.** See note on 40:1. **the grave.** The exile is likened to death itself. Death would devour with a ferocious appetite all who had turned away from God, both "nobles" (v. 14; see note on 2:10) and common people ("masses"; vv. 13–14). **So . . . exalted.** See notes on 2:9, 11 and 17. **LORD Almighty.** See note on 1:9. **justice.** See note on 1:17. **holy.** See note on 4:3. **righteousness.** See note on 1:17.
5:18–19 The third woe condemned purposeful and harmful theological corruption. **Woe.** Introduces a dire threat.
5:20 The fourth woe concerned pride and moral corruption. **Woe.** Introduces a dire threat. **light.** See note on 2:5. **darkness.** See note on verse 30.
5:21 The fifth woe condemned spiritual corruption. **Woe.** Introduces a dire threat. **wise in their own eyes.** An expression for arrogant self-reliance. Revelation from God, who alone knows all things, is the only firm foundation for all true knowledge (see Pr 3:7; 26:5,12; 28:11).
5:22–25 The sixth woe condemned social corruption.
5:22 Woe. Introduces a dire threat. **wine.** See note on 24:11. **mixing drinks.** Wine and beer with spices added. Over-indulgence, as in verse 11.
5:23 bribe. See note on 1:23. Injustice and greed, as in verse 8. **justice.** Literally, "righteousness" (see note on 1:17). See *WLC* 145.

so their roots will decay[s]
and their flowers blow away like dust;
for they have rejected the law of the LORD Almighty
and spurned the word[t] of the Holy One of Israel.
25 Therefore the LORD's anger[u] burns against his people;
his hand is raised and he strikes them down.
The mountains shake,
and the dead bodies are like refuse[v] in the streets.

Yet for all this, his anger is not turned away,[w]
his hand is still upraised.[x]

26 He lifts up a banner for the distant nations,
he whistles[y] for those at the ends of the earth.[z]
Here they come,
swiftly and speedily!
27 Not one of them grows tired or stumbles,
not one slumbers or sleeps;
not a belt is loosened at the waist,[a]
not a sandal thong is broken.[b]
28 Their arrows are sharp,[c]
all their bows[d] are strung;
their horses' hoofs seem like flint,
their chariot wheels like a whirlwind.
29 Their roar is like that of the lion,[e]
they roar like young lions;
they growl as they seize[f] their prey
and carry it off with no one to rescue.[g]
30 In that day they will roar over it
like the roaring of the sea.[h]
And if one looks at the land,
he will see darkness and distress;[i]
even the light will be darkened[j] by the clouds.

Isaiah's Commission

6 In the year that King Uzziah[k] died,[l] I saw the Lord[m] seated on a throne,[n] high and
exalted, and the train of his robe filled the temple. 2 Above him were seraphs,[o] each
with six wings: With two wings they covered their faces, with two they covered their
feet,[p] and with two they were flying. 3 And they were calling to one another:

"Holy, holy, holy is the LORD Almighty;
the whole earth is full of his glory."[q]

4 At the sound of their voices the doorposts and thresholds shook and the temple was
filled with smoke.

5:24 [s]Job 18:16 [t]Isa 8:6; 30:9,12
5:25 [u]2Ki 22:13 [v]2Ki 9:37 [w]Jer 4:8; Da 9:16 [x]Isa 9:12, 17,21; 10:4
5:26 [y]Isa 7:18; Zec 10:8 [z]Dt 28:49; Isa 13:5; 18:3
5:27 [a]Job 12:18 [b]Joel 2:7-8
5:28 [c]Ps 45:5 [d]Ps 7:12
5:29 [e]Jer 51:38; Zep 3:3; Zec 11:3 [f]Isa 10:6; 49:24-25 [g]Isa 42:22; Mic 5:8
5:30 [h]Lk 21:25 [i]Isa 8:22; Jer 4:23-28 [j]Joel 2:10
6:1 [k]2Ch 26:22,23 [l]2Ki 15:7 [m]Jn 12:41 [n]Rev 4:2
6:2 [o]Rev 4:8 [p]Eze 1:11
6:3 [q]Ps 72:19; Rev 4:8

5:24 fire. See note 4:5. **LORD Almighty.** See note on 1:9. **the Holy One of Israel.** See note on 1:4.
5:25 mountains shake. At the revelation of God's anger, nature quakes (2:19,21; 13:4,13; 24:18–19). For a contrasting image of redemption, see 54:10. **streets.** See note on 24:11. **his anger . . . upraised.** God had not been reconciled to his people, and his wrath was hanging over them (cf. 9:12,17,21, 10:4, 31:3).
5:26–30 This description of the Assyrian army so closely matches its portrayal on excavated Assyrian reliefs that it suggests the prophet must have been in close contact with Assyrian atrocities.
5:26 banner. The signal flag (11:10,12; 18:3; 49:22; 62:10). The Divine Warrior appointed Gentiles to execute his judgment (10:5). **distant nations.** Perhaps a reference to the fact that the Assyrian army was composed of mercenaries hired from all over the Assyrian Empire.
5:30 In that day. See note on 2:11. **darkness.** A metaphor for judgment (5:20; 8:22; 29:15; 42:7; 47:5; 60:2). All who twisted justice by living in darkness (5:20; 29:15; 47:5) would suffer the darkness of God's judgment. But the light of God would dawn on the humble (9:2; 29:18; 42:7; 49:9; 58:10; 60:1–2). The Lord is sovereign over both (45:7). **light.** See note on 2:5.
■ **6:1–13** *Isaiah's Mission of Judgment and Restoration.* This last cycle closes with a record of the prophet's call and the relationship of the messages of judgment and restoration to each other in God's mission for Isaiah's life.
6:1 Uzziah. This leprous king (2Ch 26:16–21) died in 740 B.C. **throne.** The Lord's throne in his earthly temple was the earthly representation of his throne in his heavenly temple (66:1). **train of his robe.** The royal majesty of God in his throne room overwhelmed Isaiah. **the temple.** God's heavenly temple and throne room intersected with the earthly temple. Isaiah is presented as being in the heavenly temple to which prophets were often taken (cf. Rev 4:1–8).
6:2–3 See *WLC* 192.
6:2 seraphs. The Hebrew term means "fiery ones" (see Nu 21:6). Angelic creatures with six wings abound in the iconography of the ancient Near East. **covered their faces.** God's glorious presence is so overwhelming that they cannot look on him. **covered their feet.** Perhaps a reference to their private areas which are not to be exposed in the presence of God (Ex 20:26). **were flying.** The seraphs fly about to perform multiple duties before the throne.
6:3 were calling to one another. The seraphs repeatedly engaged in this heavenly ritual, revealing that they were overwhelmed by God's holiness and glory. **Holy, holy, holy.** A chant. See note on 1:4. **LORD Almighty.** See note on 1:9. **whole earth.** The grandeur of God in his throne room leaves no doubt that he is King of all the world (2:19,21; 11:4,9,12; 42:1,4–5; 65:17; 66:1,22; see Lk 2:14). **glory.** See note on 4:2. See *WCF* 2.1; *WLC* 7,11.
6:4 A theophany, a visible manifestation of God. God's coming is

6:5 [r]Jer 9:3-8 [s]Jer 51:57
6:7 [t]Jer 1:9 [u]1Jn 1:7
6:8 [v]Ac 9:4

5 "Woe to me!" I cried. "I am ruined! For I am a man of unclean lips, and I live among
a people of unclean lips,[r] and my eyes have seen the King,[s] the LORD Almighty."
6 Then one of the seraphs flew to me with a live coal in his hand, which he had taken
with tongs from the altar. 7 With it he touched my mouth and said, "See, this has touched
your lips;[t] your guilt is taken away and your sin atoned for.[u]"
8 Then I heard the voice[v] of the Lord saying, "Whom shall I send? And who will go
for us?"
And I said, "Here am I. Send me!"

---

attended by the radical rearrangement of the cosmos, in this case expressing judgment against Israel (vv. 9–13), demonstrated in the quaking of the earth and the presence of smoke and often fire (13:13; 24:17–18; 29:6; 30:26–31; Ex 19:18–19; 1Ki 19:11–13; Ps 18:7–15; Eze 20:47–48; Mic 1:3–4; Na 1:3b–8; Hab 3:3–15).

6:5 Woe. Introduces a dire threat. Isaiah feared that his own sins and those of the people would cause the holy King to bring judgment against him. **LORD Almighty.** See note on 1:9. See *WLC* 11.

6:6 altar. The altar from which the "live coal" was taken is not identified, but coals were taken into the Most Holy Place once each year on the Day of Atonement (Lev 26:12).

6:7 my mouth. The prophet admitted his own sinfulness and inadequacy as a prophet but asserted that he was qualified to speak because God had purified his mouth (see Jer 1:9).

6:8 us? Refers to the Lord and the counsel of the heavenly court. Like other prophets, Isaiah served in God's court and proclaimed what he had heard and seen there both to kings and to common people (see 1Ki 22:19–20; Jer 23:18,22). In pagan religions only gods typically served as messengers from the heavenly court, whereas in the Old Testament human prophets served this function. See *WLC* 11.

Divine and Human Holiness: What Is Holiness?

IN the Scriptures the concept of holiness is associated with a group of closely related words ("holy," "sanctified," "consecrated," "holiness," "sanctification," "consecration") which have the basic meaning of "separation" or "set apart" because of some special quality, status or function. Human holiness is different from divine holiness in some senses ("O Lord . . . you alone are holy"; Rev 15:4) but similar to it in others ("I am the LORD your God . . . be holy, because I am holy"; Lev 11:44). In order to obey God's command to be holy as he is holy, we must understand what the Bible says about both divine and human holiness.

When the Scriptures call God "holy" (e.g., Lev 11:44–45; Jos 24:19; 1Sa 2:2; Ps 99:9; Isa 1:4; 6:3; 41:14,16,20; 57:15; Eze 39:7; Am 4:2; Jn 17:11; Ac 5:3–4,32; Rev 15:4), the word signifies everything about God that sets him apart from his creation and makes him an object of awe, adoration and fear. In traditional Reformed theology it has been common to speak of God's holiness in terms of his moral perfection and transcendent greatness.

On the one hand, God is holy in the sense that he is morally perfect: He has no sin (Hab 1:13); he is pure light (Jas 1:17; 1Jn 1:5) and he is good (Pss 25:7; 34:8: 100:5; 119:68; 135:3; Jer 33:11; Mk 10:18; Lk 18:19; 1Pe 2:3). Sinful worshipers fear his judgment (Lev 10:1–2; Isa 6:5) because they do not belong in his presence. God's moral perfection is the cause of much adoration and praise, as well as fear, in people's worship of him.

On the other hand, even the sinless seraphim serving in God's throne room adore him because of his holiness. They bow before him in humility and cry, "Holy, Holy, Holy is the LORD Almighty" (Isa 6:3; cf. Rev 4:8). These creatures do not humble themselves before God because his moral perfection contrasts so strongly with theirs—they too are sinless. Instead, they bow before God as holy because of his transcendent greatness. God is the Creator, distinct and separated from his creation, and that also makes him holy (cf. Isa 41:20; 43:15).

Although it is impossible for any aspect of creation to break through the Creator/creature distinction, God's holiness extends to things and people who have been separated from the world and brought into closer contact with him. Nothing is holy in itself, but people and things become holy by their consecration to God's special service.

For instance, God declared the ground near the burning bush holy because he made use of it (Ex 3:5). Similarly, the tabernacle and temple were holy buildings (Ex 40:9; 1Ch 29:3; Pss 5:7; 11:4). The Sabbath is holy because it is devoted to God (Ex 20:8–11). The ceremonies and the instruments of ceremonies were holy for similar reasons (Ex 29:37; 30:10,25; 40:10; 1Ki 8:4).

Levites and Nazirites were holy (Ex 29:1; Lev 8:12,30; 21:7; 22:9; Nu 6:5; 2Ch 23:6) because they were separated from ordinary people as special servants of God. Israel was also holy because of her special covenant relationship with the Lord (Ex 19:6). It is in this sense that the unbelieving spouses of believers are "sanctified" and the children of believers are "holy" (1Co 7:14). They are distinguished from the world and set apart to God, even though they are not yet believers. Therefore, holiness for human beings implies, in part, a separation from the corruption of this sinful world in order to live closer to God and to serve him in a way that is more special than the actions of the unsanctified world.

At the same time, holiness also refers to the moral dimension of human existence. People are holy when they are obedient to God's commands. Moral holiness or sanctification is to be the constant goal of our lives because without it we will not see God (Heb 12:14). The call to holiness of life is as constant in the New Testament as it was in the Old (Dt 30:1–10; Mt 5:48; Eph 4:17—5:14; 1Pe 1:13–22). Reformed theologians usually call this development of holiness in all areas of life our sanctification (*BC* 24; *WCF* 13; *WLC* 75; see theological article "Sanctification" at Tit 3).

9 He said, "Go[w] and tell this people:

"'Be ever hearing, but never understanding;
be ever seeing, but never perceiving.'[x]
10 Make the heart of this people calloused;[y]
make their ears dull
and close their eyes.[a]
Otherwise they might see with their eyes,
hear with their ears,[z]
understand with their hearts,
and turn and be healed."[a]

11 Then I said, "For how long, O Lord?"[b]
And he answered:

"Until the cities lie ruined[c]
and without inhabitant,
until the houses are left deserted
and the fields ruined and ravaged,
12 until the LORD has sent everyone far away[d]
and the land is utterly forsaken.[e]
13 And though a tenth remains[f] in the land,
it will again be laid waste.
But as the terebinth and oak
leave stumps when they are cut down,
so the holy seed will be the stump in the land."[g]

The Sign of Immanuel

7 When Ahaz son of Jotham, the son of Uzziah, was king of Judah, King Rezin[h] of
Aram[i] and Pekah[j] son of Remaliah king of Israel marched up to fight against Jerusalem, but they could not overpower it.
2 Now the house of David[k] was told, "Aram has allied itself with[b] Ephraim[l]"; so the
hearts of Ahaz and his people were shaken, as the trees of the forest are shaken by the
wind.
3 Then the LORD said to Isaiah, "Go out, you and your son Shear-Jashub,[c] to meet Ahaz
at the end of the aqueduct of the Upper Pool, on the road to the Washerman's Field.[m]
4 Say to him, 'Be careful, keep calm[n] and don't be afraid.[o] Do not lose heart[p] because of
these two smoldering stubs[q] of firewood—because of the fierce anger[r] of Rezin and
Aram and of the son of Remaliah. 5 Aram, Ephraim and Remaliah's son have plotted your

6:9 [w]Eze 3:11 [x]Mt 13:15*; Lk 8:10*
6:10 [y]Dt 32:15; Ps 119:70 [z]Jer 5:21 [a]Mt 13:13-15; Mk 4:12*; Ac 28:26-27*
6:11 [b]Ps 79:5 [c]Lev 26:31
6:12 [d]Dt 28:64 [e]Jer 4:29
6:13 [f]Isa 1:9 [g]Job 14:7
7:1 [h]2Ki 15:37 [i]2Ch 28:5 [j]2Ki 15:25
7:2 [k]ver 13; Isa 22:22 [l]Isa 9:9
7:3 [m]2Ki 18:17; Isa 36:2
7:4 [n]Isa 30:15 [o]Isa 35:4 [p]Dt 20:3 [q]Zec 3:2 [r]Isa 10:24

[a] *9,10* Hebrew; Septuagint *'You will be ever hearing, but never understanding; / you will be ever seeing, but never perceiving.' / [10]This people's heart has become calloused; / they hardly hear with their ears, / and they have closed their eyes* [b] *2* *Or has set up camp in* [c] *3* *Shear-Jashub* means *a remnant will return.*

6:9–10 Isaiah's mission was two-sided, as was Jesus' mission (Mt 13:13–15; Ro 11:7–10,25). The prophetic word was to be delivered in a way that left many without understanding (29:9–12), but it would also reveal truth to the humble whom God had chosen. See *WCF* 5.6.

6:11 how long . . . ? The prophet longed to speak plainly so the people would repent, but his desire was contrary to God's plan to purify the nation through the judgment of exile. He wondered when God's determination to judge his people might end.

6:13 leave stumps. Either a new shoot from the stump (11:1) or new growth from the trunk of a tree whose leaves had fallen off (1:30). **holy seed.** Or "holy Seed"; that is, the Messiah. As in the previous section, which focused on restoration (4:2–6), a purified remnant connected with the Messiah would receive the blessings of restoration through him after exile (see also 11:1).

■ **7:1—39:8** *Isaiah's Response to the Assyrian Judgment.* These chapters summarize the prophet's ministry during the period of Assyrian judgment. They are divided into three large sections: the Syrian-Israelite coalition (7:1—12:6), international upheaval during the period (13:1—27:13) and Sennacherib's invasion of Judah (28:1—39:8).

■ **7:1—12:6** *The Syrian-Israelite Coalition.* Isaiah revealed God's involvement in the events surrounding the Syrian-Israelite coalition against Assyria (see "Introduction: Time and Place of Writing"). He warned of severe judgment against Israel and Judah through Assyrian aggression but also assured his listeners of eventual restoration. These chapters focus on the signs of Isaiah's sons (7:1—8:18), the future of the northern kingdom of Israel (8:19—10:4) and the future of the southern kingdom of Judah (10:5—12:6).

■ **7:1—8:18** *The Assyrian Judgment and Isaiah's Sons.* Isaiah had two sons who served as signs of the judgment to come against Israel and Judah in connection with Assyria's response to the Syrian-Israelite coalition.

7:1 king of Judah. See 2 Kings 16:5–18 and 2 Chronicles 28:16–21. The Syrian-Israelite alliance (736–734 B.C.) posed a serious threat to Ahaz (See "Introduction to the Prophetic Books"). King Rezin of Syria (Aram) and King Pekah of Israel offered King Ahaz of Judah the choice of joining them against the Assyrians or of suffering their attacks.

7:2 the house of David. Ahaz was the rightful heir of David's dynastic promise (2Sa 7:12–16; 1Ch 17:10–14). **shaken . . . shaken.** Ahaz and the people of Judah were terrified by the threat of Syria and Israel.

7:3 Shear-Jashub. The name means "a remnant will return" (see 10:20–22), but it is two-sided in its implication. Positively, it promised salvation and life for the faithful remnant beyond the imminent doom of Assyrian aggression. Negatively, it indicated that God's people would suffer such severe judgment that only a remnant would return from exile.

7:4 don't be afraid. See note on 35:4. The prophet encouraged Ahaz to lift his eyes above the political situation and embrace the protection of God. **two smoldering stubs.** Both Syria (Aram) and Israel were about to be destroyed by the Assyrians: Damascus by Tiglath-Pileser III (732 B.C.) and Samaria by Sargon II (722 B.C.).

ruin, saying, 6“Let us invade Judah; let us tear it apart and divide it among ourselves, and
make the son of Tabeel king over it.” 7Yet this is what the Sovereign LORD says:

“ ‘It will not take place,
it will not happen,[s]
8for the head of Aram is Damascus,[t]
and the head of Damascus is only Rezin.
Within sixty-five years
Ephraim will be too shattered[u] to be a people.
9The head of Ephraim is Samaria,
and the head of Samaria is only Remaliah’s son.
If you do not stand firm in your faith,[v]
you will not stand at all.’ ”[w]

10Again the LORD spoke to Ahaz, 11“Ask the LORD your God for a sign, whether in the
deepest depths or in the highest heights.”
12But Ahaz said, “I will not ask; I will not put the LORD to the test.”
13Then Isaiah said, “Hear now, you house of David! Is it not enough to try the patience
of men? Will you try the patience of my God[x] also? 14Therefore the Lord himself will give
you[a] a sign: The virgin will be with child and will give birth to a son,[y] and[b] will call him
Immanuel.[c][z] 15He will eat curds and honey[a] when he knows enough to reject the wrong
and choose the right. 16But before the boy knows[b] enough to reject the wrong and
choose the right, the land of the two kings you dread will be laid waste.[c] 17The LORD will
bring on you and on your people and on the house of your father a time unlike any since
Ephraim broke away[d] from Judah—he will bring the king of Assyria.[e]”
18In that day the LORD will whistle[f] for flies from the distant streams of Egypt and for
bees from the land of Assyria.[g] 19They will all come and settle in the steep ravines and
in the crevices[h] in the rocks, on all the thornbushes and at all the water holes. 20In that
day the Lord will use[i] a razor hired from beyond the River[d]—the king of Assyria[j]—to
shave your head and the hair of your legs, and to take off your beards also. 21In that day,

7:7 [s]Isa 8:10; Ac 4:25
7:8 [t]Ge 14:15 [u]Isa 17:1-3
7:9 [v]2Ch 20:20 [w]Isa 8:6-8; 30:12-14
7:13 [x]Isa 25:1
7:14 [y]Lk 1:31 [z]Isa 8:8, 10; Mt 1:23*
7:15 [a]ver 22
7:16 [b]Isa 8:4 [c]Isa 17:3; Hos 5:9,13; Am 1:3-5
7:17 [d]1Ki 12:16 [e]2Ch 28:20
7:18 [f]Isa 5:26 [g]Isa 13:5
7:19 [h]Isa 2:19
7:20 [i]Isa 10:15 [j]Isa 8:7; 10:5

[a] *14* The Hebrew is plural. [b] *14* Masoretic Text; Dead Sea Scrolls *and he* or *and they* [c] *14* *Immanuel* means *God with us.* [d] *20* That is, the Euphrates

7:6 Tabeel. This Aramaic name, which means “goodness of God,” is parodied in Hebrew as Tabal, which means “good for nothing.”
7:7 it will not happen. The Lord assured Ahaz of protection from Syria (Aram) and Israel (8:9–10; 40:23–24; Pss 2:4; 33:10–11; 56:4,11).
7:8 sixty-five years. The Assyrians settled foreign peoples in the territories of the northern kingdom by c. 670 B.C. These newcomers intermarried with the Israelites who remained in the land and thus formed the “Samaritans,” a racially mixed people well known from the Gospels.
7:9 faith. God required Ahaz to trust him. See note on 1:21.
7:11 a sign. A sign authenticated prophetic messages concerning the future by revealing God’s determination to carry through with the prediction (see 37:30; 38:7). **deepest depths . . . highest heights.** God offered to show Ahaz practically any kind of sign to convince the king to trust him during this difficult time.
7:12 put the LORD to the test. See Exodus 17:2 and Deuteronomy 6:16. As Isaiah’s reaction demonstrated (v. 13), Ahaz merely feigned piety. He did not ask for a sign because he wanted to avoid increasing his culpability for refusing to believe.
7:13 house of David! See note on 7:1–2.
7:14 the Lord himself. Ahaz refused to choose a sign, so God selected one for him. **sign.** See note on 7:11. **virgin.** The Hebrew word *`almah* signifies a maiden of marriageable age, with connotations of virginity (see Ge 24:43); it occurs seven times, never clearly of a maiden who had lost virginity. The Septuagint (the Greek translation of the OT) strongly supports the translation “virgin,” as does the New Testament (Mt 1:23). Nevertheless, the sign did not specify that such a woman would conceive while still a virgin (see below). **Immanuel.** Literally, “God with us.” This name was symbolic; it was not the child’s actual name (cf. 9:6). The implication was that the child would symbolize God’s willingness to accompany Judah in battle against Syria, Israel and Assyria (see 2Ch 13:12). God offered to protect Judah from the Syrian-Israelite coalition and from Assyria, but Ahaz rejected the offer. Thus the Immanuel child to be born would later display the folly of rejecting God’s gracious offer. The New Testament identifies Jesus’ virgin birth as the fulfillment of this sign (Mt 1:23), but Christians have taken different views as to how this fulfillment is to be understood. The traditional Christian understanding is that Isaiah himself had in mind the supernatural birth of the Messiah and directly pointed to this event in the distant future as a sign against Ahaz’s disbelief. The principal difficulties with this view are that this sign was directed to Ahaz, who died hundreds of years before the birth of Christ, and that the birth of the Immanuel child was to take place before the destruction of Syria (Aram) and Israel (v. 16), which happened shortly after the prophecy was given. Second, a number of interpreters have held that Isaiah was referring to a virgin to whom he was betrothed (cf. 8:3), his first wife having died. In this view the child he had in mind was Maher-Shalal-Hash-Baz, who is described in the next chapter (cf. 7:15–16 and 8:3–4). From this perspective, the woman and child of Isaiah’s day were types or foreshadowings of Jesus’ virgin birth. As the child of Isaiah’s time was a sign of the redemption of God’s people as well as of judgment against unbelief, so Jesus was the ultimate sign that God would rescue his faithful people and bring judgment against unbelief among the Jews who rejected God’s offer of salvation in him. See *BC* 10,17; *HC* 15.
7:15 curds and honey. This is not the normal food of infants. This diet stands in contrast to bread and wine. The latter, from cultivated fields, represents a time of prosperity and peace before the Assyrian invasion; the former a time when the land was desolated (see v. 22; Dt. 32:13–14). Thus the child would be born during a time of trouble for God’s people. Curds to sustain a family required at the least “a young cow and two goats” (see v. 21). **when he knows enough to reject.** The Hebrew more often means “in order to know to reject.” The child would barely come to full moral maturity before the Assyrians would destroy Syria and Israel.
7:16 But before. Compare 8:4. Ahaz had already heard that Ephraim would be destroyed (see 7:8). Now he learned that it would be destroyed before the child reached full moral maturity. With his enemy annihilated, the child would stand as a sign of judgment against Ahaz for rejecting the offer of protection from God.
7:18 In that day. See note on 2:11. **flies . . . bees.** Both insects come in great numbers and here signify the coming hordes of invaders.
7:19 steep ravines . . . water holes. Traditional hiding places would provide no escape (cf. 2:19).
7:20 In that day. See note on 2:11. **razor.** The Assyrians would bring disgrace to the people of God. **hired.** Ironically, Ahaz paid for Assyria to come (2Ki 16:8).
7:21 In that day. See note on 2:11.

a man will keep alive a young cow and two goats. 22 And because of the abundance of the
milk they give, he will have curds to eat. All who remain in the land will eat curds and
honey. 23 In that day, in every place where there were a thousand vines worth a thousand
silver shekels,[a] there will be only briers and thorns.[k] 24 Men will go there with bow and
arrow, for the land will be covered with briers and thorns. 25 As for all the hills once cultivated by the hoe, you will no longer go there for fear of the briers and thorns; they will
become places where cattle are turned loose and where sheep run.[l]

Assyria, the LORD's Instrument

8 The LORD said to me, "Take a large scroll[m] and write on it with an ordinary pen: Maher-Shalal-Hash-Baz.[b][n] 2 And I will call in Uriah[o] the priest and Zechariah son of
Jeberekiah as reliable witnesses for me."
3 Then I went to the prophetess, and she conceived and gave birth to a son. And the
LORD said to me, "Name him Maher-Shalal-Hash-Baz. 4 Before the boy knows[p] how to say
'My father' or 'My mother,' the wealth of Damascus and the plunder of Samaria will be
carried off by the king of Assyria.[q]"
5 The LORD spoke to me again:

6 "Because this people has rejected[r]
the gently flowing waters of Shiloah[s]
and rejoices over Rezin
and the son of Remaliah,[t]
7 therefore the Lord is about to bring against them
the mighty floodwaters[u] of the River[c]—
the king of Assyria[v] with all his pomp.
It will overflow all its channels,
run over all its banks
8 and sweep on into Judah, swirling over it,
passing through it and reaching up to the neck.
Its outspread wings will cover the breadth of your land,
O Immanuel[d]!"[w]

9 Raise the war cry,[e][x] you nations, and be shattered!
Listen, all you distant lands.
Prepare[y] for battle, and be shattered!
Prepare for battle, and be shattered!
10 Devise your strategy, but it will be thwarted;[z]
propose your plan, but it will not stand,[a]
for God is with us.[f][b]

Fear God

11 The LORD spoke to me with his strong hand upon me,[c] warning me not to follow[d]
the way of this people. He said:

12 "Do not call conspiracy[e]
everything that these people call conspiracy[g];

7:23 [k]Isa 5:6
7:25 [l]Isa 5:17
8:1 [m]Isa 30:8; Hab 2:2 [n]ver 3; Hab 2:2
8:2 [o]2Ki 16:10
8:4 [p]Isa 7:16 [q]Isa 7:8
8:6 [r]Isa 5:24 [s]Jn 9:7 [t]Isa 7:1
8:7 [u]Isa 17:12-13 [v]Isa 7:20
8:8 [w]Isa 7:14
8:9 [x]Isa 17:12-13 [y]Joel 3:9
8:10 [z]Job 5:12 [a]Isa 7:7 [b]Isa 7:14; Ro 8:31
8:11 [c]Eze 3:14 [d]Eze 2:8
8:12 [e]Isa 7:2; 30:1

[a] *23* That is, about 25 pounds (about 11.5 kilograms) [b] *1* *Maher-Shalal-Hash-Baz* means *quick to the plunder, swift to the spoil*; also in verse 3. [c] *7* That is, the Euphrates [d] *8* *Immanuel* means *God with us.* [e] *9* Or *Do your worst* [f] *10* Hebrew *Immanuel* [g] *12* Or *Do not call for a treaty / every time these people call for a treaty*

7:22 curds and honey. See notes on verses 14–15.
8:1 large scroll. Better, "a tablet," a flat piece of wood (Eze 37:16) or metal (see "mirrors" at 3:23) that served as a placard. The purpose of writing "Maher-Shalal-Hash-Baz" on the placard was to announce the birth and the impending fulfillment of God's word. The significance of the name is given in verse 4.
8:2 witnesses. Priestly and prophetic associates of the apostate King Ahaz (2Ki 16:10–11) were forced to observe the sign of Immanuel's birth (see 7:10–14).
8:3 prophetess. A designation for Isaiah's wife (see note on 7:14). It could be that she also served God in a prophetic role (Jdg 4:4; 2Ki 22:14). **Maher-Shalal-Hash-Baz.** See NIV text note on verse 1. The name signifies that God would bring rapid devastation to Syria, Israel and Judah (vv. 8,10).
8:5–10 The prophet explained why Judah would suffer judgment through Assyrian aggression.
8:6 this people. Judah. **waters of Shiloah.** Perhaps a small stream and aqueduct (see 7:3) that carried water from the Gihon (2Ch 32:30). The reference is used here as a figure of the Lord's sustaining presence. **waters.** See note on 1:30. The people looked forward to the fall of Syria (King Rezin) without applying the word of judgment to Judah.
8:7 the mighty floodwaters. The Lord would unleash Assyria against Judah like a flood. **the River.** The Euphrates River is a figure for the royal Assyrian forces.
8:8 the neck. At the height of the Assyrian invasion of Judah in 701 B.C., only Jerusalem survived (see note on 1:7–9). Assyria would bring much devastation but not the complete annihilation of Judah. **O Immanuel!** See note on 7:14 (cf. v. 10). The prophet cried in regret over the nation that would stand in need of God's presence in battle.
8:9–10 you nations. Syria (Aram) and Israel. **God is with us.** Or Immanuel. See note on 7:14 (cf. v. 8).
8:11 strong hand upon me. The experience of inner compulsion from the Spirit of God (Eze 1:3; 3:14; 37:1; 40:1).
8:12–13 conspiracy. The people considered Isaiah a traitor be-

8:12 [f]1Pe 3:14*
8:13 [g]Nu 20:12 [h]Isa 29:23
8:14 [i]Isa 4:6; Eze 11:16 [j]Lk 2:34; Ro 9:33*; 1Pe 2:8* [k]Isa 24:17-18
8:15 [l]Isa 28:13; 59:10; Lk 20:18; Ro 9:32
8:16 [m]Isa 29:11-12
8:17 [n]Hab 2:3 [o]Dt 31:17; Isa 54:8
8:18 [p]Heb 2:13* [q]Lk 2:34 [r]Ps 9:11
8:19 [s]1Sa 28:8 [t]Isa 29:4
8:20 [u]Isa 1:10; Lk 16:29 [v]Mic 3:6
8:21 [w]Rev 16:11
8:22 [x]ver 20; Isa 5:30
9:1 [y]2Ki 15:29
9:2 [z]Eph 5:8

do not fear what they fear,
  and do not dread it.[f]
13 The LORD Almighty is the one you are to regard as holy,[g]
  he is the one you are to fear,
  he is the one you are to dread,[h]
14 and he will be a sanctuary;[i]
  but for both houses of Israel he will be
a stone that causes men to stumble
  and a rock that makes them fall.[j]
And for the people of Jerusalem he will be
  a trap and a snare.[k]
15 Many of them will stumble;[l]
  they will fall and be broken,
  they will be snared and captured."
16 Bind up the testimony
  and seal[m] up the law among my disciples.
17 I will wait[n] for the LORD,
  who is hiding[o] his face from the house of Jacob.
I will put my trust in him.

18 Here am I, and the children the LORD has given me.[p] We are signs[q] and symbols in
Israel from the LORD Almighty, who dwells on Mount Zion.[r]
19 When men tell you to consult[s] mediums and spiritists, who whisper and mutter,[t]
should not a people inquire of their God? Why consult the dead on behalf of the living?
20 To the law[u] and to the testimony! If they do not speak according to this word, they have
no light[v] of dawn. 21 Distressed and hungry, they will roam through the land; when they
are famished, they will become enraged and, looking upward, will curse[w] their king and
their God. 22 Then they will look toward the earth and see only distress and darkness and
fearful gloom, and they will be thrust into utter darkness.[x]

To Us a Child Is Born

9 Nevertheless, there will be no more gloom for those who were in distress. In the past
he humbled the land of Zebulun and the land of Naphtali,[y] but in the future he will
honor Galilee of the Gentiles, by the way of the sea, along the Jordan—

2 The people walking in darkness
  have seen a great light;[z]

---

cause he spoke against Ahaz and his reliance on Assyria. **fear . . . dread.** Not humans (v. 12) but the Lord (v. 13) should be the object of fear, for it is to God that we must render an account (11:2–3; 12:2; 33:6; 35:4; 50:10; 51:7,12; 57:11; 59:19; Pss 25:12–15; 34:7, 11–14; Pr 1:7). See note on 7:4. See *WLC* 104.

8:14 sanctuary. A place of refuge. **both houses.** Judah and Israel. **stone . . . snare.** The stone may be the "tested stone" (28:16). The Lord is that stone for the faithful, but others take offense at him (see Ps 118:22; Lk 10:17–18; Ro 9:33; 1Pe 2:6–8). God is also known as the Rock of Israel (17:10; 26:4; 30:29; 44:8), a royal figure of sure protection over against the false securities of humans (2:10,19,21).

8:16 disciples. Isaiah's faithful followers. See *WCF* 5.6.

8:17 wait for . . . put my trust. A response of faith and hope when trials still remained (25:9; 26:8; 30:18; 33:2; 40:31; 49:23; 64:4). **hiding his face.** The opposite of looking with favor on his people (54:8; 64:7; Dt 31:18; 32:20; 2Ch 7:14).

8:18 Here am I. Compare 6:8. Isaiah stated forthrightly the significance of the previous accounts of his sons. **children.** See 7:3 and 8:3. **symbols.** Isaiah's sons' names carried theological significance (see notes on 1:1; 7:3; 8:3). For "Shear-Jashub," see note on 7:3; for "Maher-Shalal-Hash-Baz," see notes on 8:1 and 3. **LORD Almighty.** See note on 1:9. **Zion.** See note on 1:8.

■ **8:19—10:4** *The Assyrian Judgment and Israel.* Having made it clear that the Assyrians would utterly destroy Israel, Isaiah spoke to the citizens of the northern kingdom about how to react to the judgment that was coming against them. He called them to inquire of God (8:19–22), place their hope in the family of David (9:1–7) and turn from their proud self-reliance (9:8—10:4).

■ **8:19–22** *The Call to Inquire of God.* The prophet called for the northern kingdom to inquire of God for understanding after the judgment had come rather than to turn to pagan mediums and spiritists.

8:19–20 See *WCF* 1.1.

8:19 consult. See note on 9:13. **mediums and spiritists.** Diviners were prohibited by God's law (Dt 18:10–11). See note on 2:6. **inquire of their God?** As the Assyrian judgment came upon the northern kingdom, the people would be tempted to remedy their situation by consulting with pagan diviners. Isaiah insisted, however, that they should seek understanding and wisdom from God alone (see, e.g., 1Sa 10:22; 22:10; 23:2,4; 30:8; see also Dt 18:9-22).

8:20 law . . . testimony! See 8:16. Probably Isaiah's own prophecies. **light.** See note on 2:5. See *WCF* 1.8; 20.2; *WLC* 3; *BC* 7.

8:21 Distressed. God is the only remedy for distress (33:2; 63:9; 65:16). **curse their king and their God.** This phrase may be translated "their King, their God," but the following passage (9:1–7) strongly suggests that the prophet had in mind both God and the human king, specifically the monarch of Judah's Davidic dynasty. The difficulties inflicted by the Assyrian aggression would lead many in the northern kingdom to reject even further the instrument of God's salvation: the throne of David.

8:22 darkness. Despair (50:10). **gloom.** Grave difficulty (see "hardship" at 30:6).

■ **9:1–7** *Israel's Hope in David's Throne.* Despite the rejection of the throne of David by those in the northern kingdom, God's future provision for their deliverance would be the great son of David to come.

9:1 In the past . . . in the future. These terms designate God's acts of judgment (past) and his salvation (future). See notes on 41:22 and 42:9. Those who returned from exile included many from the northern tribes (1Ch 9:3), but the New Testament notes that Jesus began the final stage of this prophecy's fulfillment with regard to the northern kingdom when he ministered in the northern regions of Israel (Mt 4:13–15). Ultimately Jesus will completely fulfill this prophecy when he returns in glory. **Zebulun . . . Naphtali.** These regions in Galilee were the first to suffer from the Assyrian wave of 732 B.C. (2Ki 15:29).

on those living in the land of the shadow of death[a] [a]
a light has dawned.[b]
3 You have enlarged the nation
and increased their joy;
they rejoice before you
as people rejoice at the harvest,
as men rejoice
when dividing the plunder.
4 For as in the day of Midian's defeat,[c]
you have shattered
the yoke[d] that burdens them,
the bar across their shoulders,[e]
the rod of their oppressor.[f]
5 Every warrior's boot used in battle
and every garment rolled in blood
will be destined for burning,[g]
will be fuel for the fire.
6 For to us a child is born,[h]
to us a son is given,[i]
and the government[j] will be on his shoulders.
And he will be called
Wonderful Counselor,[b] [k] Mighty God,[l]
Everlasting Father, Prince of Peace.[m]
7 Of the increase of his government and peace
there will be no end.[n]
He will reign on David's throne
and over his kingdom,
establishing and upholding it
with justice[o] and righteousness
from that time on and forever.
The zeal[p] of the LORD Almighty
will accomplish this.

The LORD's Anger Against Israel

8 The Lord has sent a message against Jacob;
it will fall on Israel.
9 All the people will know it—
Ephraim and the inhabitants of Samaria[q]—
who say with pride

9:2 [a]Lk 1:79 [b]Mt 4:15-16*
9:4 [c]Jdg 7:25 [d]Isa 14:25 [e]Isa 10:27 [f]Isa 14:4; 49:26; 51:13; 54:14
9:5 [g]Isa 2:4
9:6 [h]Isa 53:2; Lk 2:11 [i]Jn 3:16 [j]Mt 28:18 [k]Isa 28:29 [l]Isa 10:21; 11:2 [m]Isa 26:3,12; 66:12
9:7 [n]Da 2:44; Lk 1:33 [o]Isa 11:4; 16:5; 32:1,16 [p]Isa 37:32; 59:17
9:9 [q]Isa 7:9

a *2* Or *land of darkness* b *6* Or *Wonderful, Counselor*

9:2 shadow of death. The deep darkness within; that is, despair (see NIV text note at Ps 23:4; see also Pss 44:19; 107:10).
9:3–4 joy. God would open a new future for the humble of the northern kingdom, where gloom had previously existed (24:11; 35:10; 51:3,11; 55:12; 61:7; 66:7). The new joy is expressed in the metaphors of harvest and victory. Contrast 5:10 and 8:1. **Midian's defeat.** See 10:26–27, as well as Judges 6:7 and 7:22–25. **yoke . . . bar.** Figures representing the oppression of the Assyrians (10:27; 14:25; 47:6; cf. Mt 11:29–30).
9:5 fire. Burning the accoutrements of war indicates that the threat of further war had ceased (cf. 2:4).
9:6–7 See *WCF* 30.1; *WLC* 42; *WSC* 23.
9:6 child . . . son. The prophet indicated how the gloom of exile would be reversed for the northern kingdom through the birth of a child. This child would be of the house of David (v. 7), whose authority the northerners had rejected for centuries. Four throne names displayed the supreme qualities of this great son of David, providing assurance that he would indeed fulfill the restoration of the northern kingdom. The names exhibit a logical progression from strategy to warfare to rule and to peace. **Wonderful Counselor.** The child-deliverer would be a wondrous strategist, orchestrating an amazing victory for his people. **Mighty God.** Literally, "God is a warrior." This name praised God for the victory the son of David would accomplish for his people. He would not stay distant from battle but would display divine power as he fought for his people (10:21; Dt 10:17; Jer 32:18). **Everlasting Father.** This throne name did not confuse the king with God the Father. In line with the customs of the ancient Near East, it designated the king as the royal father of the nation. This child would always be the royal father of the nation; his paternal care for his subjects would never end (40:9–11; 65:17–25; Mt 6:25–26; 11:27–30; 18:12–14; 23:9–12; Lk 23:34; Ro 8:15–17). **Prince of Peace.** The child's government would be so effective that it would usher in peace (2:4; 11:6–9; Ps 72:7; Mic 5:5; Zec 9:10; Lk 2:14). Although all faithful sons of David strove to reach these ideals, the grand royal child of this prophecy would be none other than Jesus Christ himself. See *WLC* 11; *HC* 15.
9:7 increase. The Messianic kingdom would not stagnate but continue to grow (Da 2:35). **David's throne.** The deliverer would be a descendant of David (see note on 7:3; 11:1). **zeal.** God guaranteed that this would be fulfilled (26:11; 37:32; 42:13; 59:17; 63:15; Zec 1:14; 8:2). **LORD Almighty.** See note on 1:9. See *WCF* 25.2.
■ **9:8—10:4** *The Condemnation of Israel's Pride.* Isaiah confronted the arrogance of those who observed God's judgment but believed they could restore the kingdom in their own way, without the intervention of the great son of David mentioned in the preceding oracle. These verses are divided into four sections by the repeated refrain in 9:12, 17 and 21 and in 10:4.
9:8–12 See 5:21.
9:9 All the people will know it. Early Assyrian aggression against the Syrian-Israelite coalition (see "Introduction: Time and Place of Writing") left little doubt that Isaiah's prophecies of destruction regarding Israel were valid, but some still believed they could rebuild in their own strength. **who say with pride.** The northern kingdom had rejected the house of David since the united kingdom had been divided (930 B.C.). Therefore Isaiah expected his words of hope in David's throne (9:6–7) to be rejected. The

9:9 [r]Isa 46:12

and arrogance[r] of heart,
10 "The bricks have fallen down,
but we will rebuild with dressed stone;
the fig trees have been felled,
but we will replace them with cedars."

9:11 [s]Isa 7:8

11 But the LORD has strengthened Rezin's[s] foes against them
and has spurred their enemies on.

9:12 [t]2Ki 16:6 [u]2Ch 28:18 [v]Ps 79:7 [w]Isa 5:25

12 Arameans[t] from the east and Philistines[u] from the west
have devoured[v] Israel with open mouth.

Yet for all this, his anger is not turned away,
his hand is still upraised.[w]

9:13 [x]Jer 5:3 [y]Isa 31:1; Hos 7:7,10

13 But the people have not returned to him who struck[x] them,
nor have they sought[y] the LORD Almighty.

9:14 [z]Isa 19:15 [a]Rev 18:8

14 So the LORD will cut off from Israel both head and tail,
both palm branch and reed[z] in a single day;[a]

9:15 [b]Isa 3:2-3

15 the elders[b] and prominent men are the head,
the prophets who teach lies are the tail.

9:16 [c]Mt 15:14; 23:16, 24 [d]Isa 3:12

16 Those who guide[c] this people mislead them,
and those who are guided are led astray.[d]

9:17 [e]Jer 18:21 [f]Isa 27:11 [g]Isa 10:6 [h]Isa 1:4 [i]Mt 12:34 [j]Isa 5:25

17 Therefore the Lord will take no pleasure in the young men,[e]
nor will he pity[f] the fatherless and widows,
for everyone is ungodly[g] and wicked,[h]
every mouth speaks vileness.[i]

Yet for all this, his anger is not turned away,
his hand is still upraised.[j]

9:18 [k]Mal 4:1 [l]Ps 83:14

18 Surely wickedness burns like a fire;[k]
it consumes briers and thorns,
it sets the forest thickets ablaze,[l]
so that it rolls upward in a column of smoke.

9:19 [m]Isa 13:9,13 [n]Isa 1:31 [o]Mic 7:2,6

19 By the wrath[m] of the LORD Almighty
the land will be scorched
and the people will be fuel for the fire;[n]
no one will spare his brother.[o]

9:20 [p]Lev 26:26 [q]Isa 49:26

20 On the right they will devour,
but still be hungry;[p]
on the left they will eat,[q]
but not be satisfied.
Each will feed on the flesh of his own offspring[a]:

9:21 [r]2Ch 28:6 [s]Isa 5:25

21 Manasseh will feed on Ephraim, and Ephraim on Manasseh;
together they will turn against Judah.[r]
Yet for all this, his anger is not turned away,
his hand is still upraised.[s]

[a] *20* Or *arm*

people of the northern kingdom were determined to secure their future in their own way, symbolized by the "dressed stone . . . cedars" (v. 10). Their motivation was self-determination, expressed by "pride and arrogance of heart" (v. 9) and the words "we will . . . we will" (v. 10).

9:11 Rezin's foes. The Assyrians (see notes on 7:1–2,20; 8:7).

9:12 Arameans . . . Philistines. The Lord had raised up many enemies against Israel. **Yet . . . upraised.** See note on 9:8—10:4 (cf. v. 21; 10:4; 31:3). Despite the hardships its people already faced, more judgment was in store for the northern kingdom.

9:13 not returned. A lack of response to the divine discipline being meted out through Assyrian aggression was anticipated (Am 4:6,8–11). **sought.** The Israelites did not seek the wisdom of God in their dire circumstances (see note on 8:19), nor did they trust in the hope of the Davidic throne (9:6–7). **LORD Almighty.** See note on 1:9.

9:14–16 head . . . tail. The leadership as explained in verse 15 (cf. 3:1–3). **head.** The community elders and leaders. **tail.** The false prophets. See note on 30:10. **palm branch . . . reed.** Applied to Egyptian leaders in 19:15. **single day.** Suddenly.

9:17 Therefore. The divine sentence for the northern kingdom's arrogance was a worsening of conditions leading to the final destruction of the nation in 722 B.C. **fatherless and widows.** Ordinarily God showed special kindness to orphans and widows, but the judgment to come would be so severe that even they would not be spared. See note on 1:16–18. **everyone is ungodly . . . every mouth speaks vileness.** A hyperbole expressing that sin had spread throughout the northern kingdom. **Yet . . . upraised.** See note on 9:8—10:4 (cf. v. 21; 10:4; 31:3).

9:19 wrath. Israel's sin aroused God's anger and resulted in condemnation and curse. See 13:13; see also notes on 10:6, 13:9 and 14:6. **LORD Almighty.** See note on 1:9.

9:20–21 devour . . . feed. Rebellion against God would lead to the destruction of covenant bonds among the tribes.

9:21 Yet . . . upraised. See note on 9:8—10:4 (cf. v. 21; 10:4; 31:3).

10

Woe to those who make unjust laws,
to those who issue oppressive decrees,[t]
2 to deprive[u] the poor of their rights
and withhold justice from the oppressed of my people,[v]
making widows their prey
and robbing the fatherless.
3 What will you do on the day of reckoning,[w]
when disaster[x] comes from afar?
To whom will you run for help?[y]
Where will you leave your riches?
4 Nothing will remain but to cringe among the captives[z]
or fall among the slain.[a]

Yet for all this, his anger is not turned away,[b]
his hand is still upraised.

God's Judgment on Assyria

5 "Woe to the Assyrian,[c] the rod of my anger,
in whose hand is the club[d] of my wrath![e]
6 I send him against a godless[f] nation,
I dispatch him against a people who anger me,[g]
to seize loot and snatch plunder,[h]
and to trample them down like mud in the streets.
7 But this is not what he intends,[i]
this is not what he has in mind;
his purpose is to destroy,
to put an end to many nations.
8 'Are not my commanders[j] all kings?' he says.
9 'Has not Calno[k] fared like Carchemish?[l]
Is not Hamath like Arpad,
and Samaria[m] like Damascus?[n]
10 As my hand seized the kingdoms of the idols,[o]
kingdoms whose images excelled those of Jerusalem and Samaria—
11 shall I not deal with Jerusalem and her images
as I dealt with Samaria and her idols?' "

12 When the Lord has finished all his work[p] against Mount Zion[q] and Jerusalem, he
will say, "I will punish the king of Assyria[r] for the willful pride of his heart and the haughty look in his eyes. 13 For he says:

" 'By the strength of my hand I have done this,[s]
and by my wisdom, because I have understanding.
I removed the boundaries of nations,
I plundered their treasures;[t]

10:1 [t]Ps 58:2
10:2 [u]Isa 3:14 [v]Isa 5:23
10:3 [w]Job 31:14; Hos 9:7 [x]Lk 19:44 [y]Isa 20:6
10:4 [z]Isa 24:22 [a]Isa 22:2; 34:3; 66:16 [b]Isa 5:25
10:5 [c]Isa 14:25; Zep 2:13 [d]Jer 51:20 [e]Isa 13:3,5,13; 30:30; 66:14
10:6 [f]Isa 9:17 [g]Isa 9:19 [h]Isa 5:29
10:7 [i]Ge 50:20; Ac 4:23-28
10:8 [j]2Ki 18:24
10:9 [k]Ge 10:10 [l]2Ch 35:20 [m]2Ki 17:6 [n]2Ki 16:9
10:10 [o]2Ki 19:18
10:12 [p]Isa 28:21-22; 65:7 [q]2Ki 19:31 [r]Jer 50:18
10:13 [s]Isa 37:24; Da 4:30 [t]Eze 28:4

10:1 Woe. Introduces a dire threat. The prophet pronounced woe against the northern kingdom because he foresaw its terrible devastation at the hands of the Assyrians.
10:2 poor . . . fatherless. See notes on 1:16–18 and 11:3–5. **justice.** See note on 1:21. **my people.** See note on 40:1.
10:3 day of reckoning. The day of the Lord (see note on 2:11). **disaster.** The collapse of the structures of Israel's society (47:11; Pr 1:27; 3:25). **from afar?** That is, from Assyria.
10:4 captives . . . slain. Those who would be exiled or killed by the Assyrians (see Jer 39:6–7). **Yet . . . upraised.** See note on 9:8—10:4 (cf. v. 21; 10:4; 31:3).
■ **10:5—12:6** *The Assyrian Judgment and Judah.* Having explained why Assyrian aggression toward the northern kingdom would end in utter defeat and exile, the prophet turned to the contrasting outcome of Assyrian aggression against Judah. These chapters divide into four main parts: a woe over Assyria (10:5–19), the return of Judah's remnant (10:20–34), Judah's hope in David's house (11:1–16) and the resulting praise of God in Zion (12:1–6).
■ **10:5–19** *Woe to Assyria.* The prophet declared judgment on Assyria for overstepping its role as God's instrument of judgment.
10:5 Woe. Introduces a dire threat. **rod of my anger . . . club of my wrath!** The Assyrians were God's instrument of judgment, but they were also responsible for overstepping their bounds and abusing this privilege. See notes on 5:25 and 7:20. See *BC* 13.
10:6–7 See *WCF* 5.2; 5.4.
10:6 godless nation. Israel (v. 10) and Judah (v. 11).
10:7–9 intends . . . purpose. Assyria's goal was self-aggrandizement and absolute power. The cities that the Assyrians destroyed are listed in geographical order from the Euphrates to Judah: Carchemish (717 B.C.), Calno (see Calneh in Am 6:2; [738 B.C.]), Arpad (740 B.C.), Hamath (738 and 720 B.C.), Damascus (732 B.C.) and Samaria (722 B.C.). See also 36:19 and 37:12–13.
10:10 my hand. Assyria boasted of autonomy (Da 4:30; Lk 12:18–19). **images excelled.** Following the values of their idolatrous religion, the Assyrians imagined Jerusalem and Samaria as weak because they had relatively few idols.
10:11 Jerusalem . . . as I dealt with Samaria. The prophet addressed the Assyrians' arrogance in attacking Jerusalem as they had Samaria and a host of other cities.
10:12 When . . . has finished. God wanted a measure of judgment to come against Zion, but he would stop short of the Assyrians' desire for complete dominance of Jerusalem. Instead he would punish the king of Assyria (Sennacherib) for his "willful pride" and "haughty look." See *WCF* 5.4.
10:13–14 A restatement of verses 5–11. For similar expressions of pride see 14:13–14 and Ezekiel 28:2–5.

like a mighty one I subdued[a] their kings.

10:14 [u]Jer 49:16; Ob 1:4 [v]Job 31:25

14 As one reaches into a nest,[u]
so my hand reached for the wealth[v] of the nations;
as men gather abandoned eggs,
so I gathered all the countries;
not one flapped a wing,
or opened its mouth to chirp.' "

10:15 [w]Isa 45:9; Ro 9:20-21 [x]ver 5

15 Does the ax raise itself above him who swings it,
or the saw boast against him who uses it?[w]
As if a rod were to wield him who lifts it up,
or a club[x] brandish him who is not wood!

10:16 [y]ver 18; Isa 17:4 [z]Isa 8:7

16 Therefore, the Lord, the LORD Almighty,
will send a wasting disease[y] upon his sturdy warriors;
under his pomp[z] a fire will be kindled
like a blazing flame.

10:17 [a]Isa 31:9 [b]Isa 37:23 [c]Nu 11:1-3 [d]Isa 9:18

17 The Light of Israel will become a fire,[a]
their Holy One[b] a flame;
in a single day it will burn and consume
his thorns[c] and his briers.[d]

10:18 [e]2Ki 19:23

18 The splendor of his forests[e] and fertile fields
it will completely destroy,
as when a sick man wastes away.

10:19 [f]Isa 21:17

19 And the remaining trees of his forests will be so few[f]
that a child could write them down.

The Remnant of Israel

10:20 [g]Isa 11:10,11 [h]2Ki 16:7 [i]2Ch 28:20 [j]Isa 17:7

20 In that day[g] the remnant of Israel,
the survivors of the house of Jacob,
will no longer rely[h] on him
who struck them down[i]
but will truly rely[j] on the LORD,
the Holy One of Israel.

10:21 [k]Isa 6:13 [l]Isa 9:6

21 A remnant[k] will return,[b] a remnant of Jacob
will return to the Mighty God.[l]

10:22 [m]Ro 9:27-28 [n]Isa 28:22; Da 9:27

22 Though your people, O Israel, be like the sand by the sea,
only a remnant will return.[m]
Destruction has been decreed,[n]
overwhelming and righteous.

10:23 [o]Isa 28:22; Ro 9:27-28*

23 The Lord, the LORD Almighty, will carry out
the destruction decreed upon the whole land.[o]

10:24 [p]Ps 87:5-6 [q]Ex 5:14

24 Therefore, this is what the Lord, the LORD Almighty, says:

"O my people who live in Zion,[p]
do not be afraid of the Assyrians,
who beat[q] you with a rod
and lift up a club against you, as Egypt did.

10:25 [r]Isa 17:14 [s]ver 5; Da 11:36

25 Very soon[r] my anger against you will end
and my wrath[s] will be directed to their destruction."

[a] *13* Or *I subdued the mighty,* [b] *21* Hebrew *shear-jashub;* also in verse 22

10:15 ax . . . club. The Assyrians foolishly thought themselves greater than the Lord, but they were actually nothing more than his tools. See note on 10:5.
10:18–19 splendor. What men counted as honorable would mean little before God's fiery judgment. **forests and fertile fields.** These symbols of Assyrian pride would disappear quickly, like thorns and briers in a fire (v. 17).
■ **10:20–34** *Judah's Remnant.* The destruction of Assyria guaranteed that a remnant would one day return from the Judahites whom the Assyrians would displace during their attacks on Judah.
10:20 In that day. See note on 2:11. **remnant . . . survivors.** See note on 1:8. **rely . . . rely.** To repel the Syrian-Israelite coalition (see notes on 7:1–25) the Judahites had relied on Assyria, which later "struck them down" (see 7:1–25). Instead of depending on Assyria and on human resources (31:1), in the future the remnant would trust in the Lord (50:10). **truly.** Literally, "in truth" (48:1) or "in faithfulness" (16:5; 42:3). See 38:3 and 18–19; see also "truth" at 59:14–15. **the Holy One of Israel.** See note on 1:4.
10:21–22 A remnant will return. See notes on 1:8 and 7:3. **remnant.** See note on 1:8. **Mighty God.** See note on 9:6. **sand by the sea.** An allusion to God's promise to Abraham (Ge 22:17; cf. 1Ki 4:20). **decreed.** God was determined in his judgment (v. 23; 28:22). **righteous.** See note on 3:10.
10:23 decreed. See note on 10:21–22.
10:24 Therefore. The conclusion derived from God's plan for the future. **my people.** See note on 40:1. **Zion.** See note on 1:8. **do not be afraid.** The Lord had decreed to bless his people after the Assyrian judgment, so he encouraged them not to fear. The Assyrians would be overcome (37:6; 41:10,13; 43:1,5; 44:2). See note on 35:4. **rod . . . club.** See note on verse 5.

26 The LORD Almighty will lash[t] them with a whip,
as when he struck down Midian[u] at the rock of Oreb;
and he will raise his staff over the waters,[v]
as he did in Egypt.
27 In that day their burden will be lifted from your shoulders,
their yoke[w] from your neck;[x]
the yoke will be broken
because you have grown so fat.[a]

28 They enter Aiath;
they pass through Migron;[y]
they store supplies at Micmash.[z]
29 They go over the pass, and say,
"We will camp overnight at Geba."
Ramah[a] trembles;
Gibeah of Saul flees.
30 Cry out, O Daughter of Gallim![b]
Listen, O Laishah!
Poor Anathoth![c]
31 Madmenah is in flight;
the people of Gebim take cover.
32 This day they will halt at Nob;[d]
they will shake their fist
at the mount of the Daughter of Zion,[e]
at the hill of Jerusalem.

33 See, the Lord, the LORD Almighty,
will lop off the boughs with great power.
The lofty trees will be felled,
the tall[f] ones will be brought low.
34 He will cut down the forest thickets with an ax;
Lebanon will fall before the Mighty One.

The Branch From Jesse

11 A shoot will come up from the stump of Jesse;[g]
from his roots a Branch[h] will bear fruit.
2 The Spirit[i] of the LORD will rest on him—
the Spirit of wisdom[j] and of understanding,
the Spirit of counsel and of power,[k]
the Spirit of knowledge and of the fear of the LORD—
3 and he will delight in the fear of the LORD.

10:26 [t]Isa 37:36-38 [u]Isa 9:4 [v]Ex 14:16
10:27 [w]Isa 9:4 [x]Isa 14:25
10:28 [y]1Sa 14:2 [z]1Sa 13:2
10:29 [a]Jos 18:25
10:30 [b]1Sa 25:44 [c]Ne 11:32
10:32 [d]1Sa 21:1 [e]Jer 6:23
10:33 [f]Am 2:9
11:1 [g]ver 10; Isa 9:7; Rev 5:5 [h]Isa 4:2
11:2 [i]Isa 42:1; 48:16, 61:1; Mt 3:16; Jn 1:32-33 [j]Eph 1:17 [k]2Ti 1:7

[a] *27* Hebrew; Septuagint *broken / from your shoulders*

10:25 anger . . . wrath. See note on 10:5. The instruments of "destruction" would themselves be destroyed.
10:26 LORD Almighty. See note on 1:9. Two examples from the history of redemption are given: the defeat of Midian (see note on 9:3–4; Oreb was the Midianite leader [Jdg 7:25]) and God's victory over Egypt by the Red Sea (Ex 14:26–28).
10:27 In that day. See note on 2:11. **burden . . . yoke.** See note on 9:3–4. **fat.** Judah would be free from Assyrian domination, as a strong and fattened ox breaks its yoke.
10:28–32 Assyria's march to Judah is portrayed as moving from north to south: an advance through Aiath, Migron, Micmash, Geba, Ramah, Gibeah, Gallim, Laishah, Anathoth, Madmenah, Gebim and finally Nob, which was within sight of Zion (cf. 10:8–9). For a similar depiction of Assyria's invasion of Judah, this time from the southwest, see notes on Micah 1:10–16.
10:33–34 The Assyrians would bring terror to Judah, but God would intervene. **boughs . . . Lebanon.** See note on verses 18–19. **great power.** Nothing else compares with God's greatness and strength. This section illustrates the truth of 2:2–22. **ax.** See verse 15.
■ **11:1–16** *Judah's Hope in David's Throne.* The prophet explained that Judah's deliverance from Assyria in 701 B.C. was only a foretaste of the glorious restoration that would one day come through the great son of David (cf. 9:1–7). Later on Isaiah would explain that Jerusalem itself would be defeated by the Babylonians (39:5–7) and that the great restoration mentioned here would follow Judah's exile to Babylon.
11:1 shoot. See note on 4:2. **stump.** The Assyrian and Babylonian aggressions would leave the family of David a mere stump. The privileged sons of David are here compared to Assyria, a tree that has been chopped down (see 10:35). In spite of the judgment on Judah and on David's house, the Lord would raise up new leadership from the dynasty of David. The New Testament teaches that this hope was fulfilled in Jesus. **Jesse.** David's father (1Sa 16:10–13). **Branch.** See note on 4:2. See *BC* 18.
11:2 Spirit of the LORD. The Spirit that established God's kingdom (see Ge 1:2; Jdg 3:10; 6:34; 1Sa 10:6 and their notes) would also empower the great son of David as he established the final stage of the kingdom of God (see 42:1; Lk 3:22). **rest on him.** The Spirit came in a powerful way on believers—especially their leaders—in the Old Testament (e.g., Moses [Nu 11:17], the elders [Nu 11:25–26], Joshua [Dt 34:9], judges [Jdg 3:10; 11:29; 13:25], kings [1Sa 10:6; 11:6; 16:13; 2Sa 23:2] and prophets [1Sa 10:10; 2Sa 23:2; 1Ki 22:24; 2Ki 2:15; Mic 3:8]). The Spirit would endow the son of David with magnificent qualities. **wisdom.** Solomon had prayed for wisdom and understanding (see 1Ki 3:9), the administrative skills needed to govern the people according to the principles of righteousness and justice. The Messiah would possess just such wisdom. **understanding.** Insight and discretion (Pr 4:5,7; 9:10; 23:23) that emanate from divine wisdom. **counsel.** The Messiah has already been called "Wonderful Counselor" (9:6). **power.** A term that alludes to "Mighty God" (9:6). **knowledge.** Wise and submissive living in accordance

He will not judge by what he sees with his eyes,[l]
or decide by what he hears with his ears;[m]
4 but with righteousness[n] he will judge the needy,
with justice[o] he will give decisions for the poor[p] of the earth.
He will strike[q] the earth with the rod of his mouth;
with the breath[r] of his lips he will slay the wicked.
5 Righteousness will be his belt
and faithfulness[s] the sash around his waist.[t]

6 The wolf will live with the lamb,[u]
the leopard will lie down with the goat,
the calf and the lion and the yearling[a] together;
and a little child will lead them.
7 The cow will feed with the bear,
their young will lie down together,
and the lion will eat straw like the ox.
8 The infant will play near the hole of the cobra,
and the young child put his hand into the viper's nest.
9 They will neither harm nor destroy[v]
on all my holy mountain,
for the earth[w] will be full of the knowledge[x] of the LORD
as the waters cover the sea.

10 In that day the Root of Jesse will stand as a banner[y] for the peoples; the nations[z]
will rally to him,[a] and his place of rest[b] will be glorious. 11 In that day[c] the Lord will reach
out his hand a second time to reclaim the remnant that is left of his people from Assyria,[d] from Lower Egypt, from Upper Egypt,[b] from Cush,[c] from Elam,[e] from Babylonia,[d]
from Hamath and from the islands[f] of the sea.

12 He will raise a banner for the nations
and gather the exiles of Israel;
he will assemble the scattered people[g] of Judah
from the four quarters of the earth.
13 Ephraim's jealousy will vanish,
and Judah's enemies[e] will be cut off;
Ephraim will not be jealous of Judah,
nor Judah hostile toward Ephraim.[h]
14 They will swoop down on the slopes of Philistia to the west;
together they will plunder the people to the east.
They will lay hands on Edom[i] and Moab,[j]
and the Ammonites will be subject to them.

11:3 [l]Jn 7:24 [m]Jn 2:25
11:4 [n]Ps 72:2 [o]Isa 9:7 [p]Isa 3:14 [q]Mal 4:6 [r]Job 4:9; 2Th 2:8
11:5 [s]Isa 25:1 [t]Eph 6:14
11:6 [u]Isa 65:25
11:9 [v]Job 5:23 [w]Ps 98:2-3; Isa 52:10 [x]Isa 45:6,14; Hab 2:14
11:10 [y]Jn 12:32 [z]Isa 49:23; Lk 2:32 [a]Ro 15:12* [b]Isa 14:3; 28:12; 32:17-18
11:11 [c]Isa 10:20 [d]Isa 19:24; Hos 11:11; Mic 7:12; Zec 10:10 [e]Ge 10:22 [f]Isa 42:4,10,12; 66:19
11:12 [g]Zep 3:10
11:13 [h]Jer 3:18; Eze 37:16-17,22; Hos 1:11
11:14 [i]Da 11:41; Joel 3:19 [j]Isa 16:14; 25:10

a *6* Hebrew; Septuagint *lion will feed* b *11* Hebrew *from Pathros* c *11* That is, the upper Nile region
d *11* Hebrew *Shinar* e *13* Or *hostility*

with the will of God (33:6; 44:19,25; 47:10; 53:11). **fear of the LORD.** Reverence for God is the source of knowledge (see note on Pr 1:7). David insisted that his sons who ruled must manifest this quality (2Sa 23:1–4).
11:3–5 delight. An elaboration on the final endowment of the Spirit in the previous verse. **judge . . . faithfulness.** The prophet focused on the justice administered by the Messiah. **judge.** See note on 2:4. **righteousness . . . needy . . . justice . . . poor.** Those who longed for divine righteousness and justice (14:30; 25:4) because of oppression by the evil rulers of this earth (3:15; 10:2; 14:32; 29:19; 32:7; 41:17; 49:13; 54:11; 61:1; 66:2) would be protected by the great King to come. **rod . . . breath.** The Messiah would command such power and authority (Pss 2:9; 82:8; Rev 6:15–17; 20:11–12) that his mere breath would destroy the wicked (see 49:2; 61:1; Heb 4:12; Rev 19:15). **his belt . . . the sash.** Paul alluded to this passage as he described the armor that Christians are to wear (Eph 6:14).
11:6–9 The images of transformed rapacious beasts effectively picture the peaceable kingdom of Christ. This vision is being fulfilled in the unity of Christ's church today and will find complete fulfillment in the new heavens and the new earth.
11:10 In that day. See note on 2:11. **root of Jesse.** See note on verse 1 (Rev 22:16). **banner.** A sign of hope, in contrast to 5:26 (see 49:22; 62:10; cf. Jn 12:32). **place of rest.** That is, the promised land.
11:11 a second time. The first time of gathering was the exodus from Egypt; the second would be the gathering from exile brought about by the Assyrians and later extended by the Babylonians (see 51:9–11). **Assyria . . . islands.** No matter where the people of God were taken in exile, the son of David would gather a remnant of them back to the land of promise (24:15; 42:4,10; 51:5; 59:18–19). Jesus inaugurated this gathering of exiled Jews on the day of Pentecost (Ac 2), and he continues to gather them as the gospel goes forth. When he returns the faithful remnant of Judah will be gathered at the new Jerusalem from above (Rev 21:1–3).
11:13 Ephraim . . . Judah. The era of restoration would witness a reunion of the 12 tribes. See notes on 7:1–2, 9:20–21 and 14:1. The postexilic community witnessed a taste of this promise when a remnant of the 12 tribes returned to the land (1Ch 9:3; Ezr 6:17; 8:35). This promise was fulfilled further in Jesus Christ when he ministered both in the north and in the south (Mt 4:13–17). It moved forward even further on the day of Pentecost when Jews were gathered from all over the world (Ac 2). Its fulfillment continues in the unity of the church today (Gal 3:28) and will be completed when Christ returns (Rev 21:12–14).
11:14 Philistia . . . Ammonites. As was true of other prophets, Isaiah predicted that the restoration of Israel and Judah would entail warfare against the nations who attacked them (e.g., Eze 38; Am 9:11–12). Instead of fighting each other, Israel and Judah would defeat those enemies and rule throughout the world. The New Testa-

15 The LORD will dry up
the gulf of the Egyptian sea;
with a scorching wind he will sweep his hand[k]
over the Euphrates River.[a][l]
He will break it up into seven streams
so that men can cross over in sandals.
16 There will be a highway[m] for the remnant of his people
that is left from Assyria,
as there was for Israel
when they came up from Egypt.[n]

Songs of Praise

12 In that day you will say:

"I will praise[o] you, O LORD.
Although you were angry with me,
your anger has turned away
and you have comforted me.
2 Surely God is my salvation;
I will trust[p] and not be afraid.
The LORD, the LORD, is my strength and my song;
he has become my salvation.[q]"
3 With joy you will draw water[r]
from the wells of salvation.

4 In that day you will say:

"Give thanks to the LORD, call on his name;[s]
make known among the nations what he has done,
and proclaim that his name is exalted.
5 Sing[t] to the LORD, for he has done glorious things;[u]
let this be known to all the world.
6 Shout aloud and sing for joy, people of Zion,
for great is the Holy One of Israel[v] among you.[w]"

A Prophecy Against Babylon

13 An oracle concerning Babylon that Isaiah son of Amoz saw:

2 Raise a banner[x] on a bare hilltop,
shout to them;

11:15 [k]Isa 19:16 [l]Isa 7:20
11:16 [m]Isa 19:23; 62:10 [n]Ex 14:26-31
12:1 [o]Isa 25:1
12:2 [p]Isa 26:3 [q]Ex 15:2; Ps 118:14
12:3 [r]Jn 4:10,14
12:4 [s]Ps 105:1, Isa 24:15
12:5 [t]Ex 15:1 [u]Ps 98:1
12:6 [v]Isa 49:26 [w]Zep 3:14-17
13:2 [x]Jer 50:2; 51:27

[a] 15 Hebrew *the River*

ment explains that this final battle against the nations of the earth is now being waged through evangelism (Ac 15:12–19) and will be completed by Christ himself when he returns in glory (Rev 19).

11:15 dry up . . . Euphrates River. As God had opened a dry path through the Red Sea in the first exodus, so he would remove all obstacles for his own during the second exodus.

11:16 highway. A level way prepared by the Lord. This is a figure for the certainty and grandeur of the gathering from exile (19:23; 35:8–9; 40:3–4; 49:11; 57:14; 62:10). **remnant.** See note on 1:8. **left from Assyria.** Restoration to the land would take place for the faithful remnant who were taken into exile by the Assyrians. This promise later extended to those taken away by the Babylonians as well (40:3–4).

■ **12:1–6** *A Song of Praise in Zion.* In contrast to the condemnation of Israel's pride (9:8—10:4), Isaiah ended his prophecies regarding Assyria and Judah by predicting that the people of Judah and Israel alike would sing praise to God in Zion because of the great restoration that would take place.

12:1 In that day. See note on 2:11. **I will praise.** The prophet spoke as a representative of the people of God, much as Moses had done at the Red Sea (Ex 15:1).

12:2 God is my salvation. See Exodus 15:2. God alone would be the source of salvation from exile (12:2–3; 26:1,18; 33:2,6; 49:6,8; 51:6,8; 52:7,10; 56:1; 59:11,17; 60:18; 62:1).

12:3 joy . . . salvation. The salvation of the Lord would bring joy (35:10; 51:3,11; 61:3) as God delivered his people from oppression. Salvation is here likened to the abundance of "water" (see 1:30; Ex 15:25–27; Pss 1:3; 65:9; 104:10; 107:35) coming from the "wells of salvation" (see 41:18; Jn 4:14).

12:4 In that day. See note on 2:11. **Give thanks . . . what he has done.** Compare Psalms 105:1 and 148:13. **is exalted.** Compare Moses' song at the Red Sea (Ex 15:1).

■ **13:1—27:13** *International Upheaval During the Assyrian Judgment.* This portion of Isaiah's prophecies during the Assyrian judgment (7:1—39:8) concerns the international disruptions that God would bring through Assyrian aggression. This section was designed to encourage God's people to trust him during these difficult times and to increase their hope in the glorious future of the kingdom of God. These chapters divide into two main parts: oracles that the prophet declared against specific nations (13:1—23:18) and an elaborate description of the judgment to come against the nations, when God's people would be restored after exile (24:1—27:13).

■ **13:1—23:18** *Oracles Concerning Specific Nations.* This section presents Isaiah's prophecies concerning God's actions toward ten specific nations who played important roles during the period of Assyrian judgment. After opening with a declaration of Assyria's eventual defeat (13:1—14:27; see note on 13:1), the prophecies predict events that would soon take place in nine other nations in connection with Assyrian military campaigns and the guidance that the faithful in Israel and Judah were to gain from these events.

■ **13:1—14:27** *Babylon (Assyria).* The prophet began with a proclamation of severe judgment to come on Babylon, or as the evidence actually suggests, on Assyria (see note on 13:1).

13:1–16 It is somewhat unclear whether Assyria (see note on v. 1) is the agent or victim of God's vengeance in this passage. If the Assyrians are the agent, the fact that they overstep their bounds in

beckon to them
to enter the gates of the nobles.

13:3 [y]Joel 3:11 [z]Ps 149:2

3 I have commanded my holy ones;
I have summoned my warriors[y] to carry out my wrath—
those who rejoice[z] in my triumph.

13:4 [a]Joel 3:14

4 Listen, a noise on the mountains,
like that of a great multitude![a]
Listen, an uproar among the kingdoms,
like nations massing together!
The LORD Almighty is mustering
an army for war.

13:5 [b]Isa 5:26 [c]Isa 24:1

5 They come from faraway lands,
from the ends of the heavens[b]—
the LORD and the weapons of his wrath—
to destroy[c] the whole country.

13:6 [d]Eze 30:2 [e]Isa 2:12; Joel 1:15

6 Wail,[d] for the day[e] of the LORD is near;
it will come like destruction from the Almighty.[a]

13:7 [f]Eze 21:7

7 Because of this, all hands will go limp,
every man's heart will melt.[f]

13:8 [g]Isa 21:4 [h]Na 2:10

8 Terror[g] will seize them,
pain and anguish will grip them;
they will writhe like a woman in labor.
They will look aghast at each other,
their faces aflame.[h]

9 See, the day of the LORD is coming
—a cruel day, with wrath and fierce anger—
to make the land desolate
and destroy the sinners within it.

13:10 [i]Isa 24:23 [j]Isa 5:30; Rev 8:12 [k]Eze 32:7; Mt 24:29*; Mk 13:24*

10 The stars of heaven and their constellations
will not show their light.
The rising sun[i] will be darkened[j]
and the moon will not give its light.[k]

13:11 [l]Isa 3:11; 11:4; 26:21

11 I will punish[l] the world for its evil,
the wicked for their sins.
I will put an end to the arrogance of the haughty
and will humble the pride of the ruthless.

13:12 [m]Isa 4:1

12 I will make man[m] scarcer than pure gold,
more rare than the gold of Ophir.

13:13 [n]Isa 34:4; 51:6; Hag 2:6

13 Therefore I will make the heavens tremble;[n]
and the earth will shake from its place

[a] 6 Hebrew *Shaddai*

executing judgment leads to their own condemnation, which begins in verse 17.

13:1 Babylon. Several factors indicate that this passage actually concerns the Assyrian kingdom rather than the Babylonian Empire. (1) From the time of Tiglath-Pileser III (c. 729 B.C.) Assyrian kings designated themselves "the king of Babylon" because Babylon was among their holdings and was such an important city in the ancient world (14:3). (2) The larger literary context of this passage is concerned with the period of Assyrian, not Babylonian, judgment. (3) Isaiah 14:24–27 explicitly names Assyria but is not separated by an introductory heading such as is given for the other nations in this context (cf. 13:1; 14:28; 15:1; 17:1; 19:1; 21:1,11,13; 22:1; 23:1). For these reasons we may be confident that this prophecy predicts the defeat of the Assyrians by the Babylonians in c. 612 B.C.

13:2–5 The Lord prepared for battle against Assyria.

13:2 banner. See note on 5:26.

13:3 holy ones . . . warriors. Either the Assyrians, whom God used for his purposes, or another army God would use to bring judgment against the Assyrians (see note on 13:1–16). **rejoice.** Whether consciously or unconsciously, the attackers would celebrate the Lord's exaltation as they carried out his judgment (see 10:6,7; 45:1–7; Joel 2:11).

13:4 noise . . . uproar. The gathering of armies would be enormous and powerful (30:30–31; 33:3; Ps 29:5–9).

13:5 faraway lands . . . ends of the heavens. The Assyrian military utilized the services of soldiers from many nations, which may be an indication that the Assyrians were the agents of God's wrath (see note on 13:1–16).

13:6–22 The terror of the day of the Lord.

13:6 the day of the LORD. Or "the day" (vv. 9,13). See note on 2:11.

13:7 limp . . . melt. Many nations were utterly helpless to resist Assyrian aggression (35:3; Jer 6:24; Eze 7:17; Zep 3:16).

13:8 Terror . . . anguish . . . woman in labor. Fear and anguish would overcome those subjected to the execution of God's wrath (26:17; Jer 4:31; 6:24).

13:9 the day of the LORD. Or "that day" (see also v. 6). **a cruel day.** The Assyrians were notorious for their brutality in war, though other nations were capable of similar violence. See notes on 9:19 and 10:5.

13:10 stars . . . moon. When God comes in severe judgment, the very cosmos is affected (24:23; Joel 2:10,31; Rev 6:12–13). **light.** See note on 2:5.

13:13 heavens tremble . . . the earth will shake. Here the prophet spoke of God's approach in judgment as a shaking of the creation. The king of Assyria is also described as one "who shook the earth" (14:16) because he was God's instrument for judging so many nations.

at the wrath of the LORD Almighty,
  in the day of his burning anger.

14 Like a hunted gazelle,
  like sheep without a shepherd,[o]
each will return to his own people,
  each will flee to his native land.[p]
15 Whoever is captured will be thrust through;
  all who are caught will fall[q] by the sword.[r]
16 Their infants[s] will be dashed to pieces before their eyes;
  their houses will be looted and their wives ravished.

17 See, I will stir up[t] against them the Medes,
  who do not care for silver
  and have no delight in gold.[u]
18 Their bows will strike down the young men;
  they will have no mercy on infants
  nor will they look with compassion on children.
19 Babylon, the jewel of kingdoms,
  the glory[v] of the Babylonians'[a] pride,
will be overthrown[w] by God
  like Sodom and Gomorrah.[x]
20 She will never be inhabited[y]
  or lived in through all generations;
no Arab[z] will pitch his tent there,
  no shepherd will rest his flocks there.
21 But desert creatures[a] will lie there,
  jackals will fill her houses;
there the owls will dwell,
  and there the wild goats will leap about.
22 Hyenas will howl in her strongholds,[b]
  jackals[c] in her luxurious palaces.
Her time is at hand,[d]
  and her days will not be prolonged.

14

The LORD will have compassion[e] on Jacob;
  once again he will choose[f] Israel
  and will settle them in their own land.
Aliens[g] will join them
  and unite with the house of Jacob.
2 Nations will take them
  and bring[h] them to their own place.
And the house of Israel will possess the nations[i]
  as menservants and maidservants in the LORD's land.
They will make captives of their captors
  and rule over their oppressors.[j]

3 On the day the LORD gives you relief[k] from suffering and turmoil and cruel bondage,
4 you will take up this taunt[l] against the king of Babylon:

How the oppressor[m] has come to an end!
  How his fury[b] has ended!

13:14 [o]1Ki 22:17 [p]Jer 50:16
13:15 [q]Jer 51:4 [r]Isa 14:19; Jer 50:25
13:16 [s]Ps 137:9
13:17 [t]Jer 51:1 [u]Pr 6:34-35
13:19 [v]Da 4:30 [w]Rev 14:8 [x]Ge 19:24
13:20 [y]Isa 14:23; 34:10-15 [z]2Ch 17:11
13:21 [a]Rev 18:2
13:22 [b]Isa 25:2 [c]Isa 34:13 [d]Jer 51:33
14:1 [e]Ps 102:13; Isa 49:10,13; 54:7-8,10 [f]Isa 41:8; 44:1; 49:7; Zec 1:17; 2:12 [g]Eph 2:12-19
14:2 [h]Isa 60:9 [i]Isa 49:7,23 [j]Isa 60:14; 61:5
14:3 [k]Isa 11:10
14:4 [l]Hab 2:6 [m]Isa 9:4

[a] *19* Or *Chaldeans'* [b] *4* Dead Sea Scrolls, Septuagint and Syriac; the meaning of the word in the Masoretic Text is uncertain.

13:17 against them. God ultimately determined to judge the Assyrians by bringing other armies against them. **Medes.** Inhabitants of the Zagros Mountains, east of Babylon and Assyria. They joined Babylon in the eventual conquest of Assyria.
13:19 Babylon. See note on 13:1. **Sodom and Gomorrah.** See note on 1:9.
14:1–2 God's compassion would be shown to Israel.
14:1 Jacob . . . Israel. The 12 tribes. See notes on 11:13 and 41:8. **choose.** The destruction of Assyria was connected to God's act of choosing Israel once again. The election described here was covenantal, or national, election; Isaiah does not have in mind here eternal election to salvation. Through exile God would set Israel aside because of widespread sin, but he would select her again to receive the blessings of restoration (41:8–9; 43:10,20; 44:1–2; 45:4; 49:7; 65:9; Ex 19:6; Dt 7:6; 14:2,21; 26:19; cf. Ro 9–11). **Aliens.** One result of the restoration of Israel and Judah would be an assimilation of Gentiles into the nation (see 2:1–5).
14:2 Israel will possess. See note on 11:14 (cf. 54:3).
14:3–21 A taunt against the king of Babylon (Assyria). See note on 13:1.
14:4 taunt. Victors frequently sang taunting songs against their vanquished foes (see v. 7; 12:1; Ex 15:1). **king of Babylon.** That is, the king of Assyria (see note on 13:1). **How the oppressor.** The beginning of the first stanza of this taunt (see 14:9–11,12–15,16–21).

14:5 [n]Ps 125:3
14:6 [o]Isa 10:14 [p]Isa 47:6
14:7 [q]Ps 98:1; 126:1-3
14:8 [r]Eze 31:16
14:9 [s]Eze 32:21
14:10 [t]Eze 32:21
14:11 [u]Isa 51:8
14:12 [v]Isa 34:4; Lk 10:18 [w]2Pe 1:19; Rev 2:28; 8:10; 9:1
14:13 [x]Da 5:23; 8:10; Mt 11:23 [y]Eze 28:2; 2Th 2:4
14:14 [z]Isa 47:8; 2Th 2:4
14:15 [a]Mt 11:23; Lk 10:15
14:16 [b]Jer 50:23
14:17 [c]Joel 2:3

5 The LORD has broken the rod of the wicked,[n]
the scepter of the rulers,
6 which in anger struck down peoples[o]
with unceasing blows,
and in fury subdued nations
with relentless aggression.[p]
7 All the lands are at rest and at peace;
they break into singing.[q]
8 Even the pine trees[r] and the cedars of Lebanon
exult over you and say,
"Now that you have been laid low,
no woodsman comes to cut us down."

9 The grave[a][s] below is all astir
to meet you at your coming;
it rouses the spirits of the departed to greet you—
all those who were leaders in the world;
it makes them rise from their thrones—
all those who were kings over the nations.
10 They will all respond,
they will say to you,
"You also have become weak, as we are;
you have become like us."[t]
11 All your pomp has been brought down to the grave,
along with the noise of your harps;
maggots are spread out beneath you
and worms[u] cover you.

12 How you have fallen[v] from heaven,
O morning star,[w] son of the dawn!
You have been cast down to the earth,
you who once laid low the nations!
13 You said in your heart,
"I will ascend[x] to heaven;
I will raise my throne[y]
above the stars of God;
I will sit enthroned on the mount of assembly,
on the utmost heights of the sacred mountain.[b]
14 I will ascend above the tops of the clouds;
I will make myself like the Most High."[z]
15 But you are brought down to the grave,
to the depths[a] of the pit.

16 Those who see you stare at you,
they ponder your fate:[b]
"Is this the man who shook the earth
and made kingdoms tremble,
17 the man who made the world a desert,[c]
who overthrew its cities
and would not let his captives go home?"

[a] *9* Hebrew *Sheol*; also in verses 11 and 15 [b] *13* Or *the north*; Hebrew *Zaphon*

14:5 rod . . . scepter. See note on 10:5.
14:7 singing. A new song of victory would be heard in response to God's judgment and deliverance (12:6; 24:14,16; 25:5; 26:1,19; 44:23; 49:13; 54:1). See note on 12:6.
14:8 pine trees . . . cedars. Nature responds to God's acts of judgment and restoration (41:19; 55:13; 60:13; contrast 2:13; 9:10; 37:24; 44:14). **no woodsman.** Assyrian kings boasted in their annals of the magnificent trees they carted off from pillaged lands.
14:9–11 This second stanza describes astonishment at Assyria's fall.
14:9 grave. See note on 5:13–16. **spirits of the departed.** The spirits of kings whom the Assyrians had killed prepared to receive the kings of Assyria into the grave.
14:12–15 This third stanza reveals the justification for Assyria's fall.
14:12 fallen from heaven. A hyperbole for being cast down from an exalted political position (see La 2:1; Lk 4:6; 10:15). **morning star, son of the dawn!** The longstanding interpretation that this passage refers to the fall of Satan is incorrect. The context clearly indicates that Isaiah was speaking of the king of Assyria. Compare the similar description of the king of Tyre in Ezekiel 28.
14:13 heaven . . . stars of God. The Assyrian kings claimed to have thrones in the heavenly realms. **mount of assembly . . . sacred mountain.** The portrait here is that of Israel's God reigning supremely over angelic powers in his heavenly court, which is symbolized in Mount Zion (see Ps 48:1–2). **mountain.** See note on 2:2.
14:15 grave . . . pit. See verse 9.
14:16–21 This fourth stanza describes the demise of Assyria.
14:16–17 Is this the man who . . . ? The prophet mocked the kings of Assyria by contrasting Assyria's former glory with its future condition once God had brought judgment against this people. They seemed invincible, but they were not.

18 All the kings of the nations lie in state,
each in his own tomb.
19 But you are cast out[d] of your tomb
like a rejected branch;
you are covered with the slain,
with those pierced by the sword,
those who descend to the stones of the pit.[e]
Like a corpse trampled underfoot,
20 you will not join them in burial,
for you have destroyed your land
and killed your people.

The offspring[f] of the wicked[g]
will never be mentioned[h] again.
21 Prepare a place to slaughter his sons
for the sins of their forefathers;[i]
they are not to rise to inherit the land
and cover the earth with their cities.

22 "I will rise up against them,"
declares the LORD Almighty.
"I will cut off from Babylon her name and survivors,
her offspring and descendants,[j]"
declares the LORD.
23 "I will turn her into a place for owls[k]
and into swampland;
I will sweep her with the broom of destruction,"
declares the LORD Almighty.

A Prophecy Against Assyria

24 The LORD Almighty has sworn,[l]

"Surely, as I have planned, so it will be,
and as I have purposed, so it will stand.[m]
25 I will crush the Assyrian[n] in my land;
on my mountains I will trample him down.
His yoke[o] will be taken from my people,
and his burden removed from their shoulders.[p]"

26 This is the plan[q] determined for the whole world;
this is the hand[r] stretched out over all nations.
27 For the LORD Almighty has purposed, and who can thwart him?
His hand is stretched out, and who can turn it back?[s]

A Prophecy Against the Philistines

28 This oracle[t] came in the year King Ahaz[u] died:

29 Do not rejoice, all you Philistines,[v]
that the rod that struck you is broken;
from the root of that snake will spring up a viper,[w]
its fruit will be a darting, venomous serpent.
30 The poorest of the poor will find pasture,
and the needy[x] will lie down in safety.[y]
But your root I will destroy by famine;[z]
it will slay[a] your survivors.

14:19
[d]Isa 22:16-18
[e]Jer 41:7-9

14:20
[f]Job 18:19 [g]Isa 1:4
[h]Ps 21:10

14:21
[i]Ex 20:5; Lev 26:39

14:22
[j]1Ki 14:10; Job 18:19

14:23
[k]Isa 34:11-15; Zep 2:14

14:24
[l]Isa 45:23
[m]Ac 4:28

14:25
[n]Isa 10:5, 12
[o]Isa 9:4 [p]Isa 10:27

14:26
[q]Isa 23:9 [r]Ex 15:12

14:27
[s]2Ch 20:6; Isa 43:13; Da 4:35

14:28
[t]Isa 13:1
[u]2Ki 16:20

14:29
[v]2Ch 26:6
[w]Isa 11:8

14:30
[x]Isa 3:15 [y]Isa 7:21-22 [z]Isa 8:21; 9:20; 51:19 [a]Jer 25:16

14:19 rejected branch. In contrast with the royal Branch of David's house, who would grow and rule to the benefit of God's people (11:1).
14:21 sons. No one would remember the king of Assyria because he would lack a decent burial (vv. 18–20) and have no offspring.
14:22 Babylon. That is, Assyria (see note on 13:1). **survivors.** Unlike Israel and Judah, Assyria had no holy remnant to be blessed by God (see v. 30; 15:9; 17:3; see also note on 1:9). The Babylonian defeat of Assyria (c. 612 B.C.) began its destruction, but this prediction will ultimately be fulfilled in the judgment at the second coming of Christ.
14:25 yoke. See note on 9:3–4. **my people.** See note on 40:1.

■ **14:28–32** *Philistia.* The prophet described how God would use the Assyrians to judge the Philistines. This oracle may refer to the attacks of Tiglath-Pileser III on the Philistines in 727 B.C., as well as the attacks of Sargon II in 716/15 B.C.
14:29 rod. God would use the Assyrians to punish the Philistines. **broken.** Refers to a temporary lapse in Assyria's domination that occurred between the reigns of Tiglath-Pileser III and Sargon II. **snake . . . darting, venomous serpent.** The empire would return to power.
14:30 poor . . . needy. See note on 11:3–5. God was with his "afflicted people" (v. 32) but was against the proud. **survivors.** See note on verse 22.

31 Wail, O gate![b] Howl, O city!
Melt away, all you Philistines!
A cloud of smoke comes from the north,[c]
and there is not a straggler in its ranks.
32 What answer shall be given
to the envoys[d] of that nation?
"The LORD has established Zion,[e]
and in her his afflicted people will find refuge.[f]"

A Prophecy Against Moab

15 An oracle concerning Moab:[g]

Ar in Moab is ruined,[h]
destroyed in a night!
Kir in Moab is ruined,
destroyed in a night!
2 Dibon goes up to its temple,
to its high places[i] to weep;
Moab wails over Nebo and Medeba.
Every head is shaved[j]
and every beard cut off.
3 In the streets they wear sackcloth;
on the roofs and in the public squares[k]
they all wail,
prostrate with weeping.[l]
4 Heshbon and Elealeh[m] cry out,
their voices are heard all the way to Jahaz.
Therefore the armed men of Moab cry out,
and their hearts are faint.

5 My heart cries out over Moab;[n]
her fugitives flee as far as Zoar,
as far as Eglath Shelishiyah.
They go up the way to Luhith,
weeping as they go;
on the road to Horonaim[o]
they lament their destruction.[p]
6 The waters of Nimrim are dried up[q]
and the grass is withered;[r]
the vegetation is gone
and nothing green is left.
7 So the wealth they have acquired[s] and stored up
they carry away over the Ravine of the Poplars.
8 Their outcry echoes along the border of Moab;
their wailing reaches as far as Eglaim,
their lamentation as far as Beer Elim.
9 Dimon's[a] waters are full of blood,
but I will bring still more upon Dimon[a]—

14:31 [b]Isa 3:26 [c]Jer 1:14
14:32 [d]Isa 37:9 [e]Ps 87:2, 5; Isa 44:28; 54:11 [f]Isa 4:6; Jas 2:5
15:1 [g]Isa 11:14 [h]Jer 48:24,41
15:2 [i]Jer 48:35 [j]Lev 21:5
15:3 [k]Jer 48:38 [l]Isa 22:4
15:4 [m]Nu 32:3
15:5 [n]Jer 48:31 [o]Jer 48:3,34 [p]Jer 4:20; 48:5
15:6 [q]Isa 19:5-7; Jer 48:34 [r]Joel 1:12
15:7 [s]Isa 30:6; Jer 48:36

[a] *9* Masoretic Text; Dead Sea Scrolls, some Septuagint manuscripts and Vulgate *Dibon*

14:31 Wail. Compare 13:6, 15:2 and 16:7. **cloud of smoke.** Reference to the dust that would be stirred up by the movements of the Assyrian invaders who would attack the Philistines. **north.** Assyria would attack from the north.

14:32 envoys. The Philistines would seek to create a coalition with Judah and other nations against the Assyrians, but God's people would have to trust in him during this time of threat rather than forming an alliance with Philistia.

■ **15:1—16:14** *Moab.* Isaiah predicted that Moab would also suffer at the hands of the Assyrians. The oracle has two parts: Moab's distress (15:1–9) and the response to that distress (16:1–14).

15:1–2 Moab. This prophecy primarily concerns the defeat of Moab in c. 715 B.C. by the Assyrian king Sargon II (see also 11:14; 25:10; Jer 48; Eze 25:8–11; Am 2:1–3; Zep 2:8–11). **Ar . . . Medeba.** Various locations in the land of Moab that the Assyrians would trouble. **weep . . . cut off.** Mourning rituals that would be performed when Moab was defeated.

15:3 sackcloth . . . weeping. Aspects of the mourning rituals (22:12; Jer 4:8; 41:5; 48:20,34; La 2:10). **roofs . . . public squares.** Mourning would take place both in private and in public.

15:4 Elealeh . . . Jahaz. Other locations in Moab that would suffer from Assyrian aggression.

15:5 cries. In contrast to Isaiah's delight in the fall of other nations, he felt sympathy for Moab, perhaps because of the kinship between Israel and Moab (see 16:11). **fugitives.** Moab would be devastated, and her people would flee further south to Zoar, as their forefather Lot had done (Ge 19:23–30).

15:6 dried up . . . nothing green is left. God's judgment against Moab would involve not only military defeat but the curse of nature as well.

15:9 lion. The fugitives from Assyrian attacks would go from trou-

a lion[t] upon the fugitives of Moab
and upon those who remain in the land.

16

Send lambs[u] as tribute
to the ruler of the land,
from Sela,[v] across the desert,
to the mount of the Daughter of Zion.[w]
2 Like fluttering birds
pushed from the nest,[x]
so are the women of Moab
at the fords of the Arnon.[y]

3 "Give us counsel,
render a decision.
Make your shadow like night—
at high noon.
Hide the fugitives,[z]
do not betray the refugees.
4 Let the Moabite fugitives stay with you;
be their shelter from the destroyer."

The oppressor[a] will come to an end,
and destruction will cease;
the aggressor will vanish from the land.
5 In love a throne[b] will be established;
in faithfulness a man will sit on it—
one from the house[a] of David[c]—
one who in judging seeks justice[d]
and speeds the cause of righteousness.

6 We have heard of Moab's[e] pride[f]—
her overweening pride and conceit,
her pride and her insolence—
but her boasts are empty.
7 Therefore the Moabites wail,[g]
they wail together for Moab.
Lament and grieve
for the men[b][h] of Kir Hareseth.[i]
8 The fields of Heshbon wither,
the vines of Sibmah also.
The rulers of the nations
have trampled down the choicest vines,
which once reached Jazer
and spread toward the desert.
Their shoots spread out
and went as far as the sea.
9 So I weep,[j] as Jazer weeps,
for the vines of Sibmah.
O Heshbon, O Elealeh,
I drench you with tears!
The shouts of joy over your ripened fruit
and over your harvests[k] have been stilled.

15:9 [t]2Ki 17:25
16:1 [u]2Ki 3:4 [v]2Ki 14:7 [w]Isa 10:32
16:2 [x]Pr 27:8 [y]Nu 21:13-14; Jer 48:20
16:3 [z]1Ki 18:4
16:4 [a]Isa 9:4
16:5 [b]Da 7:14; Mic 4:7 [c]Lk 1:32 [d]Isa 9:7
16:6 [e]Am 2:1; Zep 2:8 [f]Ob 1:3; Zep 2:10
16:7 [g]Jer 48:20 [h]1Ch 16:3 [i]2Ki 3:25
16:9 [j]Isa 15:3 [k]Jer 40:12

[a] 5 Hebrew *tent* [b] 7 Or *"raisin cakes,"* a wordplay

ble to trouble (cf. Am 5:19) in their flight southward. They would finally turn to Judah in the west for asylum (16:1–5).
16:1 lambs as tribute. The Moabites were sheepherders (Nu 32:4) and sent lambs as tokens of their submission (cf. 2Ki 3:4). **from Sela.** The fugitives were either at Sela, a naturally fortified site (in Edom, near Petra), or at a mountain stronghold (*Sela* means "rock"). The tribute was sent from their outpost to Judah.
16:3–4 counsel. Moab would request asylum from the Assyrians in Judah. See note on 11:2. **shadow . . . shelter.** Protection from the Assyrian aggression. See notes on 2:2–4 and 30:2.
16:4 you. In Hebrew the form is feminine singular, a reference to the "Daughter of Zion" (16:1). **oppressor . . . aggressor.** That is, Assyria.
16:5 In love. God had established a loving bond of covenant with the house of David (55:3; 2Sa 7; 22:51; 1Ch 17; Pss 89:28; 132). See note on 54:8. In Jesus, the son of David, all nations will finally find shelter (Ac 15:16–17). **throne . . . house of David.** Hope for the Moabites was in the Lord and in his promises to David (see 9:2–7; 11:1–9). David's kingdom would one day be restored, and some Moabite survivors would join this renewed kingdom (see note on 14:1). **throne will be established.** See 9:1–7, 11:1–5, Amos 9:11–12 and Acts 15:16–17.
16:7 men. The text should probably read "raisin cakes" (see NIV text note); i.e., the food of celebration.
16:8–10 Isaiah empathized with the desolation of the fine vineyards of Moab.

[10] Joy and gladness are taken away from the orchards;[l]
no one sings or shouts in the vineyards;
no one treads[m] out wine at the presses,[n]
for I have put an end to the shouting.
[11] My heart laments for Moab[o] like a harp,
my inmost being[p] for Kir Hareseth.
[12] When Moab appears at her high place,
she only wears herself out;
when she goes to her shrine[q] to pray,
it is to no avail.[r]

[13] This is the word the LORD has already spoken concerning Moab. [14] But now the LORD says: "Within three years, as a servant bound by contract would count them, Moab's splendor and all her many people will be despised,[s] and her survivors will be very few and feeble."[t]

An Oracle Against Damascus

17 An oracle concerning Damascus:[u]

"See, Damascus will no longer be a city
but will become a heap of ruins.[v]
[2] The cities of Aroer will be deserted
and left to flocks,[w] which will lie down,
with no one to make them afraid.[x]
[3] The fortified city will disappear from Ephraim,
and royal power from Damascus;
the remnant of Aram will be
like the glory[y] of the Israelites,"[z]
declares the LORD Almighty.

[4] "In that day the glory of Jacob will fade;
the fat of his body will waste[a] away.
[5] It will be as when a reaper gathers the standing grain
and harvests[b] the grain with his arm—
as when a man gleans heads of grain
in the Valley of Rephaim.
[6] Yet some gleanings will remain,[c]
as when an olive tree is beaten,[d]
leaving two or three olives on the topmost branches,
four or five on the fruitful boughs,"
declares the LORD, the God of Israel.

[7] In that day men will look[e] to their Maker
and turn their eyes to the Holy One[f] of Israel.
[8] They will not look to the altars,
the work of their hands,[g]
and they will have no regard for the Asherah poles[a]
and the incense altars their fingers have made.

16:10 [l]Isa 24:7-8 [m]Jdg 9:27 [n]Job 24:11
16:11 [o]Isa 15:5 [p]Isa 63:15; Hos 11:8; Php 2:1
16:12 [q]Isa 15:2 [r]1Ki 18:29
16:14 [s]Isa 25:10; Jer 48:42 [t]Isa 21:17
17:1 [u]Ge 14:15; Jer 49:23; Ac 9:2 [v]Isa 25:2; Am 1:3; Zec 9:1
17:2 [w]Isa 7:21; Eze 25:5 [x]Jer 7:33; Mic 4:4
17:3 [y]ver 4; Hos 9:11 [z]Isa 7:8,16; 8:4
17:4 [a]Isa 10:16
17:5 [b]ver 11; Jer 51:33; Joel 3:13; Mt 13:30
17:6 [c]Dt 4:27; Isa 24:13 [d]Isa 27:12
17:7 [e]Isa 10:20 [f]Mic 7:7
17:8 [g]Isa 2:18,20; 30:22

[a] *8* That is, symbols of the goddess Asherah

16:11 My heart laments . . . my inmost being. A deeply felt sorrow (v. 9; 21:3–4; cf. Jer 48:36). See note on 15:5.
16:13–14 word the LORD has already spoken. The prophet summarized Moab's distress in prose by referring either to other revelations in the past or to the oracles in 15:1–9 or 15:1—16:12. **Within three years.** The desolation of Moab was imminent. This is probably a reference to the quelling of the rebellion against Sargon II, king of Assyria, in 716/715 B.C.
■ **17:1–14** *Damascus.* This oracle concerning Damascus refers to the Assyrian military response to the Syrian-Israelite coalition in 734–732 B.C.
17:1 oracle. See 13:1. **Damascus.** The capital of Syria and a commercial hub along the trade routes from Mesopotamia to Egypt and into Arabia. Damascus was captured by Tiglath-Pileser III in 732 B.C.
17:3 fortified . . . Ephraim. The "strong cities" (v. 9) of Israel were severely reduced by 732 B.C. and destroyed in 722 B.C. (see note on 9:1). **remnant.** Survivors from Syria would be extremely rare, just as the glory of Israel would dwindle (v. 4).
17:4–6 The prophet shifted from Syria to the northern kingdom of Israel, which had closely allied itself with Syria.
17:4 In that day. See note on 2:11. **the glory.** Whatever remained would be minimal in comparison with Israel's former splendor. See note on 4:2. The images are of an undernourished body (v. 4), gleanings of grain (v. 5) and the few olives left after a tree has been beaten (v. 6).
17:5 Valley of Rephaim. A lush valley southwest of Jerusalem; the gateway to the Shephelah, or western plains (Jos 15:8; 18:16; 2Sa 5:18,22; 1Ch 14:9).
17:7–8 In that day. See note on 2:11. **Maker . . . made.** The Hebrew contrasts the work of God ("Maker"; v. 7) with the accomplishments of humans ("work . . . made"; v. 8). See note on 2:8. **Asherah poles.** See NIV text note. The goddess Asherah, the consort of El, was a Canaanite fertility goddess; worship of this goddess involved fertility symbols of sacred groves and poles (27:9; Ex 34:13; Dt 16:21; Jdg 2:13).

[9]In that day their strong cities, which they left because of the Israelites, will be like
places abandoned to thickets and undergrowth. And all will be desolation.

[10]You have forgotten[h] God your Savior;[i]
you have not remembered the Rock, your fortress.
Therefore, though you set out the finest plants
and plant imported vines,
[11]though on the day you set them out, you make them grow,
and on the morning[j] when you plant them, you bring them to
bud,
yet the harvest will be as nothing[k]
in the day of disease and incurable pain.[l]

[12]Oh, the raging of many nations—
they rage like the raging sea![m]
Oh, the uproar of the peoples—
they roar like the roaring of great waters!
[13]Although the peoples roar like the roar of surging waters,
when he rebukes[n] them they flee[o] far away,
driven before the wind like chaff[p] on the hills,
like tumbleweed before a gale.[q]
[14]In the evening, sudden terror!
Before the morning, they are gone![r]
This is the portion of those who loot us,
the lot of those who plunder us.

A Prophecy Against Cush

18 Woe to the land of whirring wings[a]
along the rivers of Cush,[b][s]
[2]which sends envoys by sea
in papyrus[t] boats over the water.

Go, swift messengers,
to a people tall and smooth-skinned,
to a people feared far and wide,
an aggressive[u] nation of strange speech,
whose land is divided by rivers.[v]

[3]All you people of the world,
you who live on the earth,
when a banner[w] is raised on the mountains,
you will see it,
and when a trumpet sounds,
you will hear it.
[4]This is what the LORD says to me:

17:10 [h]Isa 51:13 [i]Ps 68:19; Isa 12:2
17:11 [j]Ps 90:6 [k]Hos 8:7 [l]Job 4:8
17:12 [m]Ps 18:4; Jer 6:23; Lk 21:25
17:13 [n]Ps 9:5 [o]Isa 13:14 [p]Isa 41:2, 15-16 [q]Job 21:18
17:14 [r]2Ki 19:35
18:1 [s]Isa 20:3-5; Eze 30:4-5, 9; Zep 2:12; 3:10
18:2 [t]Ex 2:3 [u]Ge 10:8-9; 2Ch 12:3 [v]ver 7
18:3 [w]Isa 5:26

[a] *1* Or *of locusts* [b] *1* That is, the upper Nile region

17:10 forgotten . . . not remembered. Israel had turned away from God (Dt 4:9,23,31; 8:11,14,18–19; 25:19; 32:18). **God your Savior.** The only Redeemer (43:3; 49:26; 62:11). **Rock.** See note on 8:14–15. **fortress.** The Lord alone is the strength of his people (see also "refuge" at 25:4; 27:5), in contrast to proposed military and political solutions (see "strong cities" at v. 9, "fortress" or "fortresses" at 23:4,11,14 and "protection" at 30:2). **finest plants . . . imported vines.** Reference to Canaanite fertility rituals.
17:11 you make them grow. Perhaps an allusion to a pagan practice of forcing potted plants to bloom as part of fertility rites.
17:12–14 God would take retribution against the northern kingdom through the Assyrians.
17:12 raging sea . . . great waters! The destructive power of the nations joining the Assyrians in their military campaign (see note 13:5) is compared to tumultuous waters.
17:13 hills. Grain was winnowed on often windy hilltops.
17:14 sudden terror! An unforeseen series of troubles (24:17–18) brought about on the day of the Lord's wrath (22:5). **loot us.** The Lord would protect Judah by punishing both the Syrians and the northern kingdom.
■ **18:1 –20:6** *Cush and Egypt.* The prophet turned to the troubles that would befall Cush and Egypt. A Cushite named Shabako took power in Egypt in 715 B.C. For this reason Cush and Egypt are closely connected in this prophecy, which predicts events that would take place as Cush/Egypt became involved in the international upheavals caused by Assyrian aggression, including the defeat of Egypt by the Assyrian king Esarhaddon in 670 B.C.
18:1–6 The prophet first declared an oracle against Cush.
18:1 Woe. See note on 1:4. **land of whirring wings.** Either "land of many insects" (see NIV text note; "of locusts") or "land of many ships" (as in some ancient translations of Isaiah). **Cush.** The region of Nubia, south of modern Egypt.
18:2 envoys . . . papyrus boats. The Nubians' effective use of speedy, lightweight boats would incite the nations to rebel against the Assyrians. **swift messengers.** Ironically, the prophet called for fleet-footed messengers to hurry to the Cushites and deliver the message of verses 3–6. **tall and smooth-skinned.** Perhaps a reference to the clean shaven Cushites and Egyptians.
18:3 people of the world. The addressees of the oracle (18:1–7) are all the nations that were destined to experience God's wrath through Assyrian aggression. They would observe what the Lord would do to Cush (and Egypt). **banner.** See note on 5:26. **trumpet.** The method for summoning troops.

"I will remain quiet and will look on from my dwelling place,[x]
like shimmering heat in the sunshine,
like a cloud of dew[y] in the heat of harvest."
5 For, before the harvest, when the blossom is gone
and the flower becomes a ripening grape,
he will cut off the shoots with pruning knives,
and cut down and take away the spreading branches.[z]
6 They will all be left to the mountain birds of prey
and to the wild animals;[a]
the birds will feed on them all summer,
the wild animals all winter.

7 At that time gifts will be brought to the LORD Almighty

from a people tall and smooth-skinned,
from a people feared far and wide,
an aggressive nation of strange speech,
whose land is divided by rivers—

the gifts will be brought to Mount Zion, the place of the Name of the LORD Almighty.[b]

A Prophecy About Egypt

19

An oracle[c] concerning Egypt:[d e]

See, the LORD rides on a swift cloud[f]
and is coming to Egypt.
The idols of Egypt tremble before him,
and the hearts of the Egyptians melt[g] within them.

2 "I will stir up Egyptian against Egyptian—
brother will fight against brother,[h]
neighbor against neighbor,
city against city,
kingdom against kingdom.[i]
3 The Egyptians will lose heart,
and I will bring their plans to nothing;
they will consult the idols and the spirits of the dead,
the mediums and the spiritists.[j]
4 I will hand the Egyptians over
to the power of a cruel master,
and a fierce king[k] will rule over them,"
declares the Lord, the LORD Almighty.

5 The waters of the river will dry up,[l]
and the riverbed will be parched and dry.
6 The canals will stink;[m]
the streams of Egypt will dwindle and dry up.[n]
The reeds and rushes will wither,[o]
7 also the plants along the Nile,

18:4 [x]Isa 26:21; Hos 5:15 [y]Isa 26:19; Hos 14:5
18:5 [z]Isa 17:10-11; Eze 17:6
18:6 [a]Isa 56:9; Jer 7:33; Eze 32:4; 39:17
18:7 [b]Ps 68:31
19:1 [c]Isa 13:1; Jer 43:12 [d]Joel 3:19 [e]Ex 12:12 [f]Ps 18:10; 104:3; Rev 1:7 [g]Jos 2:11
19:2 [h]Jdg 7:22; Mt 10:21,36 [i]2Ch 20:23
19:3 [j]Isa 8:19; 47:13; Da 2:2,10
19:4 [k]Isa 20:4; Jer 46:26; Eze 29:19
19:5 [l]Jer 51:36
19:6 [m]Ex 7:18 [n]Isa 37:25; Eze 30:12 [o]Isa 15:6

18:4 I will remain quiet . . . my dwelling place. The Lord would patiently observe the activities of Cush and Egypt for a while before reacting (Pss 2:1–4; 33:13–17; 80:14).
18:5–6 These verses contain two images of God's judgment through Assyrian attacks on Cush and Egypt: the pruning of vines before harvest and a carcass on which animals feed.
18:7 gifts. As other prophecies in this context indicate, God's judgment through the Assyrians against the Cushites (and the Egyptians) would eventually lead to a time when some of them would submit to Israel's God (see notes on 13:4; 16:1). **tall and smooth-skinned.** See verse 2. **Zion.** See note on 1:8. **the place.** The temple. **Name.** The Lord's accessible special presence was in the temple of Jerusalem (see theological article "The Presence of God" at 1Ki 8). This prediction was fulfilled in part as Gentiles were included among the returnees in 539–538 B.C., but it will come to final fruition in Christ, who brings large numbers of Gentiles into the kingdom of God.
19:1—20:6 The prophet turned toward Egypt (see note on 18:1—20:6). Isaiah declared the future victory of the Assyrian king Esarhaddon over Egypt in 670 B.C., as well as the effects his victory would have on Egypt and the lesson to be learned from this defeat.
19:1 oracle. See note on 13:1. **rides on a swift cloud.** The Lord would be exalted over all other gods as he engaged the Egyptians in battle through the Assyrian aggression of 670 B.C. (Pss 18:10; 68:33; 104:3).
19:2–15 The prophet revealed the frailty of Egypt before the Assyrian judgment.
19:2 Egyptian against Egyptian. See 9:21. The violence and turmoil of this period would be extensive, as God's judgment would come not only from outside Egypt but also from within (see Jdg 7:22; 2Ch 20:22).
19:3 consult the idols . . . mediums and the spiritists. The power of God displayed in the success of Esarhaddon's campaign would be a demonstration of God's power over the impotent Egyptian idols.
19:4 cruel master . . . fierce king. Expressions of the tyranny of Assyrian dominance over Egypt.
19:5–6 river . . . plants along the Nile. God's judgment against Egypt would result not only in military defeat but in curses involving nature as well.

at the mouth of the river.
Every sown field[p] along the Nile
will become parched, will blow away and be no more.
8 The fishermen[q] will groan and lament,
all who cast hooks[r] into the Nile;
those who throw nets on the water
will pine away.
9 Those who work with combed flax will despair,
the weavers of fine linen[s] will lose hope.
10 The workers in cloth will be dejected,
and all the wage earners will be sick at heart.

11 The officials of Zoan[t] are nothing but fools;
the wise counselors of Pharaoh give senseless advice.
How can you say to Pharaoh,
"I am one of the wise men,[u]
a disciple of the ancient kings"?
12 Where are your wise men[v] now?
Let them show you and make known
what the LORD Almighty
has planned[w] against Egypt.
13 The officials of Zoan have become fools,
the leaders of Memphis[a][x] are deceived;
the cornerstones of her peoples
have led Egypt astray.
14 The LORD has poured into them
a spirit of dizziness;[y]
they make Egypt stagger in all that she does,
as a drunkard staggers around in his vomit.
15 There is nothing Egypt can do—
head or tail, palm branch or reed.[z]

16 In that day the Egyptians will be like women.[a] They will shudder with fear[b] at the
uplifted hand[c] that the LORD Almighty raises against them. 17 And the land of Judah will
bring terror to the Egyptians; everyone to whom Judah is mentioned will be terrified, because of what the LORD Almighty is planning[d] against them.
18 In that day five cities in Egypt will speak the language of Canaan and swear allegiance[e] to the LORD Almighty. One of them will be called the City of Destruction.[b]
19 In that day there will be an altar[f] to the LORD in the heart of Egypt, and a monument[g] to the LORD at its border. 20 It will be a sign and witness to the LORD Almighty in

a 13 Hebrew *Noph* b 18 Most manuscripts of the Masoretic Text; some manuscripts of the Masoretic Text, Dead Sea Scrolls and Vulgate *City of the Sun* (that is, Heliopolis)

19:7 [p] Isa 23:3
19:8 [q] Eze 47:10 [r] Hab 1:15
19:9 [s] Pr 7:16; Eze 27:7
19:11 [t] Nu 13:22 [u] 1Ki 4:30; Ac 7:22
19:12 [v] 1Co 1:20 [w] Isa 14:24, Ro 9:17
19:13 [x] Jer 2:16; Eze 30:13,16
19:14 [y] Mt 17:17
19:15 [z] Isa 9:14
19:16 [a] Jer 51:30; Na 3:13 [b] Heb 10:31 [c] Isa 11:15
19:17 [d] Isa 14:24
19:18 [e] Zep 3:9
19:19 [f] Jos 22:10 [g] Ge 28:18

19:8–10 fishermen . . . flax . . . all the wage earners. God's judgment through the Assyrians would also ruin Egypt's commerce: the fishing (cf. Nu 11:5; Eze 29:4) and linen industries in particular.
19:11–12 Zoan. Or Tanis, a city in the Nile delta (v. 13; Nu 13:22; Ps 78:12,43) and Egypt's capital at the time. **fools.** God would turn the wisdom of Egypt into folly. **counselors . . . senseless advice.** See note on 11:2. **wise men, a disciple of the ancient kings?** A sarcastic remark on Egypt's claim to wisdom (cf. 1Ki 4:30).
19:12 wise men now? God mocked the failing wisdom of Egypt.
19:13–15 officials . . . cornerstones. Political, economic and religious leaders. The leadership—"head or tail, palm branch or reed" (v. 15)—would lead the people "astray" (v. 13). Only the Lord could save Egypt (see vv. 16–25). See note on 9:16. **Zoan.** See note on verses 11–12. **Memphis.** A city in Lower Egypt and Egypt's ancient capital (see note on "Zoan" at verses 11–12). **spirit of dizziness.** Confusion, in contrast to wisdom.
19:16–25 The trouble that would befall Egypt by means of Assyrian aggression would eventually lead to the spread of the fear and worship of the Lord in Egypt. This prophecy first found its fulfillment during the time when Israelites were exiled to Egypt and some learned of God from Jews living within their borders. The gospel ministry of the church from the day of Pentecost (Ac 2) until now has furthered this process. When Christ returns many Egyptians will be among the redeemed.
19:16 In that day. See note on 2:11. **shudder with fear.** Some in Egypt would perceive that the Lord, who used Assyria as his instrument of wrath, was greater than their own gods (Jos 2:9,11). **uplifted hand.** See note on 14:26–27.
19:17 terror . . . planning against them. The Egyptians would not fear Judah as such. Instead, as a result of the display of God's power through the Assyrians, the promise that God would ultimately give victory to his people against all who had oppressed them in the past would instill terror and impel some Egyptians to worship the God of Israel. The New Testament explains that this prediction is fulfilled as the nations come to Christ because they understand that Jews who follow Christ and Gentiles who have joined them in the church receive victory in Christ both now and at Christ's return.
19:18 In that day. See note on 2:11. **five cities.** Probably connotes "many," as opposed to precisely five. **language of Canaan.** An expression for the radical nature of the transformation, as Canaan had formerly been an abomination to the Egyptians (see Ge 43:32; 46:34). **swear allegiance.** Many Egyptians would express complete submission to the true God. **City of Destruction.** Probably Heliopolis (i.e., "City of the Sun"; see NIV text note), which was later destroyed by Nebuchadnezzar (Jer 43:12–13).
19:19–20 In that day. See note on 2:11. **altar.** The prediction of the construction of an altar to God in Egypt is fulfilled by the presence of the church, the temple of God, in that country. God will deliver believing Egyptians from all oppression through salvation in Christ.

19:20 [h]Isa 49:24-26
19:21 [i]Isa 11:9 [j]Isa 56:7; Mal 1:11
19:22 [k]Heb 12:11 [l]Isa 45:14; Hos 14:1 [m]Dt 32:39
19:23 [n]Isa 11:16 [o]Isa 27:13
19:25 [p]Ps 100:3 [q]Isa 29:23; 45:11; 60:21; 64:8; Eph 2:10 [r]Hos 2:23
20:1 [s]2Ki 18:17
20:2 [t]Isa 13:1 [u]Zec 13:4; Mt 3:4 [v]Eze 24:17, 23 [w]1Sa 19:24 [x]Mic 1:8
20:3 [y]Isa 8:18 [z]Isa 37:9; 43:3
20:4 [a]Isa 19:4 [b]Isa 47:3; Jer 13:22,26
20:5 [c]2Ki 18:21; Isa 30:5
20:6 [d]Isa 10:3 [e]Jer 30:15-17; Mt 23:33; 1Th 5:3; Heb 2:3
21:1 [f]Isa 13:21; Jer 51:43 [g]Zec 9:14

the land of Egypt. When they cry out to the LORD because of their oppressors, he will send
them a savior and defender, and he will rescue[h] them. 21So the LORD will make himself
known to the Egyptians, and in that day they will acknowledge[i] the LORD. They will worship[j] with sacrifices and grain offerings; they will make vows to the LORD and keep them.
22The LORD will strike[k] Egypt with a plague; he will strike them and heal them. They will
turn[l] to the LORD, and he will respond to their pleas and heal[m] them.

23In that day there will be a highway[n] from Egypt to Assyria. The Assyrians will go to
Egypt and the Egyptians to Assyria. The Egyptians and Assyrians will worship[o] together. 24In that day Israel will be the third, along with Egypt and Assyria, a blessing on the
earth. 25The LORD Almighty will bless them, saying, "Blessed be Egypt my people,[p] Assyria my handiwork,[q] and Israel my inheritance.[r]"

A Prophecy Against Egypt and Cush

20 In the year that the supreme commander,[s] sent by Sargon king of Assyria,
came to Ashdod and attacked and captured it— 2at that time the LORD spoke
through Isaiah son of Amoz.[t] He said to him, "Take off the sackcloth[u] from your body
and the sandals[v] from your feet." And he did so, going around stripped[w] and barefoot.[x]

3Then the LORD said, "Just as my servant Isaiah has gone stripped and barefoot for
three years, as a sign[y] and portent against Egypt and Cush,[a][z] 4so the king[a] of Assyria will
lead away stripped and barefoot the Egyptian captives and Cushite exiles, young and old,
with buttocks bared—to Egypt's shame.[b] 5Those who trusted in Cush and boasted in
Egypt[c] will be afraid and put to shame. 6In that day the people who live on this coast will
say, 'See what has happened to those we relied on, those we fled to for help[d] and deliverance from the king of Assyria! How then can we escape?[e]' "

A Prophecy Against Babylon

21 An oracle concerning the Desert[f] by the Sea:

Like whirlwinds sweeping through the southland,[g]
  an invader comes from the desert,
  from a land of terror.

[a] 3 That is, the upper Nile region; also in verse 5

19:21 make himself known . . . acknowledge the LORD. The Lord would reveal himself to Egyptians so that they too could fully participate in the covenant (Ps 87:4). **in that day.** See note on 2:11. See *WCF* 21.5; 22.5; *WLC* 108.

19:22 strike . . . with a plague . . . heal. Divine punishment in the form of Assyrian oppression and its extension in the repression brought about by evil throughout the centuries was intended to draw the Egyptians to the Lord (30:26; Hos 6:1; 14:1–2,4).

19:23 In that day. See note on 2:11. **highway.** Symbolizes the removal of barriers between the redeemed in Israel and these Gentile nations (see note on 11:16). **Egypt to Assyria.** The redeemed from within the borders of the two great enemy nations of Isaiah's day would find their identity and unity with God's people in a common commitment to the Lord. Christ fulfills this prediction as he brings people from these nations into his church.

19:24–25 In that day. See note on 2:11. **blessing on the earth . . . bless them.** In the future Israel, Egypt and Assyria would share together in the patriarchal promises (Ge 12:2–3). Three expressions signify that each will share in full covenant membership: "people" (cf. 10:24; 43:6–7; Ps 100:3; Jer 11:4; Hos 1:10; 2:23; see note on 40:1), "handiwork" (60:21; 64:8; Pss 119:73; 138:8) and "inheritance" (Dt 32:9). The fulfillment of this hope is evidenced by the international character of the church today and will ultimately be revealed in the new heavens and the new earth.

20:1–6 Isaiah described the Assyrian destruction of Ashdod (c. 713 B.C.), which the Nubians (Cush/Egypt) had encouraged to rebel against Assyria (see notes on 18:1–2). Given that the support of Egypt had not helped Ashdod, the Judahites would have been foolish to rely on Egypt in their own struggle against the Assyrians.

20:1 supreme commander. One of the three highest ranking Assyrian officers (see note on 36:2). **Sargon.** Sargon II, king of Assyria (721–705 B.C.). **Ashdod.** A Philistine city that had rebelled against Assyria with the encouragement of Shabako, the Nubian king of the 25th Dynasty of Egypt (see note 18:1) in 713 B.C. It fell in 711. An inscription mentioning Sargon by name has been discovered there.

20:2 sackcloth . . . barefoot. The Lord ordered Isaiah to be partially clad, like a captive going into exile, as a sign of what would happen to Egypt and Cush. This sign demonstrated that the Assyrian victory over Egypt and Cush in c. 610 B.C. had been a direct result of God's judgment. **sackcloth.** A garment of mourning and fasting (15:3; 22:12; 32:11; 37:1–2; 58:5; Ge 37:24) or the distinctive prophetic garment (2Ki 1:8; Zec 13:4).

20:3 my servant. A trusted and highly placed individual in God's administration. Moses was God's friend and servant (Ex 14:31; Nu 12:7–8; Dt 34:5). This designation was also given to individuals such as Abraham (Ps 105:42), Jacob (Eze 28:25), Joshua (Jos 24:29), David (37:35; 2Sa 3:18; Ps 132:10) and the suffering Servant (52:13—53:12), as well as to groups of people such as the prophets (44:26) and a restored Israel (41:8–9; 42:1,19; 43:10; 44:1–2,21; 45:4; 48:20; 49:3,5–7). God's servants may suffer, but they are promised a great heritage as "servants of the LORD" (54:17; 63:17; 65:8–9,13–15; 66:14). **three years.** In Hebrew calculation a period of at least 14 months. It designated either the length of Isaiah's walking about as a sign or the duration of time before the sign would be fulfilled. **sign and portent.** The prophetic sign (8:18; cf. Dt 13:1–2; 28:46; Jer 32:20) pointed out the folly of relying on Egypt and Cush because they, like many other nations, would crumble before the Assyrians.

20:4 king of Assyria. Esarhaddon fulfilled this prophecy in c. 670 B.C.

20:5 trusted . . . boasted. Hezekiah began to rely on Egypt to help him against the Assyrians, but Isaiah persuaded him to trust in God instead (30:1–2; 31:2). The sign was intended to lead the people of Judah to realize that the Cush/Egypt coalition was frail and that it would be foolish to rely on its political or military power for help against Assyria.

20:6 In that day. See note on 2:11. **relied on.** Since Egypt had not been able to rescue Ashdod from Assyria, how could anyone hope to escape God's judgment to be meted out through Assyria?

■ **21:1–10** *Babylon.* At this point the prophet spoke about the Babylonian Empire (see note on 13:1—14:27). Babylon was defeated by the Assyrians in 689 B.C., but it in turn defeated Nineveh (Assyria) in c. 612 B.C., before subjugating Judah. Babylon ultimately fell in 539 B.C. to the Persian Empire. In light of the context of the surrounding oracles, it seems most likely that Isaiah predicted the Assyrian defeat of Babylon in 689 B.C. in order to demonstrate the folly of relying on Babylon for help against Assyria. Hezekiah turned to the

2 A dire[h] vision has been shown to me:
The traitor betrays,[i] the looter takes loot.
Elam,[j] attack! Media, lay siege!
I will bring to an end all the groaning she caused.

3 At this my body is racked with pain,
pangs seize me, like those of a woman in labor;[k]
I am staggered by what I hear,
I am bewildered by what I see.
4 My heart falters,
fear makes me tremble;
the twilight I longed for
has become a horror to me.

5 They set the tables,
they spread the rugs,
they eat, they drink![l]
Get up, you officers,
oil the shields!

6 This is what the Lord says to me:

"Go, post a lookout
and have him report what he sees.
7 When he sees chariots[m]
with teams of horses,
riders on donkeys
or riders on camels,
let him be alert,
fully alert."

8 And the lookout[a] [n] shouted,

"Day after day, my lord, I stand on the watchtower;
every night I stay at my post.
9 Look, here comes a man in a chariot
with a team of horses.
And he gives back the answer:
'Babylon[o] has fallen,[p] has fallen!
All the images of its gods[q]
lie shattered on the ground!' "

10 O my people, crushed on the threshing floor,[r]
I tell you what I have heard
from the LORD Almighty,
from the God of Israel.

A Prophecy Against Edom

11 An oracle concerning Dumah[b]:[s]

21:2 [h]Ps 60:3 [i]Isa 33:1 [j]Isa 22:6; Jer 49:34
21:3 [k]Ps 48:6; Isa 26:17
21:5 [l]Jer 51:39, 57; Da 5:2
21:7 [m]ver 9
21:8 [n]Hab 2:1
21:9 [o]Rev 14:8 [p]Jer 51:8; Rev 18:2 [q]Isa 46:1; Jer 50:2; 51:44
21:10 [r]Jer 51:33
21:11 [s]Ge 25:14

[a] *8* Dead Sea Scrolls and Syriac; Masoretic Text *A lion* [b] *11* *Dumah* means *silence* or *stillness*, a wordplay on *Edom*.

Babylonians for help against Assyria in c. 701 B.C., and Isaiah severely rebuked him for this lack of faith in the Lord (39:1–8).
21:1 oracle. See note on 13:1. **Desert by the Sea.** A sarcastic reference to Babylon. Babylon's southern region on the Persian Gulf was known as "The Land of the Sea," but it would become a desert and/or prove to be a desert to anyone looking for salvation from that locale. **whirlwinds.** A desert wind (Hos 13:15). Babylon would be desolate like a desert, and all who relied on her would fall with her.
21:2 dire vision. The prophet was overwhelmed by what he saw. **traitor . . . loot.** Acts of warfare. **Elam . . . Media.** Elam was a major region of Persia. It was allied with Media in 700 B.C. Perhaps as a part of Assyria's imperial army, this alliance helped defeat Babylon in 689 B.C. See notes on 11:11 and 13:7. **attack! . . . lay siege!** A command to the nations to attack Babylon. **she.** The indefinite subject probably refers to Babylon's groaning under Assyria.
21:3–4 my body . . . fear. Expressions of great psychological suffering by the prophet (16:8–11; 22:4; cf. Da 8:27; 10:16–17). The report of Babylon's fall may have distressed Isaiah because now none could rescue Judah from Assyria (see Da 8:27). **staggered . . . bewildered.** Isaiah was overwhelmed by what he had seen and heard. **twilight.** The light of the morning had become a dread because the prophet did not know what the new day would bring.
21:5 oil the shields! A preparation for battle.
21:7 chariots . . . camels. A reference to an approaching army.
21:9 Babylon . . . has fallen! Babylon suffered defeat at the hands of the Assyrians in 689 B.C. John later employed this language as a description of the fall of the evil kingdoms of the world that oppose God and his people (Rev 14:8; 18:2).
21:10 my people, crushed. God's people would be crushed by the Assyrians in a manner suggestive of grain under the threshing sledge (28:27–28; 41:15–16; Am 1:3). Babylon could not help. **heard from the LORD.** Isaiah did not invent this prediction of Babylon's fate to support his opinion of those in Judah who might look for help from Babylon during the Assyrian judgment (39:1–8). He simply reported what he had heard from God.

Someone calls to me from Seir,[t]
"Watchman, what is left of the night?
Watchman, what is left of the night?"
12 The watchman replies,
"Morning is coming, but also the night.
If you would ask, then ask;
and come back yet again."

A Prophecy Against Arabia

13 An oracle[u] concerning Arabia:

You caravans of Dedanites,
who camp in the thickets of Arabia,
14 bring water for the thirsty;
you who live in Tema,[v]
bring food for the fugitives.
15 They flee[w] from the sword,
from the drawn sword,
from the bent bow
and from the heat of battle.

16 This is what the Lord says to me: "Within one year, as a servant bound by contract[x]
would count it, all the pomp[y] of Kedar[z] will come to an end. 17 The survivors of the bow-
men, the warriors of Kedar, will be few.[a]" The LORD, the God of Israel, has spoken.

A Prophecy About Jerusalem

22 An oracle[b] concerning the Valley[c] of Vision:

What troubles you now,
that you have all gone up on the roofs,
2 O town full of commotion,
O city of tumult and revelry?[d]
Your slain were not killed by the sword,
nor did they die in battle.
3 All your leaders have fled together;
they have been captured without using the bow.
All you who were caught were taken prisoner together,
having fled while the enemy was still far away.
4 Therefore I said, "Turn away from me;
let me weep[e] bitterly.
Do not try to console me
over the destruction of my people."[f]

5 The Lord, the LORD Almighty, has a day
of tumult and trampling and terror[g]

21:11 [t]Ge 32:3
21:13 [u]Isa 13:1
21:14 [v]Ge 25:15
21:15 [w]Isa 13:14
21:16 [x]Isa 16:14 [y]Isa 17:3 [z]Ps 120:5; Isa 60:7
21:17 [a]Isa 10:19
22:1 [b]Isa 13:1 [c]Ps 125:2; Jer 21:13; Joel 3:2, 12, 14
22:2 [d]Isa 32:13
22:4 [e]Isa 15:3; Lk 19:41 [f]Jer 9:1
22:5 [g]La 1:5

■ **21:11–12** *Edom.* Isaiah announced relief and trouble for Edom.
21:11 oracle. See note on 13:1. **Dumah.** An oasis at the intersection of two roads: One led from the Red Sea to Palmyra and the other from the Persian Gulf to Petra in Edom (see 34:5–17). **Seir.** Or Edom. The Edomites rhetorically asked the prophet what the future held.
21:12 Morning . . . night. The Assyrians had troubled the Edomites, and the future held both hope and judgment for them. They would experience some relief from Assyria, but this would be followed by oppression from Babylonia.
■ **21:13–17** *Arabia.* The prophet announced that Arabia would suffer at the hands of the Assyrians.
21:13 oracle. See note on 13:1. **Arabia.** The Arabian wilderness. The Assyrians began repeated attacks against the Arabs in 732 B.C. **caravans.** They carried the goods from east to west and from north to south.
21:14 water for the thirsty . . . food for the fugitives. The Arabs aided those oppressed by the Assyrians.
21:16–17 Within one year. Arabia would also suffer Assyrian aggression, along with the many fugitives who had fled to this region. **Kedar.** An oasis of the Bedouins in Arabia (Jer 49:28–29). **survivors . . . few.** The desolation of war would affect the heartland of the desert.
■ **22:1–25** *Jerusalem.* The occasion of this oracle was Sennacherib's siege of Jerusalem in 701 B.C. (see note on 22:15). The prophet rebuked the people and their leaders for not taking seriously the threat of Assyria. Their calm reflected self-assurance, not sincere faith in the Lord.
22:1 oracle. See note on 13:1. **Valley of Vision.** The meaning of this expression is unclear. It may be a sarcastic description of Jerusalem as a valley with little vision of reality. **gone up on the roofs.** The citizens of Jerusalem foolishly thought themselves to be invincible. They gathered on the housetops for purposes of celebrating (see v. 13). It would appear that Shebna was chief among those who reveled (see v. 15).
22:2 full of commotion . . . tumult and revelry? The noisy and excited citizenry had not witnessed what the prophet had seen. **not killed by the sword.** Isaiah foresaw what would happen to Jerusalem. Many would die of disease and hardship caused by the severe impending siege of Jerusalem by the Assyrians.
22:3 your leaders have fled. When the Assyrians would destroy much of Judah, the leaders would abandon the people. Elsewhere the prophet was highly critical of human leadership and of the people who had no "vision" of what was happening around them (see 1:10,23–26; 3:1–3,13–15; 7:1–2; 9:6,14–16; 11:1; 19:13–15; 28:7–11, 14; 29:15).
22:4 Do not try to console me. The prophet expressed his despair over the danger Jerusalem faced.

in the Valley of Vision,
a day of battering down walls
and of crying out to the mountains.
6 Elam[h] takes up the quiver,[i]
with her charioteers and horses;
Kir[j] uncovers the shield.
7 Your choicest valleys are full of chariots,
and horsemen are posted at the city gates;[k]
8 the defenses of Judah are stripped away.

And you looked in that day
to the weapons[l] in the Palace of the Forest;[m]
9 you saw that the City of David
had many breaches in its defenses;
you stored up water
in the Lower Pool.[n]
10 You counted the buildings in Jerusalem
and tore down houses to strengthen the wall.
11 You built a reservoir between the two walls[o]
for the water of the Old Pool,[p]
but you did not look to the One who made it,
or have regard for the One who planned it long ago.

12 The Lord, the LORD Almighty,
called you on that day
to weep[q] and to wail,
to tear out your hair[r] and put on sackcloth.[s]
13 But see, there is joy and revelry,
slaughtering of cattle and killing of sheep,
eating of meat and drinking of wine![t]
"Let us eat and drink," you say,
"for tomorrow we die!"[u]

14 The LORD Almighty has revealed this in my hearing:[v] "Till your dying day this sin will not be atoned[w] for," says the Lord, the LORD Almighty.

15 This is what the Lord, the LORD Almighty, says:

"Go, say to this steward,
to Shebna,[x] who is in charge of the palace:
16 What are you doing here and who gave you permission
to cut out a grave[y] for yourself here,
hewing your grave on the height
and chiseling your resting place in the rock?

22:6 [h]Isa 21:2 [i]Jer 49:35 [j]2Ki 16:9
22:7 [k]2Ch 32:1-2
22:8 [l]2Ch 32:5 [m]1Ki 7:2
22:9 [n]2Ch 32:4
22:11 [o]2Ki 25:4; Jer 39:4 [p]2Ch 32:4
22:12 [q]Joel 2:17 [r]Mic 1:16 [s]Joel 1:13
22:13 [t]Isa 5:22; 28:7-8; 56:12; Lk 17:26-29 [u]1Co 15:32*
22:14 [v]Isa 5:9 [w]Isa 13:11; 26:21; 30:13-14; Eze 24:13
22:15 [x]2Ki 18:18; Isa 36:3
22:16 [y]Mt 27:60

22:5 a day. The day of the Lord that would take place when the Assyrians laid siege to Jerusalem. See note on 2:11. **tumult.** Desolation and destruction (Dt 7:23; 28:20; 1Sa 5:9; Eze 7:7; 22:5; Am 3:9; Zec 14:13). **battering down . . . crying out.** A reference to frenzied anxiety and screams of anguish.
22:6 Elam . . . Kir. See notes on 11:11 and 21:2. These nations, situated to the east of Babylon, would join Assyria in the siege of Jerusalem. Jerusalem would be completely surrounded and defenseless.
22:8 in that day. See note on 2:11. **Palace of the Forest.** A complex adjacent to the temple (1Ki 7:2–6) that was used for storage of weapons (39:2). When it became apparent that the Assyrian threat was serious, Hezekiah frantically prepared for the approaching invaders.
22:9 Lower Pool. This reservoir of water and its connecting tunnel had been constructed by Hezekiah in preparation for this invasion by Sennacherib. It was also known as the Pool of Siloam (Ne 3:15; Lk 13:4; Jn 9:7,11). See also verse 11.
22:10 to strengthen the wall. A survey of the buildings in Jerusalem was made in preparation for battle. Some were deliberately demolished and the materials used to strengthen the wall (see 2Ch 32:5).
22:11 Old Pool. Probably the Gihon spring (7:3; 36:2). **did not look . . . or have regard.** While busying themselves with planning and fortifying Jerusalem, the people forgot the Lord. **the One who made it . . . the One who planned.** God had made the city that Hezekiah was trying so desperately to defend, and he had planned its siege. It was utterly foolish, therefore, to ignore God in this time of trouble.
22:12 weep . . . wail . . . tear ... sackcloth. God called the people to repentance, not to frantic preparation for a futile defense against the Sennacherib threat. The Lord demanded that they turn to him rather than trusting in their own plans.
22:13 there is joy and revelry. Isaiah pointed to the foolish and misguided confidence of the people. They should instead turn to the Lord in humility. **"Let us eat and drink . . . for tomorrow we die!"** A statement evidencing a foolish disregard for the warning the prophet had made about preparing properly for impending judgment (1Co 15:32; cf. Lk 12:19). See *WLC* 113.
22:14 not be atoned for. God would not overlook Jerusalem's refusal to turn to him. The threat of Jerusalem's destruction stood.
22:15–25 The prophet spoke directly to Shebna, who boldly disregarded the serious circumstances Jerusalem faced.
22:15 Shebna. Perhaps a foreigner, he was a high official in Jerusalem who apparently did not take seriously Isaiah's warning regarding Assyrian aggression.
22:16 grave . . . resting place in the rock? Isaiah questioned why Shebna was busy caring for himself rather than leading the city in repentance. Shebna's rock-cut tomb has been excavated.

17 "Beware, the LORD is about to take firm hold of you
and hurl you away, O you mighty man.
18 He will roll you up tightly like a ball
and throw[z] you into a large country.
There you will die
and there your splendid chariots will remain—
you disgrace to your master's house!
19 I will depose you from your office,
and you will be ousted from your position.

20 "In that day I will summon my servant, Eliakim[a] son of Hilkiah. 21 I will clothe him
with your robe and fasten your sash around him and hand your authority over to him.
He will be a father to those who live in Jerusalem and to the house of Judah. 22 I will place
on his shoulder the key[b] to the house of David;[c] what he opens no one can shut, and
what he shuts no one can open.[d] 23 I will drive him like a peg[e] into a firm place;[f] he will
be a seat[a] of honor[g] for the house of his father. 24 All the glory of his family will hang on
him: its offspring and offshoots—all its lesser vessels, from the bowls to all the jars.

25 "In that day," declares the LORD Almighty, "the peg[h] driven into the firm place will
give way; it will be sheared off and will fall, and the load hanging on it will be cut down."
The LORD has spoken.[i]

A Prophecy About Tyre

23 An oracle concerning Tyre:[j]

Wail, O ships[k] of Tarshish![l]
For Tyre is destroyed
and left without house or harbor.
From the land of Cyprus[b]
word has come to them.
2 Be silent, you people of the island
and you merchants of Sidon,
whom the seafarers have enriched.
3 On the great waters
came the grain of the Shihor;
the harvest of the Nile[c][m] was the revenue of Tyre,[n]
and she became the marketplace of the nations.

4 Be ashamed, O Sidon,[o] and you, O fortress of the sea,
for the sea has spoken:
"I have neither been in labor nor given birth;
I have neither reared sons nor brought up daughters."
5 When word comes to Egypt,
they will be in anguish at the report from Tyre.

6 Cross over to Tarshish;
wail, you people of the island.

22:18 [z]Isa 17:13
22:20 [a]2Ki 18:18; Isa 36:3
22:22 [b]Rev 3:7 [c]Isa 7:2 [d]Job 12:14
22:23 [e]Zec 10:4 [f]Ezr 9:8 [g]1Sa 2:7-8; Job 36:7
22:25 [h]ver 23 [i]Isa 46:11; Mic 4:4
23:1 [j]Jos 19:29; 1Ki 5:1; Jer 47:4; Eze 26, 27,28; Joel 3:4-8; Am 1:9-10; Zec 9:2-4 [k]1Ki 10:22 [l]Ge 10:4; Isa 2:16 *fn*
23:3 [m]Isa 19:7 [n]Eze 27:3
23:4 [o]Ge 10:15,19

[a] 23 Or *throne* [b] 1 Hebrew *Kittim* [c] 2,3 Masoretic Text; one Dead Sea Scroll *Sidon, / who cross over the sea; / your envoys* 3*are on the great waters. / The grain of the Shihor, / the harvest of the Nile,*

22:17 mighty man. An ironic expression of Shebna's presumption. **22:18 roll you . . . throw you.** The Lord threatened to remove Shebna (see Jer 22:26). **large country.** A figure for exile. **chariots.** Evidence of Shebna's luxurious lifestyle. **disgrace.** God's judgment on an ambitious man.
22:19 I will depose you. By the time of the siege itself, Shebna had already been demoted to serving as secretary, and Eliakim had assumed Shebna's former office (36:3,22).
22:20 In that day. See note on 2:11. **my servant.** See note on 20:3. God regarded Eliakim (cf. 36:3,11,22; 37:2) as his "servant," a special designation for one close to God.
22:21 father. A godly leader who served his people well.
22:22 key to the house of David. The key allowed access to an audience with the king and so was a symbol of authority (cf. Mt 16:19; Rev 3:7).
22:25 In that day. See note on 2:11. **LORD Almighty.** See note on 1:9. **peg . . . will give way.** Although Eliakim was faithful at that time, even he would eventually fall from power.
■ **23:1–18** *Tyre.* The prophet condemned the commercial system of Tyre that did not reckon with God. The language is stylized, general, symbolic and not historically specific. Isaiah predicted the attack of the Assyrians in c. 732 B.C., but the Babylonians and Greeks also attacked the city.
23:1 oracle. See note on 13:1. **Tyre.** A prominent Phoenician port on the Mediterranean coast. Judah had enjoyed a longstanding relationship with Tyre, as Solomon had traded with Hiram of Tyre (1Ki 5:8–9) and Phoenician sailors had manned Solomon's fleet (1Ki 9:27). **ships of Tarshish!** Large vessels of the merchant fleet (1Ki 10:22; 22:48; Ps 48:7; Jn 1:3) that traversed great distances to the Phoenician colonies along the Mediterranean coasts. **Tyre is destroyed.** Tyre did not completely fall to the Assyrians, but it was severely harmed.
23:2 island. That is, the coastland. **Sidon.** A port city north of Tyre that was also affected by the attack on Tyre.
23:3 Shihor. That is, Egypt (cf. 19:7).
23:4 the sea has spoken. Yam ("sea"), the Phoenician sea god, is portrayed as lamenting the bereavement of the port cities attacked by the Assyrians.

7 Is this your city of revelry,[p]
the old, old city,
whose feet have taken her
to settle in far-off lands?
8 Who planned this against Tyre,
the bestower of crowns,
whose merchants are princes,
whose traders are renowned in the earth?
9 The LORD Almighty planned it,
to bring low[q] the pride of all glory
and to humble[r] all who are renowned[s] on the earth.

10 Till[a] your land as along the Nile,
O Daughter of Tarshish,
for you no longer have a harbor.
11 The LORD has stretched out his hand[t] over the sea
and made its kingdoms tremble.
He has given an order concerning Phoenicia[b]
that her fortresses be destroyed.[u]
12 He said, "No more of your reveling,[v]
O Virgin Daughter[w] of Sidon, now crushed!

"Up, cross over to Cyprus[c];
even there you will find no rest."
13 Look at the land of the Babylonians,[d]
this people that is now of no account!
The Assyrians[x] have made it
a place for desert creatures;
they raised up their siege towers,
they stripped its fortresses bare
and turned it into a ruin.[y]

14 Wail, you ships of Tarshish;[z]
your fortress is destroyed!

15 At that time Tyre[a] will be forgotten for seventy years, the span of a king's life. But
at the end of these seventy years, it will happen to Tyre as in the song of the prostitute:

16 "Take up a harp, walk through the city,
O prostitute forgotten;
play the harp well, sing many a song,
so that you will be remembered."

17 At the end of seventy years, the LORD will deal with Tyre. She will return to her hire
as a prostitute[b] and will ply her trade with all the kingdoms on the face of the earth.
18 Yet
her profit and her earnings will be set apart for the LORD;[c] they will not be stored up or
hoarded. Her profits will go to those who live before the LORD,[d] for abundant food and
fine clothes.

23:7 [p]Isa 22:2; 32:13
23:9 [q]Job 40:11 [r]Isa 13:11 [s]Isa 5:13; 9:15
23:11 [t]Ex 14:21 [u]Isa 25:2; Zec 9:3-4
23:12 [v]Rev 18:22 [w]Isa 47:1
23:13 [x]Isa 10:5 [y]Isa 10:7
23:14 [z]Isa 2:16 *fn*
23:15 [a]Jer 25:22
23:17 [b]Eze 16:26; Na 3:4; Rev 17:1
23:18 [c]Ex 28:36; Ps 72:10 [d]Isa 60:5-9; Mic 4:13

[a] *10* Dead Sea Scrolls and some Septuagint manuscripts; Masoretic Text *Go through* [b] *11* Hebrew *Canaan* [c] *12* Hebrew *Kittim* [d] *13* Or *Chaldeans*

23:6 Tarshish. Perhaps Tartessus in Spain. Nations who depended on Tyre joined in the lament.
23:7 whose feet. A personification of Tyre's influence in the Mediterranean world.
23:8 Who planned this . . . ? The nations needed to recognize that it was the Lord who had done this (v. 9).
23:10 Till your land. Tarshish was to look for other economic resources. **Daughter of Tarshish.** A personification of Tarshish (see v. 12).
23:11 stretched out his hand. The Lord had executed his plan. **sea . . . kingdoms.** God's sovereignty extends over land and sea.
23:12 Virgin Daughter. A personification of Sidon (see v. 10).
23:13 Babylonians . . . place for desert creatures. The Assyrians conquered Babylon in 689 B.C. If Babylon fell, how much more easily would Tyre.
23:15–17 See *WLC* 139.
23:15 seventy years. A standard period of time used in Israelite (see Jer 25:11; 29:10) and Assyrian literature to indicate a time of divine judgment. It could be shortened or lengthened by a number of factors (see notes on Da 9). **song of the prostitute.** The title of a street song concerning a forgotten prostitute who longed to be remembered.
23:17 the LORD will deal. The Lord had more planned for Tyre. **prostitute.** In the future Tyre would return to profiting by prostituting herself to other nations.
23:18 for the LORD. When the full restoration of God's people after exile took place, the wealth of Tyre (along with some of her citizens) would be incorporated into God's kingdom (cf. 45:14; 60:5,11; 61:6; 66:12; Hag 2:7–8; Rev 21:26).

The LORD's Devastation of the Earth

24

See, the LORD is going to lay waste the earth[e]
and devastate it;
he will ruin its face
and scatter its inhabitants—
2 it will be the same
for priest as for people,[f]
for master as for servant,
for mistress as for maid,
for seller as for buyer,[g]
for borrower as for lender,
for debtor as for creditor.[h]
3 The earth will be completely laid waste
and totally plundered.[i]
The LORD has spoken this word.

4 The earth dries up and withers,
the world languishes and withers,
the exalted[j] of the earth languish.
5 The earth is defiled[k] by its people;
they have disobeyed[l] the laws,
violated the statutes
and broken the everlasting covenant.
6 Therefore a curse consumes the earth;
its people must bear their guilt.
Therefore earth's inhabitants are burned up,[m]
and very few are left.
7 The new wine dries up and the vine withers;[n]
all the merrymakers groan.[o]
8 The gaiety of the tambourines[p] is stilled,
the noise[q] of the revelers has stopped,
the joyful harp[r] is silent.[s]
9 No longer do they drink wine[t] with a song;
the beer is bitter[u] to its drinkers.
10 The ruined city lies desolate;
the entrance to every house is barred.
11 In the streets they cry out for wine;

24:1 [e]ver 20; Isa 2:19-21; 33:9
24:2 [f]Hos 4:9 [g]Eze 7:12 [h]Lev 25:35-37; Dt 23:19-20
24:3 [i]Isa 6:11-12
24:4 [j]Isa 2:12
24:5 [k]Ge 3:17; Nu 35:33 [l]Isa 10:6; 59:12
24:6 [m]Isa 1:31
24:7 [n]Joel 1:10-12 [o]Isa 16:8-10
24:8 [p]Isa 5:12 [q]Jer 7:34; 16:9; 25:10; Hos 2:11 [r]Rev 18:22 [s]Eze 26:13
24:9 [t]Isa 5:11,22 [u]Isa 5:20

■**24:1—27:13** *The Goal of International Upheaval.* These chapters provide a large-scale portrait of how God will deal with the troubled world within which his people live. This material is often called Isaiah's "Little Apocalypse" because it describes the future in universal and cosmic rather than in historical and political terms. The day of the Lord will bring devastating judgment on all the nations who oppose God and his people and will grant a new world to the faithful people of God scattered among the nations. The prophet predicted judgment as the path to joy for God's people (24:1–23), offered his own song of praise to God for his faithfulness (25:1–8) and intervention in history (25:9—26:8), and predicted the waiting time and the final outcome of God's great judgments and blessings on the earth (26:9—27:13). These chapters summarize and combine the descriptions of the preceding chapters into a grand portrait of the cosmic significance of the widespread Assyrian judgment (see 13:1—23:18). Yet this elaborate description of God's purposes for the Assyrian judgment anticipates the actual physical changes that will take place when God brings an ultimate end to evil in the world and fully rewards his people with their inheritance. This destiny of the cosmos will be completely fulfilled by Christ when he returns in glory.

■**24:1–23** *Judgment Leading to Joy.* The prophet declared the ultimate, forthcoming hope for the people of God by summarizing the portraits of judgment found in the preceding chapters (13:1—23:18). Despite their present sufferings at the hands of evil nations, the future would be wondrous for Israel and Judah. This material divides into four sections: the widespread judgment (vv. 1–13), the tension between future joy and present woe (vv. 14–16), the resolution of future judgment (vv. 17–20) and the establishment of God's kingdom (vv. 21–23).

24:1–13 The prophet first described the widespread scope of God's judgment.

24:1 lay waste the earth. The prophets often used the language of cosmic upheaval to describe the dramatic significance of a historical event such as the attack of an army as the instrument of God's wrath (see notes on 2:10,19,21; 5:25; 13:10; 14:18). Here Isaiah declared that God would deal with the rebellion of his people and the nations around them. This spectacular depiction of divine judgment was fulfilled in the military campaigns of Assyria in the days of the Old Testament, but it also points to the manner in which God will finally judge wickedness and redeem his people in Christ.

24:2 priest . . . creditor. Social class will make no difference; God will judge everyone without exception.

24:4 dries up . . . withers. Nature will suffer as in a drought (see 15:6; 34:4; see note on 1:30–31). **exalted.** God's wrath is intended to humble the defiant and proud.

24:5 defiled . . . broken. God's judgment is occasioned by human defilement of his creation and rebellion against his creation ordinances. **laws . . . everlasting covenant.** All nations are under obligation to God at least through his covenant with Noah (Ge 9:1–17), but all have flagrantly violated the terms of this covenant and therefore deserve divine judgment.

24:6 curse . . . guilt. Human rebellion will bring international judgment (see 13:9). **left.** The Hebrew word is also translated "remnant" (see 1:9; 7:3; 10:20–21). A redeemed people will be drawn out from all nations.

24:7–9 dries up . . . withers. See note on verse 4. **groan.** The prophet explained that there will be sorrow instead of laughter (vv. 8–11; see notes on 22:2,13). The musicians will stop in the middle of their merrymaking (cf. 5:12).

24:10 ruined city. Literally, "city of chaos" (see also "formless" at Ge 1:2). The great cities of human civilization will be thrown into pandemonium. **house.** A place of private security and enjoyment of life (3:7; 5:9; 6:11; 13:16,21; 31:2; 32:13).

all joy turns to gloom,[v]
all gaiety is banished from the earth.
12 The city is left in ruins,
its gate is battered to pieces.
13 So will it be on the earth
and among the nations,
as when an olive tree is beaten,[w]
or as when gleanings are left after the grape harvest.

14 They raise their voices, they shout for joy;[x]
from the west they acclaim the LORD's majesty.
15 Therefore in the east give glory[y] to the LORD;
exalt[z] the name of the LORD, the God of Israel,
in the islands of the sea.
16 From the ends of the earth we hear singing:
"Glory[a] to the Righteous One."

But I said, "I waste away, I waste away!
Woe to me!
The treacherous betray!
With treachery the treacherous betray![b]"
17 Terror and pit and snare[c] await you,
O people of the earth.
18 Whoever flees at the sound of terror
will fall into a pit;
whoever climbs out of the pit
will be caught in a snare.

The floodgates of the heavens[d] are opened,
the foundations of the earth shake.[e]
19 The earth is broken up,
the earth is split asunder,[f]
the earth is thoroughly shaken.
20 The earth reels like a drunkard,[g]
it sways like a hut in the wind;
so heavy upon it is the guilt of its rebellion[h]
that it falls—never to rise again.

21 In that day the LORD will punish[i]
the powers in the heavens above
and the kings on the earth below.
22 They will be herded together
like prisoners[j] bound in a dungeon;[k]
they will be shut up in prison
and be punished[a] after many days.[l]

24:11 [v]Isa 16:10; 32:13; Jer 14:3
24:13 [w]Isa 17:6
24:14 [x]Isa 12:6
24:15 [y]Isa 66:19 [z]Isa 25:3; Mal 1:11
24:16 [a]Isa 28:5 [b]Isa 21:2; Jer 5:11
24:17 [c]Jer 48:43
24:18 [d]Ge 7:11 [e]Ps 18:7
24:19 [f]Dt 11:6
24:20 [g]Isa 19:14 [h]Isa 1:2, 28; 43:27
24:21 [i]Isa 10:12
24:22 [j]Isa 10:4 [k]Isa 42:7, 22 [l]Eze 38:8

a 22 Or *released*

24:11 streets. The public places in the cities (5:25; 10:6; 15:3; 33:7; 42:2). **wine . . . gaiety.** In this situation music and revelry represent the bankruptcy of human civilization (vv. 7,9; 5:11–12,22; 22:13).
24:13 earth . . . nations. The judgment of God will not be limited to Judah and Israel but will be widespread. **olive tree . . . gleanings.** See note on 17:4–6.
24:14–16 The prophet described the future joy of God's redeemed people, as he had in the preceding chapters (14:1–21; 18:7; 19:19–25), but acknowledged that this joy was not a present reality.
24:14 raise their voices. The new song is in response to God's act of salvation (cf. 12:1–6; 35:6; 42:10–13; 44:23; 45:8; 49:13; 52:8–9; 54:1; 61:7; 65:14). See 12:6 and 14:7. **majesty.** They sing of the greatness of the Lord as over against the pride of humans. See note on 2:10.
24:15–16 east . . . ends of the earth. The nations, too, will join in. See note on 11:2. **glory . . . exalt.** A call to give God the recognition that is due him as the divine warrior (25:3; 43:20; Ps 22:23; Rev 4:8—5:13). **But I.** Isaiah was filled with apprehension as he looked forward to God's salvation, because he also observed the rampant corruption around him. **Woe.** Introduces a dire threat. **treacherous.** As Isaiah looked at the world of his day, he noted that treachery and deception were everywhere. Joy could not yet be found.
24:17–20 The resolution to Isaiah's woe over current conditions (v. 16) will be the dramatic intervention of God's judgment against all nations.
24:17–18 Terror. See note on 2:10. **floodgates.** Imagery from Genesis 7:11 (see note on Isa 24:5). **foundations . . . shake.** The imagery of an earthquake is further developed in verses 19–20 in connection with God's judgment (Ps 18:7,15; see notes on 6:4; 13:13).
24:20 drunkard . . . hut. Two images of humanity's realization of guilt when faced with the dramatic judgment God was about to bring.
24:21–23 The prophet completed his depiction of God's judgment throughout the world as the means by which God would establish his glorious kingdom.
24:21 In that day. See note on 2:11. **powers . . . kings.** All of Satan's hosts, as well as depraved human powers (cf. Eph 6:11–12), are reserved for punishment and will be cast out from God's presence (2Pe 2:4; Rev 9:2,11; 11:7; 17:8).

24:23
[m]Isa 13:10
[n]Rev 22:5
[o]Heb 12:22
[p]Isa 60:19

23 The moon will be abashed, the sun[m] ashamed;
for the LORD Almighty will reign[n]
on Mount Zion[o] and in Jerusalem,
and before its elders, gloriously.[p]

Praise to the LORD

25

25:1
[q]Ps 98:1 [r]Nu 23:19

25:2
[s]Isa 17:1 [t]Isa 17:3
[u]Isa 13:22

25:3
[v]Isa 13:11

25:4
[w]Isa 4:6; 17:10;
27:5; 33:16
[x]Isa 29:5; 49:25

25:5
[y]Jer 51:55

25:6
[z]Isa 2:2 [a]Isa 1:19;
Mt 8:11; 22:4
[b]Pr 9:2

25:7
[c]2Co 3:15-16;
Eph 4:18

25:8
[d]Hos 13:14;
1Co 15:54-55*
[e]Isa 30:19; 35:10;
51:11; 65:19;
Rev 7:17; 21:4
[f]Mt 5:11; 1Pe 4:14

25:9
[g]Isa 40:9 [h]Ps 20:5;
Isa 33:22; 35:4;
49:25-26; 60:16

O LORD, you are my God;
I will exalt you and praise your name,
for in perfect faithfulness
you have done marvelous things,[q]
things planned[r] long ago.
2 You have made the city a heap of rubble,[s]
the fortified[t] town a ruin,
the foreigners' stronghold[u] a city no more;
it will never be rebuilt.
3 Therefore strong peoples will honor you;
cities of ruthless[v] nations will revere you.
4 You have been a refuge[w] for the poor,
a refuge for the needy in his distress,
a shelter from the storm
and a shade from the heat.
For the breath of the ruthless[x]
is like a storm driving against a wall
5 and like the heat of the desert.
You silence[y] the uproar of foreigners;
as heat is reduced by the shadow of a cloud,
so the song of the ruthless is stilled.

6 On this mountain[z] the LORD Almighty will prepare
a feast[a] of rich food for all peoples,
a banquet of aged wine—
the best of meats and the finest of wines.[b]
7 On this mountain he will destroy
the shroud[c] that enfolds all peoples,
the sheet that covers all nations;
8 he will swallow up death[d] forever.
The Sovereign LORD will wipe away the tears[e]
from all faces;
he will remove the disgrace[f] of his people
from all the earth.
The LORD has spoken.

9 In that day they will say,

"Surely this is our God;[g]
we trusted in him, and he saved[h] us.

24:23 reign. God alone will be king when he restores his people from exile and conquers all of his enemies (32:1; 33:17,22; 41:21; 43:21; 44:6; 52:7; 1Co 15:24; Rev 4:1—5:14). See note on 52:7. **Zion.** See note on 1:8. **gloriously.** See note on 4:2.

■ **25:1–8** *Praise for God's Faithfulness.* The realization that God would eventually extend his kingdom to the ends of the earth moved Isaiah to praise the Lord for his faithfulness to his people.

25:1–5 The prophet praised God for his destruction of the wicked nations.

25:1 my God. A personal affirmation of confidence in God (7:13; 49:4–5; 57:21). **exalt . . . praise.** See note on 12:1. **faithfulness.** Isaiah praised God for keeping his covenant promises of victory and inheritance for his people. See 11:3–5.

25:2 city. A figure for the strength of nations that rebel against God and his purposes. See 24:10. **never be rebuilt.** Once the kingdom of God comes in its fullness, the cities of God's enemies will never again stand in defiance against him.

25:3 honor. The nations will acknowledge the Lord (see 2:2–4; 19:23–25; 24:14–16).

25:4 refuge. See note on 17:10. **poor . . . needy.** See note on 11:3–5. **refuge . . . shade.** See notes on 4:6 and 30:2. **storm . . . heat.** Metaphors for oppression and persecution.

25:6–8 The prophet delighted in the grand banquet to be held in celebration of God's victory over the nations.

25:6 mountain. The mountain of the Lord (vv. 7,10). See note on 2:2. **feast . . . banquet.** This festive banquet will celebrate the kingship of God (see 1Ki 1:25). **rich food . . . wines.** The finest foods and drinks will be enjoyed as a reflection of the grandeur of the event (Ps 23:5; Mt 8:11; Lk 13:29; Rev 19:9). **for all peoples.** The guests will come from all nations (Rev 14:6). See note on 24:14–16.

25:7–8 shroud . . . sheet. All mourning, "tears" (30:19; 35:10; 61:2–5; Rev 7:17; 21:4) and "disgrace"—including "death" and the sting of death (1Co 15:54)—will be removed when God reigns over the earth from Zion. **swallow up death.** Paradoxically, the enlarged mouth of death (see 5:24), from which none escape, will itself be swallowed up. **Sovereign LORD.** The Master-King-Savior (cf. 28:16; 40:10; 52:4; 65:13). See *BC* 37.

■ **25:9—26:8** *Praise in the Future.* Isaiah anticipated how the redeemed will celebrate when judgment has come and they enjoy salvation in Zion.

25:9–12 The people of God will rejoice in God's faithfulness to his people.

25:9 In that day. See note on 2:11. **our God.** The celebrants will

This is the LORD, we trusted in him;
let us rejoice[i] and be glad in his salvation."

10 The hand of the LORD will rest on this mountain;
but Moab[j] will be trampled under him
as straw is trampled down in the manure.
11 They will spread out their hands in it,
as a swimmer spreads out his hands to swim.
God will bring down[k] their pride[l]
despite the cleverness[a] of their hands.
12 He will bring down your high fortified walls
and lay them low;[m]
he will bring them down to the ground,
to the very dust.

A Song of Praise

26 In that day this song will be sung in the land of Judah:

We have a strong city;[n]
God makes salvation
its walls[o] and ramparts.
2 Open the gates
that the righteous[p] nation may enter,
the nation that keeps faith.
3 You will keep in perfect peace
him whose mind is steadfast,
because he trusts in you.
4 Trust[q] in the LORD forever,
for the LORD, the LORD, is the Rock eternal.
5 He humbles those who dwell on high,
he lays the lofty city low;
he levels it to the ground[r]
and casts it down to the dust.
6 Feet trample it down—
the feet of the oppressed,
the footsteps of the poor.[s]

7 The path of the righteous is level;
O upright One, you make the way of the righteous smooth.[t]
8 Yes, LORD, walking in the way of your laws,[b][u]
we wait for you;
your name[v] and renown
are the desire of our hearts.
9 My soul yearns for you in the night;

25:9 [i]Isa 35:2,10
25:10 [j]Am 2:1-3
25:11 [k]Isa 5:25; 14:26; 16:14 [l]Job 40:12
25:12 [m]Isa 15:1
26:1 [n]Isa 14:32 [o]Isa 60:18
26:2 [p]Isa 54:14; 58:8; 62:2
26:4 [q]Isa 12:2; 50:10
26:5 [r]Isa 25:12
26:6 [s]Isa 3:15
26:7 [t]Isa 42:16
26:8 [u]Isa 56:1 [v]Isa 12:4

[a] *11* The meaning of the Hebrew for this word is uncertain. [b] *8* Or *judgments*

acknowledge that they belong to the God who has brought great victory. **trusted.** The redeemed of the earth will be glad that they have trusted God to be faithful to his promises (see notes on 2:22; 7:2; 8:12,17; 12:2). Trust in God is necessary because the threats of wicked nations appear so strong. **rejoice . . . salvation.** See notes on 12:1–3.

25:10 hand . . . trampled. God's hand of blessing and protection will be on Zion, the capital of his kingdom, but his foot will trample his enemies. **Moab.** Probably representative of all rebellious nations, as is Edom in 34:5–17 and 63:1–6.

25:11 pride . . . cleverness. The pretense of the nations as they oppose God and his people.

26:1–8 In the future God's people will lift to him a song of praise celebrating the wonder of Jerusalem.

26:1 In that day. See note on 2:11. **city.** Jerusalem (see 1:21,25–26; 2:2; 24:10; 25:2; 60:18). **salvation its walls and ramparts.** The prophet was speaking metaphorically of the defenses of the city. Salvation, deliverance from enemies and divine judgment will surround the people of God when Jerusalem is exalted (see 2:2).

26:2 Open the gates. The celebrants will call for the city gates to be opened so that all those who are righteous and faithful may enter and enjoy the protection of God's salvation.

26:3–4 See *WSC* 86.

26:3 perfect peace. The peace of God that the righteous receive and promote (v. 12; 32:17–18; 48:18; 54:10,13; 55:12; 66:12) but from which the wicked will be excluded (48:22; 57:21; 59:8; 60:17). **trusts.** See 25:9.

26:4 Trust. See verse 3. **Rock.** A royal metaphor for God as he provides stable and reliable protection. See 8:14–15. See *WLC* 104.

26:5 lofty city. All cities and nations that defy God.

26:6 Feet trample it down—the feet of the oppressed. See 1:24 and 21:10. Ironically, those who were once abused by the proud of the earth will celebrate God's victory over evil.

26:7–8 path of the righteous . . . desire of our hearts. The blessings of God will come to those who walk according to his commands. A magnificent expression of what God desires: people who do his will and wait trustingly for his full salvation.

■ **26:9—27:13** *Waiting for the Future.* Having described the celebrations that will take place once judgment and salvation have finally come, Isaiah turned to the problem of the waiting period the people of God will have to endure.

26:9–10 The prophet expressed his own longing to see God's promised judgment against the nations.

in the morning my spirit longs[w] for you.
When your judgments come upon the earth,
the people of the world learn righteousness.[x]
10 Though grace is shown to the wicked,
they do not learn righteousness;
even in a land of uprightness they go on doing evil[y]
and regard[z] not the majesty of the LORD.
11 O LORD, your hand is lifted high,
but they do not see[a] it.
Let them see your zeal for your people and be put to shame;
let the fire[b] reserved for your enemies consume them.

12 LORD, you establish peace for us;
all that we have accomplished you have done for us.
13 O LORD, our God, other lords[c] besides you have ruled over us,
but your name alone do we honor.[d]
14 They are now dead,[e] they live no more;
those departed spirits do not rise.
You punished them and brought them to ruin;[f]
you wiped out all memory of them.
15 You have enlarged the nation, O LORD;
you have enlarged the nation.
You have gained glory for yourself;
you have extended all the borders[g] of the land.

16 LORD, they came to you in their distress;[h]
when you disciplined them,
they could barely whisper a prayer.[a]
17 As a woman with child and about to give birth[i]
writhes and cries out in her pain,
so were we in your presence, O LORD.
18 We were with child, we writhed in pain,
but we gave birth[j] to wind.
We have not brought salvation[k] to the earth;
we have not given birth to people of the world.
19 But your dead[l] will live;
their bodies will rise.
You who dwell in the dust,
wake up and shout for joy.

26:9 [w]Ps 63:1; 78:34; Isa 55:6 [x]Mt 6:33
26:10 [y]Isa 32:6 [z]Isa 22:12-13; Hos 11:7; Jn 5:37-38; Ro 2:4
26:11 [a]Isa 44:9,18 [b]Heb 10:27
26:13 [c]Isa 2:8; 10:5,11 [d]Isa 63:7
26:14 [e]Dt 4:28 [f]Isa 10:3
26:15 [g]Isa 33:17
26:16 [h]Hos 5:15
26:17 [i]Jn 16:21
26:18 [j]Isa 33:11; 59:4 [k]Ps 17:14
26:19 [l]Isa 25:8; Eph 5:14

a *16* The meaning of the Hebrew for this clause is uncertain.

26:9 night . . . morning. The prophet constantly yearned for God to complete his intervention in history and bless his faithful people.
26:10 grace. The prophet acknowledged that God had shown common grace (cf. Mt 5:45) to the wicked nations by blessing them with prosperity. Yet they neither turned to him in righteousness nor even acknowledged him (see Ac 14:14–17; Ro 1:18–32). See *WLC* 151.
26:11 hand is lifted. God's hand was about to strike the nations, as chapters 13–23 illustrate. **Let them see.** The prophet prayed that God would act soon to demonstrate his "zeal" (blessing) for his own people and bring shame (judgment) on the oppressive nations.
26:12–15 The prophet described the final outcome of God's judgment, for which he longed.
26:12 peace. See note on verse 3. **you have done for us.** The goodness to be enjoyed by God's people is a free gift of his grace.
26:13 other lords . . . have ruled. The Assyrians had oppressed God's people for a long time, but the faithful had continued to honor only the Lord.
26:14 dead . . . departed. A past-tense description of the future as though the events had already taken place. **do not rise.** Compare 14:22 and 30, as well as 26:19. **memory.** Their names, dynasty and memorials were forgotten. See note on 14:21.
26:15 enlarged . . . extended. One expectation of blessing after the exile was the extension of Israel's borders. This hope was realized as Christ opened the way for his followers to reach the ends of the earth. It will finally be fulfilled at the return of Christ when he reigns over all the earth.
26:16–19 Isaiah spoke of the failure of God's people to fulfill their purpose in the world and of how God himself would intervene to see that this purpose is accomplished.
26:16 disciplined. God was chastising his people through the Assyrian judgment, and he would do so again through the Babylonian judgment. His purpose for this discipline was to bring about the kind of repentance described here.
26:17–18 with child . . . birth to wind. Israel and Judah are likened to a woman trying, but failing, to give birth. The people of God had possessed great potential after settling in the land of promise, but this potential had been lost because of rebellion. **salvation to the earth.** God had established his people for the purpose of bringing salvation to the world by spreading the kingdom of God (see Ge 12:1–3). This purpose continues to be the goal of God's people (Mt 28:18–19). The rebellion of God's chosen nation brought failure, but God would fulfill its destiny through the judgments and blessings envisioned in these chapters. The redemption of a remnant of Israel opened the way for Israel's purpose to be fulfilled; this goal would ultimately be realized in Christ's work in his first coming, in the continuing work of the church today and in his second coming.
26:19 dead . . . bodies. A message of hope for the future, in contrast to verse 14. The new life given to Israel and Judah in the restoration would lead to renewed opportunity and success in fulfilling the goal of the nation (see Eze 37:11–12). This renewal to life would be fulfilled in part in the restoration of the nation after exile and in the inward renewal brought by Christ; ultimately it will be fulfilled in the resurrection of the bodies of believers upon Christ's return (see Da 12:2; Hos 13:14). **dwell in the dust.** The discouraged, humiliated and deceased people of God (Ps 22:15). **dew . . . birth.** Expressions representing life and a new beginning (Ps 133:3; Hos 14:5).

Your dew is like the dew of the morning;
  the earth will give birth to her dead.[m]
20 Go, my people, enter your rooms
  and shut the doors[n] behind you;
hide[o] yourselves for a little while
  until his wrath has passed by.[p]
21 See, the LORD is coming[q] out of his dwelling[r]
  to punish[s] the people of the earth for their sins.
The earth will disclose the blood[t] shed upon her;
  she will conceal her slain no longer.

Deliverance of Israel

27 In that day,

the LORD will punish with his sword,[u]
  his fierce, great and powerful sword,
Leviathan[v] the gliding serpent,
  Leviathan the coiling serpent;
he will slay the monster[w] of the sea.

2 In that day—

"Sing about a fruitful vineyard:[x]
3   I, the LORD, watch over it;
  I water[y] it continually.
I guard it day and night
  so that no one may harm it.
4   I am not angry.
If only there were briers and thorns confronting me!
  I would march against them in battle;
  I would set them all on fire.[z]
5 Or else let them come to me for refuge;[a]
  let them make peace[b] with me,
  yes, let them make peace with me."
6 In days to come Jacob will take root,
  Israel will bud and blossom[c]
  and fill all the world with fruit.[d]

7 Has ⌊the LORD⌋ struck her
  as he struck[e] down those who struck her?
Has she been killed
  as those were killed who killed her?
8 By warfare[a] and exile[f] you contend with her—
  with his fierce blast he drives her out,
  as on a day the east wind blows.

26:19 [m]Eze 37:1-14; Da 12:2
26:20 [n]Ex 12:23 [o]Ps 91:1,4 [p]Ps 30:5; Isa 54:7-8
26:21 [q]Jude 1:14 [r]Mic 1:3 [s]Isa 13:9, 11; 30:12-14 [t]Job 16:18; Lk 11:50-51
27:1 [u]Isa 34:6; 66:16 [v]Job 3:8 [w]Ps 74:13
27:2 [x]Jer 2:21
27:3 [y]Isa 58:11
27:4 [z]Isa 10:17; Mt 3:12; Heb 6:8
27:5 [a]Isa 25:4 [b]Job 22:21; Ro 5:1; 2Co 5:20
27:6 [c]Hos 14:5-6 [d]Isa 37:31
27:7 [e]Isa 37:36-38
27:8 [f]Isa 50:1; 54:7

[a] *8* See Septuagint; the meaning of the Hebrew for this word is uncertain.

26:20–21 The prophet exhorted God's people to wait patiently for the fulfillment of God's promises, even as he had expressed his own longings for the fulfillment of these promises (26:9–19).
26:20 my people. Isaiah spoke on God's behalf to his faithful people (vv. 7–9). **enter . . . hide.** The remnant needed to await God's salvation. **little while.** Although it appeared that God would never punish the Assyrians and the other nations surrounding Israel, it would eventually become apparent that punishment had not been long in coming. Present suffering is not worthy to be compared to the eternal glory that will follow (see v. 19; 54:7; Ps 30:5; 2Co 4:17; 2Pe 3:9).
27:1–13 The prophet once again described that for which he and the people of God were waiting: the destruction of evil power (v. 1), the renewal of God's people (vv. 2–6) and the redemption through judgment (vv. 7–13).
27:1 In that day. See note on 2:11. **Leviathan . . . monster.** The Old Testament employs this imagery to denote demonic forces behind oppressive political powers (see notes on 30:6–7; 51:9; cf. Job 3:8; 41:1; Pss 74:14; 84; Rev 12:7–10).
27:2–6 The song of the vineyard stands in sharp contrast to the parable of 5:1–7. For vine/vineyard imagery, see 3:14, 5:1, 61:5 and 65:21.
27:2 In that day. See note on 2:11. **fruitful vineyard.** After God's judgment the restored remnant would be responsive to God's grace (cf. 5:1–7).
27:3 watch. The Lord would care for his people. **water . . . day and night.** God would provide for all the needs of the restored nation.
27:4 briers and thorns. The Lord would protect the vineyard from unwelcome intruders.
27:5 come . . . make peace. God would gladly welcome all who wished to be reconciled to him (cf. 9:6; 11:1–16; 26:3).
27:6 take root . . . with fruit. The nation restored after oppression and exile would produce the fruit of righteousness and joy. **fill all the world.** The people of God would fulfill their purpose: the spreading of God's kingdom to all nations (see notes on 26:17–19).
27:7–13 Isaiah explained that the oppression and exile of God's people was not simply for judgment but also for their renewal and salvation.
27:7 Has . . . ? Although outwardly it appeared as though God treated his own people as he dealt with other nations by subjecting them to the Assyrian judgment, his purpose for them was very different from that for other nations.
27:8 blast . . . wind. The east wind that carried dust and scorch-

9 By this, then, will Jacob's guilt be atoned for,
and this will be the full fruitage of the removal of his sin:[g]
When he makes all the altar stones
to be like chalk stones crushed to pieces,
no Asherah poles[a][h] or incense altars
will be left standing.
10 The fortified city stands desolate,[i]
an abandoned settlement, forsaken like the desert;
there the calves graze,
there they lie down;[j]
they strip its branches bare.
11 When its twigs are dry, they are broken off
and women come and make fires with them.
For this is a people without understanding;[k]
so their Maker has no compassion on them,
and their Creator[l] shows them no favor.[m]

12 In that day the LORD will thresh from the flowing Euphrates[b] to the Wadi of Egypt,[n]
and you, O Israelites, will be gathered[o] up one by one. 13 And in that day a great trumpet[p] will sound. Those who were perishing in Assyria and those who were exiled in
Egypt[q] will come and worship the LORD on the holy mountain in Jerusalem.

Woe to Ephraim

28

Woe to that wreath, the pride of Ephraim's[r] drunkards,
to the fading flower, his glorious beauty,
set on the head of a fertile valley[s]—
to that city, the pride of those laid low by wine![t]
2 See, the Lord has one who is powerful[u] and strong.
Like a hailstorm[v] and a destructive wind,[w]
like a driving rain and a flooding[x] downpour,
he will throw it forcefully to the ground.
3 That wreath, the pride of Ephraim's[y] drunkards,
will be trampled underfoot.
4 That fading flower, his glorious beauty,
set on the head of a fertile valley,[z]
will be like a fig[a] ripe before harvest—

27:9 [g]Ro 11:27* [h]Ex 34:13
27:10 [i]Isa 32:14; Jer 26:6 [j]Isa 17:2
27:11 [k]Dt 32:28; Isa 1:3; Jer 8:7 [l]Dt 32:18; Isa 43:1,7,15; 44:1-2,21,24 [m]Isa 9:17
27:12 [n]Ge 15:18 [o]Dt 30:4; Isa 11:12; 17:6
27:13 [p]Lev 25:9; Mt 24:31 [q]Isa 19:21,25
28:1 [r]ver 3; Isa 9:9 [s]ver 4 [t]Hos 7:5
28:2 [u]Isa 40:10 [v]Isa 30:30; Eze 13:11 [w]Isa 29:6 [x]Isa 8:7
28:3 [y]ver 1
28:4 [z]ver 1 [a]Hos 9:10; Na 3:12

[a] 9 That is, symbols of the goddess Asherah [b] 12 Hebrew *River*

ing heat from the desert depicted the severity of the judgment enacted upon God's people through warfare and exile.

27:9 guilt . . . sin. The severe judgments against God's people were the means by which the nation could be restored (see 40:2). This temporary process of atonement anticipated the eternal atonement accomplished when God cursed Jesus on behalf of his people.

27:12 In that day. See note on 2:11. **thresh.** Either grain by flailing (Ru 2:17) or olives by beating the branches (Dt 24:20). **Euphrates . . . Egypt.** The territory of Canaan granted by promise to Abraham (Ge 15:18) is here closely associated with the primeval garden of Eden (see Ge 2:10-14). **gathered up one by one.** God promised to restore his people with meticulous, individual care. Representatives of those who had been taken into exile would be gathered back to the promised land. The fulfillment of this expectation began in the Old Testament with the gathering of the tribes after the exile (1Ch 9:1–34). The final stage of this gathering began on the day of Pentecost (Ac 2), continues through the ministry of the gospel today and will ultimately be accomplished at Christ's return.

27:13 trumpet. The call of God's holy army to strike against his enemies, the Assyrians (13:1—14:32). In due course this promise will be completely fulfilled when Christ returns in glory (see 1Co 15:42; 1Th 4:16). **perishing in Assyria.** This reference to Assyria demonstrates that the prophet had in mind first the end of Assyrian judgment. The complete listing of judgments and blessings mentioned here, however, will not take place until Christ returns (see theological article "The Kingdom of God" at Mt 4). **worship . . . in Jerusalem.** This promise of revived worship in Jerusalem was fulfilled in part when Zerubbabel completed the temple (Ezr 6:13–18). Jesus' earthly ministry in Jerusalem began to move the fulfillment into its final stages (Jn 2:13–22; see note on Jn 1:14). It continues today in Christ, who is in Jerusalem above (Gal 4:26), and will come to full realization at his second coming (Rev 21:2–3).

■ **28:1—39:8** *Sennacherib's Invasion.* The third section of Isaiah's ministry during Assyrian judgment (7:1—39:8) concerns Sennacherib's invasion of Judah. These chapters divide into two main parts: the prophet's oracles related to Hezekiah (28:1—35:10) and the invasion and its aftermath (36:1—39:8).

■ **28:1—35:10** *Oracles Relating to the Invasion.* The prophet had much to say during the times surrounding the Sennacherib invasion. His words were especially important for Judah and King Hezekiah. This collection of oracles concerns three main subjects: a comparison of Samaria and Jerusalem (28:1—29:24), the problem of Egypt (30:1—32:20) and the future of Assyria and Jerusalem (33:1—35:10). The oracles contain six woes (28:1; 29:1; 29:15; 30:1; 31:1; 33:1).

■ **28:1—29:24** *Samaria and Jerusalem.* Isaiah drew attention to the similarities between Samaria and Jerusalem. These verses pronounce woe against Samaria (28:1–13), the lesson to be learned by Jerusalem (28:14–29), woe against Jerusalem (29:1–16) and a word of hope (29:17–24).

■ **28:1–13** *Woe Against Samaria* These words may have been spoken first in association with the fall of the city in 722 B.C. or may be the prophet's reflection on the event as a tragedy in the past. Here they are used as the basis of a lesson for Judah (vv. 14–29).

28:1 Woe. Introduces a dire threat. **wreath.** Or "crown" (as in v. 5), a symbol of royalty (Eze 21:31) or deity (2Sa 12:30). A reference to Samaria and its debauched leadership. **drunkards . . . wine!** See note on 24:11. **glorious.** See note on 4:2. **beauty.** See note on 4:2. **pride.** Human arrogance in Samaria stood in opposition to the majesty of the Lord (26:10).

28:2 hailstorm . . . downpour. Assyria is likened to a powerful gale (cf. 7:2; 17:13; 28:17; 29:6; 30:30; 32:19; 57:13).

28:4 glorious. See note on 4:2. **beauty.** See note on 4:2. **ripe before harvest.** The June figs were delightful because they foreshad-

as soon as someone sees it and takes it in his hand,
he swallows it.

5 In that day the LORD Almighty
will be a glorious crown,[b]
a beautiful wreath
for the remnant of his people.
6 He will be a spirit of justice[c]
to him who sits in judgment,[d]
a source of strength
to those who turn back the battle[e] at the gate.

7 And these also stagger from wine[f]
and reel[g] from beer:
Priests[h] and prophets[i] stagger from beer
and are befuddled with wine;
they reel from beer,
they stagger when seeing visions,[j]
they stumble when rendering decisions.
8 All the tables are covered with vomit[k]
and there is not a spot without filth.

9 "Who is it he is trying to teach?[l]
To whom is he explaining his message?
To children weaned[m] from their milk,[n]
to those just taken from the breast?
10 For it is:
Do and do, do and do,
rule on rule, rule on rule[a];
a little here, a little there."

11 Very well then, with foreign lips and strange tongues[o]
God will speak to this people,[p]
12 to whom he said,
"This is the resting place, let the weary rest";[q]
and, "This is the place of repose"—
but they would not listen.
13 So then, the word of the LORD to them will become:
Do and do, do and do,
rule on rule, rule on rule;
a little here, a little there—
so that they will go and fall backward,
be injured[r] and snared and captured.[s]

14 Therefore hear the word of the LORD,[t] you scoffers
who rule this people in Jerusalem.
15 You boast, "We have entered into a covenant with death,
with the grave[b] we have made an agreement.

28:5 [b]Isa 62:3
28:6 [c]Isa 11:2-4; 32:1, 16 [d]Jn 5:30 [e]2Ch 32:8
28:7 [f]Isa 22:13 [g]Isa 56:10-12 [h]Isa 24:2 [i]Isa 9:15 [j]Isa 29:11; Hos 4:11
28:8 [k]Jer 48:26
28:9 [l]ver 26; Isa 30:20; 48:17; 50:4; 54:13 [m]Ps 131:2 [n]Heb 5:12-13
28:11 [o]Isa 33:19 [p]1Co 14:21*
28:12 [q]Isa 11:10; Mt 11:28-29
28:13 [r]Mt 21:44 [s]Isa 8:15
28:14 [t]Isa 1:10

[a] *10* Hebrew / *sav lasav sav lasav / kav lakav kav lakav* (possibly meaningless sounds; perhaps a mimicking of the prophet's words); also in verse 13 [b] *15* Hebrew *Sheol*; also in verse 18

owed the September harvest (Hos 9:10; Mic 7:1; Na 3:12). Ephraim, with all her possibilities of achievement, would be exiled, and the fruit of her labors would be enjoyed by the Assyrians.
28:5 Although the destruction would be devastating, a remnant would survive. This righteous minority would be blessed despite God's judgment. **In that day.** See note on 2:11. **glorious . . . beautiful.** See note on 4:2. **crown . . . wreath.** See verse 1. **remnant.** See note on 1:8.
28:6 spirit. The Spirit of transformation (32:15; 44:3–5; 59:21; 61:1). See notes on 4:4 and 11:2. The spirit of justice would prevail in the age of the restoration under the rule of the Messiah after the exile (11:1–5; 42:1–4). **justice.** See note on 1:21.
28:7 wine . . . beer. See verse 1. See note on 24:11. **Priests and prophets.** The leaders of God's people were sensual, hard of heart and sarcastic (29:9–14; cf. Zep 3:4). See NIV text note on verse 10.
28:9–10 Who . . . ? See note on 27:7. The hardened, discrediting leaders were speaking against Isaiah. **weaned . . . breast?** A reference to young children (see "young child" at 11:8; cf. Ps 131:2). **Do . . . rule.** A reference to a nursery rhyme or a mimicking of the prophets. It demonstrates the hardness of heart that led to the destruction of the northern kingdom.
28:11–12 foreign lips. The Assyrians would become Israel's teachers due to Israel's failures to remain faithful (see 33:19). Paul used this fact to explain the purpose of New Testament speaking in tongues (see 1Co 14:21). **resting place.** The Israelites had been offered rest in the promised land but refused to serve the Lord faithfully.
28:13 word of the LORD. The word of the Lord would come to Israel through the discipline of foreigners with stammering lips, who would teach Israel morals. **Do and do.** Isaiah threw the taunts of the religious leaders back at them. **fall backward.** The effect of God's word would be hardening (6:9–10).
■ **28:14–29** *A Lesson for Jerusalem.* Isaiah turned to Jerusalem to explain the significance of Samaria's fall.
28:14 Therefore. The prophet drew lessons for Jerusalem from Samaria's experience. **scoffers who rule.** Foolish and wicked rulers who declined to believe the truth of God (Pr 1:22; 29:8).
28:15 covenant . . . an agreement. The Judahites had allied

When an overwhelming scourge sweeps by,[u]
it cannot touch us,
for we have made a lie[v] our refuge
and falsehood[a] our hiding place.[w]"

16 So this is what the Sovereign LORD says:

"See, I lay a stone in Zion,
a tested stone,[x]
a precious cornerstone for a sure foundation;
the one who trusts will never be dismayed.[y]
17 I will make justice[z] the measuring line
and righteousness the plumb line;[a]
hail will sweep away your refuge, the lie,
and water will overflow your hiding place.
18 Your covenant with death will be annulled;
your agreement with the grave will not stand.[b]
When the overwhelming scourge sweeps by,[c]
you will be beaten down[d] by it.
19 As often as it comes it will carry you away;[e]
morning after morning, by day and by night,
it will sweep through."

The understanding of this message
will bring sheer terror.[f]
20 The bed is too short to stretch out on,
the blanket too narrow to wrap around you.[g]
21 The LORD will rise up as he did at Mount Perazim,[h]
he will rouse himself as in the Valley of Gibeon[i]—
to do his work,[j] his strange work,
and perform his task, his alien task.
22 Now stop your mocking,
or your chains will become heavier;
the Lord, the LORD Almighty, has told me
of the destruction decreed[k] against the whole land.[l]

23 Listen and hear my voice;
pay attention and hear what I say.
24 When a farmer plows for planting, does he plow continually?
Does he keep on breaking up and harrowing the soil?
25 When he has leveled the surface,
does he not sow caraway and scatter cummin?[m]
Does he not plant wheat in its place,[b]
barley in its plot,[b]
and spelt[n] in its field?
26 His God instructs him
and teaches him the right way.

27 Caraway is not threshed with a sledge,
nor is a cartwheel rolled over cummin;
caraway is beaten out with a rod,
and cummin with a stick.

28:15 [u]ver 2, 18; Isa 8:7-8; 30:28; Da 11:22 [v]Isa 9:15 [w]Isa 29:15
28:16 [x]Ps 118:22; Isa 8:14-15; Mt 21:42; Ac 4:11; Eph 2:20 [y]Ro 9:33*; 10:11*; 1Pe 2:6*
28:17 [z]Isa 5:16 [a]2Ki 21:13
28:18 [b]Isa 7:7 [c]ver 15 [d]Da 8:13
28:19 [e]2Ki 24:2 [f]Job 18:11
28:20 [g]Isa 59:6
28:21 [h]1Ch 14:11 [i]Jos 10:10, 12; 1Ch 14:16 [j]Isa 10:12; Lk 19:41-44
28:22 [k]Isa 10:22 [l]Isa 10:23
28:25 [m]Mt 23:23 [n]Ex 9:32

[a] 15 Or *false gods* [b] 25 The meaning of the Hebrew for this word is uncertain.

themselves with Egypt for the purpose of remaining independent, but their choice would prove deadly. **lie . . . hiding place.** Their confidence was unfounded (see note on 4:6).

28:16 stone . . . sure foundation. See note on 8:14–15. The sure foundation of the Davidic throne, which is ultimately fulfilled in Christ Jesus (cf. Ps 118:22; Ro 9:33; 10:11; 1Co 3:11; Eph 2:20; 1Pe 2:4–8). **trusts.** David's throne is the hope of God's people. See *BC* 24.

28:17 justice. See note on 1:21. **righteousness.** See note on 1:21. **hail . . . water.** See note on 28:2. **refuge.** See note on 4:6.

28:19 As often as. The Assyrian army would tramp through Israel repeatedly. **sheer terror.** Divine judgment was coming against Jerusalem.

28:20 short . . . narrow. The people of God would not be ready to face Assyria.

28:21 Perazim . . . Gibeon. In the past the Lord had struck the Philistines (2Sa 5:20) and the Canaanites (Jos 10:11) in these places. **work . . . alien task.** This time the Lord would turn against his own people.

28:22 stop your. The leaders in Jerusalem mocked the idea that their city might be destroyed as Samaria had been.

28:23–29 An analogy from the way of the wise farmer. The fact that God had not already destroyed Judah was a matter of his timing.

28:23 Listen . . . hear. The call of wisdom (1:2; Pr 1:8; 4:1; 5:1).

28:25 caraway. Black cumin (v. 27). **spelt.** Summer wheat (Ex 9:32). Common sense dictates a natural order of plowing: breaking up the clods, harrowing and sowing.

[28] Grain must be ground to make bread;
so one does not go on threshing it forever.
Though he drives the wheels of his threshing cart over it,
his horses do not grind it.
[29] All this also comes from the LORD Almighty,
wonderful in counsel[o] and magnificent in wisdom.[p]

Woe to David's City

29

Woe[q] to you, Ariel, Ariel,[r]
the city where David settled!
Add year to year
and let your cycle of festivals[s] go on.
[2] Yet I will besiege Ariel;
she will mourn and lament,[t]
she will be to me like an altar hearth.[a]
[3] I will encamp against you all around;
I will encircle[u] you with towers
and set up my siege works against you.
[4] Brought low, you will speak from the ground;
your speech will mumble[v] out of the dust.
Your voice will come ghostlike from the earth;
out of the dust your speech will whisper.

[5] But your many enemies will become like fine dust,
the ruthless hordes like blown chaff.[w]
Suddenly,[x] in an instant,
[6] the LORD Almighty will come
with thunder and earthquake[y] and great noise,
with windstorm and tempest and flames of a devouring fire.
[7] Then the hordes of all the nations[z] that fight against Ariel,
that attack her and her fortress and besiege her,
will be as it is with a dream,[a]
with a vision in the night—
[8] as when a hungry man dreams that he is eating,
but he awakens,[b] and his hunger remains;
as when a thirsty man dreams that he is drinking,
but he awakens faint, with his thirst unquenched.
So will it be with the hordes of all the nations
that fight against Mount Zion.
[9] Be stunned and amazed,
blind yourselves and be sightless;
be drunk,[c] but not from wine,[d]
stagger, but not from beer.
[10] The LORD has brought over you a deep sleep:
He has sealed your eyes[e] (the prophets);[f]
he has covered your heads (the seers).[g]

[11] For you this whole vision is nothing but words sealed[h] in a scroll. And if you give
the scroll to someone who can read, and say to him, "Read this, please," he will answer,

28:29 [o]Isa 9:6 [p]Ro 11:33
29:1 [q]Isa 22:12-13 [r]2Sa 5:9 [s]Isa 1:14
29:2 [t]Isa 3:26; La 2:5
29:3 [u]Lk 19:43-44
29:4 [v]Isa 8:19
29:5 [w]Isa 17:13 [x]Isa 17:14; 1Th 5:3
29:6 [y]Mt 24:7; Mk 13:8; Lk 21:11; Rev 11:19
29:7 [z]Mic 4:11-12; Zec 12:9 [a]Job 20:8
29:8 [b]Ps 73:20
29:9 [c]Isa 51:17 [d]Isa 51:21-22
29:10 [e]Ps 69:23; Isa 6:9-10; Ro 11:8* [f]Mic 3:6 [g]1Sa 9:9
29:11 [h]Isa 8:16; Mt 13:11; Rev 5:1-2

[a] *2* The Hebrew for *altar hearth* sounds like the Hebrew for *Ariel.*

28:29 wonderful in counsel. See 9:6, where this characteristic is attributed to the great son of David. See *WLC* 18; *WSC* 11.

■ **29:1–16** *Woe Against Jerusalem.* Jerusalem would face severe threats from Assyria that would be averted during Hezekiah's day but later fulfilled by the Babylonians.

29:1 Woe. See note on 1:4. **Ariel.** This reference to Jerusalem may mean "Lion of God" (Ge 49:9) or "altar hearth" (see NIV text note; see also v. 2; cf. Eze 43:15). The Lord would desecrate Jerusalem, the place of his altar. **year . . . festivals.** The repetitious and tiresome observance of empty rituals. See note on 1:11–17.

29:3 siege works. A reference to Assyria's siege of Jerusalem in 701 B.C.

29:4 low . . . whisper. Refers to the experience of humiliation. See 2:10. **whisper.** See 8:19.

29:5 dust . . . chaff. Imagery of judgment ("fine dust" [see 5:24; Dt 28:24; Eze 26:10] and "chaff" [see 17:13; Job 21:18; Ps 1:4; Hos 13:3; Zep 2:2]). **ruthless.** See note on 29:20. **Suddenly.** Conveys God's power in retributive justice (see 10:16; 37:36–38).

29:6 thunder . . . devouring fire. This kind of language often describes God as he approaches in holy war (see Ex 19:16–19; Jdg 5:4–5; Ps 18:7–15; Hab 3:3–7; see notes on 6:4; 26:21). **fire.** See note on 4:5.

29:7 all the nations. See note on 5:26.

29:9–10 The Assyrian judgment against Jerusalem would come suddenly and unexpectedly. **drunk . . . stagger.** See note on 28:7–11. **deep sleep . . . covered.** Inability to discern (6:10; Ex 7:13; Ro 1:24; 11:8; 1Co 2:14).

29:11–12 vision . . . sealed. The message of the prophet was concealed from the rebellious of Jerusalem and Judah (cf. Rev 5:1).

"I can't; it is sealed." 12Or if you give the scroll to someone who cannot read, and say, "Read this, please," he will answer, "I don't know how to read."

13The Lord says:

"These people come near to me with their mouth
and honor me with their lips,
but their hearts are far from me.[i]
Their worship of me
is made up only of rules taught by men.[a][j]
14Therefore once more I will astound these people
with wonder upon wonder;[k]
the wisdom of the wise[l] will perish,
the intelligence of the intelligent will vanish.[m]"
15Woe to those who go to great depths
to hide their plans from the LORD,
who do their work in darkness and think,
"Who sees us?[n] Who will know?"[o]
16You turn things upside down,
as if the potter were thought to be like the clay!
Shall what is formed say to him who formed it,
"He did not make me"?
Can the pot say of the potter,[p]
"He knows nothing"?
17In a very short time, will not Lebanon be turned into a fertile field[q]
and the fertile field seem like a forest?[r]
18In that day the deaf[s] will hear the words of the scroll,
and out of gloom and darkness
the eyes of the blind will see.[t]
19Once more the humble[u] will rejoice in the LORD;
the needy[v] will rejoice in the Holy One of Israel.
20The ruthless will vanish,
the mockers[w] will disappear,
and all who have an eye for evil[x] will be cut down—
21those who with a word make a man out to be guilty,
who ensnare the defender in court[y]
and with false testimony deprive the innocent of justice.[z]

22Therefore this is what the LORD, who redeemed Abraham,[a] says to the house of Jacob:

"No longer will Jacob be ashamed;[b]
no longer will their faces grow pale.

29:13 [i]Eze 33:31 [j]Mt 15:8-9*; Mk 7:6-7*; Col 2:22
29:14 [k]Hab 1:5 [l]Jer 8:9; 49:7 [m]Isa 6:9-10; 1Co 1:19*
29:15 [n]Ps 10:11-13; 94:7; Isa 57:12 [o]Job 22:13
29:16 [p]Isa 45:9; 64:8; Ro 9:20-21*
29:17 [q]Ps 84:6 [r]Isa 32:15
29:18 [s]Mk 7:37 [t]Isa 32:3; 35:5; Mt 11:5
29:19 [u]Isa 61:1; Mt 5:5; 11:29 [v]Isa 14:30; Mt 11:5; Jas 1:9; 2:5
29:20 [w]Isa 28:22 [x]Isa 59:4; Mic 2:1
29:21 [y]Am 5:10,15 [z]Isa 5:23; 32:7
29:22 [a]Isa 41:8; 63:16 [b]Isa 49:23

[a] 13 Hebrew; Septuagint *They worship me in vain; / their teachings are but rules taught by men*

I can't . . . don't know how. The Judahites might as well have been incompetent and illiterate.
29:13–14 come near . . . far from me. The people of Judah and Jerusalem had the trappings of true faith (in the temple and its services), but God desired their hearts, not mere formalism (Mt 15:8–9; Mk 7:6; 1Co 1:19; Col 2:22). **astound . . . wonder.** God would confound their wisdom and foil their plans (cf. 29:15–24; 30:1–7; 31:1–3). See *WCF* 16.1; *BC* 32; *HC* 91.
29:15–16 Woe. A second woe against Jerusalem. **plans . . . think.** In opposition to the plans, works and thoughts of God (Pss 10:11; 64:5–6; see note on 11:2). They tried to manipulate God rather than submit to him. **darkness.** See note on 5:30. **potter . . . clay!** They foolishly believed they could criticize what the Lord had said as though they were his superiors. See note on 27:10–11.
■ **29:17–24** *Hope for the Future.* Despite the troubles that had come upon Samaria and were threatening Jerusalem, the Lord would one day intervene to restore his blessing to his people.
29:17 Lebanon. Known for its large forests, Lebanon is perhaps a figure for Assyria, which will be reduced to a mere fertile field by divine judgment.
29:18 In that day. See note on 2:11. **deaf.** Israel had formerly been unattuned to the message of God (35:5; 42:18–19; 43:8; cf. 6:10; 29:9), but when God intervened by destroying Israel's oppressors and restoring the nation the Israelite remnant would hear God's word. **scroll.** See note on verses 11–12. **gloom and darkness.** See notes on 5:30 and 8:21—9:1. **blind.** Israelites who had formerly wandered and failed to discern the ways of God (35:5; 42:7,16,18–19; 43:8; 56:10; 59:10; La 4:14). This prophecy of restoration from exile is fulfilled in Jesus Christ (see 61:1).
29:19 humble . . . needy. See note on 11:3–5 and 25:3–4.
29:20 ruthless. The powerful and tyrannical oppressors of this world (13:11; 25:3–5; 29:5; see "fierce" at 49:25; cf. Pss 37:35; 86:14; Eze 28:7; 30:11; 32:12). **mockers.** A wisdom designation for the hardened, cynical fool (28:14; Ps 1:1; Pr 1:22; 3:34; 9:7–8; 21:11,24). **an eye for evil.** Explained in verse 21.
29:21 defender . . . innocent. Regarding God's justice, see notes on 1:11–17, 21, 23, 25–26, 3:11–15, 5:7, 18–19, 23, 30, 9:7, 10:1–2, 11:3–5, 16:4–5, 26:5 and 28:6 and 17.
29:22 Therefore. This begins the conclusion to 28:1—29:21. **redeemed Abraham.** The patriarch was delivered from his pagan origins (cf. Ge 12:1; Jos 24:14; Ac 7:2–4). **ashamed.** See note on 1:29.
29:23 children. Great privileges and responsibilities extend to the children of those bonded to God by covenant (45:11; 49:20–22; 54:1,13; 65:23; 66:7; see notes on Ac 2:38; 1Co 7:14). **holy . . . awe.** Submission to God's holy will (Mt 6:9; see note on 4:3). **God of Israel.** See note on 37:16.

23 When they see among them their children,[c]
the work of my hands,[d]
they will keep my name holy;
they will acknowledge the holiness of the Holy One of Jacob,
and will stand in awe of the God of Israel.
24 Those who are wayward[e] in spirit will gain understanding;[f]
those who complain will accept instruction."[g]

Woe to the Obstinate Nation

30 "Woe[h] to the obstinate children,"[i]
declares the LORD,
"to those who carry out plans that are not mine,
forming an alliance,[j] but not by my Spirit,
heaping sin upon sin;
2 who go down to Egypt[k]
without consulting[l] me;
who look for help to Pharaoh's protection,[m]
to Egypt's shade for refuge.
3 But Pharaoh's protection will be to your shame,
Egypt's shade will bring you disgrace.[n]
4 Though they have officials in Zoan[o]
and their envoys have arrived in Hanes,
5 everyone will be put to shame
because of a people[p] useless to them,
who bring neither help nor advantage,
but only shame and disgrace."

6 An oracle concerning the animals of the Negev:

Through a land of hardship and distress,[q]
of lions and lionesses,
of adders and darting snakes,[r]
the envoys carry their riches on donkeys' backs,
their treasures[s] on the humps of camels,
to that unprofitable nation,
7 to Egypt, whose help is utterly useless.
Therefore I call her
Rahab the Do-Nothing.

8 Go now, write it on a tablet for them,
inscribe it on a scroll,[t]
that for the days to come
it may be an everlasting witness.

29:23 [c]Isa 49:20-26 [d]Isa 19:25
29:24 [e]Isa 28:7; Heb 5:2 [f]Isa 41:20; 60:16 [g]Isa 30:21
30:1 [h]Isa 29:15 [i]Isa 1:2 [j]Isa 8:12
30:2 [k]Isa 31:1 [l]Nu 27:21 [m]Isa 36:9
30:3 [n]Isa 20:4-5; 36:6
30:4 [o]Isa 19:11
30:5 [p]ver 7
30:6 [q]Ex 5:10,21; Isa 8:22; Jer 11:4 [r]Dt 8:15 [s]Isa 15:7
30:8 [t]Isa 8:1; Hab 2:2

29:24 understanding . . . instruction. The desire to know and practice the will of God, as in 2:2–5 (cf. 32:4).

■ **30:1—32:20** *The Problem of Egypt.* Hezekiah sought help against the Assyrian forces from the Egyptians. Like Ahaz before him (ch. 7) he relied more on other nations than on the Lord. Isaiah condemned Hezekiah's actions. These verses divide into nine sections that cluster around the contrasting themes of trust in Egypt and trust in the Lord: Isaiah (1) warned against relying on Egypt (30:1–7); (2) accused Judah of not trusting in God (30:8–14); (3) called for repentance (30:15–18); (4) proclaimed that only the Lord could bring blessing and joy (30:19–26); (5) stressed that Assyria would be destroyed (30:27–33); (6) announced woe on those who relied on Egypt (31:1–3); (7) demonstrated that God's intervention was Judah's only hope (31:4–9); (8) declared that all would be well when God brought righteous rulers to replace those who had failed to lead in Hezekiah's day (32:1–8); and (9) called the people away from their false confidence to hope in the Spirit of God (32:9–20).

■ **30:1–7** *Woe Against the Obstinate.* To rely on Egypt was to trust in something that could not offer support or deliverance from Assyrian power.

30:1 Woe. Introduces a dire threat. **obstinate children.** Hezekiah's court (see note on 1:2). **plans.** See note on 11:2. **alliance.** Reliance on other nations by forming alliances with them demonstrated a failure to depend on God. **not by my Spirit.** Hezekiah's plans were not from the Spirit of God. **sin upon sin.** Not only had the Judahites turned from the law of God; they had added to this sin a refusal to rely upon God (see 1:2–4).

30:2 to Egypt . . . for refuge. In 701 B.C. Judah counted on Egyptian troops for help against Sennacherib. Only after Isaiah's repeated appeals did Hezekiah turn to God (see 20:5 and 2Ki 8:21). **protection.** See note on 17:10. **shade.** God alone is able to provide his people with protection from danger (v. 3; 4:6; 16:3; 25:4–5; 32:2; 49:2; 51:16; cf. Pss 17:8; 36:7; 91:1; 121:5).

30:3 protection . . . shade. See note on verse 2. **shame.** The experience of utter failure, from which God promises to deliver those who trust in him (v. 5; 42:17; 54:4; 61:7). **disgrace.** See 45:16 and 50:6 ("mocking"), as well as 61:7.

30:4 officials. Perhaps Judah's ambassadors who went from Zoan in the delta (see note on 19:11–12) to Hanes, 50 miles south of Cairo.

30:6–7 animals. They vainly carried Judah's gifts through the difficult wilderness to Egypt (see vv. 7–11). **Negev.** The southern desert was the scene of shuttle diplomacy between Judah and Egypt. **Rahab the Do-Nothing.** An allusion to an ancient Near Eastern myth detailing the victory of the gods over chaos (51:9; cf. Job 9:13; 26:12; Pss 87:4; 89:9–10; see notes on 27:1; 51:9–10). The Lord was victorious, and Egypt would fail Judah's expectations.

■ **30:8–14** *Accusations Against Judah.* Isaiah accused the Judahites of rejecting prophecy during this time. They would suffer severely for this.

30:8 tablet . . . scroll. These oracles concerning the folly of dependence upon Egypt were to be written down as a witness. **everlasting.** They would serve as a reminder to future generations.

30:9 [u]Isa 28:15; 59:3-4 [v]Isa 1:10
30:10 [w]Jer 11:21; Am 7:13 [x]1Ki 22:8 [y]Eze 13:7; Ro 16:18
30:11 [z]Job 21:14
30:12 [a]Isa 5:24 [b]Isa 5:7
30:13 [c]Ps 62:3 [d]1Ki 20:30 [e]Isa 29:5
30:14 [f]Ps 2:9; Jer 19:10-11
30:15 [g]Isa 32:17
30:16 [h]Isa 31:1,3
30:17 [i]Lev 26:8; Jos 23:10 [j]Lev 26:36; Dt 28:25
30:18 [k]Isa 42:14; 2Pe 3:9,15 [l]Isa 5:16 [m]Isa 25:9

9 These are rebellious people, deceitful[u] children,
children unwilling to listen to the LORD's instruction.[v]
10 They say to the seers,
"See no more visions[w]!"
and to the prophets,
"Give us no more visions of what is right!
Tell us pleasant things,[x]
prophesy illusions.[y]
11 Leave this way,
get off this path,
and stop confronting[z] us
with the Holy One of Israel!"

12 Therefore, this is what the Holy One of Israel says:

"Because you have rejected this message,[a]
relied on oppression[b]
and depended on deceit,
13 this sin will become for you
like a high wall,[c] cracked and bulging,
that collapses[d] suddenly,[e] in an instant.
14 It will break in pieces like pottery,[f]
shattered so mercilessly
that among its pieces not a fragment will be found
for taking coals from a hearth
or scooping water out of a cistern."

15 This is what the Sovereign LORD, the Holy One of Israel, says:

"In repentance and rest is your salvation,
in quietness and trust[g] is your strength,
but you would have none of it.
16 You said, 'No, we will flee on horses.'[h]
Therefore you will flee!
You said, 'We will ride off on swift horses.'
Therefore your pursuers will be swift!
17 A thousand will flee
at the threat of one;
at the threat of five[i]
you will all flee[j] away,
till you are left
like a flagstaff on a mountaintop,
like a banner on a hill."

18 Yet the LORD longs[k] to be gracious to you;
he rises to show you compassion.
For the LORD is a God of justice.[l]
Blessed are all who wait for him![m]

30:9 rebellious. A word used infrequently in Isaiah but more commonly in Ezekiel (see Eze 2:5–8; 3:9,26–27; 12:2–3,9,25; 17:12; 24:3; 44:6). **children.** See note on 1:2. **instruction.** They rejected godly wisdom through Isaiah (cf. Pr 2:1).

30:10–11 seers . . . prophets. The preaching of many prophets conformed to the expectations of the people (9:15; 28:7; 29:10; 44:25; 1Ki 22:8; Jer 6:14; 14:13–16; 20:9–10; 28:8–9; Eze 13; Hos 9:7–9; Am 2:12; 7:12,16; Mic 2:6–11; 3:5,11). In contrast, others like Isaiah spoke by inspiration of the Spirit and under compulsion of a divine vision, bringing words of judgment. **what is right! . . . pleasant things.** An expression of the optimistic message the people desired in opposition to the truth.

30:12 Therefore. Since they refused to listen to God's prophets, they would hear from God himself in judgment. **message.** The word of God through Isaiah (vv. 8–9). **oppression . . . deceit.** The pragmatism of Jerusalem's leadership that often employed deceitful means and resulted in oppression.

30:13–14 sin. Their stubborn resistance to the Lord and dependence on Egypt would precipitate their sudden downfall. **like a high wall . . . like pottery.** Figures for sudden and utter destruction, respectively.

■ **30:15–18** *Call to Repentance.* Judah was called to repent of failing to trust in God.

30:15 repentance . . . trust. Repentance, as demonstrated by radical faith in the Lord. **rest . . . quietness.** Only the Lord could give his people what they searched for in Egypt. **salvation . . . strength.** The Lord is the strength of his people, and he will be victorious. See notes on 11:2 and 12:2.

30:16 horses. Hezekiah and Judah depended upon military strength and stratagems instead of on the Lord (31:1,3; Ps 37:17). See note on 2:7.

30:17 thousand . . . one. A reversal (Dt 32:30) of God's promise to give his people victory (Lev 26:7–8; Jos 23:10).

30:18 gracious . . . compassion. God's continuing desire was that Judah repent so that he could continue to show grace and compassion. See notes on 14:1 and 27:11. **justice.** In his justice God will not overlook sin forever. By sending Christ to be the propitiation for our sins, God's justice is forever satisfied (Ro 3:21–26). See note on 1:21. **Blessed.** Encouraging words to the godly in Judah (cf. notes on vv. 19–33).

19O people of Zion, who live in Jerusalem, you will weep no more.[n] How gracious he
will be when you cry for help! As soon as he hears, he will answer[o] you. 20Although the
Lord gives you the bread[p] of adversity and the water of affliction, your teachers will be
hidden[q] no more; with your own eyes you will see them. 21Whether you turn to the right
or to the left, your ears will hear a voice[r] behind you, saying, "This is the way; walk in
it." 22Then you will defile your idols[s] overlaid with silver and your images covered with
gold; you will throw them away like a menstrual cloth and say to them, "Away with you!"

23He will also send you rain[t] for the seed you sow in the ground, and the food that
comes from the land will be rich and plentiful. In that day your cattle will graze in broad
meadows.[u] 24The oxen and donkeys that work the soil will eat fodder and mash, spread
out with fork[v] and shovel. 25In the day of great slaughter, when the towers[w] fall, streams
of water will flow[x] on every high mountain and every lofty hill. 26The moon will shine like
the sun,[y] and the sunlight will be seven times brighter, like the light of seven full days,
when the LORD binds up the bruises of his people and heals[z] the wounds he inflicted.

27See, the Name[a] of the LORD comes from afar,
  with burning anger[b] and dense clouds of smoke;
his lips are full of wrath,[c]
  and his tongue is a consuming fire.
28His breath[d] is like a rushing torrent,
  rising up to the neck.[e]
He shakes the nations in the sieve[f] of destruction;
  he places in the jaws of the peoples
  a bit[g] that leads them astray.
29And you will sing
  as on the night you celebrate a holy festival;
your hearts will rejoice
  as when people go up with flutes
to the mountain[h] of the LORD,
  to the Rock of Israel.
30The LORD will cause men to hear his majestic voice
  and will make them see his arm coming down
with raging anger and consuming fire,
  with cloudburst, thunderstorm and hail.
31The voice of the LORD will shatter Assyria;[i]
  with his scepter he will strike[j] them down.
32Every stroke the LORD lays on them
  with his punishing rod
will be to the music of tambourines and harps,
  as he fights them in battle with the blows of his arm.[k]
33Topheth[l] has long been prepared;
  it has been made ready for the king.
Its fire pit has been made deep and wide,
  with an abundance of fire and wood;

30:19 [n]Isa 60:20; 61:3 [o]Ps 50:15; Isa 58:9; 65:24; Mt 7:7-11
30:20 [p]1Ki 22:27 [q]Ps 74:9; Am 8:11
30:21 [r]Isa 29:24
30:22 [s]Ex 32:4
30:23 [t]Isa 65:21-22 [u]Ps 65:13
30:24 [v]Mt 3:12; Lk 3:17
30:25 [w]Isa 2:15 [x]Isa 41:18
30:26 [y]Isa 24:23; 60:19-20; Rev 21:23; 22:5 [z]Dt 32:39; Isa 1:5
30:27 [a]Isa 59:19 [b]Isa 66:14 [c]Isa 10:5
30:28 [d]Isa 11:4 [e]Isa 8:8 [f]Am 9:9 [g]2Ki 19:28; Isa 37:29
30:29 [h]Ps 42:4
30:31 [i]Isa 10:5,12 [j]Isa 11:4
30:32 [k]Isa 11:15; Eze 32:10
30:33 [l]2Ki 23:10

■ **30:19–26** *Restoration of Blessing and Joy.* Isaiah assured the people of Jerusalem that they would receive God's blessing if they were to repent and call out to God in faith.
30:19 weep. See note on 25:7–8 (cf. Rev 7:17; 21:4). **hears ... answer.** In response to their prayers (59:1; 65:24; see Jdg 2:18).
30:20 water. See note on 1:30–31. **teachers.** Possibly a reference to prophets, but more probably to God as "teacher," since the Hebrew could be understood as singular. For God's instruction, see 28:9–13 and 29:11–12.
30:21 right ... way. Unlike the rebels, they would walk in the way of the Lord (v. 11).
30:22 See *WCF* 15.2; *WLC* 76,108.
30:23 rain ... food. In response to their prayers God would send refreshing rain that would yield food in abundance (v. 20; cf. Dt 28:11–12). **In that day.** See note on 2:11.
30:24 oxen and donkeys. Work animals would also enjoy God's goodness.
30:25 day of great slaughter. The day of the Lord (cf. 2:11; 27:7; 34:2,6; 12:3; 19:6; 46:10; Eze 26:15; Zep 1:7–8). **towers.** Symbols of human pride (2:12–17). **streams ... lofty hill.** God's abundant blessings would fall to his children (cf. Joel 3:18; Am 9:13). **water.** See note on 1:30–31.
30:26 brighter. God is with his people (42:16; 60:19; 61:1; Rev 21:22–23). See note on 2:5. **binds up ... heals.** God disciplines, but he also cares for (61:1; Ps 147:3) and heals (19:22; 57:18–19; Jer 3:22; 30:17; Hos 11:3; but cf. Isa 6:10) the wounds he has inflicted. See note on 19:22.
■ **30:27–33** *Assyria's Certain End.* This section speaks of the certainty that Assyria's desolation was by God's power and not by Egypt's (see notes on 6:4; 28:2).
30:27 Name of the LORD. God's name in this sense is his powerful, imminent presence in the world. **comes.** The appearance of the Divine Warrior. See note on 35:4.
30:29 sing ... flutes. Celebration, as in one of the pilgrimage feasts. **mountain.** See note on 2:2. **Rock.** See note on 8:14–15.
30:30 cloudburst ... hail. See note on 28:2.
30:31 will shatter Assyria. The prophecy does not make it clear when or precisely how this would happen, but it was certain that Assyria would not survive the wrath of God.
30:33 Topheth. Probably a deep, wide pit on the south side of Jerusalem that contained a blazing fire in which children were burned as an offering to the god Molech (see 57:4; 2Ki 23:10; Jer 7:31–32; 19:6,11–14). **breath ... ablaze.** God determined when the judgment would commence.

the breath of the LORD,
like a stream of burning sulfur,[m]
sets it ablaze.

Woe to Those Who Rely on Egypt

31 Woe to those who go down to Egypt[n] for help,
who rely on horses,
who trust in the multitude of their chariots[o]
and in the great strength of their horsemen,
but do not look to the Holy One of Israel,
or seek help from the LORD.[p]
2 Yet he too is wise[q] and can bring disaster;[r]
he does not take back his words.[s]
He will rise up against the house of the wicked,[t]
against those who help evildoers.
3 But the Egyptians[u] are men and not God;[v]
their horses are flesh and not spirit.
When the LORD stretches out his hand,[w]
he who helps will stumble,
he who is helped[x] will fall;
both will perish together.

4 This is what the LORD says to me:

"As a lion[y] growls,
a great lion over his prey—
and though a whole band of shepherds
is called together against him,
he is not frightened by their shouts
or disturbed by their clamor—
so the LORD Almighty will come down[z]
to do battle on Mount Zion and on its heights.
5 Like birds hovering overhead,
the LORD Almighty will shield[a] Jerusalem;
he will shield it and deliver[b] it,
he will 'pass over' it and will rescue it."

6 Return to him you have so greatly revolted against, O Israelites. 7 For in that day every one of you will reject the idols of silver and gold[c] your sinful hands have made.

8 "Assyria[d] will fall by a sword that is not of man;
a sword, not of mortals, will devour[e] them.
They will flee before the sword
and their young men will be put to forced labor.[f]
9 Their stronghold[g] will fall because of terror;
at sight of the battle standard their commanders will panic,"
declares the LORD,
whose fire[h] is in Zion,
whose furnace is in Jerusalem.

30:33 [m]Ge 19:24
31:1 [n]Dt 17:16; Isa 30:2,5 [o]Isa 2:7 [p]Ps 20:7; Da 9:13
31:2 [q]Ro 16:27 [r]Isa 45:7 [s]Nu 23:19 [t]Isa 32:6
31:3 [u]Isa 36:9 [v]Eze 28:9; 2Th 2:4 [w]Isa 9:17,21 [x]Isa 30:5-7
31:4 [y]Nu 24:9; Hos 11:10; Am 3:8 [z]Isa 42:13
31:5 [a]Ps 91:4 [b]Isa 37:35; 38:6
31:7 [c]Isa 2:20; 30:22
31:8 [d]Isa 10:12 [e]Isa 14:25; 37:7 [f]Ge 49:15
31:9 [g]Dt 32:31,37 [h]Isa 10:17

■ **31:1–3** *Woe Against Reliance on Egypt.* The great sin of Hezekiah at this time was turning away from reliance on God and trusting in Egypt.
31:1 Woe. Introduces a dire threat. **Egypt . . . horsemen.** Judah relied on Egyptian horses and chariots (see 30:2). This is an argument against dependency on human structures, as in 30:1–18. **trust.** See note on 12:2. **seek.** See note on 9:13. Seeking the Lord entailed consulting and obeying his prophets (29:9–10; 30:1; 1Ki 22:18).
31:2 he too is wise. Prophetic sarcasm ridiculing the royal counselors for presuming to know better than God. **disaster.** God is sovereign in judgment (45:7).
31:3 Egyptians . . . not spirit. They were mortal, in contrast to the Lord (cf. 2:22; Ps 56:4,11; Hos 11:9). **stretches out.** See note on 5:25.
■ **31:4–9** *God's Salvation and Judgment.* Isaiah restated the certainty that God alone could bring salvation to Zion and judgment on Assyria.
31:4–5 See *WLC* 63.
31:4 lion . . . not frightened. Assyrian kings likened themselves to lions, but here the Lord is compared to a lion in his determination to bless his people and destroy the Assyrians.
31:5 shield Jerusalem . . . rescue. The Lord would care for his people like a mother bird (Ex 12:13,23; 19:4; Dt 32:11).
31:6 Return. Eventually Hezekiah repented and Jerusalem was delivered (see 37:1–7; Jer 26:17–19).
31:7 in that day. See note on 2:11. **reject.** See 30:22.
31:8 fall. Assyria would come to an end by God's hand and in God's timing, not by human strategies (see 37:36).

The Kingdom of Righteousness

32

See, a king[i] will reign in righteousness
and rulers will rule with justice.[j]
2 Each man will be like a shelter[k] from the wind
and a refuge from the storm,
like streams of water in the desert
and the shadow of a great rock in a thirsty land.
3 Then the eyes of those who see will no longer be closed,[l]
and the ears of those who hear will listen.
4 The mind of the rash will know and understand,[m]
and the stammering tongue will be fluent and clear.
5 No longer will the fool[n] be called noble
nor the scoundrel be highly respected.
6 For the fool speaks folly,[o]
his mind is busy with evil:
He practices ungodliness[p]
and spreads error[q] concerning the LORD;
the hungry he leaves empty[r]
and from the thirsty he withholds water.
7 The scoundrel's methods are wicked,[s]
he makes up evil schemes[t]
to destroy the poor with lies,
even when the plea of the needy[u] is just.
8 But the noble man makes noble plans,
and by noble deeds[v] he stands.

The Women of Jerusalem

9 You women who are so complacent,
rise up and listen[w] to me;
you daughters who feel secure,[x]
hear what I have to say!
10 In little more than a year
you who feel secure will tremble;
the grape harvest will fail,[y]
and the harvest of fruit will not come.
11 Tremble, you complacent women;
shudder, you daughters who feel secure!
Strip off your clothes,[z]
put sackcloth around your waists.
12 Beat your breasts[a] for the pleasant fields,
for the fruitful vines
13 and for the land of my people,
a land overgrown with thorns and briers[b]—
yes, mourn for all houses of merriment
and for this city of revelry.[c]

32:1 [i]Eze 37:24 [j]Ps 72:1-4; Isa 9:7
32:2 [k]Isa 4:6
32:3 [l]Isa 29:18
32:4 [m]Isa 29:24
32:5 [n]1Sa 25:25
32:6 [o]Pr 19:3 [p]Isa 9:17 [q]Isa 9:16 [r]Isa 3:15
32:7 [s]Jer 5:26-28 [t]Mic 7:3 [u]Isa 61:1
32:8 [v]Pr 11:25
32:9 [w]Isa 28:23 [x]Isa 47:8; Am 6:1; Zep 2:15
32:10 [y]Isa 5:5-6; 24:7
32:11 [z]Isa 47:2
32:12 [a]Na 2:7
32:13 [b]Isa 5:6 [c]Isa 22:2

■ **32:1–8** *The Coming Righteous Rulers.* Isaiah closed this section on the problem of Egypt by reminding the Judahites of the future blessings that would come when the leaders in Jerusalem were no longer so foolish.
32:1–2 See *WSC* 26.
32:1 king . . . rulers. The great son of David would reign (9:1–7; 11:1–9; 28:16; Jn 10:11,16), and godly leaders will serve beneath him (see note on 1:25–26; 1Pe 5:2). **righteousness.** See note on 1:21. **justice.** See note on 1:21.
32:2 shelter . . . great rock. By the dependence of the Judahites on God (see note on 4:6)—in contrast to their reliance on Egypt for help—the day would come when Judah would rely entirely on the Lord. That would be a time of unprecedented blessings (see 28:7; 29:9–10; 30:1–2,12; 31:1–2). **shadow.** See note on 30:2.
32:3–4 eyes . . . ears. In contrast with 6:9–10, 28:7–8, 29:9–10,14, 30:1–2 and 31:1. See note on 29:18. **mind . . . tongue.** In fulfillment of 29:24.
32:5–7 fool . . . scoundrel. A shortsighted, narrow-minded, base fellow. These are subtle references to the leader of Judah, who misled the people into dependence on Egypt rather than on the Lord (cf. Ps 14:1; Pr 17:7; Jer 17:11; Lk 12:20). **water.** See note on 1:30.
32:8 noble man. In contrast to the fool (vv. 5–7). **stands.** He has a future and reward because of God (Ps 1:5–6).
■ **32:9–20** *Call Away From False Confidence.* This section closes with Isaiah calling on the people to put their confidence in the Spirit of God rather than in the strategies followed by their leaders.
32:9 women . . . secure. The people were confident of the success of their scheming (vv. 5–7; cf. 3:16–24; Am 6:1; Zec 1:15). The term "complacent" is the same word rendered "confidence" in verse 17 and "secure" in verse 18. The false security based on confidence in Egypt is contrasted with the true security based on trust in God.
32:10 year. A sudden change from security to despair. **harvest . . . fruit.** A poor harvest is an image of God's judgment.
32:11–12 Tremble . . . Beat. Behavior that corresponds to the reality and severity of adversity (vv. 13–14).
32:13–14 land . . . city. Everything would become a wasteland because the people invested their confidence apart from the Lord (cf. 5:5–6; 16:8–10; 24:4–9; 34:13–15). **my people.** See note on

[14] The fortress[d] will be abandoned,
the noisy city deserted;[e]
citadel and watchtower[f] will become a wasteland
forever,
the delight of donkeys,[g] a pasture for flocks,
[15] till the Spirit[h] is poured upon us from on high,
and the desert becomes a fertile field,[i]
and the fertile field seems like a forest.[j]
[16] Justice will dwell in the desert
and righteousness live in the fertile field.
[17] The fruit of righteousness will be peace;[k]
the effect of righteousness will be quietness and confidence[l]
forever.
[18] My people will live in peaceful dwelling places,
in secure homes,
in undisturbed places of rest.[m]
[19] Though hail[n] flattens the forest[o]
and the city is leveled[p] completely,
[20] how blessed you will be,
sowing[q] your seed by every stream,
and letting your cattle and donkeys range free.[r]

Distress and Help

33

Woe to you, O destroyer,
you who have not been destroyed!
Woe to you, O traitor,
you who have not been betrayed!
When you stop destroying,
you will be destroyed;[s]
when you stop betraying,
you will be betrayed.[t]

[2] O LORD, be gracious to us;
we long for you.
Be our strength[u] every morning,
our salvation[v] in time of distress.
[3] At the thunder of your voice, the peoples flee;
when you rise up,[w] the nations scatter.
[4] Your plunder, O nations, is harvested as by young locusts;
like a swarm of locusts men pounce on it.

[5] The LORD is exalted,[x] for he dwells on high;
he will fill Zion with justice[y] and righteousness.[z]
[6] He will be the sure foundation for your times,
a rich store of salvation[a] and wisdom and knowledge;
the fear[b] of the LORD is the key to this treasure.[a]

32:14 [d]Isa 13:22 [e]Isa 6:11; 27:10 [f]Isa 34:13 [g]Ps 104:11
32:15 [h]Isa 11:2; Joel 2:28 [i]Ps 107:35; Isa 35:1-2 [j]Isa 29:17
32:17 [k]Ps 119:165; Ro 14:17; Jas 3:18 [l]Isa 30:15
32:18 [m]Hos 2:18-23
32:19 [n]Isa 28:17; 30:30 [o]Isa 10:19; Zec 11:2 [p]Isa 24:10; 27:10
32:20 [q]Ecc 11:1 [r]Isa 30:24
33:1 [s]Hab 2:8; Mt 7:2 [t]Isa 21:2
33:2 [u]Isa 40:10; 51:9; 59:16 [v]Isa 25:9
33:3 [w]Isa 59:16-18
33:5 [x]Ps 97:9 [y]Isa 28:6 [z]Isa 1:26
33:6 [a]Isa 51:6 [b]Isa 11:2-3; Mt 6:33

[a] 6 Or *is a treasure from him*

40:1. **thorns and briers.** See note on 5:5–6. **houses.** See note on 24:10. **revelry.** See note on 22:2, 12–14. **donkeys . . . flocks.** See note on 5:17.
32:15 Spirit. The people were to rely on God because he alone had the power to restore the fortunes of Israel. After the threats of enemies were no longer a concern, the Holy Spirit would transform Israel to God's order. He is the Spirit of restoration. See 11:2, 28:6, 42:1, 61:1, Jer 31:33, Eze 36:27 and Joel 2:28–29. **from on high.** In contrast to earthly powers.
32:16–18 Justice. See note on 1:21. **righteousness.** See note on 1:21. **peace . . . confidence.** See notes on 26:3, 28:11–12 and 30:15. **My people.** See note on 40:1.
32:19 forest . . . city. Although the day of the Lord would be terrible in many ways, the children of God would receive God's protection (31:5) and blessing (30:23–26).
■ **33:1—35:10** *The Future of Assyria and Jerusalem.* Isaiah brought his message about the Assyrian crisis in Hezekiah's day to an end by looking forward to the final outcomes of that struggle.
■ **33:1–12** *Assyria's Judgment and Zion's Salvation.* Assyria's judgment was pronounced, but the people of God were still instructed to pray to see it fulfilled.
33:1 This is the sixth section of woes in chapters 28–33. See note on 1:4. **destroyer . . . traitor.** Isaiah was referring to Assyria (see 10:5,12–19,24–25; 14:24–27; 30:31–33; 31:8–9; 2Ki 18:13–37), but similar statements may also be made of all powers opposed to God at any time.
33:2–4 Isaiah led the people of God in a prayer for God's judgment to come against Assyria. **thunder.** See note on 13:2–3; see also 30:27–33. This was a prayer for mercy during the hour of judgment, for submission and for hope in the fullness of salvation (see note on 12:2).
33:5–13 God would respond to Israel's prayers; he would destroy Assyria and exalt his people.
33:5 exalted. See note on 2:11. **dwells on high.** See note on 32:15. **Zion.** See note on 1:8. **justice.** See note on 1:21. **righteousness.** See note on 1:21.
33:6 foundation. See notes on 1:21 and 11:3–5. **salvation.** See note on 12:2. **wisdom . . . fear.** See note on 11:2.

7 Look, their brave men cry aloud in the streets;
the envoys[c] of peace weep bitterly.
8 The highways are deserted,
no travelers are on the roads.[d]
The treaty is broken,
its witnesses[a] are despised,
no one is respected.
9 The land mourns[b][e] and wastes away,
Lebanon[f] is ashamed and withers;[g]
Sharon is like the Arabah,
and Bashan and Carmel drop their leaves.

10 "Now will I arise,[h]" says the LORD.
"Now will I be exalted;
now will I be lifted up.
11 You conceive[i] chaff,
you give birth[j] to straw;
your breath is a fire[k] that consumes you.
12 The peoples will be burned as if to lime;
like cut thornbushes they will be set ablaze.[l]"

13 You who are far away,[m] hear[n] what I have done;
you who are near, acknowledge my power!
14 The sinners in Zion are terrified;
trembling[o] grips the godless:
"Who of us can dwell with the consuming fire?[p]
Who of us can dwell with everlasting burning?"
15 He who walks righteously[q]
and speaks what is right,[r]
who rejects gain from extortion
and keeps his hand from accepting bribes,
who stops his ears against plots of murder
and shuts his eyes[s] against contemplating evil—
16 this is the man who will dwell on the heights,
whose refuge[t] will be the mountain fortress.[u]
His bread will be supplied,
and water will not fail[v] him.

17 Your eyes will see the king[w] in his beauty
and view a land that stretches afar.[x]
18 In your thoughts you will ponder the former terror:[y]
"Where is that chief officer?
Where is the one who took the revenue?

33:7 [c]2Ki 18:37
33:8 [d]Jdg 5:6; Isa 35:8
33:9 [e]Isa 3:26 [f]Isa 2:13; 35:2 [g]Isa 24:4
33:10 [h]Ps 12:5; Isa 2:21
33:11 [i]Ps 7:14; Isa 59:4; Jas 1:15 [j]Isa 26:18 [k]Isa 1:31
33:12 [l]Isa 10:17
33:13 [m]Ps 48:10; 49:1 [n]Isa 49:1
33:14 [o]Isa 32:11 [p]Isa 30:30; Heb 12:29
33:15 [q]Isa 58:8 [r]Ps 15:2; 24:4 [s]Ps 119:37
33:16 [t]Isa 25:4 [u]Isa 26:1 [v]Isa 49:10
33:17 [w]Isa 6:5 [x]Isa 26:15
33:18 [y]Isa 17:14

[a] *8* Dead Sea Scrolls; Masoretic Text / *the cities* [b] *9* Or *dries up*

33:7–12 When all Judah's false hopes had vanished (vv. 7–9), the Lord responded (v. 10) by destroying Assyria (vv. 11–12).
33:7–9 brave men. Perhaps a sarcastic comment on the three officials whoconferred with Assyria (see 36:3,22). **cry . . . weep.** Human ploys had failed, and international trade, diplomacy and military expeditions had come to an end. The Assyrians treacherously accepted the gifts but continued the siege. **streets.** See note on 24:11. **land . . . Carmel.** The verdant areas had become desolate. See notes on 2:12–16, 29:17 and 32:13–14. For the transformation, see 35:1–2.
33:10 Now. The time for divine intervention and for the glorious establishment of God's kingdom. **exalted.** The Lord rules by bringing judgment on his enemies (vv. 11–12) and full salvation to his people who wait for him (vv. 13–24). See notes on 2:2 and on 26:20 and 21.
33:11 fire. The principle of retribution. See notes on 4:5 and 29:5.
33:12 lime . . . thornbushes. Two similes speak, respectively, of the completeness and swiftness of Assyria's destruction (see 27:4; Am 2:1).
■ **33:13–24** *The Future People and King of Zion.* Isaiah responded to fears and questions that the people of God had about the future of Jerusalem. What kinds of people would inhabit the city? What kind of king would there be?
33:13 far away . . . near. Everyone, both Jews and Gentiles (57:19). **hear . . . acknowledge.** The people would confess that God's judgments in history are wise and powerful and submit to his sovereignty (cf. 1Co 15:25). **power!** See note on 11:2.
33:14–16 In the future Zion would be inhabited by those who lived righteously. This hope is ultimately fulfilled at Christ's return (cf. Rev 21:1–8).
33:14 sinners . . . godless. See note on 1:27–28. **Zion.** See note on 1:8. **consuming fire?** As in 30:27 and 30. See notes 4:5 and 10:6. **Who of us can dwell . . . ?** The Judahites were challenged to repent and live in harmony with God's holy presence (Pss 15:1; 24:3). See *WLC* 128.
33:15 walks . . . shuts his eyes. Conduct proper for the godly (cf. Pss 1:1–2; 15:2–5; 24:4; Gal 5:22–25; Eph 5:1; Jas 3:13–18). **righteously.** See note on 1:21. **bribes.** See note on 1:23.
33:16 dwell on the heights. With God (v. 5). **mountain fortress . . . water.** Enjoying divine protection (see note on 4:6; cf. Ps 18:1–3) and provision (49:10; 55:1–2,10; 62:9; 65:13; cf. 30:20).
33:17–24 A vision of the presence of the glorious King among his people.
33:17 king. The coming of God's kingdom and of his Messiah in greater splendor than any previous manifestation (cf. Ps 45:3–4). See note on 32:1.

Where is the officer in charge of the towers?"

33:19 [z]Isa 28:11; Jer 5:15

19 You will see those arrogant people no more,
those people of an obscure speech,
with their strange, incomprehensible tongue.[z]

33:20 [a]Isa 32:18 [b]Ps 46:5; 125:1-2

20 Look upon Zion, the city of our festivals;
your eyes will see Jerusalem,
a peaceful abode,[a] a tent that will not be moved;[b]
its stakes will never be pulled up,
nor any of its ropes broken.

33:21 [c]Isa 41:18; 48:18; 66:12

21 There the LORD will be our Mighty One.
It will be like a place of broad rivers and streams.[c]
No galley with oars will ride them,
no mighty ship will sail them.

33:22 [d]Isa 11:4 [e]Isa 2:3; Jas 4:12 [f]Ps 89:18 [g]Isa 25:9

22 For the LORD is our judge,[d]
the LORD is our lawgiver,[e]
the LORD is our king;[f]
it is he who will save[g] us.

33:23 [h]2Ki 7:8 [i]2Ki 7:16

23 Your rigging hangs loose:
The mast is not held secure,
the sail is not spread.
Then an abundance of spoils will be divided
and even the lame[h] will carry off plunder.[i]

33:24 [j]Isa 30:26 [k]Jer 50:20; 1Jn 1:7-9

24 No one living in Zion will say, "I am ill";[j]
and the sins of those who dwell there will be forgiven.[k]

Judgment Against the Nations

34:1 [l]Isa 41:1; 43:9 [m]Ps 49:1 [n]Dt 32:1

34 Come near, you nations, and listen;
pay attention, you peoples![l]
Let the earth[m] hear, and all that is in it,
the world, and all that comes out of it![n]

34:2 [o]Isa 13:5 [p]Isa 30:25

2 The LORD is angry with all nations;
his wrath is upon all their armies.
He will totally destroy[a][o] them,
he will give them over to slaughter.[p]

34:3 [q]Joel 2:20; Am 4:10 [r]ver 7; Eze 14:19; 35:6; 38:22

3 Their slain will be thrown out,
their dead bodies will send up a stench;[q]
the mountains will be soaked with their blood.[r]

34:4 [s]Isa 13:13; 2Pe 3:10 [t]Eze 32:7-8 [u]Joel 2:31; Mt 24:29*; Rev 6:13

4 All the stars of the heavens will be dissolved[s]
and the sky rolled up[t] like a scroll;
all the starry host will fall[u]
like withered leaves from the vine,
like shriveled figs from the fig tree.

a *2* The Hebrew term refers to the irrevocable giving over of things or persons to the LORD, often by totally destroying them; also in verse 5.

33:18–19 terror . . . incomprehensible tongue. Designations for oppression and adversity that are characteristic of human kingdoms (cf. 1Co 1:20). See note on 2:9 and 11, 14:3 and 28:11–12.
33:20 Zion. See note on 1:8. **festivals.** Celebrated from the heart (30:29), not perfunctorily (29:1). **peaceful.** See note on 26:3 (cf. 32:17–18). **tent . . . ropes.** An image of the stability and prosperity of Zion (54:2; cf. Rev 21:1–2).
33:21 Mighty One. See 10:33–34. **broad rivers and streams.** God will meet all the needs of the citizens of his kingdom (41:18; 48:18). **galley . . . mighty ship.** The kingdoms of this world will no longer intimidate and harass God's people.
33:22 See notes on 2:3–4 and 12:2 (cf. 44:6; 51:4; Pss 46; 48; 96–99; Zep 3:15,17). See *WLC* 45; *WSC* 26.
33:23 Your rigging . . . sail. Salvation is the Lord's. His people are here likened to a drifting ship.
33:24 living . . . dwell. See note on verse 14. **Zion.** See note on 1:8. **ill.** With the Lord is healing and strength (65:20). See note on 30:26. **sins . . . forgiven.** See note on 4:4.
■**34:1–17** *The Future Day of Vengeance.* Isaiah gave his audience a vision of the great future that lay ahead. God would intervene in such a powerful way that he would judge all nations (including Assyria) who had troubled his people.
34:1 A call to prepare for God's universal judgment (cf. v. 2). See note on 6:3.
34:2 angry . . . wrath. See notes on 5:25 and 10:5. **totally destroy . . . to slaughter.** They are "devoted to destruction" (Jos 7:12), as the Canaanites were (Jos 6:17). See note on 30:25.
34:3 slain . . . blood. The blood of the slain will be so prevalent that it will create mudslides. This is imagery of the day of the Lord on Earth (34:4; see note on 2:11).
34:4 stars . . . starry host. God's judgments will extend to every part of his created order, even into outer space. The host of heaven was associated with the pagan pantheon. See 13:10 and 13, 24:21 and 51:6 (see also Eze 32:4–8; Joel 2:10,30–31; Mt 24:29; Mk 13:24; Rev 6:13–14; 14:11; 19:3). **rolled up.** The old world will give way to the new (see Mt 24:29; Rev 6:13–14; 21:1). This vision of the demise of the old pagan religious and political structures to make way for God's kingdom in the new age merges with the revelation of the final replacement of the original cosmos with the new (see 13:10; 2Pe 3:10–13). **fall.** The pagan pantheons, which appear so enduring, will lose their political ascendancy (see 14:12). **withered leaves . . . shriveled figs.** See note on 24:4.

5 My sword[v] has drunk its fill in the heavens;
see, it descends in judgment on Edom,[w]
the people I have totally destroyed.[x]
6 The sword of the LORD is bathed in blood,
it is covered with fat—
the blood of lambs and goats,
fat from the kidneys of rams.
For the LORD has a sacrifice in Bozrah
and a great slaughter in Edom.
7 And the wild oxen will fall with them,
the bull calves and the great bulls.[y]
Their land will be drenched with blood,
and the dust will be soaked with fat.
8 For the LORD has a day of vengeance,[z]
a year of retribution, to uphold Zion's cause.
9 Edom's streams will be turned into pitch,
her dust into burning sulfur;
her land will become blazing pitch!
10 It will not be quenched night and day;
its smoke will rise forever.[a]
From generation to generation it will lie desolate;[b]
no one will ever pass through it again.
11 The desert owl[a][c] and screech owl[a] will possess it;
the great owl[a] and the raven will nest there.
God will stretch out over Edom
the measuring line of chaos
and the plumb line[d] of desolation.
12 Her nobles will have nothing there to be called a kingdom,
all her princes[e] will vanish[f] away.
13 Thorns will overrun her citadels,
nettles and brambles her strongholds.[g]
She will become a haunt for jackals,[h]
a home for owls.
14 Desert creatures will meet with hyenas,[i]
and wild goats will bleat to each other;
there the night creatures will also repose
and find for themselves places of rest.
15 The owl will nest there and lay eggs,
she will hatch them, and care for her young under the shadow
of her wings;
there also the falcons[j] will gather,
each with its mate.

16 Look in the scroll[k] of the LORD and read:

None of these will be missing,
not one will lack her mate.

34:5 [v]Dt 32:41-42; Jer 46:10; Eze 21:5 [w]Am 1:11-12 [x]Isa 24:6; Mal 1:4
34:7 [y]Ps 68:30
34:8 [z]Isa 63:4
34:10 [a]Rev 14:10-11; 19:3 [b]Isa 13:20; 24:1; Eze 29:12; Mal 1:3
34:11 [c]Zep 2:14; Rev 18:2 [d]2Ki 21:13; La 2:8
34:12 [e]Jer 27:20; 39:6 [f]Isa 41:11-12
34:13 [g]Isa 13:22; 32:13 [h]Ps 44:19; Jer 9:11; 10:22
34:14 [i]Isa 13:22
34:15 [j]Dt 14:13
34:16 [k]Isa 30:8

a *11* The precise identification of these birds is uncertain.

34:5 descends. The Lord's avenging sword moves from demolishing the pantheon of heaven to executing retributive justice in Edom. **Edom.** Representative of the nations (vv. 5–8; 25:10–12; 63:1–6; cf. Eze 35:1–15; Ob 11–14; Rev 18:2). See notes on 25:10 and 33:1.
34:6 sword of the LORD. See Revelation 19:15. **blood . . . slaughter.** These terms link Edom's destruction in particular with that of the nations in general. See note on 30:25; see also 63:3. **Bozrah.** An Edomite city located some 25 miles southeast of the Dead Sea (cf. Jer 49:13,22).
34:7 wild oxen . . . great bulls. Designations for the Edomite leaders.
34:8 vengeance. The Hebrew term rendered "vengeance" signifies that the Sovereign Lord keeps his community whole by delivering his oppressed people while punishing their oppressors, who defy his rule. The day of the Lord refers to the time during which the Lord establishes his kingdom on Earth by delivering and glorifying his faithful people and by avenging the wicked and the oppressors of his people (35:4; 47:3; 49:8; 59:17–18; 61:2; 63:4). See notes on 2:11 and 10:3. **Zion's.** See note on 1:8.
34:9 pitch . . . blazing pitch! Imagery derived from the fall of Sodom and Gomorrah (Ge 19:24–28; Ps 11:6; Jer 49:18; Rev 14:10–11).
34:10 night and day . . . generation to generation. God's judgment is everlasting (66:24; Mt 18:8–9; 25:41,46; Mk 9:43,48; Rev 19:3).
34:11–14 desert owl . . . creatures. See note on 40:3. For the desert animals, see note on 13:20–22.
34:11 measuring line . . . plumb line. God, like a builder, has an exacting standard for measuring how far people and nations may deviate from his norms (cosmic order). **chaos . . . desolation.** The same Hebrew words are rendered "formless and empty" in Genesis 1:2. God has decreed the desolation of powers that oppose his order, and he brings disorder on those who have wrought havoc with that order.
34:16 scroll of the LORD. This scroll is either a record of divine

34:16 [l]Isa 1:20; 58:14
34:17 [m]Isa 17:14; Jer 13:25 [n]ver 10

For it is his mouth[l] that has given the order,
and his Spirit will gather them together.
17 He allots their portions;[m]
his hand distributes them by measure.
They will possess it forever
and dwell there from generation to generation.[n]

Joy of the Redeemed

35:1 [o]Isa 27:10; 41:18-19 [p]Isa 51:3
35:2 [q]Isa 25:9; 55:12 [r]Isa 32:15 [s]SS 7:5 [t]Isa 25:9

35

The desert[o] and the parched land will be glad;
the wilderness will rejoice and blossom.[p]
Like the crocus, 2 it will burst into bloom;
it will rejoice greatly and shout for joy.[q]
The glory of Lebanon[r] will be given to it,
the splendor of Carmel[s] and Sharon;
they will see the glory of the LORD,
the splendor of our God.[t]

35:3 [u]Job 4:4; Heb 12:12
35:4 [v]Isa 1:24; 34:8

3 Strengthen the feeble hands,
steady the knees[u] that give way;
4 say to those with fearful hearts,
"Be strong, do not fear;
your God will come,
he will come with vengeance;[v]
with divine retribution
he will come to save you."

35:5 [w]Mt 11:5; Jn 9:6-7 [x]Isa 29:18; 50:4
35:6 [y]Mt 15:30; Jn 5:8-9; Ac 3:8 [z]Isa 32:4; Mt 9:32-33; 12:22; Lk 11:14 [a]Isa 41:18; Jn 7:38
35:7 [b]Isa 49:10 [c]Isa 13:22

5 Then will the eyes of the blind be opened[w]
and the ears of the deaf[x] unstopped.
6 Then will the lame[y] leap like a deer,
and the mute tongue[z] shout for joy.
Water will gush forth in the wilderness
and streams[a] in the desert.
7 The burning sand will become a pool,
the thirsty ground bubbling springs.[b]
In the haunts where jackals[c] once lay,
grass and reeds and papyrus will grow.

35:8 [d]Isa 11:16; 33:8; Mt 7:13-14 [e]Isa 4:3; 1Pe 1:15 [f]Isa 52:1
35:9 [g]Isa 30:6 [h]Isa 34:14

8 And a highway[d] will be there;
it will be called the Way of Holiness.[e]
The unclean[f] will not journey on it;
it will be for those who walk in that Way;
wicked fools will not go about on it.[a]
9 No lion[g] will be there,
nor will any ferocious beast[h] get up on it;
they will not be found there.

[a] 8 Or / *the simple will not stray from it*

judgment and reward (Pss 40:7; 139:16; Da 7:10; Mal 3:16; Rev 20:12) or the prophecy found in verses 1–15. **mouth . . . Spirit.** The Word of God discloses his decree, and the Spirit confirms the Word. See *WLC* 156.

34:17 allots. As God distributed the promised land by lot (see Jos 18:10), so he would divide Edom among the unclean animals.

■ **35:1–10** *The Wonder of Returning to Zion.* The Assyrians had already exiled the northern kingdom and many in Judah by the time they had reached Jerusalem. Here Isaiah portrayed as a magnificent event the return of these and any others who had earlier departed.

35:1–10 This promise of restoration forms a fitting conclusion to 1:2—34:17. Similarly, see 11:12–16 and 27:12–13.

35:1–2 desert. See note on 40:3. Wherever God's Spirit of restoration (see note on 32:15) is present, he transforms nature and people, even though they have inevitably been affected by this sinful world. God would renew "Lebanon . . . Sharon" (v. 2), which had become like a desert (see note on 33:7–9), so that they would again be habitable for humans. **glory . . . glory.** See note on 4:2. **splendor.** See note on 2:10. **our God.** See note on 25:9. For the revelation of God's kingdom, see notes on 6:3 and 33:17 and 21–22.

35:3 feeble hands . . . knees. See note on 13:7 (cf. Heb 12:12).

35:4 Be strong. God's word of encouragement (cf. Jos 1:6,9,18). **do not fear.** An assurance of salvation (7:4; 10:24; 37:6; 40:9; 41:10,13–14; 43:5; 44:2,8; 51:7; 54:4). See note on 8:12. **God will come.** See 29:6, 30:27, 40:10, 59:19, 62:11 and 66:18. **vengeance . . . divine retribution.** He would establish justice on Earth (see note on 34:8). **save.** He would also bring complete deliverance to the oppressed.

35:5–7 blind . . . deaf. See note on 29:18. **lame . . . mute.** These changes evidence a supernatural restoration and are associated with the ministry of Jesus Christ (Mt 11:5; 12:22; Mk 7:37; Lk 7:22; Ac 3:8; 26:18). **Water.** See note on 1:30. **haunts where jackals.** In contrast to 34:13. **reeds and papyrus.** In contrast to 19:5–6.

35:8–9 highway. See note on 11:16 and 40:3. In contrast to 33:8. **Way of Holiness.** Only those who were cleansed and consecrated would be privileged to walk on the road of salvation that led to Zion. See notes on 4:3–4 and 29:23. **lion . . . ferocious beast.** In contrast to 13:21–22 and 34:11–15. **redeemed.** The people who were blind, deaf and lame would receive sight, hearing and the ability to walk, respectively (51:10; 62:12). They would also receive forgiveness, become the objects of God's compassion and await the fullness of redemption (see 12:1–6; 30:19; 33:2) from the Lord, their Redeemer (41:14; 43:14; 44:6,24; 47:4; 48:17; 49:7,26; 54:5,8; 59:20; 60:16; 63:16; cf. Lk 2:30).

But only the redeemed[i] will walk there,
10 and the ransomed of the LORD will return.
They will enter Zion with singing;
everlasting joy[j] will crown their heads.
Gladness and joy will overtake them,
and sorrow and sighing will flee away.[k]

Sennacherib Threatens Jerusalem

36 In the fourteenth year of King Hezekiah's reign, Sennacherib[l] king of Assyria attacked all the fortified cities of Judah and captured them. 2Then the king of Assyria sent his field commander with a large army from Lachish to King Hezekiah at Jerusalem. When the commander stopped at the aqueduct of the Upper Pool, on the road
to the Washerman's Field,[m] 3Eliakim[n] son of Hilkiah the palace administrator, Shebna[o]
the secretary, and Joah son of Asaph the recorder went out to him.
4The field commander said to them, "Tell Hezekiah,

" 'This is what the great king, the king of Assyria, says: On what are you basing
this confidence of yours? 5You say you have strategy and military strength—but you
speak only empty words. On whom are you depending, that you rebel[p] against me?
6Look now, you are depending on Egypt,[q] that splintered reed[r] of a staff, which
pierces a man's hand and wounds him if he leans on it! Such is Pharaoh king of
Egypt to all who depend on him. 7And if you say to me, "We are depending on the
LORD our God"—isn't he the one whose high places and altars Hezekiah removed,[s]
saying to Judah and Jerusalem, "You must worship before this altar"?[t]
8" 'Come now, make a bargain with my master, the king of Assyria: I will give
you two thousand horses—if you can put riders on them! 9How then can you repulse one officer of the least of my master's officials, even though you are depending on Egypt[u] for chariots and horsemen?[v] 10Furthermore, have I come to attack
and destroy this land without the LORD? The LORD himself told[w] me to march
against this country and destroy it.' "

11Then Eliakim, Shebna and Joah said to the field commander, "Please speak to your
servants in Aramaic,[x] since we understand it. Don't speak to us in Hebrew in the hearing of the people on the wall."
12But the commander replied, "Was it only to your master and you that my master
sent me to say these things, and not to the men sitting on the wall—who, like you, will
have to eat their own filth and drink their own urine?"

35:9 [i]Isa 51:11; 62:12; 63:4
35:10 [j]Isa 25:9 [k]Isa 30:19; 51:11; Rev 7:17; 21:4
36:1 [l]2Ch 32:1
36:2 [m]Isa 7:3
36:3 [n]Isa 22:20-21 [o]2Ki 18:18
36:5 [p]2Ki 18:7
36:6 [q]Isa 30:2,5 [r]Eze 29:6-7
36:7 [s]2Ki 18:4 [t]Dt 12:2-5
36:9 [u]Isa 31:3 [v]Isa 30:2-5
36:10 [w]1Ki 13:18
36:11 [x]Ezr 4:7

35:10 return . . . enter. Entrance into and dwelling in the city of God. See note on 33:16. **Zion.** See note on 1:8. **singing . . . joy.** Joy in the Lord (see notes on 9:3–4; 12:3,6; 24:14–16; 26:19), unlike the revelry of the city of man (see notes on 22:13; 24:7–9). **sorrow and sighing.** See note on 25:7–8; see also 51:11.

■ **36:1—39:8** *The Account of Sennacherib's Invasion.* These chapters provide an account of Sennacherib's invasion of Judah in c. 601 B.C. Much within them directly parallels 2 Kings 18:13—20:19, and they form a historical bridge between chapters 1–35 and 40–66. The section includes three parts: the first encounter with the Assyrian army (36:1—37:8), the second encounter (37:9–38) and the aftermath of Hezekiah's fatal choice (38:1—39:8).

■ **36:1—37:8** *The First Encounter.* The prophet described the first stage of the crisis posed by the Assyrian invasion by recording the Assyrians' success (36:1–3), the field commander's challenge (36:4–20), reactions to the challenge (36:21—37:7) and the departure of the Assyrian army (37:8).

■ **36:1–3** *Assyria's Military Success.* The Assyrians were triumphant in this military campaign. Having conquered most of Judah, they threatened Jerusalem itself.

36:1 fourteenth year. 701 B.C.; Hezekiah first ruled as coregent with his father, Ahaz (729–715 B.C.), after which he reigned alone (715–686 B.C.). Some explain the 14th year as a textual corruption for the 24th year, while others determine that Isaiah was referencing Hezekiah's independent rule. **Sennacherib.** King of Assyria (705–681 B.C.). **fortified cities.** Sennacherib listed 46 of them in his annals (see note on 2Ki 18:14).

36:2 field commander. The royal counselor. According to 2 Kings 18:17 the king also sent his "supreme commander" (cf. Isa 20:1) and his "chief officer." **large army.** More than 185,000 troops (see 37:36). **Lachish.** A fortress town in the Shephelah, the western plains, guarding an important road that led into the hill country south of Jerusalem (cf. Jer 34:7). **Upper Pool.** The place where Isaiah had earlier met Ahaz (7:3).

36:3 Eliakim . . . administrator. See note on 22:19–20. **Shebna . . . secretary.** See note on 22:19–20. **Joah . . . recorder.** An important officeholder.

■ **36:4–20** *The Field Commander's Challenge.* The commander of the Assyrian army made speeches to the leaders and people of Jerusalem in an attempt to persuade them to surrender.

36:4 great king. A respectful reference to the Assyrian king. See note at verses 13–14.

36:5 strategy . . . strength. See note on 11:2. **depending.** The challenge of determining whether to devote loyalty to Assyria, to other powers or to the Lord is the central message in this portion of the book of Isaiah (see note on 12:2).

36:6 Egypt. Hezekiah had depended on Egypt for support (20:1–6; see notes on 28:1—33:24; 30:2,6–7,13,15; 31:1,3; 32:2), but as Isaiah had argued by revelation, Egypt, also under divine judgment, could never deliver Judah (19:1–15; 30:3,7; 31:3).

36:7 high places and altars. Hezekiah had removed many pagan and idolatrous sites in Judah (2Ki 18:4; 2Ch 31:1); no doubt to the dismay and anger of many Judahites who had mixed their faith with other religions. The Assyrians assumed that this action also angered the Lord because many of these syncretistic altars were in his name. **this altar?** Hezekiah had removed other altars because God had ordained that worship should take place exclusively at the temple Solomon had built.

36:8 horses . . . riders. The Assyrians had sophisticated and superior forces against Judah.

36:9 one officer. Assyrian logic and logistics were opposed to the wisdom of God.

36:10 The LORD himself told me. An appeal to the religious people of Judah.

36:11 Eliakim. See note on 22:19–20. **Aramaic.** The international language for diplomacy and commerce. **Hebrew.** The language of Judah.

36:13 [y]2Ch 32:18 13 Then the commander stood and called out in Hebrew,[y] "Hear the words of the great
king, the king of Assyria! 14 This is what the king says: Do not let Hezekiah deceive you.
He cannot deliver you! 15 Do not let Hezekiah persuade you to trust in the LORD when he
36:15 [z]Isa 37:10 says, 'The LORD will surely deliver us; this city will not be given into the hand of the king
of Assyria.'[z]

36:16 [a]1Ki 4:25; Zec 3:10 [b]Pr 5:15 16 "Do not listen to Hezekiah. This is what the king of Assyria says: Make peace with
me and come out to me. Then every one of you will eat from his own vine and fig tree[a]
and drink water from his own cistern,[b] 17 until I come and take you to a land like your
own—a land of grain and new wine, a land of bread and vineyards.

18 "Do not let Hezekiah mislead you when he says, 'The LORD will deliver us.' Has the
god of any nation ever delivered his land from the hand of the king of Assyria? 19 Where
36:20 [c]1Ki 20:23 are the gods of Hamath and Arpad? Where are the gods of Sepharvaim? Have they rescued Samaria from my hand? 20 Who of all the gods[c] of these countries has been able to
save his land from me? How then can the LORD deliver Jerusalem from my hand?"

36:21 [d]Pr 9:7-8; 26:4 21 But the people remained silent and said nothing in reply, because the king had commanded, "Do not answer him."[d]

22 Then Eliakim son of Hilkiah the palace administrator, Shebna the secretary, and
Joah son of Asaph the recorder went to Hezekiah, with their clothes torn, and told him
what the field commander had said.

Jerusalem's Deliverance Foretold

37 When King Hezekiah heard this, he tore his clothes and put on sackcloth and
went into the temple of the LORD. 2 He sent Eliakim the palace administrator,
37:2 [e]Isa 1:1 Shebna the secretary, and the leading priests, all wearing sackcloth, to the prophet Isaiah son of Amoz.[e] 3 They told him, "This is what Hezekiah says: This day is a day of dis-
37:3 [f]Isa 26:18; 66:9; Hos 13:13 tress and rebuke and disgrace, as when children come to the point of birth[f] and there
is no strength to deliver them. 4 It may be that the LORD your God will hear the words of
37:4 [g]Isa 36:13,18-20 [h]Isa 1:9 the field commander, whom his master, the king of Assyria, has sent to ridicule the living God, and that he will rebuke him for the words the LORD your God has heard.[g] There-
fore pray for the remnant[h] that still survives."

37:6 [i]Isa 7:4 5 When King Hezekiah's officials came to Isaiah, 6 Isaiah said to them, "Tell your
master, 'This is what the LORD says: Do not be afraid[i] of what you have heard—those
words with which the underlings of the king of Assyria have blasphemed me. 7 Listen! I
37:7 [j]ver 9 am going to put a spirit in him so that when he hears a certain report,[j] he will return to
his own country, and there I will have him cut down with the sword.'"

37:8 [k]Nu 33:20 8 When the field commander heard that the king of Assyria had left Lachish, he withdrew and found the king fighting against Libnah.[k]

37:9 [l]ver 7 9 Now Sennacherib received a report[l] that Tirhakah, the Cushite[a] king ⌞of Egypt⌟, was
marching out to fight against him. When he heard it, he sent messengers to Hezekiah

[a] 9 That is, from the upper Nile region

36:13–14 the great king . . . Hezekiah. In contrast to the stress placed on the royalty of Sennacherib, Hezekiah was named without title.
36:15 trust . . . deliver. Testimony to Hezekiah's public expression of faith in God's word. "Trust in the LORD" has been at the heart of Isaiah's preaching in chapters 7–35 (cf. note on 2Ki 18:5).
36:16 Make peace. Literally, "make a blessing." An appeal to renew the covenant with Assyria. By contrast, see note on 27:5. **eat . . . drink.** A challenge to enjoy basic human sustenance (see note on 37:30). **vine and fig tree.** Also promised by the Lord (Mic 4:4). The Assyrians projected an ideal and happy life, but the Lord alone was in a position to fulfill what they were promising.
36:17 take you. The Assyrians made it a policy to remove rebellious populations from their homelands (cf. 2Ki 15:29).
36:18–20 god of any nation . . . Samaria. See note on 10:7–9. The field commander was uninformed on the historic and religious ties between Samaria and Jerusalem.
■ **36:21—37:7** *Response to the Assyrian Challenge.* The prophet reported the response of the people, the royal court.
37:1 heard . . . temple of the LORD. Expressions of mourning or repentance that signify humility, dependence and the need for fellowship with God.
37:2 Eliakim . . . Shebna. See 22:20–25 and 36:3. **leading priests.** Representatives of the leading priestly families (Jer 19:1).
37:3 distress . . . disgrace. A time of adversity, during which the loyalty of people would be tested (cf. 5:30; 8:22; 9:1; 25:4; 26:16; 33:2). **birth . . . no strength.** An admission of the futility of human strategies. See 26:17–18.
37:4 the living God. An expression of Hezekiah's renewed faith and zeal for the Lord. **rebuke.** He trusted that the Lord would defend his glorious name. **pray.** The prophet remained faithful and undeterred by stratagems and pragmatic solutions. **remnant.** The country was decimated (1:9; 6:11; 10:20; see note on 1:8).
37:5–7 Do not be afraid. See notes on 7:4, 10:24 and 35:4. **spirit.** An inclination. **return . . . cut down.** See verses 36–37. Isaiah encouraged Hezekiah to trust the Lord, even as he had earlier encouraged Ahaz (7:4).
■ **37:8** *Withdrawal of Assyrian Army.* The Lord fulfilled the prophetic word by having the field commander go to Sennacherib, who had left Lachish for Libnah.
37:8 Libnah. An unidentified city in the foothills of Judah (cf. 2Ki 8:22).
■ **37:9–38** *The Second Encounter.* It was not long before Sennacherib set his sights on Jerusalem again. This record divides into Sennacherib's letter (vv. 9–13), the response to this challenge (vv. 14–35) and the Assyrian departure (vv. 36–38).
■ **37:9–13** *Sennacherib's Challenge.* Sennacherib renewed his attempt at persuading Hezekiah to submit to, and depend on, Assyria. By denigrating gods of the nations, he challenged Hezekiah to stop trusting in the Lord.
37:9 Cushite king of Egypt. An anachronistic note, since he was still a prince and commander of the Egyptian troops by 701 B.C. and did not become king until 689 B.C.

with this word: 10“Say to Hezekiah king of Judah: Do not let the god you depend on deceive you when he says, ‘Jerusalem will not be handed over to the king of Assyria.’[m]
11Surely you have heard what the kings of Assyria have done to all the countries, destroying them completely. And will you be delivered?[n] 12Did the gods of the nations that were
destroyed by my forefathers[o] deliver them—the gods of Gozan, Haran,[p] Rezeph and the
people of Eden who were in Tel Assar? 13Where is the king of Hamath, the king of Arpad,
the king of the city of Sepharvaim, or of Hena or Ivvah?”

Hezekiah’s Prayer

14Hezekiah received the letter from the messengers and read it. Then he went up to
the temple of the LORD and spread it out before the LORD. 15And Hezekiah prayed to the
LORD: 16“O LORD Almighty, God of Israel, enthroned between the cherubim, you alone are
God[q] over all the kingdoms of the earth. You have made heaven and earth. 17Give ear,
O LORD, and hear;[r] open your eyes, O LORD, and see;[s] listen to all the words Sennacher-
ib has sent to insult the living God.

18“It is true, O LORD, that the Assyrian kings have laid waste all these peoples and their
lands.[t] 19They have thrown their gods into the fire and destroyed them,[u] for they were
not gods[v] but only wood and stone, fashioned by human hands. 20Now, O LORD our God,
deliver us from his hand, so that all kingdoms on earth may know that you alone,
O LORD, are God.[a][w]”

Sennacherib’s Fall

21Then Isaiah son of Amoz[x] sent a message to Hezekiah: “This is what the LORD, the
God of Israel, says: Because you have prayed to me concerning Sennacherib king of Assyria, 22this is the word the LORD has spoken against him:

“The Virgin Daughter of Zion
  despises and mocks you.
The Daughter of Jerusalem
  tosses her head[y] as you flee.
23 Who is it you have insulted and blasphemed?[z]
  Against whom have you raised your voice
and lifted your eyes in pride?[a]
  Against the Holy One of Israel!
24 By your messengers
  you have heaped insults on the Lord.
And you have said,
  ‘With my many chariots
I have ascended the heights of the mountains,
  the utmost heights of Lebanon.[b]
I have cut down its tallest cedars,
  the choicest of its pines.

37:10 [m]Isa 36:15
37:11 [n]Isa 36:18-20
37:12 [o]2Ki 18:11 [p]Ge 11:31; 12:1-4; Ac 7:2
37:16 [q]Dt 10:17; Ps 86:10; 136:2-3
37:17 [r]2Ch 6:40 [s]Da 9:18
37:18 [t]2Ki 15:29; Na 2:11-12
37:19 [u]Isa 26:14 [v]Isa 41:24,29
37:20 [w]Ps 46:10
37:21 [x]ver 2
37:22 [y]Job 16:4
37:23 [z]ver 4 [a]Isa 2:11
37:24 [b]Isa 14:8

a *20* Dead Sea Scrolls (see also 2 Kings 19:19); Masoretic Text *alone are the LORD*

37:10–11 god . . . deceive you. A direct assault on the Lord’s ability to deliver (see note on v. 4). **depend on.** See note on 12:2.
37:12 forefathers. A claim that his god was with him, based on that fact that the Assyrian string of successes went back several generations. **Gozan . . . Eden.** Cities in Mesopotamia.
37:13 Hamath . . . Ivvah? Cities in Aram (cf. 36:18–19; see note on 10:7–9).
■ **37:14–35** *Response to Sennacherib’s Challenge.* Hezekiah and Isaiah responded to the Assyrian threat in ways that demonstrated their trust in the Lord.
■ **37:14–20** *Hezekiah’s Prayer.* Hezekiah did not respond to Sennacherib’s boast but instead turned to the Lord in prayer. Unlike Ahaz Hezekiah prayed, confessing his radical trust in the Lord as King, Creator and Redeemer. The theological emphases summarize Isaiah’s vision of God (38:2).
37:16 LORD Almighty. See note on 1:9. **God of Israel.** The Lord was the God of the 12 tribes (represented by Samaria and Jerusalem) by covenant (cf. v. 21; 17:6; 21:17; 24:15; 29:23; 41:17; 45:3; 48:2; 52:12). **enthroned between the cherubim.** God was with his people and ruled over them (1Sa 4:4; 2Sa 6:2; Pss 80:1; 99:1), as was represented by his presence in the temple in the Most Holy Place, which contained the ark of the covenant (God’s footstool) beneath the two cherubim. **you alone are God.** An exclusive and unique claim to deity (44:8; 45:5–6,14,22; 46:9). **kingdoms.** See note on 13:4. **made heaven and earth.** A distinct emphasis on the Lord as the sovereign and absolute Creator of everything (42:5; 45:8,12,18; see 27:10–11).
37:17 Give ear . . . listen. Unlike the gods of Assyria, the Lord could see, hear and act (cf. 1Ki 8:52). **living God.** See 36:20.
37:19 On Isaiah’s polemic against idolatry, see 2:8.
37:20 our God. Contrast with verse 4. See note on 25:9. **kingdoms.** See note on 13:4. **you alone, O LORD, are God.** See note on verse 16.
■ **37:21–35** *Isaiah’s Prophecy.* The Lord gave Isaiah a message to encourage Hezekiah and the people.
37:21 the God of Israel. See note on verse 16.
37:22 Virgin Daughter. Hebrew literary convention speaks of cities and people as beautiful young women (cf. 47:1; La 2:10; Am 5:2). **Zion.** See note on 1:8. **despises . . . tosses her head.** An expression of rejection and derision (Ps 22:7; Jer 18:16). This taunt song in verses 22–29 is similar to the one in 14:4–21.
37:23 insulted . . . in pride? Assyria had exalted herself against the Lord. **the Holy One of Israel!** See note on 1:4.
37:24 many chariots. Assyria’s pride was in her military arsenal and ability. **ascended the heights.** A poetic expression of superiority and pride (14:13–14) that was usually reserved for deity. See note on 2:12–16. **Lebanon.** See 33:9 and 35:2. **cut down.** See 14:8.

I have reached its remotest heights,
the finest of its forests.
25 I have dug wells in foreign lands[a]
and drunk the water there.
With the soles of my feet
I have dried up all the streams of Egypt.[c]'

37:25 [c]Dt 11:10

26 "Have you not heard?
Long ago I ordained[d] it.
In days of old I planned[e] it;
now I have brought it to pass,
that you have turned fortified cities
into piles of stone.[f]
27 Their people, drained of power,
are dismayed and put to shame.
They are like plants in the field,
like tender green shoots,
like grass sprouting on the roof,[g]
scorched[b] before it grows up.

37:26 [d]Ac 2:23; 4:27-28; 1Pe 2:8 [e]Isa 10:6; 25:1 [f]Isa 25:2
37:27 [g]Ps 129:6

28 "But I know where you stay
and when you come and go[h]
and how you rage[i] against me.
29 Because you rage against me
and because your insolence[j] has reached my ears,
I will put my hook in your nose[k]
and my bit in your mouth,
and I will make you return
by the way you came.[l]

37:28 [h]Ps 139:1-3 [i]Ps 2:1
37:29 [j]Isa 10:12 [k]Isa 30:28; Eze 38:4 [l]ver 34

30 "This will be the sign for you, O Hezekiah:

"This year you will eat what grows by itself,
and the second year what springs from that.
But in the third year sow and reap,
plant vineyards and eat their fruit.
31 Once more a remnant of the house of Judah
will take root below and bear fruit[m] above.
32 For out of Jerusalem will come a remnant,
and out of Mount Zion a band of survivors.
The zeal[n] of the LORD Almighty
will accomplish this.

37:31 [m]Isa 27:6
37:32 [n]Isa 9:7

33 "Therefore this is what the LORD says concerning the king of Assyria:

"He will not enter this city
or shoot an arrow here.
He will not come before it with shield
or build a siege ramp against it.

[a] *25* Dead Sea Scrolls (see also 2 Kings 19:24); Masoretic Text does not have *in foreign lands.*
[b] *27* Some manuscripts of the Masoretic Text, Dead Sea Scrolls and some Septuagint manuscripts (see also 2 Kings 19:26); most manuscripts of the Masoretic Text *roof / and terraced fields*

37:25 I have dug . . . dried up. An absolute claim to authority over creation, which constituted an insult to God's prerogatives.
37:26 Have you not heard? A rhetorical device, as in 40:21. **Long ago I ordained.** Assyria was nothing but a pawn in God's plans. **planned.** Assyria accomplished God's will among the kingdoms of this world (10:5–19; 40:6–8; Ps 37:1–2; Mic 4:9–13). See note on 27:10–11.
37:28 I know where . . . how. God was sovereign over the Assyrians. They could never escape his scrutiny (cf. Ps 139).
37:29 rage . . . insolence. God saw what the Assyrians had done, held them responsible and declared their punishment. **hook.** The Assyrians dragged away exiles with hooks in their noses (cf. 2Ch 33:11).
37:30 sign. A witness to God's fidelity to work out his plans: the overthrow of Assyria and the restoration of a remnant (see notes on 7:11,14). **This year . . . third year.** Within three years. In Hebrew calendrical calculation, this could mean as little as 14 months. **eat their fruit.** What Assyria had promised could in reality be fulfilled by the Lord alone (36:16).
37:31 remnant. See note on 1:8. **root . . . fruit.** In fulfillment of God's promise of the restoration of his vineyard (see note on 27:6). This began in 701 B.C. and still continues, as all who are in Jesus Christ are grafted into the vine and enjoy the benefits of belonging to God's vineyard (Jn 15:1–8).
37:32 remnant. See note on 1:8. **Zion.** See note on 1:8. **zeal.** See note on 9:7. **LORD Almighty.** See note on 1:9.
37:33–35 defend . . . save. See notes on 27:3 and 31:5. Sennacherib did not succeed in his siege of Jerusalem. The Lord fought for his people because of his fidelity to the promise made to David (8:8,10; 2Sa 7:16). **servant!** See note on 20:3.

34 By the way that he came he will return;[o]
he will not enter this city,"
declares the LORD.

35 "I will defend[p] this city and save it,
for my sake[q] and for the sake of David[r] my servant!"

36 Then the angel of the LORD went out and put to death a hundred and eighty-five
thousand men in the Assyrian[s] camp. When the people got up the next morning—there
were all the dead bodies! 37 So Sennacherib king of Assyria broke camp and withdrew.
He returned to Nineveh[t] and stayed there.

38 One day, while he was worshiping in the temple of his god Nisroch, his sons Adrammelech and Sharezer cut him down with the sword, and they escaped to the land of Ararat.[u] And Esarhaddon his son succeeded him as king.

Hezekiah's Illness

38 In those days Hezekiah became ill and was at the point of death. The prophet
Isaiah son of Amoz[v] went to him and said, "This is what the LORD says: Put your
house in order,[w] because you are going to die; you will not recover."

2 Hezekiah turned his face to the wall and prayed to the LORD, 3 "Remember, O LORD,
how I have walked[x] before you faithfully and with wholehearted devotion[y] and have
done what is good in your eyes.[z]" And Hezekiah wept[a] bitterly.

4 Then the word of the LORD came to Isaiah: 5 "Go and tell Hezekiah, 'This is what the
LORD, the God of your father David, says: I have heard your prayer and seen your tears;
I will add fifteen years[b] to your life. 6 And I will deliver you and this city from the hand of
the king of Assyria. I will defend[c] this city.

7 " 'This is the LORD's sign[d] to you that the LORD will do what he has promised: 8 I will
make the shadow cast by the sun go back the ten steps it has gone down on the stairway of Ahaz.' " So the sunlight went back the ten steps it had gone down.[e]

9 A writing of Hezekiah king of Judah after his illness and recovery:

10 I said, "In the prime of my life[f]
must I go through the gates of death[a][g]
and be robbed of the rest of my years?[h]"
11 I said, "I will not again see the LORD,
the LORD, in the land of the living;[i]
no longer will I look on mankind,
or be with those who now dwell in this world.[b]
12 Like a shepherd's tent[j] my house
has been pulled down[k] and taken from me.
Like a weaver I have rolled[l] up my life,
and he has cut me off from the loom;[m]
day and night[n] you made an end of me.
13 I waited patiently till dawn,

37:34 [o]ver 29
37:35 [p]Isa 31:5; 38:6 [q]Isa 43:25; 48:9, 11 [r]2Ki 20:6
37:36 [s]Isa 10:12
37:37 [t]Ge 10:11
37:38 [u]Ge 8:4; Jer 51:27
38:1 [v]Isa 37:2 [w]2Sa 17:23
38:3 [x]Ne 13:14; Ps 26:3 [y]1Ch 29:19 [z]Dt 6:18 [a]Ps 6:8
38:5 [b]2Ki 18:2
38:6 [c]Isa 31:5; 37:35
38:7 [d]Isa 7:11,14
38:8 [e]Jos 10:13
38:10 [f]Ps 102:24 [g]Ps 107:18; 2Co 1:9 [h]Job 17:11
38:11 [i]Ps 27:13; 116:9
38:12 [j]2Co 5:1,4; 2Pe 1:13-14 [k]Job 4:21 [l]Heb 1:12 [m]Job 7:6 [n]Ps 73:14

a *10* Hebrew *Sheol* b *11* A few Hebrew manuscripts; most Hebrew manuscripts *in the place of cessation*

■ **37:36–38** *The Assyrian Defeat.* The prophet described the Lord's judgment against the Assyrian army.
37:36 angel of the LORD . . . dead bodies! Jerusalem's deliverance came about by supernatural means, as had the death of the firstborn in Egypt (Ex 12:12; 2Sa 24:16).
37:37–38 Sennacherib . . . the temple. The heart of Sennacherib remained unchanged. His death in the temple of Nisroch contrasts with the life Hezekiah had found in the temple of the Lord (see vv. 1,14). **cut him down.** Twenty years later Sennacherib was murdered by his own sons (681 B.C.). **Ararat.** The mountainous region of Urartu. **Esarhaddon.** King over Assyria from 681–669 B.C.
■ **38:1—39:8** *Hezekiah's Blessing and Curse.* Because of Hezekiah's prayer God allowed him to survive his sickness (38:1–22), but the king failed when he sought to establish an alliance with Babylon (39:1–8).
■ **38:1–22** *Hezekiah's Healing.* Hezekiah became ill, prayed and received healing from the Lord.
38:1 In those days. This may have been before or after Jerusalem's siege (701 B.C.). Some hold that Hezekiah died in 696 B.C. and date his sickness to the beginning of his sole rule (711 B.C.). See note on 36:1. **Put your house in order . . . die.** Prepare for the orderly succession of kingship (cf. 1Ki 2:1–9). See *WLC* 141.
38:2 prayed. A second prayer (cf. 37:14–20) in which the king confided his confidence in God's righteousness.
38:3 Remember . . . good. A moving expression of loyalty to the Lord (see 33:14–16). **faithfully.** See 10:20. **wept bitterly.** Hezekiah was apparently without a male heir. He lived an additional 15 years after this incident (v. 5). Manasseh, his successor to the throne, was 12 years old when Hezekiah died (2Ki 20:21—21:1). See *WLC* 192.
38:5 heard . . . seen. See note on 37:17. **fifteen years.** From 701–686 B.C.
38:6 deliver . . . defend. See 37:33–35.
38:7 sign. See 7:11–14, 37:30 and 38:21–22.
38:8 go back. Symbolized the divine reprieve of Hezekiah's life. **stairway of Ahaz.** See note on 7:11.
38:9 A writing of Hezekiah. A hymn with a mixture of lament (vv. 10–14) and thanksgiving (vv. 15–20). Compare 2 Chronicles 29:30 and Proverbs 25:1.
38:10 my life . . . my years? Hezekiah expressed his anguish over the reality and sting of death (Ps 55:4). **death.** See note on 5:13–16.
38:11 see the LORD . . . mankind. Not a denial of an afterlife but a celebration of the joys of physical, human life (Ps 6:5).
38:12–13 pulled down . . . made an end of me. Hezekiah offered many similes to express his vexation with the brevity of life, as though God were his enemy (cf. Pss 22; 32:3–4).

38:13 [o]Ps 51:8 [p]Job 10:16; Da 6:24
38:14 [q]Isa 59:11 [r]Job 17:3
38:15 [s]Ps 39:9 [t]1Ki 21:27 [u]Job 7:11
38:16 [v]Ps 119:25
38:17 [w]Ps 30:3 [x]Jer 31:34 [y]Isa 43:25; Mic 7:19
38:18 [z]Ecc 9:10 [a]Ps 6:5; 88:10-11; 115:17 [b]Ps 30:9
38:19 [c]Dt 6:7; Ps 118:17; 119:175 [d]Dt 11:19
38:20 [e]Ps 68:25 [f]Ps 33:2 [g]Ps 116:2 [h]Ps 116:17-19
39:1 [i]2Ch 32:31
39:2 [j]2Ch 32:31 [k]2Ki 18:15

but like a lion he broke[o] all my bones;[p]
day and night you made an end of me.
14 I cried like a swift or thrush,
I moaned like a mourning dove.[q]
My eyes grew weak as I looked to the heavens.
I am troubled; O Lord, come to my aid!"[r]

15 But what can I say?
He has spoken to me, and he himself has done this.[s]
I will walk humbly[t] all my years
because of this anguish of my soul.[u]
16 Lord, by such things men live;
and my spirit finds life in them too.
You restored me to health
and let me live.[v]
17 Surely it was for my benefit
that I suffered such anguish.
In your love you kept me
from the pit[w] of destruction;
you have put all my sins[x]
behind your back.[y]
18 For the grave[a][z] cannot praise you,
death cannot sing your praise;[a]
those who go down to the pit[b]
cannot hope for your faithfulness.
19 The living, the living—they praise[c] you,
as I am doing today;
fathers tell their children[d]
about your faithfulness.

20 The LORD will save me,
and we will sing[e] with stringed instruments[f]
all the days of our lives[g]
in the temple[h] of the LORD.

21 Isaiah had said, "Prepare a poultice of figs and apply it to the boil, and he will recover."
22 Hezekiah had asked, "What will be the sign that I will go up to the temple of the LORD?"

Envoys From Babylon

39 At that time Merodach-Baladan son of Baladan king of Babylon[i] sent Hezekiah letters and a gift, because he had heard of his illness and recovery. 2 Hezekiah received the envoys[j] gladly and showed them what was in his storehouses—the silver, the gold,[k] the spices, the fine oil, his entire armory and everything found among his treasures. There was nothing in his palace or in all his kingdom that Hezekiah did not show them.

a *18* Hebrew *Sheol*

38:14–17 I am troubled . . . anguish. A determination to remain faithful and an abandonment to the Lord's mysterious will, painful though it was. **restored . . . live.** Renewal and health are in God's hands. **pit of destruction.** Death (cf. v. 18). **sins.** Restoration and forgiveness of sins are interrelated (53:5; Pss 32:3–5; 103:12; Mic 7:19; Mt 8:14–17; Lk 5:17–26).

38:18–19 grave . . . pit. Synonyms for death. **praise . . . praise.** The emphasis is on communal and personal praise in response to God's acts of salvation in this life. Praise for healing is offered only in the land of the living. **cannot hope.** Hope for temporal life does not extend beyond death, but hope for eternal life does (see 52:13; Ps 22:22–31; 2Ti 1:10; Heb 2:10–12; 1Jn 5:11–12). **faithfulness.** See notes on 1:21 and 10:20. **fathers tell their children.** The story of God's acts of redemption were to be told from generation to generation.

38:20 save me . . . all the days of our lives. Hope was alive (cf. Pss 6:9; 22:22–24), as Hezekiah expected to join in the communal praise (see note on vv. 18–19). **sing.** See 12:1–6. **stringed instruments.** Music accompanied the singing of psalms (cf. Pss 33:1–3; 150). **temple.** God's dwelling place from Solomon's time to that of the apostolic community.

38:21–22 Two notes pertaining to Hezekiah's illness and recovery: (1) a poultice of figs (cf. 2Ki 20:7) and (2) the request of a sign (1Ki 20:8). **poultice.** All healing is of God, although he may mediate it through medicine. God forbids relying on medicine without accompanying faith (2Ch 16:12). See *WLC* 135.

■ **39:1–8** *Hezekiah's Failure and Judgment.* These verses describe Hezekiah's infidelity and the exile of Judah (cf. 2Ki 20:12–19).

39:1 At that time. After Hezekiah's illness. See note on 38:1. **Merodach-Baladan.** Ruled over Babylon from 721–710 B.C. and again from 705–703 B.C. **recovery.** The astronomically minded Babylonians (see 2Ch 32:31) would have had a special interest in the sun's retrograde movement, the sign given at Hezekiah's recovery (see 38:8).

39:2 silver . . . treasures. Hezekiah offered evidence of his ability to support Babylon in rebellion against Assyria. He was attempting to form an alliance.

3Then Isaiah the prophet went to King Hezekiah and asked, "What did those men say,
and where did they come from?"
"From a distant land,[l]" Hezekiah replied. "They came to me from Babylon."
4The prophet asked, "What did they see in your palace?"
"They saw everything in my palace," Hezekiah said. "There is nothing among my treasures that I did not show them."
5Then Isaiah said to Hezekiah, "Hear the word of the LORD Almighty: 6The time will
surely come when everything in your palace, and all that your fathers have stored up until this day, will be carried off to Babylon.[m] Nothing will be left, says the LORD. 7And some
of your descendants, your own flesh and blood who will be born to you, will be taken
away, and they will become eunuchs in the palace of the king of Babylon.[n]"
8"The word of the LORD you have spoken is good," Hezekiah replied. For he thought,
"There will be peace and security in my lifetime.[o]"

Comfort for God's People

40

Comfort, comfort[p] my people,
says your God.
2Speak tenderly[q] to Jerusalem,
and proclaim to her
that her hard service has been completed,[r]
that her sin has been paid for,
that she has received from the LORD's hand
double[s] for all her sins.

3A voice of one calling:
"In the desert prepare
the way[t] for the LORD[a];
make straight in the wilderness
a highway for our God.[b][u]

39:3 [l]Dt 28:49
39:6 [m]2Ki 24:13; Jer 20:5
39:7 [n]2Ki 24:15; Da 1:1-7
39:8 [o]2Ch 32:26
40:1 [p]Isa 12:1; 49:13; 51:3,12; 52:9; 61:2; 66:13; Jer 31:13; Zep 3:14-17; 2Co 1:3
40:2 [q]Isa 35:4 [r]Isa 41:11-13; 49:25 [s]Isa 61:7; Jer 16:18; Zec 9:12; Rev 18:6
40:3 [t]Mal 3:1 [u]Mt 3:3*; Mk 1:3*; Jn 1:23*

[a] 3 Or *A voice of one calling in the desert: / "Prepare the way for the LORD* [b] 3 Hebrew; Septuagint *make straight the paths of our God*

39:3–4 Isaiah . . . Hezekiah. Isaiah came as God's spokesperson and interrogated Hezekiah ("What . . . where . . . What . . . ?"). **show them.** His action demonstrated that he sought help against future troubles from an alliance with Babylon rather than from the Lord.
39:5 Hear the word. The prophetic charge and judgment. **LORD Almighty.** See note on 1:9.
39:6 carried off. The prediction of the Babylonian exile.
39:7 See 2 Kings 24:15. **eunuchs.** See 56:4 and Daniel 1:3–6.
39:8 word. See note on v. 5. **good . . . in my lifetime.** A negative note, as the king showed little concern for his own descendants or for his people. Although an end did come to the Babylonian exile, the prophetic word was clear that "there is no peace . . . for the wicked" (48:22; 57:21); yet God's peace would extend to the children of Zion (66:12).
▪ **40:1—66:24** *Isaiah and the Babylonian Judgment.* The prophecies in this section were originally addressed primarily to the exiles in Babylon to encourage them to flee their captors and return by faith to the promised land (e.g., see 47:20–21). The encouragement of these chapters is based in part on their supernatural character (e.g., see 41:21–28). These prophecies, delivered more than a century and a half beforehand (see "Introduction: Author"), predicted astonishing details of Israel's deliverance, including the role of the Persian emperor Cyrus (e.g., see 44:24—45:13) and the remarkable role of the suffering Servant (see 42:1–7; 49:1–13; 50:4–11; 52:13—53:12). These chapters divide into four major sections: Isaiah's call to proclaim restoration (40:1–11), God's ability and determination to bring about restoration for his people from Babylon (41:12—44:23), God's twin instruments of restoration (44:24—55:13) and the path of repentance and restoration that Israel had to walk in order to enjoy restoration (56:1—66:24).
▪ **40:1–11** *Isaiah's Call to Proclaim Restoration.* As God had previously called Isaiah to a ministry of judgment (see notes on 7:11–13), Isaiah now reported how God had called him to assure the people of God's deliverance from the Babylonian exile, which the prophet had predicted in the days of Hezekiah (39:5–7). These verses divide into four parts: God's call to comfort (vv. 1–2), the message (vv. 3–5), Isaiah's hesitation (vv. 6–8) and a final call to proclamation (vv. 9–11).
▪ **40:1–2** *The Call to Comfort.* The prophet reported God's message of comfort to the exiles.
40:1 Comfort, comfort. This command is plural. God was addressing the court of heaven, where many were participating in the events taking place (see v. 6; 44:26). The repetition indicates the intensity of God's desire for this message of comfort to be delivered (cf. 51:9,17; 52:1,11; 57:14; 62:10; 65.1). **my people.** Although they had rebelled and would be temporarily disowned (Hos 1:8), God would lead out of captivity a remnant who represented the continuation of Israel (Hos 1:10; 2:1). This phrase occurs frequently in Isaiah as an affectionate designation for the people of God (1:3; 3:12,15; 5:13; 14:25; 26:20; 32:13,18; 43:20; 51:4,16; 53:8; 58:1; 61:7; 65:10,22).
40:2 Speak . . . proclaim. The commands continue to be plural (see note on v. 1). **tenderly.** Literally, "to the heart." This message was to touch the innermost longings of the faithful in exile. **Jerusalem.** The city stood for the faithful as the center of God's blessing. **hard service . . . sin.** The suffering on account of sin; the exile of Israel and Judah. **paid for.** The righteous remnant could not and would not pay for their own sins, so as to render Christ's death unnecessary to satisfy the just wrath of God. Rather, they would endure the time of chastisement and in this sense find temporary atonement for their violations of the covenant. **double for all her sins.** "Double" means "the equivalent," "the right amount." Justice had been satisfied (51:19), and God was ready to forgive (43:24; 44:22; 48:9; Rev 1:5).
▪ **40:3–5** *The Message of Comfort.* The prophet reported hearing a heavenly voice proclaiming the content of the message of comfort.
40:3 voice. Another voice, perhaps that of a heavenly herald (see vv. 6,9), conveyed the content of the message of comfort. Upon hearing this, Isaiah himself delivered this message to God's people. The Gospels refer to this passage and identify John the Baptist as one who also proclaimed this message in the days of Jesus, the ultimate fulfillment of the prophecy of release from captivity (Mt 3:3; Mk 1:3; Lk 1:76; 3:4–5; Jn 1:23). **desert . . . wilderness.** A road or highway stretching from Babylon to Jerusalem that passed directly through the deserts separating the two. This road of salvation was metaphorical but corresponded to the geographical realities facing the people of God. **prepare . . . make straight.** "Prepare" means "remove the obstacles" (57:14). The metaphor of a road continues; the journey from Babylon to Jerusalem would not be difficult but miraculous and glorious. **way for the LORD.** This road was the counterpart of the Way of Marduk, a Babylonian ceremonial highway into the city. The Lord would travel out of Babylon and into Jerusalem in victory over his enemies, much as the Babylonians celebrated the victories of their god Marduk as they marched into their city.

40:4 [v]Isa 45:2,13

4 Every valley shall be raised up,
every mountain and hill made low;
the rough ground shall become level,[v]
the rugged places a plain.

40:5 [w]Isa 52:10; Lk 3:4-6* [x]Isa 1:20; 58:14

5 And the glory of the LORD will be revealed,
and all mankind together will see it.[w]
For the mouth of the LORD has spoken."[x]

6 A voice says, "Cry out."
And I said, "What shall I cry?"

40:6 [y]Job 14:2

"All men are like grass,[y]
and all their glory is like the flowers of the field.

40:7 [z]Job 41:21

7 The grass withers and the flowers fall,
because the breath[z] of the LORD blows on them.
Surely the people are grass.

40:8 [a]Isa 55:11; 59:21 [b]Mt 5:18; 1Pe 1:24-25*

8 The grass withers and the flowers fall,
but the word[a] of our God stands forever.[b]"

40:9 [c]Isa 52:7-10; 61:1; Ro 10:15 [d]Isa 25:9

9 You who bring good tidings[c] to Zion,
go up on a high mountain.
You who bring good tidings to Jerusalem,[a]
lift up your voice with a shout,
lift it up, do not be afraid;
say to the towns of Judah,
"Here is your God!"[d]

40:10 [e]Rev 22:7 [f]Isa 59:16 [g]Isa 9:6-7 [h]Isa 62:11; Rev 22:12

10 See, the Sovereign LORD comes[e] with power,
and his arm[f] rules[g] for him.
See, his reward[h] is with him,
and his recompense accompanies him.

40:11 [i]Eze 34:23; Mic 5:4; Jn 10:11

11 He tends his flock like a shepherd:[i]
He gathers the lambs in his arms
and carries them close to his heart;
he gently leads those that have young.

40:12 [j]Job 38:10 [k]Pr 30:4 [l]Heb 1:10-12

12 Who has measured the waters[j] in the hollow of his hand,[k]
or with the breadth of his hand marked off the heavens?[l]

[a] 9 Or *O Zion, bringer of good tidings, / go up on a high mountain. / O Jerusalem, bringer of good tidings*

40:4 valley . . . rugged places. This verse elaborates on the figure of building a superhighway (see v. 3): Valleys are filled in, high places are cut down and rugged places are smoothed over. The return from exile would not be fraught with difficulties and trials but would be a wondrous, supernatural event. Although this prophecy saw a measure of fulfillment in the return to the land in 539 B.C. and in the first coming of Christ, it will be fulfilled fully when Christ returns in glory.
40:5 glory. See note on 4:2. **revealed.** The restoration from exile in 539 B.C. was a manifestation of God's glory, as was the first coming of Christ (Jn 1:14) and as will be his second coming. **all mankind together.** At some stage the final restoration will be plain and visible to all creation; this will ultimately be fulfilled in the new heavens and the new earth (Ge 9:17; cf. Mt 2:1–11; 16:27; 24:30; Ac 28:28; 2Co 3:18).
■ **40:6–8** *The Prophet's Reluctance.* Isaiah hesitated when he heard the call to announce comfort because he anticipated how terribly the nation would suffer in exile. The judgment of God would be severe. What could he say to convince the people that God had not utterly deserted them?
40:6 voice. See notes on verses 1 and 3. **Cry out.** The form is singular because the angelic voice addressed Isaiah (see 6:6–9). **What . . . ?** The prophet had predicted the destruction of Judah and Jerusalem, and he wrote here for those who would witness the devastation. In light of the severity of God's judgment, he wondered what he could proclaim. **grass . . . flowers.** Expressions of the brevity and impotence of human existence in general, but here especially a description of human life under the curse of destruction and exile (34:4; 37:27; 51:12; Job 4:19–20; Pss 90:2–6; 103:14–15; Jas 1:10–11; 1Pe 1:24–25).
40:7 breath. God's wrath is likened to the destructive east desert wind as it blows and dries up grass (Ps 103:16; Jer 4:11; Eze 17:10; Lk 12:55).
40:8 word. Despite the severity of the judgment of exile, the promises of God could be trusted. As far back as Moses (see Dt 4:29–31; Lev 26:40–45) the Lord had promised to return his people, and his word would not be broken. Peter equated this reliable word about restoration from exile with the word that Christians preach (1Pe 1:24–25): the announcement of salvation through the shed blood of Jesus Christ (see 40:1–11).
■ **40:9–11** *The Call to Proclaim.* Having been assured of God's trustworthiness, Isaiah was now commanded to proclaim boldly the good news of deliverance from exile.
40:9 good tidings. This verse constitutes the prophetic background of the New Testament term "gospel." The message about Christ is called "gospel," or "good news," because Christ ultimately fulfilled this passage's promise of release from exile (see also 52:7). **Zion.** See note on 1:8. **voice.** See note on verse 3. **do not be afraid.** See note on 35:4. **"Here is your God!"** God is present to help, deliver and defend his people. This gospel message in a nutshell receives further development in verses 10–11.
40:10 Sovereign LORD. See note on 25:7–8. God would come to inaugurate his kingdom on Earth (41:20; 43:15; 44:6; 52:7–10). See note on 35:4. **power . . . rules.** The Lord would establish sovereignty over his creation by subduing the enemy and caring for his people, for he is the divine Warrior-King (see notes on 13:4; 42:13; 59:17). **arm.** Designation of the power of God, manifested in his acts of deliverance and vengeance (v. 11; 44:12; 48:14; 51:5,9; 53:1; 59:16; 63:5,12; see Ex 15:16; Pss 44:3; 89:13; 98:1; 136:12). **reward.** The spoils of victory; here, the delivered people themselves.
40:11 flock . . . . leads. Expressions of the tender, shepherding care of the Warrior-King (Pss 23:1–4; 78:52; 80:1; Jer 31:10; Eze 34:11–16; Mic 2:12; Jn 10:11). **arms.** God would strike his enemies with his mighty arm but hold his people tenderly. See note on verse 10. See *WLC* 172.
■ **40:12—44:23** *God's Power to Restore His People.* These chapters

Who has held the dust of the earth in a basket,
or weighed the mountains on the scales
and the hills in a balance?
13 Who has understood the mind[a] of the LORD,
or instructed him as his counselor?[m]
14 Whom did the LORD consult to enlighten him,
and who taught him the right way?
Who was it that taught him knowledge[n]
or showed him the path of understanding?

15 Surely the nations are like a drop in a bucket;
they are regarded as dust on the scales;
he weighs the islands as though they were fine dust.
16 Lebanon is not sufficient for altar fires,
nor its animals[o] enough for burnt offerings.
17 Before him all the nations[p] are as nothing;[q]
they are regarded by him as worthless
and less than nothing.[r]

18 To whom, then, will you compare God?[s]
What image[t] will you compare him to?
19 As for an idol,[u] a craftsman casts it,
and a goldsmith[v] overlays it with gold[w]
and fashions silver chains for it.
20 A man too poor to present such an offering
selects wood that will not rot.
He looks for a skilled craftsman
to set up an idol that will not topple.[x]

21 Do you not know?
Have you not heard?
Has it not been told[y] you from the beginning?
Have you not understood[z] since the earth was founded?[a]
22 He sits enthroned above the circle of the earth,
and its people are like grasshoppers.[b]
He stretches out the heavens like a canopy,[c]
and spreads them out like a tent[d] to live in.
23 He brings princes[e] to naught
and reduces the rulers of this world to nothing.[f]
24 No sooner are they planted,
no sooner are they sown,

40:13 [m]Ro 11:34*; 1Co 2:16*
40:14 [n]Job 21:22; Col 2:3
40:16 [o]Ps 50:9-11; Mic 6:7; Heb 10:5-9
40:17 [p]Isa 30:28 [q]Isa 29:7 [r]Da 4:35
40:18 [s]Ex 8:10; 1Sa 2:2; Isa 46:5 [t]Ac 17:29
40:19 [u]Ps 115:4 [v]Isa 41:7; Jer 10:3 [w]Isa 2:20
40:20 [x]1Sa 5:3
40:21 [y]Ps 19:1; 50:6; Ac 14:17 [z]Ro 1:19 [a]Isa 48:13; 51:13
40:22 [b]Nu 13:33; Ps 104:2; Isa 42:5 [c]Job 22:14 [d]Job 36:29
40:23 [e]Isa 34:12 [f]Job 12:21; Ps 107:40

a *13* Or *Spirit*; or *spirit*

touch on a number of subjects, but a central motif, presented from different perspectives, is God's power to restore the nation from captivity. The prophet's announcements were designed to assure the Israelites in exile that they did not need to fear that God would be unable to carry out his pledge to fulfill this covenant promise. These chapters divide into 13 main parts: a disputation over God's power (40:12–31); a courtroom speech against the nations (41:1–7); salvation for Israel (41:8–20); a courtroom speech against idols (41:21–29); salvation for Israel (42:1–17); a disputation over God's blindness and deafness (42:18–25); salvation for Israel (43:1–7); a courtroom speech against nations and idols (43:8–13); salvation for Israel (43:14–21); a disputation over God's righteousness (43:22–28); salvation for Israel (44:1–5); a courtroom speech against nations and idols (44:6–20); and salvation for Israel (44:21–23). After an introductory speech (40:12–31) each prophecy, with one exception (42:10–17), alternates between negative words against those who opposed Isaiah's message and positive announcements reassuring the righteous remnant of Israel's coming salvation from exile.

■ **40:12–31** *Disputation Over God's Power.* Anticipating the responses of some in exile, Isaiah disputed the idea that the Lord lacked the power to conquer the nations and their idols, whom these skeptics thought might resist Israel's return to the land.

40:12–14 Who . . . ? The beginning of a series of rhetorical questions (vv. 12–14,18,21,25–28). See note on 27:7. The interrogative functions as an emphatic expression, as if to say, "No one has . . ." **measured . . . weighed.** God is inscrutable and sovereign over all his creation. **mind . . . counselor?** He is all-wise (i.e., omniscient; cf. Ro 11:34; 1Co 2:16). See *WCF* 7.1; *BC* 1.

40:15 nations . . . islands. The Creator-King is sovereign over all human powers, and they (vv. 6,17) are to be regarded as nothing ("drop . . . fine dust"; 2:22).

40:16 Lebanon. A region known for its cedars. See notes on 2:12–16 and 10:33–34.

40:17 nothing . . . nothing. Rebellious nations are of so little importance that they cannot hinder God's purposes.

40:18–25 See *BC* 1; *HC* 96.

40:18 compare. The Lord is the Incomparable One (cf. v. 25; 46:5), far superior to any idol. See *WLC* 105; *BC* 1.

40:19 silver chains. To keep it from toppling over, since an idol cannot even stand up on its own.

40:21 know . . . understood. A charge of unbelief in God's revelation. See note on 52:6. **beginning . . . founded?** God's glory and power are revealed in nature (Ro 1:20).

40:22 enthroned . . . spreads them out. The Lord is the King over all creation (66:1). **circle.** Probably a reference to the horizon that encircles human experience on Earth. **tent.** An image for the sky stretched above the earth. (42:5; 44:24; 51:13; Pss 18:11; 19:4; 104:2).

40:23–24 princes . . . rulers. Humans and their leaders alike (v. 17; 2:22). **planted . . . whirlwind.** Development of verses 6–7. **chaff.** See notes on 17:12–13 and 29:5.

no sooner do they take root in the ground,
than he blows[g] on them and they wither,
and a whirlwind sweeps them away like chaff.

25 "To whom will you compare me?[h]
Or who is my equal?" says the Holy One.
26 Lift your eyes and look to the heavens:[i]
Who created[j] all these?
He who brings out the starry host[k] one by one,
and calls them each by name.
Because of his great power and mighty strength,
not one of them is missing.[l]

27 Why do you say, O Jacob,
and complain, O Israel,
"My way is hidden from the LORD;
my cause is disregarded by my God"?[m]
28 Do you not know?
Have you not heard?[n]
The LORD is the everlasting[o] God,
the Creator of the ends of the earth.
He will not grow tired or weary,
and his understanding no one can fathom.[p]
29 He gives strength to the weary[q]
and increases the power of the weak.
30 Even youths grow tired and weary,
and young men[r] stumble and fall;
31 but those who hope[s] in the LORD
will renew their strength.[t]
They will soar on wings like eagles;[u]
they will run and not grow weary,
they will walk and not be faint.[v]

The Helper of Israel

41

"Be silent[w] before me, you islands![x]
Let the nations renew their strength!
Let them come forward[y] and speak;
let us meet together[z] at the place of judgment.

2 "Who has stirred[a] up one from the east,[b]
calling him in righteousness to his service[a]?
He hands nations over to him
and subdues kings before him.
He turns them to dust[c] with his sword,
to windblown chaff[d] with his bow.

40:24 [g]Isa 41:16
40:25 [h]ver 18
40:26 [i]Isa 51:6 [j]Ps 89:11-13; Isa 42:5 [k]Ps 147:4 [l]Isa 34:16
40:27 [m]Job 27:2; Lk 18:7-8
40:28 [n]ver 21 [o]Ps 90:2 [p]Ps 147:5; Ro 11:33
40:29 [q]Isa 50:4; Jer 31:25
40:30 [r]Isa 9:17; Jer 6:11; 9:21
40:31 [s]Lk 18:1 [t]2Co 4:16 [u]Ex 19:4; Ps 103:5 [v]2Co 4:1; Heb 12:1-3
41:1 [w]Hab 2:20; Zec 2:13 [x]Isa 11:11 [y]Isa 48:16 [z]Isa 1:18; 34:1; 50:8
41:2 [a]Ezr 1:2 [b]ver 25; Isa 45:1,13 [c]2Sa 22:43 [d]Isa 40:24

[a] 2 Or / *whom victory meets at every step*

40:26 Lift . . . look. Humans are responsible for discerning the revelation of God in creation (Ro 1:18–32). **heavens . . . starry host.** The Babylonians worshiped the gods of the heavens and of the planets. Since the Lord had created the cosmos, the powers are wrongly attributed to the gods. **created.** See note on 4:5. **calls . . . mighty strength.** The Lord upholds and knows his creation intimately; he cannot be overcome. See *BC* 12.
40:27 Jacob . . . Israel. The remnant in exile. See note on 41:8. **hidden . . . disregarded.** In his wrath God had hidden his face from them (49:14; 54:8), but in his favor he would be powerful to deliver them. See note on 8:17.
40:28 know . . . heard? See notes on verse 21 and on 52:6. **everlasting God . . . Creator of the ends of the earth.** The Creator-King is sovereign over time and space (9:6; 40:22). God does "not grow tired or weary," unlike the worthless idols and those who depend on them (44:11–18). See *BC* 1.
40:29 weary . . . weak. All those who no longer find joy in this world and long for the coming of God's kingdom. See *WLC* 172.
40:31 hope. See notes on 8:17 and 26:8–9. **strength.** From the Lord and not from humans (vv. 26,29). **eagles.** Proverbial of vigor (Ex 19:4; Ps 103:5). The verbs "soar," "run" and "walk" express that God would do more than narrowly free his people from their oppressor; he would empower them to new life and joy, accomplishing his promise of a grand restoration for his people through Christ. See *WLC* 172.
■ 41:1–7 *Courtroom Speech Against the Nations.* Isaiah's response to objections about God's ability to restore Israel was in the form of a courtroom speech against the nations.
41:1 silent . . . meet. All nations are called upon to acknowledge the Lord's sovereignty and discern the hand of the Lord in history. **islands . . . nations.** See notes on 24:13 and 14–16, as well as on 40:15. These regions include Lydia in Asia Minor, which was conquered by Cyrus. **their strength!** A contrast between their unassisted strength and the strength mediated by faith (40:31).
41:2 one from the east. Cyrus the Great of Persia (559–530 B.C.). See notes on verse 25 and 44:28—45:1. **righteousness.** Cyrus was victorious in establishing a new order (44:24—45:5,13; 46:11; see note on 1:21). **hands . . . subdues.** It was the Lord's doing. **nations . . . kings.** The nations were under the Lord's authority, and they would play whatever part he assigned them in the redemption of Israel from exile (45:1; 49:7,22–23; 52:15; 60:3,16). **hands nations over.** As a ransom for Israel (see 43:3). **sword . . . bow.** Expressions of military force. **windblown chaff.** See 40:23–24.
41:3 pursues . . . moves. Cyrus's conquests were rapid (cf. 46:11).

3 He pursues them and moves on unscathed,
by a path his feet have not traveled before.
4 Who has done this and carried it through,
calling forth the generations from the beginning?[e]
I, the LORD—with the first of them
and with the last[f]—I am he."
5 The islands[g] have seen it and fear;
the ends of the earth tremble.
They approach and come forward;
6 each helps the other
and says to his brother, "Be strong!"
7 The craftsman encourages the goldsmith,[h]
and he who smooths with the hammer
spurs on him who strikes the anvil.
He says of the welding, "It is good."
He nails down the idol so it will not topple.

8 "But you, O Israel, my servant,
Jacob, whom I have chosen,
you descendants of Abraham[i] my friend,[j]
9 I took you from the ends of the earth,[k]
from its farthest corners I called you.
I said, 'You are my servant';
I have chosen[l] you and have not rejected you.
10 So do not fear, for I am with you;[m]
do not be dismayed, for I am your God.
I will strengthen you and help[n] you;
I will uphold you with my righteous right hand.

11 "All who rage[o] against you
will surely be ashamed and disgraced;[p]
those who oppose[q] you
will be as nothing and perish.[r]
12 Though you search for your enemies,
you will not find them.[s]
Those who wage war against you
will be as nothing[t] at all.
13 For I am the LORD, your God,
who takes hold of your right hand[u]
and says to you, Do not fear;
I will help[v] you.
14 Do not be afraid, O worm Jacob,
O little Israel,

41:4 [e]ver 26; Isa 46:10 [f]Isa 44:6; 48:12; Rev 1:8,17; 22:13
41:5 [g]Eze 26:17-18
41:7 [h]Isa 40:19
41:8 [i]Isa 29:22; 51:2; 63:16 [j]2Ch 20:7; Jas 2:23
41:9 [k]Isa 11:12 [l]Dt 7:6
41:10 [m]Jos 1:9; Isa 43:2,5; Ro 8:31 [n]ver 13-14; Isa 44:2; 49:8
41:11 [o]Isa 17:12 [p]Isa 45:24 [q]Ex 23:22 [r]Isa 29:8
41:12 [s]Ps 37:35-36 [t]Isa 17:14
41:13 [u]Isa 42:6; 45:1 [v]ver 10

41:4 Who . . . ? A rhetorical question. See notes on 27:7 and 40:12. **beginning?** God has ordered human history and creation (see notes on 11:2; 40:21). **I, the LORD . . . I am he.** A most significant formula for divine self-identification (43:10,13; 46:4). "I am he" is a shortened form of "I (am the) LORD" (41:13; 42:8; 43:3,15; 44:24; 45:3,5–6; 48:17; 49:23; 51:15; 60:22; cf. the use of "I am" in Jn 6:35; 8:12,58; 9:5; 10:7,9,11,14; 11:25; 14:6; 15:1,5). The Lord is the God of the patriarchs. As such he has promised to be with his people; he is the God of past, present and future, and he will fulfill his promises (cf. Ex 3:14–15; 6:6–8; Eze 20:5,7; Rev 4:8). **first . . . last.** An assurance that everything is under the Lord's control (v. 27; 44:6; 48:12; cf. Heb 13:8; Rev 1:8,17; 2:8; 21:6; 22:13).

41:5–6 fear . . . helps. Fear led to rebellion in response to the Lord's challenge of verse 1.

41:7 On Isaiah's polemic against idolatry, see 2:8.

■ **41:8–20** *Salvation for Israel.* Isaiah's first assurance of Israel's salvation in this section (40:12—44:23) focuses on the nation's role as God's servant in the world.

41:8 Israel . . . Jacob. Parallel expressions for the godly children of Abraham (v. 14; 40:27; 42:24; 43:1,22,28; 44:1,5,21,23; 45:4; 46:3; 48:1,12; cf. Lk 1:54). **servant.** See notes on 20:3 and 42:1–4. In Isaiah 40–55 the title "servant" is bestowed implicitly on Cyrus (45:1–4), explicitly on God's prophets (44:26), on the nation (here) and on the Messiah (42:1–4). These applications often blend together, although they must at times be kept distinct, as when old Israel proved to be blind and deaf (42:18) and a rebel (46:3,8,12) in need of salvation from the alert and obedient Servant (49:5; 50:4–5; 53:6). **chosen.** See note on 14:1. **Abraham.** See 51:2, 63:16, Hebrews 2:16 and James 2:23.

41:9 servant. See notes on 20:3 and 42:1–4. **chosen.** See note on 14:1.

41:10 do not fear. See note on 35:4. **I am with you.** God promised to be with his people, fight their battles and deliver them (8:8,10; 43:2,5; 45:14; cf. 2Ch 20:17; Ac 18:9–10). **do not be dismayed.** Contrast verses 5–6, and see note on 10:24. **I am your God.** The core covenant promise (41:13–14; 43:1,5; 44:2,8; 51:12; Ge 17:7; 21:17; 26:24; Dt 20:1; 31:6,8; Lev 26:12; Jer 32:38; Eze 37:27; 2Co 6:16). **strengthen . . . uphold.** The Lord would be present in graciously delivering, exalting and vindicating his children (v. 13; 42:1; 44:2; 48:13; 49:8; 50:7; 63:12). See note on 40:31. **righteous right hand.** He would establish order on Earth with power, as he had done at the exodus (63:12; Ex 15:6).

41:11 ashamed. See note on 1:29.

41:13 I am the LORD. See note on 41:4. **right hand.** See note on verse 10. **Do not fear.** See note on 35:4. **help.** See note on 40:10.

41:14 Do not be afraid. Compare verse 13. **worm.** Lowly and despised. **Jacob . . . Israel.** See note on 41:8. **help.** See note on verse

for I myself will help you," declares the LORD,
your Redeemer, the Holy One of Israel.

41:15 [w]Mic 4:13

15 "See, I will make you into a threshing sledge,[w]
new and sharp, with many teeth.
You will thresh the mountains and crush them,
and reduce the hills to chaff.

41:16 [x]Jer 51:2 [y]Isa 45:25

16 You will winnow[x] them, the wind will pick them up,
and a gale will blow them away.
But you will rejoice in the LORD
and glory[y] in the Holy One of Israel.

41:17 [z]Isa 43:20 [a]Isa 30:19

17 "The poor and needy search for water,[z]
but there is none;
their tongues are parched with thirst.
But I the LORD will answer[a] them;
I, the God of Israel, will not forsake them.

41:18 [b]Isa 30:25 [c]Isa 43:19 [d]Isa 35:7

18 I will make rivers flow[b] on barren heights,
and springs within the valleys.
I will turn the desert[c] into pools of water,
and the parched ground into springs.[d]
19 I will put in the desert
the cedar and the acacia, the myrtle and the olive.

41:19 [e]Isa 60:13

I will set pines in the wasteland,
the fir and the cypress together,[e]
20 so that people may see and know,
may consider and understand,

41:20 [f]Job 12:9

that the hand of the LORD has done this,
that the Holy One of Israel has created[f] it.

41:21 [g]Isa 43:15

21 "Present your case," says the LORD.
"Set forth your arguments," says Jacob's King.[g]

41:22 [h]Isa 43:9; 45:21 [i]Isa 46:10

22 "Bring in ⌞your idols⌟ to tell us
what is going to happen.[h]
Tell us what the former things were,
so that we may consider them
and know their final outcome.
Or declare to us the things to come,[i]

41:23 [j]Isa 42:9; 44:7-8; 45:3 [k]Jer 10:5

23 tell us what the future holds,
so we may know[j] that you are gods.
Do something, whether good or bad,[k]
so that we will be dismayed and filled with fear.

41:24 [l]Isa 37:19; 44:9; 1Co 8:4 [m]Ps 115:8

24 But you are less than nothing[l]
and your works are utterly worthless;
he who chooses you is detestable.[m]

41:25 [n]ver 2

25 "I have stirred up one from the north,[n] and he comes—
one from the rising sun who calls on my name.

---

10. **Redeemer.** See note on 35:8–9. The Hebrew term designates the family protector. For a distressed family member this "avenger of blood," among other things, would avenge a murder (see Nu 35:19) and redeem a slave (Lev 25:27–49). **the Holy One of Israel.** See note at 1:4. The Holy God stoops to deliver his own people (43:14–15; 45:11; 47:4; 48:17; 49:7; 54:5; 57:15).
41:15 threshing sledge. An agricultural implement (28:27; Am 1:3; Mic 4:13; Hab 3:12). The weak (v. 14) will become strong. **mountains . . . hills.** Metaphor for the many enemies (vv. 11–12; cf. 42:15). See note at 2:12–16. **chaff.** See note at 40:23–24.
41:17-20 The Lord promises restoration and transformation to the needy and humble.
41:17 poor and needy. The returning exiles and all who seek God's favor. See note at 11:3–5. **water.** A figure for God's salvation. See note at 1:30. **God of Israel.** See note at 37:16.
41:18-19 Images of water (rivers . . . springs) and of abundant vegetation (cedar . . . cypress) picture the transformation of creation and, hence, of the renewal of the Lord's covenant commitment. See note at 12:3. Also see 35:1–2 and 5–7 (cf. 43:18–20; 48:21; 49:9–11; 55:13). Contrast 33:7–9. **water.** See note at 1:30. **desert.** See note at 40:3.
■ **41:21-29** *Courtroom Speech Against Idols.* This second speech against unbelief in Israel in this section (see vv. 1–7) is a courtroom speech that focuses on the idols who represented the supernatural powers behind the Gentile nations (cf. Ps 82). In the ancient world it was commonly held that a conquered nation's patron deity fell subject to that of the nation that had captured it. Isaiah argued that this was not the case with Israel's captivity. On Isaiah's polemics against idolatry, see 2:8.
41:21 case . . . arguments. A renewal of the challenge of verse 1.
41:22–23 to happen . . . final outcome. The Lord alone plans, declares and executes. See note on 11:2. **former things.** Prophecies of past events, especially of God's abandonment of Israel and Judah, such as those recorded in chapters 1–35 (see 42:9; 43:9,18; 46:9; 48:3; 65:7,17). **things to come.** Prophecies of the "future" (v. 23) era of the Lord's favor and the full establishment of his kingdom, such as those given in chapters 40–66 (see 42:23; 44:7; 45:11; 46:10). This era was offered to Israel when the restoration from exile first took place in 539 B.C. It was inaugurated in the work of Christ and will be consummated at his return. **good or bad.** Isaiah taunted the gods to do anything at all, but they were totally impotent.
41:24 nothing . . . detestable. God condemned those who did not depend on him (cf. v. 29; 44:9).
41:25–29 It would soon become evident that the Lord, not the

He treads[o] on rulers as if they were mortar,
as if he were a potter treading the clay.
26 Who told of this from the beginning, so we could know,
or beforehand, so we could say, 'He was right'?
No one told of this,
no one foretold it,
no one heard any words[p] from you.
27 I was the first to tell[q] Zion, 'Look, here they are!'
I gave to Jerusalem a messenger of good tidings.[r]
28 I look but there is no one[s]—
no one among them to give counsel,[t]
no one to give answer when I ask them.
29 See, they are all false!
Their deeds amount to nothing;[u]
their images are but wind[v] and confusion.

The Servant of the Lord

42

"Here is my servant, whom I uphold,
my chosen one[w] in whom I delight;
I will put my Spirit[x] on him
and he will bring justice to the nations.
2 He will not shout or cry out,
or raise his voice in the streets.
3 A bruised reed he will not break,
and a smoldering wick he will not snuff out.
In faithfulness he will bring forth justice;[y]
4 he will not falter or be discouraged
till he establishes justice on earth.
In his law the islands will put their hope."[z]

5 This is what God the Lord says—
he who created the heavens and stretched them out,
who spread out the earth and all that comes out of it,[a]
who gives breath[b] to its people,
and life to those who walk on it:
6 "I, the Lord, have called[c] you in righteousness;[d]
I will take hold of your hand.
I will keep[e] you and will make you

41:25 [o]2Sa 22:43
41:26 [p]Hab 2:18-19
41:27 [q]Isa 48:3,16 [r]Isa 40:9
41:28 [s]Isa 50:2; 59:16; 63:5 [t]Isa 40:13-14
41:29 [u]ver 24 [v]Jer 5:13
42:1 [w]Isa 43:10; Lk 9:35; 1Pe 2:4,6 [x]Isa 11:2; Mt 3:16-17; Jn 3:34
42:3 [y]Ps 72:2
42:4 [z]Ge 49:10; Mt 12:18-21*
42:5 [a]Ps 24:2 [b]Ac 17:25
42:6 [c]Isa 43:1 [d]Jer 23:6
42:6 [e]Isa 26:3

---

idols, is the omnipotent God who carries out his purposes as he pleases.
41:25 stirred up . . . he comes. Cyrus (see v. 2). Cyrus came from Persia in the east. He conquered Media in 549 B.C., making him master of territories to Babylon's north. This king perhaps inadvertently executed the Lord's will (45:4–5; see 2Ch 36:23; Ezr 1:1–4). **potter.** See note on 27:10–11.
41:26 Who . . . ? A rhetorical question (v. 4). See notes on 27:7 and 40:12. **told . . . foretold.** See note on 52:6. **beginning . . . beforehand.** See notes on 11:2, 40:21 and 41:4 and 22.
41:27 first. See note on 41:4. **Zion.** See note on 1:8. **messenger.** Probably Isaiah (see note on 40:1). **good tidings.** See note on 40:9.
41:28 no one . . . no one. The nations and their idols were impotent. **give counsel.** See note on 11:2.
41:29 false . . . wind and confusion. The Lord's negative assessment of idols was that they were worthless (see 40:18–20; 41:7,21–24; 44:9), having no power to keep Israel in captivity.
■ **42:1–17** *Salvation for Israel Through God's Servant.* This is the second time in this section (40:12—44:23) that Isaiah assured Israel of her salvation. Here he celebrated the ideal, royal servant (see 49:1–9; 50:4–11; 52:13—53:12; cf. 61:1–11). This material divides into three parts: the announcement of salvation (vv. 1–9), an intervening song of praise (vv. 10–13) and the completion of the announcement of salvation (vv. 14–17).
42:1–9 The Servant would bring salvation to Israel.
42:1 servant. See note on 20:3. The servant imagery finds its focus in Jesus (Mt 12:18–21). The term applied to faithful Israel (see note on 41:8) before his coming and to the apostles (Ac 26:23) and the church after his advent (1Pe 2:21–22). The first of four servant songs (42:1–4; 49:1–7; 50:4–9; 52:13—53:12). The servant was to be distinguished from unfaithful Israel (vv. 18–22). **uphold.** See note on 41:10. **chosen.** See note on 14:1. **delight.** An expression of love and favor (56:7; 58:5; 60:10; 61:2; 62:4; Mt 3:17; Mk 1:11; Lk 9:35). **my Spirit.** The Spirit of power and wisdom. See notes on 11:2, 61:1 and Luke 3:21–23. **justice . . . nations.** God's universal kingdom of justice and righteousness. See note on 1:21. "Justice" is emphatically repeated three times in verses 1–4, implying that the servant of this passage was seen as a royal figure, one who would bring about justice. See *WCF* 8.1.
42:2 not shout . . . raise. No loud clamor, but the spirit of gentleness and patience. These terms connote "to cry out in the distress." **streets.** See note on 24:11.
42:3 bruised reed. A poignant figure for the poor and needy. **not break.** A negative understatement, equivalent to the positive statement "mend." **smoldering wick.** Another touching figure, this time for people who have nearly lost faith and hope. **faithfulness.** See note on 10:20. **justice.** See note on 1:21.
42:4 justice . . . law. The practice of godliness on Earth. See note on 1:21 (cf. 2:2–4). The Servant would be greater than Moses (see Dt 18:15–18; Ac 3:21–36) because he would mediate a new covenant that would eventually ensure that all believers would keep his law perfectly (see v. 6; Jer 31:31; 2Co 3:3; Heb 8:7–13). This will take place when Jesus returns to complete the restoration of the heavens and the earth (Rev 21:1–5; see theological article "The Kingdom of God" at Mt 4). **hope.** See notes on 8:17 and 26:8–9.
42:5–9 The mission of the servant was to bear God's light of salvation to both Jews and Gentiles.
42:5 God the Lord. The Lord is the God of all creation, including all the nations. **created the heavens . . . earth.** He is Lord by virtue of his having created everything. See note on 4:5. **stretched them out.** See note on 51:13. **breath . . . life.** The Creator and Sustainer of human life (Ps 104:30; Ac 17:24–25) would enable the Servant to transform the earth with new spiritual life.
42:6 called . . . keep. Parallel expressions to those in verse 1.

42:6
[f]Isa 49:8 [g]Lk 2:32; Ac 13:47

42:7
[h]Isa 35:5 [i]Isa 49:9; 61:1 [j]Lk 4:19; 2Ti 2:26; Heb 2:14-15

42:8
[k]Ex 3:15 [l]Isa 48:11

42:10
[m]Ps 33:3; 40:3; 98:1 [n]Isa 49:6 [o]1Ch 16:32; Ps 96:11

42:11
[p]Isa 32:16 [q]Isa 60:7 [r]Isa 52:7; Na 1:15

42:12
[s]Isa 24:15

42:13
[t]Isa 9:6 [u]Isa 26:11 [v]Hos 11:10 [w]Isa 66:14

42:15
[x]Eze 38:20 [y]Isa 50:2; Na 1:4-6

42:16
[z]Lk 1:78-79 [a]Isa 32:3

to be a covenant[f] for the people
and a light for the Gentiles,[g]
7 to open eyes that are blind,[h]
to free[i] captives from prison[j]
and to release from the dungeon those who sit in darkness.

8 "I am the LORD; that is my name![k]
I will not give my glory to another[l]
or my praise to idols.
9 See, the former things have taken place,
and new things I declare;
before they spring into being
I announce them to you."

Song of Praise to the LORD

10 Sing to the LORD a new song,[m]
his praise from the ends of the earth,[n]
you who go down to the sea, and all that is in it,[o]
you islands, and all who live in them.
11 Let the desert[p] and its towns raise their voices;
let the settlements where Kedar[q] lives rejoice.
Let the people of Sela sing for joy;
let them shout from the mountaintops.[r]
12 Let them give glory[s] to the LORD
and proclaim his praise in the islands.
13 The LORD will march out like a mighty[t] man,
like a warrior he will stir up his zeal;[u]
with a shout[v] he will raise the battle cry
and will triumph over his enemies.[w]

14 "For a long time I have kept silent,
I have been quiet and held myself back.
But now, like a woman in childbirth,
I cry out, I gasp and pant.
15 I will lay waste[x] the mountains and hills
and dry up all their vegetation;
I will turn rivers into islands
and dry up[y] the pools.
16 I will lead[z] the blind[a] by ways they have not known,
along unfamiliar paths I will guide them;

righteousness. See note on 1:21. **covenant for the people.** The Servant, Jesus Christ, would effect a new covenant by his vicarious death for the sins of his people (see 53:4–6; Jer 31:34; Heb 8:6–13; 9:15; see chart "Major Covenants in the Bible," on p. 25). With their consciences cleansed by his blood, they would know God (Heb 9:9–14). Moreover, his Spirit would write God's law upon their hearts in a perfect way, far exceeding the manner in which he had written it on believers' hearts in the past (see notes on 59:21; Jer 31:33; 2Co 3:3) and in this way binding Israel to the Lord (49:6–8). The prophets referred to this as a "new covenant" (Jer 31:31), a "covenant of peace" (Isa 54:10), an "everlasting covenant" (55:3) and simply, as here, as a "covenant." **light for the Gentiles.** The recipients of God's light constitute a new community of light bearers in a dark world (9:2; 49:6; 51:4; 60:1–3; Mt 5:14–16; Lk 2:31–32; Ac 26:17–18,23). **light.** The light of the kingdom of God, including his full salvation (49:6). See note on 2:5. See *WCF* 7.3; *WLC* 32.

42:7 to open . . . darkness. This is figurative language drawn from dungeon prisons, which were totally devoid of light. Behind the figure stands the Babylonian exile. Israel's salvation from that exile prefigured her spiritual deliverance through Jesus Christ from the blindness, bondage and darkness of sin. See notes on 5:30; 29:18, 32:3, 35:10 and 51:14.

42:8 I am the LORD. See note on 41:4. **glory.** See note on 4:2. See also 43:11–13 and *WCF* 26.3.

42:9 former things. The judgments on Damascus, Samaria, Nineveh and Judah. See note on 41:22. **new things.** Renewal of the covenant, restoration to the land, the Messianic kingdom, inclusion of the Gentiles and the new heavens and the new earth. See note on 41:22. **declare . . . announce.** God plans, proclaims and executes, and his word will come to pass (40:8). See note on 11:2.

42:10–12 Praise for God's promised victory over the nations interrupts the announcement of what God was going to do.

42:10–11 new song. The redeemed would sing a new (victory) song, as Moses and Miriam had done when they had witnessed God's acts of salvation (Ex 15:1,21; cf. Ps 149:1; Rev 5:9; 14:3). See notes on 12:1–6. **ends of the earth . . . Sela.** Wherever God's children could be found (11:12). **Kedar.** See note on 21:16–17 (see 60:7; Ps 120:5; Jer 2:10; 49:28–29). **Sela.** See 16:1.

42:12 glory. The Lord receives acclaim from his subjects (v. 8; 1Pe 2:9). See notes on 4:2 and 24:14–16.

42:13 mighty man . . . warrior. See Exodus 15:3. This is imagery of the Lord as the divine warrior in whom lies hope (see notes on 1:9; 5:26; 9:6; 13:4; 40:11). **shout.** The Hebrew word rendered "shout" is different from the one translated the same way in verse 2. The verb used here connotes a shout of joy, not of distress. **zeal.** See note on 9:7. Assurance that the Lord would accomplish his plan.

42:14–17 The return to the first person ("I") indicates the connection with verses 1–9. The Lord now completed his promise to act in the future.

42:14 kept silent . . . quiet. The progress of God's kingdom may be slow, but the Lord will bring it in its fullness (cf. 63:15; 64:12). **But now.** Introduces a new act of God of restoration from exile (43:1,19; 44:1; 48:6–7,16; 49:5,19). **woman in childbirth.** Imagery of a pregnant woman who is about to deliver and is anxious to bring forth a new baby.

42:15 lay waste . . . dry up. Images of judgment on the day of the Lord that are reminiscent of the exodus and of Israel's crossing through the Red Sea and the Jordan River (Ex 14:16–29; Jos 3:14–17; Ps 66:6). See notes on 24:4, 24:7–9, 30:25 and 34:3.

42:16 lead . . . not forsake. During the judgment the Lord would

I will turn the darkness into light before them
and make the rough places smooth.[b]
These are the things I will do;
I will not forsake[c] them.
17 But those who trust in idols,
who say to images, 'You are our gods,'
will be turned back in utter shame.[d]

Israel Blind and Deaf

18 "Hear, you deaf;[e]
look, you blind, and see!
19 Who is blind[f] but my servant,[g]
and deaf like the messenger[h] I send?
Who is blind like the one committed[i] to me,
blind like the servant of the LORD?
20 You have seen many things, but have paid no attention;
your ears are open, but you hear nothing."[j]
21 It pleased the LORD
for the sake of his righteousness
to make his law[k] great and glorious.
22 But this is a people plundered and looted,
all of them trapped in pits[l]
or hidden away in prisons.[m]
They have become plunder,
with no one to rescue them;
they have been made loot,
with no one to say, "Send them back."

23 Which of you will listen to this
or pay close attention[n] in time to come?
24 Who handed Jacob over to become loot,
and Israel to the plunderers?
Was it not the LORD,
against whom we have sinned?
For they would not follow[o] his ways;
they did not obey his law.
25 So he poured out on them his burning anger,
the violence of war.
It enveloped them in flames,[p] yet they did not understand;
it consumed them, but they did not take it to heart.[q]

Israel's Only Savior

43

But now, this is what the LORD says—
he who created you, O Jacob,
he who formed[r] you, O Israel:[s]
"Fear not, for I have redeemed[t] you;
I have summoned you by name;[u] you are mine.

42:16 [b]Lk 3:5 [c]Heb 13:5
42:17 [d]Ps 97:7; Isa 1:29; 44:11; 45:16
42:18 [e]Isa 35:5
42:19 [f]Isa 43:8; Eze 12:2 [g]Isa 41:8-9 [h]Isa 44:26 [i]Isa 26:3
42:20 [j]Jer 6:10
42:21 [k]ver 4
42:22 [l]Isa 24:18 [m]Isa 24:22
42:23 [n]Isa 48:18
42:24 [o]Isa 30:15
42:25 [p]2Ki 25:9 [q]Isa 29:13; 47:7; 57:1,11; Hos 7:9
43:1 [r]ver 7 [s]Ge 32:28; Isa 44:21 [t]Isa 44:2,6 [u]Isa 42:6; 45:3-4

---

be with his people and lead them as he had led Israel in the wilderness (Ex 13:21–22). See note on 35:8–9. **blind.** See notes on 29:18 and 35:5–7. **darkness into light.** An echo of the exodus from Egypt (see Ex 13:21,22). See note on 2:5.
42:17 trust. See note on 12:2. **shame.** See note on 30:3. On Isaiah's polemic against idolatry, see 2:8.
■ **42:18–25** *Disputation Over God's Sight and Hearing.* This passage reflects an imaginary dispute between the prophet and the skeptics in Israel. It is Isaiah's third response to disbelief in this section (40:12—44:23). The implicit accusation of the doubters was that God was blind and deaf to his people's condition in exile. Isaiah's response was that the Israelites, not God, were blind and deaf to the degree to which they deserved the judgment of exile.
42:18–19 deaf. Because they refused to listen (v. 23). **blind.** Because they declined to see the hand of God in their history (see v. 20; 48:3–6). This is repeated three times for emphasis. See note on 29:18. **Who . . . ?** A rhetorical question in response to an implicit accusation that God was blind and deaf (vv. 23–24; 43:9). See note on 27:7 and 40:12. **servant.** Here refers to the people taken into exile. See notes on 20:3, 41:8 and 42:1–4. **messenger.** For the mission, see 40:1–4 and 6–7.
42:21 righteousness. See note on 1:21. **law great and glorious.** To extend his kingdom on Earth (see note on v. 4).
42:22 plundered and looted . . . in prisons. Because they had rebelled against the Lord (v. 24). **prisons.** See note on 42:7, and see 51:14.
42:24 Jacob . . . Israel. See note on 41:8.
42:25 anger. See note on 10:5. **war.** The Divine Warrior came against his own people through the Assyrian and Babylonian devastations of Samaria. **did not take it to heart.** Despite the severity of God's judgment, the accusation to which Isaiah referred (see v. 19) indicates that Israel had not learned repentance and humility before God. See *WLC* 105.
■ **43:1–7** *Salvation for Israel.* Despite his harsh words against unbelief in Israel, Isaiah assured his readers for the third time in this section (40:12—44:23) that the Lord was committed to his promise of establishing a new community in the land of promise.
43:1 this is what the LORD says. An emphatic statement of the

2 When you pass through the waters,[v]
I will be with you;[w]
and when you pass through the rivers,
they will not sweep over you.
When you walk through the fire,[x]
you will not be burned;
the flames will not set you ablaze.[y]
3 For I am the LORD, your God,[z]
the Holy One of Israel, your Savior;
I give Egypt for your ransom,
Cush[a][a] and Seba in your stead.[b]
4 Since you are precious and honored in my sight,
and because I love[c] you,
I will give men in exchange for you,
and people in exchange for your life.
5 Do not be afraid,[d] for I am with you;[e]
I will bring your children[f] from the east
and gather you from the west.
6 I will say to the north, 'Give them up!'
and to the south,[g] 'Do not hold them back.'
Bring my sons from afar
and my daughters[h] from the ends of the earth—
7 everyone who is called by my name,[i]
whom I created for my glory,
whom I formed and made.[j]"

8 Lead out those who have eyes but are blind,[k]
who have ears but are deaf.[l]
9 All the nations gather together[m]
and the peoples assemble.
Which of them foretold[n] this
and proclaimed to us the former things?
Let them bring in their witnesses to prove they were right,
so that others may hear and say, "It is true."
10 "You are my witnesses," declares the LORD,
"and my servant[o] whom I have chosen,
so that you may know and believe me
and understand that I am he.
Before me no god[p] was formed,
nor will there be one after me.
11 I, even I, am the LORD,
and apart from me there is no savior.[q]
12 I have revealed and saved and proclaimed—

43:2 [v]Isa 8:7 [w]Dt 31:6,8 [x]Isa 29:6; 30:27 [y]Ps 66:12; Da 3:25-27
43:3 [z]Ex 20:2 [a]Isa 20:3 [b]Pr 21:18
43:4 [c]Isa 63:9
43:5 [d]Isa 44:2 [e]Jer 30:10-11 [f]Isa 41:8
43:6 [g]Ps 107:3 [h]2Co 6:18
43:7 [i]Isa 56:5; 63:19; Jas 2:7 [j]ver 1,21; Ps 100:3;; Eph 2:10
43:8 [k]Isa 6:9-10 [l]Isa 42:20; Eze 12:2
43:9 [m]Isa 41:1 [n]Isa 41:26
43:10 [o]Isa 41:8-9 [p]Isa 44:6,8
43:11 [q]Isa 45:21

a *3* That is, the upper Nile region

divine origin of the promise (vv. 14,16; 44:2,6,24; 45:1,11,14,18; 48:17; 49:7–8; 49:25; 50:1; 52:3; 56:1; 56:4; 65:8; 66:1,12). **created.** See note on 4:5. **Jacob . . . Israel.** See note on 41:8. **formed.** See note on 27:10–11. **Fear not.** See notes on 10:24 and 41:10. **redeemed.** See note on 35:8–9. **summoned you by name.** The Lord had called them to be his people and knew them each by name (45:3–5; 48:1,19; 49:1; 56:5; 62:2,4; 65:15; 66:22; Ex 33:12,17). **mine.** The people of God (Ex 19:5–6).
43:2 waters . . . flames. Metaphors for affliction (Ps 66:6,12). **I will be with you.** Confirmation of God's presence signified that he would fight for them and protect them. See note on 41:10. **fire.** See note on 4:5, and compare Daniel 3:25–27.
43:3–5 See *WCF* 5.7.
43:3 I am the LORD. See note on 41:4. **the Holy One of Israel.** See note on 1:4. **Savior.** Or Redeemer. See note on 35:8–9. **Egypt . . . Seba.** Territories conquered by the Persians (see 18:1–7; 19:1—20:6).
43:4 precious and honored. God's people are exalted by election (45:4; 49:5; 54:12; Ex 19:5; Dt 7:6–8). **I love you.** See 54:10, 63:9 and Exodus 19:4.
43:5–6 afraid . . . I am with you. See verses 1 and 3, as well as notes on 10:24 and 35:4. **east . . . west . . . north . . . south.** Wherever the children of God may be found, including those in the time of the exile. **the ends of the earth.** See note on 24:14–16.
43:7 name. See verse 1. **created.** See note on 4:5. **glory.** See note on 4:2. **formed.** See note on 27:10–11.
■ **43:8–13** *Courtroom Speech Against Nations and Their Idols.* In a fourth address against unbelief in this section (40:12—44:23), the prophet called for the spiritually blind and deaf Israelites to observe his courtroom speech against the nations and their idols and to learn the error of their ways.
43:8 blind . . . deaf. Those in Israel who persisted in disbelief. See notes on 29:18 and 42:18–19.
43:9 gather . . . assemble. Courtroom language depicting the scene of the Lord speaking against the nations in his heavenly court, which Israel was to witness. **Which . . . ?** The Lord demonstrated to Israel his superiority over the other nations and their gods (v. 8; see also 42:19,23–24). **former things?** See notes on 41:22 and 42:9.
43:10 witnesses . . . servant. The Lord ushered his special people into the courtroom so that they could be made aware of the truth and trust him to deliver them from exile. See notes on 20:3, 41:8 and 42:1–4. **I am he.** See note on 41:4. See *WLC* 104.
43:11–12 revealed . . . proclaimed. The Lord's claim to deity lies in his power to decree, to reveal and to act (41:4,22,26; 42:9). See note on 11:2. **witnesses.** See verse 10. See *HC* 29.

I, and not some foreign god[r] among you.
You are my witnesses,[s]" declares the LORD, "that I am God.
13 Yes, and from ancient days[t] I am he.
No one can deliver out of my hand.
When I act, who can reverse it?"[u]

God's Mercy and Israel's Unfaithfulness

14 This is what the LORD says—
your Redeemer, the Holy One of Israel:
"For your sake I will send to Babylon
and bring down as fugitives[v] all the Babylonians,[a][w]
in the ships in which they took pride.
15 I am the LORD, your Holy One,
Israel's Creator, your King."

16 This is what the LORD says—
he who made a way through the sea,
a path through the mighty waters,[x]
17 who drew out[y] the chariots and horses,
the army and reinforcements together,[z]
and they lay there, never to rise again,
extinguished, snuffed out like a wick:
18 "Forget the former things;
do not dwell on the past.
19 See, I am doing a new thing![a]
Now it springs up; do you not perceive it?
I am making a way in the desert[b]
and streams in the wasteland.
20 The wild animals honor me,
the jackals[c] and the owls,
because I provide water[d] in the desert
and streams in the wasteland,
to give drink to my people, my chosen,
21 the people I formed for myself
that they may proclaim my praise.[e]

22 "Yet you have not called upon me, O Jacob,
you have not wearied yourselves for me, O Israel.[f]
23 You have not brought me sheep for burnt offerings,
nor honored[g] me with your sacrifices.[h]
I have not burdened you with grain offerings
nor wearied you with demands[i] for incense.[j]

43:12 [r]Dt 32:12; Ps 81:9 [s]Isa 44:8
43:13 [t]Ps 90:2 [u]Job 9:12; Isa 14:27
43:14 [v]Isa 13:14-15 [w]Isa 23:13
43:16 [x]Ps 77:19; Isa 11:15; 51:10
43:17 [y]Ps 118:12; Isa 1:31 [z]Ex 14:9
43:19 [a]2Co 5:17; Rev 21:5 [b]Ex 17:6; Nu 20:11
43:20 [c]Isa 13:22 [d]Isa 48:21
43:21 [e]Ps 102:18; 1Pe 2:9
43:22 [f]Isa 30:11
43:23 [g]Zec 7:5-6; Mal 1:6-8 [h]Am 5:25 [i]Jer 7:22 [j]Ex 30:35; Lev 2:1

a *14* Or *Chaldeans*

43:13 ancient days. The Lord alone had from of old willed the redemption of his people (40:21; 41:4,26). **I am he.** See notes on 41:4. **deliver out of my hand.** See Deuteronomy 32:39. **reverse.** The Lord's decrees stand (40:6; cf. Am 1:3,6,9,11,13).
■ **43:14–21** *Salvation for Israel.* For the fourth time in this section (40:12—44:23) Isaiah assured Israel of salvation from exile by explaining that God was about to do something even greater than he had done in the exodus under Moses.
43:14 This is what the LORD says. See note on 43:1. **Redeemer.** See note on 35:8–9 and 41:14. **the Holy One of Israel.** See note on 1:4. **bring down . . . Babylonians . . . ships . . . pride.** Interpretations vary greatly because of questions about the Hebrew text and its translation. The sense seems to be that the Lord would liberate his people from their oppressors. See *WCF* 5.7.
43:15 I am the LORD. See note on 41:4. **Creator.** See note on 4:5. **King.** See note on 52:7.
43:16–17 sea . . . mighty waters. A reference to the crossing of the Red Sea (Ex 14–15). See notes on 10:26, 17:12–13 and 19:5–6. **chariots . . . horses . . . army . . . reinforcements.** The greatest opposition had been put down by the Lord (cf. 31:1).
43:18–19 former . . . past. See notes on 41:22 and 42:9. **I.** Literally, "here am I." See note on 52:6. **new thing!** The exodus was of less importance and was less spectacular than the new era of redemption would be. Even Moses predicted that the restoration after exile would entail greater blessings than those ever before received (Dt 30:5). See notes on 42:9 and 10–11. **Now.** See note on 42:14. **way.** See note on 11:16. **desert . . . wasteland.** See note on 40:3. **streams.** See note on 41:18–19.
43:20–21 wild animals . . . owls. Creatures associated with desolation (34:11–15). See note on 13:20–22. The imagery of water goes back to God's provision in the wilderness (Ex 15:22–26). See note on 1:30. **my people.** See note on 40:1. **chosen.** See note on 14:1. **formed.** See note on 27:10–11. Nature would declare the Lord's praise along with the redeemed, who would constitute a new community of "praise" (42:12). See notes on 12:1, 4, 5 and 6.
■ **43:22–28** *Disputation Over God's Requirements.* For the fifth time in this section (40:12—44:23) Isaiah disputed objections from skeptics that God would fail to keep his word by pointing out that Israel had not met God's requirements for restoration.
43:22–24 not called . . . not wearied. Instead of presenting offerings and sacrifices out of devotion to the Lord, the people were hardened in their sins. **me.** The Lord was not accusing them of failing to worship at all but of failing to worship him. **Jacob . . . Israel.** See note on 41:8. The people "wearied" (v. 22) God (1:12–14) by their multiplicity of offerings that he had not required (cf. Am 5:22–26; Mic 6:1–8). **calamus.** A fragrance used in anointing oil (see "fragrant cinnamon" at Ex 30:23; cf. Jer 6:20). **sins . . . offenses.** See note on 1:4. See *WLC* 105; *BC* 26.

43:24 [k]Ex 30:23 [l]Isa 1:14; 7:13 [m]Mal 2:17

43:25 [n]Ac 3:19 [o]Isa 37:35; Eze 36:22 [p]Isa 38:17; Jer 31:34

43:26 [q]Isa 1:18 [r]Isa 41:1; 50:8

43:27 [s]Isa 9:15; 28:7; Jer 5:31

43:28 [t]Jer 24:9; Eze 5:15

44:1 [u]ver 21; Jer 30:10; 46:27-28

44:2 [v]Isa 41:10 [w]Dt 32:15

44:3 [x]Joel 3:18 [y]Joel 2:28; Ac 2:17 [z]Isa 61:9; 65:23

44:4 [a]Lev 23:40 [b]Job 40:22

44:5 [c]Ex 13:9 [d]Zec 8:20-22

44:6 [e]Isa 41:21 [f]Isa 43:1

24 You have not bought any fragrant calamus[k] for me,
or lavished on me the fat of your sacrifices.
But you have burdened me with your sins
and wearied[l] me with your offenses.[m]

25 "I, even I, am he who blots out
your transgressions,[n] for my own sake,[o]
and remembers your sins no more.[p]
26 Review the past for me,
let us argue the matter together;[q]
state the case[r] for your innocence.
27 Your first father sinned;
your spokesmen[s] rebelled against me.
28 So I will disgrace the dignitaries of your temple,
and I will consign Jacob to destruction[a]
and Israel to scorn.[t]

Israel the Chosen

44 "But now listen, O Jacob, my servant,[u]
Israel, whom I have chosen.
2 This is what the LORD says—
he who made you, who formed you in the womb,
and who will help[v] you:
Do not be afraid, O Jacob, my servant,
Jeshurun,[w] whom I have chosen.
3 For I will pour water[x] on the thirsty land,
and streams on the dry ground;
I will pour out my Spirit[y] on your offspring,
and my blessing on your descendants.[z]
4 They will spring up like grass in a meadow,
like poplar trees[a] by flowing streams.[b]
5 One will say, 'I belong to the LORD';
another will call himself by the name of Jacob;
still another will write on his hand,[c] 'The LORD's,'[d]
and will take the name Israel.

The LORD, Not Idols

6 "This is what the LORD says—
Israel's King[e] and Redeemer,[f] the LORD Almighty:

[a] *28* The Hebrew term refers to the irrevocable giving over of things or persons to the LORD, often by totally destroying them.

43:25 blots . . . remembers. The Lord is the God who forgives sin, as Israel had experienced after the incident with the golden calf (Ex 34:6; cf. Lk 5:21). **for my own sake.** The Lord would forgive graciously in order to establish his word (37:35; 42:21; 48:9,11; cf. 37:35).
43:26 past . . . case. God openly challenged the people to dispute his claims. Israel stood condemned, unable to refute God's charge.
43:27 first father. Jacob, the father of the 12 tribes (Hos 12:3). **sinned . . . rebelled.** See notes on 1:4 and 5–9. **spokesmen.** The religious leadership; that is, the prophets and priests.
43:28 dignitaries . . . scorn. Judah suffered disgrace by the destruction of her temple and the exile of her people (44:26; 63:18; cf. 2Ki 25:18–21). **Jacob . . . Israel.** See note on 41:8.
■ **44:1–5** *Salvation for Israel.* For the fifth time in this section (40:12—44:23) Isaiah assured the nation of salvation from exile.
44:1–3 See *HC* 73.
44:1 But now. See note on 42:14. **Jacob . . . Israel.** See note on 41:8. **servant.** Here the servant was Judah, who had been chosen for a special service to God. See notes on 20:3, 41:8 and 42:1–4. **chosen.** See note on 14:1.
44:2 This is what the LORD says. See note on 43:1. **formed.** See note on 27:10–11. **in the womb.** God likened himself to a mother who has conceived and will bring forth a child (v. 24; see notes on 42:14; 66:9). **help.** See note on 40:10. **Do not be afraid.** See notes on 10:24 and 35:4. **servant.** The nation of Judah (see v. 1). See notes on 20:3, 41:8 and 42:1–4. **Jeshurun.** A poetic name for Israel (Dt 32:15). **chosen.** See note on 14:1.
44:3 water . . . thirsty land . . . streams . . . dry ground. Imagery of restoration from exile because God's people will receive many blessings in nature (43:19–21). **pour . . . Spirit . . . offspring.** Development of the promises in 28:6 and 32:15. The Spirit of God is the power by which God brings his will to pass. He would work mightily in the future blessing of nature as he had done in the primeval ordering of nature (cf. Ge 1:3). The New Testament sees the fulfillment of this promise in Jesus' miraculous work through the power of the Spirit, the Spirit's renewal in the church today (Joel 2:28; Ac 2:38–39) and the coming glorious new heavens and new earth. **blessing.** The Spirit also confirms God's promises. For the combination of water and the Spirit, see Mark 1:8–10. See *CD* 3–4. VI.
44:5 One . . . still another. Many would participate in the new age of restoration, as Gentiles and Jews together would confess the name of the Lord (cf. Ps 87:6). **Jacob . . . Israel.** See note on 41:8. **take the name Israel.** Contrast 41:14. This prophecy is fulfilled in part by the identification of Gentiles and Jews in the Christian church as "the Israel of God" (Gal 6:16).
■ **44:6–20** *Courtroom Speech Against Nations and Idols.* For the sixth time in this section (40:12—44:23) Isaiah attacked disbelief in Israel. Once again, he did this by revealing God's speech in the heavenly court against Gentile nations and their idols.
44:6 This is what the LORD says. See note on 43:1. **King.** See note on 52:7. **Redeemer.** See note on 35:8–9. **LORD Almighty.** See note on 1:9. **first . . . last.** See note on 41:4. **no God.** See note on 37:16. See *WLC* 101.

I am the first and I am the last;[g]
apart from me there is no God.
7 Who then is like me? Let him proclaim it.
Let him declare and lay out before me
what has happened since I established my ancient people,
and what is yet to come—
yes, let him foretell[h] what will come.
8 Do not tremble, do not be afraid.
Did I not proclaim this and foretell it long ago?
You are my witnesses. Is there any God[i] besides me?
No, there is no other Rock;[j] I know not one."

9 All who make idols are nothing,
and the things they treasure are worthless.[k]
Those who would speak up for them are blind;
they are ignorant, to their own shame.
10 Who shapes a god and casts an idol,
which can profit him nothing?[l]
11 He and his kind will be put to shame;[m]
craftsmen are nothing but men.
Let them all come together and take their stand;
they will be brought down to terror and infamy.[n]

12 The blacksmith[o] takes a tool
and works with it in the coals;
he shapes an idol with hammers,
he forges it with the might of his arm.[p]
He gets hungry and loses his strength;
he drinks no water and grows faint.
13 The carpenter[q] measures with a line
and makes an outline with a marker;
he roughs it out with chisels
and marks it with compasses.
He shapes it in the form of man,[r]
of man in all his glory,
that it may dwell in a shrine.[s]
14 He cut down cedars,
or perhaps took a cypress or oak.
He let it grow among the trees of the forest,
or planted a pine, and the rain made it grow.
15 It is man's fuel[t] for burning;
some of it he takes and warms himself,
he kindles a fire and bakes bread.
But he also fashions a god and worships it;
he makes an idol and bows[u] down to it.
16 Half of the wood he burns in the fire;
over it he prepares his meal,
he roasts his meat and eats his fill.
He also warms himself and says,
"Ah! I am warm; I see the fire."
17 From the rest he makes a god, his idol;
he bows down to it and worships.
He prays[v] to it and says,

44:6 [g]Isa 41:4; Rev 1:8, 17; 22:13
44:7 [h]Isa 41:22, 26
44:8 [i]Isa 43:10 [j]Dt 4:35; 1Sa 2:2
44:9 [k]Isa 41:24
44:10 [l]Isa 41:29; Jer 10:5; Ac 19:26
44:11 [m]Isa 1:29 [n]Isa 42:17
44:12 [o]Isa 40:19; 41:6-7 [p]Jer 10:3-5; Ac 17:29
44:13 [q]Isa 41:7 [r]Ps 115:4-7 [s]Jdg 17:4-5
44:15 [t]ver 19 [u]2Ch 25:14
44:17 [v]1Ki 18:26

44:7 These rhetorical questions demonstrate that the Lord is sovereign over the past, present and future. See notes on 11:2, 27:7 and 40:12. **like me?** See note on 40:18.
44:8 do not be afraid. See note on 35:4. **proclaim . . . foretell.** See note on 11:2; also see 40:1—55:13 and 41:21–28. **witnesses.** See note on 43:10. **God besides me?** See note on 37:16. **Rock.** See note on 8:14–15; also see Deuteronomy 32:4, 15 and 31.
44:9 nothing . . . worthless. See notes on 41:24 and 29. **speak up for them.** That is, witness on their behalf, in contrast to the witnesses for the Lord (v. 8). **shame.** See note on 1:29.
44:11 shame. See note on 1:29. **come together . . . stand.** In a court of law. See 41:21.
44:12 takes . . . forges. Although an idol may be a work of art, the finest craftsman is but a human who gets tired ("hungry . . . grows faint"). In contrast, see 40:28.
44:13 measures . . . in the form of man. Similarly, the carpenter only imitates the image of God in humans as he forms and shapes an idol (cf. Dt 4:16; Ro 1:23). **glory.** See note on 4:2.
44:14–17 burning . . . fashions. Many woods ("cedars . . . pine" [v. 14]) are used for different purposes by the idol maker ("warms himself . . . prepares his meal . . . makes a god" [vv. 15–17]), including worship of the wooden idol ("prays to it" [v. 17]). The prophet employed irony in an argument that led to the absurd. Only the Lord is God, as only he can hear and save.

44:17 [w]Isa 45:20

"Save[w] me; you are my god."

44:18 [x]Isa 1:3 [y]Isa 6:9-10

18 They know nothing, they understand[x] nothing;
their eyes[y] are plastered over so they cannot see,
and their minds closed so they cannot understand.

44:19 [z]Isa 5:13; 27:11; 45:20 [a]Dt 27:15

19 No one stops to think,
no one has the knowledge or understanding[z] to say,
"Half of it I used for fuel;
I even baked bread over its coals,
I roasted meat and I ate.
Shall I make a detestable[a] thing from what is left?
Shall I bow down to a block of wood?"

44:20 [b]Ps 102:9 [c]Job 15:31; Ro 1:21-23,28; 2Th 2:11; 2Ti 3:13 [d]Isa 59:3,4,13; Ro 1:25

20 He feeds on ashes,[b] a deluded[c] heart misleads him;
he cannot save himself, or say,
"Is not this thing in my right hand a lie?[d]"

44:21 [e]Isa 46:8; Zec 10:9 [f]ver 1-2 [g]Isa 49:15

21 "Remember[e] these things, O Jacob,
for you are my servant, O Israel.
I have made you, you are my servant;[f]
O Israel, I will not forget you.[g]

44:22 [h]Isa 43:25; Ac 3:19 [i]Isa 55:7 [j]1Co 6:20

22 I have swept away[h] your offenses like a cloud,
your sins like the morning mist.
Return[i] to me,
for I have redeemed[j] you."

44:23 [k]Isa 42:10 [l]Ps 148:7 [m]Ps 98:8 [n]Isa 61:3

23 Sing for joy,[k] O heavens, for the LORD has done this;
shout aloud, O earth[l] beneath.
Burst into song, you mountains,[m]
you forests and all your trees,
for the LORD has redeemed Jacob,
he displays his glory[n] in Israel.

Jerusalem to Be Inhabited

44:24 [o]Isa 43:14 [p]Isa 42:5

24 "This is what the LORD says—
your Redeemer,[o] who formed you in the womb:

I am the LORD,
who has made all things,
who alone stretched out the heavens,[p]
who spread out the earth by myself,

44:25 [q]Ps 33:10 [r]Isa 47:13 [s]1Co 1:27 [t]2Sa 15:31; 1Co 1:19-20

25 who foils[q] the signs of false prophets
and makes fools of diviners,[r]
who overthrows the learning of the wise[s]
and turns it into nonsense,[t]

44:18–19 know nothing . . . understand nothing. That is, they are utterly foolish (cf. 6:9–10). **detestable thing . . . block of wood?** Negative expressions for the practice of idolatry (cf. Ac 17:29).

44:20 feeds on ashes. An idol can be burned to ashes, as will the hopes of all who depend on it. **deluded heart.** A foolish and stubborn way of life leads to destruction (Pr 7:22–23). **lie?** The climactic conclusion: An idol is nothing but a deception.

▪ **44:21–23** *Salvation for Israel.* For the sixth and final time in this section (40:12—44:23) Isaiah assured Israel of salvation from exile.

44:21 Jacob . . . Israel. See note on 41:8. **servant.** See notes on 20:3, 41:8 and 42:1–4. **made.** See note on 27:10–11.

44:22 swept away. An expression for forgiveness. See note on 43:25. **cloud . . . morning mist.** These are momentary in comparison with the Lord's forgiveness. **Return.** A call to repentance (see Jer 31:28). **redeemed.** The Lord alone is the Redeemer, since idols cannot save. See notes on 35:8–9 and 41:14.

44:23 Sing . . . Burst. In this magnificent conclusion to this section (43:14—44:23; cf. Rev 8:20), Isaiah called for all of creation to delight in God's redemption of Israel from exile. A similar theme appears in Romans 8:22, where Paul stated that all of creation waits for the redemption of the children of God at Christ's return. See notes on 12:1–6 and 14:7. **heavens . . . trees.** All of creation. See notes on 1:2 and 42:5. **redeemed.** See note on 35:8–9. **Jacob . . . Israel.** See note on 41:8. **glory.** He would glorify the redeemed, who in turn would lead many to praise the Lord for his mighty acts (49:3; 55:5; 60:21; 61:3). See note on 4:2.

▪ **44:24—55:13** *God's Instruments of His Sure Salvation.* Many motifs appear in these chapters, but they cluster around the revelation of God's instruments for bringing deliverance from exile. The prophet first elaborated on God's instrument Cyrus (44:24—48:22) and then focused on the royal servant to come (49:1—55:13).

▪ **44:24—48:22** *God's Plan for Cyrus.* Cyrus, the emperor of Persia, is mentioned both by name and by implication throughout this passage. Cyrus has already been mentioned in 41:1 and following. He would be God's shepherd for his people (44:28), God's anointed one (45:1), the one whom God raised up (45:13), a bird of prey from the east to do God's purpose (46:11) and God's chosen ally against Babylon (48:14). Beyond these explicit statements, the topic of God's choice of Cyrus is implicit throughout these chapters.

▪ **44:24–28** *The Lord's Hymn of Self-Glorification.* This section (44:24—55:13) begins with a surprising revelation: God would set his people free from Babylon through the Persian king Cyrus.

44:24 This is what the LORD says. See note on 43:1. **Redeemer.** See notes on 35:8–9 and 41:14. **formed.** See note on 27:10–11. **womb.** See note on v. 2. **I am the LORD.** The Creator-Redeemer-King. See note on 41:4. **stretched out . . . heavens . . . earth.** See note on v. 5. See *HC* 26. **by myself.** See note on 40:19.

44:25 false prophets. Literally, "braggers" (see Jer 50:36). **diviners.** People who sought to discover information by magical or idolatrous means (see notes on 2:6,8; 8:19). **overthrows . . . nonsense.** History reveals how the Lord overturns human cultures, powers and learning (cf. 17:1–14; 29:14; 47:10–15; cf. 1Co 1:20). See notes on 11:2 and 29:13–14. **wise.** Those who were wise in their own eyes but who were sought out by God for judgment (Pr 3:5; 26:5).

26 who carries out the words[u] of his servants
and fulfills[v] the predictions of his messengers,
who says of Jerusalem, 'It shall be inhabited,'
of the towns of Judah, 'They shall be built,'
and of their ruins, 'I will restore them,'[w]
27 who says to the watery deep, 'Be dry,
and I will dry up your streams,'
28 who says of Cyrus,[x] 'He is my shepherd
and will accomplish all that I please;
he will say of Jerusalem,[y] "Let it be rebuilt,"
and of the temple,[z] "Let its foundations be laid." '

45

"This is what the LORD says to his anointed,
to Cyrus, whose right hand I take hold[a] of
to subdue nations[b] before him
and to strip kings of their armor,
to open doors before him
so that gates will not be shut:
2 I will go before you
and will level[c] the mountains[a];
I will break down gates of bronze
and cut through bars of iron.[d]
3 I will give you the treasures[e] of darkness,
riches stored in secret places,[f]
so that you may know[g] that I am the LORD,
the God of Israel, who summons you by name.[h]
4 For the sake of Jacob my servant,[i]
of Israel my chosen,
I summon you by name
and bestow on you a title of honor,
though you do not acknowledge[j] me.
5 I am the LORD, and there is no other;[k]
apart from me there is no God.[l]
I will strengthen you,[m]
though you have not acknowledged me,
6 so that from the rising of the sun
to the place of its setting[n]
men may know there is none besides me.[o]
I am the LORD, and there is no other.

44:26 [u]Zec 1:6 [v]Isa 55:11; Mt 5:18 [w]Isa 49:8-21
44:28 [x]2Ch 36:22 [y]Isa 14:32 [z]Ezr 1:2-4
45:1 [a]Ps 73:23; Isa 41:13; 42:6 [b]Jer 50:35
45:2 [c]Isa 40:4 [d]Ps 107:16; Jer 51:30
45:3 [e]Jer 50:37 [f]Jer 41:8 [g]Isa 41:23 [h]Ex 33:12; Isa 43:1
45:4 [i]Isa 41:8,9 [j]Ac 17:23
45:5 [k]Isa 44:8 [l]Ps 18:31 [m]Ps 18:39
45:6 [n]Isa 43:5; Mal 1:11 [o]ver 5,18

[a] *2* Dead Sea Scrolls and Septuagint; the meaning of the word in the Masoretic Text is uncertain.

44:26 words . . . predictions. The revelation of his plan. See notes on 11:2 and 40:1. **servants.** See notes on 20:3, 41:8 and 42:1–4. **Jerusalem . . . ruins.** The regions devastated by Babylon. **built . . . restore.** The restoration from Babylon was the beginning of a new era in the history of redemption.
44:27 watery deep . . . streams. Redemption is couched in the language of Israel's crossing through the Red Sea (see notes on 43:16–17,18–19), which is closely connected with the metaphor of the Lord's victory over the monster (see notes on 51:9–10). The prophecy may have found a literal fulfillment when Cyrus dried up the Euphrates River that fed the moats surrounding Babylon (see note on 45:2).
44:28 Cyrus. The Persian ruler. See note on 41:2. **my shepherd.** Designation for a king (2Sa 5:2; Jer 3:15; Mic 5:4; cf. Jer 27:6). Cyrus would rule by God's decree. **Jerusalem . . . temple.** They would be rebuilt by Cyrus's royal decree (Ezr 1:2–4; 6:3–5). The thought that a pagan king would free God's people and be responsible for the restoration of Jerusalem and the temple would have been difficult for many in the early days of the exile to believe.
■ **45:1–8** *Royal Oracle Concerning Cyrus.* The Lord raised up Cyrus to accomplish his purposes in redemptive history. He spoke of him in some remarkable ways.
45:1 This is what the LORD says. See note on 43:1. **his anointed.** The Hebrew word is often translated "messiah." This is the one time in Scripture that a foreign king is designated as the Lord's anointed. This term is usually reserved for the patriarchs (Ps 105:15), for prophets, priests and kings, for the new community (Hab 3:13) and especially for the Messiah of David's line (Da 9:25). It would have shocked Isaiah's faithful audience to hear that Cyrus would be God's anointed king (see notes on vv. 9–10). **right hand . . . to strip.** Cyrus would rule by the Lord's authority (41:2; 48:14; cf. Pss 2:8–9; 110:1). **nations . . . kings.** See note on 41:2.
45:2–4 I. Emphatic. **level . . . cut.** Nothing would withstand Cyrus, the Lord's servant (cf. Ps 107:16). **gates of bronze.** Babylon had 100 gates of bronze. **gates.** The prophecy may have found a literal fulfillment when Cyrus found the gates connected with Babylon's defensive moats open (see note on 44:27). **darkness . . . secret.** Precious metals were excavated from mines tunneled deep into the earth. Cyrus plundered the fabulous wealth of Lydia in 546 B.C. **know.** See note on 52:6. **I am the LORD.** See note on 41:4. **God of Israel.** See note on 37:16. **summons you by name.** The Lord would raise up Cyrus and know him, even as he knows his children by name. See note on 43:1. **servant.** See notes on 20:3, 41:8 and 42:1–4. **chosen.** See note on 14:1. As "servant" and "anointed," Cyrus would have a title of honor (44:1,28). See note on 43:4. **not acknowledge me.** Despite his pivotal role in the outworking of God's plan for his people, Cyrus would remain an unbeliever.
45:4–5 See *WLC* 45.
45:5 I am the LORD. See note on 41:4. **no other.** See note on 37:16.
45:6–7 rising . . . setting. The whole earth from east to west. **know.** See note on 52:6. **I am the LORD.** See note on 41:4. The Lord is sovereign over creation and history, over adversity and prosperity, over judgment and redemption; therefore, he can do what-

45:7 [p]Isa 31:2; Am 3:6

45:8 [q]Ps 72:6; Joel 3:18 [r]Ps 85:11; Isa 60:21; 61:10, 11; Hos 10:12 [s]Isa 12:3

45:9 [t]Job 15:25 [u]Isa 29:16; Ro 9:20-21*

45:11 [v]Isa 19:25

45:12 [w]Ge 2:1; Isa 42:5 [x]Ne 9:6

45:13 [y]2Ch 36:22; Isa 41:2 [z]Isa 52:3

45:14 [a]Isa 14:1-2

7 I form the light and create darkness,
I bring prosperity and create disaster;[p]
I, the LORD, do all these things.

8 "You heavens above, rain[q] down righteousness;[r]
let the clouds shower it down.
Let the earth open wide,
let salvation[s] spring up,
let righteousness grow with it;
I, the LORD, have created it.

9 "Woe to him who quarrels[t] with his Maker,
to him who is but a potsherd among the potsherds on the ground.
Does the clay say to the potter,[u]
'What are you making?'
Does your work say,
'He has no hands'?
10 Woe to him who says to his father,
'What have you begotten?'
or to his mother,
'What have you brought to birth?'

11 "This is what the LORD says—
the Holy One of Israel, and its Maker:
Concerning things to come,
do you question me about my children,
or give me orders about the work of my hands?[v]
12 It is I who made the earth
and created mankind upon it.
My own hands stretched out the heavens;[w]
I marshaled their starry hosts.[x]
13 I will raise up Cyrus[a][y] in my righteousness:
I will make all his ways straight.
He will rebuild my city
and set my exiles free,
but not for a price or reward,[z]
says the LORD Almighty."

14 This is what the LORD says:

"The products of Egypt and the merchandise of Cush,[b]
and those tall Sabeans—
they will come over to you
and will be yours;
they will trudge behind you,
coming over to you in chains.[a]
They will bow down before you

[a] *13* Hebrew *him* [b] *14* That is, the upper Nile region

ever he pleases. **no other.** See note on 37:16. **form.** See note on 27:10–11. **light . . . darkness.** Explicated by "prosperity . . . disaster." **light.** See note on 2:5. **create . . . create.** See note on 4:5. **darkness.** See note on 5:30 (cf. Ex 10:21–23). See *BC* 13.

45:8 heavens . . . earth. Creation was to prepare itself for the Lord's new act of redemption, which is described by two synonyms: "righteousness" (see note on 1:21) and "salvation" (see notes on 12:2 and 26:17–18). In Isaiah's world Earth's fertility and society's order depended on the king's right relationship with the deity. Because Cyrus would be the Lord's anointed, heaven would shower its blessings on Earth when he ruled (see 49:8). **created.** See note on 4:5.

■ **45:9–14** *Woe to Disputers.* Having announced that Cyrus would be God's anointed servant, Isaiah now warned once again against disbelief.

45:9–10 Woe. Introduces a dire threat. **Maker . . . potter.** See notes on 17:7–8, 22:11, 27:10–11 and 29:16. The Israelites had no right to argue with God over how he would redeem his people. If he wanted to use Cyrus and call him his "anointed one," then Israel should accept his sovereign will. See Romans 9:20.

45:11 This is what the LORD says. See note on 43:1.

45:13 not for a price. Although the Lord would give Cyrus a handsome reward (v. 3) to ransom his people (43:3; 45:14), this would not be the reason Cyrus liberated them.

45:14 This is what the LORD says. See note on 43:1. **Egypt . . . Sabeans.** After the Lord had given these nations to Cyrus as a ransom for Israel (43:3–4) they would hand themselves over to the Lord and to Israel. **bow down . . . plead.** In submission to the Lord (v. 14) and in recognition of his presence with his people (2:2–4; cf. Ps 68:31). **no other.** See note on 37:16.

■ **45:15–17** *Acceptance of God's Plan.* Isaiah responded to God's declaration of his way of saving Israel through Cyrus by affirming his acceptance of God's mysterious plan.

45:15 God who hides himself. God had just revealed that he would redeem Israel from exile in an unexpected way. This revelation still remains mysterious and difficult to understand.

and plead[b] with you, saying,
'Surely God is with you,[c] and there is no other;
there is no other god.' "

15 Truly you are a God who hides[d] himself,
O God and Savior of Israel.
16 All the makers of idols will be put to shame and disgraced;[e]
they will go off into disgrace together.
17 But Israel will be saved[f] by the LORD
with an everlasting salvation;[g]
you will never be put to shame or disgraced,
to ages everlasting.

18 For this is what the LORD says—
he who created the heavens,
he is God;
he who fashioned and made the earth,
he founded it;
he did not create it to be empty,[h]
but formed it to be inhabited[i]—
he says:
"I am the LORD,
and there is no other.[j]
19 I have not spoken in secret,[k]
from somewhere in a land of darkness;
I have not said to Jacob's descendants,[l]
'Seek me in vain.'
I, the LORD, speak the truth;
I declare what is right.[m]

20 "Gather together[n] and come;
assemble, you fugitives from the nations.
Ignorant[o] are those who carry[p] about idols of wood,
who pray to gods that cannot save.[q]
21 Declare what is to be, present it—
let them take counsel together.
Who foretold[r] this long ago,
who declared it from the distant past?
Was it not I, the LORD?
And there is no God apart from me,[s]
a righteous God and a Savior;
there is none but me.

22 "Turn[t] to me and be saved,[u]
all you ends of the earth;[v]
for I am God, and there is no other.
23 By myself I have sworn,[w]
my mouth has uttered in all integrity[x]
a word that will not be revoked:[y]
Before me every knee will bow;
by me every tongue will swear.[z]

45:14 [b]Jer 16:19; Zec 8:20-23 [c]1Co 14:25
45:15 [d]Ps 44:24
45:16 [e]Isa 44:9,11
45:17 [f]Ro 11:26 [g]Isa 26:4
45:18 [h]Ge 1:2 [i]Ge 1:26; Isa 42:5 [j]ver 5
45:19 [k]Isa 48:16 [l]Isa 41:8 [m]Dt 30:11
45:20 [n]Isa 43:9 [o]Isa 44:19 [p]Isa 46:1; Jer 10:5 [q]Isa 44:17; 46:6-7
45:21 [r]Isa 41:22 [s]ver 5
45:22 [t]Zec 12:10 [u]Nu 21:8-9; 2Ch 20:12 [v]Isa 49:6,12
45:23 [w]Ge 22:16 [x]Heb 6:13 [y]Isa 55:11 [z]Ps 63:11; Isa 19:18; Ro 14:11*; Php 2:10-11

45:17 everlasting salvation . . . ages everlasting. God is unlike humans and idols, who can never secure the future for themselves or for others (cf. Heb 5:9). Isaiah affirmed that the Lord's plan for Cyrus to deliver Israel would surely bring a great salvation to God's people.

■ **45:18–25** *The Lord Is Able.* Isaiah attacked Israel's doubts about the Lord's plan to use Cyrus to save them.

45:18 this is what the LORD says. See note on 43:1. **created . . . create.** See note on 4:5. **heavens . . . earth.** See note on 42:5. **fashioned . . . formed.** See note on 27:10–11. **empty.** This is the same word translated "formless" in Genesis 1:2 (describing the primordial chaos at the time of creation) and "vain" in Isaiah 45:19. As the One who created all, God was able to carry through with his plan. **I am the LORD.** See notes on 41:4 and 45:6–7. His intention was not to keep Israel in the desolate condition in which the Assyrians and Babylonians had left it. **no other.** See note on 37:16.

45:19 in secret . . . land of darkness. Unlike pagan oracles, which were obscure and ambiguous, the Lord's revelation was clear and public, although the outworking of his promises might not conform to human expectations (48:16). **Seek me.** God's invitation to be found was sincere (55:3). **truth.** Or "righteousness." See note on 1:21. **right.** God's words promise and establish order in his kingdom (Pss 96:10; 98:9; 99:4).

45:21 foretold this. A reference to the salvation begun with Cyrus's decree that the Israelites return home (see notes on 40:1—55:13; 44:24—45:13).

45:22 ends of the earth. A development of verses 14–17. See note on 24:14–16. **no other.** See note on 37:16.

45:23 By myself I have sworn. God's promises were ratified by his oath (see 62:8; Ge 22:16; Ex 32:13; Heb 6:13–18). See note on 14:24. **mouth.** See note on 1:20. **integrity.** Or "righteousness." See note on 1:21. **word.** The promise of full restoration, including

45:24 [a]Jer 33:16 [b]Isa 41:11
45:25 [c]Isa 41:16
46:1 [d]Isa 21:9; Jer 50:2; 51:44 [e]Isa 45:20
46:2 [f]Jdg 18:17-18; 2Sa 5:21
46:3 [g]ver 12
46:4 [h]Ps 71:18 [i]Isa 43:13
46:5 [j]Isa 40:18,25
46:6 [k]Isa 40:19 [l]Isa 44:17
46:7 [m]ver 1 [n]Isa 44:17; Isa 45:20
46:8 [o]Isa 44:21
46:9 [p]Dt 32:7 [q]Isa 45:5, 21
46:10 [r]Isa 45:21 [s]Pr 19:21; Ac 5:39

24 They will say of me, 'In the LORD alone
are righteousness[a] and strength.' "
All who have raged against him
will come to him and be put to shame.[b]
25 But in the LORD all the descendants of Israel
will be found righteous and will exult.[c]

Gods of Babylon

46

Bel[d] bows down, Nebo stoops low;
their idols are borne by beasts of burden.[a]
The images that are carried[e] about are burdensome,
a burden for the weary.
2 They stoop and bow down together;
unable to rescue the burden,
they themselves go off into captivity.[f]

3 "Listen[g] to me, O house of Jacob,
all you who remain of the house of Israel,
you whom I have upheld since you were conceived,
and have carried since your birth.
4 Even to your old age and gray hairs[h]
I am he,[i] I am he who will sustain you.
I have made you and I will carry you;
I will sustain you and I will rescue you.

5 "To whom will you compare me or count me equal?
To whom will you liken me that we may be compared?[j]
6 Some pour out gold from their bags
and weigh out silver on the scales;
they hire a goldsmith[k] to make it into a god,
and they bow down and worship it.[l]
7 They lift it to their shoulders and carry[m] it;
they set it up in its place, and there it stands.
From that spot it cannot move.
Though one cries out to it, it does not answer;
it cannot save[n] him from his troubles.

8 "Remember[o] this, fix it in mind,
take it to heart, you rebels.
9 Remember the former things, those of long ago;[p]
I am God, and there is no other;
I am God, and there is none like me.[q]
10 I make known the end from the beginning,
from ancient times,[r] what is still to come.
I say: My purpose will stand,[s]
and I will do all that I please.
11 From the east I summon a bird of prey;
from a far-off land, a man to fulfill my purpose.
What I have said, that will I bring about;
what I have planned, that will I do.

a *1* Or *are but beasts and cattle*

judgment and vindication (40:8; 55:10–11). **every knee . . . every tongue.** The goal of redemptive history (Ro 14:11; 1Co 15:25; Php 2:10–11). See *WLC* 104.
45:25 See *BC* 14.
■ **46:1–13** *Babylon's Certain Fate.* Isaiah called for Israel to hear and believe that God would carry through with his plan to destroy Babylon through one "from the east" (v. 11).
46:1–2 Bel. Or "Lord," a name for Marduk. **bows . . . stoop.** An ironic presentation of the utter helplessness of the idols and the foolishness of trusting in them. Babylon's gods would fail her. On Isaiah's polemic against idolatry, see 2:8. **Nebo.** The son of Marduk.
46:3–7 The Lord, the Incomparable One, is present with his people.
46:3 Listen to me. See note on 51:1. **Jacob . . . Israel.** See note on 41:8. **remain.** Or "remnant." See note on 1:8. **conceived . . . birth.** The Lord is like a human mother in his care for his people (49:5; cf. Ex 19:4; Dt 1:31; Hos 11:3–4). See notes on 42:14 and 44:2.
46:4 old age . . . gray hairs. The Lord is constant in his care (Ps 71:9,18), unlike the idols (vv. 1–2). **I am he.** See note on 41:4.
46:9 former . . . long ago. See notes on 41:22 and 42:9. **no other.** See note on 37:16.
46:10 end. The goal of redemptive history. **beginning . . . ancient times.** See note on 41:4. **purpose.** Or "counsel." See note on 11:2.
46:11 east . . . man. Cyrus (see 41:2). This was the element of Isaiah's message that now caused such disbelief. But God declared his freedom and determination to use Cyrus to destroy Babylon.

12 Listen[t] to me, you stubborn-hearted,
you who are far from righteousness.[u]
13 I am bringing my righteousness near,
it is not far away;
and my salvation will not be delayed.
I will grant salvation to Zion,
my splendor[v] to Israel.

The Fall of Babylon

47

"Go down, sit in the dust,
Virgin Daughter[w] of Babylon;
sit on the ground without a throne,
Daughter of the Babylonians.[a x]
No more will you be called
tender or delicate.[y]
2 Take millstones[z] and grind[a] flour;
take off your veil.[b]
Lift up your skirts,[c] bare your legs,
and wade through the streams.
3 Your nakedness[d] will be exposed
and your shame[e] uncovered.
I will take vengeance;[f]
I will spare no one."

4 Our Redeemer—the LORD Almighty is his name[g]—
is the Holy One of Israel.

5 "Sit in silence, go into darkness,[h]
Daughter of the Babylonians;
no more will you be called
queen of kingdoms.[i]
6 I was angry[j] with my people
and desecrated my inheritance;
I gave them into your hand,[k]
and you showed them no mercy.
Even on the aged
you laid a very heavy yoke.
7 You said, 'I will continue forever—
the eternal queen!'[l]
But you did not consider these things
or reflect[m] on what might happen.[n]

8 "Now then, listen, you wanton creature,
lounging in your security[o]
and saying to yourself,
'I am, and there is none besides me.[p]
I will never be a widow[q]
or suffer the loss of children.'

46:12 [t]ver 3 [u]Ps 119:150; Isa 48:1; Jer 2:5
46:13 [v]Isa 44:23
47:1 [w]Isa 23:12 [x]Ps 137:8; Jer 50:12; 51:33; Zec 2:7 [y]Dt 28:56
47:2 [z]Ex 11:5; Mt 24:41 [a]Jdg 16:21 [b]Ge 24:65 [c]Isa 32:11
47:3 [d]Eze 16:37; Na 3:5 [e]Isa 20:4 [f]Isa 34:8
47:4 [g]Jer 50:34
47:5 [h]Isa 13:10 [i]Isa 13:19
47:6 [j]2Ch 28:9 [k]Isa 10:13
47:7 [l]ver 5; Rev 18:7 [m]Isa 42:23,25 [n]Dt 32:29
47:8 [o]Isa 32:9 [p]Isa 45:6; Zep 2:15 [q]Rev 18:7

[a] *1* Or *Chaldeans*; also in verse 5

46:12 Listen to me. See note on 51:1. **stubborn-hearted.** The rebels of verse 8. They refused to accept God's revealed plan for Israel's restoration.
46:13 righteousness. See note on 1:21. "Righteousness" is a synonym of "salvation . . . splendor." The order of the Lord would bring the fullness of redemption (cf. Lk 2:32; see notes on 12:2; 26:17–18) and bestow glory (see note on 4:2) on those in Zion. **Zion.** See note on 1:8.
■ **47:1–15** *Judgment Against Babylon.* The affirmation of God's ability to carry through with his plan for Cyrus led to an oracle assuring Babylon's fall.
47:1–4 Babylon, the queen of nations, would be commanded to descend from her throne and become a menial slave girl. In contrast, Zion, a captive slave girl, would be commanded to ascend her throne (see 52:1–2).
47:1 Virgin Daughter of Babylon. A personification of Babylon. **tender or delicate.** Spoiled (cf. Dt 28:56).
47:2–3 take off . . . wade. All privileges and status would be removed. **shame.** See note on 30:3. **vengeance.** See note on 34:8.
47:4 Redeemer. See notes on 35:8–9 and 41:14. **LORD Almighty.** See note on 1:9.
47:5 queen of kingdoms. Babylon would not remain the greatest of all nations.
47:6 my people. See note on 40:1. **my inheritance.** The people of his possession (Jer 12:7). See note on 19:24–25. **no mercy . . . yoke.** A reference to the harsh treatment of Israel by Babylon (49:24–25; 51:13,19; La 5:12,14). **yoke.** See note on 9:3–4.
47:7 forever . . . eternal queen! Babylon's blasphemous boast was based on her contempt for the truths that God ruled history and would judge her for her cruelty (see v. 6). All her structures were self-perpetuating and devoid of any regard of God (cf. Rev 18:7).
47:8 widow. Contrast "Daughter" in verses 1 and 5. **loss of children.** Loss of hope in the future, resulting in consignment to slavery and death. Contrast 49:21–23 and 54:1–6.

9 Both of these will overtake you
in a moment,[r] on a single day:
loss of children[s] and widowhood.
They will come upon you in full measure,
in spite of your many sorceries[t]
and all your potent spells.[u]
10 You have trusted[v] in your wickedness
and have said, 'No one sees me.'[w]
Your wisdom[x] and knowledge mislead[y] you
when you say to yourself,
'I am, and there is none besides me.'
11 Disaster will come upon you,
and you will not know how to conjure it away.
A calamity will fall upon you
that you cannot ward off with a ransom;
a catastrophe you cannot foresee
will suddenly[z] come upon you.

12 "Keep on, then, with your magic spells
and with your many sorceries,[a]
which you have labored at since childhood.
Perhaps you will succeed,
perhaps you will cause terror.
13 All the counsel you have received has only worn you out![b]
Let your astrologers[c] come forward,
those stargazers who make predictions month by month,
let them save[d] you from what is coming upon you.
14 Surely they are like stubble;[e]
the fire will burn them up.
They cannot even save themselves
from the power of the flame.[f]
Here are no coals to warm anyone;
here is no fire to sit by.
15 That is all they can do for you—
these you have labored with
and trafficked[g] with since childhood.
Each of them goes on in his error;
there is not one that can save you.

Stubborn Israel

48

"Listen to this, O house of Jacob,
you who are called by the name of Israel
and come from the line of Judah,
you who take oaths in the name of the LORD
and invoke[h] the God of Israel—
but not in truth[i] or righteousness—
2 you who call yourselves citizens of the holy city[j]
and rely[k] on the God of Israel—
the LORD Almighty is his name:
3 I foretold the former things[l] long ago,

47:9 [r]Ps 73:19; 1Th 5:3; Rev 18:8-10 [s]Isa 13:18 [t]Na 3:4 [u]Rev 18:23
47:10 [v]Ps 52:7; 62:10 [w]Isa 29:15 [x]Isa 5:21 [y]Isa 44:20
47:11 [z]1Th 5:3
47:12 [a]ver 9
47:13 [b]Isa 57:10; Jer 51:58 [c]Isa 44:25 [d]ver 15
47:14 [e]Isa 5:24; Na 1:10 [f]Isa 10:17; Jer 51:30,32,58
47:15 [g]Rev 18:11
48:1 [h]Isa 58:2 [i]Jer 4:2
48:2 [j]Isa 52:1 [k]Isa 10:20; Mic 3:11; Ro 2:17
48:3 [l]Isa 41:22

47:9 moment . . . single day. Sudden catastrophe on the day of the Lord (see note on 13:9). **loss of children and widowhood.** Robbed of her confidence (v. 8). **in full measure.** Babylon would be unable to circumvent or protect herself from God's judgment. **sorceries . . . spells.** A reference to Babylon's numerous magic practices by which she tried to flex her power and manipulate her enemies (v. 12). For practices of divination, see note on 44:25.
47:10 wisdom . . . knowledge. Babylon's religious, magic, mantic (related to divination) and intellectual traditions. In contrast, see note on 11:2. **I am.** In brazen self-deification, Babylon usurped the name of God (see 45:5–6,18,21–22; 46:9).
47:12–13 spells . . . sorceries. See verse 9 and 44:25. **counsel . . . stargazers.** Babylon depended on the omens from the heavenly bodies for her self-determination (cf. Da 2:10).
47:14 stubble . . . flame. Compare Revelation 18:17. Babylon's astrologers (v. 13) practiced their craft in an attempt to defend Babylon against these prophecies, but they could not even save themselves (see Da 2:10).
■ **48:1–22** *The Call to Listen and Leave.* This passage twice calls for Israel to listen and believe God's word of promise. It then calls for demonstration of that faith by leaving Babylon in the confidence that God would restore his people.
48:1–2 Listen. A final and urgent appeal to deaf and blind Israel (see vv. 6,8; cf. 42:18–22; 46:3–12) to observe God's ways in creation and history (vv. 12,16). See note on 51:1. **Jacob . . . Israel.** See note on 41:8. **not in truth.** See 66:1–4. Contrast 10:20, 65:16 and John 4:23. **call yourselves.** See Romans 9:6.
48:3 foretold. See note on 52:6. **former.** See notes on 41:22 and 42:9. **mouth.** See note on 1:20.

my mouth announced[m] them and I made them known;
then suddenly I acted, and they came to pass.
4 For I knew how stubborn[n] you were;
the sinews of your neck[o] were iron,
your forehead[p] was bronze.
5 Therefore I told you these things long ago;
before they happened I announced them to you
so that you could not say,
'My idols did them;[q]
my wooden image and metal god ordained them.'
6 You have heard these things; look at them all.
Will you not admit them?

"From now on I will tell you of new things,
of hidden things unknown to you.
7 They are created now, and not long ago;
you have not heard of them before today.
So you cannot say,
'Yes, I knew of them.'
8 You have neither heard nor understood;
from of old your ear has not been open.
Well do I know how treacherous you are;
you were called a rebel[r] from birth.
9 For my own name's sake I delay my wrath;[s]
for the sake of my praise I hold it back from you,
so as not to cut you off.[t]
10 See, I have refined you, though not as silver;
I have tested you in the furnace[u] of affliction.
11 For my own sake,[v] for my own sake, I do this.
How can I let myself be defamed?[w]
I will not yield my glory to another.[x]

Israel Freed

12 "Listen[y] to me, O Jacob,
Israel, whom I have called:
I am he;
I am the first and I am the last.[z]
13 My own hand laid the foundations of the earth,[a]
and my right hand spread out the heavens;[b]
when I summon them,
they all stand up together.[c]

14 "Come together,[d] all of you, and listen:
Which of ⌊the idols⌋ has foretold these things?
The LORD's chosen ally
will carry out his purpose[e] against Babylon;
his arm will be against the Babylonians.[a]
15 I, even I, have spoken;
yes, I have called[f] him.
I will bring him,
and he will succeed in his mission.

48:3 [m]Isa 45:21
48:4 [n]Dt 31:27 [o]Ex 32:9; Ac 7:51 [p]Eze 3:9
48:5 [q]Jer 44:15-18
48:8 [r]Dt 9:7,24; Ps 58:3
48:9 [s]Ps 78:38; Isa 30:18 [t]Ne 9:31
48:10 [u]1Ki 8:51
48:11 [v]1Sa 12:22; Isa 37:35 [w]Dt 32:27; Jer 14:7,21; Eze 20:9,14,22,44 [x]Isa 42:8
48:12 [y]Isa 46:3 [z]Isa 41:4; Rev 1:17; 22:13
48:13 [a]Heb 1:10-12 [b]Ex 20:11 [c]Isa 40:26
48:14 [d]Isa 43:9 [e]Isa 46:10-11
48:15 [f]Isa 45:1

[a] *14* Or *Chaldeans*; also in verse 20

48:4 iron . . . bronze. Metaphors for rebelliousness (Jer 6:28).
48:5 told. See note on 52:6. **long ago . . . before they happened.** The Lord alone decrees and executes his will according to his word.
48:6 heard . . . look. The evidence spoke for itself, if only they would believe God's word. **new things . . . hidden things.** The glory of the new era of salvation and kingdom righteousness that began with the restoration from exile finds its focus in Christ's first advent and will continue until the fullness of the kingdom of our Lord (45:15; cf. Rev 1:19). See note on 43:18–19.
48:8 neither heard nor understood. God's methods of restoring his people were difficult for them to accept (cf. 40:21,24,28).
48:10 refined . . . tested. The exile was designed to be a period of refining (1:22,25; cf. Eze 22:18–22; 1Pe 1:7). **not as silver.** Unlike silver that is refined by purging heat, Israel had not been refined by her afflictions in exile. **furnace of affliction.** The exile was like the bondage in Egypt (Dt 4:20; Jer 11:4).
48:11 For my own sake. See note on 43:25. **glory.** See note on 4:2 and note the parallel with verse 9.
48:12 I am he. Contrast 47:8 and 10.
48:13 laid the foundations . . . earth . . . heavens. All of creation. See note on 42:5. **right hand.** See note on 41:10.
48:14 listen. See verse 1. **foretold.** See note on 52:6. **chosen ally.** Another designation for Cyrus (see notes on 41:2,25; 45:3–4; 46:11). **purpose.** The end of Babylon and the beginning of restoration. God again affirmed that his plan to use Cyrus would succeed.
48:15 I, even I. Emphatic. **called . . . succeed.** The status and special success of Cyrus would be of the Lord.

48:16 [g]Isa 41:1 [h]Isa 45:19 [i]Zec 2:9,11

16 "Come near[g] me and listen to this:

"From the first announcement I have not spoken in secret;[h]
at the time it happens, I am there."

And now the Sovereign LORD has sent[i] me,
with his Spirit.

48:17 [j]Isa 49:7 [k]Isa 43:14 [l]Isa 49:10 [m]Ps 32:8

17 This is what the LORD says—
your Redeemer,[j] the Holy One[k] of Israel:
"I am the LORD your God,
who teaches you what is best for you,
who directs[l] you in the way[m] you should go.

48:18 [n]Dt 32:29 [o]Ps 119:165; Isa 66:12 [p]Isa 45:8

18 If only you had paid attention[n] to my commands,
your peace[o] would have been like a river,
your righteousness[p] like the waves of the sea.

48:19 [q]Ge 22:17 [r]Isa 56:5; 66:22

19 Your descendants would have been like the sand,
your children like its numberless grains;[q]
their name would never be cut off[r]
nor destroyed from before me."

48:20 [s]Jer 50:8; 51:6,45; Zec 2:6-7; Rev 18:4 [t]Isa 49:13 [u]Isa 52:9; 63:9

20 Leave Babylon,
flee[s] from the Babylonians!
Announce this with shouts of joy[t]
and proclaim it.
Send it out to the ends of the earth;
say, "The LORD has redeemed[u] his servant Jacob."

48:21 [v]Isa 41:17 [w]Isa 30:25 [x]Ex 17:6; Nu 20:11; Ps 105:41; Isa 35:6

21 They did not thirst[v] when he led them through the deserts;
he made water flow[w] for them from the rock;
he split the rock
and water gushed out.[x]

48:22 [y]Isa 57:21

22 "There is no peace," says the LORD, "for the wicked."[y]

The Servant of the LORD

49:1 [z]Isa 44:24; 46:3; Mt 1:20 [a]Isa 7:14; 9:6; 44:2; Jer 1:5; Gal 1:15

49

Listen to me, you islands;
hear this, you distant nations:
Before I was born[z] the LORD called[a] me;
from my birth he has made mention of my name.

49:2 [b]Isa 11:4; Rev 1:16

2 He made my mouth like a sharpened sword,[b]
in the shadow of his hand he hid me;
he made me into a polished arrow
and concealed me in his quiver.

48:16 Come near me. God called his people to come near and trust his word to them. **the first announcement.** The announcement about Cyrus was proclaimed in 41:25–27 and then elaborated in these chapters. **sent me . . . Spirit.** See 11:2 and 42:1.
48:17 Redeemer. See notes on 35:8–9 and 41:14. **the Holy One of Israel.** See note on 1:4. **I am the LORD.** See note on 41:4. **teaches . . . directs.** Through Moses and the prophets (40:11; 55:12; 63:13; Dt 5:27; 29:5–6; Pss 23:2; 27:11; 139:10,24).
48:18–19 If only. God wished that his people had already entered into his rest. These verses bear out the responsibility of God's people in hastening the day of redemption. **peace.** See note on 26:3. **river . . . waves of the sea.** These represent abundant life and a constant and increasing state, respectively (cf. 66:12; Am 5:24). **righteousness.** See note on 1:21. Peace would come to the restored community only as righteousness prevailed among God's people (see 9:7; 32:17; 54:13–14; 60:17; Ps 85:10; Heb 7:2). **descendants . . . grains.** A promise of numerous offspring (Ge 12:2; 22:17). See note on 51:2. **name.** See note on 43:1.
48:20 Leave . . . flee. A warning not to become entangled in the structures of Babylon, because she was about to fall (cf. Rev 18:4). See notes on 20:3 and 42:1–4.
48:21 thirst . . . gushed out. The restoration would be like the exodus in that God would provide for his people (41:17–20; 43:19–21; 44:3; cf. Ex 17:6; Dt 5:15; Ps 105:41).
48:22 peace. See note on 26:3.
■ **49:1—55:13** *God's Plan for His Servant.* The second major instrument of Israel's restoration to blessing was the great son of David, the Servant. This royal servant has already been mentioned and named God's servant (42:1–4), but here his role is explained in much more detail. These chapters divide into eight parts: a royal oracle (49:1–13), disputation against unbelief (49:14—50:3), the Servant's psalm (50:4–11), a disputation over God's compassion and righteousness (51:1–8), a lament to God and his responses (51:9—52:12), the suffering and exalted Servant (52:13—53:12), a call to praise (54:1–17) and an invitation (55:1–13).
■ **49:1–13** *Royal Oracle About the Servant.* This section contains the second of four servant songs (42:1–4; 49:1–7; 50:4–9; 52:13—53:12) that explicitly connect the great Servant with the royal house of Judah.
49:1 Listen. See 48:16. **born . . . birth.** For the special relationship between the Lord and his servant, see notes on 42:1–4, 44:2 and 46:3 (cf. Ge 3:15; Jer 1:5; Gal 1:15). **called . . . name.** The faithful Servant is called "Israel" (see v. 3) because he would represent faithful Israel as he fulfilled what Israel was designed to be (see notes on 43:1; 44:2,24; 45:3; 51:1–16). It is made clear that the Servant is not Israel itself, for he is distinct from unfaithful Israel (see vv. 5–6; notes on 42:18–22; 46:3–12; 48:1–10).
49:2 mouth. The Servant would announce God's message of salvation and judgment. The effectiveness of his word is portrayed as a "sharpened sword" and a "polished arrow" (see also Eph 6:17; Heb 4:12; Rev 1:16; 2:12,16; 19:15). See 40:8, 45:19 and 55:10–11 for similar notions. **shadow . . . quiver.** Protection in the process of ministry. See note on 30:2. For both aspects, see 51:16.

3 He said to me, "You are my servant,[c]
Israel, in whom I will display my splendor.[d]"
4 But I said, "I have labored to no purpose;
I have spent my strength in vain[e] and for nothing.
Yet what is due me is in the LORD's hand,
and my reward[f] is with my God."
5 And now the LORD says—
he who formed me in the womb to be his servant
to bring Jacob back to him
and gather Israel[g] to himself,
for I am honored[h] in the eyes of the LORD
and my God has been my strength—
6 he says:
"It is too small a thing for you to be my servant
to restore the tribes of Jacob
and bring back those of Israel I have kept.
I will also make you a light for the Gentiles,[i]
that you may bring my salvation to the ends of the earth."[j]
7 This is what the LORD says—
the Redeemer and Holy One of Israel[k]—
to him who was despised[l] and abhorred by the nation,
to the servant of rulers:
"Kings[m] will see you and rise up,
princes will see and bow down,
because of the LORD, who is faithful,
the Holy One of Israel, who has chosen you."

Restoration of Israel

8 This is what the LORD says:
"In the time of my favor[n] I will answer you,
and in the day of salvation I will help you;[o]
I will keep[p] you and will make you
to be a covenant for the people,[q]
to restore the land[r]
and to reassign its desolate inheritances,
9 to say to the captives,[s] 'Come out,'
and to those in darkness, 'Be free!'
"They will feed beside the roads
and find pasture on every barren hill.[t]
10 They will neither hunger nor thirst,[u]
nor will the desert heat or the sun beat upon them.[v]
He who has compassion[w] on them will guide them
and lead them beside springs[x] of water.
11 I will turn all my mountains into roads,
and my highways[y] will be raised up.[z]

49:3 [c]Zec 3:8 [d]Isa 44:23
49:4 [e]Isa 65:23 [f]Isa 35:4
49:5 [g]Isa 11:12 [h]Isa 43:4
49:6 [i]Lk 2:32 [j]Ac 13:47*
49:7 [k]Isa 48:17 [l]Ps 22:6; 69:7-9 [m]Isa 52:15
49:8 [n]Ps 69:13 [o]2Co 6:2* [p]Isa 26:3 [q]Isa 42:6 [r]Isa 44:26
49:9 [s]Isa 42:7; 61:1; Lk 4:19 [t]Isa 41:18
49:10 [u]Isa 33:16 [v]Ps 121:6; Rev 7:16 [w]Isa 14:1 [x]Isa 35:7
49:11 [y]Isa 11:16 [z]Isa 40:4

49:3 servant. See note on 20:3. **display my splendor.** The great son of David would display God's wonder in the world. Christ revealed God's glory in his earthly ministry and will do so to an even greater extent at his return. See note on 44:23.
49:4 labored to no purpose. The Servant's complaint implies his rejection by national Israel and his suffering (see 42:2). This situation will not exist in the new creation (see 65:17). **reward.** See 40:10 and Genesis 15:1. The Servant would be vindicated (see 50:8) and rewarded with seed after his death (see 53:8) and resurrection (see 53:10).
49:5–6 formed. See note on 27:10–11. **womb.** See verse 1 and note on 44:2. **servant.** See notes on 20:3, 41:8 and 42:1–4. **bring . . . gather.** One aspect of the Servant's mission was the reconciliation of the Jews with their God (see note on 42:7). **Jacob . . . Israel.** See note on 41:8. **honored.** See note on 43:4. **strength.** See note on 12:2. **light for the Gentiles.** A second aspect of the Servant's mission would be bringing the nations into the service of God (cf. Lk 2:32; Ac 13:47; 26:23). He would fulfill the call of Abraham (see Ge 12:3; 22:18) and of national Israel (Ex 19:5–6). Today the ascended Christ fulfills this aspect of his mission through his body, the church (Mt 28:18–20; Ac 13:47; 26:23; 1Pe 2:9–10).
49:7 This is what the LORD says. The first of two (see 49:8) elaborations on the previous expectations for the Servant. See note on 43:1. **Redeemer.** See note on 41:14. **despised.** See notes on 42:2, 49:4 and 53:3. **servant of rulers.** Paradoxically, the King who would humble himself to become the servant of rulers would be given homage by them (see 4:2; 45:24; 52:15).
49:8 This is what the LORD says. See note on 49:7. **favor.** In contrast to the day of vengeance (see notes on 12:2; 34:8; cf. 35:4; 59:17–18; 61:2; 63:4; Lk 2:14; 2Co 6:2). **salvation.** See 52:7. **help.** See note on 40:10. **keep you . . . covenant.** The Servant is still in view as the One who would fulfill David's covenant and usher in a new covenant for the latter days after the exile (see note on 42:6). **restore . . . reassign.** Beginning with the restoration from exile (44:26). See note on 45:8.
49:9 captives. See notes on 42:7, 51:14 and 61:1. **Come out.** Compare 48:20. **darkness.** See note on 5:30. **feed.** The Servant is Israel's Shepherd-King (cf. 40:11; 48:22).
49:10 guide. An allusion to the first exodus (cf. 42:16; 48:21; Ex 15:13).

49:12 [a]Isa 43:5-6
49:13 [b]Isa 44:23 [c]Isa 40:1
49:15 [d]Isa 44:21
49:16 [e]SS 8:6 [f]Ps 48:12-13; Isa 62:6
49:17 [g]Isa 10:6
49:18 [h]Isa 43:5; 54:7; Isa 60:4 [i]Isa 45:23 [j]Isa 52:1
49:19 [k]Isa 54:1,3 [l]Isa 5:6 [m]Zec 10:10
49:20 [n]Isa 54:1-3
49:21 [o]Isa 5:13 [p]Isa 1:8
49:22 [q]Isa 11:10

12 See, they will come from afar[a]—
some from the north, some from the west,
some from the region of Aswan.[a]"

13 Shout for joy, O heavens;
rejoice, O earth;
burst into song, O mountains![b]
For the LORD comforts[c] his people
and will have compassion on his afflicted ones.

14 But Zion said, "The LORD has forsaken me,
the Lord has forgotten me."

15 "Can a mother forget the baby at her breast
and have no compassion on the child she has borne?
Though she may forget,
I will not forget you![d]
16 See, I have engraved[e] you on the palms of my hands;
your walls[f] are ever before me.
17 Your sons hasten back,
and those who laid you waste[g] depart from you.
18 Lift up your eyes and look around;
all your sons gather[h] and come to you.
As surely as I live,[i]" declares the LORD,
"you will wear[j] them all as ornaments;
you will put them on, like a bride.

19 "Though you were ruined and made desolate[k]
and your land laid waste,[l]
now you will be too small for your people,[m]
and those who devoured you will be far away.
20 The children born during your bereavement
will yet say in your hearing,
'This place is too small for us;
give us more space to live in.'[n]
21 Then you will say in your heart,
'Who bore me these?
I was bereaved and barren;
I was exiled and rejected.[o]
Who brought these up?
I was left[p] all alone,
but these—where have they come from?' "

22 This is what the Sovereign LORD says:

"See, I will beckon to the Gentiles,
I will lift up my banner[q] to the peoples;

a *12* Dead Sea Scrolls; Masoretic Text *Sinim*

49:11 roads . . . highways. See note on 11:16.
49:12 come from afar . . . west. The salvation of all Israel is in view (see notes on 11:11–12; 43:5–6). **Aswan.** Ancient Syene, where the Jews established a colony during the exile (see NIV text note; cf. Eze 29:10; 30:6).
49:13 Shout . . . burst. See notes on 12:6 and 14:7. **heavens . . . mountains!** See note on 42:5. **comforts.** See notes on 12:1 and 40:1. **compassion.** See verse 10. **afflicted ones.** See note on 11:3–5 (cf. 2Co 7:6).
■ **49:14—50:3** *Disputations Against Israel's Unbelief.* Isaiah reacted to the anticipated unbelief among Israelites in exile. They would find it hard to believe that God would remember them because they felt so forsaken by him (49:14–23), nor would they think it possible to overcome the fierce warriors of Babylon (49:24—50:3).
49:14–23 Isaiah disputed unbelief by answering the objection that God would so forsake his people in exile that he would forget them.
49:14 It was expected that some Israelites in exile would distrust the promises of restoration because they would feel so forsaken by God. **Zion.** See note on 1:8. **forsaken . . . forgotten.** In exile (40:27; 54:7).
49:15 forget . . . forget. See Psalm 27:10. The Lord likened himself to a mother who could not forget her nursing child. Although human mothers occasionally do the unthinkable and abandon or neglect their children, God would never forget his chosen people. There would always be a remnant of Israel who would experience the salvation of God.
49:19–21 desolate. A different word from that in verse 8. This one means "childless." **too small.** Moses promised that the restored nation would be far more numerous than it had been before (Dt 30:5). Isaiah announced that Jerusalem would be too small to include all who would be redeemed from God's judgment. Needless to say, this prophecy was hardly fulfilled when the Israelites returned after the Cyrus edict in 539 B.C. That repopulation effort failed because the returnees failed to serve the Lord. It is only in Christ's kingdom that Jerusalem and the promised land will fail to contain all of the redeemed.
49:22 Gentiles. The numbers of God's people would be great be-

they will bring your sons in their arms
and carry your daughters on their shoulders.[r]
23 Kings[s] will be your foster fathers,
and their queens your nursing mothers.[t]
They will bow down before you with their faces to the ground;
they will lick the dust[u] at your feet.
Then you will know that I am the LORD;[v]
those who hope in me will not be disappointed."

24 Can plunder be taken from warriors,[w]
or captives rescued from the fierce[a]?

25 But this is what the LORD says:

"Yes, captives[x] will be taken from warriors,[y]
and plunder retrieved from the fierce;
I will contend with those who contend with you,
and your children I will save.[z]
26 I will make your oppressors[a] eat[b] their own flesh;
they will be drunk on their own blood,[c] as with wine.
Then all mankind will know[d]
that I, the LORD, am your Savior,
your Redeemer, the Mighty One of Jacob."

Israel's Sin and the Servant's Obedience

50 This is what the LORD says:

"Where is your mother's certificate of divorce[e]
with which I sent her away?
Or to which of my creditors
did I sell[f] you?
Because of your sins you were sold;[g]
because of your transgressions your mother was sent away.
2 When I came, why was there no one?
When I called, why was there no one to answer?[h]
Was my arm too short[i] to ransom you?
Do I lack the strength[j] to rescue you?
By a mere rebuke I dry up the sea,[k]
I turn rivers into a desert;
their fish rot for lack of water
and die of thirst.
3 I clothe the sky with darkness
and make sackcloth[l] its covering."

4 The Sovereign LORD has given me an instructed tongue,[m]
to know the word that sustains the weary.[n]

49:22 [r]Isa 60:4
49:23 [s]Isa 60:3, 10-11 [t]Isa 60:16 [u]Ps 72:9 [v]Mic 7:17
49:24 [w]Mt 12:29; Lk 11:21
49:25 [x]Isa 14:2 [y]Jer 50:33-34 [z]Isa 25:9; 35:4
49:26 [a]Isa 9:4 [b]Isa 9:20 [c]Rev 16:6 [d]Eze 39:7
50:1 [e]Dt 24:1; Jer 3:8; Hos 2:2 [f]Ne 5:5; Mt 18:25 [g]Dt 32:30; Isa 52:3
50:2 [h]Isa 41:28 [i]Nu 11:23; Isa 59:1 [j]Ge 18:14 [k]Ex 14:22; Jos 3:16
50:3 [l]Rev 6:12
50:4 [m]Ex 4:12 [n]Mt 11:28

a *24* Dead Sea Scrolls, Vulgate and Syriac (see also Septuagint and verse 25); Masoretic Text *righteous*

cause after the restoration from exile God would also call many Gentiles to himself. This vision of the future restoration was inaugurated in the first coming of Christ, is continued in the gospel ministry today and will find ultimate fulfillment at Christ's return (49:6; Ac 9:15; 10:45; Gal 3:14; Rev 7:9–17). See *BC* 28.
49:23 Kings. In the restoration period and after a time of war (see notes on Eze 38; Am 9:11–13), nations that formerly oppressed Israel will serve the Messiah and so find salvation (see Ge 12:3). See notes on verses 4 and 7. **bow down.** Contrast 45:14. **lick the dust.** In Assyrian art Jehu king of Israel is shown licking the dust at the feet of an Assyrian ruler. **hope.** See 40:31. See *WCF* 20.4; 23.3; 31.2; *WLC* 124; *BC* 36.
49:24—50:3 Isaiah responded to the objection that Babylon's warriors were too fierce to overcome.
49:24–26 warriors . . . fierce? Isaiah proclaimed that God would rescue his people from those who conquered them. Doubts would remain in the minds of many Israelites as they wondered whether the terrifying armies of Babylon could be overcome. **contend . . . save.** The Lord would take up the case of the needy and be just in his retribution (v. 26; cf. Rev 16:6; 18:20). **know.** See note on 52:6. **Redeemer.** See notes on 35:8–9 and 41:14. **Mighty One.** See note on 1:24. This is the vindication of the people of God. God himself would fight for his people and redeem them from their adversity.
50:1 mother's. That is, the inhabitants of Jerusalem who went into the Babylonian exile. **certificate of divorce.** Isaiah referred to the Mosaic legislation on divorce (Dt 24:1–4). It is difficult to know precisely what this prophecy means. God had divorced the northern kingdom (Jer 3:1,8) and sent Judah away (Isa 54:6–7). Perhaps God here denied that he was the cause of the divorce. In any event, God never utterly rejected every single Israelite or Judahite; there was always to be a remnant whom God would not forget. **creditors.** Had the Lord sold Israel because he owed money, he would have lost authority over his people's destiny (cf. Ex 21:7; 2Ki 4:1; Ne 5:5). **Because of your sins.** Israel was sold in payment for the debt of her sins; in this sense the Redeemer had the responsibility to buy his people back (see 41:14; 52:3).
50:2–3 These verses elaborate on the fact that Judah was sent into exile because of her sin. The Lord had come to Israel through his prophets before her exile and had earlier redeemed Israel from Egypt, but his people had refused to turn to him. For this reason, the nation had been sent into exile.

He wakens me morning by morning,[o]
wakens my ear to listen like one being taught.
5 The Sovereign LORD has opened my ears,[p]
and I have not been rebellious;[q]
I have not drawn back.
6 I offered my back to those who beat[r] me,
my cheeks to those who pulled out my beard;
I did not hide my face
from mocking and spitting.[s]
7 Because the Sovereign LORD helps[t] me,
I will not be disgraced.
Therefore have I set my face like flint,[u]
and I know I will not be put to shame.
8 He who vindicates me is near.
Who then will bring charges against me?[v]
Let us face each other![w]
Who is my accuser?
Let him confront me!
9 It is the Sovereign LORD who helps[x] me.
Who is he that will condemn me?
They will all wear out like a garment;
the moths[y] will eat them up.

10 Who among you fears the LORD
and obeys the word of his servant?[z]
Let him who walks in the dark,
who has no light,
trust[a] in the name of the LORD
and rely on his God.
11 But now, all you who light fires
and provide yourselves with flaming torches,[b]
go, walk in the light of your fires[c]
and of the torches you have set ablaze.
This is what you shall receive from my hand:
You will lie down in torment.[d]

Everlasting Salvation for Zion

51

"Listen[e] to me, you who pursue righteousness[f]
and who seek the LORD:
Look to the rock from which you were cut
and to the quarry from which you were hewn;
2 look to Abraham,[g] your father,
and to Sarah, who gave you birth.
When I called him he was but one,
and I blessed him and made him many.[h]
3 The LORD will surely comfort[i] Zion
and will look with compassion on all her ruins;[j]

50:4 [o]Ps 5:3; 119:147; 143:8
50:5 [p]Isa 35:5 [q]Mt 26:39; Jn 8:29; 14:31; 15:10; Ac 26:19; Heb 5:8
50:6 [r]Isa 53:5; Mt 27:30; Mk 14:65; 15:19; Lk 22:63 [s]La 3:30; Mt 26:67
50:7 [t]Isa 42:1 [u]Eze 3:8-9
50:8 [v]Isa 43:26; Ro 8:32-34 [w]Isa 41:1
50:9 [x]Isa 41:10 [y]Job 13:28; Isa 51:8
50:10 [z]Isa 49:3 [a]Isa 26:4
50:11 [b]Pr 26:18 [c]Jas 3:6 [d]Isa 65:13-15
51:1 [e]Isa 46:3 [f]ver 7; Ps 94:15; Ro 9:30-31
51:2 [g]Isa 29:22; Ro 4:16; Heb 11:11 [h]Ge 12:2
51:3 [i]Isa 40:1 [j]Isa 52:9

■ **50:4–11** *The Servant's Psalm of Confidence.* The third of four servant songs (see notes on 42:1–4; 49:1–7; 50:4–11; 52:13—53:12). The reproach of men against believing Israel in the exile (see 51:7) anticipated the rejection of Jesus Christ.
50:4–6 Sovereign LORD. See note 25:7–8. **instructed . . . taught.** The Lord taught his Servant how to speak through suffering. **tongue . . . face.** His whole being was in the Lord's service. **word.** See notes on 45:23 and 49:2. **weary.** See 42:3 and Jeremiah 31:25. **wakens my ear.** Contrast 42:18–19. **not been rebellious.** Contrast 1:2. **my back.** The backs of fools were to be struck (see Pr 10:13; 19:29; 26:3). Jesus Christ in his own beating fulfilled this prophecy of injustice (see 42:2; 49:4; 53:12; Mt 27:26; Jn 19:1). **pulled out my beard.** A sign of contempt (see 2Sa 10:4–5; Ne 13:25). **mocking.** See note on 30:3.
50:7 like flint. A simile for resolute determination in the face of opposition (see Jer 1:8; Eze 3:8–9; Lk 9:51). **not be put to shame.** A figure meaning "to be honored" (see note on 42:3; cf. 49:7; 52:13).
50:10 See *WCF* 18.3; 18.4; *WLC* 172.
50:11 light fires . . . flaming torches. The self-reliant, who lived without the light of the Lord and his servant (see 2:5; 42:6).
■ **51:1–8** *Disputation Over God's Compassion and Righteousness.* Isaiah addressed the problem of disbelief concerning God's willingness to show compassion (v. 3) and righteousness (v. 5). The motifs of fear and reproach suggest that this passage was addressing disputes that were taking place between the faithful and unfaithful over these matters (v. 7).
51:1 Listen. The call to listen (see also v. 4) implies a controversy or dispute. **you who pursue righteousness.** Isaiah assured the remnant of those who were seeking to be faithful that God would not fail to restore them. **rock . . . quarry.** Figures for Abraham and Sarah, respectively (see v. 2). The mention of God's love for these ancient ancestors was meant to assure the Israelites in exile of God's continuing love for them.
51:2 but one . . . many. The prophet argued from the lesser to the greater. If God had blessed Abraham when he was only one person, how much more would he bless the innumerable offspring of Abraham who were living in the prophet's day.

he will make her deserts like Eden,[k]
her wastelands like the garden of the LORD.
Joy and gladness[l] will be found in her,
thanksgiving and the sound of singing.

4 "Listen to me, my people;[m]
hear me, my nation:
The law will go out from me;
my justice[n] will become a light to the nations.[o]
5 My righteousness draws near speedily,
my salvation is on the way,[p]
and my arm[q] will bring justice to the nations.
The islands will look to me
and wait in hope for my arm.
6 Lift up your eyes to the heavens,
look at the earth beneath;
the heavens will vanish like smoke,[r]
the earth will wear out like a garment[s]
and its inhabitants die like flies.
But my salvation will last forever,
my righteousness will never fail.

7 "Hear me, you who know what is right,[t]
you people who have my law in your hearts:[u]
Do not fear the reproach of men
or be terrified by their insults.[v]
8 For the moth will eat them up like a garment;[w]
the worm will devour them like wool.
But my righteousness will last forever,[x]
my salvation through all generations."

9 Awake, awake! Clothe yourself with strength,[y]
O arm of the LORD;
awake, as in days gone by,
as in generations of old.[z]
Was it not you who cut Rahab to pieces,
who pierced that monster[a] through?
10 Was it not you who dried up the sea,[b]
the waters of the great deep,
who made a road in the depths of the sea
so that the redeemed might cross over?
11 The ransomed[c] of the LORD will return.
They will enter Zion with singing;
everlasting joy will crown their heads.
Gladness and joy[d] will overtake them,
and sorrow and sighing will flee away.[e]

51:3 [k]Ge 2:8 [l]Isa 25:9; 66:10
51:4 [m]Ps 50:7 [n]Isa 2:4 [o]Isa 42:4,6
51:5 [p]Isa 46:13 [q]Isa 40:10; 63:1,5
51:6 [r]Mt 24:35; 2Pe 3:10 [s]Ps 102:25-26
51:7 [t]ver 1 [u]Ps 37:31 [v]Mt 5:11; Ac 5:41
51:8 [w]Isa 50:9 [x]ver 6
51:9 [y]Isa 52:1 [z]Dt 4:34 [a]Ps 74:13
51:10 [b]Ex 14:22
51:11 [c]Isa 35:9 [d]Jer 33:11 [e]Rev 7:17

51:3 comfort . . . compassion. See notes on 12:1 and 40:1. **Zion.** See note on 1:8. **ruins . . . wastelands.** As described in 49:19. **deserts.** See note on 40:3. For commentary on "Eden" as the garden of God, see Genesis 2:8, Ezekiel 28:13 and 31:8–9. This image represents transformation from curse to blessing. There would be "gladness and joy" instead of sorrow (v. 11), and God's people would regain the lost Paradise of God (see notes on 9:3–4; 12:3).
51:4 Listen. See note on verse 1. **my people.** See note on 40:1. **my nation.** Only in 51:4. **law . . . a light.** This was to be accomplished through the Servant in the last days (see 2:2–4; 42:1–4,6; 49:6). See notes on 2:3 and 42:1.
51:5 To those in exile the Lord announced that restoration was near. At that time the righteousness and justice of God would be demonstrated to all.
51:6 Lift up your eyes. See 40:26. **heavens . . . earth.** All of creation is in the service of God's redemption. **like smoke . . . like a garment.** Similes for the transience of creation (50:9; Pss 68:2; 102:3,26; Hos 13:3; cf. Isa 24:4; 34:4; Heb 1:10–11; 2Pe 3:10). **my salvation.** See note on 12:2. **righteousness.** See note on 1:21.
51:7 my law in your hearts. The spiritual reality of the covenant (Ps 40:8; Jer 31:31; Eze 36:27), in contrast to 29:13. See note on 32:15. **fear.** See notes on 8:12 and 35:4. **reproach.** See note on 50:4–11. Those who were faithful faced challenges to their belief that God would keep his promise to restore the nation.
■ **51:9—52:12** *Lament and Responses.* The prophet first reported the cry of Israel to God: "Awake, awake!" (51:9). God responded that he would do so (51:9–16). Then, with a touch of irony, God called back to Israel two different times, "Awake, awake!" (51:17; 52:1), making it clear that it was Israel, not God, who was asleep.
51:9–16 Isaiah anticipated that some exiles would accuse God of failing to act on their behalf because he was asleep. Isaiah used the form of a lament and divine response.
51:9 Awake, awake! Double imperatives, as in verse 17, 40:1, 52:1 and 11, 57:14, 62:10 and 65:1. The command implies the accusation that the Lord did not care because he was asleep (see 40:27; Ps 44:23). **Rahab.** See notes on 27:1 and 30:6–7. **monster.** A metaphor for opposition to God (see Job 7:12; Ps 74:13–14; Eze 29:3–5; 32:2–6). This borrowed imagery represents the Lord's conquest of Egypt, which resisted the birth of Israel. It links the first exodus from Egypt and the second exodus from Babylon with God's creative act of bringing a cosmos out of "the depths" (v. 10), the primeval chaotic waters at the time of the creation (see Ge 1:2 and its note). Israel's exodus is portrayed on the broader canvas of God's victory over all evil.

12 "I, even I, am he who comforts[f] you.
Who are you that you fear mortal men,[g]
the sons of men, who are but grass,[h]
13 that you forget[i] the LORD your Maker,[j]
who stretched out the heavens[k]
and laid the foundations of the earth,
that you live in constant terror[l] every day
because of the wrath of the oppressor,
who is bent on destruction?
For where is the wrath of the oppressor?
14 The cowering prisoners will soon be set free;
they will not die in their dungeon,
nor will they lack bread.[m]
15 For I am the LORD your God,
who churns up the sea[n] so that its waves roar—
the LORD Almighty is his name.
16 I have put my words in your mouth[o]
and covered you with the shadow of my hand[p]—
I who set the heavens in place,
who laid the foundations of the earth,
and who say to Zion, 'You are my people.' "

The Cup of the LORD's Wrath

17 Awake, awake![q]
Rise up, O Jerusalem,
you who have drunk from the hand of the LORD
the cup of his wrath,[r]
you who have drained to its dregs
the goblet that makes men stagger.[s]
18 Of all the sons[t] she bore
there was none to guide her;[u]
of all the sons she reared
there was none to take her by the hand.
19 These double calamities[v] have come upon you—
who can comfort you?—
ruin and destruction, famine[w] and sword—
who can[a] console you?
20 Your sons have fainted;
they lie at the head of every street,[x]
like antelope caught in a net.
They are filled with the wrath of the LORD
and the rebuke of your God.

21 Therefore hear this, you afflicted one,
made drunk,[y] but not with wine.
22 This is what your Sovereign LORD says,
your God, who defends[z] his people:

51:12 [f]2Co 1:4 [g]Ps 118:6; Isa 2:22 [h]Isa 40:6-7; 1Pe 1:24
51:13 [i]Isa 17:10 [j]Isa 45:11 [k]Ps 104:2; Isa 48:13 [l]Isa 7:4
51:14 [m]Isa 49:10
51:15 [n]Jer 31:35
51:16 [o]Dt 18:18; Isa 59:21 [p]Ex 33:22
51:17 [q]Isa 52:1 [r]Job 21:20; Rev 14:10; 16:19 [s]Ps 60:3
51:18 [t]Ps 88:18 [u]Isa 49:21
51:19 [v]Isa 47:9 [w]Isa 14:30
51:20 [x]Isa 5:25; Jer 14:16
51:21 [y]ver 17; Isa 29:9
51:22 [z]Isa 49:25

a *19* Dead Sea Scrolls, Septuagint, Vulgate and Syriac; Masoretic Text / *how can I*

51:12 I, even I. Emphatic, as in verse 15. The double pronoun corresponds to the double command to "awake" (v. 9). **comforts.** See notes on 12:1 and 40:1. **fear.** See note on 8:12. Human lives are fleeting, like the "grass" (cf. 40:6; Ps 90:5).
51:14 prisoners . . . dungeon. A metaphor for exile and for all those who would experience the darkness of alienation and the gloom of the day of the Lord (cf. 42:7,22; 49:9,24–25; 52:2; 61:1).
51:15 I am. An emphatic proclamation that God is none other than the Lord. See note on 41:4. **churns up the sea . . . waves roar.** Power over the sea is representative of God's power over all of his creation (Jer 31:35; cf. Job 26:12; Ps 107:25). **LORD Almighty.** See note on 1:9.
51:16 your mouth . . . covered you. God had richly blessed his people in the past. He now addressed Jerusalem: "You are my people." The nation was being renewed in covenant with God (see Hos 1:10—2:3).
51:17–23 God responded to the implied accusation that he had been asleep by repeating Israel's accusation back to her. She was the one who slept and needed to move forward toward restoration to the promised land.
51:17 Awake, awake! Double imperatives, as in verses 1 and 9, as well as in 52:1 and 11 (cf. Eph 5:14). See note on verse 9. **Jerusalem.** Probably a reference not just to the city itself but also to the exiled Israelites who belonged there. **hand.** See note on 40:2. **cup of his wrath . . . goblet.** An image of God's judgment (29:9; 63:6; Ps 75:8; Jer 25:15–31; Eze 23:31–34; Zec 12:2; Jn 18:11; Rev 14:10; 16:19).
51:18 she bore . . . she reared. Jerusalem is personified as a mother (cf. 50:1).
51:19 double calamities. Namely, desolation of the land and the death of the people (cf. "loss of children and widowhood" at 47:9). **comfort.** See notes on 12:1 and 40:1.
51:20 fainted . . . head of every street. See Lamentations 2:11 and 19. **antelope caught in a net.** The siege of Jerusalem. **wrath . . . rebuke.** See notes on 5:25, 10:5 and 37:3.

"See, I have taken out of your hand
the cup[a] that made you stagger;
from that cup, the goblet of my wrath,
you will never drink again.
23 I will put it into the hands of your tormentors,[b]
who said to you,
'Fall prostrate[c] that we may walk[d] over you.'
And you made your back like the ground,
like a street to be walked over."

52

Awake, awake,[e] O Zion,
clothe yourself with strength.[f]
Put on your garments of splendor,[g]
O Jerusalem, the holy city.[h]
The uncircumcised and defiled
will not enter you again.[i]
2 Shake off your dust;[j]
rise up, sit enthroned, O Jerusalem.
Free yourself from the chains on your neck,
O captive Daughter of Zion.

3 For this is what the LORD says:

"You were sold for nothing,[k]
and without money[l] you will be redeemed."

4 For this is what the Sovereign LORD says:

"At first my people went down to Egypt[m] to live;
lately, Assyria has oppressed them.

5 "And now what do I have here?" declares the LORD.
"For my people have been taken away for nothing,
and those who rule them mock,[a]"
declares the LORD.
"And all day long
my name is constantly blasphemed.[n]
6 Therefore my people will know[o] my name;
therefore in that day they will know
that it is I who foretold it.
Yes, it is I."

7 How beautiful on the mountains
are the feet of those who bring good news,[p]
who proclaim peace,[q]
who bring good tidings,
who proclaim salvation,
who say to Zion,
"Your God reigns!"[r]

51:22 [a]ver 17
51:23 [b]Isa 49:26; Jer 25:15-17,26, 28; 49:12 [c]Zec 12:2 [d]Jos 10:24
52:1 [e]Isa 51:17 [f]Isa 51:9 [g]Ex 28:2,40; Ps 110:3; Zec 3:4 [h]Ne 11:1; Mt 4:5; Rev 21:2 [i]Na 1:15; Rev 21:27
52:2 [j]Isa 29:4
52:3 [k]Ps 44:12 [l]Isa 45:13
52:4 [m]Ge 46:6
52:5 [n]Eze 36:20; Ro 2:24*
52:6 [o]Isa 49:23
52:7 [p]Isa 40:9; Ro 10:15* [q]Na 1:15; Eph 6:15 [r]Ps 93:1

[a] *5* Dead Sea Scrolls and Vulgate; Masoretic Text *wail*

51:23 tormentors. The Babylonians (La 1:4–5,12; 3:32) and all those who persecuted and oppressed God's children.
52:1–12 God once again called the exiles to awaken (cf. 51:17). Rather than complaining and accusing God, they should rejoice in the wonder that God would deliver his people.
52:1 Awake, awake. Double imperatives, as in 40:1, 51:9 and 17, 52:11, 57:14, 62:10 and 65:1. **Zion.** See note on 1:8. As in 51:17 the prophet had in mind both the city itself and the exiles who had called it home. **clothe . . . garments.** Jerusalem is pictured as magnificently attired as a royal wife (cf. 61:10; Rev 3:4–5,18; 4:4). Contrast 47:1–4 (see its note). **strength . . . splendor.** See notes on 4:2 and 12:2. By her consecration to the Lord, Jerusalem was the "holy city" (48:2; see Joel 3:17; Rev 21:2; cf. Mt 4:5). See notes on 4:3 and 35:8–9. **uncircumcised and defiled.** The wicked would have no share in the city of God (48:22; Na 1:15; Rev 21:27; 22:14–15).
52:3 sold for nothing. See note on 50:1. **without money.** Salvation is free (see 45:13; 55:1).
52:4 live. Or "sojourn." Israel was dependent on Egypt's promised hospitality, but Egypt betrayed that trust.
52:5 here? That is, Babylon. **for nothing.** That is, without cause. Israel had not wronged Egypt, Assyria or Babylon.
52:6 know my name. An allusion to Exodus 3:13–14 and 6:2. God would demonstrate in action that he was the Lord. **in that day.** See note on 2:11.
52:7 How beautiful on the mountains. The picture is that of a herald on a mountainside scanning the horizon and then running to report good news to those anxiously awaiting information regarding the battle's outcome (see Ps 125:2). **feet.** Refers to the feet of the messenger who would run across the mountains with the good news that the exile was over because God was reigning over his enemies (see 2Sa 18:26). **"Your God reigns!"** This and other passages in Isaiah provide the background of the term "gospel" in the New Testament. The essence of the gospel in both Testaments is that God reigns over all and that his kingdom has come (6:5; 24:23; 33:20; 40:10; 41:21; 43:15,21; 44:6; 60:17; cf. Pss 47:8; 93:1; 97:1; 99:1; Rev 19:6).

52:8 [s]Isa 62:6

8 Listen! Your watchmen[s] lift up their voices;
together they shout for joy.
When the LORD returns to Zion,
they will see it with their own eyes.

52:9 [t]Ps 98:4 [u]Isa 51:3 [v]Isa 48:20

9 Burst into songs of joy[t] together,
you ruins[u] of Jerusalem,
for the LORD has comforted his people,
he has redeemed Jerusalem.[v]

52:10 [w]Isa 66:18 [x]Ps 98:2-3; Lk 3:6

10 The LORD will lay bare his holy arm
in the sight of all the nations,[w]
and all the ends of the earth will see
the salvation[x] of our God.

52:11 [y]Isa 48:20 [z]Isa 1:16; 2Co 6:17* [a]2Ti 2:19

11 Depart,[y] depart, go out from there!
Touch no unclean thing![z]
Come out from it and be pure,[a]
you who carry the vessels of the LORD.

52:12 [b]Ex 12:11 [c]Mic 2:13 [d]Ex 14:19

12 But you will not leave in haste[b]
or go in flight;
for the LORD will go before you,[c]
the God of Israel will be your rear guard.[d]

The Suffering and Glory of the Servant

52:13 [e]Isa 42:1 [f]Isa 57:15; Php 2:9

13 See, my servant[e] will act wisely[a];
he will be raised and lifted up and highly exalted.[f]
14 Just as there were many who were appalled at him[b]—
his appearance was so disfigured beyond that of any man
and his form marred beyond human likeness—
15 so will he sprinkle many nations,[c]
and kings will shut their mouths because of him.
For what they were not told, they will see,
and what they have not heard, they will understand.[g]

52:15 [g]Ro 15:21*; Eph 3:4-5

53:1 [h]Ro 10:16* [i]Jn 12:38*

53

Who has believed our message[h]
and to whom has the arm of the LORD been revealed?[i]
2 He grew up before him like a tender shoot,
and like a root out of dry ground.

[a] *13* Or *will prosper* [b] *14* Hebrew *you* [c] *15* Hebrew; Septuagint *so will many nations marvel at him*

52:8–9 watchmen. Those who longed for God's righteousness (51:1; cf. 62:6). **lift up . . . Burst into songs of joy.** A response of faith in the coming kingdom (cf. 44:23; 49:13; 55:12). **the LORD returns.** The renewal of the covenant and of God's favor to his people. **Zion.** See note on 1:8. **ruins of Jerusalem.** Restoration began with the rebuilding of Jerusalem's ruins (Ezr 3:8–13; Ne 6:15—7:3) and was further manifested in Jesus Christ (Lk 2:38).

52:11–12 See *BC* 28.

52:11 Depart, depart. Double imperatives, as in 51:9 and 17 and in 52:1. **go out from there! Touch no unclean thing! . . . you who carry the vessels.** Those who were to return to Jerusalem and serve God as priests were to be consecrated for holy service (cf. 2Co 6:17; Heb 12:14; 13:13; 1Pe 2:1–12; Rev 18:4). **carry the vessels.** In the first exodus Israel had carried the precious metals for the vessels; in the second exodus (the return from exile) the priests and Levites would bear the vessels (see 2Ki 25:14–15; Ezr 1:7–11; 5:14–15).

52:12 before you . . . rear guard. An allusion to the pillar of cloud and fire that had protected Israel in its flight from Egypt (see 42:16; 49:10; 58:8; Ex 13:21–22; 14:19–20). God's presence would guide his people into the fullness and brilliance of his everlasting kingdom (4:5,6; 42:16; 49:10; 58:8; cf. Ex 13:21–22; 14:19–20).

■ **52:13—53:12** *The Suffering and Exalted Servant.* This section contains the fourth of four servant songs (see 42:1–4; 49:1–7; 50:4–9; 52:13—53:12). The New Testament confirms that the suffering Servant is Jesus Christ (Mt 8:17; 26:63,67; 27:14; Mk 9:12; 14:60; 15:4–5; Lk 22:37; 23:33; 24:27,46; Jn 1:29; 12:38; Ac 3:13; 8:32–33; Ro 4:25; 5:19; 10:16; 15:21; 1Co 5:7; 15:3; Heb 9:28; 1Pe 1:11; 2:22–25; Rev 5:6,12; 13:8). This is the most frequently cited Old Testament passage in the New Testament. Because of his vicarious suffering, all who believe on him—Jews and Gentiles—have hope of life and of sharing his rewards.

52:13–15 The Lord's vindication and glorification of his Servant. See *WLC* 48.

52:13 my servant. See notes on 41:8 and 42:1. **act wisely.** The Hebrew term connotes that the Servant would succeed and be rewarded for possessing insight into and doing God's will (cf. Jer 23:5). **raised . . . exalted.** The Hebrew verbs signify that three successive events in the Servant's exaltation are in view: resurrection, ascension and glorification. **raised . . . up.** From death (see 53:8–10).

52:14 appalled . . . marred. The suffering and disgraced Servant would not be recognized as human (cf. Ps 22:6).

52:15 sprinkle. Ritual purification for transferring the recipient from death to life: of lepers (Lev 14:7; 16:27), of the unclean by contagion with a carcass (Nu 19:4,18–19) and of all Israel on the Day of Atonement (Lev 16:14–15,19). **shut their mouths.** Out of respect. **what they have not heard.** The report given in 53:1–12 (see note on 53:1).

53:1–12 See *WCF* 11.3; *WLC* 31,71; *WSC* 27; *HC* 17,19,37,44.

53:1–3 Isaiah described the humiliation and suffering of the Servant to come (see Mk 9:12; Lk 24:27,46).

53:1 Who . . . to whom . . . ? Rhetorical questions expecting negative answers (see Jn 12:38; Ro 10:16). Although many nations would believe (see 52:15), most would not. **our.** A reference to the elect, converted Israel. **message.** A translation of the same Hebrew root rendered "heard" in 52:15.

53:2 tender shoot. A shoot rising from a plant's stem or root alongside the main plant. Elsewhere Isaiah had stated that the Messiah would grow out of the "stump of Jesse" (11:1; see 4:2). The metaphor indicates that the Servant would come from Israel and be born in humility. **root out of dry ground.** Most unpromising. **no beauty or majesty.** In human terms, the Servant would not cut an impressive figure.

He had no beauty or majesty to attract us to him,
nothing in his appearance[j] that we should desire him.
3 He was despised and rejected by men,
a man of sorrows, and familiar with suffering.[k]
Like one from whom men hide their faces
he was despised,[l] and we esteemed him not.

4 Surely he took up our infirmities
and carried our sorrows,[m]
yet we considered him stricken by God,[n]
smitten by him, and afflicted.
5 But he was pierced for our transgressions,[o]
he was crushed for our iniquities;
the punishment that brought us peace was upon him,
and by his wounds we are healed.[p]
6 We all, like sheep, have gone astray,
each of us has turned to his own way;
and the LORD has laid on him
the iniquity of us all.

7 He was oppressed and afflicted,
yet he did not open his mouth;[q]
he was led like a lamb to the slaughter,
and as a sheep before her shearers is silent,
so he did not open his mouth.
8 By oppression[a] and judgment he was taken away.
And who can speak of his descendants?
For he was cut off from the land of the living;[r]
for the transgression[s] of my people he was stricken.[b]
9 He was assigned a grave with the wicked,
and with the rich[t] in his death,
though he had done no violence,[u]
nor was any deceit in his mouth.[v]

10 Yet it was the LORD's will[w] to crush[x] him and cause him to
suffer,[y]
and though the LORD makes[c] his life a guilt offering,
he will see his offspring[z] and prolong his days,
and the will of the LORD will prosper in his hand.

53:2 [j]Isa 52:14
53:3 [k]ver 4, 10; Lk 18:31-33 [l]Ps 22:6; Jn 1:10-11
53:4 [m]Mt 8:17* [n]Jn 19:7
53:5 [o]Ro 4:25; 1Co 15:3; Heb 9:28 [p]1Pe 2:24-25
53:7 [q]Mk 14:61
53:8 [r]Da 9:26; Ac 8:32-33* [s]ver 12
53:9 [t]Mt 27:57-60 [u]Isa 42:1-3 [v]1Pe 2:22*
53:10 [w]Isa 46:10 [x]ver 5 [y]ver 3 [z]Ps 22:30

[a] *8* Or *From arrest* [b] *8* Or *away. / Yet who of his generation considered / that he was cut off from the land of the living / for the transgression of my people, / to whom the blow was due?* [c] *10* Hebrew *though you make*

53:3 despised and rejected. Christ was alienated from humans (49:7; Ps 22:6; La 1:1–3; 2:15–16). **sorrows . . . suffering.** Our Savior experienced the pain and anguish of human existence. **hide . . . despised.** He was in fact loathed by many people.
53:4–6 Expresses the vicarious nature of Christ's suffering. See *WCF* 11.3; *WLC* 71; *HC* 38.
53:4 our infirmities . . . our sorrows. Or "griefs . . . pains" that result from the fall of Adam, as well as personal sins. Christ vicariously suffered the punishment for the sins of God's own people (see v. 1) and removed sin's consequences from them (see vv. 6,11–12). Even so, this passage does not guarantee perfect health for believers during the present age. Christ will completely heal his people when he raises them from the dead in glorified bodies (1Co 15:42–44; Heb 9:28). **we considered him.** The majority of the Jewish people in the days of Jesus believed that he deserved his suffering. **stricken by God.** The law stipulated that "anyone who is hung on a tree is under God's curse" (Dt 21:23; cf. Gal 3:13), but Jesus' pain and anguish (v. 3) was for the sake of others (Mt 8:17; cf. Ro 4:25; 1Pe 2:24).
53:5 pierced. See Psalm 22:16, Zechariah 12:10 and John 19:34. **our transgressions.** He suffered for the sins of the elect. **we are healed.** A confession of faith in the Servant's vicarious sufferings and death. The New Testament explains that the Servant guarantees spiritual healing now and eventually physical restoration when he returns in glory (1Pe 2:24). Because all God's saints have been healed, they can count themselves as dead to sin and free to serve the cause of righteousness (Ro 6:6; 1Pe 2:24). See *BC* 21.
53:6 We all . . . us all. The Servant's death is efficacious for all his own people. All that the Father gives to the Son come to him (Jn 6:37). **We all.** Although God's people are primarily in view here, all humans are under divine judgment. (see note on Ge 8:21). **sheep . . . astray.** See 1 Peter 2:25. Israel's straying brought the judgment of exile. **laid.** A figure depicting God as laying the sins of his people on Christ and making him a sacrifice in their stead (see Lev 16:21; 1Pe 2:24). See *HC* 8.
53:7 oppressed and afflicted . . . lamb . . . sheep. Jesus Christ was indeed the Lamb of God (Jn 1:29; 1Co 5:7; Rev 5:6,12; 13:8) in terms of his obedience and silent submission (cf. Mt 26:63; 27:12,14; 1Pe 2:23), and he continues to be so in his glorified status (Rev 5:12; 13:8). See *BC* 21.
53:8 oppression and judgment. Jesus was judged inhumanely and unfairly and executed unjustly. He died without children ("descendants") as One judged by God (cf. 14:22). See verse 10. **descendants?** God's Son had no physical children but "begot" many spiritual "offspring" after his death (see v. 10). **transgression . . . stricken.** See NIV text note. **my people.** See note on 40:1.
53:9 wicked . . . rich. The wealthy, unrighteous Israelites trusted in themselves (see Ps 49:6,13; Pr 18:11; 28:11 and their notes) and often obtained their wealth unjustly (Pr 11:16; Jer 9:23; 17:11; Mic 6:12; Mt 12:23; Jas 5:21). **violence . . . deceit.** The Servant, though wise and righteous, died being reckoned as a criminal (1Pe 2:22). See *HC* 15,41.
53:10 the LORD's will. This amazing prophecy reveals that Christ was delivered up to death "by God's set purpose and foreknowledge" (Ac 2:23). **crush . . . suffer.** See verse 5. **guilt offering.** The guilt offering made restitution for damage done against God (Lev 5:14—6:7; 7:1–7; 14:12; 19:21). **offspring.** The seed is spiritual, for it was begotten after Christ's death (see v. 8; Gal 3:26–29). See *WCF* 8.1; *WLC* 49; *CD* 2.1.

11 After the suffering[a] of his soul,
he will see the light ⌞of life⌟[a] and be satisfied[b];
by his knowledge[c] my righteous servant will justify[b] many,
and he will bear their iniquities.
12 Therefore I will give him a portion among the great,[d][c]
and he will divide the spoils with the strong,[e]
because he poured out his life unto death,[d]
and was numbered with the transgressors.[e]
For he bore the sin of many,
and made intercession for the transgressors.

The Future Glory of Zion

54 "Sing, O barren woman,
you who never bore a child;
burst into song, shout for joy,
you who were never in labor;
because more are the children[f] of the desolate woman
than of her who has a husband,[g]"
says the LORD.

2 "Enlarge the place of your tent,[h]
stretch your tent curtains wide,
do not hold back;
lengthen your cords,
strengthen your stakes.[i]
3 For you will spread out to the right and to the left;
your descendants will dispossess nations
and settle in their desolate[j] cities.

4 "Do not be afraid; you will not suffer shame.
Do not fear disgrace; you will not be humiliated.
You will forget the shame of your youth
and remember no more the reproach[k] of your widowhood.
5 For your Maker is your husband[l]—
the LORD Almighty is his name—
the Holy One of Israel is your Redeemer;[m]
he is called the God of all the earth.[n]
6 The LORD will call you back[o]
as if you were a wife deserted[p] and distressed in spirit—
a wife who married young,
only to be rejected," says your God.
7 "For a brief moment[q] I abandoned you,
but with deep compassion I will bring you back.[r]
8 In a surge of anger[s]
I hid my face from you for a moment,

53:11 [a]Jn 10:14-18 [b]Ro 5:18-19
53:12 [c]Php 2:9 [d]Mt 26:28,38,39,42 [e]Mk 15:27*; Lk 22:37*; 23:32
54:1 [f]Isa 49:20 [g]1Sa 2:5; Gal 4:27*
54:2 [h]Isa 49:19-20 [i]Ex 35:18; 39:40
54:3 [j]Isa 49:19
54:4 [k]Isa 51:7
54:5 [l]Jer 3:14 [m]Isa 48:17 [n]Isa 6:3
54:6 [o]Isa 49:14-21 [p]Isa 50:1-2; 62:4,12
54:7 [q]Isa 26:20 [r]Isa 49:18
54:8 [s]Isa 60:10

a *11* Dead Sea Scrolls (see also Septuagint); Masoretic Text does not have *the light ⌞of life⌟.*
b *11* Or (with Masoretic Text) *[11]He will see the result of the suffering of his soul / and be satisfied*
c *11* Or *by knowledge of him*
d *12* Or *many*
e *12* Or *numerous*

53:11 knowledge. A reference to the Messiah's priestly knowledge; Christ had insight into the divine plan (see note on 52:13). **righteous.** See Romans 5:19. **justify.** To declare one acquitted of guilt (see notes on 53:4–6). **many.** See note on 52:15. **bear . . . iniquities.** An instrument of forgiveness (v. 12). See *HC* 12.
53:12 Therefore I. As the great King, the Lord divided the spoils of victory with his triumphant Servant (see 41:8; 52:13). **great . . . strong.** The Servant's triumph after death contrasts strikingly with his humiliation before and in death. **poured out his life.** He gave himself vicariously and extravagantly, in a sense "pouring himself out" for the sins of others (53:4; Lk 22:37; Heb 9:28; 1Pe 2:24). **transgressors.** The same Hebrew word translated "rebelled" in 1:2 (see note at 1:2). See Matthew 27:38, Luke 22:37 and 23:33. **intercession.** Our Savior-Mediator prayed for sinners (Lk 23:34; Heb 7:25).
■ **54:1–17** *Call for Jerusalem to Praise.* Isaiah called for Jerusalem to rejoice in praise to God for the salvation he would bring.
54:1 Sing . . . shout. See notes on 12:6 and 14:7. **barren woman . . . desolate woman.** While in exile Judah and Israel would be forsaken by God and would not experience his blessing. The New Testament applies this verse to the "heavenly Jerusalem" (Heb 12:22), "our mother" (see Gal 4:26). **children.** See 49:21 and 53:10.
54:2 Enlarge . . . strengthen. The enlargement of the tent is a metaphor of the great blessings (cf. 26:15; 33:20); in contrast, see Jeremiah 10:20. See note on 49:19–21.
54:3 right . . . settle. The expansion would be so great that they would possess the cities of their enemies (Ge 22:17; 28:14). See note on 11:14.
54:4 shame of your youth. Israel's infidelity led to its oppression by Egypt in the nation's youth (see 52:4; Jer 31:19; Eze 16:1–6). **reproach of your widowhood.** The Assyrian and Babylonian exiles came after Israel and Judah had matured (see vv. 6–8).
54:5 LORD Almighty . . . Holy One of Israel . . . Redeemer . . . God of all the earth. The piling up of titles for God demonstrates that Israel and Judah did not go into exile because of God's weakness (see 50:1–3). **distressed . . . rejected.** See notes on 40:27, 49:14 and 50:1.
54:7–10 See *WCF* 18.4; *WLC* 81,172.
54:7 brief moment. See 26:20 and Psalm 30:5.

but with everlasting kindness[t]
I will have compassion on you,"
says the LORD your Redeemer.

9 "To me this is like the days of Noah,
when I swore that the waters of Noah would never again cover the earth.[u]
So now I have sworn not to be angry[v] with you,
never to rebuke you again.
10 Though the mountains be shaken[w]
and the hills be removed,
yet my unfailing love for you will not be shaken[x]
nor my covenant[y] of peace be removed,"
says the LORD, who has compassion[z] on you.

11 "O afflicted[a] city, lashed by storms[b] and not comforted,[c]
I will build you with stones of turquoise,[a][d]
your foundations[e] with sapphires.[b]
12 I will make your battlements of rubies,
your gates of sparkling jewels,
and all your walls of precious stones.
13 All your sons will be taught by the LORD,[f]
and great will be your children's peace.[g]
14 In righteousness you will be established:
Tyranny[h] will be far from you;
you will have nothing to fear.
Terror will be far removed;
it will not come near you.
15 If anyone does attack you, it will not be my doing;
whoever attacks you will surrender[i] to you.

16 "See, it is I who created the blacksmith
who fans the coals into flame
and forges a weapon fit for its work.
And it is I who have created the destroyer to work havoc;
17 no weapon forged against you will prevail,[j]
and you will refute[k] every tongue that accuses you.
This is the heritage of the servants of the LORD,
and this is their vindication from me,"
declares the LORD.

Invitation to the Thirsty

55 "Come, all you who are thirsty,[l]
come to the waters;
and you who have no money,
come, buy[m] and eat!
Come, buy wine and milk[n]
without money and without cost.[o]

54:8 [t]ver 10
54:9 [u]Ge 8:21 [v]Isa 12:1
54:10 [w]Ps 46:2 [x]Isa 51:6 [y]Ps 89:34 [z]ver 8
54:11 [a]Isa 14:32 [b]Isa 28:2; 29:6 [c]Isa 51:19 [d]1Ch 29:2; Rev 21:18 [e]Isa 28:16; Rev 21:19-20
54:13 [f]Jn 6:45* [g]Isa 48:18
54:14 [h]Isa 9:4
54:15 [i]Isa 41:11-16
54:17 [j]Isa 29:8 [k]Isa 45:24-25
55:1 [l]Jn 4:14; 7:37 [m]La 5:4; Mt 13:44; Rev 3:18 [n]SS 5:1 [o]Hos 4:14; Mt 10:8; Rev 21:6

a *11* The meaning of the Hebrew for this word is uncertain. b *11* Or *lapis lazuli*

54:9 days of Noah. When the Lord renewed his covenant with creation, symbolized by the rainbow (Ge 9:1–17). **swore.** See note on 14:24. **not . . . never.** Negatives express the emphatic commitment of the Lord to fulfill his covenant with his people.
54:10 mountains . . . hills. The Lord's commitment to his covenants with Israel was greater than that to his covenant with creation (51:6; cf. Pss 46:2–3; 114:4,6). **unfailing love . . . covenant of peace.** Isaiah had in mind here the renewal of the covenant with Israel after the exile (see 42:6; 53:5; see also Eze 34:25; 37:26), which is also known as the "new covenant" (see note on Jer 31:31).
54:11–12 afflicted city. See note on 11:3–5. The city of Jerusalem suffered severely during the exile. **storms.** A metaphor for the day of the Lord's wrath (see note on 2:11). **build . . . sapphires.** Metaphors for the dazzling beauty and glory of Zion, the eternal city of God (cf. Rev 21:19).
54:17 heritage. A reference to the covenant and its promises, especially the promise of God's protection and "vindication" (lit., "righteousness" [v. 14]; see note on 1:21).
■ **55:1–13** *The Invitation to Come.* In light of the promises reaffirmed in the previous passage, Isaiah reported that God was calling his people to find blessing in him.
55:1–5 See *WCF* 8.1; *BC* 26.
55:1 all. The free offer of the gospel extends to all who hear the word of salvation. **thirsty . . . no money.** Reference to the needy, who hunger and thirst for that which money cannot acquire (Dt 8:3; Pss 42:2; 63:1; Pr 9:5–6; Mt 5:6; Jn 4:10–11; 7:37–38; Rev 21:6; 22:17). Isaiah frequently used the imagery of water when speaking of the era of salvation and the kingdom and of divine blessings after the exile. See note on 1:30. **no money . . . buy.** A paradox signifying that salvation is a free gift for those who desire it (see 52:3; Dt 8:3; Ro 6:23). **wine and milk.** Symbols of complete satisfaction. See *WLC* 171.

2 Why spend money on what is not bread,
and your labor on what does not satisfy?[p]
Listen, listen to me, and eat what is good,[q]
and your soul will delight in the richest of fare.
3 Give ear and come to me;
hear me, that your soul may live.[r]
I will make an everlasting covenant[s] with you,
my faithful love[t] promised to David.[u]
4 See, I have made him a witness to the peoples,
a leader and commander[v] of the peoples.
5 Surely you will summon nations[w] you know not,
and nations that do not know you will hasten to you,
because of the LORD your God,
the Holy One of Israel,
for he has endowed you with splendor."[x]

6 Seek the LORD while he may be found;[y]
call[z] on him while he is near.
7 Let the wicked forsake his way
and the evil man his thoughts.[a]
Let him turn[b] to the LORD, and he will have mercy[c] on him,
and to our God, for he will freely pardon.[d]

8 "For my thoughts are not your thoughts,
neither are your ways my ways,"[e]
declares the LORD.
9 "As the heavens are higher than the earth,[f]
so are my ways higher than your ways
and my thoughts than your thoughts.
10 As the rain[g] and the snow
come down from heaven,
and do not return to it
without watering the earth
and making it bud and flourish,
so that it yields seed for the sower and bread for the eater,[h]
11 so is my word that goes out from my mouth:
It will not return to me empty,[i]
but will accomplish what I desire
and achieve the purpose[j] for which I sent it.
12 You will go out in joy
and be led forth in peace;[k]
the mountains and hills
will burst into song before you,
and all the trees[l] of the field
will clap their hands.[m]
13 Instead of the thornbush will grow the pine tree,
and instead of briers[n] the myrtle[o] will grow.
This will be for the LORD's renown,[p]
for an everlasting sign,
which will not be destroyed."

55:2 [p]Ps 22:26; Ecc 6:2; Hos 8:7 [q]Isa 1:19
55:3 [r]Lev 18:5; Ro 10:5 [s]Isa 61:8 [t]Isa 54:8 [u]Ac 13:34*
55:4 [v]Jer 30:9; Eze 34:23-24
55:5 [w]Isa 49:6 [x]Isa 60:9
55:6 [y]Ps 32:6; Isa 49:8; 2Co 6:1-2 [z]Isa 65:24
55:7 [a]Isa 32:7; 59:7 [b]Isa 44:22 [c]Isa 54:10 [d]Isa 1:18; 40:2
55:8 [e]Isa 53:6
55:9 [f]Ps 103:11
55:10 [g]Isa 30:23 [h]2Co 9:10
55:11 [i]Isa 45:23 [j]Isa 44:26
55:12 [k]Isa 54:10,13 [l]1Ch 16:33 [m]Ps 98:8
55:13 [n]Isa 5:6 [o]Isa 41:19 [p]Isa 63:12

55:3 everlasting covenant. In the Davidic covenant God promised David an eternal offspring, throne and kingdom (see 2Sa 7:12–16; 1Ki 8:23–26; Ps 89:27–37; Jer 31:21–22; cf. Ge 9:16; 17:7, 13,19; Nu 18:19). David's house would rule over the nations (cf. Zec 9:10). These promises are fulfilled in Christ (see notes on 4:2; 7:14; 9:6; 11:1–3). **you.** The promises of the Davidic covenant are now extended to all who "come" to God through Christ (Ac 13:34). See notes on 1:21 and 54:6–8. See *WSC* 85.
55:4 witness. Especially by raising Jesus Christ of the house of David from the dead (see 43:10,12; 44:8; Ac 13:34). **leader and commander.** See 42:6, 59:6, Daniel 9:25 and Hebrews 2:10 and 12:2.
55:7 wicked . . . evil man. God requires living faith, including acts of repentance. **mercy . . . freely pardon.** Despite the requirement of repentance, salvation is entirely an act of divine mercy apart from human merit. **our God.** See note on 25:9. See *WCF* 15.4.
55:8 my thoughts are not your thoughts. God is able to assure those who come to him for salvation because his word is so different from that of ordinary humans. His thoughts are infinitely greater and higher than those of people.
55:10–11 rain . . . bread. Just as the patterns of nature established by God are reliable, God's word is sure to have its intended effect. See *WCF* 5.3.
55:12 go out. The exodus from Babylon began the restoration of God's people, but the fulfillment of deliverance from exile is accomplished in Christ (see 48:20–21; 52:11–12). **joy.** See note on 12:3. **peace.** See note on 26:3. **mountains . . . trees.** Representative of all creation. See notes on 14:8 and 54:10. **burst into song . . . clap.** The joy of creation in God's acts of redemption (44:23; 49:13; Ps 96:11–13).
55:13 Instead of. A figure for the replacement of judgment by salvation (see 5:6; 32:13; 41:19). **everlasting sign.** When the

Salvation for Others

56 This is what the LORD says:

"Maintain justice[q]
and do what is right,
for my salvation[r] is close at hand
and my righteousness will soon be revealed.
2 Blessed[s] is the man who does this,
the man who holds it fast,
who keeps the Sabbath[t] without desecrating it,
and keeps his hand from doing any evil."

3 Let no foreigner who has bound himself to the LORD say,
"The LORD will surely exclude me from his people."
And let not any eunuch[u] complain,
"I am only a dry tree."

4 For this is what the LORD says:

"To the eunuchs who keep my Sabbaths,
who choose what pleases me
and hold fast to my covenant—
5 to them I will give within my temple and its walls[v]
a memorial and a name
better than sons and daughters;
I will give them an everlasting name
that will not be cut off.[w]
6 And foreigners who bind themselves to the LORD
to serve[x] him,
to love the name of the LORD,
and to worship him,
all who keep the Sabbath[y] without desecrating it
and who hold fast to my covenant—
7 these I will bring to my holy mountain[z]
and give them joy in my house of prayer.
Their burnt offerings and sacrifices[a]
will be accepted on my altar;
for my house will be called
a house of prayer for all nations.[b]"[c]
8 The Sovereign LORD declares—
he who gathers the exiles of Israel:

56:1 [q]Isa 1:17 [r]Ps 85:9
56:2 [s]Ps 119:2 [t]Ex 20:8, 10; Isa 58:13
56:3 [u]Jer 38:7 *fn*; Ac 8:27
56:5 [v]Isa 26:1; 60:18 [w]Isa 48:19; 55:13
56:6 [x]Isa 60:7, 10; 61:5 [y]ver 2, 4
56:7 [z]Isa 2:2 [a]Ro 12:1; Heb 13:15 [b]Mt 21:13*; Lk 19:46* [c]Mk 11:17*

restoration is completed in Christ's return in glory, the blessings given to God's people will include the permanent renewal of nature in the new heavens and the new earth (Rev 21:1). Compare the rainbow (Ge 9:8-17).

■ **56:1—66:24** *Israel's Sin, Repentance and Restoration.* The prophet closed his book with messages he had given during different periods of his ministry, all focusing on Israel's need for repentance as the only avenue for experiencing the glorious restoration from exile. This section divides into two main parts: the importance of the Sabbath of justice (56:1—58:14) and repentance leading to restoration (59:1—66:24). These chapters summarize the prophet's message to the exiles. The exiles needed to acknowledge the importance of justice and righteousness, and their hope of a glorious worldwide restoration depended on their humble repentance.

■ **56:1—58:14** *The Importance of the Sabbath of Justice.* In these chapters Isaiah focused on the keeping of the Sabbath as the provision for justice and righteousness in Israel. This material divides into three main parts: Jews and Gentiles and the Sabbath (56:1–8), the division between the righteous and wicked in Israel (56:9—57:21) and the need to keep the Sabbath as a day of justice (58:1–14).

■ **56:1–8** *The Decisive Importance of Sabbath Keeping.* To stress the importance of repentance for the exiles, Isaiah indicated that justice and righteousness were to be exhibited among the people of God. This requirement is so central that even Gentiles and eunuchs who keep the Sabbath as it was connected with justice will be included in the blessings of the restoration after exile.

56:1 justice . . . right. Justice—the godly and righteous treatment of others—was a central concern of Isaiah. God through his prophet condemned Judah to exile because of injustice and held forth justice as a characteristic of the period of restoration (1:21,27; 5:7,16,23; 9:7; 10:2; 11:4; 16:5; 28:6,17,21; 29:21; 30:18; 32:1,16; 33:5; 42:1,3–4; 51:4–5; 56:1; 59:4,8–9,11,14–15; 61:8). **for.** God used repentance over injustice as a criterion for determining who would enter the age of blessing after exile. **my salvation.** Although this term refers to the restoration from exile that God brought in 539 B.C., the final stage of God's salvation comes in Christ (see theological article "The Plan of the Ages" at Heb 7). **close at hand.** Isaiah spoke from the perspective of those in exile. See 50:8, 51:5 and Php 4:5.

56:2 Blessed. The prophet did not propose salvation by keeping the law. He simply spoke of keeping the Sabbath of justice as a crucial expression of saving faith. **Sabbath.** Observance of this sign of the covenant (see Ex 31:13–17) signified loyalty to the Lord and to his covenant (58:13; Eze 20:20). Since the Sabbath was observed for the benefit of human beings (Dt 5:4–5), it was closely associated with righteousness and justice. **hand . . . evil.** The practice of godliness (cf. 58:7–9). See *WCF* 21.7; *WLC* 116.

56:3 foreigner. The non-Israelite. **eunuch.** One usually excluded from full participation in the covenant community in the Old Testament (Dt 23:1).

56:4 See *WCF* 21.7; *WLC* 116.

56:5 everlasting name. That is, everlasting life in God's temple (see v. 7; 2:2; Ac 8:27,38–40).

56:6–7 See *WCF* 21.6; 21.7; *WLC* 116.

56:7 house of prayer. See Matthew 21:13. God intended to include faithful Gentiles in communion with himself (2:2–4; Ps 15:1; cf. 1Ki 8:41–43; Mk 11:17). See note on 2:2.

56:8 Sovereign LORD. See note on 25:7–8. **gathers the exiles . . .**

"I will gather[d] still others to them
besides those already gathered."

God's Accusation Against the Wicked

9 Come, all you beasts of the field,[e]
come and devour, all you beasts of the forest!
10 Israel's watchmen[f] are blind,
they all lack knowledge;
they are all mute dogs,
they cannot bark;
they lie around and dream,
they love to sleep.[g]
11 They are dogs with mighty appetites;
they never have enough.
They are shepherds[h] who lack understanding;[i]
they all turn to their own way,
each seeks his own gain.[j]
12 "Come," each one cries, "let me get wine!
Let us drink our fill of beer!
And tomorrow will be like today,
or even far better."[k]

57

The righteous perish,[l]
and no one ponders it in his heart;[m]
devout men are taken away,
and no one understands
that the righteous are taken away
to be spared from evil.[n]
2 Those who walk uprightly[o]
enter into peace;
they find rest as they lie in death.

3 "But you—come here, you sons of a sorceress,
you offspring of adulterers[p] and prostitutes![q]
4 Whom are you mocking?
At whom do you sneer
and stick out your tongue?
Are you not a brood of rebels,
the offspring of liars?
5 You burn with lust among the oaks
and under every spreading tree;[r]
you sacrifice your children[s] in the ravines
and under the overhanging crags.
6 ⌞The idols⌟[t] among the smooth stones of the ravines are your portion;
they, they are your lot.
Yes, to them you have poured out drink offerings[u]

56:8 [d]Isa 11:12; 60:3-11; Jn 10:16
56:9 [e]Isa 18:6; Jer 12:9
56:10 [f]Eze 3:17 [g]Na 3:18
56:11 [h]Eze 34:2 [i]Isa 1:3 [j]Isa 57:17; Eze 13:19; Mic 3:11
56:12 [k]Ps 10:6; Lk 12:18-19
57:1 [l]Ps 12:1 [m]Isa 42:25 [n]2Ki 22:20
57:2 [o]Isa 26:7
57:3 [p]Mt 16:4 [q]Isa 1:21
57:5 [r]2Ki 16:4 [s]Lev 18:21; Ps 106:37-38; Eze 16:20
57:6 [t]Jer 3:9 [u]Jer 7:18

---

others. After the exile the Lord would gather both Jews and non-Jews into one community (11:11–12; cf. Jn 10:16).

■ **56:9—57:21** *The Righteous and Wicked in Israel.* After emphasizing justice (and the Sabbath) by indicating that Gentiles who exhibited commitment to this ideal would receive salvation, Isaiah warned that among the Israelites in exile there would be those who were righteous and those who were wicked. Repentance would be the key for determining the fate of individual Israelites.

56:9 beasts of the field. A metaphor for hostile nations (see 18:6; Jer 12:8–9; Eze 34:5,8,25; 1Co 15:32).

56:10–11 See *WLC* 130.

56:10 watchmen. Watchers who warned the city of approaching danger; in this context a figure for prophets (see 21:6; 57:11; Jer 6:17; Eze 3:17; 33:2–7) who served in a leadership capacity (see v. 11). **blind.** Even Israel's prophets often refused to see what they should have seen. See note on 29:18. **lie . . . sleep.** The Hebrew word for "sleep" sounds like that for "seer" (an ancient term for "prophet"). See 29:9–10.

56:11 dogs. In Isaiah's world dogs were vicious and despised scavengers that represented uncleanness. The dog is used here as a figure for insatiable greed. **shepherds.** A figure for rulers (see notes on v. 10; 40:11; Eze 34:1–6). **turn to their own way.** See note on 53:6.

56:12 Come . . . Let us. See note on 22:13. **wine!** See notes on 24:11 and 28:7–11.

57:1–2 See *WLC* 85,86; *WSC* 37.

57:3 sorceress. See 2:6 and Deuteronomy 18:10. **offspring.** See 1:4 and Ezekiel 16:3 and 45. **adulterers . . . prostitutes!** An allusion to Canaanite fertility rites (cf. Eze 16:3,45).

57:4 Whom . . . Are you . . . ? Rhetorical questions (see notes on 27:7; 40:12). **mocking . . . tongue?** The ungodly are filled with sarcasm and criticism (cf. 5:18–19; 28:9–10; 37:3).

57:5 oaks . . . spreading tree. Sacred trees (cf. Dt 12:2; Eze 6:13). See note on 1:29–30. **children.** Child sacrifice was practiced in the worship of Molech (v. 9; cf. 2Ki 23:10; Ps 106:37–38; Jer 7:31; Eze 20:28,31; Mic 6:7). **ravines . . . crags.** Secret hiding places (2:21). See note on 7:19.

57:6 idols . . . lot. Instead of the Lord being their lot and portion (Dt 4:19–20; 9:26; Pss 16:5; 142:5; Jer 10:16), idols had become their covenant partners.

and offered grain offerings.
In the light of these things, should I relent?[v]
7 You have made your bed on a high and lofty hill;[w]
there you went up to offer your sacrifices.
8 Behind your doors and your doorposts
you have put your pagan symbols.
Forsaking me, you uncovered your bed,
you climbed into it and opened it wide;
you made a pact with those whose beds you love,[x]
and you looked on their nakedness.[y]
9 You went to Molech[a] with olive oil
and increased your perfumes.
You sent your ambassadors[b][z] far away;
you descended to the grave[c] itself!
10 You were wearied by all your ways,
but you would not say, 'It is hopeless.'[a]
You found renewal of your strength,
and so you did not faint.

11 "Whom have you so dreaded and feared[b]
that you have been false to me,
and have neither remembered[c] me
nor pondered this in your hearts?
Is it not because I have long been silent[d]
that you do not fear me?
12 I will expose your righteousness and your works,[e]
and they will not benefit you.
13 When you cry out[f] for help,
let your collection ⌞of idols⌟ save you!
The wind will carry all of them off,
a mere breath will blow them away.
But the man who makes me his refuge
will inherit the land[g]
and possess my holy mountain."[h]

Comfort for the Contrite

14 And it will be said:

"Build up, build up, prepare the road!
Remove the obstacles out of the way of my people."[i]
15 For this is what the high and lofty[j] One says—
he who lives forever,[k] whose name is holy:
"I live in a high and holy place,
but also with him who is contrite[l] and lowly in spirit,[m]
to revive the spirit of the lowly
and to revive the heart of the contrite.[n]
16 I will not accuse forever,
nor will I always be angry,[o]

57:6 [v]Jer 5:9,29; 9:9
57:7 [w]Jer 3:6; Eze 16:16
57:8 [x]Eze 16:26; 23:7 [y]Eze 23:18
57:9 [z]Eze 23:16,40
57:10 [a]Jer 2:25; 18:12
57:11 [b]Pr 29:25 [c]Jer 2:32; 3:21 [d]Ps 50:21
57:12 [e]Isa 29:15; Mic 3:2-4,8
57:13 [f]Jer 22:20; 30:15 [g]Ps 37:9 [h]Isa 65:9-11
57:14 [i]Isa 62:10; Jer 18:15
57:15 [j]Isa 52:13 [k]Dt 33:27 [l]Ps 147:3 [m]Ps 34:18; 51:17; Isa 66:2 [n]Isa 61:1
57:16 [o]Ps 85:5; 103:9; Mic 7:18

[a] 9 Or *to the king* [b] 9 Or *idols* [c] 9 Hebrew *Sheol*

57:7 bed . . . high and lofty hill. A reference to immoral and idolatrous practices at the shrines (Hos 4:13).
57:8 doors . . . bed. Further elaboration of verse 7. **pact . . . nakedness.** The ungodly had made a covenant with immorality and lust.
57:9 Molech. An Ammonite god (v. 5). **sent . . . descended.** A reference to extreme efforts, taking place over an extended area, at placating the gods. **grave.** Hyperbole to express the depths to which these people had sunk.
57:10 renewal of your strength. The ungodly found a counterfeit life in immorality and idolatry—but one that ultimately led to death.
57:11 feared . . . neither remembered. See 51:12–13. **silent.** See 42:14 and 2 Peter 3:9.
57:12 expose your righteousness. Their righteousness was not genuine (see 58:2–3; 64:6).
57:13 wind. See note on 28:2. **refuge.** See note on 4:6. **inherit the land.** See Jesus' Beatitude regarding the meek (v. 15; cf. Mt 5:5). **holy mountain.** An expression of fellowship with God and of inclusion in his kingdom (33:16).
57:14 Isaiah reminded Israel that a time of restoration was coming. **Build up, build up.** A double imperative for emphasis, as in 40:1, 51:9 and 17, 52:1 and 11, 62:10 and 65:1. **road . . . way.** See notes on 11:16 and 40:2 and 3. **obstacles.** The idolatry and immorality described in verses 3–13. **my people.** See note on 40:1.
57:15 high . . . lofty One. An epithet for the Lord (6:1). See notes on 2:2 and 11. **holy.** See note on 4:3. **with . . . contrite and lowly.** Having exposed the sinfulness of the exiles, Isaiah made it clear that God would live with those who humbly repented (see Pss 34:17–18; 51:17; 1Pe 5:6) and be present with all who walked discreetly before him (Mic 6:8). See *HC* 90.
57:16 not accuse forever. Rather, in sovereign grace God would grant forgiveness and salvation to the repentant in exile (see 54:9; 57:19; Ge 8:21–22; Ps 130:3–4).

for then the spirit of man would grow faint before me—
the breath of man that I have created.
17 I was enraged by his sinful greed;[p]
I punished him, and hid my face in anger,
yet he kept on in his willful ways.[q]
18 I have seen his ways, but I will heal[r] him;
I will guide him and restore comfort[s] to him,
19 creating praise on the lips[t] of the mourners in Israel.
Peace, peace,[u] to those far and near,"[v]
says the LORD. "And I will heal them."
20 But the wicked[w] are like the tossing sea,
which cannot rest,
whose waves cast up mire and mud.
21 "There is no peace,"[x] says my God, "for the wicked."[y]

True Fasting

58

"Shout it aloud,[z] do not hold back.
Raise your voice like a trumpet.
Declare to my people their rebellion[a]
and to the house of Jacob their sins.
2 For day after day they seek[b] me out;
they seem eager to know my ways,
as if they were a nation that does what is right
and has not forsaken the commands of its God.
They ask me for just decisions
and seem eager for God to come near[c] them.
3 'Why have we fasted,'[d] they say,
'and you have not seen it?
Why have we humbled ourselves,
and you have not noticed?'[e]

"Yet on the day of your fasting, you do as you please[f]
and exploit all your workers.
4 Your fasting ends in quarreling and strife,[g]
and in striking each other with wicked fists.
You cannot fast as you do today
and expect your voice to be heard[h] on high.
5 Is this the kind of fast[i] I have chosen,
only a day for a man to humble[j] himself?
Is it only for bowing one's head like a reed
and for lying on sackcloth and ashes?[k]
Is that what you call a fast,
a day acceptable to the LORD?

6 "Is not this the kind of fasting I have chosen:
to loose the chains of injustice[l]

57:17 [p]Isa 56:11 [q]Isa 1:4
57:18 [r]Isa 30:26 [s]Isa 61:1-3
57:19 [t]Isa 6:7; Heb 13:15 [u]Eph 2:17 [v]Ac 2:39
57:20 [w]Job 18:5-21
57:21 [x]Isa 59:8 [y]Isa 48:22
58:1 [z]Isa 40:6 [a]Isa 48:8
58:2 [b]Isa 48:1; Tit 1:16; Jas 4:8 [c]Isa 29:13
58:3 [d]Lev 16:29 [e]Mal 3:14 [f]Isa 22:13; Zec 7:5-6
58:4 [g]1Ki 21:9-13; Isa 59:6 [h]Isa 59:2
58:5 [i]Zec 7:5 [j]1Ki 21:27 [k]Job 2:8
58:6 [l]Ne 5:10-11

57:17 See *WLC* 151.
57:18–19 heal . . . restore comfort. The Lord is the consummate physician (see note on 30:26), teacher (see note on 49:10) and evangelist (see notes on 12:1; 40:1). **creating.** See 4:5. **mourners.** Those who lamented Jerusalem's destruction (see 66:1). See note on 25:7–8. **Peace, peace.** A repetition once again for emphasis. See note on 26:3. **far and near.** Wherever the exiles were to be found, the humble and repentant among them would be restored (Ac 2:39; Eph 2:13,17). See notes on 33:13 and 56:8.
57:20–21 wicked. Those described in 56:10–12. The outcome for the wicked in Israel is contrasted with that of those who humbly served God. **tossing sea.** Constantly in motion, restless and troublesome (cf. Jude 13). See notes on 39:8 and 48:22.
▪ **58:1–14** *Observing Sabbath and Justice.* Having already mentioned the blessing given to Gentiles and eunuchs who observed the Sabbath, as well as the importance of humble repentance among the exiles, Isaiah applied these themes directly to the Israelites by calling on them to observe the Sabbath properly.
58:1 Shout . . . like a trumpet. Isaiah was summoned by God to condemn the people as loudly and clearly as a trumpet (see Ex 19:19; 20:18; Hos 8:1; 1Co 14:8).
58:2 The hypocrisy of the Israelites was exposed. Although they seemed pious, they were not.
58:3–10 See *WLC* 151; *HC* 111.
58:3 not seen it? The anticipated complaint of the exiles was that though they had fasted and humbled themselves, God had not answered them with deliverance from exile. **please and exploit.** They were not concerned with the rights of, or the justice shown toward, others (cf. 1:15–17; 59:2; Hos 6:4–6; Am 5:23–24; Zec 7:8–12). Instead of setting aside the day so that all could devote themselves to rest and worship, they exploited and struck the laborer who did not work.
58:4 quarreling . . . striking. Expressions of pride and hatred. **heard on high.** God does not receive favorably prayer that is not spoken in the spirit of love.
58:5 fast I have chosen. God contrasted his concept of fasting with that of the wicked in Israel (see 1:10–15; Am 5:21–23; Mic 6:7). **humble . . . lying.** God was looking for expressions of inner humility and brokenness before him, not for devotion to rituals (cf. Mt 6:16). **bowing . . . ashes?** Mourning ceremonies that accompanied fasting (see 2Sa 12:16; Joel 1:13,14).
58:6 fasting I have chosen. A clear definition of the kind of fast-

and untie the cords of the yoke,
to set the oppressed[m] free
and break every yoke?
7 Is it not to share your food with the hungry[n]
and to provide the poor wanderer with shelter[o]—
when you see the naked, to clothe[p] him,
and not to turn away from your own flesh and blood?[q]
8 Then your light will break forth like the dawn,[r]
and your healing[s] will quickly appear;
then your righteousness[a] will go before you,
and the glory of the LORD will be your rear guard.[t]
9 Then you will call,[u] and the LORD will answer;
you will cry for help, and he will say: Here am I.

"If you do away with the yoke of oppression,
with the pointing finger[v] and malicious talk,[w]
10 and if you spend yourselves in behalf of the hungry
and satisfy the needs of the oppressed,[x]
then your light[y] will rise in the darkness,
and your night will become like the noonday.[z]
11 The LORD will guide you always;
he will satisfy your needs[a] in a sun-scorched land
and will strengthen your frame.
You will be like a well-watered garden,[b]
like a spring[c] whose waters never fail.
12 Your people will rebuild the ancient ruins[d]
and will raise up the age-old foundations;[e]
you will be called Repairer of Broken Walls,
Restorer of Streets with Dwellings.

13 "If you keep your feet from breaking the Sabbath[f]
and from doing as you please on my holy day,
if you call the Sabbath a delight[g]
and the LORD's holy day honorable,
and if you honor it by not going your own way
and not doing as you please or speaking idle words,
14 then you will find your joy[h] in the LORD,
and I will cause you to ride on the heights[i] of the land
and to feast on the inheritance of your father Jacob."
The mouth of the LORD has spoken.[j]

Sin, Confession and Redemption

59 Surely the arm of the LORD is not too short[k] to save,
nor his ear too dull to hear.[l]

58:6 [m]Jer 34:9
58:7 [n]Eze 18:16; Lk 3:11 [o]Isa 16:4; Heb 13:2 [p]Job 31:19-20; Mt 25:36 [q]Ge 29:14; Lk 10:31-32
58:8 [r]Job 11:17 [s]Isa 30:26 [t]Ex 14:19
58:9 [u]Ps 50:15 [v]Pr 6:13 [w]Ps 12:2; Isa 59:13
58:10 [x]Dt 15:7-8 [y]Isa 42:16 [z]Job 11:17
58:11 [a]Ps 107:9 [b]SS 4:15 [c]Jn 4:14
58:12 [d]Isa 49:8 [e]Isa 44:28
58:13 [f]Isa 56:2 [g]Ps 84:2, 10
58:14 [h]Job 22:26 [i]Dt 32:13 [j]Isa 1:20
59:1 [k]Nu 11:23; Isa 50:2 [l]Isa 58:9; 65:24

[a] 8 Or *your righteous One*

---

ing an unjust nation was to perform: Its citizens were to deny themselves in order to rescue the oppressed and provide for the needy (cf. Job 31:17–20; Mt 25:35–36).
58:7 own flesh. See 1 Timothy 5:8.
58:8 Then. Expresses the connection between responsibility and the coming of God's kingdom. **light . . . glory.** The glorious kingdom of God (see 9:2; 60:1–3; Lk 1:78–79) would dawn with God's blessing and protection (cf. 60:1–3; see note on 2:5), with transformation (see note on 30:26), with the establishment of a new order (see note on 1:21) and with the presence of the God of glory (see note on 4:2). **glory.** A reference to the pillar of cloud and fire in the desert (see 4:5,6; Ex 13:21; 14:20).
58:9 call . . . cry. Then God would answer prayer (30:19; 65:24; cf. v. 4). **Here am I.** See note on 52:6. **oppression . . . malicious talk.** Unrighteous acts, contempt (Pr 6:13) and improper speech (cf. v. 4).
58:10 hungry . . . oppressed. A summons to "spend" (or expend) oneself in caring for the needy (v. 7). **then.** See verse 8. **light . . . noonday.** The dawning of the new age in ever greater brightness (see notes on 2:5; 5:30).
58:11 well-watered garden . . . spring. Greatly blessed and productive (cf. Jn 7:38; see note on 1:30).
58:12 rebuild the ancient ruins. The restored exiles lacked the spiritual and economic resources to rebuild (see 44:26,28; 61:2,4; Eze 36:10; Am 9:14–15; Hag 1:2–9; cf. Ac 15:15–17).
58:13 Sabbath . . . holy day. Fasting in general was now connected closely with the Sabbath. The Lord did not reject ritual as such; it was the sign of the covenant. See note on 56:2. **own way . . . speaking.** Acts and speech aimed at social prestige, financial gain and political domination (see note on 33:15). See *WCF* 21.8; *WLC* 99,117,119; *WSC* 61.
■ **59:1—66:24** *Repentance and Restoration.* Having established that the repentant and humble would experience the blessings of salvation when God restored his people, Isaiah closed his book with two parallel scenarios of repentance leading to God's reassuring promise of restoration (59:1—63:6; 63:7—66:24). This repeated structure finds its roots in the traditional, liturgical order of lament followed by a proclamation of salvation (see "Psalms: Introduction"; see also notes on 2Ch 20). As such, it provided the readers of Isaiah with a pattern of response to the book as a whole. The exiles who heard the message of the prophet were to humble themselves in repentance and cry out to God for help in complete assurance of a return to the land and to a world of God's blessings described as nothing less than "new heavens and a new earth" (65:17; see 66:22).

59:2 [m]Isa 1:15; 58:4
59:3 [n]Isa 1:15
59:4 [o]Job 15:35; Ps 7:14
59:5 [p]Job 8:14
59:6 [q]Isa 28:20 [r]Isa 58:4
59:7 [s]Pr 6:17 [t]Mk 7:21-22 [u]Ro 3:15-17*
59:8 [v]Isa 57:21; Lk 1:79
59:9 [w]Isa 5:30; 8:20
59:10 [x]Dt 28:29 [y]Isa 8:15 [z]La 3:6
59:11 [a]Isa 38:14; Eze 7:16
59:12 [b]Ezr 9:6 [c]Isa 3:9
59:13 [d]Pr 30:9; Mt 10:33; Tit 1:16

2 But your iniquities have separated
you from your God;
your sins have hidden his face from you,
so that he will not hear.[m]
3 For your hands are stained with blood,[n]
your fingers with guilt.
Your lips have spoken lies,
and your tongue mutters wicked things.
4 No one calls for justice;
no one pleads his case with integrity.
They rely on empty arguments and speak lies;
they conceive trouble and give birth to evil.[o]
5 They hatch the eggs of vipers
and spin a spider's web.[p]
Whoever eats their eggs will die,
and when one is broken, an adder is hatched.
6 Their cobwebs are useless for clothing;
they cannot cover themselves with what they make.[q]
Their deeds are evil deeds,
and acts of violence[r] are in their hands.
7 Their feet rush into sin;
they are swift to shed innocent blood.[s]
Their thoughts are evil thoughts;[t]
ruin and destruction mark their ways.[u]
8 The way of peace they do not know;
there is no justice in their paths.
They have turned them into crooked roads;
no one who walks in them will know peace.[v]

9 So justice is far from us,
and righteousness does not reach us.
We look for light, but all is darkness;[w]
for brightness, but we walk in deep shadows.
10 Like the blind[x] we grope along the wall,
feeling our way like men without eyes.
At midday we stumble[y] as if it were twilight;
among the strong, we are like the dead.[z]
11 We all growl like bears;
we moan mournfully like doves.[a]
We look for justice, but find none;
for deliverance, but it is far away.

12 For our offenses[b] are many in your sight,
and our sins testify[c] against us.
Our offenses are ever with us,
and we acknowledge our iniquities:
13 rebellion and treachery against the LORD,
turning our backs[d] on our God,

▪ **59:1—63:6** *Repentance and Response.* This first section was designed to guide the readers toward response to Isaiah's prophecies. It divides into two main sections: a call for the people to repent (59:1–13) and a description of what the Lord would do in response (59:14—63:6).

▪ **59:1–13** *Call to Repentance.* The prophet moved from exposing the sins of God's people in captivity to calling them to repent so they could return from exile.

59:1 God is able to save his people. **arm.** See note on 40:10. **ear.** Unlike people (6:10), God hears (30:19).

59:2 See *WLC* 181.

59:3 The continuing sins of God's people separated them from him so that he was not ready to save them. **blood . . . guilt.** Violence and injustice. See note on 1:15. **lies . . . wicked.** Unfair speech.

59:4 justice. Or "righteousness." See note on 1:21. **integrity.** See notes on 1:21 and 11:3–5. See *WLC* 145.

59:5–6 vipers . . . spider's web. Poignant metaphors for those in Israel who had corrupted and poisoned the nation. **cobwebs.** Their power structures were of no ultimate value (Job 8:14–15).

59:7–8 rush . . . swift. Such people had broken God's laws with little forethought (Pr 1:16). Their actions arose from their wicked hearts and resulted in discord and chaos (Ro 3:15–17). **way of peace.** Thoughts, actions and words that promote harmony. See note on 26:3. **justice.** See note on 1:21. **know peace.** In strict justice, those who deny others peace will themselves fail to know it (see 57:21).

59:9 from us. At this point (vv. 9–13) the prophecy moves from describing Israel in the second and third persons ("you," "they") to doing so in the first person ("us," "we," "our"). The readers were led to accept God's judgment and to confess their failures.

59:10 blind. See note on 29:18. **feeling our way . . . stumble.** The experience of God's curse (Dt 28:29; cf. Job 5:14).

59:11 growl . . . bears. An expression of frustration. **moan . . . doves.** Laments about their condition (cf. 38:14; Na 2:7). **justice.** See note on 1:21. **deliverance.** See note on 12:2.

59:12 offenses . . . iniquities. The people were led to confess their sin (see note on 64:5–7); this is further explicated in verse 13.

59:13 See *WLC* 145.

fomenting oppression[e] and revolt,
uttering lies[f] our hearts have conceived.
14 So justice is driven back,
and righteousness[g] stands at a distance;
truth[h] has stumbled in the streets,
honesty cannot enter.
15 Truth is nowhere to be found,
and whoever shuns evil becomes a prey.

The LORD looked and was displeased
that there was no justice.
16 He saw that there was no one,[i]
he was appalled that there was no one to intervene;
so his own arm worked salvation[j] for him,
and his own righteousness sustained him.
17 He put on righteousness as his breastplate,[k]
and the helmet[l] of salvation on his head;
he put on the garments[m] of vengeance
and wrapped himself in zeal[n] as in a cloak.
18 According to what they have done,
so will he repay
wrath to his enemies
and retribution to his foes;
he will repay the islands their due.
19 From the west,[o] men will fear the name of the LORD,
and from the rising of the sun,[p] they will revere his glory.
For he will come like a pent-up flood
that the breath of the LORD drives along.[a]

20 "The Redeemer will come to Zion,
to those in Jacob who repent of their sins,"[q]
declares the LORD.

21 "As for me, this is my covenant with them," says the LORD. "My Spirit,[r] who is on
you, and my words that I have put in your mouth will not depart from your mouth, or
from the mouths of your children, or from the mouths of their descendants from this time
on and forever," says the LORD.

The Glory of Zion

60 "Arise,[s] shine, for your light[t] has come,
and the glory of the LORD rises upon you.
2 See, darkness covers the earth
and thick darkness[u] is over the peoples,
but the LORD rises upon you
and his glory appears over you.

59:13 [e]Isa 5:7 [f]Mk 7:21-22
59:14 [g]Isa 1:21 [h]Isa 48:1
59:16 [i]Isa 41:28 [j]Ps 98:1; Isa 63:5
59:17 [k]Eph 6:14 [l]Eph 6:17; 1Th 5:8 [m]Isa 63:3 [n]Isa 9:7
59:19 [o]Isa 49:12 [p]Ps 113:3
59:20 [q]Ac 2:38-39; Ro 11:26-27*
59:21 [r]Isa 11:2; 44:3
60:1 [s]Isa 52:2 [t]Eph 5:14
60:2 [u]Jer 13:16; Col 1:13

a 19 Or *When the enemy comes in like a flood, / the Spirit of the LORD will put him to flight*

■ **59:14—63:6** *God's Response of Salvation.* Having led the readers to confess their sins, Isaiah now assured them that God would respond to their helpless condition and deliver Israel from exile.

■ **59:14—60:22** *Evil Will Be Overcome.* Evil had prevailed over the Israelites in exile to the point that they had been entirely overcome.

59:16 no one. See 63:5, which parallels this verse. The Israelites themselves were powerless to remedy their situation, so God determined to mediate on their behalf. **no one to intervene.** Contrast the intercession of the Servant (see 53:12). **arm.** See note on 40:10. **righteousness.** The Servant's victorious salvation (see 46:13; 51:6,8; 56:1).

59:17 put on . . . wrapped himself. The Divine Warrior would accomplish the defeat of his enemies and the restoration of his faithful people (42:13; 49:25; 52:10; Ex 15:3). **breastplate . . . helmet.** Between the first and second comings of Christ, Christians put on this armor of God as they continue the spiritual dimension of the great battle described here (see Eph 6:14–17).

59:20 Redeemer. The New Testament teaches that God the Redeemer came to Jerusalem in the person of Jesus Christ. This promise is confirmed by Paul (Ro 11:26–27). See note on 35:8–9. **Zion.** See note on 1:8.

59:21 covenant. The restoration from exile involved renewal of the Lord's covenant with Israel. See note on 42:6. **them.** The repentant of verse 20. **Spirit.** The covenant would be internalized by the Spirit of God (4:4; 32:15–20; 44:3–4; Jer 31:31–34; Eze 37:1–14; Zec 12:10), so that the Word and the Spirit would apply and confirm it from generation to generation. (see note on 61:8). See note on 11:2. See *WCF* 1.5; 25.3; *WLC* 2,62; *HC* 54.

60:1—63:6 These magnificent prophecies about Jerusalem's golden future find their fulfillment today in the heavenly Jerusalem (i.e., "the Jerusalem that is above"; Gal 4:26) and will be ultimately fulfilled in the new heavens and the new earth when Christ returns (Rev 21:1–27).

60:1 Arise. The form is feminine singular, as it is addressed to Zion (see v. 14; 1:8). **shine.** As opposed to suffering the gloom of destruction and oppression, Zion would rise up and shine with joy and happiness (cf. Lk 1:78–79; Eph 5:14; Rev 21:11). **light . . . glory of the LORD.** The Lord would come with the glorious blessings of salvation (see vv. 19–20).

60:2 darkness covers . . . LORD rises. As at the exodus from Egypt, God's light is on his people, while darkness is on the rest of

[3] Nations[v] will come to your light,
and kings[w] to the brightness of your dawn.

[4] "Lift up your eyes and look about you:
All assemble[x] and come to you;
your sons come from afar,
and your daughters[y] are carried on the arm.[z]
[5] Then you will look and be radiant,
your heart will throb and swell with joy;
the wealth on the seas will be brought to you,
to you the riches of the nations will come.
[6] Herds of camels will cover your land,
young camels of Midian[a] and Ephah.[b]
And all from Sheba[c] will come,
bearing gold and incense[d]
and proclaiming the praise[e] of the LORD.
[7] All Kedar's[f] flocks will be gathered to you,
the rams of Nebaioth will serve you;
they will be accepted as offerings on my altar,
and I will adorn my glorious temple.[g]

[8] "Who are these[h] that fly along like clouds,
like doves to their nests?
[9] Surely the islands[i] look to me;
in the lead are the ships of Tarshish,[a][j]
bringing[k] your sons from afar,
with their silver and gold,
to the honor of the LORD your God,
the Holy One of Israel,
for he has endowed you with splendor.[l]

[10] "Foreigners[m] will rebuild your walls,
and their kings[n] will serve you.
Though in anger I struck you,
in favor I will show you compassion.[o]
[11] Your gates[p] will always stand open,
they will never be shut, day or night,
so that men may bring you the wealth of the nations[q]—
their kings[r] led in triumphal procession.
[12] For the nation or kingdom that will not serve[s] you will perish;
it will be utterly ruined.

[13] "The glory of Lebanon[t] will come to you,
the pine, the fir and the cypress together,[u]

60:3 [v]Isa 45:14; Rev 21:24 [w]Isa 49:23
60:4 [x]Isa 11:12 [y]Isa 43:6 [z]Isa 49:20-22
60:6 [a]Ge 25:2 [b]Ge 25:4 [c]Ps 72:10 [d]Isa 43:23; Mt 2:11 [e]Isa 42:10
60:7 [f]Ge 25:13 [g]ver 13; Hag 2:3,7,9
60:8 [h]Isa 49:21
60:9 [i]Isa 11:11 [j]Isa 2:16 *fn* [k]Isa 14:2; 43:6 [l]Isa 55:5
60:10 [m]Isa 14:1-2 [n]Isa 49:23; Rev 21:24 [o]Isa 54:8
60:11 [p]ver 18; Isa 62:10; Rev 21:25 [q]ver 5; Rev 21:26 [r]Ps 149:8
60:12 [s]Isa 14:2
60:13 [t]Isa 35:2 [u]Isa 41:19

[a] 9 Or *the trading ships*

the land (see Ex 10:23). **his glory.** See verse 1, 4:5, 40:5, John 1:14 and Revelation 21:11.

60:3 Nations will come. In 2:3 the nations came to be taught; here to bring tribute. The prophecy finds fulfillment today as the kingdom of God spreads to the nations and they worship the Son of God (see notes on 2:2–4). **kings to the brightness.** The leaders of nations would submit to Christ (see 42:6; 49:6).

60:5 wealth . . . will be brought. See Haggai 2:7 and Zechariah 14:14. The fulfillment of this prophecy began with Darius's contribution to the temple (see Ezr 6:8–9). Its greater fulfillment has come in connection with the ascended Christ inhabiting his heavenly temple as he rules in the hearts of nations. It will find its consummation in the future new Jerusalem when Christ returns and possesses all things (see Heb 11:39–40; 13:14–15).

60:6 Midian. A desert tribe famous for its caravans and trade (see Ge 37:28,38; Jdg 6:5). **Ephah.** Related to Midian (Ge 25:4). **Sheba.** A country renowned for its wealth (1Ki 10:2). **praise.** See verse 18 and 1 Kings 10:9.

60:7 Kedar's. See note on 21:16–17. **Nebaioth.** Related to the Ishmaelites (Ge 25:13), who were also known as Nabateans.

60:9 islands look to me. The distant lands would give back Israelites who lived there in exile or as escapees. See also 11:11, 43:5–7 and 14, 49:18 and 51:5. **ships of Tarshish.** See note on 23:5. The blessings of the restoration are described in terms of Solomon's glorious kingdom (see 1Ki 10:22). **silver and gold.** See Haggai 2:7–9.

60:10 Foreigners. As Hiram, king of Tyre, had helped construct the original temple (see 1Ki 5:1–18), and as Cyrus and Darius, kings of Persia, would assist with building the second (Ezr 6), so today it is predominately Gentiles who are building up the church, the temple of the Lord (see Eph 2:11–22). **kings will serve.** The exiles were promised that the kings would depart (49:17); now it is predicted that they would serve Mount Zion (Ac 2:29–36; Heb 12:22) and worship the ascended Christ (see notes on 52:13–15).

60:11 gates . . . day or night. Instead of attacking, the nations would bring tribute (Rev 21:25–26).

60:12 perish. See Genesis 12:3, John 3:18 and Hebrews 2:3, 9:27 and 10:27.

60:13 Lebanon. See note on 35:1–2. **pine . . . cypress.** See notes on 41:18–19 and 44:14. **sanctuary.** Their precious wood glorified Solomon's temple (see 1Ki 5:10,18). This is another connection between the former and latter glory (see notes on vv. 6–7). **place of my feet.** In ever-widening concentric circles, God is said to place his feet on the ark (see 1Ch 28:2; Ps 13:7), the temple (Eze 43:7) and the whole world (66:1).

to adorn the place of my sanctuary;
and I will glorify the place of my feet.[v]
14 The sons of your oppressors[w] will come bowing before you;
all who despise you will bow down[x] at your feet
and will call you the City of the LORD,
Zion[y] of the Holy One of Israel.

15 "Although you have been forsaken[z] and hated,
with no one traveling[a] through,
I will make you the everlasting pride[b]
and the joy[c] of all generations.
16 You will drink the milk of nations
and be nursed[d] at royal breasts.
Then you will know that I, the LORD, am your Savior,
your Redeemer,[e] the Mighty One of Jacob.
17 Instead of bronze I will bring you gold,
and silver in place of iron.
Instead of wood I will bring you bronze,
and iron in place of stones.
I will make peace your governor
and righteousness your ruler.
18 No longer will violence be heard in your land,
nor ruin or destruction within your borders,
but you will call your walls Salvation[f]
and your gates Praise.
19 The sun will no more be your light by day,
nor will the brightness of the moon shine on you,
for the LORD will be your everlasting light,[g]
and your God will be your glory.[h]
20 Your sun[i] will never set again,
and your moon will wane no more;
the LORD will be your everlasting light,
and your days of sorrow[j] will end.
21 Then will all your people be righteous[k]
and they will possess[l] the land forever.
They are the shoot I have planted,[m]
the work of my hands,[n]
for the display of my splendor.[o]
22 The least of you will become a thousand,
the smallest a mighty nation.
I am the LORD;
in its time I will do this swiftly."

The Year of the LORD's Favor

61 The Spirit[p] of the Sovereign LORD is on me,
because the LORD has anointed[q] me
to preach good news to the poor.[r]
He has sent me to bind up[s] the brokenhearted,
to proclaim freedom for the captives[t]
and release from darkness for the prisoners,[a]

60:13 [v]1Ch 28:2; Ps 132:7
60:14 [w]Isa 14:2 [x]Isa 49:23; Rev 3:9 [y]Heb 12:22
60:15 [z]Isa 1:7-9; 6:12 [a]Isa 33:8 [b]Isa 4:2 [c]Isa 65:18
60:16 [d]Isa 49:23; 66:11, 12 [e]Isa 59:20
60:18 [f]Isa 26:1
60:19 [g]Rev 22:5 [h]Zec 2:5; Rev 21:23
60:20 [i]Isa 30:26 [j]Isa 35:10
60:21 [k]Rev 21:27 [l]Ps 37:11,22; Isa 57:13; 61:7 [m]Mt 15:13 [n]Isa 19:25; 29:23; Eph 2:10 [o]Isa 52:1
61:1 [p]Isa 11:2 [q]Ps 45:7 [r]Mt 11:5; Lk 7:22 [s]Isa 57:15 [t]Isa 42:7; 49:9

a *1* Hebrew; Septuagint *the blind*

60:14 oppressors . . . who despise. All enmity would cease. **City of the LORD.** The Lord would exalt his people by establishing his kingship in their midst. **Zion.** See note on 1:8.
60:15 everlasting. The glory of the heavenly Mount Zion will outshine that of the old because it is eternal (vv. 15–16), richer (v. 17a) and spiritual (vv. 17b–18).
60:16 nursed at royal breasts. Literally, "nursed at breasts of kings." This figurative language signifies that wealth would be brought by kings to Zion.
60:17 wood . . . bronze, and iron . . . stones. The substitution of precious metals for wood and stones demonstrates the surpassing greatness of the new temple in comparison to Solomon's. Although a temple was built by the early returnees (Ezr 3:1–13), this temple fell far short of the glory predicted by the prophet. The New Testament explains that the glorious temple of the restoration is fulfilled in Christ (Jn 2:21), in the church (1Co 3:16; 6:19) and in God and Christ's presence in the new heavens and the new earth (Rev 22:21). This hyperbole expresses the exceedingly great and enduring wealth of the heavenly temple to which the church now comes. **governor . . . ruler.** See note on 52:7.
60:18 violence . . . destruction. Associated with war and exile (59:9–11). **walls.** See note on 26:1. God's salvation and Israel's praise constitute the defense of the spiritual temple, Christ and his church (cf. Zec 2:4–5). **Salvation.** See note on 12:2.
60:19 everlasting light. A reference to God's presence among his people (see v. 1; Rev 21:11,23; 22:5). **glory.** See note on 4:2.
■ **61:1–11** *The Year of the Lord's Favor Proclaimed.* Isaiah continued to report how the Lord will respond to the repentance of his

61:2
[u]Isa 49:8; Lk 4:18-19* [v]Isa 34:8 [w]Isa 57:18; Mt 5:4

61:3
[x]Isa 60:20-21

61:4
[y]Isa 49:8; Eze 36:33; Am 9:14

61:5
[z]Isa 14:1-2

61:6
[a]Ex 19:6; 1Pe 2:5 [b]Isa 60:11

61:7
[c]Isa 40:2; Zec 9:12

61:8
[d]Ps 11:7; Isa 5:16 [e]Isa 55:3

61:10
[f]Isa 25:9; Hab 3:18

2 to proclaim the year of the LORD's favor[u]
and the day of vengeance[v] of our God,
to comfort[w] all who mourn,
3 and provide for those who grieve in Zion—
to bestow on them a crown of beauty
instead of ashes,
the oil of gladness
instead of mourning,
and a garment of praise
instead of a spirit of despair.
They will be called oaks of righteousness,
a planting of the LORD
for the display of his splendor.[x]

4 They will rebuild the ancient ruins[y]
and restore the places long devastated;
they will renew the ruined cities
that have been devastated for generations.
5 Aliens[z] will shepherd your flocks;
foreigners will work your fields and vineyards.
6 And you will be called priests[a] of the LORD,
you will be named ministers of our God.
You will feed on the wealth[b] of nations,
and in their riches you will boast.

7 Instead of their shame
my people will receive a double[c] portion,
and instead of disgrace
they will rejoice in their inheritance;
and so they will inherit a double portion in their land,
and everlasting joy will be theirs.

8 "For I, the LORD, love justice;[d]
I hate robbery and iniquity.
In my faithfulness I will reward them
and make an everlasting covenant[e] with them.
9 Their descendants will be known among the nations
and their offspring among the peoples.
All who see them will acknowledge
that they are a people the LORD has blessed."

10 I delight greatly in the LORD;
my soul rejoices[f] in my God.
For he has clothed me with garments of salvation

---

people (see note on 59:1—63:6). The time of God's favor will come to his people as he brings them out of exile and into unprecedented blessings.
61:1 Spirit. See 11:2, 42:1, 48:16 and Luke 3:22. **Sovereign LORD.** Literally, "the Master, the Lord" (see notes on 25:7–8; 50:4). **anointed me.** The great Son of David, whom the New Testament identifies as Jesus (see Lk 4:17–21). He is associated with an everlasting covenant (see v. 8; 42:6; 49:8). This Servant, Jesus Christ, is the same One described in 42:1, 49:1, 50:4 and 52:13 (see notes). He would refer to God as Master (see v. 1; 50:4), receive the Spirit (see v. 1; 42:1), bring healing and liberation (vv. 1–3; 42:7; 49:9; 50:4; 53:4) and proclaim the year of the Lord (v. 3; 49:8). Apart from Elisha (see 1Ki 9:16), the Scriptures record the anointing only of kings and high priests (see 45:1). **good news.** Proclamation is good news because of the Lord's favor (v. 2; see note on 52:7). **poor.** Those who hope confidently in God despite present distress (see note on 11:3–5). **proclaim freedom.** As in the year of Jubilee (Lev 25:10). **captives.** Those in bondage in exile (see 58:6; cf. 51:14). **prisoners.** The Septuagint (the Greek translation of the OT) reads "blind" (see NIV text note) and is the source for Luke 4:18. See *HC* 25,31.
61:2 year of the LORD's favor. The year of God's favor is the basis for the proclamation of the good news. Ultimately, the reason for God's favor lies in the ministry of Jesus Christ (Mt 11:5; Lk 4:18; 7:22; Ac 10:38). His ministry is continued by all who proclaim salvation through faith in Jesus Christ (Ac 26:18). **day of vengeance.** The new age of restoration is not only the age of salvation but also that of judgment. In terms of the New Testament fulfillment of these hopes, Christ's first advent emphasized healing, while his second will emphasize both judgment and healing (see 1Th 1:7–10). See note on 34:8. **our God.** See note on 25:9. **comfort.** See notes on 12:1 and 40:1 (cf. Mt 5:4).
61:3 oil of gladness. Lavished by a host upon his guest (see Pss 23:5; 43:7; Lk 7:46). **planting.** See 60:21
61:4 They. Jews (58:12) and Gentiles (60:10).
61:6 priests . . . ministers. Extension of priestly privileges to all of God's people (66:21; cf. 1Pe 2:5,9; Rev 1:6; 5:10). **our God.** See note on 25:9. **wealth of nations.** See note on 60:5. **riches.** See note on 4:2.
61:7 shame . . . disgrace. Experienced in exile. See notes on 30:3 and 50:4–6. **my people.** See note on 40:1. **double.** A different Hebrew word from that used in 40:2, but it probably has the same sense (see note on 40:2).
61:8 everlasting covenant. See notes on 42:6 and 55:3.
61:9 descendants. See note on 59:21. In the age of restoration, covenantal blessings would be extended to the children, as they had always been in Biblical history (see Ex 20:6; see chart, "Major Covenants in the Bible, on p. 25). **blessed.** An allusion to the promise to Abraham (see 41:8; 51:2; Ge 12:3).
61:10 I. Zion is personified. **clothed.** The sign of entering into a new status or condition (see 47:2; 52:1; 59:17).

and arrayed me in a robe of righteousness,[g]
as a bridegroom adorns his head like a priest,
and as a bride[h] adorns herself with her jewels.
11 For as the soil makes the sprout come up
and a garden causes seeds to grow,
so the Sovereign LORD will make righteousness[i] and praise
spring up before all nations.

Zion's New Name

62

For Zion's sake I will not keep silent,
for Jerusalem's sake I will not remain quiet,
till her righteousness[j] shines out like the dawn,
her salvation like a blazing torch.
2 The nations[k] will see your righteousness,
and all kings your glory;
you will be called by a new name[l]
that the mouth of the LORD will bestow.
3 You will be a crown[m] of splendor in the LORD's hand,
a royal diadem in the hand of your God.
4 No longer will they call you Deserted,[n]
or name your land Desolate.
But you will be called Hephzibah,[a]
and your land Beulah[b];
for the LORD will take delight[o] in you,
and your land will be married.[p]
5 As a young man marries a maiden,
so will your sons[c] marry you;
as a bridegroom rejoices over his bride,
so will your God rejoice[q] over you.

6 I have posted watchmen[r] on your walls, O Jerusalem;
they will never be silent day or night.
You who call on the LORD,
give yourselves no rest,
7 and give him no rest[s] till he establishes Jerusalem
and makes her the praise of the earth.

8 The LORD has sworn by his right hand
and by his mighty arm:
"Never again will I give your grain[t]
as food for your enemies,
and never again will foreigners drink the new wine
for which you have toiled;
9 but those who harvest it will eat it
and praise the LORD,
and those who gather the grapes will drink it
in the courts of my sanctuary."

61:10 [g]Ps 132:9; Isa 52:1 [h]Isa 49:18; Rev 21:2
61:11 [i]Ps 85:11
62:1 [j]Isa 1:26
62:2 [k]Isa 52:10; 60:3 [l]ver 4,12
62:3 [m]Isa 28:5; Zec 9:16; 1Th 2:19
62:4 [n]Isa 54:6 [o]Jer 32:41; Zep 3:17 [p]Jer 3:14; Hos 2:19
62:5 [q]Isa 65:19
62:6 [r]Isa 52:8; Eze 3:17
62:7 [s]Mt 15:21-28; Lk 18:1-8
62:8 [t]Dt 28:30-33; Isa 1:7; Jer 5:17

[a] 4 *Hephzibah* means *my delight is in her.* [b] 4 *Beulah* means *married.* [c] 5 Or *Builder*

■ **62:1–12** *Glorious Jerusalem to Come.* Jerusalem comes into focus as Isaiah described God's promises of salvation from exile.
62:1 Zion's. See note on 1:8. **not keep silent . . . not remain quiet.** The proclamation would continue to be made as long as the Lord was not silent (v. 6; 42:14; 57:11; 64:12; 65:6). **righteousness.** See note on 1:21. **salvation.** See note on 12:2. **blazing torch.** As developed in 58:8 and 60:1–3. See note on 4:5. See also *BC* 31.
62:2 nations . . . kings. Witnesses to the confirmation of the promises (2:2–4; 52:10; 60:3; 61:11; Dt 26:19). See note on 41:2. **righteousness.** See note on 1:21. **glory.** See note on 4:2. **a new name.** Like new clothes (see note on 61:10) this signifies a renewed relationship and enhanced level of privilege (vv. 4,12; cf. 1:26; 56:5; 58:12; 60:14,18; cf. Ge 17:5,15; Hos 2:22–23; Rev 2:17; 3:12). See note on 43:1. **mouth.** See note on 1:20.
62:3 crown of splendor. See notes on 28:1 and 5. The Lord would share his splendor with his people. **splendor.** See note on 4:2. **a royal diadem in the hand.** Similarly, an inscription concerning the god of Babylon describes a certain city as "your tiara." Jerusalem was God's crown, his delight above all other cities.
62:4 Deserted. Or rejected (v. 12; cf. 54:6; 60:15). See note on 1:4. The names in this verse are symbolic. **name.** See note on 43:1. **Desolate.** Uninhabited and useless (49:8,19; 54:1). **Hephzibah.** Means "my delight is in her." **Beulah.** Means "married."
62:5 sons. Or "builder" (see NIV text note). See 49:17 and Psalm 147:2.
62:6 watchmen. A figure for prophets (see 56:10). **give yourselves no rest.** The exhortation is based on God's promise in verse 1 (see note; cf. 64:12; 65:6).
62:8–9 sworn. See note on 14:24. **by his right hand and by his mighty arm.** By himself (cf. 40:10; 41:10; 51:9; 52:10; 53:1; Ex 6:6; Dt 5:15). See notes on 12:2 and 40:10. **food for your enemies.** Through war or taxation. The covenantal curse (Lev 26:16; Dt 28:33) would be replaced with blessing. **never again.** Compare 65:13 and 21–23, and contrast Deuteronomy 28:33. **praise . . . sanctuary.** In response to God's goodness (cf. Lev 23:39–41; Dt 14:22–26). The certainty of redemption.

62:10 [u]Isa 60:11 [v]Isa 57:14 [w]Isa 11:16 [x]Isa 11:10

10 Pass through, pass through the gates![u]
Prepare the way for the people.
Build up, build up the highway![v w]
Remove the stones.
Raise a banner[x] for the nations.

62:11 [y]Zec 9:9; Mt 21:5 [z]Rev 22:12 [a]Isa 40:10

11 The LORD has made proclamation
to the ends of the earth:
"Say to the Daughter of Zion,[y]
'See, your Savior comes![z]
See, his reward is with him,
and his recompense accompanies him.' "[a]

62:12 [b]ver 4 [c]1Pe 2:9 [d]Isa 35:9 [e]Isa 42:16

12 They will be called[b] the Holy People,[c]
the Redeemed[d] of the LORD;
and you will be called Sought After,
the City No Longer Deserted.[e]

God's Day of Vengeance and Redemption

63:1 [f]Am 1:12 [g]Zep 3:17

63 Who is this coming from Edom,
from Bozrah,[f] with his garments stained crimson?
Who is this, robed in splendor,
striding forward in the greatness of his strength?

"It is I, speaking in righteousness,
mighty to save."[g]

2 Why are your garments red,
like those of one treading the winepress?

63:3 [h]Rev 14:20; 19:15 [i]Isa 22:5 [j]Rev 19:13

3 "I have trodden the winepress[h] alone;
from the nations no one was with me.
I trampled them in my anger
and trod them down in my wrath;[i]
their blood spattered my garments,[j]
and I stained all my clothing.
4 For the day of vengeance was in my heart,
and the year of my redemption has come.

63:5 [k]Isa 41:28 [l]Ps 44:3; 98:1 [m]Isa 59:16

5 I looked, but there was no one[k] to help,
I was appalled that no one gave support;
so my own arm[l] worked salvation for me,
and my own wrath sustained me.[m]

63:6 [n]Isa 29:9 [o]Isa 34:3

6 I trampled the nations in my anger;
in my wrath I made them drunk[n]
and poured their blood[o] on the ground."

Praise and Prayer

63:7 [p]Isa 54:8

7 I will tell of the kindnesses[p] of the LORD,
the deeds for which he is to be praised,

62:10 Pass through, pass through . . . Build up, build up. These double imperatives (see also 40:1; 51:9,17; 52:1; 57:14; 65:1) emphatically encourage the people to worship in the glory of the restored Jerusalem. **gates!** Leading into the court of the sanctuary (see v. 9). **Prepare.** See notes on 40:3. A metaphor for encouraging people to come to the sanctuary to worship. **stones.** The impediments to worship (see 57:14). **Raise a banner.** See 5:26.

62:11 your Savior. See 40:9, Zechariah 9:9 and Matthew 21:5. **reward.** See note on 40:10.

■ **63:1–6** *Judgment on the Nations.* Alongside the glory of Jerusalem would be the defeat and judgment of all who had opposed God.

63:1 coming. The same One who would come with salvation for his people (62:11) would also come in judgment against others. **Edom.** Representative of the ungodly and proud nations (21:11–12; 34:1–17; Ps 137:7; Jer 49:7–22; La 4:21–22; Eze 25:12–14; Joel 3:19; Am 1:11–12; Ob 14–15; Mal 1:2–5; see note on Isa 25:10). **Bozrah.** See note on 34:6.

63:3 I. This passage is applied to Christ in Revelation 19:15 because his second coming will be the culmination of God's judgment against his enemies. **winepress . . . stained.** This extended metaphor of the day of the Lord (La 1:15; Joel 3:13; Rev 14:17–20; 19:15) implies that the wine press represents the battle; the juice, "blood." **anger.** See note on 10:5.

63:4 day of vengeance . . . the year of my redemption. Judgment and redemption go hand in hand. One cannot take place completely without the other.

63:5 arm. See note on 40:10 and note the similarity to 59:16.

■ **63:7—66:24** *Repentance and Response.* At this point Isaiah repeated the basic pattern of repentance in lament followed by God's reassurance that he would restore his people. The two main sections are the lament (63:7—64:12) and God's response (65:1—66:24).

■ **63:7—64:12** *Lament and Repentance.* Isaiah provided an exemplary lament to guide the exiles toward repentance.

63:7 I will tell. Isaiah made public proclamation of the Lord's mighty acts in the past (Pss 51:13–15; 89:1; 145:7). These acts are also spoken of as "kindnesses" (see 55:3; Ps 89:1; see note on 54:6–8), "deeds . . . to be praised" (i.e., laudable; 60:6; Pss 77; 78; 135; 136), "all . . . done" (i.e., rewards; Pss 13:6; 16:7), "good things" (i.e., acts of covenant fidelity; Ps 23:6) and "compassion" (i.e., mercy; see note on 14:1).

according to all the LORD has done for us—
yes, the many good things he has done
for the house of Israel,
according to his compassion[q] and many kindnesses.
8 He said, "Surely they are my people,[r]
sons who will not be false to me";
and so he became their Savior.
9 In all their distress he too was distressed,
and the angel of his presence[s] saved them.
In his love and mercy he redeemed[t] them;
he lifted them up and carried[u] them
all the days of old.
10 Yet they rebelled[v]
and grieved his Holy Spirit.[w]
So he turned and became their enemy[x]
and he himself fought against them.
11 Then his people recalled[a] the days of old,
the days of Moses and his people—
where is he who brought them through the sea,[y]
with the shepherd of his flock?
Where is he who set
his Holy Spirit[z] among them,
12 who sent his glorious arm of power
to be at Moses' right hand,
who divided the waters[a] before them,
to gain for himself everlasting renown,
13 who led[b] them through the depths?
Like a horse in open country,
they did not stumble;[c]
14 like cattle that go down to the plain,
they were given rest by the Spirit of the LORD.
This is how you guided your people
to make for yourself a glorious name.
15 Look down from heaven[d] and see
from your lofty throne,[e] holy and glorious.
Where are your zeal[f] and your might?
Your tenderness and compassion[g] are withheld from us.
16 But you are our Father,
though Abraham does not know us
or Israel acknowledge[h] us;
you, O LORD, are our Father,
our Redeemer[i] from of old is your name.
17 Why, O LORD, do you make us wander from your ways
and harden our hearts so we do not revere[j] you?
Return[k] for the sake of your servants,
the tribes that are your inheritance.
18 For a little while your people possessed your holy place,
but now our enemies have trampled down your sanctuary.[l]

63:7 [q]Ps 51:1; Eph 2:4
63:8 [r]Isa 51:4
63:9 [s]Ex 33:14 [t]Dt 7:7-8 [u]Dt 1:31
63:10 [v]Ps 78:40 [w]Ps 51:11; Ac 7:51; Eph 4:30 [x]Ps 106:40
63:11 [y]Ex 14:22,30 [z]Nu 11:17
63:12 [a]Ex 14:21-22; Isa 11:15
63:13 [b]Dt 32:12 [c]Jer 31:9
63:15 [d]Dt 26:15; Ps 80:14 [e]Ps 123:1 [f]Isa 9:7; 26:11 [g]Jer 31:20; Hos 11:8
63:16 [h]Job 14:21 [i]Isa 41:14; 44:6
63:17 [j]Isa 29:13 [k]Nu 10:36
63:18 [l]Ps 74:3-8

a *11* Or *But may he recall*

63:8 my people. See note on 40:1. **sons . . . not be false.** Faithful "sons" (Ex 4:22; Dt 14:1), unlike 1:2–4. **Savior.** Or Redeemer. See note on 35:8–9.
63:9 distress. Israel's sufferings in Egypt (see Ex 2:25). **angel of his presence.** See Exodus 14:19 and 23:20–23. **carried.** See Exodus 19:4, Deuteronomy 1:31 and 32:10–12. See *WLC* 45.
63:10 rebelled. See note on 1:2. **grieved his Holy Spirit.** When God's people rebel against him, it brings sadness and pain to God's Spirit (cf. Ps 106:33, Ac 7:51; Eph 4:30).
63:11 days of old. The period of the exodus and the wilderness wanderings. **sea.** The Red Sea (Ex 14:21—15:21). Moses was a "shepherd of his flock." Jesus is our Shepherd (Heb 13:20). **set his Holy Spirit.** An allusion to Numbers 11:17 and 25.
63:12 glorious arm. An allusion to Exodus 15:6 (see 51:9). **divided.** See Exodus 14:16 and 21, as well as Psalm 78:13.
63:13 depths? See Exodus 15:5 and 8 and Psalm 106:9.
63:14–16 See *WCF* 5.1; *WLC* 18,189.
63:16 our Father. God has always been the Father of his people (64:8; Dt 32:6; Jer 3:4,19); they are his children by adoption (Ex 4:22–23; cf. Jn 8:41). **Abraham.** See 51:2. **Redeemer.** He alone can deliver (vv. 5,8). See note on 35:8–9.
63:17 make us wander. God causes those who reject him to stray (see Ro 1:20–24). **harden.** The Lord confirms them in their sin (see 6:10; Ex 4:21; Ps 95:8). See *WCF* 17.3.
63:18 holy place. The temple. **enemies.** Babylonians. See Psalm 74:4–9.

19 We are yours from of old;
but you have not ruled over them,
they have not been called by your name.[a]

64

Oh, that you would rend the heavens[m] and come down,[n]
that the mountains[o] would tremble before you!
2 As when fire sets twigs ablaze
and causes water to boil,
come down to make your name known to your enemies
and cause the nations to quake[p] before you!
3 For when you did awesome[q] things that we did not expect,
you came down, and the mountains trembled before you.
4 Since ancient times no one has heard,
no ear has perceived,
no eye has seen any God besides you,
who acts on behalf of those who wait for him.[r]
5 You come to the help of those who gladly do right,[s]
who remember your ways.
But when we continued to sin against them,
you were angry.
How then can we be saved?
6 All of us have become like one who is unclean,
and all our righteous[t] acts are like filthy rags;
we all shrivel up like a leaf,[u]
and like the wind our sins sweep us away.
7 No one[v] calls on your name
or strives to lay hold of you;
for you have hidden[w] your face from us
and made us waste away[x] because of our sins.
8 Yet, O LORD, you are our Father.[y]
We are the clay, you are the potter;[z]
we are all the work of your hand.
9 Do not be angry[a] beyond measure, O LORD;
do not remember our sins[b] forever.
Oh, look upon us, we pray,
for we are all your people.
10 Your sacred cities have become a desert;
even Zion is a desert, Jerusalem a desolation.
11 Our holy and glorious temple,[c] where our fathers praised you,
has been burned with fire,
and all that we treasured[d] lies in ruins.
12 After all this, O LORD, will you hold yourself back?[e]
Will you keep silent[f] and punish us beyond measure?

Judgment and Salvation

65

"I revealed myself to those who did not ask for me;
I was found by those who did not seek me.[g]

64:1 [m]Ps 18:9; 144:5 [n]Mic 1:3 [o]Ex 19:18
64:2 [p]Ps 99:1; Jer 5:22; 33:9
64:3 [q]Ps 65:5
64:4 [r]Isa 30:18; 1Co 2:9*
64:5 [s]Isa 26:8
64:6 [t]Isa 46:12; 48:1 [u]Ps 90:5-6
64:7 [v]Isa 59:4 [w]Dt 31:18; Isa 1:15; 54:8 [x]Isa 9:18
64:8 [y]Isa 63:16 [z]Isa 29:16
64:9 [a]Isa 57:17; 60:10 [b]Isa 43:25
64:11 [c]Ps 74:3-7 [d]La 1:7, 10
64:12 [e]Ps 74:10-11; Isa 42:14 [f]Ps 83:1
65:1 [g]Hos 1:10; Ro 9:24-26; 10:20*

a *19* Or *We are like those you have never ruled, / like those never called by your name*

63:19 called by your name. Signifies ownership (see Dt. 28:10; Jer 14:9).
64:1–5 See *WCF* 17.3; *WLC* 191.
64:2 fire. Evidence of divine presence (Ex 19:18; Heb 12:18), especially in judgment (Heb 12:29). See note 4:5. **name.** See note on 12:2.
64:3 awesome things. A reflection on the exodus (Dt 10:21; Pss 66:3–6; 106:22).
64:4 God besides you. Because depraved humanity fabricates gods, religious prohibitions (e.g., Ex 20:3) assume their existence. But theological statements acknowledge no other true god but the Lord (see 43:11; Dt 4:35).
64:6 All of us . . . filthy rags. Confession of rebellion (53:6) and of uncleanness (Lev 13:45; Hag 2:13–14). **unclean.** They were not fit for God's presence. **filthy rags.** The term is unique. Some ancient versions understood it to refer to garments stained by menstruation. If so, it is a fitting parallel to "unclean" (see Lev 15:19–24; Eze 36:17). **shrivel up . . . sweep us away.** Experience of God's righteous judgment (1:30; 40:7,24). See *WCF* 16.5; *WLC* 78; *BC* 24; *HC* 62.
64:7 calls . . . strives. See notes on 65:1–2. **hidden your face.** See note on 8:17. See *WCF* 16.3; 17.3.
64:8 our Father. See note on 63:16. **clay . . . work of your hand.** See notes on 17:7–8, 22:11, 27:10–11, 29:16 and 45:9–10 and 11. See also Romans 9:20–21.
64:9 Do not be angry. Based on the promise in 54:7–8. **do not remember.** Based on the promise in 43:25. See *WCF* 17.3; *WLC* 189.
64:10 sacred cities. The cities in Judah (cf. Ps 78:54). **desert.** See note on 40:3. **Zion.** See note on 1:8.
64:11 our fathers praised you. The speakers were at least a generation removed from the fall of the temple in 586 B.C.
64:12 keep silent. Compare note on 62:1.

To a nation[h] that did not call on my name,
  I said, 'Here am I, here am I.'
2 All day long I have held out my hands
  to an obstinate people,[i]
who walk in ways not good,
  pursuing their own imaginations[j]—
3 a people who continually provoke me
  to my very face,[k]
offering sacrifices in gardens[l]
  and burning incense on altars of brick;
4 who sit among the graves
  and spend their nights keeping secret vigil;
who eat the flesh of pigs,[m]
  and whose pots hold broth of unclean meat;
5 who say, 'Keep away; don't come near me,
  for I am too sacred[n] for you!'
Such people are smoke in my nostrils,
  a fire that keeps burning all day.

6 "See, it stands written before me:
  I will not keep silent[o] but will pay back[p] in full;
  I will pay it back into their laps[q]—
7 both your sins[r] and the sins of your fathers,"[s]
  says the LORD.
"Because they burned sacrifices on the mountains
  and defied me on the hills,[t]
I will measure into their laps
  the full payment for their former deeds."

8 This is what the LORD says:

"As when juice is still found in a cluster of grapes
  and men say, 'Don't destroy it,
  there is yet some good in it,'
so will I do in behalf of my servants;
  I will not destroy them all.
9 I will bring forth descendants[u] from Jacob,
  and from Judah those who will possess[v] my mountains;
my chosen people will inherit them,
  and there will my servants live.[w]
10 Sharon[x] will become a pasture for flocks,
  and the Valley of Achor[y] a resting place for herds,
  for my people who seek[z] me.

65:1 [h]Eph 2:12
65:2 [i]Isa 1:2,23; Ro 10:21* [j]Ps 81:11-12; Isa 66:18
65:3 [k]Job 1:11 [l]Isa 1:29
65:4 [m]Lev 11:7
65:5 [n]Mt 9:11; Lk 7:39; 18:9-12
65:6 [o]Ps 50:3 [p]Jer 16:18 [q]Ps 79:12
65:7 [r]Isa 22:14 [s]Ex 20:5 [t]Isa 57:7
65:9 [u]Isa 45:19 [v]Am 9:11-15 [w]Isa 32:18
65:10 [x]Isa 35:2 [y]Jos 7:26 [z]Isa 51:1

■ **65:1—66:24** *God's Response of Judgment and Salvation.* Isaiah conveyed the manner in which God would respond to the cry for help from the repentant exiles. These chapters divide into two main parts: judgment and salvation (65:1—66:17) and the new world of blessing (66:18–24).
■ **65:1—66:17** *Judgment and Salvation to Come.* God promised to deliver his people and to destroy all who opposed him from all over the world.
65:1 I was found. Contrast 64:7. **a nation that did not call on my name.** A reference to Gentiles (see 42:1; 49:6; 52:15; 66:8). Paul's ministry fulfilled this prophecy (Ro 10:20). Those who were formerly not God's people are today his holy nation (see 1Pe 2:9–10). **Here am I.** Repeated for emphasis. God's presence guarantees salvation.
65:2 held out my hands. Unlike the people (1:15), the Lord reached out with eagerness and love.
65:3–5 See *WLC* 109.
65:3 to my very face. The ungodly did not hide their offensive religious acts. **sacrifices in gardens.** A reference to the fertility religions. See note on 1:29–30. **incense . . . brick.** A pagan worship practice perhaps associated with the worship of the Queen of Heaven (cf. Jer 44:17–19). **altars of brick.** Literally, "on bricks." Babylonians offered incense to "all the starry hosts [of heaven]" (Jer 19:13) on bricks or tile roofs.
65:4 among the graves. For the purpose of consulting the spirits of the dead (8:19; 29:4). **flesh of pigs . . . unclean meat.** Since eating pork was prohibited (66:3,17; Lev 11:7–8; Dt 14:8), God was displeased with their communal sacrifices.
65:5 too sacred. These idolaters, like the Pharisees at the time of Jesus, thought themselves better than others (see Lk 18:9–14). Jesus called the Pharisees children of the devil (see Jn 8:44). **smoke . . . fire.** Figures for provoking God's wrath.
65:6 stands written. As royal courts kept records of unpunished crimes, so the heavenly book records sin (cf. Ex 32:32; Mal 3:16). **pay back.** The principle of retribution (Ob 15; Gal 6:7; 1Pe 1:17; Rev 20:12–13; 22:12). See notes on 33:11–12 and 34:8.
65:7 sins of your fathers. See Exodus 20:5 and Ezekiel 18:20. **burned sacrifices.** On the high places (57:7; Hos 4:13).
65:8–16 The promise of God's blessing on his servants and the assurance of judgment on the apostate.
65:8 juice . . . cluster of grapes. Juice represents faithful servants of the Lord, while the cluster of grapes symbolizes apostate Israelites. **servants.** The remnant (see 1:2) and foreigners (see 56:6). See note on 54:17. **not destroy.** See notes on 1:8 and 9 and Genesis 18:22–30.
65:9 descendants. Literally, "seed," a collective singular form (cf. Jer 31:36). The prophecy finds fulfillment in the remnant that returned from exile, but Christ and those baptized in him are the final fulfillment (see Gal 3:16,26–29). **possess . . . inherit.** The kingdom will be theirs (14:25; 57:13; cf. Ob 19–21). **chosen.** See note on 14:1.
65:10 Sharon. A valley lush with vegetation; located by the Mediterranean Sea and to the west of Mount Carmel. It is here a

65:11 [a]Dt 29:24-25; Isa 1:28
65:12 [b]Isa 27:1 [c]Pr 1:24-25; Isa 41:28; 66:4 [d]2Ch 36:15-16; Jer 7:13
65:13 [e]Isa 1:19 [f]Isa 41:17 [g]Isa 44:9
65:14 [h]Mt 8:12; Lk 13:28
65:15 [i]Zec 8:13
65:16 [j]Ps 31:5 [k]Isa 19:18
65:17 [l]Isa 66:22; 2Pe 3:13 [m]Isa 43:18; Jer 3:16
65:18 [n]Ps 98:1-9; Isa 25:9
65:19 [o]Isa 35:10; 62:5 [p]Isa 25:8; Rev 7:17

11 "But as for you who forsake[a] the LORD
and forget my holy mountain,
who spread a table for Fortune
and fill bowls of mixed wine for Destiny,
12 I will destine you for the sword,[b]
and you will all bend down for the slaughter;
for I called but you did not answer,[c]
I spoke but you did not listen.[d]
You did evil in my sight
and chose what displeases me."

13 Therefore this is what the Sovereign LORD says:

"My servants will eat,[e]
but you will go hungry;
my servants will drink,
but you will go thirsty;[f]
my servants will rejoice,
but you will be put to shame.[g]
14 My servants will sing
out of the joy of their hearts,
but you will cry out[h]
from anguish of heart
and wail in brokenness of spirit.
15 You will leave your name
to my chosen ones as a curse;[i]
the Sovereign LORD will put you to death,
but to his servants he will give another name.
16 Whoever invokes a blessing in the land
will do so by the God of truth;[j]
he who takes an oath in the land
will swear[k] by the God of truth.
For the past troubles will be forgotten
and hidden from my eyes.

New Heavens and a New Earth

17 "Behold, I will create
new heavens and a new earth.[l]
The former things will not be remembered,[m]
nor will they come to mind.
18 But be glad and rejoice[n] forever
in what I will create,
for I will create Jerusalem to be a delight
and its people a joy.
19 I will rejoice[o] over Jerusalem
and take delight in my people;
the sound of weeping and of crying[p]
will be heard in it no more.
20 "Never again will there be in it
an infant who lives but a few days,

metaphor for the Lord's transformation of creation. See notes on 33:7–9 and 35:1–2. **Valley of Achor.** A valley to the west of Jericho (Jos 7:24; Hos 2:15). **my people.** See note on 40:1. **seek.** See notes on verse 1 and on 9:13.

65:11 forsake . . . fill. The rebellious people (vv. 1–7). **mountain.** Instead of true worship of the Lord (see note on 2:2), they submitted themselves to the gods of fate. **Fortune.** The false god of good luck. **Destiny.** The false god of fate. See *WLC* 109.

65:12 sword . . . slaughter. Conventional language for death.

65:15 chosen ones as a curse. The chosen (see v. 9) will use the names of the apostate as a curse formula in invoking judgment upon others. **another name.** See note on 62:2.

65:16 God of truth. Literally, "God of Amen" (cf. 2Co 1:20; Rev 3:14). The Lord will demonstrate himself to be faithful to his word. See *WCF* 22.2.

65:17 create. See note on 4:5. **new heavens and a new earth.** The new act of God is experienced now in his blessings. See notes at 42:9, 43:18–19, 48:6, 60:19–22 (cf. 2Pe 3:13; Rev 21:1). **former things.** The adversities and disgrace. See notes at 41:22 and 42:9. **remembered . . . come to mind.** See verse 16.

65:18 be glad. Saints are to celebrate now the coming salvation (see 66:10). **forever.** See notes on 61:8. **create Jerusalem.** Isaiah alluded to the language of Genesis 1:1 to draw attention to the radical renovation of the world that will take place when the restoration of his people is complete (cf. Ro 8:18–25).

65:19 no more. See 25:8, 35:10 and 51:11.

65:20 infant . . . old man. Poetic understatements expressing the unending life that will come in the climax of the restoration from exile. They promise a meaningful and blessed life for all, in contrast to the sickness and early death that resulted from God's curse (Dt 28:20–22).

or an old man who does not live out his years;[q]
he who dies at a hundred
will be thought a mere youth;
he who fails to reach[a] a hundred
will be considered accursed.
21 They will build houses[r] and dwell in them;
they will plant vineyards and eat their fruit.[s]
22 No longer will they build houses and others live in them,
or plant and others eat.
For as the days of a tree,[t]
so will be the days[u] of my people;
my chosen ones will long enjoy
the works of their hands.
23 They will not toil in vain
or bear children doomed to misfortune;
for they will be a people blessed[v] by the LORD,
they and their descendants[w] with them.
24 Before they call[x] I will answer;
while they are still speaking[y] I will hear.
25 The wolf and the lamb[z] will feed together,
and the lion will eat straw like the ox,
but dust will be the serpent's[a] food.
They will neither harm nor destroy
on all my holy mountain,"
says the LORD.

Judgment and Hope

66 This is what the LORD says:

"Heaven is my throne,[b]
and the earth is my footstool.[c]
Where is the house[d] you will build for me?
Where will my resting place be?
2 Has not my hand made all these things,[e]
and so they came into being?"
declares the LORD.

"This is the one I esteem:
he who is humble and contrite in spirit,[f]
and trembles at my word.[g]
3 But whoever sacrifices a bull[h]
is like one who kills a man,
and whoever offers a lamb,
like one who breaks a dog's neck;
whoever makes a grain offering
is like one who presents pig's blood,
and whoever burns memorial incense,[i]
like one who worships an idol.
They have chosen their own ways,[j]
and their souls delight in their abominations;

65:20 [q]Ecc 8:13
65:21 [r]Isa 32:18 [s]Isa 37:30; Am 9:14
65:22 [t]Ps 92:12-14 [u]Ps 21:4; 91:16
65:23 [v]Dt 28:3-12; Isa 61:9 [w]Ac 2:39
65:24 [x]Isa 55:6 [y]Da 9:20-23; 10:12
65:25 [z]Isa 11:6 [a]Ge 3:14; Mic 7:17
66:1 [b]Mt 23:22 [c]1Ki 8:27; Mt 5:34-35 [d]2Sa 7:7; Jn 4:20-21; Ac 7:49*; 17:24
66:2 [e]Isa 40:26; Ac 7:50* [f]Isa 57:15; Mt 5:3-4; Lk 18:13-14 [g]Ezr 9:4
66:3 [h]Isa 1:11 [i]Lev 2:2 [j]Isa 57:17

[a] 20 Or / *the sinner who reaches*

65:22 others live in them. See 62:8.
65:23 not toil . . . or bear. A reversal of God's judgment on human existence (Ge 3:16–18). **children . . . blessed.** Both they and their offspring will be blessed by the Lord (cf. 61:9).
65:24 Before . . . answer. A figure to signify that there will be no time for sorrow between prayer and praise (see 30:19; 58:9). See *HC* 129.
65:25 wolf . . . serpent's. Peace in creation signifies peace for the redeemed community (11:6–9). **dust will be the serpent's food.** An allusion to Genesis 3:14. The curse on Satan will be consummated. **harm . . . destroy.** Signifies the absence of all evil or harm. See note on 11:6–9. **holy.** See note on 4:3. **mountain.** See note on 2:2.
66:1 earth is my footstool. Since the new cosmos in its entirety will be God's temple and Earth will be part of that cosmic temple (see note on 60:13), there will be no need for a man-made temple on Earth. **resting place.** An image of the temple (see 1Ch 28:2; Ps 132:8,14). See *HC* 48.
66:2 humble . . . trembles. Terminology found elsewhere only in Ezra 9:4 and 10:13. Equivalent to "spirit and truth" (see Jn 4:24; cf. Php 2:12; 1Jn 2:17). See *WCF* 14.2; 21.5; *WLC* 157; *HC* 117.
66:3–4 The Lord hates empty religious expressions as much as he does paganism (cf. 1:11–14; 65:3–5).
66:3 kills a man. Perhaps a reference to child sacrifice. **breaks a dog's neck.** A Carthaginian worship practice (see 56:12). **pig's blood.** See 65:4. **their own ways.** Although they offered a bull, a lamb and grain, the sacrifice was not made from a contrite heart.

66:4 [k]Pr 10:24 [l]Pr 1:24; Jer 7:13 [m]2Ki 21:2,4,6 [n]Isa 65:12

4 so I also will choose harsh treatment for them
and will bring upon them what they dread.[k]
For when I called, no one answered,[l]
when I spoke, no one listened.
They did evil[m] in my sight
and chose what displeases me."[n]

66:5 [o]Ps 38:20; Isa 60:15 [p]Lk 13:17

5 Hear the word of the LORD,
you who tremble at his word:
"Your brothers who hate[o] you,
and exclude you because of my name, have said,
'Let the LORD be glorified,
that we may see your joy!'
Yet they will be put to shame.[p]

66:6 [q]Isa 65:6; Joel 3:7

6 Hear that uproar from the city,
hear that noise from the temple!
It is the sound of the LORD
repaying[q] his enemies all they deserve.

66:7 [r]Isa 54:1 [s]Rev 12:5

7 "Before she goes into labor,[r]
she gives birth;
before the pains come upon her,
she delivers a son.[s]

66:8 [t]Isa 64:4

8 Who has ever heard of such a thing?
Who has ever seen[t] such things?
Can a country be born in a day
or a nation be brought forth in a moment?
Yet no sooner is Zion in labor
than she gives birth to her children.

66:9 [u]Isa 37:3

9 Do I bring to the moment of birth[u]
and not give delivery?" says the LORD.
"Do I close up the womb
when I bring to delivery?" says your God.

66:10 [v]Dt 32:43; Ro 15:10 [w]Ps 26:8

10 "Rejoice[v] with Jerusalem and be glad for her,
all you who love[w] her;
rejoice greatly with her,
all you who mourn over her.

66:11 [x]Isa 60:16

11 For you will nurse[x] and be satisfied
at her comforting breasts;
you will drink deeply
and delight in her overflowing abundance."

66:12 [y]Isa 48:18 [z]Ps 72:3; Isa 60:5; 61:6 [a]Isa 60:4

12 For this is what the LORD says:

"I will extend peace to her like a river,[y]
and the wealth[z] of nations like a flooding stream;
you will nurse and be carried[a] on her arm
and dandled on her knees.

66:13 [b]Isa 40:1; 2Co 1:4

13 As a mother comforts her child,
so will I comfort[b] you;
and you will be comforted over Jerusalem."

14 When you see this, your heart will rejoice
and you will flourish like grass;

66:4 what they dread. See verses 15–16 and 24. **when I called.** See 65:12.
66:5 who hate you. Intensifies the opposition recorded in chapter 65. **Let . . . joy!** A reference to hypocritical righteousness (see v. 17; 64:6; 65:6). **put to shame.** The fate of the persecutors. For the destiny of the persecuted, see verse 10. See *BC* 37.
66:6 repaying his enemies. This prophecy against self-righteous idolaters in Israel who persecute God's servants found fulfillment throughout the centuries when Israel was oppressed by foreign powers. The fall of the temple in A.D. 70 (see Mt 24:1–2) and Christ's return also fulfill this judgment (see 2Th 1:7–10).
66:7 Before . . . birth. The birth of the new community would come so quickly and dramatically that it would be painless (see 65:25).
66:8 nation. See note on 65:1.
66:10 Rejoice. See note on 65:18. **mourn.** Until she gives birth to the new age.
66:11 nurse . . . satisfied. See note on 60:16. **comforting.** See notes on 12:1 and 40:1. **overflowing.** See note on 4:2.
66:12 her. Jerusalem is personified as the mother of the people of God (see vv. 8,10). **you.** The true worshipers and their offspring (see v. 22).
66:13 mother. The Lord likened his tender love to that of a mother. See note on 20:3. **comfort.** See notes on 12:1 and 40:1 (cf. 2Co 1:3–4).
66:14 rejoice. See 60:5.

the hand of the LORD will be made known to his servants,
but his fury[c] will be shown to his foes.
15 See, the LORD is coming with fire,
and his chariots[d] are like a whirlwind;
he will bring down his anger with fury,
and his rebuke[e] with flames of fire.
16 For with fire[f] and with his sword[g]
the LORD will execute judgment upon all men,
and many will be those slain by the LORD.

17 "Those who consecrate and purify themselves to go into the gardens,[h] following the
one in the midst of[a] those who eat the flesh of pigs[i] and rats and other abominable
things—they will meet their end[j] together," declares the LORD.
18 "And I, because of their actions and their imaginations, am about to come[b] and
gather all nations and tongues, and they will come and see my glory.
19 "I will set a sign[k] among them, and I will send some of those who survive to the nations—to Tarshish,[l] to the Libyans[c] and Lydians[m] (famous as archers), to Tubal[n] and
Greece, and to the distant islands[o] that have not heard of my fame or seen my glory.[p]
They will proclaim my glory among the nations. 20 And they will bring all your brothers,
from all the nations, to my holy mountain in Jerusalem as an offering to the LORD—on
horses, in chariots and wagons, and on mules and camels," says the LORD. "They will
bring them, as the Israelites bring their grain offerings, to the temple of the LORD in ceremonially clean vessels.[q] 21 And I will select some of them also to be priests[r] and Levites,"
says the LORD.

22 "As the new heavens and the new earth[s] that I make will endure before me," declares the LORD, "so will your name and descendants endure.[t] 23 From one New Moon to
another and from one Sabbath[u] to another, all mankind will come and bow down[v] before me," says the LORD. 24 "And they will go out and look upon the dead bodies of those
who rebelled against me; their worm[w] will not die, nor will their fire be quenched,[x] and
they will be loathsome to all mankind."

a 17 Or *gardens behind one of your temples, and* b 18 The meaning of the Hebrew for this clause is uncertain. c 19 Some Septuagint manuscripts *Put* (Libyans); Hebrew *Pul*

66:14 [c]Isa 10:5
66:15 [d]Ps 68:17 [e]Ps 9:5
66:16 [f]Isa 30:30 [g]Isa 27:1
66:17 [h]Isa 1:29 [i]Lev 11:7 [j]Ps 37:20; Isa 1:28
66:19 [k]Isa 11:10; 19:22 [l]Isa 2:16 [m]Eze 27:10 [n]Ge 10:2 [o]Isa 11:11 [p]1Ch 16:24; Isa 24:15
66:20 [q]Isa 52:11
66:21 [r]Ex 19:6; Isa 61:6; 1Pe 2:5,9
66:22 [s]Isa 65:17; Heb 12:26-27; 2Pe 3:13; Rev 21:1 [t]Jn 10:27-29; 1Pe 1:4-5
66:23 [u]Eze 46:1-3 [v]Isa 19:21
66:24 [w]Isa 14:11 [x]Isa 1:31; Mk 9:48*

66:15–16 fire . . . chariots. Light and storm clouds, respectively (see Dt 33:26; Pss 18:10, 63.18), both common symbols of God's coming in judgment (see 10:17–18; 29:6; 30:27–28; 64:1–3). Isaiah prayed for God to intervene in such judgment and salvation (64:1–3). **fire.** See note on 4:5. **like a whirlwind.** With the speed and ferocity of a storm (see Jer 4:13). **anger.** See note on 10:5. **sword.** The Lord is the Divine Warrior (27:1; 31:8; 34:5; Rev 19:11-18). See notes at 9:6, 13:4, 24:14–16, 40:10 and 42:13.
66:16 all men. Literally, "all flesh"; the false worshipers (contrast v. 23; see Jer 9:2).
66:17 gardens . . . pigs . . . abominable things. See verse 3 and 65:2–5.
■**66:18–24** *The Glorious New World.* Isaiah closed his book with a prophecy describing the climax of God's judgment and salvation: the new heavens and the new earth.
66:18 their actions and their imaginations. Probably the right acts and true spirit of acceptable worshipers. God uses such saints to evangelize the world (see v. 19). **come.** See note on 35:4. **all nations and tongues.** A reference to universal acknowledgment of the Lord's kingdom (cf. Zec 8:23; Rev 7:9).
66:19 sign. The Lord's acts of judgment on the false worshipers and his deliverance of the true. **who survive.** The true worshipers who survive persecution (see v. 5; Mt 24:9–14) will bring God's glory to the nations (v. 18) and give birth to the new age (vv. 7–11). **Tarshish.** See note on 23.5. **Libyans and Lydians.** Peoples in North Africa. **Tubal.** A region southeast of the Black Sea (Eze 38:2; 39:1). **Greece.** That is, the people of Asia Minor or Greece (cf. Eze 27:13,19; Joel 3:6). **proclaim . . . nations.** Nations will submit themselves to the Lord and rejoice in his mighty acts. See note on 24:14–16.
66:20 they will bring all your brothers. The Gentiles will bring dispersed, ethnic Israel back to the temple (see 43:5; 60:4,9; Ro 11:13).
66:22 new heavens . . . new earth. See note on 65:17 (cf. 2Pe 3:13; Rev 21:1). **name and descendants.** A promise of continuity of the people of God (65:18–19; cf. Jer 31:35–36). See note on 43:1.
66:23 New Moon . . . Sabbath. Universal worship of God at his appointed times (cf. Zec 14:16). See *WLC* 117; *WSC* 60; *HC* 103.
66:24 worm . . . fire. This imagery from Jerusalem's garbage dump, where unclean corpses were burned, became symbolic of perpetual punishment and anguish (cf. 48:22; 57:20; Mk 9:47–48).

JEREMIAH

Introduction

Overview

Author: Jeremiah and Baruch, his student and/or scribe

Purpose: To remind the exiles of the reasons for their trials and to assure them that, upon repentance, God's people would return to the land of promise with enormous blessings

Date: 580–539 B.C.

Key Truths:

- The people of Judah and Jerusalem deserved their exile to Babylon because of continuing sin.
- The temple in Jerusalem could not protect the Judahites from God's judgment against them for their hypocrisy.
- False prophets proclaiming peace and safety must be rejected in favor of the message of the true prophets.
- The judgment of exile would be followed by a grand restoration under a new covenant.

Author

The superscription of the book states that it contains "the words of Jeremiah son of Hilkiah" (1:1). The composition itself is complicated, as might be expected from the length and variety of Jeremiah's ministry alone (25:3). The material was presumably compiled and arranged by someone who wanted to convey the full breadth and force of that ministry from the perspective of the fulfillment of the prophet's repeated warnings of coming punishment (see "Introduction: Purpose and Distinctives"). Jeremiah himself could have been closely involved in the compilation process with help from Baruch, who may also have composed the third-person narratives.

A clue to the procedure by which the various prophecies and sermons may have been collected into a single book is given in chapter 36, where it is said that Baruch wrote down all the words of the prophet spoken up to that point and read them publicly. When the scroll was destroyed by Jehoiakim, another, more comprehensive, one was made (see 51:60).

Jeremiah prophesied during the reigns of the last kings of Judah: Josiah (640–609 B.C.), Jehoahaz (609 B.C.), Jehoiakim (609–598 B.C.), Jehoiachin (598–597 B.C.) and Zedekiah (597–586 B.C.). The northern kingdom of Israel had already disappeared in exile to Assyria in 722 B.C. Assyria then fell to Babylon in 612 B.C. The southern kingdom of Judah fell when most of its people were exiled to Babylon as a result of deportations beginning as early as 605 B.C. (see note on Da 1:1) and two invasions (597 and 586 B.C.) by King Nebuchadnezzar (see note on 21:2). Jeremiah announced these approaching judgments from God on his people and then saw them fulfilled.

Jeremiah was a priest from the priestly town of Anathoth in the territory of Benjamin (see note on 1:1). A lonely figure by reason of his unpopular message (15:17), Jeremiah was forbidden by God to marry as a sign of the imminent cessation of normal life due to the exile (16:2). On the basis of his God-given message he also found himself opposed to the authorities in the land and to virtually all classes of people (26:8). As a result, his life was in serious danger more than once (11:18–23; 18:18; 26:8; 36:19; 38:6). The prophet was sought out especially by King Zedekiah because of his commentary on the likely outcome of the final onslaught of the encroaching Babylonian armies (37:3, 17). Politically, it was a turbulent time as Egypt and Babylon contested the region. Jeremiah repeatedly prophesied a Babylonian victory, proclaiming that the Lord was using Nebuchadnezzar as his scourge. When Jerusalem fell, the Babylonian commander had a special commission from Nebuchadnezzar to care for the prophet, whose fame had spread to the heart of the empire (39:11–14).

Jeremiah remained in the land, but after the governor Gedaliah was murdered many Jews feared Babylonian reprisal. So they fled to Egypt, even though Jeremiah had warned against this move (42:1ff.), compelling Jeremiah to accompany them (43:1ff.). While in Egypt Jeremiah preached the word of God to the Jews. At that time Jeremiah was at least 70 years old, and he likely died soon afterward in Egypt.

Time and Place of Writing

The background to this book is the long struggle in Judah between the idolatrous worship of foreign gods and the true and exclusive worship of the Lord, which Josiah attempted to restore in his reform (see 2Ki 22–23). Josiah's reform began in 628 B.C. (see note on 2Ch 34:3) and was given fresh impetus by the discovery of the Book of the Law in 621 B.C. (2Ki 22:8). Jeremiah's call came in 626 B.C. (see note on 1:2), so his early ministry coincided with Josiah's reform. His prophecy testifies, however, to the reform's failure to make a lasting impact on the people's lives. Jeremiah warned that the continued waywardness of Judah would finally lead to exile, but he also held out hope of an eventual return to the land. The final editing of the book probably took place during the exile, which is the latest historical point it records.

Purpose and Distinctives

Jeremiah's message moves through phases that do not correspond exactly to the structure of the book.

(1) He called Judah to repent in order to avoid the judgment that would otherwise come (e.g., 7:1–15).

(2) He announced that the time for repentance was past and that judgment was now determined against the people (see notes on 19:10–11). Judgment is the dominant note in the book and is understood as the invocation of the final curse of the covenant; namely, loss of the promised land (Lev 26:31–33; Dt 28:49–68).

(3) The Lord would save his people, or a remnant of them, through the exile (see notes on 24:4–7). Although the Babylonians would prevail over Judah at the Lord's command, this would be for a limited time only. Babylon would fall in its turn (25:9,11–12), which occurred in 539 B.C. to an alliance of Persians and Medes under Cyrus, paving the way for the exiles to return (50:3; 51:1,27–28; 2Ch 36:20–23). This was Jeremiah's answer to the false prophets who had continually challenged his message of judgment (28:2–4).

Jeremiah also had a message of salvation, but it was intended only for those on the other side of the judgment (29:11–14). That message was crystallized in the prophecy of the new covenant (see especially 31:31–34). The new covenant prophecy was constructed around the main ingredients of the Mosaic covenant at Sinai, which spoke of God's desire to have a relationship with his chosen people and of the requirement that they reciprocate with obedience (Ex 19:3–6; Dt 7:6–11). The new covenant speaks of the empowerment of God's people to obey him (see notes on 31:33; 32:39–40), and the New Testament boldly declares that this promise is fulfilled only in Christ (see note on 31:33; cf. Lk 22:20; 1Co 11:25; Heb 8:6; 9:15; 12:24).

Jeremiah revealed his personal involvement with his message more than did the other prophets (Isa 15:7; 22:4; Mic 1:8–9); he sensed the agony of the people at the approach of the Babylonian armies even before they had experienced it themselves (4:19–21; 10:19–22; 14:19–22). He also felt the passion of the Lord about the sin he witnessed (see notes on 8:21—9:3). His role, which was mediatorial in nature, was revealed most poignantly in the series of passages often (inappropriately) known as the prophet's "confessions" (11:18–23; 12:1–6; 15:10–21; 17:12–18; 18:19–23; 20:7–18). In these passages he expressed his anguish at the overwhelming burden of his prophetic calling, prayed for vengeance on his personal enemies and even accused the Lord of having coerced or deceived him (15:18; 20:7). Some of these prayers elicited answers from God combining rebuke with reassurance (12:5–6; 15:19–21). God's encouragement to Jeremiah in 15:19–21 was later echoed in a prayer of Ephraim, which received its own answer (31:18–20). The Lord's good intentions for Jeremiah therefore became a pledge of his intended faithfulness to the whole people, both through and beyond the coming judgment.

The book's variety of materials sometimes makes it difficult for readers to follow the progression of Jeremiah's argument. Much of the work is in the form of poetic oracles that were spoken by the prophet (e.g., chs. 2–6). At other times the prophet developed his argument in a sermonic or prosaic style (e.g., 7:1–15). There is also third-person narrative about Jeremiah, presumably added by someone else (e.g., chs. 37–45), as well as an editorial appendix (e.g., ch. 52; see also 51:64).

The contents of the book are not in chronological order but rather are arranged thematically. Thus, chapters 21–24 are framed by prophecies concerning each of Josiah's successors up to, but excluding, Zedekiah. Similarly, chapters 35–36 revert backward to Jehoiakim after scenes involving Zedekiah, his successor. Many of the individual oracles are impossible to date.

Christ in Jeremiah

Jeremiah's message anticipates Christ primarily with respect to the prophet's certainty of restoration after the exile. The prophet made it clear both that the exile was coming and that afterward the people of God would enter a new covenant period replete with blessings from God. Jesus is the Lord of the new covenant (Lk 22:20; Heb 8:8; 9:5; 12:24), the son of David and the priest who ushered in the wonders of the last days through his earthly ministry. He continues this restoration work today and will complete it when he returns in glory (see theological article "The Kingdom of God" at Mt 4).

Outline

I. Superscription (1:1–3)	*Jeremiah was an inspired, authoritative prophet of the Lord who ministered to God's people for many years.*
II. Jeremiah's Call (1:4–19)	*Jeremiah was called by God to prophesy despite his reticence.*
III. Opening Case Against Judah (2:1—3:5)	*Jeremiah reported how God had declared Judah guilty of serious violations.*
IV. Judah's Sins and Judgments (3:6—6:30) A. Judah Worse Than Israel (3:6—4:4) B. Judgment of Invasion (4:5–31) C. Sinful Jerusalem (5:1–13) D. Judgment of Jerusalem's Destruction (5:14–19) E. Sins of Judah (5:20–31) F. Judgment of Exile (6:1–30)	*Judah's sins would lead to the judgment of exile.*

V. The Temple (7:1—10:25) A. Solomon's Temple and Shiloh (7:1—8:3) B. Judah's Sins and Judgment (8:4—9:26) C. Idolatry or the Lord (10:1–25)	*Jeremiah rejected the widespread assumption that the temple would protect Jerusalem from destruction.*
VI. The Broken Covenant (11:1—13:27) A. Curse of the Covenant (11:1–17) B. Judgment for Jeremiah's Opponents (11:18—12:17) 1. Complaint About a Deadly Plot (11:18–23) 2. Complaint About Wicked Opposition (12:1–17) C. Curse of the Covenant Confirmed (13:1–27)	*Judah had so violated the covenant that the nation deserved to be sent into exile.*
VII. The Judgment of Drought (14:1—15:21) A. Severe Drought (14:1–6) B. Prayer and Response (14:7—15:21)	*Jeremiah dealt with a severe drought brought about by God's judgment.*
VIII. Symbols of Coming Judgment (16:1—17:18) A. Symbolic Actions (16:1–18) B. Prayers and Response (16:19—17:18)	*Jeremiah performed symbolic actions that confirmed his prophetic message.*
IX. A Sermon About the Sabbath (17:19–27)	*Judah deserved judgment because of violations of the Sabbath.*
X. The Divine Potter (18:1—20:18) A. At the Potter's House (18:1–17) B. Opposition to Jeremiah (18:18–23) C. Symbolic Breaking of Pot (19:1–15) D. More Opposition to Jeremiah (20:1–6) E. Jeremiah's Lament (20:7–18)	*Jeremiah conveyed lessons learned at the potter's house.*
XI. Judgment and Hope in Judah's Last Days (21:1—24:10) A. Rulers of Judah (21:1—23:8) B. False Prophets (23:9–40) C. A Distinction and the Future Hope (24:1–10)	*Judah's future judgment was certain despite denials by others.*
XII. Severity and Length of Exile (25:1—29:32) A. Seventy Years of Exile Predicted (25:1–38) B. Reaction to Prediction of Exile (26:1–24) C. Rejection of False Prophecies (27:1–22) D. Confrontation With Hananiah (28:1–17) E. Letter to Exiles About False Prophecy (29:1–32)	*Jeremiah predicted a lengthy exile, which false prophets rejected.*
XIII. Certainty of Restoration (30:1—33:26) A. The Book of Restoration (30:1—31:40) B. Symbolic Purchase (32:1–44) C. Predictions of Restoration (33:1–26)	*Despite the impending exile, Jeremiah reaffirmed the promise that God's people would return from captivity.*
XIV. Representative Violations and Judgments (34:1—36:32) A. Judgment Against Zedekiah (34:1–22) B. Judgment for Falling Short of the Recabites' Example (35:1–19) C. Judgment Against Jehoiakim (36:1–32)	*Several selected events depicted the kinds of sins that caused Judah's troubles.*
XV. Final Encounters and Jerusalem's Fall (37:1—39:18) A. Jeremiah and Zedekiah (37:1–21) B. Jeremiah and the Officials (38:1–13)	*Jeremiah had several encounters with the king and his officials just before the fall of Jerusalem.*

C. Jeremiah and Zedekiah and His Officials (38:14–28) D. Jerusalem's Fall (39:1–18)	
XVI. Aftermath of Jerusalem's Fall (40:1—45:5) A. Gedaliah (40:1—41:10) B. Jeremiah's Flight to Egypt (41:11—44:30) C. Promise to Baruch (45:1–5)	*A sequence of important events took place after the fall of Jerusalem.*
XVII. Oracles Against the Nations (46:1—51:64) A. Against Egypt (46:1–28) B. Against Philistia (47:1–7) C. Against Moab (48:1–47) D. Against Ammon (49:1–6) E. Against Edom (49:7–22) F. Against Damascus (49:23–27) G. Against Arabian Tribes (49:28–33) H. Against Elam (49:34–39) I. Against Babylon (50:1—51:64)	*Jeremiah declared numerous prophecies against other nations. Many had already been fulfilled, demonstrating that his future predictions would be fulfilled as well.*
XVIII. Exile and Release From Prison (52:1–34)	*Although God's people went into exile, evidence of a future of blessing could be seen in events that took place in Babylon.*

1 The words of Jeremiah son of Hilkiah, one of the priests at Anathoth[a] in the territory of Benjamin. 2 The word of the LORD came to him in the thirteenth year of the
reign of Josiah son of Amon king of Judah, 3 and through the reign of Jehoiakim[b] son of
Josiah king of Judah, down to the fifth month of the eleventh year of Zedekiah[c] son of Josiah king of Judah, when the people of Jerusalem went into exile.[d]

The Call of Jeremiah

4 The word of the LORD came to me, saying,

5 "Before I formed you in the womb I knew[a][e] you,
before you were born[f] I set you apart;
I appointed you as a prophet to the nations.[g]"

6 "Ah, Sovereign LORD," I said, "I do not know how to speak;[h] I am only a child."[i]
7 But the LORD said to me, "Do not say, 'I am only a child.' You must go to everyone I
send you to and say whatever I command you. 8 Do not be afraid[j] of them, for I am with
you[k] and will rescue you," declares the LORD.
9 Then the LORD reached out his hand and touched[l] my mouth and said to me, "Now,

1:1 [a]Jos 21:18; 1Ch 6:60; Jer 32:7-9
1:3 [b]2Ki 23:34 [c]2Ki 24:17; Jer 39:2 [d]Jer 52:15
1:5 [e]Ps 139:16 [f]Isa 49:1 [g]ver 10; Jer 25:15-26
1:6 [h]Ex 4:10; 6:12 [i]1Ki 3:7
1:8 [j]Eze 2:6 [k]Jos 1:5; Jer 15:20
1:9 [l]Isa 6:7

[a] 5 Or *chose*

■ **1:1–3** *Superscription.* Jeremiah prophesied over a 40-year period that ended during the Babylonian exile of the people of Judah (see "Introduction: Author" and "Time and Place of Writing"). During this time the word of the Lord came to him repeatedly (see 25:3 and its note).
1:1 words of Jeremiah. These "words" include the various oracles he uttered (cf. Dt 1:1; Am 1:1). **priests at Anathoth.** Anathoth was a priestly city from early times (Jos 21:17–18; cf. Jer 11:21–23). Jeremiah was both a prophet and a priest.
1:2 The word of the LORD came to him. This phrase often opens a prophetic book (cf. Hos 1:1; Joel 1:1; Mic 1:1). Jeremiah's recorded words, therefore, are God's words. **thirteenth year.** 626 B.C. **Josiah.** He was a godly king who undertook a major religious reform beginning in 628 B.C. (2Ki 22–23; 2Ch 34–35). Jeremiah approved of him (22:15–16), although he made few specific references to the reform itself.
1:3 Jehoiakim . . . Zedekiah. Jehoahaz and Jehoiachin reigned between Jehoiakim and Zedekiah but are not mentioned here. Each, in his own way, rejected Jeremiah's words (see chs. 24; 36).
■ **1:4–19** *Jeremiah's Call.* The book begins with an account of Jeremiah's authorization. God called Jeremiah to his prophetic ministry of announcing divine judgment on Judah for idolatry.
1:4 The word . . . to me. This phrase frequently introduces an oracle in the book (cf. v. 11).
1:5 I formed you . . . knew you. God's creation and election of Jeremiah belong together (for the verb "know" in the sense of "choose," see also Ge 18:19; Am 3:2). God's choice before birth was the ground of Jeremiah's prophetic standing. Note also Moses, whose birth narrative (Ex 2) has the same significance, as well as Paul (Gal 1:15). **appointed.** In the sense of consecration. **prophet.** In general, a prophet was one who spoke God's words. The prototypical prophet was Moses (Dt 18:14–22). By Jeremiah's day the term *prophet* had come to bear the significance of a representative of God, the King, to his servants. **to the nations.** Jeremiah's message was chiefly for Judah, but he had words of judgment for other nations as well (25:8–37; chs. 46–51).
1:6 not know how to speak. Moses had made the same protest (Ex 4:10). Thus Jeremiah, like Moses, was humble and not self-assertive. **child.** This image denotes a disqualifying immaturity (1Ki 3:7).
1:8 Do not be afraid. The reassurance recurs (10:5; 30:10; cf. Isa 43:1; Lk 12:32). **I am with you.** These words constitute the Lord's promise to accompany his people in times of war and, as in Jeremiah's case, trouble (Ex 3:12; Isa 7:14; Mt 1:23; 28:20).
1:9 touched my mouth. This expression is a figurative sign of consecration for the voicing of the Lord's words (Isa 6:7). **words in your mouth.** See Exodus 4:15 and 2 Peter 1:21.

I have put my words in your mouth.[m] 10 See, today I appoint you over nations and kingdoms to uproot and tear down, to destroy and overthrow, to build and to plant."[n]
11 The word of the LORD came to me: "What do you see, Jeremiah?"[o]
"I see the branch of an almond tree," I replied.
12 The LORD said to me, "You have seen correctly, for I am watching[a] to see that my
word is fulfilled."
13 The word of the LORD came to me again: "What do you see?"[p]
"I see a boiling pot, tilting away from the north," I answered.
14 The LORD said to me, "From the north disaster will be poured out on all who live in
the land. 15 I am about to summon all the peoples of the northern kingdoms," declares
the LORD.

"Their kings will come and set up their thrones
  in the entrance of the gates of Jerusalem;
they will come against all her surrounding walls
  and against all the towns of Judah.[q]
16 I will pronounce my judgments on my people
  because of their wickedness[r] in forsaking me,[s]
in burning incense to other gods[t]
  and in worshiping what their hands have made.

17 "Get yourself ready! Stand up and say to them whatever I command you. Do not be
terrified[u] by them, or I will terrify you before them. 18 Today I have made you[v] a fortified
city, an iron pillar and a bronze wall to stand against the whole land—against the kings
of Judah, its officials, its priests and the people of the land. 19 They will fight against you
but will not overcome you, for I am with you[w] and will rescue[x] you," declares the LORD.

Israel Forsakes God

2 The word of the LORD came to me: 2 "Go and proclaim in the hearing of Jerusalem:

" 'I remember the devotion of your youth,[y]
  how as a bride you loved me
and followed me through the desert,[z]
  through a land not sown.
3 Israel was holy[a] to the LORD,[b]
  the firstfruits[c] of his harvest;
all who devoured[d] her were held guilty,[e]
  and disaster overtook them,' "
declares the LORD.

1:9 [m]Ex 4:12
1:10 [n]Jer 18:7-10; 24:6; 31:4,28
1:11 [o]Jer 24:3; Am 7:8
1:13 [p]Zec 4:2
1:15 [q]Jer 4:16; 9:11
1:16 [r]Dt 28:20 [s]Jer 17:13 [t]Jer 7:9; 19:4
1:17 [u]Eze 2:6
1:18 [v]Isa 50:7
1:19 [w]Jer 20:11 [x]ver 8
2:2 [y]Eze 16:8-14,60; Hos 2:15 [z]Dt 2:7
2:3 [a]Dt 7:6 [b]Ex 19:6 [c]Jas 1:18; Rev 14:4 [d]Isa 41:11; Jer 30:16 [e]Jer 50:7

[a] *12* The Hebrew for *watching* sounds like the Hebrew for *almond tree.*

1:10 uproot . . . plant. These images stress Jeremiah's destructive message but also foreshadow the Lord's reconstruction. The call narrative prepares for the prophet's ministry in its varied entirety. He would pronounce words of judgment leading to destruction and exile but also speak hopeful words of return and restoration after exile.

1:11 word. Connected with vision (Am 7:8).

1:13–14 boiling . . . poured out. The second vision, like the first, affirmed the coming judgment. Jeremiah needed to believe the message in order to proclaim it.

1:14 north. Although Babylon lay to the east, its armies would advance upon Judah from the north, because that was the natural approach.

1:16 judgments. Judgment was the work of God in relation to his covenant people (11:2) by which he invoked the curses of the covenant (Dt 28:15–68). **forsaking me . . . other gods.** Judah had turned away from the true God to serve idols. Jeremiah returned to this theme time and again. **burning incense.** See note on 11:12. **hands have made.** The meaning of this ironic polemic is plain enough. Worshiping gods fashioned by human hands was the height of folly (Isa 46:6).

1:17 Get yourself ready! Literally, "Gird up your loins!" The phrase was used of preparation for battle or other vigorous labor (1Ki 18:46; cf. Isa 5:27). Jeremiah was about to enter an extremely difficult ministry.

1:18 fortified city . . . bronze wall. Symbols of the kind of strength the prophet would need. **kings . . . land.** Jeremiah's accusation would embrace the whole society of Judah, from greatest to least.

1:19 fight against you . . . I am with you. The prophet was about to enter a personal war, but God promised to accompany him into battle (see note on v. 8). He had no need to fear failure.

2:1—33:26 The primary themes of the prophet's ministry appear in these chapters. He pronounced God's word concerning impending judgments, exile and restoration from exile.

2:1—6:30 This collection of the prophet's speeches is from his ministry during the reign of Josiah (3:6). These polemics pointed to the continuing sins of Judah (2:1—3:5) that led to divine judgments and finally to foreign invasion (3:6—6:30).

■ **2:1—3:5** *Opening Case Against Judah.* These prophecies are set within the framework of the court of heaven, from which summons and charges are made. As in many such lawsuits, God highlighted the sins of the people by stressing how good he had been to them. The prophet employed a number of vivid sexual images to draw attention to the Judahites' involvement in Canaanite fertility rituals.

2:1 See note on 1:2.

2:2 Jerusalem. Cities are regarded as feminine in the Hebrew language, causing the poet to personify Jerusalem as a woman (see note on 7:29). **I.** God himself spoke as the accuser; later he would speak as the judge. **devotion.** Denotes faithfulness within a relationship—personal or covenantal—such as that between the Lord and Israel/Judah (see note on La 3:22). **youth . . . bride.** Israel's earliest relationship with the Lord (in the desert, after her escape from Egypt) is remembered as pure and devoted, like a bride's with her bridegroom (cf. Hos 2:14–16).

2:3 holy . . . firstfruits. These terms are drawn from the life of worship. Israel was "holy"; i.e., dedicated to the Lord (Eze 22:26). Offerings to the Lord were to be made from the "firstfruits" (Dt

4 Hear the word of the LORD, O house of Jacob,
all you clans of the house of Israel.

5 This is what the LORD says:

"What fault did your fathers find in me,
that they strayed so far from me?
They followed worthless idols
and became worthless[f] themselves.
6 They did not ask, 'Where is the LORD,
who brought us up out of Egypt[g]
and led us through the barren wilderness,
through a land of deserts[h] and rifts,[i]
a land of drought and darkness,[a]
a land where no one travels and no one lives?'
7 I brought you into a fertile land
to eat its fruit and rich produce.[j]
But you came and defiled my land
and made my inheritance detestable.[k]
8 The priests did not ask,
'Where is the LORD?'
Those who deal with the law did not know me;[l]
the leaders rebelled against me.
The prophets prophesied by Baal,[m]
following worthless idols.[n]

9 "Therefore I bring charges[o] against you again,"
declares the LORD.
"And I will bring charges against your children's children.
10 Cross over to the coasts of Kittim[b] and look,
send to Kedar[c] and observe closely;
see if there has ever been anything like this:
11 Has a nation ever changed its gods?
(Yet they are not gods[p] at all.)
But my people have exchanged their[d] Glory[q]
for worthless idols.
12 Be appalled at this, O heavens,
and shudder with great horror,"
declares the LORD.
13 "My people have committed two sins:
They have forsaken me,
the spring of living water,[r]
and have dug their own cisterns,
broken cisterns that cannot hold water.
14 Is Israel a servant, a slave[s] by birth?
Why then has he become plunder?

2:5 [f]2Ki 17:15
2:6 [g]Hos 13:4 [h]Dt 8:15 [i]Dt 32:10
2:7 [j]Nu 13:27; Dt 8:7-9; 11:10-12 [k]Ps 106:34-39; Jer 16:18
2:8 [l]Jer 4:22 [m]Jer 23:13 [n]Jer 16:19
2:9 [o]Eze 20:35-36; Mic 6:2
2:11 [p]Isa 37:19; Jer 16:20 [q]Ps 106:20; Ro 1:23
2:13 [r]Ps 36:9; Jn 4:14
2:14 [s]Ex 4:22

[a] *6* Or *and the shadow of death* [b] *10* That is, Cyprus and western coastlands [c] *10* The home of Bedouin tribes in the Syro-Arabian desert [d] *11* Masoretic Text; an ancient Hebrew scribal tradition *my*

26:2; Hos 9:10), which were considered superior in quality. **guilty.** The guilt resulted from unauthorized handling of holy things.
2:4 Hear. This common prophetic summons introduced a call to God's heavenly tribunal and possibly to judgment (7:2; 17:20; 19:3; Isa 1:10; Hos 4:1; Am 7:16).
2:5 This is what the LORD says. A typical messenger formula for prophets (cf. Isa 7:7; Eze 2:4), it constituted the prophet's claim to be speaking God's word.
2:7 fertile land. Note the contrast between desert and fertile land in Deuteronomy 8:7–10 and 15–16. **defiled my land . . . my inheritance.** See Deuteronomy 21:23. God's holy people (Dt 7:6) dwelled in the land given to them by God as an inheritance. The land could be defiled, or made "unclean," by sin that took place within it. **detestable.** See 7:21.
2:8 priests . . . Those who deal with the law. These may be the same people (18:18; Dt 31:9), or the latter may be a scribal group (8:8). **leaders.** Literally, "shepherds," a term often used for rulers (23:1–4). **prophets.** An official group that Jeremiah frequently opposed for its apostasy (23:9–40; 28). **worthless idols.** Literally, "unprofitable." This is a different word from that used in verse 5. See *WLC* 151.
2:9 I bring charges. The courtroom metaphor is resumed (v. 5; cf. Hos 4:1; Mic 6:1–2).
2:10 Kittim . . . Kedar. These locations represent east and west, respectively. God found it unthinkable that, while other nations were faithful to their false gods, Judah was unfaithful to him.
2:11 See *BC* 26.
2:12 O heavens. See also Isaiah 1:2. Jeremiah appealed to both heaven and Earth as witnesses in the court (Dt 30:19; 31:28; 32:1).
2:13 two sins. Jeremiah stressed the seriousness of Judah's sin. The Judahites had forsaken God and replaced him with other gods. **water.** God alone provides life-giving water (Isa 55:1; Jn 4:10; 7:37–39). **cisterns.** Where the plaster lining of "cisterns" was broken, the cisterns failed. Similarly, false gods could not provide for the people's needs. See *BC* 1.

2:15 [t]Jer 4:7; 50:17 [u]Isa 1:7
2:16 [v]Isa 19:13 [w]Jer 43:7-9
2:17 [x]Jer 4:18
2:18 [y]Isa 30:2 [z]Jos 13:3
2:19 [a]Jer 3:11,22 [b]Isa 3:9; Hos 5:5 [c]Job 20:14; Am 8:10 [d]Ps 36:1
2:20 [e]Lev 26:13 [f]Isa 57:7; Jer 17:2 [g]Dt 12:2
2:21 [h]Ex 15:17 [i]Ps 80:8 [j]Isa 5:4
2:23 [k]Pr 30:12 [l]Jer 9:14 [m]Jer 7:31 [n]ver 33; Jer 31:22
2:24 [o]Jer 14:6

15 Lions[t] have roared;
they have growled at him.
They have laid waste[u] his land;
his towns are burned and deserted.
16 Also, the men of Memphis[a][v] and Tahpanhes[w]
have shaved the crown of your head.[b]
17 Have you not brought this on yourselves[x]
by forsaking the LORD your God
when he led you in the way?
18 Now why go to Egypt[y]
to drink water from the Shihor[c]?[z]
And why go to Assyria
to drink water from the River[d]?
19 Your wickedness will punish you;
your backsliding[a] will rebuke[b] you.
Consider then and realize
how evil and bitter[c] it is for you
when you forsake the LORD your God
and have no awe[d] of me,"
declares the Lord, the LORD Almighty.

20 "Long ago you broke off your yoke[e]
and tore off your bonds;
you said, 'I will not serve you!'
Indeed, on every high hill[f]
and under every spreading tree[g]
you lay down as a prostitute.
21 I had planted[h] you like a choice vine[i]
of sound and reliable stock.
How then did you turn against me
into a corrupt,[j] wild vine?
22 Although you wash yourself with soda
and use an abundance of soap,
the stain of your guilt is still before me,"
declares the Sovereign LORD.
23 "How can you say, 'I am not defiled;[k]
I have not run after the Baals'?[l]
See how you behaved in the valley;[m]
consider what you have done.
You are a swift she-camel
running[n] here and there,
24 a wild donkey[o] accustomed to the desert,
sniffing the wind in her craving—
in her heat who can restrain her?
Any males that pursue her need not tire themselves;
at mating time they will find her.

[a] *16* Hebrew *Noph* [b] *16* Or *have cracked your skull* [c] *18* That is, a branch of the Nile [d] *18* That is, the Euphrates

---

2:15 Lions. Probably refers to enemies (cf. 4:7), an introductory picture of desolation at enemy hands.
2:16 Memphis . . . Tahpanhes. Cities of Egypt. Canaan was disputed territory between Egypt and Babylon from 609 to 605 B.C. **crown.** Possibly a reference to Josiah, who was killed by Pharaoh Neco at Megiddo in 609 B.C. (2Ki 23:29).
2:18 Egypt . . . Assyria. Israel and Judah's besetting sin was seeking help from political alliances rather than from the Lord. See Isaiah 7:3–9. **water.** In 2 Kings 18:31 the Assyrian field commander boasted that Assyria was more reliable than the Lord as a provider of basic needs.
2:19 backsliding. This word speaks of a repeated turning back to other gods. This is the opposite of turning to the Lord, the heart of repentance. See "waywardness" at Hosea 14:4, where the same Hebrew word is used.
2:20 high hill . . . spreading tree. Typical sites of shrines to the gods of Canaan (see Dt 12:2; 1Ki 14:23). **prostitute.** As Canaanite worship involved ritual prostitution, so Judah herself is portrayed as a prostitute, unfaithful to the Lord (cf. Eze 23:1–8; Hos 3:1–5; 4:10–14). See *WLC* 151.
2:21 choice vine . . . wild vine? Vine imagery is frequently used for Israel (Ps 80:8–16; Isa 5:1–7; Eze 17:1–10). Jesus Christ is the true vine, and those who abide in him are the branches (Jn 15:1–8). **wild.** Literally, "foreign," where foreignness connotes pagan religious practices.
2:22 wash. The washing away of sin must be accompanied by faith and true repentance, on the basis of the blood of the everlasting covenant (Isa 53:4–6; Heb 9:11–15; 13:20).
2:23 the valley. Probably refers to the Hinnom Valley, immediately south of Jerusalem, where abominable worship practices occurred (cf. 7:31). **she-camel.** That is, a young female camel, characteristically irresolute, ready to follow any fresh impulse.
2:24 wild donkey . . . craving. Jeremiah properly characterized the waywardness of the Judahites as lustful cravings because they followed after the indecent, sensual, immoral Canaanite fertility practices.

25 Do not run until your feet are bare
and your throat is dry.
But you said, 'It's no use!
I love foreign gods,[p]
and I must go after them.'
26 "As a thief is disgraced[q] when he is caught,
so the house of Israel is disgraced—
they, their kings and their officials,
their priests and their prophets.
27 They say to wood, 'You are my father,'
and to stone,[r] 'You gave me birth.'
They have turned their backs to me
and not their faces;[s]
yet when they are in trouble,[t] they say,
'Come and save us!'
28 Where then are the gods[u] you made for yourselves?
Let them come if they can save you
when you are in trouble![v]
For you have as many gods
as you have towns,[w] O Judah.

29 "Why do you bring charges against me?
You have all[x] rebelled against me,"
declares the LORD.
30 "In vain I punished your people;
they did not respond to correction.
Your sword has devoured your prophets[y]
like a ravening lion.

31 "You of this generation, consider the word of the LORD:

"Have I been a desert to Israel
or a land of great darkness?[z]
Why do my people say, 'We are free to roam;
we will come to you no more'?
32 Does a maiden forget her jewelry,
a bride her wedding ornaments?
Yet my people have forgotten me,
days without number.
33 How skilled you are at pursuing love!
Even the worst of women can learn from your ways.
34 On your clothes men find
the lifeblood[a] of the innocent poor,
though you did not catch them breaking in.[b]
Yet in spite of all this
35 you say, 'I am innocent;
he is not angry with me.'
But I will pass judgment[c] on you
because you say, 'I have not sinned.'[d]
36 Why do you go about so much,
changing[e] your ways?
You will be disappointed by Egypt[f]
as you were by Assyria.
37 You will also leave that place
with your hands on your head,[g]
for the LORD has rejected those you trust;
you will not be helped[h] by them.

2:25 [p]Dt 32:16; Jer 3:13; 14:10
2:26 [q]Jer 48:27
2:27 [r]Jer 3:9 [s]Jer 18:17; 32:33 [t]Jdg 10:10; Isa 26:16
2:28 [u]Isa 45:20 [v]Dt 32:37 [w]2Ki 17:29; Jer 11:13
2:29 [x]Jer 5:1; 6:13; Da 9:11
2:30 [y]Ne 9:26; Ac 7:52; 1Th 2:15
2:31 [z]Isa 45:19
2:34 [a]2Ki 21:16 [b]Ex 22:2
2:35 [c]Jer 25:31 [d]1Jn 1:8, 10
2:36 [e]Jer 31:22 [f]Isa 30:2, 3, 7
2:37 [g]2Sa 13:19 [h]Jer 37:7

2:27–28 See *WLC* 105.
2:28 as many gods as . . . towns. A distinguishing feature of pagan religion.
2:32 maiden . . . bride. Such forgetfulness is virtually impossible, yet Judah had done something even more unthinkable: She had forgotten God. **days without number.** God's complaint was not simply that the Judahites had sinned, but that they had forgotten God for a prolonged period of time, even after repeated warnings. See *WLC* 105.
2:33 skilled . . . love! The metaphor persists of Judah as an unfaithful female lover (v. 25).
2:34 lifeblood . . . poor. This terminology refers to the persecution of the weak by the strong—a prominent theme in Amos (Am 2:6–8; 4:1).
2:35 See *WLC* 145.
2:37 hands on your head. A posture for captives of war.

3

"If a man divorces[i] his wife
and she leaves him and marries another man,
should he return to her again?
Would not the land be completely defiled?
But you have lived as a prostitute with many lovers[j]—
would you now return to me?"
declares the LORD.

2 "Look up to the barren heights and see.
Is there any place where you have not been ravished?
By the roadside[k] you sat waiting for lovers,
sat like a nomad[a] in the desert.
You have defiled the land[l]
with your prostitution and wickedness.
3 Therefore the showers have been withheld,[m]
and no spring rains[n] have fallen.
Yet you have the brazen look of a prostitute;
you refuse to blush with shame.[o]
4 Have you not just called to me:
'My Father,[p] my friend from my youth,[q]
5 will you always be angry?[r]
Will your wrath continue forever?'
This is how you talk,
but you do all the evil you can."

Unfaithful Israel

6During the reign of King Josiah, the LORD said to me, "Have you seen what faithless
Israel has done? She has gone up on every high hill and under every spreading tree[s] and
has committed adultery[t] there. 7I thought that after she had done all this she would return to me but she did not, and her unfaithful sister[u] Judah saw it. 8I gave faithless Israel her certificate of divorce and sent her away because of all her adulteries. Yet I saw
that her unfaithful sister Judah had no fear;[v] she also went out and committed adultery.
9Because Israel's immorality mattered so little to her, she defiled the land[w] and committed adultery with stone[x] and wood.[y] 10In spite of all this, her unfaithful sister Judah did
not return to me with all her heart, but only in pretense,[z]" declares the LORD.
11The LORD said to me, "Faithless Israel is more righteous[a] than unfaithful[b] Judah.
12Go, proclaim this message toward the north:[c]

" 'Return,[d] faithless Israel,' declares the LORD,
'I will frown on you no longer,
for I am merciful,' declares the LORD,
'I will not be angry[e] forever.
13 Only acknowledge[f] your guilt—
you have rebelled against the LORD your God,
you have scattered your favors to foreign gods[g]

3:1 [i]Dt 24:1-4 [j]Jer 2:20,25; Eze 16:26,29
3:2 [k]Ge 38:14; Eze 16:25 [l]Jer 2:7
3:3 [m]Lev 26:19 [n]Jer 14:4 [o]Jer 6:15; 8:12; Zep 3:5
3:4 [p]ver 19 [q]Jer 2:2
3:5 [r]Ps 103:9; Isa 57:16
3:6 [s]Jer 17:2 [t]Jer 2:20
3:7 [u]Eze 16:46
3:8 [v]Eze 16:47; 23:11
3:9 [w]ver 2 [x]Isa 57:6 [y]Jer 2:27
3:10 [z]Jer 12:2
3:11 [a]Eze 16:52; 23:11 [b]ver 7
3:12 [c]2Ki 17:3-6 [d]ver 14; Jer 31:21, 22; Eze 33:11 [e]Ps 86:15
3:13 [f]Dt 30:1-3; Jer 14:20; 1Jn 1:9 [g]Jer 2:25

[a] 2 Or *an Arab*

3:1 divorces his wife. The bridal metaphor (2:2) now gives way to one of divorce. The underlying law is Deuteronomy 24:1–4. Its point—the finality of divorce—is also the force of the argument here.
3:2–5 God accused Judah of infidelity in every way imaginable in order to stress the seriousness of the nation's turning away from him.
3:3 brazen look of a prostitute. Judah was unrelenting and unrepentant. See *WLC* 151.
3:4 My Father, my friend. God mocked the hypocrisy of the Judahites as they pleaded with him to circumvent his judgment, all the while turning away from him to every kind of evil they could imagine.
■ **3:6—6:30** *Judah's Sins and Judgments.* The prophet leveled two sets of accusations, followed by announcements of defeat and exile given in the days of Josiah. Judah had sinned more grievously than had northern Israel (3:6—4:4) and would suffer invasion (4:5–31). Jerusalem, a thoroughly corrupt city (5:1–13), would experience defeat and exile (5:14–19). The sins of Judah were exposed (5:20–31), and God would send its inhabitants into exile (6:1–30).
■ **3:6—4:4** *Judah Worse Than Israel.* Jeremiah compared the inhabitants of Judah with those of Israel. Although Israel had gone into exile, God was even more displeased with Judah.
3:6 King Josiah. See "Introduction: Author" and "Time and Place of Writing"; see also note on 1:2. **faithless.** Literally, "backsliding" or turning away from the Lord, the opposite of repentance. **Israel.** The prophet drew attention to the destruction of the sinful northern kingdom in 722 B.C.
3:8–11 Jeremiah explained his reason for focusing on northern Israel: Judah had failed to learn from Israel's exile and had actually become more corrupt than Israel had been.
3:8 certificate of divorce. See note on 3:1. **sent her away.** Into exile in Assyria in 722 B.C.
3:9 stone and wood. A reference to idols.
3:12 toward the north. To those already exiled in Assyria. **Return, faithless Israel.** The prophet's words were full of irony as he announced God's favor toward the northern tribes, even as he declared the impending doom of Judah. See note on 29:14. **I am merciful.** Alludes to the Lord's covenant love. **I will not be angry forever.** This answers the question of 3:5 (cf. 31:20; Ex 34:6-7).
3:13 scattered your favors. Another use of the prostitution metaphor (cf. 2:20).

under every spreading tree,[h]
and have not obeyed[i] me,' "
declares the LORD.

14"Return,[j] faithless people," declares the LORD, "for I am your husband. I will choose
you—one from a town and two from a clan—and bring you to Zion. 15Then I will give you
shepherds[k] after my own heart, who will lead you with knowledge and understanding.
16In those days, when your numbers have increased greatly in the land," declares the
LORD, "men will no longer say, 'The ark of the covenant of the LORD.' It will never enter
their minds or be remembered;[l] it will not be missed, nor will another one be made. 17At
that time they will call Jerusalem The Throne[m] of the LORD, and all nations will gather
in Jerusalem to honor[n] the name of the LORD. No longer will they follow the stubbornness of their evil hearts.[o] 18In those days the house of Judah will join the house of Israel,[p] and together[q] they will come from a northern[r] land to the land[s] I gave your forefathers as an inheritance.

19"I myself said,

" 'How gladly would I treat you like sons
and give you a desirable land,
the most beautiful inheritance of any nation.'
I thought you would call me 'Father'[t]
and not turn away from following me.
20But like a woman unfaithful to her husband,
so you have been unfaithful to me, O house of Israel,"
declares the LORD.

21A cry is heard on the barren heights,[u]
the weeping and pleading of the people of Israel,
because they have perverted their ways
and have forgotten the LORD their God.

22"Return,[v] faithless people;
I will cure[w] you of backsliding."

"Yes, we will come to you,
for you are the LORD our God.
23Surely the ⌊idolatrous⌋ commotion on the hills
and mountains is a deception;
surely in the LORD our God
is the salvation[x] of Israel.
24From our youth shameful[y] gods have consumed
the fruits of our fathers' labor—
their flocks and herds,
their sons and daughters.
25Let us lie down in our shame,[z]
and let our disgrace cover us.
We have sinned against the LORD our God,
both we and our fathers;
from our youth[a] till this day
we have not obeyed the LORD our God."

3:13 [h]Dt 12:2 [i]ver 25
3:14 [j]Hos 2:19
3:15 [k]Ac 20:28
3:16 [l]Isa 65:17
3:17 [m]Jer 17:12; Eze 43:7 [n]Isa 60:9 [o]Jer 11:8
3:18 [p]Hos 1:11 [q]Isa 11:13; Jer 50:4 [r]Jer 16:15; 31:8 [s]Am 9:15
3:19 [t]ver 4; Isa 63:16
3:21 [u]ver 2
3:22 [v]Hos 14:4 [w]Jer 33:6; Hos 6:1
3:23 [x]Ps 3:8; Jer 17:14
3:24 [y]Hos 9:10
3:25 [z]Ezr 9:6 [a]Jer 22:21

3:14 husband. The Hebrew word *ba'al,* customarily meaning "lord" or "master," often refers to a "husband," in contrast to the associations called to mind by the identical name of the infamous false god. See also Hosea 2:16–17. **choose . . . one . . . two.** God offered to elect and preserve a remnant from the various tribes, clans and towns of the exiled community (see notes on 23:3; Isa 10:20–22; cf. Dt 7:6–11). **Zion.** The book of Chronicles makes it clear that representatives of northern Israel were among the returnees to Jerusalem in 539 B.C. (see 1Ch 9:3).
3:16 In those days. Jeremiah had in mind the blessings offered in the days of restoration after the exile that find their final fulfillment in the New Testament Messianic age. **numbers have increased.** The promise to Abraham (Ge 15:5), fulfilling the blessing to Adam (Ge 1:26–28), would come to fruition in the restoration. **The ark . . . be remembered.** The symbols of the times before restoration would be replaced by the realities they symbolized.
3:17–18 Compare the promises in 31:31–33.
3:17 Throne. The ark is no longer in view (Ex 25:22; 1Sa 4:4). Rather, Jerusalem itself becomes the picture of the Lord's rule in the whole earth and the locus of his authoritative presence (Zec 2:11). In the great age of salvation after exile, the whole earth would become God's throne room.
3:19 How gladly. God continued to express the sincerity of his desire for his people to repent in order that he might bless them.
3:20 a woman unfaithful. See 3:1 and Hosea 1–3.
3:22 Return . . . backsliding. This parallels Hosea 14:4. If the Israelites would repent, God would cure his people. See *WSC* 87.
3:24 consumed . . . daughters. This is the antithesis of blessing (Dt 7:13). Children were often sacrificed to pagan gods (Jer 7:31).

4

"If you will return[b], O Israel,
return to me,"
declares the LORD.
"If you put your detestable idols[c] out of my sight
and no longer go astray,
2 and if in a truthful, just and righteous way
you swear,[d] 'As surely as the LORD lives,'[e]
then the nations will be blessed[f] by him
and in him they will glory."

3 This is what the LORD says to the men of Judah and to Jerusalem:

"Break up your unplowed ground[g]
and do not sow among thorns.[h]
4 Circumcise yourselves to the LORD,
circumcise your hearts,[i]
you men of Judah and people of Jerusalem,
or my wrath[j] will break out and burn like fire
because of the evil you have done—
burn with no one to quench[k] it.

Disaster From the North

5 "Announce in Judah and proclaim in Jerusalem and say:
'Sound the trumpet throughout the land!'
Cry aloud and say:
'Gather together!
Let us flee to the fortified cities!'[l]
6 Raise the signal to go to Zion!
Flee for safety without delay!
For I am bringing disaster from the north,[m]
even terrible destruction."

7 A lion[n] has come out of his lair;
a destroyer of nations has set out.
He has left his place
to lay waste[o] your land.
Your towns will lie in ruins[p]
without inhabitant.
8 So put on sackcloth,[q]
lament and wail,
for the fierce anger[r] of the LORD
has not turned away from us.

9 "In that day," declares the LORD,
"the king and the officials will lose heart,
the priests will be horrified,
and the prophets will be appalled."[s]

10 Then I said, "Ah, Sovereign LORD, how completely you have deceived[t] this people
and Jerusalem by saying, 'You will have peace,'[u] when the sword is at our throats."
11 At that time this people and Jerusalem will be told, "A scorching wind[v] from the barren heights in the desert blows toward my people, but not to winnow or cleanse; 12 a wind
too strong for that comes from me.[a] Now I pronounce my judgments[w] against them."

4:1 [b]Jer 3:1,22; Joel 2:12 [c]Jer 35:15
4:2 [d]Dt 10:20; Isa 65:16 [e]Jer 12:16 [f]Ge 22:18; Gal 3:8
4:3 [g]Hos 10:12 [h]Mk 4:18
4:4 [i]Dt 10:16; Jer 9:26; Ro 2:28-29 [j]Zep 2:2 [k]Am 5:6
4:5 [l]Jos 10:20; Jer 8:14
4:6 [m]Jer 1:13-15; 50:3
4:7 [n]2Ki 24:1; Jer 2:15 [o]Isa 1:7 [p]Jer 25:9
4:8 [q]Isa 22:12; Jer 6:26 [r]Jer 30:24
4:9 [s]Isa 29:9
4:10 [t]2Th 2:11 [u]Jer 14:13
4:11 [v]Eze 17:10; Hos 13:15
4:12 [w]Jer 1:16

a 12 Or *comes at my command*

4:1–2 See *WCF* 22.3; 22.4; *WLC* 112; *HC* 99,101.
4:4 Circumcise . . . hearts. Jeremiah insisted that the ideals of the Mosaic covenant were to be fulfilled in those who wished to return from exile. The outward signs of ownership by the Lord were of no avail unless they corresponded to an inner reality (31:31–34; cf. Dt 10:16; 30:6.). **wrath . . . burn.** The word "wrath" carries the connotation of heat (cf. Isa 1:31).
■**4:5–31** *Judgment of Invasion.* Jeremiah announced again that Judah would be invaded and destroyed.
4:5 Sound the trumpet. An early warning (cf. Joel 2:1; Am 3:6). **flee to the fortified cities!** Jeremiah announced destruction at the hand of a foe from the north. His cry here bespeaks the panic that would drive country-dwellers to the cities for safety.
4:7 lion . . . destroyer. Compare 2:15 and 6:26.
4:8 sackcloth . . . wail. Actions of lamentation (cf. Jnh 3:5).
4:9 In that day. A day of reckoning, when the events prophesied would come to pass (cf. Isa 2:11–12).
4:11–12 not to winnow . . . too strong for that. There would be no beneficial effects of this wind (as in winnowing).
4:11 scorching wind. The sirocco—a hot, dry desert wind.

13 Look! He advances like the clouds,[x]
his chariots[y] come like a whirlwind,[z]
his horses are swifter than eagles.[a]
Woe to us! We are ruined!
14 O Jerusalem, wash[b] the evil from your heart and be saved.
How long will you harbor wicked thoughts?
15 A voice is announcing from Dan,[c]
proclaiming disaster from the hills of Ephraim.
16 "Tell this to the nations,
proclaim it to Jerusalem:
'A besieging army is coming from a distant land,
raising a war cry[d] against the cities of Judah.
17 They surround[e] her like men guarding a field,
because she has rebelled[f] against me,' "
declares the LORD.

18 "Your own conduct and actions[g]
have brought this upon you.[h]
This is your punishment.
How bitter[i] it is!
How it pierces to the heart!"

19 Oh, my anguish, my anguish![j]
I writhe in pain.
Oh, the agony of my heart!
My heart pounds within me,
I cannot keep silent.[k]
For I have heard the sound of the trumpet;
I have heard the battle cry.[l]
20 Disaster follows disaster;[m]
the whole land lies in ruins.
In an instant my tents[n] are destroyed,
my shelter in a moment.
21 How long must I see the battle standard
and hear the sound of the trumpet?

22 "My people are fools;[o]
they do not know me.[p]
They are senseless children;
they have no understanding.
They are skilled in doing evil;[q]
they know not how to do good."[r]

23 I looked at the earth,
and it was formless and empty;[s]
and at the heavens,
and their light was gone.
24 I looked at the mountains,
and they were quaking;[t]
all the hills were swaying.
25 I looked, and there were no people;
every bird in the sky had flown away.[u]
26 I looked, and the fruitful land was a desert;
all its towns lay in ruins
before the LORD, before his fierce anger.

4:13 [x]Isa 19:1 [y]Isa 66:15 [z]Isa 5:28 [a]Dt 28:49; Hab 1:8
4:14 [b]Jas 4:8
4:15 [c]Jer 8:16
4:16 [d]Eze 21:22
4:17 [e]2Ki 25:1,4 [f]Jer 5:23
4:18 [g]Ps 107:17; Isa 50:1 [h]Jer 2:17 [i]Jer 2:19
4:19 [j]Isa 16:11; 22:4; Jer 9:10 [k]Jer 20:9 [l]Nu 10:9
4:20 [m]Ps 42:7; Eze 7:26 [n]Jer 10:20
4:22 [o]Jer 10:8 [p]Jer 2:8 [q]Jer 13:23; 1Co 14:20 [r]Ro 16:19
4:23 [s]Ge 1:2
4:24 [t]Isa 5:25; Eze 38:20
4:25 [u]Jer 9:10; 12:4; Zep 1:3

4:13 clouds . . . whirlwind . . . eagles. Images drawn from nature that indicate the strength and speed of the enemy.
4:17 like men guarding a field. As though they already owned it.
4:19–26 These verses comprise a brief interlude in which the prophet expressed his own despair over the future of Jerusalem and Judah.
4:21 How long . . . ? A common cry in psalms of lament (e.g., Ps 13:1; see "Introduction to Psalms: Structure: *Genres*"). The prophet cried out because he envisioned disaster after disaster in store for Judah.
4:22 My people are fools. These could be God's words or Jeremiah's, because the prophet identified strongly not only with the people but also with God. **fools.** See Proverbs 1:7. **skilled.** Their wickedness was a learned and ingrained habit (cf. 9:5). See *WLC* 105.
4:23 formless and empty . . . heavens . . . light was gone. Compare Genesis 1:2 and 14–15. The order of creation would be undone by this judgment.
4:25 no people. This same phrase is used in Genesis 2:5. Creation would be returned to its original chaos.
4:26 fruitful land . . . a desert. Covenant blessings would now be reversed (Dt 8:7–16).

4:27 [v]Jer 5:10,18; 12:12; 30:11; 46:28

4:28 [w]Jer 12:4,11; 14:2; Hos 4:3 [x]Isa 5:30; 50:3 [y]Nu 23:19 [z]Jer 23:20; 30:24

4:29 [a]Jer 6:23 [b]2Ki 25:4 [c]ver 7

4:30 [d]Isa 10:3-4 [e]Eze 23:40 [f]2Ki 9:30 [g]La 1:2; Eze 23:9,22

4:31 [h]Jer 13:21 [i]Isa 42:14 [j]Isa 1:15; La 1:17

27 This is what the LORD says:

"The whole land will be ruined,
though I will not destroy[v] it completely.
28 Therefore the earth will mourn[w]
and the heavens above grow dark,[x]
because I have spoken and will not relent,[y]
I have decided and will not turn back.[z]"

29 At the sound of horsemen and archers[a]
every town takes to flight.[b]
Some go into the thickets;
some climb up among the rocks.
All the towns are deserted;[c]
no one lives in them.

30 What are you doing,[d] O devastated one?
Why dress yourself in scarlet
and put on jewels[e] of gold?
Why shade your eyes with paint?[f]
You adorn yourself in vain.
Your lovers[g] despise you;
they seek your life.

31 I hear a cry as of a woman in labor,[h]
a groan as of one bearing her first child—
the cry of the Daughter of Zion gasping for breath,[i]
stretching out her hands[j] and saying,
"Alas! I am fainting;
my life is given over to murderers."

Not One Is Upright

5:1 [k]2Ch 16:9; Eze 22:30 [l]Ge 18:32 [m]Ge 18:24

5:2 [n]Jer 4:2

5:3 [o]2Ch 16:9 [p]Isa 9:13 [q]Jer 2:30; Zep 3:2 [r]Jer 7:26; 19:15; Eze 3:8-9

5:4 [s]Jer 8:7

5:5 [t]Mic 3:1,9 [u]Ps 2:3; Jer 2:20

5

"Go up and down[k] the streets of Jerusalem,
look around and consider,
search through her squares.
If you can find but one person[l]
who deals honestly and seeks the truth,
I will forgive[m] this city.
2 Although they say, 'As surely as the LORD lives,'[n]
still they are swearing falsely."
3 O LORD, do not your eyes[o] look for truth?
You struck[p] them, but they felt no pain;
you crushed them, but they refused correction.[q]
They made their faces harder than stone[r]
and refused to repent.
4 I thought, "These are only the poor;
they are foolish,
for they do not know[s] the way of the LORD,
the requirements of their God.
5 So I will go to the leaders[t]
and speak to them;
surely they know the way of the LORD,
the requirements of their God."
But with one accord they too had broken off the yoke
and torn off the bonds.[u]
6 Therefore a lion from the forest will attack them,

4:27 The Lord spoke again.
4:30 dress yourself . . . paint? A vivid reprise of the harlot metaphor. **lovers . . . seek your life.** An expression of the ironic truth of Judah's self-deception. See *WLC* 139.
4:31 Daughter of Zion. Jerusalem is personified (see note on La 1:6). **Alas . . . murderers.** Jeremiah heard her pathetic, dying breath.
■ **5:1–13** *Sinful Jerusalem.* The prophet returned to the subject of sin by focusing especially on evil in Jerusalem.
5:1 If you can find . . . this city. An allusion to Abraham's prayer for Sodom (Ge 18:22–32) and an implicit answer to Jeremiah's prayer for the city (which was later declined; 7:16). Not one honest person could be found.
5:3 made their faces harder than stone. The people's determination not to repent was the prophet's chief frustration (cf. Eze 3:7–9). See *WLC* 105,151.
5:4–5 See *WLC* 151.
5:6 lion . . . wolf . . . leopard. Such a breach of God's covenant

a wolf from the desert will ravage them,
a leopard[v] will lie in wait near their towns
to tear to pieces any who venture out,
for their rebellion is great
and their backslidings many.[w]

7 "Why should I forgive you?
Your children have forsaken me
and sworn[x] by gods that are not gods.[y]
I supplied all their needs,
yet they committed adultery[z]
and thronged to the houses of prostitutes.
8 They are well-fed, lusty stallions,
each neighing for another man's wife.[a]
9 Should I not punish them for this?"[b]
declares the LORD.
"Should I not avenge myself
on such a nation as this?

10 "Go through her vineyards and ravage them,
but do not destroy them completely.[c]
Strip off her branches,
for these people do not belong to the LORD.
11 The house of Israel and the house of Judah
have been utterly unfaithful[d] to me,"
declares the LORD.

12 They have lied about the LORD;
they said, "He will do nothing!
No harm will come to us;[e]
we will never see sword or famine.[f]
13 The prophets[g] are but wind
and the word is not in them;
so let what they say be done to them."

14 Therefore this is what the LORD God Almighty says:

"Because the people have spoken these words,
I will make my words in your mouth[h] a fire[i]
and these people the wood it consumes.
15 O house of Israel," declares the LORD,
"I am bringing a distant nation[j] against you—
an ancient and enduring nation,
a people whose language[k] you do not know,
whose speech you do not understand.
16 Their quivers are like an open grave;
all of them are mighty warriors.
17 They will devour[l m] your harvests and food,
devour[n o] your sons and daughters;
they will devour[p] your flocks and herds,
devour your vines and fig trees.
With the sword they will destroy
the fortified cities in which you trust.[q]

5:6 [v]Hos 13:7 [w]Jer 30:14
5:7 [x]Jos 23:7; Zep 1:5 [y]Dt 32:21; Jer 2:11; Gal 4:8 [z]Nu 25:1
5:8 [a]Jer 29:23; Eze 22:11
5:9 [b]ver 29; Jer 9:9
5:10 [c]Jer 4:27
5:11 [d]Jer 3:20
5:12 [e]Jer 23:17 [f]2Ch 36:16; Jer 14:13
5:13 [g]Jer 14:15
5:14 [h]Jer 1:9; Hos 6:5 [i]Jer 23:29
5:15 [j]Dt 28:49; Isa 5:26; Jer 4:16 [k]Isa 28:11
5:17 [l]Jer 8:16 [m]Lev 26:16 [n]Jer 50:7,17 [o]Dt 28:32 [p]Dt 28:31 [q]Dt 28:33

would call down the covenant curses on the people (Lev 26:22). **backslidings.** See note on 2:19.
5:7 Why should I forgive you? This question continues the topic from verse 1. **I supplied . . . adultery.** The motive for following false gods was the delusion that these idols possessed the power to make the land fertile. The Lord claimed even this as his sphere (see notes on Hos 2:8–9). **houses of prostitutes.** These houses were intended specifically for religious prostitution. See *WCF* 22.2; *WLC* 113,139.
5:8 lusty stallions . . . neighing. Religious prostitution slipped over into straightforward adultery. See similar imagery in 2:23–24.
5:9 Should I not. Again the courtroom metaphor is used; an appeal to witnesses is implied. The Lord's justice would be accomplished.
5:10 not . . . completely. This hint that punishment would not be final is one of several such in the early part of the book (cf. 12:14–17; 16:14–15; see note on 23:3). **do not belong to the LORD.** In the same breath Judah's covenant status was annulled (see note on Hos 1:9). The apparently irreconcilable needs for judgment and salvation are both evident here.
5:12 They have lied. Mistaken belief about God was related to untruth in every part of society (cf. 9:3–6). **He will do nothing!** This was the message of the false prophets (cf. 28:2–4).
5:13 prophets. Not Jeremiah, but the false prophets so prevalent in those days.
■ **5:14–19** *Judgment of Jerusalem's Destruction.* In response to the corruption of Jerusalem, God would bring invaders against the city to destroy it.
5:15 a distant nation. The Babylonians.

5:18 [r]Jer 4:27
5:19 [s]Dt 29:24-26; 1Ki 9:9 [t]Jer 16:13 [u]Dt 28:48
5:21 [v]Isa 6:10; Eze 12:2 [w]Mt 13:15; Mk 8:18
5:22 [x]Dt 28:58
5:23 [y]Dt 21:18
5:24 [z]Ps 147:8; Joel 2:23 [a]Ge 8:22; Ac 14:17
5:26 [b]Ps 10:8; Pr 1:11
5:27 [c]Jer 9:6 [d]Jer 12:1
5:28 [e]Dt 32:15 [f]Zec 7:10 [g]Isa 1:23; Jer 7:6
5:30 [h]Jer 23:14; Hos 6:10
5:31 [i]Eze 13:6; Mic 2:11

18 "Yet even in those days," declares the LORD, "I will not destroy[r] you completely.
19 And when the people ask, [s]'Why has the LORD our God done all this to us?' you will tell
them, 'As you have forsaken me and served foreign gods[t] in your own land, so now you
will serve foreigners[u] in a land not your own.'

20 "Announce this to the house of Jacob
  and proclaim it in Judah:
21 Hear this, you foolish and senseless people,
  who have eyes[v] but do not see,
  who have ears but do not hear:[w]
22 Should you not fear[x] me?" declares the LORD.
  "Should you not tremble in my presence?
I made the sand a boundary for the sea,
  an everlasting barrier it cannot cross.
The waves may roll, but they cannot prevail;
  they may roar, but they cannot cross it.
23 But these people have stubborn and rebellious[y] hearts;
  they have turned aside and gone away.
24 They do not say to themselves,
  'Let us fear the LORD our God,
who gives autumn and spring rains[z] in season,
  who assures us of the regular weeks of harvest.'[a]
25 Your wrongdoings have kept these away;
  your sins have deprived you of good.

26 "Among my people are wicked men
  who lie in wait[b] like men who snare birds
  and like those who set traps to catch men.
27 Like cages full of birds,
  their houses are full of deceit;[c]
they have become rich[d] and powerful
28 and have grown fat[e] and sleek.
Their evil deeds have no limit;
  they do not plead the case of the fatherless[f] to win it,
  they do not defend the rights of the poor.[g]
29 Should I not punish them for this?"
  declares the LORD.
"Should I not avenge myself
  on such a nation as this?

30 "A horrible[h] and shocking thing
  has happened in the land:
31 The prophets prophesy lies,[i]
  the priests rule by their own authority,
and my people love it this way.
  But what will you do in the end?

Jerusalem Under Siege

6

"Flee for safety, people of Benjamin!
  Flee from Jerusalem!

5:17 devour . . . devour . . . devour. The invading army would be absolutely vicious. Its atrocities were the antithesis of covenantal blessing. See Deuteronomy 7:13 for the promise of the very things now to be consumed.
5:18–19 Jeremiah explained the reason for his stress on the announcement of judgment against Judah: He wanted the exiles who read his book to discern how they were to react. They were to perceive that God had done these terrible things to them because of idolatry.
■ **5:20–31** *Sins of Judah.* Jeremiah rehearsed once again the sins of God's people in Judah in order to explain why the exile would take place.
5:21 foolish. See Proverbs 1:7. **who have eyes . . . do not hear.** See note on Isaiah 6:10.
5:22 Should you not fear me? Jeremiah argued from God's power in creation (cf. Job 38–41; Ro 1:18–20).
5:24 See *HC* 27.
5:25 good. Here the prophet summed up the blessings of the covenant ("that we might always prosper" [Dt 6:24] is lit., "for our good always"). See *WLC* 193.
5:26 wicked men . . . set traps to catch men. The nature of wickedness is to entice even the innocent with its wiles. See Proverbs 2:12–19 for its blandishments.
5:27–28 rich and powerful. Jeremiah moved from a discussion of specific religious sin to the ethical sphere (although the two are closely related). **fat and sleek.** Symbolizes self-centered wealth (cf. Ps 73:7). **fatherless . . . poor.** See Exodus 23:6 and Deuteronomy 14:29.
5:29 Notice the literary repetition from verse 9.
5:31 my people love it this way. Not only were the offices of prophet and priest corrupt, but the people of Judah enjoyed the fact and wanted the situation to stay that way.

Sound the trumpet in Tekoa![j]
Raise the signal over Beth Hakkerem![k]
For disaster looms out of the north,[l]
even terrible destruction.
2 I will destroy the Daughter of Zion,
so beautiful and delicate.
3 Shepherds[m] with their flocks will come against her;
they will pitch their tents around[n] her,
each tending his own portion."
4 "Prepare for battle against her!
Arise, let us attack at noon![o]
But, alas, the daylight is fading,
and the shadows of evening grow long.
5 So arise, let us attack at night
and destroy her fortresses!"

6 This is what the LORD Almighty says:

"Cut down the trees[p]
and build siege ramps[q] against Jerusalem.
This city must be punished;
it is filled with oppression.
7 As a well pours out its water,
so she pours out her wickedness.
Violence[r] and destruction[s] resound in her;
her sickness and wounds are ever before me.
8 Take warning, O Jerusalem,
or I will turn away[t] from you
and make your land desolate
so no one can live in it."

9 This is what the LORD Almighty says:

"Let them glean the remnant of Israel
as thoroughly as a vine;
pass your hand over the branches again,
like one gathering grapes."
10 To whom can I speak and give warning?
Who will listen to me?
Their ears are closed[a] [u]
so they cannot hear.
The word[v] of the LORD is offensive to them;
they find no pleasure in it.
11 But I am full of the wrath[w] of the LORD,
and I cannot hold it in.[x]
"Pour it out on the children in the street
and on the young men[y] gathered together;
both husband and wife will be caught in it,
and the old, those weighed down with years.

6:1 [j] 2Ch 11:6 [k] Ne 3:14 [l] Jer 4:6
6:3 [m] Jer 12:10 [n] 2Ki 25:4; Lk 19:43
6:4 [o] Jer 15:8
6:6 [p] Dt 20:19-20 [q] Jer 32:24
6:7 [r] Ps 55:9; Eze 7:11, 23 [s] Jer 20:8
6:8 [t] Eze 23:18; Hos 9:12
6:10 [u] Ac 7:51 [v] Jer 20:8
6:11 [w] Jer 7:20 [x] Job 32:20; Jer 20:9 [y] Jer 9:21

[a] *10* Hebrew *uncircumcised*

■ **6:1–30** *Judgment of Exile.* Jeremiah followed his announcement of Judah's sin with a final declaration of impending exile.
6:1 Flee . . . Flee. The approaching Babylonians would terrify everyone in Judah. There would be no place to hide. **north.** See note on 1:14.
6:2 Daughter of Zion . . . beautiful and delicate. See note on 2:2. Although a personification of Jerusalem (see note on 4:31), the image also had the city's refined women in mind (Isa 3:16–26; Am 4:1). The prophet's sadness was expressed by his nostalgic gaze at the city he loved.
6:3 Shepherds with their flocks. Babylonian leaders with their troops, taking possession of Jerusalem (cf. 4:15).
6:4–5 let us attack. Literally, "let us go up." Ironically, these were the same words used by the Israelites when going up to worship in Jerusalem (31:6). Here the image of holy war is reversed: The Lord would fight against his people. **at noon . . . at night.** These were unusual times to attack, revealing that the enemy's strength was such that the outcome would be the same no matter what time they chose.
6:6–7 God addressed the Babylonians, giving them instructions on how to punish Jerusalem. **oppression.** Against its own people. **As a well . . . wickedness.** As a well flows with water, so Jerusalem overflowed with evil.
6:9 Let them glean the remnant. Farmers were not to glean thoroughly but were to leave some produce for the poor (Dt 24:19–22); Babylon, however, would "glean" Judah meticulously. Contrast 5:10. The Lord had deeper purposes behind the permission he gave (see note on 23:3). The expression is hyperbolic; God did spare a remnant to fulfill his covenant of redemption. See note on 11:23.
6:11 children . . . young men . . . husband . . . wife . . . the old. The prophet used exaggeration to indicate that the destruction of Jerusalem would be massive.

12 Their houses will be turned over to others,[z]
together with their fields and their wives,[a]
when I stretch out my hand[b]
against those who live in the land,"
declares the LORD.

13 "From the least to the greatest,
all are greedy for gain;[c]
prophets and priests alike,
all practice deceit.[d]
14 They dress the wound of my people
as though it were not serious.
'Peace, peace,' they say,
when there is no peace.[e]
15 Are they ashamed of their loathsome conduct?
No, they have no shame at all;
they do not even know how to blush.[f]
So they will fall among the fallen;
they will be brought down when I punish them,"
says the LORD.

16 This is what the LORD says:

"Stand at the crossroads and look;
ask for the ancient paths,[g]
ask where the good way[h] is, and walk in it,
and you will find rest[i] for your souls.
But you said, 'We will not walk in it.'
17 I appointed watchmen[j] over you and said,
'Listen to the sound of the trumpet!'
But you said, 'We will not listen.'[k]
18 Therefore hear, O nations;
observe, O witnesses,
what will happen to them.
19 Hear, O earth:[l]
I am bringing disaster on this people,
the fruit of their schemes,[m]
because they have not listened to my words
and have rejected my law.[n]
20 What do I care about incense from Sheba
or sweet calamus[o] from a distant land?
Your burnt offerings are not acceptable;[p]
your sacrifices[q] do not please me."[r]

21 Therefore this is what the LORD says:

"I will put obstacles before this people.
Fathers and sons alike will stumble[s] over them;
neighbors and friends will perish."

22 This is what the LORD says:

"Look, an army is coming
from the land of the north;[t]
a great nation is being stirred up
from the ends of the earth.
23 They are armed with bow and spear;

6:12 [z]Dt 28:30 [a]Jer 8:10; 38:22 [b]Isa 5:25
6:13 [c]Isa 56:11 [d]Jer 8:10
6:14 [e]Jer 4:10; 8:11; Eze 13:10
6:15 [f]Jer 3:3; 8:10-12
6:16 [g]Jer 18:15 [h]Ps 119:3 [i]Mt 11:29
6:17 [j]Eze 3:17 [k]Jer 11:7-8; 25:4
6:19 [l]Isa 1:2; Jer 22:29 [m]Pr 1:31 [n]Jer 8:9
6:20 [o]Ex 30:23 [p]Am 5:22 [q]Ps 50:8-10; Jer 7:21; Mic 6:7-8 [r]Isa 1:11
6:21 [s]Isa 8:14
6:22 [t]Jer 1:15; 10:22

6:12 See Deuteronomy 28:30.

6:13 See *WLC* 193.

6:14 wound. See note on 6:7. **'Peace, peace' . . . no peace.** The easily welcomed message of the false prophets could not bring true peace (Mic 2:6), whose counterpart is righteousness.

6:16 ancient paths. The true ways laid down by Moses. **the good way.** Literally, "the way to good"; namely, the path to peace and prosperity. **rest for your souls.** See Matthew 11:29. See also *WLC* 151.

6:17 watchmen. A name for the prophets (Isa 21:11; Eze 3:17; Hab 2:1).

6:18 hear, O nations . . . O witnesses. See 2:4 and Micah 1:2.

6:20 incense . . . calamus. Expensive ingredients used in rituals (Ex 30:23–38). **burnt offerings . . . do not please me.** This strain is important in the psalms and prophets (Ps 40:6–8; Isa 1:11–15; Mic 6:6–8). See Matthew 23:23.

6:23 armed with bow and spear . . . on their horses. See the description of Babylon in Habakkuk 1:6–11. Although the Babylonians were God's instrument, he did not approve of their cruelty.

they are cruel and show no mercy.[u]
They sound like the roaring sea
as they ride on their horses;[v]
they come like men in battle formation
to attack you, O Daughter of Zion."

24 We have heard reports about them,
and our hands hang limp.
Anguish[w] has gripped us,
pain like that of a woman in labor.[x]
25 Do not go out to the fields
or walk on the roads,
for the enemy has a sword,
and there is terror on every side.[y]
26 O my people, put on sackcloth[z]
and roll in ashes;[a]
mourn with bitter wailing
as for an only son,[b]
for suddenly the destroyer
will come upon us.

27 "I have made you a tester[c] of metals
and my people the ore,
that you may observe
and test their ways.
28 They are all hardened rebels,[d]
going about to slander.[e]
They are bronze and iron;[f]
they all act corruptly.
29 The bellows blow fiercely
to burn away the lead with fire,
but the refining goes on in vain;
the wicked are not purged out.
30 They are called rejected silver,
because the LORD has rejected them."[g]

False Religion Worthless

7 This is the word that came to Jeremiah from the LORD: 2 "Stand[h] at the gate of the
LORD's house and there proclaim this message:
" 'Hear the word of the LORD, all you people of Judah who come through these gates
to worship the LORD. 3 This is what the LORD Almighty, the God of Israel, says: Reform your
ways[i] and your actions, and I will let you live in this place. 4 Do not trust in deceptive[j]
words and say, "This is the temple of the LORD, the temple of the LORD, the temple of the
LORD!" 5 If you really change your ways and your actions and deal with each other justly,[k] 6 if you do not oppress the alien, the fatherless or the widow and do not shed innocent blood[l] in this place, and if you do not follow other gods[m] to your own harm, 7 then

6:23 [u]Isa 13:18 [v]Jer 4:29
6:24 [w]Jer 4:19 [x]Jer 4:31; 50:41-43
6:25 [y]Jer 49:29
6:26 [z]Jer 4:8 [a]Jer 25:34; Mic 1:10 [b]Zec 12:10
6:27 [c]Jer 9:7
6:28 [d]Jer 5:23 [e]Jer 9:4 [f]Eze 22:18
6:30 [g]Ps 119:119; Jer 7:29; Hos 9:17
7:2 [h]Jer 17:19
7:3 [i]Jer 18:11; 26:13
7:4 [j]Mic 3:11
7:5 [k]Jer 22:3
7:6 [l]Jer 2:34; 19:4 [m]Dt 8:19

6:25 terror on every side. Jeremiah spoke this way to indicate how horrific the destruction of Jerusalem would be (see 20:10; 46:5; 49:29).
6:27–30 God spoke to Jeremiah about his role.
6:27 tester. The Lord called on Jeremiah to test Judah as a refiner tests metals to see how pure they are. Elsewhere in the book the Lord himself is the tester, both of the people (9:7; 17:10; 20:12) and of Jeremiah (11:20; 12:3). The prophet's mediatorial role is evident here.
6:29–30 lead . . . silver. Lead is used in the process of refining silver. The process of "refining" Judah had yielded nothing of value.
■ **7:1—10:25** *The Temple.* The Judahites mistakenly believed that the Babylonians would not be able to destroy Jerusalem because it was the location of the temple of God. Jeremiah dispelled this false confidence. The focus on this question divides into three sections: Jeremiah's speech at the temple (7:1—8:3), as well as supporting speeches recounting Judah's guilt (8:4—9:26) and the sin of idolatry within Judah (10:1–25).
■ **7:1—8:3** *Solomon's Temple and Shiloh.* In this speech Jeremiah attacked the false presumption that the mere presence of the temple would secure Jerusalem against her enemies.
7:1 This is the word . . . from the LORD. A typical introductory formula (cf. 11:1).
7:2 gate. Probably the gate leading into the inner court of the temple. Jeremiah stood in the central place of Judah's worship to proclaim the hypocrisy of the worshipers. The power of this action was heightened by the fact that he was himself a priest. **all you people . . . to worship the LORD.** It is likely that this speech occurred during one of the important annual feasts (Ex 23:14–18), a time when "all Israel" (Dt 31:11) was required to be present. **gates.** These gates led into the outer court of the temple.
7:3 this place. The prophet reminded the people that their assurance of living in the promised land had never been unconditional.
7:4 deceptive words . . . the temple of the LORD. The repetition indicates that the people fervently appealed to the temple as confirmation that no more harm could befall the city. Appeals to the temple for safety were deceptive because they were in vain apart from repentance and fidelity to God (vv. 5–6). See *WLC* 113.
7:6 shed innocent blood. Evidently, murder of the innocent was actually occurring, though Jeremiah did not provide details. He may have been referring to the sacrificing of children in pagan worship (cf. 19:4; 32:35).

I will let you live in this place, in the land[n] I gave your forefathers for ever and ever. 8But look, you are trusting in deceptive words that are worthless.

9" 'Will you steal and murder, commit adultery and perjury,[a] burn incense to Baal[o] and follow other gods[p] you have not known, 10and then come and stand before me in this house,[q] which bears my Name, and say, "We are safe"—safe to do all these detestable things? 11Has this house,[r] which bears my Name, become a den of robbers[s] to you? But I have been watching![t] declares the LORD.

12" 'Go now to the place in Shiloh[u] where I first made a dwelling for my Name, and see what I did[v] to it because of the wickedness of my people Israel. 13While you were doing all these things, declares the LORD, I spoke to you again and again,[w] but you did not listen;[x] I called you, but you did not answer.[y] 14Therefore, what I did to Shiloh I will now do to the house that bears my Name,[z] the temple you trust in, the place I gave to you and your fathers. 15I will thrust you from my presence, just as I did all your brothers, the people of Ephraim.'[a]

16"So do not pray for this people nor offer any plea[b] or petition for them; do not plead with me, for I will not listen to you. 17Do you not see what they are doing in the towns of Judah and in the streets of Jerusalem? 18The children gather wood, the fathers light the fire, and the women knead the dough and make cakes of bread for the Queen of Heaven.[c] They pour out drink offerings[d] to other gods to provoke[e] me to anger. 19But am I the one they are provoking? declares the LORD. Are they not rather harming themselves, to their own shame?[f]

20" 'Therefore this is what the Sovereign LORD says: My anger[g] and my wrath will be poured out on this place, on man and beast, on the trees of the field and on the fruit of the ground, and it will burn and not be quenched.

21" 'This is what the LORD Almighty, the God of Israel, says: Go ahead, add your burnt offerings to your other sacrifices[h] and eat[i] the meat yourselves! 22For when I brought your forefathers out of Egypt and spoke to them, I did not just give them commands about burnt offerings and sacrifices,[j] 23but I gave them this command: Obey[k] me, and I will be your God and you will be my people.[l] Walk in all the ways I command you, that it may go well[m] with you. 24But they did not listen or pay attention;[n] instead, they followed the stubborn inclinations of their evil hearts. They went backward and not forward. 25From the time your forefathers left Egypt until now, day after day, again and again I sent you my servants the prophets.[o] 26But they did not listen to me or pay attention. They were stiff-necked and did more evil than their forefathers.'[p]

27"When you tell[q] them all this, they will not listen[r] to you; when you call to them, they will not answer. 28Therefore say to them, 'This is the nation that has not obeyed the LORD its God or responded to correction. Truth has perished; it has vanished from their

7:7 nDt 4:40
7:9 oJer 11:13,17 pEx 20:3
7:10 qJer 32:34; Eze 23:38-39
7:11 rIsa 56:7 sMt 21:13*; Mk 11:17*; Lk 19:46* tJer 29:23
7:12 uJos 18:1 v1Sa 4:10-11,22; Ps 78:60-64
7:13 w2Ch 36:15 xIsa 65:12 yJer 35:17
7:14 z1Ki 9:7
7:15 aPs 78:67
7:16 bEx 32:10; Dt 9:14; Jer 15:1
7:18 cJer 44:17-19 dJer 19:13 e1Ki 14:9
7:19 fJer 9:19
7:20 gJer 42:18; La 2:3-5
7:21 hIsa 1:11; Am 5:21-22 iHos 8:13
7:22 j1Sa 15:22; Ps 51:16; Hos 6:6
7:23 kEx 19:5 lLev 26:12 mEx 15:26
7:24 nPs 81:11-12; Jer 11:8
7:25 oJer 25:4
7:26 pJer 16:12
7:27 qEze 2:7 rEze 3:7

a 9 Or *and swear by false gods*

7:8–10 See *WLC* 113,151.
7:9 Will you steal . . . gods you have not known. Notice the allusion to five of the Ten Commandments (cf. Hos 4:2), with a stress on the first (Ex 20:3).
7:10 this house, which bears my Name. The "place" (Dt 12:5) that bears God's Name is identified in 1 Kings 8:43 as the Jerusalem temple. When the Lord put his name there, he signified that his special presence was there (1Ki 8:27; see theological article "The Presence of God" at 1Ki 8). **safe—safe to do . . . ?** Jeremiah's sarcasm was appropriate. The people took the privilege of access to the presence of God as a license for rebellion.
7:11 den of robbers. See Matthew 21:13. **watching.** Even if they were to hide (as in a den), they would still be seen by the Lord.
7:12 Shiloh . . . my Name. The central place of worship for all Israel before David made Jerusalem his capital (Jos 18:1; 1Sa 1:9). Since Shiloh no longer existed (it had probably been destroyed by the Philistines), the reference well illustrated Jeremiah's point—that a place at which the Lord's Name dwelled was not immune to his judgment.
7:13 again and again. A common phrase in the book (25:3–4; 26:5), indicating the patience God showed toward his people before confining them to judgment. **you did not listen.** This theme is repeated often in the book (6:17; 11:7–8; 25:3; cf. 2Ki 17:13–14).
7:14 See *WLC* 113.
7:16 So do not pray. This was an ominous prohibition because one of the roles of a prophet was to intercede. See references to Abraham (Ge 20:7) and Moses (Ex 32:11–14) as intercessors. God instructed Jeremiah not to pray (11:14; see 15:1) because the fate of Jerusalem was nearly sealed. But see verses 5–6 (see also 1Sa 7:8; 12:19; 1Jn 5:16).
7:18–20 See *WLC* 110.
7:18 children . . . fathers . . . women. A picture of the universal hold idolatry had on the people. **Queen of Heaven.** Possibly a Babylonian title for the goddess Ishtar (see 44:19,25), but the identification is uncertain.
7:20 Therefore. The beginning of sentencing following the lengthy accusations of verses 1–19. **man and beast . . . fruit of the ground.** Divine judgment disrupts the relationships among God, his people and all of creation (cf. Hos 2:18).
7:21 Go ahead . . . eat the meat yourselves! The mere quantity of sacrifices meant nothing to the Lord (1Sa 15:22–23). He had so little interest in the sacrifices per se that the worshipers might as well have committed the offense of eating the flesh of the burnt offering (Lev 1:9).
7:22–23 These verses underscore the truth that the sacrifice of animals was unacceptable apart from obedience rising naturally from faith and contrition (Mic 6:6–8; Heb 11:4,6; see notes on Ge 4:4–5).
7:23 I will be your God . . . my people. This formula appears frequently and emphasizes the solidarity and loyalty that existed between God and his people in their covenant relationship (Lev 26:12). See *WLC* 104.
7:24 followed . . . their evil hearts. Compare 3:17 and Genesis 6:5. The portrayal of Judah in the book of Jeremiah, as elsewhere in Scripture, strongly suggests an inner disposition toward evil in the human heart.

lips. 29Cut off[s] your hair and throw it away; take up a lament on the barren heights, for
the LORD has rejected and abandoned[t] this generation that is under his wrath.

The Valley of Slaughter

30" 'The people of Judah have done evil in my eyes, declares the LORD. They have set
up their detestable idols[u] in the house that bears my Name and have defiled[v] it. 31They
have built the high places of Topheth[w] in the Valley of Ben Hinnom to burn their sons
and daughters[x] in the fire—something I did not command, nor did it enter my mind.[y]
32So beware, the days are coming, declares the LORD, when people will no longer call it
Topheth or the Valley of Ben Hinnom, but the Valley of Slaughter,[z] for they will bury[a]
the dead in Topheth until there is no more room. 33Then the carcasses of this people will
become food[b] for the birds of the air and the beasts of the earth, and there will be no one
to frighten them away. 34I will bring an end to the sounds[c] of joy and gladness and to the
voices of bride and bridegroom[d] in the towns of Judah and the streets of Jerusalem, for
the land will become desolate.[e]

8 " 'At that time, declares the LORD, the bones of the kings and officials of Judah, the
bones of the priests and prophets, and the bones of the people of Jerusalem will be
removed from their graves. 2They will be exposed to the sun and the moon and all the
stars of the heavens, which they have loved and served[f] and which they have followed
and consulted and worshiped. They will not be gathered up or buried, but will be like refuse lying on the ground. 3Wherever I banish them, all the survivors of this evil nation
will prefer death to life,[g] declares the LORD Almighty.'

Sin and Punishment

4"Say to them, 'This is what the LORD says:

" 'When men fall down, do they not get up?[h]
When a man turns away, does he not return?
5Why then have these people turned away?
Why does Jerusalem always turn away?
They cling to deceit;[i]
they refuse to return.[j]
6I have listened attentively,
but they do not say what is right.
No one repents[k] of his wickedness,
saying, "What have I done?"
Each pursues his own course[l]
like a horse charging into battle.
7Even the stork in the sky
knows her appointed seasons,
and the dove, the swift and the thrush
observe the time of their migration.
But my people do not know[m]
the requirements of the LORD.

8" 'How can you say, "We are wise,

7:29 [s]Job 1:20; Isa 15:2; Mic 1:16 [t]Jer 6:30
7:30 [u]Eze 7:20-22 [v]Jer 32:34
7:31 [w]2Ki 23:10 [x]Ps 106:38 [y]Jer 19:5
7:32 [z]Jer 19:6 [a]Jer 19:11
7:33 [b]Dt 28:26
7:34 [c]Isa 24:8; Eze 26:13 [d]Rev 18:23 [e]Lev 26:34
8:2 [f]2Ki 23:5; Ac 7:42
8:3 [g]Job 3:22; Rev 9:6
8:4 [h]Pr 24:16
8:5 [i]Jer 5:27 [j]Jer 7:24; 9:6
8:6 [k]Rev 9:20 [l]Ps 14:1-3
8:7 [m]Isa 1:3; Jer 5:4-5

7:29 Cut off your hair. The prophet addressed Jerusalem, picturing the city as a woman (see 2:1 and its note). The cutting of her hair may allude to the renewal of a Nazirite vow, for such action was necessary after becoming ritually unclean (Nu 6:5–9).
7:30 in the house. Here is evidence of a foreign cult having been set up in the temple itself, as had been done by Manasseh (2Ki 21:7). Josiah had removed it, but it had returned, possibly in the time of Jehoiakim (see "Introduction"). Ezekiel also knew of such defilement (Eze 8:3–12). The resurgence of such practices confirmed Jeremiah's analysis of Judah's persistent rebelliousness.
7:31 high places. A common name for pagan cult centers (2Ki 23:8–9). **Topheth.** Literally, "a place of fire." This gruesome pit was located in the Hinnom Valley, where child sacrifices were offered to the foreign god Molech. The offering of firstborn children was known in the ancient world, but in Israel they were to be "redeemed" by animal sacrifices (Ex 13:1–16; 34:19–20). Child sacrifice was expressly prohibited (Lev 18:21; 20:2–5; see also 2Ki 23:10 and its note). **Valley of Ben Hinnom.** Located south and west of Jerusalem. From its abbreviated name ("Valley of Hinnom"; Hebrew, *ge' hinnom*) came "Gehenna" (Greek, *geenna*), translated "hell" (Mt 18:9). See *WLC* 113.
7:33 carcasses. See the covenant curse in Deuteronomy 28:26. **frighten.** Lack of burial was the most terrible of fates in ancient times.
8:1 bones . . . removed from their graves. A step further than 7:33 (see 2Ki 23:16,18).
8:2 exposed to the sun . . . moon . . . stars. This is heavy irony because God's people had worshiped these (2Ki 21:3–5) even though they are merely created things (Isa 40:25–26).
8:3 will prefer death. Jeremiah closed this section by announcing that death would be preferable to the suffering of defeat and exile.
■ **8:4—9:26** *Judah's Sins and Judgment.* Having demonstrated in the previous section that the temple provided no guarantee of protection against the wrath of God, the prophet here expounds upon the sins of Jerusalem that would bring the judgment of destruction and exile to the holy city.
8:5 Jerusalem. The prophet continued to reflect on the city in which the temple stood—Judah's last hope against the invading forces from Babylon.
8:6 pursues. This additional use of the word "turned" (v. 5) describes the habitual manner of the people's quest for wickedness as a headlong rush.

for we have the law[n] of the LORD,"
when actually the lying pen of the scribes
has handled it falsely?
9 The wise[o] will be put to shame;
they will be dismayed and trapped.
Since they have rejected the word[p] of the LORD,
what kind of wisdom do they have?
10 Therefore I will give their wives to other men
and their fields to new owners.[q]
From the least to the greatest,
all are greedy for gain;[r]
prophets and priests alike,
all practice deceit.
11 They dress the wound of my people
as though it were not serious.
"Peace, peace," they say,
when there is no peace.[s]
12 Are they ashamed of their loathsome conduct?
No, they have no shame[t] at all;
they do not even know how to blush.
So they will fall among the fallen;
they will be brought down when they are punished,[u]
says the LORD.[v]

13 " 'I will take away their harvest,
declares the LORD.

There will be no grapes on the vine.[w]
There will be no figs[x] on the tree,
and their leaves will wither.[y]
What I have given them
will be taken[z] from them.[a]' "

14 "Why are we sitting here?
Gather together!
Let us flee to the fortified cities[a]
and perish there!
For the LORD our God has doomed us to perish
and given us poisoned water[b] to drink,
because we have sinned[c] against him.
15 We hoped for peace[d]
but no good has come,
for a time of healing
but there was only terror.[e]
16 The snorting of the enemy's horses
is heard from Dan;[f]
at the neighing of their stallions
the whole land trembles.
They have come to devour
the land and everything in it,
the city and all who live there."

17 "See, I will send venomous snakes[g] among you,

8:8 [n]Ro 2:17
8:9 [o]Jer 6:15 [p]Jer 6:19
8:10 [q]Jer 6:12 [r]Isa 56:11
8:11 [s]Jer 6:14
8:12 [t]Jer 3:3 [u]Ps 52:5-7; Isa 3:9 [v]Jer 6:15
8:13 [w]Joel 1:7 [x]Lk 13:6 [y]Mt 21:19 [z]Jer 5:17
8:14 [a]Jer 4:5; Jer 35:11 [b]Dt 29:18; Jer 9:15; 23:15 [c]Jer 14:7,20
8:15 [d]ver 11 [e]Jer 14:19
8:16 [f]Jer 4:15
8:17 [g]Nu 21:6; Dt 32:24

[a] *13* The meaning of the Hebrew for this sentence is uncertain.

8:8 wise . . . scribes. The term "wise" is meant to designate a group that may be identical with the latter ("scribes"). Scribes are mentioned for the first time as a group that handled the Law of Moses (see also 1Ch 2:55).

8:9 The wise . . . what kind of wisdom. There is, of course, a true wisdom, as expounded in Proverbs. The wisdom of these scribes, however, was empty, devoid of any real knowledge of the Lord's word. See 3:13–15 and Deuteronomy 4:6; *WCF* 20.2.

8:13 no grapes on the vine. The vine represents Judah (2:21). However, the imagery also connotes a deprivation of fertility. Fertility was a covenant blessing that the people wrongly attributed to other gods (Hos 2:8–9).

8:14 Gather together! The same Hebrew word is translated "harvest" in verse 13. Ironically, what the people intended as a gathering for safety would become a gathering for judgment. **fortified cities.** See note on 4:5. **poisoned water.** Symbolizes a disappointing perversion of the blessings of covenant, just as the people were a disappointing fruit (9:14; Isa 5:4).

8:17 The Lord spoke. **venomous snakes . . . vipers.** This may be taken either literally, as a kind of plague (cf. "poisoned water"; v. 14), or figuratively, as the enemy.

vipers that cannot be charmed,[h]
and they will bite you,"
declares the LORD.

18 O my Comforter[a] in sorrow,
my heart is faint[i] within me.
19 Listen to the cry of my people
from a land far away:[j]
"Is the LORD not in Zion?
Is her King no longer there?"

"Why have they provoked me to anger with their images,
with their worthless foreign idols?"[k]

20 "The harvest is past,
the summer has ended,
and we are not saved."

21 Since my people are crushed, I am crushed;
I mourn,[l] and horror grips me.
22 Is there no balm in Gilead?[m]
Is there no physician there?
Why then is there no healing[n]
for the wound of my people?

9 1 Oh, that my head were a spring of water
and my eyes a fountain of tears!
I would weep[o] day and night
for the slain of my people.[p]
2 Oh, that I had in the desert
a lodging place for travelers,
so that I might leave my people
and go away from them;
for they are all adulterers,[q]
a crowd of unfaithful people.

3 "They make ready their tongue
like a bow, to shoot lies;[r]
it is not by truth
that they triumph[b] in the land.
They go from one sin to another;
they do not acknowledge me,"
declares the LORD.

4 "Beware of your friends;
do not trust your brothers.[s]
For every brother is a deceiver,[c][t]
and every friend a slanderer.
5 Friend deceives friend,
and no one speaks the truth.
They have taught their tongues to lie;
they weary themselves with sinning.

8:17 [h]Ps 58:5
8:18 [i]La 5:17
8:19 [j]Jer 9:16 [k]Dt 32:21
8:21 [l]Jer 14:17
8:22 [m]Ge 37:25 [n]Jer 30:12
9:1 [o]Jer 13:17; La 2:11,18 [p]Isa 22:4
9:2 [q]Jer 5:7-8; 23:10; Hos 4:2
9:3 [r]Ps 64:3
9:4 [s]Mic 7:5-6 [t]Ge 27:35

[a] *18* The meaning of the Hebrew for this word is uncertain. [b] *3* Or *lies; / they are not valiant for truth*
[c] *4* Or *a deceiving Jacob*

8:18–19 Jeremiah lamented at the thought of what would happen to Jerusalem and her inhabitants. **O my Comforter.** This is a difficult text to translate (see NIV text note). Possibly it means "My grief has overwhelmed me." **Is the LORD not in Zion? Is her King no longer there?** This cry of the exiles is reminiscent of the expectation that the mere presence of the temple would protect the inhabitants of Jerusalem. The temple was the earthly palace of the Lord, the King of Israel. Jeremiah's opponents would be shocked at the defeat of Jerusalem because it would signify that the divine King had deserted his temple and was no longer there. **Why have they provoked me . . . ?** At this point God was speaking.
8:20 we are not saved. The people of the exile would cry out.
8:21 I am crushed; I mourn. Jeremiah would participate in their suffering (14:2).
8:22 no balm in Gilead? Gilead was known for its medicinal products (46:11). **no physician . . . no healing . . . ?** For reference to the healing metaphor and false healers, see 8:11. The craving for a physician was an appeal to God as such. He would come at the right time (30:17).
9:1 I would weep. Jeremiah was akin to Jesus in his sympathy for the people (Lk 19:41).
9:3 make ready their tongue like a bow. A military image underlies the verse. Their bow was falsehood, and they went out wielding it, as though to battle. **declares the LORD.** The Lord has been speaking, so 8:21—9:3 takes on new meaning. God also longed for the desert, so that he could cast off his people and no longer have fellowship with them (2:2–3). The portrayal of the Lord's feelings through the prophet is evident in this passage. See *WLC* 145.
9:5 See *WLC* 145.

6 You[a] live in the midst of deception;[u]
in their deceit they refuse to acknowledge me,"
declares the LORD.

7 Therefore this is what the LORD Almighty says:

"See, I will refine[v] and test[w] them,
for what else can I do
because of the sin of my people?
8 Their tongue[x] is a deadly arrow;
it speaks with deceit.
With his mouth each speaks cordially to his neighbor,
but in his heart he sets a trap[y] for him.
9 Should I not punish them for this?"
declares the LORD.
"Should I not avenge[z] myself
on such a nation as this?"

10 I will weep and wail for the mountains
and take up a lament concerning the desert pastures.
They are desolate and untraveled,
and the lowing of cattle is not heard.
The birds of the air[a] have fled
and the animals are gone.

11 "I will make Jerusalem a heap of ruins,
a haunt of jackals;[b]
and I will lay waste the towns of Judah
so no one can live there."[c]

12 What man is wise[d] enough to understand this? Who has been instructed by the LORD
and can explain it? Why has the land been ruined and laid waste like a desert that no one
can cross?
13 The LORD said, "It is because they have forsaken my law, which I set before them;
they have not obeyed me or followed my law.[e] 14 Instead, they have followed[f] the stubbornness of their hearts;[g] they have followed the Baals, as their fathers taught them."
15 Therefore, this is what the LORD Almighty, the God of Israel, says: "See, I will make this
people eat bitter food[h] and drink poisoned water.[i] 16 I will scatter them among nations[j]
that neither they nor their fathers have known,[k] and I will pursue them with the sword[l]
until I have destroyed them."[m]

17 This is what the LORD Almighty says:

"Consider now! Call for the wailing women[n] to come;
send for the most skillful of them.
18 Let them come quickly
and wail over us
till our eyes overflow with tears
and water streams from our eyelids.[o]
19 The sound of wailing is heard from Zion:
'How ruined[p] we are!
How great is our shame!
We must leave our land
because our houses are in ruins.' "

9:6 [u]Jer 5:27
9:7 [v]Isa 1:25 [w]Jer 6:27
9:8 [x]ver 3 [y]Jer 5:26
9:9 [z]Jer 5:9,29
9:10 [a]Jer 4:25; 12:4; Hos 4:3
9:11 [b]Isa 34:13 [c]Isa 25:2; Jer 26:9
9:12 [d]Ps 107:43; Hos 14:9
9:13 [e]2Ch 7:19; Ps 89:30-32
9:14 [f]Jer 2:8,23 [g]Jer 7:24
9:15 [h]La 3:15 [i]Jer 8:14
9:16 [j]Lev 26:33 [k]Dt 28:64 [l]Eze 5:2 [m]Jer 44:27; Eze 5:12
9:17 [n]2Ch 35:25; Ecc 12:5; Am 5:16
9:18 [o]Jer 14:17
9:19 [p]Jer 4:13

[a] 6 That is, Jeremiah (the Hebrew is singular)

9:8 cordially. Literally, "peace." This would have been a true basis for society and a product of covenant faithfulness; its opposite is falsehood—the actual basis of this society.
9:10 I will weep. As Jeremiah wept, so the Lord would weep (see note on v. 1), particularly for the desolation of the land he had given his people. It was meant to be rich and populated, but instead it was desolate. See Micah 1:8 and Matthew 23:27–28.
9:11 a haunt of jackals. Its lack of inhabitants marked the curse on the land. This is a common motif in Scripture (Ps 44:19; Isa 13:21–22).
9:12 wise . . . understand. This is reminiscent of wisdom, terminology for God-given knowledge (Pr 1:2–5). See Deuteronomy 4:6, where the idea of wisdom as a recommendation of Israel was now overturned.
9:13 forsaken my law. Jeremiah was especially concerned about the practices of idolatry (v. 14). **which I set before them.** See Deuteronomy 4:8.
9:16 scatter them. See the curse in Deuteronomy 28:64. The picture of total destruction is for effect (contrast Isa 4:27).
9:17 wailing women. The weeping motif is taken up again (vv. 1,10). This is the Old Testament's clearest allusion to professional wailing women, who were employed to lead in mourning for the dead (cf. Am 5:16).

20 Now, O women, hear the word of the LORD;
open your ears to the words of his mouth.
Teach your daughters how to wail;
teach one another a lament.[q]
21 Death has climbed in through our windows
and has entered our fortresses;
it has cut off the children from the streets
and the young men[r] from the public squares.

22 Say, "This is what the LORD declares:

" 'The dead bodies of men will lie
like refuse[s] on the open field,
like cut grain behind the reaper,
with no one to gather them.' "

23 This is what the LORD says:

"Let not the wise man boast of his wisdom[t]
or the strong man boast of his strength[u]
or the rich man boast of his riches,[v]
24 but let him who boasts boast[w] about this:
that he understands and knows me,
that I am the LORD,[x] who exercises kindness,[y]
justice and righteousness[z] on earth,
for in these I delight,"
declares the LORD.

25 "The days are coming," declares the LORD, "when I will punish all who are circumcised only in the flesh— 26 Egypt, Judah, Edom, Ammon, Moab and all who live in the
desert in distant places.[a] [b] For all these nations are really uncircumcised, and even the
whole house of Israel is uncircumcised in heart.[c]"

God and Idols

10 Hear what the LORD says to you, O house of Israel. 2 This is what the LORD says:

"Do not learn the ways of the nations[d]
or be terrified by signs in the sky,
though the nations are terrified by them.
3 For the customs of the peoples are worthless;
they cut a tree out of the forest,
and a craftsman[e] shapes it with his chisel.
4 They adorn it with silver and gold;

9:20 [q] Isa 32:9-13
9:21 [r] 2Ch 36:17
9:22 [s] Jer 8:2
9:23 [t] Ecc 9:11 [u] 1Ki 20:11 [v] Eze 28:4-5
9:24 [w] 1Co 1:31*; Gal 6:14 [x] 2Co 10:17* [y] Ps 51:1; Mic 7:18 [z] Ps 36:6
9:25 [a] Ro 2:8-9
9:26 [b] Jer 25:23 [c] Lev 26:41; Ac 7:51; Ro 2:28
10:2 [d] Lev 20:23
10:3 [e] Isa 40:19

[a] 26 Or *desert and who clip the hair by their foreheads*

9:21 Death. Death is here personified, like the Canaanite god Mot (meaning "death"). **fortresses.** These were now hollow and fragile. **children . . . young men.** See 6:11, Lamentations 5:13–15 and their notes.
9:23–24 See *HC* 122.
9:23 wisdom . . . strength . . . riches. These are not negative things when they are God's gifts. Note Solomon's preference of wisdom over riches and God's gift of both (1Ki 3; cf. also Dt 8:17; Ps 20:7; Pr 8:8–21).
9:24 boast. Following Jeremiah's lead Paul summarized this passage when he exhorted the Corinthians not to rejoice in their own talents and abilities but to take joy in the wonder of knowing God (1Co 1:31). **understands and knows me.** See verse 12, which introduced the idea of wisdom into this chapter. Wisdom is rooted in knowing God (cf. Pr 9:10). **kindness, justice and righteousness.** These are the three most characteristic qualities of the Lord as revealed and exercised in the covenant. **kindness.** This is loyalty to the terms of the covenant. See 2:2, where the same Hebrew word is translated "devotion" (see La 3:22–23 and its note). **justice.** Upholding the rights of those in the covenant relationship by punishing the aggressor and relieving the oppressed (Ps 7:8). **righteousness.** Upholding covenant standards by doing right with respect to all its partners. These qualities are also required of the covenant partner (4:2).
9:25–26 circumcised only in the flesh. See 4:4. The people of God would be subjected to the Babylonian judgment because they were not genuinely devoted to the Lord. God warned that membership in the visible nation of Israel would not exempt them from his judgment. From the days of Moses God had called all Israelites to be circumcised inwardly, to love and serve him as the natural response of inward transformation (Dt 10:16). God promised through Moses that this ideal would be reached in the last days when Israel returned from exile (Dt 30:6). Jeremiah's prophecy makes clear that the vast majority of Israelites in his day had not reached this ideal. See Romans 2:25–29, 4:9–12, 9:8 and Galatians 5:6 and 6:15. **Egypt, Judah, Edom, Ammon, Moab . . . desert in distant places.** The Babylonian army troubled and conquered many nations other than Judah.
■ **10:1–25** *Idolatry or the Lord.* This material focuses on the sin of idolatry, an appropriate theme in the context of Judah's hypocritical reliance on the temple for protection (see ch. 7). The Judahites hoped for safety in the temple while corrupting their worship with idolatry.
10:2 signs in the sky. Refers to the worship of heavenly bodies. See 8:2 and its note. **terrified.** Terror characterizes the worship of false gods. Worship of heavenly bodies carries with it special fears because of the potential for unusual phenomena. Biblical creation theology undermines such fears by showing that such occurrences are merely manifestations of God's created order (Ge 1; Isa 40:26).
10:3 worthless. This word, used elsewhere by Jeremiah for idols, here conveys emptiness (2:5). **they cut a tree.** This phrase begins a scathing passage about the folly of idolatry. See also Isaiah 44:9–20.

10:4 [f]Isa 41:7
10:5 [g]1Co 12:2 [h]Ps 115:5,7 [i]Isa 41:24; 46:7
10:6 [j]Ps 48:1
10:7 [k]Ps 22:28; Rev 15:4
10:8 [l]Isa 40:19; Jer 4:22
10:9 [m]Ps 115:4; Isa 40:19
10:10 [n]Ps 76:7
10:11 [o]Ps 96:5; Isa 2:18
10:12 [p]Ge 1:1,8; Job 9:8; Isa 40:22
10:13 [q]Job 36:29 [r]Ps 135:7
10:15 [s]Isa 41:24; Jer 14:22
10:16 [t]Dt 32:9; Ps 119:57

they fasten it with hammer and nails
so it will not totter.[f]
5 Like a scarecrow in a melon patch,
their idols cannot speak;[g]
they must be carried
because they cannot walk.[h]
Do not fear them;
they can do no harm
nor can they do any good."[i]

6 No one is like you, O LORD;
you are great,[j]
and your name is mighty in power.
7 Who should not revere you,
O King of the nations?[k]
This is your due.
Among all the wise men of the nations
and in all their kingdoms,
there is no one like you.
8 They are all senseless and foolish;[l]
they are taught by worthless wooden idols.
9 Hammered silver is brought from Tarshish
and gold from Uphaz.
What the craftsman and goldsmith have made[m]
is then dressed in blue and purple—
all made by skilled workers.
10 But the LORD is the true God;
he is the living God, the eternal King.
When he is angry, the earth trembles;
the nations cannot endure his wrath.[n]

11 "Tell them this: 'These gods, who did not make the heavens and the earth, will perish[o] from the earth and from under the heavens.' "[a]

12 But God made the earth by his power;
he founded the world by his wisdom
and stretched out the heavens[p] by his understanding.
13 When he thunders,[q] the waters in the heavens roar;
he makes clouds rise from the ends of the earth.
He sends lightning with the rain[r]
and brings out the wind from his storehouses.

14 Everyone is senseless and without knowledge;
every goldsmith is shamed by his idols.
His images are a fraud;
they have no breath in them.
15 They are worthless,[s] the objects of mockery;
when their judgment comes, they will perish.
16 He who is the Portion[t] of Jacob is not like these,

[a] *11* The text of this verse is in Aramaic.

10:4 silver and gold. Wooden idols were plated with these precious metals (v. 9).
10:7 revere. Literally, "fear." In the Bible the fear of God often involves more than the dread of God's judgment. It includes awe, reverence, honor and adoration in response to God's majesty and holiness (see, e.g., Ps 2:11–12). **O King.** This counters claims to kingship by false deities; for example, Bel-Marduk in Babylon (cf. Isa 43:15; 46:1). **wise men.** Perhaps these were magicians and sorcerers, like those in Daniel (Da 2:12). Their "wisdom" is here contrasted with the Lord's (10:12). See *WCF* 21.1.
10:8 senseless . . . foolish . . . taught. The language is again like wisdom language. See Deuteronomy 11:2 and Proverbs 3:11, where the Hebrew word for "taught" is translated "discipline." For "folly," see, for example, Proverbs 15:2, 5 and 7. See *HC* 98.
10:9 Tarshish . . . Uphaz. The former is located in modern Spain, while the latter is unknown.
10:10 true . . . living God. See Deuteronomy 5:26. **eternal King.** See note on verse 7 (see also Ex 15:18; 2Sa 7:13). In 2 Samuel 7:13 the eternity of God's kingdom is affirmed, even though the reign of the house of David was about to cease for several centuries. See *WCF* 2.1; *WLC* 8; *WSC* 5.
10:11 Perhaps for dramatic effect and international usage this pronouncement of judgment against other gods is written in Aramaic. Other passages in Aramaic appear in the Old Testament (see Ezr 6:18; 7:12–26; Da 2:4–7:28).
10:12 power . . . wisdom . . . understanding. The power of the true God in creation is used again in this polemic against foreign gods. For creation by his wisdom, see Proverbs 8:22–31, a passage that foreshadows Christ as the preexistent wisdom of God (Col 1:15; 2:3). See *WCF* 4.1.
10:13 When he thunders . . . from his storehouses. See Psalms 29:3–4 and 135:5–7. This statement of the Lord's control of the rain takes direct aim at similar claims made for the Canaanite god Baal (see 1Ki 17:1).

for he is the Maker of all things,[u]
including Israel, the tribe of his inheritance[v]—
the LORD Almighty is his name.[w]

Coming Destruction

17 Gather up your belongings[x] to leave the land,
you who live under siege.
18 For this is what the LORD says:
"At this time I will hurl[y] out
those who live in this land;
I will bring distress on them
so that they may be captured."

19 Woe to me because of my injury!
My wound[z] is incurable!
Yet I said to myself,
"This is my sickness, and I must endure[a] it."
20 My tent[b] is destroyed;
all its ropes are snapped.
My sons are gone from me and are no more;[c]
no one is left now to pitch my tent
or to set up my shelter.
21 The shepherds are senseless
and do not inquire of the LORD;
so they do not prosper
and all their flock is scattered.[d]
22 Listen! The report is coming—
a great commotion from the land of the north!
It will make the towns of Judah desolate,
a haunt of jackals.[e]

Jeremiah's Prayer

23 I know, O LORD, that a man's life is not his own;
it is not for man to direct his steps.[f]
24 Correct me, LORD, but only with justice—
not in your anger,[g]
lest you reduce me to nothing.[h]
25 Pour out your wrath on the nations[i]
that do not acknowledge you,
on the peoples who do not call on your name.[j]
For they have devoured[k] Jacob;
they have devoured him completely
and destroyed his homeland.[l]

10:16 [u]ver 12 [v]Ps 74:2 [w]Jer 31:35; 32:18
10:17 [x]Eze 12:3-12
10:18 [y]1Sa 25:29
10:19 [z]Jer 14:17 [a]Mic 7:9
10:20 [b]Jer 4:20 [c]Jer 31:15; La 1:5
10:21 [d]Jer 23:2
10:22 [e]Jer 9:11
10:23 [f]Pr 20:24
10:24 [g]Ps 6:1; 38:1 [h]Jer 30:11
10:25 [i]Zep 3:8 [j]Job 18:21; Ps 14:4 [k]Ps 79:7; Jer 8:16 [l]Ps 79:6-7

The Covenant Is Broken

11 This is the word that came to Jeremiah from the LORD: 2 "Listen to the terms of
this covenant and tell them to the people of Judah and to those who live in Je-

10:16 Portion of Jacob . . . his inheritance. Initially Scripture referred to the Lord as an "inheritance" peculiar to the Levites (Nu 18:20). Here the Lord as "portion" and "inheritance" is extended to the nation. The two metaphors together bespeak the relationship between the Lord and Israel in covenant. For the people as "the LORD's portion" see Deuteronomy 32:9.
10:19 Woe to me . . . incurable! Compare Jeremiah's cry in 4:19–21. The medical metaphor is a favorite of this prophet (6:7; 14:17; 30:12–13,15,17).
10:20 My sons are gone. The tragic effects of childlessness in general become a picture of the desolation of exile. Jeremiah would himself be doomed to childlessness to allow him forcefully to make this point (16:2).
10:21 shepherds are senseless. The motif of senselessness is now applied to the leaders in particular (see notes on 2:8; 10:8; cf. 10:14). **do not inquire of the LORD.** They resorted to the incantation of the "wise" pagans (see notes on 8:2; 10:7).
10:23–25 The prophet prayed for divine justice against those who would attack Judah and Jerusalem.
10:23 I know . . . his steps. This kind of statement is in the tradition of Biblical Wisdom Literature (see Pr 16:9).
10:25 This verse closely resembles Psalm 79:6–7 and may be a citation of it. Yet in its new context its intent may not be as well motivated as in the psalm. Even though the chapter emphasizes Judah's moral similarity to the nations, it ends (ironically) with Judah's plea for the Lord's wrath on the nations. See *WCF* 21.6.
■ **11:1—13:27** *The Broken Covenant.* These chapters begin with an explicit focus on Judah's flagrant violation of the covenant, a violation that condemned the nation to the ultimate covenant curse of exile. Several narratives and speeches follow this initial focus, confirming the judgment as inevitable. This material divides into three sections: the curse of the covenant (11:1–17), judgment for Jeremiah's opponents (11:18—12:17) and the curse of the covenant confirmed (13:1–27).
■ **11:1–17** *Curse of the Covenant.* The Lord reminded the Judahites that the terms of his covenant with them included the curse of exile for those who continued in flagrant violation of his commands.
11:2 terms. Literally, "words," meaning the commands of God and the structures of blessing and cursing attached to those com-

rusalem. **3**Tell them that this is what the LORD, the God of Israel, says: 'Cursed[m] is the
man who does not obey the terms of this covenant— **4**the terms I commanded your forefathers when I brought them out of Egypt, out of the iron-smelting furnace.[n]' I said,
'Obey[o] me and do everything I command you, and you will be my people,[p] and I will be
your God. **5**Then I will fulfill the oath I swore[q] to your forefathers, to give them a land
flowing with milk and honey'—the land you possess today."

I answered, "Amen, LORD."

6The LORD said to me, "Proclaim all these words in the towns of Judah and in the
streets of Jerusalem: 'Listen to the terms of this covenant and follow[r] them. **7**From the
time I brought your forefathers up from Egypt until today, I warned them again and
again,[s] saying, "Obey me." **8**But they did not listen or pay attention;[t] instead, they followed the stubbornness of their evil hearts. So I brought on them all the curses[u] of the
covenant I had commanded them to follow but that they did not keep.' "

9Then the LORD said to me, "There is a conspiracy[v] among the people of Judah and
those who live in Jerusalem. **10**They have returned to the sins of their forefathers,[w] who
refused to listen to my words. They have followed other gods[x] to serve them. Both the
house of Israel and the house of Judah have broken the covenant I made with their forefathers. **11**Therefore this is what the LORD says: 'I will bring on them a disaster[y] they cannot escape. Although they cry[z] out to me, I will not listen[a] to them. **12**The towns of Judah and the people of Jerusalem will go and cry out to the gods to whom they burn
incense,[b] but they will not help them at all when disaster[c] strikes. **13**You have as many
gods as you have towns, O Judah; and the altars you have set up to burn incense[d] to that
shameful[e] god Baal are as many as the streets of Jerusalem.'

14"Do not pray[f] for this people nor offer any plea or petition for them, because I will
not listen[g] when they call to me in the time of their distress.

15"What is my beloved doing in my temple
as she works out her evil schemes with many?
Can consecrated meat avert ⌊your punishment⌋?
When you engage in your wickedness,
then you rejoice.[a]"

16The LORD called you a thriving olive tree
with fruit beautiful in form.
But with the roar of a mighty storm
he will set it on fire,[h]
and its branches will be broken.[i]

17The LORD Almighty, who planted[j] you, has decreed disaster for you, because the house
of Israel and the house of Judah have done evil and provoked me to anger by burning incense to Baal.[k]

11:3 [m]Dt 27:26; Gal 3:10
11:4 [n]Dt 4:20; 1Ki 8:51 [o]Ex 24:8 [p]Jer 7:23; 31:33
11:5 [q]Ex 13:5; Dt 7:12; Ps 105:8-11
11:6 [r]Dt 15:5; Ro 2:13; Jas 1:22
11:7 [s]2Ch 36:15
11:8 [t]Jer 7:26 [u]Lev 26:14-43
11:9 [v]Eze 22:25
11:10 [w]Dt 9:7 [x]Jdg 2:12-13
11:11 [y]2Ki 22:16 [z]Jer 14:12; Eze 8:18 [a]ver 14; Pr 1:28; Isa 1:15; Zec 7:13
11:12 [b]Jer 44:17 [c]Dt 32:37
11:13 [d]Jer 7:9 [e]Jer 3:24
11:14 [f]Ex 32:10 [g]ver 11
11:16 [h]Jer 21:14 [i]Isa 27:11; Ro 11:17-24
11:17 [j]Isa 5:2; Jer 12:2 [k]Jer 7:9

a *15* Or *Could consecrated meat avert your punishment? / Then you would rejoice*

mands. **covenant.** The term for the relationship into which God freely entered first with all of humanity in the days of Noah (Ge 9:1–17); then with Abraham, as the father of Israel (Ge 17:1–21); with Israel at Sinai (Ex 19–24); with David (2Sa 7:12–16; Ps 89:3); and finally in the new covenant (see notes on 31:31–34). See chart, "Major Covenants in the Bible," on page 25.
11:3 Cursed is the man. See Deuteronomy 27:15–26.
11:4 out of Egypt . . . iron-smelting furnace. A direct allusion to Deuteronomy 4:20. **Obey me and do everything I command you.** "Obey" is literally "hear." These are common ideas in Deuteronomy (e.g., 4:1–2; 5:1; 6:3). **you will be my people . . . your God.** See 7:23.
11:5 fulfill the oath I swore. One aspect of God's covenant with Abraham was the promise that his descendants would one day inherit the land of Canaan (Ge 15:17–21; Dt 4:31). This promise was but the early stage of a greater expectation of inheriting the entire world (Ro 4:13–17). Under the sovereign control of God, how and when this promise was to be fulfilled depended upon the faithfulness of God's people. The Israelites so violated the covenant that they were actually cast out of the land. In overflowing mercy Christ—as the representative of God's people—secured their inheritance in the new heavens and the new earth to come by his perfect obedience (Rev 21:7). **a land flowing with milk and honey.** See Exodus 3:8 and Deuteronomy 6:3. **Amen.** Indicates acceptance of the terms laid down (see Dt 27:15–26). The word was uttered here by Jeremiah.
11:9 conspiracy. This could signify resistance to Jeremiah's words, to Josiah's reform or even to Nebuchadnezzar, which, because he was the Lord's instrument of wrath, was tantamount to conspiracy against the Lord (27:8).
11:10 their forefathers. The prophet may have had in mind all the previous generations who had turned away from God, but he more likely was referring to the first generation of wilderness wanderers, with whom the covenant at Sinai was made and who perished in the wilderness.
11:13 burn incense. This was a common feature both of ancient pagan worship and of the worship of the Lord (1:16; 7:9; 18:15; Ex 30:7–9). The deity to whom incense was burned made all the difference.
11:15 my beloved. Here the term refers to Judah, as also in 12:7. Compare Isaiah 5:1, where it refers to Israel. This is in line with the courtship and bridal imagery of 2:2 and 3:1, which can also lead to the language of divorce (Hos 2:2–13). **in my temple.** See 7:10–11 and Ezekiel 8:6–13. **Can consecrated meat . . . rejoice.** The Hebrew is obscure, but the criticism was of ritualistic worship that produced a falsely based joy in God's salvation.
11:16 a thriving olive tree . . . broken. Similar to the vine imagery in Psalm 80:8–13.
■ **11:18—12:17** *Judgment for Jeremiah's Opponents.* The announcement that the ultimate covenant curse of exile was coming to Judah sparked opposition to the prophet. God promised to punish his opponents.

Plot Against Jeremiah

18 Because the LORD revealed their plot to me, I knew it, for at that time he showed me
what they were doing. 19 I had been like a gentle lamb led to the slaughter; I did not realize that they had plotted[l] against me, saying,

"Let us destroy the tree and its fruit;
  let us cut him off from the land of the living,[m]
  that his name be remembered[n] no more."
20 But, O LORD Almighty, you who judge righteously
  and test the heart and mind,[o]
let me see your vengeance upon them,
  for to you I have committed my cause.

21 "Therefore this is what the LORD says about the men of Anathoth who are seeking
your life[p] and saying, 'Do not prophesy in the name of the LORD or you will die[q] by our
hands'— 22 therefore this is what the LORD Almighty says: 'I will punish them. Their young
men[r] will die by the sword, their sons and daughters by famine. 23 Not even a remnant[s]
will be left to them, because I will bring disaster on the men of Anathoth in the year of
their punishment.[t] '"

Jeremiah's Complaint

12

You are always righteous,[u] O LORD,
  when I bring a case before you.
Yet I would speak with you about your justice:
  Why does the way of the wicked prosper?[v]
  Why do all the faithless live at ease?
2 You have planted[w] them, and they have taken root;
  they grow and bear fruit.
You are always on their lips
  but far from their hearts.[x]
3 Yet you know me, O LORD;
  you see me and test[y] my thoughts about you.
Drag them off like sheep to be butchered!
  Set them apart for the day of slaughter![z]
4 How long will the land lie parched[a][a]
  and the grass in every field be withered?[b]
Because those who live in it are wicked,
  the animals and birds have perished.[c]
Moreover, the people are saying,
  "He will not see what happens to us."

God's Answer

5 "If you have raced with men on foot
  and they have worn you out,
  how can you compete with horses?
If you stumble in safe country,[b]
  how will you manage in the thickets[d] by[c] the Jordan?
6 Your brothers, your own family—

11:19 [l]Jer 18:18; 20:10 [m]Job 28:13; Isa 53:8 [n]Ps 83:4
11:20 [o]Ps 7:9
11:21 [p]Jer 12:6 [q]Jer 26:8, 11; 38:4
11:22 [r]Jer 18:21
11:23 [s]Jer 6:9 [t]Jer 23:12
12:1 [u]Ezr 9:15 [v]Jer 5:27-28
12:2 [w]Jer 11:17 [x]Isa 29:13; Jer 3:10; Mt 15:8; Tit 1:16
12:3 [y]Ps 7:9; 11:5; 139:1-4; Jer 11:20 [z]Jer 17:18
12:4 [a]Jer 4:28 [b]Joel 1:10-12 [c]Jer 4:25; 9:10
12:5 [d]Jer 49:19; 50:44

a 4 Or *land mourn*   b 5 Or *If you put your trust in a land of safety*   c 5 Or *the flooding of*

■ **11:18–23** *Complaint About a Deadly Plot.* God promised to curse Jeremiah's enemies who had risen from within his own family. This material is the first of the sections often designated as Jeremiah's "confessions" (11:18–23; 12:1–4; 15:10–21; 17:12–18; 18:18–23; 20:7–18; see "Introduction: Purpose and Distinctives").

11:19 like a gentle lamb led to the slaughter. Jeremiah described his naïveté about his enemies in terms of a sacrifice. See Psalm 44:11. Jeremiah often used the language of the lament psalms (see "Introduction to the Psalms: Structure: *Genres*"). In this way he prefigured Christ's suffering (cf. Isa 53:7). **tree and its fruit.** This could refer to Jeremiah and his message or emphatically to his very life. **cut him off . . . remembered no more.** Not to be remembered because of lack of descendants. This was considered the worst of fates. The irony, however, is that the book itself is a memorial to Jeremiah, while his enemies remain nameless (cf. Ru 4:1–6, where the nearer kinsmen was not named, although he sought to preserve his inheritance).

11:20 test the heart and mind. See 9:7.

11:21 the men of Anathoth. This was Jeremiah's hometown (1:1). The details of the plot reveal that his most intense opposition came from those closest to him (cf. Ps 69:7–9; Mt 10:36 [citing Mic 7:6]; 13:57).

11:23 Not even a remnant. This threat of total extinction contrasts the fate of Jeremiah's personal enemies with that of Judah in general. See 4:27, 5:10, 6:9 and their notes.

■ **12:1–17** *Complaint About Wicked Opposition.* The violation of the covenant and personal threats against him led Jeremiah to lament over the unbridled wickedness in Judah. God responded with words of assurance. This material is often called Jeremiah's second "confession" (see note on 11:18–23).

12:2 You have planted them. These words make further ironic allusion to Psalm 1:3.

12:5 God's response began with a warning that Jeremiah's troubles would only increase in the future.

even they have betrayed you;
they have raised a loud cry against you.[e]
Do not trust them,
though they speak well of you.[f]

7 "I will forsake my house,
abandon[g] my inheritance;
I will give the one I love
into the hands of her enemies.
8 My inheritance has become to me
like a lion in the forest.
She roars at me;
therefore I hate her.[h]
9 Has not my inheritance become to me
like a speckled bird of prey
that other birds of prey surround and attack?
Go and gather all the wild beasts;
bring them to devour.[i]
10 Many shepherds[j] will ruin my vineyard
and trample down my field;
they will turn my pleasant field
into a desolate wasteland.[k]
11 It will be made a wasteland,
parched and desolate before me;[l]
the whole land will be laid waste
because there is no one who cares.
12 Over all the barren heights in the desert
destroyers will swarm,
for the sword of the LORD[m] will devour
from one end of the land to the other;[n]
no one will be safe.
13 They will sow wheat but reap thorns;
they will wear themselves out but gain nothing.[o]
So bear the shame of your harvest
because of the LORD's fierce anger."[p]

14 This is what the LORD says: "As for all my wicked neighbors who seize the inheritance I gave my people Israel, I will uproot[q] them from their lands and I will uproot the
house of Judah from among them. 15 But after I uproot them, I will again have compassion and will bring[r] each of them back to his own inheritance and his own country. 16 And
if they learn well the ways of my people and swear by my name, saying, 'As surely as the
LORD lives'[s]—even as they once taught my people to swear by Baal[t]—then they will be
established among my people.[u] 17 But if any nation does not listen, I will completely uproot and destroy[v] it," declares the LORD.

A Linen Belt

13 This is what the LORD said to me: "Go and buy a linen belt and put it around your
waist, but do not let it touch water." 2 So I bought a belt, as the LORD directed,
and put it around my waist.

12:6 [e]Pr 26:24-25; Jer 9:4 [f]Ps 12:2
12:7 [g]Jer 7:29
12:8 [h]Hos 9:15; Am 6:8
12:9 [i]Isa 56:9; Jer 15:3; Eze 23:25
12:10 [j]Jer 23:1 [k]Isa 5:1-7
12:11 [l]ver 4; Isa 42:25; Jer 23:10
12:12 [m]Jer 47:6 [n]Jer 3:2
12:13 [o]Lev 26:20; Dt 28:38; Mic 6:15; Hag 1:6 [p]Jer 4:26
12:14 [q]Zec 2:7-9
12:15 [r]Am 9:14-15
12:16 [s]Jer 4:2 [t]Jos 23:7 [u]Isa 49:6; Jer 3:17
12:17 [v]Isa 60:12

12:6 Your brothers, your own family. See 11:21–23.
12:7 my house. The term in this context relates to "family" (lit., "house of your father") in verse 6. Since Jeremiah's "house" had forsaken him, the Lord would forsake his house (i.e., Judah). **inheritance.** This term primarily refers to the land given to Israel (Dt 4:21) but can also embrace the people themselves (see vv. 8–9; 2:7). **the one I love.** See 11:15 and its note.
12:8 like a lion. This is the first of a series of similes (cf. vv. 9–10) showing how Judah had become dehumanized. **I hate her.** Hatred, in this context, is the reversal of the love mentioned in verse 7. It includes God's wrath and intention to inflict covenant curses (cf. Lev 26:30).
12:10 shepherds. Refers here to foreign rulers (cf. 6:3). The image is now combined with that of the vineyard (see 2:21 and its note; see also 5:10; 6:9). Shepherding was a literal threat to vineyards. **pleasant field.** See Isaiah 5:7.
12:12 Over all the barren heights . . . no one will be safe. The last phrase is literally "there is no peace for anyone." The verse denounces false proclamations of peace (6:14).
12:14 wicked neighbors. Although Judah's enemies would be used by the Lord to punish her, they themselves would be judged. **uproot . . . uproot.** Recalls 1:10. The second "uprooting" would be a plucking of Judah from the midst of her enemies in the salvation that lay beyond judgment. This idea is developed in chapters 30–33.
12:15 after I uproot them . . . own country. An astonishing turn that anticipates a restoration that would include salvation for Gentile nations. With other prophets Jeremiah anticipated the inclusion of the Gentiles in God's salvation (16:19; 46:26; 48:47; 49:6; Isa 40:5; 42:6).
12:16 And if they learn . . . among my people. Continues the same thought as in verse 15. See Isaiah 19:25 for an equally surprising use of "my people" for Egypt.
■ **13:1–27** *Curse of the Covenant Confirmed.* After affirming that God would judge those who wished to harm the prophet, these

3Then the word of the LORD came to me a second time: 4"Take the belt you bought and
are wearing around your waist, and go now to Perath[a] and hide it there in a crevice in
the rocks." 5So I went and hid it at Perath, as the LORD told me.[w]
6Many days later the LORD said to me, "Go now to Perath and get the belt I told you
to hide there." 7So I went to Perath and dug up the belt and took it from the place where
I had hidden it, but now it was ruined and completely useless.
8Then the word of the LORD came to me: 9"This is what the LORD says: 'In the same way
I will ruin the pride of Judah and the great pride[x] of Jerusalem. 10These wicked people,
who refuse to listen to my words, who follow the stubbornness of their hearts[y] and go
after other gods[z] to serve and worship them, will be like this belt—completely useless!
11For as a belt is bound around a man's waist, so I bound the whole house of Israel and
the whole house of Judah to me,' declares the LORD, 'to be my people for my renown[a] and
praise and honor.[b] But they have not listened.'[c]

Wineskins

12"Say to them: 'This is what the LORD, the God of Israel, says: Every wineskin should
be filled with wine.' And if they say to you, 'Don't we know that every wineskin should
be filled with wine?' 13then tell them, 'This is what the LORD says: I am going to fill with
drunkenness[d] all who live in this land, including the kings who sit on David's throne, the
priests, the prophets and all those living in Jerusalem. 14I will smash them one against
the other, fathers and sons alike, declares the LORD. I will allow no pity or mercy or compassion[e] to keep me from destroying[f] them.' "

Threat of Captivity

15 Hear and pay attention,
do not be arrogant,
for the LORD has spoken.
16 Give glory[g] to the LORD your God
before he brings the darkness,
before your feet stumble[h]
on the darkening hills.
You hope for light,
but he will turn it to thick darkness
and change it to deep gloom.[i]
17 But if you do not listen,[j]
I will weep in secret
because of your pride;
my eyes will weep bitterly,
overflowing with tears,[k]
because the LORD's flock[l] will be taken captive.[m]

18 Say to the king and to the queen mother,
"Come down from your thrones,
for your glorious crowns
will fall from your heads."
19 The cities in the Negev will be shut up,

13:5 [w]Ex 40:16
13:9 [x]Lev 26:19
13:10 [y]Jer 11:8; 16:12 [z]Jer 9:14
13:11 [a]Jer 32:20; 33:9 [b]Ex 19:5-6 [c]Jer 7:26
13:13 [d]Ps 60:3; 75:8; Isa 51:17; 63:6; Jer 51:57
13:14 [e]Jer 16:5 [f]Dt 29:20; Eze 5:10
13:16 [g]Jos 7:19 [h]Jer 23:12 [i]Isa 59:9
13:17 [j]Mal 2:2 [k]Jer 9:1 [l]Ps 80:1; Jer 23:1 [m]Jer 14:18

[a] 4 Or possibly *the Euphrates*; also in verses 5–7

chapters confirm Jeremiah's previous condemnation of the nation by symbolic acts involving a linen belt (vv. 1–11) and wineskins (vv. 12–14), as well as by a series of speeches (vv. 15–27).
13:1 linen belt. A loincloth, symbolizing the intimate relationship intended by the Lord for himself and his people. Linen was worn by priests (Ex 28:39), so here is a hint of Israel's role as a kingdom of priests (Ex 19:6).
13:4 Perath. That is, the Euphrates River. A nearer location may actually have been intended—possibly Parah (Jos 18:23), which was close to Anathoth; its similarity of name nevertheless suggests the Euphrates and therefore the Babylonian exile.
13:6 Many days later. The extended time that the belt remained buried in Perath probably symbolized the prolonged duration of the exile.
13:7 ruined and completely useless. As a result of its burial (either in the riverbank or in the riverbed itself). Its ruin depicted the corruption of the people, who were no longer fit for a relationship with the Lord.
13:11 I bound the whole house . . . to me. The Lord spelled out the meaning of the symbolic act as an illustration of his covenant with all Israel.
13:12–13 Every wineskin . . . fill with drunkenness. Wine is often used as a symbol of God's wrath (e.g., 25:15–29).
13:15 See *WLC* 105.
13:16 darkness . . . light . . . thick darkness . . . deep gloom. The concepts of light and darkness are commonly employed for salvation and judgment, respectively (Isa 9:2; Am 5:18–20). "Thick darkness" translates the same Hebrew word as that for "shadow of death" in Psalm 23:4.
13:18 to the king and to the queen mother. Probably Jehoiachin and his mother, Nehushta (2Ki 24:8). The oracle was thus close in time to Nebuchadnezzar's attack on Jerusalem in 597 B.C. (see "Introduction: Author" and "Time and Place of Writing"). **your glorious crowns will fall.** See 22:24–26. This curse complied with the threat of judgment against particular sons of David according to the Davidic covenant (2Ch 6:16). It was not irreversible but allowed for later, faithful kings to arise (2Sa 7; Pss 89; 132).
13:19 The cities in the Negev. Cities in the arid southern por-

13:19
[n]Jer 20:4; 52:30
13:20
[o]Jer 6:22; Hab 1:6
[p]Jer 23:2
13:21
[q]Jer 38:22
[r]Jer 4:31
13:22
[s]Jer 9:2-6; 16:10-12 [t]Eze 16:37; Na 3:5-6
13:24
[u]Ps 1:4 [v]Lev 26:33
13:25
[w]Job 20:29; Mt 24:51
13:26
[x]La 1:8; Eze 16:37; Hos 2:10
13:27
[y]Jer 2:20 [z]Eze 6:13
[a]Hos 8:5
14:2
[b]Isa 3:26; Jer 8:21

and there will be no one to open them.
All Judah[n] will be carried into exile,
carried completely away.

20 Lift up your eyes and see
those who are coming from the north.[o]
Where is the flock[p] that was entrusted to you,
the sheep of which you boasted?
21 What will you say when ⌞the LORD⌟ sets over you
those you cultivated as your special allies?[q]
Will not pain grip you
like that of a woman in labor?[r]
22 And if you ask yourself,
"Why has this happened to me?"—
it is because of your many sins[s]
that your skirts have been torn off
and your body mistreated.[t]
23 Can the Ethiopian[a] change his skin
or the leopard its spots?
Neither can you do good
who are accustomed to doing evil.

24 "I will scatter you like chaff[u]
driven by the desert wind.[v]
25 This is your lot,
the portion[w] I have decreed for you,"
declares the LORD,
"because you have forgotten me
and trusted in false gods.
26 I will pull up your skirts over your face
that your shame may be seen[x]—
27 your adulteries and lustful neighings,
your shameless prostitution![y]
I have seen your detestable acts
on the hills and in the fields.[z]
Woe to you, O Jerusalem!
How long will you be unclean?"[a]

Drought, Famine, Sword

14 This is the word of the LORD to Jeremiah concerning the drought:

2 "Judah mourns,[b]
her cities languish;
they wail for the land,
and a cry goes up from Jerusalem.
3 The nobles send their servants for water;

[a] *23* Hebrew *Cushite* (probably a person from the upper Nile region)

---

tion of the land. They were important for fortification against satellite allies of Babylon (e.g., Moab; 2Ki 24:2) but were unable to prevent the sack of Judah. They served as examples of Judah's "pride" (v. 17) in that Judah relied on these cities, rather than on God, for protection.
13:20 the north. See 4:6. Judah was militarily vulnerable from both the north and the south (v. 19).
13:22 your skirts . . . mistreated. An image of public shame, as of a prostitute, possibly implying rape.
13:23 Can the Ethiopian . . . its spots? These are rhetorical questions, perhaps using hyperbole. It was typical of Jeremiah to assert that Judah had become so corrupt by this time that repentance was impossible—hence his hope in the new covenant (see notes on 31:31–34).
13:24 like chaff. This image is used of the wicked in Psalm 1:4.
13:25 lot. This originally signified the lot cast for the division of the land (Jos 14:2). Now it indicated expulsion from the same land.
13:27 adulteries and lustful neighings. See 5:8 and its note. **How long . . . ?** This was typically asked by the worshiper who sought God's action (12:4; cf. psalms of lament, e.g., Ps 13:1); here the form was ironically directed back to the people by the Lord. The question may also have indicated that the opportunity for Judah to repent still remained.
■ **14:1—15:21** *The Judgment of Drought.* These chapters declare that the Judahites were so hardened in their sin that God would not answer even Jeremiah's prayer for deliverance from the punishment of drought. In answer to Jeremiah's question in 14:19—Had God rejected Judah completely?—God replied that coming judgment was inevitable because of Judah's sin, but he also assured Jeremiah of personal deliverance from his enemies. This material divides into two sections: a description of the drought (14:1–6) and Jeremiah's three prayers and God's response (14:7—15:21).
■ **14:1–6** *Severe Drought.* Jeremiah delivered these words during an unspecified period of devastating drought in Judah.
14:1 drought. Along with other curses on nature, drought was one of the judgments threatened by the Law of Moses (Lev 26:19–20; Dt 28:22–24). Natural disasters like this were also associated with war, as here.

they go to the cisterns
but find no water.[c]
They return with their jars unfilled;
dismayed and despairing,
they cover their heads.[d]
4 The ground is cracked
because there is no rain in the land;[e]
the farmers are dismayed
and cover their heads.
5 Even the doe in the field
deserts her newborn fawn
because there is no grass.[f]
6 Wild donkeys stand on the barren heights[g]
and pant like jackals;
their eyesight fails
for lack of pasture."

7 Although our sins testify[h] against us,
O LORD, do something for the sake of your name.
For our backsliding[i] is great;
we have sinned[j] against you.
8 O Hope[k] of Israel,
its Savior in times of distress,
why are you like a stranger in the land,
like a traveler who stays only a night?
9 Why are you like a man taken by surprise,
like a warrior powerless to save?[l]
You are among[m] us, O LORD,
and we bear your name;[n]
do not forsake us!

10 This is what the LORD says about this people:

"They greatly love to wander;
they do not restrain their feet.[o]
So the LORD does not accept[p] them;
he will now remember[q] their wickedness
and punish them for their sins."[r]

11 Then the LORD said to me, "Do not pray[s] for the well-being of this people. 12 Although
they fast, I will not listen to their cry;[t] though they offer burnt offerings[u] and grain offerings,
I will not accept[v] them. Instead, I will destroy them with the sword, famine and plague."
13 But I said, "Ah, Sovereign LORD, the prophets keep telling them, 'You will not see
the sword or suffer famine.[w] Indeed, I will give you lasting peace in this place.' "
14 Then the LORD said to me, "The prophets are prophesying lies[x] in my name. I have
not sent[y] them or appointed them or spoken to them. They are prophesying to you false
visions,[z] divinations,[a] idolatries[a] and the delusions of their own minds. 15 Therefore, this

14:3 [c]2Ki 18:31; Job 6:19-20 [d]2Sa 15:30
14:4 [e]Jer 3:3
14:5 [f]Isa 15:6
14:6 [g]Job 39:5-6; Jer 2:24
14:7 [h]Hos 5:5 [i]Jer 5:6 [j]Jer 8:14
14:8 [k]Jer 17:13
14:9 [l]Isa 50:2 [m]Jer 8:19 [n]Isa 63:19; Jer 15:16
14:10 [o]Ps 119:101; Jer 2:25 [p]Jer 6:20; Am 5:22 [q]Hos 9:9 [r]Jer 44:21-23; Hos 8:13
14:11 [s]Ex 32:10
14:12 [t]Isa 1:15; Jer 11:11 [u]Jer 7:21 [v]Jer 6:20
14:13 [w]Jer 5:12
14:14 [x]Jer 27:14 [y]Jer 23:21,32 [z]Jer 23:16 [a]Eze 12:24

a 14 Or *visions, worthless divinations*

14:3 cover their heads. A sign of mourning.

14:4 no rain. Canaan depended on rainfall for its water; the Lord either gave it or withheld it (Dt 11:10–15; 28:12).

■ **14:7—15:21** *Prayer and Response.* This section alternates between Jeremiah's prayers and God's answers. The prophet prayed on behalf of the people in hopes of finding forgiveness (14:7–9), but God responded with words of judgment (14:10–12). Jeremiah prayed again (14:13), and God responded with condemnation for the false prophets (14:14–18). The prophet prayed for a third time (14:19–22), and God told him that prayer would do no good (15:1–9). Jeremiah prayed again (15:10), and God responded with words about Jeremiah and Judah (15:11–14). The prophet prayed one last time (15:15–18), and God answered him with encouragement and warning (15:19–21).

14:7–9 Jeremiah cried out for deliverance from the drought. See *WLC* 194.

14:8 Hope. The word also means "pool," a striking suggestion in a time of drought. **Savior.** Or "Deliverer," with military connotations.

14:9 we bear your name. This explains the power of the motivation in verse 7. The Lord's honor was at stake in the fortunes of his people. See *WCF* 12.

14:10–12 God answered Jeremiah's prayer with a rejection of his request.

14:10 this people. Significantly, God did not say "my people."

14:11–12 A further response of the Lord, elaborating on verse 10. **Do not pray.** See 7:16 and its note. Here the prohibition follows the intercession in verses 7–9.

14:12 fast . . . burnt offerings and grain offerings. A typical criticism of ritual for its own sake (cf. Isa 1:11–17; Mic 6:6–8). **sword, famine and plague.** This is the first of 13 appearances of this combination in Jeremiah (e.g., 15:2). It is a typical summation of the horrors that judgment can bring (Dt 32:24–25).

14:13 Jeremiah pleaded on behalf of the people, claiming that they had been misled. **the prophets.** Those who falsely prophesied peace and security (6:1–4; 8:11).

14:14–18 God responded to Jeremiah's prayer in verse 13, stating that the prophets were false and should have been recognized as such by their idolatry (see Dt 13:1–5; 18:20). See *WLC* 158.

is what the LORD says about the prophets who are prophesying in my name: I did not send
them, yet they are saying, 'No sword or famine will touch this land.' Those same prophets will perish[b] by sword and famine.[c] 16 And the people they are prophesying to will be
thrown out into the streets of Jerusalem because of the famine and sword. There will be
no one to bury[d] them or their wives, their sons or their daughters.[e] I will pour out on
them the calamity they deserve.[f]

17 "Speak this word to them:

" 'Let my eyes overflow with tears[g]
night and day without ceasing;
for my virgin daughter—my people—
has suffered a grievous wound,
a crushing blow.[h]
18 If I go into the country,
I see those slain by the sword;
if I go into the city,
I see the ravages of famine.[i]
Both prophet and priest
have gone to a land they know not.' "

19 Have you rejected Judah completely?[j]
Do you despise Zion?
Why have you afflicted us
so that we cannot be healed?[k]
We hoped for peace
but no good has come,
for a time of healing
but there is only terror.[l]
20 O LORD, we acknowledge our wickedness
and the guilt of our fathers;
we have indeed sinned[m] against you.
21 For the sake of your name[n] do not despise us;
do not dishonor your glorious throne.[o]
Remember your covenant with us
and do not break it.
22 Do any of the worthless idols of the nations bring rain?[p]
Do the skies themselves send down showers?
No, it is you, O LORD our God.
Therefore our hope is in you,
for you are the one who does all this.

15 Then the LORD said to me: "Even if Moses[q] and Samuel[r] were to stand before
me, my heart would not go out to this people.[s] Send them away from my presence![t] Let them go! 2 And if they ask you, 'Where shall we go?' tell them, 'This is what the
LORD says:

" 'Those destined for death, to death;
those for the sword, to the sword;[u]
those for starvation, to starvation;[v]
those for captivity, to captivity.'[w]

3 "I will send four kinds of destroyers[x] against them," declares the LORD, "the sword
to kill and the dogs to drag away and the birds[y] of the air and the beasts of the earth to
devour and destroy.[z] 4 I will make them abhorrent[a] to all the kingdoms of the earth[b] because of what Manasseh[c] son of Hezekiah king of Judah did in Jerusalem.

14:15 [b]Eze 14:9 [c]Jer 5:12-13
14:16 [d]Ps 79:3 [e]Jer 7:33 [f]Pr 1:31
14:17 [g]Jer 9:1 [h]Jer 8:21
14:18 [i]Eze 7:15
14:19 [j]Jer 7:29 [k]Jer 30:12-13 [l]Jer 8:15
14:20 [m]Da 9:7-8
14:21 [n]ver 7 [o]Jer 3:17
14:22 [p]Ps 135:7
15:1 [q]Ex 32:11; Nu 14:13-20 [r]1Sa 7:9 [s]Jer 7:16; Eze 14:14,20 [t]2Ki 17:20
15:2 [u]Jer 43:11 [v]Jer 14:12 [w]Rev 13:10
15:3 [x]Lev 26:16 [y]Dt 28:26 [z]Lev 26:22; Eze 14:21
15:4 [a]Jer 24:9; 29:18 [b]Dt 28:25 [c]2Ki 21:2; 23:26-27

14:19–22 Jeremiah prayed, confessing Judah's sins and asking God to respond for his own glory. See *WLC* 104.
14:19 cannot be healed . . . healing. See 3:22 and 30:17. Healing would ultimately be both moral and physical. **We hoped for peace.** This misguided expectation was due to the false prophets' teaching (see v. 13 and its note).
14:21 For the sake of your name. See verse 7 and its note. **your glorious throne.** The temple is in view (see 2Ki 19:15; but cf. 1Ki 8:27). **your covenant.** Jeremiah recalled God's covenant with Abraham, Isaac and Jacob (Ge 15:12–21; 26:3–5; 28:13–15; Lev 26:42–45).
15:1–9 God responded to Jeremiah's prayer by informing him that further prayer was now useless.
15:1 Moses and Samuel. God called to mind Israel's great intercessors (Ex 32:11–14; 1Sa 12:23). Note also Elijah in 1 Kings 17:1, where "whom I serve" is literally "before whom I stand." Prayer for the people was again prohibited, and the one just uttered (14:19–22) was specifically rejected (7:16; 11:14).
15:3 sword . . . dogs . . . birds . . . beasts. A different foursome from that in verse 2. The last three played on the people's fear of their corpses not receiving burial (7:33; 14:16; cf. 1Ki 21:23).
15:4 Manasseh. This son of Hezekiah, the reforming king (2Ki

5 "Who will have pity[d] on you, O Jerusalem?
Who will mourn for you?
Who will stop to ask how you are?
6 You have rejected[e] me," declares the LORD.
"You keep on backsliding.
So I will lay hands[f] on you and destroy you;
I can no longer show compassion.
7 I will winnow them with a winnowing fork
at the city gates of the land.
I will bring bereavement and destruction on my people,[g]
for they have not changed their ways.
8 I will make their widows more numerous
than the sand of the sea.
At midday I will bring a destroyer[h]
against the mothers of their young men;
suddenly I will bring down on them
anguish and terror.
9 The mother of seven will grow faint[i]
and breathe her last.
Her sun will set while it is still day;
she will be disgraced and humiliated.
I will put the survivors to the sword[j]
before their enemies,"
declares the LORD.

10 Alas, my mother, that you gave me birth,[k]
a man with whom the whole land strives and contends![l]
I have neither lent[m] nor borrowed,
yet everyone curses me.

11 The LORD said,

"Surely I will deliver you[n] for a good purpose;
surely I will make your enemies plead[o] with you
in times of disaster and times of distress.
12 "Can a man break iron—
iron from the north[p]—or bronze?
13 Your wealth and your treasures
I will give as plunder, without charge,[q]
because of all your sins
throughout your country.[r]
14 I will enslave you to your enemies
in[a] a land you do not know,[s]
for my anger will kindle a fire[t]
that will burn against you."

15 You understand, O LORD;
remember me and care for me.
Avenge me on my persecutors.[u]

15:5 [d]Isa 51:19; Jer 13:14; 21:7; Na 3:7
15:6 [e]Jer 6:19; 7:24 [f]Zep 1:4
15:7 [g]Jer 18:21
15:8 [h]Jer 6:4
15:9 [i]1Sa 2:5 [j]Jer 21:7
15:10 [k]Job 3:1 [l]Jer 1:19 [m]Lev 25:36
15:11 [n]Jer 40:4 [o]Jer 21:1-2; 37:3; 42:1-3
15:12 [p]Jer 28:14
15:13 [q]Ps 44:12 [r]Jer 17:3
15:14 [s]Dt 28:36; Jer 16:13 [t]Dt 32:22; Ps 21:9
15:15 [u]Jer 12:3

a *14* Some Hebrew manuscripts, Septuagint and Syriac (see also Jer. 17:4); most Hebrew manuscripts *I will cause your enemies to bring you / into*

20:21), was ironically one of the most wicked. Despite the later reforms of his grandson Josiah, Judah's punishment and exile were particularly linked with his offenses (2Ki 23:26). See "Introduction: Author" and "Time and Place of Writing."
15:6 backsliding. See 3:22. **I can no longer show compassion.** For the time being, but not forever (cf. 31:20).
15:7 winnow. See 4:11, where the image is used slightly differently. Here it means punishment (cf. Isa 41:16).
15:8 widows . . . sand of the sea. Notice the ironic transformation of promise into dire threat (Ge 22:17; cf. Isa 10:22).
15:9 mother of seven. This picture of great blessing (Ps 127:5) is again reversed. **put the survivors to the sword.** Even the remnant left by the destruction would, in its turn, succumb. See Isaiah 6:13, where a similar thought is finally softened by the promise of the "holy seed."
15:10–21 This is often described as Jeremiah's third "confession" (see note on 11:18–23).
15:10 Jeremiah prayed again, expressing his despair over the strength of his opponents.
15:11–14 God responded to Jeremiah, promising deliverance from his adversaries.
15:12 Can a man break iron . . . ? How could Jeremiah have expected to change Judah's stubborn heart? See 13:23 and its note. **from the north.** This implies again an analogy between the hardness of Jeremiah's personal enemies and that of Judah's enemy, Babylon (cf. 6:1).
15:14 enslave you to your enemies. This was fulfilled for Jeremiah in 43:4–7.
15:15–18 Jeremiah prayed, complaining further about God allowing him to be mistreated.

15:15 [v]Ps 69:7-9
15:16 [w]Eze 3:3; Rev 10:10 [x]Ps 119:72,103 [y]Jer 14:9
15:17 [z]Ps 1:1; 26:4-5; Jer 16:8
15:18 [a]Jer 30:15; Mic 1:9 [b]Job 6:15
15:19 [c]Zec 3:7
15:20 [d]Jer 20:11; Eze 3:8
15:21 [e]Jer 50:34 [f]Ge 48:16
16:2 [g]1Co 7:26-27
16:3 [h]Jer 6:21
16:4 [i]Jer 25:33 [j]Ps 83:10; Jer 9:22 [k]Ps 79:1-3; Jer 15:3; 34:20
16:6 [l]Eze 9:5-6 [m]Lev 19:28 [n]Jer 41:5; 47:5
16:7 [o]Eze 24:17; Hos 9:4

You are long-suffering—do not take me away;
think of how I suffer reproach for your sake.[v]
16 When your words came, I ate[w] them;
they were my joy and my heart's delight,[x]
for I bear your name,[y]
O LORD God Almighty.
17 I never sat[z] in the company of revelers,
never made merry with them;
I sat alone because your hand was on me
and you had filled me with indignation.
18 Why is my pain unending
and my wound grievous and incurable?[a]
Will you be to me like a deceptive brook,
like a spring that fails?[b]

19 Therefore this is what the LORD says:

"If you repent, I will restore you
that you may serve[c] me;
if you utter worthy, not worthless, words,
you will be my spokesman.
Let this people turn to you,
but you must not turn to them.
20 I will make you a wall to this people,
a fortified wall of bronze;
they will fight against you
but will not overcome you,
for I am with you
to rescue and save you,"[d]
declares the LORD.

21 "I will save you from the hands of the wicked
and redeem[e] you from the grasp of the cruel."[f]

Day of Disaster

16 Then the word of the LORD came to me: 2 "You must not marry[g] and have sons
or daughters in this place." 3 For this is what the LORD says about the sons and
daughters born in this land and about the women who are their mothers and the men
who are their fathers:[h] 4 "They will die of deadly diseases. They will not be mourned or
buried[i] but will be like refuse lying on the ground.[j] They will perish by sword and famine, and their dead bodies will become food for the birds of the air and the beasts of the
earth."[k]
5 For this is what the LORD says: "Do not enter a house where there is a funeral meal;
do not go to mourn or show sympathy, because I have withdrawn my blessing, my love
and my pity from this people," declares the LORD. 6 "Both high and low will die in this
land.[l] They will not be buried or mourned, and no one will cut[m] himself or shave[n] his
head for them. 7 No one will offer food to comfort those who mourn[o] for the dead—not
even for a father or a mother—nor will anyone give them a drink to console them.

15:16 your words . . . I ate them. This is the sweet side of the bitter-sweet task of receiving God's words (see Eze 3:1–3). **I bear your name.** This is stated of the people in 14:9.
15:17 I sat alone. No doubt this was literally true, partly due to Jeremiah's celibacy (16:2). But there would also have been a profound sense of loneliness for the unwelcome prophet. Compare Elijah (1Ki 19:10) and Jesus (Mt 26:37–38). **your hand was on me.** The compulsion to prophesy was often crushing.
15:18 wound . . . incurable? The wound is Judah's in 14:17. The whole phrase is applied to Judah in 30:12, together with a promise of healing (vv. 16–17). See also 10:19, where it is used of Jeremiah. **a deceptive brook.** Contrast 2:13 and compare 20:7.
15:19–21 God responded to Jeremiah, assuring him of deliverance but warning him to repent of his own sins.
15:21 I will save you . . . the cruel. The promise of Jeremiah's deliverance was a foretaste of Judah's. This has been an important function of the "confession" (see "Introduction: Purpose and Distinctives"), coupled with the Lord's responses.
■ **16:1—17:18** *Symbols of Coming Judgment.* Jeremiah was prohibited from taking part in some normal activities in order to symbolize the coming judgment (16:1–18). His prayer and the divine response drew a sharp contrast between the destinies of those who trusted in human beings and those who trusted in God (16:19—17:18).
■ **16:1–18** *Symbolic Actions.* God commanded Jeremiah to refrain from marriage, funeral meals and feasts in order to symbolize the imminence and severity of the coming judgment.
16:2 You must not marry. The prohibition was related exclusively to Jeremiah's role as a foreteller of Judah's fate. His celibacy entailed childlessness (see 1Co 7:26). **in this place.** The prophet's lack of offspring was a sign, especially for Judah and Jerusalem.
16:3–4 The sign of childlessness implied that there would be no future for the next generation. **deadly diseases.** Contrast Deuteronomy 7:15. **not be . . . buried.** See note on 7:33. **refuse.** See 8:2. **sword and famine.** See 14:12.
16:5 Do not . . . a funeral meal. It was customary to extend mourning by providing meals for those who attended the funeral services.
16:7 offer food . . . give them a drink to console them. This relates to a mourning custom, perhaps especially pertaining to the death of parents.

8"And do not enter a house where there is feasting and sit down to eat and drink.[p]
9For this is what the LORD Almighty, the God of Israel, says: Before your eyes and in your
days I will bring an end to the sounds[q] of joy and gladness and to the voices of bride and
bridegroom in this place.[r]

10"When you tell these people all this and they ask you, 'Why has the LORD decreed
such a great disaster against us? What wrong have we done? What sin have we committed against the LORD our God?'[s] 11then say to them, 'It is because your fathers forsook me,'
declares the LORD, 'and followed other gods and served and worshiped them. They forsook
me and did not keep my law.[t] 12But you have behaved more wickedly than your fathers.[u]
See how each of you is following the stubbornness of his evil heart[v] instead of obeying me.
13So I will throw you out of this land into a land neither you nor your fathers have
known,[w] and there you will serve other gods[x] day and night, for I will show you no favor.'[y]

14"However, the days are coming," declares the LORD, "when men will no longer say,
'As surely as the LORD lives, who brought the Israelites up out of Egypt,'[z] 15but they will
say, 'As surely as the LORD lives, who brought the Israelites up out of the land of the north
and out of all the countries where he had banished them.'[a] For I will restore[b] them to
the land I gave their forefathers.

16"But now I will send for many fishermen," declares the LORD, "and they will catch
them.[c] After that I will send for many hunters, and they will hunt[d] them down on every
mountain and hill and from the crevices of the rocks.[e] 17My eyes are on all their ways; they
are not hidden[f] from me, nor is their sin concealed from my eyes.[g] 18I will repay them double[h] for their wickedness and their sin, because they have defiled my land[i] with the lifeless forms of their vile images and have filled my inheritance with their detestable idols."

19O LORD, my strength and my fortress,
my refuge in time of distress,
to you the nations will come[j]
from the ends of the earth and say,
"Our fathers possessed nothing but false gods,[k]
worthless idols that did them no good.
20Do men make their own gods?
Yes, but they are not gods!"[l]

21"Therefore I will teach them—
this time I will teach them
my power and might.
Then they will know
that my name is the LORD.

17

"Judah's sin is engraved with an iron tool,[m]
inscribed with a flint point,
on the tablets of their hearts[n]
and on the horns of their altars.

16:8 [p]Ecc 7:2-4; Jer 15:17
16:9 [q]Isa 24:8; Eze 26:13; Hos 2:11 [r]Rev 18:23
16:10 [s]Dt 29:24; Jer 5:19
16:11 [t]Dt 29:25-26; 1Ki 9:9; Ps 106:35-43; Jer 22:9
16:12 [u]Jer 7:26 [v]Ecc 9:3; Jer 13:10
16:13 [w]Dt 28:36; Jer 5:19 [x]Dt 4:28 [y]Jer 15:5
16:14 [z]Dt 15:15; Jer 23:7-8
16:15 [a]Isa 11:11; Jer 23:8 [b]Jer 24:6
16:16 [c]Am 4:2; Hab 1:14-15 [d]Am 9:3; Mic 7:2 [e]1Sa 26:20
16:17 [f]1Co 4:5; Heb 4:13 [g]Pr 15:3
16:18 [h]Isa 40:2; Rev 18:6 [i]Nu 35:34; Jer 2:7
16:19 [j]Isa 2:2; Jer 3:17 [k]Ps 4:2
16:20 [l]Ps 115:4-7; Isa 37:19; Jer 2:11
17:1 [m]Job 19:24 [n]Pr 3:3; 2Co 3:3

16:8 do not enter . . . feasting. Yet a third prohibition was given, symbolizing the fact that Judah was not in a time in her history when she should have been celebrating.
16:9 bring an end . . . bride and bridegroom. Sounds typical of a period of peace and hope (see Mt 24:38–39; cf. Jer 33:10–11; see also 7:34).
16:12 more wickedly than your fathers. Although the present generation shared guilt with its forefathers (14:20), it was responsible for its own sin (31:29–30; Eze 18:2–4).
16:13 throw you out of this land. That is, send them into exile (see Dt 28:36,64). **serve other gods.** Through a punishment appropriate to their crime, they would finally discover their own hollowness.
16:14–16 The prophet contrasted the praise of God for his past mercy in bringing Israel out of captivity in Egypt with the greater praise he would receive after returning his people from exile. This return to the land would be greater than the first return in the days of Moses, though Jeremiah did not at this point provide supporting details for this assertion. He later specified that in the ideal restoration the people would never again fall into sin (see notes on 31:31–34).
16:16 But now. See "the days are coming" in verse 14. This referred to the relatively distant future, when a restoration would take place. But the immediate prospect was of exile. **fishermen . . . hunters.** Judah is pictured as the prey of the Lord. **every mountain and hill . . . crevices of the rocks.** There would be no escape (23:24; Isa 2:19).
16:18 double. See 17:18 and Isaiah 40:2. The exile was an appropriate punishment for the sins of the people.
■ **16:19—17:18** *Prayers and Response.* This passage begins and ends with Jeremiah's prayers (16:19–20; 17:12–18), with God's response in between (16:21—17:11).
16:19–20 The prophet acknowledged his own allegiance to God and the future conversion of the Gentile nations. See *BC* 26.
16:19 my . . . my . . . my. The prophet spoke of himself in contrast with the rest of the nation. **nations will come.** Jeremiah affirmed the hope that after the exile Gentiles would come to the Lord in large numbers (see notes on 15:12).
16:21—17:11 The Lord responded to the prophet's prayerful affirmation in the previous section.
16:21 teach . . . teach . . . know. In Hebrew, these are forms of the same word. Judah could not know unless the Lord taught her (cf. 31:18). **know that my name is the LORD.** This implies not only factual but also experiential knowledge, which the Judahites would have when they witnessed God acting in the exile and restoration.
17:1 on the tablets of their hearts. This recalls tablets for writing laws. Judah's sin had become so great that it had reached the hearts of God's people. By contrast, in 31:33 the law, rather than sin, would be written on the hearts of God's people when the restoration from exile occurred. See Proverbs 3:3 and 7:3. **on the horns of their altars.** These should have commemorated atonement for sin, but instead they would only call the sin to the Lord's mind.

[2] Even their children remember
their altars and Asherah poles[a] [o]
beside the spreading trees
and on the high hills.[p]
[3] My mountain in the land
and your[b] wealth and all your treasures
I will give away as plunder,[q]
together with your high places,[r]
because of sin throughout your country.[s]
[4] Through your own fault you will lose
the inheritance[t] I gave you.
I will enslave you to your enemies[u]
in a land[v] you do not know,
for you have kindled my anger,
and it will burn[w] forever."

[5] This is what the LORD says:

"Cursed is the one who trusts in man,[x]
who depends on flesh for his strength
and whose heart turns away from the LORD.
[6] He will be like a bush in the wastelands;
he will not see prosperity when it comes.
He will dwell in the parched places of the desert,
in a salt[y] land where no one lives.

[7] "But blessed is the man who trusts[z] in the LORD,
whose confidence is in him.
[8] He will be like a tree planted by the water
that sends out its roots by the stream.
It does not fear when heat comes;
its leaves are always green.
It has no worries in a year of drought[a]
and never fails to bear fruit."[b]

[9] The heart[c] is deceitful above all things
and beyond cure.
Who can understand it?

[10] "I the LORD search the heart[d]
and examine the mind,[e]
to reward[f] a man according to his conduct,
according to what his deeds deserve."[g]

[11] Like a partridge that hatches eggs it did not lay
is the man who gains riches by unjust means.
When his life is half gone, they will desert him,
and in the end he will prove to be a fool.[h]

[12] A glorious throne,[i] exalted from the beginning,
is the place of our sanctuary.

17:2 [o]2Ch 24:18 [p]Jer 2:20
17:3 [q]2Ki 24:13 [r]Jer 26:18; Mic 3:12 [s]Jer 15:13
17:4 [t]La 5:2 [u]Dt 28:48; Jer 12:7 [v]Jer 16:13 [w]Jer 7:20; 15:14
17:5 [x]Isa 2:22; 30:1-3
17:6 [y]Dt 29:23; Job 39:6
17:7 [z]Ps 34:8; 40:4; Pr 16:20
17:8 [a]Jer 14:1-6 [b]Ps 1:3; 92:12-14
17:9 [c]Ecc 9:3; Mt 13:15; Mk 7:21-22
17:10 [d]1Sa 16:7; Rev 2:23 [e]Ps 17:3; 139:23; Jer 11:20; 20:12; Ro 8:27 [f]Ps 62:12; Jer 32:19 [g]Ro 2:6
17:11 [h]Lk 12:20
17:12 [i]Jer 3:17

[a] *2* That is, symbols of the goddess Asherah [b] *2,3* Or *hills* / [3]*and the mountains of the land. / Your*

17:2 their altars and Asherah poles. See Exodus 34:13 and Deuteronomy 7:5. **spreading trees . . . high hills.** See 2:20.
17:3 My mountain. Mount Zion, the home of the temple, was plundered by Nebuchadnezzar (52:17–23).
17:4 the inheritance I gave you. The promised land. See 2:7.
17:5–8 See *HC* 125.
17:5 Cursed. See 11:3. The curse came in the context of the breach of covenant loyalty. See *WLC* 105; *BC* 26; *HC* 94.
17:6 prosperity. Literally, "good"; i.e., full life and all the requisite means of its support (15:11; Dt 6:24). **salt land.** See Deuteronomy 29:23, where this is a curse.
17:7 trusts . . . confidence. These two words are based on the same Hebrew word. The Lord repays trust because he is by nature trustworthy (Isa 7:9). The close similarity between verses 7–8 and Psalm 1:1–3 suggests that trust in the Lord must be guided by his law (Jas 2:17). See *BC* 26; *HC* 94.
17:8 a tree planted by the water. A potent symbol of strength in a dry land (Ps 1:3; Isa 44:4).
17:9 The heart. In the Old Testament this signifies more than the seat of emotion, representing the deepest recesses of the inner person and the basis of character, embracing the mind, will and emotions (4:19; see note on Pr 2:2). See *WCF* 6.2; *HC* 5; *CD* 3–4.III.
17:10 search . . . examine. See 9:7 and compare 11:20. **mind.** Literally, "kidneys." This word is translated "hearts" in 12:2. The two terms here are parallel.
17:11 The verse consists of two proverbs found in 8:4 and 7. **Like a partridge . . . means.** The proverb tellingly reveals the real hurt of injustice. See Nathan's rebuke of David in 2 Samuel 12:1–7. **When his life . . . fool.** On the transience of riches, see Proverbs 23:4–5.
17:12–18 Jeremiah cried to God once again because of the trials he faced when serving as a faithful prophet. This is the fourth of Jeremiah's "confessions" (see note on 11:18–23).

13 O LORD, the hope[j] of Israel,
all who forsake[k] you will be put to shame.
Those who turn away from you will be written in the dust
because they have forsaken the LORD,
the spring of living water.

14 Heal me, O LORD, and I will be healed;
save me and I will be saved,
for you are the one I praise.[l]
15 They keep saying to me,
"Where is the word of the LORD?
Let it now be fulfilled!"[m]
16 I have not run away from being your shepherd;
you know I have not desired the day of despair.
What passes my lips is open before you.
17 Do not be a terror[n] to me;
you are my refuge[o] in the day of disaster.
18 Let my persecutors be put to shame,
but keep me from shame;
let them be terrified,
but keep me from terror.
Bring on them the day of disaster;
destroy them with double destruction.[p]

Keeping the Sabbath Holy

19 This is what the LORD said to me: "Go and stand at the gate of the people, through
which the kings of Judah go in and out; stand also at all the other gates of Jerusalem.[q] 20 Say
to them, 'Hear the word of the LORD, O kings of Judah and all people of Judah and everyone living in Jerusalem[r] who come through these gates.[s] 21 This is what the LORD says: Be
careful not to carry a load on the Sabbath[t] day or bring it through the gates of Jerusalem.
22 Do not bring a load out of your houses or do any work on the Sabbath, but keep the Sabbath day holy, as I commanded your forefathers.[u] 23 Yet they did not listen or pay attention;[v] they were stiff-necked[w] and would not listen or respond to discipline.[x] 24 But if you
are careful to obey me, declares the LORD, and bring no load through the gates of this city
on the Sabbath, but keep the Sabbath day holy by not doing any work on it, 25 then kings
who sit on David's throne[y] will come through the gates of this city with their officials. They
and their officials will come riding in chariots and on horses, accompanied by the men of
Judah and those living in Jerusalem, and this city will be inhabited forever. 26 People will
come from the towns of Judah and the villages around Jerusalem, from the territory of Benjamin and the western foothills, from the hill country and the Negev,[z] bringing burnt offerings and sacrifices, grain offerings, incense and thank offerings to the house of the LORD.
27 But if you do not obey[a] me to keep the Sabbath day holy by not carrying any load as you
come through the gates of Jerusalem on the Sabbath day, then I will kindle an unquenchable fire[b] in the gates of Jerusalem that will consume her fortresses.'"[c]

17:13 [j]Jer 14:8 [k]Isa 1:28; Jer 2:17
17:14 [l]Ps 109:1
17:15 [m]Isa 5:19; 2Pe 3:4
17:17 [n]Ps 88:15-16 [o]Jer 16:19; Na 1:7
17:18 [p]Ps 35:1-8
17:19 [q]Jer 7:2; 26:2
17:20 [r]Jer 19:3 [s]Jer 22:2
17:21 [t]Nu 15:32-36; Ne 13:15-21; Jn 5:10
17:22 [u]Ex 20:8; 31:13; Isa 56:2-6; Eze 20:12
17:23 [v]Jer 7:26 [w]Jer 19:15 [x]Jer 7:28
17:25 [y]2Sa 7:13; Isa 9:7; Jer 22:2,4; Lk 1:32
17:26 [z]Jer 32:44; 33:13; Zec 7:7
17:27 [a]Jer 22:5 [b]Jer 7:20 [c]2Ki 25:9; Am 2:5

17:12 A glorious throne. See note on 14:21 and compare Psalm 99:1. **from the beginning.** This implies that Zion had been chosen as God's throne even before Solomon's temple had been constructed (cf. Ex 15:17).
17:13 the hope of Israel. See 14:8 and 22. The juxtaposition of this thought with the celebration of the temple in verse 12 may imply that hope was to be placed only in God, not in the temple. **written in the dust.** Literally, "earth." Sometimes this indicates either the underworld or death (Job 7:21). Contrast the thought of Exodus 32:32. **spring of living water.** Contrast 15:18.
17:15 Where is the word of the LORD? Jeremiah's enemies accused him of being a false prophet. This allegation presumably was made prior to the first Babylonian invasion in 605 B.C. (Dt 18:21–22). After the invasion Jeremiah would not have been so easily dismissed. See Micah 7:10 and 2 Peter 3:4.
17:18 terrified . . . terror. Prayer for his enemies' discomfiture is typical of the "confessions" of Jeremiah (11:20; 12:3; 15:15; see "Introduction: Purpose and Distinctives"). The terms here are reminiscent of his call (1:17). **double.** See 16:18 for an application of this term to Judah's punishment. Here it applies to the punishment of Jeremiah's enemies. See Isaiah 40:2 and its note.
■ **17:19–27** *A Sermon About the Sabbath.* Jeremiah exhorted the people to keep the Sabbath holy, making it clear that disobedience in this matter would bring utter destruction to Jerusalem. Why this sermon is placed here is uncertain. It may serve as background to the events of the next section, which concentrates on God's judgment against the temple and its personnel (18:1—20:18).
17:19 gate of the people. This is possibly a temple gate (as in 7:2), although the message is to be repeated at the city gates ("the other gates").
17:20–26 See *WLC* 117,118,119,121; *WSC* 61.
17:20 who come through these gates. The message is given at the gates because of their role in commerce (see Ne 13:15,19).
17:21 carry a load. The prophet spoke of doing commerce on the Sabbath, not simply of lifting objects. The Sabbath had been turned into a day of intense commerce in the city.
17:22 keep the Sabbath day holy . . . forefathers. Specific appeal was made to the Sabbath commandment (Ex 20:8–11; Dt 5:12–15; Ne 10:31; Isa 56:2).
17:25–26 This is a picture (partly repeated in 22:4) of what would happen if the people would observe the Sabbath properly. See also 23:5–6, 30:9 and 33:14–26. All that was threatened for Judah could therefore have been reversed.
17:27 gates. In the case of failure to obey, the center of the Sabbath breach would be the first to be destroyed. **kindle an unquenchable fire . . . fortresses.** Compare Amos 1:4, 7 and 10. See *WLC* 119.

At the Potter's House

18 This is the word that came to Jeremiah from the LORD: 2"Go down to the potter's house, and there I will give you my message." 3So I went down to the potter's house, and I saw him working at the wheel. 4But the pot he was shaping from the clay was marred in his hands; so the potter formed it into another pot, shaping it as seemed best to him.

5Then the word of the LORD came to me: 6"O house of Israel, can I not do with you as this potter does?" declares the LORD. "Like clay[d] in the hand of the potter, so are you in my hand, O house of Israel. 7If at any time I announce that a nation or kingdom is to be uprooted,[e] torn down and destroyed, 8and if that nation I warned repents of its evil, then I will relent[f] and not inflict on it the disaster[g] I had planned. 9And if at another time I announce that a nation or kingdom is to be built[h] up and planted, 10and if it does evil[i] in my sight and does not obey me, then I will reconsider[j] the good I had intended to do for it.

11"Now therefore say to the people of Judah and those living in Jerusalem, 'This is what the LORD says: Look! I am preparing a disaster[k] for you and devising a plan against you. So turn[l] from your evil ways,[m] each one of you, and reform your ways and your actions.' 12But they will reply, 'It's no use.[n] We will continue with our own plans; each of us will follow the stubbornness of his evil heart.' "

13Therefore this is what the LORD says:

"Inquire among the nations:
  Who has ever heard anything like this?[o]
A most horrible[p] thing has been done
  by Virgin Israel.
14Does the snow of Lebanon
  ever vanish from its rocky slopes?
Do its cool waters from distant sources
  ever cease to flow?[a]
15Yet my people have forgotten me;
  they burn incense to worthless idols,[q]
which made them stumble in their ways
  and in the ancient paths.[r]
They made them walk in bypaths
  and on roads not built up.[s]
16Their land will be laid waste,[t]
  an object of lasting scorn;[u]
all who pass by will be appalled
  and will shake their heads.[v]
17Like a wind[w] from the east,

18:6 [d]Isa 45:9; Ro 9:20-21
18:7 [e]Jer 1:10
18:8 [f]Jer 26:13; Jnh 3:8-10 [g]Eze 18:21; Hos 11:8-9
18:9 [h]Jer 1:10; 31:28
18:10 [i]Eze 33:18 [j]1Sa 2:29-30
18:11 [k]Jer 4:6 [l]2Ki 17:13; Isa 1:16-19 [m]Jer 7:3
18:12 [n]Isa 57:10; Jer 2:25
18:13 [o]Isa 66:8; Jer 2:10 [p]Jer 5:30
18:15 [q]Jer 10:15 [r]Jer 6:16 [s]Isa 57:14; 62:10
18:16 [t]Jer 25:9 [u]Jer 19:8 [v]Ps 22:7
18:17 [w]Jer 13:24

[a] *14* The meaning of the Hebrew for this sentence is uncertain.

■ **18:1—20:18** *The Divine Potter.* This material centers on the theme of the Lord acting as a potter. It divides into five parts: Jeremiah's lesson at the potter's house (18:1–17), attacks against Jeremiah (18:18–23), his symbolic act of breaking a pot (19:1–15), more persecution from opponents (20:1–6) and Jeremiah's lament to God (20:7–18).

■ **18:1–17** *At the Potter's House.* In this section Jeremiah learned a lesson about God's dealings with Israel and other nations by observing the work of a potter.

18:2 the potter's house. Apparently this was in the Hinnom Valley, which was near (appropriately) the Potsherd Gate (19:2), hence the command to "go down." See also 7:31.

18:3 wheel. Actually there were two stone wheels on an upright shaft. See the non-canonical book of Ecclesiasticus (38:29–30) for a description of its method.

18:4 marred. See 13:7 for the "ruin" (same Hebrew word) of the linen belt. **as seemed best to him.** The potter had autonomy with respect to his craft. The spoiling of his first attempt was not necessarily final.

18:6 O house of Israel. The analogy with Israel follows. The use of the term "Israel" recalls God's historic purposes of election for the whole people (to which Judah was now heir).

18:7–10 The point of the potter illustration: If the Lord announces his intention to punish or bless a nation, that purpose may be revoked by the nation's response. Judgments and blessings may be reversed, lessened or postponed (see Ex 32:14; Jdg 10:8–18; 2Ch 12:1–12; Jnh 3:10). The potter's (God's) change of intentions based on repentance does not contradict the immutability of his divine decrees (see "Introduction to the Prophetic Books"). This passage does not speak of eternal, divine decrees but of God's providential interactions with historical events that take place "necessarily, freely, or contingently" (*WCF* 5.2). God's intent to destroy or to bless is part of his eternal plan; the repentance or rebellion of the people and the providential change of divine intention is also included in the immutable plan of God (see theological article "Providence" on next page). See *WLC* 99.

18:11–12 The prophet's hope was that the people would hear that repentance could reverse the anticipated judgment, but he had experienced enough of their reactions to realize that they would only harden themselves and thus condemn themselves to judgment.

18:13 most horrible thing. A strong term used for idolatry (cf. 5:30).

18:14 Does the snow . . . cease to flow? Jeremiah used a further argument from nature. See 8:4 and 7; see also 17:11 and its note.

18:15 Yet my people have forgotten me. Compare 2:32. **burn incense.** See note on 11:12. **ancient paths . . . bypaths . . . roads not built up.** See note on 6:16. The metaphor is sustained here, for "bypaths" could refer to dangerous roads.

Providence: Who Is in Control of the World?

REFORMED theology is often confused with fatalism because it has emphasized that God has foreordained everything that comes to pass (*WCF* 3.1). To many observers, prayer, evangelism, and human choices in general seem to have no genuine significance because God's immutable and eternal decrees have already established everything that will happen. In reality, however, Reformed theology has always affirmed the importance of prayer, evangelism and human choices of every kind because it understands God's control of the world from two perspectives. The first is the well-known view from the angle of his eternal, sovereign decrees of foreordination, but the second is just as important: the perspective of providence.

God did not just create a universe that would necessarily play out precisely as he had eternally decreed. Rather, he formed a cosmos in which he could interact with his creation. It is true that God foreordained even his own involvement with creation, as well as every means to every end, but this does not make his involvement or these means any less real or necessary. It is God's interaction with creation at every moment of history that Reformed theologians refer to as "providence." As the *Westminster Confession of Faith* puts it,

> God the great Creator of all things doth uphold, direct, dispose, and govern all creatures, actions, and things, from the greatest even to the least, by His most wise and holy providence, according to His infallible foreknowledge, and the free and immutable counsel of His own will (*WCF* 5.1).

In creation God exercised his divine power to cause the world to be; in providence he continues to exercise that same power to sustain all creation, to involve himself in all events and to direct all things to their appointed ends.

Other Christian traditions have diminished the significance of divine providence by suggesting that God merely foreknows rather than controls, that he upholds indirectly without becoming intimately involved and that he manages only general directions rather than specific details of history. Yet the evidence of Scripture is clear about the nature and extent of divine providence. Louis Berkhof summarized God's present governance of creation as follows:

> The Bible clearly teaches God's providential control (1) over the universe at large, Ps 103:19; Da 4:35; Eph 1:11; (2) over the physical world, Job 37; Pss 104:14; 135:6; Mt 5:45; (3) over the brute creation, Ps 104:21,28; Mt 6:26; 10:29; (4) over the affairs of nations, Job 12:23; Ps 22:28; 66:7; Ac 17:26; (5) over man's birth and lot in life, 1Sa 16:1; Ps 139:16; Isa 45:5; Gal 1:15,16; (6) over the outward successes and failures of men's lives, Ps 75:6,7; Lk 1:52; (7) over things seemingly accidental or insignificant, Pr 16:33; Mt 10:30; (8) in the protection of the righteous, Pss 4:8; 5:12; 63:8; 121:3; Ro 8:28; (9) in supplying the wants of God's people, Ge 22:8,14; Dt 8:3; Php 4:19; (10) in giving answers to prayer, 1 Sa 1:19; Isa 20:5,6; 2 Ch 33:13; Ps 65:2; Mt 7:7; Lk 18:7,8; and (11) in the exposure and punishment of the wicked, Pss 7:12,13; 11:6. (L. Berkhof, *Systematic Theology* [Grand Rapids: Wm. B. Eerdmans Publishing Co., 1996], p. 168)

Divine providence controls even morally evil events. In this regard, however, Reformed theology has added a number of qualifications: (1) while God permits moral evil, he does not directly author it (Ac 14:16); (2) God punishes evil with evil (Ps 81:11–12; Ro 1:26–32); (3) God brings good out of evil (Ge 50:20; Ac 2:23; 4:27–28; 13:27); (4) God uses evil to test and discipline those he loves (Mt 4:1–11; Heb 12:4–14); and (5) one day God will redeem his people from the power and presence of evil altogether (Rev 21:27; 22:14–15).

Although God is in absolute, sovereign control over all things, Reformed theology has also affirmed the significance of human choice by emphasizing that God's providence is a wonderfully varied reality. In the first place, God interacts with different aspects of his creation according to their specific natures. He deals differently with volitional creatures such as angels and human beings than he does with creatures that have no will and with inanimate creation. For instance, God accomplishes many of his plans through the means of human choice, but he simply manipulates rocks and trees. In the second place, God varies his providential involvement in the world so that he ordinarily makes use of second (created) causes such as human actions, even though he also acts without, above and against created causes (*WCF* 5.3), as in miracles and other cases where he overrides the normal workings of the universe. In the third place, as God works out his sovereign plan in history he orders the interactions of created causes in different ways (*WCF* 5.2). Some events are necessary, the direct and inevitable results of other events. Some events take place freely, with no apparent necessity in the created order. Still other events occur contingently, in that the choices of human beings and angels have effects on the course of history, such as when God brings things to pass in response to our obedience or disobedience. These instances in no way diminish the doctrine of divine providence but rather stress the significance of human activities such as prayer and evangelism.

The doctrine of providence is a precious truth of Scripture for believers. It teaches us that we are never in the grip of blind forces (fortune, chance, luck, fate), but always in the hands of our loving, merciful heavenly Father. Each event comes as a new summons to trust, obey and rejoice, with the sure knowledge that everything that happens to us and through us is for our eternal good (Ro 8:28).

18:17 [x]Jer 2:27
18:18 [y]Jer 11:19 [z]Mal 2:7 [a]Jer 5:13 [b]Ps 52:2
18:20 [c]Ps 35:7; 57:6 [d]Ps 106:23
18:21 [e]Jer 11:22 [f]Ps 109:9
18:22 [g]Jer 6:26 [h]Ps 140:5
18:23 [i]Jer 11:21 [j]Ps 109:14
19:1 [k]Jer 18:2 [l]Nu 11:17
19:2 [m]Jos 15:8
19:3 [n]Jer 17:20 [o]Jer 6:19 [p]1Sa 3:11
19:4 [q]Dt 28:20; Isa 65:11 [r]Lev 18:21 [s]2Ki 21:16; Jer 2:34
19:5 [t]Lev 18:21; Ps 106:37-38 [u]Jer 7:31; 32:35
19:6 [v]Jos 15:8 [w]Jer 7:32
19:7 [x]Lev 26:17; Dt 28:25 [y]Jer 16:4; 34:20 [z]Ps 79:2
19:8 [a]Jer 18:16
19:9 [b]Lev 26:29; Dt 28:49-57; La 4:10

I will scatter them before their enemies;
I will show them my back and not my face[x]
in the day of their disaster."

18 They said, "Come, let's make plans[y] against Jeremiah; for the teaching of the law
by the priest[z] will not be lost, nor will counsel from the wise, nor the word from the
prophets.[a] So come, let's attack him with our tongues[b] and pay no attention to anything
he says."

19 Listen to me, O LORD;
hear what my accusers are saying!
20 Should good be repaid with evil?
Yet they have dug a pit[c] for me.
Remember that I stood before you
and spoke in their behalf[d]
to turn your wrath away from them.
21 So give their children over to famine;[e]
hand them over to the power of the sword.
Let their wives be made childless and widows;[f]
let their men be put to death,
their young men slain by the sword in battle.
22 Let a cry[g] be heard from their houses
when you suddenly bring invaders against them,
for they have dug a pit to capture me
and have hidden snares[h] for my feet.
23 But you know, O LORD,
all their plots to kill[i] me.
Do not forgive[j] their crimes
or blot out their sins from your sight.
Let them be overthrown before you;
deal with them in the time of your anger.

19 This is what the LORD says: "Go and buy a clay jar from a potter.[k] Take along
some of the elders[l] of the people and of the priests 2 and go out to the Valley of
Ben Hinnom,[m] near the entrance of the Potsherd Gate. There proclaim the words I tell
you, 3 and say, 'Hear the word of the LORD, O kings[n] of Judah and people of Jerusalem.
This is what the LORD Almighty, the God of Israel, says: Listen! I am going to bring a disaster[o] on this place that will make the ears of everyone who hears of it tingle.[p] 4 For they
have forsaken[q] me and made this a place of foreign gods; they have burned sacrifices[r]
in it to gods that neither they nor their fathers nor the kings of Judah ever knew, and they
have filled this place with the blood of the innocent.[s] 5 They have built the high places
of Baal to burn their sons[t] in the fire as offerings to Baal—something I did not command
or mention, nor did it enter my mind.[u] 6 So beware, the days are coming, declares the
LORD, when people will no longer call this place Topheth or the Valley of Ben Hinnom,[v]
but the Valley of Slaughter.[w]
7 " 'In this place I will ruin[a] the plans of Judah and Jerusalem. I will make them fall by
the sword before their enemies,[x] at the hands of those who seek their lives, and I will give
their carcasses[y] as food[z] to the birds of the air and the beasts of the earth. 8 I will devastate this city and make it an object of scorn;[a] all who pass by will be appalled and will
scoff because of all its wounds. 9 I will make them eat[b] the flesh of their sons and daugh-

a 7 The Hebrew for *ruin* sounds like the Hebrew for *jar* (see verses 1 and 10).

18:17 wind from the east. Compare 4:11. **my back and not my face.** See Exodus 33:23 and its note. The meaning here, however, is a withholding of favor, the opposite of finding the face of God (see 2Ch 7:14).

■ **18:18–23** *Opposition to Jeremiah.* This is the fifth of Jeremiah's "confessions" (see note on 11:18–23). He lamented the opposition he had endured and would continue to endure for telling the truth to Judah.

18:20 good be repaid with evil? Compare Psalm 35:12 and 1 Peter 2:19–24. **dug a pit.** Symbolic of a murderous intention (v. 22). See Jeremiah's actual experiences in 37:16 and 38:6. **stood before you . . . their behalf.** See note on 15:1.

18:21 famine . . . sword . . . death. This is the typical judgment triad (14:12), since "death" probably means "plague" here. Jeremiah called for the announced judgment to fall on his own enemies.

18:22 pit. See verse 20 and its note. **snares.** Compare Psalms 140:5 and 141:9.

■ **19:1–15** *Symbolic Breaking of Pot.* God instructed Jeremiah to buy and destroy a pot to illustrate the destruction that was coming to Jerusalem and the temple.

19:2 Valley of Ben Hinnom. See 18:2. **Potsherd Gate.** The gate led out of the city to the south. Possibly the Dung Gate (Ne 2:13).

19:3 a disaster . . . make the ears . . . tingle. The words closely resemble 2 Kings 21:12, a passage which also concerns the Babylonian judgment on Judah and Jerusalem. The public character of the judgment is in view.

ters, and they will eat one another’s flesh during the stress of the siege imposed on them
by the enemies[c] who seek their lives.’
10“Then break the jar[d] while those who go with you are watching, 11and say to them,
‘This is what the LORD Almighty says: I will smash[e] this nation and this city just as this
potter’s jar is smashed and cannot be repaired. They will bury[f] the dead in Topheth until there is no more room. 12This is what I will do to this place and to those who live here,
declares the LORD. I will make this city like Topheth. 13The houses[g] in Jerusalem and
those of the kings of Judah will be defiled like this place, Topheth—all the houses where
they burned incense on the roofs to all the starry hosts[h] and poured out drink offerings[i]
to other gods.’ ”
14Jeremiah then returned from Topheth, where the LORD had sent him to prophesy,
and stood in the court[j] of the LORD’s temple and said to all the people, 15“This is what
the LORD Almighty, the God of Israel, says: ‘Listen! I am going to bring on this city and
the villages around it every disaster I pronounced against them, because they were stiff-
necked[k] and would not listen to my words.’ ”

Jeremiah and Pashhur

20 When the priest Pashhur son of Immer,[l] the chief officer[m] in the temple of the
LORD, heard Jeremiah prophesying these things, 2he had Jeremiah the prophet
beaten[n] and put in the stocks[o] at the Upper Gate of Benjamin[p] at the LORD’s temple. 3The
next day, when Pashhur released him from the stocks, Jeremiah said to him, “The LORD’s
name for you is not Pashhur, but Magor-Missabib.[a][q] 4For this is what the LORD says: ‘I will
make you a terror to yourself and to all your friends; with your own eyes[r] you will see them
fall by the sword of their enemies. I will hand[s] all Judah over to the king of Babylon, who
will carry[t] them away to Babylon or put them to the sword. 5I will hand over to their enemies all the wealth[u] of this city—all its products, all its valuables and all the treasures
of the kings of Judah. They will take it away[v] as plunder and carry it off to Babylon. 6And
you, Pashhur, and all who live in your house will go into exile to Babylon. There you will
die and be buried, you and all your friends to whom you have prophesied[w] lies.’ ”

Jeremiah’s Complaint

7O LORD, you deceived[b] me, and I was deceived[b];
you overpowered me and prevailed.
I am ridiculed all day long;
everyone mocks me.
8Whenever I speak, I cry out
proclaiming violence and destruction.[x]
So the word of the LORD has brought me
insult and reproach[y] all day long.
9But if I say, “I will not mention him

19:9 [c]Isa 9:20
19:10 [d]ver 1
19:11 [e]Ps 2:9; Isa 30:14 [f]Jer 7:32
19:13 [g]Jer 32:29; 52:13 [h]Dt 4:19; Ac 7:42 [i]Jer 7:18; Eze 20:28
19:14 [j]2Ch 20:5; Jer 26:2
19:15 [k]Ne 9:16; Jer 7:26; 17:23
20:1 [l]1Ch 24:14 [m]2Ki 25:18
20:2 [n]Jer 1:19 [o]Job 13:27 [p]Jer 37:13; 38:7; Zec 14:10
20:3 [q]ver 10
20:4 [r]Jer 29:21 [s]Jer 21:10 [t]Jer 52:27
20:5 [u]Jer 17:3 [v]2Ki 20:17
20:6 [w]Jer 14:15; La 2:14
20:8 [x]Jer 6:7 [y]2Ch 36:16; Jer 6:10

[a] 3 *Magor-Missabib* means *terror on every side.* [b] 7 Or *persuaded*

19:9 eat the flesh . . . one another’s flesh. Cannibalism occurred during the siege of 586 B.C. (see La 2:20 and its note), as also earlier (2Ki 6:28–29) and in the Roman siege of Jerusalem in A.D. 70.
19:10 Then break the jar. This climax of the scene is another symbolic, prophetic action. See 13:1–11 and its notes. This jar, having set, was no longer malleable (contrast 18:4) and was fit only to be broken. See Psalm 2:9.
19:11 cannot be repaired. Judah, hardened in sin, could not be reshaped but could only be destroyed. **They will bury . . . no more room.** See 7:32.
19:13 defiled like this place. Josiah had defiled Topheth (2Ki 23:10). **on the roofs.** See 32:29 and 2 Kings 23:12. **starry hosts.** See 8:2 and its note; see also 2 Kings 23:4–5.
■ 20:1–6 *More Opposition to Jeremiah.* The priest (Pashhur) reacted strongly to Jeremiah’s symbolic act, and Jeremiah responded with further threats from God.
20:1 Pashhur. The name was apparently common. See 21:1 and 38:1—possibly each text referring to a different man. Note that senior priests had been among Jeremiah’s hearers in the valley (19:1); perhaps Pashhur had been among them. **chief officer.** See 29:26.
20:2 had Jeremiah . . . beaten. Perhaps in the line of his duty, as in 29:26 (see also Dt 25:2–3). The incident in 15:18 demonstrates that faithful prophetic preaching was dangerous (see Ge 3:15; 2Co 1:5–7; 2Ti 3:12). **the prophet.** This affirms Jeremiah’s status as a true prophet, despite the legal action against him.
20:3 Magor-Missabib. See 6:25. In Pashhur’s symbolic renaming he was likened to the enemies of Judah, since he represented Judah’s official rejection of the saving, prophetic word. See 26:7–9.
20:4 a terror to yourself and to all your friends. Pashhur intended his actions and so-called ministry to benefit Judah, but the actual outcome would be exile and death. **king of Babylon.** Nebuchadnezzar was perhaps already at the gates at the time of the first invasion of Judah in 605 B.C. (see “Introduction: Author” and “Time and Place of Writing”).
20:6 you and all your friends . . . lies. Pashhur was a false prophet (14:13). The punishment was that of the ruling classes in general (see 2Ki 24:14).
■ 20:7–18 *Jeremiah’s Lament.* This is the sixth of Jeremiah’s “confessions” (see note on 11:18–23). The prophet complained again about the opposition he faced as he brought God’s word to Judah. Although lament is a legitimate form of prayer (see “Introduction to Psalms”), here Jeremiah may have gone beyond the bounds of acceptable complaint before God. In any event, he was in utter despair because he had been so mistreated by his opponents.
20:7 deceived me . . . was deceived. This could be translated “persuaded” (see NIV text note). Jeremiah had not foreseen the trials that his task would bring, and he saw his call (especially perhaps 1:7–8) as an overpowering commission. See 4:10.
20:8 Whenever I speak . . . destruction. Jeremiah could not overcome the divine call to utter his message of coming wrath.
20:9 But if I say . . . in his name. This is an insight into Jeremiah’s profound reluctance. But the compulsion to speak apparently

20:9 [z]Ps 39:3 [a]Job 32:18-20; Ac 4:20

or speak any more in his name,"
his word is in my heart like a fire,[z]
a fire shut up in my bones.
I am weary of holding it in;[a]
indeed, I cannot.

20:10 [b]Ps 31:13; Jer 6:25 [c]Isa 29:21 [d]Ps 41:9 [e]Lk 11:53-54 [f]1Ki 19:2

10 I hear many whispering,
"Terror[b] on every side!
Report[c] him! Let's report him!"
All my friends[d]
are waiting for me to slip,[e] saying,
"Perhaps he will be deceived;
then we will prevail[f] over him
and take our revenge on him."

20:11 [g]Jer 1:8; Ro 8:31 [h]Jer 17:18 [i]Jer 15:20 [j]Jer 23:40

11 But the LORD[g] is with me like a mighty warrior;
so my persecutors[h] will stumble and not prevail.[i]
They will fail and be thoroughly disgraced;[j]
their dishonor will never be forgotten.

20:12 [k]Jer 17:10 [l]Ps 54:7; 59:10 [m]Ps 62:8; Jer 11:20

12 O LORD Almighty, you who examine the righteous
and probe the heart and mind,[k]
let me see your vengeance[l] upon them,
for to you I have committed[m] my cause.

20:13 [n]Ps 35:10

13 Sing to the LORD!
Give praise to the LORD!
He rescues[n] the life of the needy
from the hands of the wicked.

20:14 [o]Job 3:3; Jer 15:10

14 Cursed be the day I was born![o]
May the day my mother bore me not be blessed!
15 Cursed be the man who brought my father the news,
who made him very glad, saying,
"A child is born to you—a son!"

20:16 [p]Ge 19:25

16 May that man be like the towns[p]
the LORD overthrew without pity.
May he hear wailing in the morning,
a battle cry at noon.

20:17 [q]Job 10:18-19

17 For he did not kill me in the womb,[q]
with my mother as my grave,
her womb enlarged forever.
18 Why did I ever come out of the womb
to see trouble and sorrow
and to end my days in shame?[r]

20:18 [r]Ps 90:9

21:1 [s]2Ki 24:18; Jer 52:1 [t]Jer 38:1 [u]2Ki 25:18; Jer 29:25; 37:3

21:2 [v]Jer 37:3,7 [w]2Ki 25:1

God Rejects Zedekiah's Request

21 The word came to Jeremiah from the LORD when King Zedekiah[s] sent to him Pashhur[t] son of Malkijah and the priest Zephaniah[u] son of Maaseiah. They said: 2 "Inquire[v] now of the LORD for us because Nebuchadnezzar[a][w] king of Babylon is attack-

[a] 2 Hebrew *Nebuchadrezzar,* of which *Nebuchadnezzar* is a variant; here and often in Jeremiah and Ezekiel

exerted a physical pressure he could not resist (see Am 3:8; 1Co 9:16; 2Co 5:14).

20:16 the towns . . . overthrew. Sodom and Gomorrah, already used proverbially (Isa 1:9; Am 4:11).

20:17 in the womb . . . mother as my grave. In expressing the wish that he had been stillborn, Jeremiah indicated his extreme displeasure at having to deliver God's message of judgment and bemoaned the suffering inflicted on him by his people in response to his prophecies (vv. 7–10). This monstrous thought (continued in v. 18) violently strikes against the appointment he received before birth (1:5).

■ **21:1—24:10** *Judgment and Hope in Judah's Last Days.* These chapters narrate the end of the Davidic dynasty, making it clear that disaster and exile would be God's judgment on the sins of Judah's kings, prophets and people. Judgment is emphasized, but the theme of hope for a future restoration is also present. These chapters divide into three main sections: Jeremiah's words regarding the rulers of Judah (21:1—23:8), the false prophets (23:9–40) and a distinction within the nation (24:1–10).

■ **21:1—23:8** *Rulers of Judah.* These chapters summarize what Jeremiah had to say about the final years of monarchy in Judah during the reign of Zedekiah, before the final Babylonian invasion and destruction in 586 B.C. This material divides into words of condemnation (21:1—23:2) and contrasting words of hope for the future of the Davidic line after the exile (23:3–8).

21:1—23:2 These chapters explain why the royal line of Judah was so severely judged by the Babylonian captivity.

21:1 Zedekiah. Means "the LORD is my righteousness." **sent to him.** Zedekiah maintained a vacillating dependence on Jeremiah, but he lacked the moral courage to obey his warnings (37:3,21; 38:5,14,19,24–26). **Pashhur.** Not the same man mentioned in the previous chapter. See note on 20:1. **Zephaniah.** Not the prophet Zephaniah (19:25,29; 37:3; 52:24).

21:2 Inquire. A request for guidance. **Nebuchadnezzar.** King of

ing us. Perhaps the LORD will perform wonders[x] for us as in times past so that he will
withdraw from us."
3But Jeremiah answered them, "Tell Zedekiah, 4'This is what the LORD, the God of Israel, says: I am about to turn[y] against you the weapons of war that are in your hands,
which you are using to fight the king of Babylon and the Babylonians[a] who are outside
the wall besieging[z] you. And I will gather them inside this city. 5I myself will fight
against you with an outstretched hand[a] and a mighty arm in anger and fury and great
wrath. 6I will strike down those who live in this city—both men and animals—and they
will die of a terrible plague.[b] 7After that, declares the LORD, I will hand over Zedekiah[c]
king of Judah, his officials and the people in this city who survive the plague, sword and
famine, to Nebuchadnezzar king of Babylon[d] and to their enemies who seek their lives.
He will put them to the sword; he will show them no mercy or pity or compassion.'[e]
8"Furthermore, tell the people, 'This is what the LORD says: See, I am setting before
you the way of life and the way of death. 9Whoever stays in this city will die by the sword,
famine or plague.[f] But whoever goes out and surrenders to the Babylonians who are besieging you will live; he will escape with his life.[g] 10I have determined to do this city
harm[h] and not good, declares the LORD. It will be given into the hands[i] of the king of Babylon, and he will destroy it with fire.'[j]
11"Moreover, say to the royal house[k] of Judah, 'Hear the word of the LORD; 12O house
of David, this is what the LORD says:

" 'Administer justice[l] every morning;
  rescue from the hand of his oppressor
  the one who has been robbed,
or my wrath will break out and burn like fire
  because of the evil you have done—
  burn with no one to quench[m] it.
13I am against[n] you, Jerusalem,
  you who live above this valley[o]
  on the rocky plateau,
declares the LORD—
you who say, "Who can come against us?
  Who can enter our refuge?"[p]
14I will punish you as your deeds[q] deserve,
declares the LORD.
I will kindle a fire[r] in your forests[s]
  that will consume everything around you.' "

Judgment Against Evil Kings

22 This is what the LORD says: "Go down to the palace of the king of Judah and proclaim this message there: 2'Hear the word of the LORD, O king of Judah, you who
sit on David's throne[t]—you, your officials and your people who come through these
gates.[u] 3This is what the LORD says: Do what is just[v] and right. Rescue from the hand of
his oppressor[w] the one who has been robbed. Do no wrong or violence to the alien, the
fatherless or the widow,[x] and do not shed innocent blood in this place. 4For if you are
careful to carry out these commands, then kings[y] who sit on David's throne will come
through the gates of this palace, riding in chariots and on horses, accompanied by their
officials and their people. 5But if you do not obey[z] these commands, declares the LORD,
I swear[a] by myself that this palace will become a ruin.' "

21:2 [x]Ps 44:1-4; Jer 32:17
21:4 [y]Jer 32:5 [z]Jer 37:8-10
21:5 [a]Jer 6:12
21:6 [b]Jer 14:12
21:7 [c]2Ki 25:7; Jer 52:9 [d]Jer 37:17; 39:5 [e]2Ch 36:17; Eze 7:9; Hab 1:6
21:9 [f]Jer 14:12 [g]Jer 38:2,17; 39:18; 45:5
21:10 [h]Jer 44:11,27; Am 9:4 [i]Jer 32:28; 38:2-3 [j]Jer 52:13
21:11 [k]Jer 13:18
21:12 [l]Jer 22:3 [m]Isa 1:31
21:13 [n]Eze 13:8 [o]Ps 125:2 [p]Jer 49:4; Ob 1:3-4
21:14 [q]Isa 3:10-11 [r]2Ch 36:19; Jer 52:13 [s]Eze 20:47
22:2 [t]Jer 17:25; Lk 1:32 [u]Jer 17:20
22:3 [v]Mic 6:8; Zec 7:9 [w]Ps 72:4; Jer 21:12 [x]Ex 22:22
22:4 [y]Jer 17:25
22:5 [z]Jer 17:27 [a]Heb 6:13

[a] *4* Or *Chaldeans*; also in verse 9

Babylon from 605–562 B.C. **is attacking us.** Zedekiah was a puppet king of Nebuchadnezzar (37:1). He later rebelled, inviting Nebuchadnezzar's attack.
21:5 I myself will fight against you . . . outstretched hand . . . mighty arm. The language is of the Lord's holy war, which was horrifyingly turned against his own people (Dt 4:34; 5:15; 7:19; Am 5:18). **anger and fury and great wrath.** See Deuteronomy 29:23.
21:8 the way of life and the way of death. See Deuteronomy 30:15 and 19. God graciously offered life to those who would forsake the false confidence that lying prophets and kings had given them in Jerusalem and its temple (see v. 13).
21:12 Administer justice. See 9:24. Justice was expected of all kings of Judah, for they served as vice-regents of the Lord, the just King of the universe (23:5; 2Sa 8:15; 1Ki 3:28; Ps 72:1–2). **rescue . . . robbed.** See 22:3. See *BC* 36.
21:13 above this valley. Jerusalem's comparatively well-fortified position (surrounded on three sides by valleys, although exposed on the north) could give rise to complacency (7:4).
21:14 as your deeds deserve. Although they were very harsh, the judgments God was about to bring against Judah were well deserved. This is a major theme in the book of Jeremiah.
22:2 O king of Judah. Perhaps a reference to Zedekiah, but it may be an address to the royal line as a whole, serving as the prelude to a demonstration of their virtually unbroken failure. **who come through these gates.** See 17:19–20 and their notes.
22:3 See *BC* 36.
22:5 I swear by myself. See Genesis 22:16, Isaiah 45:23 and their notes. **this palace . . . a ruin.** As the temple (7:14), so the palace would also meet with disaster. See 17:27.

[6]For this is what the LORD says about the palace of the king of Judah:

"Though you are like Gilead to me,
like the summit of Lebanon,
I will surely make you like a desert,[b]
like towns not inhabited.
[7]I will send destroyers[c] against you,
each man with his weapons,
and they will cut[d] up your fine cedar beams
and throw them into the fire.

[8]"People from many nations will pass by this city and will ask one another, 'Why has the LORD done such a thing to this great city?'[e] [9]And the answer will be: 'Because they have forsaken the covenant of the LORD their God and have worshiped and served other gods.[f]' "

[10]Do not weep for the dead[g] ⌊king⌋ or mourn[h] his loss;
rather, weep bitterly for him who is exiled,
because he will never return
nor see his native land again.

[11]For this is what the LORD says about Shallum[a][i] son of Josiah, who succeeded his father as king of Judah but has gone from this place: "He will never return. [12]He will die[j] in the place where they have led him captive; he will not see this land again."

[13]"Woe to him who builds[k] his palace by unrighteousness,
his upper rooms by injustice,
making his countrymen work for nothing,
not paying[l] them for their labor.
[14]He says, 'I will build myself a great palace[m]
with spacious upper rooms.'
So he makes large windows in it,
panels it with cedar[n]
and decorates it in red.

[15]"Does it make you a king
to have more and more cedar?
Did not your father have food and drink?
He did what was right and just,[o]
so all went well[p] with him.
[16]He defended the cause of the poor and needy,[q]
and so all went well.
Is that not what it means to know me?"
declares the LORD.
[17]"But your eyes and your heart
are set only on dishonest gain,
on shedding innocent blood[r]
and on oppression and extortion."

[18]Therefore this is what the LORD says about Jehoiakim son of Josiah king of Judah:

22:6 [b]Mic 3:12
22:7 [c]Jer 4:7 [d]Isa 10:34
22:8 [e]Dt 29:25-26; 1Ki 9:8-9; Jer 16:10-11
22:9 [f]2Ki 22:17; 2Ch 34:25
22:10 [g]Ecc 4:2 [h]ver 18
22:11 [i]2Ki 23:31
22:12 [j]2Ki 23:34
22:13 [k]Mic 3:10; Hab 2:9 [l]Lev 19:13; Jas 5:4
22:14 [m]Isa 5:8-9 [n]2Sa 7:2
22:15 [o]2Ki 23:25 [p]Ps 128:2; Isa 3:10
22:16 [q]Ps 72:1-4, 12-13
22:17 [r]2Ki 24:4

[a] *11* Also called *Jehoahaz*

22:6 Gilead . . . Lebanon. Fertile places (see note on 8:22). Lebanon was well watered and richly forested, especially with cedars, which were used for the Jerusalem temple (1Ki 5:6–10); hence the next verse.
22:7 send. Literally, "consecrate." Shockingly, holy war imagery is used of the Babylonian army coming against God's people. See 6:4–5 and 21:4–5.
22:10 the dead king . . . him who is exiled. The dead king was Josiah and the exiled king his son Jehoahaz (identified in the next verse). The latter reigned briefly and was exiled to Egypt in 609 B.C. (2Ki 23:30–34).
22:11 Shallum son of Josiah. An alternate name of Jehoahaz (v. 10; 1Ch 3:15).
22:13–19 This section attacks Jehoiakim (see v. 18; 2Ki 23:35—24:7).
22:13 palace. Literally, "house." It primarily refers to the king's palace but may also refer to the royal dynasty. **making his countrymen . . . their labor.** Contrary to Deuteronomy 24:14–15 (see also 1Sa 8:10–18).
22:15 Does it make you a king . . . well with him. The contrast here is between kings: One reigned as an exercise of justice (Josiah), another as an opportunity for gaining wealth (Jehoiakim). The picture is of the covenantal harmony between obedience and blessing (Dt 7:12–13; 6:24–25).
22:16 He defended . . . the poor and needy. Elaborates on "right and just" in verse 15. **to know me?** Knowledge of the Lord is characterized by faithfulness to his commands (Mic 6:6–8; Jn 14:15,17).
22:17 your. Refers to Jehoiakim (see v. 18). **dishonest gain . . . innocent blood . . . oppression.** Jehoiakim was personally guilty of all the evils Jeremiah condemned (6:13; 7:6; 19:4; 21:12; cf. 26:20–23).
22:18 They will not mourn. Contrast 2 Chronicles 34:24–25 (also implied in v. 10).

"They will not mourn for him:
'Alas, my brother! Alas, my sister!'
They will not mourn for him:
'Alas, my master! Alas, his splendor!'
19 He will have the burial of a donkey—
dragged away and thrown[s]
outside the gates of Jerusalem."

20 "Go up to Lebanon and cry out,
let your voice be heard in Bashan,
cry out from Abarim,[t]
for all your allies are crushed.
21 I warned you when you felt secure,
but you said, 'I will not listen!'
This has been your way from your youth;[u]
you have not obeyed[v] me.
22 The wind will drive all your shepherds away,
and your allies will go into exile.
Then you will be ashamed and disgraced
because of all your wickedness.
23 You who live in 'Lebanon,[a]'
who are nestled in cedar buildings,
how you will groan when pangs come upon you,
pain[w] like that of a woman in labor!

24 "As surely as I live," declares the LORD, "even if you, Jehoiachin[b][x] son of Jehoiakim
king of Judah, were a signet ring on my right hand, I would still pull you off. 25 I will hand
you over[y] to those who seek your life, those you fear—to Nebuchadnezzar king of Babylon and to the Babylonians.[c] 26 I will hurl[z] you and the mother who gave you birth into
another country, where neither of you was born, and there you both will die. 27 You will
never come back to the land you long to return to."

28 Is this man Jehoiachin a despised, broken pot,[a]
an object no one wants?
Why will he and his children be hurled[b] out,
cast into a land[c] they do not know?
29 O land,[d] land, land,
hear the word of the LORD!
30 This is what the LORD says:
"Record this man as if childless,[e]
a man who will not prosper[f] in his lifetime,
for none of his offspring will prosper,
none will sit on the throne[g] of David
or rule anymore in Judah."

The Righteous Branch

23 "Woe to the shepherds[h] who are destroying and scattering[i] the sheep of my pasture!"[j] declares the LORD. 2 Therefore this is what the LORD, the God of Israel, says

22:19 [s]Jer 36:30
22:20 [t]Nu 27:12
22:21 [u]Jer 3:25; 32:30 [v]Jer 7:23-28
22:23 [w]Jer 4:31
22:24 [x]2Ki 24:6,8; Jer 37:1
22:25 [y]2Ki 24:16; Jer 34:20
22:26 [z]2Ki 24:8; 2Ch 36:10
22:28 [a]Ps 31:12; Jer 48:38; Hos 8:8 [b]Jer 15:1 [c]Jer 17:4
22:29 [d]Jer 6:19; Mic 1:2
22:30 [e]1Ch 3:18; Mt 1:12 [f]Jer 10:21 [g]Ps 94:20
23:1 [h]Jer 10:21; Eze 34:1-10; Zec 11:15-17 [i]Isa 56:11 [j]Eze 34:31

[a] *23* That is, the palace in Jerusalem (see 1 Kings 7:2) [b] *24* Hebrew *Coniah,* a variant of *Jehoiachin;* also in verse 28 [c] *25* Or *Chaldeans*

22:19 burial of a donkey. That is, no burial (see 7:33 and its note; cf. 15:3).
22:20 Lebanon . . . Bashan . . . Abarim. Mountainous regions to the north, northeast and southeast, respectively. Jerusalem is pictured wailing for help to former allies (v. 22; e.g., Egypt and Assyria; 2:36) that were now powerless before Babylon, leaving Jerusalem to wail alone.
22:23 Lebanon. Refers to the palace, which was built with cedar from Lebanon (see note on v. 6). The palace in Jerusalem had been called "the Palace of the Forest of Lebanon" (1Ki 7:2).
22:24–30 This is against Jehoiachin, during whose reign the first major deportations to Babylon occurred.
22:24 signet ring. Such a ring represented its owner; its rejection is shocking. The promise of a renewal of the Davidic kingdom would later be extended in the same language—then to Zerubbabel, the descendant of Jehoiachin (Hag 2:23).
22:26 you and the mother. See 13:18 and its note. **into another country.** This reference to Babylon was fulfilled in 597 B.C. (29:2; 2Ki 24:15).
22:28 Jehoiachin . . . broken pot . . . ? See 19:10–11. Jehoiachin and his children are now linked specifically with that sign. The answer to the rhetorical question is given in verse 30.
22:29 O land, land, land. In the personification of the land, we hear the Lord's grief over his inheritance, which had been defiled by Judah's sin (see 2:7 and its note; 12:4).
22:30 Record this man as if childless. Although Jehoiachin had children (1Ch 3:17–18), none of them would reign on the throne of David. A reversal of this curse was graciously offered to Zerubbabel (Hag 2:23; see also note on 22:24) but did not take place until Jesus, a descendant of Jehoiachin (see Mt 1:12, where Jehoiachin is called Jeconiah), began to reign on David's throne (Lk 1:32–33).

to the shepherds who tend my people: “Because you have scattered my flock and driv-
en them away and have not bestowed care on them, I will bestow punishment on you
for the evil[k] you have done,” declares the LORD. 3 “I myself will gather the remnant[l] of my
flock out of all the countries where I have driven them and will bring them back to their
pasture, where they will be fruitful and increase in number. 4 I will place shepherds[m] over
them who will tend them, and they will no longer be afraid[n] or terrified, nor will any be
missing,[o]” declares the LORD.

5 “The days are coming,” declares the LORD,
“when I will raise up to David[a] a righteous Branch,[p]
a King who will reign[q] wisely
and do what is just and right[r] in the land.
6 In his days Judah will be saved
and Israel will live in safety.
This is the name[s] by which he will be called:
The LORD Our Righteousness.[t]

7 “So then, the days are coming,” declares the LORD, “when people will no longer say, ‘As
surely as the LORD lives, who brought the Israelites up out of Egypt,’[u] 8 but they will say,
‘As surely as the LORD lives, who brought the descendants of Israel up out of the land of
the north and out of all the countries where he had banished them.’ Then they will live
in their own land.”[v]

Lying Prophets

9 Concerning the prophets:

My heart is broken within me;
all my bones tremble.
I am like a drunken man,
like a man overcome by wine,
because of the LORD
and his holy words.[w]
10 The land is full of adulterers;[x]
because of the curse[b] the land lies parched[c]
and the pastures[y] in the desert are withered.[z]
The ⌊prophets⌋ follow an evil course
and use their power unjustly.

11 “Both prophet and priest are godless;[a]
even in my temple[b] I find their wickedness,”
declares the LORD.
12 “Therefore their path will become slippery;[c]
they will be banished to darkness
and there they will fall.
I will bring disaster on them
in the year they are punished,[d]”
declares the LORD.

23:2 [k]Jer 21:12
23:3 [l]Isa 11:10-12; Jer 32:37; Eze 34:11-16
23:4 [m]Jer 3:15; 31:10; Eze 34:23 [n]Jer 30:10; 46:27-28 [o]Jn 6:39
23:5 [p]Isa 4:2 [q]Isa 9:7 [r]Isa 11:1; Zec 6:12
23:6 [s]Jer 33:16; Mt 1:21-23 [t]Ro 3:21-22; 1Co 1:30
23:7 [u]Jer 16:14
23:8 [v]Isa 43:5-6; Am 9:14-15
23:9 [w]Jer 20:8-9
23:10 [x]Jer 9:2 [y]Ps 107:34; Jer 9:10 [z]Hos 4:2-3
23:11 [a]Jer 6:13; 8:10; Zep 3:4 [b]Jer 7:10
23:12 [c]Ps 35:6; Jer 13:16 [d]Jer 11:23

[a] 5 Or *up from David’s line* [b] 10 Or *because of these things* [c] 10 Or *land mourns*

23:3–9 Jeremiah predicted that an exodus from Babylon would lead to the restoration of David’s kingdom.
23:3 I myself. Because of the failure of the kings, the Lord himself would take control in a new way (see note on 24:7). **remnant.** Essentially, the gathering of the remnant shows the continuing care of the Lord for his people and his determination to fulfill his covenantal purposes. In the present context, the doctrine of the remnant suggests the breaking off of certain of Judah’s branches (cf. Ro 11:17–24) following the king’s neglect and the ensuing punishment. **bring them back to their pasture.** The Lord himself would now be their shepherd (Ps 23). **be fruitful and increase in number.** Compare Exodus 1:7.
23:4 I will place shepherds over them. Under God, the divine Shepherd, other true shepherds would faithfully administer the kingdom in the age after the exile (Mic 5:5).
23:5–6 raise up to David. 2 Samuel 7:12 underlies this promise. The Messianic promise is a fulfillment of the promise to David (Mt 1:1,17; 12:23). **righteous Branch.** A Messianic term reflecting the fact that the final Anointed One of David’s line would be perfectly righteous (Isa 4:2; 11:1). This term set the standard for all leaders of God’s people (see Zec 6:12, where Zerubbabel is described this way). **righteous.** See 9:24. **name.** Names in ancient times were designations of character, not always labels of identification. See “Immanuel” in Isaiah 7:14, as well as the names in Isaiah 9:6. See *HC* 19.
23:6 Judah . . . Israel. The reunited people would be one mark of the Messianic age (Eze 37:15–22). **in safety.** The blessings of the Messianic kingdom would ultimately embrace both physical and spiritual dimensions. **The LORD Our Righteousness.** A measure of irony appears here. Zedekiah, who was the object of Jeremiah’s earlier condemnation (chs. 21–22), means “The LORD is my righteousness,” but he did not live up to that name. The great Son of David, who would restore the kingdom after exile, would succeed in being the righteousness of all those in his kingdom. He would reign in righteousness and establish the same in all his people.
■ **23:9–40** *False Prophets.* Jeremiah turned to the lying prophets and condemned them for misleading the people. See *WCF* 11.1; *BC* 22; *HC* 15.
23:9 the prophets. Refers here to false or lying prophets.
23:11 prophet and priest are godless. Jeremiah was himself a prophet and a priest (see “Introduction: Author”). See *WLC* 113.

13 "Among the prophets of Samaria
I saw this repulsive thing:
They prophesied by Baal[e]
and led my people Israel astray.
14 And among the prophets of Jerusalem
I have seen something horrible:[f]
They commit adultery and live a lie.[g]
They strengthen the hands of evildoers,[h]
so that no one turns from his wickedness.
They are all like Sodom[i] to me;
the people of Jerusalem are like Gomorrah."[j]

15 Therefore, this is what the LORD Almighty says concerning the prophets:

"I will make them eat bitter food
and drink poisoned water,[k]
because from the prophets of Jerusalem
ungodliness has spread throughout the land."

16 This is what the LORD Almighty says:

"Do not listen[l] to what the prophets are prophesying to you;
they fill you with false hopes.
They speak visions[m] from their own minds,
not from the mouth[n] of the LORD.
17 They keep saying to those who despise me,
'The LORD says: You will have peace.'[o]
And to all who follow the stubbornness[p] of their hearts
they say, 'No harm[q] will come to you.'
18 But which of them has stood in the council of the LORD
to see or to hear his word?
Who has listened and heard his word?
19 See, the storm[r] of the LORD
will burst out in wrath,
a whirlwind swirling down
on the heads of the wicked.
20 The anger[s] of the LORD will not turn back[t]
until he fully accomplishes
the purposes of his heart.
In days to come
you will understand it clearly.
21 I did not send[u] these prophets,
yet they have run with their message;
I did not speak to them,
yet they have prophesied.
22 But if they had stood in my council,
they would have proclaimed my words to my people
and would have turned[v] them from their evil ways
and from their evil deeds.
23 "Am I only a God nearby,[w]"
declares the LORD,
"and not a God far away?
24 Can anyone hide[x] in secret places
so that I cannot see him?"
declares the LORD.

23:13 [e]Jer 2:8
23:14 [f]Jer 5:30 [g]Jer 29:23 [h]Eze 13:22 [i]Ge 18:20 [j]Isa 1:9-10; Jer 20:16
23:15 [k]Jer 8:14; 9:15
23:16 [l]Jer 27:9-10, 14; Mt 7:15 [m]Jer 14:14 [n]Jer 9:20
23:17 [o]Jer 8:11 [p]Jer 13:10 [q]Jer 5:12; Am 9:10; Mic 3:11
23:19 [r]Jer 25:32; 30:23
23:20 [s]2Ki 23:26 [t]Jer 30:24
23:21 [u]Jer 14:14; 27:15
23:22 [v]Jer 25:5; Zec 1:4
23:23 [w]Ps 139:1-10
23:24 [x]Job 22:12-14

23:14 They commit adultery . . . his wickedness. Right belief and right action are inseparable in the Old Testament. It was no accident that those who had not heard God's word actively encouraged evil. See 29:21–23. **like Sodom . . . like Gomorrah.** See 20:16, Isaiah 1:9 and their notes. The prophet drew this parallel to shock his listeners, hoping to turn them toward the Lord.
23:18 stood in the council of the LORD. God is several times pictured as sitting in a council of heavenly beings, with whom he deliberates (1Ki 22:19–22; Job 1:6; Isa 6:1–8). The Old Testament phenomenon of a man standing in the heavenly court is unique in ancient Near Eastern literature. Instead of divine beings sent as messengers of the gods, the prophet was sent as the Lord's authoritative representative.
23:21 I did not send. See 14:14. **yet they have run . . . prophesied.** The false prophets zealously propagated their lies.
23:23–24 See *WCF* 2.1; *HC* 27,48,121.
23:23 nearby . . . far away? The point is that nothing, near or far, can escape God's knowledge (Ps 139:2; Am 9:2–3). See Deuteronomy 30:11–14 for a different use of this contrast.
23:24 See theological article "The Presence of God" at 1 Kings 8.

23:24 [y]1Ki 8:27
23:25 [z]Jer 14:14 [a]ver 28, 32; Jer 29:8
23:26 [b]1Ti 4:1-2
23:27 [c]Dt 13:1-3; Jer 29:8 [d]Jdg 3:7; 8:33-34
23:29 [e]Jer 5:14
23:30 [f]Ps 34:16 [g]Dt 18:20; Jer 14:15
23:31 [h]ver 17
23:32 [i]ver 25 [j]Jer 7:8; La 2:14
23:33 [k]Mal 1:1 [l]ver 39
23:34 [m]La 2:14 [n]Zec 13:3
23:35 [o]Jer 33:3; 42:4
23:36 [p]Gal 1:7-8; 2Pe 3:16
23:39 [q]Jer 7:15
23:40 [r]Jer 20:11; Eze 5:14-15
24:1 [s]2Ki 24:16; 2Ch 36:9; Jer 29:2 [t]Am 8:1-2
24:2 [u]Isa 5:4
24:3 [v]Jer 1:11; Am 8:2
24:6 [w]Jer 29:10; Eze 11:17 [x]Jer 33:7; 42:10

"Do not I fill heaven and earth?"[y]
declares the LORD.

25"I have heard what the prophets say who prophesy lies[z] in my name. They say, 'I
had a dream![a] I had a dream!' 26How long will this continue in the hearts of these lying
prophets, who prophesy the delusions[b] of their own minds? 27They think the dreams they
tell one another will make my people forget[c] my name, just as their fathers forgot[d] my
name through Baal worship. 28Let the prophet who has a dream tell his dream, but let
the one who has my word speak it faithfully. For what has straw to do with grain?" declares the LORD. 29"Is not my word like fire,"[e] declares the LORD, "and like a hammer that
breaks a rock in pieces?
30"Therefore," declares the LORD, "I am against[f] the prophets[g] who steal from one another words supposedly from me. 31Yes," declares the LORD, "I am against the prophets
who wag their own tongues and yet declare, 'The LORD declares.'[h] 32Indeed, I am against
those who prophesy false dreams,[i]" declares the LORD. "They tell them and lead my people astray with their reckless lies, yet I did not send or appoint them. They do not benefit[j] these people in the least," declares the LORD.

False Oracles and False Prophets

33"When these people, or a prophet or a priest, ask you, 'What is the oracle[a][k] of the
LORD?' say to them, 'What oracle?[b] I will forsake[l] you, declares the LORD.' 34If a prophet
or a priest or anyone else claims, 'This is the oracle[m] of the LORD,' I will punish[n] that man
and his household. 35This is what each of you keeps on saying to his friend or relative:
'What is the LORD's answer?'[o] or 'What has the LORD spoken?' 36But you must not mention 'the oracle of the LORD' again, because every man's own word becomes his oracle
and so you distort[p] the words of the living God, the LORD Almighty, our God. 37This is
what you keep saying to a prophet: 'What is the LORD's answer to you?' or 'What has the
LORD spoken?' 38Although you claim, 'This is the oracle of the LORD,' this is what the LORD
says: You used the words, 'This is the oracle of the LORD,' even though I told you that you
must not claim, 'This is the oracle of the LORD.' 39Therefore, I will surely forget you and
cast[q] you out of my presence along with the city I gave to you and your fathers. 40I will
bring upon you everlasting disgrace[r]—everlasting shame that will not be forgotten."

Two Baskets of Figs

24 After Jehoiachin[c][s] son of Jehoiakim king of Judah and the officials, the craftsmen and the artisans of Judah were carried into exile from Jerusalem to Babylon
by Nebuchadnezzar king of Babylon, the LORD showed me two baskets of figs[t] placed in
front of the temple of the LORD. 2One basket had very good figs, like those that ripen early; the other basket had very poor[u] figs, so bad they could not be eaten.
3Then the LORD asked me, "What do you see,[v] Jeremiah?"
"Figs," I answered. "The good ones are very good, but the poor ones are so bad they
cannot be eaten."
4Then the word of the LORD came to me: 5"This is what the LORD, the God of Israel,
says: 'Like these good figs, I regard as good the exiles from Judah, whom I sent away from
this place to the land of the Babylonians.[d] 6My eyes will watch over them for their good,
and I will bring them back[w] to this land. I will build[x] them up and not tear them down;

[a] *33* Or *burden* (see Septuagint and Vulgate) (The Hebrew for *oracle* and *burden* is the same.)
[b] *33* Hebrew; Septuagint and Vulgate *'You are the burden.*
[c] *1* Hebrew *Jeconiah,* a variant of *Jehoiachin*
[d] *5* Or *Chaldeans*

---

hide . . . so that I cannot see him? See Psalm 139:7–12. **fill heaven and earth?** See Isaiah 6:3. In this context the lies of the false prophets could not be hidden from the Lord.

23:25 dream . . . dream! A dream was one way in which a revelation might come to a prophet (Nu 12:6; cf. Joel 2:28). Yet claims of revelation were always to be treated with due suspicion (Dt 13:1–3).

23:28 dream . . . word . . . straw . . . grain? The (false) dream was to the true prophetic word as straw is to grain—there was a world of difference between them. See *WLC* 159.

23:29 fire . . . hammer. These similes make clear that there could be no mistaking the true word because of its inevitable effects.

23:30–32 I am against. Repeated three times for strong emphasis.

23:30 who steal . . . words supposedly from me. For a case of prophetic jealousy, see 1 Kings 22:24.

23:31 declares the LORD . . . The LORD declares. The repetition stresses the disrespect of their false claims.

23:34–38 See *WLC* 113.

23:39 forget. A suitable response to the fact that the people had forgotten him; each case had been a deliberate action.

■ **24:1–10** *A Distinction and the Future Hope.* A vision of two basketsful of figs—one representing those exiled to Babylon, the other those who would resist exile and thus the Lord's purpose of judgment and salvation. The perspective of this prophecy is after the fact, when it had become too late to avert the exile by repentance. See 21:9; see also "Introduction: Purpose and Distinctives."

24:1 Jehoiachin . . . exile. 597 B.C. was the date of the first major deportation (2Ki 24:14–16).

24:2 very good figs . . . very poor figs. The vision of good and bad figs is reminiscent of the drought, which had been one consequence of Judah's disobedience (12:4; 14:1; cf. 8:13).

24:5–7 The "good figs" are likened to the exiles. It was through those taken into exile in Babylon that the restoration of God's people would come. Christ himself was descended from those who returned from exile in Babylon.

I will plant them and not uproot them. 7 I will give them a heart to know me, that I am
the LORD. They will be my people,[y] and I will be their God, for they will return[z] to me with
all their heart.[a]
8 " 'But like the poor[b] figs, which are so bad they cannot be eaten,' says the LORD, 'so
will I deal with Zedekiah king of Judah, his officials[c] and the survivors[d] from Jerusalem,
whether they remain in this land or live in Egypt.[e] 9 I will make them abhorrent[f] and an
offense to all the kingdoms of the earth, a reproach and a byword,[g] an object of ridicule
and cursing,[h] wherever I banish[i] them. 10 I will send the sword,[j] famine and plague[k]
against them until they are destroyed from the land I gave to them and their fathers.' "

Seventy Years of Captivity

25 The word came to Jeremiah concerning all the people of Judah in the fourth year
of Jehoiakim[l] son of Josiah king of Judah, which was the first year of Nebuchadnezzar[m] king of Babylon. 2 So Jeremiah the prophet said to all the people of Judah[n] and
to all those living in Jerusalem: 3 For twenty-three years—from the thirteenth year of Josiah[o] son of Amon king of Judah until this very day—the word of the LORD has come to
me and I have spoken to you again and again,[p] but you have not listened.[q]
4 And though the LORD has sent all his servants the prophets[r] to you again and again,
you have not listened or paid any attention. 5 They said, "Turn now, each of you, from
your evil ways and your evil practices, and you can stay in the land the LORD gave to you
and your fathers for ever and ever. 6 Do not follow other gods[s] to serve and worship them;
do not provoke me to anger with what your hands have made. Then I will not harm you."
7 "But you did not listen to me," declares the LORD, "and you have provoked me with
what your hands have made,[t] and you have brought harm[u] to yourselves."
8 Therefore the LORD Almighty says this: "Because you have not listened to my words,
9 I will summon[v] all the peoples of the north[w] and my servant[x] Nebuchadnezzar king of
Babylon," declares the LORD, "and I will bring them against this land and its inhabitants
and against all the surrounding nations. I will completely destroy[a] them and make
them an object of horror and scorn,[y] and an everlasting ruin. 10 I will banish from them
the sounds[z] of joy and gladness, the voices of bride and bridegroom,[a] the sound of millstones[b] and the light of the lamp.[c] 11 This whole country will become a desolate waste
land,[d] and these nations will serve the king of Babylon seventy years.[e]
12 "But when the seventy years[f] are fulfilled, I will punish the king of Babylon and his
nation, the land of the Babylonians,[b] for their guilt," declares the LORD, "and will make
it desolate[g] forever. 13 I will bring upon that land all the things I have spoken against it,
all that are written in this book and prophesied by Jeremiah against all the nations.
14 They themselves will be enslaved[h] by many nations[i] and great kings; I will repay[j] them
according to their deeds and the work of their hands."

24:7 [y]Isa 51:16; Jer 31:33; Heb 8:10 [z]Jer 32:40 [a]Eze 11:19
24:8 [b]Jer 29:17 [c]Jer 39:6 [d]Jer 39:9 [e]Jer 44:1, 26
24:9 [f]Jer 15:4; 34:17 [g]Dt 28:25; 1Ki 9:7 [h]Jer 29:18 [i]Dt 28:37
24:10 [j]Isa 51:19 [k]Jer 27:8
25:1 [l]2Ki 24:2; Jer 36:1 [m]2Ki 24:1
25:2 [n]Jer 18:11
25:3 [o]Jer 1:2 [p]Jer 11:7; 26:5 [q]Jer 7:26
25:4 [r]Jer 7:25
25:6 [s]Dt 8:19
25:7 [t]Dt 32:21 [u]2Ki 21:15
25:9 [v]Isa 13:3-5 [w]Jer 1:15 [x]Jer 27:6 [y]Jer 18:16
25:10 [z]Isa 24:8; Eze 26:13 [a]Jer 7:34 [b]Ecc 12:3-4 [c]Rev 18:22-23
25:11 [d]Jer 4:26-27; 12:11-12 [e]2Ch 36:21
25:12 [f]Jer 29:10 [g]Isa 13:19-22; 14:22-23
25:14 [h]Jer 27:7 [i]Jer 50:9; 51:27-28 [j]Jer 51:6

a 9 The Hebrew term refers to the irrevocable giving over of things or persons to the LORD, often by totally destroying them. b 12 Or *Chaldeans*

24:7 I will give them a heart to know me. Those in exile were not better or more likely to believe than those who remained behind. The Lord's answer to his people's inability to maintain their part of the covenant relationship was that the Lord himself would intervene, creating a new capacity in them for knowing him. **They will be my people, and I will be their God.** The covenant formula (32:38; Lev 26:12) shows that this answer is nothing less than the new covenant. The theology introduced here is developed in 31:31–34.

24:8 like the poor figs. Those who remained in the land thought they would be safe from the wrath of God, but Jeremiah made it clear that this would not be the case. Those remaining would be chastened even further.

■ **25:1—29:32** *Severity and Length of Exile.* In these chapters Jeremiah predicted 70 years of Babylonian captivity for Judah as judgment for persistent sin and warned that the destruction would be massive (25:1–38). His message continued to be met with opposition from false prophets, priests and the people (26:1—29:32).

■ **25:1–38** *Seventy Years of Exile Predicted.* The prophet predicted that Jerusalem would lie in ruins for 70 years. After that time God would judge the nations and the exiles would return and rebuild.

25:1 fourth year of Jehoiakim. 605 B.C. was the year of preliminary Babylonian pillaging (see Da 1:1 and its note).

25:3 thirteenth year of Josiah. See 1:2.

25:4 again and again. See verse 3. Jeremiah's persistence was merely an echo of the whole prophetic mission to Israel, as was his failure to obtain the desired response (see 7:13 and its note).

25:9 peoples of the north. Babylon and her allies (1:15; 6:1). **my servant Nebuchadnezzar.** See also 27:6. The foreign king was God's "servant" only in the sense of having been appointed an agent of his judgment. In the same way Cyrus would be called God's "anointed" for the purpose of releasing the exiles back to their land (Isa 45:1). **the surrounding nations.** See verses 19–26. The judgment on Judah would be part of a larger judgment, as the Babylonians would destroy many nations. The description of the Babylonian invasion is very similar to that found in Zephaniah 1:1—3:8. **object of horror and scorn.** See 24:9, where the wicked in Judah are in view.

25:11–12 seventy years. See 29:10. Seventy years was a standard formula in ancient Near Eastern cultures to describe the duration of a god's displeasure with his people. It could be lengthened or shortened, depending on how the people reacted to the judgment. In Daniel 9 this prophecy of 70 years was extended seven times because the people had not repented in exile (see note on Da 9:24). The number 70 also roughly corresponds to the number of years between the first deportation in 605 B.C. (v. 1; Da 1:1) and 538 B.C., when the exiles began to return home following Cyrus's decree. The writer of Chronicles (2Ch 36:20–23) and the prophet Zechariah (Zec 1:12) associated this prophecy with the return and rebuilding of Jerusalem, which began in 539/538 B.C. **punish the king of Babylon.** Elaborated on in chapters 50–51. The agent of punishment would in turn be punished for his own sins (50:18; cf. Isa 10:5–7,12).

25:13 in this book. The Septuagint (the Greek translation of the OT) places the material in chapters 46–51 after this phrase. The subject matter in both places is comparable.

25:14 many nations and great kings. Refers to Media, Persia and their allies, the conquerors of Babylon.

The Cup of God's Wrath

15 This is what the LORD, the God of Israel, said to me: "Take from my hand this cup[k]
filled with the wine of my wrath and make all the nations to whom I send you drink it.
16 When they drink it, they will stagger[l] and go mad[m] because of the sword I will send
among them."
17 So I took the cup from the LORD's hand and made all the nations to whom he sent[n]
me drink it: 18 Jerusalem and the towns of Judah, its kings and officials, to make them a
ruin and an object of horror and scorn and cursing,[o] as they are today;[p] 19 Pharaoh king
of Egypt, his attendants, his officials and all his people, 20 and all the foreign people there;
all the kings of Uz;[q] all the kings of the Philistines (those of Ashkelon,[r] Gaza, Ekron, and
the people left at Ashdod); 21 Edom, Moab and Ammon;[s] 22 all the kings of Tyre and Sidon;[t] the kings of the coastlands[u] across the sea; 23 Dedan, Tema, Buz and all who are
in distant places[a];[v] 24 all the kings of Arabia[w] and all the kings of the foreign people who
live in the desert; 25 all the kings of Zimri, Elam[x] and Media; 26 and all the kings of the
north,[y] near and far, one after the other—all the kingdoms on the face of the earth. And
after all of them, the king of Sheshach[b][z] will drink it too.
27 "Then tell them, 'This is what the LORD Almighty, the God of Israel, says: Drink, get
drunk[a] and vomit, and fall to rise no more because of the sword[b] I will send among you.'
28 But if they refuse to take the cup from your hand and drink, tell them, 'This is what the
LORD Almighty says: You must drink it! 29 See, I am beginning to bring disaster[c] on the
city that bears my Name,[d] and will you indeed go unpunished?[e] You will not go unpunished, for I am calling down a sword upon all[f] who live on the earth, declares the LORD
Almighty.'
30 "Now prophesy all these words against them and say to them:

"'The LORD will roar[g] from on high;
he will thunder[h] from his holy dwelling
and roar mightily against his land.
He will shout like those who tread the grapes,
shout against all who live on the earth.
31 The tumult will resound to the ends of the earth,
for the LORD will bring charges[i] against the nations;
he will bring judgment on all mankind
and put the wicked to the sword,'"
declares the LORD.

32 This is what the LORD Almighty says:

"Look! Disaster is spreading
from nation to nation;[j]
a mighty storm[k] is rising
from the ends of the earth."

33 At that time those slain[l] by the LORD will be everywhere—from one end of the earth to
the other. They will not be mourned or gathered[m] up or buried,[n] but will be like refuse
lying on the ground.

25:15 [k]Isa 51:17; Ps 75:8; Rev 14:10
25:16 [l]Na 3:11 [m]Jer 51:7
25:17 [n]Jer 1:10
25:18 [o]Jer 24:9 [p]Jer 44:22
25:20 [q]Job 1:1 [r]Jer 47:5
25:21 [s]Jer 49:1
25:22 [t]Jer 47:4 [u]Jer 31:10
25:23 [v]Jer 9:26; 49:32
25:24 [w]2Ch 9:14
25:25 [x]Ge 10:22
25:26 [y]Jer 50:3,9 [z]Jer 51:41
25:27 [a]ver 16,28; Hab 2:16 [b]Eze 21:4
25:29 [c]Jer 13:12-14 [d]1Pe 4:17 [e]Pr 11:31 [f]ver 30-31
25:30 [g]Isa 16:10; 42:13 [h]Joel 3:16; Am 1:2
25:31 [i]Hos 4:1; Joel 3:2; Mic 6:2
25:32 [j]Isa 34:2 [k]Jer 23:19
25:33 [l]Isa 66:16; Eze 39:17-20 [m]Jer 16:4 [n]Ps 79:3

[a] 23 Or *who clip the hair by their foreheads* [b] *26 Sheshach* is a cryptogram for Babylon.

25:15 cup . . . of my wrath. A cup of wine is often used as a metaphor for judgment (25:17,28; 49:12; 51:7; Isa 51:17,22; Eze 23:31–33).
25:16 stagger . . . because of the sword. The image of staggering from drunkenness turns abruptly into that of staggering from a fatal blow.
25:18 Jerusalem and . . . Judah. God's people would be judged first, as befits those who are most privileged (25:29; Am 3:2). **ruin . . . cursing.** See verses 9 and 11, as well as 18:16.
25:20 the foreign people. Refers to any group not native to a region or nation (Ne 13:3). **Ashkelon . . . people left at Ashdod.** Gath, the fifth city of the Philistines, is omitted, as it apparently had already been destroyed (as also in Am 1:6–8). Ashdod was probably partially reduced by the Egyptians during the seventh century B.C. See also 47:1–7.
25:21 Edom, Moab and Ammon. See 48:1—49:22.
25:22 Tyre and Sidon. Refers to the region of Phoenicia (see Eze 28:1–23). **coastlands across the sea.** Refers to Phoenician maritime trading outposts.
25:23 Dedan, Tema. Located in Arabia (cf. Isa 21:13–14). **Buz.** An unknown location.
25:24 Arabia. See 49:28–33.
25:25 Zimri. Unknown. **Elam.** See 49:34–39. **Media.** One of the conquerors of Babylon. See 51:11 and 28.
25:26 Sheshach. This word is a cryptogram (a coded allusion) to Babylon, using "Babel," but substituting the last letter of the alphabet for the first, the next to last for the second, etc. See also 51:1.
25:29 city that bears my Name. Jerusalem (see notes on 7:10–15). The Lord would not punish his own people while ignoring the wickedness of other nations. This is an important aspect of the theology of judgment against the nations. The honor of his own name was at stake in the fate of his people.
25:31 bring charges. A legal metaphor by which the Lord claimed his right to punish the guilty (see note on 2:9).
25:32 spreading from nation to nation. Literally, "going out," as if to war. The Babylonians would be God's instrument of judgment throughout the known world.

34 Weep and wail, you shepherds;
roll[o] in the dust, you leaders of the flock.
For your time to be slaughtered[p] has come;
you will fall and be shattered like fine pottery.
35 The shepherds will have nowhere to flee,
the leaders of the flock no place to escape.[q]
36 Hear the cry of the shepherds,
the wailing of the leaders of the flock,
for the LORD is destroying their pasture.
37 The peaceful meadows will be laid waste
because of the fierce anger of the LORD.
38 Like a lion[r] he will leave his lair,
and their land will become desolate
because of the sword[a] of the oppressor
and because of the LORD's fierce anger.

Jeremiah Threatened With Death

26 Early in the reign of Jehoiakim[s] son of Josiah king of Judah, this word came from
the LORD: 2 "This is what the LORD says: Stand in the courtyard[t] of the LORD's house
and speak to all the people of the towns of Judah who come to worship in the house of
the LORD. Tell[u] them everything I command you; do not omit[v] a word. 3 Perhaps they will
listen and each will turn[w] from his evil way. Then I will relent[x] and not bring on them the
disaster I was planning because of the evil they have done. 4 Say to them, 'This is what the
LORD says: If you do not listen[y] to me and follow my law,[z] which I have set before you, 5 and
if you do not listen to the words of my servants the prophets, whom I have sent to you
again and again (though you have not listened[a]), 6 then I will make this house like Shiloh[b]
and this city an object of cursing[c] among all the nations of the earth.' "
7 The priests, the prophets and all the people heard Jeremiah speak these words in the
house of the LORD. 8 But as soon as Jeremiah finished telling all the people everything the
LORD had commanded him to say, the priests, the prophets and all the people seized him
and said, "You must die! 9 Why do you prophesy in the LORD's name that this house will
be like Shiloh and this city will be desolate and deserted?"[d] And all the people crowded
around Jeremiah in the house of the LORD.
10 When the officials of Judah heard about these things, they went up from the royal
palace to the house of the LORD and took their places at the entrance of the New Gate of
the LORD's house. 11 Then the priests and the prophets said to the officials and all the people, "This man should be sentenced to death[e] because he has prophesied against this
city. You have heard it with your own ears!"
12 Then Jeremiah said to all the officials[f] and all the people: "The LORD sent me to
prophesy[g] against this house and this city all the things you have heard.[h] 13 Now reform[i]
your ways and your actions and obey the LORD your God. Then the LORD will relent and
not bring the disaster he has pronounced against you. 14 As for me, I am in your hands;[j]
do with me whatever you think is good and right. 15 Be assured, however, that if you put
me to death, you will bring the guilt of innocent blood on yourselves and on this city and
on those who live in it, for in truth the LORD has sent me to you to speak all these words
in your hearing."
16 Then the officials[k] and all the people said to the priests and the prophets, "This man
should not be sentenced to death![l] He has spoken to us in the name of the LORD our God."

25:34 [o]Jer 6:26 [p]Isa 34:6; Jer 50:27
25:35 [q]Job 11:20
25:38 [r]Jer 4:7
26:1 [s]2Ki 23:36
26:2 [t]Jer 19:14 [u]Jer 1:17; Mt 28:20; Ac 20:27 [v]Dt 4:2
26:3 [w]Jer 36:7 [x]Jer 18:8
26:4 [y]Lev 26:14 [z]1Ki 9:6
26:5 [a]Jer 25:4
26:6 [b]Jos 18:1 [c]2Ki 22:19
26:9 [d]Jer 9:11
26:11 [e]Dt 18:20, Jer 18:23; 38:4; Mt 26:66; Ac 6:11
26:12 [f]Jer 1:18 [g]Am 7:15; Ac 4:18-20; 5:29 [h]ver 2,15
26:13 [i]Jer 7:5; Joel 2:12-14
26:14 [j]Jer 38:5
26:16 [k]Ac 23:9 [l]Ac 5:34-39; 23:29

[a] *38* Some Hebrew manuscripts and Septuagint (see also Jer. 46:16 and 50:16); most Hebrew manuscripts *anger*

25:37 peaceful meadows. "Meadows" is the same word as "land" in verse 30. **peaceful.** Has connotations of prosperity (cf. "safe country" in 12:5).
25:38 Like a lion. See note on 2:15. Here Jeremiah referred to the Lord (cf. Am 3:8).
■**26:1–24** *Reaction to Prediction of Exile.* In this chapter Jeremiah's earlier temple sermon (see ch. 7) is summarized (vv. 2–6) and the response to the sermon recorded (vv. 7–24).
26:1 Early in the reign of Jehoiakim. Possibly during his first year (609–608 B.C.). The fuller account of the temple sermon (7:1–15) is not dated. The dating here brings Jehoiakim into the foreground as one who rejected Jeremiah's words (ch. 36).
26:2 the courtyard. Probably the inner courtyard. For use of "gate," see 7:2.
26:7 priests, the prophets and all the people. Stress is placed on the numbers and kinds of people in order to demonstrate that nearly the entire city rejected Jeremiah.
26:8 You must die! This was normally uttered as the sentence for a serious crime (e.g., Ex 21:15–17; Dt 18:20). Jeremiah was evidently held to be a false prophet because of the people's complacent belief that God's temple could never be destroyed (v. 9; cf. 7:4).
26:9 in the LORD's name. The phrase implies a charge of blasphemy.
26:10 the officials of Judah. They had special legal responsibility in the royal administration. Their arrival meant that a proper legal proceeding was taking the place of a public affair. **New Gate.** The gates were the normal locations for court hearings (Ru 4:1; Pr 31:23).
26:15–16 See *WLC* 135.
26:16 This man should not be sentenced to death! Contrast

17 Some of the elders of the land stepped forward and said to the entire assembly of
people, 18 "Micah[m] of Moresheth prophesied in the days of Hezekiah king of Judah. He
told all the people of Judah, 'This is what the LORD Almighty says:

" 'Zion[n] will be plowed like a field,
Jerusalem will become a heap of rubble,[o]
the temple hill[p] a mound overgrown with thickets.'[a][q]

19 "Did Hezekiah king of Judah or anyone else in Judah put him to death? Did not Hezekiah[r] fear the LORD and seek his favor? And did not the LORD relent,[s] so that he did not
bring the disaster[t] he pronounced against them? We are about to bring a terrible disaster[u] on ourselves!"

20 (Now Uriah son of Shemaiah from Kiriath Jearim[v] was another man who prophesied
in the name of the LORD; he prophesied the same things against this city and this land as
Jeremiah did. 21 When King Jehoiakim[w] and all his officers and officials heard his words,
the king sought to put him to death. But Uriah heard of it and fled[x] in fear to Egypt. 22 King
Jehoiakim, however, sent Elnathan[y] son of Acbor to Egypt, along with some other men.
23 They brought Uriah out of Egypt and took him to King Jehoiakim, who had him struck
down with a sword and his body thrown into the burial place of the common people.)

24 Furthermore, Ahikam[z] son of Shaphan supported Jeremiah, and so he was not
handed over to the people to be put to death.

Judah to Serve Nebuchadnezzar

27 Early in the reign of Zedekiah[b][a] son of Josiah king of Judah, this word came to
Jeremiah from the LORD: 2 This is what the LORD said to me: "Make a yoke[b] out
of straps and crossbars and put it on your neck. 3 Then send word to the kings of Edom,
Moab, Ammon,[c] Tyre and Sidon through the envoys who have come to Jerusalem to Zedekiah king of Judah. 4 Give them a message for their masters and say, 'This is what the
LORD Almighty, the God of Israel, says: "Tell this to your masters: 5 With my great power
and outstretched arm[d] I made the earth and its people and the animals that are on it,
and I give[e] it to anyone I please. 6 Now I will hand all your countries over to my servant[f]
Nebuchadnezzar[g] king of Babylon; I will make even the wild animals subject to him.[h] 7 All
nations will serve[i] him and his son and his grandson until the time[j] for his land comes;
then many nations and great kings will subjugate[k] him.

8 " ' "If, however, any nation or kingdom will not serve Nebuchadnezzar king of Babylon or bow its neck under his yoke, I will punish that nation with the sword, famine and
plague, declares the LORD, until I destroy it by his hand. 9 So do not listen to your prophets, your diviners, your interpreters of dreams, your mediums[l] or your sorcerers who tell
you, 'You will not serve the king of Babylon.' 10 They prophesy lies[m] to you that will only
serve to remove you far from your lands; I will banish you and you will perish. 11 But if
any nation will bow its neck under the yoke[n] of the king of Babylon and serve him, I will
let that nation remain in its own land to till it and to live there, declares the LORD." ' "

26:18 [m]Mic 1:1 [n]Isa 2:3 [o]Ne 4:2; Jer 9:11 [p]Mic 4:1; Zec 8:3 [q]Jer 17:3
26:19 [r]2Ch 32:24-26; Isa 37:14-20 [s]Ex 32:14; 2Sa 24:16 [t]Jer 44:7 [u]Hab 2:10
26:20 [v]Jos 9:17
26:21 [w]1Ki 19:2 [x]Mt 10:23
26:22 [y]Jer 36:12,25
26:24 [z]2Ki 22:12
27:1 [a]2Ch 36:11
27:2 [b]Jer 28:10,13
27:3 [c]Jer 25:21
27:5 [d]Dt 9:29 [e]Ps 115:16
27:6 [f]Jer 25:9 [g]Jer 21:7; Eze 29:18-20 [h]Jer 28:14; Da 2:37-38
27:7 [i]2Ch 36:20 [j]Jer 25:12 [k]Jer 25:14; Da 5:28
27:9 [l]Dt 18:11
27:10 [m]Jer 23:25
27:11 [n]Jer 21:9

[a] *18* Micah 3:12 [b] *1* A few Hebrew manuscripts and Syriac (see also Jer. 27:3,12 and 28:1); most Hebrew manuscripts *Jehoiakim* (Most Septuagint manuscripts do not have this verse.)

---

verse 11. This was a remarkable vindication of Jeremiah's authenticity as a prophet.

26:18–19 Micah of Moresheth. Micah had lived a century earlier. His case was cited in support of the judgment just given. His prophecy that Jerusalem would fall (Mic 3:12) led Hezekiah and the people to repent, and Jerusalem was spared from defeat by the Assyrians (Isa 37:14–38). Like Micah, Jeremiah prophesied the destruction of Jerusalem to warn the people of their need to repent. The proper reaction to his words was not to seek his death but to solicit the mercy of God.

26:20–23 The story of Uriah demonstrates that Jeremiah was not alone in his preaching; it also stresses that Jeremiah's escape was not the most important point of this chapter. Rather, the prophet made it clear that the Judahites deserved the exile because they rejected the word of God, even to the point of killing a prophet of the Lord. See the contrasting fates of the heroes of faith in Hebrews 11:32–38.

26:22 Elnathan son of Acbor. Contrast his action on Jeremiah's behalf in 36:12 and 25. This evidence of shifting roles must have made Jeremiah's existence seem highly precarious.

26:23 burial place of the common people. This was probably located in the Kidron Valley, east of Jerusalem (2Ki 23:6).

26:24 Ahikam son of Shaphan supported Jeremiah. An official under Josiah (2Ki 22:12,14). His support may have been decisive in Jeremiah's deliverance.

■ **27:1–22** *Rejection of False Prophecies.* This chapter depicts how Jeremiah opposed the false prophecies that all would be well with Judah.

27:1 Early in the reign of Zedekiah. 593 B.C. (see 28:1 and its note).

27:3 send word. Jeremiah was, after all, a "prophet to the nations" (1:5). **Edom . . . Sidon.** See 25:21–22. They were also under the Lord's judgment. **envoys who have come . . . to Zedekiah.** In league with Egypt, they had probably come to discuss the possibility of rebellion against Nebuchadnezzar.

27:5 great power and outstretched arm. See 21:5. **I made the earth . . . give it to anyone I please.** Using an argument from creation, the Lord claimed rights over all nations. See Daniel 2:38 and 4:25, which also pertain to Nebuchadnezzar. See *BC* 36.

27:9 prophets . . . sorcerers. All of them were in error insofar as they served merely to bolster the political system, in this case with the exhortation not to submit to Babylon. Some (diviners, mediums, sorcerers), however, were explicitly forbidden whether or not they told the truth (14:14; Lev 19:26; Dt 18:10–11).

27:11 I will let that nation remain in its own land. For Judah's neighbors submission to Babylon would not entail exile.

12 I gave the same message to Zedekiah king of Judah. I said, "Bow your neck under the yoke of the king of Babylon; serve him and his people, and you will live. 13 Why will you and your people die[o] by the sword, famine and plague with which the LORD has threatened any nation that will not serve the king of Babylon? 14 Do not listen to the words of the prophets who say to you, 'You will not serve the king of Babylon,' for they are prophesying lies[p] to you. 15 'I have not sent[q] them,' declares the LORD. 'They are prophesying lies in my name.[r] Therefore, I will banish you and you will perish,[s] both you and the prophets who prophesy to you.' "

16 Then I said to the priests and all these people, "This is what the LORD says: Do not listen to the prophets who say, 'Very soon now the articles[t] from the LORD's house will be brought back from Babylon.' They are prophesying lies to you. 17 Do not listen to them. Serve the king of Babylon, and you will live. Why should this city become a ruin? 18 If they are prophets and have the word of the LORD, let them plead[u] with the LORD Almighty that the furnishings remaining in the house of the LORD and in the palace of the king of Judah and in Jerusalem not be taken to Babylon. 19 For this is what the LORD Almighty says about the pillars, the Sea,[v] the movable stands and the other furnishings[w] that are left in this city, 20 which Nebuchadnezzar king of Babylon did not take away when he carried[x] Jehoiachin[a][y] son of Jehoiakim king of Judah into exile from Jerusalem to Babylon, along with all the nobles of Judah and Jerusalem— 21 yes, this is what the LORD Almighty, the God of Israel, says about the things that are left in the house of the LORD and in the palace of the king of Judah and in Jerusalem: 22 'They will be taken[z] to Babylon and there they will remain until the day[a] I come for them,' declares the LORD. 'Then I will bring[b] them back and restore them to this place.' "

The False Prophet Hananiah

28 In the fifth month of that same year, the fourth year, early in the reign of Zedekiah[c] king of Judah, the prophet Hananiah son of Azzur, who was from Gibeon,[d] said to me in the house of the LORD in the presence of the priests and all the people: 2 "This is what the LORD Almighty, the God of Israel, says: 'I will break the yoke[e] of the king of Babylon. 3 Within two years I will bring back to this place all the articles[f] of the LORD's house that Nebuchadnezzar king of Babylon removed from here and took to Babylon. 4 I will also bring back to this place Jehoiachin[a][g] son of Jehoiakim king of Judah and all the other exiles from Judah who went to Babylon,' declares the LORD, 'for I will break the yoke of the king of Babylon.' "

5 Then the prophet Jeremiah replied to the prophet Hananiah before the priests and all the people who were standing in the house of the LORD. 6 He said, "Amen! May the LORD do so! May the LORD fulfill the words you have prophesied by bringing the articles of the LORD's house and all the exiles back to this place from Babylon. 7 Nevertheless, listen to what I have to say in your hearing and in the hearing of all the people: 8 From early times the prophets who preceded you and me have prophesied war, disaster and plague[h] against many countries and great kingdoms. 9 But the prophet who prophesies peace will be recognized as one truly sent by the LORD only if his prediction comes true.[i]"

10 Then the prophet Hananiah took the yoke[j] off the neck of the prophet Jeremiah and broke it, 11 and he said[k] before all the people, "This is what the LORD says: 'In the same way will I break the yoke of Nebuchadnezzar king of Babylon off the neck of all the nations within two years.' " At this, the prophet Jeremiah went on his way.

12 Shortly after the prophet Hananiah had broken the yoke off the neck of the prophet Jeremiah, the word of the LORD came to Jeremiah: 13 "Go and tell Hananiah, 'This is what the LORD says: You have broken a wooden yoke, but in its place you will get a yoke

27:13 [o]Eze 18:31
27:14 [p]Jer 14:14
27:15 [q]Jer 23:21 [r]Jer 29:9 [s]Jer 6:15
27:16 [t]2Ki 24:13; 2Ch 36:7,10; Jer 28:3; Da 1:2
27:18 [u]1Sa 7:8
27:19 [v]2Ki 25:13 [w]Jer 52:17-23
27:20 [x]2Ch 36:10; Jer 24:1 [y]Jer 22:24
27:22 [z]2Ki 25:13 [a]2Ch 36:21 [b]Ezr 1:7; 7:19
28:1 [c]Jer 27:1,3 [d]Jos 9:3
28:2 [e]Jer 27:12
28:3 [f]2Ki 24:13
28:4 [g]Jer 22:24-27
28:8 [h]Lev 26:14-17; Isa 5:5-7
28:9 [i]Dt 18:22
28:10 [j]Jer 27:2
28:11 [k]Jer 14:14; 27:10

[a] 20,4 Hebrew *Jeconiah,* a variant of *Jehoiachin*

27:12 serve him . . . you will live. Jeremiah had shown that exile was part of God's plan for Judah's ultimate salvation (24:5).
27:15 I have not sent them. See 14:14 and 23:21.
27:16 Very soon now. Refers to the message of Hananiah (28:1–3). **articles from the LORD's house.** These were carried off, some in 605 B.C. (Da 1:1–2) and some in 597 B.C. (2Ki 24:13).
27:22 They will be taken . . . day I come for them. The perspective of an exile with a fixed time frame (25:11; 27:7) was now applied to the fate of the temple vessels.
■ **28:1–17** *Confrontation With Hananiah.* Jeremiah confronted a prominent false prophet over the question of Jerusalem's final destruction.
28:1 that same year. 593 B.C. (see note on 27:1). **prophet.** No doubt Hananiah held this status. The issue was whether or not his message was true.
28:2 This is what the LORD . . . says. The false message was introduced just as the genuine one had been (e.g., 9:7). **yoke.** Hananiah directly challenged Jeremiah (27:2), and his message contradicted Jeremiah's (27:16–22).
28:3 Within two years. A negligible period of time that implies no judgment at all. Contrast Jeremiah's 70 years (25:11–12).
28:6 Amen! Jeremiah did not oppose Hananiah straightaway; rather, his love for land and people emerged in this wish. His exclamation was laced with sarcasm.
28:8 From early times . . . plague. Jeremiah reminded Hananiah that the true prophetic tradition was to stress judgment so that repentance could take place, rather than assuring security without repentance.

of iron. 14This is what the LORD Almighty, the God of Israel, says: I will put an iron yoke[l]
on the necks of all these nations to make them serve[m] Nebuchadnezzar king of Babylon,
and they will serve him. I will even give him control over the wild animals.[n]' "
15Then the prophet Jeremiah said to Hananiah the prophet, "Listen, Hananiah! The
LORD has not sent[o] you, yet you have persuaded this nation to trust in lies.[p] 16Therefore,
this is what the LORD says: 'I am about to remove you from the face of the earth.[q] This
very year you are going to die, because you have preached rebellion[r] against the LORD.' "
17In the seventh month of that same year, Hananiah the prophet died.

A Letter to the Exiles

29 This is the text of the letter that the prophet Jeremiah sent from Jerusalem to the
surviving elders among the exiles and to the priests, the prophets and all the
other people Nebuchadnezzar had carried into exile from Jerusalem to Babylon.[s] 2(This
was after King Jehoiachin[a][t] and the queen mother, the court officials and the leaders of
Judah and Jerusalem, the craftsmen and the artisans had gone into exile from Jerusalem.)
3He entrusted the letter to Elasah son of Shaphan and to Gemariah son of Hilkiah, whom
Zedekiah king of Judah sent to King Nebuchadnezzar in Babylon. It said:

4This is what the LORD Almighty, the God of Israel, says to all those I carried[u]
into exile from Jerusalem to Babylon: 5"Build[v] houses and settle down; plant gardens and eat what they produce. 6Marry and have sons and daughters; find wives
for your sons and give your daughters in marriage, so that they too may have sons
and daughters. Increase in number there; do not decrease. 7Also, seek the peace
and prosperity of the city to which I have carried you into exile. Pray[w] to the LORD
for it, because if it prospers, you too will prosper." 8Yes, this is what the LORD Almighty, the God of Israel, says: "Do not let the prophets and diviners among you
deceive[x] you. Do not listen to the dreams you encourage them to have.[y] 9They are
prophesying lies[z] to you in my name. I have not sent them," declares the LORD.
10This is what the LORD says: "When seventy years[a] are completed for Babylon,
I will come to you and fulfill my gracious promise to bring you back[b] to this
place. 11For I know the plans[c] I have for you," declares the LORD, "plans to prosper you and not to harm you, plans to give you hope and a future. 12Then you will
call upon me and come and pray to me, and I will listen[d] to you. 13You will seek[e]
me and find me when you seek me with all your heart.[f] 14I will be found by you,"
declares the LORD, "and will bring you back[g] from captivity.[b] I will gather you from
all the nations and places where I have banished you," declares the LORD, "and will
bring you back to the place from which I carried you into exile."[h]
15You may say, "The LORD has raised up prophets for us in Babylon," 16but this
is what the LORD says about the king who sits on David's throne and all the people who remain in this city, your countrymen who did not go with you into exile—
17yes, this is what the LORD Almighty says: "I will send the sword, famine and
plague[i] against them and I will make them like poor figs[j] that are so bad they can-

[a] 2 Hebrew *Jeconiah*, a variant of *Jehoiachin* [b] 14 Or *will restore your fortunes*

28:14 [l]Dt 28:48 [m]Jer 25:11 [n]Jer 27:6
28:15 [o]Jer 29:31 [p]Jer 20:6; 29:21; La 2:14; Eze 13:6
28:16 [q]Ge 7:4 [r]Dt 13:5; Jer 29:32
29:1 [s]2Ch 36:10
29:2 [t]2Ki 24:12; Jer 22:24-28
29:4 [u]Jer 24:5
29:5 [v]ver 28
29:7 [w]Ezr 6:10; 1Ti 2:1-2
29:8 [x]Jer 37:9 [y]Jer 23:27
29:9 [z]Jer 14:14; 27:15
29:10 [a]2Ch 36:21; Jer 25:12; Da 9:2 [b]Jer 21:22
29:11 [c]Ps 40:5
29:12 [d]Ps 145:19
29:13 [e]Mt 7:7 [f]Dt 4:29; Jer 24:7
29:14 [g]Dt 30:3; Jer 30:3 [h]Jer 23:3-4
29:17 [i]Jer 27:8 [j]Jer 24:8-10

28:13 wooden yoke . . . yoke of iron. The Lord will not be frustrated by an empty symbolic act. Judah's resistance to the message, so well summed up in Hananiah, would only make the inevitable servitude harsher.

28:16 remove. This is the same word as "sent" (v. 15), an ironic play on words. This "sending" was one to punishment by death. **rebellion.** Although the rebellion was ostensibly against Babylon, it was really against God (Dt 13:5).

■ **29:1–32** *Letter to Exiles About False Prophecy.* These verses summarize a letter Jeremiah sent to Judahites in exile. He encouraged them to accept the lengthy exile as God's just punishment against the nation. By doing so, they would be ready for the restoration to come.

29:3 Elasah son of Shaphan. Possibly he was of the same family that was sympathetic to Jeremiah (26:24). **Zedekiah . . . sent to king Nebuchadnezzar.** Although for an unnamed purpose, we may suppose that some form of regular contact continued between Jerusalem and Babylon (51:59).

29:4 This is what the LORD . . . says. The letter was the word of God just as much as the spoken prophecies were. See theological article "The Word of God" on next page.

29:5 Build houses and settle down. An act of commitment to their new lives, thus reflecting acceptance of the Lord's judgment and acknowledgment of the justice of a lengthy exile (Eze 8:1).

29:7 peace . . . prosperity . . . prospers . . . prosper. The Hebrew word for all these is *shalom* ("peace"; see 6:14 and its note). The false peace lightly promised (8:11) would give way to a true peace (cf. Jn 14:27). This instruction models the kind of actions that believers are to take in relation to the nations of the world in which they live. **Pray . . . for it.** The Lord's blessing can come on any nation through the prayer and the actions of his people (e.g., Abraham [Ge 20:17], Joseph [Ge 37–50] and Daniel [Da 1–6]).

29:8–9 prophets and diviners . . . prophesying lies. False prophets in Jerusalem claimed that the troubles from Babylon would soon be over (e.g., 28:2–4). See 20:21.

29:10 seventy years. Jeremiah again predicted that the exile would last 70 years (see note on 25:11–12). An entire generation would pass.

29:11–14 This verse echoes Deuteronomy 30:3–5 (which is similar to Dt 4:29–30).

29:14 bring you back from captivity. See NIV text note. The phrase implies a restoration of the relationship between the Lord and his people. It is typical of Jeremiah's "book of consolation" (chs. 33–36). See 30:3 and 18, 31:23, 32:44, 33:7, 11 and 26, 48:47 and 49:6 and 39.

29:16 the king. Zedekiah. That Zedekiah still ruled (albeit as a puppet) in Jerusalem may have been a focus of false hope for the exiles.

not be eaten. 18 I will pursue them with the sword, famine and plague and will
make them abhorrent[k] to all the kingdoms of the earth and an object of cursing
and horror,[l] of scorn and reproach, among all the nations where I drive them.
19 For they have not listened to my words,"[m] declares the LORD, "words that I sent
to them again and again by my servants the prophets.[n] And you exiles have not
listened either," declares the LORD.
20 Therefore, hear the word of the LORD, all you exiles whom I have sent[o] away
from Jerusalem to Babylon. 21 This is what the LORD Almighty, the God of Israel,
says about Ahab son of Kolaiah and Zedekiah son of Maaseiah, who are prophesying lies[p] to you in my name: "I will hand them over to Nebuchadnezzar king of
Babylon, and he will put them to death before your very eyes. 22 Because of them,
all the exiles from Judah who are in Babylon will use this curse: 'The LORD treat you
like Zedekiah and Ahab, whom the king of Babylon burned[q] in the fire.' 23 For they

29:18 [k]Jer 15:4 [l]Dt 28:25; Jer 42:18
29:19 [m]Jer 6:19 [n]Jer 25:4
29:20 [o]Jer 24:5
29:21 [p]ver 9; Jer 14:14
29:22 [q]Da 3:6

29:19 they have not listened. Zedekiah and those remaining in Jerusalem would be punished further because they had not yet learned the lesson of the Babylonian trials. They refused to repent of sin and turn to the Lord for help. **you . . . have not listened.** The exiles to whom Jeremiah wrote were in the same condition as those remaining in the land. Neither group had grasped the need for full repentance.

29:22 this curse. God's judgment against Zedekiah and Jerusalem would be so great that they would be used as the model of what a cursed person would experience. **in the fire.** A method of execution in Babylon (see Da 3:6).

The Word of God: Scripture as Revelation: Is the Bible the Word of God?

REFORMED Theology emphasizes the fact that God is transcendent over his creation. His transcendence forms such distance between him and humanity that we can know God only if he condescends to reveal himself to us, which he does in many ways, both through typical aspects of the creation (general revelation) and through providential interactions with people like his authoritative prophets and apostles who wrote the Scriptures (special revelation). Reformed theology seeks to rest squarely on God's revelation of himself and not on human speculation about God, and it trusts in Scripture alone as the only infallible standard by which all revelation is to be judged.

Other books, especially ancient ones associated with Israel, have much value for Christians. Even so, from its beginning Reformed theology has received the 66 books of the Bible as the only absolutely unquestionable record, interpretation and explanation of God's self-disclosure. We call this collection of books the Canon ("Canon" means "measurement" or "standard").

In one sense the Scriptures are the faithful testimony of godly people to the God they loved and served. In another sense, however, they are God's own revelation of himself given through the inspiration of the Holy Spirit (2Ti 3:16). The church calls these writings the Word of God because God himself is their ultimate author.

The belief that divine revelation came to people in written form reaches as far back as the ancient Near Eastern practice of priests recording words of the gods in writing. In Israel itself written revelation began at least as early as the time when God inscribed the Ten Commandments on stone tablets and prompted Moses to write the laws and history of the first five books of the Bible (Ex 32:15–16; 34:1,27–28; Nu 33:2; Dt 31:9).

Living according to written revelation was always central to true devotion in Israel for both leaders and ordinary people (Jos 1:7–8; 2Ki 17:13; 22:8–13; 1Ch 22:12–13; Ne 8; Ps 119). The same principle that all of life must be governed by the Scriptures now informs Christianity.

There are many reasons Christians believe that the Bible is the Word of God (*WCF* 1.5). Crucial support comes from the testimony of Christ and his apostles. We know about Christ and his apostles from the Bible, but they also testified to the authority of the Bible. Jesus viewed his Bible (our OT) as his heavenly Father's written instruction, which he was obligated to obey (Mt 4:4,7,10; 5:17–20; 19:4–6; 26:31,52–54; Lk 4:16–21; 16:17; 18:31–33; 22:37; 24:25–27,45–47; Jn 10:35) and fulfill (Mt 26:24; Jn 5:46). Paul described the Old Testament as entirely "God-breathed" and written to teach the Christian faith (2Ti 3:15–17; see also Ro 15:4; 1Co 10:11). Peter affirmed the divine origin of Biblical teaching in 1 Peter 1:10–12 and 2 Peter 1:21, and the writer of Hebrews quoted the Old Testament in ways that demonstrate its authority (Heb 1:5–13; 3:7; 4:3; 10:5–7,15–17; cf. Ac 4:25; 28:25–27).

Since the apostles' teaching about Christ is revealed truth (1Co 2:12–13), the church rightly regards the apostolic teachings collected in the New Testament as completing the Scriptures. Peter placed Paul's letters on an equal footing with the rest of Scripture (2Pe 3:15–16), and Paul apparently quoted Luke's gospel as Scripture in 1 Timothy 5:18 (Lk 10:7).

What Scripture says, God says. As a result, all of its varied contents—histories, prophecies, poems, songs, wisdom writings, sermons, statistics, letters, etc.—should be received as from God, and all that the Biblical writers taught should be revered as God's authoritative instruction. This belief was the focus of the Reformation doctrine *Sola Scriptura* (Scripture Alone), the belief that the Bible is the only absolute, unquestionable, authoritative revelation for God's people. Christians should be grateful to God for the gift of his written Word and conscientious in basing their faith and lives on its truth.

29:23 [r]Jer 23:14 [s]Heb 4:13

have done outrageous things in Israel; they have committed adultery[r] with their
neighbors' wives and in my name have spoken lies, which I did not tell them to do.
I know[s] it and am a witness to it," declares the LORD.

Message to Shemaiah

29:25 [t]2Ki 25:18; Jer 21:1
29:26 [u]2Ki 9:11; Hos 9:7; Jn 10:20 [v]Jer 20:2
29:28 [w]ver 1 [x]ver 10 [y]ver 5

24 Tell Shemaiah the Nehelamite, 25 "This is what the LORD Almighty, the God of Israel, says: You sent letters in your own name to all the people in Jerusalem, to Zephaniah[t] son of Maaseiah the priest, and to all the other priests. You said to Zephaniah, 26 'The
LORD has appointed you priest in place of Jehoiada to be in charge of the house of the
LORD; you should put any madman[u] who acts like a prophet into the stocks[v] and neck-
irons. 27 So why have you not reprimanded Jeremiah from Anathoth, who poses as a
prophet among you? 28 He has sent this message[w] to us in Babylon: It will be a long time.[x]
Therefore build[y] houses and settle down; plant gardens and eat what they produce.' "
29 Zephaniah the priest, however, read the letter to Jeremiah the prophet. 30 Then the
word of the LORD came to Jeremiah: 31 "Send this message to all the exiles: 'This is what
the LORD says about Shemaiah[z] the Nehelamite: Because Shemaiah has prophesied to
you, even though I did not send[a] him, and has led you to believe a lie, 32 this is what the
LORD says: I will surely punish Shemaiah the Nehelamite and his descendants.[b] He will
have no one left among this people, nor will he see the good[c] things I will do for my people, declares the LORD, because he has preached rebellion[d] against me.' "

29:31 [z]ver 24 [a]Jer 14:14; 28:15
29:32 [b]1Sa 2:30-33 [c]ver 10 [d]Jer 28:16

Restoration of Israel

30:2 [e]Isa 30:8
30:3 [f]Jer 29:14 [g]Jer 16:15

30 This is the word that came to Jeremiah from the LORD: 2 "This is what the LORD, the
God of Israel, says: 'Write[e] in a book all the words I have spoken to you. 3 The days
are coming,' declares the LORD, 'when I will bring[f] my people Israel and Judah back from
captivity[a] and restore[g] them to the land I gave their forefathers to possess,' says the LORD."
4 These are the words the LORD spoke concerning Israel and Judah: 5 "This is what the
LORD says:

30:5 [h]Jer 6:25
30:6 [i]Jer 4:31
30:7 [j]Isa 2:12; Joel 2:11 [k]Zep 1:15 [l]ver 10

" 'Cries of fear[h] are heard—
terror, not peace.
6 Ask and see:
Can a man bear children?
Then why do I see every strong man
with his hands on his stomach like a woman in labor,[i]
every face turned deathly pale?
7 How awful that day[j] will be!
None will be like it.
It will be a time of trouble[k] for Jacob,
but he will be saved[l] out of it.

30:8 [m]Isa 9:4 [n]Eze 34:27
30:9 [o]Isa 55:3-4; Lk 1:69; Ac 2:30; 13:23 [p]Eze 34:23-24; 37:24; Hos 3:5

8 " 'In that day,' declares the LORD Almighty,
'I will break the yoke[m] off their necks
and will tear off their bonds;
no longer will foreigners enslave them.[n]
9 Instead, they will serve the LORD their God
and David[o] their king,[p]
whom I will raise up for them.

[a] 3 *Or will restore the fortunes of my people Israel and Judah*

29:24 Tell Shemaiah. This false prophet was among the exiles, and Jeremiah opposed him directly.
29:28 a long time. The 70 years of 25:11–12 and 29:10. **build houses . . . plant gardens.** Shemaiah cited Jeremiah's letter (v. 5).
29:31–32 Compare the threat against Shemaiah with that made against Hananiah (28:15–16). **nor will he see the good things.** Ironic justice for one who would announce the "good things" too quickly and without knowledge of the mind of the Lord.
■ **30:1—33:26** *Certainty of Restoration.* Commonly referred to as Jeremiah's "book of consolation," these chapters contain promises of the restoration of Israel and Judah after the 70 years of exile. This material divides into a book of restoration (30:1—31:40), Jeremiah's purchase of a field (32:1–44) and predictions of restoration (33:1–26).
■ **30:1—31:40** *The Book of Restoration.* God called Jeremiah to write a collection of his prophecies concerning the restoration of God's people after the exile. The prophet's vision of the future spoke of a glorious outlook for the people of God.
30:3 days are coming. In this context the prophet referred to the end of exile as the time toward which "the days are coming" (31:27,38; 33:14; see also "time is coming" at 31:31).
30:6 Can a man . . . woman in labor . . . ? The anguish of childbirth is a picture of the suffering the people would experience under the Babylonian armies (4:19,31). Perhaps men would act like women in childbirth because of sickness or hunger.
30:7 that day. The day of the Lord (see note on 30:3; see also Am 5:18; 8:9). Amos's generation thought it a day of deliverance, but they had to learn that it would bring judgment. Here it refers primarily to the judgment against Jerusalem that was about to be experienced. See "Introduction to Zechariah."
30:8 that day. Here and elsewhere the day of the Lord refers to the time when God would strike out against the enemies of Israel in order to deliver his own people (cf. v. 7). See "Introduction to Zechariah."

10 " 'So do not fear,[q] O Jacob my servant;[r]
do not be dismayed, O Israel,'
declares the LORD.
'I will surely save[s] you out of a distant place,
your descendants from the land of their exile.
Jacob will again have peace and security,[t]
and no one will make him afraid.
11 I am with you and will save you,'
declares the LORD.
'Though I completely destroy all the nations
among which I scatter you,
I will not completely destroy[u] you.
I will discipline[v] you but only with justice;
I will not let you go entirely unpunished.'[w]

12 "This is what the LORD says:

" 'Your wound is incurable,
your injury beyond healing.[x]
13 There is no one to plead your cause,
no remedy for your sore,
no healing[y] for you.
14 All your allies[z] have forgotten you;
they care nothing for you.
I have struck you as an enemy[a] would
and punished you as would the cruel,[b]
because your guilt is so great
and your sins[c] so many.
15 Why do you cry out over your wound,
your pain that has no cure?
Because of your great guilt and many sins
I have done these things to you.

16 " 'But all who devour[d] you will be devoured;
all your enemies will go into exile.[e]
Those who plunder[f] you will be plundered;
all who make spoil of you I will despoil.
17 But I will restore you to health
and heal your wounds,'
declares the LORD,
'because you are called an outcast,[g]
Zion for whom no one cares.'

18 "This is what the LORD says:

" 'I will restore the fortunes[h] of Jacob's tents
and have compassion[i] on his dwellings;
the city will be rebuilt[j] on her ruins,
and the palace will stand in its proper place.
19 From them will come songs[k] of thanksgiving[l]
and the sound of rejoicing.[m]
I will add to their numbers,[n]
and they will not be decreased;
I will bring them honor,[o]
and they will not be disdained.
20 Their children[p] will be as in days of old,
and their community will be established[q] before me;
I will punish all who oppress them.
21 Their leader[r] will be one of their own;
their ruler will arise from among them.

30:10 [q]Isa 43:5; Jer 46:27-28 [r]Isa 44:2 [s]Jer 29:14 [t]Isa 35:9
30:11 [u]Jer 4:27; 46:28 [v]Jer 10:24 [w]Am 9:8
30:12 [x]Jer 15:18
30:13 [y]Jer 8:22; 14:19; 46:11
30:14 [z]Jer 22:20; La 1:2 [a]Job 13:24 [b]Job 30:21 [c]Jer 5:6
30:16 [d]Isa 33:1; Jer 2:3; 10:25 [e]Isa 14:2; Joel 3:4-8 [f]Jer 50:10
30:17 [g]Jer 33:24
30:18 [h]ver 3; Jer 31:23 [i]Ps 102:13 [j]Jer 31:4,24,38
30:19 [k]Isa 35:10; 51:11 [l]Isa 51:3 [m]Ps 126:1-2; Jer 31:4 [n]Jer 33:22 [o]Isa 60:9
30:20 [p]Isa 54:13; Jer 31:17 [q]Isa 54:14
30:21 [r]ver 9

30:10 do not fear, O Jacob my servant. See Isaiah 41:8 and 10, 43:1 and 44:1–2. In 32:39 fear of the Lord is compatible with this command. **no one will make him afraid.** Contrast verse 5. See Leviticus 26:6, where lack of fear is a fulfillment of covenant blessing. **30:20 as in days of old.** In light of verse 9, this is probably an allusion to the time of David. **community.** A technical term denoting the political or religious assembly of the covenant people (1Ki 12:20). **30:21 Their leader . . . ruler . . . from among them.** This contrasts with the imposed Babylonian rule that Judah had yet to en-

30:21 [s]Nu 16:5

I will bring him near[s] and he will come close to me,
for who is he who will devote himself
to be close to me?'
declares the LORD.

22 " 'So you will be my people,
and I will be your God.' "

30:23 [t]Jer 23:19

23 See, the storm[t] of the LORD
will burst out in wrath,
a driving wind swirling down
on the heads of the wicked.

30:24 [u]Jer 4:8 [v]Jer 4:28 [w]Jer 23:19-20

24 The fierce anger[u] of the LORD will not turn back[v]
until he fully accomplishes
the purposes of his heart.
In days to come
you will understand[w] this.

31:1 [x]Jer 30:22

31 "At that time," declares the LORD, "I will be the God[x] of all the clans of Israel,
and they will be my people."
2 This is what the LORD says:

31:2 [y]Nu 14:20 [z]Ex 33:14

"The people who survive the sword
will find favor[y] in the desert;
I will come to give rest[z] to Israel."

31:3 [a]Dt 4:37 [b]Hos 11:4

3 The LORD appeared to us in the past,[a] saying:

"I have loved[a] you with an everlasting love;
I have drawn[b] you with loving-kindness.
4 I will build you up again
and you will be rebuilt, O Virgin Israel.
Again you will take up your tambourines
and go out to dance with the joyful.[c]

31:4 [c]Jer 30:19

31:5 [d]Jer 50:19 [e]Isa 65:21; Am 9:14

5 Again you will plant vineyards
on the hills of Samaria;[d]
the farmers will plant them
and enjoy their fruit.[e]
6 There will be a day when watchmen cry out
on the hills of Ephraim,
'Come, let us go up to Zion,
to the LORD our God.' "[f]

31:6 [f]Isa 2:3; Jer 50:4-5; Mic 4:2

7 This is what the LORD says:

31:7 [g]Dt 28:13; Isa 61:9 [h]Ps 14:7; 28:9 [i]Isa 37:31

"Sing with joy for Jacob;
shout for the foremost[g] of the nations.
Make your praises heard, and say,
'O LORD, save[h] your people,
the remnant[i] of Israel.'

31:8 [j]Jer 3:18; 23:8 [k]Dt 30:4; Eze 34:12-14

8 See, I will bring them from the land of the north[j]
and gather[k] them from the ends of the earth.

[a] 3 Or *LORD has appeared to us from afar*

---

dure. It is to be understood in the light of verse 9 and speaks ultimately of a new (Messianic) order of leadership.

31:2 people who survive the sword. The remnant through whom God's purposes would continue (v. 7; see notes on 6:9; 23:3). Contrast 15:2. **desert.** As the exodus from Egypt was through a desert, so also would be the return from Babylon (the present-day Arabian Desert). For the same analogy see Isaiah 40:3–4 and 43:19–20. Like the first exodus, the restoration from exile would be a model of the Lord's power to save.

31:3 in the past. Probably a reference to Sinai (Ex 19–24). **loved . . . everlasting love.** The Lord's love for Israel was the ground for his election of his people (Dt 7:6–7). The everlasting character of the covenant is affirmed in Genesis 17:7. **loving-kindness.** Another token of the reestablishment of the broken covenant. See note on 9:24 and contrast 16:5. See *WCF* 17.2; *WLC* 79.

31:4 Virgin Israel. Contrast 18:13–15, where Israel's "virginity" was squandered. See also 2:20 and 22. In the age of restoration after the exile, the indelible stain of defilement would finally be cleansed.

31:5 plant vineyards . . . enjoy their fruit. Signifies the covenant blessing in nature (Dt 7:13; 28:4,30). **Samaria.** The capital of the northern kingdom. Its people had been exiled to Assyria in 722 B.C. The renewal after exile would be so great that even the northern kingdom would be restored. As with the restoration of Judah, the restoration of Samaria also failed to be realized completely due to infidelity.

31:6 watchmen. Perhaps they were responsible for knowing the times of annual feasts by observing the moon. **hills of Ephraim . . . let us go up to Zion.** In the restoration period the people would no longer attend the apostate northern shrines of Jeroboam at Bethel and Dan (1Ki 12:26–33). They would come to Zion instead.

Among them will be the blind[l] and the lame,[m]
expectant mothers and women in labor;
a great throng will return.
9 They will come with weeping;[n]
they will pray as I bring them back.
I will lead[o] them beside streams of water
on a level[p] path where they will not stumble,
because I am Israel's father,[q]
and Ephraim is my firstborn son.

10 "Hear the word of the LORD, O nations;
proclaim it in distant coastlands:[r]
'He who scattered Israel will gather[s] them
and will watch over his flock like a shepherd.'[t]
11 For the LORD will ransom Jacob
and redeem[u] them from the hand of those stronger[v] than they.
12 They will come and shout for joy on the heights[w] of Zion;
they will rejoice in the bounty[x] of the LORD—
the grain, the new wine and the oil,[y]
the young of the flocks and herds.
They will be like a well-watered garden,[z]
and they will sorrow[a] no more.
13 Then maidens will dance and be glad,
young men and old as well.
I will turn their mourning[b] into gladness;
I will give them comfort and joy[c] instead of sorrow.
14 I will satisfy[d] the priests with abundance,
and my people will be filled with my bounty,"
declares the LORD.

15 This is what the LORD says:

"A voice is heard in Ramah,[e]
mourning and great weeping,
Rachel weeping for her children
and refusing to be comforted,[f]
because her children are no more."[g]

16 This is what the LORD says:

"Restrain your voice from weeping
and your eyes from tears,[h]
for your work will be rewarded,[i]"
declares the LORD.

"They will return[j] from the land of the enemy.
17 So there is hope for your future,"
declares the LORD.

"Your children will return to their own land.

18 "I have surely heard Ephraim's moaning:
'You disciplined[k] me like an unruly calf,[l]
and I have been disciplined.
Restore[m] me, and I will return,
because you are the LORD my God.
19 After I strayed,[n]
I repented;

31:8 [l]Isa 42:16 [m]Eze 34:16; Mic 4:6
31:9 [n]Ps 126:5 [o]Isa 63:13 [p]Isa 49:11 [q]Ex 4:22; Jer 3:4
31:10 [r]Isa 66:19; Jer 25:22 [s]Jer 50:19 [t]Isa 40:11; Eze 34:12
31:11 [u]Isa 44:23; 48:20 [v]Ps 142:6
31:12 [w]Eze 17:23; Mic 4:1 [x]Joel 3:18 [y]Hos 2:21-22 [z]Isa 58:11 [a]Isa 65:19; Jn 16:22; Rev 7:17
31:13 [b]Isa 61:3 [c]Ps 30:11; Isa 51:11
31:14 [d]ver 25
31:15 [e]Jos 18:25 [f]Ge 37:35 [g]Jer 10:20; Mt 2:17-18*
31:16 [h]Isa 25:8; 30:19 [i]Ru 2:12 [j]Jer 30:3; Eze 11:17
31:18 [k]Job 5:17 [l]Hos 4:16 [m]Ps 80:3
31:19 [n]Eze 36:31

31:8 See *CD* 3–4.VI.
31:9 weeping. Perhaps they would weep with joy (v. 16). **lead . . . streams of water.** See Psalm 23:2, Isaiah 48:21 and 49:10. **level path.** See Isaiah 40:4. **father . . . son.** See 3:4, 31:20, Exodus 4:22 and Hosea 11:1–4.
31:11 ransom. Literally, "liberate by paying a ransom" (e.g., "buy it back" in Lev 27:27). The term is also used of the Lord's liberation of Israel from Egypt (Dt 7:8; 9:26). **redeem.** This is used in a literal sense for the redemption of a family member's forfeited property by a "kinsman-redeemer" (Ru 3:9; see Lev 25:25–28; Jer 32:7–8). This term is also used of the redemption of Israel from Egypt (Ex 6:6), implying deliverance into kin-relationship with him (Ex 6:7). The two ideas (payment of a price and kinship obligation and relationship) come together in the New Testament theology of atonement.
31:15 A voice . . . in Ramah . . . Rachel weeping. Ramah was in the tribe of Benjamin, in the former northern kingdom. Rachel was the grandmother of Ephraim and Manasseh (progenitors of the major northern tribes). She is pictured as weeping over the destruction of the north in 722 B.C. The image is applied in Matthew 2:18 to Herod's slaughter of the innocents because Israel was still under the tyranny of foreign (Roman) powers at the time of Jesus' birth.
31:17–19 See *WCF* 15.2; *WLC* 76,104,192; *WSC* 87; *BC* 12.

after I came to understand,
  I beat[o] my breast.
I was ashamed and humiliated
  because I bore the disgrace of my youth.'
20 Is not Ephraim my dear son,
  the child in whom I delight?
Though I often speak against him,
  I still remember[p] him.
Therefore my heart yearns for him;
  I have great compassion[q] for him,"
declares the LORD.

21 "Set up road signs;
  put up guideposts.
Take note of the highway,[r]
  the road that you take.
Return,[s] O Virgin[t] Israel,
  return to your towns.
22 How long will you wander,[u]
  O unfaithful[v] daughter?
The LORD will create a new thing on earth—
  a woman will surround[a] a man."

23 This is what the LORD Almighty, the God of Israel, says: "When I bring them back
from captivity,[b][w] the people in the land of Judah and in its towns will once again use
these words: 'The LORD bless you, O righteous dwelling,[x] O sacred mountain.'[y] 24 People
will live[z] together in Judah and all its towns—farmers and those who move about with
their flocks. 25 I will refresh the weary and satisfy the faint."[a]
26 At this I awoke[b] and looked around. My sleep had been pleasant to me.
27 "The days are coming," declares the LORD, "when I will plant[c] the house of Israel
and the house of Judah with the offspring of men and of animals. 28 Just as I watched over
them to uproot and tear down, and to overthrow, destroy and bring disaster,[d] so I will
watch over them to build and to plant,"[e] declares the LORD. 29 "In those days people will
no longer say,

'The fathers[f] have eaten sour grapes,
  and the children's teeth are set on edge.'[g]

30 Instead, everyone will die for his own sin;[h] whoever eats sour grapes—his own teeth
will be set on edge.

31 "The time is coming," declares the LORD,
  "when I will make a new covenant[i]
with the house of Israel
  and with the house of Judah.

31:19 [o]Eze 21:12; Lk 18:13
31:20 [p]Hos 4:4; 11:8 [q]Isa 55:7; 63:15; Mic 7:18
31:21 [r]Jer 50:5 [s]Isa 52:11 [t]ver 4
31:22 [u]Jer 2:23 [v]Jer 3:6
31:23 [w]Jer 30:18 [x]Isa 1:26 [y]Ps 48:1; Zec 8:3
31:24 [z]Zec 8:4-8
31:25 [a]Jn 4:14
31:26 [b]Zec 4:1
31:27 [c]Eze 36:9-11; Hos 2:23
31:28 [d]Jer 18:8; 44:27 [e]Jer 1:10
31:29 [f]La 5:7 [g]Eze 18:2
31:30 [h]Isa 3:11; Gal 6:7
31:31 [i]Jer 32:40; Eze 37:26; Lk 22:20; Heb 8:8-12*; 10:16-17

a *22* Or *will go about* ⌞*seeking*⌟; or *will protect* b *23* Or *I restore their fortunes*

31:21 Set up road signs. An exhortation to the exiles to remember the promised land, to let this memory inspire their repentance and to return to the promised land during the restoration.
31:22 unfaithful daughter? See 3:14 and 22. The new salvation would not diminish the need for the Lord's appeal for faithfulness. **new thing.** See Isaiah 42:9. **a woman . . . a man.** The meaning is obscure, but possibly this saying evokes the image of a mother protecting her male child (i.e., a picture of security). It may also be a metaphor of Israel, the Lord's bride, embracing him in utter fidelity (see Hos 2:16).
31:29 The fathers . . . set on edge. This proverb was used by the exiles to blame previous generations for the disaster of the exile, possibly based on a misunderstanding of Exodus 20:5 and Numbers 14:18 (see also Eze 18:2).
31:30 everyone will die for his own sin. During the restoration period the people would be judged individually. See the elaborate discussion in Ezekiel 18:4–32 (see also Dt 24:16). The point is that this generation fully deserved the punishment, even though the nation's guilt had been continuous (7:13; 11:7–8).
31:31–34 Picking up themes first expounded by Moses (see Dt 30:1–10 and their notes), Jeremiah prophesied that God would make a new covenant with his people. As the institution of the old covenant (Ex 19–24) had followed the redemption from Egypt (Ex 12–15), so the formulation of the new covenant would follow the redemption from exile (v. 34). This passage is quoted in Hebrews 8:8–12 (cf. notes on those verses). See *WCF* 7.6; *HC* 122.
31:31 time is coming. The prophet had in mind the period of restoration after the exile, when God would richly bless his people. **new covenant.** The concept is of a renewed covenant rather than a replacement covenant. See theological article "The Covenants of Works and Grace" at Genesis 6 and the chart "Major Covenants in the Bible" on page 25. New Testament passages (e.g., 1Co 11:25; 2Co 3:6; Heb 9:15; 12:24) reveal that the new covenant is fulfilled in Christ, who brought to fruition the Lord's desire for a renewed covenant relationship with his people. Even so, Christ in his first coming only inaugurated the new covenant. He continues to establish it during the time between his first and second comings and will establish it fully only at his return in glory. **with the house of Israel and with the house of Judah.** Here the continuity of God's covenant people is stressed; but see also 23:3 and its note. The Israel of the new covenant would be Abraham's seed, but as the Old Testament prophets and the New Testament indicate, believing Gentiles would be included as well (Gal 3:16,26–29).

32 It will not be like the covenant[j]
I made with their forefathers[k]
when I took them by the hand
to lead them out of Egypt,
because they broke my covenant,
though I was a husband to[a] them,[b]"
declares the LORD.
33 "This is the covenant I will make with the house of Israel
after that time," declares the LORD.
"I will put my law in their minds
and write it on their hearts.[l]
I will be their God,
and they will be my people.[m]
34 No longer will a man teach[n] his neighbor,
or a man his brother, saying, 'Know the LORD,'
because they will all know[o] me,
from the least of them to the greatest,"
declares the LORD.
"For I will forgive[p] their wickedness
and will remember their sins[q] no more."
35 This is what the LORD says,
he who appoints[r] the sun
to shine by day,
who decrees the moon and stars
to shine by night,[s]
who stirs up the sea
so that its waves roar—
the LORD Almighty is his name:[t]
36 "Only if these decrees[u] vanish from my sight,"
declares the LORD,
"will the descendants[v] of Israel ever cease
to be a nation before me."
37 This is what the LORD says:

31:32 [j]Ex 24:8 [k]Dt 5:3

31:33 [l]2Co 3:3 [m]Jer 24:7; Heb 10:16

31:34 [n]1Jn 2:27 [o]Jn 6:45 [p]Isa 54:13; Jer 33:8; 50:20 [q]Ro 11:27; Mic 7:19; Heb 10:17*

31:35 [r]Ps 136:7-9 [s]Ge 1:16 [t]Jer 10:16

31:36 [u]Isa 54:9-10; Jer 33:20-26 [v]Ps 89:36-37

[a] *32* Hebrew; Septuagint and Syriac / *and I turned away from* [b] *32* Or *was their master*

31:32 not . . . like the covenant . . . because they broke my covenant. The new covenant to be enacted would stand in contrast to the old covenant in that, ultimately, the new would not be broken as the old had been (v. 32; Heb 8:7–8). Elsewhere this contrast is traced to the grace mediated by the righteous Servant who, through his once-for-all sacrifice, would secure the covenant blessings for his people (e.g., Isa 53:4–5,8,10–12; cf. Heb 9:12–15; 10:1–4,10–18). Although much has been accomplished by Christ already (i.e., before his return in glory to establish the new covenant in its fullness), our situation as individuals and groups is much like that during the old covenant (1Co 10:1–11). As believers today it is still possible for us to be part of the visible church (the new covenant community) and break covenant so severely that we receive the judgment or discipline of God (see Heb 10:29). See theological article "The Perseverance and Preservation of Believers" at Philippians 1. This possibility will not be removed until Christ returns. **a husband to them.** See 2:2. Compare Christ's relationship to the church (Eph 5:25–27; Rev 19:7; 21:2,9).
31:33 after that time. The prophet was speaking of a time after the exile but was not otherwise specific. The New Testament shows the time to have been ushered in by Christ. **in their minds . . . on their hearts.** Unbelieving Jews in Jeremiah's day had reduced the law to an external standard, much as many Jews did in Jesus' day and in the time of the early church. The idea of the law being on the mind and in the heart was not new. It was the ideal of the old covenant that was realized to some extent in true believers in the Old Testament (Dt 6:5; 26:16; 32:46; 30:1,14). When the new covenant comes in its fullness at Christ's return, the law of God will be written on the heart of every person in the covenant in such a way that they simply cannot disobey it. Until that time, believers will find this promise fulfilled only in part, so that our attempts to internalize and love God's law will be only somewhat successful. **I will be their God, and they . . . my people.** This is the old covenant formula (Lev 26:12; cf. 7:23). The new covenant would not abolish the old but renew it and fulfill its ideals (see v. 31 and its note). See *WCF* 19.7; *CD* 3–4.VI.
31:34 Know the LORD. This exhortation summarizes the obligation of the law (e.g., 22:16–17; 1Ch 28:9). The old covenant required God's people to know him, but during the exile the knowledge of God in Israel had barely survived. In the fullness of the new covenant when Jesus returns, every person involved will know God. **because they will all know me.** Under the new covenant God will bring about what he had commanded under the old. He promises to give his people a heart to know him (24:7). Needless to say, although Christ has inaugurated the new covenant in his death and resurrection, not all who participate in the new covenant (the visible church) know the Lord in a saving way. Believers today must still teach each other to know the Lord. Jeremiah's words will not be completely realized until Christ returns. **For I will forgive.** The basis of the promises in verses 32–33 is here identified as a new work of redemption that began in Christ at his first coming and will reach its fullness at his return (see Heb 10:1–17). **remember . . . no more.** In the Old Testament the word "remember" involves taking action based on a prior commitment (see Ge 8:1 and its note). Hence this promise looked forward to a time when God would act no more to judge his people for their sins, as he had done under his prior commitment in the old covenant—a time after the sacrificial system of the old covenant had ceased, since it provided a constant reminder of sins (Heb 10:3–4,11). The words "no more" underscore that the satisfaction made for sins in the redemption to come would be final and perfect, eliminating the need for further sacrifices for sin.
31:35–36 appoints the sun . . . moon and stars. See Genesis 1:14–18. Israel's covenantal unfaithfulness had once brought judgment on creation itself (see 4:23–26 and their notes). Now the durability of God's creation was made the measure of his commitment to his people in the new covenant. See also 33:20–21 and 25–26. See *WCF* 5.2; *BC* 27.

“Only if the heavens above can be measured[w]
and the foundations of the earth below be searched out
will I reject[x] all the descendants of Israel
because of all they have done,”
declares the LORD.

38 “The days are coming,” declares the LORD, “when this city will be rebuilt[y] for me
from the Tower of Hananel[z] to the Corner Gate.[a] 39 The measuring line will stretch from
there straight to the hill of Gareb and then turn to Goah. 40 The whole valley[b] where dead
bodies[c] and ashes are thrown, and all the terraces out to the Kidron Valley[d] on the east
as far as the corner of the Horse Gate,[e] will be holy[f] to the LORD. The city will never again
be uprooted or demolished.”

Jeremiah Buys a Field

32 This is the word that came to Jeremiah from the LORD in the tenth[g] year of Zedekiah king of Judah, which was the eighteenth[h] year of Nebuchadnezzar. 2 The
army of the king of Babylon was then besieging Jerusalem, and Jeremiah the prophet was
confined in the courtyard of the guard[i] in the royal palace of Judah.
3 Now Zedekiah king of Judah had imprisoned him there, saying, “Why do you prophesy[j] as you do? You say, ‘This is what the LORD says: I am about to hand this city over to
the king of Babylon, and he will capture[k] it. 4 Zedekiah king of Judah will not escape[l] out
of the hands of the Babylonians[a] but will certainly be handed over to the king of Babylon,
and will speak with him face to face and see him with his own eyes. 5 He will take[m] Zedekiah to Babylon, where he will remain until I deal with him, declares the LORD. If you
fight against the Babylonians, you will not succeed.’ ”[n]
6 Jeremiah said, “The word of the LORD came to me: 7 Hanamel son of Shallum your uncle is going to come to you and say, ‘Buy my field at Anathoth, because as nearest relative it is your right and duty[o] to buy it.’
8 “Then, just as the LORD had said, my cousin Hanamel came to me in the courtyard
of the guard and said, ‘Buy my field at Anathoth in the territory of Benjamin. Since it is
your right to redeem it and possess it, buy it for yourself.’
“I knew that this was the word of the LORD; 9 so I bought the field at Anathoth from
my cousin Hanamel and weighed out for him seventeen shekels[b] of silver.[p] 10 I signed and
sealed the deed, had it witnessed,[q] and weighed out the silver on the scales. 11 I took the
deed of purchase—the sealed copy containing the terms and conditions, as well as the
unsealed copy— 12 and I gave this deed to Baruch[r] son of Neriah,[s] the son of Mahseiah,
in the presence of my cousin Hanamel and of the witnesses who had signed the deed and
of all the Jews sitting in the courtyard of the guard.
13 “In their presence I gave Baruch these instructions: 14 ‘This is what the LORD Almighty, the God of Israel, says: Take these documents, both the sealed and unsealed copies of the deed of purchase, and put them in a clay jar so they will last a long time. 15 For
this is what the LORD Almighty, the God of Israel, says: Houses, fields and vineyards will
again be bought in this land.’[t]
16 “After I had given the deed of purchase to Baruch son of Neriah, I prayed to the
LORD:

17 “Ah, Sovereign LORD,[u] you have made the heavens and the earth by your great
power and outstretched arm.[v] Nothing is too hard[w] for you. 18 You show love[x] to

31:37 [w]Jer 33:22 [x]Jer 33:24-26; Ro 11:1-5
31:38 [y]Jer 30:18 [z]Ne 3:1 [a]2Ki 14:13; Zec 14:10
31:40 [b]Jer 7:31-32 [c]Jer 8:2 [d]2Sa 15:23; Jn 18:1 [e]2Ki 11:16 [f]Joel 3:17; Zec 14:21
32:1 [g]2Ki 25:1 [h]Jer 25:1; 39:1
32:2 [i]Ne 3:25; Jer 37:21
32:3 [j]Jer 26:8-9 [k]ver 28; Jer 34:2-3
32:4 [l]Jer 38:18,23; 39:5-7; 52:9
32:5 [m]Jer 39:7; Eze 12:13 [n]Jer 21:4
32:7 [o]Lev 25:24-25; Ru 4:3-4; Mt 27:10*
32:9 [p]Ge 23:16
32:10 [q]Ru 4:9
32:12 [r]ver 16; Jer 36:4; 43:3,6; 45:1 [s]Jer 51:59
32:15 [t]ver 43-44; Jer 30:18; Am 9:14-15
32:17 [u]Jer 1:6 [v]2Ki 19:15; Ps 102:25 [w]Mt 19:26
32:18 [x]Dt 5:10

a *4* Or *Chaldeans;* also in verses 5, 24, 25, 28, 29 and 43 b *9* That is, about 7 ounces (about 200 grams)

31:38 this city. Jerusalem was rebuilt under the leadership of Zerubbabel and Nehemiah (Ezr 1; Ne 1–12), but that restoration program failed because of continuing sin. The New Testament sees this promise fulfilled in the new Jerusalem that will appear when Christ returns (Rev 21:2,10). **Tower of Hananel . . . Corner Gate.** Opposite ends of the city, signifying its entirety (see 2Ch 26:9; Zec 14:10–11).
31:39 measuring line. See Ezekiel 40:3, Zechariah 1:16 and 2:1. **Gareb . . . Goah.** Unknown locations in Jerusalem.
31:40 valley. That is, the Hinnom Valley. See 7:32–33. **Horse Gate.** See Nehemiah 3:28.
■ **32:1–44** *Symbolic Purchase.* God commanded Jeremiah to purchase a field just before the destruction of Jerusalem and the exile. This transaction symbolized the prophet's certainty of restoration from exile.
32:1 tenth year of Zedekiah. 587 B.C. The final siege on Jerusalem began in 588 B.C. This is the first of several exchanges between Jeremiah and Zedekiah during this period (see 21:3–7; 34:1–7; 37:3–8,17–20; 38:14–28).
32:2 confined. Jeremiah was kept under arrest until Jerusalem fell.
32:7 Anathoth. This was Jeremiah's hometown, the site of his family inheritance (see 1:1). **your right and duty to buy it.** Hanamel may have been obligated to sell because of debt, and Jeremiah was the kinsman-redeemer (see note on 31:11). The purchase of a field in the face of the loss of the whole land was, by normal standards, absurd.
32:9 seventeen shekels of silver. This was probably a customary price, although given the circumstances the field was valueless.
32:15 Houses, fields and vineyards . . . in this land. The significance of the purchase was that Judah would again possess its historic land and enjoy normal life within it. It therefore symbolizes that aspect of the new covenant promise (see 29:14 and its note; 31:38–40).
32:16–20 See *HC* 122.

thousands but bring the punishment for the fathers' sins into the laps of their children[y] after them. O great and powerful God, whose name is the LORD Almighty,[z]
19great are your purposes and mighty are your deeds.[a] Your eyes are open to all
the ways of men;[b] you reward everyone according to his conduct and as his
deeds deserve.[c] **20**You performed miraculous signs and wonders in Egypt[d] and
have continued them to this day, both in Israel and among all mankind, and have
gained the renown that is still yours. **21**You brought your people Israel out of Egypt
with signs and wonders, by a mighty hand[e] and an outstretched arm and with
great terror.[f] **22**You gave them this land you had sworn to give their forefathers,
a land flowing with milk and honey.[g] **23**They came in and took possession[h] of it,
but they did not obey you or follow your law;[i] they did not do what you commanded them to do. So you brought all this disaster[j] upon them.
24"See how the siege ramps are built up to take the city. Because of the sword,
famine and plague,[k] the city will be handed over to the Babylonians who are attacking it. What you said[l] has happened, as you now see. **25**And though the city
will be handed over to the Babylonians, you, O Sovereign LORD, say to me, 'Buy the
field with silver and have the transaction witnessed.' "

26Then the word of the LORD came to Jeremiah: **27**"I am the LORD, the God of all mankind.[m] Is anything too hard for me? **28**Therefore, this is what the LORD says: I am about
to hand this city over to the Babylonians and to Nebuchadnezzar[n] king of Babylon, who
will capture it.[o] **29**The Babylonians who are attacking this city will come in and set it on
fire; they will burn it down,[p] along with the houses[q] where the people provoked me to
anger by burning incense on the roofs to Baal and by pouring out drink offerings[r] to other gods.
30"The people of Israel and Judah have done nothing but evil in my sight from their
youth;[s] indeed, the people of Israel have done nothing but provoke[t] me with what their
hands have made,[u] declares the LORD. **31**From the day it was built until now, this city has
so aroused my anger and wrath that I must remove[v] it from my sight. **32**The people of Israel and Judah have provoked me by all the evil[w] they have done—they, their kings and
officials, their priests and prophets, the men of Judah and the people of Jerusalem. **33**They
turned their backs[x] to me and not their faces; though I taught[y] them again and again,
they would not listen or respond to discipline. **34**They set up their abominable idols in the
house that bears my Name and defiled[z] it. **35**They built high places for Baal in the Valley of Ben Hinnom to sacrifice their sons and daughters[a] to Molech,[a] though I never commanded, nor did it enter my mind,[b] that they should do such a detestable thing and so
make Judah sin.
36"You are saying about this city, 'By the sword, famine and plague[c] it will be handed
over to the king of Babylon'; but this is what the LORD, the God of Israel, says: **37**I will surely gather[d] them from all the lands where I banish them in my furious anger and great
wrath; I will bring them back to this place and let them live in safety.[e] **38**They will be my
people,[f] and I will be their God. **39**I will give them singleness[g] of heart and action, so that
they will always fear me for their own good and the good of their children after them. **40**I
will make an everlasting covenant[h] with them: I will never stop doing good to them, and
I will inspire them to fear me, so that they will never turn away from me.[i] **41**I will rejoice
in doing them good[j] and will assuredly plant[k] them in this land with all my heart and soul.

32:18 [y]Ex 20:5 [z]Jer 10:16
32:19 [a]Isa 28:29 [b]Pr 5:21; Jer 16:17 [c]Jer 17:10; Mt 16:27
32:20 [d]Ex 9:16
32:21 [e]Ex 6:6; 1Ch 17:21; Da 9:15 [f]Dt 26:8
32:22 [g]Ex 3:8; Jer 11:5
32:23 [h]Ps 44:2; 78:54-55 [i]Ne 9:26; Jer 11:8 [j]Da 9:14
32:24 [k]Jer 14:12 [l]Dt 4:25-26; Jos 23:15-16
32:27 [m]Nu 16:22
32:28 [n]2Ch 36:17 [o]ver 3
32:29 [p]2Ch 36:19; Jer 21:10; 37:8,10; 52:13 [q]Jer 19:13 [r]Jer 44:18
32:30 [s]Jer 22:21 [t]Jer 8:19 [u]Jer 25:7
32:31 [v]2Ki 23:27; 24:3
32:32 [w]Isa 1:4-6; Da 9:8
32:33 [x]Jer 2:27; Eze 8:16 [y]Jer 7:13
32:34 [z]Jer 7:30
32:35 [a]Lev 18:21 [b]Jer 7:31; 19:5
32:36 [c]ver 24
32:37 [d]Jer 23:3,6 [e]Dt 30:3; Eze 34:28
32:38 [f]Jer 24:7; 2Co 6:16*
32:39 [g]Eze 11:19
32:40 [h]Isa 55:3 [i]Jer 24:7
32:41 [j]Dt 30:9 [k]Jer 24:6; 31:28; Am 9:15

a *35* Or *to make their sons and daughters pass through* ⌞*the fire*⌟

32:20 signs and wonders. See Exodus 7:3. **and among all mankind.** This stresses the lordship of God in the whole world.
32:21 Repeated from Deuteronomy 26:8 (see also v. 20; Ex 15:14–16).
32:29 burn it down. The phrase recurs in the threats to Zedekiah in 21:10, 34:2 and 37:8. **provoked me to anger . . . burning incense on the roofs to Baal . . . drink offerings.** A mixture of typical elements in Jeremiah's accusation of Judah. See 1:16, 7:18 and 19:13 (cf. Dt 31:29).
32:33 again and again. See 7:13. **would not listen or respond to discipline.** See 2:30, 5:3, 7:24 and 11:8.
32:35 Molech. The god of the Ammonites. See 49:1 and 3 and Leviticus 18:21.
32:36 The Lord summed up his message about Jerusalem's imminent fate, which Jeremiah had been repeating, but ended it on a hopeful note. The whole chapter expresses the pattern of God's plans: judgment followed by salvation (see "Introduction: Purpose and Distinctives"). The suddenness of this offer of blessing and its contrast to the preceding tirade of verses 26–35 is explained by the rhetorical question "Is anything too hard for me?" (v. 27; cf. v. 17). **You.** The expression is plural; the population of Judah was in mind.
32:37 Jeremiah reaffirmed Moses' promise of restoration from exile (Dt 30:3–5).
32:38 my people . . . their God. See 30:22 and 31:33.
32:39 See *WLC* 112.
32:40 everlasting covenant. The new covenant will never be replaced by another; it represents the final stage of salvation history (Isa 55:3; Eze 16:60; 37:26). **never stop doing good . . . never turn away from me.** When the new covenant comes in its fullness at the return of Christ, everyone bound to this covenant will be glorified, which will entail their being made perfect and purged of the ability and desire to sin. In their glorified state they will enjoy the blessings of God for all eternity. Prior to the return of Christ not all in the new covenant community possess saving faith, and those who do not will come under the judgment of God (see notes on 31:31–34; see also theological article "The Perseverance and Preservation of Believers" at Php 1). See *WCF* 17.2; 18.4; *WLC* 79.

42"This is what the LORD says: As I have brought all this great calamity on this people, so I will give them all the prosperity I have promised[l] them. 43Once more fields will
be bought[m] in this land of which you say, 'It is a desolate waste, without men or animals, for it has been handed over to the Babylonians.' 44Fields will be bought for silver,
and deeds[n] will be signed, sealed and witnessed in the territory of Benjamin, in the villages around Jerusalem, in the towns of Judah and in the towns of the hill country, of
the western foothills and of the Negev,[o] because I will restore[p] their fortunes,[a] declares
the LORD."

Promise of Restoration

33 While Jeremiah was still confined in the courtyard[q] of the guard, the word of the
LORD came to him a second time: 2"This is what the LORD says, he who made the
earth,[r] the LORD who formed it and established it—the LORD is his name:[s] 3'Call[t] to me
and I will answer you and tell you great and unsearchable things you do not know.' 4For
this is what the LORD, the God of Israel, says about the houses in this city and the royal
palaces of Judah that have been torn down to be used against the siege[u] ramps[v] and the
sword 5in the fight with the Babylonians[b]: 'They will be filled with the dead bodies of the
men I will slay in my anger and wrath.[w] I will hide my face[x] from this city because of all
its wickedness.

6" 'Nevertheless, I will bring health and healing to it; I will heal my people and will
let them enjoy abundant peace and security. 7I will bring Judah[y] and Israel back from
captivity[c][z] and will rebuild them as they were before.[a] 8I will cleanse[b] them from all the
sin they have committed against me and will forgive[c] all their sins of rebellion against
me. 9Then this city will bring me renown, joy, praise[d] and honor[e] before all nations on
earth that hear of all the good things I do for it; and they will be in awe and will tremble
at the abundant prosperity and peace I provide for it.'

10"This is what the LORD says: 'You say about this place, "It is a desolate waste, without men or animals."[f] Yet in the towns of Judah and the streets of Jerusalem that are deserted, inhabited by neither men nor animals, there will be heard once more 11the
sounds of joy and gladness,[g] the voices of bride and bridegroom, and the voices of those
who bring thank offerings[h] to the house of the LORD, saying,

> "Give thanks to the LORD Almighty,
> for the LORD is good;[i]
> his love endures forever."[j]

For I will restore the fortunes of the land as they were before,' says the LORD.

12"This is what the LORD Almighty says: 'In this place, desolate[k] and without men or
animals—in all its towns there will again be pastures for shepherds to rest their flocks.[l]
13In the towns of the hill country, of the western foothills and of the Negev,[m] in the territory of Benjamin, in the villages around Jerusalem and in the towns of Judah, flocks will
again pass under the hand[n] of the one who counts them,' says the LORD.

14" 'The days are coming,' declares the LORD, 'when I will fulfill the gracious promise[o]
I made to the house of Israel and to the house of Judah.

> 15" 'In those days and at that time
> I will make a righteous[p] Branch[q] sprout from David's line;
> he will do what is just and right in the land.

32:42 [l]Jer 31:28
32:43 [m]ver 15
32:44 [n]ver 10 [o]Jer 17:26 [p]Jer 33:7,11,26
33:1 [q]Jer 32:2-3; 37:21; 38:28
33:2 [r]Jer 10:16 [s]Ex 3:15; 15:3
33:3 [t]Isa 55:6; Jer 29:12
33:4 [u]Eze 4:2 [v]Jer 32:24; Hab 1:10
33:5 [w]Jer 21:4-7 [x]Isa 8:17
33:7 [y]Jer 32:44 [z]Jer 30:3; Am 9:14 [a]Isa 1:26
33:8 [b]Heb 9:13-14 [c]Jer 31:34; Mic 7:18; Zec 13:1
33:9 [d]Jer 13:11 [e]Isa 62:7; Jer 3:17
33:10 [f]Jer 32:43
33:11 [g]Isa 51:3 [h]Lev 7:12 [i]1Ch 16:8; Ps 136:1 [j]1Ch 16:34; 2Ch 5:13; Ps 100:4-5
33:12 [k]Jer 32:43 [l]Isa 65:10; Eze 34:11-15
33:13 [m]Jer 17:26 [n]Lev 27:32
33:14 [o]Jer 29:10
33:15 [p]Ps 72:2 [q]Isa 4:2; 11:1; Jer 23:5

[a] 44 Or *will bring them back from captivity* [b] 5 Or *Chaldeans* [c] 7 Or *will restore the fortunes of Judah and Israel*

32:43 you. See note on 32:36.

32:44 deeds will be signed . . . and witnessed. This promise explains why God directed Jeremiah to purchase a field before the destruction of Jerusalem began (see v. 10). **Benjamin . . . Negev.** These geographical regions once spanned north and south, representing the complete repopulation of Israel.

■**33:1–26** *Predictions of Restoration.* While under arrest and awaiting the imminent destruction of Jerusalem, Jeremiah received reassuring prophecies of the restoration from exile.

33:1 a second time. The first revelation, while the prophet was under arrest, appears in chapter 32.

33:2 who made the earth. See note on 10:12. God's creation of all things demonstrates his ability to carry through with the restoration of his people from exile (32:17).

33:3 great and unsearchable things you do not know. A similar phrase in Isaiah 48:6 also speaks of salvation as new creation (see Da 2:47).

33:4–5 The prophet announced the horror of the destruction of Jerusalem.

33:6 Nevertheless. Literally, "look" or "behold." The sense is clear: God would bring his people back, despite the destruction of the city and the exile (cf. 30:8,16; 32:36).

33:9 bring me renown, joy, praise and honor. God would bring restoration from exile not only for the benefit of the people of Israel but also for his own glory among all the peoples of the earth (Ro 11:36).

33:10 You. See note on 32:36.

33:11 joy and gladness . . . bride and bridegroom. Contrast 7:34 and 16:9.

33:13 Compare the geographical references in 32:44. The entire promised land is in view.

33:15–16 This refrain is repeated from 23:5–6. See *BC* 18.

16 In those days Judah will be saved[r]
and Jerusalem will live in safety.
This is the name by which it[a] will be called:
The LORD Our Righteousness.’[s]
17 For this is what the LORD says: ‘David will never fail[t] to have a man to sit on the throne
of the house of Israel, 18 nor will the priests, who are Levites,[u] ever fail to have a man to
stand before me continually to offer burnt offerings, to burn grain offerings and to present sacrifices.[v]’ ”
19 The word of the LORD came to Jeremiah: 20 “This is what the LORD says: ‘If you can
break my covenant with the day[w] and my covenant with the night, so that day and night
no longer come at their appointed time, 21 then my covenant[x] with David my servant—
and my covenant with the Levites who are priests ministering before me—can be broken and David will no longer have a descendant to reign on his throne.[y] 22 I will make
the descendants of David my servant and the Levites who minister before me as countless[z] as the stars of the sky and as measureless as the sand on the seashore.’ ”
23 The word of the LORD came to Jeremiah: 24 “Have you not noticed that these people
are saying, ‘The LORD has rejected the two kingdoms[b][a] he chose’? So they despise[b] my
people and no longer regard them as a nation.[c] 25 This is what the LORD says: ‘If I have
not established my covenant with day and night[d] and the fixed laws of heaven and
earth,[e] 26 then I will reject[f] the descendants of Jacob[g] and David my servant and will not
choose one of his sons to rule over the descendants of Abraham, Isaac and Jacob. For I
will restore their fortunes[c][h] and have compassion on them.’ ”

Warning to Zedekiah

34 While Nebuchadnezzar king of Babylon and all his army and all the kingdoms
and peoples[i] in the empire he ruled were fighting against Jerusalem[j] and all its
surrounding towns, this word came to Jeremiah from the LORD: 2 “This is what the LORD,
the God of Israel, says: Go to Zedekiah[k] king of Judah and tell him, ‘This is what the LORD
says: I am about to hand this city over to the king of Babylon, and he will burn it down.[l]
3 You will not escape from his grasp but will surely be captured and handed over[m] to him.
You will see the king of Babylon with your own eyes, and he will speak with you face to
face. And you will go to Babylon.
4 “ ‘Yet hear the promise of the LORD, O Zedekiah king of Judah. This is what the LORD
says concerning you: You will not die by the sword; 5 you will die peacefully. As people
made a funeral fire[n] in honor of your fathers, the former kings who preceded you, so they
will make a fire in your honor and lament, “Alas,[o] O master!” I myself make this promise, declares the LORD.’ ”
6 Then Jeremiah the prophet told all this to Zedekiah king of Judah, in Jerusalem,
7 while the army of the king of Babylon was fighting against Jerusalem and the other cit-

33:16 [r] Isa 45:17 [s] 1Co 1:30
33:17 [t] 2Sa 7:13; 1Ki 2:4; Ps 89:29-37; Lk 1:33
33:18 [u] Dt 18:1 [v] Heb 13:15
33:20 [w] Ps 89:36
33:21 [x] Ps 89:34 [y] 2Ch 7:18
33:22 [z] Ge 15:5
33:24 [a] Eze 37:22 [b] Ne 4:4 [c] Jer 30:17
33:25 [d] Jer 31:35-36 [e] Ps 74:16-17
33:26 [f] Jer 31:37 [g] Isa 14:1 [h] ver 7
34:1 [i] Jer 27:7 [j] 2Ki 25:1; Jer 39:1
34:2 [k] 2Ch 36:11 [l] ver 22; Jer 32:29; 37:8
34:3 [m] 2Ki 25:7; Jer 21:7; 32:4
34:5 [n] 2Ch 16:14; 21:19 [o] Jer 22:18

[a] 16 Or *he* [b] 24 Or *families* [c] 26 Or *will bring them back from captivity*

33:17 See 23:5 and 30:9. The prophecy alludes to 2 Samuel 7:12–16 and Psalms 89:3–4 and 132:11–12. It refers to the restoration of the Davidic monarchy after the exile, which was fulfilled by Jesus.

33:18 the priests, who are Levites. The priest’s role was essential to the administration of the covenant (Ex 28–29; Dt 10:8; 18:1). Priests also had a covenant of their own with the Lord (Nu 25:12–13; 1Sa 2:30,35). God did not ignore the promise of a perpetual priestly ministry by the Levites when he ended their service at the time of Christ’s death, burial, resurrection and ascension. Rather, he kept the promise by giving his people something far better than what he had initially offered—Christ’s royal priesthood. Jesus perfectly fulfills the priestly service that the Levites only foreshadowed by their services in the tabernacle and the temple (Heb 5:6–10; 7:11–25).

33:20–21 covenant with the day and . . . with the night. Perhaps an allusion to the Noahic covenant (cf. Ge 8:22) or to a covenant implicitly made during creation (cf. Ge 1:14–18). The permanence of the institutions here envisaged is in stark contrast with the temporary character of the original temple (7:1–15). Such permanence is comprehensible in the framework of the new covenant, although the need for faithfulness is never set aside (see 32:40 and its note).

33:22 countless . . . sand on the seashore. In these promises about the Messianic kingdom, the promises to Abraham are also fulfilled (Ge 22:17; contrast Ge 15:8).

33:24 these people are saying, “The LORD has rejected . . . ?” The Lord’s own honor was bound up with his people (v. 9); the new covenant would again bring him due honor.

33:25 God again appealed to the permanence of the cosmic order (see note on vv. 20–21).

33:26 Abraham, Isaac and Jacob. The restoration after exile, which entails the reign of David’s Son, would fulfill the covenant with Abraham (see note on v. 22).

■ **34:1—36:32** *Representative Violations and Judgments.* These chapters contain representative scenes of rejection of the word of the Lord that led to final judgment on Judah. This material divides into four sections: Zedekiah’s condemnation for going back on his promise to free slaves (34:1–22), the Judahites’ judgment for failing to follow the example of the faithful Recabites (35:1–19) and King Jehoiakim’s condemnation for burning the prophet’s scroll (36:1–32).

■ **34:1–22** *Judgment Against Zedekiah.* This section focuses on Jeremiah delivering prophecies of judgment against Zedekiah for breaking his promise to free slaves in Jerusalem.

34:1 peoples in the empire . . . fighting against Jerusalem. It was often a treaty stipulation that subject nations had to fight for the overlord.

34:4–5 not die by the sword . . . die peacefully. Zedekiah’s precise fate was left obscure in 21:4–7 and 32:3–5 (but see 52:11). The point here is that he would not die in battle.

ies of Judah that were still holding out—Lachish[p] and Azekah.[q] These were the only fortified cities left in Judah.

Freedom for Slaves

8The word came to Jeremiah from the LORD after King Zedekiah had made a covenant with all the people[r] in Jerusalem to proclaim freedom[s] for the slaves. **9**Everyone was to free his Hebrew slaves, both male and female; no one was to hold a fellow Jew in bondage.[t] **10**So all the officials and people who entered into this covenant agreed that they would free their male and female slaves and no longer hold them in bondage. They agreed, and set them free. **11**But afterward they changed their minds and took back the slaves they had freed and enslaved them again.

12Then the word of the LORD came to Jeremiah: **13**"This is what the LORD, the God of Israel, says: I made a covenant with your forefathers[u] when I brought them out of Egypt, out of the land of slavery. I said, **14**'Every seventh year each of you must free any fellow Hebrew who has sold himself to you. After he has served you six years, you must let him go free.'[a][v] Your fathers, however, did not listen to me or pay attention[w] to me. **15**Recently you repented and did what is right in my sight: Each of you proclaimed freedom to his countrymen.[x] You even made a covenant before me in the house that bears my Name.[y] **16**But now you have turned around[z] and profaned[a] my name; each of you has taken back the male and female slaves you had set free to go where they wished. You have forced them to become your slaves again.

17"Therefore, this is what the LORD says: You have not obeyed me; you have not proclaimed freedom for your fellow countrymen. So I now proclaim 'freedom' for you,[b] declares the LORD—'freedom' to fall by the sword, plague and famine. I will make you abhorrent to all the kingdoms of the earth.[c] **18**The men who have violated my covenant and have not fulfilled the terms of the covenant they made before me, I will treat like the calf they cut in two and then walked between its pieces.[d] **19**The leaders of Judah and Jerusalem, the court officials,[e] the priests and all the people of the land who walked between the pieces of the calf, **20**I will hand over[f] to their enemies who seek their lives.[g] Their dead bodies will become food for the birds of the air and the beasts of the earth.[h]

21"I will hand Zedekiah[i] king of Judah and his officials[j] over to their enemies who seek their lives, to the army of the king of Babylon, which has withdrawn[k] from you. **22**I am going to give the order, declares the LORD, and I will bring them back to this city. They will fight against it, take[l] it and burn[m] it down. And I will lay waste the towns of Judah so no one can live there."

The Recabites

35 This is the word that came to Jeremiah from the LORD during the reign of Jehoiakim[n] son of Josiah king of Judah: **2**"Go to the Recabite[o] family and invite them to come to one of the side rooms[p] of the house of the LORD and give them wine to drink."

3So I went to get Jaazaniah son of Jeremiah, the son of Habazziniah, and his brothers and all his sons—the whole family of the Recabites. **4**I brought them into the house of the LORD, into the room of the sons of Hanan son of Igdaliah the man of God.[q] It was

34:7 [p]Jos 10:3 [q]Jos 10:10; 2Ch 11:9
34:8 [r]2Ki 11:17 [s]Ex 21:2; Lev 25:10,39-41; Ne 5:5-8
34:9 [t]Lev 25:39-46
34:13 [u]Ex 24:8
34:14 [v]Ex 21:2 [w]Dt 15:12; 2Ki 17:14
34:15 [x]ver 8 [y]Jer 7:10-11; 32:34
34:16 [z]Eze 3:20; 18:24 [a]Ex 20:7; Lev 19:12
34:17 [b]Mt 7:2; Gal 6:7 [c]Dt 28:25,64; Jer 29:18
34:18 [d]Ge 15:10
34:19 [e]Zep 3:3-4
34:20 [f]Jer 21:7 [g]Jer 11:21 [h]Dt 28:26; Jer 7:33; 19:7
34:21 [i]Jer 32:4 [j]Jer 39:6; 52:24-27 [k]Jer 37:5
34:22 [l]Jer 39:1-2 [m]Jer 39:8
35:1 [n]2Ch 36:5
35:2 [o]2Ki 10:15; 1Ch 2:55 [p]1Ki 6:5
35:4 [q]Dt 33:1

[a] *14* Deut. 15:12

34:7 Lachish and Azekah. Major fortified cities of Judah (2Ch 11:5,9). This verse provides a glimpse of the last days of Judah. Jerusalem knew that the enemy was closing in as the outlying cities fell one by one. A pottery fragment dating from 588 B.C. bears a message to the commander at Lachish: "We are watching for the fire-signals of Lachish . . . for we cannot see Azekah."

34:8–11 See *WLC* 151.

34:8 proclaim freedom for the slaves. In accordance with the laws (Ex 21:2–11; Lev 25:39–55; Dt 15:12–18), slaves were to be released in the last year of a seven-year cycle. Zedekiah had not enforced this practice and now sought to appease God by doing so. The king's undertaking reflected his ambivalence between listening to Jeremiah and to his political advisers.

34:14 Every seventh year. The Lord recalled Deuteronomy 15:12.

34:15–16 repented . . . turned around. These two verbs (the same Hebrew word repeated) effectively portray Judah's fickleness (see notes on 3:6,14). The Judahites turned one way and then the other. There is, however, no such thing as moral neutrality. **profaned my name.** The blatant disregard of the law for the release of slaves was in effect a repudiation of the Lord himself.

34:17 freedom . . . freedom. The ironic repetition reflects the manner in which the people brought judgment upon themselves (7:5–6; 23:12).

34:18 like the calf . . . between its pieces. See Genesis 15:18 and its note. This action often accompanied the ratification of a covenant and was a solemn self-malediction (1Ki 19:2). The one walking among the carnage swore, "May the same happen to me as to this animal if I break my covenant." The Lord here pledged to allow the curse to have its effect.

34:21–22 The Lord determined to hand over Zedekiah and his officials to the Babylonians because of Zedekiah's violation of God's law and of his covenant with God.

■ **35:1–19** *Judgment for Falling Short of the Recabites' Example.* The prophet condemned the Judahites for failing to follow the Recabite example of faithfulness.

35:2 the Recabite family. Most of what is known of them is found in this chapter. They were apparently a nomadic tribe closely related to the Kenites (1Ch 2:55). Their faithfulness stood in sharp contrast to the lack of this quality among the children of Abraham. **side rooms of the house of the LORD.** Used for storage (see 1Ki 6:5; Ne 13:4–5).

35:3 Jeremiah, the son of Habazziniah. Not the prophet. The name was evidently common at the time (40:8).

next to the room of the officials, which was over that of Maaseiah son of Shallum[r] the doorkeeper.[s] 5Then I set bowls full of wine and some cups before the men of the Recabite family and said to them, "Drink some wine."

6But they replied, "We do not drink wine, because our forefather Jonadab[t] son of Recab gave us this command: 'Neither you nor your descendants must ever drink wine.[u] 7Also you must never build houses, sow seed or plant vineyards; you must never have any of these things, but must always live in tents.[v] Then you will live a long time in the land[w] where you are nomads.' 8We have obeyed everything our forefather[x] Jonadab son of Recab commanded us. Neither we nor our wives nor our sons and daughters have ever drunk wine 9or built houses to live in or had vineyards, fields or crops.[y] 10We have lived in tents and have fully obeyed everything our forefather Jonadab commanded us. 11But when Nebuchadnezzar king of Babylon invaded[z] this land, we said, 'Come, we must go to Jerusalem[a] to escape the Babylonian[a] and Aramean armies.' So we have remained in Jerusalem."

12Then the word of the LORD came to Jeremiah, saying: 13"This is what the LORD Almighty, the God of Israel, says: Go and tell the men of Judah and the people of Jerusalem, 'Will you not learn a lesson[b] and obey my words?' declares the LORD. 14'Jonadab son of Recab ordered his sons not to drink wine and this command has been kept. To this day they do not drink wine, because they obey their forefather's command. But I have spoken to you again and again,[c] yet you have not obeyed[d] me. 15Again and again I sent all my servants the prophets[e] to you. They said, "Each of you must turn[f] from your wicked ways and reform[g] your actions; do not follow other gods to serve them. Then you will live in the land[h] I have given to you and your fathers." But you have not paid attention or listened[i] to me. 16The descendants of Jonadab son of Recab have carried out the command their forefather[j] gave them, but these people have not obeyed me.'

17"Therefore, this is what the LORD God Almighty, the God of Israel, says: 'Listen! I am going to bring on Judah and on everyone living in Jerusalem every disaster[k] I pronounced against them. I spoke to them, but they did not listen;[l] I called to them, but they did not answer.' "[m]

18Then Jeremiah said to the family of the Recabites, "This is what the LORD Almighty, the God of Israel, says: 'You have obeyed the command of your forefather Jonadab and have followed all his instructions and have done everything he ordered.' 19Therefore, this is what the LORD Almighty, the God of Israel, says: 'Jonadab son of Recab will never fail[n] to have a man to serve[o] me.' "

Jehoiakim Burns Jeremiah's Scroll

36 In the fourth year of Jehoiakim[p] son of Josiah king of Judah, this word came to Jeremiah from the LORD: 2"Take a scroll[q] and write on it all the words I have spoken to you concerning Israel, Judah and all the other nations from the time I began speaking to you in the reign of Josiah[r] till now. 3Perhaps[s] when the people of Judah hear[t] about every disaster I plan to inflict on them, each of them will turn[u] from his wicked way; then I will forgive[v] their wickedness and their sin."

4So Jeremiah called Baruch[w] son of Neriah, and while Jeremiah dictated[x] all the words the LORD had spoken to him, Baruch wrote them on the scroll.[y] 5Then Jeremiah told Baruch, "I am restricted; I cannot go to the LORD's temple. 6So you go to the house of the LORD on a day of fasting[z] and read to the people from the scroll the words of the LORD that you wrote as I dictated. Read them to all the people of Judah who come in from their towns. 7Perhaps they will bring their petition before the LORD, and each will turn[a]

[a] 11 Or *Chaldean*

35:4 [r]1Ch 9:19 [s]2Ki 12:9
35:6 [t]2Ki 10:15 [u]Lev 10:9; Nu 6:2-4; Lk 1:15
35:7 [v]Heb 11:9 [w]Ex 20:12; Eph 6:2-3
35:8 [x]Pr 1:8; Col 3:20
35:9 [y]1Ti 6:6
35:11 [z]2Ki 24:1 [a]Jer 8:14
35:13 [b]Jer 6:10; 32:33
35:14 [c]Jer 7:13; 25:3 [d]Isa 30:9
35:15 [e]Jer 7:25 [f]Jer 26:3 [g]Isa 1:16-17; Jer 4:1; 18:11; Eze 18:30 [h]Jer 25:5 [i]Jer 7:26
35:16 [j]Mal 1:6
35:17 [k]Jos 23:15; Jer 21:4-7 [l]Pr 1:24; Ro 10:21 [m]Isa 65:12; 66:4; Jer 7:13
35:19 [n]Jer 33:17 [o]Jer 15:19
36:1 [p]2Ch 36:5
36:2 [q]Ex 17:14; Jer 30:2; Hab 2:2 [r]Jer 1:2; 25:3
36:3 [s]ver 7; Eze 12:3 [t]Mk 4:12 [u]Jer 26:3; Jnh 3:8; Ac 3:19 [v]Jer 18:8
36:4 [w]Jer 32:12 [x]ver 18 [y]Eze 2:9
36:6 [z]ver 9
36:7 [a]Jer 26:3

35:4 man of God. Another name for a prophet (1Ki 12:22). **Maaseiah.** See 21:1, which possibly refers to the same person.
35:6–7 The vow taken by Jonadab son of Recab committed his descendants to a nomadic lifestyle characterized by impermanent housing and abstention from wine. This was a voluntary commitment—not required by Mosaic Law (Dt 6:10–11; 7:13)—that was similar to a Nazirite vow (Nu 6:2–3,20; Jdg 13:4–7).
35:19 never fail to have a man to serve me. See 33:17–18. Such a promise was expected of the king, and even of the priests, but not of the obscure Recabites. It is used here to contrast ominously with what Jehoiakim and the historical Davidic dynasty could expect.
■**36:1–32** *Judgment Against Jehoiakim.* King Jehoiakim had so resisted the prophetic word that he actually burned one of Jeremiah's scrolls. His actions brought upon himself the judgment of God.
36:1 fourth year of Jehoiakim. This was the year of Nebuchadnezzar's first attack on Jerusalem (605 B.C.). Jehoiakim's intransigence is even more striking against this background.
36:2 Take a scroll and write on it. This account is an important guide for understanding how prophetic books came to be written. Jeremiah's oracles were spoken over a long period (25:3) but were here collected for a continuous reading (see Isa 8:16 and its note).
36:4 Baruch. This is the second appearance of Jeremiah's scribe (32:12). His activity here suggests that he may have had a role in compiling the book of Jeremiah as we have it (see "Introduction").
36:5 I am restricted. This probably means that he was banned from the temple area because of his unpopularity with the authorities (26:2–11).

36:7 [b]Dt 31:17 from his wicked ways, for the anger[b] and wrath pronounced against this people by the
LORD are great.”
8 Baruch son of Neriah did everything Jeremiah the prophet told him to do; at the
36:9 LORD's temple he read the words of the LORD from the scroll. 9 In the ninth month[c] of the
[c]ver 22 [d]2Ch 20:3 fifth year of Jehoiakim son of Josiah king of Judah, a time of fasting[d] before the LORD was
36:10 proclaimed for all the people in Jerusalem and those who had come from the towns of
[e]Jer 52:25 [f]Jer 26:10 Judah. 10 From the room of Gemariah son of Shaphan the secretary,[e] which was in the
upper courtyard at the entrance of the New Gate[f] of the temple, Baruch read to all the
people at the LORD's temple the words of Jeremiah from the scroll.
11 When Micaiah son of Gemariah, the son of Shaphan, heard all the words of the LORD
36:12 from the scroll, 12 he went down to the secretary's room in the royal palace, where all the
[g]Jer 26:22 officials were sitting: Elishama the secretary, Delaiah son of Shemaiah, Elnathan[g] son
of Acbor, Gemariah son of Shaphan, Zedekiah son of Hananiah, and all the other offi-
36:14 cials. 13 After Micaiah told them everything he had heard Baruch read to the people from
[h]ver 21 the scroll, 14 all the officials sent Jehudi[h] son of Nethaniah, the son of Shelemiah, the son
of Cushi, to say to Baruch, “Bring the scroll from which you have read to the people and
come.” So Baruch son of Neriah went to them with the scroll in his hand. 15 They said to
him, “Sit down, please, and read it to us.”
So Baruch read it to them. 16 When they heard all these words, they looked at each
other in fear and said to Baruch, “We must report all these words to the king.” 17 Then
they asked Baruch, “Tell us, how did you come to write all this? Did Jeremiah dic-
36:18 tate it?”
[i]ver 4 18 “Yes,” Baruch replied, “he dictated[i] all these words to me, and I wrote them in ink
36:19 on the scroll.”
[j]1Ki 17:3 19 Then the officials said to Baruch, “You and Jeremiah, go and hide.[j] Don't let anyone know where you are.”
36:21 20 After they put the scroll in the room of Elishama the secretary, they went to the
[k]ver 14 [l]2Ki 22:10 king in the courtyard and reported everything to him. 21 The king sent Jehudi[k] to get the
scroll, and Jehudi brought it from the room of Elishama the secretary and read it to
36:22 the king[l] and all the officials standing beside him. 22 It was the ninth month and the king
[m]Am 3:15 was sitting in the winter apartment,[m] with a fire burning in the firepot in front of him.
23 Whenever Jehudi had read three or four columns of the scroll, the king cut them off
36:23 with a scribe's knife and threw them into the firepot, until the entire scroll was burned
[n]1Ki 22:8 in the fire.[n] 24 The king and all his attendants who heard all these words showed no
36:24 fear,[o] nor did they tear their clothes.[p] 25 Even though Elnathan, Delaiah and Gemariah
[o]Ps 36:1 urged the king not to burn the scroll, he would not listen to them. 26 Instead, the king
[p]Ge 37:29; 2Ki 22:11; Isa 37:1 commanded Jerahmeel, a son of the king, Seraiah son of Azriel and Shelemiah son of
36:26 Abdeel to arrest[q] Baruch the scribe and Jeremiah the prophet. But the LORD had hid-
[q]Mt 23:34 [r]Jer 15:21 den[r] them.
27 After the king burned the scroll containing the words that Baruch had written at
36:27 [s]ver 4 Jeremiah's dictation,[s] the word of the LORD came to Jeremiah: 28 “Take another scroll
and write on it all the words that were on the first scroll, which Jehoiakim king of Judah burned up. 29 Also tell Jehoiakim king of Judah, ‘This is what the LORD says: You
36:29 burned that scroll and said, “Why did you write on it that the king of Babylon would
[t]Isa 30:10 certainly come and destroy this land and cut off both men and animals from it?”[t]
36:30 30 Therefore, this is what the LORD says about Jehoiakim king of Judah: He will have no
[u]Jer 22:19 one to sit on the throne of David; his body will be thrown out[u] and exposed to the heat
by day and the frost by night. 31 I will punish him and his children and his attendants
for their wickedness; I will bring on them and those living in Jerusalem and the peo-
36:31 [v]Pr 29:1 ple of Judah every disaster[v] I pronounced against them, because they have not listened.’ ”
36:32 32 So Jeremiah took another scroll and gave it to the scribe Baruch son of Neriah, and
[w]ver 4 [x]Ex 34:1 as Jeremiah dictated,[w] Baruch wrote[x] on it all the words of the scroll that Jehoiakim king
[y]ver 23 of Judah had burned[y] in the fire. And many similar words were added to them.

36:9 the ninth month of the fifth year. December 604 B.C. **from the towns.** See verse 6.
36:12 Elnathan son of Acbor. See 26:22 and its note.
36:18 he dictated. This does not imply that the words originally came to Jeremiah in some mechanical way, yet Jeremiah's ability to remember them in such detail shows that, once given, they were indelibly imprinted upon his mind.
36:21 Jehudi. Baruch was no longer the reader, for he was presumably in hiding (v. 19). With the absence of Jeremiah and Baruch, Jehoiakim's response was focused on the words themselves.
36:23 the king cut them off . . . until the entire scroll was burned in the fire. The contrast with Josiah could not be stronger (2Ki 22:11–13). The destruction of the scroll may have been a superstitious attempt to invalidate its words.
36:28 Take another scroll. God's word cannot be invalidated by the destruction of a scroll.
36:30 Jehoiakim . . . will have no one to sit on the throne of David. His son Jehoiachin's rule was short-lived (2Ki 24:8; Jer 22:30).

Jeremiah in Prison

37 Zedekiah[z] son of Josiah was made king[a] of Judah by Nebuchadnezzar king of
Babylon; he reigned in place of Jehoiachin[a][b] son of Jehoiakim. **2**Neither he nor
his attendants nor the people of the land paid any attention[c] to the words the LORD had
spoken through Jeremiah the prophet.
3King Zedekiah, however, sent Jehucal son of Shelemiah with the priest Zephaniah[d]
son of Maaseiah to Jeremiah the prophet with this message: "Please pray[e] to the LORD
our God for us."
4Now Jeremiah was free to come and go among the people, for he had not yet been
put in prison.[f] **5**Pharaoh's army had marched out of Egypt,[g] and when the Babylonians[b]
who were besieging Jerusalem heard the report about them, they withdrew[h] from Jerusalem.[i]
6Then the word of the LORD came to Jeremiah the prophet: **7**"This is what the LORD,
the God of Israel, says: Tell the king of Judah, who sent you to inquire[j] of me, 'Pharaoh's
army, which has marched out to support you, will go back to its own land, to Egypt.[k]
8Then the Babylonians will return and attack this city; they will capture it and burn[l] it
down.'
9"This is what the LORD says: Do not deceive[m] yourselves, thinking, 'The Babylonians
will surely leave us.' They will not! **10**Even if you were to defeat the entire Babylonian[c]
army that is attacking you and only wounded men were left in their tents, they would
come out and burn this city down."
11After the Babylonian army had withdrawn[n] from Jerusalem because of Pharaoh's
army, **12**Jeremiah started to leave the city to go to the territory of Benjamin to get his
share of the property[o] among the people there. **13**But when he reached the Benjamin
Gate, the captain of the guard, whose name was Irijah son of Shelemiah, the son of Hananiah, arrested him and said, "You are deserting to the Babylonians!"
14"That's not true!" Jeremiah said. "I am not deserting to the Babylonians." But Irijah would not listen to him; instead, he arrested[p] Jeremiah and brought him to the officials. **15**They were angry with Jeremiah and had him beaten[q] and imprisoned in the
house[r] of Jonathan the secretary, which they had made into a prison.
16Jeremiah was put into a vaulted cell in a dungeon, where he remained a long time.
17Then King Zedekiah sent for him and had him brought to the palace, where he asked[s]
him privately,[t] "Is there any word from the LORD?"
"Yes," Jeremiah replied, "you will be handed over[u] to the king of Babylon."
18Then Jeremiah said to King Zedekiah, "What crime[v] have I committed against you
or your officials or this people, that you have put me in prison? **19**Where are your prophets who prophesied to you, 'The king of Babylon will not attack you or this land'? **20**But
now, my lord the king, please listen. Let me bring my petition before you: Do not send
me back to the house of Jonathan the secretary, or I will die there."
21King Zedekiah then gave orders for Jeremiah to be placed in the courtyard of the
guard and given bread from the street of the bakers each day until all the bread[w] in the
city was gone.[x] So Jeremiah remained in the courtyard of the guard.[y]

Jeremiah Thrown Into a Cistern

38 Shephatiah son of Mattan, Gedaliah son of Pashhur, Jehucal[d][z] son of Shelemiah, and Pashhur son of Malkijah heard what Jeremiah was telling all the people when he said, **2**"This is what the LORD says: 'Whoever stays in this city will die by the
sword, famine or plague,[a] but whoever goes over to the Babylonians[e] will live. He will

37:1 [z]2Ki 24:17 [a]Eze 17:13 [b]2Ki 24:8, 12; 2Ch 36:10; Jer 22:24
37:2 [c]2Ki 24:19; 2Ch 36:12, 14
37:3 [d]Jer 29:25; 52:24 [e]1Ki 13:6; Jer 21:1-2; 42:2
37:4 [f]ver 15; Jer 32:2
37:5 [g]Eze 17:15 [h]Jer 34:21 [i]2Ki 24:7
37:7 [j]2Ki 22:18 [k]Jer 2:36; La 4:17
37:8 [l]Jer 34:22; 39:8
37:9 [m]Jer 29:8
37:11 [n]ver 5
37:12 [o]Jer 32:9
37:14 [p]Jer 40:4
37:15 [q]Jer 20:2 [r]Jer 38:26
37:17 [s]Jer 15:11 [t]Jer 38:16 [u]Jer 21:7
37:18 [v]1Sa 26:18; Jn 10:32; Ac 25:8
37:21 [w]Isa 33:16; Jer 38:9 [x]2Ki 25:3; Jer 52:6 [y]Jer 32:2; 38:6, 13, 28
38:1 [z]Jer 37:3
38:2 [a]Jer 34:17

[a] *1* Hebrew *Coniah,* a variant of *Jehoiachin* [b] *5* Or *Chaldeans*; also in verses 8, 9, 13 and 14
[c] *10* Or *Chaldean*; also in verse 11 [d] *1* Hebrew *Jucal,* a variant of *Jehucal* [e] *2* Or *Chaldeans*; also in verses 18, 19 and 23

■ **37:1—39:18** *Final Encounters and Jerusalem's Fall.* These chapters recount Jeremiah's last days of ministry before the fall of Jerusalem and his imprisonments on account of his unpopular message. His repeated advice to surrender to the Babylonians was ignored, and he remained imprisoned until the fall of Jerusalem. This material divides into four sections: encounters between Jeremiah and Zedekiah (37:1–21), Jeremiah and the officials (38:1–13), Jeremiah and Zedekiah and his officials (38:14–28) and the fall of Jerusalem (39:1–18).
■ **37:1–21** *Jeremiah and Zedekiah.* King Zedekiah rejected the prophet's message and imprisoned him.
37:1 Zedekiah . . . was made king . . . in place of Jehoiachin. See 2 Kings 24:17–18. The year was 597 B.C.
37:5 Egypt . . . Babylonians. See 34:10–11. Egypt and Babylon were in contention for the region (see "Introduction"). Many in Judah were looking to Egypt for support (24:8), for the Babylonians would have withdrawn to deal with the Egyptian threat.
37:15 had him beaten. This is the second such punishment (20:2). **and imprisoned.** Jeremiah remained incarcerated in a succession of locations until the city fell (38:28).
37:21 the courtyard of the guard. The courtyard was less unpleasant than the "dungeon" (v. 16). See 32:2. Zedekiah here manifested respect for God's prophet.
■ **38:1–13** *Jeremiah and the Officials.* Zedekiah permitted some of his officials to cast Jeremiah into a cistern because he continued to prophesy that the Babylonians would conquer Jerusalem.

escape with his life; he will live.'[b] **3**And this is what the LORD says: 'This city will certainly be handed over to the army of the king of Babylon, who will capture it.' "[c]

4Then the officials[d] said to the king, "This man should be put to death.[e] He is discouraging the soldiers who are left in this city, as well as all the people, by the things he is saying to them. This man is not seeking the good of these people but their ruin."

5"He is in your hands," King Zedekiah answered. "The king can do nothing to oppose you."

6So they took Jeremiah and put him into the cistern of Malkijah, the king's son, which was in the courtyard of the guard.[f] They lowered Jeremiah by ropes into the cistern; it had no water in it, only mud, and Jeremiah sank down into the mud.

7But Ebed-Melech,[g] a Cushite,[a] an official[b][h] in the royal palace, heard that they had put Jeremiah into the cistern. While the king was sitting in the Benjamin Gate,[i] **8**Ebed-Melech went out of the palace and said to him, **9**"My lord the king, these men have acted wickedly in all they have done to Jeremiah the prophet. They have thrown him into a cistern, where he will starve to death when there is no longer any bread[j] in the city."

10Then the king commanded Ebed-Melech the Cushite, "Take thirty men from here with you and lift Jeremiah the prophet out of the cistern before he dies."

11So Ebed-Melech took the men with him and went to a room under the treasury in the palace. He took some old rags and worn-out clothes from there and let them down with ropes to Jeremiah in the cistern. **12**Ebed-Melech the Cushite said to Jeremiah, "Put these old rags and worn-out clothes under your arms to pad the ropes." Jeremiah did so, **13**and they pulled him up with the ropes and lifted him out of the cistern. And Jeremiah remained in the courtyard of the guard.[k]

Zedekiah Questions Jeremiah Again

14Then King Zedekiah sent for Jeremiah the prophet and had him brought to the third entrance to the temple of the LORD. "I am going to ask you something," the king said to Jeremiah. "Do not hide[l] anything from me."

15Jeremiah said to Zedekiah, "If I give you an answer, will you not kill me? Even if I did give you counsel, you would not listen to me."

16But King Zedekiah swore this oath secretly[m] to Jeremiah: "As surely as the LORD lives, who has given us breath,[n] I will neither kill you nor hand you over to those who are seeking your life."[o]

17Then Jeremiah said to Zedekiah, "This is what the LORD God Almighty, the God of Israel, says: 'If you surrender to the officers of the king of Babylon, your life will be spared and this city will not be burned down; you and your family will live.[p] **18**But if you will not surrender to the officers of the king of Babylon, this city will be handed over[q] to the Babylonians and they will burn[r] it down; you yourself will not escape[s] from their hands.' "

19King Zedekiah said to Jeremiah, "I am afraid[t] of the Jews who have gone over[u] to the Babylonians, for the Babylonians may hand me over to them and they will mistreat me."

20"They will not hand you over," Jeremiah replied. "Obey[v] the LORD by doing what I tell you. Then it will go well with you, and your life[w] will be spared. **21**But if you refuse to surrender, this is what the LORD has revealed to me: **22**All the women[x] left in the palace of the king of Judah will be brought out to the officials of the king of Babylon. Those women will say to you:

> " 'They misled you and overcame you—
> those trusted friends of yours.
> Your feet are sunk in the mud;
> your friends have deserted you.'

38:2 [b]Jer 21:9; 39:18; 45:5
38:3 [c]Jer 21:4,10; 32:3
38:4 [d]Jer 36:12 [e]Jer 26:11
38:6 [f]Jer 37:21
38:7 [g]Jer 39:16 [h]Ac 8:27 [i]Job 29:7
38:9 [j]Jer 37:21
38:13 [k]Jer 37:21
38:14 [l]1Sa 3:17
38:16 [m]Jer 37:17 [n]Isa 42:5; 57:16 [o]ver 4
38:17 [p]2Ki 24:12; Jer 21:9
38:18 [q]ver 3; Jer 34:3 [r]Jer 37:8 [s]Jer 24:8; 32:4
38:19 [t]Isa 51:12; Jn 12:42 [u]Jer 39:9
38:20 [v]Jer 11:4 [w]Isa 55:3
38:22 [x]Jer 6:12

[a] 7 Probably from the upper Nile region [b] 7 Or *a eunuch*

38:4 See *WLC* 145.
38:6 cistern. This was probably a huge cavity with only a small opening in the top. **no water in it.** Whether it was empty due to the water shortage or from disuse is unclear. It seems certain that the intention was to kill Jeremiah.
38:7 Ebed-Melech. The name means "servant of the king." It is unclear whether the term "Melech" (Hebrew for "king") marks him as the servant of Zedekiah or of the Lord—perhaps the latter, as suggested by his actions on the behalf of Jeremiah. **king was sitting in the Benjamin Gate.** He was probably hearing civil suits (2Sa 15:2–4).
38:12 rags . . . to pad the ropes. A touching glimpse of Ebed-Melech's kindness.
■ **38:14–28** *Jeremiah and Zedekiah and His Officials.* Jeremiah offered Zedekiah a last chance to save his life and spare the city from utter destruction. Zedekiah refused.
38:14 third entrance. This is not otherwise mentioned and was perhaps private to the king. The whole encounter breathes secrecy.
38:22 women . . . brought out to the officials. The loss of his harem was a humiliating forfeiture in a king's defeat in war. **those trusted friends.** Literally, "men of your peace." This included the officials who had counseled war (vv. 1,4) and the false prophets (8:11). The expression ironically confirms Jeremiah's criticism of them.

23 “All your wives and children[y] will be brought out to the Babylonians. You yourself will not escape from their hands but will be captured[z] by the king of Babylon; and this city will[a] be burned down.”

24 Then Zedekiah said to Jeremiah, “Do not let anyone know about this conversation, or you may die. 25 If the officials hear that I talked with you, and they come to you and say, ‘Tell us what you said to the king and what the king said to you; do not hide it from us or we will kill you,’ 26 then tell them, ‘I was pleading with the king not to send me back to Jonathan’s house[a] to die there.’ ”

27 All the officials did come to Jeremiah and question him, and he told them everything the king had ordered him to say. So they said no more to him, for no one had heard his conversation with the king.

28 And Jeremiah remained in the courtyard of the guard[b] until the day Jerusalem was captured.

The Fall of Jerusalem

39 This is how Jerusalem was taken: 1 In the ninth year of Zedekiah king of Judah, in the tenth month, Nebuchadnezzar king of Babylon marched against Jerusalem with his whole army and laid siege[c] to it. 2 And on the ninth day of the fourth month of Zedekiah’s eleventh year, the city wall was broken through. 3 Then all the officials[d] of the king of Babylon came and took seats in the Middle Gate: Nergal-Sharezer of Samgar, Nebo-Sarsekim[b] a chief officer, Nergal-Sharezer a high official and all the other officials of the king of Babylon. 4 When Zedekiah king of Judah and all the soldiers saw them, they fled; they left the city at night by way of the king’s garden, through the gate between the two walls, and headed toward the Arabah.[c]

5 But the Babylonian[d] army pursued them and overtook Zedekiah[e] in the plains of Jericho. They captured him and took him to Nebuchadnezzar king of Babylon at Riblah[f] in the land of Hamath, where he pronounced sentence on him. 6 There at Riblah the king of Babylon slaughtered the sons of Zedekiah before his eyes and also killed all the nobles of Judah. 7 Then he put out Zedekiah’s eyes[g] and bound him with bronze shackles to take him to Babylon.[h]

8 The Babylonians[e] set fire[i] to the royal palace and the houses of the people and broke down the walls[j] of Jerusalem. 9 Nebuzaradan commander of the imperial guard carried into exile to Babylon the people who remained in the city, along with those who had gone over to him, and the rest of the people.[k] 10 But Nebuzaradan the commander of the guard left behind in the land of Judah some of the poor people, who owned nothing; and at that time he gave them vineyards and fields.

11 Now Nebuchadnezzar king of Babylon had given these orders about Jeremiah through Nebuzaradan commander of the imperial guard: 12 “Take him and look after him; don’t harm[l] him but do for him whatever he asks.” 13 So Nebuzaradan the commander of the guard, Nebushazban a chief officer, Nergal-Sharezer a high official and all the other officers of the king of Babylon 14 sent and had Jeremiah taken out of the courtyard of the guard.[m] They turned him over to Gedaliah son of Ahikam,[n] the son of Shaphan, to take him back to his home. So he remained among his own people.[o]

15 While Jeremiah had been confined in the courtyard of the guard, the word of the LORD came to him: 16 “Go and tell Ebed-Melech[p] the Cushite, ‘This is what the LORD Almighty, the God of Israel, says: I am about to fulfill my words against this city through disaster,[q] not prosperity. At that time they will be fulfilled before your eyes. 17 But I will rescue[r] you on that day, declares the LORD; you will not be handed over to those you fear. 18 I will save you; you will not fall by the sword[s] but will escape with your life,[t] because you trust[u] in me, declares the LORD.’ ”

38:23 [y]2Ki 25:6 [z]Jer 41:10
38:26 [a]Jer 37:15
38:28 [b]Jer 37:21; 39:14
39:1 [c]2Ki 25:1; Jer 52:4; Eze 24:2
39:3 [d]Jer 21:4
39:5 [e]Jer 32:4 [f]2Ki 23:33
39:7 [g]Eze 12:13 [h]Jer 32:5
39:8 [i]Jer 38:18 [j]Ne 1:3
39:9 [k]Jer 40:1
39:12 [l]Pr 16:7; 1Pe 3:13
39:14 [m]Jer 38:28 [n]2Ki 22:12 [o]Jer 40:5
39:16 [p]Jer 38:7 [q]Jer 21:10; Da 9:12
39:17 [r]Ps 41:1-2
39:18 [s]Jer 45:5 [t]Jer 21:9; 38:2 [u]Jer 17:7

[a] 23 Or *and you will cause this city to* [b] 3 Or *Nergal-Sharezer, Samgar-Nebo, Sarsekim* [c] 4 Or *the Jordan Valley* [d] 5 Or *Chaldean* [e] 8 Or *Chaldeans*

38:27 everything the king had ordered. Jeremiah obeyed the king’s order and did not tell the officials everything that had been discussed between himself and Zedekiah.

■ **39:1–18** *Jerusalem’s Fall.* This chapter describes the fall of Jerusalem to the Babylonians.

39:1 ninth year of Zedekiah . . . tenth month. This was on the tenth day of the tenth month (52:4; 2Ki 25:1). It was January 588 B.C.

39:2 ninth day . . . fourth month . . . eleventh year. July 586 B.C. The siege lasted two and a half years.

39:3 took seats in the Middle Gate. In fulfillment of 1:15. The officials’ names were formed by using those of Babylonian gods (Nebo, Nergal).

39:11–12 Nebuchadnezzar . . . had given these orders about Jeremiah. Jeremiah was clearly an international figure (1:5). How much of the prophet’s message the king knew is unclear; he may have regarded him as a Babylonian sympathizer (but see 25:12).

39:15–18 This section closes with a return to Jeremiah in prison, thus tying this chapter to chapters 37–38. God promised to protect Jeremiah from the Babylonians.

Jeremiah Freed

40 The word came to Jeremiah from the LORD after Nebuzaradan commander of the imperial guard had released him at Ramah. He had found Jeremiah bound in chains among all the captives from Jerusalem and Judah who were being carried into exile to Babylon. 2When the commander of the guard found Jeremiah, he said to him, "The LORD your God decreed this disaster for this place.[v] 3And now the LORD has brought it about; he has done just as he said he would. All this happened because you people sinned[w] against the LORD and did not obey[x] him. 4But today I am freeing you from the chains on your wrists. Come with me to Babylon, if you like, and I will look after you; but if you do not want to, then don't come. Look, the whole country lies before you; go wherever you please."[y] 5However, before Jeremiah turned to go,[a] Nebuzaradan added, "Go back to Gedaliah[z] son of Ahikam, the son of Shaphan, whom the king of Babylon has appointed over the towns of Judah, and live with him among the people, or go anywhere else you please."[a]

Then the commander gave him provisions and a present and let him go. 6So Jeremiah went to Gedaliah son of Ahikam at Mizpah[b] and stayed with him among the people who were left behind in the land.

Gedaliah Assassinated

7When all the army officers and their men who were still in the open country heard that the king of Babylon had appointed Gedaliah son of Ahikam as governor over the land and had put him in charge of the men, women and children who were the poorest[c] in the land and who had not been carried into exile to Babylon, 8they came to Gedaliah at Mizpah[d]—Ishmael[e] son of Nethaniah, Johanan and Jonathan the sons of Kareah, Seraiah son of Tanhumeth, the sons of Ephai the Netophathite,[f] and Jaazaniah[b] the son of the Maacathite,[g] and their men. 9Gedaliah son of Ahikam, the son of Shaphan, took an oath to reassure them and their men. "Do not be afraid to serve[h] the Babylonians,[c]" he said. "Settle down in the land and serve the king of Babylon, and it will go well with you.[i] 10I myself will stay at Mizpah[j] to represent you before the Babylonians who come to us, but you are to harvest the wine, summer fruit and oil, and put them in your storage jars, and live in the towns you have taken over."[k]

11When all the Jews in Moab,[l] Ammon, Edom and all the other countries heard that the king of Babylon had left a remnant in Judah and had appointed Gedaliah son of Ahikam, the son of Shaphan, as governor over them, 12they all came back to the land of Judah, to Gedaliah at Mizpah, from all the countries where they had been scattered.[m] And they harvested an abundance of wine and summer fruit.

13Johanan son of Kareah and all the army officers still in the open country came to Gedaliah at Mizpah[n] 14and said to him, "Don't you know that Baalis king of the Ammonites[o] has sent Ishmael son of Nethaniah to take your life?" But Gedaliah son of Ahikam did not believe them.

15Then Johanan son of Kareah said privately to Gedaliah in Mizpah, "Let me go and kill Ishmael son of Nethaniah, and no one will know it. Why should he take your life and cause all the Jews who are gathered around you to be scattered and the remnant of Judah to perish?"

16But Gedaliah son of Ahikam said to Johanan son of Kareah, "Don't do such a thing! What you are saying about Ishmael is not true."

41 In the seventh month Ishmael[p] son of Nethaniah, the son of Elishama, who was of royal blood and had been one of the king's officers, came with ten men to Gedaliah son of Ahikam at Mizpah. While they were eating together there, 2Ishmael[q] son of Nethaniah and the ten men who were with him got up and struck down Gedaliah son of Ahikam, the son of Shaphan, with the sword, killing the one whom the king of Bab-

40:2 [v]Jer 50:7
40:3 [w]Da 9:11 [x]Dt 29:24-28; Ro 2:5-9
40:4 [y]Ge 13:9; Jer 39:11-12
40:5 [z]2Ki 25:22 [a]Jer 39:14
40:6 [b]Jdg 20:1; 1Sa 7:5-17
40:7 [c]Jer 39:10
40:8 [d]ver 13 [e]ver 14; Jer 41:1,2 [f]2Sa 23:28 [g]Dt 3:14
40:9 [h]Jer 27:11 [i]Jer 38:20
40:10 [j]ver 6 [k]Dt 1:39
40:11 [l]Nu 25:1
40:12 [m]Jer 43:5
40:13 [n]ver 8
40:14 [o]2Sa 10:1-19; Jer 25:21; 41:10
41:1 [p]Jer 40:8
41:2 [q]Ps 41:9; 109:5

[a] 5 Or *Jeremiah answered* [b] 8 Hebrew *Jezaniah,* a variant of *Jaazaniah* [c] 9 Or *Chaldeans;* also in verse 10

■ **40:1—45:5** *Aftermath of Jerusalem's Fall.* These chapters cover several important events that took place after the fall of the city. Three topics are particularly in view: events in the life of Gedaliah (40:1—41:10), Jeremiah's flight to Egypt (41:11—44:30) and God's promise to Baruch (45:1–5).

■ **40:1—41:10** *Gedaliah.* This section narrates the governorship and assassination of Gedaliah.

40:1 Jeremiah . . . among all the captives. It seems that Jeremiah was not immediately recognized by the Babylonian authorities.

40:5 Gedaliah son of Ahikam. See 26:24. Gedaliah was receptive to Jeremiah's understanding of events.

40:10 harvest the wine, summer fruit and oil. In the moment of judgment we are given a first glimpse of future blessing in the land. Contrast the drought conditions during parts of Jeremiah's earlier preaching (see 14:1–6 and its note).

41:1 While they were eating together. This emphasizes the treachery of Ishmael.

ylon had appointed[r] as governor over the land.[s] 3 Ishmael also killed all the Jews who
were with Gedaliah at Mizpah, as well as the Babylonian[a] soldiers who were there.
4 The day after Gedaliah's assassination, before anyone knew about it, 5 eighty men
who had shaved off their beards,[t] torn their clothes and cut themselves came from Shechem,[u] Shiloh[v] and Samaria,[w] bringing grain offerings and incense with them to the
house of the LORD.[x] 6 Ishmael son of Nethaniah went out from Mizpah to meet them,
weeping[y] as he went. When he met them, he said, "Come to Gedaliah son of Ahikam."
7 When they went into the city, Ishmael son of Nethaniah and the men who were with
him slaughtered them and threw them into a cistern. 8 But ten of them said to Ishmael,
"Don't kill us! We have wheat and barley, oil and honey, hidden in a field."[z] So he let
them alone and did not kill them with the others. 9 Now the cistern where he threw all
the bodies of the men he had killed along with Gedaliah was the one King Asa[a] had made
as part of his defense[b] against Baasha[c] king of Israel. Ishmael son of Nethaniah filled it
with the dead.

10 Ishmael made captives of all the rest of the people[d] who were in Mizpah—the king's
daughters along with all the others who were left there, over whom Nebuzaradan commander of the imperial guard had appointed Gedaliah son of Ahikam. Ishmael son of
Nethaniah took them captive and set out to cross over to the Ammonites.[e]

11 When Johanan[f] son of Kareah and all the army officers who were with him heard
about all the crimes Ishmael son of Nethaniah had committed, 12 they took all their men
and went to fight Ishmael son of Nethaniah. They caught up with him near the great
pool[g] in Gibeon. 13 When all the people[h] Ishmael had with him saw Johanan son of Kareah and the army officers who were with him, they were glad. 14 All the people Ishmael had taken captive at Mizpah turned and went over to Johanan son of Kareah. 15 But Ishmael son of Nethaniah and eight of his men escaped[i] from Johanan and fled to the
Ammonites.

Flight to Egypt

16 Then Johanan son of Kareah and all the army officers who were with him led away
all the survivors[j] from Mizpah whom he had recovered from Ishmael son of Nethaniah
after he had assassinated Gedaliah son of Ahikam: the soldiers, women, children and
court officials he had brought from Gibeon. 17 And they went on, stopping at Geruth Kimham[k] near Bethlehem on their way to Egypt[l] 18 to escape the Babylonians.[b] They were
afraid[m] of them because Ishmael son of Nethaniah had killed Gedaliah[n] son of Ahikam,
whom the king of Babylon had appointed as governor over the land.

42

Then all the army officers, including Johanan[o] son of Kareah and Jezaniah[c] son
of Hoshaiah, and all the people from the least to the greatest[p] approached 2 Jeremiah the prophet and said to him, "Please hear our petition and pray[q] to the LORD your
God for this entire remnant.[r] For as you now see, though we were once many, now only
a few[s] are left. 3 Pray that the LORD your God will tell us where we should go and what
we should do."[t]

4 "I have heard you," replied Jeremiah the prophet. "I will certainly pray[u] to the LORD
your God as you have requested; I will tell you everything the LORD says and will keep
nothing back from you."[v]

5 Then they said to Jeremiah, "May the LORD be a true and faithful witness[w] against
us if we do not act in accordance with everything the LORD your God sends you to tell us.
6 Whether it is favorable or unfavorable, we will obey the LORD our God, to whom we are
sending you, so that it will go well[x] with us, for we will obey[y] the LORD our God."

7 Ten days later the word of the LORD came to Jeremiah. 8 So he called together Johanan son of Kareah and all the army officers[z] who were with him and all the people from

41:2 [r]Jer 40:5 [s]2Sa 3:27; 20:9-10
41:5 [t]Lev 19:27 [u]Ge 33:18; Jdg 9:1-57; 1Ki 12:1 [v]Jos 18:1 [w]1Ki 16:24 [x]2Ki 25:9
41:6 [y]2Sa 3:16
41:8 [z]Isa 45:3
41:9 [a]1Ki 15:22; 2Ch 16:6 [b]Jdg 6:2 [c]2Ch 16:1
41:10 [d]Jer 40:7, 12 [e]Jer 40:14
41:11 [f]Jer 40:8
41:12 [g]2Sa 2:13
41:13 [h]ver 10
41:15 [i]Job 21:30; Pr 28:17
41:16 [j]Jer 43:4
41:17 [k]2Sa 19:37 [l]Jer 42:14
41:18 [m]Isa 51:12; Jer 42:16; Lk 12:4-5 [n]Jer 40:5
42:1 [o]Jer 40:13; 41:11 [p]Jer 6:13; 44:12
42:2 [q]Jer 36:7; Ac 8:24; Jas 5:16 [r]Isa 1:9 [s]Lev 26:22; La 1:1
42:3 [t]Ps 86:11; Pr 3:6
42:4 [u]Ex 8:29; 1Sa 12:23 [v]1Ki 22:14; 1Sa 3:17
42:5 [w]Ge 31:50
42:6 [x]Dt 5:29; 6:3; Jer 7:23 [y]Ex 24:7; Jos 24:24
42:8 [z]ver 1

[a] *3* Or *Chaldean* [b] *18* Or *Chaldeans* [c] *1* Hebrew; Septuagint (see also 43:2) *Azariah*

41:5 shaved off their beards . . . cut themselves. Signs of mourning, no doubt for the fall of Jerusalem. **from Shechem, Shiloh and Samaria.** These were important cultic centers in the former northern kingdom, which had fallen in 722 B.C. These men clearly represent a residue of the Israelite population there who had made pilgrimages to Jerusalem for the great feasts (in accordance with Ex 23:14–17). It was the time of year (the "seventh month"; v. 1) for celebrating the Feast of Tabernacles. **the house of the LORD.** Although the temple was no longer standing, the site was still regarded as holy.
41:7 the city. Mizpah. **a cistern.** See 38:6.
41:9 the cistern . . . King Asa had made. See 1 Kings 15:22.
41:10 the king's daughters. Female members of Zedekiah's court. **Ammonites.** Part of the former alliance against Babylon (27:3). The Ammonite action was itself under God's judgment (27:8; 49:1–6).
■ **41:11—44:30** *Jeremiah's Flight to Egypt.* Jeremiah was taken to Egypt by Jewish survivors in the region who fled to escape possible Babylonian reprisal. Jeremiah prophesied there, and his message was one of judgment against the Jews for their repeated involvement in idolatry, this time while in Egypt (44:1–30).
41:15 eight of his men escaped. Two were presumably lost in the skirmish (v. 2).
41:17 Geruth Kimham near Bethlehem. Far south of Mizpah, this was along the route to Egypt.
42:5–6 See *WLC* 151.

the least to the greatest. [9]He said to them, "This is what the LORD, the God of Israel, to
whom you sent me to present your petition, says:[a] [10]'If you stay in this land, I will
build[b] you up and not tear you down; I will plant[c] you and not uproot you,[d] for I am
grieved over the disaster I have inflicted on you.[e] [11]Do not be afraid of the king of Babylon,[f] whom you now fear.[g] Do not be afraid of him, declares the LORD, for I am with you
and will save[h] you and deliver you from his hands.[i] [12]I will show you compassion so that
he will have compassion on you and restore you to your land.'[j]
[13]"However, if you say, 'We will not stay in this land,' and so disobey[k] the LORD your
God, [14]and if you say, 'No, we will go and live in Egypt,[l] where we will not see war or hear
the trumpet or be hungry for bread,' [15]then hear the word of the LORD, O remnant of Judah. This is what the LORD Almighty, the God of Israel, says: 'If you are determined to go
to Egypt and you do go to settle there, [16]then the sword[m] you fear will overtake you
there, and the famine you dread will follow you into Egypt, and there you will die. [17]In-
deed, all who are determined to go to Egypt to settle there will die by the sword, famine
and plague;[n] not one of them will survive or escape the disaster I will bring on them.'
[18]This is what the LORD Almighty, the God of Israel, says: 'As my anger and wrath[o] have
been poured out on those who lived in Jerusalem,[p] so will my wrath be poured out on
you when you go to Egypt. You will be an object of cursing and horror,[q] of condemnation and reproach; you will never see this place again.'[r]
[19]"O remnant of Judah, the LORD has told you, 'Do not go to Egypt.'[s] Be sure of this:
I warn you today [20]that you made a fatal mistake[a] when you sent me to the LORD your
God and said, 'Pray to the LORD our God for us; tell us everything he says and we will do
it.'[t] [21]I have told you today, but you still have not obeyed the LORD your God in all he sent
me to tell you.[u] [22]So now, be sure of this: You will die by the sword, famine and plague[v]
in the place where you want to go to settle."[w]

43

When Jeremiah finished telling the people all the words of the LORD their God—
everything the LORD had sent him to tell them[x]— [2]Azariah son of Hoshaiah and
Johanan[y] son of Kareah and all the arrogant men said to Jeremiah, "You are lying! The
LORD our God has not sent you to say, 'You must not go to Egypt to settle there.' [3]But Baruch son of Neriah is inciting you against us to hand us over to the Babylonians,[b] so they
may kill us or carry us into exile to Babylon."[z]
[4]So Johanan son of Kareah and all the army officers and all the people disobeyed the
LORD's command[a] to stay in the land of Judah.[b] [5]Instead, Johanan son of Kareah and all
the army officers led away all the remnant of Judah who had come back to live in the land
of Judah from all the nations where they had been scattered.[c] [6]They also led away all the
men, women and children and the king's daughters whom Nebuzaradan commander of
the imperial guard had left with Gedaliah son of Ahikam, the son of Shaphan, and Jeremiah the prophet and Baruch son of Neriah. [7]So they entered Egypt in disobedience to
the LORD and went as far as Tahpanhes.[d]
[8]In Tahpanhes[e] the word of the LORD came to Jeremiah: [9]"While the Jews are watching, take some large stones with you and bury them in clay in the brick pavement at the
entrance to Pharaoh's palace in Tahpanhes. [10]Then say to them, 'This is what the LORD
Almighty, the God of Israel, says: I will send for my servant[f] Nebuchadnezzar king of Babylon, and I will set his throne over these stones I have buried here; he will spread his royal canopy above them. [11]He will come and attack Egypt,[g] bringing death to those destined for death, captivity to those destined for captivity, and the sword to those destined
for the sword.[h] [12]He[c] will set fire to the temples of the gods[i] of Egypt; he will burn their
temples and take their gods captive. As a shepherd wraps[j] his garment around him, so
will he wrap Egypt around himself and depart from there unscathed. [13]There in the temple of the sun[d] in Egypt he will demolish the sacred pillars and will burn down the temples of the gods of Egypt.' "

42:9 [a]2Ki 22:15
42:10 [b]Jer 24:6 [c]Jer 31:28 [d]Eze 36:36 [e]Jer 18:8
42:11 [f]Jer 27:11 [g]Nu 14:9 [h]Isa 43:5 [i]Jer 1:8; Ro 8:31
42:12 [j]Ps 106:44-46
42:13 [k]Jer 44:16
42:14 [l]Nu 11:4-5
42:16 [m]Eze 11:8
42:17 [n]ver 22; Jer 44:13
42:18 [o]Dt 29:18-20; Jer 7:20 [p]2Ch 36:19; Jer 39:1-9 [q]Jer 29:18 [r]Jer 22:10
42:19 [s]Dt 17:16; Isa 30:7
42:20 [t]ver 2
42:21 [u]Eze 2:7; Zec 7:11-12
42:22 [v]ver 17; Eze 6:11 [w]Hos 9:6
43:1 [x]Jer 26:8; 42:9-22
43:2 [y]Jer 42:1
43:3 [z]Jer 38:4
43:4 [a]Jer 42:5-6 [b]Jer 42:10
43:5 [c]Jer 40:12
43:7 [d]Jer 2:16; 44:1
43:8 [e]Jer 2:16
43:10 [f]Isa 44:28; Jer 25:9; 27:6
43:11 [g]Jer 46:13-26; Eze 29:19-20 [h]Jer 15:2; 44:13; Zec 11:9
43:12 [i]Jer 46:25; Eze 30:13 [j]Ps 104:2; 109:18-19

a 20 Or *you erred in your hearts* b 3 Or *Chaldeans* c 12 Or *I* d 13 Or *in Heliopolis*

42:10 If you stay in this land. This was a new aspect of Jeremiah's message. See 40:6–9. **build . . . not uproot you.** See 31:4 and 28 and 33:7. **I am grieved.** See Genesis 6:6 and its note.
42:11 Do not be afraid. As before, Jeremiah called on these people not to fear foreign invaders but to trust in the Lord to deliver them.
42:13–16 The Lord's word was still against refuge in Egypt (Dt 17:16). The issue, as ever, was false trust and the delusion of safety in human power and calculation. See 22:20 and 22 and 30:14.
42:20–21 See *WLC* 151.
43:7–8 Egypt. Jeremiah's prophetic ministry continued even in Egypt. **Tahpanhes.** See 2:16. Tahpanhes probably lay in the eastern delta region.
43:9 take some large stones . . . bury them. A prophetic, symbolic action designed to show that the word would surely come to pass.
43:10 my servant Nebuchadnezzar. See note on 25:9.
43:13 temple of the sun. Probably refers to ancient Heliopolis ("city of the sun" in Greek). **sacred pillars.** Probably obelisks, which were characteristic of Egypt.

Disaster Because of Idolatry

44 This word came to Jeremiah concerning all the Jews living in Lower Egypt—in
Migdol,[k] Tahpanhes[l] and Memphis[a][m]—and in Upper Egypt[b]:[n] 2“This is what
the LORD Almighty, the God of Israel, says: You saw the great disaster I brought on Jerusalem and on all the towns of Judah. Today they lie deserted and in ruins[o] 3because of
the evil they have done. They provoked me to anger by burning incense and by worshiping other gods[p] that neither they nor you nor your fathers[q] ever knew. 4Again and again[r]
I sent my servants the prophets,[s] who said, ‘Do not do this detestable thing that I hate!’
5But they did not listen or pay attention; they did not turn from their wickedness or stop
burning incense to other gods.[t] 6Therefore, my fierce anger was poured out; it raged
against the towns of Judah and the streets of Jerusalem and made them the desolate ruins they are today.

7“Now this is what the LORD God Almighty, the God of Israel, says: Why bring such
great disaster[u] on yourselves by cutting off from Judah the men and women,[v] the children and infants, and so leave yourselves without a remnant? 8Why provoke me to anger with what your hands have made,[w] burning incense to other gods in Egypt, where
you have come to live?[x] You will destroy yourselves and make yourselves an object of
cursing and reproach[y] among all the nations on earth. 9Have you forgotten the wickedness committed by your fathers and by the kings and queens of Judah and the wickedness committed by you and your wives in the land of Judah and the streets of Jerusalem?[z]
10To this day they have not humbled themselves or shown reverence, nor have they followed my law[a] and the decrees I set before you and your fathers.[b]

11“Therefore, this is what the LORD Almighty, the God of Israel, says: I am determined
to bring disaster[c] on you and to destroy all Judah. 12I will take away the remnant[d] of Judah who were determined to go to Egypt to settle there. They will all perish in Egypt; they
will fall by the sword or die from famine. From the least to the greatest, they will die by
sword or famine.[e] They will become an object of cursing and horror, of condemnation
and reproach.[f] 13I will punish those who live in Egypt with the sword, famine and
plague,[g] as I punished Jerusalem. 14None of the remnant of Judah who have gone to live
in Egypt will escape or survive to return to the land of Judah, to which they long to return and live; none will return except a few fugitives.”[h]

15Then all the men who knew that their wives were burning incense to other gods,
along with all the women who were present—a large assembly—and all the people living in Lower and Upper Egypt,[c] said to Jeremiah, 16“We will not listen[i] to the message
you have spoken to us in the name of the LORD! 17We will certainly do everything we said
we would:[j] We will burn incense to the Queen of Heaven[k] and will pour out drink offerings to her just as we and our fathers, our kings and our officials did in the towns of Judah and in the streets of Jerusalem. At that time we had plenty of food and were well off
and suffered no harm.[l] 18But ever since we stopped burning incense to the Queen of
Heaven and pouring out drink offerings to her, we have had nothing and have been perishing by sword and famine.[m]”

19The women added, “When we burned incense to the Queen of Heaven[n] and poured
out drink offerings to her, did not our husbands know that we were making cakes like
her image and pouring out drink offerings to her?”

20Then Jeremiah said to all the people, both men and women, who were answering
him, 21“Did not the LORD remember[o] and think about the incense[p] burned in the towns
of Judah and the streets of Jerusalem[q] by you and your fathers,[r] your kings and your officials and the people of the land? 22When the LORD could no longer endure your wicked actions and the detestable things you did, your land became an object of cursing[s] and
a desolate waste without inhabitants, as it is today.[t] 23Because you have burned incense
and have sinned against the LORD and have not obeyed him or followed his law or his decrees or his stipulations, this disaster[u] has come upon you, as you now see.”[v]

24Then Jeremiah said to all the people, including the women,[w] “Hear the word of the

44:1 [k]Ex 14:2 [l]Jer 43:7, 8 [m]Isa 19:13 [n]Isa 11:11; Jer 46:14
44:2 [o]Isa 6:11; Jer 9:11; 34:22
44:3 [p]ver 8; Dt 13:6-11; 29:26 [q]Dt 32:17; Jer 19:4
44:4 [r]Jer 7:13 [s]Jer 7:25; 25:4; 26:5
44:5 [t]Jer 11:8-10
44:7 [u]Jer 26:19 [v]Jer 51:22
44:8 [w]Jer 25:6-7 [x]1Co 10:22 [y]Jer 42:18
44:9 [z]ver 17,21
44:10 [a]Jos 1:7 [b]1Ki 9:6-9
44:11 [c]Jer 21:10; Am 9:4
44:12 [d]ver 7 [e]Isa 1:28 [f]Jer 29:18; 42:15-18
44:13 [g]Jer 42:17
44:14 [h]ver 28; Jer 22:24-27; Ro 9:27
44:16 [i]Jer 11:8-10
44:17 [j]Dt 23:23 [k]ver 25; Jer 7:18 [l]Hos 2:5-13
44:18 [m]Mal 3:13-15
44:19 [n]Jer 7:18
44:21 [o]Isa 64:9; Jer 14:10 [p]Jer 11:13 [q]ver 9 [r]Ps 79:8
44:22 [s]Jer 25:18 [t]Ge 19:13; Ps 107:33-34
44:23 [u]Jer 40:2 [v]1Ki 9:9; Jer 7:13-15; Da 9:11-12
44:24 [w]ver 15

[a] *1* Hebrew *Noph* [b] *1* Hebrew *in Pathros* [c] *15* Hebrew *in Egypt and Pathros*

44:4 this detestable thing. That is, idolatrous worship of other gods.
44:7 without a remnant? A possible threat that the predictions of 5:10 and 23:3 might not be carried out.
44:9 Have you forgotten the wickedness . . . in the land of Judah . . . Jerusalem? Jeremiah wanted the people to remember not only the wickedness but also the resulting judgment. Recalling prior judgments might encourage later compliance. Compare the use of the judgment of the northern kingdom as a warning to Judah before her fall in 2 Kings 17:18–20.
44:17 See *WLC* 109.
44:19 Queen of Heaven. See note on 7:18. **did not our husbands know . . . ?** See Numbers 30:6–15. The women evidently had a prominent role in the worship of this pagan goddess.
44:23 law . . . decrees . . . stipulations. The requirements of the Mosaic covenant (Dt 11:1,32; 12:1).

LORD, all you people of Judah in Egypt.[x] 25 This is what the LORD Almighty, the God of Israel, says: You and your wives have shown by your actions what you promised when you
said, 'We will certainly carry out the vows we made to burn incense and pour out drink
offerings to the Queen of Heaven.'[y]
"Go ahead then, do what you promised! Keep your vows![z] 26 But hear the word of the
LORD, all Jews living in Egypt: 'I swear[a] by my great name,' says the LORD, 'that no one
from Judah living anywhere in Egypt will ever again invoke my name or swear, "As surely as the Sovereign LORD lives."[b] 27 For I am watching over them for harm,[c] not for good;
the Jews in Egypt will perish by sword and famine until they are all destroyed. 28 Those
who escape the sword and return to the land of Judah from Egypt will be very few.[d] Then
the whole remnant of Judah who came to live in Egypt will know whose word will
stand—mine or theirs.[e]
29 " 'This will be the sign to you that I will punish you in this place,' declares the LORD,
'so that you will know that my threats of harm against you will surely stand.'[f] 30 This is
what the LORD says: 'I am going to hand Pharaoh[g] Hophra king of Egypt over to his enemies who seek his life, just as I handed Zedekiah[h] king of Judah over to Nebuchadnezzar king of Babylon, the enemy who was seeking his life.' "[i]

A Message to Baruch

45 This is what Jeremiah the prophet told Baruch[j] son of Neriah in the fourth year
of Jehoiakim[k] son of Josiah king of Judah, after Baruch had written on a scroll
the words Jeremiah was then dictating: 2 "This is what the LORD, the God of Israel, says
to you, Baruch: 3 You said, 'Woe to me! The LORD has added sorrow to my pain; I am worn
out with groaning[l] and find no rest.' "
4 ⌊The LORD said,⌋ "Say this to him: 'This is what the LORD says: I will overthrow what
I have built and uproot what I have planted,[m] throughout the land.[n] 5 Should you then
seek great things for yourself? Seek them not.[o] For I will bring disaster on all people, declares the LORD, but wherever you go I will let you escape with your life.' "[p]

A Message About Egypt

46 This is the word of the LORD that came to Jeremiah the prophet concerning the
nations:[q]

2 Concerning Egypt:

This is the message against the army of Pharaoh Neco[r] king of Egypt, which was defeated at Carchemish[s] on the Euphrates River by Nebuchadnezzar king of Babylon in the
fourth year of Jehoiakim[t] son of Josiah king of Judah:

3 "Prepare your shields,[u] both large and small,
and march out for battle!
4 Harness the horses,
mount the steeds!
Take your positions
with helmets on!
Polish[v] your spears,
put on your armor![w]
5 What do I see?
They are terrified,

44:24 [x]Jer 43:7
44:25 [y]ver 17 [z]Eze 20:39
44:26 [a]Ge 22:16; Isa 48:1; Heb 6:13-17 [b]Dt 32:40; Ps 50:16
44:27 [c]Jer 31:28
44:28 [d]ver 13-14; Isa 10:19 [e]ver 17, 25-26
44:29 [f]Pr 19:21
44:30 [g]Jer 46:26; Eze 30:21 [h]2Ki 25:1-7 [i]Jer 39:5
45:1 [j]Jer 32:12; 36:4, 18,32 [k]2Ch 36:5
45:3 [l]Ps 69:3
45:4 [m]Jer 11:17 [n]Isa 5:5-7; Jer 18:7-10
45:5 [o]Mt 6:25-27,33 [p]Jer 21:9; 38:2; 39:18
46:1 [q]Jer 1:10; 25:15-38
46:2 [r]2Ki 23:29 [s]2Ch 35:20 [t]Jer 45:1
46:3 [u]Isa 21:5; Jer 51:11-12
46:4 [v]Eze 21:9-11 [w]1Sa 17:5,38; 2Ch 26:14; Ne 4:16

44:25–26 See *WCF* 22.6.
44:29–30 Pharaoh Hophra (598–570 B.C.) was killed by enemies during a power struggle. His death was viewed as a sign that all the Lord's prophecies against the refugees in Egypt would come to pass.
■ **45:1–5** *Promise to Baruch.* This chapter contains God's promise to Baruch, which had been made many years earlier, to spare his life.
45:1 fourth year of Jehoiakim. The year in which Baruch prepared the first scroll of Jeremiah's words for public reading (36:1–3). The prophecy here falls chronologically between the writing of the scroll (36:1–8) and its reading before the people and Jehoiakim (36:9–32).
45:3 my pain. Baruch had evidently suffered along with Jeremiah as a result of the latter's prophetic commission (e.g., 11:18–23). See 36:19, 43:3 and their notes. **groaning.** See Psalm 6:6. **rest.** See Deuteronomy 12:9 and Psalm 95:11.
45:5 escape with your life. Baruch's faithfulness led to this great blessing from God.
■ **46:1—51:64** *Oracles Against the Nations.* This section of Jeremiah is comprised of a series of messages of judgment against surrounding nations. The prophet mentioned Egypt (46:1–28), Philistia (47:1–7), Moab (48:1–47), Ammon (49:1–6), Edom (49:7–22), Damascus (49:23–27), Arabian tribes (49:28–33), Elam (49:34–39) and Babylon (50:1—51:64).
■ **46:1–28** *Against Egypt.* This chapter contains Jeremiah's prediction of judgment against Egypt, which was fulfilled by the Babylonians prior to the composition of this book.
46:2 Carchemish. One of the decisive battles of antiquity was fought here. It was here that Babylon defeated Egypt (605 B.C.), putting an end to Egypt's claims to rule in Canaan and Syria (Aram). **fourth year of Jehoiakim.** See 36:1 and 45:1. The ascendancy of Babylon over Egypt was critical for Judah in her final years (see "Introduction: Author" and "Time and Place of Writing").
46:3–4 Prepare your shields . . . put on your armor! Addressed to Egypt, this imperative mocks her military pretensions.

they are retreating,
their warriors are defeated.
They flee[x] in haste
without looking back,
and there is terror[y] on every side,"
declares the LORD.

6 "The swift cannot flee[z]
nor the strong escape.
In the north by the River Euphrates
they stumble and fall.[a]

7 "Who is this that rises like the Nile,
like rivers of surging waters?[b]
8 Egypt rises like the Nile,
like rivers of surging waters.
She says, 'I will rise and cover the earth;
I will destroy cities and their people.'
9 Charge, O horses!
Drive furiously, O charioteers![c]
March on, O warriors—
men of Cush[a] and Put who carry shields,
men of Lydia[d] who draw the bow.
10 But that day[e] belongs to the Lord, the LORD Almighty—
a day of vengeance, for vengeance on his foes.
The sword will devour[f] till it is satisfied,
till it has quenched its thirst with blood.
For the Lord, the LORD Almighty, will offer sacrifice[g]
in the land of the north by the River Euphrates.

11 "Go up to Gilead and get balm,[h]
O Virgin[i] Daughter of Egypt.
But you multiply remedies in vain;
there is no healing[j] for you.
12 The nations will hear of your shame;
your cries will fill the earth.
One warrior will stumble over another;
both will fall[k] down together."

13 This is the message the LORD spoke to Jeremiah the prophet about the coming of Nebuchadnezzar king of Babylon to attack Egypt:[l]

14 "Announce this in Egypt, and proclaim it in Migdol;
proclaim it also in Memphis[b] and Tahpanhes:[m]
'Take your positions and get ready,
for the sword devours those around you.'
15 Why will your warriors be laid low?
They cannot stand, for the LORD will push them down.[n]
16 They will stumble[o] repeatedly;
they will fall[p] over each other.
They will say, 'Get up, let us go back
to our own people and our native lands,
away from the sword of the oppressor.'
17 There they will exclaim,
'Pharaoh king of Egypt is only a loud noise;
he has missed his opportunity.[q]'

18 "As surely as I live," declares the King,[r]
whose name is the LORD Almighty,

46:5 [x]ver 21 [y]Jer 49:29
46:6 [z]Isa 30:16 [a]ver 12, 16; Da 11:19
46:7 [b]Jer 47:2
46:9 [c]Jer 47:3 [d]Isa 66:19
46:10 [e]Joel 1:15 [f]Dt 32:42 [g]Zep 1:7
46:11 [h]Jer 8:22 [i]Isa 47:1 [j]Jer 30:13; Mic 1:9
46:12 [k]Isa 19:4; Na 3:8-10
46:13 [l]Isa 19:1
46:14 [m]Jer 43:8
46:15 [n]Isa 66:15-16
46:16 [o]Lev 26:37 [p]ver 6
46:17 [q]Isa 19:11-16
46:18 [r]Jer 48:15

[a] 9 That is, the upper Nile region [b] 14 Hebrew *Noph;* also in verse 19

46:6 by the River Euphrates. That is, at Carchemish (see note on v. 2).
46:9 Cush . . . Put . . . Lydia. Mercenaries from these locations in Greece and Africa testified to Egypt's power.
46:11 Gilead. See note on 8:22. **Virgin Daughter of Egypt.** An image of vulnerability and innocence, although it can be used ironically. See its use of Israel in 14:17 and 18:13.
46:14 Migdol . . . Memphis . . . Tahpanhes. See 2:16, 43:8 and 44:1.
46:18 As surely as I live. See Genesis 22:15. **the King.** For refer-

46:18 [s]Jos 19:22 [t]1Ki 18:42
46:19 [u]Isa 20:4
46:20 [v]ver 24; Jer 47:2
46:21 [w]2Ki 7:6 [x]ver 5 [y]Ps 37:13
46:23 [z]Jdg 7:12
46:24 [a]Jer 1:15
46:25 [b]Eze 30:14; Na 3:8 [c]Jer 43:12 [d]Isa 20:6
46:26 [e]Jer 44:30 [f]Eze 32:11 [g]Eze 29:11-16
46:27 [h]Isa 41:13; 43:5 [i]Isa 11:11; Jer 50:19
46:28 [j]Isa 8:9-10 [k]Jer 4:27
47:1 [l]Ge 10:19; Am 1:6; Zec 9:5-7
47:2 [m]Isa 8:7; 14:31

"one will come who is like Tabor[s] among the mountains,
  like Carmel[t] by the sea.
19 Pack your belongings for exile,[u]
  you who live in Egypt,
for Memphis will be laid waste
  and lie in ruins without inhabitant.

20 "Egypt is a beautiful heifer,
  but a gadfly is coming
  against her from the north.[v]
21 The mercenaries[w] in her ranks
  are like fattened calves.
They too will turn and flee[x] together,
  they will not stand their ground,
for the day[y] of disaster is coming upon them,
  the time for them to be punished.
22 Egypt will hiss like a fleeing serpent
  as the enemy advances in force;
they will come against her with axes,
  like men who cut down trees.
23 They will chop down her forest,"
  declares the LORD,
"dense though it be.
They are more numerous than locusts,[z]
  they cannot be counted.
24 The Daughter of Egypt will be put to shame,
  handed over to the people of the north.[a]"

25 The LORD Almighty, the God of Israel, says: "I am about to bring punishment on Amon god of Thebes,[a][b] on Pharaoh, on Egypt and her gods[c] and her kings, and on those who rely[d] on Pharaoh. 26 I will hand them over[e] to those who seek their lives, to Nebuchadnezzar king[f] of Babylon and his officers. Later, however, Egypt will be inhabited[g] as in times past," declares the LORD.

27 "Do not fear,[h] O Jacob my servant;
  do not be dismayed, O Israel.
I will surely save you out of a distant place,
  your descendants from the land of their exile.[i]
Jacob will again have peace and security,
  and no one will make him afraid.
28 Do not fear, O Jacob my servant,
  for I am with you,"[j] declares the LORD.
"Though I completely destroy[k] all the nations
  among which I scatter you,
  I will not completely destroy you.
I will discipline you but only with justice;
  I will not let you go entirely unpunished."

A Message About the Philistines

47 This is the word of the LORD that came to Jeremiah the prophet concerning the Philistines before Pharaoh attacked Gaza:[l]

2 This is what the LORD says:

"See how the waters are rising in the north;[m]
  they will become an overflowing torrent.

[a] *25* Hebrew *No*

ence to God as King, see 8:19, 10:7 and 10, 48:15, 51:57 and Deuteronomy 33:5. In the oracles against the nations, true kingship is contrasted with the vain pretensions of earthly kings. **Tabor . . . Carmel.** These are high mountains in northern Israel. The latter is associated with battle in Judges 4:6.

46:20 heifer. Perhaps this is an allusion to Egyptian bull worship. **gadfly.** A fly that bites livestock. Here it refers to Nebuchadnezzar, who would trouble Egypt. **from the north.** See 6:1.

46:25 Amon god of Thebes. Amon was the chief Egyptian god. Thebes was in the south, suggesting even deeper penetration by Babylon.

■ **47:1–7** *Against Philistia.* Jeremiah's words of condemnation for the Philistines were fulfilled by the Egyptians prior to the composition of this book (cf. Isa 14:28–32; Eze 25:15–17; Am 1:6–8; Zep 2:4–7).

47:1 Pharaoh. It is unclear which pharaoh Jeremiah had in mind.

They will overflow the land and everything in it,
the towns and those who live in them.
The people will cry out;
all who dwell in the land will wail
3 at the sound of the hoofs of galloping steeds,
at the noise of enemy chariots
and the rumble of their wheels.
Fathers will not turn to help their children;
their hands will hang limp.
4 For the day has come
to destroy all the Philistines
and to cut off all survivors
who could help Tyre[n] and Sidon.[o]
The LORD is about to destroy the Philistines,[p]
the remnant from the coasts of Caphtor.[a][q]
5 Gaza will shave[r] her head in mourning;
Ashkelon[s] will be silenced.
O remnant on the plain,
how long will you cut yourselves?

6 " 'Ah, sword[t] of the LORD,' you cry,
'how long till you rest?
Return to your scabbard;
cease and be still.'
7 But how can it rest
when the LORD has commanded it,
when he has ordered it
to attack Ashkelon and the coast?"

47:4 [n]Am 1:9-10; Zec 9:2-4 [o]Jer 25:22 [p]Ge 10:14; Joel 3:4 [q]Dt 2:23
47:5 [r]Jer 41:5; Mic 1:16 [s]Jer 25:20
47:6 [t]Jer 12:12

A Message About Moab

48

Concerning Moab:

This is what the LORD Almighty, the God of Israel, says:

"Woe to Nebo,[u] for it will be ruined.
Kiriathaim[v] will be disgraced and captured;
the stronghold[b] will be disgraced and shattered.
2 Moab will be praised[w] no more;
in Heshbon[c][x] men will plot her downfall:
'Come, let us put an end to that nation.'
You too, O Madmen,[d] will be silenced;
the sword will pursue you.
3 Listen to the cries from Horonaim,[y]
cries of great havoc and destruction.
4 Moab will be broken;
her little ones will cry out.[e]
5 They go up the way to Luhith,[z]
weeping bitterly as they go;
on the road down to Horonaim
anguished cries over the destruction are heard.

48:1 [u]Nu 32:38 [v]Nu 32:37
48:2 [w]Isa 16:14 [x]Nu 21:25
48:3 [y]Isa 15:5
48:5 [z]Isa 15:5

[a] *4* That is, Crete [b] *1* Or / *Misgab* [c] *2* The Hebrew for *Heshbon* sounds like the Hebrew for *plot.*
[d] *2* The name of the Moabite town Madmen sounds like the Hebrew for *be silenced.* [e] *4* Hebrew; Septuagint / *proclaim it to Zoar*

47:4 day has come. See 46:21. **who could help Tyre and Sidon.** The Phoenician cities afforded natural protection to the Philistines farther down the coast, although it is not known whether alliances ever existed between them. **from . . . Caphtor.** This was the Philistines' place of origin, usually identified as Crete.

■ **48:1–47** *Against Moab.* Jeremiah predicted destruction for Moab (cf. Isa 15–16; Eze 25:8–11; Am 2:1–3).

48:1 Moab. For reference to Moab as an enemy of Israel, see Judges 3:12–14 and 2 Kings 3:4–27. Moab occupied parts of the land originally given to Israel (see note on v. 1) and was one of her allies against Babylon (27:3). Still, this nation supplied troops for Nebuchadnezzar against Jehoiakim (2Ki 2). Its defeat by Nebuchadnezzar may have come in 582 B.C. following a rebellion. **Nebo . . . Kiriathaim.** Originally these towns had been allocated to the tribe of Reuben (Nu 32:3,37–38; Jos 13:15,19).

48:2 Heshbon. This was also assigned to Reuben (Nu 32:37; Jos 13:17).

48:3 Horonaim. Probably located at the southern end of the Dead Sea; the whole length of Moabite territory was encompassed.

48:5 Luhith. Location unknown. See Isaiah 5:15.

48:7 Chemosh. The god of Moab. He was worshiped by Solomon (1Ki 11:7,33; 2Ki 23:13). Images of "defeated" gods were often carried off into exile.

6 Flee! Run for your lives;
 become like a bush[a] in the desert.[a]
7 Since you trust in your deeds and riches,
 you too will be taken captive,
and Chemosh[b] will go into exile,[c]
 together with his priests and officials.
8 The destroyer will come against every town,
 and not a town will escape.
The valley will be ruined
 and the plateau destroyed,
 because the LORD has spoken.
9 Put salt on Moab,
 for she will be laid waste[b];
her towns will become desolate,
 with no one to live in them.

10 "A curse on him who is lax in doing the LORD's work!
 A curse on him who keeps his sword[d] from bloodshed![e]

11 "Moab has been at rest[f] from youth,
 like wine left on its dregs,[g]
not poured from one jar to another—
 she has not gone into exile.
So she tastes as she did,
 and her aroma is unchanged.
12 But days are coming,"
 declares the LORD,
"when I will send men who pour from jars,
 and they will pour her out;
they will empty her jars
 and smash her jugs.
13 Then Moab will be ashamed[h] of Chemosh,
 as the house of Israel was ashamed
 when they trusted in Bethel.

14 "How can you say, 'We are warriors,[i]
 men valiant in battle'?
15 Moab will be destroyed and her towns invaded;
 her finest young men will go down in the slaughter,[j]"
 declares the King,[k] whose name is the LORD Almighty.[l]
16 "The fall of Moab is at hand;[m]
 her calamity will come quickly.
17 Mourn for her, all who live around her,
 all who know her fame;
say, 'How broken is the mighty scepter,
 how broken the glorious staff!'

18 "Come down from your glory
 and sit on the parched ground,[n]
 O inhabitants of the Daughter of Dibon,[o]
for he who destroys Moab
 will come up against you
 and ruin your fortified cities.[p]
19 Stand by the road and watch,
 you who live in Aroer.[q]
Ask the man fleeing and the woman escaping,
 ask them, 'What has happened?'

48:6 [a]Jer 17:6
48:7 [b]Nu 21:29 [c]Isa 46:1-2; Jer 49:3
48:10 [d]Jer 47:6 [e]1Ki 20:42; 2Ki 13:15-19
48:11 [f]Zec 1:15 [g]Zep 1:12
48:13 [h]Hos 10:6
48:14 [i]Ps 33:16
48:15 [j]Jer 50:27 [k]Jer 46:18 [l]Jer 51:57
48:16 [m]Isa 13:22
48:18 [n]Isa 47:1 [o]Nu 21:30; Jos 13:9 [p]ver 8
48:19 [q]Dt 2:36

[a] 6 Or *like Aroer* [b] 9 Or *Give wings to Moab, / for she will fly away*

48:8 The destroyer. Probably refers to Nebuchadnezzar.

48:9 Put salt on Moab. This action would render its fertile land barren.

48:10 See *WLC* 136.

48:11–12 This image of wine left to mature and therefore improve represents Moab's complacency. This would be rapidly cut short when the bottles of fermenting wine were poured out.

48:13 Bethel. Possibly the name used for the Lord in Jeroboam's apostate cult at Bethel (1Ki 12:28–30). That cult had not prevented the Assyrian depredations of 722 B.C. (2Ki 18:9–12).

48:19 Aroer. Southeast of Dibon, this border fortress was on the Arnon River (v. 20). It is here pictured as anxiously watching the flight of the refugees.

20 Moab is disgraced, for she is shattered.
Wail[r] and cry out!
Announce by the Arnon[s]
that Moab is destroyed.
21 Judgment has come to the plateau—
to Holon, Jahzah[t] and Mephaath,[u]
22 to Dibon,[v] Nebo and Beth Diblathaim,
23 to Kiriathaim, Beth Gamul and Beth Meon,[w]
24 to Kerioth[x] and Bozrah—
to all the towns of Moab, far and near.
25 Moab's horn[a][y] is cut off;
her arm[z] is broken,"
declares the LORD.

26 "Make her drunk,[a]
for she has defied the LORD.
Let Moab wallow in her vomit;
let her be an object of ridicule.
27 Was not Israel the object of your ridicule?[b]
Was she caught among thieves,
that you shake your head[c] in scorn[d]
whenever you speak of her?
28 Abandon your towns and dwell among the rocks,
you who live in Moab.
Be like a dove[e] that makes its nest
at the mouth of a cave.[f]

29 "We have heard of Moab's pride[g]—
her overweening pride and conceit,
her pride and arrogance
and the haughtiness of her heart.
30 I know her insolence but it is futile,"
declares the LORD,

"and her boasts accomplish nothing.
31 Therefore I wail[h] over Moab,
for all Moab I cry out,
I moan for the men of Kir Hareseth.[i]
32 I weep for you, as Jazer weeps,
O vines of Sibmah.[j]
Your branches spread as far as the sea;
they reached as far as the sea of Jazer.
The destroyer has fallen
on your ripened fruit and grapes.
33 Joy and gladness are gone
from the orchards and fields of Moab.
I have stopped the flow of wine[k] from the presses;
no one treads them with shouts of joy.[l]
Although there are shouts,
they are not shouts of joy.

34 "The sound of their cry rises
from Heshbon to Elealeh[m] and Jahaz,[n]
from Zoar[o] as far as Horonaim[p] and Eglath Shelishiyah,
for even the waters of Nimrim are dried up.[q]
35 In Moab I will put an end
to those who make offerings on the high places[r]
and burn incense[s] to their gods,"
declares the LORD.

36 "So my heart laments[t] for Moab like a flute;

48:20 [r]Isa 16:7 [s]Nu 21:13
48:21 [t]Nu 21:23; Isa 15:4 [u]Jos 13:18
48:22 [v]Jos 13:9,17
48:23 [w]Jos 13:17
48:24 [x]Am 2:2
48:25 [y]Ps 75:10 [z]Ps 10:15; Eze 30:21
48:26 [a]Jer 25:16,27
48:27 [b]Jer 2:26 [c]Job 16:4; Jer 18:16 [d]Mic 7:8-10
48:28 [e]Ps 55:6-7 [f]Jdg 6:2
48:29 [g]Job 40:12; Isa 16:6
48:31 [h]Isa 15:5-8 [i]2Ki 3:25
48:32 [j]Isa 16:8-9
48:33 [k]Isa 16:10 [l]Joel 1:12
48:34 [m]Nu 32:3 [n]Isa 15:4 [o]Ge 13:10 [p]Isa 15:5 [q]Isa 15:6
48:35 [r]Isa 15:2; 16:12 [s]Jer 11:13
48:36 [t]Isa 16:11

a 25 *Horn* here symbolizes strength.

48:20 Arnon. The most important river in Moab.
48:27 See *WLC* 145.
48:28 dwell among the rocks. See Isaiah 2:10.
48:32 Jazer . . . Sibmah . . . the sea. See Isaiah 16:8.

it laments like a flute for the men of Kir Hareseth.
The wealth they acquired[u] is gone.
37 Every head is shaved[v]
and every beard cut off;
every hand is slashed
and every waist is covered with sackcloth.[w]
38 On all the roofs in Moab
and in the public squares
there is nothing but mourning,
for I have broken Moab
like a jar[x] that no one wants,"
declares the LORD.

39 "How shattered she is! How they wail!
How Moab turns her back in shame!
Moab has become an object of ridicule,
an object of horror to all those around her."

40 This is what the LORD says:

"Look! An eagle is swooping[y] down,
spreading its wings[z] over Moab.
41 Kerioth[a] will be captured
and the strongholds taken.
In that day the hearts of Moab's warriors
will be like the heart of a woman in labor.[a]
42 Moab will be destroyed[b] as a nation[c]
because she defied[d] the LORD.
43 Terror and pit and snare[e] await you,
O people of Moab,"
declares the LORD.

44 "Whoever flees[f] from the terror
will fall into a pit,
whoever climbs out of the pit
will be caught in a snare;
for I will bring upon Moab
the year[g] of her punishment,"
declares the LORD.

45 "In the shadow of Heshbon
the fugitives stand helpless,
for a fire has gone out from Heshbon,
a blaze from the midst of Sihon;[h]
it burns the foreheads of Moab,
the skulls[i] of the noisy boasters.
46 Woe to you, O Moab![j]
The people of Chemosh are destroyed;
your sons are taken into exile
and your daughters into captivity.

47 "Yet I will restore[k] the fortunes of Moab
in days to come,"
declares the LORD.

Here ends the judgment on Moab.

A Message About Ammon

49 Concerning the Ammonites:[l]

This is what the LORD says:

a 41 Or *The cities*

48:36 [u]Isa 15:7
48:37 [v]Isa 15:2; Jer 41:5 [w]Ge 37:34
48:38 [x]Jer 22:28
48:40 [y]Dt 28:49; Hab 1:8 [z]Isa 8:8
48:41 [a]Isa 21:3
48:42 [b]Ps 83:4; Isa 16:14 [c]ver 2 [d]ver 26
48:43 [e]Isa 24:17
48:44 [f]1Ki 19:17; Isa 24:18 [g]Jer 11:23
48:45 [h]Nu 21:21,26-28 [i]Nu 24:17
48:46 [j]Nu 21:29
48:47 [k]Jer 12:15; 49:6,39
49:1 [l]Am 1:13; Zep 2:8-9

48:38 roofs in Moab. These were places for burning incense (see 2Ki 23:12).
48:40 eagle. Nebuchadnezzar (as in Eze 17:3).
48:43 Terror and pit and snare. See Isaiah 24:17.
48:45–46 Derived from Numbers 21:28–29, this passage states that Balaam's ancient oracle was about to be fulfilled. **Sihon.** During the time of Moses he was king of the Amorites, whose capital was Heshbon (Nu 21:21–30).

"Has Israel no sons?
Has she no heirs?
Why then has Molech[a] taken possession of Gad?
Why do his people live in its towns?
2 But the days are coming,"
declares the LORD,
"when I will sound the battle cry[m]
against Rabbah[n] of the Ammonites;
it will become a mound of ruins,
and its surrounding villages will be set on fire.
Then Israel will drive out
those who drove her out,[o]"
says the LORD.
3 "Wail, O Heshbon, for Ai[p] is destroyed!
Cry out, O inhabitants of Rabbah!
Put on sackcloth and mourn;
rush here and there inside the walls,
for Molech will go into exile,[q]
together with his priests and officials.
4 Why do you boast of your valleys,
boast of your valleys so fruitful?
O unfaithful daughter,
you trust in your riches[r] and say,
'Who will attack me?'[s]
5 I will bring terror on you
from all those around you,"
declares the Lord, the LORD Almighty.
"Every one of you will be driven away,
and no one will gather the fugitives.
6 "Yet afterward, I will restore[t] the fortunes of the Ammonites,"
declares the LORD.

A Message About Edom

7 Concerning Edom:[u]

This is what the LORD Almighty says:

"Is there no longer wisdom in Teman?[v]
Has counsel perished from the prudent?
Has their wisdom decayed?
8 Turn and flee, hide in deep caves,
you who live in Dedan,[w]
for I will bring disaster on Esau
at the time I punish him.
9 If grape pickers came to you,
would they not leave a few grapes?
If thieves came during the night,
would they not steal only as much as they wanted?
10 But I will strip Esau bare;
I will uncover his hiding places,

49:2 [m]Jer 4:19 [n]Dt 3:11 [o]Isa 14:2; Eze 21:28-32; 25:2-11
49:3 [p]Jos 8:28 [q]Jer 48:7
49:4 [r]Jer 9:23; 1Ti 6:17 [s]Jer 21:13
49:6 [t]ver 39; Jer 48:47
49:7 [u]Ge 25:30; Eze 25:12 [v]Ge 36:11, 15, 34
49:8 [w]Jer 25:23

[a] *1* Or *their king*; Hebrew *malcam*; also in verse 3

■ **49:1–6** *Against Ammon.* Ammon lay to the east of the Jordan, north of Moab. It was an old enemy of Israel (Jdg 11:4–33; 1Sa 11:1–11; 2Sa 10; 1Ki 4:13–19) which was, with Moab, part of the anti-Babylonian alliance (27:3), although like Moab it supplied troops to Nebuchadnezzar against Judah (2Ki 24:2). Its hostility to Gedaliah (40:13—41:3) suggests that it rebelled against Babylon, probably leading to an attack that virtually ended its existence as an autonomous nation. Compare Amos 1:13–15 and Ezekiel 25:1–7.
49:1 Molech. Or Milcom, the chief god of the Ammonites (see 1Ki 11:5 and NIV text note).
49:2 Rabbah. Identified with modern Amman.
49:3 Heshbon. As a border town, it may have belonged to Ammon at one time (Jdg 11:26). **Ai.** Not the Israelite Ai. Its location is unknown.
■ **49:7–22** *Against Edom.* Edom was a long-time enemy of Israel (2Sa 8:13–14). Their enmity reflected the division between Jacob, who inherited Canaan by usurping Esau's birthright, and his twin brother Esau, who settled in Edom (cf. Ge 27; 32; 36). Israel felt a particular bitterness toward Edom also because Edom had given assistance to Babylon against Judah (cf. Isa 21:11–12; Eze 25:12–14; Am 1:11–12; Ob 1–16; see also Jer 27:3 and note on 49:1–6).
49:7 Teman. An important Edomite town located south of the Dead Sea.
49:8 Esau. The brother of Jacob, who was called by another name in Edom (Ge 25:29–30; see also Ob 10).

so that he cannot conceal himself.
49:10 [x]Mal 1:2-5 — His children, relatives and neighbors will perish,
and he will be no more.[x]
49:11 [y]Hos 14:3 — 11 Leave your orphans;[y] I will protect their lives.
Your widows too can trust in me."

49:12 [z]Jer 25:15 [a]Jer 25:28-29 — 12 This is what the LORD says: "If those who do not deserve to drink the cup[z] must drink
it, why should you go unpunished?[a] You will not go unpunished, but must drink it. 13 I
49:13 [b]Ge 22:16 [c]Ge 36:33; Isa 34:6 — swear[b] by myself," declares the LORD, "that Bozrah[c] will become a ruin and an object of
horror, of reproach and of cursing; and all its towns will be in ruins forever."

14 I have heard a message from the LORD:
An envoy was sent to the nations to say,
"Assemble yourselves to attack it!
Rise up for battle!"

15 "Now I will make you small among the nations,
despised among men.
16 The terror you inspire
and the pride of your heart have deceived you,
you who live in the clefts of the rocks,
who occupy the heights of the hill.
49:16 [d]Job 39:27; Am 9:2 — Though you build your nest[d] as high as the eagle's,
from there I will bring you down,"
declares the LORD.
49:17 [e]ver 13 [f]Jer 50:13; Eze 35:7 — 17 "Edom will become an object of horror;[e]
all who pass by will be appalled and will scoff
49:18 [g]Ge 19:24; Dt 29:23 [h]ver 33 — because of all its wounds.[f]
18 As Sodom and Gomorrah[g] were overthrown,
along with their neighboring towns,"
says the LORD,
"so no one will live there;
no man will dwell[h] in it.

49:19 [i]Jer 12:5 [j]Jer 50:44 — 19 "Like a lion coming up from Jordan's thickets[i]
to a rich pastureland,
I will chase Edom from its land in an instant.
Who is the chosen one I will appoint for this?
Who is like me and who can challenge me?[j]
And what shepherd can stand against me?"
49:20 [k]Isa 14:27 [l]Jer 50:45 [m]Mal 1:3-4 — 20 Therefore, hear what the LORD has planned against Edom,
what he has purposed[k] against those who live in Teman:
The young of the flock[l] will be dragged away;
he will completely destroy[m] their pasture because of them.
49:21 [n]Eze 26:15 [o]Jer 50:46; Eze 26:18 — 21 At the sound of their fall the earth will tremble;[n]
their cry[o] will resound to the Red Sea.[a]
49:22 [p]Hos 8:1 [q]Isa 13:8; Jer 48:40-41 — 22 Look! An eagle will soar and swoop[p] down,
spreading its wings over Bozrah.
In that day the hearts of Edom's warriors
will be like the heart of a woman in labor.[q]

A Message About Damascus

49:23 [r]Ge 14:15; 2Ch 16:2; Ac 9:2 [s]Isa 10:9; Am 6:2; Zec 9:2 [t]2Ki 18:34 — 23 Concerning Damascus:[r]

"Hamath[s] and Arpad[t] are dismayed,
for they have heard bad news.

[a] *21* Hebrew *Yam Suph*; that is, Sea of Reeds

49:13 swear by myself. See note on Genesis 22:16. **Bozrah.** Different from Moabite Bozrah (48:24). Identified as modern Buseira, it was the capital of Edom in Jeremiah's day.
49:22 eagle. Probably refers to Nebuchadnezzar (as 48:40), although the Edomites were more definitively subjugated by Nabatean Arabs during the sixth century B.C.
■ **49:23–27** *Against Damascus.* Syria (Aram) impinged chiefly on the northern kingdom of Israel in the Assyrian period (1Ki 20; Am 1:3–5). The three states named here had fallen to Assyria in the eighth century B.C. It is not known how they may have affected the history of Judah during the Babylonian period. See 2 Kings 24:2.
49:23 Damascus: Hamath and Arpad. Major Aramaean city-states.

They are disheartened,
troubled like[a] the restless sea.[u]
24 Damascus has become feeble,
she has turned to flee
and panic has gripped her;
anguish and pain have seized her,
pain like that of a woman in labor.
25 Why has the city of renown not been abandoned,
the town in which I delight?
26 Surely, her young men will fall in the streets;
all her soldiers will be silenced[v] in that day,"
declares the LORD Almighty.
27 "I will set fire[w] to the walls of Damascus;
it will consume the fortresses of Ben-Hadad.[x]"

49:23 [u]Ge 49:4; Isa 57:20
49:26 [v]Jer 50:30
49:27 [w]Jer 43:12; Am 1:4 [x]1Ki 15:18

A Message About Kedar and Hazor

28 Concerning Kedar[y] and the kingdoms of Hazor, which Nebuchadnezzar king of Babylon attacked.

49:28 [y]Ge 25:13 [z]Jdg 6:3

This is what the LORD says:

"Arise, and attack Kedar
and destroy the people of the East.[z]
29 Their tents and their flocks will be taken;
their shelters will be carried off
with all their goods and camels.
Men will shout to them,
'Terror on every side!'[a]
30 "Flee quickly away!
Stay in deep caves, you who live in Hazor,"
declares the LORD.
"Nebuchadnezzar king of Babylon has plotted against you;
he has devised a plan against you.
31 "Arise and attack a nation at ease,
which lives in confidence,"
declares the LORD,
"a nation that has neither gates nor bars;[b]
its people live alone.
32 Their camels will become plunder,
and their large herds will be booty.
I will scatter to the winds those who are in distant places[b][c]
and will bring disaster on them from every side,"
declares the LORD.
33 "Hazor will become a haunt of jackals,
a desolate[d] place forever.
No one will live there;
no man will dwell[e] in it."

49:29 [a]Jer 6:25; 46:5
49:31 [b]Eze 38:11
49:32 [c]Jer 9:26
49:33 [d]Jer 10:22 [e]ver 18; Jer 51:37

A Message About Elam

34 This is the word of the LORD that came to Jeremiah the prophet concerning Elam,[f]
early in the reign of Zedekiah[g] king of Judah:

49:34 [f]Ge 10:22 [g]2Ki 24:18

[a] 23 Hebrew *on* or *by* [b] 32 Or *who clip the hair by their foreheads*

■ **49:28–33** *Against Arabian Tribes.* Arab nomadic tribes posed a periodic threat to settled communities (Jdg 6:1–6). The reference of the present oracle may be to an Arab uprising against Nebuchadnezzar in 599/598 B.C.

49:28 Kedar. This was a well-known Arab tribe during the Old Testament period (see Ge 25:13; Isa 21:16–17; 42:11). **Hazor.** Also in the Arabian Desert (not the well-known Hazor in northern Israel). This was possibly a name for a number of Arab settlements that may have included Teman, Buz and Dedan (25:23–24). **people of the East.** Another designation for Arab tribal peoples (see Jdg 6:3; 7:12; Job 1:3).

49:31 at ease . . . in confidence . . . neither gates nor bars. These nomadic peoples typically lived in unwalled towns, and their lifestyle was independent of fortified cities. See the description of Laish in Judges 18:7; in each case the dwellers were no match for a well-armed invader.

■ **49:34–39** *Against Elam.* Elam was an important power to the east of Babylon that was subjugated by Assyria but resurgent in the Babylonian period. The oracle probably relates to a Babylonian containment campaign against Elam in 596/594 B.C.

49:35 [h]Isa 22:6

35 This is what the LORD Almighty says:

“See, I will break the bow[h] of Elam,
the mainstay of their might.

49:36 [i]ver 32

36 I will bring against Elam the four winds[i]
from the four quarters of the heavens;
I will scatter them to the four winds,
and there will not be a nation
where Elam’s exiles do not go.

49:37 [j]Jer 30:24 [k]Jer 9:16

37 I will shatter Elam before their foes,
before those who seek their lives;
I will bring disaster upon them,
even my fierce anger,”[j]
declares the LORD.

“I will pursue them with the sword[k]
until I have made an end of them.
38 I will set my throne in Elam
and destroy her king and officials,”
declares the LORD.

49:39 [l]Jer 48:47

39 “Yet I will restore[l] the fortunes of Elam
in days to come,”
declares the LORD.

A Message About Babylon

50:1 [m]Ge 10:10; Isa 13:1

50 This is the word the LORD spoke through Jeremiah the prophet concerning Babylon[m] and the land of the Babylonians[a]:

50:2 [n]Jer 4:16 [o]Jer 51:31 [p]Isa 46:1 [q]Jer 51:47

2 “Announce and proclaim[n] among the nations,
lift up a banner and proclaim it;
keep nothing back, but say,
‘Babylon will be captured;[o]
Bel[p] will be put to shame,
Marduk[q] filled with terror.
Her images will be put to shame
and her idols filled with terror.’

50:3 [r]ver 13; Isa 14:22-23 [s]Zep 1:3

3 A nation from the north will attack her
and lay waste her land.
No one will live[r] in it;
both men and animals[s] will flee away.

50:4 [t]Jer 3:18; Hos 1:11 [u]Ezr 3:12; Jer 31:9 [v]Hos 3:5

4 “In those days, at that time,”
declares the LORD,
“the people of Israel and the people of Judah together[t]
will go in tears[u] to seek[v] the LORD their God.

50:5 [w]Jer 33:7 [x]Isa 55:3; Jer 32:40; Heb 8:6-10

5 They will ask the way to Zion
and turn their faces toward it.
They will come[w] and bind themselves to the LORD
in an everlasting covenant[x]
that will not be forgotten.

50:6 [y]Isa 53:6; Mt 9:36; 10:6

6 “My people have been lost sheep;[y]
their shepherds have led them astray
and caused them to roam on the mountains.

[a] *1* Or *Chaldeans*; also in verses 8, 25, 35 and 45

■ **50:1—51:64** *Against Babylon.* This lengthy oracle brings the book of Jeremiah to a close. The oracles up to this point served Jeremiah’s purpose of showing that Babylon would prevail over “all nations” (27:7), at least for a period of time. Babylon has appeared thus far as the instrument of God’s wrath. Finally, however (as in 25:17–26), judgment is uttered against Babylon itself to show that the time would come for its own demise (25:11–12). The Hebrew text of Jeremiah has allowed the oracles to stand at this point in the book so that this judgment on Babylon occupies its present climactic position. The length of this section confirms Babylon’s importance in Jeremiah’s overall argument. The oracle was uttered in 593 B.C. (see 51:59; cf. Isa 13:1—14:23; 21:1–9).

50:2 Bel . . . Marduk. Marduk, the creator-god of the Babylonian creation epic, was “king of the gods.” Bel, although originally separate, became a name for Marduk. See also Isaiah 46:1.

50:3 nation from the north. See 1:14 and 6:1. The tables were now turned. The nation in question is not specified, but see 51:27–28.

50:5 everlasting covenant. See 31:31–34, 32:40 and 33:20–21. See *WLC* 174.

They wandered over mountain and hill[z]
and forgot their own resting place.[a]
7 Whoever found them devoured them;
their enemies said, 'We are not guilty,[b]
for they sinned against the LORD, their true pasture,
the LORD, the hope[c] of their fathers.'

8 "Flee[d] out of Babylon;
leave the land of the Babylonians,
and be like the goats that lead the flock.
9 For I will stir up and bring against Babylon
an alliance of great nations from the land of the north.
They will take up their positions against her,
and from the north she will be captured.
Their arrows will be like skilled warriors
who do not return empty-handed.
10 So Babylonia[a] will be plundered;
all who plunder her will have their fill,"
declares the LORD.

11 "Because you rejoice and are glad,
you who pillage my inheritance,[e]
because you frolic like a heifer threshing grain
and neigh like stallions,
12 your mother will be greatly ashamed;
she who gave you birth will be disgraced.
She will be the least of the nations—
a wilderness, a dry land, a desert.
13 Because of the LORD's anger she will not be inhabited
but will be completely desolate.
All who pass Babylon will be horrified and scoff[f]
because of all her wounds.[g]

14 "Take up your positions around Babylon,
all you who draw the bow.[h]
Shoot at her! Spare no arrows,
for she has sinned against the LORD.
15 Shout[i] against her on every side!
She surrenders, her towers fall,
her walls[j] are torn down.
Since this is the vengeance[k] of the LORD,
take vengeance on her;
do to her[l] as she has done to others.
16 Cut off from Babylon the sower,
and the reaper with his sickle at harvest.
Because of the sword[m] of the oppressor
let everyone return to his own people,[n]
let everyone flee to his own land.[o]

17 "Israel is a scattered flock
that lions[p] have chased away.
The first to devour him
was the king[q] of Assyria;
the last to crush his bones
was Nebuchadnezzar[r] king[s] of Babylon."

18 Therefore this is what the LORD Almighty, the God of Israel, says:

"I will punish the king of Babylon and his land
as I punished the king[t] of Assyria.[u]

50:6 [z]Jer 3:6; Eze 34:6 [a]ver 19
50:7 [b]Jer 2:3 [c]Jer 14:8
50:8 [d]Isa 48:20; Jer 51:6; Rev 18:4
50:11 [e]Isa 47:6
50:13 [f]Jer 18:16 [g]Jer 49:17
50:14 [h]ver 29,42
50:15 [i]Jer 51:14 [j]Jer 51:44,58 [k]Jer 51:6 [l]Ps 137:8; Rev 18:6
50:16 [m]Jer 25:38 [n]Isa 13:14 [o]Jer 51:9
50:17 [p]Jer 2:15 [q]2Ki 17:6 [r]2Ki 24:10,14 [s]2Ki 25:7
50:18 [t]Isa 10:12 [u]Eze 31:3

a *10* Or *Chaldea*

50:9 I will stir up . . . against Babylon . . . from the land of the north. See Isaiah 41:25, where Cyrus is mentioned (cf. Isa 45:1). Members of the alliance are named in 51:27–28.

50:12 your mother. The city of Babylon is personified. **least of the nations.** She was the greatest and seemed invincible.

50:19 [v]Jer 31:10; Eze 34:13 [w]Jer 31:5; 33:12

19 But I will bring[v] Israel back to his own pasture
and he will graze on Carmel and Bashan;
his appetite will be satisfied
on the hills[w] of Ephraim and Gilead.

50:20 [x]Mic 7:18,19 [y]Jer 31:34 [z]Isa 1:9

20 In those days, at that time,"
declares the LORD,
"search will be made for Israel's guilt,
but there will be none,
and for the sins[x] of Judah,
but none will be found,
for I will forgive[y] the remnant[z] I spare.

50:21 [a]Eze 23:23

21 "Attack the land of Merathaim
and those who live in Pekod.[a]
Pursue, kill and completely destroy[a] them,"
declares the LORD.

50:22 [b]Jer 4:19-21; 51:54

"Do everything I have commanded you.
22 The noise[b] of battle is in the land,
the noise of great destruction!

50:23 [c]Isa 14:16

23 How broken and shattered
is the hammer of the whole earth!
How desolate[c] is Babylon
among the nations!

50:24 [d]Da 5:30-31 [e]Jer 51:31 [f]Job 9:4

24 I set a trap[d] for you, O Babylon,
and you were caught before you knew it;
you were found and captured[e]
because you opposed[f] the LORD.

50:25 [g]Isa 13:5 [h]Jer 51:25,55

25 The LORD has opened his arsenal
and brought out the weapons[g] of his wrath,
for the Sovereign LORD Almighty has work to do
in the land of the Babylonians.[h]

50:26 [i]Isa 14:22-23

26 Come against her from afar.
Break open her granaries;
pile her up like heaps of grain.
Completely destroy[i] her
and leave her no remnant.
27 Kill all her young bulls;
let them go down to the slaughter!
Woe to them! For their day has come,
the time for them to be punished.

50:28 [j]Isa 48:20; Jer 51:10 [k]ver 15

28 Listen to the fugitives and refugees from Babylon
declaring in Zion[j]
how the LORD our God has taken vengeance,[k]
vengeance for his temple.

50:29 [l]ver 14 [m]Rev 18:6 [n]Jer 51:56 [o]Isa 47:10

29 "Summon archers against Babylon,
all those who draw the bow.[l]
Encamp all around her;
let no one escape.
Repay[m] her for her deeds;[n]
do to her as she has done.
For she has defied[o] the LORD,
the Holy One of Israel.

a *21* The Hebrew term refers to the irrevocable giving over of things or persons to the LORD, often by totally destroying them; also in verse 26.

50:19 Carmel . . . Bashan . . . hills of Ephraim and Gilead. Fertile parts of Judah's land.

50:21 Merathaim . . . Pekod. Puns on Babylonian place-names (Marratu, Puqudu). The Hebrew words mean "double rebellion" and "punishment." **completely destroy.** See NIV text note.

50:24 caught before you knew it. The Persian defeat of Babylon was unexpected.

50:27 young bulls. Babylon's fighting men are in view.

50:28 fugitives and refugees. Jewish escapees from Babylon returned to Jerusalem. **vengeance for his temple.** The burning of the temple was the definitive destruction of Jerusalem, and the Lord tied his vengeance on Babylon specifically to it.

50:29 the Holy One of Israel. This name of God is frequent in Isaiah (see note on Isa 1:4; see theological article "Divine and Human Holiness" at Isa 6).

30 Therefore, her young men[p] will fall in the streets;
all her soldiers will be silenced in that day,"
declares the LORD.
31 "See, I am against[q] you, O arrogant one,"
declares the Lord, the LORD Almighty,
"for your day has come,
the time for you to be punished.
32 The arrogant one will stumble and fall
and no one will help her up;
I will kindle a fire[r] in her towns
that will consume all who are around her."

33 This is what the LORD Almighty says:

"The people of Israel are oppressed,[s]
and the people of Judah as well.
All their captors hold them fast,
refusing to let them go.[t]
34 Yet their Redeemer is strong;
the LORD Almighty[u] is his name.
He will vigorously defend their cause[v]
so that he may bring rest[w] to their land,
but unrest to those who live in Babylon.

35 "A sword[x] against the Babylonians!"
declares the LORD—
"against those who live in Babylon
and against her officials and wise[y] men!
36 A sword against her false prophets!
They will become fools.
A sword against her warriors![z]
They will be filled with terror.
37 A sword against her horses and chariots[a]
and all the foreigners in her ranks!
They will become women.[b]
A sword against her treasures!
They will be plundered.
38 A drought on[a] her waters!
They will dry[c] up.
For it is a land of idols,[d]
idols that will go mad with terror.

39 "So desert creatures and hyenas will live there,
and there the owl will dwell.
It will never again be inhabited
or lived in from generation to generation.[e]
40 As God overthrew Sodom and Gomorrah[f]
along with their neighboring towns,"
declares the LORD,
"so no one will live there;
no man will dwell in it.

41 "Look! An army is coming from the north;[g]
a great nation and many kings
are being stirred up from the ends of the earth.[h]
42 They are armed with bows[i] and spears;
they are cruel and without mercy.[j]
They sound like the roaring sea[k]
as they ride on their horses;
they come like men in battle formation
to attack you, O Daughter of Babylon.[l]

50:30 [p]Isa 13:18; Jer 49:26
50:31 [q]Jer 21:13
50:32 [r]Jer 21:14; 49:27
50:33 [s]Isa 58:6 [t]Isa 14:17
50:34 [u]Jer 51:19 [v]Jer 15:21; 51:36 [w]Isa 14:7
50:35 [x]Jer 47:6 [y]Da 5:7
50:36 [z]Jer 49:22
50:37 [a]Jer 51:21 [b]Jer 51:30; Na 3:13
50:38 [c]Jer 51:36 [d]ver 2
50:39 [e]Isa 13:19-22; 34:13-15; Jer 51:37; Rev 18:2
50:40 [f]Ge 19:24
50:41 [g]Jer 6:22 [h]Isa 13:4; Jer 51:22-28
50:42 [i]ver 14 [j]Isa 13:18 [k]Isa 5:30 [l]Jer 6:23

[a] *38* Or *A sword against*

50:34 Redeemer. See note on 31:11.

43 The king of Babylon has heard reports about them,
and his hands hang limp.
Anguish has gripped him,
pain like that of a woman in labor.
44 Like a lion coming up from Jordan's thickets
to a rich pastureland,
I will chase Babylon from its land in an instant.
Who is the chosen[m] one I will appoint for this?
Who is like me and who can challenge me?[n]
And what shepherd can stand against me?"
45 Therefore, hear what the LORD has planned against Babylon,
what he has purposed[o] against the land of the Babylonians:
The young of the flock will be dragged away;
he will completely destroy their pasture because of them.
46 At the sound of Babylon's capture the earth will tremble;
its cry[p] will resound among the nations.

51

This is what the LORD says:

"See, I will stir up the spirit of a destroyer
against Babylon and the people of Leb Kamai.[a]
2 I will send foreigners to Babylon
to winnow[q] her and to devastate her land;
they will oppose her on every side
in the day of her disaster.
3 Let not the archer string his bow,[r]
nor let him put on his armor.[s]
Do not spare her young men;
completely destroy[b] her army.
4 They will fall[t] down slain in Babylon,[c]
fatally wounded in her streets.[u]
5 For Israel and Judah have not been forsaken[v]
by their God, the LORD Almighty,
though their land[d] is full of guilt[w]
before the Holy One of Israel.

6 "Flee[x] from Babylon!
Run for your lives!
Do not be destroyed because of her sins.[y]
It is time for the LORD's vengeance;[z]
he will pay[a] her what she deserves.
7 Babylon was a gold cup[b] in the LORD's hand;
she made the whole earth drunk.
The nations drank her wine;
therefore they have now gone mad.
8 Babylon will suddenly fall[c] and be broken.
Wail over her!
Get balm[d] for her pain;
perhaps she can be healed.

9 " 'We would have healed Babylon,
but she cannot be healed;
let us leave[e] her and each go to his own land,
for her judgment[f] reaches to the skies,
it rises as high as the clouds.'

10 " 'The LORD has vindicated[g] us;
come, let us tell in Zion
what the LORD our God has done.'[h]

50:44 [m]Nu 16:5 [n]Job 41:10; Isa 46:9; Jer 49:19
50:45 [o]Ps 33:11; Isa 14:24; Jer 51:11
50:46 [p]Rev 18:9-10
51:2 [q]Isa 41:16; Jer 15:7; Mt 3:12
51:3 [r]Jer 50:29 [s]Jer 46:4
51:4 [t]Isa 13:15 [u]Jer 49:26; 50:30
51:5 [v]Isa 54:6-8 [w]Hos 4:1
51:6 [x]Jer 50:8 [y]Nu 16:26; Rev 18:4 [z]Jer 50:15 [a]Jer 25:14
51:7 [b]Jer 25:15-16; Rev 14:8-10; 17:4
51:8 [c]Isa 21:9; Rev 14:8 [d]Jer 46:11
51:9 [e]Isa 13:14; Jer 50:16 [f]Rev 18:4-5
51:10 [g]Mic 7:9 [h]Jer 50:28

[a] *1* *Leb Kamai* is a cryptogram for Chaldea, that is, Babylonia. [b] *3* The Hebrew term refers to the irrevocable giving over of things or persons to the LORD, often by totally destroying them. [c] *4* Or *Chaldea* [d] *5* Or / *and the land* ⌊*of the Babylonians*⌋

51:10 See *BC* 22.

11 "Sharpen the arrows,[i]
take up the shields![j]
The LORD has stirred up the kings of the Medes,[k]
because his purpose[l] is to destroy Babylon.
The LORD will take vengeance,
vengeance for his temple.[m]
12 Lift up a banner against the walls of Babylon!
Reinforce the guard,
station the watchmen,
prepare an ambush!
The LORD will carry out his purpose,
his decree against the people of Babylon.
13 You who live by many waters[n]
and are rich in treasures,[o]
your end has come,
the time for you to be cut off.
14 The LORD Almighty has sworn by himself:[p]
I will surely fill you with men, as with a swarm of locusts,[q]
and they will shout[r] in triumph over you.

15 "He made the earth by his power;
he founded the world by his wisdom
and stretched[s] out the heavens by his understanding.
16 When he thunders,[t] the waters in the heavens roar;
he makes clouds rise from the ends of the earth.
He sends lightning with the rain
and brings out the wind from his storehouses.[u]

17 "Every man is senseless and without knowledge;
every goldsmith is shamed by his idols.
His images are a fraud;[v]
they have no breath in them.
18 They are worthless,[w] the objects of mockery;
when their judgment comes, they will perish.
19 He who is the Portion of Jacob is not like these,
for he is the Maker of all things,
including the tribe of his inheritance—
the LORD Almighty is his name.

20 "You are my war club,[x]
my weapon for battle—
with you I shatter[y] nations,
with you I destroy kingdoms,
21 with you I shatter horse and rider,[z]
with you I shatter chariot and driver,
22 with you I shatter man and woman,
with you I shatter old man and youth,
with you I shatter young man and maiden,[a]
23 with you I shatter shepherd and flock,
with you I shatter farmer and oxen,
with you I shatter governors and officials.[b]

24 "Before your eyes I will repay[c] Babylon and all who live in Babylonia[a] for all the wrong they have done in Zion," declares the LORD.

25 "I am against you, O destroying mountain,
you who destroy the whole earth,"
declares the LORD.

51:11 [i]Jer 50:9 [j]Jer 46:4 [k]ver 28 [l]Jer 50:45 [m]Jer 50:28
51:13 [n]Rev 17:1,15 [o]Isa 45:3; Hab 2:9
51:14 [p]Am 6:8 [q]ver 27; Na 3:15 [r]Jer 50:15
51:15 [s]Ge 1:1; Job 9:8; Ps 104:2
51:16 [t]Ps 18:11-13 [u]Ps 135:7; Jnh 1:4
51:17 [v]Isa 44:20; Hab 2:18-19
51:18 [w]Jer 18:15
51:20 [x]Isa 10:5 [y]Mic 4:13
51:21 [z]Ex 15:1
51:22 [a]2Ch 36:17; Isa 13:17-18
51:23 [b]ver 57
51:24 [c]Jer 50:15

a *24* Or *Chaldea*; also in verse 35

51:11 Medes. Babylon was conquered by an alliance of Medes and Persians (see "Introduction: Purpose and Distinctives"; see also Isa 13:17; 21:2).
51:13 by many waters. Babylon was renowned for its irrigation channels, which were fed by the Euphrates.
51:14 sworn by himself. See Genesis 22:16 and its note.
51:20 You are my war club. Apparently addressed to Babylon (50:23), verses 20–23 are therefore to be taken together with verses 24–26. The passage then means that Babylon was in turn God's "hammer" of the nations and subject to his wrath for her own sin.

"I will stretch out my hand against you,
roll you off the cliffs,
and make you a burned-out mountain.[d]
26 No rock will be taken from you for a cornerstone,
nor any stone for a foundation,
for you will be desolate[e] forever,"
declares the LORD.

27 "Lift up a banner[f] in the land!
Blow the trumpet among the nations!
Prepare the nations for battle against her;
summon against her these kingdoms:[g]
Ararat,[h] Minni and Ashkenaz.[i]
Appoint a commander against her;
send up horses like a swarm of locusts.
28 Prepare the nations for battle against her—
the kings of the Medes,[j]
their governors and all their officials,
and all the countries they rule.
29 The land trembles and writhes,
for the LORD's purposes against Babylon stand—
to lay waste the land of Babylon
so that no one will live there.[k]
30 Babylon's warriors[l] have stopped fighting;
they remain in their strongholds.
Their strength is exhausted;
they have become like women.[m]
Her dwellings are set on fire;
the bars[n] of her gates are broken.
31 One courier[o] follows another
and messenger follows messenger
to announce to the king of Babylon
that his entire city is captured,
32 the river crossings seized,
the marshes set on fire,
and the soldiers terrified.[p]"

33 This is what the LORD Almighty, the God of Israel, says:

"The Daughter of Babylon is like a threshing floor[q]
at the time it is trampled;
the time to harvest[r] her will soon come."

34 "Nebuchadnezzar[s] king of Babylon has devoured us,
he has thrown us into confusion,
he has made us an empty jar.
Like a serpent he has swallowed us
and filled his stomach with our delicacies,
and then has spewed us out.
35 May the violence done to our flesh[a] be upon Babylon,"
say the inhabitants of Zion.
"May our blood be on those who live in Babylonia,"
says Jerusalem.[t]

36 Therefore, this is what the LORD says:

"See, I will defend your cause[u]
and avenge[v] you;

51:25 [d]Zec 4:7
51:26 [e]ver 29; Isa 13:19-22; Jer 50:12
51:27 [f]Isa 13:2; Jer 50:2 [g]Jer 25:14 [h]Ge 8:4 [i]Ge 10:3
51:28 [j]ver 11
51:29 [k]ver 43; Isa 13:20
51:30 [l]Jer 50:36 [m]Isa 19:16 [n]Isa 45:2; La 2:9; Na 3:13
51:31 [o]2Sa 18:19-31
51:32 [p]Jer 50:36
51:33 [q]Isa 21:10 [r]Isa 17:5; Hos 6:11
51:34 [s]Jer 50:17
51:35 [t]ver 24; Ps 137:8
51:36 [u]Ps 140:12; Jer 50:34; La 3:58 [v]ver 6; Ro 12:19

a *35* Or *done to us and to our children*

51:27 Lift up a banner . . . Blow the trumpet. See 4:5–6 and its note. **these kingdoms.** The Medes and their allies. **Ararat.** See note on Genesis 8:4. **Minni.** Located in Armenia. **Ashkenaz.** See note on Genesis 10:3.
51:30 dwellings are set on fire. See 21:10. Babylon's sacking of Judah is being described.
51:33 Daughter of Babylon. This both personifies Babylon and alludes to its women, who were made vulnerable by defeat (see 50:42; see also La 1:6 and its note).
51:36 I will defend your cause. See 50:34. **avenge.** See 50:15. The metaphors of revenge and courtroom judgment are mixed here.

I will dry up[w] her sea
and make her springs dry.
37 Babylon will be a heap of ruins,
a haunt[x] of jackals,
an object of horror and scorn,
a place where no one lives.[y]
38 Her people all roar like young lions,
they growl like lion cubs.
39 But while they are aroused,
I will set out a feast for them
and make them drunk,
so that they shout with laughter—
then sleep forever and not awake,"
declares the LORD.[z]

40 "I will bring them down
like lambs to the slaughter,
like rams and goats.

41 "How Sheshach[a] [a] will be captured,[b]
the boast of the whole earth seized!
What a horror Babylon will be
among the nations!
42 The sea will rise over Babylon;
its roaring waves[c] will cover her.
43 Her towns will be desolate,
a dry and desert land,
a land where no one lives,
through which no man travels.[d]
44 I will punish Bel[e] in Babylon
and make him spew out[f] what he has swallowed.
The nations will no longer stream to him.
And the wall[g] of Babylon will fall.

45 "Come out[h] of her, my people!
Run[i] for your lives!
Run from the fierce anger of the LORD.
46 Do not lose heart or be afraid[j]
when rumors[k] are heard in the land;
one rumor comes this year, another the next,
rumors of violence in the land
and of ruler against ruler.
47 For the time will surely come
when I will punish the idols[l] of Babylon;
her whole land will be disgraced[m]
and her slain will all lie fallen within her.
48 Then heaven and earth and all that is in them
will shout[n] for joy over Babylon,
for out of the north[o]
destroyers will attack her,"
declares the LORD.

49 "Babylon must fall because of Israel's slain,
just as the slain in all the earth
have fallen because of Babylon.[p]
50 You who have escaped the sword,
leave[q] and do not linger!
Remember[r] the LORD in a distant land,
and think on Jerusalem."

51:36 [w]Jer 50:38
51:37 [x]Isa 13:22; Rev 18:2 [y]Jer 50:13, 39
51:39 [z]ver 57
51:41 [a]Jer 25:26 [b]Isa 13:19
51:42 [c]Isa 8:7
51:43 [d]ver 29, 62; Isa 13:20; Jer 2:6
51:44 [e]Isa 46:1 [f]ver 34 [g]ver 58; Jer 50:15
51:45 [h]Rev 18:4 [i]ver 6, Isa 48:20; Jer 50:8
51:46 [j]Jer 46:27 [k]2Ki 19:7
51:47 [l]ver 52; Isa 46:1-2; Jer 50:2 [m]Jer 50:12
51:48 [n]Isa 44:23; Rev 18:20 [o]ver 11
51:49 [p]Ps 137:8; Jer 50:29
51:50 [q]ver 45 [r]Ps 137:6

[a] *41 Sheshach* is a cryptogram for Babylon.

51:41 Sheshach. See 25:26.
51:44 Bel. See 50:2 and Isaiah 46:1. **what he has swallowed.** Refers to the nations taken into exile and to their treasures. The latter were also restored to Judah as a result of Cyrus's decree (Ezr 1:5–11). **wall of Babylon.** This was an enormously wide double wall, which was further protected by a moat.

51:51 [s]Ps 44:13-16; 79:4 [t]La 1:10

51 "We are disgraced,[s]
for we have been insulted
and shame covers our faces,
because foreigners have entered
the holy places of the LORD's house."[t]

51:52 [u]ver 47

52 "But days are coming," declares the LORD,
"when I will punish her idols,[u]
and throughout her land
the wounded will groan.

51:53 [v]Ge 11:4; Isa 14:13-14 [w]Jer 49:16

53 Even if Babylon reaches the sky[v]
and fortifies her lofty stronghold,
I will send destroyers[w] against her,"
declares the LORD.

51:54 [x]Jer 50:22

54 "The sound of a cry comes from Babylon,
the sound of great destruction[x]
from the land of the Babylonians.[a]
55 The LORD will destroy Babylon;
he will silence her noisy din.

51:55 [y]Ps 18:4

Waves[y] ⌊of enemies⌋ will rage like great waters;
the roar of their voices will resound.

51:56 [z]ver 48 [a]Ps 46:9 [b]ver 6; Ps 94:1-2; Hab 2:8

56 A destroyer[z] will come against Babylon;
her warriors will be captured,
and their bows will be broken.[a]
For the LORD is a God of retribution;
he will repay[b] in full.

51:57 [c]Ps 76:5; Jer 25:27 [d]Jer 46:18; 48:15

57 I will make her officials and wise men drunk,
her governors, officers and warriors as well;
they will sleep[c] forever and not awake,"
declares the King,[d] whose name is the LORD Almighty.

51:58 [e]ver 44 [f]ver 64 [g]Hab 2:13

58 This is what the LORD Almighty says:

"Babylon's thick wall[e] will be leveled
and her high gates set on fire;
the peoples[f] exhaust themselves for nothing,
the nations' labor is only fuel for the flames."[g]

51:59 [h]Jer 36:4 [i]Jer 52:1 [j]Jer 28:1
51:60 [k]Jer 30:2; 36:2
51:62 [l]Isa 13:20; Jer 50:13,39
51:64 [m]ver 58 [n]Job 31:40

59 This is the message Jeremiah gave to the staff officer Seraiah son of Neriah,[h] the son
of Mahseiah, when he went to Babylon with Zedekiah[i] king of Judah in the fourth[j] year
of his reign. 60 Jeremiah had written on a scroll[k] about all the disasters that would come
upon Babylon—all that had been recorded concerning Babylon. 61 He said to Seraiah,
"When you get to Babylon, see that you read all these words aloud. 62 Then say, 'O LORD,
you have said you will destroy this place, so that neither man nor animal will live in it;
it will be desolate[l] forever.' 63 When you finish reading this scroll, tie a stone to it and
throw it into the Euphrates. 64 Then say, 'So will Babylon sink to rise no more because of
the disaster I will bring upon her. And her people[m] will fall.' "

The words of Jeremiah end[n] here.

The Fall of Jerusalem

52:1 [o]2Ki 24:17

52 Zedekiah[o] was twenty-one years old when he became king, and he reigned in Jerusalem eleven years. His mother's name was Hamutal daughter of Jeremiah;

[a] 54 Or *Chaldeans*

51:51 The exiles expressed their grief over the occupation of the temple by Nebuchadnezzar in 586 B.C., perhaps feeling that this defilement could never be rectified.
51:53 Even if Babylon reaches the sky. Probably a reference to its lofty ziggurats, symbols of its religious pride (Ge 11:4).
51:58 high gates. The Ishtar Gate was known for its great height. **the nations' labor.** That is, the labor of subject nations in building Babylon's fortifications.
51:59 Seraiah son of Neriah. An official in Zedekiah's administration, he was responsible for this expedition's billeting en route. He was the brother of Baruch, Jeremiah's scribe (32:12). **went to Babylon with Zedekiah . . . fourth year of his reign.** That is, in 594/593 B.C. The expedition may have been undertaken in answer to a summons to explain Zedekiah's part in the uprising against Nebuchadnezzar (see note on 27:3).
51:60 a scroll. It may have contained the oracles in chapters 50–51. See 36:2.
51:63–64 This final, prophetic, symbolic act (see note on 13:1–11) reinforced the last recorded word of Jeremiah, namely, that Babylon would fall.
■ **52:1–34** *Exile and Release From Prison.* The final chapter of Jeremiah describes the fall of Jerusalem and recalls how many of Jere-

she was from Libnah.[p] 2He did evil in the eyes of the LORD, just as Jehoiakim[q] had done.
3It was because of the LORD's anger that all this happened to Jerusalem and Judah,[r] and
in the end he thrust them from his presence.
Now Zedekiah rebelled[s] against the king of Babylon.
4So in the ninth year of Zedekiah's reign, on the tenth[t] day of the tenth month, Nebuchadnezzar king of Babylon marched against Jerusalem[u] with his whole army. They
camped outside the city and built siege works all around it.[v] 5The city was kept under
siege until the eleventh year of King Zedekiah.
6By the ninth day of the fourth month the famine in the city had become so severe
that there was no food for the people to eat.[w] 7Then the city wall was broken through,
and the whole army fled. They left the city at night through the gate between the two
walls near the king's garden, though the Babylonians[a] were surrounding the city. They
fled toward the Arabah,[b] 8but the Babylonian[c] army pursued King Zedekiah and overtook him in the plains of Jericho. All his soldiers were separated from him and scattered,
9and he was captured.[x]
He was taken to the king of Babylon at Riblah[y] in the land of Hamath,[z] where he pronounced sentence on him. 10There at Riblah the king of Babylon slaughtered the sons[a]
of Zedekiah before his eyes; he also killed all the officials of Judah. 11Then he put out Zedekiah's eyes, bound him with bronze shackles and took him to Babylon, where he put
him in prison till the day of his death.[b]
12On the tenth day of the fifth[c] month, in the nineteenth year of Nebuchadnezzar king
of Babylon, Nebuzaradan[d] commander of the imperial guard, who served the king of
Babylon, came to Jerusalem. 13He set fire[e] to the temple[f] of the LORD, the royal palace
and all the houses of Jerusalem. Every important building he burned down. 14The whole
Babylonian army under the commander of the imperial guard broke down all the walls[g]
around Jerusalem. 15Nebuzaradan the commander of the guard carried into exile some
of the poorest people and those who remained in the city, along with the rest of the
craftsmen[d] and those who had gone over to the king of Babylon. 16But Nebuzaradan left
behind[h] the rest of the poorest people of the land to work the vineyards and fields.
17The Babylonians broke up the bronze pillars,[i] the movable stands[j] and the bronze
Sea[k] that were at the temple of the LORD and they carried all the bronze to Babylon.[l]
18They also took away the pots, shovels, wick trimmers, sprinkling bowls, dishes and all
the bronze articles used in the temple service.[m] 19The commander of the imperial guard
took away the basins, censers,[n] sprinkling bowls, pots, lampstands, dishes and bowls
used for drink offerings—all that were made of pure gold or silver.
20The bronze from the two pillars, the Sea and the twelve bronze bulls under it, and
the movable stands, which King Solomon had made for the temple of the LORD, was more
than could be weighed.[o] 21Each of the pillars was eighteen cubits high and twelve cubits
in circumference[e]; each was four fingers thick, and hollow.[p] 22The bronze capital[q] on top
of the one pillar was five cubits[f] high and was decorated with a network and pomegranates of bronze all around. The other pillar, with its pomegranates, was similar. 23There
were ninety-six pomegranates on the sides; the total number of pomegranates[r] above
the surrounding network was a hundred.
24The commander of the guard took as prisoners Seraiah[s] the chief priest, Zephaniah[t] the priest next in rank and the three doorkeepers. 25Of those still in the city, he took
the officer in charge of the fighting men, and seven royal advisers. He also took the secretary who was chief officer in charge of conscripting the people of the land and sixty of
his men who were found in the city. 26Nebuzaradan[u] the commander took them all and
brought them to the king of Babylon at Riblah. 27There at Riblah, in the land of Hamath,
the king had them executed.

52:1 [p]Jos 10:29; 2Ki 8:22
52:2 [q]Jer 36:30
52:3 [r]Isa 3:1 [s]Eze 17:12-16
52:4 [t]Zec 8:19 [u]2Ki 25:1-7; Jer 39:1 [v]Eze 24:1-2
52:6 [w]Isa 3:1
52:9 [x]Jer 32:4 [y]Nu 34:11 [z]Nu 13:21
52:10 [a]Jer 22:30
52:11 [b]Eze 12:13
52:12 [c]Zec 7:5; 8:19 [d]Jer 39:9
52:13 [e]2Ch 36:19; Ps 74:8; La 2:6 [f]Ps 79:1; Mic 3:12
52:14 [g]Ne 1:3
52:16 [h]Jer 40:6
52:17 [i]1Ki 7:15 [j]1Ki 7:27-37 [k]1Ki 7:23 [l]Jer 27:19-22
52:18 [m]Ex 27:3; 1Ki 7:45
52:19 [n]1Ki 7:50
52:20 [o]1Ki 7:47
52:21 [p]1Ki 7:15
52:22 [q]1Ki 7:16
52:23 [r]1Ki 7:20
52:24 [s]2Ki 25:18 [t]Jer 21:1; 37:3
52:26 [u]ver 12

[a] *7* Or *Chaldeans*; also in verse 17 [b] *7* Or *the Jordan Valley* [c] *8* Or *Chaldean*; also in verse 14
[d] *15* Or *populace* [e] *21* That is, about 27 feet (about 8.1 meters) high and 18 feet (about 5.4 meters) in circumference [f] *22* That is, about 7 1/2 feet (about 2.3 meters)

---

miah's prophecies had already been fulfilled. Despite its message of divine judgment for sin, this material is closely parallel to 2 Kings 24:18—25:21 and 27–30. It is likely that both books used a common source, although Jeremiah is more detailed at times. In this way, the book of Jeremiah ends (like 2 Kings) on a hopeful note by calling attention to the mercy shown to Jehoiachin, king of Judah, while in exile in Babylon (52:31–34; cf. 2Ki 25:27–30).
52:1 Jeremiah. Not the prophet.
52:12 the tenth day. The parallel in 2 Kings 25:8 has "the seventh day." One of these represents a mistake in copying the text.
52:22 five. The parallel in the Hebrew text of 2 Kings 25:17 lists the measurement as three cubits, which is "four and a half feet." See note on verse 12.
52:25 seven. The parallel in 2 Kings 25:19 refers to "five." See note on verse 12.
52:28–30 These verses refer to the two main deportations of Jews to Babylon: the first in 597 B.C. ("the seventh year") and the second in 586 B.C. (the "eighteenth year"; contrast the "nineteenth year" of v. 12; the discrepancy is due to an alternative way of counting). A third and smaller deportation is also mentioned; this was no doubt

52:27 [v]Jer 20:4 — So Judah went into captivity, away[v] from her land. 28 This is the number of the peo-
52:28 [w]2Ki 24:14-16; 2Ch 36:20 — ple Nebuchadnezzar carried into exile:[w]

> in the seventh year, 3,023 Jews;
> 29 in Nebuchadnezzar's eighteenth year,
> 832 people from Jerusalem;
> 30 in his twenty-third year,
> 745 Jews taken into exile by Nebuzaradan the commander of the imperial guard.
> There were 4,600 people in all.

Jehoiachin Released

31 In the thirty-seventh year of the exile of Jehoiachin king of Judah, in the year Evil-
Merodach[a] became king of Babylon, he released Jehoiachin king of Judah and freed him
from prison on the twenty-fifth day of the twelfth month. 32 He spoke kindly to him and
gave him a seat of honor higher than those of the other kings who were with him in Bab-
52:33 [x]2Sa 9:7 — ylon. 33 So Jehoiachin put aside his prison clothes and for the rest of his life ate regularly at the king's table.[x] 34 Day by day the king of Babylon gave Jehoiachin a regular allow-
52:34 [y]2Sa 9:10 — ance[y] as long as he lived, till the day of his death.

[a] 31 Also called *Amel-Marduk*

the result of some offense no longer known. The numbers here (smaller than in 2 Kings 24:14,16) may include only adult males.

52:31 twenty-fifth. The parallel in 2 Kings 25:27 stipulates "twenty-seventh." See note on verse 12.

52:33–34 Jehoiachin's release from prison may have been considered an indication that Jeremiah's prophecies about restoration could still be fulfilled (see especially chs. 31–33).

LAMENTATIONS

Introduction

Overview

Author: Unknown

Purpose: To express and to guide others in expressing laments over the terrible conditions brought on Jerusalem and God's people by the Babylonians

Date: c. 586–516 B.C.

Key Truths:

- Judah and Jerusalem deserved the divine judgment they had received.
- The pain of destruction and exile was greater than the people could bear without the outlet of lament.
- The only hope for deliverance from the suffering of exile was to call on God to be compassionate.

Author

Lamentations is traditionally attributed to the prophet Jeremiah. This has been true at least since the third century B.C., as evidenced by the fact that the Septuagint (Greek translation of the OT) contains a note about the prophet's authorship of the book as a heading before the first verse. The idea that Jeremiah was the author may have been encouraged by 2 Chronicles 35:25, which relates that the prophet composed laments for King Josiah. There is no direct evidence in Lamentations itself that Jeremiah was its author, although there are distinct echoes of Jeremiah's style and expressions in the book, especially in chapter 3 (e.g., vv. 48–51; cf. Jer 14:17). However, since Lamentations consists of five poems that vary somewhat in style and appear sometimes to be spoken by an individual (ch. 3) and sometimes by the community (ch. 5), the book may have been compiled from various sources rather than composed by a single author.

Time and Place of Writing

The setting of Lamentations is clearly Judah, particularly Jerusalem. The contents of the book, especially the lament concerning the loss of Judah's king (2:2,9), places it after the fall of the kingdom of Judah to the Babylonians in 586 B.C. and before the rebuilding of the temple c. 516 B.C. This setting during the period of the Babylonian exile makes Lamentations a fitting sequel to the book of Jeremiah; Jeremiah foretold the fall of Jerusalem, while the writer of Lamentations expressed the pain endured in the fulfillment of that prophecy.

Purpose and Distinctives

The purpose of Lamentations was fulfilled in its very execution and then in its adoption by others as a means of coming to terms with the destruction of Zion. It presents three harmonious perspectives on the wrath God poured out against Judah through the Babylonians.

First, the book affirms that the destruction and exile were deserved consequences for sin. The prophets had warned Judah repeatedly that judgment would come if the people continued to violate God's covenant with them. Long before Jeremiah Amos spoke of a day of the Lord against his people (Am 5:18), and that day had come (La 1:12). The prophets had drawn on the principles of the covenant, expressed most forcefully in Deuteronomy, which made an emphatic connection between the people's faithfulness to the Lord and their continuance in the land. The book's purpose, in part, was to justify God's punishment of Judah and to vindicate the prophets who had announced the judgment beforehand.

Second, the author expressed strong emotional resistance to the judgment on Judah. Was God's punishment of his people excessive (2:20–22)? Could it be right for him to behave as the enemy of his own people (2:4ff.)? These honest expressions made the book powerful in its day and make it compelling today, when a sense of anguish and forsakenness is once again pervasive.

Third, the book affirms that the Lord is still a God of mercy and faithfulness (see 3:22–36). Lamentations expresses sincere faith that the exile will end, as well as hope that there will be satisfaction for Judah's guilt and judgment on her enemies for their crimes against her. This hope reflects an understanding of the sovereignty of God over all the nations, a sovereignty that ensured the fulfillment of all his covenant promises (see 3:37–39).

The five chapters of Lamentations comprise five distinct poems. These poems are laments, which are also present in other books of the Old Testament, principally the Psalms (see "Introduction to Psalms: Structure: *Genres:* 2. *Laments*"). Laments (both of the community and of the individual) share typical characteristics: complaint about adversity, confession of trust, appeal for deliverance and confidence in God's response—often including the assurance that enemies and persecutors would, in turn, meet his wrath (e.g., Ps 74). Lamentations exhibits these usual distinctives but includes some variations as well.

The book shares with other laments a certain poetic style, namely the so-called *qinah* meter. This poetic rhythm consists of lines in which the first phrase has three points of stress (in the Hebrew) and the second has two.

Lamentations also makes extensive use of the acrostic form. In an acrostic, each successive unit, such as a line or a verse, begins with a consecutive letter of the Hebrew alphabet, which contains 22 letters (e.g., Ps 34). Lamentations conforms very closely to this pattern in chapters 1, 2 and 4. Chapter 3 varies the pattern. It includes 22 stanzas, each with three verses that begin with the same letter. Chapter 5 is not an acrostic at all, though it is also comprised of 22 verses. In the Old Testament, the acrostic form probably represented the complete expression of a sentiment or theme. The poet's artistic labor, furthermore, was an act of devotion to the Lord. In devotional meditation the acrostic produces a delicate balance between extreme emotion and disciplined restraint.

Christ in Lamentations

Lamentations points beyond the situation of the exile to Christ in several important ways. In his humiliation, Jesus suffered a type of exile through his substitutionary atonement for God's people. In the days before his own cry of abandonment as part of his redemptive suffering (Mt 27:46), Jesus spoke his own lament over Jerusalem (Mt 23:37–39; Lk 13:34–35). Christ's exaltation began the end of the suffering of God's people. He took his throne and will continue to reign, finally overcoming all his enemies. Lamentations also provides followers of Christ with a means of expressing their own laments over the conditions of life for God's people in the present. Although Christ has inaugurated the kingdom of God and the exaltation of God's people, the church continues to suffer deprivation and exile (1Pe 1:2). Lamentations asserts that in a world of pain and injustice God is still good and that he will one day bring all goodness "to those whose hope is in him" (3:25).

Outline

I. Zion Lies Devastated With No Comfort (1:1–22)	*The suffering of exile left Judah with no comfort.*
II. The Lord's Anger Against Judah (2:1–22)	*The wrath of God against his people was terrifying.*
III. A Lament and Consolation (3:1–66)	*An individual expressed lament on behalf of the people and found some consolation.*
IV. Zion's Present and Future (4:1–22)	*The poet expressed Judah's desperate appeal to God for deliverance.*
V. Judah's Appeal for God's Help (5:1–22)	*Judah's condition was horrible, but the future would hold better days for the nation.*

1[a]

How deserted lies the city,
once so full of people!
How like a widow[a] is she,
who once was great[b] among the nations!
She who was queen among the provinces
has now become a slave.[c]

2 Bitterly she weeps[d] at night,
tears are upon her cheeks.
Among all her lovers[e]
there is none to comfort her.
All her friends have betrayed[f] her;
they have become her enemies.[g]

1:1 [a]Isa 47:8 [b]1Ki 4:21 [c]Isa 3:26; Jer 40:9

1:2 [d]Ps 6:6 [e]Jer 3:1 [f]Jer 4:30; Mic 7:5 [g]ver 16

[a] This chapter is an acrostic poem, the verses of which begin with the successive letters of the Hebrew alphabet.

■ **1:1–22** *Zion Lies Devastated With No Comfort.* Lamentations opens with a lament describing Jerusalem, the capital of Judah, the city of God's glorious presence, in horrific ruin.

1:1 How deserted. The first verse sets the theme of this lament. Jerusalem, the city once favored but now desolate, had lost her greatness because of the Babylonian depredations (cf. Isa 1:21–26). **full . . . great.** Jerusalem's former greatness is emphasized by the twofold use of the Hebrew word translated by two English words in this verse, "full" and "great." The city was wealthy and highly populated and had been a microcosm foreshadowing the glory of the entire new creation to come (cf. Rev 21). **widow.** Widowhood and solitude (cf. Jer 15:17) pictured forsakenness or absence of blessing. **slave.** Slavery was the antithesis of God's plan for Israel, released into freedom from the slavery of Egypt (Lev 26:13). See Jeremiah 2:14 for the rejection of the concept of Israel as slave, as well as Deuteronomy 15:12–18, which applies Israel's essential freedom to social legislation by calling for the emancipation every seventh year of all Israelites held as slaves. Exile was the worst of the covenant curses (see chart, "Major Covenants in the Bible," on p. 25).

1:2 lovers. An ironic figure for Judah's idolatrous neighbors with whom she willingly consorted (cf. Jer 3:1). Like a rightfully jealous husband, God was angered by Judah's infidelity. In the view of Hosea the exile constituted God's divorce from Israel (Hos 2). **none to comfort.** This phrase appears five times in this first poem, making it a dominant theme (1:9,16,17,21; see also 2:13). The situation was so appalling that the exiles could find no consolation.

3 After affliction and harsh labor,
Judah has gone into exile.[h]
She dwells among the nations;
she finds no resting place.[i]
All who pursue her have overtaken her
in the midst of her distress.

4 The roads to Zion mourn,
for no one comes to her appointed feasts.
All her gateways are desolate,[j]
her priests groan,
her maidens grieve,
and she is in bitter anguish.[k]

5 Her foes have become her masters;
her enemies are at ease.
The LORD has brought her grief[l]
because of her many sins.
Her children have gone into exile,[m]
captive before the foe.

6 All the splendor has departed
from the Daughter of Zion.[n]
Her princes are like deer
that find no pasture;
in weakness they have fled
before the pursuer.

7 In the days of her affliction and wandering
Jerusalem remembers all the treasures
that were hers in days of old.
When her people fell into enemy hands,
there was no one to help her.[o]
Her enemies looked at her
and laughed at her destruction.

8 Jerusalem has sinned[p] greatly
and so has become unclean.
All who honored her despise her,
for they have seen her nakedness;[q]
she herself groans[r]
and turns away.

9 Her filthiness clung to her skirts;
she did not consider her future.[s]
Her fall[t] was astounding;
there was none to comfort[u] her.
"Look, O LORD, on my affliction,[v]
for the enemy has triumphed."

1:3 [h]Jer 13:19 [i]Dt 28:65
1:4 [j]Jer 9:11 [k]Joel 1:8-13
1:5 [l]Jer 30:15 [m]Jer 39:9; 52:28-30
1:6 [n]Jer 13:18
1:7 [o]Jer 37:7; La 4:17
1:8 [p]ver 20; Isa 59:2-13 [q]Jer 13:22,26 [r]ver 21,22
1:9 [s]Dt 32:28-29; Isa 47:7; Eze 24:13 [t]Jer 13:18 [u]Ecc 4:1; Jer 16:7 [v]Ps 25:18

1:3 Judah has gone. For accounts of Jerusalem's fall see 2 Kings 24:20—25:30, as well as Jeremiah 39–45 and 52. **exile.** the worst-case covenant curse against the covenant people. Judah's exile meant her removal from the place of God's blessing and salvation (see theological article "The Presence of God" at 1Ki 8). **no resting place.** The opposite of covenant blessing, which brought rest from enemies (Dt 12:9, 2Sa 7:1; cf. Dt 28:65).

1:4 roads to Zion. Roads taken in pilgrimage to the temple by those who lived at a distance (cf. Ps 84:5). **appointed feasts.** The main annual gatherings for worship (especially Passover, Pentecost and Harvest; Ex 23:14–17), when Jerusalem was crowded and priests presided over the jubilant celebration. **maidens grieve.** A sign of defeat; contrast Jeremiah 31:13.

1:5 The LORD has brought her grief. Because of her unfaithfulness Judah's sorrows came as the prophets had foretold. See other complaints; for example, Psalm 73 and Jeremiah 12:1. **her many sins.** The complaint was accompanied by a brief confession of sin.

1:6 Daughter of Zion. A personification of Jerusalem that appears eight times in Lamentations alone and many times in all of the prophetic materials (see 1:6; 2:1,4,8,10,13,18; 4:22; see also Jer 6:2; Mic 1:13).

1:7 Jerusalem remembers. The bitter present contrasted with an earlier, happier time, possibly that of David and Solomon. **no one to help her.** A further contrast with conquering David. See note on verse 2. See *WLC* 121.

1:8 Jerusalem has sinned. The cause of the exile. **unclean.** A reference to menstruation (see notes on Lev 15:19–33), which caused ritual impurity and prevented a woman from gaining access to the temple. The result of Judah's sin was similar, if more traumatic and harrowing; namely, a total and perpetual cutting off from the temple, the place where God had manifested his special presence (see theological article "The Presence of God" at 1Ki 8), as well as humiliation (see Jer 13:22,26). The entire city, not simply some individuals, had become unclean in God's eyes and would not be cleansed for many years.

1:9 filthiness. A further statement of ritual uncleanness (cf. v. 8). **Look, O LORD.** Personified Zion now speaks for herself and introduces the element of appeal that is a vital part of this lament. **none to comfort.** See note on verse 2.

1:10 [w]Isa 64:11 [x]Ps 74:7-8; Jer 51:51 [y]Dt 23:3

10 The enemy laid hands
 on all her treasures;[w]
she saw pagan nations
 enter her sanctuary[x]—
those you had forbidden[y]
 to enter your assembly.

1:11 [z]Ps 38:8 [a]Jer 52:6

11 All her people groan[z]
 as they search for bread;[a]
they barter their treasures for food
 to keep themselves alive.
"Look, O LORD, and consider,
 for I am despised."

1:12 [b]Jer 18:16 [c]ver 18 [d]Isa 13:13; Jer 30:24

12 "Is it nothing to you, all you who pass by?[b]
 Look around and see.
Is any suffering like my suffering[c]
 that was inflicted on me,
that the LORD brought on me
 in the day of his fierce anger?[d]

1:13 [e]Job 30:30 [f]Jer 44:6 [g]Hab 3:16

13 "From on high he sent fire,
 sent it down into my bones.[e]
He spread a net for my feet
 and turned me back.
He made me desolate,[f]
 faint[g] all the day long.

1:14 [h]Dt 28:48; Isa 47:6 [i]Jer 32:5

14 "My sins have been bound into a yoke[a];[h]
 by his hands they were woven together.
They have come upon my neck
 and the Lord has sapped my strength.
He has handed me over[i]
 to those I cannot withstand.

1:15 [j]Jer 37:10 [k]Isa 41:2 [l]Isa 28:18; Jer 18:21

15 "The Lord has rejected
 all the warriors in my midst;[j]
he has summoned an army[k] against me
 to[b] crush my young men.[l]
In his winepress the Lord has trampled
 the Virgin Daughter of Judah.

1:16 [m]La 2:11, 18; 3:48-49 [n]Ps 69:20; Ecc 4:1 [o]ver 2; Jer 13:17; 14:17

16 "This is why I weep
 and my eyes overflow with tears.[m]
No one is near to comfort[n] me,
 no one to restore my spirit.
My children are destitute
 because the enemy has prevailed."[o]

1:17 [p]Jer 4:31

17 Zion stretches out her hands,[p]
 but there is no one to comfort her.

a 14 Most Hebrew manuscripts; Septuagint *He kept watch over my sins* b 15 Or *has set a time for me / when he will*

1:10 pagan nations enter her sanctuary. A reference to the loss of Judah's place of worship and access to the presence of God (see note on v. 8). The desecration of the holy place by invaders contrasts with the intended function of the temple in drawing the nations to worship the God of Israel (1Ki 8:41–43). The destruction of the temple is probably also implied, since Nebuchadnezzar destroyed it in 586 B.C. just after desecrating it (see notes on 2Ki 25:8–9). The ruin of the temple, where God had sat enthroned, demonstrated how utterly God had deserted his people because of their sins.
1:11 All her people . . . search for bread. The desolation of the city entailed desperate food shortages. **Look, O LORD.** See note on verse 9.
1:12 Is any suffering like my suffering? Although the writer recognized that Judah's punishment was deserved (vv. 5,8), he was overwhelmed by its magnitude. He called upon onlookers to witness the extremity of God's punishment and to sympathize with Judah's plight. **the day of his fierce anger.** An allusion to "the day of the LORD" (see "Introduction to Zephaniah"), which describes any instance in which the Lord intervenes dramatically in history to destroy his enemies and to deliver his people. Jerusalem's destruction, however, revealed that God had, at least for the time being, become Judah's enemy.
1:13 he sent fire. The people of Zion realized that the Lord had used the Babylonians to afflict them so terribly (see Ps 88:13–18).
1:15 The Lord has rejected. The Lord, formerly a warrior on Israel's behalf (Dt 9:1–3), had turned his might and fury against his own people.
1:16 No one . . . to comfort. See note on 1:2.

The LORD has decreed for Jacob
that his neighbors become his foes;
Jerusalem has become
an unclean thing among them.

18 "The LORD is righteous,
yet I rebelled[q] against his command.
Listen, all you peoples;
look upon my suffering.[r]
My young men and maidens
have gone into exile.[s]

19 "I called to my allies
but they betrayed me.
My priests and my elders
perished[t] in the city
while they searched for food
to keep themselves alive.

20 "See, O LORD, how distressed[u] I am!
I am in torment[v] within,
and in my heart I am disturbed,
for I have been most rebellious.
Outside, the sword bereaves;
inside, there is only death.[w]

21 "People have heard my groaning,[x]
but there is no one to comfort me.[y]
All my enemies have heard of my distress;
they rejoice[z] at what you have done.
May you bring the day[a] you have announced
so they may become like me.

22 "Let all their wickedness come before you;
deal with them
as you have dealt with me
because of all my sins.[b]
My groans are many
and my heart is faint."

2[a] How the Lord has covered the Daughter of Zion
with the cloud of his anger[b]![c]
He has hurled down the splendor of Israel
from heaven to earth;
he has not remembered his footstool[d]
in the day of his anger.

1:18 [q]1Sa 12:14 [r]ver 12 [s]Dt 28:32,41
1:19 [t]Jer 14:15; La 2:20
1:20 [u]Jer 4:19 [v]La 2:11 [w]Dt 32:25; Eze 7:15
1:21 [x]ver 8 [y]ver 4 [z]La 2:15 [a]Isa 47:11; Jer 30:16
1:22 [b]Ne 4:5
2:1 [c]La 3:44 [d]Ps 99:5; 132:7

[a] This chapter is an acrostic poem, the verses of which begin with the successive letters of the Hebrew alphabet. [b] *1* Or *How the Lord in his anger / has treated the Daughter of Zion with contempt*

1:17 no one to comfort her. The repetition of this phrase (see note on 1:2) marks it as a dominant theme of this lament. There was no relief or consolation in sight for Jerusalem. **Jacob.** One of the historic names for Israel, from the name of the patriarch. **unclean.** Not the normal word for "ceremonially unclean," but the term for menstrual rags or filth (see note on v. 8). Even the nations, who did not respect the Lord's holy ceremonial standards, despised Judah as abhorrent. This was in stark contrast to the hope God had extended to his people through his offers of covenant blessing (see Ex 19:5–6).
1:18 The LORD is righteous. Despite the difficulties that overwhelmed the writer, he briefly acknowledged the Lord's justice in punishing Judah's sins. Yet the thought shifts quickly again to her unbearable condition.
1:19 allies. Judah's objects of false confidence, which angered God (see Isa 7:1–9).
1:21 no one to comfort me. See note on 1:2. **my enemies . . . rejoice.** An appeal to the Lord because of the enemies' gloating, which was deeply offensive to Judah as God's covenant people—and therefore to God himself. **day.** The day of the Lord (see "Introduction to Zephaniah") would become a day of terror for Zion's enemies. The lament followed the prophetic pattern of judgment first through enemies and ultimately on those enemies (cf. Jer 25:15–38).
1:22 deal with them. Zion's enemies merited judgment as thoroughly as Jerusalem did. **My groans.** Even the just punishment of her enemies would not diminish Zion's deep distress.
■ **2:1–22** *The Lord's Anger Against Judah.* This chapter is the second lament over Jerusalem's state. Its focus is on God's judgment and wrath against the nation.
2:1 the cloud of his anger. A reference to the glory cloud resting over Jerusalem, this time in wrath rather than in protection (see Isa 4:5; Eze 1). See NIV text note. **he has not remembered.** That is, he had not acted on behalf of the city. Astonishingly to Judah, God's promise to David appeared to be void (see Ps 89, especially vv. 38–51). Isaiah had given assurance about God's protection of Zion (e.g., 37:35), and Judah had behaved as though this promise were unconditional, forgetting her obligation to keep covenant with God. **his footstool.** An image depicting the ark of the covenant (1Ch 28:2; see note on Ps 132:7) and Zion, (Ps 99:5,9; see also Isa 66:1, where the figure refers to Jerusalem as well).

2:2
[e]La 3:43 [f]Ps 21:9
[g]Ps 89:39-40;
Mic 5:11
[h]Isa 25:12

2:3
[i]Ps 75:5,10
[j]Ps 74:11
[k]Isa 42:25;
Jer 21:4-5,14

2:4
[l]Job 16:13;
La 3:12-13
[m]Eze 24:16,25
[n]Isa 42:25;
Jer 7:20

2:5
[o]Jer 30:14 [p]ver 2
[q]Jer 9:17-20

2:6
[r]Jer 52:13 [s]La 1:4;
Zep 3:18 [t]La 4:16

2:7
[u]Ps 74:7-8;
Isa 64:11;
Jer 33:4-5

2:8
[v]2Ki 21:13;
Isa 34:11 [w]Isa 3:26

2:9
[x]Ne 1:3 [y]Dt 28:36;
2Ki 24:15
[z]2Ch 15:3

2 Without pity[e] the Lord has swallowed[f] up
all the dwellings of Jacob;
in his wrath he has torn down
the strongholds[g] of the Daughter of Judah.
He has brought her kingdom and its princes
down to the ground[h] in dishonor.

3 In fierce anger he has cut off
every horn[a][i] of Israel.
He has withdrawn his right hand[j]
at the approach of the enemy.
He has burned in Jacob like a flaming fire
that consumes everything around it.[k]

4 Like an enemy he has strung his bow;[l]
his right hand is ready.
Like a foe he has slain
all who were pleasing to the eye;[m]
he has poured out his wrath like fire[n]
on the tent of the Daughter of Zion.

5 The Lord is like an enemy;[o]
he has swallowed up Israel.
He has swallowed up all her palaces
and destroyed her strongholds.[p]
He has multiplied mourning and lamentation
for the Daughter of Judah.[q]

6 He has laid waste his dwelling like a garden;
he has destroyed his place of meeting.[r]
The LORD has made Zion forget
her appointed feasts and her Sabbaths;[s]
in his fierce anger he has spurned
both king and priest.[t]

7 The Lord has rejected his altar
and abandoned his sanctuary.
He has handed over to the enemy
the walls of her palaces;[u]
they have raised a shout in the house of the LORD
as on the day of an appointed feast.

8 The LORD determined to tear down
the wall around the Daughter of Zion.
He stretched out a measuring line[v]
and did not withhold his hand from destroying.
He made ramparts and walls lament;
together they wasted away.[w]

9 Her gates[x] have sunk into the ground;
their bars he has broken and destroyed.
Her king and her princes are exiled[y] among the nations,
the law[z] is no more,

[a] *3* Or / *all the strength*; or *every king*; *horn* here symbolizes strength.

2:2 strongholds. The destruction of Judah's cities represented God's curse on their infidelity (Lev 26:31,33).
2:3 horn. A metaphor for strength and prosperity (contrast v. 17; cf. note on 1Sa 2:1).
2:4–5 Like an enemy. God used Judah's enemies as his instruments in rendering judgment on his disobedient covenant people (cf. 1:15). **strung his bow.** See Genesis 9:13–14 and Deuteronomy 32:42. **poured out his wrath.** Holy war imagery, most frequently used of God's judgment on the nations (Ps 69:24). In the prophets, Judah (and Israel) were the targets (cf. Hos 5:10; see Jer 6:11; 7:20). **Daughter of Judah.** Synonymous with "Daughter of Zion" (see note on 1:6).
2:6 his dwelling . . . his place of meeting. The temple.
2:7 his altar . . . his sanctuary. God's judgment had destroyed not only the place of his dwelling but the means of Israel's approach to him in worship. The shouts of triumphant enemies replaced those of worshiping assemblies.

2:8 stretched out a measuring line. As though surveying the city for destruction (cf. Isa 34:11; Am 7:7ff.).

2:9 the law is no more. Because the king and people had been exiled and lived in servitude, they were no longer able to observe many commandments of the law. The law itself had not been abrogated (cf. Mt 5:17–19). **prophets . . . visions.** Not only had the temple been destroyed, but prophetic vision had also ceased (see 1Sa 3:1; Jer 8:8–10; 18:18).

and her prophets no longer find
visions[a] from the LORD.

10 The elders of the Daughter of Zion
sit on the ground in silence;
they have sprinkled dust on their heads[b]
and put on sackcloth.[c]
The young women of Jerusalem
have bowed their heads to the ground.[d]

11 My eyes fail from weeping,[e]
I am in torment within,[f]
my heart is poured out[g] on the ground
because my people are destroyed,
because children and infants faint[h]
in the streets of the city.

12 They say to their mothers,
"Where is bread and wine?"
as they faint like wounded men
in the streets of the city,
as their lives ebb away
in their mothers' arms.[i]

13 What can I say for you?
With what can I compare you,
O Daughter of Jerusalem?
To what can I liken you,
that I may comfort you,
O Virgin Daughter of Zion?[j]
Your wound is as deep as the sea.[k]
Who can heal you?

14 The visions of your prophets
were false and worthless;
they did not expose your sin
to ward off your captivity.[l]
The oracles they gave you
were false and misleading.[m]

15 All who pass your way
clap their hands at you;[n]
they scoff[o] and shake their heads
at the Daughter of Jerusalem:
"Is this the city that was called
the perfection of beauty,[p]
the joy of the whole earth?"[q]

16 All your enemies open their mouths
wide against you;[r]
they scoff and gnash their teeth[s]
and say, "We have swallowed her up.[t]
This is the day we have waited for;
we have lived to see it."

17 The LORD has done what he planned;
he has fulfilled his word,

2:9 [a]Jer 14:14
2:10 [b]Job 2:12 [c]Isa 15:3 [d]Job 2:13; Isa 3:26
2:11 [e]La 1:16; 3:48-51 [f]La 1:20 [g]ver 19; Ps 22:14 [h]La 4:4
2:12 [i]La 4:4
2:13 [j]Isa 37:22 [k]Jer 14:17; La 1:12
2:14 [l]Isa 58:1 [m]Jer 2:8; 23:25-32, 33-40; 29:9; Eze 13:3; 22:28
2:15 [n]Eze 25:6 [o]Jer 19:8 [p]Ps 50:2 [q]Ps 48:2
2:16 [r]Ps 56:2; La 3:46 [s]Job 16:9 [t]Ps 35:25

2:10 The elders . . . dust . . . sackcloth . . . bowed their heads. A typical Old Testament picture of mourning (see 1:4; Job 2:12ff.).
2:11–12 My eyes fail from weeping. An expression of the poet's empathy for the agony of God's people (cf. Jer 4:19; 9; Mic 1:8). **children and infants . . . lives ebb away.** These images of devastation focus on suffering and dying children (cf. v. 20).
2:13 What can I say for you? The import of this question is unclear. It may mean What can I say on your behalf? or What can I say about the calamities endured by Judah? **comfort.** See note on 1:2.
2:14 The visions . . . worthless. An elaboration of verse 9. False prophecy was and continued to be a critical issue in Israel's history (e.g., Dt 18:21ff.; Jer 5:12ff.; 23:9–40; 28).
2:15 the joy of the whole earth. The beauty of God's chosen place is extravagantly expressed (see Pss 48:2; 50:2)—by those who mock the ruin and agony of Jerusalem.
2:16 swallowed her up. God (vv. 2,5) used Judah's enemies to bring judgment against his disobedient people. The nations erroneously attributed their victory to their own strength.
2:17 fulfilled his word . . . decreed long ago. God's purposes of judgment had long ago been declared in the curses of the cov-

2:17 [u]Dt 28:15-45 [v]ver 2; Eze 5:11 [w]Ps 89:42
2:18 [x]Ps 119:145 [y]La 1:16 [z]Jer 9:1 [a]La 3:49
2:19 [b]1Sa 1:15; Ps 62:8 [c]Isa 26:9 [d]Isa 51:20
2:20 [e]Dt 28:53; Jer 19:9 [f]La 4:10 [g]Ps 78:64; Jer 14:15
2:21 [h]2Ch 36:17; Ps 78:62-63; Jer 6:11 [i]Jer 13:14; La 3:43; Zec 11:6
2:22 [j]Ps 31:13; Jer 6:25 [k]Hos 9:13
3:1 [l]Job 19:21; Ps 88:7

which he decreed long ago.[u]
He has overthrown you without pity,[v]
he has let the enemy gloat over you,
he has exalted the horn[a] of your foes.[w]

18 The hearts of the people
cry out to the Lord.[x]
O wall of the Daughter of Zion,
let your tears[y] flow like a river
day and night;[z]
give yourself no relief,
your eyes no rest.[a]

19 Arise, cry out in the night,
as the watches of the night begin;
pour out your heart[b] like water
in the presence of the Lord.[c]
Lift up your hands to him
for the lives of your children,
who faint[d] from hunger
at the head of every street.

20 "Look, O LORD, and consider:
Whom have you ever treated like this?
Should women eat their offspring,[e]
the children they have cared for?[f]
Should priest and prophet be killed[g]
in the sanctuary of the Lord?

21 "Young and old lie together
in the dust of the streets;
my young men and maidens
have fallen by the sword.[h]
You have slain them in the day of your anger;
you have slaughtered them without pity.[i]

22 "As you summon to a feast day,
so you summoned against me terrors[j] on every side.
In the day of the LORD's anger
no one escaped or survived;
those I cared for and reared,[k]
my enemy has destroyed."

3[b]

I am the man who has seen affliction
by the rod of his wrath.[l]
2 He has driven me away and made me walk

[a] 17 *Horn* here symbolizes strength. [b] This chapter is an acrostic poem; the verses of each stanza begin with the successive letters of the Hebrew alphabet, and the verses within each stanza begin with the same letter.

---

enant (see Lev 26:23–39; Dt 28:15–68); God had kept his word. See note at verse 3.

2:18 O wall. The wall is personified; the symbol of the city's strength was called to weep for the suffering of its people. The impact of this image is intensified by the irony that the wall built to protect the city was helpless to do anything but weep. **day and night.** See Deuteronomy 28:67.

2:19 children. See verse 12.

2:20 Should women eat their offspring? The theme of suffering reaches its climax here in abhorrent cannibalism within Judahite families (see note on Jer 19:9). The poet is shocked not only by the depravity of the Judahites in eating their children, but also by God's willingness to bring such an extreme curse upon Judah. The power of this appeal to God is magnified when God's own paternal relationship with his chosen people is considered.

2:21 Young and old. An allusion to the particular tragedy of death in one's youth or prime, as opposed to the blessing of attaining a good age (Job 42:17).

2:22 As . . . to a feast day. Calamities rather than celebrants flock to the city. The picture of terrors feasting on Judah continues the imagery of cannibalism (v. 19) and the swallowing up of God's people (vv. 2,5,16). **terrors.** See Jeremiah 6:25 and 20:10. **day of the LORD's anger.** The poem ends where it began, without alleviation of the dark picture.

■ **3:1–66** *A Lament and Consolation.* This poem records the words of an individual expressing grief for and on behalf of the entire Judahite community, and especially the citizens of Jerusalem (see vv. 22,40–47).

3:1 I am the man. This poem of acrostic triads is mostly written in the first-person singular. On the possible identification of the poet with Jeremiah, see the notes that follow, as well as "Introduction: Author." For the idea of the Lord as the One who afflicted the speaker, compare Job 19:21, Psalm 88:7 and 15 and Jeremiah 15:17–18. **rod of his wrath.** Perhaps a reference to Babylon, the nation God was using to bring judgment against Judah and Jerusalem (see "Introduction: Time and Place of Writing" and "Purpose and Distinctives").

3:2 in darkness rather than light. Contrast Isaiah 9:2. Darkness

in darkness[m] rather than light;
3 indeed, he has turned his hand against me[n]
again and again, all day long.

4 He has made my skin and my flesh grow old
and has broken my bones.[o]
5 He has besieged me and surrounded me
with bitterness[p] and hardship.[q]
6 He has made me dwell in darkness
like those long dead.[r]

7 He has walled me in so I cannot escape;[s]
he has weighed me down with chains.[t]
8 Even when I call out or cry for help,
he shuts out my prayer.[u]
9 He has barred my way with blocks of stone;
he has made my paths crooked.[v]

10 Like a bear lying in wait,
like a lion in hiding,
11 he dragged me from the path and mangled[w] me
and left me without help.
12 He drew his bow[x]
and made me the target[y] for his arrows.[z]

13 He pierced my heart
with arrows from his quiver.[a]
14 I became the laughingstock[b] of all my people;
they mock me in song[c] all day long.
15 He has filled me with bitter herbs
and sated me with gall.[d]

16 He has broken my teeth with gravel;[e]
he has trampled me in the dust.
17 I have been deprived of peace;
I have forgotten what prosperity is.
18 So I say, "My splendor is gone
and all that I had hoped from the LORD."[f]

19 I remember my affliction and my wandering,
the bitterness and the gall.
20 I well remember them,
and my soul is downcast[g] within me.[h]
21 Yet this I call to mind
and therefore I have hope:

22 Because of the LORD's great love we are not consumed,
for his compassions never fail.[i]
23 They are new every morning;

3:2 [m]Jer 4:23
3:3 [n]Isa 5:25
3:4 [o]Ps 51:8; Isa 38:13; Jer 50:17
3:5 [p]ver 19 [q]Jer 23:15
3:6 [r]Ps 88:5-6
3:7 [s]Job 3:23 [t]Jer 40:4
3:8 [u]Job 30:20; Ps 22:2
3:9 [v]Isa 63:17; Hos 2:6
3:11 [w]Hos 6:1
3:12 [x]La 2:4 [y]Job 7:20 [z]Ps 7:12-13; 38:2
3:13 [a]Job 6:4
3:14 [b]Jer 20:7 [c]Job 30:9
3:15 [d]Jer 9:15
3:16 [e]Pr 20:17
3:18 [f]Job 17:15
3:20 [g]Ps 42:5 [h]Ps 42:11
3:22 [i]Ps 78:38; Mal 3:6

was a metaphor for the distress that came from the judgment of God, while light stood for its opposite—salvation and blessing. Compare Amos 5:18.
3:4 skin . . . bones. Pictures of physical distress, perhaps on the basis of age or illness (see Job 13:28; Isa 38:13).
3:6 those long dead. The distresses and diseases of life were so extreme for the speaker that he portrayed his experience as being like death itself. For more on the concept of death as a shadowy existence, see Job 3:11–19 and Isaiah 14:18 and following. Similar views of death are expressed in Psalms 6:5 and 115:17. Other Old Testament passages offer hope that transcends physical death (Pss 49:15; 73:24).
3:7–9 walled me in . . . weighed me down . . . barred my way . . . made my paths crooked. See significant parallels in Psalm 88. Concerning unheard prayer, see Psalms 10:1, 13:1 and 22:2. Crooked paths make travel difficult and tedious (contrast Isa 40:3).
3:10–12 Like a bear . . . arrows. Mention of specific hazards that could overtake a traveler provided vivid expression of terror and distress.
3:14 laughingstock. See Jeremiah 20:7. **my people.** The poet's abuse at the hands of the people becomes, ironically, part of the picture of distress through which he depicts their suffering (see note on 3:1–66).
3:17 deprived of peace. Peace and prosperity summarize the covenant blessings; both are absent from the current scene.
3:18 My splendor . . . all that I had hoped from the LORD. A climactic expression of hopelessness.
3:19 I remember. The poet's personal experience is a reminder of the people's corporate memory of God's past covenant mercies (see note on 3:1–66).
3:21 Yet this I call to mind. Memories that had discouraged the writer (v. 19) now encouraged him (see Ps 77:3–9,10–15). From a standpoint of hopelessness, recollection of God's prior devotion to his people brought hope.
3:22–24 The lament form generally includes turning points at which the experience of rejection by God gives way to confidence (see "Introduction to Psalms: Structure: *Genres:* 2. *Laments*"). The poet expressed his assurance that God's love for his people would comfort those who had experienced Jerusalem's fall. No matter how difficult the situation had become, God would not fail to show love to his repentant people.
3:22 great love. Often translated "steadfast love," the central

3:23 [j]Zep 3:5
3:24 [k]Ps 16:5
3:25 [l]Isa 25:9; 30:18
3:26 [m]Ps 37:7; 40:1
3:28 [n]Jer 15:17
3:29 [o]Jer 31:17
3:30 [p]Job 16:10; Isa 50:6
3:31 [q]Ps 94:14; Isa 54:7
3:32 [r]Ps 78:38; Hos 11:8
3:33 [s]Eze 33:11
3:36 [t]Jer 22:3; Hab 1:13
3:37 [u]Ps 33:9-11
3:38 [v]Job 2:10; Isa 45:7; Jer 32:42
3:39 [w]Jer 30:15; Mic 7:9
3:40 [x]2Co 13:5 [y]Ps 119:59; 139:23-24
3:41 [z]Ps 25:1; 28:2

great is your faithfulness.[j]
24 I say to myself, "The LORD is my portion;[k]
therefore I will wait for him."

25 The LORD is good to those whose hope is in him,
to the one who seeks him;[l]
26 it is good to wait quietly
for the salvation of the LORD.[m]
27 It is good for a man to bear the yoke
while he is young.

28 Let him sit alone in silence,[n]
for the LORD has laid it on him.
29 Let him bury his face in the dust—
there may yet be hope.[o]
30 Let him offer his cheek to one who would strike him,[p]
and let him be filled with disgrace.

31 For men are not cast off
by the Lord forever.[q]
32 Though he brings grief, he will show compassion,
so great is his unfailing love.[r]
33 For he does not willingly bring affliction
or grief to the children of men.[s]

34 To crush underfoot
all prisoners in the land,
35 to deny a man his rights
before the Most High,
36 to deprive a man of justice—
would not the Lord see such things?[t]

37 Who can speak and have it happen
if the Lord has not decreed it?[u]
38 Is it not from the mouth of the Most High
that both calamities and good things come?[v]
39 Why should any living man complain
when punished for his sins?[w]

40 Let us examine our ways and test them,[x]
and let us return to the LORD.[y]
41 Let us lift up our hearts and our hands
to God in heaven,[z] and say:

---

characteristic of God expressed here is his covenant relationship with Israel. The term describes his devotion to his people. **compassions.** God's covenantal devotion is joined with his compassion, a term for God's profound emotion that finds expression in mercy and blessing. God's wrath toward his people would end because his compassion for the remnant of his people could not end (cf. 4:22; Hos 11:8).

3:23 every morning. God's love would usher in the new dawn of salvation (see Ps 90:14; Mal 4:2; Lk 1:78). **faithfulness.** A term for the unqualified reliability of God—that which makes him worthy of our trust (see Hab 2:4).

3:24 my portion. This expression recalls the territorial allocations to the Israelite tribes (see notes on Nu 26:53ff.). The priests and Levites, who were landless, had the Lord as their portion (Nu 18:20ff.). Although God had allotted land to his people, they were never to allow that inheritance to substitute for personal love and devotion to God himself.

3:25 The LORD . . . seeks him. God's movement toward his people in love demands their corresponding movement toward him (see 1Ch 28:9). The threefold good (see v. 26ff.) expressed here focuses on God's goodness (cf. v. 17, where the Hebrew word for "good" is rendered "prosperity"). Nevertheless, the experience of good cannot be separated from seeking, waiting quietly (v. 26) and enduring trials and suffering while young (v. 27).

3:27 while he is young. Refers apparently to the author's suffering in early and middle life, possibly signifying relief in his old age; by transference to the community, it may signify a similar relief for the people lying beyond their present trials.

3:28–30 Let him. An exhortation to bear suffering, especially in light of the affirmation in verses 31–33. **sit alone.** See 1:1.

3:30 Let him offer his cheek. The humiliation of Israel foreshadowed that of Christ, who willingly took upon himself God's righteous judgment against his people (see Isa 50:6; Mt 26:67). Jesus appears to have alluded to this passage in his teachings (see Mt 5:39; Lk 6:29).

3:31–33 For men are not cast off . . . forever. Since God is compassionate, the experience of his wrath by his people must be short-lived (see Ps 30:5; Isa 54:7; Hos 6:1). God's compassion is inseparable from his unfailing love (3:22). See *WCF* 12.

3:34–36 would not the Lord see such things? The implication was that God could not approve of such calamities happening to his people (see Job 8:3). Yet God had approved these very tragedies.

3:37–38 Is it not from the mouth of the Most High . . . ? All that happens is by God's Word—calamity as well as blessing (see Isa 45:7; Am 3:6).

3:39 when punished for his sins. Dreadful though God's judgment was, it was undeniably deserved as a result of sin (see 2:20–22). See *WCF* 6.6; *WLC* 27,152; *WSC* 19,84.

3:40–47 Let us . . . our. The speaker uses the first-person plural throughout this section. Since the entire chapter is a unified speech, either others join him in verses 1–39 or he invites others to join him and speaks alone on their behalf.

3:40 Let us examine. A call to repentance and acknowledgment of sin.

42 "We have sinned and rebelled[a]
and you have not forgiven.[b]

43 "You have covered yourself with anger and pursued us;
you have slain without pity.[c]
44 You have covered yourself with a cloud[d]
so that no prayer[e] can get through.
45 You have made us scum[f] and refuse
among the nations.

46 "All our enemies have opened their mouths
wide against us.[g]
47 We have suffered terror and pitfalls,[h]
ruin and destruction.[i]"
48 Streams of tears flow from my eyes[j]
because my people are destroyed.[k]

49 My eyes will flow unceasingly,
without relief,[l]
50 until the LORD looks down
from heaven and sees.[m]
51 What I see brings grief to my soul
because of all the women of my city.

52 Those who were my enemies without cause
hunted me like a bird.[n]
53 They tried to end my life in a pit[o]
and threw stones at me;
54 the waters closed over my head,[p]
and I thought I was about to be cut off.

55 I called on your name, O LORD,
from the depths of the pit.[q]
56 You heard my plea:[r] "Do not close your ears
to my cry for relief."
57 You came near when I called you,
and you said, "Do not fear."[s]

58 O Lord, you took up my case;[t]
you redeemed my life.[u]
59 You have seen, O LORD, the wrong done to me.[v]
Uphold my cause!
60 You have seen the depth of their vengeance,
all their plots against me.[w]

61 O LORD, you have heard their insults,
all their plots against me—
62 what my enemies whisper and mutter
against me all day long.[x]
63 Look at them! Sitting or standing,
they mock me in their songs.

64 Pay them back what they deserve, O LORD,

3:42 [a]Da 9:5 [b]Jer 5:7-9
3:43 [c]La 2:2,17,21
3:44 [d]Ps 97:2 [e]ver 8
3:45 [f]1Co 4:13
3:46 [g]La 2:16
3:47 [h]Jer 48:43 [i]Isa 24:17-18; 51:19
3:48 [j]La 1:16 [k]La 2:11
3:49 [l]Jer 14:17
3:50 [m]Isa 63:15
3:52 [n]Ps 35:7
3:53 [o]Jer 37:16
3:54 [p]Ps 69:2; Jnh 2:3-5
3:55 [q]Ps 130:1; Jnh 2:2
3:56 [r]Ps 55:1
3:57 [s]Isa 41:10
3:58 [t]Jer 51:36 [u]Ps 34:22; Jer 50:34
3:59 [v]Jer 18:19-20
3:60 [w]Jer 11:20; 18:18
3:62 [x]Eze 36:3

3:42 you have not forgiven. This unexpected statement could be acquiescing to the justice of God in declining to forgive. The following verses suggest the possibility that the whole speech is a complaint triggered by the thought that Judah deserved her suffering (v. 39). See *WLC* 189.
3:43–45 among the nations. A contrast with the actions of God in the exodus, when he was angry on Israel's behalf and killed the Egyptians. This was a time when a cloud was the sign of his favor and when Israel was precious in his sight among the nations. Compare 2:1.
3:48 Streams of tears flow from my eyes. The writer returns to the first-person singular to speak of the close association between his own pain and the people's grief.
3:49 will flow unceasingly. Familiar lament language (see Pss 6:6; 42:3; Jer 9:1).
3:52 enemies without cause. See Psalm 35:19 and John 15:25.
3:53 in a pit. See Psalms 28:1 and 88:6. The life of Jeremiah may be in view (see Jer 38:6).
3:55 I called . . . pit. Compare Psalm 30:1 and the experience of Jonah (Jnh 2:2–7).
3:56 You heard my plea. In this turning point of the lament, the poet expressed assurance that the Lord had heard his prayer (see Ps 6:8–10).
3:57 Do not fear. A common exhortation in Isaiah 40–55 (e.g., Isa 41:10; see also Mark 6:50).
3:58–60 my case . . . redeemed my life . . . my cause! Verses 58–66 take up the Biblical theme of the vindication of the innocent, a motif ultimately fulfilled in Christ. See Jeremiah 50:34 where the Lord, Judah's Redeemer, pleaded his people's cause.
3:61–66 Pay them back what they deserve. The poet cries for vengeance on his enemies.

for what their hands have done.[y]
65 Put a veil over their hearts,[z]
and may your curse be on them!
66 Pursue them in anger and destroy them
from under the heavens of the LORD.

4 [a]

How the gold has lost its luster,
the fine gold become dull!
The sacred gems are scattered
at the head of every street.[a]

2 How the precious sons of Zion,
once worth their weight in gold,
are now considered as pots of clay,
the work of a potter's hands!

3 Even jackals offer their breasts
to nurse their young,
but my people have become heartless
like ostriches in the desert.[b]

4 Because of thirst the infant's tongue
sticks to the roof of its mouth;[c]
the children beg for bread,
but no one gives it to them.[d]

5 Those who once ate delicacies
are destitute in the streets.
Those nurtured in purple[e]
now lie on ash heaps.[f]

6 The punishment of my people
is greater than that of Sodom,[g]
which was overthrown in a moment
without a hand turned to help her.

7 Their princes were brighter than snow
and whiter than milk,
their bodies more ruddy than rubies,
their appearance like sapphires.[b]

8 But now they are blacker[h] than soot;
they are not recognized in the streets.
Their skin has shriveled on their bones;[i]
it has become as dry as a stick.

9 Those killed by the sword are better off
than those who die of famine;
racked with hunger, they waste away
for lack of food from the field.[j]

3:64 [y]Ps 28:4
3:65 [z]Isa 6:10
4:1 [a]Eze 7:19
4:3 [b]Job 39:16
4:4 [c]Ps 22:15 [d]La 2:11, 12
4:5 [e]Jer 6:2 [f]Am 6:3-7
4:6 [g]Ge 19:25
4:8 [h]Job 30:28 [i]Ps 102:3-5
4:9 [j]Jer 15:2; 16:4

[a] This chapter is an acrostic poem, the verses of which begin with the successive letters of the Hebrew alphabet. [b] 7 Or *lapis lazuli*

■ **4:1–22** *Zion's Present and Future.* This poem contains the most vivid portrait in Lamentations of Judah's agonies, but it also assures that the devastation will end.

4:1 the gold . . . sacred gems. A reference to the precious metals, gems and rich furnishings of Solomon's temple, now laid waste by Nebuchadnezzar (2Ki 25:9).

4:2 the precious sons . . . weight in gold. The image of gold is quickly transferred to the people, who were infinitely more valuable than the temple's riches. As God's "treasured possession" (see note on Ex 19:5), they were exceedingly precious, but they were being treated as common and insignificant.

4:3 Even jackals. See Isaiah 1:2–3. **ostriches.** Proverbially known for careless parenting (see Job 39:16). Harsh treatment of children by parents is a theme of the chapter (cf. v. 10), echoing 2:20.

4:5 delicacies. The rich and delicately bred suddenly falling into the most desperate want and danger was predicted by the prophets (e.g., Jer 6:2; Am 4:1–3; 6:1).

4:6 punishment. The Hebrew word can be translated either "punishment" or "iniquity," according to the context, because the two ideas are causally linked. The connection is strong in this chapter, where the extreme suffering of Judah is linked unremittingly to her sin. The comparison of Jerusalem with Sodom is striking because of the comparable sin and judgment of the two cities (see Isa 1:10; cf. the comparison of the Israelite city Gibeah with Sodom and Gomorrah in Judges 19:22–30 [see notes there]).

4:7 princes. Literally, "separated ones." **whiter . . . ruddy.** Colors associated with vitality and beauty in the human body.

4:8 not recognized. No one was earmarked any longer as special; common suffering had obliterated all social distinctions.

4:9 Those killed . . . better off. Death by starvation was not a form of summary, instant judgment but was characterized by lingering pain and a violation of human dignity. It was unnatural, the curse of God at its starkest.

10 With their own hands compassionate women
have cooked their own children,[k]
who became their food
when my people were destroyed.

11 The LORD has given full vent to his wrath;
he has poured out his fierce anger.
He kindled a fire[l] in Zion
that consumed her foundations.[m]

12 The kings of the earth did not believe,
nor did any of the world's people,
that enemies and foes could enter
the gates of Jerusalem.[n]

13 But it happened because of the sins of her prophets
and the iniquities of her priests,[o]
who shed within her
the blood of the righteous.

14 Now they grope through the streets
like men who are blind.[p]
They are so defiled with blood[q]
that no one dares to touch their garments.

15 "Go away! You are unclean!" men cry to them.
"Away! Away! Don't touch us!"
When they flee and wander about,
people among the nations say,
"They can stay here no longer."[r]

16 The LORD himself has scattered them;
he no longer watches over them.[s]
The priests are shown no honor,
the elders[t] no favor.

17 Moreover, our eyes failed,
looking in vain[u] for help;[v]
from our towers we watched
for a nation[w] that could not save us.

18 Men stalked us at every step,
so we could not walk in our streets.
Our end was near, our days were numbered,
for our end had come.[x]

19 Our pursuers were swifter
than eagles[y] in the sky;
they chased us[z] over the mountains
and lay in wait for us in the desert.

20 The LORD's anointed,[a] our very life breath,
was caught in their traps.[b]
We thought that under his shadow
we would live among the nations.

4:10 [k]Lev 26:29; Dt 28:53-57; Jer 19:9; La 2:20; Eze 5:10
4:11 [l]Jer 17:27 [m]Dt 32:22; Jer 7:20; Eze 22:31
4:12 [n]1Ki 9:9; Jer 21:13
4:13 [o]Jer 5:31; 6:13; Eze 22:28; Mic 3:11
4:14 [p]Isa 59:10 [q]Jer 2:34; 19:4
4:15 [r]Lev 13:46
4:16 [s]Isa 9:14-16 [t]La 5:12
4:17 [u]Isa 20:5; Eze 29:16 [v]La 1:7 [w]Jer 37:7
4:18 [x]Eze 7:2-12; Am 8:2
4:19 [y]Dt 28:49 [z]Isa 5:26-28
4:20 [a]2Sa 19:21 [b]Jer 39:5; Eze 12:12-13; 19:4,8

4:10 women . . . children. See notes on verse 3.
4:11 wrath. The focus returns to God's wrath; the explanation even for these ills lies in Judah's sin.
4:12 The kings of the earth. Possibly a reference to the assumed impregnability of Zion, reinforced by the dramatic failure of the Assyrians to take the city following Sennacherib's defeat of the rest of Judah in 701 B.C. (see 2Ki 18:13—19:37).
4:14 grope through the streets. See Deuteronomy 28:28–29. **defiled with blood.** A reference to murder and to making the city unclean. Elsewhere the phrase refers to the victim's blood on the hands of the murderer (cf. Isa 59:3). Ironically, the blood that defiles the blind wanderers in this verse is that of their murdered compatriots, though the wanderers are not the ones who slew them.
4:15 unclean! See Leviticus 13:45. **When they flee.** The curse of Deuteronomy 28:65–66 is fulfilled.
4:17 a nation. Israel and Judah characteristically sought help in political alliances rather than in the Lord (see Isa 7; 30:1–5; Jer 24).
4:19 swifter than eagles. See Jeremiah 4:13.
4:20 The LORD's anointed. A reference to the last Davidic king, Zedekiah, who had been deported from Judah by Nebuchadnezzar (2Ki 25:7); no such king was reigning at the time this poem was written. Nevertheless, Josiah's earlier reforms (2Ki 22–23), though religious, had asserted Judah's independence and seemed to confirm God's ancient promises to David (2Sa 7), leaving hope that one day God would restore the Davidic dynasty, specifically through the righteous Branch of David (see Jer 23:5–8).

21 Rejoice and be glad, O Daughter of Edom,
you who live in the land of Uz.
But to you also the cup[c] will be passed;
you will be drunk and stripped naked.[d]

22 O Daughter of Zion, your punishment will end;[e]
he will not prolong your exile.
But, O Daughter of Edom, he will punish your sin
and expose your wickedness.[f]

4:21 [c]Jer 25:15 [d]Isa 34:6-10; Am 1:11-12; Ob 1:16
4:22 [e]Isa 40:2; Jer 33:8 [f]Ps 137:7; Mal 1:4

5

Remember, O LORD, what has happened to us;
look, and see our disgrace.[g]
2 Our inheritance[h] has been turned over to aliens,
our homes[i] to foreigners.
3 We have become orphans and fatherless,
our mothers like widows.[j]
4 We must buy the water we drink;
our wood can be had only at a price.[k]
5 Those who pursue us are at our heels;
we are weary[l] and find no rest.
6 We submitted to Egypt and Assyria[m]
to get enough bread.
7 Our fathers sinned and are no more,
and we bear their punishment.[n]
8 Slaves[o] rule over us,
and there is none to free us from their hands.[p]
9 We get our bread at the risk of our lives
because of the sword in the desert.
10 Our skin is hot as an oven,
feverish from hunger.[q]
11 Women have been ravished[r] in Zion,
and virgins in the towns of Judah.
12 Princes have been hung up by their hands;
elders are shown no respect.[s]
13 Young men toil at the millstones;
boys stagger under loads of wood.
14 The elders are gone from the city gate;
the young men have stopped their music.[t]

5:1 [g]Ps 44:13-16; 89:50
5:2 [h]Ps 79:1 [i]Zep 1:13
5:3 [j]Jer 15:8; 18:21
5:4 [k]Isa 3:1
5:5 [l]Ne 9:37
5:6 [m]Hos 9:3
5:7 [n]Jer 14:20; 16:12
5:8 [o]Ne 5:15 [p]Zec 11:6
5:10 [q]La 4:8-9
5:11 [r]Zec 14:2
5:12 [s]La 4:16
5:14 [t]Isa 24:8; Jer 7:34

4:21–22 O Daughter of Edom. The historic enmity between Edom and Judah was scandalous because of an ancient affinity of blood (*Edom* was another name for Esau, Jacob's brother; Ge 25:30). Edom rejoiced at Jerusalem's fall but would fall as well (see Jer 49:7–22; Am 9:20; Ob). **punishment will end.** In 3:22 the same verb for "end" is rendered "consumed." Because of God's mercy and compassion he would terminate his people's punishment and deliver them; this would not, however, be the case with Edom. See Isaiah 40:2 and Jeremiah 49:7–22.

5:1–22 *Judah's Appeal for God's Help.* Lamentations closes with a poem that climaxes in the exiled Judahites' desperate call for relief from their difficulties. This is the only poem in the book that is not an acrostic (see "Introduction: Purpose and Distinctives").

5:1 Remember . . . us. A common opening for a communal lament. Zion was no longer in the immediate throes of siege and depredation (as in ch. 4). Time has passed, replete with harsh and humiliating experiences.

5:2 Our inheritance. The promised land, Israel's inheritance from God (cf. Dt 4:21; 12:9), specifically the territory of Judah (Jos 15:20–63). **aliens . . . foreigners.** An outrageous thought, considering that God had given the land expressly to the Israelites and had required them to drive out foreigners in order to possess it.

5:3 orphans . . . widows. Those whose social position left them dependent on others for protection and provision. God had commanded Israel to care for such people, to apportion to them a share of the land's goodness (Dt 14:28–29). The Israelites had failed in this duty and so God was denying them, by exile, the good things of the land.

5:4 We must buy. A reversal of the language in Deuteronomy 6:10–11 (see also 8:7–10; Jos 9:21–23).

5:5 no rest. Another reversal (cf. v. 4) of language originally used to offer blessing (Dt 12:9). Rest is an indispensable part of the enjoyment of God's blessing (see note on 1:3).

5:6 Egypt and Assyria. An acknowledgement of the treaties Judah had made with these nations against the will of God (see note on 4:17; see 2Ki 18:14).

5:7 Our fathers sinned . . . we bear their punishment. A similar description of solidarity is found in Exodus 20:5. The misunderstanding that children are punished for their fathers' sins is prevented by passages such as Deuteronomy 2:16, Jeremiah 31:29–30 and Ezekiel 18. Those who share in their father's judgment do so because they also share in his sins. See verse 16. See also notes on Romans 5:12 and 18–19.

5:8 Slaves. An ironic reference to the Babylonians, implying that current circumstances belied the true relationships among God, Israel and the nations. Israel was in truth a nation freed from slavery (Dt 15:12–18). See 1:1 and note.

5:9 sword in the desert. Possibly that of marauders who had taken advantage of the weakened community.

5:11–13 Women have been ravished . . . and virgins. As in 2 Samuel 13:14 and 13:32, the Hebrew word translated "ravished" implies rape (cf. Jdg 20:5). The loss of virginity outside marriage brought shame on a woman and her family and could have serious consequences (Dt 22:13–21). **Princes.** Hanging was a degradation adding the sting of humiliation to the horror of execution. (Dt 21:22–23; 1Sa 31:10). **Young men . . . millstones.** Humiliating work for a young man (see Jdg 16:21); this kind of labor was traditionally reserved for women.

5:14 elders . . . young men. An allusion to aspects of normal life in Judah that had ceased. The gate, where legal and social functions had taken place, was deserted. The harshness of life as a conquered people obliterated the former light-heartedness of the young men.

15 Joy is gone from our hearts;
our dancing has turned to mourning.[u]
16 The crown[v] has fallen from our head.
Woe to us, for we have sinned![w]
17 Because of this our hearts[x] are faint,
because of these things our eyes[y] grow dim
18 for Mount Zion, which lies desolate,[z]
with jackals prowling over it.

19 You, O LORD, reign forever;
your throne endures[a] from generation to generation.
20 Why do you always forget us?[b]
Why do you forsake us so long?
21 Restore[c] us to yourself, O LORD, that we may return;
renew our days as of old
22 unless you have utterly rejected us
and are angry with us beyond measure.[d]

5:15 [u]Jer 25:10

5:16 [v]Ps 89:39 [w]Isa 3:11

5:17 [x]Isa 1:5 [y]Ps 6:7

5:18 [z]Mic 3:12

5:19 [a]Ps 45:6; 102:12, 24-27

5:20 [b]Ps 13:1; 44:24

5:21 [c]Ps 80:3

5:22 [d]Isa 64:9

5:16 The crown. Some take this to refer to Jerusalem in particular (cf. 1:1; 2:15; 5:18), but it more likely symbolized the glory of Judah among the nations (cf. Ex 19:6). **Woe . . . sinned!** See note on verse 7.

5:18 Mount Zion . . . desolate. The poet came full circle, back to 1:1, resuming the theme of the scandal of the chosen city of God lying destroyed and abandoned.

5:19–20 You, O LORD, reign forever. Although the throne of Judah had been vacated, the Lord's kingship was not threatened. This collection of poems assumed this closing affirmation throughout. **Why . . . ?** The note of lament was struck once again (see note on 1:22). There was no easy panacea from the pain expressed; the affirmation of the Lord's reign arose from the midst of that pain.

5:21 Restore . . . return. The prophets never envisaged a restoration to the promised land apart from repentance toward God. For a parallel to the thought, see Jeremiah 31:18.

5:22 unless. The poet declined to finish the lament on a high note. As with other laments, the expressions of hope are found in the middle. The conclusion voiced not despair but petition. This is the essential character of all the poems in Lamentations: They were spurred by acute grief over God's judgment and expressed the yearning that God's compassion would move him to deliver his people.

EZEKIEL

Introduction

Overview

Author: The prophet Ezekiel

Purpose: To encourage the exiles to remain faithful to the Lord so that he would fulfill his offer to restore them to the promised land and rebuild the temple and Jerusalem to new heights of glory

Date: c. 593–570 B.C.

Key Truths:

- Judah and Jerusalem deserved the judgment of total destruction and exile.
- Judgment comes on those who have themselves flagrantly violated the law of God.
- God will judge the nations who have turned against his people.
- God would bring great blessings to his people after the exile.
- The center of the restored people of God would be Jerusalem and its temple.

Author

The opening verses of Ezekiel (1:1–3) anticipate that the book consists largely of texts written by Ezekiel from an autobiographical perspective (v. 1). Third-person materials also appear (vv. 2–3), giving the impression that Ezekiel himself or someone close to him wove these independent autobiographical sections into a unified whole.

We have no information about Ezekiel beyond that contained in this book bearing his name, which means "God makes strong, hardens" (see note on 3:7–8). If Ezekiel was 30 years old when he began his prophetic ministry (1:1) and this date corresponds to the fifth year of the exile of King Jehoiachin (1:2–3), Ezekiel was about 26 when taken into exile. The latest date mentioned in the book (29:17) shows that his ministry spanned at least 23 years, at which time he would have been about 50 years old. The circumstances of his death are unknown.

Ezekiel was a priest (1:3). Priests ordinarily began their temple service at age 30. However, Ezekiel was living among the exiles 700 miles from Jerusalem, and during the period of his preaching the temple was in ruins. In the year in which he would have begun his temple service God called him to become a prophet.

Ezekiel was taken into exile as a captive in 597 B.C., after Nebuchadnezzar had captured Jerusalem and carried away Jehoiachin, the royal family and the leading citizens and skilled artisans (2Ki 24:14). Ezekiel lived in the vicinity of Nippur (1:1). He was married, but his wife died during the captivity, shortly before the city of Jerusalem was destroyed in 586 B.C. (24:18). His prophetic role was recognized by the leaders among the exiles (8:1; 20:1).

In the book God commonly addressed the prophet by the phrase "son of man," basically meaning "person, human being." The term emphasized human frailty and insignificance as compared with the transcendence of God. At a later time in Jewish history the same term took on much greater significance. See note on 2:1, as well as Daniel 7:13.

Time and Place of Writing

Ezekiel witnessed much of the decline and fall of the once mighty Assyrian Empire. The armies of Babylon, under Nebuchadnezzar, emerged as the dominant power in the ancient Near East. The Babylonian forces and the armies of Pharaoh Neco of Egypt periodically skirmished over the territory formerly subject to the Assyrians; the kings of Judah in Jerusalem were caught in the middle.

Jehoiakim was placed on the throne of Jerusalem by Neco (2Ki 23:34) in 609 B.C. After the defeat of the Egyptians at Carchemish in 605 B.C., Jehoiakim switched his allegiance and became a vassal of Nebuchadnezzar. He remained subject to Nebuchadnezzar for three years, until he switched allegiance once again to Egypt (2Ki 24:1). In the same month Nebuchadnezzar set out to punish Judah for its infidelity Jehoiakim died, and his son Jehoiachin succeeded him. Jehoiachin was left to face Nebuchadnezzar's wrath. After a brief siege in 597 B.C. Nebuchadnezzar took Jehoiachin captive, along with much of the population of Jerusalem, including Ezekiel (2Ki 24:8–12). Nebuchadnezzar installed Jehoiachin's uncle, Zedekiah, as ruler in his place; Zedekiah ruled until the destruction of Jerusalem in 586 B.C. Though some have called Zedekiah the last king of Judah, Jehoiachin was the last legitimate ruler. Dates in the book of Ezekiel are all referenced in terms of the years of Jehoiachin's exile. Zedekiah's reign was characterized by a vacillation similar to Jehoiakim's between alliances with Egypt and Babylon (17:15–19).

The captives and many of the people remaining in Jerusalem hoped that the exile would be short, that those who had been deported would soon be returned to the city and that Jerusalem would be spared further disaster. The false prophets encouraged this belief. Since the Lord had chosen Jerusalem as his dwelling and had defended the city in the past, it was popularly believed that Jerusalem was inviolable. Much of Ezekiel's preaching was devoted to warning the exiles that a worse fate was yet in store for Jerusalem—the city would be destroyed.

No other prophetic book contains as many chronological notices. Ezekiel was conscious of the relevance of his message to the immediate historical situation. Dates help orient the reader to the contemporary scene. See chart to follow. As for the accuracy of the dates in the chart, chronology for the latter half of the first millennium B.C. (including the time of Ezekiel) is firm due to availability and agreement of chronological records both from the Bible and from extra-Biblical documents in a variety of ancient Near Eastern languages. Astronomical observations recorded by ancient scribes enable correlation of the ancient and modern calendars with a high degree of confidence. Though it is conceivable that some of the dates will be adjusted in the light of further discovery, major changes are unlikely.

Reference	Yr./Mo./Day	Julian calendar	Event
1:1	30/4/5	July 31, 593	Call narrative
1:2	5/4(?)/5	July 31, 593	Call narrative
8:1	6/6/5	Sept. 17, 592	Vision of events in Jerusalem
20:1	7/5/10	Aug. 14, 591	Elders come to inquire
24:1	9/10/10	Jan. 15, 588	Siege of Jerusalem begun
26:1	11/-/1	Between Apr., 587 and Apr., 586	Oracle against Tyre
29:1	10/10/12	Jan. 7, 587	Oracle against Egypt
29:17	27/1/1	Apr. 26, 571	Egypt instead of Tyre
30:20	11/1/7	Apr. 29, 587	Oracle against Pharaoh
31:1	11/3/1	June 21, 587	Oracle against Pharaoh
32:1	12/12/1	Mar. 3, 585	Oracle against Pharaoh
32:17	12/-/15	Between Apr., 586 and Apr., 585	Oracle against Egypt
33:21	12/10/5	Jan. 8, 585	Escapee from Jerusalem arrives
40:1	25/1/10	Apr. 28, 573	Vision of restored Jerusalem

The latest date noted in Ezekiel is 571 B.C. (29:17). The book could not have reached its final composition until that time. Other portions may have been written earlier and compiled toward the end of Ezekiel's life. There is no significant evidence for placing any substantial portion of the book after his lifetime.

Purpose and Distinctives

The book of Ezekiel is unique in that, with occasional exceptions, it is entirely autobiographical, written in the first person from the viewpoint of Ezekiel himself. The book is divided into three parts. In the first two Ezekiel announced judgment on Jerusalem (chs. 1–24) and other foreign nations (chs. 25–32). After a messenger had arrived reporting the destruction of Jerusalem (33:21–22), Ezekiel's preaching became dominated by the promises of restoration and mercy for the future (chs. 33–48). The part announcing judgment on Jerusalem and the part prophesying restoration both begin with oracles concerning Ezekiel's role as a watchman (3:16–21; 33:1–20).

Ezekiel records a larger number of symbolic actions than any other prophetic book (3:22–26; 4:1–3; 4:4–8; 4:9–11; 4:12–14; 5:1–3; 12:10–16; 12:17–20; 21:6–7; 21:18–24; 24:15–24; 37:15–28; see note on 4:1–3). Ezekiel identified closely with his own message, enduring extreme hardships in order to provide signs that might spur the nation to repentance (e.g., lying on his side for over a year [4:4–7]). Ezekiel also used parables (chs. 15; 16; 17; 19; 23) and proverbs (12:21–22; 16:44; 18:2–3).

Christ in Ezekiel

Christ's prophetic ministry was anticipated as Ezekiel announced that God would destroy Jerusalem and send its population into exile because of continued unbelief. Judgment against the apostates among the covenant people extended to the ministry of Jesus as well. Jesus called for repentance among the Jews, and a remnant responded in faith. Yet Jesus announced that the destruction of the temple and Jerusalem would reoccur after his departure (Mt 24; Jn 2:19). Ezekiel also announced judgments against the Gentile nations who troubled the people of God (29:19; 30:25; 38:21–23). These judgments occurred to some degree in the inauguration of Christ's kingdom (Mt 24:34; Lk 11:32,51) but will be brought to fullness in the judgment that will come when Christ returns (Rev 11:18; 14:7; 15:1).

Christ's work was anticipated as Ezekiel announced that God would one day end the exile (chs. 33–48), establish a covenant of peace (34:5; 37:6) and restore Jerusalem to greater glory than ever before (ch. 48). In line with these hopes, Jesus' death, resurrection and ascension took place near the city (Mt 16:21). The outpouring of the Spirit occurred there as thousands of exiles came to faith in the Messiah on the Day of Pentecost (Ac 2). Furthermore, between his first and second comings the Jerusalem in heaven where Christ is becomes an important aspect of the Christian faith (Jn 3:31; Col 1:5). The New Testament also made Jerusalem the centerpiece of the new heavens and the new earth to be established when Christ returns (Rev 21:2).

Christ himself was anticipated as Ezekiel mentioned the "prince" in 34:24, 37:25, 44:3, 45:7, 16, 17 and 22, and 46:2, 4, 8, 10, 12, 16, 17 and 18. This prince would be the son of David, who would rule over the people of God after the exile. No royal figure from David's house ruled over Israel from the time of the exile until Jesus (Lk 1:32–33). Thus Jesus fulfills the hopes Ezekiel had for the restoration of the house of David after exile. See note on 37:24.

Ezekiel rested many of his hopes for Israel's future on the restoration of the temple and its priesthood (chs. 40–48). As the incarnate Son of God Jesus is the ultimate fulfillment of both the temple of God (Jn 2:19–22; Rev 21:22) and the priesthood (Heb 7:1—8:6). His death was an atoning sacrifice (Ro 3:25; Heb 2:17), and he now ministers before the throne of God in heaven, making intercession for the saints (see theological article "The Ascension and Session of Jesus" at Heb 8). When he returns in glory Christ will sanctify the new heavens and the new earth into a holy dwelling for God (Rev 21:22–23), replacing the temple as the place of his special presence (see theological article "The Presence of God" at 1Ki 8).

Outline

I. Judgment on Judah and Jerusalem (1:1—24:27)

Ezekiel proclaimed that Judah and Jerusalem would be destroyed by the Babylonians because of the continuing sins of those remaining in Jerusalem.

- A. Ezekiel's First Set of Visions, Commission, Symbolic Acts and Related Speeches (1:1—7:27)
  1. Vision and Commission (1:1—3:27)
     - a. Vision of God's Chariot (1:1–28)
     - b. Ezekiel's Commission (2:1—3:27)
  2. Symbolic Acts (4:1—5:4)
     - a. Clay Tablet (4:1–3)
     - b. Lying on His Side (4:4–8)
     - c. Rationed Food Cooked Over Excrement (4:9–17)
     - d. Burning Hair (5:1–4)
  3. Related Speeches (5:5—7:27)
     - a. Explanatory Oracles of Judgment (5:5–17)
     - b. First Judgment Oracle Against Idolatry (6:1–14)
     - c. Second Judgment Oracle Against Idolatry (7:1–27)
- B. Ezekiel's Second Set of Visions, Commission, Symbolic Acts and Related Speeches (8:1—24:27)
  1. Visions and Commission (8:1—11:25)
     - a. Transport to Jerusalem (8:1–4)
     - b. Idolatry in the Temple (8:5–18)
     - c. Executioners for the Unrepentant (9:1–11)
     - d. Chariot of Glory Departs From the Temple (10:1–22)
     - e. Jerusalem's Evil Leaders Executed (11:1–21)
     - f. Transport to Babylon (11:22–25)
  2. Symbolic Acts (12:1–20)
     - a. Packed Belongings (12:1–16)
     - b. Eating and Drinking (12:17–20)
  3. Related Speeches (12:21—24:27)
     - a. A False Proverb (12:21–28)
     - b. False Prophets and Prophetesses (13:1–23)
     - c. Consequences of Idolatry (14:1–23)
     - d. A Parable of the Vine (15:1–8)
     - e. Jerusalem as a Child and a Harlot (16:1–63)
     - f. A Parable of Two Eagles (17:1–24)
     - g. Individual Responsibility (18:1–32)
     - h. Dirge Allegory for Israel's Kings (19:1–14)
     - i. The Nation's History and Future (20:1–49)
     - j. Babylon, God's Sword (21:1–32)
     - k. The Sins of Jerusalem (22:1–31)
     - l. A Parable of Two Lewd Sisters (23:1–49)
     - m. A Cooking Pot (24:1–14)
     - n. The Death of Ezekiel's Wife (24:15–27)

II. Oracles Against the Nations (25:1—32:32)

Ezekiel announced that God would bring devastation to the nations that had troubled his people.

- A. Ammon (25:1–7)
- B. Moab (25:8–11)
- C. Edom (25:12–14)
- D. Philistia (25:15–17)

- E. Phoenicia (26:1—28:26)
  1. Judgment Oracle Against Tyre (26:1–21)
  2. Lament for Tyre (27:1–36)
  3. Judgment Oracle Against Tyre's King (28:1–10)
  4. Lament for Tyre's King (28:11–19)
  5. Judgment Oracle Against Sidon (28:20–26)
- F. Egypt (29:1—32:32)
  1. Judgment Against Egypt (29:1–16)
  2. A Second Judgment Against Egypt (29:17–21)
  3. Lament Over Egypt (30:1–19)
  4. A Third Judgment Against Egypt (30:20–26)
  5. A Fourth Judgment Against Egypt (31:1–18)
  6. Lament for Pharaoh (32:1–16)
  7. Lament for Egypt and Pharaoh (32:17–32)

III. Future Blessings for Judah and Jerusalem (33:1—48:35)

Ezekiel explained that after the exile had come to an end, the temple and Jerusalem would be gloriously restored and the people of God would be gathered and blessed as never before.

- A. Judah's Fall and Restoration (33:1—39:29)
  1. Ezekiel Recommissioned as a Watchman (33:1–20)
  2. Judah's Fall and Two Groups of Israelites (33:21–33)
  3. Shepherds of the Past and Future (34:1–31)
  4. Edom's Condemnation (35:1–15)
  5. A Prophecy to the Mountains of Israel (36:1–38)
  6. The Resurrection of Dry Bones (37:1–14)
  7. Joining of Two Sticks (37:15–28)
  8. Victory in the Future Battle (38:1—39:29)
- B. A Vision of Restored Jerusalem (40:1—48:35)
  1. Visionary Transport to Jerusalem (40:1–4)
  2. The Temple Structures (40:5—42:20)
     - a. The Temple Courtyards and Gates (40:5–49)
     - b. The Sanctuary (41:1–26)
     - c. Rooms for the Priests (42:1–20)
  3. Return of God's Glory (43:1–27)
  4. The Sacred Personnel (44:1—46:24)
     - a. The Prince, Levites and Priests (44:1–31)
     - b. The Sacred Area of the Land (45:1–12)
     - c. Offerings and Holy Days (45:13—46:24)
  5. The River, the Land and the City (47:1—48:35)
     - a. A Life-giving River (47:1–12)
     - b. Restoration of the Land (47:13—48:29)
     - c. Restoration of the City (48:30–35)

1:1 [a]Eze 11:24-25 [b]Mt 3:16; Ac 7:56 [c]Ex 24:10
1:2 [d]2Ki 24:15
1:3 [e]2Ki 3:15; Eze 3:14,22
1:4 [f]Jer 1:14

The Living Creatures and the Glory of the Lord

1 In the[a] thirtieth year, in the fourth month on the fifth day, while I was among the
exiles[a] by the Kebar River, the heavens were opened[b] and I saw visions[c] of God.
2On the fifth of the month—it was the fifth year of the exile of King Jehoiachin[d]— 3the
word of the Lord came to Ezekiel the priest, the son of Buzi,[b] by the Kebar River in the
land of the Babylonians.[c] There the hand of the Lord was upon him.[e]
4I looked, and I saw a windstorm coming out of the north[f]—an immense cloud with
flashing lightning and surrounded by brilliant light. The center of the fire looked like

[a] *1* Or ⌞*my*⌟ [b] *3* Or *Ezekiel son of Buzi the priest* [c] *3* Or *Chaldeans*

▪ **1:1—24:27** *Judgment on Judah and Jerusalem.* The first major division of the book focuses on the judgment against Judah and the final destruction of Jerusalem by the Babylonians. These events and oracles took place between 593 B.C. (1:2) and 588 B.C. (24:1). These chapters divide into two sets of visions connected by Ezekiel's commission, symbolic acts and oracles (1:1—7:27; 8:1—24:27).

▪ **1:1—7:27** *Ezekiel's First Set of Visions, Commission, Symbolic Acts and Related Speeches.* This first section of the prophet's focus on Judah and Jerusalem's judgment divides into three parts: his visions and commission (1:1—3:27), his symbolic acts (4:1—5:4) and his speeches (5:5—7:27).

▪ **1:1—3:27** *Vision and Commission.* The book begins with Ezekiel's record of his vision of God's spectacular chariot (1:1–28) and the commission he received from God (2:1—3:27).

▪ **1:1–28** *Vision of God's Chariot.* In his inaugural vision Ezekiel witnessed a theophany (appearance of God): God as the divine warrior approaching in his battle chariot.

1:1–3 thirtieth year. See "Introduction: Author" and "Time and Place of Writing." The book has a double superscription, one in the first person (v. 1) and the other in the third (vv. 2–3). The dates in Ezekiel are ordinarily given in terms of the corresponding year of the reign of Jehoiachin. However, this is not the case for this first date in the book. Verses 2–3 date Ezekiel's inaugural vision to the fifth year of Jehoiachin, whereas verse 1 specifies an unidentified thirtieth year. Most likely this date referred to Ezekiel's age at the time of his call as a prophet, so that Ezekiel's thirtieth year was also the fifth year of Jehoiachin. Ordinarily priests assumed their full responsibilities at age 30 (Nu 4:3), but Ezekiel was in exile far from the temple in Jerusalem, unable to fulfill his calling as a priest. **Kebar River.** The Jews living outside the promised land commonly established their places of worship along waterways (Ps 137:1; Ac 16:13). Two cuneiform texts from Nippur mention a "Great River," probably the Kebar River; this was the name of the large irrigation canal that drew water from the Euphrates near Babylon. **fifth year.** Jehoiachin went into exile in 597 B.C., and Nebuchadnezzar appointed Zedekiah to rule in Jerusalem in Jehoiachin's place (2Ki 24:15–17; 2Ch 36:10). Jehoiachin, however, was still the rightful king of Judah (2Ki 25:27–30), even in exile, and the dates in Ezekiel (1:2–3; 3:16; 8:1; 20:1; 24:1; 26:1; 29:1,17; 30:20; 31:1; 32:1,17; 33:21; 40:1) were given in terms of the years of his reign. Assuming that the date in 1:2 is also in the fourth month (1:1) of Jehoiachin's fifth year, this vision took place in July 593 B.C.

1:4—3:15 I looked, and I saw. Compare Ezekiel's inaugural vision to other call narratives: Moses (Ex 3), Gideon (Jdg 6), Isaiah (Isa 6) and Jeremiah (Jer 1). Like Moses, the model prophet (Dt 18:15,18), those who followed him ordinarily began their prophetic careers by inauguration into the divine presence. Each was admit-

The Glory of God: Who Gets the Glory?

THE glory of God is that honor and splendor he has possessed from all eternity apart from anything he receives back from his creation. In Scripture the glory of God is portrayed primarily by the radiant brilliance of God's appearance. Thus the *shekinah,* the dazzling cloud that could look like fire (Ex 24:17), was itself called the glory of God. God appeared with this cloud of glory at significant moments in history (Ex 33:22; 34:5; cf. Ex 16:7,10; 24:15–17; 40:34–35; Lev 9:23–24; 1Ki 8:10–11; Eze 1:28; 8:4; 9:3; 10:4; 11:22–23; Mt 17:5; Lk 2:9; Ac 1:9; 1Th 4:17; Rev 1:7). His brilliance is the visible display of the wonder of his transcendence over all creation. As the "glory" of humans pertains to their wealth and admirable qualities, the glory of God is his incomparable greatness, splendor and honor as Creator of all things. David reflected on this idea in 1 Chronicles 29:10–11: "Praise be to you, O Lord, God of our father Israel, from everlasting to everlasting. Yours, O Lord, is the greatness and the power and the glory and the majesty and the splendor, for everything in heaven and earth is yours. Yours, O Lord, is the kingdom; you are exalted as head over all."

The glory of God is also the purpose for which all things were created. As the apostle Paul put it, "From him and through him and to him are all things. To him be the glory forever" (Ro 11:36). The ultimate purpose for which all things were created was that God would receive glory through his creation. Nature declares the glory of God (Ps 8:3–9), the defeat of evil brings him honor (1Jn 2:13–14) and the redemption of his people magnifies his name (Eph 1:13–14). In this sense the glory of God is the inevitable end of all things.

Bringing glory to God is the moral responsibility of human beings. Honoring God in all we do renders him respect and acknowledges his power, goodness and dignity. Human beings are to live in submission to God's commands, thereby acknowledging his incomparable greatness to all other creatures. Paul presented this goal as the motivation for choices in life: "Whether you eat or drink or whatever you do, do it all for the glory of God" (1Co 10:31). As the Westminster Shorter Catechism so memorably puts it, "Man's chief end is to glorify God and to enjoy him forever" (*WSC* 1).

The glory God receives from human beings is the highest form of honor creation can confer upon him. God originally blessed people with "glory and honor" (Ps 8:5) by placing us as his honorable images in the world (see theological article "Human Beings in God's Image" at Ge 1). Our fall into sin marred the glory of humanity, but our redemption in Christ will reach its climax when we are glorified with Christ at his return (Ro 8:17–23). As glorified images of God we will then be enabled to more fully venerate the Son and the Father, to whom all glory is due (1Co 15:42–44; Rev 5:12). In the words of the Reformers, "Glory to God alone" (*soli Deo gloria*).

glowing metal,[g] 5and in the fire was what looked like four living creatures.[h] In appearance their form was that of a man,[i] 6but each of them had four faces[j] and four wings.
7Their legs were straight; their feet were like those of a calf and gleamed like burnished
bronze.[k] 8Under their wings on their four sides they had the hands of a man.[l] All four of
them had faces and wings, 9and their wings touched one another. Each one went
straight ahead; they did not turn as they moved.[m]
10Their faces looked like this: Each of the four had the face of a man, and on the right
side each had the face of a lion, and on the left the face of an ox; each also had the face
of an eagle.[n] 11Such were their faces. Their wings[o] were spread out upward; each had
two wings, one touching the wing of another creature on either side, and two wings covering its body. 12Each one went straight ahead. Wherever the spirit would go, they
would go, without turning as they went. 13The appearance of the living creatures was like
burning coals of fire or like torches. Fire moved back and forth among the creatures; it
was bright, and lightning[p] flashed out of it. 14The creatures sped back and forth like
flashes of lightning.[q]
15As I looked at the living creatures, I saw a wheel on the ground beside each creature with its four faces. 16This was the appearance and structure of the wheels: They
sparkled like chrysolite,[r] and all four looked alike. Each appeared to be made like a
wheel intersecting a wheel. 17As they moved, they would go in any one of the four directions the creatures faced; the wheels did not turn[s] about[a] as the creatures went. 18Their
rims were high and awesome, and all four rims were full of eyes[t] all around.
19When the living creatures moved, the wheels beside them moved; and when the living creatures rose from the ground, the wheels also rose. 20Wherever the spirit would go,
they would go,[u] and the wheels would rise along with them, because the spirit of the living creatures was in the wheels. 21When the creatures moved, they also moved; when
the creatures stood still, they also stood still; and when the creatures rose from the
ground, the wheels rose along with them, because the spirit of the living creatures was
in the wheels.[v]
22Spread out above the heads of the living creatures was what looked like an expanse,[w] sparkling like ice, and awesome. 23Under the expanse their wings were
stretched out one toward the other, and each had two wings covering its body. 24When
the creatures moved, I heard the sound of their wings, like the roar of rushing waters,
like the voice[x] of the Almighty,[b] like the tumult of an army.[y] When they stood still, they
lowered their wings.
25Then there came a voice from above the expanse over their heads as they stood
with lowered wings. 26Above the expanse over their heads was what looked like a
throne of sapphire,[c][z] and high above on the throne was a figure like that of a man.[a] 27I
saw that from what appeared to be his waist up he looked like glowing metal, as if full
of fire, and that from there down he looked like fire; and brilliant light surrounded him.[b]
28Like the appearance of a rainbow[c] in the clouds on a rainy day, so was the radiance
around him.[d]
This was the appearance of the likeness of the glory[e] of the LORD. When I saw it, I fell
facedown,[f] and I heard the voice of one speaking.

1:4 [g]Eze 8:2
1:5 [h]Rev 4:6 [i]ver 26
1:6 [j]Eze 10:14
1:7 [k]Da 10:6; Rev 1:15
1:8 [l]Eze 10:8
1:9 [m]Eze 10:22
1:10 [n]Eze 10:14; Rev 4:7
1:11 [o]Isa 6:2
1:13 [p]Rev 4:5
1:14 [q]Ps 29:7
1:16 [r]Eze 10:9-11; Da 10:6
1:17 [s]ver 9
1:18 [t]Eze 10:12; Rev 4:6
1:20 [u]ver 12
1:21 [v]Eze 10:17
1:22 [w]Eze 10:1
1:24 [x]Eze 10:5; 43:2; Da 10:6; Rev 1:15; 19:6 [y]2Ki 7:6
1:26 [z]Ex 24:10; Eze 10:1 [a]Rev 1:13
1:27 [b]Eze 8:2
1:28 [c]Ge 9:13; Rev 10:1 [d]Rev 4:2 [e]Eze 8:4 [f]Eze 3:23; Da 8:17; Rev 1:17

[a] 17 Or *aside* [b] 24 Hebrew *Shaddai* [c] 26 Or *lapis lazuli*

ted to the heavenly court of God, where he heard firsthand the words of God. The prophets who reported their call experiences did so not to furnish autobiographical information but to authenticate their prophetic authority; in at least some cases this experience distinguished true prophets from false (1Ki 22:19–28; Jer 23:16–18).

1:4 windstorm. For other references to storms as theophanies, see 2 Kings 2:1 and 11, Job 38:1, 40:6, Psalms 77:18, 83:15, 148:8, Isaiah 29:6, 66:15, Jeremiah 4:13, 23:19, 30:23, Nahum 1:3 and Zechariah 9:14.

1:5–9 four living creatures. Cherubim (10:1,15,17,20). Compare them to the seraphim who attended God at Isaiah's call (Isa 6:2) and to John's vision of the divine throne (Rev 4:6). That their wings "touched one another" (v. 9) recalls the cherubim that stood above the ark in the Most Holy Place of the temple (1Ki 6:27; 2Ch 3:11–12); the Chronicler also described the ark as the divine chariot (1Ch 28:18).

1:10 Their faces. The four faces represented the highest life forms in various realms of creation. Each human face, as supreme, faced outward. The ox represented domestic animals, the lion wild animals and the eagle birds.

1:11 each had two wings. See note on 1:5–9. See Isaiah 6:2.

1:13–14 coals . . . fire . . . torches . . . lightning. Fire was a primary mode of theophany (appearing of God) in the Old Testament (Ge 15:17; Ex 3:2; 13:21–22; 14:24; 19:18; 24:17; Nu 11:1; Dt 1:33; 4:11–12,24,33,36; 5:22–26; 9:3; Pss 18:8; 78:14,21; 89:46).

1:24 I heard the sound. An auditory component was a common element in theophanies (appearances of God) involving the divine army (2Sa 5:24; 2Ki 7:6; 1Ch 14:15; 13:4; 66:6; Joel 2:5; cf. Ge 3:8; Ex 19:19; Isa 6:4). See particularly Ezekiel 3:12–13 and 10:5.

1:26–28 on the throne was a figure. Ezekiel turned cautiously to describe the rider in the chariot.

1:27 brilliant light surrounded him. The light radiating from the divine presence was overwhelming (cf. Da 7:9–10), for God dwells in unapproachable light (1Ti 6:16).

1:28 Like . . . a rainbow. The rainbow not only reflects the splendor surrounding God but also reminds people of his dominion over the sea, as well as of his promise never again to destroy the whole world with a flood (Ge 9:16–17). God's appearance is terrifying, but the rainbow, as a reminder of God's covenant, provides some assurance of his compassion and goodwill. Nevertheless, it also brings to memory the devastating judgment that God rendered against unbelief and disobedience in the flood.

Ezekiel's Call

2 He said to me, "Son of man, stand[g] up on your feet and I will speak to you." 2 As he
spoke, the Spirit came into me and raised me[h] to my feet, and I heard him speaking to me.
3 He said: "Son of man, I am sending you to the Israelites, to a rebellious nation that
has rebelled against me; they and their fathers have been in revolt against me to this very
day.[i] 4 The people to whom I am sending you are obstinate and stubborn.[j] Say to them,
'This is what the Sovereign LORD says.' 5 And whether they listen or fail to listen[k]—for
they are a rebellious house[l]—they will know that a prophet has been among them.[m]
6 And you, son of man, do not be afraid[n] of them or their words. Do not be afraid,
though briers and thorns[o] are all around you and you live among scorpions. Do not be
afraid of what they say or terrified by them, though they are a rebellious house.[p] 7 You
must speak my words to them, whether they listen or fail to listen, for they are rebellious.[q] 8 But you, son of man, listen to what I say to you. Do not rebel like that rebellious
house;[r] open your mouth and eat[s] what I give you."
9 Then I looked, and I saw a hand[t] stretched out to me. In it was a scroll, 10 which he un-
rolled before me. On both sides of it were written words of lament and mourning and woe.[u]
3 And he said to me, "Son of man, eat what is before you, eat this scroll; then go and
speak to the house of Israel." 2 So I opened my mouth, and he gave me the scroll to eat.
3 Then he said to me, "Son of man, eat this scroll I am giving you and fill your stomach with it." So I ate[v] it, and it tasted as sweet as honey[w] in my mouth.
4 He then said to me: "Son of man, go now to the house of Israel and speak my words
to them. 5 You are not being sent to a people of obscure speech and difficult language,[x]
but to the house of Israel— 6 not to many peoples of obscure speech and difficult language, whose words you cannot understand. Surely if I had sent you to them, they would
have listened to you.[y] 7 But the house of Israel is not willing to listen to you because they
are not willing to listen to me, for the whole house of Israel is hardened and obstinate.[z]
8 But I will make you as unyielding and hardened as they are.[a] 9 I will make your forehead
like the hardest stone, harder than flint. Do not be afraid of them or terrified by them,
though they are a rebellious house.[b]"
10 And he said to me, "Son of man, listen carefully and take to heart all the words I
speak to you. 11 Go now to your countrymen in exile and speak to them. Say to them, 'This
is what the Sovereign LORD says,' whether they listen or fail to listen.[c]"
12 Then the Spirit lifted me up,[d] and I heard behind me a loud rumbling sound—May
the glory of the LORD be praised in his dwelling place!— 13 the sound of the wings of the
living creatures brushing against each other and the sound of the wheels beside them,
a loud rumbling sound.[e] 14 The Spirit then lifted me up and took me away, and I went in
bitterness and in the anger of my spirit, with the strong hand of the LORD upon me. 15 I
came to the exiles who lived at Tel Abib near the Kebar River.[f] And there, where they
were living, I sat among them for seven days[g]—overwhelmed.

Warning to Israel

16 At the end of seven days the word of the LORD came to me:[h] 17 "Son of man, I have

2:1 [g]Da 10:11
2:2 [h]Eze 3:24; Da 8:18
2:3 [i]Jer 3:25; Eze 20:8-24
2:4 [j]Eze 3:7
2:5 [k]Eze 3:11 [l]Eze 3:27 [m]Eze 33:33
2:6 [n]Jer 1:8,17 [o]Isa 9:18; Mic 7:4 [p]Eze 3:9
2:7 [q]Jer 1:7; Eze 3:10-11
2:8 [r]Isa 50:5 [s]Jer 15:16; Rev 10:9
2:9 [t]Eze 8:3
2:10 [u]Rev 8:13
3:3 [v]Jer 15:16 [w]Ps 19:10; Ps 119:103; Rev 10:9-10
3:5 [x]Isa 28:11; Jnh 1:2
3:6 [y]Mt 11:21-23
3:7 [z]Eze 2:4; Jn 15:20-23
3:8 [a]Jer 1:18
3:9 [b]Isa 50:7; Eze 2:6; Mic 3:8
3:11 [c]Eze 2:4-5,7
3:12 [d]Eze 8:3; Ac 8:39
3:13 [e]Eze 1:24; 10:5,16-17
3:15 [f]Ps 137:1 [g]Job 2:13
3:16 [h]Jer 42:7

■ **2:1—3:27** *Ezekiel's Commission.* God called Ezekiel to proclaim his word to the Israelites in exile, as well as to those remaining in Judah. He instructed the prophet to proclaim trials and destruction for the people as evidence of his judgment against them.

2:1-8 He said to me. In other call narratives, after the judge or prophet was initiated into the divine presence God announced his commission, which ordinarily included the statement that God was sending him (2:3; Ex 3:10; Jdg 6:14; Isa 6:8; Jer 1:7). Whereas the commissions of Moses and Jeremiah were centered around announcing divine judgment upon Gentile nations (Ex 3:10; Jer 1:10), Ezekiel was sent to preach judgment against Israel.

2:1 Son of man. God spoke to Ezekiel using this form of address more than 90 times. The phrase means "person" or "human being" and emphasized Ezekiel's humanity and frailty, all the more pronounced in this proximity to his vision of the glory of God on his chariot throne. This use of "son of man" is distinct from its appearance over 75 times in the Gospels as the favored self-designation of Jesus (e.g., Mt 8:20; 9:6; 10:23; 11:19; 12:8,32,40; 13:37,41). Jesus' use of the phrase depended upon Daniel 7:13–14 (see notes on those verses).

2:2 the Spirit came into me. In the Old Testament the Spirit of God was preeminently the Spirit of prophecy, the Spirit that enabled the prophet to become the channel of revelation (Nu 11:25–26,29; 1Sa 10:6; 19:20; 1Ki 22:23–24; 2Ki 2:15; Joel 2:28; Zec 7:12).

2:6 briers... thorns ... scorpions. Figures for the persecutors of those who imparted God's holy word against popular wishes (cf. 1Ki 18:4; Jer 20:7–18; Mt 23:29–31,34,37).

2:9—3:3 eat this scroll. Once a prophet had received his commission, God often provided a sign to confirm it (Ex 3:12; Jdg 6:17–22; Jer 1:11–14). Moses had stated that God would put his word into the mouths of the prophets (Dt 18:18), and here that is portrayed graphically. What food was for the body, the word of God would be for Ezekiel's ministry.

2:10 both sides. Scrolls usually had writing only on one side, but compare also Zechariah 5:3 and Revelation 5:1. **words of lament and mourning and woe.** The first half of Ezekiel contains, almost exclusively, oracles of judgment against Judah (chs. 1–24) and foreign nations (chs. 25–32).

3:7-8 to you . . . to me. Because the messenger is the representative of the sender, to reject the messenger is to reject the sender. Compare Luke 10:16, John 8:42 and 47, 13:20 and 16:18. **hardened.** Verses 7–8 may contain a pun on Ezekiel's name, which in Hebrew means "God makes strong, hardens."

3:12 Spirit lifted me up. In his visions Ezekiel was often transported by the Spirit (3:12,14; 8:3; 11:1,24; 40:1–3; 43:5; cf. 2Ki 2:11,16). Compare 2 Corinthians 12:1–2.

3:15 Tel Abib. The precise location of this site along the Kebar Canal is unknown. Despite the similarity in name, this ancient site

made you a watchman[i] for the house of Israel; so hear the word I speak and give them
warning from me. 18When I say to a wicked man, 'You will surely die,' and you do not
warn him or speak out to dissuade him from his evil ways in order to save his life, that
wicked man will die for[a] his sin, and I will hold you accountable for his blood.[j] 19But if
you do warn the wicked man and he does not turn from his wickedness or from his evil
ways, he will die for his sin; but you will have saved yourself.[k]
20"Again, when a righteous man turns from his righteousness and does evil, and I put
a stumbling block before him, he will die. Since you did not warn him, he will die for his
sin. The righteous things he did will not be remembered, and I will hold you accountable
for his blood.[l] 21But if you do warn the righteous man not to sin and he does not sin, he
will surely live because he took warning, and you will have saved yourself.[m]"
22The hand of the LORD[n] was upon me there, and he said to me, "Get up and go[o] out
to the plain,[p] and there I will speak to you." 23So I got up and went out to the plain. And
the glory of the LORD was standing there, like the glory I had seen by the Kebar River,[q]
and I fell facedown.[r]
24Then the Spirit came into me and raised me[s] to my feet. He spoke to me and said:
"Go, shut yourself inside your house. 25And you, son of man, they will tie with ropes; you
will be bound so that you cannot go out among the people.[t] 26I will make your tongue
stick to the roof of your mouth so that you will be silent and unable to rebuke them,
though they are a rebellious house.[u] 27But when I speak to you, I will open your mouth
and you shall say to them, 'This is what the Sovereign LORD says.'[v] Whoever will listen
let him listen, and whoever will refuse let him refuse; for they are a rebellious house.[w]

Siege of Jerusalem Symbolized

4 "Now, son of man, take a clay tablet, put it in front of you and draw the city of Jerusalem on it. 2Then lay siege to it: Erect siege works against it, build a ramp[x] up
to it, set up camps against it and put battering rams around it.[y] 3Then take an iron pan,
place it as an iron wall between you and the city and turn your face toward it. It will be
under siege, and you shall besiege it. This will be a sign[z] to the house of Israel.[a]
4"Then lie on your left side and put the sin of the house of Israel upon yourself.[b] You
are to bear their sin for the number of days you lie on your side. 5I have assigned you the
same number of days as the years of their sin. So for 390 days you will bear the sin of the
house of Israel.

3:17 [i]Isa 52:8; Jer 6:17; Eze 33:7-9
3:18 [j]ver 20; Eze 33:6
3:19 [k]2Ki 17:13; Eze 14:14, 20; Ac 18:6; 20:26; 1Ti 4:14-16
3:20 [l]Ps 125:5; Eze 18:24; 33:12, 18
3:21 [m]Ac 20:31
3:22 [n]Eze 1:3 [o]Ac 9:6 [p]Eze 8:4
3:23 [q]Eze 1:1 [r]Eze 1:28
3:24 [s]Eze 2:2
3:25 [t]Eze 4:8
3:26 [u]Eze 2:5; 24:27; 33:22
3:27 [v]ver 11 [w]Eze 12:3; 24:27; 33:22
4:2 [x]Jer 6:6 [y]Eze 21:22
4:3 [z]Isa 8:18; 20:3; Eze 12:3-6; 24:24, 27 [a]Jer 39:1

[a] *18* Or *in*; also in verses 19 and 20 [b] *4* Or *your side*

was not modern Tel Aviv. **overwhelmed.** The Bible records similar periods of silence or incapacity on the part of others (Ezr 9:4; Job 2:13; Jer 23:9; Da 8:27; Ac 9:9).

3:16 word of the LORD came. This phrase occurs 50 times in Ezekiel—more than in any other prophetic book.

3:17 watchman. Ezekiel elaborated on his role as a watchman in 33:1–9. This role entailed responsibility for those to whom he ministered and a duty to warn them of an impending threat. Failure to issue the warning would make him accountable for the deaths that resulted; if the warning went unheeded Ezekiel would be exonerated. It was unthinkable that the residents of a city would ignore the warning cry of a watchman, but Ezekiel's word was largely disregarded (3:6–7; cf. Isa 22:1–14).

3:22 hand of the LORD. Ezekiel used this phrase to describe the revelatory state in 1:3, 3:14, 8:1, 33:22, 37:1 and 40:1. **plain.** The word refers to an open area between mountains and hence can be translated either "valley" or, as here, "plain." The term occurs one other time in Ezekiel, in the context of the prophet's vision of the valley of dry bones (37:1); perhaps that later vision took place in the same locale.

3:24–27 you will be silent. The length and nature of Ezekiel's mute condition is one of the most debated issues about the book. Regardless of when it began, he was mute until word reached the exiles that the city of Jerusalem had been destroyed (24:27; 33:22; cf. 29:21). Ezekiel's voiceless condition must have been partial in that he was not continuously silent (cf. 3:27) but spoke when he received revelation from God. Ezekiel delivered many oracles to the exiles in the six years between his call and the destruction of Jerusalem. His mute state conveyed the idea that he would not be interceding with God on the nation's behalf—the decree of destruction was irreversible.

3:27 Whoever will listen let him listen. See Matthew 11:15 and 13:9–17 and 43.

■ **4:1—5:4** *Symbolic Acts.* Ezekiel's initial response to his divine commission was to perform a number of interconnected symbolic actions representing God's judgment against Jerusalem. Four phases of action are recorded: One involved a clay tablet (4:1–3); a second Ezekiel lying on his side (4:4–8); a third food cooked over excrement (4:9–17); and a fourth burning hair (5:1–4). Speeches closely related to these actions followed (5:5—7:27).

■ **4:1–3** *Clay Tablet.* Ezekiel illustrated his message on a clay tablet; such object lessons are called "symbolic actions" (cf. 1Ki 11:30; 22:11; 2Ki 13:17; Isa 20:2–4; Jer 13:1–14; 19:1–10). Excavations in several locations in Mesopotamia have yielded bricks or clay tablets with maps or architectural drawings inscribed on them. Ezekiel depicted the siege that would be set against Jerusalem in 597 B.C. and would lead to its destruction.

4:3 iron pan. This was a large, flat griddle on which bread was baked. Since Ezekiel represented God in this miniature drama, the iron pan standing on edge represented God's decision to separate himself from Jerusalem. Its people's prayers would not reach him, and he would not intervene on their behalf.

■ **4:4–8** *Lying on His Side.* Ezekiel lay on his side for a prolonged period of time one way and then another to illustrate the length of the coming judgments.

4:4 put the sin . . . upon yourself. The dual nature of the prophetic office—representing God to the people and mediating before God on behalf of the people—is seen in the second half of this symbolic action. Ezekiel represented the people and bore their sin (cf. Ex 32:30–32; Ro 9:3).

4:5–6 390 days . . . 40 days. Each day represented one year (cf. Nu 14:34; Da 9:24–27). The period or periods to which the figures corresponded may have been consecutive (for a total of 430 years) or concurrent (390 years total). Some think the 390-year figure reflects judgment for Israel's sin from the time Israel occupied Jerusalem or from the time the temple was dedicated until its destruction. Others regard the total of 430 years as symbolic of the length of Israel's sojourn in Egypt (Ex 12:40–41). The question is complicated further by the Septuagint (Greek translation of the OT), which renders the figure at only 150.

6“After you have finished this, lie down again, this time on your right side, and bear
the sin of the house of Judah. I have assigned you 40 days, a day for each year.[b] 7Turn
your face toward the siege of Jerusalem and with bared arm prophesy against her. 8I will
tie you up with ropes so that you cannot turn from one side to the other until you have
finished the days of your siege.[c]
9“Take wheat and barley, beans and lentils, millet and spelt;[d] put them in a storage
jar and use them to make bread for yourself. You are to eat it during the 390 days you
lie on your side. 10Weigh out twenty shekels[a] of food to eat each day and eat it at set
times. 11Also measure out a sixth of a hin[b] of water and drink it at set times. 12Eat the food
as you would a barley cake; bake it in the sight of the people, using human excrement[e]
for fuel.” 13The LORD said, “In this way the people of Israel will eat defiled food among
the nations where I will drive them.”[f]
14Then I said, “Not so, Sovereign LORD![g] I have never defiled myself. From my youth
until now I have never eaten anything found dead[h] or torn by wild animals. No unclean
meat has ever entered my mouth.[i]”
15“Very well,” he said, “I will let you bake your bread over cow manure instead of human excrement.”
16He then said to me: “Son of man, I will cut off[j] the supply of food in Jerusalem. The
people will eat rationed food in anxiety and drink rationed water in despair,[k] 17for food
and water will be scarce. They will be appalled at the sight of each other and will waste
away because of[c] their sin.[l]

5 “Now, son of man, take a sharp sword and use it as a barber’s razor[m] to shave[n] your
head and your beard.[o] Then take a set of scales and divide up the hair. 2When the
days of your siege come to an end, burn a third of the hair with fire inside the city. Take
a third and strike it with the sword all around the city. And scatter a third to the wind.
For I will pursue them with drawn sword.[p] 3But take a few strands of hair and tuck them
away in the folds of your garment.[q] 4Again, take a few of these and throw them into the
fire and burn them up. A fire will spread from there to the whole house of Israel.
5“This is what the Sovereign LORD says: This is Jerusalem, which I have set in the center of the nations, with countries all around her. 6Yet in her wickedness she has rebelled
against my laws and decrees more than the nations and countries around her. She has
rejected my laws and has not followed my decrees.[r]
7“Therefore this is what the Sovereign LORD says: You have been more unruly than
the nations around you and have not followed my decrees or kept my laws. You have not
even[d] conformed to the standards of the nations around you.[s]
8“Therefore this is what the Sovereign LORD says: I myself am against you, Jerusalem,
and I will inflict punishment on you in the sight of the nations.[t] 9Because of all your detestable idols, I will do to you what I have never done before and will never do again.[u]
10Therefore in your midst fathers will eat their children, and children will eat their fa-

4:6 [b]Nu 14:34; Da 9:24-26; 12:11-12
4:8 [c]Eze 3:25
4:9 [d]Isa 28:25
4:12 [e]Isa 36:12
4:13 [f]Hos 9:3
4:14 [g]Jer 1:6; Eze 9:8; 20:49 [h]Lev 11:39 [i]Ex 22:31; Dt 14:3; Ac 10:14
4:16 [j]Ps 105:16; Eze 5:16 [k]ver 10-11; Lev 26:26; Isa 3:1; Eze 12:19
4:17 [l]Lev 26:39; Eze 24:23; 33:10
5:1 [m]Isa 7:20 [n]Eze 44:20 [o]Lev 21:5
5:2 [p]ver 12; Lev 26:33
5:3 [q]Jer 39:10
5:6 [r]Jer 11:10; Eze 16:47-51; Zec 7:11
5:7 [s]2Ch 33:9; Jer 2:10-11; Eze 16:47
5:8 [t]Eze 15:7
5:9 [u]Da 9:12; Mt 24:21

[a] *10* That is, about 8 ounces (about 0.2 kilogram) [b] *11* That is, about 2/3 quart (about 0.6 liter)
[c] *17* Or *away in* [d] *7* Most Hebrew manuscripts; some Hebrew manuscripts and Syriac *You have*

4:8 tie you up with ropes. Ezekiel most likely was not totally immobilized for the 430 days but only for an unspecified period of time each day; at the very least he got up to make meals (4:8–13) and probably tended to other business.

■ **4:9–17** *Rationed Food Cooked Over Excrement.* To continue his symbolic representation of Jerusalem’s destruction, Ezekiel subsisted on starvation rations during his enactment of the siege of Jerusalem (Dt 28:52–57; 2Ki 6:25; 7:12; Jer 15:2; 19:9).

4:10 twenty shekels. Eight ounces of mixed-grain bread.

4:11 sixth of a hin. Just over a pint, or 0.6 liter. See note on 45:24.

4:12–15 human excrement for fuel. The niceties of ceremonial cleanliness were all but impossible to observe during a siege, even for a priest like Ezekiel. Human excrement was considered impure (Dt 23:13), and Ezekiel was repulsed by God’s command, protesting that he had never violated the dietary laws (44:31; Ex 22:31; Lev 7:19–24; 11:8,39–40; 22:8; Dt 14:3,8). God permitted him to heat his food using cattle manure, still a widely used fuel in parts of the Near East; compare 2 Kings 18:27.

■ **5:1–4** *Burning Hair.* Ezekiel gathered up the hair he had cut and divided it into thirds: one-third he burned, one-third he chopped into stubble and one-third he dispersed with the wind, tucking away a few strands in the folds of his tunic. Even a few of the strands held back were then burned. These actions demonstrated the severity with which God was about to judge Jerusalem.

5:1 razor. God prohibited Israelite men from shaving or cutting parts of their beards (Lev 19:27). This law was reiterated for priests (Lev 21:5), and Ezekiel was a priest (1:1). Cutting facial hair could be a matter of great personal shame (2Sa 10:4–5; 1Ch 19:5; Isa 7:20; 50:6) or a sign of mourning (Ezr 9:3; Isa 15:2; Jer 7:29; 41:5; 48:37).

■ **5:5—7:27** *Related Speeches.* The Lord gave Ezekiel words to speak about the coming destruction of Jerusalem. This section consists of three oracles of judgment—the first (5:5–17) closely connected with the preceding symbolic acts and the others focused on idolatry (6:1–14; 7:1–27).

■ **5:5–17** *Explanatory Oracles of Judgment.* The first oracle was closely connected with the symbolic actions that had preceded it (cf. vv. 1–4 and vv. 10–13).

5:5 center of the nations. A phrase largely responsible for the notion that Jerusalem was the “navel of the earth” (cf. 38:12; “center of the land”). Ancient and medieval cartographers often centered their maps around the location of Jerusalem.

5:10–13 A third . . . a third . . . a third. Ezekiel interpreted the symbolism of verses 1–4: The hairs burned in fire represented the people who would die of plague or famine during the siege; those chopped with a sword were those who would die in battle outside Jerusalem’s walls; the hairs dispersed by the wind represented people who would go into exile. It is striking that Ezekiel did not elaborate on the significance of the few hairs retained in the folds of his garment; they symbolized the survivors who would remain in Jerusalem (Jer 40:7–12).

5:10 eat their children. Cannibalism was often a consequence of

thers. [v] I will inflict punishment on you and will scatter all your survivors to the winds. [w]
11 Therefore as surely as I live, declares the Sovereign LORD, because you have defiled my
sanctuary with all your vile images [x] and detestable practices, [y] I myself will withdraw my
favor; I will not look on you with pity or spare you. [z] 12 A third of your people will die of
the plague or perish by famine inside you; a third will fall by the sword outside your walls;
and a third I will scatter to the winds and pursue with drawn sword. [a]
13 "Then my anger will cease and my wrath [b] against them will subside, and I will be
avenged. [c] And when I have spent my wrath upon them, they will know that I the LORD
have spoken in my zeal.
14 "I will make you a ruin and a reproach among the nations around you, in the sight
of all who pass by. [d] 15 You will be a reproach and a taunt, a warning and an object of horror to the nations around you when I inflict punishment on you in anger and in wrath
and with stinging rebuke. [e] I the LORD have spoken. [f] 16 When I shoot at you with my deadly and destructive arrows of famine, I will shoot to destroy you. I will bring more and
more famine upon you and cut off your supply of food. [g] 17 I will send famine and wild
beasts against you, and they will leave you childless. Plague and bloodshed [h] will sweep
through you, and I will bring the sword against you. I the LORD have spoken. [i]"

A Prophecy Against the Mountains of Israel

6 The word of the LORD came to me: 2 "Son of man, set your face against the mountains [j] of Israel; prophesy against them 3 and say: 'O mountains of Israel, hear the
word of the Sovereign LORD. This is what the Sovereign LORD says to the mountains and
hills, to the ravines and valleys: [k] I am about to bring a sword against you, and I will destroy your high places. [l] 4 Your altars will be demolished and your incense altars [m] will be
smashed; and I will slay your people in front of your idols. 5 I will lay the dead bodies of
the Israelites in front of their idols, and I will scatter your bones [n] around your altars.
6 Wherever you live, the towns will be laid waste and the high places demolished, so that
your altars will be laid waste and devastated, your idols [o] smashed and ruined, your incense altars [p] broken down, and what you have made wiped out. [q] 7 Your people will fall
slain among you, and you will know that I am the LORD.
8 " 'But I will spare some, for some of you will escape [r] the sword when you are scattered among the lands and nations. [s] 9 Then in the nations where they have been carried
captive, those who escape will remember me—how I have been grieved [t] by their adulterous hearts, which have turned away from me, and by their eyes, which have lusted
after their idols. [u] They will loathe themselves for the evil they have done and for all their
detestable practices. [v] 10 And they will know that I am the LORD; I did not threaten in vain
to bring this calamity on them.
11 " 'This is what the Sovereign LORD says: Strike your hands together and stamp
your feet and cry out "Alas!" because of all the wicked and detestable practices of the
house of Israel, for they will fall by the sword, famine and plague. [w] 12 He that is far
away will die of the plague, and he that is near will fall by the sword, and he that survives and is spared will die of famine. So will I spend my wrath upon them. [x] 13 And they
will know that I am the LORD, when their people lie slain among their idols around
their altars, on every high hill and on all the mountaintops, under every spreading tree
and every leafy oak [y]—places where they offered fragrant incense to all their idols. [z]
14 And I will stretch out my hand [a] against them and make the land a desolate waste

5:10 [v]Lev 26:29; La 2:20 [w]Lev 26:33; Ps 44:11; Eze 12:14; Zec 2:6
5:11 [x]Eze 7:20 [y]2Ch 36:14; Eze 8:6 [z]Eze 7:4,9
5:12 [a]ver 2,17; Jer 15:2; 21:9; Eze 6:11-12; 12:14
5:13 [b]Eze 21:17; 36:6 [c]Isa 1:24
5:14 [d]Lev 26:32; Ne 2:17; Ps 74:3-10; 79:1-4
5:15 [e]1Ki 9:7; Jer 22:8-9; 24:9 [f]Eze 25:17
5:16 [g]Dt 32:24
5:17 [h]Eze 38:22 [i]Eze 14:21
6:2 [j]Eze 36:1
6:3 [k]Eze 36:4 [l]Lev 26:30
6:4 [m]2Ch 14:5
6:5 [n]Jer 8:1-2
6:6 [o]Mic 1:7; Zec 13:2 [p]Lev 26:30 [q]Isa 6:11; Eze 5:14
6:8 [r]Jer 44:28 [s]Isa 6:13; Jer 44:14; Eze 12:16; 14:22
6:9 [t]Ps 78:40; Isa 7:13 [u]Eze 20:7,24 [v]Eze 20:43; 36:31
6:11 [w]Eze 5:12; 21:14, 17; 25:6
6:12 [x]Eze 5:12
6:13 [y]Isa 57:5 [z]1Ki 14:23; Jer 2:20; Eze 20:28; Hos 4:13
6:14 [a]Isa 5:25

a protracted siege; Moses had warned that this atrocity would occur if the nation failed to obey (Dt 28:53–57; 2Ki 6:26–29; La 2:20).

■ **6:1–14** *First Judgment Oracle Against Idolatry.* Ezekiel announced the inevitability of massive judgment on Judah because of the idolatry practiced on its hillsides.

6:1–3 O mountains of Israel. That Ezekiel spoke to the mountains and hills of Israel as though he were present there prompts some to suggest that one phase of his ministry was actually carried out in Israel instead of in Babylon. The hills and mountains of Israel represented the exiles, to whom the oracle was actually delivered. They were familiar with the terrain of their homeland, and their hearts were there.

6:3 high places. Hilltops where the Canaanites had worshiped their idols. God had commanded the Israelites to eradicate the high places when they had entered the land (Nu 33:52; Dt 12:1–3; 33:29). However, the high places continued to flourish even after the temple was built; the people worshiped Canaanite gods there or used the shrines in mixing idolatry with the worship of the Lord. The continued existence of the high places particularly offended the writer of the book of Kings (1Ki 11:7; 12:31–32; 13:2,32; 14:23; 2Ki 12:3; 14:4; 15:4,35; 17:29; 23:5,8,13,15,19–20; cf. Jer 7:31; 19:5; 32:35; 48:35; Eze 16:16).

6:5 dead bodies. Human corpses would desecrate the shrines (9:7; Nu 19:16,18; 1Ki 13:2; 2Ki 23:14–16; 2Ch 23:14–15; 34:5).

6:7 you will know that I am the LORD. Ezekiel made frequent use of this "recognition formula" (cf. 7:4,9; 11:10,12; 12:20). To know God in this sense was to be convinced by the Babylonian destruction that God is indeed the Lord over creation.

6:8 some of you will escape. Ezekiel introduced the remnant motif (9:8; 11:12–13; 12:16; 14:22–23; 20:39–44). The remnant represented the few who, though experiencing a degree of calamity, ordinarily in judgment for sin, still survived to become the nucleus for the continuation of the group: They embodied its hopes and inherited God's promises afresh. Not all who would be spared would remain faithful to the Lord, but the Lord would purge the remnant during the exile so that a pure people would emerge from it.

from the desert to Diblah[a]—wherever they live. Then they will know that I am the LORD.[b]' "

The End Has Come

7 The word of the LORD came to me: 2"Son of man, this is what the Sovereign LORD says to the land of Israel: The end![c] The end has come upon the four corners[d] of the land. 3The end is now upon you and I will unleash my anger against you. I will judge you according to your conduct and repay you for all your detestable practices. 4I will not look on you with pity[e] or spare you; I will surely repay you for your conduct and the detestable practices among you. Then you will know that I am the LORD.

5"This is what the Sovereign LORD says: Disaster![f] An unheard-of[b] disaster is coming. 6The end has come! The end has come! It has roused itself against you. It has come! 7Doom has come upon you—you who dwell in the land. The time has come, the day is near;[g] there is panic, not joy, upon the mountains. 8I am about to pour out my wrath[h] on you and spend my anger against you; I will judge you according to your conduct and repay you for all your detestable practices.[i] 9I will not look on you with pity or spare you; I will repay you in accordance with your conduct and the detestable practices among you. Then you will know that it is I the LORD who strikes the blow.

10"The day is here! It has come! Doom has burst forth, the rod[j] has budded, arrogance has blossomed! 11Violence has grown into[c] a rod to punish wickedness; none of the people will be left, none of that crowd—no wealth, nothing of value.[k] 12The time has come, the day has arrived. Let not the buyer rejoice nor the seller grieve, for wrath is upon the whole crowd.[l] 13The seller will not recover the land he has sold as long as both of them live, for the vision concerning the whole crowd will not be reversed. Because of their sins, not one of them will preserve his life.[m] 14Though they blow the trumpet and get everything ready, no one will go into battle, for my wrath is upon the whole crowd.

15"Outside is the sword, inside are plague and famine; those in the country will die by the sword, and those in the city will be devoured by famine and plague.[n] 16All who survive and escape will be in the mountains, moaning like doves[o] of the valleys, each because of his sins.[p] 17Every hand will go limp,[q] and every knee will become as weak as water. 18They will put on sackcloth and be clothed with terror.[r] Their faces will be covered with shame and their heads will be shaved.[s] 19They will throw their silver into the streets, and their gold will be an unclean thing. Their silver and gold will not be able to save them in the day of the LORD's wrath.[t] They will not satisfy their hunger or fill their stomachs with it, for it has made them stumble[u] into sin.[v] 20They were proud of their beautiful jewelry and used it to make their detestable idols and vile images.[w] Therefore I will turn these into an unclean thing for them. 21I will hand it all over as plunder to foreigners and as loot to the wicked of the earth, and they will defile it.[x] 22I will turn my face[y] away from them, and they will desecrate my treasured place; robbers will enter it and desecrate it.

23"Prepare chains, because the land is full of bloodshed[z] and the city is full of violence. 24I will bring the most wicked of the nations to take possession of their houses; I will put an end to the pride of the mighty, and their sanctuaries[a] will be desecrated.[b] 25When terror comes, they will seek peace, but there will be none.[c] 26Calamity upon calamity[d] will come, and rumor upon rumor. They will try to get a vision from the prophet; the teaching of the law by the priest will be lost, as will the counsel of the elders.[e]

6:14 [b]Eze 14:13
7:2 [c]Am 8:2, 10 [d]Rev 7:1; 20:8
7:4 [e]Eze 5:11
7:5 [f]2Ki 21:12
7:7 [g]Eze 12:23; Zep 1:14
7:8 [h]Isa 42:25; Eze 9:8; 14:19; Na 1:6 [i]Eze 20:8, 21; 36:19
7:10 [j]Ps 89:32; Isa 10:5
7:11 [k]Jer 16:6; Zep 1:18
7:12 [l]ver 7; Isa 5:13-14; Eze 30:3
7:13 [m]Lev 25:24-28
7:15 [n]Dt 32:25; Jer 14:18; La 1:20; Eze 5:12
7:16 [o]Isa 59:11 [p]Ezr 9:15; Eze 6:8
7:17 [q]Isa 13:7; Eze 21:7; 22:14
7:18 [r]Ps 55:5 [s]Isa 15:2-3; Eze 27:31; Am 8:10
7:19 [t]Eze 13:5; Zep 1:7, 18 [u]Eze 14:3 [v]Pr 11:4
7:20 [w]Jer 7:30
7:21 [x]2Ki 24:13
7:22 [y]Eze 39:23-24
7:23 [z]2Ki 21:16
7:24 [a]Eze 24:21 [b]2Ch 7:20; Eze 28:7
7:25 [c]Eze 13:10, 16
7:26 [d]Jer 4:20 [e]Isa 47:11; Eze 20:1-3; Mic 3:6

a *14* Most Hebrew manuscripts; a few Hebrew manuscripts *Riblah* b *5* Most Hebrew manuscripts; some Hebrew manuscripts and Syriac *Disaster after* c *11* Or *The violent one has become*

6:14 Diblah. A locality otherwise unknown; since Ezekiel probably intended a place well known to his audience, a copying error is possible. See NIV text note.

■ **7:1–27** *Second Judgment Oracle Against Idolatry.* Ezekiel returned to the theme of judgment against idolatry, using stronger language than before. He spoke of the coming judgment as catastrophic, involving all the nations.

7:6 The end has come! This chapter did not predict the end of the world as in the return of Christ in glory but the end of Jerusalem and of Judah with the final Babylonian invasion in 586 B.C. The judgment that the people of Israel suffered at that time, as in all other Old Testament judgments, prefigured the kind of suffering that will take place at Christ's return.

7:7 the day. The Old Testament prophets often spoke of "the day" or "the day of the LORD" (30:1–9; Isa 2:12–17; 13:1–22; 34:1–17; 61:1–3; 63:1–6; Joel 2:1—3:21; Am 5:18–20; Ob 8,15; Zep 1:1—2:3; Zec 14:1–21; Mal 3:13—4:6). This day would be characterized by the coming of the Lord as the divine warrior to judge his enemies and to bless his people (see "Introduction to Zephaniah"). The day of the Lord could be a blessing or a curse for Israel. The ultimate day of the Lord will be the day of eschatological judgment, the outpouring of his wrath against unrighteousness. See the New Testament use of the same motifs for final judgment (Ro 2:16; 1Co 1:8; 5:5; 2Co 1:14; Php 1:6,10; 2:16; 2Ti 1:12,18; 4:8; Heb 10:25; 2Pt 2:9; 3:12; Rev 16:14).

7:10–13 the rod has budded. Aaron's rod that budded had been a sign to the rebellious (Nu 17:10). Violence and arrogance that played such a role in commerce would now be met with the rod of God's own wrath.

7:22–27 they will desecrate my treasured place. Because the Lord had chosen Jerusalem as his dwelling and had fought on its behalf in the past (2Ki 18–19; 2Ch 32; Isa 36–37), the populace assumed as theological doctrine that the city was inviolable. Ezekiel's contemporary, Jeremiah, was also warning the inhabitants of the city not to trust in the existence of the temple as a guarantee of their security (Jer 7:1–15; 26:1–19). A holy God no longer ignored their conduct but would judge them for their sin (v. 27).

27 The king will mourn, the prince will be clothed with despair,[f] and the hands of the people of the land will tremble. I will deal with them according to their conduct,[g] and by their own standards I will judge them. Then they will know that I am the LORD.[h]"

Idolatry in the Temple

8 In the sixth year, in the sixth month on the fifth day, while I was sitting in my house and the elders[i] of Judah were sitting before[j] me, the hand of the Sovereign LORD came upon me there.[k] 2 I looked, and I saw a figure like that of a man.[a] From what appeared to be his waist down he was like fire, and from there up his appearance was as bright as glowing metal.[l] 3 He stretched out what looked like a hand and took me by the hair of my head. The Spirit lifted me up[m] between earth and heaven and in visions of God he took me to Jerusalem, to the entrance to the north gate of the inner court, where the idol that provokes to jealousy[n] stood. 4 And there before me was the glory[o] of the God of Israel, as in the vision I had seen in the plain.[p]

5 Then he said to me, "Son of man, look toward the north." So I looked, and in the entrance north of the gate of the altar I saw this idol[q] of jealousy.

6 And he said to me, "Son of man, do you see what they are doing—the utterly detestable[r] things the house of Israel is doing here, things that will drive me far from my sanctuary? But you will see things that are even more detestable."

7 Then he brought me to the entrance to the court. I looked, and I saw a hole in the wall. 8 He said to me, "Son of man, now dig into the wall." So I dug into the wall and saw a doorway there.

9 And he said to me, "Go in and see the wicked and detestable things they are doing here." 10 So I went in and looked, and I saw portrayed all over the walls all kinds of crawling things and detestable animals and all the idols of the house of Israel.[s] 11 In front of them stood seventy elders of the house of Israel, and Jaazaniah son of Shaphan was standing among them. Each had a censer[t] in his hand, and a fragrant cloud of incense[u] was rising.

12 He said to me, "Son of man, have you seen what the elders of the house of Israel are doing in the darkness, each at the shrine of his own idol? They say, 'The LORD does not see[v] us; the LORD has forsaken the land.' " 13 Again, he said, "You will see them doing things that are even more detestable."

14 Then he brought me to the entrance to the north gate of the house of the LORD, and I saw women sitting there, mourning for Tammuz. 15 He said to me, "Do you see this, son of man? You will see things that are even more detestable than this."

16 He then brought me into the inner court of the house of the LORD, and there at the entrance to the temple, between the portico and the altar,[w] were about twenty-five men.

7:27 [f]Ps 109:19; Eze 26:16 [g]Eze 18:20 [h]ver 4
8:1 [i]Eze 14:1 [j]Eze 33:31 [k]Eze 1:1-3
8:2 [l]Eze 1:4,26-27
8:3 [m]Eze 3:12; 11:1 [n]Ex 20:5; Dt 32:16
8:4 [o]Eze 1:28 [p]Eze 3:22
8:5 [q]Ps 78:58; Jer 32:34
8:6 [r]Eze 5:11
8:10 [s]Ex 20:4
8:11 [t]Nu 16:17 [u]Nu 16:35
8:12 [v]Ps 10:11; Isa 29:15; Eze 9:9
8:16 [w]Joel 2:17

[a] 2 *Or saw a fiery figure*

■ **8:1—24:27** *Ezekiel's Second Set of Visions, Commission, Symbolic Acts and Related Speeches.* A second section roughly paralleling the previous one (see note on 1:1—7:27) gives a record of visions, commission, actions and speeches (8:1—11:25; 12:1–20; 12:21—24:27).

■ **8:1—11:25** *Visions and Commission.* Ezekiel experienced a vision of Jerusalem in which he witnessed the sins of the people and was commissioned to prophesy against them (11:4). When the vision ended he told the exiles all he had seen (11:24–25). The punishment of Jerusalem was not over; the destruction of 586 B.C. was still ahead. These chapters divide into six parts: Ezekiel's transport to Jerusalem (8:1–4), his vision of idolatry in the temple (8:5–18), executioners for the unrepentant (9:1–11), the departure of God's glory from the temple (10:1–22), the execution of evil leaders in Jerusalem (11:1–21) and Ezekiel's transport back to Babylon (11:22–25).

■ **8:1–4** *Transport to Jerusalem.* A vision of the divine chariot appeared to Ezekiel as it had before (v. 4). This time, however, a hand reached out, grabbed Ezekiel and carried him to Jerusalem so that he could see why the city and its temple had to be destroyed.

8:2 figure like that of a man. See 1:27.

8:3 to Jerusalem. Some suggest that Ezekiel was physically transferred to Jerusalem by God's Spirit or that he made an actual trip there (see note on 6:1–3). This was unnecessary: Ezekiel experienced a visionary transport not unlike other experiences he would have and similar to the experiences of others (3:12,14; 37:1; 40:1; 2Ki 5:26; 6:32–33; 2Co 12:2). **north gate.** This led from the outer to the inner court of the temple.

■ **8:5–18** *Idolatry in the Temple.* Ezekiel was shown four different types of idolatry flourishing in the city: (1) worship of the "idol of jealousy" (vv. 5–6); (2) worship of "animals" (vv. 7–13); (3) the "Tammuz" cult (vv. 14–15); and (4) worship of the "sun" (v. 16). All segments of society were involved: the elders (vv. 11–12), the women (v. 14) and the priests (v. 16). See *WLC* 106.

8:5–6 See *WLC* 150; *WSC* 48,83.

8:5 idol of jealousy. Defined in verse 3 as the "idol that provokes to jealousy"; that is, provoked the wrath of God, who was jealous for his own honor (Ex 20:5). God's glory belonged there (v. 4); the idol did not. This idol was probably an Asherah, an image of a Canaanite goddess possibly viewed as the Lord's consort (see 2Ki 21:7; 23:6).

8:10 animals. Worshiping animals was an act of worshiping the creature rather than the Creator (Ro 1:25). Animals over which humankind had been given dominion had instead become objects of veneration (see Ge 1:28).

8:11–15 See *WLC* 150,151; *WSC* 83.

8:11 Jaazaniah son of Shaphan. Shaphan had been instrumental in Josiah's reforms (2Ki 22:3–14; 2Ch 34:8,15–20). Burning incense in the temple was a rite reserved for the priests (Ex 30:1–10; Nu 16:40; 18:1–7; 2Ch 26:16–21).

8:14 Tammuz. Worshiped as a fertility god and as the lord of the netherworld. Rites were tied to the annual cycles of death and the rejuvenation of vegetation. When vegetation failed under the heat of the summer sun, Tammuz was thought to have died and descended to the netherworld, and people mourned his passing. The reappearance of vegetation was viewed as the return of Tammuz; fertility rites sought to ensure the productivity of the land. See Deuteronomy 28:11–12 and 17–24, Psalm 104:10–30, Joel 2:18–27, Amos 9:13–15, Haggai 1:10–11, 2:15–19 and Zechariah 8:10–12.

8:16 twenty-five men. Probably priests, since access to the area between the altar and the portico of the temple was ordinarily restricted to priests. The temple faced east. Rather than face the temple to lament and mourn their sins and to intercede for the nation as they should have done (9:4; cf. Joel 2:17), these men literally turned their backs on the house of God and the Lord enthroned there above the cherubim (10:3) in order to worship the rising sun (2Ki 21:5;

With their backs toward the temple of the LORD and their faces toward the east, they were
bowing down to the sun in the east.[x]
17 He said to me, "Have you seen this, son of man? Is it a trivial matter for the house
of Judah to do the detestable things they are doing here? Must they also fill the land with
violence[y] and continually provoke me to anger?[z] Look at them putting the branch to
their nose! 18 Therefore I will deal with them in anger; I will not look on them with pity[a]
or spare them. Although they shout in my ears, I will not listen[b] to them."

Idolaters Killed

9 Then I heard him call out in a loud voice, "Bring the guards of the city here, each
with a weapon in his hand." 2 And I saw six men coming from the direction of the
upper gate, which faces north, each with a deadly weapon in his hand. With them was
a man clothed in linen[c] who had a writing kit at his side. They came in and stood beside
the bronze altar.
3 Now the glory[d] of the God of Israel went up from above the cherubim,[e] where it had
been, and moved to the threshold of the temple. Then the LORD called to the man
clothed in linen who had the writing kit at his side 4 and said to him, "Go throughout the
city of Jerusalem and put a mark[f] on the foreheads of those who grieve and lament[g] over
all the detestable things that are done in it.[h]"
5 As I listened, he said to the others, "Follow him through the city and kill, without
showing pity[i] or compassion. 6 Slaughter old men, young men and maidens, women and
children, but do not touch anyone who has the mark. Begin at my sanctuary." So they
began with the elders[j] who were in front of the temple.[k]
7 Then he said to them, "Defile the temple and fill the courts with the slain. Go!" So
they went out and began killing throughout the city. 8 While they were killing and I was
left alone, I fell facedown,[l] crying out, "Ah, Sovereign LORD! Are you going to destroy the
entire remnant of Israel in this outpouring of your wrath on Jerusalem?[m]"
9 He answered me, "The sin of the house of Israel and Judah is exceedingly great; the
land is full of bloodshed and the city is full of injustice.[n] They say, 'The LORD has forsak-
en the land; the LORD does not see.'[o] 10 So I will not look on them with pity[p] or spare them,
but I will bring down on their own heads what they have done.[q]"
11 Then the man in linen with the writing kit at his side brought back word, saying, "I
have done as you commanded."

The Glory Departs From the Temple

10 I looked, and I saw the likeness of a throne[r] of sapphire[a][s] above the expanse[t]
that was over the heads of the cherubim. 2 The LORD said to the man clothed in
linen,[u] "Go in among the wheels[v] beneath the cherubim. Fill[w] your hands with burning
coals from among the cherubim and scatter them over the city." And as I watched, he
went in.
3 Now the cherubim were standing on the south side of the temple when the man
went in, and a cloud filled the inner court. 4 Then the glory of the LORD[x] rose from above
the cherubim and moved to the threshold of the temple. The cloud filled the temple, and
the court was full of the radiance of the glory of the LORD. 5 The sound of the wings of the

[a] 1 Or *lapis lazuli*

8:16 [x]Dt 4:19; 17:3; Job 31:28; Jer 2:27; Eze 11:1,12
8:17 [y]Eze 9:9 [z]Eze 16:26
8:18 [a]Eze 9:10; 24:14 [b]Isa 1:15; Jer 11:11; Mic 3:4; Zec 7:13
9:2 [c]Lev 16:4; Eze 10:2; Rev 15:6
9:3 [d]Eze 10:4 [e]Eze 11:22
9:4 [f]Ex 12:7; 2Co 1:22; Rev 7:3; 9:4 [g]Ps 119:136; Jer 13:17; Eze 21:6 [h]Ps 119:53
9:5 [i]Eze 5:11
9:6 [j]Eze 8:11-13,16 [k]2Ch 36:17; Jer 25:29; 1Pe 4:17
9:8 [l]Jos 7:6 [m]Eze 11:13; Am 7:1-6
9:9 [n]Eze 22:29 [o]Job 22:13; Eze 8:12
9:10 [p]Eze 7:4; 8:18 [q]Isa 65:6; Eze 11:21
10:1 [r]Rev 4:2 [s]Ex 24:10 [t]Eze 1:22
10:2 [u]Eze 9:2 [v]Eze 1:15 [w]Rev 8:5
10:4 [x]Eze 1:28; 9:3

23:11). Astral cults were common in the ancient Near East; they were prominent in Mesopotamia but also indigenous to Canaan.
8:17 violence. The sins denounced in this chapter primarily, but not exclusively, involved corrupt religious practice. Corrupt religion was inevitably accompanied by corrupt relations between people, so that the entire land is described as full of violence or lawlessness, a theme developed further in 9:9 and 11:6. **branch to their nose.** Some Assyrian reliefs portray individuals holding branches to their noses in a gesture of reverence and worship; this may be a reference to that practice or to a similar worship rite.
■ **9:1–11** *Executioners for the Unrepentant.* Ezekiel continued to observe events in Jerusalem through his vision, as he saw God call for executioners to slay the unrepentant.
9:1 guards. Described as human (vv. 1–2), but probably angelic warriors (Ex 12:23–30; 1Ch 21:15–20) assigned to execute the idolaters.
9:2 clothed in linen. Linen garments were the attire of priests (Ex 28:29–42), but angels and those in the presence of God were also described as wearing them (Da 10:5; 12:6–7; Rev 15:6; 19:8,14). **writing kit at his side.** A scribe apparently charged with keeping the heavenly record (Ex 32:32–33; Pss 69:28; 139:16; Da 12:1; Php 4:3; Rev 3:5; 13:8; 17:8; 20:12,15; 21:27). Ezekiel's vision was a reminder that idolaters had no place in the city of God (1Co 5:11; 6:9; Eph 5:5; Col 3:5; Rev 21:8; 22:15; cf. 2Ch 15:12–13).
9:3 the glory. The glory cloud that symbolized the divine presence dwelt above the Most Holy Place in the temple; the cloud began a journey visually portraying the way in which God would forsake Jerusalem (10:18–19; 11:22–23).
9:4 mark on the foreheads. This symbolism may have influenced John's vision or writing in Revelation 7:3 and 14:9. The mark is reminiscent of the blood on the houses of the Israelites during the first Passover—the sign kept all the firstborn safe from death (Ex 12:12–13).
9:9 injustice. The indictments in chapter 8 concentrated on idolatry and worship violations; here the issue is social justice. Ezekiel elaborated on the violence and lawlessness mentioned in 8:17.
■ **10:1–22** *Chariot of Glory Departs From the Temple.* The glory of God left the temple and traveled east, in Ezekiel's vision, symbolizing that the temple was so defiled by sin that God would not remain there.
10:1 cherubim. The "living creatures" of 1:5, 13–15, 17, 19–22 and 3:13 are identified as cherubim (10:15,17,20).

cherubim could be heard as far away as the outer court, like the voice[y] of God Almighty[a]
when he speaks.
6When the LORD commanded the man in linen, "Take fire from among the wheels,
from among the cherubim," the man went in and stood beside a wheel. 7Then one of the
cherubim reached out his hand to the fire that was among them. He took up some of it
and put it into the hands of the man in linen, who took it and went out. 8(Under the wings
of the cherubim could be seen what looked like the hands of a man.)[z]
9I looked, and I saw beside the cherubim four wheels, one beside each of the cherubim; the wheels sparkled like chrysolite.[a] 10As for their appearance, the four of them
looked alike; each was like a wheel intersecting a wheel. 11As they moved, they would
go in any one of the four directions the cherubim faced; the wheels did not turn about[b]
as the cherubim went. The cherubim went in whatever direction the head faced, without turning as they went. 12Their entire bodies, including their backs, their hands and
their wings, were completely full of eyes,[b] as were their four wheels.[c] 13I heard the
wheels being called "the whirling wheels." 14Each of the cherubim[d] had four faces:[e] One
face was that of a cherub, the second the face of a man, the third the face of a lion, and
the fourth the face of an eagle.[f]
15Then the cherubim rose upward. These were the living creatures[g] I had seen by the
Kebar River. 16When the cherubim moved, the wheels beside them moved; and when the
cherubim spread their wings to rise from the ground, the wheels did not leave their side.
17When the cherubim stood still, they also stood still; and when the cherubim rose, they
rose with them, because the spirit of the living creatures was in them.[h]
18Then the glory of the LORD departed from over the threshold of the temple and
stopped above the cherubim.[i] 19While I watched, the cherubim spread their wings and
rose from the ground, and as they went, the wheels went with them.[j] They stopped at
the entrance to the east gate of the LORD's house, and the glory of the God of Israel was
above them.
20These were the living creatures I had seen beneath the God of Israel by the Kebar
River,[k] and I realized that they were cherubim. 21Each had four faces[l] and four wings,[m]
and under their wings was what looked like the hands of a man. 22Their faces had the
same appearance as those I had seen by the Kebar River. Each one went straight ahead.

Judgment on Israel's Leaders

11 Then the Spirit lifted me up and brought me to the gate of the house of the LORD
that faces east. There at the entrance to the gate were twenty-five men, and I
saw among them Jaazaniah son of Azzur and Pelatiah son of Benaiah, leaders of the people.[n] 2The LORD said to me, "Son of man, these are the men who are plotting evil and giving wicked advice in this city. 3They say, 'Will it not soon be time to build houses?[c] This
city is a cooking pot,[o] and we are the meat.'[p] 4Therefore prophesy[q] against them;
prophesy, son of man."
5Then the Spirit of the LORD came upon me, and he told me to say: "This is what the LORD
says: That is what you are saying, O house of Israel, but I know what is going through your
mind.[r] 6You have killed many people in this city and filled its streets with the dead.[s]
7"Therefore this is what the Sovereign LORD says: The bodies you have thrown there
are the meat and this city is the pot, but I will drive you out of it.[t] 8You fear the sword,

[a] 5 Hebrew *El-Shaddai* [b] 11 Or *aside* [c] 3 Or *This is not the time to build houses.*

10:5 [y]Job 40:9; Eze 1:24
10:8 [z]Eze 1:8
10:9 [a]Eze 1:15-16; Rev 21:20
10:12 [b]Rev 4:6-8 [c]Eze 1:15-21
10:14 [d]1Ki 7:36 [e]Eze 1:6 [f]Eze 1:10; Rev 4:7
10:15 [g]Eze 1:3,5
10:17 [h]Eze 1:20-21
10:18 [i]Ps 18:10
10:19 [j]Eze 11:1,22
10:20 [k]Eze 1:1
10:21 [l]Eze 41:18 [m]Eze 1:6
11:1 [n]Eze 8:16; 10:19; 43:4-5
11:3 [o]Jer 1:13; Eze 24:3 [p]ver 7,11
11:4 [q]Eze 3:4,17
11:5 [r]Jer 17:10
11:6 [s]Eze 7:23; 22:6
11:7 [t]Eze 24:3-13; Mic 3:2-3

10:7 reached out. The cherub reached into the fire among the wheels to retrieve the burning coals that would devour the city.
10:12 eyes. Compare Deuteronomy 11:12, 2 Chronicles 16:9, Proverbs 15:3, Zechariah 3:9, 4:10 and Revelation 4:8.
10:14 face . . . of a cherub. Replaced the ox or bull in the earlier vision (1:10; see note on v. 22).
10:18 glory of the LORD departed. From the temple toward the east (v. 4; 9:3).
10:22 Their faces had the same appearance. Since the face of the ox was replaced by the face of a cherub (v. 14), Ezekiel probably did not mean that all the faces looked the same as they had previously appeared. Presumably he referred only to their human faces—those that "went straight ahead" (cf. 1:9–10).
■ **11:1–21** *Jerusalem's Evil Leaders Executed.* Ezekiel's vision continued as he saw leaders in Jerusalem judged by God.
11:1 twenty-five men. Probably not the same people as the 25 sun worshipers (8:16); these appear to be political leaders instead of priests. **Jaazaniah son of Azzur.** Not identified with Jaazaniah son of Shaphan (8:11).
11:3 cooking pot . . . meat. The leadership of Jerusalem had been deported by Nebuchadnezzar in 597 B.C.; that deportation included much of the royal family, the leaders of the military and the skilled crafts workers, leaving "only the poorest people of the land" (2Ki 24:13–16). Those who rose to prominence in the absence of the earlier ruling class had delusions of grandeur. The analogy they proposed with a cooking pot and meat suggests that they considered those deported leaders as the offal, the waste of a butchered animal, with themselves as the choice portions.
11:4 prophesy . . . prophesy. The implicit repetition of Ezekiel's commission throughout this section is made explicit. When he returned to the exiles he continued to proclaim what he had seen (vv. 11:14–25).
11:5 See *WCF* 2.2.
11:7 meat. These plotters had murdered those better than themselves—the murdered victims had been the real "meat" of the city, and the present leadership was the offal, fit only to be discarded. See verse 3.

and the sword is what I will bring against you, declares the Sovereign LORD.[u] **9**I will drive
you out of the city and hand you over[v] to foreigners and inflict punishment on you.[w]
10You will fall by the sword, and I will execute judgment on you at the borders of Israel.[x] Then you will know that I am the LORD. **11**This city will not be a pot[y] for you, nor will
you be the meat in it; I will execute judgment on you at the borders of Israel. **12**And you
will know that I am the LORD, for you have not followed my decrees[z] or kept my laws but
have conformed to the standards of the nations around you.[a]"

13Now as I was prophesying, Pelatiah[b] son of Benaiah died. Then I fell facedown and
cried out in a loud voice, "Ah, Sovereign LORD! Will you completely destroy the remnant
of Israel?[c]"

14The word of the LORD came to me: **15**"Son of man, your brothers—your brothers who
are your blood relatives[a] and the whole house of Israel—are those of whom the people
of Jerusalem have said, 'They are[b] far away from the LORD; this land was given to us as
our possession.'[d]

Promised Return of Israel

16"Therefore say: 'This is what the Sovereign LORD says: Although I sent them far away
among the nations and scattered them among the countries, yet for a little while I have
been a sanctuary[e] for them in the countries where they have gone.'

17"Therefore say: 'This is what the Sovereign LORD says: I will gather you from the nations and bring you back from the countries where you have been scattered, and I will
give you back the land of Israel again.'[f]

18"They will return to it and remove all its vile images[g] and detestable idols.[h] **19**I will
give them an undivided heart[i] and put a new spirit in them; I will remove from them their
heart of stone[j] and give them a heart of flesh.[k] **20**Then they will follow my decrees and
be careful to keep my laws.[l] They will be my people, and I will be their God.[m] **21**But as
for those whose hearts are devoted to their vile images and detestable idols, I will bring
down on their own heads what they have done, declares the Sovereign LORD.[n]"

22Then the cherubim, with the wheels beside them, spread their wings, and the glory of the God of Israel was above them.[o] **23**The glory[p] of the LORD went up from within
the city and stopped above the mountain[q] east of it. **24**The Spirit[r] lifted me up and
brought me to the exiles in Babylonia[c] in the vision[s] given by the Spirit of God.

Then the vision I had seen went up from me, **25**and I told the exiles everything the
LORD had shown me.[t]

The Exile Symbolized

12 The word of the LORD came to me: **2**"Son of man, you are living among a rebellious people. They have eyes to see but do not see and ears to hear but do not
hear, for they are a rebellious people.[u]

3"Therefore, son of man, pack your belongings for exile and in the daytime, as they
watch, set out and go from where you are to another place. Perhaps[v] they will understand,[w] though they are a rebellious house.[x] **4**During the daytime, while they watch,

a *15* Or *are in exile with you* (see Septuagint and Syriac) b *15* Or *those to whom the people of Jerusalem have said, 'Stay* c *24* Or *Chaldea*

11:8 [u]Pr 10:24
11:9 [v]Ps 106:41 [w]Dt 28:36; Eze 5:8
11:10 [x]2Ki 14:25
11:11 [y]ver 3
11:12 [z]Lev 18:4; Eze 18:9 [a]Eze 8:10
11:13 [b]ver 1 [c]Eze 9:8
11:15 [d]Eze 33:24
11:16 [e]Ps 90:1; 91:9; Isa 8:14
11:17 [f]Jer 3:18; 24:5-6; Eze 28:25; 34:13
11:18 [g]Eze 5:11 [h]Eze 37:23
11:19 [i]Jer 32:39 [j]Zec 7:12 [k]Eze 18:31; 36:26; 2Co 3:3
11:20 [l]Ps 105:45 [m]Eze 14:11; 36:26-28
11:21 [n]Eze 9:10; 16:43
11:22 [o]Eze 10:19
11:23 [p]Eze 8:4; 10:4 [q]Zec 14:4
11:24 [r]Eze 8:3 [s]2Co 12:2-4
11:25 [t]Eze 3:4,11
12:2 [u]Isa 6:10; Eze 2:6-8; Mt 13:15
12:3 [v]Jer 36:3 [w]Jer 26:3 [x]2Ti 2:25-26

11:13 Pelatiah. Means "The Lord provides escape." When this man died unexpectedly during Ezekiel's vision, Ezekiel feared that all hope of escape had died with him. The prophet interceded with the Lord again on behalf of the remnant. See notes on 3:24–27 and 6:8; compare 9:8.
11:15 blood relatives. A kinsman was obligated to redeem a relative or the relative's property if the relative was reduced to servitude or to selling family land (Lev 25:25–55; Ru 4). But the exile gave those remaining in Jerusalem the chance to seize their deported relatives' property. Compare 45:9–12 and 46:16–18.
11:16 sanctuary for them. In the absence of the temple in Jerusalem, God himself would be their sanctuary. Jesus himself later took the place of the temple (Mt 26:61; 27:40; Jn 2:19), and his Spirit in turn made his followers a temple (1Co 3:16–17; 2Co 6:16; 1Pe 2:5).
11:18–21 an undivided heart and . . . a new spirit. God's goal in the exile was to produce a purified people who would obey his commands. Ezekiel returned to the theme of a new heart and spirit in 18:31 and 36:26. The fulfillment of this hope for a completely renewed people of God after the exile was initially fulfilled with the first coming of Jesus; it continues as the latter days extend through the centuries and will reach completion when Christ returns in glory (see notes on Jer 30:3; 31:31–34; 2Co 3:3).
11:19 See *WCF* 10.1; *WLC* 67.

■ **11:22–25** *Transport to Babylon.* In correspondence with the opening of this section (8:1–4; cf. note on 8:1—11:25), Ezekiel saw the glory cloud depart from Jerusalem and move east across the Kidron Valley to the Mount of Olives. But God had not forsaken the city forever; later Ezekiel described the glory of God returning to Jerusalem (ch. 43). See 47:1–12, Zechariah 14:4 and Acts 1:11.
■ **12:1–20** *Symbolic Acts.* In parallel with 4:1—5:17 Ezekiel performed two symbolic actions related to departing for exile. He packed belongings (vv. 1–16) and ate and drank (vv. 17–20).
■ **12:1–16** *Packed Belongings.* Another symbolic action (see note on 4:1–3); Ezekiel enacted the eventual exile of those who still remained in Jerusalem.
12:2 rebellious. See 2:3–8 and 3:9 and 26–27. **eyes . . . hear.** Compare Deuteronomy 29:4, Proverbs 20:12, Isaiah 6:10, 32:3, Jeremiah 5:21, Matthew 13:15–16, Mark 8:18, Acts 28:26 and Romans 11:8. The entire section makes frequent allusion to seeing (vv. 4–7,12–13).
12:3 pack. An exile could carry only the minimum necessities: perhaps a cloak, a couple of containers of food and water and a few personal items. The remaining goods were plunder for the conqueror. Neither a quick and safe escape nor the difficult journey into exile would have been possible if luxuries had been carried (see Mt 10:9–10; Lk 10:4; 22:35–36).

bring out your belongings packed for exile. Then in the evening, while they are watching, go out like those who go into exile.[y] 5While they watch, dig through the wall and
take your belongings out through it. 6Put them on your shoulder as they are watching
and carry them out at dusk. Cover your face so that you cannot see the land, for I have
made you a sign[z] to the house of Israel."
7So I did as I was commanded.[a] During the day I brought out my things packed for
exile. Then in the evening I dug through the wall with my hands. I took my belongings
out at dusk, carrying them on my shoulders while they watched.
8In the morning the word of the LORD came to me: 9"Son of man, did not that rebellious house of Israel ask you, 'What are you doing?'[b]
10"Say to them, 'This is what the Sovereign LORD says: This oracle concerns the
prince in Jerusalem and the whole house of Israel who are there.' 11Say to them, 'I am a
sign to you.'

"As I have done, so it will be done to them. They will go into exile as captives.[c]
12"The prince among them will put his things on his shoulder at dusk[d] and leave, and
a hole will be dug in the wall for him to go through. He will cover his face so that he cannot see the land.[e] 13I will spread my net[f] for him, and he will be caught in my snare;[g] I
will bring him to Babylonia, the land of the Chaldeans, but he will not see[h] it, and there
he will die.[i] 14I will scatter to the winds all those around him—his staff and all his
troops—and I will pursue them with drawn sword.[j]
15"They will know that I am the LORD, when I disperse them among the nations and
scatter them through the countries. 16But I will spare a few of them from the sword, famine and plague, so that in the nations where they go they may acknowledge all their detestable practices. Then they will know that I am the LORD.[k]"
17The word of the LORD came to me: 18"Son of man, tremble as you eat your food,[l] and
shudder in fear as you drink your water. 19Say to the people of the land: 'This is what the
Sovereign LORD says about those living in Jerusalem and in the land of Israel: They will
eat their food in anxiety and drink their water in despair, for their land will be stripped
of everything[m] in it because of the violence of all who live there.[n] 20The inhabited
towns will be laid waste and the land will be desolate. Then you will know that I am the
LORD.[o]' "
21The word of the LORD came to me: 22"Son of man, what is this proverb you have in
the land of Israel: 'The days go by and every vision comes to nothing'?[p] 23Say to them,
'This is what the Sovereign LORD says: I am going to put an end to this proverb, and they
will no longer quote it in Israel.' Say to them, 'The days are near when every vision will
be fulfilled.[q] 24For there will be no more false visions or flattering divinations[r] among the
people of Israel. 25But I the LORD will speak what I will, and it shall be fulfilled without
delay. For in your days, you rebellious house, I will fulfill whatever I say, declares the Sovereign LORD.[s]' "
26The word of the LORD came to me: 27"Son of man, the house of Israel is saying, 'The
vision he sees is for many years from now, and he prophesies about the distant future.'[t]
28"Therefore say to them, 'This is what the Sovereign LORD says: None of my words
will be delayed any longer; whatever I say will be fulfilled, declares the Sovereign LORD.' "

12:4 [y]ver 12; Jer 39:4
12:6 [z]ver 12; Isa 8:18; 20:3; Eze 4:3; 24:24
12:7 [a]Eze 24:18; 37:10
12:9 [b]Eze 17:12; 20:49; 24:19
12:11 [c]2Ki 25:7; Jer 15:2; 52:15
12:12 [d]Jer 39:4 [e]Jer 52:7
12:13 [f]Eze 17:20; 19:8; Hos 7:12 [g]Isa 24:17-18 [h]Jer 39:7 [i]Jer 52:11; Eze 17:16
12:14 [j]2Ki 25:5; Eze 5:10,12
12:16 [k]Jer 22:8-9; Eze 6:8-10; 14:22
12:18 [l]La 5:9; Eze 4:16
12:19 [m]Eze 6:6-14; Mic 7:13; Zec 7:14 [n]Eze 4:16; 23:33
12:20 [o]Isa 7:23-24; Jer 4:7
12:22 [p]Eze 11:3; Am 6:3; 2Pe 3:4
12:23 [q]Ps 37:13; Joel 2:1; Zep 1:14
12:24 [r]Jer 14:14; Eze 13:23; Zec 13:2-4
12:25 [s]Isa 14:24; Hab 1:5
12:27 [t]Da 10:14

12:4 evening. The departure at evening was intended to facilitate a furtive escape under cover of darkness, also symbolized by digging through the wall of the house. Ezekiel portrayed Zedekiah's thwarted effort to escape from besieged Jerusalem (vv. 10–11; 2Ki 25:3–7).
12:6 Cover your face. A gesture both of shame and of grief (24:17,22; Lev 13:45; 2Sa 19:4; Est 6:12; 7:8; Pss 44:15; 69:7). It also suggested that the exiles would never again see Jerusalem and particularly that Zedekiah would lose his sight (vv. 12–13; 2Ki 25:7).
12:12 a hole will be dug. Though the walls of Jerusalem had been breached at the time of Zedekiah, the king and his retinue managed to escape through a gate (2Ki 25:4).
12:13 I will spread my net. God is depicted as a hunter or trapper (17:20; 32:3; Job 19:6; Ps 91:3; Pr 6:5; Isa 8:14; 24:18; 51:20; Jer 50:24; La 1:13; Hos 7:12).
▪ **12:17–20** *Eating and Drinking.* Another symbolic action. Ezekiel's food and water were presumably the starvation rations he had been allotted in 4:9–11. His physical weakness and trembling represented the lot of all those remaining in Jerusalem.
▪ **12:21—24:27** *Related Speeches.* In parallel with the previous section of speeches (5:5—7:27; see "Introduction: Outline"), Ezekiel gave a number of oracles concerning what his preceding symbolic acts had portrayed. These materials divide into: a false proverb (12:21–28), false prophets and prophetesses (13:1–23), idolatry (14:1–23), a parable of the vine (15:1–8), Jerusalem as child and harlot (16:1–63), a parable of two eagles (17:1–24), the importance of individual responsibility (18:1–32), a dirge allegory for Israel's kings (19:1–14), the nation's past and future (20:1–49), Babylon as God's sword (21:1–32), the sins of Jerusalem (22:1–31), a parable of two lewd sisters (23:1–49), a cooking pot (24:1–14) and the death of Ezekiel's wife (24:15–27).
▪ **12:21–28** *A False Proverb.* God directed Ezekiel to address the issue of a proverb that was circulating among those left in Jerusalem. That fallacious proverb had likely been started by false prophets who insisted that threats of destruction and exile for Jerusalem were unfounded.
12:22 days go by. The allegation was that despite the predictions of the prophets, nothing had happened. (A similar resistance to the prophetic word was predicted in 2Pe 3:3–4.)
12:25 it shall be fulfilled without delay. Fulfillment of prophecies had sometimes been postponed because of people's responses, but Ezekiel made it clear that his threats of destruction to Jerusalem would see imminent realization (see "Introduction to the Prophetic Books").
12:27 distant future. Some concluded that Ezekiel must be referring to some time period other than their own. It was important for false prophets, perhaps for reasons of economic gain (e.g., by prolonging their employment), to assure a skittish population that ruin was not about to take place.

False Prophets Condemned

13 The word of the LORD came to me: 2"Son of man, prophesy against the prophets of Israel who are now prophesying. Say to those who prophesy out of their
own imagination: 'Hear the word of the LORD![u] 3This is what the Sovereign LORD says:
Woe to the foolish[a] prophets[v] who follow their own spirit and have seen nothing![w] 4Your
prophets, O Israel, are like jackals among ruins. 5You have not gone up to the breaks in
the wall to repair[x] it for the house of Israel so that it will stand firm in the battle on the
day of the LORD.[y] 6Their visions are false and their divinations a lie. They say, "The LORD
declares," when the LORD has not sent them; yet they expect their words to be fulfilled.[z]
7Have you not seen false visions and uttered lying divinations when you say, "The LORD
declares," though I have not spoken?

8" 'Therefore this is what the Sovereign LORD says: Because of your false words and
lying visions, I am against you, declares the Sovereign LORD. 9My hand will be against the
prophets who see false visions and utter lying divinations. They will not belong to the
council of my people or be listed in the records[a] of the house of Israel, nor will they enter the land of Israel. Then you will know that I am the Sovereign LORD.[b]

10" 'Because they lead my people astray,[c] saying, "Peace," when there is no peace,
and because, when a flimsy wall is built, they cover it with whitewash,[d] 11therefore tell
those who cover it with whitewash that it is going to fall. Rain will come in torrents, and
I will send hailstones hurtling down, and violent winds will burst forth.[e] 12When the wall
collapses, will people not ask you, "Where is the whitewash you covered it with?"

13" 'Therefore this is what the Sovereign LORD says: In my wrath I will unleash a violent wind, and in my anger hailstones[f] and torrents of rain will fall with destructive
fury.[g] 14I will tear down the wall you have covered with whitewash and will level it to the
ground so that its foundation[h] will be laid bare. When it[b] falls,[i] you will be destroyed in
it; and you will know that I am the LORD. 15So I will spend my wrath against the wall and
against those who covered it with whitewash. I will say to you, "The wall is gone and so
are those who whitewashed it, 16those prophets of Israel who prophesied to Jerusalem and
saw visions of peace for her when there was no peace, declares the Sovereign LORD.[j]" '

17"Now, son of man, set your face against the daughters[k] of your people who prophesy out of their own imagination. Prophesy against them[l] 18and say, 'This is what the Sovereign LORD says: Woe to the women who sew magic charms on all their wrists and make
veils of various lengths for their heads in order to ensnare people. Will you ensnare the lives
of my people but preserve your own? 19You have profaned[m] me among my people for a few
handfuls of barley and scraps of bread. By lying to my people, who listen to lies, you have
killed those who should not have died and have spared those who should not live.[n]

20" 'Therefore this is what the Sovereign LORD says: I am against your magic charms
with which you ensnare people like birds and I will tear them from your arms; I will set
free the people that you ensnare like birds. 21I will tear off your veils and save my people from your hands, and they will no longer fall prey to your power. Then you will know
that I am the LORD.[o] 22Because you disheartened the righteous with your lies, when I had
brought them no grief, and because you encouraged the wicked not to turn from their
evil ways and so save their lives,[p] 23therefore you will no longer see false visions or prac-

13:2 [u]ver 17; Jer 23:16; 37:19
13:3 [v]La 2:14 [w]Jer 23:25-32
13:5 [x]Isa 58:12; Eze 22:30 [y]Eze 7:19
13:6 [z]Jer 28:15; Eze 22:28
13:9 [a]Jer 17:13 [b]Eze 20:38
13:10 [c]Jer 50:6 [d]Eze 7:25; 22:28
13:11 [e]Eze 38:22
13:13 [f]Rev 11:19; 16:21 [g]Ex 9:25; Isa 30:30
13:14 [h]Mic 1:6 [i]Jer 6:15
13:16 [j]Isa 57:21; Jer 6:14
13:17 [k]Rev 2:20 [l]ver 2
13:19 [m]Eze 20:39; 22:26 [n]Pr 28:21
13:21 [o]Ps 91:3
13:22 [p]Jer 23:14; Eze 33:14-16

[a] 3 Or *wicked* [b] 14 Or *the city*

■ **13:1–23** *False Prophets and Prophetesses.* Chapter 13 is divided into two oracles: the first against false prophets (vv. 1–16) and the second against false prophetesses (vv. 17–23). The main theme is the conflict between Ezekiel and those who prophesied falsely over the destruction of Jerusalem.

13:4 like jackals. As scavengers, the jackals had no concept of what the ruins had previously been; they existed only for their own convenience and profit, with no interest in how their actions affected the city or its inhabitants.

13:5 not gone up to the breaks. The focus was the conduct of the prophets: A true prophet so identified with God's people as to expose himself to risk on their behalf. When a wall was breached by an attacking army, the station involving the greatest danger was in the break, and the difficult decision was whether to guard or to repair it. Given that the threatened battle was to take place "on the day of the LORD," the invader would seem to be God himself bringing judgment on his rebellious people. The false prophets had not sought to protect the people from God's judgment either by guarding the breaks (i.e., interceding with God on behalf of the people) or repairing them (i.e., encouraging the people to repent). Compare 22:30.

13:9 records. Probably the census lists and civil registers of the people of Israel, the earthly counterpart of the heavenly records. See note on 9:2.

13:10–12 a flimsy wall. The image of the breach in the wall (v. 5) may have prompted this further description of the actions of the false prophets. Their bogus visions and lying divinations were a wall of shoddy construction—when plastered over or whitewashed, it might look substantial, but it could not withstand the weather, much less the day of the Lord's judgment. Paul used the same figure to indicate the hypocrisy of the high priest (Ac 23:3), though he subsequently apologized; Jesus used a similar figure to indicate the hypocrisy of the scribes and Pharisees (Mt 23:27).

13:17–23 prophesy out of their own imagination. The Bible records the actions of several true prophetesses—Miriam, Deborah, Huldah, Anna (Ex 15:20; Jdg 4:4; 2Ki 22:14; 2Ch 34:22; Lk 2:36)—and some false prophetesses (Ne 6:14; Rev 2:20). These latter women here were engaged in magic and sorcery, practices forbidden for Israel; see note on 12:21—14:11. They made their living by selling amulets or other charms to ward off evil, bolstered by the false confidence that their customers would fail to heed the cry of the watchman and so would die (see note on 3:17). The false prophetesses were likened to huntresses who trapped or ensnared people; see note on 12:13. See *WLC* 113,151.

tice divination.[q] I will save my people from your hands. And then you will know that I
am the LORD.[r]' "

Idolaters Condemned

14 Some of the elders of Israel came to me and sat down in front of me.[s] **2**Then the
word of the LORD came to me: **3**"Son of man, these men have set up idols in their
hearts and put wicked stumbling blocks[t] before their faces. Should I let them inquire of
me at all?[u] **4**Therefore speak to them and tell them, 'This is what the Sovereign LORD says:
When any Israelite sets up idols in his heart and puts a wicked stumbling block before
his face and then goes to a prophet, I the LORD will answer him myself in keeping with
his great idolatry. **5**I will do this to recapture the hearts of the people of Israel, who have
all deserted[v] me for their idols.'[w]
6"Therefore say to the house of Israel, 'This is what the Sovereign LORD says: Repent!
Turn from your idols and renounce all your detestable practices![x]
7" 'When any Israelite or any alien[y] living in Israel separates himself from me and sets
up idols in his heart and puts a wicked stumbling block before his face and then goes to
a prophet to inquire of me, I the LORD will answer him myself. **8**I will set my face against[z]
that man and make him an example and a byword.[a] I will cut him off from my people.
Then you will know that I am the LORD.
9" 'And if the prophet[b] is enticed[c] to utter a prophecy, I the LORD have enticed that
prophet, and I will stretch out my hand against him and destroy him from among my
people Israel.[d] **10**They will bear their guilt—the prophet will be as guilty as the one who
consults him. **11**Then the people of Israel will no longer stray[e] from me, nor will they defile themselves anymore with all their sins. They will be my people, and I will be their
God, declares the Sovereign LORD.[f]' "

Judgment Inescapable

12The word of the LORD came to me: **13**"Son of man, if a country sins against me by being unfaithful and I stretch out my hand against it to cut off its food supply[g] and send
famine upon it and kill its men and their animals,[h] **14**even if these three men—Noah,[i]
Daniel[a][j] and Job[k]—were in it, they could save only themselves by their righteousness,[l]
declares the Sovereign LORD.
15"Or if I send wild beasts[m] through that country and they leave it childless and it becomes desolate so that no one can pass through it because of the beasts,[n] **16**as surely as
I live, declares the Sovereign LORD, even if these three men were in it, they could not save
their own sons or daughters. They alone would be saved, but the land would be desolate.[o]
17"Or if I bring a sword[p] against that country and say, 'Let the sword pass throughout the land,' and I kill its men and their animals,[q] **18**as surely as I live, declares the Sovereign LORD, even if these three men were in it, they could not save their own sons or
daughters. They alone would be saved.
19"Or if I send a plague into that land and pour out my wrath[r] upon it through
bloodshed, killing its men and their animals,[s] **20**as surely as I live, declares the Sovereign
LORD, even if Noah, Daniel and Job were in it, they could save neither son nor daughter.
They would save only themselves by their righteousness.[t]
21"For this is what the Sovereign LORD says: How much worse will it be when I send
against Jerusalem my four dreadful judgments—sword and famine and wild beasts and
plague—to kill its men and their animals![u] **22**Yet there will be some survivors—sons and
daughters who will be brought out of it.[v] They will come to you, and when you see their

13:23 [q]ver 6; Eze 12:24 [r]Mic 3:6
14:1 [s]Eze 8:1; 20:1
14:3 [t]ver 7; Eze 7:19 [u]Isa 1:15; Eze 20:31
14:5 [v]Zec 11:8 [w]Jer 2:11
14:6 [x]Isa 2:20; 30:22
14:7 [y]Ex 12:48; 20:10
14:8 [z]Eze 15:7 [a]Eze 5:15
14:9 [b]Jer 14:15 [c]Jer 4:10 [d]1Ki 22:23
14:11 [e]Eze 48:11 [f]Eze 11:19-20; 37:23
14:13 [g]Lev 26:26 [h]Eze 5:16; 6:14; 15:8
14:14 [i]Ge 6:8 [j]ver 20; Eze 28:3; Da 1:6; 6:13 [k]Job 1:1 [l]Job 42:9; Jer 15:1; Eze 18:20
14:15 [m]Eze 5:17 [n]Lev 26:22
14:16 [o]Eze 18:20
14:17 [p]Lev 26:25; Eze 5:12; 21:3-4 [q]Eze 25:13; Zep 1:3
14:19 [r]Eze 7:8 [s]Eze 38:22
14:20 [t]ver 14
14:21 [u]Jer 15:3; Eze 5:17; 33:27; Am 4:6-10; Rev 6:8
14:22 [v]Eze 12:16

[a] 14 Or *Danel;* the Hebrew spelling may suggest a person other than the prophet Daniel; also in verse 20.

■ **14:1–23** *Consequences of Idolatry.* Ezekiel confronted idolatry among the exiles.
14:3 idols in their hearts. May refer to secret idolatry (see vv. 4,7). These idols had captured the hearts of God's people. **wicked stumbling blocks.** A common phrase in Ezekiel (vv. 4,7; 7:19; 18:30; 44:12).
14:5–6 See *WLC* 76,105.
14:9 I . . . enticed . . . I will stretch out my hand. One of numerous Biblical passages affirming both the sovereignty of God and human moral responsibility in such a way that the will of God can never be used as an excuse for moral evil (Est 4:12 14; Joel 2:32; Mt 26:24; Ac 2:23). A false prophet, though enticed by God, would bear the responsibility for his wrongdoing. See 1 Kings 22:19–25. See *BC* 13.
14:14 even if. The Lord addressed the view espoused by some that the presence of a certain number of righteous people in Jerusalem would protect the city from God's wrath (cf. Ge 18:17–33). **Noah, Daniel and Job.** Though Noah was righteous and blameless among those of his generation (Ge 6:9), the world was not spared because of his presence. Job too was blameless and upright (Job 1:1), but this did not spare his family. The identity of the Daniel mentioned here is much debated. Some interpreters suggest Daniel of Biblical fame, one of Ezekiel's contemporaries in exile. In opposition to this view is the different Hebrew spelling of the name. The reference may be to a heroic figure in a text from ancient Ugarit, a king named Dan'el, identified as a righteous ruler (cf. 28:3) concerned with the plight of widows and orphans. These three people would then have had in common that they were non-Israelites known from antiquity for their uprightness. Even the prayers of such people could not turn back the wrath of the Lord.

conduct[w] and their actions, you will be consoled regarding the disaster I have brought upon Jerusalem—every disaster I have brought upon it. [23]You will be consoled when you see their conduct and their actions, for you will know that I have done nothing in it without cause, declares the Sovereign LORD.[x]"

Jerusalem, A Useless Vine

15 The word of the LORD came to me: [2]"Son of man, how is the wood of a vine[y] better than that of a branch on any of the trees in the forest? [3]Is wood ever taken from it to make anything useful? Do they make pegs from it to hang things on? [4]And after it is thrown on the fire as fuel and the fire burns both ends and chars the middle, is it then useful for anything?[z] [5]If it was not useful for anything when it was whole, how much less can it be made into something useful when the fire has burned it and it is charred?

[6]"Therefore this is what the Sovereign LORD says: As I have given the wood of the vine among the trees of the forest as fuel for the fire, so will I treat the people living in Jerusalem. [7]I will set my face against[a] them. Although they have come out of the fire, the fire will yet consume them. And when I set my face against them, you will know that I am the LORD.[b] [8]I will make the land desolate[c] because they have been unfaithful,[d] declares the Sovereign LORD."

An Allegory of Unfaithful Jerusalem

16 The word of the LORD came to me: [2]"Son of man, confront Jerusalem with her detestable practices[e] [3]and say, 'This is what the Sovereign LORD says to Jerusalem: Your ancestry[f] and birth were in the land of the Canaanites; your father was an Amorite and your mother a Hittite.[g] [4]On the day you were born[h] your cord was not cut, nor were you washed with water to make you clean, nor were you rubbed with salt or wrapped in cloths. [5]No one looked on you with pity or had compassion enough to do any of these things for you. Rather, you were thrown out into the open field, for on the day you were born you were despised.

[6]" 'Then I passed by and saw you kicking about in your blood, and as you lay there in your blood I said to you, "Live!"[a][i] [7]I made you grow[j] like a plant of the field. You grew up and developed and became the most beautiful of jewels.[b] Your breasts were formed and your hair grew, you who were naked and bare.[k]

[8]" 'Later I passed by, and when I looked at you and saw that you were old enough for love, I spread the corner of my garment[l] over you and covered your nakedness. I gave you my solemn oath and entered into a covenant with you, declares the Sovereign LORD, and you became mine.[m]

[9]" 'I bathed[c] you with water and washed[n] the blood from you and put ointments on you. [10]I clothed you with an embroidered[o] dress and put leather sandals on you. I dressed you in fine linen[p] and covered you with costly garments.[q] [11]I adorned you with jewelry:[r] I put

14:22 [w]Eze 20:43
14:23 [x]Jer 22:8-9
15:2 [y]Isa 5:1-7; Jer 2:21; Hos 10:1
15:4 [z]Eze 19:14; Jn 15:6
15:7 [a]Ps 34:16; Eze 14:8 [b]Isa 24:18; Am 9:1-4
15:8 [c]Eze 14:13 [d]Eze 17:20
16:2 [e]Eze 20:4; 22:2
16:3 [f]Eze 21:30 [g]ver 45
16:4 [h]Hos 2:3
16:6 [i]Ex 19:4
16:7 [j]Dt 1:10 [k]Ex 1:7
16:8 [l]Ru 3:9 [m]Jer 2:2; Hos 2:7, 19-20
16:9 [n]Ru 3:3
16:10 [o]Ex 26:36
16:10 [p]Eze 27:16 [q]ver 18
16:11 [r]Eze 23:40

[a] 6 A few Hebrew manuscripts, Septuagint and Syriac; most Hebrew manuscripts *"Live!" And as you lay there in your blood I said to you, "Live!"* [b] 7 Or *became mature* [c] 9 Or *I had bathed*

■**15:1–8** *A Parable of the Vine.* Ezekiel likened Israel to a vine that had been pruned. The wood that was cut off was not useful for anything but fuel (cf. Jn 15:2,6).
15:3 useful. The wood of the vine was unfit to make any worthwhile object, not even a lowly peg. God reminded the exiles that his choice of the Israelites as his people was not because of any intrinsic worth in them but solely a matter of his grace (Dt 7:6–8).
15:4 burns. The "charring" of Israel probably referred to the partial exile that had taken place in 597 B.C., with the deportation of Jehoiachin and most of Jerusalem's upper class. See note on 1:1–3. Now that the wood/city was damaged, it was worth even less. The prophet Zechariah alluded to this representation of the exile as a fire when he later described the high priest as a branch snatched from the fire (Zec 3:2).
15:6 fire. John the Baptist later used similar imagery with reference to Jerusalem, when the judgment of exile would be fulfilled to an even greater extent under the judgment rendered by the Messiah (Lk 3:9).
■**16:1–63** *Jerusalem as a Child and a Harlot.* Ezekiel told the story of an unwanted child, her rescue, marriage and infidelity. Hosea, too, used marriage as an analogy for the covenant relationship between God and Israel (Hos 1–3), and this comparison was also used in the New Testament (Eph 5:22–33; Rev 19:7; 21:2,9). Ezekiel's speech appears to have had a judicial setting; he recounted God's charge against the nation from its earliest days to his own time.
16:3 ancestry. Jerusalem had a pagan pedigree; the pre-Israelite inhabitants were variously described as Amorites, Canaanites, Jebusites and Hittites (v. 45; Ge 10:15–16; Jos 10:5; Jdg 19:11–12; 2Sa 5:6). In this respect the city was not unlike the patriarchs themselves, who were of pagan Aramean stock (Dt 26:5; Jos 24:14).
16:5 thrown out. Abandoned to die. According to documents from the ancient Near East, desertion and exposure of infants to the elements were common practices in the ancient world, especially when the infants were unwanted, malformed or sickly. These atrocities were condemned in Israel.
16:7 I made you grow. The unwanted child grew to beautiful maturity. The development of breasts (cf. Eze 23:3) and pubic hair signaled her puberty; later she attained marriageable age.
16:8 spread the corner of my garment. A man covering a woman with his garment symbolized marriage (Ru 3:9). The woman would remain covered to all but her husband (cf. Dt 22:30, where the phrase "dishonor his father's bed" translates a Hebrew phrase meaning literally, "lift off the corner of his father's garment"). **I gave you my solemn oath . . . you became mine.** Probably an allusion to the basic formulation of the covenant relationship: "I will be your God, and you will be my people" (Lev 26:12; Jer 7:12; 11:4; 30:22; Eze 36:28; Hos 1:9). For the divine oath see Genesis 15:7–21, 26:3 and Deuteronomy 1:8.
16:9–14 rose to be a queen. The foundling received all the care she had lacked at birth and far more. Her life, her status, her wealth and beauty all derived from the gracious gift of the One who had chosen her. Compare Revelation 17:4.

bracelets[s] on your arms and a necklace[t] around your neck, 12and I put a ring on your
nose,[u] earrings on your ears and a beautiful crown[v] on your head. 13So you were adorned
with gold and silver; your clothes were of fine linen and costly fabric and embroidered cloth.
Your food was fine flour, honey and olive oil.[w] You became very beautiful and rose to be
a queen.[x] 14And your fame[y] spread among the nations on account of your beauty,[z] because
the splendor I had given you made your beauty perfect, declares the Sovereign LORD.
15" 'But you trusted in your beauty and used your fame to become a prostitute. You
lavished your favors on anyone who passed by[a] and your beauty became his.[a] [b] 16You
took some of your garments to make gaudy high places, where you carried on your prostitution.[c] Such things should not happen, nor should they ever occur. 17You also took the
fine jewelry I gave you, the jewelry made of my gold and silver, and you made for yourself male idols and engaged in prostitution with them.[d] 18And you took your embroidered
clothes to put on them, and you offered my oil and incense before them. 19Also the food
I provided for you—the fine flour, olive oil and honey I gave you to eat—you offered as
fragrant incense before them. That is what happened, declares the Sovereign LORD.[e]
20" 'And you took your sons and daughters[f] whom you bore to me[g] and sacrificed
them as food to the idols. Was your prostitution not enough?[h] 21You slaughtered my children and sacrificed them[b] to the idols.[i] 22In all your detestable practices and your prostitution you did not remember the days of your youth,[j] when you were naked and bare,
kicking about in your blood.[k]
23" 'Woe! Woe to you, declares the Sovereign LORD. In addition to all your other
wickedness, 24you built a mound for yourself and made a lofty shrine[l] in every public
square.[m] 25At the head of every street you built your lofty shrines and degraded your
beauty, offering your body with increasing promiscuity to anyone who passed by.[n]
26You engaged in prostitution with the Egyptians, your lustful neighbors, and provoked[o]
me to anger with your increasing promiscuity.[p] 27So I stretched out my hand[q] against
you and reduced your territory; I gave you over to the greed of your enemies, the daughters of the Philistines,[r] who were shocked by your lewd conduct. 28You engaged in prostitution with the Assyrians[s] too, because you were insatiable; and even after that, you
still were not satisfied. 29Then you increased your promiscuity to include Babylonia,[c] [t] a
land of merchants, but even with this you were not satisfied.
30" 'How weak-willed you are, declares the Sovereign LORD, when you do all these
things, acting like a brazen prostitute![u] 31When you built your mounds at the head of every street and made your lofty shrines[v] in every public square, you were unlike a prostitute, because you scorned payment.
32" 'You adulterous wife! You prefer strangers to your own husband! 33Every prostitute receives a fee, but you give gifts[w] to all your lovers, bribing them to come to you from
everywhere for your illicit favors.[x] 34So in your prostitution you are the opposite of others; no one runs after you for your favors. You are the very opposite, for you give payment
and none is given to you.
35" 'Therefore, you prostitute, hear the word of the LORD! 36This is what the Sovereign
LORD says: Because you poured out your wealth[d] and exposed your nakedness in your
promiscuity with your lovers, and because of all your detestable idols, and because you
gave them your children's blood,[y] 37therefore I am going to gather all your lovers, with
whom you found pleasure, those you loved as well as those you hated. I will gather them
against you from all around and will strip you in front of them, and they will see all your

a *15* Most Hebrew manuscripts; one Hebrew manuscript (see some Septuagint manuscripts) *by. Such a thing should not happen* b *21* *Or and made them pass through ⌞the fire⌟* c *29* Or *Chaldea* d *36* Or *lust*

16:11
[s]Isa 3:19; Eze 23:42
[t]Ge 41:42

16:12
[u]Isa 3:21 [v]Isa 28:5; Jer 13:18

16:13
[w]1Sa 10:1
[x]Dt 32:13-14; 1Ki 4:21

16:14
[y]1Ki 10:24 [z]La 2:15

16:15
[a]ver 25 [b]Isa 57:8; Jer 2:20; Eze 23:3; 27:3

16:16
[c]2Ki 23:7

16:17
[d]Eze 7:20

16:19
[e]Hos 2:8

16:20
[f]Jer 7:31 [g]Ex 13:2
[h]Ps 106:37-38; Isa 57:5; Eze 23:37

16:21
[i]2Ki 17:17; Jer 19:5

16:22
[j]Jer 2:2; Hos 11:1
[k]ver 6

16:24
[l]ver 31; Isa 57:7
[m]Ps 78:58; Jer 2:20; 3:2; Eze 20:28

16:25
[n]ver 15; Pr 9:14

16:26
[o]Eze 8:17
[p]Eze 20:8; 23:19-21

16:27
[q]Eze 20:33
[r]2Ch 28:18

16:28
[s]2Ki 16:7

16:29
[t]Eze 23:14-17

16:30
[u]Jer 3:3

16:31
[v]ver 24

16:33
[w]Isa 30:6; 57:9
[x]Hos 8:9-10

16:36
[y]Jer 19:5; Eze 23:10

16:15–19 to become a prostitute. All that the queen had received from her loving husband and king was turned to use in wantonness and promiscuity. Contrast "you became mine" (v. 8) with "your beauty became his" (v. 15). Her actions demonstrate the irrationality of sin: There could be no sound reason for such behavior. See Deuteronomy 6:10–12.

16:20–21 See *WCF* 25.2.

16:20 sacrificed. On child sacrifice in Israel and neighboring states, see verse 36, 20:31, Genesis 22:2 and 13, Leviticus 18:21, 20:2–5, Deuteronomy 12:31, 18:10, 2 Kings 16:3, 17:17, 21:6, 23:10, 2 Chronicles 28:3, 33:6, Psalm 106:37–38, Jeremiah 32:35 and Micah 6:7. In Jerusalem these practices were associated with the Valley of Hinnom, south of the city.

16:26–29 prostitution . . . lewd conduct . . . prostitution . . . promiscuity. Israel's failure to obey God was not in the area of idolatry alone. Foreign alliances evidenced failure to trust God in periods of political difficulty and represented a breach in Israel's exclusive allegiance to the Lord. Compare 23:7, 29:16, Isaiah 7–8, 30–31, Jeremiah 2:36–37, 22:20–22, Lamentations 1:19 and Hosea 7:11–13 and 8:9. The Chronicler was particularly concerned to make this point in his history of Israel (2Ch 14:9–15; 16:1–9; 19:1–2; 20:1–37; 25:6–8; 28:1–36). See *WLC* 110.

16:26 lustful. Literally, "the ones with large flesh." Fertility icons and statues from the ancient Near East frequently display exaggerated genitalia. See 23:20.

16:37 gather them against. Jerusalem sought the loyalty and affection of her lovers, but they would be the instruments of her humiliation and punishment. Compare Revelation 17:15–17. The nations dealt treacherously with Jerusalem. Though they were the agents by which God punished his people, they would be punished for their actions (ch. 25; Isa 10:5,12; Zec 1:14–15); see note on 14:9. **strip you.** Compare verse 39. Public degradation by exposing the nakedness of prostitutes or adulteresses is also mentioned in Jeremiah 13:22 and 26, Hosea 2:10 and Nahum 3:5.

nakedness.[z] **38**I will sentence you to the punishment of women who commit adultery and
who shed blood;[a] I will bring upon you the blood vengeance of my wrath and jealous anger.[b] **39**Then I will hand you over to your lovers, and they will tear down your mounds
and destroy your lofty shrines. They will strip you of your clothes and take your fine jewelry and leave you naked and bare.[c] **40**They will bring a mob against you, who will stone[d]
you and hack you to pieces with their swords. **41**They will burn down[e] your houses and
inflict punishment on you in the sight of many women.[f] I will put a stop[g] to your prostitution, and you will no longer pay your lovers. **42**Then my wrath against you will subside and my jealous anger will turn away from you; I will be calm and no longer angry.[h]
43“ ‘Because you did not remember[i] the days of your youth but enraged me with all
these things, I will surely bring down[j] on your head what you have done, declares the
Sovereign LORD. Did you not add lewdness to all your other detestable practices?[k]
44“ ‘Everyone who quotes proverbs will quote this proverb about you: “Like mother,
like daughter.” **45**You are a true daughter of your mother, who despised her husband and
her children; and you are a true sister of your sisters, who despised their husbands and
their children. Your mother was a Hittite and your father an Amorite.[l] **46**Your older sister
was Samaria, who lived to the north of you with her daughters; and your younger sister,
who lived to the south of you with her daughters, was Sodom.[m] **47**You not only walked in
their ways and copied their detestable practices, but in all your ways you soon became
more depraved than they.[n] **48**As surely as I live, declares the Sovereign LORD, your sister
Sodom and her daughters never did what you and your daughters have done.[o]
49“ ‘Now this was the sin of your sister Sodom:[p] She and her daughters were arrogant,[q]
overfed and unconcerned; they did not help the poor and needy.[r] **50**They were haughty
and did detestable things before me. Therefore I did away with them as you have seen.[s]
51Samaria did not commit half the sins you did. You have done more detestable things
than they, and have made your sisters seem righteous by all these things you have done.[t]
52Bear your disgrace, for you have furnished some justification for your sisters. Because
your sins were more vile than theirs, they appear more righteous than you. So then, be
ashamed and bear your disgrace, for you have made your sisters appear righteous.
53“ ‘However, I will restore[u] the fortunes of Sodom and her daughters and of Samaria and her daughters, and your fortunes along with them, **54**so that you may bear your
disgrace[v] and be ashamed of all you have done in giving them comfort. **55**And your sisters, Sodom with her daughters and Samaria with her daughters, will return to what they
were before; and you and your daughters will return to what you were before.[w] **56**You
would not even mention your sister Sodom in the day of your pride, **57**before your wickedness was uncovered. Even so, you are now scorned by the daughters of Edom[a][x] and
all her neighbors and the daughters of the Philistines—all those around you who despise
you. **58**You will bear the consequences of your lewdness and your detestable practices,
declares the LORD.[y]
59“ ‘This is what the Sovereign LORD says: I will deal with you as you deserve, because
you have despised my oath by breaking the covenant.[z] **60**Yet I will remember the covenant I made with you in the days of your youth, and I will establish an everlasting covenant[a] with you. **61**Then you will remember your ways and be ashamed[b] when you receive your sisters, both those who are older than you and those who are younger. I will
give them to you as daughters, but not on the basis of my covenant with you. **62**So I will
establish my covenant with you, and you will know that I am the LORD.[c] **63**Then, when I
make atonement[d] for you for all you have done, you will remember and be ashamed and
never again open your mouth[e] because of your humiliation, declares the Sovereign
LORD.[f]’ ”

16:37 [z]Jer 13:22
16:38 [a]Eze 23:45 [b]Lev 20:10; Eze 23:25
16:39 [c]Eze 23:26; Hos 2:3
16:40 [d]Jn 8:5,7
16:41 [e]Dt 13:16 [f]Eze 23:10 [g]Eze 23:27,48
16:42 [h]Isa 54:9; Eze 5:13; 39:29
16:43 [i]Ps 78:42 [j]Eze 22:31 [k]ver 22; Eze 11:21
16:45 [l]Eze 23:2
16:46 [m]Ge 13:10-13; Eze 23:4
16:47 [n]2Ki 21:9; Eze 5:7
16:48 [o]Mt 10:15; 11:23-24
16:49 [p]Ge 13:13 [q]Ps 138:6 [r]Eze 18:7,12,16; Lk 12:16-20
16:50 [s]Ge 18:20-21; 19:5
16:51 [t]Jer 3:8-11
16:53 [u]Isa 19:24-25
16:54 [v]Jer 2:26; Eze 14:22
16:55 [w]Mal 3:4
16:57 [x]2Ki 16:6
16:58 [y]Eze 23:49
16:59 [z]Eze 17:19
16:60 [a]Jer 32:40; Eze 37:26
16:61 [b]Eze 20:43
16:62 [c]Jer 24:7; Eze 20:37,43-44; Hos 2:19-20
16:63 [d]Ps 65:3; 79:9 [e]Ro 3:19 [f]Ps 39:9; Da 9:7-8

[a] *57* Many Hebrew manuscripts and Syriac; most Hebrew manuscripts, Septuagint and Vulgate *Aram*

16:38 punishment . . . adultery. On the wrath of a jealous husband, see Proverbs 6:34. The woman's "lovers" would take her wealth and garments, leaving her as naked and bare as when the story began. She would be covered with the blood, not of her birth (v. 6), but of her wounds. The maximum penalty for adultery was death by stoning (Lev 20:10; Dt 22:21–24; cf. Jn 7:53—8:11).

16:41 burn down your houses. See 23:47. A large part of Jerusalem was burned by the Babylonian army (Jer 39:8; cf. Jer 32:29; 34:22; 37:8; 38:18).

16:44 proverbs. Ezekiel was fond of basing oracles on popular proverbs (12:21–28; 18:1–2). **Like mother, like daughter.** Generation after generation, Jerusalem's inhabitants were unfaithful to the Lord.

16:45 Hittite . . . Amorite. Assumed the moral depravity of the Hittites and Amorites; compare verse 3.

16:49 Sodom. People usually think of the sins of Sodom as sexual transgressions (Ge 19:5–9), but Ezekiel indicted the city for its materialism and neglect of the needy (although "detestable things" [v. 50] might include sexual sins). Jesus made a similar comparison with Capernaum in Matthew 11:23–24. The sins of Jerusalem had exceeded those of both her sisters, Samaria and Judah (Sodom). See *WLC* 139.

16:60 an everlasting covenant. Jerusalem would again have more influence than her sisters. God would renew his covenant with her, and in doing so he would vastly increase the blessings he would provide under it.

Two Eagles and a Vine

17 The word of the LORD came to me: 2"Son of man, set forth an allegory and tell
the house of Israel a parable.[g] 3Say to them, 'This is what the Sovereign LORD
says: A great eagle[h] with powerful wings, long feathers and full plumage of varied colors came to Lebanon.[i] Taking hold of the top of a cedar, 4he broke off its topmost shoot
and carried it away to a land of merchants, where he planted it in a city of traders.
5" 'He took some of the seed of your land and put it in fertile soil. He planted it like
a willow by abundant water,[j] 6and it sprouted and became a low, spreading vine. Its
branches turned toward him, but its roots remained under it. So it became a vine and
produced branches and put out leafy boughs.
7" 'But there was another great eagle with powerful wings and full plumage. The vine
now sent out its roots toward him from the plot where it was planted and stretched out
its branches to him for water.[k] 8It had been planted in good soil by abundant water so
that it would produce branches, bear fruit and become a splendid vine.'
9"Say to them, 'This is what the Sovereign LORD says: Will it thrive? Will it not be uprooted and stripped of its fruit so that it withers? All its new growth will wither. It will
not take a strong arm or many people to pull it up by the roots. 10Even if it[l] is transplanted, will it thrive? Will it not wither completely when the east wind strikes it—wither away
in the plot where it grew?' "
11Then the word of the LORD came to me: 12"Say to this rebellious house, 'Do you not
know what these things mean?[m]' Say to them: 'The king of Babylon went to Jerusalem
and carried off her king and her nobles,[n] bringing them back with him to Babylon.[o]
13Then he took a member of the royal family and made a treaty with him, putting him
under oath.[p] He also carried away the leading men of the land, 14so that the kingdom
would be brought low,[q] unable to rise again, surviving only by keeping his treaty. 15But
the king rebelled[r] against him by sending his envoys to Egypt to get horses and a large
army.[s] Will he succeed? Will he who does such things escape? Will he break the treaty
and yet escape?[t]
16" 'As surely as I live, declares the Sovereign LORD, he shall die[u] in Babylon, in the
land of the king who put him on the throne, whose oath he despised and whose treaty
he broke.[v] 17Pharaoh[w] with his mighty army and great horde will be of no help to him
in war, when ramps[x] are built and siege works erected to destroy many lives.[y] 18He despised the oath by breaking the covenant. Because he had given his hand in pledge[z] and
yet did all these things, he shall not escape.
19" 'Therefore this is what the Sovereign LORD says: As surely as I live, I will bring
down on his head my oath that he despised and my covenant that he broke.[a] 20I will
spread my net[b] for him, and he will be caught in my snare. I will bring him to Babylon
and execute judgment[c] upon him there because he was unfaithful to me. 21All his fleeing troops will fall by the sword,[d] and the survivors[e] will be scattered to the winds.[f] Then
you will know that I the LORD have spoken.
22" 'This is what the Sovereign LORD says: I myself will take a shoot from the very top
of a cedar and plant it; I will break off a tender sprig from its topmost shoots and plant
it on a high and lofty mountain.[g] 23On the mountain heights of Israel I will plant it; it will
produce branches and bear fruit and become a splendid cedar. Birds of every kind will
nest in it; they will find shelter in the shade of its branches.[h] 24All the trees of the field[i]

17:2 [g]Eze 20:49
17:3 [h]Hos 8:1 [i]Jer 22:23
17:5 [j]Dt 8:7-9; Isa 44:4
17:7 [k]Eze 31:4
17:10 [l]Hos 13:15
17:12 [m]Eze 12:9 [n]2Ki 24:15 [o]Eze 24:19
17:13 [p]2Ch 36:13
17:14 [q]Eze 29:14
17:15 [r]Jer 52:3 [s]Dt 17:16 [t]Jer 34:3; 38:18
17:16 [u]Jer 52:11; Eze 12:13 [v]2Ki 24:17
17:17 [w]Jer 37:7 [x]Eze 4:2 [y]Isa 36:6; Jer 37:5; Eze 29:6-7
17:18 [z]1Ch 29:24
17:19 [a]Eze 16:59
17:20 [b]Eze 12:13; 32:3 [c]Jer 2:35; Eze 20:36
17:21 [d]Eze 12:14 [e]2Ki 25:11 [f]2Ki 25:5
17:22 [g]Jer 23:5; Eze 20:40; 36:1, 36; 37:22
17:23 [h]Ps 92:12; Isa 2:2; Eze 31:6; Da 4:12; Hos 14:5-7; Mt 13:32
17:24 [i]Ps 96:12

16:61–63 See *WCF* 15.3.

■ **17:1–24** *A Parable of Two Eagles.* This oracle is not dated, but it probably came between the dates given in 8:1 and 20:1, which speak of the sixth and seventh years of the exile of Jehoiachin (592–590 B.C.). Nebuchadnezzar set siege to Jerusalem in 588 B.C. and removed Zedekiah from the throne in 586 (v. 20).

17:3 A great eagle. In Ezekiel's allegory, the imperial might of Babylon led by Nebuchadnezzar. **top of a cedar.** The kingdom of Judah and the dynasty of David that had endured by this time for over 300 years.

17:4 broke off its topmost shoot. A reference to the exile and captivity of Jehoiachin in Babylon. The exiles continued to regard Jehoiachin as the legitimate king of Judah; see note on 1:1–3.

17:6 low, spreading vine. Jerusalem under Zedekiah, who had been installed by Nebuchadnezzar after he had deported Jehoiachin (2Ki 24:15–17); the vine prospered, though on a humbler scale.

17:7 another great eagle. Egypt, led by Psammetichus II (595–589 B.C.) or Hophra (589–570 B.C.). Zedekiah shifted allegiance (vv. 15–17), resulting in Jerusalem's destruction.

17:10 east wind. See note on 19:12.

17:15 Egypt. Although the Old Testament historians did not mention Zedekiah's appeal to Egypt for help, Jeremiah did (Jer 37:5–11; 44:30). One of the Lachish letters, written on broken pottery during the last days of the kingdom of Judah, also reports that a commander of the army went to Egypt, perhaps to solicit assistance. See 16:26–29, 29:6–7 and 30:20–26.

17:16–19 See *WCF* 22.4; *WLC* 113,151.

17:20–21 he will be caught. See 2 Kings 25:4–7.

17:22 a shoot. The Bible often used a shoot, branch or tree as a symbol of royalty (Da 4:9–12,19–22). Ezekiel announced that God would restore a descendant of Jehoiachin ("the top of a cedar"; vv. 3,22) to kingship in Judah. This prediction was and will be fulfilled by Jesus the Messiah, the Branch of David (Isa 4:2; 11:1; 53:2; 60:21; Jer 23:5; 33:15; Zec 6:12).

17:23 Birds of every kind. Rather than be threatened by other kingdoms (birds such as eagles), this splendid cedar would become a haven for birds of all kinds (cf. Da 4:12,21; Mt 13:31–32). This tree would be fruitful (2Ki 19:30; Isa 11:1; 37:31; Jer 17:8; Jn 15:4,5, 8,16).

will know that I the LORD bring down the tall tree and make the low tree grow tall. I dry up the green tree and make the dry tree flourish.

"'I the LORD have spoken, and I will do it.[j]'"

17:24 [j]Eze 19:12; 21:26; 22:14; Am 9:11

The Soul Who Sins Will Die

18 The word of the LORD came to me: [2]"What do you people mean by quoting this proverb about the land of Israel:

"'The fathers eat sour grapes,
and the children's teeth are set on edge'?[k]

18:2 [k]Isa 3:15; Jer 31:29; La 5:7

[3]"As surely as I live, declares the Sovereign LORD, you will no longer quote this proverb in Israel. [4]For every living soul belongs to me, the father as well as the son—both alike belong to me. The soul who sins is the one who will die.[l]

18:4 [l]ver 20; Isa 42:5; Ro 6:23

[5]"Suppose there is a righteous man
who does what is just and right.
[6]He does not eat at the mountain[m] shrines
or look to the idols[n] of the house of Israel.
He does not defile his neighbor's wife
or lie with a woman during her period.
[7]He does not oppress[o] anyone,
but returns what he took in pledge[p] for a loan.
He does not commit robbery
but gives his food to the hungry
and provides clothing for the naked.[q]
[8]He does not lend at usury
or take excessive interest.[a][r]
He withholds his hand from doing wrong
and judges fairly[s] between man and man.
[9]He follows my decrees
and faithfully keeps my laws.
That man is righteous;[t]
he will surely live,[u]
declares the Sovereign LORD.

18:6 [m]Eze 22:9 [n]Dt 4:19; Eze 6:13; 20:24

18:7 [o]Ex 22:21 [p]Ex 22:26; Dt 24:12 [q]Dt 15:11; Mt 25:36

18:8 [r]Ex 22:25; Lev 25:35-37; Dt 23:19-20 [s]Zec 8:16

18:9 [t]Hab 2:4 [u]Lev 18:5; Eze 20:11; Am 5:4

[10]"Suppose he has a violent son, who sheds blood[v] or does any of these other things[b] [11](though the father has done none of them):

"He eats at the mountain shrines.
He defiles his neighbor's wife.
[12]He oppresses the poor[w] and needy.
He commits robbery.
He does not return what he took in pledge.
He looks to the idols.
He does detestable things.[x]
[13]He lends at usury and takes excessive interest.[y]

Will such a man live? He will not! Because he has done all these detestable things, he will surely be put to death and his blood will be on his own head.[z]

18:10 [v]Ex 21:12

18:12 [w]Am 4:1 [x]2Ki 21:11; Isa 59:6-7; Jer 22:17; Eze 8:6, 17

18:13 [y]Ex 22:25 [z]Eze 33:4-5

[a] 8 Or *take interest*; similarly in verses 13 and 17 [b] 10 Or *things to a brother*

■ **18:1–32** *Individual Responsibility.* The spiritual condition of the Israelites, both those in the land and those taken from the land, was so mixed that Ezekiel had to focus on calling individuals to responsibility. The exile was not the result of the sins of a single generation. Rather, the disobedience that had been endemic "from the day their forefathers came out of Egypt unto this day" (2Ki 21:15) brought judgment on both Israel and Judah. God judged their cumulative guilt in the events that led to the destruction of Jerusalem. The exiles' response was to question the justice of God. The popular proverb (v. 2; cf. Jer 31:29) in effect said, "It's not our fault—we are being punished for what we did not do. Our ancestors sinned, and we are paying the price." Ezekiel replied by emphasizing that God responded according to the acts of each individual and generation. The exiles could not evade their guilt; they were suffering for their own sins as well as for those of their ancestors.

18:2,4 See *HC* 14.

18:6 eat at the mountain shrines. A reference to sacrificial meals at the high places (6:13; 20:28; 22:9; 34:6; Ex 32:5–6). **during her period.** The law forbade sexual intercourse during this time (22:10; 36:17; Lev 12:2; 15:16–33; 18:19).

18:7 returns . . . pledge. See verses 12 and 16, Exodus 22:26, Deuteronomy 24:10–13 and 17, Proverbs 20:16, 27:13 and Amos 2:8. On an ostracon (a piece of broken pottery with writing on it) from late in the seventh century B.C., a field worker complained to a village official that his employer had taken his garment and had not returned it.

18:8 usury. See verses 13 and 17, Exodus 22:25, Leviticus 25:35–37 and Deuteronomy 23:19–20.

18:10 a violent son. Having a righteous father did not guarantee that an unrighteous son would escape punishment for his sin.

14 "But suppose this son has a son who sees all the sins his father commits, and though
he sees them, he does not do such things:[a]

15 "He does not eat at the mountain shrines
or look to the idols of the house of Israel.
He does not defile his neighbor's wife.
16 He does not oppress anyone
or require a pledge for a loan.
He does not commit robbery
but gives his food to the hungry
and provides clothing for the naked.[b]
17 He withholds his hand from sin[a]
and takes no usury or excessive interest.
He keeps my laws and follows my decrees.

He will not die for his father's sin; he will surely live.
18 But his father will die for his own
sin, because he practiced extortion, robbed his brother and did what was wrong among
his people.

18:14 [a]2Ch 34:21; Pr 23:24

18:16 [b]Ps 41:1; Isa 58:10

[a] *17* Septuagint (see also verse 8); Hebrew *from the poor*

18:14 son . . . things. On the other hand, having an unrighteous father would not bring judgment on a righteous son (see note on v. 10; see also Dt 24:16; 2Ki 14:6; 2Ch 25:4).
18:18 See *WLC* 136.

The Will of God: How Can I Know God's Will?

THE Scriptures speak of the will of God in a variety of ways. Even human wills are complex, so we should not be surprised to find that the divine will is multi-faceted. Reformed theology has traditionally stressed two senses in which we should understand God's will. Some Reformed theologians also speak of a third sense.

In the first place the Scriptures tell us of God's *decretive* will. This is his eternal decree of all that must take place in history, "his eternal purpose, according to the counsel of his will, whereby, for his own glory, he hath foreordained whatsoever comes to pass" (*WSC* 7). In this sense God's will is unchanging and cannot in any way be thwarted. What God has decreed will come to pass precisely as he has ordained.

The decretive will of God cannot be known ahead of time, except in glimpses revealed in the relatively few prophecies that God confirms by promise or oath. Even in these rare prophecies only the most general parameters can be discerned. The rest of God's eternal plan by which he orders the universe is hidden from human beings until it actually unfolds in history. For this reason we are called upon to trust the goodness of God that somehow he will work all things for our good (Ro 8:28).

In the second place, we may speak of God's *preceptive* will; that is, his will expressed in precepts or commands. This consists of God's moral requirements revealed in his general and special revelation. The preceptive will of God is the subject of many portions of Scripture (1Ch 13:2; Ezr 7:18; Ro 12:2; Eph 5:17; Col 1:9; 1Th 4:3-6; 5:16–18). This sense of God's will is already known in part through natural or general revelation. It can be known more fully by the study of Scripture, where it is recorded. In fact, one of the main purposes of revelation is to teach us the preceptive will of God.

Finally, many Christian traditions speak of God's *desiderative* will as his desire for things that will never come to pass and his regret over things that have already happened. Sometimes this concept is coupled with the idea that God cannot do whatever he pleases, which is clearly contrary to Scripture (Ps 115:3). Nevertheless, at times God truly expresses just such desire and regret (e.g., Ge 6:6–7; 2Sa 24:16; Eze 18:23,32; 33:11).

These expressions are not contrary to his decretive will—God is not compelled to bring some things to pass against his will or desire. Rather, God's desiderative will is closely related to his preceptive will in that it reveals his earnest desire that his precepts be obeyed. God's expressions of desire and regret also demonstrate his mercy and gracious intent toward his creatures, even when they rebel against him. For instance, God told Moses to move aside because he was going to destroy Israel (Ex 32:9–10). After hearing Moses' prayer, however, God relented and "did not bring on his people the disaster he had threatened" (Ex 32:14). God also told Ezekiel that he did not take pleasure in the death of the wicked (Eze 33:11); he desired repentance instead. This desire is frequently expressed at those times when the free offer of the gospel is in view (1Ti 2:4). God even expressed his concern for the wicked, pagan city of Nineveh (Jn 4:11), and Jesus told a personified Jerusalem that he would have gathered her under his wings had she been receptive (Mt 23:37). Some interpreters have also taken passages such as 1 Timothy 2:4 and 2 Peter 3:17 as expressions of God's desiderative will.

It is possible to know much about the desiderative will of God; it is revealed in his emotions, actions, instructions and providence. We may learn from his character and precepts what God desires of and for us. When we discern God's desires in these ways we should be moved to grateful and sincere service.

19 “Yet you ask, ‘Why does the son not share the guilt of his father?’ Since the son has
done what is just and right and has been careful to keep all my decrees, he will surely live.[c]
20 The soul who sins is the one who will die. The son will not share the guilt of the father,
nor will the father share the guilt of the son. The righteousness of the righteous man will
be credited to him, and the wickedness of the wicked will be charged against him.[d]
21 “But if a wicked man turns away from all the sins he has committed and keeps all my
decrees and does what is just and right, he will surely live; he will not die.[e] 22 None of the offenses he has committed will be remembered against him. Because of the righteous things
he has done, he will live.[f] 23 Do I take any pleasure in the death of the wicked? declares the
Sovereign LORD. Rather, am I not pleased[g] when they turn from their ways and live?[h]
24 “But if a righteous man turns from his righteousness and commits sin and does the
same detestable things the wicked man does, will he live? None of the righteous things
he has done will be remembered. Because of the unfaithfulness he is guilty of and because of the sins he has committed, he will die.[i]
25 “Yet you say, ‘The way of the Lord is not just.’ Hear, O house of Israel: Is my way unjust?[j] Is it not your ways that are unjust? 26 If a righteous man turns from his righteousness and commits sin, he will die for it; because of the sin he has committed he will die.
27 But if a wicked man turns away from the wickedness he has committed and does what
is just and right, he will save his life.[k] 28 Because he considers all the offenses he has committed and turns away from them, he will surely live; he will not die. 29 Yet the house of
Israel says, ‘The way of the Lord is not just.’ Are my ways unjust, O house of Israel? Is it
not your ways that are unjust?
30 “Therefore, O house of Israel, I will judge you, each one according to his ways, declares the Sovereign LORD. Repent![l] Turn away from all your offenses; then sin will not
be your downfall.[m] 31 Rid yourselves of all the offenses you have committed, and get a
new heart[n] and a new spirit. Why will you die, O house of Israel?[o] 32 For I take no pleasure in the death of anyone, declares the Sovereign LORD. Repent and live![p]

A Lament for Israel's Princes

19 “Take up a lament[q] concerning the princes[r] of Israel 2 and say:

“ ‘What a lioness was your mother
among the lions!
She lay down among the young lions
and reared her cubs.
3 She brought up one of her cubs,
and he became a strong lion.
He learned to tear the prey
and he devoured men.
4 The nations heard about him,
and he was trapped in their pit.
They led him with hooks
to the land of Egypt.[s]

5 “ ‘When she saw her hope unfulfilled,
her expectation gone,
she took another of her cubs
and made him a strong lion.[t]

18:19 [c]Ex 20:5; Dt 5:9; Jer 15:4; Zec 1:3-6
18:20 [d]Dt 24:16; 1Ki 8:32; 2Ki 14:6; Isa 3:11; Mt 16:27; Ro 2:9
18:21 [e]Eze 33:12,19
18:22 [f]Ps 18:20-24; Isa 43:25; Mic 7:19
18:23 [g]Ps 147:11 [h]Eze 33:11; 1Ti 2:4
18:24 [i]1Sa 15:11; 2Ch 24:17-20; Eze 3:20; 20:27; 2Pe 2:20-22
18:25 [j]Ge 18:25; Jer 12:1; Eze 33:17; Zep 3:5; Mal 2:17; 3:13-15
18:27 [k]Isa 1:18
18:30 [l]Mt 3:2 [m]Eze 7:3; 33:20; Hos 12:6
18:31 [n]Ps 51:10 [o]Isa 1:16-17; Eze 11:19; 36:26
18:32 [p]Eze 33:11
19:1 [q]Eze 26:17; 27:2, 32 [r]2Ki 24:6
19:4 [s]2Ki 23:33-34; 2Ch 36:4
19:5 [t]2Ki 23:34

18:24 commits sin. God would not allow himself to be merely an escape hatch in times of trouble; he cannot be looked to as Savior without also being received as Lord.
18:28 See *WLC* 76.
18:30–32 each one according to his ways. A summary statement. Sin can never be taken lightly in one's relationship with God. Yet in the solemn warnings about the gravity of sin and the threat it represents, there remains the assurance that God does not desire or delight in the death of any. Repentance is the way to life (2Ch 6:37; Isa 30:15; 59:20; Jer 18:8; Mt 3:2,8; 4:17: Mk 1:4,15; 6:12; Lk 5:32; 13:3,5; 15:7,10; 24:47; Ac 3:19; 8:22; 17:30; 2Co 7:10). God's repeated call for his people to repent of their sins indicates that despite his eternal decree some will not respond. God usually desires repentance—when he determines otherwise it is noted (e.g., Isa 6:10). See theological article “The Will of God” on page 1327. See *WCF* 15.2; *WLC* 76.
18:31 get a new heart and a new spirit. The gift of God (36:26) rather than the product of human effort (cf. Eph 2:8–9). Ezekiel exhorted the members of his audience to repent in order that God might grant them this blessing (v. 32).
■ **19:1–14** *Dirge Allegory for Israel's Kings.* Ezekiel presented an allegory in a form of Hebrew poetry ordinarily used for funeral dirges or laments. This kind of poetry has a special rhythm or meter that his listeners would immediately identify. Ezekiel used this same rhythm in 26:17–18, 27:12–19, 28:12–19 and 32:2–8.
19:2 lioness. The nation of Israel or the city of Jerusalem, which produced these cubs/kings; on Jerusalem as a mother, see Psalm 87:5, Isaiah 49:21, 50:1, 54:1 and Galatians 4:26–27. The lion image was frequently associated with Davidic kingship (Ge 49:9; 1Ki 10:20; Mic 5:8). The New Testament looked forward to the appearance of the Lion of the tribe of Judah to reestablish the final stages of the kingdom of God (Rev 5:5).
19:3 one of her cubs. Likely Jehoahaz, son of Josiah, who reigned for only three months before he was taken to Egypt as a captive of Pharaoh Neco in 609 B.C. (2Ki 23:30–35; 2Ch 36:2–4).
19:5 another of her cubs. Likely Jehoiachin. Ezekiel did not in-

6 He prowled among the lions,
for he was now a strong lion.
He learned to tear the prey
and he devoured men.[u]
7 He broke down[a] their strongholds
and devastated[v] their towns.
The land and all who were in it
were terrified by his roaring.
8 Then the nations[w] came against him,
those from regions round about.
They spread their net for him,
and he was trapped in their pit.[x]
9 With hooks they pulled him into a cage
and brought him to the king of Babylon.[y]
They put him in prison,
so his roar was heard no longer
on the mountains of Israel.[z]

10 " 'Your mother was like a vine in your vineyard[b]
planted by the water;
it was fruitful and full of branches
because of abundant water.[a]
11 Its branches were strong,
fit for a ruler's scepter.
It towered high
above the thick foliage,
conspicuous for its height
and for its many branches.[b]
12 But it was uprooted[c] in fury
and thrown to the ground.
The east wind made it shrivel,
it was stripped of its fruit;
its strong branches withered
and fire consumed them.[d]
13 Now it is planted in the desert,[e]
in a dry and thirsty land.[f]
14 Fire spread from one of its main[c] branches
and consumed[g] its fruit.
No strong branch is left on it
fit for a ruler's scepter.'[h]

This is a lament and is to be used as a lament."

Rebellious Israel

20 In the seventh year, in the fifth month on the tenth day, some of the elders of
Israel came to inquire of the LORD, and they sat down in front of me.[i]
2 Then the word of the LORD came to me: 3 "Son of man, speak to the elders of Israel
and say to them, 'This is what the Sovereign LORD says: Have you come to inquire[j] of me?
As surely as I live, I will not let you inquire of me, declares the Sovereign LORD.[k]'
4 "Will you judge them? Will you judge them, son of man? Then confront them with

19:6 [u]2Ki 24:9; 2Ch 36:9
19:7 [v]Eze 30:12
19:8 [w]2Ki 24:2 [x]2Ki 24:11
19:9 [y]2Ch 36:6 [z]2Ki 24:15
19:10 [a]Ps 80:8-11
19:11 [b]Eze 31:3; Da 4:11
19:12 [c]Eze 17:10 [d]Isa 27:11; Eze 28:17; Hos 13:15
19:13 [e]Eze 20:35 [f]Hos 2:3
19:14 [g]Eze 20:17 [h]Eze 15:4
20:1 [i]Eze 8:1
20:3 [j]Eze 14:3 [k]Mic 3:7

[a] *7* Targum (see Septuagint); Hebrew *He knew* [b] *10* Two Hebrew manuscripts; most Hebrew manuscripts *your blood* [c] *14* Or *from under its*

clude mention of Jehoiakim in his book. Second Kings does not mention exile for Jehoiachin (2Ki 23:36—24:7; cf. 2Ch 36:5–8); he apparently died in Jerusalem.

19:9 put him in prison. The wrath of Nebuchadnezzar fell on Jehoiachin for the rebellion of his father, Jehoiakim. Ezekiel described Jehoiachin's deportation in 597 B.C. after a reign of only three months (2Ki 24:8–16; 2Ch 36:9–10); Jehoiachin was imprisoned in Babylon until the reign of Evil-Merodach (562–560 B.C.; 2Ki 25:27–30).

19:12 east wind. As in 17:9–10. The east wind was an instrument of the Lord's will (Ex 10:13; 14:21; Ps 78:26; Hos 13:15; Jnh 4:8). Here it is a figure for Nebuchadnezzar and the Babylonians who plundered the land and subjected the people.

19:14 No strong branch. The kingdom of Judah ended when the vine was uprooted (v. 12) and no branch was left from which to fashion a ruler's scepter (v. 14). For commentary on the branch as a symbol of the Messianic king, see note on 17:22. Compare the preaching of John the Baptist (Lk 3:9).

■ **20:1–49** *The Nation's History and Future.* The elders gathered about a year later than the date last mentioned (8:1; cf. 14:1) to seek instruction from Ezekiel. Ezekiel explained why Israel was in its current condition and what could be expected in the future.

20:1 seventh year . . . fifth month . . . tenth day. The tenth of Ab, August 14, 591 B.C., five years to the day before Jerusalem was put to the torch (Jer 52:12).

the detestable practices of their fathers[l] 5and say to them: 'This is what the Sovereign
LORD says: On the day I chose[m] Israel, I swore with uplifted hand to the descendants of
the house of Jacob and revealed myself to them in Egypt. With uplifted hand I said to
them, "I am the LORD your God.[n]" 6On that day I swore to them that I would bring them
out of Egypt into a land I had searched out for them, a land flowing with milk and honey,[o] the most beautiful of all lands.[p] 7And I said to them, "Each of you, get rid of the vile
images[q] you have set your eyes on, and do not defile yourselves with the idols of Egypt.
I am the LORD your God.[r]"

8" 'But they rebelled against me and would not listen to me; they did not get rid of the
vile images they had set their eyes on, nor did they forsake the idols of Egypt.[s] So I said
I would pour out my wrath on them and spend my anger against them in Egypt.[t] 9But
for the sake of my name I did what would keep it from being profaned in the eyes of the
nations they lived among and in whose sight I had revealed myself to the Israelites by
bringing them out of Egypt.[u] 10Therefore I led them out of Egypt and brought them into
the desert.[v] 11I gave them my decrees and made known to them my laws, for the man
who obeys them will live by them.[w] 12Also I gave them my Sabbaths as a sign[x] between
us, so they would know that I the LORD made them holy.

13" 'Yet the people of Israel rebelled[y] against me in the desert. They did not follow my
decrees but rejected my laws—although the man who obeys them will live by them—and
they utterly desecrated my Sabbaths. So I said I would pour out my wrath[z] on them and
destroy them in the desert.[a] 14But for the sake of my name I did what would keep it from
being profaned in the eyes of the nations in whose sight I had brought them out.[b]
15Also with uplifted hand I swore to them in the desert that I would not bring them into
the land I had given them—a land flowing with milk and honey, most beautiful of all
lands[c]— 16because they rejected my laws and did not follow my decrees and desecrated my Sabbaths. For their hearts[d] were devoted to their idols.[e] 17Yet I looked on them
with pity and did not destroy them or put an end to them in the desert. 18I said to their
children in the desert, "Do not follow the statutes of your fathers[f] or keep their laws or
defile yourselves with their idols. 19I am the LORD your God;[g] follow my decrees and be
careful to keep my laws.[h] 20Keep my Sabbaths holy, that they may be a sign between us.
Then you will know that I am the LORD your God.[i]"

21" 'But the children rebelled against me: They did not follow my decrees, they were
not careful to keep my laws—although the man who obeys them will live by them—and
they desecrated my Sabbaths. So I said I would pour out my wrath on them and spend
my anger against them in the desert. 22But I withheld[j] my hand, and for the sake of my
name I did what would keep it from being profaned in the eyes of the nations in whose
sight I had brought them out. 23Also with uplifted hand I swore to them in the desert that
I would disperse them among the nations and scatter[k] them through the countries, 24be-
cause they had not obeyed my laws but had rejected my decrees and desecrated my Sabbaths,[l] and their eyes ⌞lusted⌟ after[m] their fathers' idols.[n] 25I also gave them over[o] to statutes that were not good and laws they could not live by;[p] 26I let them become defiled
through their gifts—the sacrifice of every firstborn[a]—that I might fill them with horror
so they would know that I am the LORD.[q]'

27"Therefore, son of man, speak to the people of Israel and say to them, 'This is what
the Sovereign LORD says: In this also your fathers blasphemed[r] me by forsaking me:[s]
28When I brought them into the land[t] I had sworn to give them and they saw any high
hill or any leafy tree, there they offered their sacrifices, made offerings that provoked me

20:4 [l]Eze 16:2; 22:2; Mt 23:32
20:5 [m]Dt 7:6 [n]Ex 6:7
20:6 [o]Ex 3:8; Jer 32:22 [p]Dt 8:7; Ps 48:2; Da 8:9
20:7 [q]Ex 20:4 [r]Ex 20:2; Lev 18:3; Dt 29:18
20:8 [s]Eze 7:8 [t]Isa 63:10
20:9 [u]Eze 36:22; 39:7
20:10 [v]Ex 13:18
20:11 [w]Lev 18:5; Dt 4:7-8; Ro 10:5
20:12 [x]Ex 31:13
20:13 [y]Ps 78:40 [z]Dt 9:8 [a]Nu 14:29; Ps 95:8-10; Isa 56:6
20:14 [b]Eze 36:23
20:15 [c]Ps 95:11; 106:26
20:16 [d]Nu 15:39 [e]Am 5:26
20:18 [f]Zec 1:4
20:19 [g]Ex 20:2 [h]Dt 5:32-33; 6:1-2; 8:1; 11:1; 12:1
20:20 [i]Jer 17:22
20:22 [j]Ps 78:38
20:23 [k]Lev 26:33; Dt 28:64
20:24 [l]ver 13 [m]Eze 6:9 [n]ver 16
20:25 [o]Ps 81:12 [p]2Th 2:11
20:26 [q]2Ki 17:17
20:27 [r]Ro 2:24 [s]Eze 18:24
20:28 [t]Ps 78:55, 58

a 26 Or *—making every firstborn pass through ⌞the fire⌟*

20:5 swore with uplifted hand. A repeated phrase in the chapter; see verses 5, 6, 15, 23, 28 and 42. God had pledged himself to Israel and would fulfill his promises. See Exodus 3:6–10 and 6:2–8.

20:8 idols of Egypt. The Pentateuch recounts no details of the religious life of the Israelites during their slavery in Egypt, but it is likely that they assimilated to the religion of the host culture there, as they would later do in Canaan. The incident of the golden calf (Ex 32) reflected the idolatry in Egypt. See 23:3 and Joshua 24:14.

20:11 my laws. God's gracious gift to Israel; a way of life (Dt 4:40; 32:46–47; Jos 1:7–8; see theological articles "The Law of God" at Ex 20 and "The Three Uses of the Law" at Ps 119).

20:12 Sabbaths. The Sabbath (20:13,16,21,24) was a law unique to Israel; it was a part that represented the whole of the law and is an important theme in Ezekiel (22:8,26; 23:38; 44:24; cf. Ne 13:18; Isa 56:2,4,6; Jer 17:19–27). See *WLC* 121.

20:13 Israel rebelled. The first generation in the wilderness rebelled against God (Ex 17:2; Nu 14:18; 16–17; 20:10,24; 25; 26:9; 27:14; Dt 1:26,43; 9:7; 31:27). **desecrated my Sabbaths.** See Numbers 15:32–36.

20:18–20 See *WLC* 121; *HC* 91.

20:23 swore to them in the desert. The threat of exile had already existed before the people entered the land (Dt 28:64–67; Lev 26:32–35); see Psalm 106:26. Moses predicted that, once in the land, they would rebel against the Lord (Dt 31:27,29; cf. 31:15–29).

20:25–26 laws they could not live by. Compare Romans 1:24–32. The law was God's gracious gift (see note on v. 11), but that law when perverted brought death. Ezekiel apparently regarded child sacrifice in Israel as a perversion of the laws regarding the firstborn in Exodus 13:1–16, 22:29, 34:19–20 and Numbers 18:15–16. The firstborn belonged to the Lord and were sacrificed (Nu 18:17–19), though children and some animals were to be redeemed. See note on 16:20–21.

to anger, presented their fragrant incense and poured out their drink offerings.[u] 29Then
I said to them: What is this high place you go to?' " (It is called Bamah[a] to this day.)

Judgment and Restoration

30"Therefore say to the house of Israel: 'This is what the Sovereign LORD says: Will you
defile yourselves[v] the way your fathers did and lust after their vile images?[w] 31When you
offer your gifts—the sacrifice of your sons[x] in[b] the fire—you continue to defile yourselves
with all your idols to this day. Am I to let you inquire of me, O house of Israel? As surely as I live, declares the Sovereign LORD, I will not let you inquire of me.[y]

32" 'You say, "We want to be like the nations, like the peoples of the world, who serve
wood and stone." But what you have in mind will never happen. 33As surely as I live, declares the Sovereign LORD, I will rule over you with a mighty hand and an outstretched
arm and with outpoured wrath.[z] 34I will bring you from the nations[a] and gather you from
the countries where you have been scattered—with a mighty hand and an outstretched
arm and with outpoured wrath.[b] 35I will bring you into the desert of the nations and
there, face to face, I will execute judgment[c] upon you. 36As I judged your fathers in the
desert of the land of Egypt, so I will judge you, declares the Sovereign LORD.[d] 37I will take
note of you as you pass under my rod,[e] and I will bring you into the bond of the covenant.[f] 38I will purge[g] you of those who revolt and rebel against me. Although I will bring
them out of the land where they are living, yet they will not enter the land of Israel. Then
you will know that I am the LORD.[h]

39" 'As for you, O house of Israel, this is what the Sovereign LORD says: Go and serve
your idols,[i] every one of you! But afterward you will surely listen to me and no longer profane my holy name with your gifts and idols.[j] 40For on my holy mountain, the high mountain of Israel, declares the Sovereign LORD, there in the land the entire house of Israel will
serve me, and there I will accept them. There I will require your offerings[k] and your
choice gifts,[c] along with all your holy sacrifices.[l] 41I will accept you as fragrant incense
when I bring you out from the nations and gather you from the countries where you have
been scattered, and I will show myself holy[m] among you in the sight of the nations.[n]
42Then you will know that I am the LORD,[o] when I bring you into the land of Israel,[p] the
land I had sworn with uplifted hand to give to your fathers. 43There you will remember
your conduct and all the actions by which you have defiled yourselves, and you will
loathe yourselves for all the evil you have done.[q] 44You will know that I am the LORD,
when I deal with you for my name's sake[r] and not according to your evil ways and your
corrupt practices, O house of Israel, declares the Sovereign LORD.[s]' "

Prophecy Against the South

45The word of the LORD came to me: 46"Son of man, set your face toward the south;
preach against the south and prophesy against[t] the forest of the southland.[u] 47Say to the
southern forest: 'Hear the word of the LORD. This is what the Sovereign LORD says: I am
about to set fire to you, and it will consume all your trees, both green and dry. The blazing flame will not be quenched, and every face from south to north will be scorched by
it.[v] 48Everyone will see that I the LORD have kindled it; it will not be quenched.[w]' "

49Then I said, "Ah, Sovereign LORD! They are saying of me, 'Isn't he just telling parables?[x]' "

20:28 [u]Eze 6:13
20:30 [v]ver 43 [w]Jer 16:12
20:31 [x]Eze 16:20 [y]Ps 106:37-39; Jer 7:31
20:33 [z]Jer 21:5
20:34 [a]2Co 6:17* [b]Isa 27:12-13;; Jer 44:6; La 2:4
20:35 [c]Jer 2:35
20:36 [d]Nu 11:1-35; 1Co 10:5-10
20:37 [e]Lev 27:32; Jer 33:13 [f]Eze 16:62
20:38 [g]Eze 34:17-22; Am 9:9-10 [h]Ps 95:11; Jer 44:14; Eze 13:9; Mal 3:3; Heb 4:3
20:39 [i]Jer 44:25 [j]Isa 1:13; Eze 43:7; Am 4:4
20:40 [k]Isa 60:7 [l]Isa 56:7; Mal 3:4
20:41 [m]Eze 28:25; 36:23 [n]Eze 11:17
20:42 [o]Eze 38:23 [p]Eze 34:13; 36:24
20:43 [q]Eze 6:9; 16:61; Hos 5:15
20:44 [r]Eze 36:22 [s]Eze 24:24
20:46 [t]Eze 21:2; Am 7:16 [u]Isa 30:6; Jer 13:19
20:47 [v]Isa 9:18-19; 13:8; Jer 21:14
20:48 [w]Jer 7:20
20:49 [x]Mt 13:13; Jn 16:25

[a] 29 *Bamah* means *high place.* [b] 31 Or *—making your sons pass through* [c] 40 Or *and the gifts of your firstfruits*

20:29 high place. The writer of Kings measured almost every king of Judah by what he did (or failed to do) about the high places around Jerusalem (e.g., Josiah's reforms in 2Ki 23).
20:32–38 want to be like the nations. Reflects 1 Samuel 8:20; the people had rejected God (vv. 7–8). But just as God had not abandoned earlier generations of his people, so through Ezekiel he promised a new exodus and a return to the wilderness experience. Just as only the faithful and obedient from those in the wilderness generation crossed into the land (Nu 14:30,38), so God would again purge the nation to bring a faithful people into it.
20:35 desert of the nations. Possibly the Arabian desert, which bordered the nations in which Israel was exiled. Israel would be judged in the desert just as the wilderness generation had been.
20:37 pass under my rod. An allusion to counting off animals for the tithe (Lev 27:32–33); it suggested that a tenth would be left (cf. Isa 6:13).
20:39 no longer profane my holy name. The goal of the catastrophes that periodically befell Israel was to produce a purified, purged and faithful remnant; see note on 6:8.
20:40 holy mountain. That is, Zion. That purified, faithful remnant would worship at God's holy mountain (Pss 43:3; 48:1; 87:1; 99:9; Isa 11:9; 27:13; 56:7; 57:13; 65:11,25; 66:20; Zec 8:3). The glory of the grace of God is that he deals with us not as our sins deserve but in mercy (20:44; Ezr 9:13; Job 33:27; Ps 103:10; La 3:22–23,31–33).
20:45–48 preach against the south. Specified as against Jerusalem in 21:1–5. Both here and in 21:4 disaster comes "from south to north," and it cannot be stopped (v. 48; 21:5). The threat came from Babylon, and Israel lay to the south. Disaster was commonly portrayed as coming from the north (Job 37:22; Isa 14:31; 41:25; Jer 1:13–15; 4:6; 6:1,22; 10:22; 13:20; 25:9; 47:2; 50:9,41; 51:48; Joel 2:20; Zec 6:8).
20:49 They are saying. Ridicule and mocking were often a prophet's lot (2Ki 2:23–24; 2Ch 36:16; Mt 20:19; 27:29; 2Pe 3:3).

Babylon, God's Sword of Judgment

21 The word of the LORD came to me: 2"Son of man, set your face against Jerusalem and preach against the sanctuary. Prophesy against[y] the land of Israel 3and say to her: 'This is what the LORD says: I am against you.[z] I will draw my sword from its scabbard and cut off from you both the righteous and the wicked.[a] 4Because I am going to cut off the righteous and the wicked, my sword will be unsheathed against everyone from south to north.[b] 5Then all people will know that I the LORD have drawn my sword from its scabbard; it will not return[c] again.'[d]

6"Therefore groan, son of man! Groan before them with broken heart and bitter grief.[e] 7And when they ask you, 'Why are you groaning?' you shall say, 'Because of the news that is coming. Every heart will melt and every hand go limp;[f] every spirit will become faint and every knee become as weak as water.' It is coming! It will surely take place, declares the Sovereign LORD."

8The word of the LORD came to me: 9"Son of man, prophesy and say, 'This is what the Lord says:

" 'A sword, a sword,
sharpened and polished—
10sharpened for the slaughter,[g]
polished to flash like lightning!

" 'Shall we rejoice in the scepter of my son ⌊Judah⌋? The sword despises every such stick.

11" 'The sword is appointed to be polished,[h]
to be grasped with the hand;
it is sharpened and polished,
made ready for the hand of the slayer.
12Cry out and wail, son of man,
for it is against my people;
it is against all the princes of Israel.
They are thrown to the sword
along with my people.
Therefore beat your breast.[i]

13" 'Testing will surely come. And what if the scepter ⌊of Judah⌋, which the sword despises, does not continue? declares the Sovereign LORD.'

14"So then, son of man, prophesy
and strike your hands[j] together.
Let the sword strike twice,
even three times.
It is a sword for slaughter—
a sword for great slaughter,
closing in on them from every side.[k]
15So that hearts may melt[l]
and the fallen be many,
I have stationed the sword for slaughter[a]
at all their gates.
Oh! It is made to flash like lightning,
it is grasped for slaughter.[m]
16O sword, slash to the right,
then to the left,
wherever your blade is turned.

21:2 [y]Eze 20:46
21:3 [z]Jer 21:13 [a]ver 9-11; Job 9:22
21:4 [b]Eze 20:47
21:5 [c]ver 30 [d]Na 1:9
21:6 [e]Isa 22:4
21:7 [f]Eze 22:14; 7:17
21:10 [g]Ps 110:5-6; Isa 34:5-6
21:11 [h]Jer 46:4
21:12 [i]Jer 31:19
21:14 [j]Nu 24:10 [k]Eze 6:11; 30:24
21:15 [l]2Sa 17:10 [m]Ps 22:14

[a] *15* Septuagint; the meaning of the Hebrew for this word is uncertain.

■ **21:1–32** *Babylon, God's Sword.* This section consists of three oracles united around the image of a sword (21:1–7,8–27,28–32). The Old Testament frequently described God as a warrior. As commander of the heavenly army he fought Israel's battles for her and guaranteed her security (Ex 15:3; Nu 10:9; Dt 7:17–24; Jos 6:15–19; Jdg 20:28; 1Sa 17:47; 2Ch 13:12; 20:15,17; 32:8; Ps 24:8; Isa 9:6; 13:2–6; 31:4; 42:13; Joel 3:9–14; Zec 14:3). His sword had been wielded against her enemies (Dt 32:41; Isa 31:8; 34:5–8; 66:16; Jer 25:31; 50:35–37; Zep 2:12), but that sword was now in the hands of the Babylonians and would be brandished against Judah and Jerusalem (cf. 1Ch 21:14–16,21). See note on 7:7.

21:8–17 A sword, a sword. Though the text does not specify this, it may be that Ezekiel again used a symbolic action (see note on 4:1–3). He may have been whirling, cutting and slashing with the sword in a dramatic dance as part of the oracle.

21:10,13 scepter. These verses are united with verse 27 in part by their allusions to Judah's scepter (Ge 49:10). A wooden scepter gave no contest against an iron sword. Judah was Nebuchadnezzar's target, and she was no match.

17 I too will strike my hands[n] together,
and my wrath[o] will subside.
I the LORD have spoken."

18 The word of the LORD came to me: 19 "Son of man, mark out two roads for the sword
of the king of Babylon to take, both starting from the same country. Make a signpost
where the road branches off to the city. 20 Mark out one road for the sword to come
against Rabbah of the Ammonites[p] and another against Judah and fortified Jerusalem.
21 For the king of Babylon will stop at the fork in the road, at the junction of the two roads,
to seek an omen: He will cast lots[q] with arrows, he will consult his idols, he will examine the liver.[r] 22 Into his right hand will come the lot for Jerusalem, where he is to set up
battering rams, to give the command to slaughter, to sound the battle cry, to set battering rams against the gates, to build a ramp and to erect siege works.[s] 23 It will seem like
a false omen to those who have sworn allegiance to him, but he will remind[t] them of
their guilt and take them captive.

24 "Therefore this is what the Sovereign LORD says: 'Because you people have brought
to mind your guilt by your open rebellion, revealing your sins in all that you do—because
you have done this, you will be taken captive.

25 " 'O profane and wicked prince of Israel, whose day has come, whose time of punishment has reached its climax,[u] 26 this is what the Sovereign LORD says: Take off the turban, remove the crown.[v] It will not be as it was: The lowly will be exalted and the exalted will be brought low.[w] 27 A ruin! A ruin! I will make it a ruin! It will not be restored until
he comes to whom it rightfully belongs; to him I will give it.'[x]

28 "And you, son of man, prophesy and say, 'This is what the Sovereign LORD says
about the Ammonites[y] and their insults:

" 'A sword,[z] a sword,
drawn for the slaughter,
polished to consume
and to flash like lightning!
29 Despite false visions concerning you
and lying divinations about you,
it will be laid on the necks
of the wicked who are to be slain,
whose day has come,
whose time of punishment has reached its climax.[a]
30 Return the sword to its scabbard.[b]
In the place where you were created,
in the land of your ancestry,[c]
I will judge you.
31 I will pour out my wrath upon you
and breathe out my fiery anger[d] against you;
I will hand you over to brutal men,
men skilled in destruction.[e]
32 You will be fuel for the fire,[f]
your blood will be shed in your land,
you will be remembered[g] no more;
for I the LORD have spoken.' "

21:17 [n]ver 14; Eze 22:13 [o]Eze 5:13
21:20 [p]Dt 3:11; Jer 49:2; Am 1:14
21:21 [q]Pr 16:33 [r]Nu 22:7; 23:23
21:22 [s]Eze 4:2; 26:9
21:23 [t]Nu 5:15
21:25 [u]Eze 35:5
21:26 [v]Jer 13:18 [w]Ps 75:7; Eze 17:24
21:27 [x]Ps 2:6; Jer 23:5-6; Eze 37:24; Hag 2:21-22
21:28 [y]Zep 2:8 [z]Jer 12:12
21:29 [a]ver 25; Eze 22:28; 35:5
21:30 [b]Jer 47:6 [c]Eze 16:3
21:31 [d]Eze 22:20-21 [e]Jer 51:20-23
21:32 [f]Mal 4:1 [g]Eze 25:10

21:18–23 mark out two roads. Ezekiel probably drew a map that looked something like an inverted *Y*, scratched into a clay tablet or in the dirt; see note on 4:1–3. Nebuchadnezzar would come from the north to a fork in the road. The left (eastern) route followed the major Transjordanian highway, commonly called the King's Highway, through Ammon. The right (western) route would take the Babylonians along the major international highway, the Via Maris, in the coastal plain not far from Jerusalem. The fork in the road was likely the intersection of these two major routes near Damascus.
21:21 omen. The Babylonians used various means to discern the will of the gods. (1) **cast lots with arrows.** (2) **consult his idols.** The idols were worship objects; it is not known how they were used to obtain oracles. (3) **examine the liver.** Divination by examining the contours and health of, as well as the markings on the livers of sheep and birds ("hepatoscopy") is widely attested in the ancient Near East. The people of Jerusalem might have wished these were false divinations (v. 23), but in this instance these lots were controlled by the Lord (Nu 23:23; Pr 16:33).
21:23 sworn allegiance. See comments on 17:18–19. Nebuchadnezzar set siege to Jerusalem by January 588 B.C. (v. 22).
21:25 prince. The profane and wicked prince was the last king of Judah, Zedekiah; see 17:1–10.
21:27 he comes to whom it rightfully belongs. An allusion to Genesis 49:10.
21:28 Ammonites. In the earlier section (vv. 18–23) it had appeared that the Babylonians would attack Jerusalem and spare Ammon. This third and last sword song corrected that misapprehension, for Ammon too would taste God's wrath in the fury of the Babylonians (Jer 25:21). Ammon had joined Jerusalem and Egypt in alliance against the Babylonians in 589 B.C. However, when Jerusalem had been attacked Ammon had taken advantage of her former ally (Jer 27:3; 40:11,14; 41:10,15; 49:2; cf. 2Ki 24:2).

Jerusalem's Sins

22 The word of the LORD came to me: 2 "Son of man, will you judge her? Will you
judge this city of bloodshed?[h] Then confront her with all her detestable practices[i] 3 and say: 'This is what the Sovereign LORD says: O city that brings on herself doom
by shedding blood[j] in her midst and defiles herself by making idols, 4 you have become
guilty because of the blood you have shed[k] and have become defiled by the idols you
have made. You have brought your days to a close, and the end of your years has come.[l]
Therefore I will make you an object of scorn to the nations and a laughingstock to all the
countries.[m] 5 Those who are near and those who are far away will mock you, O infamous
city, full of turmoil.

6 " 'See how each of the princes of Israel who are in you uses his power to shed blood.[n]
7 In you they have treated father and mother with contempt;[o] in you they have oppressed the alien and mistreated the fatherless and the widow.[p] 8 You have despised my
holy things and desecrated my Sabbaths.[q] 9 In you are slanderous men[r] bent on shedding blood; in you are those who eat at the mountain shrines[s] and commit lewd acts.[t]
10 In you are those who dishonor their fathers' bed; in you are those who violate women
during their period, when they are ceremonially unclean.[u] 11 In you one man commits a
detestable offense with his neighbor's wife, another shamefully defiles his daughter-in-
law,[v] and another violates his sister,[w] his own father's daughter. 12 In you men accept
bribes[x] to shed blood; you take usury and excessive interest[a] and make unjust gain from
your neighbors[y] by extortion. And you have forgotten me, declares the Sovereign LORD.

13 " 'I will surely strike my hands[z] together at the unjust gain[a] you have made and at
the blood[b] you have shed in your midst. 14 Will your courage endure or your hands be
strong in the day I deal with you? I the LORD have spoken,[c] and I will do it.[d] 15 I will disperse you among the nations and scatter[e] you through the countries; and I will put an
end to your uncleanness.[f] 16 When you have been defiled[b] in the eyes of the nations, you
will know that I am the LORD.' "

17 Then the word of the LORD came to me: 18 "Son of man, the house of Israel has become dross[g] to me; all of them are the copper, tin, iron and lead left inside a furnace.
They are but the dross of silver.[h] 19 Therefore this is what the Sovereign LORD says: 'Because you have all become dross, I will gather you into Jerusalem. 20 As men gather silver, copper, iron, lead and tin into a furnace to melt it with a fiery blast, so will I gather
you in my anger and my wrath and put you inside the city and melt you.[i] 21 I will gather
you and I will blow on you with my fiery wrath, and you will be melted inside her. 22 As
silver is melted[j] in a furnace, so you will be melted inside her, and you will know that I
the LORD have poured out my wrath upon you.' "[k]

23 Again the word of the LORD came to me: 24 "Son of man, say to the land, 'You are a
land that has had no rain or showers[c] in the day of wrath.'[l] 25 There is a conspiracy[m] of
her princes[d] within her like a roaring lion tearing its prey; they devour people,[n] take treasures and precious things and make many widows[o] within her. 26 Her priests do violence
to my law[p] and profane my holy things; they do not distinguish between the holy and the
common;[q] they teach that there is no difference between the unclean and the clean;[r] and
they shut their eyes to the keeping of my Sabbaths, so that I am profaned among them.[s]
27 Her officials within her are like wolves tearing their prey; they shed blood and kill people to make unjust gain.[t] 28 Her prophets whitewash[u] these deeds for them by false visions
and lying divinations. They say, 'This is what the Sovereign LORD says'—when the LORD

22:2 [h]Eze 24:6,9; Na 3:1 [i]Eze 16:2
22:3 [j]ver 6,13,27; Eze 23:37,45
22:4 [k]2Ki 21:16 [l]Eze 21:25 [m]Eze 5:14
22:6 [n]Isa 1:23
22:7 [o]Dt 5:16; 27:16 [p]Ex 22:21-22
22:8 [q]Eze 23:38-39
22:9 [r]Lev 19:16 [s]Eze 18:11 [t]Hos 4:10,14
22:10 [u]Lev 18:8,19
22:11 [v]Lev 18:15 [w]Lev 18:9; 2Sa 13:14
22:12 [x]Dt 27:25; Mic 7:3 [y]Lev 19:13
22:13 [z]Eze 21:17 [a]Isa 33:15 [b]ver 3
22:14 [c]Eze 24:14 [d]Eze 17:24; 21:7
22:15 [e]Dt 4:27; Zec 7:14 [f]Eze 23:27
22:18 [g]Ps 119:119; Isa 1:22 [h]Jer 6:28-30
22:20 [i]Mal 3:2
22:22 [j]Isa 1:25 [k]Eze 20:8, 33
22:24 [l]Eze 24:13
22:25 [m]Jer 11:9 [n]Hos 6:9 [o]Jer 15:8
22:26 [p]Mal 2:7-8 [q]Eze 44:23 [r]Lev 10:10 [s]1Sa 2:12-17; Jer 2:8,26; Hag 2:11-14
22:27 [t]Isa 1:23
22:28 [u]Eze 13:10

[a] 12 Or *usury and interest* [b] 16 Or *When I have allotted you your inheritance* [c] 24 Septuagint; Hebrew *has not been cleansed or rained on* [d] 25 Septuagint; Hebrew *prophets*

■ **22:1–31** *The Sins of Jerusalem.* This chapter consists of three oracles (vv. 1–16,17–22,23–31), each introduced by the phrase "the word of the LORD came to me" (vv. 1,17,23). All three serve to indict Jerusalem for her crimes.

22:1–16 city of bloodshed. This, the first of three oracles, revolved around the repeated use of the term *blood* (vv. 2,3,4,6,9, 12,13; cf. 22:27). Jerusalem was indicted for both moral and ritual crimes.

22:7 father and mother. They abused their own parents (Dt 5:16; Mic 7:6; Mt 10:21; Ro 1:30; Eph 6:1; Col 3:20; 2Ti 3:2). **the alien . . . the fatherless and the widow.** These were the ones "without" in ancient Israel: without political rights, parents and providers. As such, they were the particular objects of God's care and protection (Dt 10:18; 14:29; 16:11,14; 24:17; 26:12–13; 27:19; Pss 68:5; 94:6; 146:9; Isa 1:17,23; 10:2; Jer 7:6; 22:3; Zec 7:10; Mal 3:5).

22:11 detestable offense. On the range of forbidden sexual relations, see Leviticus 18:6–23 and 20:10–21; compare Deuteronomy 22:30 and 27:20.

22:12 usury. See 18:8. See *WLC* 142.

22:18 dross . . . left inside a furnace. The periodic outpouring of divine judgment upon Israel was designed to purge her of her sins and to produce a pure people; see note on 6:8. Just as Israel's experience in Egypt was likened to time in a furnace (Dt 4:20; 1Ki 8:51; Jer 11:4), so too the exile would be the refiner's furnace. Refining is a common image for purgation (Pss 66:10; 119:119; Pr 17:3; 25:4; 27:21; Isa 1:25; 48:10; Jer 9:7; Zec 13:9; Mal 3:2–3; 1Co 3:12–15; 1Pe 1:7).

22:21 blow. God would blow on the flame, his breath a bellows to stoke the fire hotter. The fear was that no silver would emerge from the furnace—there would only be dross.

22:26 See *WLC* 119,121; *WSC* 61.

has not spoken.[v] 29 The people of the land practice extortion and commit robbery; they oppress the poor and needy and mistreat the alien,[w] denying them justice.[x]
30 "I looked for a man among them who would build up the wall[y] and stand before me
in the gap on behalf of the land so I would not have to destroy it, but I found none.[z] 31 So
I will pour out my wrath on them and consume them with my fiery anger, bringing
down[a] on their own heads all they have done, declares the Sovereign LORD.[b]"

Two Adulterous Sisters

23 The word of the LORD came to me: 2 "Son of man, there were two women,
daughters of the same mother.[c] 3 They became prostitutes in Egypt,[d] engaging
in prostitution[e] from their youth. In that land their breasts were fondled and their virgin bosoms caressed. 4 The older was named Oholah, and her sister was Oholibah. They
were mine and gave birth to sons and daughters. Oholah is Samaria, and Oholibah is Jerusalem.
5 "Oholah engaged in prostitution while she was still mine; and she lusted after her
lovers, the Assyrians[f]—warriors[g] 6 clothed in blue, governors and commanders, all of
them handsome young men, and mounted horsemen. 7 She gave herself as a prostitute
to all the elite of the Assyrians and defiled herself with all the idols of everyone she lusted after.[h] 8 She did not give up the prostitution she began in Egypt,[i] when during her
youth men slept with her, caressed her virgin bosom and poured out their lust upon her.[j]
9 "Therefore I handed her over[k] to her lovers, the Assyrians, for whom she lusted.[l]
10 They stripped[m] her naked, took away her sons and daughters and killed her with the
sword. She became a byword among women,[n] and punishment was inflicted on her.[o]
11 "Her sister Oholibah saw this, yet in her lust and prostitution she was more depraved than her sister.[p] 12 She too lusted after the Assyrians—governors and commanders, warriors in full dress, mounted horsemen, all handsome young men.[q] 13 I saw that
she too defiled herself; both of them went the same way.
14 "But she carried her prostitution still further. She saw men portrayed on a wall,[r] figures of Chaldeans[a] portrayed in red,[s] 15 with belts around their waists and flowing turbans on their heads; all of them looked like Babylonian chariot officers, natives of Chaldea.[b] 16 As soon as she saw them, she lusted after them and sent messengers to them in
Chaldea. 17 Then the Babylonians came to her, to the bed of love, and in their lust they
defiled her. After she had been defiled by them, she turned away from them in disgust.
18 When she carried on her prostitution openly and exposed her nakedness, I turned
away[t] from her in disgust, just as I had turned away from her sister.[u] 19 Yet she became
more and more promiscuous as she recalled the days of her youth, when she was a prostitute in Egypt. 20 There she lusted after her lovers, whose genitals were like those of donkeys and whose emission was like that of horses. 21 So you longed for the lewdness of your
youth, when in Egypt your bosom was caressed and your young breasts fondled.[c][v]
22 "Therefore, Oholibah, this is what the Sovereign LORD says: I will stir up your lovers against you, those you turned away from in disgust, and I will bring them against you
from every side[w]— 23 the Babylonians[x] and all the Chaldeans, the men of Pekod[y] and
Shoa and Koa, and all the Assyrians with them, handsome young men, all of them governors and commanders, chariot officers and men of high rank, all mounted on horses.[z]

a *14* Or *Babylonians* b *15* Or *Babylonia*; also in verse 16 c *21* Syriac (see also verse 3); Hebrew *caressed because of your young breasts*

22:28 [v]Eze 13:2,6-7
22:29 [w]Ex 22:21; 23:9 [x]Isa 5:7
22:30 [y]Eze 13:5 [z]Ps 106:23; Jer 5:1
22:31 [a]Eze 16:43 [b]Eze 7:8-9; 9:10; Ro 2:8
23:2 [c]Jer 3:7; Eze 16:45
23:3 [d]Jos 24:14 [e]Lev 17:7
23:5 [f]2Ki 16:7; Hos 5:13 [g]Hos 8:9
23:7 [h]Hos 5:3; 6:10
23:8 [i]Ex 32:4 [j]Eze 16:15
23:9 [k]2Ki 18:11 [l]Hos 11:5
23:10 [m]Hos 2:10 [n]Eze 16:41 [o]Eze 16:36
23:11 [p]Jer 3:8-11; Eze 16:51
23:12 [q]2Ki 16:7-15; 2Ch 28:16
23:14 [r]Eze 8:10 [s]Jer 22:14
23:18 [t]Ps 78:59; 106:40; Jer 6:8 [u]Jer 12:8; Am 5:21
23:21 [v]Eze 16:26
23:22 [w]Eze 16:37
23:23 [x]2Ki 20:14-18 [y]Jer 50:21 [z]2Ki 24:2

22:29 See *WLC* 142.
22:30 gap. See 13:5.
■ **23:1–49** *A Parable of Two Lewd Sisters.* An allegory in which Ezekiel presented Samaria and Jerusalem as two lewd sisters. "Oholah" represented Samaria, the capital of the northern kingdom, while "Oholibah" signified Jerusalem, capital of the southern kingdom (20:4). Ezekiel described Oholah first (vv. 4–10) and then her sister (vv. 11–35); he summarized their history and pronounced their sentence (vv. 36–49).
23:3 prostitutes. Though Ezekiel emphasized that each individual and generation would bear responsibility for its own sin (see note on 18:1–32), he also saw guilt as cumulative and punishment as deferred. Here the sins for which the two kingdoms are to be judged began with their prostitution in Egypt. See 16:26 and 20:4–9.
23:4 mine. The sisters were the Lord's "wives"; that is, they had a covenant relationship with him.
23:5 lovers. Foreign alliances broke Israel's oath of exclusive allegiance to the Lord as much as idolatry had done (vv. 5–10; 16:26–29 note; cf. Hos 8:9). Her prostitution did not secure the admiration or affection of her Assyrian lovers—quite the contrary (23:9–10). Assyria destroyed the northern kingdom (2Ki 17:5–6).
23:11 more depraved. Rather than learn from Samaria's experience, Jerusalem did even worse. After the destruction of the northern kingdom Assyria was the dominant political force in Judah for the next century (2Ki 15:29; 16:7–10; 17:3–6; 18–19; 2Ch 28:16–21; 30:6; 32:1–22; 33:11). Extra-Biblical texts also confirm contacts with the kings of Assyria on the part of both Israel and Judah.
23:14–16 See *WLC* 139.
23:14 still further. Judah entered into anti-Assyrian alliances with the Babylonians (2Ki 20:12–18; 23:29; 2Ch 33:11; Isa 39:1). The pro-Babylonian policy occasionally became anti-Babylonian (23:17) and included overtures to Egypt (23:19–21).
23:20 genitals. See note at 16:26. **like those of donkeys . . . horses.** An allusion to bestiality, a capital offense in Israel (see Ex 22:19).
23:23 Pekod and Shoa and Koa. Identified with Aramean tribes that occupied areas east of the Tigris River. Tribes with names approximately the equivalent of these are known from that region from Assyrian and Babylonian inscriptions.

24 They will come against you with weapons,[a] chariots and wagons[a] and with a throng of people; they will take up positions against you on every side with large and small shields and with helmets. I will turn you over to them for punishment,[b] and they will punish you according to their standards. 25 I will direct my jealous anger against you, and they will deal with you in fury. They will cut off your noses and your ears, and those of you who are left will fall by the sword. They will take away your sons and daughters,[c] and those of you who are left will be consumed by fire.[d] 26 They will also strip[e] you of your clothes and take your fine jewelry.[f] 27 So I will put a stop[g] to the lewdness and prostitution you began in Egypt. You will not look on these things with longing or remember Egypt anymore.

28 "For this is what the Sovereign LORD says: I am about to hand you over[h] to those you hate, to those you turned away from in disgust. 29 They will deal with you in hatred and take away everything you have worked for. They will leave you naked and bare, and the shame of your prostitution will be exposed. Your lewdness and promiscuity[i] 30 have brought this upon you, because you lusted after the nations and defiled yourself with their idols.[j] 31 You have gone the way of your sister; so I will put her cup[k] into your hand.[l]

32 "This is what the Sovereign LORD says:

"You will drink your sister's cup,
a cup large and deep;
it will bring scorn and derision,
for it holds so much.[m]
33 You will be filled with drunkenness and sorrow,
the cup of ruin and desolation,
the cup of your sister Samaria.[n]
34 You will drink it[o] and drain it dry;
you will dash it to pieces
and tear your breasts.

I have spoken, declares the Sovereign LORD.

35 "Therefore this is what the Sovereign LORD says: Since you have forgotten[p] me and thrust me behind your back,[q] you must bear the consequences of your lewdness and prostitution."

36 The LORD said to me: "Son of man, will you judge Oholah and Oholibah? Then confront[r] them with their detestable practices,[s] 37 for they have committed adultery and blood is on their hands. They committed adultery with their idols; they even sacrificed their children, whom they bore to me,[b] as food for them.[t] 38 They have also done this to me: At that same time they defiled my sanctuary and desecrated my Sabbaths. 39 On the very day they sacrificed their children to their idols, they entered my sanctuary and desecrated[u] it. That is what they did in my house.[v]

40 "They even sent messengers for men who came from far away,[w] and when they arrived you bathed yourself for them, painted your eyes[x] and put on your jewelry.[y] 41 You sat on an elegant couch,[z] with a table[a] spread before it on which you had placed the incense and oil that belonged to me.

42 "The noise of a carefree crowd was around her; Sabeans[c] were brought from the desert along with men from the rabble, and they put bracelets[b] on the arms of the woman and her sister and beautiful crowns on their heads.[c] 43 Then I said about the one worn out by adultery, 'Now let them use her as a prostitute,[d] for that is all she is.' 44 And they slept with her. As men sleep with a prostitute, so they slept with those lewd women, Oholah and Oholibah. 45 But righteous men will sentence them to the punishment of women who commit adultery and shed blood, because they are adulterous and blood is on their hands.[e]

46 "This is what the Sovereign LORD says: Bring a mob[f] against them and give them over to terror and plunder. 47 The mob will stone them and cut them down with their swords; they will kill their sons and daughters and burn[g] down their houses.[h]

23:24 [a]Jer 47:3; Eze 26:7, 10; Na 2:4 [b]Jer 39:5-6
23:25 [c]ver 47 [d]Eze 20:47-48
23:26 [e]Jer 13:22 [f]Isa 3:18-23; Eze 16:39
23:27 [g]Eze 16:41
23:28 [h]Jer 34:20
23:29 [i]Dt 28:48
23:30 [j]Eze 6:9
23:31 [k]Jer 25:15 [l]2Ki 21:13
23:32 [m]Ps 60:3; Isa 51:17; Jer 25:15
23:33 [n]Jer 25:15-16
23:34 [o]Ps 75:8; Isa 51:17
23:35 [p]Isa 17:10; Jer 3:21 [q]1Ki 14:9
23:36 [r]Eze 16:2 [s]Isa 58:1; Eze 22:2; Mic 3:8
23:37 [t]Eze 16:36
23:39 [u]2Ki 21:4 [v]Jer 7:10
23:40 [w]Isa 57:9 [x]2Ki 9:30 [y]Jer 4:30; Eze 16:13-19
23:41 [z]Est 1:6; Pr 7:17; Am 6:4 [a]Isa 65:11; Eze 44:16
23:42 [b]Ge 24:30 [c]Eze 16:11-12
23:43 [d]ver 3
23:45 [e]Lev 20:10; Eze 16:38; Hos 6:5
23:46 [f]Eze 16:40
23:47 [g]2Ch 36:19 [h]2Ch 36:17; Eze 16:40-41

a *24* The meaning of the Hebrew for this word is uncertain. b *37* Or *even made the children they bore to me pass through* ⌊*the fire*⌋ c *42* Or *drunkards*

23:29 naked and bare. See 16:35–41.

23:31–34 cup. A common metaphor in the Bible, sometimes symbolic of God's blessings (Pss 16:5; 23:5; 116:13; 1Co 10:16), sometimes of his fury and anger (75:7–8; Isa 51:17–20; Jer 25:12–29; 49:12; 51:7; La 4:21; Hab 2:16; Zec 12:2; Rev 14:9–11). The cup of God's wrath was the cup about which Jesus prayed in the Garden of Gethsemane (Mt 26:39,42) and was a focal point in John's account of the crucifixion (Jn 18:11; 19:28–30).

23:37–39 See *WLC* 119,151; *WSC* 61.

23:40 put on your jewelry. Compare 16:11 and 17, 2 Kings 9:30, Jeremiah 4:30 and Hosea 2:13. See *WLC* 139.

[48]"So I will put an end to lewdness in the land, that all women may take warning and
not imitate you.[i] [49]You will suffer the penalty for your lewdness and bear the consequences of your sins of idolatry. Then you will know that I am the Sovereign LORD.[j]"

The Cooking Pot

24 In the ninth year, in the tenth month on the tenth day, the word of the LORD
came to me:[k] [2]"Son of man, record this date, this very date, because the king
of Babylon has laid siege to Jerusalem this very day.[l] [3]Tell this rebellious house[m] a parable[n] and say to them: 'This is what the Sovereign LORD says:

" 'Put on the cooking pot;[o] put it on
and pour water into it.
[4]Put into it the pieces of meat,
all the choice pieces—the leg and the shoulder.
Fill it with the best of these bones;
[5]take the pick of the flock.[p]
Pile wood beneath it for the bones;
bring it to a boil
and cook the bones in it.[q]

[6]" 'For this is what the Sovereign LORD says:

" 'Woe to the city of bloodshed,[r]
to the pot now encrusted,
whose deposit will not go away!
Empty it piece by piece
without casting lots[s] for them.

[7]" 'For the blood she shed is in her midst:
She poured it on the bare rock;
she did not pour it on the ground,
where the dust would cover it.[t]
[8]To stir up wrath and take revenge
I put her blood on the bare rock,
so that it would not be covered.

[9]" 'Therefore this is what the Sovereign LORD says:

" 'Woe to the city of bloodshed!
I, too, will pile the wood high.
[10]So heap on the wood
and kindle the fire.
Cook the meat well,
mixing in the spices;
and let the bones be charred.
[11]Then set the empty pot on the coals
till it becomes hot and its copper glows
so its impurities may be melted
and its deposit burned away.[u]
[12]It has frustrated all efforts;
its heavy deposit has not been removed,
not even by fire.

[13]" 'Now your impurity is lewdness. Because I tried to cleanse you but you would not

23:48 [i]2Pe 2:6
23:49 [j]Eze 7:4; 9:10; 20:38
24:1 [k]Eze 8:1
24:2 [l]2Ki 25:1; Jer 39:1; 52:4
24:3 [m]Isa 1:2; Eze 2:3,6 [n]Eze 17:2; 20:49 [o]Jer 1:13; Eze 11:3
24:5 [p]Jer 52:10 [q]Jer 52:24-27
24:6 [r]Eze 22:2 [s]Ob 1:11; Na 3:10
24:7 [t]Lev 17:13
24:11 [u]Jer 21:10; Eze 22:15

■ **24:1–14** *A Cooking Pot.* Ezekiel described a cooking pot (vv. 3–5), then in two oracles applied its significance (vv. 6–8,9–14). He introduced each oracle with the phrase "this is what the Sovereign LORD says, 'Woe to the city of bloodshed' " (24:6,9).

24:1 ninth year . . . tenth month . . . tenth day. Of Jehoiachin's reign; January 15, 588 B.C., the beginning of the siege of Jerusalem by Nebuchadnezzar. The date is also known from 2 Kings 25:1 and Jeremiah 52:4. It was commemorated annually with a fast among the exiles (Zec 8:19). God revealed to Ezekiel information about events taking place hundreds of miles away in Jerusalem.

24:3 the cooking pot. Jerusalem; an image used in 11:2–12 (cf. Jer 1:13–14; Mic 3:3). Preparations were made for a festive meal, the best meats were to be cooked.

24:6 deposit. Ezekiel looked at the corrosion in the pot or the baked-on remains of its contents and likened it to the bloodshed and guilt in Jerusalem. Though its occupants were removed piece by piece and dispersed to the far corners of the world, its guilt remained like corrosion in the bottom of the pot. Compare the denunciation of the bloodshed in the city in 22:1–16, 35:6, 36:18, 2 Kings 21:16, 24:4, Isaiah 5:7, 26:21, 59:7, Lamentations 4:13, Hosea 4:2, Joel 3:21 and Micah 3:10.

24:7 cover. Blood, shed and uncovered, cried out to be avenged; compare the same concept in Genesis 4:10 and Job 16:18.

24:11 hot. The pot was emptied in an effort to cleanse it, but the corrosion was so great that even heating the pot until it glowed could not purify it. God would destroy Jerusalem.

be cleansed from your impurity, you will not be clean again until my wrath against you
has subsided.[v]
[14]" 'I the LORD have spoken. The time has come for me to act. I will not hold back; I
will not have pity, nor will I relent. You will be judged according to your conduct and your
actions,[w] declares the Sovereign LORD.[x]' "

Ezekiel's Wife Dies

[15]The word of the LORD came to me: [16]"Son of man, with one blow I am about to take
away from you the delight of your eyes. Yet do not lament or weep or shed any tears.[y]
[17]Groan quietly; do not mourn for the dead. Keep your turban fastened and your sandals
on your feet; do not cover the lower part of your face or eat the customary food ⌞of
mourners⌟.[z]"
[18]So I spoke to the people in the morning, and in the evening my wife died. The next
morning I did as I had been commanded.
[19]Then the people asked me, "Won't you tell us what these things have to do
with us?[a]"
[20]So I said to them, "The word of the LORD came to me: [21]Say to the house of Israel,
'This is what the Sovereign LORD says: I am about to desecrate my sanctuary—the
stronghold in which you take pride, the delight of your eyes,[b] the object of your affection. The sons and daughters[c] you left behind will fall by the sword.[d] [22]And you will do
as I have done. You will not cover the lower part of your face or eat the customary food
⌞of mourners⌟.[e] [23]You will keep your turbans on your heads and your sandals on your
feet. You will not mourn[f] or weep but will waste away because of[a] your sins and groan
among yourselves.[g] [24]Ezekiel will be a sign[h] to you; you will do just as he has done. When
this happens, you will know that I am the Sovereign LORD.'
[25]"And you, son of man, on the day I take away their stronghold, their joy and glory,
the delight of their eyes, their heart's desire, and their sons and daughters[i] as well— [26]on
that day a fugitive will come to tell you[j] the news. [27]At that time your mouth will be
opened; you will speak with him and will no longer be silent. So you will be a sign to
them, and they will know that I am the LORD.[k]"

A Prophecy Against Ammon

25 The word of the LORD came to me: [2]"Son of man, set your face against the Ammonites[l] and prophesy against them.[m] [3]Say to them, 'Hear the word of the Sovereign LORD. This is what the Sovereign LORD says: Because you said "Aha![n]" over my
sanctuary when it was desecrated and over the land of Israel when it was laid waste and
over the people of Judah when they went into exile,[o] [4]therefore I am going to give you
to the people of the East[p] as a possession. They will set up their camps and pitch their
tents among you; they will eat your fruit and drink your milk.[q] [5]I will turn Rabbah[r] into
a pasture for camels and Ammon into a resting place for sheep.[s] Then you will know that

24:13 [v]Jer 6:28-30; Eze 16:42; 22:24
24:14 [w]Eze 36:19 [x]Eze 18:30
24:16 [y]Jer 13:17; 16:5; 22:10
24:17 [z]Jer 16:7
24:19 [a]Eze 12:9; 37:18
24:21 [b]Ps 27:4 [c]Eze 23:25 [d]Jer 7:14,15; Eze 23:47
24:22 [e]Jer 16:7
24:23 [f]Job 27:15 [g]Ps 78:64
24:24 [h]Isa 20:3; Eze 4:3; 12:11
24:25 [i]Jer 11:22
24:26 [j]1Sa 4:12; Job 1:15-19
24:27 [k]Eze 3:26; 33:22
25:2 [l]Eze 21:28; Zep 2:8-9 [m]Jer 49:1-6
25:3 [n]Eze 26:2; 36:2 [o]Pr 17:5
25:4 [p]Jdg 6:3 [q]Dt 28:33, 51; Jdg 6:33
25:5 [r]Dt 3:11; Eze 21:20 [s]Isa 17:2

[a] *23* Or *away in*

■ **24:15–27** *The Death of Ezekiel's Wife.* Customary mourning rites included lamenting and weeping (27:31; Ge 23:2; 37:34; 50:10; 2Sa 1:12; 19:1; Ne 8:9; Est 4:3; Ps 35:14; Jer 22:10; 31:15; Am 5:16; 8:10; Mk 5:38; 16:10; Rev 18:19); removing headgear and covering the head with dust and ashes (Jos 7:6; 1Sa 4:12; Job 2:12); removing sandals (2Sa 15:30; Isa 20:2; Mic 1:8); covering the head or face (2Sa 15:30; Est 6:12; Jer 14:3–4; 48:36); and eating such food as was offered by well-wishers to console those who grieved (Jer 6:7). Ezekiel would do none of those things; his refusal signified what the inhabitants of Jerusalem would soon do.

24:22 you will do as I have done. Those who escaped death would be taken captive and would not be allowed to perform the customary rituals of mourning.

24:27 no longer be silent. See 3:24–27 and its note. Ezekiel's message would be vindicated when word reached the exiles that Jerusalem had been destroyed and he was released from the mute condition God had imposed on him.

■ **25:1—32:32** *Oracles Against the Nations.* Between his oracles forewarning the destruction of Jerusalem (chs. 1–24) and his prophecies of hope and restoration (chs. 33–48) Ezekiel included a section of oracles against other nations. He indicted seven nations, just as Amos had spoken against seven nations before taking up his charges against Israel (Am 1:3—2:5).

Israel's prophets played an important role in warfare, often providing oracles concerning particular battles (1Sa 22:5; 28:6; 1Ki 20:13–14,22; 22:6–7; 2Ki 3:11; 6:12,16; 9:6–7; 20:14; 2Ch 16:7; 18:5; 20:14,20; 28:9; Isa 39:3; Jer 28:8; 38:14). The oracles against foreign nations in the prophetic books reflect this function; they resemble the battlefield oracles given by the prophets during the course of actual war but in these instances were uttered instead in prediction of battles to come. Archaeological evidence from the cultures surrounding Israel attests to ceremonies in which enemy powers were ritually denounced or symbolically destroyed; some of the oracles in the Biblical prophets may have had such a setting.

Ezekiel presented his oracles in geographical order, starting in the northeast with Ammon and proceeding clockwise to the south and around to the Phoenician states in the north, then jumping back to the major power in the south, Egypt. Most of the states of the ancient Near East were the objects of these oracles or were at least mentioned in them, with one notable exception—Babylon (see note on 38:2). Babylon was the instrument of God's punishment against most of these nations.

■ **25:1–7** *Ammon.* Ezekiel had already spoken against Ammon (21:28–32). The history of Israel's relationship with the Ammonites had been long and varied but was primarily a record of conflict (Dt 2:19,37; 3:11; 23:3–4; Jdg 3:13; 10:6–18; 11:4–33; 1Sa 11:1–11; 14:47; 2Sa 8:12; 10:1—11:1; 12:26,31; 1Ki 11:7,33; 2Ki 23:13; 24:2; 1Ch 19:7–19; 20:1,3; 2Ch 20:1,10,22–23; 26:8; 27:5; Jer 27:3; 40:11). Oracles against this nation are also found in Jeremiah 49:1–6, Amos 1:13 and Zephaniah 2:8–9.

25:5 you will know that I am the LORD. Several of these oracles against foreign nations end with the "recognition formula" (vv.

I am the LORD. 6 For this is what the Sovereign LORD says: Because you have clapped your
hands and stamped your feet, rejoicing with all the malice of your heart against the land
of Israel,[t] 7 therefore I will stretch out my hand[u] against you and give you as plunder to
the nations. I will cut you off from the nations and exterminate you from the countries.
I will destroy[v] you, and you will know that I am the LORD.[w]' "

A Prophecy Against Moab

8 "This is what the Sovereign LORD says: 'Because Moab[x] and Seir said, "Look, the
house of Judah has become like all the other nations," 9 therefore I will expose the flank
of Moab, beginning at its frontier towns—Beth Jeshimoth[y], Baal Meon[z] and Kiriathaim[a]—the glory of that land. 10 I will give Moab along with the Ammonites to the people
of the East as a possession, so that the Ammonites will not be remembered[b] among the
nations; 11 and I will inflict punishment on Moab. Then they will know that I am the
LORD.' "

A Prophecy Against Edom

12 "This is what the Sovereign LORD says: 'Because Edom[c] took revenge on the house
of Judah and became very guilty by doing so, 13 therefore this is what the Sovereign LORD
says: I will stretch out my hand against Edom and kill its men and their animals.[d] I will
lay it waste, and from Teman to Dedan[e] they will fall by the sword. 14 I will take vengeance
on Edom by the hand of my people Israel, and they will deal with Edom in accordance
with my anger[f] and my wrath; they will know my vengeance, declares the Sovereign
LORD.' "

A Prophecy Against Philistia

15 "This is what the Sovereign LORD says: 'Because the Philistines[g] acted in vengeance and took revenge with malice in their hearts, and with ancient hostility sought
to destroy Judah, 16 therefore this is what the Sovereign LORD says: I am about to stretch
out my hand against the Philistines,[h] and I will cut off the Kerethites[i] and destroy those
remaining along the coast. 17 I will carry out great vengeance on them and punish them
in my wrath. Then they will know that I am the LORD, when I take vengeance on them.' "

A Prophecy Against Tyre

26 In the eleventh year, on the first day of the month, the word of the LORD came
to me: 2 "Son of man, because Tyre[j] has said of Jerusalem, 'Aha![k] The gate to the

25:6 [t]Ob 1:12; Zep 2:8
25:7 [u]Zep 1:4 [v]Eze 21:31 [w]Am 1:14-15
25:8 [x]Jer 48:1; Am 2:1
25:9 [y]Nu 33:49 [z]Nu 32:3; Jos 13:17 [a]Nu 32:37; Jos 13:19
25:10 [b]Eze 21:32
25:12 [c]2Ch 28:17
25:13 [d]Eze 29:8 [e]Jer 25:23
25:14 [f]Eze 35:11
25:15 [g]2Ch 28:18
25:16 [h]Jer 47:1-7 [i]1Sa 30:14; Zep 2:4-5
26:2 [j]2Sa 5:11; Isa 23 [k]Eze 25:3

7,11,17); see note on 6:7. The nations would recognize the universal sovereignty of the Lord.

25:6–7 Because . . . therefore. The punishment fit the crime: For rejoicing at the harm done to Jerusalem, the Ammonites would themselves become prey to a foreign power. Though many of the small states in the area escaped the destruction during the Babylonian invasion of 587–586 B.C., extra-Biblical sources indicate that Nebuchadnezzar decimated both Ammon and Moab in 582 B.C. Ezekiel made this same point in 21:28–32.

■ **25:8–11** *Moab.* Israel's relationships with Moab were also largely a history of conflict (Ex 15:15; Nu 21:11–29; 22:1–36; 23:6–17; 24:17; 25:1; Dt 2:8–9,18,29; 23:3; 34:5–6; Jdg 3:12–30; 11:15–18; Ru 1:1–2; 1Sa 12:9; 14:47; 22:3–4; 2Sa 8:2; 1Ki 11:1,7; 2Ki 1:1; 3:4–26; 13:20; 24:2; 1Ch 18:2; 2Ch 20:1,10,22–23). Other prophets also included oracles against this nation (Isa 15:1–9; 16:2–14; Jer 48:1–47; Am 2:1–2; Zep 2:8–9). Moab would share Ammon's fate.

■ **25:12–14** *Edom.* Edom made incursions into Judah at the time of Jerusalem's fall (35:15; 36:5; Ps 137:7–9; La 4:21–22). The tensions between Israel and Edom began in the relationship between Jacob and Esau, the twin sons of Isaac, from whom these nations, respectively, were descended (Ge 25:23,30; cf. Ge 36:1,8–9; Nu 20:14–21; 24:18; Dt 23:7; Jdg 11:17–18; 1Sa 14:47; 2Sa 8:13–14; 1Ki 11:14–17; 22:47; 2Ki 3:8–26; 8:20–22; 14:7,10; 16:6; 2Ch 20:2; 21:8–10; 25:14,19–20; 28:17). Although the brothers were eventually reconciled (Ge 33), tensions between their peoples continually resurfaced. Ezekiel included a second oracle against Edom, in chapter 35; other prophets made pronouncements against Edom in Isaiah 34:5–11, Jeremiah 49:7–22, Lamentations 4:21–22, Amos 1:11, Obadiah and Malachi 1:3–5.

■ **25:15–17** *Philistia.* The nations mentioned thus far were on the other side of the Jordan from Judah. However, the Philistines occupied the coastal plain on the western side of the Jordan and controlled a long segment of the vital international coastal highway. Conflicting territorial claims and competing strategic interests made for a history of unfriendly relations with Israel; Ezekiel had already spoken of this enmity (16:27,57). The Philistines played an important role in the Biblical record of the judges and of the united monarchy (Ge 21:34; 26:1,8,14–15; Ex 15:14; Jos 13:2–3; Jdg 3:3,31; 10:7; 13:1,5; 14:4; 15:20; 16:28; 1Sa 4:1–17; 5:1–11; 7:7–14; 9:16; 13:3–5,19–23; 14:13,31–47; 17:1–55; 18:25–30; 19:8; 23:1–5; 27:1,7; 28:1–5; 29:1–4; 31:1–2,7; 2Sa 1:20; 3:18; 5:17–25; 8:1; 21:15–19; 23:9–16; 1Ki 4:21; 15:27; 16:15; 2Ki 18:8; 1Ch 14:16; 18:1; 2Ch 9:26; 17:11; 21:16; 26:6–7; 28:18). Other prophets also included oracles against the Philistines (Isa 14:29–31; Jer 47:1–7; Joel 3:4; Am 1:6–8; Zep 2:4–7; Zec 9:5–6). There is no further information on the actions of the Philistines at the time of Jerusalem's fall.

25:16 Philistines. The Philistines appear to have entered Canaan en masse in the latter half of the second millennium B.C. as part of a large migration of ethnic groups from Mediterranean areas; Egyptian records call them the "sea peoples." **Kerethites.** The Kerethites may have been a group or tribe of the Philistines. Their name probably designates their ancestors as Cretans. The Kerethites are frequently associated with the Pelethites (possibly Philistines); they were hired as mercenary soldiers in David's army (2Sa 8:18; 15:18; 20:7,23; 1Ki 1:39,44; 1Ch 18:17). See 1 Samuel 30:14 and its note.

■ **26:1—28:26** *Phoenicia.* These chapters are devoted to oracles against Israel's Phoenician neighbors, primarily Tyre (26:1—28:19) but also Sidon (28:20–26). The chapters divide into five subsections, each introduced by the phrase "the word of the LORD came to me" (26:1; 27:1; 28:1,11,20): a judgment oracle against Tyre (26:1–21), a lament for Tyre (27:1–36), a judgment against Tyre's king (28:1–10), a lament for Tyre's king (28:11–19) and a judgment oracle against Sidon (28:20–26). Though there was occasional military conflict between Israel and the Phoenicians, the Bible mentions Tyre and Sidon primarily as the source of pagan cults, especially the Baal worship of Jezebel, a Phoenician princess (Jdg 10:6; 1Ki 11:1,5,33; 16:31; 2Ki 23:13). The Phoenicians provided Israel with trade and expert labor (2Sa 5:11; 1Ki 5:1,6; 7:13–14; 9:11–12; 1Ch 14:1; 22:4, 2Ch 2:3,11,14; Ezr 3:7; Ne 13:16; Ps 45:12; Joel 3:3–6; Am 1:9; Ac 12:20). Other prophetic books also include oracles against Tyre and Sidon (Isa 23:1–22; Joel 3:4; Am 1:9–10; Zec 9:2–3).

nations is broken, and its doors have swung open to me; now that she lies in ruins I will
prosper,' 3therefore this is what the Sovereign LORD says: I am against you, O Tyre, and
I will bring many nations against you, like the sea[l] casting up its waves. 4They will destroy[m] the walls of Tyre[n] and pull down her towers; I will scrape away her rubble and
make her a bare rock. 5Out in the sea[o] she will become a place to spread fishnets, for I
have spoken, declares the Sovereign LORD. She will become plunder[p] for the nations,
6and her settlements on the mainland will be ravaged by the sword. Then they will know
that I am the LORD.

7"For this is what the Sovereign LORD says: From the north I am going to bring
against Tyre Nebuchadnezzar[a][q] king of Babylon, king of kings,[r] with horses and chariots,[s] with horsemen and a great army. 8He will ravage your settlements on the mainland
with the sword; he will set up siege works[t] against you, build a ramp[u] up to your walls
and raise his shields against you. 9He will direct the blows of his battering rams against
your walls and demolish your towers with his weapons. 10His horses will be so many that
they will cover you with dust. Your walls will tremble at the noise of the war horses, wagons and chariots[v] when he enters your gates as men enter a city whose walls have been
broken through. 11The hoofs[w] of his horses will trample all your streets; he will kill your
people with the sword, and your strong pillars[x] will fall to the ground.[y] 12They will plunder your wealth and loot your merchandise; they will break down your walls and demolish your fine houses and throw your stones, timber and rubble into the sea.[z] 13I will put
an end[a] to your noisy songs, and the music of your harps[b] will be heard no more.[c] 14I
will make you a bare rock, and you will become a place to spread fishnets. You will never be rebuilt,[d] for I the LORD have spoken, declares the Sovereign LORD.

15"This is what the Sovereign LORD says to Tyre: Will not the coastlands[e] tremble[f] at
the sound of your fall, when the wounded groan and the slaughter takes place in you?
16Then all the princes of the coast will step down from their thrones and lay aside their
robes and take off their embroidered garments. Clothed[g] with terror, they will sit on the
ground, trembling[h] every moment, appalled[i] at you. 17Then they will take up a lament[j]
concerning you and say to you:

" 'How you are destroyed, O city of renown,
peopled by men of the sea!
You were a power on the seas,
you and your citizens;
you put your terror
on all who lived there.[k]
18Now the coastlands tremble
on the day of your fall;
the islands in the sea
are terrified at your collapse.'[l]

19"This is what the Sovereign LORD says: When I make you a desolate city, like cities
no longer inhabited, and when I bring the ocean depths over you and its vast waters cover you,[m] 20then I will bring you down with those who go down to the pit,[n] to the people
of long ago. I will make you dwell in the earth below, as in ancient ruins, with those who
go down to the pit, and you will not return or take your place[b] in the land of the living.[o]
21I will bring you to a horrible end and you will be no more. You will be sought, but you
will never again be found, declares the Sovereign LORD."[p]

26:3 [l]Isa 5:30; Jer 50:42; 51:42
26:4 [m]Isa 23:1,11 [n]Am 1:10
26:5 [o]Eze 27:32 [p]Eze 29:19
26:7 [q]Jer 27:6 [r]Ezr 7:12; Da 2:37 [s]Eze 23:24; Na 2:3-4
26:8 [t]Jer 6:6 [u]Eze 21:22
26:10 [v]Jer 4:13
26:11 [w]Isa 5:28 [x]Jer 43:13 [y]Isa 26:5
26:12 [z]Isa 23:8; Eze 27:3-27; 28:8
26:13 [a]Jer 7:34 [b]Isa 14:11 [c]Jer 25:10; Rev 18:22
26:14 [d]Job 12:14; Mal 1:4
26:15 [e]Eze 27:35 [f]Jer 49:21
26:16 [g]Job 8:22 [h]Hos 11:10 [i]Eze 32:10
26:17 [j]Eze 19:1; 27:32 [k]Isa 14:12
26:18 [l]Isa 23:5; 41:5; Eze 27:35
26:19 [m]Isa 8:7-8
26:20 [n]Eze 32:18; Am 9:2; Jnh 2:2,6 [o]Eze 32:24,30
26:21 [p]Eze 27:36; 28:19; Rev 18:21

[a] 7 Hebrew *Nebuchadrezzar,* of which *Nebuchadnezzar* is a variant; here and often in Ezekiel and Jeremiah
[b] 20 Septuagint; Hebrew *return, and I will give glory*

■ **26:1–21** *Judgment Oracle Against Tyre.* Ezekiel offered a judgment oracle against Tyre.
26:1 eleventh year. Does not mention the month of the year, as do the other date formulas.
26:2 I will prosper. Tyre would benefit from Jerusalem's fall. Judah at various times controlled a long segment of the vital international highway through the coastal plain to Egypt and routes to the port of Ezion Geber, connecting with the lucrative trade from Arabia and Africa. The misfortune of Jerusalem would eliminate negotiations with a powerful middle party and would increase commercial benefit to Tyre.
26:4 Tyre . . . rock. The prophet employed a pun: *Tyre* in Hebrew is like the word *rock,* and God would leave the island as a bare rock (26:4,14).
26:7 Tyre. Shortly after the fall of Jerusalem Nebuchadnezzar set siege to Tyre. The mainland part of the city was occupied quickly, in 585 B.C., but the island fortress defied the armies of Babylon for 13 years, until it fell in 572 B.C. (cf. 29:17–18).
26:19–20 waters . . . pit. Ezekiel described the mythological waters of chaos engulfing the island and its inhabitants. Waters and a pit were common Biblical metaphors for death or the realm of the dead (waters: Ex 14:26; 15:5,8,10; Job 26:5; Pss 18:16; 32:6; 69:2,14; La 3:54; Jnh 2:5; Lk 8:24; pit: 32:18,23–24,30; Job 33:18–30; Pss 28:1; 30:3,9; 40:2; 55:23; 69:15; 88:4,6; 103:4; 143:7; Pr 1:12; Isa

A Lament for Tyre

27 The word of the LORD came to me: 2“Son of man, take up a lament concerning
Tyre. 3Say to Tyre, situated at the gateway to the sea,[q] merchant of peoples on
many coasts, ‘This is what the Sovereign LORD says:

“ ‘You say, O Tyre,
“I am perfect in beauty.[r]”
4 Your domain was on the high seas;
your builders brought your beauty to perfection.
5 They made all your timbers
of pine trees from Senir[a];[s]
they took a cedar from Lebanon
to make a mast for you.
6 Of oaks[t] from Bashan
they made your oars;
of cypress wood[b] from the coasts of Cyprus[c][u]
they made your deck, inlaid with ivory.
7 Fine embroidered linen from Egypt was your sail
and served as your banner;
your awnings were of blue and purple[v]
from the coasts of Elishah.
8 Men of Sidon and Arvad[w] were your oarsmen;
your skilled men, O Tyre, were aboard as your seamen.[x]
9 Veteran craftsmen of Gebal[d][y] were on board
as shipwrights to caulk your seams.
All the ships of the sea and their sailors
came alongside to trade for your wares.
10 “ ‘Men of Persia,[z] Lydia and Put[a]
served as soldiers in your army.
They hung their shields and helmets on your walls,
bringing you splendor.
11 Men of Arvad and Helech
manned your walls on every side;
men of Gammad
were in your towers.
They hung their shields around your walls;
they brought your beauty to perfection.

12“ ‘Tarshish[b] did business with you because of your great wealth of goods;[c] they exchanged silver, iron, tin and lead for your merchandise.
13“ ‘Greece, Tubal and Meshech[d] traded with you; they exchanged slaves[e] and articles of bronze for your wares.
14“ ‘Men of Beth Togarmah[f] exchanged work horses, war horses and mules for your
merchandise.
15“ ‘The men of Rhodes[e][g] traded with you, and many coastlands[h] were your customers; they paid you with ivory[i] tusks and ebony.
16“ ‘Aram[f][j] did business with you because of your many products; they exchanged

27:3 [q]ver 33 [r]Eze 28:2
27:5 [s]Dt 3:9
27:6 [t]Nu 21:33; Jer 22:20; Zec 11:2 [u]Ge 10:4; Isa 23:12
27:7 [v]Ex 25:4; Jer 10:9
27:8 [w]Ge 10:18 [x]1Ki 9:27
27:9 [y]Jos 13:5; 1Ki 5:18
27:10 [z]Eze 38:5 [a]Eze 30:5
27:12 [b]Ge 10:4 [c]ver 18, 33
27:13 [d]Ge 10:2; Isa 66:19; Eze 38:2 [e]Rev 18:13
27:14 [f]Ge 10:3; Eze 38:6
27:15 [g]Ge 10:7 [h]Jer 25:22 [i]1Ki 10:22; Rev 18:12
27:16 [j]Jdg 10:6; Isa 7:1-8

[a] *5* That is, Hermon [b] *6* Targum; the Masoretic Text has a different division of the consonants. [c] *6* Hebrew *Kittim* [d] *9* That is, Byblos [e] *15* Septuagint; Hebrew *Dedan* [f] *16* Most Hebrew manuscripts; some Hebrew manuscripts and Syriac *Edom*

14:15; 30:33; 38:18; Eze 31:14,16; Jnh 2:6). The two images are combined in Psalm 69:15, Ezekiel 28:8 and Jonah 2:6.

■ **27:1–36** *Lament for Tyre.* To demonstrate the severity of the coming judgment against Tyre, Ezekiel offered a lament on behalf of the ruined city.

27:3 I am perfect. The ship metaphor was particularly apt for the island city of Tyre. No expense was spared in her construction (vv. 3–9). She was built of the finest materials, without regard for cost, finished with luxurious detail and manned by an experienced crew.

27:5 Senir. The Amorite name for Mount Hermon (Dt 3:9).

27:7 Elishah. Probably a region on Cyprus.

27:8 Arvad. A town on the Mediterranean coast north of Byblos.

27:9 Gebal. An ancient name for Byblos on the Mediterranean coast north of Tyre.

27:10 soldiers. Tyre's mercenary armies came from Persia, Lydia (a region on the western end of the Anatolian peninsula) and Put (a part of Libya).

27:11 Helech. Cilicia, at the northeastern corner of the Mediterranean. **Gammad.** Its identity is less certain, but it was probably a region in north Syria.

27:12–24 Tarshish . . . Kilmad. The list of trading partners is in geographical order, starting in the far west with Tarshish (Tartessus in Spain) and proceeding to Rhodes (v. 15) in the eastern Mediterranean. Then it starts in the south with Edom (v. 16; NIV “Aram”) and moves north to Damascus (v. 18) and finally to Arabia and Mesopotamia.

27:13 Tubal and Meshech. Peoples (32:26; 38:2–3; 39:1; Ge 10:2; 1Ch 1:5) in Asia Minor, in the region of the northeastern corner of the Mediterranean; they are also known from Assyrian inscriptions. **slaves.** On Tyre's slave trade, see Joel 3:3–8.

27:14 Beth Togarmah. A region of northeastern Asia Minor.

turquoise,[k] purple fabric, embroidered work, fine linen, coral and rubies for your merchandise.
17“ ‘Judah and Israel traded with you; they exchanged wheat from Minnith[l] and con-
fections,[a] honey, oil and balm for your wares.
18“ ‘Damascus,[m] because of your many products and great wealth of goods, did
business with you in wine from Helbon and wool from Zahar.
19“ ‘Danites and Greeks from Uzal bought your merchandise; they exchanged
wrought iron, cassia and calamus for your wares.
20“ ‘Dedan traded in saddle blankets with you.
21“ ‘Arabia and all the princes of Kedar[n] were your customers; they did business with
you in lambs, rams and goats.
22“ ‘The merchants of Sheba[o] and Raamah traded with you; for your merchandise
they exchanged the finest of all kinds of spices[p] and precious stones, and gold.
23“ ‘Haran,[q] Canneh and Eden[r] and merchants of Sheba, Asshur and Kilmad traded
with you. 24In your marketplace they traded with you beautiful garments, blue fabric,
embroidered work and multicolored rugs with cords twisted and tightly knotted.

25“ ‘The ships of Tarshish[s] serve
as carriers for your wares.
You are filled with heavy cargo
in the heart of the sea.
26 Your oarsmen take you
out to the high seas.
But the east wind[t] will break you to pieces
in the heart of the sea.
27 Your wealth,[u] merchandise and wares,
your mariners, seamen and shipwrights,
your merchants and all your soldiers,
and everyone else on board
will sink into the heart of the sea
on the day of your shipwreck.
28 The shorelands will quake[v]
when your seamen cry out.
29 All who handle the oars
will abandon their ships;
the mariners and all the seamen
will stand on the shore.
30 They will raise their voice
and cry bitterly over you;
they will sprinkle dust[w] on their heads
and roll[x] in ashes.[y]
31 They will shave their heads because of you
and will put on sackcloth.
They will weep[z] over you with anguish of soul
and with bitter mourning.[a]
32 As they wail and mourn over you,
they will take up a lament[b] concerning you:
“Who was ever silenced like Tyre,
surrounded by the sea?”
33 When your merchandise went out on the seas,
you satisfied many nations;

27:16 [k]Eze 28:13
27:17 [l]Jdg 11:33
27:18 [m]Ge 14:15; Eze 47:16-18
27:21 [n]Ge 25:13; Isa 60:7
27:22 [o]Ge 10:7,28; 1Ki 10:1-2; Isa 60:6 [p]Ge 43:11
27:23 [q]2Ki 19:12 [r]Isa 37:12
27:25 [s]Isa 2:16 *fn*
27:26 [t]Ps 48:7; Jer 18:17
27:27 [u]Pr 11:4
27:28 [v]Eze 26:15
27:30 [w]2Sa 1:2 [x]Jer 6:26 [y]Rev 18:18-19
27:31 [z]Isa 16:9 [a]Isa 22:12; Eze 7:18
27:32 [b]Eze 26:17

[a] *17* The meaning of the Hebrew for this word is uncertain.

27:17 traded with you. As a maritime power, Tyre was probably not agriculturally self-sufficient; the Bible several times mentions her trade with Israel for foodstuffs (1Ki 5:9–11; 2Ch 2:10; Ezr 3:7; Ne 13:16; Ac 12:20). **Minnith.** Located east of the Jordan near Rabbah of the Ammonites (modern Amman), though the site for this town has not been identified with certainty (Jdg 11:33).
27:18 Helbon. A town northwest of Damascus. Akkadian texts and Greek historians mention the wine from this region. **Zahar.** Probably near Helbon, but not otherwise known.
27:19 Danites and Greeks. These two terms represent a much debated textual difficulty. In place of “Danites” some scholars read “Vedan”; in place of “Greeks” some scholars read “Javan” (cf. Ge 10:2,4; 1Ch 1:5,7). **Uzal.** A region in southern Arabia (Ge 10:27; 1Ch 1:21).
27:22 Raamah. A region in southern Arabia (Ge 10:7; 1Ch 1:9).
27:23 Canneh. Probably an alternative spelling of Calneh, a city in northern Syria (Isa 10:9, “Calno”; Am 6:2, “Calneh”). **Eden.** That is, Beth Eden, a city between the Euphrates and Balikh Rivers (Am 1:5; 2Ki 19:12; Isa 37:12). **Kilmad.** This is not otherwise identified and may represent a textual error for “all of Media.”
27:25–36 will sink into the heart of the sea. It was unthinkable that the metaphoric ship, Tyre, could sink. But her strength, wealth and skill were no match for seas that obeyed the command of God. Tyre’s fate would be a warning to other nations.

with your great wealth[c] and your wares
you enriched the kings of the earth.
34 Now you are shattered by the sea
in the depths of the waters;
your wares and all your company
have gone down with you.[d]
35 All who live in the coastlands[e]
are appalled at you;
their kings shudder with horror
and their faces are distorted with fear.
36 The merchants among the nations hiss at you;[f]
you have come to a horrible end
and will be no more.[g]' "

A Prophecy Against the King of Tyre

28 The word of the LORD came to me: 2"Son of man, say to the ruler of Tyre, 'This
is what the Sovereign LORD says:

" 'In the pride of your heart
you say, "I am a god;
I sit on the throne[h] of a god
in the heart of the seas."
But you are a man and not a god,
though you think you are as wise as a god.[i]
3 Are you wiser than Daniel[a]?[j]
Is no secret hidden from you?
4 By your wisdom and understanding
you have gained wealth for yourself
and amassed gold and silver
in your treasuries.[k]
5 By your great skill in trading
you have increased your wealth,
and because of your wealth
your heart has grown proud.[l]

6" 'Therefore this is what the Sovereign LORD says:

" 'Because you think you are wise,
as wise as a god,
7 I am going to bring foreigners against you,
the most ruthless of nations;[m]
they will draw their swords against your beauty and wisdom
and pierce your shining splendor.
8 They will bring you down to the pit,[n]
and you will die a violent death
in the heart of the seas.[o]
9 Will you then say, "I am a god,"
in the presence of those who kill you?
You will be but a man, not a god,
in the hands of those who slay you.
10 You will die the death of the uncircumcised[p]
at the hands of foreigners.

I have spoken, declares the Sovereign LORD.' "

27:33 [c]ver 12; Eze 28:4-5
27:34 [d]Zec 9:4
27:35 [e]Eze 26:15
27:36 [f]Jer 18:16; 19:8; 49:17; 50:13; Zep 2:15 [g]Ps 37:10, 36; Eze 26:21
28:2 [h]Isa 14:13 [i]Ps 9:20; 82:6-7; Isa 31:3; 2Th 2:4
28:3 [j]Da 1:20; 5:11-12
28:4 [k]Zec 9:3
28:5 [l]Job 31:25; Ps 52:7; 62:10; Hos 12:8; 13:6
28:7 [m]Eze 30:11; 31:12; 32:12; Hab 1:6
28:8 [n]Eze 32:30 [o]Eze 27:27
28:10 [p]Eze 31:18; 32:19, 24

[a] 3 Or *Danel*; the Hebrew spelling may suggest a person other than the prophet Daniel.

■ **28:1–10** *Judgment Oracle Against Tyre's King.* Ezekiel continued his announcements of judgment on Tyre, but this time he drew attention to Tyre's king.
28:2 a god in the heart of the seas. In the mythology of much of the ancient Near East, the watery depths or the primeval ocean symbolized death and chaos. In a number of the creation accounts unearthed by archaeologists, a god or gods slay a dragon/sea monster called "the Sea" as part of creation, thus subduing the threat of chaos to the created order. The gods then rule over the sea. In the Bible the sea is no threat to God; God controls it with ease. In Ezekiel's description the king of Tyre, due to the island's immense wealth, prowess and security, viewed himself as a god ruling over the sea (cf. Ps 29:10; Rev 17:1,15). But the sea (as a symbol of death) would swallow him (Eze 28:8). See note on 26:19–20.
28:3 Daniel. See 14:12–23.
■ **28:11–19** *Lament for Tyre's King.* The judgment predicted against Tyre's king led to laments for him.

28:12 [q]Eze 19:1 [r]Eze 27:2-4
28:13 [s]Ge 2:8 [t]Eze 31:8-9 [u]Eze 27:16
28:14 [v]Ex 30:26; 40:9 [w]Ex 25:17-20
28:16 [x]Hab 2:17 [y]Ge 3:24
28:17 [z]Eze 31:10
28:18 [a]Mal 4:3
28:19 [b]Jer 51:64; Eze 26:21; 27:36
28:21 [c]Eze 6:2 [d]Ge 10:15; Jer 25:22
28:22 [e]Eze 39:13 [f]Eze 30:19

11The word of the LORD came to me: 12"Son of man, take up a lament[q] concerning the king of Tyre and say to him: 'This is what the Sovereign LORD says:

" 'You were the model of perfection,
full of wisdom and perfect in beauty.[r]
13 You were in Eden,[s]
the garden of God;[t]
every precious stone adorned you:
ruby, topaz and emerald,
chrysolite, onyx and jasper,
sapphire,[a] turquoise[u] and beryl.[b]
Your settings and mountings[c] were made of gold;
on the day you were created they were prepared.
14 You were anointed[v] as a guardian cherub,[w]
for so I ordained you.
You were on the holy mount of God;
you walked among the fiery stones.
15 You were blameless in your ways
from the day you were created
till wickedness was found in you.
16 Through your widespread trade
you were filled with violence,[x]
and you sinned.
So I drove you in disgrace from the mount of God,
and I expelled you, O guardian cherub,[y]
from among the fiery stones.
17 Your heart became proud[z]
on account of your beauty,
and you corrupted your wisdom
because of your splendor.
So I threw you to the earth;
I made a spectacle of you before kings.
18 By your many sins and dishonest trade
you have desecrated your sanctuaries.
So I made a fire come out from you,
and it consumed you,
and I reduced you to ashes[a] on the ground
in the sight of all who were watching.
19 All the nations who knew you
are appalled at you;
you have come to a horrible end
and will be no more.[b]' "

A Prophecy Against Sidon

20The word of the LORD came to me: 21"Son of man, set your face against[c] Sidon;[d]
prophesy against her 22and say: 'This is what the Sovereign LORD says:

" 'I am against you, O Sidon,
and I will gain glory[e] within you.
They will know that I am the LORD,
when I inflict punishment[f] on her
and show myself holy within her.
23 I will send a plague upon her

[a] *13* Or *lapis lazuli* [b] *13* The precise identification of some of these precious stones is uncertain.
[c] *13* The meaning of the Hebrew for this phrase is uncertain.

28:12 lament. See note on 19:1–14. **king of Tyre.** The king of Tyre was Ethbaal. Ezekiel described God's favor to Ethbaal by portraying him as a primeval being, a figure like Adam, the crown and epitome of creation, living in the garden paradise that God had made. The glorious king remained there until wickedness was found in him (v. 15). Some interpreters view Ezekiel as describing the king of Tyre as though he were Satan, a glorious being who fell from grace (1Ti 3:6).
28:13–14 garden . . . mount. Ezekiel conjoined two images regarding the dwelling place of God: a garden (Ge 2–3) and a mountain (Ex 19:23; Dt 33:2; Pss 43:3; 48:1; 87:1; 99:9; Isa 27:13; 56:7; 57:13; 66:20; Eze 20:40; Rev 21:10). The temple integrated these themes: It was located on Mount Zion and decorated with the floral motifs of a garden (1Ki 6:29,32,35; 7:18,20,22,36,42; 2Ch 3:5; Eze 40:16,22,26,31,34,37; 41:18–20,25–27).
■ **28:20–26** *Judgment Oracle Against Sidon.* Sidon was commonly paired with her trading partner, Tyre, located 25 miles further south on the Mediterranean coast.

and make blood flow in her streets.
The slain will fall within her,
with the sword against her on every side.
Then they will know that I am the LORD.[g]

24 " 'No longer will the people of Israel have malicious neighbors who are painful briers and sharp thorns.[h] Then they will know that I am the Sovereign LORD.
25 " 'This is what the Sovereign LORD says: When I gather[i] the people of Israel from the
nations where they have been scattered,[j] I will show myself holy[k] among them in the
sight of the nations. Then they will live in their own land, which I gave to my servant Jacob.[l] 26 They will live there in safety[m] and will build houses and plant vineyards; they will
live in safety when I inflict punishment on all their neighbors who maligned them. Then
they will know that I am the LORD their God.[n]' "

A Prophecy Against Egypt

29 In the tenth year, in the tenth month on the twelfth day, the word of the LORD
came to me:[o] 2 "Son of man, set your face against Pharaoh king of Egypt[p] and
prophesy against him and against all Egypt.[q] 3 Speak to him and say: 'This is what the
Sovereign LORD says:

" 'I am against you, Pharaoh[r] king of Egypt,
you great monster[s] lying among your streams.
You say, "The Nile is mine;
I made it for myself."
4 But I will put hooks[t] in your jaws
and make the fish of your streams stick to your scales.
I will pull you out from among your streams,
with all the fish sticking to your scales.[u]
5 I will leave you in the desert,
you and all the fish of your streams.
You will fall on the open field
and not be gathered or picked up.
I will give you as food
to the beasts of the earth and the birds of the air.[v]

6 Then all who live in Egypt will know that I am the LORD.

" 'You have been a staff of reed[w] for the house of Israel. 7 When they grasped you with
their hands, you splintered[x] and you tore open their shoulders; when they leaned on
you, you broke and their backs were wrenched.[a][y]
8 " 'Therefore this is what the Sovereign LORD says: I will bring a sword against you and
kill your men and their animals.[z] 9 Egypt will become a desolate wasteland. Then they will
know that I am the LORD.
" 'Because you said, "The Nile is mine; I made it,[a]" 10 therefore I am against you and
against your streams, and I will make the land of Egypt a ruin and a desolate waste from

28:23 [g]Eze 38:22
28:24 [h]Nu 33:55; Jos 23:13; Eze 2:6
28:25 [i]Ps 106:47; Jer 32:37 [j]Isa 11:12 [k]Eze 20:41 [l]Jer 23:8; Eze 11:17; 34:27; 37:25
28:26 [m]Jer 23:6 [n]Isa 65:21; Jer 32:15; Eze 38:8; Am 9:14-15
29:1 [o]ver 17; Eze 26:1
29:2 [p]Jer 25:19 [q]Isa 19:1-17; Jer 46:2; Eze 30:1-26; 31:1-18; 32:1-32
29:3 [r]Jer 44:30 [s]Ps 74:13; Isa 27:1; Eze 32:2
29:4 [t]2Ki 19:28 [u]Eze 38:4
29:5 [v]Jer 7:33; 34:20; Eze 32:4-6; 39:4
29:6 [w]2Ki 18:21; Isa 36:6
29:7 [x]Isa 36:6 [y]Eze 17:15-17
29:8 [z]Eze 14:17; 32:11-13
29:9 [a]Eze 30:7-8,13-19

a 7 Syriac (see also Septuagint and Vulgate); Hebrew *and you caused their backs to stand*

28:25 gather. God would bring his people back to their land. Israel would flourish, since the nations that had been her adversaries would be eliminated.

28:26 vineyards. The prophets often described God's future blessing of Israel in terms of agricultural prosperity (36:29–30; 1Ki 4:25; 2Ki 18:31; Isa 36:16; 65:21–22; Jer 32:15; Joel 3:18; Am 9:13–15; Mic 4:4; Zec 3:10).

■ **29:1—32:32** *Egypt.* In these four chapters Ezekiel prophesied against Egypt, one of the great empires of the ancient world. All the prophecies are dated (29:1,17; 30:20; 31:1; 32:1,17), with the exception of the oracle beginning in 30:1. The chapters follow the general pattern seen in the previous section—judgment oracles followed by laments—and divide into seven parts: a first judgment against Egypt (29:1–16), a second judgment (29:17–21), a lament over Egypt (30:1–19), a third judgment (30:20–26), a fourth judgment (31:1–18), a lament for Pharaoh (32:1–16) and a lament over Egypt and Pharaoh (32:17–32).

■ **29:1–16** *Judgment Against Egypt.* Ezekiel condemned Egypt to destruction.

29:1 tenth year . . . tenth month . . . twelfth day. Of Jehoiachin's reign; January 587 B.C., about a year after Nebuchadnezzar had set siege to Jerusalem. See note on 24:1.

29:3 monster. Ezekiel likened Egypt to a sea monster (vv. 2–5). The term used could designate both the abundant crocodiles of the Nile and the sea monster that represented chaos in the mythology of the ancient Near East. The Bible calls this mythological creature "monster," "leviathan," or "Rahab" (32:2; Job 3:8; 7:12; 9:13; 26:12–13; 41:1; Pss 74:13–14; 89:10; Isa 27:1; 30:7; 51:9; cf. Rev 12:15; 20:2); the term *Rahab* was also a poetic designation for Egypt (Ps 87:4; Isa 30:7). In the mythology of the cultures surrounding Israel, this sea monster was a god who rivaled other gods, but in the Bible it was simply another creature living in submission to the command of Yahweh.

29:4 hooks. God would pluck this monster from the sea as easily as fishers hauled in pan fish, but he would leave it rotting on the shore. See 28:2–10.

29:5 food to the beasts. The birds and animals were given to humankind as food (Ge 1:30; 9:2); the reversal of this relationship was a common covenant curse (32:4; Dt 28:26; Ps 79:2; Isa 17:4–6; Jer 7:33; 15:3; 16:4; 19:7; 34:20).

29:6 reed. Ezekiel's description of Egypt as a splintered reed recalls the Assyrian field commander's similar comments to Hezekiah (2Ki 18:21,24).

Migdol to Aswan,[b] as far as the border of Cush.[a] 11No foot of man or animal will pass
through it; no one will live there for forty years.[c] 12I will make the land of Egypt desolate
among devastated lands, and her cities will lie desolate forty years among ruined cities. And
I will disperse the Egyptians among the nations and scatter them through the countries.[d]
13" 'Yet this is what the Sovereign LORD says: At the end of forty years I will gather the
Egyptians from the nations where they were scattered. 14I will bring them back from captivity and return them to Upper Egypt,[b][e] the land of their ancestry. There they will be a
lowly[f] kingdom. 15It will be the lowliest of kingdoms and will never again exalt itself
above the other nations.[g] I will make it so weak that it will never again rule over the nations. 16Egypt will no longer be a source of confidence[h] for the people of Israel but will
be a reminder of their sin in turning to her for help. Then they will know that I am the
Sovereign LORD.[i]' "

17In the twenty-seventh year, in the first month on the first day, the word of the LORD
came to me:[j] 18"Son of man, Nebuchadnezzar[k] king of Babylon drove his army in a hard
campaign against Tyre; every head was rubbed bare[l] and every shoulder made raw. Yet
he and his army got no reward from the campaign he led against Tyre. 19Therefore this
is what the Sovereign LORD says: I am going to give Egypt to Nebuchadnezzar king of Babylon, and he will carry off its wealth. He will loot and plunder the land as pay for his
army.[m] 20I have given him Egypt as a reward for his efforts because he and his army did
it for me, declares the Sovereign LORD.[n]
21"On that day I will make a horn[c][o] grow for the house of Israel, and I will open your
mouth[p] among them. Then they will know that I am the LORD.[q]"

A Lament for Egypt

30 The word of the LORD came to me: 2"Son of man, prophesy and say: 'This is what
the Sovereign LORD says:

" 'Wail[r] and say,
"Alas for that day!"
3For the day is near,[s]
the day of the LORD[t] is near—
a day of clouds,
a time of doom for the nations.
4A sword will come against Egypt,
and anguish will come upon Cush.[d]
When the slain fall in Egypt,
her wealth will be carried away
and her foundations torn down.[u]
5Cush and Put,[v] Lydia and all Arabia, Libya[e] and the people[w] of the covenant land will
fall by the sword along with Egypt.
6" 'This is what the LORD says:

" 'The allies of Egypt will fall
and her proud strength will fail.
From Migdol to Aswan[x]
they will fall by the sword within her,
declares the Sovereign LORD.

29:10 [b]Eze 30:6
29:11 [c]Eze 32:13
29:12 [d]Jer 46:19; Eze 30:7,23,26
29:14 [e]Eze 30:14 [f]Eze 17:14
29:15 [g]Zec 10:11
29:16 [h]Isa 36:4,6 [i]Isa 30:2; Hos 8:13
29:17 [j]Eze 24:1
29:18 [k]Jer 27:6; Eze 26:7-8 [l]Jer 48:37
29:19 [m]Jer 43:10-13; Eze 30:4,10,24-25
29:20 [n]Isa 10:6-7; 45:1; Jer 25:9
29:21 [o]Ps 132:17 [p]Eze 33:22 [q]Eze 24:27
30:2 [r]Isa 13:6
30:3 [s]Eze 7:7; Joel 2:1,11; Ob 1:15 [t]ver 18; Eze 7:12,19
30:4 [u]Eze 29:19
30:5 [v]Eze 27:10 [w]Jer 25:20
30:6 [x]Eze 29:10

[a] *10* That is, the upper Nile region [b] *14* Hebrew *to Pathros* [c] *21 Horn* here symbolizes strength.
[d] *4* That is, the upper Nile region; also in verses 5 and 9 [e] *5* Hebrew *Cub*

29:10 Migdol to Aswan. That is, from north to south. Migdol was in northern Egypt, probably in the eastern Nile delta; it was a site on the route of the exodus (Ex 14:2; cf. Eze 30:6; Nu 33:7; Jer 44:1; 46:14). Aswan was in southern Egypt at the first cataract on the Nile; it was the terminus point of deep-water navigation on the Nile and represented Egypt's southern frontier.
29:11 forty years. It is difficult to fix a definite historical period of 40 years for an Egyptian exile; the number may have been symbolic rather than intended as a definite period.
29:15 lowliest of kingdoms. Egypt has never regained the military might and prowess that characterized her history in the Biblical period.
■ **29:17–21** *A Second Judgment Against Egypt.* Ezekiel gave a second lengthy speech against Egypt.
29:17 twenty-seventh year . . . first month . . . first day. Of Jehoiachin's reign. The day of the new year, April 571 B.C., 16 years later than the preceding oracle (29:1) and the latest date mentioned in the book.
29:18 no reward. Nebuchadnezzar's siege of Tyre had lasted for 13 years (see note on 26:7), ending probably during the year before Ezekiel made this prophecy (572 B.C.). It had been protracted and expensive, and its rewards were not worth the effort.
29:21 horn. A symbol for political power (Dt 33:17; 1Sa 2:10; 2Sa 22:3; Pss 18:2; 75:4–5,10; 89:24; 92:10; 112:9; 132:17; 148:14; Jer 48:25; La 2:3,17; Da 7:7–8,20–21; Zec 1:18–21; Rev 17:12). This oracle against Egypt ended with hope for Israel; compare 28:24–26. **open your mouth.** See notes on 24:27 and 33:22.
■ **30:1–19** *Lament Over Egypt.* Ezekiel's only non-dated oracle against Egypt. He may have given it between January and April 587 B.C. (29:1; 30:20).

[7]“ ‘They will be desolate
among desolate lands,
and their cities will lie
among ruined cities.[y]
[8]Then they will know that I am the LORD,
when I set fire to Egypt
and all her helpers are crushed.

[9]“ ‘On that day messengers will go out from me in ships to frighten Cush[z] out of her
complacency. Anguish[a] will take hold of them on the day of Egypt’s doom, for it is sure
to come.[b]

[10]“ ‘This is what the Sovereign LORD says:

“ ‘I will put an end to the hordes of Egypt
by the hand of Nebuchadnezzar king of Babylon.[c]
[11]He and his army—the most ruthless of nations[d]—
will be brought in to destroy the land.
They will draw their swords against Egypt
and fill the land with the slain.
[12]I will dry up[e] the streams of the Nile[f]
and sell the land to evil men;
by the hand of foreigners
I will lay waste the land and everything in it.

I the LORD have spoken.

[13]“ ‘This is what the Sovereign LORD says:

“ ‘I will destroy the idols[g]
and put an end to the images in Memphis.[a][h]
No longer will there be a prince in Egypt,[i]
and I will spread fear throughout the land.
[14]I will lay[j] waste Upper Egypt,[b]
set fire to Zoan[k]
and inflict punishment on Thebes.[c][l]
[15]I will pour out my wrath on Pelusium,[d]
the stronghold of Egypt,
and cut off the hordes of Thebes.
[16]I will set fire to Egypt;
Pelusium will writhe in agony.
Thebes will be taken by storm;
Memphis will be in constant distress.
[17]The young men of Heliopolis[e][m] and Bubastis[f]
will fall by the sword,
and the cities themselves will go into captivity.
[18]Dark will be the day at Tahpanhes
when I break the yoke of Egypt;[n]
there her proud strength will come to an end.
She will be covered with clouds,
and her villages will go into captivity.[o]
[19]So I will inflict punishment on Egypt,
and they will know that I am the LORD.’ ”

[20]In the eleventh year, in the first month on the seventh day, the word of the LORD
came to me:[p] [21]“Son of man, I have broken the arm[q] of Pharaoh king of Egypt. It has not
been bound up for healing[r] or put in a splint so as to become strong enough to hold a

30:7 [y]Eze 29:12
30:9 [z]Isa 18:1-2 [a]Isa 23:5 [b]Eze 32:9-10
30:10 [c]Eze 29:19
30:11 [d]Eze 28:7
30:12 [e]Isa 19:6 [f]Eze 29:9
30:13 [g]Jer 43:12 [h]Isa 19:13 [i]Zec 10:11
30:14 [j]Eze 29:14 [k]Ps 78:12,43 [l]Jer 46:25
30:17 [m]Ge 41:45
30:18 [n]Lev 26:13 [o]ver 3
30:20 [p]Eze 26:1; 29:17; 31:1
30:21 [q]Jer 48:25 [r]Jer 30:13; 46:11

[a] *13* Hebrew *Noph*; also in verse 16 [b] *14* Hebrew *waste Pathros* [c] *14* Hebrew *No*; also in verses 15 and 16 [d] *15* Hebrew *Sin*; also in verse 16 [e] *17* Hebrew *Awen* (or *On*) [f] *17* Hebrew *Pi Beseth*

30:14 Zoan. In the eastern Nile delta; also known as Tanis.
30:15 Pelusium. A fortress on the Mediterranean coast and Egypt’s northeastern frontier.
30:17 Heliopolis. Near the southern vertex of the Nile delta; an important religious center. **Bubastis.** Mentioned only here in the Bible; located in the eastern delta and a capital city during the twenty-third and twenty-second Egyptian dynasties (950–750 B.C.).

■ **30:20–26** *A Third Judgment Against Egypt.* Again God declared that he would destroy Egypt.
30:20 eleventh year . . . first month . . . seventh day. Of Jehoiachin’s reign; April 587 B.C.
30:21 broken the arm. A symbol of broken military might. Pharaoh Hophra sent an army to assist Zedekiah, but it was repulsed (Jer 37:1–10; cf. Eze 29:6–7; 17:15–17). Besieged Jerusalem and the

sword. 22 Therefore this is what the Sovereign LORD says: I am against Pharaoh king of
Egypt.[s] I will break both his arms, the good arm as well as the broken one, and make the
sword fall from his hand.[t] 23 I will disperse the Egyptians among the nations and scatter
them through the countries.[u] 24 I will strengthen[v] the arms of the king of Babylon and
put my sword[w] in his hand, but I will break the arms of Pharaoh, and he will groan before him like a mortally wounded man. 25 I will strengthen the arms of the king of Babylon, but the arms of Pharaoh will fall limp. Then they will know that I am the LORD, when
I put my sword into the hand of the king of Babylon and he brandishes it against Egypt.
26 I will disperse the Egyptians among the nations and scatter them through the countries. Then they will know that I am the LORD.[x]"

A Cedar in Lebanon

31 In the eleventh year,[y] in the third month on the first day, the word of the LORD
came to me:[z] 2 "Son of man, say to Pharaoh king of Egypt and to his hordes:

" 'Who can be compared with you in majesty?
3 Consider Assyria, once a cedar in Lebanon,
with beautiful branches overshadowing the forest;
it towered on high,
its top above the thick foliage.[a]
4 The waters nourished it,
deep springs made it grow tall;
their streams flowed
all around its base
and sent their channels
to all the trees of the field.
5 So it towered higher
than all the trees of the field;
its boughs increased
and its branches grew long,
spreading because of abundant waters.[b]
6 All the birds of the air
nested in its boughs,
all the beasts of the field
gave birth under its branches;
all the great nations
lived in its shade.[c]
7 It was majestic in beauty,
with its spreading boughs,
for its roots went down
to abundant waters.
8 The cedars[d] in the garden of God
could not rival it,
nor could the pine trees
equal its boughs,
nor could the plane trees
compare with its branches—
no tree in the garden of God
could match its beauty.[e]
9 I made it beautiful
with abundant branches,
the envy of all the trees of Eden[f]
in the garden of God.[g]

30:22 [s]Jer 46:25 [t]Ps 37:17
30:23 [u]Eze 29:12
30:24 [v]Zec 10:6,12 [w]Eze 21:14; Zep 2:12
30:26 [x]Eze 29:12
31:1 [y]Jer 52:5 [z]Eze 30:20
31:3 [a]Isa 10:34
31:5 [b]Eze 17:5
31:6 [c]Eze 17:23; Mt 13:32
31:8 [d]Ps 80:10 [e]Ge 2:8-9
31:9 [f]Ge 2:8 [g]Ge 13:10; Eze 28:13

exiles had hoped that Egypt would defeat Babylon, but this oracle denied that hope. Instead, Babylon would render Egypt powerless.

■ **31:1–18** *A Fourth Judgment Against Egypt.* Ezekiel described the judgment that would come on Egypt despite her glories.

31:1 eleventh year . . . third month . . . first day. Of Jehoiachin's reign; June 587 B.C. Jerusalem was in the final weeks of the siege that would end with the destruction of the city.

31:3 Assyria. Ezekiel used the fate of Assyria as a warning to Egypt; the mighty Assyrian Empire had collapsed during the years from 640 to 609 B.C. Some scholars regard it as improbable that in an oracle against Egypt (vv. 2,18) the primary focus should be Assyria (vv. 3–17). Altering one consonant in the text could change the translation "Assyria" (1) to "cypress," or (2) "to what shall I liken you?"—a fitting parallel to the last clause in verse 2. Either rendering explains what appears to be a misplaced reference to Assyria. **cedar.** Great trees that tower hundreds of feet and live for millennia provide apt metaphors for kingdoms and dynasties. Ezekiel had used a similar image earlier (see 17:22–24). This tree resembled the one in Nebuchadnezzar's dream (Da 4:1–12,19–27). Compare Ezekiel's lavish description of this tree to his extravagant depiction of Tyre as a ship (27:3–11).

10" 'Therefore this is what the Sovereign LORD says: Because it towered on high, lifting its top above the thick foliage, and because it was proud[h] of its height, 11I handed it
over to the ruler of the nations, for him to deal with according to its wickedness. I cast
it aside,[i] 12and the most ruthless of foreign nations[j] cut it down and left it. Its boughs fell
on the mountains and in all the valleys;[k] its branches lay broken in all the ravines of the
land. All the nations of the earth came out from under its shade and left it.[l] 13All the birds
of the air settled on the fallen tree, and all the beasts of the field were among its branches.[m] 14Therefore no other trees by the waters are ever to tower proudly on high, lifting
their tops above the thick foliage. No other trees so well-watered are ever to reach such
a height; they are all destined for death,[n] for the earth below, among mortal men, with
those who go down to the pit.[o]

15" 'This is what the Sovereign LORD says: On the day it was brought down to the
grave[a] I covered the deep springs with mourning for it; I held back its streams, and its
abundant waters were restrained. Because of it I clothed Lebanon with gloom, and all
the trees of the field withered away. 16I made the nations tremble[p] at the sound of its fall
when I brought it down to the grave with those who go down to the pit. Then all the
trees[q] of Eden, the choicest and best of Lebanon, all the trees that were well-watered,
were consoled[r] in the earth below.[s] 17Those who lived in its shade, its allies among the
nations, had also gone down to the grave with it, joining those killed by the sword.[t]

18" 'Which of the trees of Eden can be compared with you in splendor and majesty?
Yet you, too, will be brought down with the trees of Eden to the earth below; you will lie
among the uncircumcised,[u] with those killed by the sword.

" 'This is Pharaoh and all his hordes, declares the Sovereign LORD.' "

A Lament for Pharaoh

32 In the twelfth year, in the twelfth month on the first day, the word of the LORD
came to me:[v] 2"Son of man, take up a lament[w] concerning Pharaoh king of
Egypt and say to him:

" 'You are like a lion[x] among the nations;
you are like a monster in the seas
thrashing about in your streams,
churning the water with your feet
and muddying the streams.[y]

3" 'This is what the Sovereign LORD says:

" 'With a great throng of people
I will cast my net over you,
and they will haul you up in my net.[z]
4I will throw you on the land
and hurl you on the open field.
I will let all the birds of the air settle on you
and all the beasts of the earth gorge themselves on you.[a]
5I will spread your flesh on the mountains
and fill the valleys[b] with your remains.
6I will drench the land with your flowing blood[c]
all the way to the mountains,
and the ravines will be filled with your flesh.
7When I snuff you out, I will cover the heavens
and darken their stars;
I will cover the sun with a cloud,
and the moon will not give its light.[d]

31:10 [h]Isa 14:13-14; Eze 28:17
31:11 [i]Da 5:20
31:12 [j]Eze 28:7 [k]Eze 32:5; 35:8 [l]Eze 32:11-12; Da 4:14
31:13 [m]Isa 18:6; Eze 29:5; 32:4
31:14 [n]Ps 82:7 [o]Ps 63:9; Eze 26:20; 32:24
31:16 [p]Eze 26:15 [q]Isa 14:8 [r]Eze 14:22; 32:31 [s]Isa 14:15; Eze 32:18
31:17 [t]Ps 9:17
31:18 [u]Jer 9:26; Eze 32:19,21
32:1 [v]Eze 31:1; 33:21
32:2 [w]Eze 19:1; 27:2 [x]Eze 19:3,6; Na 2:11-13 [y]Eze 29:3; 34:18
32:3 [z]Eze 12:13
32:4 [a]Isa 18:6; Eze 31:12-13
32:5 [b]Eze 31:12
32:6 [c]Isa 34:3
32:7 [d]Isa 13:10; 34:4; Eze 30:3; Joel 2:2, 31; 3:15; Mt 24:29; Rev 8:12

a 15 Hebrew *Sheol*; also in verses 16 and 17

■ **32:1–16** *Lament for Pharaoh.* In response to the predictions of doom, Ezekiel lamented on behalf of Pharaoh.
32:1 twelfth year . . . twelfth month . . . first day. March 585 B.C., two months after the exiles had received news of the destruction of Jerusalem (33:21).
32:2 monster. In the mythology of much of the ancient Near East, the ordered universe emerged from chaos after a cosmic battle between a god and a great sea monster or dragon having the name "Sea." After the battle, parts of the universe were fashioned from the carcass of the slain sea monster. Ezekiel had used elements of this ancient myth in his other oracles against Egypt (29:3–5), and he would do so again (38:18–23). Here he likened Egypt to the great sea monster which the Lord subdued.
32:6–8 darken their stars. See note on 7:7. Language similar to that used of the day of the Lord in Isaiah 13:10, Joel 2:30–31, 3:15 and Amos 8:9. The appearance of the divine warrior would be accompanied by paroxysms in the cosmos, and the universe would revert to primeval chaos. Such rich imagery and extravagant hyperbole in connection with significant national events is common throughout the Old Testament.

8 All the shining lights in the heavens
I will darken over you;
I will bring darkness over your land,
declares the Sovereign LORD.
9 I will trouble the hearts of many peoples
when I bring about your destruction among the nations,
among[a] lands you have not known.
10 I will cause many peoples to be appalled at you,
and their kings will shudder with horror because of you
when I brandish my sword before them.
On the day[e] of your downfall
each of them will tremble
every moment for his life.[f]

11 " 'For this is what the Sovereign LORD says:
" 'The sword of the king of Babylon[g]
will come against you.
12 I will cause your hordes to fall
by the swords of mighty men—
the most ruthless of all nations.[h]
They will shatter the pride of Egypt,
and all her hordes will be overthrown.[i]
13 I will destroy all her cattle
from beside abundant waters
no longer to be stirred by the foot of man
or muddied by the hoofs of cattle.[j]
14 Then I will let her waters settle
and make her streams flow like oil,
declares the Sovereign LORD.
15 When I make Egypt desolate
and strip the land of everything in it,
when I strike down all who live there,
then they will know that I am the LORD.[k]'

16 "This is the lament[l] they will chant for her. The daughters of the nations will chant
it; for Egypt and all her hordes they will chant it, declares the Sovereign LORD."

17 In the twelfth year, on the fifteenth day of the month, the word of the LORD came to
me:[m] 18 "Son of man, wail for the hordes of Egypt and consign[n] to the earth below both
her and the daughters of mighty nations, with those who go down to the pit.[o] 19 Say to
them, 'Are you more favored than others? Go down and be laid among the uncircumcised.'[p] 20 They will fall among those killed by the sword. The sword is drawn; let her be
dragged[q] off with all her hordes. 21 From within the grave[b][r] the mighty leaders will say
of Egypt and her allies, 'They have come down and they lie with the uncircumcised, with
those killed by the sword.'

22 "Assyria is there with her whole army; she is surrounded by the graves of all her
slain, all who have fallen by the sword. 23 Their graves are in the depths of the pit[s] and
her army lies around her grave. All who had spread terror in the land of the living are
slain, fallen by the sword.

24 "Elam[t] is there, with all her hordes around her grave. All of them are slain, fallen
by the sword.[u] All who had spread terror in the land of the living[v] went down uncircumcised to the earth below. They bear their shame with those who go down to the pit.[w] 25 A

32:10 [e]Jer 46:10 [f]Eze 26:16; 27:35
32:11 [g]Jer 46:26
32:12 [h]Eze 28:7 [i]Eze 31:11-12
32:13 [j]Eze 29:8,11
32:15 [k]Ex 7:5; 14:4,18; Ps 107:33-34; Eze 6:7
32:16 [l]2Sa 1:17; 2Ch 35:25; Eze 26:17
32:17 [m]ver 1
32:18 [n]Jer 1:10 [o]Eze 31:14,16; Mic 1:8
32:19 [p]ver 29-30; Eze 28:10; 31:18
32:20 [q]Ps 28:3
32:21 [r]Isa 14:9
32:23 [s]Isa 14:15
32:24 [t]Ge 10:22 [u]Jer 49:37 [v]Job 28:13 [w]Eze 26:20

[a] 9 Hebrew; Septuagint *bring you into captivity among the nations, / to* [b] 21 Hebrew *Sheol*; also in verse 27

32:11 sword. God would subdue the sea monster, Egypt, by bringing the armies of Babylon against her (see note on v. 2). The sword of the king of Babylon was the sword of the Lord (21:1–32; 30:25).
■ **32:17–32** *Lament for Egypt and Pharaoh.* Ezekiel closed his oracles against the nations with a final lament for the troubles Egypt would face.
32:17 twelfth year . . . fifteenth day. Presumably the twelfth month of the year, as in the preceding oracle (v. 1), so that this oracle followed two weeks later in the spring of 585 B.C.
32:18 consign to the earth below. Describes Egypt's descent to the netherworld, where that proud empire became just one more among the great and small states that had preceded her (Assyria, v. 22; Elam, v. 24; Meshech and Tubal, v. 26; Edom, v. 29; Sidon and the northern princes, v. 30). The mythology and religion of these cultures portrayed the netherworld ("Sheol" or "the grave") as a vast burial chamber where the dead shared a shadowy and joyless existence. Compare Genesis 37:35, 42:38, Job 3:17–19, 7:9, 10:20–22, 17:13, 40:13, Psalms 31:17, 88:5 and 11, 115:17, Proverbs 1:12, 5:5, 7:27, 9:18, Ecclesiastes 9:10, Isaiah 5:14, 14:9–11, 38:18 and Habakkuk 2:5.

bed is made for her among the slain, with all her hordes around her grave. All of them
are uncircumcised, killed by the sword. Because their terror had spread in the land of
the living, they bear their shame with those who go down to the pit; they are laid among
the slain.
26 "Meshech and Tubal[x] are there, with all their hordes around their graves. All of
them are uncircumcised, killed by the sword because they spread their terror in the land
of the living. 27 Do they not lie with the other uncircumcised warriors who have fallen,
who went down to the grave with their weapons of war, whose swords were placed under their heads? The punishment for their sins rested on their bones, though the terror
of these warriors had stalked through the land of the living.
28 "You too, O Pharaoh, will be broken and will lie among the uncircumcised, with
those killed by the sword.
29 "Edom[y] is there, her kings and all her princes; despite their power, they are laid
with those killed by the sword. They lie with the uncircumcised, with those who go down
to the pit.[z]
30 "All the princes of the north[a] and all the Sidonians[b] are there; they went down with
the slain in disgrace despite the terror caused by their power. They lie uncircumcised
with those killed by the sword and bear their shame with those who go down to the pit.
31 "Pharaoh—he and all his army—will see them and he will be consoled[c] for all his
hordes that were killed by the sword, declares the Sovereign LORD. 32 Although I had him
spread terror in the land of the living, Pharaoh and all his hordes will be laid among the
uncircumcised, with those killed by the sword, declares the Sovereign LORD."

Ezekiel a Watchman

33 The word of the LORD came to me: 2 "Son of man, speak to your countrymen and
say to them: 'When I bring the sword[d] against a land, and the people of the land
choose one of their men and make him their watchman,[e] 3 and he sees the sword coming
against the land and blows the trumpet[f] to warn the people, 4 then if anyone hears the
trumpet but does not take warning[g] and the sword comes and takes his life, his blood will
be on his own head.[h] 5 Since he heard the sound of the trumpet but did not take warning,
his blood will be on his own head. If he had taken warning, he would have saved himself.
6 But if the watchman sees the sword coming and does not blow the trumpet to warn the
people and the sword comes and takes the life of one of them, that man will be taken away
because of his sin, but I will hold the watchman accountable for his blood.'[i]
7 "Son of man, I have made you a watchman for the house of Israel; so hear the word
I speak and give them warning from me.[j] 8 When I say to the wicked, 'O wicked man, you
will surely die,[k]' and you do not speak out to dissuade him from his ways, that wicked
man will die for[a] his sin, and I will hold you accountable for his blood.[l] 9 But if you do
warn the wicked man to turn from his ways and he does not do so, he will die for his sin,
but you will have saved yourself.[m]
10 "Son of man, say to the house of Israel, 'This is what you are saying: "Our offenses
and sins weigh us down, and we are wasting away[n] because of[b] them. How then can we
live?[o]" ' 11 Say to them, 'As surely as I live, declares the Sovereign LORD, I take no pleasure in the death of the wicked, but rather that they turn from their ways and live.[p] Turn!
Turn from your evil ways! Why will you die, O house of Israel?'[q]
12 "Therefore, son of man, say to your countrymen, 'The righteousness of the righteous man will not save him when he disobeys, and the wickedness of the wicked man
will not cause him to fall when he turns from it. The righteous man, if he sins, will not
be allowed to live because of his former righteousness.'[r] 13 If I tell the righteous man that
he will surely live, but then he trusts in his righteousness and does evil, none of the righ-

32:26 [x]Ge 10:2; Eze 27:13
32:29 [y]Isa 34:5-15; Jer 49:7; Eze 35:15; Ob 1:1 [z]Eze 25:12-14
32:30 [a]Jer 25:26; Eze 38:6; 39:2 [b]Jer 25:22; Eze 28:21
32:31 [c]Eze 14:22; 31:16
33:2 [d]Jer 12:12 [e]Eze 3:11
33:3 [f]Hos 8:1
33:4 [g]2Ch 25:16 [h]Jer 6:17; Eze 18:13; Zec 1:4; Ac 18:6
33:6 [i]Eze 3:18
33:7 [j]Jer 26:2; Eze 3:17
33:8 [k]ver 14 [l]Eze 18:4
33:9 [m]Eze 3:17-19
33:10 [n]Eze 24:23 [o]Lev 26:39; Eze 4:17
33:11 [p]Eze 18:32; 2Pe 3:9 [q]Eze 18:23
33:12 [r]2Ch 7:14; Eze 3:20

[a] *8* Or *in*; also in verse 9 [b] *10* Or *away in*

32:26 Meshech and Tubal. See note on 27:13.

■ **33:1—48:35** *Future Blessings for Judah and Jerusalem.* This chapter begins the third major section of Ezekiel. In the first Ezekiel had been primarily concerned with Jerusalem's past and present (1:1—24:27); in the second he had focused on the destruction of other nations (25:1—32:32). In this third section he concentrated on the future blessings of restoration Judah would enjoy after exile. This section divides into two major parts: Judah's fall and restoration (33:1—39:29) and a vision of Jerusalem restored (40:1—48:35).

■ **33:1—39:29** *Judah's Fall and Restoration.* Ezekiel traced the theme of Judah's future after exile in eight main sections: his own recommissioning as a watchman (33:1–20), the spiritual division among Israelites (33:21–33), shepherds of the past and future (34:1–31), Edom condemned (35:1–15), prophecies to the mountains of Israel (36:1–38), the resurrection of dry bones (37:1–14), joining of two sticks (37:15–28) and victory in a great future battle (38:1—39:29).

■ **33:1–20** *Ezekiel Recommissioned as a Watchman.* Ezekiel indicated his recommissioning by repeating two important themes from an earlier portion: (1) reiterating his call as watchman (vv. 1–9; cf. 3:16–21) and (2) emphasizing the doctrine of individual moral responsibility (vv. 10–20; ch. 18). The exiles heard the news of the destruction of Jerusalem (v. 21); the remainder of Ezekiel's utterances about Jerusalem anticipated her restoration.

teous things he has done will be remembered; he will die for the evil he has done.[s] 14 And
if I say to the wicked man, 'You will surely die,' but he then turns away from his sin and
does what is just[t] and right— 15 if he gives back what he took in pledge for a loan, returns
what he has stolen,[u] follows the decrees that give life, and does no evil, he will surely
live; he will not die.[v] 16 None of the sins he has committed will be remembered against
him. He has done what is just and right; he will surely live.[w]
17 "Yet your countrymen say, 'The way of the Lord is not just.' But it is their way that
is not just. 18 If a righteous man turns from his righteousness and does evil, he will die
for it.[x] 19 And if a wicked man turns away from his wickedness and does what is just and
right, he will live by doing so. 20 Yet, O house of Israel, you say, 'The way of the Lord is
not just.' But I will judge each of you according to his own ways."

Jerusalem's Fall Explained

21 In the twelfth year of our exile, in the tenth month on the fifth day, a man who had
escaped[y] from Jerusalem came to me and said, "The city has fallen![z]" 22 Now the evening
before the man arrived, the hand of the LORD was upon me,[a] and he opened my mouth[b]
before the man came to me in the morning. So my mouth was opened and I was no longer silent.[c]
23 Then the word of the LORD came to me: 24 "Son of man, the people living in those ruins[d] in the land of Israel are saying, 'Abraham was only one man, yet he possessed the
land. But we are many; surely the land has been given to us as our possession.'[e] 25 Therefore say to them, 'This is what the Sovereign LORD says: Since you eat meat with the
blood[f] still in it and look to your idols and shed blood, should you then possess the land?[g]
26 You rely on your sword, you do detestable things, and each of you defiles his neighbor's
wife.[h] Should you then possess the land?'
27 "Say this to them: 'This is what the Sovereign LORD says: As surely as I live, those
who are left in the ruins will fall by the sword, those out in the country I will give to the
wild animals to be devoured, and those in strongholds and caves will die of a plague.[i]
28 I will make the land a desolate waste, and her proud strength will come to an end, and
the mountains of Israel will become desolate so that no one will cross them. 29 Then they
will know that I am the LORD, when I have made the land a desolate waste because of all
the detestable things they have done.'
30 "As for you, son of man, your countrymen are talking together about you by the
walls and at the doors of the houses, saying to each other, 'Come and hear the message
that has come from the LORD.' 31 My people come to you, as they usually do, and sit before[j] you to listen to your words, but they do not put them into practice. With their
mouths they express devotion, but their hearts are greedy for unjust gain.[k] 32 Indeed, to
them you are nothing more than one who sings love songs with a beautiful voice and
plays an instrument well, for they hear your words but do not put them into practice.[l]
33 "When all this comes true—and it surely will—then they will know that a prophet
has been among them.[m]"

Shepherds and Sheep

34 The word of the LORD came to me: 2 "Son of man, prophesy against the shepherds of Israel; prophesy and say to them: 'This is what the Sovereign LORD says:

33:13 [s]Eze 18:24; Heb 10:38; 2Pe 2:20-21
33:14 [t]Eze 18:27
33:15 [u]Ex 22:1-4; Lev 6:2-5 [v]Eze 20:11; Lk 19:8
33:16 [w]Isa 43:25; Eze 18:22
33:18 [x]Eze 3:20; Eze 18:26
33:21 [y]Eze 24:26 [z]2Ki 25:4,10; Jer 39:1-2; Eze 32:1
33:22 [a]Eze 1:3 [b]Lk 1:64 [c]Eze 3:26-27; 24:27
33:24 [d]Eze 36:4 [e]Isa 51:2; Jer 40:7; Eze 11:15; Ac 7:5
33:25 [f]Ge 9:4; Dt 12:16 [g]Jer 7:9-10; Eze 22:6,27
33:26 [h]Eze 22:11
33:27 [i]1Sa 13:6; Isa 2:19; Jer 42:22; Eze 39:4
33:31 [j]Eze 8:1 [k]Ps 78:36-37; Isa 29:13; Eze 22:27; Mt 13:22; 1Jn 3:18
33:32 [l]Mk 6:20
33:33 [m]1Sa 3:20; Jer 28:9; Eze 2:5

■ **33:21–33** *Judah's Fall and Two Groups of Israelites.* Jerusalem's destruction left Ezekiel with two groups to address: those living in the ruins and those in exile. Neither group was faring well in the eyes of God.
33:21 twelfth year . . . tenth month . . . fifth day. Jerusalem was destroyed by fire during the fifth month of the eleventh year of Jehoiachin's rule (2Ki 25:8–9; Jer 52:12). If news did not reach the exiles until the twelfth year, tenth month, then it took over a year and a half for it to arrive—far longer than the journey would have required (cf. Ezr 7:9); less than six months is far more probable. Thus, many prefer to follow the reading in a few Hebrew texts and an ancient Syriac translation in which the news is said to have reached the exiles in the eleventh year instead of the twelfth; the difference in the two readings is a single Hebrew consonant.
33:22 opened my mouth. Ezekiel had been silent for a sustained period; see notes on 3:24–27 and 24:27. News of Jerusalem's destruction was about to reach the exiles, and he could now speak. Ezekiel addressed (1) those who remained in Judah (vv. 23–29) and (2) those with him in exile (vv. 30–33).
33:24 people living in those ruins. Those who remained in Judah.
33:25 you eat meat with the blood. A practice forbidden in Genesis 9:4, Leviticus 7:26–27, 17:10 and Deuteronomy 12:16 and 23.
33:26 wife. See 18:6, 11 and 15.
33:30–32 See *WLC* 119.
33:30 talking together. Ezekiel had been ignored and even ridiculed, but now that events had confirmed the truth of his words he had become popular. But the people were still not listening with the kind of care that resulted in repentance and obedience (v. 11).
33:32 love songs. No longer dismissing him as the prattler of parables (see note on 20:49), the exiles saw Ezekiel as a source of entertainment. Listening to him became a way to fill an idle afternoon or evening.
■ **34:1–31** *Shepherds of the Past and Future.* Ezekiel drew attention to the terrible leadership in the past and to God's plan to replace that leadership with his own direct care through a future son of David (34:24). This prophecy was and will be fulfilled in Christ, the great Shepherd of the sheep (Jn 10:11–14).
34:2–10 Woe to the shepherds of Israel. Sheep that are weak, injured or ill are the particular objects of a shepherd's attention; considerable effort is directed to caring for them. In the ancient world one ideal for kingship was to care for the people like a shepherd. The poor and the oppressed were to be the particular object

Woe to the shepherds of Israel who only take care of themselves! Should not shepherds
take care of the flock?[n] 3You eat the curds, clothe yourselves with the wool and slaughter the choice animals, but you do not take care of the flock.[o] 4You have not strengthened the weak or healed the sick or bound up the injured. You have not brought back
the strays or searched for the lost. You have ruled them harshly and brutally.[p] 5So they
were scattered because there was no shepherd,[q] and when they were scattered they became food for all the wild animals.[r] 6My sheep wandered over all the mountains and on
every high hill. They were scattered over the whole earth, and no one searched or
looked for them.[s]

7" 'Therefore, you shepherds, hear the word of the LORD: 8As surely as I live, declares
the Sovereign LORD, because my flock lacks a shepherd and so has been plundered and
has become food for all the wild animals, and because my shepherds did not search for
my flock but cared for themselves rather than for my flock, 9therefore, O shepherds, hear
the word of the LORD: 10This is what the Sovereign LORD says: I am against[t] the shepherds
and will hold them accountable for my flock. I will remove them from tending the flock
so that the shepherds can no longer feed themselves. I will rescue[u] my flock from their
mouths, and it will no longer be food for them.[v]

11" 'For this is what the Sovereign LORD says: I myself will search for my sheep and
look after them. 12As a shepherd[w] looks after his scattered flock when he is with them,
so will I look after my sheep. I will rescue them from all the places where they were scattered on a day of clouds and darkness.[x] 13I will bring them out from the nations and gather them from the countries, and I will bring them into their own land. I will pasture them
on the mountains of Israel, in the ravines and in all the settlements in the land.[y] 14I will
tend them in a good pasture, and the mountain heights of Israel[z] will be their grazing
land. There they will lie down in good grazing land, and there they will feed in a rich pasture[a] on the mountains of Israel.[b] 15I myself will tend my sheep and have them lie down,
declares the Sovereign LORD.[c] 16I will search for the lost and bring back the strays. I will
bind up the injured and strengthen the weak,[d] but the sleek and the strong I will destroy.
I will shepherd the flock with justice.[e]

17" 'As for you, my flock, this is what the Sovereign LORD says: I will judge between one
sheep and another, and between rams and goats.[f] 18Is it not enough for you to feed on the
good pasture? Must you also trample the rest of your pasture with your feet? Is it not
enough for you to drink clear water? Must you also muddy the rest with your feet? 19Must
my flock feed on what you have trampled and drink what you have muddied with your feet?

20" 'Therefore this is what the Sovereign LORD says to them: See, I myself will judge
between the fat sheep and the lean sheep. 21Because you shove with flank and shoulder,
butting all the weak sheep with your horns[g] until you have driven them away, 22I will
save my flock, and they will no longer be plundered. I will judge between one sheep and
another.[h] 23I will place over them one shepherd, my servant David, and he will tend[i]
them; he will tend them and be their shepherd. 24I the LORD will be their God,[j] and my
servant David will be prince among them. I the LORD have spoken.[k]

25" 'I will make a covenant of peace with them and rid the land of wild beasts[l] so that
they may live in the desert and sleep in the forests in safety.[m] 26I will bless[n] them and
the places surrounding my hill.[a] I will send down showers in season;[o] there will be show-

34:2 [n]Ps 78:70-72; Isa 40:11; Jer 3:15; 23:1; Mic 3:11; Jn 10:11; 21:15-17
34:3 [o]Isa 56:11; Eze 22:27; Zec 11:16
34:4 [p]Zec 11:15-17
34:5 [q]Nu 27:17 [r]ver 28; Isa 56:9
34:6 [s]Ps 142:4; 1Pe 2:25
34:10 [t]Jer 21:13 [u]Ps 72:14 [v]1Sa 2:29-30; Zec 10:3
34:12 [w]Isa 40:11; Jer 31:10; Lk 19:10 [x]Eze 30:3
34:13 [y]Jer 23:3
34:14 [z]Eze 20:40 [a]Ps 23:2 [b]Eze 36:29-30
34:15 [c]Ps 23:1-2
34:16 [d]Mic 4:6 [e]Isa 10:16; Lk 5:32
34:17 [f]Mt 25:32-33
34:21 [g]Dt 33:17
34:22 [h]Ps 72:12-14; Jer 23:2-3
34:23 [i]Isa 40:11
34:24 [j]Eze 36:28 [k]Jer 30:9
34:25 [l]Lev 26:6 [m]Isa 11:6-9; Hos 2:18
34:26 [n]Ge 12:2 [o]Ps 68:9

[a] 26 Or *I will make them and the places surrounding my hill a blessing*

of royal care. See note on 22:7. However, Jerusalem's kings, instead of relieving oppression and exploitation, all too often were numbered among the chief oppressors.
34:2–4 See *WLC* 130; *WSC* 65.
34:11 I myself. Having set aside those unfaithful undershepherds, God took upon himself the role of shepherd; see note on verses 2–10. Compare the parable of the good shepherd who searched for his lost sheep (Lk 15:3–7).
34:12 clouds and darkness. Language ordinarily associated with the day of the Lord (Joel 2:2; Zep 1:15; cf. Ex 20:18,21; Dt 4:11; 5:22–23; 1Ki 8:12; Ps 97:2; Isa 60:2; Jer 13:16; 23:12; Am 5:18–20). See note on 7:7.
34:17 rams and goats. God's judgment was not confined to the shepherds alone but would also include the cattle. Some of the cattle in the herd had been bullying others; these were probably members of the powerful and wealthy classes of Jerusalem society who had oppressed the poorer classes. Compare the situation in the restoration community (Ne 5).
34:23 David. This promise of restoration (vv. 6,10–16) looks forward to a Messianic kingdom. God's servant, one like David, would rule in peace, righteousness and prosperity exceeding that known during the rule of the historical David. No descendant of David in the restoration period fulfilled Ezekiel's prophetic description of Israel's future; the New Testament writers identified Jesus as that good shepherd (see note on vv. 2–10).
34:24 David will be prince. As the prophets repeated time and again, the future of Israel was directly tied to the future of David's line. After the exile the great son of David would rise and rule over Israel and eventually over the entire earth (cf. Am 9:11–15). **prince.** See note on 37:24.
34:25 covenant of peace. The imagery of Paradise restored. The verses that follow spell out what this covenant would entail; it would include safety and agricultural bounty. This covenant after exile is identical with "the new covenant" promised by Jeremiah (see notes on Jer 31:31). **safety.** The subjugation of wild animals was reminiscent of the original status of humanity in the garden. Wild animals were a particular danger when covenant curses came to fruition, and safety from them was an important covenant blessing (Lev 26:6; Dt 33:20; Jdg 14:5–6; 1Sa 17:34–37; 1Ki 13:24–28; 20:36; 2Ki 2:24; 17:25–26; Pss 7:2; 10:9; 17:12; Pr 28:15; Isa 31:4; Jer 5:6; La 3:10; Hos 13:8; Am 3:4,8,12; 5:19; Mic 5:8; cf. Isa 11:6–9; 65:25).
34:26 bless them. Agricultural prosperity was a common theme

ers of blessing.[p] 27 The trees of the field will yield their fruit and the ground will yield its
crops; the people will be secure in their land. They will know that I am the LORD, when
I break the bars of their yoke[q] and rescue them from the hands of those who enslaved
them.[r] 28 They will no longer be plundered by the nations, nor will wild animals devour
them. They will live in safety, and no one will make them afraid.[s] 29 I will provide for them
a land renowned[t] for its crops, and they will no longer be victims of famine[u] in the land
or bear the scorn[v] of the nations.[w] 30 Then they will know that I, the LORD their God, am
with them and that they, the house of Israel, are my people, declares the Sovereign
LORD.[x] 31 You my sheep, the sheep of my pasture,[y] are people, and I am your God, declares the Sovereign LORD.' "

A Prophecy Against Edom

35 The word of the LORD came to me: 2 "Son of man, set your face against Mount
Seir; prophesy against it 3 and say: 'This is what the Sovereign LORD says: I am
against you, Mount Seir, and I will stretch out my hand[z] against you and make you a desolate waste.[a] 4 I will turn your towns into ruins and you will be desolate. Then you will
know that I am the LORD.[b]

5 " 'Because you harbored an ancient hostility and delivered the Israelites over to the
sword at the time of their calamity, the time their punishment reached its climax,[c]
6 therefore as surely as I live, declares the Sovereign LORD, I will give you over to bloodshed and it will pursue you.[d] Since you did not hate bloodshed, bloodshed will pursue
you. 7 I will make Mount Seir a desolate waste and cut off from it all who come and go.
8 I will fill your mountains with the slain; those killed by the sword will fall on your hills
and in your valleys and in all your ravines.[e] 9 I will make you desolate forever; your towns
will not be inhabited. Then you will know that I am the LORD.[f]

10 " 'Because you have said, "These two nations and countries will be ours and we will
take possession[g] of them," even though I the LORD was there, 11 therefore as surely as I
live, declares the Sovereign LORD, I will treat you in accordance with the anger[h] and jealousy you showed in your hatred of them and I will make myself known among them
when I judge you.[i] 12 Then you will know that I the LORD have heard all the contemptible
things you have said against the mountains of Israel. You said, "They have been laid
waste and have been given over to us to devour.[j]" 13 You boasted against me and spoke
against me without restraint, and I heard it.[k] 14 This is what the Sovereign LORD says:
While the whole earth rejoices, I will make you desolate.[l] 15 Because you rejoiced[m]
when the inheritance of the house of Israel became desolate, that is how I will treat you.
You will be desolate, O Mount Seir,[n] you and all of Edom.[o] Then they will know that I
am the LORD.' "

A Prophecy to the Mountains of Israel

36 "Son of man, prophesy to the mountains of Israel and say, 'O mountains of Israel, hear the word of the LORD. 2 This is what the Sovereign LORD says: The enemy said of you, "Aha![p] The ancient heights[q] have become our possession.[r]" ' 3 Therefore prophesy and say, 'This is what the Sovereign LORD says: Because they ravaged and
hounded you from every side so that you became the possession of the rest of the nations
and the object of people's malicious talk and slander,[s] 4 therefore, O mountains of Israel, hear the word of the Sovereign LORD: This is what the Sovereign LORD says to the
mountains and hills, to the ravines and valleys,[t] to the desolate ruins and the deserted
towns that have been plundered and ridiculed by the rest of the nations around you[u]—
5 this is what the Sovereign LORD says: In my burning zeal I have spoken against the rest
of the nations, and against all Edom, for with glee and with malice in their hearts they
made my land their own possession so that they might plunder its pastureland.'[v] 6 Therefore prophesy concerning the land of Israel and say to the mountains and hills, to the ravines and valleys: 'This is what the Sovereign LORD says: I speak in my jealous wrath because you have suffered the scorn of the nations.[w] 7 Therefore this is what the Sovereign
LORD says: I swear with uplifted hand that the nations around you will also suffer scorn.

34:26 [p]Dt 11:13-15; Isa 44:3
34:27 [q]Lev 26:13 [r]Jer 30:8
34:28 [s]Jer 30:10; Eze 39:26
34:29 [t]Isa 4:2 [u]Eze 36:29 [v]Eze 36:6 [w]Eze 36:15
34:30 [x]Eze 14:11; 37:27
34:31 [y]Ps 100:3; Jer 23:1
35:3 [z]Jer 6:12 [a]Eze 25:12-14
35:4 [b]ver 9
35:5 [c]Ps 137:7; Eze 21:29
35:6 [d]Isa 63:2-6
35:8 [e]Eze 31:12
35:9 [f]Jer 49:13
35:10 [g]Ps 83:12; Eze 36:2,5
35:11 [h]Eze 25:14 [i]Ps 9:16; Mt 7:2
35:12 [j]Jer 50:7
35:13 [k]Da 11:36
35:14 [l]Jer 51:48
35:15 [m]Ob 1:12 [n]ver 3 [o]Isa 34:5-6,11; Jer 50:11-13; La 4:21
36:2 [p]Eze 25:3 [q]Dt 32:13 [r]Eze 35:10
36:3 [s]Ps 44:13-14
36:4 [t]Eze 6:3 [u]Dt 11:11; Ps 79:4; Eze 34:28
36:5 [v]Jer 50:11; Eze 25:12-14; 35:10,15
36:6 [w]Ps 123:3-4; Eze 34:29

---

concerning the latter days (vv. 25–29). See theological article "The Plan of the Ages" at Hebrews 7.

34:30 Then they will know. See note on 6:7. **with them . . . my people.** God's covenant with the Israelites was that he would be their God and they would be his people (11:20; 36:28; Ex 6:7; Lev 26:12; Dt 7:6; 14:2,21; 27:9; 29:13; Ps 50:7; Isa 51:22; Jer 7:23; 11:4; 30:22; Joel 2:27). Mutual love and loyalty bound God to his repentant people.

■ **35:1–15** *Edom's Condemnation.* An oracle against Mount Seir; that is, Edom (Ge 32:3; 36:8–9; Nu 24:18; 2Ch 20:2,10; 25:14).

35:2 Mount Seir. Used as a synonym for Edom. Edom was located along the margin of arable land southeast of the Dead Sea; Seir was the chief mountain range in the country (35:15; Ge 32:3; 36:8–9; Dt 2:8; Jdg 5:4; 2Ch 20:10,22–23; 25:14).

8 " 'But you, O mountains of Israel, will produce branches and fruit[x] for my people Israel, for they will soon come home. 9 I am concerned for you and will look on you with
favor; you will be plowed and sown, 10 and I will multiply the number of people upon you,
even the whole house of Israel. The towns will be inhabited and the ruins rebuilt.[y] 11 I will
increase the number of men and animals upon you, and they will be fruitful and become
numerous. I will settle people on you as in the past[z] and will make you prosper more
than before.[a] Then you will know that I am the LORD. 12 I will cause people, my people Israel, to walk upon you. They will possess you, and you will be their inheritance;[b] you will
never again deprive them of their children.

13 " 'This is what the Sovereign LORD says: Because people say to you, "You devour
men[c] and deprive your nation of its children," 14 therefore you will no longer devour men
or make your nation childless, declares the Sovereign LORD. 15 No longer will I make you
hear the taunts of the nations, and no longer will you suffer the scorn of the peoples or
cause your nation to fall, declares the Sovereign LORD.[d] ' "

16 Again the word of the LORD came to me: 17 "Son of man, when the people of Israel
were living in their own land, they defiled it by their conduct and their actions. Their conduct was like a woman's monthly uncleanness in my sight.[e] 18 So I poured out[f] my wrath
on them because they had shed blood in the land and because they had defiled it with
their idols. 19 I dispersed them among the nations, and they were scattered[g] through the
countries; I judged them according to their conduct and their actions.[h] 20 And wherever
they went among the nations they profaned[i] my holy name, for it was said of them, 'These
are the LORD's people, and yet they had to leave his land.'[j] 21 I had concern for my holy
name, which the house of Israel profaned among the nations where they had gone.[k]

22 "Therefore say to the house of Israel, 'This is what the Sovereign LORD says: It is not
for your sake, O house of Israel, that I am going to do these things, but for the sake of my
holy name, which you have profaned[l] among the nations where you have gone.[m] 23 I will
show the holiness of my great name, which has been profaned among the nations, the
name you have profaned among them. Then the nations will know that I am the LORD, declares the Sovereign LORD, when I show myself holy[n] through you before their eyes.[o]

24 " 'For I will take you out of the nations; I will gather you from all the countries and
bring you back into your own land.[p] 25 I will sprinkle[q] clean water on you, and you will
be clean; I will cleanse[r] you from all your impurities and from all your idols.[s] 26 I will give
you a new heart[t] and put a new spirit in you; I will remove from you your heart of stone
and give you a heart of flesh.[u] 27 And I will put my Spirit[v] in you and move you to follow
my decrees and be careful to keep my laws. 28 You will live in the land I gave your forefathers; you will be my people,[w] and I will be your God.[x] 29 I will save you from all your
uncleanness. I will call for the grain and make it plentiful and will not bring famine[y]
upon you. 30 I will increase the fruit of the trees and the crops of the field, so that you will
no longer suffer disgrace among the nations because of famine.[z] 31 Then you will remember your evil ways and wicked deeds, and you will loathe yourselves for your sins and detestable practices.[a] 32 I want to know that I am not doing this for your sake, declares
the Sovereign LORD. Be ashamed and disgraced for your conduct, O house of Israel![b]

36:8 [x]Isa 27:6
36:10 [y]ver 33; Isa 49:17-23
36:11 [z]Mic 7:14 [a]Jer 31:28; Eze 16:55
36:12 [b]Eze 47:14,22
36:13 [c]Nu 13:32
36:15 [d]Ps 89:50-51; Eze 34:29
36:17 [e]Jer 2:7
36:18 [f]2Ch 34:21
36:19 [g]Dt 28:64 [h]Eze 39:24
36:20 [i]Ro 2:24 [j]Isa 52:5; Jer 33:24; Eze 12:16
36:21 [k]Ps 74:18; Isa 48:9
36:22 [l]Ro 2:24* [m]Ps 106:8
36:23 [n]Eze 20:41 [o]Ps 126:2; Isa 5:16
36:24 [p]Eze 34:13; 37:21
36:25 [q]Heb 9:13; 10:22 [r]Ps 51:2,7 [s]Zec 13:2
36:26 [t]Jer 24:7 [u]Ps 51:10; Eze 11:19
36:27 [v]Eze 37:14
36:28 [w]Jer 30:22 [x]Eze 14:11; 37:14, 27
36:29 [y]Eze 34:29
36:30 [z]Lev 26:4-5; Eze 34:27; Hos 2:21-22
36:31 [a]Eze 6:9; 20:43
36:32 [b]Dt 9:5

35:10 two nations. Israel and Judah. **ours.** Contrast Deuteronomy 2:2–8, in which Israel was forbidden to take the territory of Edom because God had given it to the descendants of Esau.

■**36:1–38** *A Prophecy to the Mountains of Israel.* The mountains of Israel, once blessed by God and now under his wrath—but their future blessing was assured.

36:2 ancient heights. Refers to the land God had promised Israel or, more narrowly, to the heights of Zion (17:23; 34:14; Dt 32:13; Pss 48:2; 78:69; Isa 31:4; 58:14; Jer 31:12).

36:12 children. Israel would prosper and be more populous than before the recent disaster (vv. 11–12; cf. Zec 2:4). Children were often the first to feel the effects of war; they lost fathers in battle and succumbed to diseases that ravaged the population in famine and siege. For this reason the prophets often described God's future blessing in terms of multitudes of children (36:12–13; 37:25; Isa 43:5; 49:20; 54:1; 59:21; 66:8; Jer 30:20; 31:17; Zec 8:5).

36:13 You devour men. Compare Numbers 13:32.

36:17 defiled. The exile resulted from God's regard for his own holiness (vv. 16–23). God would graciously preserve a remnant according to his promises to the patriarchs and to David, but his commands could not be transgressed with impunity. See 6:8. **monthly uncleanness.** Menstrual period. See 18:6 and 22:9–10.

36:21–23 See *WLC* 114.

36:22 not for your sake . . . my holy name. The ultimate purpose of all things in history, including Israel's exile, was and is the glory and honor of God. See *BC* 23.

36:25–27 See *WCF* 7.3; 16.3; *WLC* 67; *WSC* 31; *HC* 70.

36:25 sprinkle clean water on you. Referred to ritual purification for removing ceremonial defilement (Ex 30:17–21; Lev 14:52; Nu 19:17–19). Sprinkling or pouring water also symbolized the impartation of God's Spirit in the anointing of kings, priests and occasionally prophets; the outpouring of God's Spirit was a sign of the Messianic age (37:14; 39:29; Isa 42:1; 44:3; 59:21; Joel 2:28–29). This rich symbolism is attached to baptism in the New Testament (see note on Heb 10:22). The language of verses 25–27 closely parallels that of Psalm 51:7–11.

36:26 new heart . . . new spirit. See 11:19 and 18:31. Instead of a heart unable to respond to the law and commands of God with love and obedience, God would grant a new heart and new spirit. Note that these would come as the result of divine initiative and grace rather than of human attainment. Jeremiah spoke similarly of a new covenant (Jer 31:33; cf. Pr 3:3; 7:3; Ro 2:15,29; 2Co 3:3; Heb 8:10; 10:16). See *WCF* 10.1; *CD* 3–4.VIII.

36:27 my Spirit. The new spirit would be God's Spirit, who would transform those in whom he dwelt and enable them to obey the law of God. Compare Romans 7:6, 8:2–18, 12:1, Galatians 5:16–18 and 22 and 1 John 3:24. See *WCF* 10.1; 10.2; 19.7; *WLC* 32,77.

36:28 my people . . . your God. See 34:30.

36:31–32 See *WCF* 15.2; 15.3; *WLC* 76,87; *BC* 23.

33 " 'This is what the Sovereign LORD says: On the day I cleanse you from all your sins,
I will resettle your towns, and the ruins will be rebuilt. 34 The desolate land will be cultivated instead of lying desolate in the sight of all who pass through it. 35 They will say,
"This land that was laid waste has become like the garden of Eden;[c] the cities that were
lying in ruins, desolate and destroyed, are now fortified and inhabited.[d]" 36 Then the nations around you that remain will know that I the LORD have rebuilt what was destroyed
and have replanted what was desolate. I the LORD have spoken, and I will do it.'[e]
37 "This is what the Sovereign LORD says: Once again I will yield to the plea of the house
of Israel and do this for them: I will make their people as numerous as sheep, 38 as numerous as the flocks for offerings[f] at Jerusalem during her appointed feasts. So will the
ruined cities be filled with flocks of people. Then they will know that I am the LORD."

The Valley of Dry Bones

37 The hand of the LORD was upon me,[g] and he brought me out by the Spirit[h] of
the LORD and set me in the middle of a valley;[i] it was full of bones.[j] 2 He led me
back and forth among them, and I saw a great many bones on the floor of the valley,
bones that were very dry. 3 He asked me, "Son of man, can these bones live?"
I said, "O Sovereign LORD, you alone know.[k]"
4 Then he said to me, "Prophesy to these bones and say to them, 'Dry bones, hear the
word of the LORD![l] 5 This is what the Sovereign LORD says to these bones: I will make
breath[a] enter you, and you will come to life.[m] 6 I will attach tendons to you and make
flesh come upon you and cover you with skin; I will put breath in you, and you will come
to life. Then you will know that I am the LORD.[n]' "
7 So I prophesied as I was commanded. And as I was prophesying, there was a noise,
a rattling sound, and the bones came together, bone to bone. 8 I looked, and tendons and
flesh appeared on them and skin covered them, but there was no breath in them.
9 Then he said to me, "Prophesy to the breath;[o] prophesy, son of man, and say to it,
'This is what the Sovereign LORD says: Come from the four winds, O breath, and breathe
into these slain, that they may live.' " 10 So I prophesied as he commanded me, and breath
entered them; they came to life and stood up on their feet—a vast army.[p]
11 Then he said to me: "Son of man, these bones are the whole house of Israel. They
say, 'Our bones are dried up and our hope is gone; we are cut off.'[q] 12 Therefore prophesy and say to them: 'This is what the Sovereign LORD says: O my people, I am going to
open your graves and bring you up from them; I will bring you back to the land of Israel.[r] 13 Then you, my people, will know that I am the LORD, when I open your graves and
bring you up from them. 14 I will put my Spirit[s] in you and you will live, and I will settle
you in your own land. Then you will know that I the LORD have spoken, and I have done
it, declares the LORD.[t]' "

One Nation Under One King

15 The word of the LORD came to me: 16 "Son of man, take a stick of wood and write on
it, 'Belonging to Judah and the Israelites[u] associated with him.[v]' Then take another stick
of wood, and write on it, 'Ephraim's stick, belonging to Joseph and all the house of Isra-

36:35 [c]Joel 2:3 [d]Isa 51:3
36:36 [e]Eze 17:22; 22:14; 37:14; 39:27-28
36:38 [f]1Ki 8:63; 2Ch 35:7-9
37:1 [g]Eze 1:3; 8:3 [h]Eze 11:24; Lk 4:1; Ac 8:39 [i]Jer 7:32 [j]Jer 8:2; Eze 40:1
37:3 [k]Dt 32:39; 1Sa 2:6; Isa 26:19
37:4 [l]Jer 22:29
37:5 [m]Ge 2:7; Ps 104:29-30
37:6 [n]Eze 38:23; Joel 2:27; 3:17
37:9 [o]Ps 104:30
37:10 [p]Rev 11:11
37:11 [q]La 3:54
37:12 [r]Dt 32:39; 1Sa 2:6; Isa 26:19; Hos 13:14; Am 9:14-15
37:14 [s]Joel 2:28-29 [t]Eze 36:27-28,36
37:16 [u]1Ki 12:20; 2Ch 10:17-19 [v]Nu 17:2-3; 2Ch 15:9

[a] 5 The Hebrew for this word can also mean *wind* or *spirit* (see verses 6–14).

36:33 ruins will be rebuilt. Compare Isaiah 44:26, 51:3, 58:12 and 61:4.

36:35 Eden. The land of Israel would become God's paradise; see notes on 28:13–14, 40:16 and 47:1–12.

■ **37:1–14** *The Resurrection of Dry Bones.* Interpreters have long discussed the issue of the relationship between Ezekiel's vision and a general resurrection at the end of time. Though accounts mention prophets restoring dead individuals to life (1Ki 17:17–24; 2Ki 4:8–37; 13:21), the Old Testament says very little about a personal or general resurrection (Job 14:14; 19:25–26; Da 12:2). Ezekiel's images clearly pertained to the situation of the exiles and their hopes for a restoration (v. 14); the vision is not about a resurrection at the end of time. Intertestamental literature, preceding the New Testament, developed the doctrine of the resurrection more fully, and Jesus confirmed that a general resurrection lay in the future (Jn 5:28–29). The image of resurrection in Ezekiel's vision aptly portrayed the spiritual renewal God's people needed if they were to be restored (cf. Eph 2:1–10).

37:1 by the Spirit. The words *breath, spirit* and *wind* in this passage are all renderings of the same Hebrew word, translated to fit the requirements of the context (vv. 1,5,6,8,9,10,14). **valley.** The same term used in 3:22; see note there. Since it is used in Ezekiel only in these two passages, the locale in this vision may have been the same as that in the prophet's call. Some suggest that the setting was the environs of Jerusalem, possibly the Kidron Valley east of the city (47:1–6; Joel 3:12; Zec 14:4).

37:4 Prophesy to these bones. The prophetic word was like God's own word at creation. God spoke and new life was created (Ge 1). Ezekiel's words were similarly effective in this vision, for they were God's words.

37:9 breathe into these slain. Recalls Genesis 2:7.

37:12 open your graves. The vision began with exposed and unburied bones (v. 2) but broadened to the opening of graves.

37:14 you will know. Israel's restoration would be God's testimony to his own power and rule.

■ **37:15–28** *Joining of Two Sticks.* Ezekiel performed another symbolic action (see note on 4:1–3). Two sticks, one bearing the name of the southern kingdom, Judah, and the other that of the northern kingdom, Ephraim (Israel), were held end to end in Ezekiel's hand so that they appeared to be joined (vv. 15–17). Zechariah 11:7 may be based on this passage.

el associated with him.' 17 Join them together into one stick so that they will become one
in your hand.[w]
18 "When your countrymen ask you, 'Won't you tell us what you mean by this?'[x] 19 say
to them, 'This is what the Sovereign LORD says: I am going to take the stick of Joseph—
which is in Ephraim's hand—and of the Israelite tribes associated with him, and join it
to Judah's stick, making them a single stick of wood, and they will become one in my
hand.'[y] 20 Hold before their eyes the sticks you have written on 21 and say to them, 'This
is what the Sovereign LORD says: I will take the Israelites out of the nations where they
have gone. I will gather them from all around and bring them back into their own
land.[z] 22 I will make them one nation in the land, on the mountains of Israel. There will
be one king over all of them and they will never again be two nations or be divided into
two kingdoms.[a] 23 They will no longer defile[b] themselves with their idols and vile images or with any of their offenses, for I will save them from all their sinful backsliding,[a] and
I will cleanse them. They will be my people, and I will be their God.[c]
24 " 'My servant David[d] will be king over them, and they will all have one shepherd.[e]
They will follow my laws and be careful to keep my decrees.[f] 25 They will live in the land
I gave to my servant Jacob, the land where your fathers lived.[g] They and their children
and their children's children will live there forever,[h] and David my servant will be their
prince forever.[i] 26 I will make a covenant of peace[j] with them; it will be an everlasting covenant. I will establish them and increase their numbers,[k] and I will put my sanctuary
among them forever.[l] 27 My dwelling place[m] will be with them; I will be their God, and
they will be my people.[n] 28 Then the nations will know that I the LORD make Israel holy,[o]
when my sanctuary is among them forever.' "

A Prophecy Against Gog

38 The word of the LORD came to me: 2 "Son of man, set your face against Gog, of
the land of Magog,[p] the chief prince of[b] Meshech and Tubal;[q] prophesy against

[a] *23* Many Hebrew manuscripts (see also Septuagint); most Hebrew manuscripts *all their dwelling places where they sinned* [b] *2* Or *the prince of Rosh,*

37:17 [w]ver 24; Isa 11:13; Jer 50:4; Hos 1:11
37:18 [x]Eze 24:19
37:19 [y]Zec 10:6
37:21 [z]Isa 43:5-6; Eze 36:24; 39:27
37:22 [a]Isa 11:13; Jer 3:18; Hos 1:11
37:23 [b]Eze 36:25; 43:7 [c]Eze 11:18; 36:28
37:24 [d]Hos 3:5 [e]Isa 40:11; Eze 34:23 [f]Ps 78:70-71
37:25 [g]Eze 28:25 [h]Am 9:15 [i]Isa 11:1
37:26 [j]Isa 55:3 [k]Jer 30:19 [l]Eze 16:62
37:27 [m]Lev 26:11; Jn 1:14 [n]2Co 6:16*
37:28 [o]Ex 31:13; Eze 20:12
38:2 [p]Ge 10:2 [q]Rev 20:8

37:18–23 one nation. Ezekiel interpreted his own actions (vv. 16–17). The descendants of Joseph's son Ephraim dominated the northern kingdom, which, therefore, was sometimes designated "Ephraim" (2Ch 25:7,10; Isa 7:2,9,17; 11:13; 17:3; Jer 31:20; Hos 4:17; 5:5; 6:4; 8:9; 9:8; 10:6; Zec 9:13). The northern kingdom had fallen to the Assyrians almost a century and a half before Ezekiel's oracle; much of its population was dispersed among other nations and absorbed by them. Ezekiel looked back to the kingdom united under David and Solomon and forward to a future, ideal restoration (33:23,24; Jer 3:18; 23:5–6; Hos 1:11; Am 9:11).

37:24 king. Ezekiel had not used the word *king* in referring to any of the historical rulers of Jerusalem, instead using the term *prince* (v. 25; 7:27; 12:10,12; 19:1; 21:12,25; 22:6; 34:24). Here, however, he described the future Davidic ruler as "king" (vv. 22,24), possibly a subtle way of distinguishing this future ruler from any that Israel had ever known. The New Testament identified this Shepherd-King as Jesus; see notes on at 34:1–31 and 2–10. Jesus reigns over a renewed people of God as their king forever (v. 25; Mt 22:44; 26:64; Mk 12:36; 14:62; 16:19; Lk 20:42; 22:69; Ac 2:33–34; 5:31; 7:56; Ro 8:34; Heb 1:3,13; 12:2; 1Pe 3:22).

37:25–28 will live there forever. Ezekiel clearly spoke of an eschatological reunification, evidenced by his repeated use of "forever" (vv. 25–26,28).

37:25 prince. See note at verse 24.

37:26 covenant of peace. Compare 34:25. **everlasting covenant.** A phrase used of the Noahic covenant (Ge 9:16; Isa 24:5), the Abrahamic covenant (Ge 17:7,13,19; 1Ch 16:17; Ps 105:10), the Davidic covenant (2Sa 23:5; Is 55:3) and the new covenant (Isa 61:8; Jer 32:40; 50:5; Eze 16:60). Compare Numbers 18:19 and 25:12–13. See theological article "The Covenants of Works and Grace" at Genesis 6.

37:27 their God . . . my people. See note on 34:30.

37:28 sanctuary is among them forever. Ezekiel looked for a renewed city of God (chs. 40–48); over 600 years later John had a similar vision (Rev 21), but of a city that needed no temple building (Rev 21:22).

▪ **38:1—39:29** *Victory in the Future Battle.* Before his description of the future city of God Ezekiel described the defeat and removal of her foes, who would oppose the restored community, just as other prophets had predicted that the nations would threaten war against the restored Israel. Some opposition did arise against early efforts to restore the nation (see Ezra and Nehemiah), but they did not amount to much because Israel did not amount to much. Here Gog, the prince of Magog, became the embodiment of ultimate opposition to the kingdom and people of God. God would come as the divine warrior, fighting Israel's battle and delivering an apocalyptic defeat against his foes, preparing the way for the renewed city. This great, final battle was postponed because of the failures of the restored community. It was begun, however, in Christ's death and resurrection, continues in the church today and will be brought to fullness when Christ returns (see notes on Am 9:11–15).

38:1–7 Ezekiel described the formation of an alliance that would take place after the Israelites had returned to the land from exile.

38:2 Gog. The identity of Gog is uncertain. He is often identified with Gyges, a king of Lydia, a land in Anatolia (Asia Minor) near the northeastern corner of the Mediterranean Sea. In Akkadian texts from the seventh century B.C., Gyges is known as an Assyrian vassal; later legend attached to him the invention of coinage. Though the name *Gog* is phonetically similar to the Akkadian word for "Gyges," identification with that historical king is by no means certain. **Magog.** This land ruled by Gog is also otherwise unknown from extant geographical lists or citations in ancient literature; it may mean no more than "land of Gog." **chief prince of Meshech and Tubal.** Though the identification of Gog and Magog remains uncertain, that of Meshech and Tubal is not in doubt (see note on 27:13). They are mentioned by the ancient historians Herodotus and Josephus and in Assyrian documents from the twelfth to the eighth centuries as tribes that lived in central and eastern Anatolia. One king of the Mushku (Meshech) in the late eighth century was known to the Assyrians as Mitas, the Midas known in the classical historians for his legendary wealth.

Considerable misunderstanding has resulted from misguided speculation regarding these geographical terms. Some interpreters have wrongly identified these locations with other sites known from contemporary geography and have proceeded to conjecture regarding future political events. Meshech is thus said to be Moscow, and Tubal is identified with the Russian city Tobolsk, both of which are geographically far removed from the region Ezekiel had in mind. Further, since the word "chief" in the phrase "chief prince" (v. 2) is the Hebrew word *ro'sh,* some have insisted that the phrase mentions instead the "prince of Russia." Even if this word were supposed to be translated as a geographical name and not as "chief," it would scarcely refer to modern Russia. The word *Russia* was brought into the region north of Kiev in the Middle Ages by

him 3and say: 'This is what the Sovereign LORD says: I am against you, O Gog, chief prince
of[a] Meshech and Tubal.[r] 4I will turn you around, put hooks[s] in your jaws and bring you
out with your whole army—your horses, your horsemen fully armed, and a great horde
with large and small shields, all of them brandishing their swords.[t] 5Persia, Cush[b][u] and
Put[v] will be with them, all with shields and helmets, 6also Gomer[w] with all its troops, and
Beth Togarmah[x] from the far north with all its troops—the many nations with you.
7" 'Get ready; be prepared,[y] you and all the hordes gathered about you, and take
command of them. 8After many days[z] you will be called to arms. In future years you will
invade a land that has recovered from war, whose people were gathered from many nations[a] to the mountains of Israel, which had long been desolate. They had been brought
out from the nations, and now all of them live in safety.[b] 9You and all your troops and
the many nations with you will go up, advancing like a storm;[c] you will be like a cloud[d]
covering the land.
10" 'This is what the Sovereign LORD says: On that day thoughts will come into your
mind and you will devise an evil scheme.[e] 11You will say, "I will invade a land of unwalled
villages; I will attack a peaceful and unsuspecting people—all of them living without
walls and without gates and bars.[f] 12I will plunder and loot and turn my hand against
the resettled ruins and the people gathered from the nations, rich in livestock and
goods, living at the center of the land." 13Sheba[g] and Dedan and the merchants of Tarshish and all her villages[c] will say to you, "Have you come to plunder? Have you gathered your hordes to loot, to carry off silver and gold, to take away livestock and goods
and to seize much plunder?[h]" '
14"Therefore, son of man, prophesy and say to Gog: 'This is what the Sovereign LORD
says: In that day, when my people Israel are living in safety,[i] will you not take notice of
it? 15You will come from your place in the far north, you and many nations with you, all
of them riding on horses, a great horde, a mighty army.[j] 16You will advance against my
people Israel like a cloud[k] that covers the land. In days to come, O Gog, I will bring you
against my land, so that the nations may know me when I show myself holy through you
before their eyes.[l]
17" 'This is what the Sovereign LORD says: Are you not the one I spoke of in former days
by my servants the prophets of Israel? At that time they prophesied for years that I would
bring you against them. 18This is what will happen in that day: When Gog attacks the
land of Israel, my hot anger will be aroused, declares the Sovereign LORD. 19In my zeal
and fiery wrath I declare that at that time there shall be a great earthquake in the land
of Israel.[m] 20The fish of the sea, the birds of the air, the beasts of the field, every crea-

38:3 [r]Eze 39:1
38:4 [s]2Ki 19:28 [t]Eze 29:4; Da 11:40
38:5 [u]Ge 10:6 [v]Eze 27:10
38:6 [w]Ge 10:2 [x]Eze 27:14
38:7 [y]Isa 8:9
38:8 [z]Isa 24:22 [a]Isa 11:11 [b]Jer 23:6
38:9 [c]Isa 28:2 [d]Jer 4:13; Joel 2:2
38:10 [e]Ps 36:4; Mic 2:1
38:11 [f]Jer 49:31; Zec 2:4
38:13 [g]Eze 27:22 [h]Isa 10:6; Jer 15:13
38:14 [i]ver 8; Zec 2:5
38:15 [j]Eze 39:2
38:16 [k]ver 9 [l]Isa 29:23; Eze 39:21
38:19 [m]Ps 18:7; Eze 5:13; Hag 2:6, 21

a 3 Or *Gog, prince of Rosh,* b 5 That is, the upper Nile region c 13 Or *her strong lions*

---

the Vikings and therefore would not have been in use in Ezekiel's time.

In describing the threats to Israel's existence the Bible commonly refers to foes coming from the north (Isa 41:25; Jer 1:13–15; 4:6; 6:22; 10:22; 13:20; 15:12; 25:9,26; 46:10,20,24; 50:3,9,41,49; Eze 26:7; 38:6,15; 39:2; Da 11; Zec 2:6; 6:6–8; cf. Isa 5:26–29; 13:1–13; Na 2:2–10; 3:1–3; Heb 1:5–11). References to these northern foes in the preexilic period were allusions to Israel's traditional enemies Assyria, Babylon and Persia; however, in the exilic and postexilic writings the foes from the north took on proportions beyond the ordinary. In his description of this final conflict with the restored community Ezekiel chose to mention tribes on the fringes of kingdoms to the north to indicate that there was to be widespread opposition to the restored kingdom of God. Rather than fuel speculation about future history, modern readers should understand that Ezekiel intended these nations as references to all powers arrayed against God's people. Notably, in his oracles against foreign nations (Eze 29–32), the book contains no judgments on Babylon, where Ezekiel and the exiles were held in captivity.

God and Magog recur in John's apocalyptic description of future conflict between good and evil. In Revelation 20:8 Gog and Magog are both geographical terms.

38:5 Persia, Cush and Put. See 27:10.

38:6 Gomer. Probably a group known to the Assyrians as the Gimirrai and to the Greeks as the Cimmerians, from the area north of the Black Sea. Gog would lead a coalition of nations not only from the north but also from regions south of Israel (Cush and Put). The picture is that of total mobilization against the people of God. Compare the divine summons to war in Joel 3:9–11. **Beth Togarmah.** See note on 27:14.

38:8–16 advancing like a storm. Ezekiel described how the alliance of nations would attack the restored people of God. His words first applied to the resistance that the early postexilic community suffered. But they also pertain to the persecution against the people of God from that point forward, especially against the church until the return of Christ.

38:8 After many days. Ezekiel spoke of a time in the future when Israel would have been regathered into the land. This gathering began in 539 B.C., when Cyrus sent back some Israelites to repopulate the land. Yet continuing sin caused this restoration to fail so that it was postponed until the time of Christ. Christ began to restore the people of God in his first coming, he continues to do so now through the ministry of the church and will completely restore them in his second coming. See "Introduction to the Prophetic Books." See also theological article "The Plan of the Ages" at Hebrews 7.

38:9 like a cloud. An innumerable foe would amass; compare Joel 2:2 and 11 and see Jeremiah 4:13.

38:11 unsuspecting people. Compare the strategy in Judges 18:7–8. Though Gog plotted against Israel, in reality God was bringing the foes to their own destruction (vv. 4,16).

38:13 Sheba. Modern Yemen, at the southwestern corner of the Arabian peninsula. The Sabeans, the people of Sheba, were noted in antiquity for their trade (23:42; 27:22; 1Ki 10:1–2; Job 6:19; Joel 3:8). **Dedan.** A territory in southern Edom (25:13; 27:20; Jer 25:23; 49:8). **Tarshish.** See 27:12.

38:17 the one I spoke of. Ezekiel referred to earlier prophecies that described a foe coming from the north (see note on v. 2). Gog is not named in any other Old Testament prophecy.

38:18–23 a great earthquake. God himself would be Israel's defender. In passages describing the appearance of the divine warrior the prophets commonly spoke also of a reflexive convulsion in the created order; of creation dissolved into primeval chaos (29:3–5; Isa 13:13; 24:18–20; Jer 4:23–26; Hag 2:6,7,21; Joel 2:10,30–31; 3:16; cf. Jdg 5:4; Pss 18:8; 46:3; 68:9; 77:19). See note on 32:6–8.

ture that moves along the ground, and all the people on the face of the earth will tremble at my presence. The mountains will be overturned, the cliffs will crumble and every
wall will fall to the ground.[n] 21 I will summon a sword[o] against Gog on all my mountains,
declares the Sovereign LORD. Every man's sword will be against his brother.[p] 22 I will execute judgment[q] upon him with plague and bloodshed; I will pour down torrents of rain,
hailstones[r] and burning sulfur on him and on his troops and on the many nations with
him. 23 And so I will show my greatness and my holiness, and I will make myself known
in the sight of many nations. Then they will know that I am the LORD.[s]'

39 "Son of man, prophesy against Gog and say: 'This is what the Sovereign LORD
says: I am against you, O Gog, chief prince of[a] Meshech and Tubal.[t] 2 I will turn
you around and drag you along. I will bring you from the far north and send you against
the mountains of Israel. 3 Then I will strike your bow[u] from your left hand and make your
arrows[v] drop from your right hand. 4 On the mountains of Israel you will fall, you and all
your troops and the nations with you. I will give you as food to all kinds of carrion birds
and to the wild animals.[w] 5 You will fall in the open field, for I have spoken, declares the
Sovereign LORD. 6 I will send fire[x] on Magog and on those who live in safety in the coastlands,[y] and they will know that I am the LORD.

7 " 'I will make known my holy name among my people Israel. I will no longer let my
holy name be profaned,[z] and the nations will know that I the LORD am the Holy One in
Israel.[a] 8 It is coming! It will surely take place, declares the Sovereign LORD. This is the
day I have spoken of.

9 " 'Then those who live in the towns of Israel will go out and use the weapons for fuel
and burn them up—the small and large shields, the bows and arrows, the war clubs and
spears. For seven years they will use them for fuel.[b] 10 They will not need to gather wood
from the fields or cut it from the forests, because they will use the weapons for fuel. And
they will plunder those who plundered them and loot those who looted them, declares
the Sovereign LORD.[c]

11 " 'On that day I will give Gog a burial place in Israel, in the valley of those who travel east toward[b] the Sea.[c] It will block the way of travelers, because Gog and all his hordes
will be buried there. So it will be called the Valley of Hamon Gog.[d][d]

12 " 'For seven months the house of Israel will be burying them in order to cleanse the
land.[e] 13 All the people of the land will bury them, and the day I am glorified[f] will be a
memorable day for them, declares the Sovereign LORD.

14 " 'Men will be regularly employed to cleanse the land. Some will go throughout the
land and, in addition to them, others will bury those that remain on the ground. At the
end of the seven months they will begin their search. 15 As they go through the land and
one of them sees a human bone, he will set up a marker beside it until the gravediggers
have buried it in the Valley of Hamon Gog. 16 (Also a town called Hamonah[e] will be there.)
And so they will cleanse the land.'

17 "Son of man, this is what the Sovereign LORD says: Call out to every kind of bird[g] and
all the wild animals: 'Assemble and come together from all around to the sacrifice I am
preparing for you, the great sacrifice on the mountains of Israel. There you will eat flesh
and drink blood. 18 You will eat the flesh of mighty men and drink the blood of the princes of the earth as if they were rams and lambs, goats and bulls—all of them fattened animals from Bashan.[h] 19 At the sacrifice I am preparing for you, you will eat fat till you are
glutted and drink blood till you are drunk. 20 At my table you will eat your fill of horses
and riders, mighty men and soldiers of every kind,' declares the Sovereign LORD.[i]

21 "I will display my glory among the nations, and all the nations will see the punishment I inflict and the hand I lay upon them.[j] 22 From that day forward the house of Isra-

38:20 [n]Hos 4:3; Na 1:5
38:21 [o]Eze 14:17 [p]1Sa 14:20; 2Ch 20:23; Hag 2:22
38:22 [q]Isa 66:16; Jer 25:31 [r]Ps 18:12; Rev 16:21
38:23 [s]Eze 36:23
39:1 [t]Eze 38:2,3
39:3 [u]Hos 1:5 [v]Ps 76:3
39:4 [w]ver 17-20; Eze 29:5; 33:27
39:6 [x]Eze 30:8; Am 1:4 [y]Jer 25:22
39:7 [z]Ex 20:7 [a]Isa 12:6; Eze 36:16,23
39:9 [b]Ps 46:9
39:10 [c]Isa 14:2; 33:1; Hab 2:8
39:11 [d]Eze 38:2
39:12 [e]Dt 21:23
39:13 [f]Eze 28:22
39:17 [g]Rev 19:17
39:18 [h]Ps 22:12; Jer 51:40
39:20 [i]Rev 19:17-18
39:21 [j]Ex 9:16; Isa 37:20; Eze 38:16

a *1* Or *Gog, prince of Rosh,* b *11* Or *of* c *11* That is, the Dead Sea d *11* *Hamon Gog* means *hordes of Gog.* e *16* *Hamonah* means *horde.*

39:9 weapons for fuel . . . seven years. Ezekiel used a vivid image to describe how large the enemy army had been and how total its defeat. Compare Psalm 46:9 and Joel 3:10.
39:11 burial place. The burial place for Gog's hordes would be on the borders of Israel, near the Dead Sea. The slaughter would be so great that the burials would require seven months, and a further burial detail would continue to search for corpses after this prolonged period (vv. 12–15).
39:14 cleanse. Contact with a corpse rendered one ceremonially unclean (Lev 11:24–28,39; 22:4), so the land would require cleansing.
39:15 Hamon Gog. The valley would be named "Valley of the Hordes of Gog."
39:17 sacrifice. See note on 29:5 and compare verse 4. Ordinarily animals were offered as sacrifices and consumed in sacrificial meals. Here the image is reversed: God made a sacrifice of his enemies, and the animals fed. This reversal of the created order (Ge 1:30; 9:2–3) is one more way in which Ezekiel illustrated the dissolution of the cosmos into chaos as part of divine judgment; see note on 38:18–23. John later made use of the same image (Rev 19:17–18; cf. Isa 34:6–7; Jer 46:10; Zep 1:7–9).
39:18 Bashan. A region east of the Sea of Galilee, known for its fine cattle (Dt 32:14; Ps 22:12; Am 4:1).
39:19 eat fat . . . drink blood. Parts of a sacrificial animal offered to God (44:15; Lev 3:17).

el will know that I am the LORD their God. 23And the nations will know that the people
of Israel went into exile for their sin, because they were unfaithful to me. So I hid my face
from them and handed them over to their enemies, and they all fell by the sword.[k] 24I
dealt with them according to their uncleanness and their offenses, and I hid my face from
them.[l]
25"Therefore this is what the Sovereign LORD says: I will now bring Jacob back from
captivity[a][m] and will have compassion[n] on all the people of Israel, and I will be zealous
for my holy name.[o] 26They will forget their shame and all the unfaithfulness they showed
toward me when they lived in safety[p] in their land with no one to make them afraid.[q]
27When I have brought them back from the nations and have gathered them from the
countries of their enemies, I will show myself holy through them in the sight of many nations.[r] 28Then they will know that I am the LORD their God, for though I sent them into
exile among the nations, I will gather them to their own land, not leaving any behind.
29I will no longer hide my face from them, for I will pour out my Spirit[s] on the house of
Israel, declares the Sovereign LORD."

The New Temple Area

40 In the twenty-fifth year of our exile, at the beginning of the year, on the tenth
of the month, in the fourteenth year after the fall of the city[t]—on that very day
the hand of the LORD was upon me[u] and he took me there. 2In visions[v] of God he took
me to the land of Israel and set me on a very high mountain,[w] on whose south side were
some buildings that looked like a city. 3He took me there, and I saw a man whose appearance was like bronze;[x] he was standing in the gateway with a linen cord and a measuring rod[y] in his hand. 4The man said to me, "Son of man, look with your eyes and hear
with your ears and pay attention to everything I am going to show you, for that is why
you have been brought here. Tell[z] the house of Israel everything you see.[a]"

The East Gate to the Outer Court

5I saw a wall completely surrounding the temple area. The length of the measuring
rod in the man's hand was six long cubits, each of which was a cubit[b] and a handbreadth.[c] He measured[b] the wall; it was one measuring rod thick and one rod high.
6Then he went to the gate facing east.[c] He climbed its steps and measured the
threshold of the gate; it was one rod deep.[d] 7The alcoves[d] for the guards were one rod

39:23 [k]Isa 1:15; 59:2; Jer 22:8-9; 44:23
39:24 [l]Jer 2:17,19; 4:18; Eze 36:19
39:25 [m]Jer 33:7; Eze 34:13 [n]Jer 30:18 [o]Isa 27:12-13
39:26 [p]1Ki 4:25 [q]Isa 17:2; Eze 34:28; Mic 4:4
39:27 [r]Eze 36:23-24; 37:21; 38:16
39:29 [s]Joel 2:28; Ac 2:17
40:1 [t]2Ki 25:7; Jer 39:1-10; 52:4-11; Eze 33:21 [u]Eze 1:3
40:2 [v]Da 7:1,7 [w]Eze 17:22; Rev 21:10
40:3 [x]Eze 1:7; Da 10:6; Rev 1:15 [y]Eze 47:3; Zec 2:1-2; Rev 11:1; 21:15
40:4 [z]Jer 26:2 [a]Eze 44:5
40:5 [b]Eze 42:20
40:6 [c]Eze 8:16
40:7 [d]ver 36

[a] *25* Or *now restore the fortunes of Jacob* [b] *5* The common cubit was about 1 1/2 feet (about 0.5 meter).
[c] *5* That is, about 3 inches (about 8 centimeters) [d] *6* Septuagint; Hebrew *deep, the first threshold, one rod deep*

39:23 went into exile. The exile did not show that God had failed in his promises—to the contrary, it demonstrated to Israel and to the nations that his sovereignty was universal. Though God had afflicted his people he had not abandoned them (vv. 25–29). After describing how God would crush his enemies (chs. 38–39) Ezekiel turned to a description of the glorious restoration of the people of God (chs. 40–48).
39:25 bring Jacob back. With the enemies destroyed, Ezekiel turned to God's purposes for his people, their restoration and blessedness.
39:29 pour out my Spirit. See note on 36:25; compare 11:19, 18:31, 36:26–27, 37:14 and Joel 2:28.
■ **40:1—48:35** *A Vision of Restored Jerusalem.* Ezekiel's vision of the restored city combined many strands of Biblical tradition. Ezekiel wove the common understanding of Jerusalem as the city where God had chosen to dwell with other images that portrayed Mount Zion in terms of Mount Sinai and the Garden of Eden. These chapters divide into five main parts: Ezekiel's visionary transport to future Jerusalem (40:1–4); the temple structures (40:5—42:20); the return of God's glory (43:1–27); the sacred personnel (44:1—46:24); and the river, land and city (47:1—48:35).

Interpretations of these chapters vary widely. Many see the blueprint and building specifications for a city that was to be built (cf. 43:10–11), either by the returnees from exile or at some future time. However, Ezekiel's restoration expectations extended beyond a mere human rebuilding effort (e.g., 47:1–12). From a Christian point of view the sixth-century restoration community failed, but God mercifully brought these predictions to even more glorious fulfillment in Christ. Christ came as God's final temple in his first coming (Jn 2:19); the church is now the temple (1Co 3:9–17; 2Co 6:16; Eph 2:19–22) and in the new heavens and the new earth there will be no temple because the whole earth will be filled with his presence (Hab 2:14; Rev 21). There is no reason to believe that this prophecy has yet to be fulfilled in terms of rebuilding an Old Testament style temple in which animal sacrifices are again to be made. Christ has done away with all of those shadows by the reality of his coming to Earth (Heb 10:1–18).
■ **40:1–4** *Visionary Transport to Jerusalem.* Ezekiel was taken to the Jerusalem of the future to see its glory so that he could encourage the exiles to hope in the future blessing of God.
40:1 twenty-fifth year . . . at the beginning. That is, 573 B.C. It was appropriate that Ezekiel's vision of the future age would occur at the new year.
40:2 visions of God. See 1:1 and 8:3. **high mountain.** Presumably Mount Zion, the site of the temple in Jerusalem (17:22–24; 20:40; cf. Ps 48:1–2; Isa 2:2; Mic 4:1). Ezekiel would tour the holy mountain just as the psalmist had (Ps 48:12–13).
40:3 a man . . . like bronze. An angelic guide. **measuring rod.** Compare the imagery of a measuring line or rod in 2 Kings 21:13, Amos 7:7–8, Zechariah 2:1–2 and Revelation 21:10 and 15.
40:4 Tell . . . everything you see. John received similar instructions (Rev 1:11).
■ **40:5—42:20** *The Temple Structures.* Ezekiel was shown how the glorious temple of the future would look. He observed the temple courtyards and gates (40:5–49), the sanctuary (41:1–26) and the rooms for the priests (42:1–20).
■ **40:5–49** *The Temple Courtyards and Gates.* Ezekiel first saw the outer structures of the future temple.
40:5 cubits. Israel knew at least two standards for the cubit: the short cubit (about 17.4 inches) and the long cubit, mentioned here (about 20.4 inches; see also 43:13; 2Ch 3:3). The rod would be a bit over ten feet long.
40:6 climbed its steps. One approached the temple by steps to the raised platform that served as the outer court. Other steps led to a yet higher platform that served as the inner court (vv. 34,37). Still another flight of stairs reached the temple building (v. 49; 41:8). The higher the elevation and the closer to the inner sanctuary, the greater the degree of sanctity.
40:7 guards. Since a wall separated the sacred precincts (v. 5) from the secular or profane areas outside, access to the temple was

Ezekiel's Temple

- **A.** Wall (40:5,16-20)
- **B.** East gate (40:6-14,16)
- **C.** Portico (40:8)
- **D.** Outer court (40:17)
- **E.** Pavement (40:17)
- **F.** Inner court (40:19)
- **G.** North gate (40:20-22)
- **H.** Inner court (40:23)
- **I.** South gate (40:24-26)
- **J.** South inner court (40:27)
- **K.** Gateway (40:28-31)
- **L.** Gateway (40:32-34)
- **M.** Gateway (40:35-38)
- **N.** Priests' rooms (40:44-45)
- **O.** Court (40:47)
- **P.** Temple portico (40:48-49)
- **Q.** Outer sanctuary (41:1-2)
- **R.** Most Holy Place (41:3-4)
- **S.** Temple walls (41:5-7,9,11)
- **T.** Base (41:8)
- **U.** Open area (41:10)
- **V.** West building (41:12)
- **W** Priests' rooms (42:1-10)
- **X.** Altar (43:13-17)
- **AA.** Rooms for preparing sacrifices (40:39-43)
- **BB.** Ovens (46:19-20)
- **CC.** Kitchens (46:21-24)

Ezekiel uses a long or "royal" cubit, c. 21 inches or 52 cm ("cubit and a handbreadth," Eze 40:5) as opposed to the standard Hebrew cubit of c. 18 inches or 45 cm.

Scripture describes a floor plan, but provides few height dimensions. This artwork shows an upward projection of the temple over the floor plan. This temple existed only in a vision of Ezekiel (Eze 40:2), and has never actually been built as were the temples of Solomon, Zerubbabel and Herod.

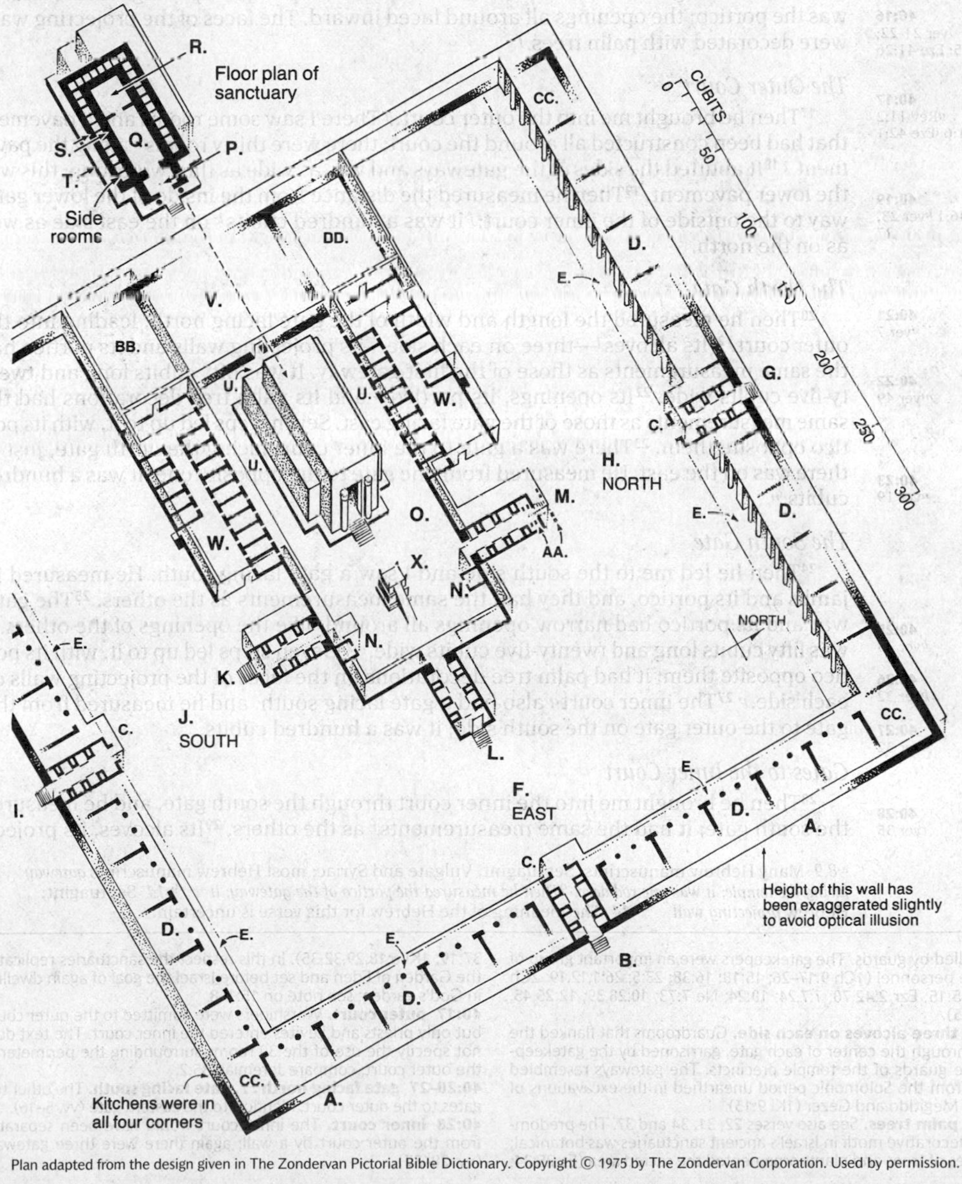

long and one rod wide, and the projecting walls between the alcoves were five cubits
thick. And the threshold of the gate next to the portico facing the temple was one rod
deep.
8 Then he measured the portico of the gateway; 9 it[a] was eight cubits deep and its
jambs were two cubits thick. The portico of the gateway faced the temple.
10 Inside the east gate were three alcoves on each side; the three had the same measurements, and the faces of the projecting walls on each side had the same measurements. 11 Then he measured the width of the entrance to the gateway; it was ten cubits
and its length was thirteen cubits. 12 In front of each alcove was a wall one cubit high, and
the alcoves were six cubits square. 13 Then he measured the gateway from the top of the
rear wall of one alcove to the top of the opposite one; the distance was twenty-five cubits from one parapet opening to the opposite one. 14 He measured along the faces of the
40:14 projecting walls all around the inside of the gateway—sixty cubits. The measurement
[e]Ex 27:9 was up to the portico[b] facing the courtyard.[c][e] 15 The distance from the entrance of the
gateway to the far end of its portico was fifty cubits. 16 The alcoves and the projecting
walls inside the gateway were surmounted by narrow parapet openings all around, as
40:16 was the portico; the openings all around faced inward. The faces of the projecting walls
[f]ver 21-22; 2Ch 3:5; Eze 41:26 were decorated with palm trees.[f]

The Outer Court

40:17 [g]Rev 11:2 17 Then he brought me into the outer court.[g] There I saw some rooms and a pavement
[h]Eze 41:6 [i]Eze 42:1 that had been constructed all around the court; there were thirty rooms[h] along the pavement.[i] 18 It abutted the sides of the gateways and was as wide as they were long; this was
40:19 the lower pavement. 19 Then he measured the distance from the inside of the lower gate-
[j]Eze 46:1 [k]ver 23, 27 way to the outside of the inner court;[j] it was a hundred cubits[k] on the east side as well
as on the north.

The North Gate

40:21 [l]ver 7 20 Then he measured the length and width of the gate facing north, leading into the
outer court. 21 Its alcoves[l]—three on each side—its projecting walls and its portico had
the same measurements as those of the first gateway. It was fifty cubits long and twen-
40:22 [m]ver 49 ty-five cubits wide. 22 Its openings, its portico[m] and its palm tree decorations had the
same measurements as those of the gate facing east. Seven steps led up to it, with its portico opposite them. 23 There was a gate to the inner court facing the north gate, just as
40:23 there was on the east. He measured from one gate to the opposite one; it was a hundred
[n]ver 19 cubits.[n]

The South Gate

24 Then he led me to the south side and I saw a gate facing south. He measured its
jambs and its portico, and they had the same measurements as the others. 25 The gate-
40:25 way and its portico had narrow openings all around, like the openings of the others. It
[o]ver 33 was fifty cubits long and twenty-five cubits wide.[o] 26 Seven steps led up to it, with its por-
40:26 tico opposite them; it had palm tree decorations on the faces of the projecting walls on
[p]ver 22 each side.[p] 27 The inner court[q] also had a gate facing south, and he measured from this
40:27 [q]ver 32 gate to the outer gate on the south side; it was a hundred cubits.

Gates to the Inner Court

40:28 28 Then he brought me into the inner court through the south gate, and he measured
[r]ver 35 the south gate; it had the same measurements[r] as the others. 29 Its alcoves, its project-

[a] *8,9* Many Hebrew manuscripts, Septuagint, Vulgate and Syriac; most Hebrew manuscripts *gateway facing the temple; it was one rod deep. 9 Then he measured the portico of the gateway; it* [b] *14* Septuagint; Hebrew *projecting wall* [c] *14* The meaning of the Hebrew for this verse is uncertain.

controlled by guards. The gatekeepers were an important group of temple personnel (1Ch 9:17–26; 15:18; 16:38; 23:5; 26:1,12,19; 2Ch 8:14; 35:15; Ezr 2:42,70; 7:7,24; 10:24; Ne 7:73; 10:28,39; 12:25,45, 47; 13:5).

40:10 three alcoves on each side. Guardrooms that flanked the path through the center of each gate, garrisoned by the gatekeepers, the guards of the temple precincts. The gateways resembled gates from the Solomonic period unearthed in the excavations of Hazor, Megiddo and Gezer (1Ki 9:15).

40:16 palm trees. See also verses 22, 31, 34 and 37. The predominant decorative motif in Israel's ancient sanctuaries was botanical; varieties of trees and plants ornamented the sacred area (Ex 25:34; 37:19; 1Ki 6:18,29,32,35). In this respect the sanctuaries replicated the Garden of Eden and set before Israel the goal of again dwelling in God's garden; see note on 15:1–8.

40:17 outer court. Worshipers were admitted to the outer court, but only priests and Levites entered the inner court. The text does not specify the use of the 30 rooms surrounding the perimeter of the outer court; compare Jeremiah 35:2.

40:20–27 gate facing north . . . gate facing south. The other two gates to the outer court, identical to the eastern gate (vv. 5–16).

40:28 inner court. The inner court would have been separated from the outer court by a wall; again there were three gateways (vv. 28–37).

ing walls and its portico had the same measurements as the others. The gateway and its
portico had openings all around. It was fifty cubits long and twenty-five cubits wide.
30(The porticoes[s] of the gateways around the inner court were twenty-five cubits wide
and five cubits deep.) **31**Its portico[t] faced the outer court; palm trees decorated its
jambs, and eight steps led up to it.

32Then he brought me to the inner court on the east side, and he measured the gateway; it had the same measurements as the others. **33**Its alcoves, its projecting walls and
its portico had the same measurements as the others. The gateway and its portico had
openings all around. It was fifty cubits long and twenty-five cubits wide. **34**Its portico[u]
faced the outer court; palm trees decorated the jambs on either side, and eight steps led
up to it.

35Then he brought me to the north gate[v] and measured it. It had the same measurements as the others, **36**as did its alcoves,[w] its projecting walls and its portico, and it had
openings all around. It was fifty cubits long and twenty-five cubits wide. **37**Its portico[a] faced
the outer court; palm trees decorated the jambs on either side, and eight steps led up to it.

The Rooms for Preparing Sacrifices

38A room with a doorway was by the portico in each of the inner gateways, where the
burnt offerings[x] were washed. **39**In the portico of the gateway were two tables on each
side, on which the burnt offerings,[y] sin offerings[z] and guilt offerings[a] were slaughtered.
40By the outside wall of the portico of the gateway, near the steps at the entrance to the
north gateway were two tables, and on the other side of the steps were two tables. **41**So
there were four tables on one side of the gateway and four on the other—eight tables in
all—on which the sacrifices were slaughtered. **42**There were also four tables of dressed
stone[b] for the burnt offerings, each a cubit and a half long, a cubit and a half wide and
a cubit high. On them were placed the utensils for slaughtering the burnt offerings and
the other sacrifices.[c] **43**And double-pronged hooks, each a handbreadth long, were attached to the wall all around. The tables were for the flesh of the offerings.

Rooms for the Priests

44Outside the inner gate, within the inner court, were two rooms, one[b] at the side of
the north gate and facing south, and another at the side of the south[c] gate and facing
north. **45**He said to me, "The room facing south is for the priests who have charge of the
temple,[d] **46**and the room facing north[e] is for the priests who have charge of the altar.[f]
These are the sons of Zadok,[g] who are the only Levites who may draw near to the LORD
to minister before him.[h]"

47Then he measured the court: It was square—a hundred cubits long and a hundred
cubits wide. And the altar was in front of the temple.

The Temple

48He brought me to the portico of the temple[i] and measured the jambs of the portico; they were five cubits wide on either side. The width of the entrance was fourteen cubits and its projecting walls were[d] three cubits wide on either side. **49**The portico[j] was
twenty cubits wide, and twelve[e] cubits from front to back. It was reached by a flight of
stairs,[f] and there were pillars[k] on each side of the jambs.

41 Then the man brought me to the outer sanctuary[l] and measured the jambs; the
width of the jambs was six cubits[g] on each side.[h] **2**The entrance was ten cubits

40:30 [s]ver 21
40:31 [t]ver 22
40:34 [u]ver 22
40:35 [v]Eze 44:4; 47:2
40:36 [w]ver 7
40:38 [x]2Ch 4:6; Eze 42:13
40:39 [y]Eze 46:2 [z]Lev 4:3, 28 [a]Lev 7:1
40:42 [b]Ex 20:25 [c]ver 39
40:45 [d]1Ch 9:23
40:46 [e]Eze 42:13 [f]Nu 18:5 [g]1Ki 2:35 [h]Nu 16:5; Eze 43:19; 44:15; 45:4; 48:11
40:48 [i]1Ki 6:2
40:49 [j]ver 22; 1Ki 6:3 [k]1Ki 7:15
41:1 [l]ver 23

[a] *37* Septuagint (see also verses 31 and 34); Hebrew *jambs* [b] *44* Septuagint; Hebrew *were rooms for singers, which were* [c] *44* Septuagint; Hebrew *east* [d] *48* Septuagint; Hebrew *entrance was* [e] *49* Septuagint; Hebrew *eleven* [f] *49* Hebrew; Septuagint *Ten steps led up to it* [g] *1* The common cubit was about 1 1/2 feet (about 0.5 meter). [h] *1* One Hebrew manuscript and Septuagint; most Hebrew manuscripts *side, the width of the tent*

40:38 burnt offerings were washed. Sacrificial animals were slaughtered in the gateways to the inner court where the altar (43:13–27) was located. After the animals were slaughtered the parts were washed (Lev 1:9,13; 2Ch 4:6).
40:43 hooks. The parts to be offered were hung on hooks.
40:45 room . . . for the priests. Inside the inner court, next to the gateways on the north and south, were rooms for the use of the priests.
40:46 Zadok. See note on 44:15.
40:48—41:4 portico . . . outer sanctuary . . . inner sanctuary. Like Solomon's temple the temple in Ezekiel's vision consisted of three rooms: a vestibule or portico (40:48–49), the outer sanctuary (41:1–2) and the inner sanctuary or Most Holy Place (41:3–4). The temple building was elevated from the surrounding courtyard by stairways leading to the portico (40:49; 41:8); see note on 40:6. Each of the entrances to the successive rooms was narrower: The vestibule was 14 cubits wide (40:48); the outer rooms ten (41:2) and the Most Holy Place six (41:3). Like the increase in height approaching the temple building, the increasing narrowness of the doorways inside represented increasing sanctity; it also served to focus the eyes of the observer on the innermost rooms of the sanctuary.
40:49 pillars. The pillars presumably resembled Jakin and Boaz, the pillars that stood outside Solomon's temple (1Ki 7:15–22).
■**41:1–26** *The Sanctuary.* Ezekiel saw inside to the holier places of the temple.

wide, and the projecting walls on each side of it were five cubits wide. He also measured
the outer sanctuary; it was forty cubits long and twenty cubits wide.[m]
3Then he went into the inner sanctuary and measured the jambs of the entrance;
each was two cubits wide. The entrance was six cubits wide, and the projecting walls on
each side of it were seven cubits wide. **4**And he measured the length of the inner sanctuary; it was twenty cubits, and its width was twenty cubits across the end of the outer
sanctuary.[n] He said to me, "This is the Most Holy Place.[o]"
5Then he measured the wall of the temple; it was six cubits thick, and each side room
around the temple was four cubits wide. **6**The side rooms were on three levels, one above
another, thirty[p] on each level. There were ledges all around the wall of the temple to
serve as supports for the side rooms, so that the supports were not inserted into the wall
of the temple.[q] **7**The side rooms all around the temple were wider at each successive level. The structure surrounding the temple was built in ascending stages, so that the rooms
widened as one went upward. A stairway[r] went up from the lowest floor to the top floor
through the middle floor.
8I saw that the temple had a raised base all around it, forming the foundation of the
side rooms. It was the length of the rod, six long cubits. **9**The outer wall of the side rooms
was five cubits thick. The open area between the side rooms of the temple **10**and the
⌊priests'⌋ rooms was twenty cubits wide all around the temple. **11**There were entrances
to the side rooms from the open area, one on the north and another on the south; and
the base adjoining the open area was five cubits wide all around.
12The building facing the temple courtyard on the west side was seventy cubits wide.
The wall of the building was five cubits thick all around, and its length was ninety cubits.
13Then he measured the temple; it was a hundred cubits long, and the temple courtyard and the building with its walls were also a hundred cubits long. **14**The width of the
temple courtyard on the east, including the front of the temple, was a hundred cubits.[s]
15Then he measured the length of the building facing the courtyard at the rear of the
temple, including its galleries[t] on each side; it was a hundred cubits.
The outer sanctuary, the inner sanctuary and the portico facing the court, **16**as well
as the thresholds and the narrow windows[u] and galleries around the three of them—everything beyond and including the threshold was covered with wood. The floor, the wall
up to the windows, and the windows were covered.[v] **17**In the space above the outside of
the entrance to the inner sanctuary and on the walls at regular intervals all around the
inner and outer sanctuary **18**were carved[w] cherubim[x] and palm trees.[y] Palm trees alternated with cherubim. Each cherub had two faces:[z] **19**the face of a man toward the palm
tree on one side and the face of a lion toward the palm tree on the other. They were
carved all around the whole temple.[a] **20**From the floor to the area above the entrance,
cherubim and palm trees were carved on the wall of the outer sanctuary.
21The outer sanctuary[b] had a rectangular doorframe, and the one at the front of the
Most Holy Place was similar. **22**There was a wooden altar[c] three cubits high and two cubits square[a]; its corners, its base[b] and its sides were of wood. The man said to me, "This
is the table[d] that is before the LORD." **23**Both the outer sanctuary[e] and the Most Holy Place
had double doors.[f] **24**Each door had two leaves—two hinged leaves[g] for each door. **25**And
on the doors of the outer sanctuary were carved cherubim and palm trees like those
carved on the walls, and there was a wooden overhang on the front of the portico. **26**On
the sidewalls of the portico were narrow windows with palm trees carved on each side.
The side rooms of the temple also had overhangs.[h]

Rooms for the Priests

42 Then the man led me northward into the outer court and brought me to the
rooms[i] opposite the temple courtyard[j] and opposite the outer wall on the north

41:2 [m]2Ch 3:3
41:4 [n]1Ki 6:20 [o]Ex 26:33; Heb 9:3-8
41:6 [p]Eze 40:17 [q]1Ki 6:5
41:7 [r]1Ki 6:8
41:14 [s]Eze 40:47
41:15 [t]Eze 42:3
41:16 [u]1Ki 6:4 [v]ver 25-26; 1Ki 6:15; Eze 42:3
41:18 [w]1Ki 6:18 [x]Ex 37:7; 2Ch 3:7 [y]1Ki 6:29; 7:36 [z]Eze 10:21
41:19 [a]Eze 10:14
41:21 [b]ver 1
41:22 [c]Ex 30:1 [d]Ex 25:23; Eze 23:41; 44:16; Mal 1:7,12
41:23 [e]ver 1 [f]1Ki 6:32
41:24 [g]1Ki 6:34
41:26 [h]ver 15-16; Eze 40:16
42:1 [i]ver 13 [j]Eze 41:12-14

[a] *22* Septuagint; Hebrew *long* [b] *22* Septuagint; Hebrew *length*

41:3 he went into the inner sanctuary. Access to the Most Holy Place was restricted to the high priest on the Day of Atonement (Lev 16; Heb 9:11–14); the angel could enter this room, but Ezekiel could not.

41:4 twenty cubits. The dimensions of the Most Holy Place in the tabernacle and in Solomon's temple had also been a cube, with equal measurements for the length, width and height (cf. Rev 21:16).

41:5–12 side rooms. Rooms were built around the north, west and south sides of the temple building; these three-story structures would apparently be used to store equipment and the wealth of the temple (cf. 42:13 and 1Ki 6:5–10). The second and third stories were offset so that each was a cubit wider than the level below.

41:18 carved. Compare 1 Kings 6:18 and 2 Chronicles 3:5–7.

41:22 altar. The table for the bread of the Presence is described as an altar in this passage, probably because the bread was consumed by the priests as though part of a sacrificial meal and because the incense set out with the bread was viewed as a memorial offering (Lev 24:5–9; 1Sa 21:3–6).

side.[k] 2 The building whose door faced north was a hundred cubits[a] long and fifty cubits
wide. 3 Both in the section twenty cubits from the inner court and in the section opposite the pavement of the outer court, gallery[l] faced gallery at the three levels.[m] 4 In front
of the rooms was an inner passageway ten cubits wide and a hundred cubits[b] long. Their
doors were on the north.[n] 5 Now the upper rooms were narrower, for the galleries took
more space from them than from the rooms on the lower and middle floors of the building. 6 The rooms on the third floor had no pillars, as the courts had; so they were smaller
in floor space than those on the lower and middle floors. 7 There was an outer wall parallel to the rooms and the outer court; it extended in front of the rooms for fifty cubits.
8 While the row of rooms on the side next to the outer court was fifty cubits long, the row
on the side nearest the sanctuary was a hundred cubits long. 9 The lower rooms had an
entrance[o] on the east side as one enters them from the outer court.

10 On the south side[c] along the length of the wall of the outer court, adjoining the temple courtyard and opposite the outer wall, were rooms[p] 11 with a passageway in front of
them. These were like the rooms on the north; they had the same length and width, with
similar exits and dimensions. Similar to the doorways on the north 12 were the doorways
of the rooms on the south. There was a doorway at the beginning of the passageway that
was parallel to the corresponding wall extending eastward, by which one enters the
rooms.

13 Then he said to me, "The north[q] and south rooms facing the temple courtyard are
the priests' rooms, where the priests who approach the LORD will eat the most holy offerings. There they will put the most holy offerings—the grain offerings, the sin offerings[r]
and the guilt offerings[s]—for the place is holy.[t] 14 Once the priests enter the holy precincts,
they are not to go into the outer court until they leave behind the garments[u] in which
they minister, for these are holy. They are to put on other clothes before they go near the
places that are for the people.[v]"

15 When he had finished measuring what was inside the temple area, he led me out
by the east gate[w] and measured the area all around: 16 He measured the east side with
the measuring rod; it was five hundred cubits.[d] 17 He measured the north side; it was five
hundred cubits[e] by the measuring rod. 18 He measured the south side; it was five hundred
cubits by the measuring rod. 19 Then he turned to the west side and measured; it was five
hundred cubits by the measuring rod. 20 So he measured[x] the area on all four sides. It had
a wall around it,[y] five hundred cubits long and five hundred cubits wide,[z] to separate
the holy from the common.[a]

The Glory Returns to the Temple

43 Then the man brought me to the gate facing east,[b] 2 and I saw the glory of the
God of Israel coming from the east. His voice was like the roar of rushing waters,[c] and the land was radiant with his glory.[d] 3 The vision I saw was like the vision I had
seen when he[f] came to destroy the city and like the visions I had seen by the Kebar River, and I fell facedown. 4 The glory[e] of the LORD entered the temple through the gate facing east.[f] 5 Then the Spirit[g] lifted me up[h] and brought me into the inner court, and the
glory of the LORD filled the temple.

6 While the man was standing beside me, I heard someone speaking to me from inside the temple. 7 He said: "Son of man, this is the place of my throne and the place for

42:1 [k]Eze 40:17
42:3 [l]Eze 41:15 [m]Eze 41:16
42:4 [n]Eze 46:19
42:9 [o]Eze 44:5; 46:19
42:10 [p]ver 1
42:13 [q]Eze 40:46 [r]Lev 10:17; 6:25 [s]Lev 14:13 [t]Ex 29:31; Lev 6:29; 7:6; 10:12-13; Nu 18:9-10
42:14 [u]Eze 44:19 [v]Ex 29:9; Lev 8:7-9
42:15 [w]Eze 43:1
42:20 [x]Eze 40:5 [y]Zec 2:5 [z]Eze 45:2; Rev 21:16 [a]Eze 22:26
43:1 [b]Eze 10:19; 42:15; 44:1; 46:1
43:2 [c]Rev 1:15 [d]Isa 6:3; Eze 11:23; Rev 18:1
43:4 [e]Eze 1:28 [f]Eze 10:19
43:5 [g]Eze 11:24 [h]Eze 3:12; 8:3

[a] *2* The common cubit was about 1 1/2 feet (about 0.5 meter). [b] *4* Septuagint and Syriac; Hebrew *and one cubit* [c] *10* Septuagint; Hebrew *Eastward* [d] *16* See Septuagint of verse 17; Hebrew *rods*; also in verses 18 and 19. [e] *17* Septuagint; Hebrew *rods* [f] *3* Some Hebrew manuscripts and Vulgate; most Hebrew manuscripts *I*

■ **42:1–20** *Rooms for the Priests.* These rooms should not be confused with those built on the perimeter of the temple building itself (41:5–12); these were built along the north and south sides of the wall separating the inner and outer courts. They were for the priests' use.

42:20 wall. The outer wall separated the sacred precincts from the secular; see note on 40:7. **five hundred cubits.** The 500 cubits consisted of the length of the outer north gateway (50) plus the length of the outer court (100) plus that of the inner north gateway (50) plus the lengths across the inner court (100), the opposite (south) inner gateway (50), the opposite side of the outer court (100) and the opposite outer (south) gateway (50).

■ **43:1–27** *Return of God's Glory.* Ezekiel had earlier seen a vision of the glory of the Lord departing from Jerusalem (10:18–22; 11:22–24); in the current vision he witnessed its return. The glory arrived from the east, the same direction to which it had departed (11:23). The glory of the Lord had also filled the tabernacle and Solomon's temple when they were dedicated (Ex 40:34–35; 1Ki 8:10–11; 2Ch 5:13–14; 7:1–2; cf. Isa 60:1–3). See note on 11:22–25. The temple of the restoration period was not built on the model of Ezekiel's vision; it was a more modest structure than Solomon's temple (Ezr 3:12–13; Hag 2:3). Yet Haggai foresaw that the glory of the second temple would exceed that of the former (Hag 2:7–9). This hope of God's glory coming to the second temple was fulfilled beyond expectation when Jesus made his dwelling among people and his glory was revealed (Jn 1:14); he was himself the radiance of God's glory, the exact representation of his being (Heb 1:3).

43:7 throne. The Jerusalem temple was the place where God had his throne; he was enthroned above the ark in the Most Holy Place (1Sa 4:4; 2Sa 6:2; 2Ki 19:15; 1Ch 13:6; Pss 80:1; 99:1; 132:13–14; Isa 37:16).

the soles of my feet. This is where I will live among the Israelites forever. The house of
Israel will never again defile my holy name—neither they nor their kings—by their
prostitution[a] and the lifeless idols[b] of their kings at their high places.[i] [8]When they
placed their threshold next to my threshold and their doorposts beside my doorposts,
with only a wall between me and them, they defiled my holy name by their detestable
practices. So I destroyed them in my anger. [9]Now let them put away from me their prostitution and the lifeless idols of their kings, and I will live among them forever.[j]
[10]"Son of man, describe the temple to the people of Israel, that they may be ashamed[k]
of their sins. Let them consider the plan, [11]and if they are ashamed of all they have done,
make known to them the design of the temple—its arrangement, its exits and entrances—its whole design and all its regulations[c] and laws. Write these down before them so
that they may be faithful to its design and follow all its regulations.[l]
[12]"This is the law of the temple: All the surrounding area[m] on top of the mountain will
be most holy. Such is the law of the temple.

The Altar

[13]"These are the measurements of the altar[n] in long cubits, that cubit being a cubit[d]
and a handbreadth[e]: Its gutter is a cubit deep and a cubit wide, with a rim of one span[f]
around the edge. And this is the height of the altar: [14]From the gutter on the ground up
to the lower ledge it is two cubits high and a cubit wide, and from the smaller ledge up
to the larger ledge it is four cubits high and a cubit wide. [15]The altar hearth is four cubits high, and four horns[o] project upward from the hearth. [16]The altar hearth is square,
twelve cubits long and twelve cubits wide. [17]The upper ledge also is square, fourteen cubits long and fourteen cubits wide, with a rim of half a cubit and a gutter of a cubit all
around. The steps[p] of the altar face east."
[18]Then he said to me, "Son of man, this is what the Sovereign LORD says: These will
be the regulations for sacrificing burnt offerings[q] and sprinkling blood[r] upon the altar
when it is built: [19]You are to give a young bull[s] as a sin offering to the priests, who are
Levites, of the family of Zadok,[t] who come near[u] to minister before me, declares the Sovereign LORD. [20]You are to take some of its blood and put it on the four horns of the altar
and on the four corners of the upper ledge[v] and all around the rim, and so purify the altar[w] and make atonement for it. [21]You are to take the bull for the sin offering and burn
it in the designated part of the temple area outside the sanctuary.[x]
[22]"On the second day you are to offer a male goat without defect for a sin offering, and
the altar is to be purified as it was purified with the bull. [23]When you have finished purifying it, you are to offer a young bull and a ram from the flock, both without defect.[y]
[24]You are to offer them before the LORD, and the priests are to sprinkle salt[z] on them and
sacrifice them as a burnt offering to the LORD.
[25]"For seven days[a] you are to provide a male goat daily for a sin offering; you are also
to provide a young bull and a ram from the flock, both without defect.[b] [26]For seven days
they are to make atonement for the altar and cleanse it; thus they will dedicate it. [27]At
the end of these days, from the eighth day[c] on, the priests are to present your burnt offerings and fellowship offerings[g][d] on the altar. Then I will accept you, declares the Sovereign LORD."

43:7 [i]Lev 26:30
43:9 [j]Eze 37:26-28
43:10 [k]Eze 16:61
43:11 [l]Eze 44:5
43:12 [m]Eze 40:2
43:13 [n]2Ch 4:1
43:15 [o]Ex 27:2
43:17 [p]Ex 20:26
43:18 [q]Ex 40:29 [r]Lev 1:5, 11; Heb 9:21-22
43:19 [s]Lev 4:3; Eze 45:18-19 [t]Eze 44:15 [u]Nu 16:40; Eze 40:46
43:20 [v]ver 17 [w]Lev 16:19
43:21 [x]Ex 29:14; Heb 13:11
43:23 [y]Ex 29:1
43:24 [z]Lev 2:13; Mk 9:49-50
43:25 [a]Lev 8:33 [b]Ex 29:37
43:27 [c]Lev 9:1 [d]Lev 17:5

[a] *7* Or *their spiritual adultery*; also in verse 9 [b] *7* Or *the corpses*; also in verse 9 [c] *11* Some Hebrew manuscripts and Septuagint; most Hebrew manuscripts *regulations and its whole design*
[d] *13* The common cubit was about 1 1/2 feet (about 0.5 meter). [e] *13* That is, about 3 inches (about 8 centimeters) [f] *13* That is, about 9 inches (about 22 centimeters) [g] *27* Traditionally *peace offerings*

43:10 plan. Like the plans for Israel's earlier sanctuaries, the blueprints for the temple in Ezekiel's vision were of divine origin. See note on 40:1—48:35. Like Moses, who had given Israel the laws for the tabernacle, Ezekiel saw the promise only from a distance, in a vision (Nu 27:12–13; Dt 32:52; 34:4).
43:12 law of the temple. Ezekiel's temple vision is the only body of ceremonial law in the Bible not from the mouth of Moses. Like Moses, Ezekiel received the law while on a high mountain (40:2; Ex 25:9,40).
43:13 long cubits. See note on 40:5. **altar.** The altar was built as a series of platforms, each smaller than the one below, reminiscent of the Mesopotamian ziggurats. The ancient rabbis had many discussions about this altar since its construction contradicted the command that the altar should not have steps (Ex 20:24–26).
43:15 hearth. See Isaiah 29:1–2.
43:18–27 regulations for sacrificing. Regulations for consecrating the altar. On the first day a young bull was offered as a sin offering (vv. 18–21) and on the second a male goat (vv. 22–24). On the remaining days a male goat, young bull and ram were offered (vv. 25–26). After this period of consecration the regular offerings could commence (v. 27). Compare the seven-day dedication of Solomon's temple (2Ch 7:8–9). The priests who were not members of the Zadok clan (v. 19) had been barred from serving as priests; see note on 44:15.

43:18 sprinkling blood. See Exodus 29:16 and Leviticus 4:6 and 5:9.

43:21 outside. See Exodus 29:14, Leviticus 4:12 and 21, 8:17, 9:11 and 16:27. The writer of Hebrews took these instructions as an aspect of Christ's offering of himself (Heb 13:11–13).

The Prince, the Levites, the Priests

44 Then the man brought me back to the outer gate of the sanctuary, the one facing east,[e] and it was shut. 2The LORD said to me, "This gate is to remain shut. It
must not be opened; no one may enter through it.[f] It is to remain shut because the LORD,
the God of Israel, has entered through it. 3The prince himself is the only one who may
sit inside the gateway to eat in the presence[g] of the LORD. He is to enter by way of the portico of the gateway and go out the same way.[h]"
4Then the man brought me by way of the north gate to the front of the temple. I
looked and saw the glory of the LORD filling the temple[i] of the LORD, and I fell facedown.[j]
5The LORD said to me, "Son of man, look carefully, listen closely and give attention to
everything I tell you concerning all the regulations regarding the temple of the LORD. Give
attention to the entrance of the temple and all the exits of the sanctuary.[k] 6Say to the rebellious house[l] of Israel, 'This is what the Sovereign LORD says: Enough of your detestable
practices, O house of Israel! 7In addition to all your other detestable practices, you
brought foreigners uncircumcised in heart[m] and flesh into my sanctuary, desecrating my
temple while you offered me food, fat and blood, and you broke my covenant.[n] 8Instead
of carrying out your duty in regard to my holy things, you put others in charge of my sanctuary.[o] 9This is what the Sovereign LORD says: No foreigner uncircumcised in heart and
flesh is to enter my sanctuary, not even the foreigners who live among the Israelites.[p]
10" 'The Levites who went far from me when Israel went astray[q] and who wandered
from me after their idols must bear the consequences of their sin.[r] 11They may serve in
my sanctuary, having charge of the gates of the temple and serving in it; they may
slaughter the burnt offerings[s] and sacrifices for the people and stand before the people
and serve them.[t] 12But because they served them in the presence of their idols and made
the house of Israel fall into sin, therefore I have sworn with uplifted hand[u] that they must
bear the consequences of their sin, declares the Sovereign LORD.[v] 13They are not to come
near to serve me as priests or come near any of my holy things or my most holy offerings;
they must bear the shame[w] of their detestable practices.[x] 14Yet I will put them in charge
of the duties of the temple and all the work that is to be done in it.[y]
15" 'But the priests, who are Levites and descendants of Zadok and who faithfully carried out the duties of my sanctuary when the Israelites went astray from me, are to come
near to minister before me; they are to stand before me to offer sacrifices of fat and blood,
declares the Sovereign LORD.[z] 16They alone are to enter my sanctuary; they alone are to
come near my table[a] to minister before me and perform my service.[b]
17" 'When they enter the gates of the inner court, they are to wear linen clothes;[c] they
must not wear any woolen garment while ministering at the gates of the inner court or
inside the temple. 18They are to wear linen turbans[d] on their heads and linen undergarments[e] around their waists. They must not wear anything that makes them perspire.[f]
19When they go out into the outer court where the people are, they are to take off the
clothes they have been ministering in and are to leave them in the sacred rooms, and put

44:1 [e]Eze 43:1
44:2 [f]Eze 43:4-5
44:3 [g]Ex 24:9-11 [h]Eze 46:2,8
44:4 [i]Isa 6:4; Rev 15:8 [j]Eze 1:28; 3:23
44:5 [k]Eze 40:4; 43:10-11
44:6 [l]Eze 3:9
44:7 [m]Lev 26:41 [n]Ge 17:14; Ex 12:48; Lev 22:25
44:8 [o]Lev 22:2; Nu 18:7
44:9 [p]Joel 3:17; Zec 14:21
44:10 [q]2Ki 23:8 [r]Nu 18:23
44:11 [s]2Ch 29:34 [t]Nu 3:5-37; 16:9; 1Ch 26:12-19
44:12 [u]Ps 106:26 [v]2Ki 16:10-16
44:13 [w]Eze 16:61 [x]Nu 18:3
44:14 [y]Nu 18:4; 1Ch 23:28-32
44:15 [z]Jer 33:18; Eze 40:46; Zec 3:7
44:16 [a]Eze 41:22 [b]Nu 18:5
44:17 [c]Ex 39:27-28; Rev 19:8
44:18 [d]Ex 28:39; Isa 3:20 [e]Ex 28:42 [f]Lev 16:4

■ **44:1—46:24** *The Sacred Personnel.* Ezekiel's visions of the sacred personnel who must lead the gloriously restored people of God. These chapters divide into three main parts: the prince, Levites and priests (44:1–31); the allotments of sacred land (45:1–12); and the offerings and holy days with which they were deeply involved (45:13—46:24). We should not expect these offices to be fulfilled today as they were in the Old Testament. The New Testament teaches that the sacred offices and their duties are fulfilled by Christ and his church, both now and in the age to come.

■ **44:1–31** *The Prince, Levites and Priests.* Ezekiel saw the sacred personnel of restored Jerusalem.

44:1 shut. Ezekiel was taken from the inner court (43:5) to the eastern gate. That gate would remain closed because the glory of the Lord had entered the temple through it (43:4; cf. Ps 24:7–10). The closed gate may imply that the Lord would never again leave the temple (43:7,9).

44:3 prince. See note on 37:24. With the gate closed the gateway would become a room; in this room the prince (i.e., the king) would eat his portion of the sacrificial meals. This provision was never put into effect for any king of Israel. In Ezekiel's vision it represented the special relationship the promised king would maintain with the temple. God had promised that David's throne would be restored after the exile, and Ezekiel built on that promise. The prince he had in mind was a son of David who would reign after the exile. The New Testament teaches that this was Christ.

44:4–9 you brought foreigners. Though foreigners had served in the temple in the past (e.g., the Carite guards; 2Ki 11:4), they would no longer be allowed to enter because the ideal arrangements would now be met. The tasks they had performed properly belonged to the Levites (Nu 1:50–53; 3:6,8,28–32; 1Ch 23:24–32; 2Ch 8:14–15). While some portions of the Old Testament emphasize restrictions on the participation of foreigners in Israel's worship (Ex 12:43; Lev 22:25; Ne 9:2; Jer 51:51), other passages anticipate the participation of foreigners (47:22–23; 1Ki 8:41,43; 2Ch 6:32–33; Isa 56:3,6; cf. Zec 14:21; Eph 2:12,19). Similar restrictions on foreigners characterize other postexilic writings (Ezr 4:1–3; 10:10–44; Ne 13:1–9; Hag 2:14). During the New Testament period a written warning at the entrance to the temple prohibited Gentiles from entering upon pain of death (cf. Ac 21:26–30). In the new Israel of the new covenant, the church, all such distinctions between Jew and Gentile have been removed (Ro 2:28–29; Php 3:3); part of the work of Christ was the destruction of those barriers (Mt 10:18; Lk 2:32; Ac 9:15; 10:28,45; 11:1,18; 13:46–48; 15:7; Ro 1:5,16; 2:10; 3:29; 10:12; 15:16; Gal 2:7; 3:8,28; Eph 2:11–18; 3:6).

44:10–14 Those priestly families that had engaged in idolatry during the preexilic period (8:6) would join their fellow Levites, but their service would be confined to slaughtering sacrificial animals, maintenance and assisting the priests. The priesthood would be restricted to the descendants of Zadok (v. 15; 40:45–46).

44:15 Zadok. Zadok had served as high priest alongside Abiathar during the reign of David (2Sa 8:17; 15:24–29); however Zadok became the sole high priest after he had supported Solomon's succession, when Abiathar had backed Adonijah (1Ki 1:8). The priesthood had earlier been restricted to the sons of Aaron among the Levites (Ex 28:1; Lev 8:2–7; 9:1–24; Nu 20:25–28; 1Ch 6:48–53), but Ezekiel foresaw a further restriction to one Aaronic family.

on other clothes, so that they do not consecrate[g] the people by means of their garments.[h]

20 " 'They must not shave their heads or let their hair grow long, but they are to keep the hair of their heads trimmed.[i] 21 No priest is to drink wine when he enters the inner court.[j] 22 They must not marry widows or divorced women; they may marry only virgins of Israelite descent or widows of priests.[k] 23 They are to teach my people the difference between the holy and the common[l] and show them how to distinguish between the unclean and the clean.[m]

24 " 'In any dispute, the priests are to serve as judges[n] and decide it according to my ordinances. They are to keep my laws and my decrees for all my appointed feasts, and they are to keep my Sabbaths holy.[o]

25 " 'A priest must not defile himself by going near a dead person; however, if the dead person was his father or mother, son or daughter, brother or unmarried sister, then he may defile himself.[p] 26 After he is cleansed, he must wait seven days.[q] 27 On the day he goes into the inner court of the sanctuary to minister in the sanctuary, he is to offer a sin offering for himself, declares the Sovereign LORD.

28 " 'I am to be the only inheritance[r] the priests have. You are to give them no possession in Israel; I will be their possession. 29 They will eat the grain offerings, the sin offerings and the guilt offerings; and everything in Israel devoted[a] to the LORD[s] will belong to them.[t] 30 The best of all the firstfruits[u] and of all your special gifts will belong to the priests. You are to give them the first portion of your ground meal[v] so that a blessing[w] may rest on your household.[x] 31 The priests must not eat anything, bird or animal, found dead or torn by wild animals.[y]

Division of the Land

45 " 'When you allot the land as an inheritance,[z] you are to present to the LORD a portion of the land as a sacred district, 25,000 cubits long and 20,000[b] cubits wide; the entire area will be holy.[a] 2 Of this, a section 500 cubits square[b] is to be for the sanctuary, with 50 cubits around it for open land. 3 In the sacred district, measure off a section 25,000 cubits[c] long and 10,000 cubits[d] wide. In it will be the sanctuary, the Most Holy Place. 4 It will be the sacred portion of the land for the priests,[c] who minister in the sanctuary and who draw near to minister before the LORD. It will be a place for their houses as well as a holy place for the sanctuary.[d] 5 An area 25,000 cubits long and 10,000 cubits wide will belong to the Levites, who serve in the temple, as their possession for towns to live in.[e][e]

6 " 'You are to give the city as its property an area 5,000 cubits wide and 25,000 cubits long, adjoining the sacred portion; it will belong to the whole house of Israel.[f]

7 " 'The prince will have the land bordering each side of the area formed by the sacred district and the property of the city. It will extend westward from the west side and eastward from the east side, running lengthwise from the western to the eastern border parallel to one of the tribal portions.[g] 8 This land will be his possession in Israel. And my princes will no longer oppress my people but will allow the house of Israel to possess the land according to their tribes.[h]

9 " 'This is what the Sovereign LORD says: You have gone far enough, O princes of Israel! Give up your violence and oppression and do what is just and right.[i] Stop dispossessing my people, declares the Sovereign LORD. 10 You are to use accurate scales,[j] an ac-

44:19 [g]Lev 6:27; Eze 46:20 [h]Lev 6:10-11; Eze 42:14
44:20 [i]Lev 21:5; Nu 6:5
44:21 [j]Lev 10:9
44:22 [k]Lev 21:7
44:23 [l]Eze 22:26 [m]Mal 2:7
44:24 [n]Dt 17:8-9; 1Ch 23:4 [o]2Ch 19:8
44:25 [p]Lev 21:1-4
44:26 [q]Nu 19:14
44:28 [r]Nu 18:20; Dt 10:9; 18:1-2; Jos 13:33
44:29 [s]Lev 27:21 [t]Nu 18:9,14
44:30 [u]Nu 18:12-13 [v]Nu 15:18-21 [w]Mal 3:10 [x]Ne 10:35-37
44:31 [y]Ex 22:31; Lev 22:8
45:1 [z]Eze 47:21-22 [a]Eze 48:8-9,29
45:2 [b]Eze 42:20
45:4 [c]Eze 40:46 [d]Eze 48:10-11
45:5 [e]Eze 48:13
45:6 [f]Eze 48:15-18
45:7 [g]Eze 48:21
45:8 [h]Nu 26:53; Eze 46:18
45:9 [i]Jer 22:3; Zec 7:9-10; 8:16
45:10 [j]Dt 25:15; Pr 11:1; Am 8:4-6; Mic 6:10-11

[a] *29* The Hebrew term refers to the irrevocable giving over of things or persons to the LORD.
[b] *1* Septuagint (see also verses 3 and 5 and 48:9); Hebrew *10,000* [c] *3* That is, about 7 miles (about 12 kilometers) [d] *3* That is, about 3 miles (about 5 kilometers) [e] *5* Septuagint; Hebrew *temple; they will have as their possession 20 rooms*

44:24 judges. On the judicial role of the priests, compare 1 Chronicles 26:29 and 2 Chronicles 19:8–11.
44:25 dead person. Contact with death rendered an individual unclean; priests, and especially the high priest, had to avoid such contact (Lev 21:1–12).
44:28 only inheritance. Compare Numbers 18:20–24, Deuteronomy 10:9, 18:1–5, Joshua 13:33 and 18:7.
44:31 must not eat. The prohibition against eating meat of an animal found dead applied to all Israel (Lev 11:39–40; Dt 14:21).
■**45:1–12** *The Sacred Area of the Land.* The allocation of the land was taken up in greater detail in chapters 47–48; here the concern is more narrowly with the sacred precincts. Ezekiel saw a sacred area in the middle of the land, a square of about eight miles (25,000 cubits) on each side, further subdivided into three strips of land; compare Revelation 21:16. The northernmost zone (about 25 square miles) was set aside for the use of the Levites. The center zone contained the sanctuary and was set apart for the priests. The southernmost zone, about half the size of the other two, was given to the city. The area to the east and west of the 64-square-mile area was given to the prince, while the areas north and south would be divided among the other tribes. Interestingly, in Ezekiel's vision the temple would be outside the city.
45:9–12 See *HC* 110.
45:10 accurate. Archaeological excavations testify to considerable variation in weights used in ancient Israel. To date no two weights of the same denomination have been discovered that actually weigh the same; the use of false weights and balances was widespread (Lev 19:35–36; Dt 25:13–16; Pr 11:1; Am 8:5; Mic 6:10–12). **ephah . . . bath.** The ephah was a dry measure and the bath a liquid measure; both amounted to about 22 liters, or a bit under six gallons. See "Table of Weights and Measures" at the back of this Bible.

curate ephah[a][k] and an accurate bath.[b] 11The ephah[l] and the bath are to be the same
size, the bath containing a tenth of a homer[c] and the ephah a tenth of a homer; the homer is to be the standard measure for both. 12The shekel[d] is to consist of twenty gerahs.[m]
Twenty shekels plus twenty-five shekels plus fifteen shekels equal one mina.[e]

Offerings and Holy Days

13" 'This is the special gift you are to offer: a sixth of an ephah from each homer of
wheat and a sixth of an ephah from each homer of barley. 14The prescribed portion of
oil, measured by the bath, is a tenth of a bath from each cor (which consists of ten baths
or one homer, for ten baths are equivalent to a homer). 15Also one sheep is to be taken
from every flock of two hundred from the well-watered pastures of Israel. These will be
used for the grain offerings, burnt offerings[n] and fellowship offerings[f] to make atonement[o] for the people, declares the Sovereign LORD. 16All the people of the land will participate in this special gift for the use of the prince in Israel. 17It will be the duty of the
prince to provide the burnt offerings, grain offerings and drink offerings at the festivals,
the New Moons and the Sabbaths[p]—at all the appointed feasts of the house of Israel. He
will provide the sin offerings, grain offerings, burnt offerings and fellowship offerings to
make atonement for the house of Israel.[q]

18" 'This is what the Sovereign LORD says: In the first month[r] on the first day you are
to take a young bull without defect[s] and purify the sanctuary.[t] 19The priest is to take
some of the blood of the sin offering and put it on the doorposts of the temple, on the
four corners of the upper ledge[u] of the altar[v] and on the gateposts of the inner court.
20You are to do the same on the seventh day of the month for anyone who sins unintentionally[w] or through ignorance; so you are to make atonement for the temple.

21" 'In the first month on the fourteenth day you are to observe the Passover,[x] a feast
lasting seven days, during which you shall eat bread made without yeast. 22On that day
the prince is to provide a bull as a sin offering for himself and for all the people of the
land.[y] 23Every day during the seven days of the Feast he is to provide seven bulls and sev-
en rams[z] without defect as a burnt offering to the LORD, and a male goat for a sin offering.[a] 24He is to provide as a grain offering[b] an ephah for each bull and an ephah for each
ram, along with a hin[g] of oil for each ephah.[c]

25" 'During the seven days of the Feast,[d] which begins in the seventh month on the
fifteenth day, he is to make the same provision for sin offerings, burnt offerings, grain
offerings and oil.[e]

46 " 'This is what the Sovereign LORD says: The gate of the inner court[f] facing east[g]
is to be shut on the six working days, but on the Sabbath day and on the day of
the New Moon[h] it is to be opened. 2The prince is to enter from the outside through the
portico[i] of the gateway and stand by the gatepost. The priests are to sacrifice his burnt
offering and his fellowship offerings.[h] He is to worship at the threshold of the gateway
and then go out, but the gate will not be shut until evening.[j] 3On the Sabbaths and New
Moons the people of the land are to worship in the presence of the LORD at the entrance
to that gateway.[k] 4The burnt offering the prince brings to the LORD on the Sabbath day
is to be six male lambs and a ram, all without defect. 5The grain offering given with the

[a] *10* An ephah was a dry measure. [b] *10* A bath was a liquid measure. [c] *11* A homer was a dry measure. [d] *12* A shekel weighed about 2/5 ounce (about 11.5 grams). [e] *12* That is, 60 shekels; the common mina was 50 shekels. [f] *15* Traditionally *peace offerings;* also in verse 17 [g] *24* That is, probably about 4 quarts (about 4 liters) [h] *2* Traditionally *peace offerings;* also in verse 12

45:10 [k]Lev 19:36
45:11 [l]Isa 5:10
45:12 [m]Ex 30:13; Lev 27:25; Nu 3:47
45:15 [n]Lev 1:4 [o]Lev 6:30
45:17 [p]Lev 23:38; Isa 66:23 [q]1Ki 8:62; 2Ch 31:3; Eze 46:4-12
45:18 [r]Ex 12:2 [s]Lev 22:20; Heb 9:14 [t]Lev 16:16, 33
45:19 [u]Eze 43:17 [v]Lev 16:18-19; Eze 43:20
45:20 [w]Lev 4:27
45:21 [x]Ex 12:11; Lev 23:5-6
45:22 [y]Lev 4:14
45:23 [z]Job 42:8 [a]Nu 28:16-25
45:24 [b]Nu 28:12-13 [c]Eze 46:5-7
45:25 [d]Dt 16:13 [e]Lev 23:34-43; Nu 29:12-38
46:1 [f]Eze 40:19 [g]1Ch 9:18 [h]ver 6; Isa 66:23
46:2 [i]ver 8 [j]ver 12; Eze 44:3
46:3 [k]Lk 1:10

45:11 homer. Ten baths or ephahs equaled a homer, about 58 gallons or six bushels. See "Table of Weights and Measures."

45:12 shekel . . . mina. A shekel was about two-fifths of an ounce; a mina of 60 shekels would be about a pound and a half. The mina ordinarily consisted of 50 shekels. See "Table of Weights and Measures."

■**45:13—46:24** *Offerings and Holy Days.* Ezekiel foresaw the crucial roles that sacred leaders would perform in the future Jerusalem.

45:17 duty of the prince. Israel's princes were also responsible to make offerings on behalf of the people (vv. 13–17). The people would donate offerings in kind to the prince, who in turn would provide them to the sanctuary. Compare 2 Chronicles 30:24 and see notes on 37:24 and 44:3.

45:18–25 In the first month . . . seventh month. Regulations covering aspects of the ceremonial observances in the first month (New Year's Day; 45:18–20) and seventh month (Passover [45:21–24] and Tabernacles [45:25]). This legislation may have represented modifications of earlier liturgical practice. Once again, like Moses, Ezekiel provided worship legislation for Israel; see notes on 43:10 and 12.

45:19 altar. Compare the consecration of the altar in Exodus 29:35–37.

45:24 hin. A hin was one-sixth of a bath, about three and two-thirds liters. See "Table of Weights and Measures" at the back of this Bible.

46:1–12 The prince is to enter. The prince was allowed to enter as far as the inner threshold of the eastern gate of the inner courtyard on festival days; on other days he entered and left among the ordinary people (vv. 9–10), unless he was making a freewill offering (v. 12). The prince also had special privileges with reference to the eastern gate in the outer courtyard (see notes on 44:1 and 3). From his vantage point at the threshold of the inner gate he would have a full view of the actions in the inner courtyard and at the great altar; however, he could not go beyond this point since entry into the inner court was restricted to priests and Levites.

46:4 burnt offering. The specifications for this offering differ from those of the Sabbath offerings in Numbers 28:9, where two lambs but no ram were required.

ram is to be an ephah,[a] and the grain offering with the lambs is to be as much as he
pleases, along with a hin[b] of oil for each ephah.[l] 6 On the day of the New Moon[m] he is to
offer a young bull, six lambs and a ram, all without defect. 7 He is to provide as a grain
offering one ephah with the bull, one ephah with the ram, and with the lambs as much
as he wants to give, along with a hin of oil with each ephah.[n] 8 When the prince enters,
he is to go in through the portico[o] of the gateway, and he is to come out the same way.[p]
9 " 'When the people of the land come before the LORD at the appointed feasts,[q] whoever enters by the north gate to worship is to go out the south gate; and whoever enters
by the south gate is to go out the north gate. No one is to return through the gate by
which he entered, but each is to go out the opposite gate. 10 The prince is to be among
them, going in when they go in and going out when they go out.[r]
11 " 'At the festivals and the appointed feasts, the grain offering is to be an ephah with
a bull, an ephah with a ram, and with the lambs as much as one pleases, along with a
hin of oil for each ephah.[s] 12 When the prince provides[t] a freewill offering[u] to the LORD—
whether a burnt offering or fellowship offerings—the gate facing east is to be opened for
him. He shall offer his burnt offering or his fellowship offerings as he does on the Sabbath day. Then he shall go out, and after he has gone out, the gate will be shut.[v]
13 " 'Every day you are to provide a year-old lamb without defect for a burnt offering
to the LORD; morning by morning you shall provide it.[w] 14 You are also to provide with it
morning by morning a grain offering, consisting of a sixth of an ephah with a third of a
hin of oil to moisten the flour. The presenting of this grain offering to the LORD is a lasting ordinance.[x] 15 So the lamb and the grain offering and the oil shall be provided morning by morning for a regular[y] burnt offering.[z]
16 " 'This is what the Sovereign LORD says: If the prince makes a gift from his inheritance
to one of his sons, it will also belong to his descendants; it is to be their property by inheritance.[a] 17 If, however, he makes a gift from his inheritance to one of his servants, the
servant may keep it until the year of freedom;[b] then it will revert to the prince. His inheritance belongs to his sons only; it is theirs. 18 The prince must not take any of the inheritance[c] of the people, driving them off their property. He is to give his sons their inheritance
out of his own property, so that none of my people will be separated from his property.' "
19 Then the man brought me through the entrance[d] at the side of the gate to the sacred rooms facing north, which belonged to the priests, and showed me a place at the
western end. 20 He said to me, "This is the place where the priests will cook the guilt offering and the sin offering and bake the grain offering, to avoid bringing them into the
outer court and consecrating[e] the people."[f]
21 He then brought me to the outer court and led me around to its four corners, and I
saw in each corner another court. 22 In the four corners of the outer court were enclosed[c]
courts, forty cubits long and thirty cubits wide; each of the courts in the four corners was
the same size. 23 Around the inside of each of the four courts was a ledge of stone, with
places for fire built all around under the ledge. 24 He said to me, "These are the kitchens
where those who minister at the temple will cook the sacrifices of the people."

The River From the Temple

47 The man brought me back to the entrance of the temple, and I saw water[g] coming out from under the threshold of the temple toward the east (for the temple

46:5 [l]ver 11; Eze 45:24
46:6 [m]ver 1; Nu 10:10
46:7 [n]Eze 45:24
46:8 [o]ver 2 [p]Eze 44:3
46:9 [q]Ex 23:14; 34:20
46:10 [r]2Sa 6:14-15; Ps 42:4
46:11 [s]ver 5
46:12 [t]Eze 45:17 [u]Lev 7:16 [v]ver 2
46:13 [w]Ex 29:38; Nu 28:3
46:14 [x]Da 8:11
46:15 [y]Ex 29:42 [z]Ex 29:38; Nu 28:5-6
46:16 [a]2Ch 21:3
46:17 [b]Lev 25:10
46:18 [c]Lev 25:23; Eze 45:8; Mic 2:1-2
46:19 [d]Eze 42:9
46:20 [e]Lev 6:27 [f]Zec 14:20
47:1 [g]Isa 55:1

[a] 5 That is, probably about 3/5 bushel (about 22 liters) [b] 5 That is, probably about 4 quarts (about 4 liters) [c] *22* The meaning of the Hebrew for this word is uncertain.

46:5 ephah. See note on 45:10–11. According to Numbers 28:9 the grain offering on the Sabbath amounted to two-tenths of an ephah. Again Ezekiel functioned as a kind of second Moses and gave ceremonial legislation for the nation's future. See notes on 43:10 and 12 and 45:18–25.

46:6 day of the New Moon. The first day of the lunar month. The specifications for this offering again differ from those of earlier legislation (Nu 28:11), which required two bulls, one ram and seven male lambs.

46:7 grain offering. Contrast Numbers 28:12.

46:9 whoever enters. In Ezekiel's vision of this ideal Israel so many would regularly worship at the temple that crowd control would be necessary to ensure orderly movement.

46:13 Every day. Whereas most of the preceding regulations concerned offerings on particular days of the Old Testament liturgical calendar, God was to be worshiped in Israel every day (vv. 13–15). **morning by morning.** These provisions for the daily offerings also differ from earlier practice (Nu 28:3–8; 2Ki 16:15; 1Ch 16:40; 2Ch 13:11; 31:3).

46:14 grain offering. Contrast Numbers 28:4–5.

46:16–18 none . . . separated from his property. See notes on 33:23–29 and 45:9–12. In redeeming the Israelites from bondage in Egypt and in Babylon God not only brought them from the place of bondage but also secured for his people an inheritance in their land. The right to the land was inalienable (Lev 25:14–17,23–24; 1Ki 21); this represented the permanence of the redemption and inheritance that God had provided (1Pe 1:4).

46:16 descendants. Ezekiel envisaged the restoration of Davidic rule. See notes on 43:10 and 12 and on 45:18–25.

46:17 year of freedom. Most likely a reference to the Year of Jubilee (Lev 25:8–17; 27:24; Isa 61:1–2).

46:20 cook. Old Testament worship combined sacrifice and prayer with eating and social activity. These regulations specified the locations where the Levites were to prepare offerings for the sacrificial meals to be eaten by worshipers.

faced east). The water was coming down from under the south side of the temple, south
of the altar.[h] 2He then brought me out through the north gate and led me around the
outside to the outer gate facing east, and the water was flowing from the south side.
3As the man went eastward with a measuring line[i] in his hand, he measured off a
thousand cubits[a] and then led me through water that was ankle-deep. 4He measured off
another thousand cubits and led me through water that was knee-deep. He measured
off another thousand and led me through water that was up to the waist. 5He measured
off another thousand, but now it was a river that I could not cross, because the water had
risen and was deep enough to swim in—a river that no one could cross.[j] 6He asked me,
"Son of man, do you see this?"
Then he led me back to the bank of the river. 7When I arrived there, I saw a great
number of trees on each side of the river.[k] 8He said to me, "This water flows toward the
eastern region and goes down into the Arabah,[b][l] where it enters the Sea.[c] When it empties into the Sea,[c] the water there becomes fresh.[m] 9Swarms of living creatures will live
wherever the river flows. There will be large numbers of fish, because this water flows
there and makes the salt water fresh; so where the river flows everything will live.[n]
10Fishermen[o] will stand along the shore; from En Gedi[p] to En Eglaim there will be places for spreading nets.[q] The fish will be of many kinds[r]—like the fish of the Great Sea.[d][s]
11But the swamps and marshes will not become fresh; they will be left for salt.[t] 12Fruit
trees of all kinds will grow on both banks of the river.[u] Their leaves will not wither, nor
will their fruit[v] fail. Every month they will bear, because the water from the sanctuary
flows to them. Their fruit will serve for food and their leaves for healing.[w]"

The Boundaries of the Land

13This is what the Sovereign LORD says: "These are the boundaries[x] by which you are
to divide the land for an inheritance among the twelve tribes of Israel, with two portions
for Joseph.[y] 14You are to divide it equally among them. Because I swore with uplifted
hand to give it to your forefathers, this land will become your inheritance.[z]

15"This is to be the boundary of the land:

[a] *3* That is, about 1,500 feet (about 450 meters) [b] *8* Or *the Jordan Valley* [c] *8* That is, the Dead Sea
[d] *10* That is, the Mediterranean; also in verses 15, 19 and 20

47:1 [h]Ps 46:4; Joel 3:18; Rev 22:1
47:3 [i]Eze 40:3
47:5 [j]Isa 11:9; Hab 2:14
47:7 [k]ver 12; Rev 22:2
47:8 [l]Dt 3:17; Jos 3:16 [m]Isa 41:18
47:9 [n]Isa 12:3; 55:1; Jn 4:14; 7:37-38
47:10 [o]Mt 4:19 [p]Jos 15:62 [q]Eze 26:5 [r]Ps 104:25; Mt 13:47 [s]Nu 34:6
47:11 [t]Dt 29:23
47:12 [u]ver 7; Rev 22:2 [v]Ps 1:3 [w]Ge 2:9; Jer 17:8
47:13 [x]Nu 34:2-12 [y]Ge 48:5
47:14 [z]Ge 12:7; Dt 1:8; Eze 20:5-6

■ **47:1—48:35** *The River, the Land and the City.* Ezekiel's angelic guide led him to the temple entrance, where the prophet saw a river forming from a trickle of water flowing out of the temple (47:1–12). This section is followed by a summary of the allocation of land and a description of the city gates (47:13—48:35).

■ **47:1–12** *A Life-giving River.* Ezekiel, in his vision, depicted the centrality of the temple, its personnel and ceremonies as a life-giving river flowing from the temple.

47:1–2 water . . . from under the threshold. The courtyard of the tabernacle had a large basin or laver where the priests washed (Ex 30:17–21). This basin was replaced in Solomon's temple by the much larger Sea (1Ki 7:23–26). The Sea was used by the priests for ritual purifications (2Ch 4:6), but, as its name implied, it also symbolized by its abundance of fresh water fullness of life in the presence of God. In Ezekiel's temple vision these earlier basins were replaced by a life-giving river (cf. Rev 21:1; 22:1–2). The tabernacle laver and the temple Sea stood south of the altar in the sanctuary courtyard; the river also originated from south of the altar. This passage should be compared with others that speak of a river in the city of God (Ps 46:4) or describe the eruption of a stream from within the city (Joel 3:17; Zec 14:3–8). Since the temple in part symbolized Paradise, this river recalls the rivers issuing from the Garden of Eden (Ge 2:10–14).

47:3–12 a great number of trees. The river would bring life everywhere it went and transform Israel into a paradisiacal garden. **empties into the Sea.** The Dead Sea. Jerusalem sits on the Judean watershed astride a ridge of hills; rainfall from the city also flows into the Kidron Valley and makes its way to the Dead Sea. Jesus appealed to the images used in this passage to describe himself. He told a Samaritan woman that he was the source of life-giving water (Jn 4:10–14). When the disciples were surprised that Jesus had deigned to talk with her, he spoke to them of an unending harvest that had already begun (Jn 4:27–38), drawing on Ezekiel's picture of trees bearing 12 crops each year. John also reported Jesus' preaching that he was the source of streams of living water, adding the comment that Jesus was speaking of God's Spirit (Jn 7:37–39).

47:10 En Gedi. Located about midway along the western shore of the Dead Sea. See Genesis 14:7, Joshua 15:62, 1 Samuel 23:29 and 2 Chronicles 20:2. **En Eglaim.** Near the northwestern corner of the Dead Sea.

47:11 swamps and marshes. The statement that the swamps and marshes would be left for salt may indicate familiarity with the tradition that the shallow southern reaches of the Dead Sea contained the sites of the ancient cities of Sodom and Gomorrah (Ge 19:27–29).

47:12 Fruit trees. A picture of agricultural bounty, a blessing of the full restoration of God's people after exile. For Christians this promise is fulfilled in part in the down payment of the Holy Spirit, who is associated with the restoration of nature (Ge 1:2; Ps 104:30) and with the inheritance of the new heavens and the new earth. See notes on 28:25 and 26 and on 34:25–26.

■ **47:13—48:29** *Restoration of the Land.* Ezekiel's vision of the future restoration included the restoration of the land to its God-ordained order.

47:13 two portions for Joseph. In Ezekiel's vision the land would be divided equally among the 12 tribes. Since the tribe of Levi had no territorial inheritance but lived on its portion of the offerings of the people, the number 12 was maintained by dividing the tribe of Joseph into two tribes, bearing the names of his sons, Ephraim and Manasseh (Ge 48:1–6).

47:14 your inheritance. The land would be that which God had promised to the patriarchs (Ge 12:7; 15:18–21; 22:17: 28:4) and which was possessed during the reigns of David and Solomon (1Ki 8:65; 1Ch 10:11; 13:5; 2Ch 9:26).

47:15 boundary. The boundaries detailed here (vv. 15–20) mention a number of sites that are not known, but they roughly correspond to other such lists (Nu 34:1–12; 1Ki 8:65). However, the allocation of the land (ch. 48) is quite different from the historical boundaries of the tribes. The eastern and western boundaries are easy to identify: On the east the boundary began in the headwaters of the Jordan south of Damascus, down the Jordan River and along the western shore of the Dead Sea; on the west the boundary was the Mediterranean Sea. The northern and southern boundaries are more difficult to establish: In the north the boundary began near Tyre and proceeded east to a point north of the Sea of Galilee; in the south it ran from a point below the Dead Sea to the Wadi of Egypt (the Wadi el-Arish) on the Mediterranean coast.

15 "On the north side it will run from the Great Sea by the Hethlon road[a] past Lebo[a] Hamath
to Zedad, 16 Berothah[b] [b] and Sibraim (which lies on the border between Damascus
and Hamath),[c] as far as Hazer Hatticon, which is on the border of Hauran. 17 The
boundary will extend from the sea to Hazar Enan,[c] along the northern border of Damascus, with the border of Hamath to the north. This will be the north boundary.[d]
18 "On the east side the boundary will run between Hauran and Damascus, along the Jordan between Gilead and the land of Israel, to the eastern sea and as far as Tamar.[d]
This will be the east boundary.
19 "On the south side it will run from Tamar as far as the waters of Meribah Kadesh,[e] then
along the Wadi ⌊of Egypt⌋[f] to the Great Sea.[g] This will be the south boundary.
20 "On the west side, the Great Sea will be the boundary to a point opposite Lebo[e] Hamath.[h] This will be the west boundary.[i]

21 "You are to distribute this land among yourselves according to the tribes of Israel.
22 You are to allot it as an inheritance for yourselves and for the aliens[j] who have settled
among you and who have children. You are to consider them as native-born Israelites;
along with you they are to be allotted an inheritance among the tribes of Israel.[k] 23 In
whatever tribe the alien settles, there you are to give him his inheritance," declares the
Sovereign LORD.

The Division of the Land

48 1 "These are the tribes, listed by name: At the northern frontier, Dan[l] will have
one portion; it will follow the Hethlon road[m] to Lebo[f] Hamath;[n] Hazar Enan and
the northern border of Damascus next to Hamath will be part of its border from the east
side to the west side.
2 "Asher[o] will have one portion; it will border the territory of Dan from east to west.
3 "Naphtali[p] will have one portion; it will border the territory of Asher from east to west.
4 "Manasseh[q] will have one portion; it will border the territory of Naphtali from east
to west.
5 "Ephraim[r] will have one portion; it will border the territory of Manasseh[s] from east
to west.[t]
6 "Reuben[u] will have one portion; it will border the territory of Ephraim from east to
west.
7 "Judah[v] will have one portion; it will border the territory of Reuben from east to west.
8 "Bordering the territory of Judah from east to west will be the portion you are to present as a special gift. It will be 25,000 cubits[g] wide, and its length from east to west will
equal one of the tribal portions; the sanctuary will be in the center of it.[w]
9 "The special portion you are to offer to the LORD will be 25,000 cubits long and
10,000 cubits[h] wide.[x] 10 This will be the sacred portion for the priests. It will be 25,000
cubits long on the north side, 10,000 cubits wide on the west side, 10,000 cubits wide
on the east side and 25,000 cubits long on the south side. In the center of it will be the
sanctuary of the LORD.[y] 11 This will be for the consecrated priests, the Zadokites,[z] who
were faithful in serving me[a] and did not go astray as the Levites did when the Israelites
went astray.[b] 12 It will be a special gift to them from the sacred portion of the land, a most
holy portion, bordering the territory of the Levites.

47:15 [a]Eze 48:1
47:16 [b]2Sa 8:8 [c]Nu 13:21; Eze 48:1
47:17 [d]Eze 48:1
47:19 [e]Dt 32:51 [f]Isa 27:12 [g]Eze 48:28
47:20 [h]Eze 48:1 [i]Nu 34:6
47:22 [j]Isa 14:1 [k]Nu 26:55-56; Isa 56:6-7; Ro 10:12; Eph 2:12-16; 3:6; Col 3:11
48:1 [l]Ge 30:6 [m]Eze 47:15-17 [n]Eze 47:20
48:2 [o]Jos 19:24-31
48:3 [p]Jos 19:32-39
48:4 [q]Jos 17:1-11
48:5 [r]Jos 16:5-9 [s]Jos 17:7-10 [t]Jos 17:17
48:6 [u]Jos 13:15-21
48:7 [v]Jos 15:1-63
48:8 [w]ver 21
48:9 [x]Eze 45:1
48:10 [y]ver 21; Eze 45:3-4
48:11 [z]2Sa 8:17 [a]Lev 8:35 [b]Eze 14:11; 44:15

[a] *15* Or *past the entrance to* [b] *15,16* See Septuagint and Ezekiel 48:1; Hebrew *road to go into Zedad, 16Hamath, Berothah* [c] *17* Hebrew *Enon,* a variant of *Enan* [d] *18* Septuagint and Syriac; Hebrew *Israel. You will measure to the eastern sea* [e] *20* Or *opposite the entrance to* [f] *1* Or *to the entrance to* [g] *8* That is, about 7 miles (about 12 kilometers) [h] *9* That is, about 3 miles (about 5 kilometers)

48:1–29 These are the tribes. In Ezekiel's visionary geography the allotment of the land among the tribes would be quite different from what it had been historically. Each tribe would be allocated a strip of land connecting with the eastern and western borders. The status of Jacob's wives and of the individual tribes seem to be the determining factors in the arrangement of the allotments; compare Numbers 2–3. The northernmost tribes (Dan, Asher and Naphtali) were traditionally located in the north; the southernmost tribe (Gad; v. 27) was historically a northern tribe. These four tribes were the descendants of Leah's servant Zilpah and of Rachel's servant Bilhah (Ge 30:3–7,10–12); as tribes descended from the servants, they would according to Ezekiel's vision be located at the outer extremities of the tribal allotments.

Looking at the other tribes north of the "sacred portion," which was in the center of the land (vv. 8–22; 45:1–8), Judah would be the closest to the sacred portion. Judah historically was a southern tribe; by placing the tribe of David with the northern tribes Ezekiel may have indicated that the north would "have a share in David" (2Sa 20:1; 1Ki 12:16; 2Ch 10:16). Judah received the place of honor that would ordinarily have belonged to the firstborn, Reuben; the territory of Reuben would be immediately north of Judah. North of Reuben would be Joseph's tribes, Ephraim and Manasseh; they were descendants of Jacob through his favored wife, Rachel.

South of and closest to the sacred portion would be Benjamin. Benjamin was historically north of the holy city. Its favored place reflected the favored status of Rachel and balanced the favored position of Joseph's tribes in the north. The remaining three southern tribes (Simeon, Issachar and Zebulun) were the descendants of Leah; Issachar and Zebulun historically held allocations in the north.

48:8–22 The special portion. The sacred portion; an elaboration of 45:1–8, in particular the southern strip of land within the sacred portion that would be set aside for the city (45:6). This inheritance too was to be inalienable; see notes on 46:16–18.

48:11 Zadokites. See note on 44:10–14.

13“Alongside the territory of the priests, the Levites will have an allotment 25,000 cubits long and 10,000 cubits wide. Its total length will be 25,000 cubits and its width
10,000 cubits.[c] 14They must not sell or exchange any of it. This is the best of the land and
must not pass into other hands, because it is holy to the LORD.[d]
15“The remaining area, 5,000 cubits wide and 25,000 cubits long, will be for the common use of the city, for houses and for pastureland. The city will be in the center of it
16and will have these measurements: the north side 4,500 cubits, the south side 4,500
cubits, the east side 4,500 cubits, and the west side 4,500 cubits.[e] 17The pastureland for
the city will be 250 cubits on the north, 250 cubits on the south, 250 cubits on the east,
and 250 cubits on the west. 18What remains of the area, bordering on the sacred portion
and running the length of it, will be 10,000 cubits on the east side and 10,000 cubits on
the west side. Its produce will supply food for the workers of the city.[f] 19The workers from
the city who farm it will come from all the tribes of Israel. 20The entire portion will be a
square, 25,000 cubits on each side. As a special gift you will set aside the sacred portion,
along with the property of the city.
21“What remains on both sides of the area formed by the sacred portion and the city
property will belong to the prince. It will extend eastward from the 25,000 cubits of the
sacred portion to the eastern border, and westward from the 25,000 cubits to the western border. Both these areas running the length of the tribal portions will belong to the
prince, and the sacred portion with the temple sanctuary will be in the center of them.[g]
22So the property of the Levites and the property of the city will lie in the center of the
area that belongs to the prince. The area belonging to the prince will lie between the border of Judah and the border of Benjamin.
23“As for the rest of the tribes: Benjamin[h] will have one portion; it will extend from
the east side to the west side.
24“Simeon[i] will have one portion; it will border the territory of Benjamin from east
to west.
25“Issachar[j] will have one portion; it will border the territory of Simeon from east to
west.
26“Zebulun[k] will have one portion; it will border the territory of Issachar from east to
west.
27“Gad[l] will have one portion; it will border the territory of Zebulun from east to west.
28“The southern boundary of Gad will run south from Tamar[m] to the waters of Meribah Kadesh, then along the Wadi ⌊of Egypt⌋ to the Great Sea.[a][n]
29“This is the land you are to allot as an inheritance to the tribes of Israel, and these
will be their portions,” declares the Sovereign LORD.

The Gates of the City

30“These will be the exits of the city: Beginning on the north side, which is 4,500 cubits long, 31the gates of the city will be named after the tribes of Israel. The three gates
on the north side will be the gate of Reuben, the gate of Judah and the gate of Levi.
32“On the east side, which is 4,500 cubits long, will be three gates: the gate of Joseph,
the gate of Benjamin and the gate of Dan.
33“On the south side, which measures 4,500 cubits, will be three gates: the gate of
Simeon, the gate of Issachar and the gate of Zebulun.
34“On the west side, which is 4,500 cubits long, will be three gates: the gate of Gad,
the gate of Asher and the gate of Naphtali.
35“The distance all around will be 18,000 cubits.
“And the name of the city from that time on will be:

THE LORD IS THERE.[o]”

48:13 [c]Eze 45:5
48:14 [d]Lev 25:34; 27:10, 28
48:16 [e]Rev 21:16
48:18 [f]Eze 45:6
48:21 [g]ver 8, 10; Eze 45:7
48:23 [h]Jos 18:11-28
48:24 [i]Ge 29:33; Jos 19:1-9
48:25 [j]Jos 19:17-23
48:26 [k]Jos 19:10-16
48:27 [l]Jos 13:24-28
48:28 [m]Ge 14:7 [n]Eze 47:19
48:35 [o]Isa 12:6; 24:23; Jer 3:17; 14:9; Jer 33:16; Joel 3:21; Zec 2:10; Rev 21:3

[a] *28* That is, the Mediterranean

■ **48:30–35** *Restoration of the City.* The city would have 12 gates, named after the 12 tribes (cf. Rev 21:12–14). However, since one gate was to be named after Levi, the tribes Ephraim and Manasseh would be combined as “Joseph” in order to keep the number at 12. The northern gates would be named after Reuben (the firstborn), Judah (the tribe of David and the royal line) and Levi (the tribe of the temple personnel). The eastern gates would be the descendants of Rachel (Joseph and Benjamin) and of one son of Rachel’s servant Bilhah (Dan). The southern gates would be named after those tribes listed in the south in verses 24–26. Those on the west would be named for the other sons of Zilpah and Bilhah. Compare the encampment of the tribes in the wilderness (Nu 2–3; see chart, “Encampment of the Tribes of Israel,” on page 205). Ezekiel’s vision of the glorious city would be fulfilled in Christ’s death and resurrection occurring near Jerusalem, in the Jerusalem above where Christ is now (Ac 2:33; 1Pe 3:22) and in the descent of the new Jerusalem when Christ returns in glory (Rev 21:1–2).

48:35 **THE LORD IS THERE.** From the beginning of the Old Testament God revealed his intention to be with his people. He walked and spoke with them in the Garden of Eden and dwelled in sanctuaries built in Israel’s midst. It is fitting that the New Testament hope in Christ reached its climax with a description of the city of God and of a time when the dwelling of God would be on Earth (Rev 21:3). Ezekiel’s hope remains that of the church throughout the ages.

DANIEL

Introduction

Overview

Author: Daniel

Purpose: To assure the exiles and early returnees to the land that God was in control of history and that his prophet Daniel spoke the truth about prolonged troubles before the final stage of God's kingdom

Date: Shortly after 539 B.C.

Key Truths:

- Daniel and his friends were loyal to God during their time in exile.
- Daniel could be trusted to tell the truth because he never compromised with his captors.
- God is in absolute control over all of history.
- Israel's exile was extended until four kingdoms ruled over God's people because of their continuing sin.
- Trials would come in Israel's future, but the Anointed One, the Christ, would come and bring salvation.

Author

The authorship of the book of Daniel has been a matter of considerable debate among interpreters. Many scholars have dated the book between 170 and 165 B.C., during the lifetime of Antiochus IV Epiphanes, well after the time of the prophet Daniel. However, this late date is contrary to the book itself, which indicates that Daniel was its principal author (9:2; 10:2) and that it was written shortly after the capture of Babylon by Cyrus in 539 B.C. Moreover, Christ himself explicitly associated the book with the prophet Daniel (Mt 24:15).

Time and Place of Writing

The controversy over dating the book of Daniel involves three basic issues: (1) the nature of prophecy, (2) alleged historical errors in Daniel and (3) the linguistic features of Hebrew and Aramaic in the book.

Generally speaking, Israel's prophets were primarily concerned with the religious and social circumstances confronting themselves and their contemporaries. When the prophets predicted future events they were concerned most often with incidents in the near term. For this reason some interpreters have held that Daniel's vision concerning the "king of the North" and the "king of the South" (11:2—12:3) is too detailed to have come from Daniel, who lived 200–300 years before the events described in his prophecy.

However, this point of view disregards the supernatural character of prophecy and the occasional practices of other prophets (e.g., 1Ki 13:2; Isa 44:28; 45:1). Although Daniel 11:2—12:3 is unusual, it was certainly not impossible for Daniel to have known these details.

Some advocates of a late date have also attributed historical errors to the book of Daniel to support their view. They have raised questions about Belshazzar's relationship to Nebuchadnezzar (see note on 5:2) and the identity of Darius the Mede (see note on 6:1). Moreover, they have identified the four kingdoms foreseen by Daniel (chs. 2; 7) as those of the Babylonians, the Medes, the Persians and the Greeks (including the Seleucids and Ptolemies). This identification is problematic because there is no evidence for an independent Median kingdom in an interval between the Babylonian and Persian kingdoms. Cyrus, the Persian king (550–530 B.C.), conquered the Medes in 549 B.C. and the Babylonians in 539 B.C. (see notes on 5:1,31).

Supporters of an early date for the book understand the sequence of the four kingdoms to be predictive of the Babylonian kingdom, the Medo-Persian kingdom, the Greek kingdom and the Roman kingdom. They are supported by the reference to "the Medes and Persians" in 5:28, which shows that the author considered the two as constituting one kingdom.

Those who date the book late argue that several Greek loanwords for musical instruments appear (see note on 3:5) and that later Hebrew and Aramaic terms also occur (see note on 2:4). Neither of these arguments is convincing. There is abundant evidence of contact between the Greeks and the peoples of the Near East prior to the time of Alexander the Great. Such contacts are sufficient to explain the use of Greek loanwords prior to the time of Alexander's conquests. The Aramaic and Hebrew of Daniel can be dated anytime between the late sixth and early second centuries B.C. In other words, the linguistic evidence does not lend much weight to either early or late proposals.

The arguments for a date in the second century B.C. contradict the Biblical statements regarding the date and authorship of the book of Daniel and do not sufficiently establish the case for a late date. A date shortly after 539 B.C. (see 1:21) accords best with the nature of prophecy, historical data and the language of the text.

Purpose and Distinctives

Daniel contains two different types of material. Six historical narratives appear in chapters 1–6 and four visions in chapters 7–12. The visions are almost exclusively predictive. Among the six narratives chapter 2 is distinct because it also contains a prediction.

Reflection on the content of the historical narratives reveals that they are independent narrative units that have been placed together for a specific purpose. The narratives provide neither a history of Israel under Babylonian or Persian rule nor a biographical account of Daniel or his friends. An overview reveals two central concerns. On the one hand the stories emphasize how the absolute sovereignty of God operates in the affairs of all nations (2:47; 3:17–18; 4:28–37; 5:18–31; 6:25–28). Jerusalem was destroyed, the temple lay in ruins, God's people were in exile and wicked rulers seemed triumphant—but God remained supreme. According to his sovereign pleasure he would intervene among the kingdoms of this world to establish a universal kingdom that would last forever.

These narratives depict Daniel and his friends as being prominent in the lands of their captors not because they compromised their loyalty to God but because they were exalted by God's blessing on them. This motif is central because it gives credibility to Daniel's prophecies, especially those related to the prolonging of Israel's suffering.

The visions (chs. 7–12) contain predictions of future times during which the truths of the narratives would prove to be of particular importance for God's people. Although the Jews were persecuted during the time of their subjection to Babylonian and Persian rulers, there was no widespread and systematic attempt to abolish their faith. This did not happen until the time of Antiochus IV Epiphanes, a ruler of the Seleucid Empire from 175–164 B.C. He attempted to eradicate the Jewish religion and to force the Jews to conform to Greek religious practices. Many Jews followed him, but others refused and suffered severe persecution. One of the major reasons for the writing of Daniel was to prepare God's people for the time of Antiochus Epiphanes and to provide encouragement for those living during that coming period of persecution. The book also looks beyond the time of Antiochus Epiphanes to the coming of Christ, who will destroy all human kingdoms and establish his eternal kingdom of righteousness and peace. All of these events are in view in the prophecies of Daniel. The book has been of great encouragement to God's people in times of persecution and continues to inspire those suffering persecution today.

Christ in Daniel

Daniel's concentration on Israel's restoration after exile draws attention rather directly to Jesus. Like other Old Testament prophets Daniel predicted a glorious future for God's people that the New Testament explains as fulfilled in the first and second comings of Christ, as well as in the entirety of church history.

Much controversy surrounds many details of the fulfillments of Daniel's predictions, but the basic structure of Daniel's vision of the future leaves no doubt that Christ fulfills the prophet's hopes. This is most clearly seen in the way Jesus identifies himself as the "Son of Man" (e.g., Mt 9:6; 10:23; 12:8). As Daniel used the term, the "son of man" was a great Davidic king who was exalted by God and represented God on Earth. Jesus, the Messiah, was the ultimate Davidic King; he alone fulfills the predictions made of the son of man in Daniel's vision (see notes on 7:13 and 14; see theological article "The Kingdom of God" at Mt 4).

Further, in chapter 9 Daniel learned that Jeremiah's prediction of 70 years for Israel's exile in Babylon would be extended to "Seventy 'sevens' " of years (9:24), or about 490 years. This prediction finds initial fulfillment in the first coming of Christ. The prolongation of exile corresponds to the series of four foreign empires that oppressed the people of God (2:1–49) and to the appearance of the "rock that . . . became a huge mountain and filled the whole earth" (2:35), which Daniel later called "a kingdom that will never be destroyed" (2:44). This great kingdom is none other than the kingdom of Christ, which began at his first coming, continues today and will reach its consummation at Christ's glorious return (see theological articles "The Kingdom of God" at Mt 4 and "The Plan of the Ages" at Heb 7).

Other, more specific events predicted by Daniel also come to the foreground in the New Testament. For example, Jesus himself referred to Daniel's prediction of "an abomination that causes desolation" (see notes on 9:27; 11:31; 12:11), which originally referred to the defilement of the temple by the Greek Antiochus IV Epiphanes (see "Introduction: Purpose and Distinctives") as a precursor to the defilement brought by the Roman general Titus in A.D. 70 (see notes on Mt 24:15; Mk 13:14). In one way or another most Christian interpreters closely associate this typology with the antichrist, whose spirit is already at work in the world (see note on 1Jn 2:18) and will come to full development, perhaps as an actual person, near the return of Christ (see note on 2Th 2:3).

Outline

I. The Narratives (1:1—6:28)
   A. Vindication of Daniel and His Friends (1:1–21)
   B. Nebuchadnezzar's First Dream (2:1–49)
   C. Deliverance From the Furnace (3:1–30)
   D. Nebuchadnezzar's Second Dream (4:1–37)
   E. Judgment on Belshazzar (5:1–31)
   F. Deliverance From the Den of Lions (6:1–28)

The stories of Daniel and his friends illustrate their faithfulness to God and his supremacy over all nations.

II. The Visions (7:1—12:13)
   A. Vision of the Four Beasts (7:1–28)
   B. Vision of the Ram and the Goat (8:1–27)
   C. Vision of the Seventy Weeks (9:1–27)

Daniel's visions depicted the future of God's people as they looked beyond the years of exile. God revealed to Daniel that four major kingdoms would control Israel and persecute the Israelites.

D. Vision of the Future of God's People (10:1—12:13)
   1. The Angel's Message to Daniel (10:1—11:1)
   2. From Daniel Until Antiochus IV Epiphanes (11:2–20)
   3. The Rule of Antiochus IV Epiphanes (11:21—12:3)
   4. A Final Message to Daniel (12:4–13)

Daniel's Training in Babylon

1 In the third year of the reign of Jehoiakim king of Judah, Nebuchadnezzar[a] king of
Babylon came to Jerusalem and besieged it.[b] 2 And the Lord delivered Jehoiakim
king of Judah into his hand, along with some of the articles from the temple of God. These
he carried off to the temple of his god in Babylonia[a] and put in the treasure house of his
god.[c]
3 Then the king ordered Ashpenaz, chief of his court officials, to bring in some of the
Israelites from the royal family and the nobility[d]— 4 young men without any physical defect, handsome, showing aptitude for every kind of learning, well informed, quick to understand, and qualified to serve in the king's palace. He was to teach them the language
and literature of the Babylonians.[b] 5 The king assigned them a daily amount of food and
wine[e] from the king's table. They were to be trained for three years, and after that they
were to enter the king's service.[f]
6 Among these were some from Judah: Daniel,[g] Hananiah, Mishael and Azariah. 7 The
chief official gave them new names: to Daniel, the name Belteshazzar;[h] to Hananiah,
Shadrach; to Mishael, Meshach; and to Azariah, Abednego.[i]
8 But Daniel resolved not to defile[j] himself with the royal food and wine, and he asked
the chief official for permission not to defile himself this way. 9 Now God had caused the

1:1 [a]2Ki 24:1 [b]2Ch 36:6
1:2 [c]2Ch 36:7; Jer 27:19-20; Zec 5:5-11
1:3 [d]2Ki 20:18; 24:15; Isa 39:7
1:5 [e]ver 8,10 [f]ver 19
1:6 [g]Eze 14:14
1:7 [h]Da 4:8; 5:12 [i]Da 2:49; 3:12
1:8 [j]Eze 4:13-14

[a] 2 Hebrew *Shinar* [b] 4 Or *Chaldeans*

■ **1:1—6:28** *The Narratives.* This first section of the book highlights both God's absolute control over the kingdoms of this world and the sincere devotion that Daniel and his friends offered to God. Daniel wanted his readers to learn that although God's people are sometimes persecuted, kings and kingdoms rise and fall according to God's purpose. Daniel also taught that God would greatly bless those who paid attention to him as God's faithful spokesman. This material divides into six separate narratives: the vindication of Daniel and his friends (1:1–21), Nebuchadnezzar's dream (2:1–49), deliverance from the furnace (3:1–30), Nebuchadnezzar's second dream (4:1–37), judgment on Belshazzar (5:1–31) and Daniel's deliverance from the den of lions (6:1–28).

■ **1:1–21** *Vindication of Daniel and His Friends.* The prophet set the context of his book by narrating his (and his companions') personal history of captivity, training, faithfulness and service to King Nebuchadnezzar.

1:1 In the third year of the reign of Jehoiakim. In 605 B.C., the same year Nebuchadnezzar defeated an Assyrian-Egyptian coalition at Carchemish and initiated Babylon's rise to international power. Subsequent to victory at Carchemish Nebuchadnezzar advanced against Jehoiakim (2Ki 24:1–2; 2Ch 36:5–7) and took Daniel and a number of other Judahites captive. This was the first of three invasions of Judah by Nebuchadnezzar. The second was in 597 B.C. (2Ki 24:10–14) and the third in 587 B.C. (2Ki 25:1–24). The apparent discrepancy between Daniel 1:1 and Jeremiah 25:1 and 46:2 (where Jeremiah placed Nebuchadnezzar's attack against Jehoiakim during Jehoiakim's fourth rather than third year) may be explained by the difference between the Babylonian and Jewish systems of chronology. Under the Babylonian system, which Daniel apparently used, the first year of a king's reign was viewed as an "accession year," and the reign itself was counted as beginning on the first of the month of Nisan in the following year. **Nebuchadnezzar king of Babylon.** Nebuchadnezzar led the Babylonians to victory at Carchemish in 605 B.C. as crown prince and commander of the army. Shortly after this victory he assumed the Babylonian throne upon the death of his father, Nabopolassar (626–605 B.C.). Nebuchadnezzar's reign (605–562 B.C.) forms the historical background for much in the books of Jeremiah, Ezekiel and Daniel.

1:2 And the Lord delivered. Israel's defeat by the Babylonians is not to be explained simply by analysis of the military and political conditions of the time. God was sovereignly at work in the affairs of the nations. He used the Babylonians to judge his own people for breaking their covenant obligations (2Ki 17:15,18–20; 21:12–15; 24:3–4). **These he carried off.** Refers to the plunder of vessels from the temple, not to the deportation of captives. **the temple of his god.** Marduk was the chief god of the Babylonian pantheon (cf. Jer 50:2).

1:4 the language and literature of the Babylonians. Babylonian literature was written in cuneiform and primarily on clay tablets. Thousands of these tablets have been discovered. Study of this literature would have introduced Daniel and his friends to the polytheistic worldview of the Babylonians, which prominently featured magic, sorcery and astrology.

1:5 from the king's table. Jehoiachin later received the same provision under the rule of the Babylonian king Evil-Merodach (2Ki 25:27–30).

1:6 Daniel, Hananiah, Mishael and Azariah. Characteristic Hebrew names. Two of them contain the Hebrew component *el,* meaning "God," and two the component *yah,* a shortened form of "Yahweh" ("the LORD"). Daniel means "My judge is God," Hananiah "Yahweh is gracious," Mishael "Who is what God is?" and Azariah "Yahweh has helped."

1:7 Belteshazzar . . . Shadrach . . . Meshach . . . Abednego. The meanings of these names are disputed. Suggestions for Belteshazzar: "Bel [another name for Marduk, the chief Babylonian god] protect his life" or "Lady, protect the king." Shadrach: "I am very fearful (of God)" or "The command of Aku [the Sumerian moon god]." Meshach: "I am of little account" or "Who is what Aku is?" Abednego: "Servant of the shining one."

1:8 resolved not to defile himself. The reason for Daniel's conclusion that the king's food would defile him and his friends is not given. Perhaps eating it involved violation of the dietary laws of the Mosaic legislation (Lev 11:1–47), which prohibited eating pork or meat from which blood had not been drained (Lev 17:10–14). It may also have involved partaking of food that had been offered to Babylonian idols.

official to show favor[k] and sympathy[l] to Daniel, 10but the official told Daniel, "I am afraid
of my lord the king, who has assigned your[a] food and drink. Why should he see you looking worse than the other young men your age? The king would then have my head because of you."
11Daniel then said to the guard whom the chief official had appointed over Daniel,
Hananiah, Mishael and Azariah, 12"Please test your servants for ten days: Give us nothing but vegetables to eat and water to drink. 13Then compare our appearance with that
of the young men who eat the royal food, and treat your servants in accordance with
what you see." 14So he agreed to this and tested them for ten days.
15At the end of the ten days they looked healthier and better nourished than any of
the young men who ate the royal food.[m] 16So the guard took away their choice food and
the wine they were to drink and gave them vegetables instead.[n]
17To these four young men God gave knowledge and understanding[o] of all kinds of
literature and learning.[p] And Daniel could understand visions and dreams of all kinds.[q]
18At the end of the time[r] set by the king to bring them in, the chief official presented
them to Nebuchadnezzar. 19The king talked with them, and he found none equal to Daniel, Hananiah, Mishael and Azariah; so they entered the king's service.[s] 20In every matter of wisdom and understanding about which the king questioned them, he found them
ten times better than all the magicians and enchanters in his whole kingdom.[t]
21And Daniel remained there until the first year of King Cyrus.[u]

Nebuchadnezzar's Dream

2 In the second year of his reign, Nebuchadnezzar had dreams;[v] his mind was troubled[w] and he could not sleep.[x] 2So the king summoned the magicians,[y] enchanters, sorcerers[z] and astrologers[b][a] to tell him what he had dreamed.[b] When they came in
and stood before the king, 3he said to them, "I have had a dream that troubles[c] me and
I want to know what it means.[c]"
4Then the astrologers answered the king in Aramaic,[d][d] "O king, live forever![e] Tell
your servants the dream, and we will interpret it."
5The king replied to the astrologers, "This is what I have firmly decided: If you do not
tell me what my dream was and interpret it, I will have you cut into pieces[f] and your
houses turned into piles of rubble.[g] 6But if you tell me the dream and explain it, you will
receive from me gifts and rewards and great honor.[h] So tell me the dream and interpret
it for me."

[a] *10* The Hebrew for *your* and *you* in this verse is plural. [b] *2* Or *Chaldeans;* also in verses 4, 5 and 10
[c] *3* Or *was* [d] *4* The text from here through chapter 7 is in Aramaic.

1:9 [k]Ge 39:21; Pr 16:7 [l]1Ki 8:50; Ps 106:46
1:15 [m]Ex 23:25
1:16 [n]ver 12-13
1:17 [o]1Ki 3:12 [p]Da 2:23; Jas 1:5 [q]Da 2:19,30; 7:1; 8:1
1:18 [r]ver 5
1:19 [s]Ge 41:46
1:20 [t]1Ki 4:30; Da 2:13, 28
1:21 [u]Da 6:28; 10:1
2:1 [v]Job 33:15,18; Da 4:5 [w]Ge 41:8 [x]Est 6:1; Da 6:18
2:2 [y]Ge 41:8 [z]Ex 7:11 [a]ver 10; Da 5:7 [b]Da 4:6
2:3 [c]Da 4:5
2:4 [d]Ezr 4:7 [e]Da 3:9; 5:10
2:5 [f]ver 12 [g]Ezr 6:11; Da 3:29
2:6 [h]ver 48; Da 5:7,16

1:15 they looked healthier and better nourished than any of the young men who ate the royal food. God blessed Daniel and his friends for their obedience to the Lord and their refusal to compromise their faith in a heathen environment (Dt 8:3; Mt 4:4).
1:17 God gave knowledge and understanding of all kinds of literature and learning. God's blessing was not limited to physical well-being but included outstanding success in intellectual development during their three years of Babylonian education. **visions and dreams of all kinds.** With a view to what follows in the book (chs. 2; 4–5) Daniel was distinguished from his companions by his ability to interpret dreams and visions, much as Joseph had been set apart by the same in the court of Pharaoh (Ge 40:8; 41:16).
1:18 At the end of the time set by the king. After the three years mentioned in verse 5.
1:20 the magicians and enchanters. The term here translated "magician" is also used in Genesis 41:8 and 24 and Exodus 7:11. The term translated "enchanters" occurs only here and in 2:2 and is sometimes rendered "conjurer" or "soothsayer." Daniel and his friends demonstrated superior insight on the matters about which they were questioned.
1:21 until the first year of King Cyrus. Babylon fell to Cyrus in 539 B.C., 66 years after Daniel had been taken captive to Babylon. Daniel lived through the entire period of the Babylonian captivity. Cyrus issued a decree in the first year of his reign that permitted the Israelites to return from captivity and to take with them the vessels from the temple that had been seized by Nebuchadnezzar (Ezr 1:7–11). The statement does not signify that Daniel died in the first year of Cyrus's reign (10:1).
■ **2:1–49** *Nebuchadnezzar's First Dream.* While in the service of Nebuchadnezzar Daniel interpreted the king's dream, revealing that Daniel was greatly blessed by God and that God was moving history toward the establishment of his kingdom.
2:1 In the second year of his reign. There is no contradiction between this statement and the completion of the three-year period of training for Daniel and his friends mentioned in 1:5 and 18–20 if one understands that the first year of training was considered Nebuchadnezzar's "accession year," while the second and third years would correspond with the "first" and "second" years of Nebuchadnezzar's reign. It was during Nebuchadnezzar's second year, according to the Babylonian system of accession-year dating, that the dream occurred (see note on 1:1). **his mind was troubled and he could not sleep.** It was widely believed in the ancient Near East that the gods spoke to human beings in dreams. Nebuchadnezzar's agitation is understandable because the dream had implications for the future of his kingdom. When a dream could not be remembered, it was believed to be a sign that the deity was angry with the person involved.
2:2 magicians, enchanters. See note on 1:20. **sorcerers.** Practitioners of divination through means such as witchcraft. Their activities were prohibited by God (Ex 22:18; Dt 18:10; Isa 47:9,12; Jer 27:9). **astrologers.** This term translates the Hebrew term for Chaldeans; it is probably used here as a designation for a class of soothsayers concerned with astrology rather than as a designation for an ethnic group. See 1:4, 3:8, 5:30, 9:1 and NIV text notes.
2:4 Aramaic. From here until the end of chapter 7 the text is written in Aramaic rather than in Hebrew (Ezr 4:8—6:18 was also written in Aramaic). It is not clear why the two languages were used, but Aramaic may have been used for the sections containing prophecies that would have been of more interest to non-Jews.
2:5 If you do not tell me what my dream was and interpret it. Nebuchadnezzar formulated a plan for testing his advisors. If they could not relate the dream back to him he would have no confidence in their interpretation (see v. 9).

7 Once more they replied, "Let the king tell his servants the dream, and we will interpret it."

8 Then the king answered, "I am certain that you are trying to gain time, because you realize that this is what I have firmly decided: 9 If you do not tell me the dream, there is just one penalty[i] for you. You have conspired to tell me misleading and wicked things, hoping the situation will change. So then, tell me the dream, and I will know that you can interpret it for me."[j]

10 The astrologers answered the king, "There is not a man on earth who can do what the king asks! No king, however great and mighty, has ever asked such a thing of any magician or enchanter or astrologer.[k] 11 What the king asks is too difficult. No one can reveal it to the king except the gods,[l] and they do not live among men."

12 This made the king so angry and furious[m] that he ordered the execution[n] of all the wise men of Babylon. 13 So the decree was issued to put the wise men to death, and men were sent to look for Daniel and his friends to put them to death.[o]

14 When Arioch, the commander of the king's guard, had gone out to put to death the wise men of Babylon, Daniel spoke to him with wisdom and tact. 15 He asked the king's officer, "Why did the king issue such a harsh decree?" Arioch then explained the matter to Daniel. 16 At this, Daniel went in to the king and asked for time, so that he might interpret the dream for him.

17 Then Daniel returned to his house and explained the matter to his friends Hananiah, Mishael and Azariah.[p] 18 He urged them to plead for mercy[q] from the God of heaven concerning this mystery,[r] so that he and his friends might not be executed with the rest of the wise men of Babylon. 19 During the night the mystery[s] was revealed to Daniel in a vision.[t] Then Daniel praised the God of heaven 20 and said:

"Praise be to the name of God for ever and ever;[u]
 wisdom and power[v] are his.
21 He changes times and seasons;[w]
 he sets up kings and deposes[x] them.
He gives wisdom[y] to the wise
 and knowledge to the discerning.
22 He reveals deep and hidden things;[z]
 he knows what lies in darkness,[a]
 and light[b] dwells with him.
23 I thank and praise you, O God of my fathers:[c]
 You have given me wisdom[d] and power,
you have made known to me what we asked of you,
 you have made known to us the dream of the king."

Daniel Interprets the Dream

24 Then Daniel went to Arioch,[e] whom the king had appointed to execute the wise men of Babylon, and said to him, "Do not execute the wise men of Babylon. Take me to the king, and I will interpret his dream for him."

25 Arioch took Daniel to the king at once and said, "I have found a man among the exiles from Judah[f] who can tell the king what his dream means."

26 The king asked Daniel (also called Belteshazzar),[g] "Are you able to tell me what I saw in my dream and interpret it?"

27 Daniel replied, "No wise man, enchanter, magician or diviner can explain to the king the mystery he has asked about,[h] 28 but there is a God in heaven who reveals mysteries.[i] He has shown King Nebuchadnezzar what will happen in days to come.[j] Your dream and the visions that passed through your mind[k] as you lay on your bed are these:

2:9 [i]Est 4:11 [j]Isa 41:22-24
2:10 [k]ver 27
2:11 [l]Da 5:11
2:12 [m]Da 3:13,19 [n]ver 5
2:13 [o]Da 1:20
2:17 [p]Da 1:6
2:18 [q]Isa 37:4 [r]Jer 33:3
2:19 [s]ver 28 [t]Job 33:15; Da 1:17
2:20 [u]Ps 113:2; 145:1-2 [v]Jer 32:19
2:21 [w]Da 7:25 [x]Job 12:19; Ps 75:6-7 [y]Jas 1:5
2:22 [z]Job 12:22; Ps 25:14; Da 5:11 [a]Ps 139:11-12; Jer 23:24; Heb 4:13 [b]Isa 45:7; Jas 1:17
2:23 [c]Ex 3:15 [d]Da 1:17
2:24 [e]ver 14
2:25 [f]Da 1:6; 5:13; 6:13
2:26 [g]Da 1:7
2:27 [h]ver 10
2:28 [i]Ge 40:8; Am 4:13 [j]Ge 49:1; Da 10:14 [k]Da 4:5

2:11 No one can reveal it to the king except the gods. The wise men were forced to confess that they were unable to do what the king asked. They claimed that only the gods have such power and that they do not reveal such things to men. See Exodus 8:18–19.
2:18 plead for mercy from the God of heaven concerning this mystery. Daniel also realized that human wisdom was insufficient to meet the king's demand (see note on 2:11). Daniel addressed God as the ruler of the stars to which the heathen astrologers looked for guidance.
2:19 mystery. Here the word denotes an enigma that can be interpreted only by God's revelation. The term was later used by Daniel as a reference to God's hidden purpose at work in history (4:9).
2:21 he sets up kings and deposes them. Daniel alluded to the content of the dream. See *BC* 36.
2:22 He reveals deep and hidden things. See note on 2:11.
2:23 I thank and praise you, O God of my fathers. Daniel was deeply grateful for God's mercy in responding to his prayer. The divine revelation he received was in stark contrast to the silence of the false deities of the heathen soothsayers. Only God knows all things and is sovereign over all creation. God chose to exalt Daniel by imparting to him special knowledge.
2:24 I will interpret his dream for him. Daniel spoke here only of the interpretation of the dream. The text assumes that he also knew the content.

29 "As you were lying there, O king, your mind turned to things to come, and the revealer of mysteries showed you what is going to happen. 30 As for me, this mystery has
been revealed[l] to me, not because I have greater wisdom than other living men, but so
that you, O king, may know the interpretation and that you may understand what went
through your mind.

31 "You looked, O king, and there before you stood a large statue—an enormous, dazzling statue,[m] awesome in appearance. 32 The head of the statue was made of pure
gold, its chest and arms of silver, its belly and thighs of bronze, 33 its legs of iron, its feet
partly of iron and partly of baked clay. 34 While you were watching, a rock was cut out,
but not by human hands.[n] It struck the statue on its feet of iron and clay and smashed
them.[o] 35 Then the iron, the clay, the bronze, the silver and the gold were broken to pieces at the same time and became like chaff on a threshing floor in the summer. The wind
swept them away[p] without leaving a trace. But the rock that struck the statue became
a huge mountain[q] and filled the whole earth.

36 "This was the dream, and now we will interpret it to the king. 37 You, O king, are the
king of kings.[r] The God of heaven has given you dominion[s] and power and might and
glory; 38 in your hands he has placed mankind and the beasts of the field and the birds
of the air. Wherever they live, he has made you ruler over them all.[t] You are that head
of gold.

39 "After you, another kingdom will rise, inferior to yours. Next, a third kingdom, one
of bronze, will rule over the whole earth. 40 Finally, there will be a fourth kingdom,
strong as iron—for iron breaks and smashes everything—and as iron breaks things to
pieces, so it will crush and break all the others.[u] 41 Just as you saw that the feet and toes
were partly of baked clay and partly of iron, so this will be a divided kingdom; yet it will
have some of the strength of iron in it, even as you saw iron mixed with clay. 42 As the toes
were partly iron and partly clay, so this kingdom will be partly strong and partly brittle.
43 And just as you saw the iron mixed with baked clay, so the people will be a mixture and
will not remain united, any more than iron mixes with clay.

44 "In the time of those kings, the God of heaven will set up a kingdom that will never be destroyed, nor will it be left to another people. It will crush[v] all those kingdoms[w]
and bring them to an end, but it will itself endure forever.[x] 45 This is the meaning of the
vision of the rock[y] cut out of a mountain, but not by human hands[z]—a rock that broke
the iron, the bronze, the clay, the silver and the gold to pieces.

"The great God has shown the king what will take place in the future. The dream is
true and the interpretation is trustworthy."

46 Then King Nebuchadnezzar fell prostrate[a] before Daniel and paid him honor and
ordered that an offering[b] and incense be presented to him. 47 The king said to Daniel,
"Surely your God is the God of gods[c] and the Lord of kings[d] and a revealer of mysteries,[e]
for you were able to reveal this mystery."

2:30 [l]Isa 45:3; Da 1:17; Am 4:13
2:31 [m]Hab 1:7
2:34 [n]Zec 4:6 [o]ver 44-45; Ps 2:9; Isa 60:12; Da 8:25
2:35 [p]Ps 1:4; 37:10; Isa 17:13 [q]Isa 2:3; Mic 4:1
2:37 [r]Eze 26:7 [s]Jer 27:7
2:38 [t]Jer 27:6; Da 4:21-22
2:40 [u]Da 7:7, 23
2:44 [v]Ps 2:9; 1Co 15:24 [w]Isa 60:12 [x]Ps 145:13; Isa 9:7; Da 4:34; 6:26; 7:14, 27; Mic 4:7; Lk 1:33
2:45 [y]Isa 28:16 [z]Da 8:25
2:46 [a]Da 8:17; Ac 10:25 [b]Ac 14:13
2:47 [c]Da 11:36 [d]Da 4:25 [e]ver 22, 28

2:28 there is a God in heaven who reveals mysteries. As Joseph had done in Egypt (Ex 40:8; 41:16), Daniel attributed his knowledge of the dream and its interpretation to divine revelation. God showed himself superior in his ability to reveal secrets and mysteries. **in days to come.** Literally, "in the after part of the days." This expression can mean "in the end times" or "in the last days," which is the time of restoration after the exile (see Dt 4:30). The phrase may also simply refer to the general future (Ge 49:1; Dt 4:30; 31:29). The Septuagint (the Greek translation of the OT) interprets it here as "in the last days," although it is difficult to determine Daniel's intended usage. The Greek expression is used five times in the New Testament, two with reference to the age begun at Pentecost (Ac 2:17; Heb 1:2) and three with regard to the end of the age preceding the second advent of Christ (2Ti 3:1; Jas 5:3; 2Pe 3:3).
2:32–33 The head . . . gold, its chest and arms . . . silver, its belly and thighs . . . bronze, its legs . . . iron, its feet partly . . . iron and partly . . . clay. Moving from the head to the feet of the image, there is a decrease in both the value and weight of the materials but a general increase in its strength. The image was clearly top heavy with fragile feet.
2:34 rock . . . not by human hands. Unlike the kingdoms represented by the statue, this rock would be formed by God himself. In the Old Testament a rock is often associated with kingship; here it is linked to the kingdom itself (see 1Co 10:4 and its note). It is likely that Daniel had in mind the Messiah, the great son of David, who would establish God's kingdom over all of the earth—including the Gentile nations (v. 35)—after the restoration from exile. See theological article "The Kingdom of God" at Matthew 4. **It struck the statue on its feet of iron and clay.** Some interpreters view the mixture of iron and clay in the feet of the image as representing a second phase of the fourth kingdom—as distinguished from the legs, which were made of solid iron (cf. vv. 41–43).
2:38–40 You are that head of gold . . . another kingdom . . . a third kingdom . . . Finally . . . a fourth kingdom. The four kingdoms represent the Babylonian, Medo-Persian, Greek and Roman Empires. The climax of the dream occurs in the time of the fourth kingdom (see "Introduction" and chart, "Visions in Daniel," at Daniel 7).
2:43 the people will be a mixture and will not remain united. The fourth kingdom would constitute a composite of peoples who would not adhere together well. Efforts to combine the diverse elements of the kingdom would not succeed.
2:44 In the time of those kings. Some interpreters surmise that "those kings" refers to the succeeding kings of the fourth kingdom. It seems best, however, to understand them as referring to the succession of the rulers of the four kingdoms previously mentioned in this chapter. **the God of heaven will set up a kingdom that will never be destroyed.** Like other prophets Daniel spoke of the kingdom of God that would be established after the exile as permanent (e.g., Isa 9:7; Joel 2:26–27; Am 9:15). The New Testament explains that the kingdom began with the first coming of Jesus and will reach its consummation at Christ's glorious return. See theological article "The Kingdom of God" at Matthew 4.
2:46 Then King Nebuchadnezzar fell prostrate before Daniel. In a remarkable reversal of roles Daniel was exalted to a position of great honor by virtue of the Lord's intervention on his behalf. Nebuchadnezzar's reaction anticipated the coming kingdom of God.
2:47 your God is the God of gods. Nebuchadnezzar's statement does not signify that he recognized Israel's God as the only true

48 Then the king placed Daniel in a high position and lavished many gifts on him. He
made him ruler over the entire province of Babylon and placed him in charge of all its
wise men.[f] 49 Moreover, at Daniel's request the king appointed Shadrach, Meshach and
Abednego administrators over the province of Babylon,[g] while Daniel himself remained
at the royal court.

The Image of Gold and the Fiery Furnace

3 King Nebuchadnezzar made an image[h] of gold, ninety feet high and nine feet[a] wide,
and set it up on the plain of Dura in the province of Babylon. 2 He then summoned
the satraps, prefects, governors, advisers, treasurers, judges, magistrates and all the other provincial officials[i] to come to the dedication of the image he had set up. 3 So the satraps, prefects, governors, advisers, treasurers, judges, magistrates and all the other provincial officials assembled for the dedication of the image that King Nebuchadnezzar had
set up, and they stood before it.
4 Then the herald loudly proclaimed, "This is what you are commanded to do, O peoples, nations and men of every language:[j] 5 As soon as you hear the sound of the horn,
flute, zither, lyre, harp, pipes and all kinds of music, you must fall down and worship the
image of gold that King Nebuchadnezzar has set up.[k] 6 Whoever does not fall down and
worship will immediately be thrown into a blazing furnace."[l]
7 Therefore, as soon as they heard the sound of the horn, flute, zither, lyre, harp and
all kinds of music, all the peoples, nations and men of every language fell down and worshiped the image of gold that King Nebuchadnezzar had set up.[m]
8 At this time some astrologers[b] [n] came forward and denounced the Jews. 9 They said
to King Nebuchadnezzar, "O king, live forever![o] 10 You have issued a decree,[p] O king, that
everyone who hears the sound of the horn, flute, zither, lyre, harp, pipes and all kinds
of music must fall down and worship the image of gold,[q] 11 and that whoever does not
fall down and worship will be thrown into a blazing furnace. 12 But there are some Jews
whom you have set over the affairs of the province of Babylon—Shadrach, Meshach and
Abednego[r]—who pay no attention[s] to you, O king. They neither serve your gods nor worship the image of gold you have set up."[t]
13 Furious[u] with rage, Nebuchadnezzar summoned Shadrach, Meshach and Abednego. So these men were brought before the king, 14 and Nebuchadnezzar said to them, "Is
it true, Shadrach, Meshach and Abednego, that you do not serve my gods[v] or worship
the image[w] of gold I have set up? 15 Now when you hear the sound of the horn, flute, zither, lyre, harp, pipes and all kinds of music, if you are ready to fall down and worship the

2:48 [f] ver 6; Da 4:9; 5:11
2:49 [g] Da 1:7
3:1 [h] Isa 46:6; Jer 16:20; Hab 2:19
3:2 [i] ver 27; Da 6:7
3:4 [j] Da 4:1; 6:25
3:5 [k] ver 10,15
3:6 [l] ver 11,15,21; Jer 29:22; Da 6:7; Mt 13:42,50; Rev 13:15
3:7 [m] ver 5
3:8 [n] Da 2:10
3:9 [o] Ne 2:3; Da 5:10; 6:6
3:10 [p] Da 6:12 [q] ver 4-6
3:12 [r] Da 2:49 [s] Da 6:13 [t] Est 3:3
3:13 [u] Da 2:12
3:14 [v] Isa 46:1; Jer 50:2 [w] ver 1

[a] *1* Aramaic *sixty cubits high and six cubits wide* (about 27 meters high and 2.7 meters wide)
[b] *8* Or *Chaldeans*

God, but he did perceive him to be superior to the deities of the Babylonian pantheon. **and the Lord of kings.** Nebuchadnezzar declared that Israel's God was supreme also over human rulers and their kingdoms. This is a unifying theme of Daniel 1:1—6:28.

2:48 ruler over the entire province of Babylon. The Babylonian Empire was divided into provinces. Daniel was appointed the ruler (cf. 3:2) of the province in which the capital city was located. For accounts of similar ascents to political power by Jews in foreign lands, see Exodus 41:37–44 (Joseph) and Esther 8:1–2 (Mordecai). Daniel's friends were similarly exalted as his assistants (v. 49). The divine approval of Daniel is another dominant theme in this portion of the book. Although prominent in Babylon, he never compromised his faith; he was a reliable prophet of God.

■ **3:1–30** *Deliverance From the Furnace.* Daniel recounted God's miraculous deliverance of his friends from the fiery furnace to instruct his readers that God's people must admire Daniel's companions and be faithful to God alone. He also illustrated that God would eventually frustrate even the mightiest kings who tempt his people to abandon their God to worship another.

3:1 an image. Opinions differ as to whether this extraordinary image was of Nebuchadnezzar himself or of a Babylonian deity or whether it was merely an obelisk. From what is known of Babylonian religious tradition, it seems likely that the image was either of Bel or of Nabu, Nebuchadnezzar's patron deity. Prostration before the image of this deity would also indicate submission to Nebuchadnezzar, the deity's representative (cf. 2:46). **gold.** Probably gold overlay, the fabrication of the image being much like that described in Isaiah 40:19, 41:7 and Jeremiah 10:3–9. **ninety feet high and nine feet wide.** The proportions are the reason some have concluded that the image was an obelisk rather than a human form (the proportions of the human body are six to one). However, the image may have stood on a pedestal or had a stylized shape. **the plain of Dura.** Its location is uncertain. It is usually associated with Tolul Dura, located about six miles south of Babylon.

3:2 satraps . . . officials. The precise responsibilities of these seven different types of officials are not known. Five of the seven terms seem to be of Persian origin, perhaps indicating that Daniel did not complete the writing of this account until after the beginning of Persian rule in 539 B.C.

3:4–6 See *WLC* 130.

3:5 horn . . . pipes. Three of the six terms used for different types of musical instruments account for the only Greek loanwords ("zither," "harp" and "pipes") in Daniel. This is not surprising, since the exchange of musicians and their instruments at royal courts has a long history. The presence of these Greek terms does not therefore constitute compelling evidence that this account was written after the conquests of Alexander the Great.

3:6 a blazing furnace. Furnaces, or kilns, were widely used in Babylon for the firing of bricks (Ge 11:3). It was not unusual to use such furnaces for execution by burning (Jer 29:22; see Herodotus, 1.86; 4.69; see also 2 Maccabees 7 [an Apocryphal book]).

3:8 astrologers. See NIV text note and note on 2:2. The term "Chaldeans" as used here is best understood as indicating nationality rather than function. The informants looked down on the Jews simply because they were Jews (v. 12; Est 3:5–6). The privileged position of Shadrach, Meshach and Abednego (2:49) heightened the Chaldeans' hostility toward them (v. 12).

3:12 Shadrach, Meshach and Abednego. See note on 1:7. Daniel was either not present or exempted from demonstrating his loyalty because of his high position (2:48).

3:15 Then what god will be able to rescue you from my hand? From Nebuchadnezzar's polytheistic, heathen perspective there was no god capable of such deliverance. Unwittingly Nebuchadnezzar challenged the power of the God of Israel.

image I made, very good. But if you do not worship it, you will be thrown immediately
into a blazing furnace. Then what god[x] will be able to rescue[y] you from my hand?"
16 Shadrach, Meshach and Abednego[z] replied to the king, "O Nebuchadnezzar, we do
not need to defend ourselves before you in this matter. 17 If we are thrown into the blazing furnace, the God we serve is able to save[a] us from it, and he will rescue[b] us from your
hand, O king. 18 But even if he does not, we want you to know, O king, that we will not
serve your gods or worship the image of gold you have set up.[c]"
19 Then Nebuchadnezzar was furious with Shadrach, Meshach and Abednego, and his
attitude toward them changed. He ordered the furnace heated seven[d] times hotter than
usual 20 and commanded some of the strongest soldiers in his army to tie up Shadrach,
Meshach and Abednego and throw them into the blazing furnace. 21 So these men,
wearing their robes, trousers, turbans and other clothes, were bound and thrown into
the blazing furnace. 22 The king's command was so urgent and the furnace so hot that the
flames of the fire killed the soldiers who took up Shadrach, Meshach and Abednego,[e]
23 and these three men, firmly tied, fell into the blazing furnace.
24 Then King Nebuchadnezzar leaped to his feet in amazement and asked his advisers, "Weren't there three men that we tied up and threw into the fire?"
They replied, "Certainly, O king."
25 He said, "Look! I see four men walking around in the fire, unbound and unharmed,
and the fourth looks like a son of the gods."
26 Nebuchadnezzar then approached the opening of the blazing furnace and shouted,
"Shadrach, Meshach and Abednego, servants of the Most High God,[f] come out! Come
here!"
So Shadrach, Meshach and Abednego came out of the fire, 27 and the satraps, prefects, governors and royal advisers[g] crowded around them.[h] They saw that the fire[i] had
not harmed their bodies, nor was a hair of their heads singed; their robes were not
scorched, and there was no smell of fire on them.
28 Then Nebuchadnezzar said, "Praise be to the God of Shadrach, Meshach and Abednego, who has sent his angel[j] and rescued his servants! They trusted[k] in him and defied
the king's command and were willing to give up their lives rather than serve or worship
any god except their own God.[l] 29 Therefore I decree[m] that the people of any nation or
language who say anything against the God of Shadrach, Meshach and Abednego be cut
into pieces and their houses be turned into piles of rubble,[n] for no other god can save[o]
in this way."
30 Then the king promoted Shadrach, Meshach and Abednego in the province of
Babylon.[p]

Nebuchadnezzar's Dream of a Tree

4 King Nebuchadnezzar,

To the peoples, nations and men of every language,[q] who live in all the world:

May you prosper greatly![r]

2 It is my pleasure to tell you about the miraculous signs[s] and wonders that the
Most High God[t] has performed for me.

3:15 [x]Isa 36:18-20 [y]Ex 5:2; 2Ch 32:15
3:16 [z]Da 1:7
3:17 [a]Ps 27:1-2 [b]Job 5:19; Jer 1:8
3:18 [c]ver 28; Jos 24:15
3:19 [d]Lev 26:18-28
3:22 [e]Da 1:7
3:26 [f]Da 4:2,34
3:27 [g]ver 2 [h]Isa 43:2; Heb 11:32-34 [i]Da 6:23
3:28 [j]Ps 34:7; Da 6:22; Ac 5:19 [k]Job 13:15; Ps 26:1; 84:12; Jer 17:7 [l]ver 18
3:29 [m]Da 6:26 [n]Ezr 6:11 [o]Da 6:27
3:30 [p]Da 2:49
4:1 [q]Da 3:4 [r]Da 6:25
4:2 [s]Ps 74:9 [t]Da 3:26

3:17–18 the God we serve is able . . . we will not serve your gods. The men did not assert that God always protects his people from physical harm (Isa 43:1–2). Although he may opt to do so, and certainly is able, the central idea is that God's people should remain obedient to their Lord no matter what the circumstances because he is far more trustworthy than any human ruler and more powerful than any force on Earth. Thus the first six chapters of Daniel exalt the prophet and his friends as men who were unflinchingly faithful to God throughout their ordeals. See *WLC* 109.

3:25 a son of the gods. In the ancient world the expression "son of the gods" could refer to various types of heavenly beings. Here it meant "angel" (v. 28). No explanation is given for why Nebuchadnezzar recognized the fourth person in the furnace as a heavenly being (see note on v. 28). Perhaps the miraculous presence of the fourth person was in itself sufficient reason for this conclusion.

3:26 the Most High God. A title for God's universal authority. As in verse 29 ("no other god can save in this way") and in 2:47, this confession on the lips of a pagan was not an acknowledgment that Daniel's Lord alone was God but rather that Daniel's God was supreme above other deities (4:2,17,34). On the lips of an Israelite the same confession implied monotheism (4:24–32; 5:18,21; 7:18–27).

3:27 See *WCF* 5.3.

3:28 angel. The angel may be identified with "the angel of the LORD," who may have represented an appearance of Christ prior to his incarnation (cf. 6:22; see notes on Ge 16:7 and Ex 3:2). God promised his presence when Israel walked through fire (Isa 43:1–3).

3:29 no other god. See note on verse 26. See also *WCF* 20.4.

3:30 the king promoted. As this narrative makes clear, their prominence resulted from their faithfulness to God, not from compromise with the Babylonians.

■ **4:1–37** *Nebuchadnezzar's Second Dream.* The prophet narrated the story of the king's second dream and its interpretation. Once again Daniel was exalted and Nebuchadnezzar humbled before God.

4:1 King Nebuchadnezzar. This is the book's final incident associated with Nebuchadnezzar. It too is placed late in the king's 43-year reign, at a time when his building projects were completed and his power was at its height (cf. vv. 4,30). At that time Nebuchadnezzar ruled over the most powerful kingdom on Earth, but he was no match for the God of Israel.

4:2 the Most High God. See notes on 2:47 and 3:26 and 28.

4:3 [u]Ps 105:27; Da 6:27 [v]Da 2:44
4:4 [w]Ps 30:6
4:5 [x]Da 2:1 [y]Da 2:28
4:6 [z]Da 2:2
4:7 [a]Ge 41:8 [b]Isa 44:25; Da 2:2 [c]Da 2:10
4:8 [d]Da 1:7 [e]Da 5:11, 14
4:9 [f]Da 2:48 [g]Da 5:11-12
4:10 [h]ver 5

> [3]How great are his signs,
> how mighty his wonders![u]
> His kingdom is an eternal kingdom;
> his dominion endures[v] from generation to generation.

[4]I, Nebuchadnezzar, was at home in my palace, contented[w] and prosperous.
[5]I had a dream[x] that made me afraid. As I was lying in my bed, the images and visions that passed through my mind[y] terrified me. [6]So I commanded that all the
wise men of Babylon be brought before me to interpret[z] the dream for me. [7]When
the magicians,[a] enchanters, astrologers[a] and diviners[b] came, I told them the
dream, but they could not interpret it for me.[c] [8]Finally, Daniel came into my presence and I told him the dream. (He is called Belteshazzar,[d] after the name of my
god, and the spirit of the holy gods[e] is in him.)
[9]I said, "Belteshazzar, chief[f] of the magicians, I know that the spirit of the holy
gods[g] is in you, and no mystery is too difficult for you. Here is my dream; interpret
it for me. [10]These are the visions I saw while lying in my bed:[h] I looked, and there

a 7 Or *Chaldeans*

4:3 How great . . . Nebuchadnezzar's confession in this verse and in verses 34–35 communicates one of the central themes of the book of Daniel; namely, the absolute sovereignty of the God of Israel over the kingdoms of the earth and their rulers.

4:6–7 See notes on 1:20 and 2:2.

4:8 Belteshazzar. See note on 1:7.

4:9 spirit of the holy gods. Although he spoke in pagan terms Nebuchadnezzar stated an important truth. The presence of God's Spirit in an individual has remarkable effects. Here his ability to give extraordinary insight into God's mystery, such as was later given to Paul and the church (1Co 2:6–16), is in view. **no mystery is too difficult for you.** See 2:47 and note on 2:19.

4:10–12 before me stood a tree. See Ezekiel 31 for an extensive description of a nation (Assyria), using the imagery of a tree. Similar imagery is found in Psalms 1:3, 37:35, 52:8, 92:12, Jeremiah 11:16–17 and 17:8 (see also Mt 13:32). **its top touched the sky.** The term "sky" may also be translated "heaven," a key term in this chapter. The tree represented Nebuchadnezzar's kingdom reaching from Earth to heaven (vv. 11,20,22) and protecting birds, which defy the separation of the two spheres (vv. 12,21). In truth the king was not only subject to the judgment of heaven for his pride (vv. 13,23,31) but also dependent on the God of heaven for his existence (vv. 15,22,25,33) and sanity (v. 34).

The Neo-Babylonian Empire

626–539 B.C.

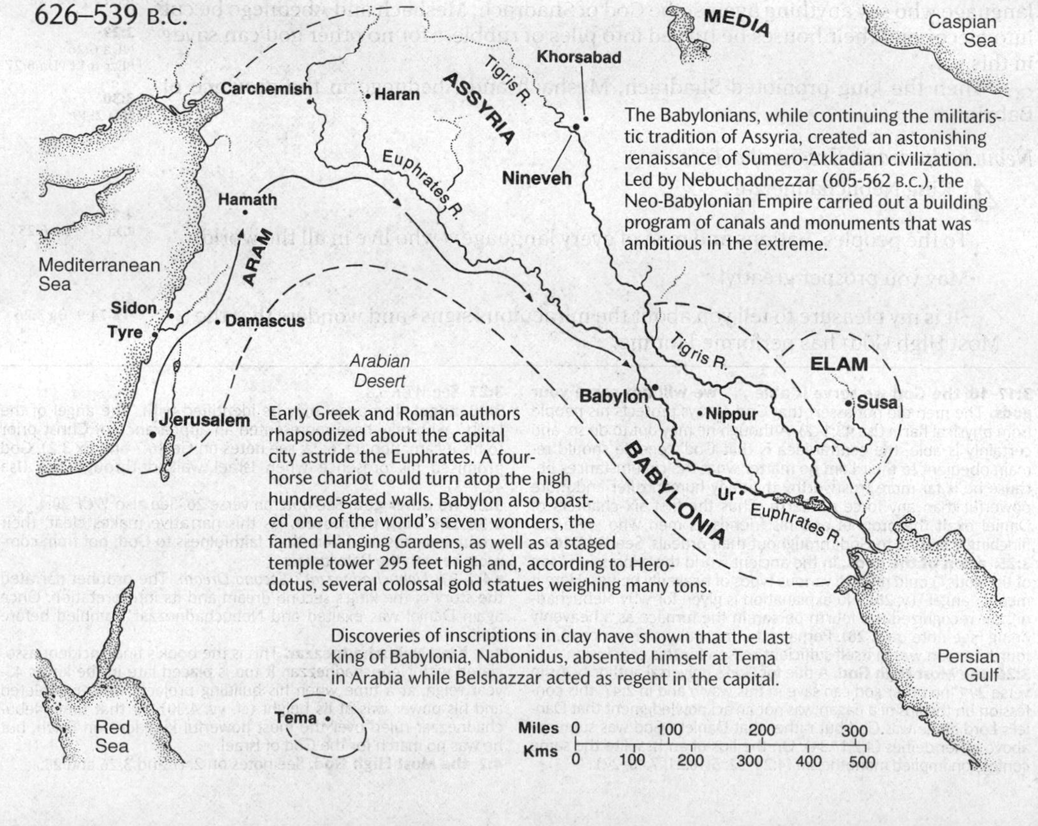

The Babylonians, while continuing the militaristic tradition of Assyria, created an astonishing renaissance of Sumero-Akkadian civilization. Led by Nebuchadnezzar (605-562 B.C.), the Neo-Babylonian Empire carried out a building program of canals and monuments that was ambitious in the extreme.

Early Greek and Roman authors rhapsodized about the capital city astride the Euphrates. A four-horse chariot could turn atop the high hundred-gated walls. Babylon also boasted one of the world's seven wonders, the famed Hanging Gardens, as well as a staged temple tower 295 feet high and, according to Herodotus, several colossal gold statues weighing many tons.

Discoveries of inscriptions in clay have shown that the last king of Babylonia, Nabonidus, absented himself at Tema in Arabia while Belshazzar acted as regent in the capital.

before me stood a tree in the middle of the land. Its height was enormous.[i] 11The
tree grew large and strong and its top touched the sky; it was visible to the ends
of the earth. 12Its leaves were beautiful, its fruit abundant, and on it was food for
all. Under it the beasts of the field found shelter, and the birds of the air lived in
its branches;[j] from it every creature was fed.
13"In the visions I saw while lying in my bed,[k] I looked, and there before me
was a messenger,[a] a holy one,[l] coming down from heaven. 14He called in a loud
voice: 'Cut down the tree and trim off its branches; strip off its leaves and scatter
its fruit. Let the animals flee from under it and the birds from its branches.[m] 15But
let the stump and its roots, bound with iron and bronze, remain in the ground, in
the grass of the field.
" 'Let him be drenched with the dew of heaven, and let him live with the animals among the plants of the earth. 16Let his mind be changed from that of a man
and let him be given the mind of an animal, till seven times[b] pass by for him.[n]
17" 'The decision is announced by messengers, the holy ones declare the verdict, so that the living may know that the Most High[o] is sovereign[p] over the kingdoms of men and gives them to anyone he wishes and sets over them the lowliest[q] of men.'
18"This is the dream that I, King Nebuchadnezzar, had. Now, Belteshazzar, tell
me what it means, for none of the wise men in my kingdom can interpret it for
me.[r] But you can,[s] because the spirit of the holy gods is in you."[t]

Daniel Interprets the Dream

19Then Daniel (also called Belteshazzar) was greatly perplexed for a time, and
his thoughts terrified[u] him. So the king said, "Belteshazzar, do not let the dream
or its meaning alarm you."
Belteshazzar answered, "My lord, if only the dream applied to your enemies
and its meaning to your adversaries! 20The tree you saw, which grew large and
strong, with its top touching the sky, visible to the whole earth, 21with beautiful
leaves and abundant fruit, providing food for all, giving shelter to the beasts of the
field, and having nesting places in its branches for the birds of the air— 22you,
O king, are that tree![v] You have become great and strong; your greatness has
grown until it reaches the sky, and your dominion extends to distant parts of the
earth.[w]
23"You, O king, saw a messenger, a holy one,[x] coming down from heaven and
saying, 'Cut down the tree and destroy it, but leave the stump, bound with iron
and bronze, in the grass of the field, while its roots remain in the ground. Let him
be drenched with the dew of heaven; let him live like the wild animals, until sev-
en times pass by for him.'[y]
24"This is the interpretation, O king, and this is the decree[z] the Most High has
issued against my lord the king: 25You will be driven away from people and will live
with the wild animals; you will eat grass like cattle and be drenched with the dew
of heaven. Seven times will pass by for you until you acknowledge that the Most
High[a] is sovereign over the kingdoms of men and gives them to anyone he wishes.[b] 26The command to leave the stump of the tree with its roots[c] means that your
kingdom will be restored to you when you acknowledge that Heaven rules.[d]
27Therefore, O king, be pleased to accept my advice: Renounce your sins by doing

4:10 [i]Eze 31:3-4
4:12 [j]Eze 17:23; Mt 13:32
4:13 [k]Da 7:1 [l]ver 23; Dt 33:2; Da 8:13
4:14 [m]Eze 31:12; Mt 3:10
4:16 [n]ver 23,32
4:17 [o]ver 2,25; Ps 83:18 [p]Jer 27:5-7; Da 2:21; 5:18-21 [q]Da 11:21
4:18 [r]Ge 41:8; Da 5:8, 15 [s]Ge 41:15 [t]ver 7-9
4:19 [u]Da 7:15,28; 8:27; 10:16-17
4:22 [v]2Sa 12:7 [w]Jer 27:7; Da 2:37-38; 5:18-19
4:23 [x]ver 13 [y]Da 5:21
4:24 [z]Job 40:12; Ps 107:40
4:25 [a]ver 17; Ps 83:18 [b]Jer 27:5; Da 5:21
4:26 [c]ver 15 [d]Da 2:37

[a] 13 Or *watchman*; also in verses 17 and 23 [b] 16 Or *years*; also in verses 23, 25 and 32

4:13 messenger. Although Nebuchadnezzar continued speaking in terms of his pagan religion, he acknowledged that he saw a holy, heavenly being in his vision. This common ancient Near Eastern belief fits well with the Biblical truth that God involves himself in Earth's affairs through revelations by angels.
4:15 Let him. It becomes clear that the dream concerned a human being and not just a tree. See note on verse 22.
4:16 let him be given the mind of an animal. Nebuchadnezzar may have suffered from a recognized mental illness called lycanthropy—which comes from the Greek words *lukos* ("wolf") and *anthropos* ("man")—in which a person is deluded into behaving like a wolf or some other animal (v. 33; see also note on 4:33). **till seven times pass by for him.** Seven periods of an unspecified duration (cf. vv. 23,25). Most interpreters conclude that "time" represents a period of one year. Verse 33 suggests that the period was longer than a day, week or month.
4:22 you, O king, are that tree! With this statement—much like that of Nathan to David (2Sa 12:7)—a direct application was made to Nebuchadnezzar.
4:25 You will be driven away from people and will live with the wild animals. In words more specific than those in verse 15 Daniel indicated the form of mental illness that God would bring upon the mighty Nebuchadnezzar. Similar symptoms occasionally afflicted King George III of England (1738–1820) and Otto of Bavaria (1848–1916). See note on 4:16. **until you acknowledge that the Most High is sovereign over the kingdoms of men.** The purpose of Nebuchadnezzar's humiliation was to compel him to recognize God's sovereignty. See *WCF* 2.2.
4:26 your kingdom will be restored to you. Nebuchadnezzar was assured that, in spite of the severity and length of his illness, he would regain the throne subsequent to his acknowledgment of God's sovereignty. **Heaven rules.** For the first time in Scripture "heaven" is used as a substitute name for God (cf. v. 37). Compare Matthew 5:3 with Luke 6:20.

what is right, and your wickedness by being kind to the oppressed.[e] It may be that then your prosperity will continue.[f]"

The Dream Is Fulfilled

28 All this happened[g] to King Nebuchadnezzar. 29 Twelve months later, as the king was walking on the roof of the royal palace of Babylon, 30 he said, "Is not this the great Babylon I have built as the royal residence, by my mighty power and for the glory of my majesty?"[h]

31 The words were still on his lips when a voice came from heaven, "This is what is decreed for you, King Nebuchadnezzar: Your royal authority has been taken from you. 32 You will be driven away from people and will live with the wild animals; you will eat grass like cattle. Seven times will pass by for you until you acknowledge that the Most High is sovereign over the kingdoms of men and gives them to anyone he wishes."

33 Immediately what had been said about Nebuchadnezzar was fulfilled. He was driven away from people and ate grass like cattle. His body was drenched with the dew of heaven until his hair grew like the feathers of an eagle and his nails like the claws of a bird.[i]

34 At the end of that time, I, Nebuchadnezzar, raised my eyes toward heaven, and my sanity was restored. Then I praised the Most High; I honored and glorified him who lives forever.[j]

His dominion is an eternal dominion;
  his kingdom endures from generation to generation.[k]
35 All the peoples of the earth
  are regarded as nothing.[l]
He does as he pleases[m]
  with the powers of heaven
  and the peoples of the earth.
No one can hold back his hand
  or say to him: "What have you done?"[n]

36 At the same time that my sanity was restored, my honor and splendor were returned to me for the glory of my kingdom.[o] My advisers and nobles sought me out, and I was restored to my throne and became even greater than before. 37 Now I, Nebuchadnezzar, praise and exalt and glorify the King of heaven, because everything he does is right and all his ways are just.[p] And those who walk in pride he is able to humble.[q]

The Writing on the Wall

5 King Belshazzar gave a great banquet[r] for a thousand of his nobles and drank wine with them. 2 While Belshazzar was drinking his wine, he gave orders to bring in the gold and silver goblets[s] that Nebuchadnezzar his father[a] had taken from the temple in Jerusalem, so that the king and his nobles, his wives and his concubines might drink from them.[t] 3 So they brought in the gold goblets that had been taken from the temple

4:27 [e]Isa 55:6-7 [f]1Ki 21:29; Ps 41:3; Eze 18:22
4:28 [g]Nu 23:19
4:30 [h]Isa 37:24-25; Da 5:20; Hab 2:4
4:33 [i]Da 5:20-21
4:34 [j]Da 12:7; Rev 4:10 [k]Ps 145:13; Da 2:44; 5:21; 6:26; Lk 1:33
4:35 [l]Isa 40:17 [m]Ps 115:3; 135:6 [n]Isa 45:9; Ro 9:20
4:36 [o]Pr 22:4
4:37 [p]Dt 32:4; Ps 33:4-5 [q]Ex 18:11; Job 40:11-12; Da 5:20,23
5:1 [r]Est 1:3
5:2 [s]2Ki 24:13; Jer 52:19 [t]Est 1:7; Da 1:2

[a] *2* Or *ancestor*; or *predecessor*; also in verses 11, 13 and 18

4:30 See *WLC* 105.
4:33 ate grass like cattle. Because Nebuchadnezzar exhibited traits characteristic of oxen, the form of his mental illness is sometimes termed boanthropy. See note on 4:16.
4:34–35,37 Although Nebuchadnezzar confessed God's sovereignty in no uncertain terms, he never explicitly affirmed the God of Israel as the only supreme Creator of the universe. See *WCF* 2.2; 5.1.
4:37 King of heaven. This unique term brings together the theme of the chapter: the rule of God from heaven (see 4:26 and its note).
■ **5:1–31** *Judgment on Belshazzar.* Daniel turned next to an account of God's judgment against Belshazzar. In this narrative the king is condemned for his impudent disregard for the holiness of Israel's God and of his temple.
5:1 King Belshazzar. Belshazzar means "Bel, protect the king." It is not to be confused with Belteshazzar, the Babylonian name given to Daniel (see note on 1:7). From Babylonian sources we know that Nabonidus, Nebuchadnezzar's son-in-law, was the last king of Babylon. Belshazzar, the eldest son of Nabonidus, was made co-regent with his father and placed in charge of affairs in Babylon while Nabonidus spent extensive periods of time at Tema in Arabia. The events of this chapter took place in 539 B.C., the year of Babylon's fall to the Persians and of the edict releasing Israelites from captivity, 42 years after the death of Nebuchadnezzar in 563 B.C. **banquet.** The banquet scene juxtaposes the splendor of the event and the divine judgment that would soon be meted out (cf. Ge 40:20–22; Mk 6:21–28).
5:2 While Belshazzar was drinking. Under the influence of wine Belshazzar committed a sacrilegious act. Even from a heathen standpoint the holy things of other religions were to be held in reverence. **the gold and silver goblets . . . from the temple in Jerusalem.** See note on 1:2. **his father.** See NIV text note. Nebuchadnezzar is called the father of Belshazzar here and in verses 11, 13 and 18, and in verse 22 Belshazzar is called the "son" of Nebuchadnezzar. Although we know that Belshazzar was the immediate son of Nabonidus, not Nebuchadnezzar, the terms *father* and *son* were often used in the ancient world in the broader sense of "ancestor" or "predecessor" and "descendant" or "successor," respectively. It is likely that Belshazzar was the grandson of Nebuchadnezzar through his mother, Nitocris.

of God in Jerusalem, and the king and his nobles, his wives and his concubines drank
from them. 4As they drank the wine, they praised the gods of gold and silver, of bronze,
iron, wood and stone.[u]
5Suddenly the fingers of a human hand appeared and wrote on the plaster of the wall,
near the lampstand in the royal palace. The king watched the hand as it wrote. 6His face
turned pale and he was so frightened[v] that his knees knocked together and his legs gave
way.[w]
7The king called out for the enchanters, astrologers[a] and diviners[x] to be brought and
said to these wise[y] men of Babylon, "Whoever reads this writing and tells me what it
means will be clothed in purple and have a gold chain placed around his neck,[z] and he
will be made the third highest ruler in the kingdom."[a]
8Then all the king's wise men came in, but they could not read the writing or tell the
king what it meant.[b] 9So King Belshazzar became even more terrified[c] and his face grew
more pale. His nobles were baffled.
10The queen,[b] hearing the voices of the king and his nobles, came into the banquet
hall. "O king, live forever!"[d] she said. "Don't be alarmed! Don't look so pale! 11There is
a man in your kingdom who has the spirit of the holy gods[e] in him. In the time of your
father he was found to have insight and intelligence and wisdom[f] like that of the gods.
King Nebuchadnezzar your father—your father the king, I say—appointed him chief of
the magicians, enchanters, astrologers and diviners.[g] 12This man Daniel, whom the king
called Belteshazzar,[h] was found to have a keen mind and knowledge and understanding, and also the ability to interpret dreams, explain riddles and solve difficult problems.[i]
Call for Daniel, and he will tell you what the writing means."
13So Daniel was brought before the king, and the king said to him, "Are you Daniel,
one of the exiles my father the king brought from Judah?[j] 14I have heard that the spirit
of the gods is in you and that you have insight, intelligence and outstanding wisdom.
15The wise men and enchanters were brought before me to read this writing and tell me
what it means, but they could not explain it. 16Now I have heard that you are able to give
interpretations and to solve difficult problems. If you can read this writing and tell me
what it means, you will be clothed in purple and have a gold chain placed around your
neck, and you will be made the third highest ruler in the kingdom."
17Then Daniel answered the king, "You may keep your gifts for yourself and give your
rewards to someone else.[k] Nevertheless, I will read the writing for the king and tell him
what it means.
18"O king, the Most High God gave your father Nebuchadnezzar sovereignty and
greatness and glory and splendor.[l] 19Because of the high position he gave him, all the
peoples and nations and men of every language dreaded and feared him. Those the king
wanted to put to death, he put to death;[m] those he wanted to spare, he spared; those
he wanted to promote, he promoted; and those he wanted to humble, he humbled. 20But
when his heart became arrogant and hardened with pride,[n] he was deposed from his
royal throne and stripped[o] of his glory.[p] 21He was driven away from people and given the
mind of an animal; he lived with the wild donkeys and ate grass like cattle; and his body
was drenched with the dew of heaven, until he acknowledged that the Most High God
is sovereign[q] over the kingdoms of men and sets over them anyone he wishes.[r]

[a] 7 Or *Chaldeans*; also in verse 11 [b] 10 Or *queen mother*

5:4 [u]Ps 135:15-18; Hab 2:19; Rev 9:20
5:6 [v]Da 4:5 [w]Eze 7:17
5:7 [x]Isa 44:25 [y]Da 4:6-7 [z]Ge 41:42 [a]Da 2:5-6,48; 6:2-3
5:8 [b]Da 2:10,27
5:9 [c]Isa 21:4
5:10 [d]Da 3:9
5:11 [e]Da 4:8-9,19 [f]ver 14; Da 1:17 [g]Da 2:47-48
5:12 [h]Da 1:7 [i]ver 14-16; Da 6:3
5:13 [j]Da 6:13
5:17 [k]2Ki 5:16
5:18 [l]Jer 27:7; Da 2:37-38
5:19 [m]Da 2:12-13; 3:6
5:20 [n]Da 4:30 [o]Jer 13:18 [p]Job 40:12; Isa 14:13-15
5:21 [q]Eze 17:24 [r]Da 4:16-17,35

5:4 praised the gods. The temple vessels were defiled not only by being put to profane use but also by being used to honor the false deities of Babylon.
5:7 the enchanters, astrologers and diviners. See notes on 1:20 and 2:2 (cf. 2:27; 4:7). **Whoever reads this writing and tells me what it means.** Once again the king demanded a double requirement: to declare the portent and then to interpret it (cf. 2:3). **third highest ruler in the kingdom.** Next in power under Nabonidus and his co-regent Belshazzar (see note on 5:1).
5:8 they could not read the writing or tell the king what it meant. See 2:2–13 and 4:7; see also Genesis 41:8.
5:10 The queen. See NIV text note. It is unlikely that she was a consort of Belshazzar since these women were already present at the banquet (vv. 2–3). She may have been the widow of Nebuchadnezzar, but it is more likely that she was Nitocris, the wife of Nabonidus, daughter of Nebuchadnezzar and mother of Belshazzar.
5:11 the spirit of the holy gods. See 4:8. It is not surprising that the queen mother was more familiar with the events of Daniel's time than was Belshazzar. It is likely that Daniel was in his 80s by 539 B.C. He had been a young man when taken to Babylon 66 years earlier in 605 B.C. (see note on 1:1).
5:12 This man . . . was found to have. This divine enablement can be described theologically as the presence of God's Spirit in an individual or as a person possessing a remarkable spirit. **Belteshazzar.** See note on 1:7.
5:16 third highest ruler in the kingdom. See note on verse 7.
5:17 You may keep your gifts. Some think that Daniel rejected Belshazzar's offer of reward not only because he did not seek such honors but also because of his consciousness that it was only by God's mercy that he had been able to respond to the king's request; he did not want to use his God-given role as a means of personal profit (Ge 14:23). Yet he had accepted such rewards before (2:48) and did so again later (v. 29). Perhaps he was avoiding any pressure to modify the ominous message (Nu 22:18; Mic 3:5,11).
5:18 the Most High God gave. See 2:37 and 4:36. **your father Nebuchadnezzar.** See note on verse 2.
5:20–21 See 4:31–33.
5:21 Most High God is sovereign. This statement summarizes the book's theology (see "Introduction: Purpose and Distinctives").

5:22 [s]Ex 10:3; 2Ch 33:23
5:23 [t]Jer 50:29 [u]Ps 115:4-8; Hab 2:19 [v]Job 12:10 [w]Job 31:4; Jer 10:23
5:26 [x]Jer 27:7 [y]Isa 13:6
5:27 [z]Ps 62:9
5:28 [a]Isa 13:17 [b]Da 6:28
5:30 [c]ver 1 [d]Isa 21:9; Jer 51:31
5:31 [e]Da 6:1; 9:1
6:1 [f]Da 5:31 [g]Est 1:1
6:2 [h]Da 2:48-49 [i]Ezr 4:22
6:3 [j]Ge 41:41; Est 10:3; Da 5:12-14
6:5 [k]Ac 24:13-16
6:6 [l]Ne 2:3; Da 2:4

22 "But you his son,[a] O Belshazzar, have not humbled[s] yourself, though you knew all
this. 23 Instead, you have set yourself up against[t] the Lord of heaven. You had the goblets from his temple brought to you, and you and your nobles, your wives and your concubines drank wine from them. You praised the gods of silver and gold, of bronze, iron,
wood and stone, which cannot see or hear or understand.[u] But you did not honor the
God who holds in his hand your life[v] and all your ways.[w] 24 Therefore he sent the hand
that wrote the inscription.
25 "This is the inscription that was written:

MENE, MENE, TEKEL, PARSIN[b]

26 "This is what these words mean:

Mene[c]: God has numbered the days[x] of your reign and brought it to an end.[y]
27 *Tekel*[d]: You have been weighed on the scales and found wanting.[z]
28 *Peres*[e]: Your kingdom is divided and given to the Medes[a] and Persians."[b]

29 Then at Belshazzar's command, Daniel was clothed in purple, a gold chain was
placed around his neck, and he was proclaimed the third highest ruler in the kingdom.
30 That very night Belshazzar,[c] king of the Babylonians,[f] was slain,[d] 31 and Darius[e] the
Mede took over the kingdom, at the age of sixty-two.

Daniel in the Den of Lions

6 It pleased Darius[f] to appoint 120 satraps[g] to rule throughout the kingdom, 2 with
three administrators over them, one of whom was Daniel.[h] The satraps were made
accountable[i] to them so that the king might not suffer loss. 3 Now Daniel so distinguished
himself among the administrators and the satraps by his exceptional qualities that the
king planned to set him over the whole kingdom.[j] 4 At this, the administrators and the
satraps tried to find grounds for charges against Daniel in his conduct of government affairs, but they were unable to do so. They could find no corruption in him, because he
was trustworthy and neither corrupt nor negligent. 5 Finally these men said, "We will never find any basis for charges against this man Daniel unless it has something to do with
the law of his God."[k]
6 So the administrators and the satraps went as a group to the king and said: "O King
Darius, live forever![l] 7 The royal administrators, prefects, satraps, advisers and gover-

[a] 22 Or *descendant*; or *successor* [b] 25 Aramaic *UPARSIN* (that is, *AND PARSIN*) [c] 26 *Mene* can mean *numbered* or *mina* (a unit of money). [d] 27 *Tekel* can mean *weighed* or *shekel*. [e] 28 *Peres* (the singular of *Parsin*) can mean *divided* or *Persia* or *a half mina* or *a half shekel*. [f] 30 Or *Chaldeans*

5:22 But you his son. See note on verse 2. **though you knew all this.** Because the king was without excuse—even more so than his father—the time of mercy had passed (see 1Ti 1:13). See *WLC* 151.
5:23 See *WLC* 105.
5:24 Therefore. The writing on the wall was God's answer to the arrogant challenge presented by Belshazzar's pride and defiance of the God who had demonstrated his existence and sovereignty in the time of Nebuchadnezzar.
5:25 MENE, MENE, TEKEL, PARSIN. Literally, "numbered, numbered, weighed, divided" or "mina [a unit of weight], mina, shekel, half shekel."
5:26 *Mene*. See NIV text note. The original script for this word could be understood as either a verb or a noun. Daniel read it as a verb meaning "numbered" or "counted" and interpreted it as signifying that the days and years of Belshazzar's reign had been determined by God and were about to end.
5:27 *Tekel*. See NIV text note. This word could also be understood as either a verb or a noun. Daniel read it as a verb meaning "weighed" and interpreted it as signifying that Belshazzar failed to measure up to God's standards of righteousness.
5:28 *Peres*. See NIV text note. Daniel construed this word as a verb meaning "divided" and interpreted it to signify that Belshazzar`s kingdom would be taken from him and given to the Medes and Persians. If, as is likely, those present at the banquet understood the three terms as nouns that simply indicated various monetary weights (*mene*, a weight equivalent to 60 Babylonian shekels; *tekel*, the shekel; *peres*, a half shekel), then it is not surprising that they failed to comprehend the significance of the inscription. **Medes and Persians.** See "Introduction: Purpose and Distinctives." See also *BC* 36.
5:29 Belshazzar's command. Like Nebuchadnezzar Belshazzar honored Daniel (2:48), but unlike Nebuchadnezzar he did not honor Daniel's God (2:46–47). The honor that Daniel and his companions had repeatedly received because of their faithfulness to God had established Daniel's credibility as a prophet. He was not a compromiser; he was faithful to God. Therefore his later prophecies (chs. 7–12) could be fully trusted.
5:30 Belshazzar . . . was slain. Ancient Near Eastern texts and the Greek historians Herodotus and Xenophon record that Babylon was taken in a surprise attack by the Persians while the Babylonians were engaged in reveling and dancing.
5:31 Darius the Mede. It has long been alleged that this and other references to "Darius the Mede" in the book of Daniel (6:1,6, 9,25,28; 9:1; 11:1) are historical errors. See note on 6:1.
5:32 See *WCF* 19.2.
■ **6:1–28** *Deliverance From the Den of Lions.* The prophet recounted his treatment under Darius the Mede, who succeeded Belshazzar. During his reign Daniel was thrown into a lions' den, and only through faith did he emerge unscathed.
6:1 Darius. See note on 5:31. While it is true that Darius the Mede is not referred to in extant historical sources outside the Scripture and that there was no interval between Belshazzar/Nabonidus (see note on 5:1) and the accession of Cyrus of Persia, this does not necessarily mean that the book of Daniel is in error. Most likely "Darius the Mede" was a throne name for Cyrus, the founder of the Persian Empire (see note on v. 28). It is also possible, but not as likely, that it was a designation for Gubaru, a general who defected from Nebuchadnezzar to Cyrus, led the Persian conquest of Babylon and was made governor by Cyrus over the territories the Persians had taken from the Babylonians.
6:3 his exceptional qualities. See 1:17, 4:8 and 5:12.
6:5 the law of his God. Daniel's adversaries affirmed not only his moral integrity but also the visible nature of his piety and commitment to the God of Israel. Thus the book's major theme of Daniel's holiness and reliability is affirmed once again.

nors[m] have all agreed that the king should issue an edict and enforce the decree that
anyone who prays to any god or man during the next thirty days, except to you, O king,
shall be thrown into the lions' den.[n] 8 Now, O king, issue the decree and put it in writing so that it cannot be altered—in accordance with the laws of the Medes and Persians,
which cannot be repealed."[o] 9 So King Darius put the decree in writing.
10 Now when Daniel learned that the decree had been published, he went home to his
upstairs room where the windows opened toward[p] Jerusalem. Three times a day he got
down on his knees[q] and prayed, giving thanks to his God, just as he had done before.[r]
11 Then these men went as a group and found Daniel praying and asking God for help.
12 So they went to the king and spoke to him about his royal decree: "Did you not publish a decree that during the next thirty days anyone who prays to any god or man except to you, O king, would be thrown into the lions' den?"

The king answered, "The decree stands—in accordance with the laws of the Medes
and Persians, which cannot be repealed."[s]

13 Then they said to the king, "Daniel, who is one of the exiles from Judah,[t] pays no
attention[u] to you, O king, or to the decree you put in writing. He still prays three times
a day." 14 When the king heard this, he was greatly distressed;[v] he was determined to rescue Daniel and made every effort until sundown to save him.
15 Then the men went as a group to the king and said to him, "Remember, O king, that
according to the law of the Medes and Persians no decree or edict that the king issues
can be changed."[w]
16 So the king gave the order, and they brought Daniel and threw him into the lions'
den.[x] The king said to Daniel, "May your God, whom you serve continually, rescue[y] you!"
17 A stone was brought and placed over the mouth of the den, and the king sealed[z] it
with his own signet ring and with the rings of his nobles, so that Daniel's situation might
not be changed. 18 Then the king returned to his palace and spent the night without eating[a] and without any entertainment being brought to him. And he could not sleep.[b]
19 At the first light of dawn, the king got up and hurried to the lions' den. 20 When he
came near the den, he called to Daniel in an anguished voice, "Daniel, servant of the living God, has your God, whom you serve continually, been able to rescue you from the
lions?"[c]
21 Daniel answered, "O king, live forever![d] 22 My God sent his angel,[e] and he shut the
mouths of the lions.[f] They have not hurt me, because I was found innocent in his sight.[g]
Nor have I ever done any wrong before you, O king."
23 The king was overjoyed and gave orders to lift Daniel out of the den. And when Daniel was lifted from the den, no wound[h] was found on him, because he had trusted[i] in his
God.
24 At the king's command, the men who had falsely accused Daniel were brought in
and thrown into the lions' den,[j] along with their wives and children.[k] And before they
reached the floor of the den, the lions overpowered them and crushed all their bones.[l]
25 Then King Darius wrote to all the peoples, nations and men of every language
throughout the land:

"May you prosper greatly![m]

6:7 [m]Da 3:2 [n]Ps 59:3; 64:2-6; Da 3:6
6:8 [o]Est 1:19
6:10 [p]1Ki 8:48-49 [q]Ps 95:6 [r]Ac 5:29
6:12 [s]Est 1:19; Da 3:8-12
6:13 [t]Da 2:25; 5:13 [u]Est 3:8; Da 3:12
6:14 [v]Mk 6:26
6:15 [w]Est 8:8
6:16 [x]ver 7 [y]Job 5:19; Ps 37:39-40
6:17 [z]Mt 27:66
6:18 [a]2Sa 12:17 [b]Est 6:1; Da 2:1
6:20 [c]Da 3:17
6:21 [d]Da 2:4
6:22 [e]Da 3:28 [f]Ps 91:11-13; Heb 11:33 [g]Ac 12:11; 2Ti 4:17
6:23 [h]Da 3:27 [i]1Ch 5:20
6:24 [j]Dt 19:18-19; Est 7:9-10; Ps 54:5 [k]Dt 24:16; 2Ki 14:6 [l]Isa 38:13
6:25 [m]Da 4:1

6:7 have all agreed. The false implication was that Daniel had concurred with the proposal. These officials were hypocritical in their seeming devotion to Darius. Their scheme was an attempt to manipulate him into securing their own designs. **who prays to any god or man . . . except to you.** The proposal would have seemed to Darius to be more political than religious and would have served to consolidate his authority over newly conquered territories.
6:8 the laws of the Medes and Persians, which cannot be repealed. See Esther 1:19 and 8:8. The irrevocable nature of Persian law is also attested in extra-Biblical writings. The effect of the decree was to create a conflict for Daniel between allegiance to the Lord and obedience to human government.
6:10 opened toward Jerusalem. See 1 Kings 8:44 and 48, as well as Psalms 5:7 and 138:2. **Three times a day.** See Psalm 55:17–18. **down on his knees.** Standing may have been a regular posture in prayer (1Ch 23:30; Ne 9), while kneeling in prostration marked a lowering of oneself, appropriate in circumstances of particular solemnity (1Ki 8:54; Ezr 9:5; see also Ps 95:6; Lk 22:41; Ac 7:60; 9:40). **just as he had done before.** Evidently Daniel's prayer habits were public knowledge, a mark of his genuine piety.
6:13 who is one of the exiles from Judah. This ethnic identification of Daniel is perhaps indicative of prejudice toward the Jews on the part of the other officials (cf. 3:8). That Daniel's ethnic identity was widely known reveals that he had not compromised his heritage in favor of success in captivity—an important lesson to the readers.
6:14 he was determined to rescue Daniel. Darius immediately perceived that he had been victimized by the intrigue of his own officials in order to trap Daniel. His appreciation for Daniel remained unshaken.
6:16 May your God . . . rescue you! Against his own will Darius was forced to comply with the decree. Nevertheless, he hoped that Daniel's God would intervene on behalf of his faithful servant.
6:17 sealed it with his own signet ring and with the rings of his nobles. Signet rings and cylinder seals were commonly used by the Assyrians, Babylonians and Persians. The ring or cylinder was rolled across impressionable clay to leave the personal mark of the owner of the seal. Breaking open whatever was sealed in this way would be a violation of the law.
6:22 My God sent his angel. Likely the angel of the Lord (see note on 3:28).
6:23 gave orders to lift Daniel out of the den. Darius could do this without violating the initial decree, since its demands had already been fulfilled.

6:26 [n]Ps 99:1-3; Da 3:29 [o]Da 2:44; 4:34

26 "I issue a decree that in every part of my kingdom people must fear and reverence the God of Daniel.[n]

"For he is the living God
and he endures forever;
his kingdom will not be destroyed,
his dominion will never end.[o]

6:27 [p]Da 4:3 [q]ver 22

27 He rescues and he saves;
he performs signs and wonders[p]
in the heavens and on the earth.
He has rescued Daniel
from the power of the lions."[q]

6:28 [r]2Ch 36:22; Da 1:21

28 So Daniel prospered during the reign of Darius and the reign of Cyrus[a] [r] the Persian.

Daniel's Dream of Four Beasts

7:1 [s]Da 5:1 [t]Da 1:17 [u]Jer 36:4

7 In the first year of Belshazzar[s] king of Babylon, Daniel had a dream, and visions
passed through his mind[t] as he was lying on his bed. He wrote[u] down the substance
of his dream.

7:2 [v]Rev 7:1 · 7:3 [w]Rev 13:1

2 Daniel said: "In my vision at night I looked, and there before me were the four winds
of heaven[v] churning up the great sea. 3 Four great beasts,[w] each different from the others, came up out of the sea.

7:4 [x]Jer 4:7 [y]Eze 17:3

4 "The first was like a lion,[x] and it had the wings of an eagle.[y] I watched until its wings
were torn off and it was lifted from the ground so that it stood on two feet like a man,
and the heart of a man was given to it.

7:5 [z]Da 2:39

5 "And there before me was a second beast, which looked like a bear. It was raised up
on one of its sides, and it had three ribs in its mouth between its teeth. It was told, 'Get
up and eat your fill of flesh!'[z]

7:6 [a]Rev 13:2

6 "After that, I looked, and there before me was another beast, one that looked like a
leopard.[a] And on its back it had four wings like those of a bird. This beast had four heads,
and it was given authority to rule.

[a] *28* Or *Darius, that is, the reign of Cyrus*

6:26–27 See 2:47, 3:17–18 and 28–29, 4:2–3 and 28–37 and 5:18–29. As in the previous narratives the Lord revealed himself to be greater than human rulers or kingdoms, for his sovereignty extends over nature and history. But this decree went far beyond those earlier confessions in acknowledging God as a living, enduring and saving deity, whose kingdom is eternal and secure.

6:26 decree. Darius's decree does not imply that he actually converted from pagan polytheism to faith in Daniel's God alone any more than did Cyrus's proclamation that God had instructed him to send the Jews home (Ezr 1:3–4; Isa 44:28; 45:4).

6:28 Daniel prospered. The major theme of God's blessing toward Daniel appears again. Daniel remained faithful, refusing to compromise. For this reason he rose in prominence under both Babylonian and Persian kings. This fact exalted Daniel as a faithful Israelite whose prophecies could be trusted. **the reign of Darius and the reign of Cyrus.** See NIV text note. The wording may be understood in two ways: (1) Daniel prospered under the rule of Gubaru (see note on v. 1) as well as under Cyrus; or (2) Daniel prospered under the reign of Darius, *even* in the reign of Cyrus. In the latter case, Darius the Mede and Cyrus are understood to be two names for the same ruler (see note on v. 1).

■ **7:1—12:13** *The Visions.* In these chapters Daniel turned from historical narrative to reports of visions. These visions depend on the two main themes set forth in the first six chapters of the book: Israel's God was in control of all nations, and Daniel could be trusted as God's uncompromising prophet. These chapters prepared an exiled Israel for the long delay of the restoration and the trials to come under the control of foreign powers. They also encouraged the people of God not to give up hope that God's kingdom would come at the end of these trials. Daniel touched on four main topics: the four beasts (7:1–28), the ram and the goat (8:1–27), the "seventy weeks" (9:1–27) and the future of God's people (10:1—12:13).

■ **7:1–28** *Vision of the Four Beasts.* Daniel reported his dream of four beasts. The dream traces the history of foreign kingdoms oppressing Israel until their earthly dominion was given to the "one like a son of man" and to the saints.

7:1 the first year of Belshazzar. See note on 5:1. It is not known whether Belshazzar's co-regency with Nabonidus began at the same time as the accession of Nabonidus (556 B.C.) or a few years later. In any case, the events of this chapter (and ch. 8) are to be placed chronologically between those of chapters 4 and 5.

7:2 great sea. Whether or not this is a reference to the Mediterranean Sea is immaterial. What is clear is that the sea is symbolic of the chaotic restlessness that characterized the sinful nations oppressing Israel. See the interpretation given in verse 17 and in Isaiah 17:12–13 and 57:20.

7:3 Four great beasts. These four beasts represent four kingdoms (vv. 17,23). It is clear that there is a close correspondence between the four kingdoms of Nebuchadnezzar's vision of the image in chapter 2 and those symbolized by the beasts in this chapter. For identification of the four kingdoms, see chart, "Visions in Daniel," on the next page.

7:4 The first was like a lion . . . wings of an eagle. The lion with "the wings of an eagle" is an appropriate symbol for the Babylonian Empire (cf. Jer 50:44; Eze 17:3). Winged lions were common Babylonian art forms often placed at the entrances of important public buildings. **wings were torn off . . . and the heart of a man was given to it.** Perhaps this is a reference to Nebuchadnezzar's humiliation and later restoration following a seven-year period of insanity (4:1–37).

7:5 a second beast . . . like a bear . . . raised up on one of its sides, and it had three ribs in its mouth. The Medo-Persian kingdom is symbolized by a beast with a voracious appetite. The raised side may represent the superior status of Persia, and the three ribs likely point to Persia's conquests over Lydia (546 B.C.), Babylon (539 B.C.) and Egypt (525 B.C.). See note on 8:3.

7:6 another beast . . . like a leopard . . . it had four wings . . . four heads. The Greek Empire is symbolized by a leopard, which is known for its speed. Alexander the Great (356–323 B.C.) conquered the Persian Empire with great rapidity. He encountered the Persians in three major battles: (1) At the Granicus River (334 B.C.) he gained entry into Asia Minor. (2) At Issus (333 B.C.), he was enabled to occupy Syria, Canaan and Egypt. (3) At Arbela (331 B.C.) he destroyed the last Persian army and pushed onward toward India. See also 8:5–8. Shortly after his premature death at age thirty-three the empire he had established divided into four parts: Macedonia under Cassander, Thrace and Asia Minor under Lysimachus, Syria under Seleucus and Egypt under Ptolemy.

7 "After that, in my vision at night I looked, and there before me was a fourth beast—
terrifying and frightening and very powerful. It had large iron[b] teeth; it crushed and devoured its victims and trampled underfoot whatever was left. It was different from all the
former beasts, and it had ten horns.[c]
8 "While I was thinking about the horns, there before me was another horn, a little[d]
one, which came up among them; and three of the first horns were uprooted before it.
This horn had eyes like the eyes of a man[e] and a mouth that spoke boastfully.[f]
9 "As I looked,

"thrones were set in place,
and the Ancient of Days took his seat.
His clothing was as white as snow;
the hair of his head was white like wool.[g]
His throne was flaming with fire,
and its wheels[h] were all ablaze.
10 A river of fire[i] was flowing,

7:7 [b]Da 2:40 [c]Rev 12:3

7:8 [d]Da 8:9 [e]Rev 9:7 [f]Ps 12:3; Rev 13:5-6

7:9 [g]Rev 1:14 [h]Eze 1:15; 10:6

7:10 [i]Ps 50:3; 97:3; Isa 30:27

7:7 a fourth beast—terrifying and frightening and very powerful. History has revealed that this unidentified beast represents Rome, the kingdom that ultimately assimilated the various parts of the divided Greek kingdom. **it had ten horns.** The ten horns symbolize ten kings or kingdoms arising from the Roman kingdom (v. 24). It is not clear whether these horns are successive or contemporaneous. Some suggest that they represent a second phase of the fourth kingdom, "a revived Roman Empire" of the last days, but there is no evidence of such a distinction.
7:8 another horn, a little one . . . three of the first horns were uprooted before it. The ten horns are prior in time to the "little horn," which uproots three of them. Here is another phase of the fourth kingdom. Many interpreters have suggested that the little horn symbolizes the rise of the antichrist (2Th 2:3–4,8). If so, this is the first Scriptural reference to the antichrist. **eyes like the eyes of a man and a mouth that spoke boastfully.** The imagery suggests that this horn represents an individual rather than a kingdom.
7:9 the Ancient of Days took his seat. The title "Ancient of Days" occurs in the Bible only in this chapter (vv. 13,22). A similar expression appears in Ugaritic texts to designate the great God *El.* It is clearly used as a designation for God, who is sitting to judge, and it implies that God is eternal or that he has ruled from ancient times. **clothing . . . hair.** Although God appeared in magnificent glory to Daniel, he still revealed himself in a recognizably human form so that Daniel could grasp what he saw. **His throne . . . and its wheels.** The depiction of God's throne resembles that of Ezekiel's vision (Eze 1:15–20). As in other parts of the ancient world the divine throne is depicted as having wheels, like a mobile chariot-throne used most notably in battle. Similar motifs lie behind the pillar of fire that led Israel during the exodus (Ex 13:21–22).

Visions in Daniel

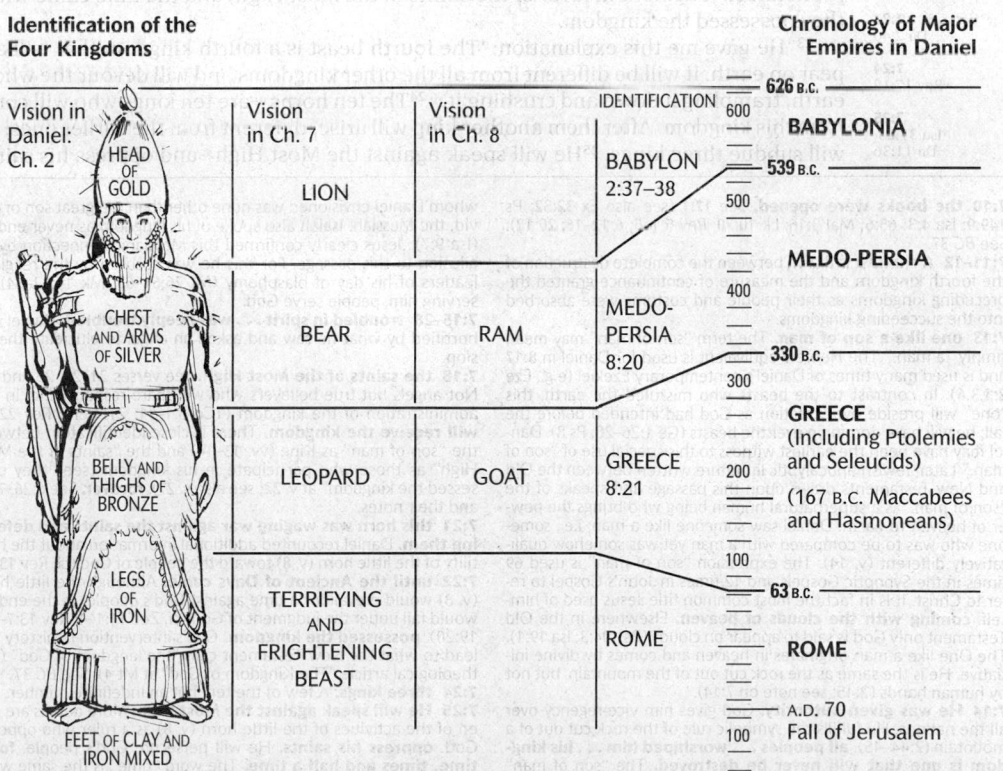

Identification of the Four Kingdoms

Vision in Daniel: Ch. 2	Vision in Ch. 7	Vision in Ch. 8	IDENTIFICATION
HEAD OF GOLD	LION		BABYLON 2:37–38
CHEST AND ARMS OF SILVER	BEAR	RAM	MEDO-PERSIA 8:20
BELLY AND THIGHS OF BRONZE	LEOPARD	GOAT	GREECE 8:21
LEGS OF IRON; FEET OF CLAY AND IRON MIXED	TERRIFYING AND FRIGHTENING BEAST		ROME

Chronology of Major Empires in Daniel

626 B.C.	
600	**BABYLONIA**
539 B.C.	
500	**MEDO-PERSIA**
400	
330 B.C.	
300	**GREECE** (Including Ptolemies and Seleucids)
200	(167 B.C. Maccabees and Hasmoneans)
100	
63 B.C.	**ROME**
100	A.D. 70 Fall of Jerusalem

7:10 [j]Dt 33:2; Ps 68:17; Rev 5:11 [k]Rev 20:11-15
7:11 [l]Rev 19:20
7:13 [m]Mt 8:20*; Rev 1:13* [n]Mt 24:30; Rev 1:7
7:14 [o]Mt 28:18 [p]Ps 72:11; 102:22; 1Co 15:27; Eph 1:22 [q]Da 2:44; Heb 12:28; Rev 11:15
7:15 [r]Da 4:19
7:16 [s]Da 8:16; 9:22; Zec 1:9
7:18 [t]Isa 60:12-14; Rev 2:26; 20:4
7:21 [u]Rev 13:7
7:23 [v]Da 2:40
7:24 [w]Rev 17:12
7:25 [x]Isa 37:23; Da 11:36

coming out from before him.[j]
Thousands upon thousands attended him;
ten thousand times ten thousand stood before him.
The court was seated,
and the books[k] were opened.

11 "Then I continued to watch because of the boastful words the horn was speaking.
I kept looking until the beast was slain and its body destroyed and thrown into the blazing fire.[l] 12 (The other beasts had been stripped of their authority, but were allowed to
live for a period of time.)
13 "In my vision at night I looked, and there before me was one like a son of man,[m]
coming with the clouds of heaven.[n] He approached the Ancient of Days and was led into
his presence. 14 He was given authority,[o] glory and sovereign power; all peoples, nations
and men of every language worshiped him.[p] His dominion is an everlasting dominion
that will not pass away, and his kingdom is one that will never be destroyed.[q]

The Interpretation of the Dream

15 "I, Daniel, was troubled in spirit, and the visions that passed through my mind disturbed me.[r] 16 I approached one of those standing there and asked him the true meaning of all this.
"So he told me and gave me the interpretation[s] of these things: 17 'The four great
beasts are four kingdoms that will rise from the earth. 18 But the saints of the Most High
will receive the kingdom and will possess it forever—yes, for ever and ever.'[t]
19 "Then I wanted to know the true meaning of the fourth beast, which was different
from all the others and most terrifying, with its iron teeth and bronze claws—the beast
that crushed and devoured its victims and trampled underfoot whatever was left. 20 I also
wanted to know about the ten horns on its head and about the other horn that came up,
before which three of them fell—the horn that looked more imposing than the others
and that had eyes and a mouth that spoke boastfully. 21 As I watched, this horn was waging war against the saints and defeating them,[u] 22 until the Ancient of Days came and
pronounced judgment in favor of the saints of the Most High, and the time came when
they possessed the kingdom.
23 "He gave me this explanation: 'The fourth beast is a fourth kingdom that will appear on earth. It will be different from all the other kingdoms and will devour the whole
earth, trampling it down and crushing it.[v] 24 The ten horns[w] are ten kings who will come
from this kingdom. After them another king will arise, different from the earlier ones; he
will subdue three kings. 25 He will speak against the Most High[x] and oppress his saints

7:10 the books were opened. See 12:1 (see also Ex 32:32; Ps 149:9; Isa 4:3; 65:6; Mal 3:16; Lk 10:20; Rev 5:1–5; 6:12–16; 20:12). See *BC* 37.

7:11–12 A contrast is drawn between the complete destruction of the fourth kingdom and the measure of continuance granted the preceding kingdoms as their people and customs were absorbed into the succeeding kingdoms.

7:13 one like a son of man. The term "son of man" may mean simply "a man." The Hebrew equivalent is used for Daniel in 8:17 and is used many times of Daniel's contemporary Ezekiel (e.g., Eze 2:1,3,6). In contrast to the beasts who misruled the earth, this "one" will preside over creation as God had intended before the fall; he will have dominion over the beasts (Ge 1:26–28; Ps 8). Daniel may have been the earliest witness to this special use of "son of man." Later Jewish apocalyptic literature written between the Old and New Testaments draws upon this passage and speaks of the "son of man" as a supernatural human being who brings the power of heaven to Earth. Daniel saw someone like a man; i.e., someone who was to be compared with a man yet was somehow qualitatively different (v. 14). The expression "son of man" is used 69 times in the Synoptic Gospels and 12 times in John's Gospel to refer to Christ. It is in fact the most common title Jesus used of himself. **coming with the clouds of heaven.** Elsewhere in the Old Testament only God is said to appear on clouds (Ps 104:3; Isa 19:1). The One like a man originates in heaven and comes by divine initiative. He is the same as the rock cut out of the mountain, but not by human hands (2:45; see note on 7:14).

7:14 He was given authority. God gives him vice-regency over all the nations. He fulfills the symbolic rule of the rock cut out of a mountain (2:44–45). **all peoples . . . worshiped him . . . his kingdom is one that will never be destroyed.** The "son of man" whom Daniel envisioned was none other than the great son of David, the Messiah. Isaiah also spoke of his kingdom as never ending (Isa 9:7). Jesus clearly confirmed this Messianic connection by an allusion to this passage. For this he was accused by the religious leaders of his day of blasphemy (Mt 26:64–65; Mk 14:62–64). In serving him, people serve God.

7:15–28 troubled in spirit . . . was deeply troubled. Daniel was horrified by what he saw and asked an angel to elucidate the vision.

7:18 the saints of the Most High. See verses 21–22, 25 and 27. Not angels but true believers who will share responsibility in the administration of the kingdom (1Co 6:1–11; 2Ti 2:12; Rev 22:5). **will receive the kingdom.** There is close identification between the "son of man" as King (vv. 13–14) and the "saints of the Most High" as those who participate in his kingdom (see "they possessed the kingdom" at v. 22; see also v. 27). **forever.** See 6:26, 7:14 and their notes.

7:21 this horn was waging war against the saints and defeating them. Daniel recounted additional information about the hostility of the little horn (v. 8) toward the people of God (cf. Rev 13:7).

7:22 until the Ancient of Days came. Although the little horn (v. 8) would prevail for a time against God's people, in the end he would fall under the judgment of God (cf. Zec 14:1–4; Rev 13:7–17; 19:20). **possessed the kingdom.** God's intervention in history will lead to what the New Testament calls "the kingdom of God" (see theological article "The Kingdom of God" at Mt 4). See *BC* 37.

7:24 three kings. A few of the ten, but an indefinite number.

7:25 He will speak against the Most High. More details are given of the activities of the little horn (v. 8) as a ruler who opposes God. **oppress his saints.** He will persecute God's people. **for a time, times and half a time.** The word "time" is the same word

and try to change the set times[y] and the laws. The saints will be handed over to him for
a time, times and half a time.[a z]
26"'But the court will sit, and his power will be taken away and completely destroyed forever. 27Then the sovereignty, power and greatness of the kingdoms under the
whole heaven will be handed over to the saints, the people of the Most High. His kingdom will be an everlasting[a] kingdom, and all rulers will worship[b] and obey him.'
28"This is the end of the matter. I, Daniel, was deeply troubled[c] by my thoughts, and
my face turned pale, but I kept the matter to myself."

Daniel's Vision of a Ram and a Goat

8 In the third year of King Belshazzar's reign, I, Daniel, had a vision, after the one that
had already appeared to me. 2In my vision I saw myself in the citadel of Susa[d] in the
province of Elam;[e] in the vision I was beside the Ulai Canal. 3I looked up,[f] and there before me was a ram with two horns, standing beside the canal, and the horns were long.
One of the horns was longer than the other but grew up later. 4I watched the ram as he
charged toward the west and the north and the south. No animal could stand against
him, and none could rescue from his power. He did as he pleased[g] and became great.
5As I was thinking about this, suddenly a goat with a prominent horn between his
eyes came from the west, crossing the whole earth without touching the ground. 6He
came toward the two-horned ram I had seen standing beside the canal and charged at
him in great rage. 7I saw him attack the ram furiously, striking the ram and shattering
his two horns. The ram was powerless to stand against him; the goat knocked him to the
ground and trampled on him,[h] and none could rescue the ram from his power. 8The goat
became very great, but at the height of his power his large horn was broken off,[i] and in
its place four prominent horns grew up toward the four winds of heaven.[j]
9Out of one of them came another horn, which started small but grew in power to the
south and to the east and toward the Beautiful Land.[k] 10It grew until it reached[l] the host
of the heavens, and it threw some of the starry host down to the earth[m] and trampled[n]

7:25 [y]Da 2:21 [z]Da 8:24; 12:7; Rev 12:14
7:27 [a]Da 2:44; 4:34; Lk 1:33; Rev 11:15; 22:5 [b]Ps 22:27; 72:11; 86:9
7:28 [c]Da 4:19
8:2 [d]Est 1:2 [e]Ge 10:22
8:3 [f]Da 10:5
8:4 [g]Da 11:3,16
8:7 [h]Da 7:7
8:8 [i]2Ch 26:16-21; Da 5:20 [j]Da 7:2; Rev 7:1
8:9 [k]Da 11:16
8:10 [l]Isa 14:13 [m]Rev 12:4 [n]Da 7:7

[a] 25 *Or for a year, two years and half a year*

used in 4:16 and 4:23 and, as there (see note on 4:16), may be understood as representing a period of one year (cf. Rev 12:14). It is best understood as symbolic of a period of time that will be shortened when God suddenly intervenes.

7:26 the court. The court of heaven (see v. 10).

7:27 will be handed over to the saints. After God's people face the trials of oppressive kingdoms they will rule over all forever. See note on 7:18. See *BC* 37.

7:28 deeply troubled . . . turned pale. Thoughts of Israel falling under repeated and prolonged oppression from foreign powers still troubled Daniel, even though the ultimate outcome would be divine intervention resulting in victory for God's people. **kept the matter to myself.** Daniel mentioned this to inform his readers that he did not delight in the prospect of such a future for God's people. Despite his authority in the Gentile courts of Babylon and Persia, no one could rightly accuse him of betraying his loyalty to God's people. He spoke of these future events with regret.

8:1—12:13 Daniel resumed use of the Hebrew language in the book's last five chapters. He had written 2:4—7:28 in Aramaic (see note on 2:4).

■ **8:1–27** *Vision of the Ram and the Goat.* The prophet recorded a vision concerning the treatment of God's people under the Medo-Persians and Greeks.

8:1 In the third year of King Belshazzar's reign. That is, two years after Daniel's dream in chapter 7 (see note on 7:1).

8:2 I saw myself. Daniel experienced a visionary journey like that of Ezekiel (Eze 3:10–15). **the citadel of Susa in the province of Elam.** In Daniel's time Susa was the capital of Elam, about 230 miles east of Babylon. It is unclear whether Elam was then independent or aligned with either Babylon or Media. Later, however, as one of three royal cities, Susa became the diplomatic and administrative capital of the Persian Empire (cf. Est 1:2; Ne 1:1). **Ulai Canal.** This canal near Susa connected two rivers that flowed into the Persian Gulf.

8:3 a ram with two horns. Verse 20 identifies the ram and its horns as a symbol for the kings of the Medo-Persian Empire. **One of the horns was longer than the other but grew up later.** Medo-Persian history clarifies the symbolism here. The Medes became strong and independent of Assyria after 631 B.C. The Persians began as an insignificant segment of the Median kingdom but eventually rose to control it when Cyrus (reigned 559–530 B.C.) of Anshan (in Elam) brought Media under his control (550 B.C.). Cyrus added to his list of titles "King of the Medes." Thus both horns were long but the one representing Persia longer because it was superior in might, and later in growing because it came to power after the other.

8:4 he charged toward the west and the north and the south. Cyrus initially took Asia Minor; afterward, both northern and southern Mesopotamia. Subsequent rulers extended Medo-Persian control far to the East. **became great.** The Persian Empire became larger and more powerful than any previous empire in ancient Near Eastern history.

8:5 a goat with a prominent horn between his eyes came from the west. Verse 21 identifies the goat as Greece and the large horn between his eyes as its first king. The symbolism is a clear depiction of the rise of the Greek Empire under the leadership of Alexander the Great (356–323 B.C.). **crossing the whole earth without touching the ground.** This depicts the amazing rapidity of Alexander's conquests (see note on 7:6). In only three years he was able to defeat the powerful Persian Empire.

8:8 The goat became very great. Alexander's empire quickly exceeded the Persian Empire in size. By 327 B.C. Alexander had moved eastward into what is today Afghanistan and then on to the Indus Valley. **but at the height of his power his large horn was broken off.** When his own troops refused to advance farther eastward Alexander returned to Babylon, where he died at the age of thirty-three. **in its place four prominent horns grew up.** Verse 22 indicates that these horns symbolize four kingdoms that emerged from Alexander's empire but were inferior in strength to its original domain. Historical records indicate that after a time of internal struggle four of Alexander's generals were able to secure portions of the former Greek Empire as their own kingdoms. See note on 7:6.

8:9 another horn, which started small. Verse 23 indicates that this horn symbolizes a wicked ruler who would arise in one of the four Greek kingdoms after an extended interval of time ("in the latter part of their reign"). The descriptions of the actions of this ruler (vv. 9–14,23–25) identify him as Antiochus IV Epiphanes, the ruler of the Seleucid kingdom from 175 to 164 B.C. This horn is not to be identified with the "little horn" of 7:8, which would arise during the Roman rather than the Greek period. **toward the Beautiful Land.** Daniel showed his love for the promised land by this expression.

8:10 the host of the heavens. Or the stars (cf. Jer 33:22), symbolizing the people of God (cf. 12:3; Ge 12:3; 15:5; Ex 12:41) and/or a

8:11 [o]Da 11:36-37 [p]Eze 46:13-14 [q]Da 11:31; 12:11
8:13 [r]Da 4:23 [s]Da 12:6 [t]Lk 21:24; Rev 11:2
8:14 [u]Da 12:11-12
8:15 [v]ver 1 [w]Da 10:16-18
8:16 [x]Da 9:21; Lk 1:19
8:17 [y]Eze 1:28; Da 2:46; Rev 1:17 [z]Hab 2:3
8:18 [a]Da 10:9 [b]Eze 2:2; Da 10:16-18
8:19 [c]Hab 2:3
8:21 [d]Da 10:20 [e]Da 11:3
8:24 [f]Da 7:25; 11:36
8:25 [g]Da 11:36 [h]Da 2:34; 11:21

on them. 11 It set itself up to be as great as the Prince of the host;[o] it took away the daily sacrifice[p] from him, and the place of his sanctuary was brought low.[q] 12 Because of rebellion, the host ⌊of the saints⌋[a] and the daily sacrifice were given over to it. It prospered
in everything it did, and truth was thrown to the ground.
13 Then I heard a holy one[r] speaking, and another holy one said to him, "How long
will it take for the vision to be fulfilled[s]—the vision concerning the daily sacrifice, the rebellion that causes desolation, and the surrender of the sanctuary and of the host that
will be trampled[t] underfoot?"
14 He said to me, "It will take 2,300 evenings and mornings; then the sanctuary will
be reconsecrated."[u]

The Interpretation of the Vision

15 While I, Daniel, was watching the vision[v] and trying to understand it, there before
me stood one who looked like a man.[w] 16 And I heard a man's voice from the Ulai calling, "Gabriel,[x] tell this man the meaning of the vision."
17 As he came near the place where I was standing, I was terrified and fell prostrate.[y]
"Son of man," he said to me, "understand that the vision concerns the time of the
end."[z]
18 While he was speaking to me, I was in a deep sleep, with my face to the ground.[a]
Then he touched me and raised me to my feet.[b]
19 He said: "I am going to tell you what will happen later in the time of wrath, because
the vision concerns the appointed time of the end.[b][c] 20 The two-horned ram that you saw
represents the kings of Media and Persia. 21 The shaggy goat is the king of Greece,[d] and
the large horn between his eyes is the first king.[e] 22 The four horns that replaced the one
that was broken off represent four kingdoms that will emerge from his nation but will
not have the same power.
23 "In the latter part of their reign, when rebels have become completely wicked, a
stern-faced king, a master of intrigue, will arise. 24 He will become very strong, but not
by his own power. He will cause astounding devastation and will succeed in whatever
he does. He will destroy the mighty men and the holy people.[f] 25 He will cause deceit to
prosper, and he will consider himself superior. When they feel secure, he will destroy
many and take his stand against the Prince of princes.[g] Yet he will be destroyed, but not
by human power.[h]

[a] 12 Or *rebellion, the armies* [b] 19 Or *because the end will be at the appointed time*

---

heavenly army (Isa 14:13; also see 2 Maccabees 9:10 [an Apocryphal book]). Antiochus's coins picture a star above his head. *Epiphanes* means "God manifest." The attack against the people of God amounted to an attack against heaven itself. **threw some of the starry host down to the earth and trampled on them.** This is a symbolic depiction of the severe persecution of God's people under Antiochus IV Epiphanes, who attempted to abolish Israel's traditional worship and way of life (see "Introduction: Purpose and Distinctives"; cf. 11:21–35; 1 Maccabees 1:10–64 [an Apocryphal book]).

8:11 as great as the Prince of the host. The "Prince" is to be understood as God, the Lord of hosts. See verse 25, where the designation is "Prince of princes." Antiochus IV took the name Epiphanes ("God manifest") and viewed himself as the incarnate manifestation of Zeus (the chief god of the Greek pantheon). **took away the daily sacrifice from him.** See verses 12–13 and 11:31. Antiochus IV ordered the cessation of all ceremonial observances related to the worship of the Lord at the Jerusalem temple and in the cities of Judah. **the place of his sanctuary was brought low.** Antiochus IV not only entered the Most Holy Place and plundered the silver and gold vessels, but he also erected an altar to Zeus on top of the altar of the Lord in the temple court and offered swine upon it (see note on 11:31).

8:12 the host of the saints and the daily sacrifice were given over to it. God's people were subjected to the power of the horn that started small (v. 9), Antiochus IV. This entailed the cessation of regular temple observances. **It prospered in everything it did.** The vision depicts the apparent success of the wicked acts of Antiochus IV (the horn that started small). That success included the destruction of copies of the Hebrew Scripture (cf. 1 Maccabees 1:56–57 [an Apocryphal book]).

8:14 It will take 2,300 evenings and mornings. The phrase "evenings and mornings" occurs in the Old Testament only here and in verse 26. Some understand it as a reference to the evening and morning sacrifices (cf. Ex 29:38–42). On that basis it would represent 1,150 days. Others view it as simply an expression for 2,300 days. Since the beginning of the persecutions of Antiochus IV could be linked with any one of a number of incidents beginning as early as 171 B.C., it is difficult to determine which understanding of the phrase is to be preferred. The number 23 may be symbolic of a fixed period, as in apocalyptic literature outside the Bible. **then the sanctuary will be reconsecrated.** The temple was cleansed and rededicated under the leadership of Judas Maccabeus on December 25, 165 B.C. (see note on 11:34; cf. Zec 9:13–17).

8:16 Gabriel. This angel is mentioned four times in Scripture (9:21; Lk 1:11,19,26). The name denotes one who is strong in the Lord (*Gabriel* means "strength of God") because of a relationship with him.

8:17 Son of man. See note on 7:13. The "strong man of God" (see note on v. 16), the angel Gabriel, was speaking to this exalted mortal. **the vision concerns the time of the end.** See also verse 19 ("the appointed time of the end"). This expression does not necessarily have to do with the absolute end of history. It occurs in 11:27 and 35 in contexts that probably refer to the end of the persecutions under Antiochus IV.

8:19 what will happen later in the time of wrath. The "time of wrath" may here refer to the time of God's judgment on his people Israel during the period of their subjection to the Babylonians, Persians and Greeks.

8:20 ram. See notes on verses 3–4.

8:21 goat . . . horn. See notes on verses 5 and 8.

8:22 four horns. See note on verse 8.

8:23–25 See notes on verses 9–14. Some interpreters have found a picture of the antichrist in the descriptions of the horn of this chapter (v. 8) by viewing Antiochus IV as a type of any powerful opponent of God's people in the future.

8:24–25 mighty . . . many. Descriptions of faithful Jews.

8:25 Prince of princes. A reference to God. **he will be destroyed, but not by human power.** Antiochus IV was not assassinated, nor did he die in battle. His death in 164 B.C. resulted from a physical or nervous disorder. For variant accounts of his death see 1 Maccabees 6:1–16 and 2 Maccabees 9:1–28 (both are Apocryphal books).

26“The vision of the evenings and mornings that has been given you is true,[i] but seal[j]
up the vision, for it concerns the distant future.”[k]
27I, Daniel, was exhausted and lay ill for several days. Then I got up and went about
the king’s business.[l] I was appalled[m] by the vision; it was beyond understanding.

Daniel’s Prayer

9 In the first year of Darius[n] son of Xerxes[a] (a Mede by descent), who was made ruler over the Babylonian[b] kingdom— 2in the first year of his reign, I, Daniel, understood from the Scriptures, according to the word of the LORD given to Jeremiah the
prophet, that the desolation of Jerusalem would last seventy[o] years. 3So I turned to the
Lord God and pleaded with him in prayer and petition, in fasting, and in sackcloth and
ashes.[p]
4I prayed to the LORD my God and confessed:

“O Lord, the great and awesome God,[q] who keeps his covenant of love[r] with
all who love him and obey his commands, 5we have sinned and done wrong.[s] We
have been wicked and have rebelled; we have turned away[t] from your commands
and laws.[u] 6We have not listened to your servants the prophets,[v] who spoke in
your name to our kings, our princes and our fathers, and to all the people of the
land.
7“Lord, you are righteous, but this day we are covered with shame[w]—the
men of Judah and people of Jerusalem and all Israel, both near and far, in all the
countries where you have scattered[x] us because of our unfaithfulness to you.[y]
8O LORD, we and our kings, our princes and our fathers are covered with shame
because we have sinned against you. 9The Lord our God is merciful and forgiving,[z]
even though we have rebelled against him;[a] 10we have not obeyed the LORD our
God or kept the laws he gave us through his servants the prophets.[b] 11All Israel
has transgressed your law and turned away, refusing to obey you.
“Therefore the curses and sworn judgments written in the Law of Moses, the
servant of God, have been poured out on us, because we have sinned[c] against you.
12You have fulfilled[d] the words spoken against us and against our rulers by bringing upon us great disaster. Under the whole heaven nothing has ever been done
like what has been done to Jerusalem.[e] 13Just as it is written in the Law of Moses,
all this disaster has come upon us, yet we have not sought the favor of the LORD
our God by turning from our sins and giving attention to your truth.[f] 14The LORD
did not hesitate to bring the disaster[g] upon us, for the LORD our God is righteous
in everything he does; yet we have not obeyed him.[h]
15“Now, O Lord our God, who brought your people out of Egypt with a mighty
hand[i] and who made for yourself a name[j] that endures to this day, we have
sinned, we have done wrong. 16O Lord, in keeping with all your righteous acts,[k]

8:26 [i]Da 10:1 [j]Rev 22:10 [k]Da 10:14
8:27 [l]Da 2:48 [m]Da 7:28
9:1 [n]Da 5:31
9:2 [o]2Ch 36:21; Jer 29:10; Zec 7:5
9:3 [p]Ne 1:4; Jer 29:12
9:4 [q]Dt 7:21 [r]Dt 7:9
9:5 [s]Ps 106:6 [t]Isa 53:6 [u]ver 11; La 1:20
9:6 [v]2Ch 36:16; Jer 44:5
9:7 [w]Ps 44:15 [x]Dt 4:27; Am 9:9 [y]Jer 3:25
9:9 [z]Ps 130:4 [a]Ne 9:17; Jer 14:7
9:10 [b]2Ki 17:13-15; 18:12
9:11 [c]Isa 1:4-6; Jer 8:5-10
9:12 [d]Isa 44:26; Zec 1:6 [e]Jer 44:2-6; Eze 5:9
9:13 [f]Isa 9:13; Jer 2:30
9:14 [g]Jer 44:27 [h]Ne 9:33
9:15 [i]Jer 32:21 [j]Ne 9:10
9:16 [k]Ps 31:1

[a] 1 Hebrew *Ahasuerus* [b] 1 Or *Chaldean*

8:26 seal up the vision. A “seal” was used either to authenticate or certify something or to close up or secure something for confidentiality or safekeeping. The second sense seems most fitting in this context (see note on 6:17). **for it concerns the distant future.** Literally, “[the vision] pertains to many days.” The conquests of Alexander (333–323 B.C.) occurred nearly two centuries after Daniel’s vision (c. 550 B.C.), while Antiochus IV was active about a century and a half after Alexander (171–164 B.C.).

■ **9:1–27** *Vision of the Seventy Weeks.* Daniel recorded an account of a revelation he received concerning Jeremiah’s prophecy about the 70 years of Jerusalem’s desolation. The vision followed Daniel’s prayer in which he confessed the justice of Jerusalem’s desolation and sought the favor of God for the restoration of the city and the temple. This vision revealed that the time of Judah’s exile was extended because the people of God had not yet repented of the sins that had brought exile upon them.

9:1 the first year of Darius son of Xerxes. See notes on 5:30–31 and 6:1. The term “Xerxes” (not the same person mentioned in Est 1:1) may be a royal title rather than a personal name. The first year of Darius’s reign was 539 B.C.

9:2 understood from the Scriptures . . . given to Jeremiah . . . that the desolation of Jerusalem would last seventy years. See Jeremiah 25:11–12 and 29:10. Daniel was concerned because the 70 years of exile had nearly come to an end but the Israelites were not ready to return to the land. Interpreters differ on the dates of the beginning and ending of the 70-year period and on whether it is to be understood as a round number, suggesting a human lifetime, or an exact time period. Some date the period from 586 B.C. (the destruction of Jerusalem by Nebuchadnezzar) to 515 B.C., when the restoration of the temple was completed under Zerubbabel (Ezr 6:13–18; Zec 1:12). Others date the beginning of the period to the year of Daniel’s own captivity (604 B.C.; see note on 1:1). Daniel was also undoubtedly aware that Isaiah had prophesied Israel’s release from exile under the Persian ruler Cyrus (Isa 44:28; 45:1–13). As Daniel apparently did here, the writer of Chronicles cited Cyrus’s release of the exiles as having taken place in 539 B.C. as the fulfillment of Jeremiah’s prophecy (2Ch 36:21). In the literature of the ancient Near East 70 years was a standard time period during which a god would punish his people for disloyalty. This period could be lengthened or shortened by the reactions of the people (see “Introduction to the Prophetic Books”). For this reason it is not surprising that there would be some flexibility in the ways different Biblical writers applied the number to Israel’s history.

9:4–19 Daniel’s prayer is rooted in a covenantal understanding of the Lord’s relation to his people (blessing for obedience and cursing for disobedience; see especially vv. 5,7,11–12,14; Lev 26:14–45; Dt 28:15–68; 30:1–5). For a similar prayer see Nehemiah 9. The prayer contains four parts: (1) worship (v. 4); (2) a confession of sin (vv. 5–11a); (3) recognition of the justice of God in his judgment on sin (vv. 11b–14); and (4) a plea for God’s mercy based on concern for his name, kingdom and will (vv. 15–19). The prayer is grounded in God’s promises (v. 2), was voiced in a spirit of contrition and humility (v. 3) and provides a model for appropriate elements of effective prayer. See *WLC* 178,180,196; *WSC* 98,107; *HC* 117.

9:16 [l]Jer 32:32 [m]Zec 8:3 [n]Eze 5:14
9:17 [o]Nu 6:24-26; Ps 80:19
9:18 [p]Ps 80:14 [q]Isa 37:17; Jer 7:10-12; 25:29
9:19 [r]Ps 44:23
9:20 [s]ver 3; Ps 145:18; Isa 58:9
9:21 [t]Da 8:16; Lk 1:19 [u]Ex 29:39
9:23 [v]Da 10:19; Lk 1:28 [w]Da 10:11-12; Mt 24:15
9:24 [x]Isa 53:10 [y]Isa 56:1
9:25 [z]Ezr 4:24 [a]Jn 4:25
9:26 [b]Isa 53:8 [c]Na 1:8

turn away your anger and your wrath from Jerusalem,[l] your city, your holy hill.[m]
Our sins and the iniquities of our fathers have made Jerusalem and your people
an object of scorn[n] to all those around us.
17"Now, our God, hear the prayers and petitions of your servant. For your sake,
O Lord, look with favor[o] on your desolate sanctuary. 18Give ear, O God, and hear;
open your eyes and see[p] the desolation of the city that bears your Name.[q] We do
not make requests of you because we are righteous, but because of your great
mercy. 19O Lord, listen! O Lord, forgive![r] O Lord, hear and act! For your sake, O my
God, do not delay, because your city and your people bear your Name."

The Seventy "Sevens"

20While I was speaking and praying, confessing my sin and the sin of my people Israel and making my request to the LORD my God for his holy hill[s]— 21while I was still in
prayer, Gabriel,[t] the man I had seen in the earlier vision, came to me in swift flight about
the time of the evening sacrifice.[u] 22He instructed me and said to me, "Daniel, I have now
come to give you insight and understanding. 23As soon as you began to pray, an answer
was given, which I have come to tell you, for you are highly esteemed.[v] Therefore, consider the message and understand the vision:[w]
24"Seventy 'sevens'[a] are decreed for your people and your holy city to finish[b] transgression, to put an end to sin, to atone[x] for wickedness, to bring in everlasting righteousness,[y] to seal up vision and prophecy and to anoint the most holy.[c]
25"Know and understand this: From the issuing of the decree[d] to restore and rebuild[z]
Jerusalem until the Anointed One,[e][a] the ruler, comes, there will be seven 'sevens,' and
sixty-two 'sevens.' It will be rebuilt with streets and a trench, but in times of trouble. 26Af-
ter the sixty-two 'sevens,' the Anointed One will be cut off[b] and will have nothing.[f] The
people of the ruler who will come will destroy the city and the sanctuary. The end will
come like a flood:[c] War will continue until the end, and desolations have been decreed.
27He will confirm a covenant with many for one 'seven.'[g] In the middle of the 'seven'[g] he
will put an end to sacrifice and offering. And on a wing ⌞of the temple⌟ he will set up an

[a] *24* Or *'weeks'*; also in verses 25 and 26 [b] *24* Or *restrain* [c] *24* Or *Most Holy Place*; or *most holy One* [d] *25* Or *word* [e] *25* Or *an anointed one*; also in verse 26 [f] *26* Or *off and will have no one*; or *off, but not for himself* [g] *27* Or *'week'*

9:21 Gabriel, the man I had seen in the earlier vision. See note on 8:16.
9:24 Seventy 'sevens.' The "seventy 'sevens'" (lit., "seventy weeks") represent 490 years (see note on 9:24–27). The 70 years of exile (v. 2) are multiplied seven times in accordance with the pattern of covenantal curses (Lev 26:14,21,24,28). God extended the exile because of Israel's continuing sinfulness. Just as the 70 years of exile predicted by Jeremiah may have followed a standard formula (see note on v. 2), the period of 490 years probably represented a standard formula as well. For instance, the intertestamental, non-canonical book Jubilees structures the whole of history into periods of 490 years. It is likely, therefore, that Daniel had in mind not a precise calculation of years but broadly defined segments of time. This extension of time was not absolute; it could be lengthened if the people continued to rebel or shortened if they repented (see "Introduction to the Prophetic Books"). **are decreed . . . to.** Six things were to be accomplished during the period of "seventy 'sevens.'" As with all Old Testament prophecies about the restoration from exile in the latter days, these six items are fulfilled in the work of Christ in bringing the kingdom of God (see theological articles "The Kingdom of God" at Mt 4 and "The Plan of the Ages" at Heb 7). The New Testament teaches that the kingdom was inaugurated in the first coming of Christ, continues now and will reach its consummation at Christ's return. Therefore, some aspects of these predictions are more closely related to Christ's first coming, others to his second coming and still others are fulfilled by both his first and second comings. See *WCF* 8.5; 11.3; *WLC* 71.
9:25–27 The "seventy weeks" of years are divided into three subunits of 49 years ("seven 'sevens'"; v. 25), 434 years ("sixty-two 'sevens'"; v. 26) and seven years ("one 'seven'"; v. 27). Interpreters differ over whether these subunits are to be viewed as a continuous sequence or as subunits separated by time intervals. Many attempts have been made to understand this chronology as precise numbers of years, but all attempts fall short of completeness due to the fact that these numbers were intended as round figures of representative periods of time. Although Daniel's calculations are not to be taken as precise, the basic pattern of his prediction may be discerned without falling into speculation. The order to rebuild Jerusalem (v. 25) was followed by "seven 'sevens'" or 49 years (v. 25), at which time the rebuilding of Jerusalem was completed (see Ezra and Nehemiah). This was followed by "sixty-two 'sevens'" or 434 years (v. 25), at which time the Messiah was cut off (v. 26; see note). The single "seven" was fulfilled during or near the time of Christ's earthly ministry (v. 27).
9:25 Anointed One, the ruler. Two interpretations of this figure are possible: (1) He is the Messiah, the Christ. (2) He is a king whom God has anointed as his instrument in accomplishing his will (cf. Isa 45:1). While most interpreters take the anointed one and the ruler in verse 25 to be the same person, there is some disagreement as to whether or not this figure is identical to the person or persons referred to as "anointed one" and "ruler" in verse 26. In verse 26 the ruler appears to act against God. If the same ruler is intended in both verses, he is most likely not to be equated with the Messiah.
9:26 the Anointed One will be cut off. This is either a reference to the crucifixion of Christ or to judgment that God would bring against a king who had overstepped his bounds as God's instrument of judgment (see note on v. 25).**The people of the ruler who will come will destroy the city and the sanctuary.** A reference either to the Greek Antiochus IV Epiphanes as a precursor to the Roman general Titus (see "Introduction: Purpose and Distinctives") or directly to Titus and/or his armies, who destroyed Jerusalem in A.D. 70. See *WCF* 8.5; 11.3; *WLC* 71; *BC* 21.
9:27 He will confirm a covenant with many for one 'seven.' The most likely antecedent of "he" is "the Anointed One" or "the ruler" (v. 26). It is popular to interpret this statement as descriptive of an agreement that the antichrist will establish with Jewish people who have re-gathered in the land of Israel during the "tribulation" period, but this outlook is less likely. **In the middle of the 'seven' he will put an end to sacrifice and offering.** This may be a reference to the termination of the Old Testament sacrificial system by the atoning death of Christ. It is also possible that it refers to the desecration of the temple by Antiochus IV Epiphanes or Titus (see note on v. 26). Some interpreters take the less likely view that this is a reference to the antichrist's prohibition of "sacri-

abomination that causes desolation, until the end that is decreed[d] is poured out on him.[a]"[b]

Daniel's Vision of a Man

10 In the third year of Cyrus[e] king of Persia, a revelation was given to Daniel (who was called Belteshazzar).[f] Its message was true[g] and it concerned a great war.[c] The understanding of the message came to him in a vision.

2At that time I, Daniel, mourned[h] for three weeks. **3**I ate no choice food; no meat or wine touched my lips; and I used no lotions at all until the three weeks were over.

4On the twenty-fourth day of the first month, as I was standing on the bank of the great river, the Tigris,[i] **5**I looked up and there before me was a man dressed in linen,[j] with a belt of the finest gold[k] around his waist. **6**His body was like chrysolite, his face like lightning,[l] his eyes like flaming torches,[m] his arms and legs like the gleam of burnished bronze,[n] and his voice like the sound of a multitude.

7I, Daniel, was the only one who saw the vision; the men with me did not see it,[o] but such terror overwhelmed them that they fled and hid themselves. **8**So I was left alone,[p] gazing at this great vision; I had no strength left,[q] my face turned deathly pale and I was helpless.[r] **9**Then I heard him speaking, and as I listened to him, I fell into a deep sleep, my face to the ground.[s]

10A hand touched me[t] and set me trembling on my hands and knees.[u] **11**He said, "Daniel, you who are highly esteemed,[v] consider carefully the words I am about to speak to you, and stand up,[w] for I have now been sent to you." And when he said this to me, I stood up trembling.

12Then he continued, "Do not be afraid, Daniel. Since the first day that you set your mind to gain understanding and to humble[x] yourself before your God, your words were heard, and I have come in response to them.[y] **13**But the prince of the Persian kingdom resisted me twenty-one days. Then Michael,[z] one of the chief princes, came to help me, because I was detained there with the king of Persia. **14**Now I have come to explain[a] to you what will happen to your people in the future, for the vision concerns a time yet to come.[b]"

15While he was saying this to me, I bowed with my face toward the ground and was speechless.[c] **16**Then one who looked like a man[d] touched my lips, and I opened my mouth and began to speak.[d] I said to the one standing before me, "I am overcome with anguish[e] because of the vision, my lord, and I am helpless. **17**How can I, your servant, talk with you, my lord? My strength is gone and I can hardly breathe."[f]

18Again the one who looked like a man touched[g] me and gave me strength. **19**"Do not be afraid, O man highly esteemed," he said. "Peace![h] Be strong now; be strong."[i]

9:27 [d]Isa 10:22
10:1 [e]Da 1:21 [f]Da 1:7 [g]Da 8:26
10:2 [h]Ezr 9:4
10:4 [i]Ge 2:14
10:5 [j]Eze 9:2; Rev 15:6 [k]Jer 10:9
10:6 [l]Mt 17:2 [m]Rev 19:12 [n]Rev 1:15
10:7 [o]2Ki 6:17-20; Ac 9:7
10:8 [p]Ge 32:24 [q]Da 8:27 [r]Hab 3:16
10:9 [s]Da 8:18
10:10 [t]Jer 1:9 [u]Rev 1:17
10:11 [v]Da 9:23 [w]Eze 2:1
10:12 [x]Da 9:3 [y]Da 9:20
10:13 [z]ver 21; Da 12:1; Jude 1:9
10:14 [a]Da 9:22 [b]Da 2:28; 8:26; Hab 2:3
10:15 [c]Eze 24:27; Lk 1:20
10:16 [d]Isa 6:7; Jer 1:9; Da 8:15-18 [e]Isa 21:3
10:17 [f]Da 4:19
10:18 [g]ver 16
10:19 [h]Jdg 6:23; Isa 35:4 [i]Jos 1:9

[a] *27* Or *it* [b] *27* Or *And one who causes desolation will come upon the pinnacle of the abominable ⌞temple⌟, until the end that is decreed is poured out on the desolated ⌞city⌟* [c] *1* Or *true and burdensome* [d] *16* Most manuscripts of the Masoretic Text; one manuscript of the Masoretic Text, Dead Sea Scrolls and Septuagint *Then something that looked like a man's hand*

fice and offering" (perhaps standing for religious practice in general) by the re-gathered Jewish people after three and a half years (Rev 11:2; 12:6,14) of the "tribulation" period. **And on a wing of the temple he will set up an abomination that causes desolation.** Daniel most likely described the destruction of the temple under either Antiochus IV Epiphanes or Titus (see note on v. 26 and "Introduction: Purpose and Distinctives"), rather than actions of a future antichrist. Phrases similar to "an abomination that causes desolation" occur in 8:13, 11:31 and 12:11 (see their notes), as well as in 1 Maccabees 1:54 (an Apocryphal book). Daniel 8:13 and 1 Maccabees 1:54 refer to the activities of Antiochus IV. Daniel used the same language to describe one who would defile the temple in the time near that of the Messiah. Jesus alluded to this abomination in Matthew 24:15 and Mark 13:14. See *WCF* 19.3.

■ **10:1—12:13** *Vision of the Future of God's People.* The prophet turned his attention to a final, lengthy vision that focused on the reign of Antiochus IV Epiphanes (see "Introduction: Purpose and Distinctives") and looked beyond that reign as well. This material divides into four main sections: the angel's announcement to Daniel (10:1—11:1), events from Daniel until Antiochus IV Epiphanes (11:2–20), the reign of Antiochus IV Epiphanes (11:21—12:3) and a final message to Daniel (12:4–13).

■ **10:1—11:1** *The Angel's Message to Daniel.* Daniel was prepared by an angelic being to receive a revelation pertaining to "a time yet to come" (10:14).

10:1 In the third year of Cyrus king of Persia. In 537 B.C. See notes on 1:21, 5:30, 6:1 and 9:1. The repatriated exiles were at this time back in the land to rebuild the temple (Ezr 1:1–4; 3:8), but they would soon have to give up the rebuilding (Ezr 4:24).

10:2 mourned. Daniel probably mourned because of the state of Jerusalem (Ne 1:4; Isa 61:3–4; 64:8–12; 66:10).

10:5 a man dressed in linen. Verses 5–6 give a detailed description of an angel, perhaps Gabriel (9:21) or the one who spoke to Gabriel (8:16). His appearance was similar to that of the glory of the Lord (Eze 1:26–28; Rev 1:12–16). For other references to angels see Judges 13:6, Ezekiel 9:2–3, 10:2 and Luke 24:4.

10:7 terror overwhelmed. See Isaiah 6:5 and Luke 5:8.

10:12 your words were heard, and I have come in response to them. The vision and revelation that Daniel received came as a direct response to his prayers.

10:13 But the prince of the Persian kingdom resisted me. In the context it is apparent that this prince refers to an evil, but powerful, spiritual being (cf. Job 1:6–12; Ps 82; Isa 24:21; Lk 11:14–26) assigned by Satan to activity pertaining to Persian rule. Similarly, the archangel Michael is called "the great prince who protects" Israel (12:1). The host of heaven are said to fight for Israel elsewhere in the Old Testament (Jdg 5:20; 2Ki 6:15–18; Ps 103:20–21). **Then Michael, one of the chief princes, came to help me.** Michael is depicted as the commander of the holy angels in Jude 9 and Revelation 12:7. Here a glimpse is given into the spiritual battles waged in the heavenly realms that affect events on Earth (cf. Eph 6:12; Rev 12:7–9).

When he spoke to me, I was strengthened and said, "Speak, my lord, since you have
given me strength."[j]
20 So he said, "Do you know why I have come to you? Soon I will return to fight against
the prince of Persia, and when I go, the prince of Greece[k] will come; 21 but first I will tell
you what is written in the Book of Truth.[l] (No one supports me against them except
11 Michael,[m] your prince. 1 And in the first year of Darius[n] the Mede, I took my
stand to support and protect him.)

The Kings of the South and the North

2 "Now then, I tell you the truth:[o] Three more kings will appear in Persia, and then a
fourth, who will be far richer than all the others. When he has gained power by his
wealth, he will stir up everyone against the kingdom of Greece.[p] 3 Then a mighty king will
appear, who will rule with great power and do as he pleases.[q] 4 After he has appeared,
his empire will be broken up and parceled out toward the four winds of heaven.[r] It will
not go to his descendants, nor will it have the power he exercised, because his empire
will be uprooted and given to others.
5 "The king of the South will become strong, but one of his commanders will become
even stronger than he and will rule his own kingdom with great power. 6 After some
years, they will become allies. The daughter of the king of the South will go to the king
of the North to make an alliance, but she will not retain her power, and he and his power[a] will not last. In those days she will be handed over, together with her royal escort and
her father[b] and the one who supported her.
7 "One from her family line will arise to take her place. He will attack the forces of the
king of the North[s] and enter his fortress; he will fight against them and be victorious. 8 He
will also seize their gods,[t] their metal images and their valuable articles of silver and gold
and carry them off to Egypt.[u] For some years he will leave the king of the North alone.
9 Then the king of the North will invade the realm of the king of the South but will retreat
to his own country. 10 His sons will prepare for war and assemble a great army, which will
sweep on like an irresistible flood[v] and carry the battle as far as his fortress.
11 "Then the king of the South will march out in a rage and fight against the king of
the North, who will raise a large army, but it will be defeated.[w] 12 When the army is carried off, the king of the South will be filled with pride and will slaughter many thousands,
yet he will not remain triumphant. 13 For the king of the North will muster another

10:19 [j]Isa 6:1-8
10:20 [k]Da 8:21; 11:2
10:21 [l]Da 11:2 [m]ver 13; Jude 1:9
11:1 [n]Da 5:31
11:2 [o]Da 10:21 [p]Da 10:20
11:3 [q]Da 8:4,21
11:4 [r]Da 7:2; 8:22
11:7 [s]ver 6
11:8 [t]Isa 37:19; 46:1-2 [u]Jer 43:12
11:10 [v]Isa 8:8; Jer 46:8; Da 9:26
11:11 [w]Da 8:7-8

[a] 6 Or *offspring* [b] 6 Or *child* (see Vulgate and Syriac)

10:20 I will return to fight against the prince of Persia. See note on verse 13. **the prince of Greece.** This is a fallen angel or demonic power assigned by Satan to participate in the affairs of the Greek kingdom (see note on v. 13; see Jn 14:30; Eph 6:12). Although both Persia and Greece would conquer God's people, Daniel was to understand that their power would be limited by the power of God, whose purposes always prevail.
10:21 the Book of Truth. A metaphor for God's knowledge and control over all of history. **No one . . . except Michael.** Michael's interest in protecting Israel (see note on v. 13; cf. 12:1) corresponded with that of the messenger, who was directly concerned about God's purposes.
11:1 in the first year of Darius the Mede. Earlier the angel who was speaking to Daniel had given assistance to Michael (see note on 10:13), perhaps in connection with the Persian decree to permit the Jews to return to their homeland.
■ **11:2–20** *From Daniel Until Antiochus IV Epiphanes.* The revelation given to Daniel in 11:2–20 concerned ancient Near Eastern history from the time of Daniel until the time of Antiochus IV Epiphanes. The prophet's vision was unusually detailed, describing intricate interconnections among events far beyond that normally given to an Israelite prophet. Such details drew the attention of early readers of this book and demonstrated Daniel's reliability.
11:2 Three more kings will appear in Persia. Cambyses (529–523 B.C.), Pseudo-Smerdis or Gaumata (523–522 B.C.) and Darius I (522–486 B.C.). **a fourth.** Xerxes I (485–464 B.C.). **his wealth.** See Esther 1:4. **he will stir up everyone against the kingdom of Greece.** Xerxes waged a number of campaigns against Greece, beginning in 480 B.C.
11:3 a mighty king will appear. Alexander the Great (336–323 B.C.). See notes on 7:6 and 8:5 and 8.
11:4 his empire will be broken up . . . toward the four winds of heaven. See notes on 7:6 and 8:8.
11:5 The king of the South. Ptolemy I Soter (323–285 B.C.). **one of his commanders will become even stronger.** Seleucus I Nicator (311–280 B.C.). Seleucus broke with Ptolemy, became king of Babylon and controlled territories from the Indus River in the east to Syria in the west.
11:6–20 Verses 6–20 contain detailed predictions of relations between the king of the North (the Seleucid kingdom) and the king of the South (the Ptolemaic kingdom). This section may be divided into three parts: (1) events concerning Laodice and Berenice (vv. 6–9), (2) the career of Antiochus III (vv. 10–19) and (3) the reign of Seleucus IV (v. 20).
11:6 The daughter of the king of the South. Berenice, the daughter of Ptolemy II Philadelphus (285–246 B.C.). **to make an alliance.** Refers to a marriage alliance (c. 250 B.C.) between Antiochus II Theos (261–246 B.C.) of Syria and Ptolemy II of Egypt. **she will not retain her power, and he and his power will not last.** Laodice, the former wife of Antiochus, instigated a conspiracy that resulted in the poisoning deaths of Berenice, Antiochus II and their infant son.
11:7 One from her family line will arise. Ptolemy III Euergetes (246–221 B.C.), the brother of Berenice (see note on v. 6). **He will attack the forces of the king of the North.** Ptolemy III attacked the Seleucid kingdom, had Laodice (see note on v. 6) put to death and returned to Egypt with considerable booty.
11:9 the king of the North will invade the realm of the king of the South. This refers to the unsuccessful campaign of Seleucus II Callinicus (246–226 B.C.), the son of Laodice, against the Ptolemaic kingdom in 240 B.C.
11:10 His sons. Seleucus III Ceraunus (226–223 B.C.) and Antiochus III the Great (223–187 B.C.). **will prepare for war and assemble a great army.** Antiochus III fought with the Ptolemies from 222–187 B.C. and for a time gained control of Canaan, as well as western Syria. **his fortress.** This probably refers to Raphia, a Ptolemaic fortress in southern Canaan. A major battle was fought there in 217 B.C.
11:11 the king of the South. Ptolemy IV Philopator (221–203 B.C.). **fight against the king of the North.** Antiochus III. He suffered great losses (over 14,000 men) at the battle of Raphia in 217 B.C.
11:13 the king of the North will muster another army. In al-

army, larger than the first; and after several years, he will advance with a huge army fully equipped.
14“In those times many will rise against the king of the South. The violent men
among your own people will rebel in fulfillment of the vision, but without success.
15Then the king of the North will come and build up siege ramps[x] and will capture a fortified city. The forces of the South will be powerless to resist; even their best troops will
not have the strength to stand. 16The invader will do as he pleases;[y] no one will be able
to stand against him.[z] He will establish himself in the Beautiful Land and will have the
power to destroy it.[a] 17He will determine to come with the might of his entire kingdom
and will make an alliance with the king of the South. And he will give him a daughter in
marriage in order to overthrow the kingdom, but his plans[a] will not succeed[b] or help
him. 18Then he will turn his attention to the coastlands[c] and will take many of them, but
a commander will put an end to his insolence and will turn his insolence back upon
him.[d] 19After this, he will turn back toward the fortresses of his own country but will
stumble and fall,[e] to be seen no more.[f]
20“His successor will send out a tax collector to maintain the royal splendor.[g] In a few
years, however, he will be destroyed, yet not in anger or in battle.
21“He will be succeeded by a contemptible[h] person who has not been given the hon-
or of royalty.[i] He will invade the kingdom when its people feel secure, and he will seize
it through intrigue. 22Then an overwhelming army will be swept away before him; both
it and a prince of the covenant will be destroyed.[j] 23After coming to an agreement with
him, he will act deceitfully,[k] and with only a few people he will rise to power. 24When the
richest provinces feel secure, he will invade them and will achieve what neither his fathers nor his forefathers did. He will distribute plunder, loot and wealth among his followers.[l] He will plot the overthrow of fortresses—but only for a time.
25“With a large army he will stir up his strength and courage against the king of the
South. The king of the South will wage war with a large and very powerful army, but he
will not be able to stand because of the plots devised against him. 26Those who eat from
the king’s provisions will try to destroy him; his army will be swept away, and many will
fall in battle. 27The two kings, with their hearts bent on evil,[m] will sit at the same table
and lie[n] to each other, but to no avail, because an end will still come at the appointed
time.[o] 28The king of the North will return to his own country with great wealth, but his
heart will be set against the holy covenant. He will take action against it and then return
to his own country.
29“At the appointed time he will invade the South again, but this time the outcome
will be different from what it was before. 30Ships of the western coastlands[b][p] will oppose
him, and he will lose heart. Then he will turn back and vent his fury against the holy covenant. He will return and show favor to those who forsake the holy covenant.

11:15 [x]Eze 4:2
11:16 [y]Da 8:4 [z]Jos 1:5; Da 8:7 [a]Da 8:9
11:17 [b]Ps 20:4
11:18 [c]Isa 66:19; Jer 25:22 [d]Hos 12:14
11:19 [e]Ps 27:2 [f]Ps 37:36; Eze 26:21
11:20 [g]Isa 60:17
11:21 [h]Da 4:17 [i]Da 8:25
11:22 [j]Da 8:10-11
11:23 [k]Da 8:25
11:24 [l]Ne 9:25
11:27 [m]Ps 64:6 [n]Ps 12:2; Jer 9:5 [o]Hab 2:3
11:30 [p]Ge 10:4

[a] *17* Or *but she* [b] *30* Hebrew *of Kittim*

liance with Philip V of Macedon, he raised an even larger army to invade the Ptolemaic kingdom. Ptolemy IV died in mysterious circumstances and was succeeded by Ptolemy V Epiphanes (203–181 B.C.), his four-year-old son.

11:15 the king of the North will come and build up siege ramps and will capture a fortified city. This refers to the victory of Antiochus III at Sidon over the Egyptian general Scopas in 198 B.C. It marked the end of Ptolemaic rule in the area only much later referred to as Palestine.

11:16 the Beautiful Land. The promised land (see vv. 41,45; 8:9).

11:17–19 See *WSC* 105.

11:17 He . . . will make an alliance with the king of the South. And he will give him a daughter in marriage. Cleopatra, the daughter of Antiochus III, was given in marriage to the boy king Ptolemy V. **his plans will not succeed or help him.** Cleopatra aligned herself with the Egyptians rather than with her father. She sought Roman help against the attempt of Antiochus III to take coastal cities in Asia Minor controlled by the Egyptians.

11:18 a commander will put an end to his insolence. The Roman general Lucius Cornelius Scipio defeated Antiochus III in several battles and forced him to cede Asia Minor to Roman control (the Peace of Apamea; 188 B.C.). At this time the second son of Antiochus III, later to be known as Antiochus IV Epiphanes, was taken hostage to Rome.

11:20 His successor. Seleucus IV Philopator (187–175 B.C.), the elder son of Antiochus III. **a tax collector.** Heliodorus (see 2 Maccabees 3:7–40 [an Apocryphal book]).

■ **11:21—12:3** *The Rule of Antiochus IV Epiphanes.* Daniel turned to the most important character in the history outlined thus far: the great Antiochus IV, who persecuted the Jews and defiled the temple. The prophet concentrated on his accession and character (11:21–24), his career (11:25–31), the conditions of God’s people during his reign (11:32–35), a summary of his religious attitudes (11:36–39), his heart’s ambition (11:40–45) and a description of his defeat (12:1–3).

11:21 a contemptible person . . . not . . . given the honor of royalty. This is the infamous Antiochus IV Epiphanes (175–164 B.C.), brother of Seleucus IV but not his legitimate successor, since Seleucus IV had a son, Demetrius Soter, also known as Demetrius I. See verses 23–24 and notes on 8:9–14.

11:22 a prince of the covenant will be destroyed. Perhaps this is a reference to the assassination of the high priest Onias III by the supporters of Antiochus IV (175–163 B.C.) in Jerusalem in 171 B.C. (cf. 2 Maccabees 4:32–43 [an Apocryphal book]).

11:25 the king of the South. Ptolemy VI Philometor (181–146 B.C.), son of Ptolemy V and Cleopatra and nephew of Antiochus (see note on v. 17). **he will not be able to stand.** Antiochus IV defeated Ptolemy VI at Pelusium, located on the border of Egypt (cf. 1 Maccabees 1:16–19 [an Apocryphal book]).

11:28 The king of the North will return . . . but his heart will be set against the holy covenant. As a result of intrigues in Jerusalem against his supporters, Antiochus IV plundered the temple on his return from Egypt to Antioch in Syria (cf. 1 Maccabees 1:20–28 [an Apocryphal book]).

11:29 he will invade the South again. Antiochus IV invaded Egypt again in 168 B.C.

11:30 Ships of the western coastlands will oppose him. Roman armies under Gaius Popilius Laenas forced Antiochus IV to re-

11:31 [q]Da 8:11-13; 9:27; Mt 24:15*; Mk 13:14*
11:32 [r]Mic 5:7-9
11:33 [s]Mal 2:7 [t]Mt 24:9; Jn 16:2; Heb 11:32-38
11:34 [u]Mt 7:15; Ro 16:18
11:35 [v]Ps 78:38; Da 12:10; Zec 13:9; Jn 15:2
11:36 [w]Rev 13:5-6 [x]Dt 10:17; Isa 14:13-14; Da 7:25; 8:11-12, 25; 2Th 2:4 [y]Isa 10:25; 26:20

31 "His armed forces will rise up to desecrate the temple fortress and will abolish the
daily sacrifice. Then they will set up the abomination that causes desolation.[q] 32 With flattery he will corrupt those who have violated the covenant, but the people who know their
God will firmly resist[r] him.
33 "Those who are wise will instruct[s] many, though for a time they will fall by the
sword or be burned or captured or plundered.[t] 34 When they fall, they will receive a little help, and many who are not sincere[u] will join them. 35 Some of the wise will stumble,
so that they may be refined,[v] purified and made spotless until the time of the end, for it
will still come at the appointed time.

The King Who Exalts Himself

36 "The king will do as he pleases. He will exalt and magnify himself above every god
and will say unheard-of things[w] against the God of gods.[x] He will be successful until the
time of wrath[y] is completed, for what has been determined must take place. 37 He will
show no regard for the gods of his fathers or for the one desired by women, nor will he
regard any god, but will exalt himself above them all. 38 Instead of them, he will honor a
god of fortresses; a god unknown to his fathers he will honor with gold and silver, with

treat from Egypt. **vent his fury against the holy covenant.** Antiochus determined to exterminate Jewish religion.

11:31 abolish the daily sacrifice . . . set up the abomination that causes desolation. The desecration of the temple in December 168 B.C. by Antiochus IV (cf. 1 Maccabees 1:54,59; 2 Maccabees 6:2 [Apocryphal books]; see notes on 8:11; 9:27; 12:11).

11:32 the people who know their God will firmly resist him. Refers to those who opposed Antiochus IV and remained faithful to the Lord even unto death (1 Maccabees 1:61–63 [an Apocryphal book]).

11:34 they will receive a little help. Possibly this is a reference to Mattathias, an elderly priest, and his five sons (John, Simon, Judas, Eleazar and Jonathan), who waged a guerrilla war against Antiochus IV. Mattathias died in 166 B.C. His sons carried on the struggle and became known as the Maccabees. Victory was achieved under Judas Maccabeus in December 165 B.C., when the temple was cleansed and the daily sacrifices restored (cf. 1 Maccabees 4:36–39 [an Apocryphal book]).

11:35 the time of the end . . . the appointed time. See note on 8:17.

11:36—12:3 At his proudest moment this king will be destroyed right at Mount Zion in the heart of the Holy Land (vv. 44–45). His defeat in 12:1–3 is described in terms of the absolute end of history. Because these prophesies have not found a historical fulfillment, it is difficult to discern how literal or metaphorical they are, and our interpretation must be guarded. Certain details in 11:36—12:3 cannot be easily harmonized with the time of Antiochus IV. For this reason many evangelical interpreters understand these verses to be descriptive of the antichrist who will persecute God's people just prior to the second advent of Christ (cf. 12:1–3). Yet this understanding requires the assumption of an extended time interval between the events depicted in 11:21–35 and those in 11:36—12:3, which the text does not communicate. It is possible that these prophesied events were averted, altered or delayed (see "Introduction to the Prophetic Books").

11:36–39 This king "will do as he pleases . . . [and] magnify himself above every god" (v. 36). He will "show no regard for the gods of his fathers" (v. 37) but will "greatly honor those who acknowledge him" (v. 39).

11:36 until the time of wrath is completed. Just as in 8:17 and 11:35, the time of persecution is subject to God's control.

Ptolemies and Seleucids

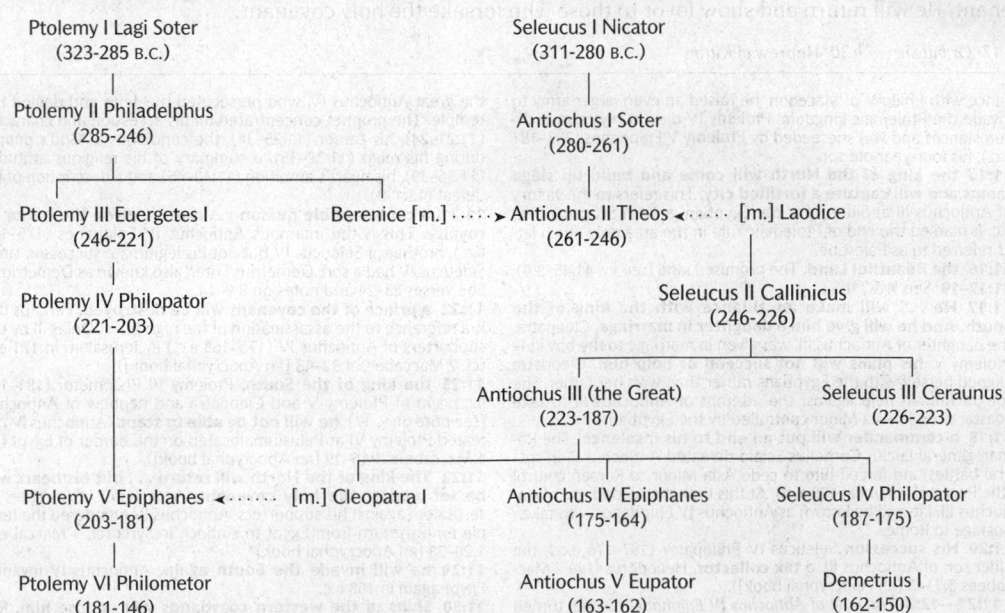

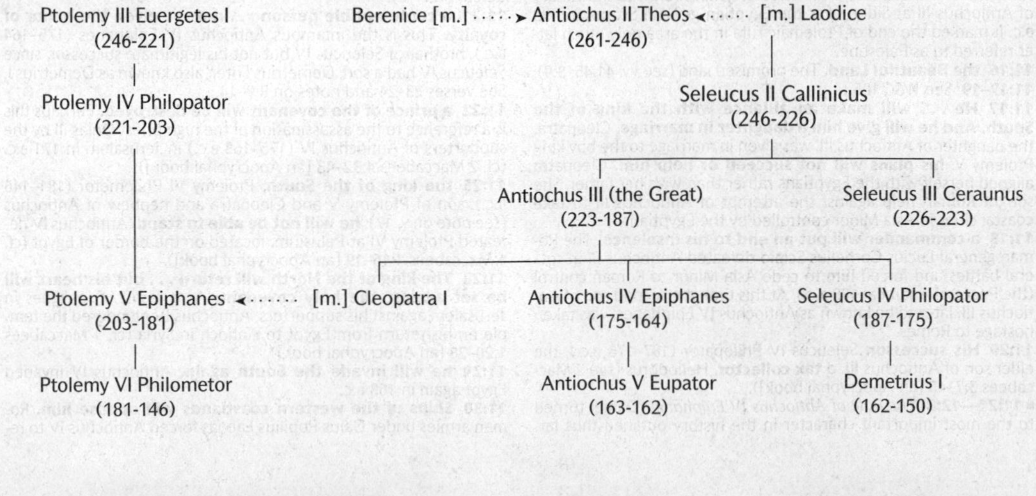

precious stones and costly gifts. 39 He will attack the mightiest fortresses with the help
of a foreign god and will greatly honor those who acknowledge him. He will make them
rulers over many people and will distribute the land at a price.[a]
40 "At the time of the end the king of the South[z] will engage him in battle, and the king
of the North will storm[a] out against him with chariots and cavalry and a great fleet of
ships. He will invade many countries and sweep through them like a flood.[b] 41 He will also
invade the Beautiful Land. Many countries will fall, but Edom,[c] Moab[d] and the leaders
of Ammon will be delivered from his hand. 42 He will extend his power over many countries; Egypt will not escape. 43 He will gain control of the treasures of gold and silver and
all the riches of Egypt,[e] with the Libyans[f] and Nubians in submission. 44 But reports from
the east and the north will alarm him, and he will set out in a great rage to destroy and
annihilate many. 45 He will pitch his royal tents between the seas at[b] the beautiful holy
mountain. Yet he will come to his end, and no one will help him.

The End Times

12 "At that time Michael,[g] the great prince who protects your people, will arise.
There will be a time of distress[h] such as has not happened from the beginning
of nations until then. But at that time your people—everyone whose name is found written in the book[i]—will be delivered.[j] 2 Multitudes who sleep in the dust of the earth will
awake: some to everlasting life, others to shame and everlasting contempt.[k] 3 Those who
are wise[c][l] will shine[m] like the brightness of the heavens, and those who lead many to
righteousness, like the stars for ever and ever.[n] 4 But you, Daniel, close up and seal[o] the

a 39 Or *land for a reward* b 45 Or *the sea and* c 3 Or *who impart wisdom*

11:40 [z]Isa 21:1 [a]Isa 5:28 [b]Eze 38:4
11:41 [c]Isa 11:14 [d]Jer 48:47
11:43 [e]Eze 30:4 [f]2Ch 12:3; Na 3:9
12:1 [g]Da 10:13 [h]Da 9:12; Mt 24:21; Mk 13:19; Rev 16:18 [i]Ex 32:32; Ps 56:8 [j]Jer 30:7
12:2 [k]Isa 26:19; Mt 25:46; Jn 5:28-29
12:3 [l]Da 11:33 [m]Mt 13:43; Jn 5:35 [n]1Co 15:42
12:4 [o]Isa 8:16

11:40 At the time of the end. See note on 0:17.
11:41 Beautiful Land. Canaan (see vv. 16,45; 8:9).
11:45 Yet he will come to his end, and no one will help him. See Joel 3 (see also Zec 14:1–4; 2Th 2:8; Rev 16:13–16; 19:11–21).
12:1 At that time. Michael, the angelic protector of Israel, will not permit God's people to be persecuted forever. He will judge those who oppress his people. **Michael, the great prince who protects your people.** See note on 10:13. **a time of distress.** See Matthew 24:21 and Mark 13:19, where Jesus drew upon these prophecies about Antiochus IV to describe the time of the Roman siege against Jerusalem in A.D. 70. **your people . . . will be delivered.** This deliverance is not necessarily from martyrdom (v. 2) but from the power of Satan (cf. Mt 6:13; 2Ti 4:18). As such the verse assures God's people that he will deliver them from Satan's temptation to apostatize during the time of distress.
12:2 will awake . . . to everlasting life . . . and everlasting contempt. This is a prediction of the bodily resurrection of the godly and ungodly prior to a final judgment (Mt 25:46; Jn 5:28–29).
■ 12:4–13 *A Final Message to Daniel.* The book concludes by setting out a future course of events and by promising Daniel rest in the eternal state.
12:4 seal the words of the scroll. The act of sealing was under-

Soon after the death of Alexander the Great in 323 B.C., his generals divided his empire into four parts, two of which—Egypt and Syria—were under the rule of the Ptolemies and Seleucids respectively. The Holy Land was controlled from Egypt by the Ptolemaic dynasty from 323 to 198, and was subsequently governed by the Seleucids of Syria from 198 to 142.

The Diadochi, as the successors of Alexander were called, struggled bitterly for power over his domain. At first Ptolemy I seized his own satrapy, Egypt and North Africa, which had splendid resources and natural defense capabilities. Seleucus gained Syria and Mesopotamia, and by 301 Lysimachus held Thrace and Asia Minor while Cassander ruled Macedon. The situation changed again by 277, when only three major Hellenistic kingdoms stabilized in Egypt, in Syria, and in Macedonia under the Antigonids (277-168). Each continued until the eventual triumph of Rome.

Daniel 11 treats the "king of the South" and the "king of the North," describing their conflicts, wars and alliances. Their hostility toward the people of God culminated in the "abomination that causes desolation" (11:31), identified historically with the reign of Antiochus IV Epiphanes (175-164). The Maccabean revolt followed, leading eventually to the founding of the Hasmonean dynasty.

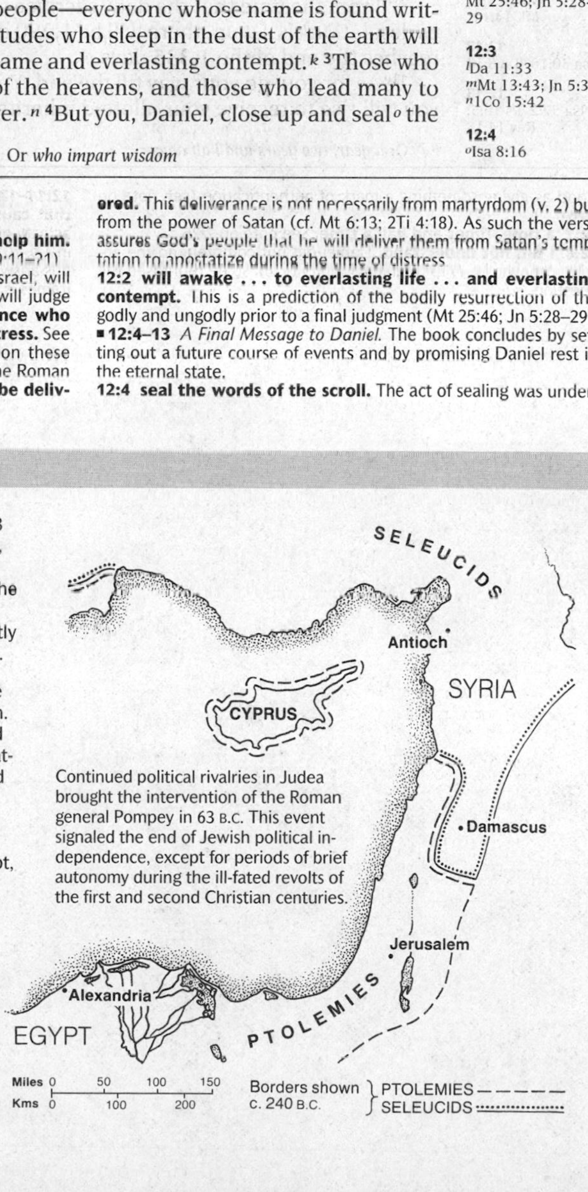

Continued political rivalries in Judea brought the intervention of the Roman general Pompey in 63 B.C. This event signaled the end of Jewish political independence, except for periods of brief autonomy during the ill-fated revolts of the first and second Christian centuries.

words of the scroll until the time of the end.[p] Many will go here and there to increase
knowledge."

[5]Then I, Daniel, looked, and there before me stood two others, one on this bank of
the river and one on the opposite bank.[q] [6]One of them said to the man clothed in linen,[r]
who was above the waters of the river, "How long will it be before these astonishing
things are fulfilled?"[s]

[7]The man clothed in linen, who was above the waters of the river, lifted his right hand
and his left hand toward heaven, and I heard him swear by him who lives forever,[t] saying, "It will be for a time, times and half a time.[a][u] When the power of the holy people[v]
has been finally broken, all these things will be completed.[w]"

[8]I heard, but I did not understand. So I asked, "My lord, what will the outcome of all
this be?"

[9]He replied, "Go your way, Daniel, because the words are closed up and sealed until the time of the end.[x] [10]Many will be purified, made spotless and refined,[y] but the wicked will continue to be wicked.[z] None of the wicked will understand, but those who are
wise will understand.[a]

[11]"From the time that the daily sacrifice is abolished and the abomination that causes desolation[b] is set up, there will be 1,290 days. [12]Blessed is the one who waits[c] for and
reaches the end of the 1,335 days.[d]

[13]"As for you, go your way till the end. You will rest,[e] and then at the end of the days
you will rise to receive your allotted inheritance.[f]"

12:4 [p]ver 9,13; Rev 22:10
12:5 [q]Da 10:4
12:6 [r]Eze 9:2 [s]Da 8:13
12:7 [t]Rev 10:5-6 [u]Da 7:25 [v]Da 8:24 [w]Lk 21:24; Rev 10:7
12:9 [x]ver 4
12:10 [y]Da 11:35 [z]Isa 32:7; Rev 22:11 [a]Hos 14:9
12:11 [b]Da 8:11; 9:27; Mt 24:15*; Mk 13:14*
12:12 [c]Isa 30:18 [d]Da 8:14
12:13 [e]Isa 57:2 [f]Ps 16:5; Rev 14:13

[a] *7* Or *a year, two years and half a year*

---

stood as giving something a mark of authentication (see note on 8:26).

12:7 a time, times and half a time. See note on 7:25.

12:8 I did not understand. Daniel did not comprehend the angel's response (v. 7) to his initial inquiry (v. 6), so he rephrased the question.

12:11–12 the daily sacrifice is abolished and the abomination that causes desolation is set up. See note on 9:27. The similar activity of Antiochus IV prefigured this activity of the Roman Titus in A.D. 70. **1,290 days . . . 1,335 days.** The angel clarified his previous answer (v. 7; see note on v. 6). The significance of these time frames is obscure.

HOSEA

Introduction

Overview

Author: The prophet Hosea

Purpose: To explain that the turmoil of the northern kingdom was God's just judgment leading to exile and to assure God's people that a great restoration would take place after the exile

Date: c. 760–722 B.C.

Key Truths:

- God is a jealous husband and his people are his bride.
- God shows great kindness to his people, but they turn against him.
- God will punish his people for flagrant violations of his covenant.
- God will never utterly forsake his people, but will restore them to the blessings of covenant life with him.

Author

Little is known about the background and training of the author of this book, the prophet Hosea, son of Beeri (1:1). Though not clearly stated in the book, Hosea's familiarity with the geography (4:15; 5:1,8; 6:8,9; 9:15; 10:5; 12:11) and history of the northern kingdom, Israel (5:13; 7:7,11; 8:4,9–14), suggests that he was a native of Israel.

Time and Place of Writing

Hosea provides a record of a prophetic ministry in the northern kingdom between about 760 B.C. and a few years before the fall of Samaria in 722 B.C. Hosea prophesied during the last years of Jeroboam II (793–753 B.C.), the third king of the Jehu dynasty, and saw that dynasty end when Jeroboam's son Zechariah was assassinated in 753 B.C. (2Ki 15:8–12; see 1:4–5). Following Zechariah three more kings of Israel were also assassinated (Shallum [2Ki 15:13–14], Pekahiah [2Ki 15:22–25] and Pekah [2Ki 15:27–30]), and one became a political prisoner (Hoshea; 2Ki 17:1–4).

Hosea also saw Assyria take control of Syria and Israel (2Ki 16:7–9) in its expansion north and west under Tiglath-Pileser III (745–727 B.C.) and his son Shalmaneser V (727–722 B.C.), who forced Hoshea, the last king of the northern kingdom, to become his vassal (2Ki 17:3). After King Hoshea rebelled, Shalmaneser laid siege to Samaria. Shalmaneser's successor, Sargon II, defeated Samaria in 722 B.C. and exiled many Israelites (2Ki 17:5–6).

Hosea's preaching reflected shifting political circumstances in the northern kingdom. In the relative calm under Jeroboam II, Hosea spoke concerning injustice and complacency and warned of impending judgment (e.g., 2:5,8,13). Other passages reveal later turmoil in domestic (e.g., 7:3–7; 13:10–11) and foreign affairs (e.g., 7:8–12; 12:1). For example, the Syro-Ephraimite war of 735–732 B.C. (2Ki 15:27–30; 16:5–9; Isa 7:1–9) was probably behind Hosea's message in 5:8–10 (perhaps even 5:8—6:6).

The text also reflects Samaria's shifting loyalties between Egypt and Assyria (5:13; 7:11; 8:9–10; 9:3; 11:5; 12:1). Hosea's political commentary explained reasons for the final attack by the Assyrians, the arrest of King Hoshea, the siege of Samaria and the end of the northern kingdom in 722 B.C.

Hosea's ethical commentary explained why God would allow his people's destruction at the hand of enemies. Israel was in spiritual and moral decline. Her ancient faith, which Hosea described so beautifully using the analogy of marital love (2:14–23), had been polluted by elements of the Canaanite fertility religion, notably sexual rites that included prostitution and drunken orgies (4:10–13). Canaanite religion worshiped Baal as the giver of rain and fertility. The worship of the Lord and that of Baal had become intermingled (2:5–13). Religious corruption extended even to the religious leaders, who in their greed and hard-heartedness failed to instruct the people in the true faith and tolerated—even sponsored—syncretistic practices (4:4–13; 5:1; 6:9).

Hosea's commentary, whether political or ethical, focused on Israel's breaches of covenant that gave rise to God's judgment. Nevertheless, Hosea balanced this message of doom with the proclamation of God's enduring love for his people and the promise of restoration after a period of exile (e.g., 1:10—2:1; 2:21–23).

Purpose and Distinctives

Hosea's book reports his experiences and words in service of God's purposes for Israel. The prophet explained the reasons for the defeat of the northern kingdom and gave God's people hope in a future restoration.

A number of other themes recur throughout the book. (1) Hosea emphasized God's unique sovereignty (12:9; 13:4) and holiness (11:9), to which adoration is the only proper response (3:5); God tolerates no rival claim. All is under his rule, whether prosperity (2:8), Israel's history (5:14,15) or the nations (10:10). (2) The theme of marital/covenantal infidelity—symbolized in Hosea's relationship with his wife, Gomer, and with his children—dominates the book (e.g., 2:2–5; 3:3; 4:10–19; 5:3–7; 6:10; 8:9; 9:1). (3) Hosea emphasized repentance, calling wayward Israel to turn to the Lord she had forsaken and to reestablish a faithful relationship with him (2:19–20). (4) Another important theme centers around what it means to *know* or *acknowledge* God (e.g., 2:8,20; 4:1,6; 5:4; 6:3,6; 13:4), words Hosea uses as technical terms for covenant intimacy, loyalty and obedience. The book teaches that true knowledge of God involves the kind of intimacy a person experiences in marriage and family situations, evidenced in worship, purity of lifestyle and loyal commitment to the covenant Lord. Hosea also warned that sin could delude people into thinking that they knew and understood God when in fact they were far from him (8:2). (5) The theme of prostitution as an illustration of religious syncretism also pervades the book (2:2–13; 4:10–19; 5:4; 9:1–10). Hosea repeatedly pointed to Israel's sin of wedding the worship of the covenant Lord to Canaanite religion. The impossibility of such union warned the people of God to remain steadfast in a culture that encouraged compromise and acceptance of principles and beliefs incompatible with Biblical doctrine.

Chapters 1–3 describe Hosea's family life—his marriage, divorce and remarriage to Gomer. Attempts at appropriate interpretation of these personal events have long perplexed readers of Hosea. In struggling to reconcile the moral issue of a holy God asking Hosea to marry a prostitute, some interpret the details about Hosea's married life allegorically. Others reason that Gomer became a prostitute only after the birth of their first child. Still others, advocating a modified literal reading, argue that Gomer was not a common prostitute but participated in prostitution related to the Baal religious cult. However, a literal reading, which makes the analogy between Hosea's relationship with his unfaithful wife and the Lord's relationship with Israel most poignant, seems to have been Hosea's intention.

Questions are also asked about Hosea's children. Their names, like that of the child born to Isaiah and the prophetess (Isa 8:1–4), had symbolic significance (cf. Isa 7:3; Eze 23:1–4). The names given to Hosea's children (Jezreel, Lo-Ruhamah and Lo-Ammi; see notes on 1:4,6,9) were purposefully ambiguous, not only to encapsulate Hosea's message about God's increasing displeasure with wayward Israel but also to convey the message of hope, renewal, love and restoration (see notes on 2:21–23).

Another interpretive problem centers on the question of the relationship between chapter 1, a biographical account of Hosea's marriage to Gomer and the subsequent birth of their children, and chapter 3, an autobiographical account of God's instructions to love an unfaithful woman. Though the first two chapters have most often been regarded as a chronologically sequential account of Hosea's marriage to Gomer, some argue that they describe two different women and two different marriages. Others suggest that the chapters are not sequential but parallel. Difficulties in the Hebrew text and in translation options underlie these various views. The debates over various details of interpretation continue, but the fundamental symbolic meaning of the prophet's marriage(s) as a picture of the Lord's relationship with Israel is clear.

Christ in Hosea

Hosea reveals Christ in at least four ways. First, the theme of Israel's impending judgment at the hands of the Assyrians anticipated the judgment that would and will yet come in Christ. Jesus' earthly ministry distinguished the faithful in Israel from the unfaithful. Jesus pronounced judgment on the covenant people who flagrantly violated their relationship with God (Mt 23:13–39). Still today the call of the gospel separates those who will be saved from those who will be judged (2Co 2:16; 1Th 5:5; 1Pe 2:9). When Christ returns the final judgment against all of God's enemies, both under and outside the covenant, will take place (Mt 25; Ac 24:25; Rev 14:7).

Hosea balanced his message of judgment with assurance of restoration after exile. This theme pointed even more directly to Christ. Hosea declared that after an exile, in "the last days" (3:5), God would forgive his people (14:1–3), renew his covenant with them (2:1) and grant them many blessings (14:4–7). The New Testament reveals that just such forgiveness (Mt 26:28; Lk 24:47), covenant renewal (Mk 14:24; Heb 8:1–13) and eternal blessings (Mt 25:46; Jn 10:28; Eph 1:14; 2Ti 2:10) are fulfilled in Christ (Ac 2:17; 2Ti 3:1; Heb 1:2; Jas 5:3; 2Pe 3:3). Paul and Peter both cited Hosea 1:9–10 as having been fulfilled in Christ, through the incorporation of Gentiles, who had been under the curse of exile (Ro 9:25–26; 1Pe 2:10), into the people of God alongside Jews.

Third, Hosea's experience of marriage, divorce and remarriage (chs. 1–3) anticipated Christ by paralleling God's experience with his covenant people. Israel's portrayal as the Lord's bride is the background against which the apostle Paul referred to the church as the bride of Christ (Eph 5:23–32; cf. Rev 19:7). The church stands in the same covenant relationship with God in which Israel stood. The blessings, judgments, privileges and responsibilities of ancient Israel anticipated what was, is and will be realized in Christ.

As a minor theme Hosea included the reestablishment of David's throne in his vision of the restoration after exile (1:10–11; 3:5). This hope was directly Messianic, a prediction that the great son of David would rule over all his people. The New Testament teaches that Jesus fulfilled this hope; he is the King of kings and Lord of lords (1Ti 6:15; Rev 19:16).

Outline

I. Superscription (1:1)	*Hosea's message came from the Lord and was to be heeded.*
II. Hosea's Prophetic Experience (1:2—3:5) A. Hosea's Wife and Children (1:2—2:1) 1. Impending Doom (1:2–9) 2. Restoration (1:10—2:1)	*Hosea's experience of marriage, divorce and remarriage to Gomer symbolized God's relationship with Israel.*

B. Punishment and Reconciliation (2:2–23)
  1. Lawsuit Against Infidelity (2:2–13)
  2. Promise of Reconciliation (2:14–23)
C. Hosea Loves Again (3:1–5)

III. Hosea's Prophetic Message (4:1—14:9)
  A. The Case, Warfare and Mourning (4:1—9:9)
    1. Two Lawsuits Against Israel (4:1—5:7)
      a. Lawsuit Against the Priests (4:1–19)
      b. Lawsuit Against Priests, the People and the Leaders (5:1–7)
    2. Impending Defeat in War (5:8—8:14)
      a. First Summons to Defeat in War (5:8–15)
      b. Hypocritical Repentance Resulting in Defeat (6:1—7:2)
      c. Political Corruption Resulting in Defeat (7:3–16)
      d. Second Summons to Defeat in War (8:1–14)
    3. Mourning Over Defeat (9:1–9)
  B. Historical Reflections and Israel's Future (9:10—13:16)
    1. Grapes and Figs (9:10–17)
    2. Spreading Vine (10:1–10)
    3. Trained Heifer (10:11–15)
    4. Growing Child (11:1—13:16)
  C. Closing Call for Repentance (14:1–9)

Israel's violations of God's covenant would lead to defeat, exile and severe mourning. Israel turned away from God despite his many wondrous blessings. This rebellion would result in severe judgment, but upon repentance great blessings would return after exile. Repentance was necessary for Israel to receive the blessings of God.

1 The word of the LORD that came to Hosea son of Beeri during the reigns of Uzziah,
Jotham, Ahaz and Hezekiah, kings of Judah,[a] and during the reign of Jeroboam[b] son
of Jehoash[a] king of Israel:[c]

1:1 [a]Isa 1:1; Mic 1:1 [b]2Ki 13:13 [c]Am 1:1

Hosea's Wife and Children

[2]When the LORD began to speak through Hosea, the LORD said to him, "Go, take to
yourself an adulterous[d] wife and children of unfaithfulness, because the land is guilty
of the vilest adultery[e] in departing from the LORD." [3]So he married Gomer daughter of
Diblaim, and she conceived and bore him a son.

1:2 [d]Jer 3:1; Hos 2:2, 5; 3:1 [e]Dt 31:16; Jer 3:14; Eze 23:3-21; Hos 5:3

[4]Then the LORD said to Hosea, "Call him Jezreel,[f] because I will soon punish the house
of Jehu for the massacre at Jezreel, and I will put an end to the kingdom of Israel. [5]In that
day I will break Israel's bow in the Valley of Jezreel.[g]"

1:4 [f]2Ki 10:1-14; Hos 2:22

1:5 [g]2Ki 15:29

[a] *1* Hebrew *Joash,* a variant of *Jehoash*

■ **1:1** *Superscription.* Hosea introduced his prophecy, specifying himself as God's messenger and indicating the time frame in which God's word came to him.
1:1 word of the LORD. God's message given through Hosea. **Hosea.** Derived from the verb "to save," the name probably means "he [Yahweh] has saved [or delivered]." Whereas four kings of Judah are named—Uzziah (c. 783–742 B.C.), Jotham (c. 742–735 B.C.), Ahaz (c. 735–715 B.C.) and Hezekiah (c. 715–687 B.C.)—the only northern king cited is Jeroboam II (c. 786–746 B.C.). Perhaps the writer thought that the succession of northern kings who reigned between Jeroboam II and the fall of the north in 722 B.C. (four of whom were assassinated) were not worthy of mention. The priority given to Judahite kings may indicate that this book was finally composed in and for the southern kingdom, even though Hosea's ministry was in the north.
■ **1:2—3:5** *Hosea's Prophetic Experience.* Hosea recounted his family experience as an illustration of God's relationship with the northern kingdom, Israel. These chapters divide into three main parts: Hosea's marriage and children (1:2—2:1), God's punishment of and reconciliation with Israel (2:2–23) and the prophet's reconciliation with his wife (3:1–5).
■ **1:2—2:1** *Hosea's Wife and Children.* Hosea recalled the beginnings of his family through which God illustrated his intention to punish adulterous Israel. This material divides into two parts: the depiction of impending divine judgment (1:2–9) and the promise of reversal of the judgment after exile (1:10—2:1).
■ **1:2–9** *Impending Doom.* Hosea married Gomer and named his children symbolically so that Israel might learn of the judgment of Assyrian aggression.
1:2 take to yourself an adulterous wife and children of unfaithfulness. See "Introduction: Purpose and Distinctives." **because the land is guilty of . . . adultery.** Hosea's marriage and children symbolized the religious adultery of the Israelites, who pursued other gods and participated in the fertility religions of Canaan.
1:3 Gomer. There is no symbolic significance in her name, unlike those of her children (see 1:4—2:1). **him.** The lack of reference to Hosea in verses 6 and 8 leaves room for the possibility but does not necessarily imply that he did not father Gomer's next two children.
1:4 Jezreel. Literally, "God sows/plants" or "has sown/planted"; a valley between the mountain ranges of Samaria and Galilee, the site of Gideon's victory over the Midianites (see Jdg 6:33). Also the name of a town at the valley's southern end, where Jehu came to power through violent revolt (1Ki 21:1; 2Ki 9–10). **soon punish the house of Jehu.** Jeroboam II, the only northern king men-

1:6 [h]ver 3 [i]Hos 2:4
1:7 [j]Ps 44:6 [k]Zec 4:6

6 Gomer[h] conceived again and gave birth to a daughter. Then the LORD said to Hosea,
"Call her Lo-Ruhamah,[a] for I will no longer show love to the house of Israel,[i] that I should
at all forgive them. 7 Yet I will show love to the house of Judah; and I will save them—not
by bow,[j] sword or battle, or by horses and horsemen, but by the LORD their God.[k]"
8 After she had weaned Lo-Ruhamah, Gomer had another son. 9 Then the LORD said,
"Call him Lo-Ammi,[b] for you are not my people, and I am not your God.

1:10 [l]Ge 22:17; Jer 33:22 [m]ver 9; Ro 9:26*
1:11 [n]Isa 11:12,13 [o]Jer 23:5-8 [p]Eze 37:15-28
2:1 [q]ver 23

10 "Yet the Israelites will be like the sand on the seashore, which cannot be measured
or counted.[l] In the place where it was said to them, 'You are not my people,' they will
be called 'sons of the living God.'[m] 11 The people of Judah and the people of Israel will be
reunited,[n] and they will appoint one leader[o] and will come up out of the land,[p] for great
will be the day of Jezreel.

2 "Say of your brothers, 'My people,' and of your sisters, 'My loved one.'[q]

Israel Punished and Restored

2:2 [r]ver 5; Isa 50:1; Hos 1:2 [s]Eze 23:45
2:3 [t]Eze 16:4,22 [u]Isa 32:13-14

2 "Rebuke your mother,[r] rebuke her,
for she is not my wife,
and I am not her husband.
Let her remove the adulterous[s] look from her face
and the unfaithfulness from between her breasts.
3 Otherwise I will strip her naked
and make her as bare as on the day she was born;[t]
I will make her like a desert,[u]

[a] 6 *Lo-Ruhamah* means *not loved.* [b] 9 *Lo-Ammi* means *not my people.*

tioned in the superscription, was of the dynasty of Jehu. Jehu had become king in a bloodbath at Jezreel (2Ki 9:14–37; cf. 1Ki 19:16–17); the event was recalled and the place of judgment predicted (v. 5) in the name of Hosea's child. Jehu's dynasty had followed the idolatry of the earlier kings of the northern kingdom and would experience God's judgment in the onslaught of Assyrian forces. See *WCF* 16.7.

1:5 Israel's bow. The war bow, symbol of Israel's military strength (Ge 49:24; 1Sa 2:4; Eze 39:3; cf. Jer 49:35). But that strength was broken by the Assyrian army under Tiglath-Pileser III, who conquered the northern territories of Israel. **the Valley of Jezreel.** Appropriately, the place of judgment in 733 B.C. (2Ki 15:29). Punishment through military defeat was one of the curses for covenant breaking (Dt 28:25,49–57; cf. Lev 26:17).

1:6 Lo-Ruhamah. Literally, "she has received no compassion"; signified the imminent withdrawal of the compassion God had shown Israel in spite of her covenant unfaithfulness. See 2:4 and the restoration of compassion in 2:23; compare also Deuteronomy 31:17 and 32:19–20.

1:7 house of Judah. Judah's short-term future faced Assyrian aggression as well, but with the striking difference that Judah would be spared. **I will save them.** Fulfilled in Jerusalem's miraculous deliverance from the Assyrians in 701 B.C. (2Ki 19:32–37; Isa 37:14, 33–38). See *WCF* 5.3.

1:9 Lo-Ammi. "Not-my-people"; marked the high point of God's judgment as he reversed the ancient covenantal formula (Ex 6:7; Lev 26:12; Dt 26:17–19) and declared that the people were consigned to covenant curses reserved for God's enemies. **I am not your God.** Literally, "I am not your 'I Am.'" Hosea used the name for God revealed to Moses in Exodus 3:14.

■ **1:10—2:1** *Restoration.* As often occurs in this book, the negative word of judgment is balanced by a word of hope. The severe oracles of judgment, symbolized in the names of the three children, would one day be reversed.

1:10 sand on the seashore. An allusion to the patriarchal promise of innumerable descendants (Ge 22:17; 32:12; cf. Ge 13:16; 15:5; 17:1; 26:24; 28:14). **You are not my people.** In contrast with verse 9 Hosea stated that Israel as a whole would one day be God's covenant people once again and that the Israelites would be heirs of God's blessings. That restoration of God's people was not only promised but stood as an ideal toward which they would strive until the promise was fulfilled. The reversal began in a small measure when remnants of Israel joined with Judah during Hezekiah's reforms (2Ch 30:11,18), as well as after the exile under Zerubbabel's leadership (1Ch 9:3; Ezr 8:35). Both restorations were short-lived because the people returned to their sinful ways. The New Testament teaches that this promise of restoration was, is and will be fulfilled in Christ. The church, composed of both Jews and Gentiles, constitutes the restored people (Ro 9:24–26; 1Pe 2:10; Rev 7:9; 21:3). **sons of the living God.** A unique expression depicting the intimate (and legitimate) relationship that God—the Giver of life—desired with Israel, as opposed to the lifeless (and illegitimate) relationship Israel had with Baal. In Isaiah 40:18–20, 41:5–10, 44:9–20 and 46:5–11, "dead" idols were contrasted with the living God. See "Introduction: Time and Place of Writing." The expression echoed Deuteronomy 14:1, but the idea that believers are sons of God would be emphasized much more in the New Testament (cf. Mt 5:9; Ro 8:14,19; Gal 3:26; Heb 2:11; 12:7).

1:11 The people . . . will be reunited. See note on verse 10. **one leader.** A prediction of complete reconciliation between both kingdoms and the Lord, under Christ, the son of David (Mt 1:23; 2:6,15). **great will be the day of Jezreel.** The prophet played with the meaning of Jezreel ("God sows/plants" or "has sown/planted"), the name of his first child, to turn it into a positive image. See notes on 1:4 and 2:21–23.

2:1 brothers . . . sisters. The hostile siblings, Israel and Judah, would be reconciled and the horrible indictments in the names Lo-Ruhamah and Lo-Ammi reversed. See NIV text notes on these names in verses 6 and 9.

■ **2:2–23** *Punishment and Reconciliation.* Hosea prophesied (in terms of his marital experience) concerning God's rejection of Israel and his purpose to punish and bring her back to himself. These verses divide into his declaration of judgment (vv. 2–13) and the announcement of reconciliation (vv. 14–23).

■ **2:2–13** *Lawsuit Against Infidelity.* In the court of heaven God announced his rejection of Israel for her continual, flagrant infidelities.

2:2–4 See *WLC* 110.

2:2 Rebuke. Literally, "make an accusation." This is legal language often used by the prophets to introduce a lawsuit that God prosecuted against his people. In the case that God brought against Israel the children were called to accuse their mother. **your mother.** In the previous chapter both the mother (Gomer) and the children (Jezreel, Lo-Ruhamah and Lo-Ammi) represented the northern kingdom. Gomer was the source of the "children of unfaithfulness" (1:2). She may more precisely have represented the unfaithful generations of Israel who brought God's wrath, and the children represented the Israelites living in the aftermath of their infidelities. Yet it is likely that Hosea did not sharply distinguish between these as he gave his oracles. **not my wife . . . not her husband.** Though the relationship was broken by unfaithfulness, reconciliation—not divorce—was the goal of God's repudiation (see notes on vv. 14–23).

2:3 strip . . . bare. If she did not repent, the unfaithful wife (Gomer/Israel) would be publicly exposed (v. 10) and left destitute—traditional punishments for adultery (Eze 16:37–39; Rev 17:16) for which the death penalty (Dt 22:22; cf. Eze 16:39–40; Na 3:5–7) was the maximum sentence.

turn her into a parched land,
and slay her with thirst.
4 I will not show my love to her children,[v]
because they are the children of adultery.
5 Their mother has been unfaithful
and has conceived them in disgrace.
She said, 'I will go after my lovers,[w]
who give me my food and my water,
my wool and my linen, my oil and my drink.'[x]
6 Therefore I will block her path with thornbushes;
I will wall her in so that she cannot find her way.[y]
7 She will chase after her lovers but not catch them;
she will look for them but not find them.[z]
Then she will say,
'I will go back to my husband as at first,[a]
for then I was better off[b] than now.'
8 She has not acknowledged[c] that I was the one
who gave her the grain, the new wine and oil,
who lavished on her the silver and gold—
which they used for Baal.[d]

9 "Therefore I will take away my grain[e] when it ripens,
and my new wine[f] when it is ready.
I will take back my wool and my linen,
intended to cover her nakedness.
10 So now I will expose her lewdness
before the eyes of her lovers;
no one will take her out of my hands.[g]
11 I will stop[h] all her celebrations:
her yearly festivals, her New Moons,
her Sabbath days—all her appointed feasts.[i]
12 I will ruin her vines[j] and her fig trees,
which she said were her pay from her lovers;
I will make them a thicket,[k]
and wild animals will devour them.[l]
13 I will punish her for the days
she burned incense to the Baals;[m]
she decked herself with rings and jewelry,[n]
and went after her lovers,[o]
but me she forgot,[p]"
declares the LORD.

14 "Therefore I am now going to allure her;

2:4 [v]Eze 8:18
2:5 [w]Jer 3:6 [x]Jer 44:17-18
2:6 [y]Job 3:23; 19:8; La 3:9
2:7 [z]Hos 5:13 [a]Jer 2:2; 3:1 [b]Eze 16:8
2:8 [c]Isa 1:3 [d]Eze 16:15-19; Hos 8:4
2:9 [e]Hos 8:7 [f]Hos 9:2
2:10 [g]Eze 16:37
2:11 [h]Jer 7:34 [i]Isa 1:14; Jer 16:9; Hos 3:4; Am 8:10
2:12 [j]Isa 7:23; Jer 8:13 [k]Isa 5:6 [l]Hos 13:8
2:13 [m]Hos 11:2 [n]Eze 16:17 [o]Hos 4:13 [p]Hos 4:6; 8:14; 13:6

2:4 children of adultery. God's love or compassion (1:6) would also be withdrawn from the children who, like their mother, were guilty of promiscuous behavior.
2:5 mother . . . unfaithful. The unfaithful mother (Israel) looked to Canaanite fertility religion and not to the Lord (vv. 8–9) to provide the staples of life. See "Introduction: Time and Place of Writing" and "Purpose and Distinctives."
2:6–7 See *WLC* 76.
2:6 Therefore. God announced his sentence against the unfaithful nation. **thornbushes.** Placing obstacles in her way would hinder and frustrate the wayward activities of the unfaithful wife (Gomer/Israel).
2:7 chase . . . look for them. Hosea stressed the woman's initiative, which represented the behavior of all Israel. **her lovers.** That is, the Baals and the participants in Baal fertility rituals. **I will go back.** The punishment would lead to repentance, which had always been the goal of covenant judgments (cf. Lev 26).
2:8 not acknowledged. The charge of ingratitude is added to infidelity. **grain . . . wine . . . silver and gold.** The Lord's agricultural and commercial gifts (Dt 7:13; 11:14; 12:17; 28:1–12,51) were credited to Baal, who was regarded as the god of the storm and the provider of rain and fertility.
2:9–13 Therefore I will take away. God announced more sentences against the nation. Though not punished with death (Dt 21:21–22; cf. Eze 16:37–40), the unfaithful and forgetful wife would be severely chastised through a series of dramatic reversals in which God's gifts would be withdrawn through failed harvests (vv. 9,12), exposure (v. 10) and the cessation of festivals (v. 11).
2:9 take away. The Hebrew term refers to a vicious or harsh action.
2:11 appointed feasts. The festivals intermingled the worship of the Lord and of Baal. See "Introduction: Time and Place of Writing."
2:12 vines . . . fig trees. See Micah 4:4 and its note. **pay from her lovers.** The Israelites credited the fertility rituals for their prosperity. The prostitute's dues—gifts from the Lord (v. 8)—would be transformed into a wilderness or consumed.
2:13 lovers. In verses 7, 10 and 12 the "lovers" were probably the Baals and the prostitutes associated with the temples of the Baals.
■ **2:14–23** *Promise of Reconciliation.* As was his habit Hosea added a word of hope to the judgments he had just announced. He spoke of restoration after exile as a courtship that would reestablish God's relationship with Israel.
2:14 allure. Even "seduce" (cf. Ex 22:16). **into the desert.** As God had brought Israel through the desert in the first exodus, he promised to guide her through another exodus from the places of captivity to the promised land (v. 16; cf. Jer 2:2). **speak tenderly to her.** Literally, "speak to the heart," an idiom used elsewhere for wooing (Ge 34:3), speaking kindly (Ru 2:13) and coaxing (Jdg 19:3).

I will lead her into the desert
and speak tenderly to her.
15 There I will give her back her vineyards,
and will make the Valley of Achor[a][q] a door of hope.
There she will sing[b][r] as in the days of her youth,[s]
as in the day she came up out of Egypt.[t]

16 "In that day," declares the LORD,
"you will call me 'my husband';
you will no longer call me 'my master.[c]'
17 I will remove the names of the Baals from her lips;[u]
no longer will their names be invoked.[v]
18 In that day I will make a covenant for them
with the beasts of the field and the birds of the air
and the creatures that move along the ground.[w]
Bow and sword and battle
I will abolish[x] from the land,
so that all may lie down in safety.[y]
19 I will betroth[z] you to me forever;
I will betroth you in[d] righteousness and justice,[a]
in[e] love and compassion.
20 I will betroth you in faithfulness,
and you will acknowledge[b] the LORD.

21 "In that day I will respond,"
declares the LORD—
"I will respond[c] to the skies,
and they will respond to the earth;
22 and the earth will respond to the grain,
the new wine and oil,[d]
and they will respond to Jezreel.[f]
23 I will plant[e] her for myself in the land;
I will show my love to the one I called 'Not my loved one.[g][f]'
I will say to those called 'Not my people,[h]' 'You are my people';[g]
and they will say, 'You are my God.[h]' "

2:15 [q]Jos 7:24,26 [r]Ex 15:1-18 [s]Jer 2:2 [t]Hos 12:9
2:17 [u]Ex 23:13; Ps 16:4 [v]Jos 23:7
2:18 [w]Job 5:22 [x]Isa 2:4 [y]Jer 23:6; Eze 34:25
2:19 [z]Isa 62:4 [a]Isa 1:27
2:20 [b]Jer 31:34; Hos 6:6; 13:4
2:21 [c]Isa 55:10; Zec 8:12
2:22 [d]Jer 31:12; Joel 2:19
2:23 [e]Jer 31:27 [f]Hos 1:6 [g]Hos 1:10 [h]Ro 9:25*; 1Pe 2:10

[a] *15* *Achor* means *trouble.* [b] *15* Or *respond* [c] *16* Hebrew *baal* [d] *19* Or *with*; also in verse 20 [e] *19* Or *with* [f] *22* *Jezreel* means *God plants.* [g] *23* Hebrew *Lo-Ruhamah* [h] *23* Hebrew *Lo-Ammi*

2:15 Valley of Achor. "Trouble Valley." The precise location is disputed, but it likely was the plain between the eastern wilderness and the fertile land west of the Jordan. **door of hope.** The valley associated with Achan's sin (Jos 7:24–26) was to be transformed. The failures of the first exodus-conquest would not be repeated. **sing.** Literally, "answer" or "respond." **as in the day.** Israel's exodus experience was cast in a positive light. As then, Israel would respond in covenant faithfulness to the Lord (Lev 26:45).

2:16 that day. That is, the day of the Lord, when he would mete out judgment on his enemies and bless his faithful people. See note on Amos 5:18. **my husband.** The Hebrew word for "man" (*'ish*) also means "husband." **my master.** The Hebrew word (*ba'al*) can also signify "husband," "lord" and the god "Baal." After the judgment of exile Israel's relationship with the Lord would outshine the one established at the first exodus. It would be as intimate as marriage (Eph 5:25–32)—in contrast to a relationship with a servant—and would not be stained with associations with Baal worship (v. 17). As early as Moses the expectation had been that God's blessings after the exile would be greater than those before it (Dt 30:5,9). This promise is the background to the New Testament teaching that blessings and judgments in Christ are greater than Old Testament blessings and judgments (Heb 3:1–19).

2:18 covenant. Jeremiah, Hosea's "posthumous disciple," explained the covenant as entailing a new heart (Jer 31:31–34). **with the beasts.** The security and peace of the future kingdom are depicted as free from the threat of wild animals (Isa 11:6–9) and invasions (Ps 46:9; Isa 9:5; Mic 4:3). Wild animals were a particular threat after invading armies had decimated a land.

2:19–20 betroth. The final step in courtship, betrothal involved paying the bride-price to the bride's father (cf. 2Sa 3:14). The qualities of righteousness, justice, love, compassion and faithfulness would constitute this bride-price and characterize the marriage relationship. **righteousness.** The word can involve salvation and deliverance, vindication and justice, and fairness and equity in covenanted relationships (10:12; Am 5:7; 6:12). **justice.** Can signify the legal decisions and relationships by which equity and fairness are established and restored (5:11; 6:5; 10:4; Am 5:7,15,24; 6:12; Mic 6:8). **love.** Denotes binding affection, devotion, loyalty, faithfulness and kindness (4:1; 6:4,6; 10:12; 12:6; Ge 20:13; Ex 34:6–7; Jos 2:12; 1Sa 15:6; 2Sa 15:20; Ps 36:7; Jer 2:2). **compassion.** Can mean mercy, heartfelt sensitivity and love (1:6; Ge 43:14; Dt 13:17; 2Sa 24:14).

2:20 faithfulness. Dependability, truthfulness, steadfastness, fidelity and responsibility in relationships. See 4:1, Psalms 88:11, 89:1–2, 5, 8 and 24, 92:2 and 98:3; also translated "steady" (Ex 17:12) and "truth" (Ps 96:13). Christ by his active obedience provided these virtues of the covenant for his people. He writes his nature on the hearts of his church by the Holy Spirit (2Co 3:3). **acknowledge.** Literally, "know"; to recognize covenant bonds between God and his people.

2:21–22 respond. The Lord would respond graciously to Israel, as she learned again to respond/sing to him (v. 15). **respond to the skies.** The Lord would show that he and not Baal commanded the cycles of nature whereby the land would become fertile and produce the crops that had been withheld (v. 9). See "Introduction: Time and Place of Writing." **respond to Jezreel.** *Jezreel* means "God plants"—the renewed land would be particularly fertile (see notes on 1:4–5). See *WCF* 5.3.

2:23 I will . . . they will. The promised restoration would come to a climax as Jezreel's shameful past (1:4–5; cf. 2:22) would be redeemed, Lo-Ruhamah (1:6) would be shown God's love and Lo-Ammi (1:9) would become God's people. **You are my God.** See "Introduction: Christ in Hosea" regarding the fulfillment of these promises.

Hosea's Reconciliation With His Wife

3 The LORD said to me, "Go, show your love to your wife again, though she is loved
by another and is an adulteress.[i] Love her as the LORD loves the Israelites, though
they turn to other gods and love the sacred raisin cakes.[j]"
2So I bought her for fifteen shekels[a] of silver and about a homer and a lethek[b] of barley. 3Then I told her, "You are to live with[c] me many days; you must not be a prostitute
or be intimate with any man, and I will live with[c] you."
4For the Israelites will live many days without king or prince,[k] without sacrifice[l] or
sacred stones, without ephod or idol.[m] 5Afterward the Israelites will return and seek the
LORD their God and David their king.[n] They will come trembling to the LORD and to his
blessings in the last days.[o]

3:1 [i]Hos 1:2 [j]2Sa 6:19
3:4 [k]Hos 13:11 [l]Da 11:31; Hos 2:11 [m]Jdg 17:5-6; Zec 10:2
3:5 [n]Eze 34:23-24 [o]Jer 50:4-5

The Charge Against Israel

4 Hear the word of the LORD, you Israelites,
because the LORD has a charge to bring
against you who live in the land:
"There is no faithfulness, no love,
no acknowledgment[p] of God in the land.
2 There is only cursing,[d] lying[q] and murder,[r]
stealing[s] and adultery;
they break all bounds,
and bloodshed follows bloodshed.
3 Because of this the land mourns,[e t]
and all who live in it waste away;[u]
the beasts of the field and the birds of the air
and the fish of the sea are dying.[v]

4:1 [p]Jer 7:28
4:2 [q]Hos 7:3; 10:4 [r]Hos 6:9 [s]Hos 7:1
4:3 [t]Jer 4:28 [u]Isa 33:9 [v]Jer 4:25; Zep 1:3

[a] *2* That is, about 6 ounces (about 170 grams) [b] *2* That is, probably about 10 bushels (about 330 liters) [c] *3* Or *wait for* [d] *2* That is, to pronounce a curse upon [e] *3* Or *dries up*

■ **3:1–5** *Hosea Loves Again.* Hosea recounts in autobiographical form his reconciliation with his wife, Gomer, after their divorce. Their reconciliation foreshadowed God's reconciliation with Israel after the exile.

3:1 Go, show your love . . . , though she is loved by another and is an adulteress. God's astounding request, patterned after his loyal, protective and bountiful love for unfaithful (and undeserving) Israel. **sacred raisin cakes.** Delicacies made from crushed dried grapes and associated with special occasions (2Sa 6:19); may have been used in Baal worship as an aphrodisiac (SS 2:5). See "Introduction: Time and Place of Writing."

3:2 shekels. The payment, roughly half in silver and half in produce, amounted to about 30 shekels and approximated the price for a slave; see Exodus 21:32. The New Testament made clear the final price of redemption for the people of God: Christ's blood (1Pe 1:18).

3:4 live . . . without. Israel's basic political and religious institutions—both legitimate (sacrifice and ephod; Ex 28:31) and illegitimate (sacred stones or pillars [Dt 16:21–22] and idols or household gods [Zec 10:2])—would be removed as punishment. **many days.** The prophetic action of verse 3 symbolized the waiting period before the great restoration. The New Testament taught that this long-awaited restoration began with the first coming of Christ and will be completed at his return (Ro 8:18–27). **without king or prince . . . sacrifice.** Deprivation (i.e., exile) would lead to restoration. The restoration could not take place without a son of David on the throne (see note on Am 9:11). Jesus fulfilled that requirement.

3:5 return and seek. Although the returnees in the days of Zerubbabel and later under the leadership of Ezra and Nehemiah did exhibit a measure of repentance, they did not do so with consistency. The restoration of scattered Israelites began to take place in earnest at Pentecost (Ac 2:38–46), continues through the preaching of the gospel throughout the world (Ro 1:16) and will be completed in the inclusion of repentant Jews in the new heavens and the new earth (Rev 7:9; cf. Ro 9:1–29). **their God and David their king.** A direct Messianic expectation. Hosea expressed the certainty that service to God in the restoration would include service to the great son of David. The New Testament indicates that Jesus is this son of David. Repentance unto life, therefore, must include an acknowledgment of Jesus as Savior and Lord. **trembling.** Knowing that God's unique sovereignty would fill the true Israel of God with reverential awe (Gal 6:15). **in the last days.** Terminology derived from Moses' outline of Israel's future in Deuteronomy 4:30. He identified "the last days" with the days of return from exile. The prophets used the term in the same way to point to the time of restoration from exile that will include a return to the land, renewed devotion, restoration of the Davidic kingship and enormous blessings (see, e.g., Isa 2:2) The New Testament applied this terminology to Christ's kingdom between his first coming and his return (Ac 2:17; 2Ti 3:1; Heb 1:2; Jas 5:3; 2Pe 3:3).

■ **4:1—14:9** *Hosea's Prophetic Message.* Hosea explicitly declared the message illustrated in his prophetic experience (1:2—3:5). He delineated the transgressions for which God would punish the northern kingdom but assured the people that God would eventually grant them repentance and reconciliation. These chapters divide into three sections: the case, the upcoming destruction of war and the resultant mourning (4:1—9:9), a series of oracles built on metaphorical historical reflections (9:10—13:16) and a final call to repentance (14:1–9).

■ **4:1—9:9** *The Case, Warfare and Mourning.* A number of Hosea's oracles are gathered into a large-scale pattern that begins with a focus on lawsuits against Israel (4:1—5:7) and moves to the destruction in warfare to come (5:8—8:14) and the mourning appropriate for that destruction (9:1–9).

■ **4:1—5:7** *Two Lawsuits Against Israel.* In two lawsuits (4:1–19; 5:1–7), both of which begin with a summons to court—"hear" (4:1; 5:1)—Hosea built a case against Israel, demonstrating that the nation deserved God's judgment.

■ **4:1–19** *Lawsuit Against the Priests.* Hosea reported the proceedings of the heavenly court (cf. 2:2–13), focusing especially on the false priests who had perverted worship and justice in the northern kingdom.

4:1–3 The Lord, the prosecutor, set out a case against Israel in verses 1–2 and then announced judgment in verse 3.

4:1 Hear. The defendants were summoned to hear the charges against them (see 5:1). **charge.** The technical, legal term for a lawsuit. Compare 2:2, where it is translated "rebuke." **faithfulness . . . love . . . acknowledgment.** See note on these terms at 2:19–20. See *WLC* 105.

4:2 cursing, lying and murder, stealing and adultery. This catalogue of sins resulting from the refusal to acknowledge God (v. 1) includes the abuse of words; cursing (Jdg 17:2; 1Sa 14:24) and lying (7:3; cf. Ex 23:1; Dt 25:13–16); theft (Ex 20:15); murder (Ex 20:13); and adultery (Ex 20:14).

4:3 the land mourns. Or "the land will mourn." God's judgment often included curses that impacted the environment, such as fire, swarms of locusts and the withholding of rain (Nu 11:1–3; 1Ki 8:35; 2Ch 7:13). The grief of the inanimate "land" contrasts with the attitude of its inhabitants who refused to mourn their demise.

4 “But let no man bring a charge,
let no man accuse another,
for your people are like those
who bring charges against a priest.[w]
5 You stumble[x] day and night,
and the prophets stumble with you.
So I will destroy your mother[y]—
6 my people are destroyed from lack of knowledge.[z]

“Because you have rejected knowledge,
I also reject you as my priests;
because you have ignored the law[a] of your God,
I also will ignore your children.
7 The more the priests increased,
the more they sinned against me;
they exchanged[a] their[b] Glory[b] for something disgraceful.[c]
8 They feed on the sins of my people
and relish their wickedness.[d]
9 And it will be: Like people, like priests.[e]
I will punish both of them for their ways
and repay them for their deeds.[f]

10 “They will eat but not have enough;[g]
they will engage in prostitution but not increase,
because they have deserted[h] the LORD
to give themselves 11 to prostitution,[i]
to old wine and new,
which take away the understanding[j] 12 of my people.
They consult a wooden idol[k]
and are answered by a stick of wood.[l]
A spirit of prostitution leads them astray;[m]
they are unfaithful to their God.
13 They sacrifice on the mountaintops
and burn offerings on the hills,
under oak,[n] poplar and terebinth,
where the shade is pleasant.[o]
Therefore your daughters turn to prostitution[p]
and your daughters-in-law to adultery.[q]

14 “I will not punish your daughters
when they turn to prostitution,

4:4 [w]Dt 17:12; Eze 3:26
4:5 [x]Eze 14:7 [y]Hos 2:2
4:6 [z]Hos 2:13; Mal 2:7-8 [a]Hos 8:1,12
4:7 [b]Hab 2:16 [c]Hos 10:1,6; 13:6
4:8 [d]Isa 56:11; Mic 3:11
4:9 [e]Isa 24:2 [f]Jer 5:31; Hos 8:13; 9:9,15
4:10 [g]Lev 26:26; Mic 6:14 [h]Hos 7:14; 9:17
4:11 [i]Hos 5:4 [j]Pr 20:1
4:12 [k]Jer 2:27 [l]Hab 2:19 [m]Isa 44:20
4:13 [n]Isa 1:29 [o]Jer 3:6; Hos 11:2 [p]Jer 2:20; Am 7:17 [q]Hos 2:13

[a] 7 Syriac and an ancient Hebrew scribal tradition; Masoretic Text *I will exchange* [b] 7 Masoretic Text; an ancient Hebrew scribal tradition *my*

4:4–9 let no man bring a charge. The priests falsely accused the people of causing God’s judgment, but God charged the priests with failing in their duty to instruct God’s people (Dt 31:9–13; 33:10; 2Ch 17:8–9; Ezr 7:6,10; Jer 18:18). They carried the responsibility for the people’s lack of knowledge of God and consequently faced judgment.
4:5 stumble day and night. Failures of the leaders led to one disaster after another. **your mother.** That is, the nation of Israel (2:2,5; Isa 50:1).
4:6 people are destroyed from lack of knowledge. Israel the nation would fall under harsh judgment through the people’s lack of covenant knowledge (4:8,12; 6:11; 11:7). Knowledge of God was inseparable from the law of God. See “Introduction: Purpose and Distinctives.” The priests would be punished for failing in their responsibility to teach the law (Dt 31:9–13; 33:10; 2Ch 17:8–9; Ezr 7:6,10; Jer 18:18), and future generations would be chastened for ignoring or forgetting it. See *WLC* 105,158.
4:7 The more the priests increased. The priests increased in numbers in the northern kingdom as syncretism flourished (see 2Ch 11:15). God insisted that this increase caused the people to sin all the more. The priests were in fact the source of the problem (cf. v. 6). **their Glory.** That is, the Lord (Isa 60:19; Jer 2:11). **something disgraceful.** That is, idols or false gods (Dt 32:15–18).
4:8 feed on the sins . . . relish their wickedness. Taken literally, the priests who ate portions of the animals that were sacrificed for sin encouraged the people to sin so that they would have more to eat (cf. Lev 6:26). Taken metaphorically, the priests were gratified by the people’s sin.
4:9 Like people, like priests. No one is spared from judgment (cf. Isa 24:1–3).
4:10 eat . . . engage in prostitution. Food would not satisfy (v. 8), and illicit sex would not produce the desired increase (cf. v. 14). The people left the Lord, the source of life, to practice prostitution/harlotry (vv. 12,18; 2:4; 6:10; 9:1). See “Introduction: Time and Place of Writing.”
4:11 take away the understanding. Literally, “take away the [people’s] heart”; that is, their ability to feel, judge and think clearly (cf. Ge 31:20). See “Introduction: Purpose and Distinctives.”
4:12 wooden idol. Literally, “its wood/tree.” Perhaps this refers to the Asherah pole (see note on 1Ki 14:15) beside a Canaanite shrine (Dt 16:21; Jdg 6:25–32), to some other deity (Hab 2:18–19) or to a sacred tree thought to give oracles (cf. Jdg 9:37). **a stick of wood.** Literally, “its staff.” Probably a divining rod (cf. Eze 21:21–22), though perhaps a small figurine of Asherah. **A spirit of prostitution.** The source of their spiritual adultery was an intoxicating and seductive power that drew them continuously into sin (cf. “spirit of dizziness” in Isa 19:14; spirit of “deep sleep” in Isa 29:10). See *WLC* 105.
4:14 I will not punish. God refused to allow the women guilty of cult prostitution and adultery to be punished because the men shared in their guilt (cf. Ge 38:24; Jn 8:4–7). **a people without un-**

nor your daughters-in-law
when they commit adultery,
because the men themselves consort with harlots[r]
and sacrifice with shrine prostitutes—
a people without understanding will come to ruin!

15 "Though you commit adultery, O Israel,
let not Judah become guilty.

"Do not go to Gilgal;[s]
do not go up to Beth Aven.[a]
And do not swear, 'As surely as the LORD lives!'
16 The Israelites are stubborn,
like a stubborn heifer.
How then can the LORD pasture them
like lambs[t] in a meadow?
17 Ephraim is joined to idols;
leave him alone!
18 Even when their drinks are gone,
they continue their prostitution;
their rulers dearly love shameful ways.
19 A whirlwind[u] will sweep them away,
and their sacrifices will bring them shame.[v]

Judgment Against Israel

5 "Hear this, you priests!
Pay attention, you Israelites!
Listen, O royal house!
This judgment is against you:
You have been a snare[w] at Mizpah,
a net spread out on Tabor.
2 The rebels are deep in slaughter.[x]
I will discipline all of them.[y]
3 I know all about Ephraim;
Israel is not hidden from me.
Ephraim, you have now turned to prostitution;
Israel is corrupt.[z]

4 "Their deeds do not permit them
to return to their God.
A spirit of prostitution[a] is in their heart;
they do not acknowledge[b] the LORD.

4:14 [r]ver 11
4:15 [s]Hos 9:15; 12:11; Am 4:4
4:16 [t]Isa 5:17; 7:25
4:19 [u]Hos 12:1; 13:15 [v]Isa 1:29
5:1 [w]Hos 6:9; 9:8
5:2 [x]Hos 4:2 [y]Hos 9:15
5:3 [z]Hos 6:10
5:4 [a]Hos 4:11 [b]Hos 4:6

a 15 *Beth Aven* means *house of wickedness* (a name for Bethel, which means *house of God*).

derstanding will come to ruin! This concluding wisdom saying pronounced judgment on the morally bankrupt nation (vv. 1–3), whose involvement in prostitution (vv. 10–14) detracted from understanding and knowledge (vv. 1,6,11–14).
4:15 let not Judah. A warning to the readers in the southern kingdom not to follow the example of the northern kingdom. **Gilgal.** An important Israelite sanctuary near Jericho, across the Jordan from Baal Peor (cf. 9:10,15) and long associated with particularly wicked, unorthodox and syncretistic religious practices (Jos 4:19—5:12; 1Sa 11:13–15; Am 4:4; 5:5; cf. Hos 9:15; 12:11). **Beth Aven.** Literally, "House of Wickedness," a contemptuous nickname for Bethel ("House of God"), the important royal sanctuary (cf. 1Ki 12:28–33; Am 4:4; 5:5; 7:13). **As surely as the LORD lives!** This oath (Jdg 8:19; Ru 3:13; 1Sa 14:39) was forbidden because the people were lying (v. 2) and/or because it was being misused when the Lord was associated with Baal in worship.
4:16 stubborn heifer. Israel was kicking against all of the Lord's efforts to care for her (cf. Jer 31:18).
4:17 Ephraim. A tribal name used of all Israel, the northern kingdom (11:8; Ge 48). **leave him alone!** The plural verb here suggests that Hosea addressed other prophets (Mic 2:6).
4:19 A whirlwind will sweep them away. Literally, "a wind/spirit has bound them up with its wings"; probably intended as a word play on the Hebrew word meaning "wind/spirit." For not only was the destructive storm wind about to sweep away the people (cf. Job 1:19), but the prostituting spirit (4:12; 5:4) was also leading them to ruin.
■ **5:1–7** *Lawsuit Against Priests, the People and the Leaders.* Worship leaders, the nobility and the people were charged with religious prostitution.
5:1 Hear this. The defendants were summoned to hear the case against them (see 4:1). **priests! . . . Israelites! . . . O royal house!** The priests were responsible for teaching the law (4:6) and the royal house for administering justice. **Israelites!** Literally, "O house of Israel." **snare.** The people fell into sin when they foolishly followed the sinful lead of the priests and royalty. **Mizpah.** Probably Mizpah in Benjamin, the site of Samuel's circuit of judging (1Sa 7:5–6; 10:17–24), not Mizpah in Gilead (Ge 31:43–55). **Tabor.** A famous mountain on the southeastern edge of the Jezreel Valley (Dt 33:19; Jdg 4:6; Ps 68). These and other sites in the northern kingdom were snares of the cult of Baal. See "Introduction: Time and Place of Writing."
5:3 Ephraim. That is, Israel (cf. 4:17; 5:5; 11:8).
5:4 spirit of prostitution. Reference to participation in Canaanite fertility rituals. Imprisoned by their evil deeds (4:10; 7:2; 9:15; 12:2) and possessed by an adulterous spirit (cf. 4:12), the adherents did not acknowledge or know the Lord (4:1,6) nor could they return or repent (cf. Jer 13:23; see theological article "Effectual Calling and Conversion" at Ac 16).

5 Israel's arrogance testifies[c] against them;
the Israelites, even Ephraim, stumble in their sin;
Judah also stumbles with them.
6 When they go with their flocks and herds
to seek the LORD,[d]
they will not find him;
he has withdrawn[e] himself from them.
7 They are unfaithful[f] to the LORD;
they give birth to illegitimate[g] children.
Now their New Moon festivals
will devour[h] them and their fields.

8 "Sound the trumpet in Gibeah,[i]
the horn in Ramah.[j]
Raise the battle cry in Beth Aven[a];[k]
lead on, O Benjamin.
9 Ephraim will be laid waste
on the day of reckoning.[l]
Among the tribes of Israel
I proclaim what is certain.[m]
10 Judah's leaders are like those
who move boundary stones.[n]
I will pour out my wrath[o] on them
like a flood of water.
11 Ephraim is oppressed,
trampled in judgment,
intent on pursuing idols.[b][p]
12 I am like a moth[q] to Ephraim,
like rot to the people of Judah.

13 "When Ephraim saw his sickness,
and Judah his sores,
then Ephraim turned to Assyria,[r]
and sent to the great king for help.[s]
But he is not able to cure[t] you,
not able to heal your sores.[u]
14 For I will be like a lion[v] to Ephraim,
like a great lion to Judah.
I will tear them to pieces and go away;
I will carry them off, with no one to rescue them.[w]

5:5 [c]Hos 7:10
5:6 [d]Mic 6:6-7 [e]Pr 1:28; Isa 1:15; Eze 8:6
5:7 [f]Hos 6:7 [g]Hos 2:4 [h]Hos 2:11-12
5:8 [i]Hos 9:9; 10:9 [j]Isa 10:29 [k]Hos 4:15
5:9 [l]Isa 37:3; Hos 9:11-17 [m]Isa 46:10; Zec 1:6
5:10 [n]Dt 19:14 [o]Eze 7:8
5:11 [p]Hos 9:16; Mic 6:16
5:12 [q]Isa 51:8
5:13 [r]Hos 7:11; 8:9 [s]Hos 10:6 [t]Hos 14:3 [u]Jer 30:12
5:14 [v]Am 3:4 [w]Mic 5:8

[a] *8 Beth Aven* means *house of wickedness* (a name for Bethel, which means *house of God*).
[b] *11* The meaning of the Hebrew for this word is uncertain.

5:5 testifies. In the case the Lord brought against his people (4:1), their own crimes witnessed against them (Dt 1:43; 1Sa 12:3; 2Sa 1:16; Eze 16:56–57).
5:6 will not find him. The Lord sentenced Israel to futility in worship. He would not be found through the people's sacrifices (4:13; 5:15; 1Sa 15:7–35; 2Ki 3:27; Isa 1:11–17; Am 5:4–5), and their corrupt worship caused God to reject them.
5:7 unfaithful . . . illegitimate children. Like an unfaithful wife and mother, Israel gave birth to religious bastards (4:6,13–14), just as her literal prostitutions and adulteries, often in the context of Baal worship, resulted in actual pregnancies and illegitimate children. **New Moon.** Festivals the people thought would confer the Lord's blessing on their wombs and crops brought judgment instead (cf. Isa 1:13; Jer 2:27).
■ **5:8—8:14** *Impending Defeat in War.* Hosea called the nation to prepare for attack by God's instrument of judgment. Hosea had in mind the many attacks during the period of judgment by Assyria (734–722 B.C.), including incursions by Judahites. Samaria's destruction by Assyria in 722 brought these words to their Old Testament fulfillment. The commands to blow a trumpet (5:8; 8:1) introduced calls to war that frame these chapters and constitute their main theme. These chapters divide into four main parts: summons to defeat in war (5:8–15), hypocrisy resulting in defeat (6:1—7:2), corrupt leaders and alliances resulting in defeat (7:3–16) and a second summons to defeat in war (8:1–14).
■ **5:8–15** *First Summons to Defeat in War.* Hosea called upon the Israelites to prepare for a war that they were sure to lose because they were under God's judgment.
5:8 Sound . . . Raise . . . lead. Three imperatives sounded the watchman's cry to warn of an approaching enemy. **Gibeah . . . Ramah . . . Beth Aven.** These Benjamite towns lay in a straight line running north from Jerusalem: Gibeah three miles, Ramah five miles and Beth Aven (i.e., Bethel) eleven miles. At various times these towns were claimed by Israel or by Judah (1Ki 15:16–22; 2Ki 16:5).
5:10 boundary stones. Judah's reckless annexation of Benjamite territory (1Ki 15:16–22) incurred God's anger; the boundary lines were sacred to the Lord, who owned the land and expected it to be distributed as he had ordered (Dt 19:14; 27:17; Job 24:2; Pr 22:28; 23:10). See *BC* 36.
5:11 See *WCF* 20.2; *WLC* 109.
5:12 moth . . . rot. Destroyers of things of value.
5:13 sickness . . . sores. Instead of turning to the Lord to heal them of miseries inflicted by an enemy (cf. Isa 1:5–6; Jer 30:12–13), the Israelites turned to Assyria. Assyrian records speak of the tribute paid by Menahem and Hoshea; compare 2 Kings 15:16–22 and 17:3. **sent.** Judah may be the subject of this verb, as in "Judah [saw] his sores" in the first part of the verse.
5:14 like a lion . . . I will tear . . . I will carry them off. Even with Assyrian aid Israel was helpless prey before the powerful and hungry lion, the Lord (cf. 13:7; Am 1:2; 3:8).

15 Then I will go back to my place
until they admit their guilt.
And they will seek my face;[x]
in their misery[y] they will earnestly seek me.[z]"

Israel Unrepentant

6 "Come, let us return to the LORD.
He has torn us to pieces[a]
but he will heal us;
he has injured us
but he will bind up our wounds.[b]
2 After two days he will revive us;[c]
on the third day he will restore us,
that we may live in his presence.
3 Let us acknowledge the LORD;
let us press on to acknowledge him.
As surely as the sun rises,
he will appear;
he will come to us like the winter rains,[d]
like the spring rains that water the earth.[e]"

4 "What can I do with you, Ephraim?[f]
What can I do with you, Judah?
Your love is like the morning mist,
like the early dew that disappears.[g]
5 Therefore I cut you in pieces with my prophets,
I killed you with the words of my mouth;[h]
my judgments flashed like lightning upon you.[i]
6 For I desire mercy, not sacrifice,[j]
and acknowledgment[k] of God rather than burnt offerings.
7 Like Adam,[a] they have broken the covenant[l]—
they were unfaithful[m] to me there.
8 Gilead is a city of wicked men,
stained with footprints of blood.
9 As marauders lie in ambush for a man,
so do bands of priests;

5:15 [x]Hos 3:5 [y]Jer 2:27 [z]Isa 64:9
6:1 [a]Hos 5:14 [b]Dt 32:39; Jer 30:17; Hos 14:4
6:2 [c]Ps 30:5
6:3 [d]Joel 2:23 [e]Ps 72:6
6:4 [f]Hos 11:8 [g]Hos 7:1; 13:3
6:5 [h]Jer 1:9-10; 23:29 [i]Heb 4:12
6:6 [j]Isa 1:11; Mt 9:13*; 12:7* [k]Hos 2:20
6:7 [l]Hos 8:1 [m]Hos 5:7

a 7 Or *As at Adam*; or *Like men*

5:15 until they admit their guilt. God would withdraw in anger to his heavenly sanctuary (contrast Dt 33:2; Jdg 5:4; Am 1:2, cf. Ps 46:4) until his people had truly repented (3:5).
■ **6:1—7:2** *Hypocritical Repentance Resulting in Defeat.* The mention of repentance as the solution to divine judgment raised the issue of Israel's hypocritical repentance. This song of repentance uses the imagery of 5:11–14 but seems superficial in tone (cf. 6:4). The Lord responded to this hypocrisy with severe judgment.
6:1 let us. Perhaps the priests were quoted here as Israel was quoted in 2:7. **return.** The call to return to the Lord is one of the central messages of the book (2:7; 3:5; 5:4,15). True repentance and conversion bring reconciliation that can encompass healing and the binding up of wounds (cf. Dt 32:39). The words that follow, however, indicated that this repentance was not genuine.
6:2 two days . . . the third. Denotes a short period of time. Hypocrisy is evident in that the people had not yet acknowledged how serious their offenses were. **restore.** The Hebrew word means "raise up"; a related form is translated "rise" in Isaiah 26:19. Paul possibly alluded to this verse in 1 Corinthians 15:4. **live in his presence.** See Psalm 16:11. A central restoration hope was that God's presence would be re-established among his people (see Jer 24:7; Eze 37:27).
6:3 acknowledge. This second call (cf. 6:1) to know and accept the covenant Lord with heart and life is central to Hosea's message (2:8,20; 4:1,6; 5:4; 6:6). See "Introduction: Purpose and Distinctives." **as the sun rises . . . like the winter rains, like the spring rains.** Metaphors comparing God's reliability to recurring events of nature.
6:4–11 God responded to the hypocritical repentance taking place in Israel.
6:4 like the morning mist, like the early dew. God lamented the temporary, transitory quality of Israel and Judah's covenant love, contrasting it with his own faithfulness (v. 3) by using more images from nature.
6:5 Therefore. The question in verse 4 is answered. **prophets.** God used the prophets to convey messages of warning and judgment. **lightning.** Literally, "light." Like the light of the sun whose rising dispels the darkness day by day, God's justice consistently and inevitably went forth (cf. Ps 37:6), exposing the sins of those who broke the covenant.
6:6 mercy . . . acknowledgment. See notes on 2:19–20; compare 4:1. **acknowledgment of God.** Covenant faithfulness—loyalty—not mechanical rituals, was required of the covenant people. See Psalm 51, Micah 6:8 and their notes.
6:7–10 God demonstrated the hypocrisy of the nation by rapidly cataloging a number of the people's sins. These verses enumerate several specific places that were infamous in Hosea's day. Though the details are now lost the record serves to indict the whole nation (v. 10).
6:7 Adam. The allusion is unclear. Three possible references are proposed, the first in the NIV text and the others in the NIV text note: (1) the first man, Adam (Ge 3); (2) a location, the ancient site Tell ed-Damiyeh on the Jordan River (Jos 3:16), parallel to Gilead in verse 8 and Shechem in verse 9 and suggested by "there" in the second half of this verse; and (3) humanity. The doctrine of God's covenant with Adam rests on factors other than the interpretation of this text: The elements of a covenant were present in God's relationship with Adam. See notes on Genesis 1–3.
6:8 Gilead. A mountainous region in northern Transjordan, but the word may refer to a city named Adam (see note on v. 7). **wicked men.** A term used frequently in the psalms of the enemies of the righteous and of the Lord. **footprints of blood.** Perhaps an allusion to the 50 men of Gilead involved in the assassination of Pekahiah (2Ki 15:25).

they murder on the road to Shechem,
committing shameful crimes.[n]
10 I have seen a horrible[o] thing
in the house of Israel.
There Ephraim is given to prostitution
and Israel is defiled.[p]

11 "Also for you, Judah,
a harvest[q] is appointed.

7

"Whenever I would restore the fortunes of my people,
1 whenever I would heal Israel,
the sins of Ephraim are exposed
and the crimes of Samaria revealed.[r]
They practice deceit,[s]
thieves break into houses,[t]
bandits rob in the streets;
2 but they do not realize
that I remember[u] all their evil deeds.
Their sins engulf them;[v]
they are always before me.

3 "They delight the king with their wickedness,
the princes with their lies.[w]
4 They are all adulterers,[x]
burning like an oven
whose fire the baker need not stir
from the kneading of the dough till it rises.
5 On the day of the festival of our king
the princes become inflamed with wine,[y]
and he joins hands with the mockers.
6 Their hearts are like an oven;[z]
they approach him with intrigue.
Their passion smolders all night;
in the morning it blazes like a flaming fire.
7 All of them are hot as an oven;
they devour their rulers.
All their kings fall,
and none of them calls[a] on me.

8 "Ephraim mixes[b] with the nations;
Ephraim is a flat cake not turned over.
9 Foreigners sap his strength,[c]
but he does not realize it.
His hair is sprinkled with gray,
but he does not notice.

6:9 [n]Jer 7:9-10; Eze 22:9; Hos 7:1
6:10 [o]Jer 5:30 [p]Hos 5:3
6:11 [q]Jer 51:33; Joel 3:13
7:1 [r]Hos 6:4 [s]ver 13 [t]Hos 4:2
7:2 [u]Jer 14:10; Hos 8:13 [v]Jer 2:19
7:3 [w]Hos 4:2; Mic 7:3
7:4 [x]Jer 9:2
7:5 [y]Isa 28:1,7
7:6 [z]Ps 21:9
7:7 [a]ver 16
7:8 [b]ver 11; Ps 106:35; Hos 5:13
7:9 [c]Isa 1:7; Hos 8:7

6:9 murder. The allusion is unclear but perhaps is a reference to the priests' role in a conspiracy against the royal family (see note on v. 8). **Shechem.** An important religious and political center (Dt 27:4,12–14; Jos 8:30; 20:7; 24:1,25; Jdg 9; 1Ki 12:1,25).
6:10 horrible thing. Compare Jeremiah 5:30–31, 18:13 and 23:14. **prostitution.** Perhaps figurative for religious or political infidelity.
6:11—7:1 harvest. A metaphor for God's judgment (Jer 51:33; Joel 3:13). **restore . . . heal.** If the people had sincerely turned to the Lord he would have forgiven them. As it was, their actions revealed their true character. **Ephraim . . . Samaria.** Both refer to the northern kingdom, of which Samaria was the capital.
7:2 they do not realize. They even deceived themselves with their hypocrisy (Gal 6:7). **always before me.** False repentance would not suffice because God knew the sins of the people. Compare Psalm 51:3.
■ **7:3–16** *Political Corruption Resulting in Defeat.* Hosea next turned to political corruption as the cause of the impending defeat in war.
7:3–7 oven . . . fire . . . baker. Metaphors Hosea used to paint a graphic picture of the self-propagating passion, treachery and wickedness that infested the political life of Israel during its last days and led to a series of violent assassinations of its kings (2Ki 15:8–30). The assassination of Pekah by Hoshea (2Ki 15:30) may have been behind this oracle.
7:3 They. Perhaps the treacherous priests who allied themselves with usurpers of the throne. **king . . . princes.** Those who were to provide moral leadership savored instead the evil and treachery of those around them (2Ki 15:8–30).
7:4 adulterers. Those unfaithful to the covenant (cf. 2:4; 4:13,14; Jer 9:2; 23:10). See "Introduction: Purpose and Distinctives."
7:5 festival of our king. This coronation or royal anniversary became an opportunity for drunkenness, which fueled wickedness (cf. 1Ki 16:9–10; Isa 28:7–10; Am 6:1–7). **inflamed with wine.** This deprived the royal house of sound judgment (Pr 31:4,5). **mockers.** Probably the priests.
7:6 Their hearts. Referred to the priests' political passions.
7:7 rulers . . . kings. Even amidst unrest that assassinated four kings in 20 years (2Ki 15:8–30), none of the leaders (who should have been exemplary) called on God.
7:8 mixes with the nations. Pointed to Israel's shifting alliances with Egypt, Philistia, Aram and Assyria. **flat cake.** Dough placed on coals or pressed to the sides of a hot oven had to be turned over or doubled over to be cooked properly. **not turned over.** Israel was like a useless, half-baked or burnt cake because she refused to turn to the Lord. This was a sarcastic figure for the nation's incompetent politics.

10 Israel's arrogance testifies against him,[d]
but despite all this
he does not return to the LORD his God
or search[e] for him.

11 "Ephraim is like a dove,[f]
easily deceived and senseless—
now calling to Egypt,
now turning to Assyria.[g]
12 When they go, I will throw my net[h] over them;
I will pull them down like birds of the air.
When I hear them flocking together,
I will catch them.
13 Woe[i] to them,
because they have strayed[j] from me!
Destruction to them,
because they have rebelled against me!
I long to redeem them
but they speak lies against me.[k]
14 They do not cry out to me from their hearts[l]
but wail upon their beds.
They gather together[a] for grain and new wine[m]
but turn away from me.[n]
15 I trained them and strengthened them,
but they plot evil[o] against me.
16 They do not turn to the Most High;
they are like a faulty bow.[p]
Their leaders will fall by the sword
because of their insolent words.
For this they will be ridiculed[q]
in the land of Egypt.[r]

Israel to Reap the Whirlwind

8 "Put the trumpet to your lips!
An eagle[s] is over the house of the LORD
because the people have broken my covenant
and rebelled against my law.[t]
2 Israel cries out to me,
'O our God, we acknowledge you!'

7:10 [d]Hos 5:5 [e]Isa 9:13
7:11 [f]Hos 11:11 [g]Hos 5:13; 12:1
7:12 [h]Eze 12:13
7:13 [i]Hos 9:12 [j]Jer 14:10; Eze 34:4-6; Hos 9:17 [k]ver 1; Mt 23:37
7:14 [l]Jer 3:10 [m]Am 2:8 [n]Hos 13:16
7:15 [o]Na 1:9,11
7:16 [p]Ps 78:9,57 [q]Eze 23:32 [r]Hos 9:3
8:1 [s]Dt 28:19; Jer 4:13 [t]Hos 4:6; 6:7

a *14* Most Hebrew manuscripts; some Hebrew manuscripts and Septuagint *They slash themselves*

7:9 sap his strength. By demanding and receiving tribute from Israel. **he does not realize it . . . does not notice.** Identical phrases in the Hebrew that stressed Israel's ignorance of how politically weak and drained she was. Lack of self-awareness followed lack of knowledge of God.
7:10 arrogance. Stubborn pride that blinded Israel and testified against the nation (cf. 5:5). Turning back to the Lord was Israel's only hope (3:5; 5:4; Am 4:6–12).
7:11–12 dove. A bird reputed to have such little sense that it was easy to trap. **Egypt . . . Assyria.** Like a witless bird Israel fluttered from one nation to another seeking security and protection. While King Menahem had submitted to Assyria and paid a vast tribute (2Ki 15:19–20), King Pekah was anti-Assyrian, forming a coalition with Syria (2Ki 15:29,37; 16:5), and King Hoshea shifted his allegiance from Assyria to Egypt (2Ki 17:3–4). **my net.** The Lord's net of judgment would come down on flitting Israel.
7:13 Woe. Introduces a dire threat. **I long to redeem them.** The complexity of God's relationship with Israel is expressed. He longed to redeem his people, as Jesus longed for the redemption of Jerusalem (Mt 23:37), but redemption could not take place because of the continuing rebellion of the people. **redeem.** A term also used in commercial law, meaning "buy back" (see Lev 27:27–31), was used of Israel's deliverance from bondage (13:14; Ex 15:13; Dt 7:8; 9:26; see note on Mic 6:4). **lies.** Perhaps a reference to the false ideas about the Lord incorporated into Israelite religion, to insincere words of repentance (6:1–3) or, more generally, to the broken promises of the covenant.
7:14 cry out . . . wail . . . gather together. Israel's cry for help, using practices adapted from Canaanite worship—crying out, wailing, gathering together or perhaps self-mutilation (see NIV text note; cf. Lev 19:28; Dt 14:1; 1Ki 18:26–29)—was of no account in light of the broken covenant. **not . . . from their hearts.** The people feigned repentance, but this pretense was not acceptable (see notes on 6:1–4).
7:16 turn. Instead of turning to God (7:14) the Israelites turned to foreign nations and Canaanite religious practices. See "Introduction: Time and Place of Writing." **faulty bow.** Compare Psalm 78:57. **fall by the sword.** The main motif throughout this section is defeat in war. **insolent words.** Directed against God and his prophets (6:5). **ridiculed in . . . Egypt.** The Egyptians would soon mock at the fall of those who had only intermittently solicited their help.
■ **8:1–14** *Second Summons to Defeat in War.* The section of Hosea focusing on judgment in warfare (5:8—8:14) closes as it began (5:8–15), with a call for Israel to make ready for a war in which it would inevitably be defeated. Hosea confronted the nation's idolatry and foreign alliances.
8:1 trumpet. The urgent alarm (cf. 5:8) reported that an eagle or vulturelike foe (cf. Dt 28:49–50; Jer 4:13; 48:40; La 4:19; Hab 1:8), Assyria, was rapidly approaching to administer God's judgment. **the house of the LORD.** Can refer to the land as well as to the temple (9:8,15). **my covenant . . . my law.** Rebellion against the terms of the covenant was tantamount to rebellion against God (4:6; 6:6–7; 7:13; 8:12).
8:2 we acknowledge you! In their cry for help the Israelites claimed knowledge of God, but their actions belied their words (see notes on 6:1–8).

3 But Israel has rejected what is good;
an enemy will pursue him.

8:4
[u]Hos 13:10
[v]Hos 2:8

4 They set up kings without my consent;
they choose princes without my approval.[u]
With their silver and gold
they make idols[v] for themselves
to their own destruction.

8:5
[w]Hos 10:5
[x]Jer 13:27

5 Throw out your calf-idol, O Samaria![w]
My anger burns against them.
How long will they be incapable of purity?[x]
6 They are from Israel!
This calf—a craftsman has made it;
it is not God.
It will be broken in pieces,
that calf of Samaria.

8:7
[y]Pr 22:8;
Isa 66:15;
Hos 10:12-13;
Na 1:3 [z]Hos 2:9

7 "They sow the wind
and reap the whirlwind.[y]
The stalk has no head;
it will produce no flour.
Were it to yield grain,
foreigners would swallow it up.[z]

8:8
[a]Jer 51:34
[b]Jer 22:28

8 Israel is swallowed up;[a]
now she is among the nations
like a worthless[b] thing.
9 For they have gone up to Assyria
like a wild donkey wandering alone.
Ephraim has sold herself to lovers.

8:10
[c]Eze 16:37; 22:20
[d]Jer 42:2

10 Although they have sold themselves among the nations,
I will now gather them together.[c]
They will begin to waste away[d]
under the oppression of the mighty king.

8:11
[e]Hos 10:1; 12:11

11 "Though Ephraim built many altars for sin offerings,
these have become altars for sinning.[e]
12 I wrote for them the many things of my law,
but they regarded them as something alien.

8:13
[f]Jer 7:21 [g]Hos 7:2
[h]Hos 4:9
[i]Hos 9:3,6

13 They offer sacrifices given to me
and they eat[f] the meat,
but the LORD is not pleased with them.
Now he will remember[g] their wickedness
and punish their sins:[h]
They will return to Egypt.[i]

8:14
[j]Dt 32:18;
Hos 2:13

14 Israel has forgotten[j] his Maker
and built palaces;

8:3 good. A comprehensive term describing all the blessings under God's covenant; it may even refer to the good One, God himself (Am 5:14–15; Mic 6:8).
8:4 kings . . . princes. Israel's independence from God in the political sphere appeared in her refusal to consult God regarding choices of leaders. This precipitated a remarkable series of conspiracies and violent assassinations (7:3–7; 2Ki 15:8–30). See "Introduction: Time and Place of Writing." **idols.** Through fashioning gods of silver and gold Israel expressed defiant rejection of the good (8:5; Ex 20:3–6; 34:17; Lev 19:4).
8:5–6 calf-idol. To judge from parallels, the calf was originally crafted as the pedestal on which a deity stood; it was established as an idol representing the Lord by Jeroboam I (1Ki 12:26–30; cf. Ex 32) and is here described as the object of worship itself. **How long.** A passionate lament expressing God's grief over Israel's sin purposefully juxtaposed with an expression of God's anger.
8:7 sow . . . reap. This proverbial saying emphasized the dire cause-and-effect relationship between sin and increased punishment (cf. 10:13; Job 4:8; Ps 126:5–6; Pr 11:18; 22:8; Gal 6:7–9).
8:8 worthless. Though Israel had once been chosen from among all the nations (Ex 19:5; Am 3:2), she no longer possessed anything useful, desirable or precious.
8:9 gone up to Assyria. Probably indicated King Hoshea's submission to Assyria in his attempt to retain the power he had seized by his murder of Pekah (cf. 7:8–12; 2Ki 15:19; 17:3). See "Introduction: Time and Place of Writing." **wild donkey.** The play on words between the Hebrew for "wild donkey" and "Ephraim" suggests that the comparison was with Ephraim (Israel) and not with Assyria. Ephraim stubbornly rejected the Lord's company and gave her favors to Assyria (2Ki 15:19; 17:3).
8:10 gather them together. Divine judgment would come on the Israelites (cf. Joel 3:2; Zep 3:8). **the mighty king.** Assyria, the power to whom Israel surrendered, would become the instrument of God's judgment.
8:11 altars. Built to deal with sin, altars in the northern kingdom became, instead, places at which to sin. See *WLC* 4.
8:13 sacrifices. In vain did the unrepentant Israelites participate in communal sacrifices (Lev 7:11–18; Dt 12:7; Jer 7:21). **return to Egypt.** Ironically, the place out of which God had lovingly called Israel (11:1) was now a place of captivity and punishment (Dt 28:68; Hos 9:3; 11:5).
8:14 palaces. Israel's confidence that buildings and fortifications brought spiritual and political-military security was misguided. **fire.** See Amos 1:4—2:5.

Judah has fortified many towns.
But I will send fire upon their cities
that will consume their fortresses."[k]

Punishment for Israel

9 Do not rejoice, O Israel;
do not be jubilant[l] like the other nations.
For you have been unfaithful[m] to your God;
you love the wages of a prostitute
at every threshing floor.
2 Threshing floors and winepresses will not feed the people;
the new wine[n] will fail them.
3 They will not remain[o] in the LORD's land;
Ephraim will return to Egypt[p]
and eat unclean[a] food in Assyria.[q]
4 They will not pour out wine offerings to the LORD,
nor will their sacrifices please[r] him.
Such sacrifices will be to them like the bread of mourners;
all who eat them will be unclean.[s]
This food will be for themselves;
it will not come into the temple of the LORD.
5 What will you do[t] on the day of your appointed feasts,[u]
on the festival days of the LORD?
6 Even if they escape from destruction,
Egypt will gather them,
and Memphis[v] will bury them.
Their treasures of silver will be taken over by briers,
and thorns[w] will overrun their tents.
7 The days of punishment[x] are coming,
the days of reckoning are at hand.
Let Israel know this.
Because your sins[y] are so many
and your hostility so great,
the prophet is considered a fool,[z]
the inspired man a maniac.
8 The prophet, along with my God,
is the watchman over Ephraim,[b]
yet snares[a] await him on all his paths,
and hostility in the house of his God.
9 They have sunk deep into corruption,
as in the days of Gibeah.[b]

8:14 [k]Jer 17:27
9:1 [l]Isa 22:12-13 [m]Hos 10:5
9:2 [n]Hos 2:9
9:3 [o]Lev 25:23 [p]Hos 8:13 [q]Eze 4:13; Hos 7:11
9:4 [r]Jer 6:20; Hos 8:13 [s]Hag 2:13-14
9:5 [t]Isa 10:3; Jer 5:31 [u]Hos 2:11
9:6 [v]Isa 19:13 [w]Isa 5:6; Hos 10:8
9:7 [x]Isa 34:8; Jer 10:15; Mic 7:4 [y]Jer 16:18 [z]Isa 44:25; La 2:14; Eze 14:9-10
9:8 [a]Hos 5:1
9:9 [b]Jdg 19:16-30; Hos 5:8; 10:9

[a] 3 That is, ceremonially unclean [b] 8 Or *The prophet is the watchman over Ephraim, / the people of my God*

■ **9:1–9** *Mourning Over Defeat.* Following his oracles about Israel's defeat in war (5:8—8:14), Hosea called for mourning over conquered Israel. The joyous celebrations of the annual fall harvest festival (cf. Ex 23:16; Dt 16:13–17; Lev 23:33–43), which had become tainted with paganism, were to be replaced with grief because of the exile (v. 3).

9:1 threshing floor. The flat, open area used for threshing wheat and barley was also a place where Israel indulged in sensual fertility rites related to the worship of Baal.

9:2 winepresses. Literally, "press"; a device used for wine and oil. The land would not feed the people any longer; they would be under a curse.

9:3 the LORD's land. Also referred to as the Lord's house (8:1; 9:15), the promised land was owned by the Lord, not by Baal or even by Israel (Lev 25:23). **return to Egypt.** See note on 11:11. See also 7:16, 8:13, 9:6, 11:5 and 11 and Deuteronomy 28:68. **unclean food.** A foreign land and the food it produced were considered unclean. See NIV text note at 9:3; see also Ezekiel 4:13 and Amos 7:17.

9:4 bread of mourners. Food in the house of mourners was considered unclean because of contact with a dead body (Nu 19:11–22; Dt 26:14; Jer 16:7). **temple of the LORD.** Sacrifices and offerings would not be presented in exile (Ex 29:40; Lev 23:13; Nu 15:1–12).

9:5 appointed feasts . . . festival days of the LORD. Probably the annual fall harvest feast of booths or tabernacles (Lev 23:33–36,39–43; Dt 16:13–15).

9:6 destruction. The Assyrian invasions (see note on 5:8—8:14). **Egypt.** The place from which Israel was once delivered would become a gathering place for destruction and death. **Memphis will bury them.** Used as a poetic pair with "Egypt," the allusion was to the city's great cemeteries, tombs and pyramids. **treasures of silver . . . tents.** The exiles would leave behind either idols of silver and tent shrines or simply their personal possessions.

9:7 prophet . . . a fool. The Israelites' sin was so great that they even considered the prophet a foolish and idle talker (cf. Pr 10:8,10). **inspired man.** Used in parallel with "prophet"; probably another expression for "man of God" (cf. 1Sa 10:6; 1Ki 18:12; 22:21–28; 2Ki 2:9,16). **maniac.** A crazy, nonsensical babbler or deranged person (1Sa 21:13–15; 2Ki 9:11; Jer 29:26).

9:8 watchman. The prophet was not a maniac but one who kept watch over Israel (5:8; 8:11; cf. Jer 6:1; Eze 3:17; 33:2,6,7). **snares.** The one who sounded the alarm found himself hunted like an animal and the object of hostility. **the house of his God.** That is, the land.

9:9 Gibeah. Infamous for the gang rape of the Levite's concubine and the series of violent and abusive acts and war that followed (Jdg 19–21). The genesis of the Israelites' sins underscored their gravity and implied the need for a complete renewal of Israel's na-

God will remember[c] their wickedness
and punish them for their sins.

10 "When I found Israel,
it was like finding grapes in the desert;
when I saw your fathers,
it was like seeing the early fruit on the fig tree.
But when they came to Baal Peor,[d]
they consecrated themselves to that shameful idol[e]
and became as vile as the thing they loved.
11 Ephraim's glory will fly away like a bird[f]—
no birth, no pregnancy, no conception.[g]
12 Even if they rear children,
I will bereave them of every one.
Woe[h] to them
when I turn away from them![i]
13 I have seen Ephraim, like Tyre,
planted in a pleasant place.[j]
But Ephraim will bring out
their children to the slayer."

14 Give them, O LORD—
what will you give them?
Give them wombs that miscarry
and breasts that are dry.[k]

15 "Because of all their wickedness in Gilgal,[l]
I hated them there.
Because of their sinful deeds,[m]
I will drive them out of my house.
I will no longer love them;
all their leaders are rebellious.[n]
16 Ephraim[o] is blighted,
their root is withered,
they yield no fruit.[p]
Even if they bear children,
I will slay[q] their cherished offspring."

17 My God will reject them
because they have not obeyed[r] him;
they will be wanderers among the nations.[s]

10

Israel was a spreading vine;[t]
he brought forth fruit for himself.
As his fruit increased,

9:9 [c]Hos 8:13
9:10 [d]Nu 25:1-5; Ps 106:28-29 [e]Jer 11:13; Hos 4:14
9:11 [f]Hos 4:7; 10:5 [g]ver 14
9:12 [h]Hos 7:13 [i]Dt 31:17
9:13 [j]Eze 27:3
9:14 [k]ver 11; Lk 23:29
9:15 [l]Hos 4:15 [m]Hos 7:2 [n]Isa 1:23; Hos 4:9; 5:2
9:16 [o]Hos 5:11 [p]Hos 8:7 [q]ver 12
9:17 [r]Hos 4:10 [s]Dt 28:65; Hos 7:13
10:1 [t]Eze 15:2

---

ture. **wickedness . . . sins.** Israel's innumerable covenantal violations called forth God's punishment (cf. 8:13).

■ **9:10—13:16** *Historical Reflections and Israel's Future.* These chapters contain a variety of oracles gathered around metaphorical reflections on Israel's past and future. The oracles speak of the Assyrian judgment and of restoration after exile. Five metaphors organize this material into four groups: grapes and figs (9:10–17), a spreading vine (10:1–10), a trained heifer (10:11–15) and a growing child (11:1—13:16).

■ **9:10–17** *Grapes and Figs.* Hosea announced that Israel was like grapes and figs that had promised a bountiful harvest but that rebellion against God had ruined the nation. The Israelites were destined for judgment.

9:10 grapes in the desert. An extraordinarily rare and delicious find. **early fruit on the fig tree.** The early fig that ripens on the previous year's sprouts is not only very tender but also quite rare (cf. Isa 28:4). These images stress the exceptional and pleasing character of the Lord's initial covenant relationship with Israel and the potential for a wonderful harvest. **Baal Peor.** A poignant allusion to the place where the Israelites rejected the Lord by succumbing to sexual and spiritual adultery (Nu 25) much like that practiced by Hosea's contemporaries. **became as vile.** By joining themselves to the god of shame, Baal, the Israelites themselves became detestable.

9:11 glory. Perhaps her historical political and military power. The context, however, suggests her large population. The blessing on Joseph/Ephraim had made the people fruitful (Ge 48:16; 49:22–26). **no birth . . . pregnancy . . . conception.** Participation in the fertility religions resulted in the curse of infertility, not the blessing of increased progeny (Dt 28:18).

9:13 slayer. Ephraim's politics would lead to destruction and death.

9:14 Give them wombs that miscarry. Hosea responded in prayer, asking that God's fertility blessings be withdrawn (Ge 49:25; Ex 23:26; Dt 28:4,11). The prophet could only concur with God's righteous judgment.

9:15 Gilgal. See note on 4:15. **drive them out.** Notice how this parallels God's banishment of the Canaanites (Ex 23:29,30; 33:2; Jos 24:18; Jdg 2:3; 6:9), who would be exiled from the promised land.

9:16 Ephraim . . . root . . . fruit. A pun; Ephraim-fruit recalled the opening metaphors of grapes and figs and ironically underscored the tragedy of Israel's fruitlessness (see NIV text note on Ge 41:52).

9:17 My God. Unlike the people, who had turned away from God (cf. 2:5; 14:4), the prophet remained faithful to the covenant. **wanderers among the nations.** Having wandered from God (7:13), the Israelites, like Cain (see Ge 4:12), were destined to be restless fugitives among the nations, separated from the paradise offered to them in Canaan.

he built more altars;[u]
as his land prospered,
he adorned his sacred stones.[v]
2 Their heart is deceitful,[w]
and now they must bear their guilt.[x]
The LORD will demolish their altars[y]
and destroy their sacred stones.[z]

3 Then they will say, "We have no king
because we did not revere the LORD.
But even if we had a king,
what could he do for us?"
4 They make many promises,
take false oaths[a]
and make agreements;[b]
therefore lawsuits spring up
like poisonous weeds in a plowed field.
5 The people who live in Samaria fear
for the calf-idol of Beth Aven.[a][c]
Its people will mourn over it,
and so will its idolatrous priests,[d]
those who had rejoiced over its splendor,
because it is taken from them into exile.[e]
6 It will be carried to Assyria[f]
as tribute for the great king.[g]
Ephraim will be disgraced;[h]
Israel will be ashamed of its wooden idols.[b]
7 Samaria and its king will float away[i]
like a twig on the surface of the waters.
8 The high places of wickedness[c][j] will be destroyed—
it is the sin of Israel.
Thorns[k] and thistles will grow up
and cover their altars.[l]
Then they will say to the mountains, "Cover us!"
and to the hills, "Fall on us!"[m]

9 "Since the days of Gibeah,[n] you have sinned, O Israel,
and there you have remained.[d]
Did not war overtake
the evildoers in Gibeah?
10 When I please, I will punish[o] them;

10:1 [u]1Ki 14:23 [v]Hos 8:11; 12:11
10:2 [w]1Ki 18:21 [x]Hos 13:16 [y]ver 8 [z]Mic 5:13
10:4 [a]Hos 4:2 [b]Eze 17:19; Am 5:7
10:5 [c]Hos 5:8 [d]2Ki 23:5 [e]Hos 8:5; 9:1,3,11
10:6 [f]Hos 11:5 [g]Hos 5:13 [h]Isa 30:3; Hos 4:7
10:7 [i]Hos 13:11
10:8 [j]1Ki 12:28-30; Hos 4:13 [k]Hos 9:6 [l]ver 2; Isa 32:13 [m]Lk 23:30*; Rev 6:16
10:9 [n]Hos 5:8
10:10 [o]Eze 5:13; Hos 4:9

a 5 *Beth Aven* means *house of wickedness* (a name for Bethel, which means *house of God*). b 6 Or *its counsel*
c 8 Hebrew *aven*, a reference to Beth Aven (a derogatory name for Bethel) d 9 Or *there a stand was taken*

■ **10:1–10** *Spreading Vine.* Hosea likened Israel to a vine that was increasing in size and fruitfulness. As increase occurred, however, the nation gave credit to idols rather than to the Lord. These verses divide into three sets each of accusations (10:1 2a,4,9a) and judgments (10:2b–3,5–8,9b–10).

10:1 spreading . . . brought forth. Israel had done well because of God's blessing. In the days of Jeroboam II (703–753 B.C.) her prosperity had been enormous. Yet as early as 922 B.C. Jeroboam I had erected idolatrous altars in Dan and Bethel, turning the people to idolatry (see 1Ki 12:25–33), the practice of which only increased as Israel continued to prosper. The credit for prosperity was not given to the Lord but to material contributions to an idolatrous cult. **vine.** A frequently used metaphor for Israel (Dt 32:32; Ps 80:8–11; Isa 1:5; Jer 2:21). Israel had turned away from God, but the remnant called out by Jesus would again become a fruitful vine (Jn 15:1–8).

10:2 heart. The Israelites needed renewal from within. **The LORD.** Literally, "he," the Hebrew pronoun substitutes for God's proper name in this context. **demolish their altars.** God would destroy the idols Israel trusted.

10:3 no king. Whether the king was still on the throne, about to be deposed or already deposed, without God's blessing he was useless.

10:4 They. Either the kings or the people. **promises.** The king's commitments could be covenants of vassalage to Assyria; they could be deemed false because they were ratified by invoking an Assyrian deity or deities (cf. v. 6). More likely, the broken obligations were those of the king to his people (cf. 2Sa 3:21; 5:3), especially his failure to maintain justice. **poisonous weeds.** Compare Amos 6:12.

10:5 Samaria. The capital city. **fear . . . mourn . . . rejoiced.** In words of judgment for the violations of verse 4, Hosea mocked the pious emotions the people manifested for an idol, which were noticeably absent for God. **calf-idol of Beth Aven.** See NIV text note and note on 8:5–6. Its sinfulness is rooted in its very origins. **idolatrous priests.** The calf and its priests (cf. 2Ki 23:5; Zep 1:4) were probably not foreign. Rather, they represented a traditional (but perverted) form of worshiping the Lord in Israel (1Ki 12:31–33).

10:7 its king. The king of Israel or, perhaps more likely, the calf-idol.

10:8 high places. See 4:13–14. **wickedness.** See NIV text note. **say to the mountains, "Cover us!" and to the hills, "Fall on us!"** Words connoting overwhelming and climactic devastation by the Lord. The people would rather die than face further judgments from him. The passage was cited by Jesus in Luke 23:30 and alluded to in Revelation 6:16, because the judgments in the latter days will also involve severe punishment for the unfaithful among the people of God.

10:9–10 I will punish. Hosea declared that Israel had sown the seeds of wickedness and would reap the fruits thereof.

10:9 Gibeah. See note on 9:9.

nations will be gathered against them
to put them in bonds for their double sin.
11 Ephraim is a trained heifer
that loves to thresh;
so I will put a yoke
on her fair neck.
I will drive Ephraim,
Judah must plow,
and Jacob must break up the ground.

10:12
[p]Pr 11:18 [q]Jer 4:3
[r]Hos 12:6 [s]Isa 45:8

12 Sow for yourselves righteousness,[p]
reap the fruit of unfailing love,
and break up your unplowed ground;[q]
for it is time to seek[r] the LORD,
until he comes
and showers righteousness[s] on you.

10:13
[t]Job 4:8; Hos 7:3; 11:12; Gal 6:7-8
[u]Ps 33:16

13 But you have planted wickedness,
you have reaped evil,[t]
you have eaten the fruit of deception.
Because you have depended on your own strength
and on your many warriors,[u]

10:14
[v]Isa 17:3
[w]Hos 13:16

14 the roar of battle will rise against your people,
so that all your fortresses will be devastated[v]—
as Shalman devastated Beth Arbel on the day of battle,
when mothers were dashed to the ground with their children.[w]
15 Thus will it happen to you, O Bethel,
because your wickedness is great.

10:15
[x]ver 7

When that day dawns,
the king of Israel will be completely destroyed.[x]

God's Love for Israel

11:1
[y]Ex 4:22; Hos 12:9,13; 13:4; Mt 2:15*

11

"When Israel was a child, I loved him,
and out of Egypt I called my son.[y]
2 But the more I[a] called Israel,
the further they went from me.[b]

[a] 2 Some Septuagint manuscripts; Hebrew *they* [b] 2 Septuagint; Hebrew *them*

10:10 double sin. Possibly the past sin at Gibeah and the present sin of Israel, or Israel's religious and political faithlessness or simply her repeated and unremitting transgressions.

■ **10:11–15** *Trained Heifer.* Hosea likened Israel to a trained heifer that was supposed to plow in order to sow righteousness but instead sowed only wickedness.

10:11 Ephraim . . . Judah. The whole nation, north and south. **trained heifer . . . loves to thresh.** A positive image of Israel's original calling as a tractable, unmuzzled animal threshing the harvested grain, free to eat as it worked (cf. 11:4; Dt 25:4; Pr 12:10; Jer 50:11). Jesus put a light yoke on his disciples (Mt 11:28–30). **fair neck.** A strong neck was capable of the arduous work of breaking and harrowing the ground under a yoke.

10:12 Sow. God chose Israel to fill the earth with righteousness. **unfailing love.** See note on "love" at 2:19–20. Sowing what is right and good would lead to a harvest of loyalty. **break up your unplowed ground.** When virgin or fallow ground is plowed it produces a particularly abundant harvest. **to seek the LORD.** To turn to him when in distress or trouble (see Dt 4:29–31). **showers righteousness.** God would grant the harvest of righteousness to the people if they would but turn to him in sincerity (1Co 3:6).

10:13 planted wickedness. Instead of cultivating a fruitful relationship with God (v. 12), Israel had planted, reaped and eaten wickedness, evil and deception or dishonesty (7:3; 10:4; 12:1). **Because you have depended on your own strength.** The punishment God would bring (military defeat; v. 14) was directly related to Israel's crime of depending on her own military power rather than on the Lord (Jer 9:23–24).

10:14 Shalman devastated Beth Arbel. An event Hosea's audience remembered as particularly brutal is not otherwise known. Shalman has been identified variously as Shalmaneser III of Assyria (859–824 B.C.), Shalmaneser V (727–722 B.C.) or Salamanu, a contemporary Moabite king. Beth Arbel is usually identified with the site of Irbid in Gilead. **mothers were dashed . . . with their children.** Such brutal atrocities were common in the ancient Near East (see 13:16; 2Ki 8:12; 15:16; Ps 137:8–9; Isa 13:16; Am 1:13; Na 3:10). Because Israel failed to persevere in her covenantal relationship she would be destroyed in a similar manner.

10:15 Bethel. Usually called Beth Aven in Hosea (4:15; 5:8; 10:5), some prefer the Septuagint (Greek translation of the OT) rendering "house of Israel." Bethel was one of the sites at which Jeroboam I had established illegitimate worship in Israel (see 1Ki 12:25–33).

■ **11:1—13:16** *Growing Child.* Hosea likened Israel to a developing child whose father loved him and tenderly cared for him. The child grew up, however, and rebelled against his father. A number of oracles of judgment and salvation are presented by this last metaphor and further united by repeated references to coming out of Egypt (11:1; 12:9,13; 13:4), mentioned in Hosea only one other time (2:15). Moreover, the last section (13:1–16) of these chapters recalls the metaphor of a child (see note on 13:13), forming a frame around the intervening material and thereby indicating its unity.

11:1–11 When Israel was a child. In language even more tender than that of the story of the lost son (Lk 15:11–32), God, the loving parent, confessed that he could not help but show compassion to his son, Israel, in spite of Israel's rebellion (9:10). Although the Lord pronounced judgment on the people he simultaneously offered hope that they would be restored and renewed, not utterly destroyed.

11:1 loved. The language of love described both the father and son relationship and the covenantal relationship between a suzerain and vassal in ancient Near Eastern treaties (cf. Dt 6:5; 7:8,13; 10:15; 23:5). **out of Egypt I called my son.** Reference here and in verse 4 to God's past deliverance of Israel from slavery in Egypt (cf. Ex 4:22). The deliverance from Egypt served as a model, or type, of salvation that was to come in Christ (see, e.g., 1Co 10:1–10). Jesus, the King of Israel and thus its representative, fulfilled this type in his own childhood (Mt 2:15).

They sacrificed to the Baals[z]
and they burned incense to images.[a]
3 It was I who taught Ephraim to walk,
taking them by the arms;[b]
but they did not realize
it was I who healed[c] them.
4 I led them with cords of human kindness,
with ties of love;[d]
I lifted the yoke[e] from their neck
and bent down to feed[f] them.

5 "Will they not return to Egypt[g]
and will not Assyria[h] rule over them
because they refuse to repent?
6 Swords[i] will flash in their cities,
will destroy the bars of their gates
and put an end to their plans.
7 My people are determined to turn from me.[j]
Even if they call to the Most High,
he will by no means exalt them.

8 "How can I give you up, Ephraim?[k]
How can I hand you over, Israel?
How can I treat you like Admah?
How can I make you like Zeboiim?[l]
My heart is changed within me;
all my compassion is aroused.
9 I will not carry out my fierce anger,[m]
nor will I turn and devastate[n] Ephraim.
For I am God, and not man[o]—
the Holy One among you.
I will not come in wrath.[a]
10 They will follow the LORD;
he will roar like a lion.
When he roars,
his children will come trembling from the west.[p]
11 They will come trembling
like birds from Egypt,
like doves from Assyria.[q]
I will settle them in their homes,"[r]
declares the LORD.

11:2 [z]Hos 2:13 [a]2Ki 17:15; Isa 65:7; Jer 18:15
11:3 [b]Dt 1:31; Hos 7:15 [c]Jer 30:17
11:4 [d]Jer 31:2-3 [e]Lev 26:13 [f]Ex 16:32; Ps 78:25
11:5 [g]Hos 7:16 [h]Hos 10:6
11:6 [i]Hos 13:16
11:7 [j]Jer 3:6-7; 8:5
11:8 [k]Hos 6:4 [l]Ge 14:8
11:9 [m]Dt 13:17; Jer 30:11 [n]Mal 3:6 [o]Nu 23:19
11:10 [p]Hos 6:1-3
11:11 [q]Isa 11:11 [r]Eze 28:26

[a] 9 Or *come against any city*

11:2 the more I called Israel. See NIV text note. **Baals.** Baal worship constituted a breach of the covenant, the basis of Israel's relationship with God.
11:3 taught Ephraim to walk. An allusion to God, who, like a parent teaching a child to walk, had led Israel through the wilderness to the promised land. **I who healed.** An allusion to God's sparing Israel from harm during that formative period (cf. Ex 15:26).
11:4 cords . . . ties . . . yoke . . . feed. The imagery returned to Israel as a work animal (cf. 10:11), but here God pampered the creature.
11:5 Egypt . . . Assyria. See notes on 8:13 and 9:3. Though deserved, the effect of this judgment would be tempered (v. 11).
11:6 their cities. Symbols of their self-reliance (8:14).
11:8 you. God now spoke directly to the Israelites rather than about them. The contrast with verses 5–7 heightens the impact of this deeply personal confession of relentless compassion. **Admah? . . . Zeboiim?** Two cities on the plain near the southern end of the Dead Sea (Ge 10:19; 14:2,8) that had been destroyed with Sodom and Gomorrah (Ge 19:23–25) and so served as examples of God's wrath (Dt 29:23; cf. Jer 49:18). **My heart is changed.** True to his faithful character God would turn from wrath against sin to compassion toward his covenant people.
11:9 I will. This verse and the rest of the chapter look to the future. **Holy One.** Holiness distinguishes God from humans. People would exact revenge, but God works salvation. **not come in wrath.** See NIV text note. God's love and wrath are both described in human terms; both are dictated, however, by his divine character.
11:10 They will follow the LORD. Restoration, not destruction, was the goal of God's judgment against his covenant people.
11:11 from Egypt . . . Assyria. God compassionately tempered the effect of the judgment pronounced in verse 5. There were Israelite refugees in Egypt as well as deportees in exile in Assyria (cf. 9:3; 11:5).
11:12—12:14 This section accuses Israel of betrayal and pronounces judgment. Recurrent themes are the past treachery of Israel (artistically linked with episodes from the life of Jacob/Israel) and Israel's rejection of the word of the Lord through the prophets.
11:12 surrounded me with lies. The northern kingdom had besieged God. **Judah is unruly against.** Or "roams, walks with" (a difficult word in Hebrew); some believe the prophet spoke of Judah's faithfulness either to God or to a Canaanite god and its "holy ones." **God.** This can also be rendered "god" or even "El," head of the Canaanite pantheon. **Holy One.** A plural form in the Hebrew, potentially referring to the "holy ones" of El.

Israel's Sin

[12] Ephraim has surrounded me with lies,[s]
the house of Israel with deceit.
And Judah is unruly against God,
even against the faithful Holy One.

12

[1] Ephraim feeds on the wind;[t]
he pursues the east wind all day
and multiplies lies and violence.
He makes a treaty with Assyria
and sends olive oil to Egypt.[u]
[2] The LORD has a charge[v] to bring against Judah;
he will punish Jacob[a] according to his ways
and repay him according to his deeds.[w]
[3] In the womb he grasped his brother's heel;[x]
as a man he struggled[y] with God.
[4] He struggled with the angel and overcame him;
he wept and begged for his favor.
He found him at Bethel[z]
and talked with him there—
[5] the LORD God Almighty,
the LORD is his name[a] of renown!
[6] But you must return to your God;
maintain love and justice,[b]
and wait for your God always.[c]

[7] The merchant uses dishonest scales;[d]
he loves to defraud.
[8] Ephraim boasts,
"I am very rich; I have become wealthy.[e]
With all my wealth they will not find in me
any iniquity or sin."

[9] "I am the LORD your God,
⌊who brought you⌋ out of[b] Egypt;[f]
I will make you live in tents[g] again,
as in the days of your appointed feasts.
[10] I spoke to the prophets,
gave them many visions
and told parables[h] through them."[i]

11:12 [s]Hos 4:2
12:1 [t]Eze 17:10 [u]2Ki 17:4
12:2 [v]Mic 6:2 [w]Hos 4:9
12:3 [x]Ge 25:26 [y]Ge 32:24-29
12:4 [z]Ge 28:12-15; 35:15
12:5 [a]Ex 3:15
12:6 [b]Mic 6:8 [c]Hos 6:1-3; 10:12; Mic 7:7
12:7 [d]Am 8:5
12:8 [e]Ps 62:10; Rev 3:17
12:9 [f]Lev 23:43; Hos 11:1 [g]Ne 8:17
12:10 [h]Eze 20:49 [i]2Ki 17:13; Jer 7:25

a *2* *Jacob* means *he grasps the heel* (figuratively, *he deceives*). b *9* Or *God / ever since you were in*

12:1 feeds on. See the use of this pastoral verb in Proverbs 15:14 and Isaiah 44:20. **wind . . . east wind.** See 8:7, 13:15, Job 15:2, Ecclesiastes 1:14, Jeremiah 18:17 and Ezekiel 17:10; images of futility and destruction applied to Israel's alliances with Assyria (5:13; 7:11; 8:9; 14:3; 2Ki 17:3) and Egypt (2Ki 17:4). Such alliances were not just examples of ill-advised foreign policy but expressions of faithlessness against the Lord. **lies.** Examples of deception include vacillating between Assyria and Egypt (7:11) and playing off the latter against the former (2Ki 17:3–4). **oil.** Gifts were often given in the process of covenant making with foreign nations.
12:2 charge. As in 4:1–3 and again in 4:4–10, the Lord (as plaintiff, judge and prosecutor in a court scene) brought a lawsuit against his people (vv. 2–15). He called for punishment (v. 2) and reconciliation (v. 6). **Jacob.** That is, Israel; see NIV text note and 10:11.
12:3 grasped. The Hebrew is the root for "Jacob" (Ge 25:26) and is translated "deceive" in Genesis 27:36. See also NIV text note on verse 2. **struggled.** The Hebrew is the root for "Israel" (Ge 32:22–32, esp. v. 29). The nation's namesake, Jacob/Israel, functioned as an example in the lawsuit. Though perhaps used positively in Hosea 12:4, the example in verse 3 is probably negative: In manhood Israel (Jacob) was no less tenacious with God than he had been with an elder brother at birth.
12:4 struggled with the angel. See Genesis 32:22–32, including NIV text note on verse 28. Jacob set a positive example by clinging to the angel for God's blessing. **He found him.** That is, God found Jacob. **Bethel.** The place where God had made himself known to Jacob (Ge 28:12–19; 35:1–15). In Hosea's day it was the most important royal sanctuary in the northern kingdom (see Am 7:13).
12:5 LORD God Almighty. A liturgical doxology not unlike those in Amos (Am 4:13; 5:8–9; 9:5–6), linking the Lord Almighty with Israel.
12:6 return to your God. Following the doxology (v. 5) Israel was summoned afresh. The nation needed to relive the career of Jacob/Israel, its namesake and ancestor (see notes on vv. 2 and 4). The message applied not only to the nation but perhaps reflected Hosea's understanding of what God had said to Jacob at Bethel (cf. v. 4). **love . . . justice.** See note on 2:19–20.
12:7 merchant. The Hebrew word is *cana'an,* which is also the word for "Canaan" and may be translated "Canaanite"—the Canaanites were so well known for trading that their name had become synonymous with "merchant." By using this word rather than another for "merchant," Hosea may have intended to imply that the merchant Ephraim/Israel (v. 8) was not merely dishonest, but also pagan. See *WLC* 193.
12:9 I am the LORD your God, who brought you out of Egypt. See NIV text notes here and on 13:4; compare Exodus 20:2 and Deuteronomy 5:6. This statement of self-presentation introduced an expression of the divine will to the covenant people. The reference to coming out of Egypt connects this material to the metaphor of the growing child (see note on 11:1—13:16). **appointed feasts.** See 2:11.
12:10 spoke to the prophets. See 6:5, 12:13, Numbers 12:6–8, Deuteronomy 18:15–22, Amos 2:11 and Hebrews 1:1. There could be no excuse of ignorance. **visions.** That is, revelations (2Sa 7:17; Pr 29:18). **parables.** Figures of speech bearing divine messages (2Sa 12:1–4; Ps 78:2; Isa 5:1–7; Eze 17:2; 24:3).

[11]Is Gilead wicked?[j]
Its people are worthless!
Do they sacrifice bulls in Gilgal?[k]
Their altars will be like piles of stones
on a plowed field.[l]
[12]Jacob fled to the country of Aram[a];[m]
Israel served to get a wife,
and to pay for her he tended sheep.[n]
[13]The LORD used a prophet to bring Israel up from Egypt,
by a prophet he cared for him.[o]
[14]But Ephraim has bitterly provoked him to anger;
his Lord will leave upon him the guilt of his bloodshed[p]
and will repay him for his contempt.[q]

The LORD's Anger Against Israel

13 When Ephraim spoke, men trembled;[r]
he was exalted[s] in Israel.
But he became guilty of Baal worship[t] and died.
[2]Now they sin more and more;
they make idols for themselves from their silver,[u]
cleverly fashioned images,
all of them the work of craftsmen.
It is said of these people,
"They offer human sacrifice
and kiss[b] the calf-idols.[v]"
[3]Therefore they will be like the morning mist,
like the early dew that disappears,[w]
like chaff[x] swirling from a threshing floor,[y]
like smoke[z] escaping through a window.
[4]"But I am the LORD your God,
⌞who brought you⌟ out of[c] Egypt.[a]
You shall acknowledge no God but me,[b]
no Savior[c] except me.
[5]I cared for you in the desert,
in the land of burning heat.

12:11 [j]Hos 6:8 [k]Hos 4:15 [l]Hos 8:11
12:12 [m]Ge 28:5 [n]Ge 29:18
12:13 [o]Ex 13:3; Isa 63:11-14
12:14 [p]Eze 18:13 [q]Da 11:18
13:1 [r]Jdg 12:1 [s]Jdg 8:1 [t]Hos 11:2
13:2 [u]Isa 46:6; Jer 10:4 [v]Isa 44:17-20
13:3 [w]Hos 6:4 [x]Isa 17:13 [y]Da 2:35 [z]Ps 68:2
13:4 [a]Hos 12:9 [b]Ex 20:3 [c]Isa 43:11; 45:21-22

[a] *12* That is, Northwest Mesopotamia [b] *2* Or *"Men who sacrifice / kiss* [c] *4* Or *God / ever since you were in*

12:11 Gilead. A place of illegal sacrifices, bloodshed and idolatry and a region conquered by Assyria in 731–732 B.C. (2Ki 15:29, cf. 6:8). **Gilgal.** See note on 4:15. **piles of stones.** When plowing, farmers piled up the stones they struck.
12:12 country of Aram. That is, Paddan-Aram (Ge 28:2,5). **pay.** Possibly Jacob's servitude for a wife (Ge 29:20–30) invited comparison with Israel's servitude to pagan sex rites. More likely Jacob's service to secure a wife from Aram illustrated God's rescue of his bride from Egypt. **tended.** Jacob's care for Laban's flock (Ge 30:31) paled in comparison to God's care for Israel through the prophet (see note on v. 13).
12:13 used a prophet. Moses (Dt 18:15; 34:10–12). **from Egypt.** Reference to the exodus from Egypt; recalled the opening metaphor of a growing child (see note on 11:1—13:16). **by a prophet.** Perhaps Moses as well, though a Mosaic prophet like Samuel (cf. Jer 15:1) or Elijah (cf. 1Ki 19:9–13) may be in view here. **cared for.** In Hebrew the same verb as "tended" in verse 12 (see its note). Israel was not to focus on frail and human Jacob but on God's provision through the Mosaic prophet, which included obedience to covenant law.
12:14 provoked. Hosea contrasted past provision (v. 13) with present punishment. Elsewhere the Lord was provoked by the worship of pagan gods (e.g., Dt 32:21), though here more factors seem to be involved. **bloodshed.** A reference either to murder (4:2; 5:2; 6:8) or, as in legal texts, to being guilty of a crime warranting capital punishment (i.e., "bloodguilt"; see Lev 20:9–27 for a similar expression: "Their blood will be on their own heads"). The verse concludes the lawsuit and in structure parallels verse 2, which introduces the section.
13:1–16 The Lord would judge idolatrous Israel, who was ripe for destruction.
13:1 Begins an announcement of judgment in which sins past (v. 1) and present (v. 2) precede the statement of the penalty (v. 3). **Ephraim.** It is ironic that the northern kingdom bore the name of the tribe of Ephraim, which had a prominent past (Ge 48:10–20; Jdg 8:1–3) and which gave rise to powerful leaders such as Joshua (Jos 24:30) and Jeroboam I (1Ki 11:26; 12:20). **Baal worship.** See 2:7–8 and 17, 9:10 and 11:2. **died.** Enslaved to sin (idolatry), Israel was subject to death and did indeed die to God: The northern kingdom was already dead in its transgressions and sins (cf. Eph 2:1).
13:2 idols . . . images . . . calf-idols. See 8:5–6 and 11:2. The first word signifies literally "molten images" (cf. Ex 32:4,8; 34:17; Lev 19:4; Dt 9:16). The collective picture is of calf statuettes made of bronze and overlaid with silver. Though Canaanite and linked with Baal, the calf was probably associated with the Lord in the minds of the idolaters (see note on Ex 32:4). **kiss.** An act of devotion, adoration or appeasement (1Ki 19:18; Ps 2:12).
13:3 mist . . . dew. Compare 6:4.
13:4 Egypt. Recalled the metaphor of a growing child (see note on 11:1—13:16). **You shall acknowledge no God but me.** In contrast to the idolatry of verse 2. The statement, reminding Israel of the exclusiveness of the covenant relationship, was cast in the language of the first of the Ten Commandments (cf. Ex 20:2–3; Dt 5:6–7; Joel 2:27) but with the added notion of acknowledging or, literally, of "knowing" God. Other gods might be worshiped, but only the one true God can be "known." See "Introduction: Purpose and Distinctives." See also notes on 12:9. For a link with 13:1–3, see Exodus 20:4–6 and Deuteronomy 5:8–10. **Savior.** A helper in time of trouble. Israel's source of aid could be none other than the God of history. Contrast Israel's reliance upon kings in 13:10, the military in 14:3 and idols in 13:2.
13:5 I cared for you. Literally, "I knew you [singular]," referring to Israel as a corporate whole. Through the covenant there had been a mutual (and genuine) relationship (see v. 4, where Israel had "known" God; also see "Introduction: Purpose and Distinc-

13:6 [d]Dt 32:12-15; Hos 2:13
13:8 [e]2Sa 17:8 [f]Ps 50:22
13:9 [g]Jer 2:17-19 [h]Dt 33:29
13:10 [i]2Ki 17:4 [j]1Sa 8:6; Hos 8:4
13:11 [k]1Ki 14:10; Hos 10:7
13:12 [l]Dt 32:34
13:13 [m]Isa 13:8; Mic 4:9-10 [n]Isa 66:9
13:14 [o]Ps 49:15; Eze 37:12-13 [p]1Co 15:55*
13:15 [q]Hos 10:1 [r]Eze 19:12

6 When I fed them, they were satisfied;
when they were satisfied, they became proud;
then they forgot me.[d]
7 So I will come upon them like a lion,
like a leopard I will lurk by the path.
8 Like a bear robbed of her cubs,[e]
I will attack them and rip them open.
Like a lion I will devour them;
a wild animal will tear them apart.[f]

9 "You are destroyed, O Israel,
because you are against me,[g] against your helper.[h]
10 Where is your king,[i] that he may save you?
Where are your rulers in all your towns,
of whom you said,
'Give me a king and princes'?[j]
11 So in my anger I gave you a king,
and in my wrath I took him away.[k]
12 The guilt of Ephraim is stored up,
his sins are kept on record.[l]
13 Pains as of a woman in childbirth[m] come to him,
but he is a child without wisdom;
when the time arrives,
he does not come to the opening of the womb.[n]

14 "I will ransom them from the power of the grave[a];[o]
I will redeem them from death.
Where, O death, are your plagues?
Where, O grave,[a] is your destruction?[p]

"I will have no compassion,
15 even though he thrives[q] among his brothers.
An east wind[r] from the LORD will come,

[a] *14* Hebrew *Sheol*

tives"). **desert.** Another positive reference to Israel's time in the wilderness; compare 2:14–15. **burning heat.** Alternatively, "drought."

13:6 I fed them. This remarkable feat (cf. v. 5) was sadly a step in the process of Israel's forgetting God (cf. Dt 32:10–18; Jer 2). **proud.** See Deuteronomy 8:10–18. **forgot.** The pitiful climax of verses 4–6; it stands in sharp contrast to former days of knowledge and intimacy (see notes on vv. 4,5). The Israelites' sins at their origin reflected the depth and gravity of their moral degeneracy (see "Introduction: Purpose and Distinctives"). See Hosea 2:13 and Deuteronomy 8:11–20.

13:7–9 The Lord, elsewhere described as a shepherd (4:16), would attack like the wild beasts that devoured the flocks. Though balanced by such passages as 11:8–11 and 14:1–9, the tone of these verses is stern.

13:7 lion. Compare 5:14. **leopard.** See Jeremiah 5:6.

13:8 bear robbed of her cubs. See Proverbs 17:12. **I will attack them and rip them open.** Literally, "I will rip open the casing of their heart." **Like a lion I will devour them.** Another interpretation is "there dogs will devour them," which possibly forms a suitable parallel with the following line. These wild animal images depicted the savagery of the attack.

13:9 helper. That the helper should turn destroyer was explained in terms of Israel's rebellion against the helper. On God's role as helper, see 11:8–11. Compare Exodus 18:4, Deuteronomy 33:26–29, Psalms 10:14, 54:4, 115:9–11, 121 and 146:5. God stated the essence of his case: To be against him was to incur destruction. See *BC* 26.

13:10 king. Which king is not specified; this may be a reference to the royal assassinations of Hosea's time (3:4; 7:7; 8:4; 10:3; cf. 2Ki 15:8–31; 17:1–6); to an early king of notoriety, such as Saul (who was given in direct response to the people's demand); or even to all of the kings of the northern kingdom (all 20 who "did evil in the eyes of the Lord"). Kings gave Israel a false sense of security; the Lord alone (their true King) was their help. **Give me a king.** On Israel's request for a monarchy see notes on 1 Samuel 8:5 and 19. For commentary on the request made later for a non-Davidic monarchy for the northern kingdom specifically, see 1 Kings 12:16–20.

13:11 gave . . . took. Though describing past action the Hebrew verb form suggests an ongoing process of giving and taking. God had always planned for the Israelites to have a human king, but because of their motivation their request constituted a rejection of God as King (see notes on 1Sa 8:1–22). **in my wrath I took him away.** Many of the northern kings fell by treachery.

13:12 guilt . . . sins. Lest they be diminished or forgotten, transgressions were written down (as though in a legal document), tied up and stored in a safe place (for future retribution); compare 7:2, 9:9 and Deuteronomy 32:34–35. **Ephraim.** The northern kingdom, Israel. **stored up.** Literally, "bound up"; see 1 Samuel 25:29, Job 14:17 and Isaiah 8:16.

13:13 without wisdom. Relates to the theme of failure to acknowledge God. See "Introduction: Purpose and Distinctives." **when the time arrives, he does not come to the opening of the womb.** The Hebrew is difficult, but the analogy and its point are nonetheless apparent: As a child dies when something goes wrong at the point of its birth (cf. 2Ki 19:3), so Israel would die for failing to respond to the punishment meant to prompt repentance and new life. This analogy connects with the opening metaphor of a growing child (see note on 11:1—13:16) and signals the end of that imagery.

13:14 I will . . . I will. To some interpreters the context of judgment in verses 12 and 15 suggests that these two lines should be rendered as questions ("Will I . . . ? will I . . . ?"), for which the answer of no is expected. In that case the next two lines beginning with "where" merely summon the weapons of death to destroy Israel. It is likely, however, that the verse anticipates the positive spirit of 14:4–7 and is one of the great affirmations of God's power over the last enemy: death. Paul's use of this verse in 1 Corinthians 15:55 applied it to the promises of restoration. Whereas God's people refused to rely on his power over death in Hosea's time, Christ and the believers in his church have experienced and will experience it. The final triumph over God's last enemy is assured by the death of Christ for sin and his resurrection from the grave. **grave.** See NIV text note. **I will have no compassion.** Unbelieving Ephraim/Israel would not be spared.

blowing in from the desert;
his spring will fail
and his well dry up.[s]
His storehouse will be plundered[t]
of all its treasures.
16 The people of Samaria must bear their guilt,[u]
because they have rebelled[v] against their God.
They will fall by the sword;[w]
their little ones will be dashed[x] to the ground,
their pregnant women[y] ripped open."

Repentance to Bring Blessing

14 Return, O Israel, to the LORD your God.
Your sins have been your downfall![z]
2 Take words with you
and return to the LORD.
Say to him:
"Forgive all our sins
and receive us graciously,[a]
that we may offer the fruit of our lips.[a][b]
3 Assyria cannot save us;
we will not mount war-horses.[c]
We will never again say 'Our gods'[d]
to what our own hands have made,
for in you the fatherless[e] find compassion."

4 "I will heal[f] their waywardness
and love them freely,[g]
for my anger has turned away from them.
5 I will be like the dew to Israel;
he will blossom like a lily.[h]
Like a cedar of Lebanon[i]
he will send down his roots;[j]
6 his young shoots will grow.
His splendor will be like an olive tree,[k]
his fragrance like a cedar of Lebanon.[l]
7 Men will dwell again in his shade.[m]
He will flourish like the grain.
He will blossom like a vine,
and his fame will be like the wine[n] from Lebanon.[o]

13:15 [s]Jer 51:36 [t]Jer 20:5
13:16 [u]Hos 10:2 [v]Hos 7:14 [w]Hos 11:6 [x]2Ki 8:12; Hos 10:14 [y]2Ki 15:16; Isa 13:16
14:1 [z]Hos 5:5
14:2 [a]Mic 7:18-19 [b]Heb 13:15
14:3 [c]Ps 33:17; Isa 31:1 [d]Hos 8:6 [e]Ps 10:14; 68:5
14:4 [f]Hos 6:1 [g]Zep 3:17
14:5 [h]SS 2:1 [i]Isa 35:2 [j]Job 29:19
14:6 [k]Ps 52:8; Jer 11:16 [l]SS 4:11
14:7 [m]Ps 91:1-4 [n]Hos 2:22 [o]Eze 17:23

a 2 Or *offer our lips as sacrifices of bulls*

13:15 he. Ephraim. **thrives.** A play on the word *Ephraim,* or "fruitful." **east wind.** See 12:1 and its note. This destructive force was a symbol for Assyria, which invaded Israel in 734 B.C., then conquered and exiled its people in 722–721 B.C. **from the LORD.** On Assyria as the Lord's instrument, see also Isaiah 10:5–19. **plundered.** See 2 Kings 17:20; compare Isaiah 17:14 and Nahum 2:9.
13:16 Samaria. The capital city and driving force behind the northern kingdom's rebellion and obstinacy. **fall . . . dashed . . . ripped.** Metaphorical language for destruction (vv. 3,8,15) gave way to concrete and chilling expression. **little ones . . . women.** See 10:14 and its note.
■ **14:1–9** *Closing Call for Repentance.* Hosea closed his book with an exhortation for the Israelites to confess and repent of their sins that they might again be blessed of God.
14:1–3 The prophet spoke to the people, urging the type of repentance the Lord promises to bless (vv. 4–8).
14:1 Return. This thematic exhortation to turn/return (2:7; 3:5; 6:1; 7:10,16; 12:6; Dt 30:1–10) was now addressed to those who had already fallen because of their sins. See "Introduction: Purpose and Distinctives."
14:2 Take words. Genuine words of confession, not halfhearted sacrifices (5:6; 6:6; 8:13), accompanied by obedience were required of a genuinely repentant people. A precise wording of the confession is given in verses 2b–3. **the fruit of our lips.** See Proverbs 12:14, 13:2 and Hebrews 13:15. See *WCF* 15.3; *WLC* 194.
14:3 Assyria . . . war-horses . . . 'Our gods.' Israel was to give up trusting in foreign political powers (e.g., 5:13; 7:11; 12:1), her own military strength (e.g., 10:13; cf. Ps 33:16–17) and unorthodox and syncretistic religion (e.g., 2:8,13; 3:1; 4:12; 8:5–6; 10:5–6; 13:2). **fatherless find compassion.** An allusion to the earlier theme of the loss and restoration of love illustrated by Hosea's marriage (3:1) and by the name of his daughter, Lo-Ruhamah (1:6–8; 2:1,23). See "Introduction: Purpose and Distinctives."
14:4 I will heal. The promise of healing began to be fulfilled when Israel returned from the exile. It is finding a much greater fulfillment in Jesus Christ and his church and will be consummated at his second coming. **waywardness.** Literally, "turning." Israel's unfaithful ways would be mended (e.g., 4:10–12; 5:4; 7:4; 11:5) as God's anger was satisfied. See "Introduction: Purpose and Distinctives." **love them freely.** In this love song we hear again the genuine affections of God for his elect. This promise of God's undeserved love exemplifies what the New Testament calls grace (e.g., Ro 5:15; Eph 2:5,8). See *WCF* 15.3.
14:5–7 like a lily. Like a cedar. In this section, resplendent with the language of love, colorful metaphors drawn from plant life—a blossoming lily (cf. 1Ki 7:26; SS 2:1,16); a deeply rooted, sprouting and fragrant cedar of Lebanon (cf. Pss 92:12; 104:16); a splendid olive tree (cf. Ps 52:8; Jer 11:16); a shady tree (cf. SS 2:3; Eze 17:22–23); flourishing grain (2:17,20); a flowering vine (10:1; Isa 5:1–7); and the celebrated fruit of the vine—depict a vigorously healthy, renowned, stable and prosperous Israel flourishing under God, who was likened to the life-giving dew (Dt 33:13).

14:8
*p*ver 3

[8] O Ephraim, what more have I[a] to do with idols?[p]
I will answer him and care for him.
I am like a green pine tree;
your fruitfulness comes from me."

14:9
*q*Ps 107:43
*r*Pr 10:29; Isa 1:28
*s*Ps 111:7-8; Zep 3:5; Ac 13:10
*t*Isa 26:7

[9] Who is wise?[q] He will realize these things.
Who is discerning? He will understand them.[r]
The ways of the LORD are right;[s]
the righteous walk[t] in them,
but the rebellious stumble in them.

[a] *8* Or *What more has Ephraim*

14:8 O Ephraim. Either an exclamation (6:4; 11:8) or a rhetorical question declaring once again the utter incompatibility of God and idols (see NIV text note). **green pine tree.** Like a tree renowned as a symbol of life (cf. Ge 3:22; Rev 22:2), God would give fruit to fruitful Ephraim (see note on 9:16; cf. Ge 41:52).
14:9 Who is wise? This epilogue challenged each generation of readers of Hosea's prophecy to consider carefully the ways of the Lord (Pss 1; 18:21; Pr 10:24,29,30; 11:3; 12:3,5,7) presented in the book. The choices between wisdom and folly, discipleship and rebellion, walking and stumbling, obedience and disobedience, life and death repeatedly presented to Israel are also presented to the reader. The wise and discerning will choose life (Dt 30:15–20).

JOEL

Introduction

Overview

Author: The prophet Joel

Purpose: To call God's people to repentance so they could escape judgment and enjoy blessings on the approaching day of the Lord

Date: Unknown

Key Truths:

- Temporary, historical judgments call for repentance.
- Temporary judgments indicate the importance of repentance for the great day of the Lord.
- God promises his repentant people salvation from judgment and unending blessings in the future.

Author

The prophet Joel is identified only as "Joel son of Pethuel" (1:1). The book gives us no other information about the prophet, and he is mentioned nowhere else in Scripture.

Time and Place of Writing

Since the book of Joel contains no clear indications as to when it was written, it is difficult to date the book. Joel's keen interest in Jerusalem—particularly in the temple and its functionaries (e.g., 1:9,13–14; 2:14–17,32; 3:1,6,16–17)—suggests that he lived in Jerusalem at a time when temple services were active. Various clues have been used for dating purposes: the book's location in the canon, its vocabulary, linguistic parallels to other prophetic books and historical allusions. Some interpreters date the book to the ninth century B.C. during the reign of Joash (c. 835 B.C.). Others place it in the years just prior to the fall of Jerusalem in 586 B.C., while still others prefer a postexilic date, either early (c. 520–500 B.C.) or late (c. 400 B.C.).

It has been noted that, compared to the long list of accusations in other prophetic books, the book of Joel does not catalog the sins that caused the disasters it mentions. This has caused some interpreters to suggest that Joel was purposefully written as a liturgical guide to be used at any time of crisis or threat to God's people. In this light Calvin's firm posture that one cannot know the date of the book may suit the situation well.

Purpose and Distinctives

Although the book's unity was challenged by critics of the late nineteenth and early twentieth centuries (they surmised that different authors had written the contemporary [1:1—2:17] and futuristic [2:18—3:21] sections of the book), most interpreters now advocate its essential unity. Such features as the repeated theme of the "day of the LORD" (1:15; 2:1,11,31; 3:14) and verbal links between the sections (e.g., 2:2 and 2:31; 2:10–11 and 3:16; 2:10 and 3:15; 2:11 and 31; 2:17 and 3:2; 2:27 and 3:17) point to this unity.

One central theological motif of Joel is the concept of the "day of the LORD." In 1:15 the day of the Lord is introduced in the context of Joel's depiction of the horrible devastation he believed foreshadowed a greater future judgment. In this first instance, then, Joel, like Amos (Am 5:18–20; cf. Zep 1:7–13), declared the day of the Lord to be a day of judgment against God's own people. Similarly, in chapter 2 Joel described the day of the Lord as a "dreadful" day (2:11), "a day of darkness and gloom, a day of clouds and blackness" (2:2), a day when the Lord would lead his army against Israel. However, in the second part of the book Joel focused on the day of the Lord as the day of judgment against the enemies of God's people, while God's people would be protected and blessed (Isa 13; Jer 46–51; Eze 25–32). On the day of the Lord the nations would be accountable for their crimes against the Lord's covenant people and would be judged accordingly (3:2–16,19). But the people of the Lord's inheritance would be protected and spiritually and physically blessed (2:28–32; 3:16–18,20–21).

A second central motif in Joel is repentance. The call to repentance is given not merely to a select number within the covenant community, but rather to all the Lord's people who were called to return to him: young and old, men and women, leaders and followers and even those who might otherwise be exempted from community responsibilities (e.g., nursing mothers and newlyweds [1:13–14; 2:15–17]). Joel called the people to a return to God that involved the whole person. Such repentance was to be manifested externally through such actions as mourning, weeping, crying out to the Lord and fasting. He called for repentance in light of the locust plague (1:13–14) and the still future day of judgment (2:15–17). However, external or ritual manifestations of repentance were inadequate, and the Lord summoned the people to demonstrate the sincerity of their repentance by returning to him with all their heart (2:12–13). Joel also reminded God's people that the proper motivation for repentance lies firmly in the nature of God: "He is gracious and compassionate, slow to anger and abounding in love" (2:13). At the same time Joel stressed that the possibility of repentance lies not with the people but with God, who is free to exercise his sovereign freedom and grace in granting forgiveness to his people.

Joel poses an interpretive difficulty with regard to one of its central images: locusts. Interpreters throughout the ages have been faced with the question of whether to interpret these locusts literally or figuratively. Although the majority of interpreters throughout history have understood the locusts as symbols of future enemies—one sixth-century manuscript of the Septuagint (the Greek translation of the OT) went so far as to read the four locusts as symbolizing the Egyptians, Assyrians, Greeks and Romans—most modern interpreters understand at least the locusts of chapter 1 in a literal way. To be sure, Joel moves quickly from a literal and remarkably accurate description of a contemporary crisis involving a devastation by locusts in chapter 1 to a description of the dreadful locust-like army of the Lord that blends the literal and figurative in chapter 2. It may be that Joel witnessed literal devastation by locusts and found in the event a picture of the destruction that would take place on the impending day of the Lord. This may have motivated him to employ the imagery of locusts in describing the coming invaders.

Christ in Joel

The book of Joel has had an important place in the life of the church. The New Testament makes it clear that Jesus and his followers were familiar with the writings of Joel, and its influence is most evident in the New Testament passages that speak of the latter days (see theological article "The Plan of the Ages" at Heb 7). These passages pick up on the graphic images used by Joel to describe the day of the Lord and the plague of locusts (e.g., Mk 13:24; Lk 21:25; Rev 6:9; 9:2). Also important are the promises in 2:28–32, which Peter quoted and claimed to have been inaugurated during the event at Pentecost (Ac 2:16–21). Paul also referred to this prophecy in Romans 10:13, where he used Joel 2:32 to substantiate his argument that "there is no difference between Jew and Gentile" (Ro 10:12). Salvation is for all; as the prophet Joel stated: "Everyone who calls on the name of the LORD will be saved" (2:32).

The church has continued to find Joel's teaching on the day of the Lord to be an important source of hope and comfort on the one hand and a word of warning on the other. In times of distress and trouble Christians have found the promises regarding the ultimate blessing, protection and vindication of the Lord's covenant community to be consoling and inspiring. At the same time Joel's vivid depiction of the dreadful aspects of the day of the Lord has served as a reminder of God's holiness and judgment and as a continuing call to wholehearted repentance and holiness of life. Ultimately, the great day of the Lord is the day of Christ's return, the day when he will judge the whole world, casting his enemies into hell and blessing believers with an eternal inheritance in the new heavens and the new earth.

Outline

I. Superscription (1:1)

Joel's message came from the Lord and was to be received as his authoritative word.

II. Crises Demanding Repentance (1:2—2:17)
- A. Recent Devastation by Locust and Drought (1:2–20)
- B. Future Devastation on the Day of the Lord (2:1–17)

A locust plague and drought foreshadowed the need for repentance for the greater, impending day of judgment.

III. Divine Responses to Repentance (2:18—3:21)
- A. Promise of Renewal (2:18–32)
  1. Renewal of the Land (2:18–27)
  2. Renewal of God's People (2:28–32)
- B. Final Judgment and Blessing (3:1–21)
  1. Judgment on the Nations (3:1–16)
  2. Blessings for God's People (3:17–21)

God responded to the repentance of his people with promises of final judgment against his enemies and with blessings for his repentant people.

1:1 [a]Jer 1:2 [b]Ac 2:16

1 The word of the LORD that came[a] to Joel[b] son of Pethuel.

An Invasion of Locusts

1:2 [c]Hos 5:1 [d]Hos 4:1

2 Hear this,[c] you elders;
listen, all who live in the land.[d]
Has anything like this ever happened in your days

■ **1:1** *Superscription.* The book begins with an identification of the prophet Joel.

1:1 The word of the LORD. This short and simple title announces that what follows is the Lord's word. It compares most closely with Jonah 1:1 (cf. the more expansive titles in Jer 1:2; Eze 1:3; Hos 1:1; Mic 1:1; Zep 1:1; Hag 1:1; Zec 1:1; Mal 1:1). **Joel.** His name means "the LORD is God." **Pethuel.** Joel's father's name is not found elsewhere.

■ **1:2—2:17** *Crises Demanding Repentance.* Two crises confronted the Judahites with the consequences of their sins: (1) the recent devastation of the land (1:2–20) by locusts (1:4–8) and drought (1:10–12,16–20); and (2) the impending assault on the land by the army of the Lord (2:1–17). If the people were to repent of their sins and return to the Lord they might be delivered from these calamities.

■ **1:2–20** *Recent Devastation by Locust and Drought.* Joel appealed to elders (v. 2), drunkards (v. 5), farmers (v. 11) and priests (v. 13) to ponder the implications of the recent locust plague and drought and to repent.

1:2 Hear . . . listen. This series of imperatives called the people

or in the days of your forefathers?[e]
3 Tell it to your children,[f]
and let your children tell it to their children,
and their children to the next generation.
4 What the locust swarm has left
the great locusts have eaten;
what the great locusts have left
the young locusts have eaten;
what the young locusts have left
other locusts[a] have eaten.[g]

5 Wake up, you drunkards, and weep!
Wail, all you drinkers of wine;[h]
wail because of the new wine,
for it has been snatched from your lips.
6 A nation has invaded my land,
powerful and without number;[i]
it has the teeth[j] of a lion,
the fangs of a lioness.
7 It has laid waste[k] my vines
and ruined my fig trees.[l]
It has stripped off their bark
and thrown it away,
leaving their branches white.

8 Mourn like a virgin[b] in sackcloth[m]
grieving for the husband[c] of her youth.
9 Grain offerings and drink offerings[n]
are cut off from the house of the LORD.
The priests are in mourning,
those who minister before the LORD.
10 The fields are ruined,
the ground is dried up[d];[o]
the grain is destroyed,
the new wine[p] is dried up,
the oil fails.
11 Despair, you farmers,[q]
wail, you vine growers;
grieve for the wheat and the barley,
because the harvest of the field is destroyed.[r]
12 The vine is dried up
and the fig tree is withered;

1:2 [e]Joel 2:2
1:3 [f]Ex 10:2; Ps 78:4
1:4 [g]Dt 28:39; Na 3:15
1:5 [h]Joel 3:3
1:6 [i]Joel 2:2,11,25 [j]Rev 9:8
1:7 [k]Isa 5:6 [l]Am 4:9
1:8 [m]ver 13; Isa 22:12; Am 8:10
1:9 [n]Hos 9:4; Joel 2:14,17
1:10 [o]Isa 24:4 [p]Hos 9:2
1:11 [q]Jer 14:3-4; Am 5:16 [r]Isa 17:11

[a] *4* The precise meaning of the four Hebrew words used here for locusts is uncertain. [b] *8* Or *young woman* [c] *8* Or *betrothed* [d] *10* Or *ground mourns*

to recognize the personal and spiritual ramifications of the invasion of the locusts. The parallelism of thought in the first and second and again in the third and fourth lines is typical of Hebrew poetry. **elders.** The religious and community leaders. The same term is used in 2:28, but there it seems to refer more specifically to chronological age; hence the translation "old men." **all who live in the land.** The entire population of Judah and Jerusalem was called to listen.

1:3 Tell . . . children . . . next generation. God's judgments, as well as his mercies, are to be passed on to future generations (cf. Dt 4:9; 6:7; 32:7; Ps 78:1–8).

1:4 locust. Poetic repetitions emphasize the thoroughness of the locusts' destruction. The four different designations for the locusts may refer to different developmental stages of locusts (as the NIV translation suggests), although color differences or differences in type or regional origin may be reflected both here and in 2:25. It is also possible that the descriptions are meant only to indicate that different swarms would be involved. In any event, when locusts were understood as an instrument of divine punishment repentance was in order (Dt 28:38; Am 7:1; Isa 33:4).

1:5 Wake up . . . weep! The first call to respond was given to the drunkards, who represented the attitude of many who were oblivious to things of spiritual significance around them. Only those who are awake are able to respond to God's judgment.

1:6 invaded . . . lion. The locusts are compared to an invading nation that has the consuming passion of a lion (cf. 2:4–9; Rev 9:7–9). Locusts and armies were often compared in ancient times. Mythic Ugaritic literature (fifteenth century B.C.) likens an army to a locust swarm in terms of size (see Jdg 6:5; 7:12; Pr 30:27; Jer 51:14,27; Na 3:15–17). **my land.** Personal pronouns are used throughout the book, pointing to the covenantal relationship that binds the Lord not only to the land and its vines and fig trees but also to his people (1:7; 2:13–14,17–18,23,26–27; 3:2–3,17).

1:7 vines . . . fig trees. The locusts' teeth effectively stripped these most valuable forms of vegetation in the Lord's land.

1:8 Mourn. The mourning was to be like that of a young woman who had lost her beloved before marriage. **sackcloth.** This coarsely woven material was often made of goat's hair and was typically worn during periods of mourning (see v. 13; Ge 37:34; 2Sa 3:31; 1Ki 21:27; Isa 32:11–12).

1:9 Grain offerings and drink offerings. These offerings, which were to be made twice daily (Ex 29:38–42; Lev 2:1–2; 23:13), were lacking because of the devastation of the crops.

1:10 dried up. Drought accompanied the locust invasion. **grain . . . new wine . . . oil.** The ingredients needed for the daily offerings traditionally appear in this order in Scripture (2:19; Hos 2:8).

1:12 vine . . . fig tree . . . pomegranate . . . palm . . . apple tree. Five kinds of trees are noted, leading up to the climactic

the pomegranate, the palm and the apple tree—
all the trees of the field—are dried up.[s]
Surely the joy of mankind
is withered away.

A Call to Repentance

13 Put on sackcloth,[t] O priests, and mourn;
wail, you who minister[u] before the altar.
Come, spend the night in sackcloth,
you who minister before my God;
for the grain offerings and drink offerings[v]
are withheld from the house of your God.
14 Declare a holy fast;[w]
call a sacred assembly.
Summon the elders
and all who live in the land
to the house of the LORD your God,
and cry out[x] to the LORD.

15 Alas for that[y] day!
For the day of the LORD[z] is near;
it will come like destruction from the Almighty.[a]

16 Has not the food been cut off[a]
before our very eyes—
joy and gladness
from the house of our God?[b]
17 The seeds are shriveled
beneath the clods.[b c]
The storehouses are in ruins,
the granaries have been broken down,
for the grain has dried up.
18 How the cattle moan!
The herds mill about
because they have no pasture;
even the flocks of sheep are suffering.

19 To you, O LORD, I call,[d]
for fire[e] has devoured the open pastures[f]
and flames have burned up all the trees of the field.
20 Even the wild animals pant for you;[g]
the streams of water have dried up[h]
and fire has devoured the open pastures.

1:12 [s]Hag 2:19
1:13 [t]Jer 4:8 [u]Joel 2:17 [v]ver 9
1:14 [w]2Ch 20:3 [x]Jnh 3:8
1:15 [y]Jer 30:7 [z]Isa 13:6, 9; Joel 2:1,11,31
1:16 [a]Isa 3:7 [b]Dt 12:7
1:17 [c]Isa 17:10-11
1:19 [d]Ps 50:15 [e]Am 7:4 [f]Jer 9:10
1:20 [g]Ps 104:21 [h]1Ki 17:7

a *15* Hebrew *Shaddai* b *17* The meaning of the Hebrew for this word is uncertain.

statement that all the trees of the field were dried up. **joy of mankind.** Joy withered with the vegetation.
1:13 Put on sackcloth . . . mourn . . . wail . . . spend the night in sackcloth. The priests were given precise instructions about how to respond personally to God's judgment. The specific instructions for the priests here and in 2:15–17 suggest that the book of Joel was designed to guide national repentance in any given situation.
1:14 Declare. The priests were also to provide leadership in the community by declaring a public fast so that the entire nation could stop all regular activities for a time (probably for a day, as in Jdg 20:26; 1Sa 14:24; Jer 36:6–9) to acknowledge God's judgment and to repent.
1:15 that day . . . the day of the LORD. The magnitude of the devastation points to an even more ominous day of judgment to come. The expression "day of the LORD" occurs five times in Joel (1:15; 2:1,11,31; 3:14) and eleven other times in the Old Testament (Isa 13:6,9; Eze 13:5; Am 5:18a,18b,20; Ob 15; Zep 1:7,14a,14b; Mal 4:5). Here (and in 2:1,11) it refers to a day of the Lord's wrath against his enemies and of blessings for the Lord's faithful people (2:31; 3:14). Most Israelites believed that their ethnic identity guaranteed that they would all be blessed when the Lord appeared in judgment, but the prophets made it clear that the unfaithful in Israel would be judged along with the unrepentant among the Gentiles. **is near.** The prophet did not envision the day of the Lord as a distant time. Instead he saw it as an imminent event (see 2:1; 3:14). **destruction from the Almighty.** This phrase may be translated "might from the Almighty," a rendering that captures the sense of the Hebrew wordplay *shod* ("destruction") from *Shaddai,* "the Almighty" (Isa 13:6).
1:16–18 Joel reinforced his point about the day of the Lord by again reminding his audience of God's judgment, the signs of which could be seen in the drought conditions all around them.
1:19–20 To you, O LORD, I call. The prophet himself began the lamentation. The devastation was from the Lord, who was also the only source of restoration. **the wild animals pant for you.** Even the animals joined Joel in his cry (Job 38:41; Pss 104:21; 147:9). **fire.** The metaphor of fire describes the effects of the drought, although in 2:3 it applies to the devastation of the locusts. Fire is often associated with God's judgment (Dt 32:22; Pss 50:3; 97:3).

An Army of Locusts

2 Blow the trumpet[i] in Zion;[j]
sound the alarm on my holy hill.
Let all who live in the land tremble,
for the day of the LORD[k] is coming.
It is close at hand[l]—
2 a day of darkness[m] and gloom,[n]
a day of clouds and blackness.
Like dawn spreading across the mountains
a large and mighty army[o] comes,
such as never was of old[p]
nor ever will be in ages to come.

3 Before them fire devours,
behind them a flame blazes.
Before them the land is like the garden of Eden,[q]
behind them, a desert waste[r]—
nothing escapes them.
4 They have the appearance of horses;[s]
they gallop along like cavalry.
5 With a noise like that of chariots[t]
they leap over the mountaintops,
like a crackling fire[u] consuming stubble,
like a mighty army drawn up for battle.

6 At the sight of them, nations are in anguish;[v]
every face turns pale.[w]
7 They charge like warriors;
they scale walls like soldiers.
They all march in line,
not swerving[x] from their course.
8 They do not jostle each other;
each marches straight ahead.
They plunge through defenses
without breaking ranks.
9 They rush upon the city;
they run along the wall.
They climb into the houses;
like thieves they enter through the windows.[y]

10 Before them the earth shakes,[z]
the sky trembles,
the sun and moon are darkened,[a]
and the stars no longer shine.[b]
11 The LORD[c] thunders
at the head of his army;
his forces are beyond number,
and mighty are those who obey his command.
The day of the LORD is great;[d]

2:1 [i]Jer 4:5 [j]ver 15 [k]Joel 1:15; Zep 1:14-16 [l]Ob 1:15
2:2 [m]Am 5:18 [n]Da 9:12 [o]Joel 1:6 [p]Joel 1:2
2:3 [q]Ge 2:8 [r]Ps 105:34-35
2:4 [s]Rev 9:7
2:5 [t]Rev 9:9 [u]Isa 5:24; 30:30
2:6 [v]Isa 13:8 [w]Na 2:10
2:7 [x]Isa 5:27
2:9 [y]Jer 9:21
2:10 [z]Ps 18:7 [a]Mt 24:29 [b]Isa 13:10; Eze 32:8
2:11 [c]Joel 1:15 [d]Zep 1:14; Rev 18:8

■ **2:1–17** *Future Devastation on the Day of the Lord.* The prophet shifted from focusing on the locusts and drought to the greater day of the Lord that was coming. Joel urged "all who live in the land" (v. 1) to prepare for an assault by the army of the Lord, the Divine Warrior. A contrite heart among the people would perhaps bring compassion and "leave behind a blessing" (v. 14).
2:1 the trumpet. This instrument, made of a ram's horn, signaled danger—here, the coming of the day of the Lord. **Zion . . . my holy hill.** Jerusalem. **tremble.** All quavered at the trumpet blast (Am 3:6; Zep 1:14–16). **close at hand.** The day of the Lord is described again as imminent (see 1:15; 3:14).
2:2 a day of darkness and gloom . . . clouds and blackness. The language describing the coming day of the Lord (cf. Am 5:18,20; Zep 1:15) corresponds to that used to describe the Lord's appearances in the past (Dt 4:11; 5:22–23; Ps 97:2). **mighty army.** The Lord's army, which was coming to judge Israel, was similar to the hordes of locusts in 1:6, but it was also like an invading armed force (vv. 4–11).
2:3 a desert waste. The invaders razed the land. The bold contrast between "the garden of Eden" and a "desert waste" (see Ge 13:10; Isa 51:3; Eze 28:13–19; 31:8–9,16–18; 36:35) underlines the horror of the inescapable invasion.
2:5 Again the army is compared with a locust invasion (Rev 9:1–11). But, like the description of the coming of the Lord in Micah 1:3–4, the language is symbolic in nature.
2:7–9 The army was disciplined, ruthless and successful. The "city" (v. 9) was finally overtaken (cf. the plague of locusts in Ex 10:6).
2:10 earth . . . sky . . . sun . . . moon . . . stars. The Lord's visitations are associated with natural reversals and the return of chaos. Depending on the severity of the divine intervention, the whole cosmos might be disrupted (v. 31; Jer 4:23–26; Eze 32:7–8; Na 1:5; Hab 3:6,10).
2:11 his army. The relentless army was the Lord's. He commanded and his forces obeyed. The day of the Lord is variously described as great (2:31; Zep 1:14), dreadful (Mal 4:5) and unbearable (Na 1:6; Mal 3:2).

2:11
[e]Eze 22:14

it is dreadful.
Who can endure it?[e]

Rend Your Heart

2:12
[f]Jer 4:1; Hos 12:6

12 "Even now," declares the LORD,
"return[f] to me with all your heart,
with fasting and weeping and mourning."

2:13
[g]Ps 34:18; Isa 57:15 [h]Job 1:20 [i]Ex 34:6 [j]Jer 18:8

13 Rend your heart[g]
and not your garments.[h]
Return to the LORD your God,
for he is gracious and compassionate,
slow to anger and abounding in love,[i]
and he relents from sending calamity.[j]

2:14
[k]Jer 26:3 [l]Hag 2:19 [m]Joel 1:13

14 Who knows? He may turn[k] and have pity
and leave behind a blessing[l]—
grain offerings and drink offerings[m]
for the LORD your God.

2:15
[n]Nu 10:2 [o]Jer 36:9 [p]Joel 1:14

15 Blow the trumpet[n] in Zion,
declare a holy fast,[o]
call a sacred assembly.[p]

2:16
[q]Ex 19:10,22 [r]Ps 19:5

16 Gather the people,
consecrate[q] the assembly;
bring together the elders,
gather the children,
those nursing at the breast.
Let the bridegroom[r] leave his room
and the bride her chamber.

2:17
[s]Eze 8:16; Mt 23:35 [t]Dt 9:26-29; Ps 44:13 [u]Ps 42:3

17 Let the priests, who minister before the LORD,
weep between the temple porch and the altar.[s]
Let them say, "Spare your people, O LORD.
Do not make your inheritance an object of scorn,[t]
a byword among the nations.
Why should they say among the peoples,
'Where is their God?[u]' "

The LORD's Answer

2:18
[v]Zec 1:14

18 Then the LORD will be jealous[v] for his land
and take pity on his people.

19 The LORD will reply[a] to them:

2:19
[w]Jer 31:12

"I am sending you grain, new wine and oil,[w]

[a] 18,19 Or *LORD was jealous . . . / and took pity . . . / 19The LORD replied*

2:12–13 See *WCF* 15.2; *WLC* 76,108; *HC* 89.
2:12 Even now . . . return. The Lord invites escape from judgment through a turning or returning to him with the whole heart—a complete reorientation of one's life toward him. **fasting and weeping and mourning.** Visible signs of repentance (Ezr 10:1–6; Est 4:3; Jnh 3:5–9). See *WCF* 21.5; *WSC* 87.
2:13 gracious . . . abounding in love. The call to return to the Lord was based on a confessional statement about the Lord's nature found in Exodus 34:6–7 and frequently repeated throughout the Old Testament (e.g., Nu 14:18; Ne 9:17; Pss 86:15; 103:8; 145:8; Jnh 4:2).
2:14 Who knows? He may . . . have pity. The characterization of God in verse 13 does not limit his sovereignty and freedom (cf. Ex 33:19; 2Sa 12:22; La 3:29; Jnh 3:9; Zep 2:3). God's reaction to repentance is not mechanical, but it is merciful. He may carry through with his threat of judgment or he may reverse it, delay it, soften it or rescue repentant individuals from it. See "Introduction to the Prophetic Books: True Prophets and Their Predictions."
2:15–16 Further instructions for returning to the Lord included a holy fast and an assembly (v. 15), as well as a gathering and consecration of all the people, including the elders, children, nursing infants and even those about to consummate marriage (v. 16). The staccato quality of the Hebrew poetry in these verses emphasizes the urgency of the situation. See *WCF* 15.2.
2:17 Specific instructions were also given to the priests, who were to weep and offer prayers of intercession (see note on 1:13). **between the temple porch and the altar.** The usual place for priestly intercession (1Ki 8:22; Eze 8:16). **your inheritance.** The priestly lament appealed to the Lord's sense of ownership and pride in his covenant people (Dt 9:26,29; Pss 44:11–14; 74:2; 79:10; 115:2; Mic 7:10).
■ **2:18—3:21** *Divine Responses to Repentance.* The Lord, the God of the covenant, promised to renew the land and his people as they responded in repentance to the crises of 1:2—2:17. The redemptive renewal of God's people will someday culminate in the ultimate devastation of Zion's enemies and the final exaltation of Zion itself. These chapters divide into two sections: God's promise of renewal (2:18–32) and final judgment and blessing (3:1–21).
■ **2:18–32** *Promise of Renewal.* Repentance would bring renewal of the blessings of God. He would bless the land (vv. 18–27) and renew his people with his Spirit (vv. 28–32).
■ **2:18–27** *Renewal of the Land.* The land that suffered under God's judgment would be blessed.
2:18 A change in subject, mood and tense takes place at this point as the Lord promised restoration.
2:19 The prayers of God's people would be answered.

enough to satisfy you fully;
never again will I make you
an object of scorn[x] to the nations.

20 "I will drive the northern army[y] far from you,
pushing it into a parched and barren land,
with its front columns going into the eastern[z] sea[a]
and those in the rear into the western sea.[b]
And its stench[a] will go up;
its smell will rise."

Surely he has done great things.[c]
21 Be not afraid,[b] O land;
be glad and rejoice.
Surely the LORD has done great things.[c]
22 Be not afraid, O wild animals,
for the open pastures are becoming green.[d]
The trees are bearing their fruit;
the fig tree and the vine yield their riches.[e]
23 Be glad, O people of Zion,
rejoice[f] in the LORD your God,
for he has given you
the autumn rains in righteousness.[d]
He sends you abundant showers,
both autumn and spring rains,[g] as before.
24 The threshing floors will be filled with grain;
the vats will overflow[h] with new wine[i] and oil.

25 "I will repay you for the years the locusts have eaten—
the great locust and the young locust,
the other locusts and the locust swarm[e]—
my great army that I sent among you.
26 You will have plenty to eat, until you are full,[j]
and you will praise[k] the name of the LORD your God,
who has worked wonders[l] for you;
never again will my people be shamed.
27 Then you will know that I am in Israel,
that I am the LORD[m] your God,
and that there is no other;
never again will my people be shamed.

The Day of the LORD

28 "And afterward,
I will pour out my Spirit[n] on all people.
Your sons and daughters will prophesy,
your old men will dream dreams,

2:19 [x]Eze 34:29
2:20 [y]Jer 1:14-15 [z]Zec 14:8 [a]Isa 34:3
2:21 [b]Isa 54:4; Zep 3:16-17 [c]Ps 126:3
2:22 [d]Ps 65:12 [e]Joel 1:18-20
2:23 [f]Ps 149:2; Isa 12:6; 41:16; Hab 3:18; Zec 10:7 [g]Lev 26:4
2:24 [h]Lev 26:10; Mal 3:10 [i]Am 9:13
2:26 [j]Lev 26:5 [k]Isa 62:9 [l]Ps 126:3; Isa 25:1
2:27 [m]Joel 3:17
2:28 [n]Eze 39:29

[a] *20* That is, the Dead Sea [b] *20* That is, the Mediterranean [c] *20* Or *rise. / Surely it has done great things."* [d] *23* Or */ the teacher for righteousness:* [e] *25* The precise meaning of the four Hebrew words used here for locusts is uncertain.

2:20 northern army. Some interpreters have understood this to be a reference to the locusts of chapter 1, although it is more likely an allusion to the foreign invaders of the Lord's vast and mighty army of chapter 2. Unlike most literal locust invasions that came from the east or south, foreign incursions often came from the north (see, e.g., Jer 1:14–15; 4:6; 6:1,22; Eze 38:6,15; 39:2).

2:21–24 The land and the wild animals were urged not to be afraid; then, together with the people of Zion, they were exhorted to be glad and rejoice in the agricultural abundance from the Lord.

2:25 See note on 1:4.

2:26 The blessings of nature would lead to praise (cf. Dt 8:10; Hos 13:5–6).

2:27 Restoration would result in a new realization that the Lord was in Israel, that he was the covenant God and that there was no other besides him.

■ **2:28–32** *Renewal of God's People.* Near the time of the great day of the Lord an unprecedented outpouring of God's Spirit would occur, bringing salvation to his people.

2:28–29 As Moses prayed for the Israelites to serve as God's prophets (Nu 11:29), Joel predicted that this desire would be experienced in Israel's glorious future. Peter proclaimed that this vision's fulfillment began at Pentecost with the advent of the Holy Spirit (Ac 2:16–21), who empowers believers to bear witness to Jesus Christ (Ac 1:8). By introducing this prophecy with the words "in the last days" (Ac 2:17), Peter connected it with other prophecies regarding Israel's Messianic future and so taught that Pentecost was critical to the inauguration of the promised new age. See theological article "The Plan of the Ages" at Hebrews 7.

2:28 afterward. Joel introduced more distant promises. **pour out.** Although the word here refers primarily to the pouring out of liquids (Ge 9:6; Ex 4:9), it is also used to describe the outpouring of the Spirit (Eze 39:29; Zec 12:10) that would occur during the restoration after the exile. **prophesy . . . dream dreams . . . see visions.** See Numbers 12:6, Jeremiah 31:31–34 and Ezekiel 36:26–29. See also *HC* 32.

your young men will see visions.
29 Even on my servants,[o] both men and women,
I will pour out my Spirit in those days.
30 I will show wonders in the heavens[p]
and on the earth,[q]
blood and fire and billows of smoke.
31 The sun will be turned to darkness[r]
and the moon to blood
before the coming of the great and dreadful day of the LORD.[s]
32 And everyone who calls
on the name of the LORD will be saved;[t]
for on Mount Zion[u] and in Jerusalem
there will be deliverance,[v]
as the LORD has said,
among the survivors[w]
whom the LORD calls.

The Nations Judged

3 "In those days and at that time,
when I restore the fortunes[x] of Judah and Jerusalem,
2 I will gather all nations
and bring them down to the Valley of Jehoshaphat.[a]
There I will enter into judgment[y] against them
concerning my inheritance, my people Israel,
for they scattered my people among the nations
and divided up my land.
3 They cast lots for my people
and traded boys for prostitutes;
they sold girls for wine[z]
that they might drink.

4 "Now what have you against me, O Tyre and Sidon[a] and all you regions of Philistia? Are you repaying me for something I have done? If you are paying me back, I will
swiftly and speedily return on your own heads what you have done.[b] 5 For you took my
silver and my gold and carried off my finest treasures to your temples.[c] 6 You sold the
people of Judah and Jerusalem to the Greeks, that you might send them far from their
homeland.
7 "See, I am going to rouse them out of the places to which you sold them,[d] and I will
return on your own heads what you have done. 8 I will sell your sons[e] and daughters to
the people of Judah,[f] and they will sell them to the Sabeans, a nation far away." The LORD
has spoken.

2:29 [o]1Co 12:13; Gal 3:28
2:30 [p]Lk 21:11 [q]Mk 13:24-25
2:31 [r]Mt 24:29 [s]Isa 13:9-10; Mal 4:1,5
2:32 [t]Ac 2:17-21*; Ro 10:13* [u]Isa 46:13 [v]Ob 1:17 [w]Isa 11:11; Mic 4:7; Ro 9:27
3:1 [x]Jer 16:15
3:2 [y]Eze 36:5
3:3 [z]Am 2:6
3:4 [a]Mt 11:21 [b]Isa 34:8
3:5 [c]2Ch 21:16-17
3:7 [d]Isa 43:5-6; Jer 23:8
3:8 [e]Isa 60:14 [f]Isa 14:2

[a] 2 *Jehoshaphat* means *the LORD judges*; also in verse 12.

2:30–31 The structure of these verses emphasizes the cosmic nature of the events that would warn of the coming of the great and terrible day. The more devastating the divine intervention, the greater the cosmic upheaval (see Isa 13:10; Eze 32:7–8; Am 8:9; Zep 1:14–17).
2:32 calls on the name of the LORD. This phrase refers to worshiping the Lord (Ge 12:8), especially to making his name known to those who either do not know him or are antagonistic toward him (1Ki 18:24; Ps 105:1; Isa 12:4; Jer 10:25; Zec 13:9). **survivors.** Those called by the Lord who have responded in faith. See *BC* 27.
■ **3:1–21** *Final Judgment and Blessing.* God's response to the cries of his people would finally climax in the day of the Lord, a day on which God would judge all his enemies (vv. 1–17) and bless his people forever (vv. 18–21).
■ **3:1–16** *Judgment on the Nations.* The impending day of the Lord would include judgment against the nations that had rebelled against God and troubled his people.
3:1 In those days. Synonymous with "at that time," this phrase marks the beginning of a further series of promises for God's people (Jer 33:15; 50:4,20). **restore the fortunes.** This can also be translated "bring back from captivity" (see NIV text note on Jer 29:14).
3:2 Restoration would include the judgment of Israel's enemies ("all nations") for their injustices against God's people and land. **Valley of Jehoshaphat.** This is the "valley of decision" mentioned in verse 14. The name means "The LORD judges" and is symbolic of what was to take place on the Day of the Lord. A specific valley is not in view. **scattered . . . divided.** Following the expulsion of the people the land was redistributed among the conquerors. The historical referent is unclear; it may refer even to small deportations involving border wars (e.g., Am 1:9–10).
3:3 Following the casting of lots for prisoners (Ob 11; Na 3:10) the defenseless children were traded and sold for purposes of debauchery (Am 2:6).
3:4 against me. The legal charge against Tyre and Sidon (i.e., coastal Phoenicia) and the regions of Philistia (i.e., coastal Palestine; Jos 13:2–3) concerns their involvement in capturing and trading Israelites as prisoners of war. Both regions had sold Israelites as slaves to the Greeks (v. 6) and to Edom (Am 1:6,9).
3:5 my silver and my gold. The land's silver and gold, as well as its inhabitants, belonged to the Lord (Hag 2:8).
3:6 The Judahites sold to the Greeks were so far from home that it was either impossible to locate them or to make the journey to buy their freedom and return them to the promised land.
3:7 them. God's restored people would mediate punishment to Tyre, Sidon and Philistia.
3:8 Sabeans. Merchants from the distant land of Sheba (1Ki 10:1–13; Jer 6:20).

9 Proclaim this among the nations:
Prepare for war![g]
Rouse the warriors![h]
Let all the fighting men draw near and attack.
10 Beat your plowshares into swords
and your pruning hooks[i] into spears.
Let the weakling[j] say,
"I am strong!"
11 Come quickly, all you nations from every side,
and assemble[k] there.

Bring down your warriors,[l] O LORD!
12 "Let the nations be roused;
let them advance into the Valley of Jehoshaphat,
for there I will sit
to judge[m] all the nations on every side.
13 Swing the sickle,
for the harvest[n] is ripe.
Come, trample the grapes,
for the winepress[o] is full
and the vats overflow—
so great is their wickedness!"

14 Multitudes, multitudes
in the valley of decision!
For the day of the LORD[p] is near
in the valley of decision.
15 The sun and moon will be darkened,
and the stars no longer shine.
16 The LORD will roar from Zion
and thunder from Jerusalem;[q]
the earth and the sky will tremble.[r]
But the LORD will be a refuge for his people,
a stronghold[s] for the people of Israel.

Blessings for God's People

17 "Then you will know that I, the LORD your God,[t]
dwell in Zion,[u] my holy hill.
Jerusalem will be holy;
never again will foreigners invade her.

18 "In that day the mountains will drip new wine,
and the hills will flow with milk;[v]
all the ravines of Judah will run with water.[w]
A fountain will flow out of the LORD's house[x]
and will water the valley of acacias.[a][y]

3:9 [g]Isa 8:9 [h]Jer 46:4
3:10 [i]Isa 2:4; Mic 4:3 [j]Zec 12:8
3:11 [k]Eze 38:15-16; Zep 3:8 [l]Isa 13:3
3:12 [m]Isa 2:4
3:13 [n]Hos 6:11; Mt 13:39; Rev 14:15-19 [o]Rev 14:20
3:14 [p]Isa 34:2-8; Joel 1:15
3:16 [q]Am 1:2 [r]Eze 38:19 [s]Jer 16:19
3:17 [t]Joel 2:27 [u]Isa 4:3
3:18 [v]Ex 3:8 [w]Isa 30:25; 35:6 [x]Rev 22:1-2 [y]Eze 47:1; Am 9:13

[a] *18* Or *Valley of Shittim*

3:9–12 Joel issued a bitterly ironic invitation into battle to those nations that would be defeated by the Lord.
3:10 plowshares . . . pruning hooks. Contrast Isaiah 2:4 and Micah 4:3.
3:11 there. The place of the great battle, the Valley of Jehoshaphat, is clarified in verse 12.
3:13 Like grain ready to be cut down with the sickle (Isa 17:5) and like grapes waiting to be pressed (Isa 63:3), the exceedingly wicked nations were ripe for harvest (cf. Rev 14:15,18,20). **winepress is full . . . vats overflow.** The full winepress and overflowing vats emphasize the enormity of the wickedness of the nations massed in the valley for judgment.
3:14 valley of decision! The Valley of Jehoshaphat is now identified as the valley of decision, the place where the Lord's judgment would be passed upon multitudes. **near.** The imminence of the great day of the Lord, a day when he will bring vengeance on the nations, is again emphasized (1:15; 2:1).
3:15 sun . . . moon . . . stars. Nature will respond to the appearance of the Lord on the day of judgment (2:10,31; Am 5:18). Cosmic language often figuratively represents events of national significance, but on the final day of the Lord the universe itself will actually be destroyed and recreated (2Pe 3:7–12; Rev 21:1).
3:16 roar . . . thunder. The earth and the sky tremble at the powerful voice of the Lord (Ps 29:3–9; Jer 25:30; Am 1:2). **refuge . . . stronghold.** In the midst of the extraordinary manifestations of the Lord's anger against the nations, God would protect the people of the covenant (Ps 46:1; Isa 25:4).
■ **3:17–21** *Blessings for God's People.* Although judgment would come against the nations, God's repentant people would be blessed forever through the day of the Lord.
3:17 I . . . dwell in Zion. Judah's experience of the Lord's protection in the midst of his wrath would deepen her knowledge of the reality of God's presence in her midst; i.e., in Zion, the Lord's holy hill (Ps 46:4; Isa 8:18; 52:1–2; Zec 2:10; 8:3). The New Testament explains that this promise will ultimately be fulfilled in the new heavens and the new earth (Rev 21:3).
3:18 The final scene of the drama is one of paradisiacal prosperity and blessing (cf. 2:19–26). **A fountain . . . out of the LORD's**

3:19 [z]Ob 1:10
3:20 [a]Am 9:15
3:21 [b]Eze 36:25

19 But Egypt will be desolate,
Edom a desert waste,
because of violence[z] done to the people of Judah,
in whose land they shed innocent blood.
20 Judah will be inhabited forever[a]
and Jerusalem through all generations.
21 Their bloodguilt, which I have not pardoned,
I will pardon.[b]"

The LORD dwells in Zion!

house. A description of the temple as the source of a life-giving stream (Ps 46:4; Eze 47:1–12) that waters even the dry and barren valley where acacias grow. The New Testament envisions the fulfillment of this prophecy at Christ's return (Rev 22:1–2).
3:19 Egypt . . . Edom. Egypt (1Ki 14:25–26; 2Ki 23:29) and Edom (Ob 9–14), historic adversaries of Israel and here representative of all Israel's enemies, would lie in ruins following the judgment.
3:20 inhabited forever. In contrast to their enemies Judah and Jerusalem would be blessed and would perpetually possess the promised land (Jer 17:25; Zec 12:6). The permanence of this blessed arrangement corresponds to the New Testament teaching on eternal life in the new heavens and the new earth (Rev 21).
3:21 pardon . . . dwells. Joel sounded a note of promise and certainty as he reminded all hearers and readers of God's eternal sovereignty. God's covenant people were therefore to continue to trust in his faithfulness (Ps 9:11–12).

AMOS

Introduction

Overview

Author: The prophet Amos

Purpose: To reveal the severity of divine judgment for covenant infidelity in Israel and Judah and to declare the hope of a great restoration after the approaching destruction and exile

Date: 760–750 B.C.

Key Truths:

- Just as the Gentile nations would be judged for their wickedness, so Israel and Judah would be judged by Assyrian aggression because of their sins.
- God's case against Israel was irrefutable and the cause of much trouble for Israel both in nature and in war.
- Amos's visions of the future confirmed that Samaria would be destroyed by Assyrian aggression.
- Although Israel and Judah would be judged along with the other nations, after the exile they would be exalted above their Gentile neighbors.

Author

Amos was from Tekoa (1:1), a village about ten miles south of Jerusalem and six miles from Bethlehem in Judah. He was a shepherd (1:1), a livestock breeder (see note on 7:14) and a dresser of sycamore-fig trees (7:14). His rural background notwithstanding, Amos clearly knew much about international history (1:3—2:3). He was also familiar with the law of God and the history of God's covenant people. He had not studied to be a prophet (7:14), but the Lord sovereignly called him to this task. He spoke primarily to the northern kingdom (7:15) but also addressed the sins of Judah (2:4–5; cf. 9:11).

Time and Place of Writing

According to 1:1 Amos prophesied during the reigns of Uzziah of Judah (792–740 B.C.) and Jeroboam II of Israel (793–753 B.C.). Amos probably delivered most, if not all, of the oracles of this book in the northern kingdom. It is certain that he fulfilled some of his prophetic ministry at Bethel (7:10–17). From his descriptions of the circumstances of Israel, most interpreters conclude that these oracles were delivered during the decade of great prosperity during the reign of Jeroboam II (760–750 B.C.). During this time there was peace between Judah and Israel. The king had restored the boundaries of Israel in accordance with the prophecy of Jonah son of Amittai (2Ki 14:25). The northern kingdom had become wealthy and was enjoying a false sense of security made possible by the weakness of Egypt, Babylon and especially Assyria, which had entered a temporary decline after the death of Adad-Nirari III (805–783 B.C.). Israel faced no serious threat from Assyrian armies for about 40 years.

Original Audience

Amos directed his ministry to the northern kingdom (Israel). At the time, many Israelites were maintaining and even exceeding the ritual requirements of the law (4:4–5). Yet the true worship of God was mixed with idolatry (5:26; 2Ki 17:14–17), which led to various forms of violence and injustice (2:6–8; 4:1). Although the Lord had already sent warnings to Israel in the form of hunger, thirst, blight, locusts, plagues and military defeat, his people had refused to see his hand in these events and had failed to repent (4:6–11).

Purpose and Distinctives

Amos vigorously challenged Israel's idolatry and social injustice, declaring that syncretistic worship denied the most basic truths about Israel's God. The Lord alone is sovereign over all that he has created (4:13; 5:8; 9:5–6). He is the one true God over the nations. As such, he is able to turn nation against nation (1:3—2:3) and to judge his covenant people through the aggression of other nations (6:14). But for all of this, he is a loving God who desires the life, not the death, of his people (5:4).

Amos indicated that because Israel had not repented, even after being judged (4:6–11), the Lord would bring more severe judgment, ending in wholesale destruction and exile (4:12—5:20). Shortly after Amos predicted that Israel would fall to the Assyrian Empire, his predictions began to be fulfilled. Under Tiglath-Pileser III (745–727 B.C.), Assyria gained strength and expanded to the north and west. Judah soon became an Assyrian vassal. Syria, located between Israel and Assyria, became part of the Assyrian Empire (2Ki 16:7–9).

Tiglath-Pileser III was succeeded by his son Shalmaneser V (727–722 B.C.), who continued his father's policy of westward expansion, forcing Hoshea, the last king of the northern kingdom, to become his vassal (2Ki 17:3). Hoshea rebelled and mistakenly hoped for help from Egypt (2Ki 17:4). As a result, Shalmaneser V of Assyria began a siege of Samaria, and the Israelite capital fell to his successor, Sargon II, in 722 B.C. (2Ki 17:5–6).

The Lord chastises those he loves, and his judgment was a sign of his commitment to his covenant people as a whole. Amos therefore affirmed God's promise never to utterly forsake his covenant people. Amos declared that after the exile "David's fallen tent" (9:11) would be restored, the royal line would conquer the nations (9:12) and God's people would be blessed beyond measure (9:13–15).

Christ in Amos

Amos's prophecies reveal Christ in three ways.

1. The major theme of Amos—judgment against the nations and against the unfaithful of Israel and Judah—foreshadows the judgment that comes in Christ. The New Testament teaches that Christ will judge those who turn against God (Jn 5:21–27; Ro 2:12–16), including people in covenant with God (Heb 10:26–30; 1Pe 4:17; Rev 2:4–5,14–16,20–23; 3:1–3,15–19). Christ ultimately fulfills the theme of judgment in Amos.

2. Amos 9:11–15 speaks of the restoration promised to Israel and Judah after exile. Following the pattern laid down by Moses (Lev 26; Dt 4:15–31; 28:1–68), Amos announced that the exile would be followed by a time of great blessings for God's people. After the failures of those who returned to the land in 539 B.C., these restoration prophecies began to be fulfilled. The New Testament explains their initial fulfillment in the giving of the Spirit as the down payment for the believers' inheritance in Christ's first coming (Eph 1:14), as well as their final fulfillment in the new heavens and the new earth when Christ returns (Rev 21:1ff.).

3. Amos spoke of the restoration of "David's fallen tent"—David's royal dynasty (9:11). This prediction indicated that sometime after the exile a son of David would lead the people of God to victory over the nations (9:12) and secure for them eternal safety (9:15). This prophecy is fulfilled by Jesus, the final, royal son of David (Mt 1:1; Lk 1:32–33; Rev 22:16). Jesus rose to the throne of the house of David in his resurrection and ascension (Ac 2:25–36). He reigns now and engages in holy war against the nations through the gospel (Ac 15:13–19; 1Co 15:23–25). Ultimately, he will defeat all of his enemies and establish a worldwide kingdom when he returns in glory (Ac 2:34–36; Rev 19:11–21; 21:1—22:5).

Outline

I. Superscription (1:1)	*The prophet and the time of his ministry are identified.*
II. God's People Judged Along With the Nations (1:2—2:16) A. The Lord Roars (1:2) B. Judgment on Aram (1:3–5) C. Judgment on Philistia (1:6–8) D. Judgment on Phoenicia (1:9–10) E. Judgment on Edom (1:11–12) F. Judgment on Ammon (1:13–15) G. Judgment on Moab (2:1–3) H. Judgment on Judah (2:4–5) I. Judgment on Israel (2:6–16)	*Amos declared that God had determined to judge Israel and Judah, along with the Gentile nations, through Assyrian aggression.*
III. Oracles Against Israel (3:1—6:14) A. The Prosecution of Israel (3:1—4:13) 1. First Covenant Lawsuit (3:1–15) 2. Second Covenant Lawsuit (4:1–13) B. The Severity of Judgment (5:1—6:7) 1. Lament for Virgin Israel (5:1–17) 2. Woe for Those Who Long (5:18–27) 3. Woe for the Complacent (6:1–7) C. The Certainty of Divine Oath (6:8–14)	*Amos delivered oracles from God that justified Israel's judgment, revealing how terrible it would be and how determined God was to carry it out.*
IV. Visions Against Israel (7:1—9:10) A. Relented Judgments (7:1–6) 1. Vision of Locusts (7:1–3) 2. Vision of Fire (7:4–6) B. Unrelented Judgments (7:7—9:10) 1. Vision of a Plumb Line (7:7–9) 2. Elaboration (7:10–17) 3. Vision of Ripe Fruit (8:1–3) 4. Elaboration (8:4–14) 5. Vision of the Altar (9:1–4) 6. Elaboration (9:5–10)	*Amos reported visions indicating that God's judgment against Israel was righteous but severe.*
V. God's People Exalted Above the Nations (9:11–15) A. Restoration of David's Victorious Dynasty (9:11–12) B. Blessing of Abundance in Nature (9:13–15)	*Amos declared that after a period of exile, God would raise Israel to victory over the nations through the son of David.*

1 The words of Amos, one of the shepherds of Tekoa[a]—what he saw concerning Israel two years before the earthquake,[b] when Uzziah[c] was king of Judah and Jeroboam[d] son of Jehoash[a] was king of Israel.[e]
2He said:

"The LORD roars[f] from Zion
and thunders from Jerusalem;[g]
the pastures of the shepherds dry up,[b]
and the top of Carmel[h] withers."[i]

Judgment on Israel's Neighbors

3This is what the LORD says:

"For three sins of Damascus,[j]
even for four, I will not turn back ⌞my wrath⌟.[k]
Because she threshed Gilead
with sledges having iron teeth,
4I will send fire[l] upon the house of Hazael
that will consume the fortresses[m] of Ben-Hadad.[n]
5I will break down the gate[o] of Damascus;
I will destroy the king who is in[c] the Valley of Aven[d]
and the one who holds the scepter in Beth Eden.
The people of Aram will go into exile to Kir,[p]"
says the LORD.

6This is what the LORD says:

"For three sins of Gaza,[q]
even for four, I will not turn back ⌞my wrath⌟.
Because she took captive whole communities

1:1 [a]2Sa 14:2 [b]Zec 14:5 [c]2Ch 26:23 [d]2Ki 14:23 [e]Hos 1:1
1:2 [f]Isa 42:13 [g]Joel 3:16 [h]Am 9:3 [i]Jer 12:4
1:3 [j]Isa 8:4; 17:1-3 [k]Am 2:6
1:4 [l]Jer 49:27 [m]Jer 17:27 [n]1Ki 20:1; 2Ki 6:24
1:5 [o]Jer 51:30 [p]2Ki 16:9
1:6 [q]1Sa 6:17; Zep 2:4

[a] *1* Hebrew *Joash,* a variant of *Jehoash* [b] *2* Or *shepherds mourn* [c] *5* Or *the inhabitants of* [d] *5* *Aven* means *wickedness.*

■ **1:1** *Superscription.* Amos introduced himself and his prophecy, specifying the time during which God's word had come to him.
1:1 The words of Amos. Oracles of prophets are sometimes introduced with this formula (cf. Jer 1:1). As a prophet, Amos was God's covenant emissary bringing God's lawsuit against Israel, who had flagrantly violated God's covenant requirements. **shepherds.** The Hebrew term refers to one who shepherds a particular kind of sheep known for their unusually fine wool. The king of Moab is identified as owning such sheep (2Ki 3:4). **Tekoa.** This village was twelve miles south of Jerusalem and six miles from Bethlehem. Because of its prime pastureland, it supported many shepherds with their flocks. **earthquake.** Since this was a memorable event in an earthquake-prone region, it would have been remembered as an act of divine judgment (cf. Zec 14:5).
■ **1:2—2:16** *God's People Judged Along With the Nations.* The book begins with a series of judgment oracles announcing God's intention to judge Israel and Judah, as well as the Gentile nations. The prophet implicitly referred to the upcoming Assyrian aggressions as the instrument of God's wrath on the nations and his own people (see "Introduction: Purpose and Distinctives"). This series of oracles begins with an introductory announcement that unites the entire section (1:2) and then divides into eight parts: Syria (1:3–5), Philistia (1:6–8), Phoenicia (1:9–10), Edom (1:11–12), Ammon (1:13–15), Moab (2:1–3) and then, ironically, Judah (2:4–5) and Israel (2:6–16).
■ **1:2** *The Lord Roars.* These first words of Amos reveal the tone of most of this book. Amos announced that God was roaring like a lion.
1:2 roars. The Hebrew may also be rendered "will roar aggressively." God is likened to a lion roaring as it is about to attack. As a shepherd, Amos probably knew this kind of roaring well (cf. 1Sa 17:34–37). **from Zion . . . Jerusalem.** The Lord established his temple in Zion. From that royal palace, the great King roared as his wrath was about to go forth (Joel 3:16; cf. Jer 25:30). **pastures . . . withers.** The Lord's judgment would come in the form of a drought (see Lev 26:19; Dt 28:22–24). It would dry up the whole land, from the pastures to the forested top of Mount Carmel, rich in orchards and vineyards. Although Amos may have been prophesying a literal drought, the verses that follow (1:3—2:16) suggest that he was referring metaphorically to the devastating onslaught of Assyrian aggression.
■ **1:3–5** *Judgment on Aram.* The prophet first announced the destruction of Aram (Syria), Israel's immediate northern neighbor. The Assyrian king Tiglath-Pileser III conquered Damascus in 732 B.C.
1:3 For three sins . . . for four. This repeated refrain (1:6,9,11,13; 2:1,4,6) is a typical example of parallelism using ascending numbers (cf. Ps 62:11; Mic 5:5). A standard device in ancient Near Eastern poetry, it is not to be taken literally but rather as meaning "for many sins." **Damascus.** David had defeated and garrisoned this royal city of Syria (2Sa 8:6). During Solomon's reign (1Ki 11:23–25) Damascus broke free, with Rezon as king. **sledges having iron teeth.** Grain was threshed by driving over the cut grain with a wooden board that had "teeth," or studs of iron or basalt embedded on the underside. An ox would pull the sledge while the driver stood upon it. The prophet accused the Syrians of treating Gilead in this manner (cf. 2Ki 13:7).
1:4 I will send fire . . . fortresses. Compare 1:7,10,12 and 14 and 2:2 and 5. The refrain was also adopted by Hosea (Hos 8:14) and Jeremiah (Jer 17:27; 21:14; 29:27; 50:32). Fire was thought in the ancient Near East to be an instrument of divine judgment. It was often used in warfare and was interpreted as a means whereby a god angrily purged his rebellious people. **Hazael.** This king of Damascus (c. 842–796 B.C.) founded a dynasty in Syria, as Elisha had predicted (2Ki 8:7–15). **fortresses.** Possibly these were the fortress-like citadels of the nobility and the wealthy. **Ben-Hadad.** This is a throne name, similar to that of "Pharaoh" in Egypt, for the king of Syria.
1:5 destroy. Literally, "cut off." The verb is often used to indicate annihilation by war (e.g., Jos 23:4; Jdg 4:24; Isa 10:7). **king.** Literally, "the enthroned one" or, less likely, "the inhabitant." The Hebrew word is used of God enthroned as King (Pss 2:4; 22:3). **Valley of Aven.** Literally, "Valley of Wickedness/Idolatry." The location in mind is uncertain. **Beth Eden.** This location was probably a district about 200 miles northeast of Damascus (not to be confused with Eden; Ge 2:8) and ruled by a Syrian vassal king. The use of parallelism here (Valley of Aven and Beth Eden) indicates that not only Damascus but also its territories would be undone. **Kir.** The original home of Aram (9:7).
■ **1:6–8** *Judgment on Philistia.* From the time of Samson, the Philistines had troubled God's people. Here Amos announced God's vengeance. The cities of Philistia revolted against Assyrian domination at different times and suffered severely for their disloyalty.
1:6 See note on verse 3. **Gaza.** This was the southernmost of the Philistines' five royal cities. The other four were Ashkelon, Ashdod,

1:6 [r]Ob 1:11
1:8 [s]2Ch 26:6 [t]Ps 81:14 [u]Eze 25:16 [v]Isa 14:28-32; Zep 2:4-7
1:9 [w]1Ki 5:1; 9:11-14; Isa 23:1-18; Jer 25:22; Joel 3:4; Mt 11:21
1:10 [x]Zec 9:1-4
1:11 [y]Nu 20:14-21; 2Ch 28:17; Jer 49:7-22 [z]Eze 25:12-14
1:12 [a]Ob 1:9-10
1:13 [b]Jer 49:1-6; Eze 21:28; 25:2-7

and sold them to Edom, [r]
7 I will send fire upon the walls of Gaza
that will consume her fortresses.
8 I will destroy the king[a] of Ashdod [s]
and the one who holds the scepter in Ashkelon.
I will turn my hand [t] against Ekron,
till the last of the Philistines [u] is dead,"
says the Sovereign LORD. [v]

9 This is what the LORD says:

"For three sins of Tyre, [w]
even for four, I will not turn back ⌊my wrath⌋.
Because she sold whole communities of captives to Edom,
disregarding a treaty of brotherhood,
10 I will send fire upon the walls of Tyre
that will consume her fortresses. [x]"

11 This is what the LORD says:

"For three sins of Edom, [y]
even for four, I will not turn back ⌊my wrath⌋.
Because he pursued his brother with a sword,
stifling all compassion,[b]
because his anger raged continually
and his fury flamed unchecked, [z]
12 I will send fire upon Teman [a]
that will consume the fortresses of Bozrah."

13 This is what the LORD says:

"For three sins of Ammon, [b]
even for four, I will not turn back ⌊my wrath⌋.

a *8* Or *inhabitants* b *11* Or *sword / and destroyed his allies*

Ekron and Gath (see v. 8). Located between Egypt and Canaan, Gaza was a natural center for trade. Sargon took Gaza in 720 B.C. when the king of Gaza joined the Egyptians. It may have been destroyed then but was certainly ravaged by Alexander the Great in 332 B.C. **whole communities.** Literally, "a complete exile or exiled group." The Philistine trade included slaves. Prisoners of war usually became slaves in the ancient Near East, but here a whole community, or population, was sold into slavery. The reference is apparently to the capture and sale of Israelites during the reign of Jehoram (2Ch 21:16–17; Joel 3:3,6; cf. Am 1:9). **to Edom.** Edom, in effect Israel's "brother" through Esau (Ge 25:25,30), received Israelites as slaves from the Philistines. For its role in this decidedly unbrotherly sin, Gaza, which stands for Philistia as a whole, was now sentenced.

1:8 Ashdod . . . Ashkelon . . . Ekron. Important cites of Philistia. Ashdod was destroyed in 711 B.C. when it revolted against Sargon. Ashkelon and Ekron revolted during the reign of Sennacherib (705–681 B.C.) and were severely punished. All four cities are mentioned in Assyrian annals as vassals of Esarhaddon (680–669 B.C.) and Ashurbanipal (668–627 B.C.). Gath, the fifth city, was unmentioned because it had already been defeated by Hazael (2Ki 12:17).

▪ **1:9–10** *Judgment on Phoenicia.* Phoenicia was at different times friend or foe of Israel. The fact that Phoenicia was a costal region made it very important to Israel.

1:9 Tyre. The name means "rock." The older of the two major Phoenician cities (the other being Sidon) mentioned in the Amarna letters (fourteenth century B.C.), Tyre was built on a rock in the sea and was virtually impregnable. It was troubled by the Assyrians, Babylonians and Persians but was not finally destroyed until Alexander the Great took the city and killed nearly all of its citizens. **she sold.** Like Gaza (v. 6), Tyre sold Israelites into slavery and thereby broke a historical succession of treaties. **whole communities . . . disregarding.** The word "disregarding" is literally "did not remember." The term "remember" is standard for "keep the terms of" in ancient international covenants or treaties (cf. Ge 9:15; Ex 2:24; Lev 26:42). Tyre did not remember its historical treaties with Israel. **treaty of brotherhood.** Literally, "of brothers." In the ancient Near East, kings entering into treaties styled themselves "brothers." So Hiram of Tyre called Solomon "my brother" (1Ki 9:13; cf. 1Ki 5:12) against a background of treaty relations with David (2Sa 5:11). Ahab later continued the close relations with Phoenicia by marrying Jezebel, the daughter of Ethbaal, king of Sidon (1Ki 16:31).

▪ **1:11–12** *Judgment on Edom.* Amos now turned his attention to the southeast. Edom had troubled God's people from early times.

1:11 See note on verse 3. **Edom.** This was Israel's "brother" in the flesh (see note on v. 6), and possibly Israel's treaty "brother" as well. **pursued . . . sword.** These events of the reign of Jehoram include Edom's revolt and collusion with the Philistines and Arabs when they attacked Judah and entered Jerusalem, plundering the palace and deporting the royal household (2Ch 21:16–17). Edom not only received its Israelite brothers as slaves from Philistia (1:6) and Tyre (1:9), but "pursued his brother with a sword." Compare Obadiah 10–14.

1:12 Teman. Teman was a grandson of Esau (Ge 36:11,15). His descendant clan apparently gave its name to a region in the south of Edom and to a village some 15 miles from Petra. The reference here is to the region. Teman was famous for his wisdom (cf. Job 2:11; Jer 49:7). **Bozrah.** The northernmost Edomite city, it was some 35 miles north of Petra. By mentioning its northernmost and southernmost regions, Amos consigned all of Edom to destruction. From the time of Amos, Edom passed to the control of one empire after another. In 300 B.C. the region of Edom fell under the attacks of the Nabateans.

▪ **1:13–15** *Judgment on Ammon.* The Ammonites descended from Ben-Ammi, the offspring of the trickery and incest of Lot's younger daughter (Ge 19:34–38). They lived between Aram and Moab. The Assyrian king Shalmaneser III (858–824 B.C.) conquered Ammon, making it an Assyrian vassal. Later Assyrian kings brought more destruction to the region. Amos predicted these events.

1:13 See note on verse 3. **Ammon.** Literally, "the sons of Ammon." **ripped open the pregnant women.** This particular atrocity was practiced by others, including Hazael of Syria (2Ki 8:12), Menahem of Israel (2Ki 15:16), and Assyria (Hos 13:16). Apparently the purpose was to eliminate descendants who might try to reclaim the land. **to extend his borders.** It was a typical boast of ancient Near Eastern kings that they had extended the borders of their land. By doing so they fancied that they had carried out the desire of their gods.

Because he ripped open the pregnant women[c] of Gilead
in order to extend his borders,
14 I will set fire to the walls of Rabbah[d]
that will consume her fortresses
amid war cries[e] on the day of battle,
amid violent winds on a stormy day.
15 Her king[a] will go into exile,
he and his officials together,"
says the LORD.

2 This is what the LORD says:

"For three sins of Moab,
even for four, I will not turn back ⌊my wrath⌋.
Because he burned, as if to lime,
the bones of Edom's king,
2 I will send fire upon Moab
that will consume the fortresses of Kerioth.[b]
Moab will go down in great tumult
amid war cries and the blast of the trumpet.
3 I will destroy her ruler[f]
and kill all her officials with him,"[g]
says the LORD.

4 This is what the LORD says:

"For three sins of Judah,[h]
even for four, I will not turn back ⌊my wrath⌋.
Because they have rejected the law[i] of the LORD
and have not kept his decrees,[j]
because they have been led astray[k] by false gods,[c][l]
the gods[d] their ancestors followed,[m]
5 I will send fire upon Judah
that will consume the fortresses of Jerusalem.[n]"

1:13 [c]Hos 13:16
1:14 [d]Dt 3:11 [e]Am 2:2
2:3 [f]Ps 2:10 [g]Isa 40:23
2:4 [h]2Ki 17:19; Hos 12:2 [i]Jer 6:19 [j]Eze 20:24 [k]Isa 9:16 [l]Isa 28:15 [m]2Ki 22:13; Jer 16:12
2:5 [n]Jer 17:27; Hos 8:14

[a] *15* Or / *Molech*; Hebrew *malcam* [b] *2* Or *of her cities* [c] *4* Or *by lies* [d] *4* Or *lies*

1:14 Rabbah. This shortened form of the fuller reference "Rabbah of the Ammonites" (Dt 3:11; 2Sa 12:26) is modern Amman, Jordan (1:14, Jer 49:2,3; Eze 21:20; 25:5). **war cries.** The shouts of troops engaging in combat. See the war cry "against Rabbah of the Ammonites" (Jer 49:2). **violent winds on a stormy day.** This figure for God's judgment storm comes in the form of tumultuous military attack (see Ps 83:15; Isa 5:28; Jer 4:13; 23:19; 25:32). The same language also describes the Lord's appearance in judgment (Isa 17:13; 29:6; 66:15; Na 1:3).
1:15 Her king. Literally, "their king." The term is used here and in Jeremiah 49:3 (where the NIV translation is "Molech"). **he and his officials together.** It was a regular Assyrian practice to take a king and his household and officials into exile together.
■ **2:1–3** *Judgment on Moab.* Moab was a vassal (servant) state to a series of Assyrian kings, from Tiglath-Pileser III to Ashurbanipal. Amos's prediction was fulfilled when Moab rebelled against Sennacherib, who then subdued the land.
2:1 See note on verse 3. **burned . . . the bones of Edom's king.** According to Hebrew tradition, these are the "bones" of the Moabite king Mesha. Such burning indicated particular contempt and was believed to deprive the dead of peace in the afterlife. Josiah similarly burned the bones of false priests on the altar at Bethel (2Ki 23:15–16).
2:2 Kerioth. This may possibly be a common noun meaning "cities" (so translates the Septuagint, the Greek translation of the OT), but it is more likely a major Moabite city and cult center, apparently the capital, named also in Jeremiah 48:41. **the trumpet.** The shofar—the war trumpet, or bugle, of ancient warfare that was made from a curved ram's horn.
2:3 I will destroy. Literally, "cut off" (i.e., kill). The destruction of both king and officials was a typical punishment for rebellious vassals in the Near East.
■ **2:4–5** *Judgment on Judah.* Amos turned his attention from Gentile nations to the covenant people.
2:4 Judah. Amos gave this series of oracles in Israel, the northern kingdom (see "Introduction: Time and Place of Writing"), and for this reason the inclusion of Judah was not entirely distasteful to his listeners. The northern and southern kingdoms had been at odds for more than a century and at war during many of those years. The northerners might have heard this oracle with some smugness, thinking themselves superior since Judah, not Israel, had been selected for punishment along with the Gentile nations. But any sense of security they may have enjoyed would soon be shattered (see v. 6). **rejected the law of the LORD.** Literally, "of Yahweh." The nations were worthy of judgment because they had violated laws of common grace known from the creation (Ro 1:18–23). But the Lord had specially revealed and codified his righteous laws to his people. For rejecting God's law, and thereby God himself, they were particularly worthy of judgment. **not kept his decrees.** Covenant terminology like this is also found in Exodus 15:26 and Deuteronomy 4:40. **their ancestors followed.** Literally, "their fathers walked after." In the ancient Near East, the idiom "to walk after" meant "to follow in obedience as a vassal [servant]." So Judah, who was properly the vassal of the great King, the Lord, had chosen instead to be a vassal to false gods, which both the Old and New Testaments (Dt 32:17; 1Co 10:20) reveal to be demons.
2:5 fire . . . consume the fortresses. Because they followed the gods of the nations, the Judahites would be punished like the inhabitants of Aram (1:4), Gaza (1:7), Tyre (1:10), Edom (1:12), Ammon (1:14) and Moab (v. 2). **Jerusalem.** The name means, ironically, "city of peace." *Peace* in Hebrew connotes not only an absence of war but also a character of wholeness. Because Judah had not sought integrity in the Lord, the nation would be visited not by peace but by destruction. This prophecy was fulfilled over 150 years later when Nebuchadnezzar II conquered Jerusalem and burned every notable building, including the king's palace (cf. 2Ki 25:8–10).

Judgment on Israel

6 This is what the LORD says:

"For three sins of Israel,
even for four, I will not turn back ⌊my wrath⌋.
They sell the righteous for silver,
and the needy for a pair of sandals.[o]
7 They trample on the heads of the poor
as upon the dust of the ground
and deny justice to the oppressed.
Father and son use the same girl
and so profane my holy name.[p]
8 They lie down beside every altar
on garments taken in pledge.[q]
In the house of their god
they drink wine[r] taken as fines.

9 "I destroyed the Amorite[s] before them,
though he was tall as the cedars
and strong as the oaks.
I destroyed his fruit above
and his roots[t] below.

10 "I brought you up out of Egypt,[u]
and I led you forty years in the desert[v]
to give you the land of the Amorites.[w]
11 I also raised up prophets[x] from among your sons
and Nazirites[y] from among your young men.
Is this not true, people of Israel?"
declares the LORD.
12 "But you made the Nazirites drink wine
and commanded the prophets not to prophesy.[z]

13 "Now then, I will crush you
as a cart crushes when loaded with grain.
14 The swift will not escape,
the strong[a] will not muster their strength,
and the warrior will not save his life.[b]

2:6 [o]Joel 3:3; Am 8:6
2:7 [p]Am 5:11-12; 8:4
2:8 [q]Ex 22:26 [r]Am 4:1; 6:6
2:9 [s]Nu 21:23-26; Jos 10:12 [t]Eze 17:9; Mal 4:1
2:10 [u]Ex 20:2; Am 3:1 [v]Dt 2:7 [w]Ex 3:8; Am 9:7
2:11 [x]Dt 18:18; Jer 7:25 [y]Nu 6:2-3; Jdg 13:5
2:12 [z]Isa 30:10; Jer 11:21; Am 7:12-13; Mic 2:6
2:14 [a]Jer 9:23 [b]Ps 33:16; Isa 30:16-17

■ **2:6–16** *Judgment on Israel.* Amos now spoke about his immediate listeners, the citizens of the northern kingdom.
2:6 Israel. Israel had consistently broken God's law, engaging in social injustice (vv. 6–7a), sexual immorality (v. 7b) and religious abuses (v. 8). **the righteous.** In this context, "righteous" carries the connotation of one who was not in debt and therefore could not legally be sold into slavery (cf. Lev 25:39–43). **the needy.** Those who were both poor and powerless. The Lord had a special concern that their rights be protected (cf. Ex 23:6; Jer 5:28). **a pair of sandals.** For such a paltry debt, the needy were being sold into slavery. Indigent slavery in Israel was legal, but it was intended to be benign and full of brotherly consideration (cf. Ex 21:2 11; Dt 15:12–18).
2:7 trample . . . the poor. One mark of a good king in the ancient Near East was that he took special care of the poor. Amos expected this to be even more true of God's people (cf. Ex 23:6–8), but in Israel this was not so (cf. Isa 3:15). **deny justice to the oppressed.** This can also be rendered "pervert the justice due to the oppressed." Compare Proverbs 17:23. **Father and son use the same girl.** Such was not only contrary to God's original intentions for sexual union (Ge 2:23–24; Mt 19:4–6) but also specifically prohibited by the law (Lev 18:7–30). This sin, too, was like that of the nations around Israel, as the Lord had warned in Leviticus 18:24. See *WCF* 24.4.
2:8 beside every altar. Apparently they conducted their illicit sex beside the altars, further profaning the Lord's name. There were many altars in Israel, including those at Bethel (3:14), Dan (8:14) and Gilgal (Hos 12:11). **garments taken in pledge.** Such garments were not to be kept overnight (Ex 22:26), nor were they to be slept on (Dt 24:12–13). **wine taken as fines.** Implicitly, the fines were unjust. Perhaps, if this continues the thought of verse 7, alcohol abuse alongside sexual indulgence is indicated.
2:9 I destroyed the Amorite before them. As the Lord had destroyed the Rephaites before the Ammonites (Dt 2:20–21) and the Horites before the sons of Esau (Dt 2:22), so he had graciously destroyed the Amorites (a term sometimes used to indicate all Canaanites, as here) before Israel: first by Moses defeating Sihon and Og east of the Jordan (Dt 2:24—3:11) and later by Joshua conquering the land west of the Jordan (Jos 21:43). **tall as the cedars.** The description recalls not only the report of the spies (Nu 13:26–33) but also God's wrath against all the arrogant (Isa 2:12–18). **fruit above . . . roots below.** This poetic language indicates that God destroyed them completely.
2:10 I brought you up out of Egypt. The Lord recalled his ancient covenant faithfulness (cf. Ge 50:24; Ex 3:8). **forty years in the desert.** The time was necessary to prepare a people who would obey the Lord and conquer the land (Dt 1:19–40). **to give you the land of the Amorites.** Literally, "to inherit the land of the Amorites"; i.e., so that they might inherit it. The covenant promise was given to Abraham (Ge 15:7) and fulfilled—as the Lord had promised—for his descendants (Dt 2:31).
2:11 I also raised up prophets. The Lord had sovereignly raised up prophets (Dt 18:15,17), judges (Jdg 2:18), priests (1Sa 2:35) and kings (2Sa 7:12). The prophets were his special covenant emissaries sent to call the people to obedience to his covenant law. **Nazirites.** These men or women were specially dedicated to the Lord and, according to the law (Nu 6:1–21), could drink no wine, wine vinegar or grape juice, nor even eat grapes or raisins. They allowed their hair to grow long as an outward sign of their dedication. The Old Testament mentions two Nazirites by name: Samson (Jdg 13:1–5) and Samuel (1Sa 1:11).
2:12 But you. In contrast to what the Lord had done ("I . . . raised up prophets"; v. 11), his people Israel had sought to defeat his purposes by commanding his lawsuit messengers not to bring suit and by making his Nazirites, who were not even to eat grapes, drink wine. So they showed their contempt for both the law and the Lord of the law.
2:13 crush. The Lord would crush Israel as a cart that has been filled crushes whatever it rolls over.

15 The archer[c] will not stand his ground,
the fleet-footed soldier will not get away,
and the horseman will not save his life.
16 Even the bravest warriors[d]
will flee naked on that day,"
declares the LORD.

2:15 [c]Eze 39:3
2:16 [d]Jer 48:41

Witnesses Summoned Against Israel

3 Hear this word the LORD has spoken against you, O people of Israel—against the whole family I brought up out of Egypt:[e]

2 "You only have I chosen[f]
of all the families of the earth;
therefore I will punish you
for all your sins.[g]"

3 Do two walk together
unless they have agreed to do so?
4 Does a lion roar in the thicket
when he has no prey?[h]
Does he growl in his den
when he has caught nothing?
5 Does a bird fall into a trap on the ground
where no snare has been set?
Does a trap spring up from the earth
when there is nothing to catch?
6 When a trumpet sounds in a city,
do not the people tremble?
When disaster comes to a city,
has not the LORD caused it?[i]

3:1 [e]Am 2:10
3:2 [f]Dt 7:6; Lk 12:47 [g]Jer 14:10
3:4 [h]Ps 104:21; Hos 5:14
3:6 [i]Isa 14:24-27; 45:7

2:14 The swift . . . the strong. Even the fleet of foot, who might have been expected to escape, and the strong, who might have been expected to stand their ground, would not survive. **the warrior.** This can be rendered "the hero"; i.e., the one who, by exemplary physique and skill, was specially suited to be a mighty warrior. Goliath was one of these (1Sa 17:51), and the term is also used of David (1Sa 16:18) and of the Messiah ("Mighty God"; literally "God the hero", Isa 9:6).
2:15 The archer . . . the fleet-footed . . . the horseman. None of those who might have been expected to escape or stand their ground in battle would do so. All would die.
2:16 will flee naked. The Hebrew word for "naked" was used of Adam and Eve (Ge 2:25). Here the bravest warriors not only jettisoned their armor and weapons but also cast off every impediment, including clothing, in a panicky but useless flight. **on that day.** This phrase is commonly used in the Prophets to indicate "the day of the LORD" (see note on 5:18), the time when God will devastate his enemies both within and outside of the covenant and bring great blessings to the faithful. In this case, it portends the approaching day of Assyrian conquest.
■ **3:1—6:14** *Oracles Against Israel.* After God through Amos had set Judah and Israel on a par with other nations as the objects of his wrath, the prophet proclaimed a number of oracles that explained the case against Israel (3:1—4:13), as well as the horrible nature (5:1—6:7) and certainty of the coming judgment (6:8–14).
■ **3:1—4:13** *The Prosecution of Israel.* The prophet built his case in two covenant lawsuits against the nation (3:1–15; 4:1–13).
■ **3:1–15** *First Covenant Lawsuit.* Amos reported what he had heard in the heavenly courtroom of God, where God was the prosecutor and judge and Israel the guilty defendant. This lawsuit established God's case for the judgment of successful Assyrian aggression against Israel.
3:1 Hear this word. This solemn command summoned the Israelites to hear what had been said of them in God's court (see 4:1; 5:1; see also Isa 1:2; Jer 2:4; Hos 4:1).
3:2 The Lord immediately raised an accusation and pronounced a preliminary sentence. **You only have I chosen.** Literally, "You only have I known." The verb *know* has a wide range of meanings in Biblical Hebrew, referring, among other things, to sexual relations (Adam "lay with [knew] his wife"; Ge 4:1); cognition (e.g., "I don't know"; Ge 4:9); and concern, especially God's unique concern for his people as his vassals (e.g., "I cared for [knew] you in the desert"; Hos 13:5). That the third sense applies here is confirmed by the presence of the adverb "only." Hosea's words echo the implications of Deuteronomy 7:7–8: "The LORD did not set his affection on you and choose you because you were more numerous . . . [but] because the LORD loved you and kept the oath he swore to your forefathers." Certainly the all-knowing God has known (has complete information about) every family of the earth, but he has known (been uniquely concerned for and related by oath to) the seed of Abraham alone among all the families of the earth. **therefore.** The Lord's love for Israel was rebuffed by his people's disobedience. Consequently, his choice of Israel actually became the basis of his judgment (cf. Hos 11:1–7).
3:3–6 God explained why Amos had announced this case against Israel. Here is a series of logical, cause-and-effect questions to which the answer in every case was so clear that no one could miss it. It was obvious to all that Amos had been speaking as the Lord's spokesperson.
3:3 walk. The Hebrew verb also has connotations of "live." The Lord's people are to "walk" (i.e., "live") in his ways (Ps 119:3). Here, implicitly, the prophet "lives" in close relationship with the Lord, desiring to be filled with his holiness and with his very self (cf. Gal 2:20).
3:4 roar. As in 1:2, this is the roar of a lion about to attack. He would not roar in this way if he saw no prey. **Does he growl . . . ?** Literally, "Does a (young) lion thunder?" The word used here for "lion" is often translated "young lion." The idiom used here for "thunder" is the same one used of the Lord's thundering in 1:2.
3:5 snare. The original meaning of the word is probably "bait" (hence, "snare"). The point is that no bird would be caught in a trap that had no bait. Compare Ecclesiastes 9:12.
3:6 trumpet. Again, the shofar, as in 2:2 (see its note). It was blown either by the attacking enemy or (as here) as a warning for the besieged. Siege was a fearful prospect in the ancient world, for it often resulted in the starvation of many of the beleaguered populace, followed by all the horrors of conquest: rape, pillage, slaughter and burning. **disaster.** Literally, "evil." The Old Testament clearly teaches that the Lord is the Creator of good and evil (Isa 45:7). However, this is not evil in the sense of moral wrong but rather "disaster," or "adversity" (as here), which the Lord may sovereignly inflict as punishment upon individuals or nations. The Biblical model of such "evil" from the Lord is seen in the curse oracles of Genesis 3:14–19. See *BC* 13.

3:7 [j]Ge 18:17; Da 9:22; Jn 15:15; Rev 10:7 [k]Jer 23:22

7 Surely the Sovereign LORD does nothing
without revealing his plan[j]
to his servants the prophets.[k]

3:8 [l]Jer 20:9; Jnh 1:1-3; 3:1-3; Ac 4:20

8 The lion has roared—
who will not fear?
The Sovereign LORD has spoken—
who can but prophesy?[l]

3:9 [m]Am 4:1; 6:1

9 Proclaim to the fortresses of Ashdod
and to the fortresses of Egypt:
"Assemble yourselves on the mountains of Samaria;[m]
see the great unrest within her
and the oppression among her people."

3:10 [n]Jer 4:22; Am 5:7; 6:12 [o]Hab 2:8 [p]Zep 1:9

10 "They do not know how to do right,[n]" declares the LORD,
"who hoard plunder[o] and loot in their fortresses."[p]

11 Therefore this is what the Sovereign LORD says:

3:11 [q]Am 2:5; 6:14

"An enemy will overrun the land;
he will pull down your strongholds
and plunder your fortresses.[q]"

12 This is what the LORD says:

3:12 [r]1Sa 17:34 [s]Am 6:4

"As a shepherd saves from the lion's[r] mouth
only two leg bones or a piece of an ear,
so will the Israelites be saved,
those who sit in Samaria
on the edge of their beds
and in Damascus on their couches.[a] [s]"

3:13 [t]Eze 2:7

13 "Hear this and testify[t] against the house of Jacob," declares the Lord, the LORD God Almighty.

3:14 [u]Am 5:5-6

14 "On the day I punish Israel for her sins,
I will destroy the altars of Bethel;[u]
the horns of the altar will be cut off
and fall to the ground.

[a] *12* The meaning of the Hebrew for this line is uncertain.

3:7 without revealing his plan. The Lord revealed his plan to and through his prophets. He graciously did this so that people could be warned and repent. For example, he disclosed his plans for Sodom and Gomorrah to Abraham (Ge 18:17), who was himself a prophet (see Ge 20:7 and its note). **his servants the prophets.** Moses, the supreme Old Testament prophet, was called "the servant of the LORD" (Dt 34:5), and subsequent prophets were characterized by the phrase "his servants the prophets" (Da 9:10; see also Jer 7:25; Eze 38:17). The term *servant* has connotations of "official" in some contexts. As applied to prophets, it may denote official emissaries of the court of God.
3:8 The lion has roared. The phrase echoes 1:2 (see note on v. 4). The Lion of Judah (see Rev 5:5) has roared. That is, God has threatened to attack his people for their sins in such a way that Amos has heard him. **who can but prophesy?** Amos came from Tekoa in Judah. He did not prophesy against the northern kingdom for personal or political reasons. He spoke because God had roared. As a true prophet, he was obligated to repeat what God told him to say (Dt 18:18; cf. Jn 7:16; 14:24).
3:9 Proclaim. The Lord summoned witnesses to the court. The command is in the plural, for it is a directive to the heavenly counsel. The royal Judge called for his court to summon Gentile nations to witness the proceedings against Israel (cf. Isa 40:1–2; Jer 5:1,10,20). **fortresses.** These royal citadels are also mentioned in 1:4. **Ashdod . . . Egypt.** The nobility of these pagan lands was summoned (via a poetic device) to look upon the injustice that reigned in Samaria. Ironically, Israel, the recipient of God's law, should have been more righteous than they. **mountains of Samaria.** The spectators were asked to view Samaria from the mountains that surrounded her. **unrest.** Or "disorders." The word appears as the opposite of peace in 2 Chronicles 15:5. The cause of the disorders is sin.
3:10 They do not know. The accusation was made against Samaria. **plunder and loot.** Literally, "violence and destruction." By a figure of speech, Amos described the people as hoarding "violence and destruction"; he was referring to the "plunder and loot" as having been obtained by these means. The rich had plundered and looted the poor.
3:11 Therefore. The prophet reported the divine sentence against Israel (vv. 11–15). **enemy.** Assyria. **overrun . . . pull down.** The thought echoes the covenantal curse that the Lord had threatened to bring upon his people if they were disobedient (Dt 28:52).
3:12 As a shepherd saves. A good shepherd protected his sheep (1Sa 17:34–37). In the ancient Near East, kings were often spoken of as the shepherds of their people. The Lord, the great King, is often characterized in this way (Ge 48:15; Ps 23:1; Isa 40:11). But now, in the midst of violent attack, the sheep of Israel, who had wandered far astray, would only be saved in a mutilated condition. In fact, the nation would be destroyed; only a remnant would remain. **in Damascus on their couches.** The rich reclined idly, enjoying the luxury they had extorted from the poor. See 6:4.
3:13 Hear this and testify. The command here (in the plural) may be to the pagans who had been summoned as witnesses or to the Lord's messengers who were commanded to summon the pagan witnesses (v. 9).
3:14 On the day I punish Israel for her sins. The phrasing harks back to the original covenant documents (Ex 32:34). **altars of Bethel.** Jeroboam I had forged a golden calf for Israel to worship at Bethel, as an alternative to worship at Jerusalem (1Ki 12:25–33), and had installed an altar there (1Ki 13:1). Josiah destroyed both the altar and the sanctuary in his efforts at reform (2Ki 23:15–16). **horns of the altar.** Grasping the horns of the altar was a means by which a fugitive might gain asylum (cf. 1Ki 1:49–51), although such impunity was not always respected (1Ki 2:28–35). Here the horns would be cut off, so that even this last resort would be denied sinful Israel.

15 I will tear down the winter house[v]
along with the summer house;[w]
the houses adorned with ivory[x] will be destroyed
and the mansions will be demolished,"
declares the LORD.

Israel Has Not Returned to God

4 Hear this word, you cows of Bashan[y] on Mount Samaria,[z]
you women who oppress the poor and crush the needy
and say to your husbands, "Bring us some drinks![a]"
2 The Sovereign LORD has sworn by his holiness:
"The time will surely come
when you will be taken away[b] with hooks,
the last of you with fishhooks.
3 You will each go straight out
through breaks in the wall,[c]
and you will be cast out toward Harmon,[a]"
declares the LORD.

4 "Go to Bethel and sin;
go to Gilgal[d] and sin yet more.
Bring your sacrifices every morning,[e]
your tithes[f] every three years.[b][g]
5 Burn leavened bread[h] as a thank offering
and brag about your freewill offerings[i]—
boast about them, you Israelites,
for this is what you love to do,"
declares the Sovereign LORD.

6 "I gave you empty stomachs[c] in every city
and lack of bread in every town,
yet you have not returned to me,"
declares the LORD.[j]

3:15 [v]Jer 36:22 [w]Jdg 3:20 [x]1Ki 22:39
4:1 [y]Ps 22:12; Eze 39:18 [z]Am 3:9 [a]Am 2:8; 5:11; 8:6
4:2 [b]Am 6:8
4:3 [c]Eze 12:5
4:4 [d]Hos 4:15 [e]Nu 28:3 [f]Dt 14:28 [g]Eze 20:39; Am 5:21-22
4:5 [h]Lev 7:13 [i]Lev 22:18-21
4:6 [j]Isa 3:1; Jer 5:3; Hag 2:17

[a] 3 Masoretic Text; with a different word division of the Hebrew (see Septuagint) *out, O mountain of oppression* [b] 4 Or *tithes on the third day* [c] 6 Hebrew *you cleanness of teeth*

3:15 winter house . . . summer house. The possession of both a summer and a winter house was a great luxury, affordable only to kings and the very wealthy. The Lord would destroy these multiple houses and lavishly decorated mansions. His instrument of judgment, Assyria, was expert at such destruction and plunder, as the vast wealth of Nineveh (cf. Na 2:9) amply testified.

■ **4:1–13** *Second Covenant Lawsuit.* Amos reported a second lawsuit against Israel that established God's case for sending the Assyrians against the northern kingdom.

4:1–5 God indicted the inhabitants of Samaria on charges of social and religious sin.

4:1 Hear this word. See note on 3:1. **cows of Bashan.** This was a description of the wealthy women of Samaria who had been pampered like the prime cattle of Bashan, a fertile area west of the Jordan. Bashan was formerly the kingdom of Og (Nu 21:33–35). **who oppress . . . and crush . . . and say.** For the form of this epithet, which describes the qualities of the women, see note on verse 13. **husbands.** Literally, "lords," a Hebrew word indicating men of high rank.

4:2 A severe sentencing against the women of Samaria. **sworn by his holiness.** See 6:8. The same phrase occurs in Psalm 89:35. It indicates the Lord's faithfulness to enforce his covenant, either for blessing or for curse. No oath could be greater or more final. The exile of these wealthy women of Samaria would be irreversible. See Hebrews 6:13–14. **hooks . . . fishhooks.** The Assyrians frequently led away prisoners of war by ropes attached to rings or hooks in their noses or lips.

4:3 You. Amos addressed the women ("you" here is a feminine plural in the Hebrew), not the entire nation. **will be cast out toward Harmon.** Agrees with some ancient versions taking Harmon as a location. See NIV text note for an alternative.

4:4 Go. Here the prophet addressed the whole population of Samaria, men and women alike. He mocked the people's religious practices, accusing them of serious sin. **Bethel . . . Gilgal.** Both Bethel (Ge 28:10–22) and Gilgal (Jos 4:19–20) were important cities in the earlier history of Israel and significant cult sites as well. Bethel was a sanctuary during the period of the judges (Jdg 20:18,26), and Samuel judged both there and at Gilgal (1Sa 7:16). Both were important centers of worship in Amos's day (cf. 5:5; Hos 4:15; 9:15; 12:11). **every three years.** Literally, "every three days." Although the Hebrew word for "day" can stand for a year, the context usually makes it clear when it is being so used. Here, three literal days seem to be meant in an ironic criticism of Israel's religious observances, which went even beyond what the law required. The people were enthusiastic about ritual but had no living relationship with God. They had a form of religion, while implicitly denying its power.

4:5 leavened bread. The covenant made it clear that the Israelites were not to burn leavened bread (Lev 2:11; 6:17; 7:12). Rather, unleavened bread was to be used, as a reminder of the unleavened bread they had prepared before leaving Egypt. Here, ironically, the people are being enjoined to continue in disobedience. **boast.** Amos pointed to the hypocrisy of the Israelites who boasted of their duplicitous piety. **what you love to do.** Literally, "For so you love." The phrase may mean "This is the way you love to do." However, in the ancient Near East, the term "to love" had special significance in covenants: It indicated a love for the sovereign that entailed obedience. (Cf. Jn 14:15: "If you love me, you will obey what I command.") So here the criticism seems to be: "This is the way you love me: by disobeying my commands."

4:6–11 This section is a historical review of what the Lord had done to warn his people and draw their attention back to him. All of the disasters mentioned were threatened in the covenant with Moses (Dt 28). Israel should have realized what was befalling her and repented. The nation did not, however; hence the refrain "Yet you have not returned to me" (4:6,8–11).

4:6 I. Literally, "and I even." The Lord emphasized his own role in warning them, as well as the lengths to which he had gone. **empty stomachs.** Literally, "cleanness of teeth." Their teeth were clean because the people had nothing to eat. The original covenant had

7 "I also withheld rain from you
when the harvest was still three months away.
I sent rain on one town,
but withheld it from another.[k]
One field had rain;
another had none and dried up.
8 People staggered from town to town for water[l]
but did not get enough to drink,
yet you have not returned[m] to me,"
declares the LORD.[n]

9 "Many times I struck your gardens and vineyards,
I struck them with blight and mildew.[o]
Locusts devoured your fig and olive trees,[p]
yet you have not returned[q] to me,"
declares the LORD.

10 "I sent plagues[r] among you
as I did to Egypt.
I killed your young men with the sword,
along with your captured horses.
I filled your nostrils with the stench of your camps,
yet you have not returned to me,"
declares the LORD.[s]

11 "I overthrew some of you
as I[a] overthrew Sodom and Gomorrah.[t]
You were like a burning stick snatched from the fire,
yet you have not returned to me,"
declares the LORD.

12 "Therefore this is what I will do to you, Israel,
and because I will do this to you,
prepare to meet your God, O Israel."

13 He who forms the mountains,[u]
creates the wind,
and reveals his thoughts[v] to man,
he who turns dawn to darkness,
and treads the high places of the earth[w]—
the LORD God Almighty is his name.[x]

4:7 [k]Ex 9:4,26; Dt 11:17; 2Ch 7:13
4:8 [l]Eze 4:16-17 [m]Jer 3:7 [n]Jer 14:4
4:9 [o]Dt 28:22 [p]Joel 1:7 [q]Jer 3:10; Hag 2:17
4:10 [r]Ex 9:3; Dt 28:27 [s]Isa 9:13
4:11 [t]Ge 19:24; Jer 23:14
4:13 [u]Ps 65:6 [v]Da 2:28 [w]Mic 1:3 [x]Isa 47:4; Am 5:8,27; 9:6

[a] *11* Hebrew *God*

warned of hunger and want (Dt 28:47–48) as a penalty for disobedience.

4:7–8 rain. The winter rains that normally fell from October through February were essential if the crops were to begin their growing cycle well. The spring or "latter" rains of March and April would provide the necessary water for mature growth. The Lord had promised these rains so long as Israel obeyed his commands (Lev 26:3–4), but he had also warned that he would withhold them if his people chose to disobey (Lev 26:18–19; Dt 28:23–24).

4:8–11 See *WLC* 151.

4:9 blight and mildew. Compare Haggai 2:17. The Lord had threatened these in the covenant (Dt 28:22). **Locusts.** In Hebrew, the singular word literally means "the shearer/cutter." The locust was a devouring, devastating insect (cf. Joel 1:4; 2:25). Ironically, the punishment described here is just like that which the Lord inflicted on Egypt (Ps 105:34–35), whose pharaoh was in a state of rebellion against God. Israel, likewise rebellious, had received the same punishment and, like Pharaoh, had not repented.

4:10 plagues . . . Egypt. The Lord had also threatened plague in his covenant with Israel (Dt 28:21), along with all the diseases of Egypt (Dt 28:60) that he had inflicted before the exodus (Ex 7:14—12:30). **killed . . . with the sword.** This phrase also has a covenantal background in Exodus 22:24, where the Lord threatened to "kill [Israel] with the sword" if his people oppressed the weak and helpless.

4:11 as I overthrew Sodom and Gomorrah. The phrase is rooted in the covenantal warning to God's people in Deuteronomy 29:23, where Sodom and Gomorrah were (as here) a model for Israel's judgment. The identical phrase is used in oracles against Babylon (Isa 13:19; Jer 50:40) and Edom (Jer 49:18). The Lord destroyed Sodom and Gomorrah in one cataclysmic outpouring of sulfurous flame because of their sin (Ge 19:24–25). God was saying that he had overthrown some of the Israelites with equal thoroughness, although by different means; namely, the covenant curses already described and fulfilled in 4:6–10. **a burning stick.** Compare Zechariah 3:2.

4:12 because I will do this to you. Or "because this is what I have done to you." The Hebrew is ambiguous and may indicate that because the Lord had already shown himself fully prepared to carry out his covenant curses, the people should have prepared themselves to meet their God. **prepare . . . God.** The phrase stems from Exodus 19:15–17, where, after a three-day period of sanctification ("Prepare yourselves . . . to meet with God"), the people came to Mount Sinai to meet with the God who was forging a covenant with them. Ironically, they would now meet with the God who was coming in retribution for their covenant breaking.

4:13 He who forms . . . his name. This verse is in the form of a hymnic series of titles or epithets praising the deeds or powers of a god or king. Here they describe the great King, who is abundantly able to carry out the curses he had originally threatened in the covenant. For the form, see Isaiah 44:24–28 and, ironically, Amos 4:1.

A Lament and Call to Repentance

5 Hear this word, O house of Israel, this lament[y] I take up concerning you:

2 "Fallen is Virgin[z] Israel,
never to rise again,
deserted in her own land,
with no one to lift her up.[a]"

3 This is what the Sovereign LORD says:

"The city that marches out a thousand strong for Israel
will have only a hundred left;
the town that marches out a hundred strong
will have only ten left.[b]"

4 This is what the LORD says to the house of Israel:

"Seek me and live;[c]
5 do not seek Bethel,
do not go to Gilgal,[d]
do not journey to Beersheba.[e]
For Gilgal will surely go into exile,
and Bethel will be reduced to nothing.[a][f]"
6 Seek[g] the LORD and live,[h]
or he will sweep through the house of Joseph like a fire;[i]
it will devour,
and Bethel[j] will have no one to quench it.

7 You who turn justice into bitterness[k]
and cast righteousness to the ground
8 (he who made the Pleiades and Orion,[l]
who turns blackness into dawn[m]
and darkens day into night,[n]

5:1 [y]Eze 19:1
5:2 [z]Jer 14:17 [a]Jer 50:32; Am 8:14
5:3 [b]Isa 6:13; Am 6:9
5:4 [c]Isa 55:3; Jer 29:13
5:5 [d]1Sa 11:14; Am 4:4 [e]Am 8:14 [f]1Sa 7:16
5:6 [g]Isa 55:6 [h]ver 14 [i]Dt 4:24 [j]Am 3:14
5:7 [k]Am 6:12
5:8 [l]Job 9:9 [m]Isa 42:16 [n]Ps 104:20; Am 8:9

[a] 5 Or *grief*; or *wickedness*; Hebrew *aven*, a reference to Beth Aven (a derogatory name for Bethel)

■ **5:1—6:7** *The Severity of Judgment.* In an oracle of lament (5:1–17) and in two oracles of woe (5:18–27; 6:1–7), Amos expressed how terrible the coming judgment would be.
5:1—6:7 See *BC* 12.
■ **5:1–17** *Lament for Virgin Israel.* Amos lamented over the fate of Samaria under Assyrian rule, as he had described it in the preceding section.
5:1 Hear this word. See note on 3:1. **lament.** Amos lamented over Israel as though she were already dead. This literary device is typical of Old Testament prophecy, especially in Ezekiel (e.g., Eze 19:1; 26:17; 27:2; 32:2). This lament consists of four parts: a description of the tragedy (vv. 2–3), a call to react (vv. 4–6), a direct address to the fallen (vv. 7–13) and a summons to mourning (vv. 16–17).
5:2 This verse begins the lament proper with a description of the tragedy. **Fallen.** This term is used in other laments (e.g., 2Sa 1:19,25,27; 3:34; La 2:21). **Virgin Israel.** This imperfectly understood personification of Israel (cf. 2Ki 19:21; Jer 18:13) is also applied to other nations; e.g., Babylon (the "Virgin Daughter of Babylon"; Isa 47:1) and Egypt (the "Virgin Daughter of Egypt"; Jer 46:11). Against the background of Ugaritic mythology, the phrase may have had connotations of the nation in question being the consort of a god, as indeed Israel was the bride of Yahweh and the church the bride of Christ (Rev 19:7; 21:2,9; 22:17).
5:3 a thousand . . . a hundred . . . a hundred . . . ten. The drastic military reversals described here echo the prophecy of such disasters in the covenant (Dt 32:28–30). The Lord warned that these calamities would come because of idolatry (Dt 32:15–18).
5:4 This verse begins the call to react. See note on verse 1. **Seek me and live.** Compare verses 6 and 14. The Lord had promised to be available to those who would seek him, even while in exile (Dt 4:29; cf. La 3:25). Tragically, the Lord's people typically did not seek him (Isa 9:13; Jer 10:21).
5:5 do not seek. The Israelites had grown accustomed to turning to their syncretistic worship sites for help in times of trouble, instead of seeking deliverance from the Lord. **Bethel . . . Gilgal.** See note on 4:4. **Beersheba.** This ancient holy place (Ge 21:31–33; 26:23–25; 46:1–5) was located some 50 miles south-southwest of Jerusalem. People from the north evidently traveled to this southern sanctuary on pilgrimage (cf. 8:14). Josiah desecrated the high places "from Geba to Beersheba" in his reform (2Ki 23:8). **go into exile . . . reduced to nothing.** God threatened to remove the people and devastate these places if repentance did not take place.
5:6 Seek the LORD and live, or he will. Assuming that this series of oracles appears roughly in chronological order, God had already sworn to punish the women of Samaria (4:2) and was about to swear to destroy Samaria (6:8). Here he threatened to do the same to other parts of the northern kingdom unless the people were to repent and seek him (see verse 15). **house of Joseph.** The term denotes the tribes of Ephraim and Manasseh and so covers the tribal areas that contained Bethel (Ephraim) and Gilgal (Manasseh). These sanctuaries in the north would be destroyed; Beersheba, in the south, would not be destroyed in the judgment fire that would sweep through the northern kingdom. **fire.** See note on 1:4. **no one to quench it.** The Lord's judgment fire cannot be extinguished (cf. Isa 1:31; Jer 4:4; Mt 3:12).
5:7 This begins the direct address to the fallen. See note on verse 1. **You who turn justice into bitterness.** This epithet follows the manner of the divine or royal epithet. As in 4:1, it is again ironic. See note on 4:13. The same phrase occurs in 6:12, and this weighs against the emendation made by some, "You who turn justice upside down." **cast righteousness to the ground.** Justice and righteousness often occur together in the Old Testament as qualities of life the Lord desires (cf. v. 24; Isa 5:7). Here the prophet rebuked the leaders of Israel for their failure to establish justice and righteousness.
5:8–9 he who made . . . ruin. For this divine epithet, see note on 4:13. This majestic series of titles for the Lord contrasts starkly with the previous verse, which describes a sinful people.
5:8 Pleiades. This is an open star cluster (denoted as M45) in the constellation Taurus; it includes seven prominent stars visible to the naked eye. **Orion.** The Hebrew name possibly means "the Fool," although in classical literature it speaks of "the Hunter." The Pleiades and Orion occur elsewhere together in the context of God's incomparable power and wisdom (Job 9:9; 38:31).

who calls for the waters of the sea
and pours them out over the face of the land—
the LORD is his name[o]—
9 he flashes destruction on the stronghold
and brings the fortified city to ruin),[p]
10 you hate the one who reproves in court[q]
and despise him who tells the truth.[r]

11 You trample on the poor[s]
and force him to give you grain.
Therefore, though you have built stone mansions,[t]
you will not live in them;
though you have planted lush vineyards,
you will not drink their wine.[u]
12 For I know how many are your offenses
and how great your sins.

You oppress the righteous and take bribes
and you deprive the poor of justice in the courts.[v]
13 Therefore the prudent man keeps quiet in such times,
for the times are evil.

14 Seek good, not evil,
that you may live.
Then the LORD God Almighty will be with you,
just as you say he is.
15 Hate evil,[w] love good;
maintain justice in the courts.
Perhaps the LORD God Almighty will have mercy[x]
on the remnant[y] of Joseph.

16 Therefore this is what the Lord, the LORD God Almighty, says:

"There will be wailing[z] in all the streets
and cries of anguish in every public square.
The farmers[a] will be summoned to weep
and the mourners to wail.
17 There will be wailing in all the vineyards,
for I will pass through[b] your midst,"
says the LORD.[c]

5:8 [o]Ps 104:6-9; Am 4:13
5:9 [p]Mic 5:11
5:10 [q]Isa 29:21 [r]1Ki 22:8
5:11 [s]Am 8:6 [t]Am 3:15 [u]Mic 6:15
5:12 [v]Isa 5:23; Am 2:6-7
5:15 [w]Ps 97:10; Ro 12:9 [x]Joel 2:14 [y]Mic 5:7,8
5:16 [z]Jer 9:17 [a]Joel 1:11
5:17 [b]Ex 12:12 [c]Isa 16:10; Jer 48:33

5:10 you hate . . . and despise. Literally, "they hate . . . and despise." This verse contrasts with the following verses (vv. 11–12), which are in the second person. However, no significant difference of tone seems to be intended by this shift, and such changes of person are common in ancient Near Eastern documents, including letters, treaties and dedicatory inscriptions. **the one who reproves . . . tells the truth.** Such people rebuke falsehood and bear true witness in a court of law. Israel had come to hate such individuals, because they threatened to prevent corruption and dishonest gain (cf. 2:6–7). **in court.** Literally, "in the gate." Much of a city's legal business was transacted in its gate, a large passage with adjacent rooms.

5:11 stone mansions. Literally, "houses of dressed stone." Such structures would have been costly to build, in contrast to the houses of mud brick in which most people lived. Compare Isaiah 9:10. **though you have built . . . you will not live . . . though you have planted . . . you will not drink.** The futility curses (i.e., curses that would render futile any of their constructive efforts) the Lord had formerly inflicted on the Canaanites would now be directed against his own people (Dt 6:10–12; see also vv. 16–17 and their note). The curse on vineyards is drawn from the covenant as stipulated in Deuteronomy 28:30 and 39.

5:12 I know. It was important for the Israelites to realize that the Lord knew what they perhaps imagined he did not (cf. Job 22:13–14; Ps 73:11; Lk 16:15). **bribes.** The kind of bribe referred to was a ransom for the life of a murderer, which was against the law (Nu 35:31).

5:13 keeps quiet. This can be rendered "will cease," since the Hebrew word is used elsewhere as a parallel with death: "Her young men will fall in the streets; all her soldiers will be silenced in that day" (Jer 49:26; 50:30). The Lord removed wise or prudent men from leadership positions as part of his judgment on a nation; e.g., Judah (Isa 3:1–4,12) and Edom (Jer 49:7; Ob 8).

5:14 Seek good, not evil. For this thought, see Isaiah 1:16–17. Compare verse 4, where God commanded his people to seek him and live. **that you may live.** While it is true that obedience to the Lord brings security and prosperity (Dt 28:1–14), this verse points to a deeper truth: To know God is the essence of life itself (cf. Jn 17:3). **with you.** Expresses the deepest need of God's people, which is anticipated also (but with different Hebrew wording) in Isaiah 7:14 ("Immanuel" means "God with us"; Mt 1:23). **as you say he is.** The Israelites, with misguided confidence, claimed that the Lord was with them, despite their rebelliousness, simply because he had made a covenant with them. For an example of a similar unfounded confidence, compare Matthew 3:9.

5:15 courts. Literally "gates," as in verse 10. **Perhaps . . . remnant of Joseph.** In Amos's day Israel was relatively prosperous and strong. The phrase anticipates a future time after God's judgment had come. If the people were to reform their ways, it was possible that God would relent from judging the entire nation. Assuming that these oracles are arranged chronologically, God had already sworn to send the wealthy women of Samaria into exile (4:2), but here the prophet offered hope, though not a guarantee ("perhaps"), that the rest of the land might be spared upon repentance. This series eventually ends with God swearing to destroy Samaria (6:8). See *WCF* 15.2.

5:16–17 These verses comprise the summons to mourning that concludes the lament (see note on v. 1). **streets . . . vineyards.** The laments over Israel would be taken up in every part of the land, since every part would be punished. **There will be wailing in all the streets.** Literally, "In all the streets they will say, 'Woe! Woe!' " For other prophetic uses of this cry, see verse 18, 6:1, Isaiah 1:4 ("Ah") and Jeremiah 22:18 ("Alas"). **I will pass through.** The same phrase appears in Exodus 12:12, where the Lord said of his impending judgment on Egypt, "I will pass through Egypt." Ironically, because his people had become as pagan as the Egyptians, he

The Day of the LORD

18 Woe to you who long
for the day of the LORD![d]
Why do you long for the day of the LORD?
That day will be darkness,[e] not light.[f]
19 It will be as though a man fled from a lion
only to meet a bear,
as though he entered his house
and rested his hand on the wall
only to have a snake bite him.[g]
20 Will not the day of the LORD be darkness, not light—
pitch-dark, without a ray of brightness?[h]

21 "I hate, I despise your religious feasts;[i]
I cannot stand your assemblies.[j]
22 Even though you bring me burnt offerings and grain offerings,
I will not accept them.
Though you bring choice fellowship offerings,[a]
I will have no regard for them.[k l]
23 Away with the noise of your songs!
I will not listen to the music of your harps.[m]
24 But let justice[n] roll on like a river,
righteousness like a never-failing stream![o]

25 "Did you bring me sacrifices[p] and offerings
forty years[q] in the desert, O house of Israel?
26 You have lifted up the shrine of your king,
the pedestal of your idols,
the star of your god[b]—
which you made for yourselves.

5:18 [d]Joel 1:15 [e]Joel 2:2 [f]Isa 5:19,30; Jer 30:7
5:19 [g]Job 20:24; Isa 24:17-18; Jer 15:2-3; 48:44
5:20 [h]Isa 13:10; Zep 1:15
5:21 [i]Lev 26:31 [j]Isa 1:11-16
5:22 [k]Am 4:4; Mic 6:6-7 [l]Isa 66:3
5:23 [m]Am 6:5
5:24 [n]Jer 22:3 [o]Mic 6:8
5:25 [p]Isa 43:23 [q]Dt 32:17

[a] *22* Traditionally *peace offerings* [b] *26* *Or lifted up Sakkuth your king / and Kaiwan your idols, / your star-gods*; Septuagint *lifted up the shrine of Molech / and the star of your god Rephan, / their idols*

would now pass through Israel in judgment, as he once passed through the land of its oppressors.

■ **5:18–27** *Woe for Those Who Long.* The prophet pronounced woe over the northern kingdom because its future was so bleak.

5:18 Woe. See note on verses 16–17. **the day of the LORD!** Refers to that time when God will come as King to judge his enemies and bless his faithful people (see Isa 2:12; 13:6–13; Ob 15; Zep 1:7,14). Every major Old Testament period of judgment may be called "the day of the LORD," just as the New Testament associates the term with Pentecost (Ac 2:20), but primarily with the still future return of Christ (1Co 1:8; 5:5; 2Co 1:14; 1Th 5:2; 2Th 2:1; 2Pe 3:10). **Why do you long for the day of the LORD?** This can also be rendered, "What good will the day of the LORD be to you?" The Israelites were so confident of their good standing with God that they believed the day of the Lord would be to their benefit. They had failed to understand that their flagrant violations of the covenant actually made them the enemies of God, the objects of his wrath. **darkness, not light.** Perhaps this is an echo of verse 8. The Lord alone has power to turn day into night, both literally and figuratively, in judgment.

5:19 Amos portrayed the futility of trying to escape the Lord's judgment. For the spirit of the verse, see Isaiah 24:17–18.

5:20 Will not. In Hebrew, the question expects the answer yes. **darkness, not light.** See note on verse 18. **brightness.** Figuratively, this represents well-being or cause for joy. But brightness is also associated with the Lord (Ps 18:12; Isa 4:5), and with the righteous (Pr 4:18; Isa 60:3; 62:1). The implication here is that there would be no light of righteousness in the land and no brightness of the Lord's (favorable) countenance. Judgment would be black and total, engulfing the whole land.

5:21–23 This is a brief critique of Israel's religious practices. The point is not that the practices themselves were wrong, for the Lord had ordained them. Rather, they were being performed in an unspiritual manner, having the form of religion but denying its power (1Ti 3:5).

5:21 I hate, I despise. Two words combine here to express one concept more forcefully than either could convey by itself. This could also be translated, "I reject with utter hatred." **cannot stand.** Literally, "will not smell." The language here comes from the realm of burnt offering. Similarly, in the original covenant the Lord had declared that, if his people were to become disobedient, he would "take no delight in [not smell] the pleasing aroma of [their] offerings" (Lev 26:31).

5:22 Even though . . . I will have no regard for them. The Lord has always been more interested in our spiritual attitude toward him (and toward others made in his image) than he has been in sacrifices (cf. Mt 5:23–24; 1Co 13:3).

5:23 noise. Literally, "din." The same word is used to describe the tumult of waters in heaven when the Lord thunders (Jer 10:13), as well as the rumble of an army's chariot wheels (Jer 47:3).

5:24 justice . . . righteousness. See note on verse 7. **river . . . never-failing stream!** Literally, "ever-flowing wadi." Wadies in the Middle East are narrow valleys through which torrents rush in the rainy season but which may be completely dry at other times. Symbolically, the Lord, the Giver of the rains, would gladly provide perpetual rains to supply the wadies of justice and righteousness—but Israel, the dry wadi, would not have it so.

5:25 Did you bring . . . ? Such offerings had, in fact, been brought to the Lord (cf. Ex 18:12; Lev 9:8–24). But the point of the rhetorical question was to emphasize that such sacrifices were not of primary importance to God. Rather, he wanted (and still wants) worship offered in spirit and in truth. **forty years in the desert.** See note on 2:10.

5:26 lifted up. Idols could be carried around. **the shrine of your king.** This can be rendered "Sakkuth, your king." The Hebrew consonant does, in fact, indicate this reading. Sakkuth was an Assyrian god of war and the chase, and the name means "king of decision" (i.e., the divine "king" who decides victory or defeat in war). The translators of the Septuagint (the Greek translation of the OT) knew nothing of this and so translated it as "tent/tabernacle" (cf. NIV text note "shrine"). They also translated "your king" as "Molech" (cf. Ac 7:42–43). **the pedestal.** This word can also be rendered "Kaiwan," a name attested in other Semitic languages (Akkadian, Syriac and Arabic) for the planet Saturn, which is next referred to as "the star of your god." **which you made for yourselves.** Old Testament polemics against idolatry often emphasized that these productions were made by human beings (cf. Isa 44:9–20; Jer 10:1–16; see note on Mic 5:10–16).

5:27
[r]Am 4:13; Ac 7:42-43*
6:1
[s]Lk 6:24 [t]Isa 32:9-11
6:2
[u]Ge 10:10
[v]2Ki 18:34
[w]2Ch 26:6 [x]Na 3:8
6:3
[y]Isa 56:12; Am 9:10
6:4
[z]Eze 34:2-3; Am 3:12
6:5
[a]Isa 5:12; Am 5:23
[b]1Ch 15:16
6:6
[c]Am 2:8 [d]Eze 9:4
6:8
[e]Ge 22:16; Heb 6:13
[f]Lev 26:30
[g]Ps 47:4 [h]Am 4:2
[i]Dt 32:19
6:9
[j]Am 5:3
6:10
[k]1Sa 31:12

27 Therefore I will send you into exile beyond Damascus,"
says the LORD, whose name is God Almighty.[r]

Woe to the Complacent

6 Woe to you[s] who are complacent in Zion,
and to you who feel secure on Mount Samaria,
you notable men of the foremost nation,
to whom the people of Israel come![t]
2 Go to Calneh[u] and look at it;
go from there to great Hamath,[v]
and then go down to Gath[w] in Philistia.
Are they better off than[x] your two kingdoms?
Is their land larger than yours?
3 You put off the evil day
and bring near a reign of terror.[y]
4 You lie on beds inlaid with ivory
and lounge on your couches.
You dine on choice lambs
and fattened calves.[z]
5 You strum away on your harps[a] like David
and improvise on musical instruments.[b]
6 You drink wine[c] by the bowlful
and use the finest lotions,
but you do not grieve[d] over the ruin of Joseph.
7 Therefore you will be among the first to go into exile;
your feasting and lounging will end.

The LORD Abhors the Pride of Israel

8 The Sovereign LORD has sworn by himself[e]—the LORD God Almighty declares:

"I abhor[f] the pride of Jacob[g]
and detest his fortresses;
I will deliver up[h] the city
and everything in it.[i]"

9 If ten[j] men are left in one house, they too will die. 10 And if a relative who is to burn
the bodies[k] comes to carry them out of the house and asks anyone still hiding there, "Is

5:27 beyond Damascus. Regarding Damascus, see note on 1:3. Exile beyond Damascus would have implied deportation to Assyria, as Amos's audience would well have understood. Banishment far from home was one of the original covenant curses (Dt 28:36,49,64–68).

■ **6:1–7** *Woe for the Complacent.* In addition to woe pronounced over those who prayed and longed for the day of the Lord, the prophet also declared woe over the complacent inhabitants of Samaria and Zion, who fancied themselves beyond harm.

6:1 Woe. See note on 5:16–17. **Zion . . . Mount Samaria.** Regarding Zion, see note on 1:2. Regarding Mount Samaria, see note on 3:9. Like his contemporaries (see, e.g., Isa 9:8–21; Hos 6:11; Mic 1:3–5), Amos was given a prophecy that addressed both kingdoms (cf. 2:4–5). **foremost nation.** The phrase occurs also in Numbers 24:20 (of Amalek). Israel had become powerful and prosperous under Jeroboam II and may have imagined herself the first among the nations.

6:2 Calneh. The identity of this city is uncertain, but it may be the Calno mentioned in Isaiah 10:9, which was conquered by Sargon II of Assyria in 710 B.C. **great Hamath.** Located north of Dan on the Orontes River in Syria, it was restored to Israelite control by Jeroboam II (2Ki 14:23–28). **Gath.** One of the five major Philistine cities (see note on 1:8). Uzziah had recaptured it from Syrian control (2Ki 12:17; 2Ch 26:6). **Are they better off . . . ? Is their land larger . . . ?** This means "Are [you] better off than these kingdoms?" The parallelism indicates the answer to both questions. The land of these cities was not larger than Israel, so the answer to the second question must be no. The implied response to the first rhetorical question must then be no as well. This was tragic, for, with God's special revelation, Israel and Judah should have been much better off than these other kingdoms. But if these pagans would not escape conquest, neither would Israel and Judah.

6:3 reign of terror. Literally, "an enthronement of violence." Israel had enthroned violence (e.g., extortion and abuse of the poor) as a way of life, while simultaneously denying that the evil day, the day of judgment (cf. 5:13), was coming.

6:4 ivory. See 3:15. **fattened calves.** Literally, "calves from the fattening stall." These choice calves were kept in stalls and fattened for special occasions. Such was the normal fare for the wealthy of Samaria.

6:5 strum away. The meaning is uncertain, but (to judge from an Arabic cognate) it may mean something like "sing frivolous songs." **like David.** This comparison is intensely ironic. David's songs were never frivolous, but he did compose many psalms to the glory of the Lord (cf. 2Sa 23:1).

6:6 by the bowlful. Literally, "from basins." The Hebrew word refers to large basins, like those used to throw blood against the altar (Lev 1:5,11). They were apparently heavy, made of valuable metal. Nahshon offered "one silver sprinkling bowl weighing seventy shekels" (Nu 7:13) for the dedication of the altar of the Mosaic tabernacle. **grieve.** Literally, "be sick [with grief]." **Joseph.** See note on 5:6.

6:7 first to go into exile. In Hebrew this phrase is a wordplay on the earlier "foremost nation" (v. 1). The leaders in Samaria and Jerusalem fancied themselves as first in importance, but they would in fact find themselves first among the exiles.

■ **6:8–14** *The Certainty of Divine Oath.* This oath is placed at the end of these oracles (3:1—6:14) because it represents the Lord's final conclusion. He swore that the city of Samaria would be destroyed, rendering this outcome inevitable. The Assyrians accomplished this in 722 B.C. (see "Introduction: Purpose and Distinctives").

6:8 sworn by himself. For essentially the same phrase, see Genesis 22:16, Exodus 32:13 and Isaiah 45:23. See also note on 4:2. Such an oath declared the matter to be irreversible (Heb 6:13–14), although some details (how? when? how much? to whom precisely? etc.) could vary. **pride of Jacob.** This may refer to his own pride, to that in which he took pride or (most likely) to both. **fortresses.** See note on 1:4.

anyone with you?" and he says, "No," then he will say, "Hush![l] We must not mention the
name of the LORD."

11 For the LORD has given the command,
and he will smash the great house[m] into pieces
and the small house into bits.[n]
12 Do horses run on the rocky crags?
Does one plow there with oxen?
But you have turned justice into poison[o]
and the fruit of righteousness into bitterness[p]—
13 you who rejoice in the conquest of Lo Debar[a]
and say, "Did we not take Karnaim[b] by our own strength?[q]"
14 For the LORD God Almighty declares,
"I will stir up a nation[r] against you, O house of Israel,
that will oppress you all the way
from Lebo[c] Hamath[s] to the valley of the Arabah."[t]

Locusts, Fire and a Plumb Line

7 This is what the Sovereign LORD showed me:[u] He was preparing swarms of locusts[v]
after the king's share had been harvested and just as the second crop was coming
up. 2 When they had stripped the land clean,[w] I cried out, "Sovereign LORD, forgive! How
can Jacob survive?[x] He is so small![y]"
3 So the LORD relented.[z]
"This will not happen," the LORD said.[a]
4 This is what the Sovereign LORD showed me: The Sovereign LORD was calling for judg-

6:10 [l] Am 8:3
6:11 [m] Am 3:15 [n] Isa 55:11
6:12 [o] Hos 10:4 [p] Am 5:7
6:13 [q] Job 8:15; Isa 28:14-15
6:14 [r] Jer 5:15 [s] 1Ki 8:65 [t] Am 3:11
7:1 [u] Am 8:1 [v] Joel 1:4
7:2 [w] Ex 10:15 [x] Isa 37:4 [y] Eze 11:13
7:3 [z] Dt 32:36; Jer 26:19; Jnh 3:10 [a] Hos 11:8

[a] 13 *Lo Debar* means *nothing.* [b] 13 *Karnaim* means *horns; horn* here symbolizes strength. [c] 14 Or *from the entrance to*

6:9 ten men . . . one house. The meaning here is unclear. Possibilities are (1) only ten men left in a large, wealthy house; (2) only ten members remaining of a household; or (3) only ten soldiers (units of ten being the smallest in the army) left in the one house still standing.
6:10 relative who is to burn the bodies. Literally, "a man's kinsman and his burner." The reference is probably to one and the same person. He came not to "burn the bodies" but to burn a fire in honor of the dead (cf. Jer 34:5). **We must not mention the name of the LORD.** This rendering understands the sentence to mean that it would be dangerous to mention the Lord. It may also be translated "not invoke the name of the LORD" (see Isa 48:1). If this later translation is correct, it means that one might invoke the Lord's name for help under normal circumstances, but that on the day of judgment one should not do so because the God of the covenant would be coming in judgment against his own people.
6:11 given the command. Literally, "is even now commanding." The Lord was rousing Assyria, his instrument of judgment, to rise up against Israel. **great house . . . small house.** The references are not to the "summer house" and the "winter house" of 3:15, since both of those houses belonged to the wealthy and might be expected to be "great." Rather, both the great houses of the wealthy and the small houses of the poor would be shattered by the coming judgment. Here, as often in the Hebrew, the word "house" might have secondary connotations of "household."
6:12 Do horses run . . . ? Does one plow . . . ? Obviously, the expected answer is an emphatic "No!" One plows in fertile soil, not on crags; nor do horses run in such a dangerous place. The emendation "Does one plow the sea with oxen?" which is sometimes adopted, requires a vowel change of the Hebrew and is attested by no ancient version. It rests on a lack of recognition of a Hebrew poetic technique, reflected here as the double-duty use of the word "crags," which is missing from the second line (but rightly included in the translation with the word "there"). **justice into poison.** See note on 5:7.
6:13 Lo Debar . . . Karnaim. The former is a border town in Gilead; the latter, a city on the plain of Bashan on the way to Damascus. Both were apparently retaken from Hazael by Jehoash (2Ki 10:32–33; 13:25) but later conquered by Assyria (2Ki 15:29). The names mean, respectively, "Nothing" and "A Pair of Horns." A wordplay is intended, by which Amos declared that Israel rejoiced in the conquest of nothing (for the conquest of Lo Debar, soon to be taken by Assyria, was ephemeral) and said, "We have taken a pair of horns [symbolic of military strength in the ancient Near East; cf. 1Ki 22:11] by our own strength." The Israelites' conquests would amount to nothing, and their strength would melt away before the Lord's judgment.
6:14 a nation. Assyria. **from Lebo Hamath . . . the valley of the Arabah.** These are the northern and southern boundaries of the kingdom as restored by Jeroboam II (2Ki 14:25).
■ **7:1—9:10** *Visions Against Israel.* In this section Amos reported a series of visions that clarified the nature of God's judgment against Israel. These visions fall into two main groups: judgments from which God relented (7:1–17) and judgments from which he did not relent (7:7—9:10).
■ **7:1–6** *Relented Judgments.* Amos saw God preparing two curses for his people, and the prophet interceded on their behalf for fear that the curses would destroy everyone in Israel.
■ **7:1–3** *Vision of Locusts.* Amos visualized God preparing a plague of locusts to curse Israel. The prophet interceded and God relented.
7:1 showed me. See verses 4 and 7 and 8:1. **locusts.** This Hebrew word, which occurs only here and in Nahum 3:17, denotes swarming hordes of newly-hatched locusts. **king's share.** Literally, "king's mowings"; i.e., the mowing that occurred before the general populace gathered crops. **second crop.** Literally, "latter crop"; i.e., the crop that began to grow after the "latter" spring rains of March and April (see note on 4:7–8).
7:2 stripped the land clean. Literally, "finished eating the vegetation of the land." The word for "vegetation" is the same as that used in Genesis 1:11; hence the reference is to all vegetation, not just to crops. In Hebrew the whole phrase echoes almost word for word Exodus 10:12 and 15 ("devour everything growing in the fields"). This deliberate echo indicates that, ironically, the Lord would punish Israel just as he had punished Egypt before the exodus. **How can Jacob survive?** Amos's concern was that none in Israel would survive. This would violate God's promise always to conserve a remnant out of which to build future generations (cf. Isa 10:22; Joel 2:32; Mic 2:12; 4:7; 5:7–8; 7:18; see also Zep 2:7; 3:13; Hag 1:12,14; Zec 8:6).
7:3 relented. Moved by intercessory appeal, the Lord was willing to redirect history or "relent" concerning his intended punishment (cf. Ex 32:12,14; Jer 18:8; Joel 2:13; Jnh 3:10). Here, as elsewhere, the perspective is one of God's interactions with creatures, not his eternal, immutable decrees.
■ **7:4–6** *Vision of Fire.* Amos observed God calling for fire. He interceded, and God again relented.
7:4 judgment by fire. See note on 1:4; See also Isaiah 66:15–16.

ment by fire;[b] it dried up the great deep and devoured[c] the land. 5 Then I cried out, "Sovereign LORD, I beg you, stop! How can Jacob survive? He is so small![d]"
6 So the LORD relented.[e]
"This will not happen either," the Sovereign LORD said.

7 This is what he showed me: The Lord was standing by a wall that had been built true
to plumb, with a plumb line in his hand. 8 And the LORD asked me, "What do you see,[f]
Amos?[g]"
"A plumb line,[h]" I replied.
Then the Lord said, "Look, I am setting a plumb line among my people Israel; I will
spare them no longer.[i]

9 "The high places of Isaac will be destroyed
and the sanctuaries[j] of Israel will be ruined;
with my sword I will rise against the house of Jeroboam.[k]"

Amos and Amaziah

10 Then Amaziah the priest of Bethel[l] sent a message to Jeroboam[m] king of Israel:
"Amos is raising a conspiracy[n] against you in the very heart of Israel. The land cannot
bear all his words.[o] 11 For this is what Amos is saying:

" 'Jeroboam will die by the sword,
and Israel will surely go into exile,
away from their native land.' "

12 Then Amaziah said to Amos, "Get out, you seer! Go back to the land of Judah. Earn
your bread there and do your prophesying there.[p] 13 Don't prophesy anymore at Bethel,
because this is the king's sanctuary and the temple of the kingdom.[q]"
14 Amos answered Amaziah, "I was neither a prophet[r] nor a prophet's son, but I was
a shepherd, and I also took care of sycamore-fig trees. 15 But the LORD took me from tend-

7:4 [b]Isa 66:16 [c]Dt 32:22
7:5 [d]ver 1-2; Joel 2:17
7:6 [e]Jnh 3:10
7:8 [f]Jer 1:11,13 [g]Isa 28:17; La 2:8; Am 8:2 [h]2Ki 21:13 [i]Jer 15:6; Eze 7:2-9
7:9 [j]Lev 26:31 [k]2Ki 15:9; Isa 63:18; Hos 10:8
7:10 [l]1Ki 12:32 [m]2Ki 14:23 [n]Jer 38:4 [o]Jer 26:8-11
7:12 [p]Mt 8:34
7:13 [q]Am 2:12; Ac 4:18
7:14 [r]2Ki 2:5; 4:38

---

great deep . . . the land. The "great deep" may refer to the Mediterranean Sea, although the same phrase is used of the ocean (Ge 7:11) and of the Red Sea at Israel's crossing (Isa 51:10). The prospect of a judgment fire that would devour the sea and the land echoes the covenant judgment warning in Deuteronomy 32:22.

7:5 See note on verse 2.

7:6 See note on verse 3.

■ **7:7—9:10** *Unrelented Judgments.* Amos reported three visions of God's coming wrath that did not prompt him to intercede for God to relent. The visions of a plumb line (7:7–9), ripe fruit (8:1–3) and the altar (9:1–4) are followed by elaborations (7:10–17; 8:4–14; 9:5–10).

■ **7:7–9** *Vision of a Plumb Line.* Amos had a vision of God measuring Israel with a plumb line that measured the pitch of individual walls to determine whether they should be torn down or remain standing.

7:7 standing by. This can also be rendered "standing above" (see 9:1; Ge 28:13). **a wall . . . true to plumb.** The wall that had been originally built true to plumb was Israel in her early, relative innocence. **with a plumb line in his hand.** Most interpret this phrase as a reference to God's covenant word (law) as his standard of judging whether or not Israel was "true to plumb." In the ancient Near East it was necessary to regularly evaluate whether walls were true to plumb. Those that were not had to be torn down and reconstructed, but those that stood properly were spared. Amos did not intercede after this vision of judgment because the salvation of a remnant was secure (cf. vv. 2,5).

7:8 A plumb line . . . a plumb line. See notes on verse 7. **spare.** Literally, "pass over." The complete idiom is "to pass over the transgression [of someone]" (see Mic 7:18; cf. Pr 19:11).

7:9 high places . . . sanctuaries. The high places were natural or man-made hills, sites of idolatrous worship (cf. Dt 12:2; 2Ki 17:10–12). The sanctuaries might have been for intended idolatrous worship or, more likely, for worship of the Lord mixed with the worship practices of other gods. See note on Micah 1:3–5. **house of Jeroboam.** The household of Jeroboam (see note on 6:11; cf. Isa 31:2). This leaves open the prospect that, although Jeroboam himself might not die by the sword, his household would be affected. Jeroboam apparently did die a natural death (2Ki 14:29); his son Zechariah, however, was assassinated (2Ki 15:10).

■ **7:10–17** *Elaboration.* This autobiographical section reports how the priest Amaziah reacted to Amos's vision of God's destruction of the high places in Israel and the house of his supporter Jeroboam. It also conveys how Amos served God faithfully despite this opposition.

7:10 the priest of Bethel. Probably refers to the high priest. **conspiracy.** Similarly, Jeremiah was wrongly considered to be treasonous because of his prophecies against Judah (Jer 26:7–11; 37:11–13; 38:1–4).

7:11 Jeroboam will die by the sword. This is an allusion to verse 9, where the Lord declared, "I will rise against the house of Jeroboam." Amaziah misquoted Amos in such a way as to make Jeroboam feel more personally threatened than Amos's prophecy warranted. **Israel . . . land.** This is an exact quote from 5:5, except that "Israel" is here substituted for "Gilgal" (which represents all Israel in the earlier quote).

7:12 Earn your bread there and do your prophesying there. Possibly this is a hendiadys (one idea expressed by two independent words or phrases connected by *and*). Here the two phrases combine to mean "Earn your living by prophesying there [in Judah]." Although it was appropriate for a prophet to be paid for his work (1Sa 9:7–8; but cf. Mic 3:5,11), Amaziah accused Amos of being merely a prophet for hire. Amaziah's command here and in the next verse is an example of the sin earlier cited by Amos: "You . . . commanded the prophets not to prophesy" (2:12).

7:13 Don't prophesy. See note on verse 12 (cf. Mic 2:6). **king's sanctuary . . . temple of the kingdom.** From the time Jeroboam I established idolatry at Bethel (see note on 3:14), the kings of Israel had a major influence on worship in the northern kingdom. Amaziah was concerned for the sanctuary of his earthly king rather than for that of the great King, the Lord. Ironically, Amaziah was the religious official who, being paid for his work, was concerned to protect earthly interests—the very charge he had levied against Amos (verse 12). A future generation of priests would likewise consign to death Jesus, the greatest of the prophets, on the basis of a misguided concern to protect their own kingdom and temple (Jn 11:48).

7:14 neither a prophet nor a prophet's son. Amos was not originally a prophet, nor was he one of the "sons of the prophets" (i.e., disciples of the prophets; 1Ki 20:35; 2Ki 2:3,5,7,15). He was not a paid professional prophet. **shepherd.** Amos was a "livestock breeder" (cf. "shepherds" at note on 1:1). **took care of . . . trees.** This describes one who treated the fruit by appropriate cutting to ensure superior sweetness once the fruit was ripe. That Amos mentioned these two callings, which are different from that of shepherding in 1:1 (see note), indicates that he was skilled in several trades.

7:15 But the LORD took me from tending the flock . . . my people Israel. Amos flatly rejected Amaziah's accusation (v. 12) and made it clear that the Lord had sovereignly called him to

ing the flock[s] and said to me, 'Go, prophesy to my people Israel.'[t] 16 Now then, hear the
word of the LORD. You say,

> " 'Do not prophesy against[u] Israel,
> and stop preaching against the house of Isaac.'

17 "Therefore this is what the LORD says:

> " 'Your wife will become a prostitute[v] in the city,
> and your sons and daughters will fall by the sword.
> Your land will be measured and divided up,
> and you yourself will die in a pagan[a] country.
> And Israel will certainly go into exile,
> away from their native land.[w]' "

7:15 [s]2Sa 7:8 [t]Jer 7:1-2; Eze 2:3-4
7:16 [u]Eze 20:46; Mic 2:6
7:17 [v]Hos 4:13 [w]2Ki 17:6; Eze 4:13; Hos 9:3

A Basket of Ripe Fruit

8 This is what the Sovereign LORD showed me: a basket of ripe fruit. 2 "What do you
see,[x] Amos?[y]" he asked.

"A basket of ripe fruit," I answered.

Then the LORD said to me, "The time is ripe for my people Israel; I will spare them no
longer.[z]

3 "In that day," declares the Sovereign LORD, "the songs in the temple will turn to wailing.[b][a] Many, many bodies—flung everywhere! Silence![b]"

> 4 Hear this, you who trample the needy
> and do away with the poor[c] of the land,[d]

5 saying,

> "When will the New Moon be over
> that we may sell grain,
> and the Sabbath be ended
> that we may market wheat?"—
> skimping the measure,
> boosting the price
> and cheating with dishonest scales,[e]
> 6 buying the poor with silver
> and the needy for a pair of sandals,
> selling even the sweepings with the wheat.[f]

8:2 [x]Jer 24:3 [y]Am 7:8 [z]Eze 7:2-9
8:3 [a]Am 5:16 [b]Am 5:23; 6:10
8:4 [c]Pr 30:14 [d]Ps 14:4; Am 2:7
8:5 [e]2Ki 4:23; Ne 13:15-16; Hos 12:7; Mic 6:10-11
8:6 [f]Am 2:6

a 17 Hebrew *an unclean* b 3 Or *"the temple singers will wail*

---

prophesy. He had not come to the northern kingdom to earn money, nor did he wish ill on Israel. He had come only because he had been called. The identical phraseology is used to relate the Lord's choice of David as king: "I took you from the pasture and from following [tending] the flock to be ruler over my people Israel" (2Sa 7:8). Amos's use of the same wording implies that the Lord had the sovereign right to choose both kings and prophets—and, implicitly, that a prophet so chosen had every right to prophecy at the "king's sanctuary" (v. 13).

7:16 Do not prophesy. See notes on 2:12, 7:12 and 7:13 (cf. 2:12).

7:17 Your wife will become a prostitute. She would stoop to this level out of desperation to provide some money once her husband's wealth had been stripped away and her children had been killed. **your sons and daughters . . . sword.** Compare Ezekiel 24:21. Sons and daughters were often punished along with their parents for covenant transgressions (Dt 28:32,53; Jer 5:17). To "fall by the sword" was a typical covenant punishment (Isa 3:25; Jer 39:18). **in a pagan country.** Literally, "in an unclean land." Exile would have been especially distasteful for Amaziah, a priest, for in a pagan land he would most likely have been forced into actions that would have made him ritually unclean (cf. Lev 11). For other prophetic judgments against disobedient priests, see 1 Samuel 2:34 (Eli's sons) and Jeremiah 20:1–6 (Pashhur). **Israel . . . land.** Amos quoted, with terrible irony, Amaziah's own summary of his prophecy (v. 11) back to him.

■ **8:1–3** *Vision of Ripe Fruit.* Amos saw a vision of ripe fruit, which illustrated Israel's condition.

8:1 ripe fruit. Literally, "summer fruit," or fruit that ripened during the summer (2Sa 16:1–2).

8:2 ripe fruit . . . time is ripe. In Hebrew this reads "summer fruit . . . the end has come." The Hebrew words for "summer fruit" and "end" are similar and are brought together here in a wordplay. The vision of summer fruit indicates that the end was fast approaching for Israel. **spare.** See note on 7:8.

8:3 that day. That is, the day of the Lord (see notes on 2:16; 5:18). **songs . . . wailing.** The temple songs, whose "din" the Lord could no longer tolerate (see note on 5:23), would give way to the wailing of bereavement when the Lord would come in judgment. **Many, many bodies.** An abundance of corpses was typical in defeated cities in the ancient Near East, especially those conquered by the Assyrians (cf. Na 3:19). **Silence!** See 6:10, where the same word is translated "Hush!"

■ **8:4–14** *Elaboration.* The prophet expanded on the vision of ripe fruit through oracles that revealed God's charges of social injustice, commercial dishonesty and indifference to holy days.

8:4 do away with the poor. The point here was not that the wealthy deliberately did away with the poor but that the oppression so deprived the needy that they could no longer afford the most basic necessities in life and therefore perished.

8:5 New Moon . . . Sabbath. The New Moon (festival) was celebrated every fourth week with various offerings (Nu 28:11–15). By custom, if not explicitly by law, buying and selling were halted during this time. The Sabbath, which was observed every week, was founded on God's acts of creation (Ex 20:8–11) and redemption (i.e., new creation; Dt 5:12–15). Work of any kind was forbidden on this day. **skimping . . . scales.** Such cheating practices were against the Lord's law (cf. Lev 19:36; Dt 25:14) and would result in his judgment. See *WLC* 99,119,121,142; *WSC* 61.

8:6 buying the poor with silver. See note on 2:6. **and the needy for a pair of sandals.** This repeats 2:6 (see its note). **the**

8:7 [g]Am 6:8 [h]Hos 8:13

7 The LORD has sworn by the Pride of Jacob:[g] "I will never forget[h] anything they have done.

8:8 [i]Hos 4:3 [j]Ps 18:7; Jer 46:8; Am 9:5

8 "Will not the land tremble[i] for this,
and all who live in it mourn?
The whole land will rise like the Nile;
it will be stirred up and then sink
like the river of Egypt.[j]

9 "In that day," declares the Sovereign LORD,

8:9 [k]Job 5:14; Isa 59:9-10; Jer 15:9; Am 5:8; Mic 3:6

"I will make the sun go down at noon
and darken the earth in broad daylight.[k]
10 I will turn your religious feasts into mourning
and all your singing into weeping.

8:10 [l]Jer 48:37 [m]Jer 6:26; Zec 12:10 [n]Eze 7:18

I will make all of you wear sackcloth[l]
and shave your heads.
I will make that time like mourning for an only son[m]
and the end of it like a bitter day.[n]

11 "The days are coming," declares the Sovereign LORD,
"when I will send a famine through the land—

8:11 [o]1Sa 3:1; 2Ch 15:3; Eze 7:26

not a famine of food or a thirst for water,
but a famine of hearing the words of the LORD.[o]
12 Men will stagger from sea to sea
and wander from north to east,

8:12 [p]Eze 20:3,31

searching for the word of the LORD,
but they will not find it.[p]

13 "In that day

8:13 [q]Isa 41:17; Hos 2:3

"the lovely young women and strong young men
will faint because of thirst.[q]

8:14 [r]1Ki 12:29 [s]Am 5:5 [t]Am 5:2

14 They who swear by the shame[a] of Samaria,
or say, 'As surely as your god lives, O Dan,'[r]
or, 'As surely as the god[b] of Beersheba[s] lives'—
they will fall,
never to rise again.[t]"

Israel to Be Destroyed

9 I saw the Lord standing by the altar, and he said:

"Strike the tops of the pillars
so that the thresholds shake.

[a] 14 Or *by Ashima;* or *by the idol* [b] 14 Or *power*

sweepings with the wheat. The estate owners sold even the chaff that had fallen to the floor when the wheat was threshed. They mixed it with the wheat, thereby cheating the buyer.
8:7 the Pride of Jacob. See note on 6:8. Here the phrase may refer to the Lord himself or to the land of Israel, which is elsewhere called "our inheritance . . . the pride of Jacob" (Ps 47:4).
8:8 Will not . . . ? This is a rhetorical question to which the obvious answer is yes. **rise like the Nile . . . sink like the river of Egypt.** Each year the Nile rose and overflowed its banks, flooding the countryside and leaving rich alluvial deposits. The imagery is used here to depict a coming flood of judgment—namely, the Assyrians (cf. Isa 8:7–8)—that would bring great upheaval with it.
8:9 that day. See notes on 2:16 and 5:18. **the sun go down.** The sun was worshiped in Judah (cf. 2Ki 23:5,11) and probably in Israel as well, since Israel was involved in astral worship (cf. 5:26), despite the fact that this practice was prohibited in the covenant (Dt 4:19). Star and sun worship were universal practices in the ancient Near East. Here the assertion that the Lord would make the sun go down affirms that he alone is God and that the sun is merely one of his creations. **the earth.** More specifically, this can be translated "the land," since the land of Israel would be punished. The phraseology directly recalls the plague of darkness that the Lord had brought upon the land of Egypt (cf. Ex 10:21–22; Ps 105:28). Here the Lord was about to judge Israel with a similar verdict. For further mention of darkness at noon on the day of judgment, see Job 5:14, Isaiah 59:10 and Jeremiah 15:9.
8:10 sackcloth. This was coarse material from which sacks were made. It was rough against the skin and not ordinarily intended for wearing, but it was worn by mourners to indicate that the pleasures of life no longer mattered (cf. Ge 37:34; 2Sa 3:31). **shave your heads.** Another sign of mourning, but one that was prohibited in the covenant (Dt 14:1), perhaps because it was viewed as a bodily disfigurement that disgraced God's image and because it was practiced by pagans (cf. Isa 15:2–3; Eze 27:30–31). **bitter.** Bitterness is the ultimate consequence of sin (cf. 2Sa 2:26; Pr 5:4).
8:11 a famine of hearing the words of the LORD. This curse stems from the covenant (Dt 4:28–29; 32:20; cf. Hos 3:4). During the period of the judges, when sin abounded (Jdg 21:25), "the word of the LORD was rare" (1Sa 3:1). Compare Luke 17:22.
8:12 from sea to sea. A standard concept in ancient Near Eastern geography that literally meant "from the Mediterranean to the Persian Gulf." Figuratively, it denoted "the ends of the earth."
8:13 young women . . . young men. Even the young and robust would be at the end of their strength (cf. Isa 51:20). **thirst.** This includes both physical (cf. 4:7–8) and spiritual (v. 11) thirst.
8:14 swear. To swear by a god in the ancient Near East meant to take that god as one's own. Idolaters swore by what were not gods (Jer 5:7), but demons (Dt 32:17). The Israelites, however, were commanded to swear by the Lord (Dt 6:13; 10:20).

Bring them down on the heads[u] of all the people;
those who are left I will kill with the sword.
Not one will get away,
none will escape.
2 Though they dig down to the depths of the grave,[a][v]
from there my hand will take them.
Though they climb up to the heavens,[w]
from there I will bring them down.[x]
3 Though they hide themselves on the top of Carmel,[y]
there I will hunt them down and seize them.[z]
Though they hide from me at the bottom of the sea,
there I will command the serpent to bite them.[a]
4 Though they are driven into exile by their enemies,
there I will command the sword[b] to slay them.
I will fix my eyes upon them
for evil[c] and not for good."[d][e]

5 The Lord, the LORD Almighty,
he who touches the earth and it melts,[f]
and all who live in it mourn—
the whole land rises like the Nile,
then sinks like the river of Egypt[g]—
6 he who builds his lofty palace[b] in the heavens
and sets its foundation[c] on the earth,
who calls for the waters of the sea
and pours them out over the face of the land—
the LORD is his name.[h]

7 "Are not you Israelites
the same to me as the Cushites[d]?"[i]
declares the LORD.
"Did I not bring Israel up from Egypt,
the Philistines from Caphtor[e][j]
and the Arameans from Kir?[k]

9:1 [u]Ps 68:21
9:2 [v]Ps 139:8 [w]Jer 51:53 [x]Ob 1:4
9:3 [y]Am 1:2 [z]Ps 139:8-10 [a]Jer 16:16-17
9:4 [b]Lev 26:33; Eze 5:12 [c]Jer 21:10 [d]Jer 39:16 [e]Jer 44:11
9:5 [f]Ps 46:2; Mic 1:4 [g]Am 8:8
9:6 [h]Ps 104:1-3, 5-6, 13; Am 5:8
9:7 [i]Isa 20:4; 43:3 [j]Dt 2:23; Jer 47:4 [k]2Ki 16:9; Isa 22:6; Am 1:5; 2:10

[a] 2 Hebrew *to Sheol* [b] 6 The meaning of the Hebrew for this phrase is uncertain. [c] 6 The meaning of the Hebrew for this word is uncertain. [d] 7 That is, people from the upper Nile region [e] 7 That is, Crete

■ **9:1–4** *Vision of the Altar.* Amos saw a vision of the Lord at the altar. In the other four visions (see 7:1—8:3), Amos was an intercessor or respondent to the Lord's questions. In this vision, however, he had no active role but simply recorded what he saw.
9:1 by the altar. This can mean, specifically, "above the altar" (see note on 7:7). It is not clear whether Amos's vision was of God at the temple in Jerusalem or at the worship center in Bethel. In any event, God called for the temple structure to fall on the people as an act of divine judgment. **Strike.** The Lord commanded not Amos but presumably an angel, perhaps the "destroying angel" (see 2Sa 24:15–16; 2Ki 19:35). **Bring them down on the heads of all the people.** This can be rendered "Cut them [the pillars] off at the top; all of them." The Hebrew is ambiguous, perhaps intentionally so. The command seems to be for someone (possibly an angel) to destroy the temple, bringing it down on the heads of those within (Jdg 16:29–30). **those who are left.** The Lord would see to the destruction of any survivors.
9:2–4 This brief section stresses the impossibility of escape from the Lord, who is omnipresent.
9:2 the depths of the grave. Literally, "Sheol," the place of death. **the heavens.** The pairing (the "depths of the grave . . . the heavens") expresses poetically the infinite nature of God's dominion (cf. Isa 7:11). For the thought here, see Psalm 139:7–12.
9:3 Carmel. See note on 1:2. **bottom of the sea.** This contrasts with the height of Carmel. Since Carmel was the westernmost point of land in Israel, further flight would lead one into the sea. **serpent.** This sea monster is perhaps the Leviathan of Isaiah 27:1. The verse poetically asserts the Lord's sovereignty over all creation; none can escape his justice.
9:4 exile. This is one of the covenant curses for disobedience (Dt 28:41). **I will fix my eyes . . . for evil and not for good.** God had determined to bring judgment against the Israelites no matter where they went (see Jer 21:10; 39:16; cf. Pss 33:18; 34:15).
■ **9:5–10** *Elaboration.* Amos expanded on his vision of destruction with a hymnic praise of God in judgment (vv. 5–6) and a disputation leading to a pronouncement of judgment (vv. 7–10).
9:5–6 This section constitutes a short, hymnic celebration of the Lord as the great Judge of all (see note on 4:13).
9:5 touches . . . melts. For similar expressions of the Lord's awesome power, see Psalms 46:6 and 104:32, as well as Nahum 1:5. **the whole land . . . Egypt.** Parallels the phrasing in 8:8.
9:6 palace. This can be rendered "temple" (see NIV text note). Compare Revelation 11:19. The Hebrew word literally means "steps," such as those used to enter the temple, particularly the eschatological temple (cf. Eze 40:6,22,26,31,34). **foundation.** Literally, "vault," a Hebrew word whose meaning in this context is not entirely clear. It seems to mean stones fitted together to form an arch. Poetically, then, it is used as a parallel concept to "temple." **who calls . . . name.** The conclusion of the title is an exact repetition of 5:8.
9:7–10 The prophet explained that Israel, who had broken covenant with God, was liable to judgment, though a remnant would be saved. See *WCF* 5.7.
9:7 Are not you . . . ? Did I not . . . ? The expected answer to these rhetorical questions is clearly yes. These questions reflect a real or imagined disputation over the uniqueness of Israel. Amos's opponents claimed that nothing so drastic as the destruction of the Lord's temple (at Bethel?) would take place because Israel was God's special people. However, as this book demonstrates in its opening section (1:1—2:16), the Israelites had become so corrupt that they were to be judged along with the Gentile nations. **Cushites.** Literally, "sons of Cushites." Cush was a son of Ham (Ge 10:6–7). **Israel up from Egypt.** The Lord had brought Israel out of Egypt. It was not that there was no difference between the Israelites' exodus from Egypt and the movements of other nations. Rather, through their flagrant and prolonged disobedience, God's people had rendered their exodus nothing special. God told Israel that the nation had become no

8 "Surely the eyes of the Sovereign LORD
are on the sinful kingdom.
I will destroy it
from the face of the earth—
yet I will not totally destroy
the house of Jacob,"
declares the LORD.[l]
9 "For I will give the command,
and I will shake the house of Israel
among all the nations
as grain[m] is shaken in a sieve,[n]
and not a pebble will reach the ground.
10 All the sinners among my people
will die by the sword,
all those who say,
'Disaster will not overtake or meet us.'[o]

9:8 [l]Jer 44:27
9:9 [m]Lk 22:31 [n]Isa 30:28
9:10 [o]Am 6:3

Israel's Restoration

11 "In that day I will restore
David's fallen tent.
I will repair its broken places,
restore its ruins,
and build it as it used to be,[p]
12 so that they may possess the remnant of Edom[q]
and all the nations that bear my name,[a][r]"
declares the LORD, who will do these things.[s]

13 "The days are coming," declares the LORD,
"when the reaper will be overtaken by the plowman[t]
and the planter by the one treading grapes.

9:11 [p]Ps 80:12
9:12 [q]Nu 24:18 [r]Isa 43:7 [s]Ac 15:16-17*
9:13 [t]Lev 26:5

[a] *12* Hebrew; Septuagint *so that the remnant of men / and all the nations that bear my name may seek* ⌞*the Lord*⌟

better than the pagans. **Caphtor.** Probably refers to Crete. **Arameans from Kir.** See note on 1:5.

9:8 eyes. See note on verse 4. **sinful kingdom.** Israel. **I will destroy . . . earth.** "Earth" in Hebrew may also be translated "land." This translation draws attention to the fact that the Lord would remove his people from the promised land, the land of their covenantal inheritance. This threat always stood over the people of the covenant (Lev 26:14–39; Dt 4:14–15; 28:64–68). **not totally destroy.** A remnant chosen according to grace would survive (see note on 7:2).

9:9 I will shake . . . among all the nations. The Lord would scatter his people among the nations. He would accomplish this by means of the Assyrians, who often resettled conquered peoples in different parts of the Assyrian Empire (see "Introduction: Purpose and Distinctives"). **as grain is shaken in a sieve.** When the grain fell through, any chaff or pebbles remained in the sieve. So the Lord would sift Israel, preserving some (cf. "I will not totally destroy"; v. 8) but binding and destroying the wicked (cf. v. 10).

9:10 sinners . . . by the sword. See note on 7:11, where it is said that the house of Jeroboam would die by the sword. **those who say.** This same terminology is used in 4:1, 6:13 and 7:16—all, as here, are cases of sinners whose words further illustrated their godlessness. **Disaster . . . us.** Denial of judgment, like denial of guilt, is characteristic of sin.

■ **9:11–15** *God's People Exalted Above the Nations.* In contrast to the opening section of this book (1:2—2:16), this closing section concerns the restoration of Israel after exile and the resulting exaltation of Israel over other nations. These verses divide into two main sections: the blessing of David's dynasty (vv. 11–12) and the blessing of nature's restoration (vv. 13–15). Amos assured his readers that once judgment of exile was complete, restoration was as certain as their dispersion.

■ **9:11–12** *Restoration of David's Victorious Dynasty.* Amos assured the Israelites that the restoration of the nation after exile would include the reestablishment of David's royal line and the defeat of the enemies of God by this royal line.

9:11 In that day. See notes on 2:16 and 5:18. Here the phrase indicates the time after the exile, when God's wrath would be poured out on his enemies. **fallen tent.** Literally, "collapsing hut." The hut represents the dynasty of David, which to the eyes of the prophet was as good as fallen. The royal power was about to depart from Israel and Judah (cf. 2:4–5). Judah, surrounded and threatened because of her sin, is compared to "a hut in a field of melons" (Isa 1:8). The term does not necessarily denote a humble structure, for it is also used of the Lord's heavenly sanctuary (Pss 18:11 ["canopy"]; 31:20 ["dwelling"]). This dilapidated "hut" of David would be rebuilt. The New Testament explains that in Jesus, the great son of David, the dynasty of David has been reestablished (Ac 15:16–17). **ruins.** Literally, "broken walls," such as typically resulted from conquest and were associated with exile (cf. 4:3; Ps 144:14).

9:12 possess. This terminology is used frequently to mean "dispossess" or "take possession by force" (e.g., Dt 2:31; 4:14). Amos had in mind here that the house of David would wage war against the nations, a theme that occurs in many prophetic portraits of the time after exile (see, e.g., Eze 38–39; Joel 3:9; Hag 2:20–32; Zec 12:1—14:21; Rev 19–20) **the remnant of Edom.** Although Edom would be subject to divine judgment (1:11–12), a remnant of Edom would be brought under the redemptive kingship of David's offspring. **Edom and all the nations.** The nations would come under the dominion of David's future son (cf. Ps 2:8,12). In Acts 15:13–17 James applied this passage to God's taking a people for himself from among the Gentiles and including them in the church (cf. NIV text note on 9:12). **that bear my name.** Literally, "over whom my name is called," indicating subordination. The phrase was also sometimes used of Israel's subordination to God's covenant lordship (Dt 28:10; Jer 14:9), and it reveals that some, but not all, from every Gentile group would come under the dominion of David's son (cf. Ps 2:12); that is, only those who bear God's name from among all the nations will be included. Accordingly, Amos foresaw that in the day when David's fallen tent is restored, the Lord will take possession of the remnant of all the nations and will reign over them in a covenantal relationship through his Messianic King. This prophecy is in agreement with the ministry of Christ in taking a people for himself from among the nations (Ac 15:13–17).

■ **9:13–15** *Blessing of Abundance in Nature.* Alongside victory in war will come the enjoyment of nature renewed.

9:13 After prophecies of disaster and want (cf. 4:6–11; 5:11,16–17)

New wine will drip from the mountains
and flow from all the hills.[u]
14 I will bring back my exiled[a] people Israel;
they will rebuild the ruined cities[v] and live in them.
They will plant vineyards and drink their wine;
they will make gardens and eat their fruit.[w]
15 I will plant[x] Israel in their own land,
never again to be uprooted
from the land I have given them,"

says the LORD your God.[y]

9:13 [u]Joel 3:18
9:14 [v]Isa 61:4 [w]Jer 30:18; 31:28; Eze 28:25-26
9:15 [x]Isa 60:21 [y]Jer 24:6; Eze 34:25-28; 37:12,25

a *14* Or *will restore the fortunes of my*

comes a prophecy of abundance—indeed more than abundance. The culmination of the Lord's redemptive work through David's son will see seasons of planting and harvest run together in an endless cycle of fruitfulness evocative of Eden and perhaps surpassing it. The curses of Genesis 3:17–19 will be lifted. For the imagery, see Joel 3:18.

9:14 I will bring back my exiled people. Literally, "I will turn the captivity of my people." This is a stock phrase in covenant lawsuit literature (cf. Jer 29:14; Eze 16:53; Hos 6:11). **they will rebuild . . . and live . . . They will plant . . . and drink . . . they will make . . . and eat.** These blessings are the opposite of the earlier futility curses ("Though you have built stone mansions, you will not live in them"; 5:11).

9:15 I will plant . . . uprooted. A promise of lasting security for God's people. This promise was an aspect of God's covenant with David (2Sa 7:10), as it also appears to be here (v. 11): David's future son would be the Israelites' security against further uprooting from their homeland. **never again.** The promise is made that once the restoration of God's people has reached its culmination, they never need fear exile again. This theme appears in a number of prophecies (see note on Joel 3:20). The early returnees failed to reach this stage of restoration, and Israel was subjugated time and again. The New Testament explains, however, that this permanent possession of Canaan will take place when Christ returns and gives to his people, Jews and Gentiles alike, permanent possession of the entire new earth (Rev 5:9–10; 21:1–7), of which Canaan was simply a type (Ro 4:13). Even now, a remnant of ethnic Israel joined with Gentiles enjoys the deposit guaranteeing that inheritance in the outpouring of the Holy Spirit (Eph 1:14). **the land I have given them.** The phrasing harks back to God's covenant with Abraham and his seed (Ge 12:1,7; 13:14–17; 15:18; 17:8; 22:16–18). Once before, God had given them the land; but they had sinned, and he had expelled them from it. Once again he will give them the land, and they will dwell in it as oaks of righteousness.

OBADIAH

Introduction

Overview

Author: The prophet Obadiah
Purpose: To encourage Judahites facing trouble from Edom to hope in divine justice and for eventual victory over all enemies
Date: c. 586 B.C.
Key Truths:

- God cares for his people when they suffer.
- God warns but will eventually judge those who persecute his people.
- God will give victory to his people.
- God's faithful people will inherit the kingdom of God in its fullness.

Author

We know nothing of the prophet Obadiah other than his name, which means "the servant [or worshiper] of the LORD." Not even his name is notable, for it was common in Israel (1Ki 18:3–16; 1Ch 3:21; 7:3; 8:38; 9:16; 12:9; 27:19; 2Ch 17:7; 34:12; Ezr 8:9; Ne 10:5; 12:25). The value and authority of the message rests not upon the renown or personality of the messenger but upon the fact that "the LORD has spoken" (v. 18).

Time and Place of Writing

Interpreters have long debated the date of composition for this book. The prophet had in view a violent ransacking of Jerusalem in which the Edomites had gleefully participated (vv. 11–14). But Obadiah did not provide clearly datable information in describing the catastrophe.

Some date the book in relation to an invasion of Judah by Philistines and Arabs during King Jehoram's reign (848–841 B.C.)—an invasion in which the Edomites presumably took part (cf. 2Ki 8:20–22; 2Ch 21:8–10,16–17). Others date the prophecy in connection with the Babylonian assaults on Judah that eventually resulted in her collapse in 586 B.C. Both Scripture (Ps 137; Eze 35:1–15) and Jewish tradition (1 Esdras 4:45 [a noncanonical book]) explicitly connect the Edomites with this final catastrophe. The text of the prophecy itself seems to refer more naturally to this event. Whatever the precise historical setting, the situation was one in which Edom prospered while Judah lay defeated, and the moral order of the world appeared to God's people to have been overthrown by chaos.

Although the striking similarities between Obadiah 1–9 and Jeremiah 49:7–22 must be more than an impressive coincidence, they do not resolve the problem of dating. We know that Jeremiah ministered from 626 to sometime after 586 B.C. (see "Introduction to Jeremiah: Time and Place of Writing"), but whether one prophet echoed the other or both relied on an earlier source has not been resolved.

Purpose and Distinctives

Obadiah's book is "about Edom" (v. 1) and is repeatedly addressed to that nation, but it was written to the Judahites as God's covenant people. Obadiah may or may not have delivered a spoken oracle to Edom prior to writing his book. God spoke against Edom for Judah's benefit, sentencing the Edomites to humiliation, looting and death in order to bolster Judah's weakened faith and morale. Edom deserved God's judgment because of her severe and prolonged mistreatment of Judah. The destruction of Edom was part of God's larger plan for judging all nations and granting his people blessings in the new earth. The purpose of the book of Obadiah, therefore, was not to warn Edom of imminent judgment but to reassure God's people of his triumphant justice at work for them. The righteous power of God, not the evil plans of the nations, determines the course of history.

Obadiah's prophecy closely follows the pattern of a covenant-lawsuit address. It begins with the scene of judgment and continues with the speech of the judge, which includes the address to the defendant, the pronouncement of guilt and the handing down of the sentence (see "Introduction: Outline" and "Introduction to the Prophetic Books: The Forms of Prophetic Literature").

Christ in Obadiah

The book of Obadiah does not contain Messianic predictions that point directly to Christ, but the theme of divine judgment against those who persecute God's people finds its final fulfillment in Christ. Jesus himself suffered at the hands of God's enemies (Ac 2:36), and he predicted that his followers would experience the same affliction (Ac 14:21–22). Yet Christ promised to keep his people in his love during these difficult times (Ro 8:28–39). When he returns in glory he will judge all those who have stood against himself and his people (Mt 25; Rev 19:1–2).

Obadiah's vision of a new order in which God's people are restored in victory over the nations also finds fulfillment in Christ. Christ began to rule over all in his resurrection and ascension (1Co 15:25), the church now spreads his kingdom throughout the earth (Mt 28:19–20; Ac 2:37–41) and he will expand it to the ends of the earth when he returns (Rev 11:15). When Christians suffer at the hands of God's enemies they need to renew their faith in the just God who reveals himself through the prophecy of Obadiah. Although it often appears as though the torment of the church will never end, God is always at work behind the veil of appearances on behalf of his people (Rev 6:9–10).

Outline

I. Title (1a)	*This vision was received by Obadiah.*
II. Scene of Judgment in War (1b)	*The scene of divine judgment in war is set.*
III. Divine Speech of Judgment and Hope (2–21)	*God spoke against Edom for Judah's benefit.*
A. Sentences Against Edom (2–9)	
1. God's Resolve to Humiliate Edom (2–4)	*God sentenced Edom to humiliation, looting and death.*
2. God's Resolve to Loot Edom (5–7)	
3. God's Resolve to Kill Edomites (8–9)	
B. Accusations Against Edom (10–14)	*Edom deserved God's judgments because of severe mistreatment of Judah.*
1. Edom's Violence (10)	
2. Edom's Cruel Indifference (11)	
3. Edom's Cruel Boasting and Attacks (12–14)	
C. Announcement of a New Order (15–21)	*The destruction of Edom is part of God's larger plan for judging all nations and granting his people blessings in a new order.*
1. International Judgment to Come (15–16)	
2. Judah's Restoration and Expansion (17–21)	

1The vision of Obadiah.

This is what the Sovereign LORD says about Edom[a]—

We have heard a message from the LORD:
An envoy[b] was sent to the nations to say,
"Rise, and let us go against her for battle"[c]—

2"See, I will make you small among the nations;
you will be utterly despised.
3The pride[d] of your heart has deceived you,
you who live in the clefts of the rocks[a]
and make your home on the heights,
you who say to yourself,
'Who can bring me down to the ground?'[e]
4Though you soar like the eagle

1 [a]Isa 63:1-6; Jer 49:7-22; Eze 25:12-14; Am 1:11-12 [b]Isa 18:2 [c]Jer 6:4-5

3 [d]Isa 16:6 [e]Isa 14:13-15; Rev 18:7

[a] 3 Or *of Sela*

■ **1a** *Title.* The book opens with a simple identification of Obadiah as the recipient of this revelation.
1a vision. This word does not necessarily imply an image. A message came to Obadiah. See note on Micah 1:1.
■ **1b** *Scene of Judgment in War.* The stage is set for the kind of judgment that would soon come against Edom.
1b This is what the Sovereign LORD says. God revealed the content of the prophecy (cf. 2Pe 1:21). Obadiah's predictions about the fate of Edom were not motivated by unholy, human desire for vengeance but by holy, divine judgment. **Edom.** The bitterness between Edom and Israel had begun during the patriarchal age. God had blessed Isaac and Rebekah with twin sons, Esau and Jacob (Ge 25:21–26; cf. Mal 1:2–4; Ro 9:10–13). The personal rivalry between the two (Ge 27)—from whom the nations of Israel and Edom descended—developed into longstanding national conflict (Ex 15:13–15; Nu 20:14–21; 24:18; 1Sa 14:47; 2Sa 8:13–14; 1Ki 11:14–15; 2Ki 8:20–22; 14:7), despite the apparent reconciliation between the brothers recounted in Genesis 33. In some passages Edom symbolically epitomizes all the enemies of God's people (Isa 63:1–6; Am 9:12). **We have heard . . . "Rise, and let us go against her for battle."** Speaking for his people the prophet saw divine significance in the news of a conspiracy against Edom. Behind the human plot the Sovereign Lord was at work. That such news reached Obadiah's ears in connection with this vision was no coincidence but a token of the prophecy's sure fulfillment.
■ **2–21** *Divine Speech of Judgment and Hope.* The rest of Obadiah's prophecy concerns the Lord's speech in his heavenly court. It divides into three main parts: sentences against Edom (vv. 2–9), accusations against Edom (vv. 10–14) and the announcement of a new order (vv. 15–21).
■ **2–9** *Sentences Against Edom.* The prophet reported a number of judgments to come against Edom. The Edomites would be humiliated (vv. 2–4), looted (vv. 5–7) and killed (vv. 8–9).
■ **2–4** *God's Resolve to Humiliate Edom.* The Edomites had been filled with pride, but they would be humbled.
3–4 The force of these verses lies in Edom's question ("Who can bring me down to the ground?"; v. 3) and in God's answer ("I will bring you down"; v. 4). In their arrogant disregard for God the Edomites had lost touch with reality.
3 of the rocks. Compare NIV text note. Sela was a fortress city in the rocky heights of Edom. The rugged mountain terrain of Edom deterred invasion from without and encouraged complacency within.
4 like the eagle . . . among the stars. The Lord progressively exaggerated his portrait of Edom's inflated self-image, as though to

and make your nest[f] among the stars,
from there I will bring you down,"[g]
declares the LORD.[h]

5 "If thieves came to you,
if robbers in the night—
Oh, what a disaster awaits you—
would they not steal only as much as they wanted?
If grape pickers came to you,
would they not leave a few grapes?[i]
6 But how Esau will be ransacked,
his hidden treasures pillaged!
7 All your allies[j] will force you to the border;
your friends will deceive and overpower you;
those who eat your bread[k] will set a trap for you,[a]
but you will not detect it.

8 "In that day," declares the LORD,
"will I not destroy[l] the wise men of Edom,
men of understanding in the mountains of Esau?
9 Your warriors, O Teman,[m] will be terrified,
and everyone in Esau's mountains
will be cut down in the slaughter.
10 Because of the violence[n] against your brother Jacob,[o]
you will be covered with shame;
you will be destroyed forever.[p]
11 On the day you stood aloof
while strangers carried off his wealth
and foreigners entered his gates
and cast lots[q] for Jerusalem,
you were like one of them.
12 You should not look down on your brother
in the day of his misfortune,
nor rejoice[r] over the people of Judah
in the day of their destruction,[s]
nor boast so much
in the day of their trouble.[t]
13 You should not march through the gates of my people
in the day of their disaster,
nor look down on them in their calamity[u]
in the day of their disaster,
nor seize their wealth
in the day of their disaster.
14 You should not wait at the crossroads
to cut down their fugitives,
nor hand over their survivors
in the day of their trouble.

4 [f] Hab 2:9 [g] Isa 14:13 [h] Job 20:6
5 [i] Dt 24:21
7 [j] Jer 30:14 [k] Ps 41:9
8 [l] Job 5:12; Isa 29:14
9 [m] Ge 36:11,34
10 [n] Joel 3:19 [o] Ps 137:7; Am 1:11-12 [p] Eze 35:9
11 [q] Na 3:10
12 [r] Eze 35:15 [s] Pr 17:5 [t] Mic 4:11
13 [u] Eze 35:5

[a] 7 The meaning of the Hebrew for this clause is uncertain.

say, "It doesn't matter how high you elevate yourselves—whether to the skies or even to the very heavens—for you cannot rise above me." To the defeated people of Judah Edom seemed invincible; but God called the Judahites to believe that no earthly power can evade his sovereign justice.

■ **5–7** *God's Resolve to Loot Edom.* God would plunder Edom's ill-gotten prosperity.

7 The conspiring nations of verse 1 turned out to be Edom's own allies attacking her from her blind side. It was a matter of justice that the Edomites should be betrayed by friends, after having repeatedly stabbed their "brother Jacob" (v. 10) in the back.

■ **8–9** *God's Resolve to Kill Edomites.* Even the wise of Edom would be destroyed.

8 wise. Edom was known for its wise men (Jer 49:7). Job's friend Eliphaz was called a Temanite (Job 5:12), a possible reference to the region of Edom.

9 Teman. The personal name of a descendant of Esau. The name was also used for the Edomite nation.

■ **10–14** *Accusations Against Edom.* The prophet shifted from emphasizing divine sentences to announcing accusations against Edom. These verses focus on Edom's violence (v. 10), cruel indifference (v. 11) and boastful attacks against Judah (vv. 12–14).

■ **10** *Edom's Violence.* Edom had been hostile toward Judah throughout her history, but especially during the days of Babylon's aggression (see Ps 137; Eze 35:13).

■ **11** *Edom's Cruel Indifference.* Edom had not come to Judah's aid during the Babylonian crisis but had rather joined forces with Judah's attacker.

11 strangers . . . foreigners. The interplay between "your brother" (v. 10) and the invading "strangers" and "foreigners" is powerful. Edom was morally obliged to fight for "brother Jacob" (v. 10) against the invaders, but she had instead acted "like one of them."

■ **12–14** *Edom's Cruel Boasting and Attacks.* The Edomites violated their familial obligations based on their kinship with Judah by demeaning and attacking the Judahites.

13 seize their wealth. Edom proved through her disregard for moral and spiritual imperatives that her true loyalty was to personal gain.

14 cut down their fugitives . . . hand over their survivors. Given Edom's perspective (see note on v. 13), no act was considered

15 “The day of the LORD is near[v]
for all nations.
As you have done, it will be done to you;
your deeds[w] will return upon your own head.
16 Just as you drank on my holy hill,
so all the nations will drink[x] continually;
they will drink and drink
and be as if they had never been.
17 But on Mount Zion will be deliverance;[y]
it will be holy,[z]
and the house of Jacob
will possess its inheritance.
18 The house of Jacob will be a fire
and the house of Joseph a flame;
the house of Esau will be stubble,
and they will set it on fire and consume[a] it.
There will be no survivors
from the house of Esau.”

The LORD has spoken.

19 People from the Negev will occupy
the mountains of Esau,
and people from the foothills will possess
the land of the Philistines.[b]
They will occupy the fields of Ephraim and Samaria,[c]
and Benjamin will possess Gilead.
20 This company of Israelite exiles who are in Canaan
will possess ˌthe landˌ as far as Zarephath;[d]
the exiles from Jerusalem who are in Sepharad
will possess the towns of the Negev.[e]
21 Deliverers will go up on[a] Mount Zion
to govern the mountains of Esau.
And the kingdom will be the LORD’S.[f]

15 [v]Eze 30:3 [w]Jer 50:29; Hab 2:8
16 [x]Jer 25:15; 49:12
17 [y]Am 9:11-15 [z]Isa 4:3
18 [a]Zec 12:6
19 [b]Isa 11:14 [c]Jer 31:5
20 [d]1Ki 17:9-10 [e]Jer 33:13
21 [f]Ps 22:28; Zec 14:9,16; Rev 11:15

[a] *21* Or *from*

too low in the process of exploiting even a brother’s vulnerability. The seeds of Edom’s moral character were sown by her ancestor Esau, who had cared more for the things of this earthly life than for the promised kingdom of God. Esau had “despised his birthright” (Ge 25:34) for a serving of stew (Ge 25:29–34). The low estimate he had placed on his spiritual heritage was also evident in his choice of Hittite women for wives (Ge 26:34–35; 27:46—28:1).

■ **15–21** *Announcement of a New Order.* The Lord’s pronouncement of judgment against Edom was part of a much larger scenario that included international upheaval (vv. 15–16) and Judah’s ultimate, victorious restoration (vv. 17–21).

■ **15–16** *International Judgment to Come.* God determined to bring judgment against all nations who had troubled his people.

15 The day of the LORD is near for all nations. For additional insight on “the day of the LORD,” see Isaiah 2:11–12, Acts 2:20 and their notes, “Introduction to Joel” and “Introduction to Zechariah.” Here the prophet set the judgment of Edom against the larger backdrop of God’s reckoning with all the nations. This episode with Edom is only a small part of God’s plan of judgment; he will not stop until he has purged his world of all his enemies. The connection between Edom and the rest of the nations was their shared rebellion against God, which the Lord would not allow to succeed. **As you have done.** The vengeance of God was his just fulfillment of the offer of protection he had long ago made to Abraham (Ge 12:3).

16 The Edomites’ drunken revelry on the sacred temple mount in Jerusalem would be answered in kind with the cup of God’s wrath forced to the lips of Edom and all the nations that had desecrated the things of God.

■ **17–21** *Judah’s Restoration and Expansion.* The climax of the new order after Judah’s defeat and exile in Babylon would not only be judgment against God’s enemies but a glorious restoration of people and nature and the extension of Judah to conquered territories. The New Testament explains that these prophetic hopes for restoration were initially fulfilled in Christ’s first coming (Lk 4:18–19), are now being fulfilled through the spread of the gospel (Ac 15:16–18) and will come to final fruition in Christ’s second advent (Rev 11:15).

17 it will be holy. No longer the degraded plaything of pillaging armies, Mount Zion will one day be holy and undefiled for God.

18 no survivors. The “survivors” (v. 14) of Judah would rise up as a blazing fire of divine wrath to consume Edom, leaving her not a single survivor. This is probably hyperbole, a common prophetic device in reference to God’s judgment. **The LORD has spoken.** Functioning like a signature, this clause emphasizes that these predictions came from God.

19–20 God’s exiled people would return to occupy the land of their inheritance, the boundaries of which would be restored and expanded.

19 God promised his people that the boundaries of the Davidic kingdom would be restored in the south (“the mountains of Esau”), the west (“the land of the Philistines”), the north (“the fields of Ephraim and Samaria”) and the east (“Gilead”).

20 The boundaries of the Davidic kingdom would be not only restored (v. 19) but also extended to reach northward to Zarephath, which was located between Tyre and Sidon. Some exiles would return from “Sepharad,” the location of which is uncertain. Proposals include Sardis in Asia Minor, Spain and Media.

21 Restored Zion would emerge supreme over Edom. **Deliverers.** God’s people, transformed from fugitives (v. 14) into deliverers, would reign over what had once been enemy-occupied territory. **the kingdom will be the LORD’s.** To be sure, the Lord is the eternal King of the entire universe (cf. Pss 47:2; 145:13). But Obadiah’s focus here is on the day when God’s enemies will be destroyed and his redeemed people will extend his reign to the ends of the earth (see theological article: “The Kingdom of God” at Mt 4). God will be all in all, and his glorious, triumphant people will reign forever with him. In this promise Judah was to find hope for a future without Edomite persecution. The Christian too may anticipate a future in which “the kingdom of the world has become the kingdom of our Lord and of his Christ” (Rev 11:15).

JONAH

Introduction

Overview

Author: Unknown

Purpose: To encourage the Israelites to embrace God's call to extend his mercy to the nations

Date: 750–613 B.C.

Key Truths:

- God calls his people to seek the repentance of the nations.
- God's people will suffer divine displeasure if they fail to extend God's mercy to the nations.
- God rightly delights in showing mercy to repentant Gentiles.

Author

The author of this narrative is unknown. This fifth book of the Minor Prophets takes its name from its principal character, Jonah, son of Amittai (1:1). Nothing is known of Amittai. Outside of this composition Jonah is mentioned only in 2 Kings, where he is described as the prophet who proclaimed God's blessing to the northern kingdom during the reign of Jeroboam II (786–746 B.C.). This monarch extended the borders of his kingdom at the expense of Syria "in accordance with the word of the LORD . . . spoken through his servant Jonah son of Amittai, the prophet from Gath Hepher" (2Ki 14:25).

Time and Place of Writing

Based on 2 Kings 14:25, the events recorded in the book of Jonah should be assigned to the eighth century B.C. However, determining the chronology of the book's composition is difficult. The book has been dated at many different points between the eighth and late third centuries B.C. Its focus on Jonah's call to Nineveh would have been particularly poignant after Israel had suffered the destruction of Samaria by Nineveh, the capitol of Assyria in 722–721 B.C. Moreover, it seems unlikely that the author would have so greatly stressed God's mercy toward Nineveh if the Babylonian defeat of the city in 612 B.C. had occurred by the time of his writing. It seems most likely, therefore, that the book was written as early as the reign of Jeroboam II (786–746 B.C.) and as late as the time just prior to Nineveh's defeat in 612 B.C.

The reign of Jeroboam II (786–746 B.C.) provides the setting for the Jonah story. This monarch was one of the strong military leaders of Israel's history. According to 2 Kings 14:25–28 Jonah supported Jeroboam by prophesying blessings on Jeroboam's kingdom, specifically the expansion of Israel's territory into Damascus and Hamath, thereby restoring Israel's northern boundary to the place it had been in the days of Solomon (1Ki 8:65). It is clear that Jeroboam's reign, together with that of his Judahite contemporary Uzziah (783–742 B.C.), ushered in a period of remarkable peace and prosperity. The kingdom enjoyed population and territorial expansion, commercial growth and flourishing industrial activity. By all outward appearances the nation was enjoying the blessing of God. The future looked bright.

Even so, the prophets Hosea and Amos declared that the kingdom of Israel was in a state of social, moral and religious decay. Their messages consisted, in part, of condemnation, indictment and judgment for religious syncretism and social injustice (Hos 1:2–8; 2:1–13; 4:1—5:14; 6:1–6; 7:11–16; 8:1—9:17; 11:1–12; 12:1–8; Am 2:6–16; 3:9–15; 5:21–27; 7:7–17).

In this historical context Jonah resisted God's call to Nineveh. He obeyed reluctantly after experiencing God's judgment and eventually learned God's outlook on the value of the Ninevites. The God of Israel intended to spread his kingdom to all nations. Yet given the unique relationship between the Lord and his covenant people, Jonah and many of his countrymen were held in the grip of intense nationalism and ethnic particularism, which blinded them to the purpose of Israel's election.

Through Jonah God offered Jeroboam the blessing of military victory in retaking lost portions of God's kingdom, including Syria (2Ki 14:25–28). The events recorded in this book, however, show that Jonah also learned the importance of repenting of his disobedience and extending the mercy of God to other nations. The readers of this narrative were to learn from Jonah's experience that they were to repent of their own disobedience and help to bring God's blessings to all nations (Ge 12:3).

Purpose and Distinctives

In addition to teaching that God's mercy and love have universal aspects, the book maintains the theme of God's universal sovereignty, presenting God as the Creator, "the God of heaven, who made the sea and the land" (1:9). Creation responds obediently to his every command (1:4,15,17; 2:10; 4:6–8), just as the Assyrians of Isaiah's day did (Isa 10:5–6,12). The book of Jonah emphasizes the universal power and sovereign control of God over humanity and nature, over life and death. (See theological articles "Divine Sovereignty" at Ps 97 and "God, the Creator of Heaven and Earth" at Ps 104.)

Four basic interpretive strategies have been posited for the book: allegory, midrash, parable and historical narrative. An allegory is a technique of creating or interpreting literature so as to convey more than one level of meaning. The text of Jonah lacks typical indications that would call for an allegorical understanding—the text is presented in the form of historical narrative.

Midrash refers to a type of interpretation of Scripture that is basically expository in nature. As applied to Jonah, this approach treats the book as a commentary on passages such as Exodus 34:6–7 (Jnh 4:2)—a commentary in which the events referred to are not necessarily historical. Such an approach is out of step with credible defenses of the book's historicity, not to mention the witness of Christ (Mt 12:39–42; Lk 11:29–32).

Interpreting Jonah as a parable is perhaps the most common approach. A parable is an extended metaphor or simile, a brief, fictitious story that illustrates moral, religious or spiritual truths. The concept of parable is best illustrated in the teachings of Jesus (e.g., Mt 13:45–46; Lk 10:29–37; 15:11–32). Second Samuel 11 is a good example of an Old Testament parable. This view understands the narrative as a moral story with a didactic aim. There are a number of objections to a parabolic interpretation, such as the unusual complexity and length of the story and the identification of its main character (Jonah) as an actual historical figure (2Ki 14:25). Most importantly, this interpretation has a tendency to deprive the book of its historical foundation, contrary to the New Testament's witness.

In spite of its surprises and sensational elements, the work should be understood as historical (prophetic) narrative. The story centers on a specific, historical figure and is presented as a trustworthy narration of a factual set of events. Jewish tradition regards the narrative as history, and Christ's allusions to the story (Mt 12:39–42; Lk 11:29–32) lend further credibility to the historicity of the work. Yet like all historical narratives in Scripture, this book was written for a purpose other than simply preserving data. Jonah was designed to teach its readers how to live faithfully before God.

Christ in Jonah

Jesus drew a connection between himself and "the sign of (the prophet) Jonah" (Mt 12:39; 16:4; Lk 11:29). At a time when many Israelites refused to obey the prophetic word given to them, Jonah's release from the huge fish after three days and nights led the Ninevites to repentance. Jesus predicted that his own upcoming release from the grave after three days would lead to the repentance of Gentiles, while many Jews would still reject his prophetic word. In a sense, then, the story of Jonah called its Jewish readers to repentance as it endorsed ministry to Gentiles, just as Jesus and his apostles did.

Outline

I. Jonah's Disobedience and God's Reaction (1:1—2:10)

God sent judgment against Jonah for refusing his call to extend God's mercy to Nineveh. Jonah repented of his disobedience and God rescued him.

- A. Jonah Flees From God's Call (1:1–3)
- B. God Sends a Great Storm (1:4–15)
- C. Jonah's Flight Is Ended (1:16–17)
- D. Jonah's Prayer and God's Response (2:1–10)
  1. Jonah Prays With Thanksgiving (2:1–9)
  2. God Answers Jonah's Prayer (2:10)

II. Jonah's Obedience and God's Reaction (3:1—4:11)

God responded favorably to Jonah's obedience to his call to Nineveh. God affirmed that it was appropriate to seek the repentance and forgiveness of the Ninevites.

- A. Jonah Obeys God's Call (3:1–4)
- B. Ninevites Repent and God Responds With Compassion (3:5–10)
- C. Jonah's Prayer and God's Response (4:1–11)
  1. Jonah Prays With Anger and God Answers (4:1–4)
  2. Jonah Receives Further Explanation From God (4:5–11)

Jonah Flees From the LORD

1 The word of the LORD came to Jonah[a] son of Amittai:[b] 2"Go to the great city of Nineveh[c] and preach against it, because its wickedness has come up before me."
3But Jonah ran[d] away from the LORD and headed for Tarshish. He went down to Jop-

1:1 [a]Mt 12:39-41 [b]2Ki 14:25
1:2 [c]Ge 10:11
1:3 [d]Ps 139:7

■ **1:1—2:10** *Jonah's Disobedience and God's Reaction.* The book of Jonah falls into two clear sections, each introduced by the sentence "The word of the LORD came to Jonah" (1:1; 3:1). This first section depicts Jonah's disobedient response to the prophetic commission and God's response in sending a storm. Ironically, the storm led not only to judgment on Jonah but to the worship of God by Gentile sailors as well. These verses divide into four main parts: Jonah's flight from God (1:1–3), the great storm (1:4–15), the end of Jonah's flight (1:16–17) and Jonah's prayer and God's response (2:1–10).

■ **1:1–3** *Jonah Flees From God's Call.* Jonah received God's call to Nineveh, but he fled in the opposite direction.

1:1 The word of the LORD came to Jonah. Literally, "The word of Yahweh was to Jonah." With some variations, this wording is used 112 times in the Old Testament to describe the giving of a divine oracle to a prophet. **Jonah son of Amittai.** The recipient of the Lord's revelation was Jonah (meaning "dove"), the son of Amittai (meaning "truth"). The prophet is identified as the historical character of 2 Kings 14:25 who proclaimed that Jeroboam II (786–746 B.C.) would recover territory from the Syrians to the north. Jonah's message to Jeroboam contrasted with the words of Amos and Hosea, his eighth-century contemporaries (see "Introduction: Time and Place of Writing").

1:2 Go to . . . Nineveh. The Lord's sovereignty over all the nations is implicit in the command to Jonah. God is the Judge of all

pa,[e] where he found a ship bound for that port. After paying the fare, he went aboard
and sailed for Tarshish to flee from the LORD.
4Then the LORD sent a great wind on the sea, and such a violent storm arose that the
ship threatened to break up.[f] 5All the sailors were afraid and each cried out to his own
god. And they threw the cargo into the sea to lighten the ship.[g]
But Jonah had gone below deck, where he lay down and fell into a deep sleep. 6The
captain went to him and said, "How can you sleep? Get up and call[h] on your god! Maybe he will take notice of us, and we will not perish."[i]
7Then the sailors said to each other, "Come, let us cast lots to find out who is responsible for this calamity."[j] They cast lots and the lot fell on Jonah.
8So they asked him, "Tell us, who is responsible for making all this trouble for us? What
do you do? Where do you come from? What is your country? From what people are you?"
9He answered, "I am a Hebrew and I worship the LORD, the God of heaven,[k] who
made the sea and the land.[l]"
10This terrified them and they asked, "What have you done?" (They knew he was running away from the LORD, because he had already told them so.)

1:3 [e]Jos 19:46; Ac 9:36,43
1:4 [f]Ps 107:23-26
1:5 [g]Ac 27:18-19
1:6 [h]Jnh 3:8 [i]Ps 107:28
1:7 [j]Jos 7:10-18; 1Sa 14:42
1:9 [k]Ac 17:24 [l]Ps 146:6

the earth (Ge 6:13; 18:25; 1Ch 16:14; Ps 82:8; Jer 25:31). **Nineveh.** A principal city and the last capital of the Assyrian Empire. The city was located on the east side of the Tigris River, directly opposite the modern city of Mosul in northern Iraq. The site has been extensively excavated and boasts a long and rich history reaching back to prehistoric times. **preach against it.** Jonah understood that his pronouncement of the Lord's judgment on the feared and hated Assyrian Empire was revocable (see note on 4:2) and that his message was a threat of judgment that also offered blessing upon repentance. **its wickedness has come up before me.** In the later prophecy of Nahum (seventh century B.C.), Nineveh (representing Assyria) was the focus of divine wrath and was depicted as the embodiment of evil and cruelty (Na 2:13; 3:4–7). The Assyrian war machine was guilty of horrendous atrocities, and, with time (612 B.C.), the empire would fall victim to its own brand of evil.

1:3 Tarshish. There are several possible understandings of the term "Tarshish" in this context. It may refer to a specific geographical location along the Mediterranean Sea, with possible sites lying between the Levantine coast and the mining port of Tartessus in southwestern Spain. The term may also be understood in a generic sense to designate distant Mediterranean coastlands. **from the LORD.** Although God's presence is even "on the far side of the sea" (Ps 139:9), Jonah sought to run as far away from God as possible.

■ **1:4–15** *God Sends a Great Storm.* In reaction to Jonah's disobedience God sent a terrible storm to prevent Jonah from escaping his call.

1:4 the LORD sent a great wind on the sea. God is the Creator and Lord of the wind and the sea (Ex 10:13–19; 14:21–22; 15:8,10; Nu 11:31; Ps 135:6–7; Am 4:13; Na 1:3). See theological article "God, the Creator of Heaven and Earth" at Psalm 104.

1:6 Get up and call. Interestingly, the captain's command represents the same Hebrew expression used by God to command Jonah to go and preach against Nineveh.

1:7 let us cast lots. The casting of lots, a device used to discern the will of a god or the gods, was a common form of divination in the ancient world. The practice was not forbidden in ancient Israel, for the Lord ruled over and through lots (Nu 26:55; 33:54; 34:13; Jos 14:2; 18:6–10; 19:1,10,17,24,32,40,51; 21:4–6,8,10; 1Ch 6:54,61,65; Pr 16:33).

1:9 I am a Hebrew. Jonah identified himself in ethnic terms. The term "Hebrew" was used by Israelites in identifying themselves to foreigners (Ge 40:15; Ex 1:19; 2:7; 3:18; 5:3; 7:16; 9:1,13; 10:3) or by non-Israelites, such as Philistines or Egyptians, as an ethnic term in contradistinction to themselves (Ge 39:14,17; 41:12; Ex 1:16; 2:6; 1Sa 4:6,9; 13:3,19; 14:11; 29:3). **I worship the LORD.** Jonah identified himself in religious terms. The Lord is not just a personal, family or clan deity; indeed he is even more than a national god. He is the supreme and sovereign God, the Creator of sea and land. See theological articles "Divine Sovereignty" at Psalm 97 and "God, the Creator of Heaven and Earth" at Psalm 104. **God of heaven.** An old epithet (Ge 24:3,7) commonly used in the Persian period after the exile (2Ch 36:23; Ezr 1:2; Ne 1: 4–5; 2:4).

The Book of Jonah

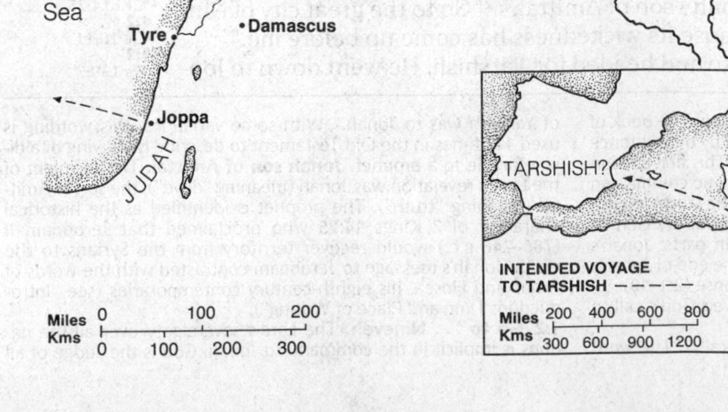

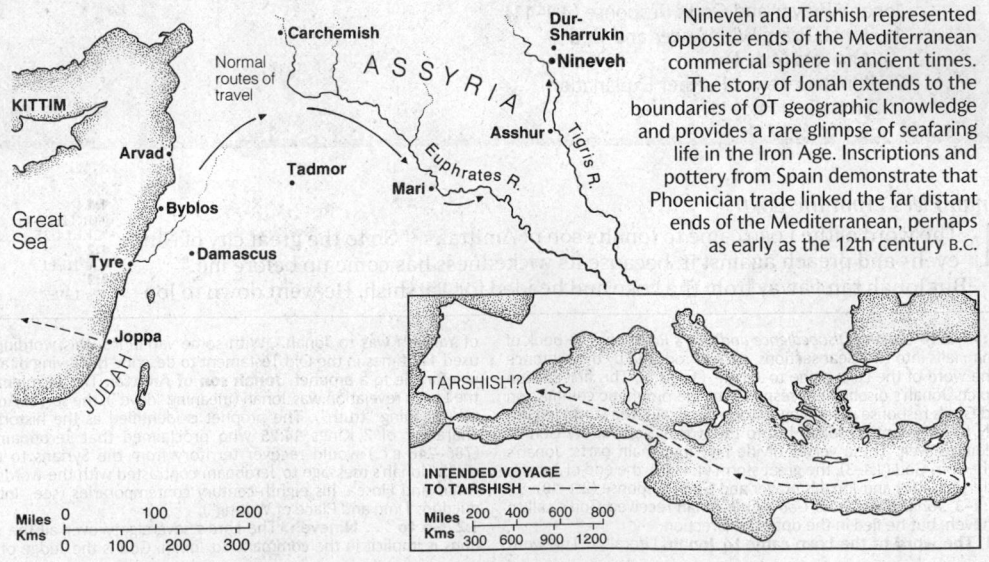

Nineveh and Tarshish represented opposite ends of the Mediterranean commercial sphere in ancient times. The story of Jonah extends to the boundaries of OT geographic knowledge and provides a rare glimpse of seafaring life in the Iron Age. Inscriptions and pottery from Spain demonstrate that Phoenician trade linked the far distant ends of the Mediterranean, perhaps as early as the 12th century B.C.

11 The sea was getting rougher and rougher. So they asked him, "What should we do
to you to make the sea calm down for us?"
12 "Pick me up and throw me into the sea," he replied, "and it will become calm. I
know that it is my fault that this great storm has come upon you."[m]
13 Instead, the men did their best to row back to land. But they could not, for the sea
grew even wilder than before.[n] 14 Then they cried to the LORD, "O LORD, please do not let
us die for taking this man's life. Do not hold us accountable for killing an innocent man,[o]
for you, O LORD, have done as you pleased."[p] 15 Then they took Jonah and threw him overboard, and the raging sea grew calm.[q] 16 At this the men greatly feared[r] the LORD, and
they offered a sacrifice to the LORD and made vows to him.
17 But the LORD provided a great fish to swallow Jonah,[s] and Jonah was inside the fish
three days and three nights.

Jonah's Prayer

2 From inside the fish Jonah prayed to the LORD his God. 2 He said:

"In my distress I called to the LORD,[t]
and he answered me.
From the depths of the grave[a] I called for help,
and you listened to my cry.
3 You hurled me into the deep,[u]
into the very heart of the seas,
and the currents swirled about me;
all your waves and breakers
swept over me.[v]
4 I said, 'I have been banished
from your sight;[w]
yet I will look again
toward your holy temple.'
5 The engulfing waters threatened me,[b]
the deep surrounded me;
seaweed was wrapped around my head.[x]
6 To the roots of the mountains I sank down;
the earth beneath barred me in forever.
But you brought my life up from the pit,
O LORD my God.

7 "When my life was ebbing away,
I remembered[y] you, LORD,

1:12 [m]2Sa 24:17; 1Ch 21:17
1:13 [n]Pr 21:30
1:14 [o]Dt 21:8 [p]Ps 115:3
1:15 [q]Ps 107:29; Lk 8:24
1:16 [r]Mk 4:41
1:17 [s]Mt 12:40; 16:4; Lk 11:30
2:2 [t]Ps 18:6; 120:1
2:3 [u]Ps 88:6 [v]Ps 42:7
2:4 [w]Ps 31:22
2:5 [x]Ps 69:1-2
2:7 [y]Ps 77:11-12

[a] 2 Hebrew *Sheol* [b] 5 Or *waters were at my throat*

1:15 sea grew calm. The scene shifts as the storm God sent (1:4) subsided.

■ **1:16–17** *Jonah's Flight Is Ended.* In the aftermath of the storm an ironic contrast appeared. The Gentile sailors feared God and honored him with vows, while God sent a great fish to swallow the insubordinate Jonah. This contrast anticipates the difference between Jonah and the Ninevites seen in chapters 3–4.

1:17 three days and three nights. Jonah's situation is ambiguous at this point. He was not simply left to drown, but he was not entirely rescued either. Jonah had some time to ponder what he had done and how he would respond to God's judgment against him. Jesus referred to this part of the Jonah story in order to communicate truths regarding his own message and mission (see "Introduction: Christ in Jonah").

■ **2:1–10** *Jonah's Prayer and God's Response.* While in the great fish Jonah prayed to God (2:1–9) and God answered his prayer (2:10).

■ **2:1–9** *Jonah Prays With Thanksgiving.* The response of the prophet to his judgment is couched in a typical psalm of thanksgiving. The literary structure is typical of a thanksgiving psalm: (1) a petition for deliverance (v. 2); (2) a review of the crisis (vv. 3–6a); (3) a review of the deliverance (vv. 6b–7); and (4) praise for the deliverance (vv. 8–9). It is likely that Jonah composed this song after his rescue as a paraphrase of his experience.

2:2 I called . . . he answered me. Through poetic parallelism Jonah's psalm is introduced in two couplets with an expression of the Lord's faithfulness in answered prayer. Twice it is said that the prophet prayed and the Lord answered. Jonah acknowledged that he was rescued "from the depths of the grave" (lit., "from the belly of Sheol"); in this instance the rescue was from a watery grave, the sea.

2:3–6 These verses contain a vivid recollection of the near-death crisis, as well as an assessment of its causes and results. Jonah's plight was brought about by his own disobedience (1:3); his near drowning was a result of the Lord's judgment on that noncompliance. His brush with a watery grave is presented with graphic imagery (e.g., his entanglement in seaweed, the silence of the deep water and the image of waves swelling high above him).

2:4 I have been banished from your sight. For the prophet the ultimate tragedy of his circumstance was that it threatened separation from the blessings of the Lord (Pss 88:4–6,10–12; 115:17). **yet I will look again toward your holy temple.** The Jerusalem temple was the place of the Lord's dwelling, the earthly location of the divine presence toward which God's people were to pray (1Ki 8:23–53; 2Ch 6:14–42). Jonah longed for the communion with God that was afforded by the temple. The prophet lamented the loss of contact with God's special presence, which earlier (1:3,10) he had sought to escape. See *WLC* 172.

2:6 I sank down . . . forever. Jonah was at death's door. His slow, silent descent through the depths, like a journey to the underworld, brought him to "the gates of death" (Ps 9:13). **But you brought my life up from the pit.** The word "pit" is used to describe the realm of death (Job 33:22–24; Pss 16:10; 49:9; 103:4; Isa 51:14). Despite the apparent hopelessness of the circumstances the repentant prophet was rescued from the realm of the dead and restored to communion with God.

2:7 I remembered you, LORD. The importance and efficacy of

2:7 [z]2Ch 30:27 [a]Ps 11:4; 18:6

and my prayer[z] rose to you,
to your holy temple.[a]

2:8 [b]2Ki 17:15; Jer 10:8

8 "Those who cling to worthless idols[b]
forfeit the grace that could be theirs.

2:9 [c]Ps 50:14, 23; Hos 14:2 [d]Ecc 5:4-5 [e]Ps 3:8

9 But I, with a song of thanksgiving,
will sacrifice[c] to you.
What I have vowed[d] I will make good.
Salvation[e] comes from the LORD."

10 And the LORD commanded the fish, and it vomited Jonah onto dry land.

Jonah Goes to Nineveh

3:1 [f]Jnh 1:1

3 Then the word of the LORD came to Jonah[f] a second time: 2 "Go to the great city of
Nineveh and proclaim to it the message I give you."
3 Jonah obeyed the word of the LORD and went to Nineveh. Now Nineveh was a very
important city—a visit required three days. 4 On the first day, Jonah started into the city.
He proclaimed: "Forty more days and Nineveh will be overturned." 5 The Ninevites believed God. They declared a fast, and all of them, from the greatest to the least, put on
sackcloth.[g]

3:5 [g]Da 9:3; Lk 11:32

6 When the news reached the king of Nineveh, he rose from his throne, took off his
royal robes, covered himself with sackcloth and sat down in the dust.[h] 7 Then he issued
a proclamation in Nineveh:

3:6 [h]Job 2:8, 13; Eze 27:30-31

"By the decree of the king and his nobles:

3:7 [i]2Ch 20:3

Do not let any man or beast, herd or flock, taste anything; do not let them eat
or drink.[i] 8 But let man and beast be covered with sackcloth. Let everyone call[j] urgently on God. Let them give up their evil ways and their violence. 9 Who knows?[k]
God may yet relent and with compassion turn[l] from his fierce anger so that we
will not perish."

3:8 [j]Ps 130:1; Jnh 1:6
3:9 [k]2Sa 12:22 [l]Joel 2:14

---

prayer is again emphasized, as in the introductory verse (cf. Heb 4:16). See *WLC* 172.

2:8 Those who cling to worthless idols. Recalling the ineffectiveness of the sailors' prayers and the helplessness of the gods to whom those prayers were addressed (1:5), Jonah condemned those who put their faith in worthless idols, forsaking covenant loyalty to the Lord.

2:9 Salvation comes from the LORD. Like Joshua before him (Jos 24:14–20), Jonah declared his loyalty to the Lord and extolled him as the only One to whom salvation and deliverance belong. Salvation belongs to the Lord and is his—and his alone—to impart. In providing salvation to Jonah, the Lord sovereignly moved the prophet from disobedience to repentance; in offering salvation to the Ninevites he sovereignly moved them from idolatry to faith (3:5–10); later, in imparting salvation to the Gentiles at large, he sovereignly moved them to faith and repentance (Ac 11:17–18).

■ **2:10** *God Answers Jonah's Prayer.* In response to Jonah's prayer God conveyed the prophet to dry land to begin his delayed journey toward Nineveh.

2:10 the LORD commanded the fish, and it vomited Jonah. The fish, which might have been God's weapon of death, became by grace God's tool of deliverance, for it saved Jonah from death in the sea.

■ **3:1—4:11** *Jonah's Obedience and God's Reaction.* In this section of the book the Lord commissioned Jonah a second time, but this time the prophet obeyed. These verses divide into three sections: Jonah preached the message as commanded (3:1–4), the Ninevites repented and received divine mercy (3:5–10) and Jonah prayed with anger and received God's answer (4:1–11).

■ **3:1–4** *Jonah Obeys God's Call.* This time Jonah obeyed the Lord's renewed commission. The text does not indicate that he was any more receptive to the prospect of Ninevite repentance but only that he complied with God's instruction.

3:3 Nineveh was. Some have suggested that the use of the past tense ("was") indicates that the city was no longer in existence at the time of writing. Given the city's destruction in 612 B.C. at the hands of the Medes and Babylonians, this interpretation would date the narrative sometime after the late seventh century B.C. The past tense does not necessarily preclude an eighth-century chronology, however. It can be understood as indicating the status of the city when the prophet arrived. **a very important city—a visit required three days.** Although posing some difficulties for translation and understanding, these two descriptive formulas emphasize Nineveh's significance and size. Many commentators understand these expressions to refer exclusively to the physical size of Nineveh (i.e., "a vast city—it took three days to cross it"). Archaeological exploration has shown that the city was between seven and eight miles in circumference with an estimated population of 120,000 people. Alternatively, the first formula could be rendered as "a very important city" (Ge 10:9; 23:6; 30:8; Ex 9:28; Ps 36:7) without reference to size. Or, more literally, it could be translated "a city important to God." The latter fits the context best. The second expression (lit., "journey of three days") could indicate the time required to take in all the features of the city.

■ **3:5–10** *Ninevites Repent and God Responds With Compassion.* Jonah's preaching brought dramatic repentance, which evoked God's mercy toward Nineveh.

3:5 The Ninevites believed. Jonah's worst fears were realized when the people believed, repented, proclaimed a fast and adorned themselves in sackcloth, the traditional mourning garb of the ancient Near East. The repentance was swift and widespread. As in the ministry of Jesus, the word "believed" should not be understood as necessarily indicating saving faith (Jn 2:23).

3:6 the news reached the king of Nineveh. It appears likely that the title "king of Nineveh" refers to the king of Assyria. Certain identification of the monarch in question is impossible. Although it is highly unlikely that Assyrian records would note this unusual occurrence, some scholars have suggested such an allusion in the religious reforms of Adad-nirari III (811–784 B.C.). Assur-dan III (773–756 B.C.) has also been suggested as a possible candidate. **he rose . . . and sat down in the dust.** The king's response was as immediate and spontaneous as that of his subjects. Regal authority gave way to penitent humility. His robes were exchanged for sackcloth; his throne for a bed of ashes (Job 12:7; Isa 58:5).

3:7–8 By the decree of the king . . . call urgently on God. With the issuing of a royal edict mandating prayer, mourning rites and a fast for man and beast, Nineveh's repentance was complete. It was a custom in the Persian period for domestic animals to participate in the rites of mourning (cf. Joel 4:19–20). **Let them give up . . . their violence.** The royal admonition that violence be rejected is of some poignancy for the period of the Neo-Assyrian Empire (eighth/seventh centuries B.C.), since physical violence and social injustice were sins characteristic of Nineveh (Na 2:13; 3:4–7).

3:9 Who knows? God may yet relent . . . so that we will not perish. The king gave personal and corporate expression to the hope that genuine repentance would avert the divine judgment.

10 When God saw what they did and how they turned from their evil ways, he had compassion[m] and did not bring upon them the destruction[n] he had threatened.[o]

Jonah's Anger at the LORD's Compassion

4 But Jonah was greatly displeased and became angry.[p] 2 He prayed to the LORD,
"O LORD, is this not what I said when I was still at home? That is why I was so quick
to flee to Tarshish. I knew[q] that you are a gracious and compassionate God, slow to anger and abounding in love,[r] a God who relents from sending calamity.[s] 3 Now, O LORD,
take away my life,[t] for it is better for me to die[u] than to live."
4 But the LORD replied, "Have you any right to be angry?"[v]
5 Jonah went out and sat down at a place east of the city. There he made himself a
shelter, sat in its shade and waited to see what would happen to the city. 6 Then the
LORD God provided a vine and made it grow up over Jonah to give shade for his head
to ease his discomfort, and Jonah was very happy about the vine. 7 But at dawn the next
day God provided a worm, which chewed the vine so that it withered.[w] 8 When the sun
rose, God provided a scorching east wind, and the sun blazed on Jonah's head so that
he grew faint. He wanted to die, and said, "It would be better for me to die than to
live."
9 But God said to Jonah, "Do you have a right to be angry about the vine?"
"I do," he said. "I am angry enough to die."
10 But the LORD said, "You have been concerned about this vine, though you did not
tend it or make it grow. It sprang up overnight and died overnight. 11 But Nineveh[x] has
more than a hundred and twenty thousand people who cannot tell their right hand from
their left, and many cattle as well. Should I not be concerned[y] about that great city?"

3:10 [m]Am 7:6 [n]Jer 18:8 [o]Ex 32:14
4:1 [p]ver 4; Lk 15:28
4:2 [q]Jer 20:7-8 [r]Ex 34:6; Ps 86:5, 15 [s]Joel 2:13
4:3 [t]1Ki 19:4 [u]Job 7:15
4:4 [v]Mt 20:11-15
4:7 [w]Joel 1:12
4:11 [x]Jnh 1:2; 3:2 [y]Jnh 3:10

God alone determines when repentance will turn his wrath aside. So, as others did in similar circumstances (2Sa 12:22; Joel 2:14), the king confessed, "Who knows?" The structure of 3:5–9 conforms to the typical pattern of reporting corporate repentance in the Old Testament (1Sa 7:3–14; 2Sa 24; Jer 36:3; Joel 1:1—2:27): the threat of judgment, the penitent response and the divine decision to withhold punishment.

3:10 When God saw . . . he . . . did not bring upon them. As in many predictions that are not specific covenant promises, the prophetic warning (v. 4) was a threat, not an absolute condemnation (see "Introduction to the Prophetic Books. True Prophets and Their Predictions"). The prediction cautioned that judgment was imminent if the city did not repent. The Ninevites met that condition: "They turned from their evil ways." The divine response was to nullify the threatened judgment in light of their genuine repentance. The Lord ordains the means as well as the ends of his sovereign plan. Thus he is free to make his own response contingent upon human response (Jer 18:7–10). Sometimes he nullifies a prediction; at other times he postpones, lessens or increases the degree of his judgment.

■ **4:1–11** *Jonah's Prayer and God's Response.* After he had observed repentance among the Ninevites Jonah grew angry; he then prayed and received an answer from God. We are not made privy to Jonah's response to this instruction.

■ **4:1–4** *Jonah Prays With Anger and God Answers.* Jonah expressed his anger that the Lord had spared the Ninevites—Israel's enemies—rather than raining judgment upon them.

4:1 But Jonah was greatly displeased and became angry. Jonah's greatest fear was that the Lord would bestow his forgiveness on Israel's most hated enemy. So he was furious at the city's response. In the Hebrew his emotion is expressed in the strongest language possible.

4:2 you are a gracious and compassionate God . . . who relents from sending calamity. Despite his blatant disobedience and narrow-mindedness Jonah understood the character of God. The wording of the text includes the phrase "who relents from sending calamity," indicating that the prophet understood God's character from Exodus 34:6–7. It is only here and in Joel 2:13 that the reference to divine repentance concludes the formula (see note on 3:9)—an inclusion altogether appropriate to the context of Nineveh's repentance and subsequent deliverance.

4:4 Have you any right . . . ? God challenged Jonah's assertiveness, asking Jonah on what moral grounds the prophet had become angry over God's demonstration of mercy to Nineveh.

■ **4:5–11** *Jonah Receives Further Explanation From God.* After challenging Jonah's right to be angry, God provided the prophet with an experience that dramatically illustrated why mercy had been shown to Nineveh.

4:5 Jonah went out and . . . made himself a shelter. Jonah was unmoved by God's brief response (v. 4). While grateful for his own deliverance, he refused to accept that of the Ninevites. Clinging to the hope that the Lord would execute judgment, he left the city for a vantage point from which to witness the falling fire and brimstone. In order to protect himself from the sun he constructed a small shelter or hut.

4:6 the LORD God provided a vine . . . to ease his discomfort. Jonah's shelter apparently was inadequate to provide protection from the sun, a serious matter in the ancient Near East. As the Lord had provided the fish to rescue Jonah, so again he made provision for the beleaguered prophet. He provided a fast-growing plant, the leaves of which would give shade. The type of vegetation is uncertain.

4:7–8 worm . . . withered . . . wind. Once again Jonah had been the undeserving recipient of God's mercy. Yet the same hand that had provided the fish and the shade plant also sent a worm to kill the plant and a hot east wind to afflict Jonah.

4:9–11 As before (v. 4) the Lord questioned Jonah's right to be angry or to complain. The prophet insisted that his anger was indeed legitimate (v. 9). **concerned about.** The Hebrew verb denotes care and compassion. Jonah pitied the plant yet showed no pity for those to whom he was called to preach.

4:11 that great city? God described the greatness of Nineveh to explain why he was inclined to have mercy on the city. It was not its wealth or glory that moved him. He listed two things. First, there were "more than" 120,000 people who could not "tell their right hand from their left." In other words there were many young children in the city who deserved special consideration because of their limited moral capacity (Dt 1:39; Isa 7:15–16). Second, there were "many cattle [or animals] as well." God, who takes no delight in the death of the wicked (Eze 18:21–23; 33:11), also delights in the animals he has created. The anticipated answer to this question is, "Yes, the Lord should have compassion for these reasons, and his people should delight to see God's mercy extended toward the Gentiles."

MICAH

Introduction

Overview

Author: The prophet Micah

Purpose: To call Judah to repentance and hope during the Assyrian crisis and to prepare Judah for the Babylonian exile by announcing God's judgments against sin and his promises of restoration

Date: 742–686 B.C.

Key Truths:

- God threatened to judge Samaria and Judah for their flagrant violations of the covenant.
- God called his people to repent of their sins in order to avert or delay judgment.
- God affirmed his promises to restore his people from defeat and exile.
- God promised to bless his restored people with victory, expansion and peace.

Author

Micah is identified by his hometown of Moresheth (1:1,14), implying that he was an outsider to Jerusalem. As a prophet who ministered alongside Isaiah, Micah had an influential ministry during a critical time in Judah's history.

Time and Place of Writing

Micah preached during the reigns of Jotham (742–735 B.C.), Ahaz (735–715 B.C.) and Hezekiah (715–686 B.C.). During this time a shocking contrast developed between the extremely rich and the oppressed poor due to the exploitation of Israel's middle class (2:8–9) by greedy landowners (2:1–5), who were supported by Israel's corrupt political and religious leaders (ch. 3). Because of this failed leadership the whole nation became morally corrupt (6:9–16; 7:1–7).

God raised up Assyria as his rod of judgment against his sinful people (Isa 10:5–11). As Micah had predicted (1:2–7), the Assyrians destroyed Samaria in 722 B.C. (2Ki 17:1–6). Judah felt the full force of God's judgment when the Assyrian king Sennacherib (705–681 B.C.) marched through Judah's western foothills and up to the gate of Jerusalem, as Micah had also foretold (1:8–16). When the city was under siege, Hezekiah finally repented, and the Lord turned back the army of Assyria (Jer 26:18–19).

Purpose and Distinctives

Micah arranged his 19 prophecies into three cycles (chs. 1–2; 3–5; 6–7). Each cycle begins with prophecies of judgment and ends with a prophecy (or prophecies) of salvation, and each opens with the same Hebrew word rendered "hear" (1:2) or "listen" (3:1; 6:1). The middle cycle includes three oracles of judgment (ch. 3) and seven oracles of salvation (chs. 4–5). Micah used clever puns and quoted his opponents, who tried to silence him (2:6–7).

In his oracles of salvation Micah foresaw that Jerusalem's salvation during the Sennacherib invasion (701 B.C.) would depend solely upon the Lord's mercy toward a remnant (2:13). He also foresaw that God would later deliver his people from Babylonian captivity (4:9–10). As a result the covenant people were to walk in the name of the Lord (4:5) and depend on God's sovereign grace (5:9), not the works of their hands (5:10–15). Throughout these trials, as well as in the future, a forgiven remnant would endure through the mercy of God because God had pledged on oath to be true to the patriarchs (7:18–20).

Christ in Micah

The book of Micah reveals Christ in at least two ways. First, Micah made many predictions of judgment and deliverance that spoke directly to the judgment of the Assyrian king Sennacherib's devastating attack on Judah and the salvation of Jerusalem. He also predicted that the Babylonians would conquer Judah. As major acts of divine judgment and salvation, these predictions and their fulfillments are shadows or types anticipating the final judgment and salvation that comes in Christ.

Second, predictions of the judgments and the blessings that would take place at the restoration of God's people after the Babylonian captivity speak more directly of Christ. According to the New Testament, Jesus inaugurated these events in his earthly ministry, continues them today and will bring them to completion at his return. Micah spoke of these events as "the last days" (4:1; see theological article "The Plan of the Ages" at Heb 7) and "that day" (2:4; 4:6; 5:10; 7:12); that is, "the day of the Lord," which the New Testament connects to the work of Christ (2Th 2:1–2; 2Pe 3:10). Perhaps the most direct prediction of Christ in Micah is found in 5:1–6 (see Mt 2:6), where God promised that the house of David would rise up after exile, defeat Judah's enemies, rule over the entire earth and bring peace to God's people.

Outline

I. Superscription (1:1)	*Micah and his historical circumstances are identified.*
II. Judgment and Deliverance in the Assyrian Crises (1:2—2:13) A. Judgment in Samaria's Downfall (1:2–7) B. Lament Over Judah's Defeat (1:8–16) C. Judgment on Greedy Landowners (2:1–5) D. Judgment Against False Prophets (2:6–11) E. Salvation of a Remnant in Zion (2:12–13)	*God threatened to judge the northern and southern kingdoms through Assyrian invasions, but a remnant would be kept safe in Jerusalem.*
III. Judgment of Leaders and Future Restoration (3:1—5:15) A. Judgment on Leaders Turned Cannibals (3:1–4) B. Judgment on Profiteering Prophets (3:5–8) C. Judgment of Zion's Destruction (3:9–12) D. Zion to Be Exalted (4:1–5) E. Future Strength of the Remnant (4:6–7) F. Zion's Future Dominion (4:8) G. Zion's Distress and Future Salvation (4:9–13) H. The Messianic Ruler (5:1–6) I. Future Rule of the Remnant (5:7–9) J. The Lord's Protection of His Empire (5:10–15)	*God threatened to judge Judah and Jerusalem with defeat and exile because her leaders were so corrupt, but both would one day be restored.*
IV. Judgment of the Nation and Future Restoration (6:1—7:20) A. Judgment for Breaking Covenant (6:1–8) B. Judgment of Curses on Jerusalem (6:9–16) C. Judgment of Social Disintegration (7:1–6) D. Micah's Confidence in God (7:7) E. Hymn of Praise for God's Victory (7:8–20)	*God threatened to judge Judah and Jerusalem with defeat and exile because the nation had flagrantly violated the covenant, but both would one day be restored.*

1 The word of the LORD that came to Micah of Moresheth[a] during the reigns of Jotham,[b] Ahaz[c] and Hezekiah, kings of Judah[d]—the vision[e] he saw concerning Samaria and Jerusalem.

2 Hear, O peoples, all of you,[f]
listen, O earth[g] and all who are in it,
that the Sovereign LORD may witness[h] against you,
the Lord from his holy temple.[i]

Judgment Against Samaria and Jerusalem

3 Look! The LORD is coming from his dwelling[j] place;
he comes down and treads the high places of the earth.[k]
4 The mountains melt[l] beneath him
and the valleys split apart,[m]

1:1 [a]Jer 26:18 [b]1Ch 3:12 [c]1Ch 3:13 [d]Hos 1:1 [e]Isa 1:1
1:2 [f]Ps 50:7 [g]Jer 6:19 [h]Ge 31:50; Dt 4:26; Isa 1:2 [i]Ps 11:4
1:3 [j]Isa 18:4 [k]Am 4:13
1:4 [l]Ps 46:2,6 [m]Nu 16:31; Na 1:5

■ **1:1** *Superscription.* Micah is introduced as an authoritative prophet of the Lord.
1:1 The word of the LORD. Micah's prophetic ministry is validated in a superscription instead of in a call narrative (3:8; cf. Isa 6). **vision.** A supernatural revelation to the prophet's inner sight or hearing.
■ **1:2—2:13** *Judgment and Deliverance in the Assyrian Crises.* Micah predicted that God would judge the northern kingdom (Israel) and the southern kingdom (Judah) through the Assyrians because of the sins of the people. He also announced God's offer to spare Jerusalem. These chapters divide into five parts: judgment on Samaria (1:2–7), judgment on Judah (1:8–16), judgment on landowners (2:1–5), judgment on false prophets (2:6–11) and deliverance for the remnant gathered in Jerusalem (2:12–13).
■ **1:2–7** *Judgment in Samaria's Downfall.* Although Micah mentioned Judah (v. 5), his first oracle concerns the Assyrian judgment on Samaria, the capital of Israel. This oracle has four parts: the summons of the nations to trial (v. 2), a vision of God's approach in battle (vv. 3–4), an accusation against Israel's capitals (v. 5) and the divine sentence to destroy Samaria (vv. 6–7).
1:2 O peoples . . . against you. God's forthcoming judgment of Samaria was to be noticed by all the nations on Earth. God will one day judge idolatry and social crimes in all nations.
1:3–5 The prophet understood that God was marching before the Assyrian armies. The language of cosmic upheaval depicts the severity of the Assyrian aggression against Israel, Judah and the other nations in the path of the Assyrian march.
1:3 high places. Pagan temples and palaces were located on heights.
1:4 mountains melt . . . valleys split. Symbolic language depicting the instability of the cosmos is typical in prophecies pertaining to events of national significance (cf. Na 1:5). Here the destruction of Samaria is most directly in view (vv. 6–7), though the threat includes judgment against Judah as well (v. 5). **fire . . . rushing**

like wax before the fire,
like water rushing down a slope.
5 All this is because of Jacob's transgression,
because of the sins of the house of Israel.
What is Jacob's transgression?
1:5 [n]Am 8:14 — Is it not Samaria?[n]
What is Judah's high place?
Is it not Jerusalem?

6 "Therefore I will make Samaria a heap of rubble,
1:6 [o]Am 5:11 [p]Eze 13:14 — a place for planting vineyards.
I will pour her stones[o] into the valley
and lay bare her foundations.[p]
1:7 [q]Eze 6:6 [r]Dt 9:21 [s]Dt 23:17-18 — 7 All her idols[q] will be broken to pieces;
all her temple gifts will be burned with fire;
I will destroy all her images.[r]
Since she gathered her gifts from the wages of prostitutes,[s]
as the wages of prostitutes they will again be used."

Weeping and Mourning

1:8 [t]Isa 15:3 — 8 Because of this I will weep[t] and wail;
I will go about barefoot and naked.
I will howl like a jackal
1:9 [u]Jer 46:11 [v]2Ki 18:13 [w]Isa 3:26 — and moan like an owl.
9 For her wound[u] is incurable;
it has come to Judah.[v]
It[a] has reached the very gate[w] of my people,
even to Jerusalem itself.
10 Tell it not in Gath[b];
weep not at all.[c]
In Beth Ophrah[d]
1:11 [x]Eze 23:29 — roll in the dust.
11 Pass on in nakedness[x] and shame,
you who live in Shaphir.[e]
Those who live in Zaanan[f]
will not come out.
Beth Ezel is in mourning;
its protection is taken from you.
1:12 [y]Jer 14:19 — 12 Those who live in Maroth[g] writhe in pain,
waiting for relief,[y]
because disaster has come from the LORD,
even to the gate of Jerusalem.

[a] 9 Or *He* [b] 10 *Gath* sounds like the Hebrew for *tell.* [c] 10 Hebrew; Septuagint may suggest *not in Acco.* The Hebrew for *in Acco* sounds like the Hebrew for *weep.* [d] 10 *Beth Ophrah* means *house of dust.* [e] 11 *Shaphir* means *pleasant.* [f] 11 *Zaanan* sounds like the Hebrew for *come out.* [g] 12 *Maroth* sounds like the Hebrew for *bitter.*

down. These words link the symbolic vision with the historical overthrow of Samaria (vv. 6–7).
1:5 Jacob's . . . Israel . . . Jacob's . . . Samaria . . . Judah's . . . Jerusalem? Jacob designates the northern kingdom, as the association with Samaria indicates. Israel designates Judah, the southern kingdom, as indicated by the association with Jerusalem. **transgression . . . Samaria . . . high place . . . Jerusalem?** Samaria and Jerusalem were accused of being the centers of rebellion against the Lord. To designate Jerusalem as a "high place" was to identify it as a pagan worship center because of the idolatry present there.
1:6 I will. The Lord himself handed down the sentence.
1:7 wages of prostitutes. The images of paganized worship in the northern kingdom came from the wages of religious prostitution. The wealth gathered from religious prostitution would be taken by the Assyrian army and used once again for prostitution.
■ **1:8–16** *Lament Over Judah's Defeat.* Micah next turned to the Assyrian aggression against Judah, which he had suggested in his previous oracle (v. 5). He did this in the form of a lament over various places in Judah that would fall to Assyria. The lament has three parts: an introduction that states Micah's resolve to mourn Judah's exile (vv. 8–9); a body that predicts—through a series of puns on the names of Judah's strongholds (see NIV text notes on vv. 10–15)—Judah's fall and exile (vv. 10–15); and a conclusion that calls the house of David to join in mourning rites because it too would go into exile (v. 16).
1:8 barefoot and naked. A symbolic act that threatened captivity (see Isa 20:2–4).
1:9 gate. Sennacherib reached Jerusalem's gate but did not take the city (see v. 12; see also "Introduction: Time and Place of Writing").
1:10 Tell it not in Gath. This call links Micah's lament over the fall of David's house with David's lament over the fall of Saul's house under similar circumstances (2Sa 1:20). Gath represents the Philistines (Judah's enemies). The prohibition here was designed to keep enemies from gloating over Judah's defeat. **roll in the dust.** A vivid expression of grief over a humiliating defeat (Jer 6:26).
1:11 Zaanan . . . out. "Going Forth Town" would cower behind its wall instead of boldly going forth into battle. **Beth Ezel . . . you.** "House of Taking Away" would remove its protection from Judah because it would be annexed by the conqueror.
1:12 Maroth. "Bitter Town" ironically expected sweet relief from Jerusalem during the Assyrian attack.

[13] You who live in Lachish,[a] [z]
harness the team to the chariot.
You were the beginning of sin
to the Daughter of Zion,
for the transgressions of Israel
were found in you.
[14] Therefore you will give parting gifts[a]
to Moresheth Gath.
The town of Aczib[b] [b] will prove deceptive[c]
to the kings of Israel.
[15] I will bring a conqueror against you
who live in Mareshah.[c] [d]
He who is the glory of Israel
will come to Adullam.[e]
[16] Shave[f] your heads in mourning
for the children in whom you delight;
make yourselves as bald as the vulture,
for they will go from you into exile.

Man's Plans and God's

2 Woe to those who plan iniquity,
to those who plot evil on their beds![g]
At morning's light they carry it out
because it is in their power to do it.
[2] They covet fields[h] and seize them,
and houses, and take them.
They defraud[i] a man of his home,
a fellowman of his inheritance.

[3] Therefore, the LORD says:

"I am planning disaster[j] against this people,
from which you cannot save yourselves.
You will no longer walk proudly,[k]
for it will be a time of calamity.
[4] In that day men will ridicule you;
they will taunt you with this mournful song:
'We are utterly ruined;[l]
my people's possession is divided up.
He takes it from me!
He assigns our fields to traitors.' "
[5] Therefore you will have no one in the assembly of the LORD
to divide the land[m] by lot.

1:13 [z]Jos 10:3
1:14 [a]2Ki 16:8 [b]Jos 15:44 [c]Jer 15:18
1:15 [d]Jos 15:44 [e]Jos 12:15
1:16 [f]Job 1:20
2:1 [g]Ps 36:4
2:2 [h]Isa 5:8 [i]Jer 22:17
2:3 [j]Jer 18:11; Am 3:1-2 [k]Isa 2:12
2:4 [l]Jer 4:13
2:5 [m]Jos 18:4

a 13 *Lachish* sounds like the Hebrew for *team.* b 14 *Aczib* means *deception.* c 15 *Mareshah* sounds like the Hebrew for *conqueror.*

1:13 team. The Hebrew literally means "swift horses," producing the ironic translation "Harness the war chariot to racing horses." **beginning of sin.** As Judah's principal stronghold, Lachish introduced the sin of trusting in human strength rather than in divine protection (5:10). **Daughter of Zion.** A personification of Jerusalem.
1:14 parting gifts. Or "dowry" (see 2Ki 16:8), a metaphor for the hated tribute paid to Assyria. Jerusalem would give up Moresheth Gath to Assyria. **town.** Or "workshops" (see 1Ch 4:21–23). The king lost revenue to the enemy by paying tribute (v. 14a) and by losing his workshops to the enemy (v. 14b).
1:15 glory of Israel. Or "men of rank" (see Isa 5:13, where the same Hebrew expression is so rendered). **Adullam.** As David fled to Adullam as an exile, so his successors would go there under similar circumstances (2Sa 22:1; 23:13). The lament begins and ends with an allusion to David (see note on v. 10).
■ **2:1–5** *Judgment on Greedy Landowners.* Having introduced the judgments coming against Samaria and Judah, the prophet explained the reasons for these judgments by pointing to the sins of landowners. The oracle has three parts: (1) the accusation that evil and violent men had wrongly seized sacred property and destroyed its owners (vv. 1–2); (2) the Lord's sentence of exile (v. 3), entailing the loss of their lands to invaders (v. 4); and (3) the conclusion that the robbers would be permanently disinherited (v. 5). The accusation and sentence are linked by a pun involving "who plot evil" (v. 1) and "I am planning disaster" (v. 3), which are virtually identical expressions in Hebrew. As the powerful took fields away from Israel's men (vv. 1–2), so the Lord would send an enemy army to wrest the promised land from them (vv. 4–5).
2:1 morning's light. Court was held when the sun rose. Ironically, instead of finding the expected justice, the oppressed were met with injustice. See *WLC* 151.
2:2 covet. Covetousness is at the heart of many sins (Ex 20:17; Ro 7:8). **inheritance.** A family's property was a permanent, sacred trust from God (Lev 25:10,13). See *WLC* 142.
2:5 assembly . . . to divide the land. The language reflects the expectation that after exile an assembly would be held to redistribute the land, as had been done in previous generations (e.g., Jos 19:51). Because of their grievous sins the landowners were threatened with permanent disinheritance.

False Prophets

[6] "Do not prophesy," their prophets say.
"Do not prophesy about these things;
disgrace[n] will not overtake us.[o]"
[7] Should it be said, O house of Jacob:
"Is the Spirit of the LORD angry?
Does he do such things?"

"Do not my words do good[p]
to him whose ways are upright?[q]
[8] Lately my people have risen up
like an enemy.
You strip off the rich robe
from those who pass by without a care,
like men returning from battle.
[9] You drive the women of my people
from their pleasant homes.[r]
You take away my blessing
from their children forever.
[10] Get up, go away!
For this is not your resting place,[s]
because it is defiled,[t]
it is ruined, beyond all remedy.
[11] If a liar and deceiver[u] comes and says,
'I will prophesy for you plenty of wine and beer,'
he would be just the prophet for this people![v]

Deliverance Promised

[12] "I will surely gather all of you, O Jacob;
I will surely bring together the remnant[w] of Israel.
I will bring them together like sheep in a pen,
like a flock in its pasture;
the place will throng with people.
[13] One who breaks open the way will go up before[x] them;
they will break through the gate and go out.
Their king will pass through before them,
the LORD at their head."

Leaders and Prophets Rebuked

3 Then I said,

"Listen, you leaders[y] of Jacob,
you rulers of the house of Israel.
Should you not know justice,

2:6 [n]Mic 6:16 [o]Am 2:12
2:7 [p]Ps 119:65 [q]Ps 15:2; 84:11
2:9 [r]Jer 10:20
2:10 [s]Dt 12:9 [t]Lev 18:25-29; Ps 106:38-39
2:11 [u]Jer 5:31 [v]Isa 30:10
2:12 [w]Mic 4:7; 5:7; 7:18
2:13 [x]Isa 52:12
3:1 [y]Jer 5:5

■ **2:6–11** *Judgment Against False Prophets.* False prophets had insisted that God would not judge his people, but Micah pronounced judgment against them for their lies. This judgment has four parts: (1) Micah rebuffed their command to stop prophesying (v. 6). (2) The Lord corrected their presumption upon his grace (v. 7) and accused the powerful of exploiting the defenseless (vv. 8–9). (3) God sentenced them to exile because they had made the land unclean (v. 10). (4) Micah rebuked the powerful for desiring liars who would support their crimes (v. 11).
2:6–7 Micah, quoting the false prophets, spoke in verses 6–7a. God, contradicting and judging the false prophets and their followers, spoke in verses 7b–11.
2:8–9 rich robe . . . pleasant homes . . . blessing from their children. The oppressed belonged to Israel's middle class.
2:8 like men returning from battle. Tragically, Israel's men were plundered in their homeland, where they felt most secure.
2:11 just the prophet for this people! The Lord mocked the people who were following false prophets because they wanted to hear only words of peace and prosperity.
■ **2:12–13** *Salvation of a Remnant in Zion.* This first positive oracle in the book concerns Jerusalem's deliverance from the Sennacherib invasion in 701 B.C., not the return from exile. Israel's divine Shepherd would gather Judah's remnant into Jerusalem for protection from Sennacherib's attack (v. 12) and then deliver them by decimating the Assyrian army (v. 13). See "Introduction: Time and Place of Writing" and "Purpose and Distinctives."
2:12 all of you . . . remnant of Israel. "All" is qualified by "remnant." The remnant was that small portion of the nation that would survive divine judgment and continue into the future as God's covenant people. As the Assyrians attacked villages and cities in Judah (1:8–16), many would run to Jerusalem for safety. **pen.** Jerusalem is likened to a sheepfold.
2:13 king. Better, "King," given the parallel to "the LORD."
■ **3:1—5:15** *Judgment of Leaders and Future Restoration.* Micah warned that Jerusalem would be destroyed, but he also promised that one day, after the exile, it would be greatly exalted. Ten oracles comprise this section. The first three build to the warning of the destruction of Jerusalem; the latter seven assure the readers of the ultimate restoration of Jerusalem.
■ **3:1–4** *Judgment on Leaders Turned Cannibals.* Judah's leaders had become so corrupt that Micah likened them to cannibals. The three judgment oracles in this chapter share common features. They address the same people: Israel's incompetent, corrupt leadership. They have a common length—four verses—and a common form—an address (vv. 1,5,9), an accusation introduced by "who" (vv. 2,5,9) and a sentence introduced by "then" (v. 4) or "there-

2 you who hate good and love evil;
who tear the skin from my people
and the flesh from their bones;[z]
3 who eat my people's flesh,[a]
strip off their skin
and break their bones in pieces;[b]
who chop them up like meat for the pan,
like flesh for the pot?[c]"

4 Then they will cry out to the LORD,
but he will not answer them.[d]
At that time he will hide his face[e] from them
because of the evil they have done.

5 This is what the LORD says:

"As for the prophets
who lead my people astray,[f]
if one feeds them,
they proclaim 'peace';
if he does not,
they prepare to wage war against him.
6 Therefore night will come over you, without visions,
and darkness, without divination.[g]
The sun will set for the prophets,[h]
and the day will go dark for them.
7 The seers will be ashamed[i]
and the diviners disgraced.[j]
They will all cover their faces
because there is no answer from God."

8 But as for me, I am filled with power,
with the Spirit of the LORD,
and with justice and might,
to declare to Jacob his transgression,
to Israel his sin.[k]
9 Hear this, you leaders of the house of Jacob,
you rulers of the house of Israel,
who despise justice
and distort all that is right;[l]
10 who build[m] Zion with bloodshed,[n]
and Jerusalem with wickedness.[o]
11 Her leaders judge for a bribe,
her priests teach for a price,
and her prophets tell fortunes for money.[p]
Yet they lean upon the LORD and say,
"Is not the LORD among us?
No disaster will come upon us."[q]
12 Therefore because of you,
Zion will be plowed like a field,

3:2 [z]Ps 53:4; Eze 22:27
3:3 [a]Ps 14:4 [b]Zep 3:3 [c]Eze 11:7
3:4 [d]Ps 18:41; Isa 1:15 [e]Dt 31:17
3:5 [f]Isa 3:12; 9:16
3:6 [g]Isa 8:19-22 [h]Isa 29:10
3:7 [i]Mic 7:16 [j]Isa 44:25
3:8 [k]Isa 58:1
3:9 [l]Ps 58:1-2; Isa 1:23
3:10 [m]Jer 22:13 [n]Hab 2:12 [o]Eze 22:27
3:11 [p]Isa 1:23; Jer 6:13; Hos 4:8,18 [q]Jer 7:4

fore" (vv. 6,12). Most importantly, they have a common theme—the miscarriage of justice for personal gain.
3:1 Then I said. An editorial suture demonstrating that Micah edited his own book (see "Introduction: Purpose and Distinctives"). **justice.** A reference to decisions in the law (Ex 21:1) and other verdicts (Dt 17:8–11) and to deciding cases (1Ki 3:28; 7:7) so that oppressors would be punished and the oppressed delivered.
3:4 not answer. As the magistrates refused to hear the cry of the oppressed, so God would refuse to hear their cry in the time of judgment.
■ **3:5–8** *Judgment on Profiteering Prophets.* Micah returned to the problem of false prophets who profited from assuring the people that they were safe.
3:6 day will go dark. The loss of prophecy and visions is likened to darkness (Ps 82:5).
3:7 disgraced. A prophet exposed as a fraud was regarded as unclean (La 4:13–15).
3:8 But as for me. Micah insisted that, in contrast to the false prophets, he was empowered by God to tell the truth about Judah's sins.
■ **3:9–12** *Judgment of Zion's Destruction.* This oracle declares the severe judgment of destruction on Jerusalem because of her corrupt leaders and prophets. Jeremiah 26:17–19 refers to verse 12 and dates Micah's ministry at the time of the reign of Hezekiah.
3:9–11 These verses repeat accusations against leaders, judges, priests and prophets. See *WCF* 18.1.
3:12 Zion will be plowed. Micah threatened that Jerusalem's destruction would be like that of Samaria (1:6). Jerusalem would be "plowed like a field . . . a heap of rubble . . . a mound overgrown with thickets." Hezekiah's repentance and prayer averted this disaster in his day (see "Introduction"), but the destruction was carried out in 586 B.C. Thus, as 4:10 indicates, the restoration oracles following this threat of destruction and exile for Jerusalem concern restoration from the Babylonian exile in 539 B.C.

3:12
[r]Jer 26:18

Jerusalem will become a heap of rubble,[r]
  the temple hill a mound overgrown with thickets.

The Mountain of the Lord

4:1
[s]Zec 8:3 [t]Eze 17:22
[u]Ps 22:27; 86:9;
Jer 3:17

4 In the last days

the mountain[s] of the Lord's temple will be established
  as chief among the mountains;
it will be raised above the hills,[t]
  and peoples will stream to it.[u]

[2]Many nations will come and say,

4:2
[v]Jer 31:6
[w]Zec 2:11; 14:16
[x]Ps 25:8-9;
Isa 54:13

"Come, let us go up to the mountain of the Lord,[v]
  to the house of the God of Jacob.[w]
He will teach us his ways,[x]
  so that we may walk in his paths."
The law will go out from Zion,
  the word of the Lord from Jerusalem.

4:3
[y]Isa 11:4 [z]Joel 3:10
[a]Isa 2:4

[3]He will judge between many peoples
  and will settle disputes for strong nations far and wide.[y]
They will beat their swords into plowshares
  and their spears into pruning hooks.[z]
Nation will not take up sword against nation,
  nor will they train for war anymore.[a]

4:4
[b]1Ki 4:25
[c]Lev 26:6
[d]Isa 1:20; Zec 3:10

[4]Every man will sit under his own vine
  and under his own fig tree,[b]
and no one will make them afraid,[c]
  for the Lord Almighty has spoken.[d]

4:5
[e]2Ki 17:29
[f]Jos 24:14-15;
Isa 26:8; Zec 10:12

[5]All the nations may walk
  in the name of their gods;[e]
we will walk in the name of the Lord
  our God for ever and ever.[f]

The Lord*'s Plan*

[6]"In that day," declares the Lord,

4:6
[g]Ps 147:2
[h]Eze 34:13,16;
37:21; Zep 3:19

"I will gather the lame;
  I will assemble the exiles[g]
  and those I have brought to grief.[h]

4:7
[i]Mic 2:12 [j]Da 7:14;
Lk 1:33; Rev 11:15

[7]I will make the lame a remnant,[i]
  those driven away a strong nation.
The Lord will rule over them in Mount Zion
  from that day and forever.[j]
[8]As for you, O watchtower of the flock,
  O stronghold[a] of the Daughter of Zion,

[a] *8* Or *hill*

■ **4:1–5** *Zion to Be Exalted.* Micah announced that the exile following Jerusalem's destruction would lead to a great restoration of the city and its people. The oracle has three parts: (1) an introduction stating that the vision was for "the last days" (v. 1); (2) a body consisting of a vision of Zion established as the chief mountain (v. 1) with nations "stream[ing]" (v. 1) to it to learn the law (v. 2a) and a reflection that as the law went out from Mount Zion, the world would be pacified (vv. 2b–4a); and (3) a conclusion, including the prophetic formula that God had generated the oracle (v. 4b) and a liturgical response by the people indicating their intention to obey the law until the prophecy had been fulfilled (v. 5).
4:1 In the last days. An expression that points to a new epoch that would begin after God's people had been restored from exile. The terminology derives from Deuteronomy 4:30, where Moses described the scenario of sin, exile and restoration in the latter days. The New Testament teaches that the latter days began at Christ's first advent (Ac 2:7; Heb 1:2) and will reach their fullness in the new heaven and the new earth (Rev 21–22). See theological article "The Plan of the Ages" at Hebrews 7. **mountain . . . temple.** Along with other Old Testament prophets Micah believed that the city and temple would be rebuilt after the exile, but the New Testament explains that the manner in which the kingdom of God came in Christ shifted this expectation. Christ embodies the temple (Jn 2:19,22), the church is the temple (1Co 3:16–17) and when Christ returns the entire creation will be the dwelling place of God's special presence (Rev 21:22–26). **chief.** Pagan gods had sacred mountains with temples. By being raised above them, God, in association with Mount Zion, would be established among the nations as the true God.
4:5 See *WLC* 112.
■ **4:6–7** *Future Strength of the Remnant.* Destruction and exile would weaken the remnant, but it would be strengthened when the restoration occurred.
4:6 In that day. Probably "the day of the Lord," the day on which God intervenes to establish his reign over his enemies and blesses his people with victory. See note on verse 1 and "Introduction to Zephaniah."
4:7 remnant. The remnant of 2:12 that survived Sennacherib's invasion would also survive the Babylonian exile. **strong nation.** Those who returned from exile in 539 B.C. never experienced this strengthening because they continued in sin. When Christ came, however, he established his church as an invincible nation (Mt 16:18; 1Pe 2:9–10).

the former dominion will be restored[k] to you;
kingship will come to the Daughter of Jerusalem."

9 Why do you now cry aloud—
have you no king?[l]
Has your counselor perished,
that pain seizes you like that of a woman in labor?[m]
10 Writhe in agony, O Daughter of Zion,
like a woman in labor,
for now you must leave the city
to camp in the open field.
You will go to Babylon;[n]
there you will be rescued.
There the LORD will redeem[o] you
out of the hand of your enemies.

11 But now many nations
are gathered against you.
They say, "Let her be defiled,
let our eyes gloat[p] over Zion!"
12 But they do not know
the thoughts of the LORD;
they do not understand his plan,[q]
he who gathers them like sheaves to the threshing floor.

13 "Rise and thresh, O Daughter of Zion,
for I will give you horns of iron;
I will give you hoofs of bronze
and you will break to pieces many nations."[r]

You will devote their ill-gotten gains to the LORD,
their wealth to the Lord of all the earth.

A Promised Ruler From Bethlehem

5 Marshal your troops, O city of troops,[a]
for a siege is laid against us.
They will strike Israel's ruler
on the cheek[s] with a rod.

2 "But you, Bethlehem[t] Ephrathah,[u]
though you are small among the clans[b] of Judah,
out of you will come for me
one who will be ruler over Israel,
whose origins[c] are from of old,[v]
from ancient times.[d]"[w]

3 Therefore Israel will be abandoned
until the time when she who is in labor gives birth

4:8 [k]Isa 1:26
4:9 [l]Jer 8:19 [m]Jer 30:6
4:10 [n]2Ki 20:18; Isa 43:14 [o]Isa 48:20
4:11 [p]La 2:16; Ob 1:12
4:12 [q]Isa 55:8; Ro 11:33-34
4:13 [r]Da 2:44
5:1 [s]La 3:30
5:2 [t]Jn 7:42 [u]Ge 48:7 [v]Ps 102:25 [w]Mt 2:6*

a *1* Or *Strengthen your walls, O walled city* b *2* Or *rulers* c *2* Hebrew *goings out* d *2* Or *from days of eternity*

■ **4:8** *Zion's Future Dominion.* Micah predicted that Jerusalem would become a fortified tower after the exile, but continuing sin among the returnees postponed the completion of this promise until the fulfillment of the kingdom of Christ in the descent of the heavenly Jerusalem in the new heavens and the new earth (Rev 21:1–2).

■ **4:9–13** *Zion's Distress and Future Salvation.* Micah acknowledged the pain Jerusalem's inhabitants would experience in the coming destruction and exile but assured them that salvation would follow. This oracle describes God's plan for Israel's present distress (the "now" of vv. 9,11) to bring glorious salvation—from the Babylonian exile to liberation (vv. 9–12).

4:9 king . . . counselor. Jerusalem would be deserted, without a king. It is possible that Micah had in mind the Lord as the King who would desert the city.

4:10 like a woman in labor. From the present affliction the remnant in Zion would give birth to a new age. **go to Babylon.** It should not be surprising that Micah anticipated an exile to Babylon. Isaiah announced to Hezekiah that the treasures of Jerusalem would be taken to Babylon because of infidelity to God (Isa 39:5–7). Once the Assyrian threat was averted, either Micah focused his prophetic judgments directly on the threat of Babylonian exile or his oracles that had originally focused on Assyria were reapplied to this new threat.

■ **5:1–6** *The Messianic Ruler.* This oracle concerns a king from David's family (the Messiah) who would establish a worldwide kingdom that would bring peace and blessings to God's faithful people. It also moves from the present distress (4:13) to the Messiah's victory (vv. 1–3) and the triumph of his leadership (vv. 4–6).

5:1 cheek. The blow on the cheek to Judah's ruler represents the climactic insult—all power to resist was gone. See *BC* 8,10.

5:2 Jesus, the long awaited son of David, fulfilled the promises made in this oracle (Mt 2:6).

5:3 will be abandoned. Israel was without a king from 586 B.C. to the advent of Christ. **rest of his brothers.** Thousands of Jews who

and the rest of his brothers return
to join the Israelites.

5:4 [x]Isa 40:11; 49:9; Eze 34:11-15,23; Mic 7:14 [y]Isa 52:13; Lk 1:32

4 He will stand and shepherd his flock[x]
in the strength of the LORD,
in the majesty of the name of the LORD his God.
And they will live securely, for then his greatness[y]
will reach to the ends of the earth.
5 And he will be their peace.[z]

5:5 [z]Isa 9:6; Lk 2:14; Col 1:19-20 [a]Isa 8:7 [b]Isa 10:24-27

Deliverance and Destruction

When the Assyrian invades[a] our land
and marches through our fortresses,
we will raise against him seven shepherds,
even eight leaders of men.[b]
6 They will rule[a] the land of Assyria with the sword,
the land of Nimrod[c] with drawn sword.[b][d]
He will deliver us from the Assyrian
when he invades our land
and marches into our borders.[e]

5:6 [c]Ge 10:8 [d]Zep 2:13 [e]Na 2:11-13

5:7 [f]Mic 2:12 [g]Isa 44:4

7 The remnant[f] of Jacob will be
in the midst of many peoples
like dew from the LORD,
like showers on the grass,[g]
which do not wait for man
or linger for mankind.
8 The remnant of Jacob will be among the nations,
in the midst of many peoples,
like a lion among the beasts of the forest,[h]
like a young lion among flocks of sheep,
which mauls and mangles[i] as it goes,
and no one can rescue.[j]

5:8 [h]Ge 49:9 [i]Mic 4:13; Zec 10:5 [j]Ps 50:22; Hos 5:14

5:9 [k]Ps 10:12

9 Your hand will be lifted up[k] in triumph over your enemies,
and all your foes will be destroyed.

10 "In that day," declares the LORD,

"I will destroy your horses from among you
and demolish your chariots.[l]
11 I will destroy the cities[m] of your land
and tear down all your strongholds.[n]
12 I will destroy your witchcraft
and you will no longer cast spells.[o]
13 I will destroy your carved images
and your sacred stones from among you;
you will no longer bow down
to the work of your hands.[p]
14 I will uproot from among you your Asherah poles[c][q]
and demolish your cities.

5:10 [l]Hos 14:3; Zec 9:10

5:11 [m]Isa 6:11 [n]Hos 10:14; Am 5:9

5:12 [o]Dt 18:10-12; Isa 2:6; 8:19

5:13 [p]Eze 6:9; Zec 13:2

5:14 [q]Ex 34:13

[a] *6* Or *crush* [b] *6* Or *Nimrod in its gates* [c] *14* That is, symbols of the goddess Asherah

had not been reckoned with the faithful remnant were converted after Pentecost (Ac 2:41,47).

5:4 reach to the ends of the earth. Jesus commanded his disciples to spread his kingdom to all nations (Mt 28:18–20; Ac 1:8). Christ will reign in heaven until all his enemies are subdued (Ps 110:1); then he will return as King over all.

5:5 seven . . . eight. In contrast to the inadequate leadership Judah had experienced in the past (3:1–11), there would be a more than sufficient supply of capable leaders to expand Christ's kingdom.

5:6 Assyria . . . land of Nimrod. This word against Assyria, which would be punished for the destruction of the northern kingdom and the troubles of Judah in the days of Hezekiah, extends to the "land of Nimrod" (the Babylonian kingdom), which finally sent Judah into exile (see Ge 10:8–11).

■ **5:7–9** *Future Rule of the Remnant.* This oracle has two parts: a prophecy that the remnant would become God's instrument of life and death (vv. 7–8) and a petition that God would defeat all his foes (v. 9). As with all restoration prophecies these predictions find initial fulfillment in Christ's first coming, continued fulfillment now and completion in his second coming.

5:7 wait for . . . linger for. Better, "look expectantly . . . count on." As rain depends on the divine initiative, so the remnant was dependent on God to refresh the earth through them.

5:9 will be lifted up. Better, "Let . . . be lifted up."

■ **5:10–15** *The Lord's Protection of His Empire.* This oracle has two parts: God would cleanse his nation (vv. 10–14) and cut off the pagan nations (v. 15), and God's salvation would not be complete until he had utterly purified his nation of all vain and false military confidences (vv. 10–11), witchcraft (v. 12) and idolatry (vv. 13–14), all of which are the works of people's hands.

5:12 witchcraft. Literally, "witchcraft of your hands."

5:14 cities. Or "idols."

15 I will take vengeance[r] in anger and wrath
upon the nations that have not obeyed me."

The LORD*'s Case Against Israel*

6 Listen to what the LORD says:

"Stand up, plead your case before the mountains;[s]
let the hills hear what you have to say.
2 Hear,[t] O mountains, the LORD's accusation;[u]
listen, you everlasting foundations of the earth.
For the LORD has a case against his people;
he is lodging a charge[v] against Israel.

3 "My people, what have I done to you?
How have I burdened[w] you? Answer me.
4 I brought you up out of Egypt
and redeemed you from the land of slavery.[x]
I sent Moses[y] to lead you,
also Aaron[z] and Miriam.[a]
5 My people, remember
what Balak[b] king of Moab counseled
and what Balaam son of Beor answered.
Remember ⌊your journey⌋ from Shittim[c] to Gilgal,[d]
that you may know the righteous acts[e] of the LORD."

6 With what shall I come before the LORD
and bow down before the exalted God?
Shall I come before him with burnt offerings,
with calves a year old?[f]
7 Will the LORD be pleased with thousands of rams,[g]
with ten thousand rivers of oil?[h]
Shall I offer my firstborn[i] for my transgression,
the fruit of my body for the sin of my soul?[j]
8 He has showed you, O man, what is good.
And what does the LORD require of you?
To act justly[k] and to love mercy
and to walk humbly[l] with your God.[m]

Israel's Guilt and Punishment

9 Listen! The LORD is calling to the city—
and to fear your name is wisdom—

5:15 [r]Isa 65:12
6:1 [s]Ps 50:1; Eze 6:2
6:2 [t]Dt 32:1 [u]Hos 12:2 [v]Ps 50:7
6:3 [w]Jer 2:5
6:4 [x]Dt 7:8 [y]Ex 4:16 [z]Ps 77:20 [a]Ex 15:20
6:5 [b]Nu 22:5-6 [c]Nu 25:1 [d]Jos 5:9-10 [e]Jdg 5:11; 1Sa 12:7
6:6 [f]Ps 40:6-8; 51:16-17
6:7 [g]Isa 40:16 [h]Ps 50:8-10 [i]Lev 18:21 [j]2Ki 16:3
6:8 [k]Isa 1:17; Jer 22:3 [l]Isa 57:15 [m]Dt 10:12-13; 1Sa 15:22; Hos 6:6

5:15 vengeance. By his vengeance the Lord himself redeemed his people from exile. He delivered his wronged subjects and punished the hypocrites among them, as well as their guilty oppressors.

■ **6:1—7:20** *Judgment of the Nation and Future Restoration.* In this third cycle of judgments and blessings Micah focused on the nation as a whole and the wonder of God's final salvation for his people. These chapters divide into five sections: judgments for breaking covenant (6:1–8), curses on Jerusalem (6:9–16), the disintegration of the nation (7:1–6), an expression of confidence in God's salvation (7:7) and a closing hymn of praise (7:8–20).

■ **6:1–8** *Judgment for Breaking Covenant.* This oracle follows the pattern of a covenant lawsuit in which God prosecutes and judges his people for flagrant violations of the covenant. After an introduction in verse 1a addressed to the book's audience, this oracle falls into three parts: (1) It begins with a judgment scene that includes the Lord as plaintiff, Micah as his envoy, the mountains as witnesses and Israel as the accused (vv. 1b–2). (2) The Lord then accuses the Israelites of ingratitude (v. 3) and calls them to remember (v. 5) his gracious, saving acts during Israel's formative period—from the exodus out of Egypt to the entrance into the promised land (vv. 4–5). (3) The Lord then demands justice as the prerequisite for atonement and access to his saving presence (vv. 6–8). This lawsuit, which is addressed to "My people" (v. 3,5), aims to restore, not to condemn.

6:1 case. The technical word for a covenant lawsuit. **mountains.** As Jacob and Laban piled up rocks as a witness to their covenant, so the Lord used the enduring mountains as witnesses to the covenant that Moses had mediated (Dt 4:26; 30:19; 31:28; 32:1).

6:4–5 Egypt . . . Gilgal. These two extremes—the exodus from Egypt and the entrance into the promised land—represent all of God's saving acts during Israel's formative period, including the Passover, the angel of the Lord, the crossing of the Red Sea, the provision of manna, water from the rock and victory over enemies.

6:5 Remember. This word denotes not merely recalling past events but bringing them to bear on present existence, making them effectual in the present through imagination and faith.

6:7–8 Although he appeared very religious by escalating the value of his sacrifice, the representative worshiper condemned himself. He manifested a profound unbelief in God's grace, for Israel's salvation (vv. 4–5) was free; a profound misunderstanding of his covenantal obligations, which entailed social justice and mercy, not mere liturgy (vv. 7–8); and a profound refusal to repent, for instead of asking God to change him he aimed at bribing God, along with Israel's magistrates, prophets and priests (3:11). His attempt to buy God led him to offer (in absurd fashion) "rivers of oil" and (in pagan fashion) his "firstborn."

6:8 humbly. The term may also be translated "prudently." The Lord actually required very little of his people (cf. Dt 30:11–14), but they nevertheless violated the covenant and stood condemned. See *WCF* 16.1; *WLC* 91,95,104,192; *WSC* 39.

■ **6:9–16** *Judgment of Curses on Jerusalem.* This oracle consists of an address to Jerusalem (v. 9); an accusation of using false measures (vv. 10–11) and false speech (v. 12); and a judicial sentence that consisted of disease and ruin in general (v. 13) and, more specifically, afflictions of the body (v. 14) and the pillaging of crops (v. 15). Verse 16 recapitulates the message: accusation and sen-

"Heed the rod and the One who appointed it.[a]
10 Am I still to forget, O wicked house,
your ill-gotten treasures
and the short ephah,[b] which is accursed?[n]
11 Shall I acquit a man with dishonest scales,[o]
with a bag of false weights?
12 Her rich men are violent;[p]
her people are liars[q]
and their tongues speak deceitfully.[r]
13 Therefore, I have begun to destroy[s] you,
to ruin you because of your sins.
14 You will eat but not be satisfied;[t]
your stomach will still be empty.[c]
You will store up but save nothing,[u]
because what you save I will give to the sword.
15 You will plant but not harvest;[v]
you will press olives but not use the oil on yourselves,
you will crush grapes but not drink the wine.[w]
16 You have observed the statutes of Omri[x]
and all the practices of Ahab's[y] house,
and you have followed their traditions.[z]
Therefore I will give you over to ruin[a]
and your people to derision;
you will bear the scorn[b] of the nations.[d]"

6:10 [n]Eze 45:9-10; Am 3:10; 8:4-6
6:11 [o]Lev 19:36; Hos 12:7
6:12 [p]Isa 1:23 [q]Isa 3:8 [r]Jer 9:3
6:13 [s]Isa 1:7; 6:11
6:14 [t]Isa 9:20 [u]Isa 30:6
6:15 [v]Dt 28:38; Jer 12:13 [w]Am 5:11; Zep 1:13
6:16 [x]1Ki 16:25 [y]1Ki 16:29-33 [z]Jer 7:24 [a]Jer 25:9 [b]Jer 51:51

Israel's Misery

7

What misery is mine!
I am like one who gathers summer fruit
at the gleaning of the vineyard;
there is no cluster of grapes to eat,
none of the early figs that I crave.
2 The godly have been swept from the land;[c]
not one upright man remains.
All men lie in wait to shed blood;[d]
each hunts his brother with a net.[e]
3 Both hands are skilled in doing evil;[f]
the ruler demands gifts,
the judge accepts bribes,
the powerful dictate what they desire—
they all conspire together.
4 The best of them is like a brier,[g]
the most upright worse than a thorn hedge.
The day of your watchmen has come,
the day God visits you.
Now is the time of their confusion.[h]
5 Do not trust a neighbor;
put no confidence in a friend.[i]
Even with her who lies in your embrace
be careful of your words.

7:2 [c]Ps 12:1 [d]Mic 3:10 [e]Jer 5:26
7:3 [f]Pr 4:16
7:4 [g]Eze 2:6 [h]Isa 22:5; Hos 9:7
7:5 [i]Jer 9:4

[a] *9* The meaning of the Hebrew for this line is uncertain. [b] *10* An ephah was a dry measure. [c] *14* The meaning of the Hebrew for this word is uncertain. [d] *16* Septuagint; Hebrew *scorn due my people*

tence. The sentence fulfilled the covenantal curses (cf. Lev 26; Dt 28).

6:9–11 See *HC* 110.

6:13 I have begun. Some ancient versions read "I will make you sick."

6:14 You will . . . sword. Many ancient versions suggest the reading "You shall come to labor but not bring forth. And even if you bear a child, I will give it to the sword."

6:16 See *WLC* 109.

■ **7:1–6** *Judgment of Social Disintegration.* This oracle has two parts: an accusation (the nation's crimes; vv. 1b–4a) and the sentence (national confusion; vv. 4b–6).

7:1 I. Micah, representing the Lord, compared himself to a vine dresser.

7:2 not one. The same Hebrew word rendered "none" in verse 1 links the interpretation (v. 2) to the allegory (v. 1).

7:4 watchmen. A figure for the prophets who announced the coming judgment.

7:5–6 Under the strain of a city under siege, the strongest ties of social solidarity would disintegrate. This passage was later used in apocalyptic literature to describe the eschatological day of the Lord (1 Enoch 56:7; 100:2; Jubilees 23:19; 4 Ezra 6:24; all three noncanonical books). Jesus used this passage to describe the disruption his kingdom brought to relationships (Mt 10:35–39; Lk 12:53).

6 For a son dishonors his father,
  a daughter rises up against her mother,[j]
a daughter-in-law against her mother-in-law—
  a man's enemies are the members of his own household.[k]
7 But as for me, I watch in hope[l] for the LORD,
  I wait for God my Savior;
  my God will hear[m] me.

Israel Will Rise

8 Do not gloat over me,[n] my enemy!
  Though I have fallen, I will rise.[o]
Though I sit in darkness,
  the LORD will be my light.[p]
9 Because I have sinned against him,
  I will bear the LORD's wrath,[q]
until he pleads my case
  and establishes my right.
He will bring me out into the light;
  I will see his righteousness.[r]
10 Then my enemy will see it
  and will be covered with shame,[s]
she who said to me,
  "Where is the LORD your God?"
My eyes will see her downfall;[t]
  even now she will be trampled[u] underfoot
  like mire in the streets.
11 The day for building your walls[v] will come,
  the day for extending your boundaries.
12 In that day people will come to you
  from Assyria and the cities of Egypt,
even from Egypt to the Euphrates
  and from sea to sea
  and from mountain to mountain.[w]
13 The earth will become desolate because of its inhabitants,
  as the result of their deeds.[x]

Prayer and Praise

14 Shepherd[y] your people with your staff,[z]
  the flock of your inheritance,
which lives by itself in a forest,
  in fertile pasturelands.[a]
Let them feed in Bashan and Gilead[a]
  as in days long ago.
15 "As in the days when you came out of Egypt,
  I will show them my wonders.[b]"
16 Nations will see and be ashamed,[c]
  deprived of all their power.
They will lay their hands on their mouths

7:6 [j]Eze 22:7 [k]Mt 10:35-36*
7:7 [l]Ps 130:5; Isa 25:9 [m]Ps 4:3
7:8 [n]Pr 24:17 [o]Ps 37:24; Am 9:11 [p]Isa 9:2
7:9 [q]La 3:39-40 [r]Isa 46:13
7:10 [s]Ps 35:26 [t]Isa 51:23 [u]Zec 10:5
7:11 [v]Isa 54:11
7:12 [w]Isa 19:23-25
7:13 [x]Isa 3:10-11
7:14 [y]Mic 5:4 [z]Ps 23:4 [a]Jer 50:19
7:15 [b]Ex 3:20; Ps 78:12
7:16 [c]Isa 26:11

a *14* Or *in the middle of Carmel*

7:7–9 See *WCF* 18.4.
■ **7:7** *Micah's Confidence in God.* This verse constitutes a brief statement of confidence in God as Savior.
7:7 watch. Micah was watching for salvation, in contrast to judgment (v. 4). See *WLC* 185.
■ **7:8–20** *Hymn of Praise for God's Victory.* This concluding liturgical hymn consists of four stanzas: (1) Lady Jerusalem in her fallen status confessed her faith in the Lord (vv. 8–10). (2) In response to this faith the prophet promised that she would become the eschatological sheepfold, offering salvation to a whole world under judgment (vv. 11–13). (3) Micah prayed that the Lord would miraculously shepherd his people (v. 14), the Lord responded that he would do so (v. 15) and Micah reflected that believing Israel would be saved but the unbelieving enemy conquered (vv. 16–17). (4) The people celebrated the wonder that God would hurl their sins into the sea in order to fulfill his covenantal promises to the patriarchs (vv. 18–20).
7:8 darkness. A dungeon without light is an apt figure for a trapped city under siege.
7:9 righteousness. The Lord's righteousness entailed faithful Israel's salvation (vv. 8–9) and her unbelieving tormenter's destruction (v. 10).
7:12 In that day. See 4:1 and 6 and 5:10–15. **from Egypt to the Euphrates.** See Genesis 15:18 (cf. Ex 23:31; Dt 11:24; 1Ki 4:21,25).
7:13 earth will become desolate. Outside of the elect's secure borders there would be universal judgment. The final judgment is ultimately in view.
7:16 lay . . . deaf. Signs of humiliation. They would no longer taunt Israel or listen to the vain boasts of others.

and their ears will become deaf.
17 They will lick dust like a snake,
like creatures that crawl on the ground.
They will come trembling out of their dens;
they will turn in fear[d] to the LORD our God
and will be afraid of you.
18 Who is a God like you,
who pardons sin[e] and forgives[f] the transgression
of the remnant[g] of his inheritance?[h]
You do not stay angry[i] forever
but delight to show mercy.[j]
19 You will again have compassion on us;
you will tread our sins underfoot
and hurl all our iniquities[k] into the depths of the sea.[l]
20 You will be true to Jacob,
and show mercy to Abraham,
as you pledged on oath to our fathers[m]
in days long ago.

7:17 [d]Isa 25:3; 49:23; 59:19
7:18 [e]Isa 43:25; Jer 50:20 [f]Ps 103:8-13 [g]Mic 2:12 [h]Ex 34:9 [i]Ps 103:9 [j]Jer 32:41
7:19 [k]Isa 43:25 [l]Jer 31:34
7:20 [m]Dt 7:8; Lk 1:72

7:18–20 See *HC* 19,56.
7:18 Who is . . . you . . . ? Micah—whose name means "Who is like the LORD?"—artfully associated God's name with his pardoning grace. Without that quality Micah's ministry would have been pointless. See *WLC* 179.
7:19 hurl . . . sea. As Israel's journey had begun by God hurling the Egyptians into the Red Sea, so God would consummate her history by hurling her iniquities into the metaphorical depths.
7:20 true to Jacob. God's loving fidelity to the patriarchs constitutes the basis of the church's hope (Ro 4:17; Gal 3:7–29).

NAHUM

Introduction

Overview

Author: The prophet Nahum

Purpose: To comfort Judah by announcing future judgments against Nineveh

Date: 663–612 B.C.

Key Truths:

- God's glory in judgment is worthy of praise.
- God would judge Nineveh, as well as other nations, for mistreating his people.
- God would keep his faithful people safe and restore them from destruction and exile.

Author

The name Nahum means "comfort" and is possibly an abbreviation of a fuller form, such as Nehemiah, which means "Yahweh comforts." This prophet's name is followed by the designation "the Elkoshite" (1:1), a possible reference to the location of his birth and/or his later prophetic activities. Attempts to provide a closer identification of Elkosh have been unsuccessful. Proposals have included locations near ancient Nineveh, in Galilee (e.g., Capernaum = town of Nahum) and in Judah. The internal witness of the book (1:12,15) supports Judah as the general vicinity of Nahum's prophetic activity.

As is the case in most prophetic books the prophet himself receded behind his message. Nahum was often incorrectly regarded as a narrow nationalist who, inspired by feelings of hatred and vengeance, proclaimed his message of judgment against Nineveh and at the same time extended the promise of unconditional salvation to the Judahites, his own people. This view overlooks the reality that this book belongs to the literary form of prophecies against foreign nations (e.g., Isa 13–23; Jer 46–51; Am 1–2; Ob). Nahum, as a true servant of God, was inspired by the knowledge of the Lord's universal dominion over all the kingdoms of this world. In this book we meet a prophet who was deeply aware of the incomparability and power of God. He was also a gifted poet, as was his predecessor Isaiah. Employing a wealth of imagery and pictorial language, he vividly portrayed the total destruction of Nineveh by an anonymous enemy and so voiced the universal relief and joy of all those who had suffered under the oppressive regime of this merciless tyrant.

Time and Place of Writing

The reference to the coming destruction of Nineveh provides the first clue to the date of this prophecy. Nahum announced this event (3:5–7) before it happened (612 B.C.). In 3:8 the prophet referred to the capture of Thebes, the once magnificent capital of Egypt, by the Assyrian armies of Ashurbanipal (668–627 B.C.) in 663 B.C. It is therefore clear that Nahum was a seventh-century prophet and roughly a contemporary of Zephaniah, Jeremiah and (possibly) Habakkuk.

A date between 663 and 627 B.C. is probable. During this period two major crises arose in the Assyrian Empire. One came from the side of the Medes and the advancing Scythians (642–638 B.C.). The first and major crisis of this period was the Babylonian Revolt (652–648 B.C.) under the leadership of Ashurbanipal's elder brother, who was supported by the Elamites and peoples from the Iranian highlands. Ripple effects of this revolt were experienced in Canaan and Syria. The revolt was eventually suppressed by a bitter fight that shook the empire. It seems more likely that Nahum's prophetic activities would have been associated with this first crisis rather than with the subsequent trouble with the Medes. At this time the destruction of Thebes would also still have been alive in the memory of his audience. Therefore, the most plausible date for Nahum's prophecy would be between 660 and 650 B.C., during the days of King Manasseh of Judah, a loyal vassal of Assyria.

Purpose and Distinctives

The book of Nahum has a double title. It is called "an oracle concerning Nineveh" and "the book of the vision of Nahum" (1:1). *Oracle* often indicates a divine message of judgment against a foreign nation (Isa 13:1). *Vision* refers to the unique prophetic experience of receiving the Lord's message. At times a prophet was instructed to write down a specific oracle (Isa 8:1–4; 30:8) or even "all the words" (Jer 36:2) that the Lord required him to proclaim (Jer 36:1–32). The written form then provided a strong additional witness to the certainty of the fulfillment of those divine pronouncements. The prophecy's double title therefore constitutes a strong affirmation of the authenticity of this oracle of doom against Nineveh and the inescapability of God's imminent judgment on the Assyrian kingdom.

This often neglected and sometimes disparaged (see "Introduction: Author") book provides us with an important key to understanding the past, present and future. History does not simply happen; it is determined by the will and power of God. In the opening hymn (1:2–8) and especially in 1:2–3 (the "text" of Nahum's sermon), we learn that the Lord's control over, and guidance of, history is in accordance with his character as the covenant God. He demands undivided submission everywhere and from everyone. Rejection of him and his government leads to chaos. Rebellion of this nature inevitably evokes his displeasure and divine anger and results in just retribution. God's patience must never be misconstrued as weakness. Neither corporate nor individual sins will be left unpunished. By his dynamic word he dictates the events of history. Thus Nahum proclaimed the destruction of Nineveh and invited his people to a joyful celebration of this event long before it took place. It is not the powers of this world that finally determine the course of history, but God and God alone (see theological article "Divine Sovereignty" at Ps 97).

The ancient city of Nineveh was a wicked, imperialistic and deceitful metropolis with an arrogant and unscrupulous hunger for power and domination (2:12; 3:1,4) that was manifested in merciless military violence. In addition to its military prowess Nineveh was also condemned for its ruthless trade practices and insatiable materialism (2:12; 3:16). It was to this evil city that Nahum delivered his message of divine vengeance and retribution (1:8,10,14–15; 2:10; 3:7–15). No earthly power that defies God ultimately escapes his judgment.

Judgment, however, is not the Lord's final word. His acts of retribution are also acts of redemptive judgment that stand in the service of his love for his people and his covenant with them (1:15; 2:2). He destroys the forces of chaos with the purpose of recreating a new world of freedom, peace (1:13) and lasting comfort. He knows and cares for those who trust in him (1:7).

Christ in Nahum

The book of Nahum contains no direct Messianic prophecies, yet the expectations of judgment against Nineveh and of salvation for God's faithful people are ultimately fulfilled by Christ. Jesus and his apostles declared salvation for God's people and judgment against his enemies. In fact, Christ began this judgment and salvation in his first coming (Jn 5:22–30). The spiritual warfare in which the church is constantly engaged (Mt 16:18; Eph 6:10–17) continues this process today. Moreover, when Christ returns in glory he will destroy all opposing powers and hand over the kingdom to his Father "so that God may be all in all" (1Co 15:24–28).

Outline

I. Title (1:1)	*Nahum is introduced as God's prophet and Nineveh as the subject of his message.*
II. Praise to the Divine Warrior (1:2–8)	*Nahum praised God for his glorious power in judgment against his enemies.*
III. Judgment for Nineveh and Salvation for God's People (1:9—2:2) A. Nineveh's Judgment (1:9–11) B. Judah's Salvation (1:12–13) C. Nineveh's Judgment (1:14) D. Judah's Salvation (1:15) E. Nineveh's Judgment (2:1) F. Judah and Israel's Salvation (2:2)	*Nahum declared God's severe judgment against Nineveh but assured God's people of their deliverance from oppression.*
IV. A Vivid Vision of Nineveh's End (2:3–10)	*Nahum vividly described the devastation of Nineveh.*
V. Mockery of Doomed Nineveh (2:11—3:19) A. Taunt Against Nineveh, the Lion (2:11–13) B. Woe Over Nineveh, a City Destroyed (3:1–7) C. Taunt Against Nineveh, a City Like Thebes (3:8–17) D. Applause Over Nineveh, a Fatally Wounded City (3:18–19)	*Nahum mocked doomed Nineveh.*

1 An oracle[a] concerning Nineveh.[b] The book of the vision of Nahum the Elkoshite.

The LORD's Anger Against Nineveh

2 The LORD is a jealous[c] and avenging God;
the LORD takes vengeance[d] and is filled with wrath.

1:1 [a]Isa 13:1; 19:1; Jer 23:33-34 [b]Jnh 1:2; Na 2:8; Zep 2:13
1:2 [c]Ex 20:5 [d]Dt 32:41; Ps 94:1

■ **1:1** *Title.* The title of the book is set forth (see "Introduction: Author" and "Time and Place of Writing").
■ **1:2-8** *Praise to the Divine Warrior.* The introductory hymn (vv. 2–8), resembling an acrostic poem (see "Introduction to Psalms: Structure: *Poetic Style and Devices*"), honors the Lord for his character and actions as the universal judge.
1:2–3 See *WCF* 2.1.
1:2 jealous. This attribute refers to God's passionate reaction against any infringement on his holiness or any attempt to divide his glory. His jealousy demands exclusive loyalty and reveals itself as wrath against any rejection of himself and his lordship. **avenging . . . vengeance . . . vengeance.** True to his nature the universal Judge leaves no sin unpunished and metes out the just deserts of the wicked. The repetition emphasizes the notion of an in-

The LORD takes vengeance on his foes
and maintains his wrath against his enemies.
3 The LORD is slow to anger[e] and great in power;
the LORD will not leave the guilty unpunished.[f]
His way is in the whirlwind and the storm,
and clouds[g] are the dust of his feet.
4 He rebukes the sea and dries it up;
he makes all the rivers run dry.
Bashan and Carmel[h] wither
and the blossoms of Lebanon fade.
5 The mountains quake[i] before him
and the hills melt away.[j]
The earth trembles at his presence,
the world and all who live in it.
6 Who can withstand his indignation?
Who can endure[k] his fierce anger?
His wrath is poured out like fire;[l]
the rocks are shattered[m] before him.
7 The LORD is good,[n]
a refuge in times of trouble.
He cares for[o] those who trust in him,
8 but with an overwhelming flood
he will make an end of ⌊Nineveh⌋;
he will pursue his foes into darkness.
9 Whatever they plot against the LORD
he[a] will bring to an end;
trouble will not come a second time.
10 They will be entangled among thorns[p]
and drunk from their wine;
they will be consumed like dry stubble.[b][q]
11 From you, ⌊O Nineveh,⌋ has one come forth
who plots evil against the LORD
and counsels wickedness.

1:3 [e]Ne 9:17 [f]Ex 34:7 [g]Ps 104:3
1:4 [h]Isa 33:9
1:5 [i]Ex 19:18 [j]Mic 1:4
1:6 [k]Mal 3:2 [l]Jer 10:10 [m]1Ki 19:11
1:7 [n]Jer 33:11 [o]Ps 1:6
1:10 [p]2Sa 23:6 [q]Isa 5:24; Mal 4:1

[a] 9 Or *What do you foes plot against the LORD? / He*
[b] 10 The meaning of the Hebrew for this verse is uncertain.

escapable and appropriate retribution. **foes . . . enemies.** This terminology is typical of the psalms and of holy war imagery. The nations that attacked God's covenant people were his enemies (e.g., Assyria in Ge 12:3), but the covenant people of Israel could also become his adversaries (e.g., Isa 63:10). Flagrant sin, not ethnicity, makes people foes of God (see Ro 5:10; 11:28). See *HC* 10.

1:3–6 The prophet poetically portrayed the power of the Lord as manifested in his control of nature in judgment. He is in the "whirlwind," "storm" and "clouds" (v. 3), all of which are under his control. Nature is not to be confused with God or worshiped as God; it is the theater of his revelation. See theological article "God, the Creator of Heaven and Earth" at Psalm 104.

1:3 slow to anger. A well-known confession of God's patience with his covenant people (Ex 34:6–7; Nu 14:18; Ne 9:17; Pss 86:15; 103:8; 145:8; Joel 2:13) that describes his treatment of Gentile nations as well (see Jn 4:2). **power . . . leave . . . unpunished.** God's patience never implies weakness or acceptance of evil.

1:4 He rebukes. God's word controls the forces of chaos, as at the crossings of the Red Sea (Ex 14) and the overflowing Jordan (Jos 3). **sea . . . rivers.** Used here as poetic parallels (Ps 74:12–15; Isa 50:2). The abundant vegetation of the fertile "Bashan," "Carmel" and "Lebanon" withers when the Lord causes the hot desert wind to blow over it (cf. Isa 2:13; 33:9; 35:2; Am 4:1).

1:5 The displeasure of the approaching Lord fills the earth and its creatures with terror. The creation seems threatened by chaos, for even the stable and permanent things—"the mountains . . . the earth" (v. 5)—are metaphorically portrayed as trembling and disappearing. On the great and final day of the Lord they will actually be destroyed (2Pe 3:7–12) and created anew (Rev 21:1). Compare Micah's description of God's judgment through the Assyrian invasion (Mic 1:3–4).

1:6 Who can . . . ? Who can . . . ? These rhetorical questions emphasize the inability of anyone, even a great nation like Assyria, to withstand or endure God's judgment.

1:7–8 Nahum's praise ends by contrasting God's treatment of those who trust him and those who resist him.

1:7 good . . . a refuge . . . He cares. The Lord's faithful people experience his awesome power as holy love. "Good" refers not only to God's character but also to his benevolence toward his faithful people; he is the source of all prosperity (Ps 73:1). When help is sorely needed he is a refuge, an impregnable fortress (Ps 46). **for those who trust him.** God's blessings do not come automatically. These words of assurance also called on the Judahite readers to place their trust, or reliance, upon God so that they might receive his blessings. Trust in God had been a requirement of the covenant people from the days of Moses (e.g., Dt 1:32). Israel was often called to faith in times of uncertainty and war (e.g., 2Ki 18:5; Isa 31:1; Zep 3:12).

1:8 flood . . . darkness. These images are often associated with judgment (e.g., Ge 6:17; Ex 10:21).

■ **1:9—2:2** *Judgment for Nineveh and Salvation for God's People.* Having distinguished between the Lord's goodness toward those who trust him and his judgment against his enemies (1:7), the prophet embarked on a series of judgment oracles against Nineveh that were interwoven with salvation oracles toward Judah. These verses divide into six short sections: judgment (1:9–11), salvation (1:12–13), judgment (1:14), salvation (1:15), judgment (2:1) and salvation (2:2).

■ **1:9–11** *Nineveh's Judgment.* God declared that the Assyrians would have no more victories over his people; they would fail and be destroyed.

1:9 plot. All Assyrian strategies would be futile. Their struggle and their plans were now deemed to be against the Lord, who had determined their destruction and would bring it about once and for all. **a second time.** Assyria had only one major victory over God's people: the destruction of Samaria in 722–721 B.C. (2Ki 17). The attempt to destroy Jerusalem in 701 B.C. failed (2Ki 18:13—19:37; Isa 36–37). Although the Assyrians held much power over

1:12
[r]Isa 10:34
[s]Isa 54:6-8; La 3:31-32

12 This is what the LORD says:

"Although they have allies and are numerous,
they will be cut off[r] and pass away.
Although I have afflicted you, ⌊O Judah,⌋
I will afflict you no more.[s]

1:13
[t]Isa 9:4

13 Now I will break their yoke[t] from your neck
and tear your shackles away."

1:14
[u]Isa 14:22
[v]Mic 5:13
[w]Eze 32:22-23

14 The LORD has given a command concerning you, ⌊Nineveh⌋:
"You will have no descendants to bear your name.[u]
I will destroy the carved images[v] and cast idols
that are in the temple of your gods.
I will prepare your grave,[w]
for you are vile."

1:15
[x]Isa 40:9; Ro 10:15
[y]Isa 52:7
[z]Lev 23:2-4
[a]Isa 52:1

15 Look, there on the mountains,
the feet of one who brings good news,[x]
who proclaims peace![y]
Celebrate your festivals,[z] O Judah,
and fulfill your vows.
No more will the wicked invade you;[a]
they will be completely destroyed.

Nineveh to Fall

2:1
[b]Jer 51:20

2

An attacker[b] advances against you, ⌊Nineveh⌋.
Guard the fortress,
watch the road,
brace yourselves,
marshal all your strength!

2:2
[c]Eze 37:23
[d]Isa 60:15

2 The LORD will restore[c] the splendor[d] of Jacob
like the splendor of Israel,
though destroyers have laid them waste
and have ruined their vines.

3 The shields of his soldiers are red;

Judah they never utterly destroyed the capital, Jerusalem. The Assyrian Empire fell to Babylon in 612 B.C. (see "Introduction").
1:11 one . . . who plots evil. Perhaps the Assyrian king Ashurbanipal (668–627 B.C.). **wickedness.** The word suggests something demonic, like the powers of chaos.
■ **1:12–13** *Judah's Salvation.* The prophet addressed Judah in the second person (". . . you, O Judah"; v.12). Although judgment against Assyria is mentioned (v. 11), the main focus is deliverance for Judah. The comforting oracle assured God's people that the downfall of Assyria would eventually end their humiliation.
1:12 This . . . says. The well-known prophetic messenger formula. Nahum spoke on behalf of God. **have allies and are numerous.** Nahum pronounced this prophecy while Assyria was still extremely powerful, probably during the reign of Ashurbanipal (668–627 B.C.).
1:13 break their yoke . . . tear your shackles. Vivid poetic images to describe Judah's emancipation (Ps 2:3; Jer 2:20). Judah would be Assyria's vassal state for many years, but the threat of utter defeat for Judah and Jerusalem was removed.
■ **1:14** *Nineveh's Judgment.* God declared an end to the Assyrian Empire.
1:14 command. Emphasizes God's authority to direct human history and the certainty of his will being done. **You . . . name.** Complete loss of power and prestige awaited the Assyrians for generations to come. **destroy . . . gods.** The temple and other objects of the Assyrians' trust and pride would also be destroyed. **grave . . . vile.** God had determined to bring the Assyrian king and his empire to an end; their mistreatment of his people had made them contemptible in his eyes.
■ **1:15** *Judah's Salvation.* Nahum announced that a watchman would bring good news of the defeat of Nineveh.
1:15 one who brings good news. See note on Isaiah 52:7. The approach of a herald bringing "good news," with his feet clearly visible on "the mountains" of Judah, initiates a new period of grateful service to the Lord. The "good news" is summarized in one meaningful word, "peace," which signified not only the end of hostilities but also the establishment of abundant living conditions and general well-being after the defeat of Assyria. Isaiah extended this hope of good news beyond the end of Assyrian trouble to the culmination of the Babylonian exile (Isa 52:7). Thus the New Testament draws upon the expression "good news" in its use of the term "gospel." The Christian gospel announces that Christ has brought peace and relief from the troubles of exile. At Christ's return all of God's enemies will be destroyed and his people exalted (Heb 10:13,27). **Celebrate . . . vows.** National crises or foreign oppression often made the celebration of the important feasts at the temple difficult, if not impossible. The vows made during the previous period of distress would now be fulfilled (Ps 116:14,17–19). **No more . . . invade you.** The offer of peace after the destruction of Assyria was postponed because of Hezekiah's ingratitude (Isa 39:5–7) and Judah's continued rebellion against the Lord. The Babylonian exile itself was extended because of continuing sin in Israel and Judah (Da 9). Christ began in his first coming the total and permanent removal of all threats against God's people, but he will bring this blessing to full realization when he returns (Rev 6:9–17).
■ **2:1** *Nineveh's Judgment.* In sharp contrast to the call for celebration in Judah, Nineveh was called to prepare for an attack.
2:1 attacker. Literally, "scatterer" or "disperser." The Assyrians, who had destroyed many nations, including Israel, by scattering their inhabitants over the face of the earth, would now experience a similar fate. In August 612 B.C. the combined forces of the Medes and Babylonians destroyed Nineveh, and shortly thereafter the final death knell was sounded over the Assyrian Empire.
■ **2:2** *Judah and Israel's Salvation.* The night of destruction and ruin would be turned into a new day of restoration and splendor for the people of God.
2:2 Jacob . . . Israel. Probably a reference to the southern and northern kingdoms, both of which would be restored. The New Testament explains that the splendors of restored Israel come to all (both Jews and Gentiles) who follow Christ faithfully (Mt 5:12; 1Co 3:11–15; Rev 11:18).
■ **2:3–10** *A Vivid Vision of Nineveh's End.* Nahum described with dramatic imagery how Nineveh would be captured and plun-

the warriors are clad in scarlet.[e]
The metal on the chariots flashes
on the day they are made ready;
the spears of pine are brandished.[a]
4 The chariots[f] storm through the streets,
rushing back and forth through the squares.
They look like flaming torches;
they dart about like lightning.

5 He summons his picked troops,
yet they stumble[g] on their way.
They dash to the city wall;
the protective shield is put in place.
6 The river gates[h] are thrown open
and the palace collapses.
7 It is decreed[b] that ⌊the city⌋
be exiled and carried away.
Its slave girls moan[i] like doves
and beat upon their breasts.[j]
8 Nineveh is like a pool,
and its water is draining away.
"Stop! Stop!" they cry,
but no one turns back.
9 Plunder the silver!
Plunder the gold!
The supply is endless,
the wealth from all its treasures!
10 She is pillaged, plundered, stripped!
Hearts melt, knees give way,
bodies tremble, every face grows pale.[k]

11 Where now is the lions' den,[l]
the place where they fed their young,
where the lion and lioness went,
and the cubs, with nothing to fear?
12 The lion killed[m] enough for his cubs
and strangled the prey for his mate,
filling his lairs with the kill
and his dens with the prey.

2:3 [e]Eze 23:14-15
2:4 [f]Jer 4:13
2:5 [g]Jer 46:12
2:6 [h]Na 3:13
2:7 [i]Isa 59:11 [j]Isa 32:12
2:10 [k]Isa 29:22
2:11 [l]Isa 5:29
2:12 [m]Jer 51:34

[a] *3* Hebrew; Septuagint and Syriac / *the horsemen rush to and fro* [b] *7* The meaning of the Hebrew for this word is uncertain.

---

dered. He stood, as it were, on the walls of Nineveh, witnessing the attack. This prediction was initially fulfilled when Babylon captured Nineveh in 612 B.C.; it will ultimately be fulfilled when Christ returns.
2:3 his. That is, of the Lord (v. 2). These warriors and chariots of the attackers belonged to the Lord and stood in his service. **red . . . scarlet.** These terms emphasize the awe-inspiring appearance of the approaching army, whether the color refers to their actual robes or to the blood stains on them. **metal . . . brandished.** The Hebrew is unclear but conveys the general impression of being ready and eager for war.
2:4 Nineveh was astir with the frantic activity of the defenders and/or attackers. **streets.** Possibly open fields or plains outside the city; if so, the verse denotes the approaching army and its chariots of war.
2:5 He summons. This could refer to the Assyrian king and his "picked troops," especially the commanding corps, or to the leader of the attackers laying siege to Nineveh.
2:6 river gates. Some accounts relate the fall of Nineveh to flooding when the enemy redirected the dams and sluices of the water system. The description is poetic, however, not literal. **gates.** Could simply refer to the five gates opening (3:13) in the direction of the Tigris River, with its tributaries and canals. The location of the palace excluded the possibility of collapse by flooding. **palace.** The seat of political and military organization.
2:7 the city. Nineveh, personified as a woman (a queen), would go into exile. Her "slave girls" (or "maid servants"), the inhabitants of the city, would mourn the fate of their mistress.
2:8 pool . . . draining away. This striking image portrays the slow defeat of a city under siege.
2:9 Plunder. This dramatic, imaginative exclamation describes the invaders' cry as they contemplated enjoying the rich spoils of victory. Babylonian records indicate that the plunder from Nineveh was copious.
2:10 Hearts . . . pale. The merciless devastation would create mortal fear and paralysis among the once mighty Ninevites.
■ **2:11—3:19** *Mockery of Doomed Nineveh.* Having given a vivid description of Nineveh's fall to the Babylonians, the book of Nahum closes with a collection of taunts, woes and laments over Nineveh. As sad as these words would have been for Ninevites, Judahites hearing and reading this section of Nahum would have rejoiced in the destruction of their enemy. These verses divide into four sections: taunt against Nineveh, the lion (2:11–13); woe over Nineveh, a city destroyed (3:1–7); taunt against Nineveh, a city like Thebes (3:8–17); and applause over Nineveh, a fatally wounded city (3:18–19).
■ **2:11–13** *Taunt Against Nineveh, the Lion.* This is a taunt song in which Nineveh is likened to a lion. The song mocks the city for its future humiliation.
2:11–12 Where . . . where . . . ? A poetic device to express how the once famous city would be reduced to oblivion.
2:12 lion . . . dens. An apt image to describe the aggressive, ruthless, rapacious and fearsome Assyrians. This menace would soon be terminated.

2:13 [n]Jer 21:13; Na 3:5 [o]Ps 46:9

13 "I am against[n] you,"
declares the LORD Almighty.
"I will burn up your chariots in smoke,[o]
and the sword will devour your young lions.
I will leave you no prey on the earth.
The voices of your messengers
will no longer be heard."

Woe to Nineveh

3:1 [p]Eze 22:2; Mic 3:10

3 Woe to the city of blood,[p]
full of lies,
full of plunder,
never without victims!
2 The crack of whips,
the clatter of wheels,
galloping horses
and jolting chariots!
3 Charging cavalry,
flashing swords
and glittering spears!
Many casualties,
piles of dead,
bodies without number,
people stumbling over the corpses[q]—

3:3 [q]2Ki 19:35; Isa 34:3

4 all because of the wanton lust of a harlot,
alluring, the mistress of sorceries,[r]
who enslaved nations by her prostitution[s]
and peoples by her witchcraft.

3:4 [r]Isa 47:9 [s]Isa 23:17; Eze 16:25-29

5 "I am against[t] you," declares the LORD Almighty.
"I will lift your skirts[u] over your face.
I will show the nations your nakedness[v]
and the kingdoms your shame.

3:5 [t]Na 2:13 [u]Jer 13:22 [v]Isa 47:3

6 I will pelt you with filth,[w]
I will treat you with contempt[x]
and make you a spectacle.[y]

3:6 [w]Job 9:31 [x]1Sa 2:30; Jer 51:37 [y]Isa 14:16

7 All who see you will flee from you and say,
'Nineveh[z] is in ruins—who will mourn for her?'[a]
Where can I find anyone to comfort[b] you?"

3:7 [z]Na 1:1 [a]Jer 15:5 [b]Isa 51:19

8 Are you better than[c] Thebes,[a][d]

3:8 [c]Am 6:2 [d]Jer 46:25

[a] *8* Hebrew *No Amon*

2:13 I am against you. From a merely human vantage point Nineveh's destruction would take place through the attack of another nation, but God revealed that Nineveh was about to confront the wrath of Israel's God. **messengers.** The voices of the Assyrian envoys dictating terms and exacting tribute would be permanently silenced on the face of the earth.

■ **3:1–7** *Woe Over Nineveh, a City Destroyed.* Nahum pronounced woe over the Assyrian capital, mocking Nineveh, for her glory would soon be overturned by the Babylonians. The pronouncement consisted of an accusation (v. 1), the judgment (vv. 2–3), an accusation (v. 4) and the judgment (vv. 5–7).

3:1 Woe. Introduces a dire threat. **city of blood.** Emphasizes the merciless cruelty about which the Assyrians openly boasted in their official records. Isaiah accused Jerusalem in a similar way (Isa 1:15). **lies.** Deceitful diplomacy characterized the Ninevites' international dealings (Isa 36:16–17). **plunder.** See 2:12–13. In their insatiable greed, the Assyrians constantly victimized more and more people.

3:2–3 Nahum described the destruction of Nineveh with one of the most vivid portrayals of a battle scene in the Old Testament. The staccato beat, word economy and gruesome detail create an image of the Assyrian armies reducing whole populations to "piles of dead" (v. 3).

3:4 because of. The prophet returned to the accusation or reason for the judgment. **harlot . . . mistress of sorceries.** The imagery changes and Nineveh is likened to a beautiful and seductive "harlot" to whom "nations" and "peoples" were enslaved. Jerusalem was also described as a harlot because of infidelity to the Lord (Eze 16; 23; Hos 1). Warfare, commerce and service of the gods were closely intertwined in the ancient world. Nahum offered an ironic characterization of the pagan religion of Nineveh (Isa 47:11–15; cf. Rev 17:5).

3:5 The prophecy returns to the judgment that is appropriate for the preceding accusation. **lift your skirts.** Refers to the public humiliation with which harlots were punished and with which the women in covenant breaking communities were threatened in inscriptions outside of the Bible (see Isa 47:2–3).

3:6 contempt . . . spectacle. The image of the harlot continues. She would be made an object of scorn and an example to deter similar conduct in others.

3:7 Nineveh is in ruins. The sight would be so terrible that neither mourner nor comforter would do what was expected from them.

■ **3:8–17** *Taunt Against Nineveh, a City Like Thebes.* Nineveh's judgment could not be averted any more than the strength of Thebes had secured this Egyptian stronghold against Assyria. Nineveh would share the fate of magnificent Thebes.

3:8 Thebes. The Hebrew reads "No Amon," which means "the city of [the god] Amon." This ancient and magnificent metropolis of Upper Egypt was conquered by the Assyrians in 663 B.C. despite its strategic position on the Nile, with the natural defense of waters from moats and canals as its walls. The mention of Thebes's defeat places Nahum's ministry after 663 B.C.

situated on the Nile,[e]
with water around her?
The river was her defense,
the waters her wall.
9 Cush[a][f] and Egypt were her boundless strength;
Put[g] and Libya[h] were among her allies.
10 Yet she was taken captive[i]
and went into exile.
Her infants were dashed[j] to pieces
at the head of every street.
Lots were cast for her nobles,
and all her great men were put in chains.
11 You too will become drunk;[k]
you will go into hiding[l]
and seek refuge from the enemy.
12 All your fortresses are like fig trees
with their first ripe fruit;
when they are shaken,
the figs[m] fall into the mouth of the eater.
13 Look at your troops—
they are all women![n]
The gates[o] of your land
are wide open to your enemies;
fire has consumed their bars.[p]

14 Draw water for the siege,[q]
strengthen your defenses![r]
Work the clay,
tread the mortar,
repair the brickwork!
15 There the fire will devour you;
the sword will cut you down
and, like grasshoppers, consume you.
Multiply like grasshoppers,
multiply like locusts![s]
16 You have increased the number of your merchants
till they are more than the stars of the sky,
but like locusts they strip the land
and then fly away.
17 Your guards are like locusts,[t]
your officials like swarms of locusts
that settle in the walls on a cold day—

3:8 [e]Isa 19:6-9
3:9 [f]2Ch 12:3 [g]Eze 27:10 [h]Eze 30:5
3:10 [i]Isa 20:4 [j]Isa 13:16; Hos 13:16
3:11 [k]Isa 49:26 [l]Isa 2:10
3:12 [m]Isa 28:4
3:13 [n]Isa 19:16; Jer 50:37 [o]Na 2:6 [p]Isa 45:2
3:14 [q]2Ch 32:4 [r]Na 2:1
3:15 [s]Joel 1:4
3:17 [t]Jer 51:27

[a] 9 That is, the upper Nile region

3:9 Thebes had at its disposal natural resources and strong political allies, but these were of no avail. **Put.** The location is uncertain.
3:10 The conquerors showed no mercy to infants and meted out harsh treatment to nobles and other notable men.
3:11 **drunk.** Probably refers to the cup of the Lord's anger from which all who defy him are forced to drink (Isa 51:17–23). In her distress Nineveh would attempt to hide and seek refuge, but only the Lord can provide safe haven in times of trouble (1:7). Compared to him the most powerful is weak and vulnerable (vv. 12–17).
3:12 **fig trees.** This telling image emphasizes both the desirability and the easy accessibility of normally impregnable fortifications.
3:13 In the face of the approaching enemy all the Assyrian troops were like women—not trained for, and therefore inept at warfare. All barriers to inhibit the progress of the enemy—like gates and bars—had been removed.
3:14 Frantic efforts would be made to "strengthen . . . defenses" and to prepare for a lengthy period of siege. The imperatives are ironic, and verses 14–17 reflect the mood of a taunt song.
3:15 Even the most strenuous efforts to avoid invasion were of no avail. The city and its people would succumb to fire and sword.
3:16 **merchants.** Nahum referred to Assyria's extensive trade and commercial activities that brought wealth to Nineveh. Under pressure from outside, the self-interest of these traders would become clear. **like locusts.** They would grab whatever they could and disappear.
3:17 **guards . . . officials.** These two terms are very unusual in Hebrew and may even be Assyrian loanwords. They probably represent important officials in the government of the vast empire who would run for safety when things became dangerous, contributing to the city's precarious situation. In the hour of distress riches, power and organization would fail miserably.
■ **3:18–19** *Applause Over Nineveh, a Fatally Wounded City.* The finality of divine judgment on the cruel oppressor would lead to rejoicing among all those peoples Assyria had oppressed. These verses form an appropriate conclusion to the mocking against Nineveh throughout this section.
3:18 **shepherds.** A well-known metaphor for rulers, it here indicates the subordinate officials of the Assyrian king. **slumber . . . lie down.** Euphemisms referring to death. **Your people . . . gather them.** The image of the shepherd is carried over to include that of the people as a flock. **people.** Refers to the army (v. 13) or to the population in general who, with the defeat and loss of its leaders, were "scattered."

but when the sun appears they fly away,
and no one knows where.

3:18
[u]Ps 76:5-6
[v]Isa 56:10
[w]1Ki 22:17

3:19
[x]Jer 30:13; Mic 1:9
[y]Job 27:23; La 2:15; Zep 2:15

18 O king of Assyria, your shepherds[a] slumber;[u]
your nobles lie down to rest.[v]
Your people are scattered[w] on the mountains
with no one to gather them.
19 Nothing can heal your wound;[x]
your injury is fatal.
Everyone who hears the news about you
claps his hands[y] at your fall,
for who has not felt
your endless cruelty?

[a] 18 Or *rulers*

3:19 Everyone . . . claps his hands. Nineveh's incurable "wound" and fatal "injury" would be received with applause by all but the Assyrians. The jealous and avenging God of Israel would finally put an end to the "endless cruelty" and wickedness that had caused suffering everywhere. The vision of Nahum came to initial fruition in 612 B.C. but awaits its ultimate fulfillment at the second coming of our Lord Jesus Christ.

HABAKKUK

Introduction

Overview

Author: The prophet Habakkuk

Purpose: To guide Israel toward faith in God during the trials of the Babylonian conquest and exile by displaying the prophet's personal struggle and resolution

Date: 605–600 B.C.

Key Truths:

- God will not tolerate severe sinfulness among his people forever.
- God may use wicked unbelievers to chastise his people.
- Believers should honestly acknowledge before God the various difficulties they face.
- Believers should learn to trust God, even when circumstances are difficult.

Author

The opening verse explicitly identifies "Habakkuk the prophet" as the author of this book. The meaning of his name is uncertain. It may be connected with the Hebrew root "to embrace" or with the name of an Assyrian plant called "hambakuku." The former meaning may refer to Habakkuk's embrace of the Lord or vice versa; the latter may suggest a penetration of Assyrian culture into Judahite society. The reference in 1:1 to Habakkuk as "the prophet" may imply that he was well known. His use of the worship and wisdom traditions of Israel in his preaching has led some interpreters to the doubtful notion that he was a prophet attached to the temple in Jerusalem. The suggestion that he simply worked in Jerusalem is more likely because he was deeply concerned with matters related to Jerusalem. What is certain is that in this book we meet Habakkuk as a true prophet with a burning zeal for the glory of the Lord. His "oracle" (1:1) is unusual in that it is not primarily a word directed to the people but an answer to his own painful questions.

Time and Place of Writing

The only objective evidence for the dating of Habakkuk's prophetic activity is provided by 1:6. The reference to the Babylonians (lit., "Chaldeans") as the threatening new world power indicates a period prior to Judah's subjugation by the armies of Nebuchadnezzar. This threat became a reality in 597 B.C., when the Babylonians captured Jerusalem and deported the young king Jehoiachin to Babylon (2Ki 24:8–17). Habakkuk lived during the period of Jehoiakim's reign (608–598 B.C.) and was a younger contemporary of Jeremiah. An important event during this period was the defeat at Carchemish of Pharaoh Neco and his Egyptian army by Prince Nebuchadnezzar of Babylonia in 605 B.C. Shortly after Babylon gained this victory over Egypt, Judah and a number of other kingdoms became subject to the powerful Babylonians. A date between 605 and 600 B.C. may therefore be an appropriate conjecture of the time in which Habakkuk had his inspired vision. During this time the Babylonians became the dominating force on the international scene, mercilessly sweeping aside any opposition (1:5–17). The evil reign of Jehoiakim formed a sad contrast to that of his father, the good king Josiah (see Jer 22:13–19,25–26). It was a period of spiritual deterioration in which the covenant people increasingly lost their unique character (1:2–4).

Original Audience

Habakkuk appears to have written to the Judahites still living in the promised land (the northern tribes had been taken into captivity in 722 B.C.). The Judahites had committed grave covenant violations, including committing violence against one another and perverting justice (1:2–4), such that God was about to judge them severely by exiling them from the promised land (exile took place in 597 B.C.).

Purpose and Distinctives

In many respects Habakkuk closely resembled his contemporary Jeremiah, for he was deeply concerned with the waywardness of God's people and the further difficulties they were about to endure. Habakkuk's concern demonstrated itself in dialogues with, and persistent appeals to, God (2:1–2; 3:2,16) rather than in prophetic preaching. The book records how the prophet moved from severe grief and doubt to trust and hope through prayer to God.

Habakkuk, a man with a burning passion for the honor of his holy God (1:12; 3:3), experienced a profound spiritual crisis because of the Lord's apparent indifference to appalling spiritual conditions among his people (1:2–4). The absence of covenant life and obedience was not only dangerous to the people of God but also an insult to, and a rejection of, the covenant Lord himself. Because only divine intervention could bring about a reversal of this lethal situation, Habakkuk urgently and persistently (but seemingly in vain) appealed to the heavenly Judge (1:2). In response the Lord revealed that the Babylonians who were then appearing on the scene of history (1:6) would be his instrument of judgment. This cure sounded even worse than the disease and added to the prophet's distress (1:5–17). How could the holy God, for whom it is impossible to tolerate wrong (1:3–13), use these wicked people for the fulfillment of his purposes? Does God really maintain the difference between evil and good in the outcome of history?

Convinced that the events of history were not determined by blind fate but by the living God of Israel, Habakkuk stationed himself in expectant waiting on the Lord until he received an answer to his painful questions (2:1). The Lord's subsequent reply or revelation (literally, "vision"; see 2:2–3) provides his people with a true perspective on the promised outcome of history. It does not resolve all the painful questions, but it does teach the secret of covenant life in the here and now of history (2:3–4); that is, perseverance, patience and hopeful expectation in waiting for the coming fulfillment of the Lord's unfailing promise. In spite of the inscrutability of his ways, God's purposes are consistent and will culminate in eternal life for the faithful and righteous but woe and death for the self-sufficient and arrogant (2:4–19). The Lord's presence in his temple affirms his lordship over history and carries the assurance that, in the end, his legitimate claim to the whole world will be universally acknowledged (2:14,20; Isa 45:21–25; 1Co 15:28).

The revelation of the Lord's purposeful guidance of history transformed Habakkuk's complaint into a hymn of prayer, praise and joy (3:2–20). Instead of passively waiting for divine intervention, he began to positively pray that the Lord would again act in accordance with his mighty deeds and with his qualities as displayed in the exodus and at Sinai. In his prayer the future moved into the present. In anticipation he celebrated the Lord's coming (3:3–7) and his conflict against (3:8–12) and triumph over all opposition in nature and history (3:13–15). Nothing, not even the possibility of the severest calamities, could any longer dampen Habakkuk's overwhelming joy in the expectation of the coming salvation guaranteed by the Lord's faithfulness to himself and to his revelation (3:17–19).

Christ in Habakkuk

When Paul, in his letter to the Romans, looked for an appropriate text on which to base his understanding of the gospel, he chose Habakkuk 2:4 in the Septuagint, the Greek translation of the Old Testament (Ro 1:17; cf. Gal 3:11; Heb 10:37–38). Like Habakkuk (ch. 1), Paul was convinced that wickedness and sin are incompatible with God's holiness and that this tension can be resolved only by divine intervention. The prophetic word to Habakkuk (ch. 2) reveals in principle the way by which God will ultimately deal through Christ with the incompatibility between sin and holiness. The cross of Christ and the final judgment at his return are fulfillments of this revelation. Paul, like Habakkuk, affirmed that true life is possible only in a relationship of total dependence on the Lord. Such dependence, based on the faithfulness of our God, transforms our very existence in this world by filling our lives with joy and hope in the expectation of the final fulfillment of all his promises (ch. 3; cf. 2:3). In this way, Habakkuk can be called the great-grandfather of the Reformation. The key concepts of his preaching, taken over by Paul, deeply influenced men like Luther and Calvin and eventually became key slogans in Reformation faith. Only faith—that persevering and obedient trust in the God of Habakkuk, the God and Father of our Lord Jesus Christ—provides the key to meaningful existence in the world during this period between Christ's first coming and his return.

Outline

I. Title (1:1)

Habakkuk introduced himself as the author.

II. First Complaint and Response (1:2–11)
- A. Habakkuk's Complaint About Judah (1:2–4)
- B. Divine Response of Babylonian Judgment (1:5–11)

Habakkuk complained that wickedness had grown in Judah with little response from God. God promised to punish Judah's wickedness by sending the Babylonians.

III. Second Complaint and Response (1:12—2:20)
- A. Habakkuk's Complaint About the Babylonians (1:12—2:1)
- B. Divine Response of Judgment for Wicked (2:2–20)
  1. A Crucial Distinction (2:2–5)
  2. Woes Against the Wicked (2:6–20)

Habakkuk complained that the Babylonians were even more wicked than the Judahites. God promised that eventually the Babylonians would be destroyed.

IV. Closing Prayer of Resolve and Faith (3:1–19)
- A. Superscription (3:1)
- B. Invocation (3:2)
- C. Divine Theophany (3:3–15)
- D. Faith's Expectation (3:16–19a)
- E. Postscript (3:19b)

Habakkuk expressed his trust that God would keep his promise. He pledged to praise him, even as the difficult times continued.

1 The oracle[a] that Habakkuk the prophet received.

Habakkuk's Complaint

2 How long, O LORD, must I call for help,
but you do not listen?[b]
Or cry out to you, "Violence!"
but you do not save?[c]
3 Why do you make me look at injustice?
Why do you tolerate[d] wrong?
Destruction and violence[e] are before me;
there is strife,[f] and conflict abounds.
4 Therefore the law[g] is paralyzed,
and justice never prevails.
The wicked hem in the righteous,
so that justice is perverted.[h]

The LORD's Answer

5 "Look at the nations and watch—
and be utterly amazed.[i]
For I am going to do something in your days
that you would not believe,
even if you were told.[j]
6 I am raising up the Babylonians,[a][k]
that ruthless and impetuous people,
who sweep across the whole earth
to seize dwelling places not their own.[l]
7 They are a feared and dreaded people;[m]
they are a law to themselves
and promote their own honor.

1:1 [a]Na 1:1
1:2 [b]Ps 13:1-2; 22:1-2 [c]Jer 14:9
1:3 [d]ver 13 [e]Jer 20:8 [f]Ps 55:9
1:4 [g]Ps 119:126 [h]Job 19:7; Isa 1:23; 5:20; Eze 9:9
1:5 [i]Isa 29:9 [j]Ac 13:41*
1:6 [k]2Ki 24:2 [l]Jer 13:20
1:7 [m]Isa 18:7; Jer 39:5-9

[a] 6 Or *Chaldeans*

■ **1:1** *Title.* The opening verse gives rise to the title of the book by introducing Habakkuk as author and prophet.
1:1 oracle. This term may mean "to lift up the voice" and is often, though not always, a technical term for an oracle of judgment against a foreign nation (e.g., Isa 13:1; 15:1; Na 1:1). **Habakkuk the prophet.** See "Introduction: Author." **received.** Literally, "saw." The word reminds the reader of the supernatural reception of divine revelation by the prophet.
■ **1:2–11** *First Complaint and Response.* The first section of the book concerns the problem of wickedness in Judah. It divides into two main sections: Habakkuk's complaint about wickedness (1:2–4) and God's response to the prophet (1:5–11).
■ **1:2–4** *Habakkuk's Complaint About Judah.* The sinfulness of many in Judah grieved and shocked the prophet. Many Judahites no longer lived according to the stipulations of the covenants with Abraham, Moses and David (see theological article "The Covenants of Works and Grace" at Ge 6). Habakkuk was even more concerned about the Lord's apparent lack of response to Judah's sin. Flagrant covenant violations required curses and judgments (Ge 18:25; Dt 28:15–68; 30:11–19). The prophet therefore appealed to the Lord in language reminiscent of the psalms of individual lament (see "Introduction to Psalms") to redress a seemingly hopeless situation.
1:2 How long . . . ? The honest question of one who has endured much suffering. This question is characteristic of the psalms of lament (Pss 13:2; 62:3; Jer 47:6), and even the martyrs in heaven ask it (Rev 6:10). With the proper motives, the question indicates faithfulness in its appeal to the Lord as the final Judge. **call for help.** This is one word in Hebrew, indicating the loud cry of someone in deep distress (e.g., Pss 22:24; 30:2). **you do not listen . . . do not save.** These words express the painful experience of the Lord's seeming indifference and inactivity in the face of undeserved suffering. **Violence!** This term summarizes the deliberate, brutal and insensitive infringement on the rights and privileges of God's people and their exploitation and oppression by some powerful Judahites.
1:3 Why . . . ? The question continues the complaint (see Ps 22:1; La 5:20). **injustice.** A reference to the misuse of power. **tolerate.** Literally, "look on" or "observe"; that is, continue to act like an unconcerned spectator. Words for seeing occur regularly and are significant in Habakkuk (e.g., vv. 5,13). **wrong.** The distress, exhaustion and despondency experienced by all those who suffered under those circumstances. **Destruction . . . me.** The festering and proliferating nature of unchecked wickedness resulted in strife and conflict and a divided community riddled with suspicions, accusations and personal attacks.
1:4 law. The divine guideline and standard for covenant life was the Law of Moses as it had been shaped by further revelation through the covenant with David. **wicked.** A collective noun, it here refers to those in Israel who spurned the Lord's law. **hem in.** A military term for acting in a hostile manner by surrounding or encircling (Jdg 20:43; Pss 22:12; 142:7). **the righteous.** Habakkuk did not have in mind moral perfection (a standard no one could meet). Rather, he was referring to those who accepted the Lord's law as the norm for their lives and strove to obey it in faith. **perverted.** Crooked or distorted. See *WLC* 145.
■ **1:5–11** *Divine Response of Babylonian Judgment.* The prophet reported that the Lord would send the Babylonians to judge his people for their wickedness. The Lord is never indifferent to the sins of his people. Rather, he is active on a universal scale to bring about the triumph of his kingdom and the downfall of the wicked. The triumph of his kingdom, however, requires the purging of the wicked within it.
1:5 Look . . . watch . . . be . . . amazed. The prophet urged the people to pay attention to the spectacle of God's just and holy method of dealing with sinful Judah. The victory of the wicked over "those more righteous" (v. 13) would pose a stumbling block to faith among Habakkuk's audience. Later, Paul used this verse to urge the Jews in his day not to stumble over the spectacle of the crucifixion of the righteous Jesus (Ac 13:41). God commonly uses wicked people to accomplish his righteous ends (e.g., Ac 4:27–28), including the judgment and discipline of his people.
1:6 I am raising up. God controls every power in history, including the military force that was appearing on the horizon of history in Habakkuk's day: the aggressive Babylonians.
1:7 law to themselves. The arrogant enemy's actions were determined only by what they judged would enhance their own importance.

1:8 [n]Jer 4:13

8 Their horses are swifter[n] than leopards,
fiercer than wolves at dusk.
Their cavalry gallops headlong;
their horsemen come from afar.
They fly like a vulture swooping to devour;
9 they all come bent on violence.
Their hordes[a] advance like a desert wind
and gather prisoners[o] like sand.

1:9 [o]Hab 2:5

1:10 [p]2Ch 36:6

10 They deride kings
and scoff at rulers.[p]
They laugh at all fortified cities;
they build earthen ramps and capture them.

1:11 [q]Jer 4:11-12 [r]Da 4:30

11 Then they sweep past like the wind[q] and go on—
guilty men, whose own strength is their god."[r]

Habakkuk's Second Complaint

1:12 [s]Isa 31:1 [t]Isa 10:6

12 O LORD, are you not from everlasting?
My God, my Holy One,[s] we will not die.
O LORD, you have appointed[t] them to execute judgment;
O Rock, you have ordained them to punish.

1:13 [u]La 3:34-36

13 Your eyes are too pure to look on evil;
you cannot tolerate wrong.[u]
Why then do you tolerate the treacherous?
Why are you silent while the wicked
swallow up those more righteous than themselves?
14 You have made men like fish in the sea,
like sea creatures that have no ruler.

1:15 [v]Isa 19:8 [w]Jer 16:16

15 The wicked foe pulls all of them up with hooks,[v]
he catches them in his net,[w]
he gathers them up in his dragnet;
and so he rejoices and is glad.

1:16 [x]Jer 44:8

16 Therefore he sacrifices to his net
and burns incense[x] to his dragnet,
for by his net he lives in luxury
and enjoys the choicest food.

1:17 [y]Isa 14:6; 19:8

17 Is he to keep on emptying his net,
destroying nations without mercy?[y]

2:1 [z]Isa 21:8 [a]Ps 48:13

2 I will stand at my watch[z]
and station myself on the ramparts;[a]

[a] 9 The meaning of the Hebrew for this word is uncertain.

1:8–9 Vivid poetic imagery portrays the speed and purposefulness of these fierce and overpowering warriors.
1:10 They . . . them. The intimidating Babylonian armies looked at obstacles as challenges and treated their opposition with contempt.
■ **1:12—2:20** *Second Complaint and Response.* Having reported how God was going to send the Babylonians to punish Judah, Habakkuk moved to a second lament over the apparent injustice of such a response from God. It is likely that some Babylonian incursion or injustice toward Judah after the first complaint and response (1:1–10) had given Habakkuk stimulus for this complaint. This section divides into two parts: the prophet's complaint about the Babylonians (1:12—2:1) and God's response (2:2–20).
■ **1:12—2:1** *Habakkuk's Complaint About the Babylonians.* The prophet wondered why the Lord would use the wicked Babylonians to chastise his own people. Did this course of action violate God's character? Habakkuk's lament reflected his deep perplexity.
1:12 everlasting. The covenant Lord was there from the very beginning. As the Lord of history and of his people, he had the freedom to choose his agents of chastisement. **My.** Habakkuk's personal relationship to an incomparable God ("Holy One") transformed his confusion into the conviction that the present painful experience would not be the end. **O Rock.** This ancient Mosaic name for God (Ge 49:24; Dt 32:4) emphasizes divine dependability and protection, often with royal connotations (see note on 1Co 10:3–4).
1:13 tolerate wrong . . . tolerate the treacherous. The prophet faced a serious theological problem: God is pure and holy; therefore, in one sense he cannot tolerate sin. Yet God used the treacherous Babylonians as his instrument of judgment. The difficulty of reconciling God's intolerance of sin with his apparent tolerance, and even use, of the wicked lies at the heart of many Biblical laments. Knowing that God is sovereign and good leads to the perplexing problem of how evil fits within his plans. As important as it is to struggle honestly with this question, it ultimately drives the true believer to humble faith and trust, as it did Habakkuk (3:1–19). See *WLC* 152.
1:14 You. A bold accusation by Habakkuk. He argued that if the Lord tolerated the evil actions of the Babylonians, he was responsible for what happened to their victims. **men like fish.** Violence robs human beings of their dignity as images of God (Ge 1:26) and treats them like the creatures that were subjected to them at creation (Ps 8:6–8).
1:15–16 hooks . . . net. Fishing imagery dominates these verses, including the relishing of a successful catch.
1:16 sacrifices. The instruments of success are idolized and worshiped. See verse 11. See also *WLC* 105.
1:17 The fishing imagery (i.e., the cruel annihilation of other nations) is explained. In Babylonia fishing was important in areas with an abundant water supply. Babylonian art also portrayed prisoners of war in nets. See Jeremiah 16:16.
2:1 Habakkuk's anguished questioning drove him back to the fount of all wisdom to wait for an answer. His words indicate his de-

I will look to see what he will say[b] to me,
and what answer I am to give to this complaint.[a][c]

The LORD's Answer

2 Then the LORD replied:

"Write[d] down the revelation
and make it plain on tablets
so that a herald[b] may run with it.
3 For the revelation awaits an appointed time;
it speaks of the end[e]
and will not prove false.
Though it linger, wait[f] for it;
it[c] will certainly come and will not delay.[g]

4 "See, he is puffed up;
his desires are not upright—
but the righteous will live by his faith[d][h]—
5 indeed, wine[i] betrays him;
he is arrogant and never at rest.
Because he is as greedy as the grave[e]
and like death is never satisfied,[j]
he gathers to himself all the nations
and takes captive all the peoples.

6 "Will not all of them taunt[k] him with ridicule and scorn, saying,

" 'Woe to him who piles up stolen goods

2:1 [b]Ps 85:8 [c]Ps 5:3

2:2 [d]Rev 1:19

2:3 [e]Da 8:17; 10:14 [f]Ps 27:14 [g]Eze 12:25; Heb 10:37-38

2:4 [h]Ro 1:17*; Gal 3:11*; Heb 10:37-38*

2:5 [i]Pr 20:1 [j]Pr 27:20; 30:15-16

2:6 [k]Isa 14:4

[a] *1* Or *and what to answer when I am rebuked* [b] *2* Or *so that whoever reads it* [c] *3* Or *Though he linger, wait for him; / he* [d] *4* Or *faithfulness* [e] *5* Hebrew *Sheol*

termination and perseverance to wait for an answer. Revelation can never be forced. **watch . . . ramparts.** Military terms picture the circumstances of Habakkuk's waiting and do not necessarily refer to a place in the temple.

■ **2:2–20** *Divine Response of Judgment for Wicked.* God responded to Habakkuk by affirming that there will be life for the righteous and woe for the wicked. God will show that he is just to those who have faith in him. The final outcome of history will be worship of the one holy and just King (v. 20). The destiny of peoples or of individual persons will be determined by their attitude toward the King. This material divides into two parts: God's revelation of a crucial distinction (2:2–5) and the movement from woe to worship (2:6–20).

■ **2:2–5** *A Crucial Distinction.* In response to the prophet's complaint about the Babylonians, the Lord revealed a crucial distinction between the righteous and the wicked.

2:2 Write. See Nahum 1:1. The preservation and transmission of God's answer required writing. This principle undergirds the doctrine of Scripture as the authoritative revelation of God. **revelation.** Literally, "vision." It consisted of words and deeds. **tablets.** The plural may indicate one large tablet. **so . . . it.** Or "so that whoever reads what was clearly written may do so swiftly"; that is, with ease and immediate understanding. See NIV text note. **herald.** The courier who was to read the message.

2:3 appointed time . . . not delay. A fixed period of time was to elapse before the revelation would be fulfilled. This lingering was not to be seen as failure or deception. Rather, it was a time that was to be met with the Lord's guarantee of approaching fulfillment. Long after Habakkuk's vision, judgment on the Babylonians was executed through Cyrus on October 29, 539 B.C.

2:4 Having told Habakkuk to record the revelation he had been given and to wait for its fulfillment (vv. 2–3), the Lord disclosed the essential distinction between the wicked (here, the Babylonians) and the righteous (here, the remnant of Judah): By their evil desires and deeds, the wicked will take a path that leads to death and defeat; by faith the righteous will take a path that leads to life and victory. This distinction was a word of comfort to Habakkuk and marked the turning point in his struggle to reconcile God's holiness with God's use of the wicked Babylonians as a rod of judgment against his people. **he.** The Babylonian king and kingdom, the embodiment of wickedness in the world. **puffed up.** Compare 1:7 and 10–11. The words describe the Babylonians' attitude of boastful pride and arrogant self-trust, the opposite of humble trust in the living God. **desires are not upright.** The whole inward disposition of the Babylonians was one that rejected what was right and what led to life. **but.** Parenthetically, the Lord contrasted the future of the righteous with that of the wicked. **the righteous will live by his faith.** Here was the awaited word of comfort for Habakkuk and the remnant. In the midst of a land filled with wickedness (1:2–4) and subject to God's wrath, the Lord promised that there would be a righteous remnant in Judah who would take a path that would lead to life by trusting in him who in his wrath still remembers mercy (3:2). The clause recalls the words of Genesis 15:6 and applies them to Habakkuk's situation. In Genesis 15:1–6, the Lord promised to give life to Abraham's as-good-as-dead body in order that he might have children (Ro 4:18–21; Heb 11:11–12). In Habakkuk, the Lord promised life (and victory) to the righteous remnant in as good-as-dead Judah, just as he had given life (and victory) to the nation of Israel through the exodus (3:13–19). As by faith Abraham had waited patiently for God to do what he had promised (Heb 6:13–15), so Habakkuk and the remnant were to wait patiently for God to do the same on their behalf (v. 3; 3:16). In Habakkuk's day, the blessing of life was secured by faith in the God who gives life to the dead. In Paul's day, that same blessing was secured by faith that explicitly focused on Jesus, who had been raised from the dead (Ro 4:24–25). The same is true in our day. See *BC* 24; *HC* 59.

2:5 wine . . . rest. This striking metaphor adds to the picture of the blind arrogance of the wicked, here typified by the Babylonians (see v. 4). Like those besotted with wine, they inexorably plunged ahead on their fatal course. **Because . . . peoples.** Pride is insatiable in its merciless passion for self-aggrandizement.

■ **2:6–20** *Woes Against the Wicked.* This section forms a distinct literary unit that is connected by verse 5 to the revelation Habakkuk received. The wicked Babylonians could not escape divine judgment. God pronounced their doom in prophetic woes (Na 3:1–19), presented here in a taunting song (see Isa 13–14), a poetic form expressing the glee of the persecuted and suffering at the demise of the tyrant. This portion divides into five separate woes: 2:6–8; 2:9–11; 2:12–14; 2:15–18; 2:19–20.

2:6–8 The first woe dooms the wicked for their unscrupulous greed for power and possessions.

2:6 all of them. Judah and all those who suffered under the Babylonian oppressor. The woe oracles are depicted in such general and proverbial colors that they acquire a future perspective and a universal applicability to the struggle of the persecuted against the persecutor. **Woe.** This cry of anguish, derived from the funeral lament, detects the odor of death in the shameless deeds of the

and makes himself wealthy by extortion![l]
How long must this go on?'
7 Will not your debtors[a] suddenly arise?
Will they not wake up and make you tremble?
Then you will become their victim.[m]
8 Because you have plundered many nations,
the peoples who are left will plunder you.[n]
For you have shed man's blood;[o]
you have destroyed lands and cities and everyone in them.

9 "Woe to him who builds[p] his realm by unjust gain
to set his nest on high,
to escape the clutches of ruin!
10 You have plotted the ruin[q] of many peoples,
shaming[r] your own house and forfeiting your life.
11 The stones[s] of the wall will cry out,
and the beams of the woodwork will echo it.

12 "Woe to him who builds a city with bloodshed[t]
and establishes a town by crime!
13 Has not the LORD Almighty determined
that the people's labor is only fuel for the fire,[u]
that the nations exhaust themselves for nothing?[v]
14 For the earth will be filled with the knowledge of the glory[w] of the
LORD,
as the waters cover the sea.[x]

15 "Woe to him who gives drink to his neighbors,
pouring it from the wineskin till they are drunk,
so that he can gaze on their naked bodies.
16 You will be filled with shame[y] instead of glory.
Now it is your turn! Drink and be exposed[b]![z]
The cup[a] from the LORD's right hand is coming around to you,
and disgrace will cover your glory.
17 The violence[b] you have done to Lebanon will overwhelm you,
and your destruction of animals will terrify you.[c]
For you have shed man's blood;[d]
you have destroyed lands and cities and everyone in them.

18 "Of what value is an idol,[e] since a man has carved it?
Or an image that teaches lies?
For he who makes it trusts in his own creation;
he makes idols that cannot speak.[f]

2:6 [l]Am 2:8
2:7 [m]Pr 29:1
2:8 [n]Isa 33:1; Zec 2:8-9 [o]ver 17
2:9 [p]Jer 22:13
2:10 [q]Jer 26:19 [r]ver 16
2:11 [s]Jos 24:27; Lk 19:40
2:12 [t]Mic 3:10
2:13 [u]Isa 50:11 [v]Isa 47:13
2:14 [w]Nu 14:21 [x]Isa 11:9
2:16 [y]ver 10 [z]La 4:21 [a]Isa 51:22
2:17 [b]Jer 51:35 [c]Jer 50:15 [d]ver 8
2:18 [e]Jer 5:21 [f]Ps 115:4-5; Jer 10:14

[a] *7* Or *creditors and stagger* [b] *16* Masoretic Text; Dead Sea Scrolls, Aquila, Vulgate and Syriac (see also Septuagint)

tyrant. **extortion.** Literally, "goods taken in pledge." The Babylonians forced conquered peoples to pay exacting tributes, taking valuable and indispensable possessions and even human hostages in pledge for certain privileges.
2:7–8 A striking description of the reversal of fortune when the wicked reap what they have sown and retribution matches their misdeeds.
2:9–11 The second woe denounces the attempted creation of an inviolable national security at the expense of others.
2:9 nest on high. Birds of prey often make their nests in high and inaccessible places. Likewise the Babylonians considered their position in world history as inviolable (Isa 14:13–14; 47:7).
2:10 Security at the expense of others brings shame, not glory; ruin, not protection.
2:11 The stones . . . will echo it. A striking personification. The outcry against the blatant injustice would emerge from the building materials illegally taken from their rightful owners.
2:12–14 The third woe pronounces judgment on the Babylonians for their ruthless but futile tyranny.
2:12 builds a city. Babylonian inscriptions confirm the high premium placed on building activities. Nebuchadnezzar took special pride in his building of Babylon (Da 4:30) and referred to the large number of subjected peoples he used as forced labor for the building of the tower of Babylon. Projects like these involved the loss of lives and were paid for with the spoils of war; i.e., bloodshed.
2:13 Has . . . nothing? History witnesses to the futility and failure of humanity's proudest efforts to perpetuate momentary glory.
2:14 glory of the LORD. The reference is to God's divine incomparability and revealed holiness.
2:15–17 The fourth woe pronounces judgment on the Babylonians for their sadistic and humiliating treatment of others and the creation.
2:15 neighbors. Possibly refers to fellow humans or former allies, thus emphasizing the callousness of the actions.
2:16 The cup . . . you. This well-known figure of speech indicates divine retributive judgment (e.g., Isa 51:17–23). What the Babylonians did to others would be done to them.
2:17 The violence . . . you. Military campaigns often involved extensive damage to flora and fauna. Trees supplied building material and firewood, while wild and domestic animals were a welcome supplement to the soldier's regular diet (Dt 20:19–20). The divine concern for the physical dimensions of his creation should be noticed.
2:18–20 The fifth woe denounces the Babylonians for their futile and foolish idolatry (see Isa 44:9–20; 57:12–13). As in all cultures, the Babylonians' religion deeply influenced their behavior. Kings ascribed their military and building achievements to their gods and rendered regular—sometimes exaggerated—accounts to them in these matters. See *HC* 98.
2:18 teaches lies. Guidance given by gods of stone and wood is untrustworthy.

[19] Woe to him who says to wood, 'Come to life!'
Or to lifeless stone, 'Wake up!'[g]
Can it give guidance?
It is covered with gold and silver;[h]
there is no breath in it.
[20] But the LORD is in his holy temple;[i]
let all the earth be silent[j] before him."

2:19 [g]1Ki 18:27 [h]Jer 10:4
2:20 [i]Ps 11:4 [j]Isa 41:1

Habakkuk's Prayer

3 A prayer of Habakkuk the prophet. On *shigionoth.*[a]

[2] LORD, I have heard[k] of your fame;
I stand in awe[l] of your deeds, O LORD.
Renew[m] them in our day,
in our time make them known;
in wrath remember mercy.[n]

[3] God came from Teman,
the Holy One from Mount Paran. *Selah*[b]
His glory covered the heavens
and his praise filled the earth.[o]
[4] His splendor was like the sunrise;
rays flashed from his hand,
where his power was hidden.
[5] Plague went before him;
pestilence followed his steps.
[6] He stood, and shook the earth;
he looked, and made the nations tremble.
The ancient mountains crumbled
and the age-old hills collapsed.[p]
His ways are eternal.
[7] I saw the tents of Cushan in distress,
the dwellings of Midian[q] in anguish.[r]

[8] Were you angry with the rivers,[s] O LORD?
Was your wrath against the streams?

3:2 [k]Ps 44:1 [l]Ps 119:120 [m]Ps 85:6 [n]Isa 54:8
3:3 [o]Ps 48:10
3:6 [p]Ps 114:1-6
3:7 [q]Jdg 7:24-25 [r]Ex 15:14
3:8 [s]Ex 7:20

[a] *1* Probably a literary or musical term also in verses 9 and 13 [b] *3* A word of uncertain meaning; possibly a musical term;

2:19 covered with gold . . . no breath. Although idols could be glorious on the outside, they sadly lacked the inward power of true life.
2:20 But. Notice the sharp contrast between lifeless idols and the living God. **temple.** Literally, "palace." The word can refer to the heavenly or earthly sanctuary. The earthly temple represented the place where God's royal footstool touched the earth, the center of his expanding reign on Earth (1Ch 29:2). **let . . . him.** The woes of judgment on the proud and wicked culminate in the universal silence of worship (v. 14) in the glorious presence of this incomparable God (Ps 46:10; Isa 45:22–23).
■ **3:1–19** *Closing Prayer of Resolve and Faith.* In hymnic style Habakkuk responded to the anticipation of the Lord's intervention on behalf of his people. As the Babylonians represented the proud and wicked (2:6–20) on their way to woe, Habakkuk typified the faithful righteous, persevering and already rejoicing in their expectation of the fulfillment of the Lord's promise of life. This prayer divides into five sections: a superscription (v. 1), an invocation (v. 2), the praise of God's appearance (vv. 3–15), the prophet's faith (vv. 16–19a) and a postscript (v. 19b).
■ **3:1** *Superscription.* The presence of a superscription strongly suggests that this hymn existed independently and was later incorporated into the book.
3:1 prayer. Here perhaps a synonym for "hymn" (Ps 72:20). **On *shigionoth.*** The precise meaning of this term is not known, but it appears to be a musical or liturgical notation resembling a characteristic feature of many psalms. See "Introduction to Psalms: Purpose and Distinctives."
■ **3:2** *Invocation.* This verse is an invocation to the hymn in which Habakkuk called on God to act again on behalf of his troubled people.
3:2 I have heard . . . deeds. Standing before the Lord (2:1), and hearing the report of the Lord's past (Ex 15:1–21) and recent activities (1:5) flooded Habakkuk's understanding and filled him with reverent fear at the realization of what the Lord had done and would do again (2:2–20). This awe inspired urgent prayer. **Renew . . . known.** Literally, "make alive"; that is, translate vision into concrete events. **wrath . . . mercy.** Boldness combined with apprehension at the prospect of the answer to his prayer. The Lord's coming would be a terrible event in which God would execute wrathful judgment against his enemies. The prophet yearned for this retribution but also desired that mercy be shown to the faithful so that they would not be swept away with the wicked.
■ **3:3–15** *Divine Theophany.* Habakkuk portrayed a divine theophany of victory in three movements: verses 3–7, verses 8–11 and verses 12–15. The description uses traditional poetic material and the characteristically metaphoric language of theophanies (e.g., Ex 19:16–20; 24:15–17; Dt 4:9–12; 33:2) and many psalms (e.g., Ps 50:2–6). The victories envisioned here are principally those over the Egyptians and Canaanites.
3:3–7 The prophet described poetically the effect on nature of the coming of the Lord from the direction of Sinai.
3:3 Teman. The name of Esau's grandson here represents the land of Edom. **Mount Paran.** Located in the well-known Paran wilderness of the Sinai peninsula.
3:5 Plague . . . steps. Habakkuk pictured the ominous dimensions of the Lord's coming (Ps 91:4–6), with horrible curses falling on his enemies.
3:6 He . . . collapsed. The metaphor of the shaking and destruction of the creation commonly represented earthly judgments, such as conquest by a foreign nation (see Isa 14:16; Mic 1:3–7).
3:7 Cushan . . . Midian. These terms are synonymous and refer to locations in the vicinity of Sinai.
3:8–11 The approaching Lord is the invincible, divine warrior por-

Did you rage against the sea
when you rode with your horses
3:8 [t]Ps 68:17 — and your victorious chariots?[t]
9 You uncovered your bow,
3:9 [u]Ps 7:12-13 — you called for many arrows.[u] *Selah*
You split the earth with rivers;
10 the mountains saw you and writhed.
3:10 [v]Ps 98:7 [w]Ps 93:3 — Torrents of water swept by;
the deep roared[v]
and lifted its waves[w] on high.

3:11 [x]Jos 10:13 [y]Ps 18:14
11 Sun and moon stood still[x] in the heavens
at the glint of your flying arrows,[y]
at the lightning of your flashing spear.
3:12 [z]Isa 41:15
12 In wrath you strode through the earth
and in anger you threshed[z] the nations.
3:13 [a]Ps 20:6; 28:8 [b]Ps 68:21; 110:6
13 You came out to deliver[a] your people,
to save your anointed one.
You crushed[b] the leader of the land of wickedness,
you stripped him from head to foot. *Selah*
3:14 [c]Jdg 7:22 [d]Ps 64:2-5
14 With his own spear you pierced his head
when his warriors stormed out to scatter us,[c]
gloating as though about to devour
the wretched[d] who were in hiding.
3:15 [e]Ex 15:8; Ps 77:19
15 You trampled the sea with your horses,
churning the great waters.[e]

16 I heard and my heart pounded,
my lips quivered at the sound;
decay crept into my bones,
and my legs trembled.
Yet I will wait patiently for the day of calamity
to come on the nation invading us.
3:17 [f]Joel 1:10-12,18 [g]Jer 5:17
17 Though the fig tree does not bud
and there are no grapes on the vines,
though the olive crop fails
and the fields produce no food,[f]
though there are no sheep in the pen
and no cattle in the stalls,[g]
3:18 [h]Isa 61:10; Php 4:4
18 yet I will rejoice in the LORD,[h]
I will be joyful in God my Savior.

3:19 [i]Dt 33:29; Ps 46:1-5 [j]Dt 32:13; 2Sa 22:34; Ps 18:33
19 The Sovereign LORD is my strength;[i]
he makes my feet like the feet of a deer,
he enables me to go on the heights.[j]

For the director of music. On my stringed instruments.

trayed in imagery reminiscent of a huge thunderstorm. At creation he subdued the forces of chaos and established his lordship over the world (Ge 1:2). Similar descriptions known from other ancient Near Eastern cultures enhance the poetic imagery. The speech changes from indirect to direct address.
3:12–15 The Lord of nature also has absolute power over the forces of history (Ps 46:2–3,6,8). His coming is for the deliverance of his people and the judgment of the wicked.
3:12 threshed. An agricultural image derived from the way in which grain was released from its husks by violent beating or trampling (Am 1:3).
3:13 You . . . one. In the past the Lord had come out of his heavenly or earthly palace for the salvation of his suffering people. This is what Habakkuk expected him to do again. **anointed.** Possibly a synonym for the people, but more likely a reference to the Davidic king, the representative head of the people of Israel. **You . . . foot.** This is what the Lord would also do in Habakkuk's day to the Babylonians and their king.
3:15 You . . . waters. Habakkuk referred again to the exodus, an event in which the Creator displayed his undisputed dominion over nature and the forces of chaos (represented by the dreaded sea).
■ **3:16–19a** *Faith's Expectation.* Habakkuk declared his expectation and jubilation.
3:16 This verse, together with verse 2, sets off the hymn of verses 3–15 with autobiographical references at the beginning and end. **I . . . trembled.** Habakkuk described in physical terms the profound effect that the vision/revelation had on him (Jer 4:19). The Lord answered his painful questions and would hear his prayer. **Yet . . . come.** Habakkuk rested in the assurance that the Lord would remain faithful to himself and judge the wicked. **invading.** That is, attacking again and again by sending raiding parties.
3:17–18 Even in a future time of the most adverse agricultural and pastoral calamities, when God's people would experience hunger and poverty, Habakkuk's trustful expectation would not be quelled. Trust and hope had transformed his fear for the future into the desire always to rejoice in his Savior-God (Ro 8:35–39; Php 4:4).
3:19a Sovereign . . . strength. Total dependence on the royal, covenant Lord was Habakkuk's key to life. **he . . . heights.** This striking figure portrays true life in its uninhibited freedom and surefooted progress in spite of challenges and dangers.
■ **3:19b** *Postscript.* A note regarding instrumentation. **For . . . instruments.** See note on verse 1. That this instrumental note appears in a postscript may indicate that similar instructions in the Psalms are also postscripts rather than superscripts.

ZEPHANIAH

Introduction

Overview

Author: The prophet Zephaniah
Purpose: To call the people of Jerusalem and Judah to repentance in the face of the Babylonian invasion and hope in a grand restoration after the time of destruction and exile
Date: 640–621 B.C.
Key Truths:

- God used the Babylonians to bring severe judgment on Judah and many other nations for their sins.
- Humbly seeking God provides hope for protection from harm.
- The destruction of other nations would one day be to Israel's advantage.
- God will purify Gentiles and Jews and grant them magnificent blessings after his judgment is complete.

Author

That Zephaniah's lineage was traced back to the fourth generation (1:1) is unique in prophetic literature. This may indicate that the Hezekiah (715–686 B.C.) mentioned in the fourth generation is the well-known king by that name. The name Zephaniah, which means, "Yahweh [the LORD] hides," is used of a priest who was a contemporary of Jeremiah (21:1; 29:25), as well as of other persons in the Old Testament (Zec 6:10,14). Although the prophet employed priestly vocabulary at several points (1:4–5,7–9; 3:4,18), there is no conclusive evidence to indicate that he was officially associated with the temple.

Time and Place of Writing

Zephaniah prophesied during the reign of Josiah (640–609 B.C.), but there is some question whether his ministry preceded or followed Josiah's reform in 621 B.C. His denunciation of syncretistic and Baal worship strongly suggests a date prior to Josiah's reforms. All that can be said with certainty is that Nineveh had not yet been destroyed (2:13–15); therefore the prophet's message was spoken prior to its annihilation in 612 B.C. Zephaniah was a contemporary of Jeremiah (whose call came in Josiah's 13th year; 627 B.C.), as well as of Nahum (663–612 B.C.) and perhaps Habakkuk (605–597 B.C.). If Zephaniah's ministry is dated at the earlier part of Josiah's reign, then Zephaniah may have been instrumental in precipitating Josiah's reforms since the sins he attacked (1:4–6) were those abolished through Josiah's reforms (2Ki 23:4; 2Ch 34:1–7).

Purpose and Distinctives

Zephaniah's terminology is often similar to that of his predecessors (cf. 1:7a with Hab 2:20; 1:14 with Joel 1:15; 1:7b with Isa 34:6), which probably indicates that he was familiar with their prophecies. He stood in continuity with prophets before him.

The focal point of his message, however, was the day of the Lord. On that day a foreign enemy, the Lord's "sword" (2:12), would inflict severe destruction upon Jerusalem (1:4). This enemy has been variously identified as the Scythians, the Assyrians or the Babylonians. Near the end of Hezekiah's reign Isaiah had already identified the Babylonians as those who would conquer Jerusalem (Isa 39:5–7). So it is most likely that Zephaniah had this threat in mind.

Zephaniah's treatment of this subject forms two cycles that move from divine judgment to the hope of salvation. The first cycle speaks of "the day of the LORD" (1:7)—the time when God would devastate his enemies both within and outside Judah (1:2–18) and bring great blessings to the faithful remnant (3:16–17). That day was near (1:7)—a day in which the wrath and anger of Israel's sovereign Lord would be directed against the wicked (1:15,18; 2:2–3). Following this announcement of judgment the prophet called on Judah and the nations to repent and seek the Lord (2:1–3). Repentance was the only hope of finding salvation from the approaching Babylonian judgment.

The second cycle begins with the prophet elaborating further on the judgment to come (2:4— 3:8). He specified that a number of other nations would be destroyed along with Judah. Then the prophet returned to the theme of the hope of salvation (3:9–20). He joyfully announced that following judgment God would purify his people and restore the fortunes of Jerusalem.

Christ in Zephaniah

The book of Zephaniah contains no direct Messianic prophecies, but the prophet's focus on "the day of the Lord" as the time of judgment and blessing connects his message with the work of Christ. The New Testament on one occasion identifies the day of the Lord with the gift of the Spirit on the day of Pentecost (Ac 2:20). Normally, however, in the New Testament the day of the Lord refers to Christ's glorious return (1Co 1:8; 5:5; 2Co 1:14; 1Th 5:2; 2Th 2:2; 2Ti 4:8; 2Pe 3:10), and describes that day as the time when Jesus will destroy all his enemies and bestow incredible blessings on his faithful followers. These connections between Zephaniah's message and New Testament teaching point in two directions.

First, Zephaniah predicted that the destruction inflicted by the Babylonians would reach far and wide.

Not only were the wicked in Judah to be judged, but the evil nations of the world would also receive God's judgment. This Babylonian judgment, however, would be only a foretaste of the eternal judgment that will come when Christ returns in glory.

Second, Zephaniah predicted that the destruction by the Babylonians would not thwart the promises of God. God would purify a people for himself from among the nations and the exiled Jews, and he would bring them in joyous celebration to the wonders of a renewed Jerusalem. This prophetic vision is fulfilled in Jesus. In Christ Gentiles are united with believing Jews into one body (Eph 2:11–16). When Christ returns redeemed men and women from every nation will bow before him in joyous praise (Rev 7:9–10) in the new Jerusalem (Rev 21:1–3).

Outline

I. Superscription (1:1)

Zephaniah's genealogy and time of ministry are identified.

II. Divine Judgment (1:2–18)
- A. Approaching Judgment (1:2–6)
  - 1. Against All Nations (1:2–3)
  - 2. Against Judah (1:4–6)
- B. The Imminent Day of the Lord (1:7–18)
  - 1. Against Judah (1:7–13)
  - 2. Against All Nations (1:14–18)

The prophet predicted that a terrible day of judgment was coming soon for Judah and the Gentile nations.

III. Hope of Salvation (2:1–3)

The only hope for protection from divine judgment was to seek God in humility.

IV. Divine Judgment (2:4—3:8)
- A. Against Philistia (2:4–7)
- B. Against Moab and Ammon (2:8–11)
- C. Against Cush (2:12)
- D. Against Assyria (2:13–15)
- E. Against Jerusalem (3:1–5)
- F. Against All Nations (3:6–8)

The prophet elaborated on the judgment that was coming soon by naming specific nations.

V. Hope of Salvation (3:9–20)
- A. Purification (3:9–13)
- B. Rejoicing in Jerusalem (3:14–17)
- C. Restoration of Jerusalem (3:18–20)

The destruction of judgment would be followed by a time of salvation for both Jews and Gentiles as God purified them from sin and granted them joyous blessings.

1:1 [a]2Ki 22:1; 2Ch 34:1-35:25

1 The word of the LORD that came to Zephaniah son of Cushi, the son of Gedaliah, the son of Amariah, the son of Hezekiah, during the reign of Josiah[a] son of Amon king of Judah:

Warning of Coming Destruction

1:2 [b]Ge 6:7

2 "I will sweep away everything
from the face of the earth,"[b]
declares the LORD.

1:3 [c]Jer 4:25

3 "I will sweep away both men and animals;
I will sweep away the birds of the air[c]
and the fish of the sea.
The wicked will have only heaps of rubble[a]

[a] 3 The meaning of the Hebrew for this line is uncertain.

■ **1:1** *Superscription.* Zephaniah's genealogy and time of ministry are established (see "Introduction: Author" and "Time and Place of Writing").

1:1 word of the LORD. A phrase frequently used to refer to revelation received from the Lord and communicated through a prophet.

■ **1:2–18** *Divine Judgment.* The prophecy begins with an extensive revelation of God's judgment against Judah and the nations through the Babylonian aggression. This chapter divides into two main parts: a dramatic description of the approaching judgment (vv. 2–6) and two oracles concerning the imminent day of the Lord (vv. 7–18).

■ **1:2–6** *Approaching Judgment.* The prophecy begins with an announcement of universal judgment (vv. 2–3) but quickly narrows its focus to Judah and Jerusalem (vv. 4–6).

■ **1:2–3** *Against All Nations.* The Lord would devastate the world with sweeping destruction caused by the Babylonian armies.

1:2 sweep away. The Hebrew expression is emphatic and may be translated "utterly (or 'completely,' 'totally') sweep away." The coming judgment was compared to that of Noah's flood by use of the phrases "men and animals" (Ge 6:7) and "birds of the air" (Ge 7:23). Although this language was hyperbolic in Zephaniah's context, it understates the future judgment of God at Christ's return (2Pe 3:3–7).

when I cut off man from the face of the earth,"[d]
declares the LORD.

Against Judah

4 "I will stretch out my hand[e] against Judah
and against all who live in Jerusalem.
I will cut off from this place every remnant of Baal,[f]
the names of the pagan and the idolatrous priests[g]—
5 those who bow down on the roofs
to worship the starry host,
those who bow down and swear by the LORD
and who also swear by Molech,[a][h]
6 those who turn back from following[i] the LORD
and neither seek[j] the LORD nor inquire[k] of him.
7 Be silent[l] before the Sovereign LORD,
for the day of the LORD[m] is near.
The LORD has prepared a sacrifice;[n]
he has consecrated those he has invited.
8 On the day of the LORD's sacrifice
I will punish[o] the princes
and the king's sons[p]
and all those clad
in foreign clothes.
9 On that day I will punish
all who avoid stepping on the threshold,[b]
who fill the temple of their gods
with violence and deceit.[q]
10 "On that day," declares the LORD,
"a cry will go up from the Fish Gate,[r]
wailing from the New Quarter,
and a loud crash from the hills.
11 Wail,[s] you who live in the market district[c];
all your merchants will be wiped out,
all who trade with[d] silver will be ruined.[t]
12 At that time I will search Jerusalem with lamps
and punish those who are complacent,[u]
who are like wine left on its dregs,[v]

1:3 [d]Hos 4:3
1:4 [e]Jer 6:12 [f]Mic 5:13 [g]Hos 10:5
1:5 [h]Jer 5:7
1:6 [i]Isa 1:4; Jer 2:13 [j]Isa 9:13 [k]Hos 7:7
1:7 [l]Hab 2:20; Zec 2:13 [m]ver 14; Isa 13:6 [n]Isa 34:6; Jer 46:10
1:8 [o]Isa 24:21 [p]Jer 39:6
1:9 [q]Am 3:10
1:10 [r]2Ch 33:14
1:11 [s]Jas 5:1 [t]Hos 9:6
1:12 [u]Am 6:1 [v]Jer 48:11

[a] 5 Hebrew *Malcam,* that is, Milcom [b] 9 See 1 Samuel 5:5. [c] 11 Or *the Mortar* [d] 11 Or *in*

1:3 cut off man. See Matthew 13:41.
■ **1:4–6** *Against Judah.* Three specific sins of Judah are denounced: idolatry (v. 4), syncretism (worship of the true God along with worship of other gods; v. 5) and religious indifference (v. 6).
1:4 stretch out my hand. This phrase refers to the power of God unleashed against his antagonists (2:13; Ex 3:20; Dt 4:34; Isa 5:25). **remnant of Baal.** That is, all that remains of Baal worship. The expression may draw a comparison between the current and previous generations. **pagan . . . priests.** These priests functioned at the high places and "burned incense to Baal, to the sun and moon, to the constellations and to all the starry hosts" (2Ki 23:5).
1:5 those who bow down on the roofs to worship the starry host. Baal worship and the worship of the stars were sins that had contributed to the demise of the northern kingdom (2Ki 17:16). Altars were apparently erected upon the roofs of houses (2Ki 23:12; Jer 19:13). **Molech.** Worship of this Ammonite god was specifically forbidden (Lev 18:21; 20:2–5). The hideous ritual of child sacrifice was part of Ammonite worship practice (see 1Ki 11:5; 2Ki 23:10; Jer 32:35).
1:6 seek the LORD. See 2:3.
■ **1:7–18** *The Imminent Day of the Lord.* The theme of judgment continues, with specific attention given to the nearness of the day of the Lord (vv. 7,14). These verses concern Judah first (vv. 7–13) but are inclusive of the other nations (vv. 14–18).
■ **1:7–13** *Against Judah.* The day of the Lord would bring severe judgment against God's covenant people.
1:7 Be silent. See Psalm 46:10, Habakkuk 2:20 and Zechariah 2:13. The prophet called for reverent submission to the sovereign, covenant God. The command to "be silent" is often linked to being in the presence of the holy God. **the day of the LORD.** Also expressed as "that day" (vv. 9–10,15; 2:2; 3:11,16) and "that time" (1:12; 3:19–20). The phrase refers to any specific time when the Lord is glorious in victory—be it against Babylon through Media (see Isa 13:1—14:27, especially 13:6), against Egypt through Babylon (see 2:3,12; Eze 30:2–4) or against Israel through Assyria (Am 5:18). This text is particularly graphic in describing that day. That day of the Lord's vengeance may be the time of Israel's deliverance (Isa 34:2—35:10), which is represented as the Lord decisively defeating all of Israel's opposition (2:3–15; 3:8–20; Joel 3:14–16). It may also be a day of destruction for those in Israel who have rebelled against the Lord, as is true in this context (see 2:1–2; Am 5:18–20). **sacrifice.** The imminent judgment coming upon Judah is compared to a sacrifice (Isa 34:6; Jer 46:10; Eze 39:17–19). **he has consecrated those he has invited.** The invited guests probably refer to the nation that serves as the instrument of divine judgment (Isa 10:5–11; Hab 1:6). Otherwise the invited guests are the covenant people who are themselves the sacrificial offerings.
1:8 I will punish the princes. "Princes" refers to the sons of the Israelite king and other royal officials. Their lack of commitment to the covenant was evidenced by their adaptation of foreign customs and attire, a sign of religious disloyalty.
1:9 threshold. That is, the threshold of a sanctuary (1Sa 5:5). A Philistine religious practice was probably being imitated.
1:11 merchants. The cries of anguish coming from all parts of the city depict the extent of the evil and the judgment. The wealthier merchant class is singled out for its greed and corrupt business practices (Am 8:4–6).
1:12 I will search. There would be no escaping the divine scruti-

1:12 [w]Eze 8:12
1:13 [x]Jer 15:13 [y]Dt 28:30,39; Am 5:11; Mic 6:15

who think, 'The LORD will do nothing,[w]
either good or bad.'
13 Their wealth will be plundered,[x]
their houses demolished.
They will build houses
but not live in them;
they will plant vineyards
but not drink the wine.[y]

1:14 [z]ver 7; Joel 1:15 [a]Eze 7:7
1:15 [b]Isa 22:5; Joel 2:2
1:16 [c]Jer 4:19 [d]Isa 2:15
1:17 [e]Isa 59:10 [f]Ps 79:3 [g]Jer 9:22
1:18 [h]Eze 7:19 [i]ver 2-3; Zep 3:8 [j]Ge 6:7

The Great Day of the LORD

14 "The great day of the LORD[z] is near[a]—
near and coming quickly.
Listen! The cry on the day of the LORD will be bitter,
the shouting of the warrior there.
15 That day will be a day of wrath,
a day of distress and anguish,
a day of trouble and ruin,
a day of darkness and gloom,
a day of clouds and blackness,[b]
16 a day of trumpet and battle cry[c]
against the fortified cities
and against the corner towers.[d]
17 I will bring distress on the people
and they will walk like blind[e] men,
because they have sinned against the LORD.
Their blood will be poured out[f] like dust
and their entrails like filth.[g]
18 Neither their silver nor their gold
will be able to save them
on the day of the LORD's wrath.[h]
In the fire of his jealousy
the whole world will be consumed,[i]
for he will make a sudden end
of all who live in the earth.[j]"

2:1 [k]2Ch 20:4; Joel 1:14 [l]Jer 3:3; 6:15
2:2 [m]Isa 17:13; Hos 13:3 [n]La 4:11
2:3 [o]Am 5:6 [p]Ps 45:4; Am 5:14-15 [q]Ps 57:1

2

Gather together,[k] gather together,
O shameful[l] nation,
2 before the appointed time arrives
and that day sweeps on like chaff,[m]
before the fierce anger[n] of the LORD comes upon you,
before the day of the LORD's wrath comes upon you.
3 Seek[o] the LORD, all you humble of the land,
you who do what he commands.
Seek righteousness, seek humility;[p]
perhaps you will be sheltered[q]
on the day of the LORD's anger.

---

ny (Ps 139:1–16,23–24; Am 9:1–4). **complacent.** Their standing before God was a matter of indifference to them. **wine left on its dregs.** In the wine-making process the sediment thickens and hardens if it is left undisturbed. It needs to be poured into another container to be strained of these impurities before they harden. These spiritually apathetic Judahites had lost faith in the living God who governs and rules the world. See *WLC* 105.

■ **1:14–18** *Against All Nations.* Zephaniah elaborated further on the day of the Lord by broadening his view to include the destruction of all nations (see note on v. 18).

1:17 they will walk like blind men. One of the curses of the covenant (Dt 28:28–29). **they have sinned.** The reason for the Lord's judgment against Judah is stated in general terms (see note on 3:1–5).

1:18 Neither their silver nor their gold will be able to save them. See Psalm 49:6–9, Proverbs 11:4, Matthew 16:26 and Luke 12:13–21. **jealousy.** See Exodus 20:5, 34:14 and Deuteronomy 4:24. God's jealousy presupposed his covenant love, which had redeemed a people to make them his personal property (see "treasured possession" at Ex 19:5) and demanded in turn their absolute loyalty. **the whole world . . . all who live in the earth.** These references indicate that Zephaniah once again had in mind the Gentile nations as well as Judah (see vv. 2–3).

■ **2:1–3** *Hope of Salvation.* The first cycle of the book ends with a call for repentance as the way of hope for salvation from the destruction of the day of the Lord.

2:1 Gather together, gather together. Using terminology that normally means "to gather sticks or stubble," the prophet ironically called for the Judahites to assemble as chaff about to be swept away (v. 2). They were called to assemble in order to hear (see Isa 34:1; Jer 4:5; Joel 2:15–16; 3:11) and to seek God's mercy (v. 3). It is an act of divine grace when people are exhorted to hear severe warnings, for warnings are designed to elicit repentance from those who hear them.

2:2 the fierce anger of the LORD. Literally, "the heat of the LORD's anger" (see Ex 32:12; Nu 32:13; Dt 13:17; Jer 4:26; 12:13; 25:37–38; Jnh 3:9; Na 1:6).

2:3 Seek the LORD. See 1:6 and Isaiah 55:6–7. In this context seeking the Lord is further delineated as an act of repentance ("seek righteousness, seek humility"). A similar pattern is to be seen in Amos 5, where the prophet commands, "Seek the LORD" (Am 5:6) and later, "Seek good, not evil" (Am 5:14). **perhaps you**

Against Philistia

4 Gaza[r] will be abandoned
and Ashkelon left in ruins.
At midday Ashdod will be emptied
and Ekron uprooted.
5 Woe to you who live by the sea,
O Kerethite[s] people;
the word of the LORD is against you,[t]
O Canaan, land of the Philistines.

"I will destroy you,
and none will be left."[u]

6 The land by the sea, where the Kerethites[a] dwell,
will be a place for shepherds and sheep pens.[v]
7 It will belong to the remnant of the house of Judah;
there they will find pasture.
In the evening they will lie down
in the houses of Ashkelon.
The LORD their God will care for them;
he will restore their fortunes.[b][w]

Against Moab and Ammon

8 "I have heard the insults[x] of Moab
and the taunts of the Ammonites,
who insulted[y] my people
and made threats against their land.
9 Therefore, as surely as I live,"
declares the LORD Almighty, the God of Israel,
"surely Moab[z] will become like Sodom,[a]
the Ammonites[b] like Gomorrah—
a place of weeds and salt pits,
a wasteland forever.
The remnant of my people will plunder[c] them;
the survivors of my nation will inherit their land.[d]"
10 This is what they will get in return for their pride,[e]
for insulting[f] and mocking the people of the LORD Almighty.
11 The LORD will be awesome[g] to them
when he destroys all the gods[h] of the land.
The nations on every shore will worship him,[i]
every one in its own land.

2:4 [r]Am 1:6,7-8; Zec 9:5-7
2:5 [s]Eze 25:16 [t]Am 3:1 [u]Isa 14:30
2:6 [v]Isa 5:17
2:7 [w]Ps 126:4; Jer 32:44
2:8 [x]Jer 48:27 [y]Eze 25:3
2:9 [z]Isa 15:1-16:14; Jer 48:1-47 [a]Dt 29:23 [b]Jer 49:1-6; Eze 25:1-7 [c]Isa 11:14 [d]Am 2:1-3
2:10 [e]Isa 16:6 [f]Jer 48:27
2:11 [g]Joel 2:11 [h]Zep 1:4 [i]Zep 3:9

[a] 6 The meaning of the Hebrew for this word is uncertain. [b] 7 Or *will bring back their captives*

---

will be sheltered. Compare Amos 5:15. The Lord's promise of eternal salvation is certain to all who truly seek him (Isa 55:7). The prophet's tentative words here expressed his hope that the "humble" remnant would find refuge from the imminent destruction of the Babylonians.

■ **2:4–3:8** *Divine Judgment.* The prophet returned to a description of how God would judge through the Babylonians. These oracles of judgment are similar to those of other prophets (see Isa 13–30; Eze 25–32; Am 1:3—2:3). He specified six nations (including Judah; 3:1–5) in five oracles and ended with a summary pronouncement of worldwide destruction (3:6–8). Words of salvation for the remnant of Judah (2:7,9), as well as a word of hope about the nations (2:11), are scattered throughout these oracles.

■ **2:4–7** *Against Philistia.* The Philistines had troubled Israel from the time of Samson (Jdg 13:1; 15:20).

2:5 Woe. This is the same word of doom later pronounced upon Jerusalem (3:1). It is a literary form used to introduce a dire threat.

2:7 the remnant of the house of Judah. Those Judahites who survived judgment and returned to the land would possess the lands of Philistia. The remaining references to the remnant in Zephaniah are in 2:9 and 3:9–13. The failures of those who returned from exile caused the fulfillment of this promise to be delayed; it did not begin to be fulfilled until Christ's first coming (Eph 1:19–23) and will not come to complete fruition until Christ returns and gives dominion to his people in the new earth (2Ti 2:11; 21:1—22:5). **he will restore their fortunes.** This widely employed phrase refers to Israel's future salvation beyond the judgment (Dt 30:3; Ps 14:7; Jer 30:3,18; 32:44; Am 9:14), which sometimes applies to her return from exile. See 3:20, where the same phrase describes Israel's future destiny after exile.

■ **2:8–11** *Against Moab and Ammon.* These nations are treated together because of their common ancestry (Ge 19:4–5,36–38).

2:8 See *WLC* 151.

2:9 like Sodom . . . like Gomorrah. These cities epitomize sin and serve as types of God's final judgment on sinners (Isa 1:9; Am 4:11; 2Pe 2:6). The comparison is fitting in light of the close association of Sodom with the ancestor of Moab and Ammon (Ge 19:4–5,36–38). **remnant of my people.** See note on verse 7.

2:10–11 See *WLC* 151.

2:11 The nations on every shore will worship him. See 3:9–10, Psalm 72:8–11 and Isaiah 56:6–7.

■ **2:12** *Against Cush.* The remote people of the upper Nile would not escape.

2:12 my sword. Compare Isaiah 10:5.

Against Cush

2:12 [j]Isa 18:1; 20:4 [k]Jer 46:10

12 "You too, O Cushites,[a][j]
will be slain by my sword.[k]"

Against Assyria

2:13 [l]Na 1:1 [m]Mic 5:6

13 He will stretch out his hand against the north
and destroy Assyria,
leaving Nineveh[l] utterly desolate
and dry as the desert.[m]
14 Flocks and herds will lie down there,
creatures of every kind.

2:14 [n]Isa 14:23

The desert owl[n] and the screech owl
will roost on her columns.
Their calls will echo through the windows,
rubble will be in the doorways,
the beams of cedar will be exposed.

2:15 [o]Isa 32:9 [p]Isa 47:8 [q]Eze 28:2 [r]Na 3:19

15 This is the carefree[o] city
that lived in safety.[p]
She said to herself,
"I am, and there is none besides me."[q]
What a ruin she has become,
a lair for wild beasts!
All who pass by her scoff[r]
and shake their fists.

The Future of Jerusalem

3:1 [s]Jer 6:6 [t]Eze 23:30

3:2 [u]Jer 22:21 [v]Jer 7:28 [w]Ps 73:28; Jer 5:3

3 Woe to the city of oppressors,[s]
rebellious and defiled![t]
2 She obeys[u] no one,
she accepts no correction.[v]
She does not trust in the LORD,
she does not draw near[w] to her God.

3:3 [x]Eze 22:27

3 Her officials are roaring lions,
her rulers are evening wolves,[x]
who leave nothing for the morning.

3:4 [y]Jer 9:4 [z]Eze 22:26

4 Her prophets are arrogant;
they are treacherous[y] men.
Her priests profane the sanctuary
and do violence to the law.[z]

3:5 [a]Dt 32:4

5 The LORD within her is righteous;
he does no wrong.[a]
Morning by morning he dispenses his justice,
and every new day he does not fail,
yet the unrighteous know no shame.

a *12* That is, people from the upper Nile region

■ **2:13–15** *Against Assyria.* The Assyrians conquered the northern kingdom in 722 B.C. and troubled the southern kingdom of Judah.
2:13 destroy Assyria. The Babylonians conquered Nineveh in 612 B.C., suggesting that Zephaniah prophesied prior to that date.
2:15 I am, and there is none besides me. Such a boast is couched in language similar to that which the Sovereign Lord alone uses (Dt 4:39; Isa 45:5–6; 47:10).
■ **3:1–5** *Against Jerusalem.* The references here to prophets, priests, the sanctuary and the law indicate that the prophet was addressing Jerusalem. This oracle presupposes the most heinous crime, since Jerusalem's sins were committed against a God who had spoken in a special way to her inhabitants and had chosen them from among all other peoples (Am 2:4–5,10–16; 3:2). People and leaders were accused of infidelity (3:1–4), in contrast to the Lord's faithfulness (v. 5). The general accusation of 1:17 now becomes specific.
3:2 She obeys no one. Literally, "She listens to no voice"; that is, to God's voice revealed either in the law (Dt 31:9–13), through the prophets (Jer 7:23–28; Hag 1:12) or through wise teachers (Dt 1:13–15). **she accepts no correction.** See verse 7. It is so critical to receive correction that failure to be receptive to it leads to death (Pr 5:23; Jer 2:30; 5:3; 7:28; 32:33) and acceptance of it to life (Pr 6:23). **she does not draw near to her God.** The phrase "draw near to her God" means "to approach God properly in worship" (cf. Lev 9:7–8; 10:4–5; 16:1ff.). Worship must come from the heart, not just from the mouth (cf. Isa 29:13; Jn 4:24).
3:3–4 See Micah 3:9–11.
3:3 roaring lions. The images of the unclean lion and wolf here describe the preying, rapacious and fierce nature of those governmental officials whose proper office was to protect and give stability to society.
3:4 Her prophets . . . Her priests. See Isaiah 28:7, Jeremiah 4:9, 5:31, 6:13, 8:10, and Hosea 4:5–6. **arrogant . . . treacherous.** See Micah 2:6–11 and 3:5–8.
3:5 within her. Zephaniah contrasted the presence of the righteous Lord within Jerusalem with that of corrupt and unrighteous leaders within her (see note on v. 3). The essence of the promise of God's covenant is his presence with his people (Ex 33:14–15; Nu 14:14; Isa 43:2). God being in the midst of ("within") Jerusalem is here considered a threat of judgment, but the same Hebrew term in verse 17 (where it is translated "with") signifies salvation.

6 "I have cut off nations;
their strongholds are demolished.
I have left their streets deserted,
with no one passing through.
Their cities are destroyed;[b]
no one will be left—no one at all.
7 I said to the city,
'Surely you will fear me
and accept correction!'
Then her dwelling would not be cut off,
nor all my punishments come upon her.
But they were still eager
to act corruptly[c] in all they did.
8 Therefore wait[d] for me," declares the LORD,
"for the day I will stand up to testify.[a]
I have decided to assemble the nations,[e]
to gather the kingdoms
and to pour out my wrath on them—
all my fierce anger.
The whole world will be consumed[f]
by the fire of my jealous anger.

9 "Then will I purify the lips of the peoples,
that all of them may call[g] on the name of the LORD
and serve[h] him shoulder to shoulder.
10 From beyond the rivers of Cush[b][i]
my worshipers, my scattered people,
will bring me offerings.[j]
11 On that day you will not be put to shame[k]
for all the wrongs you have done to me,
because I will remove from this city
those who rejoice in their pride.
Never again will you be haughty
on my holy hill.
12 But I will leave within you
the meek[l] and humble,
who trust[m] in the name of the LORD.
13 The remnant[n] of Israel will do no wrong;[o]
they will speak no lies,[p]

3:6
[b]Lev 26:31
3:7
[c]Hos 9:9
3:8
[d]Ps 27:14 [e]Joel 3:2
[f]Zep 1:18
3:9
[g]Zep 2:11
[h]Isa 19:18
3:10
[i]Ps 68:31 [j]Isa 60:7
3:11
[k]Joel 2:26-27
3:12
[l]Isa 14:32 [m]Na 1:7
3:13
[n]Isa 10:21; Mic 4:7
[o]Ps 119:3
[p]Rev 14:5

[a] *8* Septuagint and Syriac; Hebrew *will rise up to plunder* [b] *10* That is, the upper Nile region

■ **3:6–8** *Against All Nations.* The enemies of God, including the wicked in Judah, would be summoned to appear and would be subject to God's anger and wrath.
3:6 cut off nations. See Joshua 24:11.
3:7 fear me and accept correction! See 3:2. **eager to act corruptly.** Note the contrast between the nation's character and God's character of dispensing justice "morning by morning" (v. 5).
3:8 pour out. See Revelation 16:1.
■ **3:9–20** *Hope of Salvation.* As the prophet had offered the possibility of protection from Babylon upon repentance (2:1–3), he now turned his attention toward the promised future beyond the days of destruction. Judgment would be the prelude to restoration and purification, both in Israel and among the nations (vv. 9,12–13). These verses divide into three parts: purification (vv. 9–13), rejoicing in Jerusalem (vv. 14–17) and the glorious restoration of Jerusalem (vv. 18–20).
■ **3:9–13** *Purification.* The judgment of the day of the Lord would lead to a purification of some from the nations and from the exiled Jews.
3:9 will I purify the lips. See Genesis 11:1–9. To "purify the lips" means either to cleanse from sin in general (cf. Isa 6:5–7) or to remove the names of foreign gods from the lips of a pagan worshiper (Hos 2:17). **of the peoples.** Gentiles would also call upon his name (Isa 52:15; 65:1). See *WLC* 191. **that all of them may call on the name of the LORD.** See Genesis 4:26, 1 Kings 18:24, Jeremiah 10:25 and Joel 2:32. This is similar to the clause "trust in the name of the LORD" in verse 12. It is in contrast to those who "swear by the LORD and who also swear by Molech" (1:5).
3:10 my scattered people. Probably a reference to the Jews who would be driven from the land by the Babylonian invasions and deportations. Zephaniah envisioned both purified Jews and Gentiles worshiping the Lord.
3:11–12 See *BC* 23.
3:11 rejoice in their pride. See Genesis 11:1–9 and Isaiah 2:6–22.
3:12 the meek and humble. These are contrasted with the proud and haughty (v. 11). **trust in the name of the LORD.** See Psalms 2:12, 31:1–2, Isaiah 57:13 and Nahum 1:7.
3:13 remnant. See note on 2:7. **will do no wrong.** When this purification after exile reached its fullness the remnant would be without sin; the law of God would be perfectly written in their hearts (Jer 31:31–33). This hope will come to ultimate fruition when Christ returns (see Rev 21:22–27). **they will speak no lies.** See 1:9, 3:4 and Revelation 14:5. **They will eat and lie down.** The Hebrew verb for "eat" literally means "graze," so that the verse metaphorically represents God's people as his flock. This is a common figure in the prophets (Isa 49:9; Jer 50:19; Eze 34:14; Mic 7:14), portraying the security that comes from trusting God and acknowledging his kingship (v. 15). The verb may also mean "pasture" if it has a direct object, which is not the case in this verse, although some interpreters believe one is implied. If their understanding is correct the verse portrays God's people as shepherds who tend their flocks in peace. **no one will make them afraid.** The days of full restoration would be without trials or troubles of any kind (see Mic 4:4). Although Christ has already introduced his people to this experience (1Jn 5:18), fear of troubles from others will utterly disappear when he returns (Rev 21:4).

nor will deceit be found in their mouths.
They will eat and lie down[q]
and no one will make them afraid.[r]"

14 Sing, O Daughter of Zion;[s]
shout aloud,[t] O Israel!
Be glad and rejoice with all your heart,
O Daughter of Jerusalem!
15 The LORD has taken away your punishment,
he has turned back your enemy.
The LORD, the King of Israel, is with you;[u]
never again will you fear[v] any harm.
16 On that day they will say to Jerusalem,
"Do not fear, O Zion;
do not let your hands hang limp.[w]
17 The LORD your God is with you,
he is mighty to save.[x]
He will take great delight[y] in you,
he will quiet you with his love,
he will rejoice over you with singing."

18 "The sorrows for the appointed feasts
I will remove from you;
they are a burden and a reproach to you.[a]
19 At that time I will deal
with all who oppressed you;
I will rescue the lame
and gather those who have been scattered.[z]
I will give them praise[a] and honor
in every land where they were put to shame.
20 At that time I will gather you;
at that time I will bring[b] you home.
I will give you honor[c] and praise
among all the peoples of the earth
when I restore your fortunes[b][d]
before your very eyes,"
says the LORD.

3:13 [q]Eze 34:15; Zep 2:7 [r]Eze 34:25-28
3:14 [s]Zec 2:10 [t]Isa 12:6
3:15 [u]Eze 37:26-28 [v]Isa 54:14
3:16 [w]Job 4:3; Isa 35:3-4; Heb 12:12
3:17 [x]Isa 63:1 [y]Isa 62:4
3:19 [z]Eze 34:16; Mic 4:6 [a]Isa 60:18
3:20 [b]Jer 29:14; Eze 37:12 [c]Isa 56:5; 66:22 [d]Joel 3:1

[a] *18* Or *"I will gather you who mourn for the appointed feasts; / your reproach is a burden to you* [b] *20* Or *I bring back your captives*

■ **3:14–17** *Rejoicing in Jerusalem.* Thoughts of the purity of Jerusalem in the future led the prophet to call for the city to rejoice.
3:14 Daughter of Zion. That is, Jerusalem. This figure of speech follows the practice of personifying inanimate objects according to the gender of the noun. As this practice applies here, the word *city* in Hebrew is feminine, and thus the prophet spoke of Zion as "Daughter."
3:15–17 King of Israel, is with you . . . mighty to save. The presence of God as King among his people means that he will fight for them and protect them from harm (see notes on vv. 5,17). The incarnation of Christ was the fullest expression of God's presence with us that brought about victory for God's people (Mt 1:23).
3:15 your punishment. The basis for the rejoicing in verse 14 is explained. Judgment was not glossed over but was dealt with by the Lord. The Babylonian exile was Jerusalem's punishment for sin. The release from guilt and punishment promised here was fulfilled when Christ died and rose again.
3:17 He will take great delight in you. See Deuteronomy 30:9, Isaiah 62:4–5, 65:18–19 and Jeremiah 32:41. The basis of this delight is the character of God, who "delight[s] to show mercy" (Mic 7:18). **he will quiet you with his love.** The phrase "quiet you" may mean "quiet himself." The translation "quiet you" follows the understanding in the Septuagint (the Greek translation of the OT), so that the phrase means "he will refresh you in his love." However, because in this context God is seen as the warrior who is "mighty to save," "quiet himself" may be the better translation, with the meaning that the Lord's former war cry (1:14) is now quieted by his love. The Lord performs a purging and transforming work of grace and creates a new people who acknowledge his rule and trust in his name (v. 12).
■ **3:18–20** *Restoration of Jerusalem.* The prophet offered assurances that the purification (vv. 9–13) and rejoicing (vv. 14–17) would be followed by a full restoration of Jerusalem, including abundant blessings for all its inhabitants.
3:19 the lame . . . scattered. Zephaniah had in mind the people of Israel who had been wounded and dispersed through the Babylonian exile. Jesus declared that his earthly ministry was the beginning of the healing and gathering of the exiled remnant (Mt 11:1–5). **I will give them praise and honor.** See verse 20. The phrase alludes to Deuteronomy 26:18–19, where Israel is offered praise and honor as God's treasured possession. As with other restoration promises, this promise is also fulfilled in the glorification of all who follow Christ (2Co 3:18; Rev 20:4).
3:20 restore your fortunes. Moses promised that after the exile God's people would be more prosperous than before (Dt 30:5). In Christ the people of God are given tremendous blessings, both now and in the future in the new heavens and the new earth (Eph 1:3; Rev 21:6–7).

HAGGAI

Introduction

Overview

Author: The prophet Haggai
Purpose: To encourage the reconstruction of the temple in hopes of bringing great blessings to Israel after the exile
Date: 520 B.C. (Haggai's ministry)
Key Truths:

- God offered many blessings to the first returnees after the exile.
- The priorities of God's kingdom must take precedence over our personal comforts.
- Servants in the kingdom of God must be undefiled.
- The hopes of God's people rest in the temple and in the house of David as they are fulfilled by Christ.
- God's people are destined to inherit the earth in Christ.

Author

The prophet Haggai (his name means "my feast") worked with the prophet Zechariah to encourage the returning Jewish exiles as they rebuilt the temple (Ezr 5:1; 6:14). We know nothing about Haggai other than what the book of Ezra mentions and what we learn from the prophet's own book. The book closes with high expectations for Zerubbabel, leaving little doubt that the book was written before the governor's restoration program failed.

Time and Place of Writing

As we might expect from our discussion of authorship, the books of Haggai and Zechariah (see "Introduction to Zechariah") have a common historical background, both prophets having begun their ministries in 520 B.C., in "the second year of King Darius" (1:1; see also Zec 1:1). The Jews had returned to the promised land under the edict of Cyrus (Ezr 1:1–4) in 538 B.C. and had begun to rebuild the temple. Opposition from the outside and discouragement from within caused them to abandon the project (Ezr 4:1–4) for 16 or 17 years. When Haggai and Zechariah began their work in 520 B.C., further opposition came from Tattenai, the Persian governor of Trans-Euphrates (see note on Ezr 4:9–10). But Darius I (Hystaspes), who ruled Persia from 522 to 486 B.C., reissued Cyrus's edict so that the temple was rebuilt within four years (Ezr 6:13–15). The second temple was dedicated on March 12, 516 B.C.

As for Haggai's oracles, we learn from his book that they were delivered between August and December 520 B.C.

Purpose and Distinctives

The book of Haggai consists of four messages, each of which is headed by the phrase "the word of the LORD came through the prophet Haggai [or "to Haggai"]" (1:1; 2:1; 2:10; 2:20). These four messages alternate between calls to repentance in light of God's continued withholding of blessings on the land (1:1–11; 2:10–19) and promises of greater blessings on the temple and through the Davidic line (2:1–9; 2:20–23).

Haggai, Zechariah and Malachi together use the title "LORD Almighty" more than 90 times (14 times in Haggai). In Hebrew it literally means "Lord of armies." The title's meaning has two aspects: It stresses the sovereign power of the Lord who reigns over Israel and the whole earth though his military power (1Sa 17:45) and emphasizes his faithfulness to his covenant people, which causes them to worship him (cf. Ps 24).

Through his "messenger" (1:13) Haggai the Lord called upon the unfaithful remnant of his covenant people to repent and rebuild his temple. God's concern was based upon his own sovereign pleasure and his desire to be honored (1:8). The people's lack of desire to build the temple revealed their deeper lack of desire for God's special presence. They were under the curses of the covenant (see notes on 1:6,9,11) but did not realize it. As a result of Haggai's ministry and of the prompting of God's Spirit (1:14) they responded with obedience (1:12).

Haggai reaffirmed that the Lord was with his people, just as he had been with them when he had brought them out of Egypt (1:13; 2:4–5). Haggai's ministry was based on the expectation that God would renew his covenant promises to his people when he brought them back into the land. Haggai's words drew on those of earlier prophets at a number of points (see notes on 2:7–8). The rebuilding of the temple was an important part of that renewal, and Haggai developed that hope by associating the temple with the renewal of the house of David. Haggai affirmed the hope that as God's anointed representative on Earth, the great son of David, the Messiah, would bring his glory, peace and prosperity to God's people (2:6–9). Zerubbabel prefigured the Messiah in Haggai's day and was the object of much hope for the nation. Ultimately, however, only Jesus the Messiah fulfills the promise made to Zerubbabel (2:23) of being God's royal ruler ("signet ring") on Earth.

Christ in Haggai

The two central themes of this book—the temple and the victory of the Davidic line—find their fulfillment in Christ. Rebuilding the temple was crucial for the restoration of the nation to the blessings of God. It was the place of prayer, worship, forgiveness, etc.

Christ is the final temple (Jn 2:21–22), but the church, his body, is the temple of the Holy Spirit (1Co 6:19–20). When Christ returns the new heavens and the new earth will be God's holy dwelling place (Rev 21:22–23).

The restoration of David's line was also an essential part of God's blessing on the restored community. The Davidic line was to lead the people in battle and secure their prosperity. Jesus is the Messiah, the final and perfect son of David (Mt 1:1; Lk 20:41–44; Ro 1:3). After his death he established his kingdom when he ascended to his throne in heaven (Ac 1:9–11). He now reigns until all of his enemies are subdued (1Co 15:25–27; 1Pe 3:22). When he returns he will rule over the heavens and the earth (Heb 2:8; Rev 1:5). The church is united with Christ in his enthronement (Ro 8:37; 1Pe 5:10), so that one day those who overcome will reign with him.

Outline

I. Call to Rebuild the Temple (1:1–15)
   A. The People's Problem: Lethargy (1:1–4)
   B. The People's Poverty: Economic and Spiritual (1:5–11)
   C. The People's Response: Repentance (1:12–15)

Haggai called the people to repent of their neglect of rebuilding the temple.

II. God's Greater Temple and Blessings (2:1–9)
   A. Encouragement From God's Presence (2:1–5)
   B. Encouragement From God's Promise of Blessing (2:6–9)

Haggai explained the blessings that would come to the nation through the reconstructed temple.

III. God's Blessing for a Defiled People (2:10–19)
   A. The Cause of Their Defilement (2:10–14)
   B. God's Reaction of Curses and Blessings (2:15–19)

Haggai reminded the returnees of their defilement but assured them of future blessings from God.

IV. Victory for God's People (2:20–23)
   A. Overthrow of the Nations (2:20–22)
   B. Enthronement of David's Son (2:23)

Haggai announced great victory over the nations for Zerubbabel, as representative of the house of David.

A Call to Build the House of the LORD

1:1 [a]Ezr 4:24 [b]Ezr 5:1 [c]Mt 1:12-13 [d]Ezr 5:3 [e]Ezr 2:2 [f]1Ch 6:15; Ezr 3:2
1:3 [g]Ezr 5:1
1:4 [h]2Sa 7:2 [i]ver 9; Jer 33:12

1 In the second year of King Darius,[a] on the first day of the sixth month, the word of
the LORD came through the prophet Haggai[b] to Zerubbabel[c] son of Shealtiel, governor[d] of Judah, and to Joshua[a][e] son of Jehozadak,[f] the high priest:
2 This is what the LORD Almighty says: "These people say, 'The time has not yet come
for the LORD's house to be built.' "
3 Then the word of the LORD came through the prophet Haggai:[g] 4 "Is it a time for you
yourselves to be living in your paneled houses,[h] while this house remains a ruin?[i]"

a 1 A variant of *Jeshua*; here and elsewhere in Haggai

■ **1:1–15** *Call to Rebuild the Temple.* Haggai's prophecies begin with a forceful call for the restored community to rebuild the temple.
■ **1:1–4** *The People's Problem: Lethargy.* This first section consists of the prophet's call for the people to stop pursuing their own needs and rebuild the Lord's temple. They were using their time to enjoy their own homes while the Lord's house was still in ruins.
1:1 the first day of the sixth month. August 29, 520 B.C. Haggai's message was publicly addressed to the leaders so that the people could respond as well (v. 12). **Zerubbabel.** Most likely he was the same as Sheshbazzar (cf. Ezr 1:8), since both are said to have rebuilt the temple. Sheshbazzar could have been his official Persian name. He was the grandson of King Jehoiachin (1Ch 3:19) and a descendant of David. **Joshua son of Jehozadak.** A descendant of Zadok the priest (see 1Ch 6:8,15). Under Persian rule Zerubbabel had responsibility over the daily civil affairs of the region. As high priest Joshua handled the ecclesiastical matters. As prophet Haggai was not appointed by men but was called by God to deliver God's word to the leaders of his people.
1:2 These people. A negative expression for God's people (2:14). Verses 1–11 are an indictment against their spiritual indifference and misplaced priorities. **The time has not yet come.** Their objection was not to the rebuilding itself but to the timing of the project. Their protests may have been economic, because their land was in trouble (cf. vv. 10–11), or theological, because (1) according to Ezekiel 37:24–27 the Messiah himself was to rebuild the temple, and (2) according to Jeremiah 25:11–14 the nation was to serve a foreign king for 70 years. The temple was destroyed in 586 B.C. The people may have reasoned that they should not start rebuilding until 516 B.C. Such excuses showed that they were not pursuing God's kingdom and righteousness (cf. Mt 6:33). **the LORD's house.** The temple was the dwelling place of God's special presence with his people, the place where his name dwelled (1Ki 8:27–30). That same presence is in the church today, prompting Paul to identify the church as God's temple (1Co 3:16–17).
1:4 paneled houses. Haggai revealed the hypocrisy of the people's objections by a rhetorical question. Those who had sufficient resources had evidently installed wooden ceilings in their homes—ceilings that were elaborate by the standards of those days (1Ki 7:3; Jer 22:14).

5Now this is what the LORD Almighty says: "Give careful thought[j] to your ways. 6You
have planted much, but have harvested little.[k] You eat, but never have enough. You
drink, but never have your fill. You put on clothes, but are not warm. You earn wages,[l]
only to put them in a purse with holes in it."
7This is what the LORD Almighty says: "Give careful thought to your ways. 8Go up into
the mountains and bring down timber and build the house, so that I may take pleasure[m]
in it and be honored," says the LORD. 9"You expected much, but see, it turned out to be
little. What you brought home, I blew away. Why?" declares the LORD Almighty. "Because
of my house, which remains a ruin,[n] while each of you is busy with his own house.
10Therefore, because of you the heavens have withheld their dew and the earth its
crops.[o] 11I called for a drought[p] on the fields and the mountains, on the grain, the new
wine, the oil and whatever the ground produces, on men and cattle, and on the labor of
your hands.[q]"

12Then Zerubbabel[r] son of Shealtiel, Joshua son of Jehozadak, the high priest, and the
whole remnant[s] of the people obeyed[t] the voice of the LORD their God and the message
of the prophet Haggai, because the LORD their God had sent him. And the people feared[u]
the LORD.
13Then Haggai, the LORD's messenger, gave this message of the LORD to the people:
"I am with[v] you," declares the LORD. 14So the LORD stirred up the spirit of Zerubbabel[w]
son of Shealtiel, governor of Judah, and the spirit of Joshua son of Jehozadak, the high
priest, and the spirit of the whole remnant[x] of the people. They came and began to work
on the house of the LORD Almighty, their God, 15on the twenty-fourth day of the sixth
month[y] in the second year of King Darius.

The Promised Glory of the New House

2 On the twenty-first day of the seventh month, the word of the LORD came through
the prophet Haggai: 2"Speak to Zerubbabel son of Shealtiel, governor of Judah, to
Joshua son of Jehozadak, the high priest, and to the remnant of the people. Ask them,
3'Who of you is left who saw this house[z] in its former glory? How does it look to you now?

1:5 [j]La 3:40
1:6 [k]Dt 28:38 [l]Hag 2:16; Zec 8:10
1:8 [m]Ps 132:13-14
1:9 [n]ver 4
1:10 [o]Lev 26:19; Dt 28:23
1:11 [p]Dt 28:22; 1Ki 17:1 [q]Hag 2:17
1:12 [r]ver 1 [s]ver 14; Isa 1:9; Hag 2:2 [t]Isa 50:10 [u]Dt 31:12
1:13 [v]Mt 28:20; Ro 8:31
1:14 [w]Ezr 5:2 [x]ver 12
1:15 [y]ver 1
2:3 [z]Ezr 3:12

■ **1:5–11** *The People's Poverty: Economic and Spiritual.* The returnees' labor was in vain. The returns on their crops were so meager because they had not gathered the proper materials and finished the temple.
1:6 You have planted much, but have harvested little. They did not realize why they were experiencing economic and social hardship: It was because they had not fully escaped the curse God had placed on the nation during the exile (Lev 26:20; Dt 11:8–15; 28:29,38–40). Because they had not yet come to full repentance, God frustrated their efforts.
1:8 so that I may take pleasure in it and be honored. God's purpose for the rebuilt temple was his own pleasure and his desire to be honored by his people. Their lack of concern for rebuilding indicated that they had neither a genuine desire to please God nor a desire to promote his honor.
1:9 each of you is busy with his own house. This was the crux of the problem. The focus of their lives was on building, not God's kingdom, but their personal fortunes.
1:11 I called for a drought. The drought on Judah's crops was God's curse on the people's agriculture, which was in keeping with his covenant (see note on 1:6; see also Dt 7:13). The word "ruin" in verse 9 sounds like the Hebrew word for "drought" that is used here. Haggai played on the similarity in sound to point out that the drought was God's response to his people's neglect of his house.
■ **1:12–15** *The People's Response: Repentance.* The people gladly responded in the fear of God and received the promise of the Lord's presence, a pledge the Lord began to fulfill immediately when his Spirit stirred up the nation, from the leaders to the common people, to resume the work on the Lord's house.
1:12 remnant. This is a common term used by the prophets (see Jer 23:3) to designate those of God's people who remained faithful to him in the midst of pervasive unbelief. Paul used the term in Romans 9–11 to designate those Jews who had embraced Christ (Ro 11:5). **obeyed.** The response on the part of the leaders and the "whole remnant of the people" was godly obedience. The outward manifestation of this response was resumption of the work of building the temple. **because the LORD their God had sent him.** The people's obedience resulted from their recognition that God's word was heard through the prophet's voice. **the people feared.** Their inward response was a new reverence for the Lord and a desire for his presence in their midst. The use here of the divine name "Yahweh" ("the LORD") may indicate that they recognized the obligations that had been laid upon them as the covenant people of God. They revered God as their gracious sovereign.
1:13 I am with you. As the people repented of their sin they received the greatest assurance possible: the presence of God. The prophets emphasized that the Lord's presence was an essential facet of the renewal of the covenant after the exile (Jer 32:38; Zec 2:11).
1:14 stirred. God himself brought about the response of his people by his presence with them. Haggai emphasized their internal response by the repeated use of "spirit." God's word worked efficaciously through the Spirit to bring about his sovereign purpose (cf. Isa 55:11).
1:15 twenty-fourth day of the sixth month. September 21, 520 B.C.
■ **2:1–9** *God's Greater Temple and Blessings.* Almost a month after Haggai's first message the Lord again spoke to the people through his prophet, but this time he did so to encourage them to continue building. Apparently the reports about the magnificence of the former temple were a source of discouragement, especially when the builders viewed the present state of the temple project. Haggai also reassured them about the future in terms of the goal of the present project. The glory of this temple would ultimately far outstrip that of Solomon's temple. Their present building would lead to the glory of the last days.
■ **2:1–5** *Encouragement From God's Presence.* The Lord first assured the returnees of the present reality: He himself was with them.
2:1 twenty-first day of the seventh month. October 17, 520 B.C. According to Leviticus 23:33–43 this was the last day of the Feast of Tabernacles, a celebration in which God's people were to rejoice in God's provision for them in the wilderness and in the blessings of the harvest. There seemed to be little reason to rejoice, however, since the harvest had been meager at best (1:11).
2:2 the remnant of the people. In chapter 1 Haggai addressed the leaders because they had to initiate the work. At this point he included the people because this message was intended to encourage them regarding the task at hand.
2:3 this house in its former glory? "This house" designates not only the building but also the institution it represented. Solomon had also dedicated the first temple in the seventh month (1Ki 8:2). The hopes of these repentant people would have been low as they looked on the incompleted, and ostensibly inferior, second temple. Verses 1–3 suggest that the people of God were discouraged by the

Does it not seem to you like nothing?[a] 4But now be strong, O Zerubbabel,' declares the
LORD. 'Be strong,[b] O Joshua son of Jehozadak, the high priest. Be strong, all you people
of the land,' declares the LORD, 'and work. For I am with[c] you,' declares the LORD Almighty. 5'This is what I covenanted with you when you came out of Egypt.[d] And my Spirit[e] remains among you. Do not fear.'
6"This is what the LORD Almighty says: 'In a little while[f] I will once more shake the
heavens and the earth,[g] the sea and the dry land. 7I will shake all nations, and the desired of all nations will come, and I will fill this house[h] with glory,' says the LORD Almighty. 8'The silver is mine and the gold is mine,' declares the LORD Almighty. 9'The
glory[i] of this present house will be greater than the glory of the former house,' says the
LORD Almighty. 'And in this place I will grant peace,' declares the LORD Almighty."

Blessings for a Defiled People

10On the twenty-fourth day of the ninth month,[j] in the second year of Darius, the
word of the LORD came to the prophet Haggai: 11"This is what the LORD Almighty says:
'Ask the priests[k] what the law says: 12If a person carries consecrated meat in the fold of
his garment, and that fold touches some bread or stew, some wine, oil or other food,
does it become consecrated?[l]' "
The priests answered, "No."
13Then Haggai said, "If a person defiled by contact with a dead body touches one of
these things, does it become defiled?"
"Yes," the priests replied, "it becomes defiled.[m]"
14Then Haggai said, " 'So it is with this people and this nation in my sight,' declares
the LORD. 'Whatever they do and whatever they offer[n] there is defiled.
15" 'Now give careful thought[o] to this from this day on[a]—consider how things were

2:3 [a]Zec 4:10
2:4 [b]1Ch 28:20; Zec 8:9; Eph 6:10 [c]2Sa 5:10; Ac 7:9
2:5 [d]Ex 29:46 [e]Ne 9:20; Isa 63:11
2:6 [f]Isa 10:25 [g]Heb 12:26*
2:7 [h]Isa 60:7
2:9 [i]Ps 85:9
2:10 [j]ver 1
2:11 [k]Lev 10:10-11; Dt 17:8-11; Mal 2:7
2:12 [l]Lev 6:27; Mt 23:19
2:13 [m]Lev 22:4-6
2:14 [n]Isa 1:13
2:15 [o]Hag 1:5

[a] *15* Or *to the days past*

temple's lack of splendor and by the difficulty of the calling they faced.

2:4 be strong. The threefold repetition of this command emphasizes the need for God's people not to give up in the Lord's work (cf. Gal 6:9). **I am with you.** The Lord's presence with them instilled confidence that the work was not in vain. God would be their sustaining strength. The cure for their discouragement was recognizing God's promise and presence.

2:5 what I covenanted with you. As God had made a covenant with his people in the exodus from Egypt, so now his covenant assured them of his presence (cf. Ex 33:12–17; Nu 11:16–17). **my Spirit remains among you.** The special presence of the Holy Spirit whetted the expectation for the age of restoration after exile (see Joel 2:28). These words indicated that God's Spirit was among the returnees as he had once been among his people during their wilderness pilgrimage.

■ **2:6–9** *Encouragement From God's Promise of Blessing.* Haggai encouraged the returnees to rebuild the temple by reminding them that the future held a glorious destiny for the people of God, for the nations' riches would be brought to God's temple.

2:6 In a little while I will once more shake. The prophet spoke of a universal shaking that would include judgment on both the natural and human worlds (2:21). Hebrews 12:26–28 says that the ultimate shaking of the created order will come at the return of Christ.

2:7 the desired of all nations. The word "desired" is probably not a reference to the One desired by all nations (i.e., the Messiah) but rather to the things desired by all nations, the things precious to them. The following context (v. 8) speaks of such precious things, and it is worth noting that the decree of King Darius, during whose reign Haggai ministered, alludes to just such priceless gifts being contributed to the temple-building project (Ezr 6:3–5,8–9). It seems best to conclude that Haggai was echoing Isaiah's promise that Israel would be made rich after the exile by the wealth of the nations (Isa 60:5). Because of the failures of the returnees the fulfillment of this prediction was delayed; it will not be fulfilled until Christ returns, when all believers will inherit the riches of the new earth (cf. Mt 5:5; 19:28–29; 25:34; 1Co 3:21; 4:8). **this house with glory.** God's intention was to honor himself by manifesting his glorious presence before "all nations." As God's presence filled the temple the nations would be drawn to the light (Isa 2:3–5; 60:3).

2:8 The silver . . . the gold. As the sovereign possessor of all things (cf. Pss 24:1; 50:9–12), God would bring about both his own glorification and his people's inheritance of the nations' wealth (Isa 60:5).

2:9 glory. Haggai could say this with confidence because this was to be the temple of the last days. Yet this promise of a greater glory is ultimately realized in Christ, the greatest manifestation of God's presence and glory (Jn 1:14). Accordingly, Ephesians 2:21 and 3:20–21 teach that Christ's glory is seen in his church, the temple of God. **in this place I will grant peace.** "Peace" implies more than the absence of conflict. It connotes prosperity and a sense of total well-being. Peace was the goal of the restoration effort. According to the New Testament Christ gives peace to believers now (Jn 14:27), but the ultimate fulfillment of this promise awaits the time when the Lord God Almighty and the Lamb will themselves be the temple (Rev 21:22) of the new Jerusalem.

■ **2:10–19** *God's Blessing for a Defiled People.* The third speech pointed out that before the people had begun to obey the Lord and put his house first in their priorities, their very blessings had become a curse. Now the Lord promised that obedience to him would bring great and unmitigated blessing. From now on the Lord would abundantly reward the labors of their hands.

■ **2:10–14** *The Cause of Their Defilement.* The restored community's sins had defiled the people and their worship. This was an issue they had not yet fully comprehended.

2:10 the twenty-fourth day of the ninth month. The sequence of time is important for interpretation: (1) The people had repented and resumed the work on September 21, 520 B.C. (1:15). (2) Haggai brought a message of encouragement on October 17, 520 B.C. (2:1–9). (3) Haggai brought another message of condemnation on December 18, 520 B.C. (here). This message of condemnation was given because the people had not yet seen the deeper issue: their defilement before the holy God. This was consistent with Zechariah's call to return to the Lord (Zec 1:3–6), a call issued after the people had begun working on the temple.

2:11–13 what the law says. Consecration required an act of setting something apart to God (Lev 20:7). People and objects could not be consecrated accidentally by touching other things that had already been set apart. In contrast, defilement was contagious; people and objects became defiled when they came into contact with something that was ritually unclean (v. 13; Nu 19:11–13). The two questions in verses 12–13 were rhetorical, and the people should have known the answers.

2:14 So it is with this people. Haggai applied the lesson learned from the preceding questions to his hearers. The fact that they were doing sacred work did not exonerate them from their sin; rather, they defiled the work of the temple and their offerings because their estrangement from God was more deep-seated than they realized. See *WCF* 16.7.

■ **2:15–19** *God's Reaction of Curses and Blessings.* In the past God had cursed the people because of their sins. Now, in light of their repentance, he was about to bless them.

before one stone was laid[p] on another in the LORD's temple.[q] 16When anyone came to a
heap of twenty measures, there were only ten. When anyone went to a wine vat to draw
fifty measures, there were only twenty.[r] 17I struck all the work of your hands[s] with
blight,[t] mildew and hail, yet you did not turn to me,' declares the LORD.[u] 18'From this day
on, from this twenty-fourth day of the ninth month, give careful thought to the day when
the foundation[v] of the LORD's temple was laid. Give careful thought: 19Is there yet any
seed left in the barn? Until now, the vine and the fig tree, the pomegranate and the olive tree have not borne fruit.

" 'From this day on I will bless you.' "

Zerubbabel the LORD's Signet Ring

20The word of the LORD came to Haggai a second time on the twenty-fourth day of the
month: 21"Tell Zerubbabel[w] governor of Judah that I will shake the heavens and the
earth. 22I will overturn royal thrones and shatter the power of the foreign kingdoms.[x] I
will overthrow chariots[y] and their drivers; horses and their riders will fall, each by the
sword of his brother.[z]

23" 'On that day,' declares the LORD Almighty, 'I will take you, my servant[a] Zerubbabel son of Shealtiel,' declares the LORD, 'and I will make you like my signet ring, for I have
chosen you,' declares the LORD Almighty."

2:15 [p]Ezr 3:10 [q]Ezr 4:24
2:16 [r]Hag 1:6
2:17 [s]Hag 1:11 [t]Dt 28:22; 1Ki 8:37; Am 4:9 [u]Am 4:6
2:18 [v]Zec 8:9
2:21 [w]Ezr 5:2
2:22 [x]Da 2:44 [y]Mic 5:10 [z]Jdg 7:22
2:23 [a]Isa 43:10

2:17 I struck . . . hail. This verse draws on the words of Amos 4:9. Such natural disasters were God's instruments to call his people to repentance. They were spoken in Deuteronomy 28:22 as curses for disobedience to the Lord's covenant.

2:19 Is there yet any seed . . . ? As in chapter 1 the lack of agricultural productivity was a sure sign of God's curse on the people. **I will bless you.** God's grace would overcome their sin and defilement. Although he chastised his people, mercy would triumph over judgment in the end.

■ **2:20–23** *Victory for God's People.* When the returnees faced threats from armies on every side, the Lord promised to eliminate the power of the nations (vv. 20–22) and to exalt his own Davidic prince, Israel's ruler, the Servant of the Lord (v. 23).

■ **2:20–22** *Overthrow of the Nations.* A great war against the returnees had been predicted (e.g., Eze 38:2; Zec 14:13). Haggai announced the blessing of the defeat of these enemy nations contingent upon Israel's faithfulness.

2:22 I will overturn. God would enter into a holy war against his enemies and emerge victorious. The military and political powers of the nations would finally submit to his lordship (see also Da 2:44; 7:27). The disobedience of the restored community eliminated them as a threat to other nations and rendered them powerless against the Greeks and Romans. It was not until Christ that the victory offered here began to be fulfilled.

■ **2:23** *Enthronement of David's Son.* Victory over enemies would come through the family of David.

2:23 On that day. This prophetic expression describes the time of God's judgment and salvation. Here the immediate focus is on enemies gathering against the returnees, but this promise finds its ultimate fulfillment in Christ in the day of final judgment (2Pe 3:10, Rev 18:8). **my servant.** Zerubbabel was God's chosen representative to accomplish his work. Isaiah spoke of a greater servant who would come, one whom Zerubbabel foreshadowed (Isa 42:10). Jesus is the perfect descendant of Zerubbabel (Mt 1:12) and the final, royal Servant of God (Ac 4:27,30). **signet ring.** A symbol of authority and power. Jeremiah 22:24 uses the term to refer to one who is precious to God.

ZECHARIAH

Introduction

Overview

Author: The prophet Zechariah

Purpose: To encourage belief in Zechariah's predictions not only of trials, but also of the great blessings for Jerusalem when the kingdom of God comes in its fullness

Date: 520–475 B.C. (Zechariah's ministry)

Key Truths:

- God offered wonderful blessings to his people after exile through Zerubbabel, the son of David, and through Joshua, the high priest.
- Despite the failures of those who returned from exile, God would not fail to complete his promises.
- God has all power to defeat his enemies and will do so one day.
- A final battle will bring ultimate victory to God's people.

Author

Zechariah 1:1 identifies the author as "Zechariah son of Berekiah, the son of Iddo." The traditional view is that this man was a sixth-century contemporary of Haggai and that the entire book was written by him. Some modern interpreters believe that what we know as one book was originally two books (chs. 1–8 and chs. 9–14). Those holding this view consider the first part to be from the sixth-century prophet and the second from an author of a later time (The Maccabean era [c. 168 B.C.] is the period most frequently suggested). Various literary and historical arguments have been used to arrive at these conclusions, but none of them provide compelling reasons to abandon the traditional view that follows the testimony of the book itself.

Time and Place of Writing

The historical background of Zechariah is the same as that of Haggai (see "Introduction to Haggai"), but their ministries differed in emphasis. Haggai's work centered on the rebuilding of the temple; Zechariah was concerned with rebuilding the temple as well, but his prophecies also encouraged God's people regarding Jerusalem's place in the long-term future of the kingdom of God.

It is helpful to keep in mind the sequence of historical events as they relate to Haggai, Zechariah and their speeches (see chart below).

Purpose and Distinctives

Zechariah contains a variety of literary forms. The visions of the first part are similar to those of Ezekiel and Daniel. The book is often taken as an example of early apocalyptic literature, and certainly methods and themes characteristic of such literature are in evidence. In chapter 14 a description is found of a final war against Jerusalem in which God comes as a victorious warrior to save his people from their enemies. Similarly the visions of the horsemen (1:7–17), the four chariots (6:1–8) and the woman in the basket (5:5–11) might also be viewed as early forms of apocalyptic literature.

The welfare and future of Jerusalem as the holy city is a pervasive theme in Zechariah. Several of the visions develop this theme (see notes on 1:7–17; 2:1–13; 5:1–4). Chapter 8 gives a picture of an idyllic Jerusalem, and the book ends with a chapter developing this theme (ch. 14). Zechariah's focus on Jerusalem reflects the theology of Zion that is found especially in Psalms 46–48 and 132.

Dates and Events in Haggai, Zechariah and Ezra

Date (B.C.)	Haggai	Zechariah	Ezra
Aug. 29, 520	Haggai's First Message (1:1–11)		
Sept. 21, 520	Rebuilding Temple Resumes (1:12–15)		
Oct. 17, 520	Haggai's Second Message (2:1–9)		
Oct./Nov. 520		Zechariah's Preaching Begins (1:1–6)	
Dec. 18, 520	Haggai's Third Message (2:10–19)		
Dec. 18, 520	Haggai's Fourth Message (2:20–23)		
519–518			Tattenai's Complaint to Darius (5:3—6:14)
Feb. 15, 519		Zechariah's Night Visions (1:7—6:8)	
Feb. 519		Joshua Crowned as High Priest (6:9–15)	
Dec. 7, 518		Zechariah Calls for Repentance (7:1—8:23)	
Mar. 12, 516			Dedication of Temple (6:15–18)
After 480		Zechariah's Later Prophecies (9:1—14:5)	

Christ in Zechariah

Zechariah spoke both to Israel's immediate future and to the distant future in Christ. As with most prophecies of Israel's restoration after exile, the predictions he made had immediate significance for Zerubbabel the son of David, for Joshua the high priest and for Jerusalem. At the same time, however, Zerubbabel was only the continuance of, not the end of, the Davidic line. Joshua was also a continuance of the priestly line and was "symbolic of things to come" (3:8). As a result, what was said about Zerubbabel and Joshua anticipated what the final son of David, the Messiah, would one day accomplish in full measure. For example, the predictions of God's blessing on Jerusalem (e.g., 2:5,11) were genuine offers to the returnees. These blessings could have been realized to some extent during the early years after the exile but were largely lost because of sin. Yet what was offered to Zerubbabel would certainly be fulfilled in the Messiah, who would bring all the hopes of David's dynasty and the priesthood to their final fulfillment by means of his perfect obedience. We may rightly say, therefore, that Zechariah provided many insights into the Messiah, Jesus. Zechariah focused on the royal family of David (Zerubbabel) and the Zadokite priesthood (Joshua) as central figures in the realization of God's restoration blessings. It is not surprising, then, that Christ's fulfillment of these two roles is tied to Zechariah's prophecies. Jesus is the King who came riding into Jerusalem in the manner predicted in 9:9–10, a passage quoted by Matthew with regard to Jesus' triumphal entry (Mt 21:1–11). Christ's betrayal and death are spoken of in 13:7. Moreover, Zechariah developed the Messianic imagery of a branch that combines the offices of a priest and king (see notes on 3:8; 6:12).

Although the Messiah is not specifically mentioned in 2:5 and 10, the promise of God's dwelling in the midst of his people is realized in Christ (Jn 1:14). Similarly, the Feast of Tabernacles celebrated in 14:16–20 will find its fullest expression in the final stage of the kingdom of the Messiah in the new heavens and the new earth (Rev 21:1–3).

Outline

I. Prophecies of More Immediate Significance (1:1—8:23)
- A. Title (1:1)
- B. Opening Message (1:2–6)
- C. The Eight Night Visions (1:7—6:8)
  1. The Man Among the Myrtle Trees (1:7–17)
  2. Four Horns and Four Craftsmen (1:18–21)
  3. A Man With a Measuring Line (2:1–13)
  4. A Clean Garment for the High Priest (3:1–10)
  5. The Gold Lampstand and the Two Olive Trees (4:1–14)
  6. The Flying Scroll (5:1–4)
  7. The Woman in a Basket (5:5–11)
  8. The Four Chariots and the High Priest (6:1–8)
- D. The Crowning of Joshua (6:9–15)
- E. The Transformation of Jerusalem (7:1—8:23)
  1. Jerusalem's Continuing Hypocrisy (7:1–14)
  2. Jerusalem's Future Blessings (8:1–23)

Zechariah declared prophecies that focused on the near future of the restored community. The people responded to Zechariah's call with repentance. Zechariah had eight visions that displayed the importance of Zerubbabel and Joshua in God's plan for the returnees. He recounted the reasons for Judah's exile and presented God's offer of great blessings to the returnees if they would turn from their hypocrisies.

II. Prophecies of More Future Significance (9:1—14:20)
- A. The First Group of Oracles (9:1—11:17)
  1. God Avenges His People (9:1–8)
  2. Israel's King Arrives in Jerusalem (9:9–17)
  3. God Gathers His People (10:1—11:3)
  4. The Shepherd of God's People (11:4–17)
- B. The Second Group of Oracles (12:1—14:21)
  1. Victory Over the Nations (12:1–9)
  2. Mourning Over the Past (12:10–14)
  3. Cleansing the Land of Judah (13:1–6)
  4. The Stricken Shepherd (13:7–9)
  5. The War Against Jerusalem (14:1–15)
  6. The Future Celebration (14:16–21)

Zechariah declared a number of prophecies that focused on the more distant future of the restored community. One group of oracles revealed that God would bring blessings to Jerusalem through David's royal line. A second revealed the complex process by which God would keep his promises to his people despite their continued failures.

A Call to Return to the LORD

1 In the eighth month of the second year of Darius,[a] the word of the LORD came to the
prophet Zechariah[b] son of Berekiah,[c] the son of Iddo:[d]
2"The LORD was very angry[e] with your forefathers. 3Therefore tell the people: This is
what the LORD Almighty says: 'Return to me,' declares the LORD Almighty, 'and I will return to you,'[f] says the LORD Almighty. 4Do not be like your forefathers,[g] to whom the earlier prophets proclaimed: This is what the LORD Almighty says: 'Turn from your evil ways[h]
and your evil practices.' But they would not listen or pay attention to me,[i] declares the
LORD. 5Where are your forefathers now? And the prophets, do they live forever? 6But did
not my words and my decrees, which I commanded my servants the prophets, overtake
your forefathers?
"Then they repented and said, 'The LORD Almighty has done to us what our ways and
practices deserve,[j] just as he determined to do.' "

The Man Among the Myrtle Trees

7On the twenty-fourth day of the eleventh month, the month of Shebat, in the second
year of Darius, the word of the LORD came to the prophet Zechariah son of Berekiah, the
son of Iddo.
8During the night I had a vision—and there before me was a man riding a red[k] horse!
He was standing among the myrtle trees in a ravine. Behind him were red, brown and
white horses.[l]
9I asked, "What are these, my lord?"
The angel[m] who was talking with me answered, "I will show you what they are."
10Then the man standing among the myrtle trees explained, "They are the ones the
LORD has sent to go throughout the earth."[n]
11And they reported to the angel of the LORD, who was standing among the myrtle trees,
"We have gone throughout the earth and found the whole world at rest and in peace."[o]
12Then the angel of the LORD said, "LORD Almighty, how long will you withhold mercy from Jerusalem and from the towns of Judah, which you have been angry with these
seventy[p] years?" 13So the LORD spoke kind and comforting words to the angel who
talked with me.[q]
14Then the angel who was speaking to me said, "Proclaim this word: This is what the
LORD Almighty says: 'I am very jealous[r] for Jerusalem and Zion, 15but I am very angry with
the nations that feel secure.[s] I was only a little angry, but they added to the calamity.'[t]

1:1 [a]Ezr 4:24; 6:15 [b]Ezr 5:1 [c]Mt 23:35; Lk 11:51 [d]ver 7; Ne 12:4
1:2 [e]2Ch 36:16
1:3 [f]Mal 3:7; Jas 4:8
1:4 [g]2Ch 36:15 [h]Ps 106:6 [i]2Ch 24:19; Ps 78:8; Jer 6:17
1:6 [j]Jer 12:14-17; La 2:17
1:8 [k]Rev 6:4 [l]Zec 6:2-7
1:9 [m]Zec 4:1,4-5
1:10 [n]Zec 6:5-8
1:11 [o]Isa 14:7
1:12 [p]Da 9:2
1:13 [q]Zec 4:1
1:14 [r]Joel 2:18; Zec 8:2
1:15 [s]Jer 48:11 [t]Ps 123:3-4; Am 1:11

■ **1:1—8:23** *Prophecies of More Immediate Significance.* These chapters contain prophecies offered to the early returnees from exile as they struggled with the challenge of rebuilding the temple. This material divides into the title (1:1) and four main parts: an introductory message (1:2–6), eight visions (1:7—6:8), the crowning of Joshua (6:9–15) and the transformation of Jerusalem (7:1—8:23).
■ **1:1** *Title.* The title identifies the prophet and the time of his ministry.
1:1 the eighth month of the second year of Darius. October–November 520 B.C. (see "Introduction: Time and Place of Writing"). Zechariah began his ministry two months after the returnees resumed the rebuilding of the temple. **Zechariah son of Berekiah.** His name means "the LORD remembers." See "Introduction: Author" and "Time and Place of Writing."
■ **1:2–6** *Opening Message.* Zechariah began his ministry by calling the returnees to repent of serious sins.
1:2 The LORD was very angry. Although the people had already responded to Haggai's call to rebuild the temple, their hearts were still far from God. The anger the Lord had shown toward the generation of the exile had continued to this day because the people had continued to rebel against him.
1:3 the LORD Almighty. The traditional translation "LORD of hosts" ("Lord of armies") was particularly relevant to the visions to follow (1:7—6:8). **Return to me . . . I will return.** The Hebrew word translated "return" may also mean "repent." Repentance involves a total turning away from sin and a turning to God. God's return would involve his turning away from judgment and turning to blessing his people (v. 16; 2:11).
1:4 the earlier prophets. The preexilic or exilic prophets (e.g., Isaiah and Jeremiah). **they would not listen or pay attention.** Their fathers showed obstinacy and rebellion (2Ki 17:13–15). Consequently, the curses of the covenant (Dt 28:15–68) came upon them for their disobedience.
1:6 my servants the prophets. See note on Isaiah 44:26. **they repented.** See Nehemiah 9:1—10:39 and Daniel 9:1–19. **what our ways and practices deserve.** The returnees confessed that their fathers deserved the exile, a prominent theme among the earlier prophets. Moreover, they also confessed that they had themselves received what they deserved from God during the disappointing early years of restoration. Admitting the justice of God's judgment was a crucial element of their repentance.
■ **1:7—6:8** *The Eight Night Visions.* Zechariah received visions from God concerning what God would do about the current difficulties the returnees faced. This material divides into eight parts: the man among the myrtle trees (1:7–17), the four horns and craftsmen (1:18–21), a measuring line (2:1–13), a clean garment for the high priest (3:1–10), the gold lampstand and the two olive trees (4:1–14), the flying scroll (5:1–4), the woman in a basket (5:5–11) and the four chariots (6:1–8).
■ **1:7–17** *The Man Among the Myrtle Trees.* These verses record the first of eight visions that Zechariah received during the course of one night (v. 8). This first vision emphasized God's commitment to his covenant people as the restorer of Jerusalem and as its protector against pagan forces. The vision called God's people to look beyond their present circumstances and to place their trust in the promises of God.
1:11 the whole world at rest and in peace. The self-assured nations are contrasted to the struggling Jewish state under Persian rule. Yet God's assurance to his people was that the nations that felt secure would experience judgment (see Edom's judgment in Ob 3,8,18).
1:12 the angel of the LORD. The messenger of God who interpreted the visions for Zechariah (see v. 19; 2:3; 3:1; 4:1). See theological article "Angels" on the following page. **seventy years?** A reference to the prophecy of Jeremiah 25:11–12, which announced the exile. Chronicles associates the end of Jeremiah's 70 years with the edict of Cyrus in 539 B.C. (2Ch 36:21). See note on 7:5.
1:13 kind and comforting words. Words that reflected God's love for his people and reaffirmed his commitment not to forsake them (Heb 13:5).
1:14 I am very jealous for Jerusalem. God's zealous love for his chosen city and people moved him to act in their behalf (8:2). A

16"Therefore, this is what the LORD says: 'I will return[u] to Jerusalem with mercy, and
there my house will be rebuilt. And the measuring line[v] will be stretched out over Jerusalem,' declares the LORD Almighty.
17"Proclaim further: This is what the LORD Almighty says: 'My towns will again overflow with prosperity, and the LORD will again comfort[w] Zion and choose[x] Jerusalem.'"[y]

1:16 [u]Zec 8:3 [v]Zec 2:1-2
1:17 [w]Isa 51:3 [x]Isa 14:1 [y]Zec 2:12

Four Horns and Four Craftsmen

18Then I looked up—and there before me were four horns! 19I asked the angel who
was speaking to me, "What are these?"
He answered me, "These are the horns[z] that scattered Judah, Israel and Jerusalem."

1:19 [z]Am 6:13

similar theme is expressed in Zephaniah 3:9–20 (see especially v. 17).
1:15 I am very angry with the nations. Notice the contrast with verse 2, where God was angry with his own people. Here God's love for his own (see v. 14) moved him to protect them by bringing judgment on the nations who had afflicted his people beyond measure.
1:17 the LORD will again . . . choose Jerusalem. A common theme in the visions (2:12; 3.2). God's choice of his people and their capital city distinguished them from the pagan nations. The result of his choice was to bring them prosperity ("My towns will again overflow with prosperity"). Haggai made similar offers of blessing to the returnees at about this same time (Hag 2:6–9). If they would rebuild the temple and repent of their wicked ways, God would bring many blessings to the newly formed community in Jerusalem.

■ **1:18–21** *Four Horns and Four Craftsmen.* Zechariah's second vision focused on four horns (i.e., animal horns). Animal horns were symbolic of power and pride in the ancient Near East and elsewhere in the Old Testament (Ps 75:4–5). In this vision the four horns represent four nations that oppressed God's people; the four craftsmen represent the nations that would destroy the horns.
1:19 These are the horns that scattered. The identification of the four horns could be the same as those of Daniel's prophecies (Da 2:36–45; 7:17–28), in which case they would correspond to Babylonia, Medo-Persia, Greece and Rome. The mention of Israel as well as Judah may indicate that the four oppressing nations were Assyria, Babylonia, Egypt and Persia (10:10–11). It is also possible that the four horns represent "the fours corners of the earth" (Rev 20:8); that is, nations from every side.

Angels: Are There Angels Around Us?

IN recent decades there has been a resurgence of interest in angels. Unfortunately, many teachings on angels are speculative at best. So it is important to know what the Scriptures teach on this subject. Reformed theology as a whole has not placed much emphasis on the subject of angels, but they are mentioned in Reformed catechisms and confessions (e.g., *WLC* 12,13,16,19).

God created two sorts of personal beings: angels (from the Greek term meaning "messenger") and human beings. There are many angels (Mt 26:53; Rev 5:11). They are intelligent, moral agents, without bodies and normally invisible, although they are able to show themselves to people in what appears as a physical form (Ge 18:2—19.22; Jn 20:10–14; Ac 12:7–10). They do not marry and are not subject to physical death (Mt 22:30; Lk 20:35–36). They can move from one point in space to another, and many of them can congregate in a tiny area (Lk 8:30, where the reference is to fallen angels; see article "Demons" at 1Co 10).

Heaven is the angels' home (Mt 18:10; 22:30; Rev 5:11), where they continuously worship God (Pss 103:20–21; 148:2). The "holy" and "elect" angels (see Mt 25:31; Mk 8:38; Lk 9:26; Ac 10:22; 1Ti 5:21; Rev 14:10) move out from there to various tasks at God's bidding (Heb 1:14). God's work of grace through Christ is continually demonstrating to these angels more of the divine wisdom and glory than they knew before (Eph 3:10; 1Pe 1:12).

Angelic activity was prominent at the great turning points in the divine plan of salvation (the days of the patriarchs; the time of the exodus and the giving of the law; the period of the exile and restoration; and the birth, resurrection and ascension of Jesus Christ) and will be so again when Christ returns (Mt 25:31; Mk 8:38).

Holy angels guard believers (Pss 34:7: 91:11), particularly the young and vulnerable (Mt 18:10), and constantly observe what goes on in the church (1Co 11:10). It may be that they are more knowledgeable about divine realities than humans generally are (Mk 13:32), and there is evidence that they have a special ministry to believers at the time of their deaths (Lk 16:22). Yet the Scriptures give only the barest information about these things. Good angels watch Christians in hope of seeing grace triumph in their lives.

The mysterious "angel of the Lord" or "angel of God" appears often in the early Old Testament. He is sometimes identified with God and at other times distinguished from him (Ge 16:7–13; 18:1–33; 22:11–18; 24:7,40; 31:11–13; 32:24–30; 48:15–16; Ex 3:2–6; 14:19; 23:20–23; 32:34—33:5; Nu 22:22–35; Jos 5:13–15; Jdg 2:1–5; 6:11–23; 9:13–23). Some scholars conclude that in some sense the angel of the Lord is a manifestion of God in which he acts as his own messenger; often he is seen as a pre-incarnate appearance of God the Son. Others believe that he is identified closely with God because he is God's representative (see notes on Ge 16:7; Ex 3:2; 14:19; Jdg 2:1).

The Scriptures honor all holy angels as glorious creatures. They are called "sons of God" (Job 1:6 [see NIV text note]; 2:1 [see NIV text note]) and "mighty ones" (Ps 29:1) and are said to be radiant and powerful (Isa 6:1–4; 2Th 1:7; 1Pe 3:22; 2Pe 2:11; Rev 15:8), even forming the victorious army of God (Ex 14:19). Yet Scripture also points to the honor and splendor of holy human beings. The Psalmist stated we were created "a little lower than the heavenly beings" (Ps 8:5), which is an honorable position. Yet the apostle Paul noted that this would not be the final order between angels and humans. He told the Corinthians that when Christ returns human beings will "judge angels" (1Co 6:3). The human race—the image of God—will one day rule not only over the earth and its creatures but also over the angels.

20Then the LORD showed me four craftsmen. 21I asked, "What are these coming
to do?"
He answered, "These are the horns that scattered Judah so that no one could raise
his head, but the craftsmen have come to terrify them and throw down these horns of
the nations who lifted up their horns[a] against the land of Judah to scatter its people."[b]

A Man With a Measuring Line

2 Then I looked up—and there before me was a man with a measuring line in his
hand! 2I asked, "Where are you going?"
He answered me, "To measure Jerusalem, to find out how wide and how long it is."[c]
3Then the angel who was speaking to me left, and another angel came to meet him
4and said to him: "Run, tell that young man, 'Jerusalem will be a city without walls[d] because of the great number[e] of men and livestock in it. 5And I myself will be a wall[f] of fire
around it,' declares the LORD, 'and I will be its glory[g] within.'
6"Come! Come! Flee from the land of the north," declares the LORD, "for I have scattered you to the four winds of heaven,"[h] declares the LORD.
7"Come, O Zion! Escape, you who live in the Daughter of Babylon!"[i] 8For this is what
the LORD Almighty says: "After he has honored me and has sent me against the nations
that have plundered you—for whoever touches you touches the apple of his eye[j]— 9I will
surely raise my hand against them so that their slaves will plunder them.[a][k] Then you will
know that the LORD Almighty has sent me.[l]
10"Shout and be glad, O Daughter of Zion.[m] For I am coming,[n] and I will live among
you,"[o] declares the LORD. 11"Many nations will be joined with the LORD in that day and
will become my people. I will live among you and you will know that the LORD Almighty
has sent me to you. 12The LORD will inherit[p] Judah as his portion in the holy land and will
again choose[q] Jerusalem. 13Be still[r] before the LORD, all mankind, because he has roused
himself from his holy dwelling."

Clean Garments for the High Priest

3 Then he showed me Joshua[b][s] the high priest standing before the angel of the LORD,
and Satan[c][t] standing at his right side to accuse him. 2The LORD said to Satan, "The

1:21 [a]Ps 75:4 [b]Ps 75:10
2:2 [c]Eze 40:3; Rev 21:15
2:4 [d]Eze 38:11 [e]Isa 49:20; Jer 30:19; 33:22
2:5 [f]Isa 26:1 [g]Rev 21:23
2:6 [h]Eze 17:21
2:7 [i]Isa 48:20
2:8 [j]Dt 32:10
2:9 [k]Isa 14:2 [l]Zec 4:9
2:10 [m]Zep 3:14 [n]Zec 9:9 [o]Lev 26:12; Zec 8:3
2:12 [p]Dt 32:9; Ps 33:12; Jer 10:16 [q]Zec 1:17
2:13 [r]Hab 2:20
3:1 [s]Hag 1:1; Zec 6:11 [t]Ps 109:6

[a] *8,9* Or *says after . . . eye:* [9]*"I . . . plunder them."* [b] *1* A variant of *Jeshua;* here and elsewhere in Zechariah [c] *1* *Satan* means *accuser.*

1:21 throw down these horns of the nations. The four craftsmen of the second vision came to overthrow the power of the oppressing nations. This symbolizes that other nations would destroy the nations that had afflicted God's people, a fulfillment of God's assurance to Abraham that he would curse those who cursed Abraham's descendants (Ge 12:3).

■ **2:1–13** *A Man With a Measuring Line.* This chapter focuses on the welfare and future of Jerusalem. It divides into two sections: the vision itself (vv. 1–5) and an appeal to the returnees (vv. 6–13).

2:1–5 Zechariah's third vision describes a man with a measuring line. It stresses that God would protect his people with his own personal presence (see note on v. 5). Jerusalem's walls were probably not yet rebuilt, and the city was subject to attack from roving bands. Thus this affirmation of God's protection came as welcome news. These prophecies would have been fulfilled in some measure had Zerubbabel and the people repented and faithfully served the Lord, but they would be fully realized only in the great son of David, Jesus.

2:1 a measuring line. An implement (v. 2) that symbolized Jerusalem's rebuilding in Jeremiah's portrait of a restored Jerusalem (Jer 31:39).

2:4 without walls . . . great number. Zechariah and other Old Testament prophets envisioned the restoration after exile as a time when Jerusalem would be the center of worship for the nations (v. 11; 8:20–23; Isa 2:1–5), and thus the city would overflow with people. **the great number of men and livestock.** See note on verse 11.

2:5 a wall of fire around it. The day of restoration was portrayed by Zechariah and Isaiah as a second exodus with the imagery of the pillar of fire (Isa 4:5–6). As God had once protected Israel from her enemies, so he would again guard her from oppressors.

2:6–13 The blessings of Zechariah's preceding vision were offered to his original audience. In this section of the chapter the prophet addressed the Jews both in Babylon (vv. 6–9) and in Jerusalem (vv. 10–13).

2:6 Come! Come! The essence of Zechariah's call was to come and begin the fulfillment of what God had promised. **I have scattered you.** A reference to God's judgment of Judah in the exile (Dt 28:36,49–50). The time of judgment was over; the time of restoration had come.

2:8 the apple of his eye. An expression used only here and in Deuteronomy 32:10. In both places it expresses God's intimate care and love for his people. We, as his people, are his "treasured possession" (Ex 19:5; Dt 7:6). Peter spoke of "a people belonging to God" (1Pe 2:9).

2:10 I will live among you. This promise assumed the sanctification of the people and land through the blood of the covenant (see notes on 3:9; 8:8).

2:11 Many nations. The vision describes a time when salvation would not be primarily limited to the Jewish nation but would extend to the world. Zerubbabel and his contemporaries saw next to nothing of this vision fulfilled because of their waywardness. Instead, that day began with Christ's inauguration of the kingdom of God.

2:12 in the holy land. An expression used only here in the Scriptures. Judah would be holy because God would dwell there. Notice that verse 11 suggests that at that time the land would hold the greatly expanded people of God, including both Jews and Gentiles. Zechariah envisioned the realization of God's promise to Abraham (Ge 15:5), which is ultimately fulfilled only in Christ.

2:13 Be still. All nations should revere God because of the great salvation spoken of in this chapter (Hab 2:20). **roused himself.** God would rise up for the purpose of judgment. In this context God would not only judge the nations that oppressed his people but would also provide a safe home for them.

■ **3:1–10** *A Clean Garment for the High Priest.* The fourth vision concerns Joshua, the high priest. This vision deals particularly with the problem of the defilement of the priesthood. It begins by showing how God would take care of the problem (vv. 4–5) and ends by depicting how God would wipe away the sin of his people (vv. 8–9).

3:1 A courtroom scene similar to that in Job (Job 1:6–12). Satan had come to accuse Joshua of his unworthiness for the priesthood. "Satan" means "the accuser" and here may not be used as a proper name. Accusation is a favored ploy of Satan against believers. It differs from the conviction of the Holy Spirit, who convinces us of our sin in order to move us to repentance and forgiveness. Satan's

LORD rebuke you,[u] Satan! The LORD, who has chosen[v] Jerusalem, rebuke you! Is not this
man a burning stick snatched from the fire?"[w]
3Now Joshua was dressed in filthy clothes as he stood before the angel. 4The angel
said to those who were standing before him, "Take off his filthy clothes."
Then he said to Joshua, "See, I have taken away your sin,[x] and I will put rich garments[y] on you."
5Then I said, "Put a clean turban[z] on his head." So they put a clean turban on his head
and clothed him, while the angel of the LORD stood by.
6The angel of the LORD gave this charge to Joshua: 7"This is what the LORD Almighty
says: 'If you will walk in my ways and keep my requirements, then you will govern my
house[a] and have charge of my courts, and I will give you a place among these standing
here.
8" 'Listen, O high priest Joshua and your associates seated before you, who are men
symbolic[b] of things to come: I am going to bring my servant, the Branch.[c] 9See, the stone
I have set in front of Joshua! There are seven eyes[a] on that one stone,[d] and I will engrave
an inscription on it,' says the LORD Almighty, 'and I will remove the sin[e] of this land in a
single day.
10" 'In that day each of you will invite his neighbor to sit under his vine and fig tree,[f]'
declares the LORD Almighty."

The Gold Lampstand and the Two Olive Trees

4 Then the angel who talked with me returned and wakened[g] me, as a man is wakened from his sleep.[h] 2He asked me, "What do you see?"[i]
I answered, "I see a solid gold lampstand[j] with a bowl at the top and seven lights[k]
on it, with seven channels to the lights. 3Also there are two olive trees[l] by it, one on the
right of the bowl and the other on its left."
4I asked the angel who talked with me, "What are these, my lord?"
5He answered, "Do you not know what these are?"
"No, my lord," I replied.[m]
6So he said to me, "This is the word of the LORD to Zerubbabel:[n] 'Not by might nor by
power, but by my Spirit,'[o] says the LORD Almighty.

3:2 [u]Jude 1:9 [v]Isa 14:1 [w]Am 4:11; Jude 1:23
3:4 [x]Eze 36:25; Mic 7:18 [y]Isa 52:1; Rev 19:8
3:5 [z]Ex 29:6
3:7 [a]Dt 17:8-11; Eze 44:15-16
3:8 [b]Eze 12:11 [c]Isa 4:2
3:9 [d]Isa 28:16 [e]Jer 50:20
3:10 [f]1Ki 4:25; Mic 4:4
4:1 [g]Da 8:18 [h]Jer 31:26
4:2 [i]Jer 1:13 [j]Ex 25:31; Rev 1:12 [k]Rev 4:5
4:3 [l]ver 11; Rev 11:4
4:5 [m]Zec 1:9
4:6 [n]Ezr 5:2 [o]Isa 11:2-4; Hos 1:7

a 9 Or *facets*

---

accusations are not always false, but his goal is destruction, not redemption.

3:2 a burning stick snatched from the fire? The fire is a metaphor for the exile from which the people of God had been snatched. Amos 4:11 uses the same expression to speak of the danger from which God had redeemed his people. See *WLC* 195.

3:3 filthy clothes. Here we see the basis for Satan's accusations that Joshua was unworthy. If the high priest was unclean, who could make atonement for sin? If he could not make atonement, how could the people be forgiven? God answered in two ways in the following verses.

3:4 Take off his filthy clothes. God made Joshua fit for the priesthood by giving him new garments. To be sure, this cleansing of the priesthood took place to some extent in the early postexilic period. Yet what happened to Joshua also pointed to the need for utter and permanent purity in Israel's priesthood, which would occur only in Christ.

3:5 a clean turban. The turban was part of the high priest's dress. A new, clean turban completed the catalog of restored garments, indicating that God had taken away the reproach on the priesthood (Ex 28:36; 39:30).

3:8 men symbolic of things to come. The Hebrew is literally "men of a sign." As important as Joshua and his associates were to the life of Israel at that time, they were not the final set of temple servants. They foreshadowed the coming Servant (the Messiah), who would fulfill their task perfectly (see note on v. 9). **my servant.** A title of honor used for Moses (Nu 12:6–8). The term became a title in Isaiah that was sometimes used for Israel (Isa 41:8; 44:1,2) and sometimes for the royal Servant (the Messiah), who would minister to Israel (Isa 42:1–7; 52:13). **the Branch.** A title for the great son of David who was anticipated by this book. It combines the offices of priest and king (see notes on 6:12; Isa 4:2).

3:9 the stone. Possibly a reference to the Messiah or to the Messianic kingdom (see Da 2:34–35,45). Several Old Testament passages about the stone (Ps 118:22; Isa 8:14; 28:16) were interpreted in the New Testament in connection with the Messiah and his kingdom (Mt 21:42; 1Pe 2:6–8). **seven eyes.** The mixture of images is difficult to interpret, but these eyes seem to be symbols of God's omniscient and watchful care (see 4:10). **remove the sin of this land.** God would take away his people's sin in one day (see note on Da 9:24). The priestly system in the Old Testament was not actually intended to cover sin but only temporarily to forestall divine wrath and to point forward to the need for a final sacrifice that would deal with sin once and for all (Heb 10:11–13). **in a single day.** The Day of Atonement (Lev 16:30, 23:28) was an annual reminder of sin (Heb 9:7–10), but Christ on one day (i.e., Good Friday) ultimately paid for the sins of all the faithful (Heb 9:11–14).

3:10 sit under his vine and fig tree. As 1 Kings 4:25 and Micah 4:4 reveal, this expression is an image of peace and prosperity. The ultimate state of God's kingdom is in view. On the same day that the sin of the land was removed (v. 9) peace and contentment would prevail.

■ **4:1–14** *The Gold Lampstand and the Two Olive Trees.* This vision focuses on how the work of rebuilding the temple would be completed. Joshua and Zerubbabel were human beings with natural limitations; the empowerment for completing the task would have to come from God. The temple that was built at this time was but a foreshadowing of the greater presence of God that would become a reality when Jesus came to Earth as God's final temple (Jn 2:21; see note on Jn 1:14) and established the church as the temple of the Spirit (1Co 6:19).

4:2 gold lampstand. The image of the lampstand was probably used to remind the people of the lampstand in the tabernacle/temple (Ex 25:31; 1Ch 28:15; 2Ch 13:11), although its shape was different. **seven lights . . . seven channels.** The significance of the numbers in this verse is not entirely clear, but they probably signify that there were seven lamps on the rim of the bowl and that a tube went from each lamp to the olive trees (v. 12).

4:3 two olive trees. See note on verse 14.

4:4 What are these . . . ? Zechariah's focus was on the olive trees, not on the lampstand. Here his question did not receive an immediate reply. It was answered, however, at the end of the vision (v. 14).

4:6 Zerubbabel. Even though the vision includes Joshua as one of the olive trees, the main figure is Zerubbabel, as is evident from the repetition of his name in verses 6–7 and 9–10. **Not by might.** God's people were repeatedly cautioned not to depend on military power and foreign alliances to accomplish their calling (Ps 20:7–9;

7“What[a] are you, O mighty mountain? Before Zerubbabel you will become level
ground.[p] Then he will bring out the capstone[q] to shouts of ‘God bless it! God bless it!’ ”
8Then the word of the LORD came to me: 9“The hands of Zerubbabel have laid the
foundation[r] of this temple; his hands will also complete it.[s] Then you will know that the
LORD Almighty has sent me[t] to you.
10“Who despises the day of small things?[u] Men will rejoice when they see the plumb
line in the hand of Zerubbabel.
“(These seven are the eyes[v] of the LORD, which range throughout the earth.)”
11Then I asked the angel, “What are these two olive trees[w] on the right and the left
of the lampstand?”
12Again I asked him, “What are these two olive branches beside the two gold pipes
that pour out golden oil?”
13He replied, “Do you not know what these are?”
“No, my lord,” I said.
14So he said, “These are the two who are anointed[x] to[b] serve the Lord of all the earth.”

The Flying Scroll

5 I looked again—and there before me was a flying scroll![y]
2He asked me, “What do you see?”
I answered, “I see a flying scroll, thirty feet long and fifteen feet wide.[c]”
3And he said to me, “This is the curse[z] that is going out over the whole land; for according to what it says on one side, every thief[a] will be banished, and according to what
it says on the other, everyone who swears falsely[b] will be banished. 4The LORD Almighty
declares, ‘I will send it out, and it will enter the house of the thief and the house of him
who swears falsely by my name. It will remain in his house and destroy it, both its timbers and its stones.[c]’ ”

The Woman in a Basket

5Then the angel who was speaking to me came forward and said to me, “Look up and
see what this is that is appearing.”
6I asked, “What is it?”
He replied, “It is a measuring basket.[d]” And he added, “This is the iniquity[e] of the people throughout the land.”

4:7 [p]Jer 51:25 [q]Ps 118:22
4:9 [r]Ezr 3:11 [s]Ezr 3:8; 6:15; Zec 6:12 [t]Zec 2:9
4:10 [u]Hag 2:3 [v]Zec 3:9; Rev 5:6
4:11 [w]ver 3; Rev 11:4
4:14 [x]Ex 29:7; 40:15; Da 9:24-26; Zec 3:1-7
5:1 [y]Eze 2:9; Rev 5:1
5:3 [z]Isa 24:6; 43:28; Mal 3:9; 4:6 [a]Ex 20:15; Mal 3:8 [b]Isa 48:1
5:4 [c]Lev 14:34-45; Hab 2:9-11; Mal 3:5

[a] 7 Or *Who* [b] 14 Or *two who bring oil and* [c] 2 Hebrew *twenty cubits long and ten cubits wide* (about 9 meters long and 4.5 meters wide) [d] 6 Hebrew *an ephah*; also in verses 7–11 [e] 6 Or *appearance*

Isa 31:1–3). **power.** A general word for strength or might. No one but God could accomplish the task before Zerubbabel. **by my Spirit.** The period of restoration after the exile was expected to be a time when the Spirit of God would be more active and effective than ever before (Nu 11:29; Joel 2:28–32). God's Spirit enabled Zerubbabel and Joshua to overcome the obstacles facing them. Isaiah spoke in similar terms about the coming Servant of God, the Messiah (Isa 11:2; 42:1; 61:1).

4:7 mountain? A figure for every obstacle Zerubbabel and Joshua faced as they led the returnees in obedience to God. **the capstone.** The last and most important stone; the presumption is that it would be ceremonially placed within the completed temple. **God bless it!** Literally, “grace to it.” The Hebrew word could denote an appreciation of its external beauty and of God's grace in bringing about the completion (see v. 9, where it is explicitly stated that Zerubbabel would complete the temple). The phrase is repeated for emphasis (see note on Isa 40:1).

4:10 the day of small things? It would have been easy to be discouraged with the meager results and progress. The people of Judah were disheartened both at the laying of the foundation of the second temple (Ezr 3:10–12) and at its reconstruction in Haggai's day (520 B.C.; Hag 2:3). The work of Zerubbabel and Joshua would constitute the mere beginning of God's kingdom, infinitesimal in comparison with the fullness of the kingdom that the Messiah would bring. **eyes of the LORD.** See note on 3:9.

4:14 anointed. Literally, “sons of fresh oil.” The reference is to Zerubbabel and Joshua. As God's chosen leaders they would be supplied by the Holy Spirit with the necessary strength to finish the temple. Together they foreshadowed the Messiah, the great Anointed One, who would unite the offices of priest and king into one person (see note on 6:12; see also “Introduction”).

■ **5:1–4** *The Flying Scroll.* The sixth vision concerns a flying scroll. Its message is that the Lord who loves and restores his people is also righteous and will still punish wickedness. This vision and the one to follow warn the returnees not to neglect their responsibilities for fear of judgment. They were to realize that God would take care of the problem of sin in the land.

5:2–4 See *WLC* 114.

5:2 thirty feet . . . fifteen feet. A large scroll that was open so that all could read its words. As the context implies, the words on the scroll were words of the law. Its large size was appropriate for its task of going out over the whole land; that is, to deal with every sin (v. 3).

5:3 curse. The curse contained in the law (Dt 28:15–68). As in Haggai 1:1–11 the prophet emphasized that obedience would bring blessings and disobedience would convey God's curses to the restored community. **on one side . . . on the other.** Like the Ten Commandments (Ex 32:15) and treaty documents in the ancient world, the scroll had writing on both sides. **every thief . . . everyone who swears falsely.** The curse was probably not directed at just these two sins; they are representative sins.

5:4 destroy it. God's word always accomplishes its intended purpose (Isa 55:11). Those who break God's law will surely suffer the consequences that this word of cursing brings. The returnees had continued in rebellion against God and would return to sin after Zechariah's ministry ended. The threat of curses still remained over them. See *WLC* 113.

■ **5:5–11** *The Woman in a Basket.* The seventh vision emphasizes the removal of wickedness from the land that would take place during the days of Zerubbabel and Joshua (see note on v. 1). This vision stresses that God would take care of the problem of wickedness.

5:6 a measuring basket. An ephah-sized container (see “Table of Weights and Measures”). The exact dimensions are unknown, but it was clearly big enough to carry a woman. **iniquity.** While some translations read “appearance” (see NIV text note), “iniquity” seems to fit the context of the vision better and has considerable support from ancient versions.

7 Then the cover of lead was raised, and there in the basket sat a woman! 8 He said,
"This is wickedness," and he pushed her back into the basket and pushed the lead cover down over its mouth.[d]
9 Then I looked up—and there before me were two women, with the wind in their
wings! They had wings like those of a stork,[e] and they lifted up the basket between heav-
en and earth.
10 "Where are they taking the basket?" I asked the angel who was speaking to me.
11 He replied, "To the country of Babylonia[a][f] to build a house[g] for it. When it is
ready, the basket will be set there in its place."[h]

Four Chariots

6 I looked up again—and there before me were four chariots[i] coming out from between two mountains—mountains of bronze! 2 The first chariot had red horses, the
second black,[j] 3 the third white,[k] and the fourth dappled—all of them powerful. 4 I asked
the angel who was speaking to me, "What are these, my lord?"
5 The angel answered me, "These are the four spirits[b][l] of heaven, going out from
standing in the presence of the Lord of the whole world. 6 The one with the black horses is going toward the north country, the one with the white horses toward the west,[c]
and the one with the dappled horses toward the south."
7 When the powerful horses went out, they were straining to go throughout the
earth.[m] And he said, "Go throughout the earth!" So they went throughout the earth.
8 Then he called to me, "Look, those going toward the north country have given my
Spirit[d] rest[n] in the land of the north."

A Crown for Joshua

9 The word of the LORD came to me: 10 "Take silver and gold from the exiles Heldai,
Tobijah and Jedaiah, who have arrived from Babylon.[o] Go the same day to the house of
Josiah son of Zephaniah. 11 Take the silver and gold and make a crown,[p] and set it on the
head of the high priest, Joshua[q] son of Jehozadak.[r] 12 Tell him this is what the LORD Almighty says: 'Here is the man whose name is the Branch,[s] and he will branch out from
his place and build the temple of the LORD.[t] 13 It is he who will build the temple of the
LORD, and he will be clothed with majesty and will sit and rule on his throne. And he will

5:8 [d]Mic 6:11
5:9 [e]Lev 11:19
5:11 [f]Ge 10:10 [g]Jer 29:5,28 [h]Da 1:2
6:1 [i]ver 5
6:2 [j]Rev 6:5
6:3 [k]Rev 6:2
6:5 [l]Eze 37:9; Mt 24:31; Rev 7:1
6:7 [m]Zec 1:10
6:8 [n]Eze 5:13; 24:13
6:10 [o]Ezr 7:14-16; Jer 28:6
6:11 [p]Ps 21:3 [q]Zec 3:1 [r]Ezr 3:2
6:12 [s]Isa 4:2; Zec 3:8 [t]Ezr 3:8-10; Zec 4:6-9

[a] 11 Hebrew *Shinar* [b] 5 Or *winds* [c] 6 Or *horses after them* [d] 8 Or *spirit*

5:7 woman! Here a woman is used as a personification of wickedness, but see women as righteous in verse 9.
5:9 two women, with the wind in their wings! These women were God's agents for removing wickedness from the land. God determined to remove sin from his people after the return from exile (Ps 103:11–12; Mic 7:19).
5:11 Babylonia. An older word in Hebrew (*Shinar;* see NIV text note) is used as a possible allusion to the tower of Babel, a symbol of opposition to God. Babylon, not Jerusalem, the dwelling place of the holy One of Israel (2:10–13; 8:3), was an appropriate symbol for iniquity. In effect, Zechariah taught his listeners that they should have left their wicked ways back in Babylon because such sinfulness had no place in the promised land.
■ **6:1–8** *The Four Chariots and the High Priest.* This vision of four chariots corresponds to the four horses of the first vision (1:7–17). The four chariots are symbolic of "the four spirits of heaven" (v. 5). It is unlikely that the order and color of the horses have any special significance. The author of Revelation drew on the imagery of these visions in his portrayal of the four horsemen (Rev 6:1–6). This section describes the successful movements of the heavenly war chariots into a position that secured the returnees from attacks from enemies to the north.
6:1 mountains of bronze! The prophet's imagery resembles ancient Near Eastern images of mountains that form the posts for the gates to heaven. In the first vision the riders went from the presence of God (1:10). Here the chariots are God's emissaries of judgment who emerge from between the bronze mountains. It is feasible that the bronze mountains correspond to the bronze pillars of the temple (1Ki 7:13–22).
6:5 the four spirits of heaven. The Hebrew word for "spirit" may mean "wind," and Zechariah may have been intentionally drawing on that ambiguity to state that as the winds cover the earth, so the angels of God cover the earth with the presence of God (cf. note on v. 8).
6:7 were straining to go throughout the earth. The eager horses portray the immediacy of God's judgment. God commanded them to go back and forth over the earth.
6:8 north country. The north is here representative of Israel's greatest threat at the time: the Persian Empire. The geography of Canaan demanded that anyone attacking from the east had to approach by way of the north. Thus an attack from the Persian Empire would have come from the north. **my Spirit.** This phrase may also be translated "my spirit" with reference to an angelic being. The idea is that the chariots had reached and secured Israel on its northern border.
■ **6:9–15** *The Crowning of Joshua.* This section focuses on the results of God's securing the restored community: the symbolic crowning of Joshua, the high priest.
6:12 the Branch. As is true of many of Zechariah's prophecies, the immediate context makes it clear that this term refers to Joshua, the high priest. On the other hand, Zechariah had earlier stated that Joshua and company were symbols of things to come later (3:8); that is, that their actions were at best the initiations of blessings and judgments that would take place with the coming of the great son of David. Thus it is not surprising that the term refers to the Messiah as well (see 3:8). Isaiah used it (Isa 4:2), as did Jeremiah (Jer 23:5–6; 33:15–16), as a title for the Davidic descendant who would rule on David's throne. Early Jewish interpreters also saw the word "Branch" as a Messianic title. The work of Joshua (as well as that of Zerubbabel) foreshadowed the work of Christ, our High Priest (Heb 4:14; 7:24; 9:11) and our King (Mt 22:41–46; Heb 1:8).
6:13 It is he who will build the temple of the LORD. Joshua worked together with Zerubbabel to rebuild the temple. This action foreshadowed the work of the Messiah. As the King of God's people, the Messiah would also build the temple. Zechariah encouraged the Jews of his day by pointing out that the actions taken in their day anticipated, and moved in the direction of, the full restoration in the Messiah. The New Testament explains that Jesus began to fulfill the rebuilding of the temple through the resurrection of his body (Mt 12:6; Jn 2:18–21), continues to fulfill it in the church (1Co 3:16–17; 2Co 6:16; Eph 2:19–22) and will ultimately fulfill it in the purification of the new heavens and the new earth as the dwelling place of God (Isa 65:17; 66:22; 2Pe 3:13; Rev 21:1—3,22).

be a priest[u] on his throne. And there will be harmony between the two.' [14]The crown will
be given to Heldai,[a] Tobijah, Jedaiah and Hen[b] son of Zephaniah as a memorial in the
temple of the LORD. [15]Those who are far away will come and help to build the temple of
the LORD,[v] and you will know that the LORD Almighty has sent me to you.[w] This will happen if you diligently obey[x] the LORD your God."

Justice and Mercy, Not Fasting

7 In the fourth year of King Darius, the word of the LORD came to Zechariah on the
fourth day of the ninth month, the month of Kislev.[y] [2]The people of Bethel had sent
Sharezer and Regem-Melech, together with their men, to entreat[z] the LORD [3]by asking
the priests of the house of the LORD Almighty and the prophets, "Should I mourn[a] and
fast in the fifth[b] month, as I have done for so many years?"

[4]Then the word of the LORD Almighty came to me: [5]"Ask all the people of the land and
the priests, 'When you fasted[c] and mourned in the fifth and seventh months for the past
seventy years, was it really for me that you fasted? [6]And when you were eating and drinking, were you not just feasting for yourselves? [7]Are these not the words the LORD proclaimed through the earlier prophets[d] when Jerusalem and its surrounding towns were
at rest[e] and prosperous, and the Negev and the western foothills[f] were settled?' "

[8]And the word of the LORD came again to Zechariah: [9]"This is what the LORD Almighty
says: 'Administer true justice;[g] show mercy and compassion to one another. [10]Do not oppress the widow or the fatherless, the alien[h] or the poor. In your hearts do not think evil
of each other.'[i]

[11]"But they refused to pay attention; stubbornly they turned their backs and stopped
up their ears.[j] [12]They made their hearts as hard as flint[k] and would not listen to the law
or to the words that the LORD Almighty had sent by his Spirit through the earlier prophets.[l] So the LORD Almighty was very angry.[m]

[13]" 'When I called, they did not listen;[n] so when they called, I would not listen,'[o] says
the LORD Almighty.[p] [14]'I scattered[q] them with a whirlwind[r] among all the nations,
where they were strangers. The land was left so desolate behind them that no one
could come or go. This is how they made the pleasant land desolate.[s]' "

The LORD Promises to Bless Jerusalem

8 Again the word of the LORD Almighty came to me. [2]This is what the LORD Almighty
says: "I am very jealous for Zion; I am burning with jealousy for her."

6:13 [u]Ps 110:4
6:15 [v]Isa 60:10 [w]Zec 2:9-11 [x]Isa 58:12; Jer 7:23; Zec 3:7
7:1 [y]Ne 1:1
7:2 [z]Jer 26:19; Zec 8:21
7:3 [a]Zec 12:12-14 [b]Jer 52:12-14; Zec 8:19
7:5 [c]Isa 58:5
7:7 [d]Zec 1:4 [e]Jer 22:21 [f]Jer 17:26
7:9 [g]Zec 8:16
7:10 [h]Ex 22:21 [i]Ex 22:22; Isa 1:17
7:11 [j]Jer 8:5; 11:10; 17:23
7:12 [k]Jer 17:1; Eze 11:19 [l]Ne 9:29 [m]Da 9:12
7:13 [n]Pr 1:24 [o]Isa 1:15; Jer 11:11; 14:12; Mic 3:4 [p]Pr 1:28
7:14 [q]Dt 4:27; 28:64-67 [r]Jer 23:19 [s]Jer 44:6

a *14* Syriac; Hebrew *Helem* b *14* Or *and the gracious one, the*

6:15 Those who are far away . . . build the temple. The prophets had already established that Gentiles would join with Israel in service to the Lord (e.g., Isa 2:2ff.; 19:25). Haggai also indicated that the wealth of the Gentiles would fill the temple (see note on Hag 2:7; cf. 1Ki 5).

■ **7:1—8:23** *The Transformation of Jerusalem.* These chapters focus on Jerusalem's present sinfulness in contrast to the future of the city. Two main topics come to the foreground: exposing continuing hypocrisy (7:1–14) and blessings in the future (8:1–23).

■ **7:1–14** *Jerusalem's Continuing Hypocrisy.* Zechariah faced squarely the sinfulness of the returnees. This chapter deals with a question from the returnees about the need to fast now that the restoration had begun. Their preoccupation with this question while injustices continued in the land shows that they still lived in the hypocritical ways that had led earlier generations into exile.

7:1 fourth year . . . fourth day . . . ninth month. December 7, 518 B.C.; that is, a little more than two years after the visions in chapters 1–6 (see "Introduction: Time and Place of Writing").

7:2–3 sent . . . to entreat the LORD by asking the priests. A delegation came from Bethel to inquire (perhaps with pride in their piety) whether they should continue to fast as a way of mourning the destruction of the temple (586 B.C.) in the fifth month (2Ki 25:8–15).

7:4 See *WLC* 141.

7:5 fifth. See note on 7:2. **seventh.** The fast that mourned the assassination of Gedaliah, the governor of Judah appointed by the Babylonians (see note on 2Ki 25:25). **seventy years.** Strictly speaking it had been 68 years since the destruction of the temple, but God was speaking in round numbers (see note on Da 9:2). **was it really for me that you fasted?** The Lord's response through Zechariah pointed out the hypocrisy of their fasting: They fasted for *themselves* (perhaps they thought that fasting would gain them merit before God or show them to be pious before other people). The same was true of their observances of Israel's festivals.

7:7 Negev . . . settled? The southern part of the land of Israel.

7:9 Their forebears had gone into exile because they had not established righteousness in the land. The returnees had not accepted this reality and continued in the evil practices of their forebears. **Administer true justice.** Zechariah called on the people to do what their fathers had not done. True justice would mean applying God's Word to the personal and social problems confronting the restored community; namely, delivering the oppressed and punishing the oppressors. Throughout the Scriptures the vision of the full deliverance of God's people and of salvation includes the establishment of justice on the earth (e.g., Isa 9:7; 42:4; Rev 6:10).

7:10 the widow or the fatherless, the alien or the poor. These groups were easily exploited. God had a special love for them (Ex 22:21; Dt 10:18) and had made provision for their care (Dt 24:17–22). God also pronounced curses on those who oppressed them (Dt 27:19). For references to injustices perpetrated upon these groups, see Psalm 94:6 and Isaiah 10:1–2. **do not think evil of each other.** The root problem of mistreatment of others is not the outward acts but the inward despising of and disregard for others (Mt 5:21–22). See *WLC* 141.

7:11–12 See *WLC* 151.

7:12 by his Spirit. God inspired his prophets to speak his words. The Scriptures give us an infallible resource for learning their inspired words.

7:13 I would not listen. God's judgment in the exile was in proportion to the people's disobedience. The prophets repeatedly emphasized that religious acts of worship were nullified by disobedience (e.g., 1Sa 15:22; Isa 1:15).

7:14 they made the pleasant land desolate. The disobedience of their forebears had brought about God's judgment. Zechariah wanted the people to understand that continued disobedience would result in further judgment.

■ **8:1–23** *Jerusalem's Future Blessings.* This chapter describes the future of Jerusalem, a time when hypocrisy would be eliminated

3 This is what the LORD says: "I will return[t] to Zion and dwell in Jerusalem.[u] Then Jerusalem will be called the City of Truth, and the mountain of the LORD Almighty will be
called the Holy Mountain."
4 This is what the LORD Almighty says: "Once again men and women of ripe old age
will sit in the streets of Jerusalem,[v] each with cane in hand because of his age. 5 The city
streets will be filled with boys and girls playing there.[w]"
6 This is what the LORD Almighty says: "It may seem marvelous to the remnant of this
people at that time,[x] but will it seem marvelous to me?[y]" declares the LORD Almighty.
7 This is what the LORD Almighty says: "I will save my people from the countries of the
east and the west.[z] 8 I will bring them back[a] to live in Jerusalem; they will be my people,[b]
and I will be faithful and righteous to them as their God."
9 This is what the LORD Almighty says: "You who now hear these words spoken by the
prophets[c] who were there when the foundation was laid for the house of the LORD Almighty, let your hands be strong[d] so that the temple may be built. 10 Before that time
there were no wages[e] for man or beast. No one could go about his business safely because of his enemy, for I had turned every man against his neighbor. 11 But now I will not
deal with the remnant of this people as I did in the past,"[f] declares the LORD Almighty.
12 "The seed will grow well, the vine will yield its fruit,[g] the ground will produce its
crops,[h] and the heavens will drop their dew.[i] I will give all these things as an inheritance[j]
to the remnant of this people. 13 As you have been an object of cursing[k] among the nations, O Judah and Israel, so will I save you, and you will be a blessing.[l] Do not be afraid,
but let your hands be strong."
14 This is what the LORD Almighty says: "Just as I had determined to bring disaster[m]
upon you and showed no pity when your fathers angered me," says the LORD Almighty,
15 "so now I have determined to do good[n] again to Jerusalem and Judah. Do not be afraid.
16 These are the things you are to do: Speak the truth[o] to each other, and render true and
sound judgment in your courts;[p] 17 do not plot evil[q] against your neighbor, and do not
love to swear falsely.[r] I hate all this," declares the LORD.
18 Again the word of the LORD Almighty came to me. 19 This is what the LORD Almighty
says: "The fasts of the fourth,[s] fifth,[t] seventh[u] and tenth[v] months will become joyful[w]
and glad occasions and happy festivals for Judah. Therefore love truth[x] and peace."
20 This is what the LORD Almighty says: "Many peoples and the inhabitants of many cities will yet come, 21 and the inhabitants of one city will go to another and say, 'Let us go
at once to entreat[y] the LORD and seek the LORD Almighty. I myself am going.' 22 And many
peoples and powerful nations will come to Jerusalem to seek the LORD Almighty and to
entreat him."[z]
23 This is what the LORD Almighty says: "In those days ten men from all languages and

8:3 [t]Zec 1:16 [u]Zec 2:10
8:4 [v]Isa 65:20
8:5 [w]Jer 30:20; 31:13
8:6 [x]Ps 118:23; 126:1-3 [y]Jer 32:17,27
8:7 [z]Ps 107:3; Isa 11:11; 43:5
8:8 [a]Zec 10:10 [b]Eze 11:19-20; 36:28; Zec 2:11
8:9 [c]Ezr 5:1 [d]Hag 2:4
8:10 [e]Hag 1:6
8:11 [f]Isa 12:1
8:12 [g]Joel 2:22 [h]Ps 67:6 [i]Ge 27:28 /Ob 1:17
8:13 [k]Jer 42:18 [l]Ge 12:2
8:14 [m]Jer 31:28; Eze 24:14
8:15 [n]ver 13; Jer 29:11; Mic 7:18-20
8:16 [o]Ps 15:2; Eph 4:25 [p]Zec 7:9
8:17 [q]Pr 3:29 [r]Pr 6:16-19
8:19 [s]Jer 39:2 [t]Jer 52:12 [u]2Ki 25:25 [v]Jer 52:4 [w]Ps 30:11 [x]ver 16
8:21 [y]Zec 7:2
8:22 [z]Ps 117:1; Isa 60:3; Zec 2:11

---

from the restored community. It is similar to Isaiah's portrayal of the future (Isa 65–66). Since the coming of Christ into the world the beginning of these blessings has appeared, but their fullest realization awaits his glorious return (Isa 65:17; Rev 21:1—22:5).

8:2 I am very jealous . . . for her. God's jealousy is born of the love and commitment he has for his people and in turn expects from them (1:14). God is jealous *for* his people, never *of* them.

8:3 City of Truth. Faithful observance of God's law was rarely the case in Israel, even in Zechariah's day. The prophet foresaw a time when God's people would perfectly reflect his character in their dealings with one another (v. 16). See also Exodus 34:6–7. **Holy Mountain.** Mount Zion will one day be holy because God's presence will dwell there in a special way and sin will be entirely removed. The prophets repeatedly emphasized the day of salvation as a day of the renewal of God's presence (2:5,11).

8:4–5 These verses reveal a picture of God's covenant blessings; long life (cf. Ex 20:12) and playing children reflect a state of peace and well-being.

8:6 marvelous. This term describes a situation or state that inspires awe in the beholder because it is impossible to attain by human strength. For other instances of this meaning see Genesis 18:14 ("hard") and Judges 13:18 ("beyond understanding"). **remnant.** Those who remained faithful to God in the midst of disobedience would be rescued by God and continue as his covenant people. Paul spoke of "a remnant chosen by grace" in Romans 11:5. The elect of God are preserved to serve him faithfully. See notes on Isaiah 1:9 and Micah 2:12.

8:7 save my people . . . the west. As the writer of Chronicles confirmed, the full restoration of God's people would involve many more of them returning from foreign lands (see Dt 30:1–5; see also notes on 1Ch 1–9; Jer 30:8–11).

8:8 they will be my people . . . their God. The bond of loyalty between God and Israel was a central dimension of covenant life (Ge 17:7) and is the focal point of the renewed covenant in Jeremiah 31:33.

8:12 The seed will grow well . . . the heavens will drop their dew. The day of God's total renewal will include the restoration of nature on a grand scale (Dt 30:9). Believers today receive the Holy Spirit as the down payment of their inheritance (Eph 1:13–14) and look forward to the total renewal of nature in the new heavens and the new earth when Christ returns (Rev 21:1—22:5).

8:16–17 truth . . . sound judgment . . . swear falsely. The people were called upon to order their lives in keeping with God's law. The godly behavior described here contrasts with the ungodliness characterizing most of Israel's history, but truth and righteousness will reign (Am 5:24). **do not plot evil.** Or "do not think evil" (7:10). See *WLC* 113,141,144; *WSC* 77.

8:19 This verse picks up on the question asked in 7:3. The fasts that the Israelites had been observing would turn into celebrations. **fourth.** This fast mourned the fall of the walls of Jerusalem, an event that marked the beginning of the end for the city (2Ki 25:3–4). On the fasts of the fifth and seventh months, see note on 7:5. **tenth.** 2 Kings 25:1 relates how Nebuchadnezzar began his siege of Jerusalem in the tenth month (Jer 39:1–10).

8:20–23 These verses picture a large-scale pilgrimage by the Gentile nations to Jerusalem. This frequent scene in the prophets (14:16–20; Isa 2:1–4; Mic 4:1–5) depicts the extension of God's kingdom beyond the borders to Israel to the world (Mal 1:5). An initial stage of this expansion was offered to Israel in the days of Zechariah, but it was not significantly realized until the ministry of Christ and his apostles. The fullness of Gentiles will join Israel only at the return of Christ in glory.

8:22 powerful nations. See notes on Isaiah 2:2–4 and Micah 4:1–3.

nations will take firm hold of one Jew by the hem of his robe and say, 'Let us go with you, because we have heard that God is with you.' "[a]

Judgment on Israel's Enemies

An Oracle

9 The word of the LORD is against the land of Hadrach
and will rest upon Damascus[b]—
for the eyes of men and all the tribes of Israel
are on the LORD—[a]
2 and upon Hamath[c] too, which borders on it,
and upon Tyre[d] and Sidon, though they are very skillful.
3 Tyre has built herself a stronghold;
she has heaped up silver like dust,
and gold like the dirt of the streets.[e]
4 But the Lord will take away her possessions
and destroy her power on the sea,
and she will be consumed by fire.[f]
5 Ashkelon will see it and fear;
Gaza will writhe in agony,
and Ekron too, for her hope will wither.
Gaza will lose her king
and Ashkelon will be deserted.
6 Foreigners will occupy Ashdod,
and I will cut off the pride of the Philistines.
7 I will take the blood from their mouths,
the forbidden food from between their teeth.
Those who are left will belong to our God
and become leaders in Judah,
and Ekron will be like the Jebusites.
8 But I will defend my house
against marauding forces.
Never again will an oppressor overrun my people,
for now I am keeping watch.[g]

8:23 [a]Isa 45:14; 1Co 14:25
9:1 [b]Isa 17:1
9:2 [c]Jer 49:23 [d]Eze 28:1-19
9:3 [e]Job 27:16; Eze 28:4
9:4 [f]Isa 23:1; Eze 26:3-5; 28:18
9:8 [g]Isa 52:1; 54:14

[a] 1 Or *Damascus. / For the eye of the LORD is on all mankind, / as well as on the tribes of Israel,*

8:23 ten men from all languages and nations. Emphasis is placed on the great numbers (see "many peoples" in v. 22) of Gentiles who would come to worship the true God. As with other restoration prophecies, the fulfillment of this vision began with Jesus in his earthly ministry (Mt 28:19–20), continues through the church today and will be completed when Jesus returns (Rev 5:9). **God is with you.** God would be with the returnees in the sense that he would stand and fight with them against their enemies (see 2Ch 13:12).

■ **9:1—14:20** *Prophecies of More Future Significance.* This second half of the book contains undated oracles that were well suited for a time slightly after the rebuilding of the temple. The prophet turned his attention to the future of God's kingdom in two major sections (9:1—11:17; 12:1—14:20).

■ **9:1—11:17** *The First Group of Oracles.* These chapters focus on the coming of God the King in judgment.

■ **9:1–8** *God Avenges His People.* These verses portray God as an avenging warrior who would take possession of his land by destroying all enemies in his path. He would come from the north to Jerusalem, an event that would lead to the call for celebration in verse 9 (cf. vv. 14–17, where God is pictured as coming from the south to Jerusalem). As elsewhere in the prophets, God is seen as avenging his people through the advance of a Gentile army (see Isa 45:1–3; Mic 1:2–7 and their notes). After the Medo-Persian Empire Alexander the Great came from the north and conquered Canaan in 333 B.C.

9:1 An Oracle/The word of the LORD. This exact expression is used only two other times in the Old Testament (12:1; Mal 1:1). **Hadrach.** The northernmost city listed in verses 1–8. It is called Hatarikka in the Assyrian cuneiform inscriptions. **Damascus.** The capital city of Aram, Israel's neighbor just to the north. **the eyes of men . . . are on the LORD.** The military campaign of Alexander would be so spectacular that all of humanity, especially God's people, would take notice of this mighty king as he meted out God's justice.

9:2 Hamath. On the Orontes River, north of Damascus. **Tyre and Sidon.** These cities on the Mediterranean coast of ancient Phoencia were commercial centers throughout the Biblical period. The description of their residents as being "very skillful" may relate to their business shrewdness. Judgment on these cities is a common theme in the Old Testament (Jer 47:1–7; Eze 28:1–23).

9:5 Askelon . . . Gaza . . . Ekron. These strong cities of Philistia would be unable to withstand God's judgment against them. They are marked out for judgment many times in the Old Testament (see Isa 14:28–32; Eze 25:15–17; Am 1:6–8).

9:7 like the Jebusites. Some of the inhabitants of Canaan who were not destroyed by the onslaught of God's judgment would be absorbed into God's people and become his servants, as Araunah the Jebusite had become a part of Judah generations before (2Sa 24:16–24; 1Ch 21:18–26).

9:8 I will defend. God announced that he would defend his city at this time. Alexander the Great did not destroy Jerusalem or the temple that Zerubbabel and Joshua had built (see 1:1—8:23). **Never again.** On a number of occasions prophets announced that once the restoration from exile had taken place in its fullness God would never again allow Gentile nations to destroy or control the land of Israel (14:11; Joel 2:19,26–27; Am 9:15; Zep 3:11,15). Here Zechariah spoke of the period of Alexander's campaign (333 B.C.), but the Greeks and Romans continued to oppress God's people for centuries after Alexander's campaign. Daniel had prophesied that a fourth kingdom (Rome) would oppress Judah (Da 2:24–45) as part of an extension of the exile due to the restored community's continued rebellion against God (Da 9). Zechariah presented the genuine offer of God that this extension of the exile could be cut short and that the Messiah's restoration could take place after the Greek occupation. It is true that the Maccabean war (166–142 B.C.) resulted in independence for Israel, but this autonomy was tarnished by the sinfulness of both the leaders and the people. In 63 B.C. Rome took over the region. Thus the restoration never came about in any large measure. The promise that God's people will

The Coming of Zion's King

9 Rejoice greatly, O Daughter of Zion!
Shout, Daughter of Jerusalem!
See, your king[a] comes to you,
righteous and having salvation,[h]
gentle and riding on a donkey,
on a colt, the foal of a donkey.[i]
10 I will take away the chariots from Ephraim
and the war-horses from Jerusalem,
and the battle bow will be broken.[j]
He will proclaim peace to the nations.
His rule will extend from sea to sea
and from the River[b] to the ends of the earth.[c][k]
11 As for you, because of the blood of my covenant[l] with you,
I will free your prisoners[m] from the waterless pit.
12 Return to your fortress,[n] O prisoners of hope;
even now I announce that I will restore twice as much to you.
13 I will bend Judah as I bend my bow
and fill it with Ephraim.[o]
I will rouse your sons, O Zion,
against your sons, O Greece,[p]
and make you like a warrior's sword.[q]

The LORD Will Appear

14 Then the LORD will appear over them;[r]
his arrow will flash like lightning.[s]
The Sovereign LORD will sound the trumpet;
he will march in the storms[t] of the south,
15 and the LORD Almighty will shield[u] them.
They will destroy
and overcome with slingstones.
They will drink and roar as with wine;
they will be full like a bowl
used for sprinkling[d] the corners[v] of the altar.
16 The LORD their God will save them on that day

9:9
[h]Isa 9:6-7; 43:3-11; Jer 23:5-6; Zep 3:14-15; Zec 2:10 [i]Mt 21:5*; Jn 12:15*

9:10
[j]Hos 1:7; 2:18; Mic 4:3; 5:10; Zec 10:4 [k]Ps 72:8

9:11
[l]Ex 24:8 [m]Isa 42:7

9:12
[n]Joel 3:16

9:13
[o]Isa 49:2 [p]Joel 3:6 [q]Jer 51:20

9:14
[r]Isa 31:5 [s]Ps 18:14; Hab 3:11 [t]Isa 21:1; 66:15

9:15
[u]Isa 37:35; Zec 12:8 [v]Ex 27:2

[a] 9 Or *King* [b] 10 That is, the Euphrates [c] 10 Or *the end of the land* [d] 15 Or *bowl, / like*

"never again" suffer defeat will be finally fulfilled only when Christ returns in glory.

■ **9:9–17** *Israel's King Arrives in Jerusalem.* These verses look forward to the victorious Messiah arriving in Jerusalem to secure the promise of verse 9. Once again the offer was given that this would take place in response to Greek oppression (v. 13). Despite the victory of Israel during the Maccabean period, the ongoing, flagrant sinfulness of Israel postponed this ultimate Messianic victory until Daniel's fourth kingdom (Rome). Even so, Zechariah's prophecy gave his original audience hope in the coming of the Messiah to destroy all enemies and to secure the restoration of Jerusalem.

9:9 O Daughter of Zion! A common title for God's holy city and people (Isa 62:11; Zep 3:14; see note on Isa 1:8). **Shout.** God's people could rejoice because the Lord had finally arrived in Jerusalem. **your king.** The supreme, royal descendant of David who had been promised repeatedly (2Sa 7:12–14; Ps 132:1,10–11; Isa 9:7; 11:1–5; Jer 23:5–6; 33:15–22; Eze 34:23–24; 37:24–28). **righteous . . . gentle.** His character and demeanor would not be like those of the kings of the world. He would uphold God's law as the kings of the Old Testament should have done (Dt 17:14–20). His gentleness would make him open and approachable (Mt 11:29; Php 2:5). **on a donkey . . . colt, the foal of a donkey.** Instead of riding on a warrior's steed at this point (cf. Rev 19:11), the great King would make his appearance in Jerusalem astride a young donkey (Mk 11:1–7). Donkey's were among the mounts preferred by royalty (see note on 1Ki 1:33) during peacetime. By riding a donkey the King would indicate his complete victory and the end of war (see v. 10). See *HC* 31.

9:10 take away the chariots . . . the war-horses. The implements of war would be abolished in the peaceful reign of the righteous King (Isa 2:1–5; 11:6–9; see note on Mic 5:10). **peace to the nations.** The great King of Israel would defeat all enemies of God and thereby usher in a universal peace (Isa 2:1–5; 9:5–7; 57:19; Mic 4:1–5; Eph 2:12–18). **His rule will extend . . . to the ends of the earth.** The universal, sovereign rule of God was foundational to Old Testament faith (Pss 22:27–28; 72:8; 96:4–6; Isa 45:22; 52:10; 66:18; Da 2:44–47; 7:13–14,27). Yet the goal of Biblical history is for God's reign to be acknowledged on Earth as it is in heaven (see theological article "The Kingdom of God" at Mt 4). Christ is the One who will bring the Father's universal dominion to Earth (Mt 12:28; Php 2:9–11; Rev 19:11–21).

9:11 blood of my covenant. A reference to God's gracious provision for the covering of sin. In the Old Testament this was the blood of animals (Ex 24:8); in the New Testament this earlier provision is superceded by the blood of the Messiah (Mt 26:28).

9:12 Return . . . O prisoners of hope. Those who remained outside the land of promise would be told that they should return to their homes in the promised land. **restore twice as much to you.** From the time of Moses it had been God's plan to bless his people after returning them from exile in ways that would exceed the blessings bestowed upon their forebears (Dt 30:5). It is on this basis that the New Testament understands God's great blessings to believers under the new covenant.

9:13 O Greece. It is possible that "Greece" is used generically for Gentile nations, but see note on verse 8.

9:14 the LORD will appear over them . . . in the storms of the south. The God of Israel is now portrayed as coming from the southern region of the desert, mounted astride the storm clouds (see 2Sa 22:8–18; Ps 18:7–15; Da 7:13). The Hebrew word translated "south" may also be the proper name "Teman" (see note on Hab 3:3). The response of God against his enemies is here portrayed in terms of the ancient memory of God moving toward the battle for Canaan in the days of Moses (see Ex 15:14–18).

9:15 the LORD Almighty will shield them. This verse envisions God protecting his people as he marches against his enemies. **They will drink and roar as with wine.** God's people would be exuberant with a holy joy.

as the flock of his people.
They will sparkle in his land
like jewels in a crown.[w]
17 How attractive and beautiful they will be!
Grain will make the young men thrive,
and new wine the young women.

9:16 [w]Isa 62:3; Jer 31:11

The LORD Will Care for Judah

10

Ask the LORD for rain in the springtime;
it is the LORD who makes the storm clouds.
He gives showers of rain to men,
and plants of the field to everyone.
2 The idols[x] speak deceit,
diviners see visions that lie;
they tell dreams that are false,
they give comfort in vain.
Therefore the people wander like sheep
oppressed for lack of a shepherd.[y]

10:2 [x]Eze 21:21 [y]Eze 34:5; Hos 3:4; Mt 9:36

3 "My anger burns against the shepherds,
and I will punish the leaders;[z]
for the LORD Almighty will care
for his flock, the house of Judah,
and make them like a proud horse in battle.
4 From Judah will come the cornerstone,
from him the tent peg,[a]
from him the battle bow,[b]
from him every ruler.
5 Together they[a] will be like mighty men
trampling the muddy streets in battle.[c]
Because the LORD is with them,
they will fight and overthrow the horsemen.[d]

10:3 [z]Jer 25:34

10:4 [a]Isa 22:23 [b]Zec 9:10

10:5 [c]2Sa 22:43 [d]Am 2:15; Hag 2:22

6 "I will strengthen the house of Judah
and save the house of Joseph.
I will restore them
because I have compassion on them.[e]
They will be as though
I had not rejected them,
for I am the LORD their God
and I will answer[f] them.
7 The Ephraimites will become like mighty men,
and their hearts will be glad as with wine.[g]
Their children will see it and be joyful;
their hearts will rejoice in the LORD.

10:6 [e]Zec 8:7-8 [f]Zec 13:9

10:7 [g]Zec 9:15

[a] *4,5* Or *ruler, all of them together. / [5]They*

9:16 the flock of his people. His people would rest secure, as sheep under his care (13:7; Eze 34:1–24; 37:24). **They will sparkle . . . like jewels in a crown.** God's people would themselves become glorious as a result of basking in his presence (2Co 3:18).
9:17 beautiful . . . Grain . . . new wine. The natural abundance that will occur after the Messiah has fully established his kingdom fulfills the hopes of creation's renewal (see Isa 65:17; Rev 21:1).
■ **10:1—11:3** *God Gathers His People.* God would not only bring victory over Israel's oppressors but would also bring his people back from exile to the land of promise. His faithfulness to this promise is contrasted with the folly of Israel's reliance on idols.
10:1 Ask the LORD for rain. The blessings spoken of in 9:17 would take place when the people of God depended on the Lord.
10:2 idols . . . diviners. In the past God's people had relied on idolatry and occult practices, but these practices had eventually led to the exile of Israel and Judah. **lack of a shepherd.** In this context the term "shepherd" refers primarily to the royal leadership of Israel and Judah. The people of God fell into idolatry because their kings failed to lead them in the ways of righteousness. As a result the exile removed Israel's failing royal shepherds. The nation lacked substantial leadership during its years of oppression, especially during the exile, but the people hoped that the great Shepherd-King would rise up and lead them in righteousness (see Eze 34:23–24). The New Testament reveals that this Messiah is none other than Jesus (Jn 10:11–16; Heb 13:20; 1Pe 5:4).
10:3 My anger burns against the shepherds . . . the LORD Almighty will care for his flock. The punishment of exile for the leaders (especially the royal leaders) of Israel (see Eze 34:1–31). **proud horse.** A horse arrayed for battle, a symbol of Judah's strength because of God's might (v. 6).
10:4 cornerstone . . . tent peg . . . battle bow . . . every ruler. References to the great son of David, the Messiah who would establish the kingdom of God in all of its fullness. Jesus was from the tribe of Judah (Heb 7:14) and came in fulfillment of the promise of a King who would overcome every other ruler (see notes on Ge 49:10; Mic 5:2).
10:6 I am the LORD their God and I will answer them. Another strong reaffirmation of the covenant bond between God and his people. God would save his people because of his covenant commitment to them (see note on 8:8; see also Jer 33:3).

8 I will signal[h] for them
and gather them in.
Surely I will redeem them;
they will be as numerous[i] as before.
9 Though I scatter them among the peoples,
yet in distant lands they will remember me.[j]
They and their children will survive,
and they will return.
10 I will bring them back from Egypt
and gather them from Assyria.[k]
I will bring them to Gilead[l] and Lebanon,
and there will not be room[m] enough for them.
11 They will pass through the sea of trouble;
the surging sea will be subdued
and all the depths of the Nile will dry up.[n]
Assyria's pride[o] will be brought down
and Egypt's scepter[p] will pass away.
12 I will strengthen them in the LORD
and in his name they will walk,[q]"
declares the LORD.

11 Open your doors, O Lebanon,[r]
so that fire may devour your cedars!
2 Wail, O pine tree, for the cedar has fallen;
the stately trees are ruined!
Wail, oaks of Bashan;
the dense forest[s] has been cut down!
3 Listen to the wail of the shepherds;
their rich pastures are destroyed!
Listen to the roar of the lions;
the lush thicket of the Jordan is ruined![t]

Two Shepherds

4 This is what the LORD my God says: "Pasture the flock marked for slaughter. 5 Their
buyers slaughter them and go unpunished. Those who sell them say, 'Praise the LORD, I
am rich!' Their own shepherds do not spare them.[u] 6 For I will no longer have pity on the
people of the land," declares the LORD. "I will hand everyone over to his neighbor[v] and
his king. They will oppress the land, and I will not rescue them from their hands."[w]
7 So I pastured the flock marked for slaughter, particularly the oppressed of the flock.
Then I took two staffs and called one Favor and the other Union, and I pastured the flock.
8 In one month I got rid of the three shepherds.

10:8 [h]Isa 5:26 [i]Jer 33:22; Eze 36:11
10:9 [j]Eze 6:9
10:10 [k]Isa 11:11 [l]Jer 50:19 [m]Isa 49:19
10:11 [n]Isa 19:5-7; 51:10 [o]Zep 2:13 [p]Eze 30:13
10:12 [q]Mic 4:5
11:1 [r]Eze 31:3
11:2 [s]Isa 32:19
11:3 [t]Jer 2:15; 50:44
11:5 [u]Jer 50:7; Eze 34:2-3
11:6 [v]Zec 14:13 [w]Isa 9:19-21; Jer 13:14; Mic 5:8; 7:2-6

10:8 signal. Literally, "whistle," a verb used by Isaiah (Isa 5:26) to denote God's use of the Assyrian army in battle. **gather.** From the foreign lands to which they had been scattered (Dt 30:1–10). **as numerous as before.** In fulfillment of God's covenant promise to Abraham in Genesis 15:5 and 17:6. In fact, Moses had promised that the restored, post-exilic nation would be even more populous than before (Dt 30:5).

10:10 from Egypt . . . Assyria. These nations represent the many areas to which God had scattered his people during the exile. **to Gilead and Lebanon . . . not be room enough.** The returnees would settle in Gilead and Lebanon. They would be so numerous that there would not be enough room for them (see note on v. 8).

10:11 sea of trouble . . . Nile. The prophet drew upon memories of the exodus under Moses to describe the gathering of the exiles. **Assyria's pride . . . Egypt's scepter.** As God's people departed the foreign nations God would bring his judgment on those nations, as he had done when the Israelites left Egypt in the first exodus.

11:1–3 These verses picture the destruction of the powerful nations that exalted themselves against God. The references to large oaks, dense forests, shepherds and ravaging lions are best taken as metaphors for the nations (e.g., cedars = Lebanon; cf. Jdg 9:15; 1Ki 5:6; Ps 29:5) and their leaders, whom God would judge as he returned his people to their land.

■ **11:4–17** *The Shepherd of God's People.* The difficulty of this section has led to many different interpretations. The main contours of the passage may be summarized in this way. First, someone was called to play the role of Israel's faithful, royal shepherd who bore two staffs representing the offer of favor and (re)union to the exiled nation. This image probably refers to Zerubbabel, the son of David whom Haggai and Zechariah hailed as the one who would begin the blessings of restoration from exile (4:6–10; Hag 2:4,21,23). Second, Israel rejected this faithful shepherd and treated him as a lowly slave (v. 8). Consequently he revoked the offer of divine favor and (re)union to the people of God. This probably refers to the failure of the returnees to carry through with the restoration program by faithfully following the lead of Zerubbabel (see "Introduction to 1 Chronicles"). Third, attention moves to a foolish and worthless shepherd who did not care for the people of Israel. He replaced the rejected shepherd as God announced woe because of the eventual destruction of this king. This scenario refers either to foreign leaders who oppressed God's people or to the leaders of Israel after Zerubbabel, perhaps those who governed during the brief independence after the Maccabean war (see notes on 9:9–10). Destruction would come upon them at a later time (v. 17).

11:4 the flock marked for slaughter. The people of Israel were like sheep bound for the slaughterhouse of exile (see Isa 65:12; Eze 21:10–28).

11:6 I will no longer have pity. These words describe the time leading up to the exile (Jer 13:14; 15:5; 21:7) and now applied to the withdrawal of divine protection after the early days of restoration.

11:7 Favor. The word also means "beauty" and is used this way of God himself (Pss 27:4; 90:17). The staff is symbolic of the favor God had shown his people in his covenant (v. 10). **Union.** The unity of the divided nation (v. 14) had been promised as part of the new covenant (Jer 30:3; 31:27,31; 33:7).

The flock detested me, and I grew weary of them 9and said, "I will not be your shepherd. Let the dying die, and the perishing perish.[x] Let those who are left eat one another's flesh."

10Then I took my staff called Favor[y] and broke it, revoking[z] the covenant I had made with all the nations. 11It was revoked on that day, and so the afflicted of the flock who were watching me knew it was the word of the LORD.

12I told them, "If you think it best, give me my pay; but if not, keep it." So they paid me thirty pieces of silver.[a]

13And the LORD said to me, "Throw it to the potter"—the handsome price at which they priced me! So I took the thirty pieces of silver and threw them into the house of the LORD to the potter.[b]

14Then I broke my second staff called Union, breaking the brotherhood between Judah and Israel.

15Then the LORD said to me, "Take again the equipment of a foolish shepherd. 16For I am going to raise up a shepherd over the land who will not care for the lost, or seek the young, or heal the injured, or feed the healthy, but will eat the meat of the choice sheep, tearing off their hoofs.

17"Woe to the worthless shepherd,[c]
who deserts the flock!
May the sword strike his arm[d] and his right eye!
May his arm be completely withered,
his right eye totally blinded!"[e]

Jerusalem's Enemies to Be Destroyed

An Oracle

12

This is the word of the LORD concerning Israel. The LORD, who stretches out the heavens,[f] who lays the foundation of the earth,[g] and who forms the spirit of man[h] within him, declares: 2"I am going to make Jerusalem a cup[i] that sends all the surrounding peoples reeling.[j] Judah[k] will be besieged as well as Jerusalem. 3On that day, when all the nations[l] of the earth are gathered against her, I will make Jerusalem an immovable rock[m] for all the nations. All who try to move it will injure[n] themselves. 4On that day I will strike every horse with panic and its rider with madness," declares the LORD. "I will keep a watchful eye over the house of Judah, but I will blind all the horses of the

11:9 [x]Jer 15:2; 43:11
11:10 [y]ver 7 [z]Ps 89:39; Jer 14:21
11:12 [a]Ex 21:32; Mt 26:15
11:13 [b]Mt 27:9-10*; Ac 1:18-19
11:17 [c]Jer 23:1 [d]Eze 30:21-22 [e]Jer 23:1
12:1 [f]Isa 42:5; Jer 51:15 [g]Ps 102:25; Heb 1:10 [h]Isa 57:16
12:2 [i]Ps 75:8 [j]Isa 51:23 [k]Zec 14:14
12:3 [l]Zec 14:2 [m]Da 2:34-35 [n]Mt 21:44

11:8 the three shepherds. Their identity is unknown. They could represent all leaders whom the faithful royal figure would remove from contention for leadership.
11:9 The prophet as shepherd expressed his disgust with the rebellion and disobedience of the flock.
11:10 revoking the covenant. The removal of God's favor from the people. **all the nations.** This phrase probably refers to the Jewish Diaspora (scattering) among the nations. After the removal of God's favor the nations could afflict the flock of God.
11:12 thirty pieces of silver. The price of a slave (Ex 21:32), which denigrated the Davidic shepherd, Zerubbabel, who had offered so much to the oppressed nation. Matthew appropriately alluded to this passage when he noted that the Jewish officials paid 30 shekels of silver for Judas's betrayal of Jesus (Mt 26:14–16). Jesus, the last royal son of David, was treated as his precursor Zerubbabel had been.
11:13 the handsome price . . . and threw them into the house of the LORD to the potter. The Lord responded sarcastically to the manner in which his royal shepherd was devalued. Judas would later throw his 30 pieces of ill-gotten silver back to the priests, perhaps unaware of the incident having been foreshadowed in Scripture (Jer 19:1–13; Mt 27:1–10).
11:14 Union, breaking the brotherhood between Judah and Israel. A reference to the abolition of the unity of the nation because of the people's rejection of the good shepherd Zerubbabel.
11:15–16 The foolish shepherd is described as one who would ravage the flock of God. Ezekiel had spoken in this way of the kings of Judah prior to the exile (Eze 34:1–10). Zechariah was referring to leaders who would come after the rejection of Zerubbabel, either from within Israel or from foreign powers.
11:17 worthless shepherd. Another name for the foolish shepherd of verse 15. The loss of the right arm and the right eye indicated loss of the power and insight necessary for leadership.
■ **12:1—14:21** *The Second Group of Oracles.* The second group of oracles in the book's latter half focuses on God's judgment against the nations. It culminates in the final salvation of Jerusalem and the celebration of the Feast of Tabernacles.
■ **12:1–9** *Victory Over the Nations.* The theme of these verses is God's judgment against other nations through the victory of Judah.
12:1 An Oracle/This is the word of the LORD. See note on 9:1.
12:2–4 See *WLC* 63.
12:2 Jerusalem a cup . . . reeling. A symbol of the pain that Jerusalem would inflict on her enemies. Other prophets spoke of God's wrath as a cup from which the nations would drink (Isa 51:17; Jer 25:15–38; Eze 23:32–34).
12:3 On that day. This phrase occurs 16 times in chapters 12–14. It is an abbreviated reference to "the day of the LORD," a phrase often used by the prophets to describe times when God intervenes in history to defeat his enemies and bless his people. Here the prophet had in mind the day of the great battle between the restored community and all the nations of the world. See "Introduction to Zephaniah." **all the nations of the earth.** Ezekiel predicted that the restored community would so threaten the nations that they would form alliances and attack (Eze 38–39). Some small resistance took place in the early days of return (Ezr 4; Ne 2:19; 4:1–23), but the weakness of Judah due to her sins led to minimal resistance. Thus the great battle was postponed. See note on 14:2. **Jerusalem an immovable rock.** This phrase parallels the cup of "reeling" in verse 2 (see note on Da 2:45). Here the prophet offered hope to the returnees that the nations attacking Jerusalem would be defeated in their attempt to destroy the city and its inhabitants. There was some resistance to the early restoration community (Ezr 4; Ne 2:19; 4:1–23), and the Maccabean revolt was successful against the Greeks, but this ultimate battle did not take place because Israel remained largely insignificant in the eyes of the world. The expectation of this ultimate battle was therefore cast into the future. The New Testament teaches that the rebuilt Jerusalem is a type of the heavenly Jerusalem in which we now live by faith (Heb 12:22–23) and of the future, final Jerusalem of the new heavens and the new earth (Rev 21:2).

nations.[o] 5Then the leaders of Judah will say in their hearts, 'The people of Jerusalem are
strong, because the LORD Almighty is their God.'
6"On that day I will make the leaders of Judah like a firepot[p] in a woodpile, like a flaming torch among sheaves. They will consume[q] right and left all the surrounding peoples,
but Jerusalem will remain intact in her place.
7"The LORD will save the dwellings of Judah first, so that the honor of the house of David and of Jerusalem's inhabitants may not be greater than that of Judah.[r] 8On that day
the LORD will shield[s] those who live in Jerusalem, so that the feeblest among them will
be like David, and the house of David will be like God,[t] like the Angel of the LORD going
before[u] them. 9On that day I will set out to destroy all the nations that attack Jerusalem.[v]

Mourning for the One They Pierced

10"And I will pour out on the house of David and the inhabitants of Jerusalem a spirit[a] of grace and supplication.[w] They will look on[b] me, the one they have pierced,[x] and
they will mourn for him as one mourns for an only child, and grieve bitterly for him as
one grieves for a firstborn son. 11On that day the weeping in Jerusalem will be great, like
the weeping of Hadad Rimmon in the plain of Megiddo.[y] 12The land will mourn,[z] each
clan by itself, with their wives by themselves: the clan of the house of David and their
wives, the clan of the house of Nathan and their wives, 13the clan of the house of Levi and
their wives, the clan of Shimei and their wives, 14and all the rest of the clans and their
wives.

Cleansing From Sin

13 "On that day a fountain[a] will be opened to the house of David and the inhabitants of Jerusalem, to cleanse[b] them from sin and impurity.
2"On that day, I will banish the names of the idols[c] from the land, and they will be remembered no more," declares the LORD Almighty. "I will remove both the prophets[d] and
the spirit of impurity from the land. 3And if anyone still prophesies, his father and mother, to whom he was born, will say to him, 'You must die, because you have told lies in
the LORD's name.' When he prophesies, his own parents will stab him.[e]
4"On that day every prophet will be ashamed[f] of his prophetic vision. He will not put
on a prophet's garment[g] of hair[h] in order to deceive. 5He will say, 'I am not a prophet.
I am a farmer; the land has been my livelihood since my youth.[c]'[i] 6If someone asks him,
'What are these wounds on your body[d]?' he will answer, 'The wounds I was given at the
house of my friends.'

12:4 [o]Ps 76:6
12:6 [p]Isa 10:17-18; Zec 11:1 [q]Ob 1:18
12:7 [r]Jer 30:18; Am 9:11
12:8 [s]Joel 3:16; Zec 9:15 [t]Ps 82:6 [u]Mic 7:8
12:9 [v]Zec 14:2-3
12:10 [w]Isa 44:3; Eze 39:29; Joel 2:28-29 [x]Jn 19:34, 37*; Rev 1:7
12:11 [y]2Ki 23:29
12:12 [z]Mt 24:30; Rev 1:7
13:1 [a]Jer 17:13 [b]Ps 51:2; Heb 9:14
13:2 [c]Ex 23:13; Eze 36:25; Hos 2:17 [d]1Ki 22:22; Jer 23:14-15
13:3 [e]Dt 13:6-11; 18:20; Jer 23:34; Eze 14:9
13:4 [f]Jer 6:15; Mic 3:6-7 [g]Mt 3:4 [h]2Ki 1:8; Isa 20:2
13:5 [i]Am 7:14

[a] *10* Or *the Spirit* [b] *10* Or *to* [c] *5* Or *farmer; a man sold me in my youth* [d] *6* Or *wounds between your hands*

12:6 Judah like a firepot in a woodpile . . . flaming torch among sheaves. More images of Judah's devouring power when led by the faithful son of David (see note on Hag 2:22–23). **Jerusalem will remain intact.** In contrast to the nations, the people of God in the holy city would be secure (Pss 46; 125:1).
12:8–9 See *WLC* 63.
12:8 like David . . . like God. The victory for God's people against the nations would be so definitive that even the weak would fight like the great warrior David. The house of David would fight like God and the angel of the Lord. Its members would destroy all the nations that attacked Jerusalem. The offer that the process of worldwide victory for Jerusalem could begin was made by the prophets as early as the time of Zerubbabel (see note on Hag 2:22–23).
■ **12:10–14** *Mourning Over the Past.* Judah's victory over the nations that would attack after the exile is set alongside spiritual renewal of the people of Judah. The former could not occur without the latter.
12:10 a spirit of grace and supplication. Probably a way of speaking about the Holy Spirit (see NIV text note), who is graciously given and produces humility in God's people. The Old Testament prophets emphasized that God's renewal of the covenant after the exile (Jer 31:31–33) would entail a renewal in his Spirit (Isa 59:21; Eze 36:26–27; 39:29; Joel 2:28–29). **supplication.** A pleading for grace from God (Ac 2:37). **look on.** Probably means "look to"; that is, as the source of salvation. Many passages in John's Gospel speak of faith as "looking" (see Jn 3:14–15). **me, the one they have pierced.** The reference is to God (cf. "I will pour out"), whom the Jews had rejected in years past. John saw this passage as fulfilled in the death of Christ (Jn 19:37), which also represented the low point of Israel's rejection of God. **a firstborn son.** The prophet indicated that at the time when the Spirit was poured out on God's people they would severely regret their past rebellions. See *WCF* 15.1; *WLC* 76,171,174,182.
■ **13:1–6** *Cleansing the Land of Judah.* The mourning in Jerusalem over past sins would bring about the cleansing of the land from its defilement.
13:1 On that day. This phrase connects chapter 13 with the mourning of 12:10–13. **fountain . . . to cleanse them from sin and impurity.** The metaphor of a fountain indicates the abundance of the forgiveness. In Jeremiah 2:13 God called himself "the spring of living water." Ultimately we find that abundance of forgiveness in Jesus and his Spirit (Jn 7:37–39). See *HC* 70.
13:2–6 These verses indicate the effects of the cleansing (v. 1). The first major outcome would be the removal of idolatry and false prophets (vv. 2–3). See *WCF* 20.4; *WLC* 109.
13:3 lies in the LORD's name. False prophecy was, among other things, either prophesying in the name of a false god or presumptuously speaking in the Lord's name (Dt 13:1–18; 18:21–22). **his own parents.** A false prophet was to die by the sword (Dt 13:15). The commitment of God's people at this time of thorough repentance and blessing would be such that parents would delight more in God than in their children.
13:4–6 The second effect of the cleansing (v. 1) would be that false prophets would be ashamed to admit their deception. They would deny being prophets for fear of retribution.
13:4 a prophet's garment of hair. A traditional symbol of a prophet (1Ki 1:8; Mt 3:4).
13:6 What are these wounds on your body? A probable reference to wounds that were self-inflicted during idolatrous worship.

The Shepherd Struck, the Sheep Scattered

7 "Awake, O sword,[j] against my shepherd,[k]
against the man who is close to me!"
declares the LORD Almighty.
"Strike the shepherd,
and the sheep will be scattered,[l]
and I will turn my hand against the little ones.
8 In the whole land," declares the LORD,
"two-thirds will be struck down and perish;
yet one-third will be left in it.[m]
9 This third I will bring into the fire;[n]
I will refine them like silver[o]
and test them like gold.
They will call[p] on my name
and I will answer[q] them;
I will say, 'They are my people,'[r]
and they will say, 'The LORD is our God.[s]'"

The LORD Comes and Reigns

14 A day of the LORD[t] is coming when your plunder will be divided among you.
2 I will gather all the nations to Jerusalem to fight against it; the city will be captured, the houses ransacked, and the women raped. Half of the city will go into exile, but
the rest of the people will not be taken from the city.[u]
3 Then the LORD will go out and fight[v] against those nations, as he fights in the day of
battle. 4 On that day his feet will stand on the Mount of Olives,[w] east of Jerusalem, and the
Mount of Olives will be split in two from east to west, forming a great valley, with half of
the mountain moving north and half moving south. 5 You will flee by my mountain valley,
for it will extend to Azel. You will flee as you fled from the earthquake[a][x] in the days of Uzziah king of Judah. Then the LORD my God will come,[y] and all the holy ones with him.[z]
6 On that day there will be no light,[a] no cold or frost. 7 It will be a unique[b] day, without daytime or nighttime[c]—a day known to the LORD. When evening comes, there will
be light.[d]
8 On that day living water[e] will flow out from Jerusalem, half to the eastern[f] sea[b] and
half to the western sea,[c] in summer and in winter.

13:7 [j]Jer 47:6 [k]Isa 40:11; 53:4; Eze 37:24 [l]Mt 26:31*; Mk 14:27*
13:8 [m]Eze 5:2-4,12
13:9 [n]Mal 3:2 [o]Isa 48:10; 1Pe 1:6-7 [p]Ps 50:15 [q]Zec 10:6 [r]Jer 30:22 [s]Jer 29:12
14:1 [t]Isa 13:9; Mal 4:1
14:2 [u]Isa 13:6; Zec 13:8
14:3 [v]Zec 9:14-15
14:4 [w]Eze 11:23
14:5 [x]Am 1:1 [y]Isa 29:6; 66:15-16 [z]Mt 16:27; 25:31
14:6 [a]Isa 13:10; Jer 4:23
14:7 [b]Jer 30:7 [c]Rev 21:23-25; 22:5 [d]Isa 30:26
14:8 [e]Eze 47:1-12; Jn 7:38; Rev 22:1-2 [f]Joel 2:20

[a] 5 Or [5]*My mountain valley will be blocked and will extend to Azel. It will be blocked as it was blocked because of the earthquake* [b] 8 That is, the Dead Sea [c] 8 That is, the Mediterranean

---

Several texts in the Old Testament suggest that such practices were customary in pagan worship rituals (Lev 19:28; 21:5; Dt 14:1; 1Ki 18:28). **wounds . . . the house of my friends.** The accused prophet would explain his wounds as the result of a fight with a friend.

■ **13:7–9** *The Stricken Shepherd.* After the rebuilding of the temple Zechariah came to understand more of what had to happen for God's people to attain the promised victory. The son of David would suffer at God's hand, and the people of God would be refined so that true believers would be separated from nonbelievers.

13:7 my shepherd . . . man . . . close to me! This is the great son of David for whom the prophets continued to hope. **Strike the shepherd . . . the sheep.** As in Isaiah 52:13—53:12 the royal figure is struck. It is possible that Zechariah had in mind the death of Zerubbabel, in whom so much hope had been placed (chs. 1–8), as well as the sufferings that would follow for Israel. This figure would then be a type of Christ. The New Testament teaches that Jesus is the Shepherd who ultimately fulfilled this prophecy and whose death distinguished the faithful from the unfaithful in Israel (Mt 26:31–35; Mk 14:27–31; Lk 22:31–34).

13:8 two-thirds . . . perish. Judgment would sift the true believers from the pretenders. That God's judgment distinguishes between the humble and the proud (Zep 3:11–12), between the true and the false sheep (Eze 34:17–24), is a common prophetic theme.

13:9 This third . . . them like gold. True believers would pass through the fire. **my people . . . our God.** The remnant who survived the judgment would be the true people of God, who would enjoy the blessing of covenant renewal. See note on 8:8; see also Genesis 17:7.

■ **14:1–15** *The War Against Jerusalem.* The city of Jerusalem would be attacked and many taken captive. Then the Lord would lead his people into great battle to defeat his and their enemies.

14:1 A day of the LORD. A day appointed by the Lord on which he comes to judge the nations and to protect his people (see "Introduction to Zephaniah"). The picture here is of the people of God who reign victorious because of the mighty God in their midst (Zep 3:17).

14:2 gather all the nations . . . fight against it. See Ezekiel 38–39. **captured . . . ransacked . . . raped.** The city and its inhabitants would be devastated by the nations that would overrun it (see 13:8–9).

14:3 the LORD will go out . . . day of battle. In the midst of devastation God would come to do battle for his people (see note on v. 5).

14:5 Azel. Clearly a place close to Jerusalem, but its precise location is unknown. **all the holy ones.** God's chosen servants, both human and angelic, will come to Jerusalem to liberate it from its pagan aggressors. This prediction will be fulfilled in the second coming of Christ, when God's people will finally be granted ultimate victory (1Th 3:13; Jude 14).

14:7 unique day . . . there will be light. God himself will be the light of the city (Isa 60:19–20; Rev 21:25; 22:5). Verse 6 is speaking of natural light from the sun. This day of battle will usher in the eternal bliss of God's special presence among his people.

14:8 living water . . . from Jerusalem. As the result of the Lord's presence a refreshing stream of water will bring healing to those who seek refuge in him. Water is often a symbol of the blessings of salvation (Isa 55:1–5; Eze 47:1–12; Jn 4:10–14), particularly of the Holy Spirit (Jn 7:37–39; Rev 22:17). Jesus spoke of the believer as both the recipient of the living water that only he can supply and the source of that water for others (Jn 7:37–39). The believer today receives life from Jesus by the Spirit through faith, and the final state holds the promise of a river flowing with the water of life (Rev 22:1–2).

9 The LORD will be king over the whole earth.[g] On that day there will be one LORD, and
his name the only name.[h]
10 The whole land, from Geba[i] to Rimmon, south of Jerusalem, will become like the
Arabah. But Jerusalem will be raised up[j] and remain in its place,[k] from the Benjamin
Gate to the site of the First Gate, to the Corner Gate, and from the Tower of Hananel to
the royal winepresses. 11 It will be inhabited; never again will it be destroyed. Jerusalem
will be secure.[l]
12 This is the plague with which the LORD will strike all the nations that fought against
Jerusalem: Their flesh will rot while they are still standing on their feet, their eyes will
rot in their sockets, and their tongues will rot in their mouths.[m] 13 On that day men will
be stricken by the LORD with great panic. Each man will seize the hand of another, and
they will attack each other.[n] 14 Judah[o] too will fight at Jerusalem. The wealth of all the
surrounding nations will be collected[p]—great quantities of gold and silver and clothing.
15 A similar plague[q] will strike the horses and mules, the camels and donkeys, and all the
animals in those camps.
16 Then the survivors from all the nations that have attacked Jerusalem will go up year
after year to worship the King, the LORD Almighty, and to celebrate the Feast of Tabernacles.[r] 17 If any of the peoples of the earth do not go up to Jerusalem to worship the King,
the LORD Almighty, they will have no rain.[s] 18 If the Egyptian people do not go up and take
part, they will have no rain. The LORD[a] will bring on them the plague he inflicts on the
nations that do not go up to celebrate the Feast of Tabernacles.[t] 19 This will be the punishment of Egypt and the punishment of all the nations that do not go up to celebrate
the Feast of Tabernacles.
20 On that day HOLY TO THE LORD will be inscribed on the bells of the horses, and the
cooking pots[u] in the LORD's house will be like the sacred bowls[v] in front of the altar. 21 Every pot in Jerusalem and Judah will be holy[w] to the LORD Almighty, and all who come to
sacrifice will take some of the pots and cook in them. And on that day[x] there will no lon
ger be a Canaanite[b][y] in the house of the LORD Almighty.[z]

14:9 [g]Dt 6:4; Isa 45:24; Rev 11:15 [h]Eph 4:5-6
14:10 [i]1Ki 15:22 [j]Jer 30:18; Am 9:11 [k]Zec 12:6
14:11 [l]Eze 34:25-28
14:12 [m]Lev 26:16; Dt 28:22
14:13 [n]Zec 11:6
14:14 [o]Zec 12:2 [p]Isa 23:18
14:15 [q]ver 12
14:16 [r]Isa 60:6-9
14:17 [s]Jer 14:4; Am 4:7
14:18 [t]ver 12
14:20 [u]Eze 46:20 [v]Zec 9:15
14:21 [w]Ro 14:6-7; 1Co 10:31 [x]Ne 8:10 [y]Zec 9:8 [z]Eze 44:9

[a] *18* Or *part, then the LORD* [b] *21* Or *merchant*

14:9 The LORD will be king over the whole earth. In verses 9–21 the results of the battle are given, the most important one being the emergence of the true God as the acknowledged Lord of the whole world. **one LORD, and his name the only name.** These words clearly draw on Deuteronomy 6:4, the foundational confession of Israel. It is only on this day of victory that the true meaning of that confession will be fully understood.
14:10 The extensive geographical description is designed to stress how the whole land of God's people will be claimed by God himself.
14:12 Another result of the Lord's kingship (as in v. 9) is described. **plague.** The plague recalls the plagues on Egypt (Ex 7–12), which were also inflicted by God because Egypt had afflicted his people.
14:14 wealth of all the surrounding nations. Compare note on Haggai 2:7.
14:15 A similar plague. The plague will extend to all living things in the possession of God's enemies. The prophet emphasized that the destruction of God's enemies will be final and complete. Even now Christians enjoy victory in faith (1Jn 5:4) and await the final subjugation of God's adversaries to Christ (1Co 15:24–28).
■ **14:16–21** *The Future Celebration.* This culminating passage of the book pictures the universal blessing that God will bestow when the restoration is finally completed. The New Testament teaches believers to look for this kind of celebration at the return of Christ (Rev 19:9).
14:16 survivors. Not all the people in the pagan nations will be destroyed. Some will be converted and come to worship the true and living God in Jerusalem (see note on Isa 2:2–4). **Feast of Tabernacles.** The worship of the Gentiles is expressed in terms of this feast because it was one of joy and thankfulness to God for his blessings (Lev 23:33–36,39–43; Nu 29:12–34; Dt 16:13–15). This feast occurred during the fall harvest season and therefore could symbolize the ingathering of people (i.e., Gentiles), as well as of crops.
14:20 HOLY TO THE LORD. Originally inscribed on the high priest's turban (Ex 28:36–38) as a statement of dedication, this phrase will one day be applied to everything in Jerusalem (horses' bells, cooking pots) because God's special presence will transform all that is around it.
14:21 Canaanite. The word could be translated "merchant" (see NIV text note; see also note on Hos 12:7), but this meaning is unlikely. This ethnic term was used to identify anyone who was unacceptable in the presence of God. The final, blessed state of God's people will involve total separation from the wicked.

MALACHI

Introduction

Overview

Author: The prophet Malachi

Purpose: To call the discouraged community living in the promised land after the exile to renewed faith by announcing the coming judgment of the Messiah

Date: 458–433 B.C.

Key Truths:

- The people of Israel were corrupted by sin during the last years of the Old Testament period.
- God offered his people forgiveness of their sins.
- God promised that the Messiah would come to purify the nation.
- The wicked will be judged and the righteous rewarded in the future judgment.

Author

The authorship of Malachi is a subject of some debate. Scholars are divided as to whether the term "Malachi" is a personal name or a title. Both the Aramaic Targum and the Septuagint (the Greek translation of the OT) suggest something other than a personal name. The former identifies Malachi with Ezra. The latter translates the phrase "by Malachi," as "by the hand of his angel [or 'messenger']." The main arguments against viewing "Malachi" as the personal name of the prophet are the absence of specific data concerning his father and the lack of any mention of his place of birth. These are not compelling reasons for rejecting "Malachi" as a personal name, however. In every other prophetic book a personal name is involved, and this should cause us to expect the same regarding this book. As with almost all the prophets, we know little about the author's personal circumstances. It is enough for us to know that the words this "messenger" brought were from God (Am 3:7).

Time and Place of Writing

Malachi is to be dated around the time of Ezra and Nehemiah. Malachi's emphasis on the law (4:4) presupposes Ezra's ministry of restoring the prominence and authority of the law (Ezr 7:14,25–26; Ne 8:18). The reference to the governor (1:8) locates the book in the Persian period. Based on this evidence some date the book between the coming of Ezra (458 B.C.) and that of Nehemiah (445 B.C.). Others place Malachi in the period between Nehemiah's two visits to Jerusalem, around 433 B.C. Although some interpreters place the prophecies of Joel after this time, it is more likely that Malachi was the last prophet of the Old Testament.

Although we cannot be more certain of the exact time of Malachi's ministry, the conditions and problems that Ezra and Nehemiah confronted also appear in Malachi. All three spoke out against marriage to foreign women (e.g., 2:11–15; Ne 13:23–27), condemned the neglect of the tithe (e.g., 3:8–10; Ne 13:10–14), castigated the evils of a degenerate priesthood (e.g., 1:6—2:9; Ne 13:7–8) and criticized the people for their social sins (e.g., 3:5; Ne 5:1–13). Ezra and Nehemiah approached these issues primarily with programs of reform, whereas Malachi's strategy was to confront them with oracles from the Lord, perhaps in support of the programs of his contemporaries.

Purpose and Distinctives

Covenant is one of the prominent themes in Malachi. There are four explicit references to covenant: the covenant of Levi (2:4–9), the covenant of the fathers (2:10), the marriage covenant (2:14) and the messenger of the covenant (3:1). In addition to these direct references the book begins with God's covenant love (1:2–5). The seriousness of priestly incompetence and unfaithfulness is seen in the erosion of the faithfulness of the common people who "profane[d] the covenant" (2:10) by breaking faith with one another in their marriages (2:11,14) and in their social and economic relationships (3:5). Unless they repented (3:7) they would fall under God's covenant curse (3:9; Lev 26:14–46; Dt 28:15–68).

Malachi spoke to a disillusioned, discouraged and doubting people whose experience was incompatible with their understanding of the Messianic age after the exile. Instead of victory in war and abundance in nature, they experienced poverty, drought and economic adversity. Malachi's word met a people skeptical of God's promises and therefore apathetic in their commitment to live in the light of those promises and to worship and serve the Lord with all their hearts. The book may serve as a catechism for times of doubt and disappointment, during which people in the visible church are tempted to disengage from their covenant God. The prophet's ministry was to light the lamp of faith in a disheartened people by reminding them of God's electing love (1:2) and to set forth the continuing obligations of the covenant to those who truly knew God (3:16–18).

Christ in Malachi

The book of Malachi points to Christ in two ways. In general terms Malachi called the returnees to repentance so that they could receive the blessings God had offered his people following exile. In much the same way Christ called for repentance so that a righteous remnant could receive these same blessings (Mk 2:15). For this reason James applied Malachi's call for repentance to the ongoing lives of believers (Jas 4:8; cf. Mal 3:7). Moreover, Malachi predicted that the worship of God would spread to all nations (1:11), and Christ and his apostles opened the door of salvation to the Gentile nations as never before (Ac 10:9–48; Eph 2:11–13).

A more specific Messianic focus also appears in Malachi. The prophet predicted that the renewal of God's people would take place through the work of "the messenger of the covenant" (3:1), who would be preceded by "the prophet Elijah" (4:5; cf. 3:1–2). The New Testament specifically identifies Jesus as this messenger and John the Baptist as the one who preceded him and who ministered in the spirit and power of Elijah (Mt 11:14; 17:10–12; Lk 1:17). Thus Jesus cleansed the temple (Jn 2:14–17) as the prophet had predicted (3:1,3) and will utterly purify the people of God and their worship when he returns in glory (Rev 21:22–27).

Outline

I. The Truth of God's Love (1:1–5)	*God affirmed his special love for the people of Israel despite the trials of the exile.*
II. Israel's Unfaithfulness (1:6—2:16) A. The Priests' Violations (1:6—2:9) 1. Defiling Worship (1:6–14) 2. Neglecting the Law (2:1–9) B. The Peoples' Violations (2:10–16) 1. Marrying Idolatrous Wives (2:10–12) 2. Divorcing Israelite Wives (2:13–16)	*The nation of Israel was in serious rebellion against God. The priests showed contempt for God's name by corrupting worship and neglecting the law. The people had broken faith by violating God's gift of marriage.*
III. God's Just Judgment (2:17—4:6) A. The Certainty of God's Justice (2:17—3:5) B. God's Offer of Blessing (3:6–12) C. The Importance of Serving God (3:13—4:6) 1. God's Distinction Among His People (3:13–18) 2. Final Judgment to Come (4:1–6)	*God was determined to judge his people in righteousness. Despite appearances Israel could be sure that God would send the Messiah to judge and purify his people. God still offered Israel the opportunity to repent and receive his blessing. Faithful service to God was of paramount importance because the righteous and wicked would be distinguished by divine judgment in the future.*

1 An oracle:[a] The word[b] of the LORD to Israel through Malachi.[a]

1:1 [a]Na 1:1 [b]1Pe 4:11

Jacob Loved, Esau Hated

2"I have loved[c] you," says the LORD.
"But you ask, 'How have you loved us?'
"Was not Esau Jacob's brother?" the LORD says. "Yet I have loved Jacob,[d] 3but Esau I
have hated, and I have turned his mountains into a wasteland[e] and left his inheritance
to the desert jackals.[f]"

1:2 [c]Dt 4:37 [d]Ro 9:13*

1:3 [e]Isa 34:10 [f]Eze 35:3-9

a *1* Malachi means *my messenger.*

■ **1:1–5** *The Truth of God's Love.* The Lord revealed a dispute between himself and Israel. He claimed to love the nation, but the Israelites who were living in the disappointing conditions after the exile doubted God's love for them. The Lord responded to these doubts by reminding them that he had chosen Jacob, their forebear, and rejected Esau, Edom's forebear. Although Israel had experienced the Lord's wrath during the exile and was still enduring it afterward, Edom was "a people always under the wrath of the LORD" (1:4). Furthermore, Israel was under the everlasting promises of its covenant Lord, which would eventually lead to blessing, but Edom would never rise to such heights.

1:1 oracle. Compare Isaiah 13:1, Nahum 1:1 and Habakkuk 1:1. Normally a prophecy of judgment, the word may point to the constraint felt by the prophet in his proclamation (see Jer 20:9; Am 3:8).

1:2–3 See *BC* 16.

1:2 I have loved you. Because God loved Jacob, he sovereignly elected him to salvation and chose his descendants as his covenant people (cf. the parallel between forms of the verbs *to choose* and *to love* in Dt 7:6–8). Because of God's hatred for the reprobate Esau, God brought curses not only upon Esau but also upon his descendants. God's love began in eternity (Jer 31:3) and was manifested in his covenantal dealings with his people (Ex 34:6–7; Dt 7:9; 1Ki 8:23). The Lord's love by which he elects individuals to salvation is distinct from but related to his love for his covenant people. His electing love will never be removed; it necessarily results in the salvation of those who are loved. His love for his covenant people is reflected in his mercy and patience toward them above all other people, but may be removed in response to their disobedience and does not necessarily result in their salvation. See theological article "Predestination and Foreknowledge" at Romans 8. **How have you loved us?** The covenant love of God was supposed to lead to reciprocal love from Israel (Ex 20:6; Dt 7:9), but it did not. Instead, God's people challenged God's claim that he loved them. **Esau Jacob's brother?** God's election of Jacob over Esau in the past continued to have relevance for his dealings with Israel during the period of Malachi's ministry. Although the nation had endured much trouble, there was sufficient evidence from God's historical dealings with Israel for his audience to be assured of his love for them. Instead, Israel's hardships led to doubt about God's love. **Jacob.** The patriarchal story of Jacob and Esau in Genesis clearly indicates that God's choice of Jacob was not based on merit (see especially Ge 25:21–34). God loves sinners, those who by nature ought to be the objects of his displeasure and wrath (Lk 15:2; Eph 2:3–5).

1:3 hated. God hates idolaters (Jer 44:4–5; Hos 9:15), evildoers (Ps 5:5), the wicked and those who love violence (Ps 11:5). See also Proverbs 6:16–19. Scripture sometimes uses the verb *hate* in a sense meaning "to love less" (see Ge 29:30–31; Dt 21:15–17; Lk

4 Edom may say, "Though we have been crushed, we will rebuild[g] the ruins."
But this is what the LORD Almighty says: "They may build, but I will demolish. They
will be called the Wicked Land, a people always under the wrath of the LORD.[h] 5 You will
see it with your own eyes and say, 'Great[i] is the LORD—even beyond the borders of Israel!'[j]

Blemished Sacrifices

6 "A son honors his father, and a servant his master. If I am a father, where is the hon-
or due me? If I am a master, where is the respect[k] due me?" says the LORD Almighty.[l] "It
is you, O priests, who show contempt for my name.
"But you ask, 'How have we shown contempt for your name?'
7 "You place defiled food[m] on my altar.
"But you ask, 'How have we defiled you?'
"By saying that the LORD's table is contemptible. 8 When you bring blind animals for
sacrifice, is that not wrong? When you sacrifice crippled or diseased animals,[n] is that not
wrong? Try offering them to your governor! Would he be pleased with you? Would he accept you?" says the LORD Almighty.[o]
9 "Now implore God to be gracious to us. With such offerings[p] from your hands, will
he accept you?"—says the LORD Almighty.
10 "Oh, that one of you would shut the temple doors, so that you would not light useless fires on my altar! I am not pleased[q] with you," says the LORD Almighty, "and I will
accept no offering[r] from your hands. 11 My name will be great among the nations, from
the rising to the setting of the sun. In every place incense[s] and pure offerings will be
brought to my name, because my name will be great among the nations," says the LORD
Almighty.

1:4 [g]Isa 9:10 [h]Eze 25:12-14
1:5 [i]Ps 35:27; Mic 5:4 [j]Am 1:11-12
1:6 [k]Isa 1:2 [l]Job 5:17
1:7 [m]ver 12; Lev 21:6
1:8 [n]Lev 22:22; Dt 15:21 [o]Isa 43:23
1:9 [p]Lev 23:33-44
1:10 [q]Hos 5:6 [r]Isa 1:11-14; Jer 14:12
1:11 [s]Isa 60:6-7; Rev 8:3

14:26). The context immediately following (vv. 3–4), however, suggests that here *hate* involves active rejection, displeasure and disfavor that is manifested in retributive justice. It is not merely that Esau (Edom) had lesser or fewer blessings than Jacob but that he suffered under God's wrathful judgment. See Paul's use of this verse in Romans 9:13. For other instances of this usage of *hate,* see, in addition to the texts cited above, 2:16, Isaiah 61:8 and Amos 5:21. **wasteland.** Most likely refers to the occupation of Edom by the Nabatean Arabs.

1:4 always under the wrath. Moses initially promoted benevolent treatment for the Edomites (Nu 20:14–19), but as they continued to persecute the people of God they became the objects of divine judgment (Isa 34:5–17; Jer 25:17–18,21; Eze 25:12–14; Ob 1). In Amos 9:11–12 Edom is seen as the object of the victorious attack of the restored house of David. As a result of this attack some Edomites who remained alive would receive salvation.

1:5 You will see. In all likelihood Malachi had in mind the defeat of Edom in the great battle between Israel and her surrounding enemies, which had earlier been prophesied (see note on v. 4). **beyond the borders of Israel!** God is the sovereign Lord of history, whose redemptive purposes were and are accomplished both inside and outside the nation of Israel (see v. 11; Ge 12:3).

■ **1:6—2:16** *Israel's Unfaithfulness.* In these verses the prophet identified some of the principal ways in which the Israelites had been unfaithful to God. Malachi's focus was in two directions: the priests' violations (1:6—2:9) and the peoples' violations (2:10–16).

■ **1:6—2:9** *The Priests' Violations.* The failure of the priesthood was a major reason for the Lord's anger against Israel. At the altar the priests offered diseased or imperfect animals, thereby perpetrating curse and defilement where they should have brought blessing and cleansing. In their teaching and judging they violated the covenant with Levi, causing many to stumble and showing partiality. If they continued to violate the priestly regulations, the Lord would repudiate them and raise up a pure priesthood—and, by implication, a pure kingdom—from among the Gentile nations. This material divides into two parts: the defiling worship in Judah (1:6–14) and the judgment of God to come against the priests (2:1–9).

■ **1:6–14** *Defiling Worship.* The priests had shown disregard for the sanctity of God's name by worshiping and sacrificing as they wished rather than by observing God's regulations.

1:6–8 See *WLC* 109,113; *WSC* 55.

1:6 father. The Old Testament speaks of God as Israel's father and of Israel as his son (e.g., Dt 8:5). **where is the honor due me?** Human fathers are honored by their children, but Israel did not honor her divine Father, who had done so much more than any human parent. As in the first disputation God spoke of his kindness to the Israelites (see v. 2) to clarify why he expected faithfulness from them. **master.** God is not only fatherly toward his people but also rules over them as their royal Father or Master. In this capacity he is not only a compassionate, gentle, forbearing and gracious King, but also the sovereign Lord who cares for his people's needs, protects their lives and preserves justice for them. In all ways he is deserving of their respect. **show contempt.** The opposite of honoring and fearing the Lord (1:7,12–13). The word is used often in Proverbs (e.g., Pr 1:7; 15:20; 23:22), where it is translated "despised" or grouped with the word "scorn" (Pr 23:9). See also 2 Samuel 12:9–10. **my name.** In the context of worship the name of God is equated with his special presence, his personal attention to the affairs of his people who approach him (see 1Ki 8:28–29). Through their careless sacrificial practices the priests of Malachi's day had shown little regard for the wonder that the God of all things would bless them by being present with them and accessible to them. **But you ask.** The Israelites challenged God's claim that they demonstrated contempt for his name. They apparently felt that their practices were acceptable. See *WLC* 104,127.

1:7 defiled food. A reference to animal sacrifices (v. 8). "Defiled" here means ceremonially unclean and therefore unacceptable. God is not offended merely by ritualistic imperfections but by the attitudes behind such imperfections (see Ge 4:3–5; Heb 11:4 and their notes). **the LORD's table.** This phrase is used in the Old Testament with reference to the altar only here and in verse 12. In the New Testament it refers to the Lord's Supper (1Co 10:21).

1:8 diseased animals. The law expressly prohibited such offerings (Lev 22:22; Dt 15:21). **to your governor!** God asserted that the Israelites would not dare to proffer such offerings to a mere human leader. He certainly deserved better treatment than that afforded a human governor. See *WLC* 151.

1:10 shut the temple doors. It would have been better for worship to stop than for it to be performed in ways that violated the law and thus offended God. God refused to accept these offerings.

1:11 My name will be great among the nations. God responded to the unacceptable sacrificial practices of the Jews in Malachi's time by stressing that he would be honored one day among the Gentiles, even if the Jews continued to rebel. The future triumph of his glorious kingdom "from the rising of the sun to the place where it sets" (Ps 50:1; see also Isa 45:6; 59:19) would lead to true worship among the Gentiles. The New Testament testifies to the beginning of such a shift because so few Jews believed in the Messiah (Mt 8:10–11; Ac 13:46–48). **In every place.** Jerusalem would remain the center of the worship of God even after the Gentiles began to participate in large numbers (Isa 2:2–4; 66:19–21; Zec 14:16–21), yet this worship would originate in every part of the world. The promise of this verse is being fulfilled now as Christ gathers his kingdom of priests from among the nations (Rev 7:9–10), and it will be consummated in the future as the nations gather to worship God in purity in the new Jerusalem (Rev 21:2,10). See *WCF* 21.6; *WLC* 191; *WSC* 54.

[12]"But you profane it by saying of the Lord's table, 'It is defiled,' and of its food,[t] 'It
is contemptible.' [13]And you say, 'What a burden!'[u] and you sniff at it contemptuously,"
says the LORD Almighty.
"When you bring injured, crippled or diseased animals and offer them as sacrifices,
should I accept them from your hands?" says the LORD. [14]"Cursed is the cheat who has
an acceptable male in his flock and vows to give it, but then sacrifices a blemished animal[v] to the Lord. For I am a great king,[w]" says the LORD Almighty, "and my name is to
be feared among the nations.

Admonition for the Priests

2 "And now this admonition is for you, O priests.[x] [2]If you do not listen, and if you do
not set your heart to honor my name," says the LORD Almighty, "I will send a curse[y]
upon you, and I will curse your blessings. Yes, I have already cursed them, because you
have not set your heart to honor me.
[3]"Because of you I will rebuke[a] your descendants[b]; I will spread on your faces the offal[z] from your festival sacrifices, and you will be carried off with it.[a] [4]And you will know
that I have sent you this admonition so that my covenant with Levi[b] may continue," says
the LORD Almighty. [5]"My covenant was with him, a covenant[c] of life and peace,[d] and I
gave them to him; this called for reverence and he revered me and stood in awe of my
name. [6]True instruction[e] was in his mouth and nothing false was found on his lips. He
walked with me in peace and uprightness, and turned many from sin.[f]
[7]"For the lips of a priest[g] ought to preserve knowledge, and from his mouth men
should seek instruction[h]—because he is the messenger[i] of the LORD Almighty. [8]But you
have turned from the way and by your teaching have caused many to stumble;[j] you have
violated the covenant with Levi," says the LORD Almighty. [9]"So I have caused you to be
despised[k] and humiliated before all the people, because you have not followed my
ways but have shown partiality in matters of the law."

Judah Unfaithful

[10]Have we not all one Father[c]?[l] Did not one God create us? Why do we profane the
covenant[m] of our fathers by breaking faith with one another?
[11]Judah has broken faith. A detestable thing has been committed in Israel and in Je-

[a] 3 Or *cut off* (see Septuagint) [b] 3 Or *will blight your grain* [c] 10 Or *father*

1:12 [t]ver 7
1:13 [u]Isa 43:22-24
1:14 [v]Lev 22:18-21 [w]1Ti 6:15
2:1 [x]ver 7
2:2 [y]Dt 28:20
2:3 [z]Ex 29:14 [a]1Ki 14:10
2:4 [b]Nu 3:12
2:5 [c]Dt 33:9 [d]Nu 25:12
2:6 [e]Dt 33:10 [f]Jer 23:22; Jas 5:19-20
2:7 [g]Jer 18:18 [h]Lev 10,11 [i]Nu 27:21
2:8 [j]Jer 18:15
2:9 [k]1Sa 2:30
2:10 [l]1Co 8:6 [m]Ex 19:5

1:12–13 See *WLC* 109,113,119; *WSC* 55,61.
1:14 Cursed is the cheat. Laws regulating voluntary offerings required the presentation of a perfect offering. This text implies an attempt to deceive the Lord and refers to what happened in the interval between the vow and its performance (Ps 76:11). See *WLC* 109,112,151; *WSC* 54. **I am a great king.** When God called himself "father" and "master" (v. 6), these terms were used in a royal sense. God is the great royal Father of Israel. The revelation of God as king permeates the Scriptures (e.g., Ex 15:18; Nu 23:21; Dt 33:5; Pss 93–100).
■ **2:1–9** *Neglecting the Law.* In addition to offering inappropriate sacrifices the priests neglected to teach and enforce the law of God. For these reasons divine judgment was coming against them.
2:2 I will send a curse upon you. See Deuteronomy 28:20. **I will curse your blessings.** "Blessings" could refer either to the blessings the priests received from the peoples' tithes (Nu 18:21) or to the priests' pronouncements of blessing at the time of the sacrifices (Nu 6:24–26). **set your heart to honor me.** Although the priests went through many of the required rituals, their hearts were not intent on honoring God. They sought instead their own honor. See *WLC* 113; *WSC* 55.
2:3 offal. The entrails of sacrificed animals that were to be burned outside the camp (see Ex 29:14; Lev 8:17; 16:27).
2:5 a covenant of life and peace. It is most likely that the covenant with Phineas is in mind here (Nu 25:10–13). In that covenant God promised Aaron's grandson that his family would always be the priestly family of Israel. **this called for reverence.** As was the case with all Biblical covenants, however, flagrant violation would lead to curses. The Levites in Malachi's day had so violated their responsibilities that curses were threatened against them.
2:7 the lips of a priest ought to preserve knowledge. See Ezra 7:10 and Hosea 4:6. Like Phineas before them (see note on v. 5) the Levites were responsible for teaching the Law of Moses (Lev 10:8,11). The connection between the priesthood and instruction in the law is vividly set forth in 2 Chronicles 15:3. See *WLC* 158.
2:8 you have turned from the way. See Nehemiah 13:29. The priests had abandoned their calling with regard to both their teaching and their practice of the truth (see Pss 1:6; 18:21–22; Ac 6:7).
2:9 you . . . have shown partiality in matters of the law. The character of God was the basis for this censure. God "shows no partiality and accepts no bribes" (Dt 10:17; cf. Lev 19:15). Possibly the priests were not applying the law indiscriminately to all but were being selective in the application with respect to the rich and powerful strata of society.
■ **2:10–16** *The Peoples' Violations.* Lack of faithfulness toward God led to the destruction of marriage. Malachi addressed two problems in this regard. He rebuked the men in his audience for their marriages to idolatrous wives (vv. 10–12) and objected to their illegitimate divorces of Israelite wives (vv. 13–16).
■ **2:10–12** *Marrying Idolatrous Wives.* God expressed dismay over the way Judahite men had broken faith by marrying idolatrous Gentile women.
2:10 one Father? Some interpret this as referring to Abraham (see NIV text note). The parallel in the second sentence ("one Father . . . one God") makes it more likely, however, that Malachi was referring to God (1:6; Ex 4:22–23; Dt 32:6; Isa 63:16; 64:8; Jer 3:4,19; 31:9). See *BC* 1.
2:11–12 See *WCF* 24.3; *WLC* 139.
2:11 broken faith. This expression is used five times in this section (vv. 10–11,14–16). It also appears in Jeremiah 3:20 with reference to marital unfaithfulness. Judah had so turned away from God that she had violated the central requirements of fidelity expressed in her covenant with him. **A detestable thing.** The Hebrew word here, prominently employed in Deuteronomy, refers to idolatrous religious practices (Dt 7:25–26; 13:13–15; 18:10–12), though it can also refer to a sexual transgression (Lev 18:22,26,29–30; Dt 24:1–4). **desecrated the sanctuary.** The word translated "sanctuary" could refer to the temple; if so, the inference is that those married to foreign women came to the temple defiled by their pagan wives. The term "sanctuary" can also refer to the people set apart for God's service. (See "holy seed" at Isa 6:13 and "holy race" at Ezr 9:2, where the same Hebrew word here translated "sanctuary" is translated "seed" and "race," respectively.) **marrying the daugh-**

rusalem: Judah has desecrated the sanctuary the LORD loves, by marrying[n] the daughter of a foreign god.[o] 12 As for the man who does this, whoever he may be, may the LORD
cut him off[p] from the tents of Jacob[a]—even though he brings offerings[q] to the LORD Almighty.
13 Another thing you do: You flood the LORD's altar with tears. You weep and wail because he no longer pays attention[r] to your offerings or accepts them with pleasure from
your hands. 14 You ask, "Why?" It is because the LORD is acting as the witness between
you and the wife of your youth,[s] because you have broken faith with her, though she is
your partner, the wife of your marriage covenant.
15 Has not ⌞the LORD⌟ made them one?[t] In flesh and spirit they are his. And why one?
Because he was seeking godly offspring.[b][u] So guard yourself in your spirit, and do not
break faith with the wife of your youth.
16 "I hate divorce,[v]" says the LORD God of Israel, "and I hate a man's covering himself[c]
with violence as well as with his garment," says the LORD Almighty.
So guard yourself in your spirit, and do not break faith.

The Day of Judgment

17 You have wearied[w] the LORD with your words.
"How have we wearied him?" you ask.
By saying, "All who do evil are good in the eyes of the LORD, and he is pleased with
them" or "Where is the God of justice?"
3 "See, I will send my messenger, who will prepare the way before me.[x] Then suddenly the Lord you are seeking will come to his temple; the messenger of the covenant,
whom you desire, will come," says the LORD Almighty.
2 But who can endure[y] the day of his coming? Who can stand when he appears? For
he will be like a refiner's fire[z] or a launderer's soap. 3 He will sit as a refiner and purifier
of silver;[a] he will purify[b] the Levites and refine them like gold and silver. Then the LORD

2:11 [n]Ne 13:23 [o]Ezr 9:1; Jer 3:7-9
2:12 [p]Eze 24:21 [q]Mal 1:10
2:13 [r]Jer 14:12
2:14 [s]Pr 5:18
2:15 [t]Ge 2:24; Mt 19:4-6 [u]1Co 7:14
2:16 [v]Dt 24:1; Mt 5:31-32; 19:4-9
2:17 [w]Isa 43:24
3:1 [x]Isa 40:3; Mt 11:10*; Mk 1:2*; Lk 7:27*
3:2 [y]Eze 22:14; Rev 6:17 [z]Zec 13:9; Mt 3:10-12
3:3 [a]Da 12:10 [b]Isa 1:25

[a] *12* Or *12May the LORD cut off from the tents of Jacob anyone who gives testimony in behalf of the man who does this*
[b] *15* Or *15But the one ⌞who is our father⌟ did not do this, not as long as life remained in him. And what was he seeking? An offspring from God* [c] *16* Or *his wife*

---

ter of a foreign god. This phrase refers to the act of marrying a woman still committed to a foreign god; that is, marrying an idolater, one outside the covenant (cf. Ge 24:3–4; Ex 34:12–16; Dt 7:1–4; Jos 23:12–13; 1Ki 11:1–10). The Old Testament did not forbid interracial or interethnic marriages (e.g., Zipporah [Ex 2:21], Rahab [Jos 2:1; Mt 1:5], Ruth [Ru 1:4; 4:10–22; Mt 1:5]), but it did forbid God's people from marrying outside of the faith. Marriages involving idolatrous women were a major problem during the postexilic period (Ezr 9:1–2; Ne 13:23–27). This instruction continues in the New Testament (1Co 7:39; cf. 2Co 6:14).
2:12 cut him off. This terminology is applied to a variety of penalties in Scripture that denote the curses of the covenant.
■ **2:13–16** *Divorcing Israelite Wives.* A second violation of marriage moves to the foreground: The men of Israel were illegitimately divorcing their Israelite wives.
2:14–15 See *WLC* 139.
2:14 wife of your youth. See verse 15 and Proverbs 5:18. **marriage covenant.** God's covenant faithfulness is to find visible expression in the marriages of his people (Pr 2:17). The apostle Paul instructed the New Testament people of God in the same manner (Eph 5:22–33).
2:15 one? See Genesis 2:24. See also *WCF* 24.2.
2:16 I hate divorce. Although divorce is never the ideal course for the faithful to follow, it is sanctioned by the Scriptures under certain conditions (see Dt 24:1–4; Isa 50:1; Mt 19:9; 1Co 7:15). See theological article "Marriage and Divorce" at Matthew 19. **divorce . . . violence.** The connection between divorce and violence may reflect the difficult and dangerous circumstances that divorce in ancient times conferred upon women. See *WLC* 139. **garment.** Entering into marriage and obtaining a wife were sometimes symbolically portrayed by the act of covering with a garment (see Ru 3:9; Eze 16:8). **do not break faith.** Malachi had already accused the Judahites of breaking faith with God through violation of the covenant (v. 11). Here he encouraged them to stop pursuing their apostasy.
■ **2:17—4:6** *God's Just Judgment.* The second half of Malachi's prophecies concentrates on the question of divine justice. Will God be just? Will he indeed punish the wicked and reward the righteous? How will he do this? Who will be judged? Who will be rewarded? These chapters divide into three sections: the certainty of God's justice (2:17—3:5), God's offer of blessing (3:6–12) and the importance of serving God (3:13—4:6).
■ **2:17—3:5** *The Certainty of God's Justice.* The cynics in Israel charged that the Lord was paying no attention to evil and injustice. God responded that he would send a messenger to prepare the way, after which he would return to his temple to judge the wicked.
2:17 wearied the LORD. See Isaiah 43:24. In Malachi the offenses revolved around the cynical rejection of God's moral government and the attendant petulant spirit that constantly put God on trial. **God of justice?** The people of Judah faced trials and threats from the peoples surrounding them and longed for justice against their enemies. Since God had not yet struck out against the Gentile nations, they questioned his justice.
3:1 my messenger. Compare 4:5 and Isaiah 40:3 (where the phrase "prepare the way" is also used). It was the practice in the Near East to send messengers in advance of a visiting king to announce his coming and to remove all impediments or obstacles. It is possible that the prophet (whose name means "my messenger") spoke of himself here as one preparing the way for the Lord, but he may also have been referring to one who would come later in the spirit of his ministry. The New Testament identifies John the Baptist as playing this preparatory role (see Mt 11:10–11; Mk 1:2,4; Lk 1:63,67,76). **suddenly.** The Hebrew word translated by this adverb is almost universally associated with an unhappy and calamitous circumstance (e.g., Nu 12:4; Isa 47:11; cf. 2Pe 3:10). Here the suddenness implied that when the Messiah came he would bring judgment against those who awaited him. **you are seeking . . . you desire.** The members of the postexilic community were not seeking God's messenger in true piety but were doing so because they believed that the coming of the messenger would lead to judgment on the nations around them. They would discover, however, that the messenger would also bring judgment against them. For a similar reversal of expectations, see Amos 5:18–27. **the messenger of the covenant.** This Messenger probably is not the same as the one identified as "my messenger" earlier in the verse. He would not merely prepare but would also be the One who would purify and judge the nation. He would accomplish a complete reformation not only of the impure sacrificial practices but also of the nation of priests itself (vv. 2–5). For this reason it is appropriate to identify this "messenger of the covenant" with the great son of David, the Messiah.
3:2 who can endure . . . stand . . . ? The nation had become so corrupt that virtually all would be condemned when God rendered his judgment.
3:3 he will purify the Levites. The messenger of the covenant

will have men who will bring offerings in righteousness, [4]and the offerings[c] of Judah and
Jerusalem will be acceptable to the LORD, as in days gone by, as in former years.[d]
[5]"So I will come near to you for judgment. I will be quick to testify against sorcerers,
adulterers and perjurers,[e] against those who defraud laborers of their wages,[f] who oppress the widows[g] and the fatherless, and deprive aliens of justice, but do not fear me,"
says the LORD Almighty.

Robbing God

[6]"I the LORD do not change.[h] So you, O descendants of Jacob, are not destroyed. [7]Ever
since the time of your forefathers you have turned away[i] from my decrees and have not
kept them. Return to me, and I will return to you,"[j] says the LORD Almighty.
"But you ask, 'How are we to return?'
[8]"Will a man rob God? Yet you rob me.
"But you ask, 'How do we rob you?'
"In tithes[k] and offerings. [9]You are under a curse—the whole nation of you—because
you are robbing me. [10]Bring the whole tithe into the storehouse,[l] that there may be food
in my house. Test me in this," says the LORD Almighty, "and see if I will not throw open
the floodgates[m] of heaven and pour out so much blessing that you will not have room
enough for it. [11]I will prevent pests from devouring your crops, and the vines in your
fields will not cast their fruit," says the LORD Almighty. [12]"Then all the nations will call
you blessed,[n] for yours will be a delightful land,"[o] says the LORD Almighty.
[13]"You have said harsh things[p] against me," says the LORD.
"Yet you ask, 'What have we said against you?'
[14]"You have said, 'It is futile[q] to serve God. What did we gain by carrying out his requirements and going about like mourners[r] before the LORD Almighty? [15]But now we call
the arrogant blessed. Certainly the evildoers[s] prosper, and even those who challenge
God escape.'"
[16]Then those who feared the LORD talked with each other, and the LORD listened and
heard.[t] A scroll[u] of remembrance was written in his presence concerning those who
feared the LORD and honored his name.

3:4 [c]2Ch 7:12; Ps 51:19; Mal 1:11 [d]2Ch 7:3
3:5 [e]Jer 7:9 [f]Lev 19:13; Jas 5:4 [g]Ex 22:22
3:6 [h]Nu 23:19; Jas 1:17
3:7 [i]Jer 7:26; Ac 7:51 [j]Zec 1:3
3:8 [k]Ne 13:10-12
3:10 [l]Ne 13:12 [m]2Ki 7:2
3:12 [n]Isa 61:9 [o]Isa 62:4
3:13 [p]Mal 2:17
3:14 [q]Ps 73:13 [r]Isa 58:3
3:15 [s]Jer 7:10
3:16 [t]Ps 34:15 [u]Ps 56:8

---

would have the task of cleansing Israel, especially the priesthood. The priests had been instrumental in leading the people astray. The work of purification would begin with them and from there spread to the whole of the nation. The Levites were the pattern for the whole nation, which was to be "a kingdom of priests" (Ex 19:6). **offerings in righteousness.** See "pure offerings" at 1:11. As a result of the work of the messenger of the covenant, proper worship would again be offered, since the hearts and lives of the givers would be purified (cf. Ps 4:5; Zep 3:9).

3:5 So I will come near to you for judgment. This section begins with the religious cynics accusing the Lord of injustice. It ends with a covenant lawsuit in which the Lord brings charges against his people. The specific sins mentioned in verse 5 were those clearly marked out by the law of God. The root cause of these sins was the absence of the fear of God.

■ **3:6–12** *God's Offer of Blessing.* Having indicated that God's just judgment was sure, the prophet addressed the topic of tithes and offerings to make it clear that God was willing to forgive and bless his people. From God's point of view withholding the tithe was tantamount to stealing from him. As a consequence the righteous Lord withheld blessing. So the Lord urged his people to put him to the test. If they did the consequent provision would be so great that the nations would see the difference and pronounce Israel blessed.

3:6 I the LORD do not change. The immutability of God's covenant promise is seen in his purpose to bless his elect people according to the terms of the covenant. Thus they were not destroyed (Ex 34:6–7; Jer 30:11). See *WCF* 2.1; *WLC* 7.

3:7 Return to me, and I will return to you. The command to repent is connected with an offer of blessing (cf. Zec 1:3; Jas 4:8). Sin separates from God and causes him to hide his face (Isa 59:2), but repentance and obedience often motivate him to bless his people (Joel 2:12–14).

3:8 In tithes and offerings. A tithe is a tenth part (Eze 45:11,14). Tithing occurred in the patriarchal accounts of Abraham (Ge 14:20) and Jacob (Ge 28:22) and received codification in the Law of Moses (Lev 27:30; Nu 18:28; Dt 12:4–19; 14:22–29; 26:12). **offerings.** Refers to portions of the animal sacrifices that were specifically to be given to the priests (Ex 29:27–28; Lev 9:22). These were gifts voluntarily offered for a specific purpose (Ex 25:1–7). See Nehemiah 13:10. See also *WLC* 109.

3:10 storehouse. This term refers to a room within the temple designated for the storage of gifts (2Ch 31:11; Ne 10:38–39; 12:44; 13:12). **Test me.** This statement is a reversal of ordinary Biblical usage describing God as testing human beings (Pss 11:5; 26:2; 66:10; Pr 17:3; Jer 11:20; 12:3; 17:10). There are only a few instances of human beings being invited to test God; that is, to prove his claims and justify his commands (e.g., Jdg 6:36–40; 1Ki 18:22–46; Isa 7:11–12). **floodgates of heaven.** See Genesis 7:11.

■ **3:13—4:6** *The Importance of Serving God.* This last section returns to the prophecy in 3:1–5 concerning the forerunner, and the coming, of God. In various ways the beginning of the section is reminiscent of a lament psalm. Here, however, the complaints were interpreted as hard words against the Lord. There were others who sensed the same injustices yet did not conclude that it was futile to serve the Lord. The first group spoke hard words and brought the Lord's response; the latter feared the Lord and caused him to write words of remembrance concerning them. God promised that this latter group would be his special possession in that great day. The reference to "the day" (v. 17) again introduces the day of final judgment, a day of destruction for the wicked but healing for the righteous (see "Introduction to Zephaniah"). The final verses return to the promised forerunner and exhort the people to keep the Law of Moses. That period before the dreadful day of the Lord will divide his people into those whose family relationships were tokens of love and those whose relationships were not. If the people as a whole did not respond to the mission of this new Elijah, the Lord would curse them.

■ **3:13–18** *God's Distinction Among His People.* God would judge his people, bringing curses against those who believed it was futile to serve him and bestowing blessings on those who remained faithful to him.

3:14 gain. A word used often of a greedy person or of one striving for unjust gain (Ex 18:21; Isa 56:11; Jer 8:10). The desire for personal gain from service is the very opposite of the longing for God's truth (Ps 119:36).

3:16 Then. The conversation and conduct of those who feared God contrasts with the murmuring and disobedience of those who spoke against him (vv. 13–15). See *WLC* 113; *WSC* 55. **feared the LORD.** See 1:6–14. **scroll of remembrance.** This exact phrase is found only here, but the reference to a special book appears elsewhere in the Old Testament (e.g., Ex 32:32; Pss 69:28; 139:16; Isa 4:3; 65:6; cf. Rev 20:12). See *WLC* 104,112.

3:17 [v]Dt 7:6 [w]Ps 103:13; Isa 26:20
3:18 [x]Ge 18:25
4:1 [y]Joel 2:31 [z]Isa 5:24; Ob 1:18
4:2 [a]Lk 1:78; Eph 5:14 [b]Isa 30:26 [c]Isa 35:6
4:3 [d]Job 40:12 [e]Eze 28:18
4:4 [f]Ps 147:19
4:5 [g]Mt 11:14; Lk 1:17 [h]Joel 2:31
4:6 [i]Lk 1:17 [j]Isa 11:4; Rev 19:15 [k]Zec 5:3

17 "They will be mine," says the LORD Almighty, "in the day when I make up my treasured possession.[a] [v] I will spare [w] them, just as in compassion a man spares his son who
serves him. 18 And you will again see the distinction between the righteous [x] and the wicked, between those who serve God and those who do not.

The Day of the LORD

4 "Surely the day is coming; [y] it will burn like a furnace. All the arrogant and every
evildoer will be stubble, [z] and that day that is coming will set them on fire," says the
LORD Almighty. "Not a root or a branch will be left to them. 2 But for you who revere my
name, the sun of righteousness [a] will rise with healing [b] in its wings. And you will go out
and leap [c] like calves released from the stall. 3 Then you will trample [d] down the wicked;
they will be ashes [e] under the soles of your feet on the day when I do these things," says
the LORD Almighty.

4 "Remember the law [f] of my servant Moses, the decrees and laws I gave him at Horeb for all Israel.

5 "See, I will send you the prophet Elijah [g] before that great and dreadful day of the
LORD comes. [h] 6 He will turn the hearts of the fathers to their children, [i] and the hearts of
the children to their fathers; or else I will come and strike [j] the land with a curse." [k]

[a] 17 Or *Almighty, "my treasured possession, in the day when I act*

3:17 They will be mine. This phrase refers to the remnant described in verse 16. **treasured possession.** In the early stage of Old Testament revelation the nation of Israel is called God's "treasured possession" (Ex 19:5; Dt 7:6; 14:2; 26:18).

3:18 you will again see the distinction between. There are six distinguishing characteristics of God's "treasured possession," in contrast with those who have turned away from him (v. 17). Those whom God will bless: honor and fear God (2:2,5; 3:16), keep the covenant (2:8; 3:14), follow him in marriage commitments (2:11–15), discern and discriminate between good and evil (3:5), honor God through the giving of money (3:9–12) and serve God (3:18).

■ **4:1–6** *Final Judgment to Come.* The coming judgment would be thorough; all evildoers would be completely destroyed, leaving only the righteous alive to enjoy God's blessings. Before executing his justice God would send a prophet to encourage the people to repent in order that they might avoid condemnation and receive blessing.

4:1 fire. Two images of fire are used to describe the Lord in Malachi: a refining fire (3:2) and a destroying fire (4:1). Compare Psalm 21:9, Isaiah 10:16, 30:27, Joel 2:1 and 3, Zephaniah 1:18, 3:8 and Hebrews 12:29. **a root or a branch.** The thought here presupposes a tree (Am 2:9) that would be consumed down to the roots; that is, totally destroyed.

4:2–3 See *WCF* 8.8.

4:2 sun of righteousness. The image of the sun is applied to the Lord in several instances (Nu 6:25; Isa 60:19; Rev 22:5). The Davidic king would "reign in righteousness" (Isa 32:1) and be called the "righteous Branch" (Jer 23:5) **healing.** See Exodus 15:26 and Deuteronomy 32:39. Healing is sometimes synonymous with forgiveness (2Ch 7:14; Ps 103:3; Isa 53:5; Jer 17:14).

4:5 See, I will send you the prophet Elijah. The connection of this verse with "my messenger" in 3:1 is clear. Both verses begin with the word "see" and use the same form of the verb *to send.* In both cases the mission is to bring repentance ("prepare the way" in 3:1 is similar to "turn" in 4:6) in light of the coming day of the Lord. The presumption is that this new Elijah is the same figure as "my messenger" (3:1). The New Testament identifies Elijah with John the Baptist (Mt 17:10–13; Mk 9:11–13; Lk 1:13,17).

4:6 turn the hearts of the fathers to their children. Repentance and turning to God bring about the restoration of family relationships (Lk 1:17). **or else I will come and strike the land with a curse.** Although Malachi begins with the announcement of God's electing love, the book ends with the threat of a curse. Malachi's dual thrust on mercy and judgment is reminiscent of Paul's pronouncement that we are to "consider therefore the kindness and sternness of God" (Ro 11:22).

From Malachi to Christ

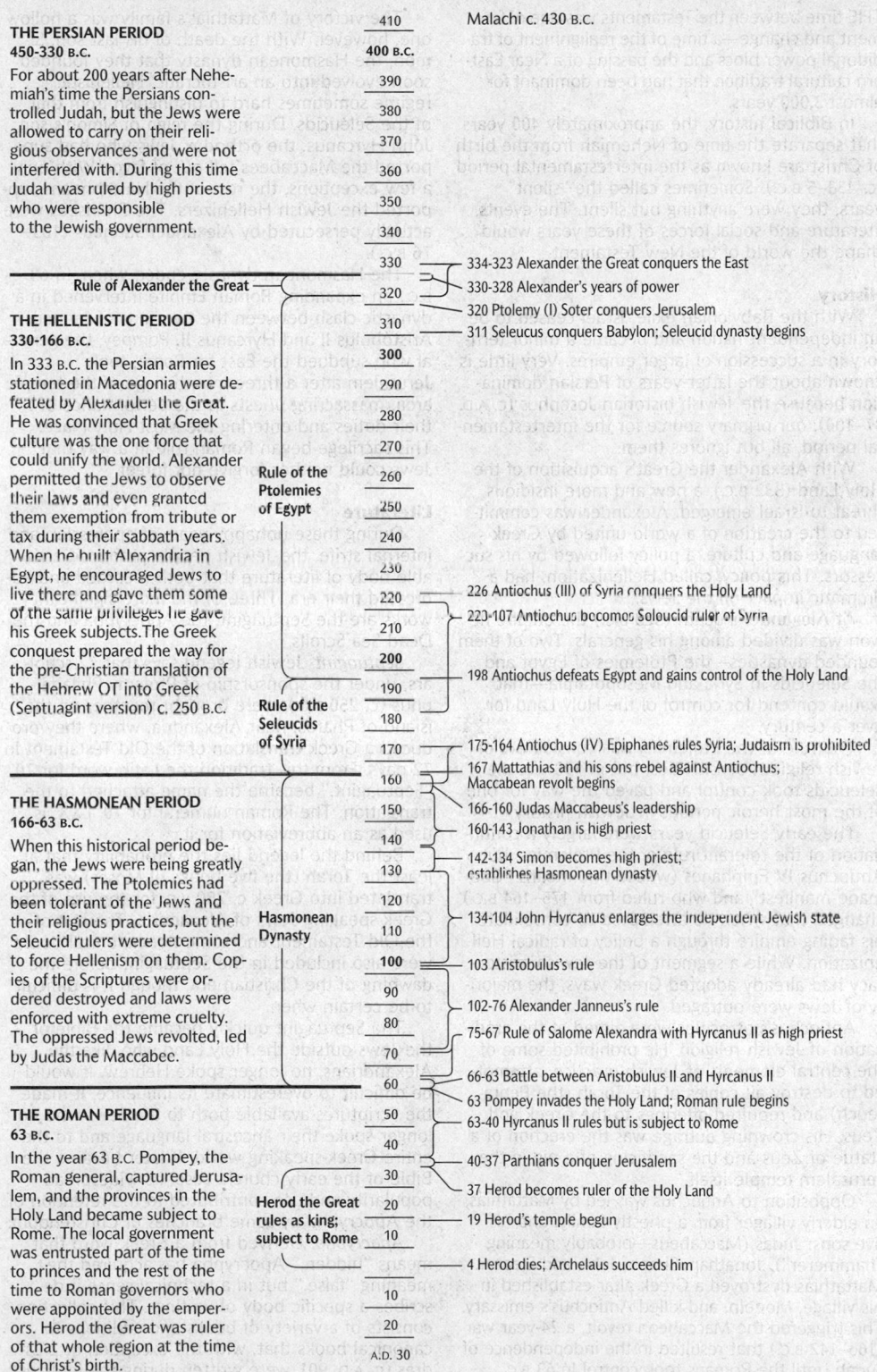

THE PERSIAN PERIOD
450-330 B.C.

For about 200 years after Nehemiah's time the Persians controlled Judah, but the Jews were allowed to carry on their religious observances and were not interfered with. During this time Judah was ruled by high priests who were responsible to the Jewish government.

THE HELLENISTIC PERIOD
330-166 B.C.

In 333 B.C. the Persian armies stationed in Macedonia were defeated by Alexander the Great. He was convinced that Greek culture was the one force that could unify the world. Alexander permitted the Jews to observe their laws and even granted them exemption from tribute or tax during their sabbath years. When he built Alexandria in Egypt, he encouraged Jews to live there and gave them some of the same privileges he gave his Greek subjects. The Greek conquest prepared the way for the pre-Christian translation of the Hebrew OT into Greek (Septuagint version) c. 250 B.C.

THE HASMONEAN PERIOD
166-63 B.C.

When this historical period began, the Jews were being greatly oppressed. The Ptolemies had been tolerant of the Jews and their religious practices, but the Seleucid rulers were determined to force Hellenism on them. Copies of the Scriptures were ordered destroyed and laws were enforced with extreme cruelty. The oppressed Jews revolted, led by Judas the Maccabee.

THE ROMAN PERIOD
63 B.C.

In the year 63 B.C. Pompey, the Roman general, captured Jerusalem, and the provinces in the Holy Land became subject to Rome. The local government was entrusted part of the time to princes and the rest of the time to Roman governors who were appointed by the emperors. Herod the Great was ruler of that whole region at the time of Christ's birth.

Timeline (410 B.C. – A.D. 30)

- Malachi c. 430 B.C.
- **400 B.C.**
- **Rule of Alexander the Great**
- 334-323 Alexander the Great conquers the East
- 330-328 Alexander's years of power
- 320 Ptolemy (I) Soter conquers Jerusalem
- 311 Seleucus conquers Babylon; Seleucid dynasty begins
- **Rule of the Ptolemies of Egypt**
- 226 Antiochus (III) of Syria conquers the Holy Land
- 223-107 Antiochus becomes Seleucid ruler of Syria
- 198 Antiochus defeats Egypt and gains control of the Holy Land
- **Rule of the Seleucids of Syria**
- 175-164 Antiochus (IV) Epiphanes rules Syria; Judaism is prohibited
- 167 Mattathias and his sons rebel against Antiochus; Maccabean revolt begins
- 166-160 Judas Maccabeus's leadership
- 160-143 Jonathan is high priest
- 142-134 Simon becomes high priest; establishes Hasmonean dynasty
- **Hasmonean Dynasty**
- 134-104 John Hyrcanus enlarges the independent Jewish state
- 103 Aristobulus's rule
- 102-76 Alexander Janneus's rule
- 75-67 Rule of Salome Alexandra with Hyrcanus II as high priest
- 66-63 Battle between Aristobulus II and Hyrcanus II
- 63 Pompey invades the Holy Land; Roman rule begins
- 63-40 Hyrcanus II rules but is subject to Rome
- 40-37 Parthians conquer Jerusalem
- 37 Herod becomes ruler of the Holy Land
- **Herod the Great rules as king; subject to Rome**
- 19 Herod's temple begun
- 4 Herod dies; Archelaus succeeds him
- A.D. 30

The Time Between the Testaments

THE time between the Testaments was one of ferment and change—a time of the realignment of traditional power blocs and the passing of a Near Eastern cultural tradition that had been dominant for almost 3,000 years.

In Biblical history, the approximately 400 years that separate the time of Nehemiah from the birth of Christ are known as the intertestamental period (c. 433–5 B.C.). Sometimes called the "silent" years, they were anything but silent. The events, literature and social forces of these years would shape the world of the New Testament.

History

With the Babylonian exile, Israel ceased to be an independent nation and became a minor territory in a succession of larger empires. Very little is known about the latter years of Persian domination because the Jewish historian Josephus (c. A.D. 37–100), our primary source for the intertestamental period, all but ignores them.

With Alexander the Great's acquisition of the Holy Land (332 B.C.), a new and more insidious threat to Israel emerged. Alexander was committed to the creation of a world united by Greek language and culture, a policy followed by his successors. This policy, called Hellenization, had a dramatic impact on the Jews.

At Alexander's death (323 B.C.) the empire he won was divided among his generals. Two of them founded dynasties—the Ptolemies of Egypt and the Seleucids in Syria and Mesopotamia—that would contend for control of the Holy Land for over a century.

The rule of the Ptolemies was considerate of Jewish religious sensitivities, but in 198 B.C. the Seleucids took control and paved the way for one of the most heroic periods in Jewish history.

The early Seleucid years were largely a continuation of the tolerant rule of the Ptolemies, but Antiochus IV Epiphanes (whose title means "God made manifest" and who ruled from 175–164 B.C.) changed that when he attempted to consolidate his fading empire through a policy of radical Hellenization. While a segment of the Jewish aristocracy had already adopted Greek ways, the majority of Jews were outraged.

Antiochus's atrocities were aimed at the eradication of Jewish religion. He prohibited some of the central elements of Jewish practice, attempted to destroy all copies of the Torah (the Pentateuch) and required offerings to the Greek god Zeus. His crowning outrage was the erection of a statue of Zeus and the sacrificing of a pig in the Jerusalem temple itself.

Opposition to Antiochus was led by Mattathias, an elderly villager from a priestly family, and his five sons: Judas (Maccabeus—probably meaning "hammerer"), Jonathan, Simon, John and Eleazar. Mattathias destroyed a Greek altar established in his village, Modein, and killed Antiochus's emissary. This triggered the Maccabean revolt, a 24-year war (166–142 B.C.) that resulted in the independence of Judah until the Romans took control in 63 B.C.

The victory of Mattathias's family was a hollow one, however. With the death of his last son, Simon, the Hasmonean dynasty that they founded soon evolved into an aristocratic, Hellenistic regime sometimes hard to distinguish from that of the Seleucids. During the reign of Simon's son, John Hyrcanus, the orthodox Jews who had supported the Maccabees fell out of favor. With only a few exceptions, the rest of the Hasmoneans supported the Jewish Hellenizers. The Pharisees were actually persecuted by Alexander Janneus (103–76 B.C.).

The Hasmonean dynasty ended when, in 63 B.C., an expanding Roman Empire intervened in a dynastic clash between the two sons of Janneus, Aristobulus II and Hyrcanus II. Pompey, the general who subdued the East for Rome, took Jerusalem after a three-month siege of the temple area, massacring priests in the performance of their duties and entering the Most Holy Place. This sacrilege began Roman rule in a way that Jews could neither forgive nor forget.

Literature

During these unhappy years of oppression and internal strife, the Jewish people produced a sizable body of literature that both recorded and addressed their era. Three of the more significant works are the Septuagint, the Apocrypha and the Dead Sea Scrolls.

Septuagint. Jewish legend says that 72 scholars, under the sponsorship of Ptolemy Philadelphus (c. 250 B.C.), were brought together on the island of Pharos, near Alexandria, where they produced a Greek translation of the Old Testament in 72 days. From this tradition the Latin word for 70, "Septuagint," became the name attached to the translation. The Roman numeral for 70, LXX, is used as an abbreviation for it.

Behind the legend lies the probability that at least the Torah (the five books of Moses) was translated into Greek c. 250 B.C. for the use of the Greek-speaking Jews of Alexandria. The rest of the Old Testament and some noncanonical books were also included in the Septuagint before the dawning of the Christian era, though it is difficult to be certain when.

The Septuagint quickly became the Bible of the Jews outside the Holy Land who, like the Alexandrians, no longer spoke Hebrew. It would be difficult to overestimate its influence. It made the Scriptures available both to the Jews who no longer spoke their ancestral language and to the entire Greek-speaking world. It later became the Bible of the early church. Also, its widespread popularity and use contributed to the retention of the Apocrypha by some branches of Christendom.

Apocrypha. Derived from a Greek word that means "hidden," Apocrypha has acquired the meaning "false," but in a technical sense it describes a specific body of writings. This collection consists of a variety of books and additions to canonical books that, with the exception of 2 Esdras (c. A.D. 90), were written during the intertestamental period. Their recognition as authoritative in Roman and Eastern Christianity is the result of a complex historical process.

The limits of the Hebrew canon of the Old Testament, also accepted by most Protestants today, were very likely established by the dawn of the second century A.D. In spite of disagreements among some of the church fathers as to which books were canonical and which were not, the Apocryphal books (which were included in the Septuagint) continued in common use by most Christians until the Reformation. During this period most Protestants decided to follow the original Hebrew canon while Rome, at the Council of Trent (1546) and more recently at the First Vatican Council (1869–70), affirmed the larger "Alexandrian" canon that includes the Apocrypha.

The Apocryphal books have retained their place primarily through the weight of ecclesiastical authority, without which they would not commend themselves as canonical literature. There is no clear evidence that Jesus or the apostles ever quoted any Apocryphal works as inspired Scripture. The Jewish community that produced them repudiated them, and the historical surveys in the apostolic sermons recorded in Acts completely ignore the period they cover. Even the sober, historical account of 1 Maccabees is tarnished by numerous errors and anachronisms.

There is nothing of theological value in the Apocryphal books that cannot be duplicated in canonical Scripture, and they contain much that runs counter to its teachings. Nonetheless, this body of literature does provide a valuable source of information for the study of the intertestamental period.

Dead Sea Scrolls. In the spring of 1947 an Arab shepherd chanced upon a cave in the hills overlooking the southwestern shore of the Dead Sea that contained what has been called "the greatest manuscript discovery of modern times." The documents and fragments of documents found in those caves, dubbed the "Dead Sea Scrolls," included Old Testament books, a few books of the Apocrypha, apocalyptic works, pseudepigrapha (books that purport to be the work of ancient heroes of the faith) and a number of books peculiar to the sect that produced them.

Approximately a third of the documents are Biblical, with Psalms, Deuteronomy and Isaiah—the books quoted most often in the New Testament—occurring most frequently. One of the most remarkable finds was a complete 24-foot-long scroll of Isaiah.

The Scrolls have made a significant contribution to the quest for a form of the Old Testament texts most accurately reflecting the original manuscripts; they provide copies 1,000 years closer to the originals than were previously known. The understanding of Biblical Hebrew and Aramaic and knowledge of the development of Judaism between the Testaments have been increased significantly. Of great importance to readers of the Bible is the demonstration of the care with which Old Testament texts were copied, thus providing objective evidence for the general reliability of those texts.

Social Developments

The Judaism of Jesus' day is, to a large extent, the result of changes that came about in response to the pressures of the intertestamental period.

Diaspora. The Diaspora (dispersion) of Israel begun in the exile accelerated during these years until a writer of the day could say that Jews filled "every land and sea."

Jews outside the Holy Land, cut off from the temple, concentrated their religious life in the study of the Torah and the life of the synagogue (see below). The missionaries of the early church began their Gentile ministries among the Diaspora, using their Greek translation of the Old Testament (the Septuagint).

Sadducees. In the Holy Land, the Greek world made its greatest impact through the party of the Sadducees. Made up of aristocrats, it became the temple party. Because of their position, the Sadducees had a vested interest in the status quo.

Relatively few in number, they wielded disproportionate political power and controlled the high priesthood. They rejected all religious writings except the Torah, as well as any doctrine (such as resurrection from the dead) not found in those five books.

Synagogue. During the Babylonian exile, Israel was cut off from the temple, divested of nationhood and surrounded by pagan religious practices. The nation's faith was threatened with extinction. Under these circumstances, the exiles turned their religious focus from what they had lost to what they retained—the Torah and the belief that they were God's people. They concentrated on the law rather than on nationhood, on personal piety rather than sacramental rectitude, and on prayer as an acceptable replacement for the sacrifices denied to them.

When they returned from the exile, they brought with them this new form of religious expression, as well as the synagogue (its center), and Judaism became a faith that could be practiced wherever the Torah could be carried. The emphases on personal piety and a relationship with God, which characterized synagogue worship, not only helped preserve Judaism but also prepared the way for the Christian gospel.

Pharisees. As the party of the synagogue, the Pharisees strove to reinterpret the law. They built a "hedge" around it to enable Jews to live righteously before God in a world that had changed drastically since the days of Moses. Although they were comparatively few in number, the Pharisees enjoyed the support of the people and influenced popular opinion, if not national policy. They were the only party to survive the destruction of the temple in A.D. 70 and were the spiritual progenitors of modern Judaism.

Essenes. An almost forgotten Jewish sect (but referred to by Josephus) until the discovery of the

The Time Between the Testaments *(continued)*

Dead Sea Scrolls, the Essenes were a small, separatist group that grew out of the conflicts of the Maccabean age. Like the Pharisees, they stressed strict legal observance, but they considered the temple priesthood corrupt and rejected much of the temple ritual and sacrificial system. Mentioned by several ancient writers, the precise nature of the Essenes is still not certain, though it is generally agreed that the Qumran community that produced the Dead Sea Scrolls was an Essene group.

Because they were convinced that they were the true remnant, these Qumran Essenes had separated themselves from Judaism at large and devoted themselves to personal purity and preparation for the final war between the "Sons of Light and the Sons of Darkness." They practiced an apocalyptic faith, looking back to the contributions of their "Teacher of Righteousness" and forward to the coming of two, and possibly three, Messiahs. The destruction of the temple in A.D. 70, however, seems to have delivered a death blow to their apocalyptic expectations.

Attempts have been made to equate aspects of the beliefs of the Qumran community with the origins of Christianity. Some have seen a prototype of Jesus in their "Teacher of Righteousness," and both John the Baptist and Jesus have been assigned membership in the sect. There is, however, only a superficial, speculative base for these conjectures.

THE
NEW TESTAMENT

Introduction to the Gospels and Acts

HISTORICAL BACKGROUND

Herod the Great, who died soon after the birth of Jesus, had designated his son Archelaus to succeed him as ruler of Judea and Samaria (Mt 2:19–22). Having inherited the faults of his father and none of his virtues, Archelaus was banished within ten years. As a result, Judea and Samaria came under the direct rule of Rome through a series of governors or prefects (later known as "procurators"), including Pontius Pilate, who held that position during the ministry of Jesus.

Herod had granted the provinces of Galilee (where Jesus spent most of his life and ministry) and Perea to another son, Herod Antipas, who is mentioned briefly in the Gospels (e.g., Mt 14:1–12; Lk 23:6–15). Antipas's reign was lengthy, but in A.D. 39 a grandson of Herod the Great named Herod Agrippa succeeded in having Antipas banished and took over Galilee and Perea. Two years later his childhood friend Claudius, then the Roman Emperor, made him king of Judea and Samaria as well. Agrippa was well loved by the Jews, but his reign was short. After having persecuted some of the apostles and receiving adulation as though he were a god, he died in A.D. 44 (Ac 12:1–4,19–23).

At that time the land reverted back to Roman governors, though Agrippa II was given rule over a small portion (Ac 25:13—26:32). The tensions between Jews and Romans became severe during this period and led eventually to a revolt in A.D. 66. This war proved disastrous for the Jewish nation, and Jerusalem was destroyed in A.D. 70.

THE CHARACTER OF NEW TESTAMENT NARRATIVE

Apart from the Pentateuch, the major historical books of the Old Testament (Joshua, Judges, 1–2 Samuel, 1–2 Kings) are called the "Former Prophets" in Jewish tradition. Their primary purpose was to serve, not as national archives, but as prophetic messages of rebuke and comfort. Similarly, the Gospels and Acts do not provide us with all of the historical details that might interest modern readers, nor can they rightly be called biographies of Jesus or the apostles. Rather, they record events that have been selected and arranged to present the message of the gospel.

When reading New Testament narratives, therefore, we should make a special effort to determine why events were included, described and arranged as they were. Details that may seem insignificant at first sight (e.g., Paul's vow recorded in Ac 18:18) may subsequently prove quite important (Ac 21:20–24). Similarly, when an event in Jesus' life is recounted by more than one Gospel, we can discern more of its significance by reading the perspective of each account.

THE SYNOPTIC PROBLEM

Even a quick reading of the four Gospels reveals that three of them (Matthew, Mark and Luke) are very much alike, especially when contrasted with John. With a few important exceptions, the events included in John (e.g., chs. 3, 9, 11 and 14) do not appear in the first three Gospels. For these reasons the first three Gospels are often referred to as the "Synoptics" (sharing one point of view).

A more detailed comparison, however, reveals differences as well as similarities among the Synoptics. Sometimes the material recorded is exactly the same; in other instances there are verbal differences. In some cases the order of events is the same, but often it is not. From a literary point of view, these facts create a problem. How did these Gospels originate? Did their authors make use of each other's work? Did they draw on other materials?

The most common answer to these questions is that Mark was the first Gospel to be written and that Matthew and Luke followed its basic outline (Mk 2:1–22; cf. Mt 9:2–17; Lk 5:18–38). But Matthew and Luke have in common some important material not found at all in Mark (e.g., Mt 7:24–27; Lk 6:47–49), so scholars suppose that a second document, no longer extant, was used by these two writers. This solution is known as the "Two-Source Theory." In addition, Matthew and Luke clearly each had access to much information found only in their respective Gospels.

This proposal cannot account for all the facts, and so alternate theories have been suggested. Some argue for the priority of Matthew rather than Mark; a few suggest instead that Luke was written first. A number of scholars place much emphasis on the oral tradition that must have preceded the writing of these documents and downplay their literary interdependence. Most New Testament specialists continue to use the Two-Source approach as a working hypothesis but recognize that many questions remain unanswered.

Although many questions remain unresolved in the study of the Gospels, our confidence in their truth should not rest on the ability of specialists to sort out literary developments, but rather on divine inspiration (2Ti 3:16–17). See *WCF* 1.5, *BC* 5.

MATTHEW

Introduction

Overview

Author: Matthew (Levi)

Purpose: To inspire Christians to grateful and faithful service in furthering the kingdom of God by presenting Jesus as the long-awaited King and by presenting the kingdom that he brought as the fulfillment of God's plan of redemption

Date: A.D. 60–70

Key Truths:

- Jesus fulfilled the Old Testament Scriptures.
- Jesus is the promised King (Messiah).
- Jesus inaugurated the kingdom of God while on Earth.
- Jesus' followers must spread the kingdom to all nations.
- Jesus' followers will suffer, but Jesus is always with them.
- Jesus will complete the kingdom of God at his return.

Author

Although this Gospel was written anonymously, some early manuscripts bear the inscription "according to Matthew," and Eusebius (*Ecclesiastical History* 3.39) tells us that the early church father Papias, writing within the first two decades of the second century, spoke of Matthew as having arranged "the oracles" about Jesus. The subsequent unanimous tradition, including that of Calvin and other early Reformers, is that the disciple named Levi (Matthew) was the author of this Gospel (9:9–13).

Not until the 18th century did scholars question this tradition. First, they pointed to Papias's apparent claim that Matthew "arranged the oracles in the Hebrew dialect." This would seem to indicate that Matthew wrote in Hebrew or Aramaic, but modern scholars point out that the Gospel of Matthew does not read like a translation from Hebrew or Aramaic. Matthew's Gospel also has a close literary affinity with the Gospel of Mark, which was originally written in Greek. The solution may be that the word "dialect" did not mean so much "language" as "literary style." Certainly Matthew has many Jewish stylistic features. It is also possible that Matthew wrote in both Hebrew and Greek, much as Calvin wrote works in both Latin and French.

Second, some have objected that Papias did not say "gospel" but "oracles," and they have identified these "oracles" as one of the sources lying behind the canonical Gospel of Matthew. But Eusebius appears to have understood "oracles" to mean "gospel," and Irenaeus (writing about A.D. 180) speaks of a "gospel" by Matthew written "for the Hebrews in their own dialect" (*Against Heresies* 3.1.1).

Other scholarly objections to Matthew's authorship are more speculative. For example, the first Gospel's supposedly late composition (see below) and its alleged dependence on Mark are adduced to cast doubt on Matthean authorship, but no better suggestion has been advanced. While some surmise that it was the product of a "school," there is no compelling reason to accept this hypothesis.

There may be subtle confirmation of Matthew's authorship in the way he speaks of himself (9:9; 10:3), but this evidence is questionable. Although it is impossible to determine the author's identity with absolute certainty, the book's early association with Matthew points to its acceptance as an eyewitness account of Jesus' life. Moreover, we hear in this Gospel the voice of its primary author, the Spirit of God himself.

Time and Place of Writing

The earliest external evidence for the existence of Matthew is a probable reference by Ignatius (*Epistle to the Smyrnaeans* 1.1), who died about A.D. 110, and the evidence of Papias, who wrote very early in the second century. Almost no one dates the book later than A.D. 100. But dating the work more specifically than this is difficult. Some scholars have dated it as early as A.D. 50, but most critics believe it was completed after the destruction of Jerusalem, probably between A.D. 80 and 100.

Some reasons for preferring a late date are quite dubious, such as the assumption that Jesus could not have predicted the future destruction of the temple or that a high Christology is Hellenistic, and therefore that the date should be late. Further, there is some internal evidence that Matthew was written *before* the destruction of Jerusalem (i.e., prior to A.D. 70). For instance, 12:5–7 and 23:16–22 imply that the temple was still standing when Matthew was written. Also, this Gospel warns against the Sadducees, a group that ceased to exist after A.D. 70.

If, in accordance with prevailing opinion, we concede that the writer of this Gospel used the Gospel of Mark as source material, and if we assume that the Gospel of Mark was composed in association with Peter in Rome, we can fix a date for the writing of Matthew sometime after A.D. 64. Even apart from this concession, it seems probable that the Gospel was composed during that decade (A.D. 60–70).

The date of the Gospel of Matthew may be difficult to fix, but it was certainly completed within 50 or 60 years after the events described. Its author could not have invented material freely, for eyewitnesses were still living to refute false claims.

Matthew's Gospel was most likely written in Antioch in Syria.

Original Audience

The Gospel of Matthew was probably addressed to the church in Antioch. Ignatius, the first church father to cite Matthew, was bishop of Antioch. Further, the congregation in Antioch was of mixed Jewish and Gentile origin (cf. Ac 15), a fact that could well have given rise to the problems of legalism and antinomianism that Matthew particularly addresses.

Purpose and Distinctives

The Gospel of Matthew presents Jesus—especially Jesus' teaching about himself and the kingdom of heaven. This kingdom is the fulfillment of God's plan of redemption and renewal that had been prophesied since the fall (Ge 3:15). In this plan, Jesus' passion and death are not a regrettable tragedy; rather, they are the means God ordained in order to accomplish his goal. Jesus' resurrection marks the beginning of history's end.

The purpose of Matthew's Gospel is to convey authoritative teaching by and about Jesus, whose coming marked the fulfillment of God's promises. It is not merely a history or biography, a theology or confession, a catechism or teaching tract; it is a combination of all these things. Matthew allows no divorce between narrative and theology or between theory and practice. The history is the only proper basis for the theology, and the theology gives the only proper meaning to the history; so, too, with theory and practice.

Matthew's Gospel is exceptional in its extensive appeal to Jesus' fulfillment of the Old Testament patterns, requirements and expectations. These are presented not simply as "predictions" and "fulfillments," but as indications of the fulfillment of all the hopes of the Old Testament and of the purpose of Israel's existence (see note on 1:23).

This concern with fulfillment is reflected not only in Matthew's citations, but also in the way certain things in the history are stressed. It is Matthew's Gospel that points out that there were *two* demoniacs and *two* blind men, in accordance with the Old Testament principle that testimony be established on the basis of at least two witnesses. It is Matthew's Gospel that clearly shows us the illegality of the Sanhedrin's actions, the perversion of the Old Testament by the scribes and Pharisees and the covenantal nature of God's dealing with his people.

Also distinctive to Matthew is its structuring of Jesus' teaching into five major discourses: ethics, discipleship and mission, the kingdom of heaven, the church, and eschatology. This structure itself may have been patterned after the five books of Moses in order to present Jesus as the "prophet like [Moses]" (Dt 18:18) who was even greater than Moses.

Most scholars today recognize these five major discourses as Matthew's key structuring device, especially since each discourse ends with a formula: "And when Jesus had finished . . ." Further, there seems to be a relationship between each discourse and the narrative material preceding it. The following outline reflects this consensus. The *narrative* sections deal primarily with the question "Who is the King?" The *discourse* material tends to focus on the King's people.

Outline

I. Prologue (1:1—2:23)

Jesus' genealogy, birth and early childhood demonstrate that he is the long-expected Messiah. God worked miraculously in the early years of Jesus' life to display him as the King of the Jews and Gentiles.

II. The Kingdom Comes (3:1—7:29)
- A. Narrative: Announcing the Kingdom (3:1—4:25)
- B. Discourse: Kingdom Law (5:1—7:29)

John the Baptist announced that Jesus is the One who brings the kingdom of heaven. Jesus' temptations in the wilderness showed him to be deserving of his Messianic role. Jesus' Sermon on the Mount exalted him as the divinely authorized lawgiver for the kingdom.

III. The Works of the Kingdom (8:1—10:42)
- A. Narrative: Healing and Calling (8:1—9:38)
- B. Discourse: Kingdom Mission (10:1–42)

Jesus performed many miracles that displayed his power to establish the kingdom. He also called, empowered and sent disciples to spread the kingdom. Jesus warned, however, that persecution and suffering will come to those who serve the kingdom of heaven.

IV. The Nature of the Kingdom (11:1—13:58)
- A. Narrative: Who Was John? Who Is Jesus? (11:1—12:50)
- B. Discourse: Kingdom Parables (13:1–58)

Jesus revealed the nature of the kingdom to John the Baptist and to the Jews. His actions and words challenged popular expectations about the Messiah and his kingdom. He offered numerous parables that explained that the kingdom comes over time and that all must repent and remain faithful to him to enter it.

V. The Authority of the Kingdom (14:1—18:35) A. Narrative: Character and Authority of Jesus (14:1—17:27) B. Discourse: Character and Authority of the Church (18:1–35)	*Jesus' miracles demonstrated his authority as the Messiah. Many testified to his supremacy as they saw him performing great works. Jesus insisted that life under his kingship is different from life in other kingdoms.*
VI. The Changes of the Kingdom (19:1—25:46) A. Narrative: Parables and Woes (19:1—23:39) B. Discourse: Kingdom Judgment (24:1—25:46)	*Jesus' actions, parables and answers to challenges revealed that his kingdom brings remarkable changes in the beliefs and practices of God's people. Jesus strongly condemned the religious leaders of Israel for their hypocrisies and warned of divine judgment.*
VII. Passion and Resurrection (26:1—28:20)	*Jesus was afflicted and died as the suffering King of the Jews, and he was exalted in his resurrection as the victorious King. Jesus revealed himself to his disciples and commissioned them to spread his kingdom to the ends of the earth.*

The Genealogy of Jesus

1 A record of the genealogy of Jesus Christ the son of David,[a] the son of Abraham:[b]

2 Abraham was the father of Isaac,[c]
Isaac the father of Jacob,[d]
Jacob the father of Judah and his brothers,[e]
3 Judah the father of Perez and Zerah, whose mother was Tamar,[f]
Perez the father of Hezron,
Hezron the father of Ram,
4 Ram the father of Amminadab,
Amminadab the father of Nahshon,
Nahshon the father of Salmon,
5 Salmon the father of Boaz, whose mother was Rahab,
Boaz the father of Obed, whose mother was Ruth,
Obed the father of Jesse,
6 and Jesse the father of King David.[g]

David was the father of Solomon, whose mother had been Uriah's wife,[h]
7 Solomon the father of Rehoboam,
Rehoboam the father of Abijah,
Abijah the father of Asa,
8 Asa the father of Jehoshaphat,
Jehoshaphat the father of Jehoram,
Jehoram the father of Uzziah,
9 Uzziah the father of Jotham,
Jotham the father of Ahaz,

1:1 [a]2Sa 7:12-16; Isa 9:6,7; 11:1; Jer 23:5,6; Mt 9:27; Lk 1:32,69; Ro 1:3; Rev 22:16 [b]Ge 22:18; Gal 3:16
1:2 [c]Ge 21:3,12 [d]Ge 25:26 [e]Ge 29:35
1:3 [f]Ge 38:27-30
1:6 [g]1Sa 16:1; 17:12 [h]2Sa 12:24

▪ **1:1—2:23** *Prologue.* Chapters 1–2 form the prologue, opening the Gospel with a genealogy and several dramatic events demonstrating that Jesus is the Messiah.
1:1 genealogy. Literally, "origin" or "beginning" (*genesis*), which in Biblical terminology could mean "account" (cf. Ge 2:4; 5:1). The word also occurs (in the better manuscripts) in 1:18, where it cannot mean "genealogy." The term could well point beyond the genealogy to the whole Gospel, which is an "account of the beginning" of Jesus Christ; i.e., the inauguration of his reign. **Christ.** Based on the Greek word for "anointed," *Christ* corresponds to the Hebrew word *mashiach,* or "Messiah," "the anointed one." In the Old Testament, anointing with oil symbolized God's designation of a person to an office. All three Old Testament offices—prophet, priest and king—were so designated (see 1Ki 19:16; Ex 29:7; 1Sa 16:13, respectively), but by the time of Jesus "Messiah" was a designation primarily used for the office of king. The Old Testament promised the coming of the righteous servant of the Lord (Isa 42:1–9), who would be a prophet like Moses (Dt 18:18–19), a priest like Melchizedek (Ps 110:4) and a king like David, the Lord's anointed (Isa 55:3–5; Jer 30:9; Eze 34:24; Hos 3:5; Zec 12:8). Israel expected a Messiah who would bring victory over its enemies and establish a rule of peace. The Gospel of Matthew claims that Jesus is the "Christ," the promised King and Deliverer—much more than the Messiah of popular expectation. Jesus himself rarely used the title because it was so misunderstood. See *HC* 35.
1:2–16 Women are not usually named in Near Eastern genealogies, but they were intrinsic to God's purpose in bringing forth the Christ. The five explicitly named in Jesus' genealogy all remind us that God often does the unexpected and chooses the unlikely. Tamar reminds us of Judah's failures (Ge 38:6–30); Rahab was a Gentile prostitute (Jos 2); Ruth was a Moabitess and thus under a special curse (cf. Dt 23:3–5); Bathsheba, the wife of Uriah the Hittite, was David's downfall (2Sa 11). Mary, the virgin, not only fulfilled Isaiah 7:14 (cf. v. 23) but also the even more important promise of Genesis 3:15 (cf. Gal 4:4).
1:2 The specifics of the genealogy differ from Luke 3:23–38, probably because the Gospel of Luke is giving the physical descent, whereas the Gospel of Matthew records the throne succession.

Ahaz the father of Hezekiah,

1:10 [i]2Ki 20:21

10 Hezekiah the father of Manasseh,[i]
Manasseh the father of Amon,
Amon the father of Josiah,

1:11 [j]2Ki 24:14-16; Jer 27:20; Da 1:1,2

11 and Josiah the father of Jeconiah[a] and his brothers at the time of the exile to Babylon.[j]

12 After the exile to Babylon:

1:12 [k]1Ch 3:17 [l]1Ch 3:19; Ezr 3:2

Jeconiah was the father of Shealtiel,[k]
Shealtiel the father of Zerubbabel,[l]
13 Zerubbabel the father of Abiud,
Abiud the father of Eliakim,
Eliakim the father of Azor,
14 Azor the father of Zadok,
Zadok the father of Akim,
Akim the father of Eliud,
15 Eliud the father of Eleazar,
Eleazar the father of Matthan,
Matthan the father of Jacob,

1:16 [m]Lk 1:27 [n]Mt 27:17

16 and Jacob the father of Joseph, the husband of Mary,[m] of whom was born Jesus, who is called Christ.[n]

17 Thus there were fourteen generations in all from Abraham to David, fourteen from David to the exile to Babylon, and fourteen from the exile to the Christ.[b]

The Birth of Jesus Christ

1:18 [o]Lk 1:35

1:19 [p]Dt 24:1

18 This is how the birth of Jesus Christ came about: His mother Mary was pledged to
be married to Joseph, but before they came together, she was found to be with child
through the Holy Spirit.[o] 19 Because Joseph her husband was a righteous man and did not
want to expose her to public disgrace, he had in mind to divorce[p] her quietly.
20 But after he had considered this, an angel of the Lord appeared to him in a dream

[a] *11* That is, Jehoiachin; also in verse 12

[b] *17* Or *Messiah.* "The Christ" (Greek) and "the Messiah" (Hebrew) both mean "the Anointed One."

1:17 fourteen generations. Matthew organizes the genealogy into three groups of 14 (or three groups of double sevens) to show that God has a purpose in history and that Israel's early history leading to David, the monarchy leading to the exile, and the post-exilic history of Israel all led up to and pointed to Christ. Jeconiah (i.e., Jehoiachin) is included in both the second and third groups of 14. This is not an error, nor is Matthew's an abbreviation of the genealogy. Jehoiachin was both a preexilic and a postexilic king. (Da 9:24), Matthew was not interested in numerology per se; he was pointing out a pattern in God's redemptive history.

1:18–23 See *WCF* 24.5; *HC* 18,35.

1:19 Joseph . . . had in mind to divorce her. Betrothal, the pledge of marriage, was as binding as marriage, and infidelity during the betrothal made divorce virtually obligatory, since not to divorce would have been a tacit admission of one's own guilt.

The Virgin Birth of Jesus: Was Mary Really a Virgin?

MATTHEW 1:18–25, Luke 1:26–56 and Luke 2:4–7 unite in witnessing to Jesus' birth as the consequence of a miraculous conception. Mary became pregnant by the Holy Spirit's creative action while she was still a virgin (Mt 1:20; Lk 1:35).

Most Christians accepted the virgin birth without hesitation until modern theology challenged miracles in the 19th century. Then the doctrine of the virgin birth became a pivotal point in the debate about Christian supernaturalism and the divinity of Jesus. Modern liberalism rejected the virgin birth along with all other Biblical miracles.

In reality, the virgin birth meshes harmoniously with the rest of the New Testament message about Jesus. He himself worked miracles and rose miraculously from the dead, so no new problem is involved in affirming that he entered the world miraculously. He left the world supernaturally, by resurrection and ascension, so a supernatural way of arriving was entirely fitting. Jesus' preincarnate dignity and glory (Jn 1:1–9; 17:5; Php 2:5–11; Col 1:15–17; Heb 1:1–3; 1Jn 1:1), as well as the glory of the work he came to do (Mt 1:21–23; Lk 1:31–35), made it only natural that his birth should be glorious and miraculous. To reject the virgin birth of Jesus is implicitly to question the entire teaching of the New Testament concerning him.

Jesus' miraculous conception points to his deity and also to the reality of the creative power that operates in our own new birth (Jn 1:13). His miraculous birth also points to his sinlessness. Although Mary was a sinner (Lk 1:43–48), she gave birth to One who was not. Through the Holy Spirit's action, Jesus' humanity avoided sin's taint, allowing Jesus to become the perfect sacrifice for human sins and the Savior of his own mother and of the rest of the true church along with her.

and said, "Joseph son of David, do not be afraid to take Mary home as your wife, because
what is conceived in her is from the Holy Spirit. 21 She will give birth to a son, and you
are to give him the name Jesus,[a][q] because he will save his people from their sins."[r]
22 All this took place to fulfill what the Lord had said through the prophet: 23 "The virgin will be with child and will give birth to a son, and they will call him Immanuel"[b][s]—
which means, "God with us."
24 When Joseph woke up, he did what the angel of the Lord had commanded him and
took Mary home as his wife. 25 But he had no union with her until she gave birth to a son.
And he gave him the name Jesus.[t]

The Visit of the Magi

2 After Jesus was born in Bethlehem in Judea,[u] during the time of King Herod,[v] Magi[c]
from the east came to Jerusalem 2 and asked, "Where is the one who has been born
king of the Jews?[w] We saw his star[x] in the east[d] and have come to worship him."
3 When King Herod heard this he was disturbed, and all Jerusalem with him. 4 When
he had called together all the people's chief priests and teachers of the law, he asked
them where the Christ[e] was to be born. 5 "In Bethlehem[y] in Judea," they replied, "for this
is what the prophet has written:

6 " 'But you, Bethlehem, in the land of Judah,
are by no means least among the rulers of Judah;
for out of you will come a ruler
who will be the shepherd of my people Israel.'[f]"[z]

7 Then Herod called the Magi secretly and found out from them the exact time the star
had appeared. 8 He sent them to Bethlehem and said, "Go and make a careful search for
the child. As soon as you find him, report to me, so that I too may go and worship him."
9 After they had heard the king, they went on their way, and the star they had seen in
the east[g] went ahead of them until it stopped over the place where the child was.
10 When they saw the star, they were overjoyed. 11 On coming to the house, they saw the
child with his mother Mary, and they bowed down and worshiped him.[a] Then they
opened their treasures and presented him with gifts[b] of gold and of incense and of
myrrh. 12 And having been warned[c] in a dream[d] not to go back to Herod, they returned
to their country by another route.

The Escape to Egypt

13 When they had gone, an angel[e] of the Lord appeared to Joseph in a dream.[f] "Get
up," he said, "take the child and his mother and escape to Egypt. Stay there until I tell
you, for Herod is going to search for the child to kill him."
14 So he got up, took the child and his mother during the night and left for Egypt,
15 where he stayed until the death of Herod. And so was fulfilled what the Lord had said
through the prophet: "Out of Egypt I called my son."[h][g]
16 When Herod realized that he had been outwitted by the Magi, he was furious, and

1:21 [q]Lk 1:31 [r]Lk 2:11; Ac 5:31; 13:23,28
1:23 [s]Isa 7:14; 8:8,10
1:25 [t]ver 21
2:1 [u]Lk 2:4-7 [v]Lk 1:5
2:2 [w]Jer 23:5; Mt 27:11; Mk 15:2; Jn 1:49; 18:33-37 [x]Nu 24:17
2:5 [y]Jn 7:42
2:6 [z]2Sa 5:2; Mic 5:2
2:11 [a]Isa 60:3 [b]Ps 72:10
2:12 [c]Heb 11:7 [d]ver 13, 19,22; Mt 27:19
2:13 [e]Ac 5:19 [f]ver 12, 19,22
2:15 [g]Ex 4:22,23; Hos 11:1

[a] *21 Jesus* is the Greek form of *Joshua,* which means *the LORD saves.* [b] *23* Isaiah 7:14 [c] *1* Traditionally *Wise Men* [d] *2* Or *star when it rose* [e] *4* Or *Messiah* [f] *6* Micah 5:2 [g] *9* Or *seen when it rose* [h] *15* Hosea 11:1

1:21 Jesus. The Greek equivalent of *Joshua,* Jesus means "Yahweh is salvation" or "Yahweh saves." See *WLC* 40,41; *BC* 21,22; *HC* 29.
1:23 virgin. The precise meaning of the Hebrew word *'almah* in Isaiah 7:14 is still debated, but Matthew clearly presents Mary as a virgin up to the conception of Jesus. The virgin conception was miraculous and as such was a sign of God's imminent redemption of his people and of his presence with them. (See theological article "The Virgin Birth of Jesus" at Mt 1.) This is the first of a number of Old Testament references Matthew uses to demonstrate that Jesus fulfilled the Old Testament (see notes on 2:6,15,18,23). In the entire Gospel there are 12 such fulfillment formulas, as well as 47 Old Testament citations. The name *Immanuel* is brought to mind again in 28:20, where Jesus promised that he would be *with* his disciples to the end of the age (see notes on Isa 7:14). See *WLC* 40; *BC* 18.
2:1 during the time of King Herod. Herod the Great died in April, 4 B.C. Therefore Jesus must have been born in 5 or 6 B.C. **Magi.** Gentile specialists in the supernatural, not kings.
2:2 star. It may have been a planetary conjunction, a supernova or something purely supernatural. Whatever the case, it alluded to the star of Jacob (Nu 24:17), which was prophesied by Balaam, another Gentile specialist in the supernatural. God often uses physical means to draw attention to spiritual realities.
2:4–5 See *WCF* 23.3; 31.2.
2:6 The second line of citation in Matthew appears formally to be the opposite of the second line of Micah 5:2 in the Hebrew, but the meanings of the verses are the same: Although Bethlehem appeared to be insignificant, it was actually wonderfully important. Although the religious experts concluded from the prophets that the Messiah was to be born in Bethlehem, not one of them bothered to make the short journey with the Magi to see the Christ.
2:11 house. Jesus was no longer in a stable. This visit occurred some time after the birth (2:1), perhaps a year or more later. Herod's order to kill infants under two years of age was based on information received from the Magi (2:16). Although the Magi could scarcely have realized the full symbolic value of their gifts, Matthew reports them to show the fulfillment of Old Testament passages that describe Gentiles bringing their wealth to Israel's king (Ps 72:10; Isa 60:6).
2:15 fulfilled. Hosea 11:1 refers to God's calling of his son Israel out of Egypt at the exodus. Matthew shows that the history of God's redemption of Israel actually pointed to Jesus, the true Son of God. Some have said that Jesus "recapitulated" the history of Israel.

he gave orders to kill all the boys in Bethlehem and its vicinity who were two years old
and under, in accordance with the time he had learned from the Magi. 17Then what was
said through the prophet Jeremiah was fulfilled:

18"A voice is heard in Ramah,
weeping and great mourning,
Rachel weeping for her children
and refusing to be comforted,
because they are no more."[a] [h]

The Return to Nazareth

19After Herod died, an angel of the Lord appeared in a dream[i] to Joseph in Egypt
20and said, "Get up, take the child and his mother and go to the land of Israel, for those
who were trying to take the child's life are dead."

21So he got up, took the child and his mother and went to the land of Israel. 22But
when he heard that Archelaus was reigning in Judea in place of his father Herod, he was
afraid to go there. Having been warned in a dream,[j] he withdrew to the district of Galilee,[k] 23and he went and lived in a town called Nazareth.[l] So was fulfilled[m] what was said
through the prophets: "He will be called a Nazarene."[n]

John the Baptist Prepares the Way

3 In those days John the Baptist[o] came, preaching in the Desert of Judea 2and saying,
"Repent, for the kingdom of heaven[p] is near." 3This is he who was spoken of
through the prophet Isaiah:

"A voice of one calling in the desert,
'Prepare the way for the Lord,
make straight paths for him.'"[b] [q]

4John's clothes were made of camel's hair, and he had a leather belt around his
waist.[r] His food was locusts[s] and wild honey. 5People went out to him from Jerusalem
and all Judea and the whole region of the Jordan. 6Confessing their sins, they were baptized by him in the Jordan River.

7But when he saw many of the Pharisees and Sadducees coming to where he was
baptizing, he said to them: "You brood of vipers![t] Who warned you to flee from the coming wrath?[u] 8Produce fruit in keeping with repentance.[v] 9And do not think you can say

2:18 [h]Jer 31:15
2:19 [i]ver 12,13,22
2:22 [j]ver 12,13,19; Mt 27:19 [k]Lk 2:39
2:23 [l]Lk 1:26; Jn 1:45, 46 [m]Mt 1:22 [n]Mk 1:24
3:1 [o]Lk 1:13,57-66; 3:2-19
3:2 [p]Da 2:44; Mt 4:17; 6:10; Lk 11:20; 21:31; Jn 3:3,5; Ac 1:3,6
3:3 [q]Isa 40:3; Mal 3:1; Lk 1:76; Jn 1:23
3:4 [r]2Ki 1:8 [s]Lev 11:22
3:7 [t]Mt 12:34; 23:33 [u]Ro 1:18; 1Th 1:10
3:8 [v]Ac 26:20

[a] *18* Jer. 31:15 [b] *3* Isaiah 40:3

2:18 Matthew cites Jeremiah 31:15, a verse taken from the middle of a prophecy about the return of Israel from exile. Rachel, the matriarch, represents Israel in her weeping, and the departure of the Lord's Christ to Egypt is like the departure of Rachel's sons Joseph and Benjamin to Egypt in Genesis. The citation in Matthew thus connects the sorrow preceding the exodus from Egypt with the sorrow in Babylon prior to the return and with Israel's sorrow at this time in Christ's life.

2:23 He will be called a Nazarene. The Old Testament has no verse that exactly corresponds to this, but it should be noted that Matthew introduces this reference to "the prophets" in more general terms than the other citations do. Matthew may have been thinking not so much of Nazareth as the place where the Christ would live as of the fact that the Christ would endure the stigma of being despised, as Nazarenes were (cf. Jn 1:46; 7:41–42,52). Isaiah 11:1, which refers to the coming Christ as a *netzer,* a "Branch" that comes from the roots of Jesse, may also have been in view.

■ **3:1—7:29** *The Kingdom Comes.* Chapters 3–7 form the second major portion of Matthew's Gospel and focus on the coming of the kingdom of heaven. These materials are divided into two sections: a narrative portion (3:1—4:25) followed by Jesus' first discourse (5:1—7:29).

■ **3:1—4:25** *Narrative: Announcing the Kingdom.* Chapters 3–4 form a narrative section that describes how John and Jesus announced the coming of the kingdom.

3:2 Repent. This was the first command of both John and Jesus (4:17). Repentance is not just sorrow for sin, but a decisive change, a turning away from one's sin and a commitment to begin a life of obedience. "Repent" translates the Old Testament prophets' call to Israel to "turn" back to God and to faithfulness to the covenant. True repentance does carry with it sorrow for sin, but contrition is indicated by a different Greek word. Judas felt remorse (27:3) but did not experience repentance. **kingdom of heaven.** Repentance is urgent because of the kingdom. This message of John introduces the theme of Jesus' teaching and work. The Gospels of Mark and Luke call it the "kingdom of God" (cf. 4:17 with Mk 1:15 and Lk 4:43). The "kingdom," or better, the "reign" of God is what the Old Testament prophets awaited: God's display of his saving power for the redemption of his people, his sovereignty and his redemption of his citizenry. Jesus' preaching that the kingdom had come (or was near) meant that the time of waiting was over and that the King himself had arrived on the scene. With the death and resurrection of Jesus and the spreading of the Good News to all nations, the Old Testament promises of God were fulfilled for us, although we still await their full realization, which will occur when Christ returns in judgment (cf. notes on chapter 13). **is near.** Can mean either "is just around the corner" or "has arrived." The term well describes the coming of the kingdom that had already been ushered in with the King's arrival on Earth but was still only partially fulfilled, awaiting his death, resurrection and ascension. Its realization is in another sense still forthcoming, awaiting his long-awaited second coming. (See theological article "The Kingdom of God" at Mt 4.)

3:3 This is he. The kingdom was at hand because the Lord was at hand. John proclaimed the coming of the Lord from Isaiah 40:3 and identified the Lord as Jesus (3:11–12,14).

3:6 Gentiles who converted to Judaism were not only circumcised but also baptized as a symbol of their death to their old Gentile lives and their cleansing from spiritual "uncleanness." The fact that John demanded that *Jews* be baptized meant that Jews were spiritually as unclean as pagans.

3:7–8 See *WLC* 153.

3:7 the coming wrath. The Old Testament promised the coming of the Lord in righteous judgment (Ps 96:13; Zep 2:1–2; Mal 3:2). John did not allow the leaders to suppose that the cup of God's wrath was only for Israel's enemies or that they themselves would escape. John was later confused because Jesus did not initiate judgment (see 11:2–3 and its note).

3:8 fruit. Refers to genuine, inward righteousness, not merely

to yourselves, 'We have Abraham as our father.' I tell you that out of these stones God
can raise up children for Abraham. 10The ax is already at the root of the trees, and every tree that does not produce good fruit will be cut down and thrown into the fire.[w]
11"I baptize you with[a] water for repentance. But after me will come one who is more
powerful than I, whose sandals I am not fit to carry. He will baptize you with the Holy Spirit[x] and with fire.[y] 12His winnowing fork is in his hand, and he will clear his threshing floor,
gathering his wheat into the barn and burning up the chaff with unquenchable fire."[z]

The Baptism of Jesus

13Then Jesus came from Galilee to the Jordan to be baptized by John.[a] 14But John tried
to deter him, saying, "I need to be baptized by you, and do you come to me?"
15Jesus replied, "Let it be so now; it is proper for us to do this to fulfill all righteousness." Then John consented.
16As soon as Jesus was baptized, he went up out of the water. At that moment heav-
en was opened, and he saw the Spirit of God[b] descending like a dove and lighting on
him. 17And a voice from heaven[c] said, "This is my Son,[d] whom I love; with him I am well
pleased."[e]

The Temptation of Jesus

4 Then Jesus was led by the Spirit into the desert to be tempted by the devil. 2After
fasting forty days and forty nights,[f] he was hungry. 3The tempter[g] came to him and
said, "If you are the Son of God,[h] tell these stones to become bread."

3:10 [w]Mt 7:19; Lk 13:6-9; Jn 15:2,6
3:11 [x]Mk 1:8 [y]Isa 4:4; Ac 2:3,4
3:12 [z]Mt 13:30
3:13 [a]Mk 1:4
3:16 [b]Isa 11:2; 42:1
3:17 [c]Mt 17:5; Jn 12:28 [d]Ps 2:7; 2Pe 1:17, 18 [e]Isa 42:1; Mt 12:18; 17:5; Mk 1:11; 9:7; Lk 9:35
4:2 [f]Ex 34:28; 1Ki 19:8
4:3 [g]1Th 3:5 [h]Mt 3:17; Jn 5:25; Ac 9:20

[a] *11* Or *in*

outward obedience. "Repentance" without any discernible change in one's life cannot be real. Since the Pharisees reckoned themselves to be the *righteous* of their day, these words of John must have cut deeply. Notice that they did not come to be baptized, which would have demonstrated acknowledgement of their unrighteousness and need of repentance, but only to see what John was doing (v. 7).

3:9 Abraham as our father. Although being Jewish includes outward covenant privileges (Ro 9:4–5), the true children of God enjoy this status by virtue of God's act alone. God can sprinkle with clean water and change hearts of stone (Eze 36:25–26). Neither a Jew by birth nor a Christian "by birth" can expect to be spared the ax of judgment apart from repentance and faith.

3:10 will be cut down. Just as the kingdom is imminent, so is judgment; the arrival of one implies the approach of the other. John did not yet realize that Jesus had come not to bring judgment, but to bear it (see note on 11:2–3).

3:11 baptize. Baptism functions symbolically in a number of ways. It represents: repentance (v. 11); the crucifixion (Lk 12:50); a sharing in Christ's crucifixion as death to the old life (Ro 6:3–4); cleansing from past sins (Ac 22:16); covenant identification with the person in whose name one is baptized (28:19; 1Co 10:2); and the bestowal of the Holy Spirit (Ac 2:38). It is the new covenant's functional equivalent to circumcision (Col 2:11–12). John's baptism is distinguished from Christian baptism not so much in that it was symbolically different but because it occurred at a different stage of redemptive history. After the resurrection and ascension of Christ, true baptism occurs as an act of the Holy Spirit (1Co 12:13). John's baptism looked forward to Spirit baptism (v. 11; Ac 1:5). Christian baptism lays claim on behalf of the one baptized to the promised gift of the Spirit. **with the Holy Spirit and with fire.** Cleansing with fire describes God's ultimate baptism, contrasted with the symbol of cleansing with water. The fire of the Spirit renovates the people of God and consumes the wicked as chaff (Isa 4:4; Zec 13:9; Mal 3:2–3; 4:1). John's witness to Jesus as the Lord who has come (v. 3) is extended. As Lord, Jesus baptizes with the Spirit and executes the last judgment. See *WCF* 27.3; 28.2; *WLC* 163,177; *WSC* 91; *BC* 34; *HC* 69,72.

3:13–15 John was reluctant to baptize Jesus because he recognized that Jesus was the one man who had no need for repentance. But in order for "all righteousness" (v. 15) to be fulfilled, Jesus had to be identified with his people in the removal of their sins. Ultimately John's baptism pointed to Jesus because it represented a death, and only Jesus' death on a cross, which Jesus called his "baptism" (Lk 12:50), could truly remove sins. Jesus' covenantal identification with us involved his baptism for us, his being anointed with the Spirit for our sake and his victory over temptation on our behalf. This incident shows that from the very beginning of his ministry—even before his baptism—Jesus knew he was to be the suffering servant of Isaiah 53 who was destined to die for his people.

3:15 righteousness. God's kingdom, his saving rule, is defined by his righteousness. Jesus taught the perfect righteousness that God requires (5:20,48), and he secured that very righteousness for sinners. His baptism pointed to his death as a ransom for many (20:28) and showed the perfect obedience by which he would fulfill all righteousness (Jer 23:5–6). Remission of sins and the garment of righteousness (22:11–12) are given through faith in Jesus (8:10; cf. 21:32). Those who lack God's righteousness but hunger and thirst for it will be filled (5:6; 6:33). Jesus calls those burdened with the load of self-righteousness to find their Sabbath-rest in him (11:28– 12:8). Those whom Christ knows as his own are those who will enter the future kingdom of glory (cf. 7:23). They will show their relation to him through the fruit of righteous deeds (7:20,23; 25:40). Matthew faithfully records Jesus' teaching as the foundational gospel. The later unfolding of revelation on the part of the glorified Christ made more specific the relationship between God's righteousness as gift and his righteous requirement, but he clearly taught both from the beginning. See *WCF* 8.4.

3:16–17 Again Jesus represents his people in his receiving of the Holy Spirit following his baptism. The accompanying testimony from heaven confirmed his identification as the servant of the Lord (Isa 42:1; cf. Ex 4:22) and tied it to his Messianic kingship (Ps 2:7). **like a dove.** Jesus "went up out of the water" (cf. Isa 43:2). The form of the dove suggests blessing beyond judgment (Ge 8:8–12; 1Pe 3:20–21). See *WCF* 2.3; 11.3; *WLC* 9,38,40; *BC* 8,9,10; *HC* 25.

4:1–11 Jesus' temptation is the counterpart to Israel's testing in the desert. As in Numbers 14:34, the 40 days represent 40 years. This event looks back to Deuteronomy 8:1–5, which Jesus cited in response to one of the temptations. Again we see Jesus presented as the true or ultimate Israel, the Son of God. Indeed, the experience of the nation of Israel was the type, the shadow that pointed to what Christ would later experience. The real ordeal and proving of Israel as the son of God was accomplished by Jesus, the ultimate Israel and Son of God. The temptations Jesus faced represent the kinds of temptations every human being experiences: those generated by physical drives, those that appeal to pride and those that stem from a desire to possess (cf. 1Jn 2:16). But each was also a uniquely Messianic temptation. Note that Satan did not merely appeal to hunger or pride in Jesus but couched the temptations in terms of a challenge to Jesus' divine right: "If you are the Son of God . . ." (vv. 3,6; cf. the taunt in 27:40). The last temptation presented Jesus with a path to kingship that would have avoided the cross. Not only was Jesus tempted in every way that we are (Heb 4:15), but his temptations were much greater than any we experience. Yet he did not sin. This triumph over temptation uniquely qualifies Jesus to represent us before God as our "merciful and faithful high priest" (Heb 2:17); the Son knows personally and experientially what it is like to endure temptation. Jesus was and is without sin. Temptation did not arise from within him, as it does

4 Jesus answered, "It is written: 'Man does not live on bread alone, but on every word
that comes from the mouth of God.'[a]"[i]
5 Then the devil took him to the holy city[j] and had him stand on the highest point of
the temple. 6 "If you are the Son of God," he said, "throw yourself down. For it is written:

"'He will command his angels concerning you,
and they will lift you up in their hands,
so that you will not strike your foot against a stone.'[b]"[k]

7 Jesus answered him, "It is also written: 'Do not put the Lord your God to the test.'[c]"[l]
8 Again, the devil took him to a very high mountain and showed him all the kingdoms
of the world and their splendor. 9 "All this I will give you," he said, "if you will bow down
and worship me."
10 Jesus said to him, "Away from me, Satan![m] For it is written: 'Worship the Lord your
God, and serve him only.'[d]"[n]
11 Then the devil left him, and angels came and attended him.[o]

Jesus Begins to Preach

12 When Jesus heard that John had been put in prison,[p] he returned to Galilee.[q]
13 Leaving Nazareth, he went and lived in Capernaum,[r] which was by the lake in the area
of Zebulun and Naphtali— 14 to fulfill what was said through the prophet Isaiah:

15 "Land of Zebulun and land of Naphtali,
the way to the sea, along the Jordan,
Galilee of the Gentiles—
16 the people living in darkness
have seen a great light;
on those living in the land of the shadow of death
a light has dawned."[e][s]

17 From that time on Jesus began to preach, "Repent, for the kingdom of heaven[t] is
near."

The Calling of the First Disciples

18 As Jesus was walking beside the Sea of Galilee,[u] he saw two brothers, Simon called
Peter[v] and his brother Andrew. They were casting a net into the lake, for they were fishermen. 19 "Come, follow me,"[w] Jesus said, "and I will make you fishers of men." 20 At once
they left their nets and followed him.
21 Going on from there, he saw two other brothers, James son of Zebedee and his
brother John.[x] They were in a boat with their father Zebedee, preparing their nets. Jesus
called them, 22 and immediately they left the boat and their father and followed him.

Jesus Heals the Sick

23 Jesus went throughout Galilee,[y] teaching in their synagogues,[z] preaching the good

4:4 [i]Dt 8:3
4:5 [j]Ne 11:1; Da 9:24; Mt 27:53
4:6 [k]Ps 91:11,12
4:7 [l]Dt 6:16
4:10 [m]1Ch 21:1 [n]Dt 6:13
4:11 [o]Mt 26:53; Lk 22:43; Heb 1:14
4:12 [p]Mt 14:3 [q]Mk 1:14
4:13 [r]Mk 1:21; Lk 4:23, 31; Jn 2:12; 4:46, 47
4:16 [s]Isa 9:1,2; Lk 2:32
4:17 [t]Mt 3:2
4:18 [u]Mt 15:29; Mk 7:31; Jn 6:1 [v]Mt 16:17,18
4:19 [w]Mk 10:21,28,52
4:21 [x]Mt 20:20
4:23 [y]Mk 1:39; Lk 4:15, 44 [z]Mt 9:35; 13:54; Mk 1:21; Lk 4:15; Jn 6:59

[a] *4* Deut. 8:3 [b] *6* Psalm 91:11,12 [c] *7* Deut. 6:16 [d] *10* Deut. 6:13 [e] *16* Isaiah 9:1,2

with us (Jas 1:14). Yet, as true man, Jesus was indeed tempted. Only one who resists temptation feels its full force. See theological article "The Full Humanity of Jesus" at Luke 3. **tempted.** See note on James 1:13. See *WLC* 48.

4:3 Son of God. See note on 16:15–16.

4:4 on every word. In Deuteronomy 8:3 this phrase refers to God's word of direction in the wilderness and his provision of manna. Unlike Israel, Jesus did not abandon his trust in God's provision. Although Jesus had the power of the Holy Spirit in full measure, he replied to each of Satan's temptations with a reference to Scripture. The power of the Spirit is God's Word (Eph 6:17), and even Jesus relied on Scripture for strength in his spiritual struggle. See *WCF* 1.1; 5.3; *WLC* 155.

4:5 the highest point of the temple. This was probably an extension of the temple wall on the edge of the Kidron ravine. Josephus (*Antiquities,* 15:410) referred to the precipitous drop from the top of this wall to the bottom of the ravine.

4:6–11 See *WLC* 99,135; *BC* 12.

4:6 Satan can also quote Scripture, but it is worth noting that he here used Psalm 91:11–12 in a way exactly opposite the psalmist's intent. Psalm 91 exhorts its hearers to trust in God; Satan attempted to replace trust with a test casting doubt on God's faithfulness and demanding sight in place of faith. Presumption does not flow from great faith but from lack of faith. It is interesting to note that Satan did not go on to quote Psalm 91:13.

4:7 Israel put God on trial at Massah/Meribah (Ex 17:1–7). See *WCF* 1.1; *WLC* 105,155; *HC* 105.

4:10 With all the zeal of true worship, Jesus rejected Messianic idolatry. He commanded Satan to depart, for Jesus had conquered the "strong man" (12:29). See *WCF* 1.1; 21.2; *WLC* 104,105,155,179; *WSC* 46; *HC* 105.

4:15–16 Galilee of the Gentiles. Matthew stresses Jesus' almost exclusive focus during his earthly ministry on the house of Israel (10:5–6), but the fact that Jesus' ministry fulfilled Isaiah 9:2 shows that 28:19 was not an afterthought. The ultimate goal has always been that all nations be enlightened. Israel was to be a light to the Gentiles (Isa 60:3), but this task could only be fulfilled in the work of Jesus, God's true Servant-Son (Isa 42:6; cf. Isa 51:4).

4:17 See note on 3:2. **From that time on.** This phrase, which also occurs in 16:21, probably marks a turning point or major shift in subject matter in Matthew. Here we are moving from the period of preparation to that of Jesus' public ministry.

4:18–19 Jesus had come to gather the scattered people of God (9:36; 12:30). He called fishermen as disciples to serve in his mission (Jer 16:16; Eze 47:10). He would provide them with better nets!

4:23 teaching . . . preaching . . . healing. Jesus' ministry involved teaching, preaching and healing. His teaching communicated the

The Kingdom of God: Is God's Kingdom Now or Later?

THE kingdom of God (also called "the kingdom of heaven," "the kingdom of Christ," "the kingdom of the LORD," "the kingdom," and so forth) undergirds the teaching of the entire Bible. The Scriptures reveal God using a number of metaphors, but the primary imagery that Biblical writers used for God was that of a divine king (see, e.g., 1Sa 8:7). Alongside the basic conviction that God is the supreme King is the belief that he reigns over creation as his kingdom (Pss 47:1–9; 83:18; Da 4:25–26; 5:21). In this general sense, then, God has always been the sovereign King who rules in heaven over all things (Pss 103:19; 113:5; Mt 5:34; Eph 1:20; Col 1:16; Heb 12:2; Rev 7:15).

At the same time, the Biblical concept of the kingdom of God also takes on a special sense. Jesus described this narrower sense of the kingdom of God in this way: "Your kingdom come, your will be done on earth as it is in heaven" (Mt 6:10). God's holiness and glory in his heavenly throne room are so overwhelming that all creatures there honor him with unqualified, voluntary service. On Earth, however, creatures rebel and refuse to acknowledge God as King, and evil kingdoms rise up to oppose his kingdom. The hope that Scripture presents from cover to cover is that this disparity between the heavenly throne room and the earth will one day be eliminated (1Ch 16:31). God will judge the wicked and bring the redeemed humanity into a new creation (Isa 65; Zec 14). When this transformation takes place, only God's kingdom will stand, and voluntary obedience to him will extend to the ends of the earth, as it does now in heaven (1Ch 16:31; Ps 97:1–2).

The Scriptures reveal, however, that God determined to accomplish this end through a long historical process. With the choice of Abraham and his descendants as God's special people (Ex 3:6–7; 6:2–8), the kingdom of God was primarily limited to the people and land of Israel. God asserted his kingship on Earth when he delivered Israel from Egypt and brought her to the promised land (Ex 15). Under David and Solomon, Israel became an empire with the sons of David sitting on the throne of God as his vice-regents (2Ch 6) and with God's royal footstool in the temple (1Ch 28:2). This ethnically and geographically limited form of the kingdom was not an end in itself. On the contrary, Old Testament Israel was established as a stage from which the kingdom of God would eventually extend to all peoples and lands of the earth (Ge 17:17–20; 18:18; Ro 4:13–17).

The flagrant rebellion of Israel and Judah eventually hurled the kingdom of God in Israel into crisis. Yet the Old Testament announced that after the exile God would remove the wicked from the earth and establish his reign without opposition over the entire planet (Mal 4). At that time, full obedience to God would spread to the ends of the earth, encompassing both Jews and Gentiles (1Ch 16:23–36; Ps 67; 97; Isa 52:7–15).

The New Testament teaches that this final worldwide stage of the kingdom of God began with the incarnation of Christ. He and John the Baptist announced the good news that the kingdom was at hand (Mt 3:2, 4.17; Mk 1:15). But contrary to common Jewish expectations, Jesus and his apostles explained that the worldwide reign of God on Earth would not come suddenly in all of its fullness. Instead, Christ inaugurated this final stage of the kingdom in his earthly ministry (Mt 2:2; 4:23; 9:35; 27:11; Mk 15:2; Lk 16:16; 23:3; Jn 18:37); it continues today in the church (Mt 24:14; Ro 14:16–17; 1Co 4:19–20; Col 4:11) and will reach its ultimate end when Christ returns in glory (1Co 15:50–58; Rev 11.15). When that day finally comes, the will of God will be done throughout the earth just as it is now done in heaven.

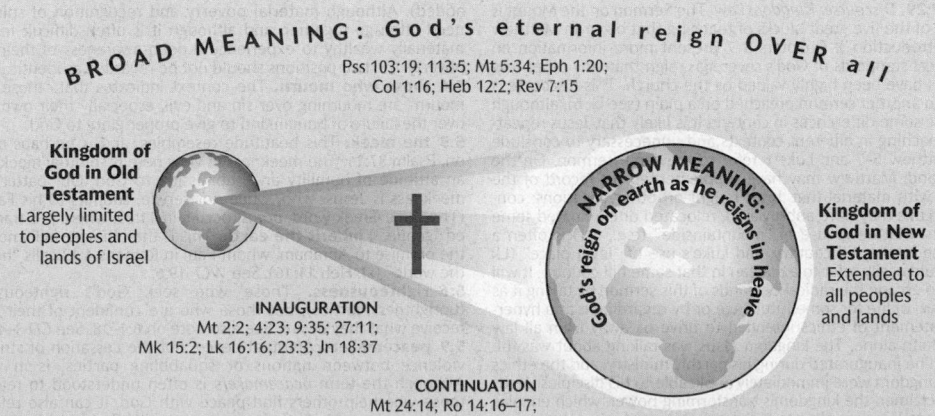

The Kingdom of God

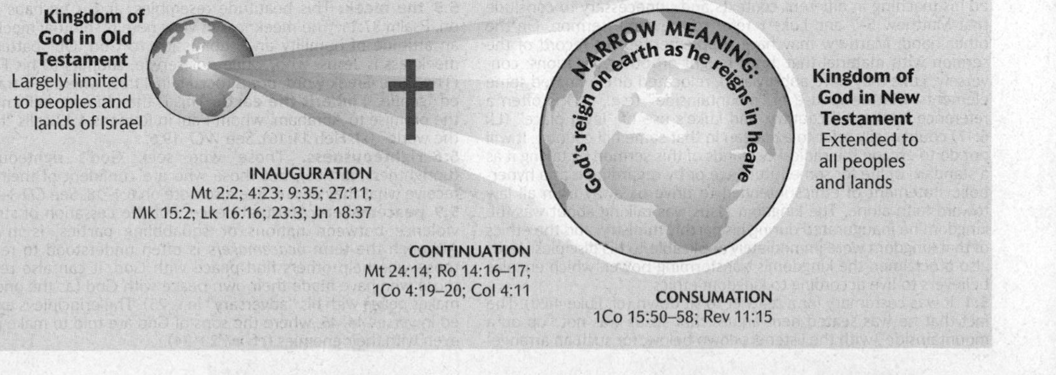

news[a] of the kingdom,[b] and healing every disease and sickness among the people.[c]
24 News about him spread all over Syria,[d] and people brought to him all who were ill with
various diseases, those suffering severe pain, the demon-possessed,[e] those having seizures,[f] and the paralyzed,[g] and he healed them. 25 Large crowds from Galilee, the Decapolis,[a] Jerusalem, Judea and the region across the Jordan followed him.[h]

The Beatitudes

5 Now when he saw the crowds, he went up on a mountainside and sat down. His disciples came to him, 2 and he began to teach them, saying:

3 "Blessed are the poor in spirit,
for theirs is the kingdom of heaven.[i]
4 Blessed are those who mourn,
for they will be comforted.[j]
5 Blessed are the meek,
for they will inherit the earth.[k]
6 Blessed are those who hunger and thirst for righteousness,
for they will be filled.[l]
7 Blessed are the merciful,
for they will be shown mercy.
8 Blessed are the pure in heart,[m]
for they will see God.[n]
9 Blessed are the peacemakers,
for they will be called sons of God.[o]
10 Blessed are those who are persecuted because of righteousness,[p]
for theirs is the kingdom of heaven.

11 "Blessed are you when people insult you,[q] persecute you and falsely say all kinds
of evil against you because of me. 12 Rejoice and be glad,[r] because great is your reward
in heaven, for in the same way they persecuted the prophets who were before you.[s]

4:23 [a]Mk 1:14 [b]Mt 3:2; Ac 20:25 [c]Mt 8:16; 15:30; Ac 10:38
4:24 [d]Lk 2:2 [e]Mt 8:16, 28; 9:32; 15:22; Mk 1:32; 5:15,16, 18 [f]Mt 17:15 [g]Mt 8:6; 9:2; Mk 2:3
4:25 [h]Mk 3:7,8; Lk 6:17
5:3 [i]ver 10,19; Mt 25:34
5:4 [j]Isa 61:2,3; Rev 7:17
5:5 [k]Ps 37:11; Ro 4:13
5:6 [l]Isa 55:1,2
5:8 [m]Ps 24:3,4 [n]Heb 12:14; Rev 22:4
5:9 [o]ver 44,45; Ro 8:14
5:10 [p]1Pe 3:14
5:11 [q]1Pe 4:14
5:12 [r]Ac 5:41; 1Pe 4:13, 16 [s]Mt 23:31,37; Ac 7:52; 1Th 2:15

[a] *25* That is, the Ten Cities

---

nature and purpose of God's kingdom. We see this in the Sermon on the Mount (chs. 5–7) and in the parables of the kingdom (ch. 13). His preaching published the Good News that God's kingdom was near, that his sovereign purposes in history were finally coming to fruition. His healing, as well as his teaching and preaching, was a sign that this kingdom had indeed arrived (cf. 11:5).

4:24 Syria. An ambiguous reference. In Roman eyes the word applied to virtually the whole of Palestine with the exception of Galilee (cf. Lk 2:2). A Galilean would probably have understood *Syria* to refer to the territory just north of Galilee from the Mediterranean to Damascus. **demon-possessed.** A distinction must be made between demon-possession and the occurrence of seizures resulting from various medical conditions. Demon-possession was not an ancient, superstitious misdiagnosis for ailments such as schizophrenia or epilepsy.

▪**5:1—7:29** *Discourse: Kingdom Law.* The Sermon on the Mount is the first of the five great blocks of teaching that occur in Matthew (see "Introduction"). Chapters 5–7 present more information on the ethical standards of God's sovereign reign than any other text and thus have been highly valued by the church. This discourse is similar to another sermon preached on a plain (see Lk 6), although there are some differences in content. It is likely that Jesus repeated his teaching in different contexts and unnecessary to conclude that Matthew 5–7 and Luke 6 refer to the same sermon. On the other hand, Matthew may have supplemented his record of the sermon with material that Jesus taught on other occasions; conversely, Luke may have abbreviated, relocated or eliminated some elements. Matthew's use of "mountainside" (e.g., 5:1) is often a reference to the hill country, and Luke's use of "level place" (Lk 6:17) could easily refer to a plateau in that same hill country. It will not do to escape the radical demands of this sermon by taking it as a standard of life for some future age or by regarding it as a hyperbolic statement of ethics intended to drive us away from all law toward faith alone. The kingdom Jesus was talking about was the kingdom he inaugurated during his earthly ministry, and the ethics of that kingdom were immediately applicable to his disciples. Jesus also proclaimed the kingdom's transforming power, which enables believers to live according to kingdom ethics.

5:1 It was customary for a teacher to sit down (cf. Luke 4:20). The fact that he was seated here argues that Jesus was not "up on a mountainside" with the listeners down below, for such an arrangement would not have worked well acoustically. A better translation is ". . . he went up into the hill country."

5:3–12 See *WLC* 172; *HC* 63,107.

5:3 Blessed. The term means more than the emotional state represented by the word *happy.* It includes spiritual well-being, basking in the approval of God, and thus anticipating a happier destiny (cf. Ps 1). **poor in spirit.** Those willing to acknowledge spiritual need are more likely than the spiritually complacent to perceive their own deficiency and to depend on God alone rather than on their own goodness. Paul noted the same principle (Ro 9:30–31). The parallel in Luke 6 renders this condition simply as "poor," without adding the phrase "in spirit." This distinction has led many to suppose that Jesus was really speaking of the materially poor. Note, however, that in Luke 6 he was addressing the disciples when he stated: "Blessed are *you* who are poor" (emphasis added). Although material poverty and recognition of spiritual need often go together, and although it is often difficult for the materially wealthy to experience a deep awareness of their true poverty, the two positions should not be regarded as identical.

5:4 those who mourn. The context indicates that "those who mourn" are mourning over sin and evil, especially their own, and over the failure of humankind to give proper glory to God.

5:5 the meek. This beatitude resembles, and is perhaps based on, Psalm 37:11. The meekness in view here is spiritual meekness, an attitude of humility and submission to God. Our pattern for meekness is Jesus, who, while not servile, submits to his Father. (The same Greek word, *praus,* occurs in 11:29, where it is translated "gentle.") **inherit the earth.** This is the ultimate fulfillment of the promise to Abraham, whom Paul in Romans 4:13 calls "heir of the world" (cf. Heb 11:16). See *WCF* 19.6.

5:6 righteousness. Those who seek God's righteousness (uprightness, justice), not those who are confident of their own, receive what they desire. See also note on 6:1–18. See *CD* 3–4.IV.

5:9 peacemakers. Spiritual peace, not the cessation of strife or violence between nations or squabbling parties, is in view. Although the term *peacemakers* is often understood to refer to those who help others find peace with God, it can also refer to those who have made their own peace with God (as the one who makes peace with his "adversary" in v. 25). The principle is extended in verses 44–45, where the sons of God are told to make peace even with their enemies (cf. vv. 23–24).

Salt and Light

13 “You are the salt of the earth. But if the salt loses its saltiness, how can it be made
salty again? It is no longer good for anything, except to be thrown out and trampled by
men.[t]
14 “You are the light of the world.[u] A city on a hill cannot be hidden. 15 Neither do people light a lamp and put it under a bowl. Instead they put it on its stand, and it gives light
to everyone in the house.[v] 16 In the same way, let your light shine before men, that they
may see your good deeds and praise[w] your Father in heaven.

The Fulfillment of the Law

17 “Do not think that I have come to abolish the Law or the Prophets; I have not come
to abolish them but to fulfill them.[x] 18 I tell you the truth, until heaven and earth disappear, not the smallest letter, not the least stroke of a pen, will by any means disappear
from the Law until everything is accomplished.[y] 19 Anyone who breaks one of the least
of these commandments[z] and teaches others to do the same will be called least in the
kingdom of heaven, but whoever practices and teaches these commands will be called
great in the kingdom of heaven. 20 For I tell you that unless your righteousness surpasses that of the Pharisees and the teachers of the law, you will certainly not enter the kingdom of heaven.

Murder

21 “You have heard that it was said to the people long ago, ‘Do not murder,[a][a] and anyone who murders will be subject to judgment.’ 22 But I tell you that anyone who is angry
with his brother[b] will be subject to judgment.[b] Again, anyone who says to his brother,
‘Raca,[c]’ is answerable to the Sanhedrin.[c] But anyone who says, ‘You fool!’ will be in danger of the fire of hell.[d]
23 “Therefore, if you are offering your gift at the altar and there remember that your
brother has something against you, 24 leave your gift there in front of the altar. First go
and be reconciled to your brother; then come and offer your gift.
25 “Settle matters quickly with your adversary who is taking you to court. Do it while
you are still with him on the way, or he may hand you over to the judge, and the judge
may hand you over to the officer, and you may be thrown into prison. 26 I tell you the
truth, you will not get out until you have paid the last penny.[d]

Adultery

27 “You have heard that it was said, ‘Do not commit adultery.’[e][e] 28 But I tell you that

5:13 [t]Mk 9:50; Lk 14:34,35
5:14 [u]Jn 8:12
5:15 [v]Mk 4:21; Lk 8:16
5:16 [w]Mt 9:8
5:17 [x]Ro 3:31
5:18 [y]Lk 16:17
5:19 [z]Jas 2:10
5:21 [a]Ex 20:13; Dt 5:17
5:22 [b]1Jn 3:15 [c]Mt 26:59 [d]Jas 3:6
5:27 [e]Ex 20:14; Dt 5:18

[a] *21* Exodus 20:13 [b] *22* Some manuscripts *brother without cause* [c] *22* An Aramaic term of contempt
[d] *26* Greek *kodrantes* [e] *27* Exodus 20:14

5:13 salt. In a society without refrigerators, salt is primarily used not as a flavoring but as a preservative. Disciples are to hinder the world's corruption or decay. The salt deposits along the Dead Sea contain not only sodium chloride but also a variety of other minerals. This salt can lose its saltiness over the years through leaching by rain, to the point that it becomes good for nothing except road building.
5:14–16 See Isaiah 60:1–3. See also *WCF* 16.2; *BC* 30; *HC* 2,86,122.
5:17–20 the Law or the Prophets. This term was a way of referring to the whole Old Testament. **not come to abolish.** The correctives of verses 21–48 should be read in the light of this opening remark. In fulfilling the law, Jesus did not alter, replace or nullify the former commands. Rather, he established their true intent and purpose in his teaching and accomplished them in his obedient life. The entire Old Testament pointed forward to Christ. See *WCF* 1.8; 8.4; 19.4; 19.5; 21.7; *WLC* 48,116.
5:18–19 least stroke of a pen. Literally, “horn,” a tiny extension on certain letters in the Hebrew alphabet. Although tiny, the “horn” distinguishes some letters from others and so can be important. Jesus defined these strokes as “one of the least of these commandments” (v. 19). **until everything is accomplished.** This refers to the totality of God's will, his purpose for renewal (6:10).
5:20 unless your righteousness surpasses. Jesus did not criticize the Pharisees for their strictness but rather for their externalism (cf. ch. 23). By focusing on obedience to externals, they avoided the real intent of the law and so lessened its real demands. The Dead Sea Scrolls refer to the Pharisees as “seekers after smooth things” because they accommodated and compromised the law to fit the “realities” of life as they saw it. Such accommodation removed awareness of the need for grace and dependence on God. In the subsequent verses Jesus restored an understanding of the true nature of God's law as demanding total, radical holiness. Our righteousness must surpass that of the Pharisees. Jesus demands a deeper obedience, not a disregard for God's commands.
5:21–48 See *WLC* 113.
5:21–25 See *WLC* 99; 135; *HC* 105.
5:21 You have heard that it was said. This clause points out that the statement to follow is not the teaching of God's law itself or of its promises, but the teaching of the law as interpreted by the scribes and Pharisees (see note on vv. 43–47).
5:22 You fool. Apparently Jewish law had sanctions against the specific insult of “Raca,” but Jesus showed that verbal abuse of any kind makes one liable to eternal damnation. **hell.** Refers here to the “Gehenna,” the “Valley of Hinnom,” which was a trash dump outside Jerusalem where fires burned constantly to incinerate waste. The place was also notorious as the location of human sacrifices by fire during the reigns of Ahaz and Manasseh (2Ch 28:3; 33:6). Jeremiah prophesied that it would be called the “Valley of Slaughter” (Jer 7:31–32), a symbol of God's fearful judgment. See *WLC* 136,151.
5:23–24 Therefore. Signifies that verses 23–24 are based on the reality that God will punish any slighting of other persons. **be reconciled.** Note that the command is given not to the plaintiff but to the accused. See *WLC* 171.
5:25 Settle matters quickly. The wisdom of settlement out of court applies above all to our relationship with God. If reconciliation with other human beings is important, how much more so our reconciliation with God.
5:27–30 See *WLC* 99,139; *WSC* 72; *HC* 94,109.

anyone who looks at a woman lustfully has already committed adultery with her in his
heart.[f] 29 If your right eye causes you to sin,[g] gouge it out and throw it away. It is better
for you to lose one part of your body than for your whole body to be thrown into hell.
30 And if your right hand causes you to sin, cut it off and throw it away. It is better for you
to lose one part of your body than for your whole body to go into hell.

Divorce

31 "It has been said, 'Anyone who divorces his wife must give her a certificate of divorce.'[a][h] 32 But I tell you that anyone who divorces his wife, except for marital unfaithfulness, causes her to become an adulteress, and anyone who marries the divorced woman commits adultery.[i]

Oaths

33 "Again, you have heard that it was said to the people long ago, 'Do not break your
oath,[j] but keep the oaths you have made to the Lord.'[k] 34 But I tell you, Do not swear at
all:[l] either by heaven, for it is God's throne;[m] 35 or by the earth, for it is his footstool; or
by Jerusalem, for it is the city of the Great King.[n] 36 And do not swear by your head, for
you cannot make even one hair white or black. 37 Simply let your 'Yes' be 'Yes,' and your
'No,' 'No';[o] anything beyond this comes from the evil one.[p]

An Eye for an Eye

38 "You have heard that it was said, 'Eye for eye, and tooth for tooth.'[b][q] 39 But I tell you,
Do not resist an evil person. If someone strikes you on the right cheek, turn to him the other also.[r] 40 And if someone wants to sue you and take your tunic, let him have your cloak
as well. 41 If someone forces you to go one mile, go with him two miles. 42 Give to the one
who asks you, and do not turn away from the one who wants to borrow from you.[s]

Love for Enemies

43 "You have heard that it was said, 'Love your neighbor[c][t] and hate your enemy.'[u]
44 But I tell you: Love your enemies[d] and pray for those who persecute you,[v] 45 that you
may be sons[w] of your Father in heaven. He causes his sun to rise on the evil and the good,
and sends rain on the righteous and the unrighteous.[x] 46 If you love those who love you,
what reward will you get?[y] Are not even the tax collectors doing that? 47 And if you greet
only your brothers, what are you doing more than others? Do not even pagans do that?
48 Be perfect, therefore, as your heavenly Father is perfect.[z]

Giving to the Needy

6 "Be careful not to do your 'acts of righteousness' before men, to be seen by them.[a]
If you do, you will have no reward from your Father in heaven.

5:28 [f]Pr 6:25
5:29 [g]Mt 18:6,8,9; Mk 9:42-47
5:31 [h]Dt 24:1-4
5:32 [i]Lk 16:18
5:33 [j]Lev 19:12 [k]Nu 30:2; Dt 23:21; Mt 23:16-22
5:34 [l]Jas 5:12 [m]Isa 66:1; Mt 23:22
5:35 [n]Ps 48:2
5:37 [o]Jas 5:12 [p]Mt 6:13; 13:19,38; Jn 17:15; 2Th 3:3; 1Jn 2:13,14; 3:12; 5:18,19
5:38 [q]Ex 21:24; Lev 24:20; Dt 19:21
5:39 [r]Lk 6:29; Ro 12:17,19; 1Co 6:7; 1Pe 3:9
5:42 [s]Dt 15:8; Lk 6:30
5:43 [t]Lev 19:18 [u]Dt 23:6
5:44 [v]Lk 6:27,28; 23:34; Ac 7:60; Ro 12:14; 1Co 4:12; 1Pe 2:23
5:45 [w]ver 9 [x]Job 25:3
5:46 [y]Lk 6:32
5:48 [z]Lev 19:2; 1Pe 1:16
6:1 [a]Mt 23:5

[a] *31* Deut. 24:1 [b] *38* Exodus 21:24; Lev. 24:20; Deut. 19:21 [c] *43* Lev. 19:18 [d] *44* Some late manuscripts *enemies, bless those who curse you, do good to those who hate you*

5:29 gouge it out. The eyes and hands are the most valuable non-vital parts of the body. The severity of the demand illustrates the radical nature of Jesus' ethic and demonstrates our need for radical surgery. Of course, Jesus was not advocating self-mutilation; it is not the eyes or hands that cause lust but the heart and mind. What we really need is spiritual surgery.
5:31–32 See the notes on 19:3ff. See *WCF* 24.5; *WLC* 139.
5:33–37 See *WLC* 99; *HC* 102.
5:34 Do not swear. Some have understood Jesus' proscription against oaths to be a universal prohibition, but Jesus himself submitted to an oath when adjured by the high priest (26:63), and Paul was not sinning when he invoked God as his witness in Romans 1:9. God himself took an oath so that we might have greater confidence (Heb 6:17). Jesus addressed the problem of a casuistry that required a specific oath to make the spoken words binding. The implication of such an approach to truth is that when we do not speak under oath, we cannot be trusted. Jesus said that we must speak as though everything we say is spoken under oath. See *WCF* 22.2.
5:37–39 See *WCF* 22.2; *WLC* 99; *HC* 99.
5:38–39 Eye for eye. The original intent of Exodus 21:24, Leviticus 24:20 and Deuteronomy 19:21 was that the punishment should be equitable and should correspond to the crime. This excluded sanctioning a greater vengeance (such as Lamech boasted of in Genesis 4:23–24) or applying varying standards to different social classes. Jesus contradicted the misinterpretation that saw in the principle a warrant for personal vengeance. **Do not resist.** The slap on the right cheek is a backhanded one—an insult as well as an injury. In this context, "Do not resist" means "Do not seek restitution in court." Jesus' words may reflect Isaiah 50:6. See *WCF* 19.4.
5:41 If someone forces. The possibility of a Roman soldier coercing a local person to serve as a guide was very real. Even if we are compelled by force to do something for someone else, we should not begrudge the service but should demonstrate our freedom by volunteering more than what was demanded.
5:43–47 hate your enemy. This statement does not appear in the Old Testament but was a false conclusion in scribal teaching that was drawn from the narrow understanding of "neighbor" as simply "fellow Jew." Jesus showed that the true intent of Leviticus 19:18 extends even to one's enemies. Compare Luke 10:29ff.; see *WLC* 99,183; *HC* 107.
5:48 Be perfect. The standard that God demands of his people is nothing less than the perfect character of God himself. It includes far more than simple justice. God's perfection includes the love of benevolent grace (v. 45). Although perfection is not attainable in this life, it is nevertheless the goal of those who have become children of the Father (cf. Php 3:12–13). See *WLC* 7.
6:1–18 acts of righteousness. Jewish piety consisted of three types of righteous acts: giving, prayer and fasting. Jesus reaffirmed the positive value of these acts, but only when they are done in submission to God and out of love for him, not as an attempt to seek honor from other people. The most important of these acts is prayer, a subject that Jesus addressed in greater detail in verses 5–15. (See theological article "Prayer" at Mt 6.)
6:1–2 See *WLC* 113.

2"So when you give to the needy, do not announce it with trumpets, as the hypocrites
do in the synagogues and on the streets, to be honored by men. I tell you the truth, they
have received their reward in full. 3But when you give to the needy, do not let your left
hand know what your right hand is doing, 4so that your giving may be in secret. Then
your Father, who sees what is done in secret, will reward you.[b]

Prayer

5"And when you pray, do not be like the hypocrites, for they love to pray standing[c]
in the synagogues and on the street corners to be seen by men. I tell you the truth, they
have received their reward in full. 6But when you pray, go into your room, close the door
and pray to your Father,[d] who is unseen. Then your Father, who sees what is done in secret, will reward you. 7And when you pray, do not keep on babbling[e] like pagans, for they
think they will be heard because of their many words.[f] 8Do not be like them, for your Father knows what you need[g] before you ask him.

9"This, then, is how you should pray:

" 'Our Father in heaven,
hallowed be your name,
10 your kingdom[h] come,
your will be done[i]
on earth as it is in heaven.
11 Give us today our daily bread.[j]
12 Forgive us our debts,
as we also have forgiven our debtors.[k]
13 And lead us not into temptation,[l]
but deliver us from the evil one.[a]'[m]

14For if you forgive men when they sin against you, your heavenly Father will also forgive you.[n] 15But if you do not forgive men their sins, your Father will not forgive your
sins.[o]

Fasting

16"When you fast, do not look somber[p] as the hypocrites do, for they disfigure their
faces to show men they are fasting. I tell you the truth, they have received their reward
in full. 17But when you fast, put oil on your head and wash your face, 18so that it will not
be obvious to men that you are fasting, but only to your Father, who is unseen; and your
Father, who sees what is done in secret, will reward you.[q]

6:4 [b]ver 6, 18; Col 3:23, 24
6:5 [c]Mk 11:25; Lk 18:10-14
6:6 [d]2Ki 4:33
6:7 [e]Ecc 5:2 [f]1Ki 18:26-29
6:8 [g]ver 32
6:10 [h]Mt 3:2 [i]Mt 26:39
6:11 [j]Pr 30:8
6:12 [k]Mt 18:21-35
6:13 [l]Jas 1:13 [m]Mt 5:37
6:14 [n]Mt 18:21-35; Mk 11:25, 26; Eph 4:32; Col 3:13
6:15 [o]Mt 18:35
6:16 [p]Isa 58:5
6:18 [q]ver 4,6

[a] *13* Or *from evil*; some late manuscripts *one, / for yours is the kingdom and the power and the glory forever. Amen.*

6:2 hypocrites. In the New Testament, the hypocrite is one who pretends to have a relationship with God and appears to love righteousness but who is actually self-seeking and self-deceived. The hypocrites denounced in chapter 23 were unaware of their hypocrisy. See *WCF* 16.7.
6:5–6 See *WCF* 16.7; 21.6; *WLC* 113.
6:7 do not keep on babbling. This does not contradict the principle that we should keep asking God for what we think is his will (Lk 18), but it does negate the idea that God is impressed with quantity of verbiage or with eloquence. Gentile incantations insult him (1Ki 18:26). Even this prayer (vv. 9–13) should not be made a mantra. See theological article "Prayer" at Matthew 6.
6:9–13 Although usually called the "Lord's Prayer," this prayer might better be termed the "Disciples' Prayer." Of its seven petitions, three ask God to glorify himself and four request his work in our lives. The entire prayer presupposes total dependence on God. It models vast brevity. See *WLC* 186; *WSC* 99; *HC* 119.
6:9 hallowed be your name. To hallow is to make holy or to treat as holy. This petition asks not just that creatures would hallow God's name, but also that God would ensure the hallowing of his name by being the holy Judge and Savior. See *WLC* 112,184, 187,189,190; *WSC* 54,100,101.
6:10 your kingdom come. See theological article "The Kingdom of God" at Matthew 4. See *WLC* 191,192; *WSC* 102,103.
6:11 daily. The Greek word translated "daily" is unique, and the phrase has been variously rendered as "daily bread," "necessary bread," "future bread," "the next day's bread" or "the coming meal of the kingdom." **bread.** There are three basic theological understandings of this "bread." The sacramental view is that it refers to the communion bread, representing the body of the Lord. The eschatological view is that the bread symbolizes life in the coming kingdom, so that the petition is an extension of "your kingdom come" (v. 10). The sustenance view understands the petition as simply looking to God for provision for daily physical needs. This last view is perhaps the most accurate; it corresponds to the development in verses 19–34 (also cf. Pr 30:8). See *WCF* 21.6; *WLC* 193; *WSC* 104.
6:12 debts. In view here are spiritual debts (vv. 14–15). We are both under obligation and totally unable on our own to make restitution to God for our sins. We must forgive because we have been forgiven (18:32–33). If we do not forgive others, we cannot claim God's forgiveness (vv. 14–15). See *WCF* 11.5; 21.3; *WLC* 194; *WSC* 105; *HC* 13.
6:13 lead us not into temptation. Sinners seek temptation. The forgiven pray this petition because they trust God and distrust themselves. The Father may prove us (4:1; see also Dt 8:2), but he does not entice us to sin (Jas 1:13–14) and will not allow us to be tempted beyond our ability to withstand (1Co 10:13). The petition also points forward to the final assaults of the evil one before Christ returns (24:21; cf. Lk 22:31–32; 2Th 3:3). See *WLC* 195,196; *WSC* 106,107.
6:14–15 See *WCF* 21.3; *WLC* 194; *HC* 126.
6:16 See *WCF* 16.7; *WLC* 113.
6:17–18 oil on your head and wash your face . . . not be obvious. Putting oil on one's head and washing one's face were traditional parts of a person's daily routine except when fasting. Declining to wash and anoint made it obvious that one was fasting and, since fasting was pious, advertised one's "piety."

6:19 [r]Pr 23:4; Heb 13:5 [s]Jas 5:2,3
6:20 [t]Mt 19:21; Lk 12:33; 18:22; 1Ti 6:19 [u]Lk 12:33
6:21 [v]Lk 12:34

Treasures in Heaven

19 "Do not store up for yourselves treasures on earth,[r] where moth and rust destroy,[s]
and where thieves break in and steal. 20 But store up for yourselves treasures in heaven,[t]
where moth and rust do not destroy, and where thieves do not break in and steal.[u] 21 For
where your treasure is, there your heart will be also.[v]
22 "The eye is the lamp of the body. If your eyes are good, your whole body will be full

---

6:19 rust. The Greek word used here refers not only to metal corrosion but also to mildew, wood rot and the like. Everything worldly is subject to decay or loss.
6:20–21 See *HC* 80.

Prayer: Why Should We Pray?

REFORMED theology has consistently insisted on the importance and effectiveness of prayer. God made us and redeemed us in order that we might have fellowship with him, and that is what prayer is: fellowship with God. God speaks to us through revelation, both the special revelation of Scripture and the general revelation of the creation. He also speaks to us as the Holy Spirit enables us to understand this revelation, convicts us of our sin and works in us to obey and to rejoice in the revelation we have received. In response, we engage in prayer to speak to God about himself, ourselves, our relationship with him and everything that exists and takes place in his creation.

There is no tension or inconsistency between the reality that God is sovereign over all things and the fact that prayer is effective. Just as God has ordained eating as a means by which hunger may be satisfied, so he has ordained prayer as a means by which events may come to pass. God has even ordained our prayers themselves, so they are fully in accord with his eternal counsel. Divine sovereignty does not contradict but affirms our responsibility to pray.

Although God has commanded us to pray, this is not the only reason we do so. We pray because we are entirely dependent on God, needing him and his fellowship. We pray because God sovereignly controls all things and can therefore do whatever he pleases, and we pray so that he will choose to do good things for us. Of all the human means that God uses to carry out his eternal plan, prayer is certainly one of the most powerful and effective because prayer calls on the all-powerful God to act on our behalf. As James put it, "The prayer of a righteous man is powerful and effective" (Jas 5:16).

Prayer takes different forms and emphases in different situations, and there are many legitimate ways to summarize the Bible's teaching on prayer. One helpful way to think of prayer is as a fourfold activity to be performed by God's people both individually (Mt 6:5–6) and with each other (Ac 1:14; 4:24): We are to (1) express adoration and praise, (2) confess our sins with contrition and seek forgiveness, (3) offer thanks for benefits received and (4) voice petitions and supplications for ourselves and others. The Lord's Prayer (Mt 6:9–13; Lk 11:2–4) embodies adoration, petition and confession; the Psalter consists of models of all four elements of prayer.

Petition is our humble acknowledgment that we both need and trust God, that we depend on his sovereign wisdom and goodness. This is perhaps the most prominent dimension of prayer as expressed throughout the Bible (e.g., Ge 18:16–33; Ex 32:31—33:17; Ezr 9:5–15; Ne 1:5–11; 4:4–5,9; 6:9,14; Da 9:4–19; Mt 7:7–11; Jn 16:23–24; 17:1–26; Eph 6:18–20; Jas 5:16–18; 1Jn 5:14–16). Petition, along with the other modes of prayer, should ordinarily be directed to the Father, as the Lord's Prayer demonstrates, but we may also direct our petitions to Christ (Jn 14:14), especially those for salvation and healing (Ac 7:59; Ro 10:8–13; 2Co 12:7–9). We may also petition the Holy Spirit, since he too is fully God, although Scripture presents no actual examples of petitions specifically addressed to him. Scripture does affirm the role of the Spirit in motivating our prayers and in praying on our behalf (Ro 8:15,26). It cannot be wrong to present petitions to God as triune or to request a spiritual blessing from any one of the three persons of the Trinity, but there is wisdom in following the New Testament pattern.

Jesus teaches that petition to the Father is to be made in the Son's name (Jn 14:13–14; 15:16; 16:23–24). This means invoking Jesus' merit as the basis for our access to the Father and looking to Jesus for support as our intercessor in the Father's presence. We can only look to Jesus for support, however, when what we ask is in accord with God's revealed will (1Jn 5:14) and when we ask with right motives (Jas 4:3).

Jesus teaches that we may properly press God with fervent persistence when we bring needs to him (Lk 11:5–13; 18:1–8) and that he will answer such prayer in positive terms. But we must remember that God, who knows what is best in a way that we cannot, may deny our specific requests as to how these needs should be met. When God doesn't give us what we request, it is because he has something better for us, as when the Lord declined to heal the thorn in Paul's flesh (2Co 12:7–9).

Christians who pray to God sincerely, reverently, humbly and penitently, with a sense of privilege and with a purified heart, will find that the Holy Spirit prompts them to pray even more and to trust in their heavenly Father implicitly (Ro 8:15; Gal 4:6). They will find themselves compelled to pray even though they may not know what thoughts or desires to express (Ro 8:26–27). The mysterious reality of the Holy Spirit's help in prayer becomes known only to those who actively engage in prayer.

of light. 23But if your eyes are bad, your whole body will be full of darkness. If then the
light within you is darkness, how great is that darkness!
24"No one can serve two masters. Either he will hate the one and love the other, or
he will be devoted to the one and despise the other. You cannot serve both God and
Money.[w]

Do Not Worry

25"Therefore I tell you, do not worry[x] about your life, what you will eat or drink; or
about your body, what you will wear. Is not life more important than food, and the body
more important than clothes? 26Look at the birds of the air; they do not sow or reap or
store away in barns, and yet your heavenly Father feeds them.[y] Are you not much more
valuable than they?[z] 27Who of you by worrying can add a single hour to his life[a]?[a]
28"And why do you worry about clothes? See how the lilies of the field grow. They do
not labor or spin. 29Yet I tell you that not even Solomon in all his splendor[b] was dressed
like one of these. 30If that is how God clothes the grass of the field, which is here today
and tomorrow is thrown into the fire, will he not much more clothe you, O you of little
faith?[c] 31So do not worry, saying, 'What shall we eat?' or 'What shall we drink?' or 'What
shall we wear?' 32For the pagans run after all these things, and your heavenly Father
knows that you need them.[d] 33But seek first his kingdom and his righteousness, and all
these things will be given to you as well.[e] 34Therefore do not worry about tomorrow, for
tomorrow will worry about itself. Each day has enough trouble of its own.

Judging Others

7 "Do not judge, or you too will be judged.[f] 2For in the same way you judge others,
you will be judged, and with the measure you use, it will be measured to you.[g]
3"Why do you look at the speck of sawdust in your brother's eye and pay no attention to the plank in your own eye? 4How can you say to your brother, 'Let me take the
speck out of your eye,' when all the time there is a plank in your own eye? 5You hypocrite, first take the plank out of your own eye, and then you will see clearly to remove the
speck from your brother's eye.
6"Do not give dogs what is sacred; do not throw your pearls to pigs. If you do, they
may trample them under their feet, and then turn and tear you to pieces.

Ask, Seek, Knock

7"Ask and it will be given to you;[h] seek and you will find; knock and the door will be
opened to you. 8For everyone who asks receives; he who seeks finds;[i] and to him who
knocks, the door will be opened.
9"Which of you, if his son asks for bread, will give him a stone? 10Or if he asks for a
fish, will give him a snake? 11If you, then, though you are evil, know how to give good gifts

6:24 [w]Lk 16:13
6:25 [x]ver 27,28,31,34; Lk 10:41; 12:11, 22; Php 4:6; 1Pe 5:7
6:26 [y]Job 38:41; Ps 147:9 [z]Mt 10:29-31
6:27 [a]Ps 39:5
6:29 [b]1Ki 10:4-7
6:30 [c]Mt 8:26; 14:31; 16:8
6:32 [d]ver 8
6:33 [e]Mt 19:29; Mk 10:29-30
7:1 [f]Lk 6:37; Ro 14:4, 10,13; 1Co 4:5; Jas 4:11,12
7:2 [g]Mk 4:24; Lk 6:38
7:7 [h]Mt 21:22; Mk 11:24; Jn 14:13,14; 15:7, 16; 16:23,24; Jas 1:5-8; 4:2,3; 1Jn 3:22; 5:14,15
7:8 [i]Pr 8:17; Jer 29:12, 13

a 27 Or *single cubit to his height*

6:23 light. Light is that by which we see, so the "light within" is that by which we interpret the world. If our basic outlook on the world is flawed, our perceptions will be distorted and misleading without our ever realizing it.
6:25–34 See *WCF* 12; 14.3; *WLC* 74,136,142; *HC* 26,121,125.
6:26 they do not sow. The point is not that birds do nothing—an adult bird does not stay in its nest with open beak—but that birds do not fret about what the future holds. Christians need not and ought not expend themselves acquiring more than they need. The attempt to stave off worst-case scenarios of the future or to add to the life God has allotted shows lack of trust in his knowledge and care (vv. 32–33).
6:27 a single hour to his life. Literally, "a single cubit [18 inches] to his height [or life span]." Since adding a foot-and-one-half to one's height would not seem to be a small thing, the NIV applies the reference to life span and construes the "cubit" to be figurative—a short distance in time rather than in space.
6:33 seek first his kingdom and his righteousness. This means making God's sovereign rule and our right relationship with him the highest priorities in life. (Cf. note on 3:15 for a definition of "righteousness.") Worry is inconsistent with these priorities, for it doubts the sovereignty or goodness of God and distracts us from the true goals of life. God will meet all the needs of those who risk all for him. See *HC* 118,123.
7:1–6 Do not judge. Jesus prohibits one kind of judging but approves another. Condemning a fellow believer for his or her faults equates to failure to exercise forgiveness (6:14–15); only a gentle and humble correction that first recognizes one's own, quite possibly greater, faults is helpful. A discerning kind of judgment that does not condemn but distinguishes unbelief from belief (v. 6) is also necessary. The method of discernment is given in verse 16. See *WLC* 145; *HC* 112.
7:6 what is sacred. Refers to the evidences of the kingdom, such as healings and exorcisms. But "what is sacred" would also include the preaching of the gospel of the kingdom. This proscription may seem strange, but we are not to continue to preach to people who have rejected the gospel with vicious contempt and scorn (cf. 10:14 and 15:14). The Christians in Acts learned to put this principle into practice (Ac 13:44–51; 18:5–6; 28:17–28). This is reiterated in Titus 3:10–11 and probably underlies Hebrews 6:4–6. See *WCF* 29.8; 30.3; *WLC* 173.
7:7–11 See *HC* 26,116,117,120.
7:11 though you are evil. Assumed here is the general sinfulness of humanity, since even those who call God "Father" are said to be evil. **good gifts.** The good gifts of God are those that Jesus had been describing as characteristic of disciples: righteousness, sincerity, purity, humility, wisdom. The one who knows his or her own needs will ask God to supply them. The parallel in Luke 11:13 focuses on the single greatest gift—the One who gives all good things, namely, the Holy Spirit. The Spirit is the best and most necessary gift we can request, and God gives his Spirit freely when we ask, so that we may have wisdom to discern without being judgmental (vv. 1–6), to enter the narrow gate that few find (vv. 13–14) and to bear good fruit (vv. 15–20). See *WLC* 184.

to your children, how much more will your Father in heaven give good gifts to those who
ask him! 12So in everything, do to others what you would have them do to you,[j] for this
sums up the Law and the Prophets.[k]

The Narrow and Wide Gates

13"Enter through the narrow gate.[l] For wide is the gate and broad is the road that
leads to destruction, and many enter through it. 14But small is the gate and narrow the
road that leads to life, and only a few find it.

A Tree and Its Fruit

15"Watch out for false prophets.[m] They come to you in sheep's clothing, but inwardly they are ferocious wolves.[n] 16By their fruit you will recognize them.[o] Do people pick
grapes from thornbushes, or figs from thistles?[p] 17Likewise every good tree bears good
fruit, but a bad tree bears bad fruit. 18A good tree cannot bear bad fruit, and a bad tree
cannot bear good fruit. 19Every tree that does not bear good fruit is cut down and
thrown into the fire.[q] 20Thus, by their fruit you will recognize them.
21"Not everyone who says to me, 'Lord, Lord,'[r] will enter the kingdom of heaven, but
only he who does the will of my Father who is in heaven.[s] 22Many will say to me on that
day,[t] 'Lord, Lord, did we not prophesy in your name, and in your name drive out demons
and perform many miracles?'[u] 23Then I will tell them plainly, 'I never knew you. Away
from me, you evildoers!'[v]

The Wise and Foolish Builders

24"Therefore everyone who hears these words of mine and puts them into practice[w]
is like a wise man who built his house on the rock. 25The rain came down, the streams
rose, and the winds blew and beat against that house; yet it did not fall, because it had
its foundation on the rock. 26But everyone who hears these words of mine and does not
put them into practice is like a foolish man who built his house on sand. 27The rain came
down, the streams rose, and the winds blew and beat against that house, and it fell with
a great crash."

28When Jesus had finished saying these things,[x] the crowds were amazed at his
teaching,[y] 29because he taught as one who had authority, and not as their teachers of
the law.

The Man With Leprosy

8 When he came down from the mountainside, large crowds followed him. 2A man
with leprosy[a][z] came and knelt before him[a] and said, "Lord, if you are willing, you
can make me clean."
3Jesus reached out his hand and touched the man. "I am willing," he said. "Be

7:12 [j]Lk 6:31 [k]Ro 13:8-10; Gal 5:14
7:13 [l]Lk 13:24
7:15 [m]Jer 23:16; Mt 24:24; Mk 13:22; Lk 6:26; 2Pe 2:1; 1Jn 4:1; Rev 16:13 [n]Ac 20:29
7:16 [o]Mt 12:33; Lk 6:44 [p]Jas 3:12
7:19 [q]Mt 3:10
7:21 [r]Hos 8:2; Mt 25:11 [s]Ro 2:13; Jas 1:22
7:22 [t]Mt 10:15 [u]1Co 13:1-3
7:23 [v]Ps 6:8; Mt 25:12, 41; Lk 13:25-27
7:24 [w]Jas 1:22-25
7:28 [x]Mt 11:1; 13:53; 19:1; 26:1 [y]Mt 13:54; Mk 1:22; 6:2; Lk 4:32; Jn 7:46
8:2 [z]Lk 5:12 [a]Mt 9:18; 15:25; 18:26; 20:20

[a] *2* The Greek word was used for various diseases affecting the skin—not necessarily leprosy.

7:12 do to others. The so-called Golden Rule was stated negatively by a number of ancient thinkers, but Jesus made it a positive obligation. It appears in the context of the discussion of God's goodness and willingness to give. Again we see the connection between righteousness in relationship to God and righteous acts that stem from that relationship. See *WLC* 122; *HC* 107,111.
7:14 narrow the road. Evangelistic efforts that obscure the fact that the gateway to life is narrow (i.e., entered exclusively by faith in Christ) succeed only in excluding people from the kingdom. Likewise, presenting a rosy picture of the Christian life and minimizing the fact that it is filled with trouble does not follow the leading of our Lord (cf. Ac 14:22). It might even be that the "false prophets" of verse 15 are specifically those who deny the narrowness and hardships of the way. See *HC* 20.
7:15–20 Describing false prophets as wolves in sheep's clothing reminds us that they look like real prophets and that their message may be very attractive and even sound orthodox. The only sure method of discernment is to allow them time to demonstrate their fruit. Some of the false prophets' fruits are mentioned in the New Testament: controversies (1Ti 1:3–4), divisiveness (1Ti 6:3–5), destruction of faith (2Ti 2:17–18) and self-destruction by heresy (2Pe 2:1). See *BC* 24; *HC* 86.
7:21–23 Lord, Lord. The doubling of a name constituted an address of intimacy (cf. Ge 22:11; 1Sa 3:10; 2Sa 18:33; Lk 22:31). It is not claims or feelings of intimacy with Jesus that matter, nor is it simply "good works," even miraculous ones; only doing the will of the Father counts. This involves knowing God—or rather, being known by him (1Co 8:2–3). See *WCF* 10.4; 18.1; *WLC* 61,68,180; *HC* 124.
7:24–27 The rain came. Storms in Judea are infrequent, but they can be violent. Although the houses of both the foolish and wise men may for a long time appear equally secure, when the storm does come, the destruction of the foolish man's house is total (cf. Isa 28:14–19). So it is with the life of the one who ignores the words of Jesus.
7:29 not as their teachers. The scribes, like the later rabbis, taught by citing what previous teachers had said. Authority was established by reference to tradition. Jesus taught directly from Scripture on the basis of his own authority and made no reference (except negatively) to tradition.
■ **8:1—10:42** *The Works of the Kingdom.* Chapters 8–10 form the third major section of Matthew's Gospel and primarily concern the works of the kingdom. They are divided into two segments: narratives (8:1—9:38) and a discourse (10:1–42).
■ **8:1—9:38** *Narrative: Healing and Calling.* This series of narratives focuses on the works of the kingdom displayed by Jesus' healing miracles and the calling of his disciples. The order of the events in these chapters differs from that in the Gospels of Mark and Luke. Matthew probably arranged events topically rather than chronologically.
8:2–3 leprosy. A variety of skin diseases may have been termed "leprosy" (cf. NIV text note), but the dominant form was Hansen's disease, a disfiguring bacterial infection that attacks the skin and nerves, often resulting in loss of feeling and muscle control. Loss of

clean!" Immediately he was cured[a] of his leprosy. 4Then Jesus said to him, "See that you
don't tell anyone.[b] But go, show yourself to the priest and offer the gift Moses commanded,[c] as a testimony to them."

The Faith of the Centurion

5When Jesus had entered Capernaum, a centurion came to him, asking for help.
6"Lord," he said, "my servant lies at home paralyzed and in terrible suffering."
7Jesus said to him, "I will go and heal him."
8The centurion replied, "Lord, I do not deserve to have you come under my roof. But
just say the word, and my servant will be healed.[d] 9For I myself am a man under authority, with soldiers under me. I tell this one, 'Go,' and he goes; and that one, 'Come,' and
he comes. I say to my servant, 'Do this,' and he does it."
10When Jesus heard this, he was astonished and said to those following him, "I tell
you the truth, I have not found anyone in Israel with such great faith.[e] 11I say to you that
many will come from the east and the west,[f] and will take their places at the feast with
Abraham, Isaac and Jacob in the kingdom of heaven.[g] 12But the subjects of the kingdom[h]
will be thrown outside, into the darkness, where there will be weeping and gnashing of
teeth."[i]
13Then Jesus said to the centurion, "Go! It will be done just as you believed it would."[j]
And his servant was healed at that very hour.

Jesus Heals Many

14When Jesus came into Peter's house, he saw Peter's mother-in-law lying in bed with
a fever. 15He touched her hand and the fever left her, and she got up and began to wait
on him.
16When evening came, many who were demon-possessed were brought to him, and
he drove out the spirits with a word and healed all the sick.[k] 17This was to fulfill[l] what
was spoken through the prophet Isaiah:

> "He took up our infirmities
> and carried our diseases."[b][m]

The Cost of Following Jesus

18When Jesus saw the crowd around him, he gave orders to cross to the other side of
the lake.[n] 19Then a teacher of the law came to him and said, "Teacher, I will follow you
wherever you go."
20Jesus replied, "Foxes have holes and birds of the air have nests, but the Son of Man[o]
has no place to lay his head."

8:4 [b]Mt 9:30; Mk 5:43; 7:36; 8:30 [c]Lev 14:2-32
8:8 [d]Ps 107:20
8:10 [e]Mt 15:28
8:11 [f]Ps 107:3; Isa 49:12; 59:19; Mal 1:11 [g]Lk 13:29
8:12 [h]Mt 13:38 [i]Mt 13:42, 50; 22:13; 24:51; 25:30; Lk 13:28
8:13 [j]Mt 9:22
8:16 [k]Mt 4:23, 24
8:17 [l]Mt 1:22 [m]Isa 53:4
8:18 [n]Mk 4:35
8:20 [o]Da 7:13; Mt 12:8, 32, 40; 16:13, 27, 28; 17:9; 19:28; Mk 2:10; 8:31

a *3* Greek *made clean* b *17* Isaiah 53:4

feeling can lead to infection and decay from unnoticed injury, while loss of muscle control can lead to atrophy and even paralysis. In advanced stages the rotting flesh can literally crumble off the extremities and even the face. This "living death" was greatly feared and served as a graphic picture of sin. Touching a leper made one ceremonially unclean. In this case, however, Jesus did not become unclean, but the leper became clean. Although the sin that resides within each of us is immeasurably more disgusting to Jesus than leprosy, he is willing to touch us also and make us clean.

8:4 don't tell anyone. The command to the leper to be silent was intended to prevent wonder seekers from inhibiting Jesus from accomplishing his main mission (cf. Mk 1:45). By showing himself to the priest, the leper would bear testimony to the fact that the Old Testament points to Jesus.

8:5–13 centurion. An officer in charge of 100 men. This man had an appreciation for Jesus' authority that surpassed that of anyone else in Israel, an awareness of his own unworthiness, and faith that Jesus could overcome the difficulty posed by that unworthiness. The centurion's faith is even more remarkable in that we have no indication up to this point that Jesus had healed anyone by a simple word. Matthew, in keeping with its condensed style, does not mention the intermediaries who appear in the parallel account in Luke 7:1–10.

8:9–10 See *WCF* 14.3; 23.2.

8:10–12 That the centurion was a Gentile provides the occasion for the prediction of Israel's hardening and the extension of the gospel of the kingdom to the Gentiles. **feast with Abraham.** This is the Messianic banquet theme of Isaiah 25:6–9. Gentiles now appear in place of the natural "sons." This theme recurs in the parables of the wicked tenants (21:33–44, specifically v. 43) and of the wedding banquet (22:1–14). We have here an example of the principle of Romans 9:30–32: Israel tried to pursue righteousness by works but failed to obtain it, while Gentiles who knew they deserved only condemnation sought and received God's mercy.

8:12 darkness . . . weeping and gnashing of teeth. Represents the extreme and hopeless dismay of those who are finally excluded from the kingdom (cf. marginal references).

8:17 He took up our infirmities. Isaiah 53:4 uses infirmities and sorrows to represent the curse of sin. "Sorrows" might also be translated "diseases" (cf. 53:5). Jesus came to bear the curse as well as the guilt of sin. He did so on the cross, but even his healing ministry was not without cost to himself (cf. Mk 5:30). When Christ returns in glory, we will receive incorruptible bodies. This verse gives no warrant for miraculous healing on demand prior to Christ's return.

8:18–22 These two events show the radical commitment Jesus demands of disciples. If we identify with Jesus, we too will be homeless, "aliens and strangers in the world" (1Pe 2:11). Burying one's parents was one of the strictest obligations in Jewish society, but Jesus demanded a greater allegiance to himself. Probably the man was requesting that he be allowed to wait for his father to die before beginning his discipleship in earnest.

8:20 Son of Man. Of the 81 occurrences of this title in the New Testament, all but three (Ac 7:56; Rev 1:13; 14:14) are Jesus' references to himself or quotations from Jesus. The term was not used as a title for Christ in the early church, but the disciples clearly remembered that it was Jesus' preferred way of referring to himself. The occurrences of this title in the Gospels may be classified into

21 Another disciple said to him, "Lord, first let me go and bury my father."
22 But Jesus told him, "Follow me,[p] and let the dead bury their own dead."

Jesus Calms the Storm

23 Then he got into the boat and his disciples followed him. 24 Without warning, a furious storm came up on the lake, so that the waves swept over the boat. But Jesus was sleeping. 25 The disciples went and woke him, saying, "Lord, save us! We're going to drown!"
26 He replied, "You of little faith,[q] why are you so afraid?" Then he got up and rebuked
the winds and the waves, and it was completely calm.[r]
27 The men were amazed and asked, "What kind of man is this? Even the winds and
the waves obey him!"

The Healing of Two Demon-possessed Men

28 When he arrived at the other side in the region of the Gadarenes,[a] two demon-possessed[s] men coming from the tombs met him. They were so violent that no one could
pass that way. 29 "What do you want with us,[t] Son of God?" they shouted. "Have you
come here to torture us before the appointed time?"[u]
30 Some distance from them a large herd of pigs was feeding. 31 The demons begged
Jesus, "If you drive us out, send us into the herd of pigs."
32 He said to them, "Go!" So they came out and went into the pigs, and the whole herd
rushed down the steep bank into the lake and died in the water. 33 Those tending the pigs
ran off, went into the town and reported all this, including what had happened to the demon-possessed men. 34 Then the whole town went out to meet Jesus. And when they saw
him, they pleaded with him to leave their region.[v]

Jesus Heals a Paralytic

9 Jesus stepped into a boat, crossed over and came to his own town.[w] 2 Some men
brought to him a paralytic,[x] lying on a mat. When Jesus saw their faith,[y] he said to
the paralytic, "Take heart,[z] son; your sins are forgiven."[a]
3 At this, some of the teachers of the law said to themselves, "This fellow is blaspheming!"[b]
4 Knowing their thoughts,[c] Jesus said, "Why do you entertain evil thoughts in your
hearts? 5 Which is easier: to say, 'Your sins are forgiven,' or to say, 'Get up and walk'? 6 But
so that you may know that the Son of Man[d] has authority on earth to forgive sins . . ."
Then he said to the paralytic, "Get up, take your mat and go home." 7 And the man got
up and went home. 8 When the crowd saw this, they were filled with awe; and they
praised God,[e] who had given such authority to men.

8:22 [p]Mt 4:19
8:26 [q]Mt 6:30 [r]Ps 65:7; 89:9; 107:29
8:28 [s]Mt 4:24
8:29 [t]Jdg 11:12; 2Sa 16:10; 1Ki 17:18; Mk 1:24; Lk 4:34; Jn 2:4 [u]2Pe 2:4
8:34 [v]Lk 5:8; Ac 16:39
9:1 [w]Mt 4:13
9:2 [x]Mt 4:24 [y]ver 22 [z]Jn 16:33 [a]Lk 7:48
9:3 [b]Mt 26:65; Jn 10:33
9:4 [c]Ps 94:11; Mt 12:25; Lk 6:8; 9:47; 11:17
9:6 [d]Mt 8:20
9:8 [e]Mt 5:16; 15:31; Lk 7:16; 13:13; 17:15; 23:47; Jn 15:8; Ac 4:21; 11:18; 21:20

[a] *28* Some manuscripts *Gergesenes*; others *Gerasenes*

---

three categories: (1) the apocalyptic Son of Man who appears at the end of the age, (2) the suffering and dying Son of Man and (3) Jesus' use of the phrase as a first-person reference to himself. The first reference to the apocalyptic Son of Man is found in Daniel 7:13–14, a passage in which the Son of Man appears before the Ancient of Days and receives world dominion and worship. This is clearly the figure in view in 24:30 and 26:64, and the allusion thus underlies the other references to the Son of Man coming in judgment. The background for the other two categories has been sought in various places. For example, the term in Ezekiel 2 (God's address to the prophet) is supposedly equivalent in Aramaic to a first-person singular pronoun. "Son of Man" would be equivalent to "human being." The likelihood is that Jesus preferred the title precisely because it was ambiguous to his audience. On the one hand, it was not a usual or expected way of referring to the Messiah. On the other, it claimed more than the title "Messiah" by itself could claim: total dominion and the prerogatives of deity. See note on 17:22–23.

8:24–27 the winds and the waves obey him. That Jesus calmed the storm demonstrates his deity, for in the Old Testament it was God who stilled the seas and was Lord of the storm (cf. Pss 29:3–4; 65:5–7; 89:9; 107:23–30). Thus, the disciples' astonished question in verse 27 was "What kind of man is this?"

8:28–29 region of the Gadarenes. This is identified in Mark and Luke as the territory around the village of Gerasa, which was in the predominantly Gentile area of the Decapolis. Gerasa was controlled by the larger town of Gadara. Probably only one of these two demoniacs was exceedingly violent. Hence, Mark and Luke mentioned the one only, whereas Matthew was concerned about the double witness of the testimony. The demons knew Jesus to be the Son of God, and they had a seemingly legitimate complaint: It was not yet the "appointed time" (v. 29), the day of judgment. But Jesus was already inaugurating the kingdom of God, and already the powers of darkness were being broken (cf. 12:28). **Son of God.** See note on 16:15–16.

8:30–32 demons. The Greek word translated "demon" is the generic term for a "god" (cf. Ac 17:18). Of course, the demons were not God; insofar as they had actual personal existence, they were "evil spirits" (10:1). They opposed the true God and wreaked havoc in the lives of people, sometimes by possession. Thus they were identified with Satan, the prince of demons (9:34, 12:24–28). Adam should have thrown Satan out of Eden; Jesus did throw out Satan's minions. Casting out demons was a sign of the arrival of the kingdom (12:28). Jesus most likely permitted the demons to enter the pigs either in consideration of the fact that the day of final judgment had not yet arrived or because the subsequent drowning demonstrated the perverse values of the people in the community, who valued their swine above the rescue of two human beings. Luke 8:31 reports the entreaty of the demons that they not be sent to the Abyss. The drowning of the pigs in the depths of the lake suggests that by granting the request of the demons, Jesus consigned them to a place prefiguring the Abyss. See *WLC* 19; *BC* 13.

9:1–3 your sins are forgiven. Forgiveness is the prerogative of the one sinned against. For Jesus to forgive sins against God was for him to claim divine authority (cf. Isa 43:25).

9:5–7 Which is easier. Ultimately, forgiving sins is much more difficult than performing a miracle, as presumably the scribes would have known since they recognized that only God can forgive sins. But forgiving sins is also empirically unverifiable. Thus Jesus performed the lesser deed to demonstrate the greater.

9:8 were filled with awe. Literally, "were afraid." Fear is a prop-

The Calling of Matthew

9 As Jesus went on from there, he saw a man named Matthew sitting at the tax collector's booth. "Follow me," he told him, and Matthew got up and followed him.
10 While Jesus was having dinner at Matthew's house, many tax collectors and "sinners" came and ate with him and his disciples. 11 When the Pharisees saw this, they asked
his disciples, "Why does your teacher eat with tax collectors and 'sinners'?"[f]
12 On hearing this, Jesus said, "It is not the healthy who need a doctor, but the sick.
13 But go and learn what this means: 'I desire mercy, not sacrifice.'[a][g] For I have not come
to call the righteous, but sinners."[h]

Jesus Questioned About Fasting

14 Then John's disciples came and asked him, "How is it that we and the Pharisees
fast,[i] but your disciples do not fast?"
15 Jesus answered, "How can the guests of the bridegroom mourn while he is with
them?[j] The time will come when the bridegroom will be taken from them; then they will
fast.[k]
16 "No one sews a patch of unshrunk cloth on an old garment, for the patch will pull
away from the garment, making the tear worse. 17 Neither do men pour new wine into
old wineskins. If they do, the skins will burst, the wine will run out and the wineskins will
be ruined. No, they pour new wine into new wineskins, and both are preserved."

A Dead Girl and a Sick Woman

18 While he was saying this, a ruler came and knelt before him[l] and said, "My daughter has just died. But come and put your hand on her,[m] and she will live." 19 Jesus got up
and went with him, and so did his disciples.
20 Just then a woman who had been subject to bleeding for twelve years came up behind him and touched the edge of his cloak.[n] 21 She said to herself, "If I only touch his
cloak, I will be healed."
22 Jesus turned and saw her. "Take heart, daughter," he said, "your faith has healed
you."[o] And the woman was healed from that moment.[p]
23 When Jesus entered the ruler's house and saw the flute players and the noisy
crowd,[q] 24 he said, "Go away. The girl is not dead[r] but asleep."[s] But they laughed at him.
25 After the crowd had been put outside, he went in and took the girl by the hand, and
she got up. 26 News of this spread through all that region.[t]

Jesus Heals the Blind and Mute

27 As Jesus went on from there, two blind men followed him, calling out, "Have mercy on us, Son of David!"[u]

9:11 [f]Mt 11:19; Lk 5:30; 15:2; Gal 2:15
9:13 [g]Hos 6:6; Mic 6:6-8; Mt 12:7 [h]1Ti 1:15
9:14 [i]Lk 18:12
9:15 [j]Jn 3:29 [k]Ac 13:2, 3; 14:23
9:18 [l]Mt 8:2 [m]Mk 5:23
9:20 [n]Mt 14:36; Mk 3:10
9:22 [o]Mk 10:52; Lk 7:50; 17:19; 18:42 [p]Mt 15:28
9:23 [q]2Ch 35:25; Jer 9:17,18
9:24 [r]Ac 20:10 [s]Jn 11:11-14
9:26 [t]Mt 4:24
9:27 [u]Mt 15:22; Mk 10:47; Lk 18:38-39

[a] *13* Hosea 6:6

er response to the claim of having authority to forgive sins (Ps 130:4).

9:11 sinners. Just as Jesus was not defiled by contact with lepers, so he is not corrupted by contact with "sinners." He is the physician who heals spiritual as well as physical sickness. But those who do not know they are sick do not go to a doctor. Lack of awareness of serious disease is often the most insidious "symptom" of all.

9:14 John's disciples. Although Luke notes that the Pharisees asked the question (Lk 5:30–33), Mark includes both John's disciples and the Pharisees among those who raised the issue of fasting.

9:15 then they will fast. Jesus explained his disciples' lack of fasting by referring to his own Messianic presence. God had earlier referred to himself as Israel's bridegroom (Isa 54:5; 62:4–5; Hos 2), and Jesus recognized a future time when the bridegroom would not be with them. This points to the fact that, from the earliest stages of his ministry, Jesus anticipated a time between his initial coming in redemption and his final coming in judgment. See *WCF* 21.5.

9:17 new wine. Wine continues to ferment, building up pressure that would burst a previously used wineskin.

9:18–25 As usual, Matthew has a more condensed form of this story than Mark and Luke. Both the surrounding story of the ruler's daughter and the nested story of the woman with a hemorrhage illustrate the power of Jesus in bringing the kingdom and the nature of faith in relation to its coming. The same point appears in the following accounts of the blind man and the mute demonic. The dead were raised, the sick healed, the unclean cleansed, the blind given sight, demons cast out, mutes enabled to speak. These works came in response to various forms of faith—not because faith empowered Jesus, but because outside the context of faith miracles were not signs of the kingdom's coming but only strange events without particular meaning.

9:20 bleeding. The woman's condition was probably chronic uterine bleeding, which must have been a common problem given that Jewish oral tradition engaged in much discussion about it. The woman may not have understood much about the kingdom of God, but she knew enough to come to Jesus, and this involved courage on her part.

9:22 faith. The woman's faith made her well because the benefits of the kingdom flow to those who look to Jesus for the solution to their problems.

9:23 flute players. They, as well as loud lamenters, were professional mourners who helped the bereaved express their grief.

9:24 not dead but asleep. This might mean that Jesus knew the girl was only comatose or cataleptic, but more likely it was a reminder from Jesus that death for believers is not permanent and irrevocable (cf. Jn 11:11–14) and that the day of waking (resurrection) is already dawning.

9:27 two blind men. The story of their healing is sometimes taken as a doublet of the blind Bartimaeus account in Mark 10:46–52. But Matthew also relates the later story (20:30–34), and since there are other differences, this should be understood as a separate incident. Jesus healed many blind people. Both Bartimaeus and these blind men expressed their faith by calling Jesus "Son of David," a Messianic title (cf. 12:23).

28When he had gone indoors, the blind men came to him, and he asked them, "Do
you believe that I am able to do this?"
"Yes, Lord," they replied.
29Then he touched their eyes and said, "According to your faith will it be done to
you";[v] 30and their sight was restored. Jesus warned them sternly, "See that no one
knows about this."[w] 31But they went out and spread the news about him all over that region.[x]
32While they were going out, a man who was demon-possessed[y] and could not talk[z]
was brought to Jesus. 33And when the demon was driven out, the man who had been
mute spoke. The crowd was amazed and said, "Nothing like this has ever been seen in
Israel."[a]
34But the Pharisees said, "It is by the prince of demons that he drives out demons."[b]

The Workers Are Few

35Jesus went through all the towns and villages, teaching in their synagogues, preaching the good news of the kingdom and healing every disease and sickness.[c] 36When he
saw the crowds, he had compassion on them,[d] because they were harassed and helpless, like sheep without a shepherd.[e] 37Then he said to his disciples, "The harvest[f] is plentiful but the workers are few.[g] 38Ask the Lord of the harvest, therefore, to send out workers into his harvest field."

Jesus Sends Out the Twelve

10 He called his twelve disciples to him and gave them authority to drive out evil[a]
spirits[h] and to heal every disease and sickness.
2These are the names of the twelve apostles: first, Simon (who is called Peter) and his
brother Andrew; James son of Zebedee, and his brother John; 3Philip and Bartholomew;
Thomas and Matthew the tax collector; James son of Alphaeus, and Thaddaeus; 4Simon
the Zealot and Judas Iscariot, who betrayed him.[i]
5These twelve Jesus sent out with the following instructions: "Do not go among the
Gentiles or enter any town of the Samaritans.[j] 6Go rather to the lost sheep of Israel.[k] 7As
you go, preach this message: 'The kingdom of heaven[l] is near.' 8Heal the sick, raise the
dead, cleanse those who have leprosy,[b] drive out demons. Freely you have received, free-

9:29 [v]ver 22
9:30 [w]Mt 8:4
9:31 [x]ver 26; Mk 7:36
9:32 [y]Mt 4:24 [z]Mt 12:22-24
9:33 [a]Mk 2:12
9:34 [b]Mt 12:24; Lk 11:15
9:35 [c]Mt 4:23
9:36 [d]Mt 14:14 [e]Nu 27:17; Eze 34:5,6; Zec 10:2; Mk 6:34
9:37 [f]Jn 4:35 [g]Lk 10:2
10:1 [h]Mk 3:13-15; Lk 9:1
10:4 [i]Mt 26:14-16,25, 47; Jn 13:2,26,27
10:5 [j]2Ki 17:24; Lk 9:52; Jn 4:4-26, 39,40; Ac 8:5,25
10:6 [k]Jer 50:6; Mt 15:24
10:7 [l]Mt 3:2

[a] 1 Greek *unclean* [b] 8 The Greek word was used for various diseases affecting the skin—not necessarily leprosy.

9:35–38 This passage functions both as a summary statement of the activity of Jesus as described in chapters 5–9 (teaching, preaching, healing) and as an introduction to the mission discourse in chapter 10. The background is found in Ezekiel 34:5–6. The implication is that Jesus is the true Shepherd who is concerned for his sheep (made explicit in John 10) and is thus identified with the Sovereign Lord of Ezekiel 34:11–16.
9:37–38 harvest. Often a metaphor for the end-time activity of God. That it is "plentiful" indicates that the "harvest" is not referring to the harvest time but to the harvest crop (as in Luke 10:2). It is not so much judgment that is in view here as the proclamation of the gospel, the eschatological announcement that precedes judgment and urges people to repent and have faith. **workers.** Not the angels sent to gather for judgment as in 13:49 but, as is made clear from what follows, the disciples who imitate Jesus by proclaiming the coming of the kingdom (10:7). It is interesting that Jesus did not yet command his disciples to go into the harvest as laborers, but to pray for God to provide laborers (v. 38). No one can do the work of the harvest unless he or she is first called to and equipped for it by God. See *WLC* 191.
■ **10:1–42** *Discourse: Kingdom Mission.* Chapter 10 comprises Jesus' second major discourse in which he announced the mission of the kingdom. At this point, Jesus sent out the Twelve to spread the kingdom of God to "the lost sheep of Israel" (v. 6).
10:2 apostles. Greek *apostolos.* Literally, "sent ones." Although *apostolos* is used in a general sense in the New Testament (e.g., "representatives" in 2Co 8:23; see also 1Th 2:6 with 1Th 1:1), when used of the special office of apostle, the term takes on the additional force of the Hebrew *shaliach,* the imperial overlord's authoritative representative whose word was that of the suzerain. Note that here the Twelve were given the authority to do exactly the things Jesus himself was doing (vv. 7–8). The apostolic lists in the Synoptic Gospels (vv. 2–4; Mk 3:16–19; Lk 6:13–16) all begin with Simon Peter and end with Judas Iscariot. The pairing in Matthew may reflect the fact that the Twelve were sent out two by two (Mk 6:7).
10:3 Thaddaeus. Probably the same as Judas, son (or brother) of James, who is mentioned in Luke 6:16.
10:4 Simon the Zealot. The same as Simon the Cananaean ("zealot" in Aramaic). Zealots advocated military action against Rome and later became a powerful political force. Probably Simon had been associated with the movement prior to his call and continued to be called "the Zealot" to distinguish him from Simon Peter. See chart "Jewish Sects" at Matthew 23.
10:5—11:1 Chapter 10 contains several lines of teaching regarding mission that are scattered throughout the other Gospels. This does not mean that Matthew invented the occasion, but it may mean that, in order to group the teachings of Jesus under five headings, Matthew brought in relevant material that may have been delivered on one or more different occasions. This is true particularly of verses 17–22, which envisions a world mission with predictions about being brought before "governors and kings" (v. 18) and seems to go beyond verse 5, which restricted the mission to Israel. Nevertheless, the future mission of the disciples to the whole world is linked to this early experience of preaching to Israel. Matthew's grouping of the material is appropriate.
10:5 Do not go. Although Jesus had already responded to Gentile faith (8:10), the focus of this first mission of the disciples, like that of Jesus before his passion and resurrection (cf. 15:24), was to the natural sons of the kingdom, the Jewish people. Note, however, that he did not *prohibit* the disciples from preaching to Gentiles whom they might encounter as they traveled. **Do not go among the Gentiles.** Literally, "Do not depart into the road of the Gentiles"; i.e., do not go to Gentile lands.
10:7–8 preach . . . Heal . . . raise . . . cleanse . . . drive out. The same signs of the coming of the kingdom that Jesus performed in chapters 8–9 are to be carried out by his disciples.
10:8–10 freely give. The kingdom was given to the disciples freely. If they marketed the message, it would insult God and obscure the nature of the gospel as a free gift. Nevertheless they would be provided for; they were not to "take along" ("procure" is a better translation) extra travel money and provisions (vv. 9–10)

ly give. 9Do not take along any gold or silver or copper in your belts;[m] 10take no bag for
the journey, or extra tunic, or sandals or a staff; for the worker is worth his keep.[n]
11"Whatever town or village you enter, search for some worthy person there and stay
at his house until you leave. 12As you enter the home, give it your greeting.[o] 13If the home
is deserving, let your peace rest on it; if it is not, let your peace return to you. 14If anyone will not welcome you or listen to your words, shake the dust off your feet[p] when you
leave that home or town. 15I tell you the truth, it will be more bearable for Sodom and
Gomorrah[q] on the day of judgment[r] than for that town.[s] 16I am sending you out like
sheep among wolves.[t] Therefore be as shrewd as snakes and as innocent as doves.[u]
17"Be on your guard against men; they will hand you over to the local councils[v] and
flog you in their synagogues.[w] 18On my account you will be brought before governors and
kings[x] as witnesses to them and to the Gentiles. 19But when they arrest you, do not worry about what to say or how to say it.[y] At that time you will be given what to say, 20for it
will not be you speaking, but the Spirit of your Father[z] speaking through you.
21"Brother will betray brother to death, and a father his child; children will rebel
against their parents[a] and have them put to death. 22All men will hate you because of
me, but he who stands firm to the end will be saved.[b] 23When you are persecuted in one
place, flee to another. I tell you the truth, you will not finish going through the cities of
Israel before the Son of Man comes.
24"A student is not above his teacher, nor a servant above his master.[c] 25It is enough
for the student to be like his teacher, and the servant like his master. If the head of the
house has been called Beelzebub,[a][d] how much more the members of his household!
26"So do not be afraid of them. There is nothing concealed that will not be disclosed,
or hidden that will not be made known.[e] 27What I tell you in the dark, speak in the daylight; what is whispered in your ear, proclaim from the roofs. 28Do not be afraid of those
who kill the body but cannot kill the soul. Rather, be afraid of the One[f] who can destroy
both soul and body in hell. 29Are not two sparrows sold for a penny[b]? Yet not one of them

10:9 [m]Lk 22:35
10:10 [n]1Ti 5:18
10:12 [o]1Sa 25:6
10:14 [p]Ne 5:13; Lk 10:11; Ac 13:51
10:15 [q]2Pe 2:6 [r]Mt 12:36; 2Pe 2:9; 1Jn 4:17 [s]Mt 11:22,24
10:16 [t]Lk 10:3 [u]Ro 16:19
10:17 [v]Mt 5:22 [w]Mt 23:34; Mk 13:9; Ac 5:40; 26:11
10:18 [x]Ac 25:24-26
10:19 [y]Ex 4:12
10:20 [z]Ac 4:8
10:21 [a]ver 35,36; Mic 7:6
10:22 [b]Mt 24:13; Mk 13:13
10:24 [c]Lk 6:40; Jn 13:16; 15:20
10:25 [d]Mk 3:22
10:26 [e]Mk 4:22; Lk 8:17
10:28 [f]Isa 8:12,13; Heb 10:31

[a] 25 Greek *Beezeboul* or *Beelzeboul*   [b] 29 Greek *an assarion*

but were to depend on God's provision. This is a paradigm of the Christian life in general.

10:14–15 shake the dust off. Jews sometimes shook the dust off their feet when returning from Gentile lands. A town that did not receive the disciples did not receive Jesus and became spiritually "pagan" and subject to judgment, just as Sodom and Gomorrah had been (cf. Ac 13:51).

10:17–20 Be on your guard. As discussed in the note on 10:5—11:1, verses 17–20 anticipate a later, more extensive mission than that presented on the immediate occasion described in verse 5. Persecution would occur at the hands of both Jewish (v. 17) and Gentile (v. 18) authorities. But Jesus' disciples were not to respond to it in the same way pagans did—by hiring professional orators as defense attorneys. Instead, the Holy Spirit would provide their defense.

10:19–20 See *HC* 127.

10:22 All men. Means "all sorts of people." The allusion is to Micah 7:6, a passage that Matthew later quotes (vv. 35–36).

10:23 you will not finish . . . before the Son of Man comes. There are several views on what the "coming" of the Son of Man in this verse is referring to. The more important are:

(1) This "coming" refers to the second coming of Christ in judgment at the end of the age. This view has the advantage of tying easily to some other references to this "coming" (24:30; 25:31; 26:64), although the reference in 16:28 speaks against it. There are three variations on this view:
  (a) The dispensational view interjects a suspension and later resumption of the mission to Israel. The main problem here is that this detaches either verse 23 or all of verses 16–23 from the context and makes this material incomprehensible both to Jesus' original audience and to the early church.
  (b) The symbolic form of this view understands the use of "Israel" here to mean the world or church. But the context gives no indication of a symbolic meaning for *Israel,* and Matthew does not use *Israel* in this way in any other passage.
  (c) A third view is that Jesus simply means that the task of evangelizing Jews will not be complete until the second coming. This may be linguistically the most natural understanding, but there seems to be a note of urgency in verse 23 that is difficult to explain.

(2) This "coming" is the exaltation of Jesus in heaven at his resurrection. The difficulty here is that there is no evidence that the disciples were persecuted with the intensity assumed in verses 17–22 prior to Jesus' resurrection.

(3) This "coming" is the sending of the Spirit at Pentecost. This explanation suffers from the lack of evidence of persecution prior to Pentecost. Further, the disciples were told to wait until *after* Pentecost before beginning their mission (Ac 1:4).

(4) The phrase "before the Son of Man comes" is a way of saying, "until I catch up with you." But once again, the persecution described in verses 17–22 then seems irrelevant. The theological significance of the "coming" of the Son of Man also makes this meaning unlikely.

(5) This "coming" refers to the destruction of Jerusalem in A.D. 70. This "coming" is then the coming in judgment against Israel as a nation, the final symbolic elimination of the old order and the fulfillment of prophecy. This view retains the note of urgency, understands "Israel" to be Israel and fits with known persecution prior to A.D. 70. Further, it would be addressed to the disciples rather than to a hypothetical generation more than 2,000 years later. It can also be tied to all other references to the "coming" of the Son of Man, for they all have to do with the great and terrible display of God's judgment. There is still a difficulty, however: Not all the occurrences of the "coming" of the Son of Man can readily be applied only to the destruction of Jerusalem. Yet, just as we can see the connection between the resurrections that occurred at Jesus' death (27:52–53), Jesus' own resurrection and the final resurrection, we can also perceive a connection between the judgment of the cross, the judgment of Jerusalem and the final judgment of the world. The destruction of Jerusalem was an "in-breaking" into the present of the final judgment of God against all unbelief.

10:25 Beelzebub. Also Beelzebul. The prince of demons, identified with Satan in 12:24–27. Its derivation might be from the Hebrew for "lord of the flies," "prince Baal" or perhaps even "lord of the dung."

10:26–31 be afraid. This injunction to be afraid of God rather than people is perhaps a development of Isaiah 8:12–13. It is supported by three arguments: (1) The acts of evil people will be shown for what they are; (2) evil people can only kill the body, not the soul, whereas God can punish both soul and body eternally; and (3) God sovereignly orders everything, even including the fall of a sparrow or the number of hairs on one's head. Fear is an appropriate response to God. There is a non-submissive fear and dread that love casts out (1Jn 4:18), but a submissive fear that recognizes God as God remains the only appropriate attitude. **soul.** In Scripture this term does not usually refer simply to the non-physical part of a human being, but to personal existence or life that

will fall to the ground apart from the will of your Father. 30 And even the very hairs of your
head are all numbered.[g] 31 So don't be afraid; you are worth more than many sparrows.[h]
32 "Whoever acknowledges me before men,[i] I will also acknowledge him before my Father in heaven. 33 But whoever disowns me before men, I will disown him before my Father in heaven.[j]
34 "Do not suppose that I have come to bring peace to the earth. I did not come to
bring peace, but a sword. 35 For I have come to turn

" 'a man against his father,
a daughter against her mother,
a daughter-in-law against her mother-in-law[k]—
36 a man's enemies will be the members of his own household.'[a][l]

37 "Anyone who loves his father or mother more than me is not worthy of me; anyone
who loves his son or daughter more than me is not worthy of me;[m] 38 and anyone who
does not take his cross and follow me is not worthy of me.[n] 39 Whoever finds his life will
lose it, and whoever loses his life for my sake will find it.[o]
40 "He who receives you receives me,[p] and he who receives me receives the one who
sent me.[q] 41 Anyone who receives a prophet because he is a prophet will receive a prophet's reward, and anyone who receives a righteous man because he is a righteous man will
receive a righteous man's reward. 42 And if anyone gives even a cup of cold water to one
of these little ones because he is my disciple, I tell you the truth, he will certainly not lose
his reward."[r]

Jesus and John the Baptist

11 After Jesus had finished instructing his twelve disciples,[s] he went on from there
to teach and preach in the towns of Galilee.[b]
2 When John heard in prison[t] what Christ was doing, he sent his disciples 3 to ask him,
"Are you the one who was to come,[u] or should we expect someone else?"
4 Jesus replied, "Go back and report to John what you hear and see: 5 The blind receive
sight, the lame walk, those who have leprosy[c] are cured, the deaf hear, the dead are
raised, and the good news is preached to the poor.[v] 6 Blessed is the man who does not
fall away on account of me."[w]
7 As John's[x] disciples were leaving, Jesus began to speak to the crowd about John:
"What did you go out into the desert to see? A reed swayed by the wind? 8 If not, what
did you go out to see? A man dressed in fine clothes? No, those who wear fine clothes
are in kings' palaces. 9 Then what did you go out to see? A prophet?[y] Yes, I tell you, and
more than a prophet. 10 This is the one about whom it is written:

10:30 g1Sa 14:45; 2Sa 14:11; Lk 21:18; Ac 27:34
10:31 hMt 12:12
10:32 iRo 10:9
10:33 jMk 8:38; 2Ti 2:12
10:35 kver 21
10:36 lMic 7:6
10:37 mLk 14:26
10:38 nMt 16:24; Lk 14:27
10:39 oLk 17:33; Jn 12:25
10:40 pMt 18:5; Gal 4:14 qLk 9:48; Jn 12:44; 13:20
10:42 rMt 25:40; Mk 9:41; Heb 6:10
11:1 sMt 7:28
11:2 tMt 14:3
11:3 uPs 118:26; Jn 11:27; Heb 10:37
11:5 vIsa 35:4-6; 61:1; Lk 4:18,19
11:6 wMt 13:21
11:7 xMt 3:1
11:9 yMt 21:26; Lk 1:76

a 36 Micah 7:6 b 1 Greek *in their towns* c 5 The Greek word was used for various diseases affecting the skin—not necessarily leprosy.

both includes and transcends physical life. It is the word translated "life" in verse 39. **hell.** Compare note on 5:22. See *WCF* 4.2; 5.1; *WLC* 17,18; *WSC* 11; *BC* 13; *HC* 1,26,27.

10:32–33 Whoever acknowledges. Jesus declared that one's relationship to God depends exclusively and eternally on one's relationship to and attitude toward Jesus (cf. Ac 4:12). See *WLC* 90; *WSC* 38; *BC* 37; *HC* 32,99.

10:34–36 not . . . peace, but a sword. Micah 7:6 addressed the rebelliousness and strife characteristic of Israel during the time of Ahaz. Just as Israel's history foreshadows Jesus' history (cf. note on 2:15), its turmoil and strife foreshadowed the strife that resulted from the coming of the Messiah, even to the division of families. Many who have been converted from non-Christian backgrounds bear testimony to the sober truth of this divisiveness. Embracing the gospel often makes life more difficult, not easier, because Jesus demands allegiance that supersedes the strongest ties of human life (vv. 37–39).

10:37–39 See *HC* 94.

10:38–39 take his cross. This does not mean that Jesus' followers are to bear some burden the Lord has imposed. Rather, it refers to their radical obedience to, and identification with, Jesus, even unto death. Hence, in verse 39 we must stress the words "for my sake."

10:40–42 prophet . . . righteous man. Refers to Old Testament spokesmen of God (cf. 13:17; 23:29), so here it simply emphasizes the principle that receiving someone as an emissary of another is equivalent to receiving the person who sent him or her (v. 40). **little ones.** Consistently refers to Jesus' disciples, not to young children.

▪ 11:1—13:58 *The Nature of the Kingdom.* Chapters 11–13 reveal the nature of the kingdom. Where is it? What is it? How is it coming? Matthew's record is divided into two parts: narratives (11:1—12:50) and discourse (13:1–52).

▪ 11:1—12:50 *Narrative: Who Was John? Who Is Jesus?* Matthew explains the nature of the kingdom by focusing on the identities and roles of John the Baptist and Jesus.

11:2–3 what Christ was doing. Literally, "the works of the Christ." Since Matthew ordinarily avoids anachronistic or premature use of the title "Christ" as a name for Jesus, this probably means "When John heard in prison about the Messianic deeds . . ." John had predicted that the coming Messiah would bring judgment, chopping down the trees of wickedness and separating the wheat from the chaff (3:10,12). But while Jesus brought kingdom blessings, he also allowed his own forerunner to be imprisoned by the wicked Herod. Where was the Messiah's deliverance of the prisoners? John asked himself (Isa 61:1–2).

11:4–6 Jesus made John's disciples witnesses of his miracles—miracles that directly fulfilled Isaiah 35:5–6. John was not to take offense at the fact that Jesus did not come at first to bring judgment but to bear the judgment.

11:8 See *WLC* 141.

11:9–10 more than a prophet. John the Baptist was greater than any other prophet because he was the most immediate forerunner of the One to whom all the prophets were pointing; hence, he pointed to Christ more clearly than the others. But He was also the object of prophecy, the fulfillment of the Elijah prophecy of Malachi 4:5–6 (see v. 14) and the announcer of the servant of the Lord (Isa 40:3; Mt 3:3).

" 'I will send my messenger ahead of you,
who will prepare your way before you.'[a][z]

11I tell you the truth: Among those born of women there has not risen anyone greater
than John the Baptist; yet he who is least in the kingdom of heaven is greater than he.
12From the days of John the Baptist until now, the kingdom of heaven has been forcefully advancing, and forceful men lay hold of it. 13For all the Prophets and the Law prophesied until John. 14And if you are willing to accept it, he is the Elijah who was to come.[a]
15He who has ears, let him hear.[b]
16"To what can I compare this generation? They are like children sitting in the marketplaces and calling out to others:

17" 'We played the flute for you,
and you did not dance;
we sang a dirge,
and you did not mourn.'

18For John came neither eating[c] nor drinking,[d] and they say, 'He has a demon.' 19The Son
of Man came eating and drinking, and they say, 'Here is a glutton and a drunkard, a
friend of tax collectors and "sinners." '[e] But wisdom is proved right by her actions."

Woe on Unrepentant Cities

20Then Jesus began to denounce the cities in which most of his miracles had been performed, because they did not repent. 21"Woe to you, Korazin! Woe to you, Bethsaida![f]
If the miracles that were performed in you had been performed in Tyre and Sidon,[g] they
would have repented long ago in sackcloth and ashes.[h] 22But I tell you, it will be more
bearable for Tyre and Sidon on the day of judgment than for you.[i] 23And you, Capernaum,[j] will you be lifted up to the skies? No, you will go down to the depths.[b][k] If the miracles that were performed in you had been performed in Sodom, it would have remained
to this day. 24But I tell you that it will be more bearable for Sodom on the day of judgment than for you."[l]

Rest for the Weary

25At that time Jesus said, "I praise you, Father,[m] Lord of heaven and earth, because
you have hidden these things from the wise and learned, and revealed them to little children.[n] 26Yes, Father, for this was your good pleasure.
27"All things have been committed to me[o] by my Father.[p] No one knows the Son except the Father, and no one knows the Father except the Son and those to whom the Son
chooses to reveal him.[q]
28"Come to me,[r] all you who are weary and burdened, and I will give you rest. 29Take

11:10 [z]Mal 3:1; Mk 1:2

11:14 [a]Mal 4:5; Mt 17:10-13; Mk 9:11-13; Lk 1:17; Jn 1:21

11:15 [b]Mt 13:9,43; Mk 4:23; Lk 14:35; Rev 2:7

11:18 [c]Mt 3:4 [d]Lk 1:15

11:19 [e]Mt 9:11

11:21 [f]Mk 6:45; Lk 9:10; Jn 12:21 [g]Mt 15:21; Lk 6:17; Ac 12:20 [h]Jnh 3:5-9

11:22 [i]ver 24; Mt 10:15

11:23 [j]Mt 4:13 [k]Isa 14:13-15

11:24 [l]Mt 10:15

11:25 [m]Lk 22:42, Jn 11:41 [n]1Co 1:26-29

11:27 [o]Mt 28:18 [p]Jn 3:35; 13:3; 17:2 [q]Jn 10:15

11:28 [r]Jn 7:37

a *10* Mal. 3:1 b *23* Greek *Hades*

11:11 greater than he. After the cross, the resurrection and Pentecost, "he who is least in the kingdom" is greater than John because such a person can point to Jesus even more clearly than John could. Of course, John is *now* in the kingdom along with all the Old Testament believers, but when they lived on Earth they could only look forward to it (cf. Heb 11:39–40). Greatness may also indicate the reception of a larger measure of blessedness in God's kingdom as it unfolds throughout history. Believers who live after Christ's death, resurrection and ascension enjoy the presence of the kingdom of God in greater measure than John did.
11:12 forcefully advancing. The Greek verb translated "forcefully advancing" can also mean "suffering violence," but in other Greek literature it almost always takes the former meaning. Further, the parallel saying in Luke 16:16 uses "the kingdom of God is being preached," which corresponds to "forcefully advancing." On the other hand, in other Greek literature the noun translated "forceful men" always means "violent people" and has a negative connotation, as the verb "lay hold of" usually does. The best understanding of this verse is that the kingdom is pressing ahead with force even though violent men (e.g., Herod, who had imprisoned John) are trying to overcome it by force. It is not the strong and forceful who obtain the kingdom but the weak and helpless who know their own weakness and thus depend on God (vv. 28–30).
11:14 he is the Elijah. See note on John 1:21.
11:19 Son of Man. See note on 8:20. **wisdom is proved right by her actions.** Luke 7:35 replaces "actions" with "children." The point is this: Just as people are known by their fruit (7:16,20), so also will a wise course be confirmed by that which flows from it.
11:21–24 See *WCF* 3.2; *WLC* 151; *BC* 37; *CD* 1.IX.
11:25–26 See *WCF* 3.7; *WLC* 13; *CD* 1.VIII.
11:25 you have hidden . . . and revealed. God is sovereign in choosing those to whom he will reveal his truth. All *human* wisdom and learning are irrelevant to the question of knowing God (1Co 1:26–31). See *BC* 27.
11:27 committed to me. Jesus here makes extraordinary claims: (1) God's sovereign disposition of all things has been committed to Jesus. As in Daniel 7, the Son of Man has received all power and dominion. (2) Jesus possesses an exclusive knowledge of the Father, and only the Father truly knows him. His knowledge is thus equal to the Father's, and his Sonship is unique. (3) Jesus' sovereignty extends even to deciding who will know the Father. This parallels verse 25, but here it is Jesus who reveals the Father. These claims are so far-reaching that many modernist scholars argue that they are inauthentic, late and Hellenistic, but research into the language and forms keeps demonstrating their Semitic and early character. The only real reason for denying that Jesus said these words is the presupposition that he could not possibly have said such things, a circular argument.
11:28–30 Because the Son is sovereign in revealing God, he has the authority to invite people to himself. Because he is gentle and humble, he extends his invitation first to the weary and burdened and secondarily to the strong and comfortable. See *WLC* 172; *BC* 26,28,29,30.

my yoke upon you and learn from me,[s] for I am gentle and humble in heart, and you will
find rest for your souls.[t] 30 For my yoke is easy and my burden is light."[u]

Lord of the Sabbath

12 At that time Jesus went through the grainfields on the Sabbath. His disciples
were hungry and began to pick some heads of grain[v] and eat them. 2 When the
Pharisees saw this, they said to him, "Look! Your disciples are doing what is unlawful
on the Sabbath."[w]
3 He answered, "Haven't you read what David did when he and his companions were
hungry?[x] 4 He entered the house of God, and he and his companions ate the consecrated bread—which was not lawful for them to do, but only for the priests.[y] 5 Or haven't you
read in the Law that on the Sabbath the priests in the temple desecrate the day[z] and yet
are innocent? 6 I tell you that one[a] greater than the temple is here.[a] 7 If you had known
what these words mean, 'I desire mercy, not sacrifice,'[b][b] you would not have condemned the innocent. 8 For the Son of Man[c] is Lord of the Sabbath."
9 Going on from that place, he went into their synagogue, 10 and a man with a shriveled hand was there. Looking for a reason to accuse Jesus, they asked him, "Is it lawful
to heal on the Sabbath?"[d]
11 He said to them, "If any of you has a sheep and it falls into a pit on the Sabbath, will
you not take hold of it and lift it out?[e] 12 How much more valuable is a man than a sheep![f]
Therefore it is lawful to do good on the Sabbath."
13 Then he said to the man, "Stretch out your hand." So he stretched it out and it was
completely restored, just as sound as the other. 14 But the Pharisees went out and plotted how they might kill Jesus.[g]

God's Chosen Servant

15 Aware of this, Jesus withdrew from that place. Many followed him, and he healed
all their sick,[h] 16 warning them not to tell who he was.[i] 17 This was to fulfill what was spoken through the prophet Isaiah:

18 "Here is my servant whom I have chosen,
the one I love, in whom I delight;[j]
I will put my Spirit on him,
and he will proclaim justice to the nations.
19 He will not quarrel or cry out;
no one will hear his voice in the streets.
20 A bruised reed he will not break,

[a] 6 Or *something*; also in verses 41 and 42 [b] 7 Hosea 6:6

11:29 [s]Jn 13:15; Php 2:5; 1Pe 2:21; 1Jn 2:6 [t]Jer 6:16
11:30 [u]1Jn 5:3
12:1 [v]Dt 23:25
12:2 [w]ver 10; Lk 13:14; 14:3; Jn 5:10; 7:23; 9:16
12:3 [x]1Sa 21:6
12:4 [y]Lev 24:5,9
12:5 [z]Nu 28:9,10; Jn 7:22,23
12:6 [a]ver 41,42
12:7 [b]Hos 6:6; Mic 6:6-8; Mt 9:13
12:8 [c]Mt 8:20
12:10 [d]ver 2; Lk 13:14; 14:3; Jn 9:16
12:11 [e]Lk 14:5
12:12 [f]Mt 10:31
12:14 [g]Mt 26:4; 27:1; Mk 3:6; Lk 6:11; Jn 5:18; 11:53
12:15 [h]Mt 4:23
12:16 [i]Mt 8:4
12:18 [j]Mt 3:17

11:29–30 yoke. Judaism bore the yoke of the law, which had become a heavy burden (Ac 15:10). Jesus offers not independence, but a different yoke. It is "easy" and "light" (v. 30), not because it is less demanding, but because it is administered by a Shepherd desiring personal relationship, rather than by the impersonal harshness of the law divorced from the Lawgiver. Jesus, the Lord of the Sabbath, offers rest (12:8).
12:1–31 See *WSC* 60.
12:1–13 See *WCF* 21.8; *WLC* 117.
12:2 unlawful. Nowhere does the Old Testament prohibit plucking grain on the Sabbath in order to eat—the disciples were not farmers doing some illicit harvesting. The Pharisees' objections were based on an oral tradition that failed to understand the true purpose of the law. **Sabbath.** Represents three aspects of a person's relationship to God: Exodus 20:11 ties it to the *creation* as a symbol of God's sovereignty over the whole created universe; Deuteronomy 5:15 grounds Sabbath observance in the remembrance of God's *redemption* of his people; and Hebrews 4:9 shows that for people on Earth the Sabbath represents the hope of eternal rest at the *consummation* of the kingdom. Jesus, as Lord of the Sabbath (v. 8), fulfills all aspects of its meaning.
12:3–6 what David did. Both the example of David and the example of the priests' work on the Sabbath (v. 5) demonstrated the Pharisaic misunderstanding. David in a sense "violated" a written law, and the priests every week "violated" the Sabbath ban on work, but there was no guilt. The law must always be interpreted in terms of the intention of the Lawgiver, and the purpose of the Sabbath is to foster the relationship of humankind to God, not to mandate arbitrary observances.
12:6 one greater than the temple. Literally, "something greater than the temple," but the NIV understands it correctly as referring to Christ himself. As the genuine needs of people are more important to God than ceremonial symbols, so the One in whom God fully dwells is greater than the symbolic dwelling place. Jesus is the true temple to whom the symbol pointed (Jn 1:14; 2:21). The disciples, who were in the presence of Jesus, had a far greater service than the priests who served in the physical temple.
12:7 I desire mercy. Attachment to ceremony and ignorance of substance were not new to Jesus' day; Hosea was familiar with the problem already in the eighth century B.C. (Hos 6:6). See *WLC* 99.
12:8 Lord of the Sabbath. The Son of Man has been given dominion over creation (cf. note on 8:20) and redemption (20:28). So too he has dominion over the Sabbath, the sign of God's sovereignty in creation and redemption. Also implicit is his lordship over the interpretation of the Scriptures. The claims Jesus made here are stupendous, and they doubtless shocked the Pharisees, furthering their resolve to kill him (v. 14).
12:9–14 This is another example of Christ's lordship of the Sabbath. Again, there is no actual Old Testament prohibition against healing on the Sabbath, and it is always lawful to do good. The problem was not that the Pharisees observed the Sabbath but that they observed it wrongly, turning what should have been a delight into a burden.
12:15–21 warning them not to tell. Isaiah 42:1–4, which relates the true nature and purpose of the Messiah (the suffering servant), is given as an explanation for why Jesus commanded people not to tell others who he was. He had come to proclaim and establish justice, but not by an ostentatious show of power and certainly not by developing a popular political or military movement. Since the Messiahship was so misunderstood among the people, Jesus had to dampen the misguided enthusiasm that inevitably sprang up.
12:20 See *WLC* 172.

and a smoldering wick he will not snuff out,
till he leads justice to victory.
21 In his name the nations will put their hope."[a] [k]

Jesus and Beelzebub

22 Then they brought him a demon-possessed man who was blind and mute, and Jesus
healed him, so that he could both talk and see.[l] 23 All the people were astonished and
said, "Could this be the Son of David?"[m]
24 But when the Pharisees heard this, they said, "It is only by Beelzebub,[b] [n] the prince
of demons, that this fellow drives out demons."[o]
25 Jesus knew their thoughts[p] and said to them, "Every kingdom divided against itself
will be ruined, and every city or household divided against itself will not stand. 26 If Satan[q] drives out Satan, he is divided against himself. How then can his kingdom stand?
27 And if I drive out demons by Beelzebub, by whom do your people[r] drive them out? So
then, they will be your judges. 28 But if I drive out demons by the Spirit of God, then the
kingdom of God has come upon you.
29 "Or again, how can anyone enter a strong man's house and carry off his possessions
unless he first ties up the strong man? Then he can rob his house.
30 "He who is not with me is against me, and he who does not gather with me scatters.[s] 31 And so I tell you, every sin and blasphemy will be forgiven men, but the blasphemy against the Spirit will not be forgiven.[t] 32 Anyone who speaks a word against the Son
of Man will be forgiven, but anyone who speaks against the Holy Spirit will not be forgiven, either in this age[u] or in the age to come.[v]
33 "Make a tree good and its fruit will be good, or make a tree bad and its fruit will be
bad, for a tree is recognized by its fruit.[w] 34 You brood of vipers,[x] how can you who are
evil say anything good? For out of the overflow of the heart the mouth speaks.[y] 35 The
good man brings good things out of the good stored up in him, and the evil man brings
evil things out of the evil stored up in him. 36 But I tell you that men will have to give account on the day of judgment for every careless word they have spoken. 37 For by your
words you will be acquitted, and by your words you will be condemned."

The Sign of Jonah

38 Then some of the Pharisees and teachers of the law said to him, "Teacher, we want
to see a miraculous sign from you."[z]
39 He answered, "A wicked and adulterous generation asks for a miraculous sign! But
none will be given it except the sign of the prophet Jonah.[a] 40 For as Jonah was three days
and three nights in the belly of a huge fish,[b] so the Son of Man[c] will be three days and
three nights in the heart of the earth.[d] 41 The men of Nineveh[e] will stand up at the judgment with this generation and condemn it; for they repented at the preaching of Jonah,[f]
and now one[c] greater than Jonah is here. 42 The Queen of the South will rise at the judgment with this generation and condemn it; for she came[g] from the ends of the earth to
listen to Solomon's wisdom, and now one greater than Solomon is here.
43 "When an evil[d] spirit comes out of a man, it goes through arid places seeking rest

12:21 [k]Isa 42:1-4
12:22 [l]Mt 4:24; 9:32-33
12:23 [m]Mt 9:27
12:24 [n]Mk 3:22 [o]Mt 9:34
12:25 [p]Mt 9:4
12:26 [q]Mt 4:10
12:27 [r]Ac 19:13
12:30 [s]Mk 9:40; Lk 11:23
12:31 [t]Mk 3:28,29; Lk 12:10
12:32 [u]Tit 2:12 [v]Mk 10:30; Lk 20:34,35; Eph 1:21; Heb 6:5
12:33 [w]Mt 7:16,17; Lk 6:43,44
12:34 [x]Mt 3:7; 23:33 [y]Mt 15:18; Lk 6:45
12:38 [z]Mt 16:1; Mk 8:11,12; Lk 11:16; Jn 2:18; 6:30; 1Co 1:22
12:39 [a]Mt 16:4; Lk 11:29
12:40 [b]Jnh 1:17 [c]Mt 8:20 [d]Mt 16:21
12:41 [e]Jnh 1:2 [f]Jnh 3:5
12:42 [g]1Ki 10:1; 2Ch 9:1

[a] *21* Isaiah 42:1–4 [b] *24* Greek *Beezeboul* or *Beelzeboul*; also in verse 27 [c] *41* Or *something*; also in verse 42 [d] *43* Greek *unclean*

12:24 Beelzebub. Compare note on 10:25.
12:25 See *WCF* 20.4.
12:28–29 ties up the strong man. Jesus' driving out of demons showed that he had "tie[d] up the strong man." From his victory over Satan in the wilderness, Jesus showed that Satan was helpless to prevent him from bringing in the kingdom. The "binding of Satan" was a symbol of the Messianic age in Jewish apocalyptic literature (*Assumption of Moses* 10:1), as we see also in Revelation 20:2. Jesus by the Holy Spirit had bound Satan and was continuing to move people, even Gentiles, from the realm of darkness into his kingdom.
12:30 He who is not with me. It is impossible to remain neutral toward Jesus.
12:31–32 blasphemy against the Spirit. See theological article "Blasphemy Against the Holy Spirit" at Mark 3. See *WLC* 151.
12:34 brood of vipers. The Pharisees referred to the work of the Spirit as the work of Satan. Because these religious leaders spoke evil like Satan the serpent (cf. Rev 12:9; 20:2), they were considered by Jesus to be Satan's offspring (cf. Jn 8:44).
12:36–37 Sometimes words are downgraded in importance in comparison with deeds, but Jesus here indicates that words, even carelessly spoken words, are eternally important. In the Bible, verbal sins such as lying, gossip and insulting are as severely condemned as adultery and murder (e.g., 5:22,37; 2Co 12:20; 1Ti 1:10; Jas 3:6; Rev 21:8). The "unforgivable sin" is verbal, at least in its expression. See *WCF* 15.4; 33.1; *BC* 37.
12:38 sign. That they asked for a sign was incredible in the face of the exorcism that Jesus had just performed. Jesus did not perform miracles on demand.
12:39 Jonah was as good as dead but was restored to life, foreshadowing the Son of Man's rising from the dead. Jesus' resurrection was the greatest sign of all that the kingdom had come. See theological article "The Resurrection of Jesus" at Luke 24.
12:40 three days and three nights. A figurative expression meaning "three days." Past days were counted inclusively, with the first and the last each being counted as full days even though only a portion of those days had actually been involved in the event. Thus there is no conflict with Luke 24:46 and 1 Corinthians 15:4, which indicate that Christ was raised on "the third day." See *WLC* 50.
12:43–45 An unoccupied house invites squatters. In other words, unless the Holy Spirit resides in the heart, unholy spirits may well

and does not find it. 44Then it says, ‘I will return to the house I left.’ When it arrives, it
finds the house unoccupied, swept clean and put in order. 45Then it goes and takes with
it seven other spirits more wicked than itself, and they go in and live there. And the final condition of that man is worse than the first.[h] That is how it will be with this wicked generation.”

12:45 [h]2Pe 2:20

Jesus’ Mother and Brothers

12:46 [i]Mt 1:18; 2:11,13, 14,20; Lk 1:43; 2:33,34,48,51; Jn 2:1,5; 19:25,26 [j]Mt 13:55; Jn 2:12; 7:3,5; Ac 1:14; 1Co 9:5; Gal 1:19

46While Jesus was still talking to the crowd, his mother[i] and brothers[j] stood outside,
wanting to speak to him. 47Someone told him, “Your mother and brothers are standing
outside, wanting to speak to you.”[a]
48He replied to him, “Who is my mother, and who are my brothers?” 49Pointing to his
disciples, he said, “Here are my mother and my brothers. 50For whoever does the will of
my Father in heaven[k] is my brother and sister and mother.”

12:50 [k]Jn 15:14

The Parable of the Sower

13:1 [l]ver 36; Mt 9:28

13:2 [m]Lk 5:3

13:8 [n]Ge 26:12

13:9 [o]Mt 11:15

13 That same day Jesus went out of the house[l] and sat by the lake. 2Such large
crowds gathered around him that he got into a boat[m] and sat in it, while all the
people stood on the shore. 3Then he told them many things in parables, saying: “A farmer went out to sow his seed. 4As he was scattering the seed, some fell along the path, and
the birds came and ate it up. 5Some fell on rocky places, where it did not have much soil.
It sprang up quickly, because the soil was shallow. 6But when the sun came up, the
plants were scorched, and they withered because they had no root. 7Other seed fell
among thorns, which grew up and choked the plants. 8Still other seed fell on good soil,
where it produced a crop—a hundred,[n] sixty or thirty times what was sown. 9He who has
ears, let him hear.”[o]
10The disciples came to him and asked, “Why do you speak to the people in parables?”
11He replied, “The knowledge of the secrets of the kingdom of heaven has been giv-
en to you,[p] but not to them. 12Whoever has will be given more, and he will have an abundance. Whoever does not have, even what he has will be taken from him.[q] 13This is why
I speak to them in parables:

13:11 [p]Mt 11:25; 16:17; 19:11; Jn 6:65; 1Co 2:10,14; Col 1:27; 1Jn 2:20, 27

13:12 [q]Mt 25:29; Lk 19:26

13:13 [r]Dt 29:4; Jer 5:21; Eze 12:2

“Though seeing, they do not see;
though hearing, they do not hear or understand.[r]

14In them is fulfilled the prophecy of Isaiah:

[a] *47* Some manuscripts do not have verse 47.

---

take up residence. Again, as in verse 30, one cannot remain neutral to Jesus and his sovereignty. Whether Jesus was referring to the Jewish nation or to individuals in general, his teaching applies. Unless one commits oneself to the King whose power he or she has experienced, this person’s final state will be worse than if the kingdom had never come. (Heb 6:4–6 is a relevant commentary.)

12:46 brothers. See note on Mark 3:31.

12:50 my brother and sister and mother. The true family of Jesus is determined by obedience to God rather than by birth.

■ **13:1–58** *Discourse: Kingdom Parables.* Chapter 13 is the third great discourse in Matthew (see “Introduction”). It describes the nature of the kingdom of heaven through the use of parables. The order that Matthew gives to the parables, the Scripture citations and the two parable interpretations may not at first be evident. One notable element in the sequence is the alternation of positive and negative material. Often the positive material is closely related to the positive material that follows, but not to the intervening negative section, and vice versa. So verses 3–9, 18–23, 31–35 and 44–46 go together, as do verses 10–17, 24–30, 36–43 and 47–50.The first three of these parables are linked by the term “seed,” which represents the message of the kingdom or its results (those who believe). See *CD* 3–4.9.

13:3 parables. “Parable” is the equivalent of the Hebrew *mashal* (cf. v. 35, citing Ps 78:2). Literally, it means a “comparison” (i.e., a figure, analogy or saying that instructs or imparts wisdom or understanding). Most of the parables of Jesus are illustrative, but they also contain an intrinsic ambiguity, such that only a right relationship to Jesus can provide a key to correct interpretation. It was only to the disciples that Jesus gave the interpretation of the parable of the sower (vv.18–23), which he had earlier told to the crowd (vv. 3–9). Likewise, the parable of the weeds (vv. 24–30) was explained only to the disciples (vv. 36–43; cf. v. 11; see also note on 13:34–35).

13:11–17 It would be difficult to escape the implication of divine election here. The ability to understand God’s message, let alone to respond to it, lies within God’s sovereignty. The “ears that hear” (Dt 29:4) are blessed by God.

13:11 to you, but not to them. Jesus’ reply was an answer to the question “Why do you speak to the people in parables?” (v. 10). The “secrets” of the kingdom are those truths that were alluded to in a veiled manner in the Old Testament but now made clear *to the disciples* with the actual coming of the kingdom. See *CD* 1.VIII.

13:12 To those who enjoy a relationship with Jesus, parables enhance understanding and foster deeper fellowship. But to those who do not experience such a relationship, parables only increase confusion and ignorance. Thus, the function of parables is both to enlighten and to obscure. This is one more way in which presumed “neutrality” is broken. No one can hear the preaching of the kingdom and remain unaffected; no one can hear the gospel and remain neutral toward Jesus. See *WCF* 5.6.

13:13–15 Though seeing. Mark states this even more strongly, indicating that Jesus spoke in parables *so that* they might never see (Mk 4:11–12). But what is explicit in Mark is here implicit: Jesus spoke in parables to fulfill Isaiah 6:9. Matthew continues with the following words: “Otherwise they might see with their eyes . . . and turn, and I would heal them” (v. 15). Jesus employed parables in order to prevent the salvation of the reprobate, those whom God has not chosen for salvation. As in the Isaiah context, God’s sovereign hardening of their hearts does not deny that such people are at the same time personally responsible for their hardness of heart—quite the contrary—but it does indicate that the willful hardening of hearts is also a function of God’s purpose. Note that in Isaiah 6:10, which Matthew quotes, the emphasis is not on the people hardening their own hearts, but on God’s servant hardening their hearts by his preaching: “*Make* the heart of this people calloused” (emphasis added).

" 'You will be ever hearing but never understanding;
you will be ever seeing but never perceiving.
15 For this people's heart has become calloused;
they hardly hear with their ears,
and they have closed their eyes.
Otherwise they might see with their eyes,
hear with their ears,
understand with their hearts
and turn, and I would heal them.'[a] [s]

16 But blessed are your eyes because they see, and your ears because they hear.[t] 17 For I
tell you the truth, many prophets and righteous men longed to see what you see[u] but did
not see it, and to hear what you hear but did not hear it.

18 "Listen then to what the parable of the sower means: 19 When anyone hears the message about the kingdom[v] and does not understand it, the evil one[w] comes and snatches
away what was sown in his heart. This is the seed sown along the path. 20 The one who
received the seed that fell on rocky places is the man who hears the word and at once receives it with joy. 21 But since he has no root, he lasts only a short time. When trouble or
persecution comes because of the word, he quickly falls away.[x] 22 The one who received
the seed that fell among the thorns is the man who hears the word, but the worries of this
life and the deceitfulness of wealth[y] choke it, making it unfruitful. 23 But the one who received the seed that fell on good soil is the man who hears the word and understands it.
He produces a crop, yielding a hundred, sixty or thirty times what was sown."[z]

The Parable of the Weeds

24 Jesus told them another parable: "The kingdom of heaven is like[a] a man who
sowed good seed in his field. 25 But while everyone was sleeping, his enemy came and
sowed weeds among the wheat, and went away. 26 When the wheat sprouted and formed
heads, then the weeds also appeared.

27 "The owner's servants came to him and said, 'Sir, didn't you sow good seed in your
field? Where then did the weeds come from?'

28 " 'An enemy did this,' he replied.

"The servants asked him, 'Do you want us to go and pull them up?'

29 " 'No,' he answered, 'because while you are pulling the weeds, you may root up the
wheat with them. 30 Let both grow together until the harvest. At that time I will tell the
harvesters: First collect the weeds and tie them in bundles to be burned; then gather
the wheat and bring it into my barn.' "[b]

The Parables of the Mustard Seed and the Yeast

31 He told them another parable: "The kingdom of heaven is like[c] a mustard seed,[d]
which a man took and planted in his field. 32 Though it is the smallest of all your seeds,
yet when it grows, it is the largest of garden plants and becomes a tree, so that the birds
of the air come and perch in its branches."[e]

33 He told them still another parable: "The kingdom of heaven is like[f] yeast that a
woman took and mixed into a large amount[b] of flour[g] until it worked all through the
dough."[h]

34 Jesus spoke all these things to the crowd in parables; he did not say anything to

13:15 [s]Isa 6:9,10; Jn 12:40; Ac 28:26, 27; Ro 11:8
13:16 [t]Mt 16:17
13:17 [u]Jn 8:56; Heb 11:13; 1Pe 1:10-12
13:19 [v]Mt 4:23 [w]Mt 5:37
13:21 [x]Mt 11:6
13:22 [y]Mt 19:23; 1Ti 6:9, 10,17
13:23 [z]ver 8
13:24 [a]ver 31,33,45,47; Mt 18:23; 20:1; 22:2; 25:1; Mk 4:26,30
13:30 [b]Mt 3:12
13:31 [c]ver 24 [d]Mt 17:20; Lk 17:6
13:32 [e]Ps 104:12; Eze 17:23; 31:6; Da 4:12
13:33 [f]ver 24 [g]Ge 18:6 [h]Gal 5:9

a *15* Isaiah 6:9,10 b *33* Greek *three satas* (probably about 1/2 bushel or 22 liters)

13:19–21 See *WCF* 10.4; 21.5; *WLC* 68; *CD* 5.VII.
13:22 Wealth appears to be, and indeed is, a blessing from God. But it is a dangerous blessing if it captivates the heart.
13:23 who hears the word and understands it. Only hearing and understanding the word (obedience being implied) results in fruit. Note that there are many kinds of hypocrites—people who think they receive the word but who fall away to avoid earthly woe or who lose their commitment in pursuit of earthly wealth. Likewise there are differing levels of fruit bearing. But there are only two kinds of ground: that which receives the word to bear fruit and that which does not. See *BC* 37.
13:24–30 Again, Jesus provided the interpretation to this parable (vv. 36–43). The field is the whole world, not just Israel or the church, and God withholds immediate judgment for the sake of the elect who are in the world. The righteous have lived in the midst of the unrighteous from the beginning. See *WCF* 25.5; *BC* 29.
13:31–32 like a mustard seed. The things of God may appear small in the world, but they produce great results. Certainly the kingdom of heaven at this point appeared insignificant in contrast to mighty Rome, but it was, and is, inherently much greater than Rome ever was. The mustard scrub may grow to a height of ten feet in Galilee. The picture of a tree with birds nesting in its branches recalls Ezekiel 17:23 and 31:6, passages in which the birds represent the Gentile nations taking refuge in the Messiah and enjoying the blessings of the covenant.
13:33 like yeast. Although yeast or leaven is often a symbol of evil (cf. 16:11), here the point is that the kingdom permeates the world. From both of these pictures, as well as from the previous parable of wheat and weeds, we see Jesus' concerns extending beyond Israel to the whole world. These pictures also provided encouragement to the disciples not to despise "the day of small things" (Zec 4:10).
13:34–35 Parables reveal as well as conceal. The citation in verse 35 is from Psalm 78:2, a psalm in which the "parables" or "hidden

Parables of Jesus

Parable	Matthew	Mark	Luke
Lamp under a bowl	5:14-15	4:21-22	8:16; 11:33
Wise and foolish builders	7:24-27		6:47-49
New cloth on an old coat	9:16	2:21	5:36
New wine in old wineskins	9:17	2:22	5:37-38
Sower and the soils	13:3-8,18-23	4:3-8,14-20	8:5-8,11-15
Weeds	13:24-30,36-43		
Mustard seed	13:31-32	4:30-32	13:18-19
Yeast	13:33		13:20-21
Hidden treasure	13:44		
Valuable pearl	13:45-46		
Net	13:47-50		
Owner of a house	13:52		
Lost sheep	18:12-14		15:4-7
Unmerciful servant	18:23-34		
Workers in the vineyard	20:1-16		
Two sons	21:28-32		
Tenants	21:33-44	12:1-11	20:9-18
Wedding banquet	22:2-14		
Fig tree	24:32-35	13:28-29	21:29-31
Faithful and wise servant	24:45-51		12:42-48
Ten virgins	25:1-13		
Talents (minas)	25:14-30		19:12-27
Sheep and goats	25:31-46		
Growing seed		4:26-29	
Watchful servants		13:35-37	12:35-40
Moneylender			7:41-43
Good Samaritan			10:30-37
Friend in need			11:5-8
Rich fool			12:16-21
Unfruitful fig tree			13:6-9
Lowest seat at the feast			14:7-14
Great banquet			14:16-24
Cost of discipleship			14:28-33
Lost coin			15:8-10
Lost (prodigal) son			15:11-32
Shrewd manager			16:1-8
Rich man and Lazarus			16:19-31
Master and his servant			17:7-10
Persistent widow			18:2-8
Pharisee and tax collector			18:10-14

them without using a parable.[i] 35So was fulfilled what was spoken through the
prophet:

> "I will open my mouth in parables,
> I will utter things hidden since the creation of the world."[a j]

The Parable of the Weeds Explained

36Then he left the crowd and went into the house. His disciples came to him and said,
"Explain to us the parable[k] of the weeds in the field."
37He answered, "The one who sowed the good seed is the Son of Man.[l] 38The field is
the world, and the good seed stands for the sons of the kingdom. The weeds are the sons
of the evil one,[m] 39and the enemy who sows them is the devil. The harvest[n] is the end
of the age,[o] and the harvesters are angels.[p]
40"As the weeds are pulled up and burned in the fire, so it will be at the end of the age.
41The Son of Man[q] will send out his angels,[r] and they will weed out of his kingdom everything that causes sin and all who do evil. 42They will throw them into the fiery furnace,
where there will be weeping and gnashing of teeth.[s] 43Then the righteous will shine like
the sun[t] in the kingdom of their Father. He who has ears, let him hear.[u]

The Parables of the Hidden Treasure and the Pearl

44"The kingdom of heaven is like[v] treasure hidden in a field. When a man found it,
he hid it again, and then in his joy went and sold all he had and bought that field.[w]
45"Again, the kingdom of heaven is like[x] a merchant looking for fine pearls. 46When
he found one of great value, he went away and sold everything he had and bought it.

The Parable of the Net

47"Once again, the kingdom of heaven is like[y] a net that was let down into the lake
and caught all kinds[z] of fish. 48When it was full, the fishermen pulled it up on the shore.
Then they sat down and collected the good fish in baskets, but threw the bad away.
49This is how it will be at the end of the age. The angels will come and separate the wicked from the righteous[a] 50and throw them into the fiery furnace, where there will be
weeping and gnashing of teeth.[b]
51"Have you understood all these things?" Jesus asked.
"Yes," they replied.
52He said to them, "Therefore every teacher of the law who has been instructed about
the kingdom of heaven is like the owner of a house who brings out of his storeroom new
treasures as well as old."

A Prophet Without Honor

53When Jesus had finished these parables,[c] he moved on from there. 54Coming to his
hometown, he began teaching the people in their synagogue,[d] and they were amazed.[e]
"Where did this man get this wisdom and these miraculous powers?" they asked. 55"Isn't
this the carpenter's son?[f] Isn't his mother's[g] name Mary, and aren't his brothers James,
Joseph, Simon and Judas? 56Aren't all his sisters with us? Where then did this man get
all these things?" 57And they took offense[h] at him.

13:34 [i]Mk 4:33; Jn 16:25
13:35 [j]Ps 78:2; Ro 16:25, 26; 1Co 2:7; Eph 3:9; Col 1:26
13:36 [k]Mt 15:15
13:37 [l]Mt 8:20
13:38 [m]Jn 8:44,45; 1Jn 3:10
13:39 [n]Joel 3:13 [o]Mt 24:3; 28:20 [p]Rev 14:15
13:41 [q]Mt 8:20 [r]Mt 24:31
13:42 [s]ver 50; Mt 8:12
13:43 [t]Da 12:3 [u]Mt 11:15
13:44 [v]ver 24 [w]Isa 55:1; Php 3:7,8
13:45 [x]ver 24
13:47 [y]ver 24 [z]Mt 22:10
13:49 [a]Mt 25:32
13:50 [b]Mt 8:12
13:53 [c]Mt 7:28
13:54 [d]Mt 4:23 [e]Mt 7:28
13:55 [f]Lk 3:23; Jn 6:42 [g]Mt 12:46
13:57 [h]Jn 6:61

a *35* Psalm 78:2

things" are a recital of the history of God's redemption of his people that reaches its climax in the giving of David as their shepherd. The redemptive *events* were not "hidden," but their *meaning* was not obvious. The psalmist made known their meaning, especially focusing on God's continued mercy in spite of Israel's rebelliousness. The history also pointed to something that was still hidden: the hope for another "David." As the psalmist revealed the meaning of God's redemptive acts by comparisons, so too did Jesus. Jesus fulfilled Psalm 78 in the same way he fulfilled Hosea 11:1 (cf. note on 2:15). Israel's history derives its ultimate meaning from Jesus' history.

13:37 Son of Man. See note on 8:20.

13:38–42 See *WCF* 8.4; *BC* 29.

13:41 weed out. The final judgment will not only be a separation of the ungodly from the godly, but also a separation of ungodliness from the godly. Note that the Son of Man will send *his* angels—Jesus unambiguously assumes the divine prerogative.

13:43 shine like the sun. An allusion to Daniel 12:3, a great promise of the future resurrection.

13:44–46 Jesus made known the hidden things of the kingdom by parables (v. 35), but most people did not see these things as precious, so they were unable to understand what had been made known. Like the man who finds treasure or the savvy pearl merchant, those who do perceive the value of the kingdom will sacrifice everything to obtain it (cf. Php 3:8).

13:47 See *WCF* 25.2; 25.5.

13:52 teacher of the law. Jesus frequently castigated teachers of the law (cf. 23:13ff), not because of their office of teaching the truth about God, but because of their hypocrisy. **has been instructed about the kingdom.** Is perhaps better rendered "has become a disciple of the kingdom of heaven." Since this statement immediately follows Jesus' asking the disciples, "Have you understood all these things?" (v. 51), the implication is that the disciples would become teachers and, like hospitable hosts, would share with others the "treasure" they had received. They had an understanding of both the old redemptive history that pointed to Christ and the new redemptive acts that marked the presence of the kingdom.

13:55 carpenter's son. The word translated "carpenter" is actually the more general term "builder." Joseph may have been a stonemason.

But Jesus said to them, "Only in his hometown and in his own house is a prophet without honor."[i]

58 And he did not do many miracles there because of their lack of faith.

John the Baptist Beheaded

14 At that time Herod[j] the tetrarch heard the reports about Jesus,[k] 2 and he said to his attendants, "This is John the Baptist;[l] he has risen from the dead! That is why miraculous powers are at work in him."

3 Now Herod had arrested John and bound him and put him in prison[m] because of Herodias, his brother Philip's wife,[n] 4 for John had been saying to him: "It is not lawful for you to have her."[o] 5 Herod wanted to kill John, but he was afraid of the people, because they considered him a prophet.[p]

6 On Herod's birthday the daughter of Herodias danced for them and pleased Herod so much 7 that he promised with an oath to give her whatever she asked. 8 Prompted by her mother, she said, "Give me here on a platter the head of John the Baptist." 9 The king was distressed, but because of his oaths and his dinner guests, he ordered that her request be granted 10 and had John beheaded[q] in the prison. 11 His head was brought in on a platter and given to the girl, who carried it to her mother. 12 John's disciples came and took his body and buried it.[r] Then they went and told Jesus.

Jesus Feeds the Five Thousand

13 When Jesus heard what had happened, he withdrew by boat privately to a solitary place. Hearing of this, the crowds followed him on foot from the towns. 14 When Jesus landed and saw a large crowd, he had compassion on them[s] and healed their sick.[t]

15 As evening approached, the disciples came to him and said, "This is a remote place, and it's already getting late. Send the crowds away, so they can go to the villages and buy themselves some food."

16 Jesus replied, "They do not need to go away. You give them something to eat."

17 "We have here only five loaves[u] of bread and two fish," they answered.

18 "Bring them here to me," he said. 19 And he directed the people to sit down on the grass. Taking the five loaves and the two fish and looking up to heaven, he gave thanks and broke the loaves.[v] Then he gave them to the disciples, and the disciples gave them to the people. 20 They all ate and were satisfied, and the disciples picked up twelve basketfuls of broken pieces that were left over. 21 The number of those who ate was about five thousand men, besides women and children.

Jesus Walks on the Water

22 Immediately Jesus made the disciples get into the boat and go on ahead of him to the other side, while he dismissed the crowd. 23 After he had dismissed them, he went up on a mountainside by himself to pray.[w] When evening came, he was there alone, 24 but the boat was already a considerable distance[a] from land, buffeted by the waves because the wind was against it.

25 During the fourth watch of the night Jesus went out to them, walking on the lake.

13:57 [i]Lk 4:24; Jn 4:44
14:1 [j]Mk 8:15; Lk 3:1, 19; 13:31; 23:7,8; Ac 4:27; 12:1 [k]Lk 9:7-9
14:2 [l]Mt 3:1
14:3 [m]Mt 4:12; 11:2 [n]Lk 3:19,20
14:4 [o]Lev 18:16; 20:21
14:5 [p]Mt 11:9
14:10 [q]Mt 17:12
14:12 [r]Ac 8:2
14:14 [s]Mt 9:36 [t]Mt 4:23
14:17 [u]Mt 16:9
14:19 [v]1Sa 9:13; Mt 26:26; Mk 8:6; Lk 24:30; Ac 2:42; 27:35; 1Ti 4:4
14:23 [w]Lk 3:21

[a] 24 Greek *many stadia*

13:58 did not do many miracles. Jesus did few miracles in Nazareth, not because he needed the faith of people to empower him, but because miracles apart from faith are counterproductive. Jesus did not perform miracles to generate belief but to direct and confirm it.

■ **14:1—18:35** *The Authority of the Kingdom.* Chapters 14–18 primarily concern authority in the kingdom. They divide into two sections: narrative (14:1—17:27) and discourse (18:1–35).

■ **14:1—17:27** *Narrative: Character and Authority of Jesus.* Chapters 14–17 display the astounding authority Jesus possessed as King by recording the miracles he performed and the reactions of those who came into contact with him.

14:3 The line of Herod the Great is confusing because of his several marriages and many children coupled with the frequent intermarriage of his descendants and their tendency to use the same names repeatedly. There is thus some uncertainty regarding the identity of the Philip to whom Herodias was formerly married. Probably this was not Philip the tetrarch of Iturea and Traconitis (Lk 3:1). Herodias was the daughter of Aristobulus, one of the sons whom Herod the Great killed, and was thus a granddaughter of Herod the Great. She married her half uncle Philip but then abandoned him for another half uncle, Herod Antipas, Philip's half brother. Marriage to a living brother's former wife is prohibited in Leviticus 18:16.

14:8 See *WLC* 130.

14:13–14 what had happened. Might refer to the death of John, making Jesus' withdrawal a response to the news of John's death. But John had actually been executed some time previously (vv. 3–12 are a digression), so Jesus' withdrawal was more likely a response to the rumors that he was a resurrected John (v. 2). Jesus sought to escape such false prominence, but his own compassion motivated his continued involvement with the people.

14:15–21 As God had miraculously provided manna for Israel in the wilderness, so Jesus provided bread for these people in a remote place. That the feeding was intended to recall the manna is indicated by the explicit mention of "twelve basketfuls" (v. 20) of leftovers—one for each tribe and disciple (cf. 19:28). There may also be a hint here of the Messianic banquet (cf. 8:11; Isa 25:6). Jesus challenged the disciples to provide for the crowd and then made them ministers of his own provision (vv. 16,19).

14:25 fourth watch. The watch from 3:00 A.M. to 6:00 A.M.

26When the disciples saw him walking on the lake, they were terrified. "It's a ghost,"[x]
they said, and cried out in fear.
27But Jesus immediately said to them: "Take courage![y] It is I. Don't be afraid."[z]
28"Lord, if it's you," Peter replied, "tell me to come to you on the water."
29"Come," he said.
Then Peter got down out of the boat, walked on the water and came toward Jesus.
30But when he saw the wind, he was afraid and, beginning to sink, cried out, "Lord,
save me!"
31Immediately Jesus reached out his hand and caught him. "You of little faith,"[a] he
said, "why did you doubt?"
32And when they climbed into the boat, the wind died down. 33Then those who were
in the boat worshiped him, saying, "Truly you are the Son of God."[b]
34When they had crossed over, they landed at Gennesaret. 35And when the men of
that place recognized Jesus, they sent word to all the surrounding country. People
brought all their sick to him 36and begged him to let the sick just touch the edge of his
cloak,[c] and all who touched him were healed.

Clean and Unclean

15 Then some Pharisees and teachers of the law came to Jesus from Jerusalem and
asked, 2"Why do your disciples break the tradition of the elders? They don't
wash their hands before they eat!"[d]
3Jesus replied, "And why do you break the command of God for the sake of your tradition? 4For God said, 'Honor your father and mother'[a][e] and 'Anyone who curses his father or mother must be put to death.'[b][f] 5But you say that if a man says to his father or
mother, 'Whatever help you might otherwise have received from me is a gift devoted to
God,' 6he is not to 'honor his father[c]' with it. Thus you nullify the word of God for the sake
of your tradition. 7You hypocrites! Isaiah was right when he prophesied about you:

8" 'These people honor me with their lips,
but their hearts are far from me.
9They worship me in vain;
their teachings are but rules taught by men.[g]'[d][h]"

10Jesus called the crowd to him and said, "Listen and understand. 11What goes into
a man's mouth does not make him 'unclean,'[i] but what comes out of his mouth, that is
what makes him 'unclean.' "[j]
12Then the disciples came to him and asked, "Do you know that the Pharisees were
offended when they heard this?"
13He replied, "Every plant that my heavenly Father has not planted[k] will be pulled up
by the roots. 14Leave them; they are blind guides.[e][l] If a blind man leads a blind man, both
will fall into a pit."[m]
15Peter said, "Explain the parable to us."[n]
16"Are you still so dull?"[o] Jesus asked them. 17"Don't you see that whatever enters the
mouth goes into the stomach and then out of the body? 18But the things that come out
of the mouth come from the heart,[p] and these make a man 'unclean.' 19For out of the
heart come evil thoughts, murder, adultery, sexual immorality, theft, false testimony,
slander.[q] 20These are what make a man 'unclean';[r] but eating with unwashed hands
does not make him 'unclean.' "

14:26 [x]Lk 24:37
14:27 [y]Mt 9:2; Ac 23:11 [z]Da 10:12; Mt 17:7; 28:10; Lk 1:13,30; 2:10; Ac 18:9; 23:11; Rev 1:17
14:31 [a]Mt 6:30
14:33 [b]Ps 2:7; Mt 4:3
14:36 [c]Mt 9:20
15:2 [d]Lk 11:38
15:4 [e]Ex 20:12; Dt 5:16; Eph 6:2 [f]Ex 21:17; Lev 20:9
15:9 [g]Col 2:20-22 [h]Isa 29:13; Mal 2:2
15:11 [i]Ac 10:14,15 [j]ver 18
15:13 [k]Isa 60:21; 61:3; Jn 15:2
15:14 [l]Mt 23:16,24; Ro 2:19 [m]Lk 6:39
15:15 [n]Mt 13:36
15:16 [o]Mt 16:9
15:18 [p]Mt 12:34; Lk 6:45; Jas 3:6
15:19 [q]Gal 5:19-21
15:20 [r]Ro 14:14

a *4* Exodus 20:12; Deut. 5:16 b *4* Exodus 21:17; Lev. 20:9 c *6* Some manuscripts *father or his mother*
d *9* Isaiah 29:13 e *14* Some manuscripts *guides of the blind*

14:30 Paying attention to life's danger and difficulty rather than focusing on Jesus can cause us to sink. But even then, when we call out to Jesus, he takes us by the hand. Peter was unconsciously living out Psalm 69:1–3.

14:33 Son of God. Recognizes the Messiahship of Jesus and his unique display of divine power. See note on 16:15–16.

15:2 tradition of the elders. The oral law, which was regarded among Pharisees as being of equal weight to the written law. In the second century it was codified and written down. It is called "Mishnah," now part of the Talmud. There is an entire tractate dealing with details of hand washing, such as how much water is to be used, how many rinsings are necessary, etc. See chart "Jewish Sects" at Matthew 23.

15:3–9 See *WCF* 16.1; 20.2; 21.1; 29.4; *WLC* 99,109,128; *WSC* 65; *BC* 7,32; *HC* 91.

15:3–6 Jesus made a sharp distinction between human traditions and the divine commands of Scripture. The Pharisees allowed their traditions to become as or perhaps more important to them than God's word. We should never let our most cherished traditional understandings supplant or obscure the Bible itself, or to elevate our customs to the level of law.

15:7 Isaiah . . . prophesied about you. Isaiah addressed not only the hypocritical externalism of his own day but condemned all such "lip service."

15:11 what comes out of his mouth. Again we see the importance of words in a person's moral life. What one says is a reflection or product of what is inside (cf. note on 12:36–37).

15:19 See *WCF* 6.4; *WLC* 25,139; *WSC* 18,72.

The Faith of the Canaanite Woman

15:21 [s]Mt 11:21 — 21 Leaving that place, Jesus withdrew to the region of Tyre and Sidon.[s] 22 A Canaanite
woman from that vicinity came to him, crying out, "Lord, Son of David,[t] have mercy on
15:22 [t]Mt 9:27 [u]Mt 4:24 — me! My daughter is suffering terribly from demon-possession."[u]
23 Jesus did not answer a word. So his disciples came to him and urged him, "Send her
15:24 [v]Mt 10:6,23; Ro 15:8 — away, for she keeps crying out after us."
24 He answered, "I was sent only to the lost sheep of Israel."[v]
25 The woman came and knelt before him.[w] "Lord, help me!" she said.
15:25 [w]Mt 8:2 — 26 He replied, "It is not right to take the children's bread and toss it to their dogs."
27 "Yes, Lord," she said, "but even the dogs eat the crumbs that fall from their masters' table."
15:28 [x]Mt 9:22 — 28 Then Jesus answered, "Woman, you have great faith![x] Your request is granted."
And her daughter was healed from that very hour.

Jesus Feeds the Four Thousand

29 Jesus left there and went along the Sea of Galilee. Then he went up on a mountainside and sat down. 30 Great crowds came to him, bringing the lame, the blind, the crip-
15:30 [y]Mt 4:23 — pled, the mute and many others, and laid them at his feet; and he healed them.[y] 31 The
15:31 [z]Mt 9:8 — people were amazed when they saw the mute speaking, the crippled made well, the lame
walking and the blind seeing. And they praised the God of Israel.[z]
15:32 [a]Mt 9:36 — 32 Jesus called his disciples to him and said, "I have compassion for these people;[a] they
have already been with me three days and have nothing to eat. I do not want to send
them away hungry, or they may collapse on the way."
33 His disciples answered, "Where could we get enough bread in this remote place to
feed such a crowd?"
34 "How many loaves do you have?" Jesus asked.
"Seven," they replied, "and a few small fish."
35 He told the crowd to sit down on the ground. 36 Then he took the seven loaves and
15:36 [b]Mt 14:19 — the fish, and when he had given thanks, he broke them[b] and gave them to the disciples,
15:37 [c]Mt 16:10 — and they in turn to the people. 37 They all ate and were satisfied. Afterward the disciples
picked up seven basketfuls of broken pieces that were left over.[c] 38 The number of those
who ate was four thousand, besides women and children. 39 After Jesus had sent the
crowd away, he got into the boat and went to the vicinity of Magadan.

The Demand for a Sign

16:1 [d]Ac 4:1 [e]Mt 12:38 — **16** The Pharisees and Sadducees[d] came to Jesus and tested him by asking him to
show them a sign from heaven.[e]
2 He replied,[a] "When evening comes, you say, 'It will be fair weather, for the sky is
red,' 3 and in the morning, 'Today it will be stormy, for the sky is red and overcast.' You
know how to interpret the appearance of the sky, but you cannot interpret the signs of
16:3 [f]Lk 12:54-56 — the times.[f] 4 A wicked and adulterous generation looks for a miraculous sign, but none
16:4 [g]Mt 12:39 — will be given it except the sign of Jonah."[g] Jesus then left them and went away.

The Yeast of the Pharisees and Sadducees

5 When they went across the lake, the disciples forgot to take bread. 6 "Be careful," Jesus
16:6 [h]Lk 12:1 — said to them. "Be on your guard against the yeast of the Pharisees and Sadducees."[h]
7 They discussed this among themselves and said, "It is because we didn't bring any
bread."

[a] *2* Some early manuscripts do not have the rest of verse 2 and all of verse 3.

15:21–28 The faith of the Canaanite woman stands in stark contrast to the response of the Pharisees.
15:24 only to the lost sheep of Israel. Prior to the resurrection, the "dividing wall" (Eph 2:14) between Jew and Gentile still stood, and at this point Jesus' mission was to "Israel" as defined according to Old Testament ordinances. Jesus had earlier responded to Gentiles who were in Jewish territory, but to respond to Gentiles in Gentile territory could have resulted in a prolonged distraction from his primary purpose. Jesus replied to the woman's request only after clear evidence that she had no thought of any *claim* to the covenant mercies; rather, she hoped to benefit from the overflow of the blessings promised to Israel. See *BC* 16.
15:29–39 Mark 7:31 indicates that this took place in "the region of the Decapolis," so the crowd was probably Gentile or at least a mix of Jews and Gentiles. Following as it does the story of the Canaanite woman's faith, this may represent an outworking of the spilling over of bread crumbs to Gentiles.
15:37 seven basketfuls. In the feeding of 5,000 Jews, there were 12 baskets of leftovers, representing abundance to the 12 tribes. Here there are seven basketfuls, perhaps representing abundance to the fullness of God's people, including Gentiles.
16:1–3 sign from heaven. Jesus referred the Pharisees to a literal sign from heaven: the sky itself. His analogy to their interpretation of the weather shows that the problem was not lack of evidences, but an unwillingness to accept their significance. Jesus had already provided plenty of signs. Evidence, whether miraculous or not, will be misinterpreted or distorted by the unbelieving mind. Jesus threw no pearls before pigs (see 7:6).
16:4 sign of Jonah. Compare note on 12:39.

8 Aware of their discussion, Jesus asked, "You of little faith,[i] why are you talking
among yourselves about having no bread? 9 Do you still not understand? Don't you remember the five loaves for the five thousand, and how many basketfuls you gathered?[j]
10 Or the seven loaves for the four thousand, and how many basketfuls you gathered?[k]
11 How is it you don't understand that I was not talking to you about bread? But be on
your guard against the yeast of the Pharisees and Sadducees." 12 Then they understood
that he was not telling them to guard against the yeast used in bread, but against the
teaching of the Pharisees and Sadducees.[l]

Peter's Confession of Christ

13 When Jesus came to the region of Caesarea Philippi, he asked his disciples, "Who
do people say the Son of Man is?"
14 They replied, "Some say John the Baptist;[m] others say Elijah; and still others, Jeremiah or one of the prophets."[n]
15 "But what about you?" he asked. "Who do you say I am?"
16 Simon Peter answered, "You are the Christ,[a] the Son of the living God."[o]
17 Jesus replied, "Blessed are you, Simon son of Jonah, for this was not revealed to you
by man,[p] but by my Father in heaven. 18 And I tell you that you are Peter,[b][q] and on this
rock I will build my church,[r] and the gates of Hades[c] will not overcome it.[d] 19 I will give
you the keys[s] of the kingdom of heaven; whatever you bind on earth will be[e] bound in
heaven, and whatever you loose on earth will be[e] loosed in heaven."[t] 20 Then he warned
his disciples not to tell anyone[u] that he was the Christ.

Jesus Predicts His Death

21 From that time on Jesus began to explain to his disciples that he must go to Jeru-

16:8 [i]Mt 6:30
16:9 [j]Mt 14:17-21
16:10 [k]Mt 15:34-38
16:12 [l]Ac 4:1
16:14 [m]Mt 3:1; 14:2 [n]Mk 6:15; Jn 1:21
16:16 [o]Mt 4:3; Ps 42:2; Jn 11:27; Ac 14:15; 2Co 6:16; 1Th 1:9; 1Ti 3:15; Heb 10:31; 12:22
16:17 [p]1Co 15:50; Gal 1:16; Eph 6:12; Heb 2:14
16:18 [q]Jn 1:42 [r]Eph 2:20
16:19 [s]Isa 22:22; Rev 3:7 [t]Mt 18:18; Jn 20:23
16:20 [u]Mk 8:30

[a] *16 Or Messiah; also in verse 20* [b] *18 Peter means rock.* [c] *18 Or hell* [d] *18 Or not prove stronger than it* [e] *19 Or have been*

16:11 not . . . about bread. Jesus frequently spoke parabolically but was misunderstood as speaking literally. His reference to his feeding of the thousands shows that he expected the disciples to grasp the symbolism of the miracles.
16:12 teaching. Like leaven in dough, false teaching can quickly permeate the church and vitiate its holiness. Jesus did not regard doctrine as unimportant.
16:13 Caesarea Philippi. Philip's Caesarea. It was a small town at the foot of Mount Hermon, about 25 miles north of Galilee and the northernmost point of Jesus' itinerary as recorded in the Gospels.
16:15–17 See *HC* 21.
16:15–16 Who do you say I am? The "you" here is plural. Peter answered on behalf of the Twelve. His declaration that Jesus is "the Christ" (v. 16) reflects his realization that Jesus was the expected eschatological King prophesied in the Old Testament (see note on "Christ" at 1:1). **Son of the living God.** The title "Son of God" (in this instance "Son of the living God") occurs in Matthew (1) in recognition by Satan or his demons (4:3; 8:29); (2) in confession by the disciples (14:33; 16:16); (3) in taunt or question by unbelieving Jews (26:63; 27:40,43); and (4) on the lips of the Gentile centurion (27:54). It is conjoined with "the Christ" in verse 16 and 26:63. God himself also testified that Jesus is his Son (3:17; 17:5). The concept is not that of a half-deity or a divine man, such as is found in pagan literature, but comes rather from the Old Testament background of the anointed king as God's son (cf. 2Sa 7:14 and Ps 2:7, both of which were rightly regarded by Jews as Messianic passages). See theological article "Jesus Christ, God and Man" at John 1. Israel as a whole was God's son in the Old Testament (e.g., Ex 4:22), and Jesus fulfilled this status of Israel (cf. note on 2:15). Yet, as applied to Jesus, the title reflects his own knowledge of the Father as the unique Son (11:27; cf. 21:38). Jesus was acknowledged by the Father as his beloved Son (3:17) in the sense of the only Son (Ge 22:2). While Peter's understanding was not yet as clear as it would later become (1Pe 3:15), it was given by the Father and went beyond what Peter could have concluded on his own (v. 17).
16:17 not revealed to you by man. The recognition of who Jesus is must come from God. See *HC* 122.
16:18 rock. The Greek word is *petra,* so there is a play on words with the name "Peter," but the exact meaning of this wordplay is disputed. The most likely options are that (1) Peter's *confession* (that Jesus is the Christ) is the "rock" upon which the church is built; (2) Jesus is the "rock," as Peter himself testifies in 1 Peter 2:5–8; (3) Peter, as the confessing and representative apostle, is foundational to the church (cf. Eph 2:20); or (4) Peter in his confession represents the type of material with which and on which the true church will be built. The first and second options are often defended by pointing out that whereas Peter's name is *petros,* the foundational rock is *petra.* But the Aramaic would have made no such distinction—in both cases it would have been *kefa'*—and even the Greek made little distinction between the two terms. The second option is also problematic because in this passage Jesus is not the foundation but the *builder* of the church. Were it not for the abuse of this passage by the Roman Catholic Church, it is unlikely that any doubt would ever have arisen that the reference here is to Peter. But the foundational rock is not Peter apart from his confession, but Peter as an apostle whose confession of Christ was revealed to him by the Father. When Peter later insisted that Jesus must not go to the cross, he was called not a "rock" of foundation, but a "stumbling block" (v. 23). Neither may Peter be separated from the Eleven. The authority given to him was also given to the other apostles, and that authority provides the foundation for the governing of Christ's church (18:18). As Peter himself declared (1Pe 2:5–8), all believers have become living stones by virtue of their association with Christ, but the apostles, represented here by the spokesman for the Twelve, are the foundation (cf. Eph 2:20–21; Rev 21:14). Of course, even if the foundation rock is interpreted as the person of Peter, there is still nothing to suggest that Peter would have "successors." **gates of Hades.** In both the Old Testament (e.g., Job 17:16; Ps 9:13) and Jewish intertestamental literature, "the gates of death" and "the gates of Hades" are used to represent death, the power of Satan. Jesus claimed that death itself will not overcome his people. See *WCF* 25.5; *BC* 27; *HC* 54,123.
16:19 keys of the kingdom. This metaphor specifies the manner in which the apostles are foundational to the church: They were given binding and loosing powers, or "keys," which locked and unlocked doors. The apostles opened the kingdom to those who shared Peter's confession and excluded those who did not receive their testimony to Christ (10:14–15). Through them Jesus revealed his own word of kingdom authority. The apostolic foundation of the church was laid in the New Testament (Eph 2:20; 3:5). The keys of Christ's authority in the church are the application of this apostolic authority (18:18). See *WCF* 23.3; 30.2; *WLC* 108; *HC* 83,84.
16:20 not to tell anyone. Compare 8:4. The popular conceptions of the Messiah were far from those that recognized his suffering ministry. To allow his disciples to proclaim his Messiahship openly would have been to instigate a political movement that would have hampered his real mission (as almost happened in John 6:15).
16:21 From that time on. This marks a new phase of Jesus' ministry. The same phrase occurs at 4:17. Here Matthew shifts from the Galilean public preaching of the kingdom to Jesus' careful instruction to his disciples regarding his death and resurrection,

salem and suffer many things[v] at the hands of the elders, chief priests and teachers of
the law, and that he must be killed and on the third day[w] be raised to life.[x]
22 Peter took him aside and began to rebuke him. "Never, Lord!" he said. "This shall
never happen to you!"
23 Jesus turned and said to Peter, "Get behind me, Satan![y] You are a stumbling block
to me; you do not have in mind the things of God, but the things of men."
24 Then Jesus said to his disciples, "If anyone would come after me, he must deny himself and take up his cross and follow me.[z] 25 For whoever wants to save his life[a] will lose
it, but whoever loses his life for me will find it.[a] 26 What good will it be for a man if he
gains the whole world, yet forfeits his soul? Or what can a man give in exchange for his
soul? 27 For the Son of Man[b] is going to come[c] in his Father's glory with his angels, and
then he will reward each person according to what he has done.[d] 28 I tell you the truth,
some who are standing here will not taste death before they see the Son of Man coming
in his kingdom."

The Transfiguration

17 After six days Jesus took with him Peter, James and John the brother of James,
and led them up a high mountain by themselves. 2 There he was transfigured before them. His face shone like the sun, and his clothes became as white as the light. 3 Just
then there appeared before them Moses and Elijah, talking with Jesus.
4 Peter said to Jesus, "Lord, it is good for us to be here. If you wish, I will put up three
shelters—one for you, one for Moses and one for Elijah."
5 While he was still speaking, a bright cloud enveloped them, and a voice from the
cloud said, "This is my Son, whom I love; with him I am well pleased.[e] Listen to him!"[f]
6 When the disciples heard this, they fell facedown to the ground, terrified. 7 But
Jesus came and touched them. "Get up," he said. "Don't be afraid."[g] 8 When they looked
up, they saw no one except Jesus.
9 As they were coming down the mountain, Jesus instructed them, "Don't tell anyone[h]
what you have seen, until the Son of Man[i] has been raised from the dead."[j]
10 The disciples asked him, "Why then do the teachers of the law say that Elijah must
come first?"
11 Jesus replied, "To be sure, Elijah comes and will restore all things.[k] 12 But I tell you,
Elijah has already come,[l] and they did not recognize him, but have done to him everything they wished.[m] In the same way the Son of Man is going to suffer[n] at their hands."
13 Then the disciples understood that he was talking to them about John the Baptist.

The Healing of a Boy With a Demon

14 When they came to the crowd, a man approached Jesus and knelt before him.
15 "Lord, have mercy on my son," he said. "He has seizures[o] and is suffering greatly. He
often falls into the fire or into the water. 16 I brought him to your disciples, but they could
not heal him."
17 "O unbelieving and perverse generation," Jesus replied, "how long shall I stay with

16:21 [v]Mk 10:34; Lk 17:25 [w]Jn 2:19 [x]Mt 17:22,23; 27:63; Mk 9:31; Lk 9:22; 18:31-33; 24:6,7
16:23 [y]Mt 4:10
16:24 [z]Mt 10:38; Lk 14:27
16:25 [a]Jn 12:25
16:27 [b]Mt 8:20 [c]Ac 1:11 [d]Job 34:11; Ps 62:12; Jer 17:10; Ro 2:6; 2Co 5:10; Rev 22:12
17:5 [e]Mt 3:17; 2Pe 1:17 [f]Ac 3:22,23
17:7 [g]Mt 14:27
17:9 [h]Mk 8:30 [i]Mt 8:20 [j]Mt 16:21
17:11 [k]Mal 4:6; Lk 1:16,17
17:12 [l]Mt 11:14 [m]Mt 14:3,10 [n]Mt 16:21
17:15 [o]Mt 4:24

a 25 The Greek word means either *life* or *soul*; also in verse 26.

---

the nature of his Messiahship and their discipleship. To this point Jesus had given only hints regarding his redemptive suffering and death. Now he began to "explain," or "show," these things to his disciples, perhaps by referring to the Old Testament Scriptures (cf. Lk 24:44–47).
16:24–26 See *HC* 124.
16:24–25 Compare note on 10:38–39. Jesus adds the mandate to "deny" oneself. To be disciples we must completely abandon our natural desire to seek the advancement of ourselves, our comfort, our esteem, our power.
16:28 will not taste death before. Although this has been taken as a reference to the transfiguration, the phrase implies a period of at least more than a week. Another option is the destruction of Jerusalem (see note on 10:23). But unlike 10:23, the context here is not specifically related to the judgment of Israel, but to Jesus' imminent death and resurrection. The most compelling view is that the "coming" mentioned here relates to the entire complex of events involved in the Son of Man's receiving of dominion, especially his resurrection, ascension, sending of the Spirit and judgment against Jerusalem. All of these events occurred while some of the disciples were still living. The transfiguration could also be included in this complex of events.
17:1 After six days. Such an exact time indicator is rare in the Gospels; it must have been included to make clear the connection between the confession at Caesarea Philippi and the transfiguration. Since the disciples had begun to recognize who Jesus is, he was ready to head toward the climactic culmination of events in Jerusalem. The transfiguration was part of Jesus' preparation for that crisis.
17:3 Moses and Elijah. The Law and the Prophets testify to Jesus. Moses, the lawgiver, and Elijah, the greatest prophet of the monarchical period, are here privileged to talk with Jesus. According to Luke 9:31, they discussed Jesus' imminent, redemptive death.
17:5–6 This is my Son. These words from heaven showed the disciples just how foolish Peter's suggestion (v. 4) was, and the disciples began to realize just who it was they had been traveling with. **my Son, whom I love.** This designation, earlier given at Jesus' baptism (3:17), means "unique, one and only son"; it is synonymous with the familiar "only begotten." **Listen to him!** The Word of God spoken through Moses and the prophets pointed to Jesus. Now the final word was being spoken by God's Son. See *BC* 7,10.
17:9 See note on 16:20.
17:11–12 Elijah comes. Compare note on John 1:21. The scribes were right, but they failed to recognize either Elijah or the Messiah when they did come (v. 12). See *WCF* 3.1; 9.1.
17:17 Compare Deuteronomy 32:20. Jesus, like Moses, came down from the mount of glory to encounter unbelief.

you? How long shall I put up with you? Bring the boy here to me." 18 Jesus rebuked the
demon, and it came out of the boy, and he was healed from that moment.
19 Then the disciples came to Jesus in private and asked, "Why couldn't we drive it
out?"
20 He replied, "Because you have so little faith. I tell you the truth, if you have faith[p]
as small as a mustard seed,[q] you can say to this mountain, 'Move from here to there' and
it will move.[r] Nothing will be impossible for you.[a]"
22 When they came together in Galilee, he said to them, "The Son of Man[s] is going to
be betrayed into the hands of men. 23 They will kill him,[t] and on the third day[u] he will
be raised to life."[v] And the disciples were filled with grief.

The Temple Tax

24 After Jesus and his disciples arrived in Capernaum, the collectors of the two-drach-
ma tax[w] came to Peter and asked, "Doesn't your teacher pay the temple tax[b]?"
25 "Yes, he does," he replied.
When Peter came into the house, Jesus was the first to speak. "What do you think,
Simon?" he asked. "From whom do the kings of the earth collect duty and taxes[x]—from
their own sons or from others?"
26 "From others," Peter answered.
"Then the sons are exempt," Jesus said to him. 27 "But so that we may not offend[y]
them, go to the lake and throw out your line. Take the first fish you catch; open its mouth
and you will find a four-drachma coin. Take it and give it to them for my tax and yours."

The Greatest in the Kingdom of Heaven

18 At that time the disciples came to Jesus and asked, "Who is the greatest in the
kingdom of heaven?"
2 He called a little child and had him stand among them. 3 And he said: "I tell you the
truth, unless you change and become like little children,[z] you will never enter the kingdom of heaven.[a] 4 Therefore, whoever humbles himself like this child is the greatest in
the kingdom of heaven.[b]
5 "And whoever welcomes a little child like this in my name welcomes me.[c] 6 But if anyone causes one of these little ones who believe in me to sin,[d] it would be better for him
to have a large millstone hung around his neck and to be drowned in the depths of the
sea.[e]
7 "Woe to the world because of the things that cause people to sin! Such things must
come, but woe to the man through whom they come![f] 8 If your hand or your foot causes
you to sin,[g] cut it off and throw it away. It is better for you to enter life maimed or crippled than to have two hands or two feet and be thrown into eternal fire. 9 And if your eye
causes you to sin,[h] gouge it out and throw it away. It is better for you to enter life with
one eye than to have two eyes and be thrown into the fire of hell.[i]

17:20 [p]Mt 21:21 [q]Mt 13:31; Mk 11:23; Lk 17:6 [r]1Co 13:2
17:22 [s]Mt 8:20
17:23 [t]Ac 2:23; 3:13 [u]Mt 16:21 [v]Mt 16:21
17:24 [w]Ex 30:13
17:25 [x]Mt 22:17-21; Ro 13:7
17:27 [y]Jn 6:61
18:3 [z]Mt 19:14; 1Pe 2:2 [a]Mt 3:2
18:4 [b]Mk 9:35
18:5 [c]Mt 10:40
18:6 [d]Mt 5:29 [e]Mk 9:42; Lk 17:2
18:7 [f]Lk 17:1
18:8 [g]Mt 5:29; Mk 9:43, 45
18:9 [h]Mt 5:29 [i]Mt 5:22

a *20* Some manuscripts *you.* *21 But this kind does not go out except by prayer and fasting.* b *24* Greek *the two drachmas*

17:20 so little faith. The disciples' faith was not little because they lacked confidence or did not expect success—they were apparently surprised by their failure—but because their expectation was not properly grounded in relationship to God. A tiny bit (like a grain of mustard seed) of *true* faith—faith rooted in submissiveness to God—is effectual. Mark 9:29 makes this clear by speaking of prayer as the key. (See theological article "Prayer" at Mt 6.)

17:22–23 This is the second prediction of Jesus' passion and resurrection in Matthew (cf. 16:21–24). The eschatological figure of the "Son of Man" (cf. note on 8:20) is here identified with the suffering servant of the Lord introduced in Isaiah 53. To our knowledge, no one before Jesus had ever identified the Old Testament Messiah, the Old Testament Son of Man and the Old Testament suffering servant as the same Redeemer-King. The disciples were so overwhelmed by their difficulty in accepting the suffering of the Messiah that they apparently failed to even hear the promise of the resurrection. At least they did not really believe it.

17:24–27 The temple tax of two drachmas or half a shekel was instituted by God in Exodus 30:13. Jesus' point here is not that we should pay taxes to the civil authority (although that is true; cf. 22:21), but that Christ and the temple he is building (his church) are greater than the physical temple, which was only a type. Yet Jesus was willing to conform to previous requirements in order to avoid giving offense. Paul's advice (Ro 14:13–21) and practice (Ac 16:3; 21:26) were similar. See *BC* 36.

■ **18:1–35** *Discourse: Character and Authority of the Church.* Chapter 18 is the fourth of the five great discourses in Matthew (see "Introduction"). The material in this chapter has to do largely with the way the people of Christ's kingdom should relate to one another—in humility and with forgiveness and mutual concern.

18:3 like little children. Not because children are supposed to be innocent, but because they are dependent and make no pretense of being otherwise.

18:5–7 whoever welcomes. Since Jesus' disciples were to become "like little children" (v. 3), the term has come to represent the disciples. A response to Jesus' disciples is a response to Jesus himself, and causing a disciple to sin is a horrible thing (v. 6). **Such things must come.** Note the ultimacy of divine sovereignty. **woe to the man through whom they come.** Yet note the reality of human responsibility. It does no good to stress one by denying the other. See *WLC* 151.

18:8–9 Compare note on 5:29.

The Parable of the Lost Sheep

10 “See that you do not look down on one of these little ones. For I tell you that their
angels[j] in heaven always see the face of my Father in heaven.[a]
12 “What do you think? If a man owns a hundred sheep, and one of them wanders
away, will he not leave the ninety-nine on the hills and go to look for the one that wandered off? 13 And if he finds it, I tell you the truth, he is happier about that one sheep than
about the ninety-nine that did not wander off. 14 In the same way your Father in heaven
is not willing that any of these little ones should be lost.

A Brother Who Sins Against You

15 “If your brother sins against you,[b] go and show him his fault,[k] just between the two
of you. If he listens to you, you have won your brother over. 16 But if he will not listen, take
one or two others along, so that ‘every matter may be established by the testimony of two
or three witnesses.’[c][l] 17 If he refuses to listen to them, tell it to the church;[m] and if he refuses to listen even to the church, treat him as you would a pagan or a tax collector.[n]
18 “I tell you the truth, whatever you bind on earth will be[d] bound in heaven, and
whatever you loose on earth will be[d] loosed in heaven.[o]
19 “Again, I tell you that if two of you on earth agree about anything you ask for, it will
be done for you[p] by my Father in heaven. 20 For where two or three come together in my
name, there am I with them.”

The Parable of the Unmerciful Servant

21 Then Peter came to Jesus and asked, “Lord, how many times shall I forgive my
brother when he sins against me?[q] Up to seven times?”[r]
22 Jesus answered, “I tell you, not seven times, but seventy-seven times.[e][s]
23 “Therefore, the kingdom of heaven is like[t] a king who wanted to settle accounts[u]
with his servants. 24 As he began the settlement, a man who owed him ten thousand talents[f] was brought to him. 25 Since he was not able to pay,[v] the master ordered that he
and his wife and his children and all that he had be sold[w] to repay the debt.
26 “The servant fell on his knees before him.[x] ‘Be patient with me,’ he begged, ‘and I
will pay back everything.’ 27 The servant’s master took pity on him, canceled the debt and
let him go.
28 “But when that servant went out, he found one of his fellow servants who owed him
a hundred denarii.[g] He grabbed him and began to choke him. ‘Pay back what you owe
me!’ he demanded.
29 “His fellow servant fell to his knees and begged him, ‘Be patient with me, and I will
pay you back.’
30 “But he refused. Instead, he went off and had the man thrown into prison until he
could pay the debt. 31 When the other servants saw what had happened, they were
greatly distressed and went and told their master everything that had happened.
32 “Then the master called the servant in. ‘You wicked servant,’ he said, ‘I canceled

18:10 [j]Ge 48:16; Ps 34:7; Ac 12:11,15; Heb 1:14
18:15 [k]Lev 19:17; Lk 17:3; Gal 6:1; Jas 5:19,20
18:16 [l]Nu 35:30; Dt 17:6; 19:15; Jn 8:17; 2Co 13:1; 1Ti 5:19; Heb 10:28
18:17 [m]1Co 6:1-6 [n]Ro 16:17; 2Th 3:6,14
18:18 [o]Mt 16:19; Jn 20:23
18:19 [p]Mt 7:7
18:21 [q]Mt 6:14 [r]Lk 17:4
18:22 [s]Ge 4:24
18:23 [t]Mt 13:24 [u]Mt 25:19
18:25 [v]Lk 7:42 [w]Lev 25:39; 2Ki 4:1; Ne 5:5,8
18:26 [x]Mt 8:2

[a] *10* Some manuscripts *heaven. 11 The Son of Man came to save what was lost.* [b] *15* Some manuscripts do not have *against you.* [c] *16* Deut. 19:15 [d] *18* Or *have been* [e] *22* Or *seventy times seven* [f] *24* That is, millions of dollars [g] *28* That is, a few dollars

18:10 their angels. Scripture teaches us that angels guard and minister to God’s people (Pss 34:7; 91:11; Heb 1:14; Rev 1:20). See *WLC* 192.

18:12–14 The concern for the one is not at the expense of the 99, but indicates God’s commitment to each disciple and his special concern for one who is straying or in danger. God elects, seeks out and preserves not only his church as a whole, but also each individual within that body. Eze 34:11–16 probably lies behind this parable. Compare also 9:36.

18:15–20 See *WCF* 23.3; 30.2; 30.4; 31.3; *WLC* 45,151; *BC* 32; *HC* 85.

18:15–17 If your brother sins. The three-stage procedure in verses 15–17 for dealing with a brother caught up in sin lies at the heart of all church discipline, whether or not the words “against you” are original (see NIV text note). The goal is to produce repentance while keeping public awareness of the sin to a minimum. At no point is the matter to be broadcast to the world at large. **church.** May appear anachronistic here, but only if the concept of “church” is divorced from its moorings in the Old Testament. The “assembly” (*qahal*) of the people of God was translated in the Greek Old Testament (the Septuagint) as *ekklesia,* or “church.” The fact that Jesus applied Deuteronomy 19:15 demonstrates that he regards *his* church as of a piece with Old Testament Israel. **treat him as you would a pagan or a tax collector.** Means cutting such a person off from the worshiping community and suspending his or her full social relations with other Christians outside the context of worship. Paul applied this discipline in 1 Corinthians 5 and 1 Timothy 1:20. See *WCF* 20.4; *WLC* 108.

18:18 Compare note on 16:19.

18:19–20 if two of you . . . agree. Verses 19–20 should be taken in the larger context of dealing with church discipline. Verse 19 is thus a further application of verse 18, and verse 20 states that Jesus is present to validate the judicial activity of the church.

18:21–35 See *WLC* 194; *WSC* 105; *BC* 31; *HC* 105,126.

18:23–35 Compare 5:7 and 7:2. Those who know God’s mercy must operate on the principle of mercy. If they do not show mercy but insist on justice, they will receive justice rather than mercy. We must not minimize the seriousness of this matter. An unforgiving heart is a heart that is subject to torment “until [its debtor] should pay back all” (v. 34) that is owed, which in the case of any human being equates to forever. A truly forgiving heart is the fruit of regeneration.

18:24 talents. About 75 pounds or 34 kilograms.

all that debt of yours because you begged me to. 33 Shouldn't you have had mercy on your
fellow servant just as I had on you?' 34 In anger his master turned him over to the jailers
to be tortured, until he should pay back all he owed.
35 "This is how my heavenly Father will treat each of you unless you forgive your brother from your heart."[y]

Divorce

19 When Jesus had finished saying these things,[z] he left Galilee and went into the
region of Judea to the other side of the Jordan. 2 Large crowds followed him, and
he healed them[a] there.
3 Some Pharisees came to him to test him. They asked, "Is it lawful for a man to divorce his wife[b] for any and every reason?"
4 "Haven't you read," he replied, "that at the beginning the Creator 'made them male
and female,'[a][c] 5 and said, 'For this reason a man will leave his father and mother and be
united to his wife, and the two will become one flesh'[b]?[d] 6 So they are no longer two, but
one. Therefore what God has joined together, let man not separate."

18:35 [y]Mt 6:14; Jas 2:13
19:1 [z]Mt 7:28
19:2 [a]Mt 4:23
19:3 [b]Mt 5:31
19:4 [c]Ge 1:27; 5:2
19:5 [d]Ge 2:24; 1Co 6:16; Eph 5:31

[a] 4 Gen. 1:27 [b] 5 Gen. 2:24

■ **19:1—25:46** *The Changes of the Kingdom.* Chapters 19–25 focus on the changes brought about by the coming of the kingdom in Christ. The material divides into two sections: narrative (with parables and woes in 19:1—23:39) and discourse (24:1— 25:46).
■ **19:1—23:39** *Narrative: Parables and Woes.* Chapters 19–23 record Jesus' last trip to Galilee and entrance into Jerusalem before his crucifixion. This passage emphasizes divergent reactions to Jesus' teaching—both acceptance and rejection.
19:3–6 Is it lawful . . . to divorce. The Pharisees' question may reflect the opinion of the rabbi Hillel, who reportedly allowed divorce even for inconsequential reasons on the basis of Deuteronomy 24:1–4. He was opposed in this matter by another rabbi, Shammai, who argued that only gross indecency constituted grounds for divorce. Jesus' answer to the question transcends this casuistic discussion of Deuteronomy and returns to the order of creation by God. Jesus views divorce as a fundamental denial of God's created order and of the nature of the marriage institution. *Every* legitimate marriage is "made in heaven" and is thus inviolate. See theological article "Marriage and Divorce," below.
19:5–9 See *WCF* 24.1; 24.6; *WLC* 139.

Marriage and Divorce: Is Divorce an Option?

MARRIAGE is an exclusive relationship in which a man and a woman commit themselves to each other in covenant for life and, on the basis of this solemn vow, become "one flesh" physically (Ge 2:24; Mal 2:14; Mt 19:4–6). As the Westminster Confession of Faith puts it, "Marriage was ordained for the mutual help of husband and wife, for the increase of mankind with a legitimate issue, and of the Church with an holy seed; and for preventing of uncleanness [sexual license and immorality]" (*WCF* 24.2; cf. Ge 1:28; 2:18; 1Co 7:2–9). God's ideal for marriage is that the man and the woman should experience completion in each other (Ge 2:23) and share in his creative work of making new people. With rare exception, marriage is for all people, but it is God's will that his own people should marry only fellow believers (1Co 7:39; cf. Ezr 9–10; Ne 13:23–27; Mt 19:10–12; 2Co 6:14). Deepest intimacy is impossible when the partners are not united in faith.

By using Christ's relationship to his church to illustrate what Christian marriage ought to be, Paul highlights the husband's special responsibility as his wife's servant-leader and protector, as well as the wife's calling to accept her husband in that role (Eph 5:21–33). The distinction of roles does not, however, imply that the wife is an inferior person. As God's image bearers, both the husband and wife have equal dignity and value, and they are to fulfill their roles on the basis of a mutual respect that is rooted in recognition of their equality in the eyes of God.

God hates divorce (Mal 2:16), yet he provided a procedure for it that protected the divorced wife (Dt 24:1–4). Jesus declared, however, that this provision was given "because your hearts were hard" (Mt 19:8). Divorce is not the ideal but a way to mitigate the damages caused by sin. In Matthew 5:31–32 and 19:8–9, Jesus taught that marital infidelity (the sin of adultery) violates the marriage covenant and warrants divorce (though reconciliation is preferable) but that a man who divorces his wife for any lesser reason becomes guilty of adultery when he remarries, and that he drives his divorced wife into adultery in her remarriage as well. In every case, divorce and remarriage involve the disruption of God's ideal for the sexual relationship. Notice that when asked "Is it lawful . . . to divorce?" (Mt 19:3), Jesus did not concede that divorce is sometimes a good alternative to remaining in an unhealthy marital relationship. Rather, he explained that because hearts sometimes continue to be hard, divorce may be permitted (Mt 19:4–6).

Paul added that a Christian who is deserted by an unbelieving partner is not "bound" (1Co 7:15). This evidently means that he or she may regard the relationship as finished. Still, the Bible leaves many questions unanswered: What behavior by an unbelieving spouse constitutes abandonment? May a professing believer ever be counted as an unbeliever in the case of abandonment? Does abandonment confer the right of remarriage on the abandoned spouse? These are issues on which Reformed theologians have long been divided.

7 “Why then,” they asked, “did Moses command that a man give his wife a certificate
of divorce and send her away?”[e]
8 Jesus replied, “Moses permitted you to divorce your wives because your hearts were
hard. But it was not this way from the beginning. 9 I tell you that anyone who divorces his
wife, except for marital unfaithfulness, and marries another woman commits adultery.”[f]
10 The disciples said to him, “If this is the situation between a husband and wife, it is
better not to marry.”
11 Jesus replied, “Not everyone can accept this word, but only those to whom it has
been given.[g] 12 For some are eunuchs because they were born that way; others were
made that way by men; and others have renounced marriage[a] because of the kingdom
of heaven. The one who can accept this should accept it.”

The Little Children and Jesus

13 Then little children were brought to Jesus for him to place his hands on them[h] and
pray for them. But the disciples rebuked those who brought them.
14 Jesus said, “Let the little children come to me, and do not hinder them, for the kingdom of heaven belongs[i] to such as these.”[j] 15 When he had placed his hands on them, he
went on from there.

The Rich Young Man

16 Now a man came up to Jesus and asked, “Teacher, what good thing must I do to get
eternal life[k]?”[l]
17 “Why do you ask me about what is good?” Jesus replied. “There is only One who is
good. If you want to enter life, obey the commandments.”[m]
18 “Which ones?” the man inquired.
Jesus replied, “ ‘Do not murder, do not commit adultery,[n] do not steal, do not give
false testimony, 19 honor your father and mother,’[b][o] and ‘love your neighbor as yourself.’[c]”[p]
20 “All these I have kept,” the young man said. “What do I still lack?”
21 Jesus answered, “If you want to be perfect,[q] go, sell your possessions and give to the
poor,[r] and you will have treasure in heaven.[s] Then come, follow me.”

19:7 [e]Dt 24:1-4; Mt 5:31
19:9 [f]Mt 5:32; Lk 16:18
19:11 [g]Mt 13:11; 1Co 7:7-9,17
19:13 [h]Mk 5:23
19:14 [i]Mt 25:34 [j]Mt 18:3; 1Pe 2:2
19:16 [k]Mt 25:46 [l]Lk 10:25
19:17 [m]Lev 18:5
19:18 [n]Jas 2:11
19:19 [o]Ex 20:12-16; Dt 5:16-20 [p]Lev 19:18; Mt 5:43
19:21 [q]Mt 5:48 [r]Lk 12:33; Ac 2:45; 4:34-35 [s]Mt 6:20

[a] *12* Or *have made themselves eunuchs* [b] *19* Exodus 20:12–16; Deut. 5:16–20 [c] *19* Lev. 19:18

19:7–8 Why then. Hearing Jesus' view of marriage, the Pharisees thought they could catch him contradicting Moses. But Jesus showed that Moses in Deuteronomy 24:1–4 was not giving reasons for divorce but making provisions in the event of divorce. Actually, Deuteronomy 24:1–4 consists of a long introductory "if" statement, ending with the prohibition against a man remarrying a woman he had earlier divorced. The situation in Israel reflected a cavalier attitude and a "hardness of heart" with respect to marriage and divorce that had to be specifically restrained by case law.

19:9 This verse is not easy to exegete, but its basic thrust is clear: Remarriage after divorce is adultery. The assumption is that in God's eyes a wrongly divorced couple is still married. Remarriage under such conditions constitutes adultery because it places the divorced partners in sexual relationships with persons outside that marital bond. Matthew 5:32 focuses on the further implication that divorcing a woman causes her to commit adultery because she is virtually bound to remarry in order to survive. The difficulty lies in the "exception clause" that is found here and in 5:32, but not in Mark 10:11. Is Jesus giving a ground for divorce, and if so, what is it? Any decision must deal with at least three basic questions. (1) What is the scope of the term translated "marital unfaithfulness" in the NIV? The Greek word *porneia* is actually fairly broad, pertaining to any number of sexual sins or other vile, indecent acts. It is not identical to *moicheia* ("adultery") used at the end of the verse, and this suggests that Jesus had something other than just adultery in mind. (2) Why does Mark not include the exception clause? To maintain the unity of Scripture, we conclude either that Mark *assumed* the exception and knew his audience would also assume it or else that the exception was only relevant to Matthew's readers. (3) How does Jesus' exception relate to the "something indecent" (Dt 24:1) that Moses conceded as a cause (not a ground) of divorce? Moses' allowance cannot mean that God maintained less stringent standards then than he does now, although it may be that the standards were imposed differently (polygamy was inherently opposed to the created order but was not explicitly condemned in the patriarchs). Jesus never corrected the law; he gave the correct interpretation of it. Whatever the solution, discussions about grounds for divorce and remarriage should not degenerate into casuistic arguments that lose sight of the main issue: Marriage is a creation ordinance and is by nature inviolable. This was the mistake that Hillel, Shammai and the other Pharisees made. See theological article "Marriage and Divorce" at Matthew 19. See *WCF* 24.5.

19:10–12 it is better not to marry. The disciples reacted rather cynically to Jesus' teaching on the inviolability of marriage. Jesus accepted their disparaging response and indicated that it may indeed be better for some not to marry (vv. 11–12), but only when this decision is made for the sake of the kingdom, not because God has a strict view of marriage. Compare 1 Corinthians 7:7–9. See *WCF* 22.7; *WLC* 139.

19:13–15 Let the little children come. The Dead Sea community excluded children from its assembly. The disciples viewed children as a distraction from the work of Jesus. But Jesus welcomed them as subjects of the kingdom and blessed them (v. 15). Since entrance into the kingdom is by God's grace, not human achievement, dependent little ones have a special claim to covenant blessing (cf. 18:1–9). See *BC* 34; *HC* 74.

19:16–22 The words used in Matthew differ from those in Mark (10:17–31) and Luke (18:18–30). It is often alleged that Matthew changed Mark's record of the young man's words ("Good teacher . . . what must I do?" in Mark 10:17) and Jesus' response ("Why do you call me good?" in Mark 10:18) to "Teacher, what good thing must I do?" (v. 16) and "Why do you ask me about what is good?" (v. 17) in order to avoid the supposed implication that Jesus did not regard himself as good. But Matthew did not differ from Mark in his view of Jesus. He highlighted the good *deed* by which the young man sought to procure eternal life. All three Gospel records focus on the mistake of thinking one can be good enough to achieve eternal life. Matthew includes the key phrase "There is only One who is good" (v. 17), while Mark and Luke record Jesus' statement as "No one is good—except God alone" (Mk 10:18; Lk 18:19), but all three imply the impossibility of obtaining eternal life by one's own goodness. Matthew's version focuses on the impossibility of good *deeds* as grounds for eternal life; Mark and Luke stress the impossibility of *being* good enough. See note on Mark 10:18. See *WSC* 41.

22 When the young man heard this, he went away sad, because he had great wealth.
23 Then Jesus said to his disciples, "I tell you the truth, it is hard for a rich man[t] to enter the kingdom of heaven. 24 Again I tell you, it is easier for a camel to go through the
eye of a needle than for a rich man to enter the kingdom of God."
25 When the disciples heard this, they were greatly astonished and asked, "Who then
can be saved?"
26 Jesus looked at them and said, "With man this is impossible, but with God all things
are possible."[u]
27 Peter answered him, "We have left everything to follow you![v] What then will there
be for us?"
28 Jesus said to them, "I tell you the truth, at the renewal of all things, when the Son
of Man sits on his glorious throne,[w] you who have followed me will also sit on twelve
thrones, judging the twelve tribes of Israel.[x] 29 And everyone who has left houses or
brothers or sisters or father or mother[a] or children or fields for my sake will receive a
hundred times as much and will inherit eternal life.[y] 30 But many who are first will be last,
and many who are last will be first.[z]

The Parable of the Workers in the Vineyard

20 "For the kingdom of heaven is like[a] a landowner who went out early in the
morning to hire men to work in his vineyard.[b] 2 He agreed to pay them a denarius for the day and sent them into his vineyard.
3 "About the third hour he went out and saw others standing in the marketplace doing nothing. 4 He told them, 'You also go and work in my vineyard, and I will pay you
whatever is right.' 5 So they went.
"He went out again about the sixth hour and the ninth hour and did the same thing.
6 About the eleventh hour he went out and found still others standing around. He asked
them, 'Why have you been standing here all day long doing nothing?'
7 " 'Because no one has hired us,' they answered.
"He said to them, 'You also go and work in my vineyard.'
8 "When evening came,[c] the owner of the vineyard said to his foreman, 'Call the workers and pay them their wages, beginning with the last ones hired and going on to the
first.'
9 "The workers who were hired about the eleventh hour came and each received a denarius. 10 So when those came who were hired first, they expected to receive more. But
each one of them also received a denarius. 11 When they received it, they began to grumble[d] against the landowner. 12 'These men who were hired last worked only one hour,'
they said, 'and you have made them equal to us who have borne the burden of the work
and the heat[e] of the day.'
13 "But he answered one of them, 'Friend,[f] I am not being unfair to you. Didn't you
agree to work for a denarius? 14 Take your pay and go. I want to give the man who was
hired last the same as I gave you. 15 Don't I have the right to do what I want with my own
money? Or are you envious because I am generous?'[g]
16 "So the last will be first, and the first will be last."[h]

Jesus Again Predicts His Death

17 Now as Jesus was going up to Jerusalem, he took the twelve disciples aside and said
to them, 18 "We are going up to Jerusalem,[i] and the Son of Man[j] will be betrayed to the

19:23 [t]Mt 13:22; 1Ti 6:9, 10
19:26 [u]Ge 18:14; Job 42:2; Jer 32:17; Zec 8:6; Lk 1:37; 18:27; Ro 4:21
19:27 [v]Mt 4:19
19:28 [w]Mt 20:21; 25:31 [x]Lk 22:28-30; Rev 3:21; 4:4; 20:4
19:29 [y]Mt 6:33; 25:46
19:30 [z]Mt 20:16; Mk 10:31; Lk 13:30
20:1 [a]Mt 13:24 [b]Mt 21:28, 33
20:8 [c]Lev 19:13; Dt 24:15
20:11 [d]Jnh 4:1
20:12 [e]Jnh 4:8; Lk 12:55; Jas 1:11
20:13 [f]Mt 22:12; 26:50
20:15 [g]Dt 15:9; Mk 7:22
20:16 [h]Mt 19:30
20:18 [i]Lk 9:51 [j]Mt 8:20

[a] 29 Some manuscripts *mother or wife*

19:21 sell your possessions. Jesus' instruction to the young man to sell all he had demonstrates that what the young man lacked was the attitude that abandons everything else (16:24) in order to cling to God's unearned grace. If our worldly riches become more important to us than Jesus, then we, too, must abandon them. We must count all things as loss for the sake of gaining Christ (Php 3:7–9).

19:23–26 Since the Jews regarded wealth as evidence of God's approval, they usually thought that the wealthy were the most likely candidates for the kingdom. Jesus turned this conception on its head. The result was not lost on the disciples, who asked, "Who then can be saved?" (v. 25). Indeed, salvation is as impossible for a human being to achieve as putting the largest animal in Palestine through a needle's eye. This is especially true for the wealthy, who are less likely to come to God without pretensions. **saved.** The phrases "get eternal life" (v. 16) and "enter the kingdom of God" (v. 24) are equivalent to "be saved."

19:28 judging. Here means governing, not sentencing to punishment.

19:29 will receive a hundred times. It is impossible to out-give God.

19:30 first will be last. There is no correlation between earthly position and heavenly approval, except sometimes a negative one. Similarly, there is no causal connection between length of earthly labor and size of heavenly reward (cf. 20:1–16).

20:1–15 This is a hard saying only for those who fail to recognize their absolute dependence on grace for *any* good thing from God's hand. There is no room for a Christian to be jealous of the good gifts God has given to another.

20:16 Compare note on 19:30.

20:17–19 Jesus' third prediction of his passion and resurrection (cf. 16:21 and note on 17:22–23).

chief priests and the teachers of the law.[k] They will condemn him to death 19and will turn
him over to the Gentiles to be mocked and flogged[l] and crucified.[m] On the third day[n]
he will be raised to life!"[o]

A Mother's Request

20Then the mother of Zebedee's sons[p] came to Jesus with her sons and, kneeling
down,[q] asked a favor of him.
21"What is it you want?" he asked.
She said, "Grant that one of these two sons of mine may sit at your right and the other at your left in your kingdom."[r]
22"You don't know what you are asking," Jesus said to them. "Can you drink the cup[s]
I am going to drink?"
"We can," they answered.
23Jesus said to them, "You will indeed drink from my cup,[t] but to sit at my right or left
is not for me to grant. These places belong to those for whom they have been prepared
by my Father."
24When the ten heard about this, they were indignant[u] with the two brothers. 25Jesus
called them together and said, "You know that the rulers of the Gentiles lord it over
them, and their high officials exercise authority over them. 26Not so with you. Instead,
whoever wants to become great among you must be your servant,[v] 27and whoever
wants to be first must be your slave— 28just as the Son of Man[w] did not come to be
served, but to serve,[x] and to give his life as a ransom[y] for many."

Two Blind Men Receive Sight

29As Jesus and his disciples were leaving Jericho, a large crowd followed him. 30Two
blind men were sitting by the roadside, and when they heard that Jesus was going by,
they shouted, "Lord, Son of David,[z] have mercy on us!"
31The crowd rebuked them and told them to be quiet, but they shouted all the louder, "Lord, Son of David, have mercy on us!"
32Jesus stopped and called them. "What do you want me to do for you?" he asked.
33"Lord," they answered, "we want our sight."
34Jesus had compassion on them and touched their eyes. Immediately they received
their sight and followed him.

The Triumphal Entry

21 As they approached Jerusalem and came to Bethphage on the Mount of Olives,[a]
Jesus sent two disciples, 2saying to them, "Go to the village ahead of you, and
at once you will find a donkey tied there, with her colt by her. Untie them and bring them
to me. 3If anyone says anything to you, tell him that the Lord needs them, and he will
send them right away."
4This took place to fulfill what was spoken through the prophet:
5"Say to the Daughter of Zion,
'See, your king comes to you,

20:18 [k]Mt 16:21; 27:1,2
20:19 [l]Mt 16:21 [m]Ac 2:23 [n]Mt 16:21 [o]Mt 16:21
20:20 [p]Mt 4:21 [q]Mt 8:2
20:21 [r]Mt 19:28
20:22 [s]Isa 51:17,22; Jer 49:12; Mt 26:39,42; Mk 14:36; Lk 22:42; Jn 18:11
20:23 [t]Ac 12:2; Rev 1:9
20:24 [u]Lk 22:24,25
20:26 [v]Mt 23:11; Mk 9:35
20:28 [w]Mt 8:20 [x]Lk 22:27; Jn 13:13-16; 2Co 8:9; Php 2:7 [y]Isa 53:10; Mt 26:28; 1Ti 2:6; Tit 2:14; Heb 9:28; 1Pe 1:18,19
20:30 [z]Mt 9:27
21:1 [a]Mt 24:3; 26:30; Mk 14:26; Lk 19:37; 21:37; 22:39; Jn 8:1; Ac 1:12

20:23 cup. Refers in Old Testament imagery to the outpouring of God's wrath. That the disciples would indeed drink of this cup means that they would experience suffering, but note that Jesus called it "*my* cup" (emphasis added). Because Jesus drank the cup of God's wrath for believers, they do not drink the wrath they deserve. In union with Christ, his followers have already undergone judgment. They are now justified in Christ and heirs of his glory (Ro 8:17). Yet it is their privilege to be identified with Christ in his sufferings (1Pe 2:21) and to know his cleansing discipline (Mal 3:2–3; 1Pe 4:16–17). See *BC* 16.
20:28 ransom. This term refers to the price paid to deliver someone from slavery or judicial punishment. The price of our freedom from sin and condemnation is Jesus' life, or, in symbolic language, his blood (1Pe 1:18–19). The New Testament never directly indicates to whom the ransom is paid, but if that from which we are liberated is the wrath of God, the ransom had to be paid to God himself (cf. Ps 49:7–9). Jesus was about to drink the "cup" (v. 23) of God's wrath, not for his own sin, but as a means of ransoming many. **for.** The Greek preposition translated "for" can also be rendered "in the place of." It expresses the substitutionary nature of Jesus' suffering. **many.** That Jesus said "many" here rather than "all men" indicates a specific or definite focus to his redemptive activity (cf. also the "many" in Isa 53:11–12). Jesus died for specific people. See notes on John 17:6–20 and 1 Timothy 2:6. See *WLC* 71.
20:29 were leaving. Luke indicates that they were entering, rather than leaving, Jericho. One possible explanation is that Matthew and Mark are referring to the older town of Jericho, while Luke is referring to the newer town of Jericho built by Herod, which was about a mile away from the older town.
20:30 Two blind men. Matthew mentions two, whereas Mark and Luke mention only one each. Compare note on 8:28–29.
21:1–11 Of the Synoptic Gospels (Matthew, Mark and Luke), only Matthew mentions the colt's mother, probably to emphasize that it was a very young colt that had not yet been weaned; it therefore had not yet been ridden (cf. Mk 11:2). The quotation from Zechariah 9:9 indicates that the coming king would ride on "a colt, the foal of a donkey." Jesus chose to make the fulfillment of the prophecy unmistakable. The triumphal entry was clearly a symbolic act on his part. Zechariah 9:9 was recognized as Messianic by Jews, and the shout "Hosanna to the Son of David" (v. 9), as well as their spreading of cloaks on the ground (cf. 2Ki 9:13), indicates that the crowd recognized Jesus' claim to be Messiah. Note David's proclamation of Solomon as his designated heir by having him ride into the city on a donkey (1Ki 1:33,38,44). The donkey also symbolized the humility of God's anointed and Jesus' dependence on God's power. **Blessed is he who comes.** Taken from Psalm 118:26.
21:3 Lord. Jesus claimed the authority of Yahweh.
21:5 See *WLC* 42; *WSC* 23; *HC* 31.

gentle and riding on a donkey,
on a colt, the foal of a donkey.' "[a][b]

[6]The disciples went and did as Jesus had instructed them. [7]They brought the donkey
and the colt, placed their cloaks on them, and Jesus sat on them. [8]A very large crowd
spread their cloaks[c] on the road, while others cut branches from the trees and spread
them on the road. [9]The crowds that went ahead of him and those that followed shouted,

"Hosanna[b] to the Son of David!"[d]

"Blessed is he who comes in the name of the Lord!"[c][e]

"Hosanna[b] in the highest!"[f]

[10]When Jesus entered Jerusalem, the whole city was stirred and asked, "Who is
this?"
[11]The crowds answered, "This is Jesus, the prophet[g] from Nazareth in Galilee."

Jesus at the Temple

[12]Jesus entered the temple area and drove out all who were buying[h] and selling there.
He overturned the tables of the money changers[i] and the benches of those selling
doves.[j] [13]"It is written," he said to them, " 'My house will be called a house of prayer,'[d][k]
but you are making it a 'den of robbers.'[e]"[l]
[14]The blind and the lame came to him at the temple, and he healed them.[m] [15]But
when the chief priests and the teachers of the law saw the wonderful things he did and
the children shouting in the temple area, "Hosanna to the Son of David,"[n] they were indignant.[o]
[16]"Do you hear what these children are saying?" they asked him.
"Yes," replied Jesus, "have you never read,

" 'From the lips of children and infants
you have ordained praise'[f]?"[p]

[17]And he left them and went out of the city to Bethany,[q] where he spent the night.

The Fig Tree Withers

[18]Early in the morning, as he was on his way back to the city, he was hungry. [19]Seeing a fig tree by the road, he went up to it but found nothing on it except leaves. Then
he said to it, "May you never bear fruit again!" Immediately the tree withered.[r]
[20]When the disciples saw this, they were amazed. "How did the fig tree wither so
quickly?" they asked.
[21]Jesus replied, "I tell you the truth, if you have faith and do not doubt,[s] not only can
you do what was done to the fig tree, but also you can say to this mountain, 'Go, throw
yourself into the sea,' and it will be done. [22]If you believe, you will receive whatever you
ask for[t] in prayer."

The Authority of Jesus Questioned

[23]Jesus entered the temple courts, and, while he was teaching, the chief priests and
the elders of the people came to him. "By what authority[u] are you doing these things?"
they asked. "And who gave you this authority?"

21:5 [b]Isa 62:11; Zec 9:9
21:8 [c]2Ki 9:13
21:9 [d]ver 15; Mt 9:27 [e]Ps 118:26; Mt 23:39 [f]Lk 2:14
21:11 [g]Lk 7:16,39; 24:19; Jn 1:21,25; 6:14; 7:40
21:12 [h]Dt 14:26 [i]Ex 30:13 [j]Lev 1:14
21:13 [k]Isa 56:7 [l]Jer 7:11
21:14 [m]Mt 4:23
21:15 [n]ver 9; Mt 9:27 [o]Lk 19:39
21:16 [p]Ps 8:2
21:17 [q]Mt 26:6; Mk 11:1; Lk 24:50; Jn 11:1, 18; 12:1
21:19 [r]Isa 34:4; Jer 8:13
21:21 [s]Mt 17:20; Lk 17:6; 1Co 13:2; Jas 1:6
21:22 [t]Mt 7:7
21:23 [u]Ac 4:7; 7:27

[a]5 Zech. 9:9 [b]9 A Hebrew expression meaning "Save!" which became an exclamation of praise; also in verse 15 [c]9 Psalm 118:26 [d]*13* Isaiah 56:7 [e]*13* Jer. 7:11 [f]*16* Psalm 8:2

21:7 Jesus sat on them. Jesus was not straddling the two animals; he actually rode the colt (cf. Mk 11:7). Perhaps "them" refers to the garments.
21:12–13 John 2:13–17 recounts a cleansing of the temple early in Jesus' ministry rather than one during Passion Week. Many scholars, including some evangelicals, maintain that either John or the Synoptics (Matthew, Mark and Luke) put the account at a different point for theological reasons. However, the descriptive details are quite different, and it is not impossible that there were two separate occasions on which Jesus drove out moneychangers. The phrase "den of robbers" (v. 13) is from Jeremiah 7:11, a passage in which the Lord denounced the notion that the physical temple somehow guaranteed God's blessing in spite of Judah's wickedness. This same superstitious notion prevailed in Jesus' time.
21:15 See *WLC* 145; *CD* 1.18.
21:16 Psalm 8 says that God ordained praise *for himself* from the lips of children. Thus, in citing Psalm 8:2 to justify the children's acclamations, Jesus indirectly claimed the prerogative of deity.
21:18–20 Matthew condenses events that actually took place on two separate days (cf. Mk 11:12–14,20–26). The fig tree's fruit ordinarily begins to appear before its leaves in the spring and, though not appetizing, the unripe fruit is edible. Jesus cursed this tree because, although it showed promise of having figs by being full of leaves, this was show only. It thus served as an analogy for hypocrisy, which God curses. The linking of this incident with the cleansing of the temple hints at God's imminent punishment of Israel's hypocrisy by the destruction of the city and the temple (cf. Jer 24:1–8). It bears a close relationship to 21:33–46 (see note below), both in its subject matter and in its probable roots in Isaiah 5:1–7.
21:21–22 This is similar to 17:20, but here the emphasis is on not doubting. Freedom from doubt is the awareness that something is truly God's will. It is not presumptive arrogance, but trust in God and submission to his sovereignty.

24 Jesus replied, "I will also ask you one question. If you answer me, I will tell you by
what authority I am doing these things. 25 John's baptism—where did it come from? Was
it from heaven, or from men?"
They discussed it among themselves and said, "If we say, 'From heaven,' he will ask,
'Then why didn't you believe him?' 26 But if we say, 'From men'—we are afraid of the peo-
21:26 [v]Mt 11:9; Mk 6:20 ple, for they all hold that John was a prophet."[v]
27 So they answered Jesus, "We don't know."
Then he said, "Neither will I tell you by what authority I am doing these things.

The Parable of the Two Sons

28 "What do you think? There was a man who had two sons. He went to the first and
21:28 [w]ver 33; Mt 20:1 said, 'Son, go and work today in the vineyard.'[w]
29 " 'I will not,' he answered, but later he changed his mind and went.
30 "Then the father went to the other son and said the same thing. He answered, 'I will,
sir,' but he did not go.
31 "Which of the two did what his father wanted?"
"The first," they answered.
21:31 [x]Lk 7:29 [y]Lk 7:50 Jesus said to them, "I tell you the truth, the tax collectors[x] and the prostitutes[y] are
21:32 [z]Mt 3:1-12 [a]Lk 3:12,13; 7:29 [b]Lk 7:36-50 [c]Lk 7:30 entering the kingdom of God ahead of you. 32 For John came to you to show you the way
of righteousness,[z] and you did not believe him, but the tax collectors[a] and the prosti-
tutes[b] did. And even after you saw this, you did not repent[c] and believe him.

The Parable of the Tenants

21:33 [d]Ps 80:8 [e]Isa 5:1-7 [f]Mt 25:14,15 33 "Listen to another parable: There was a landowner who planted[d] a vineyard. He put
a wall around it, dug a winepress in it and built a watchtower.[e] Then he rented the vine-
yard to some farmers and went away on a journey.[f] 34 When the harvest time ap-
21:34 [g]Mt 22:3 proached, he sent his servants[g] to the tenants to collect his fruit.
21:35 [h]2Ch 24:21; Mt 23:34,37; Heb 11:36,37 35 "The tenants seized his servants; they beat one, killed another, and stoned a third.[h]
36 Then he sent other servants[i] to them, more than the first time, and the tenants treat-
ed them the same way. 37 Last of all, he sent his son to them. 'They will respect my son,'
he said.
21:36 [i]Mt 22:4 38 "But when the tenants saw the son, they said to each other, 'This is the heir.[j] Come,
let's kill him[k] and take his inheritance.'[l] 39 So they took him and threw him out of the
21:38 [j]Heb 1:2 [k]Mt 12:14 [l]Ps 2:8 vineyard and killed him.
40 "Therefore, when the owner of the vineyard comes, what will he do to those tenants?"
41 "He will bring those wretches to a wretched end,"[m] they replied, "and he will rent
21:41 [m]Mt 8:11,12 [n]Ac 13:46; 18:6; 28:28 the vineyard to other tenants,[n] who will give him his share of the crop at harvest time."
42 Jesus said to them, "Have you never read in the Scriptures:

" 'The stone the builders rejected
has become the capstone[a];
the Lord has done this,
21:42 [o]Ps 118:22,23; Ac 4:11; 1Pe 2:7 and it is marvelous in our eyes'[b]?[o]

21:43 [p]Mt 8:12 43 "Therefore I tell you that the kingdom of God will be taken away from you[p] and giv-
en to a people who will produce its fruit. 44 He who falls on this stone will be broken to
21:44 [q]Lk 2:34 pieces, but he on whom it falls will be crushed."[c][q]
45 When the chief priests and the Pharisees heard Jesus' parables, they knew he was

a *42* Or *cornerstone* b *42* Psalm 118:22,23 c *44* Some manuscripts do not have verse 44.

21:33–46 This parable is based on Isaiah 5:1–7 and probably also reflects Psalm 80:8–18. Most of the metaphorical correspondences are explicit or obvious: The landowner is God. The vineyard is the kingdom of God (v. 43). The servants are the prophets. The son is Jesus. The tenants are the Jews who opposed Jesus. The killing of the son is the crucifixion. The removal of the tenants is the transferal of the kingdom to a new people of God that includes Gentiles. On the other hand, not all the details have necessary correspondences—e.g., the winepress, the watchtower and the journey. See *WLC* 151.

21:42 Psalm 118:22–23, from which this citation is taken, alludes to David as the paradigm for the coming Messiah (see note on "Christ" at 1:1). David was one whom the worldly-wise overlooked but whom God chose. Jesus, even more than David, was rejected by the self-designated leadership of Israel. He responded to this challenge to his authority (v. 23) by showing the consequences of rejecting it.

21:44 This verse combines the prophecies of Isaiah 8:14 ("for both houses of Israel he will be a stone that causes men to stumble") and Daniel 2:34 and 44, a passage in which the rock strikes the statue of Nebuchadnezzar's dream, crushes all the worldly kingdoms and then becomes a great worldwide kingdom that never ends. Thus, Jesus claimed to be the destroyer of earthly kingdoms and the founder of God's kingdom on Earth and at the same time pointed out that the Jewish leaders were by divine plan opposed to this kingdom. Jesus' citation of Psalm 118 and his allusion to Isaiah 8:14 and Daniel 2 provide the ground for the "stone" designation that appears frequently in the New Testament (Ac 4:11; Ro 9:33; 1Pe 2:6–8 and many other references).

talking about them. 46They looked for a way to arrest him, but they were afraid of the
crowd because the people held that he was a prophet.[r]

The Parable of the Wedding Banquet

22 Jesus spoke to them again in parables, saying: 2"The kingdom of heaven is like[s]
a king who prepared a wedding banquet for his son. 3He sent his servants[t] to
those who had been invited to the banquet to tell them to come, but they refused to come.
4"Then he sent some more servants[u] and said, 'Tell those who have been invited that
I have prepared my dinner: My oxen and fattened cattle have been butchered, and everything is ready. Come to the wedding banquet.'
5"But they paid no attention and went off—one to his field, another to his business.
6The rest seized his servants, mistreated them and killed them. 7The king was enraged.
He sent his army and destroyed those murderers[v] and burned their city.
8"Then he said to his servants, 'The wedding banquet is ready, but those I invited did
not deserve to come. 9Go to the street corners[w] and invite to the banquet anyone you
find.' 10So the servants went out into the streets and gathered all the people they could
find, both good and bad,[x] and the wedding hall was filled with guests.
11"But when the king came in to see the guests, he noticed a man there who was not
wearing wedding clothes. 12'Friend,'[y] he asked, 'how did you get in here without wedding clothes?' The man was speechless.
13"Then the king told the attendants, 'Tie him hand and foot, and throw him outside,
into the darkness, where there will be weeping and gnashing of teeth.'[z]
14"For many are invited, but few are chosen."[a]

Paying Taxes to Caesar

15Then the Pharisees went out and laid plans to trap him in his words. 16They sent
their disciples to him along with the Herodians.[b] "Teacher," they said, "we know you are
a man of integrity and that you teach the way of God in accordance with the truth. You
aren't swayed by men, because you pay no attention to who they are. 17Tell us then, what
is your opinion? Is it right to pay taxes[c] to Caesar or not?"
18But Jesus, knowing their evil intent, said, "You hypocrites, why are you trying to trap
me? 19Show me the coin used for paying the tax." They brought him a denarius, 20and
he asked them, "Whose portrait is this? And whose inscription?"
21"Caesar's," they replied.
Then he said to them, "Give to Caesar what is Caesar's,[d] and to God what is God's."
22When they heard this, they were amazed. So they left him and went away.[e]

Marriage at the Resurrection

23That same day the Sadducees,[f] who say there is no resurrection,[g] came to him with
a question. 24"Teacher," they said, "Moses told us that if a man dies without having children, his brother must marry the widow and have children for him.[h] 25Now there were
seven brothers among us. The first one married and died, and since he had no children,
he left his wife to his brother. 26The same thing happened to the second and third
brother, right on down to the seventh. 27Finally, the woman died. 28Now then, at the resurrection, whose wife will she be of the seven, since all of them were married to her?"

21:46 [r]ver 11,26
22:2 [s]Mt 13:24
22:3 [t]Mt 21:34
22:4 [u]Mt 21:36
22:7 [v]Lk 19:27
22:9 [w]Eze 21:21
22:10 [x]Mt 13:47,48
22:12 [y]Mt 20:13; 26:50
22:13 [z]Mt 8:12
22:14 [a]Rev 17:14
22:16 [b]Mk 3:6
22:17 [c]Mt 17:25
22:21 [d]Ro 13:7
22:22 [e]Mk 12:12
22:23 [f]Ac 4:1 [g]Ac 23:8; 1Co 15:12
22:24 [h]Dt 25:5,6

22:1–14 Although this parable resembles the one found in Luke 14:16–24, there are very few actual verbal similarities—and some notable differences. The two should be understood as different parables delivered on different occasions. This parable has two parts. (1) Verses 1–10 continue the theme begun in the previous chapter that those who ought to have received the kingdom have wickedly rejected it, resulting in the kingdom being offered to others. The inclusion not only of "the tax collectors and the prostitutes" (21:31), but also of Gentiles is here envisioned. Verse 9 implies that God's servants have the task of offering the gospel to all men and women. (2) Verses 11–14 speak of the fact that receiving an invitation to God's kingdom does not guarantee inclusion; one must be properly clothed, and, according to Galatians 3:27, this clothing is Christ himself. Although everyone who hears the gospel has been invited, and although many may actually pretend to be in the kingdom, only those endued with Christ's righteousness are actually presentable to God. The two parts are tied together by verse 14, which concisely expresses the theme of God's elective sovereignty. Both Jew and Gentile are called, but only those who are chosen will be present at the marriage supper of the Lamb, and this election does not depend on any previous status (cf. 8:11–12). Those who "chose themselves" end up being thrown out.

22:2 wedding banquet. A symbol for the consummation, at which time the King's Son, the Bridegroom (Jesus), will be fully united with his people.

22:5 See *WLC* 109.

22:13 outside, into the darkness, where there will be weeping and gnashing of teeth. A description of eternal punishment in hell.

22:14 See *WCF* 10.4; *WLC* 61,68.

22:16–17 taxes. The hated poll tax symbolized submission to Rome. If Jesus had simply answered "Yes, pay the tax," he would have alienated the majority of the people. If he had said no, the Herodians would have had grounds for accusing him of treason. Jesus' answer transcends the question by focusing on the major issue: one's relationship to God. The coin bore Caesar's image; we bear God's image. Jesus also laid the foundation for his disciples' relation to civil government.

22:21 See *WLC* 127; *BC* 36; *HC* 104.

22:24–31 See *WCF* 1.10; *WLC* 16,113.

22:24 Compare Deuteronomy 25:5–6.

29 Jesus replied, "You are in error because you do not know the Scriptures[i] or the power of God. 30 At the resurrection people will neither marry nor be given in marriage;[j] they
will be like the angels in heaven. 31 But about the resurrection of the dead—have you not
read what God said to you, 32 'I am the God of Abraham, the God of Isaac, and the God
of Jacob'[a]?[k] He is not the God of the dead but of the living."
33 When the crowds heard this, they were astonished at his teaching.[l]

The Greatest Commandment

34 Hearing that Jesus had silenced the Sadducees,[m] the Pharisees got together. 35 One
of them, an expert in the law,[n] tested him with this question: 36 "Teacher, which is the
greatest commandment in the Law?"
37 Jesus replied: " 'Love the Lord your God with all your heart and with all your soul
and with all your mind.'[b][o] 38 This is the first and greatest commandment. 39 And the second is like it: 'Love your neighbor as yourself.'[c][p] 40 All the Law and the Prophets hang on
these two commandments."[q]

Whose Son Is the Christ?

41 While the Pharisees were gathered together, Jesus asked them, 42 "What do you
think about the Christ[d]? Whose son is he?"
"The son of David,"[r] they replied.
43 He said to them, "How is it then that David, speaking by the Spirit, calls him 'Lord'?
For he says,

> 44 " 'The Lord said to my Lord:
> "Sit at my right hand
> until I put your enemies
> under your feet." '[e][s]

45 If then David calls him 'Lord,' how can he be his son?" 46 No one could say a word in
reply, and from that day on no one dared to ask him any more questions.[t]

Seven Woes

23 Then Jesus said to the crowds and to his disciples: 2 "The teachers of the law[u]
and the Pharisees sit in Moses' seat. 3 So you must obey them and do everything
they tell you. But do not do what they do, for they do not practice what they preach.
4 They tie up heavy loads and put them on men's shoulders, but they themselves are not
willing to lift a finger to move them.[v]
5 "Everything they do is done for men to see:[w] They make their phylacteries[f][x] wide and
the tassels on their garments[y] long; 6 they love the place of honor at banquets and the
most important seats in the synagogues;[z] 7 they love to be greeted in the marketplaces and
to have men call them 'Rabbi.'[a]
8 "But you are not to be called 'Rabbi,' for you have only one Master and you are all
brothers. 9 And do not call anyone on earth 'father,' for you have one Father,[b] and he is
in heaven. 10 Nor are you to be called 'teacher,' for you have one Teacher, the Christ.[g] 11 The

22:29 [i]Jn 20:9
22:30 [j]Mt 24:38
22:32 [k]Ex 3:6; Ac 7:32
22:33 [l]Mt 7:28
22:34 [m]Ac 4:1
22:35 [n]Lk 7:30; 10:25; 11:45; 14:3
22:37 [o]Dt 6:5
22:39 [p]Lev 19:18; Mt 5:43; 19:19; Gal 5:14
22:40 [q]Mt 7:12
22:42 [r]Mt 9:27
22:44 [s]Ps 110:1; Ac 2:34, 35; 1Co 15:25; Heb 1:13; 10:13
22:46 [t]Mk 12:34; Lk 20:40
23:2 [u]Ezr 7:6,25; Ne 8:4
23:4 [v]Lk 11:46; Ac 15:10; Gal 6:13
23:5 [w]Mt 6:1,2,5,16 [x]Ex 13:9; Dt 6:8 [y]Nu 15:38; Dt 22:12
23:6 [z]Lk 11:43; 14:7; 20:46
23:7 [a]ver 8; Mk 9:5; 10:51; Jn 1:38,49
23:9 [b]Mal 1:6; Mt 7:11

[a] *32* Exodus 3:6 [b] *37* Deut. 6:5 [c] *39* Lev. 19:18 [d] *42* Or *Messiah* [e] *44* Psalm 110:1
[f] *5* That is, boxes containing Scripture verses, worn on forehead and arm [g] *10* Or *Messiah*

22:31 have you not read. Jesus cited the Pentateuch (Ex 3:6), the only portion of Scripture accepted by the Sadducees. That God is (not was) the God of the patriarchs proves the resurrection because the living God would not name himself as the God of the dead and gone. The eternal God calls his saints to an eternal relationship with himself. God made covenant promises to the patriarchs, promises that were not fulfilled during their earthly lives and yet are still in force. All this implies that God will restore the patriarchs to life. See *WCF* 1.10.

22:37–40 See *WCF* 19.2; *WLC* 98,99,122,141; *WSC* 42; *HC* 93,94,107.

22:40 All the Law and the Prophets. This is a way of referring to the entire Old Testament. Love fulfills the law because it both sums up God's commandments and motivates our obedience to them (Ro 13:8–10; 1Co 13). It does not dissolve God's norms for conduct but illumines and deepens them (cf. 5:17; Ro 8:4).

22:41–46 What do you think. The Pharisees had tested Jesus; now Jesus tested them. He focused on the crucial issue of the identity of the Messiah (the Christ), and his quotation from Psalm 110 (in v. 44) shows that the common concept of the Messiah was too limited. See note on "Christ" at 1:1.

23:1–39 Some regard this chapter as another discourse (bringing the total number to six rather than five; see "Introduction") or as part of the eschatological discourse in chapters 24–25. However, chapter 23 does not conclude with the phrase "When Jesus had finished saying these things"—or a similar phrase—which closes the other discourses (see 7:28; 11:1; 13:53; 19:1; 26:1). Further, unlike the other five discourses, the latter part of this speech is addressed to Jesus' opponents. Chapter 23 should rather be seen as a narrative portion, demonstrating Jesus' prophetic activity in delivering "woe oracles" to the unfaithful leaders of Israel (cf. note on 23:13). It is related to the following discourse, however, in that it provides the reason for the doom of Jerusalem, which is announced in the language of Old Testament judgment prophecy.

23:2 sit in Moses' seat. Greek, "sat in Moses' seat." They have arrogated to themselves Moses' authority. See *WLC* 130.

23:3–4 See *WCF* 16.7; *WLC* 130.

23:8–10 See *WCF* 20.2; 25.6; *BC* 31.

23:9 do not call anyone on earth "father." Jews did not call their living teachers "father" but did refer to the venerated teachers of earlier generations as "fathers." No earthly teacher of any age is the progenitor of true spiritual understanding; this role belongs solely to God himself. See *WLC* 105.

greatest among you will be your servant.[c] 12For whoever exalts himself will be humbled,
and whoever humbles himself will be exalted.[d]
13"Woe to you, teachers of the law and Pharisees, you hypocrites![e] You shut the kingdom of heaven in men's faces. You yourselves do not enter, nor will you let those enter
who are trying to.[a][f]
15"Woe to you, teachers of the law and Pharisees, you hypocrites! You travel over land
and sea to win a single convert,[g] and when he becomes one, you make him twice as
much a son of hell[h] as you are.
16"Woe to you, blind guides![i] You say, 'If anyone swears by the temple, it means noth-

23:11 [c]Mt 20:26; Mk 9:35
23:12 [d]Lk 14:11
23:13 [e]ver 15,23,25,27, 29 [f]Lk 11:52
23:15 [g]Ac 2:11; 6:5; 13:43 [h]Mt 5:22
23:16 [i]ver 24; Mt 15:14

a *13* Some manuscripts *to.* *14Woe to you, teachers of the law and Pharisees, you hypocrites! You devour widows' houses and for a show make lengthy prayers. Therefore you will be punished more severely.*

23:13–36 Woe to you. Luke 11:37–54 records an earlier proclamation of six woes. This series of seven woes was a prophetic pronouncement; it involved bringing God's covenant lawsuit (*a rîb*) against his people and announcing the imminent realization of the covenant curses. Compare the six woes given by Isaiah (Isa 5:8–23); the five by Habakkuk (Hab 2:6–20); and others by Isaiah, Jeremiah, Ezekiel and several minor prophets. Such oracles are not vindictive but stem from God's concern for his people and from his desire that they repent (cf. vv. 37–39).
23:13 shut the kingdom. By turning people away from Christ and his righteousness. The disciples were to do the opposite by using the keys of the gospel (see 16:19). **hypocrites.** See note on 6:2. See also *WLC* 109.
23:14 See *WLC* 113.
23:15 hell. See note on 5:22. Proselytes to *Pharisaism* (not just Judaism) were converts to *legalism* and were thus insulated from receiving the righteousness that is by faith. See *WLC* 151.
23:16–22 If anyone swears. Compare 5:33–37. The casuistry of oaths bears a resemblance to children swearing while crossing their fingers behind their backs. Such trickery does not make a promise or an oath any less binding in God's eyes. God desires truth in all our words (5:37). See *HC* 102.

Jewish Sects

Pharisees Their roots can be traced to Hasidim of the the second century B.C. (see note on Mk 2:16).	1. Along with the Torah, they accepted as equally inspired and authoritative all material contained within the oral tradition. 2. On free will and determination, they held to a mediating view that made it impossible for either free will or the sovereignty of God to cancel out the other. 3. They accepted a rather developed hierarchy of angels and demons. 4. They believed in the resurrection of the dead. 5. They believed in the immortality of the soul and in reward and retribution after death. 6. They were champions of human equality. 7. The emphasis of their teaching was ethical rather than theological.
Sadducees They probably had their beginning during the Hasmonean period (166-63 B.C.). Their demise occurred c. A.D. 70 with the fall of Jerusalem and the destruction of the temple.	1. They denied that the oral law was authoritative and binding. 2. They interpreted the Mosaic law more literally than did the Pharisees. 3. They were very exacting in Levitical purity. 4. They attributed everything to free will. 5. They argued that there is neither resurrection of the dead nor a future life. 6. They rejected belief in angels and demons. 7. They rejected the idea of a spiritual world. 8. They considered only the books of Moses to be canonical Scripture.
Essenes They probably originated among the Hasidim, along with the Pharisees, from whom they later separated (I Maccabees 2:42; 7:13). They were a group of very strict and zealous Jews who took part with the Maccabeans in a revolt against the Syrians, c. 165-155 B.C.	1. They strictly observed the purity laws of the Torah. 2. They practiced communal ownership of property. 3. They had a strong sense of mutual responsibility. 4. Daily worship was an important feature along with daily study of their sacred scriptures. 5. Solemn oaths of piety and obedience had to be taken. 6. Sacrifices were offered on holy days and during sacred seasons. 7. Marriage was not condemned in principle but was avoided. 8. They attributed everything that happened to fate.
Zealots They originated during the reign of Herod the Great c. 6 B.C. and were exterminated at Masada in A.D. 73.	1. They opposed payment of tribute for taxes to a pagan emperor because they believed that allegiance was due to God alone. 2. They were fiercely loyal to Jewish tradition. 3. They believed in violence as long as it accomplished a good end. 4. They were opposed to the use of the Greek language in the Holy Land.

ing; but if anyone swears by the gold of the temple, he is bound by his oath.’[j] 17You blind
fools! Which is greater: the gold, or the temple that makes the gold sacred?[k] 18You also
say, ‘If anyone swears by the altar, it means nothing; but if anyone swears by the gift on
it, he is bound by his oath.’ 19You blind men! Which is greater: the gift, or the altar that
makes the gift sacred?[l] 20Therefore, he who swears by the altar swears by it and by everything on it. 21And he who swears by the temple swears by it and by the one who
dwells[m] in it. 22And he who swears by heaven swears by God’s throne and by the one
who sits on it.[n]

23“Woe to you, teachers of the law and Pharisees, you hypocrites! You give a tenth[o]
of your spices—mint, dill and cummin. But you have neglected the more important matters of the law—justice, mercy and faithfulness.[p] You should have practiced the latter,
without neglecting the former. 24You blind guides![q] You strain out a gnat but swallow
a camel.

25“Woe to you, teachers of the law and Pharisees, you hypocrites! You clean the outside of the cup and dish,[r] but inside they are full of greed and self-indulgence.[s] 26Blind
Pharisee! First clean the inside of the cup and dish, and then the outside also will be clean.

27“Woe to you, teachers of the law and Pharisees, you hypocrites! You are like whitewashed tombs,[t] which look beautiful on the outside but on the inside are full of dead
men’s bones and everything unclean. 28In the same way, on the outside you appear to
people as righteous but on the inside you are full of hypocrisy and wickedness.

29“Woe to you, teachers of the law and Pharisees, you hypocrites! You build tombs
for the prophets[u] and decorate the graves of the righteous. 30And you say, ‘If we had lived
in the days of our forefathers, we would not have taken part with them in shedding the
blood of the prophets.’ 31So you testify against yourselves that you are the descendants
of those who murdered the prophets.[v] 32Fill up, then, the measure[w] of the sin of your
forefathers!

33“You snakes! You brood of vipers![x] How will you escape being condemned to
hell?[y] 34Therefore I am sending you prophets and wise men and teachers. Some of them
you will kill and crucify;[z] others you will flog in your synagogues[a] and pursue from town
to town.[b] 35And so upon you will come all the righteous blood that has been shed on
earth, from the blood of righteous Abel[c] to the blood of Zechariah son of Berekiah,[d]
whom you murdered between the temple and the altar.[e] 36I tell you the truth, all this will
come upon this generation.[f]

37“O Jerusalem, Jerusalem, you who kill the prophets and stone those sent to you,[g]
how often I have longed to gather your children together, as a hen gathers her chicks under her wings, but you were not willing. 38Look, your house is left to you desolate.[h] 39For
I tell you, you will not see me again until you say, ‘Blessed is he who comes in the name
of the Lord.’[a]”[i]

Signs of the End of the Age

24 Jesus left the temple and was walking away when his disciples came up to him
to call his attention to its buildings. 2“Do you see all these things?” he asked. “I

23:16 [j]Mt 5:33-35
23:17 [k]Ex 30:29
23:19 [l]Ex 29:37
23:21 [m]1Ki 8:13; Ps 26:8
23:22 [n]Ps 11:4; Mt 5:34
23:23 [o]Lev 27:30 [p]Mic 6:8; Lk 11:42
23:24 [q]ver 16
23:25 [r]Mk 7:4 [s]Lk 11:39
23:27 [t]Lk 11:44; Ac 23:3
23:29 [u]Lk 11:47,48
23:31 [v]Ac 7:51-52
23:32 [w]1Th 2:16
23:33 [x]Mt 3:7; 12:34 [y]Mt 5:22
23:34 [z]2Ch 36:15,16; Lk 11:49 [a]Mt 10:17 [b]Mt 10:23
23:35 [c]Ge 4:8; Heb 11:4 [d]Zec 1:1 [e]2Ch 24:21
23:36 [f]Mt 10:23; 24:34
23:37 [g]2Ch 24:21; Mt 5:12
23:38 [h]1Ki 9:7,8; Jer 22:5
23:39 [i]Ps 118:26; Mt 21:9

[a] 39 Psalm 118:26

23:24 gnat. The smallest of unclean animals. **camel.** The largest of unclean animals. In Aramaic this also involved wordplay: “You strain out a gnat [*qamla’*] but swallow a camel [*gamla’*].”
23:25 See *WLC* 142.
23:26 Compare 15:11.
23:33 See *BC* 37.
23:34 I am sending. Compare Luke 11:49, where “God in his wisdom” (or “the wisdom of God”) sends. Jesus fills the role of wisdom.
23:35 By persecuting Christians, the unbelieving Pharisees became identified with their murdering forebears. Note that Jesus said, “Zechariah . . . whom *you* murdered” (emphasis added). **Abel . . . Zechariah.** Abel was the first person to be killed for righteousness’ sake (Ge 4:8). The identity of Zechariah is problematic, and all suggested solutions have difficulties. The best possibilities are: (1) The prophet Zechariah (Zec 1:1), who was the “son of Berekiah” but of whose martyrdom we have no knowledge. (2) Zechariah son of Baruch, who was killed by Zealots and was mentioned by Josephus (*Jewish War* 4.334–44). He was killed in the temple area, but probably not between the sanctuary and the altar. (3) The son of Jehoiada, the last martyr mentioned in the Old Testament according to the arrangement of the Hebrew Bible (2Ch 24:20–22), who was killed in the temple courtyard by Joash’s command. If it were not for the words “son of Berekiah,” this last option would be the most likely, since then the phrase “Abel to Zechariah” would refer to the first and last martyrs in the Hebrew canon. It is remotely possible that the words “son of Berekiah” were an insertion on the part of an early copyist (Lk 11:51 does not include them) or that Jehoiada was actually Zechariah’s grandfather and that his father was a Berekiah not named in Chronicles.
23:36 this generation. The punishment they experienced was probably the destruction of Jerusalem and the temple in A.D. 70. Compare note on 24:34.
23:37 Compare Deuteronomy 32:11; Psalms 36:7; 91:4.
23:39 again. Literally, “from now.” This is associated with the second coming (26:29,64). The Messiah of Israel will not be seen by unrepentant Israel until he comes again in glory and every tongue confesses him as Lord (Php 2:10–11).
■ **24:1—25:46** *Discourse: Kingdom Judgment.* Chapters 24–25 comprise the last of Jesus’ five great discourses in Matthew and focus on kingdom judgment. This section is generally called the “eschatological discourse” for its content or the “Olivet discourse” because Jesus delivered it on the Mount of Olives. Most of it is also recorded in Mark 13. It is difficult to interpret because the language

tell you the truth, not one stone here will be left on another;[j] every one will be thrown
down."
3As Jesus was sitting on the Mount of Olives,[k] the disciples came to him privately.
"Tell us," they said, "when will this happen, and what will be the sign of your coming and
of the end of the age?"
4Jesus answered: "Watch out that no one deceives you. **5**For many will come in my
name, claiming, 'I am the Christ,[a]' and will deceive many.[l] **6**You will hear of wars and
rumors of wars, but see to it that you are not alarmed. Such things must happen, but the
end is still to come. **7**Nation will rise against nation, and kingdom against kingdom.[m]
There will be famines[n] and earthquakes in various places. **8**All these are the beginning
of birth pains.
9"Then you will be handed over to be persecuted[o] and put to death,[p] and you will be
hated by all nations because of me. **10**At that time many will turn away from the faith and
will betray and hate each other, **11**and many false prophets[q] will appear and deceive
many people. **12**Because of the increase of wickedness, the love of most will grow cold,
13but he who stands firm to the end will be saved.[r] **14**And this gospel of the kingdom[s] will
be preached in the whole world[t] as a testimony to all nations, and then the end will
come.
15"So when you see standing in the holy place[u] 'the abomination that causes desolation,'[b][v] spoken of through the prophet Daniel—let the reader understand— **16**then let
those who are in Judea flee to the mountains. **17**Let no one on the roof of his house[w] go
down to take anything out of the house. **18**Let no one in the field go back to get his cloak.
19How dreadful it will be in those days for pregnant women and nursing mothers![x] **20**Pray
that your flight will not take place in winter or on the Sabbath. **21**For then there will be
great distress, unequaled from the beginning of the world until now—and never to be
equaled again.[y] **22**If those days had not been cut short, no one would survive, but for the
sake of the elect[z] those days will be shortened. **23**At that time if anyone says to you, 'Look,
here is the Christ!' or, 'There he is!' do not believe it.[a] **24**For false Christs and false prophets will appear and perform great signs and miracles[b] to deceive even the elect—if that
were possible. **25**See, I have told you ahead of time.

24:2 [j]Lk 19:44
24:3 [k]Mt 21:1
24:5 [l]ver 11,23,24; 1Jn 2:18
24:7 [m]Isa 19:2 [n]Ac 11:28
24:9 [o]Mt 10:17 [p]Jn 16:2
24:11 [q]Mt 7:15
24:13 [r]Mt 10:22
24:14 [s]Mt 4:23 [t]Lk 2:1; 4:5; Ac 11:28; 17:6; Ro 10:18; Col 1:6,23; Rev 3:10; 16:14
24:15 [u]Ac 6:13 [v]Da 9:27; 11:31; 12:11
24:17 [w]1Sa 9:25; Mt 10:27; Lk 12:3; Ac 10:9
24:19 [x]Lk 23:29
24:21 [y]Da 12:1; Joel 2:2
24:22 [z]ver 24,31
24:23 [a]Lk 17:23; 21:8
24:24 [b]2Th 2:9-11; Rev 13:13

[a] *5* Or *Messiah*; also in verse 23 [b] *15* Daniel 9:27; 11:31; 12:11

is symbolic and because it deals with a complex of events, not just a single incident. There are three basic interpretive approaches: (1) All or most of chapter 24 (at least up through verse 35) is concerned exclusively with the destruction of Jerusalem, and the "coming" is the exaltation of Jesus in heaven. (2) All of this sermon is concerned with the final coming in judgment. (3) This sermon contains a mixture of near-future and far-future events or deals with Jerusalem as symbolic of world judgment in such a way that it is difficult to separate them sharply. This third interpretation may account best for the presence of language with both near and distant foci.
24:2 not one stone. The temple was destroyed in A.D. 70. Not a single stone was left upon another.
24:3 The disciples were correct in understanding that the destruction of Jerusalem and Jesus' coming in judgment are closely related, but they incorrectly assumed that the two events would occur at the same time. We should not assume that all events in this discourse are chronologically concurrent or *necessarily* sequential.
24:4–14 Wars, earthquakes, persecutions and false prophets are all Messianic "birth pains" (v. 8) or signs of Jesus' coming, but they are only indications *that* Jesus is coming in judgment, not indications of *when* he is coming. Note that such things must happen, but that "the end is still to come" (v. 6) and that these things are the "beginning of birth pains" (v. 8). These signs characterize the entire period between Jesus' resurrection and his coming in judgment. Knowing when their Lord would return would lead his disciples to laziness and laxity in their watchfulness. The only *when* that Jesus gives is task oriented: after the gospel has been preached to the whole world.
24:15–21 Although some interpreters have taken this passage, along with the rest of the sermon, to refer exclusively to the second coming in judgment, certain elements contain unmistakable references to the destruction of Jerusalem in A.D. 70. That this is in view is clear from the parallel account in Luke 21:20–24. This section deals with the first of the disciples' questions (v. 3). The destruction of Jerusalem, however, was a typical foretaste of the final judgment and so serves as a sign of the coming wrath. It stands as a unique declaration of the annihilation of the old age and is thus a specific and uniquely important "birth pain" (v. 8).
24:15 abomination that causes desolation. Literally, "the abomination of desolation." The phrase could be understood as the abomination that results from desolation. If so, it perhaps should be read in the light of 23:38. The abominable siege of Jerusalem that resulted in its being left desolate ensued on account of the people's stubborn and unrepentant refusal to submit to God (cf. Jer 12:7; 22:5). This interpretation coincides well with Luke, who substitutes for "abomination that causes desolation" the warning "When you see Jerusalem being surrounded by armies" (Lk 21:20). It would also correspond with Daniel 8:13, where the rebelliousness of God's people resulted in the desolation of the temple. On the other hand, although "holy place" here might mean the city, it most naturally would mean the temple area, and by the time the Romans stood in the temple, it was too late to flee. So most understand "abomination" to refer to some catalyst that brought about the outpouring of God's temporal judgment on Jerusalem, not the judgment itself. Perhaps the Zealots' appropriation (and thus desecration) of the temple precincts during the war is the abomination in view. The term picks up on the phrase "abomination that causes desolation" in Daniel 8:13 (where "rebellion that causes desolation" is used), 9:27, 11:31 and 12:11. Daniel 9:27 occurs at the climax of the seventy-weeks vision; its interpretation is controversial. Daniel 11:31 makes reference to the abomination by the arch-typical antichrist, generally recognized to have been Antiochus Epiphanes, who desecrated the temple by offering sacrifices to Zeus in it in 168 B.C. Daniel 12:11 may refer to the destruction of Jerusalem, to the wicked acts of the final antichrist or perhaps to both. **let the reader understand.** Probably a comment made not by Matthew, but by Jesus. In either case, the meaning is not "let the reader of this *Gospel* understand," but "let the reader of *Daniel* understand what the prophet was ultimately speaking about."
24:16 flee to the mountains. According to the early church historian Eusebius, the Christians did flee Jerusalem during the Jewish war "in obedience to a prophecy" (*Ecclesiastical History* 3.5.).
24:22 those days. Although this is usually taken with verses 15–21, it is also possible to understand it as reverting to the general birth pains of verses 4–14. **no one.** Literally, "not all flesh," a Semitic way of referring to "no human being in the world."
24:24 if that were possible. Indicates that, although deceit of the elect is the intent of the false prophets, it is only their intention

26"So if anyone tells you, 'There he is, out in the desert,' do not go out; or, 'Here he
is, in the inner rooms,' do not believe it. 27For as lightning[c] that comes from the east is
visible even in the west, so will be the coming of the Son of Man.[d] 28Wherever there is a
carcass, there the vultures will gather.[e]
29"Immediately after the distress of those days

" 'the sun will be darkened,
and the moon will not give its light;
the stars will fall from the sky,
and the heavenly bodies will be shaken.'[a][f]

30"At that time the sign of the Son of Man will appear in the sky, and all the nations
of the earth will mourn. They will see the Son of Man coming on the clouds of the sky,[g]
with power and great glory. 31And he will send his angels[h] with a loud trumpet call,[i] and
they will gather his elect from the four winds, from one end of the heavens to the other.
32"Now learn this lesson from the fig tree: As soon as its twigs get tender and its leaves
come out, you know that summer is near. 33Even so, when you see all these things, you
know that it[b] is near, right at the door.[j] 34I tell you the truth, this generation[c] will certainly not pass away until all these things have happened.[k] 35Heaven and earth will pass
away, but my words will never pass away.[l]

The Day and Hour Unknown

36"No one knows about that day or hour, not even the angels in heaven, nor the Son,[d]
but only the Father.[m] 37As it was in the days of Noah,[n] so it will be at the coming of the
Son of Man. 38For in the days before the flood, people were eating and drinking, marrying and giving in marriage,[o] up to the day Noah entered the ark; 39and they knew nothing about what would happen until the flood came and took them all away. That is how
it will be at the coming of the Son of Man. 40Two men will be in the field; one will be tak-
en and the other left.[p] 41Two women will be grinding with a hand mill; one will be tak-
en and the other left.[q]
42"Therefore keep watch, because you do not know on what day your Lord will
come.[r] 43But understand this: If the owner of the house had known at what time of night
the thief was coming,[s] he would have kept watch and would not have let his house be
broken into. 44So you also must be ready,[t] because the Son of Man will come at an hour
when you do not expect him.
45"Who then is the faithful and wise servant,[u] whom the master has put in charge of
the servants in his household to give them their food at the proper time? 46It will be good
for that servant whose master finds him doing so when he returns.[v] 47I tell you the truth,
he will put him in charge of all his possessions.[w] 48But suppose that servant is wicked
and says to himself, 'My master is staying away a long time,' 49and he then begins to beat
his fellow servants and to eat and drink with drunkards.[x] 50The master of that servant
will come on a day when he does not expect him and at an hour he is not aware of. 51He

24:27 [c]Lk 17:24 [d]Mt 8:20
24:28 [e]Lk 17:37
24:29 [f]Isa 13:10; 34:4; Eze 32:7; Joel 2:10, 31; Zep 1:15; Rev 6:12,13; 8:12
24:30 [g]Da 7:13; Rev 1:7
24:31 [h]Mt 13:41 [i]Isa 27:13; Zec 9:14; 1Co 15:52; 1Th 4:16; Rev 8:2; 10:7; 11:15
24:33 [j]Jas 5:9
24:34 [k]Mt 16:28; 23:36
24:35 [l]Mt 5:18
24:36 [m]Ac 1:7
24:37 [n]Ge 6:5; 7:6-23
24:38 [o]Mt 22:30
24:40 [p]Lk 17:34
24:41 [q]Lk 17:35
24:42 [r]Mt 25:13; Lk 12:40
24:43 [s]Lk 12:39
24:44 [t]1Th 5:6
24:45 [u]Mt 25:21,23
24:46 [v]Rev 16:15
24:47 [w]Mt 25:21,23
24:49 [x]Lk 21:34

[a] *29* Isaiah 13:10; 34:4 [b] *33* Or *he* [c] *34* Or *race* [d] *36* Some manuscripts do not have *nor the Son.*

and not a real possibility. However, the warning is still real because people can *think* they are elect without actually being so. See *CD* 1.VI.

24:27 as lightning. The coming of Christ will be evident, unambiguous and clear to all.

24:28 Wherever there is a carcass. Compare Job 39:30. Just as the carcass inevitably results in the gathering of carrion birds, so will the wickedness of people certainly result in their judgment. Or perhaps the proverb simply means that the sign of Jesus' coming will be as clear as the fact that carrion is around where vultures gather. Compare the parallel in Luke 17:37. See *BC* 28.

24:29–31 Some have understood these verses to represent the defeat of Satan's minions, the Son of Man's vindication and the spread of the gospel to all the world, which occurred symbolically at the destruction of Jerusalem. But the language of verse 31 parallels other passages (13:41; 16:27; 25:31; 1Co 15:52; 1Th 4:14–17). It is therefore difficult not to take this passage as a reference to Christ's final coming in judgment. Every interpretation has its difficulties, and it is best to focus on Jesus' main message in this chapter: Always be on guard against Satan and ready for judgment.

24:30 sign. The military banner of Christ coming to conquer and judge. The tribes of Earth mourning is an allusion to Zechariah 12:10–12, and the coming on the clouds refers to Christ's assumption of dominion prophesied in Daniel 7:13–14. See *WLC* 56; *BC* 37.

24:34 this generation. Often understood to mean "this race" or "this kind of people" (i.e., wicked and adulterous people; cf. 12:39), but the phrase more naturally means the people who were alive when Jesus spoke. **all these things.** Refers to the "all these things" of verse 33, which are distinguished from the consummation itself. They are the birth pains and signs that lead up to and point to the final coming of Christ, including the greatest birth pain: the siege and fall of Jerusalem. All of the elements of this prophecy, save only the consummation itself, occurred in some form before the disciples died. See note on Luke 21:32.

24:36 No one knows. All attempts at predicting the time of Christ's return are here condemned. If it were possible to deduce the time from Scripture, was not Jesus a good enough student of Scripture to ascertain it? As Jesus was fully human as well as fully divine, without any commingling of the two natures, it is not surprising that his human mind remained ignorant of some matters. (See theological article "Jesus Christ, God and Man" at Jn 1.) This verse is difficult for those who deny that Jesus considered himself the "Son," since it is extremely unlikely that the early church would have invented a saying that appeared to limit Jesus' knowledge. See *WCF* 33.3; *WLC* 16,88; *BC* 37.

24:42–51 keep watch. Active stewardship, not lazy waiting. See *WCF* 33.3; *WLC* 88.

will cut him to pieces and assign him a place with the hypocrites, where there will be
weeping and gnashing of teeth.[y]

The Parable of the Ten Virgins

25 "At that time the kingdom of heaven will be like[z] ten virgins who took their
lamps[a] and went out to meet the bridegroom.[b] 2 Five of them were foolish and
five were wise.[c] 3 The foolish ones took their lamps but did not take any oil with them.
4 The wise, however, took oil in jars along with their lamps. 5 The bridegroom was a long
time in coming, and they all became drowsy and fell asleep.[d]
6 "At midnight the cry rang out: 'Here's the bridegroom! Come out to meet him!'
7 "Then all the virgins woke up and trimmed their lamps. 8 The foolish ones said to the
wise, 'Give us some of your oil; our lamps are going out.'[e]
9 " 'No,' they replied, 'there may not be enough for both us and you. Instead, go to
those who sell oil and buy some for yourselves.'
10 "But while they were on their way to buy the oil, the bridegroom arrived. The virgins who were ready went in with him to the wedding banquet.[f] And the door was shut.
11 "Later the others also came. 'Sir! Sir!' they said. 'Open the door for us!'
12 "But he replied, 'I tell you the truth, I don't know you.'
13 "Therefore keep watch, because you do not know the day or the hour.[g]

The Parable of the Talents

14 "Again, it will be like a man going on a journey,[h] who called his servants and entrusted his property to them. 15 To one he gave five talents[a] of money, to another two talents, and to another one talent, each according to his ability.[i] Then he went on his journey. 16 The man who had received the five talents went at once and put his money to work
and gained five more. 17 So also, the one with the two talents gained two more. 18 But the
man who had received the one talent went off, dug a hole in the ground and hid his master's money.
19 "After a long time the master of those servants returned and settled accounts with
them.[j] 20 The man who had received the five talents brought the other five. 'Master,' he
said, 'you entrusted me with five talents. See, I have gained five more.'
21 "His master replied, 'Well done, good and faithful servant! You have been faithful
with a few things; I will put you in charge of many things.[k] Come and share your master's happiness!'
22 "The man with the two talents also came. 'Master,' he said, 'you entrusted me with
two talents; see, I have gained two more.'
23 "His master replied, 'Well done, good and faithful servant! You have been faithful
with a few things; I will put you in charge of many things.[l] Come and share your master's happiness!'
24 "Then the man who had received the one talent came. 'Master,' he said, 'I knew that
you are a hard man, harvesting where you have not sown and gathering where you have
not scattered seed. 25 So I was afraid and went out and hid your talent in the ground. See,
here is what belongs to you.'
26 "His master replied, 'You wicked, lazy servant! So you knew that I harvest where I
have not sown and gather where I have not scattered seed? 27 Well then, you should have
put my money on deposit with the bankers, so that when I returned I would have received it back with interest.
28 " 'Take the talent from him and give it to the one who has the ten talents. 29 For everyone who has will be given more, and he will have an abundance. Whoever does not
have, even what he has will be taken from him.[m] 30 And throw that worthless servant outside, into the darkness, where there will be weeping and gnashing of teeth.'[n]

The Sheep and the Goats

31 "When the Son of Man comes[o] in his glory, and all the angels with him, he will sit

24:51 [y]Mt 8:12
25:1 [z]Mt 13:24 [a]Lk 12:35-38; Ac 20:8; Rev 4:5 [b]Rev 19:7; 21:2
25:2 [c]Mt 24:45
25:5 [d]1Th 5:6
25:8 [e]Lk 12:35
25:10 [f]Rev 19:9
25:13 [g]Mt 24:42,44; Mk 13:35; Lk 12:40
25:14 [h]Mt 21:33; Lk 19:12
25:15 [i]Mt 18:24,25
25:19 [j]Mt 18:23
25:21 [k]ver 23; Mt 24:45,47; Lk 16:10
25:23 [l]ver 21
25:29 [m]Mt 13:12; Mk 4:25; Lk 8:18; 19:26
25:30 [n]Mt 8:12
25:31 [o]Mt 16:27; Lk 17:30

[a] *15* A talent was worth more than a thousand dollars.

25:1–13 By their readiness, the wise distinguish themselves from the foolish during the delay of Christ's return. Being "ready" (v. 10) includes being prepared for a long delay; short-lived zeal is inadequate. See *BC* 37.
25:15 talent. A talent (about 75 pounds or 34 kilograms) of gold would be the equivalent of 20 years' wages for a day laborer. Even a talent of silver would come to more than a year's pay.
25:21–30 See *WCF* 5.6; 16.6; 33.2; *WSC* 38.
25:24–25 I knew that you are a hard man. The third servant was unwilling to invest his efforts into developing the talent for the benefit of another. His attitude was not one of stewardship or service.
25:31–46 See *WCF* 3.3; 6.6; 16.7; 33.2; *WLC* 27,87,88,89,90,135,136,152; *WSC* 19,84; *BC* 12,37; *HC* 11,32,52.
25:31 Son of Man. Compare note on 8:20. See *WLC* 16,56; *BC* 37.

on his throne[p] in heavenly glory. 32All the nations will be gathered before him, and he
will separate[q] the people one from another as a shepherd separates the sheep from the
goats.[r] 33He will put the sheep on his right and the goats on his left.
34"Then the King will say to those on his right, 'Come, you who are blessed by my Father; take your inheritance, the kingdom[s] prepared for you since the creation of the
world.[t] 35For I was hungry and you gave me something to eat, I was thirsty and you gave
me something to drink, I was a stranger and you invited me in,[u] 36I needed clothes and
you clothed me,[v] I was sick and you looked after me,[w] I was in prison and you came to
visit me.'[x]
37"Then the righteous will answer him, 'Lord, when did we see you hungry and feed
you, or thirsty and give you something to drink? 38When did we see you a stranger and
invite you in, or needing clothes and clothe you? 39When did we see you sick or in prison and go to visit you?'
40"The King will reply, 'I tell you the truth, whatever you did for one of the least of
these brothers of mine, you did for me.'[y]
41"Then he will say to those on his left, 'Depart from me,[z] you who are cursed, into
the eternal fire[a] prepared for the devil and his angels.[b] 42For I was hungry and you gave
me nothing to eat, I was thirsty and you gave me nothing to drink, 43I was a stranger and
you did not invite me in, I needed clothes and you did not clothe me, I was sick and in
prison and you did not look after me.'
44"They also will answer, 'Lord, when did we see you hungry or thirsty or a stranger
or needing clothes or sick or in prison, and did not help you?'
45"He will reply, 'I tell you the truth, whatever you did not do for one of the least of
these, you did not do for me.'[c]
46"Then they will go away to eternal punishment, but the righteous to eternal life."[d][e]

The Plot Against Jesus

26 When Jesus had finished saying all these things,[f] he said to his disciples, 2"As
you know, the Passover[g] is two days away—and the Son of Man will be handed over to be crucified."
3Then the chief priests and the elders of the people assembled[h] in the palace of the
high priest, whose name was Caiaphas,[i] 4and they plotted to arrest Jesus in some sly way
and kill him.[j] 5"But not during the Feast," they said, "or there may be a riot[k] among the
people."

Jesus Anointed at Bethany

6While Jesus was in Bethany[l] in the home of a man known as Simon the Leper, 7a
woman came to him with an alabaster jar of very expensive perfume, which she poured
on his head as he was reclining at the table.
8When the disciples saw this, they were indignant. "Why this waste?" they asked.
9"This perfume could have been sold at a high price and the money given to the poor."
10Aware of this, Jesus said to them, "Why are you bothering this woman? She has
done a beautiful thing to me. 11The poor you will always have with you,[m] but you will
not always have me. 12When she poured this perfume on my body, she did it to prepare
me for burial.[n] 13I tell you the truth, wherever this gospel is preached throughout the
world, what she has done will also be told, in memory of her."

25:31 [p]Mt 19:28
25:32 [q]Mal 3:18 [r]Eze 34:17,20
25:34 [s]Mt 3:2; 5:3,10,19; 19:14; Ac 20:32; 1Co 15:50; Gal 5:21; Jas 2:5 [t]Heb 4:3; 9:26; Rev 13:8; 17:8
25:35 [u]Job 31:32; Isa 58:7; Eze 18:7; Heb 13:2
25:36 [v]Isa 58:7; Eze 18:7; Jas 2:15,16 [w]Jas 1:27 [x]2Ti 1:16
25:40 [y]Pr 19:17; Mt 10:40,42; Heb 6:10; 13:2
25:41 [z]Mt 7:23 [a]Isa 66:24; Mt 3:12;; 5:22; Mk 9:43,48; Lk 3:17; Jude 7 [b]2Pe 2:4
25:45 [c]Pr 14:31; 17:5
25:46 [d]Mt 19:29; Jn 3:15,16,36; 17:2,3; Ro 2:7; Gal 6:8; 5:11,13,20 [e]Da 12:2; Jn 5:29; Ac 24:15; Ro 2:7,8; Gal 6:8
26:1 [f]Mt 7:28
26:2 [g]Jn 11:55; 13:1
26:3 [h]Ps 2:2 [i]ver 57; Jn 11:47-53; 18:13,14,24,28
26:4 [j]Mt 12:14
26:5 [k]Mt 27:24
26:6 [l]Mt 21:17
26:11 [m]Dt 15:11
26:12 [n]Jn 19:40

25:32 the people. Literally, "them." The division concerns individuals, not nations, as the Greek pronoun "them" makes clear. **sheep.** The image of Christ's elect as sheep is based on Ezekiel 34 and has already appeared in Jesus' teaching (10:16; 18:12). For this context, note Ezekiel 34:17.

25:40 these brothers of mine. Christ's disciples (cf. 10:42; 12:48–49; 18:14), as opposed to all Jews or the poor and needy in general. The judgment of the nations depends on how they respond to Christians and thus to the gospel (10:40–42), not only because it is through the testimony of Christians that the Gentiles can hear and believe (Ro 10:14), but also because Christ identifies so closely with his people that their suffering is his suffering, and compassion shown to them is compassion shown to him.

■ **26:1—28:20** *Passion and Resurrection.* Chapters 26–28 form the last major section of Matthew's Gospel. They portray the drama of Jesus' death and resurrection, as well as his appearances and ascension. These final chapters exalt Jesus by drawing attention to his decisive sacrifice on the cross, his victory over death and his commission for the church to continue expanding the kingdom of God until he returns.

26:1—27:66 See *WCF* 8.4.

26:5 not during the Feast. Although the officials intended to postpone the murder of Jesus until after Passover, God purposed (v. 2) that this pivotal event take place on or just before the Feast (see note on v. 17).

26:6–13 Mark 14:3–9 is an exact parallel; John 12:1–8 differs chronologically, but none of the details conflict, and it probably refers to the same incident. John states that the woman anointed Jesus' *feet*—this may indicate that she poured on so much that it ran down even to his feet. This is not the same incident as that recorded in Luke 7:36–38, which bears only superficial similarity to this story.

26:8–9 they were indignant. John reports the hypocritical objection of Judas (Jn 12:4–5). Matthew indicates that other disciples joined in the objection.

26:11 The poor you will always have with you. Concern for the poor is a Scriptural priority, but it is not as high a priority as love for Jesus. The words of Jesus reveal his amazing claim to worship and make care for the poor the concern of all those who cannot now anoint his feet. See *BC* 19,35.

Judas Agrees to Betray Jesus

14 Then one of the Twelve—the one called Judas Iscariot[o]—went to the chief priests
15 and asked, "What are you willing to give me if I hand him over to you?" So they counted out for him thirty silver coins.[p] 16 From then on Judas watched for an opportunity to
hand him over.

The Lord's Supper

17 On the first day of the Feast of Unleavened Bread,[q] the disciples came to Jesus and
asked, "Where do you want us to make preparations for you to eat the Passover?"
18 He replied, "Go into the city to a certain man and tell him, 'The Teacher says: My
appointed time[r] is near. I am going to celebrate the Passover with my disciples at your
house.' " 19 So the disciples did as Jesus had directed them and prepared the Passover.
20 When evening came, Jesus was reclining at the table with the Twelve. 21 And while
they were eating, he said, "I tell you the truth, one of you will betray me."[s]
22 They were very sad and began to say to him one after the other, "Surely not I, Lord?"
23 Jesus replied, "The one who has dipped his hand into the bowl with me will betray
me.[t] 24 The Son of Man will go just as it is written about him.[u] But woe to that man who
betrays the Son of Man! It would be better for him if he had not been born."
25 Then Judas, the one who would betray him, said, "Surely not I, Rabbi?"[v]
Jesus answered, "Yes, it is you."[a]
26 While they were eating, Jesus took bread, gave thanks and broke it,[w] and gave it to
his disciples, saying, "Take and eat; this is my body."
27 Then he took the cup, gave thanks and offered it to them, saying, "Drink from it, all
of you. 28 This is my blood of the[b] covenant,[x] which is poured out for many for the forgiveness of sins.[y] 29 I tell you, I will not drink of this fruit of the vine from now on until
that day when I drink it anew with you[z] in my Father's kingdom."
30 When they had sung a hymn, they went out to the Mount of Olives.[a]

26:14 [o]ver 25,47; Mt 10:4
26:15 [p]Ex 21:32; Zec 11:12
26:17 [q]Ex 12:18-20
26:18 [r]Jn 7:6,8,30; 12:23; 13:1; 17:1
26:21 [s]Lk 22:21-23; Jn 13:21
26:23 [t]Ps 41:9; Jn 13:18
26:24 [u]Isa 53; Da 9:26; Mk 9:12; Lk 24:25-27,46; Ac 17:2,3; 26:22,23
26:25 [v]Mt 23:7
26:26 [w]Mt 14:19; 1Co 10:16
26:28 [x]Ex 24:6-8; Heb 9:20 [y]Mt 20:28; Mk 1:4
26:29 [z]Ac 10:41
26:30 [a]Mt 21:1; Mk 14:26

[a] *25* Or *"You yourself have said it"* [b] *28* Some manuscripts *the new*

26:15 Compare note on 27:4.
26:17 the first day of the Feast. The day of preparation for Passover, presumably Thursday, 14 Nisan. Thus, Jesus ate the Passover that evening (which was the beginning of Friday, 15 Nisan, Passover Day) and was crucified in the afternoon of Passover Day. The problem here is that John seems in some places (Jn 18:28; 19:14, 31) to present Jesus as crucified on 14 Nisan, the day *before* Passover, in which case the Lord's Supper was not a Passover meal (unless Jesus ate the Passover a day early). But although John presents Jesus as the Passover Lamb, he does not say that Jesus was killed *at the same time* as the lambs in the temple, and the relevant passages in John do not necessarily prove 14 Nisan as the crucifixion date. Calvin understood "Preparation Day" to be the day before the Passover celebration and argued that since 15 Nisan fell on a Friday, the Jews according to some tradition combined the Passover with the weekly Sabbath and thus celebrated Passover on 16 Nisan. If so, the reference in 27:62 is to the Preparation Day that the Jewish leadership observed. There is some difficulty, however, in seeing how Jesus' disciples could have had their lamb slaughtered in advance of the officially accepted Day of Preparation, and Mark 14:12 unambiguously indicates that Jesus arranged for Passover preparation on the day when the lambs were customarily slaughtered. Whatever the solution, Matthew here makes it plain that it was a Passover meal that Jesus ate with his disciples on the eve of his crucifixion. (See also note on Jn 19:14.)
26:18 My appointed time. Jesus emphasized again that all the terrible events that were soon to take place were totally under God's sovereign control.
26:24 Son of Man. See note on 8:20. **as it is written about him.** Points out that Judas's betrayal was ordained by God. Even sins are foreordained, but their *sinfulness* comes not from God but from the evil intent of the human perpetrator. God's foreordination does not relieve the sinner of responsibility for his or her sin (cf. Ro 9:19–20). The question arises as to where Judas's betrayal is prophesied in the Old Testament. While there is no obvious prophecy that fits, the New Testament sees the psalms, especially those of David, as Messianic words. Passages like Psalms 41:9 and 55:12–14 express the horror of betrayal by a close companion in a way that indirectly prophesies Judas's betrayal, and Peter applied Psalms 69:25 and 109:8 to Judas (see Ac 1:16–20).
26:26–30 See *WCF* 27.2; 27.3; 29.2; 29.3; 29.5; *WLC* 162,164,168, 169,170,171,176; *WSC* 93; *BC* 33,35; *HC* 66,75.
26:26–29 That Jesus transformed his last Passover meal to institute the Lord's Supper shows the unity of God's redemption and revelation: It demonstrates the essential continuity between the old and new covenants. It claims that the true meaning of the Passover lay in the fact that it pointed to Jesus Christ. It shows the essential relationship between Jesus' death and the forgiveness of sins, as well as the connection of both to the Passover sacrifice. It looks forward to the Messianic banquet at the consummation. **this is my body.** These words have aroused much discussion that misses the force of the figure. It is clearly an instance of metonymy, a figure of speech that calls something by the name of that which represents it; e.g., "He is loyal to the *crown*" or "His *pen* is full of invective" or "His *heart* was broken." Jesus spoke these words in the body, and his declaration presents the bread as representing his body. Our feeding upon Christ's flesh and blood is not some kind of cannibalism, but a spiritual partaking of Christ, an identification of ourselves with him (see Jn 6:53–58). See *HC* 78.
26:28 my blood of the covenant. This is Jesus' fulfillment of the representative blood of the covenant described in Exodus 24:8. Probably Jews already understood the wine of Passover to represent the blood of the covenant (recorded in the Mishnaic tractate Pesahim 10:6). Christ's death, symbolized by his blood, truly establishes God's relationship with his people, by which he remits their sins. Luke 22:17–20 and 1 Corinthians 11:23–25 record the fact that Jesus called the cup of his blood the "new covenant." Thus, the renewal of God's covenant with his people, as foretold in passages such as Jeremiah 31:31–34, is also in view. **covenant.** The Greek New Testament term for "covenant" (*diatheke*) is not the usual word for an agreement between equal parties (a contract, *suntheke*). It is a testament or disposition by one person, formally declaring the terms of a relationship. Its ordinary use was in reference to a will (cf. Heb 9:16–22). The reason for using this term lies in the Old Testament concept of covenant, whereby God formally declared the nature, terms and sanctions (blessings for obedience and curses for disobedience) of his relationship with Israel. God never negotiated a covenant. He simply announced and implemented it. Covenants were ratified by a symbolic death, which represented the curse that would fall upon those who broke the covenant. The new covenant, however, is the consummation of God's covenants with his people. It was not ratified by a *symbolic* death but by the *real* death of Jesus, who endured the curse for us. See *WLC* 170,171,172,174.

Jesus Predicts Peter's Denial

31 Then Jesus told them, "This very night you will all fall away on account of me,[b] for
it is written:

> " 'I will strike the shepherd,
> and the sheep of the flock will be scattered.'[a] [c]

32 But after I have risen, I will go ahead of you into Galilee."[d]
33 Peter replied, "Even if all fall away on account of you, I never will."
34 "I tell you the truth," Jesus answered, "this very night, before the rooster crows, you
will disown me three times."[e]
35 But Peter declared, "Even if I have to die with you,[f] I will never disown you." And
all the other disciples said the same.

Gethsemane

36 Then Jesus went with his disciples to a place called Gethsemane, and he said to
them, "Sit here while I go over there and pray." 37 He took Peter and the two sons of Zebedee[g] along with him, and he began to be sorrowful and troubled. 38 Then he said to
them, "My soul is overwhelmed with sorrow[h] to the point of death. Stay here and keep
watch with me."[i]
39 Going a little farther, he fell with his face to the ground and prayed, "My Father, if
it is possible, may this cup[j] be taken from me. Yet not as I will, but as you will."[k]
40 Then he returned to his disciples and found them sleeping. "Could you men not
keep watch with me[l] for one hour?" he asked Peter. 41 "Watch and pray so that you will
not fall into temptation.[m] The spirit is willing, but the body is weak."
42 He went away a second time and prayed, "My Father, if it is not possible for this cup
to be taken away unless I drink it, may your will be done."
43 When he came back, he again found them sleeping, because their eyes were heavy.
44 So he left them and went away once more and prayed the third time, saying the same
thing.
45 Then he returned to the disciples and said to them, "Are you still sleeping and resting? Look, the hour[n] is near, and the Son of Man is betrayed into the hands of sinners.
46 Rise, let us go! Here comes my betrayer!"

Jesus Arrested

47 While he was still speaking, Judas, one of the Twelve, arrived. With him was a large
crowd armed with swords and clubs, sent from the chief priests and the elders of the people. 48 Now the betrayer had arranged a signal with them: "The one I kiss is the man; arrest him." 49 Going at once to Jesus, Judas said, "Greetings, Rabbi!"[o] and kissed him.
50 Jesus replied, "Friend,[p] do what you came for."[b]
Then the men stepped forward, seized Jesus and arrested him. 51 With that, one of
Jesus' companions reached for his sword,[q] drew it out and struck the servant of the high
priest, cutting off his ear.[r]
52 "Put your sword back in its place," Jesus said to him, "for all who draw the sword
will die by the sword.[s] 53 Do you think I cannot call on my Father, and he will at once put
at my disposal more than twelve legions of angels?[t] 54 But how then would the Scriptures
be fulfilled[u] that say it must happen in this way?"

26:31 [b]Mt 11:6 [c]Zec 13:7; Jn 16:32
26:32 [d]Mt 28:7,10,16
26:34 [e]ver 75; Jn 13:38
26:35 [f]Jn 13:37
26:37 [g]Mt 4:21
26:38 [h]Jn 12:27 [i]ver 40, 41
26:39 [j]Mt 20:22 [k]ver 42; Ps 40:6-8; Isa 50:5; Jn 5:30; 6:38
26:40 [l]ver 38
26:41 [m]Mt 6:13
26:45 [n]ver 18
26:49 [o]ver 25
26:50 [p]Mt 20:13; 22:12
26:51 [q]Lk 22:36,38 [r]Jn 18:10
26:52 [s]Ge 9:6; Rev 13:10
26:53 [t]2Ki 6:17; Da 7:10; Mt 4:11
26:54 [u]ver 24

[a] *31* Zech. 13:7 [b] *50* Or *"Friend, why have you come?"*

26:31 I will strike the shepherd. In the context of Zechariah 13:7, Yahweh strikes the shepherd, the man who is close to him. As a result, God's "little ones" (Zec 13:7) are scattered, but they are subsequently renewed and truly become God's people. The disciples' forthcoming abandonment of Jesus is representative of the nation's apostasy, and their return represents the remnant that God will save.

26:32 I will go ahead of you into Galilee. The fulfillment is recorded in 28:16.

26:34 before the rooster crows. The apparent disagreement with Mark (Mk 14:30,72, according to most manuscripts) is a pseudo-problem. Matthew simply presents a condensed account and does not make a point of mentioning two crows of the rooster. It was clearly one particular rooster crow that convicted Peter.

26:36–46 See *WCF* 8.4; *WLC* 37,192; *WSC* 22; *HC* 44.

26:39 cup. In Scripture, "cup" frequently refers to the cup of God's wrath (cf., e.g., Ps 75:8; Isa 51:17,22; Jer 25:15–16). Jesus was horrified at the prospect of enduring his Father's wrath. We are able to face death knowing that God is with us, but Jesus had to face death knowing that his Father would be pitted against him in wrath and condemnation. See *WLC* 185; *WSC* 103.

26:41 Watch and pray. Even in his agony, Jesus' concern was for his disciples. See *WLC* 195; *WSC* 106; *HC* 127.

26:52 Put your sword back. Physical swords were inappropriate for defending Jesus, who has more power at his disposal than we could imagine. Likewise, military force is inappropriate to defending the gospel. This passage cannot be used in defense of pacifism, in opposition to capital punishment or in denying the *state* the use of physical warfare or force. If anything, Jesus' words appear to be based on the principle of Genesis 9:6 that he who kills a man is himself to be killed, thus explicitly empowering the state to execute murderers. More to the point, this passage deals with *spiritual*, not physical, warfare. Spiritual battles must be waged with spiritual weapons, with the sword of the Spirit, the two-edged sword that is the Word of God (cf. 2Co 10:3–6; Heb 4:12). See *HC* 105.

26:54,56 be fulfilled. Jesus is committed to the fulfillment of the

55At that time Jesus said to the crowd, "Am I leading a rebellion, that you have come
out with swords and clubs to capture me? Every day I sat in the temple courts teaching,[v]
and you did not arrest me. 56But this has all taken place that the writings of the prophets might be fulfilled."[w] Then all the disciples deserted him and fled.

Before the Sanhedrin

57Those who had arrested Jesus took him to Caiaphas,[x] the high priest, where the
teachers of the law and the elders had assembled. 58But Peter followed him at a distance,
right up to the courtyard of the high priest.[y] He entered and sat down with the guards[z]
to see the outcome.
59The chief priests and the whole Sanhedrin[a] were looking for false evidence against
Jesus so that they could put him to death. 60But they did not find any, though many false
witnesses[b] came forward.
Finally two[c] came forward 61and declared, "This fellow said, 'I am able to destroy the
temple of God and rebuild it in three days.'"[d]
62Then the high priest stood up and said to Jesus, "Are you not going to answer? What
is this testimony that these men are bringing against you?" 63But Jesus remained silent.[e]
The high priest said to him, "I charge you under oath[f] by the living God:[g] Tell us if
you are the Christ,[a] the Son of God."
64"Yes, it is as you say," Jesus replied. "But I say to all of you: In the future you will
see the Son of Man sitting at the right hand of the Mighty One[h] and coming on the clouds
of heaven."[i]
65Then the high priest tore his clothes[j] and said, "He has spoken blasphemy! Why do
we need any more witnesses? Look, now you have heard the blasphemy. 66What do you
think?"
"He is worthy of death,"[k] they answered.
67Then they spit in his face and struck him with their fists.[l] Others slapped him
68and said, "Prophesy to us, Christ. Who hit you?"[m]

Peter Disowns Jesus

69Now Peter was sitting out in the courtyard, and a servant girl came to him. "You
also were with Jesus of Galilee," she said.
70But he denied it before them all. "I don't know what you're talking about," he said.
71Then he went out to the gateway, where another girl saw him and said to the people there, "This fellow was with Jesus of Nazareth."
72He denied it again, with an oath: "I don't know the man!"
73After a little while, those standing there went up to Peter and said, "Surely you are
one of them, for your accent gives you away."
74Then he began to call down curses on himself and he swore to them, "I don't know
the man!"
Immediately a rooster crowed. 75Then Peter remembered the word Jesus had spoken:
"Before the rooster crows, you will disown me three times."[n] And he went outside and
wept bitterly.

[a] *63* Or *Messiah*; also in verse 68

26:55 [v]Mk 12:35; Lk 21:37; Jn 7:14, 28; 18:20
26:56 [w]ver 24
26:57 [x]ver 3
26:58 [y]Jn 18:15 [z]Jn 7:32, 45,46
26:59 [a]Mt 5:22
26:60 [b]Ps 27:12; 35:11; Ac 6:13 [c]Dt 19:15
26:61 [d]Jn 2:19
26:63 [e]Mt 27:12,14 [f]Lev 5:1 [g]Mt 16:16
26:64 [h]Ps 110:1 [i]Da 7:13; Rev 1:7
26:65 [j]Mk 14:63
26:66 [k]Lev 24:16; Jn 19:7
26:67 [l]Mt 16:21; 27:30
26:68 [m]Lk 22:63-65
26:75 [n]ver 34; Jn 13:38

Scriptures, for they set forth the decrees of God (cf. Lk 22:37). Some commentators suggest that Zechariah 13:7 is still in view (v. 31), but it is more probable that Jesus had in mind the whole complex of his passion, death and resurrection, as well as the subsequent giving of the Spirit and the mission to the world (cf. Lk 24:44–46). See *WLC* 49.

26:59–61 Apparently the Sanhedrin had difficulty getting even the pretext of evidence from more than one witness. Finally a trivial charge that was a perversion of something Jesus actually did say (Jn 2:19) was extricated from two witnesses, the requisite number for action. The incredible number of irregularities in this trial has often been noted. This is evidence not of historical unreliability but of the extreme anxiety of the Jewish leaders to rid themselves of Jesus. See *WLC* 145.

26:63–64 I charge you under oath. Since the offense "proven" was still not a capital offense, Caiaphas had to provoke Jesus. **Son of God.** Here used as an equivalent to "Messiah" (see note on 16:15–16). The high priest's adjuration put Jesus under legal obligation to answer truthfully to prevent the possibility of his denying that he was the Messiah. But Jesus, in order to tell the whole truth, could not simply acknowledge that he was the Messiah without further definition of who the Messiah was. It was his further claim to be the divine "Son of Man" of Daniel 7—and more, the One who will come on the clouds and reign with God Almighty (Ps 110:1)—that elicited the charge of blasphemy (v. 65). See theological article "Jesus Christ, God and Man" at John 1. **you will see.** Jesus' coming in judgment is the only event that can here be meant, for no unbelieving Jews witnessed either the resurrection or the ascension. Some have argued that the judgment in view is the destruction of the temple and city, but it is more natural to understand Jesus as referring to the final judgment, for it is doubtful that many unbelieving Jews "*saw*" Jesus as the One punishing Israel in A.D. 70.

26:69–75 he denied. Peter's three denials are recorded in all four Gospels (see also Mk 14:66–72; Lk 22:54–62; Jn 18:15–18,25–27), but the accounts differ in detail. The differences are neither great nor irreconcilable (for example, John may have reversed the second and third denials). **oath.** Not "cuss words," but calls upon God as witness with a self-curse if he were lying. That all the Gospels record this incident shows how deeply it was impressed on the mind of the early church. It stood as a testimony both to the inadequacy of human strength and to the greatness of God's mercy. **crowed.** Regarding the rooster crowing twice, see note on verse 34. See *WCF* 11.5; 17.3; 18.4; *WLC* 195.

Judas Hangs Himself

27 Early in the morning, all the chief priests and the elders of the people came to
the decision to put Jesus to death.[o] 2 They bound him, led him away and handed him over[p] to Pilate, the governor.[q]
3 When Judas, who had betrayed him,[r] saw that Jesus was condemned, he was seized
with remorse and returned the thirty silver coins[s] to the chief priests and the elders. 4 "I
have sinned," he said, "for I have betrayed innocent blood."
"What is that to us?" they replied. "That's your responsibility."[t]
5 So Judas threw the money into the temple[u] and left. Then he went away and hanged
himself.[v]
6 The chief priests picked up the coins and said, "It is against the law to put this into
the treasury, since it is blood money." 7 So they decided to use the money to buy the potter's field as a burial place for foreigners. 8 That is why it has been called the Field of
Blood[w] to this day. 9 Then what was spoken by Jeremiah the prophet was fulfilled:[x] "They
took the thirty silver coins, the price set on him by the people of Israel, 10 and they used
them to buy the potter's field, as the Lord commanded me."[a][y]

Jesus Before Pilate

11 Meanwhile Jesus stood before the governor, and the governor asked him, "Are you
the king of the Jews?"[z]
"Yes, it is as you say," Jesus replied.
12 When he was accused by the chief priests and the elders, he gave no answer.[a]
13 Then Pilate asked him, "Don't you hear the testimony they are bringing against you?"[b]
14 But Jesus made no reply,[c] not even to a single charge—to the great amazement of the
governor.
15 Now it was the governor's custom at the Feast to release a prisoner[d] chosen by the
crowd. 16 At that time they had a notorious prisoner, called Barabbas. 17 So when the
crowd had gathered, Pilate asked them, "Which one do you want me to release to you:
Barabbas, or Jesus who is called Christ?"[e] 18 For he knew it was out of envy that they had
handed Jesus over to him.
19 While Pilate was sitting on the judge's seat,[f] his wife sent him this message: "Don't
have anything to do with that innocent[g] man, for I have suffered a great deal today in a
dream[h] because of him."
20 But the chief priests and the elders persuaded the crowd to ask for Barabbas and
to have Jesus executed.[i]
21 "Which of the two do you want me to release to you?" asked the governor.
"Barabbas," they answered.
22 "What shall I do, then, with Jesus who is called Christ?"[j] Pilate asked.
They all answered, "Crucify him!"
23 "Why? What crime has he committed?" asked Pilate.
But they shouted all the louder, "Crucify him!"
24 When Pilate saw that he was getting nowhere, but that instead an uproar[k] was
starting, he took water and washed his hands[l] in front of the crowd. "I am innocent of
this man's blood,"[m] he said. "It is your responsibility!"[n]

27:1 [o]Mt 12:14; Mk 15:1; Lk 22:66
27:2 [p]Mt 20:19 [q]Mk 15:1; Lk 13:1; Ac 3:13; 1Ti 6:13
27:3 [r]Mt 10:4 [s]Mt 26:14,15
27:4 [t]ver 24
27:5 [u]Lk 1:9,21 [v]Ac 1:18
27:8 [w]Ac 1:19
27:9 [x]Mt 1:22
27:10 [y]Zec 11:12,13; Jer 32:6-9
27:11 [z]Mt 2:2
27:12 [a]Mt 26:63; Mk 14:61; Jn 19:9
27:13 [b]Mt 26:62
27:14 [c]Mk 14:61
27:15 [d]Jn 18:39
27:17 [e]ver 22; Mt 1:16
27:19 [f]Jn 19:13 [g]ver 24 [h]Ge 20:6; Nu 12:6; 1Ki 3:5; Job 33:14-16; Mt 1:20; 2:12, 13,19,22
27:20 [i]Ac 3:14
27:22 [j]Mt 1:16
27:24 [k]Mt 26:5 [l]Ps 26:6 [m]Dt 21:6-8 [n]ver 4

[a] *10* See Zech. 11:12,13; Jer. 19:1–13; 32:6–9.

27:3 remorse. Judas's remorse was not the same as repentance (see note on "Repent" at 3:2). It is possible that he had been trying to force Jesus into a display of power and was shocked when things turned out as they did. Even if this was his motive, it was one of unbelief, an unwillingness to do things Jesus' way and a presumption that he knew better than his Lord did.

27:4 innocent blood. They cannot claim indifference to the question of innocent blood for which they paid the price. Their attempt at passing responsibility is about as effective as Pilate's in verse 24. See *WLC* 28,49,83.

27:5 hanged himself. Acts 1:18 says that Judas bought the field, that he fell headlong and that his visceral organs fell out. It is possible that the word "hanged" here means that he was impaled and that Matthew uses the more general term "hanged" to bring out the parallel with Ahithophel (2Sa 17:23). Alternatively, since his suicide occurred on a feast day and the following week was a holy week, his body may have been left to rot for some time, so that when it fell down or was released, his abdomen burst. The difference as to who bought the field is easily reconciled. The priests would have bought the field in Judas's name since they, as priests, could not own land or buy it in the temple's interest.

27:9–10 spoken by Jeremiah. The bulk of the words in the citation (vv. 9–10) are from Zechariah 11:12–13, but the content is also closely related to Jeremiah 19:1–13, which is a prophecy of judgment for the shedding of innocent blood (Mt 27:4) that describes Topheth as the "Valley of Slaughter" (Jer 19:6), a burial ground (Jer 19:11). Matthew reveals in Judas's and the priests' actions a fulfillment of the judgment prophecies of Zechariah and Jeremiah, inasmuch as Judas's betrayal represents the betrayal of the good Shepherd by the nation of Israel—especially that of its leadership, who "handed him over" (v. 26; the same Greek word is translated "betray") to be crucified. This betrayal by the nation is in turn the ultimate expression of the pattern of apostasy, unbelief and rejection of God's sovereign claim that characterized Israel throughout its history and was expressed in the days of Jeremiah and Zechariah. Judas's "Field of Blood" (v. 8) thus stands as a warning of the coming judgment on the house of Israel.

27:12–14 Jesus' silence fulfilled Isaiah 53:7.

27:24 It is your responsibility! Compare verse 4.

25All the people answered, "Let his blood be on us and on our children!"[o]
26Then he released Barabbas to them. But he had Jesus flogged,[p] and handed him
over to be crucified.

The Soldiers Mock Jesus

27Then the governor's soldiers took Jesus into the Praetorium[q] and gathered the
whole company of soldiers around him. 28They stripped him and put a scarlet robe on
him,[r] 29and then twisted together a crown of thorns and set it on his head. They put a
staff in his right hand and knelt in front of him and mocked him. "Hail, king of the Jews!"
they said.[s] 30They spit on him, and took the staff and struck him on the head again and
again.[t] 31After they had mocked him, they took off the robe and put his own clothes on
him. Then they led him away to crucify him.[u]

The Crucifixion

32As they were going out,[v] they met a man from Cyrene,[w] named Simon, and they
forced him to carry the cross.[x] 33They came to a place called Golgotha (which means The
Place of the Skull).[y] 34There they offered Jesus wine to drink, mixed with gall;[z] but after
tasting it, he refused to drink it. 35When they had crucified him, they divided up his
clothes by casting lots.[a][a] 36And sitting down, they kept watch[b] over him there. 37Above
his head they placed the written charge against him: THIS IS JESUS, THE KING OF THE JEWS.
38Two robbers were crucified with him,[c] one on his right and one on his left. 39Those who
passed by hurled insults at him, shaking their heads[d] 40and saying, "You who are going
to destroy the temple and build it in three days,[e] save yourself![f] Come down from the
cross, if you are the Son of God!"[g]
41In the same way the chief priests, the teachers of the law and the elders mocked
him. 42"He saved others," they said, "but he can't save himself! He's the King of Israel![h]
Let him come down now from the cross, and we will believe[i] in him. 43He trusts in God.
Let God rescue him[j] now if he wants him, for he said, 'I am the Son of God.'" 44In the
same way the robbers who were crucified with him also heaped insults on him.

The Death of Jesus

45From the sixth hour until the ninth hour darkness[k] came over all the land. 46About
the ninth hour Jesus cried out in a loud voice, *"Eloi, Eloi,*[b] *lama sabachthani?"*—which
means, "My God, my God, why have you forsaken me?"[c][l]

27:25 [o]Jos 2:19; Ac 5:28
27:26 [p]Isa 53:5; Jn 19:1
27:27 [q]Jn 18:28,33; 19:9
27:28 [r]Jn 19:2
27:29 [s]Isa 53:3; Jn 19:2,3
27:30 [t]Mt 16:21; 26:67
27:31 [u]Isa 53:7
27:32 [v]Heb 13:12 [w]Ac 2:10; 6:9; 11:20; 13:1 [x]Mk 15:21; Lk 23:26
27:33 [y]Jn 19:17
27:34 [z]ver 48; Ps 69:21
27:35 [a]Ps 22:18
27:36 [b]ver 54
27:38 [c]Isa 53:12
27:39 [d]Ps 22:7; 109:25; La 2:15
27:40 [e]Mt 26:61; Jn 2:19 [f]ver 42 [g]Mt 4:3,6
27:42 [h]Jn 1:49; 12:13 [i]Jn 3:15
27:43 [j]Ps 22:8
27:45 [k]Am 8:9
27:46 [l]Ps 22:1

[a] 35 A few late manuscripts *lots that the word spoken by the prophet might be fulfilled: "They divided my garments among themselves and cast lots for my clothing"* (Psalm 22:18) [b] 46 Some manuscripts *Eli, Eli* [c] 46 Psalm 22:1

27:25 his blood be on us. This verse has often been read as an anti-Semitic judgment on the part of the author of Matthew. But quite aside from the fact that Matthew was reporting a historical incident, denunciation of Israel for its collective guilt was something that Old Testament prophets did with regularity, and these Jewish prophets were certainly not anti-Semitic. The judgment is *ethical,* not racial, and there always remains a faithful remnant within the unfaithful nation.
27:26–50 See *WLC* 49,145; *BC* 19; *HC* 44.
27:26 flogged. The scourging by Romans was incredibly cruel, with bits of bone tied into the multi-stranded whip. Frequently men died of shock from the scourging alone. We cannot begin to realize what awful suffering Christ endured for our iniquities (Isa 53:5; 1Pe 2:24).
27:27–31 Compare Isaiah 53:3.
27:28 robe. Probably a Roman soldier's cloak. Matthew described the robe as "scarlet," although Mark and John both called it "purple" (Mk 15:20; Jn 19:2). It is doubtful that Matthew changed the color to symbolize blood and suffering; color differentiation is often highly subjective.
27:32–37 Crucifixion was a slow and unspeakably agonizing form of execution. Probably the wrists rather than the palms were nailed or roped to the crosspiece. The force of gravity made breathing laborious and painful, and involuntary efforts by the legs to ease the pressure greatly increased pain in the feet. This continued until total exhaustion resulted in asphyxiation. The dying process could last for days.
27:34 gall. Can refer to any of several bitter herbs; Mark mentions myrrh (Mk 15:23). The combination of myrrh and wine is often thought by modern commentators to be narcotic; had this been the case, Jesus would have refused because he wished to be fully conscious. But the offer of galled wine was probably not a gesture of compassion but of further torment, as in Psalm 69:21, which is here fulfilled. Jesus' thirst would have been very great, but the gall would have made the wine undrinkable.
27:35 they divided up his clothes. This fulfilled Psalm 22:18, as is made explicit in John 19:23–24 and some later manuscripts of Matthew (see text footnote). That which was figuratively done to David was literally done to Jesus. The crucifixion of Jesus involved numerous literal as well as figurative fulfillments of Psalm 22 (cf. notes on 27:43 and 46, below).
27:37 THE KING OF THE JEWS. The placard at the head named the crime. Pilate was throwing an insult at the Jewish leaders, but the irony of its truth was apparent to the early church.
27:38 Compare Isaiah 53:12. The term translated "robbers" is the word Josephus used for insurrectionists. Robbers were not ordinarily crucified. Perhaps these two were cohorts of Barabbas (cf. Mk 15:7).
27:40 Note the irony. By *not* coming down from the cross, Jesus was destroying the temple (his body, but also the literal temple; cf. v. 51) and rebuilding it in three days (his physical body and his metaphorical body, the church). **Son of God.** See note on 16:15–16. The crowd's taunt ("If you are the Son of God") echoes Satan's (4:3,6).
27:43 Let God rescue him. A fulfillment of Psalm 22:8.
27:45 From the sixth hour until the ninth hour. From noon until 3:00 P.M.
27:46 *Eloi.* Most manuscripts have "*Eli*" (Hebrew for "my God") instead of "*Eloi*" (Aramaic), but a few of the best render this as "*Eloi*"(as in Mark). The rest of the cry is in Aramaic. If Jesus did use the Hebrew "*Eli,*" the confusion with "Elijah" may be somewhat more understandable. **why have you forsaken me?** Jesus' cry of dereliction was a fulfillment of Psalm 22:1, but it was also far more. It reflected the depth of Jesus' distress as he endured the pangs of separation from his Father. Later the apostles realized that Jesus was enduring the curse of God's judgment on sin—the full, furious

47 When some of those standing there heard this, they said, "He's calling Elijah."
48 Immediately one of them ran and got a sponge. He filled it with wine vinegar,[m] put
it on a stick, and offered it to Jesus to drink. 49 The rest said, "Now leave him alone. Let's
see if Elijah comes to save him."
50 And when Jesus had cried out again in a loud voice, he gave up his spirit.[n]
51 At that moment the curtain of the temple[o] was torn in two from top to bottom. The
earth shook and the rocks split.[p] 52 The tombs broke open and the bodies of many holy
people who had died were raised to life. 53 They came out of the tombs, and after Jesus'
resurrection they went into the holy city[q] and appeared to many people.
54 When the centurion and those with him who were guarding[r] Jesus saw the earthquake and all that had happened, they were terrified, and exclaimed, "Surely he was the
Son[a] of God!"[s]
55 Many women were there, watching from a distance. They had followed Jesus from
Galilee to care for his needs.[t] 56 Among them were Mary Magdalene, Mary the mother of
James and Joses, and the mother of Zebedee's sons.[u]

The Burial of Jesus

57 As evening approached, there came a rich man from Arimathea, named Joseph,
who had himself become a disciple of Jesus. 58 Going to Pilate, he asked for Jesus' body,
and Pilate ordered that it be given to him. 59 Joseph took the body, wrapped it in a clean
linen cloth, 60 and placed it in his own new tomb[v] that he had cut out of the rock. He
rolled a big stone in front of the entrance to the tomb and went away. 61 Mary Magdalene
and the other Mary were sitting there opposite the tomb.

The Guard at the Tomb

62 The next day, the one after Preparation Day, the chief priests and the Pharisees
went to Pilate. 63 "Sir," they said, "we remember that while he was still alive that deceiver said, 'After three days I will rise again.'[w] 64 So give the order for the tomb to be made
secure until the third day. Otherwise, his disciples may come and steal the body and tell
the people that he has been raised from the dead. This last deception will be worse than
the first."
65 "Take a guard,"[x] Pilate answered. "Go, make the tomb as secure as you know how."
66 So they went and made the tomb secure by putting a seal[y] on the stone[z] and posting
the guard.[a]

The Resurrection

28 After the Sabbath, at dawn on the first day of the week, Mary Magdalene and
the other Mary[b] went to look at the tomb.
2 There was a violent earthquake,[c] for an angel[d] of the Lord came down from heav-
en and, going to the tomb, rolled back the stone and sat on it. 3 His appearance was like
lightning, and his clothes were white as snow.[e] 4 The guards were so afraid of him that
they shook and became like dead men.
5 The angel said to the women, "Do not be afraid,[f] for I know that you are looking for
Jesus, who was crucified. 6 He is not here; he has risen, just as he said.[g] Come and see
the place where he lay. 7 Then go quickly and tell his disciples: 'He has risen from the

27:48 [m]ver 34; Ps 69:21
27:50 [n]Jn 19:30
27:51 [o]Ex 26:31-33; Heb 9:3,8 [p]ver 54
27:53 [q]Mt 4:5
27:54 [r]ver 36 [s]Mt 4:3; 17:5
27:55 [t]Lk 8:2,3
27:56 [u]Mk 15:47; Lk 24:10; Jn 19:25
27:60 [v]Mt 27:66; 28:2; Mk 16:4
27:63 [w]Mt 16:21
27:65 [x]ver 66; Mt 28:11
27:66 [y]Da 6:17 [z]ver 60; Mt 28:2 [a]Mt 28:11
28:1 [b]Mt 27:56
28:2 [c]Mt 27:51 [d]Jn 20:12
28:3 [e]Da 10:6; Mk 9:3; Jn 20:12
28:5 [f]ver 10; Mt 14:27
28:6 [g]Mt 16:21

[a] *54* Or *a son*

---

and dreadful wrath of Almighty God. This was all the more agonizing to Jesus, who had enjoyed the closest love relationship with the Father from all eternity. See *WCF* 8.4; *WLC* 49; *WSC* 27; *BC* 21.
27:48–49 Another fulfillment of Psalm 69:21. Compare note on 27:34.
27:51 curtain of the temple. The curtain that separated the Most Holy Place from the larger sanctuary. It symbolized the unapproachable nature of God (Heb 9:8). Jesus' death was his sacrifice at the heavenly altar (Heb 9:12,24–25), opening the way to God for us (Heb 10:19–20). The symbolic veil in the earthly copy of the heavenly tabernacle was torn because the true spiritual barrier had been removed. Heaven had been opened to a new and royal priesthood in Christ (1Pe 2:9). The phrase "from top to bottom" implies a divine action. Jesus' death rendered the old covenant ceremonial system obsolete and "destroy[ed] this temple" (John 2:19). The tearing of the veil foreshadowed the impending destruction of the earthly temple. Not only was the veil torn, but the earth shook, rocks split and tombs broke open. Everything that separated God from his people—even death—was destroyed by Jesus' death.
27:52 were raised to life. The resurrection of the "many holy people," although mentioned here to show the connection to the rending of the veil, is materially joined to Jesus' resurrection (v. 53). It would have seemed strange for them to be resurrected and then to wait in their tombs until Jesus was raised. Whatever the case, this resurrection was a symbolic prefulfillment of Daniel 12:2. It accomplishes little to speculate about who these people were or whether they died again or were translated.
27:54 Surely he was the Son of God. Whether or not the centurion and the soldiers understood the Messianic import included in the title "Son of God" (see note on 16:15–16), their words show that while most of the natural heirs of the covenant were deriding their Messiah, Gentiles made an appropriate confession.
27:57 a rich man. Only Matthew informs us that Joseph was rich. Joseph's provision of a tomb completed Jesus' fulfillment of Isaiah 53:9.
27:62–66 Matthew includes this as background for 28:11–15.
27:62 Preparation Day. The term for Friday. Had the word "Sabbath" been used, it would have been ambiguous, since that Friday was also a kind of Sabbath (Passover Day). Compare note on 26:17.
28:7 Compare 26:32.

dead and is going ahead of you into Galilee.[h] There you will see him.' Now I have told
you."
8 So the women hurried away from the tomb, afraid yet filled with joy, and ran to tell
his disciples. 9 Suddenly Jesus met them.[i] "Greetings," he said. They came to him,
clasped his feet and worshiped him. 10 Then Jesus said to them, "Do not be afraid. Go and
tell my brothers[j] to go to Galilee; there they will see me."

The Guards' Report

11 While the women were on their way, some of the guards[k] went into the city and reported to the chief priests everything that had happened. 12 When the chief priests had
met with the elders and devised a plan, they gave the soldiers a large sum of money,
13 telling them, "You are to say, 'His disciples came during the night and stole him away
while we were asleep.' 14 If this report gets to the governor,[l] we will satisfy him and keep
you out of trouble." 15 So the soldiers took the money and did as they were instructed.
And this story has been widely circulated among the Jews to this very day.

The Great Commission

16 Then the eleven disciples went to Galilee, to the mountain where Jesus had told
them to go.[m] 17 When they saw him, they worshiped him; but some doubted. 18 Then Jesus
came to them and said, "All authority in heaven and on earth has been given to me.[n]
19 Therefore go and make disciples of all nations,[o] baptizing them in[a] the name of the Father and of the Son and of the Holy Spirit,[p] 20 and teaching[q] them to obey everything I
have commanded you. And surely I am with you[r] always, to the very end of the age."[s]

28:7 [h]ver 10,16; Mt 26:32
28:9 [i]Jn 20:14-18
28:10 [j]Jn 20:17; Ro 8:29; Heb 2:11-13,17
28:11 [k]Mt 27:65,66
28:14 [l]Mt 27:2
28:16 [m]ver 7,10; Mt 26:32
28:18 [n]Da 7:13,14; Lk 10:22; Jn 3:35; 17:2; 1Co 15:27; Eph 1:20-22; Php 2:9,10
28:19 [o]Mk 16:15,16; Lk 24:47; Ac 1:8; 14:21 [p]Ac 2:38; 8:16; Ro 6:3,4
28:20 [q]Ac 2:42 [r]Mt 18:20; Ac 18:10 [s]Mt 13:39

[a] *19* Or *into*; see Acts 8:16; 19:5; Romans 6:3; 1 Cor. 1:13; 10:2 and Gal. 3:27.

28:10 my brothers. Jesus was referring to all his disciples (cf. 12:49–50; 25:40).

28:11–15 This incident demonstrates that the most blatant and clear empirical evidence in the world has no effect on those who are committed to unbelief. That the story of a body theft was still circulated in the days of Justin Martyr indicates something of the desperation felt by Jewish leaders to explain the empty tomb.

28:17 but some. This translation of a Greek idiom means "but some others." **doubted.** A rare Greek word that probably means something like "were uncertain about what to think."

28:18–20 See *WCF* 7.6; 25.3; 25.5; 27.3; 28.1; 28.2; 30.1; *WLC* 35,42,53,62,154,176; *WSC* 88; *HC* 22,25,31,47,65,68.

28:18 All authority. Jesus now wields complete authority. The Son of Man has come before the Ancient of Days and received the promised dominion (Da 7:13–14). The end of history has begun, but it will not be completed until his return to Earth in glory (26:64). See *WCF* 8.3; *BC* 26,27; *HC* 50.

28:19 Therefore go . . . The Great Commission proceeds from Christ's authority. Since the new age has begun, the gospel must go out to the whole world. The authority of Jesus in his direct and unequivocal command is our primary reason for evangelism and missions. **go.** Although the word is not a command in form, it shares in the imperative force of the verb upon which it depends, as in verse 7, where the same syntactic form for "go" is certainly meant as a command. **make disciples.** The verb here is typically rendered "teach" or "train." In one sense, only God "makes disciples," but he does send us forth as teachers and trainers to those whom he effectually calls. This training of disciples involves "baptizing them" and "teaching them to obey" (v. 20). **nations.** The same word is often translated "Gentiles." No longer is the gospel aimed toward Israel alone (contrast 10:5–6). Rather, the great promise that in Abraham all the nations would be blessed (Ge 12:3) is now to be fulfilled as Jesus' disciples spread the kingdom to all nations. **baptizing.** Compare note on 3:11. Here, those who become disciples are baptized in (lit., "into") the triune name. It is one name (not "in the names of") and one baptism because the Father, Son and Spirit are one God. Disciples are baptized "into" this name because they have believed "into" (i.e., placed themselves at the disposal of and trusted themselves to) the Father, the Son and the Holy Spirit, and they are brought "into" the new covenant that the three persons of the Trinity have ratified. See *WCF* 2.3; 21.5; 27.1; 27.4; 28.1; 28.4; *WLC* 9,11,35,108,162,164,165,166,176; *WSC* 6,93,94; *BC* 8,9,11,33,34; *HC* 53,71.

28:20 teaching them to obey. Disciples are not just taught cold truth; they are taught to *obey*. Of course in order to obey, one must know what Jesus taught, so it is also necessary to know the truth. Doctrine and obedience cannot be divorced. **with you always, to the very end of the age.** Jesus did not lay on his disciples the responsibility of discipling the world without promising his presence in their endeavor. We have the confidence that we are not deserted, even in the most discouraging moments, because he is with us "always." Jesus' final words in Matthew's Gospel draw attention to the great hope of all those who follow Christ. Jesus has inaugurated the kingdom and sent us to spread it far and wide. Yet the greater goal in which we place all our hope is that the kingdom will bring an end to this age and usher in the fullness of Christ's glorious kingdom when he returns. See *WLC* 108; *WSC* 50; *BC* 19,27,29,33; *HC* 47.

MARK

Introduction

Overview

Author: John Mark

Purpose: To present the Good News about Jesus to a substantially Gentile audience by recounting the witness of Jesus' disciples concerning the salient facts of his life, death and resurrection.

Date: A.D. 62–69 or earlier

Key Truths:

- Jesus was Israel's long-awaited Messiah.
- Jesus revealed himself in special ways to his 12 disciples.
- Jesus showed that he was the divine Son of God.
- Jesus resisted public recognition to suffer and die on behalf of his people.
- Jesus showed keen interest in extending salvation to the Gentiles.
- The spread of the Good News about Jesus exerts power over evil.

Author

All four Gospels are anonymous, perhaps to honor Jesus' intention to give the church an authorized, collective witness of his person and work through the apostles (a theme so often underlined in Mark; see notes on 3:14; 4:10; 5:37; 6:7,30; 8:32; 9:2,31,34–35,38; 13:3; 14:10,17,72; 16:7). It is conceivable that the Twelve would have employed fellow workers such as John Mark (who would not have placed their names on the work) to put this apostolic witness into writing.

External considerations point to Mark as the author of the Gospel that traditionally bears his name. First, the title, "According to Mark," appears in all the ancient canonical lists and many ancient manuscripts. Although this title is not original to the work, it is thought to have been added very early in the history of the textual tradition. Second, church fathers such as Papias (A.D. 140), Justin Martyr (A.D. 150), Irenaeus (A.D. 185) and Clement of Alexandria (A.D. 195) affirm Marcan authorship of the second Gospel. Papias included the note that Mark was Peter's interpreter. Third, the authenticity of this ascription to Mark is confirmed by the fact that in the second and third centuries of the church it was common to ascribe noncanonical books to well-known apostles, not to secondary figures such as Mark. Internally, Mark's signature is perhaps to be seen in the strangely oblique reference to a young man fleeing from the soldiers who came to arrest Jesus (see notes on 14:51,52) and in the simplified chronological order of events that mirrors Peter's preaching in Acts (Ac 10:36–43; cf. Ac 1:21–22; 3:13–14; see also "Purpose and Distinctives"). For Mark's relationship to the apostles, see Acts 12:12,25; 13:5,13; Colossians 4:10; 2 Timothy 4:11; Philemon 24.

Time and Place of Writing

If the Gospel of Mark was used as a reference by Matthew and Luke, then it is the earliest of the Synoptic Gospels. Since it is generally thought that the Gospels of Matthew and Luke come from the period A.D. 80–90, perhaps Mark is to be dated around A.D. 70. However, if Luke antedates Acts (Acts being the second volume of Luke's work), and if Acts was finished shortly after A.D. 62 (when its narrative ends), then Mark should be dated even earlier.

The church fathers place the writing of Mark in Rome or, more generally, in Italy. This view is corroborated by (1) Mark's association with Peter, who also addressed Christians in Babylon/Rome (1Pe 5:13); (2) many "Latinisms" in the Greek text (4:21; 5:9,15; 6:27,37; 7:4; 12:14; 15:15,39,44); and (3) the probable reference to members of the Roman church (15:21; cf. Ro 16:13).

Original Audience

Beyond the specific destination of Rome or, more generally, Italy (see "Time and Place of Writing"), the translation of Semitic terms (3:17; 5:41; 15:22,34) and the explanation of Jewish customs (7:2–4; 15:42) suggest that a Gentile readership is anticipated, though not to the exclusion of Jewish followers of Christ.

Purpose and Distinctives

Mark's primary purpose was to present in writing the witness of the Twelve to the salient facts of the life, death and resurrection of Jesus. Mark considered this the essence of the gospel (1:1). He did not intend to write a biography or a complete account of Jesus' public ministry. He had simplified the historical record to its barest minimum and to a minimal, threefold structure: (1) the inauguration of the ministry with John the Baptist, (2) the public ministry of Jesus in "Gentile" Galilee (Mt 4:15) and surrounding regions, and (3) the final journey to "Jewish" Judea and Jerusalem for the ultimate sacrifice on the cross. The Gospel of John shows that, in fact, Jesus made at least five visits to Jerusalem. The Gospels of Matthew and Luke record much more of Jesus' actual teaching. But Mark's goal was manifestly different. By limiting historical details, he sought simply to give an enlarged account of what the apostles preached regarding the centrality of the death and resurrection of Jesus Christ (see 1Co 2:2; see also Ac 1:21–22; 2:22–24; 5:29–32; 10:39–41; 13:26–31).

The Gospel of Mark highlights several features of Jesus' life.

1. Mark shows that Jesus was the true Israelite (1:9–12), whose whole life demonstrated the necessity of submission to the written Word of God (1:13; 8:31; cf. 7:6–13; 12:24,35–37). No doubt in the light of present or future persecution, Jesus presented himself as the model for his disciples (8:34—9:1; 9:35—10:31; 10:42–45).

2. Mark demonstrates the divinity of Jesus as the Son of God and the Son of Man (1:11; 2:10,28; 3:11; 5:7; 9:7; 14:62; 15:39) as it shines through the state of humiliation inherent in Jesus' earthly Messianic calling (the so-called Messianic secret; see 1:34,44; 3:12; 5:43; 7:36–37; 8:26,30; 9:9).

3. Mark emphasizes the importance of the preaching/teaching of the gospel not just as theological truth, but as "the power of God" (Ro 1:16; cf. Mk 12:24) over evil and sickness (1:27; see also 16:15–18).

4. Mark shows Jesus' interest in the Gentiles in order to support and guide the church's mission to non-Jews. This can be seen in the Gospel's basic structure (see above), in the explanation of Jewish terms and customs, in the presence of "Latinisms" (see "Time and Place of Writing"), in the declaration that the temple was to be "a house of prayer for all nations" (11:17) and in the Gospel's final high Christological confession from the mouth of a Gentile (15:39). See also note on 5:19.

Outline

I. The Beginning of Jesus' Ministry (1:1–13)
- A. Witness of Prophecy (1:1–8)
- B. Witness at Baptism (1:9–11)
- C. Witness in the Wilderness (1:12–13)

Several events near the beginning of Jesus' ministry demonstrated that he was Israel's long-awaited Messiah.

II. Jesus' Galilean Ministry (1:14—9:50)
- A. The Call of the First Disciples (1:14–20)
- B. Ministry in Capernaum (1:21–34)
- C. Ministry Around Galilee (1:35–45)
- D. Healing in Capernaum (2:1–12)
- E. The Call of Levi (2:13–17)
- F. Controversies With Authorities (2:18—3:12)
- G. The Call of the Twelve (3:13–19)
- H. Accusations in Capernaum (3:20–35)
- I. Kingdom Parables (4:1–34)
- J. Incursion Into the Decapolis (4:35—5:20)
- K. More Ministry in Galilee (5:21—6:6)
- L. The Galilean Mission of the Twelve (6:7–30)
- M. Feeding the Five Thousand (6:31–44)
- N. Visit to Gennesaret (6:45—7:23)
- O. Tyre, Sidon and the Decapolis (7:24—8:9)
- P. The Vicinity of Caesarea Philippi (8:10—9:32)
- Q. The Return to Capernaum (9:33–50)

Jesus revealed his concern for extending salvation to the Gentiles by spending much of his public ministry in the northern regions, where many Gentiles lived. He entered into controversies with religious leaders, performed many miracles and taught large crowds his ways. Jesus resisted public acclamation and devoted much of his time to preparing the 12 disciples for his death and resurrection as well as for their future ministries.

III. Jesus' Judean Ministry (10:1—16:20)
- A. Teaching on the Way (10:1–45)
- B. The Healing in Jericho (10:46–52)
- C. The Triumphal Entry Into Jerusalem (11:1–11)
- D. Cleansing the Temple (11:12–26)
- E. Controversies at the Temple (11:27—12:44)
- F. Prophecies on the Mount of Olives (13:1–37)
- G. Anointing at Bethany (14:1–11)
- H. The Passover Meal in Jerusalem (14:12–31)
- I. Desertion, Trial and Death (14:32—15:47)
- J. Resurrection and Vindication (16:1–20)

The climax of Jesus' ministry was in Judea and, more specifically, in Jerusalem, the place of his death and resurrection. Jesus challenged the failing religious authorities and institutions of Jerusalem. He revealed himself even more fully to the 12 disciples. His disciples deserted him as he suffered and died, but Jesus was vindicated to them by his resurrection from the dead.

John the Baptist Prepares the Way

1 The beginning of the gospel about Jesus Christ, the Son of God.[a] [a]

2 It is written in Isaiah the prophet:

"I will send my messenger ahead of you,
who will prepare your way"[b] [b]—
3 "a voice of one calling in the desert,
'Prepare the way for the Lord,
make straight paths for him.' "[c] [c]

4 And so John[d] came, baptizing in the desert region and preaching a baptism of repentance[e] for the forgiveness of sins.[f] 5 The whole Judean countryside and all the people of
Jerusalem went out to him. Confessing their sins, they were baptized by him in the Jordan River. 6 John wore clothing made of camel's hair, with a leather belt around his waist,
and he ate locusts[g] and wild honey. 7 And this was his message: "After me will come one
more powerful than I, the thongs of whose sandals I am not worthy to stoop down and
untie.[h] 8 I baptize you with[d] water, but he will baptize you with the Holy Spirit."[i]

The Baptism and Temptation of Jesus

9 At that time Jesus came from Nazareth[j] in Galilee and was baptized by John in the
Jordan. 10 As Jesus was coming up out of the water, he saw heaven being torn open and
the Spirit descending on him like a dove.[k] 11 And a voice came from heaven: "You are my
Son,[l] whom I love; with you I am well pleased."

1:1 [a]Mt 4:3
1:2 [b]Mal 3:1; Mt 11:10; Lk 7:27
1:3 [c]Isa 40:3; Jn 1:23
1:4 [d]Mt 3:1 [e]Ac 13:24 [f]Lk 1:77
1:6 [g]Lev 11:22
1:7 [h]Ac 13:25
1:8 [i]Isa 44:3; Joel 2:28; Ac 1:5; 2:4; 11:16; 19:4-6
1:9 [j]Mt 2:23
1:10 [k]Jn 1:32
1:11 [l]Mt 3:17

[a] *1* Some manuscripts do not have *the Son of God.* [b] *2* Mal. 3:1 [c] *3* Isaiah 40:3 [d] *8* Or *in*

■ **1:1–13** *The Beginning of Jesus' Ministry.* Mark opened his Gospel with several short accounts of remarkable events that occurred at the beginning of Jesus' ministry. These three events included (1) the prophetic witness through John the Baptist (vv. 1–8), (2) the witness of the Father and the Spirit at Jesus' baptism (vv. 9–11) and (3) the witness of the Spirit and angels in the wilderness during Jesus' period of tempting by Satan (vv. 12–13).

■ **1:1–8** *Witness of Prophecy.* Mark pointed out that John the Baptist fulfilled Isaiah's prophecy that a messenger would precede the return of the Lord's grace to his people. Mark also noted that John announced that the Lord's grace would come through Jesus.

1:1 The beginning. Unlike the Gospels of Matthew and Luke, Mark does not contain an account of Jesus' birth. The "beginning" (Ge 1:1; Jn 1:1) is identified with the ministry of John the Baptist (cf. Ac 1:22) and with the Old Testament prophecies announcing John's coming. **gospel.** A term belonging to the domain of historical reporting, meaning either "good news" (2Sa 4:10; 1Ki 1:42) or simply "news" (1Sa 4:17; Jer 20:15). The Greeks used the word for significant events, like the birth of an emperor or a major military victory. The gospel of Jesus is the announcement of God's salvation accomplished by Christ. **about Jesus Christ.** The original has the more (intentionally) ambiguous form "of Jesus Christ." While the content of Mark's Gospel is "about" Jesus Christ, this Gospel is also "of" him in that it emanates from him (Ro 1:9; 1Co 9:12; 2Co 10:14). The Gospel of Mark thereby lays claim to divine authority and implicitly demands to be received as the Word of Christ through his apostles to the church (cf. Rev 1:1). **Jesus.** *Jesus* is the Greek form of the Hebrew *Joshua,* which means "the LORD saves" (Mt 1:21). **Christ.** See note on Matthew 1:1. **Son of God.** While this can be taken simply as another Messianic title (as Ps 2:7 applied it to David's dynasty), Mark was surely presenting Jesus at the beginning of his Gospel as the divine, eternal Son (see notes on 12:37; 13:32; 14:36; 15:39).

1:2 It is written. The Greek tense suggests a meaning such as "it stands written," expressing the unchanging character of God-inspired Scripture. By citing Isaiah 40:3 and Malachi 3:1, Mark showed the unified progress of revelation under the divine Lord of history. The Gospel's beginning and source is the Old Testament, and it is the inspired interpretation of the Old Testament's message in the light of the person and work of Jesus Christ. **Isaiah the prophet.** The citation consists of a chain of texts concerning messengers God sent to prepare his people (Ex 23:20; Isa 40:3; Mal 3:1).

1:4 John. The Old Testament citations teach us to situate John not in some insignificant sectarian movement as some suggest, but in the center of God's plan for dealing with his people. **in the desert.** John preached in the desert to distinguish himself from the corruption of the religious leaders in Jerusalem and symbolically to remind Israel of the exodus (cf. Jer 2:2ff.) and the promised return from exile (Isa 40:1ff.). **baptism of repentance.** The Qumran community, with which John may have had contact in his youth, practiced ritual cleansings/baptisms. Gentile converts to Judaism were also baptized. For John, baptism was not only a sign of radical repentance and of turning away from sin and toward good, but it was also an identification with the true remnant of Israel prepared for the Messiah's kingdom. **for the forgiveness of sins.** John did not actually bestow forgiveness of sins. Here the Greek preposition "for" signifies "in preparation for" or "with a view to." Definitive forgiveness of sins belongs to the new covenant (Jer 31:34), which the Messiah would bring. See *WCF* 28.1; *WLC* 165.

1:5 whole . . . all. Mark used hyperbole to indicate that the covenant people went out to John in remarkably large numbers, no doubt as entire families (see notes on 4:1; 6:44; cf. Mt 14:21).

1:6 camel's hair. John's clothing and food identified him with the practices of Old Testament prophets (2Ki 1:8; Zec 13:4).

1:7 his message. Who is the One whom John announced and before whom he did not even feel worthy to kneel? The Old Testament prophecies already cited are clear: He is the "Lord . . . [who] will come to his temple; the messenger of the covenant" (Mal 3:1). Earlier in Malachi 3:1 the Lord identified this messenger as "my messenger."

1:8 Holy Spirit. The Son possessed the Holy Spirit in full measure (Isa 42:1; 61:1). The new covenant also brought a greater outpouring of the Holy Spirit to God's people than that given in the Old Testament (Eze 37:14; cf. Jer 31:33–34; Joel 2:28–29; also theological article "The Holy Spirit" at Acts 2).

1:9–11 *Witness at Baptism.* When John baptized Jesus, the Father revealed Jesus' unique status as the divine Son of God by sending his Holy Spirit to descend upon him like a dove.

1:9 At that time. According to John 2:20, one of Jesus' earliest acts of public ministry following his baptism took place when the rebuilding of the temple was in its 46th year. Since Herod began the temple's construction in 19 B.C., we can conclude that Jesus was baptized in A.D. 26 or 27. **Nazareth.** A small town in Galilee, a region that was despised (Jn 7:41,52) as "Gentiles" (Mt 4:15) because of its ethnically mixed population. **baptized by John.** Jesus knew this to be part of the divine plan ("all righteousness"; Mt 3:15) by which he identified fully with the human condition and began his work of salvation.

1:10 As. The NIV frequently does not render this small but important Greek word (*euthus*) that is characteristic of this Gospel (12 times in the rest of the NT, but 42 times in Mark). It generally means "at once" or "immediately" (1:12,18,20,23,29,42,43), though here not speed but rather the sureness and inevitability of God's sovereign plan may be in view, recalling that God ordered Jesus' ministry and that Jesus followed that divine plan without hesitation. **Spirit descending.** This visible token of the Spirit's unction is a sign of Jesus' Messiahship (see note on v. 8). In Jesus' baptism, as later in Christian baptism (Mt 28:19), all three persons of the Trini-

12 At once the Spirit sent him out into the desert, 13 and he was in the desert forty days,
being tempted by Satan.[m] He was with the wild animals, and angels attended him.

The Calling of the First Disciples

14 After John was put in prison, Jesus went into Galilee,[n] proclaiming the good news
of God.[o] 15 "The time has come,"[p] he said. "The kingdom of God is near. Repent and believe the good news!"[q]

16 As Jesus walked beside the Sea of Galilee, he saw Simon and his brother Andrew
casting a net into the lake, for they were fishermen. 17 "Come, follow me," Jesus said, "and
I will make you fishers of men." 18 At once they left their nets and followed him.

19 When he had gone a little farther, he saw James son of Zebedee and his brother John
in a boat, preparing their nets. 20 Without delay he called them, and they left their father
Zebedee in the boat with the hired men and followed him.

Jesus Drives Out an Evil Spirit

21 They went to Capernaum, and when the Sabbath came, Jesus went into the synagogue and began to teach.[r] 22 The people were amazed at his teaching, because he taught
them as one who had authority, not as the teachers of the law.[s] 23 Just then a man in their
synagogue who was possessed by an evil[a] spirit cried out, 24 "What do you want with us,[t]
Jesus of Nazareth?[u] Have you come to destroy us? I know who you are—the Holy One
of God!"[v]

[a] *23* Greek *unclean*; also in verses 26 and 27

1:13 [m]Mt 4:10
1:14 [n]Mt 4:12 [o]Mt 4:23
1:15 [p]Gal 4:4; Eph 1:10 [q]Ac 20:21
1:21 [r]Mt 4:23; Mk 10:1
1:22 [s]Mt 7:28,29
1:24 [t]Mt 8:29 [u]Mt 2:23; Lk 24:19; Ac 24:5 [v]Lk 1:35; Jn 6:69; Ac 3:14

ty are involved. We see the initiative of the Father, the vicarious work of the Son and the glorifying, enabling power of the Spirit.

1:11 You are my Son. The mystery of the person of Jesus finds expression in this divine declaration. He is the second person of the Godhead, the representative believer and the one true and faithful son of Israel. He pleases the Father, and the Father acknowledges him as Son in both a personal and an official, royal sense (Ps 2:7; Isa 42:1; see note on 1:1). **whom I love.** This phrase describes the unique relationship between the Father and the Son (see Ge 22:2,12,16, where the same phrase is used in the Greek OT). It is underlined by the repetition of the definite article in the original, which, reproduced literally, would be "the son of me, the beloved one."

■ **1:12–13** *Witness in the Wilderness.* Jesus' unique character was further demonstrated by the Holy Spirit's sending him into the wilderness, where he not only faced Satan, but also received the ministrations of angels.

1:12 At once. See note on 1:10. **the Spirit sent him.** The original is much stronger, literally, "the Spirit drove him." In the choice of these terms one should see the idea of divine necessity. After Jesus' baptism, the Spirit drove him into the desert. In the same way, Israel, God's "son" (Ex 4:23), was "baptized into Moses in the cloud and in the sea" (1Co 10:2; see also Ex 14:13–31), was led from there into the wilderness (Ex 15:22) and was tested not only then (Ex 15:25) but also for 40 years thereafter (e.g., Ex 16:4; 20:20). At many points, Jesus' life recapitulated important events in Israel's history.

1:13 forty days. Granting the above parallels to Israel's experience, a counterpart to the 40 years of Israel's desert wandering (Dt 1:3) is certainly to be found here. **tempted.** The Greek verb can mean either "testing" (a beneficial experience to which God exposes his people) or "tempting" (a malicious ruse of the devil to turn God's servants from their Lord). God's sovereign power turns "tempting" into "testing." **wild animals.** Since the fall, wild animals threaten human life (Lev 26:22). This detail underscores the fact that the desert symbolizes a place of curse far removed from paradise. **angels attended.** Angels also accompanied Israel in the first exodus (Ex 14:19; 23:20 [cited in Mk 1:2]; 32:34; 33:2). The presence of angels reminds us that God always cares for his people in times of temptation and testing.

■ **1:14—9:50** *Jesus' Galilean Ministry.* Mark divided Jesus' ministry into two stages. Before turning to Jesus' work in Judea and Jerusalem, Mark first described how Jesus did much of his work in Galilee, a northern area known as a Gentile region because so many Gentiles lived there. By drawing attention to the Gentile focus of Jesus' ministry, Mark touched on the interests of his Gentile readers who followed Christ.

■ **1:14–20** *The Call of the First Disciples.* Mark first recorded how Jesus began his ministry by calling disciples in Galilee. Mark emphasized this because he was deeply concerned with the role that the disciples would later play as witnesses to Jesus.

1:15 The time has come. This could also be translated "the time is fulfilled." Events in past times, especially God's acts of salvation for his people Israel, reached their climax in this time of salvation through Jesus. **The kingdom of God is near.** Ultimately, the kingdom of God is that final state of affairs wherein God reigns unopposed over the transformed universe and his redeemed people are glorified. The kingdom is near in the sense that the coming of Jesus has begun to bring about its full realization. God requires repentance and belief from all those who hope to enjoy life in this kingdom (see note on v. 4). See theological article "The Kingdom of God" at Matthew 4. See *WCF* 15.1.

1:16 Sea of Galilee. An inland lake twelve miles long and six miles wide. It is also known in the New Testament as the Lake of Gennesaret or the Sea of Tiberias.

1:17 Come, follow me . . . fishers of men. Mark's Gospel immediately draws attention to the fact that Jesus called his disciples in order that they would call others. Seeking the lost became a primary goal of the embryonic church.

1:19 James . . . and his brother John. That James and John were fishermen underscores the priority that Jesus gave to "fishing" for people. In this light it is interesting to note that Jesus did not recruit religiously educated individuals but those from ordinary walks of life.

1:20 hired men. Indicates a small, prosperous business.

■ **1:21–34** *Ministry in Capernaum.* Mark reported how Jesus amazed many by his teaching and miracles in Capernaum.

1:21 Sabbath. *Shabbath* (Hebrew) means "rest"; thus the Sabbath is the day of rest, a day consecrated to God (Ge 2:2–3). God's plan for the coming of his kingdom does not contradict previous revelation requiring the consecration of the Sabbath (Dt 5:15) and the regular meeting together of his people (Ex 23:14–17; Ps 68:26). Ultimately, it fulfills them. Jesus commonly taught and healed in the synagogues on the Sabbath (3:1-5; 6:2; Lk 13:10-16), and participated in worship (Lk 4:15-16). **teach.** Teaching in the synagogue was a custom reserved for respected rabbis.

1:22 one who had authority. Unlike the Gospels of Matthew and Luke, Mark's account does not develop the specifics of this teaching but merely indicates Jesus' general style in contrast to that of the scribes. Jesus' teaching was not mere human opinion but the authoritative teaching of the Son of God.

1:24 What do you want with us . . . ? An idiomatic phrase implying displeasure, rejection or a desire to dissociate. The only other occurrence of this idiom in the New Testament is in Jesus' rebuke of Mary (Jn 2:4). In the Septuagint (the Greek translation of the Hebrew OT), this phrase appears in such passages as Judges 11:12, 2 Samuel 16:1, 1 Kings 17:18, 2 Kings 3:13 and Hosea 14:8. **Nazareth.** Literally, "Nazarene." Nazareth, which was located west of the Sea of Galilee, was Jesus' hometown. **Holy One of God.** Applied to Aaron (Ps 106:16) and to Samson (Jdg 13:7; 16:17) in the sense of "one specially consecrated to God." In the Gospels, this description of Jesus is unique to this incident (see also Lk 4:34), but the apostles so describe him in Acts 2:27 and 13:35 (in quotations from Ps 16:10) and in Acts 3:14. The demons quake in the presence of divine holiness.

1:25 [w]ver 34 — 25 “Be quiet!” said Jesus sternly. “Come out of him!”[w] 26 The evil spirit shook the man
violently and came out of him with a shriek.[x]
1:26 [x]Mk 9:20 — 27 The people were all so amazed[y] that they asked each other, “What is this? A new
teaching—and with authority! He even gives orders to evil spirits and they obey him.”
1:27 [y]Mk 10:24,32 — 28 News about him spread quickly over the whole region[z] of Galilee.

Jesus Heals Many

1:28 [z]Mt 9:26 — 29 As soon as they left the synagogue,[a] they went with James and John to the home of
1:29 [a]ver 21,23 — Simon and Andrew. 30 Simon’s mother-in-law was in bed with a fever, and they told Jesus
about her. 31 So he went to her, took her hand and helped her up.[b] The fever left her and
1:31 [b]Lk 7:14 — she began to wait on them.
32 That evening after sunset the people brought to Jesus all the sick and demon-pos-
1:32 [c]Mt 4:24 — sessed.[c] 33 The whole town gathered at the door, 34 and Jesus healed many who had various diseases.[d] He also drove out many demons, but he would not let the demons speak
1:34 [d]Mt 4:23 [e]Mk 3:12; Ac 16:17,18 — because they knew who he was.[e]

Jesus Prays in a Solitary Place

1:35 [f]Lk 3:21 — 35 Very early in the morning, while it was still dark, Jesus got up, left the house and
went off to a solitary place, where he prayed.[f] 36 Simon and his companions went to look
for him, 37 and when they found him, they exclaimed: “Everyone is looking for you!”
38 Jesus replied, “Let us go somewhere else—to the nearby villages—so I can preach
1:38 [g]Isa 61:1 — there also. That is why I have come.”[g] 39 So he traveled throughout Galilee, preaching in
1:39 [h]Mt 4:23 [i]Mt 4:24 — their synagogues[h] and driving out demons.[i]

A Man With Leprosy

1:40 [j]Mk 10:17 — 40 A man with leprosy[a] came to him and begged him on his knees,[j] “If you are willing,
you can make me clean.”
41 Filled with compassion, Jesus reached out his hand and touched the man. “I am
willing,” he said. “Be clean!” 42 Immediately the leprosy left him and he was cured.
43 Jesus sent him away at once with a strong warning: 44 “See that you don’t tell this
1:44 [k]Mt 8:4 [l]Lev 13:49 [m]Lev 14:1-32 — to anyone.[k] But go, show yourself to the priest[l] and offer the sacrifices that Moses commanded for your cleansing,[m] as a testimony to them.” 45 Instead he went out and began
to talk freely, spreading the news. As a result, Jesus could no longer enter a town open-
1:45 [n]Lk 5:15,16 [o]Mk 2:13; Lk 5:17; Jn 6:2 — ly but stayed outside in lonely places.[n] Yet the people still came to him from everywhere.[o]

Jesus Heals a Paralytic

2:2 [p]ver 13; Mk 1:45 — **2** A few days later, when Jesus again entered Capernaum, the people heard that he
had come home. 2 So many[p] gathered that there was no room left, not even out-
side the door, and he preached the word to them. 3 Some men came, bringing to him a

[a] *40* The Greek word was used for various diseases affecting the skin—not necessarily leprosy.

1:25 Be quiet! Or “be muzzled.” In the Judaism of Jesus’ day, this was a technical expression denoting the presence of God’s power to establish his kingdom in the face of evil.
1:30 Simon’s mother-in-law. The fact that Peter was married indicates that marriage, not celibacy (which is nevertheless a legitimate possibility; see Mt 19:12; 1Co 7:7–8,32), is normal for Christian leaders (cf. 1Co 9:5).
1:32 after sunset. Jesus was already healing on the Sabbath day (vv. 21ff.), though in private (cf. 3:1–6). Not daring to break the traditional Jewish Sabbath practices, the people waited until sunset to carry their sick to Jesus.
1:34 many demons. The large extent of demon possession in Galilee (v. 32) may have been due to the Gentile/pagan influence in that region, especially its openness to the occult (see also theological article “Demons” at 1 Corinthians 10). **he would not let the demons speak.** This is the first time that Jesus warned others not to announce his Messiahship (see v. 43; 3:12; 4:10–11; 5:19; 9:9; see also note on 5:19). Jesus was not uncertain of his mission. Rather, he maintained secrecy so that premature, popular Messianic fervor would not compromise God’s plan for his Son’s suffering and death.
■ **1:35–45** *Ministry Around Galilee.* Jesus traveled about Galilee, preaching and performing many miracles. Enthusiastic crowds followed him everywhere he went, but Jesus resisted them so that he could complete the task God had given him.
1:35 solitary place. Literally, “desert place,” where Jesus fought his spiritual battle (v. 12; cf. v. 3). It is also, as with ancient Israel, symbolic of the present Christian walk (1Co 10:1–11; Heb 13:12–13).
1:38 That is why I have come. Jesus stated his program of evangelistic preaching with compelling clarity (v. 14; Lk 19:10).
1:40–44 leprosy. This term was used to refer to a variety of skin diseases. In the Old Testament, leprosy made people not only physically, but also ceremonially, unclean, which then excluded them from communal life (Lev 13:46). Jesus respected the Mosaic legislation (“as a testimony”; v. 44) but showed that, as the great high priest of another line (Heb 7:11—8:13), his ministry to lepers went beyond Old Testament confines. He touched the man and brought him the healing power promised in the final stages of the kingdom of God.
1:43 strong warning. See note on verse 34. The original verb expresses very deep emotion, as in the case of Jesus before the tomb of Lazarus (Jn 11:33,38).
1:45 talk freely. Literally, “preaching a lot.” This was not the time for unbridled proclamation (see v. 34), although after the resurrection, open preaching about Jesus as Messiah would be the proper order of the day (Mt 10:27; Lk 12:2–3; cf. Ac 2:29ff.; 4:13; 28:31). **lonely places.** Literally, “desert places.” See note on verse 35.
■ **2:1–12** *Healing in Capernaum.* Mark showed that Jesus’ pronouncements of forgiveness were secure by reporting Jesus’ healing of a paralytic in Capernaum.
2:1 home. Since Jesus’ original home was in Nazareth (some 20 miles away), Simon Peter’s house (1:29) may have served as Jesus’ home in Capernaum, a village more centrally situated and with direct access to the Sea of Galilee.

Miracles of Jesus

Healing Miracles	Matthew	Mark	Luke	John
Man with leprosy	8:2-4	1:40-42	5:12-13	
Roman centurion's servant	8:5-13		7:1-10	
Peter's mother-in-law	8:14-15	1:30-31	4:38-35	
Two men from Gadara	8:28-34	5:1-15	8:26-35	
Paralyzed man	9:2-7	2:3-12	5:18-25	
Woman with bleeding	9:20-22	5:25-29	8:43-48	
Two blind men	9:27-31			
Mute, demon-possessed man	9:32-33			
Man with a shriveled hand	12:10-13	3:1-5	6:6-10	
Blind, mute, demon-possessed man	12:22		11:14	
Canaanite woman's daughter	15:21-28	7:24-30		
Boy with a demon	17:14-18	9:17-29	9:38-43	
Two blind men (including Bartimaeus)	20:29-34	10:46-52	18:35-43	
Deaf mute		7:31-37		
Possessed man in synagogue		1:23-26	4:33-35	
Blind man at Bethsaida		8:22-26		
Crippled woman			13:11-13	
Man with dropsy			14:1-4	
Ten men with leprosy			17:11-19	
The high priest's servant			22:50-51	
Official's son at Capernaum				4:46-54
Sick man at pool of Bethesda				5:1-9
Man born blind				9:1-7
Miracles showing power over nature				
Calming the storm	8:23-27	4:37-41	8:22-25	
Walking on water	14:25	6:48-51		6:19-21
Feeding of the 5,000	14:15-21	6:35-44	9:12-17	6:6-13
Feeding of the 4,000	15:32-38	8:1-9		
Coin in fish	17:24-27			
Fig tree withered	21:18-22	11:12-14,20-25		
Large catch of fish			5:4-11	
Water turned into wine				2:1-11
Another large catch of fish				21:1-11
Miracles of raising the dead				
Jairus's daughter	9:18-19,23-25	5:22-24,38-42	8:41-42,49-56	
Widow's son at Nain			7:11-15	
Lazarus				11:1-44

paralytic,[q] carried by four of them. 4Since they could not get him to Jesus because of
the crowd, they made an opening in the roof above Jesus and, after digging through it,
lowered the mat the paralyzed man was lying on. 5When Jesus saw their faith, he said
to the paralytic, "Son, your sins are forgiven."[r]
6Now some teachers of the law were sitting there, thinking to themselves, 7"Why does
this fellow talk like that? He's blaspheming! Who can forgive sins but God alone?"[s]
8Immediately Jesus knew in his spirit that this was what they were thinking in their
hearts, and he said to them, "Why are you thinking these things? 9Which is easier: to say
to the paralytic, 'Your sins are forgiven,' or to say, 'Get up, take your mat and walk'? 10But
that you may know that the Son of Man[t] has authority on earth to forgive sins . . ." He
said to the paralytic, 11"I tell you, get up, take your mat and go home." 12He got up, took
his mat and walked out in full view of them all. This amazed everyone and they praised
God,[u] saying, "We have never seen anything like this!"[v]

The Calling of Levi

13Once again Jesus went out beside the lake. A large crowd came to him,[w] and he began to teach them. 14As he walked along, he saw Levi son of Alphaeus sitting at the tax
collector's booth. "Follow me,"[x] Jesus told him, and Levi got up and followed him.
15While Jesus was having dinner at Levi's house, many tax collectors and "sinners"
were eating with him and his disciples, for there were many who followed him. 16When
the teachers of the law who were Pharisees[y] saw him eating with the "sinners" and tax
collectors, they asked his disciples: "Why does he eat with tax collectors and 'sinners'?"[z]
17On hearing this, Jesus said to them, "It is not the healthy who need a doctor, but
the sick. I have not come to call the righteous, but sinners."[a]

Jesus Questioned About Fasting

18Now John's disciples and the Pharisees were fasting.[b] Some people came and
asked Jesus, "How is it that John's disciples and the disciples of the Pharisees are fasting, but yours are not?"
19Jesus answered, "How can the guests of the bridegroom fast while he is with them?

2:3 [q]Mt 4:24
2:5 [r]Lk 7:48
2:7 [s]Isa 43:25
2:10 [t]Mt 8:20
2:12 [u]Mt 9:8 [v]Mt 9:33
2:13 [w]Mk 1:45; Lk 5:15; Jn 6:2
2:14 [x]Mt 4:19
2:16 [y]Ac 23:9 [z]Mt 9:11
2:17 [a]Lk 19:10; 1Ti 1:15
2:18 [b]Mt 6:16-18; Ac 13:2

2:4 opening in the roof. This action was possible because houses then had flat roofs made of branches and hardened clay, supported by transversal beams.
2:5 their faith. The sick man was hardly an unwilling beneficiary, and there is collective faith here that Jesus recognized. **your sins are forgiven.** An extraordinary response because Jesus assumed for himself the power to forgive sins, a prerogative which in the entire Bible is attributed only to God (Ex 34:7; Isa 1:18; Hos 11:8–9). The teachers of the law present in the house immediately drew what would have been the right conclusion had Jesus been a mere man, and they cried, "He's blaspheming!" (v. 7; see note on 3:29).
2:9 Which is easier . . . ? Jesus asked the scribes to reconsider their judgment of his words in the light of his power to heal (cf. Jn 5:36; 10:25,38), which was ultimately an act of God (Ps 41:1; Jer 3:22; Hos 14:4).
2:10 Son of Man. Jesus' most common title for himself constituted an implicit claim that he fulfilled in his ministry the role of the celestial "son of man" of Daniel 7:13–14. See verse 28, 8:31, 9:31, 10:33 and 45, 13:26; see also "Introduction to the Gospels."
▪ **2:13–17** *The Call of Levi.* Mark described Jesus' calling of Levi (Matthew), the tax collector, to introduce his Gentile readers to Jesus' commitment to serving those who were disdained by the hypocritical Jewish religious authorities.
2:14 Levi son of Alphaeus. In the parallel account in Matthew 9:9–13, this person is called Matthew. Since Matthew appears in Mark's list of apostles (3:18) and there is no mention of Levi, most scholars assume that Levi, like Simon, took or preferred another name once he became a disciple/apostle of Jesus. **tax collector's booth.** They were set up on highways, at bridges and at canals to collect tolls, and at the lakeside to tax the fishing industry. Beyond the people's general dislike for tax officials, Levi and his Jewish colleagues were hated as collaborators with the occupying pagan forces, and as cheats who extorted beyond what the authorities required. For these reasons they were excluded from the religious life of the synagogue and the temple. **Levi got up.** Matthew's action of getting up and leaving his tax office parallels that of the paralytic getting up, picking up his bed and walking. Matthew's response was a miraculous demonstration of Jesus' saving power.
2:15 sinners. In the New Testament this term is often used as a Pharisaic designation of disdain for anyone who did not carefully follow Jewish traditions. **eating with.** Dining with sinners put Jesus in the same category as sinners, since rabbinic regulations specifically prohibited all teachers of the law from such table fellowship. On the other hand, the "sinners" would have seen this as a gesture of friendship and acceptance.
2:16 Pharisees. Adherents to a strong Jewish tradition that descended from the Hasidim of the second century B.C. The Pharisees sought meticulous faithfulness to the law against Greco-Roman influence in Palestine. At the time of Jesus, the strict practice of the law, and especially ritual purity, was rendered possible by reference to "the tradition of the elders" (7:3), a body of interpretations from earlier teachers (rabbis). The difficulty of being familiar with the endless interpretations of the law created a divide between a more or less intellectual religious elite ("the righteous") and the general population ("the sinners").
2:17 I have . . . come. Note Jesus' clear declaration of the priority of his mission (cf. 1:38). There is both truth and biting irony in Jesus' words. Tax collectors, prostitutes and the like were indeed spiritually "sick," but in reality the Pharisees were "sick" too. Jesus adopted the Pharisees' outlook that they were "healthy" in order to refute their hypocrisy. As the Old Testament teaches, all are sinners (1Ki 8:46; Ps 14:1–3), and righteousness is first and foremost a gift of God to repentant sinners (Ps 51:1–18; cf. Lk 18:9–14; 19:9; Ro 3:22).
▪ **2:18—3:12** *Controversies With Authorities.* In order to develop in his readers a high regard for the teachings of Jesus, Mark recorded several instances in which Jesus faced theological controversies with Jewish religious authorities.
2:18 fasting. The Old Testament required only one annual national fast, which was to be on the Day of Atonement (Lev 16:29–31). Nevertheless, as a sign of severe need, contrition and penitence, associated with prayer, fasting had been part of Old Testament spirituality from the time of the judges (Jdg 20:26; cf. 1Ki 21:27). It is not surprising (see Mt 6:16) that the Pharisees and their adherents fasted, apparently twice a week (Lk 18:12). Inasmuch as the message of John the Baptist centered on repentance (Mt 3:11), fasting certainly was appropriate for his disciples. What is unusual is that Jesus, whose own message included repentance, did not insist upon fasting during his earthly ministry.
2:19 Jesus answered. Jesus set himself apart from all that had gone on before him, for the "bridegroom" (v. 20) had now come, and the "new" (vv. 21–22) was present. By using the image of himself as the bridegroom, Jesus affirmed the presence of the kingdom's joy. Now was the time for celebration, as at a wedding.

They cannot, so long as they have him with them. 20 But the time will come when the
bridegroom will be taken from them,[c] and on that day they will fast.
21 "No one sews a patch of unshrunk cloth on an old garment. If he does, the new
piece will pull away from the old, making the tear worse. 22 And no one pours new wine
into old wineskins. If he does, the wine will burst the skins, and both the wine and the
wineskins will be ruined. No, he pours new wine into new wineskins."

Lord of the Sabbath

23 One Sabbath Jesus was going through the grainfields, and as his disciples walked
along, they began to pick some heads of grain.[d] 24 The Pharisees said to him, "Look, why
are they doing what is unlawful on the Sabbath?"[e]
25 He answered, "Have you never read what David did when he and his companions
were hungry and in need? 26 In the days of Abiathar the high priest,[f] he entered the house
of God and ate the consecrated bread, which is lawful only for priests to eat.[g] And he also
gave some to his companions."[h]
27 Then he said to them, "The Sabbath was made for man,[i] not man for the Sabbath.[j]
28 So the Son of Man[k] is Lord even of the Sabbath."
3 Another time he went into the synagogue,[l] and a man with a shriveled hand was
there. 2 Some of them were looking for a reason to accuse Jesus, so they watched
him closely[m] to see if he would heal him on the Sabbath.[n] 3 Jesus said to the man with
the shriveled hand, "Stand up in front of everyone."
4 Then Jesus asked them, "Which is lawful on the Sabbath: to do good or to do evil,
to save life or to kill?" But they remained silent.
5 He looked around at them in anger and, deeply distressed at their stubborn hearts,
said to the man, "Stretch out your hand." He stretched it out, and his hand was completely restored. 6 Then the Pharisees went out and began to plot with the Herodians[o]
how they might kill Jesus.[p]

Crowds Follow Jesus

7 Jesus withdrew with his disciples to the lake, and a large crowd from Galilee followed.[q] 8 When they heard all he was doing, many people came to him from Judea, Jerusalem, Idumea, and the regions across the Jordan and around Tyre and Sidon.[r] 9 Because of the crowd he told his disciples to have a small boat ready for him, to keep the

2:20 [c]Lk 17:22
2:23 [d]Dt 23:25
2:24 [e]Mt 12:2
2:26 [f]1Ch 24:6; 2Sa 8:17 [g]Lev 24:5-9 [h]1Sa 21:1-6
2:27 [i]Ex 23:12; Dt 5:14 [j]Col 2:16
2:28 [k]Mt 8:20
3:1 [l]Mt 4:23; Mk 1:21
3:2 [m]Mt 12:10 [n]Lk 14:1
3:6 [o]Mt 22:16; Mk 12:13 [p]Mt 12:14
3:7 [q]Mt 4:25
3:8 [r]Mt 11:21

Thus, Jesus ate and drank with sinners, bringing joy and salvation to the house (Lk 19:6,9).

2:20 will fast. The present celebration (v. 19) was temporary, for Jesus still had to suffer and die. Moreover, his followers also faced a future period of trouble and suffering (13:13; 14:27). For this reason, it would later be proper for Jesus' disciples to fast (Ac 13:2; 14:23; 2Co 6:5; 11:27).

2:21–22 new piece . . . new wineskins. These images again emphasize the new situation brought about by the coming of the kingdom and of its king. (See theological article "The Kingdom of God" at Mt 4.) These images demonstrate the inappropriateness of fasting in this new situation.

2:23 One Sabbath . . . they began to pick some heads of grain. The extent of legalism among the Pharisees is highlighted in this account. In reality, their views contradicted the Law of Moses. The disciples were not stealing since their action was allowed by the law (Dt 23:25), nor were they farming since they were not putting a sickle to standing grain, which would have constituted both stealing and (technically) farmwork, which Exodus 34:21 forbids. Thus, by the standard of the Old Testament, the Pharisees' accusation of Sabbath work was inappropriate.

2:25 He answered, "Have you never read . . . ?" Jesus' reply raised the debate to a level the Pharisees undoubtedly did not expect, especially since the phrase "have you never read" suggested an ironic criticism of their superficial knowledge of Scripture (see Jn 3:10; 5:39,47). Jesus did not justify himself by laying aside the Old Testament. Rather, he showed the depth of his understanding. **David.** Executing a divine mission (1Sa 21:5) as the Lord's anointed (*Messiah*), he ate the "bread of the Presence" (Ex 25:30), which was normally reserved for the priests. Hence, David's greatest son (Jesus) and Jesus' disciples were perfectly justified in their action.

2:26 Abiathar. 1 Samuel 21:1–6 states that it was Abiathar's father, Ahimelech, who gave David the bread of the Presence. It is evident from Samuel's record that Abiathar was alive, and perhaps even present, when this incident occurred. So the phrase "in the days of Abiathar the high priest" is technically correct. Probably Jesus was referring to Abiathar as a general, temporal reference because Abiathar was well known as one of David's chief supporters.

2:28 Lord even of the Sabbath. Again (cf. 2:10) Jesus declared his authority as the Son of Man who brings blessings, this time as sovereign interpreter of the Old Testament's beneficent teaching concerning the Sabbath (v. 25). This claim was made against the Pharisaic traditions (see note on v. 16), which had turned the life-promoting fourth commandment (Ex 20:8–11) into an oppressive, unbearable burden (3:1–5). Jesus also identified himself as the Lord to whom the Sabbath belonged (Ex. 20:10).

3:1 shriveled hand. Literally, "dried up," indicating a long process, not a life-or-death illness for which even the Pharisees would have accepted healing on the Sabbath. Jesus' action appears to have been a deliberate provocation as well as an act of mercy.

3:2 they watched him closely. They (no doubt the Pharisees; see v. 6) made Jesus' action a test case, as Jesus evidently wanted them to do.

3:4 Which is lawful . . . ? Jesus anticipated their criticism by reiterating the Sabbath teaching he had begun in 2:25–28. The Pharisees held that only essential aid to the sick was lawful on the Sabbath. Jesus showed that their interpretation actually went against the purpose of the commandment, which existed for the promotion of good (2:27).

3:6 began to plot. The Pharisees were motivated not by the power of God and good, but by the power of evil and hypocrisy, for while Jesus was promoting life by healing on the Sabbath, they were plotting on the Sabbath to kill him. **Herodians.** Unlike the Pharisees, the Herodians were a non-religious political group supporting the Herodian dynasty (which had a non-Jewish origin). Like the Herods, this group collaborated with Rome. The Pharisees showed their hypocrisy by joining forces with the Herodians (cf. Dt 7:2; 17:15). For more on this conspiracy, see 8:15, 12:13 and Acts 4:27.

3:8–9 many people . . . crowd. Apparently one emphasis of verses 7–12 is that Jesus' public ministry was becoming a mass movement despite the opposition of the ruling elite (v. 6). Jesus was overwhelmed and had to take refuge in a small boat. Geographically, people were coming to Galilee from everywhere to hear him: from the south (Jerusalem, Judea and Idumea), from the east (regions across the Jordan) and from the north (Tyre and

3:10 [s]Mt 4:23 [t]Mt 9:20
3:11 [u]Mt 4:3; Mk 1:23, 24
3:12 [v]Mt 8:4; Mk 1:24, 25,34; Ac 16:17, 18
3:13 [w]Mt 5:1
3:14 [x]Mk 6:30
3:15 [y]Mt 10:1
3:16 [z]Jn 1:42

people from crowding him. **10**For he had healed many,[s] so that those with diseases were
pushing forward to touch him.[t] **11**Whenever the evil[a] spirits saw him, they fell down before him and cried out, "You are the Son of God."[u] **12**But he gave them strict orders not
to tell who he was.[v]

The Appointing of the Twelve Apostles

13Jesus went up on a mountainside and called to him those he wanted, and they came
to him.[w] **14**He appointed twelve—designating them apostles[b][x]—that they might be
with him and that he might send them out to preach **15**and to have authority to drive out
demons.[y] **16**These are the twelve he appointed: Simon (to whom he gave the name Peter);[z] **17**James son of Zebedee and his brother John (to them he gave the name Boaner-
ges, which means Sons of Thunder); **18**Andrew, Philip, Bartholomew, Matthew, Thomas, James son of Alphaeus, Thaddaeus, Simon the Zealot **19**and Judas Iscariot, who
betrayed him.

a *11* Greek *unclean*; also in verse 30 b *14* Some manuscripts do not have *designating them apostles.*

Sidon). Galilee was replacing Jerusalem as the center of true religious life.

3:11 Whenever the evil spirits saw him. The verb translated "saw" suggests a repeated event. Jesus was continually meeting people with evil spirits. **the Son of God.** In the presence of Jesus, demons were exposed, and they in turn exposed the true identity of Jesus. See notes on 1:1 and 15:39.

3:12 strict orders. See 1:34 and 1:43–44.

▪ **3:13–19** *The Call of the Twelve.* Mark reported how Jesus appointed 12 apostles to minister with his authority so that his readers would recognize the importance of the apostles' ministries in their day.

3:13 those he wanted. Mark underlined this particular act of Jesus to emphasize its origin in Jesus' determined purpose.

3:14 He appointed twelve. The significance of the number 12 could hardly be missed (Mt 19:28; Lk 22:29–30). **designating them apostles.** Most, but not all, early manuscripts include this phrase. Mark only uses the term "apostles" one other time (6:30). The Eleven (the faithful apostles) received their full apostolic status in John 20:22, and the Twelve—newly constituted with the addition of Matthias (Ac 1:26)—received their full apostolic gifting when they received the outpouring of the Spirit in Acts 2. Often in the New Testament the meaning of "apostle" derives from the traditional rabbinic term *shaliach* ("sent one"). As "sent ones" the apostles bore the full representative authority of the One who sent them, namely, Christ. **that they might be with him.** The Twelve were unique in regard to the time they spent with the earthly Jesus (cf. "with me"; Jn 15:26–27). **preach.** Again (see 1:14,17) the priority was mission preaching coupled with exorcism. The time of preparation had a markedly practical emphasis.

3:18 Thaddaeus. Mark and Matthew (Mt 10:2–4) have identical lists. The parallel list in Luke (Lk 6:12–16) is identical except that the name "Thaddaeus" does not occur, and in its place is "Judas son of James" (not Judas Iscariot). The only reasonable explanation of this anomaly is that Thaddaeus had a second name, Judas. **Zealot.** A member of a religious political party whose goal was national independence and whose means included armed rebellion. See the chart titled "Jewish Sects" located at Matthew 23.

3:19 Iscariot. Some believe that Judas was also a Zealot (see note on v. 18) because the name "Iscariot" may have derived from the Latin *sicarius* ("dagger"). More likely, since it was also the name of his father (Jn 6:71), the word has a Semitic origin: *Ish* ("man [of]") joined with "Kerioth," a town in Israel close to Hebron (Jos 15:25).

Blasphemy Against the Holy Spirit: Can I Be Forgiven?

JESUS taught that every kind of sin can be forgiven except blasphemy against the Holy Spirit (Mt 12:31–32; Mk 3:28–29; Lk 12:10). If anyone blasphemes against the Holy Spirit, that person demonstrates that he or she is not among the elect—that person will never be saved ("a tree is recognized by its fruit"; Mt 12:33). But what exactly is blasphemy against the Holy Spirit? How can we know if we have committed this unforgivable sin?

Generally, "blasphemy" is "speaking impiously," "slandering" or "using abusive language." When the Pharisees insisted that he exorcised demons by being in league with Satan (Beelzebub), Jesus warned them that blasphemy against the Holy Spirit is unpardonable, both in this age and in the next (Mt 12:32; Mk 3:29–30). By denying that the Holy Spirit was the power behind the exorcism, by attributing that power to Satan, the Pharisees spoke against the Holy Spirit. On this basis, theologians have commonly understood blasphemy against the Holy Spirit to be attributing the work of the Holy Spirit to Satan or to other demonic forces.

Even this definition, however, needs refining. In responding to the Pharisees, Jesus also made the point that the work he did was obviously from the Holy Spirit (according to the logic of his argument in Mt 12:25–29 and Mk 3:23–27). There was no reasonable explanation for the exorcism other than the power of the Holy Spirit, and this should have been evident to all. The Pharisees' rejection of the Holy Spirit was thus informed and willful; they had not simply made a mistake. Speaking from the evil of their hearts (Mt 12:34–35), they had intentionally blasphemed what they knew to be the power of the Holy Spirit.

Blasphemy against the Holy Spirit is informed and intentional, motivated by evil. Because it is unforgivable, it cannot be committed by a Christian or by someone who is not yet a Christian but who later will come to faith. Even so, sincere Christians sometimes fear that they have blasphemed the Holy Spirit. Usually these people have simply misunderstood the nature of such blasphemy or have misjudged their own actions. In any event, since the reprobate (those who will never come to faith) cannot truly repent of their sin (cf. Ac 11:18), Christians who fear that they may have committed this unpardonable sin generally show by their very anxiety and repentance that they have not done so.

Jesus and Beelzebub

20 Then Jesus entered a house, and again a crowd gathered,[a] so that he and his disciples were not even able to eat.[b] 21 When his family heard about this, they went to take
charge of him, for they said, "He is out of his mind."[c]
22 And the teachers of the law who came down from Jerusalem[d] said, "He is possessed
by Beelzebub[a]![e] By the prince of demons he is driving out demons."[f]
23 So Jesus called them and spoke to them in parables:[g] "How can Satan[h] drive out
Satan? 24 If a kingdom is divided against itself, that kingdom cannot stand. 25 If a house
is divided against itself, that house cannot stand. 26 And if Satan opposes himself and is
divided, he cannot stand; his end has come. 27 In fact, no one can enter a strong man's
house and carry off his possessions unless he first ties up the strong man. Then he can
rob his house.[i] 28 I tell you the truth, all the sins and blasphemies of men will be forgiv-
en them. 29 But whoever blasphemes against the Holy Spirit will never be forgiven; he is
guilty of an eternal sin."[j]
30 He said this because they were saying, "He has an evil spirit."

Jesus' Mother and Brothers

31 Then Jesus' mother and brothers arrived.[k] Standing outside, they sent someone in
to call him. 32 A crowd was sitting around him, and they told him, "Your mother and
brothers are outside looking for you."
33 "Who are my mother and my brothers?" he asked.
34 Then he looked at those seated in a circle around him and said, "Here are my mother and my brothers! 35 Whoever does God's will is my brother and sister and mother."

The Parable of the Sower

4 Again Jesus began to teach by the lake.[l] The crowd that gathered around him was
so large that he got into a boat and sat in it out on the lake, while all the people were
along the shore at the water's edge. 2 He taught them many things by parables,[m] and in
his teaching said: 3 "Listen! A farmer went out to sow his seed.[n] 4 As he was scattering the
seed, some fell along the path, and the birds came and ate it up. 5 Some fell on rocky places, where it did not have much soil. It sprang up quickly, because the soil was shallow.
6 But when the sun came up, the plants were scorched, and they withered because they
had no root. 7 Other seed fell among thorns, which grew up and choked the plants, so

3:20 [a]ver 7 [b]Mk 6:31
3:21 [c]Jn 10:20; Ac 26:24
3:22 [d]Mt 15:1 [e]Mt 10:25; 11:18; 12:24; Jn 7:20; 8:48,52; 10:20 [f]Mt 9:34
3:23 [g]Mk 4:2 [h]Mt 4:10
3:27 [i]Isa 49:24,25
3:29 [j]Mt 12:31,32; Lk 12:10
3:31 [k]ver 21
4:1 [l]Mk 2:13; 3:7
4:2 [m]ver 11; Mk 3:23
4:3 [n]ver 26

a 22 Greek *Beezeboul* or *Beelzeboul*

■ **3:20–35** *Accusations in Capernaum.* Mark related two accusations against Jesus: (1) that he was mad and (2) that he was demon possessed. The Jews saw a general connection between madness and demon possession (Jn 10:20). Moreover, the accusations appear together. The account of the intervention of Jesus' family begins in verse 21 and is completed in verses 31ff. In between is the account of the verbal attack on Jesus by the "teachers of the law" (vv. 22–30). Diabolical attacks on Jesus came both from the religious leaders and from Jesus' own family (see Jn 7:5), as they would also come from within Jesus' inner circle of the Twelve (Mt 16:23; Jn 13:27).

3:21 his family. This phrase is slightly ambiguous in the original, so certain translations render it "family," while others propose "associates" or "friends." However, this group is clearly identified in verse 34 as his mother and brothers. **out of his mind.** This phrase reveals that Jesus' brothers considered him, at least temporarily, mentally impaired. It may imply either disdain or concern.

3:22 Beelzebub. The Greek has *Beelzeboul,* which occurs only here and in the parallel accounts in Matthew 12:24–29 and Luke 11:14–22. The corresponding Hebrew term *Baal-Zebub,* "lord of the flies," is apparently a parody of Baal-Zabul, the god of Ekron (2Ki 1:2), which means "Baal is Prince." The Pharisees used it here as a name for Satan and accused Jesus of casting out demons by the power of Satan.

3:23–27 parables. See the chart "Parables of Jesus" at Matthew 13. This parable illustrates the claim of Jesus that the kingdom had come (Mt 12:28), for one stronger than the "strong man" (Satan) was present. Jesus was able to bind Satan and free his people from the power of this demonic lord.

3:29 whoever blasphemes against the Holy Spirit. For the various forms of blasphemy, see Exodus 22:28, Leviticus 24:10–16, Ezekiel 35:12–13, Mark 2:7, Mark 14:64, John 10:33–36 and Acts 6:11. Here the unforgivable blasphemy is specified as the act of deliberately associating the power and work of Jesus (Jn 10:21), who was full of the Holy Spirit, with the work of Satan.

3:31 mother and brothers. See verse 21. Roman Catholic commentators, for whom the eternal virginity of Mary is a dogma, stress the fact that "brother" can refer to wider family relations, pointing to Genesis 13:8, 14:16, 29:15, Leviticus 10:4 and 1 Chronicles 23:22. However, elsewhere in Mark the term always seems to imply siblings from the same parents. Further, Matthew 1:25 indicates clearly that after Jesus' birth Mary and Joseph engaged in normal marital relations, giving added meaning to Luke's designation of Jesus as Mary's "firstborn" (Lk 2:7).

3:35 Whoever does God's will. The arrival of the kingdom of God disrupts normal life. At times mothers, brothers, houses and land must be left behind for the sake of the kingdom (10:17–31). Although the kingdom of God will ultimately heal human life, the process of healing prior to Jesus' return involves strife and judgment against sinners, as well as trials and suffering for believers (Ro 5:3; Jas 1:2; 1Pe 1:6).

■ **4:1–34** *Kingdom Parables.* Mark turned to a series of parables Jesus taught by the Sea of Galilee. These parables explain that the kingdom of God will not come suddenly, as the Jews commonly expected. Rather it is a kingdom that grows slowly through the spread of the gospel. (See theological article "The Kingdom of God" at Mt 4.)

4:1 crowd . . . so large. Mark again stressed that Jesus' public ministry was a mass movement. In chapter 6 the miraculous feeding probably involved a crowd of some 15,000, since the 5,000 (6:44) were men (Lk 9:14). Perhaps only the heads of families were counted, for Matthew's Gospel adds the phrase "besides women and children" (Mt 14:21).

4:2 parables. The Greek word for "parables" translates the Hebrew word for proverbs, figurative sayings and riddles. See notes on verse 11 and Matthew 13:3; see also the chart, "Parables of Jesus," at Matthew 13.

4:3–8 A farmer . . . was scattering the seed. This was not a wasteful or inexperienced farmer. In Palestine sowing precedes plowing. Thus, thorny areas will be plowed up. Rocky places that are covered by a thin layer of soil will only become visible after plowing.

that they did not bear grain. 8 Still other seed fell on good soil. It came up, grew and produced a crop, multiplying thirty, sixty, or even a hundred times."[o]
9 Then Jesus said, "He who has ears to hear, let him hear."[p]
10 When he was alone, the Twelve and the others around him asked him about the
parables. 11 He told them, "The secret of the kingdom of God[q] has been given to you. But
to those on the outside[r] everything is said in parables 12 so that,

" 'they may be ever seeing but never perceiving,
and ever hearing but never understanding;
otherwise they might turn and be forgiven!'[a]"[s]

13 Then Jesus said to them, "Don't you understand this parable? How then will you understand any parable? 14 The farmer sows the word.[t] 15 Some people are like seed along
the path, where the word is sown. As soon as they hear it, Satan[u] comes and takes away
the word that was sown in them. 16 Others, like seed sown on rocky places, hear the word
and at once receive it with joy. 17 But since they have no root, they last only a short time.
When trouble or persecution comes because of the word, they quickly fall away. 18 Still
others, like seed sown among thorns, hear the word; 19 but the worries of this life, the deceitfulness of wealth[v] and the desires for other things come in and choke the word, making it unfruitful. 20 Others, like seed sown on good soil, hear the word, accept it, and produce a crop—thirty, sixty or even a hundred times what was sown."

A Lamp on a Stand

21 He said to them, "Do you bring in a lamp to put it under a bowl or a bed? Instead,
don't you put it on its stand?[w] 22 For whatever is hidden is meant to be disclosed, and
whatever is concealed is meant to be brought out into the open.[x] 23 If anyone has ears
to hear, let him hear."[y]
24 "Consider carefully what you hear," he continued. "With the measure you use, it
will be measured to you—and even more.[z] 25 Whoever has will be given more; whoever
does not have, even what he has will be taken from him."[a]

The Parable of the Growing Seed

26 He also said, "This is what the kingdom of God is like.[b] A man scatters seed on the
ground. 27 Night and day, whether he sleeps or gets up, the seed sprouts and grows,
though he does not know how. 28 All by itself the soil produces grain—first the stalk, then
the head, then the full kernel in the head. 29 As soon as the grain is ripe, he puts the sickle to it, because the harvest has come."[c]

4:8 [o]Jn 15:5; Col 1:6
4:9 [p]ver 23; Mt 11:15
4:11 [q]Mt 3:2 [r]1Co 5:12, 13; Col 4:5; 1Th 4:12; 1Ti 3:7
4:12 [s]Isa 6:9,10; Mt 13:13-15
4:14 [t]Mk 16:20; Lk 1:2; Ac 4:31; 8:4; 16:6; 17:11; Php 1:14
4:15 [u]Mt 4:10
4:19 [v]Mt 19:23; 1Ti 6:9, 10,17; 1Jn 2:15-17
4:21 [w]Mt 5:15
4:22 [x]Jer 16:17; Mt 10:26; Lk 8:17; 12:2
4:23 [y]ver 9; Mt 11:15
4:24 [z]Mt 7:2; Lk 6:38
4:25 [a]Mt 13:12; 25:29
4:26 [b]Mt 13:24
4:29 [c]Rev 14:15

[a] *12* Isaiah 6:9,10

4:9–10 See *WCF* 21.1.
4:9 He who has ears. This phrase may indicate that serious attention and reflection are required to grasp the parable's meaning (v. 2; cf. Ps 115:6; Mt 11:15; 13:9,43; Mk 4:23; 7:16; Lk 8:8; 14:35; Rev 2:7). Ultimately, however, it is the Holy Spirit who gives people ears to hear spiritual truth (1Co 2:14, 1Th 1:5).
4:10 When he was alone. Jesus often isolated himself with his disciples, particularly with the Twelve (see note on 3:14). His choice of some as special recipients of this blessing is an essential component of his earthly ministry in all the Gospels. The same Greek term occurs in Luke 9:18, prior to Peter's confession that Jesus is the Christ. See also Matthew 10:26–27, 11:25, Luke 12:2–3 and John 16:29.
4:11 secret . . . parables. The "secret," or "mystery," means special, divine revelation (Ro 16:25; 1Co 2:1; Eph 1:9; 3:3,9) and derives from the Old Testament notion of the prophet who by the Spirit was present in God's deliberative council. What he heard constituted his authoritative, divinely inspired message for the people (1Ki 22:19; Jer 23:18; Am 3:7; cf. Ex 24:15–18; Dt 33:2; Isa 6:1–13). Such revelation reached its fulfillment in the apostolic gospel, which Paul would later call "the mystery of Christ" (Eph 3:4; Col 4:3) or "the mystery of the gospel" (Eph 6:19). It begins with what Jesus communicated to the Twelve, those who had been divinely chosen first for salvation and then for service. Here, the secret of the kingdom (vv. 13–20) was the fact that the kingdom actually arrived with Jesus because he is the King. This "secret," which was revealed to the disciples, was contrasted with the parables told to "those on the outside" (i.e., those who were not genuine followers). Without the "secret," the parable was a riddle (Jn 16:29) that kept them from understanding (as the Scripture had prophesied; see 4:12, citing Isaiah 6:9–10).
4:13 How then will you understand any parable? This explanation of the function of parables applies to all parables. Thus the secret here given is the key to all the parables; that is, all the parables reveal something about Jesus the King and about the manner in which he brings the kingdom of God. See chart "Parables of Jesus" at Matthew 13.
4:14–20 The difficulty of the parable seems not to have resided in the moral teaching (which was actually quite clear) on the hardness of human hearts. The difficulty, or "secret," is to be found in the fact that the announcement of the final stages of God's kingdom was like a fragile seed, and that the Son of Man who exercises all authority on Earth (2:11,27) appeared as Jesus, a humble sower. At that time, the coming of the kingdom and of its King was marked by ambiguity. Those on the outside had unreceptive hearts, while those who followed Jesus to the end would bear much fruit. For those with ears to hear, the parable unveiled a great secret about the history of redemption.
4:19 deceitfulness of wealth. Compare Ephesians 4:22. See *WLC* 195.
4:21–25 These verses constitute the conclusion to the explanations of parables given to the disciples (vv. 10–20).
4:22 whatever is hidden. During Jesus' earthly ministry, many truths that were to be revealed later remained hidden (see also Mt 10:26–27; Lk 12:2–3).
4:24 With the measure. Publishing the mystery of the kingdom will be rewarded in direct measure to one's faithfulness to the task.
4:25 given more. This principle is perfectly illustrated in the parables of the talents (Mt 25:14–30) and of the ten minas (Lk 19:11–27).

The Parable of the Mustard Seed 4:30
30 Again he said, "What shall we say the kingdom of God is like,[d] or what parable shall [d]Mt 13:24
we use to describe it? 31 It is like a mustard seed, which is the smallest seed you plant in
the ground. 32 Yet when planted, it grows and becomes the largest of all garden plants,
with such big branches that the birds of the air can perch in its shade."
33 With many similar parables Jesus spoke the word to them, as much as they could 4:33
understand.[e] 34 He did not say anything to them without using a parable.[f] But when he [e]Jn 16:12
was alone with his own disciples, he explained everything. 4:34

Jesus Calms the Storm [f]Jn 16:25
35 That day when evening came, he said to his disciples, "Let us go over to the other 4:36
side." 36 Leaving the crowd behind, they took him along, just as he was, in the boat.[g] [g]ver 1; Mk 3:9; 5:2,
There were also other boats with him. 37 A furious squall came up, and the waves broke 21; 6:32,45
over the boat, so that it was nearly swamped. 38 Jesus was in the stern, sleeping on a cush-
ion. The disciples woke him and said to him, "Teacher, don't you care if we drown?"
39 He got up, rebuked the wind and said to the waves, "Quiet! Be still!" Then the wind
died down and it was completely calm. 4:40
40 He said to his disciples, "Why are you so afraid? Do you still have no faith?"[h] [h]Mt 14:31;
41 They were terrified and asked each other, "Who is this? Even the wind and the Mk 16:14
waves obey him!"

The Healing of a Demon-possessed Man
5 They went across the lake to the region of the Gerasenes.[a] 2 When Jesus got out of 5:2
the boat,[i] a man with an evil[b] spirit[j] came from the tombs to meet him. 3 This man [i]Mk 4:1 [j]Mk 1:23
lived in the tombs, and no one could bind him any more, not even with a chain. 4 For he
had often been chained hand and foot, but he tore the chains apart and broke the irons
on his feet. No one was strong enough to subdue him. 5 Night and day among the tombs
and in the hills he would cry out and cut himself with stones.
6 When he saw Jesus from a distance, he ran and fell on his knees in front of him. 7 He 5:7
shouted at the top of his voice, "What do you want with me,[k] Jesus, Son of the Most High [k]Mt 8:29 [l]Mt 4:3;
God?[l] Swear to God that you won't torture me!" 8 For Jesus had said to him, "Come out Lk 1:32; 6:35;
of this man, you evil spirit!" Ac 16:17; Heb 7:1
9 Then Jesus asked him, "What is your name?" 5:9
"My name is Legion,"[m] he replied, "for we are many." 10 And he begged Jesus again [m]ver 15
and again not to send them out of the area.

[a] *1* Some manuscripts *Gadarenes*; other manuscripts *Gergesenes* [b] *2* Greek *unclean*; also in verses 8 and 13

4:30–32 The secret revealed in the parable of the mustard seed was the ambiguity of the kingdom's manifestation in Jesus' earthly ministry. What was small and apparently insignificant would become the greatest thing of all.
4:32 birds of the air. See Daniel 4:21, where the nearly identical image describes the worldwide dominion of Nebuchadnezzar.
4:33–34 See verses 10–12.
▪ **4:35—5:20** *Incursion Into the Decapolis.* Mark reported that Jesus moved into the territory of the Decapolis, a highly pagan region. Mark did this to demonstrate that Jesus' power had no geographical boundaries and that pagan powers could not resist his will.
4:35 the other side. According to 3:7, Jesus was in Galilee at this time. The region of the Gerasenes (in the Decapolis) was on the "other side" of the lake (5:1).
4:36 other boats. This detail provides added realism and indicates an eyewitness account lying behind Mark's narrative.
4:37 furious squall. The Sea of Galilee (a lake) is 660 feet below sea level, 12 miles long and 7 1/2 miles wide. At its southern end is a deep, cliff-lined valley, known as the Ghor. The wind, funneling through the surrounding hills and through this valley, can cause sudden, violent storms on the lake.
4:38 Jesus was . . . sleeping. Jesus had been teaching all day and was exhausted (cf. Jn 4:6; 11:35,38). This fact underlines his full humanity; our Lord took on genuine human flesh, though without the dreadful propensity to sin inherited from Adam (Ro 8:3; cf. Ro 5:12ff.; 2Co 5:21). See theological article "The Full Humanity of Christ" at Luke 3.
4:39 Quiet! Be still! While on Earth, Jesus revealed his authority to forgive sins (2:10), his lordship over the Sabbath (2:28), his authority in teaching (1:22) and his authority over demons (1:27). Here he demonstrated his authority over nature. This calming of the storm resembled Jesus' exorcisms. The expression of violence (1:26; 5:4,13), the command to "be still" (1:25) and the resultant calm (5:15; 7:38) draw these accounts together. Thus Jesus again binds "the strong man" (3:27), reclaiming from him the physical creation, which will one day know the glorious liberty of the sons of God (cf. Ro 8:19–21).
5:1 the region of the Gerasenes. Some early manuscripts substitute "Gadarenes," but the region of Gerasa, which is some 35 miles southeast of the lake, seems likely since it contains the kinds of escarpment and tombs described in the story. However, the town of Gadara was much closer to the water, being only ten miles south of the lake. Mark's Gospel depicts Jesus moving deliberately into the heavily pagan territory of the Decapolis (a political association of ten independent Greek city-states). Moreover, the herd of pigs portrays these events as taking place in a thoroughly pagan environment.
5:2 came from the tombs. This demon-possessed man (according to Mt 8:28, there were two) had cut himself off from normal human contact, leaving his village and his family (v. 19).
5:3 no one could bind him. Violence and unusual physical strength (v. 5; 9:22) often seem to characterize those with demons (1:26; 9:18–26; see note on 5:13), but before the spiritual strength of Jesus the demons cowered and fled.
5:7 What do you want with me . . . ? See 1:24.
5:9 What is your name? Naming someone appears to have been a way of gaining power over the person, but this was not the method Jesus used in every exorcism (e.g., 7:26–29). The demon(s) had already identified Jesus (v. 7), as they had in 1:24 and generally did (1:34), but by this question Jesus revealed his superior power. **Legion.** The demons were forced to unmask themselves before Jesus. There was not one demon, but many (a Roman legion numbered 6,000 men). It is unclear whether this response was offered

11 A large herd of pigs was feeding on the nearby hillside. 12 The demons begged Jesus, "Send us among the pigs; allow us to go into them." 13 He gave them permission, and the evil spirits came out and went into the pigs. The herd, about two thousand in number, rushed down the steep bank into the lake and were drowned.

14 Those tending the pigs ran off and reported this in the town and countryside, and the people went out to see what had happened. 15 When they came to Jesus, they saw the man who had been possessed by the legion[n] of demons,[o] sitting there, dressed and in his right mind; and they were afraid. 16 Those who had seen it told the people what had happened to the demon-possessed man—and told about the pigs as well. 17 Then the people began to plead with Jesus to leave their region.

18 As Jesus was getting into the boat, the man who had been demon-possessed begged to go with him. 19 Jesus did not let him, but said, "Go home to your family and tell them[p] how much the Lord has done for you, and how he has had mercy on you." 20 So the man went away and began to tell in the Decapolis[a][q] how much Jesus had done for him. And all the people were amazed.

A Dead Girl and a Sick Woman

21 When Jesus had again crossed over by boat to the other side of the lake,[r] a large crowd gathered around him while he was by the lake.[s] 22 Then one of the synagogue rulers,[t] named Jairus, came there. Seeing Jesus, he fell at his feet 23 and pleaded earnestly with him, "My little daughter is dying. Please come and put your hands on[u] her so that she will be healed and live." 24 So Jesus went with him.

A large crowd followed and pressed around him. 25 And a woman was there who had been subject to bleeding[v] for twelve years. 26 She had suffered a great deal under the care of many doctors and had spent all she had, yet instead of getting better she grew worse. 27 When she heard about Jesus, she came up behind him in the crowd and touched his cloak, 28 because she thought, "If I just touch his clothes,[w] I will be healed." 29 Immediately her bleeding stopped and she felt in her body that she was freed from her suffering.[x]

30 At once Jesus realized that power[y] had gone out from him. He turned around in the crowd and asked, "Who touched my clothes?"

31 "You see the people crowding against you," his disciples answered, "and yet you can ask, 'Who touched me?' "

32 But Jesus kept looking around to see who had done it. 33 Then the woman, knowing what had happened to her, came and fell at his feet and, trembling with fear, told him the whole truth. 34 He said to her, "Daughter, your faith has healed you.[z] Go in peace[a] and be freed from your suffering."

5:15 [n]ver 9 [o]ver 16,18; Mt 4:24
5:19 [p]Mt 8:4
5:20 [q]Mt 4:25; Mk 7:31
5:21 [r]Mt 9:1 [s]Mk 4:1
5:22 [t]ver 35,36,38; Lk 13:14; Ac 13:15; 18:8,17
5:23 [u]Mt 19:13; Mk 6:5; 7:32; 8:23; 16:18; Lk 4:40; 13:13; Ac 6:6
5:25 [v]Lev 15:25-30
5:28 [w]Mt 9:20
5:29 [x]ver 34
5:30 [y]Lk 5:17; 6:19
5:34 [z]Mt 9:22 [a]Ac 15:33

[a] *20* That is, the Ten Cities

by the demoniac or by a demon representing the entire legion.

5:10 he begged. As in verse 9, it is unclear whether the begging was done by the demoniac himself or by a demon representing the legion. The begging included invoking God's name as a form of protection (v. 7) because Jesus had absolute power over demons to do with them as he willed.

5:13 He gave them permission. Jesus did not banish the demons to the Abyss (i.e., hell; cf. Lk 8:31), but permitted them to enter the pigs, who hurled themselves over the cliff. This was a dramatic demonstration of Jesus' power over evil (see the effects of this event in vv. 14,16) and of the presence of the kingdom already at work in his ministry (see Lk 11:20). The reason for this "permission" seems to be that Jesus' victory over evil was just beginning. This act was therefore one of the signs of the kingdom. But the kingdom would come "with power" (9:1), and the power of evil would be broken at the cross (Col 2:14–15; cf. Php 2:8–10; Rev 12:1–14; 20:1–3).

5:15 sitting there. In comparison with his previous personal violence and the recent destruction of the pigs, the man, "sitting there, dressed and in his right mind," gave eloquent expression to the notion of calm and life and to the restoration that comes from the power of Jesus (cf. 4:39; 9:26–27).

5:19 Go home. This man would become the first Gentile missionary. While among Jews, Jesus demanded silence (1:34,44; 3:12; 8:30; 9:9,30). But in the pagan Decapolis, the preparation of the soil for the future mission of the church could already begin.

■ **5:21—6:6** *More Ministry in Galilee.* Mark reported events in Galilee that showed the importance of faith for the success of Jesus' ministry. Mark did this to encourage faith in his readers as they sought Christ's blessings in their own day.

5:22 one of the synagogue rulers. An ambiguous phrase that could mean "the ruler of one of the synagogues" or "one of the rulers of the synagogue." Though he was a layman, a ruler's responsibilities were socially and religiously very important, including not only the upkeep of the building, but also the good order of the service and the choice of Torah readings.

5:25 bleeding. Literally, "a flow of blood." The text is not more specific, but in Leviticus 20:18 in the Septuagint (Greek translation of the OT) the same term designates menstrual bleeding, which would have rendered the woman ceremonially "unclean" (Lev 15:25–33). Her hemorrhaging condition "grew worse" (v. 26), no doubt disqualifying her not only from marriage (Lev 20:18), but also from most aspects of Jewish religious life.

5:29 Immediately. See note on 1:10.

5:30 power had gone out from him. This phrase occurs only here. **Who touched my clothes?** Jesus noticed the touch of faith even though, in such a dense crowd, all kinds of people were probably jostling him.

5:32 Jesus kept looking around. Because the woman had been a social outcast for many years, the healing was complete only when Jesus had publicly identified her, commended her for her faith and declared to all that she had been healed (v. 34) and thus cleansed.

5:34 your faith. Mark stressed the role of faith in Jesus in the furtherance of Jesus' ministry. This woman had faith; Jairus was told to "just believe" (v. 36); but Jesus' hometown demonstrated a "lack of faith" (6:6). **healed.** Literally, "saved." The double meaning of this verb (also used in v. 28)—"heal" (the body) and "save" (the person)—and the place of faith in the healing process indicate

35 While Jesus was still speaking, some men came from the house of Jairus, the synagogue ruler.[b] "Your daughter is dead," they said. "Why bother the teacher any more?"
36 Ignoring what they said, Jesus told the synagogue ruler, "Don't be afraid; just believe."
37 He did not let anyone follow him except Peter, James and John the brother of
James.[c] 38 When they came to the home of the synagogue ruler,[d] Jesus saw a commotion,
with people crying and wailing loudly. 39 He went in and said to them, "Why all this commotion and wailing? The child is not dead but asleep."[e] 40 But they laughed at him.
After he put them all out, he took the child's father and mother and the disciples who
were with him, and went in where the child was. 41 He took her by the hand[f] and said to
her, "*Talitha koum!*" (which means, "Little girl, I say to you, get up!").[g] 42 Immediately the
girl stood up and walked around (she was twelve years old). At this they were completely astonished. 43 He gave strict orders not to let anyone know about this,[h] and told them
to give her something to eat.

A Prophet Without Honor

6 Jesus left there and went to his hometown,[i] accompanied by his disciples. 2 When
the Sabbath came,[j] he began to teach in the synagogue,[k] and many who heard him
were amazed.[l]
"Where did this man get these things?" they asked. "What's this wisdom that has
been given him, that he even does miracles! 3 Isn't this the carpenter? Isn't this Mary's
son and the brother of James, Joseph,[a] Judas and Simon?[m] Aren't his sisters here with
us?" And they took offense at him.[n]
4 Jesus said to them, "Only in his hometown, among his relatives and in his own house
is a prophet without honor."[o] 5 He could not do any miracles there, except lay his hands
on[p] a few sick people and heal them. 6 And he was amazed at their lack of faith.

Jesus Sends Out the Twelve

Then Jesus went around teaching from village to village.[q] 7 Calling the Twelve to him,[r]
he sent them out two by two[s] and gave them authority over evil[b] spirits.[t]
8 These were his instructions: "Take nothing for the journey except a staff—no bread,
no bag, no money in your belts. 9 Wear sandals but not an extra tunic. 10 Whenever you
enter a house, stay there until you leave that town. 11 And if any place will not welcome

5:35 [b]ver 22
5:37 [c]Mt 4:21
5:38 [d]ver 22
5:39 [e]Mt 9:24
5:41 [f]Mk 1:31 [g]Lk 7:14; Ac 9:40
5:43 [h]Mt 8:4
6:1 [i]Mt 2:23
6:2 [j]Mk 1:21 [k]Mt 4:23 [l]Mt 7:28
6:3 [m]Mt 12:46 [n]Mt 11:6; Jn 6:61
6:4 [o]Lk 4:24; Jn 4:44
6:5 [p]Mk 5:23
6:6 [q]Mt 9:35; Mk 1:39; Lk 13:22
6:7 [r]Mk 3:13 [s]Dt 17:6; Lk 10:1 [t]Mt 10:1

[a] 3 Greek *Joses*, a variant of *Joseph* [b] 7 Greek *unclean*

that the goal of Jesus' healings was to bring people to faith and to full salvation (1:40–41; 2:5,9).
5:36 just believe. See note on verse 34.
5:37 Peter, James and John. There were numerous disciples (4:10), of whom 12 were appointed apostles (3:13ff.). Among the Twelve, some (Peter, James and John, and sometimes Andrew) enjoyed greater intimacy with Jesus, most notably at the transfiguration (9:2ff.) and in Gethsemane (14:32).
5:38 wailing. In oriental countries, wailing is still a customary expression of grief, even to the extent of hiring professional mourners.
5:40 put them all out. Jesus was not interested in producing a grand spectacle of healing. Rather he was concerned for the suffering of the girl, for the faith of her parents (see also v. 19 regarding Jesus' respect for family) and for the ultimate goal of his mission (v. 43).
5:41 *Talitha koum!* Aramaic for "Rise, little girl." Aramaic was the popular language spoken in Palestine. Mark gave Aramaic equivalents for other terms (3:17; 7:11; 10:46; 14:36), apparently to increase vividness.
5:43 strict orders. See note on verse 19.
6:1 hometown. Nazareth, which is some 25 miles southwest of Capernaum and the Sea of Galilee (cf. Mt 2:23). **his disciples.** The Twelve (6:7; see also 1:16ff.; 3:14; 6:30; 9:2ff.; 14:17).
6:2 amazed. See 1:22, 7:37, 10:26 and 11:18.
6:3 carpenter. Could also mean house builder, which might partially explain Jesus' use of the building image in his teaching and in the description of his own ministry (Mt 7:24; 16:18; 21:33; Mk 14:58; 15:29; Lk 12:18; 17:28). The remark concerning manual labor was probably not intended to be derogatory, for all rabbis were expected to have a trade. The accusation was that Jesus, who taught with "wisdom" (v. 2), was only a carpenter/builder without rabbinic training and credentials. The people of Nazareth knew this because Jesus had lived there all his life and had never attended the rabbinic schools in Jerusalem. **Mary's son.** See 3:31.
6:4 own house. Jesus was rejected not only by the people of the town and the wider circle of relatives there, but also by his own immediate family (3:31).
6:5 could not do any miracles. It was not that Jesus lacked power to perform miracles. Rather, he had chosen to tie his kingdom miracles to the faith of his people, much as he has tied salvation to faith (Eph 2:8–9).
6:6 lack of faith. See note on 5:34.
■ **6:7–30** *The Galilean Mission of the Twelve.* Mark turned to the sending of the apostles to show that their ministry was an extension of Jesus' ministry from the very beginning (vv. 7–13,30). He inserted an account of the death of John the Baptist (vv. 14–29) to demonstrate that the mission of Jesus and his disciples superseded the ministry of John and his disciples.
6:7 the Twelve. Having already been appointed to be with Jesus (see note on 3:14) and to receive special revelation concerning the mystery of his person and role (see notes on 4:10,11), the Twelve were now permitted to share his ministry and authority. **sent them out.** The Greek verb has the same root as the noun translated "apostle," and it underlines the Twelve's link with Jesus as his representatives (see note on 3:14). **two by two.** The Biblical principle that testimony should be given by at least two witnesses (Nu 35:30; Dt 17:6; 19:15; Mt 18:16; Jn 8:17; 2Co 13:1; 1Ti 5:19; Heb 10:28) was also applied in the missionary ministry of the early church. It can be seen with Peter and John (Ac 3:1; 4:1), with Paul and Barnabas (Ac 13:2) and with Paul and Silas (Ac 15:40).
6:8 no bread. Matthew 10:10 gives the reason: "The worker is worth his keep."
6:9 Wear sandals. In Matthew Jesus prohibited the wearing of sandals (Mt 10:10), a detail some take as a contradiction in the Biblical record. Common sense, however, would suggest the unlikelihood of Jesus requiring his disciples to go barefooted when both he himself (Mk 1:7; Jn 1:27) and his great predecessor Moses (Ac 7:33)

6:11 [u]Mt 10:14 you or listen to you, shake the dust off your feet[u] when you leave, as a testimony against
them."
6:12 [v]Lk 9:6 12 They went out and preached that people should repent.[v] 13 They drove out many demons and anointed many sick people with oil[w] and healed them.

6:13 [w]Jas 5:14

John the Baptist Beheaded

6:14 14 King Herod heard about this, for Jesus' name had become well known. Some were
[x]Mt 3:1 saying,[a] "John the Baptist[x] has been raised from the dead, and that is why miraculous
6:15 powers are at work in him."
[y]Mal 4:5 [z]Mt 21:11 15 Others said, "He is Elijah."[y]
[a]Mt 16:14; Mk 8:28 And still others claimed, "He is a prophet,[z] like one of the prophets of long ago."[a]
16 But when Herod heard this, he said, "John, the man I beheaded, has been raised
from the dead!"
6:17 17 For Herod himself had given orders to have John arrested, and he had him bound
[b]Mt 4:12; 11:2; Lk 3:19,20 and put in prison.[b] He did this because of Herodias, his brother Philip's wife, whom he
had married. 18 For John had been saying to Herod, "It is not lawful for you to have your
6:18 brother's wife."[c] 19 So Herodias nursed a grudge against John and wanted to kill him.
[c]Lev 18:16; 20:21 But she was not able to, 20 because Herod feared John and protected him, knowing him
6:20 to be a righteous and holy man.[d] When Herod heard John, he was greatly puzzled[b]; yet
[d]Mt 11:9; 21:26 he liked to listen to him.
6:21 21 Finally the opportune time came. On his birthday Herod gave a banquet[e] for his
[e]Est 1:3; 2:18 [f]Lk 3:1 high officials and military commanders and the leading men of Galilee.[f] 22 When the
daughter of Herodias came in and danced, she pleased Herod and his dinner guests.
The king said to the girl, "Ask me for anything you want, and I'll give it to you." 23 And
6:23 he promised her with an oath, "Whatever you ask I will give you, up to half my king-
[g]Est 5:3,6; 7:2 dom."[g]
24 She went out and said to her mother, "What shall I ask for?"
"The head of John the Baptist," she answered.
25 At once the girl hurried in to the king with the request: "I want you to give me right
now the head of John the Baptist on a platter."
26 The king was greatly distressed, but because of his oaths and his dinner guests, he
did not want to refuse her. 27 So he immediately sent an executioner with orders to bring
John's head. The man went, beheaded John in the prison, 28 and brought back his head
on a platter. He presented it to the girl, and she gave it to her mother. 29 On hearing of
this, John's disciples came and took his body and laid it in a tomb.

Jesus Feeds the Five Thousand

6:30 [h]Mt 10:2; Lk 9:10; 17:5; 22:14; 24:10; Ac 1:2,26 [i]Lk 9:10
30 The apostles[h] gathered around Jesus and reported to him all they had done and
taught.[i] 31 Then, because so many people were coming and going that they did not even
6:31 have a chance to eat,[j] he said to them, "Come with me by yourselves to a quiet place and
[j]Mk 3:20 get some rest."
6:32 32 So they went away by themselves in a boat[k] to a solitary place. 33 But many who saw
[k]ver 45; Mk 4:36 them leaving recognized them and ran on foot from all the towns and got there ahead

[a] *14* Some early manuscripts *He was saying* [b] *20* Some early manuscripts *he did many things*

wore sandals. It is more likely that the text of Matthew presupposes the idea of "extra" sandals, as is explicitly the case for tunics.

6:11 shake the dust off. Strict Jews shook the dust off their shoes after traveling through pagan, "unclean," territories. Refusal to accept the gospel brings a similar accusatory "testimony."

6:14 King Herod heard. Herod Antipas, son of Herod the Great, of Idumean Arab descent, was actually the "tetrarch," or ruler, of Galilee and Perea. The mission of the Twelve, which included healings and exorcisms accomplished in the name of Jesus, caused Herod to "hear."

6:15 one of the prophets. Speculation about the prophetic identity of Jesus naturally leads into the account of the miraculous feedings (vv. 30ff.; 8:1ff.) and the walk on water (vv. 47ff.), all of which point to something higher—namely, Jesus' personal divinity. But first Mark's Gospel sets the record straight concerning John the Baptist, with whom Herod and others had identified Jesus.

6:18 brother's wife. Aristobulus, one of the sons of Herod the Great (37–4 B.C.), was the father of Herodias. Herod Antipas and Herod Philip were Aristobulus's half brothers, also sons of Herod the Great. After marrying her half uncle Herod Philip, Herodias left him for an incestuous relationship with his brother Herod Antipas. Such were the loose morals, typical of the Herodian dynasty, against which John the Baptist preached with Scriptural support (Lev 18:16,20). See *WCF* 24.4; *WLC* 139.

6:22–26 See *WCF* 22.7; *WLC* 113,130,139.

6:30 The apostles. See note on verse 7. Mark encapsulated his account of John's death within that of the mission of Jesus' apostles. He then linked the apostles' mission to the specific role they would later play in Jesus' feeding of the 5,000, in order to show the superiority of Jesus' ministry over John's.

■ **6:31–44** *Feeding the Five Thousand.* The priority of Jesus' ministry over John's was proven when Jesus and his apostles fed the 5,000. This incident also shows Jesus' great concern for the daily needs of his people, concerns expressed first in his decision to teach them and afterward in his determination to feed them.

6:31 by yourselves. Being alone with Jesus—who initiated them into the mystery of the kingdom (4:10–11)—was part of the disciples' preparation for future ministry (4:34; 9:2,28; 13:3; cf. Jn 13:1; 16:29).

6:32 solitary place. Literally, "desert place" (see note on 1:12). Jesus was about to perform a very significant miracle in the desert. This entire event recalled Israel's beginnings, when the people were led by manifestations of the Spirit, tested by experiences of need and sustained by God's miraculous intervention.

of them. 34 When Jesus landed and saw a large crowd, he had compassion on them, be- 6:34
cause they were like sheep without a shepherd.[l] So he began teaching them many [l]Mt 9:36
things.
35 By this time it was late in the day, so his disciples came to him. "This is a remote
place," they said, "and it's already very late. 36 Send the people away so they can go to
the surrounding countryside and villages and buy themselves something to eat."
37 But he answered, "You give them something to eat."[m] 6:37
They said to him, "That would take eight months of a man's wages[a]! Are we to go and [m]2Ki 4:42-44
spend that much on bread and give it to them to eat?"
38 "How many loaves do you have?" he asked. "Go and see."
When they found out, they said, "Five—and two fish."[n] 6:38
39 Then Jesus directed them to have all the people sit down in groups on the green [n]Mt 15:34; Mk 8:5
grass. 40 So they sat down in groups of hundreds and fifties. 41 Taking the five loaves and 6:41
the two fish and looking up to heaven, he gave thanks and broke the loaves.[o] Then he [o]Mt 14:19
gave them to his disciples to set before the people. He also divided the two fish among
them all. 42 They all ate and were satisfied, 43 and the disciples picked up twelve basketfuls of broken pieces of bread and fish. 44 The number of the men who had eaten was five
thousand.

Jesus Walks on the Water

6:45

45 Immediately Jesus made his disciples get into the boat[p] and go on ahead of him to [p]ver 32 [q]Mt 11:21
Bethsaida,[q] while he dismissed the crowd. 46 After leaving them, he went up on a moun- 6:46
tainside to pray.[r] [r]Lk 3:21
47 When evening came, the boat was in the middle of the lake, and he was alone on
land. 48 He saw the disciples straining at the oars, because the wind was against them. 6:49
About the fourth watch of the night he went out to them, walking on the lake. He was [s]Lk 24:37
about to pass by them, 49 but when they saw him walking on the lake, they thought he 6:50
was a ghost.[s] They cried out, 50 because they all saw him and were terrified. [t]Mt 14:27
Immediately he spoke to them and said, "Take courage! It is I. Don't be afraid."[t] 6:51
51 Then he climbed into the boat[u] with them, and the wind died down.[v] They were com- [u]ver 32 [v]Mk 4:39
pletely amazed, 52 for they had not understood about the loaves; their hearts were hard- 6:52
ened.[w] [w]Mk 8:17-21
53 When they had crossed over, they landed at Gennesaret and anchored there.[x] 6:53
54 As soon as they got out of the boat, people recognized Jesus. 55 They ran throughout that [x]Jn 6:24,25
whole region and carried the sick on mats to wherever they heard he was. 56 And wher-

[a] 37 Greek *take two hundred denarii*

6:34 had compassion. An attitude typical of Jesus regarding the lostness and confusion of the people of God. Jesus did what God had promised to do in Ezekiel 34:11–14: "I myself will search for my sheep and look after them . . . I will tend them in a good pasture." Jesus thus acted as the Shepherd Messiah, like Moses (Nu 27:15–17; Ps 77:20), David (Ps 78:70–72) and God himself (Pss 23:1; 74:1; 78:52–53; 80:1; Eze 34:15). **sheep without a shepherd.** In the Old Testament Israel, abandoned by unfaithful leaders, was also described in this way (Jer 50:6; Eze 34:1–10).

6:39 green grass. The mention of grass, abundant in the winter and spring in Galilee, suggests that Mark's idea behind the term "desert" was not aridity as such, but isolation and separateness.

6:40 groups of hundreds and fifties. This detail recalls the formation of ancient Israel in the desert under Moses (Ex 18:21).

6:42 They all ate and were satisfied. In unspectacular language, Mark recounts an amazing miracle. This also recalls the miraculous provision of manna/bread in the desert under Moses (Ex 16:1–36) and the fact that everyone was able to eat as much as was needed (Ex 16:16).

6:43 the disciples picked up. This detail alludes to the manna miracle, where nothing was to be left until the morning (Ex 16:19). **twelve basketfuls.** This detail recalls the twelve-fold structure of ancient Israel and suggests the important role that the Twelve would play in the constitution of the new Israel from Jesus' followers (see note on 3:14).

6:44 men . . . five thousand. Mark did not use the generic term for "men," which can also mean "human beings," but a term that distinguishes men from women (cf. Ex 18:21). Perhaps the idea of "heads of family" is intended, especially since Matthew 14:21 adds the phrase "besides women and children." The crowd could easily have numbered between 15,000 and 20,000 people.

■ **6:45—7:23** *Visit to Gennesaret.* Mark reported Jesus' work in Gennesaret to give further insight into the character of the apostles and Jesus' care for them. Jesus rescued them from a storm (vv. 45–56) and defended them against hypocritical religious authorities (7:1–23).

6:45 John 6:14–15 gives the reason for this immediate withdrawal. The symbolism of the miracle erroneously convinced some in the crowd that it was time to make Jesus "king" by force as the prelude to a political insurrection. As Jesus would later teach his disciples, "the Son of Man [would] suffer many things and . . . be killed and after three days rise again" (8:31).

6:48 fourth watch. 3:00 A.M. to 6:00 A.M. The Romans divided the night (from 6:00 P.M. to 6:00 A.M.) into four periods.

6:49 a ghost. Literally, "phantasm," an extremely rare word in the Bible (in the entire NT, used only here and in the Matthew parallel). It evokes the notion of superstitious imagination (see Isa 28:7).

6:50 It is I. The Greek phrase is also the Septuagint (Greek translation of the Hebrew OT) rendering of the divine name "I AM," which was revealed to Moses at the time of the exodus (Ex 3:14; see also Dt 32:39; Isa 41:4; 43:10,13,25; 45:18; 52:6; Hos 13:4; Joel 2:27). Mark drew attention to Jesus' divinity by including all the usual marks of God's appearing (human dread, divine identification, word of assurance).

6:52 they had not understood about the loaves. This remark indicates that the miracle of the feeding contained the same mystery concerning Jesus as did his walking on water and his using the divine name. Jesus, as to his humanity, was indeed the new Moses, but he was also God, the One who provided bread from heaven (Ex 16:4). (See theological article "Jesus Christ, God and Man" at Jn 1.) See *WCF* 17.3. **their hearts were hardened.** All forms of sin and spiritual failure are products of willfully hardened hearts (7:21; see also Ex 8:15; Eph 4:18).

6:53 Gennesaret. A place on the western shore of the Sea of Galilee (also called the Lake of Gennesaret; see Lk 5:1).

6:56 ever he went—into villages, towns or countryside—they placed the sick in the market-
[y]Mt 9:20 places. They begged him to let him touch even the edge of his cloak,[y] and all who
touched him were healed.

Clean and Unclean

7 The Pharisees and some of the teachers of the law who had come from Jerusalem
gathered around Jesus and **2**saw some of his disciples eating food with hands that
7:2 [z]Ac 10:14,28; were "unclean,"[z] that is, unwashed. **3**(The Pharisees and all the Jews do not eat unless
11:8; Ro 14:14 they give their hands a ceremonial washing, holding to the tradition of the elders.[a]
7:3 [a]ver 5,8,9,13; **4**When they come from the marketplace they do not eat unless they wash. And they ob-
Lk 11:38 serve many other traditions, such as the washing of cups, pitchers and kettles.[a])[b]
5So the Pharisees and teachers of the law asked Jesus, "Why don't your disciples live
7:4 [b]Mt 23:25; according to the tradition of the elders[c] instead of eating their food with 'unclean'
Lk 11:39 hands?"
7:5 **6**He replied, "Isaiah was right when he prophesied about you hypocrites; as it is writ-
[c]ver 3; Gal 1:14; ten:
Col 2:8

" 'These people honor me with their lips,
but their hearts are far from me.
7They worship me in vain;
7:7 [d]Isa 29:13 their teachings are but rules taught by men.'[b][d]

7:8 [e]ver 3 **8**You have let go of the commands of God and are holding on to the traditions of men."[e]
9And he said to them: "You have a fine way of setting aside the commands of God in
7:9 [f]ver 3 order to observe[c] your own traditions![f] **10**For Moses said, 'Honor your father and your
mother,'[d][g] and, 'Anyone who curses his father or mother must be put to death.'[e][h] **11**But
7:10 [g]Ex 20:12; Dt 5:16 you say[i] that if a man says to his father or mother: 'Whatever help you might otherwise
[h]Ex 21:17; have received from me is Corban' (that is, a gift devoted to God), **12**then you no longer
Lev 20:9 let him do anything for his father or mother. **13**Thus you nullify the word of God[j] by your
7:11 tradition[k] that you have handed down. And you do many things like that."
[i]Mt 23:16,18 **14**Again Jesus called the crowd to him and said, "Listen to me, everyone, and under-
7:13 [j]Heb 4:12 [k]ver 3 stand this. **15**Nothing outside a man can make him 'unclean' by going into him. Rather,
it is what comes out of a man that makes him 'unclean.'[f]"
7:17 **17**After he had left the crowd and entered the house, his disciples asked him[l] about
[l]Mk 9:28 this parable. **18**"Are you so dull?" he asked. "Don't you see that nothing that enters a man
from the outside can make him 'unclean'? **19**For it doesn't go into his heart but into his
7:19 [m]Ro 14:1-12; stomach, and then out of his body." (In saying this, Jesus declared all foods[m] "clean.")[n]
Col 2:16; 1Ti 4:3-5 **20**He went on: "What comes out of a man is what makes him 'unclean.' **21**For from
[n]Ac 10:15 within, out of men's hearts, come evil thoughts, sexual immorality, theft, murder, adul-

[a] *4* Some early manuscripts *pitchers, kettles and dining couches* [b] *6,7* Isaiah 29:13 [c] *9* Some manuscripts *set up* [d] *10* Exodus 20:12; Deut. 5:16 [e] *10* Exodus 21:17; Lev. 20:9 [f] *15* Some early manuscripts *'unclean.' [16]If anyone has ears to hear, let him hear.*

7:1 Pharisees. See note on 2:16. **teachers of the law.** Literally, "scribes." They were professional legal specialists from many different Jewish theological movements (e.g., Pharisees, Sadducees, Essenes and others). See the chart titled "Jewish Sects" located at Matthew 23.

7:2 unclean. This had no more to do with hygiene than picking up 12 basketfuls of crumbs had to do with tidiness (6:43). Rather, it concerned Old Testament ceremonial law (Ex 30:17–21; 40:12). Jesus was radically critical of this because (1) the idea of ceremonial cleanness had been so twisted that it had actually become an excuse for transgressing the moral law (vv. 9ff.), and (2) his cross would radically alter the way the ceremonial law was to be observed.

7:3 ceremonial washing. By their tradition, the Pharisees applied Old Testament injunctions originally designed for priestly washing at the moment of temple sacrifice (Ex 30:19; 40:13) to the whole of life and to all Jews. **tradition of the elders.** The Pharisees believed that in addition to the written words of the law, Moses had received oral law that was passed on by word of mouth from teacher to teacher. Thus, the Pharisees appealed to differing and even contradictory authorities. In his arguments with Pharisees, Jesus appealed constantly to Scripture as the only absolute authority and always returned to the true meaning of the text (vv. 6ff.).

7:4 See *WCF* 28.3.

7:5 Why don't your disciples . . . ? As a teacher, Jesus did not conform to accepted practice. In addition to never having had formal rabbinic training, he ate with sinners and did not require his disciples to practice the Pharisees' traditions of ceremonial washing.

7:6 Isaiah. Once again Jesus demonstrated his desire to bring people back into conformity with Scripture.

7:7 See *BC* 7.

7:8 You have let go of the commands of God. The verb translated "let go" is strong and can mean "cancel," "forsake" or "neglect" (cf. v. 13). Jesus was not against the Old Testament law itself. Like the psalmist, he was consumed with longing for the law of God (Ps 119:20), which he fulfilled, protected (Mt 5:17–20) and defended (here). He was not even against tradition per se, but only against that which annulled Scripture (e.g., the following verses).

7:11 Corban. An Aramaic word that Mark explained in Greek, thus showing that Mark wrote at least in part to Gentile readers (cf. v. 34). Jesus was referring to a tradition that effectively annulled the commandment to honor parents. By a simple vow to give money to the temple (which was not necessarily carried out afterward), a person could avoid the responsibility of parental support.

7:19 In saying this. In this aside Mark underlined the radical nature of Jesus' words (which were not understood by his own disciples until much later; see Ac 10:9–16). By this teaching, Jesus declared the end of the Old Testament dietary restrictions.

7:20 What comes out of a man. See Romans 1:24–32 and 2:17–24. Jesus was generalizing about the way in which fallen human nature expresses itself. **unclean.** Jesus went to the heart of the matter, that is, to moral uncleanness, which ceremonial uncleanness symbolized.

7:21–22 See *WLC* 193.

tery, **22**greed,[o] malice, deceit, lewdness, envy, slander, arrogance and folly. **23**All these
evils come from inside and make a man 'unclean.' "

The Faith of a Syrophoenician Woman

24Jesus left that place and went to the vicinity of Tyre.[a][p] He entered a house and did
not want anyone to know it; yet he could not keep his presence secret. **25**In fact, as soon
as she heard about him, a woman whose little daughter was possessed by an evil[b] spirit[q] came and fell at his feet. **26**The woman was a Greek, born in Syrian Phoenicia. She
begged Jesus to drive the demon out of her daughter.
27"First let the children eat all they want," he told her, "for it is not right to take the
children's bread and toss it to their dogs."
28"Yes, Lord," she replied, "but even the dogs under the table eat the children's
crumbs."
29Then he told her, "For such a reply, you may go; the demon has left your daughter."
30She went home and found her child lying on the bed, and the demon gone.

The Healing of a Deaf and Mute Man

31Then Jesus left the vicinity of Tyre[r] and went through Sidon, down to the Sea of Galilee[s] and into the region of the Decapolis.[c][t] **32**There some people brought to him a man
who was deaf and could hardly talk,[u] and they begged him to place his hand on[v] the
man.
33After he took him aside, away from the crowd, Jesus put his fingers into the man's
ears. Then he spit[w] and touched the man's tongue. **34**He looked up to heaven[x] and with
a deep sigh[y] said to him, *"Ephphatha!"* (which means, "Be opened!"). **35**At this, the man's
ears were opened, his tongue was loosened and he began to speak plainly.[z]
36Jesus commanded them not to tell anyone.[a] But the more he did so, the more they
kept talking about it. **37**People were overwhelmed with amazement. "He has done everything well," they said. "He even makes the deaf hear and the mute speak."

Jesus Feeds the Four Thousand

8 During those days another large crowd gathered. Since they had nothing to eat,
Jesus called his disciples to him and said, **2**"I have compassion for these people;[b]
they have already been with me three days and have nothing to eat. **3**If I send them home
hungry, they will collapse on the way, because some of them have come a long distance."
4His disciples answered, "But where in this remote place can anyone get enough
bread to feed them?"
5"How many loaves do you have?" Jesus asked.
"Seven," they replied.
6He told the crowd to sit down on the ground. When he had taken the seven loaves
and given thanks, he broke them and gave them to his disciples to set before the people, and they did so. **7**They had a few small fish as well; he gave thanks for them also and
told the disciples to distribute them.[c] **8**The people ate and were satisfied. Afterward the
disciples picked up seven basketfuls of broken pieces that were left over.[d] **9**About four
thousand men were present. And having sent them away, **10**he got into the boat with his
disciples and went to the region of Dalmanutha.

7:22 [o]Mt 20:15
7:24 [p]Mt 11:21
7:25 [q]Mt 4:24
7:31 [r]ver 24; Mt 11:21 [s]Mt 4:18 [t]Mt 4:25; Mk 5:20
7:32 [u]Mt 9:32; Lk 11:14 [v]Mk 5:23
7:33 [w]Mk 8:23
7:34 [x]Mk 6:41; Jn 11:41 [y]Mk 8:12
7:35 [z]Isa 35:5,6
7:36 [a]Mt 8:4
8:2 [b]Mt 9:36
8:7 [c]Mt 14:19
8:8 [d]ver 20

[a] *24* Many early manuscripts *Tyre and Sidon* [b] *25* Greek *unclean* [c] *31* That is, the Ten Cities

■ **7:24—8:9** *Tyre, Sidon and the Decapolis.* Jesus moved once again into Gentile territory to extend his ministry even farther beyond the borders of Israel.
7:24 Tyre. An ancient port city in Phoenicia (modern Lebanon). Jesus apparently sought respite there from the conflicts he had endured on Jewish soil.
7:26 Greek. She was a non-Jewish, Greek-speaking person, probably of Arab descent from Syrian Phoenicia.
7:27 First. Though in pagan territory, Jesus maintained the priority of Israel ("the children") in the divine plan of salvation, as would Paul later on (Ro 1:16; 2:10; cf. Ac 1:8; 13:46–47). **dogs.** The term was usually derogatory (Mt 7:6; Php 3:2; Rev 22:15). Jesus used the imagery of table fellowship to explain the plan of salvation; that is, that "salvation is from the Jews" (Jn 4:22). Certainly the woman took it in this sense, as Jesus' reply indicates.
7:31 the Decapolis. See note on 5:1. Jesus remained in Gentile territory, going first north to Sidon and then southeast to the Decapolis.
7:34 ***Ephphatha!*** An Aramaic word meaning "be opened." Mark's translation into Greek indicates again that he wrote with non-Jewish readers in mind (see also v. 11).
7:35 speak plainly. Usually a deaf person learns spoken language only over a period of time.
7:36 not to tell. Regarding Jesus' command of secrecy, see notes on 1:34 and 5:19.
8:1–10 A second miraculous feeding. Jesus later pointed to the deep theological significance of the two feedings (vv. 18–21).
8:2 I have compassion. Since this feeding probably took place in the Decapolis (7:31), it is evident that Jesus extended his compassion beyond the lost sheep of Israel (6:34) to the Gentiles, as his healing of the Syrophoenician woman's daughter (7:24–30) and his ministry in Gentile territory (7:31–37) also suggest. By recording these facts, Mark pointed to the worldwide mission of the church.
8:4 where in this remote place . . . ? In view of what Jesus had previously done in similar circumstances, his reproach of the disciples for asking this question (vv. 17–18) was justified. Following "remote" is the Greek phrase "desert" or "solitary place" (see notes on 1:35; 6:32).
■ **8:10—9:32** *The Vicinity of Caesarea Philippi.* Mark reported that Jesus visited in the vicinity of Caesarea Philippi, where he performed miracles, encountered controversy and instructed his disci-

11 The Pharisees came and began to question Jesus. To test him, they asked him for
a sign from heaven.[e] 12 He sighed deeply[f] and said, "Why does this generation ask for a
miraculous sign? I tell you the truth, no sign will be given to it." 13 Then he left them, got
back into the boat and crossed to the other side.

The Yeast of the Pharisees and Herod

14 The disciples had forgotten to bring bread, except for one loaf they had with them
in the boat. 15 "Be careful," Jesus warned them. "Watch out for the yeast[g] of the Pharisees[h] and that of Herod."[i]
16 They discussed this with one another and said, "It is because we have no bread."
17 Aware of their discussion, Jesus asked them: "Why are you talking about having no
bread? Do you still not see or understand? Are your hearts hardened?[j] 18 Do you have eyes
but fail to see, and ears but fail to hear? And don't you remember? 19 When I broke the
five loaves for the five thousand, how many basketfuls of pieces did you pick up?"
"Twelve,"[k] they replied.
20 "And when I broke the seven loaves for the four thousand, how many basketfuls of
pieces did you pick up?"
They answered, "Seven."[l]
21 He said to them, "Do you still not understand?"[m]

The Healing of a Blind Man at Bethsaida

22 They came to Bethsaida,[n] and some people brought a blind man[o] and begged Jesus to
touch him. 23 He took the blind man by the hand and led him outside the village. When he
had spit[p] on the man's eyes and put his hands on[q] him, Jesus asked, "Do you see anything?"
24 He looked up and said, "I see people; they look like trees walking around."
25 Once more Jesus put his hands on the man's eyes. Then his eyes were opened, his
sight was restored, and he saw everything clearly. 26 Jesus sent him home, saying, "Don't
go into the village.[a]"

Peter's Confession of Christ

27 Jesus and his disciples went on to the villages around Caesarea Philippi. On the way
he asked them, "Who do people say I am?"
28 They replied, "Some say John the Baptist;[r] others say Elijah;[s] and still others, one
of the prophets."
29 "But what about you?" he asked. "Who do you say I am?"
Peter answered, "You are the Christ.[b]"[t]
30 Jesus warned them not to tell anyone about him.[u]

8:11 [e]Mt 12:38
8:12 [f]Mk 7:34
8:15 [g]1Co 5:6-8 [h]Lk 12:1 [i]Mt 14:1; Mk 12:13
8:17 [j]Isa 6:9,10; Mk 6:52
8:19 [k]Mt 14:20; Mk 6:41-44; Lk 9:17; Jn 6:13
8:20 [l]ver 6-9; Mt 15:37
8:21 [m]Mk 6:52
8:22 [n]Mt 11:21 [o]Mk 10:46; Jn 9:1
8:23 [p]Mk 7:33 [q]Mk 5:23
8:28 [r]Mt 3:1 [s]Mal 4:5
8:29 [t]Jn 6:69; 11:27
8:30 [u]Mt 8:4; 16:20; 17:9; Mk 9:9; Lk 9:21

[a] *26* Some manuscripts *Don't go and tell anyone in the village* [b] *29* Or *Messiah.* "The Christ" (Greek) and "the Messiah" (Hebrew) both mean "the Anointed One."

---

ples about their roles and about the importance of his death and resurrection.

8:10 Dalmanutha. No doubt a village on the western shore of the Sea of Galilee. Its exact location is unknown.

8:11 Pharisees. See note on 2:16. **sign from heaven.** Jesus did not perform signs on demand, especially for skeptics who were testing him. This same verb is used of the devil's testing (Mt 4:1).

8:14 one loaf. This phrase ties together this passage and the two feeding miracles (vv. 15–21).

8:15 yeast of the Pharisees and that of Herod. Jesus made symbolic use of an everyday ingredient for the making of bread (see also Mt 16:6; Lk 12:1). What seemed like an innocent, legitimate request for a sign (Lk 23:8) was actually a rejection of his entire ministry and of all his previous signs. Here Jesus was not only warning his disciples against superficial conceptions of his role, but also preparing them for the teaching he would give them concerning the true meaning of his coming and his cross (vv. 27,31). Such teaching would remain incomprehensible to many Jews (1Co 1:22–23).

8:17 no bread? The disciples were still deeply concerned with material preoccupations. They were blind to the true vocation of their master and open to being tempted by the "yeast" of the Pharisees (see note on v. 15).

8:21 Do you still not understand? Here Jesus' role in teaching and training the Twelve comes to the fore (see note on 3:14). His question to them was a reproach—not for having failed to understand all the theological symbolism in the two feedings, but for failing to realize that the Lord who had miraculously provided first for 5,000 and later for 4,000 men (with their families) was capable of taking care of the physical needs of 12 men (see notes on vv. 14,17). Jesus had proven himself worthy of their complete trust in all that he would reveal to them.

8:22 Bethsaida. A fishing town on the northern shore of the Sea of Galilee and the home of Philip, Andrew and Peter.

8:24 trees walking around. A blind man could know trees from physical contact and from hearing about them. Mark's purpose here was to tell us that this restoration of sight was gradual.

8:26 Don't go into the village. Jesus had led him out of the village (v. 23), so it is likely that this miracle was intended in part as a lesson for his disciples. They needed to realize that Jesus was gradually healing their spiritual sight and that while they "still [did] not understand" (v. 21) who Jesus was, they, like the blind man, were about to see "clearly" (v. 25) the mystery of his person (vv. 27ff.).

8:27 Caesarea Philippi. A town at the foot of Mount Hermon and close to the source of the Jordan River. Here Herod the Great built a marble temple in honor of Caesar Augustus. Philip, the son of Herod the Great, changed the town's name from Paneas to Caesarea. To distinguish it from the other Caesarea, the well-known Mediterranean port, it was known as Philip's Caesarea.

8:29 But what about you? Again Jesus showed that the 12 disciples were a special concern of his ministry (see notes on 3:14; 8:21). Jesus dismissed what "people" said (v. 27) but affirmed the confession of the Twelve. **the Christ.** Literally, "the Anointed One"; in Hebrew *māšiyah*, "the Messiah." Peter spoke on behalf of the Twelve. He used the definite article to indicate that Jesus is the anointed One of God par excellence. This is the first time in the narrative of Mark's Gospel that the name "Christ" appears (though it is also included in the Gospel's title; 1:1). Peter's confession, along with the ensuing event of the transfiguration (9:2–13), con-

Jesus Predicts His Death

31He then began to teach them that the Son of Man[v] must suffer many things[w] and
be rejected by the elders, chief priests and teachers of the law,[x] and that he must be
killed[y] and after three days[z] rise again.[a] 32He spoke plainly[b] about this, and Peter took
him aside and began to rebuke him.

33But when Jesus turned and looked at his disciples, he rebuked Peter. "Get behind
me, Satan!"[c] he said. "You do not have in mind the things of God, but the things of men."

34Then he called the crowd to him along with his disciples and said: "If anyone
would come after me, he must deny himself and take up his cross and follow me.[d] 35For
whoever wants to save his life[a] will lose it, but whoever loses his life for me and for the
gospel will save it.[e] 36What good is it for a man to gain the whole world, yet forfeit his
soul? 37Or what can a man give in exchange for his soul? 38If anyone is ashamed of me
and my words in this adulterous and sinful generation, the Son of Man[f] will be ashamed
of him[g] when he comes[h] in his Father's glory with the holy angels."

9 And he said to them, "I tell you the truth, some who are standing here will not taste
death before they see the kingdom of God come[i] with power."[j]

The Transfiguration

2After six days Jesus took Peter, James and John[k] with him and led them up a high
mountain, where they were all alone. There he was transfigured before them. 3His
clothes became dazzling white,[l] whiter than anyone in the world could bleach them.
4And there appeared before them Elijah and Moses, who were talking with Jesus.

5Peter said to Jesus, "Rabbi,[m] it is good for us to be here. Let us put up three shelters—one for you, one for Moses and one for Elijah." 6(He did not know what to say, they
were so frightened.)

8:31 [v]Mt 8:20 [w]Mt 16:21 [x]Mt 27:1,2 [y]Ac 2:23; 3:13 [z]Mt 16:21 [a]Mt 16:21
8:32 [b]Jn 18:20
8:33 [c]Mt 4:10
8:34 [d]Mt 10:38; Lk 14:27
8:35 [e]Jn 12:25
8:38 [f]Mt 8:20 [g]Mt 10:33; Lk 12:9 [h]1Th 2:19
9:1 [i]Mk 13:30; Lk 22:18 [j]Mt 24:30; 25:31
9:2 [k]Mt 4:21
9:3 [l]Mt 28:3
9:5 [m]Mt 23:7

[a] 35 The Greek word means either *life* or *soul*; also in verse 36.

---

stituted a high point in the revelation of Jesus' person. From this moment on, Jesus' teaching concentrated on his coming death, and he would soon begin to move south toward Jerusalem.

8:30 not to tell. See notes on 5:19 and 7:36, compare 9:9. Strangely, at this high point of Jesus' self-disclosure, he gave the order to keep this information secret. Jesus would not allow socio-political notions of him as conquering revolutionary leader to compromise his true vocation as the suffering Messiah.

8:31—10:52 This section constitutes the watershed of Jesus' earthly ministry (see note on 8:29). It consists of (1) three predictions of Jesus' death and resurrection (8:31; 9:31; 10:33–34); (2) the beginning of his journey to Jerusalem and the cross; and (3) the sustained, plain (8:32) teaching concerning true Messiahship and true discipleship. All of this was especially directed to the Twelve.

8:31 Son of Man. See note on 2:10. **must.** Jesus indicated that his role as the suffering Messiah was necessitated by the weight of Scriptural prophecy and by God's sovereign decree (9:31; see also Lk 22:37; 24:7,26,44). Jesus' predictions concerning his death and resurrection derived largely from his understanding of the Old Testament Scriptures. **suffer many things.** The idea of a suffering Messiah comes particularly from Isaiah 52:13—53:12 (see also Zec 9:9; 12:10; 13:7) but also from widespread Old Testament teaching about the suffering of the righteous (e.g., Pss 22; 34:15ff.). **elders.** Lay members of the Sanhedrin. This 71-member court that governed Jewish affairs was made up of elders, chief priests and teachers of the law. **chief priests.** This is the first mention of them in Mark's Gospel (except for the temporal reference in 2:26). Jesus here predicted that the wealthy high priestly families, drawn from the Sadducees, would also be involved in his death. **after three days.** A typically Semitic expression for "a short period" (see Hos 6:2). **rise again.** See Isaiah 52:13 and 53:10; compare Psalm 110:1 and Daniel 7:13–14.

8:32 He spoke plainly. Jesus normally spoke to the public in parables (4:10–11), but the Twelve received private, plain instruction (cf. Jn 16:25,29). Jesus' straightforward communication in private would become the basis for his disciples' plain speaking in public after the resurrection (Ac 2:29; 4:13,29,31; 28:31). **Peter . . . began to rebuke him.** Even Peter, the leader among the Twelve, could not believe that the Messiah had to suffer. This indicates that Jesus maintained great discretion and secrecy regarding his Messianic office.

8:33 Get behind me, Satan! Satan was now at work even in Peter, whose well-meaning but ill-advised intervention could have annulled the plan of redemption and thus accomplished Satan's goal.

8:34 take up his cross. A condemned prisoner was generally compelled to carry the crossbar of his cross to the site of his execution (cf. 15:21). The image suggests an active willingness to suffer for and with Christ.

8:37 exchange for his soul. The same Greek word is translated here as "soul" and in verse 35 as "life." The idea behind this word is that of a created, living being (see 1Co 15:45, which uses the same word). No monetary or material value can be placed on a "life" (Ps 49:7–9).

8:38 ashamed of me and my words. See 13:9–13. Either fidelity or infidelity in the face of persecution reveals the true character of a follower of Jesus. **in his Father's glory.** Though in his earthly time of humiliation the Son of Man had no place to lay his head (Mt 8:20), one day he will be revealed with a divine splendor that will show him to be the honored Son of God (12:6–11; 14:62; cf. Da 7:13). See *WLC* 19,113.

9:1 kingdom of God come with power. This coming of the kingdom in power seems to be associated with Jesus' resurrection. It would be witnessed by "some who [were] standing [t]here," and the resurrection would come with the power of the Holy Spirit (Ro 1:4). The transfiguration, which followed this utterance, was a foretaste of the fulfillment of Jesus' words and anticipated the manifestation of resurrection power and divine glory. See note on Matthew 16:28; see also theological article "The Resurrection of Jesus" at Luke 24.

9:2 After six days. Several parallels exist between Jesus' transfiguration and the events of Exodus 24:9–18. Luke's Gospel actually uses the word "departure" (in Greek, *exodos* or "exodus") in its parallel account (Lk 9:31). Six days was the time allotted for preparation when receiving revelation and witnessing divine glory (Ex 24:16). **Peter, James and John.** The three represented the Twelve, just as the elders represented the people in Exodus 24:9–18. **a high mountain.** Both Moses and Elijah saw God on high mountains—Mount Sinai in Exodus 24 and Mount Horeb in 1 Kings 19. Moses and the elders also ascended the mountain prior to God's revelation to Moses in Exodus 24:9–18. **transfigured.** Literally, "changed in form." This same verb is used by Paul to describe the present work of the Spirit in believers (Ro 12:2; 2Co 3:18). This work in believers will be completed when this same Spirit glorifies believers' "mortal bodies" (Ro 8:11) in the same way he momentarily glorified Jesus' body at the transfiguration and eternally glorified Jesus' body when Jesus rose from the dead.

9:4 Elijah and Moses. The transfiguration ties the old covenant to the new. Moses and Elijah, representatives of the Old Testament Law and Prophets, are linked with Jesus and his apostles, the new covenant messengers of revelation.

9:5 Let us put up three shelters. Peter wished to prolong the

7Then a cloud appeared and enveloped them, and a voice came from the cloud:[n]
"This is my Son, whom I love. Listen to him!"[o]
8Suddenly, when they looked around, they no longer saw anyone with them except
Jesus.
9As they were coming down the mountain, Jesus gave them orders not to tell anyone[p]
what they had seen until the Son of Man[q] had risen from the dead. 10They kept the matter to themselves, discussing what "rising from the dead" meant.
11And they asked him, "Why do the teachers of the law say that Elijah must come
first?"
12Jesus replied, "To be sure, Elijah does come first, and restores all things. Why then
is it written that the Son of Man[r] must suffer much[s] and be rejected?[t] 13But I tell you,
Elijah has come,[u] and they have done to him everything they wished, just as it is written about him."

The Healing of a Boy With an Evil Spirit

14When they came to the other disciples, they saw a large crowd around them and the
teachers of the law arguing with them. 15As soon as all the people saw Jesus, they were
overwhelmed with wonder and ran to greet him.
16"What are you arguing with them about?" he asked.
17A man in the crowd answered, "Teacher, I brought you my son, who is possessed
by a spirit that has robbed him of speech. 18Whenever it seizes him, it throws him to the
ground. He foams at the mouth, gnashes his teeth and becomes rigid. I asked your disciples to drive out the spirit, but they could not."
19"O unbelieving generation," Jesus replied, "how long shall I stay with you? How long
shall I put up with you? Bring the boy to me."
20So they brought him. When the spirit saw Jesus, it immediately threw the boy into
a convulsion. He fell to the ground and rolled around, foaming at the mouth.[v]
21Jesus asked the boy's father, "How long has he been like this?"
"From childhood," he answered. 22"It has often thrown him into fire or water to kill
him. But if you can do anything, take pity on us and help us."
23" 'If you can'?" said Jesus. "Everything is possible for him who believes."[w]
24Immediately the boy's father exclaimed, "I do believe; help me overcome my unbelief!"
25When Jesus saw that a crowd was running to the scene,[x] he rebuked the evil[a] spirit. "You deaf and mute spirit," he said, "I command you, come out of him and never enter him again."
26The spirit shrieked, convulsed him violently and came out. The boy looked so
much like a corpse that many said, "He's dead." 27But Jesus took him by the hand and
lifted him to his feet, and he stood up.
28After Jesus had gone indoors, his disciples asked him privately,[y] "Why couldn't we
drive it out?"
29He replied, "This kind can come out only by prayer.[b]"

9:7 [n]Ex 24:16 [o]Mt 3:17
9:9 [p]Mk 8:30 [q]Mt 8:20
9:12 [r]Mt 8:20 [s]Mt 16:21 [t]Lk 23:11
9:13 [u]Mt 11:14
9:20 [v]Mk 1:26
9:23 [w]Mt 21:21; Mk 11:23; Jn 11:40
9:25 [x]ver 15
9:28 [y]Mk 7:17

[a] *25* Greek *unclean* [b] *29* Some manuscripts *prayer and fasting*

glory and thus to avoid the suffering of which Jesus had already spoken (8:31–33).
9:7 This is my Son, whom I love. This heavenly declaration was a high point of divine revelation concerning the identity of Jesus. Just as God had revealed himself visibly on Sinai as "the LORD, the compassionate and gracious God" (Ex 34:6), so here he revealed himself as the One who, through his beloved Son (Jn 1:17; 3:16; Heb 1:2), makes his love known to us. **Listen to him!** This phrase was no doubt a rebuke of Peter as well as a declaration concerning the authority of the Son as head of the new covenant. These words echo Deuteronomy 18:15 and thus identify Jesus as the great prophet like Moses.
9:9 gave them orders not to tell. See notes on 1:34 and 8:30. **until the Son of Man had risen from the dead.** Public testimony to Jesus' glory was to be withheld until after the full accomplishment of redemption.
9:10 discussing what "rising from the dead" meant. The Jews anticipated a general resurrection at history's end, but Jesus' reference to his own individual resurrection (v. 9) challenged the disciples' understanding. See theological article "The Resurrection of Jesus" at Luke 24.
9:12 Elijah does come first. There is no reason to interpret this statement woodenly. John the Baptist was not Elijah risen from the dead (6:14–16; cf. Jn 1:21). Instead, Jesus taught that Elijah prefigured John the Baptist's ministry.
9:13 they have done to him. Just as Elijah suffered at the hands of Ahab and Jezebel (1Ki 19:1–10), so John suffered at the hands of Herod and Herodias (see notes on 6:14–29). John restored all things in the sense of refocusing the long-blurred issues of repentance and godliness. If John was put to death, it should not be surprising that the Son of Man faced the same fate (v. 12).
9:17 possessed by a spirit. Demon possession is clearly distinguished from mere illness (see 7:31–37), although the cases here and in 7:31–37 both involved persons who could not speak. See notes on 1:24–25; 5:2,3,7,9,10,13,15.
9:19 O unbelieving generation. Jesus grew impatient with the disciples' lack of faith, as well as with the general scene of incredulity as he returned from the Mount of Transfiguration. This event is reminiscent of Moses coming down from Mount Sinai to find unbelief and unfaithfulness in the Israelite camp (Ex 32).
9:24 See *WCF* 18.3.
9:25 a crowd was running. The situation was still volatile. The enthusiasm of the crowd constantly placed Jesus in the dilemma of wanting to minister to the people while being compelled to restrain himself so as not to jeopardize the overarching plan of redemption. **I command you.** Jesus demonstrated his full authority over the demon.

30 They left that place and passed through Galilee. Jesus did not want anyone to
know where they were, 31 because he was teaching his disciples. He said to them, "The
Son of Man[z] is going to be betrayed into the hands of men. They will kill him,[a] and after three days[b] he will rise."[c] 32 But they did not understand what he meant[d] and were
afraid to ask him about it.

Who Is the Greatest?

33 They came to Capernaum.[e] When he was in the house,[f] he asked them, "What were
you arguing about on the road?" 34 But they kept quiet because on the way they had argued about who was the greatest.[g]

35 Sitting down, Jesus called the Twelve and said, "If anyone wants to be first, he must
be the very last, and the servant of all."[h]

36 He took a little child and had him stand among them. Taking him in his arms,[i] he
said to them, 37 "Whoever welcomes one of these little children in my name welcomes
me; and whoever welcomes me does not welcome me but the one who sent me."[j]

Whoever Is Not Against Us Is for Us

38 "Teacher," said John, "we saw a man driving out demons in your name and we told
him to stop, because he was not one of us."[k]

39 "Do not stop him," Jesus said. "No one who does a miracle in my name can in the
next moment say anything bad about me, 40 for whoever is not against us is for us.[l] 41 I
tell you the truth, anyone who gives you a cup of water in my name because you belong
to Christ will certainly not lose his reward.[m]

Causing to Sin

42 "And if anyone causes one of these little ones who believe in me to sin,[n] it would
be better for him to be thrown into the sea with a large millstone tied around his neck.[o]
43 If your hand causes you to sin,[p] cut it off. It is better for you to enter life maimed than
with two hands to go into hell,[q] where the fire never goes out.[a][r] 45 And if your foot causes you to sin,[s] cut it off. It is better for you to enter life crippled than to have two feet and
be thrown into hell.[b][t] 47 And if your eye causes you to sin,[u] pluck it out. It is better for you
to enter the kingdom of God with one eye than to have two eyes and be thrown into hell,[v]
48 where

> " 'their worm does not die,
> and the fire is not quenched.'[c][w]

49 Everyone will be salted[x] with fire.

9:31 [z]Mt 8:20 [a]ver 12; Ac 2:23; 3:13 [b]Mt 16:21 [c]Mt 16:21
9:32 [d]Lk 2:50; 9:45; 18:34; Jn 12:16
9:33 [e]Mt 4:13 [f]Mk 1:29
9:34 [g]Lk 22:24
9:35 [h]Mt 18:4; 20:26; Mk 10:43; Lk 22:26
9:36 [i]Mk 10:16
9:37 [j]Mt 10:40
9:38 [k]Nu 11:27-29
9:40 [l]Mt 12:30; Lk 11:23
9:41 [m]Mt 10:42
9:42 [n]Mt 5:29 [o]Mt 18:6; Lk 17:2
9:43 [p]Mt 5:29 [q]Mt 5:30; 18:8 [r]Mt 25:41
9:45 [s]Mt 5:29 [t]Mt 18:8
9:47 [u]Mt 5:29 [v]Mt 5:29; 18:9
9:48 [w]Isa 66:24; Mt 25:41
9:49 [x]Lev 2:13

a 43 Some manuscripts *out,* 44*where / " 'their worm does not die, / and the fire is not quenched.'* b 45 Some manuscripts *hell,* 46*where / " 'their worm does not die, / and the fire is not quenched.'* c 48 Isaiah 66:24

9:31 teaching his disciples. Again, Jesus gave priority to the training of the Twelve. For emphasis and because the lesson was still unlearned, Jesus repeated what he had taught in 8:31ff.

▪ **9:33–50** *The Return to Capernaum.* Mark closed his account of Jesus' ministry in the region of Galilee by focusing on two events in Capernaum that revealed both the disciples' desire for rewards and the required extent of their faithfulness to him. Thus Jesus established two important priorities for the Twelve.

9:34 who was the greatest. In the hierarchical culture of the time, social status played a very significant role (10:35–45). Yet the disciples were ashamed of their pursuit of honor and power. Jesus emphasized humility and service in his kingdom, without destroying the notion of appropriate authority. Thus Peter represented the Twelve (8:27ff.; see also Mt 16:16ff.); Peter, James and John formed an intimate inner circle with Jesus (5:37; 9:2; cf. Jn 13:23), and the Twelve had a special (hierarchical) place relative to Jesus' many other disciples (see note on v. 35).

9:35 Jesus called the Twelve. Again the Twelve were singled out (see 3:14) and their position of leadership explicitly recognized. **If anyone wants to be first.** Jesus did not attack leadership of every sort, but he showed the way in which such roles should be exercised. **the very last, and the servant of all.** This principle is exemplified in Jesus himself, who "did not come to be served, but to serve, and to give his life as a ransom for many" (10:45). The selfless, giving manner in which Jesus fulfilled his Messianic role was a model for his disciples for whatever secondary leadership roles they might exercise in the kingdom of God.

9:36 a little child. Literally, "infant." The God-given dignity of every human being is exemplified in a little child. This weakest and greatest of human beings must be respected and ministered to (see note on v. 35).

9:38 not one of us. This phrase probably does not mean that the man was not a follower of Jesus. He exorcised demons in Jesus' name and spoke well of Jesus (v. 39). This phrase simply indicates that he was not one of the Twelve and had not received their official commission (6:7). Perhaps sensing pride among the Twelve (see note on v. 35; see also 10:35–45), Jesus declined to reject this man's initiative. Instead, he affirmed the principle that all who are behind his cause should be gratefully acknowledged.

9:41 anyone who gives you a cup of water in my name. All acts of mercy, care and healing that are done under Jesus' authority and intended for his glory are eternally acknowledged as evidences of true discipleship.

9:42 little ones. Refers either to infants (v. 36) or to the apparently insignificant believer (v. 39).

9:43–48 See *WLC* 29,83.

9:43 cut it off. This should be taken as hyperbole. See also verses 45 and 47. Jesus was talking about costly renunciations of sinful habits.

9:44,46 See NIV text notes. These two verses do not appear in some important early manuscripts, and their content is found in verse 48.

9:49 salted with fire. This text is best linked with what follows. It means that all believers will be given favor. Their godly character will become more pronounced either through enduring the fiery ordeal of persecution or perhaps through the momentary torment of surrendering evil behaviors to be purged by grace (vv. 43–47). Jesus' imagery is derived from the Old Testament sacrifices that were consumed by fire and accompanied by salt (Lev 2:13; Eze 43:24).

50 “Salt is good, but if it loses its saltiness, how can you make it salty again?[y] Have salt
in yourselves,[z] and be at peace with each other.”[a]

Divorce

10 Jesus then left that place and went into the region of Judea and across the Jordan.[b] Again crowds of people came to him, and as was his custom, he taught
them.[c]
2 Some Pharisees[d] came and tested him by asking, “Is it lawful for a man to divorce
his wife?”
3 “What did Moses command you?” he replied.
4 They said, “Moses permitted a man to write a certificate of divorce and send her
away.”[e]
5 “It was because your hearts were hard[f] that Moses wrote you this law,” Jesus replied.
6 “But at the beginning of creation God ‘made them male and female.’[a][g] 7 ‘For this reason a man will leave his father and mother and be united to his wife,[b] 8 and the two will
become one flesh.’[c][h] So they are no longer two, but one. 9 Therefore what God has joined
together, let man not separate.”
10 When they were in the house again, the disciples asked Jesus about this. 11 He answered, “Anyone who divorces his wife and marries another woman commits adultery
against her.[i] 12 And if she divorces her husband and marries another man, she commits
adultery.”[j]

The Little Children and Jesus

13 People were bringing little children to Jesus to have him touch them, but the disciples rebuked them. 14 When Jesus saw this, he was indignant. He said to them, “Let the
little children come to me, and do not hinder them, for the kingdom of God belongs to
such as these.[k] 15 I tell you the truth, anyone who will not receive the kingdom of God like
a little child will never enter it.”[l] 16 And he took the children in his arms,[m] put his hands
on them and blessed them.

The Rich Young Man

17 As Jesus started on his way, a man ran up to him and fell on his knees[n] before him.
“Good teacher,” he asked, “what must I do to inherit eternal life?”[o]
18 “Why do you call me good?” Jesus answered. “No one is good—except God alone.

9:50 [y]Mt 5:13; Lk 14:34,35 [z]Col 4:6 [a]Ro 12:18; 2Co 13:11; 1Th 5:13
10:1 [b]Mk 1:5; Jn 10:40; 11:7 [c]Mt 4:23; Mk 2:13; 4:2; 6:6, 34
10:2 [d]Mk 2:16
10:4 [e]Dt 24:1-4; Mt 5:31
10:5 [f]Ps 95:8; Heb 3:15
10:6 [g]Ge 1:27; 5:2
10:8 [h]Ge 2:24; 1Co 6:16
10:11 [i]Mt 5:32; Lk 16:18
10:12 [j]Ro 7:3; 1Co 7:10, 11
10:14 [k]Mt 25:34
10:15 [l]Mt 18:3
10:16 [m]Mk 9:36
10:17 [n]Mk 1:40 [o]Lk 10:25; Ac 20:32

[a] *6* Gen. 1:27 [b] *7* Some early manuscripts do not have *and be united to his wife.* [c] *8* Gen. 2:24

9:50 Have salt in yourselves. The image of salt is picked up again to describe true discipleship. Here Jesus was asking his disciples to be “salty”—to stand out from the world and to apply his principles of leadership and service, principles that are so different from those of the world. See Matthew 5:13.

■ **10:1—16:20** *Jesus’ Judean Ministry.* As important as Jesus’ ministry in the north was to Mark, he presented Jesus’ Judean ministry as the climax of our Lord’s earthly life. At this point, Jesus moved toward his death and resurrection, as he had predicted.

■ **10:1–45** *Teaching on the Way.* Mark recorded how Jesus both taught the crowds and gave further insight to the Twelve concerning the humble service required in his kingdom.

10:1 region of Judea. The southern region of Palestine centered around Jerusalem. This journey into Judea was actually the beginning of the process that would lead Jesus to his death (cf. Lk 9:51). It began with the descent from the Mount of Transfiguration (9:2–13) and ended on the hill of crucifixion (15:22ff.). **across the Jordan.** Jesus went into the region of Perea (modern Jordan), where Herod Antipas was tetrarch (6:14).

10:2 Pharisees. See note on 2:16. **Is it lawful . . . to divorce . . . ?** The question was strange because Deuteronomy 24:1–4 had already indicated that the answer could be yes or no, depending on circumstances. Perhaps the Pharisees wanted to draw Jesus into the debate about Herod Antipas and his “unlawful” wife (Lev 18:16; see notes on Mk 6:18).

10:6–8 male and female . . . one flesh. Monogamous marriage is to be received and cherished as God’s intended and authoritative design for creation, as shown by the original marriage between Adam and Eve.

10:6 at the beginning. As usual, Jesus did not argue from tradition (see notes on 7:1,2,3,5,8,11) but sought to uncover the true meaning of Scripture (Mt 5:20–22,27–28,31–32). Regarding marriage, Jesus showed that the present earthly manifestation of the new covenant, in spite of the continuing presence of sin, seeks to re-establish the ideal conditions of life prior to the fall.

10:10 in the house. Again the disciples received private teaching (see note on 9:35). **Anyone who divorces.** This is a simple generalization concerning the inviolability of marriage, which Jewish practice had often disregarded. However, Jesus did specify one valid ground for divorce (Mt 5:32; 19:9)—marital infidelity. Paul specified desertion as a particular form of infidelity (1Co 7:12–16). See theological article “Marriage and Divorce” at Matthew 19.

10:13–16 See *WCF* 28.4.

10:13 little children. Literally, “infants” (see 9:36). That their parents brought them and that Jesus took them in his arms (v. 16) suggest that they were quite young.

10:14 belongs to such as these. Jesus was expressing the frequent Old Testament notion of the covenant community. These small children were part of the covenant people and as such were the expected heirs of the kingdom.

10:16 blessed them. That they received God’s blessing means that they were expected heirs to the full blessings of the covenant (Ge 22:16–18; Dt 7:13).

10:17 a man. Luke’s Gospel says the man was a ruler (Lk 18:18), Matthew states that he was young and wealthy (Mt 19:20,22) and Mark notes that he had great wealth (v. 22). The man had “everything,” yet he lacked a human being’s most important possession: eternal life. **what must I do to inherit . . . ?** The man placed the two verbs translated “doing” and “inheriting” together. The list of his moral achievements and his understanding of goodness (see note on v. 18) reveal that his confidence was based on works righteousness.

10:18 Why do you call me good? Jesus did not deny that he was good. Rather, he wanted to stress that “no one is good—except God alone.” Jesus spoke in this way so that the man would realize that he was incapable of earning eternal life. See *BC* 1,26.

19You know the commandments: 'Do not murder, do not commit adultery, do not steal,
do not give false testimony, do not defraud, honor your father and mother.'[a] [p]
20"Teacher," he declared, "all these I have kept since I was a boy."
21Jesus looked at him and loved him. "One thing you lack," he said. "Go, sell everything you have and give to the poor,[q] and you will have treasure in heaven.[r] Then come,
follow me."[s]
22At this the man's face fell. He went away sad, because he had great wealth.
23Jesus looked around and said to his disciples, "How hard it is for the rich[t] to enter
the kingdom of God!"
24The disciples were amazed at his words. But Jesus said again, "Children, how hard
it is[b] to enter the kingdom of God![u] 25It is easier for a camel to go through the eye of a
needle than for a rich man to enter the kingdom of God."[v]
26The disciples were even more amazed, and said to each other, "Who then can be
saved?"
27Jesus looked at them and said, "With man this is impossible, but not with God; all
things are possible with God."[w]
28Peter said to him, "We have left everything to follow you!"[x]
29"I tell you the truth," Jesus replied, "no one who has left home or brothers or sisters or mother or father or children or fields for me and the gospel 30will fail to receive
a hundred times as much[y] in this present age (homes, brothers, sisters, mothers, children and fields—and with them, persecutions) and in the age to come,[z] eternal life.[a]
31But many who are first will be last, and the last first."[b]

Jesus Again Predicts His Death

32They were on their way up to Jerusalem, with Jesus leading the way, and the disciples were astonished, while those who followed were afraid. Again he took the Twelve[c]
aside and told them what was going to happen to him. 33"We are going up to Jerusalem,"[d] he said, "and the Son of Man[e] will be betrayed to the chief priests and teachers
of the law.[f] They will condemn him to death and will hand him over to the Gentiles,
34who will mock him and spit on him, flog him[g] and kill him.[h] Three days later[i] he will
rise."[j]

The Request of James and John

35Then James and John, the sons of Zebedee, came to him. "Teacher," they said, "we
want you to do for us whatever we ask."
36"What do you want me to do for you?" he asked.
37They replied, "Let one of us sit at your right and the other at your left in your glory."[k]
38"You don't know what you are asking,"[l] Jesus said. "Can you drink the cup[m] I drink
or be baptized with the baptism I am baptized with?"[n]

10:19 [p]Ex 20:12-16; Dt 5:16-20
10:21 [q]Ac 2:45 [r]Mt 6:20; Lk 12:33 [s]Mt 4:19
10:23 [t]Ps 52:7; 62:10; 1Ti 6:9,10,17
10:24 [u]Mt 7:13,14
10:25 [v]Lk 12:16-20
10:27 [w]Mt 19:26
10:28 [x]Mt 4:19
10:30 [y]Mt 6:33 [z]Mt 12:32 [a]Mt 25:46
10:31 [b]Mt 19:30
10:32 [c]Mk 3:16-19
10:33 [d]Lk 9:51 [e]Mt 8:20 [f]Mt 27:1,2
10:34 [g]Mt 16:21 [h]Ac 2:23; 3:13 [i]Mt 16:21 [j]Mt 16:21
10:37 [k]Mt 19:28
10:38 [l]Job 38:2 [m]Mt 20:22 [n]Lk 12:50

[a] *19* Exodus 20:12–16; Deut. 5:16–20 [b] *24* Some manuscripts *is for those who trust in riches*

10:21 One thing you lack. The young man's love of riches (v. 22) and his refusal to give them up to follow Jesus show that he had broken the "greatest commandment" (Mt 22:36): "Love the LORD your God with all your heart and with all your soul and with all your strength" (Dt 6:5; cf. Mt 22:37). Lacking the total righteousness that God requires, the man stood condemned. His imperfect works of righteousness failed him at the point of his greatest need.
10:23 How hard it is for the rich to enter the kingdom of God! This is not because riches in themselves are evil and thus disqualify those who possess them. Like all fallen people, the rich reject God in favor of things in their lives that they love more (Lk 16:13; Jas 4:4). Wealth provides a particularly strong temptation to reject God because it offers so many pleasing benefits. Apart from God's gracious intervention changing their hearts, the rich would love their money above all and die in their sins.
10:25 camel . . . eye of a needle. There is no evidence to support the suggestion that there existed a small gate called "The Needle's Eye" through which camels passed only with great difficulty. Jesus spoke of impossibility, not of mere difficulty (v. 27).
10:26 Who then can be saved? This question shows that the disciples understood Jesus to mean that nobody can be good enough to be saved.
10:27 With man this is impossible. Because we are sinful, salvation simply is not a human possibility. Salvation is from the Lord, through sovereign and divine initiative and empowerment (Jn 2:9; cf. Pss 3:8; 68:19–20).
10:28 We have left everything. While salvation cannot be merited, receiving salvation results in radical commitment.
10:30 this present age . . . the age to come. Jewish tradition divided history into these two ages. "This age" referred to the present age of sin and death, while "the age to come" looked ahead to the future age of salvation brought by the Messiah. In New Testament theology, these two ages overlap between the first and second comings of Christ. Followers of Christ now experience many blessings of the age to come, but they also suffer the trials of this age. Thus in the present age there is "a hundred times as much" blessing, but also "persecutions." For Christ's disciples, salvation will be fully realized only when they enter into full possession of "eternal life" at his return.
10:33 the Son of Man will be betrayed. See notes on 8:31 and 9:9. **Gentiles.** The new element in this third prediction of Jesus' death is the mention of the Gentiles (in this case, the Romans) and thus the implicit prediction of death by crucifixion.
10:35 James and John. See 1:19 and 3:17. In Matthew 20:20, it was their mother who made the request. Perhaps the whole family was involved.
10:37 sit at your right. James and John had not taken to heart Jesus' teaching on greatness (see notes on 9:34,35).
10:38 drink the cup. An Old Testament symbol for suffering and wrath (Ps 75:8; Isa 51:17–22; Jer 25:15; Eze 23:31–34; cf. Mk 14:36). **baptism.** This sacrament is associated with both judgment and salvation (Ro 6:3ff.; 1Co 10:2; Col 2:11–13).

39 “We can,” they answered.
Jesus said to them, “You will drink the cup I drink and be baptized with the baptism
10:39 [o]Ac 12:2; Rev 1:9 I am baptized with,[o] 40 but to sit at my right or left is not for me to grant. These places belong to those for whom they have been prepared.”
41 When the ten heard about this, they became indignant with James and John.
42 Jesus called them together and said, “You know that those who are regarded as rulers of the Gentiles lord it over them, and their high officials exercise authority over them.
10:43 43 Not so with you. Instead, whoever wants to become great among you must be your ser-
[p]Mk 9:35 vant,[p] 44 and whoever wants to be first must be slave of all. 45 For even the Son of Man did
10:45 [q]Mt 20:28 [r]Mt 20:28 not come to be served, but to serve,[q] and to give his life as a ransom for many.”[r]

Blind Bartimaeus Receives His Sight

46 Then they came to Jericho. As Jesus and his disciples, together with a large crowd,
were leaving the city, a blind man, Bartimaeus (that is, the Son of Timaeus), was sitting
10:47 by the roadside begging. 47 When he heard that it was Jesus of Nazareth,[s] he began to
[s]Mk 1:24 [t]Mt 9:27 shout, “Jesus, Son of David,[t] have mercy on me!”
48 Many rebuked him and told him to be quiet, but he shouted all the more, “Son of
David, have mercy on me!”
49 Jesus stopped and said, “Call him.”
So they called to the blind man, “Cheer up! On your feet! He’s calling you.” 50 Throwing his cloak aside, he jumped to his feet and came to Jesus.
10:51 51 “What do you want me to do for you?” Jesus asked him.
[u]Mt 23:7 The blind man said, “Rabbi,[u] I want to see.”
10:52 52 “Go,” said Jesus, “your faith has healed you.”[v] Immediately he received his sight and
[v]Mt 9:22 [w]Mt 4:19 followed[w] Jesus along the road.

The Triumphal Entry

11:1 [x]Mt 21:17 [y]Mt 21:1 11 As they approached Jerusalem and came to Bethphage and Bethany[x] at the
Mount of Olives,[y] Jesus sent two of his disciples, 2 saying to them, “Go to the vil-
11:2 lage ahead of you, and just as you enter it, you will find a colt tied there, which no one
[z]Nu 19:2; Dt 21:3; 1Sa 6:7 has ever ridden.[z] Untie it and bring it here. 3 If anyone asks you, ‘Why are you doing this?’
tell him, ‘The Lord needs it and will send it back here shortly.’ ”
11:4 [a]Mk 14:16 4 They went and found a colt outside in the street, tied at a doorway.[a] As they untied
it, 5 some people standing there asked, “What are you doing, untying that colt?” 6 They
answered as Jesus had told them to, and the people let them go. 7 When they brought the
colt to Jesus and threw their cloaks over it, he sat on it. 8 Many people spread their cloaks

---

10:40 not for me to grant. Jesus revealed that there are areas over which only the Father has authority (see also 13:32). Such “places” are decided according to the divine plan of redemption and in accordance with the principle that Jesus gave concerning service (9:35).

10:43 Not so with you. Probably the other ten were indignant, not because John and James had failed to put Jesus’ teaching into practice, but because they themselves wanted the same places of honor. Jesus’ earlier teaching (see notes on 9:35), here repeated, was intended to eliminate these worldly notions of power and authority.

10:45 the Son of Man did not come to be served. Beyond the statement of the principle, what finally broke down the stony hearts of Jesus’ disciples was the example he himself had given. The Son of Man, to whom “authority, glory and sovereign power” (Da 7:14) has been given, had actually come as a servant, fulfilling the prophecy of Isaiah 52:13—53:12 to give his own life “as a ransom for many.” **ransom.** The price paid to pardon the guilty from their sentence (Ex 21:30) or absolve debtors of their debt (Ex 30:12; cf. Isa 53:10). **many.** See Isaiah 53:12. In the Dead Sea Scrolls of Qumran, the term “many” refers to the entire community (Ro 5:15,19).

■ **10:46–52** *The Healing in Jericho.* Mark recalled an earlier portion of his Gospel (5:34) by focusing on another miracle that revealed the importance of faith. He did this in order to instruct his original audience on the significance of faith in Christ in their own day.

10:46 Jericho. A city situated some 800 feet below sea level and 15 miles northeast of Jerusalem. The first settlement was built on the site in 6000 B.C. A new town center, located farther south, was built by Herod the Great in the first century B.C. **Son of Timaeus.** The explanation that the Semitic name *Bartimaeus* means “Son of Timaeus” shows that Mark was writing, at least in part, to a Gentile audience (see 7:34 and its note).

10:47 Son of David. A popular Messianic title (11:10; 12:35) drawn from the Old Testament (Isa 11:1–3; Jer 23:5–6; Eze 34:23–24).

10:49 Call him. One of the noticeable marks of Jesus’ ministry was that he found time to give to suffering individuals (see 5:30–34).

■ **11:1–11** *The Triumphal Entry Into Jerusalem.* Mark turned to the final stage of Jesus’ earthly ministry, the Passion Week in Jerusalem, first by describing Jesus’ triumphal entry into the city. (See chart “Passion Week” at Mk 14.) It is at this point that the center of the Christian gospel message comes into focus.

11:1 As they approached Jerusalem. The journey that began in 10:1 reaches its climax here. Jesus’ decision to come to Jerusalem was determined by his understanding of the Old Testament and was in accord with his own prophecies (see notes on 8:31). **Bethphage.** Modern Kefr-et-Tur, a small village east of Jerusalem. **Bethany.** Identified with present-day El-Azariet, two or three miles east of Jerusalem. **Mount of Olives.** East of Jerusalem and rising to a height of 2,700 feet, this “mount” commands a spectacular view of the city and, in Jesus’ day, especially of the temple. At the time it was covered with olive trees.

11:2 you will find. Jesus may have known this by supernatural means (cf. Jn 1:48–50), but he was also familiar with this region and had been here before. **colt.** A young donkey (Mt 21:2; Jn 12:15). The Old Testament again anticipated Jesus’ actions (Zec 9:9)—which in this case were unmistakably Messianic—for Zechariah prophesied the coming of a righteous and gentle king who would bring salvation.

11:8 cloaks on the road. A recognition of Jesus’ royal dignity. **branches.** See Psalm 118:27. This Messianic psalm celebrates the

on the road, while others spread branches they had cut in the fields. 9 Those who went
ahead and those who followed shouted,

"Hosanna![a]"

"Blessed is he who comes in the name of the Lord!"[b][b]

10 "Blessed is the coming kingdom of our father David!"

"Hosanna in the highest!"[c]

11 Jesus entered Jerusalem and went to the temple. He looked around at everything,
but since it was already late, he went out to Bethany with the Twelve.[d]

Jesus Clears the Temple

12 The next day as they were leaving Bethany, Jesus was hungry. 13 Seeing in the distance a fig tree in leaf, he went to find out if it had any fruit. When he reached it, he found
nothing but leaves, because it was not the season for figs.[e] 14 Then he said to the tree,
"May no one ever eat fruit from you again." And his disciples heard him say it.
15 On reaching Jerusalem, Jesus entered the temple area and began driving out those
who were buying and selling there. He overturned the tables of the money changers and
the benches of those selling doves, 16 and would not allow anyone to carry merchandise
through the temple courts. 17 And as he taught them, he said, "Is it not written:

" 'My house will be called
a house of prayer for all nations'[c]?[f]

But you have made it 'a den of robbers.'[d]"[g]
18 The chief priests and the teachers of the law heard this and began looking for a way
to kill him, for they feared him,[h] because the whole crowd was amazed at his teaching.[i]
19 When evening came, they[e] went out of the city.[j]

The Withered Fig Tree

20 In the morning, as they went along, they saw the fig tree withered from the roots.

11:9 [b]Ps 118:25,26; Mt 23:39
11:10 [c]Lk 2:14
11:11 [d]Mt 21:12,17
11:13 [e]Lk 13:6-9
11:17 [f]Isa 56:7 [g]Jer 7:11
11:18 [h]Mt 21:46; Mk 12:12; Lk 20:19 [i]Mt 7:28
11:19 [j]Lk 21:37

[a] 9 A Hebrew expression meaning "Save!" which became an exclamation of praise; also in verse 10
[b] 9 Psalm 118:25,26 [c] 17 Isaiah 56:7 [d] 17 Jer. 7:11 [e] 19 Some early manuscripts *he*

---

procession of the royal Messiah, "the stone the builders rejected [that] has become the capstone" (Ps 118:22)—a text that Jesus cited just after the temple cleansing (12:10). Jesus ascended to the temple amid the festive throng's cries of "Hosanna!" (v. 9; see Ps 118:19–21).

11:9–10 Hosanna! The Greek transliteration of the Hebrew *hoshi'a na,* which means "Save [us]!" (see Ps 118.25). The crowd was shouting phrases from Psalm 118.

11:11 he went out to Bethany. According to Matthew 21:12–22, on arriving at the temple Jesus proceeded to cleanse it, and the next day he cursed the fig tree. According to Mark, Jesus returned to Bethany for the night, and in the morning, on the way to the temple for the second time, he first cursed the fig tree and then cleansed the temple. Matthew probably treated the material topically (there is no specific time reference for the cleansing; Mt 21:12), while Mark (who liked to place stories within stories; see also 5:21–43; 6:7–30) treated it chronologically. **with the Twelve.** Once again Mark stressed that all these great Messianic events were first and foremost experienced by the Twelve.

■ **11:12–26** *Cleansing the Temple.* Mark presented the cursing of the fig tree and the cleansing of the temple as Jesus' first actions in Jerusalem. His account reveals how directly Jesus challenged the hypocrisy and failure of the most important religious institution in Jerusalem. This record is a fitting prelude to Jesus' death and resurrection, events that would do away with the corrupt earthly temple altogether.

11:12 The next day. Monday of Passion Week. See chart titled "Passion Week" at Mark 14.

11:13 not the season for figs. The fig season begins in June, while the Passover takes place at the end of March. Some fig trees bear fruit out of season. The sign of such fruit is the presence of leaves. This fig tree reminded Jesus of hypocrites because it bore signs of having fruit (leaves had appeared), but had none.

11:14 May no one ever eat fruit from you again. This account, coming immediately before that of the cleansing of the temple, has symbolic meaning. Jesus cursed this tree for being impressive but fruitless, just as he would judge the temple (vv. 15–17) and predict its destruction (13:2). He implied that the full restoration of the physical temple in Jerusalem would no longer be a goal of redemptive history.

11:15 temple area. The court of the Gentiles, the only area where Gentiles were allowed. These events were of particular interest to Mark's Gentile readers. **began driving out.** John's Gospel places a description of Jesus cleansing the temple at the beginning of Jesus' ministry (Jn 2:12–22), while all three Synoptics (Matthew, Mark and Luke) place this event at the end of his ministry (as here). It is possible that Jesus cleansed the temple twice, since (1) John's account is specifically dated (Jn 2:20; see note on Mk 1:9). (2) The accounts are by no means identical, and the Old Testament Scriptures cited are quite different—in John, Psalm 69:9 and Zechariah 14:21 are cited; in the Synoptics, Isaiah 56:7 and Jeremiah 7:11. (3) In John, Jesus came alone, whereas in the Synoptics he came in triumphal, Messianic glory. (4) Jesus, who in the latter cleansing cited Jeremiah, was no doubt aware that the prophet Jeremiah had twice cursed the temple (Jer 7:1–14; 26:2–6), the second time using the symbol of figs (Jer 24:1–10; see Mk 11:12–14). **money changers.** Exchanging money was a necessary service, since the temple tax and offerings had to be paid in the local currency. Unfair practices led Jesus to describe the scene as "a den of robbers" (v. 17). Jesus judged the Sadducean high priestly families who benefited from this abuse and who had lost all sense of the holiness of the temple (12:18–27).

11:16 not allow anyone to carry merchandise. The court of the Gentiles had become a bustling marketplace. Mark saw in Jesus' gesture the defense of Gentile rights and perhaps an indication of their future ingathering.

11:18 chief priests and teachers of the law. Jesus' action directly provoked those who would eventually kill him (8:31). **amazed at his teaching.** See note on 1:22.

11:20 In the morning. Tuesday morning of Passion Week. See chart titled "Passion Week" at Mark 14. **withered from the roots.** This phrase indicates complete destruction. See note on verse 14.

11:21 [k]Mt 23:7 21 Peter remembered and said to Jesus, "Rabbi,[k] look! The fig tree you cursed has withered!"
22 "Have[a] faith in God," Jesus answered. 23 "I tell you the truth, if anyone says to this
11:23 [l]Mt 21:21 mountain, 'Go, throw yourself into the sea,' and does not doubt in his heart but believes
that what he says will happen, it will be done for him.[l] 24 Therefore I tell you, whatever
11:24 [m]Mt 7:7 you ask for in prayer, believe that you have received it, and it will be yours.[m] 25 And when
you stand praying, if you hold anything against anyone, forgive him, so that your Father
11:25 [n]Mt 6:14 in heaven may forgive you your sins.[b]"[n]

The Authority of Jesus Questioned

27 They arrived again in Jerusalem, and while Jesus was walking in the temple courts,
the chief priests, the teachers of the law and the elders came to him. 28 "By what authority are you doing these things?" they asked. "And who gave you authority to do this?"
29 Jesus replied, "I will ask you one question. Answer me, and I will tell you by what
authority I am doing these things. 30 John's baptism—was it from heaven, or from men?
Tell me!"
31 They discussed it among themselves and said, "If we say, 'From heaven,' he will ask,
11:32 'Then why didn't you believe him?' 32 But if we say, 'From men' . . ." (They feared the peo-
[o]Mt 11:9 ple, for everyone held that John really was a prophet.)[o]
33 So they answered Jesus, "We don't know."
Jesus said, "Neither will I tell you by what authority I am doing these things."

The Parable of the Tenants

12:1 [p]Isa 5:1-7 **12** He then began to speak to them in parables: "A man planted a vineyard.[p] He put
a wall around it, dug a pit for the winepress and built a watchtower. Then he
rented the vineyard to some farmers and went away on a journey. 2 At harvest time he
sent a servant to the tenants to collect from them some of the fruit of the vineyard. 3 But
they seized him, beat him and sent him away empty-handed. 4 Then he sent another servant to them; they struck this man on the head and treated him shamefully. 5 He sent still
another, and that one they killed. He sent many others; some of them they beat, others
they killed.
12:6 6 "He had one left to send, a son, whom he loved. He sent him last of all,[q] saying, 'They
[q]Heb 1:1-3 will respect my son.'
7 "But the tenants said to one another, 'This is the heir. Come, let's kill him, and the
inheritance will be ours.' 8 So they took him and killed him, and threw him out of the vineyard.
9 "What then will the owner of the vineyard do? He will come and kill those tenants
and give the vineyard to others. 10 Haven't you read this scripture:

" 'The stone the builders rejected
12:10 [r]Ac 4:11 has become the capstone[c];[r]

[a] 22 Some early manuscripts *If you have* [b] 25 Some manuscripts *sins.* *26But if you do not forgive, neither*
will your Father who is in heaven forgive your sins. [c] 10 Or *cornerstone*

11:24 See *WCF* 21.3; *WLC* 185.
11:25 anything against anyone. See Matthew 5:23–24.
▪ **11:27—12:44** *Controversies at the Temple.* Mark revealed Jesus' authority to challenge the failing religious authorities and institutions of Jerusalem. By this means, he established Jesus as the exclusive center of faith and salvation for Jews and Gentiles throughout the world.
11:27 chief priests. See note on verse 18.
11:28 who gave you authority. . . ? The Jerusalem authorities sought to reveal Jesus as an upstart with no official status to act within the temple.
11:30 John's baptism—was it from heaven, or from men? Jesus' brilliant answer silenced these officeholders and professional theologians, for it showed that all "official" human authority must bow to the authority God delegates to his prophets. It implies that prophetic authority, which Jesus (implicitly) claimed to use, by definition cannot have a human source (cf. Gal 1:11–12). Prophetic authority is not conferred by human mediation. It is recognized as ultimate and self-attesting, and it demands submission. So Jesus left before his hearers (and Mark, before his readers) the unspoken question: "Do you recognize and submit to my authority?"
12:1 them. This personal pronoun no doubt refers to the chief priests and teachers of the law since it is linked with the "they" of verse 12 (those who were looking for a way to arrest him). This is another example of provocation (see 11:18). **parables.** See note on 4:11. **vineyard.** This parable is based on the Song of the Vineyard (Isa 5:1–5), which pictures Israel and her unfaithfulness.
12:2 servant. Often used as a term for the prophets (Ex 14:31; 2Ch 1:3; Isa 20:3; Am 3:7) whom God had sent to call Israel to faithfulness and who frequently suffered death as a direct result of their incriminating statements (Mt 23:37). **tenants.** Those with "official" authority over the people of God. The parable was told for their benefit.
12:6 a son, whom he loved. In the Synoptics, the theme of Jesus as God's beloved Son is rare (1:11; 9:7; cf. Mt 16:16), but here it is unmistakably present.
12:9 give the vineyard to others. Matthew's Gospel states this as "will be . . . given to a people who will produce its fruit" (Mt 21:43), suggesting both the community of disciples forming around Jesus (Lk 22:29–30) and the coming in of the Gentiles (Mt 8:11–12; Ro 9:22–26).
12:10 The stone the builders rejected. After the cleansing of the temple, Jesus cited Psalm 118:22–23, which celebrates the victory God gives to his king. Jesus showed his trust in his Father and in the Father's word, the Old Testament Scriptures. He had just predicted his own death—"they took him and killed him" (v. 8). Now, in the presence of his very murderers, he was already celebrating the promised victory.

11 the Lord has done this,
and it is marvelous in our eyes'[a]?"[s]

12 Then they looked for a way to arrest him because they knew he had spoken the parable against them. But they were afraid of the crowd;[t] so they left him and went away.[u]

Paying Taxes to Caesar

13 Later they sent some of the Pharisees and Herodians[v] to Jesus to catch him[w] in his
words. 14 They came to him and said, "Teacher, we know you are a man of integrity. You
aren't swayed by men, because you pay no attention to who they are; but you teach the
way of God in accordance with the truth. Is it right to pay taxes to Caesar or not?
15 Should we pay or shouldn't we?"
But Jesus knew their hypocrisy. "Why are you trying to trap me?" he asked. "Bring me
a denarius and let me look at it." 16 They brought the coin, and he asked them, "Whose
portrait is this? And whose inscription?"
"Caesar's," they replied.
17 Then Jesus said to them, "Give to Caesar what is Caesar's and to God what is
God's."[x]
And they were amazed at him.

Marriage at the Resurrection

18 Then the Sadducees,[y] who say there is no resurrection,[z] came to him with a question. 19 "Teacher," they said, "Moses wrote for us that if a man's brother dies and leaves
a wife but no children, the man must marry the widow and have children for his brother.[a] 20 Now there were seven brothers. The first one married and died without leaving any
children. 21 The second one married the widow, but he also died, leaving no child. It was
the same with the third. 22 In fact, none of the seven left any children. Last of all, the woman died too. 23 At the resurrection[b] whose wife will she be, since the seven were married
to her?"
24 Jesus replied, "Are you not in error because you do not know the Scriptures[b] or the
power of God? 25 When the dead rise, they will neither marry nor be given in marriage;
they will be like the angels in heaven.[c] 26 Now about the dead rising—have you not read
in the book of Moses, in the account of the bush, how God said to him, 'I am the God of
Abraham, the God of Isaac, and the God of Jacob'[c]?[d] 27 He is not the God of the dead, but
of the living. You are badly mistaken!"

12:11 [s]Ps 118:22,23
12:12 [t]Mk 11:18 [u]Mt 22:22
12:13 [v]Mt 22:16; Mk 3:6 [w]Mt 12:10
12:17 [x]Ro 13:7
12:18 [y]Ac 4:1 [z]Ac 23:8; 1Co 15:12
12:19 [a]Dt 25:5
12:24 [b]2Ti 3:15-17
12:25 [c]1Co 15:42,49,52
12:26 [d]Ex 3:6

[a] *11* Psalm 118:22,23 [b] *23* Some manuscripts *resurrection, when men rise from the dead,*
[c] *26* Exodus 3:6

12:12 they were afraid of the crowd. Compare 11:32. The contrast to Jesus is clear: These religious authorities (11:27) were weak, corrupt politicians who were apparently incapable of acting out of principle.
12:13 Pharisees and Herodians. The old (3:6) but strange alliance between the religious elite (the Pharisees) and the politicians of survival (the Herodians) had again reared its head. This alliance was possible because both parties accepted the Roman occupation, the former as divine punishment, the latter as political advantage. In this both were opposed to the Zealots, who sought the defeat of the occupying Roman forces. See chart "Jewish Sects" at Matthew 23.
12:14 you pay no attention to who they are. The Greek renders this, "you do not look at men's faces." **taxes to Caesar.** In addition to numerous customs taxes, tolls and other charges, each Roman province was obliged to pay the imperial tribute. The same sum was exacted from all citizens, rich and poor alike. The Zealots saw in this tax a further example of national humiliation, and they refused to pay it.
12:15 Why are you trying to trap me? Because opinions varied among the Jews on this matter, Jesus knew that a simple answer would discredit him with one group or the other. **denarius.** Numerous currencies were in circulation. Jesus asked for the Roman denarius, worth a day's wages. It carried on one side the effigy of Caesar (either Augustus or his adopted son Tiberius) and on the other a scene glorifying his reign.
12:17 Give to Caesar. In spite of the many injustices in Roman taxation and in the government in general, Jesus affirmed the legitimacy of Rome's political power and at his trial declared that it was from God (Jn 19:11). The early church followed this teaching of Jesus (Ro 13:1–7; Col 1:16; 1Ti 2:1–6; Tit 3:1–2; 1Pe 2:13–17).
12:18 Sadducees. This is the first explicit mention of this group in Mark's Gospel. They were members of the high priestly families at the time of Jesus, and they accepted as canonical only the first five books of Moses (the Pentateuch). They also denied the resurrection, on the basis that it was not taught in the Pentateuch. Their name probably derived from Zadok, David's high priest (2Sa 8:17; 1Ch 15:11; cf. 1Ch 29:22), the appointed officer over the Aaronic priestly line (1Ch 27:17), who had exclusive rights to the high priestly function (Eze 40:46; cf. Eze 43:19). See chart titled "Jewish Sects" at Matthew 23. See *BC* 37.
12:19 Moses wrote. The story they told to Jesus (vv. 19–23) was based on the Levirate or kinsman-redeemer law of Deuteronomy 25:5–10, which, in the event of premature death, provided for a family line to be perpetuated by the nearest of kin (see also Ru 3–4).
12:24 Are you not in error because you do not know the Scriptures . . . ? As in chapter 7 (see especially the note on 7:3), Jesus claimed to know the true sense of the Scripture over against the false understanding of the Jewish leaders (cf. Jn 5:39–40). **the power of God?** Jesus was probably referring to the ongoing work of God, as well as to God's powerful future manifestations (including resurrection) through his Messiah (Lk 22:69; Ro 1:16; 1Co 1:18,24)—manifestations to which the Sadducees had closed their minds.
12:25 neither marry. In the final resurrection (the transformation of the physical universe; Ro 8:21; 1Co 15:52–53), the creational mandate of marriage and reproduction (Ge 1:27–28; 2:24) will no longer be appropriate. Again the Sadducees revealed their ignorance of the "power of God" (v. 24) and of the end of world history.
12:26–27 the book of Moses. See note on verse 18. **the account of the bush.** See Exodus 3:1–6. To prove them wrong, Jesus cited a text they accepted as canonical. The God who appeared with miraculous power in the burning bush took his name not from fad-

The Greatest Commandment

28 One of the teachers of the law[e] came and heard them debating. Noticing that Jesus
had given them a good answer, he asked him, "Of all the commandments, which is the
most important?"
29 "The most important one," answered Jesus, "is this: 'Hear, O Israel, the Lord our
God, the Lord is one.[a] 30 Love the Lord your God with all your heart and with all your soul
and with all your mind and with all your strength.'[b][f] 31 The second is this: 'Love your
neighbor as yourself.'[c][g] There is no commandment greater than these."
32 "Well said, teacher," the man replied. "You are right in saying that God is one and
there is no other but him.[h] 33 To love him with all your heart, with all your understanding and with all your strength, and to love your neighbor as yourself is more important
than all burnt offerings and sacrifices."[i]
34 When Jesus saw that he had answered wisely, he said to him, "You are not far from
the kingdom of God."[j] And from then on no one dared ask him any more questions.[k]

Whose Son Is the Christ?

35 While Jesus was teaching in the temple courts,[l] he asked, "How is it that the teachers of the law say that the Christ[d] is the son of David?[m] 36 David himself, speaking by the
Holy Spirit,[n] declared:

" 'The Lord said to my Lord:
"Sit at my right hand
until I put your enemies
under your feet." '[e][o]

37 David himself calls him 'Lord.' How then can he be his son?"
The large crowd[p] listened to him with delight.
38 As he taught, Jesus said, "Watch out for the teachers of the law. They like to walk
around in flowing robes and be greeted in the marketplaces, 39 and have the most important seats in the synagogues and the places of honor at banquets.[q] 40 They devour widows' houses and for a show make lengthy prayers. Such men will be punished most
severely."

The Widow's Offering

41 Jesus sat down opposite the place where the offerings were put[r] and watched the
crowd putting their money into the temple treasury. Many rich people threw in large
amounts. 42 But a poor widow came and put in two very small copper coins,[f] worth only
a fraction of a penny.[g]

12:28 [e]Lk 10:25-28; 20:39
12:30 [f]Dt 6:4,5
12:31 [g]Lev 19:18; Mt 5:43
12:32 [h]Dt 4:35,39; Isa 45:6,14; 46:9
12:33 [i]1Sa 15:22; Hos 6:6; Mic 6:6-8; Heb 10:8
12:34 [j]Mt 3:2 [k]Mt 22:46; Lk 20:40
12:35 [l]Mt 26:55 [m]Mt 9:27
12:36 [n]2Sa 23:2 [o]Ps 110:1; Mt 22:44
12:37 [p]Jn 12:9
12:39 [q]Lk 11:43
12:41 [r]2Ki 12:9; Jn 8:20

[a] *29* Or *the Lord our God is one Lord* [b] *30* Deut. 6:4,5 [c] *31* Lev. 19:18 [d] *35* Or *Messiah*
[e] *36* Psalm 110:1 [f] *42* Greek *two lepta* [g] *42* Greek *kodrantes*

ed memories ("the dead"), but from living men of faith who are bound to him in an eternal covenant of grace. The teaching on resurrection is not based solely on Scriptures that speak of it more explicitly (e.g., Ps 16:9–11; Isa 53:11; Da 12:2; Hos 6:2; cf. Job 14:14; 19:25–27; Pss 17:15; 73:24–26; Isa 26:19; Eze 37:1–14; Hos 13:14), but is ultimately grounded in the person of the living and life-giving God. See theological article "The Resurrection of Jesus" at Luke 24. **You are badly mistaken!** This phrase could also be translated more strongly: "You are completely in error" or "You are greatly misled [or deceived]."

12:29 Hear, O Israel. Again the debate was centered around Scripture, a subject of which Jesus showed himself to be a consummate master. He cited Deuteronomy 6:4, known as the *Shema* (Hebrew for "Hear"), which had already become the great confession of Judaism's monotheistic faith.

12:31 The second. Here Jesus joined Leviticus 19:18, a text James calls "the royal law" (Jas 2:8), to Deuteronomy 6:4–5 (the *Shema*).

12:33 burnt offerings. The teacher of the law approved Jesus' answer and added Scriptural proof of his own—1 Samuel 15:22 and Hosea 6:6. See *WCF* 21.1.

12:34 not far from the kingdom. Compare this teacher of the law with the rich young ruler ("One thing you lack . . ."; 10:21) and Nicodemus (Jn 3:1ff.). In each case the need of new birth into eternal life was evident. (See theological article "Regeneration and New Birth" at Jn 3.) Here Jesus had in mind the fully consummated kingdom that will be enjoyed only by the redeemed on the basis of the death and resurrection of the Son of Man (Jn 3:3,14–15). According to Acts 6:7, many teachers of the law inherited the kingdom after Pentecost.

12:35 temple courts. See note on 11:15. In addition to the court of the Gentiles, there was also the court of women (beyond which women could not go) and the court of Israel, which was reserved for Jewish men.

12:36 David himself. Jesus' words and his interpretation were dependant on the Davidic authorship of this psalm. **speaking by the Holy Spirit.** Jesus attributed full divine inspiration to David and his writing, as did his disciples later on (Ac 1:16; 4:25).

12:37 David himself calls him "Lord." Jesus argued that while the Messiah does come from the Davidic line, his royal dignity and power far surpass David's, for David addressed this king as "my Lord" (Ps 110:1), and in the exercise of rule this king is uniquely associated with the LORD Yahweh (Ps 110:2). Jesus' lucid, fresh and faithful interpretation of Scripture produced "delight" among his listeners (cf. Lk 24:32).

12:38 Watch out for the teachers of the law. Jesus' opponents had the appearance of profundity, but they were "badly mistaken" (v. 27). A similar warning is found in 8:15 (see note).

12:40 devour widows' houses. The teachers of the law did not receive a fixed salary and so sought their support from the people, among whom widows, no doubt, were easy prey. **lengthy prayers.** See Matthew 6:5–6 for a similar judgment of ostentatious and hypocritical spirituality.

12:41 temple treasury. Appropriately, the offering boxes were situated in the court of women, which thus gave access to all.

12:42 two very small copper coins. This coin, the lepton, was the smallest in circulation. **a fraction of a penny.** Literally, "a quadrans," a Roman coin worth 1/64 of a denarius (which equaled one day's average wage). Again Mark gave the translation for his Gentile readers (see note on 7:34).

43 Calling his disciples to him, Jesus said, "I tell you the truth, this poor widow has put
more into the treasury than all the others. 44 They all gave out of their wealth; but she,
out of her poverty, put in everything—all she had to live on."[s]

Signs of the End of the Age

13 As he was leaving the temple, one of his disciples said to him, "Look, Teacher!
What massive stones! What magnificent buildings!"
2 "Do you see all these great buildings?" replied Jesus. "Not one stone here will be left
on another; every one will be thrown down."[t]
3 As Jesus was sitting on the Mount of Olives[u] opposite the temple, Peter, James, John[v]
and Andrew asked him privately, 4 "Tell us, when will these things happen? And what will
be the sign that they are all about to be fulfilled?"
5 Jesus said to them: "Watch out that no one deceives you.[w] 6 Many will come in my
name, claiming, 'I am he,' and will deceive many. 7 When you hear of wars and rumors
of wars, do not be alarmed. Such things must happen, but the end is still to come. 8 Nation will rise against nation, and kingdom against kingdom. There will be earthquakes
in various places, and famines. These are the beginning of birth pains.
9 "You must be on your guard. You will be handed over to the local councils and
flogged in the synagogues.[x] On account of me you will stand before governors and kings
as witnesses to them. 10 And the gospel must first be preached to all nations. 11 Whenever you are arrested and brought to trial, do not worry beforehand about what to say. Just
say whatever is given you at the time, for it is not you speaking, but the Holy Spirit.[y]
12 "Brother will betray brother to death, and a father his child. Children will rebel
against their parents and have them put to death.[z] 13 All men will hate you because of
me,[a] but he who stands firm to the end will be saved.[b]
14 "When you see 'the abomination that causes desolation'[a][c] standing where it[b]
does not belong—let the reader understand—then let those who are in Judea flee to
the mountains. 15 Let no one on the roof of his house go down or enter the house to

12:44 [s]2Co 8:12
13:2 [t]Lk 19:44
13:3 [u]Mt 21:1 [v]Mt 4:21
13:5 [w]ver 22; Jer 29:8; Eph 5:6; 2Th 2:3, 10-12; 1Ti 4:1; 2Ti 3:13; 1Jn 4:6
13:9 [x]Mt 10:17
13:11 [y]Mt 10:19,20; Lk 12:11,12
13:12 [z]Mic 7:6; Mt 10:21; Lk 12:51-53
13:13 [a]Jn 15:21 [b]Mt 10:22
13:14 [c]Da 9:27; 11:31; 12:11

a *14* Daniel 9:27; 11:31; 12:11   b *14* Or *he*; also in verse 29

■ 13:1–37 *Prophecies on the Mount of Olives.* Mark continued to explain how Jesus challenged the religious authorities and institutions in Jerusalem. Jesus warned of divine judgment to come against the city and predicted his own glorious return. This chapter is known as the "little apocalypse" or the "Olivet discourse." It divides into three sections: (1) prediction of the destruction of the temple (vv. 1–4), (2) future persecutions (vv. 5–25) and (3) the coming(s) of the Son of Man (vv. 26–37). For the three prominent approaches to this chapter by Reformed theologians, see note on Matthew 24:1—25:46.

13:1 What massive stones! What magnificent buildings! Herod the Great began rebuilding the temple in 19 B.C., using much marble and gold. The outer court measured 500 yards (457 meters) long by 300 yards (274 meters) wide, and it was bordered by walls of massive white stones, some of which were 37 feet (11 meters) long, 12 feet (3.7 meters) high and 18 feet (5.5 meters) wide. On top of these were magnificent cloisters, or covered walkways, with richly carved wooden ceilings. See chart titled "Herod's Temple" at Luke 2.

13:2 Not one stone. Jesus predicted the time when Jerusalem would be sacked and the temple burned and destroyed. This took place in A.D. 70 at the hand of the Roman general Titus, who later became emperor.

13:3 Peter, James, John and Andrew asked him privately. Mark's Gospel informs us that this teaching was part of the special revelation given to the Twelve (4:10–11; 8:29; 9:35).

13:4 when will these things happen? The disciples' question had in view the predicted destruction of the temple. Jesus' reply seems to have taken in both that immediate event and the time leading up to the coming of the Son of Man (v. 26; cf. Mt 24:3). As in many prophetic announcements, events separated by extended periods of time are compressed together. The events surrounding the destruction of the temple seem to anticipate those associated with the return of Christ, insofar as both sets of events include severe divine judgment. See note on Matthew 24:1—25:46 for alternate interpretations.

13:6 Many will come. Many claimed to be the Messiah. In A.D. 70, Josephus hailed the Romans as the Messiah. In A.D. 130, Bar Kokhba, the leader of a Jewish rebellion against the Romans, claimed to be the Messiah. Many others could be added to the list.

13:7 the end. According to the parallel text (Mt 24:3), "the end" is "the end of the age" (see note on 10:30).

13:8 birth pains. The Jews expected a time of suffering before the coming of the Messiah and described it in this way, as did Paul in Romans 8:22.

13:9 local councils. Synagogue councils had the right to prescribe floggings, limited to 40 strokes (Dt 25:1–3). The book of Acts (Ac 4:21; 5:18,40) and the letters of Paul (2Co 6:9; 11:23–24) speak of imprisonments and floggings that the apostles underwent.

13:10 preached to all nations. The time between the resurrection of Christ and his second coming is not simply one of suffering and persecution, but also of grace and evangelization to the ends of the earth (a fulfillment of the prophecy of Isa 49:6).

13:11 what to say. This general promise of assistance by the Holy Spirit for public witness is to be distinguished from the special ministry of the Spirit among the Twelve for establishing the apostolic word concerning the facts of the person and work of Jesus (Jn 14:25–26; 15:26–27; 16:12–14).

13:13 stands firm to the end. It is likely that this expression was intended to have a double meaning. The "end" may refer to the end of one's life (Ro 8:18–25; 12:12; Heb 10:32; 12:2; 1Pe 2:20), but for those who are still alive when Jesus returns it will mean "the end of the age." See note on verse 7. **will be saved.** Perseverance does not merit salvation but is the proof that true salvation has already taken place (Ro 8:24), leading to its future completion at the return of Christ (Ro 8:23–25).

13:14 the abomination that causes desolation. Daniel 11:31 predicts the coming of the king of the north, who will desecrate the temple. This prediction was first fulfilled in 168 B.C., when Antiochus Epiphanes set up a pagan altar and sacrificed a pig in the Most Holy Place. The desecration during the destruction of Jerusalem in A.D. 70 is a later fulfillment. See note on Matthew 24:15. **let the reader understand.** This could be Mark's comment to his readers, indicating that the destruction of the temple had already occurred (see note on v. 2). It is much more likely, however, that this was Jesus' instruction to the readers of Daniel 9:25–27 and 11:31 (see Mk 2:25; 12:10,26), especially in light of the fact that this comment also appears in Matthew 24:15. **flee to the mountains.** When the Romans sacked the Qumran community on its way to Jerusalem in A.D. 69, its members hid their precious manuscripts, and no doubt themselves, in caves high up in the mountains overlooking the Dead Sea. The fourth-century church historian Eusebius stated that the Christians left Jerusalem at that time and founded the church at Pella in the region of Perea. Jesus' prediction here concerns this historical event.

take anything out. 16 Let no one in the field go back to get his cloak. 17 How dreadful it
will be in those days for pregnant women and nursing mothers![d] 18 Pray that this will
not take place in winter, 19 because those will be days of distress unequaled from the
beginning, when God created the world,[e] until now—and never to be equaled again.[f]
20 If the Lord had not cut short those days, no one would survive. But for the sake of
the elect, whom he has chosen, he has shortened them. 21 At that time if anyone says
to you, 'Look, here is the Christ[a]!' or, 'Look, there he is!' do not believe it.[g] 22 For false
Christs and false prophets[h] will appear and perform signs and miracles[i] to deceive the
elect—if that were possible. 23 So be on your guard;[j] I have told you everything ahead
of time.

24 "But in those days, following that distress,

"'the sun will be darkened,
and the moon will not give its light;
25 the stars will fall from the sky,
and the heavenly bodies will be shaken.'[b][k]

26 "At that time men will see the Son of Man coming in clouds[l] with great power and
glory. 27 And he will send his angels and gather his elect from the four winds, from the
ends of the earth to the ends of the heavens.[m]

28 "Now learn this lesson from the fig tree: As soon as its twigs get tender and its leaves
come out, you know that summer is near. 29 Even so, when you see these things happening, you know that it is near, right at the door. 30 I tell you the truth, this generation[c][n] will
certainly not pass away until all these things have happened.[o] 31 Heaven and earth will
pass away, but my words will never pass away.[p]

The Day and Hour Unknown

32 "No one knows about that day or hour, not even the angels in heaven, nor the Son,
but only the Father.[q] 33 Be on guard! Be alert[d]![r] You do not know when that time will
come. 34 It's like a man going away: He leaves his house and puts his servants[s] in charge,
each with his assigned task, and tells the one at the door to keep watch.

35 "Therefore keep watch because you do not know when the owner of the house will
come back—whether in the evening, or at midnight, or when the rooster crows, or at
dawn. 36 If he comes suddenly, do not let him find you sleeping. 37 What I say to you, I say
to everyone: 'Watch!' "[t]

13:17 [d]Lk 23:29
13:19 [e]Mk 10:6 [f]Da 9:26; 12:1; Joel 2:2
13:21 [g]Lk 17:23; 21:8
13:22 [h]Mt 7:15 [i]Jn 4:48; 2Th 2:9,10
13:23 [j]2Pe 3:17
13:25 [k]Isa 13:10; 34:4; Mt 24:29
13:26 [l]Da 7:13; Mt 16:27; Rev 1:7
13:27 [m]Zec 2:6
13:30 [n]Lk 17:25 [o]Mk 9:1
13:31 [p]Mt 5:18
13:32 [q]Ac 1:7; 1Th 5:1,2
13:33 [r]1Th 5:6
13:34 [s]Mt 25:14
13:37 [t]Lk 12:35-40

[a] *21* Or *Messiah* [b] *25* Isaiah 13:10; 34:4 [c] *30* Or *race* [d] *33* Some manuscripts *alert and pray*

13:19 distress unequaled from the beginning. Josephus and the Roman historian Tacitus both described the destruction of the temple in A.D. 70 as a catastrophe of supernatural dimensions, complete with armies in the sky and heavenly voices. This event no doubt anticipates divine judgment at the end of the world (see note on v. 4).
13:20 cut short. This may refer to the limited period surrounding the destruction of the temple, to a similar period before the return of Christ in glory or to both (see note on v. 4). **the elect.** The people of God. See verses 22 and 27.
13:21 Look, here is the Christ! See note on verse 6.
13:22 signs and miracles. Jesus indicated that false signs and miracles would take place to compete with true Messianic manifestations.
13:24 in those days. This is a technical Old Testament term for the last days (Jer 3:16; Joel 3:1; Zec 8:23). Jesus may have been speaking here of the "end" (v. 7), especially since verse 26 refers to Christ's return. **the sun will be darkened.** The phrases in verses 24–25 appear in Old Testament threats of national judgment (Isa 13:10; 34:4; Joel 2:10,31), which were types or foreshadowings of the coming cosmic and final judgment.
13:26 coming in clouds. Clouds signify divine presence (e.g., Ex 19:9; 24:15–18). Although the first coming of the Son of Man into this world was characterized by suffering and humiliation (see note on 8:31), his future coming at the "end" will be an open ("men will see") and unambiguous declaration of his divine glory. This anticipated coming recalls the theophanies of the Old Testament (Ex 19:16; 34:5; Eze 1:4; 10:3–4), with the difference that this arrival will be universally visible. But verses 24–27 may point not to Christ's appearing for universal judgment, but to the human realization that Jesus is indeed reigning in the kingdom the Father has given him (Da 7:13), a recognition triggered by the fall of Jerusalem, God's final judgment on that city. If this is the case, verse 27 refers to the worldwide spread of the gospel that followed this event, and the "angels" depict the church-planting messengers of the gospel. (*Angel* comes from the Greek word for "messenger," whether human or angelic.) Based on this view, Jesus' first reference to "the end" (his reappearing) does not occur until verse 32 ("that day").
13:27 from the four winds. A poetic way of affirming that the new people of God will be composed of members from all people groups (Rev 5:9).
13:28 fig tree. There seems here to be no symbolic sense to this image (e.g., the flowering of the nation of Israel), especially since the parallel passage in Luke 21:29 adds "and all the trees." Jesus was simply saying that, just as there are signs of what is to come in the natural realm, so there are indicators in the spiritual realm.
13:30 this generation. For the anticipatory event of the destruction of the temple, the phrase must refer to the generation contemporaneous with Jesus. **all these things.** Essentially means the same as "everything" in verse 23. When all "these things" have happened, the end will be "near, right at the door" (v. 29), but the second coming will still be forthcoming. See note on Matthew 24:34.
13:31 Heaven and earth will pass away. Jesus placed his own words on a par with those of Scripture with regard to their eternal value (Mt 5:18).
13:32 nor the Son. Jesus acknowledged that he did not know the time of his own return. He made this admission with respect to his human nature only. With regard to his divine nature, Jesus was omniscient. See theological article "Jesus Christ, God and Man" at John 1.
13:33–37 See *WCF* 33.3; *HC* 127.

Jesus Anointed at Bethany

14 Now the Passover[u] and the Feast of Unleavened Bread were only two days
away, and the chief priests and the teachers of the law were looking for some
sly way to arrest Jesus and kill him.[v] 2"But not during the Feast," they said, "or the people may riot."
3While he was in Bethany,[w] reclining at the table in the home of a man known as Simon the Leper, a woman came with an alabaster jar of very expensive perfume, made
of pure nard. She broke the jar and poured the perfume on his head.[x]
4Some of those present were saying indignantly to one another, "Why this waste of
perfume? 5It could have been sold for more than a year's wages[a] and the money given
to the poor." And they rebuked her harshly.
6"Leave her alone," said Jesus. "Why are you bothering her? She has done a beautiful thing to me. 7The poor you will always have with you, and you can help them any time
you want.[y] But you will not always have me. 8She did what she could. She poured perfume on my body beforehand to prepare for my burial.[z] 9I tell you the truth, wherever
the gospel is preached throughout the world,[a] what she has done will also be told, in
memory of her."
10Then Judas Iscariot, one of the Twelve,[b] went to the chief priests to betray Jesus to
them.[c] 11They were delighted to hear this and promised to give him money. So he
watched for an opportunity to hand him over.

The Lord's Supper

12On the first day of the Feast of Unleavened Bread, when it was customary to sacrifice the Passover lamb,[d] Jesus' disciples asked him, "Where do you want us to go and
make preparations for you to eat the Passover?"
13So he sent two of his disciples, telling them, "Go into the city, and a man carrying

14:1 [u]Jn 11:55; 13:1 [v]Mt 12:14
14:3 [w]Mt 21:17 [x]Lk 7:37-39
14:7 [y]Dt 15:11
14:8 [z]Jn 19:40
14:9 [a]Mt 24:14; Mk 16:15
14:10 [b]Mk 3:16-19 [c]Mt 10:4
14:12 [d]Ex 12:1-11; Dt 16:1-4; 1Co 5:7

[a] 5 Greek *than three hundred denarii*

■ **14:1–11** *Anointing at Bethany.* Mark described Jesus' anointing in Bethany as a prelude for the upcoming Passover and the Feast of Unleavened Bread—the time of Jesus' death and resurrection. Mark's emphasis on the preeminence of Jesus over all other concerns of life takes center stage as he seeks to instruct Christians that Christ must be exalted in all circumstances throughout the world.

14:1 the Passover. The Passover is one of the central feasts of the Jewish calendar. It celebrates the deliverance from Egypt when the angel of death "passed over" the homes of the people of Israel (Ex 12:13ff). At the time of Jesus, the Passover was celebrated on the 15th day of the first month of the Jewish calendar (Nisan—corresponding to April), which was the last day before the full moon of the spring equinox. On that day, when the paschal lambs were killed and eaten, all leaven (symbolizing sin) was to be removed from one's house, and only unleavened bread was to be eaten for seven days (Ex 12:15–20; cf. Mk 14:12). **two days away.** John 12:1 says that Jesus ate this meal six days before the Passover. This seeming discrepancy may well be explained by the two different calendars in use at the time: (1) the official one that was followed by the Jerusalem authorities and by the Gospel of John and (2) the Old Testament calendar that was followed by strict Jewish groups such as the Qumran community and by the writers of the Synoptic Gospels. **chief priests.** See note on 8:31. **teachers of the law.** See note on 7:1.

14:2 not during the Feast. The Passover drew to Jerusalem enormous numbers of pilgrims. Josephus estimated that the population of fifty thousand increased during this time each year to three million! Though his figures are generally considered exaggerated, they indicate the reason for the authorities' fears.

14:3 Bethany. See note on 11:1. **reclining.** In the ancient world, people did not sit at tables but reclined on couches, leaning on their left elbows (cf. Jn 13:23). **Simon the Leper.** It is likely that he had been healed by Jesus and had become an important member of the wider circle of disciples since it was at his house that Jesus chose to observe the sacred meal. **a woman.** According to John 12:3, this woman was Mary, the sister of Lazarus and Martha. **alabaster.** A type of marble that in its pure form is white or translucent. It was found in limestone regions in caves and at the exits of springs. It was used for making luxurious ointment jars. **pure nard.** A rare perfume made from the dried root of a plant grown in the Himalayas. **broke the jar.** Mary broke it because it was sealed shut. According to John 12:3, the jar contained about a pound of perfume. It must have completely covered Jesus.

14:6 a beautiful thing. Jesus approved what others saw as a waste, for by this gesture Mary demonstrated the inestimable worth of Jesus and of his death (v. 8). This gesture recalled the precious ointment poured over Aaron the high priest, which the psalmist compared to the priceless blessing of the fellowship of believers (Ps 133).

14:7 The poor you will always have. Jesus did not downplay the plight of the poor (Mt 11:5; Mk 10:21,46ff.; Lk 14:13). Instead, he stressed that spiritual poverty and the spiritual richness his death would bring were even more important.

14:8 prepare for my burial. Jesus was alluding to the anointing of dead bodies with spices and perfume, a practice that was widely observed at that time and in that climate. He was not referring to embalming, which was a pagan custom used to ensure better conditions in the afterlife. He attributed prophetic symbolism to the woman's act, viewing it as an announcement of his forthcoming death.

14:9 wherever the gospel is preached throughout the world. Jesus' words indicate Mark's deeper concern in this passage that the anointing of Jesus is to be remembered throughout the world for all time as the gospel goes forth. Followers of Christ must always take to heart the supremacy of Jesus over all other concerns, even during times of suffering and hardship (like those the disciples were about to face).

14:10 Judas Iscariot. He would receive 30 silver coins—not even half the value of the perfume (vv. 4–5)—for his betrayal of Jesus (v. 11). According to John 12:4–5, he was one of those criticizing Mary's expression of the incalculable worth to her of her Savior. **the Twelve.** See note on 3:14.

14:11 They were delighted. Judas's initiative simplified the chief priests' task and changed their minds regarding the opportune moment for seizing Jesus (v. 2).

■ **14:12–31** *The Passover Meal in Jerusalem.* Mark now turned to the Passover meal that Jesus observed with his disciples. During this meal Jesus revealed to his disciples more of the significance of his imminent death and resurrection. Moreover, he established the sacrament of the Lord's Supper so that his followers would remember the significance of these events throughout the world for all time.

14:12 the Feast of Unleavened Bread. This feast symbolized the removal of sin in the life of Israelite believers (Ex 12:14–20). The Passover meal fell on the first day of this Feast (Ex 12:14–15; see also note on v. 1), which was the 14th day after the beginning of the Jewish year (Ex 12:6). **sacrifice the Passover lamb.** It is noteworthy that Jesus died at the time of Passover, for this feast celebrates the moment when the blood of the lamb saved the people in Egypt from God's punitive wrath. Jesus' own death thus

a jar of water will meet you. Follow him. 14Say to the owner of the house he enters, 'The
Teacher asks: Where is my guest room, where I may eat the Passover with my disciples?'
14:15 [e]Ac 1:13
15He will show you a large upper room,[e] furnished and ready. Make preparations for us
there."
16The disciples left, went into the city and found things just as Jesus had told them.
So they prepared the Passover.
17When evening came, Jesus arrived with the Twelve. 18While they were reclining at
the table eating, he said, "I tell you the truth, one of you will betray me—one who is eating with me."
19They were saddened, and one by one they said to him, "Surely not I?"
14:20 [f]Jn 13:18-27
20"It is one of the Twelve," he replied, "one who dips bread into the bowl with me.[f]
21The Son of Man[g] will go just as it is written about him. But woe to that man who be-
14:21 [g]Mt 8:20
trays the Son of Man! It would be better for him if he had not been born."
14:22 [h]Mt 14:19
22While they were eating, Jesus took bread, gave thanks and broke it,[h] and gave it to
his disciples, saying, "Take it; this is my body."
14:23 [i]1Co 10:16
23Then he took the cup, gave thanks and offered it to them, and they all drank
from it.[i]
14:24 [j]Mt 26:28
24"This is my blood of the[a] covenant,[j] which is poured out for many," he said to them.
25"I tell you the truth, I will not drink again of the fruit of the vine until that day when I
14:25 [k]Mt 3:2
drink it anew in the kingdom of God."[k]
26When they had sung a hymn, they went out to the Mount of Olives.[l]

14:26 [l]Mt 21:1

Jesus Predicts Peter's Denial

27"You will all fall away," Jesus told them, "for it is written:

14:27 [m]Zec 13:7

" 'I will strike the shepherd,
and the sheep will be scattered.'[b][m]

14:28 [n]Mk 16:7
28But after I have risen, I will go ahead of you into Galilee."[n]
29Peter declared, "Even if all fall away, I will not."
14:30 [o]ver 66-72; Lk 22:34; Jn 13:38
30"I tell you the truth," Jesus answered, "today—yes, tonight—before the rooster
crows twice[c] you yourself will disown me three times."[o]
14:31 [p]Lk 22:33; Jn 13:37
31But Peter insisted emphatically, "Even if I have to die with you,[p] I will never disown
you." And all the others said the same.

[a] *24* Some manuscripts *the new* [b] *27* Zech. 13:7 [c] *30* Some early manuscripts do not have *twice.*

shows the profound continuity in the divine plan of redemption (cf. 1Co 5:7). The fact that the Passover sacrifice preceded the celebration of Unleavened Bread indicates that God's gracious act of salvation precedes human works of righteousness.

14:13 a man carrying a jar of water. Women usually carried water jars. For Jesus' knowledge of other events distant in time and space, see 11:1–2 and John 1:48; compare 1 Samuel 9:19—10:7. With regard to his divine nature, Jesus was omniscient. With regard to his human nature, he was a gifted and inspired prophet. See note on 13:32; see also theological article "Jesus Christ, God and Man" at John 1.

14:17 with the Twelve. All four Gospels, including John (though implicitly), record that those present at this high point in Jesus' ministry were the Twelve whom he had chosen at the beginning (3:14). According to Luke 22:30, it was at this moment that Jesus announced their future ministry as judges of the new people of God. Here they witnessed the inauguration of the new covenant. See *BC* 35.

14:20 one of the Twelve. It was a painful irony for Jesus that one of the Twelve would betray him. His prediction no doubt came not only from his intimate knowledge of Judas, but also his profound understanding of the Scriptures, especially Psalm 41:9. This is also suggested in the following verse. **dips bread into the bowl.** What it was that was dipped into the bowl is not stated in the Greek. It could have been either bread or meat dipped into a central bowl of sauce, or the reference could be to a hand reaching into the common plate of food. Whatever view is taken, this detail underlines the deeply personal nature of Judas's betrayal. Table fellowship was a token of intimate friendship.

14:21 The Son of Man will go just as it is written about him. See note on 8:31.

14:22–24 See *WCF* 29.3; 29.4; *WLC* 169; *BC* 35; *HC* 75.

14:22 While they were eating. The sacramental meal of the new covenant grew out of the Old Testament; see the parallels between this text and Exodus 24:9–11. Jesus took two of the elements of the paschal meal—unleavened bread and wine (the other elements being bitter herbs, sauce and lamb)—to express his new work of redemption. **this is my body.** The broken bread, which is shared, vividly portrays Jesus' sacrifice of his own body in death for the benefit of "many" (v. 24).

14:24 my blood. Jesus' words about the wine must be understood in the light of the history of Passover, in which the blood of the slain lamb covered or protected the people from God's wrath against their sin and rebellion (Ex 12:29–30). **blood of the covenant.** This phrase comes from Exodus 24:8 and recalls the fact that Biblical covenants were sealed in blood (Ge 15: 9–21; 17:9–14; Ex 24:4–8). A number of ancient manuscripts refer to "new covenant," in agreement with Luke 22:20 and 1 Corinthians 11:25. Whatever the original reading, the meaning is clearly the same. **poured out for many.** Jesus was alluding to Isaiah 53:12, a passage in which the servant of the Lord "poured out his life unto death" and "bore the sins of many."

14:25 I will not drink again. Jesus was predicting the imminence of his death. Literally, he would die before he drank another cup of wine in the context of a meal. **drink it anew.** By this phrase Jesus expressed his faith in God, who would not in the final analysis abandon him in death. Jesus will celebrate a great feast with his followers in the new heaven and the new earth (Rev 19:7–9).

14:26 had sung a hymn. This mention of singing recalls the context of the Passover liturgy that Jesus followed. He and his disciples probably sang Psalms 115–118, which still today traditionally terminate the Passover meal. **Mount of Olives.** See note on 11:1.

14:27 it is written. Jesus' prediction of the falling away of the Twelve came from his knowledge of the book of Zechariah (Zec 13:7), which had already anticipated his entry into Jerusalem (see note on 11:2).

14:28 into Galilee. The angel at the tomb recalled this promise and alluded to Peter's denial (16:7).

14:30 before the rooster crows twice. For other examples of Jesus' supernatural knowledge of specific future events, see note on 14:13, but this expression could also be a poetic way of saying "before dawn."

Gethsemane

32They went to a place called Gethsemane, and Jesus said to his disciples, "Sit here
while I pray." 33He took Peter, James and John[q] along with him, and he began to be deeply distressed and troubled. 34"My soul is overwhelmed with sorrow to the point of
death,"[r] he said to them. "Stay here and keep watch."
35Going a little farther, he fell to the ground and prayed that if possible the hour[s]
might pass from him. 36"*Abba*,[a] Father,"[t] he said, "everything is possible for you. Take this
cup[u] from me. Yet not what I will, but what you will."[v]
37Then he returned to his disciples and found them sleeping. "Simon," he said to Peter, "are you asleep? Could you not keep watch for one hour? 38Watch and pray so that
you will not fall into temptation.[w] The spirit is willing, but the body is weak."[x]
39Once more he went away and prayed the same thing. 40When he came back, he
again found them sleeping, because their eyes were heavy. They did not know what to
say to him.
41Returning the third time, he said to them, "Are you still sleeping and resting?
Enough! The hour[y] has come. Look, the Son of Man is betrayed into the hands of sinners. 42Rise! Let us go! Here comes my betrayer!"

Jesus Arrested

43Just as he was speaking, Judas,[z] one of the Twelve, appeared. With him was a crowd
armed with swords and clubs, sent from the chief priests, the teachers of the law, and
the elders.
44Now the betrayer had arranged a signal with them: "The one I kiss is the man; arrest him and lead him away under guard." 45Going at once to Jesus, Judas said, "Rabbi!"[a]
and kissed him. 46The men seized Jesus and arrested him. 47Then one of those standing
near drew his sword and struck the servant of the high priest, cutting off his ear.
48"Am I leading a rebellion," said Jesus, "that you have come out with swords and
clubs to capture me? 49Every day I was with you, teaching in the temple courts,[b] and you
did not arrest me. But the Scriptures must be fulfilled."[c] 50Then everyone deserted him
and fled.[d]
51A young man, wearing nothing but a linen garment, was following Jesus. When they
seized him, 52he fled naked, leaving his garment behind.

14:33 [q]Mt 4:21
14:34 [r]Jn 12:27
14:35 [s]ver 41; Mt 26:18
14:36 [t]Ro 8:15; Gal 4:6 [u]Mt 20:22 [v]Mt 26:39
14:38 [w]Mt 6:13 [x]Ro 7:22, 23
14:41 [y]ver 35; Mt 26:18
14:43 [z]Mt 10:4
14:45 [a]Mt 23:7
14:49 [b]Mt 26:55 [c]Isa 53:7-12; Mt 1:22
14:50 [d]ver 27

a *36* Aramaic for *Father*

■ **14:32—15:47** *Desertion, Trial and Death.* Mark reported numerous details of Jesus' sufferings during his trials and crucifixion, not the least of which was the desertion of his disciples. Yet Mark also made clear that Jesus suffered as an innocent man according to God's plan for the redemption of his people.
14:32 Gethsemane. In Hebrew the word means "oil press," referring to the oil that comes from olives. Since Jesus had just set out in the direction of the Mount of Olives, it no doubt refers to a garden of olive trees in that general vicinity (see Jn 18:2).
14:33 Peter, James and John. See note on 5:37. **to be deeply distressed.** In the New Testament, the verb translated by this phrase is found only in Mark's Gospel (cf. 9:15; 16:5,6). It expresses deep emotional disturbance.
14:34 overwhelmed with sorrow to the point of death. As he faced the dreadful experience of becoming the sacrifice for human sin, Jesus felt himself dying from the burden of sorrow.
14:36 ***Abba.*** A colloquial and intimate Aramaic word for "father," which here expressed Jesus' intimate relationship with God the Father. The depth of emotion expressed in verse 34 is suggested, but not explicitly or exhaustively expressed, here. (Mark again preserved in his Greek text the Semitic original; compare 5:41; 7:34; 11:9; 14:45; 15:22,34). **cup.** See note on 10:38.
14:37 found them sleeping. The incongruity between the disciples' sleeping and the emotional agony of Jesus confronting the prospect of God's wrath recalls Israel's dancing before the golden calf while, on the mountain, the Lord of heaven and earth was writing for them on stone tablets a covenant of love and grace (Ex 32). **one hour?** Despite his noble intentions (vv. 29–31), Peter was incapable even of staying awake for a mere hour.
14:38 Watch. This exhortation recalls the warning to be vigilant and alert with regard to the coming of the Son of Man (13:32–37). It is also an instruction to remain alert in the face of "temptation." This event was a Satanic attempt to cause God's people (in this case, the Twelve) to fall and, if possible, to bring to nothing the plan of redemption. **The spirit is willing, but the body is weak.** The believer must watch and pray; that is, remain alert and attuned to God because our human nature is weak. Sincere intentions are important, but not good enough in themselves (vv. 29, 31).
14:41 third time. See Jesus' prediction that Peter would deny him three times (v. 30).
14:43 Judas. See note on 3:19. **a crowd armed.** This was no doubt a force sent by the Sanhedrin, since the three categories of its membership—chief priests, teachers of the law and elders—are mentioned and since Jesus was taken to this assembly (v. 53).
14:44 kiss. A sign of respect that disciples showed to teachers. After eating from the same dish, also a sign of friendship (see note on v. 20), Judas now hypocritically feigned submission and respect.
14:47 one of those standing near. See John 18:10. After his failure in Gethsemane (v. 37), Peter apparently wanted to prove that his commitment was not one of mere words (vv. 29,31).
14:48 leading a rebellion. The Greek term rendered here as "lead(er) of a rebellion" can mean either "robber" or "insurrectionist," but in view of the situation and the charges brought against Jesus at his trial (Luke 23:2), the latter sense is preferred.
14:49 the Scriptures must be fulfilled. In view of the following phrase (v. 50), the particular Scripture that Jesus had in mind may well have been Zechariah 13:7 (see v. 27). Regarding Jesus' fulfillment of the Scriptures, see notes on Matthew 1:23; 2:6,11,15,18,23; 3:13–15; 4:15–16; 11:4–6; 13:13–15,34–35; 21:1–11; 26:28,32,54,56; 27:12–14,34,35,43,46,48–49,57.
14:51 A young man. It is certainly valid to wonder whether in this cryptic detail, as in the mention of a linen garment (a sign of wealth), Mark may have been making an oblique reference to himself. He was a member of a well-to-do family in Jerusalem (Ac 12:12).
14:52 fled naked. For a Jew, such nakedness was shameful (Isa 20:4; 47:3; Mic 1:11; Rev 3:17–18). But added to the shame of flight and cowardice, the shame of nakedness must have forever marked the conscience of this young man who, like everyone else, deserted Jesus (v. 50).

Passion Week

Bethany,
the Mount of Olives
and Jerusalem

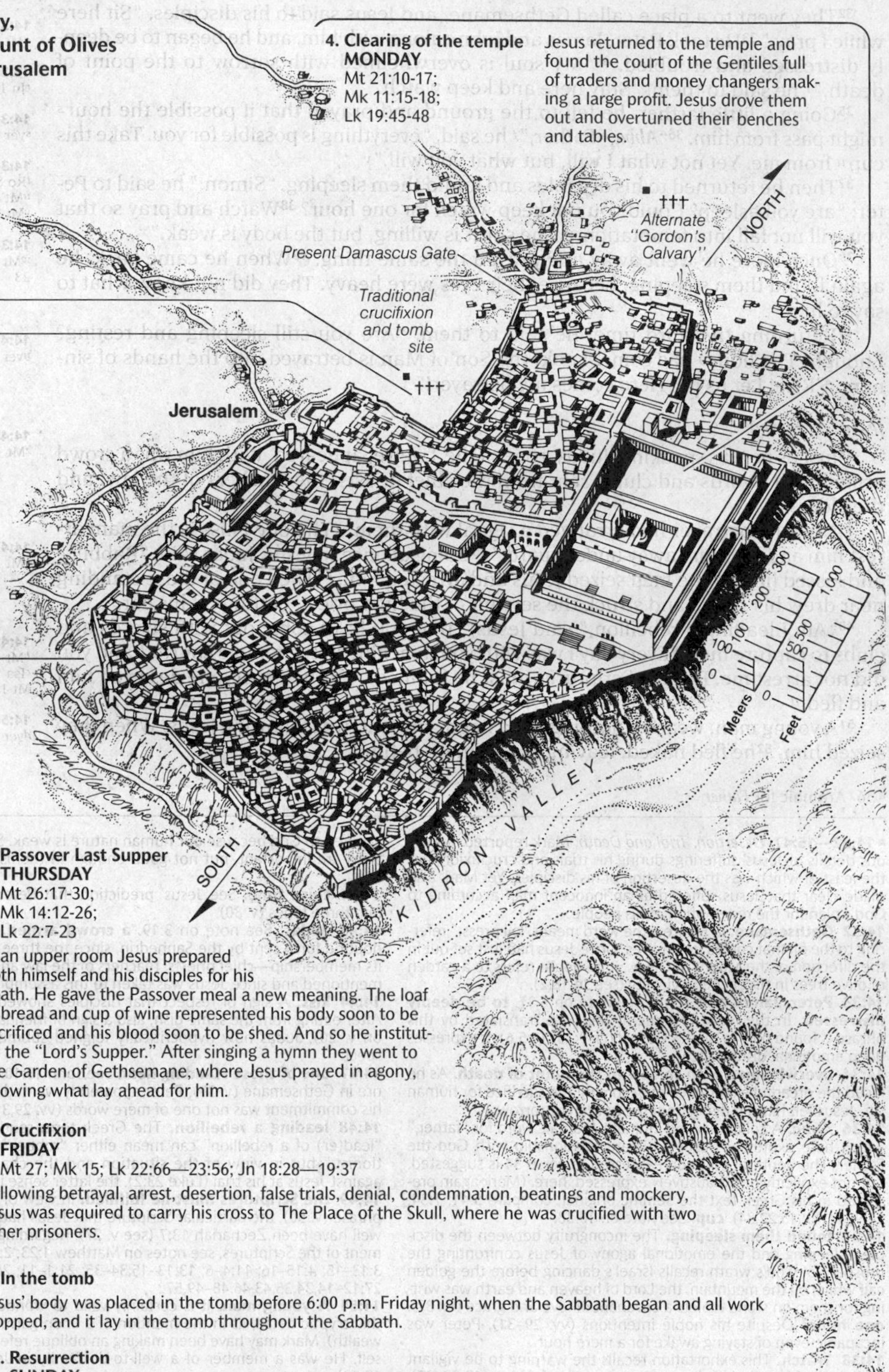

4. Clearing of the temple
MONDAY
Mt 21:10-17;
Mk 11:15-18;
Lk 19:45-48

Jesus returned to the temple and found the court of the Gentiles full of traders and money changers making a large profit. Jesus drove them out and overturned their benches and tables.

7. Passover Last Supper
THURSDAY
Mt 26:17-30;
Mk 14:12-26;
Lk 22:7-23

In an upper room Jesus prepared both himself and his disciples for his death. He gave the Passover meal a new meaning. The loaf of bread and cup of wine represented his body soon to be sacrificed and his blood soon to be shed. And so he instituted the "Lord's Supper." After singing a hymn they went to the Garden of Gethsemane, where Jesus prayed in agony, knowing what lay ahead for him.

8. Crucifixion
FRIDAY
Mt 27; Mk 15; Lk 22:66—23:56; Jn 18:28—19:37

Following betrayal, arrest, desertion, false trials, denial, condemnation, beatings and mockery, Jesus was required to carry his cross to The Place of the Skull, where he was crucified with two other prisoners.

9. In the tomb

Jesus' body was placed in the tomb before 6:00 p.m. Friday night, when the Sabbath began and all work stopped, and it lay in the tomb throughout the Sabbath.

10. Resurrection
SUNDAY
Mt 28:1-10; Mk 16:1-8; Lk 24:1-49; Jn 20

Early in the morning, women went to the tomb and found that the stone closing the tomb's entrance had been rolled back. An angel told them Jesus was alive and gave them a message. Jesus appeared to Mary Magdalene in the garden, to Peter, to two disciples on the road to Emmaus, and later that day to all the disciples but Thomas.

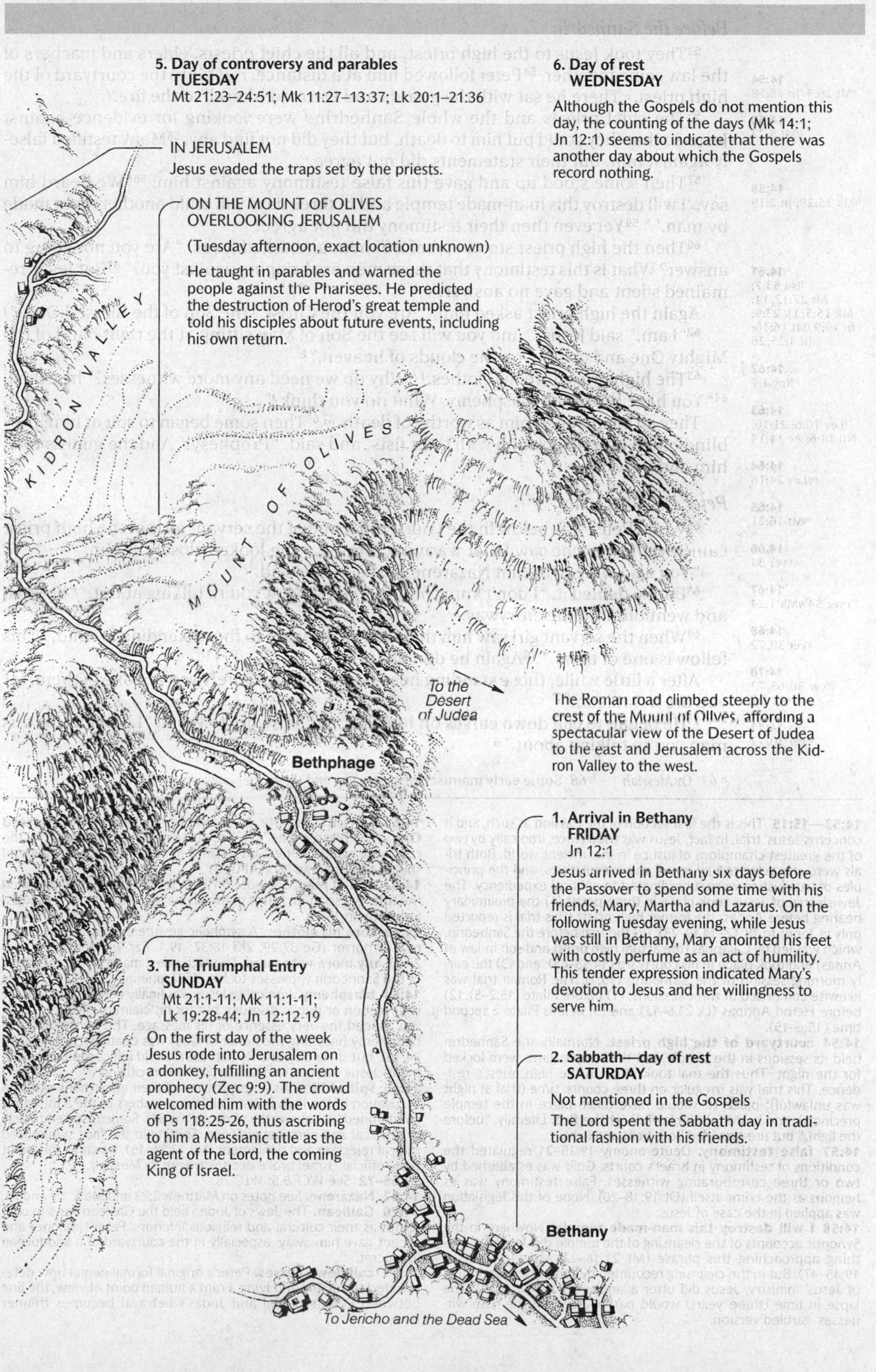
5. Day of controversy and parables
TUESDAY
Mt 21:23–24:51; Mk 11:27–13:37; Lk 20:1–21:36
IN JERUSALEM
Jesus evaded the traps set by the priests.
ON THE MOUNT OF OLIVES OVERLOOKING JERUSALEM
(Tuesday afternoon, exact location unknown)
He taught in parables and warned the people against the Pharisees. He predicted the destruction of Herod's great temple and told his disciples about future events, including his own return.
6. Day of rest
WEDNESDAY
Although the Gospels do not mention this day, the counting of the days (Mk 14:1; Jn 12:1) seems to indicate that there was another day about which the Gospels record nothing.
KIDRON VALLEY
MOUNT OF OLIVES
To the Desert of Judea
The Roman road climbed steeply to the crest of the Mount of Olives, affording a spectacular view of the Desert of Judea to the east and Jerusalem across the Kidron Valley to the west.
Bethphage
1. Arrival in Bethany
FRIDAY
Jn 12:1
Jesus arrived in Bethany six days before the Passover to spend some time with his friends, Mary, Martha and Lazarus. On the following Tuesday evening, while Jesus was still in Bethany, Mary anointed his feet with costly perfume as an act of humility. This tender expression indicated Mary's devotion to Jesus and her willingness to serve him.
3. The Triumphal Entry
SUNDAY
Mt 21:1-11; Mk 11:1-11; Lk 19:28-44; Jn 12:12-19
On the first day of the week Jesus rode into Jerusalem on a donkey, fulfilling an ancient prophecy (Zec 9:9). The crowd welcomed him with the words of Ps 118:25-26, thus ascribing to him a Messianic title as the agent of the Lord, the coming King of Israel.
2. Sabbath—day of rest
SATURDAY
Not mentioned in the Gospels
The Lord spent the Sabbath day in traditional fashion with his friends.
Bethany
To Jericho and the Dead Sea

Before the Sanhedrin

53 They took Jesus to the high priest, and all the chief priests, elders and teachers of
the law came together. 54 Peter followed him at a distance, right into the courtyard of the
high priest.[e] There he sat with the guards and warmed himself at the fire.[f]
55 The chief priests and the whole Sanhedrin[g] were looking for evidence against
Jesus so that they could put him to death, but they did not find any. 56 Many testified falsely against him, but their statements did not agree.
57 Then some stood up and gave this false testimony against him: 58 "We heard him
say, 'I will destroy this man-made temple and in three days will build another,[h] not made
by man.' " 59 Yet even then their testimony did not agree.
60 Then the high priest stood up before them and asked Jesus, "Are you not going to
answer? What is this testimony that these men are bringing against you?" 61 But Jesus remained silent and gave no answer.[i]
Again the high priest asked him, "Are you the Christ,[a] the Son of the Blessed One?"[j]
62 "I am," said Jesus. "And you will see the Son of Man sitting at the right hand of the
Mighty One and coming on the clouds of heaven."[k]
63 The high priest tore his clothes.[l] "Why do we need any more witnesses?" he asked.
64 "You have heard the blasphemy. What do you think?"
They all condemned him as worthy of death.[m] 65 Then some began to spit at him; they
blindfolded him, struck him with their fists, and said, "Prophesy!" And the guards took
him and beat him.[n]

Peter Disowns Jesus

66 While Peter was below in the courtyard,[o] one of the servant girls of the high priest
came by. 67 When she saw Peter warming himself,[p] she looked closely at him.
"You also were with that Nazarene, Jesus,"[q] she said.
68 But he denied it. "I don't know or understand what you're talking about,"[r] he said,
and went out into the entryway.[b]
69 When the servant girl saw him there, she said again to those standing around, "This
fellow is one of them." 70 Again he denied it.[s]
After a little while, those standing near said to Peter, "Surely you are one of them, for
you are a Galilean."[t]
71 He began to call down curses on himself, and he swore to them, "I don't know this
man you're talking about."[u]

14:54 [e]Mt 26:3 [f]Jn 18:18
14:55 [g]Mt 5:22
14:58 [h]Mk 15:29; Jn 2:19
14:61 [i]Isa 53:7; Mt 27:12,14; Mk 15:5; Lk 23:9; Jn 19:9 [j]Mt 16:16; Jn 4:25,26
14:62 [k]Rev 1:7
14:63 [l]Lev 10:6; 21:10; Nu 14:6; Ac 14:14
14:64 [m]Lev 24:16
14:65 [n]Mt 16:21
14:66 [o]ver 54
14:67 [p]ver 54 [q]Mk 1:24
14:68 [r]ver 30,72
14:70 [s]ver 30,68,72 [t]Ac 2:7
14:71 [u]ver 30,72

[a] *61* Or *Messiah* [b] *68* Some early manuscripts *entryway and the rooster crowed*

14:53—15:15 This is the first section of the Passion as such, and it concerns Jesus' trial. In fact, Jesus was tried twice, ironically by two of the greatest champions of justice in the ancient world. Both trials were characterized by errors and irregularities, and the principles of true justice were subordinated to political expediency. The Jewish trial of Jesus took place in three parts: (1) the preliminary hearing before Annas, the former high priest (this trial is reported only in John; Jn 18:12–14,19–23); (2) the trial before the Sanhedrin, which was led by Caiaphas (the actual high priest and son-in-law of Annas) and took place in his courtyard (14:53–65); and (3) the early morning session of the Sanhedrin (15:1). The Roman trial was likewise comprised of three sessions: (1) before Pilate (15:2–5), (2) before Herod Antipas (Lk 23:6–12) and (3) before Pilate a second time (15:6–15).
14:54 courtyard of the high priest. Normally the Sanhedrin held its sessions in the temple, but the temple gates were locked for the night. Thus the trial took place in the high priest's residence. This trial was irregular on three counts: time (trial at night was unlawful); place (it should have taken place in the temple precincts); and haste (also unlawful). **at the fire.** Literally, "before the light," but fire provided both heat and light.
14:57 false testimony. Deuteronomy 19:15–21 regulated the conditions of testimony in Israel's courts. Guilt was established by two or three corroborating witnesses. False testimony was as heinous as the crime itself (Dt 19:18–20). None of this legislation was applied in the case of Jesus.
14:58 I will destroy this man-made temple. Nowhere in the Synoptic accounts of the cleansing of the temple did Jesus say anything approaching this phrase (Mt 21:18–22; Mk 11:12–18; Lk 19:45–47). But in the cleansing recounted by John at the beginning of Jesus' ministry, Jesus did utter a similar phrase (Jn 2:19). The lapse in time (three years) would partially explain the false witnesses' garbled version.
14:61 Christ. See note on Matthew 1:1. **Son of the Blessed One.** "The Blessed One" is a circumlocution for "God" used by the rabbis to avoid taking God's name in vain. The title in general should thus be read "Son of God."
14:62 Son of Man. See note on 2:10. Jesus immediately modified the title "Messiah" in terms of the divine figure of Daniel 7. **clouds.** See note on 13:26.
14:63 tore his clothes. A symbolic gesture expressing great sorrow or horror (Ge 37:29; 2Ki 18:37; 19:1; Ezr 9:3; Jer 36:24; Joel 2:13). **any more witnesses.** The high priest made all the members of the Sanhedrin witnesses to Jesus' blasphemy.
14:64 blasphemy. Ironically, Jesus was finally condemned not for insurrection or public disorder, but for his claim to divinity, which was indeed the very essence of his message. The punishment for blasphemy (insulting the honor of God) was death by stoning (Lev 24:16), but since only the Roman court could inflict capital punishment, Jesus was put to death by Roman crucifixion.
14:65 spit at him. As an expression of their agreement with the accusation of the high priest, "all [the members of the Sanhedrin] condemned him as worthy of death" (v. 64). Some resorted to acts of physical and personal violence. Spitting in the face symbolized radical rejection and defilement (Nu 12:14–15). It was at this point that "official" Israel broke decisively with its Messiah.
14:66–72 See *WCF* 5.5; *WLC* 78.
14:67 Nazarene. See notes on Matthew 2:23 and Mark 1:9 and 24.
14:70 Galilean. The Jews of Judea held the Galilean Jews in contempt as their cultural and religious inferiors. Peter's manner and accent gave him away, especially in the courtyard of a Sadducean aristocrat.
14:71 call down curses. Peter's original formal denial now deteriorated to cursing and lying. From a human point of view, the line between Peter's denial and Judas's betrayal becomes thinner here.

72Immediately the rooster crowed the second time.[a] Then Peter remembered the
word Jesus had spoken to him: "Before the rooster crows twice[b] you will disown me three
times."[v] And he broke down and wept.

Jesus Before Pilate

15 Very early in the morning, the chief priests, with the elders, the teachers of the
law[w] and the whole Sanhedrin,[x] reached a decision. They bound Jesus, led him
away and handed him over to Pilate.[y]

2"Are you the king of the Jews?"[z] asked Pilate.
"Yes, it is as you say," Jesus replied.

3The chief priests accused him of many things. 4So again Pilate asked him, "Aren't
you going to answer? See how many things they are accusing you of."

5But Jesus still made no reply,[a] and Pilate was amazed.

6Now it was the custom at the Feast to release a prisoner whom the people requested. 7A man called Barabbas was in prison with the insurrectionists who had committed
murder in the uprising. 8The crowd came up and asked Pilate to do for them what he
usually did.

9"Do you want me to release to you the king of the Jews?"[b] asked Pilate, 10knowing
it was out of envy that the chief priests had handed Jesus over to him. 11But the chief
priests stirred up the crowd to have Pilate release Barabbas[c] instead.

12"What shall I do, then, with the one you call the king of the Jews?" Pilate asked them.

13"Crucify him!" they shouted.

14"Why? What crime has he committed?" asked Pilate.
But they shouted all the louder, "Crucify him!"

15Wanting to satisfy the crowd, Pilate released Barabbas to them. He had Jesus
flogged,[d] and handed him over to be crucified.

The Soldiers Mock Jesus

16The soldiers led Jesus away into the palace[e] (that is, the Praetorium) and called together the whole company of soldiers. 17They put a purple robe on him, then twisted together a crown of thorns and set it on him. 18And they began to call out to him, "Hail,

14:72 [v]ver 30,68
15:1 [w]Mt 27:1; Lk 22:66 [x]Mt 5:22 [y]Mt 27:2
15:2 [z]ver 9,12,18,26; Mt 2:2
15:5 [a]Mk 14:61
15:9 [b]ver 2
15:11 [c]Ac 3:14
15:15 [d]Isa 53:6
15:16 [e]Jn 18:28,33; 19:9

[a] *72* Some early manuscripts do not have *the second time.* [b] *72* Some early manuscripts do not have *twice.*

14:72 wept. Jesus' ministry of preparation of the Twelve (see note on 3:14) would appear to be a veritable disaster. In this crucial chapter, they slept at a time when his suffering was unbearable (v. 37), one of them betrayed him to the Sanhedrin (vv. 44–45), all deserted him (v. 50) and one denied all knowledge of him (v. 71). Little wonder there was shame (see note on v. 52) and weeping. The later radical change in the Eleven (excluding Judas) can only be explained adequately by Jesus' resurrection.
15:1 Very early in the morning. Probably at dawn. It appears that the Sanhedrin met again (so soon after the night session) in order to give legality to their proceedings. Nevertheless, the accusation of blasphemy, which had been established the previous night, would hardly have impressed the Roman civil court, so the second session may well have had the further goal (Lk 23:2 confirms this) of formulating a civil charge. **Pilate.** The phrase in the Apostles' Creed "suffered under Pontius Pilate" ties the Christian faith to a verifiable historical event. A large stone belonging to an official building in Caesarea of the first century bears Pilate's name and rank. Pilate was the Roman governor of Judea from A.D. 26 to 36. As supreme magistrate, only he had the legal right to pronounce a sentence of capital punishment (see note on 14:64).
15:2 king of the Jews? This term is ambiguous. In a mere political sense, the Herods were Jewish kings and Jesus was not. Nevertheless, Jesus was king in the sense that he ushered in the kingdom of God and fulfilled Old Testament Messianic hopes. **Yes, it is as you say.** The original is much more vague. Jesus literally replied to Pilate, "You say." Pilate did not follow up on Jesus' response but asked why Jesus did not answer (v. 4), perhaps indicating that Jesus had purposefully made an ambiguous or unintelligible reply.
15:3 Aren't you going to answer? No doubt Pilate wanted to make Jesus realize that, before the law, silence implied acquiescence.
15:7 Barabbas. In view of the information in this verse, it would be safe to conclude that Barabbas was a Zealot seeking the military overthrow of Rome (see note on 3:18). His name probably means "son of a rabbi." Ironically, some early manuscripts of Matthew 27:16 give Barabbas's first name as Jesus, a common name during this period and another form of Joshua, which means "savior." The option that Pilate proposed to the crowd (v. 9) was thus an unwittingly poignant choice between two kinds of saviors: (1) Jesus Barabbas, the would-be political savior of Israel; or (2) Jesus of Nazareth, the suffering servant of the Lord who would save his people from their sins (Mt 1:21).
15:13 Crucify. Of Persian origin and adopted first by the Carthaginians and then by the Romans, this cruel and shameful form of capital punishment was illegal for the execution of Roman citizens and was used mainly for slaves and insurrectionists (Ac 5:37). Metal spikes were driven through the wrists or hands (Jn 20:25) and the heels of the victim, who slowly bled in excruciating pain. Breaking the victim's legs (Jn 19:33) caused death to come more quickly by suffocation and loss of blood to the brain, because the victim could not use his legs to lift his torso to aid breathing. As Paul noted, the crucifixion of Jesus brought God's Son publicly under the Father's curse (Gal 3:13).
15:15 Wanting to satisfy the crowd. The illegality of the Roman trial (cf. note on 14:54) consisted in the fact that Pilate, though implicitly declaring Jesus innocent (v. 14; cf. Jn 18:38), still handed him over to be crucified, merely to please the crowd. **flogged.** According to Roman custom, flogging always preceded crucifixion.
15:16 Praetorium. Originally the word was used for military headquarters, but it had also come to mean "barracks." **whole company.** Literally, "cohort" (a tenth part of a Roman legion) or 600 men, though not all were necessarily present.
15:17 purple robe. Due to the difficulty of its production and its high cost, purple was a mark of high rank and dignity (Est 1:6; Pr 31:22; Lk 16:19; Rev 17:4) and thus of royalty (SS 3:10; 7:5; cf. 2Ch 2:7,14; 3:14). The robe placed on Jesus had no doubt seen better days. **crown of thorns.** That Jesus wore a crown of thorns symbolized his bearing the divine curse (see note on v. 13) of the ground, of which thorns are the immediate result (Ge 3:17–18).
15:18 Hail. The salutation, spitting and feigned homage (v. 19) were mock expressions of the kind of respect due to royalty. The sadism of the soldiers was unprovoked, for they were not even Jews. Their attitude can perhaps best be explained by the fact that they were Syrian Arabs who were capable of communicating with Jesus, doubtless in Aramaic, and who thus used the occasion to humiliate a perceived Jewish Messianic pretender.

15:18 [f]ver 2 — king of the Jews!"[f] 19 Again and again they struck him on the head with a staff and spit
on him. Falling on their knees, they paid homage to him. 20 And when they had mocked
15:20 — him, they took off the purple robe and put his own clothes on him. Then they led him
[g]Heb 13:12 — out[g] to crucify him.

15:21 [h]Mt 27:32 —
The Crucifixion

[i]Ro 16:13 [j]Mt 27:32; — 21 A certain man from Cyrene,[h] Simon, the father of Alexander and Rufus,[i] was pass-
Lk 23:26 — ing by on his way in from the country, and they forced him to carry the cross.[j] 22 They
15:23 — brought Jesus to the place called Golgotha (which means The Place of the Skull). 23 Then
[k]ver 36; Ps 69:21; — they offered him wine mixed with myrrh,[k] but he did not take it. 24 And they crucified
Pr 31:6 — him. Dividing up his clothes, they cast lots[l] to see what each would get.
15:24 [l]Ps 22:18 — 25 It was the third hour when they crucified him. 26 The written notice of the charge
against him read: THE KING OF THE JEWS.[m] 27 They crucified two robbers with him, one on
15:26 [m]ver 2 — his right and one on his left.[a] 29 Those who passed by hurled insults at him, shaking their
heads[n] and saying, "So! You who are going to destroy the temple and build it in three
15:29 [n]Ps 22:7; 109:25 — days,[o] 30 come down from the cross and save yourself!"
[o]Mk 14:58; Jn 2:19 — 31 In the same way the chief priests and the teachers of the law mocked him[p] among
15:31 [p]Ps 22:7 — themselves. "He saved others," they said, "but he can't save himself! 32 Let this Christ,[b][q]
this King of Israel,[r] come down now from the cross, that we may see and believe." Those
15:32 [q]Mk 14:61 [r]ver 2 — crucified with him also heaped insults on him.

15:33 [s]Am 8:9 —
The Death of Jesus

33 At the sixth hour darkness came over the whole land until the ninth hour.[s] 34 And
15:34 [t]Ps 22:1 — at the ninth hour Jesus cried out in a loud voice, *"Eloi, Eloi, lama sabachthani?"*—which
means, "My God, my God, why have you forsaken me?"[c][t]
15:36 [u]ver 23; Ps 69:21 — 35 When some of those standing near heard this, they said, "Listen, he's calling Elijah."
36 One man ran, filled a sponge with wine vinegar,[u] put it on a stick, and offered it to
15:37 [v]Jn 19:30 — Jesus to drink. "Now leave him alone. Let's see if Elijah comes to take him down," he said.
15:38 — 37 With a loud cry, Jesus breathed his last.[v]
[w]Heb 10:19,20 — 38 The curtain of the temple was torn in two from top to bottom.[w] 39 And when the cen-

[a] *27* Some manuscripts *left, [28] and the scripture was fulfilled which says, "He was counted with the lawless ones"* (Isaiah 53:12) [b] *32* Or *Messiah* [c] *34* Psalm 22:1

15:21 Cyrene. An important city of Lydia. A large Jewish settlement existed there (Ac 6:9), and Simon was probably a Jew in Jerusalem for the Passover (Ac 2:10). **Alexander and Rufus.** Simon's sons were members of the Christian community to which Mark wrote, probably in Rome (see Ro 16:13). **carry the cross.** Usually the condemned man would carry at least the crossbar, weighing 30 to 40 pounds. Simon, taking up the cross of Jesus, became a visual image of the devotion Jesus demands of his followers (8:34).
15:22 Place of the Skull. A macabre but chillingly appropriate name that probably referred to the shape of the hill that was the site of the execution.
15:23 wine mixed with myrrh. A primitive form of painkiller. Myrrh was an expensive spice extracted from the leaves of the cistus or labdanum tree and was used as a cosmetic ointment. It was offered to Jesus at his birth as a gift for the king (Mt 2:11), as well as applied to his body for his anointing after death (Jn 19:39–40).
15:24 Dividing up his clothes. These were the spoils reserved for the execution squad. These men had no qualms about dividing up the prisoner's clothing before he was dead. This seemingly unimportant detail is in fact a remarkable fulfillment of Psalm 22:18, which graphically describes the agony of a violent and undeserved death (see Ps 22:16). Jesus later (v. 34) cited this psalm to express the degree of his suffering.
15:25 third hour. 9:00 A.M.
15:26 the charge. Called the *titulus* in Latin, it was a traditional part of crucifixion. The official charge was written down, carried before the prisoner on his way to the site of execution and affixed behind his head to his cross. It was Pilate (Jn 19:19–22), not the Jews, who insisted on this particular inscription.
15:27 two robbers. Though the Greek word often means "robber," it can carry the more general sense of "criminal," which was the case here since robbery was not punishable by crucifixion (see note on 14:48).
15:28 See *BC* 21.
15:29 See note on 14:58.
15:30 come down. This was both an insult and a diabolical temptation similar to those proposed to Jesus at the beginning of his ministry (Mt 4:2–6). Note also the mockery of the Jewish leaders and even of those crucified with Jesus (vv. 31–32). The devil was still at work, seeking to subvert the work of redemption at the very moment it was being accomplished, which was also the moment of Jesus' greatest physical and no doubt emotional weakness (14:38).
15:33 sixth hour. Noon. **darkness.** This recalls the darkness in Egypt, which lasted three days at the time of the death of the firstborn sons (Ex 10:22). See also the prophecy of Amos, where the Lord promised to "make the sun go down at noon and darken the earth in broad daylight." This occurrence is described by the prophet as a "time like mourning for an only son" (Am 8:9–10). **ninth hour.** 3:00 P.M.
15:34 *Eloi, Eloi.* Jesus cited in Aramaic the first verse of Psalm 22. Even in the jaws of death, Jesus revealed his love for Scripture. See note on 12:37.
15:35 Elijah. Some in the crowd mistook "*Eloi*" for "Elijah," especially since in some circles it was believed that Elijah would return (6:15; 8:28). See note on Matthew 27:46.
15:36 wine vinegar. Literally, "sour." The term referred to cheap wine that had almost become vinegar. The offer of wine vinegar was not the same as the offer of wine and myrrh (v. 23). This was likely no humanitarian act to relieve suffering but rather a cruel offering intended to prolong suffering by reviving Jesus in order to see whether "Elijah" would indeed come at his call.
15:37 loud cry. Jesus had been hanging on the cross, undergoing mental and physical agony, for six hours (vv. 25,34). Crucifixion could last two or three days when there was a seat and/or footrest to facilitate the circulation of blood. Whatever the length of time, the victim, before expiring, would slowly lose consciousness due to a loss of blood. This did not happen in Jesus' case, indicating that the manner of his dying was unusual.
15:38 The curtain of the temple was torn in two. The death of Jesus was the final and definitive sacrifice for sin (Heb 7:27). The Old Testament administration of the covenant of grace was brought to a decisive end. No longer would the high priest need to enter into the Most Holy Place behind the curtain to atone for the sins of the people (Ex 26:31–33; cf. Heb 9:1–10). Jesus has become the new and eternal high priest (Heb 8:1), the perfect sacrificial

turion,[x] who stood there in front of Jesus, heard his cry and[a] saw how he died, he said,
"Surely this man was the Son[b] of God!"[y]
40Some women were watching from a distance.[z] Among them were Mary Magdalene,
Mary the mother of James the younger and of Joses, and Salome.[a] 41In Galilee these
women had followed him and cared for his needs. Many other women who had come up
with him to Jerusalem were also there.[b]

The Burial of Jesus

42It was Preparation Day (that is, the day before the Sabbath).[c] So as evening approached, 43Joseph of Arimathea, a prominent member of the Council,[d] who was himself
waiting for the kingdom of God,[e] went boldly to Pilate and asked for Jesus' body. 44Pilate was
surprised to hear that he was already dead. Summoning the centurion, he asked him if Jesus
had already died. 45When he learned from the centurion[f] that it was so, he gave the body
to Joseph. 46So Joseph bought some linen cloth, took down the body, wrapped it in the lin-
en, and placed it in a tomb cut out of rock. Then he rolled a stone against the entrance of
the tomb.[g] 47Mary Magdalene and Mary the mother of Joses[h] saw where he was laid.

The Resurrection

16 When the Sabbath was over, Mary Magdalene, Mary the mother of James, and
Salome bought spices[i] so that they might go to anoint Jesus' body. 2Very early on
the first day of the week, just after sunrise, they were on their way to the tomb 3and they
asked each other, "Who will roll the stone away from the entrance of the tomb?"[j]
4But when they looked up, they saw that the stone, which was very large, had been
rolled away. 5As they entered the tomb, they saw a young man dressed in a white robe[k]
sitting on the right side, and they were alarmed.
6"Don't be alarmed," he said. "You are looking for Jesus the Nazarene,[l] who was crucified. He has risen! He is not here. See the place where they laid him. 7But go, tell his disciples and Peter, 'He is going ahead of you into Galilee. There you will see him,[m] just as
he told you.' "[n]

15:39 [x]ver 45 [y]Mk 1:1, 11; 9:7; Mt 4:3
15:40 [z]Ps 38:11 [a]Mk 16:1; Lk 24:10; Jn 19:25
15:41 [b]Mt 27:55,56; Lk 8:2,3
15:42 [c]Mt 27:62; Jn 19:31
15:43 [d]Mt 5:22 [e]Mt 3:2; Lk 2:25,38
15:45 [f]ver 39
15:46 [g]Mk 16:3
15:47 [h]ver 40
16:1 [i]Lk 23:56; Jn 19:39,40
16:3 [j]Mk 15:46
16:5 [k]Jn 20:12
16:6 [l]Mk 1:24
16:7 [m]Jn 21:1-23 [n]Mk 14:28

[a] 39 Some manuscripts do not have *heard his cry and* [b] 39 Or *a son*

victim (Heb 9:14) who has obtained for his people "eternal redemption" (Heb 9:12).

15:39 centurion. A Roman officer responsible for 100 men. This man was no doubt responsible for the detachment that put Jesus to death. Thus, he was well situated to observe the death of Jesus (see note on v. 37). **Son of God!** It is unlikely that a Roman pagan would see in this term the Jewish/Old Testament notion of the Messiah or the Christian Trinitarian concept of the eternal Son. Rather, the title would connote for him the Hellenistic idea of a special human being who was favored by the gods. This is confirmed by the ambiguity of the Greek, which could also be translated "a son of God." Nevertheless Mark, who wrote to Gentile Christians, revealed in the centurion's confession the irony that a Roman Gentile attributed this title to Jesus while the Jews denied that he was the Son of God. The centurion's confession stands as the climax of Mark's Gospel, which had begun with the following words: "The beginning of the gospel about Jesus Christ, the Son of God" (1:1).

15:40 Mary Magdalene. From Magdala, a village on the southwestern shore of the Sea of Galilee. See 16:9 and Luke 8:2. **Mary the mother of James the younger and of Joses.** See verse 47; 16:1 and note on Luke 24:10. Only known from the crucifixion account recorded here and in Matthew 27:56 and perhaps Luke 24:10. **Salome.** The mother of James and John (Mt 27:56; cf. Mt 20:20–21).

15:41 Many other women. All the men—except for John, the beloved disciple—had fled (Jn 19:26,35).

15:42 Preparation Day. The day before the Sabbath (Friday). Food was prepared before sunset, at which time the Sabbath began. In this particular case, Joseph would have to have bought the linen, made arrangements for Jesus' burial and readied the tomb (vv. 43–46) during the three hours between Jesus' death and sunset. See *WLC* 121.

15:43 Joseph of Arimathea. From Ramah (in Judea), 20 miles northwest of Jerusalem, the city of the prophet Samuel (1Sa 1:1). He was no doubt a pious Pharisee but also a secret follower of Jesus. **Council.** The Sanhedrin. **kingdom of God.** See theological article "The Kingdom of God" at Matthew 4. **went boldly.** This was a great act of faith, and it came at a time when all of Jesus' other disciples had fled. Joseph put himself in conflict with the decision of the Sanhedrin and jeopardized his entire future in Judaism.

15:44 Pilate was surprised. Pilate's surprise again confirms the unusual character of Jesus' death. See note on verse 37.

15:46 tomb cut out of a rock. According to Matthew 27:60, the tomb belonged to Joseph and his family. Such a family burial site typically consisted of an ornately painted vestibule from which a passageway led to individual, drawer-like crypts cut into the rock. Each crypt was sealed by a heavy rolling stone that was fitted into a groove hewn into the rock.

■ **16:1–20** *Resurrection and Vindication.* Mark closed his Gospel with an account of the resurrection and appearances of Christ. (See chart titled "Resurrection Appearances" at Lk 24.) Jesus' new life vindicated his entire ministry and encouraged his disciples to fulfill the worldwide ministry to which he had called them.

16:1 the Sabbath was over. Sunset (6:00 P.M.) on Saturday evening, a time appropriate for buying spices but not typically for visiting tombs. **anoint.** This is not a reference to embalming. Embalming was a process developed by the Egyptians in the hope of ensuring survival in the next world (see note on 14:8). Anointing, in contrast, was a way of showing affection for the one who had died.

16:3 Who will roll the stone away . . . ? Having seen the "very large" (v. 4) stone put in its place (15:47), they realized it would be difficult to move it out of the groove in which it was lodged (see note on 15:46).

16:5 As they entered the tomb. Strictly speaking, they entered the vestibule of the burial chamber, at the far end of which was the individual tomb where Jesus' body had been laid. See note on 15:46. **young man.** No ordinary young man would have caused such alarm, trembling and bewilderment (vv. 6,8) in these adult women. Thus Mark's Gospel corroborates Matthew's, which specifies that he was in fact an angel (Mt 28:2).

16:6 Nazarene. See note on 14:67. **He has risen!** If the Gospel of Mark reaches its climax in the confession of Jesus as the Son of God (see note on 15:39), a second climax is reached with the declaration of Jesus' resurrection, which confirms that his preaching concerning the coming of the kingdom in power was true (see notes on 1:15; 9:1). See theological article "The Resurrection of Jesus" at Luke 24.

16:7 and Peter. These two words make all the difference in the subsequent history of redemption and in the enormous role that Peter would play in it. By their use Mark indicated, as he brought

8 Trembling and bewildered, the women went out and fled from the tomb. They said
nothing to anyone, because they were afraid.

[The earliest manuscripts and some other ancient witnesses
do not have Mark 16:9–20.]

9 When Jesus rose early on the first day of the week, he appeared first to Mary Magdalene,[o] out of whom he had driven seven demons. 10 She went and told those who had
been with him and who were mourning and weeping. 11 When they heard that Jesus was
alive and that she had seen him, they did not believe it.[p]
12 Afterward Jesus appeared in a different form to two of them while they were walking in the country.[q] 13 These returned and reported it to the rest; but they did not believe
them either.
14 Later Jesus appeared to the Eleven as they were eating; he rebuked them for their
lack of faith and their stubborn refusal to believe those who had seen him after he had
risen.[r]
15 He said to them, "Go into all the world and preach the good news to all creation.[s]
16 Whoever believes and is baptized will be saved, but whoever does not believe will be
condemned.[t] 17 And these signs will accompany those who believe: In my name they will
drive out demons;[u] they will speak in new tongues;[v] 18 they will pick up snakes[w] with
their hands; and when they drink deadly poison, it will not hurt them at all; they will
place their hands on[x] sick people, and they will get well."
19 After the Lord Jesus had spoken to them, he was taken up into heaven[y] and he sat
at the right hand of God.[z] 20 Then the disciples went out and preached everywhere, and
the Lord worked with them and confirmed his word by the signs that accompanied it.

16:9 [o]Jn 20:11-18
16:11 [p]ver 13,14; Lk 24:11
16:12 [q]Lk 24:13-32
16:14 [r]Lk 24:36-43
16:15 [s]Mt 28:18-20; Lk 24:47,48
16:16 [t]Jn 3:16,18,36; Ac 16:31
16:17 [u]Mk 9:38; Lk 10:17; Ac 5:16; 8:7; 16:18; 19:13-16 [v]Ac 2:4; 10:46; 19:6; 1Co 12:10, 28,30
16:18 [w]Lk 10:19; Ac 28:3-5 [x]Ac 6:6
16:19 [y]Lk 24:50,51; Jn 6:62; Ac 1:9-11; 1Ti 3:16 [z]Ps 110:1; Ro 8:34; Col 3:1; Heb 1:3; 12:2

---

his Gospel to an end (see note on vv. 9–20), that Jesus' preparation of the Twelve would not have been for nothing. **He is going ahead.** See note on 14:28.
16:8 afraid. If verses 9–20 are not original (see note on vv. 9–20), then the Gospel of Mark ends with the word "afraid." Note, however, that the word means "reverential fear" and that the same state of mind was produced in the disciples at the sight of the transfigured Jesus (9:6)—a sort of anticipated resurrection appearance. But the women's initial silence was in fact disobedience (v. 7).
16:9–20 These verses do not appear in some of the most important early manuscripts. Their absence as well as their different style and vocabulary raise serious doubts about their authenticity.
16:9 Mary Magdalene. See note on 15:40.
16:12 two of them. Compare Luke 24:13–35.
16:14 See *WCF* 17.3.
16:15–16 See *WCF* 7.3; 28.4; *WLC* 60,63; *HC* 71.
16:15 Go into all the world. Compare. Matthew 28:19. See *WLC* 35.
16:17 signs. All of the events predicted here (except drinking deadly poison) are recorded in the New Testament, especially in the book of Acts (see also Ro 15:19; Heb 2:3–4).
16:19 right hand of God. A position of executive authority that Jesus shares with God the Father (Php 2:7; cf. Pss 14:62; 110:1). See *WCF* 8.4; *WLC* 51; *WSC* 28; *BC* 35.
16:20 confirmed his word by the signs. See note on verse 17.

LUKE

Introduction

Overview

Author: Luke

Purpose: To present a true and orderly account that establishes the facts of Jesus' ministry and their importance in salvation history and to guide the church as it preaches repentance and forgiveness in Jesus' name to all nations.

Date: c. A.D. 60–63

Key Truths:

- Jesus' was Israel's Messiah.
- Jesus brought the kingdom of God.
- Jesus consciously controlled the events in his life to fulfill his ministry and to render himself as an offering for sin in the crucifixion.
- The facts of the gospel are historically verified. Jesus Christ truly was born, crucified, buried, rose from the grave and ascended into heaven.
- Salvation is available to all people, including the socially disenfranchised. Accordingly, Christians must welcome and honor all who come to Christ.
- Prayer is an important element in every believer's life.

Author

It is commonly accepted that the same man wrote both Luke and Acts (see "Introduction to Acts"). The style and vocabulary are similar, and both books are addressed to Theophilus. Although the author never identifies himself by name, some passages in Acts use the pronoun "we" (Ac 16:10–17; 20:5–16; 21:1–18; 27:1—28:16), indicating that the author was Paul's companion on some of his travels. Only a few individuals are named in the letters Paul wrote from Rome (where the "we" sections end; see Ac 28:16) but not named in Acts. Of these people, the most likely author of these two books is Luke. This view is supported by tradition, which unanimously ascribes the book to Luke.

The preface makes clear that the writer was not an eyewitness of the things he recorded. Both the Gospel of Luke and Acts reveal that the author was a man of culture who had researched the information he needed for his writing but who was not one of the original followers of Jesus. An objection to Lukan authorship is that the theology, especially of Acts, has different emphases from those of Paul. But there is no reason why Luke should simply repeat what Paul said. Nor is it likely that Luke was one of Paul's converts. The writer does not contradict Paul, even though he does not quote him.

Nothing is known of Luke other than what we can glean from his two books and from the scant references to him in Paul's letters (Col 4:14; 2Ti 4:11; Phm 24). There is a tradition that he came from Antioch, and Colossians 4:14 indicates that he was a physician. Lukan authorship has sometimes been defended by noting medical language in Luke and Acts, but it has been shown that medical men in New Testament times used the ordinary language of laypeople and did not have a technical language of their own. There is nothing inconsistent with the tradition, however, and the author certainly shows an interest in the sick.

Time and Place of Writing

The Gospel of Luke may have been written around A.D. 63. Luke was written before Acts (see Ac 1:1; cf. Lk 1:1–4), and Acts ends with Paul in prison in Rome. Paul's Roman imprisonment ended in A.D. 63, and it is reasonable to hold that if Luke had known of Paul's release or death, he would have mentioned it. This points to a date of composition for Acts by A.D. 63 and a somewhat earlier date for Luke. Also, since Luke noted in Acts 11:28 the fulfillment of Agabus's prophecy, he likely would have noted the same with respect to Jesus' prophecy regarding the destruction of Jerusalem (Lk 21:20) if he had written after A.D. 70. Those who argue for a date of A.D. 75–85 hold that some of Luke's wording presupposes the destruction of Jerusalem (e.g., 19:43; 21:20,24). But these passages speak of what was customary in sieges of the time, and if we grant that Jesus predicted that current policies would mean eventual disaster, not much can be made of them. A few critics have argued for a date in the second century, but there is little evidence to support this view.

Original Audience

Luke directly addressed Theophilus (1:3) as the recipient of his Gospel. *Theophilus* means "lover of God," so some interpreters have suggested that the name refers not to a specific man but to dedicated disciples. The appellation "most excellent" (1:3), however, supports the view that Theophilus was a real person. Nevertheless, what was primarily directed to him would be secondarily directed to every other believer as well.

Purpose and Distinctives

The preface to Luke's Gospel explains that Luke wrote primarily to give "an orderly account" (1:3) so that Theophilus might "know the certainty of the things" (1:4) he had heard. In a word, Luke intended to tell the truth about what Jesus had done. Yet his main concern was not mere historical reporting; he was primarily interested in explaining the history of salvation. Luke presented his record to display what God had done in Jesus to bring the historical accomplishment of salvation to its final stages. In this respect he presented Jesus as the Messiah who introduced the kingdom of God (12:35–48; 17:22–37; 21:25–26).

At the same time, Luke did not neglect the personal and human side of Jesus' life. Luke concerned himself with many people who would have been neglected by most writers of his day: children, women and poor people. Although many regarded these people as insignificant, Luke demonstrated Jesus' special concern for them.

Luke was clearly a cultured individual who was able to write in a variety of styles. His opening paragraph resembles older, sophisticated Greek, but at other times his language evokes memories of the simpler language of the Septuagint (the Greek translation of the OT). Clearly he saw this as a suitable style for the religious writing in which he was engaged.

Luke's descriptions of Jesus' journey toward Jerusalem and the sacrifice on the cross (9:51—19:44) are prominent in the literary structure of the Gospel. The sovereignty of God in Jesus' ministry and death is highlighted as Jesus moved toward the city where he would die for sinners (9:22; 17:25; 18:31–33; cf. Ac 4:28).

Luke also stressed the importance of prayer. He recorded that Jesus prayed before crucial occasions of his ministry. Nine prayers of Jesus are included in the Gospel (seven of which are found only in Luke), along with parables on prayer recorded only in Luke.

Luke was also interested in emotional reactions to Jesus. For instance, only his Gospel includes the magnificent songs of joy that accompanied the birth of the Messiah (1:46–55,68–79; 2:14,29–32).

Outline

I. Preface (1:1–4)

Luke identified his recipient and his desire to write a reliable history of Jesus.

II. Preparations for Jesus' Public Ministry (1:5—4:13)
- A. Two Mothers, Two Infants (1:5—2:52)
- B. John's Ministry as Forerunner (3:1–20)
- C. Jesus' Initiation (3:21—4:13)

Luke reported important events before Jesus' public ministry began. He stressed that the roles of John and Jesus were intertwined. God was intervening to bring salvation to his people.

III. Jesus' Public Ministry in Galilee (4:14—9:50)
- A. The Sermon at Nazareth (4:14–30)
- B. Teaching and Miracles (4:31—6:11)
- C. Choosing the Twelve (6:12–16)
- D. The Sermon on the Plain (6:17–49)
- E. Healing Miracles (7:1–17)
- F. John the Baptist (7:18–35)
- G. Jesus and a Woman (7:36–50)
- H. More Teaching and Miracles (8:1–56)
- I. Jesus Prepares the Twelve (9:1–50)

Luke described many events that took place when Jesus ministered in the region of Galilee. He recorded that Jesus announced his ministry of proclaiming the year of the Lord's favor (4:21). A Gentile himself, Luke wrote about these events to show how Jesus was deeply concerned not just with the Jews in Judea, but also with the Jews from all the tribes, as well as with the Gentiles.

IV. Jesus' Public Ministry From Galilee to Jerusalem (9:51—19:27)
- A. Teaching on Discipleship (9:51—10:42)
- B. Teaching on Prayer (11:1–13)
- C. Jesus and Evil Spirits (11:14–26)
- D. Blessing and Judgment (11:27—13:9)
- E. Healing a Woman on the Sabbath (13:10–17)
- F. The Kingdom of God (13:18—14:24)
- G. Teaching on Discipleship (14:25–35)
- H. Three Parables About the Lost (15:1–32)
- I. Money and Service (16:1—17:10)
- J. Ten Lepers (17:11–19)
- K. The Coming of the Kingdom (17:20–37)
- L. Parables About Prayer (18:1–14)
- M. Jesus and Children (18:15–17)
- N. The Rich Young Ruler (18:18–30)
- O. A Prophecy of the Passion (18:31–34)
- P. Sight to the Blind (18:35–43)
- Q. A Tax Collector Named Zacchaeus (19:1–10)
- R. Parable on the Minas (19:11–27)

When Jesus left Galilee, many things happened as he traveled toward Jerusalem. He taught crowds of people and performed many miracles. Luke stressed Jesus' mercy as Jesus ministered to women, children and sinners, and he also emphasized the cost of being Jesus' disciple.

V. Jesus' Public Ministry in Jerusalem (19:28—21:38) A. The Triumphal Entry (19:28–44) B. Cleansing the Temple (19:45–46) C. Teaching at the Temple (19:47—21:4) D. The Olivet Discourse (21:5–38)	*Luke reported how Jesus entered Jerusalem and faced conflict at the temple. Jesus came face-to-face with the central religious institution of the Old Testament: the temple. Jesus declared that the temple would be destroyed because of the sins of God's people.*
VI. Jesus' Climactic Last Days in Jerusalem (22:1—24:53) A. The Conspiracy to Betray Jesus (22:1–6) B. The Upper Room (22:7–38) C. Gethsemane (22:39–53) D. Peter's Denials (22:54–62) E. The Trials of Jesus (22:63—23:25) F. The Crucifixion (23:26–56) G. The Resurrection (24:1–49) H. The Ascension (24:50–53)	*Luke reported Jesus' death and also gave much attention to his resurrection. Jesus commissioned his disciples to be his witnesses once they had received power from above. Then they would preach repentance and forgiveness in his name throughout the world. Luke closed this volume of his history with the apostles praising God at the temple day after day in Jerusalem.*

Introduction

1 Many have undertaken to draw up an account of the things that have been fulfilled[a]
among us, 2just as they were handed down to us by those who from the first[a] were
eyewitnesses[b] and servants of the word.[c] 3Therefore, since I myself have carefully investigated everything from the beginning, it seemed good also to me to write an orderly account[d] for you, most excellent[e] Theophilus,[f] 4so that you may know the certainty of the
things you have been taught.[g]

The Birth of John the Baptist Foretold

5In the time of Herod king of Judea[h] there was a priest named Zechariah, who belonged to the priestly division of Abijah;[i] his wife Elizabeth was also a descendant of Aaron. 6Both of them were upright in the sight of God, observing all the Lord's commandments and regulations blamelessly.[j] 7But they had no children, because Elizabeth was
barren; and they were both well along in years.
8Once when Zechariah's division was on duty and he was serving as priest before
God,[k] 9he was chosen by lot, according to the custom of the priesthood, to go into the
temple of the Lord and burn incense.[l] 10And when the time for the burning of incense
came, all the assembled worshipers were praying outside.[m]

1:2 [a]Mk 1:1; Jn 15:27; Ac 1:21,22 [b]Heb 2:3; 1Pe 5:1; 2Pe 1:16; 1Jn 1:1 [c]Mk 4:14
1:3 [d]Ac 11:4 [e]Ac 24:3; 26:25 [f]Ac 1:1
1:4 [g]Jn 20:31
1:5 [h]Mt 2:1 [i]1Ch 24:10
1:6 [j]Ge 7:1; 1Ki 9:4
1:8 [k]1Ch 24:19; 2Ch 8:14
1:9 [l]Ex 30:7,8; 1Ch 23:13; 2Ch 29:11
1:10 [m]Lev 16:17

[a] *1* Or *been surely believed*

▪ **1:1–4** *Preface.* Luke wrote the opening paragraph in a classical style of Greek. It is the kind of introduction one would expect in a literary book written for a wide circulation. Luke addressed Theophilus as though he were his patron, and he explained why he had written.
1:1 Many. Many writings of the early church have been lost. **fulfilled.** The purpose of God was worked out in the things of which they wrote.
1:2 eyewitnesses. There was reliable evidence for what was written. **servants of the word.** People who preached the message God gave. Luke regarded preaching the word (Ac 8:4) as preaching Jesus (see Ac 9:20, where "preach" literally reads in the Greek "preached Jesus").
1:3–4 See *WCF* 1.1.
1:3 carefully investigated. Luke was not an eyewitness. He made inquiries and declared that his information was reliable. His investigation had been thorough. **from the beginning.** Luke had gone back in his research to the beginning of the Christian movement. **most excellent.** The appropriate address for a person of high rank in Hellenistic culture (Ac 23:26; 24:3).
1:4 the certainty. The Christian faith is well grounded.
▪ **1:5—4:13** *Preparations for Jesus' Public Ministry.* Luke began his account with several events that opened the way for a supernatural beginning of Jesus' earthly life. Jesus is shown to be anything but ordinary.
▪ **1:5—2:52** *Two Mothers, Two Infants.* The Christian story about Jesus' origins is closely linked with the miraculous birth of John the Baptist, the forerunner of Jesus.
1:5 Luke began with the announcement of John's birth. **Herod.** Herod the Great reigned from 4 B.C.–A.D. 37. What Luke described occurred toward the end of Herod's reign. **priestly division.** There was only one temple, and priests served in it according to a roster or schedule. **division of Abijah.** The eighth of the 24 divisions (1Ch 24:10); each division ministered for a week twice a year. **Elizabeth.** It was a special blessing for a priest to have a wife of priestly stock. Luke consistently paid attention to the roles women played in his history (e.g., 1:42; 2:36–38; 7:37–50; 8:1–3,43–56; 10:38–42; 11:27–28; 13:11–21; 21:23; 23:27–29,49–56; 24:1–24).
1:6 blamelessly. This strong expression does not mean that they never sinned, but rather that they were godly and upright people. See *WCF* 15.2; *WLC* 76.
1:7 no children. Children were seen as God's reward for faithful service (Ps 127:3–5), so this couple must have grieved the fact that they were childless.
1:9 burn incense. One priestly duty was to keep incense burning on the altar before the Most Holy Place (see chart "Herod's Temple" at Lk 2). Fresh incense was brought before every morning sacrifice and after every evening sacrifice. The large number of priests serving a single temple meant that a priest had few opportunities to take part in the ritual. No priest could offer incense more than once in his life (some priests never had the privilege). This was to be the high point in Zechariah's career. He would go into the Holy Place with other priests, but they would withdraw and he alone would offer the incense.

11 Then an angel[n] of the Lord appeared to him, standing at the right side of the altar
of incense.[o] 12 When Zechariah saw him, he was startled and was gripped with fear.[p]
13 But the angel said to him: "Do not be afraid,[q] Zechariah; your prayer has been heard.
Your wife Elizabeth will bear you a son, and you are to give him the name John.[r] 14 He
will be a joy and delight to you, and many will rejoice because of his birth,[s] 15 for he will
be great in the sight of the Lord. He is never to take wine or other fermented drink,[t] and
he will be filled with the Holy Spirit even from birth.[a][u] 16 Many of the people of Israel will
he bring back to the Lord their God. 17 And he will go on before the Lord,[v] in the spirit
and power of Elijah,[w] to turn the hearts of the fathers to their children[x] and the disobedient to the wisdom of the righteous—to make ready a people prepared for the Lord."

18 Zechariah asked the angel, "How can I be sure of this? I am an old man and my wife
is well along in years."[y]

19 The angel answered, "I am Gabriel.[z] I stand in the presence of God, and I have been
sent to speak to you and to tell you this good news. 20 And now you will be silent and not
able to speak[a] until the day this happens, because you did not believe my words, which
will come true at their proper time."

21 Meanwhile, the people were waiting for Zechariah and wondering why he stayed
so long in the temple. 22 When he came out, he could not speak to them. They realized
he had seen a vision in the temple, for he kept making signs[b] to them but remained unable to speak.

23 When his time of service was completed, he returned home. 24 After this his wife Elizabeth became pregnant and for five months remained in seclusion. 25 "The Lord has done
this for me," she said. "In these days he has shown his favor and taken away my disgrace[c]
among the people."

The Birth of Jesus Foretold

26 In the sixth month, God sent the angel Gabriel[d] to Nazareth,[e] a town in Galilee, 27 to
a virgin pledged to be married to a man named Joseph,[f] a descendant of David. The virgin's name was Mary. 28 The angel went to her and said, "Greetings, you who are highly favored! The Lord is with you."

29 Mary was greatly troubled at his words and wondered what kind of greeting this
might be. 30 But the angel said to her, "Do not be afraid,[g] Mary, you have found favor with
God. 31 You will be with child and give birth to a son, and you are to give him the name
Jesus.[h] 32 He will be great and will be called the Son of the Most High.[i] The Lord God will
give him the throne of his father David, 33 and he will reign over the house of Jacob forever; his kingdom[j] will never end."[k]

[a] *15* Or *from his mother's womb*

1:11 [n]Ac 5:19 [o]Ex 30:1-10
1:12 [p]Jdg 6:22,23; 13:22
1:13 [q]ver 30; Mt 14:27 [r]ver 60,63
1:14 [s]ver 58
1:15 [t]Nu 6:3; Jdg 13:4; Lk 7:33 [u]Jer 1:5; Gal 1:15
1:17 [v]ver 76 [w]Mt 11:14 [x]Mal 4:5,6
1:18 [y]ver 34; Ge 17:17
1:19 [z]ver 26; Da 8:16; 9:21; Mt 18:10
1:20 [a]Eze 3:26
1:22 [b]ver 62
1:25 [c]Ge 30:23; Isa 4:1
1:26 [d]ver 19 [e]Mt 2:23
1:27 [f]Mt 1:16,18,20; Lk 2:4
1:30 [g]ver 13; Mt 14:27
1:31 [h]Isa 7:14; Mt 1:21,25; Lk 2:21
1:32 [i]ver 35,76; Mk 5:7
1:33 [j]Mt 28:18 [k]Da 2:44; 7:14,27; Mic 4:7; Heb 1:8

1:11 the right side. Probably the south side. The angel would have been between the incense altar and the golden candlestick.
1:13 your prayer. This may have been a prayer for a son, but perhaps (more probably at such a moment) it was for the redemption of Israel. Either way, the answer to the prayer would be realized in the birth of a son. **John.** The name means "the Lord is gracious."
1:14 joy and delight. It is natural that a son would be a joy and delight to his parents, but this child would be special, and many would be glad because of him.
1:15 wine. That he was to abstain from alcoholic drinks leads many scholars to surmise that John was to take the vow of a Nazirite (Nu 6:1–4), but Luke does not specify this. It is more likely that John had a unique position, neither as a priest nor as a Nazirite. **filled with the Holy Spirit even from birth.** In the entire New Testament only John is described in this way, thus showing how special he was in the history of salvation. When he exalted Jesus above himself, John raised Jesus to the greatest possible honor. Reformed theology has also seen in this verse an indication that God may regenerate infants in an extraordinary manner, apart from the outward call of the gospel. See *WCF* 10.3.
1:17 in the spirit and power of Elijah. See Malachi 3:1 and 4:5. **turn the hearts of the fathers to their children.** This may mean remedying disunity in families or, if the fathers are understood as the great ancestors of the people, inducing the people to live so as to receive the approval of their great forefathers. **prepared.** The climax is that John would prepare the way for the Lord. It is that fulfillment of prophecy for which he is especially remembered.
1:19–20 Gabriel. Literally, "man of God." Gabriel is one of only two angels named in Scripture (Michael is the other). That he stands in God's presence indicates his greatness. Such a one should be believed. **tell you this good news.** The verb employed here would later characteristically refer to preaching the gospel. **you will be silent.** Temporarily revoking Zechariah's ability to speak was not only disciplinary, but also a sign of assurance that the angel's words were true (cf. v. 18). See *WCF* 11.5.
1:21 temple. The people were also in the temple, waiting for Zechariah to come out and pronounce the blessing. Offering incense did not take long, so the delay was puzzling. When the priest did not speak but made signs, the people concluded that he had seen a vision (v. 22).
1:24 As the angel promised, Elizabeth became pregnant, a situation in which she recognized the hand of the Lord. Childlessness was thought of as a divine punishment, but Elizabeth would bear that reproach no more (cf. Ge 30:23).
1:26 the sixth month. That is, the sixth month of Elizabeth's pregnancy.
1:27 pledged. This was much more binding than a modern engagement and was virtually a stage of marriage. The couple did not yet live together, but a divorce was required in order to break the relationship. See *WCF* 8.2; *WLC* 37,46; *WSC* 22.
1:28–29 Luke turned to the announcement of Jesus' birth. Mary was a humble girl and did not understand why an angel should refer to her as "highly favored" (a correct translation of a word sometimes rendered "full of grace"). The term indicates that she was the recipient of grace, not that she was the source of grace to others.
1:31 Jesus. The name means "Yahweh is salvation." See *BC* 21.
1:32 great. There is a fuller meaning to "great" in this verse than in verse 15, where the term was applied to John. Jesus is "the Son of the Most High." **the throne of his father.** David foretold that the Messiah would be his descendant (2Sa 7:12–16; Ps 89:29). See *BC* 27.

34“How will this be,” Mary asked the angel, “since I am a virgin?”
35The angel answered, “The Holy Spirit will come upon you,[l] and the power of the
Most High[m] will overshadow you. So the holy one[n] to be born will be called[a] the Son of
God.[o] 36Even Elizabeth your relative is going to have a child in her old age, and she who
was said to be barren is in her sixth month. 37For nothing is impossible with God.”[p]
38“I am the Lord’s servant,” Mary answered. “May it be to me as you have said.” Then
the angel left her.

Mary Visits Elizabeth

39At that time Mary got ready and hurried to a town in the hill country of Judea,[q]
40where she entered Zechariah’s home and greeted Elizabeth. 41When Elizabeth heard
Mary’s greeting, the baby leaped in her womb, and Elizabeth was filled with the Holy
Spirit. 42In a loud voice she exclaimed: “Blessed are you among women,[r] and blessed is
the child you will bear! 43But why am I so favored, that the mother of my Lord should
come to me? 44As soon as the sound of your greeting reached my ears, the baby in my
womb leaped for joy. 45Blessed is she who has believed that what the Lord has said to
her will be accomplished!”

Mary’s Song

46And Mary said:

“My soul glorifies the Lord[s]
47 and my spirit rejoices in God my Savior,[t]
48for he has been mindful
of the humble state of his servant.[u]
From now on all generations will call me blessed,[v]
49 for the Mighty One has done great things[w] for me—
holy is his name.[x]
50His mercy extends to those who fear him,
from generation to generation.[y]
51He has performed mighty deeds with his arm;[z]
he has scattered those who are proud in their inmost thoughts.
52He has brought down rulers from their thrones
but has lifted up the humble.
53He has filled the hungry with good things[a]
but has sent the rich away empty.
54He has helped his servant Israel,
remembering to be merciful[b]
55to Abraham and his descendants[c] forever,
even as he said to our fathers.”

56Mary stayed with Elizabeth for about three months and then returned home.

1:35 [l]Mt 1:18 [m]ver 32, 76 [n]Mk 1:24 [o]Mt 4:3
1:37 [p]Mt 19:26
1:39 [q]ver 65
1:42 [r]Jdg 5:24
1:46 [s]Ps 34:2,3
1:47 [t]1Ti 1:1; 2:3
1:48 [u]Ps 138:6 [v]Lk 11:27
1:49 [w]Ps 71:19 [x]Ps 111:9
1:50 [y]Ex 20:6; Ps 103:17
1:51 [z]Ps 98:1; Isa 40:10
1:53 [a]Ps 107:9
1:54 [b]Ps 98:3
1:55 [c]Ge 17:19; Ps 132:11; Gal 3:16

[a] *35* Or *So the child to be born will be called holy,*

1:33 The kingdom without end must be the kingdom of God (see Isa 9:7), the establishment of God’s reign over all the earth. See theological article “The Kingdom of God” at Matthew 4. See also *WCF* 8.1.
1:34 A married woman might expect to bear a child. Since Mary was about to be married, her question is puzzling. Evidently she understood the angel to mean a miraculous event—birth without insemination by a human father.
1:35 See *WCF* 8.2; *WLC* 36,37; *WSC* 21,22; *BC* 9,18; *HC* 35.
1:36 your relative. This is taken by some to mean that Jesus was not a physical descendant of David (of the tribe of Judah), for Elizabeth was a descendant of Aaron (of the tribe of Levi; v. 5). This is not, however, a necessary conclusion. It is possible that one of her parents was of Aaronic descent and the other of Davidic descent.
1:39 hurried. Mary must have left right away. Elizabeth was in her sixth month of pregnancy (v. 36); Mary stayed for three months (v. 56) and apparently went home before John’s birth (v. 57).
1:41 filled with the Holy Spirit. The Holy Spirit enabled Elizabeth to interpret the movement of the child in her womb as a leap for joy at the coming of the mother of the Lord (see note on 1:15).
1:42 See *WLC* 37; *WSC* 22; *BC* 18.
1:45 she who has believed. Notice the tribute to Mary’s faith. Mary expressed confidence in God’s promise, much as her forebear Abram had done (Ge 15:6).
1:46–55 This song of praise, later called the Magnificat (from its opening word in Latin), expresses God’s concern for the humble and weak, along with his rejection of the proud. Note that Mary drew from Hannah’s similar words in 1 Samuel 2:1–10. Including this song early in his account is one of a number of ways that Luke patterned his Gospel after 1 and 2 Samuel. See *HC* 122.
1:48 servant. The word means “slave” and expresses lowly servitude. Mary emphasized God’s mercy to the poor, his power and his holiness. **call me blessed.** History has born out Mary’s prediction that all future generations would honor her.
1:51–53 Many translations of these verbs use the present tense, but the verbal form Luke used might have referred to great things God had done in the past, or more probably to what he would do in days to come. Accepted expectations of privilege for the rich are rejected as Mary sings of what God will do for the poor.
1:54–55 See *BC* 18.
1:55 Abraham. Mary called to mind that the birth of her son was to be the fulfillment of the covenant God had made with Abraham. Paul was of the same opinion (Gal 3:16).

The Birth of John the Baptist

57 When it was time for Elizabeth to have her baby, she gave birth to a son. 58 Her neighbors and relatives heard that the Lord had shown her great mercy, and they shared her joy.
59 On the eighth day they came to circumcise[d] the child, and they were going to name him
after his father Zechariah, 60 but his mother spoke up and said, "No! He is to be called John."[e]
61 They said to her, "There is no one among your relatives who has that name."
62 Then they made signs[f] to his father, to find out what he would like to name the child.
63 He asked for a writing tablet, and to everyone's astonishment he wrote, "His name is
John."[g] 64 Immediately his mouth was opened and his tongue was loosed, and he began to
speak,[h] praising God. 65 The neighbors were all filled with awe, and throughout the hill country of Judea[i] people were talking about all these things. 66 Everyone who heard this wondered
about it, asking, "What then is this child going to be?" For the Lord's hand was with him.[j]

Zechariah's Song

67 His father Zechariah was filled with the Holy Spirit and prophesied:[k]

68 "Praise be to the Lord, the God of Israel,[l]
because he has come and has redeemed his people.[m]
69 He has raised up a horn[a][n] of salvation for us
in the house of his servant David[o]
70 (as he said through his holy prophets of long ago),[p]
71 salvation from our enemies
and from the hand of all who hate us—
72 to show mercy to our fathers[q]
and to remember his holy covenant,[r]
73 the oath he swore to our father Abraham:[s]
74 to rescue us from the hand of our enemies,
and to enable us to serve him[t] without fear
75 in holiness and righteousness[u] before him all our days.

76 And you, my child, will be called a prophet[v] of the Most High;[w]
for you will go on before the Lord to prepare the way for him,[x]
77 to give his people the knowledge of salvation
through the forgiveness of their sins,[y]
78 because of the tender mercy of our God,
by which the rising sun[z] will come to us from heaven
79 to shine on those living in darkness
and in the shadow of death,[a]
to guide our feet into the path of peace."

80 And the child grew and became strong in spirit;[b] and he lived in the desert until he
appeared publicly to Israel.

The Birth of Jesus

2 In those days Caesar Augustus[c] issued a decree that a census should be taken of the
entire Roman world.[d] 2 (This was the first census that took place while Quirinius was
governor of Syria.)[e] 3 And everyone went to his own town to register.

1:59 [d]Ge 17:12; Lev 12:3; Lk 2:21; Php 3:5
1:60 [e]ver 13,63
1:62 [f]ver 22
1:63 [g]ver 13,60
1:64 [h]ver 20
1:65 [i]ver 39
1:66 [j]Ge 39:2; Ac 11:21
1:67 [k]Joel 2:28
1:68 [l]Ps 72:18 [m]Ps 111:9; Lk 7:16
1:69 [n]1Sa 2:1,10; Ps 18:2; 89:17; 132:17; Eze 29:21 [o]Mt 1:1
1:70 [p]Jer 23:5
1:72 [q]Mic 7:20 [r]Ps 105:8,9; 106:45; Eze 16:60
1:73 [s]Ge 22:16-18
1:74 [t]Heb 9:14
1:75 [u]Eph 4:24
1:76 [v]Mt 11:9 [w]ver 32, 35 [x]ver 17; Mal 3:1
1:77 [y]Jer 31:34; Mk 1:4
1:78 [z]Mal 4:2
1:79 [a]Isa 9:2; 59:9; Mt 4:16; Ac 26:18
1:80 [b]Lk 2:40,52
2:1 [c]Mt 22:17; Lk 3:1 [d]Mt 24:14
2:2 [e]Mt 4:24

[a] *69 Horn* here symbolizes strength.

1:59 the eighth day. Jewish boys were circumcised on the eighth day of their life (Ge 17:12), but this is the first evidence of the custom of naming a son on that day.
1:62 signs. Zechariah may have been deaf as well as mute.
1:63 writing tablet. A board covered by wax.
1:64 tongue was loosed. Obedience to God resulted in the blessing of speech. Zechariah's first words were praise to God, the only appropriate response to such a grand, divine intervention.
1:68–75 See *WCF* 20.3; *WLC* 38,93,97,101; *WSC* 44; *HC* 122.
1:68 Praise be. This could be translated "Blessed be," a common way of beginning an expression of thanksgiving (Pss 72:18; 124:6).
1:69 horn. The metaphor of a horn refers to an animal horn lifted up as a symbol of strength, here indicating that salvation is a mighty act of God. **his servant David.** This phrase shows that Zechariah praised God for his own son because this son would be the forerunner of David's son, the Messiah. John served Jesus in much the same way that Samuel served David (1Sa 1–12).
1:72–75 There are several covenants mentioned in the Old Testament, but Israel always saw the covenant with Abraham as especially significant because it was the first covenant that set them apart from other peoples (Ge 15; 17). See "Major Covenants in the Bible" on page 25.
1:76–79 The language is similar to that of Isaiah 40:1 and Malachi 3:1, and it presupposes that Jesus, for whom John would prepare the way, is himself God.
1:77 See *BC* 22.
1:78 the rising sun. This phrase refers to the Messiah (Mal 4:2), but the Greek word *anatole* means simply "rising," and some think instead of the metaphor of a shoot from Jesse (Isa 11:1). A reference to the sun, however, is more likely. In the ancient Near East it was not uncommon to refer to the enthronement of a new king as the dawning of the sun.
1:80 lived in the desert. John grew up in the wilderness, where he may have had contact with any number of religious communities such as the one at Qumran, a community made up of people who left Jerusalem in objection to the corruption of religious authorities there and best known in modern times for its preservation of the Dead Sea Scrolls.

4 So Joseph also went up from the town of Nazareth in Galilee to Judea, to Bethlehem[f]
the town of David, because he belonged to the house and line of David. 5 He went there
to register with Mary, who was pledged to be married to him and was expecting a child.
6 While they were there, the time came for the baby to be born, 7 and she gave birth to her
firstborn, a son. She wrapped him in cloths and placed him in a manger, because there
was no room for them in the inn.

The Shepherds and the Angels

8 And there were shepherds living out in the fields nearby, keeping watch over their
flocks at night. 9 An angel[g] of the Lord appeared to them, and the glory of the Lord shone
around them, and they were terrified. 10 But the angel said to them, "Do not be afraid.[h]
I bring you good news of great joy that will be for all the people. 11 Today in the town of
David a Savior[i] has been born to you; he is Christ[a][j] the Lord. 12 This will be a sign[k] to you:
You will find a baby wrapped in cloths and lying in a manger."

13 Suddenly a great company of the heavenly host appeared with the angel, praising
God and saying,

> 14 "Glory to God in the highest,
> and on earth peace[l] to men on whom his favor rests."

15 When the angels had left them and gone into heaven, the shepherds said to one another, "Let's go to Bethlehem and see this thing that has happened, which the Lord has
told us about."

16 So they hurried off and found Mary and Joseph, and the baby, who was lying in the
manger. 17 When they had seen him, they spread the word concerning what had been
told them about this child, 18 and all who heard it were amazed at what the shepherds
said to them. 19 But Mary treasured up all these things and pondered them in her heart.[m]
20 The shepherds returned, glorifying and praising God[n] for all the things they had heard
and seen, which were just as they had been told.

Jesus Presented in the Temple

21 On the eighth day, when it was time to circumcise him,[o] he was named Jesus, the
name the angel had given him before he had been conceived.[p]

2:4 [f]Jn 7:42
2:9 [g]Lk 1:11; Ac 5:19
2:10 [h]Mt 14:27
2:11 [i]Mt 1:21; Jn 4:42; Ac 5:31 [j]Mt 1:16; 16:16,20; Jn 11:27; Ac 2:36
2:12 [k]1Sa 2:34; 2Ki 19:29; Isa 7:14
2:14 [l]Lk 1:79; Ro 5:1; Eph 2:14,17
2:19 [m]ver 51
2:20 [n]Mt 9:8
2:21 [o]Lk 1:59 [p]Lk 1:31

[a] *11* Or *Messiah.* "The Christ" (Greek) and "the Messiah" (Hebrew) both mean "the Anointed One"; also in verse 26.

2:1–3 Caesar Augustus. We have no further information about a worldwide census under Augustus, but this emperor reorganized the administration of the empire and did conduct censuses. Luke seems to be referring to an administrative direction from the emperor. **Quirinius.** The governor of Syria when a census was carried out in A.D. 6. He also was active in that area from 10–7 B.C. It seems to have been the custom to conduct a census at intervals of 14 years, so Quirinius would have been in the area at the time about which Luke wrote.
2:3 register. People returned to their ancestral homes for registration.
2:4 Bethlehem. Since Joseph was a descendant of David, his place of registration was the traditional ancestral home for the family of David.
2:5 pledged to be married to him. See note on 1:27. We have no information to suggest that Mary was required to register. Perhaps Joseph did not care to leave her alone at Nazareth at such a time.
2:7 she gave birth. The birth of Jesus is described simply. Mary herself wrapped him, indicating that she was probably not attended by a midwife. The strips of cloth were long strips commonly used to wrap a baby. That the child was placed in a manger may mean that the birth occurred in a stable. There is an ancient tradition that Jesus was born in a cave (which could have been used as a stable). Mangers were often located out of doors, and it is possible that Jesus was born in the open air. Another suggestion is that the place was the home of poor people, where the animals would have been under the same roof as the family. See *WLC* 47; *WSC* 27. **there was no room for them in the inn.** This may mean either that the innkeeper did not want to have them there or that Joseph had arrived too late to secure accommodation.
2:8 shepherds living out in the fields. That the flocks were in the open fields does not mean that it could not have been winter, for the animals to be used for the temple sacrifices were kept in the open in that area, even in winter. We have no information at all about the time of year. Shepherds were a despised class because their work prevented them from keeping the ceremonial law. As they moved about the country, it was common for them to become thieves. They were considered unreliable and were not permitted to give evidence in the courts.
2:10 Do not be afraid. In a traditional style, the angel began by reassuring the frightened men (cf. 1:13,30) and went on to use strong terms for the great joy and the Good News he was heralding. **the people.** Normally a term used for the people Israel. While this Good News would in time go to all the world, it came first to God's covenant nation.
2:11 Savior. Jesus is called "Savior" only twice in the four Gospels (see also Jn 4:42). **Christ.** Means "Messiah," Hebrew for "anointed one." **Lord.** Regularly used to refer to God in the Greek translation of the Old Testament. See *HC* 18.
2:12 The sign would enable them to find the baby and would verify the truth of what the angel had said.
2:13 the heavenly host. "Host" is a military term designating an army. The angelic army announced peace, but peace comes only after enemies have been destroyed. That God's army announced the peace implies that the peace referred to here is primarily the end of hostility between God and man. However, the restoration of the kingdom under Jesus also includes inner peace (Php 4:6-7) and peace with one another (Mk 9:50).
2:14 on whom his favor rests. The peace of the Messiah is not for everyone. It is only for those whom God has chosen; that is, his people.
2:15–20 The shepherds went to see the baby, found him as the angels had said, and returned, praising God. Luke often mentioned praise to God (5:25–26; 7:16; 13:13) to inspire his readers to appreciate the wonder of these events.
2:21–24 Jesus was circumcised on the eighth day, as the law prescribed (Ge 17:12; cf. Gal 4:4–5). The need for purification arose from the fact that a mother was ceremonially unclean for seven days after the birth of a son (Lev 12:2). For another 33 days, she was to keep away from holy things (the time periods were doubled after

2:22 [q]Lev 12:2-8
2:23 [r]Ex 13:2,12,15; Nu 3:13
2:24 [s]Lev 12:8
2:25 [t]Lk 1:6 [u]ver 38; Isa 52:9; Lk 23:51
2:27 [v]ver 22
2:29 [w]ver 26 [x]Ac 2:24
2:30 [y]Isa 52:10; Lk 3:6
2:32 [z]Isa 42:6; 49:6; Ac 13:47; 26:23

22 When the time of their purification according to the Law of Moses[q] had been completed, Joseph and Mary took him to Jerusalem to present him to the Lord 23 (as it is written in the Law of the Lord, "Every firstborn male is to be consecrated to the Lord"[a]),[r]
24 and to offer a sacrifice in keeping with what is said in the Law of the Lord: "a pair of
doves or two young pigeons."[b][s]
25 Now there was a man in Jerusalem called Simeon, who was righteous and devout.[t]
He was waiting for the consolation of Israel,[u] and the Holy Spirit was upon him. 26 It had
been revealed to him by the Holy Spirit that he would not die before he had seen the
Lord's Christ. 27 Moved by the Spirit, he went into the temple courts. When the parents
brought in the child Jesus to do for him what the custom of the Law required,[v] 28 Simeon took him in his arms and praised God, saying:

29 "Sovereign Lord, as you have promised,[w]
you now dismiss[c] your servant in peace.[x]
30 For my eyes have seen your salvation,[y]
31 which you have prepared in the sight of all people,
32 a light for revelation to the Gentiles
and for glory to your people Israel."[z]

[a] *23* Exodus 13:2,12 [b] *24* Lev. 12:8 [c] *29* Or *promised, / now dismiss*

---

the birth of a daughter; Lev 12:1–5). She was then to offer a lamb and a dove or pigeon. If she was poor, her offering was to be two doves or pigeons (Lev 12:6–8). Mary's offering was that of the poor. Only the first male child of every mother was presented to the Lord (Ex 13:2).

2:25 the consolation of Israel. This refers to the comfort the Messiah would bring. Led by the Spirit, Simeon entered the temple courts just at this time, took the baby in his arms and sang his song (cf. Isa 52:8-10).

2:30 your salvation. Jesus embodied God's salvation of his people.

2:31 all people. This term is plural ("all the peoples") and refers to the Gentile nations as well as to Israel (cf. v. 32). Simeon understood that in the latter days of history, salvation would reach the ends of the earth (see theological article "The Kingdom of God" at

Herod's Temple

20 B.C.–A.D. 70

Begun in 20 B.C., Herod's new structure towered 15 stories high, following the floor dimensions of the former temples in the Holy Place and the Most Holy Place. The high sanctuary shown here in a cutaway view was built on the site of the former temples of Solomon and Zerubbabel.

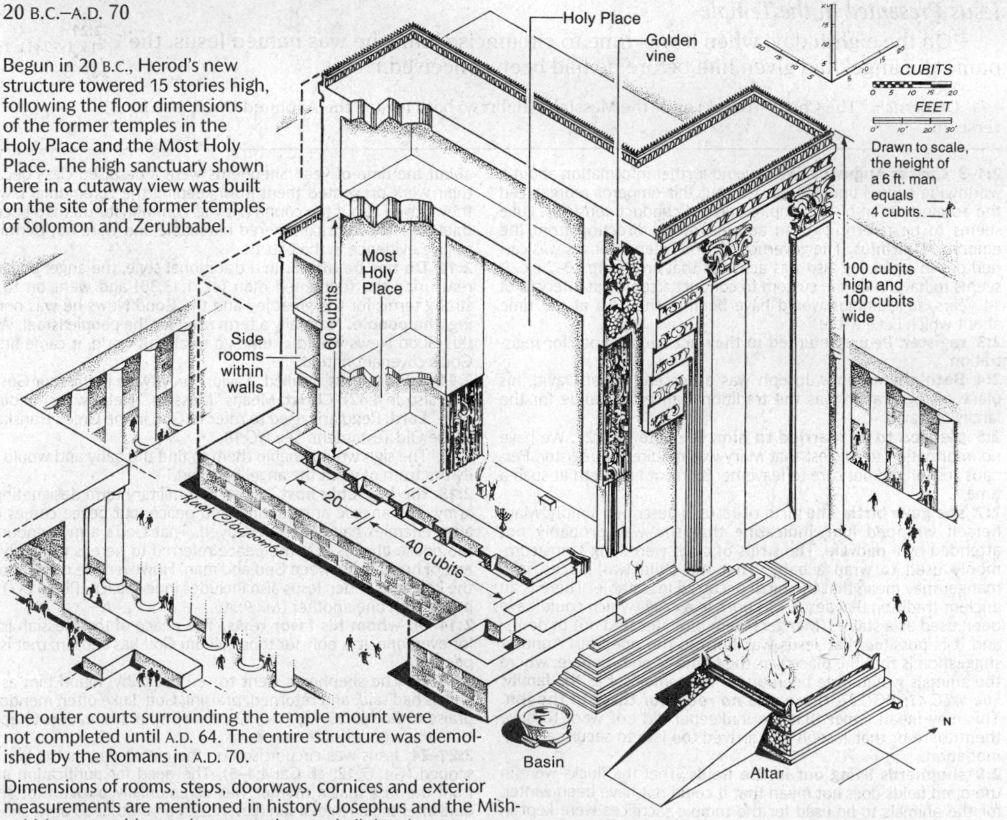

The outer courts surrounding the temple mount were not completed until A.D. 64. The entire structure was demolished by the Romans in A.D. 70.

Dimensions of rooms, steps, doorways, cornices and exterior measurements are mentioned in history (Josephus and the Mishnah) but are subject to interpretation, and all drawings vary.

33The child's father and mother marveled at what was said about him. 34Then Simeon blessed them and said to Mary, his mother:[a] "This child is destined to cause the falling[b] and rising of many in Israel, and to be a sign that will be spoken against, 35so that
the thoughts of many hearts will be revealed. And a sword will pierce your own soul too."
36There was also a prophetess,[c] Anna, the daughter of Phanuel, of the tribe of Asher. She was very old; she had lived with her husband seven years after her marriage,
37and then was a widow until she was eighty-four.[a][d] She never left the temple but worshiped night and day, fasting and praying.[e] 38Coming up to them at that very moment,
she gave thanks to God and spoke about the child to all who were looking forward to the
redemption of Jerusalem.[f]
39When Joseph and Mary had done everything required by the Law of the Lord, they
returned to Galilee to their own town of Nazareth.[g] 40And the child grew and became
strong; he was filled with wisdom, and the grace of God was upon him.[h]

The Boy Jesus at the Temple

41Every year his parents went to Jerusalem for the Feast of the Passover.[i] 42When he
was twelve years old, they went up to the Feast, according to the custom. 43After the
Feast was over, while his parents were returning home, the boy Jesus stayed behind in
Jerusalem, but they were unaware of it. 44Thinking he was in their company, they traveled on for a day. Then they began looking for him among their relatives and friends.
45When they did not find him, they went back to Jerusalem to look for him. 46After three
days they found him in the temple courts, sitting among the teachers, listening to them
and asking them questions. 47Everyone who heard him was amazed[j] at his understanding and his answers. 48When his parents saw him, they were astonished. His mother[k]
said to him, "Son, why have you treated us like this? Your father[l] and I have been anxiously searching for you."
49"Why were you searching for me?" he asked. "Didn't you know I had to be in my Father's house?"[m] 50But they did not understand what he was saying to them.[n]
51Then he went down to Nazareth with them[o] and was obedient to them. But his
mother treasured all these things in her heart.[p] 52And Jesus grew in wisdom and stature,
and in favor with God and men.[q]

John the Baptist Prepares the Way

3 In the fifteenth year of the reign of Tiberius Caesar—when Pontius Pilate[r] was governor of Judea, Herod[s] tetrarch of Galilee, his brother Philip tetrarch of Iturea and
Traconitis, and Lysanias tetrarch of Abilene—2during the high priesthood of Annas and

2:34 [a]Mt 12:46 [b]Isa 8:14; Mt 21:44; 1Co 1:23; 2Co 2:16; 1Pe 2:7,8
2:36 [c]Ac 21:9
2:37 [d]1Ti 5:9 [e]Ac 13:3; 14:23; 1Ti 5:5
2:38 [f]ver 25; Isa 40:2; Lk 1:68; 24:21
2:39 [g]ver 51; Mt 2:23
2:40 [h]ver 52; Lk 1:80
2:41 [i]Ex 23:15; Dt 16:1-8
2:47 [j]Mt 7:28
2:48 [k]Mt 12:46 [l]Lk 3:23; 4:22
2:49 [m]Jn 2:16
2:50 [n]Mk 9:32
2:51 [o]ver 39; Mt 2:23 [p]ver 19
2:52 [q]ver 40; 1Sa 2:26; Lk 1:80
3:1 [r]Mt 27:2 [s]Mt 14:1

[a] 37 *Or widow for eighty-four years*

Matthew 4). Luke, who was most likely a Gentile, held firmly to this truth.

2:33 father. Luke had previously recorded the virginal conception (1:35–37), so this refers to Joseph's legal position (cf. v. 27).

2:34 falling and rising. If the "falling and rising" refers to one group, the people must be humbled in repentance before they can rise into salvation. If it refers to two groups, there will be those who reject Jesus and therefore fall eternally, and those who accept him and rise to be with God (see the similar theme in Mary's song; 1:52).

2:35 sword. The sword imagery presages the fact that all these events would have a cost for Mary, for she would see her son rejected and crucified.

2:36–38 prophetess. Prophets were rare in Israel in those days, but the aged Anna was a prophetess (see Ac 21:9). Luke did not specify what it was for which she gave thanks, but her praise was likely connected with the redemption the child would bring to Israel. Luke consistently paid much attention to the role of women in his history (e.g., 1:42; 7:37–50; 8:1–3,43–56; 10:38–42; 11:27–28; 13:11–21; 21:23; 23:27–29,49–56; 24:1–24).

2:41 All Jewish men were to observe the Passover in Jerusalem (Ex 23:14–15; 34:23).

2:42 twelve years old. Jesus may have gone up to Jerusalem with his parents every year. In Jewish tradition it was common for a boy to be taken to the feast a year or two before he was thirteen years of age. At thirteen he would be made a "son of the covenant" and be counted as an adult.

2:43–45 Luke does not say why Jesus stayed behind or how Joseph and Mary came to leave him behind, but in a large caravan it would have been easy to miss one boy. If later custom was followed, the women and small children went ahead and the men followed. Each parent might have assumed that a twelve-year-old boy was with the other parent.

2:46–48 The temple courts were commonly used for teaching. Jesus both listened and asked questions, which demonstrates a determination to learn. In Jewish education there was an emphasis on discussion of problems, which is perhaps behind the reference to his understanding and his answers. But Joseph and Mary did not understand, for there is a note of reproach in Mary's words.

2:49 my Father's house. Already at twelve years of age, Jesus was conscious of a special relationship to the heavenly Father.

2:51 obedient. Despite his understanding of his relationship to the heavenly Father, Jesus was a dutiful son on Earth and was obedient to Joseph and Mary as he developed. **his mother treasured.** Luke's mention that Mary did not forget may indicate that she or someone close to her had told Luke this story (1:2).

2:52 grew. Luke closed his record of Jesus' childhood by noting Jesus' well-rounded personal development—intellectual, physical and spiritual. It is a testimony to Jesus' true humanity hat he grew in these ways (see theological articles "The Full Humanity of Christ" at Lk 3 and "Jesus Christ, God and Man" at Jn 1). His deity had already been indicated in 1:76.

■ **3:1–20** *John's Ministry as Forerunner.* Having sketched events in Jesus' childhood, Luke continued to treat John and Jesus together by turning to John's ministry as Jesus' forerunner.

3:1 Luke's elaborate dating comes at the beginning of John's ministry rather than at the beginning of Jesus' ministry, marking the importance of John in Luke's Gospel. This date was probably about A.D. 27–29. **Pontius Pilate.** In his will, Herod the Great left Judea to Archelaus and tetrarchies to Philip and Antipas. But Archelaus ruled so badly that the Romans removed him and appointed their own governor, Pontius Pilate. **tetrarch.** A tetrarch was technically the ruler over a fourth part, but the term was used of petty princes in general. Herod here is Herod Antipas. Philip's region was north-

Caiaphas,[t] the word of God came to John[u] son of Zechariah[v] in the desert. [3]He went into
all the country around the Jordan, preaching a baptism of repentance for the forgiveness
of sins.[w] [4]As is written in the book of the words of Isaiah the prophet:

> "A voice of one calling in the desert,
> 'Prepare the way for the Lord,
> make straight paths for him.
> [5]Every valley shall be filled in,
> every mountain and hill made low.
> The crooked roads shall become straight,
> the rough ways smooth.
> [6]And all mankind will see God's salvation.' "[a][x]

[7]John said to the crowds coming out to be baptized by him, "You brood of vipers![y]
Who warned you to flee from the coming wrath?[z] [8]Produce fruit in keeping with repentance. And do not begin to say to yourselves, 'We have Abraham as our father.'[a] For I tell
you that out of these stones God can raise up children for Abraham. [9]The ax is already
at the root of the trees, and every tree that does not produce good fruit will be cut down
and thrown into the fire."[b]
[10]"What should we do then?"[c] the crowd asked.
[11]John answered, "The man with two tunics should share with him who has none,
and the one who has food should do the same."[d]
[12]Tax collectors also came to be baptized.[e] "Teacher," they asked, "what should
we do?"
[13]"Don't collect any more than you are required to,"[f] he told them.
[14]Then some soldiers asked him, "And what should we do?"
He replied, "Don't extort money and don't accuse people falsely[g]—be content with
your pay."
[15]The people were waiting expectantly and were all wondering in their hearts if
John[h] might possibly be the Christ.[b][i] [16]John answered them all, "I baptize you with[c] water.[j] But one more powerful than I will come, the thongs of whose sandals I am not worthy to untie. He will baptize you with the Holy Spirit and with fire.[k] [17]His winnowing fork[l]
is in his hand to clear his threshing floor and to gather the wheat into his barn, but he
will burn up the chaff with unquenchable fire."[m] [18]And with many other words John exhorted the people and preached the good news to them.
[19]But when John rebuked Herod[n] the tetrarch because of Herodias, his brother's wife,

3:2 [t]Mt 26:3; Jn 18:13; Ac 4:6 [u]Mt 3:1 [v]Lk 1:13
3:3 [w]ver 16; Mk 1:4
3:6 [x]Ps 98:2; Isa 40:3-5; 42:16; 52:10; Lk 2:30
3:7 [y]Mt 12:34; 23:33 [z]Ro 1:18
3:8 [a]Isa 51:2; Lk 19:9; Jn 8:33, 39; Ac 13:26; Ro 4:1, 11, 12, 16, 17; Gal 3:7
3:9 [b]Mt 3:10
3:10 [c]ver 12, 14; Ac 2:37; 16:30
3:11 [d]Isa 58:7
3:12 [e]Lk 7:29
3:13 [f]Lk 19:8
3:14 [g]Ex 23:1; Lev 19:11
3:15 [h]Mt 3:1 [i]Jn 1:19, 20; Ac 13:25
3:16 [j]ver 3; Mk 1:4 [k]Jn 1:26, 33; Ac 1:5; 11:16; 19:4
3:17 [l]Isa 30:24 [m]Mt 13:30; 25:41
3:19 [n]ver 1

[a] *6* Isaiah 40:3–5 [b] *15* Or *Messiah* [c] *16* Or *in*

---

east of the Sea of Galilee. Nothing more is known of this Lysanias, but his Abilene was north of the other regions.

3:2 The Jews had only one high priest at a time. The Romans had deposed Annas and appointed Caiaphas, Annas's son-in-law, as the high priest. The Romans saw to it that Caiaphas exercised the official functions, but many Jews still viewed Annas as the true high priest. **the word of God came.** John's message was not his own but the dynamic word of God himself.

3:3 baptism. By this time, the ritual washings associated with temple worship (e.g., Ex 30:18–21; Nu 19:9ff.) had been extended to at least two other uses. First, Jews baptized Gentiles who wished to be circumcised and join Israel's covenant community. Second, some radical Jewish groups required washings for entry into their remnant communities. John called for the remnant of Israel following him to be baptized to demonstrate repentance.

3:4–6 A voice . . . all mankind . . . God's salvation. All four Gospels apply Isaiah 40:3 to John and his ministry. Only Luke's Gospel includes Isaiah 40:4–5 (cited at Lk 3:5–6), which focuses on the fact that all humanity will see the salvation God brings to his people. The theme of Christ's awareness of the Gentiles was important to Luke (e.g., 2:32; 4:24–27; 24:47).

3:7–8 A strong warning was directed at those who claimed Abraham as father. Being a Jew would not deliver them from the coming wrath.

3:9 ax is already at the root. This phrase points to certain and speedy judgment. **fire.** A symbol of judgment (e.g., Dt 32:22; Isa 26:11). Like his contemporaries, John expected the Messiah simultaneously to bring salvation for God's people and judgment against God's enemies. When Jesus did not do this, serious questions were raised in John's mind (Mt 11:3). Jesus explained that the kingdom of God was coming in a way that had not been previously foreseen (see theological article "The Kingdom of God" at Mt 4).

3:11 tunics. The tunic was an undergarment. Normally only one was worn. John suggested that the man who had two should give the spare to someone without one, and the prophet applied the same principle to food.

3:12 Tax collectors. The agents of Roman taxation (men who bid for the taxing rights of a city). They would pay the Romans what they bid and collect more for themselves. There was a strong temptation for them to enrich themselves by collecting much more than the amount due.

3:14 Don't extort. John admonished all to be honest. All four Gospels include an account of the ministry of John the Baptist as he called people to repentance in preparation for the coming of Jesus. Only Luke's Gospel tells us of John's answers to questioners who were uncertain about what all this meant to them. See *WCF* 23.3; *HC* 110.

3:15 Messianic speculations were in the air, but John stated clearly that he himself was not the Messiah. One greater than John was coming.

3:16–17 The Christ would baptize with the Holy Spirit and with fire. The Holy Spirit represented God's blessing as well as fire, which points to judgment (see note on v. 9). The winnowing fork also implied judgment. It was used to throw the crop into the air after it had been trodden by oxen. This separated the chaff (which was then burned) from the grain.

3:16 not worthy to untie. In the rabbinic schools, a student did not pay his teacher. He was required to perform services—but not the loosing of the sandal, which was considered too menial. John took a lowly place.

3:19–20 Herod Antipas divorced his wife and married his niece Herodias, who had been married to his own brother (see note on Mk 6:18). John denounced this immoral act, so Herod confined him in prison in the fortress of Machaerus, east of the Dead Sea.

and all the other evil things he had done, 20 Herod added this to them all: He locked John
up in prison.[o]

The Baptism and Genealogy of Jesus

21 When all the people were being baptized, Jesus was baptized too. And as he was
praying,[p] heaven was opened 22 and the Holy Spirit descended on him[q] in bodily form
like a dove. And a voice came from heaven: "You are my Son,[r] whom I love; with you I
am well pleased."[s]

23 Now Jesus himself was about thirty years old when he began his ministry.[t] He was
the son, so it was thought, of Joseph,[u]

3:20 [o]Mt 14:3,4; Mk 6:17-18
3:21 [p]Mt 14:23; Mk 1:35; 6:46; Lk 5:16; 6:12; 9:18,28; 11:1
3:22 [q]Isa 42:1; Jn 1:32, 33; Ac 10:38 [r]Mt 3:17 [s]Mt 3:17
3:23 [t]Mt 4:17; Ac 1:1 [u]Lk 1:27

■ **3:21—4:13** *Jesus' Initiation.* Luke reported that before Jesus entered his public ministry he submitted himself to John's baptism and underwent temptation in the wilderness. These events prepared him for the public work to follow.
3:21–22 See *HC* 31.
3:22 descended on him. All four Gospels tell us that the Holy Spirit came on Jesus at the time of his baptism. The dove was normally a symbol of Israel, but here it was the outward sign of the coming of the Holy Spirit on Jesus. The heavenly voice approved Jesus as he began his public ministry.
3:23–38 Luke's genealogy differs from Matthew's, partly in that Matthew goes back to Abraham and Luke to Adam. They also differ in that some of the names are different. Some suggest that Matthew's traces Joseph's line and Luke's Mary's, but Luke's specifically starts with "Joseph," the son of Heli (v. 23). It may be that Luke's genealogy gives us the physical line of Joseph and Matthew's the

The Full Humanity of Christ: What Kind of Man Was Jesus?

THE Scriptures clearly present Jesus as both fully human and fully divine. He is one person, but he has two natures: one human and the other divine.

Affirming the full humanity of Christ is critical to the Christian faith. In fact, the apostle John strongly condemned those who deny that "Jesus Christ has come in the flesh" (1Jn 4:2; see also 2Jn 7). These words spoke against an early form of a heresy known as Docetism (from the Greek word *dokeo,* "seem"). Docetists taught that Jesus was divine (though not God himself) but that he only seemed to be human. In reality, they alleged, he was a kind of phantom, a teacher who did not actually live and die as a human being.

The Scriptures make it clear that Jesus was a man. He experienced human limitations such as hunger (Mt 4:2), weariness (Jn 4:6) and ignorance (Mk 13:32; Lk 8:45–47). He experienced the pain of weeping (Jn 11:35,38), agonizing (Mk 14:32–42; Lk 12:50; Heb 5:7–10) and suffering on the cross (Mt 27:46; Mk 15:34). Being divine, Jesus could not sin (see theological article "The Sinlessness of Jesus" at Heb 4); but because he was human, he could still be genuinely tempted (Heb 4:15). Jesus could not conquer temptation without a struggle, but he always resisted and fought it until he had overcome (Mt 4:1–11). From Gethsemane we may infer that his struggles were sometimes more acute and agonizing than any we will ever know (Mt 26:36ff.).

The book of Hebrews stresses that if Jesus had not been fully human, he would not be qualified to help us as we go through the trials of human existence (Heb 2:17–18; 4:15–16; 5:2,7–9). As it is, his human experience guarantees that in our every trouble we may be confident that he sympathetically intercedes for us before the Father (Heb 7:25).

Unfortunately, many well-meaning Christians focus on Jesus' deity almost to the exclusion of his humanity, believing that they honor him by minimizing his human nature. Modern forms of the early heresy of Monophysitism (the idea that Jesus had only one nature) also tend to downplay the fact that Jesus was fully human. It is assumed by some that Jesus only pretended to be ignorant of facts; he was, after all, divine and omniscient (knowing everything). Similarly, some deny that Jesus was ever actually hungry and weary, believing that his divinity supernaturally and continually energized his human body.

The Biblical doctrine of the incarnation, however, asserts that the Son of God lived his divine-human life in and through his human mind and body at every point, maximizing his identification and empathy with those he had come to save.

The idea that Jesus alternated between his two natures, so that he sometimes acted in his humanity and sometimes in his divinity, is also mistaken. He endured all his sufferings, including those on the cross, and eventually died in the unity of his divine-human person. Nevertheless, some of Jesus' characteristics and actions are rightly attributed to his divine nature, while others stem from his human nature. The Council of Chalcedon (A.D. 451) expressed this doctrine as "the peculiar property of each nature being preserved and being united in one person and subsistence" (NPNF2, vol. 14, p. 265). For example, while Jesus was ignorant in his humanity, he was at the same time omniscient in his divinity, as difficult as that may be for us to understand.

Acknowledgement of the full humanity of Jesus is essential to the Christian faith because of the special role God gave the human race as his image bearers. Humanity was ordained as the means by which God determined to display his glory and extend his kingdom over all the earth (see theological article "The Kingdom of God" at Mt 4). Even after the fall into sin, God still declared that the descendants of Eve would crush the seed of the serpent under their feet (Ge 3:15). This early promise is fulfilled in Jesus because he was a fully human being who served God faithfully and received in reward a name greater than any other. Through Christ the victory of humanity over evil is assured.

the son of Heli, 24the son of Matthat,
the son of Levi, the son of Melki,
the son of Jannai, the son of Joseph,
25the son of Mattathias, the son of Amos,
the son of Nahum, the son of Esli,
the son of Naggai, 26the son of Maath,
the son of Mattathias, the son of Semein,
the son of Josech, the son of Joda,
3:27 27the son of Joanan, the son of Rhesa,
[v]Mt 1:12 the son of Zerubbabel,[v] the son of Shealtiel,
the son of Neri, 28the son of Melki,
the son of Addi, the son of Cosam,
the son of Elmadam, the son of Er,
29the son of Joshua, the son of Eliezer,
the son of Jorim, the son of Matthat,
the son of Levi, 30the son of Simeon,
the son of Judah, the son of Joseph,
the son of Jonam, the son of Eliakim,
3:31 31the son of Melea, the son of Menna,
[w]2Sa 5:14; 1Ch 3:5 the son of Mattatha, the son of Nathan,[w]
the son of David, 32the son of Jesse,
the son of Obed, the son of Boaz,
the son of Salmon,[a] the son of Nahshon,
3:33 33the son of Amminadab, the son of Ram,[b]
[x]Ru 4:18-22; 1Ch 2:10-12 the son of Hezron, the son of Perez,[x]
the son of Judah, 34the son of Jacob,
the son of Isaac, the son of Abraham,
3:34 [y]Ge 11:24,26 the son of Terah, the son of Nahor,[y]
35the son of Serug, the son of Reu,
the son of Peleg, the son of Eber,
the son of Shelah, 36the son of Cainan,
3:36 [z]Ge 11:12 the son of Arphaxad,[z] the son of Shem,
[a]Ge 5:28-32 the son of Noah, the son of Lamech,[a]
37the son of Methuselah, the son of Enoch,
the son of Jared, the son of Mahalalel,
the son of Kenan, 38the son of Enosh,
3:38 the son of Seth, the son of Adam,
[b]Ge 5:1,2,6-9 the son of God.[b]

The Temptation of Jesus

4:1 [c]ver 14,18 [d]Lk 3:3, 21 [e]Lk 2:27
4 Jesus, full of the Holy Spirit,[c] returned from the Jordan[d] and was led by the Spirit[e]
in the desert, 2where for forty days[f] he was tempted by the devil. He ate nothing dur-
4:2 [f]Ex 34:28; 1Ki 19:8
ing those days, and at the end of them he was hungry.
3The devil said to him, "If you are the Son of God, tell this stone to become bread."
4:4 [g]Dt 8:3
4Jesus answered, "It is written: 'Man does not live on bread alone.'[c]"[g]
5The devil led him up to a high place and showed him in an instant all the kingdoms
4:5 [h]Mt 24:14
of the world.[h] 6And he said to him, "I will give you all their authority and splendor, for
it has been given to me,[i] and I can give it to anyone I want to. 7So if you worship me, it
4:6 [i]Jn 12:31; 14:30; 1Jn 5:19
will all be yours."

[a] *32* Some early manuscripts *Sala* [b] *33* Some manuscripts *Amminadab, the son of Admin, the son of Arni;* other manuscripts vary widely. [c] *4* Deut. 8:3

legal line to David's throne, but we cannot be certain. What is clear is that both Gospels defend the fact that Jesus descended from David.

4:1 full of the Holy Spirit. That Jesus was full of the Holy Spirit and was led by the Spirit shows that the temptation had its place in the plan of God. Right at the beginning of his ministry, Jesus faced the question of what sort of Messiah he would be.

4:3–13 The devil sought to deflect Jesus from his divinely appointed Messianic mission. In his victory over Satan, Jesus bound the strong man and proceeded to plunder his possessions (11:21–22). Luke's account highlights the parallel between Jesus' temptation experience and the experience of Old Testament Israel in the wilderness. Jesus was tempted for 40 days in the desert, while Israel wandered for 40 years in the wilderness (Nu 14:34). But the difference in outcome is also crucial: Jesus was fully obedient to the Father, whereas Israel failed the test of obedience.

4:5–8 all the kingdoms of the world. This temptation comes third in Matthew. The reason for the different order is not known. The temptation was for Jesus to set up a mighty world empire, but it would have been at the cost of worshiping Satan. Jesus rejected the temptation by citing Scripture (Dt 6:13). Satan was able to offer Jesus the Gentile nations because he had gained strong power and influence over them, especially through their idolatrous worship (cf. notes on Da 10:13,20). Nevertheless, one of Jesus' primary tasks was to break Satan's hold on the Gentile nations (see Rev 20:1–3).

8Jesus answered, "It is written: 'Worship the Lord your God and serve him only.'[a]"[j]
9The devil led him to Jerusalem and had him stand on the highest point of the temple. "If you are the Son of God," he said, "throw yourself down from here. **10**For it is written:

" 'He will command his angels concerning you
to guard you carefully;
11they will lift you up in their hands,
so that you will not strike your foot against a stone.'[b]"[k]

12Jesus answered, "It says: 'Do not put the Lord your God to the test.'[c]"[l]
13When the devil had finished all this tempting,[m] he left him[n] until an opportune time.

Jesus Rejected at Nazareth

14Jesus returned to Galilee[o] in the power of the Spirit, and news about him spread through the whole countryside.[p] **15**He taught in their synagogues,[q] and everyone praised him.

16He went to Nazareth,[r] where he had been brought up, and on the Sabbath day he went into the synagogue,[s] as was his custom. And he stood up to read. **17**The scroll of the prophet Isaiah was handed to him. Unrolling it, he found the place where it is written:

18"The Spirit of the Lord is on me,[t]
because he has anointed me
to preach good news to the poor.
He has sent me to proclaim freedom for the prisoners
and recovery of sight for the blind,
to release the oppressed,
19to proclaim the year of the Lord's favor."[d][u]

20Then he rolled up the scroll, gave it back to the attendant and sat down.[v] The eyes of everyone in the synagogue were fastened on him, **21**and he began by saying to them, "Today this scripture is fulfilled in your hearing."

22All spoke well of him and were amazed at the gracious words that came from his lips. "Isn't this Joseph's son?" they asked.[w]

23Jesus said to them, "Surely you will quote this proverb to me: 'Physician, heal yourself! Do here in your hometown[x] what we have heard that you did in Capernaum.' "[y]

24"I tell you the truth," he continued, "no prophet is accepted in his hometown.[z] **25**I assure you that there were many widows in Israel in Elijah's time, when the sky was shut for three and a half years and there was a severe famine throughout the land.[a] **26**Yet Elijah was not sent to any of them, but to a widow in Zarephath in the region of Sidon.[b] **27**And there were many in Israel with leprosy[e] in the time of Elisha the prophet, yet not one of them was cleansed—only Naaman the Syrian."[c]

4:8 [j]Dt 6:13
4:11 [k]Ps 91:11,12
4:12 [l]Dt 6:16
4:13 [m]Heb 4:15 [n]Jn 14:30
4:14 [o]Mt 4:12 [p]Mt 9:26
4:15 [q]Mt 4:23
4:16 [r]Mt 2:23 [s]Mt 13:54
4:18 [t]Jn 3:34
4:19 [u]Lev 25:10; Isa 61:1,2
4:20 [v]ver 17; Mt 26:55
4:22 [w]Mt 13:54,55; Jn 6:42; 7:15
4:23 [x]ver 16 [y]Mk 1:21-28; 2:1-12
4:24 [z]Mt 13:57; Jn 4:44
4:25 [a]1Ki 17:1; 18:1; Jas 5:17,18
4:26 [b]1Ki 17:8-16; Mt 11:21
4:27 [c]2Ki 5:1-14

[a] *8* Deut. 6:13 [b] *11* Psalm 91:11,12 [c] *12* Deut. 6:16 [d] *19* Isaiah 61:1,2 [e] *27* The Greek word was used for various diseases affecting the skin—not necessarily leprosy.

4:9 the highest point. This location may have been the top of the temple wall overlooking the Kidron ravine or perhaps the highest point of the temple structure itself. Here Jesus was tempted to perform a public display of miraculous power, but he responded by again quoting Scripture (Dt 6:16). This too recalls Israel's wilderness experience. Jesus did not rebel against God as Israel had. He succeeded where the nation had failed, in this way accomplishing all righteousness.

4:13 See *WLC* 48.

■ **4:14—9:50** *Jesus' Public Ministry in Galilee.* Luke reported that once Jesus had passed the test in the wilderness, he went on to minister in Galilee. Galilee was known as a region that included many Gentiles. Jesus' extensive work in this region indicates that his kingdom is not only for Jews, but for Gentiles as well.

■ **4:14–30** *The Sermon at Nazareth.* Of the four Gospel writers, only Luke reported this event. Jesus' announcement that he proclaimed "good news" (v. 18), or "gospel," was of particular importance to Luke because of the content of that Good News.

4:14–19 See *HC* 31.

4:14–15 Jesus evidently did not return immediately to Nazareth. Matthew 4:12 seems to indicate that he returned to Galilee after John had been imprisoned, and John 3:23–24 implies that some time elapsed between Jesus' baptism and John's imprisonment. During this time, Jesus may have had time to minister in Judea. He also seems to have visited other towns in Galilee before returning to Nazareth. His ministry was extensive enough that news about him spread around the countryside before he returned to Nazareth.

4:16–21 This is the oldest known account of a synagogue service. It is unlikely that there were appointed readings; either Jesus or the ruler of the synagogue may have chosen Isaiah 61:1–2 and 58:6. In later synagogue directories it was customary to stand through the reading and to sit for the sermon. The reading chosen shows Jesus' deep concern for the poor. See *WCF* 21.6; *WLC* 117; *WSC* 60.

4:18 good news. The Good News (gospel) that Jesus proclaimed is quoted from Isaiah 61:1–2, which predicted a glorious end to Israel's exile. Jesus declared that he was the beginning of the end of Israel's exile (see theological article "The Kingdom of God" at Mt 4). See *WLC* 42; *HC* 25.

4:21–27 This account of rejection at Nazareth, presented at the beginning of Jesus' ministry, highlights certain critical characteristics of his ministry: (1) the response of wonder at his teachings coupled with persistent unbelief and rejection (vv. 22,28); (2) his ministry as the fulfillment of Scripture (v. 21); (3) his concern for the poor and oppressed (vv. 18–19); and (4) his ultimate aim of including Gentiles in the people of God (vv. 26–27). See *WLC* 42.

28All the people in the synagogue were furious when they heard this. 29They got up,
drove him out of the town,[d] and took him to the brow of the hill on which the town was
built, in order to throw him down the cliff. 30But he walked right through the crowd and
went on his way.[e]

Jesus Drives Out an Evil Spirit

31Then he went down to Capernaum,[f] a town in Galilee, and on the Sabbath began
to teach the people. 32They were amazed at his teaching,[g] because his message had authority.[h]

33In the synagogue there was a man possessed by a demon, an evil[a] spirit. He cried
out at the top of his voice, 34"Ha! What do you want with us,[i] Jesus of Nazareth?[j] Have
you come to destroy us? I know who you are[k]—the Holy One of God!"[l]

35"Be quiet!" Jesus said sternly.[m] "Come out of him!" Then the demon threw the man
down before them all and came out without injuring him.

36All the people were amazed[n] and said to each other, "What is this teaching? With
authority[o] and power he gives orders to evil spirits and they come out!" 37And the news
about him spread throughout the surrounding area.[p]

Jesus Heals Many

38Jesus left the synagogue and went to the home of Simon. Now Simon's mother-in-
law was suffering from a high fever, and they asked Jesus to help her. 39So he bent over
her and rebuked[q] the fever, and it left her. She got up at once and began to wait on them.

40When the sun was setting, the people brought to Jesus all who had various kinds
of sickness, and laying his hands on each one,[r] he healed them.[s] 41Moreover, demons
came out of many people, shouting, "You are the Son of God!"[t] But he rebuked[u] them
and would not allow them to speak,[v] because they knew he was the Christ.[b]

42At daybreak Jesus went out to a solitary place. The people were looking for him and
when they came to where he was, they tried to keep him from leaving them. 43But he
said, "I must preach the good news of the kingdom of God[w] to the other towns also, because that is why I was sent." 44And he kept on preaching in the synagogues of Judea.[c][x]

The Calling of the First Disciples

5 One day as Jesus was standing by the Lake of Gennesaret,[d] with the people crowding around him and listening to the word of God,[y] 2he saw at the water's edge two
boats, left there by the fishermen, who were washing their nets. 3He got into one of the
boats, the one belonging to Simon, and asked him to put out a little from shore. Then
he sat down and taught the people from the boat.[z]

4When he had finished speaking, he said to Simon, "Put out into deep water, and let
down[e] the nets for a catch."[a]

5Simon answered, "Master,[b] we've worked hard all night and haven't caught anything.[c] But because you say so, I will let down the nets."

4:29 [d]Nu 15:35; Ac 7:58; Heb 13:12
4:30 [e]Jn 8:59; 10:39
4:31 [f]ver 23; Mt 4:13
4:32 [g]Mt 7:28 [h]ver 36; Mt 7:29
4:34 [i]Mt 8:29 [j]Mk 1:24 [k]Jas 2:19 [l]ver 41; Mk 1:24
4:35 [m]ver 39,41; Mt 8:26; Lk 8:24
4:36 [n]Mt 7:28 [o]ver 32; Mt 7:29; Mt 10:1
4:37 [p]ver 14; Mt 9:26
4:39 [q]ver 35,41
4:40 [r]Mk 5:23 [s]Mt 4:23
4:41 [t]Mt 4:3 [u]ver 35 [v]Mt 8:4
4:43 [w]Mt 3:2
4:44 [x]Mt 4:23
5:1 [y]Mk 4:14; Heb 4:12
5:3 [z]Mt 13:2
5:4 [a]Jn 21:6
5:5 [b]Lk 8:24,45; 9:33, 49; 17:13 [c]Jn 21:3

[a] *33* Greek *unclean*; also in verse 36 [b] *41* Or *Messiah* [c] *44* Or *the land of the Jews*; some manuscripts *Galilee* [d] *1* That is, Sea of Galilee [e] *4* The Greek verb is plural.

■ **4:31—6:11** *Teaching and Miracles.* Luke reported a number of miraculous events interspersed with Jesus' teachings. All the Gospels follow this pattern because Jesus' teachings and miracles support and explain each other. As the Messiah, Jesus not only taught truth but also brought redemption to his people, as exemplified by his miracles.

4:32 amazed. In contrast to the Pharisees and teachers of the law who appealed to tradition and previous teachers, Jesus did not cite authorities. This deviation from the accepted norm amazed the people.

4:33–35 This demon was cast out on the Sabbath. Luke's Gospel tells of five exorcisms and healings Jesus performed on the Sabbath (here; v. 38; 6:6; 13:14; 14:1), compared with two recorded by John (Jn 5:8–9; 9:14).

4:33 There are few examples of demon possession either in the Old Testament or in the New Testament after the Gospels. In Scripture such possession is defined as evil opposition to the coming of God's Son.

4:34 The demon recognized Jesus as the "Holy One of God"—a term that denotes Jesus' special relationship to God and his empowerment by the Spirit (Jn 6:69). Luke's Gospel makes it clear that part of Jesus' mission was to defeat the powers of evil.

4:38–39 Matthew and Mark both report this miracle, but only Luke speaks of a high fever, a possible indication of Luke's medical interest. That Jesus rebuked the fever may mean that he saw Satan being behind it in some way.

4:41 You are the son of God! Again it is the demons who discern that Jesus is the Son of God. People might have seen no more in Jesus than they saw in other men, but the forces of evil recognized God's Son. **the Christ.** This is the Greek form of the Hebrew word *Messiah*, meaning "the anointed one" (i.e., the One marked by God for special service).

4:43 I must. This phrase points to the divine compulsion in the mission of Jesus. The kingdom was central. **kingdom of God.** This is Luke's first mention of the kingdom of God, which was Jesus' most frequent topic. See "Introduction to the Gospels," on page 1539 and theological article "The Kingdom of God" at Matthew 4.

5:1 Lake of Gennesaret. Luke always referred to this body of water as a lake (the other Gospel writers called it a sea); it is usually named the "Sea of Galilee" ("Gennesaret" occurs only here). **the word of God.** That which comes from God and tells of God.

5:2 washing their nets. After each fishing trip the nets were checked, mended and cleaned for the next use. The boats were not in use, so Jesus could sit in Simon's boat and escape the press of the crowd.

5:5 Master. This word is used only by Luke and always of Jesus. More generally, it means anyone in authority.

6When they had done so, they caught such a large number of fish that their nets began to break.[d] 7So they signaled their partners in the other boat to come and help them,
and they came and filled both boats so full that they began to sink.
8When Simon Peter saw this, he fell at Jesus' knees and said, "Go away from me, Lord;
I am a sinful man!"[e] 9For he and all his companions were astonished at the catch of fish
they had taken, 10and so were James and John, the sons of Zebedee, Simon's partners.
Then Jesus said to Simon, "Don't be afraid;[f] from now on you will catch men." 11So
they pulled their boats up on shore, left everything and followed him.[g]

The Man With Leprosy

12While Jesus was in one of the towns, a man came along who was covered with leprosy.[a][h] When he saw Jesus, he fell with his face to the ground and begged him, "Lord,
if you are willing, you can make me clean."
13Jesus reached out his hand and touched the man. "I am willing," he said. "Be clean!"
And immediately the leprosy left him.
14Then Jesus ordered him, "Don't tell anyone,[i] but go, show yourself to the priest and
offer the sacrifices that Moses commanded[j] for your cleansing, as a testimony to them."
15Yet the news about him spread all the more,[k] so that crowds of people came to hear
him and to be healed of their sicknesses. 16But Jesus often withdrew to lonely places and
prayed.[l]

Jesus Heals a Paralytic

17One day as he was teaching, Pharisees and teachers of the law,[m] who had come
from every village of Galilee and from Judea and Jerusalem, were sitting there. And the
power of the Lord was present for him to heal the sick.[n] 18Some men came carrying a
paralytic on a mat and tried to take him into the house to lay him before Jesus. 19When
they could not find a way to do this because of the crowd, they went up on the roof and
lowered him on his mat through the tiles into the middle of the crowd, right in front of
Jesus.
20When Jesus saw their faith, he said, "Friend, your sins are forgiven."[o]
21The Pharisees and the teachers of the law began thinking to themselves, "Who is
this fellow who speaks blasphemy? Who can forgive sins but God alone?"[p]
22Jesus knew what they were thinking and asked, "Why are you thinking these things
in your hearts? 23Which is easier: to say, 'Your sins are forgiven,' or to say, 'Get up and
walk'? 24But that you may know that the Son of Man[q] has authority on earth to forgive
sins . . ." He said to the paralyzed man, "I tell you, get up, take your mat and go home."
25Immediately he stood up in front of them, took what he had been lying on and went
home praising God. 26Everyone was amazed and gave praise to God.[r] They were filled
with awe and said, "We have seen remarkable things today."

The Calling of Levi

27After this, Jesus went out and saw a tax collector by the name of Levi sitting at his
tax booth. "Follow me,"[s] Jesus said to him, 28and Levi got up, left everything and followed
him.[t]
29Then Levi held a great banquet for Jesus at his house, and a large crowd of tax collectors[u] and others were eating with them. 30But the Pharisees and the teachers of the

5:6 [d]Jn 21:11
5:8 [e]Ge 18:27; Job 42:6; Isa 6:5
5:10 [f]Mt 14:27
5:11 [g]ver 28; Mt 4:19
5:12 [h]Mt 8:2
5:14 [i]Mt 8:4 [j]Lev 14:2-32
5:15 [k]Mt 9:26
5:16 [l]Mt 14:23; Lk 3:21
5:17 [m]Mt 15:1; Lk 2:46 [n]Mk 5:30; Lk 6:19
5:20 [o]Lk 7:48,49
5:21 [p]Isa 43:25
5:24 [q]Mt 8:20
5:26 [r]Mt 9:8
5:27 [s]Mt 4:19
5:28 [t]ver 11; Mt 4:19
5:29 [u]Lk 15:1

[a] *12* The Greek word was used for various diseases affecting the skin—not necessarily leprosy.

5:8 sinful man! Peter knew fishing and saw in this event the hand of God. In the presence of God, he was convicted of his sinfulness (cf. Ge 18:27; Job 42:6; Isa 6:5).
5:12 leprosy. Several different diseases, varying in severity and prognosis, were referred to as "leprosy." In its worst form the condition was defiling (the leper was considered ceremonially "unclean"), disfiguring and fatal. The only known defense was quarantine of the sufferer.
5:14 to the priest. The priest would certify that a leper had been cured, as well as offer the appropriate sacrifices for this situation (Lev 14).
5:17 Pharisees. Josephus indicated that there were over 6,000 Pharisees in his day. They saw themselves as God's "separated ones" and sought to serve him well. Many were godly men, but their emphasis on outward acts and taboos often made them hardened and formal. Such men opposed Jesus vigorously. (See chart "Jewish Sects" at Mt 23.) **teachers of the law.** Scribes whose work centered on the law of God. Many were Pharisees.
5:19 up on the roof. Houses often had flat roofs with external staircases leading up to them.
5:20 their faith. Jesus included the faith of the bearers as well as that of the patient.
5:21 Who is this fellow . . . ? See note on Mark 2:5.
5:24 that you may know. Jesus linked the power to forgive with the power to heal (see note on Mk 2:9). **the Son of Man.** Jesus' favorite self-designation, used over 80 times in the Gospels and almost always by Jesus himself. It refers to his heavenly origin and vocation (Da 7:13–14). See "Introduction to the Gospels" on page 1539.
5:27 tax collector. See note on 3:12.
5:28 left everything. Levi either left his records and money in his booth or he permanently abandoned his job as tax collector.
5:30 The Pharisees would have been outside. They regarded table fellowship with "sinners" as especially defiling.

5:30 [v]Ac 23:9 [w]Mt 9:11 law who belonged to their sect[v] complained to his disciples, "Why do you eat and drink
with tax collectors and 'sinners'?"[w]
5:32 [x]Jn 3:17 [31]Jesus answered them, "It is not the healthy who need a doctor, but the sick. [32]I have
not come to call the righteous, but sinners to repentance."[x]

Jesus Questioned About Fasting

5:33 [y]Lk 7:18; Jn 1:35; 3:25,26 [33]They said to him, "John's disciples[y] often fast and pray, and so do the disciples of
the Pharisees, but yours go on eating and drinking."
5:34 [z]Jn 3:29 [34]Jesus answered, "Can you make the guests of the bridegroom[z] fast while he is with
5:35 [a]Lk 9:22; 17:22; Jn 16:5-7 them? [35]But the time will come when the bridegroom will be taken from them;[a] in those
days they will fast."
[36]He told them this parable: "No one tears a patch from a new garment and sews it
on an old one. If he does, he will have torn the new garment, and the patch from the new
will not match the old. [37]And no one pours new wine into old wineskins. If he does, the
new wine will burst the skins, the wine will run out and the wineskins will be ruined.
[38]No, new wine must be poured into new wineskins. [39]And no one after drinking old wine
wants the new, for he says, 'The old is better.' "

Lord of the Sabbath

6:1 [b]Dt 23:25 **6** One Sabbath Jesus was going through the grainfields, and his disciples began to
pick some heads of grain, rub them in their hands and eat the kernels.[b] [2]Some of
the Pharisees asked, "Why are you doing what is unlawful on the Sabbath?"[c]
6:2 [c]Mt 12:2 [3]Jesus answered them, "Have you never read what David did when he and his com-
6:3 [d]1Sa 21:6 panions were hungry?[d] [4]He entered the house of God, and taking the consecrated
bread, he ate what is lawful only for priests to eat.[e] And he also gave some to his com-
6:4 [e]Lev 24:5,9 panions." [5]Then Jesus said to them, "The Son of Man[f] is Lord of the Sabbath."
[6]On another Sabbath[g] he went into the synagogue and was teaching, and a man was
6:5 [f]Mt 8:20 there whose right hand was shriveled. [7]The Pharisees and the teachers of the law were
looking for a reason to accuse Jesus, so they watched him closely[h] to see if he would heal
6:6 [g]ver 1 on the Sabbath.[i] [8]But Jesus knew what they were thinking[j] and said to the man with the
shriveled hand, "Get up and stand in front of everyone." So he got up and stood there.
6:7 [h]Mt 12:10 [i]Mt 12:2 [9]Then Jesus said to them, "I ask you, which is lawful on the Sabbath: to do good or
to do evil, to save life or to destroy it?"
6:8 [j]Mt 9:4 [10]He looked around at them all, and then said to the man, "Stretch out your hand."
6:11 He did so, and his hand was completely restored. [11]But they were furious[k] and began to
[k]Jn 5:18 discuss with one another what they might do to Jesus.

The Twelve Apostles

[12]One of those days Jesus went out to a mountainside to pray, and spent the night
6:12 [l]Lk 3:21 praying to God.[l] [13]When morning came, he called his disciples to him and chose twelve
6:13 [m]Mk 6:30 of them, whom he also designated apostles:[m] [14]Simon (whom he named Peter), his
brother Andrew, James, John, Philip, Bartholomew, [15]Matthew,[n] Thomas, James son of
6:15 [n]Mt 9:9 Alphaeus, Simon who was called the Zealot, [16]Judas son of James, and Judas Iscariot,
who became a traitor.

5:33 The only fast required by the law was the one mandated for the Day of Atonement, but religious people fasted on other days (e.g., Zec 7:3,5). Jesus did not command fasts, though he himself fasted (4:2) and permitted the practice among his followers (Mt 6:16–18).

5:36–38 A new patch on an old garment spoils both—the new is ruined because the patch is torn from the flimsy garment; the old is marred because the patch does not match. New wine in old wineskins ferments and bursts the skins; thus both the wine and the skins are lost.

6:1 One Sabbath. A principal source of controversy between Jesus and the Pharisees was the correct use of the Sabbath. They hedged the day with repressive regulations so as to avoid the possibility of breaking the Sabbath. Jesus did not so much argue that the regulations should be relaxed as that the Pharisees had misunderstood the intent of the Sabbath—it was a day on which good deeds should be done. **pick some heads of grain.** This activity was permitted in the law (Dt 23:25); only the fact that it was done on the Sabbath was seen by the Pharisees as unlawful.

6:4 the consecrated bread. Bread prepared in a special way for use in temple service. It was to be eaten only by priests (Lev 24:5–9), although in a time of need David had used it for his companions (1Sa 21:3–6).

6:5 Lord of the Sabbath. The Sabbath was instituted by God (Ge 2:3; Ex 20:8–11) and belonged exclusively to him (Isa 58:13). In claiming that he was Lord over it, Jesus indicated his own deity and divine authority to interpret the law.

6:9 which is lawful . . . ? Jesus presented a choice between doing good and doing evil on the Sabbath, not between doing good and doing nothing. He saw the failure to do good as evil in itself.

6:11 furious. The Pharisees wanted to kill Jesus (Jn 5:18), but he had publicly asked a relevant question and they had not answered it. They could not bring an action against him.

■**6:12–16** *Choosing the Twelve.* After Luke had provided examples of Jesus' teachings and miracles, he enumerated a list of Jesus' 12 disciples, the men Jesus also designated as apostles (see note on v. 13).

6:12 spent the night praying. Prolonged prayer preceded the important selection of the Twelve.

6:13 apostles. The word means "messenger" or "someone sent." It is not often used in the Gospels ("the Twelve" is more common) but is frequent in later books.

6:14 Simon. Luke has until now spoken of "Simon," but from this point on he regularly refers to this disciple as "Peter."

Blessings and Woes

17 He went down with them and stood on a level place. A large crowd of his disciples
was there and a great number of people from all over Judea, from Jerusalem, and from
the coast of Tyre and Sidon,[o] 18 who had come to hear him and to be healed of their diseases. Those troubled by evil[a] spirits were cured, 19 and the people all tried to touch him,[p]
because power was coming from him and healing them all.[q]
20 Looking at his disciples, he said:

"Blessed are you who are poor,
for yours is the kingdom of God.[r]
21 Blessed are you who hunger now,
for you will be satisfied.[s]
Blessed are you who weep now,
for you will laugh.[t]
22 Blessed are you when men hate you,
when they exclude you[u] and insult you[v]
and reject your name as evil,
because of the Son of Man.[w]

23 "Rejoice in that day and leap for joy,[x] because great is your reward in heaven. For
that is how their fathers treated the prophets.[y]

24 "But woe to you who are rich,[z]
for you have already received your comfort.[a]
25 Woe to you who are well fed now,
for you will go hungry.[b]
Woe to you who laugh now,
for you will mourn and weep.[c]
26 Woe to you when all men speak well of you,
for that is how their fathers treated the false prophets.[d]

Love for Enemies

27 "But I tell you who hear me: Love your enemies, do good to those who hate you,[e]
28 bless those who curse you, pray for those who mistreat you.[f] 29 If someone strikes you
on one cheek, turn to him the other also. If someone takes your cloak, do not stop him
from taking your tunic. 30 Give to everyone who asks you, and if anyone takes what belongs to you, do not demand it back.[g] 31 Do to others as you would have them do to you.[h]
32 "If you love those who love you, what credit is that to you?[i] Even 'sinners' love those
who love them. 33 And if you do good to those who are good to you, what credit is that
to you? Even 'sinners' do that. 34 And if you lend to those from whom you expect repay-
ment, what credit is that to you?[j] Even 'sinners' lend to 'sinners,' expecting to be repaid
in full. 35 But love your enemies, do good to them,[k] and lend to them without expecting
to get anything back. Then your reward will be great, and you will be sons[l] of the Most
High,[m] because he is kind to the ungrateful and wicked. 36 Be merciful,[n] just as your Father[o] is merciful.

6:17 [o]Mt 4:25; Mt 11:21; Mk 3:7,8
6:19 [p]Mt 9:20 [q]Mt 14:36; Mk 5:30; Lk 5:17
6:20 [r]Mt 25:34
6:21 [s]Isa 55:1,2; Mt 5:6 [t]Isa 61:2,3; Mt 5:4; Rev 7:17
6:22 [u]Jn 9:22; 16:2 [v]Isa 51:7 [w]Jn 15:21
6:23 [x]Mt 5:12 [y]Mt 5:12
6:24 [z]Jas 5:1 [a]Lk 16:25
6:25 [b]Isa 65:13 [c]Pr 14:13
6:26 [d]Mt 7:15
6:27 [e]ver 35; Mt 5:44; Ro 12:20
6:28 [f]Mt 5:44
6:30 [g]Dt 15:7,8,10; Pr 21:26
6:31 [h]Mt 7:12
6:32 [i]Mt 5:46
6:34 [j]Mt 5:42
6:35 [k]ver 27 [l]Ro 8:14 [m]Mk 5:7
6:36 [n]Jas 2:13 [o]Mt 5:48; 6:1; Lk 11:2; 12:32; Ro 8:15; Eph 4:6; 1Pe 1:17; 1Jn 1:3; 3:1

a *18* Greek *unclean*

■ **6:17–49** *The Sermon on the Plain.* Luke summarized Jesus' sermon on the plain (see note on vv. 20–49). This sermon contained essential elements of Jesus' teaching about the kingdom of God.
6:17 a level place. This accounts for the sermon being called "the sermon on the plain." Luke speaks of a ministry of teaching and healing that had wide appeal.
6:20–49 This sermon resembles the Sermon on the Mount (Mt 5–7), and some see it as a variant account of the same sermon. But this sermon is much shorter than the Sermon on the Mount, and Luke elsewhere includes parallels to other parts of Matthew 5–7. It is more likely that Jesus used the same or similar material on a number of occasions.
6:20 Blessed. This word implies more than *fortunate* or *happy;* it is a religious term that refers to those who enjoy the favor of God. **you who are poor.** This means "you disciples, poor as you are," not "the poor" as such. Poverty can be a curse (Pr 30:8–9), and Jesus' followers knew that they must rely on God for all things. They had no resources of their own, but God had blessed them with the kingdom.
6:21 Those who are hungry realize their need and look to God for satisfaction. Those who weep mourn over the world's evil.
6:22–23 A blessing for the persecuted is most unexpected. It is not suffering in general that is pronounced blessed, but suffering "because of the Son of Man."
6:24–26 This "woe" section corresponds to the previous "blessed" section (vv. 20–22). Those who do not realize their spiritual poverty but rely on their own achievement will in the end reap disaster. **woe.** Often introduced a prophetic oracle of doom (e.g., Eze 34:2).
6:30 Love for possessions should not prevent generosity. There may be reasons why some gifts are not given, but this must not reflect a determination to keep all that one has. See *WLC* 141.
6:31 The negative form of the Golden Rule, that we should not do to others as we would not want them to do to us, is sometimes found before the time of Jesus. Jesus is the first person known to have rendered the principle in this positive form.
6:32–34 The world's standards are not to guide the followers of Jesus.
6:35 Believers are to love even their enemies; they are to have for them a love like God's love. **sons of the Most High.** God's people are to be like God; they are to be merciful, just as he is merciful. See *HC* 110.
6:36 See *HC* 107.

Judging Others

6:37 [p]Mt 7:1 [q]Mt 6:14
6:38 [r]Ps 79:12; Isa 65:6, 7 [s]Mt 7:2; Mk 4:24
6:39 [t]Mt 15:14
6:40 [u]Mt 10:24; Jn 13:16

37“Do not judge, and you will not be judged.[p] Do not condemn, and you will not be
condemned. Forgive, and you will be forgiven.[q] 38Give, and it will be given to you. A good
measure, pressed down, shaken together and running over, will be poured into your
lap.[r] For with the measure you use, it will be measured to you.”[s]
39He also told them this parable: “Can a blind man lead a blind man? Will they not
both fall into a pit?[t] 40A student is not above his teacher, but everyone who is fully trained
will be like his teacher.[u]
41“Why do you look at the speck of sawdust in your brother’s eye and pay no attention to the plank in your own eye? 42How can you say to your brother, ‘Brother, let me
take the speck out of your eye,’ when you yourself fail to see the plank in your own eye?
You hypocrite, first take the plank out of your eye, and then you will see clearly to remove
the speck from your brother’s eye.

A Tree and Its Fruit

6:44 [v]Mt 12:33
6:45 [w]Pr 4:23; Mt 12:34, 35; Mk 7:20

43“No good tree bears bad fruit, nor does a bad tree bear good fruit. 44Each tree is recognized by its own fruit.[v] People do not pick figs from thornbushes, or grapes from briers. 45The good man brings good things out of the good stored up in his heart, and the
evil man brings evil things out of the evil stored up in his heart. For out of the overflow
of his heart his mouth speaks.[w]

The Wise and Foolish Builders

6:46 [x]Jn 13:13 [y]Mal 1:6; Mt 7:21
6:47 [z]Lk 8:21; 11:28; Jas 1:22-25

46“Why do you call me, ‘Lord, Lord,’[x] and do not do what I say?[y] 47I will show you
what he is like who comes to me and hears my words and puts them into practice.[z] 48He
is like a man building a house, who dug down deep and laid the foundation on rock.
When a flood came, the torrent struck that house but could not shake it, because it was
well built. 49But the one who hears my words and does not put them into practice is like
a man who built a house on the ground without a foundation. The moment the torrent
struck that house, it collapsed and its destruction was complete.”

The Faith of the Centurion

7:1 [a]Mt 7:28
7:7 [b]Ps 107:20

7 When Jesus had finished saying all this[a] in the hearing of the people, he entered Capernaum. 2There a centurion’s servant, whom his master valued highly, was sick
and about to die. 3The centurion heard of Jesus and sent some elders of the Jews to him,
asking him to come and heal his servant. 4When they came to Jesus, they pleaded earnestly with him, “This man deserves to have you do this, 5because he loves our nation
and has built our synagogue.” 6So Jesus went with them.
He was not far from the house when the centurion sent friends to say to him: “Lord,
don’t trouble yourself, for I do not deserve to have you come under my roof. 7That is why
I did not even consider myself worthy to come to you. But say the word, and my servant
will be healed.[b] 8For I myself am a man under authority, with soldiers under me. I tell
this one, ‘Go,’ and he goes; and that one, ‘Come,’ and he comes. I say to my servant, ‘Do
this,’ and he does it.”
9When Jesus heard this, he was amazed at him, and turning to the crowd following

---

6:37 Do not judge, and you will not be judged. Jesus taught that his disciples must sometimes confront the evil actions of others (Mt 18:15–17) and that the character of a person’s heart can be recognized by the fruit, or actions, that flow from that heart (vv. 43–45). Here Jesus condemned the hypocrisy of those who denounce in others the very sins of which they themselves are guilty (vv. 41–42), as well as the censorious failure to show mercy (v. 36). **you will be forgiven.** We do not earn forgiveness. But if we fail to forgive others, we do not have genuine repentance and faith, and thus we exclude ourselves from the possibility of forgiveness. See *HC* 112.

6:38 See *WLC* 141.

6:39–42 In quick succession Jesus presented three vivid, but unrelated, images dealing with the attitudes of disciples. In them he highlighted the danger of following (or being) a blind leader (v. 39); the importance of a disciple’s deference to his teacher (i.e., Christ; v. 40); and the danger of hypocrisy, as portrayed in the illustration of the speck and the plank (vv. 41–42).

6:43–45 The fruit reveals the tree’s real identity, just as actions expose a person’s inner character. See *HC* 64.

6:46–49 To call Jesus “Lord” is to say that he should be obeyed.

■ **7:1–17** *Healing Miracles.* Luke recorded two miracles Jesus performed that revealed his glory to many in Galilee and Judea.

7:2 centurion’s. Originally the commander of 100 soldiers, although at this time the number of soldiers varied. The centurion was roughly the equivalent of a captain in a modern army. A centurion in the New Testament was assumed to be a man of good character (7:4; 23:47; Ac 10:2; 27:43). **servant.** The Greek means “slave.” This centurion was a humane man who was concerned about the well-being of his slaves.

7:3 elders of the Jews. Leading men among the Jews. That they would plead his case demonstrates their high regard for the centurion.

7:5 loves our nation. This was an attitude unusual in a conqueror. **built our synagogue.** The centurion was interested in Jewish worship. He may even have been a “God-fearer” (a Gentile who attached himself loosely to the synagogue and worshiped the true God but who was not circumcised and had not become a Jew in the full sense).

7:6–8 In Matthew 8:5, the man comes in person. Matthew implies that what a man does through his agents he does himself. In Luke, the messengers are important because they show the man’s humility (vv. 6–7).

7:8 under authority. The centurion was familiar with the concept of authority exercised at a distance.

7:9 amazed. Only twice in the Gospel accounts is Jesus said to

him, he said, "I tell you, I have not found such great faith even in Israel." 10Then the men
who had been sent returned to the house and found the servant well.

Jesus Raises a Widow's Son

11Soon afterward, Jesus went to a town called Nain, and his disciples and a large crowd
went along with him. 12As he approached the town gate, a dead person was being carried
out—the only son of his mother, and she was a widow. And a large crowd from the town
was with her. 13When the Lord[c] saw her, his heart went out to her and he said, "Don't cry."
14Then he went up and touched the coffin, and those carrying it stood still. He said,
"Young man, I say to you, get up!"[d] 15The dead man sat up and began to talk, and Jesus
gave him back to his mother.
16They were all filled with awe[e] and praised God.[f] "A great prophet[g] has appeared
among us," they said. "God has come to help his people."[h] 17This news about Jesus
spread throughout Judea[a] and the surrounding country.[i]

Jesus and John the Baptist

18John's[j] disciples[k] told him about all these things. Calling two of them, 19he sent them
to the Lord to ask, "Are you the one who was to come, or should we expect someone else?"
20When the men came to Jesus, they said, "John the Baptist sent us to you to ask, 'Are
you the one who was to come, or should we expect someone else?' "
21At that very time Jesus cured many who had diseases, sicknesses[l] and evil spirits, and
gave sight to many who were blind. 22So he replied to the messengers, "Go back and report to John what you have seen and heard: The blind receive sight, the lame walk, those
who have leprosy[b] are cured, the deaf hear, the dead are raised, and the good news is
preached to the poor.[m] 23Blessed is the man who does not fall away on account of me."
24After John's messengers left, Jesus began to speak to the crowd about John: "What
did you go out into the desert to see? A reed swayed by the wind? 25If not, what did you
go out to see? A man dressed in fine clothes? No, those who wear expensive clothes and
indulge in luxury are in palaces. 26But what did you go out to see? A prophet?[n] Yes, I tell
you, and more than a prophet. 27This is the one about whom it is written:

> " 'I will send my messenger ahead of you,
> who will prepare your way before you.'[c][o]

28I tell you, among those born of women there is no one greater than John; yet the one
who is least in the kingdom of God[p] is greater than he."
29(All the people, even the tax collectors, when they heard Jesus' words, acknowledged that God's way was right, because they had been baptized by John.[q] 30But the
Pharisees and experts in the law[r] rejected God's purpose for themselves, because they
had not been baptized by John.)

7:13 [c]ver 19; Lk 10:1; 13:15; 17:5; 22:61; 24:34; Jn 11:2
7:14 [d]Mt 9:25; Mk 1:31; Lk 8:54; Jn 11:43; Ac 9:40
7:16 [e]Lk 1:65 [f]Mt 9:8 [g]ver 39; Mt 21:11 [h]Lk 1:68
7:17 [i]Mt 9:26
7:18 [j]Mt 3:1 [k]Lk 5:33
7:21 [l]Mt 4:23
7:22 [m]Isa 29:18,19; 35:5,6; 61:1,2; Lk 4:18
7:26 [n]Mt 11:9
7:27 [o]Mal 3:1; Mt 11:10; Mk 1:2
7:28 [p]Mt 3:2
7:29 [q]Mt 21:32; Mk 1:5; Lk 3:12
7:30 [r]Mt 22:35

[a] *17* Or *the land of the Jews* [b] *22* The Greek word was used for various diseases affecting the skin—not necessarily leprosy. [c] *27* Mal. 3:1

---

have been amazed: here at the faith of a foreigner and in Mark 6:6 at the unbelief in Nazareth.
7:13 the Lord. In all four Gospels people addressed Jesus as "Lord," but this is the first time Luke as the narrator used this title. He employed the term a number of times in passages not paralleled in Mark. John also used this title occasionally, but Mark and Matthew did not. The title was evidently not often used of Jesus during his lifetime, but it was consistently applied to him by the apostolic church. **saw her.** The mother would have been walking in front of the bier, so Jesus would have met her first. Nobody asked him to help, but he took action out of compassion.
7:14 coffin. This would have been an open bier according to Jewish custom.
7:15 The first of three instances of Jesus' raising of the dead (8:40–56; Jn 11:1–44); such miracles were powerful Messianic signs (v. 22). These "resurrections" differed markedly from that of Christ, however, for these three persons were only temporarily reunited with their mortal bodies, eventually to die once more. As the first to be clothed with an imperishable, spiritual body (1Co 15:42–44), Jesus is indeed the "firstborn from among the dead" (Col 1:18; cf. 1Co 15:20).
7:16 A great prophet. Although inadequate, this was probably the highest title they knew. At any rate, they recognized God's presence among them.
■ **7:18–35** *John the Baptist.* Luke reported a question raised by John the Baptist when John saw that Jesus had not brought the kingdom of God in its fullness as he had hoped (see note on 3:9). Jesus dealt with two matters: how he had begun kingdom blessings through his ministry and how so many in Israel failed to believe.
7:18–19 Since John had borne witness to Jesus (3:16–17), these questions from John seem surprising. Some think John's faith had failed in the harsh conditions of Herod's prison, others that his patience had given out and he was suggesting that Jesus should actively bring in the kingdom. More probably, John looked for Jesus to bring judgment, a theme John had stressed in his ministry. He failed to comprehend why Jesus did not punish sinners but constantly performed deeds of mercy. John wondered whether someone else would come to fulfill his prophecy of judgment.
7:21–23 See Isaiah 35:5–6 and 61:1.
7:24–28 Jesus' answer might suggest that he was disowning his forerunner. This was not so, and Jesus proceeded to make it clear that John was the greatest of men. Despite his questions, John was no weakling. He was a prophet and more, for he was also the fulfillment of prophecy (Mal 3:1). Great as he was, John belonged to the era that preceded the kingdom under Christ, so he was "less" than those who belonged to the new era of the kingdom.
7:29 when they heard Jesus' words. Literally, "when they heard." Some translate verses 29–30 as a parenthesis; others view these verses as a continuation of Jesus' speech.
7:30 experts in the law. This is a translation of a Greek word (*nomikos*) that is found six times in Luke but only once in the other three Gospels combined. It means "lawyers."

31 "To what, then, can I compare the people of this generation? What are they like?
32 They are like children sitting in the marketplace and calling out to each other:

" 'We played the flute for you,
and you did not dance;
we sang a dirge,
and you did not cry.'

7:33 [s]Lk 1:15 — 33 For John the Baptist came neither eating bread nor drinking wine,[s] and you say, 'He
7:34 [t]Lk 5:29,30; 15:1,2 — has a demon.' 34 The Son of Man came eating and drinking, and you say, 'Here is a glutton and a drunkard, a friend of tax collectors and "sinners." '[t] 35 But wisdom is proved
right by all her children."

Jesus Anointed by a Sinful Woman

36 Now one of the Pharisees invited Jesus to have dinner with him, so he went to the
Pharisee's house and reclined at the table. 37 When a woman who had lived a sinful life
in that town learned that Jesus was eating at the Pharisee's house, she brought an alabaster jar of perfume, 38 and as she stood behind him at his feet weeping, she began to
wet his feet with her tears. Then she wiped them with her hair, kissed them and poured
perfume on them.

7:39 [u]ver 16; Mt 21:11 — 39 When the Pharisee who had invited him saw this, he said to himself, "If this man
were a prophet,[u] he would know who is touching him and what kind of woman she is—
that she is a sinner."

40 Jesus answered him, "Simon, I have something to tell you."

"Tell me, teacher," he said.

41 "Two men owed money to a certain moneylender. One owed him five hundred denarii,[a] and the other fifty. 42 Neither of them had the money to pay him back, so he canceled the debts of both. Now which of them will love him more?"

43 Simon replied, "I suppose the one who had the bigger debt canceled."

"You have judged correctly," Jesus said.

7:44 [v]Ge 18:4; 19:2; 43:24; Jdg 19:21; Jn 13:4-14; 1Ti 5:10 — 44 Then he turned toward the woman and said to Simon, "Do you see this woman? I
came into your house. You did not give me any water for my feet,[v] but she wet my feet
with her tears and wiped them with her hair. 45 You did not give me a kiss,[w] but this wom-
7:45 [w]Lk 22:47,48; Ro 16:16 — an, from the time I entered, has not stopped kissing my feet. 46 You did not put oil on my
head,[x] but she has poured perfume on my feet. 47 Therefore, I tell you, her many sins have
7:46 [x]Ps 23:5; Ecc 9:8 — been forgiven—for she loved much. But he who has been forgiven little loves little."

48 Then Jesus said to her, "Your sins are forgiven."[y]

7:48 [y]Mt 9:2 — 49 The other guests began to say among themselves, "Who is this who even forgives
sins?"

7:50 [z]Mt 9:22; Mk 5:34; Lk 8:48 [a]Ac 15:33 — 50 Jesus said to the woman, "Your faith has saved you;[z] go in peace."[a]

The Parable of the Sower

8:1 [b]Mt 4:23 — 8 After this, Jesus traveled about from one town and village to another, proclaiming
the good news of the kingdom of God.[b] The Twelve were with him, 2 and also some
8:2 [c]Mt 27:55,56 — women who had been cured of evil spirits and diseases: Mary (called Magdalene)[c] from
whom seven demons had come out; 3 Joanna the wife of Cuza, the manager of Herod's[d]

8:3 [d]Mt 14:1

[a] 41 A denarius was a coin worth about a day's wages.

7:32 like children. Jesus drew attention to the childishness that sometimes rejects playmates no matter what they do, and went on to point out the unreasonableness of people who rejected John because he was too stern and Jesus because he was too cheerful.

■ **7:36–50** *Jesus and a Woman.* In contrast to the majority of Jews, but similar to the centurion and widow (vv. 1–16), this prostitute was praised for her humility and faith.

7:37–38 At a dinner like this, the house would have been left open, and bystanders would have come in to observe. A sinful woman (probably a prostitute) would not have been welcome; it took courage for her to come in. Diners reclined on couches, with their heads toward the table. They leaned on their left arms and used their right hands to pick up food.

7:37 alabaster. A translucent stone used to make containers for costly perfumes.

7:38 weeping. The woman's tears and her act of anointing Jesus' feet demonstrated her penitence and humility.

7:39 he would know. A Pharisee would have no contact with "sinful" people and believed that no prophet would do so either. Because Jesus did not dismiss the woman, Simon assumed that Jesus either did not know or did not care that she was sinful. In either case, in Simon's view Jesus could not have been a prophet.

7:44–46 Simon had omitted the courtesies normally accorded to guests. But the woman made up for his lack of hospitality.

7:47 for. This indicates the evidence of, not the reason for, her forgiveness. It was faith that brought forgiveness (v. 50), not love, but her love demonstrated that she had been forgiven.

7:48–50 Again Jesus authoritatively declared sins to be forgiven, an act that aroused comment. But his concern was for the woman.

■ **8:1–56** *More Teachings and Miracles.* Luke marked a shift in his narrative by collecting and recording a number of remarkable things Jesus had said and done as he had traveled from place to place.

8:2 Rabbis refused to teach women, so Jesus' attitude in accepting them into his group of followers was unusual. **Magdalene.** From the town of Magdala.

8:3 out of their own means. This phrase provides a glimpse of the way Jesus and his band were supported throughout his ministry.

household; Susanna; and many others. These women were helping to support them out
of their own means.
4While a large crowd was gathering and people were coming to Jesus from town after town, he told this parable: 5"A farmer went out to sow his seed. As he was scattering the seed, some fell along the path; it was trampled on, and the birds of the air ate it
up. 6Some fell on rock, and when it came up, the plants withered because they had no
moisture. 7Other seed fell among thorns, which grew up with it and choked the plants.
8Still other seed fell on good soil. It came up and yielded a crop, a hundred times more
than was sown."
When he said this, he called out, "He who has ears to hear, let him hear."[e]
9His disciples asked him what this parable meant. 10He said, "The knowledge of the secrets of the kingdom of God has been given to you,[f] but to others I speak in parables, so that,

" 'though seeing, they may not see;
though hearing, they may not understand.'[b][g]

11"This is the meaning of the parable: The seed is the word of God.[h] 12Those along the
path are the ones who hear, and then the devil comes and takes away the word from their
hearts, so that they may not believe and be saved. 13Those on the rock are the ones who
receive the word with joy when they hear it, but they have no root. They believe for a
while, but in the time of testing they fall away.[i] 14The seed that fell among thorns stands
for those who hear, but as they go on their way they are choked by life's worries, riches[j]
and pleasures, and they do not mature. 15But the seed on good soil stands for those with
a noble and good heart, who hear the word, retain it, and by persevering produce a crop.

A Lamp on a Stand

16"No one lights a lamp and hides it in a jar or puts it under a bed. Instead, he puts it
on a stand, so that those who come in can see the light.[k] 17For there is nothing hidden that
will not be disclosed, and nothing concealed that will not be known or brought out into
the open.[l] 18Therefore consider carefully how you listen. Whoever has will be given
more; whoever does not have, even what he thinks he has will be taken from him."[m]

Jesus' Mother and Brothers

19Now Jesus' mother and brothers came to see him, but they were not able to get near
him because of the crowd. 20Someone told him, "Your mother and brothers[n] are stand
ing outside, wanting to see you."
21He replied, "My mother and brothers are those who hear God's word and put it into
practice."[o]

Jesus Calms the Storm

22One day Jesus said to his disciples, "Let's go over to the other side of the lake." So
they got into a boat and set out. 23As they sailed, he fell asleep. A squall came down on
the lake, so that the boat was being swamped, and they were in great danger.

8:8 [e]Mt 11:15
8:10 [f]Mt 13:11 [g]Isa 6:9; Mt 13:13,14
8:11 [h]Heb 4:12
8:13 [i]Mt 11:6
8:14 [j]Mt 19:23; 1Ti 6:9, 10,17
8:16 [k]Mt 5:15; Mk 4:21; Lk 11:33
8:17 [l]Mt 10:26; Mk 4:22; Lk 12:2
8:18 [m]Mt 13:12; 25:29; Lk 19:26
8:20 [n]Jn 7:5
8:21 [o]Lk 6:47; 11:28; Jn 14:21

b *10* Isaiah 6:9

8:4 parable. From this point in Luke, Jesus' parables feature more strongly. Crowds were coming to Jesus, but he looked for more than casual contact. Parables forced people to think carefully about what he was saying in order to catch his underlying meaning. See note on Matthew 13:3.
8:5 the path. Seed was first sown and then plowed into the soil. Paths ran through fields, and these, of course, were not plowed. Seed that fell on hard-packed paths was lost because it had no chance of sinking into the soil.
8:6 on rock. That is, on rock covered with a shallow layer of soil not deep enough to hold moisture.
8:7 thorns. Prickly plants that were unsown and marked by vigorous growth.
8:8 a hundred times more. Matthew and Mark also speak of yields of 30 and 60 times more, but Luke concentrates on the crop of greatest abundance. **let him hear.** Jesus challenged the hearer to think.
8:10 secrets. The Greek word is that from which we get our word *mystery.* It refers to truths we could never before have understood, but which God has now made known. **others.** These are the kind of people of whom Isaiah's prophecy referred—in this case, they did not respond to Jesus' teaching. They heard the story but failed to comprehend its meaning. **so that.** Jesus taught that his speaking in parables had a twofold purpose: to reveal the mysteries of the kingdom to those who had "ears to hear" (v. 8) and to conceal that truth from those who did not. See notes on Matthew 13:13 and Mark 4:11.
8:13 They believe for a while. One test of a true and living faith is perseverance. Those who depart from the way of truth reveal that they were never actually saved (1Jn 2:19).
8:15 See *WLC* 160; *WSC* 90.
8:16–18 The whole purpose of lighting a lamp is to give light. Jesus' teaching is to be made known. Because his teaching is the only gospel with the power to save, and because on the judgment day nothing will be kept hidden, it is important to understand Jesus' teaching rightly. Anyone who understands the truth of his words will find that his or her stock of truth keeps growing. See *WLC* 160.
8:19 brothers. See note on Mark 3:31.
8:21 Jesus' words were not a repudiation of his earthly family (he took care of Mary even as he hung on the cross; Jn 19:26–27). Rather, he was saying that the service of God is more important than anything else.
8:22–23 This lake is 660 feet (201 meters) below sea level and adjacent to mountains, so cool air from high places often sweeps down and whips up sudden storms.

8:24 [p]Lk 5:5 [q]Lk 4:35, 39,41 [r]Ps 107:29; Jnh 1:15

24 The disciples went and woke him, saying, "Master, Master,[p] we're going to drown!"
He got up and rebuked[q] the wind and the raging waters; the storm subsided, and all
was calm.[r] 25 "Where is your faith?" he asked his disciples.
In fear and amazement they asked one another, "Who is this? He commands even the
winds and the water, and they obey him."

The Healing of a Demon-possessed Man

26 They sailed to the region of the Gerasenes,[a] which is across the lake from Galilee.
27 When Jesus stepped ashore, he was met by a demon-possessed man from the town. For
a long time this man had not worn clothes or lived in a house, but had lived in the tombs.
8:28 [s]Mt 8:29 [t]Mk 5:7
28 When he saw Jesus, he cried out and fell at his feet, shouting at the top of his voice,
"What do you want with me,[s] Jesus, Son of the Most High God?[t] I beg you, don't torture
me!" 29 For Jesus had commanded the evil[b] spirit to come out of the man. Many times it
had seized him, and though he was chained hand and foot and kept under guard, he had
broken his chains and had been driven by the demon into solitary places.
30 Jesus asked him, "What is your name?"
8:31 [u]Rev 9:1,2,11; 11:7; 17:8; 20:1,3
"Legion," he replied, because many demons had gone into him. 31 And they begged
him repeatedly not to order them to go into the Abyss.[u]
32 A large herd of pigs was feeding there on the hillside. The demons begged Jesus to
8:33 [v]ver 22,23
let them go into them, and he gave them permission. 33 When the demons came out of
the man, they went into the pigs, and the herd rushed down the steep bank into the lake[v]
and was drowned.
34 When those tending the pigs saw what had happened, they ran off and reported this
in the town and countryside, 35 and the people went out to see what had happened. When
they came to Jesus, they found the man from whom the demons had gone out, sitting at
8:35 [w]Lk 10:39
Jesus' feet,[w] dressed and in his right mind; and they were afraid. 36 Those who had seen
8:36 [x]Mt 4:24
it told the people how the demon-possessed[x] man had been cured. 37 Then all the people of the region of the Gerasenes asked Jesus to leave them,[y] because they were over-
8:37 [y]Ac 16:39
come with fear. So he got into the boat and left.
38 The man from whom the demons had gone out begged to go with him, but Jesus
sent him away, saying, 39 "Return home and tell how much God has done for you." So the
man went away and told all over town how much Jesus had done for him.

A Dead Girl and a Sick Woman

40 Now when Jesus returned, a crowd welcomed him, for they were all expecting him.
8:41 [z]ver 49; Mk 5:22
41 Then a man named Jairus, a ruler of the synagogue,[z] came and fell at Jesus' feet, pleading with him to come to his house 42 because his only daughter, a girl of about twelve,
was dying.
8:43 [a]Lev 15:25-30
As Jesus was on his way, the crowds almost crushed him. 43 And a woman was there
who had been subject to bleeding[a] for twelve years,[c] but no one could heal her. 44 She
8:44 [b]Mt 9:20
came up behind him and touched the edge of his cloak,[b] and immediately her bleeding
stopped.
45 "Who touched me?" Jesus asked.

[a] *26* Some manuscripts *Gadarenes*; other manuscripts *Gergesenes*; also in verse 37 [b] *29* Greek *unclean*
[c] *43* Many manuscripts *years, and she had spent all she had on doctors*

8:24 rebuked. This may imply an association between the sea and evil forces (cf. Ps 106:9).
8:26 Gerasenes. The manuscripts of all three Synoptic Gospels are divided, with "Gadarenes" and "Gerasenes" the most likely readings. But both towns were some miles away from the lake. See notes on Matthew 8:28 and Mark 5:1.
8:27 demon-possessed. Demon possession shows itself in many ways. This case manifested similarly to madness.
8:28 Like the demoniac of 4:34, this one knew who Jesus was (cf. the disciples in v. 25).
8:30 Legion. There may have been a great number of demons in the man (a Roman legion was comprised of about 6,000 soldiers).
8:31 the Abyss. The place of confinement for evil spirits (Rev 20:1–3). See *BC* 12.
8:32–33 We do not know how or why demons enter animals. Jesus did not send them into the pigs; he only gave permission for them to enter the herd. Nor did he instruct the demons to drive the pigs into the water.
8:37 Fear caused these people to reject the most wonderful opportunity of their lives. They may have been afraid of the power they saw in the healing of the man or of the loss of money involved in the destruction of the pigs.
8:38–39 With Jesus gone, it was most important that the man work for God in that region. Notice that what "God has done" is much the same as what "Jesus had done."
8:41 a ruler of the synagogue. The man responsible for arranging the service (e.g., choosing those who would read Scripture or lead in prayer).
8:43 subject to bleeding. The woman's bleeding problem made her ceremonially "unclean" (Lev 15:25). This meant she was cut off from many social relationships.
8:44 the edge of his cloak. Perhaps the tassel of Numbers 15:37–39.
8:45–48 It was important that the cure should be known publicly; otherwise the woman would not have been accepted back into normal social life. This is the only woman Jesus is known to have addressed as "daughter"—a tender statement.

When they all denied it, Peter said, "Master,[c] the people are crowding and pressing
against you."
46 But Jesus said, "Someone touched me;[d] I know that power has gone out from me."[e]
47 Then the woman, seeing that she could not go unnoticed, came trembling and fell
at his feet. In the presence of all the people, she told why she had touched him and how
she had been instantly healed. 48 Then he said to her, "Daughter, your faith has healed
you.[f] Go in peace."[g]
49 While Jesus was still speaking, someone came from the house of Jairus, the synagogue ruler.[h] "Your daughter is dead," he said. "Don't bother the teacher any more."
50 Hearing this, Jesus said to Jairus, "Don't be afraid; just believe, and she will be
healed."
51 When he arrived at the house of Jairus, he did not let anyone go in with him except
Peter, John and James,[i] and the child's father and mother. 52 Meanwhile, all the people
were wailing and mourning[j] for her. "Stop wailing," Jesus said. "She is not dead but
asleep."[k]
53 They laughed at him, knowing that she was dead. 54 But he took her by the hand and
said, "My child, get up!"[l] 55 Her spirit returned, and at once she stood up. Then Jesus told
them to give her something to eat. 56 Her parents were astonished, but he ordered them
not to tell anyone what had happened.[m]

Jesus Sends Out the Twelve

9 When Jesus had called the Twelve together, he gave them power and authority to
drive out all demons[n] and to cure diseases,[o] 2 and he sent them out to preach the
kingdom of God[p] and to heal the sick. 3 He told them: "Take nothing for the journey—
no staff, no bag, no bread, no money, no extra tunic.[q] 4 Whatever house you enter, stay
there until you leave that town. 5 If people do not welcome you, shake the dust off your
feet when you leave their town, as a testimony against them."[r] 6 So they set out and went
from village to village, preaching the gospel and healing people everywhere.
7 Now Herod[s] the tetrarch heard about all that was going on. And he was perplexed,
because some were saying that John[t] had been raised from the dead,[u] 8 others that Elijah had appeared,[v] and still others that one of the prophets of long ago had come back
to life.[w] 9 But Herod said, "I beheaded John. Who, then, is this I hear such things about?"
And he tried to see him.[x]

Jesus Feeds the Five Thousand

10 When the apostles[y] returned, they reported to Jesus what they had done. Then he
took them with him and they withdrew by themselves to a town called Bethsaida,[z] 11 but
the crowds learned about it and followed him. He welcomed them and spoke to them
about the kingdom of God,[a] and healed those who needed healing.
12 Late in the afternoon the Twelve came to him and said, "Send the crowd away so
they can go to the surrounding villages and countryside and find food and lodging, because we are in a remote place here."

8:45 [c]Lk 5:5
8:46 [d]Mt 14:36; Mk 3:10 [e]Lk 5:17; 6:19
8:48 [f]Mt 9:22 [g]Ac 15:33
8:49 [h]ver 41
8:51 [i]Mt 4:21
8:52 [j]Lk 23:27 [k]Mt 9:24; Jn 11:11, 13
8:54 [l]Lk 7:14
8:56 [m]Mt 8:4
9:1 [n]Mt 10:1 [o]Mt 4:23; Lk 5:17
9:2 [p]Mt 3:2
9:3 [q]Lk 10:4; 22:35
9:5 [r]Mt 10:14
9:7 [s]Mt 14:1 [t]Mt 3:1 [u]ver 19
9:8 [v]Mt 11:14 [w]ver 19; Jn 1:21
9:9 [x]Lk 23:8
9:10 [y]Mk 6:30 [z]Mt 11:21
9:11 [a]ver 2; Mt 3:2

8:51 Note Jesus' consideration for people. When he cured the hemorrhaging woman, he insisted on full publicity because she needed it to facilitate her return to society. Here, on the other hand, privacy was in order.

8:52 all the people. This certainly would have included family and friends, as well as, most likely, people from the neighborhood and professional mourners (there were flute players present according to Mt 9:23). Mourning was normally demonstrative, and there would have been much wailing. Jesus forbade the public show and pronounced that the girl was "asleep." This does not mean that she had not died, but that Jesus was prepared to awaken her from death.

8:54 get up! Luke described the miracle simply. Mark retained the Aramaic terminology Jesus used (Mk 5:41), but Luke translated the words, probably for his Gentile readers.

8:56 The effect of the miracle was amazement. This time Jesus forbade publicity. As was often the case, he did not want news of his miracles to spread (see note on Mk 1:34).

■ **9:1–50** *Jesus Prepares the Twelve.* Luke closed his account of Jesus' ministry in Galilee by recounting several ways Jesus prepared his apostles for their future task.

9:1–2 The Twelve were evidently not together all of the time (some had homes and families). But Jesus gathered them for this important mission. He "gave them power and authority" over demons and sickness and commissioned them to continue his work of preaching and healing.

9:3 They were to take with them on the journey only the barest minimum of supplies, relying instead on God's provision. **no staff.** The Markan account allows a staff (Mk 6:8). Matthew 10:9–10 states that they were not to procure a staff, presumably beyond the one each might already have possessed. **bag.** The usual bag a traveler would pack for his journey.

9:4 The disciples were to rely on hospitality. The stipulation to stay in only one house limited the length of time they would remain in any one place.

9:5 shake the dust off your feet. Strict Jews removed defiling dust from their feet when they returned from Gentile lands. The disciples' action symbolized that those who rejected the preachers were excluded from God's covenantal blessings.

9:7 Herod. Herod Antipas, who ruled Galilee. **John had been raised from the dead.** This eventually became Herod's view (Mk 6:16), but at this time he simply reflected that John was dead. Herod himself had arranged for John to be beheaded.

9:8 Elijah. See the prophecy of Malachi 4:5.

9:10–17 The one miracle, apart from the resurrection, recorded in all four Gospels.

9:10 withdrew by themselves. They retired to a private place, evidently to report to Jesus and to relax after the preaching tour. **Bethsaida.** This must mean "in the vicinity of Bethsaida," for it was "a remote place" (v. 12).

9:11 welcomed them. This was a gracious act since Jesus was looking for a time of relaxation.

13He replied, "You give them something to eat."
They answered, "We have only five loaves of bread and two fish—unless we go and
buy food for all this crowd." 14(About five thousand men were there.)
But he said to his disciples, "Have them sit down in groups of about fifty each." 15The
disciples did so, and everybody sat down. 16Taking the five loaves and the two fish and
looking up to heaven, he gave thanks and broke them.[b] Then he gave them to the disciples to set before the people. 17They all ate and were satisfied, and the disciples picked
up twelve basketfuls of broken pieces that were left over.

Peter's Confession of Christ

18Once when Jesus was praying[c] in private and his disciples were with him, he asked
them, "Who do the crowds say I am?"
19They replied, "Some say John the Baptist;[d] others say Elijah; and still others, that
one of the prophets of long ago has come back to life."[e]
20"But what about you?" he asked. "Who do you say I am?"
Peter answered, "The Christ[a] of God."[f]
21Jesus strictly warned them not to tell this to anyone.[g] 22And he said, "The Son of
Man[h] must suffer many things[i] and be rejected by the elders, chief priests and teachers
of the law,[j] and he must be killed[k] and on the third day[l] be raised to life."[m]
23Then he said to them all: "If anyone would come after me, he must deny himself and
take up his cross daily and follow me.[n] 24For whoever wants to save his life will lose it,
but whoever loses his life for me will save it.[o] 25What good is it for a man to gain the
whole world, and yet lose or forfeit his very self? 26If anyone is ashamed of me and my
words, the Son of Man will be ashamed of him[p] when he comes in his glory and in the
glory of the Father and of the holy angels.[q] 27I tell you the truth, some who are standing
here will not taste death before they see the kingdom of God."

The Transfiguration

28About eight days after Jesus said this, he took Peter, John and James[r] with him and
went up onto a mountain to pray.[s] 29As he was praying, the appearance of his face
changed, and his clothes became as bright as a flash of lightning. 30Two men, Moses and
Elijah, 31appeared in glorious splendor, talking with Jesus. They spoke about his departure,[t] which he was about to bring to fulfillment at Jerusalem. 32Peter and his companions were very sleepy,[u] but when they became fully awake, they saw his glory and the
two men standing with him. 33As the men were leaving Jesus, Peter said to him, "Master,[v] it is good for us to be here. Let us put up three shelters—one for you, one for Moses and one for Elijah." (He did not know what he was saying.)
34While he was speaking, a cloud appeared and enveloped them, and they were afraid
as they entered the cloud. 35A voice came from the cloud, saying, "This is my Son,
whom I have chosen;[w] listen to him."[x] 36When the voice had spoken, they found that
Jesus was alone. The disciples kept this to themselves, and told no one at that time what
they had seen.[y]

9:16 [b]Mt 14:19
9:18 [c]Lk 3:21
9:19 [d]Mt 3:1 [e]ver 7,8
9:20 [f]Jn 1:49; 6:66-69; 11:27
9:21 [g]Mt 16:20; Mk 8:30
9:22 [h]Mt 8:20 [i]Mt 16:21 [j]Mt 27:1,2 [k]Ac 2:23; 3:13 [l]Mt 16:21 [m]Mt 16:21
9:23 [n]Mt 10:38; Lk 14:27
9:24 [o]Jn 12:25
9:26 [p]Mt 10:33; Lk 12:9; 2Ti 2:12 [q]Mt 16:27
9:28 [r]Mt 4:21 [s]Lk 3:21
9:31 [t]2Pe 1:15
9:32 [u]Mt 26:43
9:33 [v]Lk 5:5
9:35 [w]Isa 42:1 [x]Mt 3:17
9:36 [y]Mt 17:9

a *20* Or *Messiah*

9:20 But what about you? This distinguishes the disciples from the crowds; the word "you" is emphatic. **Christ.** This word means "anointed" (i.e., set apart for special service). When *the* is added (i.e., "the Christ"), the reference is to the One God has chosen above all people, the One who will bring salvation, "the anointed one." Peter's answer was a penetrating assessment; it was not a human discovery but a revelation from God (Mt 16:17).

9:21 strictly warned. The disciples would almost certainly have been misunderstood if they had told anyone; people would have thought they were proclaiming a political deliverer. Jesus went on to explain that his role as the Christ required suffering, rejection and death.

9:23–25 take up his cross. To renounce selfish ambition, implying the death of an entire way of life.

9:26 See *WLC* 156.

9:27 see the kingdom of God. Suggestions as to the meaning of this phrase include the following: the transfiguration, Jesus' resurrection and ascension, Pentecost, the spread of the gospel, the destruction of Jerusalem or the second coming. See note on Matthew 16:28; see also theological article "The Kingdom of God" at Matthew 4.

9:28–29 Luke mentioned much about Jesus' prayers, and he made it clear that Jesus prayed often. On this particular occasion, Jesus' appearance changed while he was praying, although the precise nature of the change is not explained.

9:28 About eight days. An expression often used to mean "about a week." **a mountain.** The location of the transfiguration is not known. Mount Tabor is the traditional site, but it is a long way from Caesarea Philippi, and it was inhabited at that time. Mount Hermon is the more likely location.

9:30 Two men. Moses, the great lawgiver, and Elijah, the representative of the prophets.

9:31 his departure. Literally, "his exodus" (i.e., his death; 2Pe 1:15 uses the same Greek word). Only Luke's Gospel tells us of this conversation. That Jesus' departure, or death, was spoken of even during this revelation of glory shows its centrality.

9:32 very sleepy. The transfiguration may have taken place at night, for verse 37 refers to "the next day," and Jesus sometimes prayed all night (6:12).

9:33 three shelters. Peter wanted to prolong the experience by building shelters to accommodate, and thereby possibly detain, the heavenly visitors.

9:34 a cloud. As in the Old Testament, the cloud is associated with the presence of God.

9:35 my Son. This phrase emphasizes both the divine relationship and the divine choice. Both mark out Jesus as different from, and superior to, Moses and Elijah. **listen to him.** Jesus' words have divine authority.

The Healing of a Boy With an Evil Spirit

37The next day, when they came down from the mountain, a large crowd met him. 38A
man in the crowd called out, "Teacher, I beg you to look at my son, for he is my only
child. 39A spirit seizes him and he suddenly screams; it throws him into convulsions so
that he foams at the mouth. It scarcely ever leaves him and is destroying him. 40I begged
your disciples to drive it out, but they could not."

41"O unbelieving and perverse generation,"[z] Jesus replied, "how long shall I stay with
you and put up with you? Bring your son here."

42Even while the boy was coming, the demon threw him to the ground in a convulsion. But Jesus rebuked the evil[a] spirit, healed the boy and gave him back to his father.
43And they were all amazed at the greatness of God.

While everyone was marveling at all that Jesus did, he said to his disciples, 44"Listen
carefully to what I am about to tell you: The Son of Man is going to be betrayed into the
hands of men."[a] 45But they did not understand what this meant. It was hidden from
them, so that they did not grasp it,[b] and they were afraid to ask him about it.

Who Will Be the Greatest?

46An argument started among the disciples as to which of them would be the greatest.[c] 47Jesus, knowing their thoughts,[d] took a little child and had him stand beside him.
48Then he said to them, "Whoever welcomes this little child in my name welcomes me;
and whoever welcomes me welcomes the one who sent me.[e] For he who is least among
you all—he is the greatest."[f]

49"Master,"[g] said John, "we saw a man driving out demons in your name and we tried
to stop him, because he is not one of us."

50"Do not stop him," Jesus said, "for whoever is not against you is for you."[h]

Samaritan Opposition

51As the time approached for him to be taken up to heaven,[i] Jesus resolutely set out
for Jerusalem.[j] 52And he sent messengers on ahead, who went into a Samaritan[k] village
to get things ready for him; 53but the people there did not welcome him, because he was
heading for Jerusalem. 54When the disciples James and John[l] saw this, they asked,
"Lord, do you want us to call fire down from heaven to destroy them[b]?"[m] 55But Jesus
turned and rebuked them, 56and[c] they went to another village.

The Cost of Following Jesus

57As they were walking along the road,[n] a man said to him, "I will follow you wherever you go."

58Jesus replied, "Foxes have holes and birds of the air have nests, but the Son of Man[o]
has no place to lay his head."

59He said to another man, "Follow me."[p]

9:41 [z]Dt 32:5
9:44 [a]ver 22
9:45 [b]Mk 9:32
9:46 [c]Lk 22:24
9:47 [d]Mt 9:4
9:48 [e]Mt 10:40 [f]Mk 9:35
9:49 [g]Lk 5:5
9:50 [h]Mt 12:30; Lk 11:23
9:51 [i]Mk 16:19 [j]Lk 13:22; 17:11; 18:31; 19:28
9:52 [k]Mt 10:5
9:54 [l]Mt 4:21 [m]2Ki 1:10,12
9:57 [n]ver 51
9:58 [o]Mt 8:20
9:59 [p]Mt 4:19

[a] *42* Greek *unclean* [b] *54* Some manuscripts *them, even as Elijah did* [c] *55,56* Some manuscripts *them. And he said, "You do not know what kind of spirit you are of, for the Son of Man did not come to destroy men's lives, but to save them." 56And*

9:37–40 Note the striking contrast between the glory on the mountaintop and the disciples' inability to defeat the forces of evil on the plain. Interestingly, they had cast out demons previously (vv. 1–6; cf. Mk 9:29).

9:41 unbelieving and perverse generation. These words were apparently addressed to the people who had come without faith and who evidently expected Jesus to be powerless to help. In contrast, the father demonstrated faith, albeit imperfect faith (Mk 9:24).

9:44 you. The word is emphatic. Over against the pervasive unbelief of the masses, the disciples were to be different. Jesus then predicted his passion in general terms, but they did not understand. See *WLC* 160.

9:45 It was hidden. This may either mean that the forces of evil prevented the disciples from understanding or that before the resurrection it was difficult for his followers to accept the truth that salvation would come by way of Jesus' death.

9:46 the greatest. Luke contrasted Jesus' concern for others with the disciples' concern about their own positions.

9:47 a little child. The child was helpless and, in antiquity, unimportant. To be concerned with such and voluntarily to assume the lowest position is to be truly great. The truly great person is humble, not self-assertive (as the disciples erroneously assumed).

9:49–50 For John, it was not enough that the man did miracles in Jesus' name; the Gospel writer thought it necessary for him to be "one of [them]." Jesus emphasized that there is no neutrality in the struggle against evil; therefore, those not against us are for us—a test we can appropriately apply to others. In 11:23 we find a test we should apply to ourselves.

■ **9:51—19:27** *Jesus' Public Ministry From Galilee to Jerusalem.* Luke's Gospel records Jesus' journey to Jerusalem. There is no large-scale parallel in the other Gospels (although there are parallels to some of the individual sections). Luke's Gospel presents a solemn progress to the capital city, where Jesus would die for sinners in accordance with the will of God.

■ **9:51—10:42** *Teaching on Discipleship.* As Jesus headed toward Jerusalem, he gave the disciples instruction that would be important for them later when they were left to carry on with Christian leadership without his physical presence.

9:52–53 Jesus' traveling party would have been large enough to strain the resources of a small village if the group had dropped in unexpectedly. Jesus gave due notice but was met with the ancient hostility of Samaritans for Jews.

9:54–55 See *WLC* 105.

9:57–58 Potential disciples were tested. The first man made a good profession, but he had not realized that discipleship could mean homelessness.

But the man replied, "Lord, first let me go and bury my father."
60 Jesus said to him, "Let the dead bury their own dead, but you go and proclaim the
kingdom of God."[q]
61 Still another said, "I will follow you, Lord; but first let me go back and say good-by
to my family."[r]
62 Jesus replied, "No one who puts his hand to the plow and looks back is fit for service in the kingdom of God."

Jesus Sends Out the Seventy-two

10 After this the Lord[s] appointed seventy-two[a] others[t] and sent them two by two[u]
ahead of him to every town and place where he was about to go.[v] 2 He told them,
"The harvest is plentiful, but the workers are few. Ask the Lord of the harvest, therefore,
to send out workers into his harvest field.[w] 3 Go! I am sending you out like lambs among
wolves.[x] 4 Do not take a purse or bag or sandals; and do not greet anyone on the road.
5 "When you enter a house, first say, 'Peace to this house.' 6 If a man of peace is there,
your peace will rest on him; if not, it will return to you. 7 Stay in that house, eating and
drinking whatever they give you, for the worker deserves his wages.[y] Do not move
around from house to house.
8 "When you enter a town and are welcomed, eat what is set before you.[z] 9 Heal the sick
who are there and tell them, 'The kingdom of God[a] is near you.' 10 But when you enter a
town and are not welcomed, go into its streets and say, 11 'Even the dust of your town that
sticks to our feet we wipe off against you.[b] Yet be sure of this: The kingdom of God is
near.'[c] 12 I tell you, it will be more bearable on that day for Sodom[d] than for that town.[e]
13 "Woe to you,[f] Korazin! Woe to you, Bethsaida! For if the miracles that were performed in you had been performed in Tyre and Sidon, they would have repented long
ago, sitting in sackcloth[g] and ashes. 14 But it will be more bearable for Tyre and Sidon at
the judgment than for you. 15 And you, Capernaum,[h] will you be lifted up to the skies?
No, you will go down to the depths.[b]
16 "He who listens to you listens to me; he who rejects you rejects me; but he who rejects me rejects him who sent me."[i]
17 The seventy-two[j] returned with joy and said, "Lord, even the demons submit to us
in your name."[k]
18 He replied, "I saw Satan[l] fall like lightning from heaven.[m] 19 I have given you authority to trample on snakes[n] and scorpions and to overcome all the power of the enemy;
nothing will harm you. 20 However, do not rejoice that the spirits submit to you, but rejoice that your names are written in heaven."[o]
21 At that time Jesus, full of joy through the Holy Spirit, said, "I praise you, Father, Lord
of heaven and earth, because you have hidden these things from the wise and learned,
and revealed them to little children.[p] Yes, Father, for this was your good pleasure.

9:60 [q]Mt 3:2
9:61 [r]1Ki 19:20
10:1 [s]Lk 7:13 [t]Lk 9:1, 2, 51, 52 [u]Mk 6:7 [v]Mt 10:1
10:2 [w]Mt 9:37, 38; Jn 4:35
10:3 [x]Mt 10:16
10:7 [y]Mt 10:10; 1Co 9:14; 1Ti 5:18
10:8 [z]1Co 10:27
10:9 [a]Mt 3:2; 10:7
10:11 [b]Mt 10:14; Mk 6:11 [c]ver 9
10:12 [d]Mt 10:15 [e]Mt 11:24
10:13 [f]Lk 6:24-26 [g]Rev 11:3
10:15 [h]Mt 4:13
10:16 [i]Mt 10:40; Jn 13:20
10:17 [j]ver 1 [k]Mk 16:17
10:18 [l]Mt 4:10 [m]Isa 14:12; Rev 9:1; 12:8, 9
10:19 [n]Mk 16:18; Ac 28:3-5
10:20 [o]Ex 32:32; Ps 69:28; Da 12:1; Php 4:3; Heb 12:23; Rev 13:8; 20:12; 21:27
10:21 [p]1Co 1:26-29

[a] *1* Some manuscripts *seventy;* also in verse 17 [b] *15* Greek *Hades*

9:59 bury my father. If this man's father was still alive, his words meant that he wanted to continue to care for him until his death. If his father were dead, Jesus' words were still shocking, for filial piety demanded that a son look after the burial arrangements for his father. Either way, Jesus was implying that the demands of the kingdom override all earthly loyalties.

9:61–62 There may have been some reluctance behind this offer of service. Jesus made it clear that the kingdom requires people to move forward when they are called, not to look behind.

10:1 seventy-two others. This mission is found only in Luke, but the instructions are similar to some of those given the Twelve in the other Gospels. As to the number sent out, available manuscripts are divided between "seventy" and "seventy-two," and there is no way of being certain which number was original. Both represent the number of nations of the world in Genesis 10 (the Hebrew text has 70 names; the Greek, 72). Both numbers indicate that Jesus used the services of many humble people as well as those of the Twelve. **two by two.** Jesus had also sent out the Twelve in pairs (Mk 6:7). This afforded mutual support, as well as the benefit of the testimony of two witnesses (cf. Dt 17:6).

10:3 lambs among wolves. The implication is of helplessness and danger.

10:4 purse. A moneybag. **bag.** A traveler's bag (as in 9:3). **sandals.** This prohibition probably forbade a spare pair, as opposed to being a command to go barefooted. **do not greet.** Salutations could be elaborate and time-consuming; the disciples' business was urgent.

10:5–7 The preachers were to expect hospitality.

10:6 it will return to you. God's peace comes only to those who respond. Where there is no response, there is no ensuing peace of God.

10:11 the dust of your town. See note on 9:5.

10:12 Sodom's wickedness was proverbial, but rejecting the preachers of God's kingdom was worse than even Sodom's deeds. **that day.** The judgment day.

10:13 Korazin! . . . Bethsaida! Having heard and rejected Jesus, these towns bore more guilt than Tyre and Sidon, towns that were well-known for their evil.

10:15 Capernaum. This town, where Jesus did much of his work, will be in great trouble at the judgment. Literally, it will "go down to Hades" (i.e., to the lowest place).

10:16 To reject God's messengers is to reject God. See *BC* 30.

10:17 with joy. Demons were not mentioned in Jesus' charge, so this may have come as a joyful surprise.

10:18 Satan fall. Seems to signify that Satan was suffering defeat in the ministry of these preachers.

10:19 authority. When sent by God, his disciples were protected from the threat of snakes and scorpions (cf. Ac 28:3–5). God's messengers were shielded to accomplish what God called them to do.

10:20 do not rejoice. The disciples needed to get their priorities right. Salvation is more important than power over spirits. See *WCF* 3.8.

22"All things have been committed to me by my Father.[q] No one knows who the Son
is except the Father, and no one knows who the Father is except the Son and those to
whom the Son chooses to reveal him."[r]
23Then he turned to his disciples and said privately, "Blessed are the eyes that see
what you see. 24For I tell you that many prophets and kings wanted to see what you see
but did not see it, and to hear what you hear but did not hear it."[s]

The Parable of the Good Samaritan

25On one occasion an expert in the law stood up to test Jesus. "Teacher," he asked,
"what must I do to inherit eternal life?"[t]
26"What is written in the Law?" he replied. "How do you read it?"
27He answered: " 'Love the Lord your God with all your heart and with all your soul
and with all your strength and with all your mind'[a];[u] and, 'Love your neighbor as yourself.'[b]"[v]
28"You have answered correctly," Jesus replied. "Do this and you will live."[w]
29But he wanted to justify himself,[x] so he asked Jesus, "And who is my neighbor?"
30In reply Jesus said: "A man was going down from Jerusalem to Jericho, when he fell
into the hands of robbers. They stripped him of his clothes, beat him and went away,
leaving him half dead. 31A priest happened to be going down the same road, and when
he saw the man, he passed by on the other side.[y] 32So too, a Levite, when he came to the
place and saw him, passed by on the other side. 33But a Samaritan,[z] as he traveled, came
where the man was; and when he saw him, he took pity on him. 34He went to him and
bandaged his wounds, pouring on oil and wine. Then he put the man on his own donkey, took him to an inn and took care of him. 35The next day he took out two silver coins[c]
and gave them to the innkeeper. 'Look after him,' he said, 'and when I return, I will re-
imburse you for any extra expense you may have.'
36"Which of these three do you think was a neighbor to the man who fell into the
hands of robbers?"
37The expert in the law replied, "The one who had mercy on him."
Jesus told him, "Go and do likewise."

At the Home of Martha and Mary

38As Jesus and his disciples were on their way, he came to a village where a woman
named Martha[a] opened her home to him. 39She had a sister called Mary,[b] who sat at the
Lord's feet[c] listening to what he said. 40But Martha was distracted by all the preparations
that had to be made. She came to him and asked, "Lord, don't you care[d] that my sister
has left me to do the work by myself? Tell her to help me!"
41"Martha, Martha," the Lord answered, "you are worried[e] and upset about many
things, 42but only one thing is needed.[d][f] Mary has chosen what is better, and it will not
be taken away from her."

Jesus' Teaching on Prayer

11 One day Jesus was praying[g] in a certain place. When he finished, one of his
disciples said to him, "Lord,[h] teach us to pray, just as John taught his disciples."

10:22 [q]Mt 28:18 [r]Jn 1:18
10:24 [s]1Pe 1:10-12
10:25 [t]Mt 19:16; Lk 18:18
10:27 [u]Dt 6:5 [v]Lev 19:18; Mt 5:43
10:28 [w]Lev 18:5; Ro 7:10
10:29 [x]Lk 16:15
10:31 [y]Lev 21:1-3
10:33 [z]Mt 10:5
10:38 [a]Jn 11:1; 12:2
10:39 [b]Jn 11:1; 12:3 [c]Lk 8:35
10:40 [d]Mk 4:38
10:41 [e]Mt 6:25-34; Lk 12:11,22
10:42 [f]Ps 27:4
11:1 [g]Lk 3:21 [h]Jn 13:13

[a] *27* Deut. 6:5 [b] *27* Lev. 19:18 [c] *35* Greek *two denarii* [d] *42* Some manuscripts *but few things are needed—or only one*

10:22 The disciples could know something of Jesus, but the deep truths about the Son are known only to God. And the only people who know the Father are those to whom the Son reveals him. The exclusivity of the claim is stressed.
10:23–24 The greatest prophets and kings of earlier days had not seen the Messiah, but these disciples had (cf. 7:24–28 and its note).
10:25 an expert in the law. A lawyer and, as "the law" was the law of God, a religious man. He stood up to test Jesus, revealing that he was not genuinely looking for information but for some statement that would enable him to make an accusation against Jesus.
10:26-28 See *WLC* 93,157.
10:27 The lawyer showed insight; Jesus himself summed up the law in much the same way (Mt 22:37–40). See *WLC* 102.
10:28 Do this. Two readings are possible: (1) Perfect love for God perfectly fulfills the law and requires no forgiveness, but since such love is impossible no one can live. (2) Love for God implies faithful reliance on God for forgiveness, which results in life.
10:29–37 This parable answers the question, Who is my neighbor? and not the question, What must one do to be saved? The Jews had varied ideas about the identity of their "neighbor," but they all reserved the term for those in Israel.
10:33–34 The audience expected a priest and a Levite to be followed by a layman of Israel in an anti-clerical story. The inclusion of the Samaritan, as well as his kindness, was totally unexpected. Oil eased pain, and wine had an antiseptic effect (the man could not have known that alcohol kills germs, but he would have been aware that wine had curative properties).
10:35 two silver coins. Literally, "two denarii" (see note on Mk 12:15). The coins would have paid for the man's room and board for up to two months.
10:38 a village. Bethany, about two miles from Jerusalem (Jn 11:1).
10:40–42 Martha's preparations may have been unnecessarily elaborate. Mary demonstrated clearly the truth Jesus was bringing out, that devotion to himself is central.
■ **11:1–13** *Teaching on Prayer.* Luke recorded Jesus' instruction on prayer. The Gospel writer may have placed this material here to

[2]He said to them, "When you pray, say:

" 'Father,[a]
11:2 [i]Mt 3:2 hallowed be your name,
your kingdom[i] come.[b]
[3]Give us each day our daily bread.
11:4 [j]Mt 18:35; Mk 11:25 [k]Mt 26:41; Jas 1:13 [4]Forgive us our sins,
for we also forgive everyone who sins against us.[c][j]
And lead us not into temptation.[d] ' "[k]

[5]Then he said to them, "Suppose one of you has a friend, and he goes to him at midnight and says, 'Friend, lend me three loaves of bread, [6]because a friend of mine on a
journey has come to me, and I have nothing to set before him.'
[7]"Then the one inside answers, 'Don't bother me. The door is already locked, and my
children are with me in bed. I can't get up and give you anything.' [8]I tell you, though he
11:8 [l]Lk 18:1-6 will not get up and give him the bread because he is his friend, yet because of the man's
boldness[e] he will get up and give him as much as he needs.[l]
11:9 [m]Mt 7:7 [9]"So I say to you: Ask and it will be given to you;[m] seek and you will find; knock and
the door will be opened to you. [10]For everyone who asks receives; he who seeks finds;
and to him who knocks, the door will be opened.
[11]"Which of you fathers, if your son asks for[f] a fish, will give him a snake instead? [12]Or
if he asks for an egg, will give him a scorpion? [13]If you then, though you are evil, know
how to give good gifts to your children, how much more will your Father in heaven give
the Holy Spirit to those who ask him!"

Jesus and Beelzebub

11:14 [n]Mt 9:32,33 [14]Jesus was driving out a demon that was mute. When the demon left, the man who
had been mute spoke, and the crowd was amazed.[n] [15]But some of them said, "By Beel-
11:15 [o]Mk 3:22 [p]Mt 9:34 zebub,[g][o] the prince of demons, he is driving out demons."[p] [16]Others tested him by asking for a sign from heaven.[q]
11:16 [q]Mt 12:38 [17]Jesus knew their thoughts[r] and said to them: "Any kingdom divided against itself
will be ruined, and a house divided against itself will fall. [18]If Satan[s] is divided against
11:17 [r]Mt 9:4 himself, how can his kingdom stand? I say this because you claim that I drive out demons
by Beelzebub. [19]Now if I drive out demons by Beelzebub, by whom do your followers
11:18 [s]Mt 4:10 drive them out? So then, they will be your judges. [20]But if I drive out demons by the finger of God,[t] then the kingdom of God[u] has come to you.
11:20 [t]Ex 8:19 [u]Mt 3:2 [21]"When a strong man, fully armed, guards his own house, his possessions are safe.

[a] 2 Some manuscripts *Our Father in heaven* [b] 2 Some manuscripts *come. May your will be done on earth as it is in heaven.* [c] 4 Greek *everyone who is indebted to us* [d] 4 Some manuscripts *temptation but deliver us from the evil one* [e] 8 Or *persistence* [f] 11 Some manuscripts *for bread, will give him a stone; or if he asks for* [g] 15 Greek *Beezeboul* or *Beelzeboul*; also in verses 18 and 19

---

connect the disciples' questions about prayer with what they had learned from the preceding events about the costs of discipleship. Luke taught his readers the importance of prayer as the church endured the troubles of this world.

11:1 Lord, teach us to pray. Religious teachers often taught their disciples how to pray.

11:2–4 The form of this prayer differs somewhat from that found in Matthew 6:9–13, but both are probably summaries of Jesus' actual words, and they were given in different contexts, so small differences are to be expected. In Matthew, Jesus included a model prayer as part of his sermon; here he responds to a question. See *WLC* 186; *WSC* 99; *BC* 26; *HC* 119.

11:2 Father. This corresponds to the Aramaic *Abba,* the word a young child of Jesus' day would have used to address his or her father but also a title of endearment an adult son or daughter might have used. **name.** An individual's name stood for the whole person; therefore, the prayer is that people will reverence God. **kingdom come.** Jesus taught often about God's kingdom, and his prayer here looks for the establishment of that kingdom. See theological article "Prayer" at Matthew 6. See *WLC* 187.

11:4 Forgive us . . . for we also forgive. Sinners seek forgiveness for the sins they commit each day. They must recognize that if they do not forgive others, they are not in a condition to receive forgiveness. See *WLC* 194; *WSC* 105.

11:7 A man in a one-room house would sleep with all his family on a raised platform, and his getting up would disturb them all.

11:8 Friendship would not be enough to make him get out of bed, but persistence on the part of the supplicant would be. Effective prayer is to be persistent.

11:9–13 See *HC* 116,120.

11:13 you are evil. Universal sinfulness is presupposed. If even earthly fathers (evil as they are) give good gifts, to how much greater an extent will God give the Holy Spirit? See *WLC* 189,196; *WSC* 100; *BC* 7.

■ **11:14–26** *Jesus and Evil Spirits.* Luke dealt with a significant attack on Jesus' character and ministry. It expressed itself in the question, Did Jesus cast out demons by the power of the devil?

11:14–15 Jesus' enemies did not deny that he expelled demons, but they ascribed his power to Beelzebub, which was previously the name of a heathen god but was used at this time as a designation for Satan (2Ki 1:2; see also note on Mt 10:25).

11:16 See note on 11:29.

11:17–18 Unity is strength and division is weakness. If Jesus had been in league with Satan but had simultaneously worked against Satan, he would have been weakening his own kingdom.

11:19 The followers of those who accused Jesus also cast out demons. If demons could only be cast out by the power of Satan, the followers of Jesus' accusers were guilty too. That the accusers did not condemn their own followers proved that their accusations were false.

11:20 the finger of God. The work of God himself (see Ex 8:19). Matthew 12:28 reads "the Spirit of God." Both phrases bring out the truth that Jesus did not drive out demons by Beelzebub. The power of God was at work in him. This points to the further truth

22 But when someone stronger attacks and overpowers him, he takes away the armor in
which the man trusted and divides up the spoils.
23 "He who is not with me is against me, and he who does not gather with me, scatters.[v]
24 "When an evil[a] spirit comes out of a man, it goes through arid places seeking rest
and does not find it. Then it says, 'I will return to the house I left.' 25 When it arrives, it
finds the house swept clean and put in order. 26 Then it goes and takes seven other spirits more wicked than itself, and they go in and live there. And the final condition of that
man is worse than the first."[w]
27 As Jesus was saying these things, a woman in the crowd called out, "Blessed is the
mother who gave you birth and nursed you."[x]
28 He replied, "Blessed rather are those who hear the word of God[y] and obey it."[z]

The Sign of Jonah

29 As the crowds increased, Jesus said, "This is a wicked generation. It asks for a miraculous sign,[a] but none will be given it except the sign of Jonah.[b] 30 For as Jonah was a
sign to the Ninevites, so also will the Son of Man be to this generation. 31 The Queen of
the South will rise at the judgment with the men of this generation and condemn them;
for she came from the ends of the earth to listen to Solomon's wisdom,[c] and now one[b]
greater than Solomon is here. 32 The men of Nineveh will stand up at the judgment with
this generation and condemn it; for they repented at the preaching of Jonah,[d] and now
one greater than Jonah is here.

The Lamp of the Body

33 "No one lights a lamp and puts it in a place where it will be hidden, or under a bowl.
Instead he puts it on its stand, so that those who come in may see the light.[e] 34 Your eye
is the lamp of your body. When your eyes are good, your whole body also is full of light.
But when they are bad, your body also is full of darkness. 35 See to it, then, that the light
within you is not darkness. 36 Therefore, if your whole body is full of light, and no part of
it dark, it will be completely lighted, as when the light of a lamp shines on you."

Six Woes

37 When Jesus had finished speaking, a Pharisee invited him to eat with him; so he
went in and reclined at the table.[f] 38 But the Pharisee, noticing that Jesus did not first
wash before the meal,[g] was surprised.
39 Then the Lord[h] said to him, "Now then, you Pharisees clean the outside of the cup

[a] 24 Greek *unclean* [b] 31 Or *something*; also in verse 32

11:23 [v]Mt 12:30; Mk 9:40; Lk 9:50
11:26 [w]2Pe 2:20
11:27 [x]Lk 23:29
11:28 [y]Heb 4:12 [z]Pr 8:32; Lk 6:47; 8:21; Jn 14:21
11:29 [a]ver 16; Mt 12:38 [b]Jnh 1:17; Mt 16:4
11:31 [c]1Ki 10:1; 2Ch 9:1
11:32 [d]Jnh 3:5
11:33 [e]Mt 5:15; Mk 4:21; Lk 8:16
11:37 [f]Lk 7:36; 14:1
11:38 [g]Mk 7:3,4
11:39 [h]Lk 7:13

that in the coming of Jesus, the kingdom of God has come. The miracles he performed were evidence for those with eyes to see that God was at work.

11:21–22 Satan is like a strong man in complete control of his house (the people under his power). But Jesus is stronger than Satan and overthrows him. This is a vivid way of saying that the kingdom of God is not simply a matter of helpful teaching; it involves the power to overcome Satan.

11:23 There can be no neutrality, and there is no middle course. The message of the kingdom entails the possibility for the individual believer to overcome evil, and anyone who rejects this message implicitly accepts the ways of evil.

11:24 Jesus made it clear that he was not referring to a moral reformation whereby a sinner puts away some evil thing but replaces it with nothing else. The demon had left him and gone to arid places (demons were commonly thought to live in deserts). Dissatisfied, the demon returned to the place he had left, and since no one had taken his place, his reentry was easy. **house I left.** Literally, "my house from which I left." The demon still referred to the place he had vacated as his own.

11:25 swept clean and put in order. The man had cleaned up his life but had done nothing more. His heart was empty and open to any evil influence. The result was that seven demons more wicked than the first took up residence there.

■ **11:27—13:9** *Blessing and Judgment.* Luke compiled a number of instances in which Jesus set up decisive contrasts between those who received God's blessing and those who received his judgment.

11:28 rather. Jesus did not deny that Mary was in fact blessed; he said that hearing and obeying God's word brings even greater blessing.

11:29 a miraculous sign. Jesus responded to the demand for a "sign from heaven" (v. 16). Such a request could only have been motivated by unbelief, especially in view of the many demonstrations of Messianic power already performed by Jesus (7:20–23). For Luke, Jesus' very presence was a "sign" of God's redemptive activity (2:34; 11:30).

11:30 Just as Jonah's three-day experience in the belly of the great fish had been a sign to the people of Nineveh, so Jesus' resurrection after three days in the tomb would be a sign to the Jews of his day.

11:31 The Queen of the South. That is, the queen of Sheba (modern Yemen), who made a long and difficult journey to visit Solomon (1Ki 10). Though a heathen, she was a favorable contrast to the people who refused to take notice of Jesus, the "one greater than Solomon," when he was with them.

11:32 men of Nineveh. The Ninevites had repented when Jonah preached (Jnh 3:6–10). As with the queen of Sheba, the argument is from the lesser to the greater. People had responded to Solomon and to Jonah; how much more should they have responded to the Son of God in their midst!

11:33 A one-room home is envisioned. A light covered with a bowl would be useless, but on a stand it would light the whole house.

11:34 the lamp of your body. When the eye is functioning correctly, the body receives the benefit of the light it takes in, or "is full of light" (cf. Ps 18:28). The people seeking a sign did not need more light; they needed to pay greater attention to the light they already had. What God was doing in Jesus was plain enough.

11:38 wash before the meal. Such washing was not for reasons of hygiene, but for ceremonial purity. The hands made contact with all sorts of things, some of which may well have been defiling. Scrupulous Jews washed before eating, because defiled hands were said to allow defilement to enter the body through the food the hands had touched.

11:39–40 Pharisees were scrupulous about the rules for ceremonial cleanness, but those rules referred to that which was outward.

and dish, but inside you are full of greed and wickedness.[i] 40You foolish people![j] Did not the one who made the outside make the inside also? 41But give what is inside ⌞the dish⌟[a] to the poor,[k] and everything will be clean for you.[l]

42"Woe to you Pharisees, because you give God a tenth[m] of your mint, rue and all other kinds of garden herbs, but you neglect justice and the love of God.[n] You should have practiced the latter without leaving the former undone.[o]

43"Woe to you Pharisees, because you love the most important seats in the synagogues and greetings in the marketplaces.[p]

44"Woe to you, because you are like unmarked graves,[q] which men walk over without knowing it."

45One of the experts in the law[r] answered him, "Teacher, when you say these things, you insult us also."

46Jesus replied, "And you experts in the law, woe to you, because you load people down with burdens they can hardly carry, and you yourselves will not lift one finger to help them.[s]

47"Woe to you, because you build tombs for the prophets, and it was your forefathers who killed them. 48So you testify that you approve of what your forefathers did; they killed the prophets, and you build their tombs.[t] 49Because of this, God in his wisdom[u] said, 'I will send them prophets and apostles, some of whom they will kill and others they will persecute.'[v] 50Therefore this generation will be held responsible for the blood of all the prophets that has been shed since the beginning of the world, 51from the blood of Abel[w] to the blood of Zechariah,[x] who was killed between the altar and the sanctuary. Yes, I tell you, this generation will be held responsible for it all.[y]

52"Woe to you experts in the law, because you have taken away the key to knowledge. You yourselves have not entered, and you have hindered those who were entering."[z]

53When Jesus left there, the Pharisees and the teachers of the law began to oppose him fiercely and to besiege him with questions, 54waiting to catch him in something he might say.[a]

Warnings and Encouragements

12 Meanwhile, when a crowd of many thousands had gathered, so that they were trampling on one another, Jesus began to speak first to his disciples, saying: "Be on your guard against the yeast of the Pharisees, which is hypocrisy.[b] 2There is nothing concealed that will not be disclosed, or hidden that will not be made known.[c] 3What you have said in the dark will be heard in the daylight, and what you have whispered in the ear in the inner rooms will be proclaimed from the roofs.

11:39 [i]Mt 23:25,26; Mk 7:20-23
11:40 [j]Lk 12:20; 1Co 15:36
11:41 [k]Lk 12:33 [l]Ac 10:15
11:42 [m]Lk 18:12 [n]Dt 6:5; Mic 6:8 [o]Mt 23:23
11:43 [p]Mt 23:6,7; Mk 12:38-39; Lk 14:7; 20:46
11:44 [q]Mt 23:27
11:45 [r]Mt 22:35
11:46 [s]Mt 23:4
11:48 [t]Mt 23:29-32; Ac 7:51-53
11:49 [u]1Co 1:24,30; Col 2:3 [v]Mt 23:34
11:51 [w]Ge 4:8 [x]2Ch 24:20,21 [y]Mt 23:35,36
11:52 [z]Mt 23:13
11:54 [a]Mt 12:10; Mk 12:13
12:1 [b]Mt 16:6,11,12; Mk 8:15
12:2 [c]Mk 4:22; Lk 8:17

a *41* Or *what you have*

People could keep them all and still be inwardly defiled by greed and other forms of wickedness.
11:41 give what is inside the dish to the poor. Literally, "Give the inward things as alms." Jesus was saying that there must be a right inward attitude when one gives to the poor. When the inside is right, all is clean.
11:42 Woe. See note on 6:24–26. **give God a tenth.** Tithing was intended as a joyful and spontaneous offering made out of love to God, but the Pharisees, with their meticulous counting up of stalks of mint and the like, had turned it into a burdensome duty.
11:43 the most important seats. Seats at the front, facing the congregation. They were reserved for the prominent. **greetings.** Elaborate salutations that showed the recipients to be important people.
11:44 unmarked graves. Not lacking an identification of the person buried, but lacking identification as a grave. To touch a grave was to be ceremonially defiled (Nu 19:16), so graves were whitewashed to warn people of their location. An unmarked grave was a hidden source of defilement.
11:45 experts in the law. Lawyers, but the law in question was the law of God, so they were religious people.
11:46 burdens they can hardly carry. The legal experts added to the law a multitude of regulations meant to ensure that the law itself would not be broken, but these strictures imposed a terrible burden.
11:47 tombs for the prophets. The experts in the law built tombs for the prophets and saw themselves as honoring those great men of God. But this was in effect a completion of the work of those who had killed them. They opposed the Christ of whom the prophets spoke.
11:49 I will send . . . persecute. This is not a quotation from the Old Testament or any other known ancient writing. Jesus may have been describing the way God providentially interacts with his people.
11:50–51 Jesus' own generation had incurred great guilt. In rejecting Jesus, it had implicitly rejected the prophets who had spoken of him. Thus, these people were guilty of the blood of righteous men. Abel was the first murder victim (Ge 4:8), while Zechariah was the last whose murder is recorded in the Old Testament (2Ch 24:21–22; see also note on Mt 23:35).
11:52 taken away the key to knowledge. Through their encumbrance of God's law with human tradition, the "experts in the law" had made it impossible for ordinary people to understand the law, let alone to follow it. The Pharisees and experts in the law even used their own traditions to evade the demands of the law (cf. Mk 7:5–13).
11:54 catch. This translates a Greek word used of hunting wild animals.
12:1 many thousands. The word strictly means "ten thousands," but it was used generally of any large number. Jesus' teaching was addressed first to his disciples, although the crowds would also have heard and profited. **yeast.** Probably the word here translated "yeast" actually refers to "leaven," an old piece of dough that became a source of yeast as it fermented. People made their own bread and were familiar with the way a little yeast or leaven slowly permeates and transforms a large mass of dough. Jesus elsewhere used the figure of yeast or leaven to illustrate the hidden working of God's kingdom (13:21), but here it describes the negative influence of the Pharisees (see note on Mk 8:15).
12:2–3 Hypocrisy can work only when some things are kept hidden. On the judgment day everything will be brought into the open; all hypocrisy will be unmasked and therefore rendered useless.
12:3 inner rooms. Mud brick walls could be dug through, so

4“I tell you, my friends,[d] do not be afraid of those who kill the body and after that can
do no more. 5But I will show you whom you should fear: Fear him who, after the killing
of the body, has power to throw you into hell. Yes, I tell you, fear him.[e] 6Are not five sparrows sold for two pennies[a]? Yet not one of them is forgotten by God. 7Indeed, the very
hairs of your head are all numbered.[f] Don’t be afraid; you are worth more than many
sparrows.[g]
8“I tell you, whoever acknowledges me before men, the Son of Man will also acknowledge him before the angels of God.[h] 9But he who disowns me before men will be disowned[i] before the angels of God. 10And everyone who speaks a word against the Son of
Man[j] will be forgiven, but anyone who blasphemes against the Holy Spirit will not be forgiven.[k]
11“When you are brought before synagogues, rulers and authorities, do not worry
about how you will defend yourselves or what you will say,[l] 12for the Holy Spirit will teach
you at that time what you should say.”[m]

The Parable of the Rich Fool

13Someone in the crowd said to him, “Teacher, tell my brother to divide the inheritance with me.”
14Jesus replied, “Man, who appointed me a judge or an arbiter between you?” 15Then
he said to them, “Watch out! Be on your guard against all kinds of greed; a man’s life
does not consist in the abundance of his possessions.”[n]
16And he told them this parable: “The ground of a certain rich man produced a good
crop. 17He thought to himself, ‘What shall I do? I have no place to store my crops.’
18“Then he said, ‘This is what I’ll do. I will tear down my barns and build bigger ones,
and there I will store all my grain and my goods. 19And I’ll say to myself, “You have plenty of good things laid up for many years. Take life easy; eat, drink and be merry.” ’
20“But God said to him, ‘You fool![o] This very night your life will be demanded from
you.[p] Then who will get what you have prepared for yourself?’[q]
21“This is how it will be with anyone who stores up things for himself but is not rich
toward God.”[r]

Do Not Worry

22Then Jesus said to his disciples: “Therefore I tell you, do not worry about your life,
what you will eat; or about your body, what you will wear. 23Life is more than food, and
the body more than clothes. 24Consider the ravens: They do not sow or reap, they have
no storeroom or barn; yet God feeds them.[s] And how much more valuable you are than
birds! 25Who of you by worrying can add a single hour to his life[b]? 26Since you cannot do
this very little thing, why do you worry about the rest?
27“Consider how the lilies grow. They do not labor or spin. Yet I tell you, not even Solomon in all his splendor[t] was dressed like one of these. 28If that is how God clothes the
grass of the field, which is here today, and tomorrow is thrown into the fire, how much
more will he clothe you, O you of little faith![u] 29And do not set your heart on what you

12:4 [d]Jn 15:14,15
12:5 [e]Heb 10:31
12:7 [f]Mt 10:30 [g]Mt 12:12
12:8 [h]Lk 15:10
12:9 [i]Mk 8:38; 2Ti 2:12
12:10 [j]Mt 8:20 [k]Mt 12:31,32; Mk 3:28-29; 1Jn 5:16
12:11 [l]Mt 10:17,19; Mk 13:11; Lk 21:12,14
12:12 [m]Ex 4:12; Mt 10:20; Mk 13:11; Lk 21:15
12:15 [n]Job 20:20; 31:24; Ps 62:10
12:20 [o]Jer 17:11; Lk 11:40 [p]Job 27:8 [q]Ps 39:6; 49:10
12:21 [r]ver 33
12:24 [s]Job 38:41; Ps 147:9
12:27 [t]1Ki 10:4-7
12:28 [u]Mt 6:30

[a] 6 Greek *two assaria* [b] 25 Or *single cubit to his height*

storerooms where valuables could be kept were well away from outside walls (and therefore secret).

12:4 friends. In the Synoptic Gospels, Jesus called his disciples “friends” only here (but see also Jn 15:14).

12:5 power to throw you into hell. Only God has this power. The Greek word for “hell” here is *ge(h)enna,* the place of final punishment—not *Hades,* often a general word used for the place of all the departed. The Greek *ge(h)enna* derives from Hebrew words meaning “Valley of Hinnom,” a valley outside Jerusalem where child sacrifices had been offered in earlier days and that was seen as accursed (Jer 7:31–33). In New Testament times this was a rubbish heap where fire burned continually, and thus *ge(h)enna* was a suitable name for a place of punishment.

12:6 five sparrows sold for two pennies. Two sparrows were sold for a penny (Mt 10:29), so one was thrown in free when two pennies’ worth were sold. Not one of them is forgotten by God (not even the free one).

12:8–9 The inevitability of judgment day is an encouragement or a warning. Acknowledging Jesus is important.

12:10 blasphemes against the Holy Spirit. A radical form of sin that attributes the work of the Holy Spirit through Christ to Satan in the face of overwhelming moral evidence to the contrary. Such deliberate rejection of the truth is also a decisive rejection of the One (the Holy Spirit) who can bring a person to repentance and faith; such sin makes forgiveness impossible. See theological article “Blasphemy Against the Holy Spirit” at Mark 3.

12:13–14 See *WCF* 31.5.

12:13 The rule for inheritance was given in Deuteronomy 21:17, and cases in dispute were often settled by rabbis. This man clearly wanted only a decision in his favor; he was not seeking a just arbitration. There is no indication that his brother was present or that he had agreed to submit the case to Jesus’ arbitration.

12:15 See *WLC* 142; *HC* 110.

12:22–34 Jesus provides four weighty arguments against anxiety. First, concern for worldly goods is foolish because life itself is more important (v. 23). Second, God will take care of his own, just as he cares for the birds of the air (v. 24). Third, anxiety accomplishes nothing (vv. 25–26). Fourth, as heirs of the inexhaustible riches of the kingdom of God, believers should not worry about earthly details (vv. 32–34). In such teaching Jesus calls us to order our priorities correctly and to focus our hearts on the kingdom (v. 34). See *HC* 26.

12:25 a single hour to his life? The Greek may also mean “add a cubit [about 18 inches] to his height.” Either one is impossible for people to accomplish.

12:27 Solomon. This king was proverbial for magnificence.

will eat or drink; do not worry about it. 30 For the pagan world runs after all such things,
and your Father[v] knows that you need them.[w] 31 But seek his kingdom,[x] and these things
will be given to you as well.[y]
32 "Do not be afraid,[z] little flock, for your Father has been pleased to give you the kingdom.[a] 33 Sell your possessions and give to the poor.[b] Provide purses for yourselves that
will not wear out, a treasure in heaven[c] that will not be exhausted, where no thief comes
near and no moth destroys.[d] 34 For where your treasure is, there your heart will be
also.[e]

Watchfulness

35 "Be dressed ready for service and keep your lamps burning, 36 like men waiting for
their master to return from a wedding banquet, so that when he comes and knocks they
can immediately open the door for him. 37 It will be good for those servants whose master finds them watching when he comes.[f] I tell you the truth, he will dress himself to
serve, will have them recline at the table and will come and wait on them.[g] 38 It will be
good for those servants whose master finds them ready, even if he comes in the second
or third watch of the night. 39 But understand this: If the owner of the house had known
at what hour the thief[h] was coming, he would not have let his house be broken into.
40 You also must be ready,[i] because the Son of Man will come at an hour when you do
not expect him."
41 Peter asked, "Lord, are you telling this parable to us, or to everyone?"
42 The Lord[j] answered, "Who then is the faithful and wise manager, whom the master puts in charge of his servants to give them their food allowance at the proper time?
43 It will be good for that servant whom the master finds doing so when he returns. 44 I tell
you the truth, he will put him in charge of all his possessions. 45 But suppose the servant
says to himself, 'My master is taking a long time in coming,' and he then begins to beat
the menservants and maidservants and to eat and drink and get drunk. 46 The master of
that servant will come on a day when he does not expect him and at an hour he is not
aware of.[k] He will cut him to pieces and assign him a place with the unbelievers.
47 "That servant who knows his master's will and does not get ready or does not do
what his master wants will be beaten with many blows.[l] 48 But the one who does not
know and does things deserving punishment will be beaten with few blows.[m] From everyone who has been given much, much will be demanded; and from the one who has
been entrusted with much, much more will be asked.

Not Peace but Division

49 "I have come to bring fire on the earth, and how I wish it were already kindled! 50 But
I have a baptism[n] to undergo, and how distressed I am until it is completed![o] 51 Do you
think I came to bring peace on earth? No, I tell you, but division. 52 From now on there
will be five in one family divided against each other, three against two and two against
three. 53 They will be divided, father against son and son against father, mother against
daughter and daughter against mother, mother-in-law against daughter-in-law and
daughter-in-law against mother-in-law."[p]

12:30 [v]Lk 6:36 [w]Mt 6:8
12:31 [x]Mt 3:2 [y]Mt 19:29
12:32 [z]Mt 14:27 [a]Mt 25:34
12:33 [b]Mt 19:21; Ac 2:45 [c]Mt 6:20 [d]Jas 5:2
12:34 [e]Mt 6:21
12:37 [f]Mt 24:42,46; 25:13 [g]Mt 20:28
12:39 [h]Mt 6:19; 1Th 5:2; 2Pe 3:10; Rev 3:3; 16:15
12:40 [i]Mk 13:33; Lk 21:36
12:42 [j]Lk 7:13
12:46 [k]ver 40
12:47 [l]Dt 25:2
12:48 [m]Lev 5:17; Nu 15:27-30
12:50 [n]Mk 10:38 [o]Jn 19:30
12:53 [p]Mic 7:6; Mt 10:21

12:31 seek his kingdom. The disciples were already in the kingdom. Therefore they should concentrate their energies on the interests of that kingdom.
12:33 Sell your possessions and give to the poor. Central to this verse is the contrast between earthly goods that are perishable and a source of anxiety and the treasures of the kingdom of God that are a lasting source of peace. Some of Jesus' followers had means (10:38; Jn 19:27), and he was not demanding that all his disciples be poor. But they were not to set their hearts on earthly possessions (v. 34).
12:35–36 See *WCF* 31.5.
12:35 dressed ready for service. Literally, "let your loins be girded about." Long, flowing robes were a hindrance to work. For effective activity, they were kept above the knees by a belt.
12:37 dress himself to serve. Literally, "gird himself." This is a reversal of roles in which the master takes the place of the servant (cf. 22:27).
12:38 second or third watch. The Jews divided the night into three watches (Jdg 7:19); the Romans, into four. Jesus used the Jewish division here. These servants watched for their master throughout the night.
12:42 faithful and wise manager. A slave who had been put in charge of the whole estate by his owner. The owner was free from the burden of administration, and the manager had considerable authority. See *WLC* 159.
12:44 all his possessions. The reward of faithful service is the opportunity to perform higher service.
12:45–46 The punishment for failing to use one's opportunities for service is rightly severe.
12:47–48 People are punished for failing to do good as well as for doing evil. Ignorance does not prevent punishment when there has been an opportunity to know what was expected. God makes his people's duty plain (Ro 1:20; 2:14–15). See *WLC* 151.
12:49 fire. The fire of judgment. In a special sense, judgment on sin was accomplished on the cross.
12:50 baptism. Jesus' death was also a "baptism," another use of imagery that points to death. Liturgically, baptism came to mean death to a way of life and rising to a whole new manner of living. Jesus accepted all of this as the divine way of bringing salvation to sinners. **completed!** On the cross, Jesus spoke of the completion of his work of rendering atonement (Jn 19:30).
12:51–53 In a very important sense, Jesus brought peace (Jn 14:27). But he also called on his hearers to take up their crosses and follow him (9:23). This requirement is not acceptable to all, and it can divide families.

Interpreting the Times

54He said to the crowd: "When you see a cloud rising in the west, immediately you say,
'It's going to rain,' and it does.[q] 55And when the south wind blows, you say, 'It's going
to be hot,' and it is. 56Hypocrites! You know how to interpret the appearance of the earth
and the sky. How is it that you don't know how to interpret this present time?[r]
57"Why don't you judge for yourselves what is right? 58As you are going with your adversary to the magistrate, try hard to be reconciled to him on the way, or he may drag
you off to the judge, and the judge turn you over to the officer, and the officer throw you
into prison.[s] 59I tell you, you will not get out until you have paid the last penny.[a]"[t]

Repent or Perish

13 Now there were some present at that time who told Jesus about the Galileans
whose blood Pilate[u] had mixed with their sacrifices. 2Jesus answered, "Do you
think that these Galileans were worse sinners than all the other Galileans because they
suffered this way?[v] 3I tell you, no! But unless you repent, you too will all perish. 4Or those
eighteen who died when the tower in Siloam[w] fell on them—do you think they were
more guilty than all the others living in Jerusalem? 5I tell you, no! But unless you repent,[x]
you too will all perish."
6Then he told this parable: "A man had a fig tree, planted in his vineyard, and he went
to look for fruit on it, but did not find any.[y] 7So he said to the man who took care of the
vineyard, 'For three years now I've been coming to look for fruit on this fig tree and
haven't found any. Cut it down![z] Why should it use up the soil?'
8" 'Sir,' the man replied, 'leave it alone for one more year, and I'll dig around it and
fertilize it. 9If it bears fruit next year, fine! If not, then cut it down.' "

A Crippled Woman Healed on the Sabbath

10On a Sabbath Jesus was teaching in one of the synagogues,[a] 11and a woman was
there who had been crippled by a spirit for eighteen years.[b] She was bent over and could
not straighten up at all. 12When Jesus saw her, he called her forward and said to her,
"Woman, you are set free from your infirmity." 13Then he put his hands on her,[c] and immediately she straightened up and praised God.
14Indignant because Jesus had healed on the Sabbath,[d] the synagogue ruler[e] said to
the people, "There are six days for work.[f] So come and be healed on those days, not on
the Sabbath."
15The Lord answered him, "You hypocrites! Doesn't each of you on the Sabbath untie his ox or donkey from the stall and lead it out to give it water?[g] 16Then should not this
woman, a daughter of Abraham,[h] whom Satan[i] has kept bound for eighteen long years,
be set free on the Sabbath day from what bound her?"
17When he said this, all his opponents were humiliated,[j] but the people were delighted with all the wonderful things he was doing.

12:54 [q]Mt 16:2
12:56 [r]Mt 16:3
12:58 [s]Mt 5:25
12:59 [t]Mt 5:26; Mk 12:42
13:1 [u]Mt 27:2
13:2 [v]Jn 9:2,3
13:4 [w]Jn 9:7,11
13:5 [x]Mt 3:2; Ac 2:38
13:6 [y]Isa 5:2; Jer 8:13; Mt 21:19
13:7 [z]Mt 3:10
13:10 [a]Mt 4:23
13:11 [b]ver 16
13:13 [c]Mk 5:23
13:14 [d]Mt 12:2; Lk 14:3 [e]Mk 5:22 [f]Ex 20:9
13:15 [g]Lk 14:5
13:16 [h]Lk 3:8; 19:9 [i]Mt 4:10
13:17 [j]Isa 66:5

[a] 59 Greek *lepton*

12:54–56 The people in the crowd knew the signs of the weather. They could recognize that a west wind (from the Mediterranean Sea) meant rain and that a south wind (from desert lands) meant heat. But they did not discern what God was doing in their midst. They were ignorant of what truly mattered.
12:57–59 In legal matters, anyone facing a trial against incriminating evidence does well to secure an out-of-court settlement before the case comes before the judge. Sinners should be reconciled with God now, for they will perish if they wait until judgment day.
13:1 Pilate. To kill people as they were offering sacrifices was seen as particularly horrible. This incident, which is otherwise unknown, no doubt contributed to Pilate's reputation for cruelty.
13:2 Disaster was commonly thought to be the result of extreme sin (Jn 9:1–2), but Jesus denied that these Galileans were especially sinful.
13:3 all perish. All are sinners. Jesus called on his hearers to repent—otherwise they would perish. Because they died suddenly, the Galileans had no extra time to repent. Jesus warned that his unrepentant hearers might also face deaths with no time to prepare. See *WCF* 15.3; *WLC* 153.
13:4 Another incident unknown to us apart from this passage. **more guilty.** Literally, "debtors more." People owe obedience to God.
13:5 See *WCF* 15.3; *WLC* 153.
13:6–9 A fig tree in a vineyard is in fertile soil, and the phrase "three years" points to an established tree. It was unlikely that this tree would ever bear fruit, and it was taking up ground that could be used for a productive tree. But it was given one more chance to bear fruit. That God does not punish sinners immediately does not mean that he approves of their sin. Rather, it shows that he is merciful and that sinners should repent while there is time. The fig tree especially depicts Israel, which is being given an extra opportunity to repent.
■ **13:10–17** *Healing a Woman on the Sabbath.* Luke turned to a time when Jesus healed a crippled woman on the Sabbath. Luke not only showed Jesus' concern for women and the weak, but he also demonstrated Jesus' understanding of the rightness of showing mercy on the Sabbath.
13:10 On a Sabbath. The right use of the Sabbath was the subject of a continuing dispute between Jesus and his enemies. This is the last time Jesus is reported to have attended a synagogue.
13:11–13 The woman did not ask for healing. Jesus took the initiative.
13:14 the synagogue ruler. See note on 8:41.
13:15 You hypocrites! The ruler and all who agreed with him. The Jews cared for their animals and looked after them on the Sabbath as on other days. That Satan kept the woman "bound" (v. 16) does not mean that she was especially sinful; it was her illness that was evil.

13:18
The Parables of the Mustard Seed and the Yeast

[k]Mt 3:2 [l]Mt 13:24 [18]Then Jesus asked, "What is the kingdom of God[k] like?[l] What shall I compare it to?
13:19 [19]It is like a mustard seed, which a man took and planted in his garden. It grew and be-
[m]Lk 17:6 [n]Mt 13:32 came a tree,[m] and the birds of the air perched in its branches."[n]
[20]Again he asked, "What shall I compare the kingdom of God to? [21]It is like yeast that
13:21 a woman took and mixed into a large amount[a] of flour until it worked all through the
[o]1Co 5:6 dough."[o]

The Narrow Door

13:22 [22]Then Jesus went through the towns and villages, teaching as he made his way to
[p]Lk 9:51 Jerusalem.[p] [23]Someone asked him, "Lord, are only a few people going to be saved?"
13:24 He said to them, [24]"Make every effort to enter through the narrow door,[q] because
[q]Mt 7:13 many, I tell you, will try to enter and will not be able to. [25]Once the owner of the house
gets up and closes the door, you will stand outside knocking and pleading, 'Sir, open the
13:25 door for us.'
[r]Mt 7:23; 25:10-12 "But he will answer, 'I don't know you or where you come from.'[r]
[26]"Then you will say, 'We ate and drank with you, and you taught in our streets.'
13:27 [27]"But he will reply, 'I don't know you or where you come from. Away from me, all you
[s]Mt 7:23; 25:41 evildoers!'[s]
13:28 [28]"There will be weeping there, and gnashing of teeth,[t] when you see Abraham, Isaac
[t]Mt 8:12 and Jacob and all the prophets in the kingdom of God, but you yourselves thrown out.
13:29 [29]People will come from east and west[u] and north and south, and will take their places
[u]Mt 8:11 at the feast in the kingdom of God. [30]Indeed there are those who are last who will be first,
13:30 [v]Mt 19:30 and first who will be last."[v]

Jesus' Sorrow for Jerusalem

13:31 [31]At that time some Pharisees came to Jesus and said to him, "Leave this place and
[w]Mt 14:1 go somewhere else. Herod[w] wants to kill you."
[32]He replied, "Go tell that fox, 'I will drive out demons and heal people today and to-
13:32 [x]Heb 2:10 morrow, and on the third day I will reach my goal.'[x] [33]In any case, I must keep going to-
13:33 day and tomorrow and the next day—for surely no prophet[y] can die outside Jerusalem!
[y]Mt 21:11 [34]"O Jerusalem, Jerusalem, you who kill the prophets and stone those sent to you,
13:34 how often I have longed to gather your children together, as a hen gathers her chicks un-
[z]Mt 23:37 der her wings,[z] but you were not willing! [35]Look, your house is left to you desolate.[a] I tell
you, you will not see me again until you say, 'Blessed is he who comes in the name of the
13:35 [a]Jer 12:17; 22:5 Lord.'[b]"[b]
[b]Ps 118:26; Mt 21:9; Lk 19:38

[a] *21* Greek *three satas* (probably about 1/2 bushel or 22 liters) [b] *35* Psalm 118:26

■ **13:18—14:24** *The Kingdom of God.* Luke reported how Jesus explained in a number of ways the unexpected process by which the kingdom of God was coming. He made clear that it was coming over time and that Gentiles would replace many Jews in the kingdom.
13:19–21 These two short parables start with the small beginnings of the kingdom and point out (1) its spread throughout the world (Jesus' disciples were small in number, but their message would permeate the world), and (2) its power to transform (yeast works invisibly but powerfully).
13:21 yeast. See note on 12:1. **a large amount.** Literally, "three satas [seahs]," the amount used by Sarah (Ge 18:6). This was about half a bushel or 22 liters.
13:22 Luke gives a picture of Jesus making unhurried progress toward Jerusalem, where the climax of his life and mission would be realized. On the way Jesus continued to meet the needs of the people he encountered.
13:23 a few people. There were discussions among the Jews as to how many people would be saved, and it was generally agreed that all Israel (except for a few especially sinful people) would be included in that number. Jesus warned against such presumption.
13:24 Make every effort. Salvation must be pursued earnestly, and diligent effort must be expended to persevere in faith (Php 2:12; 2Pe 1:10). **narrow door.** The way into salvation.
13:25 closes the door. There is a time limit to the offer of salvation. It must be accepted while the offer is being presented. **I don't know you.** See Matthew 7:23 and 25:12.
13:26–27 Having social fellowship with Jesus and hearing his teaching were not enough. The people's attitude was superficial; they had never embraced the lordship of Christ. No specific sin is mentioned here. There is only the general condemnation of "evildoers" (v. 27).
13:28 weeping . . . gnashing. There will be weeping (in grief) and gnashing of teeth (in anger) as they see the great ones (with whom they had always classified themselves) in bliss, while they themselves are thrown out (which indicates God's active opposition to all that is evil).
13:29 east . . . west . . . north . . . south. The saved will include people from all over the world, including Gentiles. **the feast.** Imagery of the Messianic banquet that will take place when Christ returns. This image reflects the great joy that will be present in the kingdom at that time (14:15; Rev 19:9). There will be a complete reversal of many ideas strongly held among humankind.
13:31 Leave this place. It appears that Jesus was in Perea, where Herod ruled. The Pharisees preferred to see him in Judea, where they had more influence.
13:32 that fox. A man who was worthless and sly. Jesus was unmoved by the threat and said he would continue with his ministry. There was a limit to the amount of time available to him, as the reference to "the third day" indicates.
13:33 Jesus was contemplating his death (note his reference to Jerusalem). **must.** There was a compelling, divine necessity to what Jesus was doing. Notice the further reference to "the third day" and the certainty that Jerusalem was the place where he would die.
13:34–35 This lament over the city was probably uttered as Jesus reached it (Mt 23:37–38), but it may be included here because of its relationship with what Jesus had just said. It is also possible that Jesus spoke the same words twice.
13:34 how often. Jesus must have been in Jerusalem more often than the Synoptic Gospels record.
13:35 your house. This may mean the temple or the city as a whole. **desolate.** The inevitable result of faithlessness. **until you say.** See note on Matthew 23:39.

Jesus at a Pharisee's House

14 One Sabbath, when Jesus went to eat in the house of a prominent Pharisee,[c] he
was being carefully watched.[d] [2]There in front of him was a man suffering from
dropsy. [3]Jesus asked the Pharisees and experts in the law,[e] "Is it lawful to heal on the
Sabbath or not?"[f] [4]But they remained silent. So taking hold of the man, he healed him
and sent him away.
[5]Then he asked them, "If one of you has a son[a] or an ox that falls into a well on the
Sabbath day, will you not immediately pull him out?"[g] [6]And they had nothing to say.
[7]When he noticed how the guests picked the places of honor at the table,[h] he told
them this parable: [8]"When someone invites you to a wedding feast, do not take the place
of honor, for a person more distinguished than you may have been invited. [9]If so, the host
who invited both of you will come and say to you, 'Give this man your seat.' Then, humiliated, you will have to take the least important place. [10]But when you are invited, take the
lowest place, so that when your host comes, he will say to you, 'Friend, move up to a better place.' Then you will be honored in the presence of all your fellow guests. [11]For everyone who exalts himself will be humbled, and he who humbles himself will be exalted."[i]
[12]Then Jesus said to his host, "When you give a luncheon or dinner, do not invite your
friends, your brothers or relatives, or your rich neighbors; if you do, they may invite you
back and so you will be repaid. [13]But when you give a banquet, invite the poor, the crippled, the lame, the blind,[j] [14]and you will be blessed. Although they cannot repay you, you
will be repaid at the resurrection of the righteous."[k]

The Parable of the Great Banquet

[15]When one of those at the table with him heard this, he said to Jesus, "Blessed is the
man who will eat at the feast[l] in the kingdom of God."[m]
[16]Jesus replied: "A certain man was preparing a great banquet and invited many
guests. [17]At the time of the banquet he sent his servant to tell those who had been invited, 'Come, for everything is now ready.'
[18]"But they all alike began to make excuses. The first said, 'I have just bought a field,
and I must go and see it. Please excuse me.'
[19]"Another said, 'I have just bought five yoke of oxen, and I'm on my way to try them
out. Please excuse me.'
[20]"Still another said, 'I just got married, so I can't come.'
[21]"The servant came back and reported this to his master. Then the owner of the
house became angry and ordered his servant, 'Go out quickly into the streets and alleys
of the town and bring in the poor, the crippled, the blind and the lame.'[n]
[22]" 'Sir,' the servant said, 'what you ordered has been done, but there is still room.'
[23]"Then the master told his servant, 'Go out to the roads and country lanes and make
them come in, so that my house will be full. [24]I tell you, not one of those men who were
invited will get a taste of my banquet.' "[o]

The Cost of Being a Disciple

[25]Large crowds were traveling with Jesus, and turning to them he said: [26]"If anyone

14:1 [c]Lk 7:36; 11:37 [d]Mt 12:10
14:3 [e]Mt 22:35 [f]Mt 12:2
14:5 [g]Lk 13:15
14:7 [h]Lk 11:43
14:11 [i]Mt 23:12; Lk 18:14
14:13 [j]ver 21
14:14 [k]Ac 24:15
14:15 [l]Isa 25:6; Mt 26:29; Lk 13:29; Rev 19:9 [m]Mt 3:2
14:21 [n]ver 13
14:24 [o]Mt 21:43; Ac 13:46

a 5 Some manuscripts *donkey*

14:1 went to eat. Dinner on the Sabbath seems to have been an important meal (the food was all prepared before the day). **carefully watched.** Evidently to detect any Sabbath-breaking conduct.
14:2 dropsy. A disease in which fluid collected in the cavities of the body (mentioned in the New Testament only here).
14:3 Is it lawful . . . ? Healing on the Sabbath was not forbidden in the Law of Moses, although it was forbidden in the scribal regulations (unless there was danger to life).
14:5 a son or an ox. The Jews would pull a child or even an ox out of a well on the Sabbath, though technically this was work. Their acts in an emergency bore witness to the truth that deeds of mercy were lawful on the Sabbath. Jesus had done a similar deed of mercy.
14:7 Places near the guest of honor were eagerly sought.
14:10 Jesus was not giving worldly advice but advocating genuine humility, as verse 11 shows (cf. 18:14; Mt 23:12).
14:12–14 Hospitality must not be given with a view to being recompensed. To invite people without resources or the ability to reciprocate is genuine hospitality. See *BC* 37.
14:15 Blessed is the man. A pious and conventional utterance, perhaps meant to change the subject.
14:16–17 Evidently those invited accepted the invitation; no one is said to have declined. A second invitation when all was ready was usual and very useful in a time when people did not have watches or calendars and when a banquet took a long time to prepare (cf. Est 5:8; 6:14).
14:18–20 The excuses are transparently dishonest. No one buys a field or oxen without prior inspection of them, and if anyone did so, there was no hurry after the fact for inspection. The man who had married might cite Deuteronomy 24:5 as the basis for his nonattendance, but that regulation freed a man from military service, not social contacts.
14:21–24 This parable is a prophecy of the extension of the gospel to those who were deemed unworthy by the Pharisees. The "poor, the crippled, the blind and the lame" (v. 21) represent the "people of the land" (despised Jews who were unable to observe the traditional laws of ritual purity), and those outside the city on the "roads and country lanes" (v. 23) represent the Gentiles. The parable concludes with a warning to the elite of Israel who would reject the Messiah. Such people would be given no second chance.
▪ **14:25–35** *Teaching on Discipleship.* Luke recounted how Jesus emphasized the cost of following him. The stakes were high, and Jesus wanted his followers to assess the matter carefully.

comes to me and does not hate his father and mother, his wife and children, his brothers and sisters—yes, even his own life—he cannot be my disciple.[p] 27And anyone who
does not carry his cross and follow me cannot be my disciple.[q]
28"Suppose one of you wants to build a tower. Will he not first sit down and estimate
the cost to see if he has enough money to complete it? 29For if he lays the foundation and
is not able to finish it, everyone who sees it will ridicule him, 30saying, 'This fellow began to build and was not able to finish.'
31"Or suppose a king is about to go to war against another king. Will he not first sit
down and consider whether he is able with ten thousand men to oppose the one coming against him with twenty thousand? 32If he is not able, he will send a delegation while
the other is still a long way off and will ask for terms of peace. 33In the same way, any of
you who does not give up everything he has cannot be my disciple.[r]
34"Salt is good, but if it loses its saltiness, how can it be made salty again?[s] 35It is fit
neither for the soil nor for the manure pile; it is thrown out.[t]
"He who has ears to hear, let him hear."[u]

The Parable of the Lost Sheep

15 Now the tax collectors[v] and "sinners" were all gathering around to hear him.
2But the Pharisees and the teachers of the law muttered, "This man welcomes
sinners and eats with them."[w]
3Then Jesus told them this parable:[x] 4"Suppose one of you has a hundred sheep and
loses one of them. Does he not leave the ninety-nine in the open country and go after the
lost sheep until he finds it?[y] 5And when he finds it, he joyfully puts it on his shoulders
6and goes home. Then he calls his friends and neighbors together and says, 'Rejoice with
me; I have found my lost sheep.'[z] 7I tell you that in the same way there will be more rejoicing in heaven over one sinner who repents than over ninety-nine righteous persons
who do not need to repent.[a]

The Parable of the Lost Coin

8"Or suppose a woman has ten silver coins[a] and loses one. Does she not light a lamp,
sweep the house and search carefully until she finds it? 9And when she finds it, she calls
her friends and neighbors together and says, 'Rejoice with me; I have found my lost
coin.'[b] 10In the same way, I tell you, there is rejoicing in the presence of the angels of God
over one sinner who repents."[c]

The Parable of the Lost Son

11Jesus continued: "There was a man who had two sons.[d] 12The younger one said to

14:26 [p]Mt 10:37; Jn 12:25
14:27 [q]Mt 10:38; Lk 9:23
14:33 [r]Php 3:7,8
14:34 [s]Mk 9:50
14:35 [t]Mt 5:13 [u]Mt 11:15
15:1 [v]Lk 5:29
15:2 [w]Mt 9:11
15:3 [x]Mt 13:3
15:4 [y]Ps 23; 119:176; Jer 31:10; Eze 34:11-16; Lk 5:32; 19:10
15:6 [z]ver 9
15:7 [a]ver 10
15:9 [b]ver 6
15:10 [c]ver 7
15:11 [d]Mt 21:28

[a] *8* Greek *ten drachmas,* each worth about a day's wages

14:26 hate. This means "love less" (see Ge 29:31,33 and Dt 21:15, where the Hebrew verb meaning "to hate" is translated as "not loved"). Discipleship means loving Jesus so much that all other loves are tantamount to hatred by comparison.
14:27 carry his cross. See note on 9:23–25.
14:28 From ordinary life we learn that evaluating the cost is important before any serious project is undertaken. **tower.** A watchtower or a building on a farm. **sit down.** Points to a careful and unhurried process.
14:31 consider. A king will not engage in a war that means certain defeat. He counts the cost before he starts. The first parable asks the listeners honestly to assess whether they can afford to follow Christ. The second perhaps asks whether they can afford to refuse his demands.
14:34 Salt. Jesus did not specify the qualities that make salt good, but it has obvious flavoring and preservative uses. The salt in use at that time was far from pure, and it was possible for the sodium chloride to be leached out of it, leaving a useless residue.
■ **15:1–32** *Three Parables About the Lost.* Luke drew together three parables Jesus taught about things that were lost. Luke focused on God's mercy in pursuing and accepting his people, as well as on the proper response to seeing the salvation of others.
15:1 tax collectors. See note on 3:12. **sinners.** People who were immoral or who followed occupations that the scribes held to be incompatible with keeping God's law. A rabbinic rule stated that "one must not associate with an ungodly man," and the rabbis would not even teach such a person. Notice that chapter 14 ends with "let him hear," and chapter 15 begins with these very "sinners" gathering around to listen to Jesus.
15:3 The rabbis agreed that God would welcome the penitent sinner, but these parables teach that God actually seeks out the sinner and that God's people should rejoice with the angels when sinners repent.
15:7 rejoicing. Heaven demonstrates the proper response to a sinner's repentance: rejoicing (cf. v. 10).
15:8 silver coins. The *drachma* (the word occurs in this passage only in the New Testament) was a laborer's wage for a day's work. The ten coins may have constituted the woman's life savings. **light a lamp.** The home probably had no windows (or perhaps only small ones), so a lamp was called for even in the daytime.
15:10 rejoicing. Again, heaven demonstrates the proper response to the repentance of a sinner: jubilation (cf. v. 7).
15:11–32 The parable of the lost (or prodigal) son is perhaps more aptly referred to as the parable of the waiting father. While the son's repentance is important to the parable, the father's willingness to forgive, coupled with his unexpected and gracious actions (see notes on v. 20; vv. 22–23), provide a striking illustration of the fatherly love of God for wayward human beings. It might also be called the "parable of the callous brother," for a major purpose of it, perhaps *the* major purpose, is to rebuke the Pharisees for failing to welcome repentant sinners (including Gentiles and other violators of the law) into their fellowship.
15:11–12 The firstborn son was entitled to two-thirds of his father's property (Dt 21:17). Sometimes the father would give the capital (which meant that he could not dispose of it himself, although the son could sell it) and retain the income (if the son sold the capital, the buyer could not procure it until after the father's death). But to give the capital to one of the sons, as in this parable, was unusual.

his father, ‘Father, give me my share of the estate.’[e] So he divided his property[f] between
them.
13“Not long after that, the younger son got together all he had, set off for a distant
country and there squandered his wealth[g] in wild living. 14After he had spent everything,
there was a severe famine in that whole country, and he began to be in need. 15So he
went and hired himself out to a citizen of that country, who sent him to his fields to feed
pigs.[h] 16He longed to fill his stomach with the pods that the pigs were eating, but no one
gave him anything.
17“When he came to his senses, he said, ‘How many of my father’s hired men have
food to spare, and here I am starving to death! 18I will set out and go back to my father
and say to him: Father, I have sinned[i] against heaven and against you. 19I am no longer
worthy to be called your son; make me like one of your hired men.’ 20So he got up and
went to his father.
“But while he was still a long way off, his father saw him and was filled with compassion for him; he ran to his son, threw his arms around him and kissed him.[j]
21“The son said to him, ‘Father, I have sinned against heaven and against you.[k] I am
no longer worthy to be called your son.[a]’
22“But the father said to his servants, ‘Quick! Bring the best robe[l] and put it on him.
Put a ring on his finger[m] and sandals on his feet. 23Bring the fattened calf and kill it. Let’s
have a feast and celebrate. 24For this son of mine was dead and is alive again;[n] he was
lost and is found.’ So they began to celebrate.[o]
25“Meanwhile, the older son was in the field. When he came near the house, he heard
music and dancing. 26So he called one of the servants and asked him what was going on.
27‘Your brother has come,’ he replied, ‘and your father has killed the fattened calf because he has him back safe and sound.’
28“The older brother became angry[p] and refused to go in. So his father went out and
pleaded with him. 29But he answered his father, ‘Look! All these years I’ve been slaving
for you and never disobeyed your orders. Yet you never gave me even a young goat so I
could celebrate with my friends. 30But when this son of yours who has squandered your
property[q] with prostitutes[r] comes home, you kill the fattened calf for him!’
31“ ‘My son,’ the father said, ‘you are always with me, and everything I have is yours.
32But we had to celebrate and be glad, because this brother of yours was dead and is
alive again; he was lost and is found.’ ”[s]

The Parable of the Shrewd Manager

16 Jesus told his disciples: “There was a rich man whose manager was accused of
wasting his possessions.[t] 2So he called him in and asked him, ‘What is this I hear
about you? Give an account of your management, because you cannot be manager any
longer.’
3“The manager said to himself, ‘What shall I do now? My master is taking away my

15:12 [e]Dt 21:17 [f]ver 30
15:13 [g]ver 30; Lk 16:1
15:15 [h]Lev 11:7
15:18 [i]Lev 26:40; Mt 3:2
15:20 [j]Ge 45:14,15; 46:29; Ac 20:37
15:21 [k]Ps 51:4
15:22 [l]Zec 3:4; Rev 6:11 [m]Ge 41:42
15:24 [n]Eph 2:1,5; 5:14; 1Ti 5:6 [o]ver 32
15:28 [p]Jnh 4:1
15:30 [q]ver 12,13 [r]Pr 29:3
15:32 [s]ver 24; Mal 3:17
16:1 [t]Lk 15:13,30

[a] *21* Some early manuscripts *son. Make me like one of your hired men.*

15:15 pigs. The pig was considered an unclean animal (Lev 11:7); no Jew would take this job willingly. The rabbis considered those who bred swine to be cursed.
15:16 pods. The seeds of the carob tree.
15:17–19 The son’s original motive for going home was not praiseworthy, but his confession is laudable and exemplary. He acknowledged his sin and sought mercy. See *WLC* 76,185.
15:20–24 See *HC* 85.
15:20 The father was apparently watching intently for his son’s return. It was considered undignified for a distinguished older man to gather up his robes and run.
15:22–23 The father’s actions indicate complete forgiveness and restoration of relationship. **best robe.** A mark of distinction. **ring.** Signified authority (Ge 41:42; Est 3:10; 8:2). **sandals.** Because slaves did not wear shoes, the sandals point to the son’s status as a free man. **fattened calf.** Reserved for special occasions.
15:24 celebrate. The father and the household servants exhibited the same response as that of the owners of the lost sheep (v. 6) and the lost coin (v. 9): joy and celebration. This mirrors the celebration and joy in heaven when a sinner repents (vv. 7,10) and thus was the appropriate response to the son’s return.
15:25–28 The older son’s attitude illustrates the judgmental spirit of the Pharisees, who were annoyed at the presence of “sinners” (vv. 1–3). It stands in stark contrast to the godly response of joy and celebration (see note on v. 24).
15:28 As with the younger son (v. 20), the father took the initiative in restoring the relationship. The parable as a whole points to the sovereign love of God, who actively seeks out unworthy sinners who do not seek him (19:10).
15:29 slaving for you. This statement indicates that the older brother viewed his relationship with the father as the reward for meritorious behavior. Like the father’s loving response to the undeserving younger son, salvation is not a reward for good works but entirely the gracious gift of God (Eph 2:8–9). **you never gave me even a young goat.** This would have been cheaper than a fattened calf.
15:31 everything I have is yours. The attitude of the older son (see note on v. 29) caused him to miss out on the rich blessings of his relationship with his father.
15:32 this brother of yours. The father did not say “this son of mine,” for he would not let the offended brother forget that both sons were members of the same family.
■ **16:1—17:10** *Money and Service.* Luke presented together a number of Jesus’ statements about priorities, wealth, power, service and humility. Receiving God’s blessing, Jesus continued to warn, was not automatic for his Jewish audience.
16:1 manager. The man who ran the estate, freeing the owner from being involved in every detail. Because he was not closely supervised, it was easy for the manager to be dishonest or lazy.

job. I'm not strong enough to dig, and I'm ashamed to beg— 4I know what I'll do so that,
when I lose my job here, people will welcome me into their houses.'
5"So he called in each one of his master's debtors. He asked the first, 'How much do
you owe my master?'
6" 'Eight hundred gallons[a] of olive oil,' he replied.
"The manager told him, 'Take your bill, sit down quickly, and make it four hundred.'
7"Then he asked the second, 'And how much do you owe?'
" 'A thousand bushels[b] of wheat,' he replied.
"He told him, 'Take your bill and make it eight hundred.'
8"The master commended the dishonest manager because he had acted shrewdly.
For the people of this world[u] are more shrewd[v] in dealing with their own kind than are
the people of the light.[w] 9I tell you, use worldly wealth[x] to gain friends for yourselves,
so that when it is gone, you will be welcomed into eternal dwellings.[y]
10"Whoever can be trusted with very little can also be trusted with much,[z] and whoever is dishonest with very little will also be dishonest with much. 11So if you have not
been trustworthy in handling worldly wealth,[a] who will trust you with true riches?
12And if you have not been trustworthy with someone else's property, who will give you
property of your own?
13"No servant can serve two masters. Either he will hate the one and love the other,
or he will be devoted to the one and despise the other. You cannot serve both God and
Money."[b]
14The Pharisees, who loved money,[c] heard all this and were sneering at Jesus.[d] 15He
said to them, "You are the ones who justify yourselves[e] in the eyes of men, but God
knows your hearts.[f] What is highly valued among men is detestable in God's sight.

Additional Teachings

16"The Law and the Prophets were proclaimed until John.[g] Since that time, the good
news of the kingdom of God is being preached,[h] and everyone is forcing his way into it.
17It is easier for heaven and earth to disappear than for the least stroke of a pen to drop
out of the Law.[i]
18"Anyone who divorces his wife and marries another woman commits adultery, and
the man who marries a divorced woman commits adultery.[j]

The Rich Man and Lazarus

19"There was a rich man who was dressed in purple and fine linen and lived in luxury every day.[k] 20At his gate was laid a beggar[l] named Lazarus, covered with sores 21and

a 6 Greek *one hundred batous* (probably about 3 kiloliters) b 7 Greek *one hundred korous* (probably about 35 kiloliters)

16:8 [u]Ps 17:14 [v]Ps 18:26 [w]Jn 12:36; Eph 5:8; 1Th 5:5
16:9 [x]ver 11,13 [y]Mt 19:21; Lk 12:33
16:10 [z]Mt 25:21,23; Lk 19:17
16:11 [a]ver 9,13
16:13 [b]ver 9,11; Mt 6:24
16:14 [c]1Ti 3:3 [d]Lk 23:35
16:15 [e]Lk 10:29 [f]1Sa 16:7; Rev 2:23
16:16 [g]Mt 11:12,13 [h]Mt 4:23
16:17 [i]Mt 5:18
16:18 [j]Mt 5:31,32; 19:9; Mk 10:11; Ro 7:2, 3; 1Co 7:10,11
16:19 [k]Eze 16:49
16:20 [l]Ac 3:2

16:5–7 See *WLC* 145.
16:6 A significant reduction in the amount the debtor owed would have made him ready to take the dismissed manager into his house (v. 4), at least for a time. This amount of oil equaled the yield of 146 olive trees, a considerable sum.
16:7 The process is repeated. The wheat seems to represent the harvest of about 100 acres.
16:8 With the original bills destroyed, the owner was in an awkward position. It would be difficult for him to establish his claim to the whole amount. His praise of the shrewdness of his manager was an acknowledgement that he had been outwitted. Jesus' point was that worldly people often use the resources at their disposal more effectively than do the people of the light—even though their aims are quite different.
16:9 Jesus' disciples were to use what material goods they possessed, not for selfish purposes, but to "gain friends" (alms for the poor were probably in view here). **you will be welcomed.** The text does not explicitly specify who is doing the welcoming. Possibilities include the poor who have been helped in this life or perhaps God himself. In either case, salvation by works is not being taught (see note on 15:29). The loving help given to others in this life is a sign of genuine discipleship and salvation already enjoyed, rather than a meritorious ground of salvation.
16:10–13 See *WLC* 142; *HC* 110.
16:10 Honesty arises from a person's character, not from the greatness or smallness of what is entrusted to him or her.
16:11 true riches? Heavenly treasures.
16:12 Our money is always a gift from God and is never our own; we lose it all at death. The only property that is truly our own is the inheritance we will fully realize in the new heaven and the new earth (Mt 25:34; Rev 21:1–5).
16:13 servant. A household slave. **serve.** To serve as a slave. It is impossible to offer the wholehearted service required of a slave to more than one person.
16:15 See *BC* 23.
16:16 The Law and the Prophets. A reference to the entire Old Testament. **proclaimed until John.** Luke here indicates that the ministry of John the Baptist lies at the threshold of the major turning point in redemptive history (see note on Mt 11:11). **everyone is forcing his way into it.** A difficult statement to translate and interpret (cf. the similar saying in Mt 11:12). Some suggest that Jesus was describing the zeal with which one must seek the kingdom (13:24); thus he was exhorting his followers. Others suggest that the Greek word translated "forcing" (*biazetai*) is to be understood in the negative sense of hostile powers fighting against the kingdom (see note on Mt 11:12).
16:17 least stroke of a pen. A tiny projection on some Hebrew letters that distinguishes them from other letters; the smallest part of a letter. The entire law came from God, and we must not neglect any part of it (Mt 5:18).
16:18 Jewish men could divorce their wives easily and for the slightest provocation. Jesus had a higher view of marriage. The law's provision for divorce (Dt 24:1–4) was permitted as a concession to the hardness of the people's hearts (Mk 10:5). Jesus saw some Jewish divorces as resulting in adultery (Mt 5:31–32; 19:9).
16:19 a rich man. The name Dives, which is sometimes given him, is Latin for "rich." **purple and fine linen.** The costly clothing that was characteristic of the rich. Purple was used for the outer garment and linen for the undergarment.
16:20 Lazarus. The only character named in Jesus' parables. Jesus pictures him as living in extreme poverty and misery.

longing to eat what fell from the rich man's table.[m] Even the dogs came and licked his
sores.
22“The time came when the beggar died and the angels carried him to Abraham's
side. The rich man also died and was buried. 23In hell,[a] where he was in torment, he
looked up and saw Abraham far away, with Lazarus by his side. 24So he called to him,
'Father Abraham,[n] have pity on me and send Lazarus to dip the tip of his finger in water and cool my tongue, because I am in agony in this fire.'[o]
25“But Abraham replied, 'Son, remember that in your lifetime you received your good
things, while Lazarus received bad things,[p] but now he is comforted here and you are
in agony.[q] 26And besides all this, between us and you a great chasm has been fixed, so
that those who want to go from here to you cannot, nor can anyone cross over from there
to us.'
27“He answered, 'Then I beg you, father, send Lazarus to my father's house, 28for I
have five brothers. Let him warn them,[r] so that they will not also come to this place of
torment.'
29“Abraham replied, 'They have Moses[s] and the Prophets;[t] let them listen to them.'
30“ 'No, father Abraham,'[u] he said, 'but if someone from the dead goes to them, they
will repent.'
31“He said to him, 'If they do not listen to Moses and the Prophets, they will not be
convinced even if someone rises from the dead.' ”

Sin, Faith, Duty

17 Jesus said to his disciples: “Things that cause people to sin[v] are bound to come,
but woe to that person through whom they come.[w] 2It would be better for him
to be thrown into the sea with a millstone tied around his neck than for him to cause one
of these little ones[x] to sin.[y] 3So watch yourselves.
“If your brother sins, rebuke him,[z] and if he repents, forgive him.[a] 4If he sins against
you seven times in a day, and seven times comes back to you and says, 'I repent,' forgive
him.”[b]
5The apostles[c] said to the Lord,[d] “Increase our faith!”
6He replied, “If you have faith as small as a mustard seed,[e] you can say to this mul-
berry tree, 'Be uprooted and planted in the sea,' and it will obey you.[f]
7“Suppose one of you had a servant plowing or looking after the sheep. Would he say
to the servant when he comes in from the field, 'Come along now and sit down to eat'?
8Would he not rather say, 'Prepare my supper, get yourself ready and wait on me[g] while
I eat and drink; after that you may eat and drink'? 9Would he thank the servant because
he did what he was told to do? 10So you also, when you have done everything you were
told to do, should say, 'We are unworthy servants; we have only done our duty.' ”[h]

16:21 [m]Mt 15:27
16:24 [n]ver 30; Lk 3:8 [o]Mt 5:22
16:25 [p]Ps 17:14 [q]Lk 6:21,24,25
16:28 [r]Ac 2:40; 20:23; 1Th 4:6
16:29 [s]Lk 24:27,44; Jn 5:45-47; Ac 15:21 [t]Lk 4:17; Jn 1:45
16:30 [u]ver 24; Lk 3:8
17:1 [v]Mt 5:29 [w]Mt 18:7
17:2 [x]Mk 10:24; Lk 10:21 [y]Mt 5:29
17:3 [z]Mt 18:15 [a]Eph 4:32; Col 3:13
17:4 [b]Mt 18:21,22
17:5 [c]Mk 6:30 [d]Lk 7:13
17:6 [e]Mt 13:31; 17:20; Lk 13:19 [f]Mt 21:21; Mk 9:23
17:8 [g]Lk 12:37
17:10 [h]1Co 9:16

[a] 23 Greek *Hades*

16:22 Abraham's side. The Greek means “bosom.” The imagery is that of being the guest of honor at a banquet (cf. Jn 13:23, where the Greek means “Jesus' bosom”).
16:23–24 See *WCF* 32.1; *WLC* 86.
16:23 In hell. The Greek is *Hades,* the abode of the departed, but in the New Testament it is never used of the saved. Here it is clearly a place of torment. It is of interest that the rich man could see Lazarus and Abraham from his position in *Hades.*
16:24 Even in Hades the rich man displays arrogance, assuming that he can have Lazarus sent to do his bidding. Notice also that even a drop of water would have given some alleviation to his agony, illustrating the severity of the torments of the wicked in the afterlife. See *WLC* 29.
16:25–26 See *WCF* 21.4; *WLC* 89.
16:25 Son. Although the tone of Abraham's address to Lazarus is tender, it cannot alter the facts. A great chasm separates the two, and there is a whole new order with a complete reversal of earthly values. **your good things.** The rich man had received what he saw as good things. He could have chosen the things of God, but he had preferred sensual pleasures.
16:27–28 For the first time, the rich man thinks of someone besides himself, though his thoughts remain focused on his own family. And he still assumes that Lazarus may be sent to do his bidding.
16:29 Moses and the Prophets. A reference to the entire Old Testament. The rich man assumed that the sending of Lazarus would be effective; Jesus said that Scripture is more effective than the appearance of such an apparition could ever be. See *WCF* 1.2; *WLC* 3.
16:31 See *WCF* 1.2; *WLC* 3.
17:1 Things that cause people to sin. The Greek, *skandalon,* is a picturesque word signifying the bait stick of a trap; it has come to mean anything that trips people up and traps them. **woe.** Those who entrap people and lead them into sin should expect to fall under condemnation.
17:2 a millstone. A heavy stone used for grinding grain. **little ones.** Children or humble believers (cf. 10:21) who are helpless apart from God's aid.
17:3–4 See *WCF* 15.6.
17:4 seven times in a day. This does not mean that an eighth offense is not to be forgiven but that forgiveness must be constant.
17:5–6 Increase our faith! Apparently the disciples thought that greater faith than they possessed was necessary to forgive according to these standards. Jesus pointed to what even small faith can bring about. Even more important than the quantity of one's faith is the object of that faith—a great and almighty God. See *WCF* 14.1.
17:7 servant. The term here means “slave.” Having accomplished what he was instructed to do, a slave has done nothing deserving of thanks. His master does not allow him to eat before he prepares the master's meal (note, however, the behavior of the master in 12:37; 22:27). To serve his master is the slave's duty. Similarly, our duty is to serve God, and we can never do more than our duty, for we are required by a perfectly just and righteous God to be perfect (Mt 5:48).
17:10 See *WCF* 7.1; 16.4; 16.5; 19.6; *BC* 24; *HC* 63.

Ten Healed of Leprosy

11 Now on his way to Jerusalem,[i] Jesus traveled along the border between Samaria and
Galilee.[j] 12 As he was going into a village, ten men who had leprosy[a][k] met him. They stood
at a distance[l] 13 and called out in a loud voice, "Jesus, Master,[m] have pity on us!"
14 When he saw them, he said, "Go, show yourselves to the priests."[n] And as they
went, they were cleansed.
15 One of them, when he saw he was healed, came back, praising God[o] in a loud voice.
16 He threw himself at Jesus' feet and thanked him—and he was a Samaritan.[p]
17 Jesus asked, "Were not all ten cleansed? Where are the other nine? 18 Was no one
found to return and give praise to God except this foreigner?" 19 Then he said to him,
"Rise and go; your faith has made you well."[q]

The Coming of the Kingdom of God

20 Once, having been asked by the Pharisees when the kingdom of God would come,[r]
Jesus replied, "The kingdom of God does not come with your careful observation, 21 nor
will people say, 'Here it is,' or 'There it is,'[s] because the kingdom of God is within[b] you."
22 Then he said to his disciples, "The time is coming when you will long to see one of
the days of the Son of Man,[t] but you will not see it.[u] 23 Men will tell you, 'There he is!' or
'Here he is!' Do not go running off after them.[v] 24 For the Son of Man in his day[c] will be
like the lightning,[w] which flashes and lights up the sky from one end to the other. 25 But
first he must suffer many things[x] and be rejected[y] by this generation.[z]
26 "Just as it was in the days of Noah,[a] so also will it be in the days of the Son of Man.
27 People were eating, drinking, marrying and being given in marriage up to the day Noah
entered the ark. Then the flood came and destroyed them all.
28 "It was the same in the days of Lot.[b] People were eating and drinking, buying and
selling, planting and building. 29 But the day Lot left Sodom, fire and sulfur rained down
from heaven and destroyed them all.
30 "It will be just like this on the day the Son of Man is revealed.[c] 31 On that day no one
who is on the roof of his house, with his goods inside, should go down to get them. Likewise, no one in the field should go back for anything.[d] 32 Remember Lot's wife![e] 33 Whoever tries to keep his life will lose it, and whoever loses his life will preserve it.[f] 34 I tell
you, on that night two people will be in one bed; one will be taken and the other left.
35 Two women will be grinding grain together; one will be taken and the other left.[d]"[g]
37 "Where, Lord?" they asked.
He replied, "Where there is a dead body, there the vultures will gather."[h]

[a] *12* The Greek word was used for various diseases affecting the skin—not necessarily leprosy.
[b] *21* Or *among* [c] *24* Some manuscripts do not have *in his day.* [d] *35* Some manuscripts *left.*
36 Two men will be in the field; one will be taken and the other left.

17:11 [i]Lk 9:51 [j]Lk 9:51, 52; Jn 4:3,4
17:12 [k]Mt 8:2 [l]Lev 13:45, 46
17:13 [m]Lk 5:5
17:14 [n]Lev 14:2; Mt 8:4
17:15 [o]Mt 9:8
17:16 [p]Mt 10:5
17:19 [q]Mt 9:22
17:20 [r]Mt 3:2
17:21 [s]ver 23
17:22 [t]Mt 8:20 [u]Mt 9:15; Lk 5:35
17:23 [v]Mt 24:23; Mk 13:21; Lk 21:8
17:24 [w]Mt 24:27
17:25 [x]Mt 16:21 [y]Lk 9:22; 18:32 [z]Mk 13:30; Lk 21:32
17:26 [a]Ge 7:6-24
17:28 [b]Ge 19:1-28
17:30 [c]Mt 10:23; 16:27; 24:3,27,37,39; 25:31; 1Co 1:7; 1Th 2:19; 2Th 1:7; 2:8; 2Pe 3:4; Rev 1:7
17:31 [d]Mt 24:17,18; Mk 13:15-16
17:32 [e]Ge 19:26
17:33 [f]Jn 12:25
17:35 [g]Mt 24:41
17:37 [h]Mt 24:28

■ **17:11–19** *Ten Lepers.* Luke reported that Jesus healed ten lepers but that only one returned to thank him appropriately. Many in Israel had been blessed by Jesus, but only a few turned from sin to thank and praise Jesus. Those who did were blessed indeed.
17:11 Jesus' journey toward Jerusalem and the cross continued (13:22). Because a group of Jews traveling toward Jerusalem would not have been welcomed by Samaritans (9:51–53), Jesus and his disciples skirted the border.
17:12 leprosy. People with leprosy were required by law to keep their distance from healthy people (Lev 13:46). These lepers came as close as they dared and called out loudly.
17:14 show yourselves. When people claimed to have been cured of any of the skin diseases lumped together under the term *leprosy,* they had to present themselves to a priest, who certified them as fit to return to ordinary society (Lev 14:1–32) after certain sacrifices had been offered. **as they went.** Jesus' command, when nothing had yet happened to the men, was a test of faith. They were healed as they went in obedience to Jesus' word.
17:15–16 Gratitude impelled one man to go straight back to Jesus, praising God for what had happened. That he was a Samaritan made this act all the more interesting, for he would not have been expected to show much gratitude to a Jewish healer.
■ **17:20–37** *The Coming of the Kingdom.* Jesus spoke regarding the timing and urgency of the coming of the glorious kingdom of God.
17:21 the kingdom of God is within you. May signify that the kingdom is present as an inward reality, something hidden in people's hearts (cf. Ro 14:17). The alternate translation, "among you" (see NIV text note), may be understood to point to the presence of the kingdom among them in the person of Jesus. See *BC* 27.
17:22 one of the days of the Son of Man. A probable reference to the full manifestation of the kingdom at the second coming of Christ (vv. 26,30). Christians will long for the coming of Christ and for the peace and justice that the second coming will bring.
17:23–25 Although some will claim that the second coming of the Messiah has arrived (21:8–9), this event will be so public that everybody will see it.
17:25 must suffer many things. The word "must" is important. It indicates the sovereign purpose of God (Ac 4:27–28).
17:26–27 Noah's generation is an example of people who carried on with the normal life of this world and neglected their opportunity to repent while it was available. Jesus assumes the sin of Noah's generation (Ge 6:5–6) and focuses on the suddenness with which judgment came upon them.
17:28 in the days of Lot. The time of Lot provides a similar example. Like the wickedness of Noah's generation, Sodom's sin was proverbial (cf. Mt 10:15; 11:23–24; Lk 10:12). Assuming the severity of their sin, Jesus concentrated on the ordinary business of life in which people were so engrossed that they missed their opportunity to repent. Noah and Lot were sinners, but they heeded God's warning and were saved. They were not wholly taken up with the concerns of this life.
17:30 is revealed. This points to the second coming of our Lord. People should not focus their primary attention on their worldly possessions. See *WCF* 28.5.
17:32 Lot's wife came as close to deliverance as was possible, but her backward look doomed her (Ge 19:26).
17:33 Jesus repeated (see 9:24) the teaching that the selfish and self-affirming life leads to spiritual death.
17:34–35 Close proximity or relationship to some saved person will not help in the day of Christ's coming.
17:37 Where there is a dead body. Jesus apparently used a

The Parable of the Persistent Widow

18 Then Jesus told his disciples a parable to show them that they should always
pray and not give up.[i] 2He said: "In a certain town there was a judge who neither feared God nor cared about men. 3And there was a widow in that town who kept
coming to him with the plea, 'Grant me justice[j] against my adversary.'
4"For some time he refused. But finally he said to himself, 'Even though I don't fear
God or care about men, 5yet because this widow keeps bothering me, I will see that she
gets justice, so that she won't eventually wear me out with her coming!' "[k]
6And the Lord[l] said, "Listen to what the unjust judge says. 7And will not God bring
about justice for his chosen ones, who cry out[m] to him day and night? Will he keep putting them off? 8I tell you, he will see that they get justice, and quickly. However, when
the Son of Man[n] comes,[o] will he find faith on the earth?"

The Parable of the Pharisee and the Tax Collector

9To some who were confident of their own righteousness[p] and looked down on everybody else,[q] Jesus told this parable: 10"Two men went up to the temple to pray,[r] one
a Pharisee and the other a tax collector. 11The Pharisee stood up[s] and prayed about[a]
himself: 'God, I thank you that I am not like other men—robbers, evildoers, adulterers
or even like this tax collector. 12I fast[t] twice a week and give a tenth[u] of all I get.'
13"But the tax collector stood at a distance. He would not even look up to heaven, but
beat his breast[v] and said, 'God, have mercy on me, a sinner.'[w]
14"I tell you that this man, rather than the other, went home justified before God. For
everyone who exalts himself will be humbled, and he who humbles himself will be exalted."[x]

The Little Children and Jesus

15People were also bringing babies to Jesus to have him touch them. When the disciples saw this, they rebuked them. 16But Jesus called the children to him and said, "Let
the little children come to me, and do not hinder them, for the kingdom of God belongs
to such as these. 17I tell you the truth, anyone who will not receive the kingdom of God
like a little child[y] will never enter it."

The Rich Ruler

18A certain ruler asked him, "Good teacher, what must I do to inherit eternal life?"[z]
19"Why do you call me good?" Jesus answered. "No one is good—except God alone.

18:1 [i]Isa 40:31; Lk 11:5-8; Ac 1:14; Ro 12:12; Eph 6:18; Col 4:2; 1Th 5:17
18:3 [j]Isa 1:17
18:5 [k]Lk 11:8
18:6 [l]Lk 7:13
18:7 [m]Ex 22:23; Ps 88:1; Rev 6:10
18:8 [n]Mt 8:20 [o]Mt 16:27
18:9 [p]Lk 16:15 [q]Isa 65:5
18:10 [r]Ac 3:1
18:11 [s]Mt 6:5; Mk 11:25
18:12 [t]Isa 58:3; Mt 9:14 [u]Mal 3:8; Lk 11:42
18:13 [v]Isa 66:2; Jer 31:19; Lk 23:48 [w]Lk 5:32; 1Ti 1:15
18:14 [x]Mt 23:12; Lk 14:11
18:17 [y]Mt 11:25; 18:3
18:18 [z]Lk 10:25

[a] *11* Or *to*

---

popular proverb to teach that just as dead bodies attract vultures, so the spiritually dead invite judgment.

■ **18:1–14** *Parables About Prayer.* Jesus spoke of two attitudes in prayer. The preceding context (17:20–37) and the reference to the second coming (v. 8) suggest that persistence and humility in prayer for the coming of Christ and his final triumph over evil are particularly in view (1Co 16:22; Rev 22:20), even if that coming is seemingly delayed. There is also a more general principle here regarding the importance of persistent, humble prayer in all matters.

18:3 The widow was a helpless person with a righteous cause (she wanted justice, not revenge).

18:5 wear me out. A picturesque expression; literally, "give me a black eye."

18:7 If even an unjust judge sometimes does what is just, how much more will the righteous God always do right? **chosen ones.** God's elect who pray to him continually. He will not, like an unjust judge, keep putting them off. Any delay will have a reason; e.g., strengthening those who pray or giving the opportunity for repentance to those for whom believers pray.

18:8 quickly. This is according to God's timetable (2Pe 3:8), not ours. **will he find faith . . . ?** This does not mean that there will be no believers, but that not all people will be believers.

18:9 See *WLC* 145.

18:10 Private prayer could be offered in the temple at any time of day, not just during formal services.

18:11 stood up. The customary posture for prayer. See *WLC* 145.

18:12 fast twice a week. The only fast prescribed in the Law of Moses was to occur on the Day of Atonement (Lev 16:29–31; 23:27), although voluntary fasting could accompany prayer (Ps 35:13), penitence (1Ki 21:27) and mourning (2Sa 1:12). In the intertestamental period, Jewish oral tradition added to the number of fasts expected of the pious. Fasting can be a useful religious exercise (5:33–35; Ac 13:2–3), but Jesus roundly condemned the practice when it was seen as a way of meriting God's favor (vv. 11–12) or when it became a display of ostentatious piety (Mt 6:16–18; cf. Isa 58:1–6).

18:13–14 See *WLC* 185.

18:13 look up to heaven. Looking upward was usual while praying, but this man was too conscious of his unworthiness to do so. He simply asked for mercy as he acknowledged his sin.

18:14 went home justified. It was the penitent, not the proud, who went home justified (i.e., reckoned as just). The Pharisee relied on his own merit, but it was not enough; he had not discovered that no human righteousness is good enough before a God who demands perfection (Mt 5:48). The tax collector relied on God's mercy and found it.

■ **18:15–17** *Jesus and Children.* Luke placed this vignette here to point further to the need for humility in the kingdom.

18:15–16 See *WCF* 10.3; 28.4; *WLC* 166.

18:16 the kingdom . . . belongs to such as these. Jesus presented young children as models for those who want to inherit the kingdom. His followers must have faith in God that resembles young children's faith in their parents.

■ **18:18–30** *The Rich Young Ruler.* Here Luke raised the problem of pride and riches and of how they may prevent a person from inheriting the kingdom. The rich young ruler stood in contrast with the childlike faith mentioned in the preceding passage.

18:18 ruler. Luke alone informs us that this man was a ruler; this term is general in nature but makes it clear that the man was from the upper classes. **Good teacher.** This was not a form of address used in Judaism; it was a form of flattery. The man assumed that his deeds would earn him eternal life.

18:19 Why do you call me good? Jesus invited the man to think about what his greeting implied. Jesus did not say it was wrong to

20 You know the commandments: 'Do not commit adultery, do not murder, do not steal,
do not give false testimony, honor your father and mother.'[a] [a]
21 "All these I have kept since I was a boy," he said.
22 When Jesus heard this, he said to him, "You still lack one thing. Sell everything you
have and give to the poor,[b] and you will have treasure in heaven.[c] Then come, follow me."
23 When he heard this, he became very sad, because he was a man of great wealth.
24 Jesus looked at him and said, "How hard it is for the rich to enter the kingdom of God![d]
25 Indeed, it is easier for a camel to go through the eye of a needle than for a rich man to
enter the kingdom of God."
26 Those who heard this asked, "Who then can be saved?"
27 Jesus replied, "What is impossible with men is possible with God."[e]
28 Peter said to him, "We have left all we had to follow you!"[f]
29 "I tell you the truth," Jesus said to them, "no one who has left home or wife or brothers or parents or children for the sake of the kingdom of God 30 will fail to receive many
times as much in this age and, in the age to come,[g] eternal life."[h]

Jesus Again Predicts His Death

31 Jesus took the Twelve aside and told them, "We are going up to Jerusalem,[i] and everything that is written by the prophets[j] about the Son of Man[k] will be fulfilled. 32 He will
be handed over to the Gentiles.[l] They will mock him, insult him, spit on him, flog him[m]
and kill him.[n] 33 On the third day[o] he will rise again."[p]
34 The disciples did not understand any of this. Its meaning was hidden from them,
and they did not know what he was talking about.[q]

A Blind Beggar Receives His Sight

35 As Jesus approached Jericho,[r] a blind man was sitting by the roadside begging.
36 When he heard the crowd going by, he asked what was happening. 37 They told him,
"Jesus of Nazareth is passing by."[s]
38 He called out, "Jesus, Son of David,[t] have mercy[u] on me!"
39 Those who led the way rebuked him and told him to be quiet, but he shouted all the
more, "Son of David, have mercy on me!"[v]
40 Jesus stopped and ordered the man to be brought to him. When he came near, Jesus
asked him, 41 "What do you want me to do for you?"
"Lord, I want to see," he replied.
42 Jesus said to him, "Receive your sight; your faith has healed you."[w] 43 Immediately
he received his sight and followed Jesus, praising God. When all the people saw it, they
also praised God.[x]

Zacchaeus the Tax Collector

19 Jesus entered Jericho[y] and was passing through. 2 A man was there by the
name of Zacchaeus; he was a chief tax collector and was wealthy. 3 He wanted

18:20 [a]Ex 20:12-16; Dt 5:16-20; Ro 13:9
18:22 [b]Ac 2:45 [c]Mt 6:20
18:24 [d]Pr 11:28
18:27 [e]Mt 19:26
18:28 [f]Mt 4:19
18:30 [g]Mt 12:32 [h]Mt 25:46
18:31 [i]Lk 9:51 [j]Ps 22; Isa 53 [k]Mt 8:20
18:32 [l]Lk 23:1 [m]Mt 16:21 [n]Ac 2:23
18:33 [o]Mt 16:21 [p]Mt 16:21
18:34 [q]Mk 9:32; Lk 9:45
18:35 [r]Lk 19:1
18:37 [s]Lk 19:4
18:38 [t]ver 39; Mt 9:27 [u]Mt 17:15; Lk 18:13
18:39 [v]ver 38
18:42 [w]Mt 9:22
18:43 [x]Mt 9:8; Lk 13:17
19:1 [y]Lk 18:35

[a] *20* Exodus 20:12–16; Deut. 5:16–20

call him good, but he called on the ruler to recognize that he was making a significant statement about Jesus. See *BC* 1.
18:22 Sell everything. The challenge to sell all revealed that the young man had not really understood the commandments. When he was faced with the choice, it became clear that his possessions came before God.
18:23–25 The wealthy are tempted to rely on earthly things (as are those whose wealth is achievement in intellectual, artistic or other fields). Great achievers often find it difficult to rely wholly on the mercy of God. **eye of a needle.** See note on Mark 10:25.
18:26–27 If the rich with all their advantages cannot easily be saved, who can be? The answer: Salvation, whether for rich or poor, is always the gift of God.
18:28–29 Jesus' answer to Peter means that God's good gifts will always surpass anything we could give up for him.
18:30 many times as much in this age. Jesus spoke of spiritual rewards and family that are worth far more than earthly counterparts. A person's sacrifices for the sake of the kingdom do not obligate God to grant him or her earthly rewards or family during this life.
▪ **18:31–34** *A Prophecy of the Passion.* Jesus predicted his suffering and death (cf. 5:35; 9:22,43–45; 12:50; 13:32–33; 17:25). This is the first time he spoke of being handed over to the Gentiles (i.e., the Romans), a special concern for Luke.
▪ **18:35–43** *Sight to the Blind.* Luke recorded an incident in which a blind man demonstrated faith in Jesus even though he was opposed by others.
18:35 Jericho. See notes on Matthew 20:29 and Mark 10:46. **a blind man.** Matthew 20:30 speaks of two blind men whom Jesus met as he left Jericho; Mark 10:46 speaks of blind Bartimaeus, whom Jesus (again) met as he left the city. One blind man may have been the spokesman for the two.
18:38 Son of David. A royal title given the Messiah as the greatest son of David.
18:42 your faith. Faith was the means by which the gift was received, not the power that produced it. **has healed you.** This might be translated "has saved you," which would fit in with his following Jesus and praising God.
▪ **19:1–10** *A Tax Collector Named Zacchaeus.* Luke recalled another time (see 18:35–43) when a man, this time a hated tax collector, had faith in Jesus despite the man's alienation from others.
19:2 chief tax collector. The term is found nowhere else in the New Testament, but it clearly indicates the head of the local taxing agents. Jericho was near a trade route, and there were famous balsam groves nearby. There was much to tax, and Zacchaeus was therefore quite rich.

to see who Jesus was, but being a short man he could not, because of the crowd. 4 So he
ran ahead and climbed a sycamore-fig[z] tree to see him, since Jesus was coming that
way.[a]
5 When Jesus reached the spot, he looked up and said to him, "Zacchaeus, come down
immediately. I must stay at your house today." 6 So he came down at once and welcomed
him gladly.
7 All the people saw this and began to mutter, "He has gone to be the guest of a 'sinner.' "[b]
8 But Zacchaeus stood up and said to the Lord,[c] "Look, Lord! Here and now I give half
of my possessions to the poor, and if I have cheated anybody out of anything,[d] I will pay
back four times the amount."[e]
9 Jesus said to him, "Today salvation has come to this house, because this man, too,
is a son of Abraham.[f] 10 For the Son of Man came to seek and to save what was lost."[g]

The Parable of the Ten Minas

11 While they were listening to this, he went on to tell them a parable, because he was
near Jerusalem and the people thought that the kingdom of God[h] was going to appear
at once.[i] 12 He said: "A man of noble birth went to a distant country to have himself appointed king and then to return. 13 So he called ten of his servants[j] and gave them ten
minas.[a] 'Put this money to work,' he said, 'until I come back.'
14 "But his subjects hated him and sent a delegation after him to say, 'We don't want
this man to be our king.'
15 "He was made king, however, and returned home. Then he sent for the servants to
whom he had given the money, in order to find out what they had gained with it.
16 "The first one came and said, 'Sir, your mina has earned ten more.'
17 " 'Well done, my good servant!'[k] his master replied. 'Because you have been trustworthy in a very small matter, take charge of ten cities.'[l]
18 "The second came and said, 'Sir, your mina has earned five more.'
19 "His master answered, 'You take charge of five cities.'
20 "Then another servant came and said, 'Sir, here is your mina; I have kept it laid
away in a piece of cloth. 21 I was afraid of you, because you are a hard man. You take out
what you did not put in and reap what you did not sow.'[m]
22 "His master replied, 'I will judge you by your own words,[n] you wicked servant! You
knew, did you, that I am a hard man, taking out what I did not put in, and reaping what
I did not sow?[o] 23 Why then didn't you put my money on deposit, so that when I came
back, I could have collected it with interest?'
24 "Then he said to those standing by, 'Take his mina away from him and give it to the
one who has ten minas.'
25 " 'Sir,' they said, 'he already has ten!'
26 "He replied, 'I tell you that to everyone who has, more will be given, but as for the

19:4 [z]1Ki 10:27; 1Ch 27:28; Isa 9:10 [a]Lk 18:37
19:7 [b]Mt 9:11
19:8 [c]Lk 7:13 [d]Lk 3:12, 13 [e]Ex 22:1; Lev 6:4,5; Nu 5:7; 2Sa 12:6
19:9 [f]Lk 3:8; 13:16; Ro 4:16; Gal 3:7
19:10 [g]Eze 34:12,16; Jn 3:17
19:11 [h]Mt 3:2 [i]Lk 17:20; Ac 1:6
19:13 [j]Mk 13:34
19:17 [k]Pr 27:18 [l]Lk 16:10
19:21 [m]Mt 25:24
19:22 [n]2Sa 1:16; Job 15:6 [o]Mt 25:26

a *13* A mina was about three months' wages.

19:4 sycamore-fig. A tree frequently planted by the roadside; it was easy to climb.
19:5 must. A strong word. Jesus saw his visit to Zacchaeus as part of the divine mission on which he was sent.
19:7 All. There was universal disapproval.
19:8 I will pay back. The Greek verb is actually in the present tense; Zacchaeus saw himself as having already started. **four times.** The law required the amount plus a fifth (Lev 6:5; Nu 5:7). Zacchaeus was refunding the amount required for theft involving the slaughter of an animal (Ex 22:1; 2Sa 12:6). He was going far beyond what the law demanded. See *WCF* 15.5; *WLC* 141,145.
19:9 salvation. While Jesus had just stated that it is hard for a rich man to be saved (18:24–25), the salvation of Zacchaeus shows that it is not impossible (18:27). **a son of Abraham.** This phrase may point to Zacchaeus as one of the lost sheep of Israel, those to whom Jesus felt he had a special mission (Mt 10:6; 15:24; cf. Lk 13:16). Alternatively, this may identify Zacchaeus as a spiritual son of Abraham (Ro 4:16–17).
19:10 the Son of Man. Jesus' favorite way of referring to himself. See Introduction to the Gospels.
■ **19:11–27** *Parable on the Minas.* The people thought Jesus was going to usher in the kingdom all at once (v. 11). This parable warns of the importance of remaining faithful even if it takes a long time for the kingdom to come in its fullness. Jesus' journey to Jerusalem was nearing its end, and some thought he would set up a magnificent earthly kingdom there.
19:12 The parable of the talents (Mt 25:14–29) resembles this one, but there the amounts are large and varied, and the servants are being tested for their fitness for more significant tasks. Here the amounts are small and equal in size. The hearers are being taught that we all have one basic task: to serve God faithfully. **a distant country.** Such practices did exist, as exemplified by the Herods who were given rule over Judea by the Roman government.
19:13 ten minas. A mina was worth 100 drachmas, and a drachma was equal to a typical day's wage.
19:14 When Herod's son Archelaus had gone to Rome seeking Herod's kingdom (about 30 years prior to Jesus' ministry), Herod's Jewish subjects sent a delegation to ask that Archelaus not be made king over them.
19:16–19 Two servants did well and were rewarded with further opportunities of service in proportion to their success. Notice their modesty ("your mina has earned") and the much greater responsibility and authority allotted to them.
19:20–21 Fear kept the third man from doing anything, although he knew his master expected much. Nothing is said about the other seven servants. The parable is concerned with two classes: those who worked and those who did not.
19:22–26 The punishment for not using what one has is to lose it, a principle of wide application. Those who use their spiritual opportunities find more, while those who do nothing with them lose what ability they had.

one who has nothing, even what he has will be taken away.[p] 27But those enemies of mine
who did not want me to be king over them—bring them here and kill them in front
of me.' "

The Triumphal Entry

28After Jesus had said this, he went on ahead, going up to Jerusalem.[q] 29As he approached Bethphage and Bethany[r] at the hill called the Mount of Olives,[s] he sent two
of his disciples, saying to them, 30"Go to the village ahead of you, and as you enter it, you
will find a colt tied there, which no one has ever ridden. Untie it and bring it here. 31If
anyone asks you, 'Why are you untying it?' tell him, 'The Lord needs it.' "
32Those who were sent ahead went and found it just as he had told them.[t] 33As they
were untying the colt, its owners asked them, "Why are you untying the colt?"
34They replied, "The Lord needs it."
35They brought it to Jesus, threw their cloaks on the colt and put Jesus on it. 36As he
went along, people spread their cloaks[u] on the road.
37When he came near the place where the road goes down the Mount of Olives,[v] the
whole crowd of disciples began joyfully to praise God in loud voices for all the miracles
they had seen:

> 38"Blessed is the king who comes in the name of the Lord!"[a][w]
>
> "Peace in heaven and glory in the highest!"[x]

39Some of the Pharisees in the crowd said to Jesus, "Teacher, rebuke your disciples!"[y]
40"I tell you," he replied, "if they keep quiet, the stones will cry out."[z]
41As he approached Jerusalem and saw the city, he wept over it[a] 42and said, "If you,
even you, had only known on this day what would bring you peace—but now it is hidden from your eyes. 43The days will come upon you when your enemies will build an embankment against you and encircle you and hem you in on every side.[b] 44They will dash
you to the ground, you and the children within your walls.[c] They will not leave one stone
on another,[d] because you did not recognize the time of God's coming[e] to you."

Jesus at the Temple

45Then he entered the temple area and began driving out those who were selling. 46"It
is written," he said to them, " 'My house will be a house of prayer'[b];[f] but you have made
it 'a den of robbers.'[c]"[g]
47Every day he was teaching at the temple.[h] But the chief priests, the teachers of the

19:26 [p]Mt 13:12; 25:29; Lk 8:18
19:28 [q]Mk 10:32; Lk 9:51
19:29 [r]Mt 21:17 [s]Mt 21:1
19:32 [t]Lk 22:13
19:36 [u]2Ki 9:13
19:37 [v]Mt 21:1
19:38 [w]Ps 118:26; Lk 13:35 [x]Lk 2:14
19:39 [y]Mt 21:15,16
19:40 [z]Hab 2:11
19:41 [a]Isa 22:4; Lk 13:34,35
19:43 [b]Isa 29:3; Jer 6:6; Eze 4:2; 26:8; Lk 21:20
19:44 [c]Ps 137:9 [d]Mt 24:2; Mk 13:2; Lk 21:6 [e]1Pe 2:12
19:46 [f]Isa 56:7 [g]Jer 7:11
19:47 [h]Mt 26:55

[a] *38* Psalm 118:26 [b] *46* Isaiah 56:7 [c] *46* Jer. 7:11

■ **19:28—21:38** *Jesus' Public Ministry in Jerusalem.* Having detailed the events of Jesus' travels from Galilee to Jerusalem, Luke turned at this point to the fourth major portion of his record. He drew attention to a number of things Jesus did prior to his death, resurrection and ascension. The central theme in this section is the relationship of Jesus to the temple in Jerusalem.

■ **19:28–44** *The Triumphal Entry.* Luke began his record of Jesus' time in Jerusalem with his entry into the city. The crowds hailed Jesus as their victorious, Messianic king, a striking contrast to what they would later do.

19:29 Bethany. A village about two miles from Jerusalem. Bethphage must have been nearby, for it was regarded as the outer limit of Jerusalem.

19:30 colt. This could refer to a horse or a donkey; however, the other Gospels make it clear that it was a donkey. That no one had ridden it meant that it had no secular use and was thus fit for sacred purposes (Nu 19:2; 1Sa 6:7).

19:35–36 threw their cloaks on the colt. The clothing evidently served as a saddle. The cloaks on the road formed a triumphal carpet.

19:37 This entry into Jerusalem fulfilled prophecy (Zec 9:9) and amounted to a public claim to Messiahship. But it was a claim to a distinctive kind of Messiahship, since the donkey was the animal of a man of peace (a conquering king would have ridden a warhorse). The people seem to have recognized the kingship but not the emphasis on peace.

19:38 A quotation from Psalm 118:26, but with an explicit reference to the king. Only Luke's Gospel adds the words about peace and glory. Luke may have substituted this for "Hosanna," which the other Gospels quote the crowd as shouting but which Luke's Gentile readers would not have understood. The word "glory" conveys the meaning.

19:39 rebuke your disciples! The Pharisees would not have wanted anything to occur that would have disturbed the peace and invited trouble from the Romans.

19:40 stones will cry out. Compare Habakkuk 2:11.

19:41–42 Only Luke recorded Jesus' lament as he drew near the city. Jesus knew that the excitement of the crowds did not correspond to genuine spiritual perception and that the courses of action being pursued would inevitably bring war, not peace.

19:43 build an embankment. A description of a typical siege of a city. The embankment was erected as a protection for the besiegers and was used as a base from which to launch attacks.

19:44 The city would be completely destroyed. The people would have to live with their rejection of God's Messiah.

■ **19:45–46** *Cleansing the Temple.* All four Gospels speak of Jesus driving traders from the temple precincts, but Matthew, Mark and Luke set this event at the end of Jesus' ministry, while John places it at the beginning. There may well have been two cleansings. The businessmen in the temple courts were money changers (only Tyrian coinage was accepted in the temple, so other coins had to be changed into this currency before an offering could be made), as well as sellers of sacrificial animals and birds. It was convenient to have them close to the temple, but their presence within the temple courts made it difficult for true worship to take place. The traders would have been in the court of the Gentiles, the only location in which Gentiles were allowed to pray.

19:46 robbers. Evidently many of the traders were dishonest.

■ **19:47—21:4** *Teaching at the Temple.* Luke continued to stress Jews and the temple by recalling what Jesus taught there.

19:47–48 The temple was the customary place for teaching. Jesus' opposition now included a new group: the leaders among

law and the leaders among the people were trying to kill him.[i] 48Yet they could not find
any way to do it, because all the people hung on his words.

The Authority of Jesus Questioned

20 One day as he was teaching the people in the temple courts[j] and preaching the
gospel,[k] the chief priests and the teachers of the law, together with the elders,
came up to him. 2"Tell us by what authority you are doing these things," they said. "Who
gave you this authority?"[l]
3He replied, "I will also ask you a question. Tell me, 4John's baptism[m]—was it from
heaven, or from men?"
5They discussed it among themselves and said, "If we say, 'From heaven,' he will ask,
'Why didn't you believe him?' 6But if we say, 'From men,' all the people[n] will stone us,
because they are persuaded that John was a prophet."[o]
7So they answered, "We don't know where it was from."
8Jesus said, "Neither will I tell you by what authority I am doing these things."

The Parable of the Tenants

9He went on to tell the people this parable: "A man planted a vineyard,[p] rented it to
some farmers and went away for a long time.[q] 10At harvest time he sent a servant to the
tenants so they would give him some of the fruit of the vineyard. But the tenants beat him
and sent him away empty-handed. 11He sent another servant, but that one also they beat
and treated shamefully and sent away empty-handed. 12He sent still a third, and they
wounded him and threw him out.
13"Then the owner of the vineyard said, 'What shall I do? I will send my son, whom I
love;[r] perhaps they will respect him.'
14"But when the tenants saw him, they talked the matter over. 'This is the heir,' they
said. 'Let's kill him, and the inheritance will be ours.' 15So they threw him out of the vineyard and killed him.
"What then will the owner of the vineyard do to them? 16He will come and kill those
tenants[s] and give the vineyard to others."
When the people heard this, they said, "May this never be!"
17Jesus looked directly at them and asked, "Then what is the meaning of that which
is written:

" 'The stone the builders rejected
has become the capstone[a]'[b]?[t]

18Everyone who falls on that stone will be broken to pieces, but he on whom it falls will
be crushed."[u]
19The teachers of the law and the chief priests looked for a way to arrest him[v] immediately, because they knew he had spoken this parable against them. But they were
afraid of the people.[w]

Paying Taxes to Caesar

20Keeping a close watch on him, they sent spies, who pretended to be honest. They

19:47 [i]Mt 12:14; Mk 11:18
20:1 [j]Mt 26:55 [k]Lk 8:1
20:2 [l]Jn 2:18; Ac 4:7; 7:27
20:4 [m]Mk 1:4
20:6 [n]Lk 7:29 [o]Mt 11:9
20:9 [p]Isa 5:1-7 [q]Mt 25:14
20:13 [r]Mt 3:17
20:16 [s]Lk 19:27
20:17 [t]Ps 118:22; Ac 4:11
20:18 [u]Isa 8:14,15
20:19 [v]Lk 19:47 [w]Mk 11:18

[a] 17 Or *cornerstone* [b] 17 Psalm 118:22

---

the people. Evidently prominent laypeople had now joined the priests and the scribes in opposing Jesus.
20:1 preaching the gospel. Jesus was bringing God's Good News at the very time his enemies were plotting against him. **chief priests . . . teachers . . . elders.** This appears to have been a delegation from the Sanhedrin.
20:2 these things. That is, acts such as driving the traders out of the temple.
20:3–4 Jesus was not avoiding their question. John had earlier testified that Jesus was the Messiah. If they had answered Jesus' question, they would have had the answer to their own question.
20:5–6 Notice that they were not concerned with the truth, but only with the consequences of their possible answers.
20:7–8 Jesus would not talk about authority with people who refused to reply to an important religious question, the answer to which they already knew.
20:9–12 The tenants, who violently rejected the servants sent to collect the rent they owed, form a vivid picture of the nation that persistently rejected the messengers of God sent to call them to repentance.
20:13 With the law on his side, a landowner who was confronted with persistent refusal to pay what was due and whose messengers had received insult and ill treatment would have taken strong measures. Like this landowner, God keeps offering sinners the opportunity for repentance.
20:14 This is the heir. In a time when title to land was often uncertain, anyone who had worked land for three years was presumed to own it. By withholding the owed rent, the tenants were refusing to acknowledge the owner, and they may have reasoned that the coming of the heir meant that the father had died. With the heir out of the way, they evidently thought that they could establish their own title to the land. Jesus was making the point that the nation of Israel had behaved outrageously toward God.
20:17 Jesus quoted Psalm 118:22, which points to a complete reversal of accepted values. **capstone.** Literally, "the head of the corner." It may refer to the cornerstone, a large stone in the foundation that is laid at the corner; it determines the position of two walls and shapes the whole building. Or it may refer to the stone at the top of the corner, binding the building together.
20:19 Again we have a picture of foiled malevolence. The religious teachers were hostile to Jesus but could find no legal way of harming him.

20:20 [x]Mt 12:10 hoped to catch Jesus in something he said[x] so that they might hand him over to the pow-
[y]Mt 27:2 er and authority of the governor.[y] 21So the spies questioned him: "Teacher, we know that
20:21 you speak and teach what is right, and that you do not show partiality but teach the way
[z]Jn 3:2 of God in accordance with the truth.[z] 22Is it right for us to pay taxes to Caesar or not?"
23He saw through their duplicity and said to them, 24"Show me a denarius. Whose
portrait and inscription are on it?"
20:25 25"Caesar's," they replied.
[a]Lk 23:2; Ro 13:7 He said to them, "Then give to Caesar what is Caesar's,[a] and to God what is God's."
26They were unable to trap him in what he had said there in public. And astonished
by his answer, they became silent.

20:27 *The Resurrection and Marriage*

[b]Ac 4:1 [c]Ac 23:8; 1Co 15:12 27Some of the Sadducees,[b] who say there is no resurrection,[c] came to Jesus with a
question. 28"Teacher," they said, "Moses wrote for us that if a man's brother dies and
20:28 leaves a wife but no children, the man must marry the widow and have children for his
[d]Dt 25:5 brother.[d] 29Now there were seven brothers. The first one married a woman and died
childless. 30The second 31and then the third married her, and in the same way the sev-
en died, leaving no children. 32Finally, the woman died too. 33Now then, at the resurrection whose wife will she be, since the seven were married to her?"
20:35 34Jesus replied, "The people of this age marry and are given in marriage. 35But those
[e]Mt 12:32 who are considered worthy of taking part in that age[e] and in the resurrection from the
20:36 dead will neither marry nor be given in marriage, 36and they can no longer die; for they
[f]Jn 1:12; 1Jn 3:1-2 are like the angels. They are God's children,[f] since they are children of the resurrection.
20:37 37But in the account of the bush, even Moses showed that the dead rise, for he calls the
[g]Ex 3:6 Lord 'the God of Abraham, and the God of Isaac, and the God of Jacob.'[a][g] 38He is not the
20:40 God of the dead, but of the living, for to him all are alive."
[h]Mt 22:46; Mk 12:34 39Some of the teachers of the law responded, "Well said, teacher!" 40And no one
dared to ask him any more questions.[h]

20:41 *Whose Son Is the Christ?*

[i]Mt 1:1 41Then Jesus said to them, "How is it that they say the Christ[b] is the Son of David?[i]
42David himself declares in the Book of Psalms:

> " 'The Lord said to my Lord:
> "Sit at my right hand
20:43 43 until I make your enemies
[j]Ps 110:1; Mt 22:44 a footstool for your feet." '[c][j]

[a] 37 Exodus 3:6 [b] 41 Or *Messiah* [c] 43 Psalm 110:1

20:20 A question on taxes might provoke Jesus to offend the Romans (who wanted the taxes paid) or the Jews (who balked against paying them). **the power and authority of the governor.** Clearly they had high hopes of Jesus' saying something that would bring about his arrest by the Romans.

20:21 The flattering approach was doubtless meant to put Jesus off guard.

20:22 Is it right . . . ? Implicit in this question is "Is it in accordance with God's law?" (It was obviously right according to Roman law.) From the point of view of the questioners, the answer would inevitably put Jesus at odds with either the Jews or the Romans. **taxes.** The tax about which they asked was the tribute that differed from customs duties in that it was levied on them by the hated outsiders, and they saw no benefit from it (customs duties at least allowed transit of goods).

20:24 a denarius. Jesus called for his detractors to produce a Roman silver coin that represented a typical day's wage for a working man and was the coinage in which the tax must be paid. It bore an image and an inscription of the emperor. There was only one answer they could give to Jesus' question, and this opened up the way for his unexpected reply. Jesus could not be accused of disloyalty either to the Jews or to the Romans. He made it clear that there are duties owed to God, but also duties we must pay to the state so that it can perform its function.

20:27 Sadducees. The Sadducees are mentioned by Luke only here. Their writings have all perished, so we know them only as their opponents saw them. They were the conservative and aristocratic party of the high priests. They rejected the oral tradition in which the Pharisees delighted and found no basis in the Old Testament for the doctrine of resurrection. See chart "Jewish Sects" at Matthew 23.

20:28–33 When a married male Jew died childless, the law required that his brother marry the widow and that the first son be reckoned as the son of the deceased (Dt 25:5–10). The Sadducees clearly thought that their story made nonsense of the doctrine of resurrection.

20:34–36 The Sadducees assumed that if there were an afterlife, it would be something like a repetition of this life. Jesus denied this misconception. Marriage is an essential part of this life but not of the next; thus, their question was invalid and irrelevant.

20:36 like the angels. At the resurrection there will be a change in nature, and believers will be clothed with glorified bodies like that of Christ (1Co 15:35–58 and its notes). Jesus' point was not that the postresurrection existence of human beings will be exactly like that of angels, but that the mode of existence of angels (particularly their immortality) provides a clue to the resurrected existence of believers (i.e., it will be characterized by immortality; 1Co 15:42,52–55). Marriage and procreation will no longer be necessary or appropriate after the general resurrection.

20:37 the account of the bush. Before the invention of chapter-and-verse divisions in the Middle Ages, passages in Scripture were referred to by their content. Jesus drew an interesting proof for the resurrection from a well-known passage of Scripture (see note on Mk 12:26–27).

20:41 How is it that they say. . . ? Earlier generations were regarded as greater and wiser than the present one, and this opened the way for Jesus to pose a question of his own. By popular definition, each of David's descendants was less important than David. How then could David call the Messiah his "Lord" (Ps 110:1)? Jesus taught by his question that the Messiah is not simply David's Son; he is the Son of God and thus David's Lord.

44David calls him 'Lord.' How then can he be his son?"
45While all the people were listening, Jesus said to his disciples, 46"Beware of the
teachers of the law. They like to walk around in flowing robes and love to be greeted in
the marketplaces and have the most important seats in the synagogues and the places
of honor at banquets.[k] 47They devour widows' houses and for a show make lengthy
prayers. Such men will be punished most severely."

The Widow's Offering

21 As he looked up, Jesus saw the rich putting their gifts into the temple treasury.[l]
2He also saw a poor widow put in two very small copper coins.[a] 3"I tell you the
truth," he said, "this poor widow has put in more than all the others. 4All these people
gave their gifts out of their wealth; but she out of her poverty put in all she had to
live on."[m]

Signs of the End of the Age

5Some of his disciples were remarking about how the temple was adorned with
beautiful stones and with gifts dedicated to God. But Jesus said, 6"As for what you see
here, the time will come when not one stone will be left on another;[n] every one of them
will be thrown down."
7"Teacher," they asked, "when will these things happen? And what will be the sign
that they are about to take place?"
8He replied: "Watch out that you are not deceived. For many will come in my name,
claiming, 'I am he,' and, 'The time is near.' Do not follow them.[o] 9When you hear of wars
and revolutions, do not be frightened. These things must happen first, but the end will
not come right away."
10Then he said to them: "Nation will rise against nation, and kingdom against kingdom.[p] 11There will be great earthquakes, famines and pestilences in various places, and
fearful events and great signs from heaven.[q]
12"But before all this, they will lay hands on you and persecute you. They will deliver you to synagogues and prisons, and you will be brought before kings and governors,
and all on account of my name. 13This will result in your being witnesses to them.[r] 14But
make up your mind not to worry beforehand how you will defend yourselves.[s] 15For I will
give you[t] words and wisdom that none of your adversaries will be able to resist or contradict. 16You will be betrayed even by parents, brothers, relatives and friends,[u] and they
will put some of you to death. 17All men will hate you because of me.[v] 18But not a hair
of your head will perish.[w] 19By standing firm you will gain life.[x]
20"When you see Jerusalem being surrounded by armies,[y] you will know that its desolation is near. 21Then let those who are in Judea flee to the mountains, let those in the
city get out, and let those in the country not enter the city.[z] 22For this is the time of punishment[a] in fulfillment[b] of all that has been written. 23How dreadful it will be in those
days for pregnant women and nursing mothers! There will be great distress in the land

20:46 [k]Lk 11:43
21:1 [l]Mt 27:6; Jn 8:20
21:4 [m]2Co 8:12
21:6 [n]Lk 19:44
21:8 [o]Lk 17:23
21:10 [p]2Ch 15:6; Isa 19:2
21:11 [q]Isa 29:6; Joel 2:30
21:13 [r]Php 1:12
21:14 [s]Lk 12:11
21:15 [t]Lk 12:12
21:16 [u]Lk 12:52,53
21:17 [v]Jn 15:21
21:18 [w]Mt 10:30
21:19 [x]Mt 10:22
21:20 [y]Lk 19:43
21:21 [z]Lk 17:31
21:22 [a]Isa 63:4; Da 9:24-27; Hos 9:7 [b]Mt 1:22

[a] 2 Greek *two lepta*

20:45–47 The religious leaders loved outward show—robes, elaborate greetings, important seats, places of honor. But they also accepted offerings from widows and extortionate charges for handling widows' affairs. Their punishment was certain.
21:1 temple treasury. Placed in the court of the women were 13 trumpet-shaped collection boxes into which donations could be placed. Each box had an inscription that showed the use to which the donations would be put.
21:2 poor. An unusual word in the Greek, used in the New Testament only in this one instance. It means "very poor." The woman's total earthly possessions amounted to two very small copper coins (*lepta* were Jewish coins of the lowest value). If we measure giving by what is left over after the gift is given, the widow clearly offered more than anyone else.
■ **21:5–38** *The Olivet Discourse.* As Luke indicated in the closing verses of this section (vv. 37–38), this discourse on the Mount of Olives was closely tied to Jesus' teaching in the temple. Here Luke summarized some of Jesus' teaching about the future of the temple and the city in relation to the near and distant future.
21:5 beautiful stones. Josephus referred to stones 45 cubits long in the temple and to decorative offerings like Herod's gift of a golden vine with "grape clusters as tall as a man" (*Jewish War,* 5.5.4).
21:6 The temple was destroyed in this manner as part of the destruction of Jerusalem in A.D. 70.
21:7 See *WCF* 33.3.
21:8 I am he. False teachers often claim to be the Christ.
21:9 the end. The end of all things. Parts of this discourse seem to have been fulfilled in the destruction of Jerusalem in A.D. 70, while other parts will be fulfilled at Jesus' coming at the end of the world (see note on Mt 24:1—25:46).
21:12 synagogues. Centers for discipline as well as places of worship.
21:13 Trouble for the church also means opportunity to bear witness.
21:14–15 In times of trouble, God would give his disciples the words they would need (Ac 4:8–13).
21:16–19 This passage is a strong affirmation of God's overriding control. For some of his followers, there would be a martyr's death; for others, deliverance. Either way, God would bring his purposes to pass. See *HC* 1.
21:20 Jerusalem. This prophecy threatens the destruction of the city, not the end of the world.
21:21 flee to the mountains. People fled to a walled city for shelter from invading armies, but Jerusalem was doomed. People should flee away from it, not try to enter it.
21:22 punishment. Not meaningless suffering, but a divine penalty.
21:23 How dreadful. In fact, the siege of Jerusalem in A.D. 70 brought extreme suffering.

and wrath against this people. 24They will fall by the sword and will be taken as prisoners to all the nations. Jerusalem will be trampled[c] on by the Gentiles until the times of
the Gentiles are fulfilled.

25"There will be signs in the sun, moon and stars. On the earth, nations will be in anguish and perplexity at the roaring and tossing of the sea.[d] 26Men will faint from terror,
apprehensive of what is coming on the world, for the heavenly bodies will be shaken.[e]
27At that time they will see the Son of Man[f] coming in a cloud[g] with power and great glory. 28When these things begin to take place, stand up and lift up your heads, because
your redemption is drawing near."[h]

29He told them this parable: "Look at the fig tree and all the trees. 30When they sprout
leaves, you can see for yourselves and know that summer is near. 31Even so, when you
see these things happening, you know that the kingdom of God[i] is near.

32"I tell you the truth, this generation[a][j] will certainly not pass away until all these
things have happened. 33Heaven and earth will pass away, but my words will never pass
away.[k]

34"Be careful, or your hearts will be weighed down with dissipation, drunkenness and
the anxieties of life,[l] and that day will close on you unexpectedly[m] like a trap. 35For it will
come upon all those who live on the face of the whole earth. 36Be always on the watch,
and pray[n] that you may be able to escape all that is about to happen, and that you may
be able to stand before the Son of Man."

37Each day Jesus was teaching at the temple,[o] and each evening he went out[p] to
spend the night on the hill called the Mount of Olives,[q] 38and all the people came early
in the morning to hear him at the temple.[r]

Judas Agrees to Betray Jesus

22 Now the Feast of Unleavened Bread, called the Passover, was approaching,[s]
2and the chief priests and the teachers of the law were looking for some way to
get rid of Jesus,[t] for they were afraid of the people. 3Then Satan[u] entered Judas, called
Iscariot,[v] one of the Twelve. 4And Judas went to the chief priests and the officers of the
temple guard[w] and discussed with them how he might betray Jesus. 5They were delighted and agreed to give him money.[x] 6He consented, and watched for an opportunity to
hand Jesus over to them when no crowd was present.

The Last Supper

7Then came the day of Unleavened Bread on which the Passover lamb had to be sacrificed.[y] 8Jesus sent Peter and John,[z] saying, "Go and make preparations for us to eat the
Passover."

21:24 [c]Isa 5:5; 63:18; Da 8:13; Rev 11:2
21:25 [d]2Pe 3:10,12
21:26 [e]Mt 24:29
21:27 [f]Mt 8:20 [g]Rev 1:7
21:28 [h]Lk 18:7
21:31 [i]Mt 3:2
21:32 [j]Lk 11:50; 17:25
21:33 [k]Mt 5:18
21:34 [l]Mk 4:19 [m]Lk 12:40,46; 1Th 5:2-7
21:36 [n]Mt 26:41
21:37 [o]Mt 26:55 [p]Mk 11:19 [q]Mt 21:1
21:38 [r]Jn 8:2
22:1 [s]Jn 11:55
22:2 [t]Mt 12:14
22:3 [u]Mt 4:10; Jn 13:2 [v]Mt 10:4
22:4 [w]ver 52; Ac 4:1; 5:24
22:5 [x]Zec 11:12
22:7 [y]Ex 12:18-20; Dt 16:5-8; Mk 14:12
22:8 [z]Ac 3:1,11; 4:13, 19; 8:14

a *32* Or *race*

21:24 the times of the Gentiles. This may mean the time when the Gentiles will have their triumph over Israel or the time when the gospel is preached to the Gentiles, or both. **fulfilled.** A divine purpose will be worked out (cf. Ro 11:1–32).
21:25–26 Attention moves to the second coming of Christ. This event will be preceded by signs that will puzzle many.
21:27 coming. Jesus will return to this earth in a cloud, with power and great glory. He will come in splendor to reign.
21:28 redemption. This word means deliverance on payment of a price. Jesus paid that price at Calvary. Here Jesus looked forward to the final fulfillment of all that his deliverance would mean. See *WCF* 33.3; *HC* 52.
21:29 The appearance of leaves on the trees announces that summer is at hand. Likewise, the signs of which Jesus spoke tell us that the kingdom is near.
21:32 generation. In the New Testament, the Greek word usually means all the people alive at a given time, although it can also signify "race" or "age." **all these things.** Like "these things" in verse 31, this probably is a reference to the signs leading up to the fall of Jerusalem or perhaps to the return of Christ. See note on Matthew 24:34.
21:34 Jesus urged his followers not to be complacent but to be on their guard against falling into sins of any kind. It is important that that day (i.e., the day of his return) not find us unprepared. See *WLC* 136,195.
21:35–36 See *WLC* 88.
21:36 watch, and pray. Watchfulness and prayer are to be Christian duties to the end of time. **to stand before the Son of Man.** This signifies salvation at the last day.
21:37–38 Jesus' last days were spent teaching in Jerusalem, while by night he lodged (the word may mean "camped out") on the nearby Mount of Olives.
■**22:1—24:53** *Jesus' Climactic Last Days in Jerusalem.* Luke related the events of the final days of Jesus' life—the time when Jesus' ministry reached its climax. Luke concentrated on Jesus' suffering on behalf of his people, also stressing the glory of Christ after his resurrection, as well as the future of the church after Christ's ascension.
■**22:1–6** *The Conspiracy to Betray.* Luke began his record of Jesus' sufferings with the dramatic tension between the Passover celebration and the plot to betray Jesus.
22:1 Feast . . . the Passover. Strictly speaking, the Feast of Unleavened Bread and the Passover were different festivals (Nu 28:26–27), but the Passover was followed immediately by the Feast of Unleavened Bread, and in New Testament times the names were used interchangeably. The feast commemorated the great deliverance of Israel from Egypt (Ex 12:17).
22:2 chief priests. The chief priests held the political power among the Jews, and it was they, not the Pharisees, who led the final opposition to Jesus.
22:3–6 Satan took over Judas (Jn 13:2), and it was Judas who sought the chief priests, not they who sought him. The officers of the temple guard were mostly Levites.
■**22:7–38** *The Upper Room.* Like the other Gospels, Luke's account includes the meal that Jesus had with his disciples not only for its historical importance, but also to guide believers in their future celebration of this sacramental meal.
22:7 Passover lamb. The Greek does not specify "lamb." The animal may have been either a lamb or a young goat (Ex 12:5). It was to be killed at "twilight" (literally, "between the evenings"; Ex 12:6).

9“Where do you want us to prepare for it?” they asked.
10He replied, “As you enter the city, a man carrying a jar of water will meet you. Follow him to the house that he enters, 11and say to the owner of the house, ‘The Teacher
asks: Where is the guest room, where I may eat the Passover with my disciples?’ 12He will
show you a large upper room, all furnished. Make preparations there.”
13They left and found things just as Jesus had told them.[a] So they prepared the Passover.
14When the hour came, Jesus and his apostles[b] reclined at the table.[c] 15And he said
to them, “I have eagerly desired to eat this Passover with you before I suffer.[d] 16For I tell
you, I will not eat it again until it finds fulfillment in the kingdom of God.”[e]
17After taking the cup, he gave thanks and said, “Take this and divide it among you.
18For I tell you I will not drink again of the fruit of the vine until the kingdom of God
comes.”
19And he took bread, gave thanks and broke it,[f] and gave it to them, saying, “This is
my body given for you; do this in remembrance of me.”
20In the same way, after the supper he took the cup, saying, “This cup is the new covenant[g] in my blood, which is poured out for you. 21But the hand of him who is going to
betray me is with mine on the table.[h] 22The Son of Man[i] will go as it has been decreed,[j]
but woe to that man who betrays him.” 23They began to question among themselves
which of them it might be who would do this.
24Also a dispute arose among them as to which of them was considered to be greatest.[k] 25Jesus said to them, “The kings of the Gentiles lord it over them; and those who
exercise authority over them call themselves Benefactors. 26But you are not to be like
that. Instead, the greatest among you should be like the youngest,[l] and the one who
rules like the one who serves.[m] 27For who is greater, the one who is at the table or the
one who serves? Is it not the one who is at the table? But I am among you as one who
serves.[n] 28You are those who have stood by me in my trials. 29And I confer on you a kingdom,[o] just as my Father conferred one on me, 30so that you may eat and drink at my table in my kingdom[p] and sit on thrones, judging the twelve tribes of Israel.[q]
31“Simon, Simon, Satan has asked[r] to sift you[a] as wheat.[s] 32But I have prayed for
you,[t] Simon, that your faith may not fail. And when you have turned back, strengthen
your brothers.”[u]
33But he replied, “Lord, I am ready to go with you to prison and to death.”[v]

[a] *31* The Greek is plural.

22:13 [a]Lk 19:32
22:14 [b]Mk 6:30 [c]Mt 26:20; Mk 14:17,18
22:15 [d]Mt 16:21
22:16 [e]Lk 14:15; Rev 19:9
22:19 [f]Mt 14:19
22:20 [g]Ex 24:8; Isa 42:6; Jer 31:31-34; Zec 9:11; 2Co 3:6; Heb 8:6; 9:15
22:21 [h]Ps 41:9
22:22 [i]Mt 8:20 [j]Ac 2:23; 4:28
22:24 [k]Mk 9:34; Lk 9:46
22:26 [l]1Pe 5:5 [m]Mk 9:35; Lk 9:48
22:27 [n]Mt 20:28; Lk 12:37
22:29 [o]Mt 25:34; 2Ti 2:12
22:30 [p]Lk 14:15 [q]Mt 19:28
22:31 [r]Job 1:6-12 [s]Am 9:9
22:32 [t]Jn 17:9,15; Ro 8:34 [u]Jn 21:15-17
22:33 [v]Jn 11:16

22:8–12 Jesus was ready to die, but it would be at the time of his and God’s choosing. This may be the reason for the way Jesus made arrangements for the feast; none of the disciples knew where they would eat it.
22:10 carrying a jar. A man carrying a jar of water was distinctive, for women usually carried water jars (men carried water skins).
22:12 furnished. Literally, “spread.” This may mean that the couches on which the diners would recline had been spread out.
22:14 the hour. The time for the Passover meal. **reclined at the table.** The normal posture at such a meal. The diners would recline, leaning on their left elbows with their heads toward the table and their feet away from it.
22:15–16 We notice Jesus’ intense desire for fellowship with his disciples at this Passover meal. Its fulfillment in the kingdom of God looks forward to the death Jesus would die as our Passover sacrifice (1Co 5:7) in fulfillment of the typology in the ancient feast.
22:17 After taking the cup. At the Passover meal, each person was required to drink four cups of red wine (even if the pauper’s fund had to supply them). The wine was diluted, usually in the proportion of three parts water to one part wine. It is not clear which cup this refers to, but perhaps it was the first. Shared as it was, it was a token of fellowship.
22:18 until the kingdom of God comes. Again Jesus was looking forward to the coming of the kingdom of God. This is an important part of the Lord’s Supper. It points beyond itself to the Lord, who is coming again (1Co 11:26).
22:19–20 See *WCF* 29.3; *WLC* 169; *BC* 35; *HC* 75.
22:19 This is my body. There has been great controversy about the way these words should be understood. We should not take the word “is” to mean “is identical with” (see note on Mt 26:26). Here it means “represents,” “signifies” or perhaps “conveys.” **given for you.** Refers to Jesus’ giving of himself on the cross. **do this.** The one thing Jesus commanded his followers to do by way of remembrance of him referred to his death, a fact that points to the centrality of the cross for the Christian faith. See *WLC* 174.
22:20 after the supper. The drinking of the cup evidently did not immediately follow the reception of the bread, but came later in the meal. **the new covenant.** *Covenant* is an important Biblical concept. In his death, Jesus made the sacrifice that renewed God’s covenant with his people (see Jer 31:31). It was a fulfillment of the Old Testament Passover and of the covenant with Israel. **poured out.** Refers to the shedding of Jesus’ blood on the cross. The whole service takes its meaning from Jesus’ impending death. See *WCF* 7.4; 7.6; *WLC* 168.
22:22–23 Jesus immediately spoke of betrayal by one of those at the table. That the betrayer was enjoying table fellowship with the Lord made his crime all the more heinous. Jesus would fulfill prophecy and go as it had been decreed, but that did not mitigate the guilt of his betrayer.
22:24–27 Only Luke’s Gospel includes the account of this dispute. It shows how far even the Twelve were from understanding what Jesus had come to do. See *WLC* 132.
22:25 Benefactors. A number of kings in antiquity took the title “Benefactor,” often with little justification. The disciples were to seek to serve, as Jesus did.
22:28–30 That the disciples were to serve rather than seek greatness does not mean that they would go unnoticed. Jesus proceeded to make it clear that he was aware of how they had stood with him and that when the Father gave him the kingdom, there would be a place for them. They were promised a wonderful future that would include judging the tribes of Israel (v. 30).
22:31–32 See *WCF* 14.3; *WLC* 195.
22:31 Simon, Simon. The repetition gives solemnity and emphasis. It is a form of intimate, personal address. **sift.** An unusual metaphor, but clearly it pointed to trouble. **you.** The word used here is plural (cf. note on v. 32). Satan had asked permission to trouble all the little band. Notice that Satan has no ability to act outside the boundaries within which God has confined him.
22:32 you. The Greek word used here is singular (cf. note on v. 31).

[34] Jesus answered, "I tell you, Peter, before the rooster crows today, you will deny
22:35 three times that you know me."
[w] Mt 10:9,10; Lk 9:3; 10:4 [35] Then Jesus asked them, "When I sent you without purse, bag or sandals,[w] did you
lack anything?"

"Nothing," they answered.

[36] He said to them, "But now if you have a purse, take it, and also a bag; and if you
22:37 don't have a sword, sell your cloak and buy one. [37] It is written: 'And he was numbered
[x] Isa 53:12 with the transgressors'[a];[x] and I tell you that this must be fulfilled in me. Yes, what is written about me is reaching its fulfillment."

[38] The disciples said, "See, Lord, here are two swords."

"That is enough," he replied.

Jesus Prays on the Mount of Olives

22:39 [y] Lk 21:37 [z] Mt 21:1 [39] Jesus went out as usual[y] to the Mount of Olives,[z] and his disciples followed him.
22:40 [40] On reaching the place, he said to them, "Pray that you will not fall into temptation."[a]
[a] Mt 6:13 [41] He withdrew about a stone's throw beyond them, knelt down[b] and prayed, [42] "Father,
22:41 if you are willing, take this cup[c] from me; yet not my will, but yours be done."[d] [43] An an-
[b] Lk 18:11 gel from heaven appeared to him and strengthened him.[e] [44] And being in anguish, he
22:42 [c] Mt 20:22 prayed more earnestly, and his sweat was like drops of blood falling to the ground.[b]
[d] Mt 26:39 [45] When he rose from prayer and went back to the disciples, he found them asleep, ex-
22:43 hausted from sorrow. [46] "Why are you sleeping?" he asked them. "Get up and pray so that
[e] Mt 4:11; Mk 1:13 you will not fall into temptation."[f]

22:46 [f] ver 40

Jesus Arrested

[47] While he was still speaking a crowd came up, and the man who was called Judas,
one of the Twelve, was leading them. He approached Jesus to kiss him, [48] but Jesus asked
him, "Judas, are you betraying the Son of Man with a kiss?"

22:49 [49] When Jesus' followers saw what was going to happen, they said, "Lord, should we
[g] ver 38 strike with our swords?"[g] [50] And one of them struck the servant of the high priest, cutting off his right ear.

22:52 [51] But Jesus answered, "No more of this!" And he touched the man's ear and healed him.
[h] ver 4 [52] Then Jesus said to the chief priests, the officers of the temple guard,[h] and the elders,
22:53 who had come for him, "Am I leading a rebellion, that you have come with swords and
[i] Mt 26:55 [j] Jn 12:27 [k] Mt 8:12; Jn 1:5; 3:20 clubs? [53] Every day I was with you in the temple courts,[i] and you did not lay a hand on
me. But this is your hour[j]—when darkness reigns."[k]

Peter Disowns Jesus

22:54 [54] Then seizing him, they led him away and took him into the house of the high
[l] Mt 26:57; Mk 14:53 priest.[l] Peter followed at a distance.[m] [55] But when they had kindled a fire in the middle
[m] Mt 26:58; Mk 14:54; Jn 18:15 of the courtyard and had sat down together, Peter sat down with them. [56] A servant girl

[a] 37 Isaiah 53:12 [b] 44 Some early manuscripts do not have verses 43 and 44.

When he had come through the trial, Peter was to strengthen others. See *WCF* 11.5; 17.2; 18.4; *WLC* 79.

22:35–36 The future would not be as easy for the disciples as the past had been.

22:36 sword. This was probably not meant literally but was a way of saying that the disciples faced a dangerous future. Jesus himself confronted the fulfillment of Isaiah 53:12, and his followers would surely experience trouble.

22:38 enough. The disciples took Jesus' words about the sword quite literally, but Jesus' reply may have meant, "Enough of that sort of talk."

■ **22:39–53** *Gethsemane.* Luke recorded the terrible suffering Jesus endured as he anticipated his death. Luke also noted the weakness of Jesus' disciples during this time.

22:40 the place. Gethsemane (Mk 14:32), an olive grove (Jn 18:1).

22:41 Luke left out Jesus' selection of Peter, James and John (all of whom slept while Jesus prayed; see Mt 26:37–45) to accompany him to Gethsemane. Luke's emphasis was on Jesus' prayer, not on the disciples' failings. People of the day generally prayed standing (18:11,13), but at this solemn time, Jesus knelt.

22:42 this cup. A symbol of suffering and divine wrath (Isa 51:17; Eze 23:33). **not my will.** As one who had taken upon himself a full human nature, it was natural for Jesus to shrink from the horror of the cross, a horror magnified by his knowledge that in death he would be forsaken by God and experience the full weight of divine wrath upon the sins of the elect. Nevertheless, Jesus was determined to follow the will of his Father. See *HC* 124.

22:43–44 Only Luke's Gospel tells us of the angel who strengthened Jesus and of Jesus' sweat, which was "like drops of blood falling to the ground" (v. 44). See *WCF* 18.4; *WLC* 149; *WSC* 27; *BC* 21; *HC* 44.

22:46 temptation. The command in verse 40 is repeated because it is important.

22:47 kiss. The kiss was a common form of greeting (1Th 5:26), but it denoted friendship and was in this case a horribly ironic form of betrayal.

22:51 Only Luke's Gospel tells us that Jesus healed the wounded ear.

22:53 A furtive arrest in the darkness suited this effort of the forces of spiritual darkness (cf. Eph 6:12; Col 1:13).

■ **22:54–62** *Peter's Denials.* Although Peter was to become a very important and positive character in Luke's next book (Acts), here Peter denied Jesus for fear of his life.

22:54 house of the high priest. Jesus was taken first to the high priest, who had taken the initiative in the arrest. All four Gospels give more space to the trial than to the crucifixion. In so doing the writers answer questions as to why the Jews condemned Jesus and why the Romans executed him, and they bring out the truths that he was in fact the Son of God and the King of the Jews.

22:55–62 servant girl. All four Gospels mention that Peter's first challenge came from a slave girl. The second challenge was either

saw him seated there in the firelight. She looked closely at him and said, "This man was
with him."
57 But he denied it. "Woman, I don't know him," he said.
58 A little later someone else saw him and said, "You also are one of them."
"Man, I am not!" Peter replied.
59 About an hour later another asserted, "Certainly this fellow was with him, for he is
a Galilean."[n]
60 Peter replied, "Man, I don't know what you're talking about!" Just as he was speaking, the rooster crowed. 61 The Lord[o] turned and looked straight at Peter. Then Peter remembered the word the Lord had spoken to him: "Before the rooster crows today, you
will disown me three times."[p] 62 And he went outside and wept bitterly.

The Guards Mock Jesus

63 The men who were guarding Jesus began mocking and beating him. 64 They blindfolded him and demanded, "Prophesy! Who hit you?" 65 And they said many other insulting things to him.[q]

Jesus Before Pilate and Herod

66 At daybreak the council[r] of the elders of the people, both the chief priests and
teachers of the law, met together,[s] and Jesus was led before them. 67 "If you are the
Christ,[a]" they said, "tell us."
Jesus answered, "If I tell you, you will not believe me, 68 and if I asked you, you would
not answer.[t] 69 But from now on, the Son of Man will be seated at the right hand of the
mighty God."[u]
70 They all asked, "Are you then the Son of God?"[v]
He replied, "You are right in saying I am."[w]
71 Then they said, "Why do we need any more testimony? We have heard it from his
own lips."

23 Then the whole assembly rose and led him off to Pilate.[x] 2 And they began to accuse him, saying, "We have found this man subverting our nation.[y] He opposes payment of taxes to Caesar[z] and claims to be Christ,[b] a king."[a]
3 So Pilate asked Jesus, "Are you the king of the Jews?"
"Yes, it is as you say," Jesus replied.
4 Then Pilate announced to the chief priests and the crowd, "I find no basis for a
charge against this man."[b]
5 But they insisted, "He stirs up the people all over Judea[c] by his teaching. He started
in Galilee[c] and has come all the way here."

22:59 [n]Lk 23:6
22:61 [o]Lk 7:13 [p]ver 34
22:65 [q]Mt 16:21
22:66 [r]Mt 5:22 [s]Mt 27:1; Mk 15:1
22:68 [t]Lk 20:3-8
22:69 [u]Mk 16:19
22:70 [v]Mt 4:3 [w]Mt 27:11; Lk 23:3
23:1 [x]Mt 27:2; Mk 15:1; Jn 18:28
23:2 [y]ver 14 [z]Lk 20:22 [a]Jn 19:12
23:4 [b]ver 14,22,41; Mt 27:23; Jn 18:38; 1Ti 6:13; 2Co 5:21
23:5 [c]Mk 1:14

[a] 67 Or *Messiah* [b] 2 Or *Messiah;* also in verses 35 and 39 [c] 5 Or *over the land of the Jews*

from the same girl (Mk 14:69), from a different slave girl (Mt 26:71) or from a man (Lk 22:58). Servants were talking around a fire in a courtyard; a challenge from any of them would have been taken up by others so that there would have been several voices challenging Peter. The threefold denial fulfilled the prediction of 22:34.

■ **22:63—23:25** *The Trials of Jesus.* Luke recounted the many injustices and poignant moments of Jesus' trials.

22:63–65 Jesus was evidently left with a guard of soldiers who made sport of his predicament.

22:66–71 None of the Gospels gives a full account of Jesus' trial. It is clear that there were two main stages: The Jews tried Jesus before the Sanhedrin and gained the verdict that he was a blasphemer deserving of death according to their law. But only the Romans could execute him, and the Romans would not execute a man for blasphemy. Jesus' detractors therefore had to arrange for a different trial before the Romans, one in which they tried to get a verdict according to Roman law.

22:66 At daybreak. Only after daybreak could a legal Jewish trial be held. Anything done earlier was unofficial. Luke's account of those present points to the Sanhedrin.

22:67–69 Luke's Gospel does not speak of a formal accusation or of a trial according to due form. The Sanhedrin simply invited Jesus to incriminate himself according to their understanding of the role and function of the Messiah. This he declined to do, as they would not have believed him anyway. But Jesus did indicate that a change was coming ("from now on") and that he would be in the place of highest honor in heaven.

22:70 the Son of God? It is not certain what they meant by asking whether Jesus was *the* Son of God (a man such as a king could be called a son of God (e.g., 1Ch 28:6), but the definite article "the" indicates an even more special relationship to God.

22:71 For the Sanhedrin, Jesus' answer ended the matter. Jesus had agreed that he was the Son of God, and as far as its members were concerned, he was guilty. Persuading the Romans would require a different approach, but Jesus was guilty in the eyes of the Sanhedrin, and it remained only for them to secure his execution.

23:1 the whole assembly. Not all were needed, but this large group would impress Pilate with its seriousness and solidarity.

23:2 subverting our nation. A curiously imprecise charge. **opposes payment of taxes to Caesar.** Jesus in fact did the opposite (20:25). **claims to be Christ, a king.** Jesus specifically refused to use the term (22:67–68) in the portion of the inquiry recorded by Luke. In Matthew 16:17, however, he had affirmed Peter's confession to that effect. This charge, then, was true in a sense, but not in the sense in which the Romans would have understood it: that Jesus claimed to be a political rival to Caesar. So this charge, like the others, was essentially false.

23:3 Yes. The word "yes" is not in the Greek (nor does it appear in the parallel accounts of Mt 26:64 or Mk 15:2). In one crucially important sense Jesus was King of the Jews, so he could not say no. But in the sense in which Pilate understood the term, he was not, so he could not say yes. His answer is essentially noncommittal, something like "So you say" (cf. Jn 18:33–38). This was enough for Pilate to understand that Jesus was no revolutionary.

23:5–7 In the Roman Empire, a trial was usually held in the province in which the offense was said to have been committed, but it could be transferred to the province from which the accused came. Pilate seized on this fine point to send Jesus to Herod. Only Luke's Gospel mentions this detail.

6 On hearing this, Pilate asked if the man was a Galilean.[d] 7 When he learned that Jesus
was under Herod's jurisdiction, he sent him to Herod,[e] who was also in Jerusalem at that
time.
8 When Herod saw Jesus, he was greatly pleased, because for a long time he had been
wanting to see him.[f] From what he had heard about him, he hoped to see him perform
some miracle. 9 He plied him with many questions, but Jesus gave him no answer.[g] 10 The
chief priests and the teachers of the law were standing there, vehemently accusing him.
11 Then Herod and his soldiers ridiculed and mocked him. Dressing him in an elegant
robe,[h] they sent him back to Pilate. 12 That day Herod and Pilate became friends[i]—before this they had been enemies.
13 Pilate called together the chief priests, the rulers and the people, 14 and said to them,
"You brought me this man as one who was inciting the people to rebellion. I have examined him in your presence and have found no basis for your charges against him.[j] 15 Neither has Herod, for he sent him back to us; as you can see, he has done nothing to
deserve death. 16 Therefore, I will punish him[k] and then release him.[a]"
18 With one voice they cried out, "Away with this man! Release Barabbas to us!"[l]
19 (Barabbas had been thrown into prison for an insurrection in the city, and for murder.)
20 Wanting to release Jesus, Pilate appealed to them again. 21 But they kept shouting,
"Crucify him! Crucify him!"
22 For the third time he spoke to them: "Why? What crime has this man committed?
I have found in him no grounds for the death penalty. Therefore I will have him punished
and then release him."[m]
23 But with loud shouts they insistently demanded that he be crucified, and their
shouts prevailed. 24 So Pilate decided to grant their demand. 25 He released the man who
had been thrown into prison for insurrection and murder, the one they asked for, and
surrendered Jesus to their will.

The Crucifixion

26 As they led him away, they seized Simon from Cyrene,[n] who was on his way in from
the country, and put the cross on him and made him carry it behind Jesus.[o] 27 A large number of people followed him, including women who mourned and wailed[p] for him. 28 Jesus
turned and said to them, "Daughters of Jerusalem, do not weep for me; weep for yourselves and for your children.[q] 29 For the time will come when you will say, 'Blessed are the
barren women, the wombs that never bore and the breasts that never nursed!'[r] 30 Then

" 'they will say to the mountains, "Fall on us!"
and to the hills, "Cover us!" '[b][s]

31 For if men do these things when the tree is green, what will happen when it is dry?"[t]
32 Two other men, both criminals, were also led out with him to be executed.[u] 33 When
they came to the place called the Skull, there they crucified him, along with the criminals—one on his right, the other on his left. 34 Jesus said, "Father,[v] forgive them, for they
do not know what they are doing."[c][w] And they divided up his clothes by casting lots.[x]

23:6 [d]Lk 22:59
23:7 [e]Mt 14:1; Lk 3:1
23:8 [f]Lk 9:9
23:9 [g]Mk 14:61
23:11 [h]Mk 15:17-19; Jn 19:2,3
23:12 [i]Ac 4:27
23:14 [j]ver 4
23:16 [k]ver 22; Mt 27:26; Jn 19:1; Ac 16:37; 2Co 11:23,24
23:18 [l]Ac 3:13,14
23:22 [m]ver 16
23:26 [n]Mt 27:32 [o]Mk 15:21; Jn 19:17
23:27 [p]Lk 8:52
23:28 [q]Lk 19:41-44; 21:23,24
23:29 [r]Mt 24:19
23:30 [s]Isa 2:19; Hos 10:8; Rev 6:16
23:31 [t]Eze 20:47
23:32 [u]Isa 53:12; Mt 27:38; Mk 15:27; Jn 19:18
23:34 [v]Mt 11:25 [w]Mt 5:44 [x]Ps 22:18

[a] *16* Some manuscripts *him.* [17] *Now he was obliged to release one man to them at the Feast.* [b] *30* Hosea 10:8
[c] *34* Some early manuscripts do not have this sentence.

23:9 gave him no answer. Herod was the only person to whom Jesus refused to speak.
23:11 Herod mocked Jesus, not taking the charge against him seriously.
23:13–24 See *BC* 38.
23:16 I will punish him. Under Roman law a man might be given a light beating and a warning to encourage him to be more careful in the future. Pilate was evidently hoping that this evidence of magisterial displeasure would placate the Jews and enable him to release a man he knew to be innocent.
23:18 The custom of releasing a prisoner at the time of the Passover has not been verified by extra-Biblical sources, but this sort of tradition was widely practiced at the time, and there is nothing improbable about Herod's offer. **Barabbas.** The crowds clamored for Barabbas, a man otherwise unknown. His name means "son of the father." Luke's Gospel tells us that his crimes were rebellion and murder. Clearly, Barabbas was a proven criminal, but to the Jerusalem mob he may well have appeared as a hero of the resistance movement.
■ **23:26–56** *The Crucifixion.* Luke recorded details of Jesus' death so that the event would never be forgotten.
23:26 Simon from Cyrene. It was customary for the condemned to carry his own cross or the crossbar to the place where the crucifixion was to take place. Jesus started to carry his cross (Jn 19:17) but may have been weakened by the heavy scourging that had preceded his crucifixion (Mk 15:15). The soldiers conscripted a passerby named Simon. He was from Cyrene (in North Africa), and his sons were later known in the church (Mk 15:21).
23:27–30 Only Luke recorded this incident. There must have been many supporters of Jesus in Jerusalem, but only a comparatively small number could have crowded around the judgment hall where the opposition was concentrated.
23:28 Daughters of Jerusalem. The reference is to local women, not pilgrims from Galilee. Jesus was concerned for them (not for himself) and turned their attention to the terrible troubles that would come upon the land. He wanted them to repent rather than to sympathize with him.
23:31 Evidently a proverbial saying, possibly suggesting that if Jesus (who was innocent) was to be crucified, worse would happen to the Jews (who were guilty).
23:33 the Skull. In Latin *calvaria,* from which we get the modern term "Calvary." All four Gospels say that Jesus was crucified between two criminals. In his death he "was numbered with the transgressors" (Isa 53:12).

35The people stood watching, and the rulers even sneered at him.[y] They said, "He
saved others; let him save himself if he is the Christ of God, the Chosen One."[z]
36The soldiers also came up and mocked him.[a] They offered him wine vinegar[b] 37and
said, "If you are the king of the Jews,[c] save yourself."
38There was a written notice above him, which read: THIS IS THE KING OF THE JEWS.[d]
39One of the criminals who hung there hurled insults at him: "Aren't you the Christ?
Save yourself and us!"[e]
40But the other criminal rebuked him. "Don't you fear God," he said, "since you are
under the same sentence? 41We are punished justly, for we are getting what our deeds
deserve. But this man has done nothing wrong."[f]
42Then he said, "Jesus, remember me when you come into your kingdom.[a]"[g]
43Jesus answered him, "I tell you the truth, today you will be with me in paradise."[h]

Jesus' Death

44It was now about the sixth hour, and darkness came over the whole land until the
ninth hour,[i] 45for the sun stopped shining. And the curtain of the temple[j] was torn in
two.[k] 46Jesus called out with a loud voice,[l] "Father, into your hands I commit my spirit."[m] When he had said this, he breathed his last.[n]
47The centurion, seeing what had happened, praised God[o] and said, "Surely this was
a righteous man." 48When all the people who had gathered to witness this sight saw what
took place, they beat their breasts[p] and went away. 49But all those who knew him, including the women who had followed him from Galilee,[q] stood at a distance,[r] watching
these things.

Jesus' Burial

50Now there was a man named Joseph, a member of the Council, a good and upright
man, 51who had not consented to their decision and action. He came from the Judean
town of Arimathea and he was waiting for the kingdom of God.[s] 52Going to Pilate, he
asked for Jesus' body. 53Then he took it down, wrapped it in linen cloth and placed it in
a tomb cut in the rock, one in which no one had yet been laid. 54It was Preparation Day,[t]
and the Sabbath was about to begin.
55The women who had come with Jesus from Galilee[u] followed Joseph and saw the
tomb and how his body was laid in it. 56Then they went home and prepared spices and
perfumes.[v] But they rested on the Sabbath in obedience to the commandment.[w]

23:35 [y]Ps 22:17 [z]Isa 42:1
23:36 [a]Ps 22:7 [b]Ps 69:21; Mt 27:48
23:37 [c]Lk 4:3,9
23:38 [d]Mt 2:2
23:39 [e]ver 35,37
23:41 [f]ver 4
23:42 [g]Mt 16:27
23:43 [h]2Co 12:3,4; Rev 2:7
23:44 [i]Am 8:9
23:45 [j]Ex 26:31-33; Heb 9:3,8 [k]Heb 10:19,20
23:46 [l]Mt 27:50 [m]Ps 31:5; 1Pe 2:23 [n]Jn 19:30
23:47 [o]Mt 9:8
23:48 [p]Lk 18:13
23:49 [q]Lk 8:2 [r]Ps 38:11
23:51 [s]Lk 2:25,38
23:54 [t]Mt 27:62
23:55 [u]ver 49
23:56 [v]Mk 16:1; Lk 24:1 [w]Ex 12:16; 20:10

[a] 42 Some manuscripts *come with your kingly power*

23:34 them. This pronoun includes both Jews and Romans. See *BC* 57. **his clothes.** The clothing of the one crucified was traditionally a spoil for those who crucified him. Thus these soldiers unwittingly fulfilled Psalm 22:18.
23:35 The rulers, not the people, were sneering. It is curious that they spoke of "the Christ" and "the Chosen One," for Jesus seemed not to have used either title with any regularity.
23:36–38 Notice the kingship motif.
23:42 into your kingdom. This indicates some measure of trust. The man was confident that Jesus was not about to be annihilated in death but was going to a heavenly kingdom.
23:43 paradise. A Persian word meaning "garden." It came to be used for the place of the blessed (2Co 12:4; Rev 2:7). See *WCF* 4.2; 32.1; *WLC* 17,82,85; *WSC* 37.
23:44 about the sixth hour. About noon; with no clocks, timekeeping in antiquity was approximate. John 19:14 indicates that Pilate pronounced sentence upon Jesus "about the sixth hour." The difference may be due to the possibility that John's timekeeping followed the Roman practice of beginning at midnight rather than at daybreak. **darkness.** Not an eclipse, for it was a full (or nearly full) moon. (Passover took place on the 14th day of the month [Lev 23:5], and months were reckoned on a lunar calendar.) During a full (or nearly full) moon, the earth is between the moon and the sun, making a solar eclipse impossible because such an eclipse occurs when the moon comes between the earth and the sun. This was a supernatural darkness connected with Jesus' death.
23:45 the curtain. Located between the Most Holy Place and the rest of the temple. Jesus' death opened the way into the very presence of God.
23:46 Matthew's and Mark's Gospels stress the terrible nature of Jesus' death on behalf of sinners. Luke's Gospel does not deny this aspect but includes Jesus' words to show that his death was in accordance with the Father's will. **breathed his last.** This was an unusual way of referring to death. None of the Gospels employ standard terminology for Jesus' death, which may indicate that the writers saw it as out of the ordinary.
23:47 a righteous man. The way Jesus died showed him to be "righteous." Matthew and Mark instead use the phrase "Son of God"(Mt 27:54; Mk 15:39). In this context, the two terms carry much the same meaning. See note on Mark 15:39.
23:48 beat their breasts. A sign of grief. The crowd had come to be entertained, but Jesus' death left them sad and pensive. Luke's Gospel does not tell us the effect of the death on the disciples who witnessed it.
23:50–51 Joseph of Arimathea is mentioned only in the accounts of the burial of Jesus, and all four Gospels agree that he took the leading part. The location of Arimathea is uncertain (see note on Mk 15:43), but in any case, Joseph seems to have come to live in Jerusalem (he had a tomb nearby). He was a member of the Sanhedrin and must have been absent when the vote to execute Jesus was taken, for "all" are said to have agreed to it (Mk 14:64). That he was "waiting for the kingdom of God" (v. 51) means that he was a follower of Jesus.
23:53 linen cloth. The linen cloth was a shroud (placed over the linen strips of Jn 19:40). **a tomb cut in the rock.** A rock tomb generally held several bodies, but there were none as yet in this tomb. See note on Mark 15:46.
23:54 Preparation Day. Friday, the day on which people prepared for the Sabbath. See *WLC* 117,121.
23:55–56 There was not enough time on Friday to do all that Jesus' followers would have liked to do for his burial. The women took note of where the body was laid, evidently so that they would know where to go to complete the burial when the Sabbath had ended. Joseph and Nicodemus placed a considerable quantity of myrrh and aloes with the body as they laid it in the tomb (Jn 19:39), but the women, wanting to make their own contribution, prepared their spices during the remainder of Friday. See *WLC* 117,121.

24:1 [x]Lk 23:56
24:3 [y]ver 23,24
24:4 [z]Jn 20:12
24:6 [a]Mt 17:22,23; Mk 9:30-31; Lk 9:22; 24:44
24:7 [b]Mt 8:20 [c]Mt 16:21
24:8 [d]Jn 2:22

The Resurrection

24 On the first day of the week, very early in the morning, the women took the spices they had prepared[x] and went to the tomb. 2 They found the stone rolled away
from the tomb, 3 but when they entered, they did not find the body of the Lord Jesus.[y]
4 While they were wondering about this, suddenly two men in clothes that gleamed like
lightning[z] stood beside them. 5 In their fright the women bowed down with their faces
to the ground, but the men said to them, "Why do you look for the living among the
dead? 6 He is not here; he has risen! Remember how he told you, while he was still with
you in Galilee:[a] 7 'The Son of Man[b] must be delivered into the hands of sinful men, be crucified and on the third day be raised again.' "[c] 8 Then they remembered his words.[d]
9 When they came back from the tomb, they told all these things to the Eleven and to

■ **24:1–49** *The Resurrection.* Each of the Gospels deals with the resurrection in its own way, although none describes how it happened. Some details are clear in all four Gospels: The tomb was empty, the disciples were slow to believe that the resurrection had happened and the women were prominent in the first appearances of the resurrected Jesus. But each Gospel records some fact or event that does not appear in the others. Luke's includes the accounts of the walk to Emmaus, Thomas's doubt and Jesus' ascension into heaven.

24:1 the first day of the week. This began at sunset on Saturday. The women would have had the hours of darkness to complete their preparations before setting out for the tomb at daybreak.

24:2–3 A stone tomb was closed by rolling a stone in front of the opening, and in this case, a seal had been placed on the stone (Mt 27:66). The women had been concerned about how they would remove the stone (see note on Mk 15:46).

24:2 See theological article "The Resurrection of Jesus" at Luke 24.

24:6 Remember how he told you. The angels reminded them of Jesus' prophecies concerning his death and resurrection (see note on 18:31–34). See *WCF* 29.6.

24:7 be raised. The use of the passive verb points to the activity of the Father, who raised Jesus by the power of the Holy Spirit.

24:9 the Eleven. Judas had ceased to be an apostle, but the others remained. **all the others.** This indefinite expression shows that

Resurrection Appearances

Appearance	Place	Time	Matthew	Mark	Luke	John	Acts	1 Cor
The empty tomb	Jerusalem	Resurrection Sunday	28:1-10	16:1-8	24:1-12	20:1-9		
To Mary Magdalene in the garden	Jerusalem	Resurrection Sunday		16:9-11		20:11-18		
To other women	Jerusalem	Resurrection Sunday	28:9-10					
To two people going to Emmaus	Road to Emmaus	Resurrection Sunday		16:12-13	24:13-32			
To Peter	Jerusalem	Resurrection Sunday			24:34			15:5
To the ten disciples in the upper room	Jerusalem	Resurrection Sunday			24:36-43	20:19-25		
To the 11 disciples in the upper room	Jerusalem	Following Sunday		16:14		20:26-31		15:5
To seven disciples fishing	Sea of Galilee	Some time later				21:1-23		
To the 11 disciples on a mountain	Galilee	Some time later	28:16-20	16:15-18				
To more than 500	Unknown	Some time later						15:6
To James	Unknown	Some time later						15:7
To his disciples at his ascension	Mount of Olives	40 days after Jesus' resurrection			24:44-49		1:3-8	
To Paul	Damascus	Several years later					9:1-19 22:3-16 26:9-18	9:1

all the others. 10It was Mary Magdalene, Joanna, Mary the mother of James, and the others with them[e] who told this to the apostles.[f] 11But they did not believe[g] the women, because their words seemed to them like nonsense. 12Peter, however, got up and ran to the
tomb. Bending over, he saw the strips of linen lying by themselves,[h] and he went away,[i]
wondering to himself what had happened.

On the Road to Emmaus

13Now that same day two of them were going to a village called Emmaus, about sev-
en miles[a] from Jerusalem.[j] 14They were talking with each other about everything that
had happened. 15As they talked and discussed these things with each other, Jesus himself came up and walked along with them;[k] 16but they were kept from recognizing him.[l]
17He asked them, "What are you discussing together as you walk along?"
They stood still, their faces downcast. 18One of them, named Cleopas,[m] asked him,
"Are you only a visitor to Jerusalem and do not know the things that have happened
there in these days?"

24:10 [e]Lk 8:1-3 [f]Mk 6:30
24:11 [g]Mk 16:11
24:12 [h]Jn 20:3-7 [i]Jn 20:10
24:13 [j]Mk 16:12
24:15 [k]ver 36
24:16 [l]Jn 20:14; 21:4
24:18 [m]Jn 19:25

a *13* Greek *sixty stadia* (about 11 kilometers)

there was a large band of followers of Jesus in Jerusalem at this time. Many may have been Galileans who were in Jerusalem for the Passover.

24:10 Mary Magdalene. This woman has the distinction of being the first to see the risen Lord (Jn 20:10–18). She is mentioned in all four Gospels in connection with the crucifixion and resurrection, but apart from this, we hear of her only in 8:2. **Joanna.** Mentioned elsewhere only in 8:3. **Mary the mother of James.** The NIV is probably right in understanding the second Mary as the mother of James (cf. Mk 15:40), although Luke literally says only "James's Mary." She was not the mother of the apostle James, the son of Zebedee, because Matthew 27:56 lists "the mother of Zebedee's sons" in addition to "the mother of James and Joses." John 19:25 states that at least three women named "Mary" were present: Jesus' mother, the wife of Clopas and Mary Magdalene. It is possible that the mother of James was the wife of Clopas, but nothing is known of her except from John 19:25, including whether or not she had children named James and Joses. Jesus' mother, however, did have children named James and Joseph (Mt 13:55; Mk 6:3), and "Joseph" may refer to the same person as "Joses," so it is possible that Mary the mother of James was Jesus' mother. Luke adds a reference to "others" (the word is feminine, signifying "other women") with them.

24:11 they did not believe the women. The testimony of women was not highly regarded by first-century Jews. Because of this the Eleven and the other males associated with them refused to believe what the women had told them.

24:13 Emmaus. The exact site is unknown.

24:14 See *WLC* 160.

24:16 they were kept. This appears to mean that God prevented them from recognizing Jesus at this time.

The Resurrection of Jesus: Why Was Jesus Resurrected?

THROUGHOUT the history of the church, the bodily resurrection of Jesus has been recognized as one of the central teachings of the Christian faith. The fact that Jesus rose physically from the dead is an essential Christian belief. The New Testament stresses the certainty of our Savior's bodily resurrection as a historical fact. All four Gospels highlight the factuality of this event, focusing on the many witnesses of the empty tomb and of Jesus' resurrection appearances (see chart titled "Resurrection Appearances" at Lk 24). The book of Acts also insists that the resurrection actually happened (Ac 1:3; 2:24–35; 3:15; 4:10; 5:30–32; 13:33–37). Paul regarded the resurrection as indisputable proof that the message about Jesus as Judge and Savior is true (Ac 17:31; 1Co 15:1–11,20).

In Reformed theology, Jesus' resurrection has been viewed with two main emphases. First, it has been treated as the validation of Christian claims about the effectiveness of his atoning death. Jesus' resurrection demonstrated his victory over death (Ac 2:24; 1Co 15:54–57), vindicated him as righteous (Jn 16:10) and confirmed his divinity (Ro 1:4). This event therefore led to his ascension, enthronement (Ac 1:9–11; 2:33–34; Php 2:9–11; cf. Isa 53:10–12) and present heavenly reign. The reality of the resurrection guarantees believers' present forgiveness and justification (Ro 4:25; 1Co 15:17; Heb 7:24–25), as well as their future hope of resurrection life when Christ returns (Jn 11:25–26; Ro 6; Eph 1:18—2:10; Col 2:9–15; 3:1–4).

Second, Jesus' resurrection has been seen as Christ's move from the judgment of this age to the glories of the age to come. Jesus was lifted out of the grave so that his body might now be glorified and deathless (Php 3:21; Heb 7:16,24). The Son of God lives eternally in heaven in and through that body. As a result, when men and women are united to Christ by faith, they are also transported from the age of sin and death to that of resurrected life (Ro 6:4–11; see also theological article "Union with Christ" at Gal 6). Christians are now empowered by the Spirit, who raised Jesus from the dead (Ro 8:11). We live in newness of life even as Jesus does (Ro 6:4). In short, Christ's resurrection was just as essential to our salvation as his death, because it is by union with his resurrection that our mortal bodies will be made imperishable on the last day (Ro 6:5; 1Co 15:42–57). Without the resurrection of Christ, our faith would be in vain because we would still be dead under the judgment of God, incapable of living eternally in resurrected bodies (1Co 15:12–20).

Paul indicated that not all Christians must die before receiving their new bodies in the last resurrection. In 1 Corinthians 15:50–54 he taught that those who are alive on Earth at the moment of Christ's return will undergo a full bodily transformation, and in 2 Corinthians 5:1–5 he explained that Christians who die before the second coming will be "clothed" (v. 2) with their new bodies—the "eternal house in heaven" (v. 1)—as a distinct event.

19"What things?" he asked.
"About Jesus of Nazareth,"[n] they replied. "He was a prophet,[o] powerful in word and
deed before God and all the people. 20The chief priests and our rulers[p] handed him over
to be sentenced to death, and they crucified him; 21but we had hoped that he was the
one who was going to redeem Israel.[q] And what is more, it is the third day[r] since all this
took place. 22In addition, some of our women amazed us.[s] They went to the tomb early
this morning 23but didn't find his body. They came and told us that they had seen a vision of angels, who said he was alive. 24Then some of our companions went to the tomb
and found it just as the women had said, but him they did not see."[t]
25He said to them, "How foolish you are, and how slow of heart to believe all that the
prophets have spoken! 26Did not the Christ[a] have to suffer these things and then enter
his glory?"[u] 27And beginning with Moses[v] and all the Prophets,[w] he explained to them
what was said in all the Scriptures concerning himself.[x]
28As they approached the village to which they were going, Jesus acted as if he were
going farther. 29But they urged him strongly, "Stay with us, for it is nearly evening; the
day is almost over." So he went in to stay with them.
30When he was at the table with them, he took bread, gave thanks, broke it[y] and began to give it to them. 31Then their eyes were opened and they recognized him,[z] and he
disappeared from their sight. 32They asked each other, "Were not our hearts burning
within us[a] while he talked with us on the road and opened the Scriptures[b] to us?"
33They got up and returned at once to Jerusalem. There they found the Eleven and
those with them, assembled together 34and saying, "It is true! The Lord has risen and has
appeared to Simon."[c] 35Then the two told what had happened on the way, and how Jesus
was recognized by them when he broke the bread.[d]

Jesus Appears to the Disciples

36While they were still talking about this, Jesus himself stood among them and said
to them, "Peace be with you."[e]
37They were startled and frightened, thinking they saw a ghost.[f] 38He said to them,
"Why are you troubled, and why do doubts rise in your minds? 39Look at my hands and
my feet. It is I myself! Touch me and see;[g] a ghost does not have flesh and bones, as you
see I have."
40When he had said this, he showed them his hands and feet. 41And while they still
did not believe it because of joy and amazement, he asked them, "Do you have anything
here to eat?" 42They gave him a piece of broiled fish, 43and he took it and ate it in their
presence.[h]
44He said to them, "This is what I told you while I was still with you:[i] Everything must
be fulfilled[j] that is written about me in the Law of Moses,[k] the Prophets and the
Psalms."[l]
45Then he opened their minds so they could understand the Scriptures. 46He told
them, "This is what is written: The Christ will suffer and rise from the dead on the third
day, 47and repentance and forgiveness of sins will be preached in his name[m] to all nations,[n] beginning at Jerusalem. 48You are witnesses[o] of these things. 49I am going to send

24:19 [n]Mk 1:24 [o]Mt 21:11
24:20 [p]Lk 23:13
24:21 [q]Lk 1:68; 2:38; 21:28 [r]Mt 16:21
24:22 [s]ver 1-10
24:24 [t]ver 12
24:26 [u]Heb 2:10; 1Pe 1:11
24:27 [v]Ge 3:15; Nu 21:9; Dt 18:15 [w]Isa 7:14; 9:6; 40:10,11; 53; Eze 34:23; Da 9:24; Mic 7:20; Mal 3:1 [x]Jn 1:45
24:30 [y]Mt 14:19
24:31 [z]ver 16
24:32 [a]Ps 39:3 [b]ver 27, 45
24:34 [c]1Co 15:5
24:35 [d]ver 30,31
24:36 [e]Jn 20:19,21,26; 14:27
24:37 [f]Mk 6:49
24:39 [g]Jn 20:27; 1Jn 1:1
24:43 [h]Ac 10:41
24:44 [i]Lk 9:45; 18:34 [j]Mt 16:21; Lk 9:22, 44; 18:31-33; 22:37 [k]ver 27 [l]Ps 2; 16; 22; 69; 72; 110; 118
24:47 [m]Ac 5:31; 10:43; 13:38 [n]Mt 28:19
24:48 [o]Ac 1:8; 2:32; 5:32; 13:31; 1Pe 5:1

a *26* Or *Messiah*; also in verse 46

24:18 Cleopas is not known apart from this incident.
24:20 chief priests and our rulers. They placed the principal responsibility for Jesus' death on their own people, not on the Romans.
24:21 redeem. The term means to set free at cost. Clearly, the two were thinking of the deliverance of their nation.
24:25–27 The two men might reasonably have been expected to understand more than they actually did. They had evidently embraced what the Scriptures said about the Messiah's glory, but not what they said about his sufferings.
24:27 all the Scriptures. A reference to the Old Testament in its entirety. See *WCF* 1.3.
24:30 took bread . . . give it to them. These were actions a host would perform at a meal (cf. 22:19).
24:31 opened. This was apparently another divine action (cf. v. 16).
24:34 The Eleven had not believed the women (v. 11), but an appearance to Simon Peter carried conviction.
24:36 The sudden appearance of Jesus among them, even though the doors were locked (Jn 20:19), indicates that the risen Lord's body was not limited as ordinary human bodies are.
24:39 my hands and my feet. That is, the marks of the nails. See *WCF* 2.1; 29.6; *WLC* 52; *BC* 19.
24:42 a piece of broiled fish. The risen body could make use of food.
24:44 Everything must be fulfilled. Notice the word "must." It is no mere accident that Scripture is fulfilled: There is divine necessity about it. **the Law of Moses, the Prophets and the Psalms.** The threefold division of the Hebrew Bible (the only place where it is explicitly mentioned in the New Testament). Jesus was saying that every part of Scripture bears witness to him. See *WCF* 1.3.
24:45 opened their minds. Jesus showed his disciples the way to understand the Bible. Christ's death and resurrection had been foretold in Scripture. See *WLC* 157.
24:47 Not only had the passion and resurrection been foretold, but also the calling of people to repentance and forgiveness based on Christ's atoning work. See *WCF* 15.1.
24:48 witnesses. The preachers were not to produce some novel concepts of their own but were to bear ear- and eyewitness to what God had done. The risen Jesus would send what his Father had promised (i.e., the gift of the Holy Spirit; Joel 2:28–32; Ac 2:1–4).

you what my Father has promised;[p] but stay in the city until you have been clothed with
power from on high."

24:49 [p]Jn 14:16; Ac 1:4

The Ascension

50 When he had led them out to the vicinity of Bethany,[q] he lifted up his hands and
blessed them. 51 While he was blessing them, he left them and was taken up into heav-
en.[r] 52 Then they worshiped him and returned to Jerusalem with great joy. 53 And they
stayed continually at the temple,[s] praising God.

24:50 [q]Mt 21:17
24:51 [r]2Ki 2:11
24:53 [s]Ac 2:46

■ **24:50–53** *The Ascension.* Luke closed his Gospel with Jesus ascending to heaven and the apostles rejoicing because of all that had happened. Luke wanted his readers to respond in like manner to all they had read.
24:50–51 See *BC* 46.
24:50 Luke gave no time indication here, but later he stated that the ascension took place 40 days after the resurrection (Ac 1:3). **Bethany.** A village on the Mount of Olives about two miles east of Jerusalem (Jn 11:18).
24:51 he left them. Luke's account of the ascension is brief but serves as a fitting conclusion to Luke's first work, which was intended to be an account of "all that Jesus began to do and to teach until the day he was taken up to heaven" (Ac 1:1–2). A more detailed ascension account is found at the beginning of Luke's second work (Ac 1:9–11). The ascension marks the end of the work Jesus came to do on Earth and the beginning of what he continues to do in and through the church. See theological article "The Ascension and Session of Jesus" at Hebrews 8.

24:52 they worshiped him. Whatever their view of Jesus in earlier days, the disciples now recognized his divinity and worshiped him. The separation did not bring sadness, but "great joy."

24:53 Luke ended his Gospel as he began it: in Jerusalem with the worship of God.

JOHN

Introduction

Overview

Author: The apostle John

Purpose: To present the life of Jesus so that unbelievers will come to faith in him and believers will grow in their faith in him as the Messiah and the Son of God descended from heaven

Date: A.D. 85–90

Key Truths:

- Jesus is the divine Word from above who became flesh.
- Jesus came to the Jews, but only a few of them received him.
- Jesus performed many public signs, demonstrating that he was the Messiah, the Son of God.
- Jesus taught that salvation was in him alone.

Author

Although this Gospel is anonymous, it contains some hints about its authorship. The author was almost certainly Jewish, for he displays an intimate knowledge of Jewish customs, festivals and beliefs. His detailed geographical knowledge suggests that he was a native of the Holy Land, and it appears that he was an eyewitness of many of the events recorded in his Gospel (19:35).

Further, this is the only Gospel that refers to one of the apostles as "the disciple whom Jesus loved" (e.g., 13:23) rather than by name. This disciple is the one identified as the eyewitness who "testifies to these things and who wrote them down" (21:24). Moreover, John son of Zebedee, who was one of the most prominent disciples, is not mentioned by name in this Gospel. It is difficult to explain this omission unless we assume that the Gospel was written by John and that modesty prevented him from identifying himself.

Early church traditions (e.g., the writings of Irenaeus in the second century) explicitly and consistently attribute this Gospel to the apostle John. Modern doubts about the reliability of that tradition have led many scholars to reject the Johannine authorship of the book, but no other view accounts as satisfactorily for the facts.

Time and Place of Writing

Early church tradition suggests that John wrote this Gospel toward the end of his life, possibly around A.D. 85–90. Some scholars in the late nineteenth and early twentieth centuries, having abandoned Johannine authorship, argued that the Gospel was composed as late as the middle of the second century. However, the discoveries of the Rylands Fragment (a piece of papyrus dated no later than A.D. 130 that contains a few verses from John 18) and the Dead Sea Scrolls (which enhanced our understanding of Palestine in the first century) have compelled most scholars to return to the Gospel's traditional date. Some specialists have gone further, dating it prior to A.D. 70.

The author himself describes his purpose: "These are written that you may believe that Jesus is the Christ, the Son of God, and that by believing you may have life in his name" (20:31). There has been considerable discussion, however, concerning whether the author had in mind initial or continued belief. Grammatically, both views are possible, and there is no need to press for one to the exclusion of the other, since the author himself did not do so.

Purpose and Distinctives

Jesus' interaction with "his own [who] did not receive him" (1:11) supplements his central focus. Jesus appeared often in Jerusalem at various Jewish feasts, which took on special importance because of the way in which he related his own work to what the feasts signified (e.g., especially 7:37–39). Despite this ministry, his own people did not receive him, a fact that John explains as symptomatic of human sin. Jesus was rejected not because he was a stranger, but because people love darkness rather than light.

It is characteristic of the style of this Gospel to emphasize contrasting concepts and themes: light and darkness (1:4–9), love and hatred (15:17–18), from above and from below (8:23), life and death (6:57–58), truth and falsehood (8:32–47) and so forth. Other characteristics include the theme of misunderstanding (see notes on 2:20; 6:51–58), the employment of double meanings (see notes on 3:14; 6:62) and the inclusion of the "I am" sayings (see note on 6:35).

John highlights the reality and magnitude of sin in various ways, but especially by emphasizing our total dependence on God for salvation. Just as our physical birth was not the result of our own effort or will, so, too, we owe our spiritual birth to God's will and the power of his Spirit (1:12–13; 3:5–8). Sinful men and women are simply unable to come to Jesus for salvation unless they are drawn by the Father (6:44). Once they come to Jesus, however, they have "eternal life and will not be condemned" (5:24); they belong to the Father, and he will not let them perish (10:27–29).

One of the most striking distinctives of this Gospel is its prologue (1:1–18). Jesus is presented as the eternally existing *Logos,* or Word (i.e., the One who alone can reveal the Father). He can do so because, as the Son, he shares in the Father's deity. He is the One who made the universe (1:3). He met the needs of the Israelites in the wilderness, and now he provides spiritual water and bread (4:13–14; 6:35). In short, he is one with the Father, the great "I am" (5:18; 8:58; 10:30–33).

Moreover, John's Gospel presents Jesus as the Lamb of God who gave his life for his people (1:29; 10:11). Although he died for them, he did not leave them alone. Before his death, Jesus promised to make his home in their hearts through the Spirit, who would bring peace and teach them all things (14:15–18,23–27). After Jesus' death, his disciples, empowered by the Spirit, were sent forth, as Jesus had been sent, to perform the great work of evangelism and to bear much fruit (14:12; 15:8; 20:21–23).

Outline

I. Prologue (1:1–18)	*John announced that the incarnation of Jesus, when the light broke into the darkness, was a new beginning.*
II. Jesus' Public Ministry (1:19—12:50)	*Jesus spent most of his time ministering to people in different areas, especially around the time of Jewish feasts.*
III. The Ministry Begins (1:19–51) A. Jesus' Witness: John the Baptist (1:19–34) B. Jesus' Witnesses: His First Disciples (1:35–51)	*John the Baptist and Jesus' first disciples recognized Jesus as the Messiah from above.*
IV. From Cana to Cana (2:1—4:54) A. The Wedding in Cana (2:1–11) B. Cleansing of the Temple (2:12–25) C. Entering the Kingdom (3:1–21) D. John's Further Testimony (3:22–36) E. A Samaritan Woman (4:1–42) F. A Royal Official in Cana (4:43–54)	*Jesus performed his first sign in Cana and later returned there to perform his second. Meanwhile, several important events introduce some of the dramatic changes Jesus brought to the world.*
V. In Jerusalem Near a Feast (5:1–47) A. A Healing at the Pool of Bethesda (5:1–15) B. Jesus, the Sabbath and the Father (5:16–47)	*Jesus performed a sign and faced conflict in Jerusalem regarding his relationship with the Father.*
VI. In Galilee Near the Passover (6:1–71) A. Feeding the Five Thousand (6:1–15) B. Walking on the Water (6:16–21) C. Teaching the Crowds (6:22–71)	*Jesus' signs and teachings in Galilee correspond to Israel's experiences of Passover, crossing the sea and receiving manna during the exodus from Egypt.*
VII. In Jerusalem Near the Feast of Tabernacles (7:1—10:21) A. Leaving for Jerusalem (7:1–13) B. Teaching the Jews (7:14—8:59) C. Healing and Teaching (9:1—10:21)	*Jesus performed signs and taught in Jerusalem around the time of the Feast of Tabernacles. Many still rejected him.*
VIII. In Jerusalem Near the Feast of Dedication (10:22–42)	*Jesus revealed himself as Israel's shepherd, but he was rejected.*
IX. Near and in Jerusalem Near Passover (11:1—12:50) A. Raising the Dead (11:1–44) B. Plotting to Kill Jesus (11:45–57) C. Anointing at Bethany (12:1–8) D. The Triumphal Entry (12:9–19) E. Reacting Gentiles (12:20–36) F. Reacting Jews (12:37–50)	*Jesus entered Jerusalem, performing signs and disclosing the reality of his future death and resurrection. He was generally admired by Gentiles, but only a few Jews received him.*
X. Jesus' Ministry to His Disciples (13:1—17:26) A. Foot Washing and Betrayal Foretold (13:1–38) B. Farewell Discourse (14:1—16:33) C. Intercessory Prayer (17:1–26)	*In his last days, Jesus focused on ministry to his disciples, preparing them for his departure by serving, comforting and praying.*

XI. The Ministry Reaches Its Climax (18:1—20:31) A. Jesus' Arrest and Trial (18:1—19:16) B. Jesus' Crucifixion, Death and Burial (19:17–42) C. Jesus' Resurrection and Appearances (20:1–31)	*Jesus' death and resurrection were climactic events that show him to be the Messiah and the Son of God.*
XII. Epilogue (21:1–25) A. Miracle at the Sea (21:1–14) B. The Confirmation of Peter (21:15–19) C. The Beloved Disciple (21:20–23) D. Closing Remarks (21:24–25)	*After his resurrection, Jesus established an order in the church for future generations to follow.*

1:1 [a]Rev 19:13 [b]Jn 17:5; 1Jn 1:2 [c]Php 2:6 **1:2** [d]Ge 1:1 **1:3** [e]1Co 8:6; Col 1:16; Heb 1:2 **1:4** [f]Jn 5:26; 11:25; 14:6 [g]Jn 8:12 **1:5** [h]Jn 3:19 **1:6** [i]Mt 3:1 **1:7** [j]ver 15,19,32 [k]ver 12 **1:9** [l]1Jn 2:8 [m]Isa 49:6 **1:10** [n]Heb 1:2 **1:12** [o]ver 7 [p]1Jn 3:23

The Word Became Flesh

1 In the beginning was the Word,[a] and the Word was with God,[b] and the Word was
God.[c] 2He was with God in the beginning.[d]
3Through him all things were made; without him nothing was made that has been
made.[e] 4In him was life,[f] and that life was the light[g] of men. 5The light shines in the darkness, but the darkness has not understood[a] it.[h]
6There came a man who was sent from God; his name was John.[i] 7He came as a witness to testify[j] concerning that light, so that through him all men might believe.[k] 8He
himself was not the light; he came only as a witness to the light. 9The true light[l] that gives
light to every man[m] was coming into the world.[b]
10He was in the world, and though the world was made through him,[n] the world did
not recognize him. 11He came to that which was his own, but his own did not receive him.
12Yet to all who received him, to those who believed[o] in his name,[p] he gave the right to

a 5 Or *darkness, and the darkness has not overcome it* b 9 Or *This was the true light that gives light to every man who comes into the world*

■ **1:1–18** *Prologue.* John began his Gospel with a lengthy preface that introduces its main themes. Jesus is the Word and the light from above. He came to the world, but most people rejected him. Yet those who received him became sons of God.

1:1–3 See *HC* 33.

1:1–2 In the beginning. Emphasizes the eternal and divine pre-existence of the Word. There is an obvious allusion here to Genesis 1:1. **the Word . . . the Word . . . the Word.** The Greek term translated "Word" is *logos,* which is also applied to Jesus in Revelation 19:13. In the past, interpreters assumed that John used *logos* in ways similar to several strands of Greek philosophy, which spoke of *logos* as "reason" or "logic" that brings order and harmony to the universe. Many speculative and erroneous ideas about Christ stemmed from this association with Greek philosophy. It is better to view John's use of *logos* as his way of drawing upon his Jewish heritage. The concept of the "word of God" appears in a variety of ways throughout the Old Testament that relate to important themes in this Gospel (e.g., see Ge 1:3; Dt 32:46–47; Pss 19:8; 33:6; 119:105,130; Hos 1:1 as they relate to Jn 1:4,7–9,13). Moreover, in the Aramaic Targums (paraphrases of the Old Testament used in Jewish synagogues), the "Word of God" is actually substituted for references to God himself in Exodus 3:12 and 19:17. John based his use of the term "Word" on these traditions. As a follower of Christ, he identified Jesus as the Word. He asserted in the strongest terms that Jesus was the Word active at creation, that he was with God and that he was God from the beginning. Then this Word became flesh. **was God.** The Word is expressly affirmed to be God. Some have attempted to avoid this by alleging that the original Greek is best translated "a god" rather than "God" since the word for "God" lacks the definite article *the.* This allegation, however, reflects a misunderstanding of the language in which the New Testament was written, for there are over 250 references to God in the Greek New Testament that are grammatically identical to this, including such passages as "to the only wise God" (Ro 16:27) and "there is no God but one" (1Co 8:4). In stating twice that the Word was "with God," John's Gospel articulates a distinction of persons in the essential unity of the Godhead. It makes it plain that Father, Son and Holy Spirit are not one person but are instead eternal, personal distinctions present from "the beginning" (v. 2). The Greek word translated "with" suggests a face-to-face relationship of close personal intimacy.

1:1 See *WCF* 8.2; *WLC* 11,36; *HC* 15,35.

1:2–3 See *WCF* 4.1.

1:3 Through him all things were made. Emphasizes the deity of the Word, since creation is a distinct activity of the Godhead (see v. 10; Col 1:16–17; *BC* 10).

1:4 In him was life. Further evidence of deity. The Son, as well as the Father, has "life in himself" (5:26). **life was the light of men.** May well be further attestation of divinity, as it references the light of creation that conquered the darkness in Genesis 1:2–4.

1:5 has not understood it. The word used here may also mean "received" or "overcome" (see NIV text note). It is characteristic of the style of this Gospel to emphasize contrasting concepts (see "Introduction: Purpose and Distinctives"). The plot of this Gospel can be seen in terms of a struggle between the forces of faith and unbelief. See *BC* 14.

1:7,9 all men . . . every man. A vivid contrast with the Jewish particularism that often restricted God's saving activity to Israel. The universal importance of the gospel is asserted (v. 7).

1:9 The true light. In this Gospel "truth" and "true" are often employed to signify that which is everlasting or heavenly as opposed to that which is merely temporal or earthly (see notes on 4:24; 6:32). **gives light.** May refer to the enlightening activity of God's common grace or to the exposing of people's evil deeds as in 3:20.

1:10–12 See *WLC* 60.

1:11–12 See *WLC* 58; *WSC* 29.

1:11 He came to that which was his own, but his own did not receive him. This sentence summarizes the public ministry of Jesus (chs. 1–12), which was characterized by rejection by "his own" (i.e., the Jews).

1:12–13 See *HC* 26.

1:12 Fallen human beings are not children of God by nature. Only those who have saving faith generated in them by the sovereign action of God (v. 13) have the privilege of being his children. See *WCF* 11.2; 12; 14.2; *WLC* 32,72–74; *WSC* 34,86; *HC* 33.

become children of God[q]— 13 children born not of natural descent,[a] nor of human decision or a husband's will, but born of God.[r]
14 The Word became flesh[s] and made his dwelling among us. We have seen his glory, the glory of the One and Only,[b] who came from the Father, full of grace and truth.[t]
15 John testifies[u] concerning him. He cries out, saying, "This was he of whom I said,
'He who comes after me has surpassed me because he was before me.' "[v] 16 From the fullness[w] of his grace we have all received one blessing after another. 17 For the law was giv-
en through Moses;[x] grace and truth came through Jesus Christ.[y] 18 No one has ever seen
God,[z] but God the One and Only,[b,c][a] who is at the Father's side, has made him known.

John the Baptist Denies Being the Christ

19 Now this was John's testimony when the Jews[b] of Jerusalem sent priests and Levites
to ask him who he was. 20 He did not fail to confess, but confessed freely, "I am not the
Christ.[d]"[c]
21 They asked him, "Then who are you? Are you Elijah?"[d]
He said, "I am not."
"Are you the Prophet?"[e]
He answered, "No."

[a] *13* Greek *of bloods* [b] *14,18* Or *the Only Begotten* [c] *18* Some manuscripts *but the only* (or *only begotten*) *Son* [d] *20* Or *Messiah.* "The Christ" (Greek) and "the Messiah" (Hebrew) both mean "the Anointed One"; also in verse 25.

1:12 [q]Gal 3:26
1:13 [r]Jn 3:6; Jas 1:18; 1Pe 1:23; 1Jn 3:9
1:14 [s]Gal 4:4; Php 2:7, 8; 1Ti 3:16; Heb 2:14 [t]Jn 14:6
1:15 [u]ver 7 [v]ver 30; Mt 3:11
1:16 [w]Eph 1:23; Col 1:19
1:17 [x]Jn 7:19 [y]ver 14
1:18 [z]Ex 33:20; Jn 6:46; Col 1:15; 1Ti 6:16 [a]Jn 3:16,18; 1Jn 4:9
1:19 [b]Jn 2:18; 5:10,16; 6:41,52
1:20 [c]Jn 3:28; Lk 3:15, 16
1:21 [d]Mt 11:14 [e]Dt 18:15

1:13 children born. This could be a precise description of the virgin birth of Christ (and was so understood in early Latin versions). Yet the plural verb rendered in English by the phrase "were born" relates this verse more properly to the new birth of believers (cf. 3.3,5,7–8). There is an analogy to Jesus' birth since, on the one hand, the Holy Spirit formed the human nature of Jesus in the Virgin Mary, and on the other hand, the Spirit implants the new life of God in those who are "dead in [their] transgressions and sins" (Eph 2:1). This is articulated more fully in John 3:1–21. In other passages, regeneration is presented as a resurrection (5:24; Ro 6:4–6; Eph 2:5–6; Col 2:13; 3:1). The sovereign and gracious action of God in salvation is emphasized without denying the human response in believing and receiving. See theological article "Regeneration and New Birth" at John 3.

1:14 The Word became flesh. The climactic assertion of the prologue, which was all but incredible to ancients. To some, gods were thought to visit in human likeness (Ac 14:11); to others, the spiritual and the divine were utterly opposed to matter and flesh. But here the chasm is bridged: The eternal Word of God did not merely *appear to be* or *seem to be* flesh, but he actually "became" flesh (i.e., he took upon himself a full and genuine human nature, including a human body). This true incarnation offended many. See theological article "Jesus Christ, God and Man" at John 1. **made his dwelling among us.** The verb translated "made his dwelling" means "made his tent" or "tabernacled." This language recalls Israel's tabernacle, which served as the place of God's presence on Earth in the days of Moses (Ex 40:34–35)—Jesus fulfilled that purpose in his incarnation. **We have seen his glory.** The Word is described in the language of the Mosaic literature. His "glory" is beheld, even as God's glory was beheld in the wilderness (Ex 16:1–10; 33:18–23), in the tabernacle (Ex 40:34–35) and later in the temple (1Ki 8:1–11). This may be a reference also to the transfiguration, since John was a witness of it (Mt 17:1–5). **glory.** Means "brilliance and wonder" and, secondarily, "honor, worth, significance." The term supremely applies to God, the Creator and Ruler of the universe before whom all people will one day bow. God's brilliance is increased and recognized when his creatures give him honor and praise. One of the mottoes of the Reformation was *Soli Deo Gloria* ("To God alone be the glory"). One of the major forms of sin, whether by Satan or by humans, is to seek to capture for self the glory that belongs to God. The Son, by contrast, being vested with divine glory (17:5), humbled himself in his incarnation and atoning death (Php 2:6–8) in order to mediate between God and fallen humanity. **the One and Only.** This phrase translates a single Greek word that highlights the supreme worth of the Word and the unique relationship between the Father and the Word. Traditionally, the alternate translation ("the Only Begotten"; see NIV text note) points to the eternal generation of the Son in the Trinity. This interpretation may make the most sense in light of verse 18. In Genesis, however, Isaac is called Abraham's "only son" (Ge 22:2,12,16)—despite the fact that Ishmael was already Abraham's son—making it apparent that the term may instead mean "special" or "unique." **full of grace and truth.** "Grace" and "truth" correspond to Old Testament terms that describe God's covenant mercy; they are often translated "love" and "faithfulness" (Ge 24:27; Ex 34:6; Pss 25:10; 26:3; Pr 16:6). The Word made flesh fully manifests the gracious covenant-making and covenant-keeping character of God. See *WCF* 2.3; 8.2–3; *WLC* 10,36–37,47; *WSC* 21; *BC* 8,10,17; *HC* 35,48.

1:15 John the Baptist's ministry preceded in time the public ministry of Jesus (Mt 3). Yet the Word, being eternal, existed before John (cf. 8:58).

1:16 his grace. The word "grace," frequent in Paul's epistles, appears only here (vv. 14,16–17) and in Revelation 1:4 in the writings of John. It emphasizes the merciful character of salvation. See *WCF* 26.1; *WLC* 174.

1:17 For the law was given through Moses; grace and truth came through Jesus Christ. The reference is one of comparison: "Grace" and "truth" derived from the writings of Moses (Ge 24:27; Ex 34:6), yet they have assumed far greater proportions in the coming of Christ (Ro 5:20).

1:18 No one has ever seen God. In the Mosaic revelation, God forbade people to look at himself, on pain of death (Ex. 33:18–23). But occasionally God showed his grace by giving to some men partial visions of himself (Ge 32:30; Ex 24:9-11; Nu 12:8). Now One who is God himself had come in the flesh to make God manifest to the human race (cf. 6:46). See *WCF* 2.3; *WLC* 10,43,47; *WSC* 24; *BC* 10; *HC* 21.

■ **1:19—12:50** *Jesus' Public Ministry.* John reported Jesus' life first in terms of his public ministry in Jerusalem, Judea and Galilee. His record focused on Jesus' geographical movements and on how he performed signs, taught his ways and encountered both rejection and acceptance. During Jesus' ministry, those who had been given to Christ by the Father (6:37) responded in faith despite the rejection he encountered from the community at large. Their stories illustrate the process of becoming a true disciple and of believing all that this Gospel reveals about Jesus. This section of John's account divides into five main parts: the beginnings of Jesus' ministry (1:19–51), events as he traveled back and forth between Cana (in Galilee) and Judea (2:1—4:54), a brief visit to Jerusalem (5:1–47), his ministry in Galilee (6:1–71) and a variety of events in and near Jerusalem during several feasts (7:1—12:50).

■ **1:19–51** *The Ministry Begins.* John opened his narrative of Jesus' life with Jesus' introduction to the public through the ministry of John the Baptist (vv. 19–34). Then he turned to Jesus' selection of his first disciples (vv. 35–51). In both sections, witness is given to Jesus' heavenly origin and God's purpose for sending him.

■ **1:19–34** *Jesus' Witness: John the Baptist.* John the Baptist denied that he was the Messiah and pointed to Jesus as the One sent by the Father to save the world.

1:21 "Are you Elijah?" . . . "I am not." Jesus, in obvious reference to Malachi 4:5, told the crowd that John was "the Elijah who was to come" (Mt 11:14). This was true insofar as John came in the spirit and power of Elijah and performed a similar role. There is no reason to believe that the Jews expected an actual reappearance or reincarnation of Elijah himself. **"Are you the Prophet?"** There were different expectations among first-century Jews concerning the great "prophet like [Moses]" (Dt 18:15). Here the priests and Levites wished to know whether John considered himself to be this prophet.

22Finally they said, "Who are you? Give us an answer to take back to those who sent
us. What do you say about yourself?"
23John replied in the words of Isaiah the prophet, "I am the voice of one calling in the
desert,[f] 'Make straight the way for the Lord.' "[a g]
24Now some Pharisees who had been sent 25questioned him, "Why then do you baptize if you are not the Christ, nor Elijah, nor the Prophet?"

1:23 [f]Mt 3:1 [g]Isa 40:3

[a] *23* Isaiah 40:3

1:23 In quoting Isaiah 40:3, John bore witness to the deity of Christ by applying to Christ what was said of Yahweh in that passage (see Mk 1:1–3).

Jesus Christ, God and Man: How Can a Man Be God?

REFORMED theology has consistently affirmed both the full humanity and full divinity of Jesus. Traditionally, this has been called the doctrine of the *hypostatic union*, a doctrine that expresses the perfect union between Jesus' divine and human natures in his one person. In this union, the second person of the Trinity (see theological article "The Trinity" at Jn 14), namely God the Son, became fully human (see theological article "The Full Humanity of Christ" at Lk 3) without losing any of his divine attributes.

That the Jewish followers of Jesus believed that Jesus was both God and man is amazing. Jesus' apostles and most of the New Testament writers were Jews who strongly believed that there is only one God and that no human is divine. Nevertheless, they all taught that Jesus the Messiah should be worshiped and trusted as God. This idea is especially observable in the writings of John, Paul, Peter and the author of Hebrews.

John revealed Jesus as the eternal, divine Word, agent of creation and source of all life and light (Jn 1:1–5,9), who, in becoming "flesh," was revealed as the Son of God, the source of grace and truth—and, indeed, as "God the One and Only" (Jn 1:14,18). John's Gospel is punctuated with Jesus' "I am" statements—these are especially significant because "I am" (see notes on Jn 8:24,28,58) was used to render God's name in the Greek translation (Septuagint) of Exodus 3:14. Examples also appear in the seven declarations of Jesus' grace as (1) the bread of life, giving spiritual food (Jn 6:35,48,51); (2) the light of the world, banishing darkness (Jn 8:12; 9:5); (3) the gate for the sheep, giving access to God (Jn 10:7,9); (4) the good shepherd, protecting from peril (Jn 10:11,14); (5) the resurrection and life, overcoming our death (Jn 11:25); (6) the way, truth and life, guiding to fellowship with the Father (Jn 14:6); and (7) the true vine, nurturing for fruitfulness (Jn 15:1,5). Climactically, Thomas worshiped Jesus, declaring, "My Lord and my God" (Jn 20:28). Jesus then pronounced a blessing on all those who shared Thomas's faith, and John urged his readers to join their number (Jn 20:29–31).

Paul quoted from an apparent hymn that declares Jesus' personal deity (Php 2:6–11). He stated that "in Christ all the fullness of the Deity lives in bodily form" (Col 2:9; cf. Col 1:19). He hailed Jesus as the Son, as the Father's image and as his agent in creating and upholding everything (Col 1:15–17). He declared him to be "Lord" (a title with divine overtones), to whom one must pray for salvation according to the exhortation in Joel 2:32 to call on God (Ro 10:9–13). He called him "God over all" (Ro 9:5) and "God and Savior" (Tit 2:13), and he prayed to him personally (2Co 12:8–9), looking to him as a source of divine grace (2Co 13:14). The testimony is explicit: Faith in Jesus' deity is central to Paul's theology.

In explaining Christ's perfect high priesthood, the author of Hebrews declared the full deity and resulting unique dignity of the Son of God (Heb 1:3,6, 8–12), whose full humanity is then celebrated in chapter 2. The perfection, and indeed the very possibility, of the high priesthood he ascribed to Christ depends on an endless, unfailing divine life in combination with a full human experience of temptation, pressure and pain (Heb 2:14–18; 4:14—5:2; 7:13–28; 12:2–3).

No less significant is Peter's use of Isaiah 8:12–13 (1Pe 3:14). He cited the Greek (Septuagint) version of the Old Testament, urging the churches not to fear what others fear, but to set apart the Lord as holy. But where the Septuagint text of Isaiah says "Set apart the Lord himself," Peter wrote, "set apart Christ as Lord" (1Pe 3:15). Peter offered the adoring fear due to the Almighty to Jesus of Nazareth, his Master and Lord.

A crucial time for the church's affirmation of the hypostatic union came at the Council of Chalcedon (A.D. 451). At that time, the church countered two errors: (1) the Nestorian idea that Jesus had two "persons" (divine and human), as well as two natures, as if he were two people bound together in one body; and (2) the Eutychian idea that Jesus had only one nature, his divinity having absorbed his humanity. Rejecting both, the Council affirmed that Jesus is one divine-human person with two natures (i.e., two sets of capacities for experience, expression, reaction and action) and that the two natures are united in his personal being without mixture, confusion, separation or division, such that each nature retains its own attributes.

The New Testament reveals the great mystery that Jesus is both fully God and fully human. All that God made us to be, as well as all that is in God himself, was, is and forever will be really and distinguishably present in the one person of Jesus. The New Testament commands the worship of Jesus and focuses consistently on the divine-human Savior and Lord as the proper object of faith, hope and love.

26“I baptize with[a] water,” John replied, “but among you stands one you do not know.
27He is the one who comes after me,[h] the thongs of whose sandals I am not worthy to
untie.”
28This all happened at Bethany on the other side of the Jordan,[i] where John was baptizing.

Jesus the Lamb of God

29The next day John saw Jesus coming toward him and said, “Look, the Lamb of God,[j]
who takes away the sin of the world! 30This is the one I meant when I said, ‘A man who
comes after me has surpassed me because he was before me.’[k] 31I myself did not know
him, but the reason I came baptizing with water was that he might be revealed to Israel.”
32Then John gave this testimony: “I saw the Spirit come down from heaven as a dove
and remain on him.[l] 33I would not have known him, except that the one who sent me to
baptize with water[m] told me, ‘The man on whom you see the Spirit come down and remain is he who will baptize with the Holy Spirit.’[n] 34I have seen and I testify that this is
the Son of God.”[o]

Jesus’ First Disciples

35The next day John[p] was there again with two of his disciples. 36When he saw Jesus
passing by, he said, “Look, the Lamb of God!”[q]
37When the two disciples heard him say this, they followed Jesus. 38Turning around,
Jesus saw them following and asked, “What do you want?”
They said, “Rabbi”[r] (which means Teacher), “where are you staying?”
39“Come,” he replied, “and you will see.”
So they went and saw where he was staying, and spent that day with him. It was
about the tenth hour.
40Andrew, Simon Peter’s brother, was one of the two who heard what John had said
and who had followed Jesus. 41The first thing Andrew did was to find his brother Simon
and tell him, “We have found the Messiah” (that is, the Christ).[s] 42And he brought him
to Jesus.
Jesus looked at him and said, “You are Simon son of John. You will be called[t] Cephas”
(which, when translated, is Peter[b]).[u]

Jesus Calls Philip and Nathanael

43The next day Jesus decided to leave for Galilee. Finding Philip,[v] he said to him, “Follow me.”[w]
44Philip, like Andrew and Peter, was from the town of Bethsaida.[x] 45Philip found Na-

1:27 [h]ver 15,30
1:28 [i]Jn 3:26; 10:40
1:29 [j]ver 36; Isa 53:7; 1Pe 1:19; Rev 5:6
1:30 [k]ver 15,27
1:32 [l]Mt 3:16; Mk 1:10
1:33 [m]Mk 1:4 [n]Mt 3:11; Mk 1:8
1:34 [o]ver 49; Mt 4:3
1:35 [p]Mt 3:1
1:36 [q]ver 29
1:38 [r]ver 49; Mt 23:7
1:41 [s]Jn 4:25
1:42 [t]Ge 17:5,15 [u]Mt 16:18
1:43 [v]Mt 10:3; Jn 6:5-7; 12:21,22; 14:8,9 [w]Mt 4:19
1:44 [x]Mt 11:21; Jn 12:21

a *26* Or *in*; also in verses 31 and 33 b *42* Both *Cephas* (Aramaic) and *Peter* (Greek) mean *rock*.

1:28 Bethany. Not the Bethany near Jerusalem (which was the home of Martha and Mary).
1:29 Look, the Lamb of God. Compare verse 36. Whether this is a reference to the Passover lamb (Ex 12:1–11) or to the servant lamb (Isa 53) cannot be easily determined. There is some evidence that the two figures were already combined in the Jewish thought of this period. **who takes away the sin of the world!** Not an affirmation of universal salvation. Rather, the term “world” is used here to designate humanity as a whole in its hostility to God—a use not uncommon in this Gospel. The Baptist did not know or say how many individuals within this hostile world will actually have their sins taken away. Regardless of how many are saved, this remnant of redeemed people will comprise the salvation of the human race. Those who are not redeemed will be removed to a place of eternal punishment where they will no longer be able to influence the affairs of the world. The Baptist made it plain that only by the sacrifice of Jesus can any human sin be forgiven.
1:31 I . . . did not know him. Though John the Baptist may have had previous personal contact with Jesus (cf. Lk 1:39–45), he did not know that Jesus was the Lamb and Son of God until the Spirit so identified him (v. 32). John the Baptist functioned as a witness who, through his ministry, pointed to the identity and significance of Jesus. Witness to Jesus is a central theme in this Gospel, and the Baptist’s witness is followed shortly by that of several others (vv. 35–51).
1:33 who will baptize with the Holy Spirit. The Old Testament anticipated the day of redemption after the exile as the day when the Spirit would be poured out on God’s people (e.g., Joel 2:28ff.). Christ gives the heavenly gift of the Spirit to his people as part of their inheritance in him (2Co 1:22; 5:5; Eph 1:13–14). Jesus promised that, after he returned to heaven, he would send this heavenly Counselor to dwell with his people on earth (14:26; 16:7). The baptism of the Holy Spirit occurs at the time of the new birth (1:12–13; 1Co 12:13) and empowers believers for Christian service (Lk 24:49; Ac 1:8). See *WCF* 28.2; *WLC* 176; *BC* 9.
1:34 this is the Son of God. John’s way of recording the heavenly voice that accompanied the heaven-sent Spirit (see Mt 3:17). While the term “son of God” was used variously by Jews (2Sa 7:14; Ps 2:7) and Gentiles (see note on Mk 15:39), the Baptist’s witness (the last of the prophets of the old order; Mt 11:11–14) is clear: Jesus is the unique Son of God, the “One and Only, who came from the Father” (v. 14). See *BC* 10.
■ **1:35–51** *Jesus’ Witnesses: His First Disciples.* Jesus’ first disciples testified that Jesus was the Messiah sent from heaven. Jesus called his first disciples. Since the apostles had unique authority from Christ to bear witness—the witness on which the church would be established (Eph 2:20)—it was necessary that they be particularly identified as having been selected by Christ himself (cf. 15:16).
1:37 they followed. They physically followed Jesus, but more is in view. Upon the Baptist’s witness, these men began the journey of becoming disciples of Jesus. The idea of “following Jesus” takes on deeper levels of meaning as the Gospel progresses (13:36–38; cf. 21:15–22).
1:39 the tenth hour. 4:00 P.M. The precise time of day would have remained indelibly impressed in the mind of one for whom this encounter was a life-changing experience. This is an argument for the view that the apostle John is the author of this Gospel.

thanael[y] and told him, "We have found the one Moses wrote about in the Law,[z] and
about whom the prophets also wrote[a]—Jesus of Nazareth,[b] the son of Joseph."[c]
46 "Nazareth! Can anything good come from there?"[d] Nathanael asked.
"Come and see," said Philip.
47 When Jesus saw Nathanael approaching, he said of him, "Here is a true Israelite,[e]
in whom there is nothing false."[f]
48 "How do you know me?" Nathanael asked.
Jesus answered, "I saw you while you were still under the fig tree before Philip called
you."
49 Then Nathanael declared, "Rabbi,[g] you are the Son of God;[h] you are the King of Israel."[i]
50 Jesus said, "You believe[a] because I told you I saw you under the fig tree. You shall
see greater things than that." 51 He then added, "I tell you[b] the truth, you[b] shall see heav-
en open,[j] and the angels of God ascending and descending[k] on the Son of Man."[l]

Jesus Changes Water to Wine

2 On the third day a wedding took place at Cana in Galilee.[m] Jesus' mother[n] was
there, 2 and Jesus and his disciples had also been invited to the wedding. 3 When the
wine was gone, Jesus' mother said to him, "They have no more wine."
4 "Dear woman,[o] why do you involve me?"[p] Jesus replied. "My time[q] has not yet
come."
5 His mother said to the servants, "Do whatever he tells you."[r]
6 Nearby stood six stone water jars, the kind used by the Jews for ceremonial washing,[s] each holding from twenty to thirty gallons.[c]
7 Jesus said to the servants, "Fill the jars with water"; so they filled them to the brim.
8 Then he told them, "Now draw some out and take it to the master of the banquet."

1:45 [y]Jn 21:2 [z]Lk 24:27 [a]Lk 24:27 [b]Mt 2:23; Mk 1:24 [c]Lk 3:23
1:46 [d]Jn 7:41,42,52
1:47 [e]Ro 9:4,6 [f]Ps 32:2
1:49 [g]ver 38; Mt 23:7 [h]ver 34; Mt 4:3 [i]Mt 2:2; 27:42; Jn 12:13
1:51 [j]Mt 3:16 [k]Ge 28:12 [l]Mt 8:20
2:1 [m]Jn 4:46; 21:2 [n]Mt 12:46
2:4 [o]Jn 19:26 [p]Mt 8:29 [q]Mt 26:18; Jn 7:6
2:5 [r]Ge 41:55
2:6 [s]Mk 7:3,4; Jn 3:25

[a] *50* Or *Do you believe . . . ?* [b] *51* The Greek is plural. [c] *6* Greek *two to three metretes* (probably about 75 to 115 liters)

1:45 the one Moses wrote about in the Law, and about whom the prophets also wrote. Faithful Jews had placed all of their hopes in the promises of the Old Testament. Philip recognized that all of the Old Testament promises, both in the Law and in the Prophets, were fulfilled by Christ (Lk 24:25–27,44–47). This method was the typical way the apostles proclaimed Christ, especially to Jewish listeners (Ac 2:29–32; 3:18,21,24; 7:52–53; 8:30–35; 26:22–23; 28:23). **the son of Joseph.** Not a denial of the Virgin Birth, of which Philip may not even have been aware. It is simply a reference indicating that Joseph became the legal, adoptive father of Jesus (Mt 1:24–25).
1:46 Can anything good come from there? It is not clear whether this was a local saying that reflected jealousy between Nathanael's hometown of Cana (21:2) and Nazareth or whether it was a reflection of skepticism that a prophet would arise from Galilee (7:52). Nazareth was utterly insignificant as a village, and it is never mentioned in the Old Testament or in Jewish literature of the period. Nathanael's incredulity may well have derived from the contrast between the exalted notion of the Messiah and the lack of distinction attached to the village. But Jesus' coming from lowly Nazareth fits with the Gospel's portrayal of his humility.
1:47 a true Israelite. The implication is possibly that Nathanael was a "true" Israelite in the sense that he was about to encounter the one whom Israel had awaited (see note on 4:24). This phrase may also allude to verses 50–51, where this "true Israelite" is promised an experience similar to that of the first Israel (i.e., Jacob; Ge 28:12ff.; 32:28), whose deceitful character was transformed by God.
1:48 I saw you. That Jesus' words convinced Nathanael of Jesus' Messiahship probably indicates that Jesus had a supernatural revelation regarding Nathanael.
1:49 "Rabbi, you are the Son of God . . . the King of Israel." Philip had perhaps already indicated to Nathanael that Jesus was the One anticipated by the Law and the Prophets (v. 45). Nathanael came to Jesus looking for reason to believe or disbelieve, and he found Jesus' knowledge convincing (see note on v. 48). **the Son of God.** Some Old Testament passages suggest that this was a title for royalty (2Sa 7:14; Pss 2:7; 89:27). It may also be that this title, even when expressed at this early point in Jesus' ministry, implied a recognition of divinity (v. 34). **King of Israel.** This was a royal title, used later on Palm Sunday (12:13), and it approximated the inscription on the cross (19:19). It was supremely fulfilled in the name "Lord of lords and King of kings" (Rev 17:14; see also Rev 19:16).
1:51 heaven open, and the angels of God ascending and descending. Alludes to Jacob's vision of a stairway that stretched between heaven and Earth, with the angels of God "ascending and descending on it" (Ge 28:10–15). In Jesus' testimony, he is the reality to which the stairway pointed. Much like John described Jesus as the tabernacle (see note on v. 14), here Jesus is described as the bridge that reunites heaven and Earth, restoring the relationship with God that was lost in the garden when Adam and Eve were banished from God's presence. Though Jacob could only dream of the reunion of heaven and Earth, Jesus Christ established that reunion. **Son of Man.** A frequent self-designation of Jesus that conveyed not only his humanity, but also, more specifically, his Messianic function and dignity (see note on Mk 2:10).
■ **2:1—4:54** *From Cana to Cana.* Beginning in Cana (2:1), and returning there after traveling about (4:46), Jesus performed signs, explained his ministry and faced both positive and negative reactions. John's record divides into six main parts (see "Introduction: Outline").
■ **2:1–11** *The Wedding in Cana.* This is the first miracle, or sign, in John's Gospel. It anticipates the transformation of the old order (signified by the stone water jars used for ceremonial washing; v. 6) into the new (the wine signifies eternal life in God's kingdom) through Jesus Christ (cf. 2Co 5:17). See Isaiah 25:6–9 for the background image of salvation as a banquet.
2:3 wine. The normal term employed in the New Testament for the fermented juice of the vine (e.g., Eph 5:18).
2:4 Dear woman. Literally, "O woman." In the original, it is a respectful way of addressing a woman, and it was the way Jesus normally addressed women (e.g., 19:26). What is unusual and without known precedent is the usage of this expression in speaking to one's own mother. In employing this expression, Jesus was not denying his relation to Mary (nor was John, who called Mary "Jesus' mother" four times in this passage). Rather, as Jesus began his public ministry, he made it clear that his heavenly Father, not any human being (including any close relative), directed his works and words (8:28–29). **My time.** Literally, "My hour." Most frequently it refers to Jesus' time of passion or suffering (12:27). However, it also can refer to his Messianic work in its entirety ("a time is coming and has now come"; 4:23). In this latter context, Jesus was asserting that under the Father's direction he, not Mary, was to control the timetable of his Messianic activity. Nevertheless, he did determine, for her sake and for ours, here to provide a foretaste of the coming Messianic banquet.

They did so, 9 and the master of the banquet tasted the water that had been turned
into wine.[t] He did not realize where it had come from, though the servants who had
drawn the water knew. Then he called the bridegroom aside 10 and said, "Everyone
brings out the choice wine first and then the cheaper wine after the guests have had too
much to drink; but you have saved the best till now."
11 This, the first of his miraculous signs,[u] Jesus performed at Cana in Galilee. He thus
revealed his glory,[v] and his disciples put their faith in him.[w]

Jesus Clears the Temple

12 After this he went down to Capernaum[x] with his mother and brothers[y] and his disciples. There they stayed for a few days.
13 When it was almost time for the Jewish Passover,[z] Jesus went up to Jerusalem.[a] 14 In
the temple courts he found men selling cattle, sheep and doves, and others sitting at tables exchanging money. 15 So he made a whip out of cords, and drove all from the temple area, both sheep and cattle; he scattered the coins of the money changers and overturned their tables. 16 To those who sold doves he said, "Get these out of here! How dare
you turn my Father's house[b] into a market!"
17 His disciples remembered that it is written: "Zeal for your house will consume me."[a][c]
18 Then the Jews demanded of him, "What miraculous sign can you show us to prove
your authority to do all this?"[d]
19 Jesus answered them, "Destroy this temple, and I will raise it again in three days."[e]
20 The Jews replied, "It has taken forty-six years to build this temple, and you are going to raise it in three days?" 21 But the temple he had spoken of was his body.[f] 22 After
he was raised from the dead, his disciples recalled what he had said.[g] Then they believed
the Scripture and the words that Jesus had spoken.
23 Now while he was in Jerusalem at the Passover Feast,[h] many people saw the miraculous signs he was doing and believed in his name.[b] 24 But Jesus would not entrust himself to them, for he knew all men. 25 He did not need man's testimony about man, for he
knew what was in a man.[i]

Jesus Teaches Nicodemus

3 Now there was a man of the Pharisees named Nicodemus,[j] a member of the Jewish ruling council.[k] 2 He came to Jesus at night and said, "Rabbi, we know you are

2:9 [t]Jn 4:46
2:11 [u]ver 23; Jn 3:2; 4:48; 6:2, 14, 26, 30; 12:37; 20:30 [v]Jn 1:14 [w]Ex 14:31
2:12 [x]Mt 4:13 [y]Mt 12:46
2:13 [z]Jn 11:55 [a]Dt 16:1-6; Lk 2:41
2:16 [b]Lk 2:49
2:17 [c]Ps 69:9
2:18 [d]Mt 12:38
2:19 [e]Mt 26:61; 27:40; Mk 14:58; 15:29
2:21 [f]1Co 6:19
2:22 [g]Lk 24:5-8; Jn 12:16; 14:26
2:23 [h]ver 13
2:25 [i]Mt 9:4; Jn 6:61, 64; 13:11
3:1 [j]Jn 7:50; 19:39 [k]Lk 23:13

a *17* Psalm 69:9 b *23* Or *and believed in him*

2:11 revealed his glory. We have already been introduced to the theme of Jesus' glory (1:14). Here, in the visible act of the miracle, that glory is made manifest. In the Old Testament, God demonstrated his glory in a variety of miraculous events, and this comment indicates that John wished his readers to recognize Jesus' divinity. **and his disciples put their faith in him.** See verse 23 and 20:30 31, where John's purpose for writing the book is disclosed.

■ **2:12–25** *Cleansing of the Temple.* John briefly interrupted his narrative to describe what Jesus did in the temple in Jerusalem. This event clearly reveals Jesus' outlook on the most central religious institution in Israel at the time and his own relationship to that temple. Jesus' actions elicited positive responses from the crowds in Jerusalem, but Jesus discerned that their reactions were superficial. Just as Jesus elsewhere brought to final expression what was only a shadow in the Old Testament (Heb 10:1), so here he indicated that he is indeed the One in whom God's presence dwells. The temple in Jerusalem could be destroyed, but not the temple that Jesus would rebuild in three days (his own body, which was to be raised from the dead). The placement of the temple cleansing immediately after the miracle at Cana offers an important key to the whole of Jesus' ministry. These events signaled the superseding of the old order (the water of ceremonial cleansing and Herod's temple) and the coming of the new (the wine of salvation [Isa 25:6–9] and the risen Lamb as the new temple [Rev 21:22]). The Gospels of Matthew, Mark and Luke report a cleansing of the temple in the last week of Jesus' life on Earth. In spite of some similarities, this may well be a different incident. It is noteworthy that Jesus' statement about destroying the temple, which John alone records (v. 19), probably was the basis for the accusation of the false witnesses (Mt 26:61; Mk 14:58) and for the taunting comment of some spectators of the crucifixion (Mt 27:40; Mk 15:29).

2:12 and brothers. See Matthew 12:46.

2:15 he made a whip out of cords. Jesus here began the fulfillment of the prophecy of Malachi 3:1–4. He came suddenly to the temple and purified the sons of Levi, demonstrating his zeal for God and for God's holy ordinances.

2:19 See *WLC* 145.

2:20 It has taken forty-six years to build this temple. In the original language, this sentence can indicate either that the temple had been completed or that it had been in the process of being built for 46 years. Josephus (*Antiquities*, 15.380) reports that the temple construction began in the 18th year of Herod the Great (around 20 or 19 B.C.). If this is the case, then 46 years of construction had indeed taken place. Josephus also reports (*Antiquities*, 20.219) that the temple was not completed until the reign of Herod Agrippa (A.D. 64). If this is correct, then the 46 years of construction had not yet brought the temple to its completion. **you are going to raise it in three days?** The Jews (and the disciples; see v. 22) misunderstood a statement by Jesus that had more than one meaning. Such initial misunderstandings are common in John's Gospel (e.g., 3:4; 6:52). Those who "received him" (1:12) were led by Jesus to understand as he revealed himself to them, while those who rejected him outright remained at the level of complete misunderstanding (see 1:5).

2:22 his disciples recalled. In the farewell discourse, Jesus explained that the Holy Spirit would bring to the disciples' remembrance what he had taught them (14:25–26).

2:23 believed in his name. In Biblical times a name summed up that person's character, activity and place in God's purpose. The name *Jesus* had been given by express divine direction (Mt 1:21). The faith of those mentioned here remained superficial, and Jesus knew it.

2:24–25 See *WLC* 11.

■ **3:1–21** *Entering the Kingdom.* Jesus' first discourse. He met with Nicodemus and discussed the nature of the new order he was initiating. Jesus' discourses typically began with someone asking a question; Jesus then answered in a way that steered the discussion into a deeper realm, often pointing out misunderstandings that

3:2 ˡJn 9:16,33 ᵐAc 2:22; 10:38
3:3 ⁿJn 1:13; 1Pe 1:23
3:5 ᵒTit 3:5

a teacher who has come from God. For no one could perform the miraculous signs[l] you
are doing if God were not with him."[m]
3In reply Jesus declared, "I tell you the truth, no one can see the kingdom of God unless he is born again.[a]"[n]
4"How can a man be born when he is old?" Nicodemus asked. "Surely he cannot enter a second time into his mother's womb to be born!"
5Jesus answered, "I tell you the truth, no one can enter the kingdom of God unless
he is born of water and the Spirit.[o] 6Flesh gives birth to flesh, but the Spirit[b] gives birth

[a] 3 Or *born from above*; also in verse 7 [b] 6 Or *but spirit*

Jesus corrected. The new understanding that was achieved enabled the believer to confess Jesus more fully and accurately.
3:2 at night. Perhaps Nicodemus was afraid of being observed and so avoided making his visit by daylight. His time choice might also indicate deference to Jesus, in that he may have resisted distracting a rabbi during the day. Understood symbolically, Nicodemus represents a person living in the darkness of this world who encounters the light (cf. 9:4; 11:10; 13:30). **Rabbi, we know you are a teacher.** Points to Nicodemus's understanding that God attests his messengers or agents of revelation by giving them power to perform miracles. But such understanding falls far short of confessing fully who Jesus is.
3:3–5 See *HC* 8.
3:3 unless he is born again. The Greek term translated "again" may also be rendered "from above." This alternate rendering accords well with the discussion of "earthly" and "heavenly" things in verse 12, and with the discussion of Jesus ascending and descending in verse 13. It is also used in other places in this Gospel (19:11,23). On the other hand, the equivalent term "rebirth" (Tit 3:5) favors the meaning "born again." It is possible that Jesus was purposefully ambiguous, implying a new birth that is also a birth from above. Such ambiguity set up Nicodemus's first misunderstanding (v. 4), which in turn spurred the rest of the conversation. See theological article "Regeneration and New Birth," below. See also *WCF* 10.3.
3:5–8 See *HC* 70.
3:5 born of water and the Spirit. This enigmatic phrase has elicited much discussion and a number of proposed solutions. (1) The "water" in view is the release of amniotic fluid that accompanies physical birth. But nowhere else in Scripture does the word

Regeneration and New Birth: Must I Be Born Again?

IN Reformed theology *regeneration*, the equivalent to being "born again," is a technical term referring to God revitalizing a person by implanting new desire, purpose and moral ability that lead to a positive response to the gospel of Christ. The Greek word (*palingenesis*) from which theologians derive the term "regeneration" appears only twice in Scripture. In Matthew 19:28 Jesus spoke of the "renewal" of the universe at his second coming as *palingenesis*. In this case, the term refers to a "second genesis" or "second beginning" for the universe, rather than the individual renewal normally indicated by the theological term "regeneration." Second, Paul described baptism as "the washing of rebirth" (Tit 3:5). Although some have taken this as a reference to the recreation of the heavens and earth that will be completed when Jesus returns, traditionally Paul has been understood as speaking of the individual regeneration of the person baptized. It is this latter meaning that theologians have adopted for technical use.

Jesus taught this concept to Nicodemus when he said, "No one can see the kingdom of God unless he is born again" (Jn 3:3), indicating the depth of the change that even religious Jews were required to undergo if they are were ever to have eternal life. The Greek expression translated "born again" can also be translated "born from above" (see text notes on Jn 3:3,7). It is likely that Jesus had both meanings in mind. On the one hand, those who are dead in sin need to be given new life in what might be thought of as "spiritual birth," so that in some sense they undergo a second birth. On the other hand, as Jesus himself came from heaven (Jn 3:13), those who enter his kingdom must receive life from God who is in heaven (Jn 3:3,7). As John put it elsewhere, we must be "born of God" (Jn 1:13; 1Jn 3:9; 4:7; 5:1,4,18). This new birth brought by the Spirit (Jn 3:8) enlivens people to the things of God and gives them new lives of service to Christ.

In all events, we may think about regeneration and being "born again" in ways very similar to the New Testament concept of the new creation. The new creation is an objective reality brought about by Christ. When individuals are joined to Christ through faith in him, they become part of the new creation (2Co 5:17). In much the same way as Jesus spoke of the regeneration ("renewal") of the universe (Mt 19:28), it is appropriate to speak of the personal regeneration ("rebirth") of those who are in Christ.

The Reformed view of regeneration may be set apart from other outlooks in at least two ways. First, classical Roman Catholicism teaches that regeneration occurs at baptism, a view known as *baptismal regeneration*. Reformed theology has insisted that regeneration may take place at any time in a person's life, even in the womb (*WCF* 10.3). It is not somehow the automatic result of baptism (*WCF* 28.1,6).

Second, it is common for many other evangelical branches of the church to speak of repentance and faith leading to regeneration (i.e., people are born again only after they exercise saving faith). By contrast, Reformed theology teaches that original sin and total depravity deprive all people of the moral ability and will to exercise saving faith. For this reason, regeneration precedes repentance and saving faith. Without regeneration, we cannot even see the kingdom of God (Jn 3:3). After we are born of God, we have the ability to believe in and follow Christ. Regeneration is entirely the work of God the Holy Spirit—we can do nothing on our own to obtain it. God alone raises the elect from spiritual death to new life in Christ (Eph 2:1–10). Regeneration is God's miraculous work taking us to conscious, intentional, active faith in Christ.

to spirit.[p] **7**You should not be surprised at my saying, 'You[a] must be born again.' **8**The
wind blows wherever it pleases. You hear its sound, but you cannot tell where it comes
from or where it is going. So it is with everyone born of the Spirit."
9"How can this be?"[q] Nicodemus asked.
10"You are Israel's teacher,"[r] said Jesus, "and do you not understand these things?
11I tell you the truth, we speak of what we know,[s] and we testify to what we have seen,
but still you people do not accept our testimony.[t] **12**I have spoken to you of earthly things
and you do not believe; how then will you believe if I speak of heavenly things? **13**No one
has ever gone into heaven[u] except the one who came from heaven[v]—the Son of Man.[b]
14Just as Moses lifted up the snake in the desert,[w] so the Son of Man must be lifted up,[x]
15that everyone who believes[y] in him may have eternal life.[c]
16"For God so loved[z] the world that he gave his one and only Son,[d] that whoever believes in him shall not perish but have eternal life.[a] **17**For God did not send his Son into
the world[b] to condemn the world, but to save the world through him.[c] **18**Whoever believes in him is not condemned,[d] but whoever does not believe stands condemned already because he has not believed in the name of God's one and only Son.[e][e] **19**This is the
verdict: Light[f] has come into the world, but men loved darkness instead of light because
their deeds were evil. **20**Everyone who does evil hates the light, and will not come into
the light for fear that his deeds will be exposed.[g] **21**But whoever lives by the truth comes
into the light, so that it may be seen plainly that what he has done has been done
through God."[f]

John the Baptist's Testimony About Jesus

22After this, Jesus and his disciples went out into the Judean countryside, where he

3:6 [p]Jn 1:13; 1Co 15:50
3:9 [q]Jn 6:52,60
3:10 [r]Lk 2:46
3:11 [s]Jn 1:18; 7:16,17 [t]ver 32
3:13 [u]Pr 30:4; Ac 2:34; Eph 4:8-10 [v]Jn 6:38,42
3:14 [w]Nu 21:8,9 [x]Jn 8:28; 12:32
3:15 [y]ver 16,36
3:16 [z]Ro 5:8; Eph 2:4; 1Jn 4:9,10 [a]ver 36; Jn 6:29,40; 11:25,26
3:17 [b]Jn 6:29,57; 10:36; 11:42; 17:8,21; 20:21 [c]Jn 12:47; 1Jn 4:14
3:18 [d]Jn 5:24 [e]1Jn 4:9
3:19 [f]Jn 1:4; 8:12
3:20 [g]Eph 5:11,13

[a] *7* The Greek is plural. [b] *13* Some manuscripts *Man, who is in heaven* [c] *15* Or *believes may have eternal life in him* [d] *16* Or *his only begotten Son* [e] *18* Or *God's only begotten Son* [f] *21* Some interpreters end the quotation after verse 15.

"water" refer to amniotic fluid. (2) The "water" here refers to the water of Christian baptism. But such a reference, which would have preceded the institution of that rite, would have been meaningless to Nicodemus. (3) The "water" is an allusion to Old Testament passages in which the terms "water" and "Spirit" are linked to express the pouring out of God's Spirit in the latter days, or end times (e.g., Isa 32:15; 44:3; Eze 36:25–27; see also theological article "The Plan of the Ages" at Heb 7). The presence of such rich Old Testament imagery would account for Jesus' reproof of Nicodemus in verse 10. (4) The "water" here refers to John's baptism. Like Christian baptism, John's baptism signified cleansing from sin. Such cleansing is coupled with the positive renewing work of the Spirit in Psalm 51:7–12 (cf. Tit. 3:5), and the Old Testament mentions the coming of water together with the Spirit in the latter days (see above). This view offers the most parallels to the Old Testament and makes sense in light of the mention of John the Baptist in chapters 1 and 3. See *WCF* 10.3; 28.6, *HC* 21,65.

3:6 See *WLC* 26; *BC* 15,35.

3:8 See *WCF* 10.3; 28.6.

3:11 I tell you . . . you people do not accept our testimony. The first "you" is singular (i.e., Nicodemus), the second plural (i.e., you and those whom you represent).

3:13 who came from heaven. Jesus asserted his qualification to speak of heavenly things: He alone had come down from heaven. Later Jesus' origin "from above" became a chief issue of dispute (6:41–42). **the Son of Man.** See notes on 1:51 and Mark 2:10. See also *WCF* 8.7; *HC* 48.

3:14 Moses. Numbers 21:4–9 records the story of the bronze serpent, which was a type of Christ. As the Israelites were saved from fiery serpents by fixing their gaze on the uplifted bronze serpent, so we are saved from eternal judgment by looking to Christ, who was lifted up. **must be lifted up.** A key term in this Gospel (8:28; 12:32,34). It carries the double meaning of crucifixion and exaltation. John's Gospel views Jesus' death on the cross, his resurrection and his glorification as aspects of one event that reveals the glory of God. The word "must" points to God's sovereign purpose. Even the crucifixion was part of God's eternal plan to save the elect (Ac 4:27–28).

3:16 so. Means "in this way" or "thus." Jesus again pointed to the parallel with Moses' situation. He did not use "so" in the sense of "so greatly" or "so dearly." **loved the world.** Some have used this phrase to suggest that Jesus' death made atonement for every human being on the basis that God loves everyone in the same way and to the same degree. It is true that the New Testament teaches the free offer of the gospel to all; everyone is invited to partake of Christ. Yet elsewhere in this Gospel Jesus makes it clear that his atonement was intended only for the elect (e.g., 6:37–40; 10:14–18; 17:9). It appears that Jesus here used the term "world" to indicate that his saving work was not limited to the Jews but was to be applied to people from all the world (i.e., from all nations). See theological articles "Definite Atonement" at John 10 and "Divine Love" at 1 John 4. **that he gave his . . . Son.** Jesus defined the love of God in terms of the atonement, as is frequent in the New Testament (15:13–14; Ro 5:8, Gal 2:20; Eph 5:2; 1 Jn 3:16; 4:9–10; Rev 1:5). **that whoever believes.** Literally, "that everyone who believes," as in verse 15, where the same Greek phrase is used. **shall not perish.** Those who do not avail themselves of the remedy God has provided are doomed; they will perish. **eternal life.** More than endless existence, it is ultimately an existence in which we are forever in the beatific presence of the triune God (17:3; Rev 21:3–4). Believers already possess unending spiritual life because their spirits cannot die and already possess fuller life because they enjoy fellowship with God. In the new heavens and the new earth, they will also enjoy unending physical life and more intimate fellowship with God in his manifest presence. See *WCF* 7.3; 8.1; *WLC* 32,55,153; *BC* 21; *HC* 17,20,37.

3:17–18 See *HC* 56.

3:17 not . . . to condemn the world. Jesus did not come to declare or make the world guilty—the world was already guilty and already stood condemned—or to execute final judgment. Rather, he came to secure salvation. Although he condemned sin (e.g., 9:39) and declared certain individuals guilty, he will not officially render final judgment and execute eternal punishment on all sinners in the world until his return (5:25–30).

3:18 See *WLC* 153; *HC* 60.

3:19 but men loved darkness instead of light. The world rejects Jesus because he is the Light who exposes sin. Those whose deeds are evil recoil from him, preferring not to have their wickedness exposed.

3:21 But whoever lives by the truth comes into the light. *Truth* is both a moral and an intellectual matter. Living by the truth is contrasted not with doing what is false, but with doing what is evil (v. 20).

■ **3:22–36** *John's Further Testimony.* John the Baptist confirmed that Jesus is from above. That is a cause for celebration, for a wedding feast. Yet Jesus was received only by those to whom understanding was given from heaven. There are three sections here. In verses 22–24 we are told that Jesus and his disciples went into Judea, where John was. This provides a convenient transition to the Baptist (vv. 25–30). In verses 25–30 the Baptist affirms once more that his own importance rests entirely in his role of preparing the way for Christ. It remains an open question whether verses

spent some time with them, and baptized.[h] 23Now John also was baptizing at Aenon near
Salim, because there was plenty of water, and people were constantly coming to be baptized. 24(This was before John was put in prison.)[i] 25An argument developed between some
of John's disciples and a certain Jew[a] over the matter of ceremonial washing.[j] 26They came
to John and said to him, "Rabbi,[k] that man who was with you on the other side of the Jordan—the one you testified[l] about—well, he is baptizing, and everyone is going to him."
27To this John replied, "A man can receive only what is given him from heaven. 28You
yourselves can testify that I said, 'I am not the Christ[b] but am sent ahead of him.'[m] 29The
bride belongs to the bridegroom.[n] The friend who attends the bridegroom waits and listens for him, and is full of joy when he hears the bridegroom's voice. That joy is mine,
and it is now complete.[o] 30He must become greater; I must become less.
31"The one who comes from above[p] is above all; the one who is from the earth belongs
to the earth, and speaks as one from the earth.[q] The one who comes from heaven is above
all. 32He testifies to what he has seen and heard,[r] but no one accepts his testimony.[s] 33The
man who has accepted it has certified that God is truthful. 34For the one whom God has
sent[t] speaks the words of God, for God[c] gives the Spirit[u] without limit. 35The Father loves
the Son and has placed everything in his hands.[v] 36Whoever believes in the Son has eternal life,[w] but whoever rejects the Son will not see life, for God's wrath remains on him."[d]

Jesus Talks With a Samaritan Woman

4 The Pharisees heard that Jesus was gaining and baptizing more disciples than
John,[x] 2although in fact it was not Jesus who baptized, but his disciples. 3When the
Lord learned of this, he left Judea[y] and went back once more to Galilee.
4Now he had to go through Samaria. 5So he came to a town in Samaria called Sychar,
near the plot of ground Jacob had given to his son Joseph.[z] 6Jacob's well was there, and
Jesus, tired as he was from the journey, sat down by the well. It was about the sixth hour.
7When a Samaritan woman came to draw water, Jesus said to her, "Will you give me
a drink?" 8(His disciples had gone into the town[a] to buy food.)
9The Samaritan woman said to him, "You are a Jew and I am a Samaritan[b] woman.
How can you ask me for a drink?" (For Jews do not associate with Samaritans.[e])
10Jesus answered her, "If you knew the gift of God and who it is that asks you for a
drink, you would have asked him and he would have given you living water."[c]
11"Sir," the woman said, "you have nothing to draw with and the well is deep. Where
can you get this living water? 12Are you greater than our father Jacob, who gave us the
well[d] and drank from it himself, as did also his sons and his flocks and herds?"

3:22 [h]Jn 4:2
3:24 [i]Mt 4:12; 14:3
3:25 [j]Jn 2:6
3:26 [k]Mt 23:7 [l]Jn 1:7
3:28 [m]Jn 1:20,23
3:29 [n]Mt 9:15 [o]Jn 16:24; 17:13; Php 2:2; 1Jn 1:4; 2Jn 12
3:31 [p]ver 13 [q]Jn 8:23; 1Jn 4:5
3:32 [r]Jn 8:26; 15:15 [s]ver 11
3:34 [t]ver 17 [u]Mt 12:18; Lk 4:18; Ac 10:38
3:35 [v]Mt 28:18; Jn 5:20, 22; 17:2
3:36 [w]ver 15; Jn 5:24; 6:47
4:1 [x]Jn 3:22,26
4:3 [y]Jn 3:22
4:5 [z]Ge 33:19; 48:22; Jos 24:32
4:8 [a]ver 5,39
4:9 [b]Mt 10:5; Lk 9:52, 53
4:10 [c]Isa 44:3; Jer 2:13; Zec 14:8; Jn 7:37, 38; Rev 21:6; 22:1, 17
4:12 [d]ver 6

[a] *25* Some manuscripts *and certain Jews* [b] *28* Or *Messiah* [c] *34* Greek *he* [d] *36* Some interpreters end the quotation after verse 30. [e] *9* Or *do not use dishes Samaritans have used*

31–36 are a continuation of the Baptist's words or an editorial comment by John the evangelist. There is no textual indication that they are an isolated comment by Jesus inserted here.

3:22 baptized. From 4:2 it is clear that baptism was administered by the disciples under Jesus' authority. This baptism presumably was not Christian baptism in the name of the Father, the Son and the Holy Spirit, but an extension of John's ministry and baptism of repentance.

3:24 before John was put in prison. John's Gospel does not record the circumstances of the Baptist's imprisonment (see Mt 14:3–12; Mk 6:17–29).

3:27 A man can receive. A statement of the comprehensive sovereignty of God. See *BC* 14.

3:29 full of joy. John encouraged his followers to share his joy in Jesus rather than to begrudge the fact that John himself was fading from the limelight.

3:31–36 See *HC* 84.

3:31 The one who comes from above. Jesus is distinguished from all other humans who are "from the earth" (see note on v. 13), but note that all who enter the kingdom of God must be born from above (see note on v. 3). See *BC* 7.

3:32 no one accepts his testimony. John's disciples were concerned because they seemed to be losing their influence, and they exaggerated their plight, saying, "everyone is going to him" (v. 26). John's concern that people were not properly responding to Jesus' ministry led him to use the forceful expression "no one accepts."

3:34 for God gives the Spirit without limit. These words could certainly apply to the Spirit-empowered earthly ministry of Jesus (Lk 3:22; 4:1), but they could also refer to the fullness of the Spirit that Jesus gives to those who serve him. Jesus is the agent who sends the Spirit (15:26). See *WCF* 8.3; *WLC* 42.

3:36 whoever rejects the Son will not see life. "Rejects" may also be translated "does not obey." Obeying the Son is parallel to believing the Son. True faith involves moral commitment to Jesus, and persistent disobedience to him signifies a lack of real belief. See *HC* 59.

■ **4:1–42** *A Samaritan Woman.* Once again, John focused on the central changes in the kingdom of God that Jesus brought. Here he identified Jesus as the One who gives eternal life, the One who replaced the temple in Jerusalem and the One through whom Samaritans could find salvation even when most Jews rejected him. The background of this incident is the profound contempt that the Jews felt for the Samaritans (v. 9). Not surprisingly, the Samaritans also disliked the Jews. When traveling between Galilee and Judea, the Jews preferred to cross the Jordan River twice rather than to pass through Samaria. Jesus, however, did not follow this practice (Lk 9:52).

4:6 tired as he was. Jesus experienced fatigue, even exhaustion, by virtue of his human nature (Mt 8:24). **the sixth hour.** Noon.

4:9 Jews do not associate with Samaritans. Could also be translated, "Jews use nothing in common with Samaritans." It refers to the legislation that forbade a Jew to use eating or drinking utensils used by Samaritans. The surprise is not so much that Jesus would speak with a Samaritan, but that he would drink from a Samaritan utensil.

4:10 the gift of God. Emphasizes that salvation is not earned but given (Eph 2:8). Jesus himself is the gift of God (3:16; Gal 2:20; Eph 5:25). **living water.** This expression can mean "running water," which was likely to be fresh and pure. In the Old Testament, it was employed metaphorically as a reference to divine blessing (Jer 2:13; Zec 14:8). See John 4:14 and 7:37–39.

4:11 living water? As the Jews and Nicodemus before her, the Samaritan woman misunderstood the key terms Jesus used (v. 15; see also 2:19–21; 3:3–10).

13 Jesus answered, "Everyone who drinks this water will be thirsty again, 14 but whoever drinks the water I give him will never thirst.[e] Indeed, the water I give him will become in him a spring of water[f] welling up to eternal life."[g]
15 The woman said to him, "Sir, give me this water so that I won't get thirsty[h] and have
to keep coming here to draw water."
16 He told her, "Go, call your husband and come back."
17 "I have no husband," she replied.
Jesus said to her, "You are right when you say you have no husband. 18 The fact is, you
have had five husbands, and the man you now have is not your husband. What you have
just said is quite true."
19 "Sir," the woman said, "I can see that you are a prophet.[i] 20 Our fathers worshiped
on this mountain,[j] but you Jews claim that the place where we must worship is in Jerusalem."[k]
21 Jesus declared, "Believe me, woman, a time is coming[l] when you will worship the
Father neither on this mountain nor in Jerusalem.[m] 22 You Samaritans worship what you
do not know;[n] we worship what we do know, for salvation is from the Jews.[o] 23 Yet a time
is coming and has now come[p] when the true worshipers will worship the Father in spirit[q] and truth, for they are the kind of worshipers the Father seeks. 24 God is spirit,[r] and
his worshipers must worship in spirit and in truth."
25 The woman said, "I know that Messiah" (called Christ)[s] "is coming. When he
comes, he will explain everything to us."
26 Then Jesus declared, "I who speak to you am he."[t]

The Disciples Rejoin Jesus

27 Just then his disciples returned[u] and were surprised to find him talking with a woman. But no one asked, "What do you want?" or "Why are you talking with her?"
28 Then, leaving her water jar, the woman went back to the town and said to the people, 29 "Come, see a man who told me everything I ever did.[v] Could this be the Christ[a]?"[w]
30 They came out of the town and made their way toward him.
31 Meanwhile his disciples urged him, "Rabbi,[x] eat something."
32 But he said to them, "I have food to eat[y] that you know nothing about."
33 Then his disciples said to each other, "Could someone have brought him food?"
34 "My food," said Jesus, "is to do the will[z] of him who sent me and to finish his work.[a]
35 Do you not say, 'Four months more and then the harvest'? I tell you, open your eyes
and look at the fields! They are ripe for harvest.[b] 36 Even now the reaper draws his wages, even now he harvests[c] the crop for eternal life,[d] so that the sower and the reaper may
be glad together. 37 Thus the saying 'One sows and another reaps'[e] is true. 38 I sent you

a 29 *Or Messiah*

4:14 [e]Jn 6:35 [f]Jn 7:38 [g]Mt 25:46
4:15 [h]Jn 6:34
4:19 [i]Mt 21:11
4:20 [j]Dt 11:29; Jos 8:33 [k]Lk 9:53
4:21 [l]Jn 5:28; 16:2 [m]Mal 1:11; 1Ti 2:8
4:22 [n]2Ki 17:28-41 [o]Isa 2:3; Ro 3:1, 2; 9:4, 5
4:23 [p]Jn 5:25; 16:32 [q]Php 3:3
4:24 [r]Php 3:3
4:25 [s]Mt 1:16
4:26 [t]Jn 8:24; 9:35-37
4:27 [u]ver 8
4:29 [v]ver 17, 18 [w]Mt 12:23; Jn 7:26, 31
4:31 [x]Mt 23:7
4:32 [y]Job 23:12; Mt 4:4; Jn 6:27
4:34 [z]Mt 26:39; Jn 6:38; 17:4; 19:30 [a]Jn 19:30
4:35 [b]Mt 9:37; Lk 10:2
4:36 [c]Ro 1:13 [d]Mt 25:46
4:37 [e]Job 31:8; Mic 6:15

4:13 will be thirsty again. Jesus contrasted temporary satisfaction with eternal satisfaction, teaching that all earthly pleasures, even if legitimate, fade.
4:14 I give. Expresses the divine origin of this blessing. **welling up.** Emphasizes its great abundance. **eternal life.** Emphasizes its endless duration and surpassing quality.
4:18 you have had five husbands. Jesus' awareness of the Samaritan woman's previous life is reminiscent of his knowledge of Nathanael (1:48).
4:20 Our fathers worshiped on this mountain. The details and dates are somewhat uncertain, but sometime after Samaria fell to Assyria (722 B.C.) a split arose between the Jews there and the Jews in Jerusalem. The Samaritans built a temple on Mount Gerizim, which was destroyed around 130 B.C. They continued to worship there even after the destruction of their temple.
4:21–24 See *HC* 80.
4:21 See *WCF* 21.6.
4:22–24 See *HC* 117.
4:22 See *WCF* 10.4; 20.2; *WLC* 60.
4:23–24 See *WCF* 21.6; *HC* 96.
4:23 a time is coming and has now come. See 5:25. Throughout Jesus' earthly ministry and prior to his death and resurrection, there was a tension between the fact that the kingdom of God and its blessings had already arrived in part and the fact that those blessings had not yet been fully manifested. Indeed, prior to Jesus' second coming, there are aspects of the kingdom that have not, and will not, yet come. On the other hand, the One who brought the kingdom of God was himself already present on Earth and had inaugurated his kingdom on Earth. See theological article "The Kingdom of God" at Matthew 4.
4:24 must worship in spirit and in truth. The expression "in truth" means "in reality"; that is, in the heavenly worship of which the earthly worship was a type. Jesus used the term "truth" here as it is employed in Hebrews 8:2 and 9:24. In Hebrews 8:2, the "true tabernacle" in heaven is not contrasted with a false one, but rather with the earthly tabernacle that was patterned after it. The earthly Jerusalem was not a false place to worship, but an earthly place. It was but a shadow, a type, a copy, of the reality of heaven and of heavenly worship. Since Jesus is the One who reunites not only God and his people, but also heaven and Earth, the hour was coming when all questions regarding the earthly location of worship would be irrelevant. That to which earthly temple worship pointed was becoming a reality for God's people (see note on Mt 27:51). **spirit.** Refers to the third person of the Trinity, the Holy Spirit, as the gift of the end times that the Old Testament had promised (Joel 2:28–29). Christian worship, therefore, is not confined to any earthly locale, but rather is oriented directly toward heaven and is offered in the fullness of the Holy Spirit. See *WCF* 2.1; *WLC* 7; *WSC* 4; *BC* 1.
4:25 See *BC* 7.
4:26 "I . . . am he." The one occasion before his trial when Jesus is recorded as designating himself as the Messiah. Perhaps the political overtones associated in the Jewish mind with this concept made it unwise for Jesus to use it often (cf. 6:14–15; see also "Introduction to the Gospels").
4:27 surprised. The disciples' attitude reflects both the contempt of the Jews for the Samaritans and the male chauvinism of the time that viewed giving instruction to a woman as a waste of time.
4:30 They came. The witness of this woman was more effective in this town than was the visit of the 12 disciples.
4:37 "One sows and another reaps." Jesus made it clear that

to reap what you have not worked for. Others have done the hard work, and you have
reaped the benefits of their labor."

Many Samaritans Believe

39 Many of the Samaritans from that town[f] believed in him because of the woman's
testimony, "He told me everything I ever did."[g] 40 So when the Samaritans came to him,
they urged him to stay with them, and he stayed two days. 41 And because of his words
many more became believers.
42 They said to the woman, "We no longer believe just because of what you said; now
we have heard for ourselves, and we know that this man really is the Savior of the
world."[h]

Jesus Heals the Official's Son

43 After the two days[i] he left for Galilee. 44 (Now Jesus himself had pointed out that a
prophet has no honor in his own country.)[j] 45 When he arrived in Galilee, the Galileans
welcomed him. They had seen all that he had done in Jerusalem at the Passover Feast,[k]
for they also had been there.
46 Once more he visited Cana in Galilee, where he had turned the water into wine.[l]
And there was a certain royal official whose son lay sick at Capernaum. 47 When this man
heard that Jesus had arrived in Galilee from Judea,[m] he went to him and begged him to
come and heal his son, who was close to death.
48 "Unless you people see miraculous signs and wonders,"[n] Jesus told him, "you will
never believe."
49 The royal official said, "Sir, come down before my child dies."
50 Jesus replied, "You may go. Your son will live."
The man took Jesus at his word and departed. 51 While he was still on the way, his servants met him with the news that his boy was living. 52 When he inquired as to the time
when his son got better, they said to him, "The fever left him yesterday at the seventh
hour."
53 Then the father realized that this was the exact time at which Jesus had said to him,
"Your son will live." So he and all his household[o] believed.
54 This was the second miraculous sign[p] that Jesus performed, having come from Judea to Galilee.

The Healing at the Pool

5 Some time later, Jesus went up to Jerusalem for a feast of the Jews. 2 Now there is
in Jerusalem near the Sheep Gate[q] a pool, which in Aramaic[r] is called Bethesda[a]
and which is surrounded by five covered colonnades. 3 Here a great number of disabled
people used to lie—the blind, the lame, the paralyzed.[b] 5 One who was there had been

4:39 [f]ver 5 [g]ver 29
4:42 [h]Lk 2:11; 1Jn 4:14
4:43 [i]ver 40
4:44 [j]Mt 13:57; Lk 4:24
4:45 [k]Jn 2:23
4:46 [l]Jn 2:1-11
4:47 [m]ver 3,54
4:48 [n]Da 4:2,3; Jn 2:11; Ac 2:43; 14:3; Ro 15:19; 2Co 12:12; Heb 2:4
4:53 [o]Ac 11:14
4:54 [p]ver 48; Jn 2:11
5:2 [q]Ne 3:1; 12:39 [r]Jn 19:13,17,20; 20:16; Ac 21:40; 22:2; 26:14

[a] *2* Some manuscripts *Bethzatha;* other manuscripts *Bethsaida* [b] *3* Some less important manuscripts *paralyzed—and they waited for the moving of the waters. 4From time to time an angel of the Lord would come down and stir up the waters. The first one into the pool after each such disturbance would be cured of whatever disease he had.*

his disciples had a responsibility distinct from his own. They were to reap the harvest of Jesus' sowing. This instruction may have deliberately anticipated a later teaching (see 12:23–24).

4:42 the Savior of the world. They recognized that Jesus is more than a prophet (vv. 19,29,39); he is the Savior (1Jn 4:14). **of the world.** See note on 3:16; *WCF* 14.2.

■ **4:43–54** *A Royal Official in Cana.* John concluded his report on Jesus' travels from Cana and back with an account of the second sign: the healing of an official's son. In the same way that many Jews self-righteously despised the Samaritans for their compromised worship and ancestry, many also despised the official for compromising with the Romans, but Jesus praised the official's faith in contrast with that of the vast majority of Jews, who rejected him.

4:44 no honor in his own country. It is not clear whether "his own country" refers to Judea (which Jesus left [4:3] in order to go to Galilee) or to Galilee. Favoring Judea are two factors: (1) Jesus was typically not well received in Judea, which is consistent with 1:11; and (2) verse 45 says that the Galileans "welcomed him." But favoring Galilee are two other factors: (1) Galilee is considered in this Gospel to be the place of Jesus' origins (1:46; 2:1; 7:42,52); and (2) though the Galileans "welcomed him," the text indicates that Jesus was displeased with their dependence on "signs and wonders" (v. 48).

4:46 a certain royal official. An officer in the service of Herod Antipas, tetrarch of Galilee (cf. Mt 14:1–12; Lk 23:7).

4:48 "Unless you people see miraculous signs and wonders . . . you will never believe." See note on verse 44.

4:50 Your son will live. A word of power to effect healing, not merely a prophecy that he would recover.

4:52 the seventh hour. 1:00 P.M.

4:54 second miraculous sign. While Jesus had performed many other signs (2:23), this is the second recorded as taking place at Cana in Galilee (cf. 2:11). The threefold reference to the son's living (vv. 50,51,53) indicates that the purpose of this sign was to show that Jesus has the power to give life. Corresponding to this is the progression of the official's faith (vv. 48,50,53). This focus on life through the power of Jesus' word prepares the reader for the following discourse on life through the Son (5:19–30).

■ **5:1–47** *In Jerusalem Near a Feast.* John's account shifts from Galilee to Jerusalem, where Jesus performed a sign, taught those around him and faced their reactions. John's account divides into two main sections (see "Introduction: Outline").

■ **5:1–15** A *Healing at the Pool of Bethesda.* The healing of the paralytic brought Jesus into conflict with the Jews over another of their central religious observances: the Sabbath. This event has four parts: the healing itself (vv. 1–9), the interrogation of the healed man by the Jews (vv. 10–13), Jesus' comments to the healed man (v. 14), and the evangelist's comment on the whole event (v. 15).

5:1 a feast of the Jews. It is not clear which feast is in view, although commentators have suggested Tabernacles, Pentecost or Passover.

an invalid for thirty-eight years. 6When Jesus saw him lying there and learned that he had
been in this condition for a long time, he asked him, "Do you want to get well?"
7"Sir," the invalid replied, "I have no one to help me into the pool when the water is
stirred. While I am trying to get in, someone else goes down ahead of me."
8Then Jesus said to him, "Get up! Pick up your mat and walk."[s] 9At once the man was
cured; he picked up his mat and walked.
The day on which this took place was a Sabbath,[t] 10and so the Jews[u] said to the man
who had been healed, "It is the Sabbath; the law forbids you to carry your mat."[v]
11But he replied, "The man who made me well said to me, 'Pick up your mat and
walk.'"
12So they asked him, "Who is this fellow who told you to pick it up and walk?"
13The man who was healed had no idea who it was, for Jesus had slipped away into
the crowd that was there.
14Later Jesus found him at the temple and said to him, "See, you are well again. Stop
sinning[w] or something worse may happen to you." 15The man went away and told the
Jews[x] that it was Jesus who had made him well.

Life Through the Son

16So, because Jesus was doing these things on the Sabbath, the Jews persecuted him.
17Jesus said to them, "My Father is always at his work[y] to this very day, and I, too, am
working." 18For this reason the Jews tried all the harder to kill him;[z] not only was he
breaking the Sabbath, but he was even calling God his own Father, making himself equal
with God.[a]
19Jesus gave them this answer: "I tell you the truth, the Son can do nothing by himself;[b] he can do only what he sees his Father doing, because whatever the Father does
the Son also does. 20For the Father loves the Son[c] and shows him all he does. Yes, to your
amazement he will show him even greater things than these.[d] 21For just as the Father
raises the dead and gives them life,[e] even so the Son gives life[f] to whom he is pleased to
give it. 22Moreover, the Father judges no one, but has entrusted all judgment to the Son,[g]
23that all may honor the Son just as they honor the Father. He who does not honor the
Son does not honor the Father, who sent him.[h]
24"I tell you the truth, whoever hears my word and believes him who sent me has eternal life and will not be condemned;[i] he has crossed over from death to life.[j] 25I tell you

5:8 [s]Mt 9:5,6; Mk 2:11; Lk 5:24
5:9 [t]Jn 9:14
5:10 [u]ver 16 [v]Ne 13:15-22; Jer 17:21; Mt 12:2
5:14 [w]Mk 2:5; Jn 8:11
5:15 [x]Jn 1:19
5:17 [y]Jn 9:4; 14:10
5:18 [z]Jn 7:1 [a]Jn 10:30, 33; 19:7
5:19 [b]ver 30; Jn 8:28
5:20 [c]Jn 3:35 [d]Jn 14:12
5:21 [e]Ro 4:17; 8:11 [f]Jn 11:25
5:22 [g]ver 27; Jn 9:39; Ac 10:42; 17:31
5:23 [h]Lk 10:16; 1Jn 2:23
5:24 [i]Jn 3:18 [j]1Jn 3:14

5:6 "Do you want to get well?" After a long period of sickness, the man had probably given up hope for healing. By this question, Jesus challenged the paralysis of the man's mind.

5:7 the invalid. The nature of the man's sickness is not specified, but it has generally been thought that he was lame, since Jesus told him to take up his mat and walk and since he needed someone to put him in the water. **when the water is stirred.** Apparently there was a belief that an angel would disturb the water, and when he did so, the water would take on healing properties. Some ancient manuscripts include mention of this customary belief as part of verse 4 (see NIV text note on v. 3).

5:8 Pick up your mat. Jewish tradition interpreted the Sabbath law so as to exclude the carrying of burdens. While Jeremiah protested against unjustifiable or unnecessary loading and unloading on the Sabbath (Jer 17:21–22), it surely was not a violation of that law for the man to gather his meager property and go home on the very day of his deliverance.

5:9 the man was cured. It is not specifically stated that faith in Jesus was required of the man, as was the case in many of Jesus' other miracles (Mt 9:22; 13:58; Mk 6:5–6).

5:10 the law forbids you to carry your mat. An unnecessarily stringent interpretation that disregarded the divine purpose of the Sabbath law.

5:14 something worse. The precise identification of the "something worse" is not made here. The man had not necessarily brought his illness on himself by some specific sin. Although sins can sometimes provoke God to physical and temporal judgment (1Co 11:28–32), many illnesses are not related to particular sins (9:3). Jesus' point was that there is something worse than being ill—namely, suffering under God's eternal judgment.

■ **5:16–47** *Jesus, the Sabbath and the Father.* Jesus debated with the Jews regarding his relation to the Sabbath and to God. In this passage, Jesus did not directly argue with the Jews about whether they correctly understood the Sabbath legislation. Rather, he argued that they would not object to him if they understood who he was. He claimed to be God by indicating some of his divine prerogatives (vv. 17–30), and he showed the attestation provided for his claim (vv. 31–47).

5:17–18 See *BC* 8,13.

5:17 "My Father is always at his work . . . and I, too, am working." Jesus appealed to God's example to defend performing works of mercy on the Sabbath. Whereas the Jews wrongly thought that the Sabbath required inactivity, Jesus rightly demonstrated that showing mercy was essential to the Sabbath.

5:18 not only was he breaking the Sabbath. This does not express John's concurrence with the Jews that Jesus did in fact break the Sabbath. Rather, it expresses their reason (however invalid) for seeking to kill him. **making himself equal with God.** The Jews correctly understood Jesus' affirmation that he was more than a "son" of God in the general sense. Jesus had claimed to be the kind of Son who had the same authority over the Sabbath as the One who gave the Sabbath law, thus making himself equal in authority to the Law Giver.

5:19 the Son can do nothing. See verse 30. This does not express personal inability (cf. 15:5) on the part of Jesus but rather his choice to submit to his heavenly Father.

5:20 greater things than these. In this context, giving life (v. 21) was a greater work than healing.

5:21 the Father raises the dead. A clear affirmation of what is expressed faintly in the Old Testament. Jesus here sided with the Pharisees and against the Sadducees, who denied the resurrection (Mt 22:23). The work of raising the dead is clearly a divine prerogative, one that Jesus claimed for himself (v. 25).

5:22–23 See *HC* 50.

5:22 See *WCF* 8.3; 33.1.

5:23 that all may honor the Son just as they honor the Father. Here the specific honor that is to be given to the Son is the holy fear that is directed toward God. The Son, no less than the Father, is the One to whom all must give an account at the judgment. **He who does not honor the Son does not honor the Father.** This strong statement does not impugn the believers of the Old Testament, but it makes plain that, after the incarnation of Jesus, a denial of Jesus' deity is an affront to the Father as well as to the Son (1Jn 2:23). See *WCF* 21.2.

5:24 whoever . . . believes . . . has eternal life. The present tense of "has" indicates that salvation is not only in the future but

the truth, a time is coming and has now come[k] when the dead will hear[l] the voice of the
Son of God and those who hear will live. 26 For as the Father has life in himself, so he has
granted the Son to have life in himself. 27 And he has given him authority to judge[m] because he is the Son of Man.
28 "Do not be amazed at this, for a time is coming[n] when all who are in their graves
will hear his voice 29 and come out—those who have done good will rise to live, and those
who have done evil will rise to be condemned.[o] 30 By myself I can do nothing;[p] I judge
only as I hear, and my judgment is just,[q] for I seek not to please myself but him who
sent me.[r]

Testimonies About Jesus

31 "If I testify about myself, my testimony is not valid.[s] 32 There is another who testifies in my favor,[t] and I know that his testimony about me is valid.
33 "You have sent to John and he has testified[u] to the truth. 34 Not that I accept human
testimony;[v] but I mention it that you may be saved. 35 John was a lamp that burned and
gave light,[w] and you chose for a time to enjoy his light.
36 "I have testimony weightier than that of John.[x] For the very work that the Father
has given me to finish, and which I am doing,[y] testifies that the Father has sent me.[z]
37 And the Father who sent me has himself testified concerning me.[a] You have never
heard his voice nor seen his form,[b] 38 nor does his word dwell in you,[c] for you do not believe the one he sent.[d] 39 You diligently study[a] the Scriptures[e] because you think that by
them you possess eternal life. These are the Scriptures that testify about me,[f] 40 yet you
refuse to come to me to have life.
41 "I do not accept praise from men,[g] 42 but I know you. I know that you do not have
the love of God in your hearts. 43 I have come in my Father's name, and you do not accept me; but if someone else comes in his own name, you will accept him. 44 How can you
believe if you accept praise from one another, yet make no effort to obtain the praise that
comes from the only God[b]?[h]
45 "But do not think I will accuse you before the Father. Your accuser is Moses,[i] on
whom your hopes are set.[j] 46 If you believed Moses, you would believe me, for he wrote
about me.[k] 47 But since you do not believe what he wrote, how are you going to believe
what I say?"[l]

Jesus Feeds the Five Thousand

6 Some time after this, Jesus crossed to the far shore of the Sea of Galilee (that is, the
Sea of Tiberias), 2 and a great crowd of people followed him because they saw the

5:25 [k]Jn 4:23 [l]Jn 8:43, 47
5:27 [m]ver 22; Ac 10:42; 17:31
5:28 [n]Jn 4:21
5:29 [o]Da 12:2; Mt 25:46
5:30 [p]ver 19 [q]Jn 8:16 [r]Mt 26:39; Jn 4:34; 6:38
5:31 [s]Jn 8:14
5:32 [t]ver 37; Jn 8:18
5:33 [u]Jn 1:7
5:34 [v]1Jn 5:9
5:35 [w]2Pe 1:19
5:36 [x]1Jn 5:9 [y]Jn 14:11; 15:24 [z]Jn 3:17; 10:25
5:37 [a]Jn 8:18 [b]Dt 4:12; 1Ti 1:17; Jn 1:18
5:38 [c]1Jn 2:14 [d]Jn 3:17
5:39 [e]Ro 2:17,18 [f]Lk 24:27,44; Ac 13:27
5:41 [g]ver 44
5:44 [h]Ro 2:29
5:45 [i]Jn 9:28 [j]Ro 2:17
5:46 [k]Ge 3:15; Lk 24:27,44; Ac 26:22
5:47 [l]Lk 16:29,31

a *39* Or *Study diligently* (the imperative) b *44* Some early manuscripts *the Only One*

is already a present reality for the believer. Compare 6:47. See *HC* 42.

5:25 See *WCF* 10.2; *WLC* 67; *BC* 24,35.

5:26 See *WCF* 2.2.

5:27–29 See *WLC* 87.

5:27 See *WCF* 8.3; 33.1.

5:28–29 See *WCF* 32.3; *WLC* 87; *BC* 37.

5:29 rise to live . . . rise to be condemned. Jesus taught that there will be a general resurrection of both the righteous to life and the unrighteous to condemnation. In a similar passage, Jesus said that this life is eternal and the judgment is eternal punishment (Mt 25:46).

5:31–47 Jesus addressed four testimonies that confirm the truthfulness of his claims: those of John the Baptist, Jesus' own works, God the Father and Scripture (specifically, Moses).

5:31 If I testify about myself, my testimony is not valid. According to Mosaic Law more than one witness was required to prove the truth of one's testimony (Dt 17:6; 19:15; see note on 8:13).

5:32,36–37 See *BC* 8,13.

5:37–38 You have never heard his voice . . . nor does his word dwell in you. Probably "voice" is a reference to the direct voice of God (as in Ex. 20:1-19), "form" to the *temunah* which Moses did see (Nu. 12:8) and the rest of Israel did not (Dt. 4:15), and "word" to the revelation through human prophets, preeminently Jesus himself. This then leads naturally into v. 39 where Scripture, the written Word, is mentioned.

5:39 the Scriptures that testify about me. Jesus did not dispute that the Old Testament directs us to eternal life (cf. 2Ti 3:15); however, he insisted that it also directs us to Christ himself. The efforts of those who refuse to find Christ in the Scriptures are vain and empty. See *WCF* 1.8; *WLC* 156.

5:44 See *WLC* 130.

5:45 Your accuser is Moses. Jesus argued that Moses would accuse them for not believing in Christ. In verse 46, Jesus said that if they had believed Moses they would have believed Jesus as well, indicating that those who claimed to believe Moses, but who rejected Christ, did not in fact believe either of them. Note also that Jesus did not refer to any single text in Moses (such as Dt 18:15), but to what "he wrote" in a general way. This is similar to Jesus' postresurrection instruction to the disciples on the road to Emmaus (Lk 24:27,44–46) and to the apostolic proclamation (Ac 3:18; 17:2–3; 18:28; 26:22–23; 28:23).

5:46 See *WCF* 1.8; *HC* 19.

■ **6:1–71** *In Galilee Near the Passover.* This chapter is a major turning point of chapters 2–12. John's account shifts from Jerusalem to Galilee. It reveals most starkly the identity of Jesus as the One sent from the Father (vv. 38,44,46,50–51,57). It also graphically distinguishes between belief and unbelief through the symbolism of eating Jesus' flesh and blood (vv. 53–58), and it chronicles the swelling rejection, motivated by unbelief, that Jesus faced (vv. 41–42, 60–66). The signs in this chapter call to mind corresponding saving events in the history of Israel, and they are to be seen as signs of the fulfillment in Jesus of the typology present in the first Passover, the exodus and the desert feedings. Readers are expected to draw on their knowledge of these Old Testament accounts in order to appreciate more fully who Jesus is affirmed to be. This material divides into three sections (see "Introduction: Outline").

■ **6:1–15** *Feeding the Five Thousand.* Jesus left Jerusalem and traveled to the far side of the Sea of Galilee at the time when the

miraculous signs[m] he had performed on the sick. 3Then Jesus went up on a mountainside[n] and sat down with his disciples. 4The Jewish Passover Feast[o] was near.
5When Jesus looked up and saw a great crowd coming toward him, he said to Philip,[p] "Where shall we buy bread for these people to eat?" 6He asked this only to test him,
for he already had in mind what he was going to do.
7Philip answered him, "Eight months' wages[a] would not buy enough bread for each
one to have a bite!"
8Another of his disciples, Andrew, Simon Peter's brother,[q] spoke up, 9"Here is a boy
with five small barley loaves and two small fish, but how far will they go among so
many?"[r]
10Jesus said, "Have the people sit down." There was plenty of grass in that place, and
the men sat down, about five thousand of them. 11Jesus then took the loaves, gave
thanks,[s] and distributed to those who were seated as much as they wanted. He did the
same with the fish.
12When they had all had enough to eat, he said to his disciples, "Gather the pieces
that are left over. Let nothing be wasted." 13So they gathered them and filled twelve baskets with the pieces of the five barley loaves left over by those who had eaten.
14After the people saw the miraculous sign[t] that Jesus did, they began to say, "Surely this is the Prophet who is to come into the world."[u] 15Jesus, knowing that they intended to come and make him king[v] by force, withdrew again to a mountain by himself.[w]

Jesus Walks on the Water

16When evening came, his disciples went down to the lake, 17where they got into a
boat and set off across the lake for Capernaum. By now it was dark, and Jesus had not
yet joined them. 18A strong wind was blowing and the waters grew rough. 19When they
had rowed three or three and a half miles,[b] they saw Jesus approaching the boat, walking on the water;[x] and they were terrified. 20But he said to them, "It is I; don't be
afraid."[y] 21Then they were willing to take him into the boat, and immediately the boat
reached the shore where they were heading.
22The next day the crowd that had stayed on the opposite shore of the lake[z] realized
that only one boat had been there, and that Jesus had not entered it with his disciples,
but that they had gone away alone.[a] 23Then some boats from Tiberias[b] landed near the
place where the people had eaten the bread after the Lord had given thanks.[c] 24Once the
crowd realized that neither Jesus nor his disciples were there, they got into the boats and
went to Capernaum in search of Jesus.

Jesus the Bread of Life

25When they found him on the other side of the lake, they asked him, "Rabbi,[d] when
did you get here?"
26Jesus answered, "I tell you the truth, you are looking for me,[e] not because you saw

6:2 [m]Jn 2:11
6:3 [n]ver 15
6:4 [o]Jn 2:13; 11:55
6:5 [p]Jn 1:43
6:8 [q]Jn 1:40
6:9 [r]2Ki 4:43
6:11 [s]ver 23; Mt 14:19
6:14 [t]Jn 2:11 [u]Dt 18:15, 18; Mt 11:3; 21:11
6:15 [v]Jn 18:36 [w]Mt 14:23; Mk 6:46
6:19 [x]Job 9:8
6:20 [y]Mt 14:27
6:22 [z]ver 2 [a]ver 15-21
6:23 [b]ver 1 [c]ver 11
6:25 [d]Mt 23:7
6:26 [e]ver 24

[a] 7 Greek *two hundred denarii* [b] 19 Greek *rowed twenty-five or thirty stadia* (about 5 or 6 kilometers)

Passover was about to be celebrated. This feast, established in Exodus 12:43–51, commemorated God's slaying of the Egyptians and his passing over the Israelites. Evidence suggests that during the days of Jesus the following Old Testament passages were read during Passover: Genesis 1–8, Exodus 11–16 and Numbers 6–14. It is possible that what Jesus said in this context constituted his commentary on these passages in light of his own person and work.

6:1 Sea of Tiberias. Herod constructed the city of Tiberias between A.D. 18 and 22. Therefore John's designation reflects a rather new designation for the Sea of Galilee.

6:2 the miraculous signs. John's Gospel has thus far reported only one healing in Galilee, that of the official's son (4:46–54). The words here suggest that Jesus had performed other miracles as well (cf. 21:25).

6:3 Jesus went up on a mountainside. This detail may have been recorded to call attention to the similarity between Jesus and Moses, who went up on Mount Sinai (see note on v. 14).

6:5 he said to Philip. Since Philip came from Bethsaida, the nearest town, it was natural for Jesus to question him. **for these people to eat?** Reminiscent of Numbers 11:13, where Moses asked God a similar question.

6:7 Eight months' wages. Literally, "two hundred denarii." A denarius was the approximate wage for one day's labor (Mt 20:2).

6:10 five thousand. This figure does not include women and children (Mt 14:21). Compare 2 Kings 4:42–44.

6:12 See *WLC* 141.

6:14 the Prophet. A reference to the prophet like Moses (Dt 18:15).

6:15 make him king by force. The kingship associated with the incarnation was spiritual, not political. While accepting the title "King of Israel" (1:49), Jesus shunned the offer of Satan (Mt 4:8–9; Lk 4:5–6) and the misguided efforts of the people.

■ **6:16–21** *Walking on the Water.* John reported the miracle of walking on water, which corresponds to the crossing of the Red Sea (Ex 15). This miracle is also recorded in Matthew 14:22–33 and in Mark 6:47–51. It should not be confused with the calming of the storm (Mt 8:23–27; Mk 4:36–41; Lk 8:22–25).

6:21 immediately. Some commentators understand this to be an additional miracle; others take it to mean that after Jesus' entrance into the boat, no further difficulties were encountered.

■ **6:22–71** *Teaching the Crowds.* Continuing with his presentation of Jesus as the fulfillment of Israel's exodus, John reported that after crossing the lake, Jesus taught about himself as the bread that had come from heaven. In this discourse, Jesus and the crowd compare and contrast the supplying of manna to the Israelites in the wilderness with Jesus' sign (feeding 5,000) and with the reality of the redemption that the feeding signifies.

6:26 not because you saw miraculous signs. Although these people saw the miracle of the feeding of the 5,000, they did not see it as a sign identifying Jesus as the Messiah but merely as an opportunity for a meal.

miraculous signs[f] but because you ate the loaves and had your fill. **27**Do not work for food
that spoils, but for food that endures[g] to eternal life,[h] which the Son of Man[i] will give
you. On him God the Father has placed his seal[j] of approval."
28Then they asked him, "What must we do to do the works God requires?"
29Jesus answered, "The work of God is this: to believe[k] in the one he has sent."[l]
30So they asked him, "What miraculous sign[m] then will you give that we may see it
and believe you?[n] What will you do? **31**Our forefathers ate the manna[o] in the desert; as
it is written: 'He gave them bread from heaven to eat.'[a]"[p]
32Jesus said to them, "I tell you the truth, it is not Moses who has given you the bread
from heaven, but it is my Father who gives you the true bread from heaven. **33**For the
bread of God is he who comes down from heaven[q] and gives life to the world."
34"Sir," they said, "from now on give us this bread."[r]
35Then Jesus declared, "I am the bread of life.[s] He who comes to me will never go hungry, and he who believes in me will never be thirsty.[t] **36**But as I told you, you have seen
me and still you do not believe. **37**All that the Father gives me[u] will come to me, and whoever comes to me I will never drive away. **38**For I have come down from heaven not to do
my will but to do the will of him who sent me.[v] **39**And this is the will of him who sent me,
that I shall lose none of all that he has given me,[w] but raise them up at the last day.[x] **40**For
my Father's will is that everyone who looks to the Son and believes in him shall have eternal life,[y] and I will raise him up at the last day."
41At this the Jews began to grumble about him because he said, "I am the bread
that came down from heaven." **42**They said, "Is this not Jesus, the son of Joseph,[z]
whose father and mother we know?[a] How can he now say, 'I came down from heav-
en'?"[b]
43"Stop grumbling among yourselves," Jesus answered. **44**"No one can come to me unless the Father who sent me draws him,[c] and I will raise him up at the last day. **45**It is written in the Prophets: 'They will all be taught by God.'[b][d] Everyone who listens to the Fa-

6:26 [f]ver 30; Jn 2:11
6:27 [g]Isa 55:2 [h]ver 54; Mt 25:46; Jn 4:14 [i]Mt 8:20 [j]Ro 4:11; 1Co 9:2; 2Co 1:22; Eph 1:13; 4:30; 2Ti 2:19; Rev 7:3
6:29 [k]1Jn 3:23 [l]Jn 3:17
6:30 [m]Jn 2:11 [n]Mt 12:38
6:31 [o]Nu 11:7-9 [p]Ex 16:4,15; Ne 9:15; Ps 78:24; 105:40
6:33 [q]ver 50
6:34 [r]Jn 4:15
6:35 [s]ver 48,51 [t]Jn 4:14
6:37 [u]ver 39; Jn 17:2,6,9,24
6:38 [v]Jn 4:34; 5:30
6:39 [w]Jn 10:28; 17:12; 18:9 [x]ver 40,44,54
6:40 [y]Jn 3:15,16
6:42 [z]Lk 4:22 [a]Jn 7:27,28 [b]ver 38,62
6:44 [c]ver 65; Jer 31:3; Jn 12:32
6:45 [d]Isa 54:13; Jer 31:33,34; Heb 8:10,11; 10:16

[a] *31* Exodus 16:4; Neh. 9:15; Psalm 78:24,25 [b] *45* Isaiah 54:13

6:27 Jesus pointed to the spiritual meaning of the miracle: God's seal of approval on his ministry and claims, which identified him as the promised Messiah (the Son of Man). See *WLC* 32,42,181.

6:28–29 The people thought that eternal life could be secured by something they could do. Jesus showed them how wrong they were: Salvation is free. It is apprehended by faith, and even that [faith] is God's work, although exercised by a responsible human agent.

6:31 The crowds expected that the coming of the Messiah would be marked by a miracle as great as, or greater than, the giving of the manna in the desert. The feeding of the 5,000 was minor in comparison to the feeding of the whole people of Israel over a 40-year period with "bread from heaven."

6:32 the true bread from heaven. The word "true" has a special meaning. Jesus was referring to that which is everlasting as opposed to that which is merely a shadow or a type. The bread God provided through Moses (Ex 16; Nu 11) was not false bread. It was truly bread, but merely material. That bread anticipated the perfect and everlasting nourishment God would provide in sending his Son, in whom is eternal life (17:3). See note on 4:24.

6:33 he who comes down from heaven. Refers to Jesus Christ, whose incarnation is described as a "coming down" (3:13,31; 6:38,41–42,50–51,58; Eph 4:9–10). **gives life to the world.** See note on 3:16.

6:34 give us this bread. Jesus' audience misinterpreted his statement on a purely physical level, even as Nicodemus (3:4) and the Samaritan woman (4:15) had done earlier.

6:35 I am the bread of life. This "I am" saying is the first of seven such sayings in this Gospel (8:12; 9:5; 10:7,9,11,14; 11:25; 14:6; 15:1,5). The words "I am" are reminiscent of Exodus 3:14 and thus constitute an implicit claim to deity (see notes on 8:58,59). **He who comes to me . . . and he who believes.** Implies that the believer's union with Christ, spoken of in verses 53–58, is a spiritual bond by faith. **hungry . . . thirsty.** Introduces the metaphors of hunger and thirst that are then developed in verses 53–58. See *WLC* 174; *HC* 76.

6:36 you have seen me and still you do not believe. In spite of the special privileges of associating with the incarnate Christ and of witnessing some of his miracles, many closed their hearts and refused to turn to him in faith. Because of their privilege, their refusal made them more culpable (Mt 11:20–24).

6:37 All that the Father gives me will come. God leads to faith all those whom he plans to redeem. The redemption of the elect is certain, and no one else has the ability to come to him. **whoever comes to me I will never drive away.** Indicates the receptivity of the Son, who promises acceptance to anyone who truly believes. Note that the verse emphasizes both divine sovereignty ("the Father gives") and human responsibility ("whoever comes"). See *WCF* 8.8; 10.1–2; *WLC* 59,63; *WSC* 30; *BC* 16.

6:38 not to do my will but to do the will of him who sent me. There is no suggestion of any competition between the will of the Son and that of the Father, nor a suggestion of any difference between their wills. Rather, this verse indicates the perfect agreement between the Sender and the One sent. It calls attention to the submission of the Son.

6:39–40 See *HC* 1.

6:39 that I shall lose none of all that he has given me, but raise them up at the last day. The Father's will is not only that Jesus make an offer to lost sinners, but that he actually raise up all who are given him by the Father and lose no one from that group. These verses assert God's gracious preservation of true believers, which ensures their ultimate salvation. See *WCF* 8.8; *WLC* 59; *WSC* 30; *CD* 1.VI.

6:40 See *HC* 76.

6:41 the Jews began to grumble about him. This response is similar to that of the Israelites in the wilderness who grumbled against Moses and Aaron (Ex 16:7; 17:3; Nu 11:1).

6:42 came down from heaven. Jesus' origin is of crucial importance in establishing his identity as Messiah and Son of God (1:1–2,14,18,45–46; 3:2,13,17,31; 5:36–38; 6:29,33,38). The reason for the present and future disputes is clear enough: Jesus is identified as the incarnate Son of God through his origin from the Father. Those confronted with this revelation must respond either in belief or in rejection. There is no middle ground.

6:44–45 See *WCF* 7.3; 10.1; *WSC* 31.

6:44 No one can come to me unless the Father who sent me draws him. No one can respond favorably to Jesus' invitation apart from the Father's activity in drawing the individual to Jesus. The native hardness of heart in humanity prevents acceptance of God's invitation, unless a special work of God's grace takes place (v. 65). See *WCF* 9.3; *WLC* 67; *BC* 14,16.

6:45 'They will all be taught by God.' The original context of this quote from Isaiah 54:13 is a promise of final redemption. Jesus, by indicating in the next sentence that those who participate in this reality are those who come to him, identified himself as the One by whom that final redemption comes. **Everyone who listens . . . comes to me.** Whoever wishes may come, but how is

ther and learns from him comes to me. 46No one has seen the Father except the one who is from God;[e] only he has seen the Father. 47I tell you the truth, he who believes has everlasting life. 48I am the bread of life.[f] 49Your forefathers ate the manna in the desert, yet they died.[g] 50But here is the bread that comes down from heaven,[h] which a man may eat and not die. 51I am the living bread that came down from heaven. If anyone eats of this bread, he will live forever. This bread is my flesh, which I will give for the life of the world."[i]

52Then the Jews began to argue sharply among themselves,[j] "How can this man give us his flesh to eat?"

53Jesus said to them, "I tell you the truth, unless you eat the flesh of the Son of Man[k] and drink his blood, you have no life in you. 54Whoever eats my flesh and drinks my blood has eternal life, and I will raise him up at the last day.[l] 55For my flesh is real food and my blood is real drink. 56Whoever eats my flesh and drinks my blood remains in me, and I in him.[m] 57Just as the living Father sent me[n] and I live because of the Father, so the one who feeds on me will live because of me. 58This is the bread that came down from heaven. Your forefathers ate manna and died, but he who feeds on this bread will live forever."[o] 59He said this while teaching in the synagogue in Capernaum.

Many Disciples Desert Jesus

60On hearing it, many of his disciples[p] said, "This is a hard teaching. Who can accept it?"

61Aware that his disciples were grumbling about this, Jesus said to them, "Does this offend you?[q] 62What if you see the Son of Man ascend to where he was before![r] 63The Spirit gives life;[s] the flesh counts for nothing. The words I have spoken to you are spirit[a] and they are life. 64Yet there are some of you who do not believe." For Jesus had known[t] from the beginning which of them did not believe and who would betray him. 65He went on to say, "This is why I told you that no one can come to me unless the Father has enabled him."[u]

66From this time many of his disciples[v] turned back and no longer followed him.

67"You do not want to leave too, do you?" Jesus asked the Twelve.[w]

68Simon Peter answered him,[x] "Lord, to whom shall we go? You have the words of eternal life. 69We believe and know that you are the Holy One of God."[y]

70Then Jesus replied, "Have I not chosen you,[z] the Twelve? Yet one of you is a devil!"[a] 71(He meant Judas, the son of Simon Iscariot, who, though one of the Twelve, was later to betray him.)

Jesus Goes to the Feast of Tabernacles

7 After this, Jesus went around in Galilee, purposely staying away from Judea because the Jews[b] there were waiting to take his life.[c] 2But when the Jewish Feast of Taber-

6:46 [e]Jn 1:18; 5:37; 7:29
6:48 [f]ver 35,51
6:49 [g]ver 31,58
6:50 [h]ver 33
6:51 [i]Heb 10:10
6:52 [j]Jn 7:43; 9:16; 10:19
6:53 [k]Mt 8:20
6:54 [l]ver 39
6:56 [m]Jn 15:4-7; 1Jn 3:24; 4:15
6:57 [n]Jn 3:17
6:58 [o]ver 49-51; Jn 3:36
6:60 [p]ver 66
6:61 [q]Mt 11:6
6:62 [r]Mk 16:19; Jn 3:13; 17:5
6:63 [s]2Co 3:6
6:64 [t]Jn 2:25
6:65 [u]ver 37,44
6:66 [v]ver 60
6:67 [w]Mt 10:2
6:68 [x]Mt 16:16
6:69 [y]Mk 8:29; Lk 9:20
6:70 [z]Jn 15:16,19 [a]Jn 13:27
7:1 [b]Jn 1:19 [c]Jn 5:18

[a] 63 Or *Spirit*

anyone to be made willing unless a work of grace is moving his or her heart to listen? See note on verse 44; *WCF* 1.6; *WLC* 67.

6:46 one who is from God. A claim to deity from the lips of Christ (1:18; 14:9).

6:48 See *BC* 35.

6:50–54 See *HC* 76.

6:51–58 Jesus' hearers continued to misunderstand his statements, for they took them on a purely literal and physical level (cf. v. 34). Taken literally, what Jesus said would be highly objectionable since it would involve cannibalism and the partaking of blood, which were strictly forbidden in the law (Ge 9:4; Lev 7:26–27; 17:10–14; Dt 12:23–24). In order to test their hearts, Jesus did not correct their misunderstanding. He used the figures of eating his flesh and drinking his blood to illustrate the surpassing intimacy of the union between Christ and the believer. This spiritual union, by which Christ imparts new life and sustenance to the believer, is portrayed later as the union of the vine and the branches (15:1–8). It is sometimes called a "mystical union" because its nature transcends our comprehension and involves an identification that goes beyond the union of husband and wife (Eph 5:32). From this union issue all the benefits of salvation as expressed in the formula "in Christ" (Gal 2:20; Eph 1:3–14). The reference to the Lord's Supper is only indirect. This passage is best understood as pointing to the spiritual reality that the Lord's Supper signifies: union with Christ and the reception of all the benefits of salvation through him.

6:51 the living bread that came down from heaven. The manna in the wilderness also came from heaven (vv. 31–33), but this bread does not perish (in contrast to the manna that spoiled in the wilderness). It gives eternal life, not merely physical life, to all who partake of it. See *BC* 35; *HC* 79.

6:53 unless you eat . . . and drink. Signifies the indispensable union with Christ through faith and the Holy Spirit. Apart from personal union with the Savior there is no hope of salvation.

6:55–56 See *HC* 76.

6:55 See *BC* 35; *HC* 79.

6:56 58 See *HC* 76.

6:62 see the Son of Man ascend. Similar to the term "lifted up" (see note on 3:14). If his disciples grumbled at the "hard teaching" (v. 60) of verses 53–58, what would be their response to the scandal of the crucifixion?

6:64–65 See *WCF* 3.6; 10.4; *WLC* 68.

6:65 no one can come to me unless. See note on verse 44.

6:66–71 Many disciples, together with the crowds, rejected Jesus in unbelief, although the faith of the Twelve deepened (as exemplified by Peter's confession).

6:67 "You do not want to leave . . . ?" Jesus' question elicited the firm confession of Peter as spokesman for the Twelve (see Mt 16:13–20; Mk 8:27–29; Lk 9:18–20).

▪ **7:1—10:21** *In Jerusalem Near the Feast of Tabernacles.* John turned to another set of events in Jesus' ministry in and around Jerusalem that centered around a time near the Feast of Tabernacles. John divides Jesus' activities into three main sections (see "Introduction: Outline").

▪ **7:1–13** *Leaving for Jerusalem.* John set the stage for the discussions that followed. The doubting of Jesus by his brothers (v. 5) and the foreboding element of Jesus needing to go privately to the

7:2 [d]Lev 23:34; Dt 16:16
7:3 [e]Mt 12:46
7:5 [f]Mk 3:21
7:6 [g]Mt 26:18
7:7 [h]Jn 15:18,19 [i]Jn 3:19,20
7:8 [j]ver 6
7:11 [k]Jn 11:56
7:12 [l]ver 40,43
7:13 [m]Jn 9:22; 12:42; 19:38
7:14 [n]ver 28; Mt 26:55
7:15 [o]Jn 1:19 [p]Ac 26:24 [q]Mt 13:54
7:16 [r]Jn 3:11; 14:24
7:17 [s]Ps 25:14; Jn 8:43
7:18 [t]Jn 5:41; 8:50,54
7:19 [u]Jn 1:17 [v]ver 1; Mt 12:14
7:20 [w]Jn 8:48; 10:20
7:22 [x]Lev 12:3

nacles[d] was near, 3 Jesus' brothers[e] said to him, "You ought to leave here and go to Judea, so that your disciples may see the miracles you do. 4 No one who wants to become
a public figure acts in secret. Since you are doing these things, show yourself to the
world." 5 For even his own brothers did not believe in him.[f]

6 Therefore Jesus told them, "The right time[g] for me has not yet come; for you any time
is right. 7 The world cannot hate you, but it hates me[h] because I testify that what it does
is evil.[i] 8 You go to the Feast. I am not yet[a] going up to this Feast, because for me the right
time[j] has not yet come." 9 Having said this, he stayed in Galilee.

10 However, after his brothers had left for the Feast, he went also, not publicly, but in
secret. 11 Now at the Feast the Jews were watching for him[k] and asking, "Where is that
man?"

12 Among the crowds there was widespread whispering about him. Some said, "He is
a good man."

Others replied, "No, he deceives the people."[l] 13 But no one would say anything publicly about him for fear of the Jews.[m]

Jesus Teaches at the Feast

14 Not until halfway through the Feast did Jesus go up to the temple courts and begin
to teach.[n] 15 The Jews[o] were amazed and asked, "How did this man get such learning[p]
without having studied?"[q]

16 Jesus answered, "My teaching is not my own. It comes from him who sent me.[r] 17 If
anyone chooses to do God's will, he will find out[s] whether my teaching comes from God
or whether I speak on my own. 18 He who speaks on his own does so to gain honor for
himself,[t] but he who works for the honor of the one who sent him is a man of truth; there
is nothing false about him. 19 Has not Moses given you the law?[u] Yet not one of you keeps
the law. Why are you trying to kill me?"[v]

20 "You are demon-possessed,"[w] the crowd answered. "Who is trying to kill you?"

21 Jesus said to them, "I did one miracle, and you are all astonished. 22 Yet, because
Moses gave you circumcision[x] (though actually it did not come from Moses, but from the

[a] 8 Some early manuscripts do not have *yet.*

Feast in order to prevent his arrest (v. 10) combine to alert the reader to the growing hostility toward Jesus.

7:2 Feast of Tabernacles. The most extended feast of the Jewish year (lasting seven days), the Feast of Tabernacles followed the Jewish New Year and the Day of Atonement (Yom Kippur; see Lev 23; Dt 16) and celebrated God's gracious provision for the Israelites in the desert and the completion of each year's harvest. Prominent among the festivities were a ceremonial water-drawing ritual (commemorating the provision of water in the desert; Nu 20:2–13) and a ceremonial lamp-lighting ritual. The first of these ceremonies provided the context for Jesus' proclamation in verses 37–38; the second, for his statement in 8:12.

7:3,5,10 brothers. Compare 2:12 (see also Mt 12:46).

7:6 The right time. See 2:4, 7:8,30, 8:20, 12:23, 13:1, 17:1, Matthew 26:18 and Mark 14:41. Such passages show the studied concern of Jesus to conform to God's schedule. Jesus' actions at specific moments in time carried redemptive significance for all time.

7:7 The world. Refers here to humanity in its opposition to God and his purpose. Jesus' brothers at that time identified with the world in their unbelief; later, at least some of them became believers (Ac 1:14). **evil.** Evildoers resent being unmasked by the good (3:19–20).

7:8 I am not yet going up to this Feast. See NIV text note. These words are not a contradiction of verse 10, for Jesus did indeed go to the Feast. Rather, his brothers asked him to do so in an open fashion, presenting himself unreservedly to the crowds there. Jesus asserted that he was not going to go there in such a fashion.

7:12 "He is a good man." A notable testimony from unprejudiced observers. Their words were truer than they knew (cf. Mk 10:18).

7:13 for fear of the Jews. The term "Jews" here is not a reference to the entire nation, much less to all those who were genetic descendants of Abraham. Rather, the term designates the Jewish leaders and officials, particularly those who were hostile toward Jesus.

■ **7:14—8:59** *Teaching the Jews.* Jesus taught the reacting crowds in a variety of settings and about a variety of topics.

7:14–24 The first discourse with the people and the first interaction with the crowds.

7:15 without having studied? Jesus had never been the disciple of a known rabbi, yet his knowledge and wisdom astounded those who heard him (cf. 3:2; Mt 7:28; Lk 2:47).

7:16 from him who sent me. Jesus indicated the source of his teaching. He was not an innovator, nor was his message original to himself but came from his Father. This is an important corrective to people (in his day and ours) who attempt to find human sources of Jesus' teaching. God the Father was the only source of the Son's teaching. This reality also confirms the divine origin of Old Testament Scripture to which Jesus so frequently referred.

7:17 will find out. A true perception of the divine nature of Christ's teaching is granted to those who earnestly desire to do God's will (i.e., to sincere believers, as contrasted with those who merely profess to be seeking God). See Psalm 25:14.

7:18 on his own. A contrast is established between self-seeking messengers and those exclusively concerned with being true to their mission (12:49). Jesus is one of the latter. **man of truth.** Literally, "true" (see 1:14,17; 14:6; 18:37; 2Co 11:10; Rev 3:7,14; 19:11 for passages where Christ and his message are identified with truth). It is notable that this term applies to God the Father (Ps 31:5; Isa 65:16; Jn 7:28; 8:26; 17:3; Ro 3:4; 1Th 1:9; 1Jn 5:20; Rev 6:10; 15:3; 16:7) and to the Holy Spirit (Jn 14:17; 15:26; 16:13; 1Jn 4:6; 5:6), as well as to the Scripture and apostolic preaching (Pss 119:30,43,138,142,151,160; Jn 17:17; Eph 1:13; Col 1:5; 2Ti 2:15; Jas 1:18). This is in sharp contrast with Satan, who is "a liar and the father of lies" (Jn 8:44). See *WLC* 130,159.

7:19 Moses . . . the law? The great blessing of receiving the law as the revelation of the will of God (cf. Ps 103:7; Ro 3:2; 9:4) becomes a liability through disobedience (Ro 7:7–12).

7:20 demon-possessed. This kind of accusation was leveled by those who had nothing further to say (cf. 8:48–52; 10:19–20; Mt 12:24). This accusation elicited one of the most frightening condemnations ever to come from Jesus' lips (Mt 12:31–32).

7:21 I did one miracle. Jesus did more than one miracle, but he was referring here to the one many in this region had witnessed: the healing of the lame man (5:1–15).

7:22 circumcision. Circumcision was prescribed in the Law of Moses (Lev 12:3), but it was already instituted by God in the days of Abraham (Ge 17:10–14). The regulation that it had to be performed on the eighth day was seen as so important that it took precedence over the law of rest on the Sabbath. This is not stipulated in Scripture, but it was obviously the practice among the Jews even in Jesus' day. Hence the argument Jesus presented here.

patriarchs),[y] you circumcise a child on the Sabbath. 23Now if a child can be circumcised
on the Sabbath so that the law of Moses may not be broken, why are you angry with me
for healing the whole man on the Sabbath? 24Stop judging by mere appearances, and
make a right judgment."[z]

Is Jesus the Christ?

25At that point some of the people of Jerusalem began to ask, "Isn't this the man they
are trying to kill? 26Here he is, speaking publicly, and they are not saying a word to him.
Have the authorities[a] really concluded that he is the Christ[a]? 27But we know where this
man is from;[b] when the Christ comes, no one will know where he is from."
28Then Jesus, still teaching in the temple courts,[c] cried out, "Yes, you know me, and
you know where I am from.[d] I am not here on my own, but he who sent me is true.[e] You
do not know him, 29but I know him[f] because I am from him and he sent me."
30At this they tried to seize him, but no one laid a hand on him,[g] because his time had
not yet come. 31Still, many in the crowd put their faith in him.[h] They said, "When the
Christ comes, will he do more miraculous signs[i] than this man?"
32The Pharisees heard the crowd whispering such things about him. Then the chief
priests and the Pharisees sent temple guards to arrest him.
33Jesus said, "I am with you for only a short time,[j] and then I go to the one who sent
me.[k] 34You will look for me, but you will not find me; and where I am, you cannot come."[l]
35The Jews said to one another, "Where does this man intend to go that we cannot
find him? Will he go where our people live scattered[m] among the Greeks,[n] and teach the
Greeks? 36What did he mean when he said, 'You will look for me, but you will not find
me,' and 'Where I am, you cannot come'?"
37On the last and greatest day of the Feast,[o] Jesus stood and said in a loud voice, "If
anyone is thirsty, let him come to me and drink.[p] 38Whoever believes in me, as[b] the Scripture has said,[q] streams of living water[r] will flow from within him."[s] 39By this he meant
the Spirit,[t] whom those who believed in him were later to receive.[u] Up to that time the
Spirit had not been given, since Jesus had not yet been glorified.[v]
40On hearing his words, some of the people said, "Surely this man is the Prophet."[w]
41Others said, "He is the Christ."
Still others asked, "How can the Christ come from Galilee?[x] 42Does not the Scripture
say that the Christ will come from David's family[c][y] and from Bethlehem,[z] the town where

7:22 [y]Ge 17:10-14
7:24 [z]Isa 11:3,4; Jn 8:15
7:26 [a]ver 48
7:27 [b]Mt 13:55; Lk 4:22
7:28 [c]ver 14 [d]Jn 8:14 [e]Jn 8:26,42
7:29 [f]Mt 11:27
7:30 [g]ver 32,44; Jn 10:39
7:31 [h]Jn 8:30 [i]Jn 2:11
7:33 [j]Jn 13:33; 16:16 [k]Jn 16:5,10,17,28
7:34 [l]Jn 8:21; 13:33
7:35 [m]Jas 1:1 [n]Jn 12:20; 1Pe 1:1
7:37 [o]Lev 23:36 [p]Isa 55:1; Rev 22:17
7:38 [q]Isa 58:11 [r]Jn 4:10 [s]Jn 4:14
7:39 [t]Joel 2:28; Ac 2:17,33 [u]Jn 20:22 [v]Jn 12:23; 13:31,32
7:40 [w]Mt 21:11; Jn 1:21
7:41 [x]ver 52; Jn 1:46
7:42 [y]Mt 1:1 [z]Mic 5:2; Mt 2:5,6; Lk 2:4

[a] *26* Or *Messiah*; also in verses 27, 31, 41 and 42 [b] *37,38* Or / *If anyone is thirsty, let him come to me. / And let him drink, 38who believes in me. / As* [c] *42* Greek *seed*

7:23 whole man. Jesus called attention to the inconsistency of his accusers. There were a number of activities permissible on the Sabbath, including circumcision. Jesus wondered how it could be right to permit an act that involved only the foreskin, yet wrong to allow one that involved the whole person.

7:25–36 In this highly ironic passage, the crowds disputed Jesus' origins (see note on 6:42).

7:27 we know where this man is from. The people thought that Jesus came from Galilee (vv. 41,52), and this seemed in opposition to both views held at that time by the Jews: that the Messiah would come from Bethlehem (v. 42; Mt 2:5–6) and that his origin would be unknown. Jesus, in response, pointed to his divine origin rather than to an earthly location. In failing to acknowledge his divine mission, Jesus' listeners showed their ignorance of God's plan in spite of the miracles that evidenced a special divine endorsement (v. 31).

7:29 See *BC* 10.

7:30 they tried to seize him. The plot against Jesus' life could not succeed until God's own time for it had come.

7:34 You will look for me, but you will not find me. This is not a contradiction of Matthew 7:7. The difference lies in the "seeking." In Matthew 7:7, Jesus was speaking about a true thirst for God (cf. v. 37) that only the Holy Spirit can generate in the sinner; but in John 7:34, he was referring to an effort to localize him, which would remain futile since the Pharisees and religious leaders could not send temple guards to heaven. Note the contrast between unbelievers (v. 34) and believers (14:3).

7:35 "Where does this man intend to go . . . ?" The Jews were puzzled as to Christ's origin, and this implied that they could not understand his destination, which was heaven. They understood the concept merely in geographical terms and were not pleased at the thought that he would exercise his ministry among the Greeks, heathens whom they despised.

7:37–38 At the climax of the Feast, Jesus gave a climactic message made emphatic by his posture (he stood) and his voice (he shouted). The message given to the Samaritan woman (4:10–14) was repeated here and explained by identifying *coming* to him with *believing* in him.

7:37 See *WLC* 171.

7:38–39 See *WCF* 20.1.

7:38 as the Scripture has said. This is not an exact quotation from the Old Testament, but it may well refer to a matrix of Old Testament passages that associate water with the eschatological gift of the Spirit (e.g., Isa 44:3; Eze 36:25–27), as well as passages using the metaphor of water to describe the blessings of the Messianic age (e.g., Isa 12:3; 58:11; Eze 47). The thrust of Jesus' proclamation is clear: In him the typology of the Feast of Tabernacles is fulfilled (see note on v. 2). **streams.** Implies great abundance that benefits not only believers, but also those around them.

7:39 the Spirit had not been given. John's inspired interpretation of this statement of Jesus makes it clear that it is a reference to the blessing of Pentecost. Although the Holy Spirit was operative in the Old Testament age, at Pentecost he entered into a more intimate relationship with all believers (14:17; 1Co 6:19). The Holy Spirit is the Messiah's gift to his people (Mt 3:11; Mk 1:8; Lk 3:16; Jn 16:7; Ac 2:1-21; cf. Eph 4:8).

7:40 the Prophet. See note on 6:14. Differing testimonies were given by those who were not blinded by their prejudice: (1) The Messiah would not do more miracles than Jesus did (v. 31). (2) Jesus could be "the Prophet" promised by Moses (v. 40). (3) Jesus was himself the "Christ," the Messiah (v. 41). (4) No one else ever spoke the way Jesus did (v. 46). An interesting study could be made of the witness given by Jesus' enemies.

7:41–43 Dispute over the identity of Jesus continued to focus on his origin (cf. vv. 25–36; see also notes on 6:42; 7:27). Similar misunderstandings occurred in Jesus' conversations with Nicodemus (3:1–15) and the Samaritan woman (4:1–26).

7:42 See *BC* 17,18.

7:43 [a]Jn 9:16; 10:19
David lived?" 43Thus the people were divided[a] because of Jesus. 44Some wanted to seize
him, but no one laid a hand on him.[b]
7:44 [b]ver 30

Unbelief of the Jewish Leaders

45Finally the temple guards went back to the chief priests and Pharisees, who asked
7:46 [c]Mt 7:28
them, "Why didn't you bring him in?"
46"No one ever spoke the way this man does,"[c] the guards declared.
7:47 [d]ver 12
47"You mean he has deceived you also?"[d] the Pharisees retorted. 48"Has any of the
rulers or of the Pharisees believed in him?[e] 49No! But this mob that knows nothing of the
7:48 [e]Jn 12:42
law—there is a curse on them."
50Nicodemus,[f] who had gone to Jesus earlier and who was one of their own number,
7:50 [f]Jn 3:1; 19:39
asked, 51"Does our law condemn anyone without first hearing him to find out what he
is doing?"
7:52 [g]ver 41
52They replied, "Are you from Galilee, too? Look into it, and you will find that a prophet[a] does not come out of Galilee."[g]

[The earliest manuscripts and many other ancient witnesses do not have John 7:53–8:11.]

53Then each went to his own home.
8:1 [h]Mt 21:1
8 But Jesus went to the Mount of Olives.[h] 2At dawn he appeared again in the temple
8:2 [i]ver 20; Mt 26:55
courts, where all the people gathered around him, and he sat down to teach them.[i]
3The teachers of the law and the Pharisees brought in a woman caught in adultery. They
made her stand before the group 4and said to Jesus, "Teacher, this woman was caught
8:5 [j]Lev 20:10; Dt 22:22
in the act of adultery. 5In the Law Moses commanded us to stone such women.[j] Now
what do you say?" 6They were using this question as a trap,[k] in order to have a basis for
8:6 [k]Mt 22:15,18 [l]Mt 12:10
accusing him.[l]
But Jesus bent down and started to write on the ground with his finger. 7When they
8:7 [m]Dt 17:7 [n]Ro 2:1, 22
kept on questioning him, he straightened up and said to them, "If any one of you is without sin, let him be the first to throw a stone[m] at her."[n] 8Again he stooped down and
wrote on the ground.
9At this, those who heard began to go away one at a time, the older ones first, until
only Jesus was left, with the woman still standing there. 10Jesus straightened up and
asked her, "Woman, where are they? Has no one condemned you?"
8:11 [o]Jn 3:17 [p]Jn 5:14
11"No one, sir," she said.
"Then neither do I condemn you,"[o] Jesus declared. "Go now and leave your life of sin."[p]

---

a 52 Two early manuscripts *the Prophet*

7:45–52 The strong prejudice of the chief priests and Pharisees is apparent in their condemnation of the temple guards (vv. 47–48), of the crowd (v. 49) and even of Nicodemus, one of their own number (v. 52).

7:46–49 See *WLC* 130.

7:52 Galilee was held in contempt by the Sanhedrin as a mixed-race region where the law was not zealously observed. If the NIV text note reading ("the Prophet") is accepted, the denial was based not on the assumption that no prophet could come from Galilee (the prophet Jonah had come from the region; 2Ki 14:25), but on the premise that "*the* Prophet" (emphasis added) surely would not come from so disreputable a region. Here again the question of Jesus' origin surfaces (see notes on 6:42; 7:27).

7:53—8:11 These verses are not found in most of the best Greek manuscripts of this Gospel. The ancient manuscripts that do contain them locate them in various places (here, after 7:36, after 21:25, after Lk 21:38 and after Lk 24:53). From 7:53 and 8:1 it is clear that the present location of this narrative is not the original one, for Jesus was not present in the meeting described in 7:45–52. This evidence suggests strongly that these verses were not part of the original manuscript of this Gospel, but in all probability they were of apostolic origin and do reflect an incident that actually occurred during Jesus' ministry.

8:5 the Law. Death for both participants was mandated for adultery (Lev 20:10; Dt 22:22), although stoning was not specified, except in the case of a betrothed virgin who fraudulently claimed to have been raped in the city (Dt 22:24). In no case was the male partner exempt from the death penalty. This shows that the accusers in this situation were not really concerned about fulfilling the Law of Moses.

8:6 a trap. If Jesus had told the accusers to proceed with the stoning, he would have violated the legislation by which Romans reserved for themselves the right to exact the death penalty in occupied lands (18:31). If Jesus had instructed them to release the woman, he would have appeared to be violating the Law of Moses by condoning adultery.

8:6 started to write. The only passage where Jesus is depicted as writing. Nothing is said about what he wrote.

8:7 Jesus' challenge disqualified the accusers as judges. Their concern was not to enforce the Mosaic Law but to entrap Jesus. In the process, they used this woman in her shame as a pawn to achieve their wicked design.

8:11 condemn. A legal term that indicates a sentence of judgment by a lawfully-constituted court (following the stipulations of the Mosaic injunctions). Jesus indicated that no such lawful procedures had been followed and that there was therefore no lawful basis for the capital punishment suggested. Jesus later admonished the woman and warned her not to continue in her sin—evidence that he did, in fact, reprove her immoral behavior.

The Validity of Jesus' Testimony

12 When Jesus spoke again to the people, he said, "I am[q] the light of the world.[r] Whoever follows me will never walk in darkness, but will have the light of life."[s]
13 The Pharisees challenged him, "Here you are, appearing as your own witness; your
testimony is not valid."[t]
14 Jesus answered, "Even if I testify on my own behalf, my testimony is valid, for I know
where I came from and where I am going.[u] But you have no idea where I come from[v] or
where I am going. 15 You judge by human standards;[w] I pass judgment on no one.[x] 16 But
if I do judge, my decisions are right, because I am not alone. I stand with the Father, who
sent me.[y] 17 In your own Law it is written that the testimony of two men is valid.[z] 18 I am
one who testifies for myself; my other witness is the Father, who sent me."[a]
19 Then they asked him, "Where is your father?"
"You do not know me or my Father,"[b] Jesus replied. "If you knew me, you would
know my Father also."[c] 20 He spoke these words while teaching[d] in the temple area near
the place where the offerings were put.[e] Yet no one seized him, because his time had not
yet come.[f]
21 Once more Jesus said to them, "I am going away, and you will look for me, and you
will die[g] in your sin. Where I go, you cannot come."[h]
22 This made the Jews ask, "Will he kill himself? Is that why he says, 'Where I go, you
cannot come'?"
23 But he continued, "You are from below; I am from above. You are of this world; I
am not of this world.[i] 24 I told you that you would die in your sins; if you do not believe
that I am ⌊the one I claim to be⌋,[a][j] you will indeed die in your sins."
25 "Who are you?" they asked.
"Just what I have been claiming all along," Jesus replied. 26 "I have much to say in
judgment of you. But he who sent me is reliable,[k] and what I have heard from him I tell
the world."[l]
27 They did not understand that he was telling them about his Father. 28 So Jesus said,
"When you have lifted up the Son of Man,[m] then you will know that I am ⌊the one I claim
to be⌋ and that I do nothing on my own but speak just what the Father has taught me.
29 The one who sent me is with me; he has not left me alone,[n] for I always do what pleases him."[o] 30 Even as he spoke, many put their faith in him.[p]

The Children of Abraham

31 To the Jews who had believed him, Jesus said, "If you hold to my teaching,[q] you are
really my disciples. 32 Then you will know the truth, and the truth will set you free."[r]

8:12 [q]Jn 6:35 [r]Jn 1:4; 12:35 [s]Pr 4:18; Mt 5:14
8:13 [t]Jn 5:31
8:14 [u]Jn 13:3; 16:28 [v]Jn 7:28; 9:29
8:15 [w]Jn 7:24 [x]Jn 3:17
8:16 [y]Jn 5:30
8:17 [z]Dt 17:6; Mt 18:16
8:18 [a]Jn 5:37
8:19 [b]Jn 16:3 [c]Jn 14:7; 1Jn 2:23
8:20 [d]Mt 26:55 [e]Mk 12:41 [f]Mt 26:18; Jn 7:30
8:21 [g]Eze 3:18 [h]Jn 7:34; 13:33
8:23 [i]Jn 3:31; 17:14
8:24 [j]Jn 4:26; 13:19
8:26 [k]Jn 7:28 [l]Jn 3:32; 15:15
8:28 [m]Jn 3:14; 5:19; 12:32
8:29 [n]ver 16; Jn 16:32 [o]Jn 4:34; 5:30; 6:38
8:30 [p]Jn 7:31
8:31 [q]Jn 15:7; 2Jn 9
8:32 [r]Ro 8:2; Jas 2:12

[a] *24* Or *I am he*; also in verse 28

8:12 I am the light of the world. During the Feast of Tabernacles, candles were lit to celebrate and signify the pillar of light that led the Israelites through the wilderness. The feast undoubtedly provided the setting for this image, since Jesus is the Light to which the pillar of fire as a type pointed. He is the glorious presence of God the Israelites saw in the wilderness (cf. 1:9). This statement amounted to a claim of deity, since only God is identified as light (1Jn 1:5). The words "I am" are reminiscent of Exodus 3:14 (see note on 6:35). **light of life.** Jesus was clearly referring to a spiritual reality.
8:13 your testimony is not valid. This discussion, which runs through verse 19, pivoted around the question of valid testimony. The laws of Deuteronomy (17:6; 19:15) required multiple witnesses. The Pharisees were not alleging that Jesus' testimony was false but that it was not legally acceptable (cf. 5:31).
8:14 my testimony is valid, for I know where I came from and where I am going. In this puzzling statement, Jesus says that whether or not the Jews receive his testimony, at least he himself knows it to be true, because unlike the Pharisees he knows his origin and destination. Again, Jesus' origin becomes the crucial point of conflict (see notes on 6:42; 7:27,41–43). Further, he implies that the Pharisees themselves should accept his self-testimony, because the Father from whom he came (v. 16), and to whom he will return (v. 21), was the second witness validating that testimony (see vv. 16,18).
8:16 I am not alone. The Father is his witness. See note on 5:31–47, where four witnesses supporting Jesus are enumerated. In any case, one who has the witness of God needs nothing more, for God is always right.
8:19 The Pharisees thought that Jesus' claim was a reference to his physical father, and they may have been eager to challenge him as a child allegedly born out of wedlock. In speaking of his Father, however, Jesus was not even making a reference to his supernatural conception by the Holy Spirit, but to his Trinitarian relation to the Father as the Son of God. Knowledge of the Father comes through the Son (1:18; 14:9; 1Jn 5:20). The Pharisees' blindness about Jesus was an index of their failure to know God in spite of their technical knowledge of the law.
8:21 I am going away. Jesus was envisioning the mystery of his death, resurrection and ascension. **you will die in your sin.** Clearly articulates the two destinies of humanity. Not all humans will be saved. Some cannot go where Jesus is (i.e., heaven). The only way of salvation is to believe (v. 24; 3:16,18).
8:23 You are from below. Jesus made a double contrast here: "from below"/"from above" (cf. 3:31) and "of this world"/"not of this world" (cf. 17:14).
8:24,28 I am the one I claim to be. Literally, "I am" (see NIV text note). Here Jesus applied Old Testament language for Yahweh to himself (Ex 3:14; Isa 43:10), an implied identification that would become unambiguous in verse 58. See *WCF* 10.4; *WLC* 60.
8:26 what I have heard from him. Jesus affirmed the divine origin and truth of his own teaching.
8:28 lifted up. See note on 3:14.
8:30 put their faith in him. From what is stated afterward (vv. 33,37,39) it is apparent that their profession was superficial. True believers are those who hold to, and remain attached to, Jesus' words (v. 31). Perseverance, or the lack of it, is one way to distinguish between those who are truly regenerated and those who have made an empty profession (15:2,6; 1Jn 2:19). We must refrain from hasty judgments in such matters, since even true believers may pass through periods of spiritual backsliding.
8:32 you will know the truth. Holding to the teaching of Christ, who himself embodies and epitomizes the truth (14:6), leads one to the truth that liberates the sinner from slavery to sin. Salvation is

33 They answered him, "We are Abraham's descendants[a] [s] and have never been slaves
of anyone. How can you say that we shall be set free?"
34 Jesus replied, "I tell you the truth, everyone who sins is a slave to sin.[t] 35 Now a slave
has no permanent place in the family, but a son belongs to it forever.[u] 36 So if the Son sets
you free, you will be free indeed. 37 I know you are Abraham's descendants. Yet you are
ready to kill me,[v] because you have no room for my word. 38 I am telling you what I have
seen in the Father's presence,[w] and you do what you have heard from your father.[b]"
39 "Abraham is our father," they answered.
"If you were Abraham's children,"[x] said Jesus, "then you would[c] do the things Abraham did. 40 As it is, you are determined to kill me, a man who has told you the truth that
I heard from God.[y] Abraham did not do such things. 41 You are doing the things your own
father does."[z]
"We are not illegitimate children," they protested. "The only Father we have is God
himself."[a]

The Children of the Devil

42 Jesus said to them, "If God were your Father, you would love me,[b] for I came from
God[c] and now am here. I have not come on my own;[d] but he sent me.[e] 43 Why is my language not clear to you? Because you are unable to hear what I say. 44 You belong to your
father, the devil,[f] and you want to carry out your father's desire.[g] He was a murderer
from the beginning, not holding to the truth, for there is no truth in him. When he lies,
he speaks his native language, for he is a liar and the father of lies.[h] 45 Yet because I tell
the truth,[i] you do not believe me! 46 Can any of you prove me guilty of sin? If I am telling
the truth, why don't you believe me? 47 He who belongs to God hears what God says.[j] The
reason you do not hear is that you do not belong to God."

8:33 [s] ver 37,39; Mt 3:9
8:34 [t] Ro 6:16; 2Pe 2:19
8:35 [u] Gal 4:30
8:37 [v] ver 39,40
8:38 [w] Jn 5:19,30; 14:10,24
8:39 [x] ver 37; Ro 9:7; Gal 3:7
8:40 [y] ver 26
8:41 [z] ver 38,44 [a] Isa 63:16; 64:8
8:42 [b] 1Jn 5:1 [c] Jn 16:27; 17:8 [d] Jn 7:28 [e] Jn 3:17
8:44 [f] 1Jn 3:8 [g] ver 38,41 [h] Ge 3:4
8:45 [i] Jn 18:37
8:47 [j] Jn 18:37; 1Jn 4:6

[a] *33* Greek *seed;* also in verse 37 [b] *38* Or *presence. Therefore do what you have heard from the Father.*
[c] *39* Some early manuscripts *"If you are Abraham's children," said Jesus, "then*

not obtained by intellectual knowledge, as the Gnostics imagined, but by a personal commitment to Jesus Christ and the truth he came to reveal (18:37). In John's writings, this is often the meaning of the verb "to know" (4:10; 7:29; 8:55; 15:21; 17:3).

8:33 We . . . have never been slaves. The Jews understood Jesus' statement as applying to external, political freedom. Even so, their claim appears strange, since Abraham's descendants were enslaved in Egypt, and after settling in Canaan, were often dominated by others, including the Philistines, the Assyrians, the Babylonians, the Persians, the Greeks, the Syrians and the Romans.

8:34–36 See *HC* 1.

8:34 everyone who sins is a slave. Rather than dispute their claim at the political level, Jesus showed that once again his statement was spiritual, not physical. He described the immense gravity of sin and the desperate predicament of humanity under sin. Deliverance cannot be achieved by one's own power, but the supernatural intervention of God is indispensable to emancipate the slaves of sin. Elsewhere, Scripture represents this condition as death (Eph 2:1). The work of God's grace is not merely a healing but is indeed a resurrection (Eph 2:5–6). See *WCF* 9.4; 20.3; *BC* 14.

8:36 the Son sets you free. Regeneration is the work of the Holy Spirit (3:3–8), accomplished on the basis of the substitutionary work of Christ (3:14–16). **free indeed.** Jesus did not have political freedom in view, nor merely a formal freedom by which we are not subject to outward coercion, for this is something that human beings as rational and responsible agents do often possess. True freedom consists in the ability to function and fulfill one's destiny in line with one's created nature. Sin deprives us of this because it obscures our minds, degrades our feelings and enslaves our wills. This is what the Reformers called radical or total depravity. The only remedy is the grace of God in regeneration. See *WCF* 9.4; *BC* 24.

8:37 Abraham's descendants. The Jews could indeed claim a genealogical continuity with Abraham, as could the Ishmaelites and the Edomites. God is not primarily interested in physical ancestry, but rather in spiritual continuity. If one is walking in the path of disobedience (Eze 18), it does not matter how good his or her ancestors have been, nor does it matter for one renewed by God's Spirit and walking in the way of faith how bad this person's ancestors have been. True parentage is revealed in the direction of one's own life rather than in genealogical records (Gal 3:29).

8:40 the truth that I heard from God. Jesus manifests here a full consciousness of his own origin and ministry. **Abraham did not do such things.** Abraham showed himself to be obedient to God's messages even when such obedience was painful. Although these Jews claimed to be Abraham's descendants, they did not act as his descendants should act. Here the accent is on obedience, the true criteria for sonship, as over against biology.

8:41 illegitimate children. This may well have been a sarcastic reference to the birth of Jesus, for the Jews considered him illegitimate. **Father . . . God.** Except in synagogue liturgy, the Jews seldom emphasized that God was their "Father." The emphasis on divine fatherhood is a feature of Jesus' teaching. It relates to those who are saved and received into God's household by adoption. God is the Father of the Son in a unique sense (3:16), but he is also the Father of those who are in Christ (20:17). See *WCF* 18.1.

8:42 you would love me. The unity between Father and Son is so profound that a diversity of attitude toward them is impossible. Again Jesus' origin is a point of contention (see notes on 6:42; 7:27,41–43).

8:43 my language. Literally, "my speech" (i.e., the very words he pronounced). The Jews had so obstinately closed their minds to Jesus' message that they had become unable even to hear him (see v. 47).

8:44 You belong to your father, the devil. The relation of truth and upright moral behavior is again reiterated. People love darkness rather than light, because their deeds are evil (3:19). The frightful contrast is apparent. Ultimately there are just two options: God or Satan. By God's grace, Abraham (vv. 39–41) walked in the way of faith and obedience. The Jews, in rejecting Jesus, were doing the opposite. Hence Christ's strong denunciation. **you want.** The predicament of sin is that it orients the will to do what is evil. Only a supernatural act of grace can reorient the will to do good. **He was a murderer . . . a liar.** Among all the sins that could be mentioned as characteristic of Satan, murder and lying are singled out—lying, because it is the direct opposite of "truth," the central emphasis of this section (vv. 32–47), and murder, because the desire to kill Jesus was already in the Pharisees' hearts (vv. 13,40). Satan contrasts sharply with Jesus, who is "the truth and the life" (14:6) and the Giver of life (10:10,28). See *WLC* 19; *BC* 12; *HC* 9,112.

8:46 Can any of you prove me guilty of sin? Jesus is free of all sin (2Co 5:21, Heb 7:26), always doing what pleases the Father (Jn 8:29). Therefore, no one could demonstrate his guilt in any matter. See theological article "The Sinlessness of Jesus" at Hebrews 4.

8:47 you do not hear. Sin paralyzes our spiritual senses. It takes an act of God's grace to enable a sinner to hear his voice (cf. v. 43; 10:3–4,16,27). See *WCF* 3.6; *BC* 29.

The Claims of Jesus About Himself

48The Jews answered him, "Aren't we right in saying that you are a Samaritan[k] and
demon-possessed?"[l]
49"I am not possessed by a demon," said Jesus, "but I honor my Father and you dishonor me. 50I am not seeking glory for myself;[m] but there is one who seeks it, and he is
the judge. 51I tell you the truth, if anyone keeps my word, he will never see death."[n]
52At this the Jews exclaimed, "Now we know that you are demon-possessed! Abraham
died and so did the prophets, yet you say that if anyone keeps your word, he will never
taste death. 53Are you greater than our father Abraham?[o] He died, and so did the prophets. Who do you think you are?"
54Jesus replied, "If I glorify myself,[p] my glory means nothing. My Father, whom you
claim as your God, is the one who glorifies me.[q] 55Though you do not know him,[r] I know
him.[s] If I said I did not, I would be a liar like you, but I do know him and keep his word.[t]
56Your father Abraham[u] rejoiced at the thought of seeing my day; he saw it[v] and was
glad."
57"You are not yet fifty years old," the Jews said to him, "and you have seen Abraham!"
58"I tell you the truth," Jesus answered, "before Abraham was born,[w] I am!"[x] 59At this,
they picked up stones to stone him,[y] but Jesus hid himself,[z] slipping away from the temple grounds.

Jesus Heals a Man Born Blind

9 As he went along, he saw a man blind from birth. 2His disciples asked him, "Rab
bi,[a] who sinned,[b] this man[c] or his parents,[d] that he was born blind?"
3"Neither this man nor his parents sinned," said Jesus, "but this happened so that the
work of God might be displayed in his life.[e] 4As long as it is day,[f] we must do the work
of him who sent me. Night is coming, when no one can work. 5While I am in the world,
I am the light of the world."[g]
6Having said this, he spit[h] on the ground, made some mud with the saliva, and put

8:48 [k]Mt 10:5 [l]ver 52; Jn 7:20
8:50 [m]ver 54; Jn 5:41
8:51 [n]Jn 11:26
8:53 [o]Jn 4:12
8:54 [p]ver 50 [q]Jn 16:14; 17:1,5
8:55 [r]ver 19 [s]Jn 7:28,29 [t]Jn 15:10
8:56 [u]ver 37,39 [v]Mt 13:17; Heb 11:13
8:58 [w]Jn 1:2; 17:5,24 [x]Ex 3:14
8:59 [y]Lev 24:16; Jn 10:31; 11:8 [z]Jn 12:36
9:2 [a]Mt 23:7 [b]ver 34; Lk 13:2; Ac 28:4 [c]Eze 18:20 [d]Ex 20:5; Job 21:19
9:3 [e]Jn 11:4
9:4 [f]Jn 11:9; 12:35
9:5 [g]Jn 1:4; 8:12; 12:46
9:6 [h]Mk 7:33; 8:23

8:48 a Samaritan. A term of contempt, possibly implying a charge that Jesus' physical father was a Samaritan who had engendered Jesus out of wedlock (see note on v. 41). **demon-possessed.** When cornered by the truth, Jesus' enemies resorted to blasphemy (Mt 12:24,31).

8:49 I am not possessed. Jesus' conduct, in honoring the Father (cf. 17:4) and declining to seek glory for himself, was precisely the opposite of what a demon-possessed person would do. Jesus was not afraid to refer the matter to God's judgment. See *WLC* 111.

8:51 if any one keeps my word, he will never see death. Biblically, death is the judicial punishment for sin (Ro 6:23). Since Jesus died as a substitute for his people, those who belong to him will never see this judicial punishment; they are freed from the penalty of their sin because Christ endured it for them. **never.** In extending the promise beyond this life, Jesus laid claim to a divine prerogative. The Jews understood the statement as promising avoidance of physical death. Earlier statements made clear what Jesus meant (5:24–29).

8:53 Are you greater than our Father Abraham? Abraham and the prophets, great as they were in the history of redemption, could not remove the curse of death. Only Christ triumphed over the grave, and he is, in this sense, far greater than Abraham and the prophets.

8:54 my glory. In the days of his earthly ministry, Jesus did not seek glory even though it belonged to him as God. This glory was evident to those who had eyes to see it (1:14). It was made apparent in his resurrection and ascension (1Ti 3:16) and will be displayed in full splendor at his second coming. Glory supremely belongs to God, and in claiming it, Jesus laid claim to deity. See *BC* 10.

8:56 Abraham . . . saw it and was glad. Abraham, albeit from a limited perspective, foresaw Christ's day as he embraced in faith many promises given to him by God, promises that could only be fulfilled by the coming of Christ. Since the context of the present discussion concerned Satan as a murderer and Jesus as the One whose substitutionary death delivers people from death, it may have special reference to God's providing the ram as a substitute when Abraham was preparing to sacrifice Isaac (Ge 22). This statement makes it clear that even in Old Testament times, believers were not saved independently of Jesus Christ but through faith in Christ, who was presented to them through the foreshadowings God provided in the law and historical acts (cf. Ac 4:12). See *WCF* 7.5.

8:57 fifty years old. Jesus was closer to 30 years old (Lk 3:23).

8:58 "before Abraham was born, I am!" A clear reference to Jesus' eternal preexistence and therefore to his deity (see notes on 1:1–2; 8:24,28; 17:5). See also *BC* 10.

8:59 they picked up stones. The Jews rightly understood Christ's words as a claim of deity, and since they would not accept this claim, they treated it as a blasphemy, for which stoning was required in the law (Lev 24:16; cf. Mt 26:65; Jn 10:31).

■ **9:1—10:21** *Healing and Teaching.* Jesus, the light of the world (8:12; 9:5), gave sight to a blind man (9:1–34) in an account that serves to introduce his condemnation of the spiritual blindness of those who reject him (9:35—10:21).

9:2 who sinned . . . ? The Jews, like Job's friends, frequently held the faulty view that every temporal misfortune represented God's punitive visitation for some specific sin. They believed that congenital defects were the result of sin committed already by the child while in the mother's womb or by the parents whose misbehavior victimized their child. Jesus dismissed these theories as improper explanations (v. 3), but his dismissal does not imply that certain trials in our lives are not God-ordained punishments for specific sin (note the life of David after he had committed adultery and murder [2Sa 12–21] and the punishment of the wicked and foolish delineated in Proverbs). Nor does Jesus here dismiss the Biblical doctrine of original sin (Ro 5:12–21), which teaches that all human suffering is tied to our corporate sin and rebellion in Adam. In the case of the sufferings of others, it is unwise and inappropriate for us to judge them as specifically punitive (Mt 7:1). The question posed to Jesus was a false dilemma. Only two options were given as the reason for the man's affliction: his own sin or that of his parents. Jesus offered a third option (v. 3).

9:3 that the work of God might be displayed. Some of our sufferings, like those of Job, are intended to display the glory of God, either through our patient endurance (1Pe 4:12–19) or through a spectacular healing, as in the present case. God in his providence uses suffering for a redemptive purpose. That purpose is not always known to us, but we have God's assurance that his objective in our affliction is always good. See *HC* 27.

9:6 he spit on the ground. In Mark 8:23–25, Jesus also used saliva as an ingredient for healing. Jesus could heal the blind without such means, though in other cases he touched the blind person in some way (Mt 9:29; 20:34). Jesus' physical touch, in addition to his word, engaged the blind person's remaining senses, giving him a vivid sense of Jesus' involvement in his healing. In this case, Jesus' procedure also provided opportunity for this man to show his faith by obeying Jesus' command (v. 7). Evidently Jesus used various means of healing, each appropriate to the particular needy person.

it on the man's eyes. 7“Go,” he told him, “wash in the Pool of Siloam”[i] (this word means
Sent). So the man went and washed, and came home seeing.[j]
8His neighbors and those who had formerly seen him begging asked, “Isn't this the
same man who used to sit and beg?”[k] 9Some claimed that he was.
Others said, “No, he only looks like him.”
But he himself insisted, “I am the man.”
10“How then were your eyes opened?” they demanded.
11He replied, “The man they call Jesus made some mud and put it on my eyes. He told
me to go to Siloam and wash. So I went and washed, and then I could see.”[l]
12“Where is this man?” they asked him.
“I don't know,” he said.

The Pharisees Investigate the Healing

13They brought to the Pharisees the man who had been blind. 14Now the day on
which Jesus had made the mud and opened the man's eyes was a Sabbath.[m] 15Therefore
the Pharisees also asked him how he had received his sight.[n] “He put mud on my eyes,”
the man replied, “and I washed, and now I see.”
16Some of the Pharisees said, “This man is not from God, for he does not keep the Sabbath.”[o]
But others asked, “How can a sinner do such miraculous signs?” So they were divided.[p]
17Finally they turned again to the blind man, “What have you to say about him? It was
your eyes he opened.”
The man replied, “He is a prophet.”[q]
18The Jews[r] still did not believe that he had been blind and had received his sight until they sent for the man's parents. 19“Is this your son?” they asked. “Is this the one you
say was born blind? How is it that now he can see?”
20“We know he is our son,” the parents answered, “and we know he was born blind.
21But how he can see now, or who opened his eyes, we don't know. Ask him. He is of age;
he will speak for himself.” 22His parents said this because they were afraid of the Jews,[s]
for already the Jews had decided that anyone who acknowledged that Jesus was the
Christ[a] would be put out[t] of the synagogue.[u] 23That was why his parents said, “He is of
age; ask him.”[v]
24A second time they summoned the man who had been blind. “Give glory to God,[b]”[w]
they said. “We know this man is a sinner.”[x]
25He replied, “Whether he is a sinner or not, I don't know. One thing I do know. I was
blind but now I see!”
26Then they asked him, “What did he do to you? How did he open your eyes?”
27He answered, “I have told you already[y] and you did not listen. Why do you want to
hear it again? Do you want to become his disciples, too?”
28Then they hurled insults at him and said, “You are this fellow's disciple! We are disciples of Moses![z] 29We know that God spoke to Moses, but as for this fellow, we don't
even know where he comes from.”[a]
30The man answered, “Now that is remarkable! You don't know where he comes
from, yet he opened my eyes. 31We know that God does not listen to sinners. He listens
to the godly man who does his will.[b] 32Nobody has ever heard of opening the eyes of a
man born blind. 33If this man were not from God,[c] he could do nothing.”

9:7 [i]ver 11; 2Ki 5:10; Lk 13:4 [j]Isa 35:5; Jn 11:37
9:8 [k]Ac 3:2,10
9:11 [l]ver 7
9:14 [m]Jn 5:9
9:15 [n]ver 10
9:16 [o]Mt 12:2 [p]Jn 6:52; 7:43; 10:19
9:17 [q]Mt 21:11
9:18 [r]Jn 1:19
9:22 [s]Jn 7:13 [t]ver 34; Lk 6:22 [u]Jn 12:42; 16:2
9:23 [v]ver 21
9:24 [w]Jos 7:19 [x]ver 16
9:27 [y]ver 15
9:28 [z]Jn 5:45
9:29 [a]Jn 8:14
9:31 [b]Ge 18:23-32; Ps 34:15,16; 66:18; 145:19,20; Pr 15:29; Isa 1:15; 59:1,2; Jn 15:7; Jas 5:16-18; 1Jn 5:14,15
9:33 [c]ver 16; Jn 3:2

a *22* Or *Messiah* b *24* A solemn charge to tell the truth (see Joshua 7:19)

9:9 he only looks like him. The transformation was so stunning that onlookers could not believe this was the same man.

9:12 I don't know. As the story developed, the healed man moved forward along the path of faith. Here, he did not know where Jesus was; later he asserted that Jesus was a prophet (v. 17); later still he raised doubts concerning the accusation that Jesus was a sinner (v. 25); and finally, after a new encounter with Jesus, he acknowledged Jesus' Messiahship (the Son of Man) and worshiped him (vv. 35–38). These steps of faith are characteristic of what the author of this Gospel desired to engender in his readers (20:31).

9:16 Sabbath. Instead of recognizing in this healing a supernatural work of the grace of God, the Pharisees began to haggle about Sabbath observance. Their concern was not specifically about the Law as given in the fourth commandment (Ex 20:8–11; Dt 5:12–15) but about their traditional interpretation of what this command required. Not one of the actions involved (spitting, applying mud, going as far as Siloam, washing one's face, healing a blind man) could be rightly considered as forbidden by the fourth commandment or any other stipulation of the Mosaic Law. Instead of saying, “Our view of the Sabbath should be modified since God evidently blesses the ministry of one who does not follow our interpretation,” they rejected Jesus and his ministry (v. 16).

9:17 What have you to say . . . ? A strange question, since they claimed to have a monopoly on the teaching of the law and yet were unprepared to accept the man's answer.

9:18–23 An inquiry directed to the blind man's parents would have verified the reality of both the sickness and the healing, but because of their cowardice they took the matter no further.

9:24–34 A second investigation of the healed man brought no new facts to light, but it did manifest a hardening of the positions. The Pharisees called Jesus “a sinner” (v. 24) and one whose origin was unknown (v. 29), and they proceeded to excommunicate the man, who taunted them with sarcastic questions (vv. 27,30). The pungency of the questions is bolstered by the facts: The man born blind had been healed (v. 30), and “God does not listen to sinners” (v. 31).

34 To this they replied, "You were steeped in sin at birth;[d] how dare you lecture us!"
And they threw him out.[e]

Spiritual Blindness

35 Jesus heard that they had thrown him out, and when he found him, he said, "Do you
believe in the Son of Man?"
36 "Who is he, sir?" the man asked. "Tell me so that I may believe in him."[f]
37 Jesus said, "You have now seen him; in fact, he is the one speaking with you."[g]
38 Then the man said, "Lord, I believe," and he worshiped him.[h]
39 Jesus said, "For judgment[i] I have come into this world,[j] so that the blind will see[k]
and those who see will become blind."[l]
40 Some Pharisees who were with him heard him say this and asked, "What? Are we
blind too?"[m]
41 Jesus said, "If you were blind, you would not be guilty of sin; but now that you claim
you can see, your guilt remains.[n]

The Shepherd and His Flock

10 "I tell you the truth, the man who does not enter the sheep pen by the gate, but
climbs in by some other way, is a thief and a robber. 2 The man who enters by
the gate is the shepherd of his sheep.[o] 3 The watchman opens the gate for him, and the
sheep listen to his voice.[p] He calls his own sheep by name and leads them out. 4 When
he has brought out all his own, he goes on ahead of them, and his sheep follow him because they know his voice. 5 But they will never follow a stranger; in fact, they will run
away from him because they do not recognize a stranger's voice." 6 Jesus used this figure
of speech,[q] but they did not understand what he was telling them.
7 Therefore Jesus said again, "I tell you the truth, I am the gate for the sheep. 8 All who
ever came before me[r] were thieves and robbers, but the sheep did not listen to them. 9 I
am the gate; whoever enters through me will be saved.[a] He will come in and go out, and
find pasture. 10 The thief comes only to steal and kill and destroy; I have come that they
may have life, and have it to the full.

9:34 [d]ver 2 [e]ver 22,35; Isa 66:5
9:36 [f]Ro 10:14
9:37 [g]Jn 4:26
9:38 [h]Mt 28:9
9:39 [i]Jn 5:22 [j]Jn 3:19 [k]Lk 4:18 [l]Mt 13:13
9:40 [m]Ro 2:19
9:41 [n]Jn 15:22,24
10:2 [o]ver 11,14
10:3 [p]ver 4,5,14,16,27
10:6 [q]Jn 16:25
10:8 [r]Jer 23:1,2

[a] 9 Or *kept safe*

9:35–38 In this second encounter with Jesus, the healed man's faith moved from a general confidence in Jesus' godly mission to a joyful acceptance of him as the Messiah and to worship of him as God.

9:39–41 In this epilogue Jesus revealed the impact of his coming: Those who were thought to have a special insight into the things of God were shown to be blind opponents of God's ways. On the other hand, others who were, like all of humanity, by nature spiritually blind were made to see when the Spirit of God opened their eyes and led them to faith.

9:39 For judgment I have come. The first coming of Jesus did not immediately precipitate the Last Judgment (3:17; 12:47), but it inevitably confronted human beings with the obligation to decide for or against him (Mt 12:30; Lk 11:23). Until the second coming of Christ, we still live in the age of redemption, during which the blind are made to see and those dead in transgressions are raised to newness of life (Eph 2:4–5).

9:41 you claim you can see. Unrepentant unbelief is not the only ground for ultimate condemnation, but it marks one of the most damaging attitudes human beings may take toward God, Christ or the Holy Spirit.

10:1 The imagery of the shepherd and the flock of sheep has roots in the Old Testament. Jacob called God his "shepherd" (Ge 48:15; 49:24), as did David (Pss 23:1; 28:9), Asaph (Pss 78:52; 80:1), Isaiah (Isa 40:11), Jeremiah (Jer 31:10), Ezekiel (Eze 34:11–16) and the author of Psalm 100. Then again, rulers over a nation were frequently compared to shepherds (Nu 27:17; 2Sa 7:7; 1Ki 22:17; Isa 56:11; Jer 23:1; 50:6; Eze 34:5; Zec 11:9,17). A prophecy in Zechariah 13:7 concerning the shepherd of Israel was applied by Jesus to himself (Mt 26:31). In the parables of the lost sheep (Mt 18:12–14; Lk 15:3–7), Jesus assumed the title, and its implications were more fully developed. Later on, Jesus is referred to as "that great Shepherd" (Heb 13:20) and "the Chief Shepherd" (1Pe 5:4), and in Revelation 7:17 we read that "the Lamb . . . will be their shepherd." Jesus in turn delegates some of these responsibilities to leaders in his church, who become undershepherds (Jn 21:15–17; Ac 20:28; 1Pe 5:2). **the sheep pen.** An enclosure with one entrance and fences that prevented not only the sheep from wandering off but also predators from entering in.

10:2 enters by the gate. A legitimate shepherd does not need to climb over the fence but is readily admitted by the watchman. The language here implies that several flocks are kept within this fold and that a proper shepherd relates specifically to his own sheep.

10:3 sheep listen. The shepherd knows his sheep by name, and the sheep readily recognize the voice of the shepherd and respond by following him. This is a graphic representation of the gracious, elective purpose of God, who has marked some people as his own in the midst of fallen humanity. **by name.** This knowledge is individual and intimate, and provision is made for the sheep's needs (vv. 4,10). See *BC* 27.

10:4 know his voice. Elective grace is also effectual grace: God who knows his sheep makes himself known to them in such a way that they will respond. He does not force them to follow him against their will but makes them willing and happy to do so. See *BC* 27,29.

10:5 they will never follow a stranger. This comforting promise does not exclude the necessity of warning believers against misleading teachers (Mk 13:22–23; 2Ti 3:5; 4:2–5; 1Jn 2:26).

10:6 this figure of speech. Figures that illustrate the truth may also confuse or perplex. In some cases the disciples themselves did not understand what Jesus was saying (Mt 13:10–17,36; 15:15).

10:7 I am the gate for the sheep. Jesus changed the metaphor from "shepherd" to "gate." As the "gate for the sheep," Jesus is the One through whom eternal life is gained (cf. 14:6; Mt 7:13–14). The "I am" formula is continued (see note on 6:35).

10:8 thieves and robbers. This surely does not refer to true Old Testament prophets sent by God (Mt 21:34–36; 23:29–36) but to false and unprincipled teachers like those castigated in Ezekiel 34 and perhaps also to the scribes and Pharisees of Jesus' time.

10:9 whoever enters through me will be saved. Here is the guarantee that salvation is always granted to those who truly trust in Christ (Ac 16:31; Ro 10:9–10). These only are saved (Jn 14:6), and Christ is necessary and sufficient for salvation (3:36). **come in and go out.** The sheep come into the fold for safety and go out to pasture, all under the shepherd's guidance. See *BC* 21,26.

10:10 that they may have life, and have it to the full. God's ultimate purpose is never to impoverish his own, but to enrich them and extend to them infinite and everlasting blessedness. See *BC* 35.

11 "I am the good shepherd.[s] The good shepherd lays down his life for the sheep.[t]
12 The hired hand is not the shepherd who owns the sheep. So when he sees the wolf coming, he abandons the sheep and runs away.[u] Then the wolf attacks the flock and scatters it. 13 The man runs away because he is a hired hand and cares nothing for the sheep.
14 "I am the good shepherd;[v] I know my sheep[w] and my sheep know me— 15 just as
the Father knows me and I know the Father[x]—and I lay down my life for the sheep. 16 I
have other sheep[y] that are not of this sheep pen. I must bring them also. They too will
listen to my voice, and there shall be one flock[z] and one shepherd.[a] 17 The reason my Father loves me is that I lay down my life[b]—only to take it up again. 18 No one takes it from
me, but I lay it down of my own accord.[c] I have authority to lay it down and authority to
take it up again. This command I received from my Father."[d]

10:11 [s]ver 14; Isa 40:11; Eze 34:11-16,23; Heb 13:20; 1Pe 5:4; Rev 7:17 [t]Jn 15:13; 1Jn 3:16
10:12 [u]Zec 11:16,17
10:14 [v]ver 11 [w]ver 27
10:15 [x]Mt 11:27
10:16 [y]Isa 56:8 [z]Jn 11:52; Eph 2:11-19 [a]Eze 37:24; 1Pe 2:25
10:17 [b]ver 11,15,18
10:18 [c]Mt 26:53 [d]Jn 15:10; Php 2:8; Heb 5:8

10:11 good shepherd. A return to the earlier metaphor of "shepherd." **lays down his life.** Christ's shepherding necessitated a sacrificial activity in which death ensued (vv. 15,17). He did more than risk his life (cf. 1Sa 17:34–36); he *gave* it, enduring death as a substitute for guilty sinners. This is intimated in the name "Lamb of God," which was given by John the Baptist (1:29) and expressed in other statements by Jesus himself (2:19; 3:14; 6:51). **for the sheep.** The intent of this sacrifice is for "the sheep" (not the goats). See John 17:2,6 and 24 and notes on 10:3,4 and 26. *BC* 27.
10:12 The hired hand. Jesus contrasts his sacrificial service with the cowardly abandonment of the sheep by those motivated by self-interest. Thieves prey on the sheep and hired hands abandon them, but Jesus lays down his life for them.
10:14–16 See *HC* 54.
10:14 I know my sheep and my sheep know me. A parallel to the mutuality between the Father and the Son in the Trinity (v. 15; cf. 17:21–23). It is clear that the verb "to know" here, as so often in Scripture, means much more than mere intellectual perception; it includes intense emotional attachment and volitional commitment. God's knowing of a person in this fashion refers to his redemptive, gracious election. See *BC* 27,29.
10:15–18 See theological article "Definite Atonement," below.
10:15–16 See *WCF* 8.8; *WLC* 59.
10:15 See *CD* 2.I; 2.VII.
10:16 other sheep. An obvious reference to the universal character of the New Testament age, in which salvation is broadly offered to all nations. See *WLC* 64; *BC* 27.
10:17 my Father loves me. The self-sacrifice of the Son is so profound an act of love and obedience to God's plan that it inevitably enhances love among the three persons of the Trinity.

Definite Atonement: For Whom Did Jesus Die?

REFORMED theology affirms the doctrine of *definite atonement*, which is sometimes called *particular redemption, effective atonement* or *limited atonement* ("limited" not in reference to the power or value of Jesus' death, but in reference to the number of people for whom Christ purchased salvation). Definite atonement is to be distinguished from two other prominent views of the atonement: *universalism* and *general ransom*. All three views, including definite atonement, affirm that Christ's sacrifice is of infinite worth. General ransom and definite atonement both affirm that the free offer of the gospel comes genuinely from God to all those who hear the Good News of Christ. Universalism insists that everyone is saved, regardless of whether or not he or she responds positively to the gospel.

These three views can be most easily distinguished by looking at two different aspects of the atonement: (1) Jesus' work on the cross by which he obtained salvation and (2) the Holy Spirit's application of salvation to individuals. Universalism claims that Christ obtained salvation for everyone in the world and that the Holy Spirit applies salvation to everyone in the world so that all are saved. General ransom holds that although Christ obtained salvation for everyone in the world, the Holy Spirit applies salvation only to those who come to faith so that only these are actually saved. Definite atonement holds that Christ obtained salvation only for the elect and that the Holy Spirit applies salvation only to the elect (see theological article "Predestination and Foreknowledge" at Ro 8).

According to general ransom, while Christ's death made salvation possible for everyone in the world (both the elect and the reprobate), it did not make anyone's salvation certain. Definite atonement, however, insists that the Holy Spirit will necessarily apply salvation to everyone for whom Christ died so that all for whom Christ died must eventually be saved.

Scripture speaks of God as having chosen for salvation a great number from the fallen human race (these are the "elect") and as having sent Christ into the world to save them (Jn 6:37–40; 10:27–29; 11:51–52; Ro 8:28–39; Eph 1:3–14; 1Pe 1:20). Christ is regularly said to have died for particular groups or persons, with the clear implication that his death fully secured their salvation (Jn 10:15–18,27–29; Ro 5:8–10; 8:32; Gal 2:20; 3:13–14; 4:4–5; 1Jn 4:9–10; Rev 1:4–6; 5:9–10). Facing his suffering on the cross, Jesus prayed only for those whom the Father had given him, not for the "world" (i.e., the rest of humanity; Jn 17:9,20).

Nevertheless, it is also important to affirm the free offer of Jesus Christ in the gospel alongside the doctrine of definite atonement. It is a certain truth that whoever comes to Christ in faith will find mercy (Jn 6:35,47–51,54–57; Ro 1:16; 10:8–13). Those whom God has chosen hear Christ's offer, and through hearing it, they are effectually called by the Holy Spirit. Both the invitation and the effectual calling flow from Christ's sin-bearing death. Those who reject the offer of Christ do so because they choose to (Mt 22:1–7; Jn 3:18), so their final perishing is their own fault. Those who receive Jesus learn to thank him for the fact that his blood fully cleansed them from all unrighteousness, for they know that without this working of his grace, all hope would have been lost.

19 At these words the Jews were again divided.[e] 20 Many of them said, "He is demon-
possessed[f] and raving mad.[g] Why listen to him?"
21 But others said, "These are not the sayings of a man possessed by a demon.[h] Can
a demon open the eyes of the blind?"[i]

The Unbelief of the Jews

22 Then came the Feast of Dedication[a] at Jerusalem. It was winter, 23 and Jesus was in
the temple area walking in Solomon's Colonnade.[j] 24 The Jews[k] gathered around him,
saying, "How long will you keep us in suspense? If you are the Christ,[b] tell us plainly."[l]
25 Jesus answered, "I did tell you,[m] but you do not believe. The miracles I do in my Father's name speak for me,[n] 26 but you do not believe because you are not my sheep.[o] 27 My
sheep listen to my voice; I know them,[p] and they follow me.[q] 28 I give them eternal life,
and they shall never perish; no one can snatch them out of my hand.[r] 29 My Father, who
has given them to me,[s] is greater than all[c];[t] no one can snatch them out of my Father's
hand. 30 I and the Father are one."[u]
31 Again the Jews picked up stones to stone him,[v] 32 but Jesus said to them, "I have
shown you many great miracles from the Father. For which of these do you stone me?"
33 "We are not stoning you for any of these," replied the Jews, "but for blasphemy, because you, a mere man, claim to be God."[w]
34 Jesus answered them, "Is it not written in your Law,[x] 'I have said you are gods'[d]?[y]

10:19 [e]Jn 7:43; 9:16
10:20 [f]Jn 7:20 [g]Mk 3:21
10:21 [h]Mt 4:24 [i]Ex 4:11; Jn 9:32,33
10:23 [j]Ac 3:11; 5:12
10:24 [k]Jn 1:19 [l]Jn 16:25, 29
10:25 [m]Jn 8:58 [n]Jn 5:36
10:26 [o]Jn 8:47
10:27 [p]ver 14 [q]ver 4
10:28 [r]Jn 6:39
10:29 [s]Jn 17:2,6,24 [t]Jn 14:28
10:30 [u]Jn 17:21-23
10:31 [v]Jn 8:59
10:33 [w]Lev 24:16; Jn 5:18
10:34 [x]Jn 8:17; Ro 3:19 [y]Ps 82:6

[a] *22* That is, Hanukkah [b] *24* Or *Messiah* [c] *29* Many early manuscripts *What my Father has given me is greater than all* [d] *34* Psalm 82:6

10:17–18 Take it up again. Refers to the resurrection of Christ, a miracle so stupendous that, like creation and salvation, it is seen as the act of the three persons of the Trinity: the Father (Ac 2:32; 3:15; 4:10; Gal 1:1), the Son (Jn 10:17–18) and the Holy Spirit (Ro 8:10–11).
10:18 No one takes it from me, but I lay it down of my own accord. Implies a claim to divinity (as even Jesus' detractors well understood; v. 33) because God alone is the Author and Giver of life. God alone has authority to give life and to take it back. This verse also underscores the active, priestly role of Jesus Christ in giving his life for sinners. It reveals that no tension exists between the will of the Father and that of the Son. Christ actively and willingly obeys the Father's will. See *WCF* 8.4; *WLC* 52.
10:19 divided. See 7:43 and 9:16.
10:20 See note on 7:20.
10:21 Jesus' words were obviously not those of a maniac, and his miracles further evidenced God's blessing rather than Satanic influence.
■ **10:22–42** *In Jerusalem Near the Feast of Dedication.* John turned briefly to a time when disbelief among the Jews was particularly strong.
10:22 Feast of Dedication. Now called Hanukkah, it is celebrated around Christmastime. It is a festival of light, commemorating events in the days of Judas Maccabeus during the Jewish revolt against Antiochus Epiphanes in 164 B.C.
10:23 Solomon's Colonnade. A portico or porch with roof and supporting columns on the east side of the court of the Gentiles in Herod's temple (Ac 3:11; 5:12).
10:24 If you are the Christ. The key point of dissension concerning Jesus' ministry. The disciples had reached the conclusion that Jesus was indeed the Christ (Mt 16:16; Mk 8:29; Lk 9:20; Jn 6:69). This same question would recur at his trial, during which the high priest would choose to view Jesus' answer as blasphemy (Mt 26:63–65; Mk 14:61–64; Lk 22:67–71).
10:25 I did tell you. Jesus had asserted this to the Samaritan woman (4:26) and to the man born blind (9:37) and had accepted the acknowledgment of the disciples (1:49; see note on 10:24). In his discussions with the Jews, he surely had implied as much (8:28,58). Here he made a categorical affirmation. **The miracles.** Literally, "the works." Jesus referred to his miracles as evidence of the trustworthiness of his claims (5:36), and he would press this point later before the disciples (14:11; 15:24). The man born blind had reasoned in like manner (9:32–33).
10:26 you do not believe. They closed their eyes to the clear evidence. **because you are not my sheep.** Only those who are Christ's sheep, whom the Father has given to him, actually do come to faith. Others are so blinded by their sinful prejudice that they refuse to believe. Unbelief is characteristic of the unregenerate. Only the regenerate believe. All of Christ's sheep believe because the Holy Spirit regenerates them. See *WCF* 3.6.
10:27 My sheep. Those who are so related to Christ do two indispensable things characteristic of faith: They listen (vv. 3–5) and follow (vv. 4–5). These acts imply a renewal of life in both orientation and commitment. See *CD* 2.I.
10:27–30 See *HC* 1,51.
10:27–28 The Lord does four things for the sheep: (1) He knows them, for he has an eternal, personal attachment to them (vv. 3,14; Ro 8:29). (2) He gives them eternal life—not merely endless existence, but life characterized by perpetual and unending intimate fellowship with God (17:2–3). (3) He protects them from ever perishing, which emphasizes the indefectible character of divine grace. (4) He sees to it that no one can snatch them out of his hand, a powerful safeguard from all external enemies. The saints persevere because God preserves them. These blessings are a great reassurance to the believer. If anyone suggests that the sheep may voluntarily jump out of the pen, it must be noted that if they jumped, they would perish; Jesus has also promised that this will not happen. The solemn warnings of Scripture against apostasy are therefore not intended to implant doubts about God's preservation of those he has already saved (cf. 1Jn 2:19). See *HC* 54.
10:28–30 See *HC* 54.
10:28–29 See *WCF* 17.1; *CD* 5.III.
10:28 See *WCF* 11.5; 17.2; *WLC* 66,79; *HC* 31.
10:29 my Father's hand. The shepherd's hand is also the Father's hand, and the supreme power of God is the ultimate guarantee of the sheep's safety. See *BC* 16.
10:30–36 See *HC* 35.
10:30 I and the Father are one. Not identical persons but one in essence (the gender of the Greek word for "one" is neuter). The Father and the Son (and the Holy Spirit) possess alike the fullness of the divine nature with all its perfection. This essential unity underlies their unity in redemptive purpose. But the verse suggests far more than a mere unity of purpose. See theological article "The Trinity" at John 14. See also *WLC* 9,36; *BC 10,19.*
10:31–33 The Jews properly understood Jesus' claim to deity and were preparing to stone him for blasphemy (8:59).
10:32 For which of these do you stone me? This ironic question underscores that, in the presence of Jesus' miracles, his accusers should not so lightly have entertained a charge of blasphemy.
10:34–38 Jesus' argument has been interpreted in various ways. It is obvious that he claimed deity in a sense far superior to the manner in which judges in the Old Testament could be called "gods" (because they were viewed as acting in God's place as his representatives or agents in administrating justice). The word "Elohim" was used not only with reference to the one true God (Yahweh), but also to denote false gods, angels and sometimes men vested with "divine" functions, such as rulers. Rather than stoning Jesus for blasphemy, the Jews should have examined his credentials and recognized his mission from God to the world, which was evidenced by his miracles.
10:34 Is it not written . . . ? A frequent way of introducing a Scripture quotation; it emphasized its definitive authority. **your Law.** This text is found in Psalm 82:6, but the term "law" was not restricted to the Pentateuch but was used with reference to any

35 If he called them 'gods,' to whom the word of God came—and the Scripture cannot be
broken— 36 what about the one whom the Father set apart[z] as his very own[a] and sent
into the world?[b] Why then do you accuse me of blasphemy because I said, 'I am God's
Son'?[c] 37 Do not believe me unless I do what my Father does.[d] 38 But if I do it, even though
you do not believe me, believe the miracles, that you may know and understand that the
Father is in me, and I in the Father."[e] 39 Again they tried to seize him,[f] but he escaped
their grasp.[g]
40 Then Jesus went back across the Jordan[h] to the place where John had been baptizing in the early days. Here he stayed 41 and many people came to him. They said, "Though
John never performed a miraculous sign,[i] all that John said about this man was true."[j]
42 And in that place many believed in Jesus.[k]

The Death of Lazarus

11 Now a man named Lazarus was sick. He was from Bethany,[l] the village of Mary
and her sister Martha.[m] 2 This Mary, whose brother Lazarus now lay sick, was
the same one who poured perfume on the Lord and wiped his feet with her hair.[n] 3 So
the sisters sent word to Jesus, "Lord, the one you love[o] is sick."
4 When he heard this, Jesus said, "This sickness will not end in death. No, it is for
God's glory[p] so that God's Son may be glorified through it." 5 Jesus loved Martha and her
sister and Lazarus. 6 Yet when he heard that Lazarus was sick, he stayed where he was
two more days.
7 Then he said to his disciples, "Let us go back to Judea."[q]
8 "But Rabbi,"[r] they said, "a short while ago the Jews tried to stone you,[s] and yet you
are going back there?"
9 Jesus answered, "Are there not twelve hours of daylight? A man who walks by day
will not stumble, for he sees by this world's light.[t] 10 It is when he walks by night that he
stumbles, for he has no light."
11 After he had said this, he went on to tell them, "Our friend[u] Lazarus has fallen
asleep;[v] but I am going there to wake him up."
12 His disciples replied, "Lord, if he sleeps, he will get better." 13 Jesus had been speaking of his death, but his disciples thought he meant natural sleep.[w]
14 So then he told them plainly, "Lazarus is dead, 15 and for your sake I am glad I was
not there, so that you may believe. But let us go to him."
16 Then Thomas[x] (called Didymus) said to the rest of the disciples, "Let us also go, that
we may die with him."

Jesus Comforts the Sisters

17 On his arrival, Jesus found that Lazarus had already been in the tomb for four days.[y]
18 Bethany[z] was less than two miles[a] from Jerusalem, 19 and many Jews had come to Mar-

10:36 [z]Jer 1:5 [a]Jn 6:69 [b]Jn 3:17 [c]Jn 5:17, 18
10:37 [d]ver 25; Jn 15:24
10:38 [e]Jn 14:10, 11, 20; 17:21
10:39 [f]Jn 7:30 [g]Lk 4:30; Jn 8:59
10:40 [h]Jn 1:28
10:41 [i]Jn 2:11; 3:30 [j]Jn 1:26, 27, 30, 34
10:42 [k]Jn 7:31
11:1 [l]Mt 21:17 [m]Lk 10:38
11:2 [n]Mk 14:3; Lk 7:38; Jn 12:3
11:3 [o]ver 5, 36
11:4 [p]ver 40; Jn 9:3
11:7 [q]Jn 10:40
11:8 [r]Mt 23:7 [s]Jn 8:59; 10:31
11:9 [t]Jn 9:4; 12:35
11:11 [u]ver 3 [v]Ac 7:60
11:13 [w]Mt 9:24
11:16 [x]Mt 10:3; Jn 14:5; 20:24-28; 21:2; Ac 1:13
11:17 [y]ver 6, 39
11:18 [z]ver 1

[a] *18* Greek *fifteen stadia* (about 3 kilometers)

part of the Old Testament, bearing witness to its legal authority (Jn 15:25).
10:35 to whom the word of God came. This is not a reference to the writing of Scripture but to the divine investiture of the judges. **the Scripture cannot be broken.** An impressive witness to the unassailable authority of Scripture. In this very serious confrontation, with death as a possible outcome, Jesus did not hesitate to base his whole argument on one word of a minor psalm of Asaph, and then to affirm its validity with this weighty statement.
10:37 what my Father does. Jesus' miracles and the whole tenor of his life attested to his claim of a heavenly origin and mission.
10:38 the Father is in me, and I in the Father. This reciprocal indwelling is characteristic of the Trinitarian, and subsequently of the regenerated, life (14:10–11,20; 17:21).
10:39 he escaped. Nothing that could thwart God's plan of redemption could happen to Jesus until God's appointed hour (7:44; 8:59).
■ **11:1—12:50** *Near and in Jerusalem Near Passover.* John reported the final events that took place in Jesus' public ministry as he came to Jerusalem. John's record divides into six parts (see "Introduction: Outline").
■ **11:1–44** *Raising the Dead.* The miracle of the raising of Lazarus from the dead serves as a climax to all the preceding signs by which God's glory had been revealed through Jesus. Here death itself, the ultimate enemy of humanity, was successfully confronted by the One who is himself "the resurrection and the life" (v. 25). Yet even this glorious sign, as had the preceding signs, divided those who witnessed into two groups: those who believed, and those who rejected the revealed glory and committed themselves to pursuing Jesus' death (vv. 46–57).
11:1 Lazarus. This Lazarus is named only in John's Gospel. He should not be confused with the Lazarus of Luke 16:20.
11:2 the same one. Mary's anointing is related in 12:1–8.
11:3 the one you love is sick. A distress call, apparently sent only shortly before Lazarus died.
11:4 This sickness will not end in death. Jesus was not denying that Lazarus would be dead for four days but that Lazarus would remain dead.
11:6 two more days. A delay the sisters would have had a hard time understanding.
11:8 the Jews tried to stone you. Jesus' execution would not be the tragic death of one who was attempting to escape but the deliberate death of a priest who would offer himself as a sacrifice. Both Jesus and his disciples knew that if he went to Jerusalem, his life would be at stake.
11:11 fallen asleep. In the New Testament, death is frequently represented as sleep (Ac 7:60; 1Co 15:51; 1Th 4:13). This language, however, does not justify constructing a doctrine of "soul-sleep" for departed saints. The term is simply a euphemism. Conscious awareness continues after death (cf. Lk 23:43; Php 1:21–24).
11:16 that we may die with him. The hostility toward Jesus had now reached such a stage that the disciples were convinced that a trip to Jerusalem would eventuate in Jesus' death. If they could not talk him out of the trip, they at least declared their willingness to die with him.
11:17 four days. This reference to the duration of time in the

tha and Mary to comfort them in the loss of their brother.[a] 20When Martha heard that
Jesus was coming, she went out to meet him, but Mary stayed at home.[b]
21"Lord," Martha said to Jesus, "if you had been here, my brother would not have
died.[c] 22But I know that even now God will give you whatever you ask."[d]
23Jesus said to her, "Your brother will rise again."
24Martha answered, "I know he will rise again in the resurrection[e] at the last day."
25Jesus said to her, "I am the resurrection and the life.[f] He who believes in me will live,
even though he dies; 26and whoever lives and believes in me will never die. Do you believe this?"
27"Yes, Lord," she told him, "I believe that you are the Christ,[a][g] the Son of God,[h] who
was to come into the world."[i]
28And after she had said this, she went back and called her sister Mary aside. "The
Teacher[j] is here," she said, "and is asking for you." 29When Mary heard this, she got up
quickly and went to him. 30Now Jesus had not yet entered the village, but was still at the
place where Martha had met him.[k] 31When the Jews who had been with Mary in the
house, comforting her,[l] noticed how quickly she got up and went out, they followed her,
supposing she was going to the tomb to mourn there.
32When Mary reached the place where Jesus was and saw him, she fell at his feet and
said, "Lord, if you had been here, my brother would not have died."[m]
33When Jesus saw her weeping, and the Jews who had come along with her also weeping, he was deeply moved[n] in spirit and troubled.[o] 34"Where have you laid him?" he
asked.
"Come and see, Lord," they replied.
35Jesus wept.[p]
36Then the Jews said, "See how he loved him!"[q]
37But some of them said, "Could not he who opened the eyes of the blind man[r] have
kept this man from dying?"[s]

Jesus Raises Lazarus From the Dead

38Jesus, once more deeply moved,[t] came to the tomb. It was a cave with a stone laid
across the entrance.[u] 39"Take away the stone," he said.
"But, Lord," said Martha, the sister of the dead man, "by this time there is a bad odor,
for he has been there four days."[v]
40Then Jesus said, "Did I not tell you that if you believed,[w] you would see the glory
of God?"[x]
41So they took away the stone. Then Jesus looked up[y] and said, "Father,[z] I thank you
that you have heard me. 42I knew that you always hear me, but I said this for the benefit of the people standing here,[a] that they may believe that you sent me."[b]
43When he had said this, Jesus called in a loud voice, "Lazarus, come out!"[c] 44The

11:19 [a]ver 31; Job 2:11
11:20 [b]Lk 10:38-42
11:21 [c]ver 32,37
11:22 [d]ver 41,42; Jn 9:31
11:24 [e]Da 12:2; Jn 5:28,29; Ac 24:15
11:25 [f]Jn 1:4
11:27 [g]Lk 2:11 [h]Mt 16:16 [i]Jn 6:14
11:28 [j]Mt 26:18; Jn 13:13
11:30 [k]ver 20
11:31 [l]ver 19
11:32 [m]ver 21
11:33 [n]ver 38 [o]Jn 12:27
11:35 [p]Lk 19:41
11:36 [q]ver 3
11:37 [r]Jn 9:6,7 [s]ver 21,32
11:38 [t]ver 33 [u]Mt 27:60; Lk 24:2; Jn 20:1
11:39 [v]ver 17
11:40 [w]ver 23-25 [x]ver 4
11:41 [y]Jn 17:1 [z]Mt 11:25
11:42 [a]Jn 12:30 [b]Jn 3:17
11:43 [c]Lk 7:14

a *27* Or *Messiah*

---

tomb, repeated in verse 39, is designed to prove that Lazarus was really dead, not merely sick.

11:21 if you had been here. The same comment is the first wistful statement by each sister (cf. v. 32). They most likely repeated this sentiment, referring to Jesus in the third person, many times during those four anguished days of waiting.

11:22 even now. Martha still expected some miracle, although it seemed that her brother was irrevocably dead. When Jesus spoke of resurrection, she related it to the distant future, the "last day." Still, her faith was better informed than that of the Sadducees, who denied the resurrection of the dead (Mt 22:23).

11:25 I am the resurrection and the life. Jesus repeats this in part in 14:6. He not only is the source and provider of resurrection and life but is so intimately connected with them that he may be said to *be* resurrection and life (cf. Ac 3:15; Heb 7:16). In a very real sense, the resurrection and life of believers is the resurrection and life of Jesus himself (Ro 6:5; Gal 2:20; see theological article "Union with Christ" at Gal 6). See notes on 6:35 and 10:27–28.

11:27 you are the Christ. A confession of faith that parallels that of Peter (Mt 16:16).

11:28 The Teacher. A characterization of Jesus' ministry. He did not disdain, as the Jews often did, to teach a woman (Lk 10:39,42).

11:33 he was deeply moved. This outward expression of sorrow did not leave Jesus unmoved. He actually shed tears (v. 35) in sympathy for the mourners.

11:34 "Where have you laid him?" John's Gospel teaches both the deity of Christ (1:1,18) and his full humanity. Being fully human (without relinquishing his deity in any way), Jesus could express both sorrow and ignorance of fact (vv. 34–35). See theological article "The Full Humanity of Christ" at Luke 3.

11:37 "Could not he . . . have kept this man from dying?" These Jews used the miraculous power of Jesus as the basis for a reproach, since he did not exercise it in time to prevent Lazarus's death. They did not reflect on the fact that the healing of the blind man had been accomplished for the glory of God (9:3), not merely for relief of a trying situation. Similarly, Lazarus was allowed to die—and the sisters to mourn—in order that God's glory might be manifested in the resurrection of this man (v. 4).

11:39 "Take away the stone." A call for human beings to do what they can, even when a work of supernatural power is about to be accomplished (cf. v. 44). Jesus' command must have appeared inappropriate and even offensive. Martha wanted to avoid the release of the stench of death.

11:40 "Did I not tell you . . . ?" Jesus rightly demanded a fuller confidence in the propriety of his directives.

11:41 Father, I thank you. Even before the actual miracle took place, Jesus returned thanks for the certain answer to his prayer. He related this miracle to his mission as Messiah.

11:43 "Lazarus, come out!" Why would a loud voice of command be addressed to a dead man? Dead people hear neither loud voices nor murmurs, but Jesus wanted the people present to witness that God's voice can raise even those who are dead (5:28–29). His divine call that gave life to the dead vividly illustrates God's effectual call to spiritual life of one who is dead in sin (Eph 2:5).

dead man came out, his hands and feet wrapped with strips of linen,[d] and a cloth
around his face.[e]
Jesus said to them, "Take off the grave clothes and let him go."

The Plot to Kill Jesus

45Therefore many of the Jews who had come to visit Mary,[f] and had seen what Jesus
did,[g] put their faith in him.[h] 46But some of them went to the Pharisees and told them
what Jesus had done. 47Then the chief priests and the Pharisees[i] called a meeting[j] of the
Sanhedrin.[k]
"What are we accomplishing?" they asked. "Here is this man performing many miraculous signs.[l] 48If we let him go on like this, everyone will believe in him, and then the
Romans will come and take away both our place[a] and our nation."
49Then one of them, named Caiaphas,[m] who was high priest that year,[n] spoke up,
"You know nothing at all! 50You do not realize that it is better for you that one man die
for the people than that the whole nation perish."[o]
51He did not say this on his own, but as high priest that year he prophesied that Jesus
would die for the Jewish nation, 52and not only for that nation but also for the scattered
children of God, to bring them together and make them one.[p] 53So from that day on they
plotted to take his life.[q]
54Therefore Jesus no longer moved about publicly among the Jews.[r] Instead he withdrew to a region near the desert, to a village called Ephraim, where he stayed with his
disciples.
55When it was almost time for the Jewish Passover,[s] many went up from the country
to Jerusalem for their ceremonial cleansing[t] before the Passover. 56They kept looking for
Jesus,[u] and as they stood in the temple area they asked one another, "What do you
think? Isn't he coming to the Feast at all?" 57But the chief priests and Pharisees had giv-
en orders that if anyone found out where Jesus was, he should report it so that they might
arrest him.

Jesus Anointed at Bethany

12 Six days before the Passover,[v] Jesus arrived at Bethany,[w] where Lazarus lived,
whom Jesus had raised from the dead. 2Here a dinner was given in Jesus' hon-
or. Martha served,[x] while Lazarus was among those reclining at the table with him.
3Then Mary took about a pint[b] of pure nard, an expensive perfume;[y] she poured it on
Jesus' feet and wiped his feet with her hair.[z] And the house was filled with the fragrance
of the perfume.
4But one of his disciples, Judas Iscariot, who was later to betray him,[a] objected,
5"Why wasn't this perfume sold and the money given to the poor? It was worth a year's
wages.[c]" 6He did not say this because he cared about the poor but because he was a thief;
as keeper of the money bag,[b] he used to help himself to what was put into it.
7"Leave her alone," Jesus replied. "⌊It was intended⌋ that she should save this perfume

11:44 [d]Jn 19:40 [e]Jn 20:7
11:45 [f]ver 19 [g]Jn 2:23 [h]Ex 14:31; Jn 7:31
11:47 [i]ver 57 [j]Mt 26:3 [k]Mt 5:22 [l]Jn 2:11
11:49 [m]Mt 26:3 [n]ver 51; Jn 18:13,14
11:50 [o]Jn 18:14
11:52 [p]Isa 49:6; Jn 10:16
11:53 [q]Mt 12:14
11:54 [r]Jn 7:1
11:55 [s]Ex 12:13,23,27; Mt 26:1,2; Mk 14:1; Jn 13:1 [t]2Ch 30:17,18
11:56 [u]Jn 7:11
12:1 [v]Jn 11:55 [w]Mt 21:17
12:2 [x]Lk 10:38-42
12:3 [y]Mk 14:3 [z]Jn 11:2
12:4 [a]Mt 10:4
12:6 [b]Jn 13:29

[a] *48* Or *temple* [b] *3* Greek *a litra* (probably about 0.5 liter) [c] *5* Greek *three hundred denarii*

■ **11:45–57** *Plotting to Kill Jesus.* The Jewish leaders responded to Jesus' miracles by seeking his death.
11:45–47 many of the Jews . . . But some. The manifest work of God had a double result: faith in some, resistance and unbelief in others (cf. Mt 13:10ff.).
11:48 The Sanhedrin, which had supreme religious authority in the land, feared that Jesus' ministry would arouse a popular upheaval that the Romans would crush by force, resulting in a tightening of Rome's control and a reduction of their own influence.
11:49 Caiaphas. A Sadducee, Caiaphas was the son-in-law of Annas, who had been deposed as high priest by the Romans but who still exercised considerable influence over the religious leaders (18:13).
11:50 In a statement grounded in crass expediency, Caiaphas suggested that the execution of one innocent person would be desirable if it secured advantage for the nation. He had forgotten the message of Proverbs 17:15: "Acquitting the guilty and condemning the innocent—the LORD detests them both."
11:51 he prophesied. By the providence of God, Caiaphas unwittingly expressed a great truth despite his misguided sentiment: It was a blessing that Jesus should die, because his death was necessary for the salvation not only of Jewish people, but also of the elect scattered throughout the whole world. God can use the words of a wicked man and give them a prophetic meaning that is quite absent from that man's thought or intention. God's objective in the death of Jesus was clearly related to those he intended to save: the children of God scattered throughout the world.
11:52 See *WLC* 64.
11:54–57 The increasing hostility of the Jewish leaders led Jesus to leave Jerusalem for a time.
■ **12:1–8** *Anointing at Bethany.* The anointing of Jesus by a sinful woman (Lk 7:36–50) is a different incident from this anointing by Mary (see Mt 26:6–12; Mk 14:3–9).
12:3 an expensive perfume. See verse 5, where Judas assessed the value of this perfume as the equivalent of a year's wages, almost three times as much as Judas would later accept for Jesus' betrayal. **on Jesus' feet.** Matthew and Mark indicate that she poured some perfume on his head, which would have been the common practice. To attend to his feet and wipe them with her hair was a special tribute of humility and devotion.
12:4–6 Judas (and the other disciples; Mt 26:8) objected strongly to Mary's gesture, calling her action a waste of money. This was inconsiderate toward Jesus and cruel toward Mary. Jesus unmasked this sudden interest in the poor as purely artificial.
12:7 "Leave her alone." Jesus was more concerned with protecting Mary's feelings than with rebuking Judas's lack of kindness toward himself. Jesus was within one week of his death and related the anointing to the service usually rendered to the dead. In anticipation of his substitutionary death for sinners, the pivotal point of God's redemptive purpose, no expense could have been too great.

for the day of my burial.[c] 8You will always have the poor among you,[d] but you will not
always have me."
9Meanwhile a large crowd of Jews found out that Jesus was there and came, not only
because of him but also to see Lazarus, whom he had raised from the dead.[e] 10So the
chief priests made plans to kill Lazarus as well, 11for on account of him[f] many of the Jews
were going over to Jesus and putting their faith in him.[g]

The Triumphal Entry

12The next day the great crowd that had come for the Feast heard that Jesus was on
his way to Jerusalem. 13They took palm branches and went out to meet him, shouting,

> "Hosanna![a]"
>
> "Blessed is he who comes in the name of the Lord!"[b] [h]
>
> "Blessed is the King of Israel!"[i]

14Jesus found a young donkey and sat upon it, as it is written,

> 15"Do not be afraid, O Daughter of Zion;
> see, your king is coming,
> seated on a donkey's colt."[c] [j]

16At first his disciples did not understand all this.[k] Only after Jesus was glorified[l] did
they realize that these things had been written about him and that they had done these
things to him.
17Now the crowd that was with him[m] when he called Lazarus from the tomb and
raised him from the dead continued to spread the word. 18Many people, because they
had heard that he had given this miraculous sign,[n] went out to meet him. 19So the Pharisees said to one another, "See, this is getting us nowhere. Look how the whole world
has gone after him!"[o]

Jesus Predicts His Death

20Now there were some Greeks[p] among those who went up to worship at the Feast.
21They came to Philip, who was from Bethsaida[q] in Galilee, with a request. "Sir," they
said, "we would like to see Jesus." 22Philip went to tell Andrew; Andrew and Philip in turn
told Jesus.
23Jesus replied, "The hour has come for the Son of Man to be glorified.[r] 24I tell you the
truth, unless a kernel of wheat falls to the ground and dies,[s] it remains only a single seed.

12:7 [c]Jn 19:40
12:8 [d]Dt 15:11
12:9 [e]Jn 11:43,44
12:11 [f]ver 17,18; Jn 11:45 [g]Jn 7:31
12:13 [h]Ps 118:25,26 [i]Jn 1:49
12:15 [j]Zec 9:9
12:16 [k]Mk 9:32 [l]Jn 2:22; 7:39; 14:26
12:17 [m]Jn 11:42
12:18 [n]ver 11
12:19 [o]Jn 11:47,48
12:20 [p]Jn 7:35; Ac 11:20
12:21 [q]Mt 11:21; Jn 1:44
12:23 [r]Jn 13:32; 17:1
12:24 [s]1Co 15:36

a *13* A Hebrew expression meaning "Save!" which became an exclamation of praise
b *13* Psalm 118:25,26 c *15* Zech. 9:9

12:8 the poor. In view of Judas's offensive remark, Jesus might have overlooked the reference to the poor. Instead, he commended the needy to the attention of his disciples. **always . . . not always.** Within a week the Lord would reach the end of the days of his flesh (Heb 5:7), and the disciples would not see him again as they had heretofore. The poor, on the other hand, would always be with them. No scheme to eradicate poverty will ever be completely successful until the new heaven and the new earth have replaced this world of sin and sorrow. Nevertheless, Jesus did not indicate that poverty was an acceptable state or that the poor could be rightly disregarded. Rather, he emphasized that the opportunity to minister to him would quickly vanish, whereas the opportunity to minister to the poor would remain.

■ **12:9–19** *The Triumphal Entry.* The crowds welcomed Jesus in the hope that he would defeat their enemies, but their enthusiasm would soon dissipate.

12:9–10 Instead of recognizing God's hand in the stupendous miracle of Lazarus's resurrection, the chief priests plotted to get Jesus out of their way—and Lazarus as well.

12:11 many of the Jews. The religious leaders were faced with progressive attrition: Nicodemus seemed to have defected (7:50–52); some Jews had believed in Christ, although superficially (8:31); some were impressed by the healing of the man born blind (10:21); Jesus seemed to be gaining adherents across the Jordan (10:41–42); and now Lazarus's resurrection led still more to faith (11:45; 12:11,17–18). All of this prepared for the acclaim Jesus received in his triumphal entry into Jerusalem, which led the Pharisees to bemoan, "the whole world has gone after him!" (v. 19).

12:12 the great crowd. Many pilgrims from Galilee who had witnessed Jesus' miracles joined residents of Jerusalem who had been won over to his side.

12:13 "Hosanna!" See NIV text note. Their salutation was borrowed in part from Psalm 118:25–26, to which they added the reference to the son of David, "the King of Israel." This was particularly disquieting to the Jewish leaders, who feared a popular upheaval under Jesus' leadership.

12:14–15 The precise circumstances had been prophesied in Zechariah 9:9. This prophecy is noted also in Matthew's narrative but was understood only in retrospect by the disciples.

■ **12:20–36** *Reacting Gentiles.* John set up a startling contrast between the responses of Gentiles to Jesus and the reactions of the Jewish authorities (vv. 37–50).

12:20 some Greeks. An ironic footnote to the statement of the Pharisees in verse 19. These "Greeks" were probably not Jews of the dispersion (the Greek word is different from that translated "Grecian Jews" in Ac 6:1). Rather, they were perhaps proselytes or, more probably, Gentile "God-fearers," who participated in synagogue worship but did not undergo circumcision and full reception into the Jewish religion (Ac 8:27; 13:26).

12:21 Philip. This disciple seemed to be especially accessible (cf. 1:43–36). His name is clearly Greek.

12:23 The hour has come. In contrast to earlier statements that his time had not yet come (2:4; 7:6,8,30; 8:20), this is the first of a number of Jesus' announcements to the effect that his death and resurrection were now impending (12:27; 13:1; 16:32; 17:1). **glorified.** This is referred to as "glorification" (although the cross and burial are clearly identified elsewhere as parts of his humiliation; Php 2:8) because they are the portals through which the Mediator entered into glory by resurrection, ascension and exaltation at the right hand of the Father (13:31–32; cf. Php 2:8–9).

12:24 a kernel of wheat. A parable of Jesus' own work. Through

Jerusalem During the Ministry of Jesus

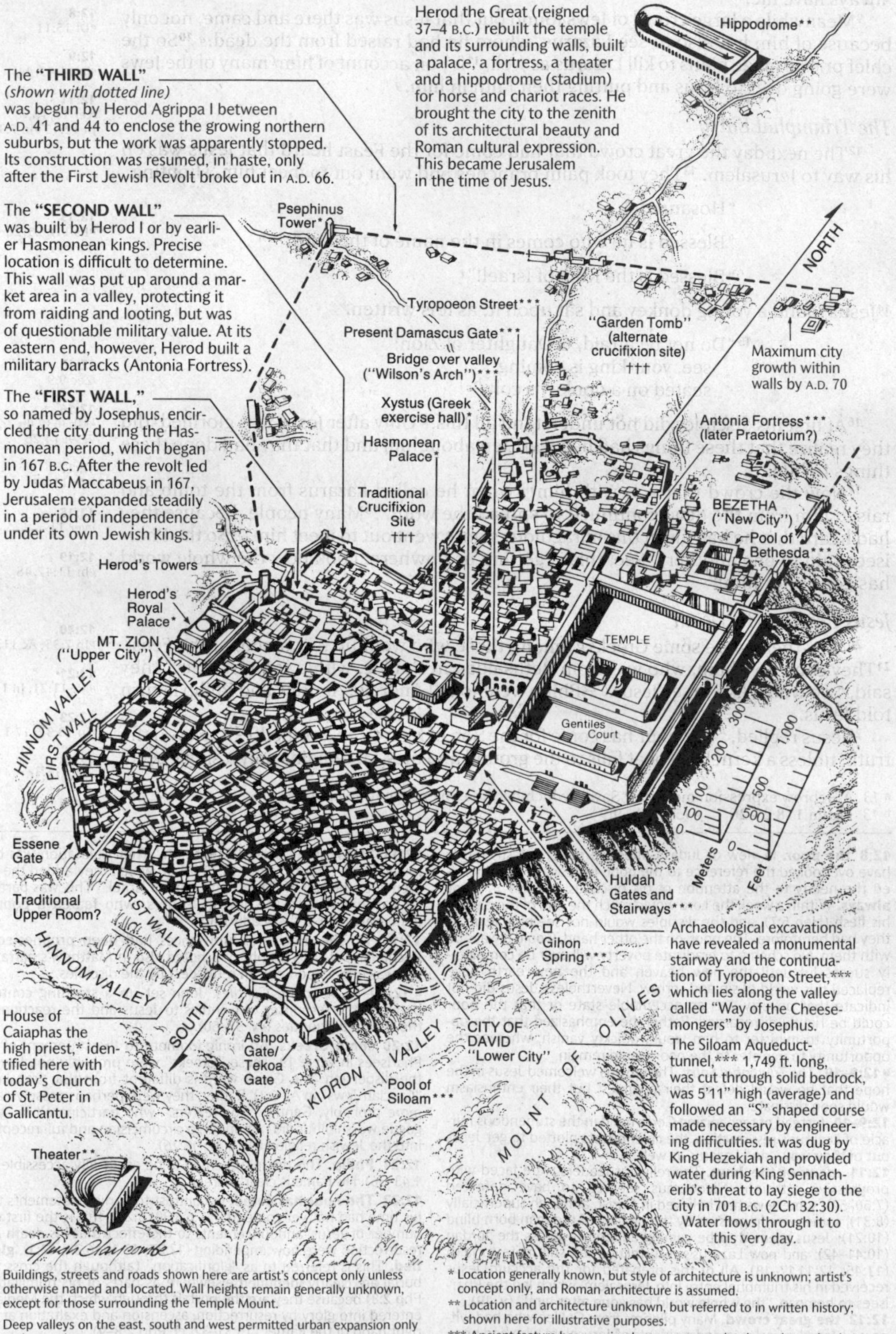

The **"THIRD WALL"** *(shown with dotted line)* was begun by Herod Agrippa I between A.D. 41 and 44 to enclose the growing northern suburbs, but the work was apparently stopped. Its construction was resumed, in haste, only after the First Jewish Revolt broke out in A.D. 66.
The **"SECOND WALL"** was built by Herod I or by earlier Hasmonean kings. Precise location is difficult to determine. This wall was put up around a market area in a valley, protecting it from raiding and looting, but was of questionable military value. At its eastern end, however, Herod built a military barracks (Antonia Fortress).
The **"FIRST WALL,"** so named by Josephus, encircled the city during the Hasmonean period, which began in 167 B.C. After the revolt led by Judas Maccabeus in 167, Jerusalem expanded steadily in a period of independence under its own Jewish kings.
Herod the Great (reigned 37–4 B.C.) rebuilt the temple and its surrounding walls, built a palace, a fortress, a theater and a hippodrome (stadium) for horse and chariot races. He brought the city to the zenith of its architectural beauty and Roman cultural expression. This became Jerusalem in the time of Jesus.
Hippodrome**
Psephinus Tower*
Tyropoeon Street***
Present Damascus Gate***
Bridge over valley ("Wilson's Arch")***
Xystus (Greek exercise hall)*
Hasmonean Palace*
Traditional Crucifixion Site
"Garden Tomb" (alternate crucifixion site)
NORTH
Maximum city growth within walls by A.D. 70
Antonia Fortress*** (later Praetorium?)
BEZETHA ("New City")
Pool of Bethesda***
Herod's Towers
Herod's Royal Palace*
MT. ZION ("Upper City")
TEMPLE
Gentiles Court
HINNOM VALLEY
FIRST WALL
Essene Gate
Traditional Upper Room?
FIRST WALL
HINNOM VALLEY
House of Caiaphas the high priest,* identified here with today's Church of St. Peter in Gallicantu.
SOUTH
Ashpot Gate/ Tekoa Gate
KIDRON VALLEY
Pool of Siloam***
CITY OF DAVID "Lower City"
MOUNT OF OLIVES
Gihon Spring***
Huldah Gates and Stairways***
Meters
Feet
0
100
200
300
0
500
1,000
Archaeological excavations have revealed a monumental stairway and the continuation of Tyropoeon Street,*** which lies along the valley called "Way of the Cheesemongers" by Josephus.
The Siloam Aqueduct-tunnel,*** 1,749 ft. long, was cut through solid bedrock, was 5'11" high (average) and followed an "S" shaped course made necessary by engineering difficulties. It was dug by King Hezekiah and provided water during King Sennacherib's threat to lay siege to the city in 701 B.C. (2Ch 32:30). Water flows through it to this very day.
Theater**
Hugh Claycombe

Buildings, streets and roads shown here are artist's concept only unless otherwise named and located. Wall heights remain generally unknown, except for those surrounding the Temple Mount.

Deep valleys on the east, south and west permitted urban expansion only to the north.

* Location generally known, but style of architecture is unknown; artist's concept only, and Roman architecture is assumed.

** Location and architecture unknown, but referred to in written history; shown here for illustrative purposes.

*** Ancient feature has remained, or appearance has been determined from evidence.

But if it dies, it produces many seeds. 25The man who loves his life will lose it, while the
man who hates his life in this world will keep it[t] for eternal life. 26Whoever serves me
must follow me; and where I am, my servant also will be.[u] My Father will honor the one
who serves me.
27"Now my heart is troubled,[v] and what shall I say? 'Father,[w] save me from this
hour'?[x] No, it was for this very reason I came to this hour. 28Father, glorify your name!"
Then a voice came from heaven,[y] "I have glorified it, and will glorify it again." 29The
crowd that was there and heard it said it had thundered; others said an angel had spoken to him.
30Jesus said, "This voice was for your benefit,[z] not mine. 31Now is the time for judgment on this world;[a] now the prince of this world[b] will be driven out. 32But I, when I am
lifted up from the earth,[c] will draw all men to myself."[d] 33He said this to show the kind
of death he was going to die.[e]
34The crowd spoke up, "We have heard from the Law that the Christ[a] will remain forever,[f] so how can you say, 'The Son of Man[g] must be lifted up'?[h] Who is this 'Son of Man'?"
35Then Jesus told them, "You are going to have the light[i] just a little while longer.
Walk while you have the light,[j] before darkness overtakes you.[k] The man who walks in
the dark does not know where he is going. 36Put your trust in the light while you have
it, so that you may become sons of light."[l] When he had finished speaking, Jesus left and
hid himself from them.[m]

The Jews Continue in Their Unbelief

37Even after Jesus had done all these miraculous signs[n] in their presence, they still
would not believe in him. 38This was to fulfill the word of Isaiah the prophet:

"Lord, who has believed our message
and to whom has the arm of the Lord been revealed?"[b][o]

39For this reason they could not believe, because, as Isaiah says elsewhere:

40"He has blinded their eyes
and deadened their hearts,
so they can neither see with their eyes,
nor understand with their hearts,
nor turn—and I would heal them."[c][p]

41Isaiah said this because he saw Jesus' glory[q] and spoke about him.[r]
42Yet at the same time many even among the leaders believed in him.[s] But because

12:25 [t]Mt 10:39; Mk 8:35; Lk 14:26
12:26 [u]Jn 14:3; 17:24; 2Co 5:8; 1Th 4:17
12:27 [v]Mt 26:38, 39; Jn 11:33, 38; 13:21 [w]Mt 11:25 [x]ver 23
12:28 [y]Mt 3:17
12:30 [z]Jn 11:42
12:31 [a]Jn 16:11 [b]Jn 14:30; 16:11; 2Co 4:4; Eph 2:2; 1Jn 4:4
12:32 [c]ver 34; Jn 3:14; 8:28 [d]Jn 6:44
12:33 [e]Jn 18:32
12:34 [f]Ps 110:4; Isa 9:7; Eze 37:25; Da 7:14 [g]Mt 8:20 [h]Jn 3:14
12:35 [i]ver 46 [j]Eph 5:8 [k]1Jn 2:11
12:36 [l]Lk 16:8 [m]Jn 8:59
12:37 [n]Jn 2:11
12:38 [o]Isa 53:1; Ro 10:16
12:40 [p]Isa 6:10; Mt 13:13, 15
12:41 [q]Isa 6:1-4 [r]Lk 24:27
12:42 [s]ver 11; Jn 7:48

[a] *34* Or *Messiah* [b] *38* Isaiah 53:1 [c] *40* Isaiah 6:10

his death the doors of salvation would be opened not only for the Jews, but also for people of every nation.

12:25 The man who loves his life. The person who is absorbed by the interests of life on Earth actually encounters ruin, while an individual detached from worldly interests will attain to eternal life through Jesus' work (Mt 10:39; Lk 17:33). It is in the service of Christ and in union with him that the truth of this statement is experienced (see chapter 14).

12:27 Now my heart is troubled. Jesus was greatly troubled by his anticipation of bearing the wrath of his holy Father in the place of sinners. Nevertheless, as a determined high priest, he accepted his role and reiterated his commitment to it.

12:28 voice came from heaven. There are three instances in Jesus' career in which the Father spoke directly from heaven: at his baptism (Mt 3:17), at the transfiguration (Mt 17:5) and in this passage. Here, for the benefit of the disciples (v. 30), the Father placed his seal of approval upon Jesus' mediatorial work.

12:29 The crowd . . . heard it. A similar situation occurred at the conversion of Paul, when the men accompanying him heard the sound of a voice but could not distinguish the words (Ac 9:7; 22:9).

12:31 Now is the time for judgment on this world. When Jesus bore the penal wrath of God for sinners and overcame the power of death, he terminated the power of sin over Adam's race. **the prince of this world.** Satan (cf. 14:30; 16:11; 2Co 4:4; Eph 2:2; 1Jn 4:4; 5:19). God permits and tolerates Satan's exercise of power in this world. Satan does not have an inalienable right to rule.

12:32 lifted up. Refers not only to the nature of the crucifixion (v. 33), but also to Jesus' ascension to the right hand of God (see note on 3:14). **I . . . will draw all.** See notes on 3:16 and 6:44. **all.** All kinds of human beings without distinction, not all members of the human race without exception.

12:34 the Law. A term used for the whole Old Testament Scripture (10:34; 15:25). It is here used as a possible reference to several Old Testament passages (Pss 89:36; 110:4; Isa 9:7; Eze 37:25; Da 7:14; Mic 5:2). **The Son of Man.** The crowd understood this title to be a claim to Messiahship. **lifted up?** Jesus' listeners interpreted this to be a reference to hanging or crucifixion and, on the basis of Scriptures such as Psalm 89:36–37, they could not reconcile Jesus' coming death with their view of the Messiah.

12:35 the light. Jesus identified himself with the light (1:4–9; 8:12; 9:5; 12:46). His impending death implied some darkness, although he delegated a ministry of enlightenment to his disciples (Mt 5:14), who could be called "sons of light" (v. 36). The walk of the unbeliever is erratic, while the believer walks in the light (Ps 119:105; Jn 8:12; 1Jn 1:7).

■ **12:37–50** *Reacting Jews.* John contrasted the reaction of the Jews to Jesus' ministry with that of the Gentiles (vv. 20–36).

12:38–40 See *WLC* 61,68.

12:38 to fulfill the word of Isaiah the prophet. Jesus' earthly public ministry is seen as a fulfillment of Isaiah's ministry. Just as Isaiah prophesied a purging judgment prior to restoration of the kingdom, so also Jesus brought judgment as he began to restore the kingdom.

12:39 they could not believe. No one will truly believe unless God renews that person's orientation by a supernatural work of the Spirit (Jn 3:3–7). See note on 10:26.

12:41 saw Jesus' glory. Isaiah supremely portrayed the majesty of the sovereign God, and John identified this with Jesus' glory, both in his humiliation and in his exaltation (see note on v. 23). See *WLC* 11.

12:42 many . . . believed in him. In spite of Isaiah's severe judgment, there were some believers even among the leaders. Most

of the Pharisees[t] they would not confess their faith for fear they would be put out of the synagogue;[u] 43for they loved praise from men more than praise from God.[v]

44Then Jesus cried out, "When a man believes in me, he does not believe in me only, but in the one who sent me.[w] 45When he looks at me, he sees the one who sent me.[x] 46I have come into the world as a light,[y] so that no one who believes in me should stay in darkness.

47"As for the person who hears my words but does not keep them, I do not judge him. For I did not come to judge the world, but to save it.[z] 48There is a judge for the one who rejects me and does not accept my words; that very word which I spoke will condemn him[a] at the last day. 49For I did not speak of my own accord, but the Father who sent me commanded me[b] what to say and how to say it. 50I know that his command leads to eternal life. So whatever I say is just what the Father has told me to say."

Jesus Washes His Disciples' Feet

13 It was just before the Passover Feast.[c] Jesus knew that the time had come[d] for him to leave this world and go to the Father.[e] Having loved his own who were in the world, he now showed them the full extent of his love.[a]

2The evening meal was being served, and the devil had already prompted Judas Iscariot, son of Simon, to betray Jesus. 3Jesus knew that the Father had put all things under his power,[f] and that he had come from God[g] and was returning to God; 4so he got up from the meal, took off his outer clothing, and wrapped a towel around his waist. 5After that, he poured water into a basin and began to wash his disciples' feet,[h] drying them with the towel that was wrapped around him.

6He came to Simon Peter, who said to him, "Lord, are you going to wash my feet?"

7Jesus replied, "You do not realize now what I am doing, but later you will understand."[i]

8"No," said Peter, "you shall never wash my feet."

Jesus answered, "Unless I wash you, you have no part with me."

9"Then, Lord," Simon Peter replied, "not just my feet but my hands and my head as well!"

10Jesus answered, "A person who has had a bath needs only to wash his feet; his whole body is clean. And you are clean,[j] though not every one of you." 11For he knew who was going to betray him, and that was why he said not every one was clean.

12When he had finished washing their feet, he put on his clothes and returned to his place. "Do you understand what I have done for you?" he asked them. 13"You call me 'Teacher'[k] and 'Lord,'[l] and rightly so, for that is what I am. 14Now that I, your Lord and Teacher, have washed your feet, you also should wash one another's feet.[m] 15I have set you an example that you should do as I have done for you.[n] 16I tell you the truth, no ser-

12:42 [t]Jn 7:13 [u]Jn 9:22
12:43 [v]Jn 5:44
12:44 [w]Mt 10:40; Jn 5:24
12:45 [x]Jn 14:9
12:46 [y]Jn 1:4; 3:19; 8:12; 9:5
12:47 [z]Jn 3:17
12:48 [a]Jn 5:45
12:49 [b]Jn 14:31
13:1 [c]Jn 11:55 [d]Jn 12:23 [e]Jn 16:28
13:3 [f]Mt 28:18 [g]Jn 8:42; 16:27,28,30
13:5 [h]Lk 7:44
13:7 [i]ver 12
13:10 [j]Jn 15:3
13:13 [k]Jn 11:28 [l]Lk 6:46; 1Co 12:3; Php 2:11
13:14 [m]1Pe 5:5
13:15 [n]Mt 11:29

[a] *1* Or *he loved them to the last*

hesitated in declaring themselves because of the influence of the Pharisees. Perhaps Nicodemus is a case in point, although he showed courage to go against the tide (7:50–52; 19:39–40).

12:44 Jesus cried out. The unity and close relationship between Jesus and the Father is stressed here in three respects: believing (v. 44), seeing (v. 45) and hearing (v. 47). See notes on 10:30 and 17:23.

■ **13:1—17:26** *Jesus' Ministry to His Disciples.* These chapters recount Jesus' ministry to the disciples in the upper room, a ministry accompanied by a meal. The other Gospels indicate at this point in the narrative that the Lord's Supper was initiated, but John does not relate this, perhaps because he viewed it as sufficiently covered in the Synoptic Gospels. The Synoptic Gospels explicitly indicate that this meal was the Passover meal (Mt 26:17–30; Mk 14:12–26; Lk 22:7–23). John, on the other hand, includes a number of statements that may indicate that this meal took place on the eve of the Passover and that Jesus' death took place at the precise time when the Passover lambs were being slaughtered (13:1,29; 18:28; 19:14,31,42). For a further discussion on this point, see notes on Matthew 26:17 and John 19:4. John's account divides into three main sections (see "Introduction: Outline").

■ **13:1–38** *Foot Washing and Betrayal Foretold.* Jesus demonstrated the type of servant ministry the disciples were to conduct after he left them, and told of his imminent betrayal by Judas Iscariot.

13:1 the full extent of his love. Great emphasis is placed on Jesus' love in chapters 13–17. Its full extent is shown in the Son's willing incarnation and substitutionary death for his own. The foot washing exemplifies the fact that the Son of God did not disdain performing the most menial tasks of a servant (Php 2:7–8).

13:2 The contrast between self-serving Judas and self-giving Jesus is vividly emphasized.

13:3 Jesus knew. Jesus' humility was not due to his forgetting his own rank and dignity; rather he willingly took the place of the lowliest slave in full perception of his origin and destiny.

13:5 wash his disciples' feet. Foot washing was an essential element of cordial hospitality in a land in which people wore sandals and no stockings (cf. Lk 7:44). This task, which demanded no special skill, was usually performed by the lowest ranking member of the household.

13:6–10 Peter, with characteristic impulsiveness, objected to Jesus' initiative in washing his feet. He failed to understand the symbolism behind Jesus' action: It anticipated the cross, through which the cleansing of God's forgiveness would be accomplished. Peter said in effect, "No, Lord," although those two words stand in sharp contradiction to each other. In response, Jesus emphasized that the spiritual washing of the soul, much more significant than physical cleanliness, can be obtained only through the shedding of his blood. This Peter would fully understand later on (cf. Ac 4:12; 1Pe 1:18–19).

13:11 he knew. Judas' betrayal was not an unforeseen or accidental development, but Jesus proceeded in full consciousness of the impending events and of Judas's role in them. This is a clear case of divine providence employing the free and responsible human decision.

13:13 'Teacher' and 'Lord.' This double title gives special significance to the mastery of Christ over the disciples' lives. Later, the word "Lord" would be used on their part as acknowledgment of Jesus' deity (20:28).

13:15 I have set you an example. Jesus' humility was to be a

vant is greater than his master,[o] nor is a messenger greater than the one who sent him.
17 Now that you know these things, you will be blessed if you do them.[p]

Jesus Predicts His Betrayal

18 "I am not referring to all of you;[q] I know those I have chosen.[r] But this is to fulfill
the scripture: 'He who shares my bread[s] has lifted up his heel[t] against me.'[a][u]
19 "I am telling you now before it happens, so that when it does happen you will believe[v] that I am He.[w] 20 I tell you the truth, whoever accepts anyone I send accepts me;
and whoever accepts me accepts the one who sent me."[x]
21 After he had said this, Jesus was troubled in spirit[y] and testified, "I tell you the truth,
one of you is going to betray me."[z]
22 His disciples stared at one another, at a loss to know which of them he meant. 23 One
of them, the disciple whom Jesus loved,[a] was reclining next to him. 24 Simon Peter motioned to this disciple and said, "Ask him which one he means."
25 Leaning back against Jesus, he asked him, "Lord, who is it?"[b]
26 Jesus answered, "It is the one to whom I will give this piece of bread when I have
dipped it in the dish." Then, dipping the piece of bread, he gave it to Judas Iscariot, son
of Simon. 27 As soon as Judas took the bread, Satan entered into him.[c]
"What you are about to do, do quickly," Jesus told him, 28 but no one at the meal understood why Jesus said this to him. 29 Since Judas had charge of the money,[d] some
thought Jesus was telling him to buy what was needed for the Feast, or to give something
to the poor. 30 As soon as Judas had taken the bread, he went out. And it was night.[e]

Jesus Predicts Peter's Denial

31 When he was gone, Jesus said, "Now is the Son of Man glorified[f] and God is glorified in him.[g] 32 If God is glorified in him,[b] God will glorify the Son in himself,[h] and will
glorify him at once.
33 "My children, I will be with you only a little longer. You will look for me, and just
as I told the Jews, so I tell you now: Where I am going, you cannot come.[i]
34 "A new command[j] I give you: Love one another.[k] As I have loved you, so you must
love one another.[l] 35 By this all men will know that you are my disciples, if you love one
another."[m]
36 Simon Peter asked him, "Lord, where are you going?"

13:16 [o]Mt 10:24; Lk 6:40; Jn 15:20
13:17 [p]Mt 7:24,25; Lk 11:28; Jas 1:25
13:18 [q]ver 10 [r]Jn 15:16, 19 [s]Mt 26:23 [t]Jn 6:70 [u]Ps 41:9
13:19 [v]Jn 14:29; 16:4 [w]Jn 8:24
13:20 [x]Mt 10:40; Lk 10:16
13:21 [y]Jn 12:27 [z]Mt 26:21
13:23 [a]Jn 19:26; 20:2; 21:7,20
13:25 [b]Jn 21:20
13:27 [c]Lk 22:3
13:29 [d]Jn 12:6
13:30 [e]Lk 22:53
13:31 [f]Jn 7:39 [g]Jn 14:13; 17:4, 1Pe 4:11
13:32 [h]Jn 17:1
13:33 [i]Jn 7:33, 34
13:34 [j]1Jn 2:7-11; 3:11 [k]Lev 19:18; 1Th 4:9; 1Pe 1:22 [l]Jn 15:12; Eph 5:2; 1Jn 4:10,11
13:35 [m]1Jn 3:14; 4:20

[a] *18* Psalm 41:9 [b] *32* Many early manuscripts do not have *If God is glorified in him.*

pattern for his disciples. The servanthood of Christ must be reflected in the Christian's life: Instead of aspiring to dominate, Christians must be eager to serve (Mt 20:26–28; Php 2:5–8; 1Pe 2:21).

13:17 if you do them. Intellectual perception is not enough. It must be backed up by a life commitment. This does not mean that our works are the ground of our acceptance by God but that they are the manifestation of a true faith, which includes a commitment to obedience.

13:18 not referring to all of you. Jesus chose Judas to be one of the Twelve, but he did not choose him for salvation. Judas was not one of the elect (Mt 26:24), but he was in no way coerced into his betrayal. **fulfill the scripture.** Jesus perceived a fulfillment of Scripture in many details of his life. He was concerned to fulfill Scripture because he viewed it for what it is: the very Word of God. Psalm 41:9, which Jesus quoted, may well be a reference to the treasonous behavior of Ahithophel (2Sa 15:31). If so, Ahithophel is a type of Judas. See *WCF* 3.4.

13:19 before it happens. The truth of prior prediction was one mark of a true prophet. **I am He.** See note on 6:35.

13:20 the one who sent me. Jesus' mission, which originated from the Father, is frequently mentioned in this Gospel, and the mission of his followers is here tied to his own work (cf. 15:20–21).

13:21 troubled in spirit. Compare 11:33 and 12:27. Even though the Lord was previously aware of Judas' treachery, the approaching hour of its wicked expression caused revulsion in Jesus' soul.

13:22 at a loss to know. Judas had hidden his intended betrayal so carefully that the other disciples had no inkling of it. Each one feared that he himself might be the weak link and asked in consternation, "Surely not I, Lord?" (Mt 26:22). Judas, too, mouthed the question (Mt 26:25), but the other disciples apparently did not overhear Jesus' response.

13:23 the disciple whom Jesus loved. This designation appears also in 19:26, 20:2 and 21:7,20. It has generally been understood as a reference to John, the author of this Gospel. It does not imply a lack of love for the other disciples (cf. 13:1) but indicates a special affinity on the part of Jesus for John (cf. 19:26–27). **reclining next to him.** See note on Luke 7:37–38.

13:26 the piece of bread. This was apparently a favor reserved for a guest of honor. That Jesus was able to pass the morsel may indicate that Judas occupied a place of honor next to Jesus. Judas remained insensitive to such favors and continued to harden his heart in his wicked resolve.

13:27 Satan entered into him. Judas's refusal to respond to Jesus' appeal opened up his heart to the control of Satan. He was still a responsible agent, but he had delivered himself to the dominion of evil (cf. 8:34). **do quickly.** Jesus was still in control of the timetable of events, and he made no further effort to check Judas on his fateful way. See *WLC* 151.

13:29 some thought. The disciples still did not have a clear understanding of Judas's treachery.

13:30 See *WLC* 151.

13:31 glorified. One would expect the opposite word—"humiliated"—for in the language of the apostle Paul, Jesus was indeed on the threshold of the deepest pit of his humiliation in his substitutionary death on the cross under the divine curse (Gal 3:13). But John's focus was on the revelation of God's glory through Jesus Christ on the cross. See note on 12:23.

13:33 You will look for me. This restriction was temporary. In time, of course, Jesus' disciples would rejoin him—after he had prepared a place for them. But for the immediate future, between Jesus' crucifixion and resurrection, they would not be able to follow him.

13:34 A new command. There is nothing new about love itself, since Leviticus 19:18 teaches us to "love [our] neighbor as [our]self." The new element is twofold: (1) the change from "neighbor" to "one another" and (2) the change from "as yourself" to "as I have loved you." Christian love has Christ's sacrificial love as its model and the community of believers as the primary context in which it is expressed (cf. Mt 25:40; Eph 5:25).

Jesus replied, "Where I am going, you cannot follow now,[n] but you will follow later."[o]
37 Peter asked, "Lord, why can't I follow you now? I will lay down my life for you."
38 Then Jesus answered, "Will you really lay down your life for me? I tell you the truth,
before the rooster crows, you will disown me three times![p]

Jesus Comforts His Disciples

14 1 "Do not let your hearts be troubled.[q] Trust in God[a]; trust also in me. 2 In my Father's house are many rooms; if it were not so, I would have told you. I am going there[r] to prepare a place for you. 3 And if I go and prepare a place for you, I will come
back and take you to be with me that you also may be where I am.[s] 4 You know the way
to the place where I am going."

Jesus the Way to the Father

5 Thomas[t] said to him, "Lord, we don't know where you are going, so how can we
know the way?"
6 Jesus answered, "I am the way[u] and the truth and the life.[v] No one comes to the Father except through me. 7 If you really knew me, you would know[b] my Father as well.[w]
From now on, you do know him and have seen him."
8 Philip said, "Lord, show us the Father and that will be enough for us."
9 Jesus answered: "Don't you know me, Philip, even after I have been among you such
a long time? Anyone who has seen me has seen the Father.[x] How can you say, 'Show us
the Father'? 10 Don't you believe that I am in the Father, and that the Father is in me?[y]
The words I say to you are not just my own.[z] Rather, it is the Father, living in me, who
is doing his work. 11 Believe me when I say that I am in the Father and the Father is in me;
or at least believe on the evidence of the miracles themselves.[a] 12 I tell you the truth, anyone who has faith[b] in me will do what I have been doing.[c] He will do even greater things
than these, because I am going to the Father. 13 And I will do whatever you ask[d] in my

13:36 [n]ver 33; Jn 14:2 [o]Jn 21:18,19; 2Pe 1:14
13:38 [p]Jn 18:27
14:1 [q]ver 27
14:2 [r]Jn 13:33,36
14:3 [s]Jn 12:26
14:5 [t]Jn 11:16
14:6 [u]Jn 10:9 [v]Jn 11:25
14:7 [w]Jn 8:19
14:9 [x]Jn 12:45; Col 1:15; Heb 1:3
14:10 [y]Jn 10:38 [z]Jn 5:19
14:11 [a]Jn 5:36; 10:38
14:12 [b]Mt 21:21 [c]Lk 10:17
14:13 [d]Mt 7:7

[a] *1* Or *You trust in God* [b] *7* Some early manuscripts *If you really have known me, you will know*

13:36 you will follow later. This is a prophecy about the martyrdom of Peter (21:18–19).
13:37 I will lay down my life for you. Undoubtedly Peter meant this, but he did not know where his own cowardice would take him.
13:38 before the rooster crows. Peter's denial took place in three clusters, not merely in one statement repeated three times.
■ **14:1—16:33** *Farewell Discourse.* John recorded a number of ways in which Jesus comforted his disciples as they faced the nearness of his death and the trials of the years to come. This material divides into five sections: mansions (14:1–4), the way (14:5–14), the Holy Spirit (14:15–31), the vine and branches (15:1–17) and comfort in persecution (15:18—16:33).
14:1 Do not let your hearts be troubled. This passage of supreme comfort was offered by Jesus in an hour of extreme pain that was darkened by the shadow of Judas's treachery and Peter's fickleness, and it was given only a few hours before the agony of Gethsemane and the torment of the cross (13:21). Yet the statement is permeated by an aura of sublime peace, and it was intended to minister to the fears of the disciples rather than to focus on Jesus' own needs.
14:2 my Father's house. A beautiful name for heaven. **many rooms.** The emphasis is more on spaciousness than on compartmentalization. While the road is narrow and the gate small that leads to life (Mt 7:14), it is also true that the number of Abraham's children is like that of the grains of sand on the beach or the stars in the sky (Ge 22:17)—"a great multitude that no one [can] count" (Rev 7:9). **prepare a place for you.** Christ prepares the place in heaven for his own, and the Holy Spirit prepares the elect on Earth for their place in heaven. See *HC* 49.
14:3 take you to be with me. Jesus had referred to himself as the One who functions as a ladder between heaven and Earth (1:51). It is he who takes his people to heaven. See *WLC* 53.
14:4 You know the way. Perhaps intended to elicit Thomas's anxious question and to introduce Jesus' sublime answer.
14:6 the truth. Not only what is conformed to reality, but also what is complete and perfect, in contrast to what is merely begun and as yet incomplete. **the life.** Not merely existence, which is endless for all humans, but fullness of life in perfect fulfillment of God's purpose (1:4). **No one comes to the Father except through me.** A strong affirmation of the exclusive character of Christianity as the way of salvation. To imagine and proclaim other ways is to mislead people and dilute the necessity of Jesus' incarnation and redemption (Ac 4:12; Ro 10:14–15; 1Jn 5:12). See *WCF* 10.4; 21.2; *WLC* 181; *BC* 26.
14:7 If you really knew me. All the blessings previously named are summed up in the knowledge of God, which is more than intellectual perception, for it involves a heart commitment. See note on 12:44.
14:8 show us the Father. Philip's request reveals misunderstanding but opens the way for the development that follows.
14:9 Anyone who has seen me has seen the Father. Not a denial of the distinctions among the persons within the Godhead, but a rejection of Philip's request for some other revelation of the Father. Jesus is the fullest revelation of the Father the world has ever seen or, indeed, needs to see. See note on 12:44. See *BC* 10.
14:11 I am in the Father and the Father is in me. This is a reference to the reciprocal indwelling announced in 10:38 (see v. 20; 17:21). There are three great unities proclaimed in Scripture: the unity of the three persons of the Trinity as the one and only God, the unity of the divine and human natures in the one person of Jesus Christ and the unity of Christ and his own people in the fulfillment of redemption. The Father and the Son work together in perfect harmony; therefore, the miracles Jesus performed are an evidence of the perfect concurrence of the Father and the Son.
14:12 He will do even greater things. History has proved that Jesus was not here affirming that each believer will perform greater miracles than he himself did. The "greater things" may refer to living in the power of the Holy Spirit that he would pour out on his own after going to the Father. It is also possible that Jesus was alluding to ministerial labor in the power of the Holy Spirit, which would be "greater" than Jesus' in its geographic and numeric extension.
14:13–14 See *WCF* 21.3; *WLC* 180; *HC* 117.
14:13 whatever you ask in my name. Not a guarantee that God will automatically grant whatever we request in a prayer to which we append the words "in Christ's name" as a kind of magical formula. To pray in Jesus' name is to pray as his representative, especially as one vested with his authority, and therefore according to his will. Primarily, Jesus was assuring the apostles, as his authoritative representatives, that God would heed the prayers they offered during the course of their ministry. This assurance applies to a lesser degree to the church, which also represents Christ on Earth (see 1Co 5:4), though with less authority than the apostles carried. See also 15:7,16. **that the Son may bring glory to the Father.** The close relationship among the persons of the

name, so that the Son may bring glory to the Father. 14You may ask me for anything in
my name, and I will do it.

Jesus Promises the Holy Spirit

15"If you love me, you will obey what I command.[e] 16And I will ask the Father, and he will

14:15 [e]ver 21,23; Jn 15:10; 1Jn 5:3

Trinity is manifested in the doctrine of prayer. Here the Son is presented as doing what is requested; elsewhere it is the Father who gives (15:16; 16:23). Here, the Father is glorified in the Son by virtue of the answers to prayer. The Holy Spirit helps us in our prayers and intercedes for us (Ro 8:26–27), and Christ Jesus also intercedes for us (Ro 8:34; Heb 7:25). These statements are all true and are not contradictory; they supplement each other. See *BC* 26; *HC* 128.

14:15 you will obey. The true proof of love is not an oral utterance but a living obedience. Persistent, willful disobedience gives good reason to doubt the reality of love, however it is professed (vv. 21,23–24).

The Trinity: One God or Three?

JUDAISM, Islam and a number of pseudo Christian cults often accuse orthodox Christians of worshiping three Gods: the Father, the Son and the Holy Spirit. This accusation reflects a serious misunderstanding of orthodox Christianity. Christianity insists that one God exists in Trinity: God has three "persons," but only one "essence."

Tertullian (c. A.D. 160–220) was the first to formulate the doctrine of the Trinity in the language of "persons" and "essence." He wrote that God exists in "three *Persons*—the Father, the Son, and the Holy Ghost: three, however, not in condition, but in degree; not in substance, but in form; not in power, but in aspect; yet of one substance, and of one condition, and of one power, inasmuch as He is one God, from whom these degrees and forms and aspects are reckoned, under the name of the Father, and of the Son, and of the Holy Ghost" (*Against Praxeas*, ch. 2).The doctrine of the Trinity was affirmed in principle at the Council of Nicea (A.D. 325) and reflected in the later Council of Constantinople (A.D. 381). These councils testified that this doctrine had been handed down through the church from the apostles themselves.

The creed most churches today recognize as the Nicene Creed (which was actually formalized by the Council of Constantinople in A.D. 381) is perhaps the most familiar early formulation of Trinitarian doctrine. It distinctly treats the Father, the Son and the Holy Spirit as individual persons within the Godhead. In its Synodical Letter of A.D. 382, the Council of Constantinople also formulated the earliest ecumenical version of this doctrine that uses the explicit terms "person" and "essence:" "There is one Godhead, Power and Substance of the Father and of the Son and of the Holy Ghost; the dignity being equal, and the majesty being equal in three perfect hypostases, i.e. three perfect persons" (NPNF 2, vol. 14.1, pp. 188–190). This is still the standard definition today.

The basic idea is that the Father, Son and Holy Spirit are coequal and coeternal centers of self-awareness, each being "I" in relation to the other two, who are "you," and each partaking of the full divine essence along with the other two. They are not three roles played by one person (*modalism*), nor are they three gods in a cluster (*tritheism*). The three persons are eternally together and cooperating. Each person is involved in everything the others do, for the Father is in the Son and the Son in him (Jn 10:38), and the Spirit is both the Spirit of God and the Spirit of Christ (Ro 8:9). But Scripture also emphasizes general distinctions among the works of the three persons, the Father initiating, the Son complying and the Spirit executing the joint will of all three. We must pay equal attention to, and give equal honor to, all three persons, while always remembering that we worship only one God in these three persons.

Although the doctrine of the Trinity is not explicitly stated in the Bible, it rightly summarizes the teaching of Scripture. The Old Testament constantly insists that there is only one God, the self-revealed Creator, who must be worshiped and loved exclusively (Dt 6:4–5; Isa 44:6—45:25). The New Testament agrees (Mk 12:29–30; 1Co 8:4, Eph 4:6; 1Ti 2:5), yet it speaks of three personal agents as fully divine: Father, Son and Holy Spirit. The New Testament affirms Jesus' divinity and the rightness of worshiping him and praying to him (Jn 1:1–5; 20:28–31; cf. Jn 1:6–18; Ac 7:59; Ro 9:5, 10:9–13; 2Co 12:7–9; Php 2:5–6; Col 1:15–17; 2:9; Heb 1:1–12; 1Pe 3.15; see also theological article "Jesus Christ, God and Man" at Jn 1). It also indicates that the Holy Spirit is a "Counselor" like Christ (Jn 14:16) and that he is at least as wonderful and valuable to the church as the incarnate Lord (Jn 14:16–17,26; 15:26–27; 16:7–15). To be as valuable to the church as Jesus is, the Holy Spirit must also be God, a fact the church has recognized from the beginning (Ac 5:3–4).

Christ himself assumed the doctrine of the Trinity when he prescribed baptism "in the name of the Father and of the Son and of the Holy Spirit" (Mt 28:19)—the three persons share one name because they are one God. We also see the doctrine of the Trinity in places that demonstrate the equal contributions of each person. For example, at Jesus' baptism the Father acknowledged the Son and the Spirit showed his presence in the Son's life and ministry (Mk 1:9–11). In Ephesians 1:3–14 we read that salvation is a work of the Trinity: the Father electing, the Son accomplishing and the Spirit applying. We also find many other passages in the New Testament that mention the Father, the Son and the Holy Spirit as equal persons (e.g., Ro 15:16; 2Co 13:14; Heb 9:14; 1Pe 1:2). Although the technical, theological language used to describe the Trinity (i.e., "three persons, one essence") does not appear in the New Testament, Trinitarian faith and thinking are present throughout its pages. Therefore, the Trinity must be acknowledged as a Biblical doctrine.

14:16 [f]Jn 15:26; 16:7
14:17 [g]Jn 15:26; 16:13; 1Jn 4:6 [h]1Co 2:14
14:18 [i]ver 3,28
14:19 [j]Jn 7:33,34; 16:16 [k]Jn 6:57
14:20 [l]Jn 10:38
14:21 [m]1Jn 5:3 [n]1Jn 2:5
14:22 [o]Lk 6:16; Ac 1:13 [p]Ac 10:41
14:23 [q]ver 15 [r]1Jn 2:24; Rev 3:20
14:24 [s]Jn 7:16
14:26 [t]Jn 15:26; 16:7 [u]Ac 2:33 [v]Jn 16:13; 1Jn 2:20,27 [w]Jn 2:22
14:27 [x]Jn 16:33; Php 4:7; Col 3:15
14:28 [y]ver 2-4,18 [z]Jn 5:18 [a]Jn 10:29; Php 2:6
14:29 [b]Jn 13:19; 16:4
14:30 [c]Jn 12:31
14:31 [d]Jn 10:18; 12:49

give you another Counselor[f] to be with you forever— **17**the Spirit of truth.[g] The world cannot accept him,[h] because it neither sees him nor knows him. But you know him, for he lives
with you and will be[a] in you. **18**I will not leave you as orphans; I will come to you.[i] **19**Before
long, the world will not see me anymore, but you will see me.[j] Because I live, you also will
live.[k] **20**On that day you will realize that I am in my Father,[l] and you are in me, and I am in
you. **21**Whoever has my commands and obeys them, he is the one who loves me.[m] He who
loves me will be loved by my Father,[n] and I too will love him and show myself to him."

22Then Judas[o] (not Judas Iscariot) said, "But, Lord, why do you intend to show yourself to us and not to the world?"[p]

23Jesus replied, "If anyone loves me, he will obey my teaching.[q] My Father will love
him, and we will come to him and make our home with him.[r] **24**He who does not love me
will not obey my teaching. These words you hear are not my own; they belong to the Father who sent me.[s]

25"All this I have spoken while still with you. **26**But the Counselor,[t] the Holy Spirit,
whom the Father will send in my name,[u] will teach you all things[v] and will remind you
of everything I have said to you.[w] **27**Peace I leave with you; my peace I give you.[x] I do not
give to you as the world gives. Do not let your hearts be troubled and do not be afraid.

28"You heard me say, 'I am going away and I am coming back to you.'[y] If you loved
me, you would be glad that I am going to the Father,[z] for the Father is greater than I.[a]
29I have told you now before it happens, so that when it does happen you will believe.[b]
30I will not speak with you much longer, for the prince of this world[c] is coming. He has
no hold on me, **31**but the world must learn that I love the Father and that I do exactly
what my Father has commanded me.[d]

"Come now; let us leave.

a *17* Some early manuscripts *and is*

14:16–19 See *HC* 47.
14:16–17 See *WCF* 17.2; *HC* 53.
14:16 I will ask the Father, and he will give. Both the Father and the Son are active in the sending of the Holy Spirit. He is called the Spirit of God the Father (Ge 1:2; Isa 11:2; Mt 10:20) and the Spirit of God the Son (Ro 8:9; Gal 4:6; Php 1:19; 1Pe 1:11). **another Counselor.** The Holy Spirit, who at Pentecost would enter into a deeper relation with believers than had previously been experienced, is here emphasized. Jesus' farewell discourse is understandably concerned with this glorious truth (v. 26; 15:26; 16:7–15). The term "Counselor" ("Paraclete") was used in legal language for the advocate for the defense (1Jn 2:1), but it implies more generally to one who is "called upon for help." Jesus had been such a help for his disciples, but after his ascension the Holy Spirit would take over that function. This term emphasizes not only the personality of the Holy Spirit as distinct from that of the Father and the Son, but also his perfect unity with them in the work of redemption. See *WCF* 8.8; *BC* 9,11; *HC* 49.
14:17 the Spirit of truth. The Spirit is in perfect association with the Father (Isa 65:16) and with the Son (v. 6). **The world.** Sinful humanity as contrasted with God's redeemed people (15:18–19; 17:9; 1Jn 2:15–17; 4:5; 5:4–5,19). **lives with you and will be in you.** The Spirit makes his dwelling place in the life, heart, body and soul of each individual believer (1Co 3:16–17; 6:19; 2Co 6:16; Eph 2:21).
14:18 I will come to you. Refers primarily to the coming of the Holy Spirit at Pentecost, but also to the blessed hope of the church: The glorious Mediator, Jesus Christ, will come back one day to take the redeemed with him (vv. 3,18,28). See *HC* 33.
14:19 Because I live, you also will live. See 11:25–26. Life is to be found only in Jesus Christ (1:4; 14:6).
14:20 I am in my Father. See notes on 10:38 and 14:11.
14:21 He who loves me will be loved. Just as there is reciprocal indwelling, there is also deep, mutual love. **I too will . . . show myself.** Love implies revelation; indifference thwarts knowledge.
14:22 to us and not to the world. Judas did understand Jesus accurately, but this disciple's Messianic expectations probably included a political triumph that would be visible to all, perhaps drawing on images from Habakkuk 3:3–15 and Zechariah 9:9–17. Jesus reinforced the necessity of obedience.
14:23 our home. The Holy Spirit, the Father and the Son all indwell the believer (Ro 8:9–11; Rev 3:20).
14:24 There is perfect harmony between the teaching of the Father and that of the Son (7:16; 14:10).
14:26 the Holy Spirit, whom the Father will send. In 15:26, it is the Son who sends the Spirit. The Father and Son concur in this sending. **will teach you all things.** That is, all things that you need to know for your mission (16:13). **will remind you of everything I have said to you.** The Holy Spirit's teaching would be fully in line with the teaching of Jesus himself. He would overcome the frailties of human memory to make sure that the words of Jesus were preserved for the instruction of God's people (Mt 24:35). These promises to the apostles were fulfilled in the apostolic preaching and the inspiration of the New Testament Scriptures. In some sense, they continue to be fulfilled as God's people are reminded and taught through the inspired Scripture. The Christian church is apostolic because the apostles, by the special assistance of the Holy Spirit, perpetuated and expounded the teaching of our Lord. See *BC* 11; *HC* 25.
14:27 Peace I leave with you. A common Hebrew phrase given as a salutation or farewell. Jesus used the clause in a new and deeper sense: His peace is the stability and security of one who has found salvation, who is now reconciled with God. This is something that the world can never give, and it was purchased by the death and resurrection of Jesus (cf. Ac 10:36; Ro 5:1; 14:17; Eph 2:14–17; Php 4:7; Col 3:15). It is the supreme remedy for all fears (v. 1) and the legacy Jesus left for us, his heirs.
14:28 you would be glad. The Lord's going away and returning complete his mediatorial work (v. 3). His going away ended the period of his humiliation (i.e., his earthly life and ministry) and began his glorification. He will receive even greater glory when he returns to conquer all his enemies and ultimately bless believers. One who loves Christ is eager to see him glorified (cf. Rev 1:5–6).**the Father is greater than I.** Should be understood in light of the clear witness of this Gospel to the full deity of the Son and to his equality and oneness with the Father (1:1; 10:30; 14:9). The context here points to the willingness of the Son to become "less" by voluntarily putting aside his glory as the divine Son of God and following the way of humble obedience to his Father through his incarnation and sacrificial death (Php 2:6–11).
14:29 I have told you. The fulfillment of Jesus' prophecies would confirm the divine origin of his mission (cf. Dt 18:22).
14:30 the prince of this world. Satan (cf. 12:31; 16:11). This refers to the momentous suffering Jesus would undergo during his arrest, trial and crucifixion. **He has no hold.** Literally, "has nothing." This is a reaffirmation of Jesus' sinlessness (v. 31; 8:29,46; 2Co 5:21; Heb 7:26–27). He is the only member of the human race about whom this may be said. The obedience that Jesus required of his disciples was supremely exemplified in his own earthly career (Ro 5:19; Php 2:8; Heb 5:8).
14:31 Come now; let us leave. This statement would appear to be most appropriate if Jesus and the disciples were leaving the upper room, but it seems that chapters 15–17 still took place in this locale. Several options are possible: (1) Jesus gave this signal, but

The Vine and the Branches

15 "I am the true vine,[e] and my Father is the gardener. 2He cuts off every branch
in me that bears no fruit, while every branch that does bear fruit he prunes[a] so
that it will be even more fruitful. 3You are already clean because of the word I have spoken to you.[f] 4Remain in me, and I will remain in you.[g] No branch can bear fruit by itself;
it must remain in the vine. Neither can you bear fruit unless you remain in me.
5"I am the vine; you are the branches. If a man remains in me and I in him, he will
bear much fruit;[h] apart from me you can do nothing. 6If anyone does not remain in me,
he is like a branch that is thrown away and withers; such branches are picked up, thrown
into the fire and burned.[i] 7If you remain in me and my words remain in you, ask whatever you wish, and it will be given you.[j] 8This is to my Father's glory,[k] that you bear much
fruit, showing yourselves to be my disciples.[l]
9"As the Father has loved me,[m] so have I loved you. Now remain in my love. 10If you
obey my commands,[n] you will remain in my love, just as I have obeyed my Father's commands and remain in his love. 11I have told you this so that my joy may be in you and that
your joy may be complete.[o] 12My command is this: Love each other as I have loved you.[p]
13Greater love has no one than this, that he lay down his life for his friends.[q] 14You are
my friends[r] if you do what I command.[s] 15I no longer call you servants, because a servant does not know his master's business. Instead, I have called you friends, for everything that I learned from my Father I have made known to you.[t] 16You did not choose

15:1 [e]Isa 5:1-7
15:3 [f]Jn 13:10; 17:17; Eph 5:26
15:4 [g]Jn 6:56; 1Jn 2:6
15:5 [h]ver 16
15:6 [i]ver 2
15:7 [j]Mt 7:7
15:8 [k]Mt 5:16 [l]Jn 8:31
15:9 [m]Jn 17:23,24,26
15:10 [n]Jn 14:15
15:11 [o]Jn 17:13
15:12 [p]Jn 13:34
15:13 [q]Jn 10:11; Ro 5:7,8
15:14 [r]Lk 12:4 [s]Mt 12:50
15:15 [t]Jn 8:26

[a] 2 The Greek for *prunes* also means *cleans.*

some time elapsed before they actually left the room. (2) They left at once, but Jesus continued his discourse on the way to Gethsemane. This would present the prayer of John 17 in very sharp contrast to the agony of the garden. (3) John arranged his material topically rather than chronologically. (4) This statement of Jesus was a challenge to meet Satan, not a signal to leave the room (i.e., "Up then, let us go to meet the foe").

15:1–27 There are two major divisions in this chapter: the discourse about the vine (vv. 1–17) and warnings about the world's hatred (vv. 18–27).

15:1–17 The union between Christ and his redeemed people is portrayed in Scripture in a variety of ways, the combination of which helps us understand the nature of this relationship: (1) the foundation and the building (1Co 3:11; Eph 2:20–22); (2) the vine and the branches (vv. 1–17); (3) the head and the body (1Co 6:15,19; 12:12; Eph 1:22–23; 4:15–16); (4) the husband and the wife (Eph 5:31–32; Rev 19:7); and (5) Adam and his descendants (Ro 5:12,18–21; 1Co 15:22,45,49). Each of these metaphors has its limitations—as does every comparison—but each also has pointed similarities with the others.

15:1–6 See *HC* 76,127.

15:1 I am the true vine. As elsewhere in this Gospel, the word "true" is not used as opposed to "false." Jesus is the final, real vine, as opposed to Israel, which as a type or precursor was referred to as God's "vine" or "vineyard" in the Old Testament (Ps 80:8–16; Jer 2:21). Although Israel was judged for not bearing fruit, Jesus actually fulfilled what the type merely signified. See the note on 4:24. This is the last of the "I am" sayings in this Gospel (see note on 6:35).

15:2 cuts off every branch in me that bears no fruit. May also be translated "lifts up every branch." Cutting or removing is appropriate for dead branches; lifting up enables fruitless live branches to bear fruit. No branch that remains fruitless is truly one of Christ's, and no branch that is truly one of Christ's remains fruitless. Those branches that genuinely belong to Christ will not only bear fruit but will also undergo the pruning necessary to bear more fruit. Israel's failure to bear fruit (Ps 80; Isa 5:1ff.; Jer 2:21) was equivalent to her failure to be covenantally obedient. Old Testament discussions of the vine's fruit, combined with the discussions of obeying Jesus' words in this chapter, indicate that the "fruit" is moral fruit—the natural outgrowth of obedience—rather than evangelistic fruit, although this is also desirable. This analogy does not carry over into the spiritual realm in every respect, for horticulturally no branch can exist at all unless it has at some point been united to the vine. If Christ meant to teach that dead branches would be removed from him, he was speaking of those who claim to be united with Christ and yet show this to be a fraudulent claim by their failure to produce the fruits of obedience.

15:3 You are . . . clean. A play on words based on the resemblance in Greek between "pruning" (*kathairô*) and "clean" (*katharos*). The pruning operation was to continue, but it had already begun in the disciples through the ministry of Jesus (13:10).

15:4–5 See *WCF* 16.3.

15:4 Remain. Jesus emphasized the importance of continuity in his relationship with the disciples. "Remain" is repeated 11 times in verses 4–10. The metaphor of a vine illustrates this point well. It is only when the sap flows freely to the branches that fruit can be borne. Similarly, it is only when the spiritual relation to Christ is intact that the Christian is healthy and fruitful. Verse 5 is even more emphatic. This radical inability of the sinner makes the intervention of grace indispensable at the start, in the development and for the culmination of salvation.

15:5 See *WCF* 9.3; *WLC* 149; *BC* 14,24; *HC* 29,64,91.

15:6 If anyone does not remain in me. Those who do not remain show that they never had a vital unity with Christ. There is, therefore, no surprise if their destiny is described here with the language of damnation (cf. Mt 3:12; 25:41; Jude 7; Rev 20:14). In this context, Jesus may have had Judas Iscariot (cf. 13:21–30) especially in mind.

15:7 If you remain in me . . . ask whatever you wish. Again, this assurance primarily applies to the 11 loyal disciples (see note on 14:13; cf. 15:16).

15:8 showing yourselves to be my disciples. The evidence of the reality of the union with Christ is the bearing of fruit (i.e., a life marked by victory over temptation and by manifesting the fruit of the Spirit; Gal 5:22). These works are in no way the ground of our acceptance by God; rather, they are the inevitable result of our vital union with Christ. They are not the cause of salvation, but rather the effect of it, an effect so indissolubly connected with it that where fruit bearing is lacking there is good reason to question whether the person is really saved. See *WCF* 16.2.

15:9 Now the emphasis falls especially on the word "love," used eight times in verses 9–13.

15:10 The connection between love and obedience is once more asserted (14:15,21,23; 15:14) and exemplified in Jesus Christ (14:31).

15:11 my joy. Many imagine that obedience to Christ is grievous, entailing as it does sacrificial self-surrender and service (Ro 12:1–2). Jesus taught the opposite, associating obedience with joy.

15:12–13 See *CD* 2.VII.

15:12 My command is this. See note on 13:34.

15:13 Greater love . . . that he lay down his life for his friends. One cannot do more for another than to sacrifice oneself for the loved person. Self-sacrifice for the ungodly (sinners, who are by nature God's enemies) is even more remarkable because of the nature of those for whom it is offered (Ro 5:7–8). See *WCF* 8.8; *BC* 21,26.

15:14 You are my friends if you do what I command. The test of friendship is obedience. If we say we love Christ, yet do not obey him, we are not his friends.

15:15 I no longer call you servants. There is no previous record of Jesus Christ calling any of the disciples "servants" (unless 12:26 is quoted to that effect), but he had a right to do so and they did rightly call him "Lord" (13:13). The word *friend,* however, connotes a closer relation, and the language of brotherhood goes still further (Heb 2:10–11). **everything . . . I have made known.** The reference is to what they were able to absorb (cf. 16:12). After his resurrection, and through the Holy Spirit after Pentecost, they would learn yet more (16:13).

me, but I chose you and appointed you[u] to go and bear fruit—fruit that will last. Then
the Father will give you whatever you ask in my name. 17This is my command: Love each
other.[v]

The World Hates the Disciples

18“If the world hates you,[w] keep in mind that it hated me first. 19If you belonged to
the world, it would love you as its own. As it is, you do not belong to the world, but I have
chosen you[x] out of the world. That is why the world hates you.[y] 20Remember the words
I spoke to you: ‘No servant is greater than his master.’[a][z] If they persecuted me, they will
persecute you also.[a] If they obeyed my teaching, they will obey yours also. 21They will
treat you this way because of my name,[b] for they do not know the One who sent me.[c]
22If I had not come and spoken to them, they would not be guilty of sin. Now, however,
they have no excuse for their sin.[d] 23He who hates me hates my Father as well. 24If I had
not done among them what no one else did,[e] they would not be guilty of sin. But now
they have seen these miracles, and yet they have hated both me and my Father. 25But
this is to fulfill what is written in their Law: ‘They hated me without reason.’[b][f]
26“When the Counselor[g] comes, whom I will send to you from the Father,[h] the Spirit of truth[i] who goes out from the Father, he will testify about me.[j] 27And you also must
testify,[k] for you have been with me from the beginning.[l]
16 “All this[m] I have told you so that you will not go astray.[n] 2They will put you out
of the synagogue;[o] in fact, a time is coming when anyone who kills you will think
he is offering a service to God.[p] 3They will do such things because they have not known
the Father or me.[q] 4I have told you this, so that when the time comes you will remember[r] that I warned you. I did not tell you this at first because I was with you.

The Work of the Holy Spirit

5“Now I am going to him who sent me,[s] yet none of you asks me, ‘Where are you going?’[t] 6Because I have said these things, you are filled with grief. 7But I tell you the truth:
It is for your good that I am going away. Unless I go away, the Counselor[u] will not come
to you; but if I go, I will send him to you.[v] 8When he comes, he will convict the world of

[a] *20* John 13:16 [b] *25* Psalms 35:19; 69:4

15:16 [u]Jn 6:70; 13:18
15:17 [v]ver 12
15:18 [w]1Jn 3:13
15:19 [x]ver 16 [y]Jn 17:14
15:20 [z]Jn 13:16 [a]2Ti 3:12
15:21 [b]Mt 10:22 [c]Jn 16:3
15:22 [d]Jn 9:41; Ro 1:20
15:24 [e]Jn 5:36
15:25 [f]Ps 35:19; 69:4
15:26 [g]Jn 14:16 [h]Jn 14:26 [i]Jn 14:17 [j]1Jn 5:7
15:27 [k]Lk 24:48; 1Jn 1:2; 4:14 [l]Lk 1:2
16:1 [m]Jn 15:18-27 [n]Mt 11:6
16:2 [o]Jn 9:22 [p]Isa 66:5; Ac 26:9,10; Rev 6:9
16:3 [q]Jn 15:21; 17:25; 1Jn 3:1
16:4 [r]Jn 13:19
16:5 [s]Jn 7:33 [t]Jn 13:36; 14:5
16:7 [u]Jn 14:16,26; 15:26 [v]Jn 7:39

See *WCF* 8.8; *WLC* 43; *WSC* 24; *BC* 7; *HC* 31.

15:16 You did not choose me, but I chose you. Jesus, of course, did not mean that his disciples exercised no volition; they had chosen to follow him. Rather, he was indicating that the initiatives and the effectual choice were his. Had he not first chosen them, they would not have chosen him. In this text, the reference is to service as apostles, but the principle applies to many other areas, including election to salvation (Eph 1:4,11). **appointed you.** Emphasizes the sovereign activity of God that is exercised apart from the human power of decision. **to go.** This verb marks the direction of Christian service (see also Mt 28:19; Ac 1:8). While specifically a missionary charge to the apostles, this typifies the general charge to the church to go and reach out to the lost wherever they may be found (Mt 28:19–20). **bear fruit.** God ordained fruitfulness, not sterility, for the apostles' ministry. The fruit refers both to individual sanctification (Gal 5:22) and to effectiveness in evangelism (Mt 13:3–8; Ro 1:13). In the same way, he ordains fruitfulness in the lives of all believers (Eph. 2:10). **fruit that will last.** The distinguishing characteristic of Christian service is that its results have eternal significance. **the Father will give you whatever you ask.** Another assurance that the apostles' prayers would be effective (14:13; 15:7). See *BC* 16; *HC* 53; *CD* 1.V.

15:17 Love each other. Repeated for the third time in this context (13:34; 15:12).

15:18–21 See *HC* 127.

15:18 the world. The opposition between the world and God's elect is articulated in the strongest terms (14:17). The world's hatred is not due to what believers do wrong, but to what they do right.

15:19 See *BC* 16.

15:21 they do not know. Ignorance of the Father is tied to disregard for the Son (16:3; 1Jn 2:23). Hatred of the Son implies hatred of the Father as well (vv. 23–24).

15:22 they would not be guilty of sin. The "sin" referred to here is the particular sin of hating Jesus and those who belong to him; the reference is not to sin in the general sense (v. 24). See *WLC* 151.

15:25 in their Law. Non-believing Jews stand condemned by the very law in which they glory. This is a quotation from the Psalms; here the term "Law" has a wider reference to the Old Testament in general, not just to the Pentateuch (see note on 10:34). Both Psalm 35:19 and Psalm 69:4 originally referred to David's experience, but they have a deeper fulfillment in the life of Christ.

15:26 the Counselor. See note on 14:16. **who goes out from the Father.** The reference is to the work of the Holy Spirit in the plan of redemption, not to his eternal relationship within the Godhead. **he will testify about me.** Since the work of Christ is central to the whole gospel, the Spirit would focus his witness on Christ. See *WCF* 2.3; *WLC* 10; *BC* 9,11; *HC* 25.

15:27 for you have been with me from the beginning. Jesus pointed to the unique witness-bearing function of the apostles. As eyewitnesses empowered by the Holy Spirit, they were to provide the foundational and authoritative witness to Christ for the church (Lk 24:48; Ac 1:21–22; Eph 2:20). The office of apostle, therefore, is not repeatable, and the church's subsequent witness to Christ is dependent on the apostolic witness of the New Testament as it is illumined by the Holy Spirit.

16:1–4 A continuation of Jesus' teaching about the world's opposition to the disciples; verses 5–15 resume his teaching about the Holy Spirit.

16:2 See *WCF* 16.1; *WLC* 105; *BC* 29.

16:4 I did not tell you this at first. While Jesus was on Earth with the disciples, he provided teaching and encouragement as the need arose. As his remaining time with them grew short, they needed to know about coming persecutions and about the ministry of the Holy Spirit.

16:5 none of you asks me. Although Peter had formally asked this and Thomas had implied as much (13:36; 14:5), their questions had been prompted merely by their sense of loss at Jesus' impending departure, rather than by a desire to understand the character and implications of his destination (v. 6). Here Jesus challenged the disciples to think about the important results of his departure—particularly the coming of the Holy Spirit.

16:6 you are filled with grief. The disciples were naturally grieved at the thought of Jesus' departure, but the coming of the Spirit at Pentecost would assure them of God's presence at their side anywhere and everywhere in the world (Mt 28:20). Jesus' presence, on the other hand, was limited to one locality during the days of his flesh. The coming of the Holy Spirit at Pentecost was conditioned upon Christ's own return to heaven.

guilt[a] in regard to sin and righteousness and judgment: 9in regard to sin,[w] because men
do not believe in me; 10in regard to righteousness,[x] because I am going to the Father,
where you can see me no longer; 11and in regard to judgment, because the prince of this
world[y] now stands condemned.
12"I have much more to say to you, more than you can now bear.[z] 13But when he, the
Spirit of truth,[a] comes, he will guide you into all truth.[b] He will not speak on his own;
he will speak only what he hears, and he will tell you what is yet to come. 14He will bring
glory to me by taking from what is mine and making it known to you. 15All that belongs
to the Father is mine.[c] That is why I said the Spirit will take from what is mine and make
it known to you.
16"In a little while[d] you will see me no more, and then after a little while you will
see me."[e]

The Disciples' Grief Will Turn to Joy

17Some of his disciples said to one another, "What does he mean by saying, 'In a little while you will see me no more, and then after a little while you will see me,'[f] and 'Because I am going to the Father'?"[g] 18They kept asking, "What does he mean by 'a little
while'? We don't understand what he is saying."
19Jesus saw that they wanted to ask him about this, so he said to them, "Are you asking one another what I meant when I said, 'In a little while you will see me no more, and
then after a little while you will see me'? 20I tell you the truth, you will weep and mourn[h]
while the world rejoices. You will grieve, but your grief will turn to joy.[i] 21A woman giving birth to a child has pain[j] because her time has come; but when her baby is born she
forgets the anguish because of her joy that a child is born into the world. 22So with you:
Now is your time of grief,[k] but I will see you again[l] and you will rejoice, and no one will
take away your joy. 23In that day you will no longer ask me anything. I tell you the truth,
my Father will give you whatever you ask in my name.[m] 24Until now you have not asked
for anything in my name. Ask and you will receive, and your joy will be complete.[n]
25"Though I have been speaking figuratively,[o] a time is coming[p] when I will no longer use this kind of language but will tell you plainly about my Father. 26In that day you
will ask in my name.[q] I am not saying that I will ask the Father on your behalf. 27No, the
Father himself loves you because you have loved me[r] and have believed that I came from

[a] 8 *Or will expose the guilt of the world*

16:9 [w]Jn 15:22
16:10 [x]Ac 3:14; 7:52; 1Pe 3:18
16:11 [y]Jn 12:31
16:12 [z]Mk 4:33
16:13 [a]Jn 14:17 [b]Jn 14:26
16:15 [c]Jn 17:10
16:16 [d]Jn 7:33 [e]Jn 14:18-24
16:17 [f]ver 16 [g]ver 5
16:20 [h]Lk 23:27 [i]Jn 20:20
16:21 [j]Isa 26:17; 1Th 5:3
16:22 [k]ver 6 [l]ver 16
16:23 [m]Mt 7:7; Jn 15:16
16:24 [n]Jn 3:29; 15:11
16:25 [o]Mt 13:34; Jn 10:6 [p]ver 2
16:26 [q]ver 23,24
16:27 [r]Jn 14:21,23

16:8–9 See *WLC* 72.
16:8 he will convict the world of guilt. Probably not a reference to the conviction that leads to repentance and salvation, but to the manifestation of humanity's inexcusable guilt.
16:9 in regard to sin. The singular gravity of unbelief is stressed without excusing other forms of sin.
16:10 in regard to righteousness. Sinners cannot be counted righteous on the basis of their own works but only by virtue of the substitutionary work of Christ. Jesus' work wipes away sins and reckons his perfect obedience to the sinner's account. It is by virtue of the resurrection (Ro 4:25) and ascension of Christ that justification for the sinner is certified.
16:11 in regard to judgment. Satan and those over whom he rules will ultimately be defeated by the divine justice of God, whose verdict has already been rendered.
16:13–14 See *WCF* 1.5; *WLC* 4.
16:13 he will guide you into all truth. This obviously refers to truths of God's salvation, not to technical mastery of every kind of information. This guidance into the truth is specifically related to the work of the apostles as vehicles of new Scripture that would take its place beside the Old Testament. The Spirit would remind them of the past (everything recorded in the Gospels; 14:26), instruct them for the present (recorded in Acts and the Epistles; 14:26; 15:26; 16:13) and reveal things to come (recorded in Revelation; 16:13). **He will not speak on his own.** The teaching work of the Spirit is not done independently of the Father and the Son but occurs as part of the plan of redemption and with the complete agreement of the three persons of the Trinity.
16:14 He will bring glory to me. Since the plan of redemption centers in Christ, this is the topic on which the Spirit concentrates his teaching (15:26).
16:15 The close interrelationship of the three persons of the Trinity is once again emphasized (17:10).
16:16 a little while . . . a little while. The first reference undoubtedly points to the crucifixion that would take Jesus away from them, while the second may refer to the resurrection, the coming of the Spirit or the second coming of Christ. The resurrection fits best for the immediacy of the prophecy; the second coming for the completeness of the joy in view.
16:17 I am going to the Father. The disciples connected what Jesus said in verse 10 with the statement of verse 16, and that made it more difficult to understand Jesus' meaning, since one statement refers to the ascension and the other to the crucifixion.
16:20 you will weep and mourn. The crucifixion of Jesus, which would appear to assure the triumph of his enemies, would deeply distress the disciples. However, since this substitutionary death secures the salvation of all believers, it becomes the subject of great rejoicing and gratitude. This is analogous to giving birth, a painful experience for the mother at the time of delivery, but a source of joy thereafter.
16:22 I will see you again. See note on verse 16. **no one will take away your joy.** The blessings that God's redemptive work affords cannot be canceled by any power, either human or satanic. The gracious purpose of God assures the perennial character of the joy of salvation (10:28; Php 1:6).
16:23 ask . . . ask. Two different Greek verbs are used here. The first ordinarily relates to inquiry; the second to petition. If we observe this distinction, we note that after the ascension, the disciples received revealed truth through the Holy Spirit. Prayers were directed mainly to the Father in Christ's name (i.e., as Christ's representatives with his delegated authority). See *WLC* 178; *WSC* 98; *HC* 117.
16:24 Until now. The disciples had previously offered prayers to God and made requests of Jesus. The difference in the future would be that they could address the Father directly with a new confidence, being vested with Christ's authority as his representatives. See *WLC* 180.
16:26 I am not saying that I will ask the Father on your behalf. Jesus is not denying the reality of his ministry of intercession (Ro 8:34; Heb 7:25; 1Jn 2:1). Rather, his meaning is that the disciples would reach a certain maturity in prayer so that he would no longer need to pray in their stead as if they were mere babes.
16:27 the Father himself loves you. The three persons of the Trinity are fully united in their common love for believers (3:16).

God. [28]I came from the Father and entered the world; now I am leaving the world and
going back to the Father."[s]
[29]Then Jesus' disciples said, "Now you are speaking clearly and without figures of
speech.[t] [30]Now we can see that you know all things and that you do not even need to
have anyone ask you questions. This makes us believe that you came from God."
[31]"You believe at last!"[a] Jesus answered. [32]"But a time is coming,[u] and has come,
when you will be scattered,[v] each to his own home. You will leave me all alone. Yet I am
not alone, for my Father is with me.[w]
[33]"I have told you these things, so that in me you may have peace.[x] In this world you
will have trouble.[y] But take heart! I have overcome[z] the world."

Jesus Prays for Himself

17 After Jesus said this, he looked toward heaven[a] and prayed:

"Father, the time has come. Glorify your Son, that your Son may glorify you.[b]
[2]For you granted him authority over all people that he might give eternal life to
all those you have given him.[c] [3]Now this is eternal life: that they may know you,
the only true God, and Jesus Christ, whom you have sent.[d] [4]I have brought you glory[e] on earth by completing the work you gave me to do.[f] [5]And now, Father, glorify me in your presence with the glory I had with you[g] before the world began.[h]

Jesus Prays for His Disciples

[6]"I have revealed you[b][i] to those whom you gave me[j] out of the world. They
were yours; you gave them to me and they have obeyed your word. [7]Now they
know that everything you have given me comes from you. [8]For I gave them the
words you gave me[k] and they accepted them. They knew with certainty that I
came from you,[l] and they believed that you sent me.[m] [9]I pray for them.[n] I am not
praying for the world, but for those you have given me, for they are yours. [10]All I

16:28 [s]Jn 13:3
16:29 [t]ver 25
16:32 [u]ver 2,25 [v]Mt 26:31 [w]Jn 8:16,29
16:33 [x]Jn 14:27 [y]Jn 15:18-21 [z]Ro 8:37; 1Jn 4:4
17:1 [a]Jn 11:41 [b]Jn 12:23; 13:31, 32
17:2 [c]ver 6,9,24; Da 7:14; Jn 6:37, 39
17:3 [d]ver 8,18,21,23, 25; Jn 3:17
17:4 [e]Jn 13:31 [f]Jn 4:34
17:5 [g]Php 2:6 [h]Jn 1:2
17:6 [i]ver 26 [j]ver 2; Jn 6:37,39
17:8 [k]ver 14,26 [l]Jn 16:27 [m]ver 3, 18,21,23,25; Jn 3:17
17:9 [n]Lk 22:32

[a] *31* Or *"Do you now believe?"* [b] *6* Greek *your name*; also in verse 26

Believers, in turn, are united in a common love for, and faith in, all three persons of the Godhead.

16:28 The incarnation is described as Jesus' coming from the Father and entering the world; the ascension, as Jesus' leaving the world and going back to the Father (17:13). This explains where Jesus was going and why the disciples would no longer see him (vv. 5–6,16–17).

16:30 you know all things. Only God is omniscient. He does not need to hear our questions in order to know what we have in mind. The disciples acknowledged both the origin and the divine nature of Christ.

16:31 "You believe at last!" Jesus did not discourage this acknowledgment of his deity. On the contrary, he accepted and endorsed it.

16:32 you will be scattered. The reference is to the forthcoming cowardice of the disciples, who would abandon Jesus at the time of his arrest (Mt 26:56). **I am not alone, for my Father is with me.** This was true for most of the period of our Lord's passion. But his cry of distress—"My God, my God, why have you forsaken me?" (Mt 27:46; Mk 15:34)—makes it clear that Jesus also accepted separation from the Father to whom he had been so wondrously united. This was what Jesus endured in order to be a sin-bearer in our stead.

16:33 peace . . . trouble. This is the contrast: in Christ, peace and joy (vv. 21–22,24); in the world, trouble and affliction. But the victory belongs to Christ.

■ **17:1–26** *Intercessory Prayer.* This chapter consists of a three-part prayer commonly known as Jesus' high priestly prayer. In verses 1–5 Jesus prayed for his own glorification. In verses 6–19 he prayed for the disciples, distinguishing them from the rest of those in the world as having been given to him in a special way by the Father (vv. 6–10). He asked the Father to protect them (vv. 11–13) and to keep them distinct from the world (vv. 14–19). In verses 20–26 Jesus prayed for those who would later come to believe in him, requesting that they be unified and one day brought to be with him.

17:1 Father. The favorite term of reference by Jesus to the first person of the Trinity (used some 109 times in this Gospel). **the time has come.** Jesus was fully conscious of his imminent ordeal. **Glorify your Son, that your Son may glorify you.** A theme announced in 1:14 and given great emphasis in this prayer. The glory of any one person of the Trinity overflows to the other two. The perfect service of the Son in his incarnation gives glory to the Godhead. The Son is glorified in his crucifixion, resurrection and enthronement at God's right hand—these events are viewed as a composite unity in this Gospel. See notes on 12:23 and 13:31.

17:2 granted . . . give . . . given. The same Greek verb is here translated as both "grant" and "give." It is used 16 times in this prayer, emphasizing what God gave to Jesus and what he in turn gave to his disciples. **eternal life.** See note on 3:16. **all those you have given him.** God's sovereign initiative is emphasized in this expression (used again in vv. 6,9,24; cf. 6:44; 10:29). See *WCF* 8.5.

17:3 that they may know you . . . and Jesus Christ. True life consists in fellowship with God, who "formed us for [himself]," so that "our hearts are restless until they find rest in [him]" (Augustine, *Confessions*). *Knowledge*, here as so often in Scripture, means more than mere intellectual understanding; it involves affection and commitment as well. By placing the Father and the Son in such a juxtaposition as the source of eternal life, Jesus affirmed his own deity. See *WCF* 10.4; *HC* 2,21,58,94,122.

17:4 by completing the work. This anticipates the cry of victory from the cross ("It is finished"; 19:30). Everything in Jesus' life was oriented toward the glory of God.

17:5 glorify me . . . with the glory. Here is a twofold claim to deity. First, Jesus affirmed as part of his petition that his glory existed "before the world began," signifying that he was preexistent and uncreated. Second, he referred to the "glory" he had—a glory that, throughout the Bible, is always associated with the true, living and only God. See *WLC* 54; *BC* 10.

17:6 revealed you. Literally, "revealed your name." The word "name" denotes God in the beauty of his perfection as revealed to humanity. **out of the world.** This indicates that the redeemed were found in the world but are destined to be removed from it. See note on 1:29. **They were yours.** Everything and everyone belongs to God by right of creation, but here the privileged possession by redemption is in view. God gave the elect to the Redeemer (cf. Heb 2:10–13). See *WCF* 8.1,8; *CD* 1.I.

17:8 The disciples are identified here in three ways: They believed Jesus' word, acknowledged his divine origin and believed in him.

17:9 I am not praying for the world. Whatever benevolence Jesus has toward the whole created order, his redeeming, priestly activity has particular reference to the elect—those whom the Father has given him (10:14–15,27–29). This verse strongly supports the doctrine of definite atonement, for it would be absurd for Jesus to die to take away the sins of those for whom he refused to pray (see theological article "Definite Atonement" at John 10). In other contexts, where Jesus' role as interceding high priest is not as immediately in view, Jesus did pray for his enemies, as we are also to do (Mt 5:44; Lk 23:34). See *WCF* 3.6; *WLC* 55,191; *WSC* 102; *BC* 16.

have is yours, and all you have is mine.[o] And glory has come to me through them.
11I will remain in the world no longer, but they are still in the world,[p] and I am
coming to you.[q] Holy Father, protect them by the power of your name—the name
you gave me—so that they may be one[r] as we are one.[s] **12**While I was with them,
I protected them and kept them safe by that name you gave me. None has been
lost[t] except the one doomed to destruction[u] so that Scripture would be fulfilled.
13"I am coming to you now, but I say these things while I am still in the world,
so that they may have the full measure of my joy[v] within them. **14**I have given them
your word and the world has hated them,[w] for they are not of the world any more
than I am of the world.[x] **15**My prayer is not that you take them out of the world but
that you protect them from the evil one.[y] **16**They are not of the world, even as I am
not of it.[z] **17**Sanctify[a] them by the truth; your word is truth.[a] **18**As you sent me into
the world,[b] I have sent them into the world.[c] **19**For them I sanctify myself, that they
too may be truly sanctified.

Jesus Prays for All Believers

20"My prayer is not for them alone. I pray also for those who will believe in me
through their message, **21**that all of them may be one, Father, just as you are in me
and I am in you.[d] May they also be in us so that the world may believe that you have
sent me.[e] **22**I have given them the glory that you gave me, that they may be one as we
are one:[f] **23**I in them and you in me. May they be brought to complete unity to let the
world know that you sent me[g] and have loved them[h] even as you have loved me.

17:10 [o]Jn 16:15
17:11 [p]Jn 13:1 [q]Jn 7:33 [r]ver 21-23 [s]Jn 10:30
17:12 [t]Jn 6:39 [u]Jn 6:70
17:13 [v]Jn 3:29
17:14 [w]Jn 15:19 [x]Jn 8:23
17:15 [y]Mt 5:37
17:16 [z]ver 14
17:17 [a]Jn 15:3
17:18 [b]ver 3,8,21,23,25 [c]Jn 20:21
17:21 [d]Jn 10:38 [e]ver 3,8,18,23,25; Jn 3:17
17:22 [f]Jn 14:20
17:23 [g]Jn 3:17 [h]Jn 16:27

[a] 17 Greek *hagiazo (set apart for sacred use* or *make holy)*; also in verse 19

17:10 all you have is mine. A manifest claim to deity. **glory has come to me through them.** It is surprising that God's glory could be associated with the actions of human beings, who are so insignificant against the scale of divine majesty. Yet the book of Job shows that humans may be God's champions, and Paul extended this principle even to the most common activities of people, such as eating and drinking (1Co 10:31). Whatever glorifies God glorifies Christ, and vice versa.

17:11 Holy Father. A form of address unique in the New Testament but well chosen to express the intimacy between God and his children, as well as the majesty of the great God who is sovereign over the whole creation. God will protect his own because he cares, and he *can* protect them because there are no limits to his power. **the power of your name.** God's revelation of himself in words and deeds (his name) is a powerful agent for sanctification (v. 17) and for protection from evil (v. 15). The Father and the Son are fully united in this revelation; thus God's name is also the "name you gave me." **that they may be one as we are one.** The pattern of the unity of persons in the Trinity is also the lofty example for the unity of believers with one another through their union with Christ (see note on 14:11). This oneness received strong emphasis in the prayer of Jesus (vv. 21–23), And this perfect unity (Eph 4:12–16), to be manifested gloriously at the day of Christ, must be ever forming and shaping God's people "so that the world may believe" (v. 21; cf. v. 23). See *WCF* 17.2.

17:12 I protected them and kept them safe. A wonderful summary of Jesus' ministry toward the apostles. The reference here is obviously to the Twelve, among whom was Judas, who in appearance seemed to be part of the group, but who never truly received the grace of God. **the one doomed to destruction.** The same term is used to denote the antichrist (2Th 2:3). This fulfills Psalm 41:9. Judas' betrayal was necessary for the fulfillment of many other passages descriptive of our Lord's passion. Jesus viewed many Scriptures as containing prophecies of various details of his Messianic career, and he stressed the point that all these would be fulfilled because they were the very Word of God. In choosing Judas, he was conscious of the role that this disciple would play in his passion, yet he included him among the Twelve. See *BC* 16.

17:13 my joy. This passage presupposes that Jesus prayed in the presence of his disciples so that they could derive joy from hearing what he said (cf. 15:11; 16:24).

17:14 I have given them your word. Refers to Jesus' teaching, which is identified with the Word of God, even as the Old Testament is God's Word (cf. Mk 7:13; Ac 10:36; Ro 9:6). **they are not of the world.** The new birth implies a radical fragmentation of humanity. Believers have their origin in the world of fallen humanity and continue to dwell there, but they do not truly belong to it (v. 16).

17:15 protect them from the evil one. Although Jesus knew that the world would hate his disciples, just as it hated him, he did not ask for the disciples to be protected from the physical or sociological afflictions of the world, but rather that they be kept from the evil one (the world's moral corruption). See also *WLC* 195.

17:17 Sanctify them by the truth. Jesus did not pray for the temporal well-being of the disciples, but rather for their sanctification. He wished above all that they should be holy and indicated the only means by which holiness may be attained: "truth." Just as error and deception are the roots of evil, so truth is the root of godliness. Those who wish to advance in holiness must submit not only to Jesus' desire that they be holy, but also to the means he has provided to make them so. **your word is truth.** This testimony, which immediately relates to the Old Testament Scriptures that the disciples already possessed, extended also to the teaching of Jesus, which is called God's "word" (v. 14), and to the message of the apostles (Lk 8:11–15,21; 11:28; Jn 17:20; Ac 4:31; 6:7; 8.14,25, 1Th 2:13). This is a powerful attestation of the authority and divine origin of both the Old and New Testament. See *WCF* 8.8; 13.1; *HC* 21.

17:18 As you sent me . . . I have sent them. Compare 20:21. As the Father appointed Jesus to his office and task and vested him with authority, so Christ in turn appointed the apostles and vested them with authority. As the Father sent his Son into the world to save sinners, so Christ sent the apostles to continue this work. Thus, Jesus is the supreme paradigm of missions. In a derivative sense, every true Christian is a missionary sent into the world to bear witness of Christ, to reach out to the lost wherever they may be found in order to lead them to the Savior. **into the world.** Not "of" the world (vv. 14,16) or "out of" the world (v. 15), but "in" the world (16:33) and "into" the world (here).

17:19 I sanctify myself. Jesus, being supremely holy, did not need to be sanctified in the sense of being made purer. His sanctification consisted of his being "set apart" for holy use. As the high priest, he consecrated himself (Ex 28:41) to his sacred task, which involved his supreme sacrifice. It follows that those who are his should be holy and dedicated to his service.

17:20 those who will believe. Jesus now embraced in his prayer the whole body of believers, even those yet to come to faith in the future ages. Every true Christian can be assured of being included in this prayer. See *WCF* 21.4; *WLC* 55,183,191; *WSC* 102; *BC* 29.

17:21–23 See *WLC* 1.

17:21 so that the world may believe that you have sent me. This prayer for unity is not merely for a spiritual (invisible) unity, but for a unity that is visible to the world, "so that the world may believe." See note on verse 11. See also *WLC* 65.

17:23 complete unity. We note here the pattern of unity that characterizes not only the relationship between the Father and the Son, but also that between the Son and the Christian. See note on 14:11.

	Father-Son	Son-Believer
Unity	vv. 21,23	vv. 21,23,26
Glory	vv. 22,24	v. 22
Love	vv. 23–24,26	13:1; 17:23,26
Mission	vv. 18,23,25	vv. 18
Knowledge	v. 25	vv. 3,8,25,26

17:24 [i]Jn 12:26
17:24 [j]Jn 1:14 [k]ver 5; Mt 25:34
17:25 [l]Jn 15:21; 16:3 [m]ver 3,8,18,21, 23; Jn 3:17; 7:29; 16:27
17:26 [n]ver 6 [o]Jn 15:9
18:1 [p]2Sa 15:23 [q]ver 26 [r]Mt 26:36
18:2 [s]Lk 21:37; 22:39
18:3 [t]Ac 1:16 [u]ver 12
18:4 [v]Jn 6:64; 13:1,11 [w]ver 7
18:7 [x]ver 4
18:9 [y]Jn 17:12
18:11 [z]Mt 20:22
18:12 [a]ver 3

24“Father, I want those you have given me to be with me where I am,[i] and to
see my glory,[j] the glory you have given me because you loved me before the creation of the world.[k]
25“Righteous Father, though the world does not know you,[l] I know you, and
they know that you have sent me.[m] 26I have made you known to them,[n] and will
continue to make you known in order that the love you have for me may be in
them[o] and that I myself may be in them.”

Jesus Arrested

18 When he had finished praying, Jesus left with his disciples and crossed the Kidron Valley.[p] On the other side there was an olive grove,[q] and he and his disciples went into it.[r]
2Now Judas, who betrayed him, knew the place, because Jesus had often met there
with his disciples.[s] 3So Judas came to the grove, guiding[t] a detachment of soldiers and
some officials from the chief priests and Pharisees.[u] They were carrying torches, lanterns
and weapons.
4Jesus, knowing all that was going to happen to him,[v] went out and asked them,
“Who is it you want?”[w]
5“Jesus of Nazareth,” they replied.
“I am he,” Jesus said. (And Judas the traitor was standing there with them.) 6When
Jesus said, “I am he,” they drew back and fell to the ground.
7Again he asked them, “Who is it you want?”[x]
And they said, “Jesus of Nazareth.”
8“I told you that I am he,” Jesus answered. “If you are looking for me, then let these
men go.” 9This happened so that the words he had spoken would be fulfilled: “I have not
lost one of those you gave me.”[a][y]
10Then Simon Peter, who had a sword, drew it and struck the high priest’s servant,
cutting off his right ear. (The servant’s name was Malchus.)
11Jesus commanded Peter, “Put your sword away! Shall I not drink the cup[z] the Father has given me?”

Jesus Taken to Annas

12Then the detachment of soldiers with its commander and the Jewish officials[a] arrested Jesus. They bound him 13and brought him first to Annas, who was the father-in-

[a] 9 John 6:39

---

loved them even as you have loved me. Relates to the love of God the Father for the redeemed (3:16), which is sometimes overlooked because of the emphasis on the love of Christ for them.

17:24 and to see my glory. Jesus’ second petition for the church was for its members to be with him in glory. He did not request temporal prosperity for either the disciples or the church; rather, he prayed for holiness and unity on Earth and for the gathering of his saints in heaven. To be with Christ is the supreme yearning of the Christian (Php 1:23; 1Th 4:17). See *WCF* 17.2; *WLC* 55,65; *HC* 49.

17:26 This prayer ends by sounding once again some of the recurrent notes heard throughout this Gospel: unity, knowledge, mission, glory and love.

■ 18:1—20:31 *The Ministry Reaches Its Climax.* All four Gospels cover the major events of the arrest, trial, execution and resurrection of Jesus. Some difficulties arise in the correlation of details, although the major elements are in complete harmony. Jesus was arrested at night. His trial before the Jewish authorities had at least two phases, and it was during this part of the trial that Peter denied his Lord three times. The trial before secular powers had three phases, and Jesus was executed by Pilate’s soldiers. He was buried in the tomb of Joseph of Arimathea, and on the first day of the week he arose from the dead and was seen alive in a variety of appearances to his disciples. None of the difficulties in the correlation of details are insuperable, but in a number of cases more than one explanation is possible, and in the absence of fuller data it is difficult to choose among them. John’s record divides into three main sections (see “Introduction: Outline”).

■ 18:1—19:16 *Jesus’ Arrest and Trial.* This section contains three major subsections: the arrest of Jesus (18:1–18), the trial before Annas (18:19–27) and the trial before Pilate (18:28—19:16).

18:1 the Kidron Valley. A valley east of the city.

18:3 officials from the chief priests. These were probably the same as the temple guards of 7:32 and 45. They obviously expected resistance to the arrest, both from Jesus and from his disciples.

18:4 knowing all . . . went out and asked them. Note here and at verses 7 and 11 that Jesus intended to undergo arrest and trial. He made no attempt to escape that which he had come to do.

18:5–6,8 “I am he.” The phrase identifies Jesus to the officials, but it also coincides with the solemn name of God in Exodus 3:14 (see note on 6:35), and the officials themselves seem to be supernaturally overwhelmed.

18:8 let these men go. Even at this crucial time, Jesus continued to show concern for his disciples (17:12).

18:9 See *BC* 16.

18:10 Peter . . . struck the high priest’s servant. An ill-conceived act of resistance that was also poorly executed since all Peter managed to do was cut off one ear. Luke alone tells us of Jesus’ healing of the man (Lk 22:51), and John alone tells us that Peter carried the sword and that Malchus was the name of the servant.

18:11 Put your sword away! Not a denial of the propriety of self-defense or of civil resistance. Jesus had come to give his life as a ransom for many, and he would not be dissuaded from this task (cf. Mt 16:21–23). **Shall I not drink the cup . . . ?** Undoubtedly the cup of the wine of God’s wrath (Ps 75:8; Isa 51:17; Jer 25:15–17, 27–38). The “cup” that Jesus chose to drink was not merely one of death, but it included the wrath of God against sin (cf. Mt 20:22; Mk 10:38).

18:13 Annas. One of the most influential Jewish leaders of that age. Although deposed by the Romans from the high priesthood, he was still known by this title. It is difficult to determine whether verse 13 and verses 19–24 represent one phase or two separate phases of Jesus’ trial before the Jewish authorities. Matthew, Mark and Luke all refer to an additional phase before the Sanhedrin. Both phases are notable for their serious irregularities and violations of the rules of judicial procedure set by the Jews themselves. For instance, the Sanhedrin was not supposed to meet at night; the death penalty could not be declared on the day of the trial; Annas and Caiaphas should have disqualified themselves as judges because of their prej-

law of Caiaphas,[b] the high priest that year. 14 Caiaphas was the one who had advised the
Jews that it would be good if one man died for the people.[c]

Peter's First Denial

15 Simon Peter and another disciple were following Jesus. Because this disciple was
known to the high priest,[d] he went with Jesus into the high priest's courtyard,[e] 16 but Peter had to wait outside at the door. The other disciple, who was known to the high priest,
came back, spoke to the girl on duty there and brought Peter in.

17 "You are not one of his disciples, are you?" the girl at the door asked Peter.

He replied, "I am not."[f]

18 It was cold, and the servants and officials stood around a fire[g] they had made to
keep warm. Peter also was standing with them, warming himself.[h]

The High Priest Questions Jesus

19 Meanwhile, the high priest questioned Jesus about his disciples and his teaching.
20 "I have spoken openly to the world," Jesus replied. "I always taught in synagogues[i]
or at the temple,[j] where all the Jews come together. I said nothing in secret.[k] 21 Why question me? Ask those who heard me. Surely they know what I said."

22 When Jesus said this, one of the officials[l] nearby struck him in the face.[m] "Is this
the way you answer the high priest?" he demanded.

23 "If I said something wrong," Jesus replied, "testify as to what is wrong. But if I spoke
the truth, why did you strike me?"[n] 24 Then Annas sent him, still bound, to Caiaphas[o] the
high priest.[a]

Peter's Second and Third Denials

25 As Simon Peter stood warming himself,[p] he was asked, "You are not one of his disciples, are you?"

He denied it, saying, "I am not."[q]

26 One of the high priest's servants, a relative of the man whose ear Peter had cut off,[r]
challenged him, "Didn't I see you with him in the olive grove?"[s] 27 Again Peter denied it,
and at that moment a rooster began to crow.[t]

Jesus Before Pilate

28 Then the Jews led Jesus from Caiaphas to the palace of the Roman governor.[u] By
now it was early morning, and to avoid ceremonial uncleanness the Jews did not enter
the palace;[v] they wanted to be able to eat the Passover.[w] 29 So Pilate came out to them
and asked, "What charges are you bringing against this man?"

18:13 [b]ver 24; Mt 26:3
18:14 [c]Jn 11:49-51
18:15 [d]Mt 26:3 [e]Mt 26:58; Mk 14:54; Lk 22:54
18:17 [f]ver 25
18:18 [g]Jn 21:9 [h]Mk 14:54,67
18:20 [i]Mt 4:23 [j]Mt 26:55 [k]Jn 7:26
18:22 [l]ver 3 [m]Mt 16:21; Jn 19:3
18:23 [n]Mt 5:39; Ac 23:2-5
18:24 [o]ver 13; Mt 26:3
18:25 [p]ver 18 [q]ver 17
18:26 [r]ver 10 [s]ver 1
18:27 [t]Jn 13:38
18:28 [u]Mt 27:2, Mk 15:1; Lk 23:1 [v]ver 33; Jn 19:9 [w]Jn 11:55

[a] *24* Or *(Now Annas had sent him, still bound, to Caiaphas the high priest.)*

udice (18:14); false evidence and false witnesses were used (Mt 26:59–60); Jesus was not guilty of blasphemy as claimed, since his statement did not blaspheme the name of God; Jesus was exposed to blows from attendants during the trial (18:22; see also Mk 14:65). In addition to all this, the Sanhedrin was not permitted to meet in a capital case on the eve of a Sabbath or a feast day. These numerous deviations from proper procedure make it plain that Jesus' condemnation by the Jewish authorities was a travesty of justice.

18:15 another disciple. Probably refers to John since, of the three closest to Jesus (James, Peter and John), he is the only one not mentioned by name in this Gospel. **known to the high priest.** He had entrance into the palace, even to the point of causing a guest to be admitted (v. 16).

18:17–27 The account of Peter's denials is interrupted in verses 19–24 by a description of one aspect of the Jewish trial. The other Gospels deal with them in one continuous paragraph. It would appear that there were three clusters of denials rather than just three negative sentences by Peter. One would expect this under the circumstances, for a number of people were coming and going and warming themselves by a fire. There are different legitimate ways of organizing these clusters so that the number three predicted by Jesus (13:38) is reached. All four Gospels agree that the first denial was in response to a question of a servant girl, identified by John as "the girl at the door" (v. 17); that is, a person of no great consequence in the household.

18:17 "I am not." Peter's denial points out the solitude of Jesus in his priestly self-offering. When he endured God's penal wrath against sin, he did so without balm, comfort or consolation. Jesus' solitude in his suffering was foreshadowed in Psalm 69:20.

18:19 the high priest questioned. This may refer to Annas or to Caiaphas in the house of Annas (v. 24). It was considered improper to question the accused until a presumption of guilt had been established by witnesses. For this reason, some refer to these proceedings as a hearing rather than a trial.

18:20 See *BC* 16.

18:22 one of the officials nearby struck him. This was highly irregular, particularly when the prisoner was bound (v. 24).

18:25 was asked. Literally, "they said to him." That there were multiple questioners probably indicates that there were multiple questions.

18:26 a relative of the man. The question by this man endangered Peter more than the previous ones, since this servant might have been seeking to avenge Malchus.

18:27 a rooster began to crow. Mark's Gospel notes that it was crowing a second time (Mk 14:72), as Jesus had predicted (Mk 14:30). The other Gospels concentrate on the crowing itself, not on how many times the rooster crowed.

18:28—19:16 John's Gospel gives us an account of the Roman trial of Jesus. There were three distinct phases: (1) the first appearance before Pilate (18:28–38); (2) the appearance before Herod (Lk 23:5–12); and (3) a second appearance before Pilate (18:39—19:16). John relates only the first and third phases, but we are given much more detail than is found in the other Gospels.

18:28 the Roman governor. Pontius Pilate. **to avoid ceremonial uncleanness.** Remarkably, the Roman praetorium, a site of hostility between the Romans and the Jews and an unclean place for Jews, was the very location at which they collaborated in putting Jesus to death. See note on 13:1—17:26.

18:29 "What charges . . . ?" A trial must begin with an indictment, but the Jews did not have any charge that would be recog-

18:32 [x]Mt 20:19; 26:2; Jn 3:14; 8:28; 12:32,33

30“If he were not a criminal,” they replied, “we would not have handed him over to
you.”
31Pilate said, “Take him yourselves and judge him by your own law.”
“But we have no right to execute anyone,” the Jews objected. 32This happened so that
the words Jesus had spoken indicating the kind of death he was going to die[x] would be
fulfilled.

18:33 [y]ver 28,29; Jn 19:9 [z]Lk 23:3; Mt 2:2

33Pilate then went back inside the palace,[y] summoned Jesus and asked him, “Are you
the king of the Jews?”[z]
34“Is that your own idea,” Jesus asked, “or did others talk to you about me?”
35“Am I a Jew?” Pilate replied. “It was your people and your chief priests who handed you over to me. What is it you have done?”

18:36 [a]Mt 3:2 [b]Mt 26:53 [c]Lk 17:21; Jn 6:15

36Jesus said, “My kingdom[a] is not of this world. If it were, my servants would fight to
prevent my arrest by the Jews.[b] But now my kingdom is from another place.”[c]
37“You are a king, then!” said Pilate.

18:37 [d]Jn 3:32 [e]Jn 8:47; 1Jn 4:6

Jesus answered, “You are right in saying I am a king. In fact, for this reason I was
born, and for this I came into the world, to testify to the truth.[d] Everyone on the side of
truth listens to me.”[e]

18:38 [f]Lk 23:4; Jn 19:4,6

38“What is truth?” Pilate asked. With this he went out again to the Jews and said, “I find
no basis for a charge against him.[f] 39But it is your custom for me to release to you one prisoner at the time of the Passover. Do you want me to release ‘the king of the Jews’?”

18:40 [g]Ac 3:14

40They shouted back, “No, not him! Give us Barabbas!” Now Barabbas had taken part
in a rebellion.[g]

Jesus Sentenced to Be Crucified

19:1 [h]Dt 25:3; Isa 50:6; 53:5; Mt 27:26

19 Then Pilate took Jesus and had him flogged.[h] 2The soldiers twisted together a
crown of thorns and put it on his head. They clothed him in a purple robe 3and

19:3 [i]Mt 27:29 [j]Jn 18:22

went up to him again and again, saying, “Hail, king of the Jews!”[i] And they struck him
in the face.[j]

19:4 [k]Jn 18:38 [l]ver 6; Lk 23:4

4Once more Pilate came out and said to the Jews, “Look, I am bringing him out[k] to you
to let you know that I find no basis for a charge against him.”[l] 5When Jesus came out wear-

19:5 [m]ver 2

ing the crown of thorns and the purple robe,[m] Pilate said to them, “Here is the man!”
6As soon as the chief priests and their officials saw him, they shouted, “Crucify! Crucify!”

---

nized in a Roman court, let alone one that would be viewed as a capital offense.

18:30 If he were not a criminal. The Jews attempted to avoid a clear answer.

18:31 Take him yourselves. A logical response. Pilate no doubt thought that if they were not willing to specify charges, they should not expect him to conduct a trial. **we have no right to execute anyone.** This was a regular limitation in a land occupied by Rome, perhaps in order to protect those who supported Rome. Compare 7:53—8:11.

18:32 indicating the kind of death. See also 12:32–33. Stoning, burning or beheading were the Jewish methods of capital punishment. Hanging and crucifixion, which are implied in the words “lifted up,” were Roman style executions. This indicates divine control over the whole procedure, even though it was blemished by flagrant injustice.

18:33 “Are you the king of the Jews?” A question based on charges recorded in Luke 23:2.

18:34 “Is that your own idea . . . ?” The distinction was important, because the answer would differ depending on the sense of the question. Jesus was not the king of the Jews in the sense that he promoted sedition against Rome, as charged by the Jewish leaders (Lk 23:2), but he was indeed the King of the Jews in the Messianic sense (Mt 2:2; Lk 1:32–33; 19:38; Jn 12:13).

18:35 “Am I a Jew?” Pilate showed some irritation at what appeared to him to be an evasive answer. Note that he did respond to Jesus’ question: The charge was not his idea.

18:36 My kingdom is not of this world. Jesus is King indeed, but at this point he made no effort to establish his kingdom by a display of physical power. This inexplicable response on the part of the accused was totally enigmatic for Pilate. See *WCF* 31.5; *HC* 20.

18:37 You are right. Pilate’s question brought about the marvelous answer of Jesus, whose kingdom and mission relate to the truth (1:14,17; 8:32; 14:6). See *BC* 29.

18:38 “What is truth?” Truth does not matter to those who, like Pilate, are motivated by expediency. Likewise, truth does not matter to those skeptics who have despaired of attaining it. Yet Jesus’ answer made it clear that he was not a political rebel who should be executed by the Roman power. **I find no basis for a charge.** Pilate found that Jesus had committed no crime (see also 19:4,6). Through his actions it is evident that Pilate was reluctant to put Jesus to death. He attempted to release Jesus (v. 39; 19:12) and had him scourged (19:1), hoping to release him after satisfying the crowd’s desire to punish him. Ironically, it was the Roman governor who wished to release Jesus, while “his own” (1:11) clamored for his death. Theologically, Pilate served the ironic role of declaring Jesus’ innocence. Jesus died a guiltless man, totally without sin; he offered himself as the Passover Lamb without blemish. See *BC* 21.

18:39 it is your custom. The practice of sparing a criminal at the time of the Passover was significant to the festival itself, which commemorated God’s sparing the Israelites from death (the Hebrew word for “Passover” is probably related to a root that sometimes means “spare”). Jesus should have been spared because he was innocent, but the Jews opted to release Barabbas instead. Most significantly, repentant sinners are spared forever the enduring penal wrath of God because Jesus endured that wrath for us.

18:40 Barabbas. Means “son of the father.” Instead of this criminal, the true Son of the Father died.

19:1 had him flogged. The Roman flogging was painful, being executed with whips of leather outfitted with metal hooks that tore the flesh. Perhaps Pilate hoped to soften the hearts of Jesus’ accusers by allowing them to witness the brutal flogging.

19:2 The soldiers showed a sadistic joy in tormenting Jesus and mocking him as the king of the Jews.

19:4 See *HC* 38.

19:5 “Here is the man!” A natural way for Pilate to introduce the accused, but providentially a most appropriate statement: Here, indeed, was the One who sums up all that humanity could and should be. He is the last Adam, the head of a new, redeemed humanity (1Co 15:45).

19:6 the chief priests . . . shouted. In their hatred of Jesus, the chief priests turned out to be the leaders of a mob. **“You . . . crucify him.”** Pilate was exasperated and either did not consider that

But Pilate answered, "You take him and crucify him.[n] As for me, I find no basis for a
charge against him."[o]
7The Jews insisted, "We have a law, and according to that law he must die,[p] because
he claimed to be the Son of God."[q]
8When Pilate heard this, he was even more afraid, 9and he went back inside the palace.[r] "Where do you come from?" he asked Jesus, but Jesus gave him no answer.[s] 10"Do
you refuse to speak to me?" Pilate said. "Don't you realize I have power either to free you
or to crucify you?"
11Jesus answered, "You would have no power over me if it were not given to you from
above.[t] Therefore the one who handed me over to you[u] is guilty of a greater sin."
12From then on, Pilate tried to set Jesus free, but the Jews kept shouting, "If you let this
man go, you are no friend of Caesar. Anyone who claims to be a king[v] opposes Caesar."
13When Pilate heard this, he brought Jesus out and sat down on the judge's seat[w] at
a place known as the Stone Pavement (which in Aramaic[x] is Gabbatha). 14It was the day
of Preparation[y] of Passover Week, about the sixth hour.[z]
"Here is your king,"[a] Pilate said to the Jews.
15But they shouted, "Take him away! Take him away! Crucify him!"
"Shall I crucify your king?" Pilate asked.
"We have no king but Caesar," the chief priests answered.
16Finally Pilate handed him over to them to be crucified.[b]

The Crucifixion

So the soldiers took charge of Jesus. 17Carrying his own cross,[c] he went out to the
place of the Skull[d] (which in Aramaic[e] is called Golgotha). 18Here they crucified him, and
with him two others[f]—one on each side and Jesus in the middle.
19Pilate had a notice prepared and fastened to the cross. It read: JESUS OF NAZARETH,[g]
THE KING OF THE JEWS.[h] 20Many of the Jews read this sign, for the place where Jesus was crucified was near the city,[i] and the sign was written in Aramaic, Latin and Greek. 21The
chief priests of the Jews protested to Pilate, "Do not write 'The King of the Jews,' but that
this man claimed to be king of the Jews."[j]
22Pilate answered, "What I have written, I have written."
23When the soldiers crucified Jesus, they took his clothes, dividing them into four

19:6 [n]Ac 3:13 [o]ver 4; Lk 23:4
19:7 [p]Lev 24:16 [q]Mt 26:63-66; Jn 5:18; 10:33
19:9 [r]Jn 18:33 [s]Mk 14:61
19:11 [t]Ro 13:1 [u]Jn 18:28-30; Ac 3:13
19:12 [v]Lk 23:2
19:13 [w]Mt 27:19 [x]Jn 5:2
19:14 [y]Mt 27:62 [z]Mk 15:25 [a]ver 19, 21
19:16 [b]Mt 27:26; Mk 15:15; Lk 23:25
19:17 [c]Ge 22:6; Lk 14:27; 23:26 [d]Lk 23:33 [e]Jn 5:2
19:18 [f]Lk 23:32
19:19 [g]Mk 1:24 [h]ver 14, 21
19:20 [i]Heb 13:12
19:21 [j]ver 14

---

the Jews could not legally carry out a crucifixion, or simply offered this statement as a retort. **I find no basis for a charge.** This is the third time Pilate proclaimed Jesus' innocence (18:38; 19:4,6), and the narrative corresponds to Luke's account (Lk 23:4,14,22).

19:7 he must die. Relates to the Jews' charge of blasphemy against Jesus (see Lev 24:16).

19:8 even more afraid. Perhaps the message from his wife (Mt 27:19) had begun to shake Pilate, now Jesus was portrayed as a supernatural figure.

19:9 but Jesus gave him no answer. It is evident here and throughout the trial that Jesus was not attempting to be released. His lack of resistance to the arrest and trial were part of his willing self-offering.

19:11 You would have no power over me. Jesus acknowledged the sovereign plan of God that included even the wickedness of his accusers and the cowardice of Pilate. Peter (Ac 2:23) and the early church (Ac 4:28) gave witness to this as well. See *WCF* 3.1; *WLC* 150.

19:12–16 See *HC* 38.

19:12 you are no friend of Caesar. A most remarkable statement for first-century Jews to make. They had been under the authority of one foreign empire after another for nearly six centuries and often had battled the Greek or Roman empires for independence (as they would again late in the first century). Their animosity toward Jesus, however, rendered them, by comparison, "friends of Caesar."

19:14 the day of Preparation of Passover Week. This is often understood as a reference to the day of preparation for the celebration of Passover (i.e., Thursday). If so, John's Gospel portrays Jesus as crucified at the same time as the Passover lambs (see note on 13:1—17:26), but this appears to conflict with the record of the Synoptic Gospels in which Jesus' crucifixion occurs on Friday. It is likely, however, that the reference here is to the day of Preparation for the weekly Sabbath of Passover Week (i.e., Friday, for the Greek word for "day of Preparation" ordinarily refers to the Friday preceding the weekly Saturday Sabbath). **"Here is your king."** To the last, Pilate referred to Jesus as the "king of the Jews." It may be that this was a last effort by Pilate to mollify the Jews; if so, it failed. Later he had this title inscribed on the cross (v. 19), perhaps as an insult to the Jews in retaliation for their having forced his hand.

19:15 no king but Caesar. From a Jew this proclamation constituted words of treason against God.

■ **19:17–42** *Jesus' Crucifixion, Death and Burial.* John recorded many details of these events to convey their importance and to help Jesus' followers always to remember what Jesus had done for them on the cross.

19:17 Carrying his own cross. Crosses had various shapes. The fact that the inscription was above the head of Jesus (Mt 27:37) gives some credence to the shape usually portrayed. Simon of Cyrene was pressed to carry Jesus' cross, perhaps because of Jesus' weakness from the fierce flogging. The Scripture does not speak about Jesus falling three times under the weight, as tradition would have it. **Golgotha.** Aramaic for "skull."

19:18 they crucified him. Crucifixion was an intensely painful form of execution, involving great suffering from nail wounds in the hands and feet, tension in the muscles and tendons of the whole body, great difficulty in breathing, atrocious headaches, burning fever and fierce thirst. It also involved the shame of being exposed naked in the public view. **two others.** Two criminals deserving of death (Lk 23;41) were crucified at the same time as Jesus, a detail that fulfilled prophecy (Isa 53:12; Lk 22:37) and afforded an opportunity for Jesus to demonstrate his saving power by reaching out and rescuing a man at the very edge of eternal death.

19:19 JESUS OF NAZARETH, THE KING OF THE JEWS. The four Gospels record Pilate's inscription with minute differences that are perhaps due to the fact that the inscription was in three languages. John's form, using the name "Jesus of Nazareth," has a Semitic flavor. It was customary to post an inscription stating the ground of the execution. More importantly, but ironically, this was an official acknowledgment of the kingship of Christ.

19:21 The chief priests . . . protested. They viewed the inscription as an offense to their nation, and perhaps Pilate meant it as such—for he stubbornly refused to change its wording. Having yielded on the main issue, he remained adamant on this detail.

shares, one for each of them, with the undergarment remaining. This garment was seamless, woven in one piece from top to bottom.
24 “Let’s not tear it,” they said to one another. “Let’s decide by lot who will get it.”
This happened that the scripture might be fulfilled[k] which said,

> “They divided my garments among them
> and cast lots for my clothing.”[a][l]

So this is what the soldiers did.
25 Near the cross[m] of Jesus stood his mother,[n] his mother’s sister, Mary the wife of Clopas, and Mary Magdalene.[o] 26 When Jesus saw his mother[p] there, and the disciple whom
he loved[q] standing nearby, he said to his mother, “Dear woman, here is your son,” 27 and
to the disciple, “Here is your mother.” From that time on, this disciple took her into his
home.

The Death of Jesus

28 Later, knowing that all was now completed,[r] and so that the Scripture would be fulfilled,[s] Jesus said, “I am thirsty.” 29 A jar of wine vinegar[t] was there, so they soaked a
sponge in it, put the sponge on a stalk of the hyssop plant, and lifted it to Jesus’ lips.
30 When he had received the drink, Jesus said, “It is finished.”[u] With that, he bowed his
head and gave up his spirit.
31 Now it was the day of Preparation,[v] and the next day was to be a special Sabbath.
Because the Jews did not want the bodies left on the crosses[w] during the Sabbath, they
asked Pilate to have the legs broken and the bodies taken down. 32 The soldiers therefore came and broke the legs of the first man who had been crucified with Jesus, and then
those of the other.[x] 33 But when they came to Jesus and found that he was already dead,
they did not break his legs. 34 Instead, one of the soldiers pierced[y] Jesus’ side with a spear,
bringing a sudden flow of blood and water.[z] 35 The man who saw it[a] has given testimony, and his testimony is true.[b] He knows that he tells the truth, and he testifies so that
you also may believe. 36 These things happened so that the scripture would be fulfilled:[c]
“Not one of his bones will be broken,”[b][d] 37 and, as another scripture says, “They will look
on the one they have pierced.”[c][e]

The Burial of Jesus

38 Later, Joseph of Arimathea asked Pilate for the body of Jesus. Now Joseph was a disciple of Jesus, but secretly because he feared the Jews. With Pilate’s permission, he came
and took the body away. 39 He was accompanied by Nicodemus,[f] the man who earlier had

19:24 [k]ver 28,36,37; Mt 1:22 [l]Ps 22:18
19:25 [m]Mt 27:55,56; Mk 15:40,41; Lk 23:49 [n]Mt 12:46 [o]Lk 24:18
19:26 [p]Mt 12:46 [q]Jn 13:23
19:28 [r]ver 30; Jn 13:1 [s]ver 24,36,37
19:29 [t]Ps 69:21
19:30 [u]Lk 12:50; Jn 17:4
19:31 [v]ver 14,42 [w]Dt 21:23; Jos 8:29; 10:26,27
19:32 [x]ver 18
19:34 [y]Zec 12:10 [z]1Jn 5:6,8
19:35 [a]Lk 24:48 [b]Jn 15:27; 21:24
19:36 [c]ver 24,28,37; Mt 1:22 [d]Ex 12:46; Nu 9:12; Ps 34:20
19:37 [e]Zec 12:10; Rev 1:7
19:39 [f]Jn 3:1; 7:50

[a] *24* Psalm 22:18 [b] *36* Exodus 12:46; Num. 9:12; Psalm 34:20 [c] *37* Zech. 12:10

19:23 garment. A woven tunic was not at all uncommon in the ancient world. The recording of this point is significant, not because of the tunic’s value, but because it manifests the depth of Jesus’ humiliation: Everything was taken from him in his self-offering. It also fulfilled the prophecy of Psalm 22:18.
19:25 Near the cross. The list given here is best understood as referring to four women. If Jesus’ mother’s sister was thought to be Mary, the wife of Cleopas, we would then have to believe that two sisters were both called Mary. It is possible that Cleopas, named here, is the Cleopas mentioned in Luke 24:18, possibly the same man as Alphaeus, the father of the apostles James and Matthew (Mt 10:3; Mk 2:14; 3:18; Lk 6:15). Note the courage of these four women. Some were present again at Jesus’ burial (Mt 27:61; Mk 15:47) and at the resurrection (Mt 28:1; Mk 16:1; Jn 20:1–18).
19:26 woman, here is your son. See note on 2:4. Jesus, in his work on the cross, was not functioning as Mary’s son but as the Mediator of the new covenant. We marvel, however, that at a time of intense physical pain and mental anguish, the Lord thought of others, as is shown in his first three statements from the cross (Lk 23:34,43; Jn 19:26–27). Jesus’ tender concern for his mother is displayed in his provision for her of a more congenial home environment than she likely could have found even with her own children (Mt 13:55–56; Jn 7:5; 19:26–27).
19:28–30 all was now completed. The fifth and sixth statements from the cross were spoken close to the actual death of Jesus. The most wrenching ordeal—the substitutionary bearing of God’s wrath against sin (Mt 27:46; Mk 15:34), which was accompanied by darkness—was over.
19:28 “I am thirsty.” It is noteworthy that under such extreme duress the Lord was still concerned with fulfilling the Scripture. In fact, two more of the seven statements from the cross have a close relation to the Old Testament (Mt 27:46 is a quotation of Ps 22:1, and Lk 23:46 quotes Ps 31:5; cf. Pss 22:15; 69:21).
19:30 “It is finished.” Corresponds to what John indicated in verse 28. Many see the burial as the *beginning* of Jesus’ exaltation since he was spared the usual Roman criminal’s fate of having his body left on the cross for days.
See *HC* 80.
19:31 the day of Preparation. See note on verse 14. **bodies left on the crosses.** This would have defiled the land (Dt 21:23). It is interesting that the Jews would have joined forces with Rome to commit murder and then turned around and become sticklers about enforcing a Jewish ceremonial law. **the legs broken.** Such an excess of pain could alone cause death. It surely made breathing very difficult, since the person could not push himself up to facilitate inhalation.
19:34 pierced Jesus’ side with a spear. John places this detail alongside those of the burial preparations in verses 39–40 and the designation of the particular tomb in verse 41 to eliminate any doubt that Jesus was really dead. Both the piercing of Jesus and the preserving of his bones unbroken fulfilled Old Testament Scripture (vv. 36–37). His death without broken bones fulfilled the ritual requirements of Numbers 9:12 and also the foreshadowing of Psalm 34:20. The piercing fulfilled Zechariah 12:10. See *WLC* 49; *BC* 34. **a sudden flow of blood and water.** John included this detail as an affidavit both for the reality of Jesus’ physical body and of his death. It may also indicate a rupturing of the heart that occurs only in cases of extreme agony. Some see symbolic significance in this and tie it with 1 John 5:6–8 (see also Zec 13:1).
19:38–42 See *HC* 41.
19:38 Joseph of Arimathea. A secret supporter of Jesus mentioned in all four Gospels in connection with Jesus’ burial. He is not mentioned elsewhere in the New Testament.
19:39 Nicodemus. Mentioned twice before in this Gospel (3:1;

visited Jesus at night. Nicodemus brought a mixture of myrrh and aloes, about seventy-
five pounds.[a] 40Taking Jesus' body, the two of them wrapped it, with the spices, in strips
of linen.[g] This was in accordance with Jewish burial customs.[h] 41At the place where Jesus
was crucified, there was a garden, and in the garden a new tomb, in which no one had
ever been laid. 42Because it was the Jewish day of Preparation[i] and since the tomb was
nearby,[j] they laid Jesus there.

The Empty Tomb

20 Early on the first day of the week, while it was still dark, Mary Magdalene[k] went
to the tomb and saw that the stone had been removed from the entrance.[l] 2So she
came running to Simon Peter and the other disciple, the one Jesus loved,[m] and said, "They
have taken the Lord out of the tomb, and we don't know where they have put him!"[n]
3So Peter and the other disciple started for the tomb.[o] 4Both were running, but the
other disciple outran Peter and reached the tomb first. 5He bent over and looked in[p] at
the strips of linen[q] lying there but did not go in. 6Then Simon Peter, who was behind him,
arrived and went into the tomb. He saw the strips of linen lying there, 7as well as the burial cloth that had been around Jesus' head.[r] The cloth was folded up by itself, separate
from the linen. 8Finally the other disciple, who had reached the tomb first,[s] also went
inside. He saw and believed. 9(They still did not understand from Scripture[t] that Jesus
had to rise from the dead.)[u]

Jesus Appears to Mary Magdalene

10Then the disciples went back to their homes, 11but Mary stood outside the tomb crying. As she wept, she bent over to look into the tomb[v] 12and saw two angels in white,[w]
seated where Jesus' body had been, one at the head and the other at the foot.
13They asked her, "Woman, why are you crying?"[x]
"They have taken my Lord away," she said, "and I don't know where they have put
him."[y] 14At this, she turned around and saw Jesus standing there,[z] but she did not realize that it was Jesus.[a]
15"Woman," he said, "why are you crying?[b] Who is it you are looking for?"
Thinking he was the gardener, she said, "Sir, if you have carried him away, tell me
where you have put him, and I will get him."
16Jesus said to her, "Mary."
She turned toward him and cried out in Aramaic,[c] "Rabboni!"[d] (which means
Teacher).

19:40 [g]Lk 24:12; Jn 11:44; 20:5,7 [h]Mt 26:12
19:42 [i]ver 14,31 [j]ver 20, 41
20:1 [k]ver 18; Jn 19:25 [l]Mt 27:60,66
20:2 [m]Jn 13:23 [n]ver 13
20:3 [o]Lk 24:12
20:5 [p]ver 11 [q]Jn 19:40
20:7 [r]Jn 11:44
20:8 [s]ver 4
20:9 [t]Mt 22:29; Jn 2:22 [u]Lk 24:26,46
20:11 [v]ver 5
20:12 [w]Mt 28:2,3; Mk 16:5; Lk 24:4; Ac 5:19
20:13 [x]ver 15 [y]ver 2
20:14 [z]Mt 28:9; Mk 16:9 [a]Lk 24:16; Jn 21:4
20:15 [b]ver 13
20:16 [c]Jn 5:2 [d]Mt 23:7

[a] *39* Greek *a hundred litrai* (about 34 kilograms)

7:50), Nicodemus brought a large amount of aromatic spices for anointing Jesus' body. The faithful women were present at this burial (Mt 27:61; Mk 15:47; Lk 23:55).

■ **20:1–31** *Jesus' Resurrection and Appearances.* After recording the discovery of the empty tomb (vv. 1–9), John recounted Jesus' appearances to Mary Magdalene (vv. 10–18), to the disciples (vv. 19–23) and to Thomas (vv. 24–31). The four Gospels have accounts of resurrection appearances that supplement each other, and, combined with Acts 1:3–8 and 1 Corinthians 15:5–8, they indicate thirteen appearances, seven in and near Jerusalem, four in Galilee, one on the Mount of Olives and one on the road to Damascus.

20:1–9 John plainly described Jesus' resurrection as both historical and bodily. Like the rest of the New Testament writers, John believed that Jesus' resurrection was essential for salvation (cf. 1Co 15:12ff.).

20:1 while it was still dark. This clause does not necessarily conflict with Mark 16:2 ("just after sunrise"). John may have been referring to the time of their departure and Mark to that of their arrival at the tomb. Or again, Mary Magdalene may have gone to the tomb earlier than the other women mentioned in Mark.

20:2 Peter and the other disciple. Peter and John. See note on 13:23. **we don't know.** "We" indicates that several women were involved, as stated also by the other Gospels. They were the same women who had kept vigil at the foot of the cross, perhaps with the exception of Mary the mother of Jesus, who is not mentioned here. **where they have put him!** Neither Mary Magdalene nor the disciples were expecting the resurrection, in spite of what Jesus had told them (cf. v. 9).

20:5–8 He . . . looked in at the strips. John had an initial cursory view and vouched for the fact that nothing had been rearranged in the tomb; then both Peter and John gave the tomb a closer inspection. The grave clothes were there in good order (v. 7). If someone had violated the tomb and removed the corpse, the linen strips would not have been left there and the burial cloth might have been flung aside, not "folded up by itself" (v. 7).

20:9 They still did not understand from Scripture. Only later, as a result of Jesus' instruction, would they understood his resurrection as a necessary fulfillment of prophecy (Lk 24:26–27,44–47; Ac 2:25–32; 13:35–37). It is clear that the disciples did not expect a resurrection, nor did they try to invent one in order to mesh with their own preconceptions.

20:10–18 Jesus appeared first to Mary, his beloved and humble servant.

20:12 two angels in white. Here the accounts of the four Gospels differ slightly (Mt 28:2 records one angel; Mk 16:5 one young man, and Lk 24:4 two men, also called "angels" in Lk 24:23). There is no necessary contradiction since the angels must have appeared in human form, and one of them may have been singled out, perhaps because he was the speaker. What Mary saw may also differ somewhat from what the other women witnessed since she remained alone at the tomb after Peter and John had left.

20:14 she . . . saw Jesus standing there. From Matthew we learn that Jesus had already appeared once to the group of women who were on their way to Jerusalem to notify the disciples about the empty tomb (Mt 28:8–10). The disciples did not believe the women (Lk 24:11,22–23), and apparently Mary could scarcely believe it herself. **she did not realize that it was Jesus.** Jesus was often not immediately recognized by people after his resurrection (v. 20; 21:4). Some may have failed to recognize him due to their skepticism and grief, while others were supernaturally kept from recognizing him (Lk 24:16,31). In addition, there are differences as well as continuities between the natural and the resurrected body, and there may have been a qualitative change in his appearance (1Co 15:35–49).

20:16 "Rabboni!" The voice of Jesus calling "Mary" revealed clearly who he was. The form of address used here strengthens the

17 Jesus said, "Do not hold on to me, for I have not yet returned to the Father. Go instead to my brothers[e] and tell them, 'I am returning to my Father[f] and your Father, to
my God and your God.' "
18 Mary Magdalene[g] went to the disciples[h] with the news: "I have seen the Lord!" And
she told them that he had said these things to her.

Jesus Appears to His Disciples

19 On the evening of that first day of the week, when the disciples were together, with
the doors locked for fear of the Jews,[i] Jesus came and stood among them and said,
"Peace[j] be with you!"[k] 20 After he said this, he showed them his hands and side.[l] The disciples were overjoyed[m] when they saw the Lord.
21 Again Jesus said, "Peace be with you![n] As the Father has sent me,[o] I am sending
you."[p] 22 And with that he breathed on them and said, "Receive the Holy Spirit.[q] 23 If you
forgive anyone his sins, they are forgiven; if you do not forgive them, they are not forgiven."[r]

Jesus Appears to Thomas

24 Now Thomas[s] (called Didymus), one of the Twelve, was not with the disciples
when Jesus came. 25 So the other disciples told him, "We have seen the Lord!"
But he said to them, "Unless I see the nail marks in his hands and put my finger where
the nails were, and put my hand into his side,[t] I will not believe it."[u]
26 A week later his disciples were in the house again, and Thomas was with them.
Though the doors were locked, Jesus came and stood among them and said, "Peace[v] be
with you!"[w] 27 Then he said to Thomas, "Put your finger here; see my hands. Reach out
your hand and put it into my side. Stop doubting and believe."[x]
28 Thomas said to him, "My Lord and my God!"
29 Then Jesus told him, "Because you have seen me, you have believed;[y] blessed are
those who have not seen and yet have believed."[z]
30 Jesus did many other miraculous signs[a] in the presence of his disciples, which are
not recorded in this book.[b] 31 But these are written that you may[a] believe[c] that Jesus is
the Christ, the Son of God,[d] and that by believing you may have life in his name.[e]

[a] *31* Some manuscripts *may continue to*

20:17 [e]Mt 28:10 [f]Jn 7:33
20:18 [g]ver 1 [h]Lk 24:10, 22,23
20:19 [i]Jn 7:13 [j]Jn 14:27 [k]ver 21,26; Lk 24:36-39
20:20 [l]Lk 24:39,40; Jn 19:34 [m]Jn 16:20,22
20:21 [n]ver 19 [o]Jn 3:17 [p]Mt 28:19; Jn 17:18
20:22 [q]Jn 7:39; Ac 2:38; 8:15-17; 19:2; Gal 3:2
20:23 [r]Mt 16:19; 18:18
20:24 [s]Jn 11:16
20:25 [t]ver 20 [u]Mk 16:11
20:26 [v]Jn 14:27 [w]ver 21
20:27 [x]ver 25; Lk 24:40
20:29 [y]Jn 3:15 [z]1Pe 1:8
20:30 [a]Jn 2:11 [b]Jn 21:25
20:31 [c]Jn 3:15; 19:35 [d]Mt 4:3 [e]Mt 25:46

---

word "Rabbi" ("my teacher"). It was used in prayer as an address to God, but since John gives us the translation "Teacher," it is unlikely that it was used to refer to Jesus' deity.

20:17 Do not hold on to me. In Matthew 28:9 the women clasped Jesus' feet, and later Jesus told Thomas to touch him (v. 27), so there was no impropriety in touching his resurrected body. The comment to Mary reminded her that he was not merely recovered but truly resurrected. She was not to "hold on to" Jesus as though he were an earthly being who had recovered; rather, she was to recognize him as One whose resurrection was the beginning of his ascension to heaven. Thus, she was prevented from showing the effusive familiarity she had displayed before his death. **my brothers.** Undoubtedly refers to Jesus' disciples (the same language is used in Mt 28:10). **my Father and your Father, to my God and your God.** Jesus articulated a distinction between his unique Sonship and the redemptive, adoptive sonship of the disciples. Similarly, his relation to the Father is different from that of redeemed humans.

20:19 the disciples. Probably refers to more than the ten apostles (twelve minus Judas Iscariot and Thomas). See Acts 1:14, where it is reported that the women, Mary (Jesus' mother), his brothers and probably others (Barsabbas and Matthias; Ac 1:23) were gathered together in the upper room after Jesus' ascension. **with the doors locked.** The impression is given that the risen Jesus could pass through locked doors (see also v. 26), not that he unlocked the doors supernaturally as in Acts 12:10. This has significance in discussions concerning the nature of the resurrected body (1Co 15:35–49). **"Peace be with you!"** A usual salutation (repeated in v. 21) and most welcome, since they might have expected a rebuke for their cowardice in abandoning Jesus at the time of his arrest.

20:20 his hands and side. Marks made by the wounds of the crucifixion (cf. v. 25). This identified Jesus and proved that he was not a ghost.

20:21–23 See *WCF* 30.2; *HC* 84.

20:21 As the Father has sent me, I am sending you. A brief encapsulation of the commission Jesus gave his disciples. (Fuller representations can be found in Mt 28:18–20; Lk 24:44–53). Jesus offers the supreme impetus for evangelism and missions.

20:22–23 See *HC* 83.

20:22 Receive the Holy Spirit. Does not refer to empowerment for ministry, which took place later at Pentecost, but to formal ordination of the 11 disciples to the office of apostle. For the Old Testament background regarding the Holy Spirit's role in official ordination, see note at Psalm 51:11.

20:23 If you forgive anyone his sins. Similar to the words of Matthew 16:19 and 18:18. The apostles, as the foundation of the church (Eph 2:20), began the process, which the church continues (1Co 5:4), of declaring on behalf of God the binding and pardoning of sin. It is in relation to the preaching of the gospel and the work of church discipline that this occurs. See *BC* 30.

20:24–31 John included the appearance of Jesus to Thomas to address the issue of doubt among Jesus' disciples.

20:25,27 See *WCF* 8.4; *BC* 19.

20:28 "My Lord and my God!" One of the clearest and simplest confessions of the deity of Christ found in the New Testament. The two words of highest possible honor, "Lord" (equivalent to the Old Testament "Yahweh") and "God," are used jointly and are manifestly addressed to Jesus as a recognition of his divine nature. Jesus accepted this acknowledgment without hesitation.

20:29 blessed are those who have not seen. While commending Thomas's faith, Jesus pronounced a blessing on those who would come to believe through the witness of the disciples (17:20; cf. 1Pe 1:8–9). This blessing introduces the reason for the writing of the Gospel (vv. 30–31).

20:30–31 See *HC* 22.

20:30 many other miraculous signs. None of the Gospels makes any claim to giving a complete or strictly chronological record (cf. 21:25). Some of the alleged difficulties could be explained by remembering this principle.

20:31 these are written that you may believe. This statement of purpose provides a capsule summary of the theology of this Gospel. Through the signs narrated, the reader is to come to faith in Jesus as more than a miracle-worker. Jesus is "the Christ, the Son of God," the eternal and fully divine Word of God. By believing we find life in him who is the very source of life itself (6:32–58). Note that true faith is elicited by, and we are blessed by, reading about Jesus' miracles, even though we have not actually witnessed them. See *WLC* 4,43; *WSC* 24; *BC* 10.

Jesus and the Miraculous Catch of Fish

21 Afterward Jesus appeared again to his disciples,[f] by the Sea of Tiberias.[a][g] It happened this way: 2 Simon Peter, Thomas[h] (called Didymus), Nathanael[i] from
Cana in Galilee,[j] the sons of Zebedee,[k] and two other disciples were together. 3 "I'm going out to fish," Simon Peter told them, and they said, "We'll go with you." So they went
out and got into the boat, but that night they caught nothing.[l]
4 Early in the morning, Jesus stood on the shore, but the disciples did not realize that
it was Jesus.[m]
5 He called out to them, "Friends, haven't you any fish?"
"No," they answered.
6 He said, "Throw your net on the right side of the boat and you will find some." When
they did, they were unable to haul the net in because of the large number of fish.[n]
7 Then the disciple whom Jesus loved[o] said to Peter, "It is the Lord!" As soon as Simon
Peter heard him say, "It is the Lord," he wrapped his outer garment around him (for he
had taken it off) and jumped into the water. 8 The other disciples followed in the boat,
towing the net full of fish, for they were not far from shore, about a hundred yards.[b]
9 When they landed, they saw a fire[p] of burning coals there with fish on it,[q] and some
bread.
10 Jesus said to them, "Bring some of the fish you have just caught."
11 Simon Peter climbed aboard and dragged the net ashore. It was full of large fish,
153, but even with so many the net was not torn. 12 Jesus said to them, "Come and have
breakfast." None of the disciples dared ask him, "Who are you?" They knew it was the
Lord. 13 Jesus came, took the bread and gave it to them, and did the same with the fish.[r]
14 This was now the third time Jesus appeared to his disciples[s] after he was raised from
the dead.

Jesus Reinstates Peter

15 When they had finished eating, Jesus said to Simon Peter, "Simon son of John, do
you truly love me more than these?"
"Yes, Lord," he said, "you know that I love you."[t]
Jesus said, "Feed my lambs."[u]
16 Again Jesus said, "Simon son of John, do you truly love me?"
He answered, "Yes, Lord, you know that I love you."
Jesus said, "Take care of my sheep."[v]
17 The third time he said to him, "Simon son of John, do you love me?"
Peter was hurt because Jesus asked him the third time, "Do you love me?"[w] He said,
"Lord, you know all things;[x] you know that I love you."

21:1 [f]Jn 20:19,26 [g]Jn 6:1
21:2 [h]Jn 11:16 [i]Jn 1:45 [j]Jn 2:1 [k]Mt 4:21
21:3 [l]Lk 5:5
21:4 [m]Lk 24:16; Jn 20:14
21:6 [n]Lk 5:4-7
21:7 [o]Jn 13:23
21:9 [p]Jn 18:18 [q]ver 10, 13
21:13 [r]ver 9
21:14 [s]Jn 20:19,26
21:15 [t]Mt 26:33,35; Jn 13:37 [u]Lk 12:32
21:16 [v]Mt 2:6; Ac 20:28; 1Pe 5:2,3
21:17 [w]Jn 13:38 [x]Jn 16:30

[a] *1* That is, Sea of Galilee [b] *8* Greek *about two hundred cubits* (about 90 meters)

▪ **21:1–25** *Epilogue.* This chapter may have been added as a postscript by the same hand that composed the Gospel (i.e., John), although another author apparently wrote verse 24 and perhaps verse 25. This chapter divides into four sections (see "Introduction: Outline").

▪ **21:1–14** *Miracle at the Sea.* Jesus appeared to his disciples while they were fishing and enabled them to catch an incredible amount of fish.

21:3 "I'm going out to fish." May indicate that Peter, having denied the Lord, thought that he had forfeited the privilege of being a witness. **but that night they caught nothing.** It was not unusual in the ancient Mediterranean world to fish at night. The circumstances are reminiscent of the miraculous catch of fish recounted in Luke 5:4–11 and are associated with the initial call of Peter and some of the other disciples (Mt 4:18–22).

21:4 but the disciples did not realize that it was Jesus. See note on 20:14.

21:7 the disciple whom Jesus loved. See note on 13:23. John was quick to recognize Jesus. **he wrapped his outer garment around him.** A surprising action for someone who was about to jump into the water. This may have been a gesture of reverence for Jesus, before whom he did not want to appear unclothed.

21:9 they saw a fire . . . with fish on it, and some bread. It is not stated where the fish came from. This may have been part of the miracle, although this is not specified.

21:11 large fish, 153. Many suggestions have been made concerning the meaning of this number. The simplest view is that this was a fisherman's way of describing an extraordinary catch.

21:14 the third time. Not the third appearance, but the third one in the presence of a group of the apostles (cf. 20:19–23,24–28)

21:15–17 See *WCF* 5.5.

▪ **21:15–19** *The Confirmation of Peter.* Because he had denied Jesus, Peter may have thought himself unfit to continue as an apostle. Jesus' affirmation of Peter in these verses confirmed Peter's apostleship.

21:15 Simon son of John. The same name Jesus used at the beginning of his solemn declaration in response to Peter's confession (Mt 16:17). **do you truly love me more than these?** It is possible to construe this question in several ways: "Do you love me more than these men love me?" "Do you love me more than you love these men?" "Do you love me more than you love these things (nets and fish)?" The Greek verb translated "love" in Jesus' question changes when he asks it the third time, while Peter's answer uses this second verb each time. Some think that some difference was intended in the denotation of the two verbs. This seems unlikely because of two considerations. First, John employed these verbs interchangeably elsewhere in his Gospel. Second, other variations of expression in this interchange seem clearly stylistic (e.g., "Feed my lambs," "Take care of my sheep," "Feed my sheep"). **"Feed my lambs."** "My lambs" and "my sheep" correspond to "my church" (10:14,26–27). Peter wrote to "fellow elders" (1Pe 5:1–2), urging them to be "shepherds of God's flock," apparently having taken to heart the words of Jesus.

21:17 The third time. Peter was not grieved because Jesus changed somewhat the vocabulary in this last question, but because the three questions about his love for Jesus no doubt reminded him of his three recent denials. Jesus kindly gave Peter an opportunity to confess his love and to reaffirm his call to serve the Lord. In grateful response, Peter called Jesus the "Chief Shepherd" (1Pe 5:4).

21:17 [y]ver 16
21:19 [z]Jn 12:33; 18:32 [a]2Pe 1:14
21:20 [b]ver 7; Jn 13:23 [c]Jn 13:25
21:22 [d]Mt 16:27; 1Co 4:5; Rev 2:25 [e]ver 19
21:23 [f]Ac 1:16
21:24 [g]Jn 15:27 [h]Jn 19:35
21:25 [i]Jn 20:30

Jesus said, "Feed my sheep.[y] 18 I tell you the truth, when you were younger you
dressed yourself and went where you wanted; but when you are old you will stretch out
your hands, and someone else will dress you and lead you where you do not want to go."
19 Jesus said this to indicate the kind of death[z] by which Peter would glorify God.[a] Then
he said to him, "Follow me!"
20 Peter turned and saw that the disciple whom Jesus loved[b] was following them. (This
was the one who had leaned back against Jesus at the supper and had said, "Lord, who
is going to betray you?")[c] 21 When Peter saw him, he asked, "Lord, what about him?"
22 Jesus answered, "If I want him to remain alive until I return,[d] what is that to you?
You must follow me."[e] 23 Because of this, the rumor spread among the brothers[f] that this
disciple would not die. But Jesus did not say that he would not die; he only said, "If I want
him to remain alive until I return, what is that to you?"
24 This is the disciple who testifies to these things[g] and who wrote them down. We
know that his testimony is true.[h]
25 Jesus did many other things as well.[i] If every one of them were written down, I
suppose that even the whole world would not have room for the books that would be
written.

21:19 the kind of death. A fairly ancient tradition holds that Peter was martyred by being crucified upside down. **"Follow me!"** Echoes the original call given by Jesus to his apostles (Mt 4:19; Lk 5:27; cf. Jn 21:22). This whole incident graciously affirmed Peter's role as an apostle.

■ **21:20–23** *The Beloved Disciple.* Jesus spoke of his future return, and John clarified that Jesus had not promised to return within John's lifetime.

21:20 disciple whom Jesus loved. See note on 13:23. The further description, when related to 13:23–25, leaves no doubt that this was John, son of Zebedee.

21:22 alive until I return. This was thought by some to be a promise of Christ's return before the end of the first century A.D. John here stipulated that no such promise was intended. But the promise of Christ's second coming, with no specification of time, is certainly expressed in these verses.

■ **21:24–25** *Closing Remarks.* These final words close the Gospel of John with an assurance that the work's contents are true but not exhaustive.

21:24 disciple who testifies. The disciple who "wrote these things" is the same disciple who was mentioned several times earlier and who was identified as the one Jesus loved (13:23)—namely John (see "Introduction: Author"). **We know.** This is the affidavit by a contemporary who was undoubtedly in a position to know John firsthand. Therefore, this whole Gospel, including chapter 21, was almost instantaneously received as canonical in the early church.

21:25 the whole world would not have room. A descriptive hyperbole, expressing clearly that each of the Gospel writers was, and indeed had to be, highly selective. Either John wrote this verse himself or it was added by the person who penned the affidavit (see note on v. 24).

ACTS

Introduction

Overview

Author: Luke, a companion of Paul

Purpose: To guide the church in its continuing mission by describing how the Holy Spirit empowered the apostles to spread their witness on Christ's behalf to the Gentile world

Date: A.D. 60–64

Key Truths:

- Christ's witnesses are empowered by the Holy Spirit.
- Christ's witnesses are to go to the ends of the earth.
- Christ's witnesses suffer persecution.
- Christ's witnesses establish churches that continue the mission

Author

Traditionally the book of Acts has been understood as having been written by Luke the physician, a companion of Paul on parts of his second and third missionary journeys and on his voyage to Rome. The early church, from the second century to the fourth century A.D., bears testimony to Luke as the author of Acts. Irenaeus (c. A.D. 130–202), Clement of Alexandria (A.D. 153–217), the Muratorian Canon (c. A.D. 170) and Eusebius (c. A.D. 325) all credit Luke as the author.

The internal evidence in Acts for this conclusion is twofold. First, the references to Theophilus in Luke 1:3 and Acts 1:1 connect Acts with the third gospel. Second, the "we" passages found in sections of the latter half of the book (16:10–17; 20:5–15; 21:1–18; 27:1—28:16) indicate that the writer was Paul's traveling companion. It appears that the narrator of Acts escorted Paul from Troas in Asia Minor to Philippi on the continent of Europe, then back again from Philippi to Troas and over to the Holy Land. He then finally escorted him from Caesarea in the Holy Land to Italy and Rome.

The author was educated, as attested by the style of Luke–Acts and the high level of Greek used. The author's Greek is sometimes fully literary, resembling that of the earlier classical period (Lk 1:1–4), pointing to a person acquainted with the non-Jewish world. In addition, the author's methodical approach to writing and his research methods (Lk 1:1–4) reveal an educated, highly trained man. Colossians 4:10–14 indicates that Luke was Gentile rather than Jewish.

Colossians 4:14 indicates that Paul had the company of his "dear friend Luke, the doctor." Some scholars, particularly in the late nineteenth and early twentieth centuries, have argued that the medical language of Luke–Acts and the author's interest in diseases (Lk 4:38; 8:43–44; Ac 3:7; 12:23; 13:11; 20:7–11; 28:3,8) point to Luke the doctor as the author. More recently, other scholars have argued that medical terms were commonly employed by a number of ancient authors and that this point cannot be used to prove that the author was a physician. Still, the interest in medical matters in Luke–Acts makes it plausible that Luke the doctor was indeed the author.

Time and Place of Writing

Three time periods have been suggested for the writing of Acts: A.D. 105–130, A.D. 80–95 and before A.D. 70. The first two views are based in part on the theory that in 5:36–37 the author of Acts (probably not Luke, according to this theory) used Josephus (*Antiquities*, 10.4–10; 20.97–98) for information about the revolutionaries Theudas and Judas. But the Theudas to whom Gamaliel referred (Ac 5:36) may well have been one of the many revolutionaries who arose about the time of Herod the Great's death, not the Theudas of A.D. 44 mentioned by Josephus. Also, the fact that both Luke and Josephus refer to a Judas of A.D. 6 does not show that either author depended on the other. Late date adherents argue that Luke (Ac 12:19–23) had access to and may have copied from Josephus's account (*Antiquities*, 19.343–350) of the death of Herod Agrippa I in A.D. 44, because the two use similar words in describing the event. The two accounts, however, differ considerably. It is also argued that the theology of Acts fits that of the second-century writer Justin Martyr. But this idea works better the other way: Justin Martyr could have received his theology from Acts.

Those favoring later dates also argue that Luke 21:20, with its mention of armies, shows that the destruction of Jerusalem had already occurred when Luke and Acts were written. We note that Mark's Gospel uses the phrase "the abomination that causes desolation" (a prophecy in Mt 24:15 and Mk 13:14 taken from Da 9:27) as an expression that the Jews would have understood. Luke, by contrast, referred to the same prophetic event but spoke of armies and therefore used a term Gentiles would have understood. In any event, the difference in terms does not prove that Jerusalem had already fallen.

The view that Luke and Acts were written prior to A.D. 70 (probably about A.D. 60–64) is the strongest. First, chapter 28 ends with Paul in semi-confinement. While he waited for his appearance before Caesar, he freely preached to all those who came to him—certainly this was before Nero blamed Christians for the Roman fire in A.D. 64. Second, there is no mention of Paul's death, which appeared to be imminent in 2 Timothy 4 and which probably occurred in A.D. 67 or 68.

Third, near the end of Acts, Luke portrayed the Roman government as benevolent toward Christianity, an attitude that changed after A.D. 64. Fourth, the use of primitive terms points to an early date for its composition. These terms include "disciple" (e.g., 9:26); "the first day of the week" (20:7), which later became "the Lord's Day" (Rev 1:10); "the people of Israel" (4:10,27), which was later changed to the term "people" to describe both Jews and Gentiles (Tit 2:14); the early title "Son of Man" (7:56); as well as archaic language involving geographical, political and territorial matters, such as details about the regional boundaries between Phrygian Iconium, Lycaonian Lystra, and Derbe.

Luke collected material from his own eyewitness experiences, from Semitic sources while he was in the Holy Land and from other sources outside of the Holy Land. He possibly gained material from people such as Sopater from Berea, Aristarchus and Secundus from Thessalonica, Gaius from Derbe, Timothy from Lystra (16:1) and Tychicus and Trophimus from the province of Asia (20:4). While in the Holy Land during Paul's two-year imprisonment, Luke gathered materials for his Gospel and for the first part of Acts. He probably talked to Mary the mother of Jesus and others who were "eyewitnesses and servants of the word" (Lk 1:2).

Original Audience

According to Luke 1:3 and Acts 1:1, Theophilus was the primary recipient of both books (see "Introduction to Luke: Original Audience"). The background of this man is not known, but he may have been Luke's patron or benefactor. Certainly he was a Gentile who received Christian instruction (Lk 1:4). As Luke's patron, Theophilus would have provided a living for Luke while the latter spent much of his time researching material and writing his two books. Compare this with Josephus, the Jewish historian (A.D. 37/38 to c. 100) who, besides indicating that the Roman generals Vespasian and Titus were his patrons (*Against Apion,* 1.50), also spoke of having another benefactor, a certain Epaphroditus (*Life,* 430; *Against Apion,* 1.1; 2.1; 2.296). Similar to what Luke said to Theophilus in Luke 1:3–4, Josephus (*Against Apion,* 2.296) said to Epaphroditus, "To you, Epaphroditus, who are a devoted lover of truth and for your sake to any who, like you, may wish to know the facts about our race, I beg to dedicate this and the preceding book."

Purpose and Distinctives

Acts presents a true historical record of the development of the early church in the middle of the first century A.D. Luke's descriptions of geographical and provincial details, of governmental officials and their official actions, of the actions of emperors and of the sea voyage to Italy with its accurate use of nautical terms, all point to a careful researcher who himself was an eyewitness to many of the events recorded in Acts 16 and succeeding chapters. Luke's Greek is excellent, and it is clear that he was in tune with his Semitic sources, for many Aramaic expressions are used in the first half of Acts.

Luke may have had several purposes for writing Acts. He stated that in his Gospel he had traced the life of Jesus until his ascension (1:1–2) and summarized his general theme for Acts by stating that the Lord was going to expand his work "in Jerusalem, and in all Judea and Samaria, and to the ends of the earth" (1:8). Acts is a road map of the progress of the church into the entire ancient world; it presents Christianity on the march. Some have also felt that Acts presents a defense of Christianity or attempts to show that Christianity was no threat to Rome. Although Acts is called the "Acts of the Apostles," Luke primarily traced the ministries of Peter (chs. 1–12) and of Paul (chs. 13–28).

The account of the day of Pentecost in Acts 2 plays a key role in Acts. Jesus told the disciples to wait in Jerusalem for the coming of the Holy Spirit because, through the power and testimony of the Spirit, the gospel was to be spread and the people of all nations were to be called to faith (Lk 24:47–49; Ac 1:4,8). Paul's role in the second half of the book continues this theme as he spread the gospel throughout the Gentile world.

Outline

I. The Apostolic Witness and the Spirit's Power (1:1—2:47)
   A. Waiting for the Spirit (1:1–26)
   B. The Outpouring of the Spirit on Pentecost (2:1–41)
   C. The Emerging Church (2:42–47)

Jesus promised the apostles that the Holy Spirit would empower them to be his witnesses in Jerusalem, Judea and Samaria, and to the ends of the earth. At Pentecost the Spirit was poured out on the apostles, and their powerful witness began.

II. The Apostolic Witness in Jerusalem (3:1—7:60)
   A. Peter's Temple Miracle and Sermon (3:1–26)
   B. Persecution From the Sanhedrin (4:1–31)
   C. Community Life Among Believers (4:32—5:11)
   D. Further Persecution From the Sanhedrin (5:12–42)
   E. Further Community Life Among Believers (6:1–7)
   F. Stephen's Persecution, Sermon and Martyrdom (6:8—7:60)

The apostles first witnessed for Christ in Jerusalem, just as he had instructed. They performed miracles and preached the gospel of Christ, but they suffered much persecution. The church grew in Jerusalem, and with that growth came internal strife. Yet the church stood strong and continued to increase in numbers in Jerusalem.

III. The Apostolic Witness in Judea and Samaria (8:1—11:18)
  A. The Witness Spreads (8:1–40)
  B. Saul's Conversion and the Growing Church (9:1–31)
  C. The Witness Spreads Farther (9:32–43)
  D. The Witness Reaches Gentiles in Samaria (10:1—11:18)
  E. The Church in Syrian Antioch (11:19–30)
  F. Persecution and Judgment in Jerusalem (12:1–25)

Persecution moved the apostolic witness beyond Jerusalem to Judea and Samaria, just as Jesus had commanded. Two significant events enabled this apostolic witness to move farther out geographically: Saul's conversion to Christianity and Peter's growth in Christianity (namely, his understanding that Gentile believers in Jesus Christ have as much right to the promises of God as do Jewish believers).

IV. The Apostolic Witness to the Ends of the Earth (13:1—28:31)
  A. Paul's First Missionary Journey (13:1—14:28)
  B. The Jerusalem Council (15:1–35)
  C. Paul's Second Missionary Journey (15:36—18:22)
  D. Paul's Third Missionary Journey (18:23—21:14)
  E. Paul's Arrest, Trial and Imprisonment in Jerusalem (21:15—26:32)
  F. Paul's Voyage to Rome (27:1—28:16)
  G. Paul's Two-Year Ministry Under House Arrest in Rome (28:17–31)

Paul, as Christ's apostolic witness, experienced the same persecution that the apostles before him endured. Through his three missionary journeys and his imprisonment, Paul carried the gospel to the ends of the earth, the Holy Spirit powerfully bearing witness to the truth of Paul's message by calling many Jews and Gentiles to faith.

Jesus Taken Up Into Heaven

1 In my former book,[a] Theophilus, I wrote about all that Jesus began to do and to
teach[b] 2 until the day he was taken up to heaven,[c] after giving instructions[d]
through the Holy Spirit to the apostles[e] he had chosen.[f] 3 After his suffering, he showed
himself to these men and gave many convincing proofs that he was alive. He appeared
to them[g] over a period of forty days and spoke about the kingdom of God. 4 On one occasion, while he was eating with them, he gave them this command: "Do not leave Jerusalem, but wait for the gift my Father promised, which you have heard me speak
about.[h] 5 For John baptized with[a] water, but in a few days you will be baptized with the
Holy Spirit."

[a] 5 Or *in*

1:1
[a]Lk 1:1-4 [b]Lk 3:23

1:2
[c]ver 9,11; Mk 16:19
[d]Mt 28:19,20
[e]Mk 6:30 [f]Jn 13:18

1:3
[g]Mt 28:17; Lk 24:34,36; Jn 20:19,26; 21:1, 14; 1Co 15:5 7

1:4
[h]Lk 24:49; Jn 14:16; Ac 2:33

■ **1:1—2:47** *The Apostolic Witness and the Spirit's Power.* After a brief introduction, Luke moved directly to the foundation of his entire history: the Holy Spirit's empowerment of the apostles as witnesses for Christ "in Jerusalem, and in all Judea and Samaria, and to the ends of the earth" (1:8). His account divides into three main sections (see "Introduction: Outline").

■ **1:1–26** *Waiting for the Spirit.* Luke reported how Jesus told the apostles to expect the Spirit to empower them for a worldwide ministry and how the apostles prepared themselves for his outpouring. This stress on the Spirit not only explains why the apostles took up the task of spreading the gospel but also displays the need for the Spirit's power for continuing its spread in every age.

1:1 my former book. Literally, "my former account" (i.e., the Gospel of Luke), as is particularly shown by the repeated reference to Theophilus (Lk 1:3). The addressee may have been the author's patron who provided the money for Luke to do his research and writing, including the distribution of the combined works of Luke and Acts (see "Introduction: Original Audience"). **all that Jesus began to do and to teach.** A fitting summary of the many events and words of Jesus that Luke recorded in his Gospel. This ministry would now be continued through the lives of the apostles, who were empowered by the Holy Spirit (v. 8).

1:2–3 See *WLC* 53.

1:2 taken up to heaven. According to Luke 24:50–52 the ascension took place in the vicinity of Bethany (on the east side of the Mount of Olives, east of Jerusalem). **instructions through the Holy Spirit.** In his postresurrection experiences with his disciples, Jesus communicated to the apostles the reality of his resurrection (Jn 20–21), the truth of his Messiahship (Lk 24:44–49), the blessing of the Holy Spirit (Jn 20:22–23) and the reality of his physically resurrected body (Lk 24:37–43). **he had chosen.** A reference to Jesus' choice of his apostles (Lk 6:12–16), one of whom Jesus knew would become a traitor (Judas).

1:3 showed himself . . . many convincing proofs. Christ's appearances after his resurrection (Mt 28; Mk 16; Lk 24; Jn 20–21; 1Co 15:5–7) were important as an outward validation of his supernatural person and work. It was important that eyewitnesses, such as the disciples (v. 22), verify his resurrection. **forty days.** The period of Jesus' postresurrection ministry. Following the ascension of Christ there were an additional ten days during which the disciples stayed in Jerusalem waiting for the promised outpouring of the Holy Spirit at Pentecost, the 50th day after Passover. **the kingdom of God.** Also called the "kingdom of heaven" (e.g., Mt 5:10). See theological article "The Kingdom of God" at Matthew 4. See also *BC* 19.

1:4 On one occasion, while he was eating with them. Jesus often communed with his friends and disciples over a meal: the feeding of the 5,000 (Lk 9:16), eating with tax collectors and sinners (Mk 2:15–16; Lk 5:29), eating at the Pharisee's house (Lk 7:37), the Last Supper (Mt 26:21,26) and eating with his disciples after the resurrection (Lk 24:42; Jn 21:9–15). **wait for the gift my Father promised.** The Holy Spirit was actually both the gift of the Father and the gift of Jesus the Son (Jn 14:1,26; 15:26).

1:5 John baptized with water. John the Baptist baptized large crowds of people (Mt 3:5–6,13–15; Mk 1:5,9; Lk 3:7–16,21). John's water baptism of repentance (Mk 1:4) pointed forward to the Messianic baptism with the Holy Spirit and fire (Lk 3:16). **in a few days.** A few days would pass before Pentecost.

6 So when they met together, they asked him, “Lord, are you at this time going to restore[i] the kingdom to Israel?”
7 He said to them: “It is not for you to know the times or dates the Father has set by
his own authority.[j] 8 But you will receive power when the Holy Spirit comes on you;[k] and
you will be my witnesses[l] in Jerusalem, and in all Judea and Samaria,[m] and to the ends
of the earth.”[n]
9 After he said this, he was taken up[o] before their very eyes, and a cloud hid him from
their sight.
10 They were looking intently up into the sky as he was going, when suddenly two men
dressed in white[p] stood beside them. 11 “Men of Galilee,”[q] they said, “why do you stand
here looking into the sky? This same Jesus, who has been taken from you into heaven,
will come back[r] in the same way you have seen him go into heaven.”

Matthias Chosen to Replace Judas

12 Then they returned to Jerusalem[s] from the hill called the Mount of Olives,[t] a Sabbath day's walk[a] from the city. 13 When they arrived, they went upstairs to the room[u]
where they were staying. Those present were Peter, John, James and Andrew; Philip and
Thomas, Bartholomew and Matthew; James son of Alphaeus and Simon the Zealot, and
Judas son of James.[v] 14 They all joined together constantly in prayer,[w] along with the
women[x] and Mary the mother of Jesus, and with his brothers.[y]
15 In those days Peter stood up among the believers[b] (a group numbering about a hundred and twenty) 16 and said, “Brothers, the Scripture had to be fulfilled[z] which the Holy
Spirit spoke long ago through the mouth of David concerning Judas,[a] who served as
guide for those who arrested Jesus— 17 he was one of our number[b] and shared in this
ministry.”[c]
18 (With the reward[d] he got for his wickedness, Judas bought a field;[e] there he fell headlong, his body burst open and all his intestines spilled out. 19 Everyone in Jerusalem heard
about this, so they called that field in their language Akeldama, that is, Field of Blood.)

a *12* That is, about 3/4 mile (about 1,100 meters) b *15* Greek *brothers*

1:6 [i]Mt 17:11
1:7 [j]Mt 24:36
1:8 [k]Ac 2:1-4 [l]Lk 24:48 [m]Ac 8:1-25 [n]Mt 28:19
1:9 [o]ver 2
1:10 [p]Lk 24:4; Jn 20:12
1:11 [q]Ac 2:7 [r]Mt 16:27
1:12 [s]Lk 24:52 [t]Mt 21:1
1:13 [u]Ac 9:37; 20:8 [v]Mt 10:2-4; Mk 3:16-19; Lk 6:14-16
1:14 [w]Ac 2:42; 6:4 [x]Lk 23:49,55 [y]Mt 12:46
1:16 [z]ver 20 [a]Jn 13:18
1:17 [b]Jn 6:70,71 [c]ver 25
1:18 [d]Mt 26:14,15 [e]Mt 27:3-10

1:6 at this time going to restore the kingdom to Israel. From what Jesus had said (Mt 19:28), the disciples thought that he might overthrow the Romans and restore the physical kingdom to Israel.
1:7 not for you to know the times or dates. That is, the specific period or the exact date or hour (which some in all ages try to predict) of the second coming of Jesus Christ to Earth (cf. 1Th 5:2). **the Father has set by his own authority.** Compare Mark 13:32. Even the Son, who in his humanity had limited knowledge (Lk 2:52), did not know the time.
1:8 Holy Spirit comes on you. The Holy Spirit would outwardly show his control of their lives by special manifestations: the blowing of a violent wind, the appearance of tongues as of fire, and speaking in foreign languages (ch. 2). **witnesses in Jerusalem, and in all Judea and Samaria, and to the ends of the earth.** The book of Acts unfolds according to this strategy. The Jerusalem witness (ch. 2) gives in miniature form God's worldwide ministry: The “Jews from every nation” (2:5) who heard and believed carried the message far and wide. The rest of Acts gives further details of how the gospel was spread to Jerusalem (3:1—8:1), to Judea and Samaria, up to Antioch of Syria (8:1—12:25) and to the ends of the earth (13:1—28:31).
1:9–11 See *WLC* 53; *HC* 46,47,76.
1:10 two men dressed in white. Persons described as dressed in white were commonly supernatural or glorified beings, such as Jesus Christ (Mt 17:2; Mk 9:3; Rev 1:14), angels (Mt 28:3; Mk 16:5; Lk 24:4; Jn 20:12) and glorified saints (Lk 9:30–31; Rev 3:4–5,18; 4:4; 7:14).
1:11 Men of Galilee. The 11 who were present were from Galilee; Judas the betrayer (who was not present) may have been from Kerioth in Judah. **in the same way.** Jesus will return in his resurrected body, coming with the clouds of heaven (Mt 24:30; 26:64; Mk 14:62; 1Th 4:16–17; Rev 1:7). See *WCF* 8.4; *WLC* 51; *WSC* 28; *BC* 19,37; *HC* 46.
1:12 The Mount of Olives. A hill beyond the Kidron Valley just east of the walled city of Jerusalem. The disciples had been with Jesus on the mount near Bethany (Lk 24:50). **a Sabbath day's walk.** From the city, a distance calculated by the rabbis as about 1,100 meters, or three-fourths of a mile.
1:13 upstairs to the room where they were staying. Probably where the disciples had been hiding for fear of the Jews. This may have been the same room in which they had celebrated the Passover and Jesus had instituted the Lord's Supper (Mk 14:15). Or it may have been a room in the house of Barnabas's aunt Mary (Ac 12:12; Col 4:10), where the Christians later held meetings (Ac 12:12). It was probably located close to the temple courts, where the visiting Jewish crowds were assembled (2:5–12). **Bartholomew.** John did not mention a disciple named Bartholomew, but he spoke of a disciple named Nathanael (Jn 1:45; 21:2). Probably these names referred to the same man, “Bartholomew” being his surname. **James son of Alphaeus.** Also known as James the younger (Mk 15:40). **Zealot.** Possibly referring to Simon's former membership in the Zealot revolutionary group. **Judas son of James.** Also known as Thaddaeus (Mt 10:3; Mk 3:18).
1:14 constantly in prayer. Jesus established a pattern of prayer in the lives of his disciples. There are many examples in Luke of Jesus praying (Lk 3:21; 5:16; 6:12; 9:18,28–29; 11:1; 22:32,41; 23:34,46). He often prayed in private. **with the women.** Groups of women followed Jesus, helped support his ministry and cared for him in his death (Mt 27:55–56; 28:1; Mk 15:40–41; Lk 8:2–3; 23:49; 24:1,22). **Mary the mother of Jesus.** This is the last reference in the New Testament to Jesus' mother. **his brothers.** The sons of Mary and Joseph (Mt 13:55; Jn 7:3,10).
1:15 In those days. The ten days between the forty days Jesus spent with the apostles (v. 3) and the day of Pentecost (2:1).
1:16 the Scripture had to be fulfilled. Psalms 69:25 and 109:8, quoted in verse 20, are applied by Peter to Judas Iscariot, who as an enemy of God had been deposed from his apostleship. Now “his place of leadership” (Ps 109:8) had to be filled again. **the Holy Spirit spoke . . . through the mouth of David.** The Holy Spirit, using the writing talents and poetic skills of David, had directed David to accurately compose the words and the truth of this message.
1:17 shared in this ministry. In his providence God allowed Judas, the enemy of the Savior, to serve for a time in the ministry of the disciples.
1:18 With the reward. The 30 silver coins (Mt 26:15), probably four drachma pieces, worth a total of 120 denarii, the value of 120 days' labor (Mt 20:2). **Judas bought a field.** Judas indirectly bought the field when he returned the bribe money to the chief priests and elders, who in turn purchased a burial place for foreigners called the “Field of Blood” (Mt 27:8). **he fell headlong . . . and all his intestines spilled out.** Matthew wrote that Judas “hanged himself” (Mt 27:5). The following represents a possible scenario: Judas hanged himself; the rope either broke or was cut down; his body then fell on the jagged rocks somewhere along the Hinnom Valley and burst open either from the violence of the fall or from eventual decomposition.

20 "For," said Peter, "it is written in the book of Psalms,

" 'May his place be deserted;
let there be no one to dwell in it,'[a][f]

and,

" 'May another take his place of leadership.'[b][g]

[a] 20 Psalm 69:25 [b] 20 Psalm 109:8

1:20 [f]Ps 69:25 [g]Ps 109:8

Evangelism: Why Should We Preach the Gospel?

IN Genesis 1:28, Adam faced a world of endless challenges. God's word to him was clear: Mere subsistence in the new creation was not enough. He was commanded to fill the earth with humanity and to be a caretaker of the plant and animal kingdoms, subduing all for God's glory and humanity's good. These tasks were not possible for Adam and Eve to complete alone—the commands were given to individuals, but the scope of the commands indicated that God intended humankind as a whole to fulfill them. The language of the dominion mandate was further extended and specified through the covenants God made with his people in the Old Testament (Ge 9:1–17; 15:1–17; 17:1–22; 22:1–18; Ex 19:5; 2Sa 7:5–29; 1Ki 8; Ps 89).

In Matthew 28:18–20, Jesus' words to his doubting disciples echoed the dominion mandate. He had already made it clear that his people were to be a loving, worshiping community (Jn 4:21–24; 13:34–35), set apart to glorify God (Mt 25:34–40; Jn 15:8), but he was not finished with his instructions. God did not simply want a community that maintained itself; he desired a conquering community, set apart for the task of multiplying disciples who would fill the earth with new covenant communities made up of baptized men, women and children from every nation (Ac 2:5; 10:35; Rev 7:9; 14:6), teaching and obeying everything that our all-powerful Lord has taught in his Word. Christ alone possesses the absolute authority (Mt 28:18; Jn 17:2; Eph 1:21–23; Col 2:10) to exercise such dominion over the world, but in commanding his people to evangelize the world and to make disciples (Mt 1:19–20; Ac 1:4–8), he has delegated a portion of that authority to the church, giving it the responsibility to preach the gospel effectively. Although this might seem an impossible task, it is not—Jesus has also assured the temporal and eternal success of the church's mission (Col 2:13–15; Rev 17:14).

But what is it that our Lord would have us teach? In the narrow sense, it is that the Biblical gospel is God's enduring message to our world. The heart of the Great Commission (Mt 28:18–20) is echoed throughout the Scriptures (Lk 19:10; Jn 13:34–35; 1Co 9:22; Php 1:27). God has committed to the whole church the task of making Christ known throughout the world. Individuals in the church may not be highly gifted in evangelism or in the associated gift of financially supporting local and world missions, but every person can pray for effective propagation of the gospel. Paul asked those in Thessalonica to "pray for us that the message of the Lord may spread rapidly and be honored, just as it was with you" (2Th 3:1).

The church's call to preach the gospel to the world is intended to combat the age-old problem of sin. Sin is comprehensive, spoiling all humankind and creation itself (1Ki 8:46; Pss 130:3; 143:2; Pr 20:9; Ecc 7:20; Ro 3:9–12; 5:12–19; 8:19–23; Gal 3:22; 1Jn 1:8–10), condemning all to the fires of hell (Mt 5:29–30; 23:32–33; Mk 9:43–47; Ro 6:23)—but God's Good News is no less so. Wherever sin reigns today, God teaches sinful people that the gospel provides a way of escape (Ro 5:8–10; 10:8–13). And the church has been called to carry this Good News to all people (Mt 28:19; Ac 1:4–8) so that all might have the opportunity to repent and be saved (Ro 10:13–15), to be reborn through God's power manifested in the preaching of the gospel (Ro 1:16; 1Co 1:17–18; 1Th 1:5).

But there is more to the gospel than converting people to Christ. Sin remains even in believers, and the Good News includes the reality that God empowers believers to avoid sin throughout their lives (Ro 8:9,13). Further, it always equips us with a way to avoid violating his commandments (1Co 10:13). By teaching one another to obey all that Jesus has commanded (Mt 28:20), we demonstrate God's means of escape from every sinful aspect of the world, the flesh and the devil's temptations, and we exhibit a positive, transforming way of life in the culture in which God has placed us.

Beyond this, the gospel is also about redeeming the whole universe (Isa 65:17; 66:22; Ro 8:19–22; Rev 21:1–5), taking back everything that was lost in humanity's fall into sin (Ge 3). We are not simply commanded to save and teach individuals and families, but to offer, by the means of the spiritual power of the gospel (2Co 6:7; 10:4), a full-scale attack on all the sinful aspects of our fallen world. It is especially in this light that the church longs for God's kingdom to be fully consummated (Mt 6:9–10; 25:1–13; Lk 12:40; see theological article "The Kingdom of God" at Mt 4) and prays for him to find a faithful covenant community upon his return. This desire for Christ's return to faithful community has been preserved in the New Testament in the Aramaic prayer "Marana tha" (1Co 16:22, see NIV footnote)—a cry to see Christian missions and evangelism fulfilled in all their glory through the submission of every nation to Jesus Christ and the destruction of all our Lord's enemies (Ps 110). Until that day, the church will continue to "wait for the blessed hope—the glorious appearing of our great God and Savior, Jesus Christ" (Tit 2:13) and to pray, "Come, Lord Jesus" (Rev 22:20). Through the power of the gospel, there will be people from every nation and every tongue to greet him on that day at "the very end of the age" (Mt 28:20).

1:22 21 Therefore it is necessary to choose one of the men who have been with us the whole
[h]Mk 1:4 [i]ver 8 time the Lord Jesus went in and out among us, 22 beginning from John's baptism[h] to the
time when Jesus was taken up from us. For one of these must become a witness[i] with us
of his resurrection."

1:24 23 So they proposed two men: Joseph called Barsabbas (also known as Justus) and
[j]Ac 6:6; 14:23 Matthias. 24 Then they prayed,[j] "Lord, you know everyone's heart.[k] Show us which of
[k]1Sa 16:7; Jer 17:10; Ac 15:8; these two you have chosen 25 to take over this apostolic ministry, which Judas left to go
Rev 2:23 where he belongs." 26 Then they cast lots, and the lot fell to Matthias; so he was added
1:26 to the eleven apostles.[l]
[l]Ac 2:14

2:1 *The Holy Spirit Comes at Pentecost*

[m]Lev 23:15,16; **2** When the day of Pentecost[m] came, they were all together[n] in one place. 2 Sudden-
Ac 20:16 [n]Ac 1:14 ly a sound like the blowing of a violent wind came from heaven and filled the whole
2:2 [o]Ac 4:31 house where they were sitting.[o] 3 They saw what seemed to be tongues of fire that separated and came to rest on each of them. 4 All of them were filled with the Holy Spirit and
2:4 [p]Mk 16:17; began to speak in other tongues[a][p] as the Spirit enabled them.
1Co 12:10 5 Now there were staying in Jerusalem God-fearing[q] Jews from every nation under
2:5 heaven. 6 When they heard this sound, a crowd came together in bewilderment, because
[q]Ac 8:2 each one heard them speaking in his own language. 7 Utterly amazed,[r] they asked: "Are
2:7 not all these men who are speaking Galileans?[s] 8 Then how is it that each of us hears
[r]ver 12 [s]Ac 1:11

[a] *4* Or *languages;* also in verse 11

1:21–22 See *BC* 7.
1:21 to choose one. The Greek contains no verb to indicate that the disciples had to "choose" a replacement. The process was designed to divine God's choice (see v. 24). **the Lord Jesus went in and out among us.** Includes the whole time of Jesus' public ministry, from his baptism to his ascension.
1:22 a witness with us of his resurrection. The resurrection of Jesus was the climax and keystone of Jesus' life and ministry. Had there been no resurrection, there would have been no meaning to his life and death (1Co 15:12–19).
1:23 proposed two men. Evidently Joseph and Matthias were recommended from a larger body of witnesses (according to v. 15, about a 120 persons were present). **Barsabbas.** The name means "son of the Sabbath." It was used for two early Christians: this particular Joseph and a certain Judas, a prophet from the Jerusalem church who was sent with Silas to Antioch (15:22,32). **Justus.** Joseph Barsabbas's Greek name. He is not referred to again in the New Testament. **Matthias.** Not mentioned elsewhere in Scripture. See *BC* 31.
1:24–25 See *WCF* 32.1; *WLC* 86,112,179.
1:26 cast lots. The apostles here used an Old Testament procedure employed to ascertain God's will. The Urim and Thummim were lots or token pieces in Aaron's breastplate (Ex 28:30) used on occasion to verify God's will (Nu 27:21). The lot was usually made of small stones or wooden pieces according to a widespread custom in the ancient Near East (e.g., Jnh 1:7). A lot was cast between Saul and Jonathan (1Sa 14:41–42; cf. 1Ch 26:13). The decisions obtained in this procedure were of the Lord (Pr 16:33). Note, however, that the apostles had already narrowed their choices according to principle. Some have suggested that the Greek word for "lots" in this verse is equivalent to another Greek word meaning a small round stone used for voting. The Greek word translated "he was added" sometimes has the meaning "chosen by vote." See *WLC* 112.
■**2:1–41** *The Outpouring of the Spirit on Pentecost.* Luke described the day of Pentecost with high drama. The apostles spoke in tongues and proclaimed the gospel of Christ to Jews gathered from all parts of the world. The apostolic witness began with spectacular, divine intervention the likes of which have never been seen again. Despite the uniqueness of this day, the ministry of the church for all generations must build on this foundation and continue to minister in the power of the outpoured Spirit.
2:1 day of Pentecost. The Greek word *pentçkostç* means "fiftieth" and refers to the 50th day after the Sabbath of the Passover week (Lev 23:4–7,15–16). Pentecost, celebrated on the first day of the week (our Sunday), was one of three great annual feasts of Israel. It was preceded by Passover (Lev 23:4–8; Nu 28:16–25) and followed four months later by the Feast of Tabernacles (Lev 23:33–43; Nu 29:12–38; cf. Jn 7:1–44). Pentecost was also called the "Feast of Weeks" because it was celebrated seven weeks after Passover (Dt 16:10), the "Feast of Harvest" because the firstfruits of the harvest were gathered (Ex 23:16), and the "day of firstfruits" (Nu 28:26). The connection between the outpouring of the Holy Spirit and the celebration of Pentecost on the day of firstfruits fits well with the teaching that the Spirit's New Testament manifestation is the "firstfruits" of the harvest of salvation in Christ (Ro 8:23). **they were all together.** All of the apostles (1:13) were present, as well as probably all of the 120 mentioned earlier (1:15). **in one place.** Possibly near the temple courts. Luke usually specified the place as temple courts (Ac 2:46; 3:2,8; 5:20–21,25,42; 24:18; 26:21), but now he referred to a house probably not far from the temple courts, for the thousands of Jews attending the Pentecost feast were close enough to hear the sound of the wind (vv. 5–11,41).
2:2 a sound . . . of a violent wind. Three signs of God's presence were witnessed: wind, fire and inspired speech (Ex 3:2; 13:21; 24:17; 40:38; 1Ki 19:11–13). The wind in particular is a symbol of the Holy Spirit's presence (Eze 37:9,13; Jn 3:8), and fire is a symbol of the Spirit's cleansing and judging power (Mt 3:11–12). The tongues spoken were not ecstatic utterances but clearly the various languages spoken by the Jews who had come from all parts of the eastern Mediterranean region, from Rome to as far east as Parthia in eastern Iran.
2:4 were filled with the Holy Spirit. They were overcome by the powerful influence of the Spirit, particularly evidenced by their speaking in other languages ("other tongues") that they had not previously learned. Acts 10:46 and 19:6 also relate instances of speaking in tongues (see 1Co 12–14 on the spiritual gift of tongues). The coming of the Spirit in the New Testament is the fulfillment of Luke 24:49 and Acts 1:5 and 8. The Holy Spirit was also present and working with God's people in the Old Testament, but now his presence is felt in much greater ways because he gifts far more people than ever before. See theological article "The Holy Spirit" at Acts 2.
2:5 God-fearing Jews. That is, devout Jews (cf. Lk 2:25; Ac 8:2; 22:12). No doubt many of these Jews had just come from foreign lands to reside temporarily in Jerusalem (v. 10) to celebrate Pentecost, while others had previously returned to take up permanent residence in the city. **from every nation under heaven.** Although this is hyperbole, Luke's expression associates this event with Old Testament prophecies that God would return the people of Israel from their exile to all nations in order to establish his kingdom (Dt 30:1–5). On this Pentecost many Jews believed and became the core of the people of God in the New Testament. In effect, Pentecost initiated the end of Israel's exile. The exile will be utterly finished when Christ returns.
2:6 each one heard . . . his own language. Some interpreters have taken this to mean that the miracle of tongues is in the hearing and not in the speaking. This seems unlikely because the apostles were accused of sounding as if they were intoxicated, probably indicating that some people heard languages they did not understand, but in any case indicating that the speakers sounded odd, while the hearers did not understand them clearly. Moreover, the Holy Spirit visibly gifted the apostles (vv. 3–4), not the crowd.
2:7 Utterly amazed. The crowd was amazed that Galileans, with their peculiar accent in speaking Aramaic and Greek, could by themselves manage to learn so many foreign languages.

The Holy Spirit: Do All Believers Have the Holy Spirit?

JESUS promised that he and the Father would send his disciples "another Counselor" (Jn 14:16; see also Jn 14:26; 15:26; 16:7). The word *Counselor* derives from the Greek word meaning one who gives support or acts as a helper, adviser, strengthener, encourager, ally and/or advocate. This Counselor is none other than the Holy Spirit, the third person of the Trinity (see theological article "The Trinity" at Jn 14).

The divinity of the Spirit appears in many ways. For example, Peter's declaration that lying to the Spirit is lying to God (Ac 5:3–4) attributes divinity to the Spirit. The close association of the Spirit with the Father and the Son in benedictions (2Co 13:14; Rev 1:4–6) and in the formula of baptism (Mt 28:19) confirms the Spirit's equality with the Father and the Son. That the Spirit is a sufficient substitute for Christ also indicates his divinity (Jn 16:7), as does his unique knowledge of the Father's mind (1Co 2:10–11). The Spirit, then, is "he," not "it," and he, along with the Father and the Son, must be obeyed, loved and adored.

Much confusion has arisen over the fact that Jesus said he would send the Spirit once he had ascended to the Father (Jn 16:7). Was the Spirit of God absent before this time? Was the Spirit's ministry unknown before this point in the New Testament?

To understand the New Testament ministry of the Spirit, it is essential to be aware that he ministered in the Old Testament period in ways that anticipated what was to come in the New Testament. He (1) brought order to the primeval chaos (e.g., Ge 1:2; Ps 33:6); (2) imparted revelation and wisdom (e.g., Dt 34:9; Mic 3:8); (3) fell upon special servants of God to enable them for service (e.g., Ex 31:2–6; Jdg 6:34; 15:14–15; Isa 11:2); and (4) brought about inward renewal in believers (e.g., Eze 36:26–27; cf. Ro 8:9–16). In these and similar ways, the Holy Spirit was revealed in the Old Testament as the power and presence of God with his people. He ministered to all of God's people and was the source of regeneration and holy living in all the faithful. But he also came in special, but very limited, ways to certain places and on certain people at particular times.

The New Testament era, however, is uniquely the age of the Spirit. One of the great expectations of Old Testament prophets was that in the last days, after Israel's exile had ended (see theological article "The Plan of the Ages" at Heb 7), God would extend his reign over all nations (Isa 2:2–5; Am 9:9–15). The glory of the Lord would one day reach from one end of the earth to the other (Pss 22:27; 48:10; 67:7; Isa 24:16). Consequently, it is not surprising that the prophet Joel predicted that in the last days the Spirit would be poured out on every class and race of people (Joel 2:28–32). This is one noteworthy way in which the Spirit's ministry in the Old Testament was less dramatic than in the New. In the Old Testament, only a select few were gifted in special ways to accomplish extraordinary tasks for God; in the New Testament, however, the Spirit gifts all believers (Ac 2:16ff.).

John the Baptist had foretold that Jesus would baptize with the Spirit (Mk 1:8; Jn 1:33), and Jesus repeated that promise (Ac 1:4–5). The outpouring of the Spirit at Pentecost began the final stages of God's special presence reaching the ends of the earth (Rev 21:1–5,23–24). Still, the work of the Spirit is not equally distributed over the entire human race, nor even over every individual within the church (1Co 12:13–30). Yet the Spirit's work is now spread much more widely than in the past, and all believers are gifted in some way (1Co 7:7; Eph 4:7; 1Pe 4:10). In this sense Jesus promised a greater distribution of the fullness of the Spirit when he promised "another Counselor" (Jn 14:16) who speaks (Ac 1:16; 8:29; 10:19; 11:12; 13:2; 28:25), teaches (Jn 14:26), witnesses (Jn 15:26), searches (1Co 2:10), determines (1Co 12:11), intercedes (Ro 8:26–27) and can be lied to (Ac 5:3) and grieved (Eph 4:30). The Spirit also enlightens us (Eph 1:17–18), regenerates us (Jn 3:5–8; Ro 8:9–11), leads and empowers us to holiness (Ro 8:14; Gal 5:16–18), transforms us (2Co 3:18; Gal 5:22–23), gives us assurance (Ro 8:16) and manifests himself in gifts for ministry (Ac 1:8; 1Co 12:4–11). All God's work in us, touching our hearts, our characters and our conduct, is accomplished by the Spirit, although aspects of it are sometimes ascribed to the Father and the Son, for whom the Spirit serves as executive.

Once the outpouring of the Spirit reached the Gentile world through the initial spread of the kingdom by the apostles, clearer distinctions were made between the ministries of the Spirit that were applied to all believers throughout the New Testament age (and, in many cases, in the Old Testament age) and those that were individualized and temporary. In the former class are the Spirit's indwelling (Ac 13:52; Ro 15:13; Eph 5:18), baptism (Mt 3:11; 28:19; Ac 1:5; 2:38; 11:16; 1Co 12:13) and sealing (2Co 1:21–22; Eph 1:13). In the latter class are the various ways he fills (Ro 12:6–8; Eph 4:8,11–13) and manifests himself (1Co 12:27–31) over time and from person to person.

The Holy Spirit's gifting is something every believer in the church should long and pray for (1Co 12:31; 14:1) in order to build up the church (1Co 12:7; 14:26). While not every claim of spiritual gifting is valid (Dt 18:20–22; Ac 19:13–16; 1Jn 4:1) or appropriately exercised (1Co 13:1–3; 14:6–19,27–31), we must not overreact to this fact by denying legitimate manifestations of the Spirit's power or by quenching his work and gifting in believers (Eph 4:30; 1Th 5:19–21). The Spirit of God is our foretaste of our future inheritance in Christ. We should long to see his ministry among us and to enjoy the fruit of the Spirit in our lives day by day (Gal 5:22–25).

2:9 [t]1Pe 1:1 [u]Ac 18:2 [v]Ac 16:6; Ro 16:5; 1Co 16:19; 2Co 1:8
2:10 [w]Ac 16:6; 18:23 [x]Ac 13:13; 15:38 [y]Mt 27:32
2:13 [z]1Co 14:23
2:15 [a]1Th 5:7
2:17 [b]Isa 44:3; Jn 7:37-39; Ac 10:45

them in his own native language? 9Parthians, Medes and Elamites; residents of Mesopotamia, Judea and Cappadocia,[t] Pontus[u] and Asia,[v] 10Phrygia[w] and Pamphylia,[x] Egypt
and the parts of Libya near Cyrene;[y] visitors from Rome 11(both Jews and converts to Judaism); Cretans and Arabs—we hear them declaring the wonders of God in our own
tongues!" 12Amazed and perplexed, they asked one another, "What does this mean?"
13Some, however, made fun of them and said, "They have had too much wine.[a]"[z]

Peter Addresses the Crowd

14Then Peter stood up with the Eleven, raised his voice and addressed the crowd: "Fellow Jews and all of you who live in Jerusalem, let me explain this to you; listen carefully to what I say. 15These men are not drunk, as you suppose. It's only nine in the morning![a] 16No, this is what was spoken by the prophet Joel:

17" 'In the last days, God says,
I will pour out my Spirit on all people.[b]

[a] *13* Or *sweet wine*

2:8–11 The list of people from 15 nations starts with one group to the east in the area of modern-day Iran and Iraq ("Parthians, Medes and Elamites [and] residents of Mesopotamia," where Jews had been taken captive to Assyria and Babylon). The list proceeds west to Judea, and then north to Asia Minor ("Cappadocia, Pontus and Asia, Phrygia and Pamphylia"), from there to North Africa ("Egypt and the parts of Libya near Cyrene"), then to Rome. Finally the list includes two widely separated areas, Arabia and the island of Crete (possibly a reference to Nabataean Jews), located to the east and south of Jerusalem. Although other Diaspora areas could have been named, Luke listed a sufficient number of representative nations from areas on all sides of Jerusalem and Judea (which as the center is mentioned fifth in the list), with an allusion to a heavy concentration of Jews having come from the east, and the rest from the north, west and south.

2:12 they asked one another. The Greek text reads "they all asked," which indicates that everyone in the crowd was amazed and perplexed, including those who made fun of the disciples and charged them with drunkenness (v. 13).

2:15 These men are not drunk. The masculine form for the word "these" need not be restricted to the 12 apostles; it could include the 120 (1:15). **only nine in the morning.** Literally, "It is the third hour." Counting the hours from 6:00 A.M. would make the time 9:00 A.M. It was customary to fast on feast days until at least the fourth hour. Thus the alleged drunkenness was most unlikely.

2:17–21 This is a quotation from the Greek Old Testament text of Joel 2:28–32 (Septuagint, Joel 3:1–5). Joel spoke authoritatively as a prophet of God, and Peter stated that what Joel said was God's Word. The words "In the last days" (cf. Isa 2:2; Hos 3:5; Mic 4:1; 2Ti 3:1) are Peter's way of associating the Hebrew and Greek words of

Countries of People Mentioned at Pentecost

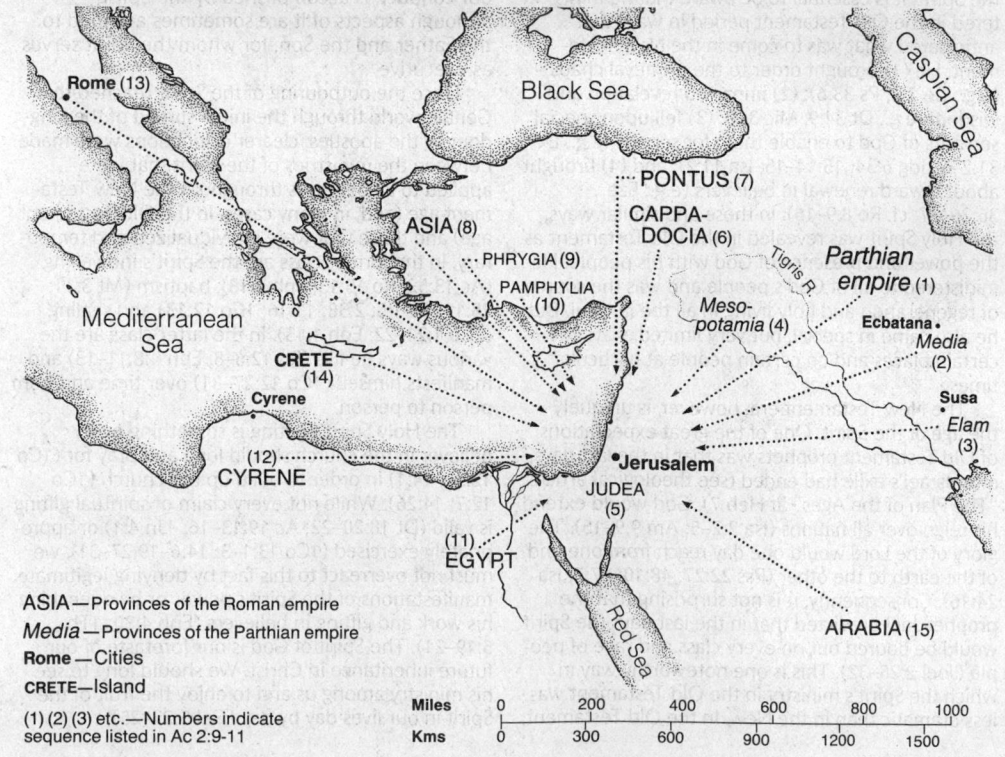

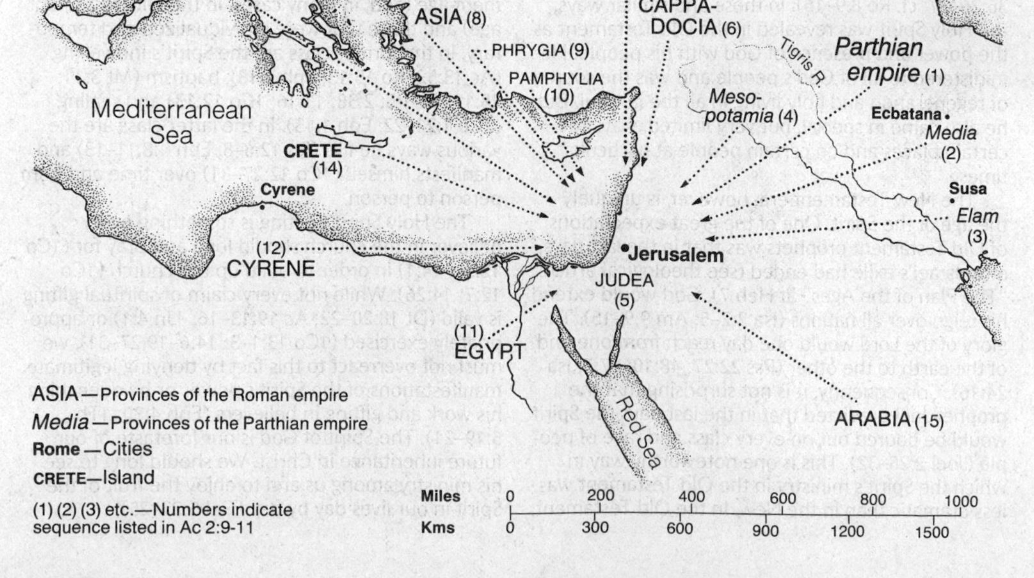

Your sons and daughters will prophesy,[c]
your young men will see visions,
your old men will dream dreams.
18 Even on my servants, both men and women,
I will pour out my Spirit in those days,
and they will prophesy.[d]
19 I will show wonders in the heaven above
and signs on the earth below,
blood and fire and billows of smoke.
20 The sun will be turned to darkness
and the moon to blood[e]
before the coming of the great and glorious day of the Lord.
21 And everyone who calls
on the name of the Lord will be saved.'[a][f]

22 "Men of Israel, listen to this: Jesus of Nazareth was a man accredited by God to
you by miracles, wonders and signs,[g] which God did among you through him,[h] as you
yourselves know. 23 This man was handed over to you by God's set purpose and foreknowledge;[i] and you, with the help of wicked men,[b] put him to death by nailing him
to the cross.[j] 24 But God raised him from the dead,[k] freeing him from the agony of
death, because it was impossible for death to keep its hold on him.[l] 25 David said about
him:

"'I saw the Lord always before me.
Because he is at my right hand,
I will not be shaken.
26 Therefore my heart is glad and my tongue rejoices;
my body also will live in hope,
27 because you will not abandon me to the grave,
nor will you let your Holy One see decay.[m]
28 You have made known to me the paths of life;
you will fill me with joy in your presence.'[c]

29 "Brothers, I can tell you confidently that the patriarch[n] David died and was buried,[o]
and his tomb is here[p] to this day. 30 But he was a prophet and knew that God had promised him on oath that he would place one of his descendants on his throne.[q] 31 Seeing
what was ahead, he spoke of the resurrection of the Christ,[d] that he was not abandoned
to the grave, nor did his body see decay.[r] 32 God has raised this Jesus to life,[s] and we are
all witnesses[t] of the fact. 33 Exalted[u] to the right hand of God,[v] he has received from the
Father[w] the promised Holy Spirit[x] and has poured out[y] what you now see and hear.
34 For David did not ascend to heaven, and yet he said,

2:17 [c]Ac 21:9
2:18 [d]Ac 21:9-12
2:20 [e]Mt 24:29
2:21 [f]Ro 10:13
2:22 [g]Jn 4:48; Ac 10:38 [h]Jn 3:2
2:23 [i]Lk 22:22; Ac 3:18; 4:28 [j]Lk 24:20; Ac 3:13
2:24 [k]ver 32; 1Co 6:14; 2Co 4:14; Eph 1:20; Col 2:12; Heb 13:20; 1Pe 1:21 [l]Jn 20:9
2:27 [m]ver 31; Ac 13:35
2:29 [n]Ac 7:8,9 [o]1Ki 2:10; Ac 13:36 [p]Ne 3:16
2:30 [q]2Sa 7:12; Ps 132:11
2:31 [r]Ps 16:10
2:32 [s]ver 24 [t]Ac 1:8
2:33 [u]Php 2:9 [v]Mk 16:19 [w]Ac 1:4 [x]Jn 7:39; 14:26 [y]Ac 10:45

[a] *21* Joel 2:28–32 [b] *23* Or *of those not having the law* (that is, Gentiles) [c] *28* Psalm 16:8–11
[d] *31* Or *Messiah.* "The Christ" (Greek) and "the Messiah" (Hebrew) both mean "the Anointed One"; also in verse 36.

Joel 2:28 ("and afterward"). Peter interpreted "and afterward" as referring to the days of the new covenant in contrast to the former days of the old covenant. See *BC* 27; *HC* 32.

2:22 Jesus of Nazareth. This title is used elsewhere by Luke (Lk 18:37; 24:19; Ac 6:14; 10:38; 22:8; 26:9). In the sermon that follows, Peter emphasized these important facts about Jesus: his death (v. 23), his bodily resurrection (vv. 24–32), his exaltation (v. 33), his coronation (vv. 34,36) and the conquest at his second coming (v. 35). **accredited by God . . . by miracles, wonders and signs.** Although the fact that Jesus came from Nazareth was a stumbling block (cf. Jn 1:46), God amply demonstrated that Jesus was the Messiah through the attestation of miracles.

2:23–33 See *WCF* 8.4; *WLC* 38,50,52,54; *WSC* 27; *BC* 9,18.

2:23 by God's set purpose and foreknowledge. Although wicked men, both Jews and Gentiles (4:27–28), had of their own will put Jesus to death, their actions were ordained within the determined purpose of God (cf. 2Ch 25:16; Jer 21:10; Da 11:36; Ac 17:26) and brought about through God's continual providential government. Although God sovereignly ordained the death of his Son, he holds people responsible for perpetrating the crime of crucifying Jesus (3:17–18; 4:27–28; 13:27). God ordains the means as well as the ends of human events without violating human freedom and responsibility. The Jews could not absolve themselves by blaming Jesus' death on the Romans; they themselves had asked the Romans to crucify Jesus. Peter taught that the Jews would be held accountable (3:15; 4:10; 5:30; 10:39). **nailing him to the cross.** Luke again emphasized that Jesus experienced Roman crucifixion. See *WCF* 3.1; 5.2; 5.4; *BC* 13,21.

2:24 freeing him from the agony of death. Although he really died (Jn 19:30), Jesus' body did not experience chemical decomposition, as Peter's quotation of Psalm 16:8–11 demonstrates (vv. 25–28). See *WLC* 46,52.

2:25–28 David said. In Psalm 16 David was speaking in part about his own human experience and suffering, but in the verses quoted here he was ultimately talking about "the Lord" Jesus (v. 25), God's Holy One whose body did not see decay (v. 27).

2:33 Exalted to the right hand of God. God's plan went beyond the resurrection of his Son. Christ also had to be exalted to the position he had occupied with the Father from eternity (Jn 17:5). **he has received from the Father . . . Holy Spirit . . . poured out.** The doctrine of the Trinity is implied. Peter showed how the Father (vv. 32–33) worked in the life, death, resurrection and exaltation of his Son Jesus and how the Holy Spirit produced the miracle of causing his servants to speak in tongues. The work of the Spirit is linked closely to the relation and purpose of the Father and the Son. See *HC* 51.

2:35 [z]Ps 110:1; Mt 22:44
2:36 [a]Lk 2:11
2:37 [b]Lk 3:10,12,14
2:38 [c]Ac 8:12,16,36, 38; 22:16 [d]Lk 24:47; Ac 3:19
2:39 [e]Isa 44:3 [f]Ac 10:45; Eph 2:13
2:40 [g]Dt 32:5
2:42 [h]Ac 1:14
2:43 [i]Ac 5:12
2:44 [j]Ac 4:32
2:45 [k]Mt 19:21
2:46 [l]Lk 24:53; Ac 5:21, 42 [m]Ac 20:7
2:47 [n]Ro 14:18 [o]ver 41; Ac 5:14
3:1 [p]Lk 22:8 [q]Ac 2:46 [r]Ps 55:17
3:2 [s]Ac 14:8

" 'The Lord said to my Lord:
"Sit at my right hand
35 until I make your enemies
a footstool for your feet." '[a] [z]

36 "Therefore let all Israel be assured of this: God has made this Jesus, whom you crucified, both Lord and Christ." [a]
37 When the people heard this, they were cut to the heart and said to Peter and the
other apostles, "Brothers, what shall we do?" [b]
38 Peter replied, "Repent and be baptized,[c] every one of you, in the name of Jesus
Christ for the forgiveness of your sins.[d] And you will receive the gift of the Holy Spirit.
39 The promise is for you and your children[e] and for all who are far off[f]—for all whom the
Lord our God will call."
40 With many other words he warned them; and he pleaded with them, "Save yourselves from this corrupt generation."[g] 41 Those who accepted his message were baptized,
and about three thousand were added to their number that day.

The Fellowship of the Believers

42 They devoted themselves to the apostles' teaching and to the fellowship, to the
breaking of bread and to prayer.[h] 43 Everyone was filled with awe, and many wonders and
miraculous signs were done by the apostles.[i] 44 All the believers were together and had
everything in common.[j] 45 Selling their possessions and goods, they gave to anyone as he
had need.[k] 46 Every day they continued to meet together in the temple courts.[l] They
broke bread[m] in their homes and ate together with glad and sincere hearts, 47 praising
God and enjoying the favor of all the people.[n] And the Lord added to their number[o] daily those who were being saved.

Peter Heals the Crippled Beggar

3 One day Peter and John[p] were going up to the temple[q] at the time of prayer—at
three in the afternoon.[r] 2 Now a man crippled from birth[s] was being carried to the

a *35* Psalm 110:1

2:36 In this climactic statement Peter stressed not only that Jesus is God's Messiah of the Old Testament (Isa 11:1; Lk 4:18–21; Ac 3:18,20; 4:26; 5:42), but also that he is the exalted Lord (Ro 10:9; Php 2:9–11) and the conquering King (1Co 15:24–25; Rev 19:16). See *WCF* 8.3.
2:37–39 See *WCF* 10.3; 28.4; *WLC* 27,155,166,172,177; *WSC* 31,87,95; *HC* 74.
2:38 Repent and be baptized. Repentance (turning from sin in sorrow) and baptism were important parts of the ministries of both John the Baptist (Mt 3:1; Mk 1:4) and Jesus (Mt 4:17; 11:20; Lk 13:3,5). They are also essential parts of the pattern for the church's preaching and teaching (Mt 28:18–19). **in the name of Jesus Christ.** Probably a summary of Matthew 28:18–19 (baptism in the name of the Father, Son and Holy Spirit). Only Jesus was mentioned here, since Peter's sermon had to do with Jesus and his ministry. **for the forgiveness of your sins.** Baptism is a sign and seal of spiritual cleansing that the Spirit effects through the forgiveness of sins (Tit 3:5). **the gift of the Holy Spirit.** The gift of the indwelling person of the Holy Spirit, as well as the gifts of forgiveness (Eph 1:7) and empowerment for ministry. Note that even in the context of the Pentecost miracle Peter did not speak of receiving the gift of tongues as a universal or necessary gift. The gifts of forgiveness and the indwelling Holy Spirit are to be thought of as essential for producing the "fruit" of the Spirit in the lives of believers (Gal 5:22–23) and for exercising the gifts that the Spirit chooses to give at different times to different believers (1Co 12:4–11). See *WCF* 28.6; *WLC* 162,166,167; *WSC* 95; *BC* 34; *HC* 66,69,73.
2:39 Peter proclaimed that salvation for the forgiveness of sins through God's Messiah is promised to the Jews who hear his message, to their covenant children and to all those far off (i.e., the Gentiles; Eph 2:11–13). Here again is the message of Acts: The gospel is for Jews and Gentiles. **for all whom the Lord our God will call.** Salvation is based on God's choice and calling (Jn 6:37; Eph 1:4–5). See *WCF* 25.2; *WLC* 62,63; *BC* 34.
2:41 See *WCF* 28.3; 28.6; *WLC* 155.
▪ **2:42–47** *The Emerging Church.* Luke closed this section on the outpouring of the Spirit with a summation of the practices of the church in Jerusalem. The first followers of Christ were somewhat unique, but their faithful practices stand as a hallmark of what believers everywhere should seek in the church. See *HC* 54,103,123.
2:42 the apostles' teaching . . . fellowship . . . the breaking of bread . . . prayer. A summary of the essential elements needed in Christian discipleship. These are elements the apostles had learned from their experience with Jesus: his teaching about his person and work (Mt 16:18–19; Lk 24:46) and their Christian responsibility as his followers (Mt 5–7); the fellowship of Christ with his disciples (Jn 13); the breaking of bread, which commonly included the Lord's Supper (Mt 26:17–30); and his prayer life for and with the disciples (Mt 6:5–13; Lk 11:1–13; Jn 17). See *WCF* 21.5; 21.6; 26.2; *WLC* 63,108,154,174,175; *WSC* 50,88; *BC* 35.
2:44–47 See *WCF* 26.2; *WLC* 154,171,175; *WSC* 88.
2:44 All the believers were together. This demonstrates the unity of the Spirit that Paul advocated (Eph 4:3).
2:45 Selling their possessions. Unified in the Spirit, the believers were attuned to the physical needs of others and voluntarily (4:34; 5:4) gave to meet those needs (4:32).
2:46 broke bread in their homes. This refers to the common daily meals shared in the homes. See *WCF* 26.2; *WLC* 175.
2:47 the Lord added. The church belongs to the Lord, and he is the One who sovereignly builds his church (Mt 16:18; 1Co 3:9). See *WCF* 25.2; *BC* 16.
▪ **3:1—7:60** *The Apostolic Witness in Jerusalem.* Having touched on the foundational events surrounding Pentecost, Luke turned to a number of events that took place as the apostolic witness spread to many in the vicinity of Jerusalem. These accounts report how the apostles succeeded in the first stage of their commission to spread the gospel to the whole world (see notes on 8:1—11:18; 13:1—28:31).
▪ **3:1–26** *Peter's Temple Miracle and Sermon.* Peter did his first miracle and preached his second sermon at the appropriate place: the temple. The temple had been the central institution of Israel's faith because it was the place where God met with his people and forgave their sins. As an apostle, Peter brought the greater presence of God in Christ to the temple by healing and announcing the gospel. Luke reported this event to demonstrate that in many ways Christ is the final temple of God (cf. Rev. 21:22).
3:1 the temple. The temple courts, and particularly that part near the gate called Beautiful (v. 2), which was possibly the so-called Nicanor Gate made of Corinthian bronze. The exact location of this gate is uncertain. It may have been located on the west side of the court of women leading into the court of Israel, or on the east side of the court of women as an entrance, or it could have

temple gate[t] called Beautiful, where he was put every day to beg[u] from those going into
the temple courts. 3When he saw Peter and John about to enter, he asked them for money. 4Peter looked straight at him, as did John. Then Peter said, "Look at us!" 5So the man
gave them his attention, expecting to get something from them.
6Then Peter said, "Silver or gold I do not have, but what I have I give you. In the name
of Jesus Christ of Nazareth,[v] walk." 7Taking him by the right hand, he helped him up, and
instantly the man's feet and ankles became strong. 8He jumped to his feet and began to
walk. Then he went with them into the temple courts, walking and jumping,[w] and
praising God. 9When all the people[x] saw him walking and praising God, 10they recognized him as the same man who used to sit begging at the temple gate called Beautiful,[y]
and they were filled with wonder and amazement at what had happened to him.

Peter Speaks to the Onlookers

11While the beggar held on to Peter and John,[z] all the people were astonished and
came running to them in the place called Solomon's Colonnade.[a] 12When Peter saw this,
he said to them: "Men of Israel, why does this surprise you? Why do you stare at us as if
by our own power or godliness we had made this man walk? 13The God of Abraham,
Isaac and Jacob, the God of our fathers,[b] has glorified his servant Jesus. You handed him
over to be killed, and you disowned him before Pilate,[c] though he had decided to let him
go.[d] 14You disowned the Holy[e] and Righteous One[f] and asked that a murderer be released to you.[g] 15You killed the author of life, but God raised him from the dead.[h] We are
witnesses of this. 16By faith in the name of Jesus, this man whom you see and know was
made strong. It is Jesus' name and the faith that comes through him that has given this
complete healing to him, as you can all see.
17"Now, brothers, I know that you acted in ignorance,[i] as did your leaders.[j] 18But this
is how God fulfilled what he had foretold[k] through all the prophets,[l] saying that his
Christ[a] would suffer.[m] 19Repent, then, and turn to God, so that your sins may be wiped
out,[n] that times of refreshing may come from the Lord, 20and that he may send the
Christ, who has been appointed for you—even Jesus. 21He must remain in heaven[o] until the time comes for God to restore everything,[p] as he promised long ago through his
holy prophets.[q] 22For Moses said, 'The Lord your God will raise up for you a prophet like
me from among your own people; you must listen to everything he tells you.[r] 23Anyone
who does not listen to him will be completely cut off from among his people.'[b][s]
24"Indeed, all the prophets[t] from Samuel on, as many as have spoken, have foretold
these days. 25And you are heirs[u] of the prophets and of the covenant[v] God made with
your fathers. He said to Abraham, 'Through your offspring all peoples on earth will be
blessed.'[c][w] 26When God raised up[x] his servant, he sent him first[y] to you to bless you by
turning each of you from your wicked ways."

Peter and John Before the Sanhedrin

4 The priests and the captain of the temple guard[z] and the Sadducees[a] came up to
Peter and John while they were speaking to the people. 2They were greatly dis-

3:2 [t]Lk 16:20 [u]Jn 9:8
3:6 [v]ver 16; Ac 4:10
3:8 [w]Ac 14:10
3:9 [x]Ac 4:16,21
3:10 [y]ver 2
3:11 [z]Lk 22:8 [a]Jn 10:23; Ac 5:12
3:13 [b]Ac 5:30 [c]Mt 27:2 [d]Lk 23:4
3:14 [e]Mk 1:24; Ac 4:27 [f]Ac 7:52 [g]Mk 15:11; Lk 23:18-25
3:15 [h]Ac 2:24
3:17 [i]Lk 23:34 [j]Ac 13:27
3:18 [k]Ac 2:23 [l]Lk 24:27 [m]Ac 17:2,3; 26:22, 23
3:19 [n]Ac 2:38
3:21 [o]Ac 1:11 [p]Mt 17:11 [q]Lk 1:70
3:22 [r]Dt 18:15,18; Ac 7:37
3:23 [s]Dt 18:19
3:24 [t]Lk 24:27
3:25 [u]Ac 2:39 [v]Ro 9:4,5 [w]Ge 12:3; 22:18; 26:4; 28:14
3:26 [x]ver 22; Ac 2:24 [y]Ac 13:46; Ro 1:16
4:1 [z]Lk 22:4 [a]Mt 3:7

[a] *18* Or *Messiah*; also in verse 20 [b] *23* Deut. 18:15,18,19 [c] *25* Gen. 22:18; 26:4

been the gate located east of the court of women on the east wall of the temple platform along Solomon's Colonnade (cf. Jn 10:23).
3:3 Peter and John about to enter. Being Jewish men, Peter and John could walk through the court of women into the court of Israel, but Gentiles were restricted to the court of the Gentiles.
3:11 Solomon's Colonnade. See note on John 10:23. Jesus taught on occasion at this location (Jn 10:23).
3:13 The God of Abraham, Isaac and Jacob. Appealing to the patriarchs was important in the sermons of Christ's servants (Ac 7:32; 13:17).
3:14–15 See *WLC* 56.
3:14 disowned the Holy and Righteous One. The phrase "the Holy One" appears a number of times in the Old Testament with reference to God. The phrase "the Holy One of Israel" occurs in Isaiah 1:4 and 5:24 (cf. Lk 1:35). Isaiah also speaks of God as "the Righteous One" (Isa 24:16; cf. Ac 7:52; 22:14). In applying this description to Jesus, Peter implied the deity of Christ.
3:16 the name of Jesus. The name of a person represented what that individual was and did (cf. Ac 4:12).
3:18 foretold through all the prophets. See Luke 24:26–27, 44–47. Peter could have cited Old Testament passages (e.g., Dt 18:15 [quoted in v. 22]; Pss 2:1–12; 16:8–11; 22:1–31; Isa 53). Compare 1 Peter 1:10–11.
3:19–21 times of refreshing . . . send the Christ . . . remain in heaven . . . God to restore everything. These phrases seem to refer to the second coming of the Messiah. See *HC* 47.
3:19 Repent . . . turn to God. Peter's sermon illustrates the inseparability of repentance, or turning aside in sorrow from sin (negative), and turning to God in faith (positive). The calls to both repentance and faith are consistent elements of the apostolic proclamation (2:38; 17:30; 20:21). **sins . . . wiped out.** In God's providence and order, repentance and faith result in forgiveness and removal of sins. See *WCF* 33.2.
3:20–24 See *WCF* 8.1; 29.6; 32.1; *WLC* 34,42,43,53,86,170; *WSC* 23; *BC* 19,35; *HC* 31.
3:25 He said to Abraham, "Through your offspring . . ." As a climax, Peter referred to the great patriarch and prophet Abraham, through whom God blessed all peoples on Earth by sending Abraham's "offspring" (singular in Greek; Gal 3:16), the Messiah.
■ **4:1–31** *Persecution From the Sanhedrin.* Luke alternated between reporting persecution against the church (4:1–31; 5:12–42) and reporting events within the Christian community (4:32—5:11; 6:1–7). From the very beginning, the Jewish religious authorities persecuted followers of Christ. They forbade Peter and John to preach the gospel, but the apostles showed the Spirit's power by refusing to submit. Their courage and faith stand as models for all believers as they face opposition.
4:1 The priests. There were a number of priests who, in serving

turbed because the apostles were teaching the people and proclaiming in Jesus the resurrection of the dead.[b] 3 They seized Peter and John, and because it was evening, they
put them in jail[c] until the next day. 4 But many who heard the message believed, and the
number of men grew[d] to about five thousand.
5 The next day the rulers,[e] elders and teachers of the law met in Jerusalem. 6 Annas the
high priest was there, and so were Caiaphas,[f] John, Alexander and the other men of the
high priest's family. 7 They had Peter and John brought before them and began to question them: "By what power or what name did you do this?"
8 Then Peter, filled with the Holy Spirit, said to them: "Rulers and elders of the people![g] 9 If we are being called to account today for an act of kindness shown to a cripple[h]
and are asked how he was healed, 10 then know this, you and all the people of Israel: It
is by the name of Jesus Christ of Nazareth, whom you crucified but whom God raised
from the dead,[i] that this man stands before you healed. 11 He is

> " 'the stone you builders rejected,
> which has become the capstone.'[a][b][j]

12 Salvation is found in no one else, for there is no other name under heaven given to men
by which we must be saved."[k]
13 When they saw the courage of Peter and John[l] and realized that they were unschooled, ordinary men,[m] they were astonished and they took note that these men had
been with Jesus. 14 But since they could see the man who had been healed standing there
with them, there was nothing they could say. 15 So they ordered them to withdraw from
the Sanhedrin[n] and then conferred together. 16 "What are we going to do with these
men?"[o] they asked. "Everybody living in Jerusalem knows they have done an outstanding miracle,[p] and we cannot deny it. 17 But to stop this thing from spreading any further
among the people, we must warn these men to speak no longer to anyone in this name."
18 Then they called them in again and commanded them not to speak or teach at all
in the name of Jesus.[q] 19 But Peter and John replied, "Judge for yourselves whether it is
right in God's sight to obey you rather than God.[r] 20 For we cannot help speaking about
what we have seen and heard."

[a] *11* Or *cornerstone* [b] *11* Psalm 118:22

4:2 [b]Ac 17:18
4:3 [c]Ac 5:18
4:4 [d]Ac 2:41
4:5 [e]Lk 23:13
4:6 [f]Mt 26:3; Lk 3:2
4:8 [g]ver 5; Lk 23:13
4:9 [h]Ac 3:6
4:10 [i]Ac 2:24
4:11 [j]Ps 118:22; Isa 28:16; Mt 21:42
4:12 [k]Mt 1:21; Ac 10:43; 1Ti 2:5
4:13 [l]Lk 22:8 [m]Mt 11:25
4:15 [n]Mt 5:22
4:16 [o]Jn 11:47 [p]Ac 3:6-10
4:18 [q]Ac 5:40
4:19 [r]Ac 5:29

their allotted week's temple service (Lk 1:8,23), were not far from Solomon's Colonnade and were able to hear Peter's declarations about Jesus as the Messiah. Alarmed at what they considered dangerous teaching against Jewish authority, they probably alerted the captain of the temple guard. This captain was the commander of the temple police force and a member of one of the important priestly families. The priests also alerted the Sadducees, who were from the priestly line. The Sadducees had held the high priesthood (Lk 22:4,52; Ac 5:24) from the time of the Maccabean revolt (168–165 B.C.) and held other prominent positions in the Sanhedrin, the Jewish council.

4:2 proclaiming in Jesus the resurrection of the dead. The Sadducees were greatly distressed because the apostles were teaching the people (an official prerogative that belonged to Sadducees, Pharisees and teachers of the law) and because they were preaching that Jesus' resurrection from the dead proved that a general resurrection would also occur (1Co 15:12–20). The Sadducees, in contrast to the Pharisees, did not believe in bodily resurrection (23:6–8). See chart "Jewish Sects" at Matthew 23.

4:3 because it was evening, they put them in jail. This action was necessary because the temple sacrifices had been concluded and the temple gates were closed. Official actions by the Sanhedrin would have to be taken the next day.

4:4 Despite the persecution, the church grew from 3,000 on the day of Pentecost to 5,000. The emphasis here is on men (Greek, *andres*), because in that ancient culture the men would have gathered together by themselves to hear the message and the women would have been by themselves in the court of women (cf. Jn 6:10). In modern Israel the men and the women are separated in their worship at the Wailing Wall.

4:5 rulers, elders and teachers of the law. These groups constituted the Jewish religious council, the Sanhedrin. Luke 22:66 describes this body as "the council of the elders of the people, both the chief priests and teachers of the law." This body included the high priest, other members of his family (v. 6), other priests who were members of the Sadducean party and other teachers, including prominent Pharisees (Mt 27:62) such as Nicodemus (who was called a ruler of the Jews and "Israel's teacher"; Jn 3:1,10) and Gamaliel (5:34; 22:3).

4:6 The men listed in this verse constituted what might be called the executive committee of the council. Caiaphas was the official high priest (Jn 18:13), but his father-in-law Annas is here called the high priest. Annas had been high priest until the Romans deposed him in A.D. 15. But because the office was held for life, many Jews probably still regarded him as high priest. As a result, he was the power behind the office. John possibly refers to Jonathan, son of Annas, who was appointed high priest in A.D. 36, or to Jonathan ben Zaccai, who became president of the Great Synagogue after the fall of Jerusalem. Nothing is known of Alexander.

4:7 By . . . what name . . . ? "By the name of Jesus Christ of Nazareth" (v. 10). There is frequent emphasis on the name of Jesus or the name of the Lord (stressing the person and work of the Lord) in Acts (2:21,38; 3:16; 4:10,12; 8:16; 9:15,28; 15:26; 16:18).

4:8 filled with the Holy Spirit. See 2:4, as well as Ephesians 5:18.

4:10–12 See *WLC* 121; *HC* 29.

4:11 stone . . . rejected . . . the capstone. In Acts, apologetics in defense of the gospel frequently include references to the fulfillment of Old Testament prophecy. Here Psalm 118:22 is quoted (also cited in Mt 21:42; 1Pe 2:7; cf. Ro 9:33). The capstone is the last, dominant stone that completes the building. The Greek word translated "capstone" here may also be translated "cornerstone," a dominant stone of the foundation.

4:12 no other name. Just as the name of Jesus had been the only hope for physical healing of the man crippled from birth, so that name is the only hope for the spiritual healing of humankind. This exclusive and total reliance upon Christ for salvation is the clear teaching of both Jesus and the New Testament generally (Jn 14:6; 1Ti 2:5). See *WCF* 10.3; 10.4; *WLC* 60,72; *BC* 21,23,26; *HC* 2.

4:13 unschooled. In the courage and ready witness of Peter and John, we see a fulfillment of Christ's promise to the disciples (Mt 10:19–20). Both the courage and the knowledge of the unschooled Galilean fishermen astonished the Sanhedrin. In taking note that "these men had been with Jesus," the council no doubt remembered how Jesus, who was also without formal rabbinic training, had surprised them with his teaching (Lk 2:46–47; Jn 7:15).

4:17–18 See *WLC* 113,130; *BC* 28.

4:19 obey you rather than God. The duty of religious worship and speech supersedes the rights of the state. The duty of a Christian conscience before God in proclaiming the gospel supersedes the rights of a religious court. The leader of the state is a servant

21 After further threats they let them go. They could not decide how to punish them,
because all the people[s] were praising God[t] for what had happened. 22 For the man who
was miraculously healed was over forty years old.

The Believers' Prayer

23 On their release, Peter and John went back to their own people and reported all that
the chief priests and elders had said to them. 24 When they heard this, they raised their
voices together in prayer to God. "Sovereign Lord," they said, "you made the heaven and
the earth and the sea, and everything in them. 25 You spoke by the Holy Spirit through
the mouth of your servant, our father David:[u]

" 'Why do the nations rage
and the peoples plot in vain?
26 The kings of the earth take their stand
and the rulers gather together
against the Lord
and against his Anointed One.[a][b][v]

27 Indeed Herod[w] and Pontius Pilate[x] met together with the Gentiles and the people[c] of
Israel in this city to conspire against your holy servant Jesus,[y] whom you anointed.
28 They did what your power and will had decided beforehand should happen.[z] 29 Now,
Lord, consider their threats and enable your servants to speak your word with great boldness.[a] 30 Stretch out your hand to heal and perform miraculous signs and wonders[b]
through the name of your holy servant Jesus."[c]

31 After they prayed, the place where they were meeting was shaken.[d] And they were
all filled with the Holy Spirit and spoke the word of God boldly.[e]

The Believers Share Their Possessions

32 All the believers were one in heart and mind. No one claimed that any of his possessions was his own, but they shared everything they had.[f] 33 With great power the apostles continued to testify[g] to the resurrection[h] of the Lord Jesus, and much grace was
upon them all. 34 There were no needy persons among them. For from time to time those
who owned lands or houses sold them,[i] brought the money from the sales 35 and put it
at the apostles' feet,[j] and it was distributed to anyone as he had need.[k]
36 Joseph, a Levite from Cyprus, whom the apostles called Barnabas[l] (which means

4:21 [s]Ac 5:26 [t]Mt 9:8
4:25 [u]Ac 1:16
4:26 [v]Ps 2:1,2; Da 9:25; Lk 4:18; Ac 10:38; Heb 1:9
4:27 [w]Mt 14:1 [x]Mt 27:2; Lk 23:12 [y]ver 30
4:28 [z]Ac 2:23
4:29 [a]ver 13,31; Ac 9:27; 14:3; Php 1:14
4:30 [b]Jn 4:48 [c]ver 27
4:31 [d]Ac 2:2 [e]ver 29
4:32 [f]Ac 2:44
4:33 [g]Lk 24:48 [h]Ac 1:22
4:34 [i]Mt 19:21; Ac 2:45
4:35 [j]ver 37; Ac 5:2 [k]Ac 2:45; 6:1
4:36 [l]Ac 9:27; 1Co 9:6

[a] *26* That is, Christ or Messiah [b] *26* Psalm 2:1,2 [c] *27* The Greek is plural.

and civil arm ordained by God to maintain peace and order (Ro 13:1–7). See *WCF* 20.2; *BC* 7,28,36.

4:24 in prayer to God. This activity was a natural result of the apostles' training with Jesus and of the habits they had formed (2:42). **Sovereign Lord.** Expresses the total creative power and control of the Lord over all of his physical creation and over the affairs of people (cf. vv. 25–26; Jer 10:12). See *HC* 26.

4:25 the Holy Spirit through the mouth of . . . David. A succinct summary of verbal inspiration. The Scripture writers spoke and wrote under the guidance of the Spirit (2Pe 1:21).

4:27–28 See *WCF* 3.1; 5.4; *WLC* 6

4:27 Herod and Pontius Pilate . . . Gentiles . . . people of Israel. The believers properly understood that both Jews and Gentiles were responsible for Jesus' crucifixion. The rulers involved (v. 26) were Herod Antipas, the son of Herod the Great and tetrarch (i.e., subordinate ruler under the Romans) of Galilee and Perea (Lk 3:1; 23:6–7), and Pontius Pilate, the Roman procurator (governor) of the area later referred to as Palestine, from A.D. 26–36 (Lk 3:1; 23:1–24). **the people of Israel.** The chief priests and elders had persuaded the people to reject Jesus and ask for the release of Barabbas (Mt 27:20–26).

4:28 what your power and will had decided beforehand. Here we have a clear affirmation that nothing—not even the wrongful death of God's Son—happens apart from God's sovereign will and control. The certainty of God's plan for the world is established by his sovereign will and ensured by his almighty power. The early chapters of Acts also teach the compatibility of divine sovereignty and human responsibility. While Jesus' murderers had acted in accord with the divine purpose, they were morally responsible agents and were held accountable (3:15). See *BC* 13.

4:29–30 See *WLC* 191.

4:29 This prayer of the believing community illustrates the way in which the church should be empowered and encouraged by God's sovereignty. In the face of the threat of physical violence, the church affirmed God's control of the situation (v. 28) and, encouraged by this, petitioned for greater boldness. **Lord.** The Greek word for "Lord" is *kurios*, used in the Septuagint (the Greek OT) to translate the divine name "Yahweh." It is used in the New Testament to refer both to God in general and to Christ specifically (2:36; 7:31).

■ **4:32—5:11** *Community Life Among Believers.* Luke turned toward internal affairs within the church in Jerusalem. For the most part, the believers in Jerusalem were richly blessed and harmonious because the apostles preached with the Spirit's power. Yet they also had to demonstrate the Spirit's power to judge when trouble rose within the Christian community. The apostles displayed unique empowerment in these events. Similar mixtures of harmony and trials and of blessing and judgment characterize the church in all ages.

4:32–35 Because the believers were "one in heart" (v. 32), they were conscious of the needy in the church; consequently, they helped by selling land and giving the proceeds to the apostles to meet those needs. This Christian giving was proportional to the real need. It was a voluntary action, not one of compulsion (5:4). See *BC* 27.

4:33 the resurrection of the Lord Jesus. The crowning proof of the salvation accomplished in Jesus Christ was Jesus' resurrection from the dead. The apostles, as chief witnesses, had to testify about this redemptive event (1:22). **grace.** In witnessing and living.

4:36 Joseph, a Levite . . . Barnabas. In the Old Testament, the Levites had not received an inheritance of land as the other tribes had, although the Levites were allotted towns (Jos 21). However, by New Testament times, a Levite such as Joseph Barnabas may well have been able to own land, especially in a country outside the Holy Land, such as Cyprus. On the other hand, the land may have belonged to his wife. This introduction of Barnabas lays the foundation for further reference to this influential believer in the lives of Jewish and Gentile churches and of Paul himself.

Son of Encouragement), 37 sold a field he owned and brought the money and put it at the
apostles' feet.[m]

Ananias and Sapphira

5 Now a man named Ananias, together with his wife Sapphira, also sold a piece of
property. 2 With his wife's full knowledge he kept back part of the money for himself, but brought the rest and put it at the apostles' feet.[n]
3 Then Peter said, "Ananias, how is it that Satan[o] has so filled your heart[p] that you
have lied to the Holy Spirit[q] and have kept for yourself some of the money you received
for the land? 4 Didn't it belong to you before it was sold? And after it was sold, wasn't the
money at your disposal? What made you think of doing such a thing? You have not lied
to men but to God."
5 When Ananias heard this, he fell down and died.[r] And great fear[s] seized all who
heard what had happened. 6 Then the young men came forward, wrapped up his body,[t]
and carried him out and buried him.
7 About three hours later his wife came in, not knowing what had happened. 8 Peter
asked her, "Tell me, is this the price you and Ananias got for the land?"
"Yes," she said, "that is the price."[u]
9 Peter said to her, "How could you agree to test the Spirit of the Lord?[v] Look! The feet
of the men who buried your husband are at the door, and they will carry you out also."
10 At that moment she fell down at his feet and died.[w] Then the young men came in
and, finding her dead, carried her out and buried her beside her husband. 11 Great fear[x]
seized the whole church and all who heard about these events.

The Apostles Heal Many

12 The apostles performed many miraculous signs and wonders[y] among the people.
And all the believers used to meet together[z] in Solomon's Colonnade.[a] 13 No one else
dared join them, even though they were highly regarded by the people.[b] 14 Nevertheless,
more and more men and women believed in the Lord and were added to their number.
15 As a result, people brought the sick into the streets and laid them on beds and mats
so that at least Peter's shadow might fall on some of them as he passed by.[c] 16 Crowds
gathered also from the towns around Jerusalem, bringing their sick and those tormented by evil[a] spirits, and all of them were healed.[d]

The Apostles Persecuted

17 Then the high priest and all his associates, who were members of the party[e] of the
Sadducees,[f] were filled with jealousy. 18 They arrested the apostles and put them in the

4:37 [m]ver 35; Ac 5:2
5:2 [n]Ac 4:35,37
5:3 [o]Mt 4:10 [p]Jn 13:2, 27 [q]ver 9
5:5 [r]ver 10 [s]ver 11
5:6 [t]Jn 19:40
5:8 [u]ver 2
5:9 [v]ver 3
5:10 [w]ver 5
5:11 [x]ver 5; Ac 19:17
5:12 [y]Ac 2:43 [z]Ac 4:32 [a]Ac 3:11
5:13 [b]Ac 2:47; 4:21
5:15 [c]Ac 19:12
5:16 [d]Mk 16:17
5:17 [e]Ac 15:5 [f]Ac 4:1

[a] *16* Greek *unclean*

4:37 sold a field he owned. As "Son of Encouragement" (v. 36), Barnabas presented a good example of a Christian who gave for the needs of others (contrasted with the selfish example of Ananias and Sapphira; 5:1–11). Barnabas also interceded for Saul (9:27), encouraged the church at Antioch in Syria (11:22), led in missionary work abroad (13:2–3) and continued in mission work despite a disagreement with Paul (15:37–39).

5:1 Ananias . . . Sapphira. The selfishness in the lives of this husband and wife stands in stark contrast to the selflessness of Barnabas, "a good man, full of the Holy Spirit and faith" (11:24).

5:2 kept back part of the money for himself. Ananias and his wife had the right to keep all of the proceeds from their land since the land and the money were theirs (v. 4), but they did not have the right to lie. The testimony of the whole church was at risk because of the sins of a few (cf. Lev 10:1–2; Nu 16:23–35; Jos 7:19–25; 2Sa 6:1–7).

5:3–4 See *WCF* 26.3; *WLC* 11,151; *HC* 53.

5:3 Satan has so filled your heart. Other examples of Satan's influence are seen in the lives of Peter (Mk 8:33) and Judas Iscariot (Lk 22:3; Jn 13:27). Later Peter warned Christians against Satan's powerful influence over them (1Pe 5:8). **lied to the Holy Spirit.** By telling Ananias that he had lied to God (v. 4), Peter indicated that the Holy Spirit is God (v. 9). See *WLC* 105,145; *BC* 11,27.

5:6 wrapped up his body. Presumably this was a simple shroud burial without a wooden coffin or stone tomb (cf. the burial of Jesus at Mt 27:59–60).

5:8–9 See *WLC* 145.

5:11 the whole church. This is the first of 23 occurrences of the word "church" (Greek, *ekklēsia*) in Acts. Stephen referred to the Old Testament *ekklēsia* ("assembly") of the people of God in 7:38, and references to the Old Testament worshiping assembly in the Septuagint (the Greek Old Testament) are often translated with this Greek word. In ancient Greece, the *ekklēsia* was the political assembly of the people (cf. 19:32, where *ekklēsia* is translated "assembly"). The New Testament generally uses the word to refer to an organized, local body of believers (8:1; 11:22; 13:1). In the Pauline writings the word is sometimes applied to the church of Jesus Christ, which is understood in a more comprehensive sense as the "body of Christ," the universal church (Eph 4:3–4; 5:25,29–30).

■ **5:12–42** *Further Persecution From the Sanhedrin.* Luke returned a second time to the persecution experienced in Jerusalem. Ironically, as crowds came to the apostles for help and healing, the Jewish religious authorities were filled with jealousy and persecuted them. In the end, the apostles rejoiced in their sufferings and continued proclaiming Christ with power. Although some aspects of these events are unique, it is apparent that Luke wanted his audience to remain faithful and to rejoice as they suffered persecution. The same is true for all time.

5:13 No one else dared join them. No insincere, superficial followers dared to identify with the church. The fear of God was strongly in evidence.

5:14 men and women believed. The true believers came forward and joined the church. Women as believers are first mentioned here in Acts. In accordance with Luke's interest in mentioning women in his Gospel (Lk 7:28; 8:2–3; 17:35; 23:27,29,49,55), he frequently refers in Acts to their activity (1:14; 8:3,12; 9:2,36; 13:50; 16:1,13–14; 17:4,12,34; 18:2; 21:5).

5:15 Peter's shadow. As when Jesus' healing power flowed from his garment at the touch of the woman who had been subject to bleeding (Mk 5:27–28), here God allowed Peter's shadow to effect a cure, as he did also through cloths and aprons that Paul had used (19:11–12).

public jail.[g] **19**But during the night an angel[h] of the Lord opened the doors of the jail[i] and
brought them out. **20**"Go, stand in the temple courts," he said, "and tell the people the
full message of this new life."[j]

21At daybreak they entered the temple courts, as they had been told, and began to
teach the people.

When the high priest and his associates[k] arrived, they called together the Sanhedrin[l]—the full assembly of the elders of Israel—and sent to the jail for the apostles. **22**But
on arriving at the jail, the officers did not find them there. So they went back and reported, **23**"We found the jail securely locked, with the guards standing at the doors; but when
we opened them, we found no one inside." **24**On hearing this report, the captain of the
temple guard and the chief priests[m] were puzzled, wondering what would come of this.

25Then someone came and said, "Look! The men you put in jail are standing in the
temple courts teaching the people." **26**At that, the captain went with his officers and
brought the apostles. They did not use force, because they feared that the people[n]
would stone them.

27Having brought the apostles, they made them appear before the Sanhedrin[o] to be
questioned by the high priest. **28**"We gave you strict orders not to teach in this name,"[p]
he said. "Yet you have filled Jerusalem with your teaching and are determined to make
us guilty of this man's blood."[q]

29Peter and the other apostles replied: "We must obey God rather than men![r] **30**The
God of our fathers[s] raised Jesus from the dead[t]—whom you had killed by hanging him
on a tree.[u] **31**God exalted him to his own right hand[v] as Prince and Savior[w] that he might
give repentance and forgiveness of sins to Israel.[x] **32**We are witnesses of these things,[y]
and so is the Holy Spirit,[z] whom God has given to those who obey him."

33When they heard this, they were furious[a] and wanted to put them to death. **34**But
a Pharisee named Gamaliel,[b] a teacher of the law,[c] who was honored by all the people, stood up in the Sanhedrin and ordered that the men be put outside for a little while.
35Then he addressed them: "Men of Israel, consider carefully what you intend to do to
these men. **36**Some time ago Theudas appeared, claiming to be somebody, and about
four hundred men rallied to him. He was killed, all his followers were dispersed, and it
all came to nothing. **37**After him, Judas the Galilean appeared in the days of the census[d]
and led a band of people in revolt. He too was killed, and all his followers were scattered. **38**Therefore, in the present case I advise you: Leave these men alone! Let them
go! For if their purpose or activity is of human origin, it will fail.[e] **39**But if it is from God,
you will not be able to stop these men; you will only find yourselves fighting against
God."[f]

40His speech persuaded them. They called the apostles in and had them flogged.[g]
Then they ordered them not to speak in the name of Jesus, and let them go.

41The apostles left the Sanhedrin, rejoicing[h] because they had been counted worthy
of suffering disgrace for the Name.[i] **42**Day after day, in the temple courts[j] and from house
to house, they never stopped teaching and proclaiming the good news that Jesus is the
Christ.[a]

5:18 [g]Ac 4:3
5:19 [h]Mt 1:20; Lk 1:11; Ac 8:26; 27:23 [i]Ac 16:26
5:20 [j]Jn 6:63,68
5:21 [k]Ac 4:5,6 [l]ver 27, 34,41; Mt 5:22
5:24 [m]Ac 4:1
5:26 [n]Ac 4:21
5:27 [o]Mt 5:22
5:28 [p]Ac 4:18 [q]Mt 23:35; 27:25; Ac 2:23,36; 3:14, 15; 7:52
5:29 [r]Ac 4:19
5:30 [s]Ac 3:13 [t]Ac 2:24 [u]Ac 10:39; 13:29; Gal 3:13; 1Pe 2:24
5:31 [v]Ac 2:33 [w]Lk 2:11 [x]Mt 1:21; Lk 24:47; Ac 2:38
5:32 [y]Lk 24:48 [z]Jn 15:26
5:33 [a]Ac 2:37; 7:54
5:34 [b]Ac 22:3 [c]Lk 2:46
5:37 [d]Lk 2:1,2
5:38 [e]Mt 15:13
5:39 [f]Pr 21:30; Ac 7:51; 11:17
5:40 [g]Mt 10:17
5:41 [h]Mt 5:12 [i]Jn 15:21
5:42 [j]Ac 2:46

a *42* Or *Messiah*

5:21 Sanhedrin. The influential Jewish religious council at Jerusalem, composed of 71 men. Under Roman occupation, this body, which included aristocratic members of the Sadducean party and learned members of the Pharisaic party and their associates, decided various religious, social and judicial cases in the area.
5:28 make us guilty of this man's blood. Peter and his associates had laid the blame for Jesus' death on the members of the Sanhedrin (2:23; 3:15–16; 4:10–11). The people had heard this accusation.
5:29 See *WCF* 20.2; *BC* 36.
5:30 God of our fathers. A phrase all the Jews listening to Peter and his fellow apostles would have understood as referring to "the God of Abraham, Isaac and Jacob" (3:13).
5:31 exalted him to his own right hand. This declaration would have been understood by the Sanhedrin as a reference to the resurrection. Such an exaltation by God would make this resurrected Jesus equal with God (cf. Jn 5:18; 10:33). See *WLC* 45.
5:34 Gamaliel. One of the most famous rabbis of his time, Gamaliel was Paul's teacher (22:3) and probably a grandson of the renowned Rabbi Hillel, the leader of one of the two great schools of Jewish legal interpretation. In contrast to the school of Shammai, Gamaliel and the school of Hillel were known for their more lenient interpretation of the law (cf. note on Mt 19:3–6).
5:36 Theudas. A man with this name is mentioned by the Jewish historian Josephus (*Antiquities*, 20, 98–99), but he lived at a later time and is different from the Theudas mentioned here (see "Introduction: Time and Place of Writing").
5:37 Judas the Galilean. Josephus (*Jewish War*, 20.118) speaks of a certain Galilean, of Gamala in Gaulanitis (*Antiquities*, 18.4), who stirred up a revolt because he resisted paying taxes and submitting to the Romans. The revolt failed but may have laid the groundwork for the party of the Zealots. The apostle Simon the Zealot (Mt 10:4; Ac 1:13) may have previously been a member of this group. **days of the census.** Not the census of Luke 2:1, which was ordered by the Emperor Augustus about 8 B.C. (but was delayed until 5 or 6 B.C.), but the census 14 years later (A.D. 6) in the time of the Procurator Coponius.
5:40 had them flogged. The apostles received the traditional "forty lashes minus one" (2Co 11:24).
5:41 the Name. The name of Jesus (see note on 4:7).
5:42 Jesus is the Christ. Constant appeal is made in sermons in Acts to Jesus as the Christ, the Messiah (2:31; 3:20; 9:22; 17:3; 18:5,28; 26:23).

The Choosing of the Seven

6 In those days when the number of disciples was increasing,[k] the Grecian Jews[l]
among them complained against the Hebraic Jews because their widows[m] were being overlooked in the daily distribution of food.[n] **2**So the Twelve gathered all the disciples together and said, "It would not be right for us to neglect the ministry of the word
of God in order to wait on tables. **3**Brothers,[o] choose seven men from among you who
are known to be full of the Spirit and wisdom. We will turn this responsibility over to
them **4**and will give our attention to prayer[p] and the ministry of the word."
5This proposal pleased the whole group. They chose Stephen,[q] a man full of faith and
of the Holy Spirit;[r] also Philip,[s] Procorus, Nicanor, Timon, Parmenas, and Nicolas from
Antioch, a convert to Judaism. **6**They presented these men to the apostles, who prayed[t]
and laid their hands on them.[u]
7So the word of God spread.[v] The number of disciples in Jerusalem increased rapidly, and a large number of priests became obedient to the faith.

Stephen Seized

8Now Stephen, a man full of God's grace and power, did great wonders and miraculous signs[w] among the people. **9**Opposition arose, however, from members of the Synagogue of the Freedmen (as it was called)—Jews of Cyrene[x] and Alexandria as well as
the provinces of Cilicia[y] and Asia.[z] These men began to argue with Stephen, **10**but they
could not stand up against his wisdom or the Spirit by whom he spoke.[a]
11Then they secretly[b] persuaded some men to say, "We have heard Stephen speak
words of blasphemy against Moses and against God."[c]
12So they stirred up the people and the elders and the teachers of the law. They seized
Stephen and brought him before the Sanhedrin.[d] **13**They produced false witnesses, who
testified, "This fellow never stops speaking against this holy place[e] and against the law.
14For we have heard him say that this Jesus of Nazareth will destroy this place and
change the customs Moses handed down to us."[f]
15All who were sitting in the Sanhedrin[g] looked intently at Stephen, and they saw that
his face was like the face of an angel.

6:1 [k]Ac 2:41 [l]Ac 9:29 [m]Ac 9:39,41 [n]Ac 4:35
6:3 [o]Ac 1:16
6:4 [p]Ac 1:14
6:5 [q]ver 8; Ac 11:19 [r]Ac 11:24 [s]Ac 8:5-40; 21:8
6:6 [t]Ac 1:24; 8:17; 13:3; 2Ti 1:6 [u]Nu 8:10; Ac 9:17; 1Ti 4:14
6:7 [v]Ac 12:24; 19:20
6:8 [w]Jn 4:48
6:9 [x]Mt 27:32 [y]Ac 15:23,41; 22:3; 23:34 [z]Ac 2:9
6:10 [a]Lk 21:15
6:11 [b]1Ki 21:10 [c]Mt 26:59-61
6:12 [d]Mt 5:22
6:13 [e]Ac 21:28
6:14 [f]Ac 15:1; 21:21; 26:3; 28:17
6:15 [g]Mt 5:22

■ **6:1–7** *Further Community Life Among Believers.* Alternating between discussions of persecution and community life, Luke returned once again to describe an event within the Christian community. Strife had risen between Palestinian and Hellenistic Jews in the church, but the apostles resolved the matter by appointing servants for the church. This solution demonstrated the need for order, leadership and service within the church.

6:1 widows were being overlooked. The Old Testament required the demonstration of concern for the poor and needy. This concern is seen in the social action set forth in 2:44–45 and 4:34–37. Here the age-old problem of discrimination had surfaced: The widows of Grecian Jews were considered outsiders by the native-born Hebraic Jews, and they were not getting their share of the food distribution (probably made available in part from the generous giving of 4:34–37).

6:2–3 See *BC* 30,31.

6:2 the Twelve. The twelve apostles including Matthias (1:26). This is a shift from the term "the Eleven" (2:14; Lk 24:9,33). **disciples.** The first of a number of times the believers are called "disciples" in Acts (e.g., 6:7; 9:1; 11:26; 13:52). Paul did not use this early term to identify Christians. **ministry of the word of God.** In Luke's discussion of the initial organization of the New Testament church he lists two important ministries: (1) the ministry of the word and prayer (v. 4) and (2) the ministry of meeting the physical needs of the believers, summarized as "waiting on tables." The Greek uses the verb *diakoneô* ("serve"), from which the English word "deacon" is derived. In 6:1 the nominal form of the same word is translated "distribution." It is also used of the apostles' "ministry" in verse 4. The qualifications of the office of deacon are described in 1 Timothy 3:8–13.

6:3 Brothers, choose seven men. The members of the church elected the seven, and then the apostles set them apart (ordained them) by prayer and the laying on of hands (v. 6). **full of the Spirit and wisdom.** There are two requirements for the ministry of service in all ages: obedience to the Spirit and action guided by wisdom.

6:5 Stephen . . . Nicholas. All of the seven men had Greek names, which may point to their being Jews from the dispersion. At this time, however, many Palestinian Jews also had Greek names (e.g., Simon *Peter*). Attributes are listed for the first and last of the seven: for Stephen ("full of faith and of the Holy Spirit") because he is featured in 6:8—7:60; and for Nicholas (a convert to Judaism from Antioch), presumably to point to the cosmopolitan nature of their service and to highlight Antioch, soon to be a target for ministry and a center of missionary activity. Philip's later ministry to Samaria and his encounter with the Ethiopian eunuch are also featured prominently (8:5–6,26–40).

■ **6:8—7:60** *Stephen's Persecution, Sermon and Martyrdom.* Stephen was the first martyr of the Christian church. He preached in ways that revealed the failure of Old Testament Israel and the hope that is offered in Christ. But preaching this message led to his murder. Luke took much delight in Stephen's courage and faith as he faced the threats of his opponents. Stephen's actions exemplified the power of the Spirit on witnesses other than the apostles.

6:8 Stephen . . . did great wonders and miraculous signs. Philip, another of the seven, later performed miracles like the apostles who had ordained them (8:6).

6:9 Synagogue of the Freedmen. Composed of Jews who had been freed from slavery. In this case they were from Cyrene, a well-known town of North Africa. **Cilicia.** A Roman province in the southeastern part of Asia Minor. Paul's hometown of Tarsus (9:11,30; 11:25) was one of its chief cities. **Asia.** A Roman province in the western part of modern-day Turkey.

6:11 secretly persuaded. Their fierce opposition to Stephen included obtaining false witnesses, stirring up the people and leaders, seizing Stephen and bringing him before the Sanhedrin. **blasphemy against Moses and against God.** Although, in the light of the gospel, he may have begun to express concern about hollow observance of the technical details of the law, all that Stephen actually said (see ch. 7) was that Moses—like Jesus and like Stephen himself—was rejected by the people (7:35,39). This should not have been taken as blasphemy against Moses and God.

6:13 against this holy place and against the law. Stephen did not speak against the temple but only declared that God is not confined to an earthly temple, since heaven is his home and throne (7:48–50). Stephen actually supported the Mosaic Law and its teaching, especially as they pointed forward to Christ (7:37–38). See *WLC* 145.

6:14 Jesus of Nazareth will destroy this place. The Jewish leadership had heard the misinterpreted quotation of Jesus (Jn 2:19), but there is no evidence that Stephen had known or used it. **customs.** Stephen had no doubt advocated that Jewish customs conform to the gospel.

Stephen's Speech to the Sanhedrin

7 Then the high priest asked him, “Are these charges true?”
2 To this he replied: “Brothers and fathers,[h] listen to me! The God of glory[i] appeared
to our father Abraham while he was still in Mesopotamia, before he lived in Haran.[j]
3 ‘Leave your country and your people,’ God said, ‘and go to the land I will show you.’[a][k]
4 “So he left the land of the Chaldeans and settled in Haran. After the death of his father, God sent him to this land where you are now living.[l] 5 He gave him no inheritance
here, not even a foot of ground. But God promised him that he and his descendants after him would possess the land,[m] even though at that time Abraham had no child. 6 God
spoke to him in this way: ‘Your descendants will be strangers in a country not their own,
and they will be enslaved and mistreated four hundred years.[n] 7 But I will punish the nation they serve as slaves,’ God said, ‘and afterward they will come out of that country and
worship me in this place.’[b][o] 8 Then he gave Abraham the covenant of circumcision.[p] And
Abraham became the father of Isaac and circumcised him eight days after his birth.[q] Later Isaac became the father of Jacob,[r] and Jacob became the father of the twelve patriarchs.[s]
9 “Because the patriarchs were jealous of Joseph,[t] they sold him as a slave into
Egypt.[u] But God was with him[v] 10 and rescued him from all his troubles. He gave Joseph
wisdom and enabled him to gain the goodwill of Pharaoh king of Egypt; so he made him
ruler over Egypt and all his palace.[w]
11 “Then a famine struck all Egypt and Canaan, bringing great suffering, and our fathers could not find food.[x] 12 When Jacob heard that there was grain in Egypt, he sent our
fathers on their first visit.[y] 13 On their second visit, Joseph told his brothers who he was,[z]
and Pharaoh learned about Joseph's family. 14 After this, Joseph sent for his father Jacob
and his whole family,[a] seventy-five in all.[b] 15 Then Jacob went down to Egypt, where he
and our fathers died.[c] 16 Their bodies were brought back to Shechem and placed in the
tomb that Abraham had bought from the sons of Hamor at Shechem for a certain sum
of money.[d]
17 “As the time drew near for God to fulfill his promise to Abraham, the number of our
people in Egypt greatly increased.[e] 18 Then another king, who knew nothing about Joseph, became ruler of Egypt.[f] 19 He dealt treacherously with our people and oppressed
our forefathers by forcing them to throw out their newborn babies so that they would
die.[g]
20 “At that time Moses was born, and he was no ordinary child.[c] For three months he
was cared for in his father's house.[h] 21 When he was placed outside, Pharaoh's daughter took him and brought him up as her own son.[i] 22 Moses was educated in all the wisdom of the Egyptians[j] and was powerful in speech and action.
23 “When Moses was forty years old, he decided to visit his fellow Israelites. 24 He saw
one of them being mistreated by an Egyptian, so he went to his defense and avenged him
by killing the Egyptian. 25 Moses thought that his own people would realize that God was
using him to rescue them, but they did not. 26 The next day Moses came upon two Israelites who were fighting. He tried to reconcile them by saying, ‘Men, you are brothers;
why do you want to hurt each other?’
27 “But the man who was mistreating the other pushed Moses aside and said, ‘Who
made you ruler and judge over us? 28 Do you want to kill me as you killed the Egyptian

7:2 [h]Ac 22:1 [i]Ps 29:3 [j]Ge 11:31; 15:7
7:3 [k]Ge 12:1
7:4 [l]Ge 12:5
7:5 [m]Ge 12:7; 17:8; 26:3
7:6 [n]Ex 12:40
7:7 [o]Ex 3:12
7:8 [p]Ge 17:9-14 [q]Ge 21:2-4 [r]Ge 25:26 [s]Ge 29:31-35; 30:5-13,17-24; 35:16-18,22-26
7:9 [t]Ge 37:4,11 [u]Ge 37:28; Ps 105:17 [v]Ge 39:2,21,23
7:10 [w]Ge 41:37-43
7:11 [x]Ge 41:54
7:12 [y]Ge 42:1,2
7:13 [z]Ge 45:1-4
7:14 [a]Ge 45:9,10 [b]Ge 46:26,27; Ex 1:5; Dt 10:22
7:15 [c]Ge 46:5-7; 49:33; Ex 1:6
7:16 [d]Ge 23:16-20; 33:18,19; 50:13; Jos 24:32
7:17 [e]Ex 1:7; Ps 105:24
7:18 [f]Ex 1:8
7:19 [g]Ex 1:10-22
7:20 [h]Ex 2:2; Heb 11:23
7:21 [i]Ex 2:3-10
7:22 [j]1Ki 4:30; Isa 19:11

[a] *3* Gen. 12:1 [b] *7* Gen. 15:13,14 [c] *20* Or *was fair in the sight of God*

7:2 The God of glory. This title recalls the divine glory that God showed his people in the time of Moses: the pillar of cloud (Ex 14:19; 16:10; Ps 105:39), the pillar of fire (Ex 14:24), the glory of the Lord on the mountain (Ex 24:15–18; 2Co 3:7) and the glory in the tabernacle (Ex 40:34–35; cf. Jn 1:14). See *WCF* 2.2; *WLC* 7.

7:4 land of the Chaldeans. The area of Babylonia in southern Mesopotamia (modern Iraq).

7:6 four hundred years. Exodus 12:40 specifies “430 years,” but Stephen was speaking in round numbers and may have been following the text of Genesis 15:13, which does state “four hundred years.”

7:8 covenant of circumcision. God established this covenant with Abraham, the father of all Israel who lived centuries before Moses came. Moses instituted the customs that Stephen's adversaries tried to protect (6:14).

7:9 See *WLC* 132.

7:14 seventy-five in all. The Hebrew text of Exodus 1:5 states “seventy.” But the Septuagint, the Greek translation of the Old Testament text, which Acts 7 basically follows, and the fragments of Exodus found among the Dead Sea Scrolls, read “seventy-five.” The explanation of the number “seventy-five” is to be found in the five additional descendants of Joseph included in the Greek translation of Genesis 46:20, which lists two sons of Manasseh, two sons of Ephraim and one grandson of Ephraim.

7:16 the tomb that Abraham had bought . . . at Shechem. Stephen condensed the events regarding the patriarchs' burial purchases. Jacob was buried in the cave of Machpelah at Hebron (Ge 50:13) and, according to Josephus (*Antiquities*, 2.199), Joseph's brothers were also buried in Hebron. But Joseph's bones were buried in the land Jacob had bought in Shechem from the sons of Hamor (Ge 33:19; 50:25; Ex 13:19; Jos 24:32). Stephen's audience knew that Jacob and his sons were buried in two different locations (Hebron and Shechem). The narrative here is highly condensed.

7:22 Moses was educated in all the wisdom of the Egyptians. Exodus 2:10 states that when the child Moses grew older, the nurse (Moses' mother) “took him to Pharaoh's daughter and he became her son.” The assumption is that as a royal prince he would have been given a full Egyptian education.

yesterday?'[a] 29 When Moses heard this, he fled to Midian, where he settled as a foreigner and had two sons.[k]
30 "After forty years had passed, an angel appeared to Moses in the flames of a burning bush in the desert near Mount Sinai. 31 When he saw this, he was amazed at the sight.
As he went over to look more closely, he heard the Lord's voice:[l] 32 'I am the God of your
fathers, the God of Abraham, Isaac and Jacob.'[b] Moses trembled with fear and did not
dare to look.[m]
33 "Then the Lord said to him, 'Take off your sandals; the place where you are standing is holy ground.[n] 34 I have indeed seen the oppression of my people in Egypt. I have
heard their groaning and have come down to set them free. Now come, I will send you
back to Egypt.'[c][o]
35 "This is the same Moses whom they had rejected with the words, 'Who made you
ruler and judge?'[p] He was sent to be their ruler and deliverer by God himself, through
the angel who appeared to him in the bush. 36 He led them out of Egypt[q] and did wonders and miraculous signs in Egypt, at the Red Sea[d][r] and for forty years in the desert.
37 "This is that Moses who told the Israelites, 'God will send you a prophet like me from
your own people.'[e][s] 38 He was in the assembly in the desert, with the angel[t] who spoke to
him on Mount Sinai, and with our fathers;[u] and he received living words[v] to pass on to us.[w]
39 "But our fathers refused to obey him. Instead, they rejected him and in their hearts
turned back to Egypt.[x] 40 They told Aaron, 'Make us gods who will go before us. As for
this fellow Moses who led us out of Egypt—we don't know what has happened to him!'[f][y]
41 That was the time they made an idol in the form of a calf. They brought sacrifices to it
and held a celebration in honor of what their hands had made.[z] 42 But God turned
away[a] and gave them over to the worship of the heavenly bodies.[b] This agrees with what
is written in the book of the prophets:

"'Did you bring me sacrifices and offerings
forty years in the desert, O house of Israel?
43 You have lifted up the shrine of Molech
and the star of your god Rephan,
the idols you made to worship.
Therefore I will send you into exile'[g][c] beyond Babylon.

44 "Our forefathers had the tabernacle of the Testimony[d] with them in the desert. It
had been made as God directed Moses, according to the pattern he had seen.[e] 45 Having
received the tabernacle, our fathers under Joshua brought it with them when they took
the land from the nations God drove out before them.[f] It remained in the land until the
time of David, 46 who enjoyed God's favor and asked that he might provide a dwelling
place for the God of Jacob.[h][g] 47 But it was Solomon who built the house for him.
48 "However, the Most High does not live in houses made by men.[h] As the prophet
says:

49 "'Heaven is my throne,
and the earth is my footstool.[i]
What kind of house will you build for me?
says the Lord.
Or where will my resting place be?
50 Has not my hand made all these things?'[i][j]

51 "You stiff-necked people,[k] with uncircumcised hearts[l] and ears! You are just like

7:29 [k]Ex 2:11-15
7:31 [l]Ex 3:1-4
7:32 [m]Ex 3:6
7:33 [n]Ex 3:5; Jos 5:15
7:34 [o]Ex 3:7-10
7:35 [p]ver 27
7:36 [q]Ex 12:41; 33:1 [r]Ex 14:21
7:37 [s]Dt 18:15,18; Ac 3:22
7:38 [t]ver 53 [u]Ex 19:17 [v]Dt 32:45-47; Heb 4:12 [w]Ro 3:2
7:39 [x]Nu 14:3,4
7:40 [y]Ex 32:1,23
7:41 [z]Ex 32:4-6; Ps 106:19,20; Rev 9:20
7:42 [a]Jos 24:20; Isa 63:10 [b]Jer 19:13
7:43 [c]Am 5:25-27
7:44 [d]Ex 38:21 [e]Ex 25:8,9,40
7:45 [f]Jos 3:14-17; 18:1; 23:9; 24:18; Ps 44:2
7:46 [g]2Sa 7:8-16; Ps 132:1-5
7:48 [h]1Ki 8:27; 2Ch 2:6
7:49 [i]Mt 5:34,35
7:50 [j]Isa 66:1,2
7:51 [k]Ex 32:9; 33:3,5 [l]Lev 26:41; Dt 10:16; Jer 4:4; 9:26

[a] *28* Exodus 2:14 [b] *32* Exodus 3:6 [c] *34* Exodus 3:5,7,8,10 [d] *36* That is, Sea of Reeds [e] *37* Deut. 18:15 [f] *40* Exodus 32:1 [g] *43* Amos 5:25–27 [h] *46* Some early manuscripts *the house of Jacob* [i] *50* Isaiah 66:1,2

7:37 a prophet like me. Stephen's first indirect reference to Moses' greater successor: Jesus, the rejected One.
7:38 the assembly in the desert. "Assembly" is a translation of the Greek word *ekklçsia* (church). It is often used in the Septuagint (Greek Old Testament) for a Hebrew word meaning "assembly" or "congregation at worship" (see note on 5:11). **the angel who spoke to him on Mount Sinai.** Although Moses received the law from God himself on Mount Sinai (Ex 20:1,21), God somehow administered it to Moses and the people through angels (Dt 33:2; Ac 7:53; Gal 3:19; Heb 2:2). **he received living words to pass on to us.** Moses, in receiving the law and passing it on in written form, became a mediator of the law of God, which was given for our correction and instruction to bring us into obedience to Christ (Gal 3:24).
7:44 tabernacle of the Testimony. The Old Testament tabernacle contained God's testimony to his presence and his promise in the form of the ark of the covenant and the tablets of the Ten Commandments, which are called "the Testimony" (the Hebrew word is related to a Babylonian word meaning "covenant stipulations"; cf. Ex 25:16,21–22; 31:7). God's presence and life-giving power were also symbolized by the table of the consecrated bread (Ex 37:10–16; Heb 9:2); the seven-branched lampstand (Ex 37:17–23; cf. Jn 8:12; Rev 1:12–18); and the altar of incense (Ex 37:25–29), which represented the prayers of God's people rising up to an ever-present God (Ps 141:2; Rev 8:3–4).
7:48–49 See *HC* 48.
7:51 You stiff-necked people, with uncircumcised hearts and

your fathers: You always resist the Holy Spirit! 52 Was there ever a prophet your fathers
did not persecute?[m] They even killed those who predicted the coming of the Righteous
One. And now you have betrayed and murdered him[n]— 53 you who have received the law
that was put into effect through angels[o] but have not obeyed it."

The Stoning of Stephen

54 When they heard this, they were furious[p] and gnashed their teeth at him. 55 But Stephen, full of the Holy Spirit, looked up to heaven and saw the glory of God, and Jesus
standing at the right hand of God.[q] 56 "Look," he said, "I see heaven open[r] and the Son
of Man[s] standing at the right hand of God."

57 At this they covered their ears and, yelling at the top of their voices, they all rushed
at him, 58 dragged him out of the city[t] and began to stone him.[u] Meanwhile, the witnesses laid their clothes[v] at the feet of a young man named Saul.[w]

59 While they were stoning him, Stephen prayed, "Lord Jesus, receive my spirit."[x]
60 Then he fell on his knees[y] and cried out, "Lord, do not hold this sin against them."[z]
When he had said this, he fell asleep.

8 And Saul[a] was there, giving approval to his death.

The Church Persecuted and Scattered

On that day a great persecution broke out against the church at Jerusalem, and all
except the apostles were scattered[b] throughout Judea and Samaria.[c] 2 Godly men buried Stephen and mourned deeply for him. 3 But Saul[d] began to destroy the church.[e] Going from house to house, he dragged off men and women and put them in prison.

Philip in Samaria

4 Those who had been scattered[f] preached the word wherever they went.[g] 5 Philip[h]
went down to a city in Samaria and proclaimed the Christ[a] there. 6 When the crowds
heard Philip and saw the miraculous signs he did, they all paid close attention to what
he said. 7 With shrieks, evil[b] spirits came out of many,[i] and many paralytics and cripples
were healed.[j] 8 So there was great joy in that city.

Simon the Sorcerer

9 Now for some time a man named Simon had practiced sorcery[k] in the city and
amazed all the people of Samaria. He boasted that he was someone great,[l] 10 and all the
people, both high and low, gave him their attention and exclaimed, "This man is the divine power known as the Great Power."[m] 11 They followed him because he had amazed
them for a long time with his magic. 12 But when they believed Philip as he preached the

7:52 [m]2Ch 36:16; Mt 5:12 [n]Ac 3:14; 1Th 2:15
7:53 [o]ver 38; Gal 3:19; Heb 2:2
7:54 [p]Ac 5:33
7:55 [q]Mk 16:19
7:56 [r]Mt 3:16 [s]Mt 8:20
7:58 [t]Lk 4:29 [u]Lev 24:14,16; Dt 13:9 [v]Ac 22:20 [w]Ac 8:1
7:59 [x]Ps 31:5; Lk 23:46
7:60 [y]Ac 9:40 [z]Mt 5:44
8:1 [a]Ac 7:58 [b]Ac 11:19 [c]Ac 9:31
8:3 [d]Ac 7:58 [e]Ac 22:4, 19; 26:10,11; 1Co 15:9; Gal 1:13, 23; Php 3:6; 1Ti 1:13
8:4 [f]ver 1 [g]Ac 15:35
8:5 [h]Ac 6:5
8:7 [i]Mk 16:17 [j]Mt 4:24
8:9 [k]Ac 13:6 [l]Ac 5:36
8:10 [m]Ac 14:11; 28:6

[a] 5 Or *Messiah* [b] 7 Greek *unclean*

---

ears! They would not listen from their hearts, nor would they obey the Lord and the Scriptures Stephen had cited. These metaphors are Old Testament figures for a spiritually stubborn and unregenerate people (Ex 32:9; 33:3,5; Dt 9:6; 10:16; 30:6; Jer 4:4). See *WLC* 105.

7:52 the Righteous One. A title used for the Lord Almighty (Isa 24:16) and for Jesus Christ (22:14; 1Jn 2:1).

7:55–57 See *WLC* 145; *HC* 80.

7:55 the glory of God. The brilliance of God's presence and his throne area (cf. Rev 15:8; 21:11,23). **standing at the right hand of God.** Usually Jesus is said to be sitting at the right hand of God because his work is finished (Ro 8:34; Col 3:1; Heb 10:12), but here he is standing to receive Stephen or to rise as his defense attorney. In this scene the Son of Man is both judge and advocate.

7:56 I see . . . the Son of Man. Stephen's vision of the Son of Man in heaven must have vividly reminded the Sanhedrin of the trial of Jesus who, in answer to their question "Are you the Christ?" had replied, "I am . . . And you will see the Son of Man sitting at the right hand of the Mighty One and coming on the clouds of heaven" (Mk 14:61–62). Stephen claimed a vision of this same Jesus now in heaven at God's right hand. This was a verification of the truth of what Stephen had been saying and a condemnation of their rejection.

7:58 laid their clothes at the feet of . . . Saul. Saul (later known as Paul) was associated with the Sanhedrin (he was a Pharisee; Php 3:5) and was possibly an instigator of Stephen's trial (8:3; 9:1–2). It is fitting at this point for Luke to introduce Saul, the second prominent figure of his book.

7:60 do not hold this sin against them. Compare the statement of Jesus in Luke 23:34. **he fell asleep.** A euphemism for "he died" (Jn 11:11–13).

▪ 8:1—11:18 *The Apostolic Witness in Judea and Samaria.* Jesus had commanded his apostles to be his witnesses in Judea and Samaria (1:8). Luke now turned to this second stage of the spread of the apostolic witness (see notes on 3:1—7:60; 13:1—28:31).

▪ 8:1–40 *The Witness Spreads.* More persecution came on the church in Jerusalem, and many believers left the city, taking the gospel of Christ with them. Luke recorded several examples of this spread of the gospel into Judea and Samaria.

8:3 Saul began to destroy the church. The Greek verb is powerful, reflecting not just harassment but personal injuries brought on by scourging and torture.

8:4 scattered preached the word. Because of persecution the message spread farther and more rapidly (11:19).

8:9 Simon. Simon the sorcerer (also known as Simon Magus) is frequently mentioned in early post-New Testament times and in ancient extrabiblical literature as an archenemy of the church and a leading proponent of the Gnostic heresy. Gnosticism taught that a person gained salvation not by the merit of Christ's atoning death for sinners but by secret knowledge about God. Justin Martyr (died c. A.D. 165), who himself was a Samaritan, stated that almost all the Samaritans considered Simon the highest god (the Samaritans called him the "Great Power"; v. 10). Irenaeus (died c. A.D. 202), who wrote extensively against the Gnostics in *Against Heresies,* indicated that Simon was one of the sources of Gnostic heresies. The non-canonical *Acts of Peter* (second century A.D.) describes the teaching and powers of Simon. Although the Simon of verse 9 could be another Simon, the church fathers equated the two, and the context of 8:9–11 (his character and the Samaritans' attitude about him) certainly points to the two as being the same person.

8:12 [n]Ac 1:3 [o]Ac 2:38
8:13 [p]ver 6; Ac 19:11
8:14 [q]ver 1 [r]Lk 22:8
8:15 [s]Ac 2:38
8:16 [t]Ac 19:2 [u]Mt 28:19; Ac 2:38
8:17 [v]Ac 6:6

good news of the kingdom of God[n] and the name of Jesus Christ, they were baptized,[o]
both men and women. 13Simon himself believed and was baptized. And he followed Philip everywhere, astonished by the great signs and miracles[p] he saw.
14When the apostles in Jerusalem heard that Samaria[q] had accepted the word of God,
they sent Peter and John[r] to them. 15When they arrived, they prayed for them that they
might receive the Holy Spirit,[s] 16because the Holy Spirit had not yet come upon any of
them;[t] they had simply been baptized into[a] the name of the Lord Jesus.[u] 17Then Peter
and John placed their hands on them,[v] and they received the Holy Spirit.
18When Simon saw that the Spirit was given at the laying on of the apostles' hands,
he offered them money 19and said, "Give me also this ability so that everyone on whom
I lay my hands may receive the Holy Spirit."
20Peter answered: "May your money perish with you, because you thought you could

[a] *16* Or *in*

8:13 Simon himself believed and was baptized. In light of the information in the note on verse 9, Simon's belief must have been based on superficial knowledge, not on true acceptance of Jesus. His interest was in the "great signs and miracles" done through Peter, not in a genuine commitment to Jesus. See *WCF* 28.5; *WLC* 161.
8:15 receive the Holy Spirit. The believing Samaritans to this point had not received evidence of the outpouring of the Holy Spirit, which was a characteristic of the New Testament era. As believers the Holy Spirit indwelled them (Ro 8:9), but the apostles laid hands on them for the special outpouring. We are not told exactly what manifestation of the Holy Spirit came upon them (e.g., tongues, gift of prophecy, etc.).
8:16–17 baptized . . . received the Holy Spirit. The granting of a separate, second blessing of baptism in the Spirit after water baptism in Jesus' name does not characterize the New Testament era. This second baptism occurred at this time because the apostles had opened a new geographical phase in the spread of the gospel by going to Samaria (see note 8:1—11:18). The normal course for the New Testament is for one baptism to be administered in the name of the Father, the Son and the Holy Spirit (Mt 28:19). Similarly extraordinary displays of the Spirit took place at several points: in Acts 2, when the first outpouring took place; here, when Peter reached Samaria; in 10:44, when Peter first preached to Gentiles; and in 19:4–7, when Paul reached Ephesus. In each case at least one apostle was present so that the Spirit's extraordinary outpouring marked a new stage in the success of the apostolic witness. See *BC* 34.
8:18 See *WLC* 109.
8:20 May your money perish with you. The Greek expression is strong: "May you and your money go to destruction" (cf. Mt 7:13; Rev 17:8).

Philip's and Peter's Missionary Journeys

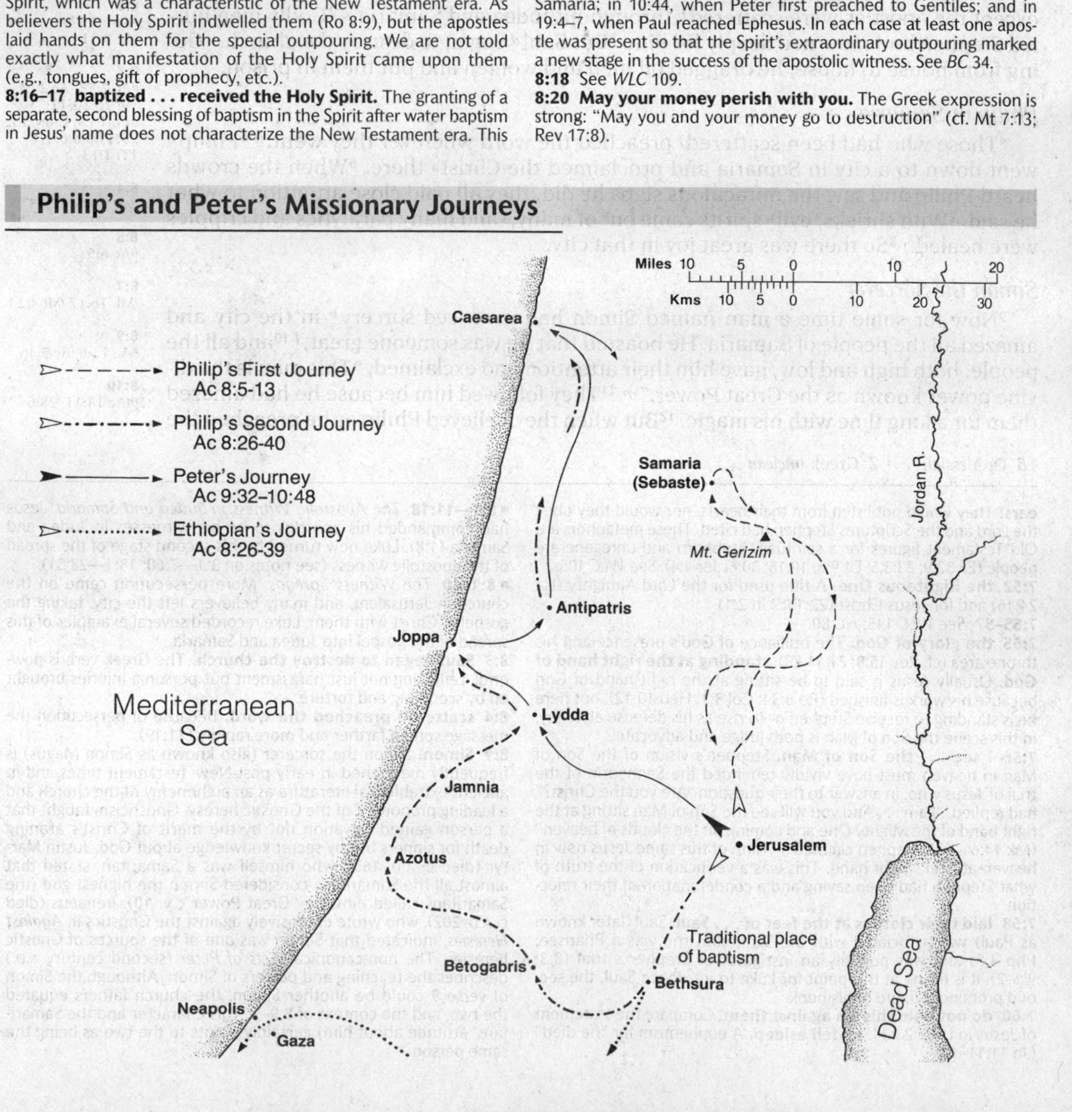

buy the gift of God with money![w] 21You have no part or share in this ministry, because
your heart is not right[x] before God. 22Repent of this wickedness and pray to the Lord.
Perhaps he will forgive you for having such a thought in your heart. 23For I see that you
are full of bitterness and captive to sin."
24Then Simon answered, "Pray to the Lord for me[y] so that nothing you have said may
happen to me."
25When they had testified and proclaimed the word of the Lord, Peter and John returned to Jerusalem, preaching the gospel in many Samaritan villages.[z]

Philip and the Ethiopian

26Now an angel[a] of the Lord said to Philip, "Go south to the road—the desert road—
that goes down from Jerusalem to Gaza." 27So he started out, and on his way he met an
Ethiopian[a][b] eunuch,[c] an important official in charge of all the treasury of Candace,
queen of the Ethiopians. This man had gone to Jerusalem to worship,[d] 28and on his way
home was sitting in his chariot reading the book of Isaiah the prophet. 29The Spirit told[e]
Philip, "Go to that chariot and stay near it."
30Then Philip ran up to the chariot and heard the man reading Isaiah the prophet.
"Do you understand what you are reading?" Philip asked.
31"How can I," he said, "unless someone explains it to me?" So he invited Philip to
come up and sit with him.
32The eunuch was reading this passage of Scripture:

> "He was led like a sheep to the slaughter,
> and as a lamb before the shearer is silent,
> so he did not open his mouth.
> 33In his humiliation he was deprived of justice.
> Who can speak of his descendants?
> For his life was taken from the earth."[b][f]

34The eunuch asked Philip, "Tell me, please, who is the prophet talking about, himself or someone else?" 35Then Philip began[g] with that very passage of Scripture[h] and told
him the good news about Jesus.
36As they traveled along the road, they came to some water and the eunuch said,
"Look, here is water. Why shouldn't I be baptized?"[c][i] 38And he gave orders to stop the
chariot. Then both Philip and the eunuch went down into the water and Philip baptized
him. 39When they came up out of the water, the Spirit of the Lord suddenly took Philip
away,[j] and the eunuch did not see him again, but went on his way rejoicing. 40Philip,
however, appeared at Azotus and traveled about, preaching the gospel in all the towns[k]
until he reached Caesarea.[l]

Saul's Conversion

9 Meanwhile, Saul was still breathing out murderous threats against the Lord's disciples.[m] He went to the high priest 2and asked him for letters to the synagogues in

8:20 [w]2Ki 5:16; Da 5:17; Mt 10:8; Ac 2:38
8:21 [x]Ps 78:37
8:24 [y]Ex 8:8; Nu 21:7; 1Ki 13:6
8:25 [z]ver 40
8:26 [a]Ac 5:19
8:27 [b]Ps 68:31; 87:4; Zep 3:10 [c]Isa 56:3-5 [d]1Ki 8:41-43; Jn 12:20
8:29 [e]Ac 10:19; 11:12; 13:2; 20:23; 21:11
8:33 [f]Isa 53:7,8
8:35 [g]Mt 5:2 [h]Lk 24:27; Ac 17:2; 18:28; 28:23
8:36 [i]Ac 10:47
8:39 [j]1Ki 18:12; 2Ki 2:16; Eze 3:12, 14; 8:3; 11:1,24; 43:5; 2Co 12:2
8:40 [k]ver 25 [l]Ac 10:1, 24; 12:19; 21:8,16; 23:23,33; 25:1,4, 6,13
9:1 [m]Ac 8:3

a *27* That is, from the upper Nile region b *33* Isaiah 53:7,8 c *36* Some late manuscripts *baptized?"* *37Philip said, "If you believe with all your heart, you may." The eunuch answered, "I believe that Jesus Christ is the Son of God."*

8:22–23 By his words and actions, Simon had proved that he was not a true believer in Christ. He was still "captive to sin" (cf. Ro 6:16; 8:8) and "full of bitterness" (cf. Dt 29:18; Ro 3:14). A profession of faith without repentance indicates the absence of true faith. See *WCF* 28.5; *WLC* 161.

8:27–39 See *WLC* 155.

8:27 Ethiopian. He was the finance minister for Ethiopia, modern Nubia, an area that extends from the modern Aswan Dam to Khartoum. **eunuch.** This word refers either to an emasculated official in the royal court or to a high official of government who was not necessarily emasculated. In the Septuagint (the Greek Old Testament) and in extrabiblical writings, it frequently means a government official. **Candace.** The title of the queen mother who ruled in secular matters in the place of her son who, as the child of the sun, was thought to be too sacred to involve himself in secular affairs of state.

8:28 reading the book of Isaiah. If the Ethiopian had been reading the passage about the Lord's mercy to eunuchs (Isa 56:3–5; cf. Dt 23:1), it would have been natural for him also to have read Isaiah 53 (see note on v. 35).

8:29 See *BC* 9,10.

8:30 heard the man. It was common practice in ancient times to read aloud. See *WLC* 157.

8:34 See *WLC* 157.

8:35 about Jesus. Philip began with Isaiah 53 and identified the servant in the passage as Jesus, the suffering servant. Luke seems to imply that Philip went on to other Old Testament passages to identify Jesus as the Messiah.

8:36–38 See *WCF* 28.4; *WLC* 166; *WSC* 95; *BC* 9,10.

8:40 Azotus. Ancient Old Testament Ashdod (1Sa 5:1), one of the five Philistine cities. It was on the coast about 20 miles north of Gaza and 60 miles south of Caesarea. Philip preached the gospel in all the towns along the coast until he reached Caesarea, a large city Herod the Great had rebuilt (near Strato's Tower). It had an excellent harbor that Herod expanded for important sea traffic (21:8), and it served as headquarters for the Roman procurators such as Pilate, Felix (23:33—24:4) and Festus (25:6). Philip may have settled in Caesarea, because years later he was still residing there (21:8).

■ **9:1–31** *Saul's Conversion and the Growing Church.* Luke recounted the dramatic conversion of the one who had led persecutions in the regions of Samaria and Galilee (7:58; 8:1) and who would

Damascus, so that if he found any there who belonged to the Way,[n] whether men or
women, he might take them as prisoners to Jerusalem. 3 As he neared Damascus on his
journey, suddenly a light from heaven flashed around him.[o] 4 He fell to the ground and
heard a voice say to him, "Saul, Saul, why do you persecute me?"
5 "Who are you, Lord?" Saul asked.
"I am Jesus, whom you are persecuting," he replied. 6 "Now get up and go into the city,
and you will be told what you must do."[p]
7 The men traveling with Saul stood there speechless; they heard the sound[q] but did
not see anyone.[r] 8 Saul got up from the ground, but when he opened his eyes he could
see nothing. So they led him by the hand into Damascus. 9 For three days he was blind,
and did not eat or drink anything.
10 In Damascus there was a disciple named Ananias. The Lord called to him in a vision,[s] "Ananias!"
"Yes, Lord," he answered.
11 The Lord told him, "Go to the house of Judas on Straight Street and ask for a man
from Tarsus[t] named Saul, for he is praying. 12 In a vision he has seen a man named Ananias come and place his hands on[u] him to restore his sight."
13 "Lord," Ananias answered, "I have heard many reports about this man and all the
harm he has done to your saints[v] in Jerusalem.[w] 14 And he has come here with authority from the chief priests[x] to arrest all who call on your name."
15 But the Lord said to Ananias, "Go! This man is my chosen instrument[y] to carry my
name before the Gentiles[z] and their kings[a] and before the people of Israel. 16 I will show
him how much he must suffer for my name."[b]
17 Then Ananias went to the house and entered it. Placing his hands on[c] Saul, he said,
"Brother Saul, the Lord—Jesus, who appeared to you on the road as you were coming
here—has sent me so that you may see again and be filled with the Holy Spirit." 18 Immediately, something like scales fell from Saul's eyes, and he could see again. He got up
and was baptized, 19 and after taking some food, he regained his strength.

Saul in Damascus and Jerusalem

Saul spent several days with the disciples[d] in Damascus.[e] 20 At once he began to
preach in the synagogues[f] that Jesus is the Son of God.[g] 21 All those who heard him were
astonished and asked, "Isn't he the man who raised havoc in Jerusalem among those
who call on this name?[h] And hasn't he come here to take them as prisoners to the chief
priests?"[i] 22 Yet Saul grew more and more powerful and baffled the Jews living in Damascus by proving that Jesus is the Christ.[a][j]
23 After many days had gone by, the Jews conspired to kill him, 24 but Saul learned of
their plan.[k] Day and night they kept close watch on the city gates in order to kill him.
25 But his followers took him by night and lowered him in a basket through an opening
in the wall.[l]
26 When he came to Jerusalem,[m] he tried to join the disciples, but they were all afraid
of him, not believing that he really was a disciple. 27 But Barnabas[n] took him and brought
him to the apostles. He told them how Saul on his journey had seen the Lord and that

9:2 [n]Ac 19:9,23; 22:4; 24:14,22
9:3 [o]1Co 15:8
9:6 [p]ver 16
9:7 [q]Jn 12:29 [r]Da 10:7; Ac 22:9
9:10 [s]Ac 10:3,17,19
9:11 [t]ver 30; Ac 21:39; 22:3
9:12 [u]Mk 5:23
9:13 [v]ver 32; Ro 1:7; 16:2,15 [w]Ac 8:3
9:14 [x]ver 2,21
9:15 [y]Ac 13:2; Ro 1:1; Gal 1:15 [z]Ro 11:13; 15:15,16; Gal 2:7,8; Eph 3:7,8 [a]Ac 25:22,23; 26:1
9:16 [b]Ac 20:23; 21:11; 2Co 11:23-27
9:17 [c]Ac 6:6
9:19 [d]Ac 11:26 [e]Ac 26:20
9:20 [f]Ac 13:5,14 [g]Mt 4:3
9:21 [h]Ac 8:3 [i]Gal 1:13,23
9:22 [j]Ac 18:5,28
9:24 [k]Ac 20:3,19
9:25 [l]1Sa 19:12; 2Co 11:32,33
9:26 [m]Ac 22:17; 26:20; Gal 1:17,18
9:27 [n]Ac 4:36

a *22* Or *Messiah*

---

become the great apostle Paul. His record demonstrates that God protected and cared for the church in those regions.

9:1 Saul. Saul was introduced in 7:58 and is the main character in 9:1–31. A third, brief glimpse of Saul appears in 11:25–30. Saul, later called Paul, is the principal character in 13:1—28:31. **still breathing out murderous threats.** Saul had helped to eliminate Stephen and now continued his attempts to stamp out the Christian faith.

9:2 the Way. A title equivalent to the following terms: "Christian" (used only in Ac 11:26; 26:28; 1Pe 4:16; see note on 11:26), "disciple" (vv. 10,19), "saints" (v. 13), "all who call on [the Lord's] name" (v. 14) and "brothers" (vv. 17,30). The term "the Way" identified the Christian cause as one composed of followers of Jesus, who is "the way" (Jn 14:6). It is used a number of times in Acts (19:9,23; 22:4; 24:14,22). Peter used the phrase "the way of truth" (2Pe 2:2; cf. Ps 119:30), an apt description of the Christian faith in contrast to "the road that leads to destruction" (Mt 7:13).

9:3 a light from heaven. A supernatural light that was brighter than that of the sun (26:13).

9:4 Saul, Saul. This repetition indicated a form of intimate personal address (cf. Ge 22:11; 46:2; Ex 3:4; 1Sa 3:10; Lk 10:41; 22:31). **persecute me?** To persecute Jesus' disciples is to persecute Jesus (Mt 5:10–12; Jn 15:19–20).

9:7 The men . . . heard the sound. Paul stated that "they did not understand the voice" (22:9). The Greek word *phone* can mean "sound" or "voice." Saul's companions heard some kind of sound but could not make out the meaning of the words.

9:15 chosen instrument . . . before the Gentiles and their kings and before the people of Israel. Paul was an apostle to the Gentiles, as Peter was to the Jews (Gal 2:7–8), but Paul also preached many times to the Jews, particularly in their synagogues (v. 20; Ro 1:16; 1Co 9:20).

9:17 Jesus, who appeared to you. Saul had not merely had a dream or a vision, but he had seen the Lord (cf. Isa 6:1,5). **be filled with the Holy Spirit.** Compare 2:38. Nothing is said about any supernatural gifts, but emphasis is placed on his powerful preaching about Jesus as the Son of God (v. 20).

9:18 something like scales fell from Saul's eyes. Luke's writings frequently call attention to physical afflictions (13:11; 28:3–8; see "Introduction: Author").

9:26 he came to Jerusalem. According to Galatians 1:18–19, Paul saw only Peter and James, the Lord's brother, at Jerusalem. The others may have declined to meet with him or may have been preaching the gospel in other areas.

the Lord had spoken to him,[o] and how in Damascus he had preached fearlessly in the
name of Jesus.[p] 28So Saul stayed with them and moved about freely in Jerusalem, speaking boldly in the name of the Lord. 29He talked and debated with the Grecian Jews,[q] but
they tried to kill him.[r] 30When the brothers[s] learned of this, they took him down to Caesarea[t] and sent him off to Tarsus.[u]
31Then the church throughout Judea, Galilee and Samaria[v] enjoyed a time of peace.
It was strengthened; and encouraged by the Holy Spirit, it grew in numbers, living in the
fear of the Lord.

Aeneas and Dorcas

32As Peter traveled about the country, he went to visit the saints[w] in Lydda. 33There
he found a man named Aeneas, a paralytic who had been bedridden for eight years.
34"Aeneas," Peter said to him, "Jesus Christ heals you.[x] Get up and take care of your
mat." Immediately Aeneas got up. 35All those who lived in Lydda and Sharon[y] saw him
and turned to the Lord.[z]
36In Joppa[a] there was a disciple named Tabitha (which, when translated, is Dorcas[a]),
who was always doing good[b] and helping the poor. 37About that time she became sick
and died, and her body was washed and placed in an upstairs room.[c] 38Lydda was near
Joppa; so when the disciples[d] heard that Peter was in Lydda, they sent two men to him
and urged him, "Please come at once!"
39Peter went with them, and when he arrived he was taken upstairs to the room. All
the widows[e] stood around him, crying and showing him the robes and other clothing
that Dorcas had made while she was still with them.
40Peter sent them all out of the room;[f] then he got down on his knees[g] and prayed.
Turning toward the dead woman, he said, "Tabitha, get up." She opened her eyes, and
seeing Peter she sat up. 41He took her by the hand and helped her to her feet. Then he
called the believers and the widows and presented her to them alive. 42This became
known all over Joppa, and many people believed in the Lord. 43Peter stayed in Joppa for
some time with a tanner named Simon.[h]

Cornelius Calls for Peter

10 At Caesarea[i] there was a man named Cornelius, a centurion in what was known
as the Italian Regiment. 2He and all his family were devout and God-fearing;[j] he
gave generously to those in need and prayed to God regularly. 3One day at about three
in the afternoon[k] he had a vision.[l] He distinctly saw an angel[m] of God, who came to him
and said, "Cornelius!"
4Cornelius stared at him in fear. "What is it, Lord?" he asked.
The angel answered, "Your prayers and gifts to the poor have come up as a memorial offering[n] before God.[o] 5Now send men to Joppa[p] to bring back a man named Simon
who is called Peter. 6He is staying with Simon the tanner,[q] whose house is by the sea."
7When the angel who spoke to him had gone, Cornelius called two of his servants and
a devout soldier who was one of his attendants. 8He told them everything that had happened and sent them to Joppa.[r]

9:27 [o]ver 3-6 [p]ver 20,22
9:29 [q]Ac 6:1 [r]2Co 11:26
9:30 [s]Ac 1:16 [t]Ac 8:40 [u]ver 11
9:31 [v]Ac 8:1
9:32 [w]ver 13
9:34 [x]Ac 3:6,16; 4:10
9:35 [y]1Ch 5:16; 27:29; Isa 33:9; 35:2; 65:10 [z]Ac 11:21
9:36 [a]Jos 19:46; 2Ch 2:16; Ezr 3:7; Jnh 1:3; Ac 10:5 [b]1Ti 2:10; Tit 3:8
9:37 [c]Ac 1:13
9:38 [d]Ac 11:26
9:39 [e]Ac 6:1
9:40 [f]Mt 9:25 [g]Lk 22:41; Ac 7:60
9:43 [h]Ac 10:6
10:1 [i]Ac 8:40
10:2 [j]ver 22,35; Ac 13:16,26
10:3 [k]Ac 3:1 [l]Ac 9:10 [m]Ac 5:19
10:4 [n]Mt 26:13 [o]Rev 8:4
10:5 [p]Ac 9:36
10:6 [q]Ac 9:43
10:8 [r]Ac 9:36

[a] *36* Both *Tabitha* (Aramaic) and *Dorcas* (Greek) mean *gazelle.*

9:31 See *HC* 53.
■ **9:32–43** *The Witness Spreads Farther.* Luke continued to report how the apostle Peter took the gospel farther into the region of Judea and Samaria.
9:35 Sharon. The news concerning the healing of the paralytic had dramatic effects as it traveled as far as the Plain of Sharon, which extends north of Joppa up the coast 40 to 50 miles.
9:36 Joppa. An ancient seaport (modern Jaffa, just south of Tel Aviv) about 38 miles northwest of Jerusalem. It was the port from which Jonah sailed (Jnh 1:3).
9:37 body was washed. Probably occurred before the anointing with spices (cf. Jn 19:40). In Jerusalem, Jesus' body had been buried on the day of his death, but outside the city a longer period was allowed (up to three days).
9:43 a tanner named Simon. Peter's willingness to stay with a tanner, a profession Jews believed to be unclean because it involved contact with dead animals (Lev 5:2), points to the way in which the message of the gospel was already beginning to break down barriers between people. This also anticipates Peter's vision in 10:9–23.
■ **10:1—11:18** *The Witness Reaches Gentiles in Samaria.* Peter was the first apostle to break the barrier between Jews and Gentiles. He did so under the direct command of God. Some Gentiles had always been counted among the people of God (e.g., Ruth in Ru 4:13–22; Kenites in 1Sa 15:6; Naaman in 2Ki 5 and Lk 4:27). But during the New Testament period, the kingdom of God was opened to Gentiles in large numbers, and full equality with Jews was granted to them. Peter began this process, but Paul would later champion the cause of the Gentiles.
10:1–2 See *WCF* 23.2.
10:1 Caesarea. Caesarea Maritima (Caesarea by the Sea) was located on the Plain of Sharon about 65 miles northwest of Jerusalem. It was a seaport greatly enhanced by Herod the Great, who rebuilt the city. **Cornelius.** A Roman army officer.
10:2 devout. Cornelius was a pious man who was given to a regular prayer life and to doing good deeds for others. **God-fearing.** Cornelius was a near-proselyte to Judaism, a Gentile who worshiped God but who objected to circumcision (13:16,26). See *WCF* 21.6; 28.5.
10:4 See *WCF* 28.4.

Peter's Vision

10:9 sMt 24:17
9About noon the following day as they were on their journey and approaching the
city, Peter went up on the roof[s] to pray. 10He became hungry and wanted something to
10:10 tAc 22:17
eat, and while the meal was being prepared, he fell into a trance.[t] 11He saw heaven
opened and something like a large sheet being let down to earth by its four corners. 12It
10:14 uAc 9:5 vLev 11:4-8, 13-20; 20:25; Dt 14:3-20; Eze 4:14
contained all kinds of four-footed animals, as well as reptiles of the earth and birds of
the air. 13Then a voice told him, "Get up, Peter. Kill and eat."
14"Surely not, Lord!"[u] Peter replied. "I have never eaten anything impure or unclean."[v]
10:15 wMt 15:11; Ro 14:14, 17, 20; 1Co 10:25; 1Ti 4:3, 4; Tit 1:15
15The voice spoke to him a second time, "Do not call anything impure that God has
made clean."[w]
16This happened three times, and immediately the sheet was taken back to heaven.
10:17 xver 7, 8
17While Peter was wondering about the meaning of the vision, the men sent by Cornelius[x] found out where Simon's house was and stopped at the gate. 18They called out,
10:19 yAc 8:29
asking if Simon who was known as Peter was staying there.
19While Peter was still thinking about the vision, the Spirit said[y] to him, "Simon,

10:9 About noon. Literally, "About the sixth hour." **on the roof to pray.** Peter probably prayed three times a day (cf. Da 6:10). Ancient Middle Eastern houses had flat roofs that were accessible by an outside stairway.
10:10 a trance. Greek, *ekstasis.* Here the word refers to a condition in which the external consciousness was suspended. It was an ideal condition in which to receive the vision and be brought to understand God's message.
10:12 all kinds of four-footed animals . . . reptiles . . . birds. Both clean and unclean animals (Lev 11).
10:13 Kill and eat. Peter was hungry but, as a good Jew, he was not willing to violate the Old Testament command of God regarding the eating of unclean animals (v. 14).
10:15 God has made clean. It would appear that one central purpose of the dietary regulations in the Old Testament was to keep Israel separated from Gentile practices. Now that God was calling unclean Gentiles to salvation in large numbers, regulations that had divided Jews from Gentiles in this way were no longer appropriate.
10:16 three times. The vision was repeated to overcome Peter's strong objections.

Timeline of Paul's Life

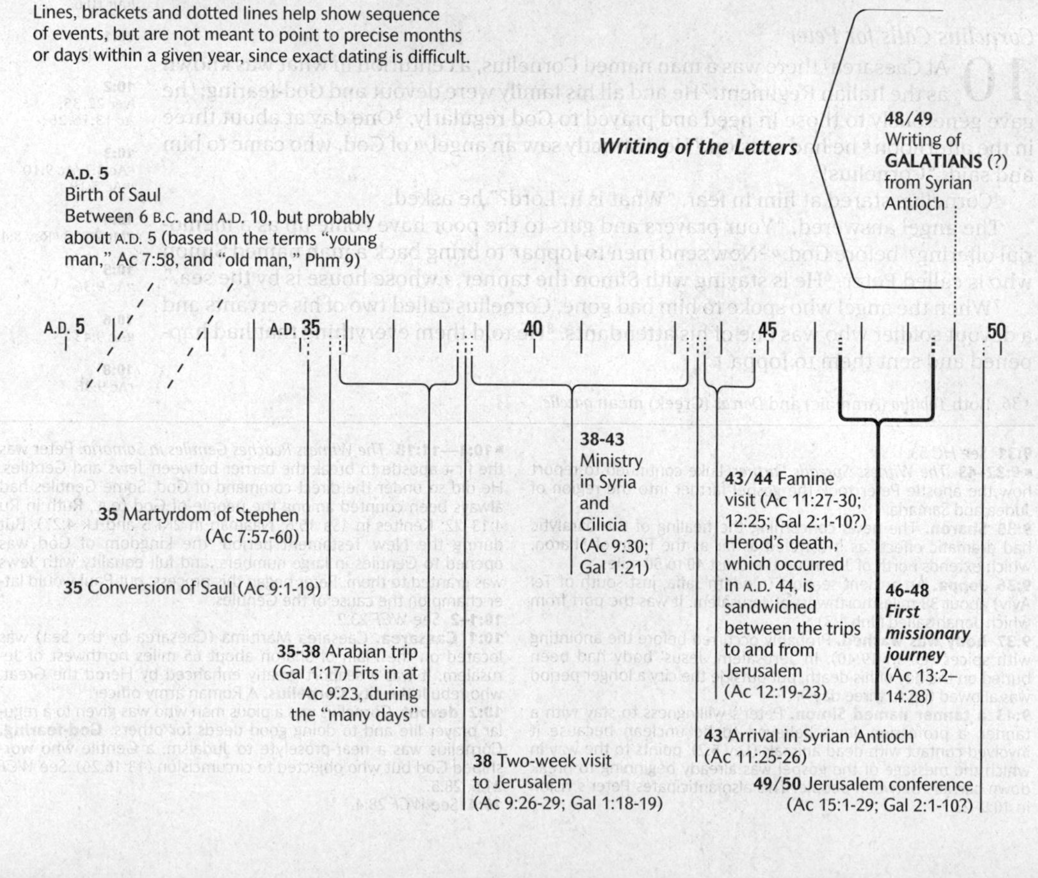

three[a] men are looking for you. 20So get up and go downstairs. Do not hesitate to go with
them, for I have sent them."[z]
21Peter went down and said to the men, "I'm the one you're looking for. Why have you
come?"
22The men replied, "We have come from Cornelius the centurion. He is a righteous
and God-fearing man,[a] who is respected by all the Jewish people. A holy angel told him
to have you come to his house so that he could hear what you have to say."[b] 23Then Peter invited the men into the house to be his guests.

Peter at Cornelius's House

The next day Peter started out with them, and some of the brothers[c] from Joppa went
along.[d] 24The following day he arrived in Caesarea.[e] Cornelius was expecting them and
had called together his relatives and close friends. 25As Peter entered the house, Cornelius met him and fell at his feet in reverence. 26But Peter made him get up. "Stand up,"
he said, "I am only a man myself."[f]
27Talking with him, Peter went inside and found a large gathering of people. 28He said
to them: "You are well aware that it is against our law for a Jew to associate with a Gentile or visit him.[g] But God has shown me that I should not call any man impure or un-

10:20 [z]Ac 15:7-9
10:22 [a]ver 2 [b]Ac 11:14
10:23 [c]Ac 1:16 [d]ver 45; Ac 11:12
10:24 [e]Ac 8:40
10:26 [f]Ac 14:15; Rev 19:10
10:28 [g]Jn 4:9; 18:28; Ac 11:3

a *19* One early manuscript *two;* other manuscripts do not have the number.

10:22 See *WCF* 28.5.
10:24 The following day. It took the group two days to travel the 30 miles from Joppa to Caesarea.
10:25–26 See *WLC* 105; *BC* 26.
10:25 Peter entered. Peter had so progressed in his spiritual understanding that he entered the house of a Gentile (v. 28). **fell at his feet in reverence.** Cornelius was overawed at Peter's presence. He had been instructed by God to send for the apostle.
10:28 God has shown me. Through the illustration of the animals being let down in the sheet and God's voice saying, "Do not call anything impure that God has made clean" (v. 15). Peter saw that the vision applied to more than dietary restrictions

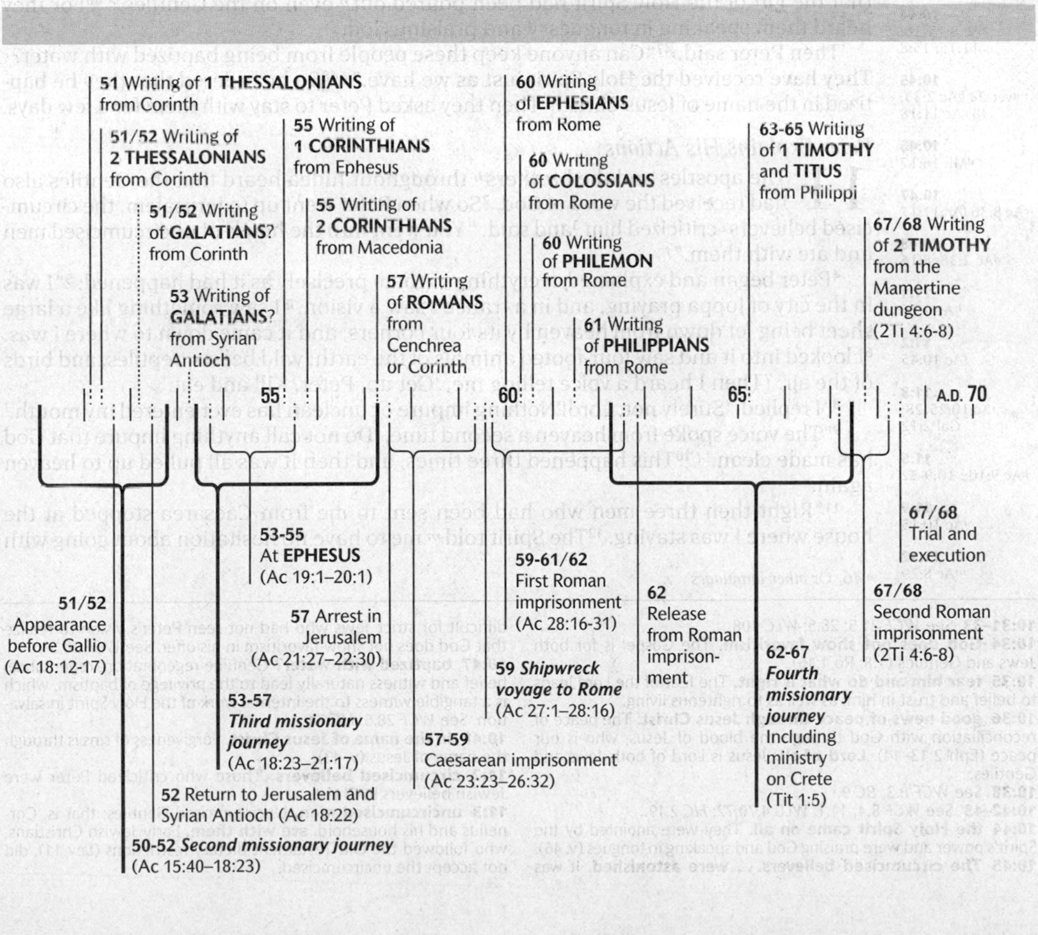

clean.[h] 29So when I was sent for, I came without raising any objection. May I ask why you
sent for me?"
30Cornelius answered: "Four days ago I was in my house praying at this hour, at three
in the afternoon. Suddenly a man in shining clothes stood before me 31and said, 'Cornelius, God has heard your prayer and remembered your gifts to the poor. 32Send to Joppa
for Simon who is called Peter. He is a guest in the home of Simon the tanner, who lives
by the sea.' 33So I sent for you immediately, and it was good of you to come. Now we are
all here in the presence of God to listen to everything the Lord has commanded you to
tell us."
34Then Peter began to speak: "I now realize how true it is that God does not show favoritism[i] 35but accepts men from every nation who fear him and do what is right.[j] 36You
know the message God sent to the people of Israel, telling the good news[k] of peace[l]
through Jesus Christ, who is Lord of all.[m] 37You know what has happened throughout
Judea, beginning in Galilee after the baptism that John preached— 38how God anointed[n] Jesus of Nazareth with the Holy Spirit and power, and how he went around doing
good and healing[o] all who were under the power of the devil, because God was with
him.[p]
39"We are witnesses[q] of everything he did in the country of the Jews and in Jerusalem. They killed him by hanging him on a tree,[r] 40but God raised him from the dead[s] on
the third day and caused him to be seen. 41He was not seen by all the people,[t] but by witnesses whom God had already chosen—by us who ate[u] and drank with him after he rose
from the dead. 42He commanded us to preach to the people[v] and to testify that he is the
one whom God appointed as judge of the living and the dead.[w] 43All the prophets testify about him[x] that everyone[y] who believes in him receives forgiveness of sins through
his name."
44While Peter was still speaking these words, the Holy Spirit came on[z] all who heard
the message. 45The circumcised believers who had come with Peter[a] were astonished
that the gift of the Holy Spirit had been poured out[b] even on the Gentiles.[c] 46For they
heard them speaking in tongues[a][d] and praising God.
Then Peter said, 47"Can anyone keep these people from being baptized with water?[e]
They have received the Holy Spirit just as we have."[f] 48So he ordered that they be baptized in the name of Jesus Christ.[g] Then they asked Peter to stay with them for a few days.

Peter Explains His Actions

11 The apostles and the brothers[h] throughout Judea heard that the Gentiles also
had received the word of God. 2So when Peter went up to Jerusalem, the circumcised believers[i] criticized him 3and said, "You went into the house of uncircumcised men
and ate with them."[j]
4Peter began and explained everything to them precisely as it had happened: 5"I was
in the city of Joppa praying, and in a trance I saw a vision.[k] I saw something like a large
sheet being let down from heaven by its four corners, and it came down to where I was.
6I looked into it and saw four-footed animals of the earth, wild beasts, reptiles, and birds
of the air. 7Then I heard a voice telling me, 'Get up, Peter. Kill and eat.'
8"I replied, 'Surely not, Lord! Nothing impure or unclean has ever entered my mouth.'
9"The voice spoke from heaven a second time, 'Do not call anything impure that God
has made clean.'[l] 10This happened three times, and then it was all pulled up to heaven
again.
11"Right then three men who had been sent to me from Caesarea stopped at the
house where I was staying. 12The Spirit told[m] me to have no hesitation about going with

10:28 [h]Ac 15:8,9
10:34 [i]Dt 10:17; 2Ch 19:7; Job 34:19; Ro 2:11; Gal 2:6; Eph 6:9; Col 3:25; 1Pe 1:17
10:35 [j]Ac 15:9
10:36 [k]Ac 13:32 [l]Lk 2:14 [m]Mt 28:18; Ro 10:12
10:38 [n]Ac 4:26 [o]Mt 4:23 [p]Jn 3:2
10:39 [q]Lk 24:48 [r]Ac 5:30
10:40 [s]Ac 2:24
10:41 [t]Jn 14:17,22 [u]Lk 24:43; Jn 21:13
10:42 [v]Mt 28:19,20 [w]Jn 5:22; Ac 17:31; Ro 14:9; 2Co 5:10; 2Ti 4:1; 1Pe 4:5
10:43 [x]Isa 53:11 [y]Ac 15:9
10:44 [z]Ac 8:15,16; 11:15; 15:8
10:45 [a]ver 23 [b]Ac 2:33, 38 [c]Ac 11:18
10:46 [d]Mk 16:17
10:47 [e]Ac 8:36 [f]Ac 11:17
10:48 [g]Ac 2:38; 8:16
11:1 [h]Ac 1:16
11:2 [i]Ac 10:45
11:3 [j]Ac 10:25,28; Gal 2:12
11:5 [k]Ac 9:10;; 10:9-32
11:9 [l]Ac 10:15
11:12 [m]Ac 8:29

[a] *46* Or *other languages*

10:31–33 See *WCF* 21.5; 28.5; *WLC* 108.
10:34 God does not show favoritism. The Gospel is for both Jews and Gentiles (1:8; Ro 1:16).
10:35 fear him and do what is right. The fear of the Lord leads to belief and trust in him, as well as to righteous living.
10:36 good news of peace through Jesus Christ. The peace of reconciliation with God through the blood of Jesus, who is our peace (Eph 2:13–14). **Lord of all.** Jesus is Lord of both Jews and Gentiles.
10:38 See *WCF* 8.3; *BC* 9.
10:42–43 See *WCF* 8.4; 11.1; *WLC* 4,70,72; *HC* 2,19.
10:44 the Holy Spirit came on all. They were anointed by the Spirit's power and were praising God and speaking in tongues (v. 46).
10:45 The circumcised believers. . . were astonished. It was difficult for strict Jews who had not seen Peter's vision to realize that God does not show favoritism in his offer. See *WCF* 28.5.
10:47 baptized with water? Genuine regeneration, repentance, belief and witness naturally lead to the privilege of baptism, which is a tangible witness to the internal work of the Holy Spirit in salvation. See *WCF* 28.5; *HC* 74.
10:48 in the name of Jesus Christ. Forgiveness of sins is through the name of Jesus (v. 43).
11:2 circumcised believers. Those who criticized Peter were Jewish believers in Christ.
11:3 uncircumcised men. Uncircumcised Gentiles; that is, Cornelius and his household. **ate with them.** Early Jewish Christians, who followed the Old Testament dietary restrictions (Lev 11), did not accept the uncircumcised.

them.[n] These six brothers also went with me, and we entered the man's house. 13He told
us how he had seen an angel appear in his house and say, 'Send to Joppa for Simon who
is called Peter. 14He will bring you a message through which you and all your household[o]
will be saved.'
15"As I began to speak, the Holy Spirit came on[p] them as he had come on us at the
beginning.[q] 16Then I remembered what the Lord had said: 'John baptized with[a] water,
but you will be baptized with the Holy Spirit.'[r] 17So if God gave them the same gift as he
gave us,[s] who believed in the Lord Jesus Christ, who was I to think that I could oppose
God?"
18When they heard this, they had no further objections and praised God, saying, "So
then, God has granted even the Gentiles repentance unto life."[t]

The Church in Antioch

19Now those who had been scattered by the persecution in connection with Stephen[u]
traveled as far as Phoenicia, Cyprus and Antioch,[v] telling the message only to Jews.
20Some of them, however, men from Cyprus[w] and Cyrene,[x] went to Antioch and began
to speak to Greeks also, telling them the good news about the Lord Jesus. 21The Lord's
hand was with them,[y] and a great number of people believed and turned to the Lord.[z]
22News of this reached the ears of the church at Jerusalem, and they sent Barnabas[a]
to Antioch. 23When he arrived and saw the evidence of the grace of God,[b] he was glad
and encouraged them all to remain true to the Lord with all their hearts.[c] 24He was a
good man, full of the Holy Spirit and faith, and a great number of people were brought
to the Lord.[d]
25Then Barnabas went to Tarsus[e] to look for Saul, 26and when he found him, he
brought him to Antioch. So for a whole year Barnabas and Saul met with the church and
taught great numbers of people. The disciples[f] were called Christians first[g] at Antioch.
27During this time some prophets[h] came down from Jerusalem to Antioch. 28One of
them, named Agabus,[i] stood up and through the Spirit predicted that a severe famine
would spread over the entire Roman world.[j] (This happened during the reign of Claudius.)[k] 29The disciples,[l] each according to his ability, decided to provide help[m] for the
brothers[n] living in Judea. 30This they did, sending their gift to the elders[o] by Barnabas
and Saul.[p]

Peter's Miraculous Escape From Prison

12 It was about this time that King Herod arrested some who belonged to the
church, intending to persecute them. 2He had James, the brother of John,[q] put
to death with the sword. 3When he saw that this pleased the Jews,[r] he proceeded to seize
Peter also. This happened during the Feast of Unleavened Bread.[s] 4After arresting him,
he put him in prison, handing him over to be guarded by four squads of four soldiers
each. Herod intended to bring him out for public trial after the Passover.
5So Peter was kept in prison, but the church was earnestly praying to God for him.[t]

11:12 [n]Ac 15:9; Ro 3:22
11:14 [o]Jn 4:53; Ac 16:15, 31-34; 1Co 1:11,16
11:15 [p]Ac 10:44 [q]Ac 2:4
11:16 [r]Mk 1:8; Ac 1:5
11:17 [s]Ac 10:45,47
11:18 [t]Ro 10:12,13; 2Co 7:10
11:19 [u]Ac 8:1,4 [v]ver 26, 27; Ac 13:1; 18:22; Gal 2:11
11:20 [w]Ac 4:36 [x]Mt 27:32
11:21 [y]Lk 1:66 [z]Ac 2:47
11:22 [a]Ac 4:36
11:23 [b]Ac 13:43; 14:26; 20:24 [c]Ac 14:22
11:24 [d]ver 21; Ac 5:14
11:25 [e]Ac 9:11
11:26 [f]Ac 6:1,2; 13:52 [g]Ac 26:28; 1Pe 4:16
11:27 [h]Ac 13:1; 15:32; 1Co 12:28,29; Eph 4:11
11:28 [i]Ac 21:10 [j]Mt 24:14 [k]Ac 18:2
11:29 [l]ver 26 [m]Ro 15:26; 2Co 9:2 [n]Ac 1:16
11:30 [o]Ac 14:23 [p]Ac 12:25
12:2 [q]Mt 4:21
12:3 [r]Ac 24:27 [s]Ex 12:15; 23:15
12:5 [t]Eph 6:18

[a] *16* Or *in*

11:14 you and all your household will be saved. God's saving grace is often extended to whole families, a concept embedded in the message of the Old Testament (e.g., Abraham, Isaac and Jacob and their families) and of the New (e.g., Lk 19:9; Ac 2:38–39; 16:31).
11:17 I could oppose God? Peter stressed God's sovereign purpose to save both Jews and Gentiles. No doubt some who were present were reminded of God's promise to Abraham: "all peoples on earth will be blessed through you" (Ge 12:3; cf. Gal 3:8).
11:18 repentance unto life. Biblical repentance includes a sorrow for sin and a change of heart that gives a new direction to one's life (26:20). It leads to trust in Jesus Christ (20:21), to forgiveness of sins (Mk 1:4; Lk 24:47), to eternal life (11:18) and to a life that manifests the fruits of repentance (26:20; Lk 3:8). See *WCF* 15.1; *WLC* 75,76; *WSC* 87.
■ **11:19–30** *The Church in Syrian Antioch.* Luke described events that took place in the church in Antioch. He not only continued his record of Paul's (Saul's) ministry, but he also showed how churches outside Jerusalem served their mother church in Jerusalem.
11:20–21 See *WLC* 76.
11:21 The Lord's hand. Although men preached the gospel, it was God who sovereignly saved many people, calling them to believe and turn to the Lord (2:38; cf. Isa 55:6–7).
11:26 called Christians. In the New Testament, the term "Christian" appears only here, in 26:28 and in 1 Peter 4:16. Josephus (*Antiquities,* 18.64) defines the term as belonging to or following Christ ("tribes of Christ"). It may have been a term the Christians first used here to distinguish themselves from followers of other religions, or it may have been a derisive label conferred on them by their enemies.
11:29–30 See *WCF* 26.2.
■ **12:1–25** *Persecution and Judgment in Jerusalem.* Luke recorded how the church in Jerusalem suffered persecution, but he also noted God's judgment against the persecutors. This material illustrates that persecutions will inevitably rise against God's faithful people but that one day judgment will come against God's enemies. Luke also continued to present background information for Paul's ministry.
12:1 about this time. The time relating to the famine relief for the brothers in Judea (11:27–30) is indefinite. The famine-relief visit (A.D. 45–47; cf. 11:28) of Barnabas and Saul could actually have occurred after the conclusion of the events of chapter 12. At that time, Barnabas and Saul returned to Antioch from Jerusalem (v. 25).
12:3 this pleased the Jews . . . seize Peter also. Here is an example of God's sovereign choices in the lives of his equally dedicated servants: James was killed by the sword, while Peter was delivered from prison (see also Jn 21:20–22). **during the Feast of Unleavened Bread.** With so many zealous Jews visiting the city for the feast, it was an opportune time to make the arrest.
12:5 See *WLC* 189; *WSC* 100.

6The night before Herod was to bring him to trial, Peter was sleeping between two soldiers, bound with two chains,[u] and sentries stood guard at the entrance. 7Suddenly an angel[v] of the Lord appeared and a light shone in the cell. He struck Peter on the side and woke him up. "Quick, get up!" he said, and the chains fell off Peter's wrists.[w]

8Then the angel said to him, "Put on your clothes and sandals." And Peter did so. "Wrap your cloak around you and follow me," the angel told him. 9Peter followed him out of the prison, but he had no idea that what the angel was doing was really happening; he thought he was seeing a vision.[x] 10They passed the first and second guards and came to the iron gate leading to the city. It opened for them by itself,[y] and they went through it. When they had walked the length of one street, suddenly the angel left him.

11Then Peter came to himself[z] and said, "Now I know without a doubt that the Lord sent his angel and rescued me[a] from Herod's clutches and from everything the Jewish people were anticipating."

12When this had dawned on him, he went to the house of Mary the mother of John, also called Mark,[b] where many people had gathered and were praying.[c] 13Peter knocked at the outer entrance, and a servant girl named Rhoda came to answer the door.[d] 14When she recognized Peter's voice, she was so overjoyed[e] she ran back without opening it and exclaimed, "Peter is at the door!"

15"You're out of your mind," they told her. When she kept insisting that it was so, they said, "It must be his angel."[f]

16But Peter kept on knocking, and when they opened the door and saw him, they were astonished. 17Peter motioned with his hand[g] for them to be quiet and described how the Lord had brought him out of prison. "Tell James[h] and the brothers[i] about this," he said, and then he left for another place.

18In the morning, there was no small commotion among the soldiers as to what had become of Peter. 19After Herod had a thorough search made for him and did not find him, he cross-examined the guards and ordered that they be executed.[j]

Herod's Death

Then Herod went from Judea to Caesarea[k] and stayed there a while. 20He had been quarreling with the people of Tyre and Sidon;[l] they now joined together and sought an audience with him. Having secured the support of Blastus, a trusted personal servant of the king, they asked for peace, because they depended on the king's country for their food supply.[m]

21On the appointed day Herod, wearing his royal robes, sat on his throne and delivered a public address to the people. 22They shouted, "This is the voice of a god, not of a man." 23Immediately, because Herod did not give praise to God, an angel of the Lord struck him down,[n] and he was eaten by worms and died.

24But the word of God continued to increase and spread.[o]

25When Barnabas[p] and Saul had finished their mission,[q] they returned from[a] Jerusalem, taking with them John, also called Mark.[r]

Barnabas and Saul Sent Off

13 In the church at Antioch[s] there were prophets[t] and teachers: Barnabas,[u] Simeon called Niger, Lucius of Cyrene, Manaen (who had been brought up with

12:6 [u]Ac 21:33
12:7 [v]Ac 5:19 [w]Ac 16:26
12:9 [x]Ac 9:10
12:10 [y]Ac 5:19; 16:26
12:11 [z]Lk 15:17 [a]Ps 34:7; Da 3:28; 6:22; 2Co 1:10; 2Pe 2:9
12:12 [b]ver 25; Ac 15:37, 39; Col 4:10; Phm 24; 1Pe 5:13 [c]ver 5
12:13 [d]Jn 18:16,17
12:14 [e]Lk 24:41
12:15 [f]Mt 18:10
12:17 [g]Ac 13:16; 19:33; 21:40 [h]Ac 15:13 [i]Ac 1:16
12:19 [j]Ac 16:27 [k]Ac 8:40
12:20 [l]Mt 11:21 [m]1Ki 5:9,11; Eze 27:17
12:23 [n]1Sa 25:38; 2Sa 24:16,17
12:24 [o]Ac 6:7; 19:20
12:25 [p]Ac 4:36 [q]Ac 11:30 [r]ver 12
13:1 [s]Ac 11:19 [t]Ac 11:27 [u]Ac 4:36; 11:22-26

[a] *25* Some manuscripts *to*

12:7 an angel of the Lord . . . a light shone. An angel was an assurance of God's presence, and the light probably reminded Peter of the Old Testament glory of the Lord (Ex 3:2; 13:22; 40:34; Ac 9:3).
12:9 prison. Probably the Antonia Fortress (rebuilt by Herod the Great and named after Mark Antony) on the north edge of the temple platform. Its easy access allowed for the public display of prisoners at the conclusion of the Passover Feast.
12:10 iron gate leading to the city. The Antonia Fortress not only had an entrance into the temple courts on the south, but it also had other entrances to the city.
12:15–16 Note the irony of the situation: The disciples prayed fervently to the sovereign God of heaven (cf. 4:23–24) to protect and deliver Peter, but then they refused to believe that the Lord in his providence had responded to their request.
12:15 his angel. A personal angelic guardian (Mt 18:10; Heb 1:14) that popular Jewish piety supposed was able to assume the appearance of the human person being protected.
12:19 executed. Roman law stipulated that if a guard were to lose a prisoner, the guard's own life was to be forfeited (cf. 16:27–28).
12:22 See *WLC* 145.
12:23 did not give praise to God. This is characteristic of humankind's depraved nature (Ro 1:21). **struck him down . . . eaten by worms.** Josephus (*Antiquities,* 19.346,349–350) indicates that Herod Agrippa I experienced intense heart pain and severe pain in his abdomen and that he died after five days. Luke said he was eaten by worms, possibly the Eastern roundworms that would actively feed on a person's alimentary canal and surrounding area. If he was struck with a disease such as appendicitis or peritonitis, he no doubt died in great agony. Herod died in A.D. 44, in the fourth year of Emperor Claudius Caesar.
12:25 Barnabas and Saul had finished their mission. The mission of bringing the Antioch famine-relief gift to Jerusalem (11:27–30). **John . . . Mark.** Possibly the young man who had fled the night of Jesus' arrest (Mk 14:51–52). Mark, the writer of the second Gospel (cf. 1Pe 5:13), accompanied Paul and Barnabas down to Antioch and on the first missionary journey (13:4). Paul considered him unfit for the second missionary journey, so Barnabas took him to Cyprus (Ac 15:36–39). Later, Paul once again appreciated and enjoyed Mark's company (Col 4:10; 2Ti 4:11; Phm 24).
■ **13:1—28:31** *The Apostolic Witness to the Ends of the Earth.* At

Herod[v] the tetrarch) and Saul. 2While they were worshiping the Lord and fasting, the
Holy Spirit said,[w] "Set apart for me Barnabas and Saul for the work[x] to which I have
called them."[y] 3So after they had fasted and prayed, they placed their hands on them[z]
and sent them off.[a]

On Cyprus

4The two of them, sent on their way by the Holy Spirit,[b] went down to Seleucia and
sailed from there to Cyprus.[c] 5When they arrived at Salamis, they proclaimed the word
of God in the Jewish synagogues.[d] John[e] was with them as their helper.
6They traveled through the whole island until they came to Paphos. There they met
a Jewish sorcerer[f] and false prophet[g] named Bar-Jesus, 7who was an attendant of the
proconsul,[h] Sergius Paulus. The proconsul, an intelligent man, sent for Barnabas and
Saul because he wanted to hear the word of God. 8But Elymas the sorcerer[i] (for that is
what his name means) opposed them and tried to turn the proconsul[j] from the faith.[k]
9Then Saul, who was also called Paul, filled with the Holy Spirit,[l] looked straight at Elymas and said, 10"You are a child of the devil[m] and an enemy of everything that is right!
You are full of all kinds of deceit and trickery. Will you never stop perverting the right
ways of the Lord?[n] 11Now the hand of the Lord is against you.[o] You are going to be blind,
and for a time you will be unable to see the light of the sun."
Immediately mist and darkness came over him, and he groped about, seeking someone to lead him by the hand. 12When the proconsul[p] saw what had happened, he believed, for he was amazed at the teaching about the Lord.

In Pisidian Antioch

13From Paphos,[q] Paul and his companions sailed to Perga in Pamphylia, where
John[r] left them to return to Jerusalem. 14From Perga they went on to Pisidian Antioch.[s]
On the Sabbath[t] they entered the synagogue[u] and sat down. 15After the reading from the
Law[v] and the Prophets, the synagogue rulers sent word to them, saying, "Brothers, if you
have a message of encouragement for the people, please speak."
16Standing up, Paul motioned with his hand[w] and said: "Men of Israel and you Gentiles who worship God, listen to me! 17The God of the people of Israel chose our fathers;
he made the people prosper during their stay in Egypt, with mighty power he led them
out of that country,[x] 18he endured their conduct[a][y] for about forty years in the desert,[z]

13:1 [v]Mt 14:1
13:2 [w]Ac 8:29 [x]Ac 14:26 [y]Ac 22:21
13:3 [z]Ac 6:6 [a]Ac 14:26
13:4 [b]ver 2,3 [c]Ac 4:36
13:5 [d]Ac 9:20 [e]Ac 12:12
13:6 [f]Ac 8:9 [g]Mt 7:15
13:7 [h]ver 8,12; Ac 19:38
13:8 [i]Ac 8:9 [j]ver 7 [k]Ac 6:7
13:9 [l]Ac 4:8
13:10 [m]Mt 13:38; Jn 8:44 [n]Hos 14:9
13:11 [o]Ex 9:3; 1Sa 5:6,7; Ps 32:4
13:12 [p]ver 7
13:13 [q]ver 6 [r]Ac 12:12
13:14 [s]Ac 14:19,21 [t]Ac 16:13 [u]Ac 9:20
13:15 [v]Ac 15:21
13:16 [w]Ac 12:17
13:17 [x]Ex 6:6,7; Dt 7:6-8
13:18 [y]Dt 1:31 [z]Ac 7:36

[a] *18* Some manuscripts *and cared for them*

---

this point, Luke described the third major stage of the spread of the gospel to the Gentile nations (see notes on 3:1—7:60; 8:1—11:18). Peter had already opened the way to the Gentiles (10:1—11:18), but now attention shifts to Paul, who continued this part of the apostolic mission.

■ **13:1—14:28** *Paul's First Missionary Journey.* These chapters describe the first of four journeys through which Paul fulfilled the apostles' mission to the nations. Paul and Barnabas reached Cyprus and Galatia.

13:1 prophets and teachers. See Ephesians 4:11. **Barnabas.** See note on 4:36. **Simeon called Niger.** A man of dark complexion (*niger* is Latin for "black") who may have come from Africa. He is possibly the Simon of Cyrene (Lk 23:26) whose sons, Alexander and Rufus, were among the Christians at Rome (Mk 15:21; cf. Ro 16:13). **Lucius of Cyrene.** Cyrene was the capital of the Roman province of Cyrenaica (in modern Libya). **Manaen.** A Christian who reportedly was raised as a foster brother with Herod Antipas. We do not know how Manaen (Greek for the Hebrew *Menahem*) heard the gospel and turned to the Lord. **Saul.** See note on 9:1.

13:2 See *BC* 31.

13:3 fasted and prayed. Fasting and especially prayer were vital in the lives of the believers in Acts (2:42; 3:1; 4:24; 6:4; 10:31; 14:23; 28:8). **placed their hands on them.** Recognizing that the Holy Spirit had set Barnabas and Saul apart, they officially placed their hands on them in recognition of what the Spirit had already done (v. 2) and of what he was going to do in sending them out (v. 4; cf. 14:23; 1Ti 4:14).

13:4 Seleucia. The port of Antioch, 16 miles west of Antioch and 4–5 miles north of the mouth of the Orontes River. **Cyprus.** An island off the coast of Phoenicia that was inhabited largely by Greeks but also by many Jews.

13:5 arrived at Salamis. They sailed directly west about 130 miles from Seleucia to Salamis on the east coast of Cyprus. Salamis was the most important city on the island at the time. The provincial capital of the island was Paphos, 90 miles southwest.

13:6 Jewish sorcerer. Greek *magos,* meaning "wise man" (Mt 2:1), "sorcerer," "magician." Although sorcery was forbidden in Judaism, some people still practiced it. Bar-Jesus (*bar* is Aramaic for "son of"; "Jesus" is from the Hebrew *Joshua*) was indeed a false prophet.

13:7 Sergius Paulus. Possibly Lucius Sergius Paulus, who had been an official during the reign of Claudius and then had become proconsul (the chief officer in a senatorial province, who answered to the Roman Senate) at Paphos in Cyprus. By contrast, the region later referred to as Palestine was an imperial province and had a procurator directly responsible to the emperor.

13:8 Elymas. Another name for Bar-Jesus. This man was in the proconsul's court. He tried to keep Paulus from believing the Christian message.

13:9 Saul . . . also called Paul. Saul was his Jewish name; Paul, his Gentile Roman name. Many Jews of the time had two names (e.g., Simon Peter). As a Roman citizen, Paul had two names, and possibly three. He used his Greek name even before Sergius Paulus was converted. Luke no longer speaks here of "Barnabas and Saul" but of "Paul and Barnabas," except when these missionaries returned to the Jerusalem church, where Barnabas would have been expected to be the leader (14:14).

13:13 sailed to Perga in Pamphylia. The city of Perga was located northwest of Cyprus in Pamphylia, an economically poor Roman province on the south coast of Asia Minor. Perga was five miles from the coast and about twelve miles northeast of the seaport Attalia.

13:14 Pisidian Antioch. This Antioch, about 100 miles north of Perga and 3,600 feet above sea level, was located in Phrygia near the border of Pisidia. To distinguish it from another Antioch in Phrygia, it was popularly called "Antioch of Pisidia."

13:15 reading from the Law and the Prophets. In the synagogue at this time, a worship service would have included the creed (Dt 6:4), the "Eighteen Blessings" prayer, one reading from the Law and one from the Prophets, an exposition and application (Lk 4:16–30) and a concluding benediction.

19he overthrew seven nations in Canaan[a] and gave their land to his people[b] as their inheritance. **20**All this took about 450 years.
"After this, God gave them judges[c] until the time of Samuel the prophet.[d] **21**Then the
people asked for a king,[e] and he gave them Saul[f] son of Kish, of the tribe of Benjamin,[g]
who ruled forty years. **22**After removing Saul,[h] he made David their king.[i] He testified
concerning him: 'I have found David son of Jesse a man after my own heart;[j] he will do
everything I want him to do.'
23"From this man's descendants[k] God has brought to Israel the Savior[l] Jesus,[m] as he
promised.[n] **24**Before the coming of Jesus, John preached repentance and baptism to all
the people of Israel.[o] **25**As John was completing his work,[p] he said: 'Who do you think I
am? I am not that one.[q] No, but he is coming after me, whose sandals I am not worthy
to untie.'[r]
26"Brothers, children of Abraham, and you God-fearing Gentiles, it is to us that this
message of salvation[s] has been sent. **27**The people of Jerusalem and their rulers did not
recognize Jesus,[t] yet in condemning him they fulfilled the words of the prophets[u] that
are read every Sabbath. **28**Though they found no proper ground for a death sentence,
they asked Pilate to have him executed.[v] **29**When they had carried out all that was written about him,[w] they took him down from the tree[x] and laid him in a tomb.[y] **30**But God
raised him from the dead,[z] **31**and for many days he was seen by those who had traveled
with him from Galilee to Jerusalem.[a] They are now his witnesses[b] to our people.
32"We tell you the good news:[c] What God promised our fathers[d] **33**he has fulfilled for
us, their children, by raising up Jesus. As it is written in the second Psalm:

> " 'You are my Son;
> today I have become your Father.[a]'[b][e]

34The fact that God raised him from the dead, never to decay, is stated in these words:

> " 'I will give you the holy and sure blessings promised to David.'[c][f]

35So it is stated elsewhere:

> " 'You will not let your Holy One see decay.'[d][g]

36"For when David had served God's purpose in his own generation, he fell asleep;
he was buried with his fathers[h] and his body decayed. **37**But the one whom God raised
from the dead did not see decay.
38"Therefore, my brothers, I want you to know that through Jesus the forgiveness of
sins is proclaimed to you.[i] **39**Through him everyone who believes is justified from everything you could not be justified from by the law of Moses.[j] **40**Take care that what the
prophets have said does not happen to you:

> **41**" 'Look, you scoffers,
> wonder and perish,
> for I am going to do something in your days
> that you would never believe,
> even if someone told you.'[e]"[k]

42As Paul and Barnabas were leaving the synagogue,[l] the people invited them to
speak further about these things on the next Sabbath. **43**When the congregation was dismissed, many of the Jews and devout converts to Judaism followed Paul and Barnabas,
who talked with them and urged them to continue in the grace of God.[m]
44On the next Sabbath almost the whole city gathered to hear the word of the Lord.
45When the Jews saw the crowds, they were filled with jealousy and talked abusively[n]
against what Paul was saying.[o]
46Then Paul and Barnabas answered them boldly: "We had to speak the word of God to

13:19 [a]Dt 7:1 [b]Jos 19:51
13:20 [c]Jdg 2:16 [d]1Sa 3:19,20
13:21 [e]1Sa 8:5,19 [f]1Sa 10:1 [g]1Sa 9:1,2
13:22 [h]1Sa 15:23,26 [i]1Sa 16:13; Ps 89:20 [j]1Sa 13:14
13:23 [k]Mt 1:1 [l]Lk 2:11 [m]Mt 1:21 [n]ver 32
13:24 [o]Mk 1:4
13:25 [p]Ac 20:24 [q]Jn 1:20 [r]Mt 3:11; Jn 1:27
13:26 [s]Ac 4:12
13:27 [t]Ac 3:17 [u]Lk 24:27
13:28 [v]Mt 27:20-25; Ac 3:14
13:29 [w]Lk 18:31 [x]Ac 5:30 [y]Lk 23:53
13:30 [z]Mt 28:6; Ac 2:24
13:31 [a]Mt 28:16 [b]Lk 24:48
13:32 [c]Ac 5:42 [d]Ac 26:6; Ro 4:13
13:33 [e]Ps 2:7
13:34 [f]Isa 55:3
13:35 [g]Ps 16:10; Ac 2:27
13:36 [h]1Ki 2:10; Ac 2:29
13:38 [i]Lk 24:47; Ac 2:38
13:39 [j]Ro 3:28
13:41 [k]Hab 1:5
13:42 [l]ver 14
13:43 [m]Ac 11:23; 14:22
13:45 [n]Ac 18:6; 1Pe 4:4; Jude 10 [o]1Th 2:16

[a] 33 Or *have begotten you* [b] 33 Psalm 2:7 [c] 34 Isaiah 55:3 [d] 35 Psalm 16:10 [e] 41 Hab. 1:5

13:20 about 450 years. About 400 years plus the 40 years in the wilderness and the period of Joshua's conquest (see note on 7:6).
13:23 See *BC* 18.
13:29 See *HC* 41.
13:33 it is written. Paul emphasized Jesus' resurrection, a crucial point of the apostles' witness (1:22). He cited three Old Testament Scriptures (Pss 2:7; 16:10; Isa 55:3). **You are my Son; today I have become your Father.** That is, "Today in raising you from the dead, I am declaring that you are my Son and I am your Father" (see note on Heb 1:5). See *HC* 35.
13:34 never to decay. See note on 2:24.
13:36–39 See *WCF* 11.1; 8.4; 32.1; *BC* 22.
13:39 The law points the sinner to Christ (Gal 3:24), for "a man is not justified by observing the law, but by faith in Jesus Christ" (Gal 2:16). To be justified is to be declared righteous by God (Ro 3:21–22) and therefore granted forgiveness of sins (Eph 1:7). See *WCF* 19.6.
13:42–46 See *WCF* 21.6; *WLC* 109,113.
13:46 the word of God to you first. Since Jesus the Messiah came through the Jews (Ge 12:3), Paul was consistent in applying

The Spread of the Gospel

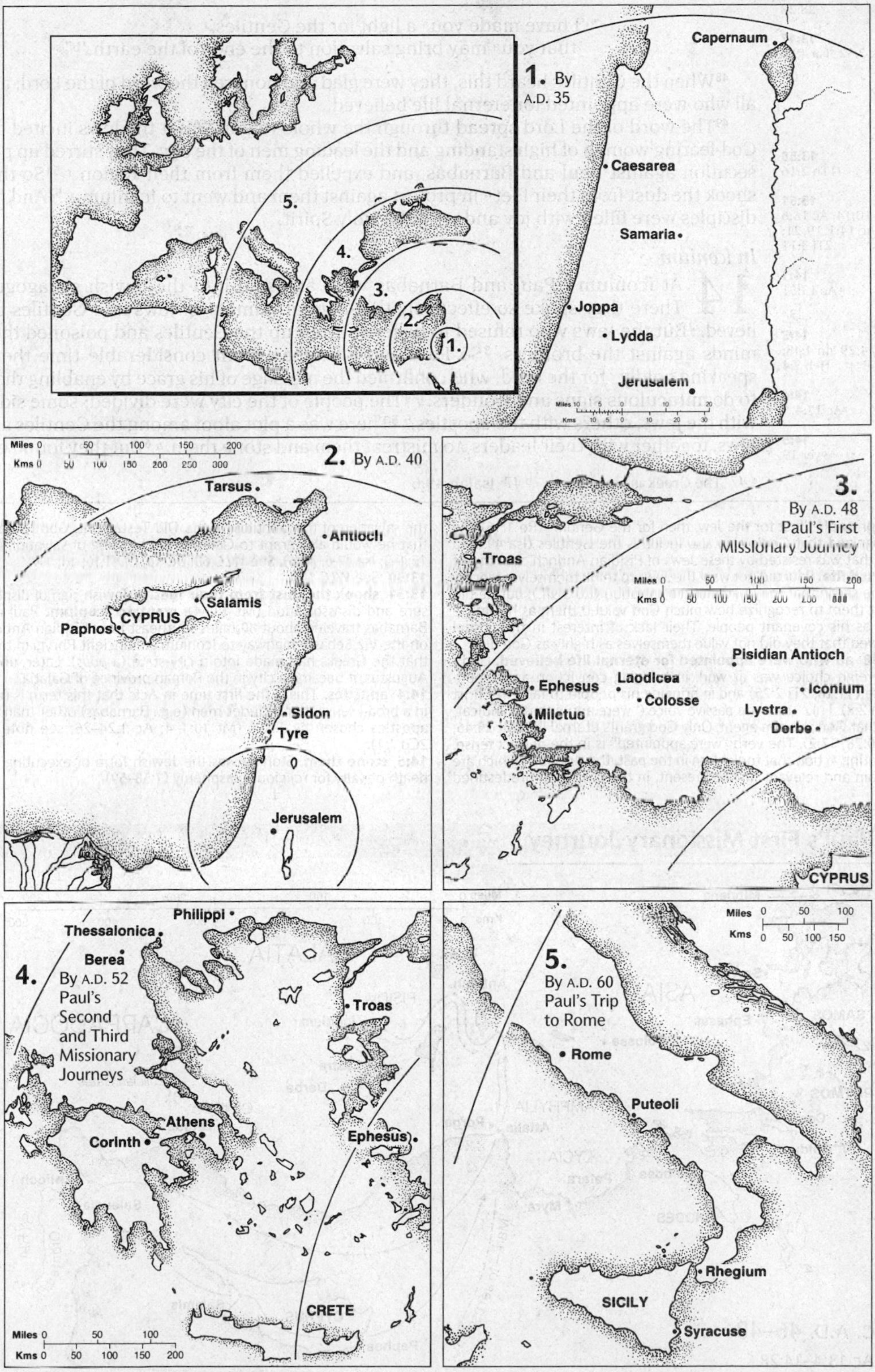

1. By A.D. 35
5.
4.
3.
2.
1.
Capernaum
Caesarea
Samaria
Joppa
Lydda
Jerusalem
Miles 10 5 0 10 20
Kms 10 5 0 10 20 30
2. By A.D. 40
Miles 0 50 100 150 200
Kms 0 50 100 150 200 250 300
Tarsus
Antioch
Salamis
CYPRUS
Paphos
Sidon
Tyre
Jerusalem
3. By A.D. 48 Paul's First Missionary Journey
Miles 0 50 100 150 200
Kms 0 50 100 150 200 250 300
Troas
Pisidian Antioch
Ephesus
Laodicea
Iconium
Colosse
Miletus
Lystra
Derbe
CYPRUS
4. By A.D. 52 Paul's Second and Third Missionary Journeys
Philippi
Thessalonica
Berea
Troas
Athens
Corinth
Ephesus
CRETE
Miles 0 50 100
Kms 0 50 100 150 200
5. By A.D. 60 Paul's Trip to Rome
Miles 0 50 100
Kms 0 50 100 150
Rome
Puteoli
Rhegium
SICILY
Syracuse

13:46 [p]ver 26; Ac 3:26 [q]Ac 18:6; 22:21; 28:28
13:47 [r]Lk 2:32 [s]Isa 49:6
13:50 [t]1Th 2:16
13:51 [u]Mt 10:14; Ac 18:6 [v]Ac 14:1,19,21; 2Ti 3:11
14:1 [w]Ac 13:51
14:3 [x]Ac 4:29 [y]Jn 4:48; Heb 2:4
14:4 [z]Ac 17:4,5
14:5 [a]ver 19

you first.[p] Since you reject it and do not consider yourselves worthy of eternal life, we now
turn to the Gentiles.[q] 47 For this is what the Lord has commanded us:

> " 'I have made you[a] a light for the Gentiles,[r]
> that you[a] may bring salvation to the ends of the earth.'[b]"[s]

48 When the Gentiles heard this, they were glad and honored the word of the Lord; and
all who were appointed for eternal life believed.
49 The word of the Lord spread through the whole region. 50 But the Jews incited the
God-fearing women of high standing and the leading men of the city. They stirred up persecution against Paul and Barnabas, and expelled them from their region.[t] 51 So they
shook the dust from their feet[u] in protest against them and went to Iconium.[v] 52 And the
disciples were filled with joy and with the Holy Spirit.

In Iconium

14 At Iconium[w] Paul and Barnabas went as usual into the Jewish synagogue.
There they spoke so effectively that a great number of Jews and Gentiles believed. 2 But the Jews who refused to believe stirred up the Gentiles and poisoned their
minds against the brothers. 3 So Paul and Barnabas spent considerable time there,
speaking boldly[x] for the Lord, who confirmed the message of his grace by enabling them
to do miraculous signs and wonders.[y] 4 The people of the city were divided; some sided
with the Jews, others with the apostles.[z] 5 There was a plot afoot among the Gentiles and
Jews, together with their leaders, to mistreat them and stone them.[a] 6 But they found out

[a] *47* The Greek is singular. [b] *47* Isaiah 49:6

the principle "first for the Jew, then for the Gentile" (Ro 1:16). He recognized that God's plan also includes the Gentiles (Isa 49:6), a fact that was resisted by these Jews of Pisidian Antioch. **worthy of eternal life.** Paul did not want the Jews to think themselves worthy in the sense that they had merited salvation (Ro 3:9ff.), but he did want them to recognize how much God valued them as his image and as his covenant people. Their lack of interest in the gospel showed that they did not value themselves as highly as God did.
13:48 all who were appointed for eternal life believed. God's sovereign choice was at work in bringing conviction and repentance (11:18; 2Ti 2:25) and in bringing his people to faith in Christ (Eph 2:8). Luke used the passive voice ("were appointed"), indicating that God was the agent. Only God grants eternal life (Mt 25:46; Jn 10:28; 17:2). The verb "were appointed" is in the perfect tense, denoting action that took place in the past, the results of which are certain and relevant for the present. In the past, God predestined the salvation of the Gentiles. In the Old Testament, God revealed that he would also grant to Gentiles the blessing of salvation (Ge 12:1–3; Isa 42:6; 49:6). See *WLC* 68; *BC* 16; *CD* 1.10; 1.I; 1.V.
13:50 See *WLC* 113.
13:51 shook the dust from their feet. A Jewish sign of displeasure and disassociation (Mt 10:14). **went to Iconium.** Paul and Barnabas traveled about 80 miles southeast from Pisidian Antioch on the Via Sebaste highway to Iconium, an ancient Phrygian town that the Greeks had made into a city-state (a *pólis*). Later, under Augustus, it became a city in the Roman province of Galatia.
14:4 apostles. This is the first time in Acts that this term is used in a broad sense that includes men (e.g., Barnabas) other than the apostles chosen by Jesus (Mt 10:1–4; Ac 1:24–26; see note on 2Co 1:1).
14:5 stone them. Stoning was the Jewish form of executing the death penalty for religious blasphemy (7:58–59).

Paul's First Missionary Journey

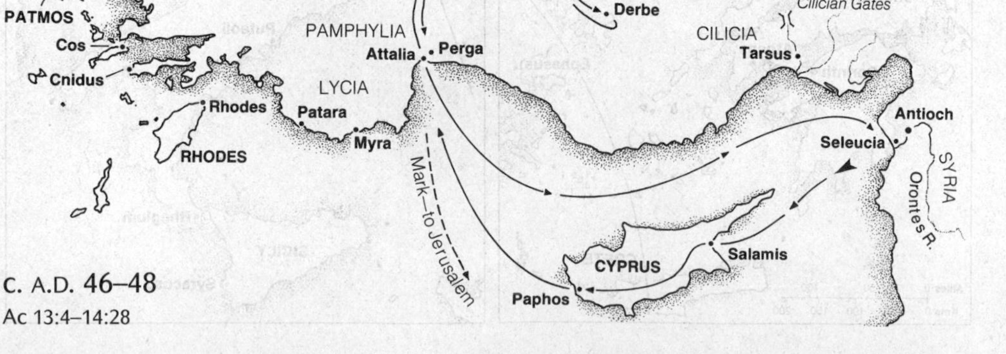

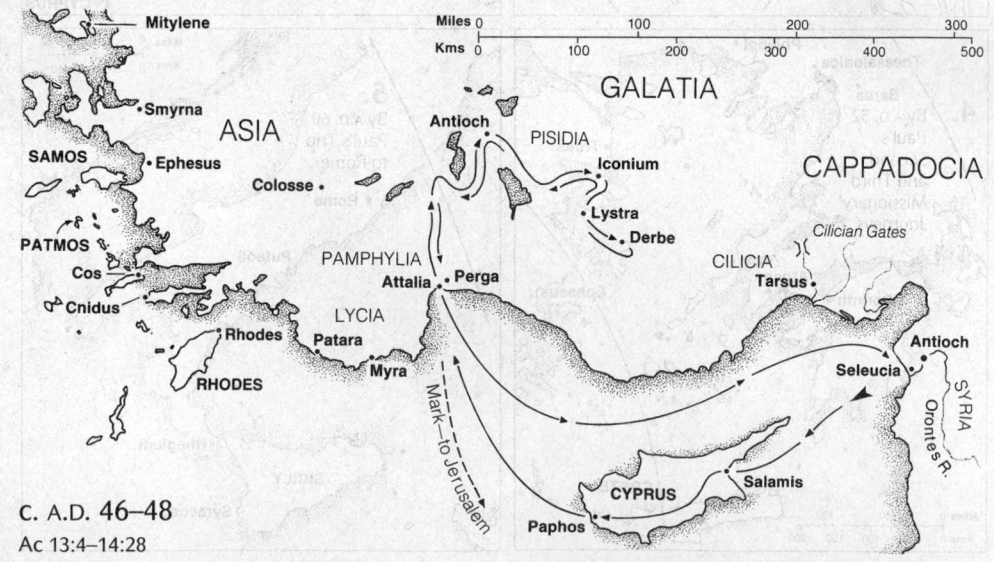

C. A.D. 46–48
Ac 13:4–14:28

about it and fled[b] to the Lycaonian cities of Lystra and Derbe and to the surrounding
country, 7where they continued to preach[c] the good news.[d]

In Lystra and Derbe

8In Lystra there sat a man crippled in his feet, who was lame from birth[e] and had never walked. 9He listened to Paul as he was speaking. Paul looked directly at him, saw that
he had faith to be healed[f] 10and called out, "Stand up on your feet!" At that, the man
jumped up and began to walk.[g]
11When the crowd saw what Paul had done, they shouted in the Lycaonian language,
"The gods have come down to us in human form!"[h] 12Barnabas they called Zeus, and
Paul they called Hermes because he was the chief speaker. 13The priest of Zeus, whose
temple was just outside the city, brought bulls and wreaths to the city gates because he
and the crowd wanted to offer sacrifices to them.
14But when the apostles Barnabas and Paul heard of this, they tore their clothes[i] and
rushed out into the crowd, shouting: 15"Men, why are you doing this? We too are only
men,[j] human like you. We are bringing you good news,[k] telling you to turn from these
worthless things[l] to the living God,[m] who made heaven and earth[n] and sea and everything in them.[o] 16In the past, he let[p] all nations go their own way.[q] 17Yet he has not left
himself without testimony:[r] He has shown kindness by giving you rain from heaven and
crops in their seasons;[s] he provides you with plenty of food and fills your hearts with joy."
18Even with these words, they had difficulty keeping the crowd from sacrificing to them.
19Then some Jews[t] came from Antioch and Iconium[u] and won the crowd over. They
stoned Paul[v] and dragged him outside the city, thinking he was dead. 20But after the disciples[w] had gathered around him, he got up and went back into the city. The next day
he and Barnabas left for Derbe.

The Return to Antioch in Syria

21They preached the good news in that city and won a large number of disciples. Then
they returned to Lystra, Iconium[x] and Antioch, 22strengthening the disciples and encouraging them to remain true to the faith.[y] "We must go through many hardships[z] to enter the kingdom of God," they said. 23Paul and Barnabas appointed elders[a][a] for them in
each church and, with prayer and fasting,[b] committed them to the Lord,[c] in whom they
had put their trust. 24After going through Pisidia, they came into Pamphylia, 25and
when they had preached the word in Perga, they went down to Attalia.
26From Attalia they sailed back to Antioch,[d] where they had been committed to the
grace of God[e] for the work they had now completed.[f] 27On arriving there, they gathered
the church together and reported all that God had done through them[g] and how he had
opened the door[h] of faith to the Gentiles. 28And they stayed there a long time with the
disciples.

The Council at Jerusalem

15 Some men[i] came down from Judea to Antioch and were teaching the brothers:
"Unless you are circumcised,[j] according to the custom taught by Moses,[k] you
cannot be saved." 2This brought Paul and Barnabas into sharp dispute and debate with

14:6 [b]Mt 10:23
14:7 [c]Ac 16:10 [d]ver 15, 21
14:8 [e]Ac 3:2
14:9 [f]Mt 9:28, 29
14:10 [g]Ac 3:8
14:11 [h]Ac 8:10; 28:6
14:14 [i]Mk 14:63
14:15 [j]Ac 10:26; Jas 5:17 [k]ver 7, 21; Ac 13:32 [l]1Sa 12:21; 1Co 8:4; 1Th 1:9 [m]Mt 16:16 [n]Ge 1:1; Jer 14:22 [o]Ps 146:6; Rev 14:7
14:16 [p]Ac 17:30 [q]Ps 81:12; Mic 4:5
14:17 [r]Ac 17:27; Ro 1:20 [s]Dt 11:14; Job 5:10; Ps 65:10
14:19 [t]Ac 13:45 [u]Ac 13:51 [v]2Co 11:25; 2Ti 3:11
14:20 [w]ver 22, 28; Ac 11:26
14:21 [x]Ac 13:51
14:22 [y]Ac 11:23; 13:43 [z]Jn 16:33; 1Th 3:3; 2Ti 3:12
14:23 [a]Ac 11:30; Tit 1:5 [b]Ac 13:3 [c]Ac 20:32
14:26 [d]Ac 11:19 [e]Ac 15:40 [f]Ac 13:1, 3
14:27 [g]Ac 15:4, 12; 21:19 [h]1Co 16:9; 2Co 2:12; Col 4:3; Rev 3:8
15:1 [i]ver 24; Gal 2:12 [j]ver 5; Gal 5:2, 3 [k]Ac 6:14

[a] *23* Or *Barnabas ordained elders;* or *Barnabas had elders elected*

14:6 Lycaonian cities of Lystra and Derbe. Although these two cities, along with Iconium, strictly belonged to the Roman province of Galatia, they were part of the subdistrict called Lycaonia. From A.D. 37–72, however, Iconium was actually counted linguistically and politically to be on the Phrygian side of the border.
14:8 Lystra. In 6 B.C. Augustus fortified this ancient Lycaonian settlement and made it into a Roman colony of the province of Galatia. He also settled the colony with Roman army veterans.
14:11 Lycaonian language. The native language of most of the people. See *WCF* 2.1.
14:12–13 An ancient legend circulated in Lystra that the Greek gods Zeus (chief of the gods) and Hermes (the spokesman of Zeus) were disguised as humans. According to the legend, they came to the Phrygian hill country seeking hospitality. Only one couple received them, and consequently their cottage was changed into a golden-roofed temple with marble columns. The rest of the people, who had refused to welcome the gods, had their houses destroyed. It may be that the Lystrans, remembering the legend, thought of Barnabas as Zeus and Paul as his messenger. To preclude divine anger, they honored them as gods.
14:14 tore their clothes. A sign of anguish.
14:15–17 The content of Paul's sermon is similar to that of his sermon at Athens (17:22–31). Both were addressed to pagan crowds who would not have understood quotations from, and explanations of, Old Testament Scriptures. Paul stressed that God's creative and providential power extended to the Lystrans. See *HC* 27.
14:15 See *WCF* 2.1; *BC* 26; *HC* 26.
14:16–17 See *WCF* 5.4; *BC* 14; *HC* 125; *CD* 3–4.V.
14:20 Derbe. Another Lycaonian border town (modern Kerti Huyuk, Turkey) in southeastern Galatia, about 65 miles southeast of Lystra.
■ **15:1–35** *The Jerusalem Council.* Paul's success in Gentile evangelism raised the question of circumcision for Gentile Christians. Luke recorded the decision of the council in order to guide the church in its mission should the matter surface again.
15:1 The reports of Paul and Barnabas's direct contact with the Gentiles on the first missionary journey may have reached Judea and Jerusalem through John Mark after he returned home (13:13). Also, others from Antioch may have brought the news during Paul and Barnabas's extended stay there. This caused the Jewish Christians to fear that their Jewish heritage was threatened; they thought that the converted Gentiles should be brought into Juda-

them. So Paul and Barnabas were appointed, along with some other believers, to go up
to Jerusalem[l] to see the apostles and elders[m] about this question. 3 The church sent them
on their way, and as they traveled through Phoenicia and Samaria, they told how the
Gentiles had been converted.[n] This news made all the brothers very glad. 4 When they
came to Jerusalem, they were welcomed by the church and the apostles and elders, to
whom they reported everything God had done through them.[o]

5 Then some of the believers who belonged to the party of the Pharisees stood up and
said, "The Gentiles must be circumcised and required to obey the law of Moses."

6 The apostles and elders met to consider this question. 7 After much discussion, Peter got up and addressed them: "Brothers, you know that some time ago God made a
choice among you that the Gentiles might hear from my lips the message of the gospel
and believe. 8 God, who knows the heart,[p] showed that he accepted them by giving the
Holy Spirit to them,[q] just as he did to us. 9 He made no distinction between us and them,[r]
for he purified their hearts by faith.[s] 10 Now then, why do you try to test God by putting
on the necks of the disciples a yoke[t] that neither we nor our fathers have been able to
bear? 11 No! We believe it is through the grace[u] of our Lord Jesus that we are saved, just
as they are."

12 The whole assembly became silent as they listened to Barnabas and Paul telling
about the miraculous signs and wonders[v] God had done among the Gentiles through
them.[w] 13 When they finished, James[x] spoke up: "Brothers, listen to me. 14 Simon[a] has described to us how God at first showed his concern by taking from the Gentiles a people
for himself. 15 The words of the prophets are in agreement with this, as it is written:

> 16 " 'After this I will return
> and rebuild David's fallen tent.
> Its ruins I will rebuild,
> and I will restore it,
> 17 that the remnant of men may seek the Lord,
> and all the Gentiles who bear my name,
> says the Lord, who does these things'[b][y]
> 18 that have been known for ages.[c]

19 "It is my judgment, therefore, that we should not make it difficult for the Gentiles
who are turning to God. 20 Instead we should write to them, telling them to abstain from
food polluted by idols,[z] from sexual immorality,[a] from the meat of strangled animals and
from blood.[b] 21 For Moses has been preached in every city from the earliest times and is
read in the synagogues on every Sabbath."[c]

The Council's Letter to Gentile Believers

22 Then the apostles and elders, with the whole church, decided to choose some of
their own men and send them to Antioch with Paul and Barnabas. They chose Judas
(called Barsabbas) and Silas,[d] two men who were leaders among the brothers. 23 With
them they sent the following letter:

The apostles and elders, your brothers,

To the Gentile believers in Antioch,[e] Syria and Cilicia:[f]

15:2 [l]Gal 2:2 [m]Ac 11:30
15:3 [n]Ac 14:27
15:4 [o]ver 12; Ac 14:27
15:8 [p]Ac 1:24 [q]Ac 10:44,47
15:9 [r]Ac 10:28,34; 11:12 [s]Ac 10:43
15:10 [t]Mt 23:4; Gal 5:1
15:11 [u]Ro 3:24; Eph 2:5-8
15:12 [v]Jn 4:48 [w]Ac 14:27
15:13 [x]Ac 12:17
15:17 [y]Am 9:11,12
15:20 [z]1Co 8:7-13; 10:14-28; Rev 2:14,20 [a]1Co 10:7,8 [b]ver 29; Ge 9:4; Lev 3:17; Dt 12:16, 23
15:21 [c]Ac 13:15; 2Co 3:14,15
15:22 [d]ver 27,32,40
15:23 [e]ver 1 [f]ver 41

[a] *14* Greek *Simeon,* a variant of *Simon;* that is, Peter [b] *17* Amos 9:11,12 [c] *17,18* Some manuscripts *things'— / 18known to the Lord for ages is his work*

ism through circumcision. Paul recognized that forcing Gentiles to be circumcised might make them think that salvation must be earned (cf. Gal 2:15–16). He knew that the Judaizers had to be opposed lest they hinder the extension of the gospel to the Gentiles (1Th 2:14–16).

15:2,4 See *WCF* 31.1; 31.2.

15:6 apostles and elders met. The church leaders took the lead in the discussion, but verse 12 indicates that the whole assembly was present. See *WCF* 31.1

15:10–11 See *WCF* 7.6; 14.2; 20.1; *WLC* 72.

15:13 James spoke up. James was the half brother of Jesus (Mt 13:55; see "Introduction to James: Author"), who by now seems to have become a prominent leader of the Jerusalem church (Gal 2:9). James added a third testimony that Gentile believers should not be burdened with keeping the law of circumcision.

15:14–18 See *WCF* 1.8; 1.9; 2.2; 3.2; 5.1; 31.3; *WLC* 6,45; *WSC* 26; *CD* 1.6.

15:19 It is my judgment. James found support in the Scriptures and in the testimonies of Simon Peter, Barnabas and Paul that God wanted Gentiles to be free from Jewish ceremonial practices and the demands of the Judaizers. He tactfully proposed that both Jews and Gentiles practice restraint. The Jewish Christians were to recognize that Gentiles were not to be bound by traditional Jewish applications of the ceremonial aspects of the law. The Gentile believers were to consider the scruples of Jewish Christians and not offend them by eating food sacrificed to idols, by eating the meat of strangled animals or by consuming blood (Lev 17:10–14; 19:26). Beyond these Jewish scruples, they were to abstain from sexual immorality, which was prevalent in pagan societies. See *WCF* 31.3.

15:21 See *WCF* 21.5; *WLC* 108.

15:22–25 See *WCF* 31.2; 31.3.

15:23 your brothers. An expression the Jewish Christian leaders used to help set the Gentile Christians at ease. They were all brothers and sisters together in the same church.

Greetings.[g]

24We have heard that some went out from us without our authorization and
disturbed you, troubling your minds by what they said.[h] 25So we all agreed to
choose some men and send them to you with our dear friends Barnabas and
Paul— 26men who have risked their lives[i] for the name of our Lord Jesus Christ.
27Therefore we are sending Judas and Silas to confirm by word of mouth what we
are writing. 28It seemed good to the Holy Spirit[j] and to us not to burden you with
anything beyond the following requirements: 29You are to abstain from food sacrificed to idols, from blood, from the meat of strangled animals and from sexual
immorality.[k] You will do well to avoid these things.

Farewell.

30The men were sent off and went down to Antioch, where they gathered the church
together and delivered the letter. 31The people read it and were glad for its encouraging
message. 32Judas and Silas, who themselves were prophets, said much to encourage and
strengthen the brothers. 33After spending some time there, they were sent off by the
brothers with the blessing of peace[l] to return to those who had sent them.[a] 35But Paul
and Barnabas remained in Antioch, where they and many others taught and preached[m]
the word of the Lord.

Disagreement Between Paul and Barnabas

36Some time later Paul said to Barnabas, "Let us go back and visit the brothers in all
the towns[n] where we preached the word of the Lord and see how they are doing." 37Bar-
nabas wanted to take John, also called Mark,[o] with them, 38but Paul did not think it wise
to take him, because he had deserted them[p] in Pamphylia and had not continued with
them in the work. 39They had such a sharp disagreement that they parted company. Barnabas took Mark and sailed for Cyprus, 40but Paul chose Silas[q] and left, commended by
the brothers to the grace of the Lord.[r] 41He went through Syria[s] and Cilicia,[t] strengthening the churches.[u]

Timothy Joins Paul and Silas

16 He came to Derbe and then to Lystra,[v] where a disciple named Timothy[w] lived,
whose mother was a Jewess and a believer, but whose father was a Greek. 2The
brothers[x] at Lystra and Iconium[y] spoke well of him. 3Paul wanted to take him along on
the journey, so he circumcised him because of the Jews who lived in that area, for they
all knew that his father was a Greek.[z] 4As they traveled from town to town, they delivered the decisions reached by the apostles and elders[a] in Jerusalem[b] for the people to
obey.[c] 5So the churches were strengthened[d] in the faith and grew daily in numbers.

Paul's Vision of the Man of Macedonia

6Paul and his companions traveled throughout the region of Phrygia[e] and Galatia,[f]

[a] 33 Some manuscripts *them,* 34*but Silas decided to remain there*

15:23 [g]Ac 23:25,26; Jas 1:1
15:24 [h]ver 1; Gal 1:7; 5:10
15:26 [i]Ac 9:23-25; 14:19
15:28 [j]Ac 5:32
15:29 [k]ver 20; Ac 21:25
15:33 [l]Mk 5:34; Ac 16:36; 1Co 16:11
15:35 [m]Ac 8:4
15:36 [n]Ac 13:4,13,14,51; 14:1,6,24,25
15:37 [o]Ac 12:12
15:38 [p]Ac 13:13
15:40 [q]ver 22 [r]Ac 11:23
15:41 [s]ver 23 [t]Ac 6:9 [u]Ac 16:5
16:1 [v]Ac 14:6 [w]Ac 17:14; 18:5, 19:22; Ro 16:21; 1Co 4:17; 2Co 1:1, 19; 1Th 3:2,6; 1Ti 1:2,18; 2Ti 1:2, 5,6
16:2 [x]ver 40 [y]Ac 13:51
16:3 [z]Gal 2:3
16:4 [a]Ac 11:30 [b]Ac 15:2 [c]Ac 15:28,29
16:5 [d]Ac 9:31; 15:41
16:6 [e]Ac 18:23 [f]Ac 18:23; Gal 1:2; 3:1

15:26 Lord Jesus Christ. This full title of Jesus was first used in 11:17. The word "Lord" refers to his sovereignty. "Jesus" is the name for "Savior" (Hebrew, *Joshua,* meaning "Yahweh saves"; Ex 17:9). "Christ" means "Messiah," "the anointed of God."
15:27–31 See *WCF* 31.3.
15:28 seemed good to the Holy Spirit and to us. As people filled with the Spirit (2:1–41; 4:8; 6:5; 9:17; 13:4), they recognized the Spirit's guidance in the debate in the assembly and in the decision that was made.
15:32 Judas and Silas . . . prophets. A primary function of the New Testament prophet (a spokesman for God) in proclaiming the Word was to bring encouragement and strength to believers. Paul chose Silas to accompany him on his second missionary journey (v. 40) and to share in the teaching of the Word.
▪ **15:36—18:22** *Paul's Second Missionary Journey.* Luke reported the second phase of Paul's outreach to the Gentile nations. After a disagreement with Barnabas, Paul visited the churches of his previous journey and continued westward into Greece.
15:39 sharp disagreement . . . parted company. This dispute was occasioned by the desire of Barnabas to take John Mark (a cousin of Barnabas; Col 4:10) on the second missionary journey, despite the fact that Mark had deserted Paul and Barnabas during the first journey (13:13). The failure of Barnabas to support the Gentile Christians (Gal 2:13) may also have contributed to the rift. Although the remainder of Acts contains no further record of Paul working with Barnabas, Paul does later mention Barnabas in a positive light (1Co 9:6). Paul's later high regard for Mark is evident (Col 4:10; 2Ti 4:11; Phm 24). **Barnabas took Mark . . . Cyprus.** Barnabas took his cousin Mark (Col 4:10) on a missionary journey to the island of Cyprus, Barnabas's home. This no doubt provided an opportunity for Barnabas to encourage (4:36) the younger man.
16:1 a disciple named Timothy. Paul found this young man, who was part Jew and part Greek, in the small Jewish community of Lystra. Like his father, Timothy had been reared as a Greek and so had not been circumcised. Since his mother was Jewish, Paul did not think he was compromising the principles of Gentile freedom by circumcising Timothy (v. 3).
16:4 See *WCF* 31.3.
16:6–7 See *CD* 3–4.V.
16:6 Phrygia and Galatia. A region in the southern portion of the province of Galatia. It included the Phrygian district, Antioch of Pisidia and the surrounding area. **Holy Spirit . . . Asia.** The province of Asia, located in the western sector of Asia Minor, included the famous city of Ephesus, where God wanted Paul to go at a later date (ch. 19). The Holy Spirit is also called the "Spirit of Jesus" (v. 7) and "God" (v. 10; cf. note on 2Co 3:17). These verses point to

16:6 [g]Ac 2:9
16:7 [h]Ro 8:9; Gal 4:6
16:8 [i]ver 11; 2Co 2:12; 2Ti 4:13
16:9 [j]Ac 9:10 [k]Ac 20:1,3
16:10 [l]ver 10-17 [m]Ac 14:7
16:11 [n]ver 8
16:12 [o]Ac 20:6; Php 1:1; 1Th 2:2 [p]ver 9
16:13 [q]Ac 13:14

having been kept by the Holy Spirit from preaching the word in the province of Asia.[g]
[7]When they came to the border of Mysia, they tried to enter Bithynia, but the Spirit of
Jesus[h] would not allow them to. [8]So they passed by Mysia and went down to Troas.[i]
[9]During the night Paul had a vision[j] of a man of Macedonia[k] standing and begging him,
"Come over to Macedonia and help us." [10]After Paul had seen the vision, we[l] got ready
at once to leave for Macedonia, concluding that God had called us to preach the gospel[m]
to them.

Lydia's Conversion in Philippi

[11]From Troas[n] we put out to sea and sailed straight for Samothrace, and the next day
on to Neapolis. [12]From there we traveled to Philippi,[o] a Roman colony and the leading
city of that district of Macedonia.[p] And we stayed there several days.
[13]On the Sabbath[q] we went outside the city gate to the river, where we expected to
find a place of prayer. We sat down and began to speak to the women who had gathered
there. [14]One of those listening was a woman named Lydia, a dealer in purple cloth from

---

the Christian doctrine of the Trinity (cf. 2Co 13:14). See theological article "The Trinity" at John 14.
16:7 border of Mysia. Having gone northwest through Phrygia and Galatia, Paul and Silas came to Mysia, a district that extended northwest to the coast, to the Hellespont (the modern Straits of Dardanelles) and Propontis (the inland Sea of Marmara). Bithynia was to the east.
16:8 they passed by Mysia . . . to Troas. Troas was an established Aegean seaport. The ancient site of famous Troy was ten miles farther inland. Important as a Greek port from about 300 B.C., Troas became a city-state and later a Roman colony that functioned as an important seaport for the region.
16:10 we. The first of the "we" passages starts here, indicating that the author accompanied Paul and Silas.
16:11 Samothrace. A prominent island in the north Aegean Sea where vessels regularly stopped. **Neapolis.** Greek for "new city" (modern Kavala), this was the seaport for Philippi, which was located ten miles inland to the northwest.
16:12 Philippi. Philip II of Macedon (Alexander the Great's father) had established a large Greek colony here and renamed it Philippi. The Romans conquered it in 167 B.C. and made it part of the province of Macedonia.
16:13 place of prayer. According to Jewish law, at least ten men were required to establish a synagogue. Failing that, a place of prayer could be established outdoors and preferably near water. **women who had gathered there.** They met informally to read and study the Scriptures, and they looked for the assistance of any Jewish teacher who happened to visit there.

Effectual Calling and Conversion: Can I Resist the Holy Spirit?

THE Reformed doctrine of *irresistible grace,* also known as *efficacious grace,* states that God regenerates and converts the elect through what is known as the *effectual call.* Effectual call is the inward call of the Holy Spirit that moves and invites the sinner to receive Christ at the same time the sinner is regenerated and renewed inwardly so as to love the Lord and willingly believe the gospel. This is to be distinguished from the outward call of the gospel, which is issued to all people indiscriminately through the preaching of the gospel, witnessing, the administration of the sacraments and other proclamations of God's Word. Nevertheless, the inward call often accompanies and works through the means of the outward call. While other traditions teach that this inward leading of the Holy Spirit may be accepted or rejected, Reformed theology insists that God's inward call is always *effectual;* that is, it never fails to save those who are so called.

The Bible speaks of God's effectual call in many places, but perhaps the passage distinguishing it most clearly from the outward call is Romans 8:29–30. There Paul indicates that the group of those who are called is identical to that of those who are predestined, justified and ultimately glorified. Clearly, this call is issued *only* to those who are saved—as well as to *all* those who are saved (cf. Ro 1:7; Jude 1; Rev 17:14).

Effectual calling is necessary because of humanity's fallen state. In our sin and spiritual deadness, we are completely unable to respond positively to the outward call of the gospel; we cannot rightly comprehend God and his message of salvation (1Co 2:12–14), and we hate God and his commandments (Ro 8:5–8). No fallen person naturally possesses the moral ability to receive Christ; only those to whom this ability has been given by God may trust in the gospel and be converted (Dt 30:6; Mt 11:25–27; 13:10–16; Jn 6:44,63–65; Ac 16:14).

In response to our inability, God has chosen to transform the hearts of the elect through his effectual calling, implanting within them new moral ability and new desires so that they unfailingly come to God when called (Jn 6:44–45; 10:1–5). It is God who initiates this process by regenerating our spirits and renewing our hearts (Dt 30:6; Jn 1:12–13; 3:5–8; Ac 16:14; Php 2:12–13; see theological article "Regeneration and New Birth" at Jn 3). He converts us by granting us saving faith as the unfailing means of our salvation (Ac 13:48; 1Co 1:22–31; Eph 2:8–9; Php 1:29; 1Jn 5:20).

God does not always issue an effectual call to the elect the first time they hear the gospel; one may be elect and still initially reject the gospel for many years. When this happens, the elect behave just as all other fallen people, necessarily rejecting the gospel because they hate God and lack the moral ability to obey him. Oftentimes, Christians wrongly assume that this means the Holy Spirit's inward, effectual call can be resisted. It is certainly true that the outward call, such as that issued by preaching and witnessing, can be effectively resisted (Ac 13:45–46,49–51; 14:1–4). In fact, the outward call is always resisted unless it is accompanied by the inward, effectual call. But the Holy Spirit's inward call always results in conversion.

the city of Thyatira,[r] who was a worshiper of God. The Lord opened her heart[s] to respond
to Paul's message. 15When she and the members of her household[t] were baptized, she
invited us to her home. "If you consider me a believer in the Lord," she said, "come and
stay at my house." And she persuaded us.

Paul and Silas in Prison

16Once when we were going to the place of prayer,[u] we were met by a slave girl who
had a spirit[v] by which she predicted the future. She earned a great deal of money for her
owners by fortune-telling. 17This girl followed Paul and the rest of us, shouting, "These
men are servants of the Most High God,[w] who are telling you the way to be saved." 18She
kept this up for many days. Finally Paul became so troubled that he turned around and
said to the spirit, "In the name of Jesus Christ I command you to come out of her!" At that
moment the spirit left her.[x]

19When the owners of the slave girl realized that their hope of making money[y] was
gone, they seized Paul and Silas[z] and dragged[a] them into the marketplace to face the
authorities. 20They brought them before the magistrates and said, "These men are Jews,
and are throwing our city into an uproar[b] 21by advocating customs unlawful for us Romans[c] to accept or practice."[d]

22The crowd joined in the attack against Paul and Silas, and the magistrates ordered them to be stripped and beaten.[e] 23After they had been severely flogged, they
were thrown into prison, and the jailer[f] was commanded to guard them carefully.
24Upon receiving such orders, he put them in the inner cell and fastened their feet in
the stocks.[g]

25About midnight Paul and Silas were praying and singing hymns[h] to God, and the
other prisoners were listening to them. 26Suddenly there was such a violent earthquake that the foundations of the prison were shaken.[i] At once all the prison doors
flew open,[j] and everybody's chains came loose.[k] 27The jailer woke up, and when he
saw the prison doors open, he drew his sword and was about to kill himself because
he thought the prisoners had escaped.[l] 28But Paul shouted, "Don't harm yourself! We
are all here!"

29The jailer called for lights, rushed in and fell trembling before Paul and Silas. 30He
then brought them out and asked, "Sirs, what must I do to be saved?"[m]

31They replied, "Believe in the Lord Jesus, and you will be saved—you and your
household."[n] 32Then they spoke the word of the Lord to him and to all the others in his
house. 33At that hour of the night[o] the jailer took them and washed their wounds; then
immediately he and all his family were baptized. 34The jailer brought them into his house
and set a meal before them; he[p] was filled with joy because he had come to believe in
God—he and his whole family.

35When it was daylight, the magistrates sent their officers to the jailer with the order:
"Release those men." 36The jailer[q] told Paul, "The magistrates have ordered that you and
Silas be released. Now you can leave. Go in peace."[r]

16:14 [r]Rev 1:11 [s]Lk 24:45
16:15 [t]Ac 11:14
16:16 [u]ver 13 [v]Dt 18:11; 1Sa 28:3,7
16:17 [w]Mk 5:7
16:18 [x]Mk 16:17
16:19 [y]ver 16; Ac 19:25, 26 [z]Ac 15:22 [a]Ac 8:3; 17:6; 21:30; Jas 2:6
16:20 [b]Ac 17:6
16:21 [c]ver 12 [d]Est 3:8
16:22 [e]2Co 11:25; 1Th 2:2
16:23 [f]ver 27,36
16:24 [g]Job 13:27; 33:11; Jer 20:2,3; 29:26
16:25 [h]Eph 5:19
16:26 [i]Ac 4:31 [j]Ac 12:10 [k]Ac 12:7
16:27 [l]Ac 12:19
16:30 [m]Ac 2:37
16:31 [n]Ac 11:14
16:33 [o]ver 25
16:34 [p]Ac 11:14
16:36 [q]ver 23,27 [r]Ac 15:33

16:14 from the city of Thyatira. About 30 miles southeast of Pergamum, Thyatira was a city in the old kingdom of Lydia until under Rome's reorganization it became part of the Roman province of Asia. Thyatira was famous for its dye industry and the purple dyes it produced (such as royal purple). **The Lord opened her heart.** Such divine illumination and persuasion is necessary if the heart, blinded by sin, is to respond to the gospel (Jer 13:23; Jn 6:44,65; Ro 9:16; 1Co 2:14). This effectual call of God ensures that all who have been chosen by God will believe (13:48; 2Th 2:13–14; 2Ti 1:9–10). See *HC* 21.

16:15 the members of her household were baptized. Throughout redemptive history it has often been God's practice to deal graciously with entire family units (e.g., Ge 17:7–14; Ac 2:38–39; 11:14; 16:31). The household baptisms of Acts are striking examples of this (10:47–48; 16:31–33; cf. 1Co 1:16). Given the fact that such household baptisms were apparently standard practice, it is probable that children and even infants were included.

16:16 a spirit by which she predicted the future. Literally, "a python spirit." The term originally referred to a mythical serpent that guarded the temple and oracle of the Greek god Apollo at Delphi. Later the phrase meant a demon-possessed person or even a ventriloquist. The people at Philippi must have thought she had a demon that told fortunes.

16:17 the Most High God. A Jew would have understood this title to apply to Yahweh (*El 'Elyon;* Nu 24:16; Ps 78:35), whereas a Gentile would have applied it to Zeus.

16:18 In the name of Jesus Christ . . . come out of her! Following the common understanding of the expression "the Most High God," everyone realized that Paul meant to convey the thought that Jesus, as deity, expelled the demon. See *BC* 30.

16:19 seized Paul and Silas. Because both Paul and Silas were Jews and leaders of the missionary team, they were seized. Their companions were Gentiles (Luke, a Gentile from Syrian Antioch, and Timothy, a half-Gentile from Lystra) and were not charged.

16:21 advocating customs unlawful for us Romans. The charge was that Paul and Silas were promulgating an illegal religion (Latin, *religio illicita*) and thus were disturbing the peace of Rome (*Pax Romana*). But this charge was inflamed by cultural and religious prejudice.

16:22 stripped and beaten. Paul and Silas were Roman citizens (v. 37) and politically exempt from such treatment. But in the mob atmosphere this was ignored.

16:24 in the inner cell . . . feet in the stocks. They were treated as common criminals and placed in a maximum-security cell.

16:27 prison doors open. See 5:19 and 12:10. **about to kill himself.** According to Roman law, if a prisoner escaped, the jailer was to die in his place (12:19).

16:28 See *WLC* 136; *WSC* 69.

16:30–31 See *WLC* 72,153,172; *HC* 60.

16:31 you and your household. For other instances of household salvation, see 2:38–39, 10:24,48, 16:15 and its note and 1 Corinthians 1:16. When a person accepted a religion, the whole family was involved (v. 34). See *WCF* 14.2; *WLC* 72; *HC* 74.

16:33 See *WCF* 28.3.

16:37 [s]Ac 22:25-29
16:38 [t]Ac 22:29
16:39 [u]Mt 8:34
16:40 [v]ver 14 [w]ver 2; Ac 1:16
17:1 [x]ver 11,13; Php 4:16; 1Th 1:1; 2Th 1:1; 2Ti 4:10
17:2 [y]Ac 9:20 [z]Ac 13:14 [a]Ac 8:35
17:3 [b]Lk 24:26; Ac 3:18 [c]Lk 24:46 [d]Ac 9:22; 18:28

37 But Paul said to the officers: "They beat us publicly without a trial, even though we
are Roman citizens,[s] and threw us into prison. And now do they want to get rid of us quietly? No! Let them come themselves and escort us out."
38 The officers reported this to the magistrates, and when they heard that Paul and Silas were Roman citizens, they were alarmed.[t] 39 They came to appease them and escorted them from the prison, requesting them to leave the city.[u] 40 After Paul and Silas came
out of the prison, they went to Lydia's house,[v] where they met with the brothers[w] and
encouraged them. Then they left.

In Thessalonica

17 When they had passed through Amphipolis and Apollonia, they came to Thessalonica,[x] where there was a Jewish synagogue. 2 As his custom was, Paul went
into the synagogue,[y] and on three Sabbath[z] days he reasoned with them from the
Scriptures,[a] 3 explaining and proving that the Christ[a] had to suffer[b] and rise from the
dead.[c] "This Jesus I am proclaiming to you is the Christ,[a]" [d] he said. 4 Some of the Jews

[a] *3* Or *Messiah*

16:37 Roman citizens. Paul strongly appealed to their Roman citizenship, which exempted them from scourging and torture. If Roman citizens were tried in a Roman court, they were given the right to appeal their case to Caesar (25:11; 26:32).
16:40 Lydia's house. Early Christians often met in private homes for Christian services (Phm 2). **met with the brothers.** The term "brother" generally refers to all believers. In this case the term included Lydia and her household; the slave girl; probably the jailer and his household; and Luke, who now stayed in Philippi.
17:1 Amphipolis and Apollonia . . . Thessalonica. Amphipolis was the capital of Macedonia's northern district from 167–142 B.C. It was about 30 miles southwest of Philippi. Apollonia was about 25 miles farther. Both cities were on the Via Egnatia highway to Thessalonica. Paul and his companions were eager to get to Thessalonica, a distance of 40 miles beyond Apollonia. Thessalonica, with a population of about 200,000, was the provincial capital of Macedonia. In Paul's day, the city served the entire province as an administrative and commercial center.
17:2 three Sabbath days. Paul may have stayed in Thessalonica much longer than three successive Sabbaths. The church at Philippi repeatedly sent him aid (Php 4:16), and he had been able to give fairly extensive doctrinal instruction to the Thessalonian Christians

Paul's Second Missionary Journey

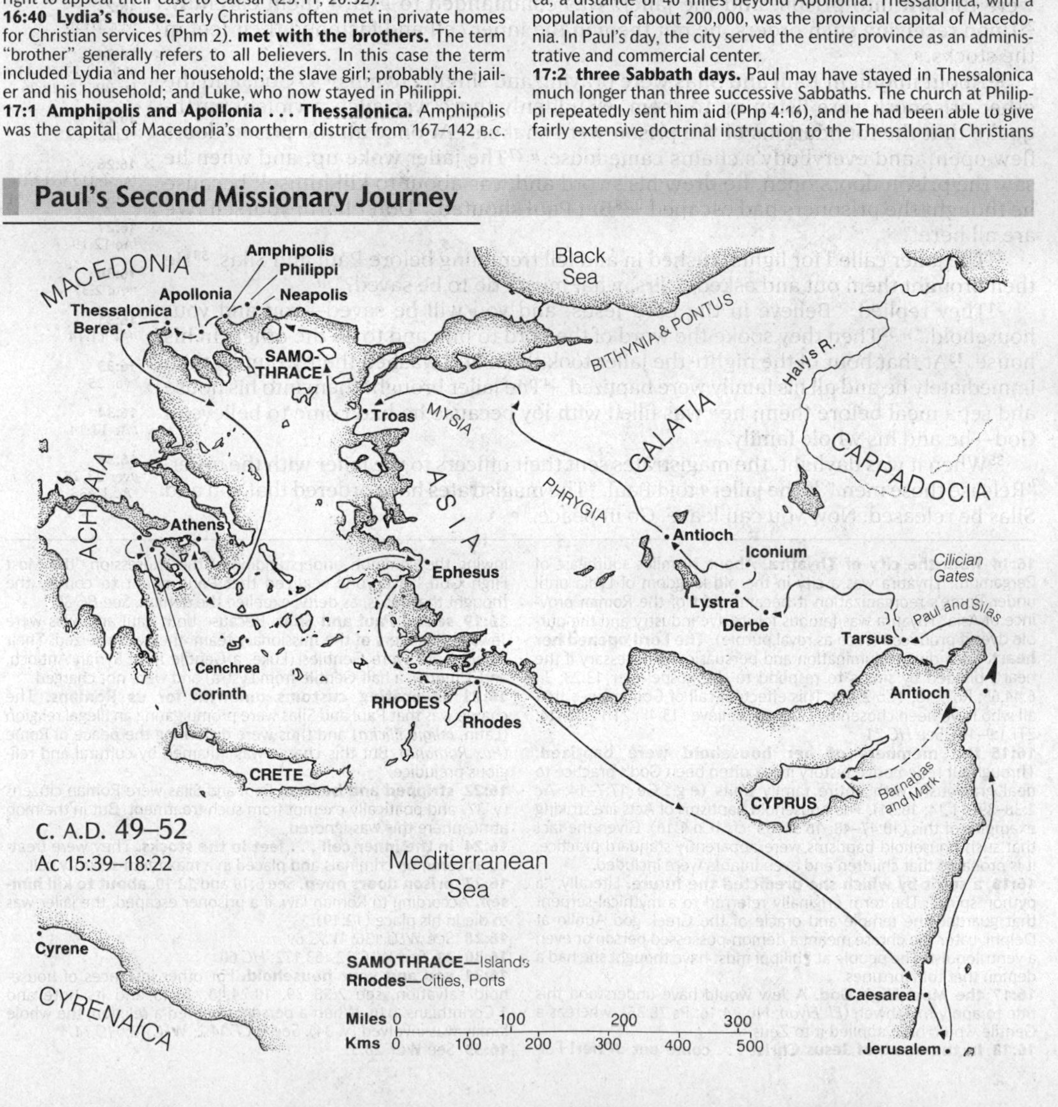

were persuaded and joined Paul and Silas,[e] as did a large number of God-fearing Greeks
and not a few prominent women.
5 But the Jews were jealous; so they rounded up some bad characters from the marketplace, formed a mob and started a riot in the city.[f] They rushed to Jason's[g] house in
search of Paul and Silas in order to bring them out to the crowd.[a] 6 But when they did not
find them, they dragged[h] Jason and some other brothers before the city officials, shouting: "These men who have caused trouble all over the world[i] have now come here,[j] 7 and
Jason has welcomed them into his house. They are all defying Caesar's decrees, saying
that there is another king, one called Jesus."[k] 8 When they heard this, the crowd and the
city officials were thrown into turmoil. 9 Then they made Jason[l] and the others post bond
and let them go.

In Berea

10 As soon as it was night, the brothers sent Paul and Silas away to Berea.[m] On arriving there, they went to the Jewish synagogue. 11 Now the Bereans were of more noble
character than the Thessalonians,[n] for they received the message with great eagerness
and examined the Scriptures[o] every day to see if what Paul said was true. 12 Many of the
Jews believed, as did also a number of prominent Greek women and many Greek men.
13 When the Jews in Thessalonica learned that Paul was preaching the word of God
at Berea, they went there too, agitating the crowds and stirring them up. 14 The brothers immediately sent Paul to the coast, but Silas[p] and Timothy[q] stayed at Berea. 15 The
men who escorted Paul brought him to Athens[r] and then left with instructions for Silas
and Timothy to join him as soon as possible.[s]

In Athens

16 While Paul was waiting for them in Athens, he was greatly distressed to see that the
city was full of idols. 17 So he reasoned in the synagogue[t] with the Jews and the God-fearing Greeks, as well as in the marketplace day by day with those who happened to be
there. 18 A group of Epicurean and Stoic philosophers began to dispute with him. Some
of them asked, "What is this babbler trying to say?" Others remarked, "He seems to be
advocating foreign gods." They said this because Paul was preaching the good news
about Jesus and the resurrection.[u] 19 Then they took him and brought him to a meeting
of the Areopagus,[v] where they said to him, "May we know what this new teaching[w] is
that you are presenting? 20 You are bringing some strange ideas to our ears, and we want
to know what they mean." 21 (All the Athenians and the foreigners who lived there spent
their time doing nothing but talking about and listening to the latest ideas.)
22 Paul then stood up in the meeting of the Areopagus and said: "Men of Athens! I see
that in every way you are very religious. 23 For as I walked around and looked carefully
at your objects of worship, I even found an altar with this inscription: TO AN UNKNOWN GOD.
Now what you worship as something unknown[x] I am going to proclaim to you.

17:4 [e]Ac 15:22
17:5 [f]ver 13; 1Th 2:16 [g]Ro 16:21
17:6 [h]Ac 16:19 [i]Mt 24:14 [j]Ac 16:20
17:7 [k]Lk 23:2; Jn 19:12
17:9 [l]ver 5
17:10 [m]ver 13; Ac 20:4
17:11 [n]ver 1 [o]Lk 16:29; Jn 5:39
17:14 [p]Ac 15:22 [q]Ac 16:1
17:15 [r]ver 16,21,22; Ac 18:1, 1Th 3:1 [s]Ac 18:5
17:17 [t]Ac 9:20
17:18 [u]ver 31,32; Ac 4:2
17:19 [v]ver 22 [w]Mk 1:27
17:23 [x]Jn 4:22

[a] 5 Or *the assembly of the people*

(see 1,2Th). The text does not indicate how much time elapsed between the third Sabbath and the forced departure of Paul and Silas.
17:6–7 See *BC* 28.
17:7 defying Caesar's decrees. A political charge was brought against Paul, who had spoken about the spiritual kingdom of God (14:22; 19:8; 20:25; 28:23,31). His opponents seemed to have distorted the message to mean political opposition to Rome. About this time Claudius Caesar (A.D. 49–50) expelled the Jews from Rome because of riots allegedly instigated by "Chrestus," a probable reference to Christ.
17:10 Berea. Berea (modern Verria) was some 50 miles southwest of Thessalonica in the foothills of the Olympian Mountains.
17:11 examined the Scriptures every day. The Bereans compared Paul's teaching with God's written Word, thus setting a good example for the church throughout history. See *WCF* 20.2; 31.4; *WLC* 157,160; *BC* 29.
17:16–17 See *WLC* 108.
17:16 Athens. This city, located five miles inland northeast from its port (Piraeus) on the Saronic Gulf, which extends west from the Aegean Sea, had a rich heritage. In the early fifth century B.C., Athens reached its zenith under the great political leader Pericles (495–429 B.C.), a period during which the Parthenon, various temples and other magnificent structures were built and the great classical poets Aeschylus, Sophocles, Euripides and Aristophanes flourished. Conquered by the Romans in 146 B.C., Athens continued to be one of the great intellectual and cultural centers of the ancient world. **full of idols.** Besides the Parthenon and temple buildings with their idol statues on the Acropolis, other public, commercial and temple buildings and statues were to be found in the marketplace below and to the west of the Acropolis.
17:18 Epicurean and Stoic. Epicurus (342–270 B.C.), the founder of the Epicurean philosophical system, taught that a person's chief end was pleasure and a life without pain, passions and fears. On the other hand, the Zeno of Citium (340–265 B.C.), the founder of Stoicism, stressed living in harmony with nature and dependence on one's reasoning and other self-sufficient powers. Both schools stressed the quest for peace of mind. Zeno viewed God pantheistically as the "world-soul." **babbler.** A derogatory term meaning a scrap collector or peddler of assorted ideas.
17:19 meeting of the Areopagus. Greek, *Areios pagos;* literally, "hill of Ares," sometimes called "Mars Hill" because the Greek god of war (Ares) was equivalent to the Roman god Mars. The term came to be applied to the council that first assembled on the hill of Ares (just northwest of the Acropolis) for murder trials. Later it served as the city council of Athens, and in Roman times it was the judicial body that supervised educational, religious and moral matters. In Paul's time, the council met in the Royal Stoa or Colonnade, which was located in the northwest corner of the marketplace. This council was to pass judgment on Paul's religious ideas.
17:22 See *WLC* 109.
17:23 TO AN UNKNOWN GOD. A reference to the Altar of the Twelve

24“The God who made the world and everything in it[y] is the Lord of heaven and earth[z]
and does not live in temples built by hands.[a] 25And he is not served by human hands, as
if he needed anything, because he himself gives all men life and breath and everything
else.[b] 26From one man he made every nation of men, that they should inhabit the whole
earth; and he determined the times set for them and the exact places where they should
live.[c] 27God did this so that men would seek him and perhaps reach out for him and find
him, though he is not far from each one of us.[d] 28‘For in him we live and move and have
our being.’[e] As some of your own poets have said, ‘We are his offspring.’

29“Therefore since we are God’s offspring, we should not think that the divine being
is like gold or silver or stone—an image made by man’s design and skill.[f] 30In the past
God overlooked[g] such ignorance,[h] but now he commands all people everywhere to repent.[i] 31For he has set a day when he will judge[j] the world with justice[k] by the man he
has appointed.[l] He has given proof of this to all men by raising him from the dead.”[m]

32When they heard about the resurrection of the dead,[n] some of them sneered, but
others said, “We want to hear you again on this subject.” 33At that, Paul left the Council. 34A few men became followers of Paul and believed. Among them was Dionysius, a
member of the Areopagus,[o] also a woman named Damaris, and a number of others.

In Corinth

18 After this, Paul left Athens[p] and went to Corinth.[q] 2There he met a Jew named
Aquila, a native of Pontus, who had recently come from Italy with his wife Priscilla,[r] because Claudius[s] had ordered all the Jews to leave Rome. Paul went to see them,
3and because he was a tentmaker as they were, he stayed and worked with them.[t] 4Ev-
ery Sabbath[u] he reasoned in the synagogue, trying to persuade Jews and Greeks.

5When Silas[v] and Timothy[w] came from Macedonia,[x] Paul devoted himself exclusively to preaching, testifying to the Jews that Jesus was the Christ.[a][y] 6But when the Jews opposed Paul and became abusive,[z] he shook out his clothes in protest and said to them,
“Your blood be on your own heads![a] I am clear of my responsibility.[b] From now on I will
go to the Gentiles.”[c]

7Then Paul left the synagogue and went next door to the house of Titius Justus, a worshiper of God.[d] 8Crispus,[e] the synagogue ruler,[f] and his entire household[g] believed in
the Lord; and many of the Corinthians who heard him believed and were baptized.

17:24 [y]Isa 42:5; Ac 14:15 [z]Dt 10:14; Mt 11:25 [a]Ac 7:48
17:25 [b]Ps 50:10-12; Isa 42:5
17:26 [c]Dt 32:8; Job 12:23
17:27 [d]Dt 4:7; Jer 23:23, 24; Ac 14:17
17:28 [e]Job 12:10; Da 5:23
17:29 [f]Isa 40:18-20; Ro 1:23
17:30 [g]Ac 14:16; Ro 3:25 [h]ver 23; 1Pe 1:14 [i]Lk 24:47; Tit 2:11, 12
17:31 [j]Mt 10:15 [k]Ps 9:8; 96:13; 98:9 [l]Ac 10:42 [m]Ac 2:24
17:32 [n]ver 18, 31
17:34 [o]ver 19, 22
18:1 [p]Ac 17:15 [q]Ac 19:1; 1Co 1:2; 2Co 1:1, 23; 2Ti 4:20
18:2 [r]Ro 16:3; 1Co 16:19; 2Ti 4:19 [s]Ac 11:28
18:3 [t]Ac 20:34; 1Co 4:12; 1Th 2:9; 2Th 3:8

[a] 5 Or *Messiah;* also in verse 28

18:4 [u]Ac 13:14 **18:5** [v]Ac 15:22 [w]Ac 16:1 [x]Ac 16:9; 17:14, 15 [y]ver 28; Ac 17:3 **18:6** [z]Ac 13:45 [a]2Sa 1:16; Eze 18:13; 33:4 [b]Ac 20:26 [c]Ac 13:46 **18:7** [d]Ac 16:14 **18:8** [e]1Co 1:14 [f]Mk 5:22 [g]Ac 11:14

Gods at Athens or to some other altar with this inscription that was erected to ensure that no god had been slighted. Paul used this point of contact to lead to his discourse on the living and personal God who has made the world, who is not carved out of stone or confined to some temple, who personally created humankind and who providentially controls the time and place where people are to live. See *WLC* 105,113.

17:24–28 See *WCF* 2.2; 4.1; 5.1; 6.3; 7.1; 21.1; *WLC* 22,101; *BC* 14; *HC* 27,28,121,125.

17:28 in him we live and move and have our being. Paul said that this God brought us into being and that we exist only by his providence. In the ancient world the three great mysteries of philosophy and science were the questions of life, motion and being. **some of your own poets.** Paul knew that the Athenians did not know the Old Testament, so he quoted from three of their own poets whose primary reference was to Zeus, the chief of the Greek gods. Paul reapplied the quotations to the living and personal God of heaven. First, Paul gave a quotation attributed to the Cretan poet Epimenides (c. 600 B.C.) in his *Cretica:* “For in you we live and move and have our being.” Then he cited Cleanthes (331–233 B.C.) in his *Hymn to Zeus,* 4, and the Cilician poet Aratus (c. 315–240 B.C.) in his *Phaenomena,* 5: “For we are also his offspring.” In spite of the distorted ideas of God that pagans have, they show that they know some things about God (Ro 1:20–21). See *WCF* 5.1; *WLC* 2,101.

17:29 See *WLC* 105,109; *HC* 96.

17:30 God overlooked such ignorance. That is, God took into consideration the limitations of their knowledge about the true God, but now Paul was revealing the truth about the living God. They were being called upon to repent of their sins. See *WCF* 15.3.

17:31 a day when he will judge . . . by the man he has appointed. The final day of judgment (Rev 20:12–15). Capricious rejection by the Athenians of the man whom God appointed would result in Jesus finally and justly rejecting them on that day of judgment. Paul stressed that God’s call to repentance and faith is not an invitation but a command. See *WCF* 8.1; 33.1; *WLC* 51,56; *WSC* 28.

18:1 Corinth. This city had been the capital of the Roman province of Achaia since 27 B.C. It was located about 50 miles southwest of Athens near the isthmus that connects Attica to the north with the Peloponnese to the south. Although Corinth was large and prosperous in the eighth to sixth centuries B.C., it declined and was captured in 338 B.C. by Philip II of Macedon. It was taken by the Romans in 196 B.C, sacked in 146 B.C. by the Romans for revolt, and finally refounded by Julius Caesar as a Roman colony in 44 B.C. In New Testament times, Corinth had a population in excess of 200,000, composed of Greeks; freedmen from Italy; Roman army veterans; businessmen; government officials; people from the Near East, including a large contingent of Jews (part of an inscription of a Jewish synagogue was found in the ruins of Corinth); and many slaves. Along with its affluence and cosmopolitan nature, Corinth was thoroughly pagan and immoral. The city was filled with pagan temples and on the south had on its high acropolis (called the Acrocorinth), a temple of the goddess Aphrodite. From the fifth century B.C. on, the expression “to Corinthianize” had meant “to be sexually immoral.”

18:2 Aquila . . . of Pontus . . . Priscilla. Aquila was a native of Pontus, a northern region of Asia Minor between Bithynia and Armenia. Priscilla is frequently listed before her husband (vv. 18–19,26; Ro 16:3; 2Ti 4:19), indicating that she may have had a higher social status than he or been more prominent in their tentmaking business.

18:6 shook out his clothes. A symbolic repudiation of the Jews’ rejection and unbelief (cf. 13:51). **Your blood be on your own heads!** They were responsible for their rejection of Christ (cf. Mt 27:25) and would bear the burden for their own sins.

18:7 house of Titius Justus, a worshiper of God. The first home of the Corinthian church. Titius Justus (both names are Roman) was a Gentile, an adherent to the faith at the synagogue and a Roman citizen. He possibly belonged to one of the families

9One night the Lord spoke to Paul in a vision: "Do not be afraid; keep on speaking,
do not be silent. 10For I am with you,[h] and no one is going to attack and harm you, because I have many people in this city." 11So Paul stayed for a year and a half, teaching
them the word of God.
12While Gallio was proconsul of Achaia,[i] the Jews made a united attack on Paul and
brought him into court. 13"This man," they charged, "is persuading the people to worship God in ways contrary to the law."
14Just as Paul was about to speak, Gallio said to the Jews, "If you Jews were making
a complaint about some misdemeanor or serious crime, it would be reasonable for me
to listen to you. 15But since it involves questions about words and names and your own
law[j]—settle the matter yourselves. I will not be a judge of such things." 16So he had them
ejected from the court. 17Then they all turned on Sosthenes[k] the synagogue ruler and
beat him in front of the court. But Gallio showed no concern whatever.

Priscilla, Aquila and Apollos

18Paul stayed on in Corinth for some time. Then he left the brothers[l] and sailed for
Syria, accompanied by Priscilla and Aquila. Before he sailed, he had his hair cut off at
Cenchrea[m] because of a vow he had taken.[n] 19They arrived at Ephesus,[o] where Paul left
Priscilla and Aquila. He himself went into the synagogue and reasoned with the Jews.
20When they asked him to spend more time with them, he declined. 21But as he left, he
promised, "I will come back if it is God's will."[p] Then he set sail from Ephesus. 22When
he landed at Caesarea,[q] he went up and greeted the church and then went down to Antioch.[r]
23After spending some time in Antioch, Paul set out from there and traveled from
place to place throughout the region of Galatia[s] and Phrygia, strengthening all the disciples.[t]
24Meanwhile a Jew named Apollos,[u] a native of Alexandria, came to Ephesus. He was
a learned man, with a thorough knowledge of the Scriptures. 25He had been instructed
in the way of the Lord, and he spoke with great fervor[a][v] and taught about Jesus accurately, though he knew only the baptism of John.[w] 26He began to speak boldly in the synagogue. When Priscilla and Aquila heard him, they invited him to their home and explained to him the way of God more adequately.
27When Apollos wanted to go to Achaia,[x] the brothers[y] encouraged him and wrote
to the disciples there to welcome him. On arriving, he was a great help to those who by
grace had believed. 28For he vigorously refuted the Jews in public debate, proving from
the Scriptures[z] that Jesus was the Christ.[a]

Paul in Ephesus

19 While Apollos was at Corinth,[b] Paul took the road through the interior and arrived at Ephesus.[c] There he found some disciples 2and asked them, "Did you receive the Holy Spirit when[b] you believed?"

[a] 25 Or *with fervor in the Spirit* [b] 2 Or *after*

18:10 [h]Mt 28:20
18:12 [i]ver 27
18:15 [j]Ac 23:29; 25:11, 19
18:17 [k]1Co 1:1
18:18 [l]Ac 1:16 [m]Ro 16:1 [n]Nu 6:2,5,18; Ac 21:24
18:19 [o]ver 21,24; 1Co 15:32
18:21 [p]Ro 1:10; 1Co 4:19; Jas 4:15
18:22 [q]Ac 8:40 [r]Ac 11:19
18:23 [s]Ac 16:6 [t]Ac 14:22; 15:32,41
18:24 [u]Ac 19:1; 1Co 1:12; 3:5,6, 22; 4:6; 16:12; Tit 3:13
18:25 [v]Ro 12:11 [w]Ac 19:3
18:27 [x]ver 12 [y]ver 18
18:28 [z]Ac 17:2 [a]ver 5; Ac 9:22
19:1 [b]Ac 18:1 [c]Ac 18:19

Julius Caesar had sent to colonize Corinth. There is reason to believe that he may be the Gaius of Romans 16:23, who is mentioned as having been baptized by Paul (1Co 1:14).
18:8 Crispus, the synagogue ruler. As synagogue ruler, Crispus was in charge of the physical arrangements for the synagogue services. It is this Crispus (and presumably his household) whom Paul baptized (1Co 1:14). **his entire household believed.** See 16:15 and its note; see also16:31–33.
18:10 I have many people in this city. Jesus guaranteed that Paul's labors in Corinth would not be without results because God's own people (i.e., those God had appointed to eternal life; 13:48) lived in this city. Even though the elect Corinthians had not yet believed the gospel, for many had not even heard Paul preach, they nevertheless belonged to God.
18:12 While Gallio was proconsul of Achaia. Luke correctly identified the administrative head of this senatorial province (Achaia) as a proconsul. An inscription found at Delphi, Greece, identifies Gallio as proconsul during Claudius's 26th acclamation as emperor (i.e., January to July of A.D. 52).
18:13 contrary to the law. That is, contrary to the Roman law forbidding the practice of religions that Rome had not legally recognized. Judaism was a legally recognized religion. Christianity was initially viewed as an offshoot of Judaism and, as such, was a legal religion (*religio licita*). See *BC* 28.
18:17 See *WLC* 130.
18:18 a vow he had taken. Although this phrase could apply to Aquila, Paul is probably in view. Because the Nazirite vow involved rigorous ceremonial purity that was impractical to implement in Gentile lands (Nu 6:1–21), the vow in question was probably a private one undertaken by Paul as a religious exercise. The cutting of the hair (which was uncut during the period of the vow) marked the conclusion of the vow and was perhaps an expression of gratitude to God.
▪ **18:23—21:14** *Paul's Third Missionary Journey.* Luke described the third phase of Paul's evangelization of Gentile nations. Once again, he traveled as far as Greece.
18:23 some time in Antioch. Presumably several months, from about the fall of A.D. 52 to the spring of A.D. 53. **Paul set out.** This is the beginning of Paul's third missionary journey. **Galatia and Phrygia.** Paul started with the nearest area of his former work, the Phrygian area of Galatia in southern Asia Minor.
18:25 See *WLC* 159.
18:28 See *WLC* 4; *BC* 7.
19:1 the interior. When he had finished his ministry in Phrygian Galatia (18:23), Paul continued westward by land through the region of Colosse, Laodicea and Hierapolis (Col 4:13) in the Lycus Valley, finally arriving at Ephesus. There he ministered for about three years (vv. 8,10), from about A.D. 53 to 56. **Ephesus.** The capital of the Roman province of Asia, Ephesus was founded in about the twelfth century B.C. by Ionians from Athens. It became a great

They answered, "No, we have not even heard that there is a Holy Spirit."
3So Paul asked, "Then what baptism did you receive?"
"John's baptism," they replied.
4Paul said, "John's baptism was a baptism of repentance. He told the people to believe in the one coming after him, that is, in Jesus."[d] **5**On hearing this, they were baptized
into[a] the name of the Lord Jesus. **6**When Paul placed his hands on them,[e] the Holy Spirit came on them,[f] and they spoke in tongues[b][g] and prophesied. **7**There were about
twelve men in all.
8Paul entered the synagogue[h] and spoke boldly there for three months, arguing per-
suasively about the kingdom of God.[i] **9**But some of them[j] became obstinate; they refused
to believe and publicly maligned the Way.[k] So Paul left them. He took the disciples[l] with
him and had discussions daily in the lecture hall of Tyrannus. **10**This went on for two

19:4 [d]Jn 1:7; Ac 13:24, 25
19:6 [e]Ac 6:6; 8:17 [f]Ac 2:4 [g]Mk 16:17; Ac 10:46
19:8 [h]Ac 9:20 [i]Ac 1:3; 28:23
19:9 [j]Ac 14:4 [k]ver 23; Ac 9:2 [l]ver 30; Ac 11:26

[a] 5 Or *in* [b] 6 Or *other languages*

---

commercial power, but the economic prosperity of the city eventually dwindled, due mainly to increasing soil erosion of the Cayster River, which resulted in the silting and clogging of the harbor. The city also derived wealth and prestige from its temple of Artemis, which was built in honor of the multi-breasted goddess of fertility. Ephesus in Paul's day had passed its zenith but was still an important commercial and religious center. **some disciples.** That is, "about twelve men" (v. 7).
19:2 receive the Holy Spirit. As followers of John the Baptist, these believers had not been instructed about the coming of the Spirit. Note that all categories of people received the baptism of the Holy Spirit: Jews, God-fearing Greeks, Samaritans and Gentiles.
19:4 baptism of repentance . . . the one coming after him . . . Jesus. John's baptism of repentance (Mk 1:4; Lk 3:3) was directed toward repentance of sins, and it looked forward to the redeeming work of Jesus, the coming One.
19:6 spoke in tongues and prophesied. The experience of these Ephesian Gentiles in receiving the Holy Spirit parallels that of believing Jews (2:4,11), Samaritans (8:14–17) and God-fearing Gentiles (10:44–46). Thus this episode represents the extension of the Pentecost experience to yet another group of people (see note on v. 2). **prophesied.** In this context, prophesying probably indicates something similar to "declaring the wonders of God" (2:11) and "praising God" (10:46).
19:9 lecture hall of Tyrannus. We know nothing about Tyrannus, whose name means "tyrant." Some manuscripts add the note "from the fifth to the tenth hour" (i.e., from 11:00 A.M. to 4:00 P.M.). Tyrannus used the room in the cool morning hours, but when the heat of the summer day became oppressive, Paul was permitted to use the hall. See *WLC* 113.

Paul's Third Missionary Journey

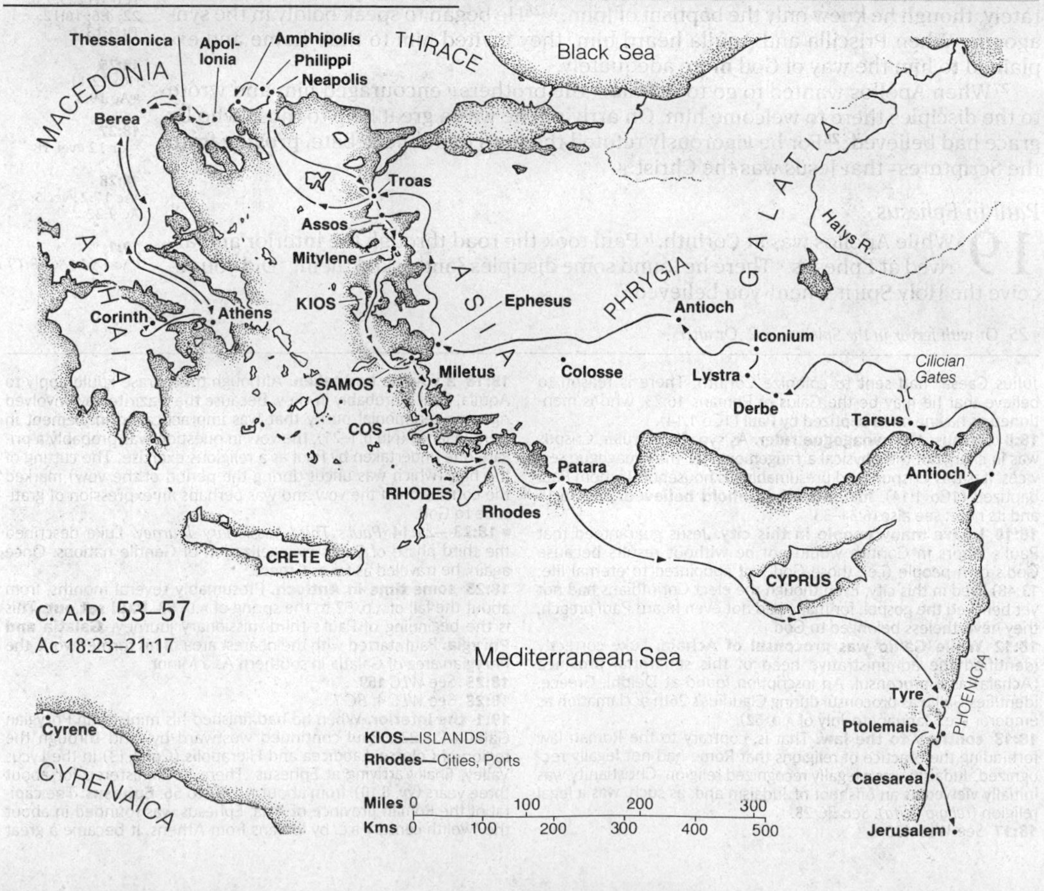

years,[m] so that all the Jews and Greeks who lived in the province of Asia[n] heard the word
of the Lord.
11God did extraordinary miracles[o] through Paul, 12so that even handkerchiefs and
aprons that had touched him were taken to the sick, and their illnesses were cured[p] and
the evil spirits left them.
13Some Jews who went around driving out evil spirits[q] tried to invoke the name of the
Lord Jesus over those who were demon-possessed. They would say, “In the name of
Jesus,[r] whom Paul preaches, I command you to come out.” 14Seven sons of Sceva, a Jewish chief priest, were doing this. 15⌊One day⌋ the evil spirit answered them, “Jesus I
know, and I know about Paul, but who are you?” 16Then the man who had the evil spirit jumped on them and overpowered them all. He gave them such a beating that they ran
out of the house naked and bleeding.
17When this became known to the Jews and Greeks living in Ephesus,[s] they were all
seized with fear,[t] and the name of the Lord Jesus was held in high honor. 18Many of those
who believed now came and openly confessed their evil deeds. 19A number who had
practiced sorcery brought their scrolls together and burned them publicly. When they
calculated the value of the scrolls, the total came to fifty thousand drachmas.[a] 20In this
way the word of the Lord spread widely and grew in power.[u]
21After all this had happened, Paul decided to go to Jerusalem,[v] passing through Macedonia[w] and Achaia.[x] “After I have been there,” he said, “I must visit Rome also.”[y] 22He
sent two of his helpers,[z] Timothy[a] and Erastus,[b] to Macedonia, while he stayed in the
province of Asia[c] a little longer.

The Riot in Ephesus

23About that time there arose a great disturbance about the Way.[d] 24A silversmith
named Demetrius, who made silver shrines of Artemis, brought in no little business for
the craftsmen. 25He called them together, along with the workmen in related trades, and
said: “Men, you know we receive a good income from this business.[e] 26And you see and
hear how this fellow Paul has convinced and led astray large numbers of people here in
Ephesus[f] and in practically the whole province of Asia. He says that man-made gods are
no gods at all.[g] 27There is danger not only that our trade will lose its good name, but also
that the temple of the great goddess Artemis will be discredited, and the goddess herself, who is worshiped throughout the province of Asia and the world, will be robbed of
her divine majesty.”
28When they heard this, they were furious and began shouting: “Great is Artemis of
the Ephesians!”[h] 29Soon the whole city was in an uproar. The people seized Gaius[i] and
Aristarchus,[j] Paul’s traveling companions from Macedonia,[k] and rushed as one man into
the theater. 30Paul wanted to appear before the crowd, but the disciples would not let
him. 31Even some of the officials of the province, friends of Paul, sent him a message begging him not to venture into the theater.
32The assembly was in confusion: Some were shouting one thing, some another.[l]
Most of the people did not even know why they were there. 33The Jews pushed Alexander to the front, and some of the crowd shouted instructions to him. He motioned[m] for

19:10 [m]Ac 20:31 [n]ver 22, 26,27
19:11 [o]Ac 8:13
19:12 [p]Ac 5:15
19:13 [q]Mt 12:27 [r]Mk 9:38
19:17 [s]Ac 18:19 [t]Ac 5:5, 11
19:20 [u]Ac 6:7; 12:24
19:21 [v]Ac 20:16,22; Ro 15:25 [w]Ac 16:9 [x]Ac 18:12 [y]Ro 15:24,28
19:22 [z]Ac 13:5 [a]Ac 16:1 [b]Ro 16:23; 2Ti 4:20 [c]ver 10, 26,27
19:23 [d]Ac 9:2
19:25 [e]Ac 16:16,19,20
19:26 [f]Ac 18:19 [g]Dt 4:28; Ps 115:4; Isa 44:10-20; Jer 10:3-5; Ac 17:29; 1Co 8:4; Rev 9:20
19:28 [h]Ac 18:19
19:29 [i]Ac 20:4; Ro 16:23; 1Co 1:14 [j]Ac 20:4; 27:2; Col 4:10; Phm 24 [k]Ac 16:9
19:32 [l]Ac 21:34
19:33 [m]Ac 12:17

[a] *19* A drachma was a silver coin worth about a day’s wages.

19:10 the province of Asia. The Roman province in the western part of Asia Minor. As a result of this teaching, groups of believers were formed in numerous places (Col 4:13,16; Rev 2–3).
19:12 handkerchiefs and aprons that had touched him. That is, sweat cloths and work aprons that Paul wore as he worked in his tentmaking trade (18:3). **taken to the sick.** This was not Paul’s doing; because of their pagan religious background, the Ephesians were used to employing superstitious means (v. 19). That God mercifully accommodated his gracious work to their ignorance in this instance does not justify the continuation of such a practice today.
19:13 driving out evil spirits. In ancient times it was common practice to use magical names to drive out evil spirits. Jews in Ephesus were trying to “invoke the name of the Lord Jesus” to imitate what Paul was doing (v. 12; 16:18). See *WLC* 113.
19:19 their scrolls. These scrolls contained the magical names and incantations used in their magical arts. **fifty thousand drachmas.** A drachma in Paul’s day was the daily wage of the common laborer. See *WLC* 142.
19:23 the Way. See note on 9:2.
19:24–25 See *WLC* 142.
19:24 A silversmith named Demetrius. An important silversmith guild had developed at Ephesus due to the large religious pilgrimage trade. This trade had developed because of the worship of the Greek goddess Artemis (Latin, *Diana*), who at Ephesus was portrayed as a grotesque, multi-breasted Near Eastern fertility mother goddess. Her “image,” which had fallen “from heaven” (v. 35), was probably a meteorite that became an object of worship. The temple of Artemis, one of the seven wonders of the ancient world, is located more than a mile northeast of the ruins of the city. Not only was it the object of religious pilgrimage, but the temple was also a banking depository for the ancient world. The making of silver shrines of the temple and images of the goddess was a major source of income.
19:27 temple of the great goddess Artemis. The archaic Ionic temple of Artemis measured 425 feet by 220 feet and had 127 marble columns 62 feet high. The lowest drums of the 36 western columns were carved with reliefs. The statue of the goddess was displayed in an inner room of the temple.
19:32 assembly. The Greek word *ekklçsia* is used here and denotes a secular assembly of people (see note on 5:11).

silence in order to make a defense before the people. 34But when they realized he was a
Jew, they all shouted in unison for about two hours: "Great is Artemis of the Ephesians!"
35The city clerk quieted the crowd and said: "Men of Ephesus,[n] doesn't all the world
know that the city of Ephesus is the guardian of the temple of the great Artemis and of
her image, which fell from heaven? 36Therefore, since these facts are undeniable, you
ought to be quiet and not do anything rash. 37You have brought these men here, though
they have neither robbed temples[o] nor blasphemed our goddess. 38If, then, Demetrius
and his fellow craftsmen have a grievance against anybody, the courts are open and
there are proconsuls.[p] They can press charges. 39If there is anything further you want to
bring up, it must be settled in a legal assembly. 40As it is, we are in danger of being
charged with rioting because of today's events. In that case we would not be able to account for this commotion, since there is no reason for it." 41After he had said this, he dismissed the assembly.

Through Macedonia and Greece

20 When the uproar had ended, Paul sent for the disciples[q] and, after encouraging them, said good-by and set out for Macedonia.[r] 2He traveled through that
area, speaking many words of encouragement to the people, and finally arrived in
Greece, 3where he stayed three months. Because the Jews made a plot against him[s] just
as he was about to sail for Syria, he decided to go back through Macedonia.[t] 4He was accompanied by Sopater son of Pyrrhus from Berea, Aristarchus[u] and Secundus from Thessalonica,[v] Gaius[w] from Derbe, Timothy[x] also, and Tychicus[y] and Trophimus[z] from the
province of Asia. 5These men went on ahead and waited for us[a] at Troas.[b] 6But we sailed
from Philippi[c] after the Feast of Unleavened Bread, and five days later joined the others
at Troas,[d] where we stayed seven days.

Eutychus Raised From the Dead at Troas

7On the first day of the week[e] we came together to break bread. Paul spoke to the people and, because he intended to leave the next day, kept on talking until midnight.
8There were many lamps in the upstairs room[f] where we were meeting. 9Seated in a window was a young man named Eutychus, who was sinking into a deep sleep as Paul talked
on and on. When he was sound asleep, he fell to the ground from the third story and was
picked up dead. 10Paul went down, threw himself on the young man[g] and put his arms
around him. "Don't be alarmed," he said. "He's alive!"[h] 11Then he went upstairs again
and broke bread[i] and ate. After talking until daylight, he left. 12The people took the
young man home alive and were greatly comforted.

Paul's Farewell to the Ephesian Elders

13We went on ahead to the ship and sailed for Assos, where we were going to take
Paul aboard. He had made this arrangement because he was going there on foot.
14When he met us at Assos, we took him aboard and went on to Mitylene. 15The next day
we set sail from there and arrived off Kios. The day after that we crossed over to Samos,

19:35 [n]Ac 18:19
19:37 [o]Ro 2:22
19:38 [p]Ac 13:7, 8, 12
20:1 [q]Ac 11:26 [r]Ac 16:9
20:3 [s]ver 19; Ac 9:23, 24; 23:12, 15, 30; 25:3; 2Co 11:26 [t]Ac 16:9
20:4 [u]Ac 19:29 [v]Ac 17:1 [w]Ac 19:29 [x]Ac 16:1 [y]Eph 6:21; Col 4:7; 2Ti 4:12; Tit 3:12 [z]Ac 21:29; 2Ti 4:20
20:5 [a]Ac 16:10 [b]Ac 16:8
20:6 [c]Ac 16:12 [d]Ac 16:8
20:7 [e]1Co 16:2; Rev 1:10
20:8 [f]Ac 1:13
20:10 [g]1Ki 17:21; 2Ki 4:34 [h]Mt 9:23, 24
20:11 [i]ver 7

19:37 neither robbed temples nor blasphemed our goddess. These were common charges of Gentiles against Jews and Jewish Christians (Josephus, *Antiquities*, 4.207; *Against Apion*, 2.237).

20:1 set out for Macedonia. Paul went up the Asia Minor coast from Ephesus, either by road or by ship, probably as far as Troas and then by ship to Macedonia (cf. 16:8–10) and on to Philippi (cf. 16:11–40), visiting groups of believers as he went. While in Macedonia, Paul may have extended his ministry as far as Illyricum (i.e., the region of modern Albania and Yugoslavia; Ro 15:19).

20:2 arrived in Greece. Paul arrived at Corinth in the province of Achaia, where he spent the winter of A.D. 56–57. It was at this time that he wrote Romans (Ro 15:26; 16:23–24).

20:4 Paul's traveling companions are listed by name. Although the text does not explicitly explain their presence, these men may have been official church representatives appointed to travel with Paul to deliver money collected for the relief of the Jerusalem church (1Co 16:1–4; 2Co 9:1–5). Sopater may be the same person as the Sosipater mentioned in Romans 16:21. Aristarchus faithfully accompanied Paul during the third missionary journey (19:29) and later to Rome (27:2), where he shared Paul's imprisonment (Col 4:10). Secundus is mentioned nowhere else in the New Testament. Gaius from Derbe in Asia Minor may be different from the Macedonian Gaius mentioned in 19:29, although some manuscripts read "Doberus" (a city in eastern Macedonia) instead of "Derbe." On Timothy, see "Introduction to 1 Timothy: Author." Tychicus would later serve as Paul's representative to various churches during the apostle's imprisonments (Eph 6:21; Col 4:7–9; 2Ti 4:12). Trophimus accompanied Paul to Jerusalem, where his presence in the city led to Paul's arrest (21:29). He apparently also traveled with Paul after the apostle's release from the first Roman imprisonment (2Ti 4:20).

20:5 waited for us. Luke again used the first person plural pronoun, indicating that he became Paul's travel companion to Jerusalem.

20:7 first day of the week. Sunday, following a Saturday Sabbath. **to break bread.** Since they were gathered together for worship on the first day of the week, the Lord's Day (Rev 1:10), this celebration is to be understood to include communion (2:42), not just a fellowship meal (2:46). **Paul spoke.** This was a Sunday evening preaching-teaching service. See *WCF* 21.7; 29.3; *WLC* 116,117,119; *WSC* 59,60,61; *BC* 35.

20:8–12 Luke recorded that Eutychus was "picked up dead," the likely result of such a fall. Paul's restoration of the young man to life is one of two such raisings of the dead by apostles recorded in Acts (9:40; cf. Lk 7:11–17; 8:49–56; Jn 11:1–44). See *WLC* 119; *WSC* 61.

20:13 sailed for Assos. Paul stayed behind at Troas and then walked 20 miles south on the Roman road to Assos, which was located on the coast opposite the island of Lesbos, whose capital city was Mitylene.

20:15 The next day . . . Kios . . . Samos . . . Miletus. They were

and on the following day arrived at Miletus.[j] 16 Paul had decided to sail past Ephesus[k]
to avoid spending time in the province of Asia, for he was in a hurry to reach Jerusalem,[l]
if possible, by the day of Pentecost.[m]
17 From Miletus, Paul sent to Ephesus for the elders[n] of the church. 18 When they arrived, he said to them: "You know how I lived the whole time I was with you,[o] from the
first day I came into the province of Asia. 19 I served the Lord with great humility and with
tears, although I was severely tested by the plots of the Jews.[p] 20 You know that I have not
hesitated to preach anything[q] that would be helpful to you but have taught you publicly and from house to house. 21 I have declared to both Jews[r] and Greeks that they must
turn to God in repentance[s] and have faith in our Lord Jesus.[t]
22 "And now, compelled by the Spirit, I am going to Jerusalem,[u] not knowing what will
happen to me there. 23 I only know that in every city the Holy Spirit warns me[v] that prison and hardships are facing me.[w] 24 However, I consider my life worth nothing to me,[x]
if only I may finish the race and complete the task[y] the Lord Jesus has given me[z]—the
task of testifying to the gospel of God's grace.
25 "Now I know that none of you among whom I have gone about preaching the kingdom will ever see me again.[a] 26 Therefore, I declare to you today that I am innocent of
the blood of all men.[b] 27 For I have not hesitated to proclaim to you the whole will of God.[c]
28 Keep watch over yourselves and all the flock of which the Holy Spirit has made you
overseers.[a][d] Be shepherds of the church of God,[b] which he bought with his own blood.
29 I know that after I leave, savage wolves[e] will come in among you and will not spare the
flock.[f] 30 Even from your own number men will arise and distort the truth in order to draw
away disciples[g] after them. 31 So be on your guard! Remember that for three years[h] I never stopped warning each of you night and day with tears.[i]
32 "Now I commit you to God[j] and to the word of his grace, which can build you up
and give you an inheritance[k] among all those who are sanctified.[l] 33 I have not coveted
anyone's silver or gold or clothing.[m] 34 You yourselves know that these hands of mine
have supplied my own needs and the needs of my companions.[n] 35 In everything I did, I
showed you that by this kind of hard work we must help the weak, remembering the
words the Lord Jesus himself said: 'It is more blessed to give than to receive.' "
36 When he had said this, he knelt down with all of them and prayed.[o] 37 They all
wept as they embraced him and kissed him.[p] 38 What grieved them most was his statement that they would never see his face again.[q] Then they accompanied him to the
ship.

On to Jerusalem

21 After we[r] had torn ourselves away from them, we put out to sea and sailed
straight to Cos. The next day we went to Rhodes and from there to Patara. 2 We
found a ship crossing over to Phoenicia,[s] went on board and set sail. 3 After sighting Cy-

[a] 28 Traditionally *bishops* [b] 28 Many manuscripts *of the Lord*

20:15
[j]ver 17; 2Ti 4:20
20:16
[k]Ac 18:19 [l]Ac 19:21
[m]Ac 2:1; 1Co 16:8
20:17
[n]Ac 11:30
20:18
[o]Ac 18:19-21; 19:1-41
20:19
[p]ver 3
20:20
[q]ver 27
20:21
[r]Ac 18:5 [s]Ac 2:38
[t]Ac 24:24; 26:18; Eph 1:15; Col 2:5; Phm 5
20:22
[u]ver 16
20:23
[v]Ac 21:4 [w]Ac 9:16
20:24
[x]Ac 21:13 [y]2Co 4:1
[z]Gal 1:1; Tit 1:3
20:25
[a]ver 38
20:26
[b]Ac 18:6
20:27
[c]ver 20
20:28
[d]1Pe 5:2
20:29
[e]Mt 7:15 [f]ver 28
20:30
[g]Ac 11:26
20:31
[h]Ac 19:10 [i]ver 19
20:32
[j]Ac 14:23
[k]Eph 1:14; Col 1:12; 3:24; Heb 9:15; 1Pe 1:4 [l]Ac 26:18
20:33
[m]1Sa 12:3; 1Co 9:12; 2Co 7:2; 11:9; 12:14-17
20:34
[n]Ac 18:3
20:36
[o]Lk 22:41; Ac 21:5
20:37
[p]Lk 15:20
20:38
[q]ver 25
21:1
[r]Ac 16:10
21:2
[s]Ac 11:19

---

sailing down the coast to Miletus, located about 30 miles farther south of Ephesus.

20:17 elders. As to position, these elders were the ordained representatives of the Ephesian congregation; as to function, they were called to be overseers and shepherds of the church of God (v. 28; cf. 1Ti 3:1–7; Tit 1:5–9). See *WCF* 30.1.

20:20 taught you publicly and from house to house. Paul's teaching ministry during his three-year stay (v. 31) in Ephesus was obviously extensive, involving both public lectures (at the synagogue and the lecture hall of Tyrannus; vv. 8–10) and more private instruction in homes.

20:21 repentance . . . faith. See note on 3:19. Both Jews and Gentiles must come to God in the same way: in repentance for sin (Lk 24:47; Ac 26:20) and through faith in Jesus Christ. See *WCF* 15.1; *WLC* 153; *WSC* 85; *BC* 10.

20:22 compelled by the Spirit. Such explicit guidance by the Holy Spirit often occurred during Paul's ministry (16:6–10).

20:25 none of you . . . will ever see me again. Paul's statement was based upon his human judgment of the situation rather than upon divine revelation. Paul considered it quite unlikely that he would again see the Ephesian elders because of the continued plots against his life by the Jews (v. 3), the divine revelation that "prison and hardships" awaited him (v. 23) and his own intention to focus his future ministry on the western Mediterranean (Ro 15:23–29). Apparently Paul did in fact later return to Ephesus after his release from prison in Rome (1Ti 1:3)

20:27 whole will of God. The whole purpose of God (i.e., the complete revelation God has given in his Son Jesus Christ, through whom the believer appropriates salvation; 2:23; 4:28), especially the gospel message (cf. Eze 3:17-21). Paul did not suppress any truths of the gospel but preached the full gospel to both Jews and Gentiles. He always used tact and discretion, but he never compromised the Good News. See *WLC* 159; *BC* 7.

20:28 he bought with his own blood. The context mentions both the Holy Spirit and God, to whom the word "blood" cannot apply. "His own" is a variant of "his beloved" or "his one and only [Son]" and refers to Jesus Christ. See *WCF* 8.7; 30.1; *WLC* 38; *HC* 54.

20:30 from your own number. Paul's prophetic warning in this verse was fulfilled in that the Ephesian church was soon to be plagued by false teachers, some of whom apparently were leaders of the church ("Introduction to 1 Timothy: Purpose and Distinctives"; 1Ti 1:3,7,19–20; 6:3–5; "Introduction to 2 Timothy: Original Audience").

20:32 See *WCF* 13.1; 14.1; *WLC* 4,43,155; *WSC* 89.

20:37 kissed him. The ancient practice of the Christian kiss (Lk 7:45; 1Th 5:26; 1Pe 5:14) is still maintained in some cultures today.

21:1 Cos . . . Rhodes . . . Patara. They sailed on a direct course among the islands off the coast of Asia Minor to the port of Pata
The small island of Cos was a free state in the province
Rhodes, the capital on the north end of the island of
famous and prosperous in the earlier Greek period
on the southwest coast of Asia Minor, was an
ancient ships sailing the eastern Mediterra
Syria, the Holy Land and Egypt into co
donia and Achaia.

21:2 Phoenicia. Syria controll

21:4 [t]Ac 11:26 [u]ver 11; Ac 20:23
21:5 [v]Ac 20:36
21:7 [w]Ac 12:20 [x]Ac 1:16
21:8 [y]Ac 8:40 [z]Ac 6:5; 8:5-40 [a]Eph 4:11; 2Ti 4:5
21:9 [b]Lk 2:36; Ac 2:17
21:10 [c]Ac 11:28
21:11 [d]ver 33 [e]1Ki 22:11
21:13 [f]Ac 20:24 [g]Ac 9:16
21:16 [h]Ac 8:40 [i]ver 3,4
21:17 [j]Ac 15:4
21:18 [k]Ac 15:13 [l]Ac 11:30
21:19 [m]Ac 14:27 [n]Ac 1:17
21:20 [o]Ac 22:3; Ro 10:2; Gal 1:14 [p]Ac 15:1,5
21:21 [q]ver 28 [r]Ac 15:19-21; 1Co 7:18,19 [s]Ac 6:14
21:23 [t]Ac 18:18
21:24 [u]ver 26; Ac 24:18 [v]Ac 18:18
21:25 [w]Ac 15:20,29
21:26 [x]Nu 6:13-20; Ac 24:18

prus and passing to the south of it, we sailed on to Syria. We landed at Tyre, where our
ship was to unload its cargo. 4Finding the disciples[t] there, we stayed with them seven
days. Through the Spirit[u] they urged Paul not to go on to Jerusalem. 5But when our time
was up, we left and continued on our way. All the disciples and their wives and children
accompanied us out of the city, and there on the beach we knelt to pray.[v] 6After saying
good-by to each other, we went aboard the ship, and they returned home.
7We continued our voyage from Tyre[w] and landed at Ptolemais, where we greeted the
brothers[x] and stayed with them for a day. 8Leaving the next day, we reached Caesarea[y]
and stayed at the house of Philip[z] the evangelist,[a] one of the Seven. 9He had four unmarried daughters who prophesied.[b]
10After we had been there a number of days, a prophet named Agabus[c] came down
from Judea. 11Coming over to us, he took Paul's belt, tied his own hands and feet with it
and said, "The Holy Spirit says, 'In this way the Jews of Jerusalem will bind[d] the owner
of this belt and will hand him over to the Gentiles.'"[e]
12When we heard this, we and the people there pleaded with Paul not to go up to Jerusalem. 13Then Paul answered, "Why are you weeping and breaking my heart? I am
ready not only to be bound, but also to die[f] in Jerusalem for the name of the Lord Jesus."[g]
14When he would not be dissuaded, we gave up and said, "The Lord's will be done."
15After this, we got ready and went up to Jerusalem. 16Some of the disciples from
Caesarea[h] accompanied us and brought us to the home of Mnason, where we were to
stay. He was a man from Cyprus[i] and one of the early disciples.

Paul's Arrival at Jerusalem

17When we arrived at Jerusalem, the brothers received us warmly.[j] 18The next day Paul
and the rest of us went to see James,[k] and all the elders[l] were present. 19Paul greeted them
and reported in detail what God had done among the Gentiles[m] through his ministry.[n]
20When they heard this, they praised God. Then they said to Paul: "You see, brother, how many thousands of Jews have believed, and all of them are zealous[o] for the law.[p]
21They have been informed that you teach all the Jews who live among the Gentiles to
turn away from Moses,[q] telling them not to circumcise their children[r] or live according
to our customs.[s] 22What shall we do? They will certainly hear that you have come, 23so
do what we tell you. There are four men with us who have made a vow.[t] 24Take these
men, join in their purification rites[u] and pay their expenses, so that they can have their
heads shaved.[v] Then everybody will know there is no truth in these reports about you,
but that you yourself are living in obedience to the law. 25As for the Gentile believers, we
have written to them our decision that they should abstain from food sacrificed to idols,
from blood, from the meat of strangled animals and from sexual immorality."[w]
26The next day Paul took the men and purified himself along with them. Then he went
to the temple to give notice of the date when the days of purification would end and the
offering would be made for each of them.[x]

21:3 Tyre. This port, famous in Old Testament times and conquered by Alexander the Great, was about 400 miles southeast of Patara, a sea journey of about five days.
21:4 Through the Spirit. Paul was not disobedient to the Spirit; the Holy Spirit was compelling him to go to Jerusalem (20:22). These urgings "through the Spirit" were the understandable response of Paul's friends to the Spirit's revelation that Paul was soon to suffer imprisonment and hardship (20:23; 21:11–12).
21:7 Ptolemais. A port (modern Acco) located 25 miles south of Tyre. The ship unlo[illegible]ded its cargo there.
21:8 Caesare[illegible] [illegible] ote on 10:1. This seaport, built by Herod the Great, wa[illegible] [illegible]al capital of Judea. It was 32 miles south of Ptole[illegible] [illegible]e **of the Seven.** One of the Seven chosen t[illegible] [illegible]ution (6:1–6). He had preached to the [illegible] eunuch and the people along the Pales- [illegible]
[illegible]**us.** The same Agabus who 15 years [illegible]ere famine in Judea and the sur- [illegible]
[illegible] the first century context of the [illegible] led directly by the Spirit to give [illegible]
[illegible] *Imprisonment in Jerusalem.* [illegible]ely accused Paul when he [illegible]ost. This series of events [illegible] strife between himself [illegible]
21:15 went up to Jerusalem. Pentecost, the 50th day after Passover, was fast approaching (the group had spent at least 36 days traveling from Philippi to Caesarea, and they had spent several days at Caesarea), and Paul wanted to be at Jerusalem for this feast.
21:20 zealous for the law. Thousands of Jewish Christians in Jerusalem strictly observed the customary Jewish application of the Mosaic Law. While many of these Jewish Christians no doubt resented the fact that Gentile Christians were not required to observe the same customs (v. 25; 15:1–31), the charge here was that Paul was encouraging *Jewish* Christians to forsake the traditional practices as well (v. 21). Such a charge may have been prompted by reports that Paul himself did not follow Jewish ceremonial practices when in Gentile company. Although Paul had no objection to Jews following their ancestral customs, he opposed any claim that such observances were in some way necessary for salvation (Ro 14:1–8; Gal 5:2–6). Always careful to avoid giving unnecessary offense, Paul's flexibility in such matters shows that the interests of the gospel were always foremost in his mind (1Co 9:19–23).
21:24 purification rites . . . expenses. This was the Nazirite vow (Nu 6:1–21), during which the devotee allowed his hair to grow. When the period of the vow was over, the Nazirite shaved off his hair, dedicated the hair to the Lord and burned it together with the sacrifice for the fellowship offering (Nu 6:18). Paul paid the expenses for four Nazirites, went to the priest with them for the sacrifices and participated in the purification rites. In this way Paul visually demonstrated that he was a law-abiding Jew.

Paul Arrested

27When the seven days were nearly over, some Jews from the province of Asia saw
Paul at the temple. They stirred up the whole crowd and seized him,[y] 28shouting, "Men
of Israel, help us! This is the man who teaches all men everywhere against our people
and our law and this place. And besides, he has brought Greeks into the temple area and
defiled this holy place."[z] 29(They had previously seen Trophimus[a] the Ephesian[b] in the
city with Paul and assumed that Paul had brought him into the temple area.)
30The whole city was aroused, and the people came running from all directions. Seizing Paul,[c] they dragged him[d] from the temple, and immediately the gates were shut.
31While they were trying to kill him, news reached the commander of the Roman troops
that the whole city of Jerusalem was in an uproar. 32He at once took some officers and
soldiers and ran down to the crowd. When the rioters saw the commander and his soldiers, they stopped beating Paul.[e]
33The commander came up and arrested him and ordered him to be bound[f] with two[g]
chains.[h] Then he asked who he was and what he had done. 34Some in the crowd shouted one thing and some another,[i] and since the commander could not get at the truth because of the uproar, he ordered that Paul be taken into the barracks.[j] 35When Paul
reached the steps,[k] the violence of the mob was so great he had to be carried by the soldiers. 36The crowd that followed kept shouting, "Away with him!"[l]

Paul Speaks to the Crowd

37As the soldiers were about to take Paul into the barracks,[m] he asked the commander, "May I say something to you?"
"Do you speak Greek?" he replied. 38"Aren't you the Egyptian who started a revolt and
led four thousand terrorists out into the desert[n] some time ago?"[o]
39Paul answered, "I am a Jew, from Tarsus[p] in Cilicia,[q] a citizen of no ordinary city.
Please let me speak to the people."
40Having received the commander's permission, Paul stood on the steps and motioned[r] to the crowd. When they were all silent, he said to them in Aramaic[a]:[s]

22
1"Brothers and fathers,[t] listen now to my defense."
2When they heard him speak to them in Aramaic,[u] they became very quiet.
Then Paul said: 3"I am a Jew,[v] born in Tarsus[w] of Cilicia, but brought up in this city.
Under[x] Gamaliel[y] I was thoroughly trained in the law of our fathers[z] and was just as zealous[a] for God as any of you are today. 4I persecuted[b] the followers of this Way to their
death, arresting both men and women and throwing them into prison,[c] 5as also the high
priest and all the Council[d] can testify. I even obtained letters from them to their brothers[e] in Damascus,[f] and went there to bring these people as prisoners to Jerusalem to be
punished.
6"About noon as I came near Damascus, suddenly a bright light from heaven flashed
around me.[g] 7I fell to the ground and heard a voice say to me, 'Saul! Saul! Why do you
persecute me?'
8" 'Who are you, Lord?' I asked.
" 'I am Jesus of Nazareth, whom you are persecuting,' he replied. 9My companions
saw the light,[h] but they did not understand the voice[i] of him who was speaking to me.
10" 'What shall I do, Lord?' I asked.
" 'Get up,' the Lord said, 'and go into Damascus. There you will be told all that you
have been assigned to do.'[j] 11My companions led me by the hand into Damascus, because the brilliance of the light had blinded me.[k]
12"A man named Ananias came to see me.[l] He was a devout observer of the law and

21:27 [y]Ac 24:18; 26:21
21:28 [z]Mt 24:15; Ac 24:5,6
21:29 [a]Ac 20:4 [b]Ac 18:19
21:30 [c]Ac 26:21 [d]Ac 16:19
21:32 [e]Ac 23:27
21:33 [f]ver 11 [g]Ac 12:6 [h]Ac 20:23; Eph 6:20; 2Ti 2:9
21:34 [i]Ac 19:32 [j]ver 37; Ac 23:10, 16, 32
21:35 [k]ver 40
21:36 [l]Lk 23:18; Jn 19:15; Ac 22:22
21:37 [m]ver 34
21:38 [n]Mt 24:26 [o]Ac 5:36
21:39 [p]Ac 9:11 [q]Ac 22:3
21:40 [r]Ac 12:17 [s]Jn 5:2
22:1 [t]Ac 7:2
22:2 [u]Ac 21:40
22:3 [v]Ac 21:39 [w]Ac 9:11 [x]Lk 10:39 [y]Ac 5:34 [z]Ac 26:5 [a]Ac 21:20
22:4 [b]Ac 8:3 [c]ver 19, 20
22:5 [d]Lk 22:66 [e]Ac 13:26 [f]Ac 9:2
22:6 [g]Ac 9:3
22:9 [h]Ac 26:13 [i]Ac 9:7
22:10 [j]Ac 16:30
22:11 [k]Ac 9:8
22:12 [l]Ac 9:17

a *40* Or possibly *Hebrew*; also in 22:2

21:29 Trophimus the Ephesian in the city with Paul. Ephesian Jews had seen Paul accompanied by Trophimus of Ephesus, whom they knew to be a Gentile Christian. They suspected that Paul had taken him into the temple area, which Gentiles were not allowed to enter. But Paul had been there with four unidentified men (vv. 23–26), and the Ephesian Jews mistakenly presumed that they were the Gentile Christians who had accompanied Paul to Jerusalem.

21:37 Do you speak Greek? The commander was surprised to hear Paul speak excellent Greek, for he thought Paul was an insurrectionist Jew from Egypt who three years before had appeared there claiming to be a prophet (Josephus, *Jewish War,* 2.261–263).

21:38 terrorists. Greek, *sikarios,* "dagger men" or "assassins." They were fanatical Jewish nationalists.

21:40 Aramaic. The common speech of the Jews in the Holy Land, although the priests and Levites in particular were acquainted with Hebrew. Greek, however, was the common language of the Roman and Mediterranean world.

22:3 Tarsus. An important commercial and university city located in Cilicia in southeastern Asia Minor. It was situated ten miles inland from the Mediterranean Sea.

22:12 Ananias. An appropriate person to meet Saul, who was a zealous Pharisee, "a Hebrew of Hebrews" (Php 3:5). Ananias became a link to other Jews in the city who had become suspicious of Paul (9:10–19).

highly respected by all the Jews living there.[m] 13He stood beside me and said, 'Brother Saul, receive your sight!' And at that very moment I was able to see him.

14"Then he said: 'The God of our fathers[n] has chosen you to know his will and to see[o] the Righteous One[p] and to hear words from his mouth. 15You will be his witness[q] to all men of what you have seen and heard. 16And now what are you waiting for? Get up, be baptized[r] and wash your sins away,[s] calling on his name.'[t]

17"When I returned to Jerusalem[u] and was praying at the temple, I fell into a trance[v] 18and saw the Lord speaking. 'Quick!' he said to me. 'Leave Jerusalem immediately, because they will not accept your testimony about me.'

19" 'Lord,' I replied, 'these men know that I went from one synagogue to another to imprison[w] and beat[x] those who believe in you. 20And when the blood of your martyr[a] Stephen was shed, I stood there giving my approval and guarding the clothes of those who were killing him.'[y]

21"Then the Lord said to me, 'Go; I will send you far away to the Gentiles.' "[z]

Paul the Roman Citizen

22The crowd listened to Paul until he said this. Then they raised their voices and shouted, "Rid the earth of him![a] He's not fit to live!"[b]

23As they were shouting and throwing off their cloaks[c] and flinging dust into the air,[d] 24the commander ordered Paul to be taken into the barracks.[e] He directed[f] that he be flogged and questioned in order to find out why the people were shouting at him like this. 25As they stretched him out to flog him, Paul said to the centurion standing there, "Is it legal for you to flog a Roman citizen who hasn't even been found guilty?"[g]

26When the centurion heard this, he went to the commander and reported it. "What are you going to do?" he asked. "This man is a Roman citizen."

27The commander went to Paul and asked, "Tell me, are you a Roman citizen?"

"Yes, I am," he answered.

28Then the commander said, "I had to pay a big price for my citizenship."

"But I was born a citizen," Paul replied.

29Those who were about to question him withdrew immediately. The commander himself was alarmed when he realized that he had put Paul, a Roman citizen,[h] in chains.

Before the Sanhedrin

30The next day, since the commander wanted to find out exactly why Paul was being accused by the Jews,[i] he released him[j] and ordered the chief priests and all the Sanhedrin[k] to assemble. Then he brought Paul and had him stand before them.

23 Paul looked straight at the Sanhedrin[l] and said, "My brothers,[m] I have fulfilled my duty to God in all good conscience[n] to this day." 2At this the high priest Ananias[o] ordered those standing near Paul to strike him on the mouth.[p] 3Then Paul said to him, "God will strike you, you whitewashed wall![q] You sit there to judge me according to the law, yet you yourself violate the law by commanding that I be struck!"[r]

4Those who were standing near Paul said, "You dare to insult God's high priest?"

5Paul replied, "Brothers, I did not realize that he was the high priest; for it is written: 'Do not speak evil about the ruler of your people.'[b]"[s]

6Then Paul, knowing that some of them were Sadducees and the others Pharisees,

[a] *20* Or *witness* [b] *5* Exodus 22:28

22:12 [m]Ac 10:22
22:14 [n]Ac 3:13 [o]1Co 9:1; 15:8 [p]Ac 7:52
22:15 [q]Ac 23:11; 26:16
22:16 [r]Ac 2:38 [s]Heb 10:22 [t]Ro 10:13
22:17 [u]Ac 9:26 [v]Ac 10:10
22:19 [w]ver 4; Ac 8:3 [x]Mt 10:17
22:20 [y]Ac 7:57-60; 8:1
22:21 [z]Ac 9:15; 13:46
22:22 [a]Ac 21:36 [b]Ac 25:24
22:23 [c]Ac 7:58 [d]2Sa 16:13
22:24 [e]Ac 21:34 [f]ver 29
22:25 [g]Ac 16:37
22:29 [h]ver 24,25; Ac 16:38
22:30 [i]Ac 23:28 [j]Ac 21:33 [k]Mt 5:22
23:1 [l]Ac 22:30 [m]Ac 22:5 [n]Ac 24:16; 1Co 4:4; 2Co 1:12; 2Ti 1:3; Heb 13:18
23:2 [o]Ac 24:1 [p]Jn 18:22
23:3 [q]Mt 23:27 [r]Lev 19:15; Dt 25:1,2; Jn 7:51
23:5 [s]Ex 22:28

22:16 be baptized. Baptism in the New Testament is, in part, an outward sign of an inward cleansing. As such, it parallels circumcision in the Old Testament (Dt 10:16; 30:6; Eze 44:7). See *BC* 34; *HC* 71.

22:24 flogged. This was to be with the Roman scourge (Latin, *flagellum*), a whip of leather thongs loaded with bits of metal or bone; it could maim for life and even kill. Jesus was scourged with this type of whip (Jn 19:1). Paul had received several Jewish beatings and beatings with rods (2Co 11:24–25), but he had never before endured this particular punishment.

22:25 stretched him out. The soldiers either stretched Paul's arms around a pole to expose his back or tied his hands with thongs and hoisted him from the ground to administer the whipping.

22:26 Roman citizen. Paul appealed again to his Roman citizenship, knowing that he was going to be punished without a trial (16:37). Roman citizenship was a highly prized status, usually conferred on those of high social and governmental position or who had performed valuable service to the state. It was then passed on to one's family.

23:2 high priest Ananias. The son of Nebedaeus, Ananias was a brutal and violent man who ruled as high priest from A.D. 48–59. He is not to be confused with the earlier Annas of John 18:13. Ananias was assassinated near the beginning of the war with Rome (A.D. 66–70).

23:3 you whitewashed wall! Tombs holding the bones of the dead were often whitewashed to make them clearly observable (Mt 23:27–28). Paul paid a fitting tribute to this corrupt official. **violate the law.** According to Jewish law, Paul had the right to a trial, and a declaration of guilt was required before he could be punished.

23:6 Sadducees . . . Pharisees. These two groups, which emerged during the intertestamental period, took different political and religious stances. Paul seized the opportunity to emphasize their religious differences by identifying himself as a Pharisee, as the son of a Pharisee and as an adherent of the Old Testament doctrine of the resurrection of the dead, which the Sadducees denied along with the existence of angels and spirits (Mt 22:23–32). See chart "Jewish Sects" at Matthew 23.

called out in the Sanhedrin, "My brothers,[t] I am a Pharisee,[u] the son of a Pharisee. I stand on trial because of my hope in the resurrection of the dead."[v] 7When he said this, a dispute broke out between the Pharisees and the Sadducees, and the assembly was divided. 8(The Sadducees say that there is no resurrection,[w] and that there are neither angels nor spirits, but the Pharisees acknowledge them all.)

9There was a great uproar, and some of the teachers of the law who were Pharisees[x] stood up and argued vigorously. "We find nothing wrong with this man,"[y] they said. "What if a spirit or an angel has spoken to him?"[z] 10The dispute became so violent that the commander was afraid Paul would be torn to pieces by them. He ordered the troops to go down and take him away from them by force and bring him into the barracks.[a]

11The following night the Lord stood near Paul and said, "Take courage![b] As you have testified about me in Jerusalem, so you must also testify in Rome."[c]

The Plot to Kill Paul

12The next morning the Jews formed a conspiracy and bound themselves with an oath not to eat or drink until they had killed Paul.[d] 13More than forty men were involved in this plot. 14They went to the chief priests and elders and said, "We have taken a solemn oath not to eat anything until we have killed Paul.[e] 15Now then, you and the Sanhedrin[f] petition the commander to bring him before you on the pretext of wanting more accurate information about his case. We are ready to kill him before he gets here."

16But when the son of Paul's sister heard of this plot, he went into the barracks[g] and told Paul.

17Then Paul called one of the centurions and said, "Take this young man to the commander; he has something to tell him." 18So he took him to the commander.

The centurion said, "Paul, the prisoner,[h] sent for me and asked me to bring this young man to you because he has something to tell you."

19The commander took the young man by the hand, drew him aside and asked, "What is it you want to tell me?"

20He said: "The Jews have agreed to ask you to bring Paul before the Sanhedrin[i] tomorrow on the pretext of wanting more accurate information about him.[j] 21Don't give in to them, because more than forty[k] of them are waiting in ambush for him. They have taken an oath not to eat or drink until they have killed him.[l] They are ready now, waiting for your consent to their request."

22The commander dismissed the young man and cautioned him, "Don't tell anyone that you have reported this to me."

Paul Transferred to Caesarea

23Then he called two of his centurions and ordered them, "Get ready a detachment of two hundred soldiers, seventy horsemen and two hundred spearmen[a] to go to Caesarea[m] at nine tonight.[n] 24Provide mounts for Paul so that he may be taken safely to Governor Felix."[o]

25He wrote a letter as follows:

26Claudius Lysias,

To His Excellency,[p] Governor Felix:

Greetings.[q]

27This man was seized by the Jews and they were about to kill him,[r] but I came with my troops and rescued him,[s] for I had learned that he is a Roman citizen.[t] 28I wanted to know why they were accusing him, so I brought him to their Sanhedrin.[u] 29I found that the accusation had to do with questions about their law,[v] but there was no charge against him[w] that deserved death or imprisonment. 30When

23:6 [t]Ac 22:5 [u]Ac 26:5; Php 3:5 [v]Ac 24:15, 21; 26:8
23:8 [w]Mt 22:23
23:9 [x]Mk 2:16 [y]ver 29; Ac 25:25; 26:31 [z]Ac 22:7,17,18
23:10 [a]Ac 21:34
23:11 [b]Ac 18:9 [c]Ac 19:21; 28:23
23:12 [d]ver 14,21,30; Ac 25:3
23:14 [e]ver 12
23:15 [f]ver 1; Ac 22:30
23:16 [g]ver 10; Ac 21:34
23:18 [h]Eph 3:1
23:20 [i]ver 1 [j]ver 14,15
23:21 [k]ver 13 [l]ver 12,14
23:23 [m]Ac 8:40 [n]ver 33
23:24 [o]ver 26,33; Ac 24:1-3,10; 25:14
23:26 [p]Lk 1:3; Ac 24:3; 26:25 [q]Ac 15:23
23:27 [r]Ac 21:32 [s]Ac 21:33 [t]Ac 22:25-29
23:28 [u]Ac 22:30
23:29 [v]Ac 18:15; 25:19 [w]ver 9; Ac 26:31

[a] *23* The meaning of the Greek for this word is uncertain.

23:9 teachers of the law who were Pharisees. These teachers (Greek, *grammateus*) were experts in interpreting the Jewish law.
23:12–21 See *WCF* 22.7; *WLC* 113,135; *BC* 12.
23:16 son of Paul's sister. Evidently some members of Paul's family were living or staying in Jerusalem. **told Paul.** Prisoners received their necessary supplies from relatives and friends who regularly visited them.
23:23–24 Heavily equipped infantry and cavalry were used to deliver Paul safely to Felix, the procurator of the imperial province of Judea. The official provincial headquarters was in Caesarea.
23:26 Governor Felix. Felix was a former slave and a freedman who had ascended to an influential position in the Roman government. In A.D. 52, Emperor Claudius sent him as governor to Caesarea. Felix was addressed as "most excellent Felix" (24:3) during his eight-year administration. The Roman historian Tacitus (c. A.D. 56–120) characterized him as cruel and rapacious, practicing "every kind of cruelty and lust, wielding the power of a king with the instincts of a slave" (*History* 5.9).

I was informed[x] of a plot[y] to be carried out against the man, I sent him to you at
once. I also ordered his accusers[z] to present to you their case against him.

31So the soldiers, carrying out their orders, took Paul with them during the night and
brought him as far as Antipatris. 32The next day they let the cavalry[a] go on with him,
while they returned to the barracks.[b] 33When the cavalry[c] arrived in Caesarea,[d] they delivered the letter to the governor[e] and handed Paul over to him. 34The governor read the
letter and asked what province he was from. Learning that he was from Cilicia,[f] 35he said,
"I will hear your case when your accusers[g] get here." Then he ordered that Paul be kept
under guard[h] in Herod's palace.

The Trial Before Felix

24 Five days later the high priest Ananias[i] went down to Caesarea with some of the
elders and a lawyer named Tertullus, and they brought their charges[j] against
Paul before the governor.[k] 2When Paul was called in, Tertullus presented his case before Felix: "We have enjoyed a long period of peace under you, and your foresight has
brought about reforms in this nation. 3Everywhere and in every way, most excellent[l] Felix, we acknowledge this with profound gratitude. 4But in order not to weary you further,
I would request that you be kind enough to hear us briefly.

5"We have found this man to be a troublemaker, stirring up riots[m] among the Jews[n]
all over the world. He is a ringleader of the Nazarene[o] sect[p] 6and even tried to desecrate
the temple;[q] so we seized him. 8By[a] examining him yourself you will be able to learn the
truth about all these charges we are bringing against him."

9The Jews joined in the accusation,[r] asserting that these things were true.

10When the governor[s] motioned for him to speak, Paul replied: "I know that for a
number of years you have been a judge over this nation; so I gladly make my defense.
11You can easily verify that no more than twelve days[t] ago I went up to Jerusalem to worship. 12My accusers did not find me arguing with anyone at the temple,[u] or stirring up
a crowd[v] in the synagogues or anywhere else in the city. 13And they cannot prove to you
the charges they are now making against me.[w] 14However, I admit that I worship the God
of our fathers[x] as a follower of the Way,[y] which they call a sect.[z] I believe everything that
agrees with the Law and that is written in the Prophets,[a] 15and I have the same hope in
God as these men, that there will be a resurrection[b] of both the righteous and the wicked.[c] 16So I strive always to keep my conscience clear[d] before God and man.

17"After an absence of several years, I came to Jerusalem to bring my people gifts for
the poor[e] and to present offerings. 18I was ceremonially clean[f] when they found me in
the temple courts doing this. There was no crowd with me, nor was I involved in any disturbance.[g] 19But there are some Jews from the province of Asia, who ought to be here
before you and bring charges if they have anything against me.[h] 20Or these who are here
should state what crime they found in me when I stood before the Sanhedrin— 21unless
it was this one thing I shouted as I stood in their presence: 'It is concerning the resurrection of the dead that I am on trial before you today.' "[i]

22Then Felix, who was well acquainted with the Way, adjourned the proceedings.
"When Lysias the commander comes," he said, "I will decide your case." 23He ordered
the centurion to keep Paul under guard[j] but to give him some freedom[k] and permit his
friends to take care of his needs.[l]

23:30 [x]ver 20,21 [y]Ac 20:3 [z]ver 35; Ac 24:19; 25:16
23:32 [a]ver 23 [b]Ac 21:34
23:33 [c]ver 23,24 [d]Ac 8:40 [e]ver 26
23:34 [f]Ac 6:9; 21:39
23:35 [g]ver 30; Ac 24:19; 25:16 [h]Ac 24:27
24:1 [i]Ac 23:2 [j]Ac 23:30, 35 [k]Ac 23:24
24:3 [l]Lk 1:3; Ac 23:26; 26:25
24:5 [m]Ac 16:20; 17:6 [n]Ac 21:28 [o]Mk 1:24 [p]ver 14; Ac 26:5; 28:22
24:6 [q]Ac 21:28
24:9 [r]1Th 2:16
24:10 [s]Ac 23:24
24:11 [t]Ac 21:27; ver 1
24:12 [u]Ac 25:8; 28:17 [v]ver 18
24:13 [w]Ac 25:7
24:14 [x]Ac 3:13 [y]Ac 9:2 [z]ver 5 [a]Ac 26:6,22; 28:23
24:15 [b]Ac 23:6; 28:20 [c]Da 12:2; Jn 5:28, 29
24:16 [d]Ac 23:1
24:17 [e]Ac 11:29,30; Ro 15:25-28,31; 1Co 16:1-4,15; 2Co 8:1-4; Gal 2:10
24:18 [f]Ac 21:26 [g]ver 12
24:19 [h]Ac 23:30
24:21 [i]Ac 23:6
24:23 [j]Ac 23:35 [k]Ac 28:16 [l]Ac 23:16; 27:3

[a] *6–8* Some manuscripts *him and wanted to judge him according to our law. 7But the commander, Lysias, came and with the use of much force snatched him from our hands 8and ordered his accusers to come before you. By*

23:27 See *WLC* 135.
23:31 Antipatris. A town built by Herod the Great in honor of his father, Antipater. It was located about 30 miles northwest of Jerusalem.
23:35 Herod's palace. The official residence Herod the Great had built. It then became a Roman praetorium or official residence that also included prison cells (Jn 18:28; Php 1:13).
24:1 Tertullus. The name is a diminutive form of "Tertius," which in Latin means "the third." Tertullus probably was a Jew from the dispersion. He knew Roman law and presumably was fluent in Latin.
24:2 See *WLC* 145.
24:5–7 The charges brought by Tertullus were threefold: (1) Paul was a chronic troublemaker, a disturber of the peace of the empire. (2) Paul was a leader of a disreputable religious sect. (3) Paul had attempted to profane the temple. Paul replied to each of these accusations in his defense before Felix (vv. 10–21).
24:5 the Nazarene sect. Christians were identified as followers of Jesus of Nazareth. The Jews may have considered "Nazareth" a term of derision (Jn 1:46). See *WLC* 145.
24:14 I worship the God of our fathers as a follower of the Way. Paul assured Felix that he stood within Judaism, a religion protected by Rome. As a follower of "the Way," Paul worshiped the "God of our fathers" and believed in the resurrection of the righteous and the wicked (Da 12:1–2; 1Th 4:13–18). See *WCF* 14.2.
24:15 See *WCF* 32.3; *WLC* 87.
24:16 See *WLC* 93.
24:21 concerning the resurrection of the dead. Paul made one critical statement that pertained not to Roman political interests but to Jewish and Christian theology. The conflict was clearly out of place in a civil court.
24:23 keep Paul under guard . . . some freedom. As a Roman citizen whose case was pending, Paul was entitled to some freedom (28:16).
24:24–25 See *WLC* 138.
24:24 Drusilla. Daughter of Herod Agrippa I (12:1–23) and sister of Herod Agrippa II (25:13; see note on 26:3) and Bernice (see note

24 Several days later Felix came with his wife Drusilla, who was a Jewess. He sent for
Paul and listened to him as he spoke about faith in Christ Jesus.[m] 25 As Paul discoursed
on righteousness, self-control[n] and the judgment[o] to come, Felix was afraid and said,
"That's enough for now! You may leave. When I find it convenient, I will send for you."
26 At the same time he was hoping that Paul would offer him a bribe, so he sent for him
frequently and talked with him.
27 When two years had passed, Felix was succeeded by Porcius Festus,[p] but because
Felix wanted to grant a favor to the Jews,[q] he left Paul in prison.[r]

The Trial Before Festus

25 Three days after arriving in the province, Festus went up from Caesarea[s] to Jerusalem, 2 where the chief priests and Jewish leaders appeared before him and
presented the charges against Paul.[t] 3 They urgently requested Festus, as a favor to them,
to have Paul transferred to Jerusalem, for they were preparing an ambush to kill him
along the way. 4 Festus answered, "Paul is being held[u] at Caesarea, and I myself am going there soon. 5 Let some of your leaders come with me and press charges against the
man there, if he has done anything wrong."
6 After spending eight or ten days with them, he went down to Caesarea, and the next
day he convened the court[v] and ordered that Paul be brought before him. 7 When Paul
appeared, the Jews who had come down from Jerusalem stood around him, bringing
many serious charges against him,[w] which they could not prove.[x]
8 Then Paul made his defense: "I have done nothing wrong against the law of the Jews
or against the temple[y] or against Caesar."
9 Festus, wishing to do the Jews a favor,[z] said to Paul, "Are you willing to go up to Jerusalem and stand trial before me there on these charges?"[a]
10 Paul answered: "I am now standing before Caesar's court, where I ought to be tried.
I have not done any wrong to the Jews, as you yourself know very well. 11 If, however, I
am guilty of doing anything deserving death, I do not refuse to die. But if the charges
brought against me by these Jews are not true, no one has the right to hand me over to
them. I appeal to Caesar!"[b]
12 After Festus had conferred with his council, he declared: "You have appealed to
Caesar. To Caesar you will go!"

Festus Consults King Agrippa

13 A few days later King Agrippa and Bernice arrived at Caesarea[c] to pay their respects
to Festus. 14 Since they were spending many days there, Festus discussed Paul's case with
the king. He said: "There is a man here whom Felix left as a prisoner.[d] 15 When I went to
Jerusalem, the chief priests and elders of the Jews brought charges against him[e] and
asked that he be condemned.
16 "I told them that it is not the Roman custom to hand over any man before he has
faced his accusers and has had an opportunity to defend himself against their charges.[f]
17 When they came here with me, I did not delay the case, but convened the court the next
day and ordered the man to be brought in.[g] 18 When his accusers got up to speak, they
did not charge him with any of the crimes I had expected. 19 Instead, they had some
points of dispute[h] with him about their own religion[i] and about a dead man named Jesus
who Paul claimed was alive. 20 I was at a loss how to investigate such matters; so I asked
if he would be willing to go to Jerusalem and stand trial there on these charges.[j] 21 When
Paul made his appeal to be held over for the Emperor's decision, I ordered him held until I could send him to Caesar."[k]
22 Then Agrippa said to Festus, "I would like to hear this man myself."
He replied, "Tomorrow you will hear him."[l]

24:24 [m]Ac 20:21
24:25 [n]Gal 5:23; 2Pe 1:6 [o]Ac 10:42
24:27 [p]Ac 25:1,4,9,14 [q]Ac 12:3; 25:9 [r]Ac 23:35; 25:14
25:1 [s]Ac 8:40
25:2 [t]ver 15; Ac 24:1
25:4 [u]Ac 24:23
25:6 [v]ver 17
25:7 [w]Mk 15:3; Lk 23:2, 10; Ac 24:5,6 [x]Ac 24:13
25:8 [y]Ac 6:13; 24:12; 28:17
25:9 [z]Ac 24:27 [a]ver 20
25:11 [b]ver 21,25; Ac 26:32; 28:19
25:13 [c]Ac 8:40
25:14 [d]Ac 24:27
25:15 [e]ver 2; Ac 24:1
25:16 [f]ver 4,5; Ac 23:30
25:17 [g]ver 6,10
25:19 [h]Ac 18:15; 23:29 [i]Ac 17:22
25:20 [j]ver 9
25:21 [k]ver 11,12
25:22 [l]Ac 9:15

on 25:13), Drusilla divorced Azizus, king of Emesa in Syria, to marry Felix, the Roman procurator. She was killed, along with her son Agrippa, in the volcanic eruption of Mount Vesuvius at Pompeii in A.D. 79.

24:27 Porcius Festus. A Roman who belonged to the Porcia clan, Festus was a member of a noble family in Rome. While Felix had been greedy and evil, Festus was wise and honorable.

25:4 Festus had to protect Paul while he was in Roman custody; therefore he refused the request of the Jews. His refusal saved Paul's life, since Paul enjoyed full protection in Caesarea. Festus noted that he himself would soon go to his headquarters in Caesarea.

25:9–11 See *WCF* 23.4.

25:11 I appeal to Caesar! Sensing that Festus was going to grant the Jews their request, Paul now exercised his right as a Roman citizen to be tried before Caesar (Nero) in Rome. At this point in his reign, Nero was under the benevolent influence of the Stoic philosopher Seneca and had not yet shown his sordid attitude toward Christianity. Paul may have hoped to be acquitted by Nero and have Christianity officially declared an accepted religion.

25:13 King Agrippa. This was Herod Agrippa II, son of Agrippa I and great-grandson of Herod the Great (see note on 26:3). **Bernice.** The eldest daughter of Herod Agrippa I, Bernice was twice widowed before entering into an incestuous relationship with her brother, Herod Agrippa II. Despite the scandal of the relationship, she was frequently presented as Herod's queen on official occasions (e.g., vv. 13,23).

Paul Before Agrippa

23 The next day Agrippa and Bernice[m] came with great pomp and entered the audience room with the high ranking officers and the leading men of the city. At the command of Festus, Paul was brought in. 24 Festus said: “King Agrippa, and all who are present with us, you see this man! The whole Jewish community[n] has petitioned me about
him in Jerusalem and here in Caesarea, shouting that he ought not to live any longer.[o]
25 I found he had done nothing deserving of death,[p] but because he made his appeal to
the Emperor[q] I decided to send him to Rome. 26 But I have nothing definite to write to
His Majesty about him. Therefore I have brought him before all of you, and especially before you, King Agrippa, so that as a result of this investigation I may have something to
write. 27 For I think it is unreasonable to send on a prisoner without specifying the
charges against him.”

26 Then Agrippa said to Paul, “You have permission to speak for yourself.”[r]
So Paul motioned with his hand and began his defense: 2 “King Agrippa, I consider myself fortunate to stand before you today as I make my defense against all the accusations of the Jews, 3 and especially so because you are well acquainted with all the
Jewish customs[s] and controversies.[t] Therefore, I beg you to listen to me patiently.
4 “The Jews all know the way I have lived ever since I was a child,[u] from the beginning
of my life in my own country, and also in Jerusalem. 5 They have known me for a long
time[v] and can testify, if they are willing, that according to the strictest sect of our religion, I lived as a Pharisee.[w] 6 And now it is because of my hope[x] in what God has promised our fathers[y] that I am on trial today. 7 This is the promise our twelve tribes[z] are hoping to see fulfilled as they earnestly serve God day and night.[a] O king, it is because of this
hope that the Jews are accusing me.[b] 8 Why should any of you consider it incredible that
God raises the dead?[c]
9 “I too was convinced[d] that I ought to do all that was possible to oppose[e] the name
of Jesus of Nazareth.[f] 10 And that is just what I did in Jerusalem. On the authority of the
chief priests I put many of the saints[g] in prison,[h] and when they were put to death, I cast
my vote against them.[i] 11 Many a time I went from one synagogue to another to have
them punished,[j] and I tried to force them to blaspheme. In my obsession against them,
I even went to foreign cities to persecute them.
12 “On one of these journeys I was going to Damascus with the authority and commission of the chief priests. 13 About noon, O king, as I was on the road, I saw a light from
heaven, brighter than the sun, blazing around me and my companions. 14 We all fell to
the ground, and I heard a voice[k] saying to me in Aramaic,[a] ‘Saul, Saul, why do you persecute me? It is hard for you to kick against the goads.’
15 “Then I asked, ‘Who are you, Lord?’
“ ‘I am Jesus, whom you are persecuting,’ the Lord replied. 16 ‘Now get up and stand
on your feet.[l] I have appeared to you to appoint you as a servant and as a witness of what
you have seen of me and what I will show you.[m] 17 I will rescue you[n] from your own people and from the Gentiles.[o] I am sending you to them 18 to open their eyes[p] and turn them
from darkness to light,[q] and from the power of Satan to God, so that they may receive
forgiveness of sins[r] and a place among those who are sanctified by faith in me.’[s]
19 “So then, King Agrippa, I was not disobedient to the vision from heaven. 20 First to
those in Damascus,[t] then to those in Jerusalem[u] and in all Judea, and to the Gentiles[v]
also, I preached that they should repent[w] and turn to God and prove their repentance

a *14* Or *Hebrew*

25:23 [m]ver 13; Ac 26:30
25:24 [n]ver 2,3,7 [o]Ac 22:22
25:25 [p]Ac 23:9 [q]ver 11
26:1 [r]Ac 9:15; 25:22
26:3 [s]ver 7; Ac 6:14 [t]Ac 25:19
26:4 [u]Gal 1:13,14; Php 3:5
26:5 [v]Ac 22:3 [w]Ac 23:6; Php 3:5
26:6 [x]Ac 23:6; 24:15; 28:20 [y]Ac 13:32; Ro 15:8
26:7 [z]Jas 1:1 [a]1Th 3:10; 1Ti 5:5 [b]ver 2
26:8 [c]Ac 23:6
26:9 [d]1Ti 1:13 [e]Jn 16:2 [f]Jn 15:21
26:10 [g]Ac 9:13 [h]Ac 8:3; 9:2,14,21 [i]Ac 22:20
26:11 [j]Mt 10:17
26:14 [k]Ac 9:7
26:16 [l]Eze 2:1; Da 10:11 [m]Ac 22:14,15
26:17 [n]Jer 1:8,19 [o]Ac 9:15
26:18 [p]Isa 35:5 [q]Isa 42:7,16; Eph 5:8; Col 1:13; 1Pe 2:9 [r]Lk 24:47; Ac 2:38 [s]Ac 20:21,32
26:20 [t]Ac 9:19-25 [u]Ac 9:26-29; 22:17-20 [v]Ac 9:15; 13:46 [w]Ac 3:19

25:25–26 Festus referred to Caesar as “Emperor” (Greek *Sebastos*, for the Latin *Augustus*, “the revered one”) and as “His Majesty” (Greek *kurios*, meaning “lord”), a term used increasingly from Nero’s time on as a title for Caesar, possibly to connote divinity.

26:3 well acquainted with all the Jewish customs and controversies. As the great-grandson of Herod the Great and the son of Herod Agrippa I, who had persecuted the church (12:1–23), Herod Agrippa II (A.D. 27–c. 100) had an intimate knowledge of Jewish matters. Although influential in Jewish religious affairs because of his political authority to appoint the high priest, Agrippa II was unpopular with the Jews because of his incestuous relationship with his sister Bernice (see note on 25:13).

26:5 strictest sect . . . I lived as a Pharisee. Based on his knowledge of Agrippa’s background, Paul stressed his dependence on the God of his fathers (24:14) and his link with Pharisaism (Php 3:5–6) to show the legitimacy of his Judaism. Paul stressed that the God of his fathers promised the resurrection of the body, which Jews (in general) and every good Pharisee (in particular) believed in and which was the basis of the charges against him.

26:6–7 See *WCF* 16.3.

26:9 See *WLC* 105.

26:12–14 Paul’s experience on the road to Damascus (9:1–19) was so important to him that he recounted it twice, once before the Jewish crowd in Jerusalem (22:6–16) and again before this mainly pagan audience in Caesarea. In this account, Paul spoke of “a light from heaven, brighter than the sun, blazing around me and my companions” (v. 13) and of the voice from heaven that spoke “in Aramaic” (v. 14). (Aramaic was the current Semitic dialect of the Holy Land, not the Greek that the pagan audience was accustomed to hearing.) He also added the remark made by the heavenly voice: “It is hard for you to kick against the goads” (v. 14). This was an expression full of meaning for a culture that relied on oxen.

26:16–18 See *WCF* 10.1; 20.1; *WLC* 67,76,155,159; *WSC* 31,89; *BC* 31.

26:20 See 2:38; 3:19 and its note; 17:20; 20:21.

by their deeds.[x] 21That is why the Jews seized me[y] in the temple courts and tried to kill
me.[z] 22But I have had God's help to this very day, and so I stand here and testify to small
and great alike. I am saying nothing beyond what the prophets and Moses said would
happen[a]— 23that the Christ[a] would suffer and, as the first to rise from the dead,[b] would
proclaim light to his own people and to the Gentiles."[c]
24At this point Festus interrupted Paul's defense. "You are out of your mind,[d] Paul!"
he shouted. "Your great learning[e] is driving you insane."
25"I am not insane, most excellent[f] Festus," Paul replied. "What I am saying is true
and reasonable. 26The king is familiar with these things,[g] and I can speak freely to him.
I am convinced that none of this has escaped his notice, because it was not done in a corner. 27King Agrippa, do you believe the prophets? I know you do."
28Then Agrippa said to Paul, "Do you think that in such a short time you can persuade
me to be a Christian?"[h]
29Paul replied, "Short time or long—I pray God that not only you but all who are listening to me today may become what I am, except for these chains."[i]
30The king rose, and with him the governor and Bernice[j] and those sitting with
them. 31They left the room, and while talking with one another, they said, "This man is
not doing anything that deserves death or imprisonment."[k]
32Agrippa said to Festus, "This man could have been set free[l] if he had not appealed
to Caesar."[m]

Paul Sails for Rome

27 When it was decided that we[n] would sail for Italy,[o] Paul and some other prisoners were handed over to a centurion named Julius, who belonged to the Imperial Regiment.[p] 2We boarded a ship from Adramyttium about to sail for ports along the
coast of the province of Asia,[q] and we put out to sea. Aristarchus,[r] a Macedonian[s] from
Thessalonica,[t] was with us.
3The next day we landed at Sidon;[u] and Julius, in kindness to Paul,[v] allowed him to
go to his friends so they might provide for his needs.[w] 4From there we put out to sea
again and passed to the lee of Cyprus because the winds were against us.[x] 5When we had
sailed across the open sea off the coast of Cilicia[y] and Pamphylia, we landed at Myra in
Lycia. 6There the centurion found an Alexandrian ship[z] sailing for Italy[a] and put us on
board. 7We made slow headway for many days and had difficulty arriving off Cnidus.
When the wind did not allow us to hold our course,[b] we sailed to the lee of Crete,[c] opposite Salmone. 8We moved along the coast with difficulty and came to a place called
Fair Havens, near the town of Lasea.
9Much time had been lost, and sailing had already become dangerous because by
now it was after the Fast.[b][d] So Paul warned them, 10"Men, I can see that our voyage is
going to be disastrous and bring great loss to ship and cargo, and to our own lives also."[e]
11But the centurion, instead of listening to what Paul said, followed the advice of the pilot and of the owner of the ship. 12Since the harbor was unsuitable to winter in, the majority decided that we should sail on, hoping to reach Phoenix and winter there. This was
a harbor in Crete, facing both southwest and northwest.

26:20 [x]Mt 3:8; Lk 3:8
26:21 [y]Ac 21:27,30 [z]Ac 21:31
26:22 [a]Lk 24:27,44; Ac 10:43; 24:14
26:23 [b]1Co 15:20,23; Col 1:18; Rev 1:5 [c]Lk 2:32
26:24 [d]Jn 10:20; 1Co 4:10 [e]Jn 7:15
26:25 [f]Ac 23:26
26:26 [g]ver 3
26:28 [h]Ac 11:26
26:29 [i]Ac 21:33
26:30 [j]Ac 25:23
26:31 [k]Ac 23:9
26:32 [l]Ac 28:18 [m]Ac 25:11
27:1 [n]Ac 16:10 [o]Ac 18:2; 25:12,25 [p]Ac 10:1
27:2 [q]Ac 2:9 [r]Ac 19:29 [s]Ac 16:9 [t]Ac 17:1
27:3 [u]Mt 11:21 [v]ver 43 [w]Ac 24:23; 28:16
27:4 [x]ver 7
27:5 [y]Ac 6:9
27:6 [z]Ac 28:11 [a]ver 1
27:7 [b]ver 4 [c]ver 12,13,21
27:9 [d]Lev 16:29-31; 23:27-29; Nu 29:7
27:10 [e]ver 21

[a] 23 Or *Messiah* [b] 9 That is, the Day of Atonement (Yom Kippur)

26:22 See *WLC* 4; *BC* 7.
26:23 Christ would suffer . . . rise from the dead. The Jews had difficulty accepting the doctrine that the Messiah would suffer and die. Jesus and his apostles taught this doctrine from the Scriptures (Lk 24:27; Ac 17:2–3; 1Co 15:3–4), yet the Jews rejected this teaching, arrested Paul and wanted to kill him.
26:27 do you believe the prophets? Agrippa faced a dilemma: If he answered negatively, he would incur the ire of the Jews. If he replied affirmatively, he would lose face because Paul would ask him to believe the gospel.
26:28 you can persuade me to be a Christian? The king used a delaying tactic, thinking that a half-hour speech was insufficient time in which to become a Christian. In the first century, the word "Christian" was a term of derision and scorn (1Pe 4:16; cf. Ac 11:26). Agrippa's question betrayed a lack of sincerity.
■ **27:1—28:16** *Paul's Voyage to Rome.* Luke reported that Paul appealed for Caesar to hear his case. The journey to Rome was treacherous, but God protected Paul and the gospel continued to spread.
27:2 Adramyttium. Located in Mysia, southeast of Troas and opposite the island of Lesbos. **we put out to sea.** This chapter is filled with nautical terms and directions, evidence that the author was an eyewitness. **Aristarchus . . . was with us.** Paul had two personal companions with him: Luke the doctor (Col 4:14) and Aristarchus (Col 4:10; Phm 24) from Thessalonica.
27:3 landed at Sidon. While the ship loaded more cargo at this Phoenician seaport town 70 miles north of Caesarea and 25 miles north of Tyre (21:3), Paul visited the group of believers there.
27:4 to the lee of Cyprus. That is, close under the eastern point of the island in order to be protected from the westerly winds of the summer and fall.
27:5 off the coast of Cilicia and Pamphylia. The ship worked its way up the Syrian coast, past Antioch of Syria and around to the west, past Attalia of Pamphilia to Myra, the most important Lycian city of Paul's day. Myra was an important port of call for grain ships sailing between Alexandria and Rome.
27:11–12 The captain and the owner wanted to reach the larger and safer harbor of Phoenix about 40 miles to the west, but in going west past Cape Matala, the ship would be exposed to winds from the northwest.

The Storm

[13]When a gentle south wind began to blow, they thought they had obtained what they
wanted; so they weighed anchor and sailed along the shore of Crete. [14]Before very long,
a wind of hurricane force,[f] called the “northeaster,” swept down from the island. [15]The
ship was caught by the storm and could not head into the wind; so we gave way to it and
were driven along. [16]As we passed to the lee of a small island called Cauda, we were
hardly able to make the lifeboat secure. [17]When the men had hoisted it aboard, they
passed ropes under the ship itself to hold it together. Fearing that they would run
aground[g] on the sandbars of Syrtis, they lowered the sea anchor and let the ship be driv-
en along. [18]We took such a violent battering from the storm that the next day they began to throw the cargo overboard.[h] [19]On the third day, they threw the ship's tackle overboard with their own hands. [20]When neither sun nor stars appeared for many days and
the storm continued raging, we finally gave up all hope of being saved.
[21]After the men had gone a long time without food, Paul stood up before them and
said: “Men, you should have taken my advice[i] not to sail from Crete;[j] then you would
have spared yourselves this damage and loss. [22]But now I urge you to keep up your courage,[k] because not one of you will be lost; only the ship will be destroyed. [23]Last night an
angel[l] of the God whose I am and whom I serve[m] stood beside me[n] [24]and said, ‘Do not
be afraid, Paul. You must stand trial before Caesar;[o] and God has graciously given you
the lives of all who sail with you.’[p] [25]So keep up your courage,[q] men, for I have faith in
God that it will happen just as he told me.[r] [26]Nevertheless, we must run aground[s] on
some island.”[t]

The Shipwreck

[27]On the fourteenth night we were still being driven across the Adriatic[a] Sea, when
about midnight the sailors sensed they were approaching land. [28]They took soundings
and found that the water was a hundred and twenty feet[b] deep. A short time later they
took soundings again and found it was ninety feet[c] deep. [29]Fearing that we would be

27:14 [f]Mk 4:37
27:17 [g]ver 26,39
27:18 [h]ver 19,38; Jnh 1:5
27:21 [i]ver 10 [j]ver 7
27:22 [k]ver 25,36
27:23 [l]Ac 5:19 [m]Ro 1:9 [n]Ac 18:9; 23:11; 2Ti 4:17
27:24 [o]Ac 23:11 [p]ver 44
27:25 [q]ver 22,36 [r]Ro 4:20,21
27:26 [s]ver 17,39 [t]Ac 28:1

[a] *27* In ancient times the name referred to an area extending well south of Italy. [b] *28* Greek *twenty orguias* (about 37 meters) [c] *28* Greek *fifteen orguias* (about 27 meters)

27:17 passed ropes. Because of the danger of violent storms on the Mediterranean Sea, ancient vessels were fitted with ropes that could be passed under the hull transversely during such emergencies. These ropes helped to undergird the hull against the stress of the wind and waves. **sea anchor.** The Greek word here means “object” or “instrument.” Fearing that the ship might be driven all the way to the sands of North Africa, the sailors apparently lowered an object that offered some resistance to the ship's forward progress as it was towed behind the vessel.

27:24 graciously given you the lives of all. In his providence and grace, God saved the physical lives of the unbelievers.

27:26 some island. The island of Malta, south of Sicily.

Paul's Journey to Rome

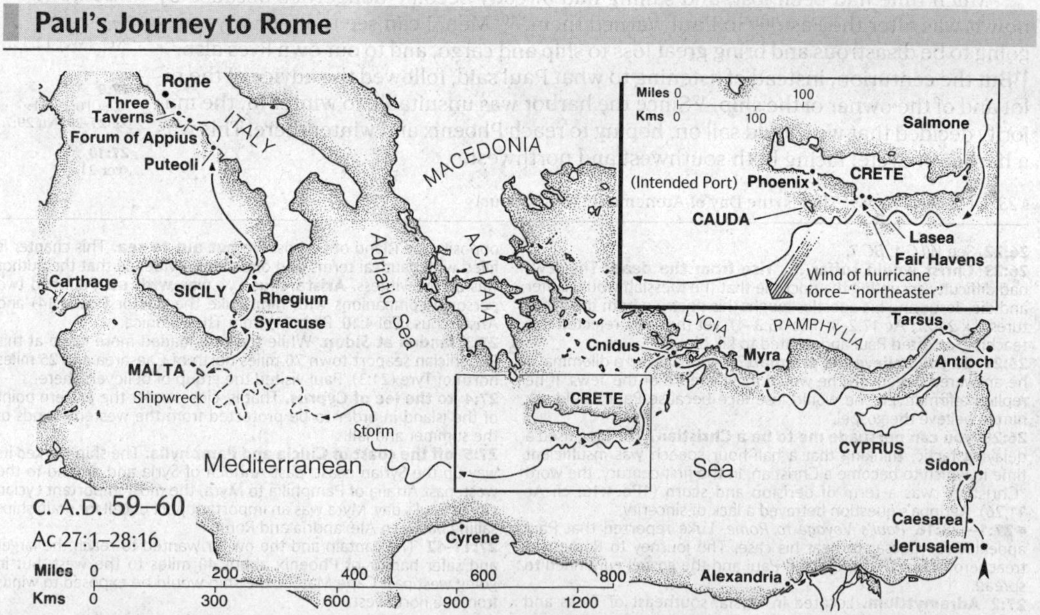

dashed against the rocks, they dropped four anchors from the stern and prayed for day- **27:30**
light. 30In an attempt to escape from the ship, the sailors let the lifeboat[u] down into the [u]ver 16
sea, pretending they were going to lower some anchors from the bow. 31Then Paul said
to the centurion and the soldiers, "Unless these men stay with the ship, you cannot be **27:31**
saved."[v] 32So the soldiers cut the ropes that held the lifeboat and let it fall away. [v]ver 24
33Just before dawn Paul urged them all to eat. "For the last fourteen days," he said,
"you have been in constant suspense and have gone without food—you haven't eaten
anything. 34Now I urge you to take some food. You need it to survive. Not one of you will **27:34**
lose a single hair from his head."[w] 35After he said this, he took some bread and gave [w]Mt 10:30
thanks to God in front of them all. Then he broke it[x] and began to eat. 36They were all **27:35**
encouraged[y] and ate some food themselves. 37Altogether there were 276 of us on board. [x]Mt 14:19
38When they had eaten as much as they wanted, they lightened the ship by throwing the **27:36**
grain into the sea.[z] [y]ver 22,25
39When daylight came, they did not recognize the land, but they saw a bay with a **27:38**
sandy beach,[a] where they decided to run the ship aground if they could. 40Cutting loose [z]ver 18; Jnh 1:5
the anchors,[b] they left them in the sea and at the same time untied the ropes that held **27:39**
the rudders. Then they hoisted the foresail to the wind and made for the beach. 41But the [a]Ac 28:1
ship struck a sandbar and ran aground. The bow stuck fast and would not move, and the **27:40**
stern was broken to pieces by the pounding of the surf.[c] [b]ver 29
42The soldiers planned to kill the prisoners to prevent any of them from swimming **27:41**
away and escaping. 43But the centurion wanted to spare Paul's life[d] and kept them from [c]2Co 11:25
carrying out their plan. He ordered those who could swim to jump overboard first and **27:43**
get to land. 44The rest were to get there on planks or on pieces of the ship. In this way [d]ver 3
everyone reached land in safety.[e] **27:44** [e]ver 22,31

Ashore on Malta

28 Once safely on shore, we[f] found out that the island[g] was called Malta. 2The is- **28:1** [f]Ac 16:10
landers showed us unusual kindness. They built a fire and welcomed us all be- [g]Ac 27:26,39
cause it was raining and cold. 3Paul gathered a pile of brushwood and, as he put it on
the fire, a viper, driven out by the heat, fastened itself on his hand. 4When the islanders **28:4**
saw the snake hanging from his hand,[h] they said to each other, "This man must be a [h]Mk 16:18
murderer; for though he escaped from the sea, Justice has not allowed him to live."[i] 5But [i]Lk 13:2,4
Paul shook the snake off into the fire and suffered no ill effects.[j] 6The people expected **28:5**
him to swell up or suddenly fall dead, but after waiting a long time and seeing nothing [j]Lk 10:19
unusual happen to him, they changed their minds and said he was a god.[k] **28:6** [k]Ac 14:11
7There was an estate nearby that belonged to Publius, the chief official of the island.
He welcomed us to his home and for three days entertained us hospitably. 8His father
was sick in bed, suffering from fever and dysentery. Paul went in to see him and, after **28:8**
prayer,[l] placed his hands on him and healed him.[m] 9When this had happened, the rest [l]Jas 5:14,15 [m]Ac 9:40
of the sick on the island came and were cured. 10They honored us in many ways and
when we were ready to sail, they furnished us with the supplies we needed.

Arrival at Rome

11After three months we put out to sea in a ship that had wintered in the island. It was **28:11**
an Alexandrian ship[n] with the figurehead of the twin gods Castor and Pollux. 12We put [n]Ac 27:6

27:31 See *WCF* 5.3.

27:34 Not one of you will lose a single hair from his head. God is in control of the most minute details of an individual's life (Lk 21:18).

27:37 of us on board. The provision of the exact number of passengers, together with the use of the word "us," indicates that Luke was an eyewitness and fellow passenger with Paul. This number of passengers on an ancient ocean-going vessel was not unusual. Some ships of the period could carry considerably more.

27:41 But the ship struck a sandbar. Literally, "But after coming into a place between two seas . . ." The "place between two seas" referred to the narrow channel in what is now called St. Paul's Bay between Malta and the island of Salmonetta, where the currents create sandbars. This sort of nautical detail indicates that Luke was an eyewitness of the event.

27:44 See *WCF* 5.3.

28:1 Malta. Ancient Melita (the name means "a place of refuge") was settled by Phoenicians who came there about 1000 B.C. In size Malta is eight miles by eighteen miles. It is located 58 miles south of Sicily and 180 miles northeast of Cyrene, North Africa.

28:3–5 Being cold-blooded, snakes can become stiff and motionless in colder weather, and Paul must have picked up the serpent along with the brush. Some have suggested that the snake was nonpoisonous, but the Greek word translated "snake" in verse 4 is one applied to dangerous animals and poisonous snakes, and there is little reason to doubt the islanders' identification of the snake as poisonous. See *WLC* 145.

28:6 they changed their minds. There is some irony in the islanders' reappraisal of Paul—from murderer destined for death to god! This recalls the events in Lystra, where the people first hailed Paul and Barnabas as gods and then nearly stoned Paul to death (14:11–20).

28:7 Publius, the chief official of the island. Emperor Octavian Augustus inaugurated a Roman governor on Malta who, according to inscriptions, was called "the chief man over all the municipality of Malta." This fits Luke's description of Publius as "the chief official of the island" (literally, "the first man of the island"). As chief official, Publius showed the visitors hospitality at his island estate.

28:8 suffering from fever and dysentery. The Greek uses the plural form of "fever" to describe repeated feverish attacks. This ailment has been speculatively diagnosed as Malta fever, which is caused by the milk of Maltese goats. Today the disease is controlled through treatment and preventive measures.

in at Syracuse and stayed there three days. 13From there we set sail and arrived at Rhegium. The next day the south wind came up, and on the following day we reached Pu-
28:14 [o]Ac 1:16 teoli. 14There we found some brothers[o] who invited us to spend a week with them. And
so we came to Rome. 15The brothers[p] there had heard that we were coming, and they
28:15 [p]Ac 1:16 traveled as far as the Forum of Appius and the Three Taverns to meet us. At the sight of
these men Paul thanked God and was encouraged. 16When we got to Rome, Paul was
28:16 [q]Ac 24:23; 27:3 allowed to live by himself, with a soldier to guard him.[q]

Paul Preaches at Rome Under Guard

28:17 [r]Ac 25:2 [s]Ac 25:5 17Three days later he called together the leaders of the Jews.[r] When they had assem-
[t]Ac 25:8 [u]Ac 6:14 bled, Paul said to them: "My brothers,[s] although I have done nothing against our people[t] or against the customs of our ancestors,[u] I was arrested in Jerusalem and handed
28:18 [v]Ac 22:24 over to the Romans. 18They examined me[v] and wanted to release me,[w] because I was not
[w]Ac 26:31,32 [x]Ac 23:9 guilty of any crime deserving death.[x] 19But when the Jews objected, I was compelled to
appeal to Caesar[y]—not that I had any charge to bring against my own people. 20For this
28:19 [y]Ac 25:11 reason I have asked to see you and talk with you. It is because of the hope of Israel[z] that
I am bound with this chain."[a]
28:20 [z]Ac 26:6,7 21They replied, "We have not received any letters from Judea concerning you, and
[a]Ac 21:33 none of the brothers[b] who have come from there has reported or said anything bad
28:21 [b]Ac 22:5 about you. 22But we want to hear what your views are, for we know that people everywhere are talking against this sect."[c]
28:22 [c]Ac 24:5,14 23They arranged to meet Paul on a certain day, and came in even larger numbers to
the place where he was staying. From morning till evening he explained and declared
28:23 [d]Ac 19:8 [e]Ac 17:3 to them the kingdom of God[d] and tried to convince them about Jesus[e] from the Law of
[f]Ac 8:35 Moses and from the Prophets.[f] 24Some were convinced by what he said, but others would
28:24 not believe.[g] 25They disagreed among themselves and began to leave after Paul had
[g]Ac 14:4 made this final statement: "The Holy Spirit spoke the truth to your forefathers when he
said through Isaiah the prophet:

> 26" 'Go to this people and say,
> "You will be ever hearing but never understanding;
> you will be ever seeing but never perceiving."
> 28:27 [h]Ps 119:70 27 For this people's heart has become calloused;[h]
> [i]Isa 6:9,10 they hardly hear with their ears,
> and they have closed their eyes.
> Otherwise they might see with their eyes,
> hear with their ears,
> understand with their hearts
> and turn, and I would heal them.'[a][i]

28:28 [j]Lk 2:30 [k]Ac 13:46 28"Therefore I want you to know that God's salvation[j] has been sent to the Gentiles,[k]
and they will listen!"[b]
30For two whole years Paul stayed there in his own rented house and welcomed all
28:31 [l]ver 23; Mt 4:23 who came to see him. 31Boldly and without hindrance he preached the kingdom of God[l]
and taught about the Lord Jesus Christ.

[a] *27* Isaiah 6:9,10 [b] *28* Some manuscripts *listen!" 29After he said this, the Jews left, arguing vigorously among themselves.*

28:16 live by himself, with a soldier. Paul lived in his own rented house while under house arrest. There he could entertain his friends and minister to groups such as the Roman Jews.

■ **28:17–31** *Paul's Two-Year Ministry Under House Arrest in Rome.* Paul explained that he had not gone against his fellow Jews, after which he boldly proclaimed the gospel. These two issues were of great importance to Luke's readers.

28:21 We have not received any letters from Judea. An honest admission of justifiable ignorance, for the Jews in Jerusalem had not sent word of their accusations to the Jews in Rome or to the Roman authorities.

28:25–27 See *WCF* 1.10; 5.6; *WLC* 11,68.

28:30–31 From A.D. 60–62 Paul spent his time under house arrest preaching, teaching and ministering to his friends, fellow Jews and any Gentiles who came to hear his message about the kingdom of God. As Luke concluded Acts, Paul had not yet been brought to trial before Nero (as the Lord had said would happen; 27:24). From what we gather elsewhere, Paul expected a positive outcome from his trial and release from his confinement (Php 1:25; 2:24; Phm 22). The release must have occurred before A.D. 64, when Nero himself set fire to Rome and then accused Christians of having done it. When released, Paul seems to have taken up his ministry again, going as far as Greece (Nicopolis, Tit 3:12; Thessalonica, 2Ti 4:10), Crete (Tit 1:5) and Asia Minor (Ephesus, 2Ti 1:18; 4:12; Troas, 2Ti 4:13; Miletus, 2Ti 4:20). Possibly he went as far west as Spain (Ro 15:23–24,28), as the early post-apostolic work *1 Clement* may indicate. About A.D. 67, he was imprisoned again by Nero and beheaded. Ominous signs had led Paul to expect the end of his life (2Ti 4:6–18).

28:31 Boldly and without hindrance. This dramatic phrase occurs at the conclusion of the Greek text of Acts. For Paul and Luke, the message about Jesus and the glorious kingdom of God was to go on in triumph.

The Epistles of the New Testament

WHY SO MANY EPISTLES?

At first glace, it may seem odd that most of the books in the New Testament are epistles (letters). The Christian faith is built on historical events described primarily in the narratives of the Old and New Testaments. Nevertheless, like their Old Testament counterparts, the Gospels and Acts often did not explicitly state all the implications of their narratives for Christian readers in different times and places. In his wisdom God ordained that epistles be written to apply the gospel message about Christ to specific needs and challenges that particular churches faced.

The New Testament epistles contain theology applied to the life of the church. They should not be viewed simply as limited personal letters. They possess an official character by virtue of their association with the apostles of Christ. Yet neither should they be treated as formal theological treatises. They are letters, written to meet relatively specific needs.

To understand New Testament epistles correctly, we must make a genuine effort to comprehend the problems that each letter addressed. Though our problems may not be identical to those of the first readers, discovering similarities between ourselves and those original readers will help us to apply the epistles to our lives in responsible ways.

PAUL'S LIFE AND EPISTLES

Saul of Tarsus, later known as Paul, became God's instrument to make known the "mystery" of the gospel, especially to the Gentiles (Eph 3:2–6). Familiar with Greek thought and thoroughly trained in Judaism, he had violently opposed the Christian faith. An extraordinary revelation of Jesus Christ, however, resulted in his conversion and subsequent ministry (Ac 9:1–22).

We know almost nothing of Paul's early ministry in the provinces of Cilicia and Syria, which lasted over a decade (Ac 9:30; 11:25–26; Gal 1:21; 2:1). In the late A.D. 40s his missionary labors began in earnest. Commissioned by the church in Antioch with Barnabas as his coworker, Paul first took the gospel to the island of Cyprus and to several cities in the province of Galatia, in the middle of Asia Minor (Ac 13–14; see map "Paul's First Missionary Journey" at Ac 14). According to some interpreters, it was upon his return to Antioch that Paul wrote his letter to the Galatians to counteract the influence of certain men known then as "the circumcision group" (Gal 2:12), who later became known as Judaizers. This group wanted to impose traditional Jewish applications of the Law of Moses on Gentile believers.

After the council of apostles and leaders met in Jerusalem (Ac 15) around A.D. 50–52, Paul set out on a second journey, this time accompanied by Silas (see map "Paul's Second Missionary Journey" at Ac 17). They visited some of the previously established churches, recruited Timothy along the way and proceeded to evangelize Europe. Churches were established in a number of important cities, such as Philippi, Thessalonica (both in the northern province of Macedonia) and Corinth (Ac 15:36—18:22). Paul resided in Corinth for a year and a half, and while there he wrote his two letters to the Thessalonians, who were in great need of encouragement and instruction as a result of severe persecution.

A third journey (c. A.D. 53–57) took Paul through the Galatian region again (see map "Paul's Third Missionary Journey" at Ac 19). He then settled for an extended period of time in Ephesus, an important metropolis on the west coast of Asia Minor (Ac 19). During this stay, Paul heard some disturbing news about a number of problems in Corinth. The important letter known as 1 Corinthians was Paul's response to this situation. Some believe that Paul also wrote Galatians around this time.

Continuing his third journey, Paul then traveled north through Macedonia, where he heard from Titus that the church in Corinth as a whole had repented. In response, the apostle penned 2 Corinthians, following this letter with a personal visit. Upon arriving in Corinth, Paul wrote his famous epistle to the Romans, in which he carefully articulated the distinctiveness of his preaching in the light of the many objections he had faced during his ministry. After three months, the apostle retraced his steps on the way back to Judea (Ac 20:1—21:16).

A riot in Jerusalem led to Paul's arrest and subsequent two-year imprisonment in Caesarea (Ac 21:27—24:27). After he had appealed his case to the emperor, he was taken to Rome, where he waited for at least another two years to see the emperor (Ac 27:1—28:31). Paul's so-called "Prison Epistles" (Ephesians, Philippians, Colossians and Philemon) were probably written from Rome in the late A.D. 50s or early 60s. Some interpreters place one or more of these letters in the period of the Caesarean imprisonment or even further back during his stay in Ephesus.

Although the book of Acts does not give us information beyond this Roman imprisonment, it is likely that Paul was released and engaged in yet a fourth missionary journey (see map "Paul's Journey to Rome" at Ac 27). He may have traveled as far west as Spain (Ro 15:24), then east to Ephesus and other regions of the Aegean (1Ti 1:3; Tit 1:5; 3:12). Both 1 Timothy and Titus, which along with 2 Timothy are known as the Pastoral Epistles, may have been written during this period. According to tradition, in the mid 60s Paul was imprisoned again, this time in Rome. From there, he wrote 2 Timothy shortly before his execution (2Ti 4:6–18).

During his remarkable career, Paul not only brought the Good News of Jesus to many places where it had not been before, but he also left behind in his epistles a treasury of Christian teaching, the depth of which the church has not yet exhausted.

THE GENERAL EPISTLES

Unfortunately, the magnitude of Paul's achievement has often led Christians to ignore the rest of New Testament epistles, but God used other individuals (James, Peter, John, Jude and the unknown author of Hebrews) to reveal truths and provide perspectives not found in the Pauline material. These letters are often known collectively as the "General Epis-

The Epistles of the New Testament *(continued)*

tles" or "Catholic Epistles" because many were written to more universal audiences than were Paul's carefully targeted letters. Unlike Paul's letters, which are called by the names of their recipients, it is traditional to refer to the General Epistles by the names of their authors. This is partly because we do not know much about the churches addressed, and partly because some of them were written to multiple churches.

Some interpreters have referred to the General Epistles as "tracts for the times" because they deal largely with issues that nearly all Christians face. All Christians are exhorted to rejoice in the midst of trials (Jas 1:2; 1Pe 4:13) and to contend for the faith delivered to us (Jude 3). We readily learn to respond to those general exhortations with faith and obedience and so to grow in the grace and knowledge of our Lord Jesus Christ (2Pe 3:18).

ROMANS

Introduction

Overview

Author: The apostle Paul
Purpose: To present Paul's gospel message to the believers in Rome and to explain how the gospel heals divisions between Jewish and Gentile believers
Date: A.D. 55–57
Key Truths:

- Jews and Gentiles are sinners under God's judgment.
- Jews and Gentiles receive justification through faith alone apart from works.
- Sanctification, which leads to glorification, takes place through dependence on the Holy Spirit.
- Jews and Gentiles have interconnected roles in history
- Jewish and Gentile Christians must learn to apply the gospel to practical living.

Author

The opening (1:1) and the biographical details (chs. 1,15–16) show that the letter to the Romans was written by the apostle Paul. The letter was already cited and listed as Paul's during the second century. Its authenticity has been disputed only rarely and never convincingly.

Time and Place of Writing

Paul wrote Romans shortly before he delivered the gift from the Gentile congregations to the church in Jerusalem (15:25; Ac 24:17). Internal indications suggest that at this time he may have been a resident of Corinth: Phoebe (16:1–2) was a member of the church at Cenchrea, the port of Corinth; Paul's host, Gaius (16:23), may have been a resident of Corinth (1Co 1:14); and Erastus had connections with Corinth (16:23; Ac 19:22; 2Ti 4:20).

Paul probably wrote this letter during the three months described in Acts 20:2–3. While it is impossible to fix a precise date, a number of factors should be considered. For instance, Paul appeared before Gallio (Ac 18:12), the proconsul (normally a one-year appointment), in Achaia in A.D. 52. Around this time, Paul was in Corinth for "some time" (Ac 18:18), presumably during the period A.D. 51–53. He then sailed to Ephesus for a brief visit and went to Caesarea and probably Jerusalem and Antioch as well (Ac 18:22). Returning through Galatia and Phrygia (Ac 18:23) to Ephesus, he resided there for about three years (Ac 19:8,10) before proceeding to Jerusalem via Macedonia and Achaia (Ac 19:21). Therefore, the earliest probable date for the writing of Romans is toward the end of A.D. 54. But a later date leaves more leeway for Paul's many activities, so the letter is more likely dated sometime between the end of A.D. 55 and the early months of A.D. 57.

Original Audience

That the faith of the Roman Christians was well known (1:8) and that Paul had desired to visit them for some time (1:13) suggest that the Christian faith had been established in Rome for a considerable period. This is supported by the statement of the Roman historian Suetonius that Claudius had expelled the Jews in A.D. 49 for rioting "at the instigation of Chrestus" (arguably a reference to Christ). Visitors from Rome were present in Jerusalem on the day of Pentecost (Ac 2:10–11) and may have been the first to bring the Good News to the city. Despite tradition stretching back through Irenaeus, it is relatively certain that neither Peter nor Paul founded the church in Rome. Paul had never visited the church prior to writing his epistle to the Romans (1:8–13), and the absence of any reference to Peter or the other apostles suggests that the Roman church had not experienced direct apostolic ministry.

Both Jews and Gentiles were members of the church(es) in Rome. Romans 1:13 indicates a predominance of Gentiles, as possibly does the warning to Gentile Christians not to be proud (11:13–24). The conflict between weak and strong (14:1—15:13) may have arisen from conflicts between Jewish and Gentile believers. It is even possible that some of the house churches in Rome were exclusively Jewish or Gentile (cf. 16:5,14–15).

Purpose and Distinctives

Paul was at a critical juncture in his ministry at the time Romans was written. He believed that he had fulfilled his ministry in the eastern Mediterranean (15:17–23) and that the time was ripe for him to move west and evangelize in Spain (15:24). He hoped to visit the Roman Christians on the way, fulfilling a long-time ambition and perhaps gaining their assistance as a supporting church (15:24). In light of this, it was essential for him to present his apostolic credentials (note the phrase "my gospel" in 2:16 and 16:25), so they would recognize the authenticity of his ministry. Paul may also have thought it necessary to defend his ministry from the false insinuations of rumormongers (3:8).

Paul's work also stood at a critical juncture in terms of his burden to see the Christian church as a mutual fellowship of Jews and Gentiles joined in the one body of Christ. This is clear from the importance he attached to the Gentile love-gift to the Jerusalem church. It also surfaces throughout Romans in the theme of the unifying of Jews and Gentiles both in sin because of Adam and through grace in Christ. Both Jews and Gentiles need the saving righteousness of the gospel, since all have sinned; it may be received by anyone, since it comes by grace through faith. The outworking of this saving righteousness in history is the key to God's ultimate purposes for both Jews and Gentiles, and this saving righteousness is to be expressed in the lives of all—personally, communally and socially—united within the body of Christ as the new people of God. The opportunity for writing while in Corinth, the pressing burden of his visit to Jerusalem and the prospect of visiting the capital of the empire before bringing the gospel to the limits of the then-known world were all factors that motivated Paul to write this letter.

Romans is Paul's most comprehensive explanation of the gospel. John Chrysostom, the fifth century's greatest preacher, had Romans read aloud to him once a week. Augustine and all of the Reformers saw Romans as crucial to a proper understanding of the rest of Scripture. In Romans Paul brought together a number of themes that have held a central role in Reformed theology: sin, law, judgment, human destiny, faith, works, grace, justification, sanctification, election, the plan of salvation, the work of Christ and of the Spirit, the Christian hope, the nature and life of the church, the place of Jews and Gentiles in the purposes of God, the meaning of the Old Testament, the duties of Christian citizenship and the principles of personal godliness and morality. However, Paul did not combine all of these topics simply for the sake of explaining Christian theology. Rather, each of these teachings contributed to his greater purposes of uniting Jews and Gentiles in the Roman church and establishing the Roman church firmly in the gospel and as a part of the Roman community. He hoped that strengthening them in these ways would not only help them mature as a church, but also better equip them to aid in his planned missionary endeavors to Spain.

Outline

I. Paul's Greetings and Longings (1:1–17)
  A. Paul's Greetings (1:1–7)
  B. Paul's Desire to Visit Rome (1:8–17)

Paul presented himself as the Apostle to the Gentiles.

II. Sinfulness of Jews and Gentiles (1:18—3:20)
  A. Gentile Sinfulness (1:18–32)
  B. Jewish Sinfulness (2:1—3:8)
  C. Universal Sinfulness (3:9–20)

In their own ways, Jews and Gentiles are both sinful and stand under the judgment of God.

III. Salvation for Jews and Gentiles (3:21—8:39)
  A. Justification (3:21—5:21)
    1. By Faith Alone (3:21–31)
    2. Abraham's Example (4:1–25)
    3. Benefits of Justification (5:1–11)
    4. Christ: The New Adam (5:12–21)
  B. Sanctification (6:1—8:39)
    1. Sin's Dominion Broken (6:1–23)
    2. Struggling With Sin (7:1–25)
    3. Living by the Spirit (8:1–39)

Salvation comes to Jews and Gentiles in the same way. Justification for all is through faith alone apart from works. Sanctification for all is through reliance on the power of the Holy Spirit.

IV. The Historical Roles of Jews and Gentiles (9:1—11:36)
  A. God's Sovereign Election (9:1–29)
  B. Unbelief and Belief in Israel (9:30—11:10)
  C. Warnings and Encouragements for Jews and Gentiles (11:11–36)

Jews and Gentiles have distinct but interconnected roles in the history of salvation.

V. Practical Instructions (12:1—15:13)
  A. Full Consecration (12:1–2)
  B. In the Body of Christ (12:3–21)
  C. In Political and Social Life (13:1–14)
  D. Among Weak and Strong (14:1—15:13)

Full devotion to Christ will lead to faithful service for Christ in the various challenges Christians face together.

VI. Final Greetings (15:14—16:27)
  A. Vision for Ministry (15:14–22)
  B. Plan to Visit Rome (15:23–33)
  C. Greetings to Christians in Rome (16:1–16)
  D. Warning Against Enemies (16:17–20)
  E. Companions Sending Greetings (16:21–24)
  F. Apostolic Doxology (16:25-27)

Paul closed with some final greetings and expressions of hope for the future.

1 Paul, a servant of Christ Jesus, called to be an apostle[a] and set apart[b] for the gospel of God[c]— 2the gospel he promised beforehand through his prophets in the Holy
Scriptures[d] 3regarding his Son, who as to his human nature[e] was a descendant of David, 4and who through the Spirit[a] of holiness was declared with power to be the Son of
God[b] by his resurrection from the dead: Jesus Christ our Lord. 5Through him and for his
name's sake, we received grace and apostleship to call people from among all the Gentiles[f] to the obedience that comes from faith.[g] 6And you also are among those who are
called to belong to Jesus Christ.[h]

7To all in Rome who are loved by God[i] and called to be saints:

Grace and peace to you from God our Father and from the Lord Jesus Christ.[j]

Paul's Longing to Visit Rome

8First, I thank my God through Jesus Christ for all of you,[k] because your faith is being reported all over the world.[l] 9God, whom I serve[m] with my whole heart in preaching the gospel of his Son, is my witness[n] how constantly I remember you 10in my prayers
at all times; and I pray that now at last by God's will the way may be opened for me to
come to you.[o]

11I long to see you[p] so that I may impart to you some spiritual gift to make you
strong— 12that is, that you and I may be mutually encouraged by each other's faith. 13I
do not want you to be unaware, brothers, that I planned many times to come to you (but
have been prevented from doing so until now)[q] in order that I might have a harvest
among you, just as I have had among the other Gentiles.

14I am obligated[r] both to Greeks and non-Greeks, both to the wise and the foolish.
15That is why I am so eager to preach the gospel also to you who are at Rome.[s]

1:1 [a]1Co 1:1 [b]Ac 9:15 [c]2Co 11:7
1:2 [d]Gal 3:8
1:3 [e]Jn 1:14
1:5 [f]Ac 9:15 [g]Ac 6:7
1:6 [h]Rev 17:14
1:7 [i]Ro 8:39 [j]1Co 1:3
1:8 [k]1Co 1:4 [l]Ro 16:19
1:9 [m]2Ti 1:3 [n]Php 1:8
1:10 [o]Ro 15:32
1:11 [p]Ro 15:23
1:13 [q]Ro 15:22,23
1:14 [r]1Co 9:16
1:15 [s]Ro 15:20

a 4 Or *who as to his spirit* b 4 Or *was appointed to be the Son of God with power*

▪ **1:1–17** *Paul's Greetings and Longings.* Paul opened this epistle, as he typically did, by identifying himself and his readers. He then immediately indicated how strongly he desired to visit the believers in Rome.

▪ **1:1–7** *Paul's Greetings.* Paul began this epistle with an elaborate introduction of himself and an acknowledgment of the Christians in Rome.

1:1 Paul. Ancient letters commonly began with the general formula "A to B sends greetings." Using his Roman name, Paul filled out this formula with Christian significance in his greeting (vv. 1–7) and in his declaration of his desire to go to Rome (vv. 8–17). **servant.** A bond servant, one who was totally at the disposal of his master. **apostle.** A messenger, someone sent by another to represent the sender. The term is used in a special, authoritative sense of the Twelve and Paul, who had been chosen as eyewitnesses of the risen Christ (Ac 1:22; 1Co 9:1; 15:7–8; Gal 1:15–16; cf. Ac 9:1–6,15). It is also used in a more general sense of messengers sent by the churches (16:7). The idea of a messenger who is sent is common to all instances, but unique authority belongs to the messengers of Christ in distinction from the messengers of the churches. **gospel.** A term meaning "good news," which is derived from Old Testament prophecy about the announcement of the reign of God and of the end of exile (Isa 41:27; 52:7). See theological article "The Gospel" at Galatians 1. **of God.** God is both the source and the theme of the message. Here and elsewhere Paul's Trinitarianism surfaces (vv. 3–4; 5:1–5; 8:3–4,9–11,16–17; 14:17–18; 15:16,30).

1:2 the gospel he promised beforehand. The gospel was announced in promise form in the preaching of the prophets, from which its apostolic presentation is drawn (see note on v. 1).

1:3–4 descendant of David . . . Son of God. Traditionally, this passage has been understood as a description of the two natures of Christ. It is better, however, to understand it primarily as a description of the Savior's ministry. Although he is the eternal second person of the Trinity, he became human in order to share humankind's weakness. He became a "descendant of David" in order to be heir to the throne of David and thereby to be Messiah. He was transformed by the "Spirit of holiness" at the resurrection and was brought into a new epoch of glorified existence as the Son of God (1Co 15:45; 2Co 13:4). Nevertheless, it is legitimate to recognize that this passage explicitly speaks of Christ as human and implicitly attributes divinity to him in the title "our Lord." See *WCF* 8.2; *WLC* 38,52; *BC* 18; *HC* 15,35.

1:5–6 Paul explained that Christ had called him to be an evangelist to the Gentiles (11:13–14; Ac 9:15; Eph 3:8).

1:5 obedience that comes from faith. Literally, "obedience of faith," perhaps indicating the obedience that flows from faith and the fact that faith itself constitutes obedient submission to the call of God (16:26).

1:7 Rome. Capital of the Roman Empire. Scholars have no specific knowledge about the founding of the Roman church(es), although visitors from Rome were among those who heard the gospel preached on the day of Pentecost (Ac 2:10). See "Introduction: Original Audience." **called to be saints.** All members of the visible church are "saints" or "holy" because they are consecrated to God. However, by using the term "called," Paul indicated that he was speaking specifically of believers within the church (cf. 8:28). Those who have saving faith are made into a new and holy people for God's glory (1Pe 2:9–10).

1:8–17 *Paul's Desire to Visit Rome.* Paul had never been to Rome, but he desired to meet the church and to minister there.

1:8 I thank my God. Gratitude for God's work of grace in others was a constant feature of Paul's life (1Co 11:4; Php 1:3; Col 1:3; 1Th 1:2; 2Th 1:3; 2Ti 1:3; Phm 4). **all over the world.** Throughout the entire empire, news had spread of the presence of Christians in the capital city. See *WLC* 144.

1:9 I remember you. Paul's constant prayerfulness was an expression of his wholehearted service and desire for spiritual usefulness. He prayed in full submission to God's will (vv. 9–12; cf. Eph 1:15–16; Php 1:9; Col 1:9; 1Th 1:3; 2Th 1:11; 2Ti 1:3). See *HC* 101.

1:11–12 See *WCF* 26.1.

1:11 spiritual gift. Here the term is not used in the functional sense of 1 Corinthians 12:1; rather, Paul had in view the results or products of spiritual gifts, namely, the benefits believers render to each other.

1:12 mutually encouraged. Ministry is for the mutual strengthening of the whole body of Christ (Eph 4:15–16).

1:13 planned many times. No record of these plans exists, but see Acts 19:21 and 23:11 for Paul's sense of divine compulsion toward Rome. **prevented.** See Acts 16:6–7 for interruptions in Paul's plans caused either by the inward counsel of the Holy Spirit or by prophetic utterance. **among the other Gentiles.** This suggests that Paul thought of the Roman church as predominantly Gentile.

1:14 obligated. Paul explained that his planning and expectations (v. 13) were rooted in a sense of obligation. He had been given the gospel for the Gentiles (11:13–14; cf. Eph 3:1–8). **Greeks . . . non-Greeks . . . wise . . . foolish.** Here the term "Greeks" referred to cultured Hellenists (the "wise"), and "non-Greeks" to "barbarians" or the uncultured ("foolish"). Paul was eager to bring the gospel to all Gentiles. See *WCF* 26.1.

16 I am not ashamed of the gospel,[t] because it is the power of God[u] for the salvation
of everyone who believes: first for the Jew,[v] then for the Gentile.[w] 17 For in the gospel a
righteousness from God is revealed,[x] a righteousness that is by faith from first to last,[a]
just as it is written: "The righteous will live by faith."[b][y]

God's Wrath Against Mankind

18 The wrath of God[z] is being revealed from heaven against all the godlessness and
wickedness of men who suppress the truth by their wickedness, 19 since what may be
known about God is plain to them, because God has made it plain to them.[a] 20 For since
the creation of the world God's invisible qualities—his eternal power and divine nature—have been clearly seen, being understood from what has been made,[b] so that men
are without excuse.

21 For although they knew God, they neither glorified him as God nor gave thanks to
him, but their thinking became futile and their foolish hearts were darkened.[c] 22 Although they claimed to be wise, they became fools[d] 23 and exchanged the glory of the
immortal God for images[e] made to look like mortal man and birds and animals and
reptiles.

24 Therefore God gave them over[f] in the sinful desires of their hearts to sexual impurity for the degrading of their bodies with one another.[g] 25 They exchanged the truth of
God for a lie,[h] and worshiped and served created things[i] rather than the Creator—who
is forever praised.[j] Amen.

26 Because of this, God gave them over[k] to shameful lusts.[l] Even their women exchanged natural relations for unnatural ones.[m] 27 In the same way the men also aban-

1:16 [t]2Ti 1:8 [u]1Co 1:18 [v]Ac 3:26 [w]Ro 2:9, 10
1:17 [x]Ro 3:21 [y]Hab 2:4; Gal 3:11; Heb 10:38
1:18 [z]Eph 5:6; Col 3:6
1:19 [a]Ac 14:17
1:20 [b]Ps 19:1-6
1:21 [c]Jer 2:5; Eph 4:17, 18
1:22 [d]1Co 1:20,27
1:23 [e]Ps 106:20; Jer 2:11; Ac 17:29
1:24 [f]Eph 4:19 [g]1Pe 4:3
1:25 [h]Isa 44:20 [i]Jer 10:14 [j]Ro 9:5
1:26 [k]ver 24,28 [l]1Th 4:5 [m]Lev 18:22,23

[a] *17* Or *is from faith to faith* [b] *17* Hab. 2:4

1:16–17 See *WCF* 14.1; *HC* 21.
1:16 I am not ashamed of the gospel. Paul affirmed his eagerness to preach the gospel with this powerful understatement. **power.** One reason for Paul's pride in the gospel was its regenerating, life-changing impact. The power of God accompanies the preaching of the gospel to overcome the weakness and spiritual inability that result from sin (5:6; 8:5–9; see Eph 2:1–10). **believes.** Salvation is unmerited but not universally enjoyed; faith is required. **first for the Jew, then for the Gentile.** Here Paul revealed one of his chief concerns in this epistle: his Christian outlook on Jews and Gentiles. The gospel came first to the Jews in terms of the history of redemption (Jn 4:22; cf. Mk 7:24–30; Ro 2:9–10), and this was also the pattern of Paul's missionary outreach. Hence, in visiting the cities of the Roman world, he began by expounding Scripture in the synagogues where possible, preaching Christ as the fulfillment of the Old Testament promises (Ac 9:20; 13:5,14; 14:1; 17:1,17; 18:4,19,26; 19:8). Throughout Romans, Paul was careful to present an appropriate outlook on the God-given privileges of the Jews and on their relationship to the Gentiles (3:1–2; 9:4–5). See *WLC* 155; *WSC* 89.
1:17 righteousness from God. Literally, "righteousness of God," a key phrase in this epistle (3:21–22; 10:3; cf. Jesus' righteousness in 5:19) that is regularly explained as "righteousness that is by faith" (3:22; 9:30; 10:6). This is the righteousness of Christ that is imputed to (reckoned by God as belonging to) the one who believes. This imputation of righteousness to sinners who believe is fully consistent with the personal righteousness of God. As a just and righteous judge (2:5–16), God justifies (declares righteous) through the death of his Son those sinners who come to true faith in Christ (3:21–26; 5:10). Luther's reading of this verse had a decisive impact on his understanding of justification. Influenced by Augustine, Luther understood this to mean "not that righteousness by which God himself is righteous" (*Commentary on Romans,* 1:17) but that righteousness God grants to us by faith. In this context "righteousness" means "meeting of the standard of God's justice." **by faith from first to last.** Paul emphasized that although believers are active in receiving the gift of salvation, they contribute no merit to it. **as it is written.** Habakkuk 2:4 provides the Old Testament basis for, and summary of, what follows, indicating that the way of life by means of faith was already known in the Old Testament. The Old Testament fully supported Paul's Christian gospel. **will live.** Both in contrast to spiritual death and in the sense of continued fellowship with God. From first to last, godly living means trusting in God and depending on his grace. See *HC* 59.
▪**1:18—3:20** *Sinfulness of Jews and Gentiles.* The gospel is needed because the whole world is guilty before God. Paul's discussion divides into three sections: the sinfulness of Gentiles (1:18–32), the sinfulness of Jews (2:1—3:8) and a summary of universal sinfulness (3:9–20).
▪**1:18–32** *Gentile Sinfulness.* Gentiles, who had not had much contact with Israel and the Scriptures, were still guilty of sin and in need of salvation because they had violated the revelation of God and his moral requirements in nature (or general revelation).
1:18 wrath. Moral evil evokes righteous anger and personal revulsion from God. Paul summed up the content of revelation in nature as "wrath"—not because nature reveals only God's wrath, but because God pours out his wrath on human beings who constantly violate God's revelation in nature. **godlessness and wickedness.** These terms jointly express the single idea of godless wickedness. The order, however, may be an implicit reminder that moral decay follows rebellion against God. **suppress the truth.** Revelation in nature (general revelation) is not merely potential knowledge of God for those who investigate nature carefully, but also truth that can be "clearly seen" by everyone (v. 20). Confronted with this truth, humanity seeks to obstruct the influence of general revelation (cf. those who love "darkness instead of light because their deeds [are] evil"; Jn 3:19). The result is that all people are "without excuse" (v. 20); none may appeal to ignorance. See *HC* 10.
1:19–20 See *WCF* 1.1; 4.1; 21.1; *WLC* 2,96; *BC* 2,14.
1:19 what may be known about God. Paul stressed the reality and universality of general revelation, which is perpetual ("since the creation") and "clearly seen" (v. 20). Divine invisibility, eternity and power are all expressed in and through the created order.
1:21–23 See *WLC* 109.
1:21 knew God. Paul stressed that even Gentiles (who did not have the Law of Moses) had the opportunity to gather true information about God and to know him personally through general revelation. Human beings refuse to acknowledge what, at some level, they all know to be true: They are aware that God exists but refuse to honor him as God or give thanks to him. As a consequence of rejecting God, "their thinking [becomes] futile and their foolish hearts [are] darkened." See *WSC* 47; *BC* 14.
1:22–23 claimed to be wise, they became fools and exchanged the glory of the immortal God. Intellectual arrogance before God displays a reversed sense of values; the worship of God is exchanged for devotion to man-made idols. The indelible instinct to worship is twisted away from the Creator and toward the creature (v. 25). See *HC* 96.
1:24 God gave them over. Rebellion against God's revelation in nature did not happen just once but continued generation after generation. As a result, God exercised his wrath by removing his restraints, both on humanity's sinful actions and on their consequences (vv. 26,28). This is how Gentile nations that had revelation in nature became so perverse and opposed to the will of God. See *WCF* 5.6; *WLC* 139.
1:25–26 See *WCF* 21.2; *WLC* 105,109; *WSC* 47.
1:26–27 natural relations . . . unnatural ones. One effect of turning away from worshiping the Creator was the perversion of

doned natural relations with women and were inflamed with lust for one another. Men
committed indecent acts with other men, and received in themselves the due penalty for
their perversion.[n]
28 Furthermore, since they did not think it worthwhile to retain the knowledge of God,
he gave them over[o] to a depraved mind, to do what ought not to be done. 29 They have
become filled with every kind of wickedness, evil, greed and depravity. They are full of
envy, murder, strife, deceit and malice. They are gossips,[p] 30 slanderers, God-haters, insolent, arrogant and boastful; they invent ways of doing evil; they disobey their parents;[q]
31 they are senseless, faithless, heartless,[r] ruthless. 32 Although they know God's righteous
decree that those who do such things deserve death,[s] they not only continue to do these
very things but also approve[t] of those who practice them.

God's Righteous Judgment

2 You, therefore, have no excuse,[u] you who pass judgment on someone else, for at
whatever point you judge the other, you are condemning yourself, because you who
pass judgment do the same things.[v] 2 Now we know that God's judgment against those
who do such things is based on truth. 3 So when you, a mere man, pass judgment on them
and yet do the same things, do you think you will escape God's judgment? 4 Or do you
show contempt for the riches[w] of his kindness,[x] tolerance[y] and patience,[z] not realizing
that God's kindness leads you toward repentance?[a]
5 But because of your stubbornness and your unrepentant heart, you are storing up
wrath against yourself for the day of God's wrath, when his righteous judgment[b] will be
revealed. 6 God "will give to each person according to what he has done."[a c] 7 To those who
by persistence in doing good seek glory, honor[d] and immortality,[e] he will give eternal life.
8 But for those who are self-seeking and who reject the truth and follow evil,[f] there will be
wrath and anger. 9 There will be trouble and distress for every human being who does evil:
first for the Jew, then for the Gentile;[g] 10 but glory, honor and peace for everyone who does
good: first for the Jew, then for the Gentile.[h] 11 For God does not show favoritism.[i]
12 All who sin apart from the law will also perish apart from the law, and all who sin
under the law[j] will be judged by the law. 13 For it is not those who hear the law who are

a 6 Psalm 62:12; Prov. 24:12

1:27 [n]Lev 18:22; 20:13
1:28 [o]ver 24,26
1:29 [p]2Co 12:20
1:30 [q]2Ti 3:2
1:31 [r]2Ti 3:3
1:32 [s]Ro 6:23 [t]Ps 50:18; Lk 11:48; Ac 8:1; 22:20
2:1 [u]Ro 1:20 [v]2Sa 12:5-7; Mt 7:1,2
2:4 [w]Ro 9:23; Eph 1:7, 18; 2:7 [x]Ro 11:22 [y]Ro 3:25 [z]Ex 34:6 [a]2Pe 3:9
2:5 [b]Jude 6
2:6 [c]Ps 62:12; Mt 16:27
2:7 [d]ver 10 [e]1Co 15:53,54
2:8 [f]2Th 2:12
2:9 [g]1Pe 4:17
2:10 [h]ver 9
2:11 [i]Ac 10:34
2:12 [j]Ro 3:19; 1Co 9:20, 21

---

basic sexual morality as evidenced in homosexuality. Homosexuality appeared in many contexts in ancient Gentile cultures, but its prevalence does not indicate that it is natural. Rather, Scripture uniformly views all homosexual actions as sinful and against the natural order of creation (Lev 18:22). The consequence is degradation of the body (v. 24), disintegration of what is truly "natural" (v. 26) and bondage to uncontrollable passions (v. 27). See *WCF* 5.6, *WLC* 28,139,151.

1:28–32 See *WLC* 145; *WLC* 105; *HC* 106,112.

1:28 did not think it worthwhile. Sin produces a disdain for godly values, and the unrepentant sinner risks abandonment by God to a spirit of licentiousness (vv. 29–31). See *WCF* 5.6; *WLC* 28; *BC* 13.

1:32 they know God's righteous decree. God's revelation in nature demonstrates his moral character and instills a sense of moral duty in all human beings. As rebellion against God continues, the threat of divine judgment no longer acts as a restraint, but spurs further rebellion in the form of encouraging and praising sin in others. This sinful condition characterizes every member of fallen humanity to some degree, but Paul emphasized that it had been particularly true of the Gentile nations throughout history. See *WCF* 1.1; 20.4; *WLC* 151.

■ **2:1—3:8** *Jewish Sinfulness.* Having established that Gentiles were guilty of rebelling against God's revelation in nature, Paul now turned to the sinful condition of Jews.

2:1–16 You, therefore, have no excuse . . . God will judge. In what follows, Paul turned to an imaginary representative of a real and identifiable group of people. Although Jews are specifically mentioned only in verse 17, Paul probably already had them in mind. They agreed with his statement about God's wrath but assumed that they stood outside of it (hence his stern warning in v. 5). But the nature of this presumption, if not its specific form, was not limited to Jews. In this context Paul depended heavily on principles of divine judgment that apply to all people. Judgment is based on truth (v. 2) and marked by righteousness (v. 5). It is according to works (v. 6), impartial in nature (v. 11) and executed through Christ (v. 16). Such judgment will bring agonizing ruin to all impenitent sinners (vv. 8–9). See *HC* 12.

2:1 no excuse. Paul unmasked those who, while agreeing with his exposition of divine wrath against Gentiles (1:18–32), assumed personal immunity to God's judgment, presumably because they were not Gentiles. **do the same things.** As different as Jews and Gentiles may have been in the ancient world, the basic directions of their lives were not radically different. See *WCF* 1.1; *WLC* 145.

2:2 based on truth. A link with 1:18. God's judgment is based on the reality of the individual's response or lack of response to him, not on other considerations.

2:4–6 See *WCF* 33.2; *HC* 13.

2:4 show contempt. They refused to acknowledge that God's beneficence was intended to produce sorrow for sin and a turning away from it. They despised the function of divine kindness and thereby showed disdain for God himself. See *WLC* 151.

2:5 storing up wrath. Religious presumption is "stubbornness." Those who resist God's grace increase their guilt even though they may protest their innocence. The "storing up" of wrath points forward to proportionate eternal punishment. See *WLC* 28,105; *BC* 37.

2:6–10 according to . . . done. Judgment will be proportionate to what people have been or done (v. 6). Paul was not denying here what he elsewhere emphasized: Salvation is a gift, not a reward (5:15,17; 6:23). Righteous people who do good works will be saved, but not on the basis of their good works. Rather, all who have saving faith demonstrate their faith in good works; they "seek glory, honor and immortality" (v. 7)—but only by God's grace and indwelling Spirit (Php 2:13). The merit that earns their salvation is Christ's alone (Col 2:13–14; 2Ti 1:9–10; Heb 9:11–15). Nevertheless, believers' eternal rewards directly correspond to their good works (Mk 9:41; Lk 19:16–19; 2Jn 8). The more good works a believer does in life, the greater his or her eternal rewards will be. Unbelievers are "self-seeking" (v. 8), not God-honoring. Moreover, while salvation is based on the good works of Christ imputed to believers, the judgment of unbelievers is based on their own sinful works (2Co 5:10). Apart from grace there is only one verdict possible, "first for the Jew, then for the Gentile" (v. 10; 1:16): *guilty.* See *WLC* 83; *BC* 21,24,37.

2:11 not show favoritism. Right standing with God is not based on ethnic background or any natural or self-generated distinctions among humanity (9:6–13; Gal 6:15).

2:12–16 apart from the law . . . under the law. The natural instinct of the self-defensive Jew (in distinction from the Gentile)

righteous in God's sight, but it is those who obey[k] the law who will be declared righteous.
14(Indeed, when Gentiles, who do not have the law, do by nature things required by the
law,[l] they are a law for themselves, even though they do not have the law, 15since they
show that the requirements of the law are written on their hearts, their consciences also
bearing witness, and their thoughts now accusing, now even defending them.) 16This will
take place on the day when God will judge men's secrets[m] through Jesus Christ,[n] as my
gospel[o] declares.

The Jews and the Law

17Now you, if you call yourself a Jew; if you rely on the law and brag about your relationship to God;[p] 18if you know his will and approve of what is superior because you are
instructed by the law; 19if you are convinced that you are a guide for the blind, a light for
those who are in the dark, 20an instructor of the foolish, a teacher of infants, because you
have in the law the embodiment of knowledge and truth— 21you, then, who teach others, do you not teach yourself? You who preach against stealing, do you steal?[q] 22You
who say that people should not commit adultery, do you commit adultery? You who abhor idols, do you rob temples?[r] 23You who brag about the law,[s] do you dishonor God by
breaking the law? 24As it is written: "God's name is blasphemed among the Gentiles
because of you."[a t]

25Circumcision has value if you observe the law,[u] but if you break the law, you have
become as though you had not been circumcised.[v] 26If those who are not circumcised
keep the law's requirements,[w] will they not be regarded as though they were circumcised?[x] 27The one who is not circumcised physically and yet obeys the law will condemn
you[y] who, even though you have the[b] written code and circumcision, are a lawbreaker.
28A man is not a Jew if he is only one outwardly,[z] nor is circumcision merely outward
and physical.[a] 29No, a man is a Jew if he is one inwardly; and circumcision is circumcision of the heart, by the Spirit,[b] not by the written code.[c] Such a man's praise is not from
men, but from God.[d]

God's Faithfulness

3 What advantage, then, is there in being a Jew, or what value is there in circumcision? 2Much in every way! First of all, they have been entrusted with the very words
of God.[e]

2:13 [k]Jas 1:22,23,25
2:14 [l]Ac 10:35
2:16 [m]Ecc 12:14 [n]Ac 10:42 [o]Ro 16:25
2:17 [p]ver 23; Mic 3:11; Ro 9:4
2:21 [q]Mt 23:3,4
2:22 [r]Ac 19:37
2:23 [s]ver 17
2:24 [t]Isa 52:5; Eze 36:22
2:25 [u]Gal 5:3 [v]Jer 4:4
2:26 [w]Ro 8:4 [x]1Co 7:19
2:27 [y]Mt 12:41,42
2:28 [z]Mt 3:9; Jn 8:39; Ro 9:6,7 [a]Gal 6:15
2:29 [b]Php 3:3; Col 2:11 [c]Ro 7:6 [d]Jn 5:44; 1Co 4:5; 2Co 10:18; 1Th 2:4; 1Pe 3:4
3:2 [e]Dt 4:8; Ps 147:19

[a] *24* Isaiah 52:5; Ezek. 36:22 [b] *27* Or *who, by means of a*

was to appeal to possession of the Law of Moses. The implication was that in this connection God does "show favoritism" (v. 11). The role of the law is a major theme in Romans (3:27–31; 4:13–15; 5:13–15; 6:14–15; 7:1–25; 13:8–10). Here in his first discussion of it, Paul showed that what pleases God is not knowledge of the law but obedience to God's will that is revealed in the law.

2:12 law. The Law of Moses, the eternal moral will of God summarized and applied to Israel in the Ten Commandments (Ex 20:1–17; Dt 5:1–22) and other legislation in the Pentateuch. **apart from the law . . . perish apart from the law.** A reference to Paul's earlier discussion of how Gentiles are judged according to their violation of the light of nature (1:18–32). **under the law . . . judged by the law.** These phrases designate the Jews who had received the special revelation of God through Moses. They were held (as is the visible church today) to the standard of special revelation. They would receive a much more severe judgment than those who did not know the law of God. See *BC* 14.

2:14–16 See *WCF* 1.1; 4.2; 6.6; 19.1; *WLC* 17,89,92,96; *WSC* 40.

2:14 do by nature things required by the law. No one can be justified on the basis of personal righteousness, but the universal presence of moral standards (albeit with various degrees of clarity) and the universal sense of obligation to such standards cannot be fully escaped. This is evidenced by "their consciences also bearing witness" (v. 15) and by the corresponding sense of self-judgment that arises.

2:16 through Jesus Christ. All judgment has been placed in his hand (Mt 7:21–23; 25:31–33; Jn 5:22; 2Co 5:10). His judgment will be infallible, penetrating to "men's secrets"; nothing will be concealed from the Judge (Heb 4:12–13). Nor will it be possible to plead that judging human beings against a divine standard is unfair, since the agent of the judgment is the incarnate Christ, who is fully human. **my gospel.** The gospel Paul preached. Judgment of sin was included in Paul's gospel because the righteous cannot receive their eternal rewards until after the wicked have been judged and removed. See *WCF* 33.1.

2:17–29 Jew. Paul spoke explicitly to the Jewish claim to special privilege, dealing in more detail with the possession of the law (vv. 17–24) and circumcision (vv. 25–29). In connection with the law, he pressed home the claim of verse 1 that the Jews were guilty of the same sins for which they condemned others. In connection with circumcision, he argued that mere outward circumcision was unimportant compared with circumcision of the heart. See *WCF* 27.3; *WLC* 109,113,151,163.

2:17–20 Paul listed the privileges that Jews thought made them superior to others.

2:21–23 The responsibilities that corresponded to privilege had not been fulfilled. Paul specified the commandments against adultery, sacrilege and theft (Ex 20:4–5,14–15). He exposed the hypocrisy of many Jews in his day; they condemned Gentiles as sinners, failing to acknowledge that they themselves fell into the same category.

2:25 Circumcision has value. Paul's argument moves to a climax. Condemnation results from failure to respond obediently to revelation of whatever kind. Jews had transgressed the Mosaic Law in particular, emptying circumcision of its real significance. Paul recognized the privileges of circumcision (3:1–2; 4:11) and of physical descent from Abraham (9:4–5), but physical circumcision was designed to symbolize the need for saving faith (v. 25; Dt 30:6).

2:29 a man is a Jew. Physical circumcision confirmed a man's membership in the covenant community of Israel. It brought him into vital contact with the promises of God's covenants with Israel. Yet circumcision alone did not secure anyone's eternal destiny. Reception of the inheritance offered in God's covenants with Israel depended on faith, not on ceremony or mere outward conformity. Paul's conclusion, though shocking to the Jews he addressed, was rooted in the teaching of the Old Testament itself (cf. 9:6).

3:1–20 Paul now moved to demonstrate that all humanity falls under God's condemnation.

3:1 What advantage. Paul's statement that "God does not show favoritism" (2:11) does not mean that there is no "advantage . . . in being a Jew." It means only that God does not exempt anyone from his righteous standard.

3:2 the very words of God. The phrase indicates that the inspi-

[3]What if some did not have faith?[f] Will their lack of faith nullify God's faithfulness?[g]
[4]Not at all! Let God be true,[h] and every man a liar.[i] As it is written:

"So that you may be proved right when you speak
and prevail when you judge."[a][j]

[5]But if our unrighteousness brings out God's righteousness more clearly, what shall
we say? That God is unjust in bringing his wrath on us? (I am using a human argument.)[k]
[6]Certainly not! If that were so, how could God judge the world?[l] [7]Someone might argue,
"If my falsehood enhances God's truthfulness and so increases his glory,[m] why am I still
condemned as a sinner?" [8]Why not say—as we are being slanderously reported as say-

3:3 [f]Heb 4:2 [g]2Ti 2:13
3:4 [h]Jn 3:33 [i]Ps 116:11 [j]Ps 51:4
3:5 [k]Ro 6:19; Gal 3:15
3:6 [l]Ge 18:25
3:7 [m]ver 4

[a] *4* Psalm 51:4

ration of the Old Testament extended beyond the ideas contained in Scripture to the words themselves (verbal inspiration). To have the words of God was a great advantage, but the privilege also intensified the judgment for disobedience. See *WCF* 1.3.

3:3–4 In the Old Testament the Jews responded to God with unbelief time and time again. Nevertheless, God remained faithful to his promises (Nu 23:19; Ro 9:6–7; 2Ti 2:13). See *BC* 7.

3:5–8 Paul responded to two closely related objections he imagined his readers might raise concerning the failures of Jews who did not have faith (v. 5). (1) If the unrighteousness of some Jews gave God opportunity to display his righteousness (v. 5), why not be unrighteous? And (2) if the falsehood of some Jews made God's truthfulness more plain (v. 7), why not lie? In short, if sin allowed God to be glorified, was it not unjust for God to bring "wrath" on his people (v. 5) or to condemn them as sinners (v. 7)? Paul answered these objections first by pointing out that if God did not judge sin in Israel, then he could not just judge sin in the world—either God is a just judge of all people or he is not a just judge at all (v. 6). Paul also argued that the logical extension of these objections would advocate sinning as often and as terribly as possible in order to provide God the greatest opportunity to display his goodness (v. 8). Such a view was repugnant to Paul and to any right-thinking Jew (v. 8). Despite their privileges, unbelieving Jews stood under God's wrath. Therefore the crucial issue to be considered was not outward circumcision, but saving faith.

3:5 human argument. Paul recognized that, taken in isolation, his statement at the beginning of verse 5 might seem to express a spirit of antagonism on his part toward God, so he explained that it was only a reflection of the way some other people might think. See *WLC* 113.

3:7 See *WLC* 113.

3:8 slanderously reported. A similar, although not identical,

Justification and Merit: Why Does God Count Me as Righteous?

ONE of the distinctive slogans of the Reformation was "Justification by Faith Alone," meaning that God counts believers as righteous (i.e., he justifies them) by means of their faith, not of their works. This idea should be clearly distinguished from the error that God counts believers as righteous on the *basis* of their faith (i.e., because they have faith). Believers do not earn righteousness by doing good works or by having faith; they are counted as if they were righteous on the basis of Christ's righteousness reckoned to them through the vehicle of faith.

The New Testament states time and again that believers are saved on the basis of Christ's work on their behalf, not on the basis of their own merit (Ro 3:22–24; 5:10–11,15–21; 8:1–4; 1Co 1:30; Gal 2:20–21; 3:27–29; 1Pe 3:18). Paul said, "I consider everything a loss . . . that I may gain Christ and be found in him, not having a righteousness of my own that comes from the law, but that which is through faith in Christ—the righteousness that comes from God and is by faith" (Php 3:8–9). Paul also clearly explained that justification is entirely of grace received through faith (Ro 3:25–30; 4:1—5:2; Gal 2:16; 3:8–14,24), referring to the example of Abraham, whom God counted as righteous by means of his faith (Ge 15:6; Ro 4:1–25; Gal 3:8–14). Paul also appealed to David's voice in Psalm 32:1–2 (Ro 4:6–8) as further Old Testament proof that God has always considered his people righteous by means of their faith, not of their works.

The idea that good works are not required to earn righteousness has not gone unchallenged. For example, the Roman Catholic Church teaches that God counts believers as righteous at least partly on the basis of the good works they perform after they come to faith. Some forms of Arminianism likewise insist that even those who are forgiven on the basis of Christ's atoning death may yet go to hell if they do not continue in faith and good works, in cooperation with the grace of God.

This subject becomes confusing for many believers because traditions like Roman Catholicism and Arminianism appeal to Scriptures that seem to contradict Paul's teaching. Whereas Paul wrote, "A man is justified by faith apart from observing the law" (Ro 3:28), James said, "A person is justified by what he does and not by faith alone" (Jas 2:24). Moreover, James also appealed to Abraham's example.

This apparent discrepancy is easily harmonized, however, by noting that "justify" (Greek, *dikaioo*) may mean either "count as righteous" (see Ro 4:5) or "prove right" (see Lk 7:35). Paul consistently referred to Abraham's faith as exercised in Genesis 15:1–6, a passage that recounts the time when God first promised Abraham a son—long before his son Isaac was born. In the Genesis 15 account, "justify" means "count as righteous": "Abram believed the LORD, and he credited it to him as righteousness" (Ge 15:6). James, however, recalled an episode (recorded in Gen 22) that took place after Isaac had been born and had grown into young adulthood (Jas 2:21). In the Genesis 22 account, "justify" means "proved right," as indicated by the fact that God was testing Abraham (Ge 22:1) and that Abraham's justification consisted in his passing the test: "Now I know that you fear God" (Ge 22:12). James agreed with Paul that Abraham was initially counted as righteous when he believed God's promise (Jas 2:22–23), but he added that Abraham's later obedience proved the earnestness of his earlier faith.

3:8 [n]Ro 6:1 ing and as some claim that we say—"Let us do evil that good may result"?[n] Their condemnation is deserved.

No One Is Righteous

[9]What shall we conclude then? Are we any better[a]? Not at all! We have already
3:9 [o]ver 19,23; Gal 3:22 made the charge that Jews and Gentiles alike are all under sin.[o] [10]As it is written:

"There is no one righteous, not even one;
[11] there is no one who understands,
no one who seeks God.
[12] All have turned away,
they have together become worthless;
3:12 [p]Ps 14:1-3 there is no one who does good,
not even one."[b][p]
3:13 [q]Ps 5:9 [r]Ps 140:3 [13] "Their throats are open graves;
their tongues practice deceit."[c][q]
"The poison of vipers is on their lips."[d][r]
3:14 [s]Ps 10:7 [14] "Their mouths are full of cursing and bitterness."[e][s]
[15] "Their feet are swift to shed blood;
[16] ruin and misery mark their ways,
[17] and the way of peace they do not know."[f]
3:18 [t]Ps 36:1 [18] "There is no fear of God before their eyes."[g][t]

3:19 [u]Jn 10:34 [v]Ro 2:12 [19]Now we know that whatever the law says,[u] it says to those who are under the law,[v]
so that every mouth may be silenced and the whole world held accountable to God.
3:20 [w]Ac 13:39; Gal 2:16 [x]Ro 7:7 [20]Therefore no one will be declared righteous in his sight by observing the law;[w] rather, through the law we become conscious of sin.[x]

Righteousness Through Faith

3:21 [y]Ro 1:17; 9:30 [z]Ac 10:43 [21]But now a righteousness from God,[y] apart from law, has been made known, to
3:22 [a]Ro 9:30 [b]Ro 10:12; Gal 3:28; Col 3:11 which the Law and the Prophets testify.[z] [22]This righteousness from God comes through
faith[a] in Jesus Christ to all who believe. There is no difference,[b] [23]for all have sinned and

a *9* Or *worse* b *12* Psalms 14:1–3; 53:1–3; Eccles. 7:20 c *13* Psalm 5:9 d *13* Psalm 140:3
e *14* Psalm 10:7 f *17* Isaiah 59:7,8 g *18* Psalm 36:1

issue arises in 5:20—6:1. In both places Paul rejected a false implication that might be drawn from his words. See *WLC* 99,105,145.
3:9–22 See *WCF* 6.2; 6.4; 9.3; *WLC* 25,149,194; *WSC* 82; *BC* 16; *HC* 2,5,60.
■ **3:9–20** *Universal Sinfulness.* The argument begun in 1:18 is now brought to a conclusion and confirmed by quotations from the Old Testament tracing sin's manifestation, its root and its ultimate cause.
3:9 Are we any better? Paul was speaking of himself and of his fellow Jews. In the final analysis, Jews and Gentiles are both under the tyranny of sin and judgment. See *WCF* 6.6; *WLC* 95.
3:10 As it is written. This is the common New Testament wording when appeal is made to the authority of Scripture (1:17; 3:4). The Biblical texts, taken together, stress the universal reign of sin and the consequent depravity and condemnation of all humankind. See *WCF* 9.3; *BC* 14,15.
3:18 no fear of God. In the Old Testament, the essence of a proper attitude to God is one of "fear," the absence of which is practical atheism.
3:19–26 See *WCF* 7.3; *WLC* 30; *WSC* 20; *HC* 115.
3:19 the law. Refers here to the Old Testament Scriptures in general. Paul's quotes come from Psalms, Ecclesiastes and Isaiah. **under the law.** Not in the sense of 6:14–15, but as in 2:12 (those who possessed the Old Testament revelation; i.e., the Jews in particular). Paul asserted that what the law said about human sinfulness certainly applied to the people to whom the law was given. **every mouth . . . silenced . . . accountable.** No one, whether Jew or Gentile, has grounds for appeal; no one can claim to be free from guilt before God. The law condemns all people, thus establishing the need for justification by faith apart from works of the law. See *WCF* 6.6; *WLC* 4; *CD* 1.1.
3:20 declared righteous . . . by observing the law. In light of what the Old Testament says about the universality of sin, it should be obvious that no one can be accepted as righteous before God simply by obeying the law. **through the law we become conscious of sin.** Instead of providing a way for us to find justification, the law reveals our sinfulness. The law, however, is not the only revealer of sin (1:18–20). See *WCF* 16.5; 19.6; *WLC* 95,97; *BC* 22; *HC* 3,62.
■ **3:21—8:39** *Salvation for Jews and Gentiles.* Having shown that both Jews and Gentiles are sinful and in need of salvation, Paul turned to an explanation of how salvation comes to all. His argument divides into two main sections: justification (3:21—5:21) and sanctification (6:1—8:39).
■ **3:21—5:21** *Justification.* Paul closed the preceding section by stating that no one can be declared righteous (justified) by the law (3:20). He here explained how justification takes place. His discussion divides into four parts: the concept of faith alone (3:21–31), the example of Abraham (4:1–25), the source and benefits of justification (5:1–11) and Christ as the new Adam (5:12–21).
■ **3:21–31** *By Faith Alone.* At this point Paul embarked on an explanation of his doctrine of justification. He clearly explained that people are declared righteous in the court of God's justice by faith in Christ alone, not by their own good works. He first explained how justification is provided in Christ (vv. 21–26) and then underlined two implications this doctrine has for the relations between Jews and Gentiles (vv. 27–31).
3:21–28 See *WCF* 7.6; 11.1; *WLC* 38,70,77,194; *WSC* 33; *HC* 21,37,60; *CD* 2.IV.
3:21 But now. This expression has special significance in Paul's writings. It is an abbreviated way of saying, "But now that Christ has come." Paul plainly argued in chapters 3–4 that the doctrine of justification by faith is taught in the Old Testament but that with the coming of the kingdom of God, beginning with the incarnation of Christ, the way of justification has been made known with greater clarity than ever before. See theological article "The Plan of the Ages" at Hebrews 7. **apart from law.** The gospel is not lawless (v. 31; 6:15; 8:3–4; 13:8,10). Nevertheless, no one can be accepted as righteous on the basis of obedience to the law because all fall short of perfection.
3:22 comes through faith in Jesus Christ to all who believe. The righteousness of God must be received now that it "has been made known" (v. 21) with such great clarity in the coming of Christ. To believe involves not only knowledge and intellectual conviction about the gospel's testimony to Christ (10:14), but also

fall short of the glory of God, 24 and are justified freely by his grace[c] through the redemption[d] that came by Christ Jesus. 25 God presented him as a sacrifice of atonement,[a][e]
through faith in his blood.[f] He did this to demonstrate his justice, because in his forbearance he had left the sins committed beforehand unpunished[g]— 26 he did it to demonstrate his justice at the present time, so as to be just and the one who justifies those who
have faith in Jesus.

27 Where, then, is boasting?[h] It is excluded. On what principle? On that of observing
the law? No, but on that of faith. 28 For we maintain that a man is justified by faith apart
from observing the law.[i] 29 Is God the God of Jews only? Is he not the God of Gentiles too?
Yes, of Gentiles too,[j] 30 since there is only one God, who will justify the circumcised by
faith and the uncircumcised through that same faith.[k] 31 Do we, then, nullify the law by
this faith? Not at all! Rather, we uphold the law.

Abraham Justified by Faith

4 What then shall we say that Abraham, our forefather, discovered in this matter? 2 If,
in fact, Abraham was justified by works, he had something to boast about—but not
before God.[l] 3 What does the Scripture say? "Abraham believed God, and it was credited to him as righteousness."[b][m]

4 Now when a man works, his wages are not credited to him as a gift,[n] but as an obligation. 5 However, to the man who does not work but trusts God who justifies the wick-

3:24 [c]Ro 4:16; Eph 2:8 [d]Eph 1:7,14; Col 1:14; Heb 9:12
3:25 [e]1Jn 4:10 [f]Heb 9:12,14 [g]Ac 17:30
3:27 [h]Ro 2:17,23; 4:2; 1Co 1:29-31; Eph 2:9
3:28 [i]ver 20,21; Ac 13:39; Eph 2:9
3:29 [j]Ro 9:24
3:30 [k]Gal 3:8
4:2 [l]1Co 1:31
4:3 [m]ver 5,9,22, Ge 15:6; Gal 3:6; Jas 2:23
4:4 [n]Ro 11:6

[a] 25 Or *as the one who would turn aside his wrath, taking away sin* [b] 3 Gen. 15:6; also in verse 22

obedient trust and reliance on him as Savior and Lord (1:5). The righteousness of God is exclusively for those who have faith "There is no difference, for all have sinned," whether Jew or Gentile (cf. 1:16–17). See *WCF* 11.1; *WLC* 70.

3:23 all. Refers specifically to those who are saved—"all who believe" (v. 22) and are being "justified" (v. 24)—with particular emphasis on the lack of distinction between Jew and Gentile. No one is saved without first being a sinner. Paul's point is based on the broader truth that every human being is guilty before God. **fall short of the glory of God.** A poignant description of the consequence of sin. Created in the image of the glorious God (Ge 1:26–27), human beings have exchanged God's glory for idolatry (1:23) and distorted their divine image. Only grace through faith (Eph 2:8–9) renews and restores that lost glory (5:2; 8:18; 1Co 15:42–49; 2Co 3:18; Eph 4:24; Php 3:20–21; Col 3:10). See *WCF* 6.2; *WLC* 23,95; *CD* 1.1.

3:24 justified. In Scripture, justification is the antithesis of condemnation (e.g., Pr 17:15). It signifies the declaration in God's heavenly court that the sinner is righteous by virtue of the imputed righteousness of Christ (the "gift of righteousness"; 5:17). Justification is final and irreversible (8:1,33–34). It is grounded in Christ's lifelong obedience (in which he fulfilled the precepts of God's law and earned perfect merit) and in his death on the cross (in which he bore the penalty of God's judgment against our sins). Believers now share the same righteous status as the risen Christ with whom they are united (2Co 5:21). **freely by his grace.** Paul's repetition of the same idea in different words emphasizes the role of divine initiative and mercy in our salvation. **redemption.** Freedom gained through the payment of a price. Here it specifically refers to the release from the former condition of bondage in sin. This is accomplished through Christ's death, the ransom-price for our salvation (Mk 10:45; 1Ti 2:6; Heb 9:15). See *WCF* 11.1; 11.3; 15.3; *WLC* 71; *BC* 22; *HC* 60.

3:25 God presented. Paul was careful to indicate that while Christ's death propitiated God's wrath by satisfying divine justice, it did not call forth God's love but was rather the fruit of it, as Paul would later emphasize (5:8; 8:32; cf. Jn 3:16). **a sacrifice of atonement.** See NIV text note. Jesus died as a propitiatory sacrifice (i.e., as a "sin offering"; 8:3) that quenched God's wrath. Since sin evokes God's wrath (1:18,24,32), the new status of justification can be bestowed only when that wrath has been fully expressed. See theological article "Definite Atonement" at John 10. **through faith.** The emphasis of verse 22 is repeated and thereby underscored. The word "through" indicates the means of being linked to the righteousness of Christ. Faith is the instrumental cause of justification. See *HC* 37.

3:26 to demonstrate his justice . . . just and the one who justifies. Paul and many of his readers were fully convinced of God's judicial righteousness (2:5; 3:5). But God's justice raised a serious problem in light of the role sin played in human history. How could God overlook human sin and remain just? Paul said that under the Mosaic sacrificial system, God exercised "forbearance" (v. 25) with sinners, as opposed to actual forgiveness. As the New Testament recognizes (Heb 9:11–15; 10:1–4), Old Testament animal sacrifices could not make sufficient atonement for the sins of humans. The real significance of these sacrifices lay in the way they pointed forward to Christ, through whom God would deal with human sin in an appropriate and final way. In view of what he would later do, God could righteously leave "the sins committed beforehand unpunished" (v. 25). Even so, a just God could not tolerate sin forever. So Christ came to make final atonement. The work of Christ reveals both the justice of God (God punished sin in the person of his own Son; 8:32) and the righteousness of God's way of salvation by "faith in Jesus." In this way, God did not compromise his own holiness but graciously provided salvation as a free gift to undeserving sinners—a salvation that human beings are incapable of accomplishing by their own efforts. In this respect, Paul saw the cross as the manifestation of the glorious wisdom of God (1Co 1:23–24). See *WCF* 8.5; 11.3.

3:27–29 See *WCF* 11.1; 11.2; *WLC* 70,73,101; *BC* 22.

3:27 Where, then, is boasting? No one, not even the Jews, has grounds for boasting (4:2–3). Indeed, boasting "is excluded" because faith alone (vv. 27–28,30), not human achievement, is the means by which God justifies sinners. That we may not even boast in our faith indicates that our faith itself is a gift from God (see theological article "Regeneration and New Birth" at Jn 3). See *WLC* 4.

3:30 there is only one God. Paul appealed to the fundamental confession of Old Testament religion: God is one (see Dt 6:4). The same God who dealt with Israel also deals with Gentiles, and he does so according to his own justice and mercy. There is only one way of salvation, both for Jews and for Gentiles. See *WCF* 7.6.

3:31 nullify the law . . . uphold the law. Paul anticipated an objection to his view. Although he rejected keeping the law on an individual basis as the way of salvation, he firmly based his doctrine of justification by faith alone on Christ's keeping of the law. Moreover, he argued for the law's continuing power to condemn those who are not in Christ. In so doing, he affirmed the law's continuing authority in both condemnation and salvation. Paul would never have accepted the Christian gospel if he could not have supported it with Old Testament teaching. See *WCF* 19.5.

■ **4:1–25** *Abraham's Example.* Paul supported his argument that justification is by grace through faith in Christ (3:22–26) by an appeal to the Old Testament narrative of the life of Abraham. As the spiritual father of the Jews (v. 1), Abraham provided a test case for Paul's thesis.

4:2–3 Contrary to the view that Abraham was considered righteous and sustained in covenant with God on the basis of his obedience and faithfulness, Paul demonstrated that the general statement in 3:27 was true of Abraham in particular. Abraham had nothing "to boast about," for Genesis 15:6 proves that it was by faith, not by keeping the law, that Abraham was justified. See *WCF* 7.6; 16.5; *BC* 22.

4:3–8 See *WCF* 11.1; *WLC* 70, 73; *BC* 22; *HC* 60.

4:4–5 credited to him as a gift. Paul focused on the word "credited," arguing that it meant for something to be given freely "as a gift." Wages are earned by work, not received "as a gift" (literally, "according to grace"). But Genesis 15:6 (see note on vv. 2–3) makes no mention of works on Abraham's part. It only mentions

ed, his faith is credited as righteousness. 6David says the same thing when he speaks of
the blessedness of the man to whom God credits righteousness apart from works:

7"Blessed are they
whose transgressions are forgiven,
whose sins are covered.
8Blessed is the man
whose sin the Lord will never count against him."[a][o]

9Is this blessedness only for the circumcised, or also for the uncircumcised?[p] We have
been saying that Abraham's faith was credited to him as righteousness.[q] 10Under what
circumstances was it credited? Was it after he was circumcised, or before? It was not after, but before! 11And he received the sign of circumcision, a seal of the righteousness
that he had by faith while he was still uncircumcised.[r] So then, he is the father[s] of all who
believe[t] but have not been circumcised, in order that righteousness might be credited
to them. 12And he is also the father of the circumcised who not only are circumcised but
who also walk in the footsteps of the faith that our father Abraham had before he was
circumcised.

13It was not through law that Abraham and his offspring received the promise[u] that
he would be heir of the world,[v] but through the righteousness that comes by faith. 14For
if those who live by law are heirs, faith has no value and the promise is worthless,[w] 15be-
cause law brings wrath.[x] And where there is no law there is no transgression.[y]

16Therefore, the promise comes by faith, so that it may be by grace[z] and may be guaranteed[a] to all Abraham's offspring—not only to those who are of the law but also to those
who are of the faith of Abraham. He is the father of us all. 17As it is written: "I have made
you a father of many nations."[b][b] He is our father in the sight of God, in whom he believed—
the God who gives life[c] to the dead and calls[d] things that are not[e] as though they were.
18Against all hope, Abraham in hope believed and so became the father of many na-

[a] *8* Psalm 32:1,2 [b] *17* Gen. 17:5

4:8 [o]Ps 32:1,2; 2Co 5:19
4:9 [p]Ro 3:30 [q]ver 3
4:11 [r]Ge 17:10,11 [s]ver 16,17; Lk 19:9 [t]Ro 3:22
4:13 [u]Gal 3:16,29 [v]Ge 17:4-6
4:14 [w]Gal 3:18
4:15 [x]Ro 7:7-25; 1Co 15:56; 2Co 3:7; Gal 3:10; Ro 7:12 [y]Ro 3:20; 7:7
4:16 [z]Ro 3:24 [a]Ro 15:8
4:17 [b]Ge 17:5 [c]Jn 5:21 [d]Isa 48:13 [e]1Co 1:28

the trust he had in God. Abraham contributed nothing to his own righteousness before God. In this sense, while faith involves human activity, it is not a human "work" (i.e., a meritorious contribution). Faith itself is a gift of God (3:27; see note on Eph 2:8; see also theological article "Regeneration and New Birth" at Jn 3). The righteousness of God was credited to Abraham (vv. 3,9), not earned by him. See *WCF* 16.5.

4:6–8 David . . . God credits . . . never count against him. Paul referred to Psalm 32:1–2 to show that David also agreed with the doctrine of justification by faith alone. Paul focused on the same Greek word translated "credit" (vv. 3–6) as it appears in Psalm 32:2 (in the Septuagint, the Greek translation of the OT), where it is translated "count." His basic point was that God credits righteousness apart from works. Blessedness, covenant fellowship with God together with all its accompaniments, and salvation are not earned but are the effects of the gift of forgiveness. We are justified only by the merit of Christ. Human merit of any sort is excluded. See *WLC* 70; *WSC* 33. See *WCF* 7.6, 16.5; *WLC* 77; *BC* 23.

4:9–12 Paul returned to drawing upon the life of Abraham by offering a response to an objection he anticipated: Even if righteousness came by grace through faith in the case of Abraham, had Paul forgotten that Abraham was the father of the circumcised (and therefore not of the uncircumcised)? The apostle responded that Genesis 15:6 describes Abraham *before* he was circumcised (v. 10). The righteousness signified and sealed for him by circumcision had already been credited to him when he was still uncircumcised, making Abraham the father of uncircumcised as well as circumcised believers. See *WCF* 7.5; 14.1; 27.1; 28.1; 28.4; 28.5; *WLC* 34,162,166,167,172,176; *BC* 33; *HC* 66.

4:13–15 not through law . . . law brings wrath. If the inheritance were dependent on obedience to the law, faith would have no place in the divine scheme of things, and the promise would be void, since the law cannot bring about the obedience it requires for its fulfillment. Only "where there is no law" is there "no transgression"; where there is law, it "brings wrath" (v. 15). Given the established truth of the sinfulness of all people (Ro 1–3), it is impossible that the promise could be received on the basis of keeping the law.

4:13 heir of the world. The Genesis record of Abraham's life does not explicitly state that Abraham would inherit the entire world. Paul probably summarized the promise to Abraham in this way for several reasons. (1) Abraham and his descendants were chosen to fulfill the original design of Adam and Eve, who were told to extend their service in Eden to the entire earth (Ge 1:26–29). (2) Abraham was promised innumerable offspring (Ge 15:5; 22:17). (3) Abraham was promised to be a blessing by extending his covenant blessing to all families of the earth (Ge 18:18; 22:18). (4) Abraham was promised to be a father of many nations (Ge 17:4–5). As Israel became a nation with a king, the vision of possessing the entire world became more prominent (e.g., Dt 2:25; Pss 22:27; 67:2; 117:1; Isa 52:10; Am 9:15–17). Christians also long for the day when they will reign with Christ in the glory of the new heavens and the new earth (Mt 5:5; Rev 22:5).

4:16–17 See *WCF* 7.6.

4:16 Therefore, the promise comes by faith. Because the promise of a great inheritance is received by faith, it is also "by grace" and "guaranteed to all Abraham's offspring." Had it been on the basis of works, the promise would have failed; had it been on the basis of circumcision, only Jews could have received it. Because it is by faith, and therefore by grace (by God's action, not humanity's), it can be "guaranteed" to come to Abraham's true spiritual offspring (i.e., to all believers, whether Jew or Gentile by birth).

4:17 As it is written. Again Paul appealed to Scripture (Ge 17:5) for confirmation of his exposition. It was already clear in Genesis that Abraham was to be not only the father of Jews (the circumcised), but also the spiritual patriarch of believers in many nations. It was not unbelievable that Gentiles should also receive the promise of God, for the One in whom Abraham believed "gives life to the dead." This was evidenced in the new life that came from the apparently dead womb of Sarah (v. 19), in the life that was given back to Isaac when he was under the sentence of death (Ge 22) and ultimately in the life restored in the resurrection of Christ (4:24–25). **calls things that are not as though they were.** This may refer to God's creation of the world out of nothing (see Ge 1; Isa 41:4; 48:13 for creation summoned into being by God's word) or to the birth of Isaac (in which a nation emerged from a barren womb). Perhaps this also alluded to the words of Hosea 1:10 and 2:23 (Ro 9:25–26).

4:18–25 See *WCF* 5.3; 7.6; 11.6; 14.3; *HC* 21,60.

4:18 Against all hope. Humanly speaking, believing that Sarah would bear his child (the first prerequisite to the realization of the promise) was futile for reasons given in verse 19. **in hope believed.** Trusting in God's power (v. 17), Abraham gained assurance that the promise would be fulfilled. Paul indicated that true faith is directed toward God and not people, toward the divine word and not toward the human situation.

tions,[f] just as it had been said to him, "So shall your offspring be."[a][g] 19Without weakening in his faith, he faced the fact that his body was as good as dead[h]—since he was about
a hundred years old[i]—and that Sarah's womb was also dead.[j] 20Yet he did not waver
through unbelief regarding the promise of God, but was strengthened in his faith and
gave glory to God,[k] 21being fully persuaded that God had power to do what he had promised.[l] 22This is why "it was credited to him as righteousness."[m] 23The words "it was credited to him" were written not for him alone, 24but also for us,[n] to whom God will credit
righteousness—for us who believe in him[o] who raised Jesus our Lord from the dead.[p]
25He was delivered over to death for our sins[q] and was raised to life for our justification.

Peace and Joy

5 Therefore, since we have been justified through faith,[r] we[b] have peace with God
through our Lord Jesus Christ, 2through whom we have gained access[s] by faith into
this grace in which we now stand.[t] And we[b] rejoice in the hope[u] of the glory of God. 3Not
only so, but we[b] also rejoice in our sufferings,[v] because we know that suffering produces perseverance;[w] 4perseverance, character; and character, hope. 5And hope[x] does not
disappoint us, because God has poured out his love into our hearts by the Holy Spirit,[y]
whom he has given us.
6You see, at just the right time,[z] when we were still powerless, Christ died for the ungodly.[a] 7Very rarely will anyone die for a righteous man, though for a good man someone might possibly dare to die. 8But God demonstrates his own love for us in this: While
we were still sinners, Christ died for us.[b]
9Since we have now been justified by his blood,[c] how much more shall we be saved
from God's wrath[d] through him! 10For if, when we were God's enemies,[e] we were reconciled[f] to him through the death of his Son, how much more, having been reconciled,
shall we be saved through his life![g] 11Not only is this so, but we also rejoice in God
through our Lord Jesus Christ, through whom we have now received reconciliation.

Death Through Adam, Life Through Christ

12Therefore, just as sin entered the world through one man,[h] and death through sin,[i]

4:18 [f]ver 17 [g]Ge 15:5 **4:19** [h]Heb 11:11,12 [i]Ge 17:17 [j]Ge 18:11 **4:20** [k]Mt 9:8 **4:21** [l]Ge 18:14; Heb 11:19 **4:22** [m]ver 3 **4:24** [n]Ro 15:4; 1Co 9:10; 10:11 [o]Ro 10:9 [p]Ac 2:24 **4:25** [q]Isa 53:5,6; Ro 5:6,8 **5:1** [r]Ro 3:28 **5:2** [s]Eph 2:18 [t]1Co 15:1 [u]Heb 3:6 **5:3** [v]Mt 5:12 [w]Jas 1:2,3 **5:5** [x]Php 1:20 [y]Ac 2:33 **5:6** [z]Gal 4:4 [a]Ro 4:25 **5:8** [b]Jn 15:13; 1Pe 3:18 **5:9** [c]Ro 3:25 [d]Ro 1:18 **5:10** [e]Ro 11:28; Col 1:21 [f]2Co 5:18,19; Col 1:20,22 [g]Ro 8:34 **5:12** [h]ver 15,16,17; 1Co 15:21,22 [i]Ge 2:17; 3:19; Ro 6:23

[a] *18* Gen. 15:5 [b] *1,2,3* Or *let us*

4:19 a hundred years old. See Genesis 17:1 and 17.

4:20 gave glory to God. Giving glory to God is a hallmark of faith, since faith is dependence on God's power and trust in his word of promise (v. 21). Abraham faithfully obeyed the standard of God's revealed attributes (cf. 1:20), and therefore God's glory was displayed in his life. It was by means of exercising this kind of faith that Abraham was justified (v. 22).

4:25 raised . . . for our justification. The proof of justification by faith in the example of Abraham led Paul back to the foundation of that justification in the work of Christ (3:24–26). Christ's death and resurrection are two aspects of the one saving event. In dying, Christ bore the legal penalty for our guilt. In rising from the dead, Christ was vindicated, and his move into new life brought about justification and new life for those who are joined to him by faith. Christ's resurrection is also critical to our justification because our justified status is maintained through his continuing intercessory work in heaven (see theological article "Ascension and Session of Jesus" at Heb 8). See *WCF* 11.4; *WLC* 38,52; *BC* 20,21; *HC* 45.

■ **5:1–11** *Benefits of Justification.* Paul expounded a number of benefits that come to those who are justified by faith. Instead of estrangement (3:10–17), there is peace (v. 1). In place of falling short of God's glory through sin (3:23), there is the hope of glory (v. 2). In lieu of suffering under judgment (2:5–6), there is joy in tribulation because of what God produces through it (v. 3). Rather than fearful uncertainty, there is assurance of God's love (vv. 6–8) and joy in him (v. 11).

5:1–2 See *WCF* 18.3; 20.1; *WLC* 55,83; *WSC* 36; *HC* 59.

5:1 we have peace. See NIV text note. While there is considerable manuscript support for "let us have," the flow of Paul's logic supports "we have." That "we have now received reconciliation" (v. 11) implies that we are already at peace with God. With peace established, we now have access to God's presence. See *WCF* 11.2; *HC* 21,90.

5:2 hope. In the New Testament, hope is the assurance that comes from knowing the certainty of our future salvation; it is not uncertain yearnings or wishful thinking. That this hope will not be frustrated is guaranteed here and now by the knowledge of the love of God that the Holy Spirit pours into believers' hearts (vv. 4–5). See *WCF* 12; 18.1.

5:3–5 See *WCF* 18.1; 18.3; *WLC* 83; *WSC* 36; *HC* 28,127; *CD* 3–4.VI.

5:4 character. The quality of being tested and approved. It confirms our confidence that the glory we hope for will one day be ours (8:17–25).

5:6 You see. The nature of this outpoured love (v. 5) is seen in the cross. There God acted "at just the right time" in the sense that the death of Jesus took place according to the immutable, foreordained divine timetable (Jn 17:1; Ac 2:23; Gal 4:4). See *WCF* 6.4; 9.3; *WLC* 25,72; *BC* 21.

5:8–11 Like 8:1–4,32, this passage highlights the qualities of particularity and effectiveness that Paul regularly ascribed to Christ's death. Christ died specifically "for us" (v. 8) who now believe and are justified through our faith, and his death actually achieved for us the "reconciliation" that "we have now received" (v. 11). See theological article "Definite Atonement" at John 10; see also *WCF* 11.3; *WLC* 71; *BC* 21,26; *CD* 5.III.

5:9 how much more. Paul argued from the greater to the lesser: If God has done for us the greater thing in the suffering and death (v. 10) of his Son, he will also do the lesser thing; that is, give us final salvation "through him [Christ]" and "through his life" (v. 10) as the resurrected, ascended Mediator. By following through with his initial purpose of love, God preserves for final salvation those who have already been justified. The decisive and more costly expression of this loving purpose was Christ's actual reconciling death, which guarantees the justification and glorification of those for whom he has died (8:32). See *BC* 21.

5:10–20 See *WCF* 7.2; *WLC* 22; *WSC* 18.

5:10 reconciled. Salvation as reconciliation appears in the Old Testament, especially in Hosea. Yet in the New Testament, Paul alone described the sin-bearing work of Christ as reconciliation (11:15; 2Co 5:18–20; Eph 2:16; Col 1:20,22). Our alienation from God is ended by the removal of the cause of alienation (our sin, guilt and condemnation) through the death of Christ (cf. 2Co 5:21). In this sense, reconciliation is objective (2Co 5:18–19). However, it must be "received" (v. 11; cf. 2Co 5:20) by the laying aside of our own alienation and hostility (i.e., by repentance and faith in Christ).

■ **5:12–21** *Christ: The New Adam.* Paul compared the sweeping significance of Adam's disobedience with that of Christ's obedience to God. This comparison relates to the preceding elaboration of the many benefits that come to those who are justified by faith in Christ (vv. 1–11). Although Adam's fall into sin affected all

and in this way death came to all men, because all sinned— 13 for before the law was giv-
en, sin was in the world. But sin is not taken into account when there is no law.[j] 14 Nevertheless, death reigned from the time of Adam to the time of Moses, even over those
who did not sin by breaking a command, as did Adam, who was a pattern of the one to
come.[k]
15 But the gift is not like the trespass. For if the many died by the trespass of the one
man,[l] how much more did God's grace and the gift that came by the grace of the one
man, Jesus Christ,[m] overflow to the many! 16 Again, the gift of God is not like the result
of the one man's sin: The judgment followed one sin and brought condemnation, but the
gift followed many trespasses and brought justification. 17 For if, by the trespass of the
one man, death[n] reigned through that one man, how much more will those who receive
God's abundant provision of grace and of the gift of righteousness reign in life through
the one man, Jesus Christ.
18 Consequently, just as the result of one trespass was condemnation for all men,[o] so
also the result of one act of righteousness was justification[p] that brings life for all men.
19 For just as through the disobedience of the one man[q] the many were made sinners, so
also through the obedience[r] of the one man the many will be made righteous.
20 The law was added so that the trespass might increase.[s] But where sin increased,
grace increased all the more,[t] 21 so that, just as sin reigned in death,[u] so also grace might
reign through righteousness to bring eternal life through Jesus Christ our Lord.

Dead to Sin, Alive in Christ

6 What shall we say, then? Shall we go on sinning so that grace may increase?[v] 2 By
no means! We died to sin;[w] how can we live in it any longer? 3 Or don't you know

5:13 [j]Ro 4:15
5:14 [k]1Co 15:22,45
5:15 [l]ver 12,18,19 [m]Ac 15:11
5:17 [n]ver 12
5:18 [o]ver 12 [p]Ro 4:25
5:19 [q]ver 12 [r]Php 2:8
5:20 [s]Ro 7:7,8; Gal 3:19 [t]1Ti 1:13,14
5:21 [u]ver 12,14
6:1 [v]ver 15; Ro 3:5,8
6:2 [w]Col 3:3,5; 1Pe 2:24

---

humanity, Paul particularly had in mind the effects of Adam's sin on those who are ultimately redeemed in Christ (cf. "we were God's enemies"; v. 10), both in the Old and New Testament eras.
5:12 just as. The beginning of a comparison that remains incomplete at this juncture. **through one man.** Paul's stress on the "one man" (Adam or Jesus) throughout the passage (vv. 12,15–17,19) indicates that he viewed both as historical individuals. In the case of Adam, the "one man" in this verse, Paul spoke of his "one sin" (v. 16), or the "one trespass" (v. 18) by which all "were made sinners" (i.e., the sinful condition was passed along to all humanity by virtue of each person's ultimate solidarity with Adam as his or her representative before God; v. 19). **death through sin.** Sin is the cause of death insofar as God punishes sin with death. The fact that all die demonstrates that all people sin. Even Jesus did not die until sin had been imputed to him (see note on 2Co 5:21). **all men.** This phrase has been traditionally understood as a reference to all humanity. This theological outlook is certainly correct, for all human beings fell under sin and death because of Adam. Nevertheless, in this context Paul's point in verses 12–21 may have been more limited. He asserted that all who are now in Christ (whether Jews or Gentiles) used to be in Adam but have been saved by Christ in the same way (i.e., through imputation; note the prominent use of "we" in vv. 1–11). In this context "all men" may mean either "every last one of us" or "all kinds of people" (cf. "all kinds of evil" at 1Ti 6:10, where "all kinds of" translates the single Greek word "all"), with specific reference being made to both Jews and Gentiles. **because all sinned.** Again, Paul's emphasis may have been that all those who are now believers were once counted among those who fell in Adam. The universal reign of death is the consequence of sin. Paul did not explain precisely how all of humanity was involved with Adam in his sinning, but simply assumed the fact. His outlook on Adam as the representative of humanity stemmed from the widespread Old Testament view that God chose to deal with people through representatives, such as ancestors (e.g., Adam, Noah, Abraham) or political leaders (e.g., Moses, David) whom he ordained as representatives of large numbers of people. See *WCF* 6.3; 15.4; 19.1; *WLC* 23,25,84; *WSC* 16,17,18; *BC* 14,15; *HC* 7,9,16; CD 3–4.I.
5:13 sin is not taken into account. Paul referred to a unique feature of the time between Adam and Moses. He did not mean that there was no personal sin for which people were held accountable during this period. Such an interpretation does not account for God's reactions to Cain (Ge 4:3–14) and the violence that had filled the earth (Ge 6:1–7). The basic principles of God's law have always been revealed to humanity (1:18–23). Nevertheless, prior to Moses the law of God was not codified or written in detail in ways that provided a clear, unified rule and guide for Israel as a nation. Paul argued that Adam's violation of the specific command in the garden (Ge 2:16–17) was similar to violations of specific commands from God through the Mosaic Law.
5:14 death reigned. Even during the time when there were very few explicit commands recorded in the Bible, death was still a universal occurrence, confirming that humanity was already sinful and sinning. **a pattern of the one to come.** Adam, the first man, was the divinely appointed representative head of the entire human race, and his sin forfeited righteousness for all those he represented. In the same way, God made Christ the representative head of a new humanity so that his obedience to death might gain their justification. All who believe ("all men" in v. 18; "the many" in vv. 15,19) were represented by Adam before coming to faith and receiving Christ's representation. Salvation in Christ reverses the effects of Adam's fall into sin (1Co 15:45–49; Heb 2:14–18). See *BC* 15.
5:15–21 See *WCF* 6.3; 11.1; *WLC* 31,70; *WSC* 33; *CD* 3–4.I.
5:15 But the gift is not like the trespass . . . how much more. Although the works of Adam and Christ resemble each other, the grace of Christ's work is greater than the sin, judgment and condemnation of Adam. Although it is true that all of humanity fell in Adam, this verse makes clear that Paul's emphasis is on those fallen individuals who have been redeemed in Christ ("the many"). See *HC* 16.
5:18–19 result . . . made sinners . . . made righteous. Paul returned to the main concern of his analogy: that there is a parallel between Adam and Christ in that condemnation and justification, respectively, are the direct fruits of their actions. Through (i.e., "on the basis of the actions of") "one man the many" are constituted either sinners or righteous. With Adam as their representative head, all those who are now believers (along with all humanity) sinned and fell when Adam sinned. With Christ as their representative head, all believers (the new humanity) are made "righteous" in Christ. See *WCF* 8.5; 11.3; 19.1; *WLC* 25,48,71; *WSC* 18; *HC* 7,9.
5:20 so that the trespass might increase. The specific, codified laws of Moses were added in the first place to guide Israel toward righteousness (Dt 6:24–25). Yet, in his infinite wisdom, God also ordained that knowledge of the law would actually increase sin in the lives of unbelievers. Awareness of its standards makes one more accountable to God (Lk 12:48) and stirs up contrary cravings in sinners' hearts (7:5,8). See theological article "The Three Uses of the Law" at Psalm 119. **grace increased all the more.** Humankind's sinfulness gave occasion to God to be even more gracious by forgiving people's sins, such that the grace expressed in Jesus' atonement outweighed the sinfulness of the new humanity (vv. 15–19). This is consistent with God's promise to Israel that even though his people would be punished with uprooting and deportation, God would show great mercy to the exiles by forgiving their sins, restoring them and blessing them more than ever before (Dt 30:1–6). The New Testament identifies Christ as the One who brings these supreme restoration blessings (including salvation) to the people of God.
■ **6:1—8:39** *Sanctification.* Having focused on justification by faith alone and on the benefits that come from Christ to those who believe, Paul turned to the Christian life, or the doctrine of sanctification. His discussion divides into three main parts: the destruc-

that all of us who were baptized[x] into Christ Jesus were baptized into his death? 4 We
were therefore buried with him through baptism into death in order that, just as Christ
was raised from the dead[y] through the glory of the Father, we too may live a new life.[z]
5 If we have been united with him like this in his death, we will certainly also be united with him in his resurrection.[a] 6 For we know that our old self[b] was crucified with him[c]
so that the body of sin[d] might be done away with,[a] that we should no longer be slaves
to sin— 7 because anyone who has died has been freed from sin.
8 Now if we died with Christ, we believe that we will also live with him. 9 For we know
that since Christ was raised from the dead,[e] he cannot die again; death no longer has
mastery over him.[f] 10 The death he died, he died to sin[g] once for all; but the life he lives,
he lives to God.
11 In the same way, count yourselves dead to sin[h] but alive to God in Christ Jesus.
12 Therefore do not let sin reign in your mortal body so that you obey its evil desires. 13 Do
not offer the parts of your body to sin, as instruments of wickedness,[i] but rather offer
yourselves to God, as those who have been brought from death to life; and offer the parts
of your body to him as instruments of righteousness.[j] 14 For sin shall not be your master,
because you are not under law,[k] but under grace.[l]

Slaves to Righteousness

15 What then? Shall we sin because we are not under law but under grace? By no
means! 16 Don't you know that when you offer yourselves to someone to obey him as
slaves, you are slaves to the one whom you obey—whether you are slaves to sin,[m] which
leads to death,[n] or to obedience, which leads to righteousness? 17 But thanks be to God[o]

6:3 [x]Mt 28:19
6:4 [y]Col 2:12 [z]Ro 7:6; Gal 6:15; Eph 4:22-24; Col 3:10
6:5 [a]2Co 4:10; Php 3:10,11
6:6 [b]Eph 4:22; Col 3:9 [c]Gal 2:20; Col 2:12, 20 [d]Ro 7:24
6:9 [e]Ac 2:24 [f]Rev 1:18
6:10 [g]ver 2
6:11 [h]ver 2
6:13 [i]ver 16,19; Ro 7:5 [j]Ro 12:1; 1Pe 2:24
6:14 [k]Gal 5:18 [l]Ro 3:24
6:16 [m]Jn 8:34; 2Pe 2:19 [n]ver 23
6:17 [o]Ro 1:8; 2Co 2:14

a 6 Or *be rendered powerless*

---

tion of sin's dominion (6:1–23), the continuing struggle with sin (7:1–25) and life in the Spirit (8:1–39).

■ **6:1–23** *Sin's Dominion Broken.* Paul concerned himself with the reality that sin remains present in the lives of believers. He explained that followers of Christ are to respond to this reality by understanding their union with Christ's death and resurrection (vv. 1–14) and by living as slaves of righteousness in him (vv. 15–23).

6:1–14 *Dead and Alive in Christ.* Paul's insistence that the increase of sin is met by the increase of grace (5:20) naturally raises the question, If sin causes grace to increase, why not sin more? Paul answered by asserting that continuing under sin's dominion contradicts the Christian's new identity in Christ.

6:1–11 See *WCF* 8.4; 13.1; 18.3; 26.1; 28.1; *WLC* 50,52,113,165,167; *WSC* 35,94; *HC* 43,45,69,70,79,88,90.

6:2 By no means! A standard phrase expressing shocked recoil and utter rejection of the idea (3:31; 6:15; 7:7,13; 9:14; 11:1,11). **We died to sin.** Believers have been united with Jesus Christ in both his death and his resurrection, so that in a spiritual and legal sense his death has become their death. As a result, believers are no longer under sin's dominion. See *BC* 29.

6:3–4 baptized into Christ . . . baptized into his death? Baptism, as the sign and seal of the new covenant, joins those who have saving faith to Christ. This union with Christ has many implications (see theological article "Union With Christ" at Gal 6), but here Paul concentrated on believers' union with Christ in his death and resurrection. Christ died with respect to sin and the curse of the law, and believers do the same. Just as Christ rose to new life, so believers rise to new life in him. See *WCF* 27.1; 28.1; *WLC* 162, 176; *BC* 34; *HC* 67,73.

6:6 we know that our old self was crucified with him. The "old self" (literally, "old man" or "old humanity") refers to Adam and to those individuals represented by him. Life in Adam is "old" for believers because they have been joined to Christ, the new man. Consequently, believers are no longer to identify themselves with Adam; that identity has been nailed to the cross. **body of sin.** The fallen material body is associated with sin because it is corrupted by sin and because the sinful life in Adam is lived in a corrupted body. Paul was not saying that the body itself is sinful. Elsewhere he taught that the corrupt body will one day be transformed into an incorruptible material body renewed by the Spirit (1Co 15:35–54). With imperishable material bodies believers will enjoy the splendor of life in the new (material) earth (Rev 21:1—22:5). **might be done away with.** Union with Christ in his death does not entirely eliminate the present corruption of the body, which will continue until Christ returns in glory. Yet already now that union ends the body's role as the place from which sin dominates believers. A Christian's body is now a member of the body of Christ (1Co 6:15), the temple of the Holy Spirit (1Co 6:19), dedicated to Christ and bearing holy fruit in his service (vv. 13,22; 7:4; 12:1). See *WCF* 13.1; *WLC* 75,77,167; *WSC* 35.

6:7 freed from sin. Literally, "justified." Paul personified sin as a monarch (5:21), as a general using various parts of the body as his weapons ("instruments"; v. 13) and as an employer who pays wages (v. 23). Deliverance from sin in this context means deliverance from the tyranny of sin, not deliverance from its presence or influence.

6:8 we will also live with him. This includes the idea of the final bodily resurrection, but even before Christ returns in glory, we experience the inward renewal of resurrection life (2Co 4:16; Eph 3:16). We become "alive to God" (v. 11).

6:11 count yourselves. Recognize, consider it true, realize that this (i.e., what has been said in vv. 1–10) is the truth about every believer. See *WLC* 167.

6:12–14 See *HC* 43.

6:12 do not let sin reign. Since the reign of sin has been broken, all attempts on sin's part to recover dominion can and must be resisted. The body (v. 13), once ruled by sinful desires, must no longer be yielded to them. See *WCF* 19.6.

6:13 offer yourselves to God. Just as believers once offered themselves fully to sin, they are now to offer themselves fully to God. A new master has taken charge. **as those who have been brought from death to life.** All this is to be done in conscious awareness, and as a deliberate expression, of our new identity in Christ. Because God was active and we were passive in this process ("have been brought"), we offer ourselves to God out of gratitude and joy for his blessings in Christ. See *HC* 2,86.

6:14 sin shall not be your master. This is a promise, not a command or an exhortation. **not under law, but under grace.** Paul did not mean that Christians have no moral obligations to the law of God (see theological article "The Three Uses of the Law" at Ps 119). On the contrary, believers are enabled by the Spirit of God to obey his law (8:1–2). In light of the context, "under law" means under the mastery and condemnation of sin as it is increased by the law in those who are "in Adam" (5:20; 6:20–23; 7:9–10). Believers are "under grace" in the sense that they are "in Christ," the One who brought the greater increase of God's grace in response to the increase of sin (5:15). They are thereby set free from the tyranny and condemnation of sin. See *WCF* 13.1; 13.3; 19.6; 20.1; *WLC* 75,77,97.

6:15–23 *Slaves to Righteousness.* That the Christian is not under law (in Adam) but under grace (in Christ) might appear to provide license for moral carelessness. Paul denied this. The reign of grace in Christ was designed to bring about righteous living. The freedom of grace is freedom from the mastery of sin and, therefore, freedom to obedience and service to God. It is not freedom to submit willingly to sin's mastery.

6:16–18 See *WCF* 10.1.

6:17 thanks be to God. While Paul did not hesitate to stress

that, though you used to be slaves to sin, you wholeheartedly obeyed the form of teaching[p] to which you were entrusted. [18]You have been set free from sin[q] and have become
slaves to righteousness.
[19]I put this in human terms[r] because you are weak in your natural selves. Just as you
used to offer the parts of your body in slavery to impurity and to ever-increasing wickedness, so now offer them in slavery to righteousness[s] leading to holiness. [20]When you
were slaves to sin,[t] you were free from the control of righteousness. [21]What benefit did
you reap at that time from the things you are now ashamed of? Those things result in
death![u] [22]But now that you have been set free from sin[v] and have become slaves to
God,[w] the benefit you reap leads to holiness, and the result is eternal life. [23]For the wages of sin is death,[x] but the gift of God is eternal life[y] in[a] Christ Jesus our Lord.

An Illustration From Marriage

7 Do you not know, brothers[z]—for I am speaking to men who know the law—that the
law has authority over a man only as long as he lives? [2]For example, by law a married woman is bound to her husband as long as he is alive, but if her husband dies, she
is released from the law of marriage.[a] [3]So then, if she marries another man while her
husband is still alive, she is called an adulteress. But if her husband dies, she is released
from that law and is not an adulteress, even though she marries another man.
[4]So, my brothers, you also died to the law[b] through the body of Christ,[c] that you
might belong to another, to him who was raised from the dead, in order that we might
bear fruit to God. [5]For when we were controlled by the sinful nature,[b] the sinful passions
aroused by the law[d] were at work in our bodies,[e] so that we bore fruit for death. [6]But
now, by dying to what once bound us, we have been released from the law so that we
serve in the new way of the Spirit, and not in the old way of the written code.[f]

Struggling With Sin

[7]What shall we say, then? Is the law sin? Certainly not! Indeed I would not have
known what sin was except through the law.[g] For I would not have known what coveting really was if the law had not said, "Do not covet."[c h] [8]But sin, seizing the opportunity afforded by the commandment,[i] produced in me every kind of covetous desire. For
apart from law, sin is dead.[j] [9]Once I was alive apart from law; but when the command-

6:17 [p]2Ti 1:13
6:18 [q]ver 7,22; Ro 8:2
6:19 [r]Ro 3:5 [s]ver 13
6:20 [t]ver 16
6:21 [u]ver 23
6:22 [v]ver 18 [w]1Co 7:22; 1Pe 2:16
6:23 [x]Ge 2:17; Ro 5:12; Gal 6:7,8; Jas 1:15 [y]Mt 25:46
7:1 [z]Ro 1:13
7:2 [a]1Co 7:39
7:4 [b]Ro 8:2; Gal 2:19 [c]Col 1:22
7:5 [d]Ro 7:7-11 [e]Ro 6:13
7:6 [f]Ro 2:29; 2Co 3:6
7:7 [g]Ro 3:20; 4:15 [h]Ex 20:17; Dt 5:21
7:8 [i]ver 11 [j]Ro 4:15; 1Co 15:56

[a] *23* Or *through* [b] *5* Or *the flesh*; also in verse 25 [c] *7* Exodus 20:17; Deut. 5:21

human activity in the Christian life ("offer yourselves" in v. 16; "obeyed" in v. 17), he gratefully traced all righteousness to the grace of God. **the form of teaching to which you were entrusted.** The antithesis of slavery to sin is commitment to the new lifestyle that grace produces. In view here are both the gospel and the kind of teaching given in chapters 12–16, perhaps with Christ himself as the model (cf. Eph 4:20–21). See *WLC* 155.

6:18 See note on verses 15–23. See *WCF* 9.4.

6:19 I put this in human terms because you are weak in your natural selves. The illustration of slavery is an inadequate representation of the Christian life, especially in the Roman context, because it connotes the harshness of human slavery and thus inadequately expresses the truth that Christ's yoke is easy (Mt 11:28–30). Nevertheless, Paul applied the metaphor, perhaps believing that the greater danger was that of failing to fulfill personal moral responsibility to the Lord.

6:21 See *WLC* 28.

6:22 set free . . . become slaves . . . holiness . . . eternal life. In these expressions Paul traced the whole process of a person's salvation. Through union with Christ we are set free from the judgment of the law and the tyranny of sin. We become slaves of righteousness because we have new lives in Christ. Our new lives lead to holiness of life, or sanctification. The final outcome of all this is the gift of eternal life. See *WCF* 9.4; 16.2; *WLC* 167.

6:23 wages . . . gift. Paul distinguished judgment (something we deserve) from salvation (something we receive entirely by grace). See *WCF* 6.6; 15.4; *WLC* 27,28,84; *WSC* 19; *CD* 1.1; 3–4.I.

■ **7:1–25** *Struggling With Sin.* Having laid the foundation of union with Christ's death and resurrection as the source of salvation, Paul wrote further about the believer's relationship with the law.

7:1–6 Paul expanded on the theme of the believer's relationship to the law. The main idea is that just as ordinary death alters legal relationships, death in Christ alters the believer's legal obligations. The penalty that the law exacts is death, but those who have died through union with Christ have already suffered this penalty. The law has already done its worst to them; it has no authority to condemn them further. In verses 2–3 this principle is illustrated from marriage. When one partner dies, the law governing the relationship ceases to apply and remarriage is not sin. In a similar way, believers' death in Christ breaks the chains of disobedience and death by which the law bound them in the flesh to condemnation in Adam (5:12–21). Now believers, raised to new life through union with Christ in his resurrection, are free to belong to Christ (free, in a sense, to marry another; v. 3) for the purpose of bearing fruit to God (v. 4). Life in Adam was life "controlled by the sinful nature" (v. 5). The word translated "sinful nature" or "flesh," refers to the compulsions of rebellious and corrupt hearts that the law constantly stimulates toward acts of sin. The offspring of that marriage was "death" (v. 5). But in Christ the old Adamic marriage to the law has ceased to exist; believers are no longer "under law" (6:14) but are "released" from it (v. 6). The new marriage, the believer's union with Christ, is an entry into a new life dominated by the Holy Spirit, who gives new power to fulfill the holy law of God. See theological article "The Three Uses of the Law" at Psalm 119. See *WCF* 6.5; 24.5.

7:3 not an adulteress. Remarriage after the death of a spouse is wholly consistent with the Christian gospel (1Ti 5:14).

7:4 body of Christ. Refers here to the physical death of Christ. **bear fruit.** The marriage metaphor is extended to the offspring of the marriage. See *WLC* 97.

7:6 what once bound us. Believers were once bound to the intermingled complex of Adam, sin, law, condemnation and death. See *WLC* 97.

7:7–25 See *HC* 3.

7:7–8 See *WCF* 6.5; *WLC* 148; *WSC* 81; *HC* 113.

7:7 Is the law sin? Paul's allusions to the law thus far have been negative in tone but narrowly focused. The negative function the law has played in fallen humanity's life is not a denigration of the law itself (note the vehement language in 3:31). The law, which brings us to know the reality of sin in our moral and spiritual system (3:20; 5:13,20), is itself "holy, righteous and good" (v. 12). See *WCF* 19.6; *WLC* 95; *HC* 115.

7:8 sin is dead. Those who do not know the particular commandments of the law sin less grievously than those who do (Lk 12:48). Also, because the law provides knowledge of more ways to sin and

ment came, sin sprang to life and I died. **10**I found that the very commandment that was
intended to bring life[k] actually brought death. **11**For sin, seizing the opportunity afforded by the commandment, deceived me,[l] and through the commandment put me to
death. **12**So then, the law is holy, and the commandment is holy, righteous and good.[m]
13Did that which is good, then, become death to me? By no means! But in order that
sin might be recognized as sin, it produced death in me through what was good, so that
through the commandment sin might become utterly sinful.
14We know that the law is spiritual; but I am unspiritual,[n] sold[o] as a slave to sin. **15**I
do not understand what I do. For what I want to do I do not do, but what I hate I do.[p]
16And if I do what I do not want to do, I agree that the law is good.[q] **17**As it is, it is no longer I myself who do it, but it is sin living in me.[r] **18**I know that nothing good lives in me,
that is, in my sinful nature.[a][s] For I have the desire to do what is good, but I cannot carry it out. **19**For what I do is not the good I want to do; no, the evil I do not want to do—
this I keep on doing.[t] **20**Now if I do what I do not want to do, it is no longer I who do it,
but it is sin living in me that does it.[u]
21So I find this law at work:[v] When I want to do good, evil is right there with me. **22**For
in my inner being[w] I delight in God's law;[x] **23**but I see another law at work in the members of my body, waging war[y] against the law of my mind and making me a prisoner of
the law of sin at work within my members. **24**What a wretched man I am! Who will rescue me from this body of death?[z] **25**Thanks be to God—through Jesus Christ our Lord!
So then, I myself in my mind am a slave to God's law, but in the sinful nature a slave
to the law of sin.

7:10 [k]Lev 18:5; Lk 10:26-28; Ro 10:5; Gal 3:12
7:11 [l]Ge 3:13
7:12 [m]1Ti 1:8
7:14 [n]1Co 3:1 [o]1Ki 21:20,25; 2Ki 17:17
7:15 [p]ver 19; Gal 5:17
7:16 [q]ver 12
7:17 [r]ver 20
7:18 [s]ver 25
7:19 [t]ver 15
7:20 [u]ver 17
7:21 [v]ver 23,25
7:22 [w]Eph 3:16 [x]Ps 1:2
7:23 [y]Gal 5:17; Jas 4:1; 1Pe 2:11
7:24 [z]Ro 6:6; 8:2

[a] 18 *Or my flesh*

because the sinful nature desires to sin, knowledge of the law produces more desires to sin. Nevertheless, although sin is less significant without the law, it is not absent.

7:9 I was alive apart from the law . . . I died. Not "alive" in the sense of possessing spiritual life (6:11), but "alive" in his own estimation. Knowing the law, which promised life for obedience (v. 10), made Paul realize that keeping its injunctions was required. Trying to obey the law made him realize that inwardly, in the desires of his heart (e.g., coveting [v. 8], the sin forbidden in the tenth commandment), he had been continually breaking the law before he realized that he was doing it, and when he saw what he was doing, he could not stop the cycle. Thus, Paul wrote that sin, the anti-God, anti-law driving force within him "deceived [him], and . . . put [him] to death" (v. 11; i.e., convinced him deep within that he was spiritually lifeless and lost). Paul offered his personal experience as an index of how sin and law relate in everyone. See *WCF* 19.6.

7:10 intended to bring life. See Leviticus 18:5 and Deuteronomy 30:15 and 19. In itself, the law marks out a path that guarantees God's favor and people's happiness. But where sin reigns, that path cannot be followed, so the law brings only misery and death.

7:11 sin . . . deceived me. Here, as elsewhere in Romans, the shadow of Eden emerges in Paul's language (Ge 3:13; cf. 2Co 11:3; 1Ti 2:14).

7:12 holy, righteous and good. The law reflects God's character ("holy"). It is the objective norm for humankind's covenantal response to God ("righteous"). And it is beneficial for human beings, who were created in the image of God ("good"). See *WCF* 2.2; 19.6; *WLC* 95,152.

7:13 Did that which is good, then, become death to me? Paul said that it was sin within him that became the cause of his spiritual death by leading him to break God's good law. Sin is thus seen to be "utterly sinful."

7:14–25 The sudden change to the present tense in verses 15–25, in contrast with the statements describing the past in verses 7–13, raises the question whether Paul was now describing his present experience. There are a variety of possible interpretations: (1) Paul was describing the experience of unregenerate people or perhaps of unbelieving Jews in particular. (2) Paul was describing a Christian in a weakened spiritual condition, one failing to draw on the indwelling Spirit's resources. (3) Paul was describing a transitional experience, possibly his own, of one who has been awakened to his or her true spiritual need but who has not yet entered the full relief of justification by grace. (4) Paul was describing, from a Christian point of view, the situation of godly people before the coming of Christ and Pentecost. (5) Paul was describing the normal condition of Christians in general, who, although they are "in Christ" and free from the condemnation of the law, do not yet perfectly fulfill the requirements of the law. The last view is the most probable interpretation and the one held by Augustine, Calvin, Luther and Melanchthon. It best accounts for Paul's shift to the present tense while his theme in verses 7–25 (God's holy law stimulating and exposing sin) continued, as well as for the presence in Paul's self-analysis here of elements found only in persons who have been united with the risen Christ to new life in the Spirit (6:4–11; 7:6; 8:4–9). Several factors reveal that this conflict was Paul's experience as a regenerate person: (1) Paul's awareness that God's law is "spiritual" in prescribing the very behavior that the Spirit prompts (v. 14); (2) Paul's delight in God's law and his desire to fulfill it fully (vv. 15–23); (3) Paul's distress that sin within him thwarted his purpose and his gratitude for the prospect of future deliverance from this frustration (v. 24; 8:23); and (4) Paul's distinction between his "mind" (which was aiming at obedience) and his "sinful nature" (which was still sinning). This profound conflict is inherent to life in Christ for every earthly believer: Christ dwells in believers (Gal 2:20), yet so does sin (vv. 17,20).

7:14–15 See *HC* 114.

7:14 the law is spiritual. A further description of the law (cf. v. 12). Far from repudiating the law (3:31), Paul declared that it is from the Holy Spirit. The law sets forth the standards (albeit specifically appropriate for Old Testament times) to which life governed by the Spirit should conform. **I am unspiritual, sold as a slave to sin.** "Unspiritual" is literally "fleshly." Because these expressions are usually reserved for unbelievers, some interpreters conclude that Paul was describing himself before his regeneration. But it is more likely that Paul simply acknowledged that even as a believer he had not fully escaped the effects of the fall. He still awaited the redemption of his flesh (8:23). See *WCF* 6.5; 19.6; *WLC* 99.

7:15 I do not understand. Paul was able to acknowledge, but not explain, the contrast between "I myself" and the "sin living in me" (vv. 17,20). There was a real and bewildering conflict between the energies of sin and of grace in his life. Even so, he knew that, while sin still accompanied his new identity in Christ in this life, his new identity would one day result in the final triumph over indwelling sin (6:2–14). See *WCF* 9.4; 16.5; *BC* 29.

7:17–19 See *WCF* 6.4; 6.5; 9.4; 13.2; 16.5; *WLC* 78,149,192; *BC* 15,18.

7:21–25 See *WCF* 19.6; *WLC* 97,195; *HC* 5,56,114,115.

7:21–23 Two laws or driving forces—the flesh and the Spirit—operate within the believer. The regenerate self, through the enabling of the Holy Spirit, loves God's law and is devoted to it; but in this present existence, the powerful force of indwelling sin continues to operate, keeping the believer from fulfilling his or her desire for undiluted obedience (Gal 5:17). See *WCF* 6.5; 9.4; 13.2; 13.3; *WLC* 78; *HC* 60,127.

7:24 Who will rescue me . . . ? This is not a cry of despair, for Paul knew and provided the answer in verse 25. **body of death.** The fallen physical body, viewed as the means by which sin is expressed. Paul's desire was not for disembodiment, as if material existence were itself evil. Instead, he was longing for the deliverance in Christ that would one day ultimately result in a glorious, resurrected body (8:23; 2Co 5:2–4; Php 3:20). See *WCF* 19.6.

7:25 So then . . . sin. Paul summarized the state of frustration he

Life Through the Spirit

8 Therefore, there is now no condemnation[a] for those who are in Christ Jesus,[a][b] **2**because through Christ Jesus the law of the Spirit of life[c] set me free[d] from the law of
sin[e] and death. **3**For what the law was powerless[f] to do in that it was weakened by the
sinful nature,[b] God did by sending his own Son in the likeness of sinful man[g] to be a sin
offering.[c][h] And so he condemned sin in sinful man,[d] **4**in order that the righteous requirements of the law might be fully met in us, who do not live according to the sinful nature
but according to the Spirit.[i]
5Those who live according to the sinful nature have their minds set on what that nature desires;[j] but those who live in accordance with the Spirit have their minds set on
what the Spirit desires.[k] **6**The mind of sinful man[e] is death, but the mind controlled by
the Spirit is life[l] and peace; **7**the sinful mind[f] is hostile to God.[m] It does not submit to
God's law, nor can it do so. **8**Those controlled by the sinful nature cannot please God.
9You, however, are controlled not by the sinful nature but by the Spirit, if the Spirit
of God lives in you.[n] And if anyone does not have the Spirit of Christ,[o] he does not belong to Christ. **10**But if Christ is in you,[p] your body is dead because of sin, yet your spirit is alive because of righteousness. **11**And if the Spirit of him who raised Jesus from the
dead[q] is living in you, he who raised Christ from the dead will also give life to your mortal bodies[r] through his Spirit, who lives in you.
12Therefore, brothers, we have an obligation—but it is not to the sinful nature, to live

a *1* Some later manuscripts *Jesus, who do not live according to the sinful nature but according to the Spirit,*
b *3* Or *the flesh*; also in verses 4, 5, 8, 9, 12 and 13 c *3* Or *man, for sin* d *3* Or *in the flesh*
e *6* Or *mind set on the flesh* f *7* Or *the mind set on the flesh*

8:1 [a]ver 34 [b]ver 39; Ro 16:3
8:2 [c]1Co 15:45 [d]Ro 6:18 [e]Ro 7:4
8:3 [f]Ac 13:39; Heb 7:18 [g]Php 2:7 [h]Heb 2:14,17
8:4 [i]Gal 5:16
8:5 [j]Gal 5:19-21 [k]Gal 5:22-25
8:6 [l]Gal 6:8
8:7 [m]Jas 4:4
8:9 [n]1Co 6:19; Gal 4:6 [o]Jn 14:17; 1Jn 4:13
8:10 [p]Gal 2:20; Eph 3:17; Col 1:27
8:11 [q]Ac 2:24 [r]Jn 5:21

---

had been describing since verse 14. **I myself.** This means "I, one and the same person." Paul totally approved of God's good law, yet sin still remained in him. See *WCF* 6.5; 19.6.

▪ **8:1–39** *Living by the Spirit.* Having acknowledged the remarkable new life believers have in Christ (6:1–23), as well as the practical reality of struggle with remaining sin (7:1–25), Paul offered the encouragement of describing the Christian life that is led by the Spirit.

8:1–17 See *HC* 1.

8:1–4 See *WCF* 19.6; *WLC* 97; *HC* 12,36,37,40,56.

8:1 Therefore. The apostle's concern here was pastoral. Paul was telling his readers, "In light of the foregoing reminder of your continuing sinfulness, you must now recall these things." **no condemnation.** Probably in both senses: the issuing of judgment and the carrying out of the sentence. See *WCF* 15.4; 18.3; 19.6; 20.1; *WLC* 97; *WSC* 35; *BC* 22; *HC* 126.

8:2 the law of the Spirit of life . . . the law of sin and death. It is possible that Paul used the term "law" here to mean "principle" as in 7:21–23. In light of verse 3, it is also possible that he had in mind the law of God. In this understanding, Paul contrasted the law of God operating within two frameworks or contexts: (1) the "law of the Spirit of life," meaning the law functioning in ("through") Christ, empowered by the Spirit and leading to life, and (2) the "law of sin and death," meaning the law, functioning in Adam, misused by sin and resulting in death. See *WCF* 10.1.

8:3 the law was powerless . . . weakened. Paul described further the law weakened by sin. He did not criticize the moral law itself but noted that because of people's sin, the law cannot bring salvation. **in the likeness of sinful man.** Literally, "in the likeness of sinful flesh." The word "likeness" (Greek, *homoioma;* 1:23; 5:14; 6:5; Php 2:7) suggests similarity to a prototype. "Sinful man" (literally, "sinful flesh") means human nature, which through the fall came to be corrupted and controlled by sin. Jesus' humanity was like ours in that he could be tempted. He lived his life as a part of a fallen world full of frailty and was exposed to vast pressures. But he did not sin, and there was no moral or spiritual corruption in him, so the likeness was only partial. Had Jesus been corrupted by sin in any way, he could not have fulfilled the Old Testament pattern that required a sin offering to be "without defect" (Lev 4:3). **condemned sin in sinful man.** Literally, "condemned sin in the flesh." Paul seems to have meant that in the crucifixion of the incarnate Son of God, sin was judged and condemned, so that now all its claims of our condemnation have become invalid. Consequently there is no condemnation remaining for those who are in Christ. See *WCF* 7.3; *WLC* 94; *BC* 20.

8:4–8 Paul's contrast between the old pattern of life and the new, between life in the flesh and that in the Spirit (7:6), is now worked out in detail in terms of two settled attitudes or mind-sets: one under the influence of the sinful nature, the other under the influence of Christ through the Spirit within believers. See *WLC* 25; *BC* 14.

8:4–5 the sinful nature . . . the Spirit. Believers are enabled to obey God, but only when they live according to the Holy Spirit by seeking and following his ministry to them. When we seek to obey God through fleshly means, we fail. Unbelievers, who do not have the Spirit, are ruled by the sinful nature and always fail to obey God. Although some of their actions conform outwardly to God's standards (cf. Mt 7:9-11), their hatred for God corrupts their motivation (v. 7), making all their actions sinful at the core.

8:4 in order that. Christ accomplished salvation for his people for the purpose of enabling believers to meet the requirements of the law. Paul's earlier discussion (chs. 6–7) makes it plain that he did not expect perfection prior to Christ's return.

8:7 hostile to God. Literally, "enmity toward God." The mindset of everyone not renewed by the Spirit is pure hostility against God (3:9–18). **does not . . . nor can it.** Human nature is so corrupt apart from Christ that not only do we refuse to serve God, but we are unable to do so. See *WCF* 6.4; 9.3; 10.2; *WLC* 192; *HC* 5.

8:8 See *WLC* 149.

8:9–11 Christians are not dominated by the sinful nature (the "flesh") in Adam but are under the rule of Christ, because the Spirit who dwells in them is the Spirit of Christ. Although death as a bodily experience continues, life prevails because those united with Christ live in the sphere of the Spirit. The duality in view here is not simply the distinction between the physical and spiritual aspects of the believer's existence, but the distinction between two spheres of existence: bodily existence in a fallen world, with its inevitable physical death, and life in the Spirit. See *WCF* 8.8; 10.3; *BC* 9,11,26.

8:10 your spirit is alive. Literally, "the spirit is life." The term "spirit" is somewhat ambiguous. It may refer to the quickened spirit of the believer, in contrast to the believer's body, which is subject to death. Alternatively, it may refer to the Holy Spirit, indicating that the corruptible body in Adam is dead but that the Spirit of God brings life. The Spirit's close association with Christ is also highlighted here. The indwelling "Spirit of God" is the "Spirit of Christ" (v. 9), and the indwelling of the Spirit is the means whereby "Christ is in you" (v. 10). Paul viewed this relationship as being so close that he could even say, "the Lord is the Spirit" (2Co 3:17; cf. 1Co 15:45). These passages do not imply that Christ and the Spirit lose their distinctive, personal identities. Rather, Christ and the Spirit function together in applying the resurrected life to believers. The Spirit's presence now is a guarantee of the future bodily resurrection of the believer (v. 11).

8:11 give life to your mortal bodies. Here Paul made it plain that the goal of salvation in Christ is not release from but renewal of the physical body. See *HC* 45.

8:12–13 See *HC* 89.

8:12 Therefore . . . an obligation. Because life comes from the Spirit and death from the sinful nature (the flesh), believers have a responsibility to live in opposition to the sinful nature. See *WCF* 18.3.

according to it. 13For if you live according to the sinful nature, you will die; but if by the
Spirit you put to death the misdeeds of the body, you will live,[s] 14because those who are
led by the Spirit of God[t] are sons of God.[u] 15For you did not receive a spirit that makes
you a slave again to fear,[v] but you received the Spirit of sonship.[a] And by him we cry,
"*Abba*,[b] Father."[w] 16The Spirit himself testifies with our spirit[x] that we are God's children.
17Now if we are children, then we are heirs[y]—heirs of God and co-heirs with Christ, if
indeed we share in his sufferings in order that we may also share in his glory.[z]

[a] 15 Or *adoption* [b] 15 Aramaic for *Father*

8:13 [s]Gal 6:8
8:14 [t]Gal 5:18 [u]Jn 1:12; Rev 21:7
8:15 [v]2Ti 1:7; Heb 2:15 [w]Mk 14:36; Gal 4:5,6
8:16 [x]Eph 1:13
8:17 [y]Ac 20:32; Gal 4:7 [z]1Pe 4:13

8:13 put to death the misdeeds of the body. The body is not evil in and of itself (see note on v. 11), but it is through our corrupt bodies that sin comes to expression, and such expressions must be put to death (i.e., terminated; 6:12–13; 12:1). See *WCF* 13.1.
8:14–17 See *WCF* 18.2; 20.1; *HC* 1,26,33; *CD* 5.10.
8:14 led by the Spirit . . . sons of God. The Holy Spirit not only enables, but also leads believers. The association between being "led" and being "sons" is derived from the conjunction of these two concepts in Israel's exodus. The Israelites were tested in the wilderness to prove their sonship by following God's leading (Dt 8:2,15; 29:5). Those who followed proved to be sons. In the New Testament the same is true of the visible church. Believers are called to prove their sonship by following the leading of the Spirit. If they do not follow, they show themselves not to be sons. See *WCF* 8.8.
8:15 Spirit of sonship. Christians have received the Spirit of adopted sonship. In addition to justification and freedom from condemnation (v. 1), believers are accepted into the family of God and inwardly persuaded by the Spirit that they belong there. The cry of the believer, "*Abba*, Father" (the intimate Aramaic word *Abba* was used by Jesus himself for God; Mk 14:36), indicates the vividness with which union with Christ was realized in the experience of the New Testament church. The cry is an expression of an assured awareness of sonship. The idea of adoption does not appear in the Old Testament legal system; Paul seems to have borrowed this apt concept from Roman law, developing it further with the Biblical theology of God's fatherhood over his people. See *WCF* 12; *WLC* 189; *WSC* 100.
8:16 It is through the cry, "*Abba*, Father," that the joint witness to our sonship (given by our own spirit and the Holy Spirit) surfaces (Gal 4:6). See *WLC* 80.
8:17–21 As all the other children in a human family are heirs of

Predestination and Foreknowledge: Are People Predestined to Heaven and Hell?

THE word *predestination* is a translation of the Greek term *proorizo*, which appears six times in the New Testament (Ac 4:28; Ro 8:29–30; 1Co 2:7; Eph 1:5,11). In some instances, it refers to God's foreordination of all the events of world history (Ac 4:28; 1Co 2:7). In others, it refers to God's decision, made before the world existed, regarding the final destiny of individual sinners—specifically of those chosen for salvation and eternal life (Ro 8:29–30; Eph 1:5,11), as opposed to those who will ultimately be condemned to eternal judgment. Many have pointed out, however, that Scripture also ascribes to God an advance decision about those who in the final analysis are not saved (Ro 9:6–29; 1Pe 2:8; Jude 4). Moreover, by predestining only some to salvation, God necessarily consigns the remainder to destruction. In light of these facts, it has become common in many circles to define God's predestination as including both his decision to save some from sin (election) and his decision to condemn the rest for their sin (reprobation).

It is difficult to deny utterly that the Scriptures teach some sort of predestination of people to salvation, since the Greek term *proorizo* does appear in Scripture (see above). Nevertheless, Christian traditions differ over the basis upon which God determined to predestine some, but not others, to eternal life. A number of branches of the church speak of predestination (or election) on the basis of God's foreknowledge of faith in certain individuals. They suppose that God knew beforehand that certain people would freely choose Christ as their Savior once they had heard the gospel, and conclude that on this basis God then predestined them to salvation. In this sense, *foreknowledge* is passive foresight on God's part of what individuals will chose of their own free will without God compelling them. God then predetermines people's destinies, responding to what he has seen will take place.

Reformed theologians, however, point out that the Greek word *proginōskō*, translated "foreknew" in Romans 8:29 and 11:2, means "foreloved" and "foreacknowledged" (cf. 1Pe 1:20, where *proginōskō* is rendered "chosen before"). Passages such as the above make it clear that *proginōskō* expresses foreknowledge of a person, not foreknowledge of mere facts about the future or a person's life choices. In effect, the New Testament teaches that God has elected on the basis of his forelove and affection for those to whom he gives eternal life.

Besides, since all people are naturally dead in sin (i.e., cut off from the life of God and unresponsive to him), no one who hears the gospel will ever come to repentance and faith without the inner quickening that only God can impart (Eph 2:4–10). Jesus said, "no one can come to me unless the Father has enabled him" (Jn 6:65; cf. Jn 6:44; 10:25–28). If God looks into the future to see what choices we will make on our own, then he sees only our firm rejection of the gospel. Sinners choose Christ only because God chose them for this choice and moved them to it by renewing their hearts.

The doctrine of predestination may be abused to support various forms of fatalism. Yet this is not the purpose for which Scripture teaches it. Indeed, Scripture repudiates fatalism by teaching that our choices and decisions are important, for they have been foreordained as God's means to accomplish his purposes (e.g., Php 2:12–13). Rather than encouraging fatalism, Scripture teaches predestination to give believers confidence that since they are in Christ, they may be sure that they are predestined to eternal life. Predestination assures us who are saved of the faithfulness of God and the certainty of our eternal destiny in Christ. We need not fear; no one can snatch us from his hand (Jn 10:28). See *WCF* 3; 10; *BC* 16; *CD* 1.

8:18 [a]2Co 4:17; 1Pe 4:13
8:20 [b]Ge 3:17-19
8:21 [c]Ac 3:21; 2Pe 3:13; Rev 21:1
8:22 [d]Jer 12:4
8:23 [e]2Co 5:5 [f]2Co 5:2, 4 [g]Gal 5:5
8:24 [h]1Th 5:8
8:26 [i]Eph 6:18
8:27 [j]Rev 2:23
8:28 [k]1Co 1:9; 2Ti 1:9
8:29 [l]Ro 11:2 [m]Eph 1:5, 11 [n]1Co 15:49; 2Co 3:18; Php 3:21; 1Jn 3:2
8:30 [o]Eph 1:5,11 [p]1Co 6:11 [q]Ro 9:23
8:31 [r]Ro 4:1 [s]Ps 118:6

Future Glory

18 I consider that our present sufferings are not worth comparing with the glory that
will be revealed in us.[a] 19 The creation waits in eager expectation for the sons of God to
be revealed. 20 For the creation was subjected to frustration, not by its own choice, but
by the will of the one who subjected it,[b] in hope 21 that[a] the creation itself will be liberated from its bondage to decay[c] and brought into the glorious freedom of the children
of God.
22 We know that the whole creation has been groaning[d] as in the pains of childbirth
right up to the present time. 23 Not only so, but we ourselves, who have the firstfruits of
the Spirit,[e] groan[f] inwardly as we wait eagerly[g] for our adoption as sons, the redemption of our bodies. 24 For in this hope we were saved.[h] But hope that is seen is no hope
at all. Who hopes for what he already has? 25 But if we hope for what we do not yet have,
we wait for it patiently.
26 In the same way, the Spirit helps us in our weakness. We do not know what we
ought to pray for, but the Spirit himself intercedes for us[i] with groans that words cannot express. 27 And he who searches our hearts[j] knows the mind of the Spirit, because
the Spirit intercedes for the saints in accordance with God's will.

More Than Conquerors

28 And we know that in all things God works for the good of those who love him,[b] who[c]
have been called[k] according to his purpose. 29 For those God foreknew[l] he also predestined[m] to be conformed to the likeness of his Son,[n] that he might be the firstborn
among many brothers. 30 And those he predestined,[o] he also called; those he called, he
also justified;[p] those he justified, he also glorified.[q]
31 What, then, shall we say in response to this?[r] If God is for us, who can be against us?[s]

[a] *20,21* Or *subjected it in hope.* [21]*For* [b] *28* Some manuscripts *And we know that all things work together for good to those who love God* [c] *28* Or *works together with those who love him to bring about what is good—with those who*

---

their father along with the oldest brother, so believers are God's heirs in and with Christ. But the receiving of the inheritance that comes to us in Christ involves sharing in his suffering, the pathway to our sharing in his "glory" (2Co 4:17). **glory.** The transforming, ennobling, joy-inducing manifestation of God in one's personal being (cf. v. 30). The glory yet to be revealed involves the sons of God being revealed in their true nature (v. 19) and the liberating of creation from its present state of imperfection and decay (vv. 20–21). The revelation of this glory will more than wipe out all the harm and loss ("frustration"; v. 20) that the created order suffered as a result of Adam's fall (Ge 3:17). The regeneration of all things (Mt 19:28; Ac 3:21; Rev 21:1) in the created order corresponds to the freedom in glory (vv. 17–18) enjoyed by the children of God and is its direct fruit. See *WCF* 12; 16.5; *WLC* 74; *WSC* 34.

8:20–22 See *WCF* 6.6; *WLC* 193.

8:22–25 The present condition of creation is not final but is akin to the pain of a mother groaning in labor pains. The entire creation possesses an eschatological destiny, and it groans for its fulfillment, as believers and the Spirit also do (vv. 23,26). Our salvation has begun—we have the Spirit as its firstfruits—but it will not be consummated until the final resurrection of our bodies (the full realization of our adoption in Christ; v. 23) at the end of time. Inevitably, therefore, the Christian life involves patient waiting in hope. See *WCF* 33.3; *HC* 52,123.

8:23 our adoption as sons, the redemption of our bodies. Full sonship means full reception of our inheritance. We will receive our full inheritance in Christ only when our bodies are redeemed. At that time, the whole creation will be renewed, and we will reign over it with Christ (Rev 21:1–5; 22:5). See *WLC* 86.

8:24 in this hope we were saved. Life for the believer, with its pain and grief over how things are (7:24–25; 8:18,36), is still permeated with expectation, patience (v. 25) and eagerness (v. 23), not with disappointment and frustration (5:5).

8:26–27 See *WLC* 179,182; *HC* 117.

8:26 In the same way. The Spirit strengthens us in our state of weakness, of which we are continuously conscious. Perplexity as to how to pray for oneself is a universal Christian experience, especially in times of despair and confusion. Even when we cannot articulate our longings, the Spirit helps us by interceding for us in our hearts, making requests that the Father will certainly answer. See *WCF* 21.3; *WLC* 178.

8:28–39 See *WCF* 3.6; *HC* 54.

8:28 And we know. The Christian assesses the present in the light of his or her assurance about the future. As "true Israelites," in whom the first and great commandment is fulfilled (Mt 22:37–38), our love for God is evoked by knowledge of his love for us (5:5–8). **called.** Brought to faith (v. 30; cf. 1:6). **according to his purpose.** The purpose of God guarantees "good" for his people in terms of the divine definition of good (i.e., conformity to Christ; vv. 17–23,29). God's providence rules in such a way as to ensure that in everything that happens to us he is working for our ultimate good. See *WCF* 5.7; 20.1; *WLC* 45; *HC* 1,26.

8:29 foreknew . . . predestined. Verses 29–30 explain God's "purpose" (v. 28), showing it to be a plan of sovereign, saving grace that entitles all who believe to trace their faith and salvation back to an eternal decision by God to bring them to glory, as well as to look forward to that glory as a guaranteed certainty. The destiny appointed for believers (conformity to Christ and glorification with him) flows from divine foreknowledge. The foreknowledge Paul mentions is of persons, not of facts or events; it refers to God's own initiative in choosing the objects of his active, saving love. *Knowing* here implies intimate personal relationship, not mere intellectual knowledge about something or someone. For example, the word *know* is translated in the Old Testament as "lay with" (Ge 4:1) and *known* as "chosen" (Am 3:2); in the New Testament *knowing* also refers to sexual union (Mt 1:25). It is virtually the equivalent of "election." See *BC* 16,22.

8:30 Those predestined are, in due time, "called" (i.e., summoned through the gospel into saving fellowship with Christ; 1:6; cf. 1Co 1:9). Note that all of those "called" are also "justified." This is not to the outward call of the gospel that many reject but the inward movement of the Holy Spirit that brings to pass what God intends. Since all those who are predestined are so called, we see that predestination involves divine determination beforehand that their destiny is to include effectual calling. Predestination is not based upon foreknowledge of a person's response to the gospel (see note on v. 29). Just as calling results from predestination, so the result of calling is justification and, subsequently, glorification. The past tense of "glorified" indicates that, from God's standpoint, the work is as good as done. He will complete it as planned. See theological article "Perseverance of Believers" at Philippians 1. See also *WCF* 3.5; 3.6; 10.1; 11.1; 11.4; *WLC* 69; *WSC* 32; *CD* 1.7; 1.II; 1.VI.

8:31–39 Paul drew the entire argument of 1:16—8:39 to a triumphal conclusion in a series of challenges to every influence that might thwart the church's confident assurance of present preservation and future glory. The passage is reminiscent of the third servant song in Isaiah 50:4–9, on which it in part depends. See *WCF* 17.2; *WLC* 55,77; *HC* 26,121; *CD* 2.VII; 5.I.

32 He who did not spare his own Son,[t] but gave him up for us all—how will he not also,
along with him, graciously give us all things? 33 Who will bring any charge[u] against those
whom God has chosen? It is God who justifies. 34 Who is he that condemns? Christ Jesus,
who died[v]—more than that, who was raised to life—is at the right hand of God[w] and is
also interceding for us.[x] 35 Who shall separate us from the love of Christ? Shall trouble or
hardship or persecution or famine or nakedness or danger or sword?[y] 36 As it is written:

> "For your sake we face death all day long;
> we are considered as sheep to be slaughtered."[a][z]

37 No, in all these things we are more than conquerors[a] through him who loved us.[b]
38 For I am convinced that neither death nor life, neither angels nor demons,[b] neither
the present nor the future, nor any powers,[c] 39 neither height nor depth, nor anything
else in all creation, will be able to separate us from the love of God[d] that is in Christ
Jesus our Lord.

God's Sovereign Choice

9 I speak the truth in Christ—I am not lying,[e] my conscience confirms[f] it in the Holy
Spirit— 2 I have great sorrow and unceasing anguish in my heart. 3 For I could wish
that I myself[g] were cursed[h] and cut off from Christ for the sake of my brothers, those of
my own race,[i] 4 the people of Israel. Theirs is the adoption as sons;[j] theirs the divine glory, the covenants,[k] the receiving of the law,[l] the temple worship[m] and the promises.[n]
5 Theirs are the patriarchs, and from them is traced the human ancestry of Christ,[o] who
is God over all,[p] forever praised![c][q] Amen.
6 It is not as though God's word had failed. For not all who are descended from Isra-

8:32 [t]Jn 3:16; Ro 4:25; 5:8
8:33 [u]Isa 50:8,9
8:34 [v]Ro 5:6-8 [w]Mk 16:19 [x]Heb 7:25; 9:24; 1Jn 2:1
8:35 [y]1Co 4:11
8:36 [z]Ps 44:22; 2Co 4:11
8:37 [a]1Co 15:57 [b]Gal 2:20; Rev 1:5; 3:9
8:38 [c]Eph 1:21; 1Pe 3:22
8:39 [d]Ro 5:8
9:1 [e]2Co 11:10; Gal 1:20; 1Ti 2:7 [f]Ro 1:9
9:3 [g]Ex 32:32 [h]1Co 12:3; 16:22 [i]Ro 11:14
9:4 [j]Ex 4:22 [k]Ge 17:2; Ac 3:25; Eph 2:12 [l]Ps 147:19 [m]Heb 9:1 [n]Ac 13:32
9:5 [o]Mt 1:1-16 [p]Jn 1:1 [q]Ro 1:25

a 36 Psalm 44:22 b 38 Or *nor heavenly rulers* c 5 Or *Christ, who is over all. God be forever praised!* Or *Christ. God who is over all be forever praised!*

8:31 What, then, shall we say in response to this? Verses 28–30 may be primarily in view here, but they should not be separated from 1:16—8:27, and especially 8:1–27. "This" embraces the whole display of free grace to lost sinners as expressed in the letter thus far. **who can be against us?** There will certainly be opposition, but Paul's point is that opposition lacks the ability to destroy faith. Since "God is for us" (i.e., on our side), victorious spiritual survival is assured. "For us" expresses the eternal commitment of almighty love that is spelled out in verses 38–39.

8:32 He who did not spare his own Son. Paul's language echoes the Septuagint (the Greek translation of the OT) rendering of Genesis 22:12 in an evocative manner. **gave him up.** The Greek word here translated "gave him up" is used elsewhere of active participation in the judicial condemnation of Christ (Mt 20:19; 26:15–16; 27:2,18,26; cf. Isa 53:6,10). **for us all.** Even for the worst of us who now believe (3:9–18; 5:6–8). Once more, as in 5:9–10, Paul reasoned from the greater to the lesser: For God to give his Son to die for us was the supreme gift, guaranteeing the subsequent gift of everything else that we need for our full and final glory (v. 30). See *WCF* 11.3; *WLC* 71; *BC* 20,21,35; *HC* 55.

8:33 It is God who justifies. The Judge has already dealt with all charges against us in the death and resurrection of Christ (4:25). Self-justification is futile. See *WCF* 3.8; *BC* 22; *CD* 1.VII.

8:34 at the right hand of God. The position of honor and executive authority (cf. Ps 110:1). There can be no condemnation for us (in either sense of the term; see note on v. 1) if our enthroned sin-bearer intercedes for us in heaven (1Jn 2:1) and the Spirit intercedes in our hearts (v. 27). See *WCF* 8.4; 8.8; *WLC* 52,54; *BC* 26; *HC* 31,46,49.

8:35 the love of Christ? The ease with which Paul used this phrase interchangeably with "the love of God . . . in Christ" (v. 39) testifies to his underlying assumption of the identity of essence between the Father and the Son.

8:36 Paul quoted Psalm 44:22, a plea to God from those who suffer innocently.

8:37 more than conquerors. The strength believers can show in enduring the hostility of persecutors and the pain of circumstances is often astonishing.

8:38–39 No aspect of the created order, nor any event or being within it (including ourselves), can terminate or disrupt our enjoyment of the active love of God to us in Christ. See *HC* 28; *CD* 5.V.

■ **9:1—11:36** *The Historical Roles of Jews and Gentiles.* Having demonstrated that Jews and Gentiles alike are sinners (1:1—3:20) who may find salvation in the same way (3:21—8:39), Paul turned to the distinct roles of Jews and Gentiles in God's plan for history. His discussion of this topic divides into three major sections: a description of divine election (9:1–29), unbelief and belief in Israel (9:30—11:10) and exhortations for Jews and Gentiles (11:11–36).

■ **9:1–29** *God's Sovereign Election.* Paul had discussed at great length the equal status that Jews and Gentiles enjoy before God. He stopped at this point to make certain that his views on Israel were properly understood. He appealed first to the Biblical principle of divine election.

9:1–5 Paul explained his loyalty and concern for his fellow Israelites.

9:1 my conscience confirms it. Scripture nowhere defines "conscience." Here and in 2:15 and 13:5 Paul spoke of it as moral self-awareness informed by divine revelation. Here Paul took a lawful oath to swear to his sincerity.

9:3 I could wish that I myself were cursed. Although he was the Apostle to the Gentiles, Paul echoed the sentiments of Moses in the face of the unbelief of the Jews (Ex 32:30–32). They were his relatives, and he agonized over them (v. 2). His willingness to suffer God's curse for his kinfolk was a radical statement of his love and concern for them.

9:4–5 Paul listed eight ways in which Israel had been blessed by God (see 3:1–2). See *WLC* 63. **adoption as sons.** From all humanity God adopted Israel as his son (Dt 8). Sonship was both a great privilege, for it opened the possibility of salvation, and a great responsibility, for it was demonstrated through testing. **divine glory.** Although God is omnipresent, he sometimes manifests his presence in a special way in a specific place. Israel received the privilege of being near the often visible, special, glorious presence of God on Sinai (Ex 19:18–20), in the tabernacle (Ex 40:34–38; 2Sa 7:5–6) and in the temple (1Ki 8:1–13; 2Ch 6). **covenants.** All of humanity was included in God's arrangement/covenant with Adam (5:12–21) and in his covenant with Noah (Ge 6:17–18; 9:9ff.), but the people of Israel were joined to God with national covenants (with Abraham [Ge 15; 17], Moses [Ex 20-24;34] and David [2Sa 7; Pss 89; 132]). See "Major Covenants in the Bible" on page 25. **the law.** The law given through Moses was a positive blessing for Israel (Ex 19:1–5), not a curse. **temple worship.** The temple was at the center of Israel's devotion to God. There sacrifices, prayers and praises were offered (1Ki 8:29ff.; 2Ch 6:19ff.). **the promises.** The nation of Israel was given many promises, but Paul probably had in mind those given to Abraham (Ge 15; 17). **the patriarchs.** The patriarchs Abraham, Isaac and Jacob, as well as Joseph and his brothers, received many blessings from God that were passed down as privileges and responsibilities for future generations. **human ancestry of Christ.** Not only was Jesus born to Israel, but he ministered among the Jews as well.

9:5 Christ, who is God over all, forever praised! Paul's words directly ascribe deity to Christ. This is the more natural rendering of the Greek, but see NIV text note for alternatives. See *WCF* 2.2; 8.2; *WLC* 36; *WSC* 21; *BC* 10,18.

9:6 God's word. His promise and plan to be the God of Abra-

el are Israel.[r] [7]Nor because they are his descendants are they all Abraham's children. On
the contrary, "It is through Isaac that your offspring will be reckoned."[a][s] [8]In other
words, it is not the natural children who are God's children,[t] but it is the children of the
promise who are regarded as Abraham's offspring. [9]For this was how the promise was
stated: "At the appointed time I will return, and Sarah will have a son."[b][u]
[10]Not only that, but Rebekah's children had one and the same father, our father
Isaac.[v] [11]Yet, before the twins were born or had done anything good or bad—in order
that God's purpose[w] in election might stand: [12]not by works but by him who calls—she
was told, "The older will serve the younger."[c][x] [13]Just as it is written: "Jacob I loved, but
Esau I hated."[d][y]
[14]What then shall we say? Is God unjust? Not at all![z] [15]For he says to Moses,

> "I will have mercy on whom I have mercy,
> and I will have compassion on whom I have compassion."[e][a]

[16]It does not, therefore, depend on man's desire or effort, but on God's mercy.[b] [17]For the
Scripture says to Pharaoh: "I raised you up for this very purpose, that I might display
my power in you and that my name might be proclaimed in all the earth."[f][c] [18]Therefore
God has mercy on whom he wants to have mercy, and he hardens whom he wants to
harden.[d]
[19]One of you will say to me:[e] "Then why does God still blame us? For who resists his
will?"[f] [20]But who are you, O man, to talk back to God? "Shall what is formed say to him
who formed it,[g] 'Why did you make me like this?' "[g][h] [21]Does not the potter have the right
to make out of the same lump of clay some pottery for noble purposes and some for common use?[i]
[22]What if God, choosing to show his wrath and make his power known, bore with
great patience[j] the objects of his wrath—prepared for destruction? [23]What if he did this
to make the riches of his glory[k] known to the objects of his mercy, whom he prepared
in advance for glory[l]— [24]even us, whom he also called,[m] not only from the Jews but also
from the Gentiles?[n] [25]As he says in Hosea:

9:6 [r]Ro 2:28,29; Gal 6:16
9:7 [s]Ge 21:12; Heb 11:18
9:8 [t]Ro 8:14
9:9 [u]Ge 18:10,14
9:10 [v]Ge 25:21
9:11 [w]Ro 8:28
9:12 [x]Ge 25:23
9:13 [y]Mal 1:2,3
9:14 [z]2Ch 19:7
9:15 [a]Ex 33:19
9:16 [b]Eph 2:8
9:17 [c]Ex 9:16
9:18 [d]Ex 4:21
9:19 [e]Ro 11:19 [f]2Ch 20:6; Da 4:35
9:20 [g]Isa 64:8 [h]Isa 29:16
9:21 [i]2Ti 2:20
9:22 [j]Ro 2:4
9:23 [k]Ro 2:4 [l]Ro 8:30
9:24 [m]Ro 8:28 [n]Ro 3:29

[a] *7* Gen. 21:12 [b] *9* Gen. 18:10,14 [c] *12* Gen. 25:23 [d] *13* Mal. 1:2,3 [e] *15* Exodus 33:19
[f] *17* Exodus 9:16 [g] *20* Isaiah 29:16; 45:9

ham's seed (Ge 17:7–8). In the Old Testament era, natural descent did not automatically guarantee inheritance of the promise. God chose who would inherit it. From a human point of view, each child was an expected heir, but to receive the promise each one had to embrace the covenant with saving faith. This principle is evident in the families of Abraham and Isaac. See *WLC* 61; *BC* 29.

9:11–13 See *CD* 1.10; 1.V.

9:11 before the twins were born or had done anything good or bad. The case of Jacob and Esau clinches the argument in three ways. (1) They were twins (i.e., as near to "natural" equals as was possible). (2) The purpose of God reversed even the "natural" distinction that did exist, since Esau, the elder, was to serve his younger brother. (3) God's purpose was stated before they were born (and was therefore not dependent on their actions). Election is not based on foreseen actions, deeds or faith. Rather, it is based on God's sovereign, predestinating grace. See *WCF* 3.2; 3.5, 10.2; *WLC* 67; *BC* 16; *HC* 102.

9:13 Jacob I loved, but Esau I hated. This distinguishing purpose of God in election (v. 11) is further confirmed by the words of Malachi 1:2–3, which speak of God's love for the nation of Israel and his hatred for the nation of Edom by explaining that God's love to Israel was rooted in his free choice of Jacob rather than Esau. **hated.** Cannot here be reduced to "loved less than," as the context of Malachi 1:3–4 makes clear. The word carries the stronger sense of rejection, antipathy and eventual judgment. See *WCF* 3.2; 3.5.

9:14–18 See *WCF* 3.1; 3.2; 3.5; 3.7; 16.7; *WLC* 12,13; *BC* 16; *CD* 1.VIII ; 3–4.IX.

9:14 What then shall we say? Compare 8:31. Paul recognized that his previous statement could not be allowed to pass without further comment. Does the distinguishing, sovereign purpose of God not throw into jeopardy his attribute of perfect righteousness? The idea is clearly unthinkable, as Paul expressed in his emphatic "Not at all!" (see also 6:2,15; 7:7). Paul explained why it was unthinkable by citing two Biblical texts (Ex 33:19; 9:16) in verses 15 and 17 that show that God is righteous in showing mercy to some while hardening the hearts of others. When God shows mercy, a person does not receive a reward earned by his or her own efforts; rather, God extends sovereign, free grace to people who are morally incapable of any acceptable effort (1:18—3:20). God owes mercy to none, so there is no injustice when mercy is not shown. The bestowal of mercy is a divine prerogative; it rests solely on God's good pleasure. When God "harden[ed]" Pharaoh's heart (v. 18), he gave Pharaoh over to his already rampant evil desires as an act of judgment, resulting eventually in God's display of power in the destruction of Pharaoh's army (Ex 14:17–18,23–28). See *WLC* 113.

9:17 the Scripture says to Pharaoh. It was God who thus spoke to Pharaoh through Moses (Ex 9:16). But Paul here pointed out that the words of Scripture and the voice and authority of God are one. See *WCF* 5.1.

9:19–22 See *WCF* 3.7; *WLC* 13,113; *BC* 16.

9:19 Then why does God still blame us? By what standard of justice can God lay the blame for their sins on those he has hardened against himself? If their rebellion conforms to the plan of God for their lives, then why does God hold them responsible?

9:20–21 Paul answered the questions in verse 19 by stating that it is irreverent for human beings to question the rightness of God's ways. The potter has every right to do as he pleases with his clay (Isa 64:8). All belong to "the same lump of clay" (i.e., fallen humanity in Adam; cf. vv. 10–13; 5:12–14). All actively sin before God hardens them in sinning (1:18–28). That God shows mercy to any from the Adamic lump and creates vessels of honor from it is a demonstration of superlative grace; that others should become vessels for common (ignoble) use is a matter of his sovereign prerogative and is itself a display of perfect justice toward them. See *WCF* 3.8; *CD* 1.18; see also theological article "Predestination and Foreknowledge" at Romans 8.

9:22–23 objects of his wrath—prepared for destruction . . . objects of his mercy, whom he prepared in advance for glory. Paul did not elaborate on the preparation in view. In both cases the use of the passive voice points to some form of divine activity. The addition of the words "in advance" in connection with the vessels of mercy may be pointing to the mercy that originates in God's good pleasure from eternity (8:29–30), while the wrath in view is directly related to actual ungodliness and unrighteousness (cf. 1:18–32). The distinction between the elect and the reprobate is grounded not in themselves (all deserve wrath) but exclusively in the will of God. Within that context, however, the objects prepared for destruction experience a wrath that is the just reward for sin. See *WCF* 3.3; 33.2; *WLC* 12; *WSC* 7.

9:24 Jews . . . Gentiles? Paul returned to the theme of God's

"I will call them 'my people' who are not my people;
and I will call her 'my loved one' who is not my loved one,"[a][o]

26 and,

"It will happen that in the very place where it was said to them,
'You are not my people,'
they will be called 'sons of the living God.' "[b][p]

27 Isaiah cries out concerning Israel:

"Though the number of the Israelites be like the sand by the sea,[q]
only the remnant will be saved.[r]
28 For the Lord will carry out
his sentence on earth with speed and finality."[c][s]

29 It is just as Isaiah said previously:

"Unless the Lord Almighty[t]
had left us descendants,
we would have become like Sodom,
we would have been like Gomorrah."[d][u]

Israel's Unbelief

30 What then shall we say? That the Gentiles, who did not pursue righteousness, have
obtained it, a righteousness that is by faith;[v] 31 but Israel, who pursued a law of righteousness,[w] has not attained it.[x] 32 Why not? Because they pursued it not by faith but as if it
were by works. They stumbled over the "stumbling stone."[y] 33 As it is written:

"See, I lay in Zion a stone that causes men to stumble
and a rock that makes them fall,
and the one who trusts in him will never be put to shame."[e][z]

10 Brothers, my heart's desire and prayer to God for the Israelites is that they may be
saved. 2 For I can testify about them that they are zealous[a] for God, but their zeal is
not based on knowledge. 3 Since they did not know the righteousness that comes from God
and sought to establish their own, they did not submit to God's righteousness.[b] 4 Christ is
the end of the law[c] so that there may be righteousness for everyone who believes.[d]
5 Moses describes in this way the righteousness that is by the law: "The man who does
these things will live by them."[f][e] 6 But the righteousness that is by faith[f] says: "Do not say in

9:25 [o]Hos 2:23; 1Pe 2:10
9:26 [p]Hos 1:10
9:27 [q]Ge 22:17; Hos 1:10 [r]Ro 11:5
9:28 [s]Isa 10:22,23
9:29 [t]Jas 5:4 [u]Isa 1:9; Dt 29:23; Isa 13:19; Jer 50:40
9:30 [v]Ro 1:17; 10:6; Gal 2:16; Php 3:9; Heb 11:7
9:31 [w]Isa 51:1; Ro 10:2,3 [x]Gal 5:4
9:32 [y]1Pe 2:8
9:33 [z]Isa 28:16; Ro 10:11
10:2 [a]Ac 21:20
10:3 [b]Ro 1:17
10:4 [c]Gal 3:24; Ro 7:1-4 [d]Ro 3:22
10:5 [e]Lev 18:5; Ne 9:29; Eze 20:11,13,21; Ro 7:10
10:6 [f]Ro 9:30

[a] *25* Hosea 2:23 [b] *26* Hosea 1:10 [c] *28* Isaiah 10:22,23 [d] *29* Isaiah 1:9 [e] *33* Isaiah 8:14; 28:16 [f] *5* Lev. 18:5

dealings with Jews and Gentiles. His point is that, as the divine Potter, God is free to choose not only Jews, but Gentiles as well. No human has any right to question God's ways.

9:25–26 not my people. Paul referred to Hosea 1:10 and 2:23, which were prophecies of Israel's restoration after exile. Under the judgment of exile, God revoked the covenant distinctive "my people" from the Israelites, but he promised to call them back as "my people" once again after exile. Paul's point was that the election of Gentiles is nothing more remarkable than the election of Jews who had been condemned as "not my people."

9:26–29 only the remnant . . . left us descendants. Paul referred to Isaiah 1:9 and 10:22 and 23, where Isaiah remarked that only a few Israelites, a small remnant, would escape the judgment of God. His point was that God did not promise universal salvation of all Israelites. He only promised that a remnant would be saved. This principle was very important to Paul's understanding of God's plan for Jewish and Gentile history. See *BC* 27.

■ **9:30—11:10** *Unbelief and Belief in Israel.* After establishing the importance of divine election rather than ethnic identity, Paul dealt with the reality of belief and unbelief in Israel.

9:30 What then shall we say? See verse 14. Having accounted for Jewish unbelief in terms of divine sovereignty, Paul now diagnosed it as due to a fatal, prior commitment to a false way of righteousness. Paul viewed divine sovereignty and the guilt of human willfulness as two aspects of reality. By God's grace and sovereignty Gentiles, who had not sought God's righteousness, had now received it through faith in Christ, but the Israelites as a people had failed to receive it because they had sought it by a road on which it could not be found. Christ had been to the Jews a stumbling stone (the image is from Isa 8:14; 28:16) over which they had fallen (vv. 32–33; 1Pe 2:8).

9:31–32 See *WLC* 60; *BC* 24.

9:31 a law of righteousness. Paul probably again had the Mosaic Law in view. The mistake the Jews made lay not in the object but in the manner of their pursuit ("not by faith but as if it were by works"; v. 32).

10:1 Brothers. A heartfelt appeal for the endorsement of his fellow Christians, the pathos of which is underlined by his recent reference to his brothers in the flesh (9:3). **that they may be saved.** Paul's concern in chapter 9 was with the salvation of the Jews, not merely with their role in redemptive history. See *WLC* 191; *WSC* 102.

10:2 zealous for God. Paul spoke here from personal experience, as to both the reality of the zeal and its wrong-headed and wrong-hearted character (Php 3:4–6). See *WCF* 16.1; *WLC* 105.

10:3–5 See *BC* 22.

10:3 they did not know the righteousness that comes from God. Paul contrasted divinely established righteousness with humankind's efforts to establish its own. **establish.** Covenant language (Ge 6:18; 17:7). Even in the context of the covenant God had made with them, they perverted his grace by relying on their own meritorious actions in keeping the law instead of on God's mercy.

10:4 Christ is the end of the law. This could mean (1) that Christ in some sense puts an end to the law, or (2) that Christ is the goal in view in the law (Gal 3:24). If the first view is correct, Paul meant that for those who believe in Christ, Christ brings to an end all wicked attempts to establish their own righteousness by means of the law. If the interpretation of verses 5–8 as suggested below (see notes on vv. 5,6–8) is followed, then the second view is correct. See *WLC* 95; *BC* 25,34; *HC* 19.

10:5 the righteousness that is by the law. Paul's quotation from Leviticus 18:5 is set originally in the context of God's redemptive grace requiring people's responsive obedience (Lev 18:2; cf. Ex 20:1–17); it is not a statement about self-established righteousness.

Legalism and Antinomianism: Why Do I Have to Obey God's Law?

CHRISTIANS are to obey God's law (Mt 28:20; Jn 14:15,21; Ro 2:13; 1Jn 2:3–6). Proper obedience is (1) according to the right standard (God's revealed will; i.e., his law; Dt 30:8–14; Mt 5:16–20; Ro 2:13); (2) from a right heart (love for God and others; Dt 30:16; Mt 22:36–40; Jn 14:15; 1Co 16:14; Gal 5:14; 2Jn 1:6); and (3) with a right goal (pleasing and glorifying God, honoring Christ, advancing his kingdom and benefiting one's neighbor; Lk 18:29–30; Ro 8:7–8; 12:1–2; Gal 1:10; Col 1:10; 1Th 2:3–4). Throughout history, however, many people have misunderstood these truths, with the result that they have generally fallen into one of two major forms of error: legalism and antinomianism.

Legalism is a broad term for certain improper perspectives on God's law. Some legalism results from skewed motives and purposes, essentially seeing good deeds as ways to earn more of God's favor than one has at the moment. Some legalism unlovingly seeks self-advancement, and some actually changes the standards of God's revelation.

In the New Testament we see both Pharisaic and Judaizing legalism. In many ways, the Pharisees were formalists, emphasizing the externals of action over motives and purposes. They thought themselves faithful law-keepers even though (1) they majored in minors, neglecting what matters most (Mt 23:23–24); (2) their casuistry negated the law's spirit and aim (Mt 15:3–9; 23:16–24); (3) they treated traditions of practice as part of God's authoritative law, thus binding consciences where God had left them free (Mk 2:16—3:6; 7:1–8); and (4) they were hypocrites at heart, angling for humanity's approval at all times (Mt 6:1–8; 23:2–7; Lk 20:45–47). Jesus was harsh with them on these points.

The Judaizers in the early church taught that Gentile believers in Christ had to perform certain good works, such as circumcision, to gain increased favor with God. Paul vigorously opposed this view in Galatians, condemning the Judaizers for obscuring and essentially denying the all-sufficient grace of the gospel revealed in Jesus (Gal 3:1–3; 4:21; 5:2–6). In Colossians he voiced a similar polemic against those who insisted that Christians needed to perform certain works in order to achieve spiritual completion (Col 2:8–23). All formulae that require us to take action in order to add to what Christ has given us are reversions to legalism and insults to Christ.

Antinomianism, which means being "anti–law," is a name that has been applied to many different views that deny the applicability or importance of God's law to the Christian's life:

Dualistic antinomianism appears to have been present in the heretics against whom Peter and Jude wrote (2Pe 2; Jude 4–19) and has arisen at other times in the history of God's people as well. This view sees salvation as for the soul only, and bodily behavior as irrelevant both to God's interest and to the soul's health. Because bodily behavior bears no eternal consequences, physical violations of God's law (e.g., sexual sins) are acceptable.

Spirit-centered antinomianism puts such trust in the Holy Spirit's inward prompting as to deny any need to be taught by the law how to live. Freedom from the law as a way of salvation is assumed to bring with it freedom from the law as a guide to conduct. In the first 150 years of the Reformation era this kind of antinomianism was common, and Paul's insistence that a truly spiritual person acknowledge the authority of God's Word (1Co 14:37; cf. 7:40) suggests that the Corinthian church was in the grip of the same mind-set in his day.

Christ-centered antinomianism argues that because believers are in Christ, who kept the law for them, God sees no sin in them—which is true. But it wrongly concludes from this fact that Christians may freely embrace sin as a way of life, so long as they continue to trust in Christ for their salvation. But 1 John 1:8—2:1 (expounding 1:7) and 3:4–10 point in a different direction, showing that it is impossible to be in Christ and at the same time to embrace sin as a way of life.

Dispensational antinomianism holds that keeping the moral law is unnecessary for Christians, since we live under a dispensation of grace, not of law. Passages such as Romans 3:31 and James 2:8–13 clearly show, however, that law-keeping is a continuing obligation for Christians.

Dialectical antinomianism, as advocated by Barth and Brunner, denies that Biblical law is God's direct command. It affirms instead that the Bible's imperative statements trigger the Word of the Spirit, which may or may not correspond exactly to the original meaning of Scripture.

Situationist antinomianism asserts that a motive and intention of love is all that God now requires of Christians, and that the specific ethical commands of Scripture are merely examples of how love was expressed in other times and places. Such examples may now be disregarded so long as one retains the motivation of love. Passages such as Romans 13:8–10, to which this view appeals, teach that without love as a motive these specific commands cannot be fulfilled, but they also maintain the importance of fulfilling the specific commands.

It must be stressed that the moral law, as summarized in the Ten Commandments and detailed in the ethical teaching of both Testaments, is one coherent law, given to be a code of practice for God's people in every age. The Spirit is given to empower law-keeping and to make us more and more like Christ, the archetypal law-keeper (Mt 5:17). This law-keeping is in fact the fulfilling of our human nature, and Scripture holds out no hope of salvation to any who do not seek to turn from sin to righteousness (1Co 6:9–11; Rev 21:8). See theological article "The Three Uses of the Law" at Psalm 119.

your heart, 'Who will ascend into heaven?'[a]"[g] (that is, to bring Christ down) 7"or 'Who will
descend into the deep?'[b]" (that is, to bring Christ up from the dead). 8But what does it say?
"The word is near you; it is in your mouth and in your heart,"[c][h] that is, the word of faith we
are proclaiming: 9That if you confess[i] with your mouth, "Jesus is Lord," and believe in your
heart that God raised him from the dead,[j] you will be saved. 10For it is with your heart that
you believe and are justified, and it is with your mouth that you confess and are saved. 11As
the Scripture says, "Anyone who trusts in him will never be put to shame."[d][k] 12For there is
no difference between Jew and Gentile[l]—the same Lord is Lord of all[m] and richly blesses
all who call on him, 13for, "Everyone who calls on the name of the Lord[n] will be saved."[e][o]

14How, then, can they call on the one they have not believed in? And how can they
believe in the one of whom they have not heard? And how can they hear without someone preaching to them? 15And how can they preach unless they are sent? As it is written, "How beautiful are the feet of those who bring good news!"[f][p]

16But not all the Israelites accepted the good news. For Isaiah says, "Lord, who has
believed our message?"[g][q] 17Consequently, faith comes from hearing the message,[r] and
the message is heard through the word of Christ.[s] 18But I ask: Did they not hear? Of
course they did:

> "Their voice has gone out into all the earth,
> their words to the ends of the world."[h][t]

19Again I ask: Did Israel not understand? First, Moses says,

> "I will make you envious[u] by those who are not a nation;
> I will make you angry by a nation that has no
> understanding."[i][v]

20And Isaiah boldly says,

> "I was found by those who did not seek me;
> I revealed myself to those who did not ask for me."[j][w]

21But concerning Israel he says,

> "All day long I have held out my hands
> to a disobedient and obstinate people."[k][x]

10:6 [g]Dt 30:12
10:8 [h]Dt 30:14
10:9 [i]Mt 10:32; Lk 12:8 [j]Ac 2:24
10:11 [k]Isa 28:16; Ro 9:33
10:12 [l]Ro 3:22,29 [m]Ac 10:36
10:13 [n]Ac 2:21 [o]Joel 2:32
10:15 [p]Isa 52:7; Na 1:15
10:16 [q]Isa 53:1; Jn 12:38
10:17 [r]Gal 3:2,5 [s]Col 3:16
10:18 [t]Ps 19:4; Mt 24:14; Col 1:6,23; 1Th 1:8
10:19 [u]Ro 11:11,14 [v]Dt 32:21
10:20 [w]Isa 65:1; Ro 9:30
10:21 [x]Isa 65:2

[a] *6* Deut. 30:12 [b] *7* Deut. 30:13 [c] *8* Deut. 30:14 [d] *11* Isaiah 28:16 [e] *13* Joel 2:32
[f] *15* Isaiah 52:7 [g] *16* Isaiah 53:1 [h] *18* Psalm 19:4 [i] *19* Deut. 32:21 [j] *20* Isaiah 65:1
[k] *21* Isaiah 65:2

Even so, in Paul's polemic against self-righteousness, Leviticus 18:5 demonstrates that absolute perfection was required of anyone who tried to use the law as a means of salvation. See *WCF* 7.2; 19.1; *WLC* 20,92,93; *WSC* 40.

10:6–8 Paul again appealed to the law to establish the way of faith. The law exhibited God's salvation as achieved not by human efforts, but by divine grace. In particular, Deuteronomy 30 set this in the context of Israel's anticipated return from exile (Dt 30:1–6; Jer 31:31–34). As expressed in the rest of the New Testament, Paul saw this restoration fulfilled in the new covenant in Christ (2Co 3:7–18). Thus, Christ was the end (goal) of the Mosaic Law. To seek a self-established righteousness now would be to attempt to do what God alone can do and has done in Christ's incarnation and resurrection. In contrast to all human efforts, God has brought near the word of salvation (and therefore the salvation it communicates). See *WCF* 7.3.

10:9–10 confess . . . believe . . . believe . . . confess. In the parallelism of verse 10, Paul reversed the order of verbs in verse 9 and thereby indicated that heart-belief and mouth-confession belong together for justification and salvation. If Paul intended here to distinguish between "justified" and "saved," the narrower term ("justified") is more properly related to faith and the broader ("saved") to the development of faith in confession, whereas in verse 9 both belief and confession are related to the more general notion of salvation. But the distinction may be only rhetorical. Both confession and belief are means by which God saves; they are not the grounds on which he saves. Although confession and belief are the normal means God uses, they are not the only means available to him (e.g., those incapable of speech may still be saved). See *WCF* 7.3; *WLC* 73; *BC* 1,22,33; *HC* 21,32,61,99.

10:11–13 See *BC* 24; *HC* 128.

10:12 there is no difference. This is confirmed not only by the unity and universal kindness of God (v. 12), but specifically by the teaching of the Old Testament (Joel 2:32—the statement fulfilled so dramatically at Pentecost in Ac 2:21). This statement lies at the core of Paul's teaching in chapters 1–11: Jews and Gentiles are both saved from the same thing in the same way; as a result, neither can claim superiority over the other. Paul hoped that by destroying elitism the church could build unity between Jewish and Gentile believers. See *WCF* 21.1.

10:13–17 See *WCF* 14.1; 20.2; 23.3; *WLC* 72,105,158; *WSC* 89,155; *BC* 24; *HC* 21,54,65,98,103,117.

10:14–15 An analysis of what is involved when anyone calls on the name of the Lord in order to be saved. See *HC* 98; *CD* 1.3.

10:14 in the one of whom. Literally, "him whom"; an indication that Paul saw Christ as the one true preacher of the gospel (cf. Jn 10:16; Eph 2:17). The ministry of preaching Christ is therefore one of great honor (cf. 2Co 3:4–11)—hence the quotation from Isaiah 52:7 in verse 15. See *WCF* 14.1; *WSC* 60,72,179.

10:18 Their voice has gone out into all the earth. The immediate context of the citation from Psalm 19:4 is that of God's general revelation (Ps 19:1–3). Paul's use of it to prove that Israel had heard the gospel of Jesus Christ may have one of two explanations: (1) Paul's quotation of this section of the psalm may carry with it the teaching of the entire psalm, which speaks of both general and special revelation. The latter takes place within the context of the former. The underlying logic may be that if those without special revelation have "heard" the message of God's glory in creation, how much more those to whom he has given special revelation. Or (2) Paul may merely be quoting the words of the psalm and applying the language to the preaching of the gospel throughout the world in a typological fashion.

10:19–21 The failure of the Jews cannot be excused on the basis either of their lack of hearing the message or the impossibility of their understanding it. Moses and Isaiah contrasted God's own people with those who lacked understanding (Dt 32:21) and with those who, while not God-seekers, were still brought to know him (Isa 65:1).

The Remnant of Israel

11 I ask then: Did God reject his people? By no means![y] I am an Israelite myself, a descendant of Abraham,[z] from the tribe of Benjamin.[a] 2God did not reject his people, whom he foreknew.[b] Don't you know what the Scripture says in the passage about Elijah—how he appealed to God against Israel: 3"Lord, they have killed your prophets and torn down your altars; I am the only one left, and they are trying to kill me"[a]?[c] 4And what was God's answer to him? "I have reserved for myself seven thousand who have not bowed the knee to Baal."[b][d] 5So too, at the present time there is a remnant[e] chosen by grace. 6And if by grace, then it is no longer by works;[f] if it were, grace would no longer be grace.[c]

7What then? What Israel sought so earnestly it did not obtain,[g] but the elect did. The others were hardened,[h] 8as it is written:

> "God gave them a spirit of stupor,
> eyes so that they could not see
> and ears so that they could not hear,[i]
> to this very day."[d][j]

9And David says:

> "May their table become a snare and a trap,
> a stumbling block and a retribution for them.
> 10May their eyes be darkened so they cannot see,
> and their backs be bent forever."[e][k]

Ingrafted Branches

11Again I ask: Did they stumble so as to fall beyond recovery? Not at all![l] Rather, because of their transgression, salvation has come to the Gentiles[m] to make Israel envious.[n] 12But if their transgression means riches for the world, and their loss means riches for the Gentiles,[o] how much greater riches will their fullness bring!

13I am talking to you Gentiles. Inasmuch as I am the apostle to the Gentiles,[p] I make much of my ministry 14in the hope that I may somehow arouse my own people to envy[q] and save[r] some of them. 15For if their rejection is the reconciliation[s] of the world, what will their acceptance be but life from the dead?[t] 16If the part of the dough offered as firstfruits[u] is holy, then the whole batch is holy; if the root is holy, so are the branches.

11:1 [y]1Sa 12:22; Jer 31:37 [z]2Co 11:22 [a]Php 3:5
11:2 [b]Ro 8:29
11:3 [c]1Ki 19:10,14
11:4 [d]1Ki 19:18
11:5 [e]Ro 9:27
11:6 [f]Ro 4:4
11:7 [g]Ro 9:31 [h]ver 25; Ro 9:18
11:8 [i]Mt 13:13-15 [j]Dt 29:4; Isa 29:10
11:10 [k]Ps 69:22,23
11:11 [l]ver 1 [m]Ac 13:46 [n]Ro 10:19
11:12 [o]ver 25
11:13 [p]Ac 9:15
11:14 [q]ver 11; Ro 10:19 [r]1Co 1:21; 1Ti 2:4; Tit 3:5
11:15 [s]Ro 5:10 [t]Lk 15:24,32
11:16 [u]Lev 23:10,17; Nu 15:18-21

[a] *3* 1 Kings 19:10,14 [b] *4* 1 Kings 19:18 [c] *6* Some manuscripts *be grace. But if by works, then it is no longer grace; if it were, work would no longer be work.* [d] *8* Deut. 29:4; Isaiah 29:10 [e] *10* Psalm 69:22,23

11:1–10 Paul here pointedly asked whether God had rejected his people. The apostle himself was evidence that God had not fully and finally rejected Israel, on whom he had set his love. Just as a believing remnant could be found in Israel in Elijah's time, so there continued in Paul's day to be a remnant formed by God's grace. By grace the elect obtain the salvation they seek; the rest are hardened.
11:1 Did God reject his people? The verb conveys the sense of vigorous pushing away from oneself. The form of the question in Greek anticipates a negative answer. **I am an Israelite myself.** See Philippians 3:5–6. Paul's impeccable lineage was traced back to Abraham, the great patriarch, but also to Benjamin, the only son of Jacob to be born in Israel. Benjamin was the tribe in whose territory Jerusalem stood, and also the tribe of Saul, the first king.
11:2 whom he foreknew. Paul hinted that God's special love and gracious choice of them made it unthinkable that he should finally reject them as a people, even though they had now broadly rejected him by denying Christ.
11:3–6 See *WCF* 3.8; 25.4; *BC* 27.
11:5 a remnant chosen by grace. In Elijah's time there was wholesale apostasy, yet the presence of a remnant of the faithful indicated that God had not fully and finally rejected his people. Paul's thinking about the remnant was rooted in the teaching of Isaiah, whose son Shear-Jashub's name meant "a remnant shall return" (Isa 7:3; cf. Isa 1:9; 6:13; 10:20–22; 11:11–16; Ro 9:27). Paul's argument here is similar to that found in 9:6–33: The proof that God did not reject his people is that he saved a remnant. See *BC* 16,24.
11:6 And if by grace, then it is no longer by works. Again the way of grace is contrasted with works of the law (3:20,27–28; 4:2,6; 9:12,32). See *CD* 1.V.
11:7–8 See *WCF* 5.6; 10.1; *WLC* 61; *CD* 5.I.
11:8–10 The passages cited (Dt 29:4; Isa 29:10; Ps 69:22–23) describe a Biblical pattern of divine activity in the judicial hardening of hearts—a pattern Paul saw repeated in his own day.

■ **11:11–36** *Warnings and Encouragements for Jews and Gentiles.* The Jews' rejection of Christ was not irreversible. Paul saw a divine pattern and purpose behind the unbelief of which the Jews were guilty. The pattern of his thought is as follows: The transgression of the Jews led to the justification of the Gentiles. The salvation of the Gentiles will lead to envy by the Jews. The envy of the Jews will draw them to the same salvation as the Gentiles.
11:11 Did they stumble so as to fall beyond recovery? Once again the form of Paul's question anticipated (and received) a negative answer.
11:12 their fullness. In the context of Paul's argument, "fullness" can only signify their reception of Christ and their restoration to God. The more difficult question is whether the term was intended to teach that each individual would be "fully restored" (roughly equivalent to "restoration," in contrast to their current "transgression" and "loss") or that the "full nation" (i.e., all the individuals within the nation, in contrast to the "remnant" of v. 5) would be restored.
11:13–14 I am talking to you Gentiles. Paul directed this teaching primarily to Gentiles, both in his role as Apostle to the Gentiles and for the sake of influencing their attitudes toward Jews. See also verses 17–24. **I make much of my ministry . . . save some of them.** Paul expressed his hope that he himself would be able to provoke the restoration of the Jewish remnant (see vv. 11–12).
11:15 life from the dead? This phrase may simply denote unprecedented blessing. The wording is slightly different from Paul's normal eschatological terminology ("resurrection from the dead"; 1:4; 1Co 15:12–13,21,42), and some have taken it to mean that the restoration of the Jewish people to the kingdom of God in Christ will be the herald of the final resurrection and so itself an end-times event.
11:16–22 See *WCF* 25.5; *HC* 20.
11:16 the whole batch is holy. Paul applied the principle that

[17]If some of the branches have been broken off,[v] and you, though a wild olive shoot,
have been grafted in among the others[w] and now share in the nourishing sap from the
olive root, [18]do not boast over those branches. If you do, consider this: You do not support the root, but the root supports you.[x] [19]You will say then, "Branches were broken off
so that I could be grafted in." [20]Granted. But they were broken off because of unbelief,
and you stand by faith.[y] Do not be arrogant,[z] but be afraid.[a] [21]For if God did not spare
the natural branches, he will not spare you either.

[22]Consider therefore the kindness[b] and sternness of God: sternness to those who fell,
but kindness to you, provided that you continue[c] in his kindness. Otherwise, you also will
be cut off.[d] [23]And if they do not persist in unbelief, they will be grafted in, for God is able
to graft them in again.[e] [24]After all, if you were cut out of an olive tree that is wild by nature, and contrary to nature were grafted into a cultivated olive tree, how much more
readily will these, the natural branches, be grafted into their own olive tree!

All Israel Will Be Saved

[25]I do not want you to be ignorant[f] of this mystery,[g] brothers, so that you may not be
conceited:[h] Israel has experienced a hardening[i] in part until the full number of the Gentiles has come in.[j] [26]And so all Israel will be saved, as it is written:

> "The deliverer will come from Zion;
> he will turn godlessness away from Jacob.
> [27]And this is[a] my covenant with them
> when I take away their sins."[b] [k]

[28]As far as the gospel is concerned, they are enemies[l] on your account; but as far as
election is concerned, they are loved on account of the patriarchs,[m] [29]for God's gifts and
his call[n] are irrevocable.[o] [30]Just as you who were at one time disobedient[p] to God have
now received mercy as a result of their disobedience, [31]so they too have now become disobedient in order that they too may now[c] receive mercy as a result of God's mercy to you

11:17 [v]Jer 11:16; Jn 15:2 [w]Ac 2:39; Eph 2:11-13
11:18 [x]Jn 4:22
11:20 [y]1Co 10:12; 2Co 1:24 [z]Ro 12:16; 1Ti 6:17 [a]1Pe 1:17
11:22 [b]Ro 2:4 [c]1Co 15:2; Heb 3:6 [d]Jn 15:2
11:23 [e]2Co 3:16
11:25 [f]Ro 1:13 [g]Ro 16:25 [h]Ro 12:16 [i]ver 7; Ro 9:18 [j]Lk 21:24
11:27 [k]Isa 27:9; Heb 8:10,12
11:28 [l]Ro 5:10 [m]Dt 7:8; 10:15; Ro 9:5
11:29 [n]Ro 8:28 [o]Heb 7:21
11:30 [p]Eph 2:2

[a] *27* Or *will be* [b] *27* Isaiah 59:20,21; 27:9; Jer. 31:33,34 [c] *31* Some manuscripts do not have *now.*

the first fruits serve as the pledge of the final harvest (cf. Nu 15:17–21). See *WCF* 25.2; *WLC* 62,166.

11:17 a wild olive shoot . . . grafted in. See Jeremiah 11:16 and Hosea 14:6 for references to Israel as an olive tree. Wild olive shoots do seem to have been grafted into cultivated trees to bring fresh vitality to them. Paul's words, however, probably intentionally stretched beyond strict horticulture. Gentiles have been grafted into the people of God "contrary to nature" (v. 24).

11:18 do not boast. Because salvation is entirely of grace, Gentile believers have no cause for boasting over or despising Jews who reject Christ. Such Gentile arrogance in relation to Jews would simply mirror the spiritual pride that led to Israel's hardening (2:17). **If you do . . . the root supports you.** Gentiles are dependent upon God's covenant with the Jewish people and therefore should not think themselves better than Jews who reject Christ ("the branches [that were] broken off"; v. 17), especially since these same branches might be grafted in once again (v. 23). Paul wanted to prevent the Gentile believers in Rome from acting arrogantly toward Jews who had rejected Christ. These same Jews might have actually been elect who would later come to faith; they might have been hardened against Christ only temporarily in order to ensure the salvation of the Gentiles (see also vv. 13–14).

11:20 While the rejoinder to Paul in verse 19 is formally true, the breaking off of the Jewish branches was God's act of righteous judgment on unbelief, and the ingrafting of the Gentiles was a matter of grace and, therefore, of faith. Their ingrafting (v. 19) was not therefore based on any superior quality in the Gentiles. **afraid.** Fear (tender-spirited awe), not arrogance, is the appropriate response to God's grace. See *WCF* 3.8.

11:22 Consider . . . the kindness and sternness of God. Gentile believers were urged to take seriously the revelation of God's character in these events of providence. God had shown them much kindness by extending to them the offer of salvation, but the threat of being cut off revealed his sternness.

11:23–24 The cutting off of unbelieving Jews was because of unbelief, not because the Gentiles were inherently better qualified for life in the olive tree. Moreover, Gentile believers should never forget that the gospel came to the Jews first (1:16–17).

11:25–32 Paul's tightly packed reasoning here has been understood in at least four different ways: (1) He was showing how God saves all of his elect people. "All Israel" in verse 26 is taken as basically synonymous with "the church"; that is, spiritual Israel, including both Jews and Gentiles. (2) Paul was showing how, or the manner in which ("and so"; v. 26), God saves those in Israel who are destined for salvation. (3) Paul was showing that God will, in the future, bring such widespread salvation to the Jewish people that it can be said that "all Israel will be saved" (v. 26). (4) Paul was referring to the immediate circumstances of his ministry in the context of the tension between Jews and Gentiles in the first-century church and expressing particular concern that Gentile believers needed to evangelize unbelieving Jews and welcome new Jewish converts. "All Israel" in this scenario is thought to refer to "all elect Jews" in Paul's day—a narrower version of (2), above.

11:25–26 See *WLC* 191.

11:25 mystery. In Paul's writings, and in Jewish thought generally, a "mystery" was a divine secret that was now being revealed (cf. 16:25). **hardening in part.** This may mean either the hardening of a limited number of Jews (all but the remnant) or a temporary hardening ("until"). **full number.** Literally, "fullness." See note on verse 12, where the same word is translated "fullness." **has come in.** An expression used infrequently by Paul but one used regularly in the Gospels to describe entrance into life or the kingdom of God (e.g., Mk 9:47). It might also be a specific reference to the ingrafting of verses 17–24.

11:26 all Israel. A critical expression at this point in Paul's argument, and one whose meaning is much debated. This statement could be understood to support view (1) from the note on verses 25–32 if "Israel" is read in a sense different from its normal use in this passage (but akin to Paul's argument in 4:12ff; 9:24–26). In support of view (2) or (4) from the same note, "all Israel" would be understood to mean "all elect Jews" (akin to Paul's argument in 9:6ff; 11:1–5). It could also be understood to refer to the nation at large, as in (3), above. **The deliverer will come from Zion.** In quoting Isaiah, Paul substituted "from" for the original preposition "to" (Isa 59:20; the Hebrew may also be rendered "for Zion"). Perhaps he was influenced by the Septuagint (the Greek translation of the OT) reading of the text ("because of Zion") or by Psalm 2:6 ("on Zion") or 14:7 ("out of Zion"), thus explaining one passage in the light of the whole of Scripture.

11:30–32 Paul's argument concludes in a manner parallel to 3:19–21, stressing that Jews and Gentiles are united in two things: the disobedience of sin and the offer of mercy from God. The wisdom and sovereignty of God's grace are demonstrated in the way in which God's purposes are fulfilled: The disobedience of the Jews

11:32 [q]Ro 3:9
11:33 [r]Ro 2:4 [s]Ps 92:5 [t]Job 11:7
11:34 [u]Isa 40:13,14; Job 15:8; 36:22; 1Co 2:16
11:35 [v]Job 35:7
11:36 [w]1Co 8:6; Col 1:16; Heb 2:10 [x]Ro 16:27
12:1 [y]Eph 4:1 [z]Ro 6:13, 16,19; 1Pe 2:5
12:2 [a]1Pe 1:14 [b]1Jn 2:15 [c]Eph 4:23 [d]Eph 5:17
12:3 [e]Ro 15:15; Gal 2:9; Eph 4:7
12:4 [f]1Co 12:12-14; Eph 4:16
12:5 [g]1Co 10:17
12:6 [h]1Co 7:7; 12:4,8-10 [i]1Pe 4:10,11
12:7 [j]Eph 4:11
12:8 [k]Ac 15:32 [l]2Co 9:5-13

32 For God has bound all men over to disobedience[q] so that he may have mercy on them all.

Doxology

33 Oh, the depth of the riches[r] of the wisdom and[a] knowledge of
God![s]
How unsearchable his judgments,
and his paths beyond tracing out![t]
34 "Who has known the mind of the Lord?
Or who has been his counselor?"[b][u]
35 "Who has ever given to God,
that God should repay him?"[c][v]
36 For from him and through him and to him are all things.[w]
To him be the glory forever! Amen.[x]

Living Sacrifices

12 Therefore, I urge you,[y] brothers, in view of God's mercy, to offer your bodies as living sacrifices,[z] holy and pleasing to God—this is your spiritual[d] act of worship. 2 Do not conform[a] any longer to the pattern of this world,[b] but be transformed by the renewing of your mind.[c] Then you will be able to test and approve what God's will is[d]—his good, pleasing and perfect will.

3 For by the grace given me[e] I say to every one of you: Do not think of yourself more highly than you ought, but rather think of yourself with sober judgment, in accordance with the measure of faith God has given you. 4 Just as each of us has one body with many members, and these members do not all have the same function,[f] 5 so in Christ we who are many form one body,[g] and each member belongs to all the others. 6 We have different gifts,[h] according to the grace given us. If a man's gift is prophesying, let him use it in proportion to his[e] faith.[i] 7 If it is serving, let him serve; if it is teaching, let him teach;[j] 8 if it is encouraging, let him encourage;[k] if it is contributing to the needs of others, let him give generously;[l] if it is leadership, let him govern diligently; if it is showing mercy, let him do it cheerfully.

[a] *33* Or *riches and the wisdom and the* [b] *34* Isaiah 40:13 [c] *35* Job 41:11 [d] *1* Or *reasonable*
[e] *6* Or *in agreement with the*

---

has led to God's mercy reaching Gentiles; the mercy of God to Gentiles will lead to the reception of mercy by Jews. There is no difference—all (Jews and Gentiles alike) have sinned (3:23), and God has mercy on both (1:16).

11:32–34 See *WCF* 5.4; 6.1.

11:33–36 Having drawn together the various strands of his argument, Paul here responded in lyrical fashion with a song of praise that reached heights that correspond to the depth of concern he had sounded in 9:2–3. God's dealings with Jews and Gentiles reveal a cross section of his majesty in which his sovereign will ("from him"), his sovereign activity ("through him") and his sovereign glory ("to him") are richly displayed (v. 36). See *WCF* 2.1; 2.2; 3.1; 3.8; *WLC* 1,12,18; *WSC* 1; *BC* 16; *HC* 122; *CD* 1.18.

■ **12:1—15:13** *Practical Instructions.* Paul had established that Jews and Gentiles are sinners, are saved in the same way and have special complementary roles in history. Now he turned to more practical matters that have many points of contact with his outlooks on Jews and Gentiles. He dealt with four subjects: the need for full consecration (12:1–2), life in the body of Christ (12:3–21), political and social responsibilities (13:1–14) and handling controversies between the spiritually weak and strong (14:1—15:13).

■ **12:1–2** *Full Consecration.* Paul encouraged his readers to respond to God's kindness with full devotion to Christ.

12:1–2 See *WLC* 91; *HC* 86,124.

12:1 God's mercy. The doctrines of grace discussed in chapters 3–11 should lead to a life motivated by gratitude, not by arrogance. **offer your bodies as living sacrifices.** Jews and Gentiles are now united as the people of God for whom the final blood sacrifice has been made (3:25). The sacrifice that remains is that of thankful response (cf. 6:17). "Bodies" implies whole persons as embodied individuals (6:12–13,19; 8:13). **spiritual act of worship.** The worship that is appropriate (possibly "reasonable worship/service") of redeemed creatures. See *HC* 32,43.

12:2 Do not conform . . . be transformed by the renewing of your mind. The Christian's mindset is to be determined and reshaped by knowledge of the gospel, by the power of the Spirit and by the concerns of the age to come (8:5–9; 13:11–14), not by the passing fashion ("pattern") of this age (2Co 4:18; 1Jn 2:17). Only by such sanctifying renewal is the Christian made sufficiently sensitive to "test and approve" (i.e., discern) the behavior that is God's will in each situation. See *WCF* 16.1; *WLC* 97.

■ **12:3–21** *In the Body of Christ.* Paul now focused on one way his readers should live in light of God's mercies: by serving other Christians.

12:3 For by the grace given me. Paul's ministry existed only because of grace (1:5), as is also true of spiritual gifts (v. 6). Realistic assessment of one's gifts ("sober judgment") is essential and involves recognition of one's "measure of faith" (not saving faith, but faith suited for the exercise of particular gifts; v. 6).

12:4–8 Paul used the analogy of the body and its various parts to illustrate the nature of the church (cf. 1Co 12). He stressed its unity (v. 5) and inherent diversity (v. 6). He also emphasized the need for each member to recognize his or her gifts and to use them appropriately (vv. 6–8). See *BC* 31; *HC* 55.

12:6 prophesying. To prophesy is to speak the word of God, but the nature of New Testament prophecy is nowhere clearly defined and is much debated. Prophecy is distinguished here and elsewhere from teaching (v. 7; Ac 13:1; 1Co 12:29; Eph 4:11), perhaps because of the greater sense of immediacy and spontaneity attached to it (Ac 13:1–3; 21:10–11). **in proportion to his faith.** "Faith" is here translated as the prophet's own faith (cf. vv. 3,6). Alternatively, it may refer to the truth content of the gospel as the standard and measure of each prophetic utterance (cf. "the pattern of sound teaching"; 2Ti 1:13).

12:7–8 Paul recognized the wide variety and practicality of these gifts and the intertwining of natural endowments with them. In employing gifts, the blessing of those ministered to must be the paramount consideration.

12:9–21 When discussing the church as the body of Christ, Paul stressed the importance of love (cf. 1Co 12–13). His series of rapid exhortations echoes Jesus' teaching style.

Love

9 Love must be sincere.[m] Hate what is evil; cling to what is good. 10 Be devoted to one another in brotherly love.[n] Honor one another above yourselves.[o] 11 Never be lacking in zeal,
but keep your spiritual fervor,[p] serving the Lord. 12 Be joyful in hope,[q] patient in affliction,[r]
faithful in prayer. 13 Share with God's people who are in need. Practice hospitality.[s]
14 Bless those who persecute you;[t] bless and do not curse. 15 Rejoice with those who
rejoice; mourn with those who mourn.[u] 16 Live in harmony with one another.[v] Do not be
proud, but be willing to associate with people of low position.[a] Do not be conceited.[w]
17 Do not repay anyone evil for evil.[x] Be careful to do what is right in the eyes of everybody.[y] 18 If it is possible, as far as it depends on you, live at peace with everyone.[z] 19 Do
not take revenge,[a] my friends, but leave room for God's wrath, for it is written: "It is mine
to avenge; I will repay,"[b][b] says the Lord. 20 On the contrary:

> "If your enemy is hungry, feed him;
> if he is thirsty, give him something to drink.
> In doing this, you will heap burning coals on his head."[c][c]

21 Do not be overcome by evil, but overcome evil with good.

Submission to the Authorities

13 Everyone must submit himself to the governing authorities,[d] for there is no authority except that which God has established.[e] The authorities that exist have
been established by God. 2 Consequently, he who rebels against the authority is rebelling
against what God has instituted, and those who do so will bring judgment on themselves.
3 For rulers hold no terror for those who do right, but for those who do wrong. Do you
want to be free from fear of the one in authority? Then do what is right and he will commend you.[f] 4 For he is God's servant to do you good. But if you do wrong, be afraid, for
he does not bear the sword for nothing. He is God's servant, an agent of wrath to bring
punishment on the wrongdoer.[g] 5 Therefore, it is necessary to submit to the authorities,
not only because of possible punishment but also because of conscience.

12:9 [m]1Ti 1:5
12:10 [n]Heb 13:1 [o]Php 2:3
12:11 [p]Ac 18:25
12:12 [q]Ro 5:2 [r]Heb 10:32,36
12:13 [s]1Ti 3:2
12:14 [t]Mt 5:44
12:15 [u]Job 30:25
12:16 [v]Ro 15:5 [w]Jer 45:5; Ro 11:25
12:17 [x]Pr 20:22 [y]2Co 8:21
12:18 [z]Mk 9:50; Ro 14:19
12:19 [a]Lev 19:18; Pr 20:22; 24:29 [b]Dt 32:35
12:20 [c]Pr 25:21,22; Mt 5:44; Lk 6:27
13:1 [d]Tit 3:1; 1Pe 2:13,14 [e]Da 2:21; Jn 19:11
13:3 [f]1Pe 2:14
13:4 [g]1Th 4:6

[a] 16 Or *willing to do menial work* [b] 19 Deut. 32:35 [c] 20 Prov. 25:21,22

12:9 sincere. Literally, "without hypocrisy." In classical Greek drama, the *hypokrites* (actors) wore masks. The Christian's loving behavior should not be contrived, as if one were acting a part or wearing a mask, but should be an authentic expression of good will.
12:10–11 See *WSC* 102.
12:10 Be devoted . . . in brotherly love. An unusual linguistic combination, combining brotherly love with the love of natural affection. The church is a family, the household of God (v. 1; 1Ti 3:15; 5:1–2). See *WLC* 126,131; *WSC* 64; *HC* 107.
12:11 There must be no apathy or laziness in Christian living. Rather, the Christian should aim at fervor and enthusiasm. See *WLC* 104,192.
12:13 hospitality. In the Greek, a compound word for "love" that has strangers in view (*philoxenia* = love of strangers). Hospitality for visiting Christians was an important part of early Christian life (Heb 13:2; 3Jn 5–8).
12:14 See Luke 6:27–28. In Scripture "bless" and "curse" express more than human emotions toward others; they involve the covenantal activity of God (Dt 27:11—30:20).
12:15–16 See *WLC* 131.
12:15 See Luke 6:31. The genuine unity of the body of Christ is especially evident in the empathy of its members in moments of high joy or deep sorrow. See *WLC* 147; *WSC* 80.
12:16 Paul's language gives the idea of Christians sharing the same thoughts with respect to one another, another indication of the strategic role of the mind in sanctification (vv. 1–2). One manifestation of this is the absence of self-conceit and pride in worldly position (Php 2:1–8). Christians should be distinguished by their readiness "to associate with people of low position" or "to do menial work" (see NIV text note). **Do not be conceited.** See Proverbs 3:7. A further focus on the thought-world. How we think determines how we live. See *WLC* 145.
12:17 Verses 17–21 describe the way Christians should react to a non-Christian environment. See *WLC* 135.
12:18 live at peace with everyone. The Christian is a peacemaker by obligation and aim. Harmony is not always possible, since truth divides as well as unites, as Paul's double qualification ("If . . . as far as") recognizes. But a failure to strive for peace in personal relations with others is inexcusable. See *HC* 107.
12:19–21 The Christian is to be free from the desire to take personal revenge. Such freedom is possible because the believer knows that God will right all wrongs in his own perfect judgment (Dt 32:35) and because Scripture urges believers to show grace to the wrongdoer as long as God remains patient with him or her (Pr 25:21–22). Refraining from taking vengeance is a prime example of how believers are to "live at peace with everyone" (v. 18). See *WLC* 135,136; *HC* 105,106,107.
12:20 heap burning coals on his head. The meaning of this phrase is not entirely clear. It may refer to providing cooking and heating coals to those who lacked them, in which case it serves as an example of overcoming "evil with good (v. 21). It may be a statement that the conscience of the enemy will burn and perhaps lead him to modify or cease his evil behavior. Or it may be a reference to God's future vengeance, the enemy being all the more culpable in the face of his victim's kindness (parallel to "leave room for God's wrath," v. 19).
■ **13:1–14** *In Political and Social Life.* Paul provided further concrete examples of what it means to "do what is right in the eyes of everybody" (12:17) and "live at peace with everyone" (12:18), specifically by submitting to the civil authorities God has ordained and living in holiness and moral purity.
13:1–8 See *WCF* 20.4; 23.1; 23.2; 23.4; *WLC* 127,129; *HC* 104.
13:1 Christians have a distinct rationale for an appropriate submission to the governing authorities: God himself is the source of the governmental structuring of society (Pr 8:15–16; Da 2:21). See *WCF* 23.4; *BC* 36.
13:2–3 Rebellion against such authority implies rebellion against God's ordinance.
13:4 God's servant to do you good. The state's authority exists for society's benefit; this is its normal function, and Paul assumed that these benefits may be realized in practical terms, even when governments are professedly non-Christian. Although Christians cannot take personal revenge (12:19), God has ordained civil governments in part to take vengeance on his behalf as his delegates. Not having to enforce civil justice helps Christians live at peace with everyone (12:18) while at the same time demonstrating mercy and love to their enemies (12:19–21). **the sword.** The power of life and death. Capital punishment is undoubtedly in view. Elsewhere Paul accepted the principle of such punishment where appropriate (Ac 25:11). **an agent of wrath.** that which the individ-

6This is also why you pay taxes, for the authorities are God's servants, who give their
full time to governing. 7Give everyone what you owe him: If you owe taxes, pay taxes;[h]
if revenue, then revenue; if respect, then respect; if honor, then honor.

Love, for the Day Is Near

8Let no debt remain outstanding, except the continuing debt to love one another, for
he who loves his fellowman has fulfilled the law.[i] 9The commandments, "Do not commit adultery," "Do not murder," "Do not steal," "Do not covet,"[a][j] and whatever other
commandment there may be, are summed up in this one rule: "Love your neighbor as
yourself."[b][k] 10Love does no harm to its neighbor. Therefore love is the fulfillment of the
law.[l]
11And do this, understanding the present time. The hour has come[m] for you to wake
up from your slumber,[n] because our salvation is nearer now than when we first believed.
12The night is nearly over; the day is almost here.[o] So let us put aside the deeds of darkness[p] and put on the armor[q] of light. 13Let us behave decently, as in the daytime, not in
orgies and drunkenness, not in sexual immorality and debauchery, not in dissension and
jealousy.[r] 14Rather, clothe yourselves with the Lord Jesus Christ,[s] and do not think about
how to gratify the desires of the sinful nature.[c]

The Weak and the Strong

14 Accept him whose faith is weak,[t] without passing judgment on disputable matters. 2One man's faith allows him to eat everything, but another man, whose
faith is weak, eats only vegetables. 3The man who eats everything must not look down
on[u] him who does not, and the man who does not eat everything must not condemn[v]
the man who does, for God has accepted him. 4Who are you to judge someone else's servant?[w] To his own master he stands or falls. And he will stand, for the Lord is able to
make him stand.
5One man considers one day more sacred than another;[x] another man considers every day alike. Each one should be fully convinced in his own mind. 6He who regards one

13:7 [h]Mt 17:25; 22:17, 21; Lk 23:2
13:8 [i]ver 10; Jn 13:34; Gal 5:14; Col 3:14
13:9 [j]Ex 20:13-15,17; Dt 5:17-19,21 [k]Lev 19:18; Mt 19:19
13:10 [l]ver 8; Mt 22:39,40
13:11 [m]1Co 7:29-31; 10:11 [n]Eph 5:14; 1Th 5:5,6
13:12 [o]1Jn 2:8 [p]Eph 5:11 [q]Eph 6:11,13
13:13 [r]Gal 5:20,21
13:14 [s]Gal 3:27; 5:16; Eph 4:24
14:1 [t]Ro 15:1; 1Co 8:9-12
14:3 [u]Lk 18:9 [v]Col 2:16
14:4 [w]Jas 4:12
14:5 [x]Gal 4:10

[a] *9* Exodus 20:13–15,17; Deut. 5:17–19,21 [b] *9* Lev. 19:18 [c] *14* Or *the flesh*

---

ual must not do (12:19) the state may legitimately do in the pursuit of justice. See *WCF* 23.2; *HC* 105.
13:6 why you pay taxes. Christian submission is a response of the conscience instructed by divine revelation. Because the task of government is divinely ordained and requires financial undergirding, Christians are to pay their taxes with a distinctive motive and spirit: The burden of paying taxes becomes an element in their devotion to God.
13:7 Give everyone what you owe him. Paul was evidently familiar with Jesus' statement (see Mt 22:21) and here indicated how it applies both to the transaction of paying taxes and to those to whom the taxes are paid. See *WLC* 141; *BC* 36.
13:8–10 Paul further applied his basic principle of Christian consecration. The connection between verses 7 and 8 is found in the exhortation of verse 7: The Christian should meet financial obligations to the state. This, however, is but the particular application of the general principle now enunciated: All obligations must be met. However, one obligation is constant: love for others. See *WCF* 19.2; 19.5; *WLC* 132,135; *WSC* 65.
13:9 Love your neighbor as yourself. See Leviticus 19:18. This is not an exhortation to self-love. Rather, the same concern assumed for oneself as created in the image of God (Ge 1:26–27) is to be exhibited to others (Lk 6:31). Paul's assumption that we naturally love ourselves implies that self-love is legitimate, indeed unavoidable, and contrary to any form of masochism. See *WLC* 148; *WSC* 81.
13:11–14 See *WLC* 113; *HC* 105.
13:11 understanding the present time. Spiritual discernment is rooted in the apprehension of divine revelation. Paul's stress on the role of the mind is again evident. **salvation.** In the sense of final redemption (8:23).
13:12 night . . . day. Paul was speaking of the present age of sin as "night" and the coming age of blessing as "day" (see theological article "The Plan of the Ages" at Heb 7). **So let us put aside . . . put on.** The metaphor "armor of light" stresses that development of positive spiritual graces, not merely rejection of vices, is essential to spiritual defense.
13:13 Let us behave decently. Paul's warning against a sinful lifestyle strikingly includes not only the traditional sins of the flesh (sexual sins and wild living), but also insidious vices that can be harbored and even paraded within the very heart of the church ("dissension and jealousy"). See *WLC* 136,139.
13:14 clothe yourselves with the Lord Jesus Christ. A further exposition of what it means to "put on the armor of light" (v. 12), indicating that those who are in Christ must live lives consistent with their new status (Eph 4:1).
■ **14:1—15:13** *Among Weak and Strong.* Paul dealt with relationships between weak and strong Christians. Much of this discussion touched on matters that could easily have divided Jewish and Gentile believers.
14:1 Accept him whose faith is weak. The Christian's basic attitude toward a fellow believer is to be one of welcome and acceptance based on God's attitude toward us in Christ (v. 3; 15:7). The weak Christian is bound by a conscience that has not yet been fully instructed by the gospel to enjoy Christian freedom (v. 2). **disputable matters.** In this instance, questions of food, drink and the observation of holy days. While Paul did not regard these controversies as insoluble, he considered the underlying issue of the unity of the church's fellowship as more immediately and fundamentally important (cf. 12:5,10,16). The particular issues in view here did not belong to the essential gospel, but to the relative strength or weakness of the individual's faith in that gospel. Where the heart of the gospel was at stake, Paul's response was different (e.g., Gal 1:6–7; 3:1–5; Php 3:2,18–19).
14:2 eats only vegetables. Vegetarianism was not required by the Old Testament, although the practice appears there (e.g., Da 1:12).
14:3 look down . . . condemn. The tendency of the strong is to despise the inhibitions of the weak as legalistic bondage; the temptation of the weak is to condemn the strong for behavior that looks like lawless license. Christians embracing these mistaken responses should yield in light of God's gracious acceptance of both weak and strong. Furthermore, a fellow believer is God's servant (not ours) and is answerable only to him. This is not a denial of proper corporate church discipline (see theological article "Church Discipline and Excommunication" at 1Co 5).
14:4 See *WCF* 20.2.
14:5 One man considers one day more sacred than another. Probably a reference to the elaborate Jewish calendar of holy days. It is unlikely that Paul had in mind here weekly Sabbath observance. Were the weekly Sabbath in view, it would have been more natural for him to say, "One man considers the Sabbath more

Christian Liberty: How Free Am I?

REFORMED theology was born in the shadow of Roman Catholic legalism, and for this reason Christian liberty has always been an important facet. This emphasis is rooted in the fact that the New Testament sees salvation in Christ as liberation from sin and corruption, and the Christian life as one of liberty—Christ has freed us for freedom (Jn 8:32,36; Gal 5:1). Christ's liberating action is not primarily a matter of sociopolitical or economic improvement, as is sometimes suggested today, but relates mainly to three specific points.

First, as Christians we have been set free from the Mosaic Law as a system of salvation. Being justified by faith in Christ, we are no longer condemned by God's law, but graciously acquitted on the basis of Jesus' merit (Ro 3:19; 6:14–15; Gal 3:23–25). This means that our standing with God (the "peace" and "access" of Ro 5:1–2) rests wholly on the fact that we have been accepted by and adopted in Christ. It does not, nor ever will, depend on what we do, nor will it ever be imperiled by what we fail to do. As long as we are in this world we live not by being perfect, but by being forgiven.

All natural religion, then, is negated, for the instinct of fallen humanity, as expressed in every form of religion that the world has ever devised, is to suppose that one gains and maintains a right relationship with ultimate reality (whether conceived as a personal God or in other terms) by disciplines of legal observance, proper ritual and asceticism. The world's faiths prescribe these disciplines as a means of establishing one's own righteousness—and Paul observed unbelieving Jews engaged in these very practices (Ro 10:3). Paul's experience had taught him the hopelessness of this enterprise. No human performance is ever good enough, for there are always wrong desires in the heart, coupled with a lack of right ones, regardless of how correct one's outward motions may be (Ro 7:7–11; cf. Php 3:6)—and it is at the heart that God looks first.

When we seek righteousness before God through keeping the law, the law arouses, exposes and condemns the sin that permeates our moral makeup, making us aware of the depth of our guilt (Ro 3:19; 1Co 15:56; Gal 3:10). So the futility of treating the law as a covenant of works, and of seeking righteousness by it, becomes plain (Gal 3:10–12; 4:21–31), as does the misery of not knowing what else to do. This is the bondage to the law from which Christ sets us free.

Second, as Christians we have been set free from sin's dominion (Jn 8:34–36; Ro 6:14–23). We have been supernaturally regenerated and made alive to God through union with Christ in his death and risen life (Ro 6:3–11), and this means that our deepest desire now is to serve God by practicing righteousness (Ro 6:18,22). Sin's domination involved not only constant acts of disobedience, but also a constant lack of zeal for law keeping that sometimes deteriorated into positive resentment and hatred toward the law. Now, however, being transformed in our hearts, motivated by gratitude for acceptance through free grace, and energized by the Holy Spirit, we "serve in the new way of the Spirit, and not in the old way of the written code" (Ro 7:6). This means that our attempts at obedience are now joyful and integrated in a way that was never true before. Sin rules them no longer. In this respect, too, we have been liberated from bondage.

Third, as Christians we have been set free from the superstition that treats matter and physical pleasure as intrinsically evil. Against this idea, Paul insisted that we are free to enjoy as God's good gifts all created things and the pleasures that they yield (1Ti 4:1–5), provided only that we do not transgress the moral law in our enjoyments nor hinder our own spiritual well-being or that of others (1Co 6:12–13; 8:7–13). The Reformers renewed this emphasis against various forms of medieval legalism.

Fourth, as Christians we are free from the regulations that others add to the teaching of Scripture in the matters of faith and worship. To submit our consciences to such human additions to Scripture—or, worse, to submit by blind obedience to such requirements—is to violate the liberty of conscience that God grants (cf. *WCF* 20). Fifth, as Christians we have been set free from self-righteousness in which we compare our behavior with that of others and judge ours to be a lot better in God's sight. Sixth, as believers we have been set free from the urge to arrange the many laws in order of importance. To do so we have to introduce more laws—laws to tell us which laws are most important. Hence, by the end of the Old Testament period there were 613 different rules or laws in addition to explanations about them.

Nevertheless, there are still ways in which believers have not yet been completely freed by God. For one thing, although we are free from the dominion and condemnation of sin, we are not free from its presence and influence. As long as we are in this life, we are continually subjected to temptation (1Ti 6:9), drawn in by the lure of the sin that continues to indwell us and surround us (Ro 7:14–25; Gal 5:17) and plagued by demonic forces (1Co 7:5; 1Ti 4:1; Rev 16:14). Our individual freedom from sin's presence awaits our release from our mortal bodies, and our complete freedom from the presence of sin in creation awaits Jesus' return and the restoration of all things in the new heavens and the new earth (Rev 21:1–5).

Nor are we free to exercise our liberty in harmful ways. For example, as Paul made clear in his discussion of questionable matters such as eating food sacrificed to idols (Ro 14; 1Co 8), believers have an obligation not to exercise their freedoms in ways that may cause other believers to fall into sin. Further, God has not freed us from obedience to the law. Although such obedience cannot merit our salvation, nor can our breaking of the law condemn us, the law is still our moral guide. Jesus himself affirmed the law's abiding validity in the life of every believer (Mt 5:17–19), and Paul went so far as to refer to it as "the law of Christ" (Gal 6:2).

day as special, does so to the Lord. He who eats meat, eats to the Lord, for he gives
thanks to God;[y] and he who abstains, does so to the Lord and gives thanks to God. 7For
none of us lives to himself alone[z] and none of us dies to himself alone. 8If we live, we live
to the Lord; and if we die, we die to the Lord. So, whether we live or die, we belong to
the Lord.[a]
9For this very reason, Christ died and returned to life[b] so that he might be the Lord
of both the dead and the living.[c] 10You, then, why do you judge your brother? Or why do
you look down on your brother? For we will all stand before God's judgment seat.[d] 11It
is written:

> " 'As surely as I live,' says the Lord,
> 'every knee will bow before me;
> every tongue will confess to God.' "[a][e]

12So then, each of us will give an account of himself to God.[f]
13Therefore let us stop passing judgment[g] on one another. Instead, make up your
mind not to put any stumbling block or obstacle in your brother's way. 14As one who is
in the Lord Jesus, I am fully convinced that no food[b] is unclean in itself.[h] But if anyone
regards something as unclean, then for him it is unclean.[i] 15If your brother is distressed
because of what you eat, you are no longer acting in love.[j] Do not by your eating destroy
your brother for whom Christ died.[k] 16Do not allow what you consider good to be spoken of as evil.[l] 17For the kingdom of God is not a matter of eating and drinking,[m] but of
righteousness, peace and joy in the Holy Spirit,[n] 18because anyone who serves Christ in
this way is pleasing to God and approved by men.[o]
19Let us therefore make every effort to do what leads to peace[p] and to mutual edification.[q] 20Do not destroy the work of God for the sake of food.[r] All food is clean, but it
is wrong for a man to eat anything that causes someone else to stumble.[s] 21It is better
not to eat meat or drink wine or to do anything else that will cause your brother to fall.[t]
22So whatever you believe about these things keep between yourself and God. Blessed
is the man who does not condemn[u] himself by what he approves. 23But the man who has
doubts[v] is condemned if he eats, because his eating is not from faith; and everything that
does not come from faith is sin.

15 We who are strong ought to bear with the failings of the weak[w] and not to
please ourselves. 2Each of us should please his neighbor for his good,[x] to build
him up.[y] 3For even Christ did not please himself[z] but, as it is written: "The insults of
those who insult you have fallen on me."[c][a] 4For everything that was written in the past
was written to teach us,[b] so that through endurance and the encouragement of the
Scriptures we might have hope.

14:6 [y]Mt 14:19; 1Co 10:30,31; 1Ti 4:3,4
14:7 [z]2Co 5:15; Gal 2:20
14:8 [a]Php 1:20
14:9 [b]Rev 1:18 [c]2Co 5:15
14:10 [d]2Co 5:10
14:11 [e]Isa 45:23; Php 2:10,11
14:12 [f]Mt 12:36; 1Pe 4:5
14:13 [g]Mt 7:1
14:14 [h]Ac 10:15 [i]1Co 8:7
14:15 [j]Eph 5:2 [k]1Co 8:11
14:16 [l]1Co 10:30
14:17 [m]1Co 8:8 [n]Ro 15:13
14:18 [o]2Co 8:21
14:19 [p]Ps 34:14; Ro 12:18; Heb 12:14 [q]Ro 15:2; 2Co 12:19
14:20 [r]ver 15 [s]1Co 8:9-12
14:21 [t]1Co 8:13
14:22 [u]1Jn 3:21
14:23 [v]ver 5
15:1 [w]Ro 14:1; Gal 6:1,2; 1Th 5:14
15:2 [x]1Co 10:33 [y]Ro 14:19
15:3 [z]2Co 8:9 [a]Ps 69:9
15:4 [b]Ro 4:23,24

[a] *11* Isaiah 45:23 [b] *14* Or *that nothing* [c] *3* Psalm 69:9

---

sacred than the other days." **Each one should be fully convinced.** See note on 4:21.

14:6–7 An appeal to what is shared by both weak and strong: the desire to honor the same Lord. That both belong to him puts minor divisions into perspective.

14:7–9 See *HC* 1.

14:9–12 Christ alone is Lord (v. 8) and Judge of his people. The immense price he paid to become such exposes the inappropriateness of believers judging or despising their brothers and sisters. Paul referred to Isaiah 45:23 as a reminder that believers must give an account of their lives to the Lord as those being judged, not as those who judge. See *WCF* 8.4; 33.1; *WLC* 45,52.

14:13—15:4 While Paul's own conscience had been liberated by the teaching of Christ (v. 14; cf. Mk 7:18–19), he recognized that not all believers had come to enjoy such freedom. Consideration for such fellow Christians ("acting in love"; 14:15) meant avoiding behavior that might distress them. Paul included two specific injunctions to this effect (14:15–16).

14:13 See *WLC* 151.

14:15 Do not by your eating destroy your brother for whom Christ died. In the Old Testament, to "destroy" means to "cut off from the covenant community" (e.g., Dt 28:21,45,48,51,61,63). To encourage weak believers to violate their consciences was to encourage them to breach their covenant with God and, in their own minds, to engage in self-destruction. At the same time, Paul did not allow tyranny to be imposed upon the church by the weaker members (i.e., forcing the stronger to submit to their every whim and scruple). See *WLC* 151.

14:16–18 The strong are urged to weigh the importance of exercising their freedom against two considerations: (1) Availing themselves of their freedom may bring division and disrepute on the church. (2) God's kingdom (and therefore our freedom) is not a matter of food and drink, but of the blessings of grace (5:1–2). Since freedom does not consist in food and drink, one cannot lose one's liberty by refraining from them.

14:17–19 See *WCF* 18.3; *WLC* 83; *WSC* 36; *HC* 58,86,90.

14:18 approved by men. See verse 16. While God alone is our judge (v. 12), the impact of our actions on others plays a vital role in fellowship and evangelism. See *BC* 10.

14:19–21 Believers are actively to promote "peace" and "mutual edification" (v. 19). For the strong, this includes both maintaining fellowship with the weak and encouraging them in the liberty that is theirs in Christ. If the Roman believers kept such aims in view, freedom to eat and drink would be willingly sacrificed for the sake of the weak; the well-being of the weaker brother or sister would take precedence over the enjoyment of meat and wine. See *WLC* 151.

14:22–23 Paul further urged the strong to enjoy their liberty of conscience in God's presence (while refraining from publicly exercising it). See *WCF* 20.2; *BC* 24.

15:1–4 We who are strong ought to bear with the failings of the weak. Paul again aligned himself with the strong, indicating the rightness of freedom. He still, however, emphasized the responsibility of the strong to support the weak.

15:2 See 14:19, 1 Corinthians 8:1 and 10:23.

15:3 Paul quoted from Psalm 69:9 (one of the most frequently quoted psalms in the New Testament). The Messiah's willingness to deny himself and to suffer for the benefit of others was to serve as an example to the Christians in Rome.

15:4 written to teach us. That the Old Testament Scriptures were written under God's providence for the benefit of Christians

5 May the God who gives endurance and encouragement give you a spirit of unity[c]
among yourselves as you follow Christ Jesus, 6 so that with one heart and mouth you may
glorify the God and Father[d] of our Lord Jesus Christ.
7 Accept one another,[e] then, just as Christ accepted you, in order to bring praise to
God. 8 For I tell you that Christ has become a servant of the Jews[a][f] on behalf of God's
truth, to confirm the promises[g] made to the patriarchs 9 so that the Gentiles[h] may glorify God[i] for his mercy, as it is written:

> "Therefore I will praise you among the Gentiles;
> I will sing hymns to your name."[b][j]

10 Again, it says,

> "Rejoice, O Gentiles, with his people."[c][k]

11 And again,

> "Praise the Lord, all you Gentiles,
> and sing praises to him, all you peoples."[d][l]

12 And again, Isaiah says,

> "The Root of Jesse[m] will spring up,
> one who will arise to rule over the nations;
> the Gentiles will hope in him."[e][n]

13 May the God of hope fill you with all joy and peace[o] as you trust in him, so that you
may overflow with hope by the power of the Holy Spirit.[p]

Paul the Minister to the Gentiles

14 I myself am convinced, my brothers, that you yourselves are full of goodness,[q] complete in knowledge[r] and competent to instruct one another. 15 I have written you quite
boldly on some points, as if to remind you of them again, because of the grace God gave
me[s] 16 to be a minister of Christ Jesus to the Gentiles[t] with the priestly duty of proclaiming the gospel of God,[u] so that the Gentiles might become an offering[v] acceptable to
God, sanctified by the Holy Spirit.
17 Therefore I glory in Christ Jesus[w] in my service to God.[x] 18 I will not venture to speak
of anything except what Christ has accomplished through me in leading the Gentiles[y]
to obey God[z] by what I have said and done— 19 by the power of signs and miracles,[a]
through the power of the Spirit.[b] So from Jerusalem[c] all the way around to Illyricum, I

15:5 [c]Ro 12:16; 1Co 1:10
15:6 [d]Rev 1:6
15:7 [e]Ro 14:1
15:8 [f]Mt 15:24; Ac 3:25, 26 [g]2Co 1:20
15:9 [h]Ro 3:29 [i]Mt 9:8 [j]2Sa 22:50; Ps 18:49
15:10 [k]Dt 32:43
15:11 [l]Ps 117:1
15:12 [m]Rev 5:5 [n]Isa 11:10; Mt 12:21
15:13 [o]Ro 14:17 [p]ver 19; 1Co 2:4; 1Th 1:5
15:14 [q]Eph 5:9 [r]2Pe 1:12
15:15 [s]Ro 12:3
15:16 [t]Ac 9:15; Ro 11:13 [u]Ro 1:1 [v]Isa 66:20
15:17 [w]Php 3:3 [x]Heb 2:17
15:18 [y]Ac 15:12; 21:19; Ro 1:5 [z]Ro 16:26
15:19 [a]Jn 4:48; Ac 19:11 [b]ver 13 [c]Ac 22:17-21

[a] *8* Greek *circumcision* [b] *9* 2 Samuel 22:50; Psalm 18:49 [c] *10* Deut. 32:43 [d] *11* Psalm 117:1
[e] *12* Isaiah 11:10

is a basic New Testament conviction (1Co 10:11; 2Ti 3:15–17; 1Pe 1:10–12). See *WCF* 1.1; 1.8; *WLC* 4,155; *WSC* 89; *BC* 7.

15:6 with one heart and mouth. See 10:9–10. Unity in the church is essential if God is to be glorified. Paul had demonstrated that humanity, which has fallen short of God's glory, is restored to it in Christ's reconciling work (1:21,23; 3:23; 5:2,11; 8:17,30).

15:8–9 Christ . . . a servant of the Jews . . . so that the Gentiles. The mutual acceptance of believers is rooted in Christ's ministry. He served the Jews in order to extend God's mercy to the Gentiles. Just as Christ served both Jews and Gentiles, Christian Jews and Christian Gentiles should devote themselves to each other. See *WCF* 27.1; *WLC* 34, 162.

15:9–12 See *WCF* 25.2; *WLC* 62.

15:9–11 Gentiles. Paul referred first to 2 Samuel 22:50 (Ps 18:49) and then to Deuteronomy 32:43, Psalm 117:1 and Isaiah 11:10. These passages all refer to the Gentiles' acknowledgment of the God of Israel. Second Samuel 22:50 and Deuteronomy 32:43 mention Gentiles praising God alongside Jews. These Old Testament passages form an appropriate ending for Paul's discussion in this section of life in the church.

15:13 What was described as the effect of Scripture in verse 4 (having hope) is now attributed to the work of the Holy Spirit. Throughout the New Testament, God's saving acts are attributed to God's Word and Spirit (e.g., sanctification in Jn 17:17; salvation in Ro 1:16; searching the heart in Heb 4:12; regeneration in 1Pe 1:23). Such passages led Calvin to speak of the "indissoluble bond" between the Word and the Holy Spirit (*Institutes of the Christian Religion* 1.9.1). They underscore the crucial importance of regular Bible reading in the life of the Christian. See *WCF* 18.3; *WLC* 194.

■ **15:14—16:27** *Final Greetings.* Paul closed his letter by touching on six matters: his vision for ministry (15:14–22), his visit to Rome (15:23–33), greetings to the Romans (16:1–16), warnings against enemies (16:17–20), greetings from companions (16:21–24) and a final doxology (16:25–27).

■ **15:14–22** *Vision for Ministry.* Paul returned to the theme of his introduction: his own ministry and his vision for the expansion and influence of the gospel (cf. 11:13–14).

15:14 my brothers. A further indication of deep emotion (1:13; 7:1,4; 11:25; 12:1). Paul graciously assured the Romans that his lengthy exposition of the gospel was not intended to raise doubts about their spiritual understanding. Their knowledge of the gospel and ability to apply it practically in mutual admonition (they were "competent to instruct one another"; cf. Col 3:16) was not in question.

15:16 minister . . . with the priestly duty. The same Greek word for "minister" is used of Christ (Heb 8:2) and of Epaphroditus (Php 2:25). Paul saw the preaching of the gospel as the means by which the Gentiles would be brought to God as a sacrificial thank offering (12:1).

15:17–20 Paul exulted in his ministry, unselfconsciously expounding the gospel in Trinitarian terms (mentioning God the Father in vv. 17–18, the Son in vv. 17–20, the Spirit in v. 19; cf. v. 16). He did not exult in his own accomplishments, but only in what Christ had done through him: "leading the Gentiles to obey God" (v. 18; cf. 1:5). See *WCF* 8.8.

15:19 signs and miracles. A phrase rooted in the authentication of Moses' ministry at the time of the exodus (Ex 7:3; Dt 4:34; 6:22; 7:19). God periodically gave such signs and miracles at critical junctures of redemptive history (e.g., the exodus, the establishing of the prophetic ministry of Elijah and Elisha, the preserving of his people in the time of Daniel and the ministry of Christ and the apostles). In Scripture, such events were unusual rather than typi-

have fully proclaimed the gospel of Christ. [20]It has always been my ambition to preach
the gospel where Christ was not known, so that I would not be building on someone
else's foundation.[d] [21]Rather, as it is written:

"Those who were not told about him will see,
and those who have not heard will understand."[a][e]

[22]This is why I have often been hindered from coming to you.[f]

Paul's Plan to Visit Rome

[23]But now that there is no more place for me to work in these regions, and since I have
been longing for many years to see you,[g] [24]I plan to do so when I go to Spain.[h] I hope to
visit you while passing through and to have you assist me on my journey there, after I
have enjoyed your company for a while. [25]Now, however, I am on my way to Jerusalem[i]
in the service[j] of the saints there. [26]For Macedonia[k] and Achaia[l] were pleased to make
a contribution for the poor among the saints in Jerusalem. [27]They were pleased to do it,
and indeed they owe it to them. For if the Gentiles have shared in the Jews' spiritual
blessings, they owe it to the Jews to share with them their material blessings.[m] [28]So after I have completed this task and have made sure that they have received this fruit, I will
go to Spain and visit you on the way. [29]I know that when I come to you,[n] I will come in
the full measure of the blessing of Christ.

[30]I urge you, brothers, by our Lord Jesus Christ and by the love of the Spirit,[o] to join
me in my struggle by praying to God for me.[p] [31]Pray that I may be rescued[q] from the unbelievers in Judea and that my service in Jerusalem may be acceptable to the saints there,
[32]so that by God's will[r] I may come to you[s] with joy and together with you be refreshed.[t]
[33]The God of peace[u] be with you all. Amen.

Personal Greetings

16 I commend[v] to you our sister Phoebe, a servant[b] of the church in Cenchrea.[w]
[2]I ask you to receive her in the Lord[x] in a way worthy of the saints and to give
her any help she may need from you, for she has been a great help to many people, including me.

[3]Greet Priscilla[c] and Aquila,[y] my fellow workers in Christ Jesus.[z] [4]They risked their lives
for me. Not only I but all the churches of the Gentiles are grateful to them.

15:20 [d]2Co 10:15,16
15:21 [e]Isa 52:15
15:22 [f]Ro 1:13
15:23 [g]Ac 19:21; Ro 1:10,11
15:24 [h]ver 28
15:25 [i]Ac 19:21 [j]Ac 24:17
15:26 [k]Ac 16:9; 2Co 8:1 [l]Ac 18:12
15:27 [m]1Co 9:11
15:29 [n]Ro 1:10,11
15:30 [o]Gal 5:22 [p]2Co 1:11; Col 4:12
15:31 [q]2Th 3:2
15:32 [r]Ac 18:21 [s]Ro 1:10,13 [t]1Co 16:18
15:33 [u]Ro 16:20; 2Co 13:11; Php 4:9; 1Th 5:23; Heb 13:20
16:1 [v]2Co 3:1 [w]Ac 18:18
16:2 [x]Php 2:29
16:3 [y]Ac 18:2 [z]ver 7,9,10

[a] *21* Isaiah 52:15 [b] *1* Or *deaconess* [c] *3* Greek *Prisca,* a variant of *Priscilla*

cal and pointed to the stages of redemptive history and the new revelation that accompanied those stages. **from Jerusalem all the way around to Illyricum.** Paul's journeys, according to Acts, had stretched from the eastern Mediterranean as far west as Macedonia. There is no record that Paul personally entered Illyricum (in the region of modern Yugoslavia and Albania). While he may have done so, it seems more likely that he meant to convey that he went as far as Macedonia. He established mission centers but did not preach personally in every village. From such centers, even Illyricum may have been reached with the gospel.

15:21 not told . . . have not heard. Paul referred to Isaiah 52:15, where the prophet spoke of the servant reaching the Gentiles. It was because of this prophetic expectation that Paul moved farther and farther into Gentile lands.

■ **15:23–33** *Plan to Visit Rome.* Paul reaffirmed his desire and plan to go to Rome.

15:23–24 Two things made the visit to Rome possible: (1) The current phase of Paul's commission had been fulfilled and (2) the new phase involving outreach to Spain was imminent. Paul sought the Roman Christians' fellowship in it.

15:24 Spain. The western extremity of the ancient world. Some suggest that Paul thought of Spain as the Tarshish of Isaiah 66:19 and saw the extension of his preaching there as significant for the Christian mission (Mt 24:14; Ac 1:8).

15:25–33 Paul disclosed his immediate plans to visit Jerusalem with the gifts that the churches had raised for the Christians there. Jerusalem was an impoverished city in general; in addition, the Christians there (who were primarily Jewish) suffered particular hardship as a suspect minority. But Paul saw a deeper significance than charity in the gift: It was a duty (v. 27), a solemn obligation of Gentile Christians in view of the privilege they had received in being grafted into God's olive tree (11:17). This conforms to the general principle that those who receive spiritual blessings should share their own material blessings (1Co 9:3–14; Gal 6:6). See *WLC* 191,196; *BC* 30.

15:29 full measure of the blessing of Christ. A striking comment in view of the manner in which Paul's aspirations were fulfilled: as a prisoner (Ac 28:11–16).

15:31 Paul's concern was twofold: (1) that he be protected from the Jewish hostility that had marked the whole of his ministry and (2) that Jewish Christians in Jerusalem respond positively to the Gentile gift, thus affirming the apostle's ministry (v. 32).

15:33 The God of peace. One of Paul's favorite designations for God (16:20; 2Co 13:11; Php 4:9; 1Th 5:23; 2Th 3:16); it was particularly appropriate here in view of his struggles (v. 30).

■ **16:1–16** *Greetings to Christians in Rome.* Paul's letters typically end with personal news and greetings. The closing chapter of Romans is remarkable for the large number of fellow believers mentioned. These verses give insight into the warmth of the apostle's personal relationships as well as the fellowship of the early Christians.

16:1 Phoebe. Probably the bearer of Paul's letter. The name *Phoebe* is common in Greek mythology and indicates a Gentile background. **servant.** Greek, *diakonos.* May also be translated "minister" (1Ti 4:6) or "deacon" (see NIV text note; see also Php 1:1; 1Ti 3:8). This language suggests that Phoebe exercised a specific ministry, but there is little agreement as to whether she held the church office of deacon or whether she served the church in an unofficial capacity. **Cenchrea.** The port of Corinth on the Saronic Gulf (see "Introduction: Time and Place of Writing").

16:2 See *HC* 123.

16:3 Priscilla and Aquila. Paul actually used the form "Prisca" (see NIV text note; 1Co 16:19; 2Ti 4:19) rather than the nickname "Priscilla" used by Luke (Ac 18:2,18,26). The couple were tentmakers (like Paul; Ac 18:3) with whom Paul resided in Corinth. They had left Rome following the decree of Claudius and had accompanied Paul to Ephesus (Ac 18:18), where they had instructed Apollos (Ac 18:24–26) prior to returning to Rome. No further information is given regarding their heroic actions on Paul's behalf.

5 Greet also the church that meets at their house.[a]
Greet my dear friend Epenetus, who was the first convert[b] to Christ in the province of Asia.
6 Greet Mary, who worked very hard for you.
7 Greet Andronicus and Junias, my relatives[c] who have been in prison with me. They are outstanding among the apostles, and they were in Christ before I was.
8 Greet Ampliatus, whom I love in the Lord.
9 Greet Urbanus, our fellow worker in Christ,[d] and my dear friend Stachys.
10 Greet Apelles, tested and approved in Christ.
Greet those who belong to the household of Aristobulus.
11 Greet Herodion, my relative.[e]
Greet those in the household of Narcissus who are in the Lord.
12 Greet Tryphena and Tryphosa, those women who work hard in the Lord.
Greet my dear friend Persis, another woman who has worked very hard in the Lord.
13 Greet Rufus, chosen in the Lord, and his mother, who has been a mother to me, too.
14 Greet Asyncritus, Phlegon, Hermes, Patrobas, Hermas and the brothers with them.
15 Greet Philologus, Julia, Nereus and his sister, and Olympas and all the saints[f] with them.[g]
16 Greet one another with a holy kiss.[h]
All the churches of Christ send greetings.

17 I urge you, brothers, to watch out for those who cause divisions and put obstacles
in your way that are contrary to the teaching you have learned.[i] Keep away from them.[j]
18 For such people are not serving our Lord Christ, but their own appetites.[k] By smooth
talk and flattery they deceive[l] the minds of naive people. 19 Everyone has heard[m] about
your obedience, so I am full of joy over you; but I want you to be wise about what is good,
and innocent about what is evil.[n]
20 The God of peace[o] will soon crush[p] Satan under your feet.
The grace of our Lord Jesus be with you.[q]
21 Timothy,[r] my fellow worker, sends his greetings to you, as do Lucius,[s] Jason[t] and
Sosipater, my relatives.[u]
22 I, Tertius, who wrote down this letter, greet you in the Lord.

16:5 [a]1Co 16:19; Col 4:15; Phm 2 [b]1Co 16:15
16:7 [c]ver 11,21
16:9 [d]ver 3
16:11 [e]ver 7,21
16:15 [f]ver 2 [g]ver 14
16:16 [h]1Co 16:20; 2Co 13:12; 1Th 5:26
16:17 [i]Gal 1:8,9; 1Ti 1:3; 6:3 [j]2Th 3:6,14; 2Jn 10
16:18 [k]Php 3:19 [l]Col 2:4
16:19 [m]Ro 1:8 [n]Mt 10:16; 1Co 14:20
16:20 [o]Ro 15:33 [p]Ge 3:15 [q]1Th 5:28
16:21 [r]Ac 16:1 [s]Ac 13:1 [t]Ac 17:5 [u]ver 7,11

16:5 Epenetus. The name means "worthy of praise." He was evidently the first of a harvest of converts in Asia.
16:6 Mary, who worked very hard for you. Otherwise unidentified. Paul recognized the devoted service of women (v. 12). Mary's work for the Roman church was known beyond her own congregation.
16:7 Andronicus and Junias. Both are translated as men's names, but early commentators believed them to be husband and wife (i.e., "Junia"). They were fellow Jews who had been converted ("in Christ") before Paul. It would be remarkable but not impossible that they were Paul's "relatives" (close family members; see also vv. 11,21), but the more general "kinsmen" is also possible (cf. 9:3 where the same word describes Paul's relationship to the entire Jewish nation). **outstanding among the apostles.** They may have been special messengers of the churches, but they did not hold the authoritative office of apostle (cf. note on 2 Co 1:1). Alternatively, the phrase may be translated "well known by the apostles."
16:8 Ampliatus. A common Roman slave name, perhaps the Ampliatus whose name appears on a tomb in the Catacomb of Domitilla, niece of the Emperor Domitian.
16:9 Urbanus . . . Stachys. Common slave names. The former was Roman; the latter, Greek.
16:10 Apelles. A common Greek name borne by one who had distinguished himself through trial and had remained faithful ("tested and approved"), a dual idea conveyed by Paul's single Greek word (12:2). **Aristobulus.** The style of Paul's greeting here (as in v. 11, but by contrast with vv. 5,14–15) may suggest that he was not included in the church. Possibly he was the grandson of Herod the Great and a friend of the Emperor Claudius.
16:11 Herodion. Perhaps a freedman of the household of Herod, since a freedman customarily took the name of his or her patron. **Narcissus.** Perhaps to be identified with Narcissus, the aide of Claudius, who was forced to commit suicide by Agrippina after Nero's accession.
16:12 Tryphena and Tryphosa . . . who work hard in the Lord. Two women with names from a common root ("gentle"/"delicate") and therefore possibly sisters or even twins. **Persis.** A common name for female slaves.
16:13 Rufus, chosen in the Lord. One of the most intriguing of the names listed in view of Mark 15:21, Mark's Gospel possibly having been written from Rome. The epithet "chosen" may reflect the unique circumstances that brought his family into contact with Christ. Paul's allusion to the mother suggests deep affection for the family.
16:16 holy kiss. The kiss was a common token of greeting in the East. Here Paul urged the believers to sanctify their greetings as symbols of fellowship.
▪ **16:17–20** *Warning Against Enemies.* Reflection on Paul's knowledge of these believers, their problems in Rome (ch. 14) and the divisive activity of Satan (v. 20) evoked an urgent summons to guard their unity (see Eph 4:3). They were to avoid those who caused divisions. Paul bluntly indicated that a divisive spirit is sinful, a mark of life in the flesh; however plausible its rationale, it is a form of self-indulgence (Gal 5:19–20). Christians must learn to discern the difference between the reality (deception; v. 18) and the appearance ("smooth talk and flattery"; v. 18); they must not be naive (1Co 14:20).
16:17 See *BC* 32.
16:19 innocent. Literally, "unmixed." The Romans needed spiritual wisdom and hearts without any alloy of evil.
16:20 Prior to the closing greetings and doxology, Paul included a promise of a prophetic nature, rooted in the first Biblical deliverance promise in Genesis 3:15. Satan is the source of division (cf. Ge 3:12). "The God of peace" (implying wholeness and integrity as well as tranquility) will act as the divine warrior to overcome Satan. This will take place "soon." Paul may have been speaking chronologically (in a short time) or eschatologically (seeing Christ's second coming as the next event on the divine calendar). **The grace of our Lord Jesus be with you.** A characteristically Pauline ending (Gal 6:18; 1Th 5:28). See *WLC* 195.
▪ **16:21–24** *Companions Sending Greetings.* Paul passed on greetings from the men who traveled with him.
16:21 Along with Silas, Timothy was Paul's closest colaborer following the disagreement with Barnabas (Ac 15:36–40), and he is mentioned in ten of Paul's letters. Lucius (whom some identify with Luke), Jason (possibly Paul's host in Thessalonica; Ac 17:5–9) and Sosipater (possibly the "Sopater" of Ac 20:4) may have been church delegates who accompanied Paul in the delivery of the collection to Jerusalem.
16:22 I, Tertius. Paul regularly used a secretary, identifying his

16:23 [v]Ac 19:22 | 16:25 [w]Eph 3:20 [x]Ro 2:16 [y]Eph 1:9; Col 1:26,27 | 16:27 [z]Ro 11:36

[23]Gaius, whose hospitality I and the whole church here enjoy, sends you his greetings.
Erastus,[v] who is the city's director of public works, and our brother Quartus send you
their greetings.[a]
[25]Now to him who is able[w] to establish you by my gospel[x] and the proclamation of
Jesus Christ, according to the revelation of the mystery[y] hidden for long ages past, [26]but
now revealed and made known through the prophetic writings by the command of the
eternal God, so that all nations might believe and obey him— [27]to the only wise God be
glory forever through Jesus Christ! Amen.[z]

[a] 23 Some manuscripts *their greetings.* [24]*May the grace of our Lord Jesus Christ be with all of you. Amen.*

letters as his own by a brief greeting written in his own handwriting (1Co 16:21; Gal 6:11; Col 4:18; 2Th 3:17).

16:23 Paul may have been residing with Gaius at the time of writing. He is presumably to be identified with the Gaius of 1 Corinthians 1:14 and may be the (Gaius?) Titius Justus of Acts 18:7. An Erastus is mentioned in Acts 19:22 and 2 Timothy 4:20, but it is not known whether these instances refer to the same man. Of greater interest is that a Christian held such a responsible post in the local government of Corinth. Of Quartus, nothing is known.

■ **16:25–27** *Apostolic Doxology.* The authenticity of this closing doxology has been questioned on the grounds of its length, its emphasis on mystery and its textual history (it is found at different points in the letter or even omitted altogether in various ancient manuscripts). Its length is perhaps appropriate, however, coming as it does at the end of this particular letter. Moreover, its themes draw to a fitting conclusion much that has already been said. In particular, Paul drew attention to his own teaching of the gospel (2:16; cf. 1Th 1:5; 2Ti 2:8) and its power to edify (1:11), to the revelation of God's mystery (11:25; cf. Eph 3:2–6), to faith and obedience among the nations (1:5) and to the wisdom of God in redemption (11:33; cf. Eph 3:10–12).

16:25 See *WLC* 155.

16:26 but now revealed and made known through the prophetic writings. Paul's "now" might suggest that he had the New Testament Scriptures in view here; however, his emphasis was that it was only now (i.e., in the light of Christ's coming) that the message already enshrined in the Old Testament was being spread to the nations. See *WCF* 14.2.

16:27 See *WCF* 2.1; *WLC* 7.

1 CORINTHIANS

Introduction

Overview

Author: The apostle Paul

Purpose: To counter defiance, divisions and lack of love that had arisen out of pride and self-importance in the Corinthian church

Date: c. A.D. 55

Key Truths:

- The church must be unified, not divided.
- Christians must look to God, not to the world, for their model of wisdom.
- Proper church courts and discipline ensure the peace and purity of the church.
- Christian liberty must be exercised in ways that protect those who are weak in faith.
- Worship and the exercise of spiritual gifts must respect and honor God and fellow believers.
- The reality of the future bodily resurrection of believers is integral to the gospel.

Author

This letter claims Paul as its author, and the Pauline authorship of the Corinthian correspondence has not been seriously questioned. Even radical scholars acknowledge that the epistle is fundamental to our understanding of Paul's ministry and message.

Time and Place of Writing

Paul wrote from Ephesus (16:8), almost certainly during his third missionary journey (c. A.D. 53–57). Since Paul stayed in Ephesus for well over two years (Ac 19:8,10), we may date the writing of 1 Corinthians about the year A.D. 55.

Original Audience

Although the book of Acts says nothing about this correspondence, Acts 18:1–11 gives us some important information about the founding of the church in Corinth during Paul's second missionary journey (c. A.D. 50–52). First, Paul arrived in Corinth after his visit to Athens (Ac 17:16–34), an experience that had reminded him of the foolishness of worldly wisdom. Second Corinthians 2:1–5 suggests that this incident with the Athenian philosophers made Paul more determined than ever to preach the simple message of the cross, however offensive it might be to some. Second, with the support of the influential Christian couple Aquila and Priscilla (16:19), Paul preached in the synagogue in Corinth until Jewish opposition forced him to focus his ministry on Gentiles. Third, the Christian congregation in Corinth, composed of both Jews and Gentiles, flourished dramatically (Ac 18:8–10). Finally, Paul's ministry in Corinth lasted more than 18 months (Ac 18:11,18). Paul had reason to expect a degree of spiritual maturity from the Corinthian Christians.

This letter reveals that after Paul left Corinth, the church developed a remarkable number of serious problems. Bickering and division, misunderstanding of the sacraments, disorder during the worship services, theological heresy and the extremes of moral laxity and unhealthy asceticism plagued the congregation. What had happened? Corinth was not only one of the largest cities in the Roman world, but also one of the most corrupt. A strategic commercial center, the city sought to provide international pleasures. It was a setting that polarized the Christians—some insisting that association with sinners was permissible and necessary, others arguing that some measure of isolation was essential to preserve holiness. These opposing tendencies spun out of control in Corinth and endangered the future of the congregation.

Purpose and Distinctives

We may infer from 5:9 that Paul had sent the church an earlier letter (which is no longer extant), exhorting its members to separate from immoral Christians. This letter must have also contained a request for an offering (16:1–4) and probably other instructions related to problems within the congregation. The troubles did not subside. Eventually, the apostle received reports that the church in Corinth was being torn apart by internal divisions, particularly as a result of some in the congregation viewing themselves as more spiritual and knowledgeable than their fellow believers (1:11–12; 3:1–4; 8:1–3). Pride also led to criticisms hurled at Paul (4:1–4), gross immorality by some church members (5:1) and lawsuits among Christians (6:1–6). Moreover, the church itself had written a letter to Paul requesting instruction about such matters as marriage and divorce, meat offered to idols, spiritual gifts and the method Paul was using for his collection (7:1,25; 8:1; 12:1; 16:1). The Corinthians also asked for a visit from Apollos (16:12). Paul was confronted with a massive task, and he wrote to deal with the problem.

The letter's contents were determined by the specific issues that had surfaced in Corinth. Many interpreters have suggested that the letter is loosely divided into two parts: the matters that had been reported to Paul (chs. 1–6) and the problems the Corinthians had raised in their letter (chs. 7–16). The Greek phrase *peri de*, generally translated "now about," appears to introduce Paul's responses to their specific questions (7:1,25; 8:1; 12:1; 16:1,12). Although such a division may not accurately reflect every section of the epistle, it does provide a valuable overview. One should note, however, that behind the great diversity of issues treated in this document lie some deep and recurring problems. Challenges to Paul's authority and a lack of love revealed that the Corinthian believers had become full of pride, thinking themselves more spiritual and insightful than other Christians. In the course of dealing with these issues, the apostle Paul set forth his teaching on a number of specific doctrines that he believed the Corinthians needed to hear.

Outline

I. Greetings and Thanksgiving (1:1–9)	*Paul identified himself and expressed thanks for the Corinthians.*
II. Report From Chloe's Household (1:10—6:20) A. Divisions in the Church (1:10—4:21) 1. Report (1:10–17) 2. The Wisdom and Power of God (1:18—3:4) 3. Ministry and Apostleship (3:5—4:21) B. Moral and Ethical Problems (5:1—6:20) 1. A Case of Incest (5:1–13) 2. Lawsuits (6:1–11) 3. Sexual Immorality (6:12–20)	*Paul responded to reports he had received from Chloe's household about troubles in the church. The wisdom of the world produces arrogance and division in the church. The Christian faith opposes the arrogance of worldly eloquence and pride. Ethical problems such as incest, lawsuits among believers and sexual immorality also result from false pride.*
III. The Corinthians' Letter (7:1—16:12) A. Marriage and Divorce (7:1–40) 1. Marital Relationships (7:1–9) 2. Divorce (7:10–24) 3. Virgins (7:25–40) B. Food Offered to Idols (8:1—11:1) 1. Central Issues (8:1–13) 2. Paul's Authority (9:1–27) 3. Old Testament Examples (10:1–22) 4. Conclusions (10:23—11:1) C. Problems in Worship (11:2–34) 1. Head Coverings (11:2–16) 2. The Lord's Supper (11:17–34) D. Spiritual Gifts (12:1—14:40) 1. Unity and Diversity (12:1–31) 2. The Supremacy of Love (13:1–13) 3. Prophecy and Tongues (14:1–25) 4. Principle of Order (14:26–40) E. Resurrection (15:1–58) 1. Christ's Resurrection (15:1–11) 2. Believers' Resurrection (15:12–34) 3. Resurrection Body (15:35–49) 4. Conclusion (15:50–58) F. Collection and Other Matters (16:1–12)	*Paul responded to questions raised in a letter from the Corinthian church. He addressed in detail specific challenges facing the Corinthians, involving marital relationships, divorce and virginity. Rampant idolatry in Corinth raised questions about involvement in pagan rituals and meat offered to idols. Paul addressed specific problems in worship, such as head coverings and the Lord's Supper. The purpose and functions of spiritual gifts in the body of Christ, including tongues and prophecy, must be set within the framework of Christian love and order.* *Contrary to pagan religion, the Christian faith insists that salvation is complete only when our physical bodies are renewed and enjoy the new heavens and the new earth. Paul mentioned several practical matters in passing, especially collections of funds for suffering Jerusalem believers.*
IV. Conclusion (16:13–24)	*Paul gave final greetings and commendations as he closed his letter.*

1
Paul, called to be an apostle[a] of Christ Jesus by the will of God,[b] and our brother
Sosthenes,[c]

2 To the church of God in Corinth,[d] to those sanctified in Christ Jesus and called[e] to
be holy, together with all those everywhere who call on the name of our Lord Jesus
Christ—their Lord and ours:

3 Grace and peace to you from God our Father and the Lord Jesus Christ.[f]

1:1 [a]Ro 1:1; Eph 1:1 [b]2Co 1:1 [c]Ac 18:17
1:2 [d]Ac 18:1 [e]Ro 1:7
1:3 [f]Ro 1:7

■ **1:1–9** *Greetings and Thanksgiving.* Paul identified himself and his readers, and he reported how he thanked God for their many blessings.
1:1 apostle. Someone commissioned directly by Christ as his authoritative messenger (see Ac 1:21–22). Paul stresses the significance of this office in 1 Corinthians (ch. 9; 15:1–11; see also 2Co 10–12; Gal 1). **Sosthenes.** Perhaps the same individual mentioned in Acts 18:17. He was the ruler of the synagogue in Corinth at the time of Paul's first visit to the city.
1:2 sanctified . . . and called to be holy. The second part of this description (literally, "called saints") is one that Paul used elsewhere to identify the Christians to whom he wrote (e.g., Ro 1:7,

Thanksgiving

4I always thank God for you[g] because of his grace given you in Christ Jesus. 5For in
him you have been enriched[h] in every way—in all your speaking and in all your knowledge[i]— 6because our testimony[j] about Christ was confirmed in you. 7Therefore you do
not lack any spiritual gift as you eagerly wait for our Lord Jesus Christ to be revealed.[k]
8He will keep you strong to the end, so that you will be blameless[l] on the day of our Lord
Jesus Christ. 9God, who has called you into fellowship with his Son Jesus Christ our
Lord,[m] is faithful.[n]

Divisions in the Church

10I appeal to you, brothers, in the name of our Lord Jesus Christ, that all of you agree
with one another so that there may be no divisions among you and that you may be perfectly united in mind and thought. 11My brothers, some from Chloe's household have informed me that there are quarrels among you. 12What I mean is this: One of you says, "I
follow Paul";[o] another, "I follow Apollos";[p] another, "I follow Cephas[a]";[q] still another,
"I follow Christ."
13Is Christ divided? Was Paul crucified for you? Were you baptized into[b] the name of
Paul?[r] 14I am thankful that I did not baptize any of you except Crispus[s] and Gaius,[t] 15so
no one can say that you were baptized into my name. 16(Yes, I also baptized the household of Stephanas;[u] beyond that, I don't remember if I baptized anyone else.) 17For Christ
did not send me to baptize,[v] but to preach the gospel—not with words of human wisdom,[w] lest the cross of Christ be emptied of its power.

Christ the Wisdom and Power of God

18For the message of the cross is foolishness to those who are perishing,[x] but to us
who are being saved it is the power of God.[y] 19For it is written:

1:4 [g]Ro 1:8
1:5 [h]2Co 9:11 [i]2Co 8:7
1:6 [j]Rev 1:2
1:7 [k]Php 3:20; Tit 2:13; 2Pe 3:12
1:8 [l]1Th 3:13
1:9 [m]1Jn 1:3 [n]Isa 49:7; 1Th 5:24
1:12 [o]1Co 3:4,22 [p]Ac 18:24 [q]Jn 1:42
1:13 [r]Mt 28:19
1:14 [s]Ac 18:8; Ro 16:23 [t]Ac 19:29
1:16 [u]1Co 16:15
1:17 [v]Jn 4:2 [w]1Co 2:1,4,13
1:18 [x]2Co 2:15 [y]Ro 1:16

[a] *12* That is, Peter [b] *13* Or *in;* also in verse 15

where it is translated "called to be saints"). The words "sanctified" (or "set apart") and "holy " (or "saintly") call attention to the readers' status as God's covenant people. These words indicate that the people were consecrated in the sense of being dedicated to God. Paul did not presume that every member of the church was regenerate, but he addressed the congregation as a whole as true believers. These terms also imply godly living. Since the Corinthians were God's people, they should have sought to please the Lord. Paul touched repeatedly on this subject because the Corinthians were plagued by ethical problems. See *WCF* 25.2; *WLC* 62,179.

1:4–9 See *WLC* 66,79,111; *WSC* 88; *HC* 54.

1:5 enriched in every way. The Corinthians were tempted to become puffed up by their gifts of "speaking and . . . knowledge" and to abuse those gifts (8:1–2; 14:23). Although Paul rebuked them for taking pride in their spiritual gifts, he did not deny or minimize the blessings these gifts constituted (v. 7).

1:8 He will keep you. Paul encouraged his readers by assuring them that God, who had begun a work of grace in them, could be trusted to complete it. Indeed, they would be presented "blameless" at Christ's return. Note the similarities between verses 8–9 and Philippians 1:6 and 10 (cf. Eph 5:26–27; 1Th 5:23–24). Later in this letter Paul warned the Corinthians not to presume their own salvation while defying God (10:1–12). His words here do not give assurance of salvation to those in rebellion against God. Instead, they express Paul's hope for the visible church in Corinth and his utter confidence in God's ability to "keep" it. See *CD* 5.II.

■**1:10—6:20** *Report From Chloe's Household.* Paul turned to some matters that had been brought to his attention by "some from Chloe's household" (1:11). He had two main concerns: divisions in the church (1:10—4:21) and moral and ethical problems (5:1—6:20).

■ **1:10—4:21** *Divisions in the Church.* Chloe's household had reported that there were very serious divisions in the church. Paul confronted this matter by reiterating the report (1:10–17), by distinguishing between Christian wisdom and the folly of the world (1:18—3:4) and by appealing to his own ministry and apostolic authority (3:5—4:21).

■**1:10–17** *Report.* Chloe's household had reported (vv. 11–12) that the unity of the Corinthian church had been severely broken. Many of the specific problems that Paul addressed in this letter reflect the spirit of dissension that had infected the community.

1:10 I appeal to you. This exhortation, which begins the body of the letter, announces Paul's primary concern and affects most of what he has to say.

1:11–13 See *WLC* 167; *HC* 30.

1:11 Chloe's household. Chloe must have been an influential Christian woman, perhaps a member of the Corinthian church. Nothing else is known about her.

1:12 I follow. Literally, "I am of" (see note on 3:21). **Apollos.** An effective preacher from Alexandria who had ministered in Ephesus and Corinth (Ac 18:24—19:1). **Cephas.** Simon Peter's Aramaic name. He was obviously popular among some groups in Corinth (perhaps among the Jewish Christians), but whether he had actually visited the church is not known.

1:13 Is Christ divided? With this question Paul anticipated one of his fundamental teachings about the church. Just as a physical body is one even though it is made up of many members, so also the church, which is the body of Christ, cannot be divided (10:16–17; 11:29; see note on 12:12). **into the name.** This expression, which is used in the baptismal formula (Mt 28:19), indicates an intimate, spiritual union. See *BC* 7.

1:14 Crispus. The synagogue ruler whose conversion is recorded in Acts 18:8. **Gaius.** Perhaps a reference to the Gaius described in Acts 19:29 as a companion of Paul, but since the name was common, it could refer to someone else.

1:16 the household of Stephanas. Paul's first converts in Corinth. They were respected for their dedication. Stephanas was one of the representatives who brought a communication from the Corinthians to Paul (16:15–17).

1:17 human wisdom. Literally, "wisdom of speech." Beneath the divisions and related problems in the Corinthian church lay an unhealthy regard for rhetorical displays. Paul would later focus attention on true wisdom (1:18—2:16; 3:18–23). Here he reminded the Corinthians that the power of his own preaching did not depend on such skills (2:1–5). **cross of Christ.** In the opinion of those who are wise according to this world's standards, proclaiming the crucified Lord is foolishness (see note on v. 23). Paul therefore treated "wisdom" and "the cross" as opposites.

■**1:18—3:4** *The Wisdom and Power of God.* The Corinthians had become enamored with the philosophical sophistry of their Greek culture. This attraction expressed a facet of their pride and false confidence. Paul addressed this matter by contrasting the wisdom and power of God with the wisdom of the world.

1:18 perishing . . . being saved. At the heart of the Biblical revelation is the inevitability of a twofold response to the gospel arising from God's elective purpose (Isa 6:9–10; Lk 2:34; Ro 9:10–12; 2Co 2:15–16). God is not to blame for the unbelief of those who perish; they perish because of their own sin and stubborn impenitence. Those who believe and are saved, on the other hand, are "those whom God has called" (see 1:24; Ro 8:28–30). See *BC* 2,22.

"I will destroy the wisdom of the wise;
the intelligence of the intelligent I will frustrate."[a z]

20Where is the wise man?[a] Where is the scholar? Where is the philosopher of this age?
Has not God made foolish[b] the wisdom of the world? 21For since in the wisdom of God
the world through its wisdom did not know him, God was pleased through the foolishness of what was preached to save those who believe. 22Jews demand miraculous signs[c]
and Greeks look for wisdom, 23but we preach Christ crucified: a stumbling block[d] to Jews
and foolishness[e] to Gentiles, 24but to those whom God has called,[f] both Jews and
Greeks, Christ the power of God and the wisdom of God.[g] 25For the foolishness[h] of God
is wiser than man's wisdom, and the weakness[i] of God is stronger than man's strength.
26Brothers, think of what you were when you were called. Not many of you were wise
by human standards; not many were influential; not many were of noble birth. 27But God
chose[j] the foolish[k] things of the world to shame the wise; God chose the weak things of
the world to shame the strong. 28He chose the lowly things of this world and the despised
things—and the things that are not[l]—to nullify the things that are, 29so that no one may
boast before him.[m] 30It is because of him that you are in Christ Jesus, who has become
for us wisdom from God—that is, our righteousness,[n] holiness and redemption.[o]
31Therefore, as it is written: "Let him who boasts boast in the Lord."[b p]

2 When I came to you, brothers, I did not come with eloquence or superior wisdom[q]
as I proclaimed to you the testimony about God.[c] 2For I resolved to know nothing
while I was with you except Jesus Christ and him crucified.[r] 3I came to you[s] in weakness
and fear, and with much trembling. 4My message and my preaching were not with wise
and persuasive words, but with a demonstration of the Spirit's power,[t] 5so that your faith
might not rest on men's wisdom, but on God's power.[u]

Wisdom From the Spirit

6We do, however, speak a message of wisdom among the mature,[v] but not the wisdom of this age[w] or of the rulers of this age, who are coming to nothing. 7No, we speak
of God's secret wisdom, a wisdom that has been hidden and that God destined for our

1:19 [z]Isa 29:14
1:20 [a]Isa 19:11,12 [b]Job 12:17; Ro 1:22
1:22 [c]Mt 12:38
1:23 [d]Lk 2:34; Gal 5:11 [e]1Co 2:14
1:24 [f]Ro 8:28 [g]ver 30; Col 2:3
1:25 [h]ver 18 [i]2Co 13:4
1:27 [j]Jas 2:5 [k]ver 20
1:28 [l]Ro 4:17
1:29 [m]Eph 2:9
1:30 [n]Jer 23:5,6; 2Co 5:21 [o]Ro 3:24; Eph 1:7,14
1:31 [p]Jer 9:23,24; 2Co 10:17
2:1 [q]1Co 1:17
2:2 [r]Gal 6:14; 1Co 1:23
2:3 [s]Ac 18:1-18
2:4 [t]Ro 15:19
2:5 [u]2Co 4:7; 6:7
2:6 [v]Eph 4:13; Php 3:15; Heb 5:14 [w]1Co 1:20

[a] *19* Isaiah 29:14 [b] *31* Jer. 9:24 [c] *1* Some manuscripts *as I proclaimed to you God's mystery*

1:20–24 See *WLC* 60.
1:20 wise man . . . scholar . . . philosopher. It is unclear whether Paul intended to express a sharp distinction among these three categories. Possibly the first one is general in character, while the other two refer respectively to Jewish scribes and Greek teachers. **this age . . . the world?** Much of Paul's theology is built on the basic opposition between "the present evil age" (Gal 1:4), or the world, which is characterized by the "flesh," and "the coming age" (1Ti 6:19), which has already dawned for those who have received the Spirit (1Co 10:11; Gal 5:16–17; Eph 1:13–14; 2:6; Php 3:20). See theological article "The Plan of the Ages" at Heb 7).
1:21 the foolishness of what was preached. This passage is filled with intense irony. Those who are wise according to the standards of the world regard the gospel as a foolish message. Even the most "foolish" thing about God, however, is far wiser than human wisdom (vv. 25,27). God can therefore use the simplicity of the gospel to demonstrate that real foolishness resides in those who oppose him (v. 27). See *WCF* 1.1; *BC* 2,22; *HC* 21.
1:23 we preach Christ crucified. This is not a full description of Paul's preaching, but this theme of his preaching appears to be what the ancient world found most offensive or problematic (cf. v. 17; 2:2). Possibly these words also reflect the reason for Paul's preconversion opposition to the gospel. That the Messiah had hung on a tree, and thus come under a divine curse (Dt 21:23; Gal 3:13), was an intolerable stumbling block to many Jews.
1:24 Christ the power of God and the wisdom of God. God's wisdom and power are not abstract forces but personal qualities that manifest themselves fully in the life, teachings, death and resurrection of Jesus Christ (v. 30; Ro 1:4; Col 2:3). See *BC* 8.
1:26 think of what you were when you were called. Literally, "look at your calling." According to the world's standards, few Corinthian Christians were wise and powerful. This demonstrates that salvation, by its very nature, does not depend on such human qualities. See *WSC* 32.
1:29 so that no one may boast before him. This principle, which Paul underscored in verse 31 by referring to Jeremiah 9:24, provides the foundation for the Biblical doctrine of salvation: It is a gracious gift from God that precludes human boasting (Eph 2:8–9).
1:30–31 See *WCF* 11.1; *HC* 61.
1:30 who has become for us wisdom. See note on verse 24. See *WCF* 8.1; *WLC* 69,77; *WSC* 32; *BC* 26; *HC* 18.
2:1 When I came to you. Paul must have been referring to his first visit to Corinth, which is recorded in Acts 18:1–17 (see "Introduction: Original Audience"). **eloquence or superior wisdom.** Influenced by Greek culture, some of the Christians in Corinth may have been critical of Paul for not using the rhetorical techniques of his contemporaries (2Co 11:5–6). See notes on 4:1,8–13, 9:3,19, 10:30 and 16:3.
2:2 Jesus Christ and him crucified. See note on 1:23. See *BC* 21.
2:3–5 Taken by themselves, these verses might suggest that Paul was a timid, uneducated preacher who was unable to speak with force and eloquence. Both the book of Acts (e.g., Ac 19:8) and the epistles (e.g., 1Co 13), however, prove otherwise. Because he knew that men and women are persuaded only "with a demonstration of the Spirit's power," Paul relied confidently on the talents and training that God had given him rather than on worldly rhetoric (2Co 3:5,12). See *WCF* 31.4; *WLC* 159; *BC* 7.
2:6–7 See *WLC* 4.
2:6 a message of wisdom. This phrase refers to the gospel, the proclamation of Christ crucified. **mature.** Literally, "perfect." Compare the use of "spiritual" in verses 13 and 15 and in 3:1, which clearly refers to the Holy Spirit. The spiritual person has the Holy Spirit and lives accordingly (see v. 14; 3:1). Since every true believer has received the Spirit, each one is spiritual and can understand God's wisdom (the gospel of Jesus Christ) to some degree, but the maturing Christian is able to grasp even more.
2:7 God's secret wisdom. Literally, "the wisdom of God in a mystery." The wisdom revealed in Paul's message, though "hidden" during the Old Testament period, had now been revealed by the Spirit (v. 10). "Mystery" in this context has a strong temporal meaning (Eph 3:2–6). It is a truth "not made known to men in other generations" (Eph 3:5) and "hidden for long ages past" (Ro 16:25). Since modern believers live in the time of fulfillment, the truth has been clearly revealed to those who have the Spirit, for it is they who experience "the fulfillment of the ages" (10:11). **destined.** Literally, "determined beforehand." A similar but more specific word ("predestined") is used in Romans 8:29 and Ephesians 1:5 to express the certainty of God's good will for his people.

glory before time began. 8None of the rulers of this age understood it, for if they had, they
would not have crucified the Lord of glory.[x] 9However, as it is written:

> "No eye has seen,
> no ear has heard,
> no mind has conceived
> what God has prepared for those who love him"[a][y]—

10but God has revealed[z] it to us by his Spirit.[a]
The Spirit searches all things, even the deep things of God. 11For who among men
knows the thoughts of a man[b] except the man's spirit[c] within him? In the same way no
one knows the thoughts of God except the Spirit of God. 12We have not received the spirit[d] of the world[e] but the Spirit who is from God, that we may understand what God has
freely given us. 13This is what we speak, not in words taught us by human wisdom[f] but
in words taught by the Spirit, expressing spiritual truths in spiritual words.[b] 14The man
without the Spirit does not accept the things that come from the Spirit of God, for they
are foolishness[g] to him, and he cannot understand them, because they are spiritually
discerned. 15The spiritual man makes judgments about all things, but he himself is not
subject to any man's judgment:

> 16"For who has known the mind of the Lord
> that he may instruct him?"[c][h]

But we have the mind of Christ.[i]

On Divisions in the Church

3 Brothers, I could not address you as spiritual[j] but as worldly[k]—mere infants[l] in
Christ. 2I gave you milk, not solid food,[m] for you were not yet ready for it.[n] Indeed,
you are still not ready. 3You are still worldly. For since there is jealousy and quarreling[o]
among you, are you not worldly? Are you not acting like mere men? 4For when one says,
"I follow Paul," and another, "I follow Apollos,"[p] are you not mere men?
5What, after all, is Apollos? And what is Paul? Only servants, through whom you came
to believe—as the Lord has assigned to each his task. 6I planted the seed,[q] Apollos wa-

2:8 [x]Ac 7:2; Jas 2:1
2:9 [y]Isa 64:4; 65:17
2:10 [z]Mt 13:11; Eph 3:3,5 [a]Jn 14:26
2:11 [b]Jer 17:9 [c]Pr 20:27
2:12 [d]Ro 8:15 [e]1Co 1:20,27
2:13 [f]1Co 1:17
2:14 [g]1Co 1:18
2:16 [h]Isa 40:13 [i]Jn 15:15
3:1 [j]1Co 2:15 [k]Ro 7:14; 1Co 2:14 [l]Heb 5:13
3:2 [m]Heb 5:12-14; 1Pe 2:2 [n]Jn 16:12
3:3 [o]1Co 1:11; Gal 5:20
3:4 [p]1Co 1:12
3:6 [q]Ac 18:4-11

[a] 9 Isaiah 64:4 [b] 13 *Or Spirit, interpreting spiritual truths to spiritual men* [c] 16 Isaiah 40:13

2:8 None of the rulers of this age understood it. Unbelievers are still part of the old age and so have not received God's wisdom (v. 14). Paul emphasized this point by focusing on the most influential members of society (1:20).
2:9–14 See *WCF* 1.1; 1.5; 1.6; 10.1; 18.3; *WLC* 11,67,80; *BC* 22; *HC* 58,65.
2:9–10 In contrast to the wise of this world who cannot even conceive the greatness of divine salvation, those who love God know and partake of his blessings. The quotation is based on Isaiah 64:4 but includes ideas found elsewhere in the Old Testament. **searches all things.** The idea of a divine searching (as in Ps 139:1; Ro 8:27) serves to emphasize God's omniscience, particularly his power to see what is invisible to humans (Jn 2:25). It does not imply that the Holy Spirit needs to seek knowledge of the Father that he otherwise lacks. The Spirit, as it were, probes the depths of divine knowledge for believers. See *WLC* 2; *BC* 2,37.
2:11 the man's spirit within him? The thrust of this verse is to point out a simple, common-sense observation, not to reveal some mystery about the makeup of human personality. The word "spirit" is a general reference to the immaterial aspect of humankind's existence, with a focus on the mental faculties (see note on v. 16).
2:13 expressing spiritual truths in spiritual words. Literally, "comparing spiritual with spiritual." The precise meaning of this clause is disputed. Paul may have been reacting to criticism that he did not use human eloquence and wisdom (see note on v. 1). If so, he may have been pointing out that the truths revealed by the Spirit must be communicated in a way that is harmonious with the Spirit, though not necessarily eloquent, like the speech of some sophisticated and articulate nonbelievers. It is also possible that he meant "explaining spiritual things to spiritual people"; that is, people who have the Spirit (see v. 14). See *WLC* 4.
2:14 without the Spirit. This expansive translation properly expresses the meaning of a Greek word often translated "natural." Paul used this word to describe the contrast between an individual who still belongs to the old age and one who is "spiritual" (see notes on 15:44,45). See *WCF* 9.3; 10.2; *WLC* 192; *BC* 14,35.
2:15 makes judgments. Literally, "examines" or "judges." Paul used the same verb three times in quick succession, but the play on words cannot be reproduced in English. It is translated "discerned" at the end of verse 14 and "not subject to any man's judgment" in verse 15. Here again, Paul may have been responding to individuals who opposed him and passed negative judgments on him (see note on v. 1).
2:16 the mind of the Lord. A quotation from Isaiah 40:13 ("the mind of the LORD"), which Paul later in the verse rendered as "the mind of Christ." To have the Spirit of Christ is to have the mind of the Lord, and Paul's opponents, who ignored this truth, were unable to instruct or examine him. By implication, those who accept the truth of Paul's teaching also have the Spirit/mind of Christ and understand the things of God.
3:1 spiritual. That is, belonging to the Holy Spirit (see note on 2:6). **worldly.** Literally, "fleshly" (not physical, but characterized by the "flesh," Paul's main word for describing the present evil age). Since many of the Corinthians had received the Spirit, they were spiritual in the most fundamental sense. Yet within the visible church at Corinth, there were those who were not believers and did not have the Spirit. Moreover, even some who did were so out of keeping with the Spirit that Paul had to treat them as though they did not.
3:2 See *WLC* 159.
3:3 jealousy and quarreling . . . mere men? See note on 1:10. The strife that existed among the Corinthians was proof that they needed to be treated as worldly (v. 1). They had become so petty and foolish that they had divided into parties loyal to various leaders.
3:4 See note 1:12.
■ **3:5—4:21** *Ministry and Apostleship.* To counter the worldly divisions that plagued the church at Corinth, Paul gave a perspective on what church leaders actually are and why they should not be objects of competing loyalties in the church.
3:5 Only servants. Jesus made it clear that leaders in his kingdom must be the lowest of servants (Mk 9:35).
3:6–8 See *WLC* 161; *BC* 31,34.
3:6 I planted. Paul's desire "to preach the gospel where Christ was not known" (Ro 15:20) led him to plant, or begin, many churches (Ac 13–20). **Apollos.** See note on 1:12. See *WSC* 91.

tered it, but God made it grow. 7So neither he who plants nor he who waters is anything,
but only God, who makes things grow. 8The man who plants and the man who waters
have one purpose, and each will be rewarded according to his own labor.[r] 9For we are
God's fellow workers;[s] you are God's field,[t] God's building.[u]
10By the grace God has given me,[v] I laid a foundation[w] as an expert builder, and
someone else is building on it. But each one should be careful how he builds. 11For no
one can lay any foundation other than the one already laid, which is Jesus Christ.[x] 12If
any man builds on this foundation using gold, silver, costly stones, wood, hay or straw,
13his work will be shown for what it is,[y] because the Day[z] will bring it to light. It will be
revealed with fire, and the fire will test the quality of each man's work. 14If what he has
built survives, he will receive his reward. 15If it is burned up, he will suffer loss; he himself will be saved, but only as one escaping through the flames.[a]
16Don't you know that you yourselves are God's temple[b] and that God's Spirit lives
in you? 17If anyone destroys God's temple, God will destroy him; for God's temple is sacred, and you are that temple.
18Do not deceive yourselves. If any one of you thinks he is wise[c] by the standards of
this age, he should become a "fool" so that he may become wise. 19For the wisdom of this
world is foolishness[d] in God's sight. As it is written: "He catches the wise in their craftiness"[a];[e] 20and again, "The Lord knows that the thoughts of the wise are futile."[b][f] 21So
then, no more boasting about men![g] All things are yours,[h] 22whether Paul or Apollos or
Cephas[c][i] or the world or life or death or the present or the future[j]—all are yours, 23and
you are of Christ,[k] and Christ is of God.

Apostles of Christ

4 So then, men ought to regard us as servants of Christ and as those entrusted[l] with
the secret things[m] of God. 2Now it is required that those who have been given a trust
must prove faithful. 3I care very little if I am judged by you or by any human court; indeed, I do not even judge myself. 4My conscience is clear, but that does not make me innocent.[n] It is the Lord who judges me. 5Therefore judge nothing[o] before the appointed
time; wait till the Lord comes. He will bring to light what is hidden in darkness and will
expose the motives of men's hearts. At that time each will receive his praise from God.[p]
6Now, brothers, I have applied these things to myself and Apollos for your benefit, so
that you may learn from us the meaning of the saying, "Do not go beyond what is written."[q] Then you will not take pride in one man over against another.[r] 7For who makes
you different from anyone else? What do you have that you did not receive?[s] And if you
did receive it, why do you boast as though you did not?

3:8 [r]Ps 62:12
3:9 [s]2Co 6:1 [t]Isa 61:3 [u]Eph 2:20-22; 1Pe 2:5
3:10 [v]Ro 12:3 [w]Ro 15:20
3:11 [x]Isa 28:16; Eph 2:20
3:13 [y]1Co 4:5 [z]2Th 1:7-10
3:15 [a]Jude 23
3:16 [b]1Co 6:19; 2Co 6:16
3:18 [c]Isa 5:21; 1Co 8:2
3:19 [d]1Co 1:20,27 [e]Job 5:13
3:20 [f]Ps 94:11
3:21 [g]1Co 4:6 [h]Ro 8:32
3:22 [i]1Co 1:12 [j]Ro 8:38
3:23 [k]1Co 15:23; 2Co 10:7; Gal 3:29
4:1 [l]1Co 9:17; Tit 1:7 [m]Ro 16:25
4:4 [n]Ro 2:13
4:5 [o]Mt 7:1,2; Ro 2:1 [p]Ro 2:29
4:6 [q]1Co 1:19,31; 3:19,20 [r]1Co 1:12
4:7 [s]Jn 3:27; Ro 12:3,6

[a] *19* Job 5:13 [b] *20* Psalm 94:11 [c] *22* That is, Peter

3:9 God's fellow workers. Paul probably meant either that Christian workers are coworkers with God or that Christians who are coworkers with one another belong to God. Paul's point is clear from the context: God alone is responsible for the success of Christian ministry. **field . . . building.** Paul shifted from the metaphor of a vineyard (vv. 6–8) to that of a building.
3:10 foundation. As one who was called to proclaim the gospel where it was not known, Paul resolved to focus his preaching on Christ crucified (see note on 1:23). **expert.** Literally, "wise." An allusion to the previous discussion of true wisdom (1:17ff; see note on 2:9–10).
3:11 See *BC* 7.
3:12–15 These verses specifically address the evaluation of Christian ministry. Some who were seeking to build God's building in Corinth but were depending on human wisdom used perishable materials ("hay or straw") that would not survive the judgment of God's fire. The builders themselves would barely escape destruction. Paul warned the members of this church that they, like Solomon's temple (1Ch 22:14–16), should be built with that which is lasting. See *BC* 24.
3:16 God's temple. Just as God indicated his presence in the temple by filling it with the cloud of his glory (1Ki 8:10–11), so too he inhabits his people by filling them with his Spirit. Paul's focus here is on God's people as a corporate whole; in 6:19 the emphasis shifts to the individual Christian's body. See *BC* 11.
3:17 God will destroy him. Paul left open the possibility that some of the "builders" in Corinth were not merely using perishable material but were actually destroying God's work. They would not be spared at the judgment.
3:18–20 Paul returned more directly to the contrast between human and divine wisdom (see notes on 1:17–31).
3:21–23 See *WCF* 26.1; *HC* 1.
3:21 no more boasting. See note on 1:29. **All things are yours.** Because Christ is of God and all believers are of Christ (v. 23), Christ's followers will all reign over the new earth when Christ returns (2Ti 2:12; Rev 2:26–27). The great inheritance that awaited the Corinthians demonstrates the absurdity of their petty quarreling over leaders ("I follow"; 1:12). Further, the "all things" that belong to all believers (see Ro 8:17; Heb 1:2) includes Christian leaders. Since all Christian leaders belong to all believers, it is foolish to be jealous over them. How little the Corinthians appreciated their Christian privileges is also pointed out in 6:2.
4:1–4 See *WCF* 23.3; *WLC* 159; *BC* 23.
4:1 ought to regard us as servants. These words and the verses that follow leave no doubt that Paul was being judged and attacked by at least some of the Corinthians (see note on 2:1). **secret things.** Literally, "mysteries." See note on 2:7. See *WCF* 27.4; *WLC* 176; *BC* 30.
4:3 I do not even judge myself. Although Paul's conscience was clear (v. 4), ultimately only God determines whether one has proved himself or herself faithful.
4:5 judge nothing. This is not an absolute prohibition against discernment and forming opinions (cf. 5:3; 6:2). It is a reference to the misconceived criticisms raised against Paul. **bring to light what is hidden.** At the judgment nothing will escape God's searching light (Mt 10:26; Mk 4:22; Lk 8:17).
4:6 the saying. These words are not in the Greek text but were added on the premise that Paul was quoting a popular proverb akin to "play by the rules." Alternatively, it is possible that Paul was asking the Corinthians to live by Scriptural principles. In that case, he may have been alluding specifically to 1:31. See *WLC* 145.
4:7 See *BC* 22,24; *CD* 3–4.IX.

8 Already you have all you want! Already you have become rich![t] You have become
kings—and that without us! How I wish that you really had become kings so that we
might be kings with you! 9 For it seems to me that God has put us apostles on display at
the end of the procession, like men condemned to die[u] in the arena. We have been made
a spectacle[v] to the whole universe, to angels as well as to men. 10 We are fools for
Christ,[w] but you are so wise in Christ![x] We are weak, but you are strong![y] You are honored, we are dishonored! 11 To this very hour we go hungry and thirsty, we are in rags,
we are brutally treated, we are homeless.[z] 12 We work hard with our own hands.[a] When
we are cursed, we bless;[b] when we are persecuted, we endure it; 13 when we are slandered, we answer kindly. Up to this moment we have become the scum of the earth, the
refuse[c] of the world.

14 I am not writing this to shame you, but to warn you, as my dear children.[d] 15 Even
though you have ten thousand guardians in Christ, you do not have many fathers, for in
Christ Jesus I became your father through the gospel.[e] 16 Therefore I urge you to imitate
me.[f] 17 For this reason I am sending to you Timothy, my son[g] whom I love, who is faithful in the Lord. He will remind you of my way of life in Christ Jesus, which agrees with
what I teach everywhere in every church.[h]

18 Some of you have become arrogant, as if I were not coming to you. 19 But I will come
to you very soon,[i] if the Lord is willing,[j] and then I will find out not only how these arrogant people are talking, but what power they have. 20 For the kingdom of God is not a
matter of talk but of power. 21 What do you prefer? Shall I come to you with a whip,[k] or
in love and with a gentle spirit?

Expel the Immoral Brother!

5 It is actually reported that there is sexual immorality among you, and of a kind that
does not occur even among pagans: A man has his father's wife.[l] 2 And you are
proud! Shouldn't you rather have been filled with grief[m] and have put out of your fellowship the man who did this? 3 Even though I am not physically present, I am with you in

4:8 [t]Rev 3:17,18
4:9 [u]Ro 8:36 [v]Heb 10:33
4:10 [w]1Co 1:18; Ac 17:18 [x]1Co 3:18 [y]1Co 2:3
4:11 [z]Ro 8:35; 2Co 11:23-27
4:12 [a]Ac 18:3 [b]1Pe 3:9
4:13 [c]La 3:45
4:14 [d]1Th 2:11
4:15 [e]1Co 9:12,14,18, 23
4:16 [f]1Co 11:1; Php 3:17; 1Th 1:6; 2Th 3:7,9
4:17 [g]1Ti 1:2 [h]1Co 7:17
4:19 [i]2Co 1:15,16 [j]Ac 18:21
4:21 [k]2Co 1:23; 13:2,10
5:1 [l]Lev 18:8; Dt 22:30
5:2 [m]2Co 7:7-11

4:8–13 In this powerful passage Paul made use of biting irony and sarcasm to point out to the Corinthians the triviality of their concerns and the unfairness of their criticisms. Paul's sufferings were comparable to the pain and public humiliation of captives condemned to die (2Co 11:23–30). In contrast, some of the Corinthians viewed themselves as superior in their faith and wisdom, but they did so only because they did not understand what it means to be fools for Christ.

4:8 Already . . . all you want . . . rich . . . kings. These words describe what some of the Corinthians thought about themselves. They believed they were so blessed that they were utterly superior to everyone else. Here Paul revealed the heart of the problem at Corinth: The believers did not recognize how weak they actually were.

4:10 We are fools . . . you are so wise. Paul was again (see note on vv. 8–13) using sarcasm. In their cultural sophistication, the arrogant Corinthians believed that they were already supremely blessed. By contrast, the apostles, Christ's authoritative leaders of the church, suffered terribly and seemed like fools. The suffering of the apostles indicated that the Corinthians were not as close to glorification as they thought they were.

4:14–16 See *WLC* 125.

4:14 not . . . to shame you. The harsh language of the previous passage was intended not simply to make them feel inferior, but also to help them see the truth of their situation.

4:15 ten thousand guardians. "Guardians" translates the Greek word *paidagōgos*, which appears in the New Testament only here and in Galatians 3:24–25. The guardian was a household slave who took charge over the master's children after they left their nurse's care and until they reached maturity. Although there is some disagreement regarding the nature of such guardians, they apparently trained children in manners and morals but not in academics, although they conducted their charges to and from school. Guardians were to protect and restrain the children, disciplining them if necessary. In Paul's analogy, "guardians" seem to be those who ministered to the Corinthian Christians after Paul's initial work in establishing their church, such as Apollos who "watered" after Paul had "planted" (3:6) and who built on the "foundation" Paul had laid (3:10). In boasting of their allegiance to Apollos, Peter and others, the Corinthians implied that they had no need for Paul. But Paul reminded them that his fatherly relationship to them was unique and that they had no good reason to attack him. Regardless of how many ministers and leaders came after Paul ("ten thousand" is clearly hyperbolic), the Corinthians should have had a special respect for Paul since he had brought them to faith. Timothy provided a proper example for Paul's other spiritual children to follow (v. 17).

4:17 I am sending to you Timothy. The verb can be translated in the past tense, and it is quite possible that Timothy had left prior to the writing of this letter (see note on 16:10).

4:18 as if I were not coming to you. Later a group of Corinthians argued that Paul was bold only when absent from them and that he would be afraid to speak authoritatively to them face-to-face (2Co 10:1–2). It is possible that such thoughts were present in Corinth even at this stage and that Paul was sending Timothy to them at this time (v. 17), rather than coming himself, in order to avoid an ugly confrontation (v. 21; 2Co 13:1–10).

■ **5:1—6:20** *Moral and Ethical Problems.* In addition to fostering divisions, the arrogance of the Corinthians had led them into a number of moral and ethical problems, which Chloe's household reported to Paul. He touched on three matters: a case of incest within the church (5:1–13), lawsuits between believers (6:1–11) and sexual immorality (6:12–20).

■ **5:1–13** *A Case of Incest.* The Corinthians had grown so sure of themselves that they failed to see how terrible it was to tolerate incest in the church.

5:1–13 See *WCF* 30.3; *WLC* 108,173.

5:1 A man has his father's wife. Whether the man's father had already died or whether the man had actually married his stepmother is not known. In any event, the sexual relationship in view was the incestuous union explicitly condemned in Leviticus 18:8. The Greek verb "has" can mean "lives in a sexual relationship with," and it is clear from Paul's reaction in this chapter that this was the meaning it carried here. Even though the Greco-Roman culture of Paul's day quietly tolerated a wide array of immoral activity, even Gentiles censured this kind of incest. See *WCF* 20.4; 24.4; *WLC* 139,151.

5:2 you are proud! The fundamental problem in Corinth was not one individual's immorality but the church's pride and false confidence in its toleration and acceptance of the incestuous man (v. 6). Its members were so proud of their tolerance that they failed not only to adhere to Biblical moral standards but also to submit to the loose moral customs of pagans (v. 1). In their arrogance they even went so far as to disregard Paul's earlier apostolic teaching to them (v. 9).

5:3–5 A very difficult passage. Although Paul was physically absent from the Corinthian community, he claimed to pass a prophetic judgment in their midst. Paul was, in effect, commanding the church to expel the offender from its fellowship ("hand this man over to Satan"). The goal of this expulsion was the man's repentance and

spirit.[n] And I have already passed judgment on the one who did this, just as if I were
present. 4When you are assembled in the name of our Lord Jesus[o] and I am with you in
spirit, and the power of our Lord Jesus is present, 5hand this man over[p] to Satan, so that
the sinful nature[a] may be destroyed and his spirit saved on the day of the Lord.
6Your boasting is not good.[q] Don't you know that a little yeast[r] works through the
whole batch of dough?[s] 7Get rid of the old yeast that you may be a new batch without
yeast—as you really are. For Christ, our Passover lamb, has been sacrificed.[t] 8Therefore
let us keep the Festival, not with the old yeast, the yeast of malice and wickedness, but
with bread without yeast,[u] the bread of sincerity and truth.
9I have written you in my letter not to associate[v] with sexually immoral people— 10not

5:3 [n]Col 2:5
5:4 [o]2Th 3:6
5:5 [p]1Ti 1:20
5:6 [q]Jas 4:16 [r]Mt 16:6, 12 [s]Gal 5:9
5:7 [t]Mk 14:12; 1Pe 1:19
5:8 [u]Ex 12:14,15; Dt 16:3
5:9 [v]Eph 5:11; 2Th 3:6,14

[a] 5 Or *that his body;* or *that the flesh*

---

ultimate salvation, but this could be achieved only if his fleshly tendencies ("the sinful nature") were overcome. According to one interpretation of 2 Corinthians 2:5–11, this man did later repent of his sin. **assembled in the name of our Lord Jesus.** The corporately gathered church carries authority delegated to it by Jesus (see note on Jn 14:13). See *WCF* 20.4; 30.4; *WLC* 45; *BC* 32; *HC* 85.

5:6–8 See *WCF* 25.4; 29.8; *WLC* 171; *WSC* 97.

5:6 boasting. See notes on 1:29 and 5:2. **yeast.** More precisely leaven, a substance used to produce fermentation in a small amount of dough. When leaven was mixed with fresh dough, the whole batch became fermented and lighter, but over a period of time, the process may have involved a health risk. As part of the purification of the annual Passover feast, the Israelites were required to remove all leaven from their houses (Ex 12:15). Accordingly, Paul here used leaven to symbolize impurity and corruption and unleavened bread to symbolize purity.

5:7 as you really are. In one sense the true believers at Corinth had genuinely been purified by Christ, and Paul continued to give the visible church as a whole the charitable judgment that its members were all true believers. Yet in tolerating incest among them, the visible church had become so corrupt that purification was necessary. The true condition of each individual would become clear only in time as their faith was examined and tested (2Co 13:5–6). See theological article "The Perseverance and Preservation of Believers" at Philippians 1. **Christ, our Passover lamb.** Paul developed this imagery of the Passover Feast by suggesting that the Passover sacrifice, as a shadow of better things to come (Heb 10:1), looked forward to its ultimate fulfillment in the death of Jesus Christ. See *WCF* 7.5; 19.3; *WLC* 34; *BC* 33.

5:8 let us keep the Festival. The final, and especially beautiful, step in Paul's argument was to draw a parallel between the Feast of Unleavened Bread and the life of purity that Christians should lead. For God's people living between the first and second comings of Christ, every day is a celebration of the festival.

5:9–13 See *WCF* 20.4; 29.8; 30.4; *BC* 29; *HC* 85,110.

5:9–11 Prior to the writing of 1 Corinthians, Paul had sent a letter (no longer extant) instructing the Corinthians to separate from believers who practiced immoral behavior. The Corinthians either misunderstood Paul (thinking he meant complete separation from the world) or tried to sidestep the issue by arguing that his request was unreasonable. Paul took this opportunity to clarify that he had in mind separation from "anyone who call[ed] himself a brother" but whose life was a blatant contradiction of the faith he professed. The injunction to ostracize offenders ("with such a man do not even eat") had primary reference to community life and probably did not mean that all personal contact was to be avoided (see 2Th 3:15).

Church Discipline and Excommunication: Who Should Be Disciplined?

THE Christian concept of discipline includes the whole range of nurturing, instructional and training procedures required in making disciples of Christ. Reformed theology has highlighted the importance of church discipline, recognizing it as a necessary mark of a true church (along with the preaching of the Word and the proper administration of the sacraments). Church discipline includes informal encouragement to learning and devotion, worship and fellowship, righteousness and service in a context of care and accountability (Mt 28:20; Jn 21:15–17; 2Ti 2:14–26; Tit 2; Heb 13:17). The New Testament also shows that formal or judicial discipline has a significant place in the maturation of churches and individuals (1Co 5:1–13; 2Co 2:5–11; 2Th 3:6,14–15; Tit 1:10–14; 3:9–11).

Judicial discipline was instituted by God in the Old Testament and is clearly evident in passages that command judicial punishment against particular crimes. For example, corresponding to modern excommunication, the punishment for many crimes in the Old Testament was that the offender be "cut off from his people" (Ge 17:14; Ex 30:33,38; 31:14; Lev 7:20–21,25,27; 17:4,9; 19:8; 23:29; Nu 9:13; 15:30). In the New Testament, Jesus assigned this power to the apostles by authorizing them to bind and to loose (i.e., prohibit and permit; Mt 18:18) and to declare sins remitted or retained (Jn 20:23). In Reformed theology the "keys of the kingdom," first given to Peter and defined as power to bind and loose (Mt 16:19), have usually been understood as the apostles' authority to establish doctrine and impose discipline infallibly. This same power is reflected, however fallibly and imperfectly, in the church's preaching of the gospel and in its authority in the duly established church courts.

In Reformed churches formal discipline ranges from admonition through exclusion from the Lord's Supper to expulsion from the congregation (excommunication), which is described as handing a person over to Satan, the prince of this world (Mt 18:15–17; 1Co 5:1–5,11; 1Ti 1:20; Tit 3:10–11). Public sins (i.e., those that are open to the whole church's view) should be publicly corrected in the church's presence (1Co 5:4–5; 1Ti 5:20; cf. Gal 2:11–14). Jesus taught an initially private procedure for dealing with those who have given personal offense; this procedure is to be used in the hope that it will not be necessary to ask for the church's public censure of such persons (Mt 18:15–17).

The ultimate purposes of church discipline in all its forms are to preserve the purity and peace of the church and to rescue those wandering from the ways of Christian faith. Even in the case of excommunication, once repentance is apparent to the duly ordained authorities, the church is to acknowledge the remission of sins and receive the offender back into full fellowship (2Co 2:6–8). See *WCF* 30; *BC* 32; *HC* 83,84,85.

at all meaning the people of this world[w] who are immoral, or the greedy and swindlers,
or idolaters. In that case you would have to leave this world. 11But now I am writing you
that you must not associate with anyone who calls himself a brother but is sexually immoral or greedy, an idolater[x] or a slanderer, a drunkard or a swindler. With such a man
do not even eat.
12What business is it of mine to judge those outside[y] the church? Are you not to judge
those inside?[z] 13God will judge those outside. "Expel the wicked man from among
you."[a a]

Lawsuits Among Believers

6 If any of you has a dispute with another, dare he take it before the ungodly for judgment instead of before the saints?[b] 2Do you not know that the saints will judge the
world?[c] And if you are to judge the world, are you not competent to judge trivial cases?
3Do you not know that we will judge angels? How much more the things of this life!
4Therefore, if you have disputes about such matters, appoint as judges even men of little account in the church![b] 5I say this to shame you.[d] Is it possible that there is nobody
among you wise enough to judge a dispute between believers?[e] 6But instead, one brother goes to law against another—and this in front of unbelievers![f]
7The very fact that you have lawsuits among you means you have been completely defeated already. Why not rather be wronged? Why not rather be cheated?[g] 8Instead, you
yourselves cheat and do wrong, and you do this to your brothers.[h]
9Do you not know that the wicked will not inherit the kingdom of God?[i] Do not be deceived:[j] Neither the sexually immoral nor idolaters nor adulterers nor male prostitutes
nor homosexual offenders 10nor thieves nor the greedy nor drunkards nor slanderers nor
swindlers will inherit the kingdom of God. 11And that is what some of you were.[k] But you
were washed,[l] you were sanctified,[m] you were justified in the name of the Lord Jesus
Christ and by the Spirit of our God.

Sexual Immorality

12"Everything is permissible for me"—but not everything is beneficial.[n] "Everything
is permissible for me"—but I will not be mastered by anything. 13"Food for the stomach

5:10 [w]1Co 10:27
5:11 [x]1Co 10:7,14
5:12 [y]Mk 4:11 [z]ver 3-5; 1Co 6:1-4
5:13 [a]Dt 13:5
6:1 [b]Mt 18:17
6:2 [c]Mt 19:28; Lk 22:30
6:5 [d]1Co 4:14 [e]Ac 1:15
6:6 [f]2Co 6:14,15
6:7 [g]Mt 5:39,40
6:8 [h]1Th 4:6
6:9 [i]Gal 5:21 [j]1Co 15:33; Jas 1:16
6:11 [k]Eph 2:2 [l]Ac 22:16 [m]1Co 1:2
6:12 [n]1Co 10:23

[a] 13 Deut 17:7; 19:19; 21:21; 22:21,24; 24:7 [b] 4 *Or matters, do you appoint as judges men of little account in the church?*

5:12–13 By quoting the frequent command in Deuteronomy to purge or expel the wicked from Israel (e.g., Dt 17:7,12), Paul drew an important parallel between the Old Testament covenant community and the Christian church (10:1–11). The visible church is to exercise discipline within its own fellowship, as Israel did within the nation in the Old Testament. Those outside the church are not to be disciplined (i.e., excluded; v. 11) by the church. Even Paul, in spite of his apostolic authority, did not "judge those outside." This does not mean that he never critiqued them or called for their repentance, but he did not try to exercise church discipline over them.

■ **6:1–11** *Lawsuits.* Another problem raised by Chloe's family was the matter of lawsuits between believers. Paul considered this a serious corruption of the church.

6:1–9 See *WCF* 33.1; *WLC* 90,113,141,142.

6:1 dare he take it before the ungodly for judgment. Paul appears to change the topic from the evils of immorality to the problem of lawsuits among Christians. It is important, however, to notice some crucial connections. In the first place, the issue of immorality (though in a different form) would surface again in 6:9, so clearly Paul had not abandoned this topic altogether. Moreover, the failings of the Corinthians with regard to lawsuits were but an expression of the same problem discussed in chapter 5: a weak doctrine of the church. Just as Christians do not have the responsibility to regulate the lives of non-Christians, so non-Christians are incapable of disciplining the church fellowship. If the Corinthians had understood the connection between the Israelite community and the Christian fellowship (see note on 5:12–13), they would have realized how absurd it was for believers to go outside the church to solve their own disputes. Who could imagine a pagan Gentile settling disputes among Israelites in the wilderness?

6:2–5 not competent . . . nobody among you wise enough. Paul's sarcasm is again evident (see notes on 4:8–13; 4:10). The Corinthians were proud and claimed to be wise beyond measure (4:10). Yet they preferred to bring their disputes to unbelieving judges rather than to believers. The absurdity of the situation in Corinth becomes clearer when one recognizes that, in the consummation of history (but not now; 5:12–13), Christians will participate with Christ in judging not only unbelievers, but even the wicked angels.

6:7 Why not rather be wronged? The point is certainly not that Christians should excuse other Christians when they inflict abuse on each other. Nor is it that Christians should always submit to injustices from other believers. That Paul recommended being wronged and cheated may indicate that he had in mind relatively minor cases that would not have had major effects on families or individuals. Otherwise, other principles, such as responsibility to family, would have come into play. The fact that cheating and injustice existed in the Corinthian church demonstrates how far the Corinthians had fallen. See *WLC* 151.

6:9–10 See *WLC* 145; *HC* 94,110.

6:9 the wicked will not inherit the kingdom of God? That the things of this world are incompatible with the kingdom of God is a recurring principle in Scripture (15:50; Gal 5:21). The question arises, however, whether anyone can be saved, since all are wicked. Paul's answer is twofold: On the one hand, God delights in justifying the wicked (Ro 4:5); on the other, those whom God justifies he also sanctifies (Ro 6:1–4). Paul strongly hoped that most of the Corinthians in the visible church were true believers who were justified in the name of Christ (see note on v. 11) and that their present misbehavior was an anomaly that could and must be corrected. Persistence in wickedness would be an indication—not absolute proof—that their faith was false. See theological article "The Perseverance and Preservation of Believers" at Philippians 1. **male prostitutes nor homosexual offenders.** The Greek words here designate passive and active partners in homosexual acts.

6:11 But you were washed. See notes on 1:2 and 5:7; see also theological article "Sanctification" at Titus 3. See *WCF* 13.1; *WLC* 75,77; *BC* 11,34; *HC* 70,73.

■ **6:12–20** *Sexual Immorality.* Paul turned to the problem of sexual immorality in a broader sense. Corinth was well known for its religious prostitution, and Paul addressed this matter directly.

6:12–13 "Everything is permissible" . . . but God. As the quotation marks indicate, Paul was apparently quoting the words of others, probably common sayings in Corinth that were used to excuse immoral behavior. The apostle's response suggests that

6:13 [o]Col 2:22 **6:14** [p]Ro 6:5; Eph 1:19, 20 **6:15** [q]Ro 12:5 **6:16** [r]Ge 2:24; Mt 19:5; Eph 5:31 **6:17** [s]Jn 17:21-23; Gal 2:20 **6:18** [t]2Co 12:21; 1Th 4:3,4; Heb 13:4 [u]Ro 6:12 **6:19** [v]Jn 2:21 [w]Ro 14:7,8 **6:20** [x]Ac 20:28; 1Co 7:23; 1Pe 1:18, 19; Rev 5:9 **7:1** [y]ver 8,26 **7:3** [z]Ex 21:10; 1Pe 3:7

and the stomach for food"—but God will destroy them both.[o] The body is not meant for
sexual immorality, but for the Lord, and the Lord for the body. [14]By his power God raised
the Lord from the dead, and he will raise us also.[p] [15]Do you not know that your bodies
are members of Christ himself?[q] Shall I then take the members of Christ and unite them
with a prostitute? Never! [16]Do you not know that he who unites himself with a prostitute
is one with her in body? For it is said, "The two will become one flesh."[a][r] [17]But he who
unites himself with the Lord is one with him in spirit.[s]

[18]Flee from sexual immorality.[t] All other sins a man commits are outside his body, but
he who sins sexually sins against his own body.[u] [19]Do you not know that your body is a
temple[v] of the Holy Spirit, who is in you, whom you have received from God? You are not
your own;[w] [20]you were bought at a price.[x] Therefore honor God with your body.

Marriage

7 Now for the matters you wrote about: It is good for a man not to marry.[b][y] [2]But since
there is so much immorality, each man should have his own wife, and each woman her own husband. [3]The husband should fulfill his marital duty to his wife,[z] and likewise the wife to her husband. [4]The wife's body does not belong to her alone but also to
her husband. In the same way, the husband's body does not belong to him alone but also

[a] *16* Gen. 2:24 [b] *1* Or "*It is good for a man not to have sexual relations with a woman.*"

---

even if there was an element of truth in these slogans, the Corinthians had perverted it. Indeed, his qualifications refuted the purposes for which these slogans were apparently used in Corinth. Rather than permitting any and all uses of bodies, Paul emphasized the noble purpose for which God had created bodies.

6:14 he will raise us also. As verses 15–17 indicate, Paul referred to the resurrection to remind the Corinthians that salvation in Christ is not merely of the soul, but of the body as well. That this will be true at Christ's return has implications for life now. Being exposed to Greek philosophies, many of the Corinthians probably had a very low view of the physical body. With such weak theology, some of them regarded sexual relationships as inherently sinful because of the bodily passions involved (7:1–5). Here, however, the opposite problem seems to have been the case. Others viewed promiscuous sexual behavior as acceptable because they believed that what one did with the body counted for nothing.

6:15–20 See *WLC* 66; *HC* 1,34,55,76,80,86,87,109.

6:15 your bodies are members of Christ. The doctrine of the believer's union with Christ is one of Paul's most fundamental teachings. This verse indicates that this union extends even to believers' present physical bodies (see Ro 12:1). The Corinthians were therefore quite wrong in thinking that sexual union with a prostitute was insignificant because it was merely physical.

6:16–17 is one with her in body? . . . is one with him in spirit. Literally, "is one body . . . is one spirit." The contrast is not that union with Christ is spiritual union while union with a prostitute is bodily. Paul had emphasized in verse 15 that union with Christ involves the body, a point that is further developed in verses 18–20. In view of verse 19, the word "spirit" in verse 17 should probably be capitalized. Through the Holy Spirit all believers (in both spirit and body) have become one with Christ, and this union precludes giving their bodies to a prostitute. If the practice condemned here has specific reference to the temple prostitutes who served the goddess Aphrodite, the religious implications of the Corinthians' immorality would have been even more obvious (10:20).

6:18 outside his body. The meaning of this passage is disputed. Certainly there are many other sins that affect a Christian's body. While some such sins are grosser and more heinous than others, believers must not think that other Christians who fall in this area are beyond forgiveness. Nevertheless, it is clear that in Paul's teaching, the physical union involved in sexual immorality has special consequences because it defiles the temple of the Christian's body just as idolatry defiles the temple of worship. Thus, it affects in a more direct way a Christian's identity as one who has been united with Christ through the Holy Spirit. It is perhaps significant that Paul's prohibition in this verse ("flee from sexual immorality") is expressed in the same way as the command against idolatry (10:14).

6:19 a temple of the Holy Spirit. Here Paul individualized the concept of the church as the new temple where God dwells (see note on 3:16). While believers must be aware of the very personal character of the Holy Spirit's indwelling, it should be remembered that the emphasis in Scripture as a whole is on the corporate identity of God's people as a holy temple and a spiritual house (Eph 2:19–22; 1Pe 2:4–5). See *HC* 53.

■ **7:1—16:12** *The Corinthians' Letter.* After dealing with matters raised by Chloe's household, Paul turned to issues raised by the church. He touched on six subjects: marriage and divorce (7:1–40), food offered to idols (8:1—11:1), worship (11:2–34), spiritual gifts (12:1—14:40), resurrection (15:1–58) and the collection for Jerusalem, as well as several other matters (16:1–12).

■ **7:1–40** *Marriage and Divorce.* The first matter discussed in this section of Paul's letter is the subject of marriage. The discussion of this subject divides into three parts: marital relationships (vv. 1–9), divorce (vv. 10–24) and virgins (vv. 25–40).

■ **7:1–9** *Marital Relationships.* The circumstances in Corinth raised important questions about sexual relationships within marriage and about singleness and remarriage.

7:1–9 See *WCF* 21.5; *WLC* 108,139; *WSC* 71; *HC* 108.

7:1 Now for the matters you wrote about. See "Introduction: Purpose and Distinctives." **It is good for a man not to marry.** Literally, "not to touch a woman." An ascetic group among the Corinthian Christians probably used this saying. Taken literally, the statement does not simply speak of marriage but refers to all sexual relations, whether within or outside marriage. Paul's opponents in this matter may have appealed to Paul's unmarried state to support their position, but this was not Paul's own opinion on sexual relations (vv. 2–5; 1Ti 2:15). Nevertheless, Paul acknowledged that there is some value in remaining unmarried under certain conditions (vv. 7–8,26), and he gave specific, valid reasons why a Christian might decide to remain single (vv. 29–35). The thrust of the paragraph, however, was intended to correct those who demanded celibacy. In a different context, Paul spoke of marriage in only positive terms (e.g., Eph 5:22–33; 1Ti 3:2) and even condemned those who had forbidden people to marry (1Ti 4:3). Moreover, Paul affirmed the Old Testament, which continually advocates godly marriage, sex and procreation as God's plan for humanity (e.g., Ge 1:28–29; 2:18).

7:2 so much immorality. Corinth was well known for its sexual immorality. Paul probably had in mind the specific matter of Christians employing prostitutes, a subject he had addressed in the preceding passage (6:15–20). Given Paul's solution to this problem ("each man should have his own wife, and each woman her own husband"), it is likely that some married partners were refusing sexual relations with their spouses and that those spouses consequently had employed prostitutes to fulfill their sexual desires. **each man should have his own wife, and each woman her own husband.** The verb "have" does not mean "possess." Rather, as in 5:1, it means "live in a sexual relationship with." Paul's solution to the problem of immorality and prostitution was that a married couple should maintain an active sexual relationship, thereby curbing the motivation for immorality. See *WCF* 22.7; 24.2; *WLC* 138.

7:3 duty. Sex within marriage is not optional. It is an obligation of both husband and wife. Paul referred to the abdication of this duty as deprivation (v. 5).

7:4 belong. This remarkable verse reveals viewpoints that were far ahead of their time: (1) a healthy perception of a woman's sexuality and (2) an understanding of the complete reciprocity that exists between a man and a woman in the most intimate area of their relationship. The Scripture gives no support whatever to the notion that the husband is the only one who should find sex satisfying or to the idea that the husband is always the one who determines whether, when and how to have sex.

to his wife. 5Do not deprive each other except by mutual consent and for a time,[a] so that
you may devote yourselves to prayer. Then come together again so that Satan[b] will not
tempt you[c] because of your lack of self-control. 6I say this as a concession, not as a command.[d] 7I wish that all men were as I am.[e] But each man has his own gift from God; one
has this gift, another has that.[f]
8Now to the unmarried and the widows I say: It is good for them to stay unmarried,
as I am.[g] 9But if they cannot control themselves, they should marry,[h] for it is better to
marry than to burn with passion.
10To the married I give this command (not I, but the Lord): A wife must not separate
from her husband.[i] 11But if she does, she must remain unmarried or else be reconciled
to her husband. And a husband must not divorce his wife.
12To the rest I say this (I, not the Lord):[j] If any brother has a wife who is not a believer and she is willing to live with him, he must not divorce her. 13And if a woman has a
husband who is not a believer and he is willing to live with her, she must not divorce him.
14For the unbelieving husband has been sanctified through his wife, and the unbelieving wife has been sanctified through her believing husband. Otherwise your children
would be unclean, but as it is, they are holy.[k]
15But if the unbeliever leaves, let him do so. A believing man or woman is not bound
in such circumstances; God has called us to live in peace.[l] 16How do you know, wife,
whether you will save[m] your husband?[n] Or, how do you know, husband, whether you
will save your wife?
17Nevertheless, each one should retain the place in life that the Lord assigned to him

7:5 [a]Ex 19:15; 1Sa 21:4,5 [b]Mt 4:10 [c]1Th 3:5
7:6 [d]2Co 8:8
7:7 [e]ver 8; 1Co 9:5 [f]Mt 19:11,12; Ro 12:6; 1Co 12:4, 11
7:8 [g]ver 1,26
7:9 [h]1Ti 5:14
7:10 [i]Mal 2:14-16; Mt 5:32; 19:3-9; Mk 10:11; Lk 16:18
7:12 [j]ver 6,10; 2Co 11:17
7:14 [k]Mal 2:15
7:15 [l]Ro 14:19; 1Co 14:33
7:16 [m]Ro 11:14 [n]1Pe 3:1

7:5–6 deprive each other . . . mutual consent. Paul indicated that to abstain from sexual relations in marriage wrongly withholds that which both parties need. Abstention should not be one-sided but requires the agreement of both parties. **for a time.** Paul allowed for the possibility that temporary abstention from sex (in a way similar to fasting) may be appropriate during intense periods of prayer. The temporary character of this precludes the legitimacy of protracted abstinence. God not only allows but commands the sexual union in marriage. **concession.** Paul allowed temporary abstention within marriage only by way of concession to those who might benefit from it. He did not command it as an occasional practice for every married couple.

7:7–8 I wish that all men were as I am. Given the circumstances in Corinth (v. 26), Paul recognized that it would be helpful to the Corinthian church if its single members remained unmarried, as he was. **each man has his own gift from God.** Paul's ability to remain single without falling into sin (see note on v. 9) was a divine blessing to him. Nevertheless, celibacy is not the only legitimate spiritual gift in the area of sexuality. The Spirit gifts his people for the benefit of the church, and no gift makes any believer superior to another. All gifts are from God and are given according to his purposes (12:4–7). By this statement Paul indicated that while he saw a benefit to singleness during Corinth's crisis, God's plan includes marriage as well as singleness. Marriage was not an inferior status for the Corinthians to hold, even in the midst of their present crisis (see note on v. 26). Moreover, Paul made it clear that it takes a special spiritual gifting for single people to resist sexual sin. He did not mean to imply that singleness itself is a gift of God, for marriage and children are covenant blessings (Ge 2:18; Lev 26:9; Dt 28:11; 30:9).

7:9 if they cannot control themselves. Literally, "if they do not control themselves." Paul recognized that refraining from marriage might cause many single people to fall into sexual sin, just as refraining from sexual relations could cause married people to fall into sin (v. 2). **it is better to marry.** Despite the benefits of singleness during Corinth's crisis (v. 26), marriage was preferable for those whom God had not gifted (v. 7) with the ability to resist sexual sin. Marriage is not a sin; sexual immorality is. Therefore, even though marriage was a less preferable state given Corinth's crisis, it was far better than falling into sin. See *WCF* 22.7; 24.2; *WLC* 138.

■ **7:10–24** *Divorce.* Paul addressed several practical matters related to divorce, including when divorce may be allowed and when divorced men and women may remarry.

7:10 not I, but the Lord. In verse 12 Paul went on to say the opposite ("I, not the Lord"). Paul was not suggesting any disagreement between himself and the Lord on these matters. With regard to the problem treated here (vv. 10–11), Jesus had given a well-known instruction during his earthly ministry (Mk 10:1–12). In verses 12–16, however, Paul discussed a difficult situation that the Lord had not directly addressed. Paul's apostolic commands, however, came by inspiration and had divine authority, as 14:37 makes clear.

7:11 if she does. In spite of the Lord's command, it appears that some of the wives in Corinth, influenced by an ascetic viewpoint (see note on v. 1), had in fact left their husbands. Because spouses are committed to each other until death (v. 39), Paul made clear that only two options were open to these women: reconcile with their husbands or remain unmarried. Paul's teaching may rightly be applied to all other situations of divorce or separation between believers that do not involve infidelity (see theological article "Marriage and Divorce" at Mt 19). The goal in all such cases should be reconciliation (Mt 19:8–9).

7:12–13 I, not the Lord. See note on verse 10. **not a believer.** This is the special circumstance about which Jesus had left no direct instructions. Should not a marriage in which only one spouse is a believer be dissolved, especially if the unbelieving spouse separates? Paul's answer is that one cannot force the unbelieving spouse to stay married (v. 15) but that the believing spouse should not initiate divorce if his or her partner is willing to remain married. See *WLC* 139.

7:14 sanctified . . . holy. A striking affirmation of an Old Testament principle regarding the special character of a home in which at least one person is a believer (see note on 1:2): The whole family is regarded as being set apart from the world and under the sanctions of God's covenant. The terms translated "sanctified" and "holy" derive from the same family of words. Although they are often used of the initial and ongoing separation unto God that occurs when people exercise saving faith, these terms also designate a covenant relationship with God that may either consist of salvation and blessings (e.g., 2Th 1:6–10) or unbelief and curses (e.g., Heb 6:4–10; 10:29). Unbelieving spouses and children come under the influence of God's work through the believing spouse or parent and become part of the visible church, the covenant community. Accordingly, this verse has been used as part of the rationale for baptizing the children of believers (see theological article "Infant or Believer's Baptism?" at Col 2). See *WCF* 25.2; 28.4; *WLC* 62,166,177; *WSC* 95; *BC* 34; *HC* 74.

7:15 is not bound. Some interpret this statement to mean that if an unbelieving spouse deserts the marriage, the believing partner may remarry. While this may be a legitimate implication of Paul's teaching here (cf. Ro 7:2–3), his actual point is simply that a Christian is not obligated to insist that the marriage remain intact. Such an insistence would prevent the man and woman from living "in peace." See *WCF* 24.6.

7:16 whether you will save. Two understandings of this passage are possible. In the light of verse 14, this statement suggests that verse 15 is somewhat parenthetical; therefore, Paul was here giving a reason why Christians should not leave their unbelieving spouses. Because the unbelieving spouses were sanctified, there was a good possibility that they would be saved. Alternatively, verse 16 may give the reason for the instruction in verse 15: The Christian spouse should let the unbelieving spouse go, because the Christian has no assurance that his or her marriage partner will be saved by being forced to remain in the marriage.

7:17–24 See *HC* 124.

7:17 [o]Ro 12:3 [p]1Co 4:17; 14:33; 2Co 8:18; 11:28
7:18 [q]Ac 15:1,2
7:19 [r]Ro 2:25-27; Gal 5:6; 6:15; Col 3:11
7:20 [s]ver 24
7:22 [t]Jn 8:32,36; Phm 16 [u]Eph 6:6
7:23 [v]1Co 6:20
7:24 [w]ver 20
7:25 [x]ver 6; 2Co 8:8 [y]2Co 4:1; 1Ti 1:13, 16
7:26 [z]ver 1,8
7:29 [a]ver 31; Ro 13:11, 12
7:31 [b]1Jn 2:17

and to which God has called him.[o] This is the rule I lay down in all the churches.[p] 18 Was
a man already circumcised when he was called? He should not become uncircumcised.
Was a man uncircumcised when he was called? He should not be circumcised.[q] 19 Circumcision is nothing and uncircumcision is nothing.[r] Keeping God's commands is what
counts. 20 Each one should remain in the situation which he was in when God called
him.[s] 21 Were you a slave when you were called? Don't let it trouble you—although if you
can gain your freedom, do so. 22 For he who was a slave when he was called by the Lord
is the Lord's freedman;[t] similarly, he who was a free man when he was called is Christ's
slave.[u] 23 You were bought at a price;[v] do not become slaves of men. 24 Brothers, each
man, as responsible to God, should remain in the situation God called him to.[w]

25 Now about virgins: I have no command from the Lord,[x] but I give a judgment as one
who by the Lord's mercy[y] is trustworthy. 26 Because of the present crisis, I think that it
is good for you to remain as you are.[z] 27 Are you married? Do not seek a divorce. Are you
unmarried? Do not look for a wife. 28 But if you do marry, you have not sinned; and if a
virgin marries, she has not sinned. But those who marry will face many troubles in this
life, and I want to spare you this.

29 What I mean, brothers, is that the time is short.[a] From now on those who have
wives should live as if they had none; 30 those who mourn, as if they did not; those who
are happy, as if they were not; those who buy something, as if it were not theirs to keep;
31 those who use the things of the world, as if not engrossed in them. For this world in its
present form is passing away.[b]

32 I would like you to be free from concern. An unmarried man is concerned about the

---

7:17 each one should retain the place in life that the Lord assigned to him and to which God has called him. Literally, "as the Lord assigned to each, as God has called each, so let him walk." The rendering of "so let him walk" as "each one should retain the place in life" can be supported on the basis of the subsequent material, although the emphasis of this verse is less on retaining a status than on total behavior ("walk"). The following verses also make clear, however, that the phrase "God has called" is not a reference to a social position but to conversion itself. Note that verses 17–24 set forth a principle that gives coherence to the whole chapter: Becoming a believer does not require one to change one's status, be it marital, ethnic or social (vv. 8,20,26). This verse has sometimes been misused as evidence that Christians should not attempt to improve their social or economic standing. On the contrary, Paul encouraged slaves to obtain their freedom if the opportunity presented itself (v. 21). See *BC* 32.
7:19 The first part of this verse is paralleled in Galatians 5:6 and 6:15. It would seem that the second part ("keeping God's commandments") is another way of saying, "faith expressing itself [literally, 'working'] through love" (Gal 5:6). Such working faith is what characterizes the "new creation" (Gal 6:15). See *WCF* 19.6.
7:20 remain in the situation. See note on verse 17. Here Paul used the language of "remain" rather than "walk," but this statement should be understood in light of the fuller explanation in verse 17. In any event, Paul's language was not a command to remain in one's present situation (if so, it would have contradicted v. 21), but an exhortation not to be troubled in any situation (see v. 21). See *WLC* 141.
7:21 Don't let it trouble you. The desire to attain a better condition is not wrong, as the rest of the verse makes clear. However, Paul did not want Christians to become troubled by situations that could not be changed. Dissatisfaction and complaining can be spiritually fatal (10:10), reflecting a lack of confidence in a sovereign God.
7:23 bought at a price. This statement supports verse 22 (cf. 6:20). If believers truly understood who they belong to, they would realize that even slavery cannot damage their privileged position in Christ. Conversely, even the greatest human master is only a humble servant before Christ. Therefore, Christians need not, and must not, "become slaves of men." See *WCF* 20.2; 22.7.
7:24 remain in the situation. See note on verse 20.
■ **7:25–40** *Virgins.* Paul's discussion of marriage and divorce in more general terms led him to address the particular issue of virgins in the church at Corinth.
7:25 Now about virgins. A new but related topic that the Corinthians had raised in their letter to Paul (see "Introduction: Purpose and Distinctives"). **I have no command from the Lord.** See note on verse 10. **I give a judgment.** This language suggests that Paul's comments were not categorical commandments concerning right or wrong moral choices, but recommendations for a particular situation. This interpretation is confirmed by the statement in verse 28 and by the choices offered in verse 38.
7:26 the present crisis. Paul was probably referring to a specific and unusual problem in Corinth. Some have argued that verse 28 ("many troubles in this life") suggests a more general idea: the predicament that every Christian faces in the present evil age (Gal 1:4). This latter interpretation is unlikely in light of several facts: (1) Paul elsewhere affirmed marriage without qualification as a general practice (11:9; Eph. 5:23–33; 1Ti 2:15; 4:3; 5:14); (2) Paul mentioned the woman's age as a significant factor (v. 36), which would have been irrelevant had the crisis been perpetual; and (3) the Old Testament affirmed marriage throughout every crisis Israel endured, despite the fact that Israel's crises were worse than the church's (i.e., because the age to come had not yet been inaugurated; see theological article "The Plan of the Ages" at Heb 7). In all probability, Paul encouraged only a temporary moratorium on marriages until the crisis in Corinth had passed. Nevertheless, his logic is applicable to many crises. At times the negative dimensions of life are so severe that it is better not to marry (assuming one has the gift of resisting sexual temptation; see note on v. 9).
7:27 married? Literally, "bound to a woman/wife." Paul's language here indicates betrothal rather than consummated marriage. **Do not seek a divorce.** A "divorce" was required to sever a betrothal. Paul's point was that betrothed couples were not to break off their commitments simply for the sake of the present crisis. While it might have been wise for them to put off marriage until the crisis had passed, Paul did not insist on such delay. In fact, even during the crisis, he was more inclined to encourage marriage in the case of older women, probably because they might age beyond their child-bearing years should the crisis be lengthy (v. 36).
7:28 troubles in this life. Literally, "troubles in the flesh." Paul did not mean that marriage is always more difficult than singleness—God ordained wives as helpers, not hindrances (Ge 2:18). Paul referred to the *kind* of troubles ("in the flesh") that could arise during the present crisis, not to the timing or duration ("in this life" or "in this age") of such troubles. He commonly used the word "flesh" to refer to the characteristics of the present evil age. This suggests that, in times of crisis, there is greater potential for suffering in marriage than in singleness (see theological article "The Plan of the Ages" at Heb 7).
7:29–31 the time is short . . . this world . . . is passing away. The Christian life must be lived in the realization that there is no time to waste. A sense of spiritual urgency should characterize the Christian's decisions (Ro 13:11–12). In times of crisis (v. 26), it is especially helpful to focus on the believer's future hope of the new heavens and the new earth, keeping in mind God's eternal kingdom rather than becoming overwhelmed by the present and its troubles.
7:32 I would like you to be free from concern. In the rest of the New Testament, the words translated "concern" and "concerned" in verses 32–34 sometimes carry a positive force ("care"; cf. 12:25; Php 2:20), but generally have a negative connotation ("worry"; cf. Mt 6:25–34; 10:19; 28:14; Lk 10:41; 12:11,22–26; Php 4:6). Since Paul wanted his readers to avoid concern, he clearly had in mind a

Lord's affairs[c]—how he can please the Lord. [33]But a married man is concerned about the
affairs of this world—how he can please his wife— [34]and his interests are divided. An unmarried woman or virgin is concerned about the Lord's affairs: Her aim is to be devoted to the Lord in both body and spirit.[d] But a married woman is concerned about the affairs of this world—how she can please her husband. [35]I am saying this for your own
good, not to restrict you, but that you may live in a right way in undivided[e] devotion to
the Lord.

[36]If anyone thinks he is acting improperly toward the virgin he is engaged to, and if
she is getting along in years and he feels he ought to marry, he should do as he wants.
He is not sinning.[f] They should get married. [37]But the man who has settled the matter
in his own mind, who is under no compulsion but has control over his own will, and who
has made up his mind not to marry the virgin—this man also does the right thing. [38]So
then, he who marries the virgin does right,[g] but he who does not marry her does even
better.[a]

[39]A woman is bound to her husband as long as he lives.[h] But if her husband dies, she
is free to marry anyone she wishes, but he must belong to the Lord.[i] [40]In my judgment,[j]
she is happier if she stays as she is—and I think that I too have the Spirit of God.

Food Sacrificed to Idols

8 Now about food sacrificed to idols:[k] We know that we all possess knowledge.[b][l]
Knowledge puffs up, but love builds up. [2]The man who thinks he knows something[m]
does not yet know as he ought to know.[n] [3]But the man who loves God is known by God.[o]

7:32 [c]1Ti 5:5
7:34 [d]Lk 2:37
7:35 [e]Ps 86:11
7:36 [f]ver 28
7:38 [g]Heb 13:4
7:39 [h]Ro 7:2,3 [i]2Co 6:14
7:40 [j]ver 25
8:1 [k]Ac 15:20 [l]Ro 15:14
8:2 [m]1Co 3:18 [n]1Co 13:8,9,12; 1Ti 6:4
8:3 [o]Ro 8:29; Gal 4:9

a 36–38 Or *[36]If anyone thinks he is not treating his daughter properly, and if she is getting along in years, and he feels she ought to marry, he should do as he wants. He is not sinning. He should let her get married. [37]But the man who has settled the matter in his own mind, who is under no compulsion but has control over his own will, and who has made up his mind to keep the virgin unmarried—this man also does the right thing. [38]So then, he who gives his virgin in marriage does right, but he who does not give her in marriage does even better.* b 1 Or *"We all possess knowledge," as you say*

---

negative meaning. Paul listed various concerns that assail both married and unmarried men and women and explained that in times of crisis marriage can compound anxiety. **An unmarried man is concerned.** Although postponing marriage during crises offers men fewer opportunities for anxiety, they are still vulnerable to worry. This anxiety may extend to the duties to which God has called them (e.g. 2Co 11:28) and even to their relationship with God (e.g., Ps 38:18).

7:33–34 a married man is concerned . . . his interests are divided. During times of crisis, a married man has more responsibilities, and hence more worries, than a single man. Not only is a married man subject to anxiety about the Lord's affairs (as is the single man; v. 32), but he also has concerns about taking adequate care of his family. **An unmarried woman or virgin is concerned.** Paul may be distinguishing between unmarried women in general and a special class of women (virgins already engaged to be married or women who had devoted themselves to a life of virginity). Opportunities for worry for unmarried women and virgins abound during times of crisis. Paul's qualification ("in both body and spirit") may call special attention not only to the strain put on their relationship with and calling from God, but also to the temptation toward sexual sin (cf. vv. 8–9). **Her aim is to be devoted.** Paul does not disparage devotion to the Lord. Rather, he points out that even devotion to God can be stressful if one does not adopt proper perspectives and priorities (cf. Lk 10:38-42). **a married woman is concerned.** During times of crisis, married women are prone to fret about matters of home and husband. Like that of all others, the sphere of their anxiety may also extend to their relationship with and calling from God.

7:34–36 See *WLC* 138; *WSC* 71.

7:35 for your own good. Paul's unmarried readers may have believed that marriage would alleviate some of their worries and troubles—as it would under more normal circumstances (Ge 2:18)—but during difficult times the responsibilities of marriage can make life more rather than less difficult. **undivided devotion.** Not a counterpart to "interests [that] are divided" (v. 34) nor a parallel to "devoted to the Lord" (v. 34). The word translated "undivided" is unrelated to the word translated "divided." Nor is the word translated "devotion" related to the words translated "interests" or "devoted." Paul's point here was not that singleness is better because it avoids multiple worries (his argument in vv. 32–34), but rather that both married and unmarried men and women should follow his teachings in order to avoid worry and to live rightly.

7:36–38 As the text note makes clear, there are two very different ways to understand this passage. The specific situation in Corinth that Paul was addressing is unknown, but two realities are clear: (1) Both marrying and delaying marriage are good options during times of crisis, even though Paul saw a particular benefit in delaying it; and (2) singleness becomes less preferable the older the bride becomes, perhaps because delaying marriage threatens to prevent the woman from ever bearing children. See *WCF* 24.3.

7:39 is bound. Marriage is clearly a life commitment. **free to marry.** A widow, no less than the others treated in this chapter, had the choice to remain unmarried or to marry. The only stipulation was that if she did remarry, the new spouse had to "belong to the Lord." See *WCF* 24.3.

7:40 she is happier if she stays as she is. Not in all circumstances, but specifically in light of the crisis in Corinth (cf. 1Ti 5:14).

■ **8:1—11:1** *Food Offered to Idols.* Greek culture was highly religious. The prominence of idolatry in the Corinthian marketplace raised serious dietary questions for the Christians in Corinth. Paul addressed this matter in four parts: the central issues (8:1–13), his authority in such matters (9:1–27), a series of Old Testament examples (10:1–22) and practical conclusions (10:23—11:1).

■ **8:1–13** *Central Issues.* This section begins Paul's discussion of the problem of idolatry that continues through chapter 10 (ch. 9 supports the larger argument). Here Paul argued strongly against eating food that had been sacrificed to idols, but not on the grounds that it was sinful in and of itself. In 10:1–22 Paul addressed more directly the evil of idolatry. Beginning with 10:25, he discussed the problem of meat sold in the market, some of which may have been involved in pagan rituals. According to some interpreters, the issues discussed in chapters 8 and 10:25–31 are one and the same. Others argue, on the basis of 8:10, that in the present chapter Paul was dealing with the more serious problem of Christians attending the pagan feasts, while in 10:25–30 he was dealing with the issue of eating food purchased in the marketplace.

8:1 Now about. The issue had been brought up by the Corinthians themselves in their letter (see "Introduction: Purpose and Distinctives"). **food sacrificed to idols.** The precise nature of their question is difficult to determine, but it clearly revolved around the association between idolatry and eating food that had been offered to idols. **we all possess knowledge.** In verses 1–3, as an introduction to the subject of eating food offered to idols, Paul addressed the sin of arrogance. These comments reveal that at least some of the Corinthians' conduct was guided not by love (cf. 13:1–8) but by pride.

8:3 known by God. The Corinthians should have been less concerned about what they knew and more concerned about who knew them (cf. 13:12).

8:4 [p]ver 1,7,10 [q]1Co 10:19 [r]Dt 6:4; Eph 4:6
8:5 [s]2Th 2:4
8:6 [t]Mal 2:10 [u]Ro 11:36 [v]Eph 4:5 [w]Jn 1:3
8:7 [x]Ro 14:14; 1Co 10:28
8:8 [y]Ro 14:17
8:9 [z]Gal 5:13 [a]Ro 14:1
8:11 [b]Ro 14:15,20
8:12 [c]Mt 18:6
8:13 [d]Ro 14:21
9:1 [e]2Co 12:12 [f]1Co 15:8 [g]1Co 3:6; 4:15
9:2 [h]2Co 3:2,3
9:4 [i]1Th 2:6
9:5 [j]1Co 7:7,8 [k]Mt 12:46
9:6 [l]Ac 4:36
9:7 [m]Dt 20:6; Pr 27:18

4So then, about eating food sacrificed to idols:[p] We know that an idol is nothing at
all in the world[q] and that there is no God but one.[r] 5For even if there are so-called gods,[s]
whether in heaven or on earth (as indeed there are many "gods" and many "lords"), 6yet
for us there is but one God, the Father,[t] from whom all things came[u] and for whom we
live; and there is but one Lord,[v] Jesus Christ, through whom all things came[w] and
through whom we live.
7But not everyone knows this. Some people are still so accustomed to idols that when
they eat such food they think of it as having been sacrificed to an idol, and since their
conscience is weak,[x] it is defiled. 8But food does not bring us near to God;[y] we are no
worse if we do not eat, and no better if we do.
9Be careful, however, that the exercise of your freedom does not become a stumbling
block[z] to the weak.[a] 10For if anyone with a weak conscience sees you who have this
knowledge eating in an idol's temple, won't he be emboldened to eat what has been sacrificed to idols? 11So this weak brother, for whom Christ died, is destroyed[b] by your
knowledge. 12When you sin against your brothers[c] in this way and wound their weak
conscience, you sin against Christ. 13Therefore, if what I eat causes my brother to fall into
sin, I will never eat meat again, so that I will not cause him to fall.[d]

The Rights of an Apostle

9 Am I not free? Am I not an apostle?[e] Have I not seen Jesus our Lord?[f] Are you not
the result of my work in the Lord?[g] 2Even though I may not be an apostle to others,
surely I am to you! For you are the seal[h] of my apostleship in the Lord.
3This is my defense to those who sit in judgment on me. 4Don't we have the right to
food and drink?[i] 5Don't we have the right to take a believing wife[j] along with us, as do
the other apostles and the Lord's brothers[k] and Cephas[a]? 6Or is it only I and Barnabas[l]
who must work for a living?
7Who serves as a soldier at his own expense? Who plants a vineyard[m] and does not
eat of its grapes? Who tends a flock and does not drink of the milk? 8Do I say this merely from a human point of view? Doesn't the Law say the same thing? 9For it is written in

[a] 5 That is, Peter

8:4 an idol is nothing. Apparently, the Corinthians' argument in favor of eating food that had been offered to idols was the doctrine of monotheism: If there is only one God, who teaches his people to disdain idols (Isa 46:6–7), why should one worry about eating food that had been offered to idols? Paul affirmed this logic (vv. 4–6) but pointed out an error in the Corinthians' application of it (v. 7). See *WCF* 2.1; *WLC* 8; *BC* 1; *HC* 25.
8:6 See *WCF* 2.1; 26.3; *WLC* 8; *BC* 1,8,10; *HC* 25.
8:7 not everyone knows this. Some believers in Corinth could not dissociate the various elements in pagan rituals (e.g., eating in a temple) from idolatry itself. When they ate food that had been offered to idols, their consciences became "defiled." Such strong language (cf. "destroyed" in v. 11) suggests that these Christians sinned not because they thought they were doing something wrong but because they were in fact becoming involved in idolatry because of their improper understanding of the situation.
8:10 weak. See note on 8:12. **eating in an idol's temple.** Eating meat at a pagan temple was roughly equivalent to eating in a modern restaurant, but with the added element that many diners considered such eating to be an act of worship. While eating in an idol's temple was not sinful in and of itself, doing so as a deliberate act of pagan worship was. See notes on verses 1 and 7 (cf. 10:18–22).
8:11–12 See *WLC* 151.
8:11 destroyed. See note on verse 7. **by your knowledge.** Some Corinthians had sufficient understanding (see v. 1) to dine in idols' temples without participating in their hearts in pagan worship. When those without sufficient knowledge observed this practice, they mistook it for idolatry and were thus encouraged to engage in idolatry themselves, perhaps thinking it compatible with Christianity.
8:12 wound their weak conscience. A common interpretation is that a weak Christian—by observing a more knowledgeable believer engaged in a practice that the weak Christian mistakenly believed to be sinful—was emboldened to sin against his or her own conscience by emulating the stronger Christian's behavior. According to this understanding, the weak Christian sinned not by doing something sinful, but by an attitude of rebellion expressed in willing engagement in an activity he or she believed to be sinful. While this is not an unreasonable interpretation, Paul's strong language suggests that the weaker believer committed the sin of idolatry in the way he or she partook of food that had been offered to idols (see notes on vv. 7,10,11). See *WLC* 151.
8:13 I will never eat meat again. This concluding comment is intended to set forth the basic principle of love: Christians are to seek the good of others above their own well-being (10:24,33; 13:5; Php 2:4).
■ **9:1–27** *Paul's Authority.* Since the apostle was not finished with his discussion of "idol food" and idolatry (10:14–33), this chapter probably relates to the same problem. The questions in verse 1 suggest that some of the Corinthians defended their conduct by questioning Paul's authority and criticizing his behavior. Here Paul responded to those objections.
9:1 Am I not free? . . . apostle? . . . seen Jesus our Lord? . . . my work . . . ? Paul was born a Roman citizen and a free man—free to make many choices for himself without consulting others. Further, he had the authority of an apostle, having met all the requirements for that office, including seeing the Lord (see theological article "The Apostles" at 2 Co 10). Moreover, the Corinthians were Paul's converts. They should never have questioned his authority.
9:3 those who sit in judgment on me. Paul had been criticized (see note on 2:1). The next ten verses contain more than a dozen rhetorical questions that reflect deep emotion on the apostle's part; they also provide clues about the historical situation. Clearly, Paul was defending his right to be supported materially by the churches, but he made his defense only in order to emphasize (vv. 15–18) that he did not choose to exercise that right. Perhaps some Corinthians inferred from his lack of patronage that Paul was not a legitimate apostle (2Co 11:7–12). Why should they then listen to his instructions about food that had been offered to idols?
9:5 a believing wife. Literally, "a sister as a wife." It is unclear whether the Corinthians themselves had raised this issue (as though the lack of a wife discredited Paul and Barnabas) or whether Paul simply used it to illustrate the distinction between having a right and exercising it. Both Paul and Barnabas were unmarried at the time of their missionary work, but it cannot be determined with certainty that neither of them had been previously married. Note that in this verse Paul took for granted that he could have been married if he had wanted to be, so long as his wife were a believer.
9:7–15 See *WCF* 19.4; *WLC* 108; *HC* 103.

the Law of Moses: "Do not muzzle an ox while it is treading out the grain."[a][n] Is it about
oxen that God is concerned?[o] 10 Surely he says this for us, doesn't he? Yes, this was written for us,[p] because when the plowman plows and the thresher threshes, they ought to
do so in the hope of sharing in the harvest.[q] 11 If we have sown spiritual seed among you,
is it too much if we reap a material harvest from you?[r] 12 If others have this right of support from you, shouldn't we have it all the more?

But we did not use this right.[s] On the contrary, we put up with anything rather than
hinder[t] the gospel of Christ. 13 Don't you know that those who work in the temple get
their food from the temple, and those who serve at the altar share in what is offered on
the altar?[u] 14 In the same way, the Lord has commanded that those who preach the gospel should receive their living from the gospel.[v]

15 But I have not used any of these rights.[w] And I am not writing this in the hope that
you will do such things for me. I would rather die than have anyone deprive me of this
boast.[x] 16 Yet when I preach the gospel, I cannot boast, for I am compelled to preach.[y]
Woe to me if I do not preach the gospel! 17 If I preach voluntarily, I have a reward;[z] if not
voluntarily, I am simply discharging the trust committed to me.[a] 18 What then is my reward? Just this: that in preaching the gospel I may offer it free of charge,[b] and so not
make use of my rights in preaching it.

19 Though I am free[c] and belong to no man, I make myself a slave to everyone,[d] to win
as many as possible.[e] 20 To the Jews I became like a Jew, to win the Jews.[f] To those under the law I became like one under the law (though I myself am not under the law), so
as to win those under the law. 21 To those not having the law I became like one not having the law[g] (though I am not free from God's law but am under Christ's law), so as to
win those not having the law. 22 To the weak I became weak, to win the weak. I have become all things to all men[h] so that by all possible means I might save some.[i] 23 I do all
this for the sake of the gospel, that I may share in its blessings.

24 Do you not know that in a race all the runners run, but only one gets the prize? Run[j]
in such a way as to get the prize. 25 Everyone who competes in the games goes into strict
training. They do it to get a crown that will not last; but we do it to get a crown that will
last forever.[k] 26 Therefore I do not run like a man running aimlessly; I do not fight like a
man beating the air. 27 No, I beat my body[l] and make it my slave so that after I have
preached to others, I myself will not be disqualified for the prize.

9:9 [n]Dt 25:4; 1Ti 5:18 [o]Dt 22:1-4
9:10 [p]Ro 4:23,24 [q]2Ti 2:6
9:11 [r]Ro 15:27
9:12 [s]Ac 18:3 [t]2Co 11:7-12
9:13 [u]Lev 6:16,26; Dt 18:1
9:14 [v]Mt 10:10; 1Ti 5:18
9:15 [w]Ac 18:3 [x]2Co 11:9,10
9:16 [y]Ro 1:14; Ac 9:15
9:17 [z]1Co 3:8,14 [a]Gal 2:7; Col 1:25
9:18 [b]2Co 11:7; 12:13
9:19 [c]ver 1 [d]Gal 5:13 [e]Mt 18:15; 1Pe 3:1
9:20 [f]Ac 16:3; 21:20-26; Ro 11:14
9:21 [g]Ro 2:12,14
9:22 [h]1Co 10:33 [i]Ro 11:14
9:24 [j]Gal 2:2; 2Ti 4:7; Heb 12:1
9:25 [k]Jas 1:12; Rev 2:10
9:27 [l]Ro 8:13

[a] *9* Deut. 25:4

9:10 Surely he says this for us, doesn't he? Paul did not deny that Deuteronomy 25:4 expressed God's concern for oxen. He merely meant that treatment of farm animals was not the only issue the law was addressing. By extension, it illustrated the principle of fairness to workers.
9:12 we did not use this right. Despite the strain caused by his having to work for pay in addition to the heavy demands of his apostolic ministry, Paul was determined not to become a burden to the churches (1Th 2:6–9). It appears from 2 Corinthians 11:7–12 that the Corinthians misinterpreted Paul's motives. For reasons that are unclear, the apostle did make an exception in the case of the Philippian church in Macedonia (Php 4:15–16).
9:14 receive their living from the gospel. This principle is reflected not only in the Old Testament priesthood (mentioned by Paul in v. 13), but also in several New Testament passages (e.g., Lk 10:7; Gal 6:6; 1Ti 5:17–18).
9:15–16 I would rather die than have anyone deprive me of this boast. Yet when I preach the gospel, I cannot boast. In the Greek the first sentence is broken off. Literally, these two sentences read, "It is good for me to die rather than . . . No one will nullify my boast, for if I preach, it is not [the grounds for] my boasting." Paul knew that he could not boast about preaching; he had been called to do it and did not have a choice in the matter. Paul had not, however, been called to preach for free. So his reward, or his ground for boasting, was that he did preach free of charge (v. 18) and did not want anyone to deprive him of the ability to follow through with this decision. Paul may have had in mind fulfilling Jesus' command to store up treasures in heaven (Mt 6:19–21).
9:19–22 See *WLC* 159.
9:19 Though I am free . . . to win as many as possible. Paul was willing to give up many rights and freedoms when he thought that retaining them would hinder his ability to preach the gospel or make people less likely to believe his message. Paul repeated this theme three other times in this passage (vv. 20,21,22).
9:20 I became like one under the law. When ministering to Jews, Paul conformed to the Old Testament ceremonial regulations and thus, from outward appearances, looked like one who was under the condemnation of the law. Paul accommodated himself behaviorally to Jewish interpretations of the law, but he did not accept Jewish theological outlooks.
9:21 I became like one not having the law. When ministering to Gentiles, Paul was willing to adopt their lifestyle, but he recognized that he was never free to disobey God. **under Christ's law.** Paul did not set Christ in opposition to Moses. The contrast here is between Christ's interpretation of Moses and the Jewish legalistic interpretation, which Paul deemed "under the law."
9:22 I became weak. A restatement of the point made in 8:13. Paul refused to exercise his freedoms when such exercise would have caused others to sin.
9:24 Run in such a way as to get the prize. Paul elsewhere used the illustration of a race and its prize to emphasize the need for single-mindedness, determination and perseverance (Php 3:12–14; 2Ti 4:7–8). This analogy is true because saving faith proves itself through perseverance. See theological article "The Perseverance and Preservation of Believers" at Philippians 1. See *HC* 115.
9:27 I beat my body. Paul did not have literal self-flagellation in mind. He continued the athletic metaphor by reminding his readers that fighters must discipline their bodies if they expect to win. Similarly, Christians must be willing to set aside their selfish interests (such as the eating of meat offered to idols; 8:13) for the sake of their primary goal. **so that . . . I myself will not be disqualified.** The words "for the prize" are not in the Greek but are added for clarification. This statement has often been used as evidence that Christians may lose their salvation. But the witness of the New Testament, and of Paul in particular, is clearly that those whom God has brought to himself are his forever (Ro 8:28–30) because the life they have is eternal in character (Jn 5:24). What God has begun he will infallibly bring to completion (Php 1:6). Those who leave the fold show thereby that they were never in God's hand (Jn 10:2–29; 1Jn 2:19). One should be careful, however, not to dismiss or minimize the force of this passage and others like it (e.g., 15:2; Php 3:11; Col 1:23) by suggesting that it is merely hypothetical or that it has to do only with rewards and not with salvation. Although Paul could express his confidence that absolutely noth-

Warnings From Israel's History

10 For I do not want you to be ignorant of the fact, brothers, that our forefathers
were all under the cloud[m] and that they all passed through the sea.[n] 2They were
all baptized into Moses in the cloud and in the sea. 3They all ate the same spiritual food
4and drank the same spiritual drink; for they drank from the spiritual rock[o] that accompanied them, and that rock was Christ. 5Nevertheless, God was not pleased with most
of them; their bodies were scattered over the desert.[p]
6Now these things occurred as examples[a] to keep us from setting our hearts on evil
things as they did. 7Do not be idolaters,[q] as some of them were; as it is written: "The people sat down to eat and drink and got up to indulge in pagan revelry."[b] [r] 8We should not
commit sexual immorality, as some of them did—and in one day twenty-three thousand
of them died.[s] 9We should not test the Lord, as some of them did—and were killed by
snakes.[t] 10And do not grumble, as some of them did[u]—and were killed[v] by the destroying angel.[w]
11These things happened to them as examples and were written down as warnings
for us, on whom the fulfillment of the ages has come.[x] 12So, if you think you are standing firm,[y] be careful that you don't fall! 13No temptation has seized you except what is
common to man. And God is faithful;[z] he will not let you be tempted beyond what you
can bear.[a] But when you are tempted, he will also provide a way out so that you can
stand up under it.

Idol Feasts and the Lord's Supper

14Therefore, my dear friends, flee from idolatry. 15I speak to sensible people; judge for
yourselves what I say. 16Is not the cup of thanksgiving for which we give thanks a participation in the blood of Christ? And is not the bread that we break a participation in

10:1 [m]Ex 13:21 [n]Ex 14:22,29
10:4 [o]Ex 17:6; Nu 20:11; Ps 78:15
10:5 [p]Nu 14:29; Heb 3:17
10:7 [q]ver 14 [r]Ex 32:4,6,19
10:8 [s]Nu 25:1-9
10:9 [t]Nu 21:5,6
10:10 [u]Nu 16:41 [v]Nu 16:49 [w]Ex 12:23
10:11 [x]Ro 13:11
10:12 [y]Ro 11:20
10:13 [z]1Co 1:9 [a]2Pe 2:9

[a] 6 Or *types;* also in verse 11 [b] 7 Exodus 32:6

ing would be able to separate him from God's love (Ro 8:38–39), he never dared presume that flagrant rebellion against God would be overlooked. No Christian (not even an apostle) can afford to take lightly such warnings of Scripture (10:12); falling away proves the absence of saving faith, and even an apostle could fall away (e.g., Judas Iscariot). See theological article "The Perseverance and Preservation of Believers" at Philippians 1.

■ **10:1–22** *Old Testament Examples.* After encouraging the Corinthians to think of their Christian life as a race, Paul explained the importance of this outlook by drawing attention to the Old Testament example of Israel in the wilderness.

10:1–5 See *WCF* 7.5; 27.5; *WLC* 174,175; *HC* 78.

10:2 They were all baptized into Moses. Because Christian baptism stresses the union of the believer with Christ, Paul used the language of baptism to draw a correspondence between Old Testament Israel and the Corinthian church (see note on 5:12–13). All the Israelites of the exodus generation went through the ordeal and deliverance of this event (which involved crossing through the water) by virtue of their identification with their leader, Moses. Note the repetition of the word "all" in verses 1–3 (also 12:13). This passage (10:1–12) serves as an illustration and explanation of the warning in 9:24–27. All the members of the visible church in Corinth had been baptized into Christ and therefore had tasted God's deliverance, but that was no guarantee that God would be pleased to save all of them. See theological article "The Church: Visible and Invisible" at 1 Peter 4. See *BC* 33.

10:3–4 ate the same spiritual food and drank the same spiritual drink. In addition to his baptismal analogy, Paul warned the Corinthians not to find false comfort in the fact that they also partook of the Lord's Supper (vv. 14–22). As the visible people of God, the Israelites had also experienced divinely given food and drink. Here the word "spiritual" does not mean "immaterial," nor does it suggest that the manna and the water had a deeper, spiritual meaning. Rather, Paul was referring to the Holy Spirit (see 2:6,14; 3:1; 15:44–46 and their notes). The Israelites were greatly privileged by receiving supernatural provisions from the Holy Spirit, just as the church receives nourishment from the Holy Spirit in the Lord's Supper. **that rock was Christ.** In the Old Testament, God is often compared to a rock because he is the King of Israel (e.g., Ge 49:24; Ps 95:1–3). Ezekiel referred to water flowing from the temple, the place of God's royal enthronement on Earth, after the restoration from exile (Eze 47:1–12). The rock that gave Israel water during the exodus fit within this royal typology. In this sense, Paul saw the water-giving rock of the wilderness as a demonstration of God's royal, life-giving care for his people. As such, the rock foreshadowed Jesus, the final, life-giving King. See *BC* 35.

10:5–14 See *WLC* 148,195; *WSC* 81; *BC* 10; *HC* 94.

10:6 examples. The Greek word is related to the English term "type" (as in v. 11). The events of the exodus mentioned here represent a pattern of deliverance that corresponds to the deliverance that Jesus brought for his people.

10:11 the fulfillment of the ages has come. Literally, "the end of the ages has come." This statement reflects Paul's conviction that the coming of Christ inaugurated "the last days" (see note on 1:20; Heb 1:2), the time when the great promises of the Old Testament come to pass. By pointing out this theme, Paul helped the Corinthians appreciate that the Old Testament events applied to them. These facts also suggest that, given their privileged position, the Corinthians should have recognized their greater responsibility (Lk 12:48). See theological article "The Plan of the Ages" at Hebrews 7. See *WLC* 155,174.

10:12 be careful that you don't fall! See note on 9:27. See *WLC* 175.

10:13 provide a way out. This well-known verse has served as a great encouragement to Christians faced with temptations. Christians should note, however, that Paul's words actually rebuke as well as assure. If God does not allow any temptation greater than the believer can withstand, then surely Christians never have a valid excuse for succumbing. Although no believer avoids sin entirely (1Ki 8:46; 1Jn 1:8–10), there is no temptation to sin that cannot be resisted. See *HC* 127; *CD* 5.11.

10:14–17 See *WCF* 29.1; *WLC* 168,171; *WSC* 97; *HC* 77,79,80.

10:14 flee from idolatry. This command does not mark a completely new thought in Paul's argument. Rather, this exhortation applies the forgoing arguments to Paul's main point in chapters 8–10 concerning food offered to idols (see note on 8:1). Specifically, Paul was grieved because some of the Corinthians engaged in idolatry when they ate in pagan temples (see notes on 8:7,10,11, 12). See *WLC* 174.

10:16 the cup of thanksgiving . . . the bread that we break. This reference to the Lord's Supper was intended to demonstrate the significance of taking part in a distinctively religious meal. Just as it would be impossible to partake of the Lord's Supper and claim that it had no religious significance, so it was naive for the Corinthians to think that participation in Greek temple feasts did not involve idolatry. Moreover, the union "in the body of Christ" that is symbolized by partaking of the bread and wine excludes union with idols. See *WCF* 27.1; 29.4; 29.7; *WLC* 162,168,170,176,177; *WSC* 96; *BC* 35; *HC* 65.

the body of Christ?[b] 17Because there is one loaf, we, who are many, are one body,[c] for
we all partake of the one loaf.
18Consider the people of Israel: Do not those who eat the sacrifices[d] participate in the
altar? 19Do I mean then that a sacrifice offered to an idol is anything, or that an idol is
anything?[e] 20No, but the sacrifices of pagans are offered to demons,[f] not to God, and I
do not want you to be participants with demons. 21You cannot drink the cup of the Lord
and the cup of demons too; you cannot have a part in both the Lord's table and the table of demons.[g] 22Are we trying to arouse the Lord's jealousy?[h] Are we stronger than he?[i]

10:16 [b]Mt 26:26-28
10:17 [c]Ro 12:5; 1Co 12:27
10:18 [d]Lev 7:6,14,15
10:19 [e]1Co 8:4
10:20 [f]Dt 32:17; Ps 106:37; Rev 9:20

10:21 [g]2Co 6:15,16 **10:22** [h]Dt 32:16,21 [i]Ecc 6:10; Isa 45:9

10:19–22 See *WLC* 110; *HC* 81.
10:20 participants with demons. Although idols are nothing (v. 19), behind pagan rituals is the reality of Satan's work, and Christians should have nothing to do with that. Paul's teaching here creates some tension with his statements in chapter 8, where he appears to allow dining in pagan temples. Perhaps the best explanation is that not all meals offered in pagan temples were intended as pagan religious feasts. Animals were regularly offered to pagan idols before being slaughtered for market, so no doubt the supply of meat flowing from pagan altars exceeded that which was used in religious feasts and ceremonies (v. 25).
10:21 cannot . . . cannot. Paul did not mean that it was physically impossible to share in the feast of demons and in the Lord's Supper at the same time. Rather, he meant that this cannot be done with impunity and should not be done. See *WCF* 27.1; 29.1; *WLC* 162,168.
10:22 Lord's jealousy? In this case, it is not jealousy for his peo-

Demons: Can I Be Possessed by a Demon?

DEMONS, or devils, are spiritual (non-physical) beings that are corrupt and hostile to both God and humanity. Demons are fallen spirits, deathless creatures in league with Satan (Jesus equated Beelzebub, their reputed prince, with Satan in Mt 12:24–29). They were cast out of heaven to await final judgment because of their sins (2Pe 2:4; Jude 6). Their minds are permanently set to oppose the honor of God and the welfare of human beings; they are beyond redemption.

The Old Testament commonly, though not exclusively, connects demons with idolatry and pagan worship practices (Lev 17:7 [see NIV text note]; Dt 32:17; Ps 106:37). They are also mentioned as holding dominion over Gentile nations (Ps 82:1; Da 10:13,20; Mt 4:8-9; Lk 4:5–7), such as those that engaged in pagan worship. For Israel to worship other nations' gods was to worship demons and Satan himself.

The severe apostasy of Israel and the tyranny of foreign powers during the centuries between the Old and New Testaments led to the infiltration of many demons into Israel during that time. As a result, Jesus exorcised demons, or drove them out of people (known as demoniacs), in large numbers. The frequency and intensity of demonic manifestations during Christ's ministry were unique; there has been no parallel either in Old Testament times or since. When Jesus came to establish the kingdom of God beginning in Israel (see theological article "The Kingdom of God" at Mt 4), Satan and his demons desperately sought to resist him (Mt 12:29). Demons were revealed as having knowledge (Mk 1:24) and strength (9:17–27). They even exploited physical and mental maladies (Mk 5:1–15; 9:17–18; Lk 11:14).

Even so, demons recognized and feared Christ. They were subject to his authority (Mk 1:25–26; 3:11–12; 9:25–26), although Jesus admitted that some were so strong that it took great effort in prayer to expel them (Mk 9:29). Christ also authorized and equipped the apostles and the 72 others to exercise demons in his name (i.e., by delegating his power and authority; Lk 9:1; 10:17; Ac 16:18), indicating that the followers of Jesus also have authority over demons so long as they exercise proper devotion and reliance on the power of the Holy Spirit (1Jn 4:4). The hold of Satan over the nations has been fundamentally broken by Christ (Mt 12:28–29; Col 2:15; 1Pe 3:21–22; Rev 20:2–3), but he and his demonic armies are not entirely impotent (Eph 6:11–12; 1Pe 5:8).

Throughout the history of the church it appears that demons have become particularly active on the frontier of God's kingdom and in those regions in which faith has been lost (once Christian lands that have subsequently denied the gospel). As in the Scriptures, demons seem to be particularly aggressive where and when the church extends itself for the first time into pagan territories. Missionaries frequently report dramatic encounters with demons. Moreover, as the example of Israel indicates (Dt 32:17; Ps 106:37; Mt 10:6-8), demonic activity seems to increase when and where serious, prolonged apostasy occurs in the church. Even so, true believers still have access to the power of Christ over these evil spirits.

Unfortunately, it is easy for well-meaning Christians to become preoccupied with this subject to the point that they identify every problem with demons. At other times, they so fear demons that they are rendered ineffective for the kingdom of God. Scripture rejects both these outlooks. Instead, the Scriptures distinguish demonic activity, which is extraordinary and supernatural, from the common difficulties caused by the fall into sin. Moreover, Scripture indicates that though demons can foment trouble of many kinds in the lives of regenerate persons, in whom the Holy Spirit dwells, they cannot take full possession of true believers (Mt 12:28–29; 1Jn 4:4), thwart God's purpose of saving his elect (Jn 10:28–29; Ro 8:38–39) or finally avoid their own eternal torment (2Pe 2:4; Jude 6). Demons are God's defeated enemies (Col 2:15), and their limited power is only prolonged for the advancement of God's glory as his people contend with them. Followers of Christ need not fear the power of demons so long as they remain faithful to Christ and rely on his power to overcome his spiritual enemies.

The Believer's Freedom

23“Everything is permissible”—but not everything is beneficial.[j] “Everything is permissible”—but not everything is constructive. 24Nobody should seek his own good, but
the good of others.[k]
25Eat anything sold in the meat market without raising questions of conscience,[l] 26for,
“The earth is the Lord's, and everything in it.”[a][m]
27If some unbeliever invites you to a meal and you want to go, eat whatever is put before you[n] without raising questions of conscience. 28But if anyone says to you, “This has
been offered in sacrifice,” then do not eat it, both for the sake of the man who told you
and for conscience' sake[b][o]— 29the other man's conscience, I mean, not yours. For why
should my freedom[p] be judged by another's conscience? 30If I take part in the meal with
thankfulness, why am I denounced because of something I thank God for?[q]
31So whether you eat or drink or whatever you do, do it all for the glory of God.[r] 32Do
not cause anyone to stumble,[s] whether Jews, Greeks or the church of God[t]— 33even as
I try to please everybody in every way.[u] For I am not seeking my own good but the good
of many, so that they may be saved.[v]

11

1Follow my example,[w] as I follow the example of Christ.

Propriety in Worship

2I praise you[x] for remembering me in everything[y] and for holding to the teachings,[c]
just as I passed them on to you.[z]
3Now I want you to realize that the head of every man is Christ,[a] and the head of the
woman is man,[b] and the head of Christ is God.[c] 4Every man who prays or prophesies with
his head covered dishonors his head. 5And every woman who prays or prophesies[d] with
her head uncovered dishonors her head—it is just as though her head were shaved.[e] 6If
a woman does not cover her head, she should have her hair cut off; and if it is a disgrace
for a woman to have her hair cut or shaved off, she should cover her head. 7A man ought
not to cover his head,[d] since he is the image[f] and glory of God; but the woman is the glo-

10:23 [j]1Co 6:12
10:24 [k]ver 33; Ro 15:1,2; 1Co 13:5; Php 2:4, 21
10:25 [l]Ac 10:15; 1Co 8:7
10:26 [m]Ps 24:1
10:27 [n]Lk 10:7
10:28 [o]1Co 8:7,10-12
10:29 [p]Ro 14:16; 1Co 9:1,19
10:30 [q]Ro 14:6
10:31 [r]Col 3:17; 1Pe 4:11
10:32 [s]Ac 24:16 [t]Ac 20:28
10:33 [u]Ro 15:2; 1Co 9:22 [v]Ro 11:14
11:1 [w]1Co 4:16
11:2 [x]ver 17,22 [y]1Co 4:17 [z]1Co 15:2,3; 2Th 2:15
11:3 [a]Eph 1:22 [b]Ge 3:16; Eph 5:23 [c]1Co 3:23
11:5 [d]Ac 21:9 [e]Dt 21:12
11:7 [f]Ge 1:26; Jas 3:9

[a] *26* Psalm 24:1 [b] *28* Some manuscripts *conscience' sake, for “the earth is the Lord's and everything in it”* [c] *2* Or *traditions* [d] *4–7* Or 4*Every man who prays or prophesies with long hair dishonors his head.* 5*And every woman who prays or prophesies with no covering ⌞of hair⌟ on her head dishonors her head—she is just like one of the “shorn women.”* 6*If a woman has no covering, let her be for now with short hair, but since it is a disgrace for a woman to have her hair shorn or shaved, she should grow it again.* 7*A man ought not to have long hair*

---

ple, but jealousy for his own holiness and the honor that is due exclusively to him and to his feast. Again Paul warned the Corinthians in the strongest terms.

■ **10:23—11:1** *Conclusions.* Paul drew a number of conclusions and practical instructions related to food offered to idols.

10:23 “Everything is permissible.” See note on 6:12–13.

10:25 Eat anything sold in the meat market. In spite of his strong words against partaking in idolatrous feasts, Paul did not want the Corinthians to be overly scrupulous. The fact that meat was offered to an idol did not change the character of the meat itself, nor did it somehow contaminate the meat with evil spirits.

10:28 then do not eat it. A different problem arose if someone else pointed out that the piece of meat had in fact been part of a pagan ritual. Presumably, such a comment would indicate that the person had some scruples about it (i.e., weak believers; 8:7–12). In that case, it would be proper for the stronger Christian to abstain “for the sake of the man who told” him or her.

10:30 why am I denounced . . . ? This question seems to indicate that Paul had been accused of eating meat offered to idols, with the implication that he had no right to forbid the Corinthians to do the same (see note on 9:19).

10:31 See *WLC* 1,112; *WSC* 1; *HC* 91.

10:33 I am not seeking my own good but the good of many. In combination with the desire to do everything for God's glory (v. 31), this principle provided Paul with his criterion for behavior. It is in fact the principle of Christian love, which “is not self-seeking” (13:5).

11:1 As the paragraph division indicates, this verse probably does not mark the beginning of a new section. Indeed, Paul's exhortation (“follow my example”) serves as a fitting conclusion to the last verse of chapter 10. Note, however, that the apostle did not set himself up as an absolute example; he asked his readers to imitate him insofar as he followed “the example of Christ.”

■ **11:2–34** *Problems in Worship.* At this point, Paul turned to another problem in the Corinthian church: the practice of worship. A number of controversial issues had been raised with respect to the way worship was conducted by the church in Corinth. Paul addressed two main issues: head coverings (vv. 2–16) and the Lord's Supper (vv. 17–34).

■ **11:2–16** *Head Coverings.* Paul's first worship-related subject was the practice of women covering their heads.

11:3 the head. The significance of this metaphor has been hotly debated by scholars. Does it indicate leadership/authority or source/origin? The evidence from Greek literature in general is somewhat ambiguous, and the present context does not clearly resolve the problem. The two ideas, however, should probably not be regarded as mutually exclusive. Sometimes when Paul spoke of Christ as head, the notion of “source” was present (cf. v. 8; Eph 4:15; Col 2:19). At other times he spoke in terms of submission and/or authority (Eph 1:22; 5:22–24; Col 1:18; 2:10). An allusion to submission as honor and respect fits the present context well (vv. 4–5,13; cf. notes on Eph 5:22,24), although authority may also be in view (v. 10).

11:4 with his head covered. What little evidence is available seems to indicate that, with few exceptions, Christian men in the first century thought it important to leave their heads uncovered while worshiping. Assuming this to be the custom in Paul's day, men who covered their heads in worship showed irreverence toward Christ. Whatever the custom in Paul's day, Paul did not argue here that such a custom ought to be observed in all places at all times. **dishonors his head.** Probably a reference to Christ as the head (v. 7).

11:5 with her head uncovered. In view of the contrast with the previous verse, this comment suggests that women in the first century worshiped with an external head covering. Some scholars have argued, however, that a particular hairstyle was in view (in Nu 5:18, loosening the hair of a woman was part of the test for an unfaithful wife; see note on 1Co 11:15). As with men with uncovered heads (v. 5), Paul did not argue that all women at all times were to cover their heads in worship. Rather, he offered this teaching in light of the circumstances current in Corinth. **just as though her head were shaved.** In verse 6 the shaving of a woman's head is pictured as analogous to having the hair cut short, presumably like a man's. It appears that Paul opposed the tendency to obliterate the distinction between the sexes. The controversy possibly reflects the general view among some of the Corinthians that they had already moved so far toward perfection that the old customs no longer applied (see “Introduction: Purpose and Distinctives”).

ry of man. 8 For man did not come from woman, but woman from man;[g] 9 neither was
man created for woman, but woman for man.[h] 10 For this reason, and because of the angels, the woman ought to have a sign of authority on her head.
11 In the Lord, however, woman is not independent of man, nor is man independent
of woman. 12 For as woman came from man, so also man is born of woman. But everything comes from God.[i] 13 Judge for yourselves: Is it proper for a woman to pray to God
with her head uncovered? 14 Does not the very nature of things teach you that if a man
has long hair, it is a disgrace to him, 15 but that if a woman has long hair, it is her glory?
For long hair is given to her as a covering. 16 If anyone wants to be contentious about this,
we have no other practice—nor do the churches of God.[j]

The Lord's Supper

17 In the following directives I have no praise for you,[k] for your meetings do more harm
than good. 18 In the first place, I hear that when you come together as a church, there are
divisions[l] among you, and to some extent I believe it. 19 No doubt there have to be differences among you to show which of you have God's approval.[m] 20 When you come together, it is not the Lord's Supper you eat, 21 for as you eat, each of you goes ahead without waiting for anybody else.[n] One remains hungry, another gets drunk. 22 Don't you
have homes to eat and drink in? Or do you despise the church of God[o] and humiliate
those who have nothing?[p] What shall I say to you? Shall I praise you[q] for this? Certainly not!
23 For I received from the Lord[r] what I also passed on to you:[s] The Lord Jesus, on the
night he was betrayed, took bread, 24 and when he had given thanks, he broke it and said,
"This is my body, which is for you; do this in remembrance of me." 25 In the same way,
after supper he took the cup, saying, "This cup is the new covenant[t] in my blood;[u] do
this, whenever you drink it, in remembrance of me." 26 For whenever you eat this bread
and drink this cup, you proclaim the Lord's death until he comes.
27 Therefore, whoever eats the bread or drinks the cup of the Lord in an unworthy
manner will be guilty of sinning against the body and blood of the Lord.[v] 28 A man ought
to examine himself[w] before he eats of the bread and drinks of the cup. 29 For anyone who
eats and drinks without recognizing the body of the Lord eats and drinks judgment on

11:8 [g]Ge 2:21-23; 1Ti 2:13
11:9 [h]Ge 2:18
11:12 [i]Ro 11:36
11:16 [j]1Co 7:17
11:17 [k]ver 2,22
11:18 [l]1Co 1:10-12; 3:3
11:19 [m]1Jn 2:19
11:21 [n]2Pe 2:13; Jude 12
11:22 [o]1Co 10:32 [p]Jas 2:6 [q]ver 2,17
11:23 [r]Gal 1:12 [s]1Co 15:3
11:25 [t]Lk 22:20 [u]1Co 10:16
11:27 [v]Heb 10:29
11:28 [w]2Co 13:5

11:10 because of the angels. Many interpretations of this phrase have been suggested, the most common being that Paul spoke either of heavenly beings who cared for the church or of messengers from other churches. All such suggestions are speculative. The difficulty of this verse indicates that Paul assumed a lot of common understanding between himself and the Corinthians. As a result, one should be especially cautious about forming universal applications from this passage (see notes on vv. 4,5,16).
11:11–12 These verses appear to be a qualification of the previous comments. With specific reference to their relationship "in the Lord," men and women are mutually dependent, since they are one in him (Gal 3:28).
11:13–14 See *WCF* 1.6.
11:14 nature of things. Many interpretations of this phrase have been suggested, but none is without problems. In light of the Old Testament's approval of long hair on men in certain circumstances (Nu 6:2–21; 2Sa 14:25–26), it seems clear that Paul was not speaking of a perpetual, universal principle. In any event, Paul expected the Corinthians to recognize and accept the fact that long hair in their setting was appropriate only for women and short hair only for men (cf. note on v. 5).
11:15 as a covering. Paul may have meant that since the woman's long hair served as a covering, the propriety of an external veil or other covering was indicated. Some argue, however, that Paul meant "in place of" a covering (thus supporting the view that Paul did not have in mind veils, but hairstyle; see note on v. 5).
11:16 we have no other practice. Paul appears to have appealed to the universal practice of the church at this point in time. He did not use exactly this kind of argument elsewhere in any of his letters, but nevertheless he expected it to settle this matter.
▪**11:17–34** *The Lord's Supper.* The second worship-related subject Paul addressed was the way the Corinthians were observing the Lord's Supper. See *HC* 82.
11:17 I have no praise for you. The contrast between these words and verse 2 indicates the seriousness of the problem with which Paul was about to deal. See *WLC* 174,175.
11:18–21 See *WLC* 151,171.
11:19 differences among you to show . . . God's approval. The Greek word translated "differences" may also be rendered "dissensions." Paul recognized that God had a perfect purpose for the divisions in the church at Corinth. Such a comment, however, only reinforced the gravity of the Corinthians' behavior; the fact of God's sovereignty can never serve as an excuse for disobedience (cf. Ac 4:27-28).
11:20 not the Lord's Supper. Their mishandling of this observance had turned it into something quite different from what it should have been. See *WCF* 26.2; 27.4; 29.3; *WLC* 164,171; *BC* 29.
11:21 One remains hungry, another gets drunk. As the next verse makes clear, Paul's concern here was not primarily with drunkenness as such but with the humiliation of the poor. A proper understanding of the rest of the passage requires that this distinction be kept in mind. The Lord's Supper symbolized, among other things, the unity of God's people (10:17). Those Corinthians who were well-off apparently prevented the less fortunate among them from eating well at the feasts where the Lord's Supper was celebrated. This behavior manifested utter selfishness and a blatant contradiction of the meaning of the ceremony.
11:23–32 See *WCF* 7.4; 21.5; 27.1; 27.4; 29.1; 29.2; 29.3; 29.4; 29.5; 29.6; 29.8; *WLC* 108,112,164,168,169,170,171,174,175,176,177; *WSC* 92,96,97; *BC* 35; *HC* 68,77,78,81,103.
11:23–25 Paul's account of the institution of the Lord's Supper is in all essentials what we find in the Gospels (Mt 26:26–29; Mk 14:22–25; Lk 22:17–20). See *WCF* 7.6; *WLC* 35,112,162,168,171; *HC* 75.
11:26 you proclaim the Lord's death until he comes. Note the connection between preaching the gospel and celebrating the Lord's Supper. Alternatively, or perhaps in addition, Paul meant that the visible demonstration of the Lord's Supper is a proclamation of the gospel. See *WLC* 174,176; *WSC* 92; *HC* 54,67,76,78.
11:27–34 It is important to take this section as a unit. Verses 33–34 make it plain that Paul still had in mind the abuses mentioned in verses 21–22. See *WCF* 30.3; *WLC* 173.
11:27 unworthy manner. See notes on verses 17, 19, 20 and 21. **sinning against the body and blood of the Lord.** Most likely refers to the sin mentioned in verse 22: despising the church, which is the body of Christ (10:17; 12:12–27), and humiliating the poor within that body. See *BC* 29,35.
11:28 examine himself. In order to make certain that he is not sinning against his fellow believers. See *WCF* 29.7; *WLC* 171,172.
11:29 recognizing the body of the Lord. The words "of the

himself. [30]That is why many among you are weak and sick, and a number of you have
fallen asleep. [31]But if we judged ourselves, we would not come under judgment.[x] [32]When
we are judged by the Lord, we are being disciplined[y] so that we will not be condemned
with the world.
[33]So then, my brothers, when you come together to eat, wait for each other. [34]If anyone is hungry,[z] he should eat at home,[a] so that when you meet together it may not result in judgment.
And when I come[b] I will give further directions.

Spiritual Gifts

12 Now about spiritual gifts,[c] brothers, I do not want you to be ignorant. [2]You know
that when you were pagans,[d] somehow or other you were influenced and led
astray to mute idols.[e] [3]Therefore I tell you that no one who is speaking by the Spirit of God
says, "Jesus be cursed,"[f] and no one can say, "Jesus is Lord,"[g] except by the Holy Spirit.[h]
[4]There are different kinds of gifts, but the same Spirit.[i] [5]There are different kinds of
service, but the same Lord. [6]There are different kinds of working, but the same God[j]
works all of them in all men.
[7]Now to each one the manifestation of the Spirit is given for the common good.[k] [8]To
one there is given through the Spirit the message of wisdom,[l] to another the message
of knowledge[m] by means of the same Spirit, [9]to another faith[n] by the same Spirit, to another gifts of healing[o] by that one Spirit, [10]to another miraculous powers,[p] to another
prophecy, to another distinguishing between spirits,[q] to another speaking in different

11:31 [x]Ps 32:5; 1Jn 1:9
11:32 [y]Ps 94:12; Heb 12:7-10; Rev 3:19
11:34 [z]ver 21 [a]ver 22 [b]1Co 4:19
12:1 [c]Ro 1:11; 1Co 14:1,37
12:2 [d]Eph 2:11,12; 1Pe 4:3 [e]Ps 115:5; Jer 10:5; Hab 2:18, 19; 1Th 1:9
12:3 [f]Ro 9:3 [g]Jn 13:13 [h]1Jn 4:2,3
12:4 [i]Ro 12:4-8; Eph 4:11; Heb 2:4
12:6 [j]Eph 4:6
12:7 [k]Eph 4:12
12:8 [l]1Co 2:6 [m]2Co 8:7
12:9 [n]Mt 17:19,20; 2Co 4:13 [o]ver 28,30
12:10 [p]Gal 3:5 [q]1Jn 4:1

Lord" are missing from the earliest manuscripts. Interpreters have understood this verse in a variety of ways. Most commonly it has been understood as a reference to recognizing Christ's presence in the bread and wine, but this is almost surely an incorrect reading. "Body" appears most naturally to refer to the church (cf. 10:17)—which is also the body of the Lord (Eph 5:23,29; Col 1:18,24)—with an emphasis on "recognizing" the importance and value of every member, including the poor (vv. 20–22; 12:12–27). See *WLC* 171,174.

11:30–32 weak and sick . . . asleep. Paul's view is not without Biblical precedence. Note the connection between illness and the Passover in 2 Chronicles 30:18–20. God does not routinely bring illness and death to Christians who partake of the Lord's Supper despite participation in known, but unconfessed, sin. The problem in Corinth was much more serious and flagrant than that: Some believers were celebrating the Lord's Supper in a way that destroyed the oneness it represented, mistreating the poor in the process. As a result, God had brought judgment into the community. God's purpose in judging these believers was to prevent them from being "condemned with the world" (v. 32). **judged ourselves.** Equivalent to "examine himself" (v. 28). Such self-judgment prevents sins against the church and thus avoids God's judgment. See *WCF* 11.5; 17.3; *WLC* 171,174,175; *WSC* 97.

11:33–34 So then . . . wait for each other. Paul intended self-examination and self-judgment to rectify the specific problem mentioned in verses 21–22, indicating again that he had in view neither recognition of Christ's presence in the bread and wine nor the confession of known sin.

■ **12:1—14:40** *Spiritual Gifts.* After dealing with two problems in worship at Corinth, Paul turned to a closely related subject: the manifestations and gifts of the Spirit in the church. Paul's discussion of this topic divides into four sections: diverse gifts within the unity of the church (12:1–31), the importance of love (13:1–13), prophecy and tongues (14:1–25) and the principle of order in the church (14:26–40).

■ **12:1–31** *Unity and Diversity.* Paul began with his main concern in this section: the need for unity and mutual respect among those representing diverse manifestations of the Spirit at Corinth.

12:1 Now about spiritual gifts. This was another subject raised by the Corinthians in their letter (see "Introduction: Purpose and Distinctives").

12:2–3 when you were pagans . . . "Jesus is Lord." As an introduction to the subject of spiritual gifts in Corinth, Paul reminded his readers of the contrast between their pagan and Christian experiences. It is not clear whether anyone was actually uttering curses against Jesus—perhaps Paul was setting up a hypothetical situation, or perhaps he referred to situations in which authorities demanded that Christians deny their Lord. In any event, the focus of this verse is on the *content* of religious utterances. In view of 14:6–19, one may infer that the apostle was anticipating his argument for intelligible speech. Pagans may also have experienced powers of utterance, but the important issue was the actual words spoken. See *BC* 18.

12:4–7 See *HC* 55.

12:4 different kinds of gifts, but the same Spirit. Apparently the Corinthians exaggerated the importance of the gift of tongues, so Paul reminded them that one and the same Spirit distributes a variety of gifts to his people. The added references to "the same Lord" and "the same God" reflect the importance of the doctrine of the Trinity and support Paul's concern for unity within diversity.

12:7 for the common good. One can completely misunderstand the purpose of the Spirit's gifts (here called the "manifestation of the Spirit") if he or she uses them for selfish reasons. Because there are differing needs within the Christian community, a variety of gifts are required. See *WCF* 26.1.

12:8–10 The list of gifts in these verses was surely not intended as a complete catalog (some others are included in v. 28). This list may reflect gifts that were especially evident or necessary in Corinth (see v. 11). One need not assume that all of the gifts were manifested in every church. The list in Romans 12:6–8, for example, includes only two of the gifts mentioned here (prophesying and faith) and omits those that one tends to think of as "miraculous" (such as healing and tongues). In seeking to determine the character of some of the gifts listed in 1 Corinthians, one is hindered by the fact that nowhere does the New Testament provide anything close to a full description of any of them. For the most part, what Paul had in mind can only be determined in very general terms. For instance, one can only guess at what may have been the difference between "the message of wisdom" and "the message of knowledge." Similarly, it is unclear why Paul listed separately the gifts of "faith" (which possibly refers to the ability to perform "supernatural" feats), "healing" and "miraculous powers." The reference to "distinguishing between spirits" perhaps should be understood in light of 14:29. Still, the inability to determine the precise function of some of these gifts does not impede one from understanding the more central issue of this passage: that unity embraces the diversity of God's endowments to his church (v. 11). **prophecy.** This gift is difficult to clearly define. It might designate (1) preaching and communicating the content of Scripture, (2) inspired prophecy like that of the great prophets of the Old Testament, (3) spontaneous exhortation or (4) divulging special information about the present or future. In a broad sense, all Christians have become "prophets" who, through the Spirit, declare "the wonders of God" (Ac 2:11; cf. Ac 2:18; 1Pe 2:9), but in typical uses prophecy and teaching are distinguished (Eph 4:11). In the New Testament, prophecy is frequently exhortation (Ac 15:32) and sometimes prediction (Ac 11:27–28; 21:10–11). The New Testament also includes prophetic literature comparable to the writings of the Old Testament prophets (e.g., Rev 1:3; 22:18–19). Such authoritatively inspired prophecy was limited to the foundational period of the first-century church (Eph 2:20; Heb 1:1–3). **speaking in different kinds of tongues.** The proper description of this gift has generated much debate. According to one view, it refers to some kind of ecstatic speech that is possibly related to "the tongues . . . of angels" (13:1), but there is little evidence for this view. On the other hand, the New Testament gives

kinds of tongues,[a] [r] and to still another the interpretation of tongues.[a] 11 All these are the
work of one and the same Spirit,[s] and he gives them to each one, just as he determines.

One Body, Many Parts

12 The body is a unit, though it is made up of many parts; and though all its parts are
many, they form one body.[t] So it is with Christ.[u] 13 For we were all baptized by[b] one Spirit[v] into one body—whether Jews or Greeks, slave or free[w]—and we were all given the
one Spirit to drink.[x]
14 Now the body is not made up of one part but of many. 15 If the foot should say, "Because I am not a hand, I do not belong to the body," it would not for that reason cease
to be part of the body. 16 And if the ear should say, "Because I am not an eye, I do not belong to the body," it would not for that reason cease to be part of the body. 17 If the whole
body were an eye, where would the sense of hearing be? If the whole body were an ear,
where would the sense of smell be? 18 But in fact God has arranged[y] the parts in the body,
every one of them, just as he wanted them to be.[z] 19 If they were all one part, where would
the body be? 20 As it is, there are many parts, but one body.[a]
21 The eye cannot say to the hand, "I don't need you!" And the head cannot say to the
feet, "I don't need you!" 22 On the contrary, those parts of the body that seem to be weaker are indispensable, 23 and the parts that we think are less honorable we treat with special honor. And the parts that are unpresentable are treated with special modesty,
24 while our presentable parts need no special treatment. But God has combined the
members of the body and has given greater honor to the parts that lacked it, 25 so that
there should be no division in the body, but that its parts should have equal concern for
each other. 26 If one part suffers, every part suffers with it; if one part is honored, every
part rejoices with it.
27 Now you are the body of Christ,[b] and each one of you is a part of it.[c] 28 And in the
church[d] God has appointed first of all apostles,[e] second prophets, third teachers, then
workers of miracles, also those having gifts of healing,[f] those able to help others, those
with gifts of administration,[g] and those speaking in different kinds of tongues.[h] 29 Are all
apostles? Are all prophets? Are all teachers? Do all work miracles? 30 Do all have gifts of

12:10 [r]Mk 16:17
12:11 [s]ver 4
12:12 [t]Ro 12:5 [u]ver 27
12:13 [v]Eph 2:18 [w]Gal 3:28; Col 3:11 [x]Jn 7:37-39
12:18 [y]ver 28 [z]ver 11
12:20 [a]ver 12,14
12:27 [b]Eph 1:23; 4:12; Col 1:18,24 [c]Ro 12:5
12:28 [d]1Co 10:32 [e]Eph 4:11 [f]ver 9 [g]Ro 12:6-8 [h]ver 10

[a] *10* Or *languages;* also in verse 28 [b] *13* Or *with;* or *in*

explicit and unequivocal evidence that the Holy Spirit granted to the early Christians the ability to speak in foreign, recognizable human languages (Ac 2:4–11). The tongues spoken in the Corinthian church required spiritual gifting to interpret (14:2,5,19,23,27–28) and sounded like foreign languages, but certainty regarding their nature cannot be attained. Although objections can be raised against this view as well (see note on 14:2), it is the more likely meaning of the term "tongues."

12:11 just as he determines. The significance of this brief clause must be fully appreciated, for it helps one to see the preceding list of gifts from the right perspective. The Spirit grants individuals and churches particular gifts according to his desires, thereby sovereignly providing for the people of God. That factor may explain why no New Testament passage gives a complete catalog of gifts or a precise definition of them, since they may vary significantly according to God's plans in changing situations. A church may appropriately pray for God to grant gifts to meet perceived needs, but such prayers must be offered in submission to his sovereign will and perfect wisdom.

12:12–27 See *WCF* 25.2; *WLC* 167; *HC* 55; *HC* 32,55.

12:12 The body is a unit. Literally, "the body is one." The description of Christ's church as a body is one of the most distinctive and significant teachings of Paul (see note on 1:13). Indeed, the apostle was given a special revelation concerning this "mystery," which was hidden for many ages: God's people, both Jews and Gentiles, constitute one body by virtue of Christ's exaltation (Eph 1:22–23; 3:2–6). Both the existence and the growth of the church derive from this unity established by Christ through the Spirit (Eph 4:3–6,11–16; Col 2:19; 3:14–15).

12:13 we were all baptized by one Spirit . . . we were all given the one Spirit to drink. The emphasis on the word "all" and the allusion to the sacraments are reminders of the similar description of the Israelites in 10:1–3. One of the truths signified and sealed by water baptism is the baptism of the Spirit (i.e., the incorporation of believers into the one body of Christ). One may call it a sign of admission into God's covenant. Similarly, partaking of the Lord's Supper indicates the believer's continued communion with the body (10:17; see notes on 11:27,29). This wonderful blessing is a privilege enjoyed by all professing Christians who have been received into the church, not just by a select and superior group. Paul stressed both this universal aspect and the unity implied by it. See *WCF* 27.3; 28.1; 29.1; *WLC* 62,161,162,165,167; *WSC* 91; *BC* 34; *HC* 76.

12:14–20 Having established the oneness of Christ's church, Paul here set forth its diversity. Paul corrected the Corinthians' error by pointing out the usefulness and necessity of the various members in the human body, all of which have different functions. As he had done in verse 11, so in verse 18 the apostle supported his point by appealing to the sovereign will of God, who "has arranged the parts in the body, every one of them, just as he wanted them to be" (v. 18). Clearly, for the Corinthians to deny the validity of certain gifts was for them to reject God's care for the body of Christ. Paul stressed unity but not uniformity.

12:22–23 weaker . . . less honorable. This comparison gives one an important clue regarding the problem Paul was addressing. It is another manifestation of the problem in Corinth that occupied him throughout most of the letter: a false sense of spiritual accomplishment and well-being. This misplaced confidence bred in some of the Corinthians an attitude of superiority and disdain for those who appeared to be weaker and less honorable. In the present context, their devaluing of certain gifts (possibly in favor of the gift of tongues) was Paul's chief concern.

12:28–29 See *WCF* 23.3; *WLC* 158.

12:28 The items listed in this verse are different from those delineated in verses 8–10. This confirms that Paul was not interested in providing an exhaustive list. Here he began with "apostles" and "prophets," whom he considered the foundation (Eph 2:20), and added as a third category "teachers," so that this list is similar to that in Ephesians 4:11. The rest of the verse literally reads, ". . . then powers, then gifts of healings, helps, governings, kinds of tongues." Although the Greek words translated "helps" and "governings" do not occur elsewhere in the New Testament, Paul probably had in mind what he elsewhere called "leadership" and "showing mercy" (Ro 12:8). See *WCF* 25.3; 30.1; *WLC* 45,108; *BC* 31.

12:29–30 The rhetorical questions in these two verses bring to a climax Paul's argument that believers should not expect everyone to have the same gifts, since God apportions them as he wills (vv. 11,18).

healing? Do all speak in tongues[a]?[i] Do all interpret? 31But eagerly desire[b][j] the greater
gifts.

Love

And now I will show you the most excellent way.
13 If I speak in the tongues[c][k] of men and of angels, but have not love, I am only a
resounding gong or a clanging cymbal. 2If I have the gift of prophecy and can
fathom all mysteries[l] and all knowledge, and if I have a faith[m] that can move mountains,[n] but have not love, I am nothing. 3If I give all I possess to the poor[o] and surrender my body to the flames,[d][p] but have not love, I gain nothing.
4Love is patient,[q] love is kind. It does not envy, it does not boast, it is not proud. 5It
is not rude, it is not self-seeking,[r] it is not easily angered, it keeps no record of wrongs.
6Love does not delight in evil[s] but rejoices with the truth.[t] 7It always protects, always
trusts, always hopes, always perseveres.
8Love never fails. But where there are prophecies,[u] they will cease; where there are
tongues,[v] they will be stilled; where there is knowledge, it will pass away. 9For we know
in part[w] and we prophesy in part, 10but when perfection comes,[x] the imperfect disappears. 11When I was a child, I talked like a child, I thought like a child, I reasoned like a
child. When I became a man, I put childish ways behind me. 12Now we see but a poor
reflection as in a mirror; then we shall see face to face.[y] Now I know in part; then I shall
know fully, even as I am fully known.[z]
13And now these three remain: faith, hope and love.[a] But the greatest of these is
love.[b]

Gifts of Prophecy and Tongues

14 Follow the way of love[c] and eagerly desire[d] spiritual gifts,[e] especially the gift of
prophecy. 2For anyone who speaks in a tongue[e][f] does not speak to men but to

12:30 [i]ver 10
12:31 [j]1Co 14:1,39
13:1 [k]ver 8
13:2 [l]1Co 14:2 [m]1Co 12:9 [n]Mt 17:20; 21:21
13:3 [o]Mt 6:2 [p]Da 3:28
13:4 [q]1Th 5:14
13:5 [r]1Co 10:24
13:6 [s]2Th 2:12 [t]2Jn 4; 3Jn 3,4
13:8 [u]ver 2 [v]ver 1
13:9 [w]ver 12; 1Co 8:2
13:10 [x]Php 3:12
13:12 [y]Ge 32:30; 2Co 5:7; 1Jn 3:2 [z]1Co 8:3
13:13 [a]Gal 5:5,6 [b]1Co 16:14
14:1 [c]1Co 16:14 [d]ver 39; 1Co 12:31 [e]1Co 12:1
14:2 [f]Mk 16:17

a *30* Or *other languages* b *31* Or *But you are eagerly desiring* c *1* Or *languages* d *3* Some early manuscripts *body that I may boast* e *2* Or *another language;* also in verses 4, 13, 14, 19, 26 and 27

12:31 desire the greater gifts. The meaning of this sentence is disputed. Some believe it refers to the more important gifts in verse 28 (especially prophecy). Others argue that it introduces the discussion of love in chapter 13. Most likely, Paul was anticipating what he would say later about "gifts that build up the church" (14:12); that is, speaking in "intelligible words to instruct others" (14:19). The verb translated as an imperative ("desire") may also be construed as a simple statement of fact. That is, Paul may have contended that the Corinthians were too concerned about the better gifts and thus misunderstood their purpose. **the most excellent way.** Before explaining what he meant by the "greater gifts" (see ch. 14), Paul first pointed out the essential condition for the proper exercise of any gift: love.

■ **13:1–13** *The Supremacy of Love.* From Paul's perspective the heart of the problems involving spiritual gifts at Corinth was the failure to love. So Paul elaborated on the nature and importance of Christian love.

13:1–7 See See *WCF* 16.7; *WLC* 144; *HC* 55,112.

13:1–3 If . . . nothing. By means of hyperbole (intended exaggeration), Paul forcefully brought home the uselessness of gifts exercised without love. In effect, he said that if he could do the utterly miraculous or unthinkable, without love his actions would amount to nothing. **tongues of men.** Probably refers to the gift of speaking in foreign languages, as in Acts 2. **and of angels.** This is best understood as hyperbole (as with "fathom all mysteries" and "move mountains"). Whether the Corinthians claimed to use angelic speech is impossible to determine (see note on 12:8–10). **surrender my body to the flames.** Literally, "give over my body so that I may burn." This may be another use of hyperbole, but some important manuscripts read, "give over my body so that I may boast," which would indicate Paul's total commitment to his apostolic ministry, with a view to godly boasting on the day of Christ (Php 2:16).

13:4–7 patient . . . kind . . . hopes . . . perseveres. Paul's description does not reduce love to mere sentiments or to mere actions. Each term describes emotion as well as behavior. To conceive of Christian love as mere feeling or mere action is to contradict the apostle's definition. See *WLC* 147; *WSC* 80.

13:5 it keeps no record of wrongs. Literally, "it does not reckon evil." This probably means that those who love do not focus their attention on the wrongs that others do to them. Alternatively, it may mean that those who love do not devise evil against others. See *WLC* 145,171.

13:7 always. Literally, "all." Paul used this word four times for rhetorical effect as he brought his description of love to a climax. In the light of his hyperbolic style here (see vv. 1–3), one should not think that love requires unlimited protection, trust, hope or perseverance toward others. Each Christian responsibility, including love, must be balanced by all other Christian responsibilities (justice, mercy, truth, etc.).

13:8 Love never fails. One could view this statement as a summary of the previous verse, especially in light of the comment that love "always perseveres" (v. 7). At the same time, the statement allowed Paul to build a contrast between love, which always remains (v. 13), and the spiritual gifts, which will cease. **prophecies . . . tongues . . . knowledge.** It is likely that Paul mentioned these three items as representative of all the spiritual gifts, which have a temporary, earthly function until the end of the age. An alternate (but less likely) interpretation is that Paul had only these three in mind because they have special revelatory functions.

13:9 See *HC* 114.

13:10 perfection. The context (especially v. 12) suggests strongly that the apostle here was referring to the second coming of Christ as the final event in God's plan of redemption and revelation. In comparison with what believers will receive then, the present blessings are only partial and thus imperfect. It was therefore a sign of immaturity for the Corinthians to attach so much significance to, and take so much pride in, the temporary, incomplete gifts of the Spirit. The view that Paul may be referring to the complete revelation contained in the New Testament Scriptures—a view that makes prophecy and other revelatory gifts obsolete—has little support from the context. Still other understandings of "perfection" have been suggested, such as the maturity in love for which the Corinthians were to aim, the maturing of the early church and the death of the individual Christian.

13:12 I shall know fully, even as I am fully known. Perhaps because the Corinthians liked to boast of how much they knew (see note on 8:1), Paul concluded by stressing the partial character of our present knowledge. The shift from the active ("know") to the passive ("am . . . known") is found elsewhere in the apostle's letters and serves to emphasize believers' dependence on God's grace (8:3; Gal 4:9; cf. 1Co 14:38). Paul did not suggest here that believers' knowledge of God would one day be comprehensive, for that would be impossible. Instead, he focused on the intimacy and immediacy of God's knowing, which believers will someday share. See *WCF* 25.5; *WLC* 86,90; *WSC* 38.

■ **14:1–25** *Prophecy and Tongues.* Having set the discussion within

God. Indeed, no one understands him; he utters mysteries[g] with his spirit.[a] 3But everyone who prophesies speaks to men for their strengthening,[h] encouragement and comfort. 4He who speaks in a tongue[i] edifies himself, but he who prophesies[j] edifies the
church. 5I would like every one of you to speak in tongues,[b] but I would rather have you
prophesy.[k] He who prophesies is greater than one who speaks in tongues,[b] unless he interprets, so that the church may be edified.

6Now, brothers, if I come to you and speak in tongues, what good will I be to you, unless I bring you some revelation[l] or knowledge or prophecy or word of instruction?[m]
7Even in the case of lifeless things that make sounds, such as the flute or harp, how will
anyone know what tune is being played unless there is a distinction in the notes?
8Again, if the trumpet does not sound a clear call, who will get ready for battle?[n] 9So it
is with you. Unless you speak intelligible words with your tongue, how will anyone know
what you are saying? You will just be speaking into the air. 10Undoubtedly there are all
sorts of languages in the world, yet none of them is without meaning. 11If then I do not
grasp the meaning of what someone is saying, I am a foreigner to the speaker, and he
is a foreigner to me. 12So it is with you. Since you are eager to have spiritual gifts, try to
excel in gifts that build up the church.

13For this reason anyone who speaks in a tongue should pray that he may interpret
what he says. 14For if I pray in a tongue, my spirit prays, but my mind is unfruitful. 15So
what shall I do? I will pray with my spirit, but I will also pray with my mind; I will sing[o]
with my spirit, but I will also sing with my mind. 16If you are praising God with your spirit, how can one who finds himself among those who do not understand[c] say "Amen"[p]
to your thanksgiving,[q] since he does not know what you are saying? 17You may be giving thanks well enough, but the other man is not edified.

18I thank God that I speak in tongues more than all of you. 19But in the church I would
rather speak five intelligible words to instruct others than ten thousand words in a
tongue.

20Brothers, stop thinking like children.[r] In regard to evil be infants,[s] but in your thinking be adults. 21In the Law[t] it is written:

> "Through men of strange tongues
> and through the lips of foreigners

14:2 [g]1Co 13:2
14:3 [h]ver 4,5,12,17,26; Ro 14:19
14:4 [i]Mk 16:17 [j]1Co 13:2
14:5 [k]Nu 11:29
14:6 [l]ver 26; Eph 1:17 [m]Ro 6:17
14:8 [n]Nu 10:9; Jer 4:19
14:15 [o]Eph 5:19; Col 3:16
14:16 [p]Dt 27:15-26; 1Ch 16:36; Ne 8:6; Ps 106:48; Rev 5:14; 7:12 [q]1Co 11:24
14:20 [r]Eph 4:14; Heb 5:12,13; 1Pe 2:2 [s]Ro 16:19
14:21 [t]Jn 10:34

[a] 2 Or *by the Spirit* [b] 5 Or *other languages*; also in verses 6, 18, 22, 23 and 39 [c] 16 Or *among the inquirers*

the proper framework of love, Paul encouraged the Corinthians to recognize the value of the spiritual gifts. Because the Corinthians had exaggerated the significance of the gift of tongues, the emphasis of chapter 14 is on the intelligible gifts (v. 19)—primarily prophecy (see note on 12:8–10), but also the interpretation of tongues (vv. 27–28).

14:1 especially the gift of prophecy. Paul seems to indicate that prophecy is the greatest gift a Christian may rightly seek. By excluding the higher gift of apostleship (12:28), he strongly implied the cessation of that authoritative office after the apostles who had already been called (see theological article "The Apostles" at 2 Co 10).

14:2 tongue. See note on 12:10. Some argue that Paul was referring to something different from human language; that is, a kind of ecstatic (perhaps uncontrolled) language used for intimate prayer. However, uninterpreted foreign language would also be an address to God rather than to people, since "no one understands him." **mysteries.** Not mysterious things, but divine truths that have not yet been disclosed. **with his spirit.** As opposed to speaking with his mind (vv. 13–15). Two understandings of this expression are possible: (1) Even the speaker does not understand what he is saying, or (2) this phrase should be translated "in the Spirit," which stresses the divine inspiration involved in uttering a mystery.

14:4 edifies himself. Implies that those speaking in an uninterpreted language, in spite of their own inability to understand the message, probably receive personal encouragement and comfort from the experience.

14:6 what good will I be to you . . . ? This principle of benefiting others by edifying them becomes the key point of the passage. Paul was applying the teaching that God has granted a diversity of gifts "for the common good" (12:7). See *WCF* 1.8; *WLC* 156.

14:7–8 These verses provide illustrations of the principle mentioned in verse 6. The people for whom musical instruments are played cannot profit from the sound unless it conveys a message.

14:9–12 See *WCF* 1.8; *WLC* 156.

14:13 should pray that he may interpret what he says. Without minimizing the significance of the gift of tongues, Paul encouraged the Corinthians to use this gift in a way that made it valuable for the congregation.

14:14 my spirit prays, but my mind is unfruitful. Whatever spiritual benefit Paul might have received from the experience, his understanding was not built up. In the next verse, Paul emphasized that it was better for believers and the church (v. 12) to have both benefits (see note on v. 2). See *WCF* 21.3.

14:15–16 See *WLC* 156,185.

14:16 say "Amen" to your thanksgiving. The members of the congregation, if they are to participate in the public worship, must be able to affirm their agreement with the message of the hymns being sung and the prayers being offered. In view here is the custom of expressing that endorsement with an audible phrase such as "Amen" or "So let it be." Others cannot do so responsibly if they do not know what has been said. See *WLC* 196; *WSC* 107.

14:18–19 It may be that some of the Corinthians justified their emphasis on the gift of tongues by arguing that Paul himself exercised this gift. Without denying the fact, the apostle put the gift in proper perspective by pointing out that it is much more valuable "to instruct others." See *WLC* 159.

14:20–25 Paul had been discussing the function of the gift of tongues among believers. But what about unbelievers who hear this phenomenon? The Corinthians had shown some spiritual immaturity by failing to consider this other aspect, so Paul admonished them by saying, "Brothers, stop thinking like children" (v. 20). See *WCF* 1.8; *WLC* 155,156; *WSC* 89.

14:21 Through men of strange tongues. Paul appealed to "the Law" (i.e., the Old Testament) as evidence that God had always planned to use the diverse languages of humanity for his purposes. Isaiah 28:11 foretold the exile of Israel through the Assyrians, who spoke a foreign tongue, and this was fulfilled with the fall of Samaria in 722 B.C. Paul applied this to the circumstance of tongues in Corinth, because the situation in Corinth paralleled that of Assyrian judgment on Israel. Through unknown tongues God once again used Gentiles speaking a variety of languages as a mark of

I will speak to this people,
but even then they will not listen to me,"[a][u]
says the Lord.
22 Tongues, then, are a sign, not for believers but for unbelievers; prophecy,[v] however, is for believers, not for unbelievers. 23 So if the whole church comes together and everyone speaks in tongues, and some who do not understand[b] or some unbelievers come
in, will they not say that you are out of your mind?[w] 24 But if an unbeliever or someone
who does not understand[c] comes in while everybody is prophesying, he will be convinced by all that he is a sinner and will be judged by all, 25 and the secrets of his heart
will be laid bare. So he will fall down and worship God, exclaiming, "God is really
among you!"[x]

Orderly Worship

26 What then shall we say, brothers? When you come together, everyone[y] has a
hymn,[z] or a word of instruction,[a] a revelation, a tongue or an interpretation. All of these
must be done for the strengthening[b] of the church. 27 If anyone speaks in a tongue, two—
or at the most three—should speak, one at a time, and someone must interpret. 28 If there
is no interpreter, the speaker should keep quiet in the church and speak to himself and
God.
29 Two or three prophets should speak, and the others should weigh carefully what is
said.[c] 30 And if a revelation comes to someone who is sitting down, the first speaker
should stop. 31 For you can all prophesy in turn so that everyone may be instructed and
encouraged. 32 The spirits of prophets are subject to the control of prophets.[d] 33 For God
is not a God of disorder[e] but of peace.
As in all the congregations of the saints,[f] 34 women should remain silent in the
churches. They are not allowed to speak, but must be in submission,[g] as the Law[h] says.
35 If they want to inquire about something, they should ask their own husbands at home;
for it is disgraceful for a woman to speak in the church.
36 Did the word of God originate with you? Or are you the only people it has reached?
37 If anybody thinks he is a prophet[i] or spiritually gifted, let him acknowledge that what
I am writing to you is the Lord's command.[j] 38 If he ignores this, he himself will be ignored.[d]
39 Therefore, my brothers, be eager[k] to prophesy, and do not forbid speaking in
tongues. 40 But everything should be done in a fitting and orderly[l] way.

14:21 [u]Isa 28:11,12
14:22 [v]ver 1
14:23 [w]Ac 2:13
14:25 [x]Isa 45:14; Zec 8:23
14:26 [y]1Co 12:7-10 [z]Eph 5:19 [a]ver 6 [b]Ro 14:19
14:29 [c]1Co 12:10
14:32 [d]1Jn 4:1
14:33 [e]ver 40 [f]Ac 9:13
14:34 [g]1Ti 2:11,12 [h]Ge 3:16
14:37 [i]2Co 10:7 [j]1Jn 4:6
14:39 [k]1Co 12:31
14:40 [l]ver 33

[a] *21* Isaiah 28:11,12 [b] *23* Or *some inquirers* [c] *24* Or *or some inquirer* [d] *38* Some manuscripts *If he is ignorant of this, let him be ignorant*

displeasure toward those who did not believe. In this sense then, uninterpreted tongues "are a sign" of judgment "for unbelievers" (v. 22). But the Corinthians' goal should have been to bring unbelievers to repentance and to the recognition that God is present in his church (v. 25). Because God uses the intelligible words of prophecy to accomplish this purpose, prophecy can be viewed as a sign "for believers" (i.e., as evidence of God's goodness to them; v. 22).

■ **14:26–40** *Principle of Order.* Paul closed his discussion of spiritual gifts by touching on a number of specific ways in which the church at Corinth needed to become more orderly.

14:26 come together, everyone has. Paul had in mind the corporate worship of the church at Corinth. When the church gathered, everyone (man and woman alike) was to be prepared for some kind of participation according to the gifts of the Holy Spirit. **for the strengthening of the church.** See note on verse 6. See also *WCF* 1.6.

14:27–28 See *WCF* 1.8; *WLC* 156.

14:27 and someone must interpret. This concern for intelligibility has informed the whole discussion (see note on v. 1).

14:29–33 Having given instructions for the proper exercise of the gift of tongues, Paul moved on to other directives that also affected the order of public worship. Since he himself had emphasized the importance of prophecy, he pointed out that even this gift should be exercised in an orderly fashion: Only "two or three prophets should speak" (during the course of, or perhaps at various points in, the service), while "the others" (perhaps referring to others with the gift of prophecy) should evaluate the message to ascertain its truth. Apparently the Corinthians were speaking in tongues and prophesying without regard either for each other or for the content of the message (see note on 12:2–3). Their disorder, another threat to the unity of the body, was incompatible with the God "of peace." See *HC* 103.

14:34—35 These verses have created heated debate among Christians, at least in part because the exact nature of the problem Paul was seeking to correct is unknown. It has even been suggested (on the basis of doubtful textual evidence) that these verses were not part of Paul's original letter. In view of 11:5 and other New Testament data (e.g., v. 26), one may be certain that Paul was not issuing an absolute prohibition (against women speaking in any church situation). Was Paul addressing a peculiar problem in Corinth, such as women creating disorder during the worship service? In view of the context (vv. 29,32), did Paul have in mind a specific function, such as the evaluation of prophecy, in which women should not participate (or more narrowly, a wife's evaluation of her own husband's prophecy)?

14:36 Did the word of God originate with you? This strongly sarcastic remark and the one that follows it clearly show that Paul was not merely giving general instructions for worship. Rather, he was addressing concrete and serious problems arising out of the Corinthians' boastful arrogance.

14:37 what I am writing to you is the Lord's command. This text identifies the written word of Paul's letter with the word of God, implying (1) the divine authority of written revelation, (2) the proper inclusion of Paul's letters within the canon of Scripture and (3) the role of these letters as a test of the validity of other forms of revelation.

14:38 ignores . . . will be ignored. See note on 13:12 for the contrast between knowing and being known. The present verse may be a warning that those who were recalcitrant would be disciplined by Paul himself or by the church (2Th 3:14), but the language suggests that they would come under direct divine judgment.

14:40 See *WCF* 1.6.

The Resurrection of Christ

15 Now, brothers, I want to remind you of the gospel[m] I preached to you, which
you received and on which you have taken your stand. 2By this gospel you are
saved,[n] if you hold firmly[o] to the word I preached to you. Otherwise, you have believed
in vain.
3For what I received[p] I passed on to you[q] as of first importance[a]: that Christ died for
our sins[r] according to the Scriptures,[s] 4that he was buried, that he was raised[t] on the
third day[u] according to the Scriptures,[v] 5and that he appeared to Peter,[b][w] and then to
the Twelve.[x] 6After that, he appeared to more than five hundred of the brothers at the
same time, most of whom are still living, though some have fallen asleep. 7Then he appeared to James, then to all the apostles,[y] 8and last of all he appeared to me also,[z] as to
one abnormally born.
9For I am the least of the apostles[a] and do not even deserve to be called an apostle,
because I persecuted[b] the church of God. 10But by the grace of God I am what I am, and
his grace to me[c] was not without effect. No, I worked harder than all of them[d]—yet not
I, but the grace of God that was with me.[e] 11Whether, then, it was I or they, this is what
we preach, and this is what you believed.

The Resurrection of the Dead

12But if it is preached that Christ has been raised from the dead, how can some of you
say that there is no resurrection of the dead?[f] 13If there is no resurrection of the dead,
then not even Christ has been raised. 14And if Christ has not been raised,[g] our preaching is useless and so is your faith. 15More than that, we are then found to be false witnesses about God, for we have testified about God that he raised Christ from the dead.[h]
But he did not raise him if in fact the dead are not raised. 16For if the dead are not raised,
then Christ has not been raised either. 17And if Christ has not been raised, your faith is
futile; you are still in your sins.[i] 18Then those also who have fallen asleep in Christ are
lost. 19If only for this life we have hope in Christ, we are to be pitied more than all men.[j]

15:1 [m]Ro 2:16
15:2 [n]Ro 1:16 [o]Ro 11:22
15:3 [p]Gal 1:12 [q]1Co 11:23 [r]Isa 53:5; 1Pe 2:24 [s]Lk 24:27; Ac 26:22,23
15:4 [t]Ac 2:24 [u]Mt 16:21 [v]Ac 2:25,30,31
15:5 [w]Lk 24:34 [x]Mk 16:14
15:7 [y]Lk 24:33,36,37; Ac 1:3,4
15:8 [z]Ac 9:3-6,17; 1Co 9:1
15:9 [a]Eph 3:8; 1Ti 1:15 [b]Ac 8:3
15:10 [c]Ro 12:3 [d]2Co 11:23 [e]Php 2:13
15:12 [f]Ac 17:32; 23:8; 2Ti 2:18
15:14 [g]1Th 4:14
15:15 [h]Ac 2:24
15:17 [i]Ro 4:25
15:19 [j]1Co 4:9

[a] 3 Or *you at the first* [b] 5 Greek *Cephas*

■ **15:1–58** *Resurrection.* At this point, Paul shifted to a new topic of great concern to him: the integrity of the gospel message with regard to the doctrine of the resurrection. Paul responded to some members of the Corinthian church who denied "the resurrection of the dead" (v. 12). This material divides into four main sections: a discussion of Christ's own resurrection (vv. 1–11), believers' resurrection on the last day (vv. 12–34), the nature of resurrection bodies (vv. 35–49) and a conclusion (vv. 50–58).

■ **15:1–11** *Christ's Resurrection.* Paul reminded the Corinthians that they already accepted the concept of physical resurrection because they affirmed Christ's resurrection. Thus, they had no basis for denying the resurrection of believers.

15:1 gospel I preached. Paul was not informing the Corinthians of a new teaching but reviewing a central element of the basic gospel message that he had already delivered and that they had already believed.

15:2 if you hold firmly. See note on 9:27. **believed in vain.** Because denying the resurrection of Christ renders one's faith useless (v. 14), Paul here alerted the Corinthians to the significance of what he was about to discuss. See *BC* 7.

15:3–5 These verses not only summarize Paul's preaching but present the early church's united confession ("what I received"): Christ's vicarious death and his resurrection were proven true by valid testimony ("Peter . . . the Twelve") and fulfilled the Old Testament message ("according to the Scriptures"). See *WCF* 8.4; *WLC* 50,51; *WSC* 27,28; *BC* 22; *HC* 41.

15:6–8 The threefold repetition of "he appeared" is an indication of Paul's burden in this passage to convey the certainty that Christ had been raised from the dead, a fact to which numerous witnesses could attest. Most of those who had witnessed the resurrection appearances were "still living" at the time Paul wrote this letter, so it was possible for anyone to check the facts. Particularly significant is the reference to "five hundred of the brothers at the same time," for it shows that the appearances cannot be explained away as hallucinations or fabrications.

15:7 James. Not the brother of John (and one of the Twelve), who was executed by Herod Agrippa (Ac 12:2), but the brother of Jesus who believed in him only after the resurrection (Jn 7:5; Ac 12:17; 15:13; Gal 1:19).

15:8 as to one abnormally born. This self-deprecating remark may reflect the sentiment of some of the Corinthians who held Paul in low esteem (see note on 2:1). What the apostle himself meant is suggested by the temporal phrase "last of all." Verse 9 also adds that Paul had previously persecuted the church. No one could have anticipated Paul's calling. The appearances of the risen Lord had ceased, while Paul was busy trying to destroy the church (Gal 1:13,23; Php 3:6; 1Ti 1:13–16). Paul was the only authoritative apostle who had not been with Jesus during his earthly ministry. Paul's language here strongly suggests that the office of apostle was a unique, foundational gift to the church (Eph 2:20) and that no more apostles would come after him.

15:10 the grace of God . . . his grace to me . . . the grace of God that was with me. Having freely admitted the irregular and undeserving character of his experience, Paul moved on to stress that this was no reason for the Corinthians to reject his message. Where sin abounds, God's grace abounds all the more (Ro 5:20); where believers are weak, God's grace becomes a showcase for his strength (2Co 12:9–10). Note, however, that divine grace is not an excuse for lethargy. On the contrary, it is the power and motivation for good works (Eph 2:8–10), and so Paul asserted that he "worked harder" than anyone else. See *BC* 30.

■ **15:12–34** *Believers' Resurrection.* Paul directly refuted the false teaching that prompted this section: the denial of the general resurrection of the dead.

15:12–23 See *WLC* 87; *HC* 15,16,45.

15:12 there is no resurrection of the dead? Some of the Corinthians, perhaps without denying specifically that Jesus had been raised, were questioning the doctrine of the general resurrection because of their unbiblical understanding of the human body (see note on v. 35). Paul needed to show them that the resurrection of Jesus is of a piece with the resurrection of those who are his (vv. 20–23). If the latter assertion is invalid, so is the former. But the consequences of denying, even by implication, that Jesus' body was raised from the tomb are catastrophic for the message of the gospel.

15:14 our preaching is useless and so is your faith. Compare verse 17. The truth of the Christian message is inextricably tied to the historical reality of Christ's death and resurrection. The apostle could not conceive of such a message having any spiritual value if it had no historical foundation.

15:19 we are to be pitied. Paul would not deny that in one sense Christians enjoy a better life than non-Christians, but this verse can only be understood when one remembers that Paul and most first-century believers paid a dear price for their faith in Christ (Php

15:20 [k]1Pe 1:3 [l]ver 23; Ac 26:23; Rev 1:5 [m]ver 6,18
15:21 [n]Ro 5:12
15:22 [o]Ro 5:14-18
15:23 [p]ver 20 [q]ver 52
15:24 [r]Da 7:14,27 [s]Ro 8:38
15:25 [t]Ps 110:1; Mt 22:44
15:26 [u]2Ti 1:10; Rev 20:14; 21:4
15:27 [v]Ps 8:6 [w]Mt 28:18
15:28 [x]Php 3:21 [y]1Co 3:23
15:30 [z]2Co 11:26
15:31 [a]Ro 8:36
15:32 [b]2Co 1:8 [c]Ac 18:19 [d]Isa 22:13; Lk 12:19
15:35 [e]Ro 9:19 [f]Eze 37:3
15:36 [g]Lk 11:40 [h]Jn 12:24

20 But Christ has indeed been raised from the dead,[k] the firstfruits[l] of those who have
fallen asleep.[m] 21 For since death came through a man,[n] the resurrection of the dead
comes also through a man. 22 For as in Adam all die, so in Christ all will be made alive.[o]
23 But each in his own turn: Christ, the firstfruits;[p] then, when he comes,[q] those who belong to him. 24 Then the end will come, when he hands over the kingdom[r] to God the Father after he has destroyed all dominion, authority and power.[s] 25 For he must reign until he has put all his enemies under his feet.[t] 26 The last enemy to be destroyed is death.[u]
27 For he "has put everything under his feet."[a][v] Now when it says that "everything" has
been put under him, it is clear that this does not include God himself, who put everything
under Christ.[w] 28 When he has done this, then the Son himself will be made subject to
him who put everything under him,[x] so that God may be all in all.[y]
29 Now if there is no resurrection, what will those do who are baptized for the dead?
If the dead are not raised at all, why are people baptized for them? 30 And as for us, why
do we endanger ourselves every hour?[z] 31 I die every day[a]—I mean that, brothers—just
as surely as I glory over you in Christ Jesus our Lord. 32 If I fought wild beasts[b] in Ephesus[c] for merely human reasons, what have I gained? If the dead are not raised,

"Let us eat and drink,
for tomorrow we die."[b][d]

33 Do not be misled: "Bad company corrupts good character." 34 Come back to your senses as you ought, and stop sinning; for there are some who are ignorant of God—I say this
to your shame.

The Resurrection Body

35 But someone may ask,[e] "How are the dead raised? With what kind of body will they
come?"[f] 36 How foolish![g] What you sow does not come to life unless it dies.[h] 37 When you

[a] *27* Psalm 8:6 [b] *32* Isaiah 22:13

1:29–30; 2Ti 3:10–12; 1Pe 4:12–19). If believers were to suffer for Christ only to discover that he had not in fact been resurrected from the dead, they were indeed to be pitied.

15:20 the firstfruits. This metaphor is based on the Old Testament requirement that the Israelites were to "bring to the priest a sheaf of the first grain" (Lev 23:10) of their harvest. Such an offering indicated the worshiper's recognition that the whole harvest was God's, and so Paul used this expression to stress, for example, that believers, in receiving the Spirit, have a guarantee of their future redemption (Ro 8:23; cf. "deposit" in 2Co 1:22; 5:5; Eph 1:13–14). The point here is that the resurrection of Jesus and the resurrection of believers are not two separate, unrelated events. Rather, Jesus was "the first to rise from the dead" (Ac 26:23), and that event makes possible the resurrection of believers. Because Christ, as the believer's representative, was raised, so also the believer has been raised spiritually (Ro 6:4–5; Eph 2:6) and will surely also be raised bodily. See *WLC* 52; *HC* 57.

15:21–22 These verses state succinctly one of Paul's most profound teachings: the twofold solidarity of believers with the first man (Adam) and the last man (Christ). By virtue of their humanity, believers are united with Adam in their present natural existence, in sin and in death; by virtue of their faith, they are united with Christ in their spiritual existence, in righteousness and in life (vv. 45–49; Ro 5:17–19). See *WCF* 6.3; *WLC* 22,52; *WSC* 16.

15:24–28 Although Paul's argument in this section includes some difficult details, the main ideas are clear and powerful. The Corinthians needed to understand that the resurrection was not some isolated, dispensable event. Rather, it was an integral and culminating stage in God's sovereign rule over history. Redemption will not be complete "until he has put all his enemies under his feet" (v. 25)—a clear allusion to an important Messianic prophecy in Psalm 110:1. Since death is "the last enemy" (v. 26), Christ's work will not be finished until death is utterly destroyed. In verses 27–28, the quotation from Psalm 8:6 led Paul to say that in the end "the Son himself will be made subject to . . . God," clearly another way of expressing the idea of verse 24 ("when he hands over the kingdom to God the Father"). Paul was not suggesting that the Son is inferior to the Father in dignity and being, but rather that, in his Messianic work, the Son subjects himself to the will of the Father. The climax of Christ's Messianic office is his total conquest over his enemies, "so that God may be all in all" (v. 28); that is, so that God's absolute supremacy may be universally acknowledged. See *WCF* 8.8; *WLC* 45,52,85; *WSC* 26; *HC* 123.

15:29 baptized for the dead? The apparent meaning of this statement is that some in Corinth were being baptized on behalf of others who had already died. If indeed there was such a widespread practice, nothing else is known about it, as neither the Bible nor any other ancient writing attests elsewhere to the practice. Because of the questions raised by this comment, numerous views have been proposed, all of them speculative and none persuasive. One should note that this verse is but the first in a series of rhetorical questions that continue for several verses. It is certainly not a theological argument as such, but rather an attempt to reflect the absurdity of the Corinthians' behavior, whatever their practice may have been. It is possibly an *ad hominem* argument by which Paul showed the logical inconsistency of his opponents' position. See *WLC* 165.

15:32 wild beasts. Probably a reference to Paul's enemies in Ephesus (from which this letter was written), who wanted to condemn him (cf. the comment about "the lion's mouth" in 2Ti 4:17). It was only because of Paul's hope of resurrection that he endured severe trials and persecutions (see note on v. 19).

15:33 Bad company corrupts good character. Derived from a comedy written by the popular Greek author Menander (342–292 B.C.), this proverb was common in the ancient world (note the comparable Jewish saying in 5:6). Those Christians in Corinth with a defective view of the resurrection not only had been influenced by the bad company they kept but were also corrupting the rest of the congregation. See *HC* 109.

15:34 some who are ignorant of God. Probably a reference to members of the church who boasted of their knowledge (see note on 8:1) but whose denial of the resurrection revealed profound ignorance regarding the things of God.

■ **15:35–49** *Resurrection Body.* At this point the apostle spoke directly of the underlying objection some in Corinth had against the resurrection of the dead (v. 12). They misunderstood the importance of the physical body.

15:35 With what kind of body will they come? It would appear that the Corinthians were influenced by a pagan dualism that contrasted the immaterial with the physical and argued that the former was good but the latter insignificant, if not evil. As a result, these Christians had developed indifference and even disdain for the human body (see note on 6:14), believing that the body was intrinsically corrupt and therefore that the doctrine of the general resurrection implied the raising of dishonorable bodies. The importance of this issue for Paul is clear from the discussion that follows. He regarded this position as foolish (v. 36) and discussed the matter extensively (vv. 36–49).

15:36 unless it dies. Because God is the Creator of the world, the processes of nature reflect, in diverse fashion, the way he works. In

sow, you do not plant the body that will be, but just a seed, perhaps of wheat or of something else. 38 But God gives it a body as he has determined, and to each kind of seed he
gives its own body.[i] 39 All flesh is not the same: Men have one kind of flesh, animals have
another, birds another and fish another. 40 There are also heavenly bodies and there are
earthly bodies; but the splendor of the heavenly bodies is one kind, and the splendor of
the earthly bodies is another. 41 The sun has one kind of splendor, the moon another and
the stars another; and star differs from star in splendor.

42 So will it be[j] with the resurrection of the dead. The body that is sown is perishable, it is raised imperishable; 43 it is sown in dishonor, it is raised in glory;[k] it is sown
in weakness, it is raised in power; 44 it is sown a natural body, it is raised a spiritual
body.[l]

If there is a natural body, there is also a spiritual body. 45 So it is written: "The first man
Adam became a living being"[a];[m] the last Adam,[n] a life-giving spirit.[o] 46 The spiritual did
not come first, but the natural, and after that the spiritual. 47 The first man was of the dust
of the earth,[p] the second man from heaven.[q] 48 As was the earthly man, so are those who
are of the earth; and as is the man from heaven, so also are those who are of heaven.[r]
49 And just as we have borne the likeness of the earthly man,[s] so shall we[b] bear the likeness of the man from heaven.[t]

50 I declare to you, brothers, that flesh and blood[u] cannot inherit the kingdom of God,
nor does the perishable inherit the imperishable. 51 Listen, I tell you a mystery:[v] We will
not all sleep, but we will all be changed[w]— 52 in a flash, in the twinkling of an eye, at the
last trumpet. For the trumpet will sound,[x] the dead[y] will be raised imperishable, and we
will be changed. 53 For the perishable must clothe itself with the imperishable,[z] and the
mortal with immortality. 54 When the perishable has been clothed with the imperishable,
and the mortal with immortality, then the saying that is written will come true: "Death
has been swallowed up in victory."[c][a]

15:38 [i]Ge 1:11
15:42 [j]Da 12:3; Mt 13:43
15:43 [k]Php 3:21; Col 3:4
15:44 [l]ver 50
15:45 [m]Ge 2:7 [n]Ro 5:14 [o]Jn 5:21; Ro 8:2
15:47 [p]Ge 2:7; 3:19 [q]Jn 3:13,31
15:48 [r]Php 3:20,21
15:49 [s]Ge 5:3 [t]Ro 8:29
15:50 [u]Jn 3:3,5
15:51 [v]1Co 13:2 [w]Php 3:21
15:52 [x]Mt 24:31 [y]Jn 5:25
15:53 [z]2Co 5:2,4
15:54 [a]Isa 25:8; Rev 20:11

[a] *45* Gen. 2:7 [b] *49* Some early manuscripts *so let us* [c] *54* Isaiah 25:8

some respects, therefore, nature is a mirror of the divine accomplishment of salvation (Isa 55:10–11). In particular, Jesus had used the picture of the seed as a pointer to spiritual truth ("if it dies, it produces many seeds"; Jn 12:24). Here Paul used the same picture to illustrate the striking difference between what is planted and what eventually grows from the seed (v. 37). The same sort of analogy can be found in Plato's *Symposium* dialogue.

15:38 to each kind of seed he gives its own body. At this point the apostle shifted the illustration to emphasize the variations among different plants. In the following verses he developed this idea by applying it to living creatures (v. 39) and heavenly bodies (vv. 40–41).

15:42–46 See *WCF* 32.2; 32.3; *WLC* 87; *WSC* 38; *HC* 57.

15:42–43 perishable . . . imperishable . . . dishonor . . . glory . . . weakness . . . power. Just as a plant arises directly from a seed, so the resurrected body is in essence the same as the body that "is sown." But Paul's emphasis is on the astounding transformation that will take place: from corruption, "dishonor" and "weakness" to incorruption, "glory" and "power."

15:44 natural body . . . spiritual body. This last contrast is somewhat difficult to understand, but it is also of great importance. Accordingly, Paul devoted several verses (vv. 45–49) to explaining what he meant. He certainly did not have in mind a contrast between physical (material) and nonphysical (immaterial). The resurrected body is definitely a physical body, not a ghostly appearance. Paul had previously used the words "natural" and "spiritual" to distinguish the individual who does not have the Holy Spirit from the one who does (see notes on 2:6,14). The former belongs to the present age (1:20), while the latter is a citizen of heaven (Php 3:20; see note on 1Co 15:20). Christians have already received the Holy Spirit and therefore may be described as "spiritual," but they have not yet received their "spiritual body" (i.e., the body that is fully compatible with existence in the age to come, the age of the Holy Spirit; see Ro 8:22–25 and its note). For this reason, it is accurate to say that Paul contrasted the natural, physical body received at birth with the spiritual (renewed by the Holy Spirit), physical body.

15:45 living being . . . life-giving spirit. Paul used a quotation from Genesis 2:7 to clarify his meaning by developing the contrast between the first man and the last man (see note on vv. 21–22). As part of his human, Messianic work, Jesus became a "life-giving Spirit" at the time of his resurrection. That is, he received his spiritual, or glorified, body and became inseparable from the Holy Spirit in his work and existence (without losing his personal identity as the Son). Note the strong connection between Christ, the Spirit and life in Romans 8:9–11 and 2 Corinthians 3:6,17–18.

15:48 earthly . . . from heaven. Here is the final and clearest contrast. It suggests that verses 42–44 refer to the distinction between earthly and heavenly human bodies. The distinction, however, is not primarily one of place, but of time (i.e., the present evil age contrasted with the coming perfect age). Believers already enjoy some of the blessings of the coming age (see note on 10:11) but still await its consummation. The crucial significance of Paul's concern has now become obvious: Until the bodily resurrection, God's work of redemption is incomplete. Just as believers bear the likeness of the first Adam, so also they will bear the likeness of the last Adam (i.e., Christ; v. 49).

15:49 See *WCF* 6.3.

■ **15:50–58** *Conclusion.* On the basis of what he had just said, Paul drew a number of conclusions regarding the resurrection of the dead.

15:50 flesh and blood. This phrase is not equivalent to "physical" (as in Mt 16:17 and Gal 1:16, where the same Greek terms are translated jointly as "man"). Rather, it brings out the weakness of mere earthly, human existence and is thus equivalent to "perishable." In this verse, Paul warned the Corinthians that without new and "imperishable" bodies they would not "inherit the kingdom of God." How then could some deny the doctrine of the resurrection?

15:51–53 See *WCF* 32.2; *WLC* 87; *BC* 37.

15:51 mystery. See note on 2:7. **We will not all sleep.** Paul recognized that one particular generation of Christians will not die but will be alive at the time of Christ's return. Even though these Christians will not be raised from the dead, they too will be transformed and receive imperishable and immortal bodies (see 1Th 4:13–18 and their notes).

15:54–57 These verses constitute one of the most eloquent and powerful passages in Scripture. With paraphrases of Isaiah and Hosea (based on the Septuagint, the Greek translation of the OT), Paul alluded to his earlier argument in verses 24–28 and vigorously insisted on the finality of death's destruction at the time of the resurrection. Somewhat unexpectedly, he further pointed out that this event will also mark the destruction of "sin" and "the law." Elsewhere Paul explained in detail how sin is the venom through which death passes to all (Ro 5:12). Paul said that the law, which itself is holy, became the instrument through which sin accomplishes deception (Ro 7:7–11). See *WCF* 20.1; *WLC* 85; *HC* 57.

55"Where, O death, is your victory?
Where, O death, is your sting?"[a][b]

56The sting of death is sin,[c] and the power of sin is the law.[d] 57But thanks be to God![e] He
gives us the victory through our Lord Jesus Christ.[f]
58Therefore, my dear brothers, stand firm. Let nothing move you. Always give yourselves fully to the work of the Lord,[g] because you know that your labor in the Lord is not
in vain.

The Collection for God's People

16 Now about the collection[h] for God's people:[i] Do what I told the Galatian[j]
churches to do. 2On the first day of every week,[k] each one of you should set
aside a sum of money in keeping with his income, saving it up, so that when I come no
collections will have to be made.[l] 3Then, when I arrive, I will give letters of introduction
to the men you approve[m] and send them with your gift to Jerusalem. 4If it seems advis-
able for me to go also, they will accompany me.

Personal Requests

5After I go through Macedonia, I will come to you[n]—for I will be going through Macedonia.[o] 6Perhaps I will stay with you awhile, or even spend the winter, so that you can
help me on my journey,[p] wherever I go. 7I do not want to see you now and make only a
passing visit; I hope to spend some time with you, if the Lord permits.[q] 8But I will stay
on at Ephesus[r] until Pentecost,[s] 9because a great door for effective work has opened to
me,[t] and there are many who oppose me.
10If Timothy[u] comes, see to it that he has nothing to fear while he is with you, for he
is carrying on the work of the Lord,[v] just as I am. 11No one, then, should refuse to accept
him.[w] Send him on his way in peace[x] so that he may return to me. I am expecting him
along with the brothers.
12Now about our brother Apollos:[y] I strongly urged him to go to you with the brothers. He was quite unwilling to go now, but he will go when he has the opportunity.
13Be on your guard; stand firm[z] in the faith; be men of courage; be strong.[a] 14Do everything in love.[b]
15You know that the household of Stephanas[c] were the first converts[d] in Achaia,[e] and
they have devoted themselves to the service of the saints. I urge you, brothers, 16to submit[f] to such as these and to everyone who joins in the work, and labors at it. 17I was glad
when Stephanas, Fortunatus and Achaicus arrived, because they have supplied what

[a] 55 Hosea 13:14

15:55 [b]Hos 13:14
15:56 [c]Ro 5:12 [d]Ro 4:15
15:57 [e]2Co 2:14 [f]Ro 8:37
15:58 [g]1Co 16:10
16:1 [h]Ac 24:17 [i]Ac 9:13 [j]Ac 16:6
16:2 [k]Ac 20:7 [l]2Co 9:4,5
16:3 [m]2Co 8:18,19
16:5 [n]1Co 4:19 [o]Ac 19:21
16:6 [p]Ro 15:24
16:7 [q]Ac 18:21
16:8 [r]Ac 18:19 [s]Ac 2:1
16:9 [t]Ac 14:27
16:10 [u]Ac 16:1 [v]1Co 15:58
16:11 [w]1Ti 4:12 [x]Ac 15:33
16:12 [y]Ac 18:24; 1Co 1:12
16:13 [z]Gal 5:1; Php 1:27; 1Th 3:8; 2Th 2:15 [a]Eph 6:10
16:14 [b]1Co 14:1
16:15 [c]1Co 1:16 [d]Ro 16:5 [e]Ac 18:12
16:16 [f]Heb 13:17

15:58 stand firm. In the face of false teaching and diverse temptations, the certain hope of the resurrection was an encouragement to the Corinthians to persevere in their faith. The exhortation to "stand," however, did not imply passivity. On the contrary, the Corinthians were to be fully active in "the work of the Lord." Although believers can become easily discouraged by thinking that their labor may come to nothing (Gal 2:2; Php 2:16; 1Th 3:5), they need only to remember the promise that when God creates the new heavens and the new earth, his people will rejoice and will long enjoy the works of their toil, for their efforts are "not in vain" (see Isa 65:17–25). See *HC* 125.

■ **16:1–12** *Collection and Other Matters.* As he neared the end of his epistle, Paul mentioned the collection of funds for Jerusalem and a number of other items.

16:1–3 See *WCF* 21.7; *WLC* 116,117; *WSC* 59; *BC* 30.

16:1 Now about the collection. On the basis of Romans 15:25–27 and 2 Corinthians 8:1–4, one may infer that one of the primary purposes of Paul's third missionary journey was the raising of an offering from among the Gentiles for Jewish Christians in Judea, who probably were experiencing poverty as a result of persecution. Apparently, Paul had already informed the Corinthians about this project in his "previous letter" (see 5:9). They, in turn, had asked for more specific information and perhaps expressed reservations (see "Introduction: Purpose and Distinctives"). **for God's people.** Literally, "for the saints" (see note on 1:2).

16:2 On the first day of every week. The reference is to Sunday, the day on which the resurrected Lord met with his disciples (Jn 20:19, 26; cf. also "the Lord's Day" in Rev 1:10). Acts 20:7 indicates that the early Christians met on Sundays "to break bread" (i.e., for worship), so it would have been appropriate to designate that day for the regular collection of the offering. See *HC* 103.

16:3 men you approve. Possibly reflects doubts among some of the Corinthians as to whether Paul should be given sole responsibility for the money (see note on 2:1).

16:5–9 These verses make clear that Paul wrote this letter from Ephesus and that he intended to visit Corinth by way of the northern land route (i.e., through the cities of Troas in Asia Minor, Philippi in Macedonia, etc.). Both Acts 20:1–2 and 2 Corinthians 2:12–13 indicate that Paul did carry out this plan. What Paul did not foresee at this time was the prior need to make a short and "painful" visit to Corinth shortly after writing this letter (2Co 1:23; 13:2; see "Introduction to 2 Corinthians: Time and Place of Writing").

16:10 If Timothy comes. Paul had mentioned earlier (4:17) that he had sent or would send Timothy to them as his delegate (Ac 19:22). Paul was concerned that his young coworker be treated with respect.

16:12 Now about our brother Apollos. Apparently the Corinthians in their letter had asked that Apollos return to them (see Ac 18:27—19:1; see also "Introduction: Purpose and Distinctives"). In spite of the dangerous attitude of the Corinthians (4:6; see note on 4:15), Paul honored their request, but Apollos was unable to go at that time.

■ **16:13–24** *Conclusion.* Paul closed this letter with some final exhortations, commendations and greetings.

16:15–18 This passage serves as a commendation of "Stephanas, Fortunatus and Achaicus," who probably were the bearers of the letter from the church in Corinth. Paul's emphasis (especially in the words "I urge you, brothers, to submit") suggests that these men, and Stephanas in particular, were the appointed leaders of the Corinthian church but that they were not receiving appropriate respect from the congregation. The phrase "what was lacking from you" does not necessarily imply a criticism (the Greek at the end of Php 2:30 is almost identical), but in this context it may suggest that the church as a whole had failed to refresh his spirit.

was lacking from you.[g] 18For they refreshed[h] my spirit and yours also. Such men deserve
recognition.[i]

Final Greetings

19The churches in the province of Asia send you greetings. Aquila and Priscilla[a][j] greet
you warmly in the Lord, and so does the church that meets at their house.[k] 20All the
brothers here send you greetings. Greet one another with a holy kiss.[l]
21I, Paul, write this greeting in my own hand.[m]
22If anyone does not love the Lord[n]—a curse[o] be on him. Come, O Lord[b]![p]
23The grace of the Lord Jesus be with you.[q]
24My love to all of you in Christ Jesus. Amen.[c]

16:17 [g]2Co 11:9; Php 2:30
16:18 [h]Phm 7 [i]Php 2:29
16:19 [j]Ac 18:2 [k]Ro 16:5
16:20 [l]Ro 16:16
16:21 [m]Gal 6:11; Col 4:18
16:22 [n]Eph 6:24 [o]Ro 9:3 [p]Rev 22:20
16:23 [q]Ro 16:20

[a] *19* Greek *Prisca,* a variant of *Priscilla* [b] *22* In Aramaic the expression *Come, O Lord* is *Marana tha.*
[c] *24* Some manuscripts do not have *Amen.*

16:19 the province of Asia. Ephesus, from which 1 Corinthians was written, was the most important city in this Roman province, which covered the southwestern section of modern Turkey. **Aquila and Priscilla.** This couple played an important role during Paul's initial visit to Corinth (Ac 18:1–3), so they were well known by the congregation.

16:20 holy kiss. Apparently a standard greeting in the early church. Although this practice was not uncommon in Judaism and Roman culture, the word "holy" indicates the significance such a greeting would have had among "the saints," since it represented the special relationship of brothers and sisters in Christ.

16:21 in my own hand. The letter up to this point would have been written by a trained scribe (Ro 16:22), but Paul himself usually appended a few words that served as his personal signature

16:22 a curse be on him. These strong words written in Paul's own hand (v. 21) assert the apostolic authority behind the whole letter. This was not a curse on unbelievers generally, but a curse on those who rejected Paul's authority and disobeyed the instructions of the letter (5:9–13; cf. Gal 1:8–9; 2Th 3:14–15). **Come, O Lord!** Instead of using Greek at this point, Paul wrote the Aramaic words *Marana tha,* reflecting the worship of the early church. It is very likely that Paul intended this phrase to be viewed in conjunction with the "curse," such that his prayer was for Christ to come in judgment against the wicked. See *WCF* 10.4.

16:24 My love to all of you. After a long letter consisting primarily of severe rebukes, these affectionate words come as a surprise. Paul had not forgotten the pastoral needs of this congregation (see note on 1:2).

2 CORINTHIANS

Introduction

Overview

Author: The apostle Paul

Purpose: To express affection and gratitude for past repentance in Corinth and to encourage further loyalty to Paul as an apostle of Christ

Date: A.D. 55

Key Truths:

- Christians should take comfort and encouragement from God's care in the midst of suffering.
- God's strength is manifested through human weakness.
- The new covenant in Christ gloriously fulfills the expectations of the old covenant.
- Christians must help meet each other's material needs.

Author

That the apostle Paul was the author of this letter (1:1) is almost universally acknowledged. See "Introduction to 1 Corinthians: Author."

Time and Place of Writing

The most likely date for the writing of 2 Corinthians is A.D. 55. Paul probably wrote this letter within a year of writing of 1 Corinthians—after he left Ephesus in Asia Minor (Ac 19:1; 20:1) but before he reached Corinth in Greece (Ac 20:2).

After founding the church in Corinth in A.D. 51–52 (Ac 18:1–18), Paul returned to Antioch, ending his second missionary journey (Ac 18:22). On his third missionary journey Paul traveled to Ephesus and stayed there for three years (Ac 19:1–41; 20:31). During his stay in Ephesus, messengers came from Corinth with questions, which Paul answered in 1 Corinthians (1Co 16:17–18). Sometime later Paul apparently heard of continuing difficulties at Corinth and made a quick voyage from Ephesus to Corinth and back. This first visit in Corinth (after his initial 18-month stay) did not go well, and Paul later referred to it as a "painful visit" (2Co 2:1). Although a later visit is not recorded in Acts, Paul wrote in 2 Corinthians that he intended to travel to Corinth a "third time" (12:14; see 13:1). We do not know many details about what made the second visit painful, but apparently one or more of the believers at Corinth opposed or seriously offended Paul (2:5,10).

Most commentators believe that after his "painful visit" Paul wrote the Corinthians what is generally referred to as a "severe letter," which has not been preserved (2:3–4; 7:8). Other interpreters hold that the letter referred to in these verses is in fact the one now called 1 Corinthians. Still others believe that the letter referred to is 2 Corinthians 10–13, which now follows 2 Corinthians 1–9 but was originally a separate letter.

While planning a second short trip to Corinth (which would be his third stay there), Paul sent Titus by sea to deliver his "severe letter," while Paul himself took the longer land route through Troas and Macedonia (2:12–13; 7:5–9,13–15; Ac 20:1–2). Paul did not know how the Corinthians would receive Titus and the letter he bore. So when he left Ephesus and traveled toward Troas, he experienced considerable anxiety regarding the Corinthian church (2:13; 7:5). Although there was an opportunity for effective ministry when he reached Troas (2:12), Paul's spirit was still deeply troubled. He left Troas and went on to Macedonia (2:13; most likely to the church in Philippi), hoping to meet Titus there. When Titus finally arrived (probably at Philippi, but perhaps at Thessalonica), Paul was overwhelmed with joy as he heard about the Corinthians' genuine repentance and deep affection and loyalty to him (7:6–15).

Paul wrote 2 Corinthians from Macedonia to express thanksgiving for the repentance and renewed obedience of the Corinthian believers (7:5–16). He also wrote to encourage them to complete their collection to aid the poor Christians in Jerusalem (chs. 8–9). Paul defended his ministry against the accusations of "false apostles" (11:13) in Corinth, who were challenging his authority and integrity (chs. 10–13; see also 3:1–6; 7:2).

Paul arrived in Corinth and remained there for three months (Ac 20:2–3). He then departed for Jerusalem with the collection that had been sent from many churches to aid the poor Christians there (Ac 20:3—21:17).

Original Audience

See "Introduction to 1 Corinthians: Original Audience."

Purpose and Distinctives

Second Corinthians is a very personal letter filled with expressions of deep emotion. As such, it affords us extraordinary insight into Paul's heart. Two chief themes appear in connection with this: divine comfort and encouragement in the midst of suffering and troubles (1:1—7:16; see especially 1:3–7; 7:4,7,13) and God's strength manifested through human weakness (10:1—13:14; see especially 12:9–10).

Other important supporting themes include the blameless nature of Paul's conduct (1:12,17–18; 6:3–10; 7:2–3), his frequent suffering for the sake of the church and for God's glory (1:5–11; 4:8–12; 6:4–10; 11:23—12:9), his strong love for all the churches and especially for the Corinthian church (2:4; 11:2,7–11; 12:14–15) and his apostolic authority to build up the church and to defeat any opposition (2:9; 10:8; 13:8–10). Other distinctive emphases include the glory of the new covenant ministry (ch. 3) and the principles of Christian stewardship and charity (chs. 8–9).

As indicated above, some scholars have suggested that 2 Corinthians was not originally a single letter. They most frequently claim that chapters 10–13 constitute a separate epistle written on a different occasion and later appended to chapters 1–9. The primary reason for thinking of chapters 10–13 as a distinct communication is that Paul's tone and attitude toward the church at Corinth seem positive and affirming in chapters 1–9, but severe and threatening in chapters 10–13. Could both sections have been written on the same occasion, and could the two be addressing the same circumstances in the same church?

The change of tone at 10:1 may be accounted for by the change of subject matter. In the earlier part of the epistle, Paul was primarily concerned with sharing his joy and thanksgiving at the repentance of the Corinthians. He also wanted to give an extensive and positive description of his own ministry of the gospel. Having accomplished that, he appealed to the Corinthians to complete the collection for the Jerusalem Christians (chs. 8–9). Finally, leaving the most distasteful task until the end, he attacked the problem of the false apostles and their accusations against him (chs. 10–13). In light of the circumstances, such a change in tone is understandable. Moreover, it is significant that from the earliest times in the history of the church there has been no indication of division in this epistle, either in the manuscript tradition or in the earliest historical writings of the church. It has been read and understood as a unified epistle, and this still seems to be the best explanation.

Other suggestions challenging the unity of 2 Corinthians, but with far fewer supporters, have been that 2:14—7:4 is a separate letter, that 6:14—7:1 is a separate paragraph inserted into 2 Corinthians and that chapters 8–9 are a distinct letter. In response to these proposals, it may be admitted that the sections in question do mark distinct changes in tone and subject matter; however, this is a frequent characteristic of Paul's writings, and these sections are not out of place in the larger argument of the epistle.

Outline

I. Salutation (1:1–2)	*Paul greeted and blessed the church in Corinth and Achaia.*
II. Explanation of Paul's Ministry (1:3—7:16) A. Thanksgiving for God's Comfort (1:3–11) B. Change of Plans Explained (1:12—2:4) C. Forgiveness of a Penitent Sinner (2:5–11) D. Journey to Troas and Macedonia (2:12–13) E. The Greatness of New Covenant Ministry (2:14—7:4) 1. Triumphal Procession (2:14–17) 2. Living Letter (3:1–3) 3. The New and Glorious Covenant (3:4—4:6) 4. Jars of Clay (4:7—5:10) 5. Ministry of Reconciliation (5:11—6:13) 6. Separation From Evil (6:14—7:4) F. Joy at the Coming of Titus (7:5–16)	*He patiently explained how his love for the Corinthians had not diminished. God had been guiding and blessing Paul's life since he last had seen them. As he described these things, Paul focused especially on the wonders of his ministry in the new covenant.*
III. Collection for Christians in Jerusalem (8:1—9:15) A. Macedonia's Example (8:1–7) B. Jesus' Example (8:8–9) C. A Reasonable Plea (8:10—9:15)	*The Corinthians had not followed through on their pledge of money for the impoverished Jerusalem church. Paul reminded them of their privilege as the body of Christ to care for believers in Jerusalem.*
IV. Defense Against False Apostles (10:1—13:10) A. Spiritual Power (10:1–12) B. Boasting (10:13—12:21) 1. Definition of Proper Boasting 10:13—11:21) 2. Boasting of Suffering and Weakness (11:22–33) 3. Boasting of Heavenly Vision (12:1–10) 4. Paul's Care for the Corinthians (12:11–21) C. Warning (13:1–10)	*False apostles had risen in Corinth and had opposed Paul. Paul defended his apostleship and severely warned that the Corinthians should follow his true teachings.*
V. Final Greeting and Benediction (13:11–14)	*Paul closed his epistle with positive words of hope for the church in Corinth.*

1 Paul, an apostle of Christ Jesus by the will of God,[a] and Timothy our brother,

To the church of God[b] in Corinth, together with all the saints throughout Achaia:[c]
2 Grace and peace to you from God our Father and the Lord Jesus Christ.[d]

The God of All Comfort

3 Praise be to the God and Father of our Lord Jesus Christ,[e] the Father of compassion
and the God of all comfort, 4 who comforts us[f] in all our troubles, so that we can comfort those in any trouble with the comfort we ourselves have received from God. 5 For just
as the sufferings of Christ flow over into our lives,[g] so also through Christ our comfort
overflows. 6 If we are distressed, it is for your comfort and salvation;[h] if we are comforted, it is for your comfort, which produces in you patient endurance of the same sufferings we suffer. 7 And our hope for you is firm, because we know that just as you share in
our sufferings,[i] so also you share in our comfort.
8 We do not want you to be uninformed, brothers, about the hardships we suffered[j]
in the province of Asia. We were under great pressure, far beyond our ability to endure,
so that we despaired even of life. 9 Indeed, in our hearts we felt the sentence of death. But
this happened that we might not rely on ourselves but on God,[k] who raises the dead.
10 He has delivered us from such a deadly peril,[l] and he will deliver us. On him we have
set our hope that he will continue to deliver us, 11 as you help us by your prayers.[m] Then
many will give thanks[n] on our[a] behalf for the gracious favor granted us in answer to the
prayers of many.

a *11* Many manuscripts *your*

1:1 [a] 1Co 1:1; Eph 1:1; Col 1:1; 2Ti 1:1 [b] 1Co 10:32 [c] Ac 18:12
1:2 [d] Ro 1:7
1:3 [e] Eph 1:3; 1Pe 1:3
1:4 [f] 2Co 7:6,7,13
1:5 [g] 2Co 4:10; Col 1:24
1:6 [h] 2Co 4:15
1:7 [i] Ro 8:17
1:8 [j] 1Co 15:32
1:9 [k] Jer 17:5,7
1:10 [l] Ro 15:31
1:11 [m] Ro 15:30; Php 1:19 [n] 2Co 4:15

■ **1:1–2** *Salutation.* As was his usual fashion, Paul began by identifying himself and the recipients of his letter.
1:1 apostle. In the greetings of his letters, Paul distinguished between himself (as an "apostle") and his close coworkers, such as Timothy (1Co 1:1; Col 1:1). The term "apostle" here denotes an official representative authorized to act on behalf of the sender. In addition to this technical sense of the term applied to the Twelve plus Paul, "apostle" is sometimes used in the New Testament in the more general sense of "messenger" or "representative" (e.g., 8:23). **by the will of God.** It is God's sovereign choice that ultimately places people in church offices and ministries—whether apostles (as here) or elders (Ac 20:28) or those whose gifts equip them for other ministries in the church (1Co 12:7,11,28). **Timothy our brother.** Timothy was apparently among Paul's most trusted and gifted coworkers (cf. 1Co 1:1; Php 1:1; Col 1:1; 1Th 1:1). **saints.** Literally, "holy or sanctified people," a term commonly used by Paul to refer to all members of the visible church (see theological article "The Church: Visible and Invisible" at 1 Pe 4). **throughout Achaia.** Although the letter was intended primarily for the church in Corinth, Paul apparently realized that it would be read by neighboring churches in the region of Achaia, which was in the southern part of modern Greece.
1:2 Grace. God's undeserved favor. Sinners need grace not only for initial forgiveness of sins, but also for ongoing forgiveness and in the vicissitudes of everyday life. **peace.** Not only external peace and freedom from persecution, but also inner peace with God (Ro 5:1–2; Php 4:7; Col 3:15).
■ **1:3—7:16** *Explanation of Paul's Ministry.* Because the Corinthians had misunderstood Paul's actions and motivations, he began this letter with an explanation of some things that had happened since he had last seen them. He touched on six main subjects: thanks for God's comfort (1:3–11), an explanation of his change in plans (1:12—2:4), concern for a penitent sinner in Corinth (2:5–11), his journey to Troas and Macedonia (2:12–13), the wonder of ministering in the new covenant (2:14—7:4) and the joy of Titus's arrival (7:5–16).
■ **1:3–11** *Thanksgiving for God's Comfort.* Paul began by expressing his gratitude for the comfort he had received from God regarding the Corinthian church.
1:3 Father of our Lord Jesus Christ. Although the three persons of the Trinity (Father, Son and Holy Spirit) have always existed and are equal in attributes and deity, they have distinct roles. The role of the Father is to initiate and direct all the actions of the Godhead and (as emphasized here) to relate to Jesus Christ, God the Son, as a father to a son. **Father of compassion . . . God of all comfort.** A prominent theme in 1:3—9:15. All true compassion and comfort (consolation and encouragement) in the world have their origin in God.
1:4 so that we can comfort. God has a sovereign purpose, both in our troubles and in the comfort that he gives us in those troubles. Those who have themselves experienced God's comfort in time of trouble may expect that God will put them in contact with others who are experiencing a similar kind of trouble, so they can share with them the comfort they have received from God.
1:5 sufferings of Christ flow over into our lives. Although believers can add nothing to Christ's full atonement for sin (Isa 53:11; Jn 19:30; Heb 9:26–28), God has called them to suffer for Christ and thereby join him in his sufferings (Ro 8:17; Col 1:24; Heb 12:2–3; 1Pe 2:21). Because believers are in union with Christ and are part of his body, both sufferings and comfort in Jesus Christ are properly seen as a result of their participation in him (Php 3:10–11). Here Paul hinted that the experiences of Christ—especially his suffering, death and resurrection—constitute the basic pattern by which Christians can understand their own experiences as members of Christ's body. Paul frequently affirmed that the Christian participates in both Christ's humiliation and his exaltation (see theological article "Union With Christ" at Gal 6).
1:6 Paul saw God's sovereign hand and good purpose in everything that happened to him, whether it brought distress or comfort.
1:7 you share in our sufferings. Believers suffer not only because they are joined to Christ (v. 5) but also because they are joined to each other—when one suffers, all suffer (1Co 12:26). The more fully this reality influences the attitudes and actions of believers toward each other, the more fully they experience satisfying fellowship through Christ with one another.
1:8 hardships we suffered in the province of Asia. Paul was apparently referring to some grave hardships (perhaps persecution, illness or injury) he had suffered since the last time he was in Corinth. These difficulties had occurred either in Ephesus (Ac 19) or during the time between his visits to Ephesus and Macedonia (not mentioned in Ac 20:1). **we suffered.** In this epistle "we" sometimes refers to Paul alone, but more frequently it refers to Paul and his coworkers (e.g., Timothy, Silas).
1:9 we felt the sentence of death. Paul was convinced that God had decided it was time for him to die and that his life was about to come to an end. **that.** God's purpose in our afflictions is often to cause us to cease trusting in our own strength and abilities and to trust more fully in him. **who raises the dead.** If God can empower even the dead to return to life, surely he can enable believers in their weaknesses. In this way, the death and resurrection of Christ are daily manifested anew in believers' lives (cf. 1Co 15:31; Gal 2:20), and their future resurrection is foreshadowed as well (Php 3:10; Col 3:1).
1:11 you help us by your prayers. Prayer has real results. Paul was convinced that God has ordained his relationship to the world in such a way that he will respond to prayer. Paul needed this kind of help from others, just as each of us does. **Then many.** The Greek term translated "then" may also be rendered "in order

Paul's Change of Plans

12Now this is our boast: Our conscience[o] testifies that we have conducted ourselves
in the world, and especially in our relations with you, in the holiness and sincerity[p] that
are from God. We have done so not according to worldly wisdom[q] but according to God's
grace. 13For we do not write you anything you cannot read or understand. And I hope
that, 14as you have understood us in part, you will come to understand fully that you can
boast of us just as we will boast of you in the day of the Lord Jesus.[r]
15Because I was confident of this, I planned to visit you[s] first so that you might benefit twice.[t] 16I planned to visit you on my way[u] to Macedonia and to come back to you
from Macedonia, and then to have you send me on my way to Judea. 17When I planned
this, did I do it lightly? Or do I make my plans in a worldly manner[v] so that in the same
breath I say, "Yes, yes" and "No, no"?
18But as surely as God is faithful,[w] our message to you is not "Yes" and "No." 19For
the Son of God, Jesus Christ, who was preached among you by me and Silas[a] and Timothy, was not "Yes" and "No," but in him it has always[x] been "Yes." 20For no matter how
many promises[y] God has made, they are "Yes" in Christ. And so through him the
"Amen"[z] is spoken by us to the glory of God. 21Now it is God who makes both us and you
stand firm in Christ. He anointed[a] us, 22set his seal of ownership on us, and put his Spirit in our hearts as a deposit, guaranteeing what is to come.[b]
23I call God as my witness[c] that it was in order to spare you[d] that I did not return to
Corinth. 24Not that we lord it over[e] your faith, but we work with you for your joy, because

1:12 [o]Ac 23:1 [p]2Co 2:17 [q]1Co 2:1,4,13
1:14 [r]1Co 1:8
1:15 [s]1Co 4:19 [t]Ro 1:11,13; 15:29
1:16 [u]1Co 16:5-7
1:17 [v]2Co 10:2,3
1:18 [w]1Co 1:9
1:19 [x]Heb 13:8
1:20 [y]Ro 15:8 [z]1Co 14:16
1:21 [a]1Jn 2:20,27
1:22 [b]2Co 5:5
1:23 [c]Ro 1:9; Gal 1:20 [d]1Co 4:21; 2Co 2:1,3; 13:2,10
1:24 [e]1Pe 5:3

[a] *19* Greek *Silvanus,* a variant of *Silas*

that." The clause depends on God's action in the beginning of verse 10 (deliverance from peril). God would continue to deliver Paul and answer prayer "in order that" many people would thank and praise God. Throughout all of human history God's desire is that many people serve and praise him (Ge 1:28–29; Rev. 7:9). Paul's ministry served this goal by redeeming many who would praise the grace of God (cf. 4:15).

■ **1:12—2:4** *Change of Plans Explained.* Some members of the Corinthian church had accused Paul of lacking integrity because he had not carried through with his earlier plans to visit them.

1:12 boast. Paul "boasted" not of his own ability, but of his clear conscience and morally upright conduct among those in Corinth (and elsewhere). These virtues were not from himself, but "from God." They were not the result of following the conventional wisdom of the world regarding how to act, but were dependent upon "God's grace." When Paul "boasted," he took no credit for himself, but gave all the glory to God. See *WCF* 18.2. **worldly wisdom . . . God's grace.** Paul introduced his denial of the charge that he had changed his plans to visit Corinth for worldly reasons.

1:13 cannot read or understand. Paul reminded the Corinthians that his writings, like his ministry, were not devious, underhanded or full of hidden meanings and concealed agendas (as perhaps some of his opponents in Corinth had claimed). Paul's writings were direct and, in the main, easy to understand. Peter's words remind us, however, that some things Paul wrote were "hard to understand" (2Pe 3:16), indicating that not everything in Paul's writings was equally clear to everyone. There is application here for the doctrine of the clarity of Scripture: All that is necessary for salvation is utterly clear in the Bible. Beyond this, believers must engage in serious study to grasp some aspects of Scripture as they seek God's help in understanding his Word (Dt 6:6–7; Pss 19:7; 119:130; 2Ti 2:15).

1:14 boast of us. That is, the Corinthians could be proud and rejoice at what God had done in Paul and his coworkers. **the day of the Lord Jesus.** Refers to "the day of the Lord"; that is, the day of Christ's return.

1:15 benefit twice. An alternative translation is "have double grace." Paul knew that his visits to the churches imparted God's grace to them.

1:17–18 See *WLC* 144.

1:17 in a worldly manner. Opponents were discrediting the apostle by charging that his word was unreliable, but they did not have all the facts.

1:18 as God is faithful. Paul called on God's faithfulness as the pattern and guarantee for his own faithfulness. **our message.** Paul reminded the Corinthians that his gospel message was absolutely reliable and had led to their salvation.

1:19 The absolute truthfulness and reliability of God's words in Christ were the standard that Paul ought to follow in his own speech. This is consistent with Paul's general pattern of deriving moral absolutes from the moral character of God.

1:20 they are "Yes" in Christ. In the final analysis, Christ fulfills all the promises of God to his people. We can rely completely on Christ's ability to grant the mercies of God to his followers. See *WLC* 57; *BC* 37; *HC* 129.

1:21–22 God . . . Christ . . . Spirit. A Trinitarian passage pointing to the role of all three divine persons in salvation. See *WCF* 18.2; *HC* 1,49,53.

1:21 stand firm. The ability to continue on in the Christian life does not come from within oneself; it is a gift from God. God always continues to give this ability to all those who are truly born again (Php 1:6; 1Pe 1:5). Those who are thus guarded by God will continue to trust in Christ throughout their lives (13:5; Col 1:23; Heb 3:14), because God's guarding of them is carried out through their faith (1:24; 1Pe 1:5). See theological article "The Perseverance and Preservation of Believers at Php 1." **anointed.** In a literal sense, to "anoint" is to pour oil on someone's head, often as a sign of divine calling and empowerment (1Sa 16:13). But God's anointing for service can come without any literal pouring of oil on the head. The one most powerfully anointed by God was Jesus Christ the Messiah (the Hebrew word "Messiah" and the Greek word "Christ" both mean "anointed one"). Christ's anointing is mentioned in Luke 4:18, Acts 4:26 27 and Acts 10:38. Here Paul used a related Greek verb as a reminder that God—just as he had anointed Jesus for service and ministry—has anointed believers, not with literal oil, but with the power of the Holy Spirit, to confirm and empower them in various ministries and areas of service (1Jn 2:20,27).

1:22 seal of ownership. An official seal marked authority or ownership and guaranteed protection (Est 8:8; Da 6:17; Mt 27:66; Rev 7:3). God has sealed believers not with a physical seal of wax or clay but with the indwelling of the Holy Spirit in their hearts (Eph 1:13; 4:30), thereby instilling faith in Christ (see theological article "Regeneration and New Birth" at Jn 3). Since this sealing is the result of an inner working of the Holy Spirit, Paul's focus does not seem to be on an outward, symbolic act, such as baptism, although some have adopted that explanation for this phrase. See *WLC* 83. **a deposit, guaranteeing what is to come.** This phrase translates a single Greek word that signifies a down payment that includes a guarantee of payment of the remaining amount. God has given us the Holy Spirit as a guarantee of the complete inheritance of all the blessings of salvation in the new heavens and the new earth (5:5; Ro 8:23; Eph 1:14).

1:23 I call God as my witness. Literally, "as witness against my life." Paul took a solemn oath to persuade the Corinthians of his truthfulness. In effect, he said, "If I am not telling the truth, I ask God to take my life." See *WCF* 22.1; 22.2; *HC* 101,102. **to spare you.** Paul wanted to give the Corinthians an opportunity to repent before he visited them (13:2–4,10). This was the reason he had not gone back to Corinth before traveling to Macedonia; his motivation had not been worldly vacillation or cowardice.

1:24 See *WCF* 20.2; 31.4; *WLC* 99,105.

1:24 [f]Ro 11:20; 1Co 15:1
2:1 [g]2Co 1:23
2:2 [h]2Co 7:8
2:3 [i]2Co 7:8,12 [j]2Co 12:21 [k]2Co 8:22; Gal 5:10
2:4 [l]2Co 7:8,12
2:5 [m]1Co 5:1,2
2:6 [n]1Co 5:4,5
2:7 [o]Gal 6:1; Eph 4:32
2:9 [p]2Co 10:6
2:11 [q]Mt 4:10 [r]Lk 22:31; 2Co 4:4; 1Pe 5:8,9
2:12 [s]Ac 16:8 [t]Ro 1:1 [u]Ac 14:27
2:13 [v]2Co 7:5 [w]2Co 7:6, 13; 12:18
2:14 [x]Ro 6:17 [y]Eph 5:2; Php 4:18
2:15 [z]1Co 1:18

2 it is by faith you stand firm.[f] 1So I made up my mind that I would not make another painful visit to you.[g] 2For if I grieve you,[h] who is left to make me glad but you
whom I have grieved? 3I wrote as I did[i] so that when I came I should not be distressed[j]
by those who ought to make me rejoice. I had confidence[k] in all of you, that you would
all share my joy. 4For I wrote you[l] out of great distress and anguish of heart and with
many tears, not to grieve you but to let you know the depth of my love for you.

Forgiveness for the Sinner

5If anyone has caused grief,[m] he has not so much grieved me as he has grieved all of
you, to some extent—not to put it too severely. 6The punishment[n] inflicted on him by the
majority is sufficient for him. 7Now instead, you ought to forgive and comfort him,[o] so
that he will not be overwhelmed by excessive sorrow. 8I urge you, therefore, to reaffirm
your love for him. 9The reason I wrote you was to see if you would stand the test and be
obedient in everything.[p] 10If you forgive anyone, I also forgive him. And what I have forgiven—if there was anything to forgive—I have forgiven in the sight of Christ for your
sake, 11in order that Satan[q] might not outwit us. For we are not unaware of his schemes.[r]

Ministers of the New Covenant

12Now when I went to Troas[s] to preach the gospel of Christ[t] and found that the Lord
had opened a door[u] for me, 13I still had no peace of mind,[v] because I did not find my
brother Titus[w] there. So I said good-by to them and went on to Macedonia.
14But thanks be to God,[x] who always leads us in triumphal procession in Christ and
through us spreads everywhere the fragrance[y] of the knowledge of him. 15For we are to
God the aroma of Christ among those who are being saved and those who are perishing.[z]

2:1 another painful visit. See "Introduction: Time and Place of Writing."

2:3 I wrote as I did. After the "painful visit" (v. 1), Paul wrote a letter of rebuke to the Corinthian church, sending it by the hand of Titus (2:13; 7:6–7,13–14).

2:4 I wrote you out of great distress. Paul continued here to talk about what many have called his "severe letter" (not preserved for us) that was sent to the Corinthian church as a rebuke after his brief, distressing visit to them (see "Introduction: Time and Place of Writing"). See *WLC* 144. **not to grieve you.** Paul's purpose in writing the severe letter was not to make the Corinthians sorrowful, but to demonstrate that his love for them was so deep that he always sought their best interests, even when that meant inflicting pain both on them and on himself.

■ **2:5–11** *Forgiveness of a Penitent Sinner.* Paul now touched on a case involving discipline in the church.

2:5 If anyone has caused grief. This passage is often taken as referring to the case of the man living with his father's wife (1Co 5:1–8). This identification is questionable because, unlike the wrongdoing spoken of here, the offense in 1 Corinthians 5 had not been committed against Paul (vv. 5,10). Also, 1 Corinthians 5 does not seem to have been written to test the Corinthians' obedience, whereas Paul explicitly intended to test the Corinthians with the situation referred to here (v. 9).

2:6–11 See *WCF* 15.6; 30.2; *HC* 85.

2:6 punishment inflicted on him by the majority. Apparently, after Paul had left Corinth or at least after Titus had come with the "severe letter" (see "Introduction: Time and Place of Writing"), the Corinthians had exercised church discipline against the offender (cf. Mt 18:15–20).

2:7 Church discipline should not continue after there has been genuine repentance for the wrong done. The goals of church discipline are the glory of Christ, the purity of the church and the restoration of the sinner. See *WLC* 173.

2:10 Paul trusted the judgment of the Corinthian congregation on this matter. **in the sight of Christ.** A common theme in this epistle. All our actions are carried out not in secrecy, but in the presence of Christ, the Lord of the church. If both Paul and Christ had forgiven the offender, the Corinthian believers should do so as well (cf. Mt 16:19; Jn 20:23).

2:11 in order that Satan might not outwit us. Satan can win a victory over us either by persuading us not to carry out church discipline at all or by convincing us to remain harsh and unforgiving after there has been a change of heart on the part of the sinner.

■ **2:12–13** *Journey to Troas and Macedonia.* Paul briefly described his travels to Troas and Macedonia, which had occurred during the time he was awaiting word from Corinth.

2:12 Troas. A city in far northwestern Asia Minor (in modern Turkey) from which Paul would sail to Philippi (in Europe). It was in Troas that Paul had previously seen the vision of the man from Macedonia imploring him to come and help (Ac 16:9). **the Lord had opened a door for me.** God had provided opportunities for preaching the gospel. Paul knew that God's sovereign work alone made evangelism effective; unless God opened a door, there would be no effective work.

2:13 I still had no peace of mind. Literally, "I did not have rest in my spirit." Paul had hoped that Titus would meet him at Troas and report that the "severe letter" (see "Introduction: Time and Place of Writing") had been well received. When Titus failed to appear, Paul was deeply troubled. **I said good-by to them.** A tremendous opportunity for effective ministry did not make Paul turn aside from his prior commitment to care for the Corinthian church and help to resolve its problems. Paul continued to feel a deep concern for all the churches (11:28–29). **to Macedonia.** Paul probably went to Philippi in Macedonia, then perhaps to Thessalonica or Berea before Titus arrived. Acts 16:8—18:1 describe Paul's previous journey along this route. At this point the narrative of his relationship with the Corinthian church is interrupted until 7:5–16, where the account of Titus's arrival is completed.

■ **2:14—7:4** *The Greatness of New Covenant Ministry.* As he described his anxiety for the Corinthian church and his disappointment at not finding Titus in Troas, Paul digressed into a lengthy reflection on the nature of his ministry. His description of his gospel ministry divides into six sections: his gospel ministry as a triumphal procession (2:14–17), his converts as living letters (3:1–3), the glory of his new covenant ministry (3:4—4:6), the treasure of the gospel in jars of clay (4:7—5:10), the goal of reconciliation (5:11—6:13) and the importance of separation from evil (6:14—7:4).

■ **2:14–17** *Triumphal Procession.* Paul began his description of his ministry in terms of a Roman triumphal procession. Despite the difficulties he had experienced as a traveling minister of the gospel, Paul knew that his work was aptly described as a victory parade.

2:14–16 See *WCF* 5.6; *WLC* 190.

2:14 triumphal procession. Paul saw himself as part of God's triumphal procession. Much as an ancient general would lead a victory parade upon returning to his own city, with vanquished captives following behind, Paul knew that God was using him to accomplish victory through the gospel. All who participate in spreading the Good News of Christ march in the victory procession of their great King, as the forces of the enemy crumble before his advance. Passing setbacks (such as Paul experienced at Troas) are temporal—the eyes of faith see the unrelenting progress of the kingdom of God. God "always leads us in triumphal procession." **fragrance.** The sweetness of the knowledge of Christ brings delight to believers' hearts.

2:15 we are to God the aroma of Christ. The fact that we are a sweet scent to God means that he delights in us and in our lives. This is a fulfillment of the Old Testament burnt offerings, the smoke of which was created "an aroma pleasing to the LORD" (Lev 1:17).

16 To the one we are the smell of death;[a] to the other, the fragrance of life. And who is
equal to such a task?[b] 17 Unlike so many, we do not peddle the word of God for profit.[c]
On the contrary, in Christ we speak before God with sincerity,[d] like men sent from God.[e]

3 Are we beginning to commend ourselves[f] again? Or do we need, like some people,
letters of recommendation[g] to you or from you? 2 You yourselves are our letter, written on our hearts, known and read by everybody.[h] 3 You show that you are a letter from
Christ, the result of our ministry, written not with ink but with the Spirit of the living God,
not on tablets of stone[i] but on tablets of human hearts.[j]

4 Such confidence[k] as this is ours through Christ before God. 5 Not that we are competent in ourselves to claim anything for ourselves, but our competence comes from
God.[l] 6 He has made us competent as ministers of a new covenant[m]—not of the letter but
of the Spirit; for the letter kills, but the Spirit gives life.[n]

The Glory of the New Covenant

7 Now if the ministry that brought death, which was engraved in letters on stone,
came with glory, so that the Israelites could not look steadily at the face of Moses because of its glory,[o] fading though it was, 8 will not the ministry of the Spirit be even more
glorious? 9 If the ministry that condemns men[p] is glorious, how much more glorious is
the ministry that brings righteousness![q] 10 For what was glorious has no glory now in

2:16 [a]Lk 2:34 [b]2Co 3:5,6
2:17 [c]2Co 4:2 [d]1Co 5:8 [e]2Co 1:12
3:1 [f]2Co 5:12; 12:11 [g]Ac 18:27
3:2 [h]1Co 9:2
3:3 [i]Ex 24:12 [j]Pr 3:3; Jer 31:33; Eze 11:19
3:4 [k]Eph 3:12
3:5 [l]1Co 15:10
3:6 [m]Lk 22:20 [n]Jn 6:63
3:7 [o]Ex 34:29-35
3:9 [p]ver 7 [q]Ro 1:17; 3:21,22

2:16 fragrance of life. True believers emit a pleasant "fragrance," not only in terms of their relationship to God but also in their interactions with those around them. On the other hand, the lives of believers frighten hardened unbelievers, who recognize that they themselves lack this sweet spiritual aroma—a warning of impending judgment (Php 1:28). **And who is equal to such a task?** To be a messenger of eternal life or death is a wondrous privilege. No one is worthy of this eternally significant task, but God qualifies believers for it nonetheless (3:6).

2:17 Unlike so many. It is tragic that, both then and now, many preach the gospel (or teach Christianity) only as a means of earning a living. Paul's goal was not his own personal benefit or financial reward, but God's glory. **before God.** The whole of Paul's ministry was carried out in the sight of God—a strong motive for keeping his conscience clear (1:12; Ac 23:1; 1Ti 1:5; 2Ti 1:3). See *WLC* 159.

■ **3:1–3** *Living Letter.* Paul's opponents used letters of recommendation to support their cause. Paul countered by referring to the Corinthians themselves as his living "letter" of recommendation.

3:1 Both questions in this verse are rhetorical and imply the answer "no." Paul did not disparage letters of recommendation generally (Ac 15:25–26; 18:27; 1Co 16:10–11), but apparently his opponents had brought some misleading reference letters to the Corinthian church. Paul showed that his letter was far superior, for he was commended by the changed lives of the Corinthian Christians (v. 2).

3:2 written on our hearts. This statement indicates that Paul and his coworkers had great affection for the Corinthian church. The alternative reading, "your hearts," though supported by fewer ancient manuscripts, is also possible and makes sense in the context. Assuming this latter reading, Paul was urging the Corinthians to recognize that their existence as a church constituted a most effective letter of recommendation for him (2:17; 1Co 9:2).

3:3 letter from Christ, the result of our ministry. The Corinthian church was a work of God's grace in which God had wonderfully used Paul and his coworkers. **with the Spirit of the living God.** This "letter" that the Corinthians constituted was superior to the ink-only letters of Paul's opponents because the work of the Spirit in the lives of the Corinthians was undeniably verifiable. The observable results in the Corinthians' lives attested to the validity (cf. "known and read by everybody"; v. 2) and superiority of Paul's ministry over that of his opponents (cf. 11:1–5; 12:11). **tablets of stone.** The Ten Commandments. **tablets of human hearts.** The "letter" composed by the lives of the Corinthians also demonstrated the validity of Paul's ministry on the basis that its glory surpassed that of Moses' ministry. Moses had given Israel the Ten Commandments on tablets of stone (Dt 9:10), and God intended for that law to be written on the hearts of his people (Dt 6:6)—indeed it was written on the hearts of some (e.g., Ps. 119:11). As a whole, however, the people of Israel had rejected God's witness through Moses and had not loved God's law or taken it to heart. As a result they were cast into exile in Assyria and Babylon. But Jeremiah 31:33 and Ezekiel 11:19 and 36:26 told of a coming day when God would restore his people from exile. In that day, all God's people would obey him in righteousness and adhere to his law. Although this promise will not be completely fulfilled until Christ returns (see theological article "The Plan of the Ages" at Heb 7), Paul indicated that it had begun to be realized even under his own ministry. For this reason, his ministry surpassed even that of Moses (vv. 6–16). See *WCF* 10.1.

■ **3:4—4:6** *The New and Glorious Covenant.* Paul continued to describe the nature of his ministry by focusing on the glory associated with his work.

3:4 Such confidence. The reference is to Paul's confidence before God that his ministry was authentic and that the Corinthians were his "letters of recommendation" (v. 1) proving it. However, Paul's confidence came not through himself, but "through Christ."

3:5 competent. This word is translated "equal to" in 2:16. Related Greek words are used for "competence" in this verse and "competent" in verse 6. Paul here answered the question of 2:16 ("Who is equal to such a task?"). Earlier he had disavowed any dependence on mere human ability (1Co 2:1–5). Unfortunately, Paul's opponents valued worldly ability more than the competence that comes from God alone. **our competence comes from God.** All ability and power in ministry come from God. See *WCF* 16.3; *WLC* 190.

3:6–18 See *WCF* 7.5; 20.1; *WLC* 33,35,157.

3:6 new covenant. The new legal relationship that God established with his people through Jesus Christ and by Christ's death (see "Major Covenants in the Bible" on p. 25). **the letter.** Although God did not give the Mosaic Law as a mere set of letters to operate without the Spirit's inward work (Dt 6:6), Jewish legalism had reduced the law to little more than an external code. As a result, the Jewish legalists relied on mere written law, which demanded perfect obedience but gave no power to obey (see theological article "Legalism and Antinomianism" at Ro 10). **the Spirit gives life.** The Spirit's work in those who follow Christ is not divorced from the moral standards of God's law, for the Holy Spirit writes God's law on believers' hearts (Jer 31:31–34; Heb 8:8–12; 9:13–14), instilling love for God's moral standards and power to obey them (Ro 8:4; 1Co 7:19). In this verse Paul was not implying that there was no spiritual life under the old covenant, but was simply emphasizing that the written law, which was characteristic of the old covenant, could not by itself produce life in God's people. But the Holy Spirit, whose powerful, life-giving ministry characterizes the new covenant, brings new life in much greater measure and with wider distribution than that which was available in the old covenant. See *WCF* 10.1; *WLC* 158.

3:7 the ministry that brought death. The law was "intended to bring life" (Ro 7:10–11), but it became an instrument of death for those without faith because it condemned them when they did not obey it. **the Israelites could not look steadily at the face of Moses.** Even in the old covenant during his ministry to faithless Israel (Nu 32:13), Moses had the radiance of God's glory shining from his face (Ex 34:29–35). The lesser covenant was still glorious.

3:8 will not the ministry of the Spirit be even more glorious? That is, will there not be a much more powerful manifestation of God's glory in the age when the Spirit is more widely and powerfully present?

3:9 brings righteousness! Believers attain righteousness in God's initial legal declaration pronouncing them to be so ("justification") at the beginning of the Christian life, in the growth in actual righteous thoughts and deeds ("sanctification") and ultimately in our future perfection ("glorification").

comparison with the surpassing glory. 11And if what was fading away came with glory,
how much greater is the glory of that which lasts!
12Therefore, since we have such a hope, we are very bold.[r] 13We are not like Moses,
who would put a veil over his face[s] to keep the Israelites from gazing at it while the radiance was fading away. 14But their minds were made dull,[t] for to this day the same veil
remains when the old covenant[u] is read.[v] It has not been removed, because only in
Christ is it taken away. 15Even to this day when Moses is read, a veil covers their hearts.
16But whenever anyone turns to the Lord,[w] the veil is taken away.[x] 17Now the Lord is the
Spirit,[y] and where the Spirit of the Lord is, there is freedom.[z] 18And we, who with unveiled faces all reflect[a][a] the Lord's glory,[b] are being transformed into his likeness[c] with
ever-increasing glory, which comes from the Lord, who is the Spirit.

Treasures in Jars of Clay

4 Therefore, since through God's mercy[d] we have this ministry, we do not lose heart.
2Rather, we have renounced secret and shameful ways;[e] we do not use deception,
nor do we distort the word of God.[f] On the contrary, by setting forth the truth plainly we
commend ourselves to every man's conscience[g] in the sight of God. 3And even if our gospel[h] is veiled,[i] it is veiled to those who are perishing.[j] 4The god[k] of this age has blinded[l] the minds of unbelievers, so that they cannot see the light of the gospel of the glory
of Christ, who is the image of God. 5For we do not preach ourselves,[m] but Jesus Christ
as Lord, and ourselves as your servants[n] for Jesus' sake. 6For God, who said, "Let light
shine out of darkness,"[b][o] made his light shine in our hearts[p] to give us the light of the
knowledge of the glory of God in the face of Christ.

3:12 [r]Eph 6:19
3:13 [s]ver 7; Ex 34:33
3:14 [t]Ro 11:7,8 [u]Ac 13:15 [v]ver 6
3:16 [w]Ro 11:23 [x]Ex 34:34
3:17 [y]Isa 61:1,2 [z]Jn 8:32
3:18 [a]1Co 13:12 [b]2Co 4:4,6 [c]Ro 8:29
4:1 [d]1Co 7:25
4:2 [e]1Co 4:5 [f]2Co 2:17 [g]2Co 5:11
4:3 [h]2Co 2:12 [i]2Co 3:14 [j]1Co 1:18
4:4 [k]Jn 12:31 [l]2Co 3:14
4:5 [m]1Co 1:13 [n]1Co 9:19
4:6 [o]Ge 1:3 [p]2Pe 1:19

a *18* Or *contemplate* b *6* Gen. 1:3

3:11 what was fading away. The old covenant was always designed to be preliminary to the final stage of God's plan for the ages: the new covenant age. **that which lasts!** That is, the new covenant.

3:12 such a hope. The splendor of the new covenant, which will not fade or pass away (v. 11), provided the apostle's hope and fueled his boldness. **we are very bold.** Paul was not at all ashamed to stand before the entire world and proclaim this excellent gospel. The reference to boldness links the discussion of verses 7–11 with Paul's defense of his apostleship (10:1–2). He was bold, not vacillating, as his opponents accused (1:17—2:4). His boldness took the form of the fearless candor so evident in this epistle, which contrasted with the deceitful selfishness of his opponents (2:17).

3:13 to keep the Israelites from gazing. Moses' veil was not worn to protect the Israelites from being harmed or frightened by the brightness of his face—he showed his face when he spoke with them (Ex 34:33). Moses wore the veil in those times between his meetings with God to keep the Israelites from seeing that the glory was "fading away," or only temporary (Ex 34:29–35). Paul stressed that Moses' glory as a minister of the old covenant was temporary and fading in contrast to the greater glory of the new covenant. Paul was not ashamed to show the world all the glory of the new covenant ministry, for that glory does not fade away. See *WCF* 20.1.

3:14 the same veil remains. Even today, Paul said, many Jewish people cannot see that, as glorious as it was, the old covenant was a temporary precursor to the new.

3:15 a veil covers their hearts. Here the metaphor shifts somewhat (as is often the case in Paul's writings). The veil no longer covers Moses face but the Israelites' hearts. Still, the effect is the same: They cannot see the fading nature of the old covenant.

3:17 the Lord is the Spirit. Paul stressed the close relationship between Christ and the Holy Spirit. By virtue of his resurrection and ascension, Christ and the life-giving Spirit are so closely identified in function (not personhood) as to be identical in the experience of the believer (1Co 15:45). Thus, in the same breath, Paul spoke of the believer as being indwelled by "the Spirit," by "the Spirit of God," by "the Spirit of Christ" and by "Christ" (Ro 8:9–11; cf. Ac 16:6–7). In speaking of this relationship, Paul did not blur the distinction among the persons of the Trinity, but merely indicated that they cooperate in their functions. Alternatively, this verse may interpret the meaning of Exodus 34:34, indicating that the "LORD" of that verse is the Holy Spirit, who worked in Moses in a manner parallel to that in which he now works in those who minister under the new covenant. **there is freedom.** That is, freedom from death, sin and obedience to the law under one's own power. See *BC* 1.

3:18 we . . . all. A characteristic experience of new covenant believers is described here. **unveiled faces.** Unlike Moses (v. 13). **reflect the Lord's glory.** "Reflect" could also be translated "behold" (as in a mirror), but the imagery of a mirror is better suited to the idea of "reflecting" in this context. Unlike Moses, who veiled his face to hide the fading of the glory, Paul openly stood before people with "unveiled" face, knowing that the new covenant glory would never diminish but only increase. Likewise, believers now stand unashamedly before the world, "reflecting" in their own lives the glory of Christ. Far from manifesting fading glory, believers reflect ever-increasing glory as they are changed more and more into the likeness of Christ. **transformed.** The other New Testament instances of this Greek word refer to Christ's transfiguration (Mt 17:2; Mk 9:2) and to believers' continual transformation by the renewing of their minds (Ro 12:2). **into his likeness.** A reference to growth throughout one's life into increasing Christlikeness. This is moral and spiritual growth, which Paul called "ever-increasing glory." Believers are being restored to greater and greater likeness to the image of God, an image that was marred at the fall of Adam. See *WCF* 13.3; *WLC* 82,155.

4:1 we do not lose heart. In spite of setbacks and discouragements, Paul did not give up hope, because the new covenant ministry in the transforming power of the Holy Spirit is so excellent and so powerful.

4:2 distort. That is, "adulterate, falsify." Paul would never water down the Word of God or attempt to modify or distort it just to please his hearers (cf. Gal. 1:10). He implied that his opponents practiced such deception and distortion. See *WLC* 159.

4:3 our gospel is veiled. See notes on 3:14 and 15.

4:4 The god of this age. Satan (cf. 1Jn 5:19). **this age.** This fallen, evil world prior to Christ's return, at which time he will fully bring in "the age to come" (Lk 18:30; cf. Gal 1:4; see theological article "The Plan of the Ages" at Heb 7). **they cannot see.** The Greek text has no term for "cannot" as it is used here. The words "do not" or "might not"(expressing purpose) are also acceptable translations. Unbelievers are not truly lucid in evaluating the claims of the gospel (unless God through the gospel enlightens them; 4:6).

4:5 we do not preach ourselves. The crucial issue was not whether people accepted or rejected Paul, but how they responded to Christ, whom Paul preached. Some preachers (such as Paul's opponents) focus so much on themselves that their own pride and self-exaltation veil Christ's glory.

4:6 For. The reason for not preaching oneself is that only God gives new, spiritual life. **made his light shine.** Paul drew upon the creation account (Ge 1:3) to point out the significance of the revelation of Christ. The coming of Christ and the salvation he brought began God's re-creative activity, inaugurating the new creation. For this reason, "the light of the knowledge of the glory of God" in Christ is as wondrous as the first light of creation (cf. 5:17; Jn 1:1–10; Rev 21:1–5). **glory of God.** In the Old Testament the glory of God was the bright light that surrounded the presence of God himself. It led the people out of Egypt as a pillar of cloud by day

7 But we have this treasure in jars of clay[q] to show that this all-surpassing power is
from God[r] and not from us. 8 We are hard pressed on every side,[s] but not crushed; perplexed, but not in despair; 9 persecuted,[t] but not abandoned;[u] struck down, but not destroyed.[v] 10 We always carry around in our body the death of Jesus, so that the life of Jesus
may also be revealed in our body.[w] 11 For we who are alive are always being given over
to death for Jesus' sake,[x] so that his life may be revealed in our mortal body. 12 So then,
death is at work in us, but life is at work in you.[y]
13 It is written: "I believed; therefore I have spoken."[a][z] With that same spirit of faith
we also believe and therefore speak, 14 because we know that the one who raised the
Lord Jesus from the dead will also raise us with Jesus[a] and present us with you in his
presence.[b] 15 All this is for your benefit, so that the grace that is reaching more and more
people may cause thanksgiving[c] to overflow to the glory of God.
16 Therefore we do not lose heart. Though outwardly we are wasting away, yet inwardly[d] we are being renewed[e] day by day. 17 For our light and momentary troubles are
achieving for us an eternal glory that far outweighs them all.[f] 18 So we fix our eyes not
on what is seen, but on what is unseen.[g] For what is seen is temporary, but what is unseen is eternal.

Our Heavenly Dwelling

5 Now we know that if the earthly[h] tent[i] we live in is destroyed, we have a building
from God, an eternal house in heaven, not built by human hands. 2 Meanwhile we
groan,[j] longing to be clothed with our heavenly dwelling,[k] 3 because when we are
clothed, we will not be found naked. 4 For while we are in this tent, we groan and are burdened, because we do not wish to be unclothed but to be clothed with our heavenly

4:7 [q]Job 4:19; 2Co 5:1 [r]1Co 2:5
4:8 [s]2Co 7:5
4:9 [t]Jn 15:20 [u]Heb 13:5 [v]Ps 37:24
4:10 [w]Ro 6:5
4:11 [x]Ro 8:36
4:12 [y]2Co 13:9
4:13 [z]Ps 116:10
4:14 [a]1Th 4:14 [b]Eph 5:27
4:15 [c]2Co 1:11
4:16 [d]Ro 7:22 [e]Col 3:10
4:17 [f]Ro 8:18; 1Pe 1:6,7
4:18 [g]Ro 8:24; Heb 11:1
5:1 [h]1Co 15:47 [i]2Pe 1:13,14
5:2 [j]ver 4; Ro 8:23 [k]1Co 15:53,54

[a] *13* Psalm 116:10

and a pillar of fire by night (Ex 13:21–22). Later, in Moses' time, it filled the tabernacle (Ex 33:8–13; 40:34–38) and still later, in Solomon's day, the temple (1Ki 8:10–11). But it departed from the temple in the time of Ezekiel because of the sins of the people (Eze 10:4,18–19; 11:23). It returned only in the presence of Jesus (Jn 1:14). In contrast to the face of Moses, from which God's glory faded (3:13), that glory forever shines brightly "in the face of Christ."

■ **4:7—5:10** *Jars of Clay.* These verses express the apostle's confidence in God. Despite the humble condition of his human existence, Paul experienced the glory of the new covenant (4:7–18) and kept his eyes fixed on what is unseen and eternal (4:18). As a result, he was able to surmount all manner of discouragements and adversities.

4:7 this treasure. The gospel ministry and the accompanying new covenant glory of the Holy Spirit. **jars of clay.** Our weak human natures, including, but not limited to, our physical bodies. This is in great contrast to the glory of the gospel. It is God's way to work through those who are weak or unimpressive in the world's eyes (cf. 12:9; 1Co 1:26–31).

4:8–9 but not. The apostle admitted that his ministry had been very difficult: He was hard pressed, perplexed, persecuted, struck down. Yet he affirmed that, despite these troubles, Christ had not failed to care for him: He was not crushed, in despair, abandoned or destroyed. Christian ministry is not easy, but its difficulties bring glory to God as he triumphs over them.

4:10 carry . . . the death of Jesus. Paul's suffering and outward troubles were evidence to all that he had no effective strength in himself. Just as Christ had died, Paul knew he was as good as "dead" in terms of his own ability to accomplish his ministry. Because Paul, like all believers, was in union with Christ, he spoke of Christ's death and resurrection as a pattern by which to understand his own experiences as an apostle of Christ. He saw his own sufferings as part of Christ's (see 1:5 and its note; see also theological article "Union With Christ" at Gal 6). **so that.** God used Paul's weakness as the vehicle for proclaiming Jesus' power.

4:12 death . . . in us, but life . . . in you. Although Paul suffered much hardship (as Jesus did), the result of his ministry was spiritual life and resurrection power in others. The recipients who benefit from a ministry may seem to fare much better in this world than the person who brings them that ministry and suffers much for the sake of the gospel. This follows the pattern of Christ (cf. 8:9).

4:13 believed . . . spoken. If faith is genuine, it normally expresses itself in words that affirm confidence in what God has promised. Paul quoted Psalm 116:10 from the Septuagint (the Greek translation of the OT). See *WCF* 8.8; 14.1; *WLC* 32,59,72.

4:15 your benefit . . . more and more people . . . to the glory of God. Paul outlined the goal of Christian ministry. The glory and honor of God are the final goal, but the steps toward reaching that goal include the benefit of those who receive ministry and the increasing numbers of people who benefit. The more people who are redeemed and the more greatly they are blessed, the more honor God receives (see note on 1:11).

4:16 we do not lose heart. This phrase repeats verse 1. God would bring glory to himself, even through the weaknesses and discouragements of Paul's ministry. **outwardly we are wasting away.** The contrast between outward and inward is not simply one between the body and the soul, but also between the old, fallen nature and the renewed humanity.

4:17 our light and momentary troubles. Although his trials were not minor by ordinary assessment (vv. 8–12; 6:4–10; 11:23–33), in comparison with the eternal glory that would one day be his, Paul saw them to be mild and transitory. Paul viewed troubles as preparation for a great future reward for believers. A believer's faith and obedience in suffering are pleasing and memorable to God (Ro 8:17–18; 1Pe 1:6–7). Not all suffering is in itself, however, pleasing to God. Only that endured in faith ("for Jesus' sake"; v. 11) will receive God's commendation.

4:18 what is unseen . . . is eternal. A frequent theme in this epistle. The unseen world is most important, because it will become the new heavens and the new earth we inherit when Christ returns. The visible world in which we now live is passing away.

5:1 tent. Our physical bodies. Even if Paul's earthly sufferings would lead ultimately to his physical death, something far greater awaited him. **we have.** Present tense, expressing certainty of a future event (i.e., "we will have"). **a building from God, an eternal house in heaven.** This probably refers to believers' resurrected bodies, although some have argued that this signifies the heavenly place that God has prepared for believers. **not built by human hands.** Unlike houses in this present age (Mk 14:58; Heb 9:24). See *WCF* 32.1; *WLC* 86; *WSC* 37.

5:2 we groan. Believers sigh in frustration at the limitations of this present life, with its sin, weakness and corruption (Ro 8:22–23).

5:3 naked. Paul referred to existence without a body as nakedness because human beings were not created to exist as mere spirits. This is as unnatural, as nakedness was after the fall of our first parents into sin (Ge 3:7). In the Biblical perspective, a human being is not a soul imprisoned in a body, but a soul united with a body. The temporary condition of the dead in Christ before the resurrection of the dead is extraordinary.

5:4 wish . . . to be clothed. Paul longed not for disembodiment, but for a future resurrected body, free of all the weaknesses and imperfections of this life. **what is mortal.** Our present physical

dwelling,[l] so that what is mortal may be swallowed up by life. 5Now it is God who has
made us for this very purpose and has given us the Spirit as a deposit, guaranteeing what
is to come.[m]
6Therefore we are always confident and know that as long as we are at home in the
body we are away from the Lord. 7We live by faith, not by sight.[n] 8We are confident, I say,
and would prefer to be away from the body and at home with the Lord.[o] 9So we make it
our goal to please him,[p] whether we are at home in the body or away from it. 10For we
must all appear before the judgment seat of Christ, that each one may receive what is
due him[q] for the things done while in the body, whether good or bad.

The Ministry of Reconciliation

11Since, then, we know what it is to fear the Lord,[r] we try to persuade men. What we
are is plain to God, and I hope it is also plain to your conscience.[s] 12We are not trying to
commend ourselves to you again,[t] but are giving you an opportunity to take pride in us,[u]
so that you can answer those who take pride in what is seen rather than in what is in the
heart. 13If we are out of our mind,[v] it is for the sake of God; if we are in our right mind,
it is for you. 14For Christ's love compels us, because we are convinced that one died for
all, and therefore all died.[w] 15And he died for all, that those who live should no longer
live for themselves[x] but for him who died for them and was raised again.
16So from now on we regard no one from a worldly[y] point of view. Though we once
regarded Christ in this way, we do so no longer. 17Therefore, if anyone is in Christ, he is
a new creation;[z] the old has gone, the new has come![a] 18All this is from God, who reconciled us to himself through Christ[b] and gave us the ministry of reconciliation: 19that
God was reconciling the world to himself in Christ, not counting men's sins against

5:4 [l]1Co 15:53,54
5:5 [m]Ro 8:23; 2Co 1:22
5:7 [n]1Co 13:12
5:8 [o]Php 1:23
5:9 [p]Ro 14:18
5:10 [q]Mt 16:27; Ro 14:10; Eph 6:8
5:11 [r]Heb 10:31; Jude 23 [s]2Co 4:2
5:12 [t]2Co 3:1 [u]2Co 1:14
5:13 [v]2Co 11:1,16,17
5:14 [w]Gal 2:20
5:15 [x]Ro 14:7-9
5:16 [y]2Co 11:18
5:17 [z]Gal 6:15 [a]Isa 65:17; Rev 21:4,5
5:18 [b]Ro 5:10; Col 1:20

bodies. **swallowed up by life.** New life in our resurrected bodies will replace our present existence.

5:5 deposit. See note on 1:22. The Holy Spirit's work in the believer's daily renewal and spiritual strengthening (3:18; 4:16) is a foretaste and guarantee of the future completion of that work (i.e., the believer's resurrected body and complete sanctification). See Ephesians 1:13–14. See also *HC* 1,49.

5:6 See *WCF* 32.1; *WLC* 86; *WSC* 37.

5:7 faith . . . sight. Paul distinguished between the unseen spiritual realm of God's manifest presence and the world visible to our physical eyes.

5:8 away from the body. The spirits of Christians who die before Christ returns go immediately into his presence and are "at home with the Lord," even though their dead bodies remain on Earth and are buried in the grave (Lk 23:43; Php 1:23). When Christ returns, the bodies of believers will be raised from the dead and reunited with their spirits (1Co 15:22–23; 1Th 4:14,16). See *WCF* 32.1; *WLC* 86; *WSC* 37.

5:10–11 See *WCF* 33.3.

5:10 may receive what is due him. Degrees of reward in heaven are taught in this verse. Although Christians are forgiven and will never suffer the punishments of hell (Ro 6:23; 8:1), all believers will nonetheless stand before Christ at the day of judgment to receive various degrees of reward for what they have done in this life (Mt 6:20; Lk 19:11–27; 1Co 3:12–15). This judgment will include an evaluation of the motives of their hearts (1Co 4:5). See *WCF* 33.1; *BC* 37.

▪ **5:11—6:13** *Ministry of Reconciliation.* Paul further described his efforts as an apostle, explaining that the goal of his ministry was reconciliation.

5:11 to fear the Lord. Not a terror of eternal condemnation, but a healthy, reverent fear of Christ's displeasure at the choices we have made, the "things done while in the body" (v. 10). Such fear would have been a healthy corrective for those Corinthians who were making trouble for Paul, and it will serve the same purposes in the lives of many careless Christians throughout history. See Proverbs 1:7, 9:10 and 15:33. **plain to God.** Again, a spiritual perspective not always evident to those in this present world.

5:12 who take pride in what is seen. This refers to the world's system of evaluation. This was contrary to that of Paul, a true apostle who endured troubles by focusing on the unseen and eternal (4:18). The false apostles at Corinth (11:13) were also typical representatives of the world's way of life, taking pride in outward appearance, relying on self and being driven by desires for money, power and prestige. **rather than in what is in the heart.** Paul presented the choice facing those in the visible church in Corinth who had been influenced by his opponents: They could focus on externals and performances that satisfied merely human standards, or they could look beyond externals to the contents of Paul's and his opponents' hearts. If they chose the latter, they would defend Paul ("answer those") against his accusers. Paul's heart contained a sincere commitment to proclaiming Christ without regard for personal gain.

5:13–15 See *WLC* 32,159.

5:13 out of our mind. This probably refers to times of worship and prayer during which Paul was caught up in intense awareness of the presence of God. The Greek word need not imply complete loss of awareness of one's surroundings, for it was used of people who were "astonished" or "amazed" at Christ's miracles (Mk 5:42; 6:51); it was also used by people to refer to Jesus (Mk 3:21). The apostle's point was clear: Whether he engaged in private worship of God or in ministry to the church, Paul lived for others, not for personal gain (v. 15). His opponents could not make the same claim.

5:14 Christ's love. Paul was here speaking of what Christ had done for him, so this phrase is best understood as meaning the love that comes from Christ (though grammatically it could also mean the love that believers give to Christ). **one died for all.** "All" refers to "all of us who died in Christ and now live in him" (see vv. 15–17; cf. 4:10–14); that is, "all believers."

5:16 Paul emphasized spiritual judgment and spiritual insight with regard to people's lives and situations. The experience of Christ's love moves believers to stop viewing others according to worldly standards and to grow in their ability to perceive others from the perspective of God's great act of salvation in Jesus Christ. The perspectives and values of the world no longer matter once participation in God's new creation is available to all who are in Christ. **we once regarded Christ in this way.** When Christ was regarded from a worldly point of view, he was rejected and crucified as a blasphemer and seditionist. But from a divine perspective, Christ is truly the Messiah and the Son of God through whom a new creation and reconciliation with God are given.

5:17–21 See *WCF* 11.1; *WLC* 70; *WSC* 33; *BC* 23,30,31; *HC* 56,60.

5:17 in Christ. Union with Christ summarizes our experience of redemption. Believers are chosen by God (Eph 1:4,11), justified (Ro 8:1), sanctified (1Co 1:2) and glorified (2Co 3:18) "in Christ" (see theological article "Union With Christ" at Gal 6). **he is a new creation.** Here Paul focused on the epochal significance of the believer's union with the Savior. Because Christ himself is the "last Adam" (1Co 15:45), the One in whom humanity is re-created (1Co 15:45; Gal 6:15; Eph 2:10) and who inaugurated the new age of Messianic blessing (Gal 1:4; cf. Mt 11:2–6), the believer's spiritual union with Christ is nothing less than participation in the "new creation." This phrase may also be translated "there is a new creation," in which case it may indicate that union with Christ proves that the new creation has been inaugurated (see theological article "The Plan of the Ages" at Heb 7). See *HC* 88.

5:18 All this is from God. Every change that takes place in people as they enter the new creation, as well as the new creation itself, is from God (see Ro 11:36).

them.[c] And he has committed to us the message of reconciliation. [20]We are therefore
Christ's ambassadors,[d] as though God were making his appeal through us. We implore
you on Christ's behalf: Be reconciled to God. [21]God made him who had no sin[e] to be sin[a]
for us, so that in him we might become the righteousness of God.[f]

6 As God's fellow workers[g] we urge you not to receive God's grace in vain. [2]For he
says,

> "In the time of my favor I heard you,
> and in the day of salvation I helped you."[b][h]

I tell you, now is the time of God's favor, now is the day of salvation.

Paul's Hardships

[3]We put no stumbling block in anyone's path,[i] so that our ministry will not be discredited. [4]Rather, as servants of God we commend ourselves in every way: in great endurance; in troubles, hardships and distresses; [5]in beatings, imprisonments[j] and riots; in
hard work, sleepless nights and hunger;[k] [6]in purity, understanding, patience and kindness; in the Holy Spirit[l] and in sincere love; [7]in truthful speech[m] and in the power of God;
with weapons of righteousness[n] in the right hand and in the left; [8]through glory and dishonor,[o] bad report and good report; genuine, yet regarded as impostors;[p] [9]known, yet
regarded as unknown; dying,[q] and yet we live on;[r] beaten, and yet not killed; [10]sorrow-
ful, yet always rejoicing;[s] poor, yet making many rich;[t] having nothing, and yet possessing everything.[u]

[11]We have spoken freely to you, Corinthians, and opened wide our hearts to you.[v]
[12]We are not withholding our affection from you, but you are withholding yours from us.
[13]As a fair exchange—I speak as to my children[w]—open wide your hearts also.

Do Not Be Yoked With Unbelievers

[14]Do not be yoked together[x] with unbelievers. For what do righteousness and wickedness have in common? Or what fellowship can light have with darkness?[y] [15]What har-

5:19 [c]Ro 4:8
5:20 [d]2Co 6:1; Eph 6:20
5:21 [e]Heb 4:15; 1Pe 2:22,24; 1Jn 3:5 [f]Ro 1:17
6:1 [g]1Co 3:9; 2Co 5:20
6:2 [h]Isa 49:8
6:3 [i]Ro 14:13,20; 1Co 9:12; 10:32
6:5 [j]2Co 11:23-25 [k]1Co 4:11
6:6 [l]1Th 1:5
6:7 [m]2Co 4:2 [n]2Co 10:4; Eph 6:10-18
6:8 [o]1Co 4:10 [p]Mt 27:63
6:9 [q]Ro 8:36 [r]2Co 1:8-10; 4:10,11
6:10 [s]2Co 7:4 [t]2Co 8:9 [u]Ro 8:32; 1Co 3:21
6:11 [v]2Co 7:3
6:13 [w]1Co 4:14
6:14 [x]1Co 5:9,10 [y]Eph 5:7,11; 1Jn 1:6

[a] *21* Or *be a sin offering* [b] *2* Isaiah 49:8

5:20 ambassadors. Paul used the technical term for the political office of one who represents one kingdom to another. He and the other apostles were ambassadors in a special, authoritative sense, but all Christians in imitation of Paul (1Th 1:5–7; Heb 6:10–12) bear the honor of representing Christ to the world. **Be reconciled to God.** If this verse was an appeal directly to the Corinthians, then Paul was imploring the members of the visible church in Corinth who were engaged in serious sin to "be reconciled to God." Theologically, this is not an impossible interpretation, for renewed reconciliation to God is something all believers need to seek each day in some sense (Mt 6:12; 1Jn 1:9). However, verses 16–21 have a broader scope than the Corinthian situation. They speak of a worldwide evangelistic ministry connected with Christ's completed work of redemption. Moreover, the word "you" in the phrase "we implore you" is not in the Greek text, making it likely that Paul was simply describing his evangelistic appeal to all people: "Be reconciled to God." Reconciliation is the restoration of loving fellowship after estrangement. See *WLC* 67; *BC* 10,31.

5:21 Christ did not actually become corrupted by sin. Rather, God as judge counted Christ as being guilty of our sin and thereby reckoned him as worthy of being punished for that sin (Isa 53:6; 1Pe 2:24). Christ was our substitute, bearing our sin and dying in our place. **we might become the righteousness of God.** Not only did God reckon our sin to Christ's account, he also reckoned Christ's perfect obedience to our account, so that we are counted as having kept the law flawlessly. This provides the basis for the progressive conforming of our moral character, thoughts and deeds to God's standard of justice, until we perfectly meet that standard when we enter into the presence of God in heaven. See *WCF* 11.1; 11.3; *WLC* 70,71; *WSC* 33; *HC* 15,17,36,38,60.

6:1–2 See *WLC* 67.

6:1 in vain. Two senses of this verse are possible. First, Paul may have meant that if the believing Corinthians allowed their church to be swept away by the "false apostles" (11:13), or if they refused to purify themselves from "everything that contaminates body and spirit" (7:1), their lives would glorify God less and less, so that the saving grace they received would bring less benefit to them in this life and fewer eternal rewards (5:10). Second, Paul may have meant that, in extreme cases, some within the visible church might prove that their faith was not saving faith (see theological article "The Church: Visible and Invisible" at 1 Pe 4). In these cases, even though they experienced the results of saving grace in their community (Heb 6:4–6), they did not receive that grace for themselves (see theological article "The Perseverance and Preservation of Believers" at Php 1).

6:2 now is the time of God's favor. When God offers help, it is wise to respond immediately, before the offer is withdrawn. "Now," in a broad sense, refers to the whole gospel age, but in a specific sense it refers to the actual time in life when an individual hears God's offer of help.

6:3 Paul's goal was never his own comfort or security or welfare, but the spread of the gospel, the salvation of the lost, the building of the church and the glory of God. He sought to defend his own ministry only in order to further those goals.

6:4 we commend ourselves. Not for his own benefit, but for the spread of the gospel. Moreover, Paul commended his ministry by actions that clearly showed that his goal was not his own welfare but the progress of the gospel (vv. 4–10).

6:6 Characteristics of the behavior of a true minister of the gospel are pure speech, pure conduct, pure motives and deep love for people. **in the Holy Spirit.** The power of the Holy Spirit was evident in Paul's ministry, whether through infusing his preaching with power, convicting unbelievers of sin (cf. Jn 16:8–11) or disseminating spiritual gifts (1Co 12:7–11). This work of the Holy Spirit was another way by which Paul's ministry was commended.

6:7 truthful speech. Paul would not compromise the sanctity of truth or tell a lie to accomplish some desirable goal. **the power of God.** Often to work miracles, bring healing or silence enemies (cf. Ac 14:3,9–10; 19:11–12; 20:10; 28:8–9; Ro 15:19). **weapons.** To be used against human and demonic opposition (cf. Ac 13:11; 16:18; 2Co 10:5–6; Eph 6:10–18).

6:8–10 A series of paradoxes again highlighting the contrast between the perspective of this world and that of the age to come, which is invisible to the natural eye but seen by the eye of faith. See 4:8–9.

6:11 opened wide our hearts to you. Paul had revealed his innermost feelings in this letter, perhaps more than in any other. His open heart revealed his love for the Corinthians.

■ **6:14—7:4** *Separation From Evil.* After revealing his tender heart to the Corinthians to assure them of his good intentions toward them, Paul wrote about a difficult matter: separation from the pagan influences surrounding them.

6:14–16 See *WCF* 29.8.

mony is there between Christ and Belial[a]? What does a believer[z] have in common with
an unbeliever? 16What agreement is there between the temple of God and idols? For we
are the temple[a] of the living God. As God has said: "I will live with them and walk among
them, and I will be their God, and they will be my people."[b] [b]

17 "Therefore come out from them[c]
and be separate,
says the Lord.
Touch no unclean thing,
and I will receive you."[c] [d]
18 "I will be a Father to you,
and you will be my sons and daughters,[e]
says the Lord Almighty."[d]

7 Since we have these promises,[f] dear friends, let us purify ourselves from everything
that contaminates body and spirit, perfecting holiness out of reverence for God.

Paul's Joy

2Make room for us in your hearts.[g] We have wronged no one, we have corrupted no
one, we have exploited no one. 3I do not say this to condemn you; I have said before that
you have such a place in our hearts[h] that we would live or die with you. 4I have great confidence in you; I take great pride in you. I am greatly encouraged; in all our troubles my
joy knows no bounds.[i]
5For when we came into Macedonia,[j] this body of ours had no rest, but we were harassed at every turn[k]—conflicts on the outside, fears within.[l] 6But God, who comforts
the downcast,[m] comforted us by the coming of Titus,[n] 7and not only by his coming but
also by the comfort you had given him. He told us about your longing for me, your deep
sorrow, your ardent concern for me, so that my joy was greater than ever.
8Even if I caused you sorrow by my letter,[o] I do not regret it. Though I did regret it—
I see that my letter hurt you, but only for a little while— 9yet now I am happy, not because you were made sorry, but because your sorrow led you to repentance. For you be-

6:15 [z]Ac 5:14
6:16 [a]1Co 3:16 [b]Lev 26:12; Jer 32:38; Eze 37:27
6:17 [c]Rev 18:4 [d]Isa 52:11
6:18 [e]Isa 43:6
7:1 [f]2Co 6:17,18
7:2 [g]2Co 6:12,13
7:3 [h]2Co 6:11,12
7:4 [i]2Co 6:10
7:5 [j]2Co 2:13 [k]2Co 4:8 [l]Dt 32:25
7:6 [m]2Co 1:3,4 [n]ver 13; 2Co 2:13
7:8 [o]2Co 2:2,4

[a] *15* Greek *Beliar,* a variant of *Belial* [b] *16* Lev. 26:12; Jer. 32:38; Ezek. 37:27 [c] *17* Isaiah 52:11; Ezek. 20:34,41 [d] *18* 2 Samuel 7:14; 7:8

6:14 yoked together. Paul saw a deeper, spiritual reality represented by the prohibition of unequal yoking conveyed in a literal sense in Deuteronomy 22:10. **with unbelievers.** Note that the false apostles in Corinth were claiming to be Christians but were in reality servants of Satan (11:13–15). To join with them would distort all life and ministry in the church. This prohibition against being yoked together with unbelievers has broader applications in situations where significant control over one's actions would be willingly yielded to an unbeliever through a voluntary partnership (such as in marriage or the submission of disputes between Christians to secular courts). However, neither Paul nor any other New Testament writer ever instructed the church not to associate with unbelievers at all (Mk 2:15–17; 1Co 5:9–10). We are told not to be "yoked together" with them in such a way that they share significantly in the direction and outcome of our activities. See *WCF* 24.3.
6:15 Belial? Meaning "wicked" and "lawless." A name for Satan derived from the Old Testament (see Dt 13:13). See *BC* 35.
6:16 we are the temple of the living God. In the Old Testament, the place of God's special dwelling on Earth was the tabernacle; later, the temple that Solomon built. When Christ came, he was the true temple, or dwelling place, of God (Jn 2:21; Col 2:9). Now, through the Holy Spirit's power and gifting, God also manifests himself in glorious ways in the church, which is the new temple of God (1Co 3:16–17; 6:19; 1Pe 2:5). **As God has said.** Paul's quotation is mostly from Leviticus 26:11–12. This Old Testament promise that God would dwell among his people as a reward for faithful obedience has become a new covenant promise of God's presence to those who trust in Christ. See *WCF* 19.6.
6:17 This quotation is mostly from Isaiah 52:11, which commanded Israel to go out from unbelieving Babylon and return to the promised land. These commands to separate have to do with breaking away from unbelievers. These verses should not be used to encourage disassociation with true believers who hold differing views on non-essential matters, nor should they be used to support the cutting off of all significant contact with unbelievers (1Co 5:9–10). The phrase "I will receive you" is from the Septuagint (the Greek translation of the OT) rendering of Ezekiel 20:34, where the same phrase is translated "I will . . . gather you." See *WCF* 19.3.
6:18 This verse refers in large part to 2 Samuel 7:14 but alludes to many passages that refer to God's presence and favor toward his people. The fulfillment of these offers depends on Christians separating themselves from moral impurity. See *WCF* 12; *WLC* 74.
7:1 these promises. The Old Testament promises quoted in 6:16–18. **let us purify ourselves.** This implies an active, vigorous role that believers must play in their sanctification (Php 2:12–13). See *WCF* 13.1; 13.3; 18.3; *WLC* 77. **everything that contaminates body and spirit.** Some sins (such as drunkenness or gluttony) defile our bodies, while others (such as bitterness or jealousy) defile our spirits. Both must be eliminated through cleansing.
7:2 A repeated plea from 6:12–13. **We have wronged no one.** Once again, in defense against those who would accuse him, Paul claimed a blameless record for his ministry.
7:3 Paul revealed how deeply he loved the church at Corinth. This was not deceitful speech, but "truthful" (6:7).
7:4 Although there was still some opposition from false apostles and perhaps from some others in the congregation, Paul's overall attitude toward the Corinthian congregation was positive.
■ **7:5–16** *Joy at the Coming of Titus.* Paul resumed the narrative of his travels, which had broken off at 2:13.
7:5 Macedonia. Northern Greece, which was on Paul's route to Corinth (see notes on 2:12,13). **conflicts on the outside, fears within.** Paul was deeply troubled about the condition of the Corinthian church as he traveled toward Macedonia and waited for news from Titus. His admission reveals the heart of one who cared deeply for the well-being of the church and of his fellow believers.
7:6 Titus had finally arrived in Macedonia with good news about the Corinthians and their response to Paul's "severe letter" (see "Introduction: Time and Place of Writing").
7:8 my letter. Paul's "severe letter" (no longer extant) was written to rebuke the Corinthians for their conduct during his "painful visit" (see notes on 2:3,4; see also "Introduction: Time and Place of Writing"). The problem was probably their failure as a church to defend Paul against the person who had wronged him. This verse provides a clear example of the fact that loving leaders of the church must sometimes rebuke and discipline those under their care, thereby causing them sorrow.

came sorrowful as God intended and so were not harmed in any way by us. [10]Godly sorrow brings repentance that leads to salvation[p] and leaves no regret, but worldly sorrow
brings death. [11]See what this godly sorrow has produced in you: what earnestness, what
eagerness to clear yourselves, what indignation, what alarm, what longing, what concern,[q] what readiness to see justice done. At every point you have proved yourselves to
be innocent in this matter. [12]So even though I wrote to you,[r] it was not on account of the
one who did the wrong[s] or of the injured party, but rather that before God you could see
for yourselves how devoted to us you are. [13]By all this we are encouraged.

In addition to our own encouragement, we were especially delighted to see how happy Titus[t] was, because his spirit has been refreshed by all of you. [14]I had boasted to him
about you,[u] and you have not embarrassed me. But just as everything we said to you was
true, so our boasting about you to Titus[v] has proved to be true as well. [15]And his affection for you is all the greater when he remembers that you were all obedient,[w] receiving him with fear and trembling.[x] [16]I am glad I can have complete confidence in you.[y]

Generosity Encouraged

8 And now, brothers, we want you to know about the grace that God has given the
Macedonian[z] churches. [2]Out of the most severe trial, their overflowing joy and their
extreme poverty welled up in rich generosity. [3]For I testify that they gave as much as they
were able,[a] and even beyond their ability. Entirely on their own, [4]they urgently pleaded with us for the privilege of sharing in this service[b] to the saints.[c] [5]And they did not
do as we expected, but they gave themselves first to the Lord and then to us in keeping
with God's will. [6]So we urged[d] Titus,[e] since he had earlier made a beginning, to bring
also to completion[f] this act of grace on your part. [7]But just as you excel in everything[g]—
in faith, in speech, in knowledge,[h] in complete earnestness and in your love for us[a]—see
that you also excel in this grace of giving.

[8]I am not commanding you,[i] but I want to test the sincerity of your love by comparing it with the earnestness of others. [9]For you know the grace of our Lord Jesus Christ,[j]
that though he was rich, yet for your sakes he became poor,[k] so that you through his poverty might become rich.

7:10 [p]Ac 11:18
7:11 [q]ver 7
7:12 [r]ver 8; 2Co 2:3,9 [s]1Co 5:1,2
7:13 [t]ver 6; 2Co 2:13
7:14 [u]ver 4 [v]ver 6
7:15 [w]2Co 2:9 [x]Php 2:12
7:16 [y]2Co 2:3
8:1 [z]Ac 16:9
8:3 [a]1Co 16:2
8:4 [b]Ac 24:17 [c]Ro 15:25; 2Co 9:1
8:6 [d]ver 17; 2Co 12:18 [e]ver 16,23 [f]ver 10, 11
8:7 [g]2Co 9:8 [h]1Co 1:5
8:8 [i]1Co 7:6
8:9 [j]2Co 13:14 [k]Mt 20:28; Php 2:6-8

[a] 7 Some manuscripts *in our love for you*

7:9 as God intended. When sin is present in the lives of Christians, God desires not that they deny it, but that they experience sincere sorrow and repentance (see theological article "The Will of God" at Ecc 10).

7:10 repentance. Turning from sin, which includes a sincere decision to forsake a specific sin (or sins) and to begin to obey God. As used here, the term does not specifically refer to initial repentance that must accompany true, saving faith (Mk 1:15; Ac 3:19; 17:30; 26:20) but to a continual turning from sin in the life of a Christian (see theological article "Repentance" at Ps 51). **leads to salvation.** As used here, this phrase refers to growth and progress in the Christian life. Godly sorrow and repentance lead to greater and greater appropriation of the blessings of salvation, culminating in the believer going to be with the Lord (cf. a similar use of the word "salvation" in 1Pe 1:9). Ordinary Christian growth will include times of profound sorrow for remaining sin. **worldly sorrow.** With no hope of forgiveness in Christ. See *HC* 89.

7:11 The Corinthians had responded to the "severe letter" brought by Titus exactly as Paul had hoped they would. See *WCF* 15.2; *WLC* 76,175; *WSC* 87.

7:12 the one who did the wrong. Probably does not refer to the man guilty of incest (as recorded in 1Co 5:1), although many have held this interpretation throughout the history of the church (see note on 2:5). **before God.** The Christian life is lived before the face of God. **devoted to us.** Their response demonstrated that they were ready to follow Paul's apostolic leadership and authority, fulfilling his hopes for the letter he had sent.

7:13 his spirit has been refreshed. There is a personal ministry of refreshment and renewal in the spiritual realm whereby, through Christian fellowship, believers' spirits become refreshed. Titus had experienced that refreshment in Corinth.

7:15 receiving him with fear and trembling. Apparently, even before Titus arrived with Paul's "severe letter," the Holy Spirit had worked repentance in the Corinthian church concerning the conduct of its members during Paul's brief visit.

7:16 Paul's confidence in the Corinthian church had been restored, even though there were matters yet to be dealt with concerning the false apostles (chs. 10–13).

■ **8:1—9:15** *Collection for Christians in Jerusalem.* At this point Paul turned to another major topic in this epistle: collecting money for the impoverished Christians in Jerusalem (see also Ac 19:21–22; Ro 15:25–28; 1Co 16:1–4). His discussion divides into three parts: the example set by the Macedonian believers (8:1–7), Jesus' example (8:8–9) and a moderate plea for help (8:10—9:15).

8:1–24 See *WCF* 26.2.

8:1–9 See *HC* 103.

■ **8:1–7** *Macedonia's Example.* Paul began his appeal for financial assistance for the church in Jerusalem by telling the Corinthians how generously believers in Macedonia had given.

8:1 grace. Their ability to give money to help other Christians in need was itself a result of God's grace, for God had granted them both the resources and the willingness to give. **Macedonian churches.** Philippi, Thessalonica, Berea.

8:3 they gave. Paul motivated the Corinthians by praising the impoverished (v. 2) churches in Macedonia (northern Greece) for their generosity when the comparatively wealthy (v. 14) Corinthian church (in Achaia, in southern Greece) had still not carried through with a contribution.

8:5 they did not do as we expected. Rather, they did much more than expected. **they gave themselves first to the Lord.** They rededicated their lives to service for the Lord, to obedience to Paul and to sharing in his ministry.

8:7 you excel in everything. The church in Corinth was strong in many ways. Its members had many spiritual gifts (1Co 12–14), including great faith, knowledge, speaking gifts, zeal and love.

■ **8:8–9** *Jesus' Example.* Paul appealed next to the example of Jesus' self-sacrifice as motivation for giving to the church in Jerusalem.

8:8 I am not commanding you. Paul preferred giving to be voluntary. Although Paul had great authority, he preferred to ask rather than to command (e.g., Phm 8–9), a good pattern for all in authority to follow.

8:9 though he was rich. In the glory and honor that were eternally his in heaven. **he became poor.** Christ gave up his heavenly glory in order to live as a man and to suffer and die. The Corinthians, like Christ, should give of themselves for the sake of others. See *WLC* 46.

■ **8:10—9:15** *A Reasonable Plea.* In the final analysis, Paul asked

10And here is my advice[l] about what is best for you in this matter: Last year you were
the first not only to give but also to have the desire to do so.[m] **11**Now finish the work, so
that your eager willingness[n] to do it may be matched by your completion of it, according to your means. **12**For if the willingness is there, the gift is acceptable according to
what one has,[o] not according to what he does not have.
13Our desire is not that others might be relieved while you are hard pressed, but that
there might be equality. **14**At the present time your plenty will supply what they need,[p]
so that in turn their plenty will supply what you need. Then there will be equality, **15**as
it is written: "He who gathered much did not have too much, and he who gathered little did not have too little."[a][q]

Titus Sent to Corinth

16I thank God,[r] who put into the heart[s] of Titus[t] the same concern I have for you.
17For Titus not only welcomed our appeal, but he is coming to you with much enthusiasm and on his own initiative.[u] **18**And we are sending along with him the brother[v] who
is praised by all the churches[w] for his service to the gospel.[x] **19**What is more, he was chosen by the churches to accompany us[y] as we carry the offering, which we administer in
order to honor the Lord himself and to show our eagerness to help.[z] **20**We want to avoid
any criticism of the way we administer this liberal gift. **21**For we are taking pains to do
what is right, not only in the eyes of the Lord but also in the eyes of men.[a]
22In addition, we are sending with them our brother who has often proved to us in
many ways that he is zealous, and now even more so because of his great confidence in
you. **23**As for Titus, he is my partner[b] and fellow worker[c] among you; as for our brothers,[d] they are representatives of the churches and an honor to Christ. **24**Therefore show
these men the proof of your love and the reason for our pride in you,[e] so that the
churches can see it.

9 There is no need[f] for me to write to you about this service to the saints.[g] **2**For I know
your eagerness to help, and I have been boasting[h] about it to the Macedonians, telling them that since last year[i] you in Achaia[j] were ready to give; and your enthusiasm has
stirred most of them to action. **3**But I am sending the brothers in order that our boasting about you in this matter should not prove hollow, but that you may be ready, as I said
you would be.[k] **4**For if any Macedonians[l] come with me and find you unprepared, we—
not to say anything about you—would be ashamed of having been so confident. **5**So I
thought it necessary to urge the brothers to visit you in advance and finish the arrangements for the generous gift you had promised. Then it will be ready as a generous gift,[m]
not as one grudgingly given.[n]

8:10 [l]1Co 7:25,40 [m]1Co 16:2,3; 2Co 9:2
8:11 [n]2Co 9:2
8:12 [o]Mk 12:43,44; Lk 21:3
8:14 [p]2Co 9:12
8:15 [q]Ex 16:18
8:16 [r]2Co 2:14 [s]Rev 17:17 [t]2Co 2:13
8:17 [u]ver 6
8:18 [v]2Co 12:18 [w]1Co 7:17 [x]2Co 2:12
8:19 [y]1Co 16:3,4 [z]ver 11,12
8:21 [a]Ro 12:17; 14:18
8:23 [b]Phm 17 [c]Php 2:25 [d]ver 18,22
8:24 [e]2Co 7:4,14; 9:2
9:1 [f]1Th 4:9 [g]2Co 8:4
9:2 [h]2Co 7:4,14 [i]2Co 8:10 [j]Ac 18:12
9:3 [k]1Co 16:2
9:4 [l]Ro 15:26
9:5 [m]Php 4:17 [n]2Co 12:17,18

a *15* Exodus 16:18

very little of the Corinthians. He encouraged them with a reasonable and practical program for collecting funds for Jerusalem.
8:10 Last year. They had begun to give in accordance with Paul's instructions in 1 Corinthians 16:1–3.
8:11 willingness . . . completion. As in all of the Christian life, so it is in giving: Actions must stem from good motives, and good motives must be demonstrated by actions.
8:12 As with the poor widow's offering in Mark 12:41–44, so it is here. The intensity of the giver's desire and willingness to give generously is pleasing to God, even when the gift is small because the donor is poor. **not according to what he does not have.** A warning against giving or promising to give an amount in excess of one's resources or ability, hoping that God will repay the amount. This is forcing a test on God (Lk 4:12). People are to give as God enables them (1Co 16:2). Yet the other (and far more common) error is that of failing to give immediately and generously when God does provide additional income. See *WCF* 16.6.
8:13 equality. The word translated "equality" can be rendered "fairness," which is the meaning it takes in Colossians 4:1 ("what is . . . fair"). It calls for equity rather than strict equality. Nowhere in Paul's writings did he indicate that he wanted all Christians to have equal possessions or equal income. Here he expressed the desire that there might be a fair distribution of the burden of caring for the poor.
8:15 Paul referred to Exodus 16:18, where those who gathered more manna shared with those who gathered less; he applied this principle to the Corinthians, who should share with those in need. See *HC* 103.
8:17 Paul sent Titus back to Corinth ahead of him.
8:18 the brother who is praised by all the churches. This Christian brother is not identified here. This may be a reference to Paul's frequent companion Luke (the most commonly proposed name), but Barnabas and Tychicus (Ac 20:4) have also been proposed, as well as several others. There is not enough information to make a definitive identification.
8:19 chosen by the churches. This suggests some congregational role in the selection of representatives to accompany Paul. **to honor the Lord himself.** The giving of money and the proper administration of that gift is not mundane or unspiritual, for in itself it honors the Lord.
8:20–21 Paul had the highest degree of personal integrity and practical wisdom. He wanted to assure the Corinthians that he would not misuse the smallest portion of the gift sent to Jerusalem. He insisted that trusted representatives from several churches accompany him (Ac 20:4), so as to avoid even the appearance of wrongdoing. These men would also have provided protection for Paul against thieves or hostile Jews (Ac 20:3).
8:22 our brother. This brother's identity is also unknown (see note on v. 18).
8:24 The Corinthians' giving would be known not only to God, but also to many other churches. This would allow other Christians to praise God for the good works done through the Corinthian believers, just as Paul and his coworkers took pride in the good works God had done and was continuing to do in the church at Corinth.
9:1–15 See *WCF* 26.2.
9:2 Achaia. Southern Greece, where Corinth was located. See *WCF* 16.2.
9:4 Paul continued to remind the Corinthians that they should complete their gift, for their giving would be seen by Titus, other church representatives, the Macedonians, Paul and ultimately God (8:23–24; 9:2,4,7).
9:5 as a generous gift. Paul wanted to preserve the motive of willing, generous giving. The actual amount he took to Jerusalem was of secondary importance to this concern.

Sowing Generously

6 Remember this: Whoever sows sparingly will also reap sparingly, and whoever sows
generously will also reap generously.[o] 7 Each man should give what he has decided in his
heart to give,[p] not reluctantly or under compulsion,[q] for God loves a cheerful giver.[r]
8 And God is able[s] to make all grace abound to you, so that in all things at all times, having all that you need,[t] you will abound in every good work. 9 As it is written:

> "He has scattered abroad his gifts to the poor;
> his righteousness endures forever."[a][u]

10 Now he who supplies seed to the sower and bread for food[v] will also supply and increase your store of seed and will enlarge the harvest of your righteousness.[w] 11 You will
be made rich[x] in every way so that you can be generous on every occasion, and through
us your generosity will result in thanksgiving to God.[y]
12 This service that you perform is not only supplying the needs[z] of God's people but is
also overflowing in many expressions of thanks to God.[a] 13 Because of the service[b] by which
you have proved yourselves, men will praise God[c] for the obedience that accompanies your
confession of the gospel of Christ,[d] and for your generosity in sharing with them and with
everyone else. 14 And in their prayers for you their hearts will go out to you, because of the
surpassing grace God has given you. 15 Thanks be to God[e] for his indescribable gift![f]

Paul's Defense of His Ministry

10 By the meekness and gentleness[g] of Christ, I appeal to you—I, Paul,[h] who am
"timid" when face to face with you, but "bold" when away! 2 I beg you that when
I come I may not have to be as bold[i] as I expect to be toward some people who think that
we live by the standards of this world. 3 For though we live in the world, we do not wage
war as the world does. 4 The weapons we fight with[j] are not the weapons of the world.
On the contrary, they have divine power[k] to demolish strongholds.[l] ■ 5 We demolish arguments and every pretension that sets itself up against the knowledge of God,[m] and we
take captive every thought to make it obedient[n] to Christ. 6 And we will be ready to punish every act of disobedience, once your obedience is complete.[o]
7 You are looking only on the surface of things.[b][p] If anyone is confident that he belongs to Christ,[q] he should consider again that we belong to Christ just as much as he.[r]

9:6 [o]Pr 11:24,25; 22:9; Gal 6:7,9
9:7 [p]Ex 25:2; 2Co 8:12 [q]Dt 15:10 [r]Ro 12:8
9:8 [s]Eph 3:20 [t]Php 4:19
9:9 [u]Ps 112:9
9:10 [v]Isa 55:10 [w]Hos 10:12
9:11 [x]1Co 1:5 [y]2Co 1:11
9:12 [z]2Co 8:14 [a]2Co 1:11
9:13 [b]2Co 8:4 [c]Mt 9:8 [d]2Co 2:12
9:15 [e]2Co 2:14 [f]Ro 5:15,16
10:1 [g]Mt 11:29 [h]Gal 5:2
10:2 [i]1Co 4:21; 2Co 13:2,10
10:4 [j]2Co 6:7 [k]1Co 2:5 [l]Jer 1:10; 2Co 13:10
10:5 [m]Isa 2:11,12, 1Co 1:19 [n]2Co 9:13
10:6 [o]2Co 2:9; 7:15
10:7 [p]Jn 7:24 [q]1Co 1:12; 3:23; 14:37 [r]2Co 11:23

[a] 9 Psalm 112:9 [b] 7 Or *Look at the obvious facts*

9:6 An agricultural metaphor—the farmer who plants much seed eventually reaps a large crop, but a small planting yields a proportionately smaller harvest. Paul assured the Corinthians that God would not overlook their generosity. What is given is not lost; it is sown. In this verse Paul spoke of sowing not in the "field" of business investments, but in the "field" of the spiritual kingdom. The expected harvest would be in this realm also. At times, God grants generous physical and material blessings to those who are generous, but such blessings are not guaranteed in this life (cf. 8:9; 11:27; Lk 6:20–21,24–25; Jas 2:5). The Holy Spirit is the only guaranteed blessing given to every believer during his or her life on this earth (1:22; 5:5; Eph 1:14).
9:7 In giving willingly, believers honor God by imitating the generosity of their Creator. **God loves a cheerful giver.** Giving can and should be joyful, for it is done as an act of obedience. Obedience is to be a matter of delight for believers.
9:8 If the Corinthians gave generously, they were not to worry about their own future needs. They would be under the blessing of the sovereign God, who would supply their needs as he saw fit (Php 4:19).
9:10 As they gave, God would increase their ability to give.
9:13–14 The benefits of giving are at least these: Needs are met, God is thanked and recipients pray for those who have given.
9:15 Our giving is only a small imitation of God's own excellent generosity to us, particularly in the giving of his Son (Jn 3:16).
■ **10:1—13:10** *Defense Against False Apostles.* In these four chapters Paul dealt with the problem of false apostles (11:13) who had opposed his authority. Even though Titus had brought good news about the resolution of previous problems at Corinth, this additional problem demanded Paul's attention. Paul had expressed confidence in the Corinthian church as a whole (7:16), but not all the Corinthians were fully persuaded to support him. Between 9:12–15 and 10:1 Paul's tone changed abruptly from hope and thanksgiving to exasperation as he found himself forced to defend the genuineness of his calling as an apostle. Paul's attention to this problem divides into three main parts: Paul's spiritual power (10:1–12), his boasting (10:13—12:21) and a solemn warning (13:1–10).
■ ***10:1–12** *Spiritual Power.* Paul challenged his opponents by calling attention to the divine power that accompanied his ministry.
10:3 as the world does. Paul was deeply concerned that the Corinthians remember the Christian view on spiritual warfare. Spiritual warfare is not waged as the nations of the world fight wars.
10:4–5 See *WLC* 155.
10:4 weapons. Prayer, the proclamation of the powerful Word of God, and authority to drive away demonic opposition (Ac 16:18; Eph 6:10–18). Moreover, there was a kind of powerful apostolic authority that one glimpses only slightly in Peter's confrontations of Ananias and Sapphira (Ac 5:1–11) and of Elymas (Ac 13:8–12). This apostolic authority had irresistible power when it was used (see note on Jn 14:13). **strongholds.** In the spiritual realm (which was what Paul was talking about), the word "strongholds" (or "fortresses") refers to centers of demonic opposition to the gospel (1Pe 5:8–9; 1Jn 5:19). Paul recognized that his opponents in Corinth were servants of Satan (11:14–15), but that knowledge did not frighten him, for the power of the Holy Spirit within him was far greater.
10:5 We demolish arguments. False wisdom and sophisticated arguments were some of the weapons used by those servants of Satan in their attack against Paul. Paul had earlier stressed the difference between the wisdom of the world and the spiritual wisdom of the message of the cross, and he had warned the Corinthians against being deluded by the world's brand of wisdom (1Co 1:18—2:16). Now Paul saw that his opponents had made such inroads with their false wisdom that he had to oppose them in the strongest terms and, at the same time, gain back the loyalty and obedience of the Corinthian Christians. **take captive every thought.** If every thought, then the whole person: every idea, motive, desire and decision.
10:6 ready to punish. If the Corinthians would join ranks in opposing these false apostles, Paul was ready to exercise [illegible] discipline directed toward the false apostles for the [illegible] brought to the church. See *BC* 36.

10:8 [s]2Co 13:10
10:10 [t]1Co 2:3; Gal 4:13, 14 [u]1Co 1:17
10:12 [v]2Co 3:1

8 For even if I boast somewhat freely about the authority the Lord gave us for building you
up rather than pulling you down,[s] I will not be ashamed of it. 9 I do not want to seem to
be trying to frighten you with my letters. 10 For some say, "His letters are weighty and
forceful, but in person he is unimpressive[t] and his speaking amounts to nothing."[u]
11 Such people should realize that what we are in our letters when we are absent, we will
be in our actions when we are present.
12 We do not dare to classify or compare ourselves with some who commend themselves.[v] When they measure themselves by themselves and compare themselves with
themselves, they are not wise. 13 We, however, will not boast beyond proper limits, but will

---

10:8 Paul knew that he must call upon the authority Christ had given him and warn the Corinthians that he was ready to exercise that authority (see note on v. 4).
10:10 his speaking amounts to nothing. Paul did not use the kind of trained oratory prized by the world and designed to elicit glory for the speaker. Those influenced by Paul's opponents devalued Paul's ministry because he lacked or chose not to use this skill (cf. notes on 1Co 1:17; 2:1).
10:11 See note on verse 4.
10:12 classify or compare ourselves. Encouraged by rival "apostles," some influential Corinthians had begun to consider these latecomers as superior to Paul. Paul was judged deficient as a speaker (v. 10; 11:5), vacillating between boldness while absent and timidity when present (vv. 10–11), unloving toward them (in refusing a monetary gift that, in their view, snubbed them as inferiors; 11:7–11; 12:14–18) and deficient in certain religious experiences of "power" (12:1–5). Paul chose to deal with this problem by declining to compare himself with his opponents in a straightforward manner because the standards of comparison chosen by the Corinthians (the wisdom of the world) were faulty. Instead, Paul compared himself with his opponents in a somewhat ironic manner, using a form of comparison, but in content showing the utter contrast between them and himself (11:16—12:10).
■ **10:13—12:21** *Boasting.* As Paul continued to defend himself

The Apostles: Can There Be Apostles Today?

REFORMED theology has consistently denied that there can be modern authoritative apostles. Some Christian traditions, however, still ordain people to the office of apostle. Roman Catholicism, for example, insists that certain elements of function and authority that once belonged to the apostles have been handed down to bishops through apostolic succession, without the personal prerogatives that the apostles themselves possessed. As a result, they believe that the bishops collectively retain the right to make authoritative judgments regarding doctrine, just as the apostles had authority to do on an individual level. In a sense, they believe in the continuation of a modified form of the office of apostle. Although some Protestant traditions also believe that the office of apostle continues, they usually distinguish modern apostles from the original apostles in one way or another.

The Bible uses the word "apostle" in two distinct senses. On the one hand, it often refers to one of "the Twelve," Jesus original 12 disciples (Mt 10:2–4), with the subsequent replacement of Judas Iscariot with Matthias (Ac 1:15–26) and the addition of Paul (e.g., Tit 1:1). This use refers to the miracle-working, Christ-commissioned, authoritative office of apostle and is the more common meaning in the New Testament. This is the meaning intended in passages describing the requirements for the office of apostle (Ac 1:15–26; 1Co 9:1–2; 15:7–8; 2Co 12:12; Gal 1:1). These requirements include the following: seeing and being taught by the Lord Jesus (Ac 1:20–26; 1Co 9:1; Gal 1:11–18); working signs, wonders and miracles (2Co 12:12); and being commissioned by God himself (Ac 1:24–26). When Reformed theologians deny the possibility of modern apostles, it is to this office that they refer.

Reformed theologians have offered a variety of reasons that there can be no authoritative apostles today. (1) Paul was the last person to whom the [illegible]n Lord appeared, and the circumstances of this event were so unusual that we should not expect them to be repeated (1Co 15:8). Since meeting the risen Lord is a qualification for the office (1Co 9:1), modern apostles are excluded. (2) The office of apostle was *foundational,* meaning that it pertained only to the period of the founding of the church (1Co 3:10–12; Eph 2:20). (3) Paul recognized apostleship as the greatest spiritual gift and encouraged believers to seek the greatest gifts (1Co 12:28–31). Nevertheless, the highest gift to which he encouraged believers to aspire was the second highest gift: prophecy (1Co 12:28; 14:1). This indicates his assumption that no one else could hold the office of apostle.

On the other hand, the Greek word translated "apostle" is also used to refer to people beyond the Twelve and Paul, such as Andronicus and Junias (Ro 16:7), Barnabas (1Co 9:5–6), unnamed brethren (translated "representatives" in 2Co 8:23), James (Gal 1:19), Epaphroditus (translated "messenger" in Php 2:25), and Silas and Timothy (1Th 2:6–7; cf. 1:1). It cannot be possible that all these others fulfilled the aforementioned requirements; Timothy, for instance, never saw the risen Lord. Moreover, the Bible provides no evidence that any of these others were called to service directly by God. The meaning of "apostle" in these instances is more general, referring to those commissioned and sent by the church for the work of the ministry or simply as messengers. These individuals did not carry the delegated authority of Christ. The distinction of this meaning from that of the authoritative office of apostle is possibly reflected in the description of Paul and Peter as apostles "of Christ Jesus" (1Co 1:1; 2Co 1:1; Eph 1:1; 1Ti 1:1; 2Ti 1:1; cf. Tit 1:1; 1Pe 1:1; 2Pe 1:1), while certain unnamed brethren were apostles or messengers "of the churches" (see 2Co 8:23, where the Greek term elsewhere translated "apostles" is rendered "representatives"). Such apostles of the churches may still exist today.

confine our boasting to the field God has assigned to us,[w] a field that reaches even to you.
14 We are not going too far in our boasting, as would be the case if we had not come to you,
for we did get as far as you[x] with the gospel of Christ.[y] 15 Neither do we go beyond our limits by boasting of work done by others.[a z] Our hope is that, as your faith continues to
grow,[a] our area of activity among you will greatly expand, 16 so that we can preach the gospel in the regions beyond you.[b] For we do not want to boast about work already done in
another man's territory. 17 But, "Let him who boasts boast in the Lord."[b c] 18 For it is not the
one who commends himself[d] who is approved, but the one whom the Lord commends.[e]

Paul and the False Apostles

11 I hope you will put up with[f] a little of my foolishness;[g] but you are already doing that. 2 I am jealous for you with a godly jealousy. I promised you to one husband,[h] to Christ, so that I might present you[i] as a pure virgin to him. 3 But I am afraid that
just as Eve was deceived by the serpent's cunning,[j] your minds may somehow be led
astray from your sincere and pure devotion to Christ. 4 For if someone comes to you and
preaches a Jesus other than the Jesus we preached,[k] or if you receive a different spirit[l]
from the one you received, or a different gospel[m] from the one you accepted, you put up
with it easily enough. 5 But I do not think I am in the least inferior to those "super-apostles."[n] 6 I may not be a trained speaker,[o] but I do have knowledge.[p] We have made this
perfectly clear to you in every way.
7 Was it a sin[q] for me to lower myself in order to elevate you by preaching the gospel
of God to you free of charge?[r] 8 I robbed other churches by receiving support from them[s]
so as to serve you. 9 And when I was with you and needed something, I was not a burden to anyone, for the brothers who came from Macedonia supplied what I needed. I
have kept myself from being a burden to you[t] in any way, and will continue to do so. 10 As
surely as the truth of Christ is in me,[u] nobody in the regions of Achaia[v] will stop this
boasting[w] of mine. 11 Why? Because I do not love you? God knows I do![x] 12 And I will keep

10:13 [w]ver 15,16
10:14 [x]1Co 3:6 [y]2Co 2:12
10:15 [z]Ro 15:20 [a]2Th 1:3
10:16 [b]Ac 19:21
10:17 [c]Jer 9:24; 1Co 1:31
10:18 [d]ver 12 [e]Ro 2:29; 1Co 4:5
11:1 [f]ver 4,19,20; Mt 17:17 [g]ver 16, 17,21; 2Co 5:13
11:2 [h]Hos 2:19; Eph 5:26,27 [i]2Co 4:14
11:3 [j]Ge 3:1-6,13; Jn 8:44; 1Ti 2:14; Rev 12:9
11:4 [k]1Co 3:11 [l]Ro 8:15 [m]Gal 1:6-9
11:5 [n]2Co 12:11; Gal 2:6
11:6 [o]1Co 1:17 [p]Eph 3:4
11:7 [q]2Co 12:13 [r]1Co 9:18
11:8 [s]Php 4:15,18
11:9 [t]2Co 12:13,14,16
11:10 [u]Ro 9:1 [v]Ac 18:12 [w]1Co 9:15
11:11 [x]2Co 12:15

a *13–15* Or *13 We, however, will not boast about things that cannot be measured, but we will boast according to the standard of measurement that the God of measure has assigned us—a measurement that relates even to you. 14 . . . 15 Neither do we boast about things that cannot be measured in regard to the work done by others.* b *17* Jer. 9:24

---

against the false teachers, he changed his tactic and began to boast. This section divides into four main issues: proper versus improper boasting (10:13—11:21), suffering and weakness (11:22–33), heavenly vision (12:1–10) and his care for the Corinthians (12:11–21).

■ **10:13—11:21** *Definition of Proper Boasting.* Paul carefully identified the kind of boasting that is acceptable in the Christian faith.

10:13 beyond proper limits. Paul engaged in "boasting" only to tell of what God had done through him, including the conversion of the Corinthians themselves. **the field God has assigned to us.** God had sent Paul to work in Corinth—something that Paul implied was not true of his opponents.

10:15 Our hope. Paul was hoping the Corinthians would repudiate the false apostles and grow even more in their faith. Then the Corinthian church would provide a perfect base from which he could launch another missionary journey farther west—to Rome and later to Spain (Ac 19:21; Ro 15:22–29). But the situation at Corinth had to be set right before he could do this.

10:17 A quotation from Jeremiah 9:24, where the prophet clarified that boasting was legitimate only in reference to knowing God's greatness. All of Paul's boasting in this epistle ultimately ends up at the only correct place: giving glory to God and thereby boasting in the Lord.

10:18 commends himself . . . the Lord commends. Once again Paul shifted the focus from the merely horizontal, human perspective to the divine perspective (cf. 5:11,16; 6:8–10).

11:2 I am jealous for you. Paul deeply longed for the Corinthians to remain loyal to him, not for his own sake, but because loyalty to him meant loyalty to Christ. In this verse Paul used the metaphors of engagement (during this life) and marriage (when Christ returns). If the Corinthians followed the false apostles, they would be spiritually unfaithful to Christ. Then they could no longer come to their Lord as a "pure virgin." In order for Paul to use this metaphor, both he and the Corinthians had to assume that God's ideal for marriage called for the absence of prior sexual relations—that a bride would come as a "pure virgin" to her husband.

11:3 I am afraid. Paul recognized the possibility that the false apostles could lead the Corinthians astray, and he warned them against this. He feared that some professing Christians in the church at Corinth would prove not to have exercised saving faith in Christ (see theological articles "The Perseverance and Preservation of Believers" at Php 1 and "The Church: Visible and Invisible" at 1 Pe 4). See *WCF* 6.1; *WLC* 21.

11:4 other than the Jesus . . . different spirit . . . different gospel. The strongholds, arguments and pretensions of the false apostles who opposed the true knowledge of God (10:4–5) so distorted the truth that their "Jesus," "spirit" and "gospel" differed radically from what Paul preached (1Co 1:18—2:16; cf. Gal 1:6–9). The "different gospel" of the opponents conformed to worldly ways of thinking to such a degree that Paul and his apostolic ministry—a ministry manifesting the death of Jesus through adversity and suffering (4:7–18; 6:4–10; cf. 1Co 4:8–13)—were despised and rejected in favor of "ministries" that better fit cultural tastes (i.e., eloquence, philosophical wisdom and spectacular displays of spiritual power; cf. 1Co 1:22–25).

11:5 "super-apostles." This is probably the sarcastic title Paul gave to the false apostles who were troubling the Corinthian church. Perhaps it was even a name they had taken for themselves. Some interpreters also believe this is a term that Paul's opponents used to refer to the Jerusalem apostles.

11:6 trained speaker. See note on 10:10.

11:7 free of charge? When Paul was in Corinth he supported himself (Ac 18:3) and accepted help from other churches as well (v. 8). Some Corinthians, however, were apparently offended by Paul's refusal to accept their gift, which was probably intended as a response to Paul's gift of preaching the gospel. In the Mediterranean cultures of Paul's day (as in some cultures today), the giving and receiving of gifts was often a way of establishing and maintaining friendships. Those operating under such a value system may have viewed Paul's refusal of their gift as a claim of superiority. But the apostle viewed his relationship with the Corinthians not from the perspective of worldly social convention (5:16) but from that of the "new creation" (5:17) of which he had been called to be an apostle and spiritual father. As a father, he could rightly give his children without expecting to receive anything (12:14–15).

11:9 from Macedonia. Probably from Philippi

11:10 the regions of Achaia. The area arou **boasting of mine.** Paul had ministered to the Co personal sacrifice and expense—unlike the false apparently were demanding support from the chur

on doing what I am doing in order to cut the ground from under those who want an opportunity to be considered equal with us in the things they boast about.
13 For such men are false apostles,[y] deceitful[z] workmen, masquerading as apostles of
Christ.[a] 14 And no wonder, for Satan himself masquerades as an angel of light. 15 It is not
surprising, then, if his servants masquerade as servants of righteousness. Their end will
be what their actions deserve.[b]

Paul Boasts About His Sufferings

16 I repeat: Let no one take me for a fool.[c] But if you do, then receive me just as you
would a fool, so that I may do a little boasting. 17 In this self-confident boasting I am not
talking as the Lord would,[d] but as a fool. 18 Since many are boasting in the way the world
does, I too will boast.[e] 19 You gladly put up with fools since you are so wise![f] 20 In fact, you
even put up with anyone who enslaves you[g] or exploits you or takes advantage of you
or pushes himself forward or slaps you in the face. 21 To my shame I admit that we were
too weak[h] for that!

What anyone else dares to boast about—I am speaking as a fool—I also dare to
boast about.[i] 22 Are they Hebrews? So am I.[j] Are they Israelites? So am I.[k] Are they Abraham's descendants? So am I. 23 Are they servants of Christ? (I am out of my mind to talk
like this.) I am more. I have worked much harder,[l] been in prison more frequently,[m]
been flogged more severely, and been exposed to death again and again. 24 Five times
I received from the Jews the forty lashes[n] minus one. 25 Three times I was beaten with
rods,[o] once I was stoned,[p] three times I was shipwrecked, I spent a night and a day in
the open sea, 26 I have been constantly on the move. I have been in danger from rivers,
in danger from bandits, in danger from my own countrymen,[q] in danger from Gentiles;
in danger in the city,[r] in danger in the country, in danger at sea; and in danger from
false brothers.[s] 27 I have labored and toiled and have often gone without sleep; I have
known hunger and thirst and have often gone without food;[t] I have been cold and naked. 28 Besides everything else, I face daily the pressure of my concern for all the
churches. 29 Who is weak, and I do not feel weak? Who is led into sin, and I do not inwardly burn?

30 If I must boast, I will boast of the things that show my weakness.[u] 31 The God and
Father of the Lord Jesus, who is to be praised forever,[v] knows that I am not lying. 32 In
Damascus the governor under King Aretas had the city of the Damascenes guarded in
order to arrest me.[w] 33 But I was lowered in a basket from a window in the wall and
slipped through his hands.[x]

11:13 [y]2Pe 2:1 [z]Tit 1:10 [a]Rev 2:2
11:15 [b]Php 3:19
11:16 [c]ver 1
11:17 [d]1Co 7:12,25
11:18 [e]Php 3:3,4
11:19 [f]1Co 4:10
11:20 [g]Gal 2:4
11:21 [h]2Co 10:1,10 [i]Php 3:4
11:22 [j]Php 3:5 [k]Ro 9:4
11:23 [l]1Co 15:10 [m]Ac 16:23; 2Co 6:4,5
11:24 [n]Dt 25:3
11:25 [o]Ac 16:22 [p]Ac 14:19
11:26 [q]Ac 9:23; 14:5 [r]Ac 21:31 [s]Gal 2:4
11:27 [t]1Co 4:11,12; 2Co 6:5
11:30 [u]1Co 2:3
11:31 [v]Ro 9:5
11:32 [w]Ac 9:24
11:33 [x]Ac 9:25

11:13 such men are false. Paul was convinced that the false teachers were servants of Satan (v. 14), not true followers of Christ.
11:15 as servants of righteousness. One of Satan's tricks is to claim to do good. Specifically, Satan may send to a church his servants who purport to be Christians but who bring only divisiveness, slander, immorality and all kinds of destructiveness (Mt 7:20; cf. Ac 20:29–30; 2Pe 2:1–22). See *HC* 127. **Their end.** Final judgment by God.
11:20–21 A description of the bold actions of the false apostles, followed by a sarcastic disclaimer.
■ **11:22–33** *Boasting of Suffering and Weakness.* Paul described his ministry in terms that could not possibly be equaled by the false apostles. In boasting about how much he had suffered for the sake of Christ, Paul employed great irony, "boasting" of things normally considered shameful, such as signs of weakness and defeats. His boasting parodied that of his opponents, who commended themselves to the Corinthians in speeches of extravagant self-praise. The topics in this section progress to a climax in which Paul dealt with what may have been uppermost in the minds of his critics: unusual religious experiences (12:1–9).
11:22 Are they Hebrews? Paul's opponents were Jews who perhaps came from Jerusalem with claims of the endorsement of the Jerusalem apostles.
11:23–27 Paul, in recounting the marks of a true servant of Christ, pointed to suffering and humiliation, thus emphasizing again (as he had in 1Co 1–4) Christ crucified.
11:23 out of my mind. Paul revealed his extreme hesitancy to speak at all on his own behalf.
11:24 forty lashes minus one. Forty lashes with a whip was the maximum degree of flogging that could be inflicted on a person according to Deuteronomy 25:3. It was Jewish practice to set the mit lower as a safeguard against miscounting.
25 beaten with rods. Once in Acts 16:22, plus two other s not mentioned in Acts. **once I was stoned.** In Lystra, on first missionary journey (Ac 14:19); the crowd on that occasion thought they had killed Paul. **three times I was shipwrecked.** A shipwreck is described in Acts 27:39–44, but 2 Corinthians was written before that incident (at the point described in Acts 20:2, when Paul was in Macedonia). These three shipwrecks must have occurred during his earlier missionary journeys. **a night and a day in the open sea.** An episode not mentioned in Acts.
11:26 in danger. Paul's goal was not his own personal safety. Many of the hardships he reported in this larger section are not recorded at all in Acts. It is hard to imagine a more hazardous existence than Paul's, yet he was obedient to God and his life was in God's hands. **false brothers.** People who were pretending to be Christians but who came into the church to stir up trouble.
11:28 the pressure of my concern. Paul felt deeply for the needs and hurts of the churches. Although his life demonstrated trust in the sovereignty of God, he did not fail to empathize with others who suffered.
11:32–33 This incident is narrated from a different perspective in Acts 9:24–25. Apparently Paul's Jewish opponents in Damascus persuaded the governor to cooperate with them in their plot against Paul. Although these two verses may seem somewhat surprising in the context, they mention Paul's first—and rather humiliating—experience of being persecuted (rather than of persecuting others) for the sake of the gospel. This account further demonstrates Paul's humiliation. The apostle was forced to escape (barely) as a common fugitive from a relatively minor civil authority. Ironic humor may be present in this context as well.
■ **12:1–10** *Boasting of Heavenly Vision.* Paul laced his recounting of his extraordinary spiritual experiences with irony. Although it was quite spectacular, this vision of paradise yielded nothing of value for ministry to others (v. 4). Instead of further glory for Paul, it brought him a painful "thorn" sent by God to keep the apostle humble (v. 7). Paul did not boast in a straightforward manner about this experience, and its results imply that it is wrong to use such experiences as a criterion for evaluating the validity of a ministry.

Paul's Vision and His Thorn

12 I must go on boasting.[y] Although there is nothing to be gained, I will go on to
visions and revelations[z] from the Lord. **2**I know a man in Christ who fourteen
years ago was caught up[a] to the third heaven.[b] Whether it was in the body or out of the
body I do not know—God knows.[c] **3**And I know that this man—whether in the body or
apart from the body I do not know, but God knows— **4**was caught up to paradise.[d] He
heard inexpressible things, things that man is not permitted to tell. **5**I will boast about
a man like that, but I will not boast about myself, except about my weaknesses. **6**Even if
I should choose to boast, I would not be a fool,[e] because I would be speaking the truth.
But I refrain, so no one will think more of me than is warranted by what I do or say.
7To keep me from becoming conceited because of these surpassingly great revelations, there was given me a thorn in my flesh,[f] a messenger of Satan, to torment me.
8Three times I pleaded with the Lord to take it away from me.[g] **9**But he said to me, "My
grace is sufficient for you, for my power[h] is made perfect in weakness." Therefore I will
boast all the more gladly about my weaknesses, so that Christ's power may rest on me.
10That is why, for Christ's sake, I delight in weaknesses, in insults, in hardships,[i] in persecutions,[j] in difficulties. For when I am weak, then I am strong.[k]

Paul's Concern for the Corinthians

11I have made a fool of myself,[l] but you drove me to it. I ought to have been commended by you, for I am not in the least inferior to the "super-apostles,"[m] even though I am
nothing.[n] **12**The things that mark an apostle—signs, wonders and miracles[o]—were
done among you with great perseverance. **13**How were you inferior to the other churches, except that I was never a burden to you?[p] Forgive me this wrong![q]
14Now I am ready to visit you for the third time,[r] and I will not be a burden to you,
because what I want is not your possessions but you. After all, children should not have
to save up for their parents,[s] but parents for their children.[t] **15**So I will very gladly spend
for you everything I have and expend myself as well.[u] If I love you more, will you love me
less? **16**Be that as it may, I have not been a burden to you.[v] Yet, crafty fellow that I am,
I caught you by trickery! **17**Did I exploit you through any of the men I sent you? **18**I urged[w]

12:1 [y]2Co 11:16,30 [z]ver 7
12:2 [a]Ac 8:39 [b]Eph 4:10 [c]2Co 11:11
12:4 [d]Lk 23:43; Rev 2:7
12:6 [e]2Co 11:16
12:7 [f]Nu 33:55
12:8 [g]Mt 26:39,44
12:9 [h]Php 4:13
12:10 [i]2Co 6:4 [j]Ro 5:3; 2Th 1:4 [k]2Co 13:4
12:11 [l]2Co 11:1 [m]2Co 11:5 [n]1Co 15:9,10
12:12 [o]Jn 4:48
12:13 [p]1Co 9:12,18 [q]2Co 11:7
12:14 [r]2Co 13:1 [s]1Co 4:14,15 [t]Pr 19:14
12:15 [u]Php 2:17; 1Th 2:8
12:16 [v]2Co 11:9
12:18 [w]2Co 8:6,16

12:2 a man in Christ. Refers to Paul himself. Paul was so hesitant to speak of his experiences—lest he appear to be boasting in himself—that he refused to identify himself explicitly. **fourteen years ago.** It is significant that for 14 years Paul had not made this amazing spiritual experience the focus of his teaching or used it as a proof of his apostleship. His emphasis was the message of Christ: "we do not preach ourselves, but Jesus Christ as Lord" (4:5). **third heaven.** The dwelling place of God. According to this enumeration, the "first heaven" is the atmosphere in which we see birds and clouds, the "second heaven" the sky in which we see stars and constellations, and the "third heaven" the place commonly referred to as "heaven," the dwelling place of God.

12:4 paradise. The Greek word for "paradise" is used with various meanings outside the New Testament, but all three Biblical occurrences refer to "heaven," the dwelling place of God (see v. 2, where it is synonymous with "third heaven"; see also Lk 23:43; Rev 2:7). This experience must have given Paul encouragement and strength in subsequent sufferings.

12:6 so no one will think more of me. Paul wanted people to evaluate him on the basis of their own firsthand impressions of him, not on the basis of what he or others said about previous experiences or ministries.

12:7–9 See *WCF* 5.5; *WLC* 195; *WSC* 106.

12:7 a thorn in my flesh. Various possibilities have been suggested for this "thorn" in the flesh: (1) a physical ailment of some sort ("in my flesh"); (2) a harassing demon ("a messenger of Satan"); or (3) the constant harassment of Jewish persecutors. Based on the known information, it is impossible to determine with certainty the identity of this "thorn." Few, if any, of God's greatest servants throughout history have been free from some kind of hindrance, weakness or opposition.

12:8 the Lord. Paul's usual way of referring to Christ, not to God the Father. Although prayers in the New Testament are most often directed to God the Father, this is one example of a prayer directed to Christ (cf. Ac 1:24; 7:59; 1Co 16:22; Rev 22:20).

12:9 my power is made perfect in weakness. Expresses one theme of this epistle: When believers recognize their own weaknesses, Christ's power will rest on them. Weakness in this regard augments, rather than diminishes, power. In 13:4 Paul tied this general principle to its source: the cross of Christ. Paul's whole response to attacks on his apostolic authority was consciously patterned on the crucified Christ, not on the so called "Jesus" or "different gospel" that his opponents foisted on the Corinthians (11:4).

12:10 I delight. Paul's insight into the true nature of his sufferings enabled him to see them as reasons for rejoicing. He knew that through them Christ's power would be at work. **I am weak . . . strong.** When difficulties destroy believers' normal self-confidence, they must rely more on Christ, who gives them strength beyond measure.

■ **12:11–21** *Paul's Care for the Corinthians.* Paul closed this part of his epistle by repeating his expression of love for the Corinthians and his intention to visit them.

12:11 you drove me to it. Paul had to "boast" about his apostolic weakness because the Corinthians, who knew him well, had not defended him against the false apostles. Instead, they had been seduced (11:1–3) by the inflated self-claims of the false apostles and the untrue criticism levied against Paul.

12:12 The things that mark an apostle. According to common understanding, the "things that mark an apostle" (or the "signs of an apostle") were miraculous deeds: "signs, wonders and miracles" such as Paul did. Yet throughout this epistle Paul pointed to other marks to confirm his apostleship: the changed lives of the Corinthians (3:2–3), the blameless character of his ministry (6:3–10; 7:2; 8:20–21), his genuine love for the churches (6:11–12; 7:3; 11:7–11) and his sacrificial endurance of suffering (6:3–10; 11:23–33). These activities are probably what he had in mind when he spoke in this verse of "the things that mark an apostle," for they clearly distinguished him from the false apostles. Sadly, the Corinthians more highly valued the spectacular works ("signs, wonders and miracles") than the other marks of apostleship, so Paul reluctantly mentioned that those spectacular works also accompanied his ministry among them.

12:14 for the third time. See "Introduction: Time and Place of Writing." The first visit was in Acts 18:1–18 on Paul's second missionary journey. The second visit is not recorded, but it must have occurred sometime during Paul's stay in Ephesus (Ac 19:1–41). **not your possessions.** Unlike those preachers whose goal was their own financial reward. See *WLC* 125.

12:15 See *WLC* 151,159.

12:16 I caught you by trickery! Perhaps Paul's opponents were saying that his apparent selflessness was merely a ploy to exploit them. Paul answered that he had never exploited them or others (v. 17).

12:18 [x]2Co 8:18
12:19 [y]Ro 9:1 [z]2Co 10:8
12:20 [a]2Co 2:1-4 [b]1Co 4:21 [c]1Co 1:11; 3:3 [d]Gal 5:20 [e]Ro 1:29 [f]1Co 14:33
12:21 [g]2Co 2:1,4 [h]2Co 13:2
13:1 [i]2Co 12:14 [j]Dt 19:15; Mt 18:16
13:2 [k]2Co 1:23 [l]2Co 12:21
13:3 [m]Mt 10:20; 1Co 5:4
13:4 [n]Php 2:7,8; 1Pe 3:18 [o]Ro 1:4; 6:4 [p]ver 9
13:5 [q]1Co 11:28 [r]Jn 6:6 [s]Ro 8:10
13:9 [t]ver 11
13:10 [u]2Co 10:8
13:11 [v]1Th 4:1; 2Th 3:1 [w]Mk 9:50 [x]Ro 15:33; Eph 6:23
13:12 [y]Ro 16:16
13:13 [z]Php 4:22
13:14 [a]Ro 16:20; 2Co 8:9 [b]Ro 5:5; Jude 21 [c]Php 2:1

Titus to go to you and I sent our brother[x] with him. Titus did not exploit you, did he? Did
we not act in the same spirit and follow the same course?
19 Have you been thinking all along that we have been defending ourselves to you? We
have been speaking in the sight of God[y] as those in Christ; and everything we do, dear
friends, is for your strengthening.[z] 20 For I am afraid that when I come[a] I may not find you
as I want you to be, and you may not find me as you want me to be.[b] I fear that there may
be quarreling,[c] jealousy, outbursts of anger, factions,[d] slander, gossip,[e] arrogance and
disorder.[f] 21 I am afraid that when I come again my God will humble me before you, and
I will be grieved[g] over many who have sinned earlier[h] and have not repented of the impurity, sexual sin and debauchery in which they have indulged.

Final Warnings

13 This will be my third visit to you.[i] "Every matter must be established by the testimony of two or three witnesses."[a][j] 2 I already gave you a warning when I was
with you the second time. I now repeat it while absent: On my return I will not spare[k]
those who sinned earlier[l] or any of the others, 3 since you are demanding proof that
Christ is speaking through me.[m] He is not weak in dealing with you, but is powerful
among you. 4 For to be sure, he was crucified in weakness,[n] yet he lives by God's power.[o] Likewise, we are weak[p] in him, yet by God's power we will live with him to serve you.
5 Examine yourselves[q] to see whether you are in the faith; test yourselves.[r] Do you not
realize that Christ Jesus is in you[s]—unless, of course, you fail the test? 6 And I trust that
you will discover that we have not failed the test. 7 Now we pray to God that you will not
do anything wrong. Not that people will see that we have stood the test but that you will
do what is right even though we may seem to have failed. 8 For we cannot do anything
against the truth, but only for the truth. 9 We are glad whenever we are weak but you are
strong; and our prayer is for your perfection.[t] 10 This is why I write these things when I
am absent, that when I come I may not have to be harsh in my use of authority—the authority the Lord gave me for building you up, not for tearing you down.[u]

Final Greetings

11 Finally, brothers,[v] good-by. Aim for perfection, listen to my appeal, be of one mind,
live in peace.[w] And the God of love and peace[x] will be with you.
12 Greet one another with a holy kiss.[y] 13 All the saints send their greetings.[z]
14 May the grace of the Lord Jesus Christ,[a] and the love of God,[b] and the fellowship
of the Holy Spirit[c] be with you all.

[a] *1* Deut. 19:15

12:18 Titus was coming ahead of Paul (8:6,16–17).
12:19 Paul again emphasized that he had not been speaking for his own reputation or glory but for the good of the church and the glory of God. This again reveals a strong consciousness of the presence of God in all he wrote and did ("in the sight of God"). See *WLC* 159.
12:20 If the false apostles were not dealt with, Paul would arrive in Corinth to find a divided, bickering church.
12:21 This verse does not imply that Paul feared a humiliating defeat before the Corinthians, for his weapons were divinely powerful (see notes on 10:3,4; see also 13:3–4,10). Rather, Paul so identified with the Corinthian believers that if he were to return and find that some of them (his "children"; v. 14) had not repented of sin, he would be humiliated, just as parents are humiliated by the misbehavior of their children. **many who have sinned earlier and have not repented.** Although the Corinthian church was strong, false apostles were not its only problem. Some individuals were still engaging in continuing sin, and Paul warned them. See *WLC* 144.
■ **13:1–10** *Warning.* Paul was so deeply concerned with the well-being of the Corinthian church that he gave serious warnings to encourage obedience in its members.
13:1 my third visit. See note on 12:14. Paul quoted Deuteronomy 19:15 here. The phrase "two or three witnesses" does not likely refer to Paul's two or three visits to Corinth (for he was still only one witness). Rather, it is most likely a reminder that when he arrived, all charges against the Corinthian believers would be considered fairly and dealt with in a just manner.
13:3 Christ is speaking through me. A strong statement of Paul's apostolic authority. Christ himself, in speaking through Paul, would powerfully silence any offenders. See *WSC* 23.
13:4 Paul's life (as that of all Christians) was united with Christ in his eath and resurrection, and Paul continued to share in Christ's resur-ion power (see theological article "Union With Christ" at Gal 6).
Examine yourselves. When those who profess the Christian faith stray into error to the degree that many of the Corinthians had, they need to examine their lives for evidence of salvation. Such evidence would include: heartfelt dependence on Christ (Col 1:23; Heb 3:6; 1Pe 1:5); morally changed lives resulting in obedience to God (Mt 7:21; 1Jn 2:3–6,29; 3:6,9–10; 5:1–3,18); continuing growth in sanctification (1Pe 1:5–11; 1Jn 3:3); the presence of the fruit of the Spirit in their lives (Gal 5:22–23), including love for other Christians (1Jn 3:14; 4:7); positive fruit in the lives of others as a result of their influence (Mt 7:15–20; Mk 4:20; Jn 15:1–8); faithful adherence to apostolic teaching (1Jn 4:6,15); and the testimony of the Holy Spirit within them (Ro 8:15–16; 1Jn 4:13). **unless, of course, you fail the test.** Paul did not believe, and was not implying, that the Corinthians could lose eternal salvation once they possessed it (see theological article "The Perseverance and Preservation of Believers" at Php 1). Instead, he wrote to the entire church in Corinth, which included both believers and unbelievers, assuring his readers of their status in Christ but warning that failing the test of living in faithful loyalty to Christ would prove that they were not truly in him (see theological article "The Church: Visible and Invisible" at 1 Pe 4). See *WLC* 171, *WSC* 97.
13:7 See *WLC* 195.
13:9 See *WLC* 195.
13:10 building you up, not for tearing you down. Like all gifts of the Spirit (1Co 12:7), Paul's apostleship was intended for the strengthening of the church. Consequently, Paul preferred to encourage rather than to rebuke. Yet he knew that in some circumstances it was necessary to be "harsh."
■ **13:11–14** *Final Greeting and Benediction.* Paul closed this epistle with some final encouraging words and a benediction.
13:13 All the saints. Refers to Christians in the church from which Paul was writing, probably Philippi, but perhaps Thessalonica or Berea (see "Introduction: Time and Place of Writing").
13:14 An early Trinitarian statement, often used as a benediction. See *WCF* 2.3; 21.2; *WLC* 9,11; *BC* 9; *HC* 25.

GALATIANS

Introduction

Overview

Author: The apostle Paul

Purpose: To help believers in Galatia resist false teachers who taught that salvation comes only to those who add the human merit of obedience to the law to their faith in Christ

Date: A.D. 49–55

Key Truths:

- Justification before God comes by faith alone.
- Sanctification in daily life comes by faith through the power of the Spirit.
- Paul's message of salvation by faith apart from works can be trusted
- The gospel of salvation by faith is taught in all the Scriptures.
- Legalism turns us away from Christ to futility and judgment.
- Freedom from legalism is freedom to live for Christ by the Spirit.
- Eternal salvation comes only to those who believe and live in the true gospel.

Author

The apostle Paul wrote Galatians (1:1). He mentioned a group of his coworkers who had some role in sending the letter (1:2), but its style and theology demonstrate that Paul was its author. A few scholars, beginning in the eighteenth century, considered the letter pseudonymous (written by someone else, using Paul's name), but their arguments are now curiosities of Biblical scholarship.

Time and Place of Writing

The question of the letter's date is intertwined with the problem of its destination. Paul named the addressees as "Galatians" (3:1; cf. 1:2), but to which Galatians was he writing? He may have been targeting his letter specifically to the Celtic people who lived in northern Galatia and who were widely known as "Galatians," or he may have been addressing churches in the entire province of Galatia. When we follow the course of Paul's first and second missionary journeys (Ac 13–14; 15:36—18:22), we discover that this question has implications for the epistle's date, as well as for its relationship to Paul's other letters. Paul visited Pisidian Antioch, Iconium, Lystra and Derbe (all cities in southern Galatia) on his first and second missionary journeys. If he wrote to southern Galatia, he may well have written to those churches early in his career, probably shortly after the first missionary journey, about the time of the Jerusalem council (c. A.D. 48; see Ac 15; cf. Gal 2:11–14). The most popular date among those who hold this view is A.D. 48–49. If they are correct, Galatians may be Paul's earliest extant epistle. It has also been suggested that Paul wrote to southern Galatia after the Jerusalem council (Ac 15) and that he referred to the council in 2:1–10, but this view seems unlikely because Paul did not rely on the decision of the council to support his views.

Many scholars believe, however, that Galatians was written to the ethnic Galatians in the north. If this view is correct, Paul probably wrote the letter after passing through "Galatia and Phrygia" (Ac 18:23) on his third missionary journey. Many who follow the "northern Galatian hypothesis" believe that Paul wrote the letter either during his two-year stay in Ephesus (Ac 19) or as he was traveling through Macedonia on his way to Greece near the end of his third missionary journey (Ac 20:1–6; cf. 2Co 2:13). If this is correct, then Galatians was probably written in A.D. 54 or 55. Theories that date the letter late in Paul's career have the merit of placing Galatians within the same period as 2 Corinthians, Romans and perhaps Philippians—letters with which Galatians bears some thematic correspondence.

Purpose and Distinctives

Galatians was written to answer specific problems within particular churches. In order to understand the epistle, some knowledge of that situation is essential. Not long after the Galatians had accepted the gospel, agitators came among them who attacked Paul personally (4:17) and preached a distorted form of Christianity (1:6–7). Their "gospel" required circumcision of Gentile Christians as a symbolic commitment to seeking salvation through works of the law (6:12). The agitators insisted that the Galatians not only had to believe in Christ for salvation, but also had to practice circumcision (2:3–5; 5:2,6,11; 6:12–13,15).

The zeal of these agitators likely reflects Jewish pressure as well as their own pride. They were attempting to turn these Gentile Christians to Jewish traditions under pressure from nationalistic Jewish groups in Judea. According to the Jewish historian Josephus, Judean Jews were becoming increasingly intolerant of contact between Jews and Gentiles during the last half of the first century.

The agitators were not content merely to preach their brand of the gospel; they also attempted to discredit Paul (4:17), who had founded the Galatian churches. Their attacks may have taken one or more of the following forms: First, they may have claimed that Paul was a renegade who had defied his superiors, the Jerusalem apostles. Paul responded to this attack i
2:1–10. Second, they may have stated that Paul h

recently argued with Peter over whether the gospel required Gentiles to become Jews in order to become Christians. Paul gave his account of the encounter with Peter in 2:11–14. Third, the agitators may have spread the notion that Paul had originally preached circumcision for salvation (5:11) but had recently changed his gospel so that he might more easily accommodate the Gentiles (1:10). Paul answered that his change of outlook resulted from a revelation received directly from Christ (1:11–24).

The Galatians, for their part, were showing interest both in the rumors about Paul and in the agitators' new form of the gospel. By the time Paul wrote to them, they were in the process of deserting the true gospel and, consequently, God himself (1:6–7). They now wanted to be "under the law" (4:21; cf. 5:1) and, specifically, to become circumcised (5:2). This transition to a "different gospel" (1:6) was not a smooth one. Dissension broke out within the community (5:15; 6:3–5).

Paul's purpose in writing was to persuade the Galatians that circumcision is not necessary in order to be saved. The "truth of the gospel" (2:5,14) is that salvation comes by faith in Jesus Christ. Anyone who seeks to violate that sacred sphere of faith by introducing other requirements corrupts the gospel and must be resisted at all costs (1:8–9).

Galatians has played a central role in Reformed theology because it clearly declares that salvation is the gift of God's grace. Salvation is unearned and undeserved (1:3,6,15; 2:19,21; 6:18) and is received by faith alone (2:15–16). Quite simply, this is "the truth of the gospel" (2:5,14). Paul showed deep anger over the agitators' denial of this truth (3:1; 5:12), warning that those who reject it cannot expect to be saved (1:8; 5:4).

Paul's emphasis on the doctrine of faith alone rises from his view of what Christ has accomplished. Christ is the One who introduced the age to come, the final stage of salvation and judgment for the world (see theological note "The Plan of the Ages" at Heb 7). He bore the curse of the law in our place on the cross (3:13; 6:14) and delivers us from this age of sin and death (1:3–4). Made one with him, we are clothed with his righteousness (3:26–27), our sure hope (5:5). Because we are united to Christ, we enter the age of the new creation (6:15), receive the rights of his Sonship (4:4–5) and are enabled by the Spirit of the Son to live lives pleasing to God (5:16–18,25). Against the proud boasting of sinners who think they can earn their own salvation by keeping God's law, Paul's boasting was only in the cross and in receiving the promise of God by faith (6:14).

Outline

I. Prescript (1:1–5)	*Paul identified himself as Jesus' apostle and greeted his readers.*
II. The Problem (1:6–10)	*A false, legalistic gospel, teaching that Gentile Christians needed to be circumcised in order to obtain salvation, had risen in Galatia. This was contrary to Paul's gospel of justification by faith alone, and anyone who taught or believed it was in serious danger.*
III. Historical Accounts (1:11—2:21) A. Call and Training (1:11–17) B. Jerusalem Leaders (1:18—2:10) C. Conflict With Peter (2:11–21)	*Several historical events support Paul's claim that his gospel of salvation by faith apart from works is the true gospel of Christ: Paul received his gospel message directly from Christ. It was not of human origin. Church leaders in Jerusalem confirmed that Paul taught the true gospel. Paul even corrected Peter for hypocrisy toward uncircumcised Gentile believers.*
IV. Theological Proofs (3:1—4:31) A. Early Experience (3:1–5) B. Abraham's Faith (3:6—4:11) C. Current Experience (4:12–20) D. Abraham's Wives and Sons (4:21–31)	*Several theological arguments support Paul's claim that his gospel of salvation by faith apart from works is the true gospel of Christ: the confirmation of Paul's gospel message by the powerful presence of the Holy Spirit, the Old Testament record of Abraham's own faith, the lost joy that the Galatians had once enjoyed, and the Old Testament record of Abraham's wives and sons.*
V. Practical Exhortations (5:1—6:10) A. Freedom in Christ (5:1–15) B. Power of the Spirit (5:16—6:6) C. Divine Judgment and Blessing (6:7–10)	*The gospel of justification by faith alone leads to a number of practical considerations: Christ has freed believers from legalistic human traditions. Believers are freed not to sin and freed to live in obedience to God as they rely on the Holy Spirit and avoid reliance on the flesh. God's blessings will come only to those who live by faith, but judgment awaits all those who turn from this true gospel.*
VI. Postscript (6:11–18)	*Paul summarized his letter and gave a closing salutation.*

1 Paul, an apostle—sent not from men nor by man, but by Jesus Christ[a] and God the
Father, who raised him from the dead[b]— 2and all the brothers with me,[c]

To the churches in Galatia:[d]

3Grace and peace to you from God our Father and the Lord Jesus Christ,[e] 4who gave
himself for our sins[f] to rescue us from the present evil age, according to the will of our
God and Father,[g] 5to whom be glory for ever and ever. Amen.[h]

No Other Gospel

6I am astonished that you are so quickly deserting the one who called[i] you by the
grace of Christ and are turning to a different gospel[j]— 7which is really no gospel at all.
Evidently some people are throwing you into confusion[k] and are trying to pervert the
gospel of Christ. 8But even if we or an angel from heaven should preach a gospel other
than the one we preached to you,[l] let him be eternally condemned![m] 9As we have already said, so now I say again: If anybody is preaching to you a gospel other than what
you accepted,[n] let him be eternally condemned!

10Am I now trying to win the approval of men, or of God? Or am I trying to please
men?[o] If I were still trying to please men, I would not be a servant of Christ.

Paul Called by God

11I want you to know, brothers,[p] that the gospel I preached is not something that man
made up. 12I did not receive it from any man,[q] nor was I taught it; rather, I received it
by revelation[r] from Jesus Christ.

13For you have heard of my previous way of life in Judaism,[s] how intensely I persecuted the church of God and tried to destroy it.[t] 14I was advancing in Judaism beyond
many Jews of my own age and was extremely zealous for the traditions of my fathers.[u]
15But when God, who set me apart from birth[a][v] and called me[w] by his grace, was

1:1 [a]Ac 9:15 [b]Ac 2:24
1:2 [c]Php 4:21 [d]Ac 16:6; 1Co 16:1
1:3 [e]Ro 1:7
1:4 [f]Mt 20:28; Ro 4:25; Gal 2:20 [g]Php 4:20
1:5 [h]Ro 11:36
1:6 [i]Gal 5:8 [j]2Co 11:4
1:7 [k]Ac 15:24; Gal 5:10
1:8 [l]2Co 11:4 [m]Ro 9:3
1:9 [n]Ro 16:17
1:10 [o]Ro 2:29; 1Th 2:4
1:11 [p]1Co 15:1
1:12 [q]ver 1 [r]ver 16
1:13 [s]Ac 26:4,5 [t]Ac 8:3
1:14 [u]Mt 15:2
1:15 [v]Isa 49:1,5; Jer 1:5 [w]Ac 9:15

a 15 Or *from my mother's womb*

■ **1:1–5** *Prescript.* Paul began this epistle with a salutation in which he identified himself and the recipients of the letter.

1:1 Paul. We know from 15 references in Acts 7–13 that Paul was also called "Saul." In his extant letters, however, he always called himself Paul, a common Roman surname. **apostle.** The word means "messenger." On occasion Paul used it to refer to an envoy such as Epaphroditus (Php 2:25), but he used it here to denote the authoritative office of one who spoke on behalf of Christ (Ac 1:21–26; 1Co 9:1). Along with the other authoritative apostles, God ordained Paul to establish the foundation of the church (1Co 3:10; 9:1; 14:37–38; Eph 2:20; 3:3–5). His authority came from God himself (1:11—2:10). **sent not from men nor by man, but by Jesus Christ.** Even during the greeting, Paul defended his apostleship as a divine commission. In distinguishing between divine and human sources of authority, he placed the name of Jesus Christ on the divine side, even though Jesus was also human (cf. vv. 10,12).

1:3 Grace and peace. Each of Paul's letters begins with a reference to these two blessings from God. "Grace" means "undeserved act of kindness." Paul used this word more often than any other New Testament writer and gave it immense theological significance. It refers to all that God has given us in Christ, none of which we have earned or can repay. "Peace" refers to the relationship that Christ's death and resurrection (1:4) have established between God and those who believe the gospel. For Paul's comments on the meanings of these two terms, see Romans 5:1–2.

1:4 from the present evil age. This expression corresponds to the common Jewish designation in Paul's day of "this age," the age of sin and judgment before the coming of the Messiah (see theological note "The Plan of the Ages" at Heb 7). Paul associated the sinful, legalistic traditions of Israel with the failures of this age, and he drew attention to the fact that Christ came to deliver his people from this age and its legalism. This expression introduces the main theme of this epistle: The Galatians must not turn away from the Christian gospel to legalism. Paul closed this epistle with the same theme, referring to the importance of the "new creation" over circumcision (6:15). See *WCF* 20.1.

■ **1:6–10** *The Problem.* Paul immediately identified the problem facing the Galatians. They had begun to follow false teachers who taught another gospel. Paul opposed this false gospel and condemned those who followed it.

1:6–8 See *WCF* 10.4.

1:6 called you by the grace. God's grace comes to us at God's initiative and by his call, not because of anything we have done to deserve it (v. 15; Ro 4:4–8; 8:30; 9:11–13).

1:7 some people. Probably refers to Jewish Christians from Jerusalem who insisted that Gentiles must not only believe in Jesus Christ to be saved but must also accept circumcision and thereby commit themselves to observing Jewish traditions as the way of salvation (2:3–5,12; 6:12–13). Various shades of this idea were widespread among early Jewish Christians (Ac 15:1; 21:20–21; Php 3:2–3).

1:8–9 eternally condemned. Literally, *anathema,* meaning "accursed by God" (Ro 9:3). Paul's usual thanksgiving for his readers is here replaced by a threatened curse. The repetition of the threat is a device used for emphasis. Those who require anything other than faith in Jesus Christ for salvation, no matter how impeccable their credentials, twist the gospel into another form. The preachers of this false gospel were under God's condemnation. See *WCF* 1.6; *WLC* 3; *BC* 7,29.

1:10 win the approval of men. Paul's opponents in Galatia had not only attacked the gospel but had also attacked its messenger, Paul. One of their charges was that Paul preached an easy form of the gospel, one that required neither circumcision nor obedience to the Sabbath laws and dietary restrictions (4:10; 5:11). See *WCF* 20.2.

■ **1:11—2:21** *Historical Accounts.* Paul defended his apostleship and gospel message by recalling several historical events: his call and training (1:11–17), his visit with the leaders in Jerusalem (1:18—2:10) and his conflict with Peter over the status of Gentiles (2:11–21).

■ **1:11–17** *Call and Training.* Paul explained that he had received his apostleship and gospel message from Christ himself.

1:11 not . . . made up. Paul defended himself against his opponents' charge that he had rebelled against the Jerusalem apostles who had given him his authority in the first place, contending that his authority came from God alone and that the Jerusalem apostles had merely confirmed it. See *BC* 7.

1:12 by revelation. See Acts 9:3–5, 22:6–10, 26:13–18 and 1 Corinthians 15:8.

1:13–14 See *WLC* 109.

1:13 persecuted the church of God. Paul's persecution of the church prior to his call was well known among early Christians (Ac 7:58; 8:3; 9:1–2). Paul himself was profoundly ashamed of this part of his past (1Co 15:9), although he looked on it as evidence that God's grace can overcome even the most rebellious of sinners (Ac 22:4–5; 26:9–11; 1Co 15:10; Php 3:6–8; 1Ti 1:13–16).

1:14 extremely zealous. Paul was fond of pointing out to his opponents that being a Jew, even a zealous Jew, is insufficient for salvation. Paul considered his own experience proof that zeal for the law cannot save (Ro 9:30—10:4; 2Co 11:22; Php 3:4-6).

1:15 apart from birth. Paul consciously echoed the call o

1:16 [x]Gal 2:9 [y]Mt 16:17
1:18 [z]Ac 9:22,23
1:18 [a]Ac 9:26,27

pleased 16 to reveal his Son in me so that I might preach him among the Gentiles, [x] I did
not consult any man, [y] 17 nor did I go up to Jerusalem to see those who were apostles before I was, but I went immediately into Arabia and later returned to Damascus.
18 Then after three years, [z] I went up to Jerusalem [a] to get acquainted with Peter[a] and

a *18* Greek *Cephas*

miah (Jer 1:5) and, perhaps, the servant of Isaiah 49 (Isa 49:1,5), both of whom, like Paul, were called to be God's messengers to the Gentiles. Paul was conscious that his apostleship stood in continuity with the Old Testament prophetic tradition (see note on v. 1). **called me by his grace.** See note on verse 6. Paul's call to be an apostle, like the faith of every believer, was the product of God's prior grace. Before our birth, and therefore before we could do anything good or bad, God chose to create faith within us (Ro 9:10–13; Eph 1:4–6). No one can earn God's call; it is a free gift.

1:16 Gentiles. The words "Gentiles" and "nations" are translated from the same Greek term. Jewish writers used this word to refer to anyone who was not a Jew. Paul was called to preach to the Gentiles (2:9; Ac 9:15; 22:21; 26:17; Ro 1:5; 15:16), but he did not regard this as a mandate to preach exclusively to Gentiles. In Acts 13–28 he frequently preached to Jews, and such passages as Romans 1:14–16, 9:1–5 and 1 Corinthians 9:20 demonstrate that he also sought to evangelize Jews. **consult any man.** Paul did, of course, meet with Ananias three days after his conversion (Ac 9:10–19; 22:12–16). The word translated "consult," however, connotes the action of laying something before someone else or submitting it to this person for approval. Paul certainly did not "consult" Ananias in this sense. Rather, Ananias's role was to baptize Paul and confirm Paul's calling to preach to the Gentiles.

1:17 Jerusalem . . . Arabia . . . Damascus. Paul's conversion and call took place near Damascus (Ac 9:3; 22:6; 26:12), and he spent several days in Damascus after his conversion (Ac 9:19). Jerusalem was the cultural and religious center of ancient Israel and the surrounding nations, as well as home to James, Peter and John, who figure prominently both in Acts and Galatians as leaders of the early Jewish-Christian community in that city (2:9). Paul stressed that his call to preach to the Gentiles came from God, not from the leaders of the Jerusalem church. Arabia was ruled by a Nabatean king, Aretas IV, who struggled with Rome for control of Damascus. At the time of Paul's conversion, Aretas's governor was in control of the city and apparently aided angry Jews in an effort to kill Paul (Ac 9:23–25; 2Co 11:32–33).

■ **1:18—2:10** *Jerusalem Leaders.* Paul supported his authority as

The Gospel: What Is Salvation and How Do I Get It?

THE Bible teaches that there is a message of Good News to all who repent and trust in Jesus Christ as their Savior. A reading of the Bible will reveal, however, a variety of legitimate (Mt 4:23; Mk 1:15; Ac 2:14–38) and illegitimate (Gal 1:9; Jude 3–19) summaries of this core teaching. Unfortunately, many believers become complacent and employ only one summary of the gospel, failing to realize that such a limit restricts not only those with whom they can share the gospel, but also the degree to which they can apply it to their own lives.

The fullest expression of the gospel message is found in Jesus Christ, the Word made flesh. Jesus Christ, the Son of God, physically became man and descended to Earth to announce the Good News that the promised kingdom of God had now come. It is this news of the kingdom that forms the foundation of the gospel message (see theological article "The Kingdom of God" at Mt 4). In establishing the kingdom by his own death, resurrection and ascension (Lk 9:21–36; Ac 1:1–11), Jesus lived out the very content of the gospel message—a message that was to be announced to the whole world (Jn 1:1–14; Ac 2:22ff.).

But what exactly is the gospel message? The gospel message may be summarized as follows: God has provided a way of escape from the eternal punishment that awaits sinners. If we have a true sense of our sin and misery and an apprehension of his mercy in Jesus Christ, and if we turn with grief and hatred away from sin and receive and rest upon Jesus Christ alone for salvation, we will be spared from God's righteous wrath against sinners. Instead, we will be united to Jesus, our sins will be forgiven, God will accept us as righteous in his sight and he will bless us abundantly for all eternity (*WSC* 86,87; *WLC* 72).

Sometimes a Christian may mistakenly assume that many other doctrines are essential to the gospel message as well, but the Bible nowhere indicates that we must possess a mature theology before we can be saved. Rather, it demonstrates the necessity of only a bare minimum of knowledge for the possession of saving faith (Lk 23:39–43; Ac 10:34–43; 16:25–34). Others err by thinking that the gospel needs to be heard only by the lost. In fact, every believer must constantly renew his or her trust in the truths of the gospel and, through ongoing faith and repentance (Php 1:25; Col 1:23; 3Jn 3), continue to be changed by the gospel's power.

All Christians are called to testify to the good news of God's work in their lives—and not just in safe environments (Mt 28:19–20; Ac 1:8; 4:20; 5:27–29; 8:4). But not everyone knows how to carry out such proclamation. One way to communicate the truths of the gospel is to begin by briefly telling our own story of God's work in our life and then to move on to a situation-appropriate summary of the content of the gospel. If someone else is struggling with a realistic sense of the meaningless of life, we can show this person how faith in God implies trusting that God sent Jesus Christ into the world to offer us a new and abundant life (Jn 7:37–38; 10:10; Gal 5:22). If this individual is grappling with his or her own weaknesses, we can demonstrate that a trusting relationship with the God of the Bible imbues us with the power to overcome loneliness, stress, fear of people and/or the future, and seemingly unbreakable negative habits (1Co 6:9–11; 1Jn 4:18). Or if such a one feels separated from God, we can confirm the reality of the alienation (Ro 3:23; 6:23) while adding the assurance that God has provided a solution in Christ (Ro 5; 1Co 1:30; 1Jn 1:7).

If God grants you the opportunity to follow up this gospel presentation by inviting people to acknowledge their need, repent of their sin, pray for God's forgiveness and embrace Jesus as Lord and Savior, then do it! God uses the power of the Holy Spirit, combined with the powerful gospel of grace, to draw his elect unto himself.

stayed with him fifteen days. 19 I saw none of the other apostles—only James,[b] the Lord's
brother. 20 I assure you before God that what I am writing you is no lie.[c] 21 Later I went
to Syria and Cilicia.[d] 22 I was personally unknown to the churches of Judea[e] that are in
Christ. 23 They only heard the report: "The man who formerly persecuted us is now
preaching the faith[f] he once tried to destroy." 24 And they praised God[g] because of me.

Paul Accepted by the Apostles

2 Fourteen years later I went up again to Jerusalem,[h] this time with Barnabas. I took
Titus along also. 2 I went in response to a revelation and set before them the gospel
that I preach among the Gentiles.[i] But I did this privately to those who seemed to be leaders, for fear that I was running or had run my race[j] in vain. 3 Yet not even Titus,[k] who was
with me, was compelled to be circumcised, even though he was a Greek.[l] 4 ⌞This matter
arose⌟ because some false brothers[m] had infiltrated our ranks to spy on[n] the freedom[o]
we have in Christ Jesus and to make us slaves. 5 We did not give in to them for a moment,
so that the truth of the gospel[p] might remain with you.
6 As for those who seemed to be important[q]—whatever they were makes no difference
to me; God does not judge by external appearance[r]—those men added nothing to my
message. 7 On the contrary, they saw that I had been entrusted with the task[s] of preaching the gospel to the Gentiles,[a][t] just as Peter[u] had been to the Jews.[b] 8 For God, who was
at work in the ministry of Peter as an apostle[v] to the Jews, was also at work in my ministry as an apostle to the Gentiles. 9 James, Peter[c][w] and John, those reputed to be pillars,[x]
gave me and Barnabas[y] the right hand of fellowship when they recognized the grace giv-
en to me.[z] They agreed that we should go to the Gentiles, and they to the Jews. 10 All they

1:19 [b]Mt 13:55
1:20 [c]Ro 9:1
1:21 [d]Ac 6:9
1:22 [e]1Th 2:14
1:23 [f]Ac 6:7
1:24 [g]Mt 9:8
2:1 [h]Ac 15:2
2:2 [i]Ac 15:4, 12 [j]1Co 9:24; Php 2:16
2:3 [k]2Co 2:13 [l]Ac 16:3; 1Co 9:21
2:4 [m]2Co 11:26 [n]Jude 4 [o]Ac 15:1; Gal 5:1, 13
2:5 [p]ver 14
2:6 [q]Gal 6:3 [r]Ac 10:34
2:7 [s]1Th 2:4; 1Ti 1:11 [t]Ac 9:15 [u]ver 9, 11, 14
2:8 [v]Ac 1:25
2:9 [w]ver 7, 11, 14 [x]1Ti 3:15 [y]Ac 4:36 [z]Ro 12:3

[a] 7 Greek *uncircumcised* [b] 7 Greek *circumcised*; also in verses 8 and 9 [c] 9 Greek *Cephas*; also in verses 11 and 14

---

an apostle by recounting his relationship with the apostles in Jerusalem.

1:18–24 Paul recorded his initial meeting with Peter and James and the initially warm reception his apostleship had received from the churches.

1:18 three years. Refers to the "many days" of Acts 9:23. Paul mentioned this time frame to show that his training under Christ was comparable to the training the other apostles had received during Jesus' three-year earthly ministry. **to Jerusalem.** Paul's first trip to Jerusalem after his conversion (Ac 9:26–30). **get acquainted.** This phrase translates a word that means visiting someone for the purpose of getting information from him or her. Paul may have interviewed Peter about Jesus' life and teaching. **Peter.** In the Greek Paul uses Peter's Aramaic name, *Cephas.* Both Cephas and Peter mean "rock."

1:19 James, the Lord's brother. See Matthew 13:55 and Mark 6:3. This James should be distinguished from the disciple of Jesus who is frequently coupled with Peter and John in the Gospels and whom Herod murdered during the church's earliest days (Ac 12:2). "James, the Lord's brother" initially did not believe in Jesus (Jn 7:5) but was later converted, perhaps as a result of having seen the risen Lord (1Co 15:7).

1:21 Syria and Cilicia. See Acts 9:30. Paul returned home to Tarsus (Ac 9:11; 21:39; 22:3), the most important city in Cilicia. Eastern Cilicia, the region in which Tarsus was located, was under the administration of the Roman province of Syria during the early first century. Paul's coupling of the two regions here is precisely correct.

1:22 Judea. Paul may have been referring to the Roman province of Judea, which included Biblical Judea, Samaria and Galilee, or to the smaller region of Biblical Judea. Jerusalem was located in Biblical Judea.

2:1–10 Paul reported a second event that displayed his authority and the veracity of his gospel: his encounter with church leaders in Jerusalem.

2:1 Fourteen years later. Either after his conversion or after his first visit to Jerusalem. **again to Jerusalem.** This may refer to Paul's second postconversion visit implied in Acts 11:27–30 or to his third visit (Ac 15:2). The purpose of the visit mentioned here corresponds well with the purpose of the Acts 15 visit. If these visits are one and the same, Paul probably omitted the Acts 11 visit from his narrative because it was irrelevant to the question of his authority. If, as some scholars believe, Galatians was written after Paul's first missionary journey (Ac 13–14) but before the Jerusalem council (Ac 15), then the journey spoken of here refers to the Acts 11 journey, and the Acts 15 journey had not yet occurred. **Barnabas.** A native of Cyprus and one of the earliest Christians (Ac 4:36). In Aramaic the name *Barnabas* means "son of encouragement," and his appearances in Acts demonstrate that he lived up to his name (Ac 4:36–37; 11:22–24,30). **Titus.** Never mentioned in Acts. He was one of Paul's trusted companions and messengers.

2:2 a revelation. If this refers to the Acts 11 visit, the revelation may have been the prophecy of Agabus (Ac 11:28). Otherwise, it probably refers to similar special revelations that Paul received from God (Ac 9:4–6; 16:9; 18:9–10; 2Co 12:1–6). **in vain.** The Jerusalem leaders were not the source of Paul's authority, but his efforts to preach the gospel would have been hindered if these influential men had opposed him.

2:3 compelled to be circumcised. See 5:12 and Acts 15:1. Circumcision was the hallmark of the Jew and had become the final step in the conversion of a male Gentile to the Jewish religion. Some Jewish Christians believed that Gentiles had to accept circumcision before they could be saved. Paul vehemently opposed this teaching, maintaining that faith in Christ is alone sufficient for salvation.

2:4–5 See *WCF* 20.2.

2:4 false brothers. Paul considered the doctrine of salvation by faith alone to be so important that he denied the salvation of all who opposed it (1:8–9; 5:2 4). **freedom.** The freedom of the believer is not freedom to sin, but freedom from human traditions and from the curse the law pronounces on sin (3:10–14; 5:1,13). **slaves.** Probably to sin (Ro 6:15–23; 7:25) and to the curse that the law pronounces on those who sin (3:10).

2:5 truth of the gospel. See note on 1:8–9; compare 2:14. Salvation comes only by the faith God graciously gives to the believer (1:15–16, cf. Eph. 2:8–9). Any attempt to add requirements, such as circumcision, is a denial of the sufficiency of faith for salvation and is therefore a perversion of the gospel.

2:6 external appearance. Just as the external mark of circumcision does not define the boundary of God's people, so external marks of prestige are unimportant to God (1Sa 16:7; Ro 2:25–29).

2:7 Gentiles. See note on 1:16. **Peter . . . to the Jews.** Peter was one of the chief spokesmen of the early Jerusalem church (Ac 1–12). Only with great reluctance did he respond to God's command to associate with, and preach the gospel to, the Gentile Cornelius (Ac 10). Although Peter recognized the necessity of evangelizing Gentiles (Ac 10:34–35; 11:17; 15:7–11), God had called him to preach the gospel specifically to Jews.

2:8 See *BC* 30.

2:9 James, Peter and John. See notes on 1:18 and 19. This trio exercised special authority in the early Jerusalem church. Peter and John were frequently coupled together (Ac 3–4), and James held a position of prominence in the Jerusalem church (Ac 12:17; 15:13; 21:18). **grace given to me.** Regarding Paul's conversion and call, see 1:15 and its note. **we should go to the Gentiles.** Barnabas, like Paul, was chiefly a missionary to the Gentiles (Ac 13–14; 15:36–41).

asked was that we should continue to remember the poor,[a] the very thing I was eager
to do.

Paul Opposes Peter

11 When Peter[b] came to Antioch,[c] I opposed him to his face, because he was clearly
in the wrong. 12 Before certain men came from James, he used to eat with the Gentiles.[d]
But when they arrived, he began to draw back and separate himself from the Gentiles
because he was afraid of those who belonged to the circumcision group.[e] 13 The other
Jews joined him in his hypocrisy, so that by their hypocrisy even Barnabas[f] was led
astray.
14 When I saw that they were not acting in line with the truth of the gospel,[g] I said to
Peter[h] in front of them all, "You are a Jew, yet you live like a Gentile and not like a Jew.[i]
How is it, then, that you force Gentiles to follow Jewish customs?
15 "We who are Jews by birth[j] and not 'Gentile sinners'[k] 16 know that a man is not justified by observing the law, but by faith in Jesus Christ.[l] So we, too, have put our faith in
Christ Jesus that we may be justified by faith in Christ and not by observing the law, because by observing the law no one will be justified.
17 "If, while we seek to be justified in Christ, it becomes evident that we ourselves are
sinners,[m] does that mean that Christ promotes sin? Absolutely not![n] 18 If I rebuild what
I destroyed, I prove that I am a lawbreaker. 19 For through the law I died to the law[o] so
that I might live for God.[p] 20 I have been crucified with Christ[q] and I no longer live, but
Christ lives in me.[r] The life I live in the body, I live by faith in the Son of God,[s] who loved
me[t] and gave himself for me.[u] 21 I do not set aside the grace of God, for if righteousness
could be gained through the law,[v] Christ died for nothing!"[a]

2:10 [a]Ac 24:17
2:11 [b]ver 7,9,14 [c]Ac 11:19
2:12 [d]Ac 11:3 [e]Ac 11:2
2:13 [f]ver 1; Ac 4:36
2:14 [g]ver 5 [h]ver 7,9,11 [i]Ac 10:28
2:15 [j]Php 3:4,5 [k]1Sa 15:18
2:16 [l]Ac 13:39; Ro 9:30
2:17 [m]ver 15 [n]Gal 3:21
2:19 [o]Ro 7:4 [p]Ro 6:10, 11,14; 2Co 5:15
2:20 [q]Ro 6:6 [r]1Pe 4:2 [s]Mt 4:3 [t]Ro 8:37 [u]Gal 1:4
2:21 [v]Gal 3:21

[a] *21* Some interpreters end the quotation after verse 14.

2:10 remember the poor. Paul had in mind economic poverty, not spiritual poverty. Some refer these words to Paul's visit to Jerusalem in Acts 11:27–30. On that visit Paul and Barnabas were commissioned to take an offering from Antioch to the Christians in Judea who were suffering because of a famine. Others believe that these words refer to Paul's collection for the Jerusalem saints (Ac 24:17; Ro 15:26; 1Co 16:1–3; 2Co 8–9), a collection to which the Galatians contributed (1Co 16:1).

■ **2:11–21** *Conflict With Peter.* Paul recalled a time when he had successfully rebuked Peter for violating the true gospel by separating himself from Gentile believers. This event supported Paul's authority as an apostle, as well as the truth of his gospel.

2:11–14 See *WLC* 78,151,195.

2:11 Antioch. Not Pisidian Antioch (Ac 13:14; 14:19,21), but the capital of the Roman province of Syria and the largest city of that province (Ac 13:1; 14:26). Antioch was home to a large Jewish community and was the first place mentioned in Acts where Jewish Christians preached the gospel to Gentiles (Ac 11:19–20; Gal 2:1). As far as we know, the church at Antioch was not only the first church to bring Jewish and Gentile Christians together in worship and fellowship, but was also the first to send missionaries to preach the gospel specifically to Gentiles (Ac 13:1–3).

2:12 draw back. Many Jewish Christians accepted God's command to receive believing Gentiles, but only after these Gentile converts submitted to the ceremonial law of Moses (Ac 10:28; 11:2–3,19; 15:1). Both Peter and Barnabas (v. 13) succumbed to pressure from a group of Jewish Christians who believed that circumcision was a necessary part of becoming a Christian.

2:14 truth of the gospel. See note on verse 5. **live like a Gentile.** Peter had previously associated freely with Gentile believers (v. 12), but he separated himself from Gentile Christians under pressure from the arriving "circumcision group" (v. 12). Paul sharply rebuked Peter for this hypocrisy.

2:15–16 These verses are central in Galatians. Paul's point is that everyone (observant Jew as well as uncircumcised Gentile) is placed in a right relationship with God through faith in Jesus Christ alone.

2:16 justified. In Greek, the noun translated "righteousness," the adjective translated "righteous" and the verb translated "justify" are all from the same root and have related meanings. In the Old Testament, God is just ("righteous"; Zep 3:5), the One who rules and judges with perfect justice (1Sa 26:23) and who pronounces his verdict of innocence or guilt. To "justify" means to "declare to be right" (Dt 25:1). But if no one living is righteous before God (Ps 143:2), how can there be hope of that verdict (Job 9:2)? Because God is the Judge whose verdict is final and just, he is also the Savior who can provide deliverance from his own judgment (Jnh 2:9). God's righteousness is revealed not just as his requirement, but also as his gift (Isa 45:24–25; 54:14–17). That gift comes at last through the Messiah (Isa 53:8; Jer 23:5–6; 33:14–16). **observing the law.** Literally, "works of the law." Paul referred specifically to those "works" that distinguish Jews from Gentiles: circumcision, dietary restrictions and Sabbath keeping (vv. 15–16). His teaching, however, extends to all efforts of fallen humanity to earn salvation by good works. **no one will be justified.** A near quotation of Psalm 143:2. No one can keep the law fully; thus legal observances such as circumcision cannot bring about a right relationship with God. Something other than the law is needed to accomplish that, and God has provided it in the gift of Christ's righteousness and the blood of his atonement. Faith does not merit God's acceptance; it accepts Christ's merit before God (Php 3:9). See *WCF* 11.1; 11.4; 19.6; *WLC* 70,73,94; *WSC* 33,86; *BC* 22; *HC* 21,60.

2:17 we ourselves are sinners. Paul either speaks of accusations of sin from the Galatian agitators and the "men . . . from James" (v. 12) for breaking Jewish dietary conventions (like the Gentiles of v. 15), or he points out that seeking salvation in Christ causes us to see and admit our true sinfulness.

2:18 If I rebuild what I destroyed. The Greek word reflected by this translation is used frequently in the New Testament to refer to the tearing down of an edifice (Mt 24:2; Mk 13:2; Lk 21:6; Ro 14:20). The metaphor probably refers to turning back to reliance on good works in order to gain a righteous standing before God. To "rebuild" is to subject oneself again to the condemnation of the law (e.g., 5:2–4). **I am a lawbreaker.** The lawbreaker is not the one who turns from the law to Christ for justification, but the one who violates his or her faith in Christ by relying on the law for justification. Only Christ can keep the law, so only those who are united to Christ by faith can be accounted law keepers. All others are accounted lawbreakers.

2:19 I died to the law. Paul died to the condemnation of the law in the death of Christ (Ro 6:5–7; 7:1–4), for he was crucified with Christ (v. 20) by his union with him, who died in his place (v. 20; 3:13; Ro 4:25; 5:6). So too, Paul was raised with Christ and therefore lived in relation to God (Col 2:12; 3:1). Death to the law does not violate the law, for Christ met its demands. It is therefore "through the law" that believers are released from its bondage and condemnation.

2:20 In Reformed theology it is usual to speak of union with Christ in two senses. First, union with Christ means that Christ represented us in his death and resurrection. By this means he atoned for our sins and guaranteed our salvation. Second, union with Christ is a vital unification with the Savior. Jesus is present with the believer. The Lord lives in inward fellowship with his own by his Spirit, and believers draw their strength from this actual union. See *WCF* 14.2; *HC* 21,90; *CD* 2.VII.

2:21 See *BC* 22.

Faith or Observance of the Law

3 You foolish Galatians! Who has bewitched you?[w] Before your very eyes Jesus Christ
was clearly portrayed as crucified.[x] 2 I would like to learn just one thing from you:
Did you receive the Spirit by observing the law, or by believing what you heard?[y] 3 Are
you so foolish? After beginning with the Spirit, are you now trying to attain your goal by
human effort? 4 Have you suffered so much for nothing—if it really was for nothing? 5 Does
God give you his Spirit and work miracles[z] among you because you observe the law, or
because you believe what you heard?
6 Consider Abraham: "He believed God, and it was credited to him as righteousness."[a][a] 7 Understand, then, that those who believe[b] are children of Abraham. 8 The Scripture foresaw that God would justify the Gentiles by faith, and announced the gospel in
advance to Abraham: "All nations will be blessed through you."[b][c] 9 So those who have
faith[d] are blessed along with Abraham, the man of faith.
10 All who rely on observing the law are under a curse, for it is written: "Cursed is everyone who does not continue to do everything written in the Book of the Law."[c][e]
11 Clearly no one is justified before God by the law, because, "The righteous will live by
faith."[d][f] 12 The law is not based on faith; on the contrary, "The man who does these things
will live by them."[e][g] 13 Christ redeemed us from the curse of the law[h] by becoming a curse
for us, for it is written: "Cursed is everyone who is hung on a tree."[f][i] 14 He redeemed us
in order that the blessing given to Abraham might come to the Gentiles through Christ
Jesus,[j] so that by faith we might receive the promise of the Spirit.[k]

The Law and the Promise

15 Brothers, let me take an example from everyday life. Just as no one can set aside or
add to a human covenant that has been duly established, so it is in this case. 16 The promises were spoken to Abraham and to his seed.[l] The Scripture does not say "and to
seeds," meaning many people, but "and to your seed,"[g] meaning one person, who is

3:1 [w]Gal 5:7 [x]1Co 1:23
3:2 [y]Ro 10:17
3:5 [z]1Co 12:10
3:6 [a]Ge 15:6; Ro 4:3
3:7 [b]ver 9
3:8 [c]Ge 12:3; Ac 3:25
3:9 [d]ver 7; Ro 4:16
3:10 [e]Dt 27:26; Jer 11:3
3:11 [f]Hab 2:4; Gal 2:16; Heb 10:38
3:12 [g]Lev 18:5; Ro 10:5
3:13 [h]Gal 4:5 [i]Dt 21:23; Ac 5:30
3:14 [j]Ro 4:9,16 [k]ver 2; Joel 2:28; Ac 2:33
3:16 [l]Lk 1:55; Ro 4:13,16

[a] *6* Gen. 15:6 [b] *8* Gen. 12:3; 18:18; 22:18 [c] *10* Deut. 27:26 [d] *11* Hab. 2:4 [e] *12* Lev. 18:5
[f] *13* Deut. 21:23 [g] *16* Gen. 12:7; 13:15; 24:7

▪ **3:1—4:31** *Theological Proofs.* Leaving his historical accounts behind, Paul turned to several theological proofs of his doctrine of justification by faith alone. His reasoning divides into four sections: the Galatians' experience when they received the gospel from Paul (3:1–5), the example of Abraham's faith (3:6—4:11), the Galatians' current experience under the influence of a false legalistic gospel (4:12–20) and the parallels between the Galatian situation and the Biblical record of Abraham's wives and sons (4:21–31).

▪ **3:1–5** *Early Experience.* Paul reminded the Galatians of the Spirit's dramatic presence when they had first received his gospel.

3:1 clearly portrayed. Perhaps in Paul's preaching. See *WLC* 113.

3:2 Spirit. Paul began by appealing to the Galatians' own experience of the Holy Spirit prior to the arrival of the agitators as proof that submitting to outmoded Jewish tradition is not a necessary part of becoming a Christian (Ac 10:47; 11:17; 15:8). They had received the Holy Spirit when they had believed the gospel, and they had done so by means of faith, not by keeping Jewish tradition.

3:3 by human effort? Literally, "in the flesh?" Perhaps Paul had in mind not only the attempt to keep the law without the Spirit (Ro 7:7—8:17), but also the attempt to gain favor with God by cutting the flesh in circumcision (Php 3:2–3). Regardless, Paul warned his readers against the attempt to win salvation by performing some work. Salvation comes only through God's grace (1:6,15–16 and their notes) by faith in Jesus Christ (2:16). See *WLC* 113.

3:5 See *BC* 24.

▪ **3:6—4:11** *Abraham's Faith.* The Genesis record of Abraham's faith in God's promises establishes that Paul's gospel of faith is true to Old Testament Scriptures.

3:6 Abraham was the father of the Jews and the person with whom God first established circumcision as a covenantal sign (Ge 17:10). Yet even this revered patriarch was placed in a right relationship with God by faith prior to his circumcision (Ro 4:11). Paul reversed the charge that he was undercutting God's covenant with Abraham. The true children of Abraham seek salvation through faith, as Abraham did, whether or not they are physically descended from him.

3:7–14 See *WCF* 7.5; 11.4; 11.6; 20.1; 28.4; *WLC* 34,97,166; *HC* 39.

3:10 Paul's point was that no one can keep the law in its entirety, and he supported this point by quoting Deuteronomy 27:26. Shortly after the passage from which Paul quotes, Deuteronomy recites the curses that will fall upon Israel for disobedience. Most Jews of Paul's day realized that Israel had broken the law and had received precisely the curses that were predicted (Dt 28:15—30:20). See *WCF* 6.6; 7.2; 19.1; *WLC* 30,93,96,152; *WSC* 19,84; *HC* 62.

3:11 See theological article "Justification and Merit" at Romans 3. See *WCF* 7.3; *WLC* 73.

3:12 The law is not based on faith. This negative assessment of the law does not reflect Paul's entire outlook. He had many positive things to say about the moral requirements of the law (e.g., Ro 7:12–16,25; 1 Ti 1:8; see also theological article "The Three Uses of the Law" at Ps 119). Here Paul spoke of the law as God's requirement apart from God's mercy. Leviticus (18:5) states this requirement and predicts the failure and curse (Lev 26:14–38). The promise is also repeated (Lev 26:40–45), for it is not voided (3:15–22). See *WCF* 7.2; 19.1; *WLC* 20,30,93; *WSC* 12.

3:13 a curse for us. Since all have broken God's covenant by violating the law, all deserve to receive the law's curse. But Christ bore the law's curse in our place, giving us peace with God (Mk 10:45; Jn 1:29; Ro 3:21–26; 4:25; 5:1–8; 2Co 5:21; Col 2:13–15; 1Pe 2:24). See *WCF* 19.6; 20.1; *WLC* 49; *HC* 37,38.

3:14 the blessing given to Abraham. See 3:8 and Genesis 18:18 and 22:18. Believing Gentiles, whose lives are marked by the indwelling Spirit, fulfill the promise that all nations would be blessed through Abraham. Elsewhere Paul called the Spirit the "deposit guaranteeing our inheritance" of salvation (Eph 1:14). See *WCF* 7.5; 7.6; 20.1; 28.4; *WLC* 34,166; *HC* 53.

3:15–18 God promised saving blessing to the nations through Abraham's "seed." That seed is Jesus Christ, who descended from Abraham in his human nature. That covenant promise was not made void by the later giving of the law. The law does not oppose the promises (v. 21) but assumes them. Its requirements show the hopelessness of earning salvation and point God's people to faith in Christ (v. 24). See *BC* 7.

3:16 "seed," meaning one person, who is Christ. Paul was aware that the noun "seed" in the singular may be used collectively as well as individually (v. 29; Ro 4:18). However, in the passage to which Paul referred, "seed" (the NIV translates the word as "offspring"; Ge 18:16–18) referred to the one person, Isaac, as indicated by singular verbs. Paul's point was that we do not receive salvation as separate individuals. Instead, the promise of salvation comes through a single representative head. As Abraham's "seed," Isaac represented all who followed him. In the same way Christ, the final individual "seed" of Abraham, represents all who believe. See *WCF* 7.6; *WLC* 31; *BC* 18.

Christ. [17]What I mean is this: The law, introduced 430 years[m] later, does not set aside
the covenant previously established by God and thus do away with the promise. [18]For if
the inheritance depends on the law, then it no longer depends on a promise;[n] but God
in his grace gave it to Abraham through a promise.

[19]What, then, was the purpose of the law? It was added because of transgressions[o]
until the Seed[p] to whom the promise referred had come. The law was put into effect
through angels[q] by a mediator.[r] [20]A mediator,[s] however, does not represent just one
party; but God is one.

[21]Is the law, therefore, opposed to the promises of God? Absolutely not![t] For if a law
had been given that could impart life, then righteousness would certainly have come by
the law.[u] [22]But the Scripture declares that the whole world is a prisoner of sin,[v] so that
what was promised, being given through faith in Jesus Christ, might be given to those
who believe.

[23]Before this faith came, we were held prisoners[w] by the law, locked up until faith
should be revealed. [24]So the law was put in charge to lead us to Christ[a][x] that we might
be justified by faith.[y] [25]Now that faith has come, we are no longer under the supervision
of the law.

Sons of God

[26]You are all sons of God[z] through faith in Christ Jesus, [27]for all of you who were baptized into Christ[a] have clothed yourselves with Christ.[b] [28]There is neither Jew nor Greek,
slave nor free,[c] male nor female, for you are all one in Christ Jesus.[d] [29]If you belong to
Christ,[e] then you are Abraham's seed, and heirs according to the promise.[f]

4 What I am saying is that as long as the heir is a child, he is no different from a slave,
although he owns the whole estate. [2]He is subject to guardians and trustees until
the time set by his father. [3]So also, when we were children, we were in slavery[g] under
the basic principles of the world.[h] [4]But when the time had fully come,[i] God sent his Son,
born of a woman,[j] born under law,[k] [5]to redeem those under law, that we might receive
the full rights[l] of sons. [6]Because you are sons, God sent the Spirit of his Son into our

3:17 [m]Ge 15:13,14; Ex 12:40
3:18 [n]Ro 4:14
3:19 [o]Ro 5:20 [p]ver 16 [q]Ac 7:53 [r]Ex 20:19
3:20 [s]Heb 8:6; 9:15; 12:24
3:21 [t]Gal 2:17 [u]Gal 2:21
3:22 [v]Ro 3:9-19; 11:32
3:23 [w]Ro 11:32
3:24 [x]Ro 10:4 [y]Gal 2:16
3:26 [z]Ro 8:14
3:27 [a]Mt 28:19; Ro 6:3 [b]Ro 13:14
3:28 [c]Col 3:11 [d]Jn 10:16; 17:11; Eph 2:14,15
3:29 [e]1Co 3:23 [f]ver 16
4:3 [g]Gal 2:4 [h]Col 2:8, 20
4:4 [i]Mk 1:15; Eph 1:10 [j]Jn 1:14 [k]Lk 2:27
4:5 [l]Jn 1:12

[a] *24* Or *charge until Christ came*

3:17 430 years later. In Exodus 12:40 this figure is given to designate the length of Israel's stay in Egypt. In the Greek (Septuagint) version of Exodus, the time of the patriarchs' stay in Canaan is included in the 430 years. Paul was not necessarily following the Septuagint in alluding to the passage. It was enough for his purpose to cite this number to show that several centuries passed before the law was given at Sinai (cf. Ge 15:13; Ac 7:6). See *WCF* 27.1.
3:19 because of transgressions. The law related to sin in a number of ways (see theological article "The Three Uses of the Law" at Ps 119). Here Paul had in mind the second use of the law as our teacher that reveals sin, condemns us and leads us to Christ. **through angels.** See Deuteronomy 33:2, Acts 7:53 and Hebrews 2:2.
3:20 mediator. Moses mediated between God and Israel when God made his covenant with Israel at Mount Sinai (Ex 19–34). The promise given to Abraham, however, was spoken directly by God himself. If God's mediated word to Moses was true, then certainly his unmediated word to Abraham was true as well. **God is one.** See Deuteronomy 6:4. God's covenant with Abraham, because it did not involve a mediator, demonstrated God's unity and sovereignty even more clearly than the covenant at Sinai.
3:21–22 See *WLC* 95; *WSC* 20.
3:21 Humanity's inability to keep the law, not the law itself, is the source of our broken relationship with God. **opposed to the promises of God?** Paul strongly denied this mistaken conclusion from his argument. The law would be in competition with the gospel only if it could impart life by delivering sinners from its own condemnation. Although the law is good and shows the kind of life that is pleasing to God (Lev 18:5; Ro 7:10), it is unable to give life to lawbreakers (2Co 3:6). The Jews, who possessed the law, were the more condemned by it. The law therefore shows that all are condemned sinners and points to the need for the promised Savior. See *WCF* 7.3; 19.7; *WLC* 30.
3:24 was put in charge to lead us. This phrase translates the Greek word *paidagôgos* (from which "pedagogue" is derived), a term Greeks applied to a slave who was responsible for a child's care and training (see note on 1Co 4:15). The law, like a teacher, points to our sin and condemns it. **to Christ.** "To" has a temporal force here, meaning "until." The law did not act as a teacher, pointing out the way, but rather it acted as a temporary guardian until Christ came (cf. 4:4). See *WCF* 19.6; *WLC* 96; *BC* 25.
3:25 no longer under the supervision of the law. Paul did not mean that Christians are not obliged to follow the law's moral requirements. Rather, the law's condemnation no longer prevents us from inheriting the blessings of the covenant (cf. 4:7).
3:26–27 You are all sons of God. We are "sons" because we are united to the one and only Son, Jesus Christ. Baptism seals our union with Christ. It is a vital union in that Christ lives in us (2:20). It is also a representative union in that Christ died and lives for us (Ro 6:5–11). To be clothed with Christ implies both: His righteousness is our robe, and we are a new creation in him (Ro 13:14; Col 3:10; Eph 4:24). See *WCF* 28.1; 28.6; *WLC* 162,165,167,17; *WSC* 94; *BC* 34; *HC* 67,73.
3:28 you are all one in Christ Jesus. The wall of separation between Jew and Gentile is removed for those united to Christ; all are Abraham's seed (Eph 2:14–16; Col 3:11). Indeed, no human distinctions avail as advantages in the matter of salvation. Paul does not utterly obliterate these distinctions (cf. 1Co 11:3; 14:34; Eph 5:23–33; 1Ti 2:11–14), but he indicates that they give no one preferential status with regard to inheriting the covenant blessings.
4:1–7 Paul had earlier compared the law to a prison warden (3:23) and a pedagogue (see note on 3:24). Now he compared the law's preparatory role to that of guardians or trustees of a minor. The full right reserved for the child who comes of age is adoption as a son and the receiving of the son's inheritance. See *WCF* 8.6; 12; 19.3; 19.6; 20.1; *WLC* 74,97; *HC* 19,26,36.
4:3 under the basic principles. The Greek phrase can refer to the basic elements that make up the world (in ancient thought: earth, wind, water and fire). Sometimes these elements were revered as deities governing the cosmos. Here Paul may have been thinking especially of the sacred calendar of the law, its seasons determined by the celestial bodies (cf. Col 2:8,20–22). The law subjected life to the control of these "basic principles."
4:4 the time had fully come. The time set by the Father (v. 2), or "the fulfillment of the ages" (1Co 10:11), when the promises of God are realized. See theological article "The Plan of the Ages" at Hebrews 7. **God sent his Son.** His eternal Son, sent to be born of a woman. **under law.** Although Christ was without sin (2Co 5:21), he was born under the law, not only as One obligated to fulfill it, but also as One identified with sinners who are under the curse of the law. His death freed us from that curse (3:10–14). See *WCF* 8.2; 8.4; 11.4; *WLC* 36,37,39,47,48; *WSC* 21,22,27; *BC* 10,17,18; *HC* 35.
4:5 to redeem. Paul's concept of redemption came from the insti-

hearts,[m] the Spirit who calls out, *"Abba,*[a] Father."[n] 7 So you are no longer a slave, but a
son; and since you are a son, God has made you also an heir.[o]

Paul's Concern for the Galatians

8 Formerly, when you did not know God,[p] you were slaves to those who by nature are
not gods.[q] 9 But now that you know God—or rather are known by God[r]—how is it that
you are turning back to those weak and miserable principles? Do you wish to be enslaved[s] by them all over again?[t] 10 You are observing special days and months and seasons and years![u] 11 I fear for you, that somehow I have wasted my efforts on you.[v]

12 I plead with you, brothers,[w] become like me, for I became like you. You have done
me no wrong. 13 As you know, it was because of an illness[x] that I first preached the gospel to you. 14 Even though my illness was a trial to you, you did not treat me with contempt or scorn. Instead, you welcomed me as if I were an angel of God, as if I were Christ
Jesus himself.[y] 15 What has happened to all your joy? I can testify that, if you could have
done so, you would have torn out your eyes and given them to me. 16 Have I now become
your enemy by telling you the truth?[z]

17 Those people are zealous to win you over, but for no good. What they want is to
alienate you ⌊from us⌋, so that you may be zealous for them. 18 It is fine to be zealous, provided the purpose is good, and to be so always and not just when I am with you.[a] 19 My
dear children,[b] for whom I am again in the pains of childbirth until Christ is formed in
you,[c] 20 how I wish I could be with you now and change my tone, because I am perplexed
about you!

Hagar and Sarah

21 Tell me, you who want to be under the law, are you not aware of what the law says?
22 For it is written that Abraham had two sons, one by the slave woman[d] and the other
by the free woman.[e] 23 His son by the slave woman was born in the ordinary way;[f] but
his son by the free woman was born as the result of a promise.[g]

24 These things may be taken figuratively, for the women represent two covenants.

4:6 [m]Ro 5:5 [n]Ro 8:15,16
4:7 [o]Ro 8:17
4:8 [p]1Co 1:21; Eph 2:12; 1Th 4:5 [q]2Ch 13:9; Isa 37:19
4:9 [r]1Co 8:3 [s]ver 3 [t]Col 2:20
4:10 [u]Ro 14:5
4:11 [v]1Th 3:5
4:12 [w]Gal 6:18
4:13 [x]1Co 2:3
4:14 [y]Mt 10:40
4:16 [z]Am 5:10
4:18 [a]ver 13,14
4:19 [b]1Co 4:15 [c]Eph 4:13
4:22 [d]Ge 16:15 [e]Ge 21:2
4:23 [f]Ro 9:7,8 [g]Ge 18:10-14; Heb 11:11

[a] 6 Aramaic for *Father*

tution of slavery. In both the Jewish and Greco-Roman worlds, a slave could buy his freedom (or someone else could buy it for him) by paying a redemption price to his owners. The price of our redemption was paid by the Father through the blood of his Son (1Pe 1:17–18) and by the Son in giving his life as a ransom for many (Mt 20:28). **those under law.** Refers not only to Jews circumcised under the Law of Moses, but also to Gentiles, for both are under the curse of the law (3:13–14). **full rights of sons.** Literally, "the adoption." While Paul has been speaking of God's people under the law as children (Ex 4:23; Isa 1:2), he now describes the only way in which that status is conferred. The word for adoption has "son" as its root. God seals our sonship by giving us the Spirit of his Son (Ro 8:9–17). See *WLC* 39.

4:6 ***Abba.*** The Aramaic term for "Father," used by Jesus himself (Mk 14:36). It was natural for Jesus, God's Son in a unique sense, to use this intimate term. Now the Spirit puts that very word on the lips of all those who have sonship in Christ. See *WCF* 2.3,12; *WLC* 10,38,74; *BC* 9; *HC* 25,53.

4:8–9 See *HC* 95.

4:8 Before their conversion, the Galatians were subject to the bondage of the "elements" of a pagan world: its false gods, its astrology, its seasonal rituals (see note on v. 3). See *WLC* 109.

4:9 known by God. Their knowledge of God was not based on *their* doing but on *his* doing. **turning back.** Amazingly, Paul likened the bondage of ceremonial legalism to that of pagan superstition. To accept circumcision as necessary for salvation was to turn from the liberty of grace to the bondage of the world with its times and seasons (v. 10; Col 2:8,20–22), whether this bondage was Jewish or Gentile.

4:10 Paul may have been referring to the observance of Jewish festivals. The Jewish agitators among the Galatians required not only circumcision for salvation, but also adoption of the whole Jewish way of life, including the observance of food laws and the keeping of Jewish festivals.

■ **4:12–20** *Current Experience.* In contrast with their experience of the Holy Spirit when they had first received the gospel (3:1–5), the Galatians were now losing the blessings of the Spirit because they were turning away from the true gospel.

4:12 become like me, for I became like you. In order to bring the gospel to the Gentile Galatians, Paul had left behind many restrictive traditional Jewish applications of the Mosaic Law (1Co 9:19–23). He had become "like" the Galatians in freedom from these applications, and he now encouraged them to be "like" him in freedom from similar legalistic bondage. **You have done me no wrong.** Paul's positive characterization of his previous relationship with the Galatian Christians (developed further in vv. 13–16) contains an implicit plea that good relations continue. Paul's depth of concern for the Galatians is evident throughout this section.

4:13 because of an illness. The identity of Paul's ailment remains uncertain. Eye difficulties (v. 15; 6:11), malaria and epilepsy have all been suggested. A possible connection with Paul's "thorn in [his] flesh" (2Co 12:7) is likewise uncertain. Paul's illness apparently necessitated a longer stay in Galatia, which offered him greater opportunity to minister in the region.

4:17 zealous. See 6:12. The source of their zeal may have been their desire to avoid persecution from false teachers who claimed to be Christians or from unbelieving Jewish nationalists who saw the inclusiveness of the Christian movement as a threat to their cause. See *WLC* 105.

4:19–20 A touching witness to the depth of Paul's feeling for those whom he had brought to faith in Christ. Paul's anger in this epistle (1:6,9; 3:1; 5:12) reflects not only the seriousness with which he regarded the task of preserving the truth of the gospel, but also the love he had for his "children" in Christ. See *WLC* 124.

■ **4:21–31** *Abraham's Wives and Sons.* Paul returned to the Genesis account of Abraham (see 3:6—4:11), but this time he pointed out how the situation in Galatia paralleled that of Sarah, Hagar, Isaac and Ishmael.

4:22 two sons. Ishmael was the older (by Hagar; Ge 16) and Isaac the younger (by Sarah; Ge 21:1–6). Hagar was Sarah's slave, while Sarah was Abraham's wife.

4:23 Ishmael, the son of Abraham and the slave woman Hagar, was born after Abraham and Sarah had despaired of having the son God had promised. Isaac was born by a miracle of the Spirit long after Sarah's childbearing years were past. God showed that no divine promise is empty (Ge 18:14; Lk 1:37). Christ is the promised Son, and in him the Gentiles are made sons and heirs (3:29). Like Isaac, the Gentiles are born of the Spirit, fulfilling God's promise to Abraham (3:16; 4:28).

4:24 figuratively. In the sense that their historical occurrence bears a deeper significance. Paul did not question the historicity of the Genesis narrative. He pointed to a theological significance of

One covenant is from Mount Sinai and bears children who are to be slaves: This is Hagar. 25Now Hagar stands for Mount Sinai in Arabia and corresponds to the present city of Jerusalem, because she is in slavery with her children. 26But the Jerusalem that is above[h] is free, and she is our mother. 27For it is written:

> "Be glad, O barren woman,
> who bears no children;
> break forth and cry aloud,
> you who have no labor pains;
> because more are the children of the desolate woman
> than of her who has a husband."[a][i]

28Now you, brothers, like Isaac, are children of promise. 29At that time the son born in the ordinary way[j] persecuted the son born by the power of the Spirit.[k] It is the same now. 30But what does the Scripture say? "Get rid of the slave woman and her son, for the slave woman's son will never share in the inheritance with the free woman's son."[b][l] 31Therefore, brothers, we are not children of the slave woman, but of the free woman.

Freedom in Christ

5 It is for freedom that Christ has set us free.[m] Stand firm,[n] then, and do not let yourselves be burdened again by a yoke of slavery.[o]

2Mark my words! I, Paul, tell you that if you let yourselves be circumcised,[p] Christ will be of no value to you at all. 3Again I declare to every man who lets himself be circumcised that he is obligated to obey the whole law.[q] 4You who are trying to be justified by law have been alienated from Christ; you have fallen away from grace.[r] 5But by faith we eagerly await through the Spirit the righteousness for which we hope.[s] 6For in Christ Jesus neither circumcision nor uncircumcision has any value.[t] The only thing that counts is faith expressing itself through love.[u]

7You were running a good race.[v] Who cut in on you[w] and kept you from obeying the truth? 8That kind of persuasion does not come from the one who calls you.[x] 9"A little yeast works through the whole batch of dough."[y] 10I am confident[z] in the Lord that you will take no other view.[a] The one who is throwing you into confusion[b] will pay the penalty, whoever he may be. 11Brothers, if I am still preaching circumcision, why am I still being persecuted?[c] In that case the offense[d] of the cross has been abolished. 12As for those agitators,[e] I wish they would go the whole way and emasculate themselves!

4:26 [h]Heb 12:22; Rev 3:12
4:27 [i]Isa 54:1
4:29 [j]ver 23 [k]Ge 21:9
4:30 [l]Ge 21:10
5:1 [m]Jn 8:32 [n]1Co 16:13 [o]Ac 15:10; Gal 2:4
5:2 [p]Ac 15:1
5:3 [q]Gal 3:10
5:4 [r]Heb 12:15; 2Pe 3:17
5:5 [s]Ro 8:23,24
5:6 [t]1Co 7:19 [u]1Th 1:3
5:7 [v]1Co 9:24 [w]Gal 3:1
5:8 [x]Ro 8:28; Gal 1:6
5:9 [y]1Co 5:6
5:10 [z]2Co 2:3 [a]Php 3:15 [b]Gal 1:7
5:11 [c]Gal 4:29; 6:12 [d]1Co 1:23
5:12 [e]ver 10

[a] *27* Isaiah 54:1 [b] *30* Gen. 21:10

the historical events. Isaac was a child born by faith in the promise of God. In this sense, Isaac was a spiritual ancestor of everyone who seeks salvation through faith in God's promises in Christ. Ishmael was born by reliance on human, fleshly effort. In this sense, Ishmael is the spiritual ancestor of all who seek salvation by human merit.

4:25 present city of Jerusalem. The earthly city of Jerusalem was the seat of Jewish legalism. For this reason, Paul associated it with Hagar, Ishmael and the way of human merit.

4:26 Jerusalem that is above. Despite the legalism that emanated from Jerusalem in Paul's day, it was still the city where God had set his name, the place of his dwelling in the midst of his people (Ps 78:68–69). In the Christian faith, however, the true Jerusalem is where Christ reigns: heaven (Heb 12:22; Rev 21:2), where believers have their citizenship (Php 3:20). For this reason, Paul associated Sarah, Isaac and the way of faith with the heavenly Jerusalem.

4:29 See *WLC* 145.

■ **5:1—6:10** *Practical Exhortations.* In this final major section of the epistle, Paul turned to practical exhortations growing out of the true gospel of justification by faith alone. This material divides into three parts: freedom in Christ (5:1–15), the power of the Spirit (5:16—6:6), and divine judgment and blessing (6:7–10).

■ **5:1–15** *Freedom in Christ.* Paul's call away from legalism raised an important question: Are Christians simply free to live as they want? Paul answered this question by pointing to the important balance between freedom and responsibility.

5:1 yoke. Jewish literature from Paul's era sometimes referred to submission to instruction in the law as being under the law's yoke. Paul was concerned that his Gentile readers not allow the law to take the place of Christ in their lives (Mt 11:29; Ac 15:10). See the theological article "Christian Liberty" at Romans 14. See *WCF* 20.1; 20.2; *BC* 32.

5:2 Regarding both Christ and circumcision as necessary for salvation is tantamount to denying the sufficiency of Christ's death for salvation. To accept circumcision as a necessity for salvation is not only to accept a standard of works righteousness that can never be met (2:21), but also to reject what Christ has done. It is to return to the dominion of sin and to the law's curse.

5:4 fallen away from grace. That is, they would be renouncing God's grace by no longer relying on it. Those who are chosen in Christ will be kept from such a renunciation of the gospel, and Paul continued to have confidence that at least some in Galatia would heed his warning (v. 10). There may have been those, however, who appeared to be true members of Christ but who demonstrated by abandoning the gospel that they were not (Ro 11:22; 1Jn 2:19). Scripture admonishes us, therefore, to be "eager to make [our] calling and election sure" (2Pe 1:10) by living in a way that demonstrates the Spirit's presence within us (5:16—6:10; 2Pe 1:5–11). See *HC* 30.

5:5 through the Spirit. The Spirit gives us eager anticipation of justification on the last day because we have already been justified in Christ (Ro 5:1–5,9–10). The Spirit is our foretaste of the heritage of glory (2Co 5:5; Eph 1:13). **the righteousness for which we hope.** The sure hope of righteousness by faith is in contrast to the vain hope of righteousness by legal works.

5:6 Paul was not arguing against circumcision itself (6:15; Ac 16:3; 1Co 7:19) but against the attempt to make the rite a requirement for salvation. The one who believes in Jesus Christ and demonstrates the reality of his belief through a sanctified life is saved, whether circumcised or not. See *WCF* 11.2; *BC* 24.

5:11 still preaching circumcision. Paul may have been referring to his life before his conversion, or he may have been refuting a false charge from his opponents that he preached the necessity of circumcision for salvation when he was with the Jerusalem apostles but left out that requirement when in the company of Gentiles (1:10). **offense of the cross.** See 1 Corinthians 1:18—2:5.

5:12 emasculate. The word means "mutilate" or "castrate" (Php 3:2). Paul's anger was a result of seeing young believers led astray.

13 You, my brothers, were called to be free. But do not use your freedom to indulge the
sinful nature[a];[f] rather, serve one another[g] in love. 14 The entire law is summed up in a
single command: "Love your neighbor as yourself."[b][h] 15 If you keep on biting and devouring each other, watch out or you will be destroyed by each other.

Life by the Spirit

16 So I say, live by the Spirit,[i] and you will not gratify the desires of the sinful nature.[j]
17 For the sinful nature desires what is contrary to the Spirit, and the Spirit what is contrary to the sinful nature.[k] They are in conflict with each other, so that you do not do
what you want.[l] 18 But if you are led by the Spirit, you are not under law.[m]
19 The acts of the sinful nature are obvious: sexual immorality,[n] impurity and debauchery; 20 idolatry and witchcraft; hatred, discord, jealousy, fits of rage, selfish ambition, dissensions, factions 21 and envy; drunkenness, orgies, and the like.[o] I warn you, as
I did before, that those who live like this will not inherit the kingdom of God.
22 But the fruit[p] of the Spirit is love,[q] joy, peace, patience, kindness, goodness, faithfulness, 23 gentleness and self-control.[r] Against such things there is no law. 24 Those who
belong to Christ Jesus have crucified the sinful nature[s] with its passions and desires.[t]
25 Since we live by the Spirit, let us keep in step with the Spirit. 26 Let us not become conceited,[u] provoking and envying each other.

Doing Good to All

6 Brothers, if someone is caught in a sin, you who are spiritual[v] should restore him
gently. But watch yourself, or you also may be tempted. 2 Carry each other's burdens, and in this way you will fulfill the law of Christ.[w] 3 If anyone thinks he is something[x]
when he is nothing, he deceives himself. 4 Each one should test his own actions. Then he
can take pride in himself, without comparing himself to somebody else, 5 for each one
should carry his own load.

5:13 [f]1Co 8:9; 1Pe 2:16 [g]1Co 9:19; Eph 5:21
5:14 [h]Lev 19:18; Mt 22:39
5:16 [i]Ro 8:2,4-6,9,14 [j]ver 24
5:17 [k]Ro 8:5-8 [l]Ro 7:15-23
5:18 [m]Ro 6:14; 1Ti 1:9
5:19 [n]1Co 6:18
5:21 [o]Ro 13:13
5:22 [p]Mt 7:16-20; Eph 5:9 [q]Col 3:12-15
5:23 [r]Ac 24:25
5:24 [s]Ro 6:6 [t]ver 16,17
5:26 [u]Php 2:3
6:1 [v]1Co 2:15
6:2 [w]Ro 15:1; Jas 2:8
6:3 [x]Ro 12:3; 1Co 8:2

[a] *13* Or *the flesh*; also in verses 16, 17, 19 and 24 [b] *14* Lev. 19:18

Jesus had some equally strong words of warning for those who dared to lead others into error (Lk 17:1–2).

5:13 freedom. Christian freedom is freedom *from* sin, not freedom *to* sin (Ro 6:1—7:6). See *WCF* 20.3.

5:14 entire law. Paul did not nullify the law; he affirmed it. Christ fulfilled the law rather than abolishing it (Mt 5:17). Many outward aspects of the law, such as its civil and dietary requirements, must be significantly reinterpreted in light of Christ's work. But the law's moral requirements continue to declare God's will for Christian behavior (Ro 8:2–8; 13:8–10). See theological article "The Three Uses of the Law" at Ps 119. **Love.** See Matthew 19:19, Romans 13:10 and 1 Corinthians 13. See also *WCF* 19.6.

5:15 See *WLC* 136.

■**5:16—6:6** *Power of the Spirit.* Paul had just called the Galatians to responsible freedom in Christ, but how were they to obey the will of God if they were not under the restrictions and threats of legalism? Relying on the Holy Spirit is the only way to live for Christ.

5:16–17 See *HC* 32.

5:16 live by the Spirit. The Holy Spirit's dwelling within the believer is a sign that the believer is an heir to the covenant promises given to Abraham (3:14; 4:6; 5:5). The Spirit's presence is also a sign that in the final day God will declare the believer to be righteous (v. 5; 2Co 1:22; 5:5). See *WCF* 19.6.

5:17 sinful nature. Literally, "flesh." Paul said in 6:13 that the agitators in Galatia wanted to circumcise the Galatians in order to "boast" in their "flesh." In 2:16 he pointed out that no one (literally, "no flesh") will be justified by observing the law. Paul used the word "flesh" in at least three ways. The broadest use referred simply to humanness. A more narrow use referred to the physical aspect of human life. The narrowest use, especially when placed in contradistinction to "Spirit," referred to the fallen, sinful nature of people, which includes both the mind and the soul. If the Galatians abandoned Christ and placed their confidence in the law, they would be turning back to reliance on the flesh and thus to existence under the law's curse. There is hope as well as warning in Paul's words. The desires of the flesh do oppose the Spirit, but the power of Christian living flows from the fact that the opposite is also true. The desires of the Spirit deliver us from the flesh and the law. See *WCF* 6.5; 9.4; 13.2; 16.4; 16.5; *WLC* 149,195; *WSC* 82; *BC* 29; *HC* 127.

5:18–24 See *WCF* 16.5; 19.6; *WLC* 32,97; *HC* 86.

5:19–21 sexual immorality . . . orgies. Paul listed gross sins that legalists would deplore (e.g., sexual immorality and idolatry) but then implicated them for the very sins that caused them to bite and devour each other (e.g., selfish ambition and factions; cf. v. 15). See *HC* 87,106; *WLC* 105,139.

5:21 will not inherit the kingdom of God. Paul uses this language several times in his letters (1Co 6:9–10; 15:50; cf. Eph 5:5). His point is that those who do not exhibit the influence of the Spirit in their lives will not take part in the consummation of God's kingdom that will take place when Christ returns.

5:22 fruit of the Spirit. In other passages Paul used the metaphor of agricultural produce to describe the conduct of the believer (Ro 6:22; Eph 5:9; Php 1:11). John the Baptist likewise claimed that true repentance would produce the "fruit" of concrete ethical behavior (Mt 3:8; Lk 3:8). The love produced by the Spirit is like the love of Christ. It goes far beyond the performance of legalistic self-righteousness (Lk 10:25–37).

5:24 have crucified the sinful nature. See 2:20, 6:14 and Romans 6:6. For the people of Christ, the cross broke the grip of the law's condemnation (2:19). Christians must by faith recognize the reality of their union with Christ in his death. So too, they must realize that they have been raised to new life in the Spirit of Christ; therefore, they must walk in the Spirit (Col 3:1,3,5). See *WCF* 13.1; *WLC* 75; *BC* 29.

5:26 See *WLC* 99,132,148; *WSC* 81.

6:1–2 See *HC* 107.

6:1 you who are spiritual. In Paul's writings the word "spiritual" frequently means "of the Holy Spirit" (e.g., Ro 1:11; 1Co 2:13; 12:1; 14:1,37; Col 1:9). Those who are in step with the Spirit (5:25) are to reach out to the believer whom sin has ensnared, but they should be cautious lest sin also ensnare them in the process.

6:2 the law of Christ. This includes loving not only one's neighbor (Mt 22:39; Gal 5:14) but one's enemy as well (Mt 5:43), using God's love as the model.

6:4 test his own actions. Paul urged the Galatian Christians to examine themselves as individuals before God rather than to draw false confidence from relative comparisons with others (cf. 2Co 13:5–6). **take pride in himself.** Literally, "have reason to boast in himself." As Paul subsequently made clear, reason for "boasting" is not to be found in one's obedience to the law. While the false teachers boasted of their success in encouraging legalism (v. 13), Paul boasted in the cross of Christ alone (v. 14; cf. 2Co 11:16—12:10).

6:5 load. In the Greek, as in the English translation, this is a different word from the one Paul used in 6:2 ("burdens"), and the shift in words indicates a shift in meaning. Paul's meaning in 6:2 is that we should help others resist the "burden" of temptation to sin.

6:6 [y]1Co 9:11,14
6:7 [z]1Co 6:9 [a]2Co 9:6
6:8 [b]Job 4:8; Hos 8:7 [c]Jas 3:18
6:9 [d]1Co 15:58 [e]Rev 2:10
6:10 [f]Pr 3:27 [g]Eph 2:19
6:11 [h]1Co 16:21

6 Anyone who receives instruction in the word must share all good things with his instructor.[y]
7 Do not be deceived:[z] God cannot be mocked. A man reaps what he sows.[a] 8 The one
who sows to please his sinful nature, from that nature[a] will reap destruction;[b] the one
who sows to please the Spirit, from the Spirit will reap eternal life.[c] 9 Let us not become
weary in doing good,[d] for at the proper time we will reap a harvest if we do not give up.[e]
10 Therefore, as we have opportunity, let us do good[f] to all people, especially to those who
belong to the family[g] of believers.

Not Circumcision but a New Creation

11 See what large letters I use as I write to you with my own hand![h]
12 Those who want to make a good impression outwardly are trying to compel you to

[a] 8 Or *his flesh, from the flesh*

Paul's meaning here is that we should not take pride in how much better we are than others, because God alone is our judge and we are, as individuals, responsible before him. Rather, we should fulfill our own calling to his glory.

6:6 See *WLC* 127.

■ **6:7–10** *Divine Judgment and Blessing.* Paul closed his practical exhortations with a severe warning and a strong encouragement. Everyone will face the final judgment of God, but believers who walk by the Spirit will reap eternal rewards.

6:9–10 See *HC* 111.

6:10 The church has a responsibility to help alleviate the suffering of those outside its fellowship, but it has a special responsibility to help brothers and sisters in Christ who are in need (1Th 3:12). See *WCF* 26.1; *WLC* 141.

■ **6:11–18** *Postscript.* Paul closed this epistle with a summary of his message and a final salutation.

6:11 Paul sometimes dictated his letters to a secretary (Ro 16:22) but customarily picked up the pen himself toward the letter's end (1Co 16:21; Col 4:18; 2Th 3:17). His "large letters" have sometimes been taken as evidence of poor eyesight (4:15).

Union With Christ: What Does it Mean to Be "in Christ"?

ONE of the doctrines most commonly referenced by the New Testament writers was that of believers' union with Christ. This doctrine lies behind the vast majority of their use of phrases such as "in Christ," "in Jesus" and "in him." Reformed theology has tended to recognize two major ideas in this union: (1) Believers are mystically united to Jesus in a vital way, such that he dwells in them and they in him; and (2) Jesus is the representative of believers before the Father, especially in Jesus' death and resurrection.

It has been common to speak of the vital union between Jesus and believers as *mystical* because the Bible does not define precisely how it takes place or what it entails. Nevertheless, the Bible does make it clear that this union involves both our bodies and our spirits (1Co 6:15–17). It is the source of our spiritual lives and will ultimately result in the resurrection and glorification of our bodies (Ro 8:9–11; Col 3:3–4). Through this union, Christ frees us from sin's mastery over our lives (Ro 6:3–11; Gal 5:24), enables and compels us to do good works (Jn 15:1–8), and demonstrates his own power through us (2Co 13:3–6). The union of Christ to believers is so close that it can even be said that believers suffer because Jesus suffers (Ro 8:17; 2Co 1:5; Php 3:10; Col 1:24)—it is not just that Jesus suffers because it hurts him to see his people in hardship, but also that his people endure new adversities as an extension of the sufferings that first fall upon Jesus. By the same means, the comfort that Jesus experiences also flows to believers (2Co 1:4–5). In fact, because he has already inaugurated the age to come (see theological article "The Plan of the Ages" at Heb 7) and begun to enjoy the blessings of that age (e.g., his resurrection in glory), believers also participate in the blessings of that future age to some degree (2Co 5:17).

Because believers are joined to Christ in this mystical way, they share not only his experiences but also his very identity, so that the Father looks upon believers as though they were Christ himself, accounting to them Jesus' status and rights (Gal 3:26–29). Thus, it is through this identification that Jesus represents believers. Some of the more significant results of this representation include the following: (1) Jesus' death is credited to believers as their own death, such that they have fully satisfied the penalty for sin and may never fall under condemnation (Ro 5:15–19; 6:3–11; 7:1–6; 8:1; 2Co 5:14). (2) Jesus' resurrection guarantees the future resurrection of all who are in him (Ro 6:3–11; 2Ti 2:11); as he merited life for himself, he also merited life for them. (3) Jesus' ascension to the right hand of the Father bestows honor and security, as well as authority, on believers (Eph 1:18–23; 2:6–7; Col 3:1; cf. Ro 5:17; 2Ti 2:12). (4) Even believers' predestination to salvation depends upon this identification and representation (Eph 1:4,11). (5) Beyond this, every other blessing of God's covenant that Christ inherits also belongs to believers—not only eternal life and forgiveness, but also permanent and ultimate comfort, joy, intimacy, love, wealth and more. Christ earned all these blessings for himself, but because believers are identified with Christ, he shares them with us (Gal 3:26–29).

Beyond these blessings that derive from our union with Christ, believers are also mystically united to one another in him (Ro 12:5; Gal 3:26–28; Eph 4:25). For this reason, we share one another's joys and pains (1Co 12:26). Moreover, regardless of our social relationships to one another according to the world's measure, we all have equal dignity in Christ (2Co 5:14–16; Gal 3:28; Col 3:11) and are to treat one another accordingly, with all patience and love (1Co 12:14–25; Col 3:12–15).

be circumcised.[i] The only reason they do this is to avoid being persecuted[j] for the cross
of Christ. 13Not even those who are circumcised obey the law,[k] yet they want you to be
circumcised that they may boast about your flesh.[l] 14May I never boast except in the
cross of our Lord Jesus Christ, through which[a] the world has been crucified to me, and
I to the world.[m] 15Neither circumcision nor uncircumcision means anything;[n] what
counts is a new creation.[o] 16Peace and mercy to all who follow this rule, even to the Israel of God.

17Finally, let no one cause me trouble, for I bear on my body the marks[p] of Jesus.
18The grace of our Lord Jesus Christ[q] be with your spirit,[r] brothers. Amen.

6:12 [i]Ac 15:1 [j]Gal 5:11
6:13 [k]Ro 2:25 [l]Php 3:3
6:14 [m]Ro 6:2,6
6:15 [n]1Co 7:19 [o]2Co 5:17
6:17 [p]Isa 44:5; 2Co 1:5
6:18 [q]Ro 16:20 [r]2Ti 4:22

[a] *14* Or *whom*

6:12 circumcised. See note on 2:3. **avoid being persecuted.** It is possible that those advocating circumcision in Galatia were doing so under pressure from extremely zealous Jewish nationalists in Judea (see note on 4:17).
6:14 boast . . . in the cross. For a more detailed outworking of this concept, see 1 Corinthians 1:18—2:5. See *WLC* 141.
6:15 circumcision. See note on 5:6. **a new creation.** In many respects, this statement sums up Paul's letter to the Galatians. Paul wanted the Galatians to leave behind matters of the fallen, old creation (including circumcision) and to embrace the wonder of the renewed creation that began with the death and resurrection of Christ. In this renewed creation, the Holy Spirit's activity in the believer's life begins to reverse the effects of the fall and to produce the new person (2Co 5:17). When Christ returns, we will take our place in the new heavens and the new earth (Rev 21:1). In the meantime, we must focus on living in the blessings of the new creation that have already become reality.
6:16 Israel of God. This phrase refers to the newly constituted people of God. Their identifying mark is the Holy Spirit rather than circumcision, and as a group they therefore include both Gentiles and Jews. Elsewhere similar phrases refer to the elect of the Jewish nation, for whose salvation Paul was deeply concerned (Ro 9:1–6; 11:12,26,31), but in the context of this letter such a reading is untenable—especially in light of verse 15, which indicates that the Israel of God contains both circumcised and uncircumcised believers.
6:17 marks. The Greek word denotes the brands used to mark a slave as the property of a certain master. The word was also used to refer to the mark that pagan priests carried to identify the god they served. It is likely that Paul was referring to the scars he had received during his missionary activity (2Co 11:23–25). These scars branded him as a slave of Christ (Ro 1:1; Php 1:1; Tit 1:1).
6:18 This benediction is a fitting conclusion to this letter, in which Paul was intensely concerned with God's grace. It summarizes Paul's hope that the gospel of God's grace would triumph among the Galatians.

EPHESIANS

Introduction

Overview

Author: The apostle Paul

Purpose: To teach the Christians at Ephesus the wonder and practical implications of being the church in Christ

Date: A.D. 60–62

Key Truths:

- The church has received wondrous blessings in union with Christ.
- The church has been brought from death to life in Christ.
- The church will extend worldwide with Jews and Gentiles joined together in Christ.
- The church must strive for unity in Christ.
- The church must live in the ways of Christ, not return to the ways of the sinful world.
- The church must find strength for spiritual warfare in Christ.

Author

The apostle Paul wrote this epistle (1:1; 3:1). Themes and language common to other Pauline letters abound in Ephesians; its verbal similarities with Colossians are especially striking.

In the modern era, however, questions have been raised about whether Paul actually wrote this epistle. Some believe that Ephesians appears to be too dependent on Colossians. It has been noticed that even though this letter resembles other letters from Paul, phrases tend to pile up more than in the earlier epistles. The letter is less didactic and more prayerful. Doctrine has given way to doxology, reasoned argument to awe. Ideas that are only implicit in his earlier letters become explicit here. Such considerations lead many to suspect that Ephesians was not written by Paul himself, but by one of his students who was attempting to carry forward some of Paul's ideas, especially those expressed in Colossians.

The language and syntax of Ephesians are certainly distinctive. They are so Pauline, however, that even if the letter did not bear the name of its author, it would be difficult to imagine the church ever crediting its authorship to anyone but Paul. It is hard to believe, as the doubters of Pauline authorship do, that a person slavishly trying to sound like Paul—even copying some verses word-for-word from Colossians—would at the same time creatively transform Paul's normal style and expand Paul's doctrine. Even less imaginable would be the early church's failure to discern that such an imitation was not an authoritative Pauline letter. It is far easier to account for the verbal similarities with Colossians by assuming that Paul wrote Ephesians shortly after having completed Colossians. It demands far less credulity to imagine Paul adopting an unusually prayerful mode to focus on the cosmic significance of Christ's church and of Christ himself.

Time and Place of Writing

The imprisonment mentioned in 3:1 and 6:20 is the same as that referred to in Colossians 4:3, 10 and 18. It probably references Paul's two-year house arrest (A.D. 60–62) in Rome, which is recounted in Acts 28.

Original Audience

Ephesus was the capital of the Roman province of Asia on the western coast of Asia Minor. A bridge city between the western and eastern halves of the Roman Empire, and among the top five cities of the empire in the first century, it was also one of the most important cities in the spread of Christianity. Paul's ministry there in A.D. 53–55 is recounted in Acts 19. During Paul's unusually long stay there, Ephesus became the center for the evangelism of the western part of Asia Minor (Ac 19:10). Paul's affectionate ties with this church are reflected in his speech to its elders as he departed for Jerusalem (Ac 20:16–38).

The city's most prominent civic monument was the temple of the goddess Artemis (Diana), one of the seven wonders of the ancient world. One inscription described the city as the "nurturer" of the goddess. Artemis, in turn, was said to have made Ephesus "most glorious" among all the Asian cities. People from this background would have appreciated the irony in Paul's words about Christ "nurturing" (NIV, "feed[ing]") his own body, the church (5:29). They would well have understood the point of contrast when Paul described Christ's goal to present his church as a glorious or "radiant" bride (5:27). It was also in Ephesus that Paul's preaching of Christ came into conflict with an economic structure dependent upon pagan worship (Ac 19:23–41) and the occult (Ac 19:17–20). Paul's exhortation to expose shameful and fruitless deeds of darkness (5:8–14) and to prepare for warfare against "spiritual forces of evil in the heavenly realms" (6:12) would have struck readers in Ephesus with special force.

There are indications that Paul wrote the letter for a broader audience than Ephesus. The oldest and best Greek manuscripts do not include "in Ephesus" (1:1) in the address of the letter, but read, "To the saints who are also faithful in Christ Jesus." Several important second- and third-century church leaders were unaware of an Ephesian address. Three verses in Ephesians (1:15; 3:2 and 4:21) fail to suggest the personal ties we know to have existed between Paul and the Ephesians. Moreover, the letter lacks the personal references and greetings Paul almost always included in his correspondence. At the same time, no manuscripts name any other city as the recipient of the epistle. As a result, many scholars believe Ephesians was written as a general letter that Paul intended to circulate among a number of churches in western Asia Minor. This would be in keeping with the sweeping content of the letter as a whole. All the same, it is hard to imagine why "in Ephesus" would have been added to the overwhelming majority of manuscripts that do include the address if it had not been there in the first place.

Accordingly, one of two theories is likely. Paul may have written originally to the Ephesians, but as the letter was spread from church to church over time the address may have begun to be omitted. Alternatively, Paul may have sent the letter in two forms: one directly to the Ephesians and the other as a circular for a more general audience.

Purpose and Distinctives

Like the letter to the Romans, Ephesians provides a unique insight into Paul's theology, for it was written when Paul had the luxury of not having to address a critical, local controversy. What stands out about Ephesians is the awe with which it contemplates the mystery of the church.

Ephesians describes the church as God's new humanity, a colony in which the Lord of history has established a foretaste of the renewed unity and dignity of the human race (1:10–14; 2:11–22; 3:6,9–11; 4:1—6:9). The church is a community in which God's power to reconcile men and women to himself is experienced and then shared in transformed relationships (2:1–10; 4:1–16; 4:32—5:2; 5:22—6:9). It is a new temple, a building of people, grounded in the sure revelation of what God has done in history and ever growing to become the place where God resides on Earth (2:19–22; 3:17–19). The church is an organism in which power and authority are exercised after the pattern of Christ himself (1:22; 5:25–27) and as a stewardship, a means of service (4:11–16; 5:22—6:9). It is an outpost in a dark world (5:3–17), under hostile attack (6:10–17) but offering light to the lost, standing against humanity's spiritual enemies and anticipating the day of final redemption. The church is a bride being prepared for the approach of her lover and husband (5:22–32).

Outline

I. Salutation (1:1–2)	*Paul identified himself and blessed the faithful church of Ephesus.*
II. The Blessings of the Church in Christ (1:3–23) A. Praise for Blessings in Christ (1:3–14) B. Prayer for Enlightenment (1:15–23)	*God has so richly blessed and honored his people that the church should praise him. God's eternal plan from before the foundation of the world was to unite us with Christ and raise us into the heavenly realms where Christ now reigns in glory. The church needs to grasp the wonder of the hope, inheritance and power that come from being united with Christ.*
III. Understanding the Blessings of the Church (2:1—3:21) A. Made Alive in Christ (2:1–10) B. Made One in Christ (2:11–22) C. Paul and the Divine Mystery (3:1–13) D. Strength for the Church (3:14–21)	*Understanding what God has done for believers is essential to strengthening the church. Believers have been resurrected from spiritual death into a new life that will lead to immeasurable blessings for them in future ages. They have been joined together through the cross of Christ to become a holy temple in which the Spirit of God dwells. A grand, divine mystery is revealed: Through the gospel Gentiles, along with Jews, have become full heirs of God's blessings. Just as God had always planned, this international church is to display God's wisdom to the evil powers that have resisted the expansion of his kingdom to all nations. Paul prayed that God would strengthen believers by enabling them to see how wondrously they have been blessed. He then praised God who does so much for his church.*
IV. Walking in the Blessings of the Church (4:1—6:20) A. Uniting in Diversity (4:1–16) B. Living in New Ways (4:17—6:9) C. Standing Strong Against the Devil (6:10–20)	*Understanding how the church is blessed will lead to living in ways that correspond to those blessings. The church must live in harmony despite its diversities. The church's varied, God-given gifts are blessings to be used for building it up in unity and love. The church must learn to live in new ways, holding to the blessings God has given and never returning to the ways of the world. Believers are to live in ways that are true to the Christian faith, because they have come to know Christ and the scope of what he has done for them. Spiritual battles are to be fought with the blessings of God. The church's victory will be certain if the armor of God is used.*

V. Final Greetings (6:21–24)

Paul's letter ends with an introduction of his associate and a blessing of peace to those who love Christ with an undying love.

1 Paul, an apostle[a] of Christ Jesus by the will of God,[b]

To the saints in Ephesus,[a] the faithful[b][c] in Christ Jesus:

[2]Grace and peace to you from God our Father and the Lord Jesus Christ.[d]

Spiritual Blessings in Christ

[3]Praise be to the God and Father of our Lord Jesus Christ,[e] who has blessed us in the
heavenly realms[f] with every spiritual blessing in Christ. [4]For he chose us in him before
the creation of the world to be holy and blameless[g] in his sight. In love[h] [5]he[c] predestined[i]
us to be adopted as his sons through Jesus Christ, in accordance with his pleasure[j] and
will— [6]to the praise of his glorious grace, which he has freely given us in the One he
loves.[k] [7]In him we have redemption[l] through his blood, the forgiveness of sins, in accordance with the riches of God's grace [8]that he lavished on us with all wisdom and understanding. [9]And he[d] made known to us the mystery[m] of his will according to his good
pleasure, which he purposed in Christ, [10]to be put into effect when the times will have
reached their fulfillment[n]—to bring all things in heaven and on earth together under one
head, even Christ.[o]

1:1 [a]1Co 1:1 [b]2Co 1:1 [c]Col 1:2
1:2 [d]Ro 1:7
1:3 [e]2Co 1:3 [f]Eph 2:6; 3:10; 6:12
1:4 [g]Eph 5:27; Col 1:22 [h]Eph 4:2, 15,16
1:5 [i]Ro 8:29,30 [j]1Co 1:21
1:6 [k]Mt 3:17
1:7 [l]Ro 3:24
1:9 [m]Ro 16:25
1:10 [n]Gal 4:4 [o]Col 1:20

[a] *1* Some early manuscripts do not have *in Ephesus.* [b] *1* Or *believers who are* [c] *4,5* Or *sight in love. 5He* [d] *8,9* Or *us. With all wisdom and understanding, 9he*

■ **1:1–2** *Salutation.* Paul began this letter by identifying himself and his apostolic office. Most early manuscripts also identify the Christians at Ephesus as the recipients (see "Introduction: Original Audience").

■ **1:3–23** *The Blessings of the Church in Christ.* Paul praised God for blessing his people and prayed that God would enlighten the Ephesians even more so that they could further appreciate these blessings.

■ **1:3–14** *Praise for Blessings in Christ.* Paul burst forth with praise to God in these verses, which form a single sentence in the Greek. This doxology is similar to the praise of God's purpose in Romans 8:28–30, although it is greatly expanded. It divides into three sections: Praise goes to the electing Father (vv. 3–6), to the redeeming Son (vv. 7–12) and to the sealing Spirit (vv. 13–14). Paul reflected on believers' election from eternity, forgiveness in the present and inheritance in the future. A central concept throughout this praise appears in the repetition of the phrases "in Christ" or "in him," which refer to the intimate union God has established between Christ and his chosen, forgiven and sealed people (see theological article "Union With Christ" at Gal 6). See *HC* 54.

1:3–6 Paul began this doxology with praise to the Father for his electing grace. See *WCF* 3.3; 3.5; 12; 18.3; *WLC* 12,13,69,74,75; *WSC* 7,20,32; *HC* 26,33; *CD* 1.7; 1.9; 1.I; 1.V.

1:3 Praise be. Literally, "blessed be," common language of praise in the Old Testament (e.g., Ge 14:20; Ex 18:10; Ru 4:14; Pss 17:47; 27:6; 30:22; 40:14; 65:20). **in the heavenly realms.** This phrase appears five times in Ephesians (1:3,20; 2:6; 3:10; 6:12; cf. 1:10; 3:15; 6:9). Two of these occurrences are similar to its meaning here. First, when Christ was raised from the dead, he was seated at the right hand of the Father "in the heavenly realms" (1:20). Second, because of their union with him, believers have been raised up and seated with Christ "in the heavenly realms" (2:6).

1:4–5 he chose us in him. God has chosen people for a relationship with himself (Ro 8:29–33; 9:6–26; 11:5,7,28; 16:13; Col 3:12; 1Th 1:4; 2Th 2:13; Tit 1:1). Some suggest that the phrase "in him" means that God chose to elect those whom he foresaw would have faith in Christ. Not only does this view add a thought that is not in the text, but elsewhere Paul taught that the very state of being "in Christ" is something to which one is chosen (1Co 1:26–31). Moreover, Paul explicitly stated that the ground of God's predestining love resides in his own good pleasure (vv. 5,9; cf. Dt 7:7–8), not in anything we have done or will do (Ro 9:11,16). The phrase "in him" means that God's choice always had in view a fallen people in union with their Redeemer (2Ti 1:9). First Peter 1:18–21 and Revelation 13:8 also shed important light on God's choice of the Redeemer and his people. **holy and blameless.** God intends to bring those whom he elects all the way from spiritual death in sin apart from God (2:1–5) to the forgiveness of their sins in Christ (v. 7) and to the elimination of sin from their experience when they are finally made completely like Christ (Ro 8:29–30). **In love.** It is uncertain whether this phrase belongs with what precedes it or with what follows it (see NIV text note). If "in love" belongs with the preceding phrase, it explains the nature of the holiness and blamelessness to which believers are called. This is consistent with the use of the phrase elsewhere in Ephesians (3:17; 4:2,15,16; 5:2). If "in love" belongs with verse 5, however, the phrase qualifies predestination as being not just an act of God's own good pleasure, but also an act of his love. This is probably the better reading and is consistent both with 2:4 and with the Hebrew understanding of "foreknew" at Romans 8:29 (i.e., virtually equivalent to "foreloved"). **adopted.** See *WCF* 3.6; *BC* 16.

1:6–7 See *WLC* 194.

1:6 The thought of God's almighty love leads to an extravagant outpouring of praise (vv. 12,14) at the overwhelming grace of a God who has not only the power, but also the will, to overcome all obstacles in bringing spiritually lifeless corpses into a living relationship with himself. This is expanded in 2:1–10. This praise is the goal of God's redemptive purpose and work. **grace . . . the One he loves.** This recalls the language of Colossians 1:13, but it also brings into view the Redeemer himself as an object of God's electing love (1Pe 1:18–21; Rev 13:8). See *WCF* 3.5; 3.8; 16.6; *WLC* 38,55.

1:7–12 Paul praised Jesus Christ for his redemptive work on behalf of believers. See *WCF* 3.5; 8.8; 10.1; *HC* 70.

1:7 redemption. Bringing about someone's deliverance (usually from slavery or captivity) by the payment of a price or ransom. In Paul's theology redemption is past, present and future. For the redemption that is yet to come, see 1:14 and 4:30 (see also note on Col 1:14). **forgiveness of sins.** See note on Colossians 2:13. See also *WCF* 11.1; 11.3; 15.3; *WLC* 70,71.

1:9 mystery. See notes on 3:5 and 6 and Colossians 1:26. See also *WCF* 3.5.

1:10 when the times will have reached their fulfillment. Literally, "the fullness of the times." By virtue of his death and resurrection, Christ has already assumed headship over the church, and, though behind the scenes, he already rules the universe (Ac 2:32–36; Col 1:15–20). But a future focus is dominant in this verse. Paul wanted to impress upon his readers that the visible unity of the church is the inauguration of Christ's eventual visible reign over all things. That is why Paul stressed the unity of Jew and Gentile in the church (vv. 11–14; 2:11–22) and the practice of love among Christians (4:2,15; 4:32—5:2; 5:21–23). Verses 9–12 are expanded in 3:2–12. See *WCF* 25.1; *WLC* 64.

11 In him we were also chosen,[a] having been predestined according to the plan of him
who works out everything in conformity with the purpose[p] of his will, 12 in order that we,
who were the first to hope in Christ, might be for the praise of his glory.[q] 13 And you also
were included in Christ when you heard the word of truth,[r] the gospel of your salvation.
Having believed, you were marked in him with a seal,[s] the promised Holy Spirit, 14 who
is a deposit guaranteeing our inheritance[t] until the redemption of those who are God's
possession—to the praise of his glory.

Thanksgiving and Prayer

15 For this reason, ever since I heard about your faith in the Lord Jesus and your love
for all the saints,[u] 16 I have not stopped giving thanks for you,[v] remembering you in my
prayers. 17 I keep asking that the God of our Lord Jesus Christ, the glorious Father,[w] may
give you the Spirit[b] of wisdom[x] and revelation, so that you may know him better. 18 I pray
also that the eyes of your heart may be enlightened[y] in order that you may know the
hope to which he has called you, the riches of his glorious inheritance in the saints, 19 and
his incomparably great power for us who believe. That power[z] is like the working of his
mighty strength,[a] 20 which he exerted in Christ when he raised him from the dead[b] and
seated him at his right hand in the heavenly realms, 21 far above all rule and authority,
power and dominion, and every title[c] that can be given, not only in the present age but
also in the one to come. 22 And God placed all things under his feet[d] and appointed him
to be head[e] over everything for the church, 23 which is his body, the fullness of him who
fills everything in every way.

Made Alive in Christ

2 As for you, you were dead in your transgressions and sins,[f] 2 in which you used to
live[g] when you followed the ways of this world and of the ruler of the kingdom of

1:11 [p]Eph 3:11; Heb 6:17
1:12 [q]ver 6,14
1:13 [r]Col 1:5 [s]Eph 4:30
1:14 [t]Ac 20:32
1:15 [u]Col 1:4
1:16 [v]Ro 1:8
1:17 [w]Jn 20:17 [x]Col 1:9
1:18 [y]Ac 26:18; 2Co 4:6
1:19 [z]Col 1:29 [a]Eph 6:10
1:20 [b]Ac 2:24
1:21 [c]Php 2:9,10
1:22 [d]Mt 28:18 [e]Eph 4:15; 5:23
2:1 [f]ver 5; Col 2:13
2:2 [g]Col 3:7

a *11* Or *were made heirs* b *17* Or *a spirit*

1:11–14 Paul anticipated what he would say in 3:6 about Jews and Gentiles being "heirs together" of the promise in Christ. Believing Jews of Paul's day, the "first to hope in Christ" (v. 12), were where they were by the will of God, and they were to the praise of God's glory. Believing Gentiles who responded to the gospel received the same promise that had been made to Israel (i.e., the reception of the Holy Spirit) and were likewise where they were to the praise of God's glory.
1:11 everything . . . his will. Paul's statement on the extent of God's will is sweeping. See *WCF* 2.1; 3.1; 3.5; 5.1; 8.5; *WLC* 12,14; *WSC* 7; *BC* 13; *HC* 26; *CD* 1.6.
1:13–14 See *WCF* 18.2; *WLC* 59; *WSC* 30; *HC* 1.
1:13 seal. Like the indelible impression made by a king's signet ring, the Holy Spirit is an inward mark of God's ownership of his people. **the promised Holy Spirit.** As Jesus said (Lk 24:49), the Holy Spirit is the promise of the Father. Remarkably, this promise is extended to Gentiles, as well as to Jews, on the basis of their trust in Christ (Eze 36:26–27; Joel 2:28; Jn 14–16; Ac 1:4–5; 2:33,38–39; Gal 3:14; 4:6). See *WLC* 72,81.
1:14 deposit. The Spirit is not only a fulfillment of God's promise to indwell his people, but he is also a guarantee that God will bring them to their final inheritance. As a down payment or first installment on their full redemption, the Spirit is both a guarantee and a foretaste of the glory of the age to come (Ro 8:18–23). For the redemption that is already enjoyed, see verse 7. **God's possession.** This recalls the Old Testament notion of God choosing a people as his inheritance (Dt 32:9; Ps 33:12) and purchasing them out of bondage to become a prized possession (Ex 19:5; Dt 7:6). Peter agreed with Paul's application of this Jewish language to Gentiles (see 1Pe 2:9). See *WCF* 8.5.
■ **1:15–23** *Prayer for Enlightenment.* Paul prayed that God would enlighten the Ephesian Christians in order that they would have greater motivation to praise God for the blessings they had received and would receive, and to unify with and minister to one another within the church.
1:15 ever since I heard. See "Introduction: Original Audience." Ephesus was a church in which Paul had ministered for over two years, although when he wrote this letter, it may have been as long as five years since he had been there. If this letter was in fact addressed to the Ephesian church, it is clear that the church had grown considerably since he had last seen it. On the other hand, his mention of people about whose faith and love he had only heard may be an indication that this was intended to be a circular letter for churches he had not visited.
1:17–20 See *WCF* 10.1; 14.1; *WLC* 67,72,190,192; *BC* 22; *CD* 3–4.VIII.
1:19–23 These verses distill the New Testament's teaching on the resurrection and enthronement of Jesus (see note on Col 1:18). But they also make two vital contributions to the New Testament understanding of Jesus' resurrection and the status of believers. First, Paul said that the same power that raised Jesus from the dead is at work in the believer (2:4–5; 3:16–17). Second, the apostle asserted that Christ enjoys his position as head over everything "for the church" (v. 22). Not only is Christ at the most exalted position in the universe, but he is there as the believers' representative (Eph 2:6; Col 3:3), governing the universe in the interest of (i.e., for the sake of) his church. The ethics of Ephesians pivot on the truth that authority exists for the sake of service. Jesus' majestic use of power and authority in the interest of his people is the Christian's model (4:1–2,7–13; 4:32—5:2; 5:22–33). All of chapter 2 was written to remind Paul's Gentile readers of two specific ways in which Christ's power had been exercised to benefit them: Christ brought them (1) from death to life (2:1–10) and (2) from alienation from God's people to membership among them (2:11–22). See *WCF* 25.1; 25.6; *WLC* 51,52,54,64,66; *WSC* 28; *BC* 29,31; *HC* 50.
1:20–21 in the heavenly realms . . . rule and authority, power and dominion, and every title. See note on 3:10.
1:21 not only in the present age but also in the one to come. See 1 Corinthians 15:24.
■ **2:1—3:21** *Understanding the Blessings of the Church.* Paul emphasized that God blesses the church by giving believers eternal life, unifying them with one another and empowering them to persevere in faith.
■ **2:1–10** *Made Alive in Christ.* These verses present in condensed form what Paul had expounded at length in Romans 1–8, namely that by God's grace through means of faith, God gives spiritual life and moral ability to helpless sinners, releasing them from future condemnation and causing them to live righteously for him.
2:1–5 See *WCF* 6.2; 6.4; 9.3; 10.1; 10.2; *WLC* 27,52,67,72,191,192; *WSC* 19; *BC* 15,24; *CD* 3–4.IV.
2:1–3 Humankind's natural state is that of a walking death. This state, often called spiritual death, has five dimensions. (1) It is universal; both Gentiles (v. 2) and Jews (v. 3) are "by nature objects of wrath" (v. 3). For Paul's view of "nature," see Romans 1. (2) It is an active rebellion against God. Note the use of the verb "live" with reference to Gentiles in verse 2 (literally, "walk"; 4:17–19) and to Jews in verse 3 (literally, "conduct one's life"). (3) It is an imprisonment to the evil rule of Satan, who is called "the ruler of the kingdom of the air" in verse 2 (see also Jn 12:31; 2Co 4:4; Gal 4:3; Eph 6:12; Col 1:13; 2:15). (4) It brings with it an utter inability to do anything about itself (Ro 8:7; 1Co 12:3; cf. Jn 1:13; 3:3,5; 6:44;

2:2 [h]Jn 12:31; Eph 6:12 [i]Eph 5:6
2:3 [j]Gal 5:16
2:5 [k]ver 1 [l]ver 8; Ac 15:11
2:6 [m]Eph 1:20 [n]Eph 1:3
2:7 [o]Tit 3:4
2:8 [p]ver 5
2:9 [q]2Ti 1:9 [r]1Co 1:29
2:10 [s]Eph 4:24 [t]Tit 2:14
2:11 [u]Col 2:11
2:12 [v]Gal 3:17 [w]1Th 4:13
2:13 [x]ver 17; Ac 2:39 [y]Col 1:20

the air,[h] the spirit who is now at work in those who are disobedient.[i] [3]All of us also lived
among them at one time, gratifying the cravings of our sinful nature[a][j] and following its
desires and thoughts. Like the rest, we were by nature objects of wrath. [4]But because of
his great love for us, God, who is rich in mercy, [5]made us alive with Christ even when we
were dead in transgressions[k]—it is by grace you have been saved.[l] [6]And God raised us
up with Christ and seated us with him[m] in the heavenly realms[n] in Christ Jesus, [7]in order that in the coming ages he might show the incomparable riches of his grace, expressed in his kindness[o] to us in Christ Jesus. [8]For it is by grace you have been saved,[p]
through faith—and this not from yourselves, it is the gift of God— [9]not by works,[q] so that
no one can boast.[r] [10]For we are God's workmanship, created[s] in Christ Jesus to do good
works,[t] which God prepared in advance for us to do.

One in Christ

[11]Therefore, remember that formerly you who are Gentiles by birth and called "uncircumcised" by those who call themselves "the circumcision" (that done in the body by
the hands of men)[u]— [12]remember that at that time you were separate from Christ, excluded from citizenship in Israel and foreigners to the covenants of the promise,[v] without hope[w] and without God in the world. [13]But now in Christ Jesus you who once were
far away have been brought near[x] through the blood of Christ.[y]

[a] 3 Or *our flesh*

8:43–44). (5) It invites the just anger of God (Ro 1:18–20; 2:5; 9:22; Eph 2:3; 5:6; Col 3:6). See *WLC* 25; *WSC* 18; *HC* 5.

2:3–9 See *WCF* 6.6; *HC* 45,49; *CD* 1.IV; 3–4.III.

2:4 But . . . God. Paul painted such a bleak portrait of the human situation precisely to highlight the contrast with God's gracious and merciful response to it. **because of his great love for us.** Paul's thought follows the pattern of Deuteronomy 7:7–8: God loves his people for no other reason than that he chooses to do so—certainly not because of any virtue within them. Men and women caught in the web of death outlined in verses 1–3 have no means of making themselves alive, of breaking away from their slavery to Satan or of averting the wrath of God. God himself, insisted Paul, brings the walking dead to life. And in offering God's own love as the ground for his doing so, Paul excluded any consideration of merit, effort or ability on the part of those who become alive. The hopeless condition of sinners apart from Christ that Paul outlined in verses 1–3 is the presupposition for understanding his teaching on God's election in 1:4–6 and on his sovereign, loving gift of life in 2:4–10. Note the summary in Romans 8:29–30.

2:5–6 made us alive . . . raised us up . . . seated us. These verbs properly refer to historical events in the life of Christ: his resurrection from the dead and enthronement at the right hand of God. But Paul assumed a union between Christ and those for whom he died—those who come to trust him (1:3; Col 3:1–4)—so that what is said of the Redeemer can also be said of the redeemed. What once historically happened to Jesus also happened to believers in a mystical, spiritual way. Moreover, these things will eventually happen to the "outward" aspect of believers as well (2Co 4:16) when they are resurrected to glory at Jesus' return (Ro 8:11; 1Co 15). For now, there is a parallel experience within the inner person: a newness of mind (Ro 12:1–2; Eph 4:23–24; Col 3:10), a new identity as God's sons and daughters (Ro 8:14–17) and a new ability to live according to God's character, free of the control of Satan (Ro 8:1–4; 2Co 5:17). See *WCF* 26.1; *WLC* 52,65,83.

2:5 In the Greek, Paul began a clause in verse 1, inserted a parenthesis in verses 2–4 to make it clear that he saw Jews to be as spiritually dead as Gentiles, and then resumed the thought in verse 5. The result is that all the more weight is thrown on the main verb ("made us alive") of verse 5. See *WCF* 9.3; 10.2; *WLC* 67; *CD* 3–4.IV.

2:6–9 See *WCF* 11.1; *WLC* 66,67.

2:7 If the ground of our salvation is God's love and mercy, its goal is the promotion of his grace and kindness (see note on 3:6). See *WCF* 11.3.

2:8–10 *WCF* 16.5; *HC* 21,60.

2:8 you have been saved. Paul's practice in his earlier letters was to refer to salvation either as a future event (Ro 5:9–10) or as a present process (1Co 1:18; 2Co 2:15). The one exception was Romans 8:24, where Paul put salvation in the past but qualified it as needing completion at Christ's return: "For in this hope we were saved." Ephesians 2:8 has come to have a special place in the vocabulary of the church because it dramatically states that salvation is a completed action that has a present effect. **through faith.** Our means of access to God's gracious gift is the exercise of faith in Christ and in his work on the cross. **and this not from yourselves, it is the gift of God.** This parenthesis is thought by many to refer to the whole complex of salvation by grace through faith as a gift of God. The thought is true enough, stating what is already clear in the passage. Others, however, take the word "this" in the parenthesis as referring to its nearest antecedent ("faith"), or more precisely, the act of believing (since Paul switched from the feminine gender of "faith" to the neuter of "this"). If this is the correct reading, it is a powerful statement of the extent of God's provision of life in Christ. Since apart from Christ we are as impotent as the image of walking death implies (vv. 1–3), then even for a believing response to Christ we are dependent on God's gracious gift. Paul appears to be making explicit here what is implicit elsewhere in the New Testament: that God is the ultimate source of saving faith (Jn 6:37,44,65; Ac 13:48; 14:27; 16:14; Php 1:29; Col 1:3–6). See *WCF* 10.2; 14.1; *WLC* 59,71; *WSC* 30; *BC* 23; *HC* 60,65; *CD* 1.5.

2:9 works. These are not the meritorious ground of acceptance by God—only faith rightly relates one to God (Ro 3:21—4:8). But good works are a vital consequence and evidence of life with God (Tit 2:14; 3:8,14; Jas 2:14–26). Just as in eternity God chose to make us holy and selected us to be his sons and daughters (1:4–5), he has now fashioned us to be his own works of art. We are new bearers of his image (4:24) who are designed for the kind of life that conforms to God's character (see 4:1—6:20).

2:10 for us to do. Literally, "that we might walk in them" (4:1; 5:2,8,15). Note the ironic comparison with verse 2; 4:17. See *WCF* 3.6; 16.2; *HC* 91.

■ **2:11–22** *Made One in Christ.* Through union with Christ believers are also united with one another. One result of this union is that Gentiles now possess the covenant blessings previously reserved for Jews.

2:11–12 See *WLC* 162.

2:11 that done in the body by the hands of men. Implicit is the idea that there is another kind of circumcision—one of the heart, not the flesh; one that is spiritual, not physical (Dt 10:16; Jer 4:4); one that is available to Gentiles as well as to Jews (Ro 2:28–29; Php 3:3; Col 2:11–13).

2:12 at that time. Contrast with the "but now" of verse 13; see also 5:8. In Romans 9:3–5, Paul listed the Jewish privileges. Here he cited the five Gentile disadvantages. **separate from Christ.** Their various cultures knew no expectation of the Messiah. **excluded from citizenship . . . and foreigners to the covenants of the promise, without hope.** They were not citizens of the nation to which God had committed himself in a covenantal relationship. And though God's relationship with Israel had involved a promise to bless the nations (Ge 12:3), Gentiles had no awareness of that hope. **without God in the world.** God had revealed himself to all humankind in nature and in the conscience. But Gentiles had suppressed what truth they did know, turning instead to idolatry (Ac 14:15–17; 17:22–31; Ro 1:18—2:16). See *WCF* 10.4; *WLC* 60,105.

2:13 in Christ Jesus . . . through the blood of Christ. There were two dimensions to these Gentiles being brought near to God. The first was their experience of union with Christ (vv. 4–10), the second the historical basis of that experience in Christ's sacrificial death (1:7; 2:14–16). **far away . . . near.** See verse 17.

14 For he himself is our peace, who has made the two one[z] and has destroyed the barrier, the dividing wall of hostility, 15 by abolishing in his flesh[a] the law with its commandments and regulations.[b] His purpose was to create in himself one[c] new man out of the
two, thus making peace, 16 and in this one body to reconcile both of them to God through
the cross,[d] by which he put to death their hostility. 17 He came and preached peace to you
who were far away and peace to those who were near.[e] 18 For through him we both have
access[f] to the Father[g] by one Spirit.[h]

19 Consequently, you are no longer foreigners and aliens,[i] but fellow citizens[j] with
God's people and members of God's household,[k] 20 built on the foundation[l] of the
apostles and prophets, with Christ Jesus himself as the chief cornerstone.[m] 21 In him the
whole building is joined together and rises to become a holy temple[n] in the Lord. 22 And
in him you too are being built together to become a dwelling in which God lives by his
Spirit.

Paul the Preacher to the Gentiles

3 For this reason I, Paul, the prisoner[o] of Christ Jesus for the sake of you Gentiles—
2 Surely you have heard about the administration of God's grace that was given to me[p]
for you, 3 that is, the mystery[q] made known to me by revelation,[r] as I have already written
briefly. 4 In reading this, then, you will be able to understand my insight[s] into the mystery
of Christ, 5 which was not made known to men in other generations as it has now been revealed by the Spirit to God's holy apostles and prophets.[t] 6 This mystery is that through the
gospel the Gentiles are heirs[u] together with Israel, members together of one body,[v] and
sharers together in the promise in Christ Jesus.

7 I became a servant of this gospel[w] by the gift of God's grace given me through the
working of his power.[x] 8 Although I am less than the least of all God's people,[y] this grace
was given me: to preach to the Gentiles the unsearchable riches of Christ, 9 and to make
plain to everyone the administration of this mystery,[z] which for ages past was kept hid-

2:14 [z]1Co 12:13
2:15 [a]Col 1:21,22 [b]Col 2:14 [c]Gal 3:28
2:16 [d]Col 1:20,22
2:17 [e]Ps 148:14; Isa 57:19
2:18 [f]Eph 3:12 [g]Col 1:12 [h]1Co 12:13
2:19 [i]ver 12 [j]Php 3:20 [k]Gal 6:10
2:20 [l]Mt 16:18; Rev 21:14 [m]1Pe 2:4-8
2:21 [n]1Co 3:16,17
3:1 [o]Ac 23:18; Eph 4:1
3:2 [p]Col 1:25
3:3 [q]Ro 16:25 [r]1Co 2:10
3:4 [s]2Co 11:6
3:5 [t]Ro 16:26
3:6 [u]Gal 3:29 [v]Eph 2:15,16
3:7 [w]1Co 3:5 [x]Eph 1:19
3:8 [y]1Co 15:9
3:9 [z]Ro 16:25

2:14–16 See 4:22–24 and its note (see also notes on Col 3:9,10, 11,12).
2:14 the barrier, the dividing wall of hostility. The controlling image is the physical arrangement of the temple in Jerusalem. A wall separated Gentiles and Jews, and signs threatened death to Gentiles who entered the Holy Place, where God was thought to dwell and where sacrifices for sin were offered.
2:15–19 See *WCF* 7.6; 19.3.
2:15 abolishing . . . the law with its commandments and regulations. Christ offered in his own body the final sacrifice to which the temple's sacrifices merely pointed. (See note on Col 2:15 for the impact of Christ's death on the law's power to condemn.) The ceremonies the law required under the old administration, the observance of which separated Jew from Gentile, were no longer appropriate in the light of their fulfillment in Christ. Approximately three years earlier, Paul had been arrested in Jerusalem because he was wrongly thought to have brought a Gentile (an Ephesian named Trophimus) into the temple area, which was reserved for Jews (Ac 21:27–33). Although Paul honored Jewish scruples, he believed that Christ's death made obsolete the sacrificial system that continued to operate. Despite the fact that sinners had been made right with God, this sacrificial system continued to divide the world into those who could draw near and those who had to stand afar.
2:17–18 Isaiah had prophesied a day when God's peace would be proclaimed to those "far and near" (Isa 57:19). Paul saw the fulfillment of Isaiah's promise in the gospel of Christ. Through the gospel the Spirit brings Gentiles ("you who were far away") and Jews ("those who were near") together before the Father. See *WCF* 21.2; *WLC* 32; *BC* 26.
2:19–22 These verses describe the reversal of the Gentile disadvantages outlined in verses 11–12 (see 3:6). The building of this new temple replaces the outmoded one in Jerusalem.
2:19 no longer foreigners. The kingdom of God is now an international one. **household.** See the expansion of the household motif in the Pastoral Epistles, especially 1 Timothy 3:15. See *WCF* 25.2.
2:20 The solidity and stability of God's house lies in its foundation having been laid once and for all by the work of the New Testament era apostles and prophets, who in turn took their bearings from the sure cornerstone, who is Christ. Compare the image in 1 Corinthians 3:10–11 (cf. Heb 1:1–2; 2:3–4). See *WCF* 1.2; 1.10; 31.4; *WLC* 3; *WSC* 2; *BC* 29.
2:21–22 rises . . . being built. The dynamism of God's house lies in the fact that it is still under construction, as living stones continue to be added and integrated (1Pe 2:5). Paul changed the image from house to temple in order to indicate that God himself dwells within this new structure of people who are organically related to one another through the Spirit. Although the *shekinah* glory, the actual presence of God, had long ago abandoned the Jerusalem temple (Eze 10–11), God has once again made his dwelling among humans in his church (1Co 3:16; Eph 3:17; 4:1–16).
■ **3:1–13** *Paul and the Divine Mystery.* Paul was ready to pray that his Gentile readers be filled with the presence of Christ and be enabled to apprehend the truths of chapter 2 about their Redeemer's love and power (vv. 14–21). But before doing so, he interrupted himself to explain the nature of his own ministry and his insight into the unity of Jew and Gentile in Christ.
3:1 prisoner. Paul was under house arrest in Rome (Ac 28:16,30).
3:3 as I have already written briefly. See 1:9–10.
3:5 as it has now been revealed. That is, to the same degree that it has now been revealed. The Old Testament's silence about Paul's mystery—radical equality and unity between Jews and Gentiles in the church (v. 6)—was relative, not absolute. A striking example of its anticipation is seen in Isaiah 19:25, where the prophet looked forward to a day when God would declare, "Blessed be Egypt my people, Assyria my handiwork, and Israel my inheritance." If the idea of unity and equality between Jews and Gentiles were altogether absent from the Old Testament, Paul could not have insisted, as he did in Romans 4, that the Abrahamic covenant included all who were of a like faith with Abraham (including Gentiles). Nor could Paul have stood before Agrippa and insisted that his proclamation of light to both Jews and Gentiles was no more than what had been promised by the prophets and Moses (Ac 26:22–23). **to God's holy apostles and prophets.** The mystery was not a private revelation received by Paul alone. Recall Peter's experience in Acts 10–11 and its implications for the question of Gentile circumcision in Acts 15:7–11.
3:6 together . . . together . . . together. Despite the Old Testament's occasional glimpses of a unified human race, it is only in the light of Christ's actual sacrifice that it becomes clear that it was God's plan all along to remove, in one magnificent and decisive blow, the enmity between himself and humankind and to eradicate the divisions that fracture humanity (2:14–18). In Romans, Paul had reflected on the unnatural manner in which God included Gentiles among the people of God: They were a wild branch grafted (contrary to normal agricultural practice) into a cultivated olive tree (Ro 11:11–24). By asserting that in Christ Gentiles share identical privileges with Jews, Paul indicated the depth of that ingrafting.
3:8 Compare the progression of Paul's self-description from 1 Corinthians 15:9 to Ephesians 3:8 to 1 Timothy 1:15–16.
3:9 See *BC* 10.

3:10 [a]1Co 2:7 [b]1Pe 1:12 [c]Eph 1:21
3:12 [d]Eph 2:18 [e]Heb 4:16
3:14 [f]Php 2:10
3:16 [g]Col 1:11 [h]Ro 7:22
3:17 [i]Jn 14:23 [j]Col 1:23
3:18 [k]Job 11:8,9
3:19 [l]Col 2:10 [m]Eph 1:23
3:20 [n]Ro 16:25
3:21 [o]Ro 11:36
4:1 [p]Eph 3:1 [q]Php 1:27; Col 1:10

den in God, who created all things. 10 His intent was that now, through the church, the
manifold wisdom of God[a] should be made known[b] to the rulers and authorities[c] in the
heavenly realms, 11 according to his eternal purpose which he accomplished in Christ
Jesus our Lord. 12 In him and through faith in him we may approach God[d] with freedom
and confidence.[e] 13 I ask you, therefore, not to be discouraged because of my sufferings
for you, which are your glory.

A Prayer for the Ephesians

14 For this reason I kneel[f] before the Father, 15 from whom his whole family[a] in heav-
en and on earth derives its name. 16 I pray that out of his glorious riches he may strength-
en you with power[g] through his Spirit in your inner being,[h] 17 so that Christ may dwell
in your hearts[i] through faith. And I pray that you, being rooted[j] and established in love,
18 may have power, together with all the saints, to grasp how wide and long and high and
deep[k] is the love of Christ, 19 and to know this love that surpasses knowledge—that you
may be filled[l] to the measure of all the fullness of God.[m]
20 Now to him who is able[n] to do immeasurably more than all we ask or imagine, according to his power that is at work within us, 21 to him be glory in the church and in
Christ Jesus throughout all generations, for ever and ever! Amen.[o]

Unity in the Body of Christ

4 As a prisoner[p] for the Lord, then, I urge you to live a life worthy[q] of the calling you
have received. 2 Be completely humble and gentle; be patient, bearing with one an-

a 15 Or *whom all fatherhood*

3:10 through the church. That is, through the incorporation of Jews and Gentiles together into one body in Christ. **should be made known . . . in the heavenly realms.** Paul had already mentioned "the ruler of the kingdom of the air" (2:2) and would return to the Christians' battle against their heavenly enemies (6:10–17). It is helpful here to recall his controversy with the false teachers in Colosse. He had argued in his epistle to that church that Jesus is Lord of all things, including the spirit world, and further, that it is in Jesus and Jesus alone that heaven and Earth are reconciled (Col 1:15–20; 2:8–23). Accordingly, Paul saw the establishment of peace between Jews and Gentiles in the church as a signal to the cosmic powers. From his cultural background, there was no deeper division in the human race than that between Jew and Gentile. That they could be radically unified with one another in Christ was testimony to the profound wisdom of God (Isa 55:8–9; 1Co 2:6–10), and it stood as proof even to the heavenly powers that Jesus is indeed Lord of the universe (1:20–23). See *WCF* 5.1.
3:12 See *WCF* 12; *WLC* 181; *BC* 26.
■ **3:14–21** *Strength for the Church.* Paul prayed that the Holy Spirit would strengthen and enlighten the Ephesian believers so that they would persevere in faith and offer greater praise to God.
3:14–20 See *WCF* 13.1; 18.3; 26.1; *WLC* 75,191,195; *BC* 9,26.
3:14 I kneel. Jews normally prayed standing (Mt 6:5; Mk 11:25; Lk 18:11,13). Kneeling appears to have been a posture of greater than usual humility and urgency (Ezr 9:5; Mt 26:39; Lk 22:41; Ac 7:59–60; Php 2:10). This verse introduces the prayer Paul had almost begun in verse 1.
3:15 his whole family. The Greek words for "Father" and "family" are similar (see NIV text note). The text note reading, if accepted, indicates that all fatherhood (i.e., family) relationships, earthly and heavenly, have their origin in one heavenly Father. **in heaven.** Jewish intertestamental and rabbinic literature refers to families of angels. See *WCF* 25.2.
3:16 in your inner being. This is some of Paul's most pointed language regarding the work of the Spirit within individuals (2Co 5:17). Much of Ephesians addresses the believers' sense of corporate identity (1:10–14; 2:14–18,21–22; 3:6,10; 4:3–6,12–16,25; 4:32—5:2; 5:19; 5:21—6:9). But Christ also dwells in individual hearts. Christianity is neither a common confession to the exclusion of individual experience, nor a private piety without corporate vision. To the extent that it is Christianity at all, it is both. See *WLC* 192.
3:17 rooted and established in love. This probably refers to believers' love for one another and is the starting point for what follows. See *WSC* 30; *BC* 35.
3:18 how wide . . . is the love of Christ. Paul may have intended for these spatial dimensions (nouns rather than adjectives in the Greek) to bring to readers' minds the temple image of 2:21. As living stones are linked in love, God's dwelling place grows and is filled with Christ himself. God uses the love that is shared among "all the saints"—Jew and Gentile alike—to build a whole that is greater than any of its individual parts and, in this setting, to give each member a greater grasp of Christ's love than any could attain individually. Alternatively, Paul may intend his spatial language to be taken less concretely (as in the NIV), perhaps as a prayer that through their love for one another believers may grow to understand even more about Christ's love for them—that it is inclusive, inexhaustible, exalting and self-sacrificing.
3:20–21 See *WLC* 196.
3:20 his power that is at work within us. See 1:19–23 and 2:5–6. The first half of the letter ends in a crescendo as it describes the overwhelming power of the God who effects his surpassingly gracious (2:7) and inscrutably wise (3:10) plan for the reconciliation of the human race.
3:21 glory. While the power comes *from* God, the glory goes *to* him. **in the church and in Christ Jesus.** Note the mutual relationship between the body and its head (1:22–23), the reconciled and the reconciler (2:14–18; 4:3), the bride and her groom (5:22–33). **throughout all generations, for ever and ever!** God is glorified in Christ and the church, both in history and throughout all eternity.
■ **4:1—6:20** *Walking in the Blessings of the Church.* The letter moves from the grand picture of redemption to the pattern of life redemption is designed to produce. God has created "one new man" in his Son (2:15); there is a twofold pattern of life that belongs to this new creation: unity and purity. Paul wanted to show how oneness can be realized in practical experience, even in the face of intimidating differences (4:1–16; 4:25—5:2; 5:22—6:9). He was also concerned that his Gentile readers adopt new mindsets and new patterns of life, befitting their new identities as bearers of the image of the righteous and holy God (4:17–24; 5:3–20), and that they guard these by relying on the Holy Spirit for strength (6:10–20). On the relationship between redemption (the "is" of the Christian life) and obedience (the "ought"), see notes on Colossians 2:6–7 and 3:1.
■ **4:1–16** *Uniting in Diversity.* Although believers possess different gifts and callings (vv. 7–12), they are united in Christ and by their common faith (vv. 4–6,15–16). Their different gifts and callings are complementary, enabling those in the church to minister to one another and to grow in maturity.
4:1–6 See *HC* 54.
4:1 The Greek expression "to walk" is rendered "to live" in the NIV (see v. 17; 5:2,8; see also note on 2:10). In fact, "walking" is a leitmotiv running through chapters 4–5. Throughout, Paul was unfolding the life, or "walk," of good works mentioned in 2:10. **calling.** In 1:18 and 4:4 Paul spoke of a *hope* to which believers are called; here he focused on the *life* to which they are called. He had already provided strong indications of its shape and significance (1:4,12,14; 2:10,22; 3:10).
4:2–4 See *WLC* 135,162; *BC* 27; *HC* 107.

other[r] in love.[s] 3Make every effort to keep the unity[t] of the Spirit through the bond of
peace. 4There is one body and one Spirit[u]—just as you were called to one hope when you
were called— 5one Lord, one faith, one baptism; 6one God and Father of all, who is over
all and through all and in all.[v]
7But to each one of us[w] grace has been given[x] as Christ apportioned it. 8This is why
it[a] says:

> "When he ascended on high,
> he led captives[y] in his train
> and gave gifts to men."[b][z]

9(What does "he ascended" mean except that he also descended to the lower, earthly regions[c]? 10He who descended is the very one who ascended higher than all the heavens,
in order to fill the whole universe.) 11It was he who gave some to be apostles,[a] some to
be prophets, some to be evangelists,[b] and some to be pastors and teachers, 12to prepare
God's people for works of service, so that the body of Christ[c] may be built up 13until we
all reach unity[d] in the faith and in the knowledge of the Son of God and become mature,[e]
attaining to the whole measure of the fullness of Christ.
14Then we will no longer be infants,[f] tossed back and forth by the waves,[g] and blown
here and there by every wind of teaching and by the cunning and craftiness of men in
their deceitful scheming.[h] 15Instead, speaking the truth in love, we will in all things grow
up into him who is the Head,[i] that is, Christ. 16From him the whole body, joined and held
together by every supporting ligament, grows[j] and builds itself up in love, as each part
does its work.

Living as Children of Light

17So I tell you this, and insist on it in the Lord, that you must no longer live as the Gentiles do, in the futility of their thinking.[k] 18They are darkened in their understanding[l] and
separated from the life of God[m] because of the ignorance that is in them due to the hard-

4:2 [r]Col 3:12,13 [s]Eph 1:4
4:3 [t]Col 3:14
4:4 [u]1Co 12:13
4:6 [v]Ro 11:36
4:7 [w]1Co 12:7,11 [x]Ro 12:3
4:8 [y]Col 2:15 [z]Ps 68:18
4:11 [a]1Co 12:28 [b]Ac 21:8
4:12 [c]1Co 12:27
4:13 [d]ver 3,5 [e]Col 1:28
4:14 [f]1Co 14:20 [g]Jas 1:6 [h]Eph 6:11
4:15 [i]Eph 1:22
4:16 [j]Col 2:19
4:17 [k]Ro 1:21
4:18 [l]Ro 1:21 [m]Eph 2:12

[a] *8* Or *God* [b] *8* Psalm 68:18 [c] *9* Or *the depths of the earth*

4:4–6 The word "one" is repeated seven times in verses 4–6 (three times of members of the Godhead and four times of aspects of our redemption). See *BC* 1,7,27,31.
4:7–12 See *WLC* 158; *BC* 19; *HC* 46,51.
4:7 But to each one of us. All Christians have a common bestowal of grace: salvation through faith (2:5,8). Each Christian is given some particular gift of grace to benefit the church (Paul spoke of his own in 3:2,8). The church's unity is nowhere more evident than in this organic interdependence within the body of Christ.
4:8 Paul saw in Psalm 68's celebration of God's triumphant march from Mount Sinai to Mount Zion and his subsequent enthronement in the temple a prefiguring of Christ's victorious ascent into heaven. **captives in his train.** The spiritual forces of darkness Christ defeated and disarmed at the cross (3:10; 6:12; Col 1:20; 2:15 and notes). While Psalm 68 envisions the victorious Lord receiving gifts from men, Paul pictures Christ as going past the reception of tribute to the sharing of his booty with men. In Jewish worship this psalm had come to be associated with Pentecost, and it may have come to Paul's mind for this reason. Upon his ascension and heavenly enthronement, Jesus received the Holy Spirit from the Father; on the day of Pentecost, he poured the Spirit out on his church (Ac 2:32–33). In 1 Corinthians Paul emphasized the way the Holy Spirit empowers the church for ministry. In Ephesians Paul wrote more in terms of individuals who enable ministry. See *WLC* 53.
4:9 In view of his overall purpose of encouraging believers to adopt a pattern of life like Christ's, Paul inserted a parenthesis to remind readers that it was through Christ's humiliation (his incarnation to "the lower, earthly regions") that the Son came to the exalted position he now enjoys (1:20–23; 5:2; Php 2:1–11).
4:10–13 See *WCF* 23.3; 25.3; 32.1; *WLC* 43,45,53,54,63,86,108.
4:11 Through special functionaries, God has provided the means for shaping the diversity he himself has placed within the body. **apostles.** Formally, those who had been with Jesus and had seen the risen Lord, who had experienced a special revelation of the risen Jesus or who had been commissioned by Jesus to be founders of the church and special bearers of revelation (Ac 1:21–22; 1Co 15:1–9). The word was also used in a broader sense of people sent out as delegates of particular churches, though this does not appear to be what Paul had in mind in this passage (2Co 8:23; Php 2:25). **prophets.** Persons who served as vehicles of direct and special revelation in the early church. Their functions included prediction, exhortation, encouragement, warning and explanation (Ac 11:27; 13:1; 15:32; 19:6; 21:9–10; Ro 12:6; 1Co 12:10; 13:2,8; 14:3,6,29–37). Because their teaching laid the foundation for the church (2:20), fundamental aspects of the apostles' and New Testament prophets' work appear to be unrepeatable. **evangelists.** People (in any age) especially gifted in the task of expanding God's flock (Ac 21:8; 1Co 1:17; 2Ti 4:5). **pastors and teachers.** Sharing a single definite article in the Greek (*the* pastors and teachers), these words refer to a single set of individuals who both shepherd and instruct God's flock.
4:12–13 It is not primarily those mentioned in verse 11 but the people they equip who do the work of the ministry. Paul's congregations did not just congregate; they ministered. Effective teachers help every believer find his or her particular way of benefiting the rest of the church. See *WCF* 9.5; *WLC* 159; *BC* 28.
4:15–16 See *WCF* 13.3; 26.1; *HC* 76.
4:16 body. Paul now used the analogy of the human body. Believers are not given gifts to be used in isolation for self-edification, nor are they to seek growth to maturity on their own. Paul's vision included all Christians (Col 1:28–29). Paul himself, though far advanced in his understanding of the deeper things of Christ, strove for a knowledge of the Son of God and a degree of maturity that would come to him only after all other believers had attained it as well.
■ **4:17—6:9** *Living in New Ways.* The new natures, identities and lives believers possess in Christ require the cessation of sin and the beginning of new behaviors that flow from and reflect the holiness and purity of Christ.
4:17–19 Strongly reminiscent of Paul's critique of Gentile culture in Romans 1. Paul had previously spoken of the Gentiles' alienation from God's people (2:12). Here he spoke of their alienation from the life of God himself (the walking death of ch. 2). Willfulness ("hardening of their hearts") gives birth to ignorance (v. 18; cf. Ro 1:21–22,28), which in turn brings the judgment of spiritual death ("separated from the life of God"; v. 18; cf. Ro 1:18,24,28). While Romans envisions God giving Gentiles over to a reckless and wanton lifestyle (Ro 1:24–31), Ephesians presents the same dynamic from the human side: "Having lost all sensitivity, they have given themselves over . . ." (v. 19). Compare Exodus, where a dominant motif is that of God hardening Pharaoh's heart (e.g., Ex 4:21; 7:3) but where Pharaoh fully cooperated by hardening his own heart (Ex 8:15,32; 9:34).See *WCF* 6.6; *WLC* 28; *BC* 14.

ening of their hearts.[n] **19**Having lost all sensitivity,[o] they have given themselves over[p] to
sensuality[q] so as to indulge in every kind of impurity, with a continual lust for more.
20You, however, did not come to know Christ that way. **21**Surely you heard of him and
were taught in him in accordance with the truth that is in Jesus. **22**You were taught, with
regard to your former way of life, to put off[r] your old self,[s] which is being corrupted by
its deceitful desires; **23**to be made new in the attitude of your minds;[t] **24**and to put on the
new self,[u] created to be like God in true righteousness and holiness.[v]

25Therefore each of you must put off falsehood and speak truthfully[w] to his neighbor,
for we are all members of one body.[x] **26**"In your anger do not sin"[a]: Do not let the sun
go down while you are still angry, **27**and do not give the devil a foothold. **28**He who has
been stealing must steal no longer, but must work,[y] doing something useful with his own
hands,[z] that he may have something to share with those in need.[a]

29Do not let any unwholesome talk come out of your mouths,[b] but only what is helpful for building others up according to their needs, that it may benefit those who listen.
30And do not grieve the Holy Spirit of God,[c] with whom you were sealed for the day of
redemption.[d] **31**Get rid of all bitterness, rage and anger, brawling and slander, along with
every form of malice.[e] **32**Be kind and compassionate to one another, forgiving each other, just as in Christ God forgave you.[f]

5 Be imitators of God,[g] therefore, as dearly loved children **2**and live a life of love, just
as Christ loved us and gave himself up for us[h] as a fragrant offering and sacrifice
to God.[i]

3But among you there must not be even a hint of sexual immorality, or of any kind of
impurity, or of greed,[j] because these are improper for God's holy people. **4**Nor should
there be obscenity, foolish talk or coarse joking, which are out of place, but rather
thanksgiving.[k] **5**For of this you can be sure: No immoral, impure or greedy person—such
a man is an idolater[l]—has any inheritance in the kingdom of Christ and of God.[b][m] **6**Let
no one deceive you with empty words, for because of such things God's wrath[n] comes
on those who are disobedient. **7**Therefore do not be partners with them.

4:18 [n]2Co 3:14
4:19 [o]1Ti 4:2 [p]Ro 1:24 [q]Col 3:5
4:22 [r]1Pe 2:1 [s]Ro 6:6
4:23 [t]Col 3:10
4:24 [u]Ro 6:4 [v]Eph 2:10
4:25 [w]Zec 8:16 [x]Ro 12:5
4:28 [y]Ac 20:35 [z]1Th 4:11 [a]Lk 3:11
4:29 [b]Col 3:8
4:30 [c]1Th 5:19 [d]Ro 8:23
4:31 [e]Col 3:8
4:32 [f]Mt 6:14,15
5:1 [g]Lk 6:36
5:2 [h]Gal 1:4 [i]2Co 2:15; Heb 7:27
5:3 [j]Col 3:5
5:4 [k]ver 20
5:5 [l]Col 3:5 [m]1Co 6:9
5:6 [n]Ro 1:18

[a] *26* Psalm 4:4 [b] *5* Or *kingdom of the Christ and God*

4:21 heard of him. Literally, "heard him" (i.e., in the message proclaimed about him). **truth that is in Jesus.** God had broken the cycle of death by giving these Gentiles an understanding of his Son and of his work on their behalf (1:13,15).
4:22–24 to put off . . . to be made new . . . and to put on. Part of what they had been taught when they first came to know Christ was that belonging to Christ involves repudiating an old life and embracing a new. The image is that of taking off frayed clothes and putting on a fresh set. On the divine side, and at God's own initiative, we are re-created in Christ's image, made alive with him even while we are dead in our transgressions and sins (2:1–10,14–16). On the human side, we respond to God's grace and seize upon this new life to make it our own. While the old form of existence in Adam (see note on Col 3:9) was subject to corruption, the new one in Christ is continually being made new. While the old life was dominated by lusts (2:2–3), the new is characterized by righteousness and holiness. While the old life was one of lies and deception, the new has taken hold of truth (vv. 21,24). See *WCF* 4.2; *WLC* 17,75; *WSC* 10,35; *BC* 14; *HC* 6,9,88; *CD* 3–4.II.
4:25—5:5 Paul outlined six concrete ways in which the "putting off and putting on" dynamic needs to take place within the Christian community: from lying to truth telling (4:25–26), from uncontrolled to controlled anger (4:26–27), from stealing to useful labor (4:28), from an unhelpful to a helpful use of speech (4:29–30), from bitterness to love in relationships (4:31—5:2) and from a warped preoccupation with sex to a thankful acknowledgment of God's good gift (5:3–5). In each case, Paul offered a sanction or reason for the change from old to new. In some cases he offered social considerations; in others, theological considerations.
4:25 See *WLC* 144; *HC* 112.
4:26 See *WLC* 135; *HC* 105.
4:27 Because practical unity among believers is God's showcase for his reconciling power (2:14–16; 3:10; 4:1–10; see note on Col 3:15), its disruption is especially prized by the doomed, but still defiant, devil (2:2; 6:11).
4:28 See *WCF* 22.7; 26.3; *WLC* 99,141,142,193; *WSC* 75; *HC* 111.
4:30–31 See *WCF* 18.4; *WLC* 136.
4:30 do not grieve. That is, by the destructive use of the mouth (v. 29). That the Holy Spirit (neuter in gender in the Greek) can be saddened is a telling indication of his identity as a personal being rather than an impersonal force. That this was not a new idea to New Testament writers is clear from Paul's citing here of the prophet Isaiah (Isa 63:10). See *WCF* 12; 17.3; 18.2; *WLC* 105,151.
4:32—5:2 just as . . . just as. Believers are expected to extend to others the same forgiveness and love that God has extended to them in Christ. The logic is similar to that of the Pentateuch: The Israelites, purchased out of slavery and bondage in Egypt, were to have a special regard for aliens, slaves and the dispossessed in their midst (Ex 22:21; 23:9; Lev 19:33–34; Dt 5:15). This redemptive, ethical logic also lies at the heart of Jesus' new commandment: "As I have loved you, so you must love one another" (Jn 13:34). See *WCF* 8.5; 11.3; *WLC* 135; *HC* 43,87.
5:1 as dearly loved children. See note on Colossians 3:12. It is a firm grasp of being genuinely loved by God and of having a secure, albeit adoptive (1:5), place in his family that motivates the self-sacrifice to which these verses call believers.
5:3–5 See *WLC* 139; *HC* 108.
5:3–4 improper . . . out of place. The trivialization of the sexual relationship on the one hand and its idolization on the other are equally out of step with our identity as "God's holy people." As those called out of the human race (1:4–6) to bear his restored image (4:24), we are able to accept with thanksgiving all his good gifts—including sex—and restore them to their proper place (Ge 1:27–28; 2:20–25; Pr 5:18–19; 1Th 4:3–8; Tit 1:15; Heb 13:4). See *WLC* 139; *WSC* 72; *HC* 109.
5:5 See NIV text note. Because "Christ" and "God" share the same definite article in the Greek (literally, "the Christ and God"), it is possible that Paul was referring to Christ as God (Tit 2:13). See *HC* 95,110.
5:6–21 Before discussing relationships in which believers' unity is to be demonstrated (5:22—6:9), Paul outlined a number of ways in which believers define themselves over against their non-Christian contemporaries.
5:6 Although the day of reckoning may be dismissed with "empty words" (see also 2Pe 3:3–4), God's judgment will make a final separation between those who are disobedient (literally, "the sons of disobedience," 2:2,3; cf. 5:5) and God's beloved children (1:4–5; 5:1; see note on v. 8). See *WLC* 152; *WSC* 84; *HC* 10.
5:7 partners with them. These words translate the same Greek expression used in 3:6 to refer to Gentiles as "sharers together" with Jews in the promise in Christ Jesus. Christians should consider the awful destiny of their non-believing contemporaries and refuse to join in their folly.
5:8–10 See *HC* 2.

8For you were once[o] darkness, but now you are light in the Lord. Live as children of
light[p] 9(for the fruit[q] of the light consists in all goodness, righteousness and truth)
10and find out what pleases the Lord. 11Have nothing to do with the fruitless deeds of
darkness, but rather expose them. 12For it is shameful even to mention what the disobedient do in secret. 13But everything exposed by the light[r] becomes visible, 14for it is light
that makes everything visible. This is why it is said:

> "Wake up, O sleeper,[s]
> rise from the dead,[t]
> and Christ will shine on you."[u]

15Be very careful, then, how you live—not as unwise but as wise, 16making the most
of every opportunity,[v] because the days are evil.[w] 17Therefore do not be foolish, but understand what the Lord's will is.[x] 18Do not get drunk on wine,[y] which leads to debauchery. Instead, be filled with the Spirit.[z] 19Speak to one another with psalms, hymns and
spiritual songs.[a] Sing and make music in your heart to the Lord, 20always giving thanks[b]
to God the Father for everything, in the name of our Lord Jesus Christ.
21Submit to one another[c] out of reverence for Christ.

Wives and Husbands

22Wives, submit to your husbands[d] as to the Lord.[e] 23For the husband is the head of
the wife as Christ is the head of the church,[f] his body, of which he is the Savior. 24Now

5:8 [o]Eph 2:2 [p]Lk 16:8
5:9 [q]Gal 5:22
5:13 [r]Jn 3:20,21
5:14 [s]Ro 13:11 [t]Jn 5:25 [u]Isa 60:1
5:16 [v]Col 4:5 [w]Eph 6:13
5:17 [x]Ro 12:2; 1Th 4:3
5:18 [y]Pr 20:1 [z]Lk 1:15
5:19 [a]Ac 16:25; Col 3:16
5:20 [b]Ps 34:1
5:21 [c]Gal 5:13
5:22 [d]Ge 3:16; 1Pe 3:1,5,6 [e]Eph 6:5
5:23 [f]1Co 11:3; Eph 1:22

5:8 once . . . but now. See 2:11 and 13. Paul wanted believers to do more than refuse partnership in the things that make God's wrath inevitable. They are "children of light" (note the cross references; see note on Col 1:13). A result of the believers' union with Christ is that he who is "the light of the world" (Jn 8:12; 9:5) has made them also "the light of the world" (Mt 5:14). By definition, light sheds light; therefore, Paul envisions believers having an impact on their world. See *BC* 14.
5:11 See *WLC* 99.
5:14 for it is light that makes everything visible. Certain aspects of non-Christian practice are so shameful that their being brought to light (whether by a believer's opposite example or by denunciation) will shame some non-Christians into repentance. Paul envisioned an evangelistic edge to a Christian's presence in this dark world. Accordingly, the apostle cited what appears to be an early Christian hymn suggestive of a number of Old Testament passages (Isa 26:19; 51:17; 52:1; 60:1) and calling upon the (spiritually) dead to rise up and receive the light of Christ (cf. 2:1–10).
5:15–17 See *WLC* 113.
5:18 drunk on wine. This is probably more than a general prohibition of drunkenness. Paul was probably referring to a wild, orgiastic form of worship with which he contrasts Christian worship. For instance, the cult of Dionysus (Bacchus), the wine god, was widespread. Worship of this god involved drunken states in which the god was thought to enter the bodies of worshipers, inspiring prophecy and frenzied dancing and music. Whether this cult specifically, or another like it, was in view, the apostle characterized such worship as "debauchery." **be filled with the Spirit.** While the sealing of the Spirit (1:13–14; 4:30) is a once-for-all initiation into the Christian life, the filling of the Spirit is not only repeatable but is to be sought after time and again. In the parallel passage in Colossians 3:15–16, Christians are told to let the "peace of Christ" govern their hearts and to allow the "word of Christ" to dwell in them richly. In Christian experience there is harmony between Christ, his Word and the Spirit (Jn 14:16,26; 16:12–15; 17:17). See *HC* 109.
5:19–21 In a series of five Greek participles ("Speak . . . sing and make music . . . giving thanks . . . submit"), Paul characterized the behavior of people who come under the Spirit's direct influence and who have the word of Christ dwelling richly within them.
5:19 to one another . . . to the Lord. In one sense, worship has an audience of one, for it is directed to God himself. A host of Old Testament psalms address God directly (e.g., Ps 65:1,5). At the same time, worship has a human audience, for edification also takes place (1Co 14). Believers remind one another of the greatness of God and of his redeeming work; they encourage one another and "spur one another on toward love and good deeds" (Heb 10:24). A number of Old Testament psalms have this horizontal thrust (e.g., Pss 29:1–2; 33:1–3; 95:1) **psalms, hymns and spiritual songs.** See note on Colossians 3:16. See also *WCF* 21.5.
5:20 See *WLC* 108.
5:21–22 See *HC* 104.
5:21 This transitional verse is last in the chain of expressions explaining what being filled with the Spirit looks like. Addressed to all Christians, regardless of social rank, this verse recalls the New Testament stress on believers patterning their relational styles on the humility and kindness of Christ (Mk 10:45; Lk 22:24–27; Jn 13:1–17,34–35; Eph 4:32—5:2; Php 2:1–11). Because the Holy Spirit is the Spirit of Christ, the Spirit resists pride, self-sufficiency and self-exaltation. Because verse 22 lacks a verb in the Greek, verse 21 is also the springboard for instruction on the shape submission and authority are to take in specific relationships. See *WLC* 126; *WSC* 64.
5:22—6:9 See 1 Corinthians 7:17–24,29–31 (see also Col 3:18—4:1; 1Ti 2:8–15; 5:1–3; 6:1–2,17–19; Tit 2:1–10; 3:1; 1Pe 2:13—3:7; 5:1–7). At least as far back as Aristotle in the fourth century B.C., Greek ethics addressed relationships within the household in terms of this pattern: husbands and wives, parents and children, masters and slaves. Consistently, the interest was to help the household head learn how most effectively to "rule" his wife, children and slaves. Dramatically, Paul (and Peter) transformed the issue from how husbands, fathers and masters "rule" to how they can mirror the love of Christ they have themselves experienced by nurturing those in their care. Simultaneously, as wives, children and slaves define their roles in terms of service to Christ, they stop being passive objects in a social world that devalues them, becoming instead active partners with God in the plan to bring unity to a race divided by gender, age and economic diversity.
5:22–33 Throughout Ephesians, Paul has emphasized the significance of headship over all in both the old and the new creations. As head of the church, Jesus embodies and empowers a new community of love: the church, his own body. Here Paul applied Christ's headship to marriage. Christ reverses the enmity that often arises between spouses as a result of the fall (Ge 3:16), restoring the original creative order in which husbands and wives complement each other. Paul's understanding of marriage was strongly grounded in creation (1Co 11:8–9; 1Ti 2:13), and he took account of the fall's lingering effects, even among Christians (1Ti 2:14). His burden in Ephesians was to flesh out the manner in which redemption in Christ restores the intimate interdependence men and women were created to enjoy in marriage. He called spouses to love one another but emphasized the husband's call to sacrificial love over that of the wife. He called both to respectful submission (Eph 5:21) but emphasized the wife's call to submission more strongly than the husband's. These different emphases have been interpreted in two main ways: (1) They reflect different problems among Paul's readers (i.e., husbands were failing to love and wives failing to submit), and (2) they reflect respective higher levels of responsibility (i.e. husbands have a greater responsibility to love than their wives, while wives have a greater responsibility to submit). These two trends in interpretation need not be exclusive of one another.
5:22 submit. A Christian wife is called to live in grateful acknowledgment of her husband's care and leadership. See also note on verse 24. **as to the Lord.** Just as all believers respect and submit to the Lord, Paul wanted wives to respect and submit to their husbands. Unlike the respect we render to Christ, the respect wives render to husbands is of necessity to be conditional. When human leaders violate divine law, we must remain loyal to God above all others (Lk 18:29–30; Ac 5:29). See note on verse 24.
5:23 head of the wife . . . head of the church. In other pas-

as the church submits to Christ, so also wives should submit to their husbands in everything.
25Husbands, love your wives,[g] just as Christ loved the church and gave himself up for
her[h] 26to make her holy, cleansing[a] her by the washing[i] with water through the word,
27and to present her to himself as a radiant church, without stain or wrinkle or any other blemish, but holy and blameless.[j] 28In this same way, husbands ought to love their
wives[k] as their own bodies. He who loves his wife loves himself. 29After all, no one ever
hated his own body, but he feeds and cares for it, just as Christ does the church— 30for
we are members of his body.[l] 31"For this reason a man will leave his father and mother
and be united to his wife, and the two will become one flesh."[b][m] 32This is a profound
mystery—but I am talking about Christ and the church. 33However, each one of you also
must love his wife[n] as he loves himself, and the wife must respect her husband.

Children and Parents

6 Children, obey your parents in the Lord, for this is right.[o] 2"Honor your father and
mother"—which is the first commandment with a promise— 3"that it may go well
with you and that you may enjoy long life on the earth."[c][p]
4Fathers, do not exasperate your children;[q] instead, bring them up in the training and
instruction of the Lord.[r]

Slaves and Masters

5Slaves, obey your earthly masters with respect[s] and fear, and with sincerity of
heart,[t] just as you would obey Christ.[u] 6Obey them not only to win their favor when their

5:25 [g]Col 3:19 [h]ver 2
5:26 [i]Ac 22:16
5:27 [j]Eph 1:4; Col 1:22
5:28 [k]ver 25
5:30 [l]1Co 12:27
5:31 [m]Ge 2:24; Mt 19:5; 1Co 6:16
5:33 [n]ver 25
6:1 [o]Col 3:20
6:3 [p]Ex 20:12
6:4 [q]Col 3:21 [r]Ge 18:19; Dt 6:7
6:5 [s]1Ti 6:1 [t]Col 3:22 [u]Eph 5:22

[a] *26* Or *having cleansed* [b] *31* Gen. 2:24 [c] *3* Deut. 5:16

sages in this letter on the subject of Christ's headship, Paul spoke of the way Christ governs the cosmos "for the church" (1:22) and serves as the source of the body's health and growth to maturity (4:14–16). This kind of benevolent headship is the model husbands are to follow. **his body.** Christ has invested his own identity in the church (vv. 28–30). **the Savior.** It is less in his role as Lord and more in his role as Savior that Christ serves as the husband's model (vv. 25–27). See *WCF* 8.1; 25.1; *WLC* 60,66.

5:24 Now as the church . . . so also wives. By respecting their husbands, wives reflect the responsive posture of the church toward Christ, her Bridegroom. Respect may be rendered even when leaders do not earn it (cf. Ac 23:2–5), and it may be rendered to human leaders in certain situations without accompanying obedience (cf. Ac 5:29). **submit.** Paul's word for "submit" in this passage does not imply blind obedience, but rather subordination of rank so that respect, deference and honor are rendered even when obedience is not given (vv. 21,24; "submit" does not appear in the Greek of v. 22). **in everything.** Paul meant "in every area of life," not "in every detail without exception." Husbands are to exemplify trustworthiness to the same extent.

5:25–26 See *WCF* 28.6.

5:25 Husbands, love. Paul's conclusion was not that the husband's headship grants him authority to govern and control, but that it obligates the husband to love. **just as Christ loved the church and gave himself up for her.** Nowhere else in the New Testament is Christ's self-sacrificing love applied more directly to a specific relationship as a pattern to be emulated.

5:26–27 In these verses Paul outlined the entire process to which Christ has committed himself in his relationship with the church: Christ has washed her from the defilement of sin and is now preparing her for a glorious destiny with himself. Husbands are called in like manner to care for their wives. See *WCF* 13.1; 25.1; *WLC* 85,90,165; *BC* 34; *HC* 78.

5:28–32 as their own bodies . . . Christ and the church. Paul called for husbands to love their wives as their own bodies because he understood that the "one flesh" of Genesis 2:24 prefigured Christ's becoming "united to his wife" (v. 31), the church. Husbands are to emulate Christ, who intimately united the church to himself, covenantally bound his own regal identity to hers and bestowed upon her pride in her place alongside himself "in the heavenly realms" (2:6). See *WCF* 25.1; *WLC* 66,135; *WSC* 68; *HC* 76.

5:33 respect. The submission wives are to render to their husbands amounts largely to an attitude of respect. This differs from the submission slaves are to render to their masters and children to their parents, which consists largely of obedience (6:1,5).

6:1–9 See *WLC* 127; *HC* 104,124.

6:1–3 God honors children by giving them partial responsibility for unifying the human race, specifically by promoting unity between generations. For Paul, part of what characterized Gentile culture as standing under God's judgment was that it was marked by children's disobedience to their parents (Ro 1:30); the evil end times are also marked by disobedience to parents (2Ti 3:2). See *WCF* 19.6; *WLC* 124,127,133; *WSC* 66.

6:1 in the Lord. This probably specifies that what is considered by thinking people in every culture to be "right"—obedience to parents—takes on a distinctly Christian sense.

6:2 the first commandment with a promise. Probably not first in chronological order but in order of rank. In Mark 12:28 the same Greek phrase for "first commandment" appears with the clear meaning "important commandment." Mark 12:28 also contains a Greek word meaning "of all," rendering the literal meaning "most important commandment of all." In Ephesians, however, "first commandment" is not modified by "of all," so that it seems to identify a very important commandment, but not necessarily the most important commandment. This difficult phrase might also be paraphrased "a very important commandment, which is accompanied by a promise." Although the law of God has lost its power to condemn (Col 2:13–14) and the observance of certain of its forms is inappropriate in the light of their fulfillment in Christ (2:15; Col 2:16–17), in "the more important matters of the law" (Mt 23:23) God's character still shines through, as do those nonnegotiable ethical principles that are dictated by conscience and accepted without question in every culture and time. One of these principles is that a key to a healthy society is children who honor their parents. See *WCF* 19.5.

6:4 Fathers. Conversely, to parents (and especially, to fathers), Paul stressed the responsibility of the authority role. **bring them up.** The Greek suggests the idea of helping to flourish (5:29). Parents are entrusted with nurturing the minds, emotions and bodies of tender bearers of God's image. Accordingly, children are not born for the benefit or enjoyment of their parents, but parents are there for children—to help them come into their own personhood before God. **training.** The shaping of the will through discipline. **instruction.** The shaping of the mind through teaching. See *WLC* 125,129,130.

6:5–8 This is the voice of a carefully considered Christology. In the first place, slaves identified with Christ when they adopted a posture of obedient submission (Php 2:1–11). All believers are called to share Christ's humiliation and sufferings in this age, in order to be exalted and glorified with him in the next (Ro 8:17). Paul was not interested in making anyone's share in that suffering worse than it needed to be (1Co 7:21); neither, however, was he interested in pretending there was an easy route around it. In the second place, as slaves served the exalted Christ rather than merely their earthly masters, they came to a radically new, Christ-centered self-understanding. The obstacle to attaining unity and brotherhood across the lines of slavery was that the very personhood of one man or woman was a commodity owned by another (slaves in antiquity were called "tools with souls"). Paul insisted that our ownership by Christ must overrule all other definitions of our per-

eye is on you, but like slaves of Christ, doing the will of God from your heart. [7]Serve
wholeheartedly, as if you were serving the Lord, not men,[v] [8]because you know that the
Lord will reward everyone for whatever good he does,[w] whether he is slave or free.
[9]And masters, treat your slaves in the same way. Do not threaten them, since you
know that he who is both their Master and yours[x] is in heaven, and there is no favoritism with him.

The Armor of God

[10]Finally, be strong in the Lord[y] and in his mighty power.[z] [11]Put on the full armor of
God[a] so that you can take your stand against the devil's schemes. [12]For our struggle is
not against flesh and blood, but against the rulers, against the authorities,[b] against the
powers[c] of this dark world and against the spiritual forces of evil in the heavenly
realms.[d] [13]Therefore put on the full armor of God, so that when the day of evil comes,
you may be able to stand your ground, and after you have done everything, to stand.
[14]Stand firm then, with the belt of truth buckled around your waist,[e] with the breastplate
of righteousness in place,[f] [15]and with your feet fitted with the readiness that comes from
the gospel of peace.[g] [16]In addition to all this, take up the shield of faith,[h] with which you
can extinguish all the flaming arrows of the evil one. [17]Take the helmet of salvation[i] and
the sword of the Spirit, which is the word of God.[j] [18]And pray in the Spirit on all occasions[k] with all kinds of prayers and requests.[l] With this in mind, be alert and always keep
on praying for all the saints.
[19]Pray also for me,[m] that whenever I open my mouth, words may be given me so that
I will fearlessly[n] make known the mystery of the gospel, [20]for which I am an ambassador[o] in chains.[p] Pray that I may declare it fearlessly, as I should.

6:7 [v]Col 3:23
6:8 [w]Col 3:24
6:9 [x]Job 31:13,14
6:10 [y]1Co 16:13 [z]Eph 1:19
6:11 [a]Ro 13:12
6:12 [b]Eph 1:21 [c]Ro 8:38 [d]Eph 1:3
6:14 [e]Isa 11:5 [f]Isa 59:17
6:15 [g]Isa 52:7
6:16 [h]1Jn 5:4
6:17 [i]Isa 59:17 [j]Heb 4:12
6:18 [k]Lk 18:1 [l]Mt 26:41; Php 1:4
6:19 [m]1Th 5:25 [n]Ac 4:29; 2Co 3:12
6:20 [o]2Co 5:20 [p]Ac 21:33

---

sonhood: "He who was a slave when he was called by the Lord is the Lord's freedman" (1Co 7:22). By rendering ungrudging service to their true heavenly owner, slaves had an extraordinary opportunity to demonstrate that what mattered was not their value in the marketplace but their value to the One who had spent his own life for their ransom. In this instruction Paul did not condone the ancient system of slavery. Rather, he merely instructed the Ephesian Christians how to function within the bounds of their existing society.

6:9 in the same way. If masters could expect to be obeyed as though they were Christ himself, then slaves could expect more from their Christian masters—to be treated the way Christ treats his own. **their Master and yours.** Earthly masters and slaves are all slaves of their heavenly master (cf. "he who was a free man when he was called is Christ's slave"; 1Co 7:22), so that earthly masters must not only manage the master-slave relationship with great patience and mercy but must actually consider and treat their slaves as equals. **no favoritism.** Earthly society might condone masters treating their slaves with harshness, but God will not. Before God, master and slave are equal; God will hold masters accountable for treating their slaves as well as they would treat all other fellow Christians.

■ **6:10–20** *Standing Strong Against the Devil.* By relying on the strength of the Holy Spirit and making use of the means of grace (e.g., Scripture and prayer), Christians can withstand spiritual warfare and demonic temptation, living godly lives and strengthening one another to do the same.

6:10–17 The Christian pursuit of unity and purity is complicated in that believers live under hostile conditions. Christ's cross and resurrection are the devil's undoing (see note on Col 2:15), and at Christ's second coming Satan's defeat will be completed and made visible (Ro 16:20). But the peace of the cross will be experienced in this interim only in the midst of intense spiritual struggle. Though the spiritual forces of darkness have already been vanquished, they are not yet harmless. See *HC* 127.

6:10 be strong . . . mighty power. These are the same terms Paul used in 1:19 to describe the power that raised Jesus from the dead and is presently at work within believers (cf. 3:16,18). Believers are not encouraged to face the evil hosts of darkness in their own strength but to do so in the strength that raised Jesus and has raised them with him (2:4–6; 3:16–19).

6:11 Put on. See 4:24. **the full armor of God.** The new set of clothes now becomes a warrior's battle gear (4:24; see notes on Col 3:10,12). **stand.** Repeated four times in verses 11 and 13–14. The "walking" image of chapters 4–5 (with 2:10 in the background) gives way to a picture of a soldier standing his ground in the midst of a heated battle. See *HC* 32.

6:12 See 1:21, 2:2 and 3:10. **rulers . . . forces.** These terms all refer to powerful spiritual beings—perhaps in terms of various ranks—making up the "kingdom of the air" (2:2) that Satan rules. **dark.** Compare 5:8–14.

6:13 the full armor of God. Paul combined a picture of the battle gear of the Roman infantryman with a number of Old Testament images of God or his Messiah as warrior. Strikingly, what is spoken of God or his Messiah in the Old Testament (cf. Isa 59:16–17) is applied to believers in Ephesians. The cumulative effect of verses 13–17 is a picture of a people who are so caught up in the victory already won for them in Jesus' conquest of the forces of darkness that they are immovable in the face of threats against God's vision to establish a community that reflects his loving and holy character.

6:14 belt of truth. The Roman warrior's leather belt supported and protected his lower abdomen, gathered his tunic together and held his sword. Paul seems to have had in mind the confidence that comes from certainty about the objective truthfulness of God's Word. **breastplate of righteousness.** Being clothed with an imputed, or alien, righteousness (Php 3:9–10), the believer can stand up under the accusations of the one whose Greek title (*diábolos* or "devil") means "slanderer" (see Ro 8:31–34). Simultaneously, as believers take on the righteous character of Christ (4:25; 5:9), their growing conformity to his image gives them confidence in resisting temptation.

6:15 feet fitted. Despite a clear allusion to Isaiah 52:7, Paul did not have in mind the barefooted messenger who takes the gospel to others. The image here is that of the Roman soldier's sturdy sandals, which gave him stability and protection in battle. Ironically, the peace that comes from the gospel readies one for war against evil (2:14–15,17).

6:16–17 See *WLC* 155.

6:16 shield of faith. A Roman infantryman carried a lengthy, oblong shield that covered his body from head to toe. It was made of wood, covered with hide and bound with iron at the top and bottom. When dipped in water before a battle, it could extinguish arrows that had been dipped in pitch, set ablaze and then shot. The evil one and his hosts continually assault believers with accusations and temptations, but by faith believers can hold firmly to the promise of forgiveness in Christ, as well as receive empowerment to resist temptation. See *WCF* 14.3.

6:17 helmet of salvation. For Paul, salvation was both a present experience (see 2:8 and its note) and a future hope (1Th 5:8). The believers' final ground of confidence is the faithfulness of God to complete in them what he has begun (Php 1:6). **sword of the Spirit, which is the word of God.** The one offensive weapon in the believer's arsenal. This was the Roman soldier's short sword. It was designed for hand-to-hand combat. See Jesus' use of Scripture in Matthew 4:1–11 and Luke 4:1–13.

6:18–20 The warrior motif issued in an equally martial call to prayer on behalf of all believers and of Paul's ministry. See 1:15–23 for Paul's dependence on prayer. See *WCF* 21.3; 21.6; *WLC* 160, 183,185,191.

Final Greetings

6:21 [q]Ac 20:4
6:22 [r]Col 4:7-9
6:23 [s]Gal 6:16; 1Pe 5:14

21Tychicus,[q] the dear brother and faithful servant in the Lord, will tell you everything, so that you also may know how I am and what I am doing. 22I am sending him
to you for this very purpose, that you may know how we are,[r] and that he may encourage you.
23Peace[s] to the brothers, and love with faith from God the Father and the Lord Jesus
Christ. 24Grace to all who love our Lord Jesus Christ with an undying love.

■ **6:21–24** *Final Greetings.* In his typical fashion, Paul closed this letter with a blessing and benediction to his readers.

6:21–24 Tychicus. See note on Colossians 4:7. Paul's lack of personal greetings may indicate the circular nature of this letter. See "Introduction: Original Audience."

PHILIPPIANS

Introduction

Overview

Author: The apostle Paul

Purpose: To thank the Philippians for their solidarity with him while he was in prison and to encourage them to unity and humble service toward each other in Christ

Date: c. A.D. 61

Key Truths:

- The gospel of Christ will go forward, even in the face of persecution.
- Suffering for Christ is a joy and leads to glory for believers.
- Believers are to display the gospel in their lives by serving each other in imitation of Christ.
- Believers are to hold fast to the truth and avoid the extremes of legalism and antinomianism (the belief that the Christian is not subject to the moral law of God).
- Supporting others in ministry is an important Christian practice.

Author

The author identified himself as Paul (1:1). This explicit claim is confirmed by the fact that the early church unanimously attributed this letter to Paul, based on its many personal references and its similarity to the other Pauline writings.

Paul's initial involvement with the church at Philippi is recorded in Acts 16. Prompted by a vision (Ac 16:6–10), Paul and his colleagues traveled to Philippi (Ac 16:12). During their brief visit, God did mighty works and a church was established (Ac 16:40), Paul's first on European soil. Paul returned on at least two other occasions to strengthen the believers there (Ac 20:1–6; 2Co 2:13).

Time and Place of Writing

Paul wrote from prison (1:12–30), but the location of the imprisonment is uncertain. Some interpreters think he wrote from Ephesus, but Acts 19 says nothing of his being imprisoned during his lengthy Ephesian ministry. It has also been suggested that he wrote this letter dur-

Philippi in the Time of Paul

The Roman colony of Philippi *(Colonia Augusta Julia Philippensis)* was an important city in Macedonia, located on the main highway leading from the eastern provinces to Rome. This road, the Via Egnatia, bisected the city's forum and was the chief cause of its prosperity and political importance. Ten miles distant on the coast was Neapolis, the place where Paul landed after sailing from Troas, in response to the Macedonian vision.

As a prominent city of the gold-producing region of Macedonia, Philippi had a proud history. Named originally after Philip II, the father of Alexander the Great, the city was later honored with the name of Julius Caesar and Augustus. Many Italian settlers from the legions swelled the ranks of citizens and made Philippi vigorous and polyglot. It grew from a small settlement to a city of dignity and privilege. Among its highest honors was the *ius Italicum,* by which it enjoyed rights legally equivalent to those of Italian cities.

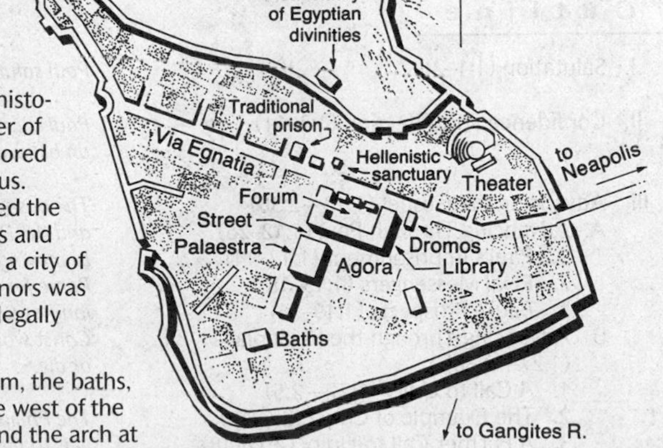

Ruins of the theater, the acropolis, the forum, the baths, and the commemorative arch (about a mile west of the city) have been found. A little farther beyond the arch at the Gangites River is the place where Paul addressed some God-fearing women and where Lydia was converted (Ac 16:13–15).

ing his imprisonment in Caesarea (Ac 23:23—26:32). It is most likely, however, in accordance with long-standing tradition, that Paul wrote Philippians while imprisoned in Rome (Ac 28) and that he did so toward the end of that period, around A.D. 61. Philippians 1:13 and 4:22 accord best with a Roman setting, and the language of 1:7–26 suggests legal proceedings at the highest level—proceedings that were similar to those Paul faced in Rome. Finally, Acts 28:16–31 (see also Php 1:12–14) speaks of Paul's freedom to preach during this confinement.

Original Audience

The city of Philippi was named for Philip of Macedon, father of Alexander the Great. One reason for its importance is that it lay on the Via Egnatia, the main road between the eastern provinces and Rome. As a Roman colony populated in part by retired Roman soldiers, its inhabitants enjoyed the privileges of Roman citizenship. The absence of Old Testament quotations and Jewish names indicates that the church of Philippi was largely Gentile.

Purpose and Distinctives

Paul wrote this letter to express both joy and concern. The epistle rings with gratitude for the way God was carrying forward his saving work among the Philippians and for the special bond that existed between Paul and his readers. At the same time, there is a gravity to the letter. The Philippians faced persecution (1:27–30) and pressures from false teachings (3:2–21). Moreover, conflicts within the church jeopardized the ministry in Philippi (1:27—2:18; 4:2–3). Paul wrote both to convey his joy and to give instruction to the Philippian believers. He focused particularly on the following topics:

1. *Paul's Affection for His Readers.* This epistle amply attests to the special bond of love Paul felt toward the Philippians (1:3–8; 4:10–19). They had been faithful in their support of Paul's ministry, and their willingness to suffer with him for Christ's sake was a source of encouragement for Paul.

2. *Joy.* Despite the circumstances of his imprisonment, Paul's letter resounds with the theme of joy. Different expressions point to joy at least 16 times in the letter. Paul's joyfulness stemmed largely from the faithfulness of the Philippians, and he wanted the same for them as an antidote to all anxiety (4:4–7).

3. *The Example of Christ's Humility.* Philippians focuses much on the humble state of Jesus' incarnation. The majestic "hymn to Christ" (see 2:6–11) offers a model for believers. In his preincarnate state, Christ Jesus was "in very nature God" (2:6). Nevertheless, he took the form of a slave and made himself nothing by taking on human nature and subjecting himself to his own creatures. Yet even in this state of humiliation, Christ did not cease being fully divine (see theological article "Jesus Christ, God and Man" at Jn 1).

4. *Justification by Grace Through Faith.* Against those who enjoined obedience to the Old Testament law as a condition for meriting salvation, Paul stressed that God has willed for his people to be saved by receiving his righteousness rather than by striving to establish their own. Although Paul had been scrupulous in his obedience to the law, he came to realize that his confidence in such obedience was a great sin, for it kept him from trusting God. Paul viewed his former boasting with disgust (3:7–8) and embraced Christ alone as his source of confidence (3:3,9).

5. *The Christian Life.* This epistle is filled with instruction on practical Christianity. Just as Christ became a servant, so also the Christian becomes the servant of Christ (1:1). Only the person enslaved to Christ is free to love and serve others (2:3–5).

Paul stressed the importance of identification with Christ in his death and resurrection. As with Christ, the believer's suffering is the prelude to resurrection (3:10–11). For the present, it is in the midst of the ongoing struggle that the Christian experiences joy and empowerment (3:10; 4:13).

Paul highlighted the importance of striving toward the goal of final salvation. Confident in God's calling, the apostle pushed forward toward the heavenly prize (3:13–14). Only as Christians work do they realize that God is working in them (2:12–13). Human effort is precisely the area in which the power of God is manifested.

Outline

I. Salutation (1:1–2)	*Paul saluted the believers in Philippi.*
II. Confidence and Affection (1:3–11)	*Paul expressed his confidence in and love for the Philippian believers.*
III. Advancing the Gospel (1:12—2:30) A. Advancing Through Paul (1:12–26) 1. Paul's Imprisonment (1:12–14) 2. Rival Messengers (1:15–18) 3. Paul's Prospects (1:19–26)	*The gospel advanced in important ways through Paul and the Philippians. Paul's life was devoted in every way to moving the gospel forward. He was imprisoned in Rome for Christ's sake, rejoiced in his rival preachers so long as Christ was exalted and expressed confidence that Christ would find honor whether Paul himself were to live or die.*
B. Advancing Through the Philippians (1:27—2:30) 1. A Call to Unity (1:27—2:5) 2. The Example of Christ (2:6–11) 3. A Further Call to Unity (2:12–18) 4. Two Examples of Service (2:19–30)	*The Philippians needed a reminder of the ways the gospel was to move forward through them. God had called them to unity in Christ and to service to each other.*

IV. Resisting Error (3:1—4:1) A. Against the Legalists (3:1–11) B. Living Now for the Future (3:12–16) C. Against the Libertines (3:17—4:1)	*Paul strongly urged the Philippians to resist legalism as well as antinomianism (see note on 3:17—4:1). They were to live in the present life with their eyes on the goal of their future at Christ's return.*
V. Exhortations (4:2–9)	*Paul called for harmony, service and love in the church at Philippi.*
VI. Thanksgiving (4:10–20) A. Contentment (4:10–13) B. Partnership (4:14–20)	*Paul thanked the Philippians for their support while he suffered imprisonment.*
VII. Final Greeting and Benediction (4:21–23)	*Paul offered some final remarks, including greetings and blessings.*

1 Paul and Timothy,[a] servants of Christ Jesus,

To all the saints[b] in Christ Jesus at Philippi,[c] together with the overseers[a][d] and deacons:[e]

2 Grace and peace to you from God our Father and the Lord Jesus Christ.[f]

Thanksgiving and Prayer

3 I thank my God every time I remember you.[g] 4 In all my prayers for all of you, I always
pray[h] with joy 5 because of your partnership[i] in the gospel from the first day[j] until now,
6 being confident of this, that he who began a good work in you will carry it on to com
pletion until the day of Christ Jesus.[k]

7 It is right[l] for me to feel this way about all of you, since I have you in my heart;[m] for
whether I am in chains[n] or defending[o] and confirming the gospel, all of you share in God's
grace with me. 8 God can testify[p] how I long for all of you with the affection of Christ Jesus.

9 And this is my prayer: that your love[q] may abound more and more in knowledge and
depth of insight, 10 so that you may be able to discern what is best and may be pure and

1:1 [a]Ac 16:1; 2Co 1:1 [b]Ac 9:13 [c]Ac 16:12 [d]1Ti 3:1 [e]1Ti 3:8
1:2 [f]Ro 1:7
1:3 [g]Ro 1:8
1:4 [h]Ro 1:10
1:5 [i]Ac 2:42; Php 4:15 [j]Ac 16:12-40
1:6 [k]ver 10; 1Co 1:8
1:7 [l]2Pe 1:13 [m]2Co 7:3 [n]ver 13,14,17; Ac 21:33 [o]ver 16
1:8 [p]Ro 1:9
1:9 [q]1Th 3:12

[a] *1* Traditionally *bishops*

■ **1:1–2** *Salutation.* Paul began this epistle in his usual manner—by identifying himself and his readers.
1:1 Paul and Timothy. Timothy, who had been present at the founding of the Philippian church (Ac 16), was known to the readers (2:22). In distinguishing between the two men, Paul called himself "an apostle" and Timothy "our brother" (2Co 1:1; Col 1:1). **servants of Christ Jesus.** Both men were called "servants" (Greek, *doulos*), a word meaning "slave" here. Timothy was like a son to Paul (2:22), but both stood under Christ the Lord. **in Christ Jesus.** One of Paul's favorite ways to describe the union of believers with Christ. This phrase (or the shorter "in Christ") occurs ten times in Philippians. Moreover, the parallel expression "in the Lord" appears nine times (see note at v. 14). See theological article "Union With Christ" at Galatians 6. **overseers and deacons.** These terms designated the twofold leadership in the church at Philippi (1Ti 3:1–13). *Episcopos* ("overseer") is sometimes translated "bishop," but in Titus 1:5–7 Paul used this term and *presbyteros* ("elder") interchangeably, indicating that both refer to the same office.
1:2 Grace and peace. This couplet, a concise expression of the nature and effect of Christ's saving work, appears in all 13 Pauline salutations. The joint source of both is "God our Father and the Lord Jesus Christ."
■ **1:3–11** *Confidence and Affection.* After initial greetings Paul immediately expressed his confidence in, as well as his encouragement, concern and affection for the Philippian Christians.
1:3–4 Paul's memory of his time with the Philippians prompted him to pray for them frequently ("in all my prayers"), comprehensively ("for all of you") and gratefully ("I thank my God").
1:4 with joy. Joy is a dominant theme in Philippians (vv. 18,26; 3:1; 4:4,10).
1:5 your partnership. The Philippians' financial support is especially in view (4:10–20). **in the gospel.** The word "gospel" was Paul's favorite way of describing his message. It occurs nine times in Philippians (proportionately more than in any other letter). Their common commitment to the gospel (v. 7) bound Paul and the Philippians to each other. **from the first day until now.** Paul had in mind the first time he had preached the gospel in Philippi (4:15; Ac 16:12–40).
1:6 he who began a good work in you will carry it on to completion. Paul was confident that God would complete the salvation of believers in Philippi. Elsewhere Paul stressed the place of human effort in persevering faith, but here he pointed out clearly that the perseverance of the saints depends upon God's own power, preserving them by grace. God's saving purpose will be consummated on "the day of Christ Jesus" (v. 10; 2:16), when Jesus returns in glory to raise his people from the dead (3:11,20–21) and to receive universal homage (2:9–11). All people who have exercised saving faith in Christ will be kept until that day. See theological article "The Perseverance and Preservation of Believers" at Philippians 1. See *WCF* 17.1.
1:7 to feel this way. The Greek verb here translated "to feel" (*phroneo*) occurs ten times in Philippians, proportionately much more often than in any other Pauline letter. The term embraces thought as well as feeling and implies a course of action upon which one's mind is set (note its usage in 2:2,5; 3:15,19). **I have you in my heart.** The words could also be rendered, "You have me in your heart." The Philippians "share[d] in God's grace" with Paul through supporting his ministry (v. 5). **defending and confirming the gospel.** The legal terms suggest apostolic witness during a trial (cf. v. 16; Mk 13:9–11).
1:8 the affection of Christ Jesus. The verb corresponding to the noun "affection" is frequently used in the Gospels to describe Jesus' compassion (e.g., Mt 9:36; 14:14). It indicates deep emotion.
1:9–10 Not only did Paul tell the Philippians that he prayed for them (v. 4), but he also reported to them the content of his prayers. In Paul's mind, Christian love leads to increasingly greater levels of knowledge, insight and discernment, and culminates in behavior that is "pure and blameless" (cf. Col 1:9–11). The absence of love demonstrates that alleged knowledge by itself is worthless (1Co 13:1–3), while love is itself knowledge of the deepest kind (1Co 8:1–3). The seriousness of Paul's prayer—that "love [would]

blameless until the day of Christ,[r] 11 filled with the fruit of righteousness[s] that comes
through Jesus Christ—to the glory and praise of God.

Paul's Chains Advance the Gospel

12 Now I want you to know, brothers, that what has happened to me has really served
to advance the gospel. 13 As a result, it has become clear throughout the whole palace
guard[a] and to everyone else that I am in chains[t] for Christ. 14 Because of my chains,[u] most
of the brothers in the Lord have been encouraged to speak the word of God more courageously and fearlessly.
15 It is true that some preach Christ out of envy and rivalry, but others out of goodwill.
16 The latter do so in love, knowing that I am put here for the defense of the gospel.[v] 17 The
former preach Christ out of selfish ambition,[w] not sincerely, supposing that they can stir
up trouble for me while I am in chains.[b][x] 18 But what does it matter? The important thing
is that in every way, whether from false motives or true, Christ is preached. And because
of this I rejoice.
Yes, and I will continue to rejoice, 19 for I know that through your prayers[y] and the help
given by the Spirit of Jesus Christ,[z] what has happened to me will turn out for my deliverance.[c] 20 I eagerly expect[a] and hope that I will in no way be ashamed, but will have sufficient courage[b] so that now as always Christ will be exalted in my body,[c] whether by life or
by death.[d] 21 For to me, to live is Christ[e] and to die is gain. 22 If I am to go on living in the
body, this will mean fruitful labor for me. Yet what shall I choose? I do not know! 23 I am
torn between the two: I desire to depart[f] and be with Christ,[g] which is better by far; 24 but
it is more necessary for you that I remain in the body. 25 Convinced of this, I know that I will
remain, and I will continue with all of you for your progress and joy in the faith, 26 so that
through my being with you again your joy in Christ Jesus will overflow on account of me.
27 Whatever happens, conduct yourselves in a manner worthy[h] of the gospel of Christ.

1:10 [r]ver 6; 1Co 1:8
1:11 [s]Jas 3:18
1:13 [t]ver 7,14,17
1:14 [u]ver 7,13,17
1:16 [v]ver 7,12
1:17 [w]Php 2:3 [x]ver 7, 13,14
1:19 [y]2Co 1:11 [z]Ac 16:7
1:20 [a]Ro 8:19 [b]ver 14 [c]1Co 6:20 [d]Ro 14:8
1:21 [e]Gal 2:20
1:23 [f]2Ti 4:6 [g]Jn 12:26; 2Co 5:8
1:27 [h]Eph 4:1

[a] *13* Or *whole palace* [b] *16,17* Some late manuscripts have verses 16 and 17 in reverse order.
[c] *19* Or *salvation*

---

abound" among the Philippians—would become more apparent later (2:1–18). See *WLC* 190.
1:11 Not only is the sinner justified through faith in Christ (3:9), but "the fruit of righteousness," or the righteous life that ensues, also "comes through Jesus Christ" by the work of his Spirit (Gal 5:22–23), "to the glory and praise of God" the Father. All three persons of the Godhead are active in the believers' sanctification. See *WCF* 16.2; *WLC* 190.
■ **1:12—2:30** *Advancing the Gospel.* Paul began the main portion of this letter with a positive presentation of the ways the gospel is advanced. His discussion divides into two parts: the gospel in his own life (1:12–26) and in the lives of the Philippians (1:27—2:18).
■ **1:12–26** *Advancing Through Paul.* In his positive presentation of the gospel, Paul described how the Good News of Christ had affected his life. He discussed his own imprisonment (vv. 12–14), other teachers (vv. 15–18) and his future prospects as a minister of the gospel (vv. 19–26).
■ **1:12–14** *Paul's Imprisonment.* Paul reveled in the fact that God had used his imprisonment to further the gospel.
1:12 served to advance the gospel. Literally, "has led to the advance of the gospel." Because of Paul's imprisonment, the gospel, itself a saving power (Ro 1:16), had moved irresistibly through the palace guard and beyond.
1:13 whole palace guard . . . everyone else. Paul's imprisonment for Christ had become known not only to the soldiers assigned to the emperor, but also to the imperial household and perhaps to the Roman populace beyond.
1:14 brothers. Following the custom of his day, Paul used this term for all people in the visible church, whether male or female. The designation, however, does not mean that those addressed were necessarily saved or members of the invisible church (see theological article "The Church: Visible and Invisible" at 1 Pe 4). **in the Lord.** This important Pauline phrase points to the believer's union with Christ and to the divine resources available through Christ to those united with him (4:13). The phrase occurs nine times in Philippians (including "in the Lord Jesus" at 2:19). By means of Paul's imprisonment, Christ the Lord strengthened and encouraged the "brothers" to proclaim the gospel fearlessly.
■ **1:15–18** *Rival Messengers.* The subject is not rival messages, for both parties preached Christ, but the motivations and attitudes of other ministers. The motive of one group was "goodwill" and "love" for Christ. The dominant motive of the other was "selfish ambition." This group preached Christ so that they themselves would be magnified, an attitude different from Paul's (vv. 20–21). They responded to Paul's successes by seeking to "stir up trouble" for him. Paul called the Philippians to follow the first motivation and to reject the second. What Paul taught, he exemplified.
1:15–17 See *WCF* 16.7; *WLC* 159,174.
1:18 Christ is preached. And because of this I rejoice. Paul showed goodwill toward his rivals because the exaltation of Christ through preaching was more important to him than focusing on the motivations of others. This did not mean, however, that he simply ignored their evil motives. See *WCF* 16.7.
■ **1:19–26** *Paul's Prospects.* Paul assured the Philippians of his expectations for his future.
1:19 Spirit of Jesus Christ. Paul identified the third person of the Trinity as both the Spirit of God and the Spirit of Christ (Ro 8:9; Gal 4:6). **deliverance.** Paul expected to be released from prison, but he was not certain of it (vv. 20–27; 2:24). God would deliver him (vv. 25–26) through his appointed agencies, both divine ("the help given by the Spirit of Jesus Christ") and human (the Philippians' prayers).
1:20 Christ will be exalted . . . whether by life or by death. Paul's passion was not his life or his death. His life and death were secondary to his desire to see Christ honored. He knew that this higher goal could be reached either through the extension of his life (Ro 12:1–2) or through his death (Php 2:17).
1:21–23 See *HC* 42,57.
1:21 For to me, to live is Christ. Christ was Paul's reason for being. His heart was so filled with passion for Christ's glory that all other motivations faded into insignificance. **to die is gain.** Paul did not consider passing from this life to the next a loss. Far from severing his union with Christ, death would usher Paul into a deeper experience of Christ and his blessings.
1:23 I am torn between the two. Paul desired both to be with Christ and to remain on Earth for further service to the Philippians and others. Therefore he was faced with a genuine dilemma. Nevertheless, Paul understood that such matters are determined by God, and he was convinced that God had further work for him to do among the Philippians (vv. 24–25). **to depart and be with Christ.** Paul's language here sheds light on the character of the intermediate state (i.e., the condition of the person between physical death and the resurrection; cf. 2Co 5:6–9). That this state is "better by far" and that "to die is gain" (v. 21) indicate that Paul expected conscious and intimate fellowship with Christ. However, fullness of fellowship awaits the reunion of the soul with the body (3:20–21). See *WCF* 32.1; *WLC* 85,86; *WSC* 37.
■ **1:27—2:30** *Advancing Through the Philippians.* Having described the gospel in relation to his own life, Paul now turned to its role in

Then, whether I come and see you or only hear about you in my absence, I will know that you stand firm[i] in one spirit, contending[j] as one man for the faith of the gospel 28 without being frightened in any way by those who oppose you. This is a sign to them that they will

1:27 [i]1Co 16:13 [j]Jude 3

---

the lives of the Philippians. His discussion divides into three parts: a call to unity (1:27—2:5), the example of Christ (2:6–11) and another call to unity (2:12–18).

■ **1:27—2:5** *A Call to Unity.* Paul's chief concern at this point was that the Philippians see unity among believers as a crucial effect of the gospel.

The Perseverance and Preservation of Believers: Can I Lose My Salvation?

REFORMED theology has generally used the twofold terminology of the *perseverance* and *preservation* of believers when addressing the question of true believers' eternal security in Christ. This terminology represents a balanced approach to the Biblical teaching that perseverance in the Christian faith is required to receive the final reward of eternal salvation but that the perseverance of all who have genuinely trusted Christ is guaranteed because of God's preservation. Believers persevere by persistence under discouragement and contrary pressure, but they are able to do so because Jesus Christ through the Spirit ensures that every true believer will endure to the end.

Many other Christian traditions diverge from Reformed theology by going in one of two directions. On the one hand, some teach that it is possible for people who have exercised saving faith, who are genuinely regenerated in Christ, to lose their salvation. They appeal to passages in Scripture that warn against turning from the faith and require obedience to receive the final reward of eternal salvation (e.g., Ps 69,28; Mt 24:13; Lk 9:62; Jn 2:23–24; 15:6; 1Co 9:27; 2Co 13:5; Heb 3:6; 6:1–8; 10:26–31; 12:14; 2Pe 2:21–22; Rev 2:7,11,17; 22:19). Reformed theology has acknowledged that these and similar passages require perseverance and indicate that a person may exercise a measure of faith and receive many blessings from God, but then suffer eternal judgment because of apostasy. The question is, What kind of faith and what kind of blessings do such people have?

On the other hand, some branches of the church teach that the only requirements for eternal salvation are a decision to receive Christ as Savior and a sincere profession of faith. They draw upon passages that stress that justification is by faith alone and that salvation is a free gift that cannot be lost (e.g., Jn 3:16; 6:37; Ac 16:31; Ro 3:28; 8:38–39; Gal 2:16). Extreme versions of this outlook are sometimes called *decisionism* or *easy believism,* meaning that the only requirement for salvation is that a person have sincerely professed faith in Christ as Savior, but not necessarily as Lord. Seldom distinguishing between the kind of faith that saves and that which does not, or between true believers and mere professors of faith, these Christians hold that while a person can lose temporal blessings because of flagrant, habitual sin, no sincere person has to fear the eternal judgment of God. Some go so far as to insist that even if one repudiates a prior confession of faith and rejects Christ, that person will still be saved.

Reformed theology strikes a balance between these two positions, embracing some aspects of both points of view and rejecting others. On the one hand, the need for perseverance is acknowledged. It is true that we are justified by faith alone, but faith that saves is never truly "alone." As James put it, "Faith by itself, if it is not accompanied by action, is dead" (Jas 2:17). For this reason, Paul exhorted the Philippian Christians to "work out [their] salvation with fear and trembling" (Php 2:12) because during the Christian life one's faith is tested to see whether the person is truly in Christ (2Co 13:5). In this sense, Reformed theologians often distinguish saving faith from seemingly sincere but temporary faith that leads to hypocrisy and apostasy.

As the parable of the sower indicates (Mt 13:18–23), there are different kinds of faith, but only faith that produces the fruit of holy living is saving faith. This is why the writer of Hebrews insisted that "without holiness no one will see the Lord" (Heb 12:14). Those with temporary faith may experience many blessings from God because of their close association with the faithful (Heb 6:1–6; 2Pe 2:21–22), but they will lose those blessings as they turn from Christ and will eventually suffer eternal judgment (Heb 10:26–31). Many who say to Jesus, "Lord, Lord," will not be acknowledged (Mt 7:21–23). Only those who show themselves to be regenerate by pursuing holiness as they pass through this world are entitled to believe themselves secure in Christ. Persevering in faith and penitence, not just in Christian formalism, is the path to glory.

Nevertheless, Reformed theology has also emphasized that God's gracious preservation must sustain true believers so that they remain faithful to Christ. Christians do not begin their walk with Christ by faith and then continue by reliance on their own efforts (Gal 3:3). Paul exhorted the Philippians to "work out [their] salvation" (Php 2:12) but then added, "for it is God who works in you to will and to act according to his good purpose" (Php 2:13). Paul also assured them, declaring that "he who began a good work in you will carry it on to completion" (Php 1:6). Jesus himself stressed his preservation of true believers when he said that believers "shall never perish; no one can snatch them out of my hand" (Jn 10:28).

Sometimes truly regenerate believers backslide and fall into gross sin. But in this they act out of character, do violence to their own new nature and make themselves deeply miserable, so that eventually they seek and find restoration to righteousness. When regenerate people act in character, they manifest a humble, grateful desire to please the God who saved them, and the knowledge that he is pledged to keep them safe forever simply increases this desire. See *WCF* 17; *BC* 24,25; *HC* 86; *CD* V.

1:29
[k]Mt 5:11,12
[l]Ac 14:22
1:30
[m]Col 2:1; 1Th 2:2
[n]Ac 16:19-40
[o]ver 13
2:1
[p]2Co 13:14
[q]Col 3:12
2:2
[r]Jn 3:29 [s]Php 4:2
[t]Ro 12:16
2:3
[u]Gal 5:26
[v]Ro 12:10; 1Pe 5:5
2:5
[w]Mt 11:29
2:6
[x]Jn 1:1 [y]Jn 5:18
2:7
[z]Mt 20:28 [a]Jn 1:14;
Heb 2:17
2:8
[b]Mt 26:39;
Jn 10:18; Heb 5:8

be destroyed, but that you will be saved—and that by God. 29 For it has been granted to
you[k] on behalf of Christ not only to believe on him, but also to suffer[l] for him, 30 since you
are going through the same struggle[m] you saw[n] I had, and now hear[o] that I still have.

Imitating Christ's Humility

2 If you have any encouragement from being united with Christ, if any comfort from
his love, if any fellowship with the Spirit,[p] if any tenderness and compassion,[q] 2 then
make my joy complete[r] by being like-minded,[s] having the same love, being one[t] in spirit and purpose. 3 Do nothing out of selfish ambition or vain conceit,[u] but in humility consider others better than yourselves.[v] 4 Each of you should look not only to your own interests, but also to the interests of others.
5 Your attitude should be the same as that of Christ Jesus:[w]

6 Who, being in very nature[a] God,[x]
did not consider equality with God[y] something to be grasped,
7 but made himself nothing,
taking the very nature[b] of a servant,[z]
being made in human likeness.[a]
8 And being found in appearance as a man,
he humbled himself
and became obedient to death[b]—
even death on a cross!

[a] 6 Or *in the form of* [b] 7 Or *the form*

1:27 worthy of the gospel. No one can be worthy to receive the gospel—or to live in perfect accordance with it. Yet to live in a manner appropriate to the wonder of the gospel is the goal of everyone who has saving faith in Christ. In this context, Paul's ideal of worthiness was expressed in several ways. **stand firm in one spirit, contending as one man.** Literally, "stand firm in one spirit, contending as one soul." The Greek words for "spirit" and "soul" do not denote separate constituent parts of the person. One very important way we are to live worthily of the gospel is to pursue unity among believers. This theme appears time and again in Paul's writings (Ro 15:5; Eph 4:3,13). **contending as one man for the faith of the gospel.** Paul also urged his readers to contend in unity against non-Christian opponents for the truth of the gospel—even if the threats from the world were frightful (v. 28). See *WLC* 112.

1:28 This is a sign. Standing in unity with each other and against the world signifies that (1) opponents of the gospel will be destroyed and (2) believers will be saved.

1:29 it has been granted. God gives believers many privileges. Here Paul identified both the honor of believing in Christ and that of suffering for him. To suffer for Christ and his gospel is an honor because it leads to great reward and eternal life (Ro 8:17–18; Php 3:10–11). See *CD* 1.5.

2:1 encouragement from being united with Christ. Paul appealed to the encouragement or hope that all believers derive from being joined with Christ through faith (see theological article "Union With Christ" at Gal 6). **if any.** The repetition of this phrase made Paul's words especially forceful. Moreover, the qualities mentioned are true of all believers to one degree or another. As a result, the appeal of verse 1 provides the basis for the exhortations of verses 2–4. If these conditions are realities to any degree (v. 1), then the results (vv. 2–4) must be in evidence as well. **comfort from his love.** Literally, "comfort from love." Paul also appealed to the fact that all believers find encouragement both from Christ's love for them and from their love for Christ. **fellowship with the Spirit.** This phrase may also be rendered "fellowship produced by the Spirit." The wonder of the Sprit's work is evident to some extent in every true believer's life. **tenderness and compassion.** These qualities have their source in God, and they find expression in Christians' conduct toward each other (1:8; Col 3:12). They are closely associated with love, a quality of life that all true believers exhibit.

2:2 then make my joy complete. Paul made a deeply personal appeal. If the Philippians had even the smallest measure of the qualities mentioned in verse 1, then Paul wanted them to go one step further and make him full of joy. **like-minded . . . same love . . . one in spirit and purpose.** The accent on unity is strong in this verse (see also 1:27). Through unity in the church, Paul would receive much joy.

2:3–4 See *WLC* 131,141.

2:3 selfish ambition . . . vain conceit. Paul added a prohibition against those qualities that destroy Christian unity. Unrighteous pride places one Christian above others and therefore promotes conflicts rather than harmony in personal relationships. By contrast, humility places each Christian beneath others in a place of service with a concern for the needs and interests of others (1:27; 2:2,4,14). Love (v. 2) is essential if believers are to relate to one another in humility (thus the prayer of 1:9; cf. 1Co 13:4–5).

2:4–11 See *WLC* 42,46; *HC* 55.

2:5 Your attitude. This verse connects the exhortations of verses 1–4 to praise of Christ in verses 6–11. Paul forged the link with the same Greek word (here translated "attitude") that he used twice in verse 2. Addressing the pride that lay at the root of the Philippians' disunity (1:27—2:4), Paul invoked Christ as the supreme example of humility. For Paul, Christ is first Lord and Savior (v. 11; 3:20), but he is surely an example as well (Ro 15:1–3; 2Co 10:1).

▪ **2:6–11** *The Example of Christ.* Paul drew upon what may have been a hymn already in use in the early church. This hymn in praise of Christ may be conveniently divided into six stanzas (represented exactly in the verse divisions of the NIV). The first three (vv. 6–8) celebrate Christ's humiliation, the latter three (vv. 9–11) his exaltation.

2:6 being in very nature God. Literally, "being in the form of God." The word "form" witnesses to the underlying reality. The phrase "the form of God" points to Jesus' deity. The participle "being" denotes not merely existence, but also possession. Christ possesses deity, a deity he did not relinquish by becoming a man (v. 7). **equality with God.** Literally, "the being equal with God." In this instance, the definite article points to something previously mentioned (namely, Christ's "being in the form of God"). To be "in the form of God" is to be equal with God. **something to be grasped.** This denotes something desirable and, in this case, already possessed. Jesus did not selfishly cling to the glory of his heavenly station but instead took the course of action described in verse 7. See *WCF* 8.2; *WLC* 36.

2:7 made himself nothing. Literally, "emptied himself." Christ is not said to have emptied himself of divine attributes. The phrase means that he gave utterly of himself, that he expended himself to the full by becoming a man. The nature of his self-emptying is defined in the three participial phrases that follow ("taking . . . being made . . . being found"). Paul here described Christ's relinquishing of his heavenly glory (see Jn 17:5), not Christ's abdication of his divine being or powers. Christ took the form of a slave without abandoning the form of God. In his incarnate state, he did not relinquish, but manifested, the being and character of God. **taking the very nature of a servant.** Literally, "the form of a slave." This language vividly expresses Christ's willingness to deprive himself of his glory. **being made in human likeness.** Christ is truly human. The word "likeness" does not deny the reality of his humanity. In order to die (v. 8), Christ had to be genuinely human. At the same time, Paul made a distinction between Christ and other, ordinary human beings. Unlike them, Christ is not sinful (2Co 5:21). And unlike them, he belongs essentially (touching his divine nature) to the transcendent world. Even in making himself nothing and hum-

9 Therefore God exalted him[c] to the highest place
and gave him the name that is above every name,[d]
10 that at the name of Jesus every knee should bow,[e]
in heaven and on earth and under the earth,[f]
11 and every tongue confess that Jesus Christ is Lord,[g]
to the glory of God the Father.

Shining as Stars

12 Therefore, my dear friends, as you have always obeyed—not only in my presence,
but now much more in my absence—continue to work out your salvation with fear and
trembling,[h] 13 for it is God who works in you[i] to will and to act according to his good purpose.
14 Do everything without complaining[j] or arguing, 15 so that you may become blameless and pure, children of God[k] without fault in a crooked and depraved generation,[l] in
which you shine like stars in the universe 16 as you hold out[a] the word of life—in order
that I may boast on the day of Christ that I did not run or labor for nothing.[m] 17 But even
if I am being poured out like a drink offering[n] on the sacrifice[o] and service coming from

a 16 Or *hold on to*

2:9 [c]Ac 2:33; Heb 2:9 [d]Eph 1:20,21
2:10 [e]Ro 14:11 [f]Mt 28:18
2:11 [g]Jn 13:13
2:12 [h]2Co 7:15
2:13 [i]Ezr 1:5
2:14 [j]1Co 10:10; 1Pe 4:9
2:15 [k]Mt 5:45,48; Eph 5:1 [l]Ac 2:40
2:16 [m]1Th 2:19
2:17 [n]2Ti 4:6 [o]Ro 15:16

---

bling himself, he remained a heavenly being (see theological article: "Jesus Christ, God and Man" at Jn 1). See *BC* 18,26; *HC* 35.

2:8 And being found in appearance as a man. These words build on verse 7. Christ did not merely appear to be a man, as though his incarnation were an illusion. He chose to reveal himself through his humanity. **he humbled himself.** The language here is parallel to the phrase "made himself nothing" in verse 7. Each act occurred by the free exercise of Christ's own will. Paul's readers were to do the same. **and became obedient to death.** Submission to the Father's will (Heb 10:5–9) is more significant for One who is equal with the Father (v. 6) than for one who is not. Paul's words embrace Christ's lifetime of utter obedience and emphasize that the supreme expression of that obedience came in his death. **even death on a cross!** The accent is on Christ's willingness to suffer the most shameful and painful of deaths, not on the atoning significance of the event (cf. Ro 3:21–26). See *WCF* 8.4; *WLC* 49; *WSC* 27; *BC* 21; *HC* 40.

2:9 Therefore God. The Father's act was a direct response to Christ's obedience. **exalted him to the highest place.** The verb "exalted" here does not mean that God granted Christ a higher station than before but that God has granted him the highest possible exaltation. Christ was restored to the glory that he had at the beginning the glory he voluntarily relinquished in order to become a human. **the name that is above every name.** See note on verse 11. See *WLC* 54.

2:10 at the name of Jesus. This may mean "the name belonging to Jesus" (i.e., "Lord," as in v. 11). But more likely Paul meant that the utterance of the name "Jesus" is the signal that "every knee should bow" to offer him worship and to acclaim him Lord. "Jesus" comes from the Greek form of the Hebrew "Joshua," which means "Yahweh is salvation." **in heaven and on earth and under the earth.** The language is comprehensive, but the subjugation of the hostile demonic powers may be especially in view (cf. Eph 1:19–21; Col 2:15).

2:11 and every tongue confess. The action that should accompany the bowing of the knee. **that Jesus Christ is Lord.** The second person of the Trinity took the name "Jesus" upon his incarnation. Consequently, in this context the name emphasizes his humility. "Christ" is a title drawn from his human office as Messiah, or king of Israel. Thus, it is as the humble One that Christ is extolled; his humility is his glory (cf. Mt 23:12). The "name that is above every name" (v. 9) is "Lord." In the Septuagint (the Greek translation of the Hebrew OT), God is represented by the title "Lord" (Greek, *kyrios*). In Isaiah 45:23, it is Yahweh before whom "every knee will bow" and by whom "every tongue will swear." In Philippians, Christ is now acclaimed to be what he has always been: God himself. In confessing that "Jesus Christ is Lord," the creatures acknowledge both the fact and the character of his deity. The ascription of praise embraces both the humanity ("Jesus Christ") and the deity ("Lord") of Christ; he is worshiped as the God-man. **to the glory of God the Father.** Jesus Christ is, by implication, the Son of the Father. Both Christ and the Father are entitled to adoration. So united are the members of the Godhead that the very act of worshiping the Son glorifies the Father. See *BC* 10.

■ **2:12–18** *A Further Call to Unity.* Having drawn attention to the wonder of Christ's humiliation as a model for Christian living, Paul once again directly exhorted the Philippians to unity and service.

2:12 Therefore. On the basis of Christ's supreme example, Paul resumed his appeal. The apostle's presence furnished incentive for the Philippians to obey, but the chief motivation came from the "God who work[ed]" in them (v. 13) so that their obedience would flourish in Paul's absence as well (1:27). **continue to work out your salvation.** Paul did not believe that salvation comes through works. That is plain enough from his other writings (Ro 4:2ff.; 9:32; Gal 2:16; 3:10; 2Ti 1:9). As in 1:28, Paul spoke here of salvation in terms of the outworking of initial salvation in the daily sanctification of believers, which leads to the eternal salvation that will come at Christ's return. All of these processes are thoroughly gracious gifts from God, but the sanctifying process uniquely calls for ongoing obedience. **with fear and trembling.** This refers to awe and reverence rather than panic and alarm. Such emotions are essential to the Christian life for many reasons, not the least of which is the prospect of judgment that comes upon those who prove they never had saving faith by turning from the gospel (see theological article "The Perseverance and Preservation of Believers" at Php 1). See *WCF* 16.3.

2:13 for it is God who works in you to will and to act. The expending of human effort (v. 12), far from violating God's sovereign will (cf. Eph 2:10), is just what God commands for achieving his saving purpose. Moreover, his work within us grants the power for believers to work out their sanctification. Having invoked the example of Christ, Paul now offered the needed assurance that the Philippians did not will and work independently, but that their wills and actions were the very areas in which God's own power manifested itself (4:13; 1Th 2:13). See *WCF* 9.4; 10.1; 16.3; *WLC* 67; *WSC* 31; *BC* 14,24; *CD* 3–4.IX.

2:14 without complaining or arguing. The Philippians were to avoid imitating the ancient Israelites (Ex 15:24; 16:7–9; 1Co 10:10). Note also the allusion to Deuteronomy 32:5 in verse 15. The Philippians may well have grumbled against church leaders, as the Israelites did against Moses (v. 29; 1Th 5:12–13).

2:15 so that you may become. The corporate witness of a united church is in view. **blameless and pure . . . without fault.** The meanings of these terms overlap considerably. Paul described the quality of life required of "children of God." Such persons will "shine like stars in the universe"—in marked contrast to their "crooked and depraved" contemporaries—but they will offer hope to their contemporaries as well (Mt 5:14–16; Ac 2:40).

2:16 as you hold out. Paul was concerned with the Philippians' fidelity to the gospel of Jesus Christ (1:27; 2:1–5), so the reading "hold on to" (see NIV text note) may be preferable. In turn, the fact that believers hold fast to the gospel by loving one another provides a powerful witness to the world (Jn 13:34–35). **the word of life.** This refers to both the gospel and the ethical teachings founded upon it (1:27; 4:8–9). **I may boast.** Paul's pride on the "day of Christ" (1:6,10) will be the Philippians' spiritual growth rather than his own (1:9–11).

2:17 even if I am being poured out. Paul here referred not to his present suffering, but to the possibility (though not the certainty) of his martyrdom. As a follower of Christ the servant (vv. 6–8), Paul was willing to expend himself to the utmost for his people (2Co 12:15). **drink offering.** A libation (normally wine, not blood) that was to accompany a sacrifice. **sacrifice and service coming from**

your faith, I am glad and rejoice with all of you. 18 So you too should be glad and rejoice
with me.

Timothy and Epaphroditus

19 I hope in the Lord Jesus to send Timothy to you soon,[p] that I also may be cheered
when I receive news about you. 20 I have no one else like him,[q] who takes a genuine interest in your welfare. 21 For everyone looks out for his own interests,[r] not those of Jesus Christ.
22 But you know that Timothy has proved himself, because as a son with his father[s] he has
served with me in the work of the gospel. 23 I hope, therefore, to send him as soon as I see
how things go with me.[t] 24 And I am confident[u] in the Lord that I myself will come soon.
25 But I think it is necessary to send back to you Epaphroditus, my brother, fellow worker[v] and fellow soldier,[w] who is also your messenger, whom you sent to take care of my
needs.[x] 26 For he longs for all of you[y] and is distressed because you heard he was ill. 27 Indeed he was ill, and almost died. But God had mercy on him, and not on him only but also
on me, to spare me sorrow upon sorrow. 28 Therefore I am all the more eager to send him,
so that when you see him again you may be glad and I may have less anxiety. 29 Welcome
him in the Lord with great joy, and honor men like him,[z] 30 because he almost died for the
work of Christ, risking his life to make up for the help you could not give me.[a]

No Confidence in the Flesh

3 Finally, my brothers, rejoice in the Lord! It is no trouble for me to write the same
things to you again, and it is a safeguard for you.
2 Watch out for those dogs,[b] those men who do evil, those mutilators of the flesh. 3 For
it is we who are the circumcision,[c] we who worship by the Spirit of God, who glory in
Christ Jesus, and who put no confidence in the flesh— 4 though I myself have reasons for
such confidence.
If anyone else thinks he has reasons to put confidence in the flesh, I have more: 5 circumcised[d] on the eighth day, of the people of Israel,[e] of the tribe of Benjamin,[f] a Hebrew
of Hebrews; in regard to the law, a Pharisee;[g] 6 as for zeal, persecuting the church;[h] as
for legalistic righteousness,[i] faultless.

2:19 [p]ver 23
2:20 [q]1Co 16:10
2:21 [r]1Co 10:24; 13:5
2:22 [s]1Co 4:17; 1Ti 1:2
2:23 [t]ver 19
2:24 [u]Php 1:25
2:25 [v]Php 4:3 [w]Phm 2 [x]Php 4:18
2:26 [y]Php 1:8
2:29 [z]1Co 16:18; 1Ti 5:17
2:30 [a]1Co 16:17
3:2 [b]Ps 22:16,20
3:3 [c]Ro 2:28,29; Gal 6:15; Col 2:11
3:5 [d]Lk 1:59 [e]2Co 11:22 [f]Ro 11:1 [g]Ac 23:6
3:6 [h]Ac 8:3 [i]Ro 10:5

---

your faith. The Philippians' gifts to Paul (4:10–20). **I am glad and rejoice.** Suffering itself is not pleasant, but Paul found reasons for joy even in the midst of suffering. It was to be the same for the Philippians (v. 18).

■ **2:19–30** *Two Examples of Service.* Paul's emphasis on humility and service as necessities of the Christian life led him to mention two important models of such service: Timothy (vv. 19–24) and Epaphroditus (vv. 25–30).

2:19 Timothy. Paul intended to send Timothy to Philippi from Rome (see 1:1) to bring greetings and to discern the state of the church there. Timothy had shown great interest in the Philippians' well-being (v. 20).

2:21 own interests. This verse echoes verse 4, where the phrase "own interests" first occurs. Timothy's life was a model of the humility to which Paul called his readers as well as an image of Christ's own humility (vv. 5–11). See *WLC* 105,130.

2:22 as a son with his father. Timothy worked closely with Paul for Christ the Lord; both were Christ's servants (1:1).

2:23 as soon as I see how things go with me. Amid difficult circumstances (1:12–30), perhaps including a forthcoming trial, Paul needed a person of Timothy's character. In verses 23–24 Paul reiterated the confidence he had expressed in 1:19–26.

2:24 confident in the Lord. The plans concerning both Timothy and Paul were submitted to the divine will (v. 19).

2:25 Epaphroditus. This fellow worker with Paul, like Timothy, was worthy of honor. Like Timothy, and like Jesus himself, he was a man devoted to others. He obeyed Christ by enlisting himself in service to other believers—both to the Philippians (4:18) and to Paul, for whose sake he risked his life (vv. 26–27,30).

2:26 distressed. Epaphroditus was more concerned that the Philippians had been saddened by news of his illness than he was about his own suffering. Paul considered this attitude exemplary of Christian service and humility.

2:29 Welcome him . . . honor men like him. Epaphroditus had come near death (v. 30), so Paul sent him home to Philippi. Paul encouraged the Philippians to honor not only Epaphroditus, but also other people who served Christ as he had.

■ **3:1—4:1** *Resisting Error.* In the second part of the main portion of his letter, Paul directed his attention toward several errors that had entered the church in Philippi. His discussion divides into three sections: concern about legalists (3:1–11), the need to press forward in the Christian life (3:12–16) and concern about libertines (3:17—4:1).

■ **3:1–11** *Against the Legalists.* These verses contain Paul's condemnation of legalists, who saw obedience to the law as the way of gaining or maintaining salvation.

3:1 rejoice in the Lord! This appeal is exactly reiterated in 4:4. Paul's intention was not to command or demand that the Philippians be joyful in the sense that sadness or discouragement must be reckoned as sin. If this were so, then Christ himself sinned (Lk 19:41; 22:44; Jn 11:35). His words were an expression of hope and encouragement that the Philippians would be happy in the good things that Christ had given them. **the same things.** This refers to what Paul was about to say in verses 2–21 (see v. 18). Here Paul repeated material he had previously communicated, either personally or by letter, as a "safeguard" against false teaching in the church.

3:2 those dogs . . . mutilators of the flesh. Paul's opponents may have been either Judaizing Christians (as in Galatians) or non-Christian Jews who championed the Law of Moses and insisted on circumcision as the badge of salvation (Ac 15:1). Although "dogs" was sometimes a Jewish term for Gentiles (cf. Mt 15:22-27; Mk 7:26-28), the metaphor was also applied to sinful Jews (cf. Isa 56:10-11), perhaps implying that they were no better than Gentiles. In Revelation 22:15 the metaphor identifies all sinners without reference to ethnicity.

3:3 we who are the circumcision. In response to the Judaizers (those in the visible church who insisted on keeping the Mosaic Law in addition to faith in Christ as a means of securing holiness and acceptance before God) and their mistaken emphasis upon the rite of circumcision, Paul asserted that Christians are the true circumcision (i.e., the true spiritual Israel; cf. Gal 3:6—4:7). **worship by the Spirit of God.** This phrase may also be translated "worship God in spirit." **who glory in Christ Jesus.** This stands in stark contrast to "confidence in the flesh." **flesh.** As used by Paul, this term often embraces all that is natural and human (e.g., Eph 6:5, where the Greek is rendered "earthly"). In this verse, however, the physical act of circumcision is probably in view (v. 5; cf. Gal 6:12–15).

3:4–9 See *WLC* 60.

3:4–6 I have more . . . faultless. These verses list Paul's sevenfold pedigree of accomplishments from his legalistic days.

3:5 circumcised on the eighth day. Paul had been circumcised in accordance with Genesis 17:12. **of the people of Israel.** See Romans 9:3–4 and 11:1. **of the tribe of Benjamin.** Paul, formerly Saul of Tarsus, may have been named for King Saul, also a Benjamite (1Sa 9:1–2). **a Hebrew of Hebrews.** This phrase may indi-

7 But whatever was to my profit I now consider loss[j] for the sake of Christ. 8 What is
more, I consider everything a loss compared to the surpassing greatness of knowing[k]
Christ Jesus my Lord, for whose sake I have lost all things. I consider them rubbish, that
I may gain Christ 9 and be found in him, not having a righteousness of my own that comes
from the law,[l] but that which is through faith in Christ—the righteousness that comes
from God and is by faith.[m] 10 I want to know Christ and the power of his resurrection and
the fellowship of sharing in his sufferings,[n] becoming like him in his death,[o] 11 and so,
somehow, to attain to the resurrection[p] from the dead.

Pressing on Toward the Goal

12 Not that I have already obtained all this, or have already been made perfect,[q] but
I press on to take hold[r] of that for which Christ Jesus took hold of me.[s] 13 Brothers, I do
not consider myself yet to have taken hold of it. But one thing I do: Forgetting what is
behind[t] and straining toward what is ahead, 14 I press on[u] toward the goal to win the
prize for which God has called[v] me heavenward in Christ Jesus.
15 All of us who are mature[w] should take such a view of things.[x] And if on some point
you think differently, that too God will make clear to you. 16 Only let us live up to what
we have already attained.
17 Join with others in following my example,[y] brothers, and take note of those who live

3:7 [j]Mt 13:44; Lk 14:33
3:8 [k]Eph 4:13; 2Pe 1:2
3:9 [l]Ro 10:5 [m]Ro 9:30
3:10 [n]Ro 8:17 [o]Ro 6:3-5
3:11 [p]Rev 20:5,6
3:12 [q]1Co 13:10 [r]1Ti 6:12 [s]Ac 9:5,6
3:13 [t]Lk 9:62
3:14 [u]Heb 6:1 [v]Ro 8:28
3:15 [w]1Co 2:6 [x]Gal 5:10
3:17 [y]1Co 4:16; 1Pe 5:3

---

cate that Hebrew (or Aramaic) was spoken in his home (Ac 6:1; 22:2), distinguishing him from other Jews of the Diaspora who no longer spoke the tongue(s) of their ethnic heritage. **in regard to the law, a Pharisee.** Paul's life was one of scrupulous obedience to the law, which included both the Torah and the Pharisaic traditions built upon it (Ac 22:3; 26:5; Gal 1:14).

3:6 as for zeal, persecuting the church. See Acts 9:13–14, 22.4–5 and 26:9–11 (see also 1Co 15:9; Gal 1:13–14). **as for legalistic righteousness.** This phrase may also be translated "as for the righteousness set forth in, or required by, the law" (cf. v. 9). **faultless.** This was not a claim of utter sinlessness (Ro 7:7–13), but one of fundamental fidelity to the Old Testament's prescribed way of life. Paul's obedience to the law was honorable, but his resultant "confidence" (the word is repeated three times in vv. 3–4) was sinful.

3:7 whatever was to my profit. Paul was obviously not thinking of his transgressions of the law but of his scrupulous obedience to its commands (v. 6). **I now consider loss.** This decision was even more meaningful because it was (at least in part) a virtue that he had renounced (it is often much harder to renounce a virtue than a vice). Yet Paul saw that the more noble one's lineage and the more virtuous one's attainments, the greater the temptation to pride and self-confidence (Lk 18:9–14; Eph 2:8–9). Paul freely discarded all sources of self-confidence and personal profit "for the sake of Christ."

3:8–11 See *HC* 60; *WLC* 172.

3:8 rubbish. The Greek word here is graphic; it is appropriately rendered "dung" in the KJV. Paul flung away in disgust whatever interfered with "the surpassing greatness of knowing Christ Jesus." See *BC* 21.

3:9–11 Verse 9 speaks of justification, verse 10 of sanctification and verse 11 of glorification. The sequence of privilege, death and exaltation suggests a connection with 2:6–11.

3:9 not having a righteousness of my own. Paul recognized that salvation is based not upon human attainments of obedience to the law, but entirely and exclusively upon "the righteousness that comes from God," which is given to those united with Christ (Ro 1:16–17; 3:21–26). **that which is through faith in Christ.** Christ is the object of faith (Gal 2:16), and now that Paul trusted Christ alone, he abandoned all reliance on his own credentials (vv. 7–8). Faith is the means, not the ground, of salvation. Paul declared that we are saved *through* faith, never that we are saved *on account of* faith. The merit of Christ is the ground of salvation. Faith is the instrument that links believers to Christ and his merit. **and is by faith.** This phrase might be translated, "given by God in response to faith." Faith receives God's gift of righteousness (Ro 3:22; 5:17), and the exercise of faith precedes God's verdict of justification (Ro 4:3; 5:1; Gal 3:6). In Reformed theology it has traditionally been said that "faith precedes justification," not in terms of time, but in terms of logical priority. One's justification is dependent upon faith, not one's faith upon justification, although the two occur simultaneously. See *WCF* 11.1; *WLC* 70,72,73; *WSC* 33,86; *BC* 22.

3:10 I want to know Christ. This was Paul's most passionate longing (1:20–24). He spoke not merely of greater mental awareness, but also of deepened personal union. The following two clauses explain how knowing Christ is presently experienced. **the power of his resurrection.** Identification with the crucified and risen Christ is fundamental to Christian living. Elsewhere (e.g., 2Co 4:7–11) Paul taught that it is through participation in the sufferings of Christ that the power of Christ's resurrection is manifested in the life of the Christian. This identification with the sufferings of Christ involves not just martyrdom (2:17) but all of life. See *WCF* 13.1; 26.1.

3:11 somehow. Paul was neither skeptical nor presumptuous. He recognized that the believer's perseverance depends on the willing and the working of the sovereign God (1:6; 2:13; 3:12–14,21). **attain to the resurrection.** Sharing in Christ's suffering is preparation for sharing in his glory at the resurrection of the dead (vv. 20–21; Ro 8:17).

■ **3:12–16** *Living Now for the Future.* Paul digressed from his attack on legalists by focusing on the challenges of living in this life for the sake of what Christ will bring in the future. Although believers have already received much in Christ, there is much yet to be experienced in him. See *HC* 114.

3:12–14 See *WLC* 77; *HC* 115.

3:12 Not that I have already obtained. Paul had not yet received all the benefits of salvation. He emphasized this point over against any idea of perfection in this life (cf. Jas 3:2; 1Jn 1:8) and to express the grandeur of his future glorification in Christ. The saving process that is to be consummated on the day of Christ (1:6,10) and the resurrection of the dead (v. 11) has already begun, but it is not yet complete. See *WCF* 13.2.

3:14 the goal. The objective of Paul's striving promised a splendid trophy: salvation in all its fullness (cf. 1:28; Ro 13:11). **God has called me heavenward.** God had already called Paul (Ro 8:30; Gal 1:15). It was because "Christ Jesus took hold of" Paul (v. 12) that he pressed forward toward the goal of life in glory (vv. 13–14).

3:15 All of us who are mature. Paul's opening words of verse 15 may have been a tribute to persons who in fact thought and lived in a mature fashion. Paul indeed used the Greek word here rendered "mature" in a favorable sense (cf. Col 1:28, where it is translated "perfect"). Alternatively, Paul may have been speaking ironically of persons who considered themselves already "perfect" (v. 12) and whose thinking Paul sought to correct. **such a view of things.** This refers to the teaching of verses 12–14. **if . . . you think differently.** These words may reinforce the preceding appeal to agree with Paul, but the repeated verbs ("take such a view . . . think") recall 2:1–5 and suggest that the apostle was also concerned that the Philippians agree with each other. **God will make clear to you.** Whether spiritual discernment and understanding or agreement among believers is in view, the grace of God is necessary (1:9–11). In the meantime, believers' conduct should accord with the degree of insight that God has already granted (v. 16).

■ **3:17—4:1** *Against the Libertines.* This paragraph is directed especially (although not exclusively) against antinomianism (the belief that the Christian is not subject to the moral law of God), which often results from an overreaction to legalism (cf. vv. 2–11). Galatians 5:13–26 also addresses this problem.

3:17 following my example. Paul's example was the opposite of that expressed in verses 18–19. Paul was faithful to the cross (Gal 6:14), Christ was his glory (v. 21; cf. v. 3), and his mind was set on heavenly things (vv. 20–21). See *WLC* 127.

3:18 [z]Ac 20:31 [a]Gal 6:12
3:19 [b]Ro 16:18 [c]Ro 6:21 [d]Ro 8:5,6
3:20 [e]Eph 2:19 [f]Col 3:1 [g]1Co 1:7
3:21 [h]Eph 1:19 [i]1Co 15:43-53 [j]Col 3:4
4:1 [k]Php 1:8 [l]1Co 16:13; Php 1:27
4:2 [m]Php 2:2
4:4 [n]Ro 12:12; Php 3:1
4:5 [o]Heb 10:37; Jas 5:8,9
4:6 [p]Mt 6:25-34 [q]Eph 6:18
4:7 [r]Isa 26:3; Jn 14:27; Col 3:15

according to the pattern we gave you. 18 For, as I have often told you before and now say
again even with tears,[z] many live as enemies of the cross of Christ.[a] 19 Their destiny is destruction, their god is their stomach,[b] and their glory is in their shame.[c] Their mind is
on earthly things.[d] 20 But our citizenship[e] is in heaven.[f] And we eagerly await a Savior
from there, the Lord Jesus Christ,[g] 21 who, by the power[h] that enables him to bring everything under his control, will transform our lowly bodies[i] so that they will be like his
glorious body.[j]

4 Therefore, my brothers, you whom I love and long for,[k] my joy and crown, that is
how you should stand firm[l] in the Lord, dear friends!

Exhortations

2 I plead with Euodia and I plead with Syntyche to agree with each other[m] in the Lord.
3 Yes, and I ask you, loyal yokefellow,[a] help these women who have contended at my side
in the cause of the gospel, along with Clement and the rest of my fellow workers, whose
names are in the book of life.

4 Rejoice in the Lord always. I will say it again: Rejoice![n] 5 Let your gentleness be evident to all. The Lord is near.[o] 6 Do not be anxious about anything,[p] but in everything,
by prayer and petition, with thanksgiving, present your requests to God.[q] 7 And the peace
of God,[r] which transcends all understanding, will guard your hearts and your minds in
Christ Jesus.

8 Finally, brothers, whatever is true, whatever is noble, whatever is right, whatever is

[a] 3 Or *loyal Syzygus*

3:18–19 This could describe all sorts of opponents (cf. 1Co 1:23), including the Judaizers (vv. 2–6; Gal 2:15–21). In this instance Paul may have been thinking especially of persons who conceived of Christ as pure spirit and who scorned the idea of his saving by means of incarnation and a "physical body through death" (Col 1:22). Such persons considered themselves to be living on an exalted spiritual plane that freed them to enjoy sensual pleasures, whether gluttonous ("their god is their stomach") or sexual ("their glory is in their shame"). Compare 1 Corinthians 6:9–10. See *HC* 95.
3:18 even with tears. Paul wept, not because he feared that someone could undo what Christ had done, but because of the destruction in store for opponents of the gospel. This destiny (v. 19) completes a destructive process initiated by their very sin (Ro 1:18–32; Gal 6:7–8).
3:20–21 See *HC* 45,52.
3:20 our citizenship is in heaven. Just as Philippi was a Roman colony (Ac 16:12), the church is a colony of heaven. Believers belong to heaven because that is where Christ now dwells. When Christ returns in glory, however, the wonder of heaven will come to Earth, and believers will find their home in the new heavens and the new earth (see Rev 21:1–5) **And we eagerly await.** This anticipation is a counterpart to the longing of 1:23. All other instances of this verb in Paul's epistles have a similar focus on the consummation of the ages at the return of Christ (Ro 8:19,23,25; 1Co 1:7; Gal 5:5). See *HC* 80.
3:21 power . . . to bring everything under his control. See 1 Corinthians 15:20–28. **transform our lowly bodies.** Rather than scorn the physical body and the physical world as some of his opponents had (see note on verses 18–19), Paul understood that salvation would be incomplete until the physical was fully transformed as well. Here Paul celebrated Christ's future transformation of our bodies (cf. 1Co 15:50–53). **like his glorious body.** Christ himself rose bodily from the grave, the "firstfruits" of a great harvest (1Co 15:20–23). The Father vindicated Christ's obedience (2:6–11), and the believers' faithfulness in affliction presages the glorious resurrection. See *WCF* 32.3; *WLC* 87; *HC* 57.
4:1 Founded upon what precedes it, this verse is a bridge between Paul's teachings in the previous chapters and his more personal comments in chapter 4. **that is how you should stand firm.** This phrase might be rendered "stand firm thus," for Paul may have been anticipating the exhortations that would follow, especially the difficult ones of verses 2–3. This helps to explain the presence of six terms of affection in verse 1. The challenge to "stand firm" harks back to 1:27 (where the same imperative occurs) and rests immediately upon the declaration of hope in 3:20–21. It is especially in view of Christ's return that Paul called his readers his "joy and crown" (cf. 1Th 2:19–20).
■ **4:2–9** *Exhortations.* Paul followed his attacks on legalism and antinomianism (the belief that the Christian is not subject to the moral law of God) with a series of specific exhortations appropriate for the church at Philippi.
4:2 I plead . . . I plead. Paul used entreaty rather than command, and his approach of addressing each woman in turn strengthened the appeal. **Euodia . . . Syntyche.** These women are mentioned nowhere else in the New Testament. Both were courageous fellow workers of Paul and apparently were persons of great influence in the church. **to agree.** From *phroneo;* see note on 1:7. Paul's main concern was not that they agree "with each other" (words lacking in the Greek), but that they both manifest the attitude commended in 2:2. Their attitudes were critical for the church's unity.
4:3 yokefellow. Refers either to a particular individual, perhaps with this name (see NIV text note), or to members of the church generally, all of whom were responsible to work for unity (1:27—2:18). The task of helping these women accords well with the metaphor. **along with Clement.** The name occurs nowhere else in the New Testament. This phrase goes with the word "contended" rather than with the more remote "help." **book of life.** The names of all God's elect are inscribed in this book (Rev 3:5; 20:15).
4:4 Rejoice. The theme of joy is prominent in Philippians. See note on 3:1.
4:5 gentleness. The Greek word denotes magnanimity, or a forgiving spirit, of which Jesus provides the supreme example (2Co 10:1). Such a person does not insist on his or her rights (2:1–4). Only such persons learn the secret of joy. **The Lord is near.** This may be understood in two ways: temporally, as referring to Christ's coming (3:20–21), which affords hope amidst the struggle; or spatially, in terms of Christ's abiding presence and the effect of being united to him (1:1).
4:6 Do not be anxious. The present imperative may suggest discontinuing a practice of worrying (due to such obstacles as conflicts and persecutions). The same verb was used in 2:20 of a loving concern for others. Here it denotes anxiety that is incompatible with trust in God (the same verb occurs in Mt 6:25). As in verse 4 (and 3:1), Paul was not laying the burden of a commandment on his readers. Not every form of anxiety is sinful (see 1Co 12:25; Php 2:20, where the same verb describes the care believers have for one another; cf. Jesus' emotions in Lk 22:44). Instead, Paul was encouraging his readers to adopt a more positive outlook on their circumstances rather than to fall into unjustified worry. **about anything, but in everything.** Paul's language was deliberately all-inclusive; there are to be no restrictions on the application. **prayer and petition, with thanksgiving . . . requests.** The four terms used here form two couplets. Paul was not defining separate types of prayer. Rather, the cluster of words reflects the importance he attached to the practice of prayer. Presenting "requests" in prayer provides an outlet for anxiety (1Pe 5:7). Doing so "with thanksgiving" is itself an antidote to worry. See *WCF* 21.3; *WLC* 104,108,178, 185,193,196; *WSC* 98.
4:7 peace of God . . . all understanding. This is the direct answer to the prayer of anxiety. That which cannot be fully comprehended can nonetheless be deeply experienced by those who are in Christ Jesus (1:2; cf. Eph 3:18–19).
4:8 Concluding these exhortations, Paul called his readers to a life of obedience, the right response to the peace of God. The virtues

pure, whatever is lovely, whatever is admirable—if anything is excellent or praiseworthy—think about such things. [9]Whatever you have learned or received or heard from me,
or seen in me—put it into practice.[s] And the God of peace[t] will be with you.

Thanks for Their Gifts

[10]I rejoice greatly in the Lord that at last you have renewed your concern for me.[u] Indeed, you have been concerned, but you had no opportunity to show it. [11]I am not saying this because I am in need, for I have learned to be content[v] whatever the circumstances. [12]I know what it is to be in need, and I know what it is to have plenty. I have
learned the secret of being content in any and every situation, whether well fed or hungry,[w] whether living in plenty or in want.[x] [13]I can do everything through him who gives
me strength.[y]
[14]Yet it was good of you to share[z] in my troubles. [15]Moreover, as you Philippians
know, in the early days[a] of your acquaintance with the gospel, when I set out from Macedonia, not one church shared with me in the matter of giving and receiving, except you
only;[b] [16]for even when I was in Thessalonica,[c] you sent me aid again and again when I
was in need.[d] [17]Not that I am looking for a gift, but I am looking for what may be credited to your account.[e] [18]I have received full payment and even more; I am amply supplied, now that I have received from Epaphroditus[f] the gifts you sent. They are a fragrant[g] offering, an acceptable sacrifice, pleasing to God. [19]And my God will meet all your
needs[h] according to his glorious riches[i] in Christ Jesus.
[20]To our God and Father[j] be glory for ever and ever. Amen.[k]

Final Greetings

[21]Greet all the saints in Christ Jesus. The brothers who are with me[l] send greetings.
[22]All the saints[m] send you greetings, especially those who belong to Caesar's household.
[23]The grace of the Lord Jesus Christ[n] be with your spirit. Amen.[a]

4:9 [s]Php 3:17 [t]Ro 15:33
4:10 [u]2Co 11:9
4:11 [v]1Ti 6:6,8
4:12 [w]1Co 4:11 [x]2Co 11:9
4:13 [y]2Co 12:9
4:14 [z]Php 1:7
4:15 [a]Php 1:5 [b]2Co 11:8,9
4:16 [c]Ac 17:1 [d]1Th 2:9
4:17 [e]1Co 9:11,12
4:18 [f]Php 2:25 [g]2Co 2:14
4:19 [h]Ps 23:1; 2Co 9:8 [i]Ro 2:4
4:20 [j]Gal 1:4 [k]Ro 11:36
4:21 [l]Gal 1:2
4:22 [m]Ac 9:13
4:23 [n]Ro 16:20

a *23* Some manuscripts do not have *Amen.*

---

listed here are not exhaustive but representative, and they come to expression in countless ways (note the repeated phrase "whatever is"). The focused thought on such things is not an end in itself, but preparation for purposeful action (v. 9). **true.** See Ephesians 4:24–25. **noble.** The underlying Greek word (*semnos*) is translated "worthy of respect" in 1 Timothy 3:8 and 11. **right.** See note on 1:11. **pure.** See 1 Timothy 5:22 and Titus 2:5. **lovely . . . admirable.** Terms used only here in the New Testament. See *WLC* 144.

4:9 The Philippians were to be guided both by Paul's teaching and by his example, especially his love for them (1:3–8; 2:12; 4:1). **the God of peace.** An even richer promise than "the peace of God" (v. 7), the fulfillment of which depends on obedience.

▪ **4:10–20** *Thanksgiving.* In these verses of thanksgiving and gratitude, Paul returned to a theme of chapter 1: the Philippians' partnership with him in the gospel (1:5), especially as expressed through their financial support. He focused on two matters: contentment (vv. 10–13) and partnership (vv. 14–20).

▪ **4:10–13** *Contentment.* Paul first focused on how God had granted him contentment within his circumstances.

4:10 you had no opportunity. The last part of the verse adds a qualification, lest the first part seem a rebuke.

4:11–13 I am in need. These verses do not deny the reality of Paul's need, but rather testify that he was content to live either in plenty or in want.

4:13 I can do everything. Granted Christ's power and attitude (2:5; 3:10), Paul was able to face all circumstances with contentment. He wanted to impress the same lesson on his readers (vv. 6–7,19). See *WCF* 16.3.

▪ **4:14–20** *Partnership.* At this point Paul offered thanks for the partnership the Philippians had established with him through their support of his ministry.

4:14 share. The Greek term is related to the word translated "fellowship" or "partnership" (1:5). **in my troubles.** The qualifications of verses 10–13 caused Paul to acknowledge that he had been in real need (1:17).

4:15–16 in the early days of your acquaintance with the gospel. Literally, "in the beginning of the gospel" (i.e., the arrival of the gospel in Philippi; 1:5). **when I set out from Macedonia.** During his second missionary journey, Paul left Macedonia to go to Athens and Achaia (Ac 16:40—18:18). Even before the apostle left Macedonia, the Philippians were extraordinarily and repeatedly generous to him.

4:17–18 As is made emphatically clear in verse 18, Paul was now amply supplied and wished to place no further strain on the church's resources. Yet the main cause of his rejoicing (v. 10) was not that his needs had been fully met but that he perceived the Philippians' gifts as an act of worship that was pleasing to God (Heb 13:15–16), for which God would richly bless them (2Co 9).

4:19 And my God will meet all your needs. This refers both to material and spiritual needs (vv. 6–7). The promise is for persons who are in Christ Jesus (1:1; 4:21).

4:20 This ascription is a response to the promise of verse 19.

▪ **4:21–23** *Final Greeting and Benediction.* Paul closed his letter in his usual fashion: with greetings and a benediction.

4:21 all the saints in Christ Jesus. See 1:1. **brothers.** Here, as elsewhere, this refers to fellow believers of both sexes. Paul frequently addressed the Philippians with this term (e.g., 1:12; 3:1). **who are with me.** See 1:1 and 14.

4:22 All the saints send you greetings. This points to the corporate solidarity of believers, both within and among local churches, in this case Philippi and Rome. **especially those who belong to Caesar's household.** Not members of the royal family, but servants in the palace. They were the Roman believers with whom Paul had the most contact (1:13).

4:23 with your spirit. The character of the Greek in this sentence (the plural "your"; the singular "spirit") is influenced by Hebrew usage. "Spirit" does not denote a segment of the self, but the whole self viewed in a particular way. This phrase (found also in Gal 6:18) is virtually equivalent to the more common "with you" (e.g., Col 4:18; 1Th 5:28). **Amen.** When "amen" introduces a statement, as it frequently does in the Gospels, it points to the authority and trustworthiness of what is about to be said (e.g., Jn 3:3). When used at the end of a statement, as here and frequently in the epistles, it expresses the response of trust and commitment to what has been said (v. 20). It is a statement that confirms the truthfulness and reliability of what has been declared.

COLOSSIANS

Introduction

Overview

Author: The apostle Paul

Purpose: To affirm and explain the supremacy and sufficiency of Christ in opposition to all other powers and attempts to gain salvation.

Date: c. A.D. 60

Key Truths:

- Christ is supreme over all of creation and over the church.
- Believers must not be confused by false pieties that mix true faith with false religions or philosophies.
- Christ is completely sufficient to bring the fullness and newness of life to believers.
- Christians must live in dependence on Christ, not on any other power.

Author

The traditional view that apostle Paul wrote Colossians is certainly correct (1:1; 4:18). Though many modern scholars have doubts, the case for Pauline authorship is strong. First, some critics argue that this letter does not demonstrate Paul's typical attention to church officers. This epistle does not speak of elders and deacons, but the letter certainly does not indicate any opposition to church offices; it merely does not mention them. Second, some object to Pauline authorship on the basis of linguistic distinctives of the letter. Yet most of the language and style in Colossians is well within the range Paul displays elsewhere. Some elements of the vocabulary of this epistle are distinctive (terms such as "fullness," "mystery," "basic principles" and "humility"), but these terms all appear elsewhere in Paul's writings. Third, the false teaching opposed in this epistle is not to be identified with second-century Gnosticism, which did not fully develop until after Paul's lifetime. A careful reading indicates that if the false teaching was related to Gnosticism, it was at most an incipient form of it. In light of the explicit affirmation of Pauline authorship and the early church's acceptance of the epistle as authentic, we may confidently state that Paul wrote this letter.

Time and Place of Writing

During Paul's first imprisonment in Rome (Ac 2:16–31), Epaphras (see "Introduction: Original Audience") joined him under house arrest (Ac 28; Col 4:12–13). He told the apostle about false teachings that threatened the church of Colosse and remained with Paul to pray for the churches of the Lycus Valley. It is most likely that Paul wrote his letter to the Colossians in response to this visit (c. A.D. 60).

Original Audience

Paul never visited Colosse (2:1). The church there had been founded by Epaphras, himself a Colossian, apparently in the wake of Paul's ministry in Ephesus (A.D. 53–55). Luke noted that Paul's message in Ephesus spread until "all the Jews and Greeks who lived in the province of Asia heard the word of the Lord" (Ac 19:10).

In earlier days, Colosse, a city on the Lycus River in southeastern Asia Minor, had been prosperous and large, enjoying a thriving wool industry and a strategic location on a main overland trade route between Ephesus, 100 miles to the west, and the Euphrates River, some 400 miles to the east. In the days of Paul, however, Colosse had declined in the face of the growth of two sister cities in the Lycus Valley: Laodicea and Hierapolis. In Paul's day, Colosse was a fairly inconsequential market town. It was easily the least significant city to which any of Paul's surviving letters was addressed.

Purpose and Distinctives

The Colossian epistle addressed Christians who had come under the influence of a false teaching that mixed elements of Greek philosophy with Judaism. In part, this movement taught that the Colossian Christians were subject to a variety of spiritual forces that needed to be placated through veneration, asceticism and the observance of special holy days.

Paul wrote to help members of the church in Colosse hold firmly to the truth that God had already accepted them by virtue of their union with Christ. While perfection, or maturity, still stood before them as a goal (1:22–23,28), they already enjoyed "fullness in Christ" (2:10), the perfect One.

It is difficult to reconstruct the precise elements of false teaching to which Paul responded because the epistle is less a critique of error than a positive statement of the sufficiency of the person and work of Christ. However, certain features of this false teaching do surface.

First, it claimed to be a "philosophy" (2:8). As was often the case in the Hellenistic period, the word *philosophy* did not refer to rational inquiry, but to occult speculations and practices based on a body of "tradition" (2:8).

Second, this false teaching appears to have been strongly dependent on Judaism. It placed much value on legal ordinances derived from the Old Testament, such as food regulations, Sabbath and New Moon observance and other prescriptions of the Jewish calendar (2:16). The mention of circumcision (2:11) also points to the Jewish nature of this false teaching, but it does not suggest that the Old Testament rite was a central issue in Colosse, as it was in Galatia (see "Introduction to Galatians: Purpose and Distinctives").

Third, the role of angelic spirits was an important element in this teaching. Three key factors point to this.

1. Paul stressed Christ's superiority to and victory over "the powers and authorities" (2:15; see also 1:15–16,19; 2:10,18–19). He wanted the Colossians to stand strong in their commitment to Christ as the Lord of all.

2. The phrase "the basic principles of this world" (2:8,20; cf. Gal 4:3) may also point to angelic beings. Although some interpreters in the past associated this expression with Jewish legalism, a pagan identification is more likely. The Greek word *stoicheia*, which the NIV translates as "principles," may also be translated "elements." In the first century this term was used in the Greek world to refer to gods of stars and planets, and even to the physical elements (earth, wind, fire and water) that were thought to control the destinies of men and women. For instance, the Phrygian god Cybele and her lover Attis are known to have been transformed by popular pagan piety (though the dating is obscure) into astral and cosmic powers. Parallel developments took place in Jewish traditions, which opened the way for mixing Judaism with these pagan beliefs. Some Jewish thinkers merged angels with astral powers thought to be protecting the planets. Moreover, intertestamental Jewish literature envisioned Israel caught in the middle of a conflict between two kingdoms led, respectively, by good and evil powers that claimed her allegiance. The victory of the good powers over the evil was the promised result of Israel's repentance, full obedience and perfect Sabbath observance. It appears that the Colossians also may have come under the influence of a syncretistic piety—partly Jewish, partly pagan—that encouraged obeisance to these astral or cosmic powers.

3. The role of angels in this false teaching is also evident in the phrase "the worship of angels" (2:18). Early Christians understood angels to be agents in creation and in the giving of the law (Ac 7:53; Gal 3:19; Heb 2:2). The teaching in Colosse confused the limited role angels legitimately have as "ministering spirits" (Heb 1:14) with the larger cosmic role being accorded them in some Jewish quarters, as well as the role attributed to astral powers outside Judaism. As a means of overcoming fear of the astral or cosmic powers, and under the guise of revelations the "philosophers" received in ecstatic states, the Colossians were being urged to pursue a regimen of asceticism, abstinence and angel veneration.

Paul wrote to oppose these false teachings, whatever their source. He rejected ceremonialism (2:16–17), asceticism (2:21,23) and angel worship (2:18). Paul exalted Christ as supreme over all and as the source of all wisdom (1:15–20; 2:2–3,9).

Outline

I. Introduction (1:1–14) A. Salutation (1:1–2) B. Report of Thanksgiving (1:3–8) C. Report of Intercession (1:9–14)	*Paul greeted the Colossians and told them of his praise and prayers to God on their behalf.*
II. Christ's Supremacy (1:15–23) A. Head Over Creation (1:15–17) B. Head Over the Church (1:18–20) C. Practical Implications (1:21–23)	*The false teaching in Colosse was discredited by the supremacy of Christ over everything, including every power both in the old and in the new creation.*
III. Paul's Ministry to the Colossians (1:24—2:7)	*Paul's ministry to the church was intended to draw the Colossians away from the false teachings among them.*
IV. The Supremacy and Sufficiency of Christ (2:8–23) A. Warning Against False Teaching (2:8) B. Fullness of Life in the Fullness of God (2:9–10) C. Circumcision and Baptism in Christ (2:11–12) D. New Life and Forgiveness in Christ (2:13–14) E. Victory In Christ Over the Hostile Powers (2:15) F. Freedom From Legalism and Asceticism (2:16–23)	*In contrast to the false teachings in Colosse, the wondrous benefits of salvation come only through Christ's sufficiency and supremacy.*

V. Living in Christ (3:1—4:6)
  A. Old Humanity, New Humanity (3:1–17)
    1. Union With Christ (3:1–4)
    2. Death to the Old Humanity (3:5–9)
    3. New Humanity in Christ (3:10–17)
  B. Practical Guidance (3:18—4:6)
    1. Authority and Submission (3:18—4:1)
    2. In Prayer (4:2–4)
    3. Among Unbelievers (4:5–6)

The believer's daily life requires continual, vital union with Christ. Many practical implications flow from the believer's dependence on Christ.

VI. Final Greetings (4:7–18)

Paul closed his letter with final greetings and words of encouragement.

1:1 [a]1Co 1:1 [b]2Co 1:1 **1** Paul, an apostle[a] of Christ Jesus by the will of God,[b] and Timothy our brother,
1:2 [c]Col 4:18 [d]Ro 1:7 2To the holy and faithful[a] brothers in Christ at Colosse:
1:3 [e]Ro 1:8 Grace[c] and peace to you from God our Father.[b][d]
1:4 [f]Gal 5:6 [g]Eph 1:15 ***Thanksgiving and Prayer***
3We always thank God,[e] the Father of our Lord Jesus Christ, when we pray for you,
1:5 [h]1Th 5:8; Tit 1:2 [i]1Pe 1:4 4because we have heard of your faith in Christ Jesus and of the love[f] you have for all the
saints[g]— 5the faith and love that spring from the hope[h] that is stored up for you in heav-
1:6 [j]Ro 10:18 [k]Jn 15:16 en[i] and that you have already heard about in the word of truth, the gospel 6that has
come to you. All over the world[j] this gospel is bearing fruit[k] and growing, just as it has
1:7 [l]Phm 23 [m]Col 4:7 been doing among you since the day you heard it and understood God's grace in all its
truth. 7You learned it from Epaphras,[l] our dear fellow servant, who is a faithful minis-
1:8 [n]Ro 15:30 ter[m] of Christ on our[c] behalf, 8and who also told us of your love in the Spirit.[n]
1:9 [o]Eph 1:15 [p]Eph 5:17 [q]Eph 1:17 9For this reason, since the day we heard about you,[o] we have not stopped praying for
you and asking God to fill you with the knowledge of his will[p] through all spiritual wis-
dom and understanding.[q] 10And we pray this in order that you may live a life worthy[r] of
1:10 [r]Eph 4:1 the Lord and may please him in every way: bearing fruit in every good work, growing in
the knowledge of God, 11being strengthened with all power[s] according to his glorious
1:11 [s]Eph 3:16 [t]Eph 4:2 might so that you may have great endurance and patience,[t] and joyfully 12giving thanks
to the Father,[u] who has qualified you[d] to share in the inheritance[v] of the saints in the
1:12 [u]Eph 5:20 [v]Ac 20:32

a 2 Or *believing* b 2 Some manuscripts *Father and the Lord Jesus Christ* c 7 Some manuscripts *your*
d 12 Some manuscripts *us*

■ **1:1–14** *Introduction.* Paul began his epistle with customary salutations (vv. 1–2) and assured the Colossians of his thanksgivings (vv. 3–8) and prayers (vv. 9–14) on their behalf.
■ **1:1–2** *Salutation.* Paul greeted the Colossians in his customary way (see note on Ro 1:1).
1:1 Timothy. See "Introduction to 1 Timothy: Author."
1:2 holy and faithful. Paul complimented the Colossians not only because they had been made "holy"—set apart from the world—in Christ, but also because they had remained "faithful" to Christ despite the false teachings that had entered their region. Paul's sincerity is established by the fact that in other circumstances he was not so positive about the condition of his readers (e.g., Gal 1:6).
■ **1:3–8** *Report of Thanksgiving.* To express his genuine appreciation of their service to Christ, Paul mentioned that he gave thanks for the work of God's grace in the lives of this church's members.
1:4 faith in Christ Jesus. A teaching that was circulating in Colosse questioned whether Christ alone is sufficient for faithful living and final salvation. In this brief expression Paul reminded his readers that what they already had "in Christ" was sufficient and complete.
1:5 faith and love . . . hope. These qualities are the grounds of Paul's thanks and are central to his understanding of the Christian life (see Ro 5:2–5; 1Co 13:13; Gal 5:5–6; 1Th 1:3; 5:8; cf. Heb 10:22–24). They are gifts of God rather than virtues springing from believers themselves. Paul underscored the sovereignty of God in the bestowal of salvation, as well as believers' security in their relationship with Christ (Eph 1:4; 2:8).
1:6 All over the world. See note on 1:23.
1:7 Epaphras. See "Introduction: Time and Place of Writing" and "Original Audience."
1:8 in the Spirit. Despite his focus on Christ, Paul expressed his firm conviction that the Holy Spirit brings about sanctification in the church (here expressed in Christian "love"). See Galatians 5:22–23; see also note on Galatians 5:22.
■ **1:9–14** *Report of Intercession.* Despite the good reports he had received, Paul understood that the Colossian Christians were in constant need of God's help. He assured them that he prayed continuously for them.
1:9–10 knowledge . . . all spiritual wisdom and understanding . . . knowledge. The Colossians had encountered false teachings that claimed to provide special insights and revelations. Paul informed them that they should receive this kind of knowledge from the Spirit. He countered this false teaching by drawing attention to the true source of understanding.
1:10–12 bearing fruit . . . joyfully giving thanks. Characteristics of the Christian life that please God. To counter the false teaching in Colosse, Paul presented a positive outlook on the Christian life. These descriptions were particularly relevant to the situation in Colosse, but they also point to characteristics that every believer should strive to manifest. See *WLC* 75.
1:10 worthy of the Lord . . . please him in every way. In a strict sense it is impossible for believers to live lives worthy of their status in Christ. Before Christ returns, we cannot and will not please God in everything we do. Yet such perfection is our goal, and we can always do better in our attempts to serve Christ faithfully.
1:11–14 See *WCF* 13.1; *WLC* 97; *BC* 33; *HC* 34,94.
1:12 qualified you. The false teaching in Colosse resulted in cowardice before cosmic beings thought to have power over believers (2:16,18,20–23). This accounts for Paul's use of the term "qualified" here. No power in the universe can cancel the credentials of those

kingdom of light. 13 For he has rescued us from the dominion of darkness[w] and brought
us into the kingdom[x] of the Son he loves,[y] 14 in whom we have redemption,[a][z] the forgiveness of sins.[a]

The Supremacy of Christ

15 He is the image[b] of the invisible God,[c] the firstborn over all creation. 16 For by him
all things were created:[d] things in heaven and on earth, visible and invisible, whether
thrones or powers or rulers or authorities;[e] all things were created by him and for him.[f]
17 He is before all things,[g] and in him all things hold together. 18 And he is the head[h] of
the body, the church; he is the beginning and the firstborn from among the dead,[i] so that
in everything he might have the supremacy. 19 For God was pleased[j] to have all his fullness[k] dwell in him, 20 and through him to reconcile[l] to himself all things, whether things
on earth or things in heaven,[m] by making peace through his blood,[n] shed on the cross.
21 Once you were alienated from God and were enemies[o] in your minds[p] because of[b]
your evil behavior. 22 But now he has reconciled you by Christ's physical body[q] through
death to present you holy in his sight, without blemish and free from accusation[r]— 23 if
you continue in your faith, established[s] and firm, not moved from the hope[t] held out in

1:13 [w]Ac 26:18 [x]Eph 6:12; 2Pe 1:11 [y]Mt 3:17
1:14 [z]Ro 3:24 [a]Eph 1:7
1:15 [b]2Co 4:4 [c]Jn 1:18
1:16 [d]Jn 1:3 [e]Eph 1:20, 21 [f]Ro 11:36
1:17 [g]Jn 1:2
1:18 [h]Eph 1:22 [i]Ac 26:23; Rev 1:5
1:19 [j]Eph 1:5 [k]Jn 1:16
1:20 [l]2Co 5:18 [m]Eph 1:10 [n]Eph 2:13
1:21 [o]Ro 5:10 [p]Eph 2:3
1:22 [q]Ro 7:4 [r]Eph 5:27
1:23 [s]Eph 3:17 [t]ver 5

a *14* A few late manuscripts *redemption through his blood* b *21* Or *minds, as shown by*

---

who are "in Christ" (vv. 2,4). See theological article "Union With Christ" at Galatians 6. See also *BC* 29.

1:13 rescued us. This language recalls God's rescue of Israel from slavery in Egypt and later from captivity in Babylon. Paul viewed humanity outside Christ as being helplessly under the "dominion of darkness," the evil rule of Satan (Eph 2:1–3; 6:11). Believers are rescued from this world order (Gal 1:4) and brought under the dominion and protection of God's Son. The image of the "kingdom of light" (v. 12) is appropriate here, for elsewhere Paul spoke of the light of the gospel shining in the darkness and penetrating the veil covering the hearts of those who are perishing (2Co 3:15; 4:4–6; 6:14; Eph 5:8–14; Php 2:15; 1Th 5:5). **the Son he loves.** Note the Synoptic Gospels' portrayal of Jesus as God's beloved (Mt 3:17; 17:5; Mk 1:11; 9:7; Lk 3:22), as well as the rich Old Testament background out of which the designation emerged (Dt 18:15; Ps 2:7; Isa 42:1). See *WCF* 9.1; 20.1.

1:14 redemption. Elsewhere Paul spoke of redemption as a future event, a time when believers will experience the emancipation of their bodies at Christ's return (Ro 8:23). Here redemption is described as something that has already been bestowed because we have already received the forgiveness of our sins (note the "formerly . . . but now" pattern of 1:21–22,26; 2:13,17,20; 3:10). **the forgiveness of sins.** See note on 2:13.

■ **1:15–23** *Christ's Supremacy.* Paul broke into a doxology in praise of the grandeur and glory of Jesus Christ. Many interpreters believe Paul was appropriating an early Christian hymn. By pointing to the supremacy of Christ both in creation (vv. 15–17) and in redemption (vv. 18–19), he indicated the missing element in the false teaching in Colosse: an adequate view of the person of Christ. With a proper view of Christ, the Colossians would be able to resist the false teachings that troubled them (vv. 20–23). Further, by writing in hymnlike fashion, Paul invited the worship of, rather than mere doctrinal allegiance to, God's Son.

■ **1:15–17** *Head Over Creation.* Paul first extolled the supremacy of Christ over everything created, including cosmic powers. See *HC* 35.

1:15 image of the invisible God. Christ is the "image of God" in the sense that he is the perfect human being, the last Adam (Ro 5:14; 1Co 15:45). Yet Christ also fits this definition in that he is God incarnate. The deity of Christ (Ro 9:5; Php 2:6; Tit 2:13) was of practical import for Paul. Being in nature God, Christ reveals God, who cannot be seen with the eye or with the understanding (1Ti 1:17; 6:16). The thought is parallel to material in John 1:1–18 and Hebrews 1:3. The Colossians were to seek God in Christ above all else, for only in him was God's image perfectly preserved.**the firstborn over all creation.** Paul did not mean that the Son was the first created being, for this would contradict verses 16–17. In light of the clear affirmations of Christ's divinity elsewhere in the New Testament (see theological article "Jesus Christ, God and Man" at Jn 1), it is best to understand the term "firstborn" to mean "the favored son who is principal heir to a family estate" (e.g., Ex 4:22; Ps 89:27). The term is used in Colossians to denote status. Because he is especially loved by his Father (v. 13) and because in him, by him and for him all things were created (vv. 16–17), Jesus exercises all authority over creation and enjoys all rights to it. See *BC* 1,8,10.

1:16 all things were created by him and for him. Because he is both the agent and goal of creation, Christ is Lord of all that is, even of the angelic hierarchy the Colossians thought they needed to placate or revere. Christ is Lord of the angels, not their peer. See *WCF* 4.1; *WLC* 11,16; *BC* 8,12.

1:17 before all things. A strong restatement of the temporal priority and cosmic supremacy of Christ, this verse makes explicit what was implicit in verse 16: Christ is temporally (in time) prior to all creation. He is not a created being. It cannot be said, as Arius (c. A.D. 250–336) was later to maintain, that "there was a time when he was not" (*NPNF* 2.14.53). The thought of Jesus' being the moment-by-moment sustainer and unifying principle of the universe is echoed in Hebrews 1:2–3. See *BC* 8.

■ **1:18–20** *Head Over the Church.* Having affirmed the supremacy of Christ over the creation, Paul turned to Christ's supremacy over the new creation, the center of which is his body, the church.

1:18–20 See *WCF* 8.3; 8.5; 26.3; *HC* 30.

1:18 head of the body, the church. Paul explained this image in Ephesians 1:21–23 and worked out its implications in Ephesians 4:15 and 5:23. **the beginning and the firstborn from among the dead.** Jesus' resurrection marked the beginning of a new creation (2Co 5:17; see note on 3:10). As the first to rise from the dead, Jesus inaugurated the new age anticipated by the Old Testament prophets (Ac 2:29–36; 13:32–35) and founded a new humanity in himself to replace the old one in Adam. His resurrection is both an anticipation and a guarantee of the resurrection all believers will one day enjoy (Ro 8:29; 1Co 15:20–28; Heb 1:6; 12:23). **so that . . . supremacy.** Without detracting from the glory the preexistent Son already had with the Father, the New Testament teaches that Christ's resurrection marked out for him an even higher standing and won for him an even greater name (Ac 13:33–34; Ro 1:4; Eph 1:20–23; Php 2:1–11; Heb 1:4–5). By virtue of his resurrection from the dead, Jesus Christ is Lord of the universe he created, sustains and has redeemed. See *WCF* 25.1; 25.6; *WLC* 52; *BC* 8; *HC* 50,54.

1:19 See 2:9.

1:20 to reconcile . . . all things. The high point of this hymnlike section. Humanity's fall into sin (see theological article "Creation, Fall, Redemption" at Ge 3) brought with it the corruption of all creation, both seen and unseen (Ge 3; Ro 5:12; 8:20; Eph 2:2; 6:12). Through Christ's incarnation and atoning death, the continuation of his kingdom and his return in glory, God's righteousness is satisfied (Ro 3:21–26), peace between God and humanity is restored (2Co 5:17–21), the eventual glorification of the created order is assured (Ro 8:18–21) and the powers of rebellious spirit beings are circumscribed (2:15) and destroyed (2Pe 2:4; Jude 6).

■ **1:21–23** *Practical Implications.* After considering Christ's majestic role in creation and in the church of the new creation, Paul refocused his discussion on the Colossian believers. Once God's enemies and alienated from his life, they had now been given peace with God and called to fidelity to Christ.

1:21–22 See *WCF* 11.4.

1:21 alienated . . . evil behavior. See NIV text note; 2:13; Eph 2:2–3; 4:17–19. The text may indicate either that mental alienation from God has a behavioral root or that it is expressed behaviorally. The point is that our thinking and actions are coconspirators against God. See *WCF* 6.4.

1:22 by Christ's physical body. Jesus' death in the flesh means that the reconciliation God has accomplished is not merely a mat-

the gospel. This is the gospel that you heard and that has been proclaimed to every creature under heaven,[u] and of which I, Paul, have become a servant.[v]

Paul's Labor for the Church

24 Now I rejoice in what was suffered for you, and I fill up in my flesh what is still lacking in regard to Christ's afflictions,[w] for the sake of his body, which is the church. 25 I have
become its servant[x] by the commission God gave me[y] to present to you the word of God
in its fullness— 26 the mystery[z] that has been kept hidden for ages and generations, but
is now disclosed to the saints. 27 To them God has chosen to make known[a] among the
Gentiles the glorious riches of this mystery, which is Christ in you, the hope of glory.
28 We proclaim him, admonishing[b] and teaching everyone with all wisdom,[c] so that
we may present everyone perfect[d] in Christ. 29 To this end I labor,[e] struggling[f] with all
his energy, which so powerfully works in me.[g]

2 I want you to know how much I am struggling[h] for you and for those at Laodicea,[i]
and for all who have not met me personally. 2 My purpose is that they may be encouraged in heart[j] and united in love, so that they may have the full riches of complete
understanding, in order that they may know the mystery of God, namely, Christ, 3 in
whom are hidden all the treasures of wisdom and knowledge.[k] 4 I tell you this so that no
one may deceive you by fine-sounding arguments.[l] 5 For though I am absent from you in
body, I am present with you in spirit[m] and delight to see how orderly[n] you are and how
firm[o] your faith in Christ is.

Freedom From Human Regulations Through Life With Christ

6 So then, just as you received Christ Jesus as Lord,[p] continue to live in him, 7 rooted[q]

1:23 [u]Ro 10:18 [v]ver 25; 1Co 3:5
1:24 [w]2Co 1:5
1:25 [x]ver 23 [y]Eph 3:2
1:26 [z]Ro 16:25
1:27 [a]Mt 13:11
1:28 [b]Col 3:16 [c]1Co 2:6, 7 [d]Eph 5:27
1:29 [e]1Co 15:10 [f]Col 2:1 [g]Eph 1:19
2:1 [h]Col 1:29; 4:12 [i]Rev 1:11
2:2 [j]Col 4:8
2:3 [k]Ro 11:33; 1Co 1:24, 30
2:4 [l]Ro 16:18
2:5 [m]1Th 2:17 [n]1Co 14:40 [o]1Pe 5:9
2:6 [p]Col 1:10
2:7 [q]Eph 3:17

---

ter of the cosmic pacification of the hostile powers. It also provides the personal renewal and purification of those who grasp and hold on to the gospel (2:13; Ro 5:6–11; Eph 2:4–10).

1:23 if you continue in your faith . . . not moved from the hope. Saving faith is persevering and enduring faith (v. 11) that is anchored in hope (v. 5). Contrary to what Paul's opponents taught, true faith and hope are in Christ alone. This relationship with Christ is confirmed by faith and hope, not by adherence to rigorous ascetic disciplines. **proclaimed to every creature.** An allusion to one of the conditions to be fulfilled before the consummation of the ages: the worldwide proclamation of the gospel (1:6; Mt 24:14; Mk 13:10). This passage speaks of this as already having been completed, much as the book of Acts does (Ac 1:8; 13:47; 28:28–31). Paul used hyperbole (an intentional exaggeration for the sake of effect) here. Still, by aiming his ministry at the urban centers of the Roman Empire, Paul saw himself (and the other apostles) as having reached the civilized world (Ac 19:10; Ro 15:18–25), thus making possible the imminent return of Christ. See *BC* 29.

■ **1:24—2:7** *Paul's Ministry to the Colossians.* Paul had reminded the Colossians of the cosmic scope of Christ's lordship (1:15–20) and of the way Christ's redemptive work had come to bear on their lives (1:21–23). Now he turned to his own role in God's redemptive plan and the relationship he hoped this letter would establish between himself and the Colossians (most of whom he had never met), in order to woo them from the captivity of the "philosophy" prevalent among them (2:8).

1:24 fill up . . . what is still lacking. Given the context of this passage, which stresses the total sufficiency of Christ, as well as what Paul said elsewhere (e.g., Ro 3:21–26; 2Co 5:17–21), Paul's words do not mean that Christ's saving work on the cross lacked sufficient merit to secure our salvation. The passage is seriously misconstrued if taken to mean that the sufferings of the church add merit beyond that achieved by Christ. Rather, Christ's suffering is "lacking" because of the divinely appointed necessity that suffering be endured by Christians, in that the church is called to suffer for and with Christ (2Co 4:7–12; 1Th 3:2–4). In a very real sense, this ongoing suffering of the church as the body of Christ is identified with the sufferings of Christ himself (cf. Ac 9:4). Paul may have had in view here the intensification of sufferings to be borne by God's people in the last days (Mt 24:21–22), the final stages of history, which were ushered in by the death and resurrection of Christ (Ro 13:11–14; 1Co 7:29). This is why Paul suffered "for the sake of" the church (2Ti 2:10; see also Eph 3:13). As a servant of the gospel, Paul rejoiced in his opportunity to participate in the sufferings of God's people.

1:26 mystery. This word was much used in the pagan religion of the first century to refer to secret insights given (usually for a fee) to a select, initiated few, so it was with some irony that Paul applied this term to the revelation of God's Son that has been freely made available to the nations (1:27; 2:2; 4:3; Eph 1:9; 3:3–4,9; 5:32; 6:19). In Paul's vocabulary, "mystery" refers to what once was hidden in the council of God but has now been revealed, namely, the manner in which the kingdom of God was extended to the Gentile nations in the New Testament period. **kept hidden.** God's saving purpose for Gentiles was for the most part hidden from them prior to the coming of Jesus. Previous generations had been allowed to "go their own way" (Ac 14:16; see Ro 1:24–32; Eph 2:12). The Old Testament did speak in shadows, signs and hints of a day when God would bring the Gentiles into the kingdom of God through the Messiah (e.g., Ge 12:3; Zec 9:9–10). Yet Paul himself had to learn that the majority of Jews would reject the gospel and that Gentiles would believe in large numbers (Ac 13:46). In this sense, the manner and degree to which the inclusion of Gentiles would take place during the New Testament period had been largely hidden. It was revealed only to, and explained by, the apostles and prophets of the New Testament (Eph 3:5–6).

1:28–29 See *WLC* 159; *BC* 31.

2:1 Laodicea. See "Introduction: Original Audience." Though Paul had not visited this church either, he expected this letter to be read there (4:16).

2:2 See *WCF* 14.3.

2:3 all the treasures of wisdom and knowledge. The false teachers who troubled Christians in the region promised secret wisdom and knowledge (see note on 1:9–10; see also "Introduction: Purpose and Distinctives"). Paul insisted, however, that wisdom and knowledge can be found only in Christ. Only through faith in, and observance of, Christ's supremacy can insights into divine revelation be gained. See *WCF* 8.3.

2:4 fine-sounding arguments. Paul admitted that his opponents were sophisticated and that they offered elaborate and impressive arguments to support their views, but here and elsewhere he warned against the dangers of relying on such sophistication (see 1Co 1:20–25).

2:6–7 just as you received . . . continue to live. The term "received" refers to the acceptance of teaching about Christ as well as the acceptance of Christ himself as one's Lord and Savior, acknowledging that one is united to him by God's grace. For further light on Paul's sense that the Good News of Jesus Christ is a divinely ordained tradition that can be received, see 1 Corinthians 11:2 and 15:1–5 (see also 1Th 2:13; 2Th 3:6). The Colossians had received the true gospel from the apostles, but they needed to continue in that manner of living. Only then would they grow in their Christian faith. **overflowing with thankfulness.** Because it would be grounded in what they had already come to know and experience of the supremacy of Christ, the Colossians' further obedience was to be motivated by thankfulness (v. 7; 3:17) rather than by frustrated, anxious guilt (see note on 3:1). See *BC* 32.

Infant or Believer's Baptism: Should We Baptize Our Children?

REFORMED theologians have differing opinions regarding who should be baptized. Should we baptize only those who profess faith in Christ (the Reformed Baptist view)? Or should we baptize believers and their children (the Reformed Paedobaptist view)? Differences of opinion are reflected in our confessions (compare *WCF* 28; *BC* 34; *LBC* 29) and have continued for so long that it seems unlikely that the various churches adhering to Reformed theology will ever come to agreement on this matter. Yet it is important for all of us to understand and appreciate the varying outlooks.

By and large, Reformed Baptists base their case on two pillars. First, all commands and examples of baptism in the New Testament are preceded by repentance and faith. The New Testament pattern is reflected in Peter's words: "Repent and be baptized . . . for the forgiveness of your sins" (Ac 2:38). Jesus himself connected teaching and baptism when he instructed, "Go and make disciples of all nations, baptizing them . . . and teaching them" (Mt 28:19–20).

Second, Reformed Baptists argue that as Biblical history moved from the Old Testament to the new covenant in Christ, a purification of the community of God's people took place. Unlike the Old Testament community that included believers as well as their unbelieving neighbors, children and servants, the community of the new covenant is restricted in principle to believers only. Jeremiah's prediction of the purity of the new covenant community illustrates the point: " 'No longer will a man teach his neighbor, or a man his brother, saying, "Know the LORD," because they will all know me, from the least of them to the greatest,' declares the LORD. 'For I will forgive their wickedness and will remember their sins no more' " (Jer 31:34). Although all Reformed Baptists agree that the church is not actually pure, they argue that we should aim for this ideal by doing our best to ensure that everyone baptized into the church makes a credible profession of saving faith.

Reformed Paedobaptists readily admit that the New Testament does not command or indisputably illustrate the baptism of children. The few references to household baptisms may have included children, but they are not explicit (Ac 10:44ff.; 16:13–15, 30–34). Moreover, Paedobaptists also affirm that the pattern in evangelism should be "repent and be baptized" (Ac 2:38). On these matters, Baptists and Paedobaptists agree for the most part.

Nevertheless, Paedobaptists argue that the children of believers should be baptized for two other reasons. First, they dispute that it is possible for the visible church to be utterly purified prior to the return of Christ and contend that it is wrong for the church to withhold membership from those who are not pure (Mt 13:24–30,36–43). Everyone agrees that each covenant in the Old Testament included both believers and unbelievers. The covenants with Noah (Ge 9), Abraham (Ge 15; 17), Moses (Ex 20–24; 34) and David (2Sa 7; Pss 89; 132) all included both believers and unbelievers. Moreover, in every Old Testament covenant a special place was given to the progeny of believers because they were the expected—though not guaranteed—heirs of the covenant promises (Ge 9:9; 15:18; 17:7; Dt 7:9; Pss 89:28–29; 132:11–12).

Paedobaptists add, however, that although we are in the age of the new covenant (Lk 22:20; 2Co 3:6; Heb 9:15; 12:24), the promises of the new covenant have not been completely fulfilled. For instance, we must still teach our neighbors, brothers and sisters, saying, "Know the Lord" (Heb 8:11), even though Jeremiah had stated that this would not be true in the new covenant period. This and other new covenant promises will not be completely fulfilled until Christ returns in glory. In fact, Jesus' parable of the wheat and the weeds (Mt 13:24–30,36–43) reveals how dangerous it is to try to rid the church of all unbelievers before the final judgment, unless there is strong evidence of apostasy. Until then, many patterns from the Old Testament community continue to be true of the new covenant community.

Peter announced one of these patterns on the day of Pentecost when he said, "The promise is for you and your children and for all who are far off—for all whom the Lord our God will call" (Ac 2:39). The order of priority is the same in the New Testament as it was in the Old. God's promises are first to believers, second to their children and third to others who are far off. In a similar way, Paul argued for the sanctification of unbelieving spouses married to believers, noting that "otherwise your children would be unclean, but as it is, they are holy" (1Co 7:14). This Old Testament pattern appears in the New Testament because the generational dimension of covenant life will not come to an end until there are no more new generations to come. It is therefore not surprising that Jesus himself laid his hands on children and infants (Lk 18:15) to confer on them a covenant blessing (Mk 10:16).

Second, Reformed Paedobaptists argue from the parallels that exist between circumcision and baptism. God ordained in Israel's national covenants that the male children of believers should be circumcised to signify that they were included under the sanctions of the covenants (see theological article "Divine Covenants" at Jer 31). Failing to do so was the equivalent of breaking the covenant (Ge 17:14). In Colossians 2:11–12 Paul pointed to the fact that New Testament baptism replaces the Old Testament sign of circumcision when he said, "In him you were also circumcised . . . having been buried with him in baptism." On these bases, Paedobaptists baptize not only those who profess faith in Christ, but their children as well.

Certainly, both camps hold many views in common. All believe that baptism does not save but signifies the introduction of a person into a special covenant relationship with God. All believe that adult church members should profess faith before receiving baptism. Baptists and Paedobaptists nurture their children in the Christian faith in similar ways: Infants are dedicated to God, either by baptism or by a dedication rite; they are brought up to live for the Lord; and they are led to the point of publicly professing faith on their own account in confirmation or baptism.

and built up in him, strengthened in the faith as you were taught, and overflowing with
thankfulness.
[8]See to it that no one takes you captive through hollow and deceptive philosophy,[r]
which depends on human tradition and the basic principles of this world[s] rather than
on Christ.
[9]For in Christ all the fullness of the Deity lives in bodily form, [10]and you have been giv-
en fullness in Christ, who is the head[t] over every power and authority. [11]In him you were
also circumcised,[u] in the putting off of the sinful nature,[a][v] not with a circumcision done
by the hands of men but with the circumcision done by Christ, [12]having been buried with
him in baptism and raised with him[w] through your faith in the power of God, who raised
him from the dead.[x]
[13]When you were dead in your sins[y] and in the uncircumcision of your sinful nature,[b]
God made you[c] alive with Christ. He forgave us all our sins, [14]having canceled the written code, with its regulations,[z] that was against us and that stood opposed to us; he took
it away, nailing it to the cross.[a] [15]And having disarmed the powers and authorities,[b] he
made a public spectacle of them, triumphing over them[c] by the cross.[d]
[16]Therefore do not let anyone judge you[d] by what you eat or drink,[e] or with regard

2:8 [r]1Ti 6:20 [s]Gal 4:3
2:10 [t]Eph 1:22
2:11 [u]Ro 2:29; Php 3:3 [v]Gal 5:24
2:12 [w]Ro 6:5 [x]Ac 2:24
2:13 [y]Eph 2:1,5
2:14 [z]Eph 2:15 [a]1Pe 2:24
2:15 [b]Eph 6:12 [c]Lk 10:18
2:16 [d]Ro 14:3,4 [e]Ro 14:17

a *11* Or *the flesh* b *13* Or *your flesh* c *13* Some manuscripts *us* d *15* Or *them in him*

■ **2:8–23** *The Supremacy and Sufficiency of Christ.* Christ is supreme over every other power in the universe. He is sufficient to save all those who trust in him and to empower them for holy living.

■ **2:8** *Warning Against False Teaching.* Paul began this section with a direct warning against the false teaching that tempted the Colossians.

2:8 hollow and deceptive philosophy. In this context the term "philosophy" referred not to the rational pursuit of truth, but to occult practices focused on discerning cosmic mysteries and powers. See "Introduction: Purpose and Distinctives." **human tradition . . . rather than on Christ** See note on 2:3. **the basic principles of this world.** This difficult terminology does not refer to Old Testament law, as has often been understood. Paul may have used the term "basic principles" to refer to cosmic powers or to gods associated with stars, planets and the elements of the physical world (cf. 2:18–20; Gal 4:8–9). The pursuit of such powers seems to have been mixed with Jewish customs in the Colossian church, but the focus remained largely pagan in its basic orientation. Alternatively, this phrase may refer to worldly means of pursuing salvation and holiness (cf. 2:20–21; Gal 4:3). See "Introduction: Purpose and Distinctives."

2:9–10 *Fullness of Life in the Fullness of God.* Paul gave a stunning rebuttal of the false teachers who encouraged submission to the "basic principles" (v. 8) as a means of overcoming fears of inadequacy before God.

2:9 fullness of the Deity. As in 1:19, Paul made it clear that insights into the divine mysteries are found in Christ because he is God incarnate. No one can offer more than he does. See *WCF* 8.2; *WLC* 36; *WSC* 21; *HC* 48.

2:10 given fullness in Christ. Because the Colossian believers were in union with Christ, who is himself God, they had "fullness," or completion, entirely in him. They required nothing more; e.g., cosmic insights and powers such as those offered by occult teachers. See theological article "Union With Christ" at Galatians 6. See *HC* 30.

2:11–13 See *HC* 74.

■ **2:11–12** *Circumcision and Baptism in Christ.* Paul continued to describe the great blessings found in Christ, now focusing on circumcision and baptism. See *WCF* 7.5; 28.1; 28.4; *WLC* 166,167; *WSC* 95; *HC* 43.

2:11 circumcision. It is often speculated that the false teachers in Colosse were commending circumcision, as had those in Galatia, and that this is why Paul brought up this matter here. While this may have been true, the fact that Paul did not directly argue against circumcision here, as he had in Galatians, suggests otherwise. The focus of these verses does reveal that the pagan philosophies troubling the Colossians had been mixed with Jewish legalism, but Paul introduced the topic of circumcision to show that an element of what the Colossians were seeking from the false teachers—power over the flesh (v. 23)—was already theirs through their union with Christ. As the initiatory rite of the old covenant, circumcision had signified the cutting away of sin, a change of heart and inclusion in the household of faith (Dt 10:16; 30:6; Jer 4:4; 9:25–26; Eze 44:7,9). Dramatically, Paul indicated that in their baptism into Christ, these Gentiles had themselves been circumcised. Called here "the circumcision done by Christ" (literally, "the circumcision of Christ"), baptism signifies such realities as the washing away of sin, personal renewal by the Spirit of God and membership in the body of Christ (Ac 2:38; Ro 6:4; 1Co 12:13; Gal 3:26–29; Col 2:13; Tit 3:5; 1Pe 3:21). This passage makes an important point about the unity of God's covenantal administration: Gentile believers are not expected to follow the old covenant mode of identifying themselves with God and his people (Ac 15). But their faith in Christ has nonetheless made them as much children of Abraham as are ethnic Jewish believers (Ro 2:28–29; Gal 3:26–29; Php 3:3). Although baptism is not identical to circumcision, it has important covenantal parallels (see theological article "Infant or Believer's Baptism" on previous page). See *BC* 33,34.

2:12 buried with him . . . raised with him. Through their union with Christ—not through the pursuit of false philosophies—believers find the fullness of God's blessings in their lives. See theological article "Union With Christ" at at Galatians 6. See also *WLC* 52,176.

■ **2:13–14** *New Life and Forgiveness in Christ.* Paul continued to oppose the false teaching by elaborating on how much Christ offers his people.

2:13 forgave us all our sins. It is more characteristic of Paul to speak of justification than of forgiveness and of sin in the singular than of sins in the plural (cf. Ro 5:12–21). Paul apparently wanted to emphasize that God has not simply overcome the general power of sin but has also eradicated the guilt that stems from particular acts by which sinners have violated his character. See *WCF* 9.3.

2:14 canceled the written code. In opposition to elements of Jewish legalism, Paul employed this vivid image from the business world that compared the law to a certificate of indebtedness written in the debtor's own hand. Jesus was "born under law" (Gal 4:4) and was therefore subject to its demands and curses. On the cross he was "made . . . to be sin for us" (2Co 5:21) and endured the law's "curse" against unrighteousness (Gal 3:13). In the death sentence that nailed Jesus to the cross, Paul saw the cancellation of the death warrant that stood against transgressors of the law. The believer no longer stands under the threat of the law's condemnation. See *WCF* 19.3; *BC* 21.

■ **2:15** *Victory in Christ Over the Hostile Powers.* Paul described yet another way in which Christ showed himself superior to the tenets of the false teaching: Our Lord conquered all evil powers.

2:15 disarmed. By taking away the power to accuse (cf. Zec 3:1; Ro 8:33–34,38; Rev 12:10). **powers and authorities.** Paul again referred to angelic and demonic powers (see 2:8). Through Jesus' death for sinners, Satan (literally, the "accuser") was robbed of his power to intimidate and control humans. Jesus' death removed for us the threat of death and eternal judgment that sin deserves and that the law requires (Eze 18; Ro 5:12; 6:23; Heb 2:14–15). Although the cosmic struggle with Satan and his legions will continue until the Lord's return in glory (2Co 4:4; Eph 6:10–18; 1Pe 5:8), the devil's power was decisively and permanently broken by the death and resurrection of Christ. **made a public spectacle.** An image of a conquering Roman general parading his vanquished and humiliated enemies behind his chariot. An invisible, cosmic struggle took place at the cross, and the prince of this age was "driven out" (Jn 12:31), "hurled down" (Rev 12:9) and "bound" (Rev 20:2). See also Matthew 12:29 and Luke 10:18. See *WCF* 8.8.

■ **2:16–23** *Freedom From Legalism and Asceticism.* Paul reminded the Colossians that Christ had set them free from their pagan practices and misuse of God's law.

2:16–17 See *WCF* 19.3.

2:16 do not let anyone judge you. Paul may have meant that

to a religious festival,[f] a New Moon celebration[g] or a Sabbath day.[h] 17 These are a shadow of the things that were to come;[i] the reality, however, is found in Christ. 18 Do not let
anyone who delights in false humility[j] and the worship of angels disqualify you for the
prize.[k] Such a person goes into great detail about what he has seen, and his unspiritual mind puffs him up with idle notions. 19 He has lost connection with the Head,[l] from
whom the whole body, supported and held together by its ligaments and sinews, grows
as God causes it to grow.[m]
20 Since you died with Christ to the basic principles of this world,[n] why, as though you
still belonged to it, do you submit to its rules:[o] 21 "Do not handle! Do not taste! Do not
touch!"? 22 These are all destined to perish[p] with use, because they are based on human
commands and teachings.[q] 23 Such regulations indeed have an appearance of wisdom,
with their self-imposed worship, their false humility and their harsh treatment of the
body, but they lack any value in restraining sensual indulgence.

Rules for Holy Living

3 Since, then, you have been raised with Christ, set your hearts on things above,
where Christ is seated at the right hand of God. 2 Set your minds on things above,
not on earthly things.[r] 3 For you died,[s] and your life is now hidden with Christ in God.
4 When Christ, who is your[a] life, appears,[t] then you also will appear with him in glory.[u]

2:16 [f]Ro 14:5 [g]1Ch 23:31 [h]Gal 4:10
2:17 [i]Heb 8:5
2:18 [j]ver 23 [k]Php 3:14
2:19 [l]Eph 1:22 [m]Eph 4:16
2:20 [n]Gal 4:3,9 [o]ver 14, 16
2:22 [p]1Co 6:13 [q]Isa 29:13; Mt 15:9; Tit 1:14
3:2 [r]Php 3:19,20
3:3 [s]Ro 6:2; 2Co 5:14
3:4 [t]1Co 1:7 [u]1Pe 1:13; 1Jn 3:2

[a] 4 Some manuscripts *our*

the observation of traditional Jewish celebrations is now optional for Christians, or that those who observe these days properly should not accept the condemnation of those who corrupt them with pagan practices. **eat or drink . . . religious festival, a New Moon . . . Sabbath.** These terms refer to traditional Jewish religious observances. Some scholars argue that the pagan asceticism in Colosse (v. 15) was mixed with these celebrations, perhaps in an attempt to placate astral powers or angels who were thought to direct the course of the stars, regulate the calendar and determine human destiny. Others insist that the celebrations were simply observed in a legalistic fashion. In either case, these practices were the very sort of bondage from which Christ came to liberate men and women. Paul did not reject proper Christian observance of feasts or the fourth commandment (see Ex 20:8–11; Ro 7:12-16; 1Ti 1:8), just as he did not reject fasting or other religious observances practiced from proper motivation.

2:17 shadow . . . reality. Even in their pure form, the Old Testament ceremonies were designed to point ahead to the greatest stage of God's kingdom that would come through Christ (Heb 10:1). Legalistic observance of selected Old Testament regulations, especially when intermingled with pagan philosophy, could not provide wisdom, knowledge or salvation. In saying this, however, Paul was not opposing the proper use of God's law given through Moses (see theological article "The Three Uses of the Law" at Ps 119). See *WCF* 7.6; 19.3; *BC* 25; *HC* 19.

2:18 false humility . . . worship of angels. In light of Paul's mention of visions, some interpreters have seen in this phrase a reference to a form of piety found among some Jewish mystics. The goal was participation in the angels' worship of God at the heavenly throne, and this ecstatic experience was said to be attained through asceticism and strict observance of Torah. In this case, the phrase "worship of angels" should be understood as "worship with angels." Nevertheless, it would appear more likely that the Colossians were tempted to false humility in the sense of cowering in inappropriate veneration ("worship") of spirit beings whom they believed stood between God and humans (see "Introduction: Purpose and Distinctives"). **disqualify you for the prize.** The prize is eternal salvation (1Co 9:24). As in all his epistles, Paul wrote to the visible church, which included more than true believers. When those who profess to be followers of Christ turn to flagrant apostasy, they demonstrate that they are not truly regenerate and disqualify themselves from the prize of salvation in Christ (see theological article "The Perseverance and Preservation of Believers" at Php 1). See *WCF* 21.2; *WLC* 105; *BC* 29.

2:19 lost connection with the Head. Paul did not mean here that salvation can be possessed and then lost. He was still referring to members of the visible body of Christ (the church), who were in covenant with God but not necessarily truly regenerate. By seeking the favor of angelic beings, they failed to give to Christ the honor that is his alone as the "fullness of the Deity" (v. 9), and they failed to enjoy the totality of the redemption won in the death and resurrection of Christ (1:20–22; 2:10–15). **Head . . . body.** This language looks back at 1:18, as well as ahead to the way Paul would develop the idea of the Christian life under Christ's headship in the context of church membership (3:1—4:6). See *WCF* 26.1; *BC* 29.

2:20–23 See *WCF* 20.2; 21.1; *WLC* 109,113.

2:20 basic principles. See note on 2:8. See also *WCF* 20.2.

■ **3:1—4:6** *Living in Christ.* The route to maturity in the Christian life does not lie along the path of esoteric, secret revelations or in self-punishing disciplines. The Colossians had an inappropriate focus on heavenly reality, a focus that ironically led them to fruitless efforts on the earthly plane. Paul's discussion divides into two parts: the new and old humanity (3:1–17) and practical guidelines for the Christian life (3:17—4:6).

■ **3:1–17** *Old Humanity, New Humanity.* Union with Christ in his death and resurrection brings believers into a new humanity, and understanding and living on the basis of this union enables them to live as God commands. This material divides into a description of the believer's union with Christ (vv. 1–4) and discussions of death to the old humanity (vv. 5–9) and life in the new (vv. 10–16).

■ **3:1–4** *Union With Christ.* The source of all maturity and spiritual growth for Christians is their union with Christ (see theological article "Union With Christ" at Gal 6). See *HC* 45,49.

3:1–3 See *WLC* 53; *HC* 80.

3:1 Since, then, you have been raised with Christ. Note the extent to which believers are joined with Christ: They have died with him (v. 3; cf. 2:11–12,20), have been raised with him (v. 1; cf. 2:12–13), are with him in heaven (v. 3; cf. Eph 2:6), will be with him at his return (v. 4) and have "taken off" the "old self" (v. 9) and "put on the new self" (v. 10). Paul's prescription for right behavior follows his description of the redemption God has richly bestowed on his people. Obedience becomes a response to, rather than a means of gaining, his favor (2:6–7). **seated at the right hand of God.** A pivotal, exultant motif in the New Testament (Ac 2:33–35; 5:31; 7:55–56; Ro 8:34; Eph 1:20; Heb 1:3,13; 8:1; 10:12; 12:2; 1Pe 3:22; Rev 3:21). See *HC* 76.

3:2 on things above . . . earthly things. Both Christ and his followers (in him) have been lifted on high (v. 2); therefore, our thoughts and affections should be on things above rather than on earthly things. In many respects, the false teaching in Colosse also encouraged attention to matters beyond this world, but, as Paul indicated, the Colossians' false practices actually hindered them from properly understanding heavenly things. Only those who exalt Christ as supreme and sufficient have the privilege of setting their minds and lives on things above, where Christ is. See *WLC* 105,142.

3:3 hidden with Christ in God. Some understand this to mean that the new life of the Christian is not obvious to others and is, in that sense, "hidden." However, the probable connection with 2:3 indicates that more is in view. Although the reality and implications of the new life in Christ are not yet fully revealed, the fact that the life of the believer "is hidden with Christ in God" points also to the security and impregnability of the new life in Christ. What God has freely given, neither human nor angel can take away (Jn 10:29).

3:4 When Christ . . . appears. Contrary to much modern interpretation of Colossians, the hope of Christ's return remains vibrant and central to the ethics of this section (vv. 5–11).

5 Put to death, therefore, whatever belongs to your earthly nature: sexual immorality, impurity, lust, evil desires and greed,[v] which is idolatry.[w] 6 Because of these, the wrath
of God[x] is coming.[a] 7 You used to walk in these ways, in the life you once lived.[y] 8 But now
you must rid yourselves[z] of all such things as these: anger, rage, malice, slander,[a] and
filthy language from your lips.[b] 9 Do not lie to each other,[c] since you have taken off your
old self with its practices 10 and have put on the new self, which is being renewed[d] in
knowledge in the image of its Creator.[e] 11 Here there is no Greek or Jew,[f] circumcised or
uncircumcised,[g] barbarian, Scythian, slave or free,[h] but Christ is all,[i] and is in all.
12 Therefore, as God's chosen people, holy and dearly loved, clothe yourselves with
compassion, kindness, humility,[j] gentleness and patience.[k] 13 Bear with each other[l]
and forgive whatever grievances you may have against one another. Forgive as the
Lord forgave you.[m] 14 And over all these virtues put on love,[n] which binds them all together in perfect unity.[o]
15 Let the peace of Christ[p] rule in your hearts, since as members of one body you were
called to peace. And be thankful. 16 Let the word of Christ[q] dwell in you richly as you
teach and admonish one another with all wisdom,[r] and as you sing psalms, hymns and
spiritual songs with gratitude in your hearts to God.[s] 17 And whatever you do,[t] whether
in word or deed, do it all in the name of the Lord Jesus, giving thanks[u] to God the Father through him.

Rules for Christian Households

18 Wives, submit to your husbands,[v] as is fitting in the Lord.

3:5 [v]Eph 5:3 [w]Eph 5:5 **3:6** [x]Ro 1:18 **3:7** [y]Eph 2:2 **3:8** [z]Eph 4:22 [a]Eph 4:31 [b]Eph 4:29 **3:9** [c]Eph 4:22,25 **3:10** [d]Ro 12:2; Eph 4:23 [e]Eph 2:10 **3:11** [f]Ro 10:12 [g]1Co 7:19 [h]Gal 3:28 [i]Eph 1:23 **3:12** [j]Php 2:3 [k]2Co 6:6; Gal 5:22,23 **3:13** [l]Eph 4:2 [m]Eph 4:32 **3:14** [n]1Co 13:1-13 [o]Eph 4:3 **3:15** [p]Jn 14:27 **3:16** [q]Ro 10:17 [r]Col 1:28 [s]Eph 5:19 **3:17** [t]1Co 10:31 [u]Eph 5:20 **3:18** [v]Eph 5:22

[a] *6* Some early manuscripts *coming on those who are disobedient*

3:5–10 See *HC* 88.
■ **3:5–9** *Death to the Old Humanity.* Paul elaborated on the lives of those who put their minds on things above. In so doing, they put off their old sinful ways.
3:5 Put to death. The first of a series of behavioral imperatives running through 4:6. Despite Paul's rejection of legalistic asceticism, he called upon believers to become in practice what they are in principle: dead to sin and alive to God (Ro 6:1–14). The apostle called for a rigorous departure from the old lifestyle, which is incompatible with life in Christ. In verse 5 Paul listed five vices—four of a sexual nature, plus greed, significantly identified with idolatry; in verse 8 he listed five more vices, all of which deal with anger and abusive speech. See *WLC* 99,105,139,148,151.
3:7 in the life you once lived. That is, before these believers had been brought "into the kingdom of the Son [God] loves" (1:13).
3:9 taken off. From the same root as "putting off of the sinful nature" (2:11) and "disarmed" (2:15). See *WLC* 145.
■ **3:10–17** *New Humanity in Christ.* Being oriented toward things above (v. 2) means not only putting to death the old humanity, but also affirming and living as part of the new humanity in Christ.
3:10 new self. In Christ, God's second Adam (1Co 15:20–28,45–49), the human race has been reconstituted. Not coincidentally, each of the attributes Paul later lists in verse 12 can be traced to the character of God generally or of Christ specifically. This demonstrates how fully Paul understood the idea of believers taking on the "image" of their Creator. See *WCF* 4.2; *WLC* 17; *WSC* 10; *HC* 6.
3:11 no Greek or Jew. Paul was probably commenting on the elitism of the Colossian false teachers, who believed their spiritual condition made them superior to others. The cross-cultural unity of all who belong to Christ is an idea that appears frequently in Paul's writings (e.g., 1Co 7; Gal 3:28). **barbarian.** Greeks viewed those who did not speak Greek as illiterate and uncivilized. **Scythian.** By reputation, a brutal and wretched slave class drawn from tribes around the Black Sea. Scythians were occasionally lampooned in Greek comedy because of their uncouth ways and speech. **slave or free.** Within the body of Christ, distinctions based on social position are irrelevant (1Co 7:17–24). At the same time, as Paul's separate instructions to slaves and slaveholders in 3:22—4:1 make clear, unity in Christ does not imply or mandate a uniformity of function or capacity. It is important to recognize that "Christ is all, and is in all." In the Pauline churches, diverse social positions continued to exist and were not subject to an indiscriminate leveling process. Rather, they became opportunities for expressing Christ's love across traditional social boundaries.
3:12–14 compassion . . . perfect unity. These verses outline the obligations all Christians have toward one another, which lead to unity. Verses 3:18—4:2 focus on opportunities for service within specified relationships. See *WLC* 135.
3:12 as God's chosen people, holy and dearly loved. Believers are entitled to a clear sense that God grounds and guarantees their relationship with him (Jn 6:37,44,65; 15:16; Eph 1:4–5; Php 1:6). They can know not only that they have been declared holy on the basis of a righteousness that is not their own (Ro 3:21–26; 1Co 1:2,30) but that God also genuinely, even passionately, loves them (Jn 3:16; Ro 8:32; Gal 2:20; Tit 3:4; 1Jn 4:9–10). Although this address is easily glossed over, it clarifies the self-understanding that properly motivates ethics. **clothe yourselves.** Paul envisioned believers taking on the character of the Lord himself. The "new self" (v. 10) is not something believers must construct by their own power. Their new identities take shape as they become better acquainted with Christ, the image of the invisible God and the One in whom all the treasures of wisdom and knowledge are hidden (1:15; 2:3). **compassion.** An emotional engagement with the hurting and broken (Mt 9:36; 14:14; Ro 12:1). **kindness.** Readiness to do good, even when such a response is undeserved by its recipients (Ro 2:4; 11:22; Tit 3:4). **humility.** A posture of lowliness and servanthood (Mk 10:45; Php 2:1–11). **gentleness.** A "soft touch" in offering help; a noncoercive approach to encouraging positive change in others (Mt 11:29; 2Co 10:1; cf. Gal 6:1; 2Ti 2:25). **patience.** A willingness to take the long view in the face of human frailty (Ro 2:4; 1Ti 1:16). See *HC* 107.
3:13–14 Forgive as the Lord. Paul grounded his ethic of forbearance, forgiveness and love in the example provided by the redemptive pattern of Christ's work (see Eph 4:32—5:2).
3:15 the peace of Christ. In its practice of love, forgiveness and graciousness, the new community is to be a showcase of the reconciliation and peace that Christ has effected between heaven and Earth (1:20–22; 2:15) and within a fractured humanity (3:11,13).
3:16 teach and admonish. The word of Christ was to motivate as effectively as the presence of the apostle himself (cf. 1:28). **psalms, hymns and spiritual songs.** In the Septuagint (the Greek translation of the OT), these terms widely overlap, so Paul may not have intended to distinguish three varieties of song. Because these same words describe the different types of compositions in the book of Psalms, some see here a reference to the Psalter (cf. Eph 5:19). **with gratitude in your hearts.** Paul spoke of admonishment in song because he envisioned a community that would be filled with thanksgiving and joy—provided the Colossians would reject the false teachers and embrace his gospel. See *WCF* 1.8; 21.5; *HC* 103.
3:17 whatever you do. Paul broadened his view from focus on the manner in which instructions ought to be given in the Christian community to the entirety of life as the new humanity. In light of the supremacy and sufficiency of Christ—a focal point in this letter—all things must be done "in the name of the Lord Jesus," that is, under his authority and for his glory. Moreover, all things must be done with "thanks to God the Father" because he has given all the blessings we have in Christ. See *WCF* 21.2; *WLC* 112,181; *HC* 99.
■ **3:18—4:6** *Practical Guidance.* After having provided an orientation toward the Christian life, Paul turned to a number of practical

19 Husbands, love your wives and do not be harsh with them.
20 Children, obey your parents in everything, for this pleases the Lord.
21 Fathers, do not embitter your children, or they will become discouraged.
22 Slaves, obey your earthly masters in everything; and do it, not only when their eye
is on you and to win their favor, but with sincerity of heart and reverence for the Lord.
23 Whatever you do, work at it with all your heart, as working for the Lord, not for men,
24 since you know that you will receive an inheritance[w] from the Lord as a reward. It is
the Lord Christ you are serving. 25 Anyone who does wrong will be repaid for his wrong,
and there is no favoritism.[x]

4 Masters, provide your slaves with what is right and fair, because you know that you
also have a Master in heaven.

Further Instructions

2 Devote yourselves to prayer,[y] being watchful and thankful. 3 And pray for us, too,
that God may open a door[z] for our message, so that we may proclaim the mystery of
Christ, for which I am in chains.[a] 4 Pray that I may proclaim it clearly, as I should. 5 Be
wise[b] in the way you act toward outsiders;[c] make the most of every opportunity.[d] 6 Let
your conversation be always full of grace,[e] seasoned with salt,[f] so that you may know
how to answer everyone.[g]

Final Greetings

7 Tychicus[h] will tell you all the news about me. He is a dear brother, a faithful minister and fellow servant[i] in the Lord. 8 I am sending him to you for the express purpose that
you may know about our[a] circumstances and that he may encourage your hearts.[j] 9 He
is coming with Onesimus,[k] our faithful and dear brother, who is one of you. They will tell
you everything that is happening here.
10 My fellow prisoner Aristarchus[l] sends you his greetings, as does Mark, the cousin
of Barnabas.[m] (You have received instructions about him; if he comes to you, welcome
him.) 11 Jesus, who is called Justus, also sends greetings. These are the only Jews among
my fellow workers for the kingdom of God, and they have proved a comfort to me. 12 Epaphras,[n] who is one of you and a servant of Christ Jesus, sends greetings. He is always
wrestling in prayer for you,[o] that you may stand firm in all the will of God, mature[p] and
fully assured. 13 I vouch for him that he is working hard for you and for those at Laodicea[q] and Hierapolis. 14 Our dear friend Luke,[r] the doctor, and Demas[s] send greetings.

3:24 [w]Ac 20:32
3:25 [x]Ac 10:34
4:2 [y]Lk 18:1
4:3 [z]Ac 14:27 [a]Eph 6:19,20
4:5 [b]Eph 5:15 [c]Mk 4:11 [d]Eph 5:16
4:6 [e]Eph 4:29 [f]Mk 9:50 [g]1Pe 3:15
4:7 [h]Ac 20:4 [i]Eph 6:21,22
4:8 [j]Eph 6:21,22
4:9 [k]Phm 10
4:10 [l]Ac 19:29 [m]Ac 4:36
4:12 [n]Col 1:7; Phm 23 [o]Ro 15:30 [p]1Co 2:6
4:13 [q]Col 2:1
4:14 [r]2Ti 4:11; Phm 24 [s]2Ti 4:10

[a] 8 Some manuscripts *that he may know about your*

matters. His instructions focused on authorities in life (3:17—4:1), on prayer (4:2–4) and on interactions with unbelievers (4:5–6).

■ **3:18—4:1** *Authority and Submission.* Paul's first area of practical concern involved the dynamics of relationships involving authority. See *HC* 104.

3:18–21 See *HC* 104.

3:18–19 See note on Ephesians 5:22–33. See *WLC* 129.

3:20–21 See notes on Ephesians 6:1–3 and 4. See *WLC* 99,130.

3:22—4:1 Slaves . . . Masters. The more extended treatment of slave and free may be due to the delicate matter of the return of Onesimus, the runaway slave, to his owner, Philemon. Onesimus was accompanying Tychicus in bringing this letter to the Colossians, and they were likely delivering Paul's letter to Philemon as well (see "Introduction to Philemon"). Onesimus's very presence with Tychicus is a living example of the subtlety, tact and wisdom Paul expected to be exercised in the relationships this section addresses.

■ **4:2–4** *In Prayer.* Another way in which Paul hoped the Colossians would live as the new humanity was by devoting themselves to prayer.

4:2–3 See *WCF* 21.3; *WLC* 183.

4:4 that I may proclaim. Paul was particularly concerned that the Colossians pray for his ministry of proclaiming the gospel—that doors might be opened to him and that he might be afforded every opportunity to explain clearly the Good News of Christ.

■ **4:5–6** *Among Unbelievers.* Paul's desire for prayer for his ministry to unbelievers raised a similar matter in the lives of the Colossian believers: living as the new humanity in their interactions with unbelievers.

4:6 full of grace, seasoned with salt. From the examples of Paul and of Christ himself, we know that this instruction does not mean that believers should always be positive or approving in their conversations with unbelievers. Graciousness and wholesomeness in speech imply patience and longsuffering, not shrinking from telling the truth (Mt 12:34; 16:23; Gal 3:1–5). See *WLC* 138; *WSC* 71.

■ **4:7–18** *Final Greetings.* The letter ends with a brief look at the complex and fluid network of leaders that tied Paul's churches together. Note the overlap of workers in Philemon 23–24.

4:7 Tychicus. The primary letter bearer of Colossians, Philemon and Ephesians (Eph 6:21–22). First mentioned as part of Paul's entourage in Acts 20:4, Tychicus was from the province of Asia on the western coast of Asia Minor, and he appears to have been one of Paul's more trusted emissaries toward the end of the apostle's ministry (2Ti 4:12; Tit 3:12).

4:9 Onesimus. See "Introduction to Philemon."

4:10 Aristarchus. A Jew from Thessalonica. He had been publicly associated with Paul's tumultuous ministry in Ephesus (Ac 19:29) and had traveled with Paul's company through Greece (Ac 20:4) and on to Jerusalem and Rome (Ac 27:2), where he now shared the apostle's imprisonment. **Mark.** The rift that had emerged 12 years previously between Paul and the cousins Barnabas and John Mark (author of the Gospel of Mark; Ac 13:13; 15:37–40) had healed (2Ti 4:11; Phm 24). Paul's mention of Mark testifies to the power of the reconciling work of Christ (1:20,22) and to the peace that is to rule within Christ's body (3:15).

4:11 Jesus, who is called Justus. Otherwise unknown.

4:12 Epaphras. See 1:7 and "Introduction: Time and Place of Writing" and "Original Audience." See also *WLC* 159.

4:13 Hierapolis. See "Introduction: Original Audience."

4:14 Luke. Luke sometimes traveled with Paul (Ac 16:10) and was with Paul on what may have been the eve of his death (2Ti 4:11). As the author of Luke and Acts, he was also Paul's chronicler. Though his writings show him to be exceptionally literate, the mention of his occupation does not necessarily mark him as a man of high social standing, since doctors were often slaves. **Demas.** The only other mention of Demas shows him abandoning Paul during his second imprisonment in Rome (2Ti 4:10).

4:15 [t]Ro 16:5
4:16 [u]2Th 3:14
4:17 [v]Phm 2 [w]2Ti 4:5
4:18 [x]1Co 16:21 [y]Heb 13:3 [z]1Ti 6:21; 2Ti 4:22; Tit 3:15; Heb 13:25

15 Give my greetings to the brothers at Laodicea, and to Nympha and the church in her
house.[t]
16 After this letter has been read to you, see that it is also read[u] in the church of the
Laodiceans and that you in turn read the letter from Laodicea.
17 Tell Archippus:[v] "See to it that you complete the work you have received in the
Lord."[w]
18 I, Paul, write this greeting in my own hand.[x] Remember[y] my chains. Grace be with
you.[z]

4:15 Nympha. If the best textual evidence is correct, Nympha was a woman who hosted a Laodicean house church. Along with other matter-of-fact references to women as patronesses or hostesses of churches or as workers in ministry (Ac 12:12; 16:13–15; Ro 16:1–2, 6–7,12–13; Php 4:2–3; 2Jn 1,5), this passage indicates that the subordination pattern of 3:18 and its parallels (1Co 14:33–35; Eph 5:22–33; 1Ti 2:11–15) are consistent with a strong sense of partnership between men and women in early church ministry. **church in her house.** There is no evidence until the middle of the third century of churches owning separate property for the purpose of worship. Until then, house churches were the norm. Those who exercised a ministry of hospitality by hosting churches in their homes were important benefactors of the early church (Ro 12:13; 1Ti 3:2; Tit 1:8; Heb 13:2; 1Pe 4:9). For mention of other house churches, see Acts 12:12, Romans 16:5, 1 Corinthians 16:19 and Philemon 2.

4:16 letter from Laodicea. Some suggest that Paul was referring to what we know as the letter to the Ephesians, which in many ancient manuscripts lacks a destination and which may have gone out as a circular letter (see "Introduction to Ephesians: Original Audience"). Since Tychicus was the bearer of Ephesians as well (Eph 6:21–22), this scenario would imply that Colossians and Ephesians were written at approximately the same time and that Tychicus traveled first to Laodicea and then on to Colosse. However, it may be more natural to assume, on the basis of the more reflective style of Ephesians, that it was written some time after Colossians and that Tychicus delivered it to the churches on a subsequent trip (if it was a circular letter). The best proposal for the identity of "the letter from Laodicea" is that Paul wrote a separate letter, which has not survived, to the Christians in Laodicea that was to be passed on to the church in Colosse.

4:17 Archippus. If Philemon hosted the house church in Colosse, which had seen the Onesimus incident, this verse may suggest that Archippus was its spiritual head.

4:18 in my own hand. Paul's general practice was to dictate the body of his letters and then close them in his own hand. These concluding sections vary, depending on the circumstances. Sometimes they include personal greetings to strengthen the bond between himself, his workers and his churches (e.g., 4:7–17; Ro 16). Sometimes they summarize the content of the letter (e.g., Gal 6:11–17), and on other occasions (as here) they provide a signature to guarantee the letter's authenticity (1Co 16:21; 2Th 3:17; Phm 19).

1 THESSALONIANS

Introduction

Overview

Author: The apostle Paul

Purpose: To assure the Thessalonians of Paul's love and to instruct them on the importance of living for Christ and properly understanding the ramifications of his return

Date: A.D. 50–51

Key Truths:

- God is to be thanked for the faithfulness of his people.
- Believers are to be commended for their faithfulness.
- Believers are to live lives pleasing to God.
- Believers who have died will rise when Christ returns.
- Believers must always be ready for the return of Christ.

Author

The author of this epistle identified himself as the apostle Paul (1:1; 2:18). Paul's authorship has occasionally been challenged, but with notable lack of success.

The possibility of contributions from Silas and Timothy with regard to the substance of the Thessalonian letters cannot be determined with any certainty. Certain peculiarities of these epistles, in comparison with the rest of the Pauline corpus, may be traceable to the influence of one or the other of these close associates of Paul.

Time and Place of Writing

Paul almost certainly wrote his first letter to the Thessalonians from Corinth, where Silas and Timothy, co-senders of the letters, were reunited with him (Ac 18:5; 2Co 1:19). This epistle was most likely written in A.D. 50 or 51, and 2 Thessalonians was written shortly thereafter. Therefore, 1 and 2 Thessalonians are among the earliest letters we have from Paul's hand, the letter to the Galatians holding the only reasonable claim to an earlier date (see "Introduction to Galatians").

Original Audience

The city of Thessalonica was named for the half-sister of Alexander the Great and was founded about 315 B.C. by her husband, King Cassander of Macedonia. In Roman times it was the provincial seat of government, and it was ruled by five or six "city officials" (Ac 17:6; from the Greek *politarch,* "city ruler").

On Paul's second missionary tour, he and his companions Silas and Timothy had come to this city of over 200,000 along the Egnatian Way after having been "insulted" at Philippi (1Th 2:2), their last base of ministry, according to the book of Acts. Paul preached and debated in the synagogue in Thessalonica for three successive Sabbaths (Ac 17:2).

The Thessalonian correspondence indicates that the makeup of the congregation was predominately Gentile, promoting the view that a successful ministry among Gentiles continued after Paul's access to the synagogue was cut off. During their abbreviated stay in Thessalonica, which cannot have lasted more than several months, the missionaries apparently received more than one small contribution for their support from the Philippian congregation (Php 4:15–16). This, combined with earnings from their own labors (2:9; 2Th 3:7–8), meant that they were able to support themselves without having to depend upon the Thessalonians for any financial remuneration. They set an example of humble, industrious behavior for a minority in the church who wanted to refrain from working for a living.

Eventually some members of the Jewish community enlisted unscrupulous men to stir up animosity against the Christians. A riot ensued, and a number of Christians, including a Jewish convert named Jason, were dragged before the authorities. Jason and the others were forced to post security money to guarantee the peaceable conduct of the new group. Paul, Silas and Timothy were summarily whisked away under cover of darkness and soon found themselves in Berea to the west (Ac 17:5–10).

Purpose and Distinctives

First Thessalonians was occasioned by a report Paul had received from Timothy regarding the state of the Thessalonian congregation (3:6–7). Paul wrote with joy and relief, for, according to this report, the Thessalonians were continuing to stand firm in the faith despite the premature departure of Paul and his coworkers and despite harassment from hostile factions.

Paul focused on two important themes in this letter:

1. *Christ's Return.* Much teaching about Christ's return runs through both Thessalonian epistles, especially in chapters 4–5 of the first letter and chapters 1–2 of the second. Paul's preaching at Athens (Ac 17) confirms that his strategy among non-Jewish audiences at this time was to stress the coming judgment (1Th 4:6), which God has placed in the hands of the risen Jesus.

The return of Christ for judgment will immediately precede a resurrection of the just for their eternal rest and salvation in the Lord's presence (4:16; 5:9; 2Th 1:7), as well as a resurrection of the unjust that Paul presupposed would be for their eternal separation from Christ (2Th 1:9). The onset of the end will be preceded by a widespread movement of apostasy and by the appearance of a diabolical "man of lawlessness" (2Th 2:3; see also 2Th 2:1–12). Since this person had not yet appeared, those in the Thessalonian congregation who had been claiming that the "day of the Lord" (2Th 2:2) had already arrived were to be silenced.

2. *The Divine Christ.* Another notable characteristic of these letters is Paul's assumption of Christ's divine status. This is all the more striking because of the early date of the letters and the spontaneous and unguarded nature of the references. Several times Jesus Christ and God his Father are linked together as the common source of divine blessing and the common object of prayer (1:1; 3:11; 2Th 1:1–2,12; 2:16; 3:5,16). Paul's use of the Old Testament expression "day of the LORD [*Yahweh*]," in which "the LORD [*Yahweh*]" is now revealed to be the Lord Jesus Christ (5:2; 2Th 2:2), also directly attributes deity to Jesus Christ (see note on 5:2). The unified work of the three Persons of the Trinity is mentioned in 2 Thessalonians 2:13–14 (see theological article "The Trinity" at Jn 14).

Outline

I. Salutation (1:1)	*Paul identified himself and greeted the Thessalonians.*
II. History (1:2—3:13) A. Paul's Thanksgiving for the Thessalonians (1:2—2:16) 1. Their Faith, Love and Hope (1:2–10) 2. Their Memory of Paul's Ministry (2:1–12) 3. Their Reception of God's Word (2:13–16) B. Paul's Absence Explained (2:17—3:10) C. Paul's Prayer (3:11–13)	*Paul addressed several aspects of his relationship with the Thessalonians: Paul thanked God for the Thessalonians because they had been faithful and had not forgotten his exemplary ministry among them. Paul explained how he yearned to see the Thessalonians and how Timothy's positive report had encouraged him. Paul prayed that God would make a visit possible and continue to bless the Thessalonians.*
III. Instructions (4:1—5:22) A. Ethical Living (4:1–12) 1. Sexual Morality (4:1–8) 2. Brotherly Love (4:9–10) 3. Work Before Outsiders (4:11–12) B. The Return of Christ (4:13—5:11) 1. The Dead in Christ (4:13–18) 2. The Day of the Lord (5:1–11) C. Final Instructions (5:12–22)	*Paul offered instructions on several subjects that were of special concern: Paul reminded the Thessalonians how he had instructed them earlier to please God by avoiding sexual immorality, to love each other increasingly, and to live honorably before unbelievers. Paul addressed two issues related to the return of Christ: Believers who have died will be raised when Christ returns, and believers must be ready for that return. Paul then briefly addressed a number of specific ethical matters.*
IV. Concluding Prayer, Exhortations and Blessing (5:23–28)	*Paul blessed the Thessalonians, instructed them and charged that his letter be read to all.*

1:1 *a*Ac 16:1; 2Th 1:1 *b*Ac 17:1 *c*Ro 1:7

1 Paul, Silas[a] and Timothy,[a]

To the church of the Thessalonians[b] in God the Father and the Lord Jesus Christ:

Grace and peace to you.[b c]

1:2 *d*Ro 1:8

Thanksgiving for the Thessalonians' Faith

2 We always thank God for all of you,[d] mentioning you in our prayers. 3 We continually remember before our God and Father your work produced by faith,[e] your labor
prompted by love, and your endurance inspired by hope in our Lord Jesus Christ.

1:3 *e*2Th 1:11

a *1* Greek *Silvanus,* a variant of *Silas* b *1* Some early manuscripts *you from God our Father and the Lord Jesus Christ*

■ **1:1** *Salutation.* Paul introduced himself and his companions and addressed the Thessalonians.

1:1 Silas. Sometimes called "Silvanus" (the Latin form of the name), Silas was a prophet of the Jerusalem church delegated to accompany Paul and Barnabas to Antioch to deliver the decision of the Jerusalem council (Ac 15:22,27,32,40) regarding expectations of Gentiles in the church (Ac 15:13–21). He was chosen by Paul to be his associate on his second missionary journey. **Timothy.** The son of a Greek father and a devout Jewish mother, Timothy was at the time of writing a relative newcomer to the Christian mission. Paul and Silas had drafted the youthful but highly regarded disciple for their ministry approximately one year earlier in Lystra (Ac 16:1). **in God the Father and the Lord Jesus Christ.** This phrase points to a unique intimacy between the Father and the Son in that the church can be said to be "in" both (see "Introduction: Purpose and Distinctives").

■ **1:2—3:13** *History.* Paul began the main body of this epistle with historical reflections. He focused on three areas: his thanks to God (1:2—2:16), an explanation of his absence from the Thessalonians (2:17—3:10) and his prayer on their behalf (3:11–13).

■ **1:2—2:16** *Paul's Thanksgiving for the Thessalonians.* Paul greatly appreciated what God had done in the lives of the Thessalonian believers. He reflected on their faith, love and hope (1:2–10); their firsthand experience of his ministry (2:11–12); and their eager reception of God's word (2:13–16).

■ **1:2–10** *Their Faith, Love and Hope.* Paul thanked the Lord for several specific aspects of the Thessalonians' exemplary behavior.

4For we know, brothers loved by God, that he has chosen you, 5because our gospel[f]
came to you not simply with words, but also with power, with the Holy Spirit and with
deep conviction. You know how we lived among you for your sake. 6You became imitators of us[g] and of the Lord; in spite of severe suffering,[h] you welcomed the message with
the joy given by the Holy Spirit.[i] 7And so you became a model to all the believers in Macedonia and Achaia. 8The Lord's message rang out from you not only in Macedonia and
Achaia—your faith in God has become known everywhere.[j] Therefore we do not need
to say anything about it, 9for they themselves report what kind of reception you gave us.
They tell how you turned to God from idols[k] to serve the living and true God, 10and to
wait for his Son from heaven, whom he raised from the dead[l]—Jesus, who rescues us
from the coming wrath.[m]

Paul's Ministry in Thessalonica

2 You know, brothers, that our visit to you[n] was not a failure. 2We had previously suffered[o] and been insulted in Philippi, as you know, but with the help of our God we
dared to tell you his gospel in spite of strong opposition. 3For the appeal we make does
not spring from error or impure motives,[p] nor are we trying to trick you. 4On the contrary, we speak as men approved by God to be entrusted with the gospel.[q] We are not
trying to please men[r] but God, who tests our hearts. 5You know we never used flattery,
nor did we put on a mask to cover up greed[s]—God is our witness.[t] 6We were not looking for praise from men, not from you or anyone else.
As apostles[u] of Christ we could have been a burden to you, 7but we were gentle
among you, like a mother caring for her little children.[v] 8We loved you so much that we
were delighted to share with you not only the gospel of God but our lives as well,[w] because you had become so dear to us. 9Surely you remember, brothers, our toil and hardship; we worked[x] night and day in order not to be a burden to anyone[y] while we
preached the gospel of God to you.
10You are witnesses,[z] and so is God, of how holy,[a] righteous and blameless we were
among you who believed. 11For you know that we dealt with each of you as a father deals
with his own children,[b] 12encouraging, comforting and urging you to live lives worthy[c]
of God, who calls you into his kingdom and glory.

1:5 [f]2Th 2:14
1:6 [g]1Co 4:16 [h]Ac 17:5-10 [i]Ac 13:52
1:8 [j]Ro 1:8; 10:18
1:9 [k]1Co 12:2; Gal 4:8
1:10 [l]Ac 2:24 [m]Ro 5:9
2:1 [n]1Th 1:5,9
2:2 [o]Ac 16:22; Php 1:30
2:3 [p]2Co 2:17
2:4 [q]Gal 2:7 [r]Gal 1:10
2:5 [s]Ac 20:33 [t]Ro 1:9
2:6 [u]1Co 9:1,2
2:7 [v]ver 11
2:8 [w]2Co 12:15; 1Jn 3:16
2:9 [x]Ac 18:3 [y]2Th 3:8
2:10 [z]1Th 1:5 [a]2Co 1:12
2:11 [b]ver 7; 1Co 4:14
2:12 [c]Eph 4:1

1:3 work produced by faith. The faith of the Thessalonians, obviously a chief concern for Paul, is referred to again in verse 8, 3:2,5–7 and 10 and 5:8. **labor prompted by love.** Their love was shown especially in the welcome they gave to the itinerants (v. 9). Paul commended their love again in 4:9–10, where he asserted that they had been "taught by God to love each other" (4:9). **endurance inspired by hope.** Paul referred to the Thessalonians' hope in the return of the Lord Jesus, who would one day deliver them from their present troubles and from God's coming wrath. For the trio of faith, love and hope, see 5:8 (see also Ro 5:2–5; 1Co 13:13; Gal 5:5–6; Col 1:4–5; Heb 6:10–12; 10:22–24; 1Pe 1:3–8, 21–22).

1:4 that he has chosen you. Literally, "your election." Election is a theme of both Thessalonian epistles (5:9; 2Th 2:13). Paul was unafraid to express his assurance of election by God to this young, predominantly Gentile congregation. He saw in these believers the fruit of God's electing grace, manifested here in their divinely effected response to the preaching of the gospel and in their early progress in sanctification (see note on 2Th 2:13).

1:6 imitators. The Thessalonian believers became imitators of the missionaries and of the Lord in that they received the word of the gospel, despite tribulation, with the joy that comes only from the Holy Spirit. The Spirit plays an especially prominent role in sustaining the believer who undergoes persecution for Christ (Mt 10:19–20; 1Pe 4:12–14). See *BC* 22.

1:7–8 Paul was writing from Achaia, after having traversed Macedonia and come through Athens to Corinth. Along his journey he found that the Christians he met not only knew of his labors in Thessalonica but had also learned of the faith of the Thessalonians. The Thessalonian Christians, babes in Christ though they were, had become examples to others of faith, love and hope.

1:9–10 These verses parallel the preaching of Paul at Athens (Ac 17:29–31). In preaching to Jews, Paul could presuppose the existence of the true God and the authority of the Old Testament Scriptures and go on to proclaim the advent of God's promised Messiah. To Gentiles uninstructed in the faith of Israel, Paul stressed the need for two behaviors: (1) acknowledging the true and living God, while forsaking the dead idols of nonexistent deities; and (2) being prepared for God's coming universal judgment to be executed by Jesus Christ, the God-man, who died and rose from the dead (4:6; Ac 17:29–31). Both emphases carry an urgent appeal for conversion. See *WCF* 2.1; *WLC* 105.

1:10 from heaven. See 4:16 (see also Ac 1:11; Php 3:20; 2Th 1:7). **Jesus, who rescues us from the coming wrath.** Jesus died to turn away God's past wrath, but the full import of this saving work will not be displayed until the judgment day. Then, through Christ's intervention, believers will be spared the condemnation and punishment their sins would otherwise deserve. See *WCF* 20.1.

■ **2:1–12** *Their Memory of Paul's Ministry.* These verses review Paul's ministry in Thessalonica. Although Paul was thankful that the believers there were aware of the conduct he had displayed when he had ministered among them, there is a polemical undertone to this passage. It appears that Paul was responding to certain doubts or criticisms implied or levied against him. He implicitly defended the source, style, substance and success of his gospel ministry among them. At the same time, by recalling the work he and his companions had done there, he gave the Thessalonians a pattern of loving service.

2:2 with the help of our God we dared. Despite having been called by God to enter the Macedonian mission field (Ac 16:9–10), Paul and Silas had been severely beaten and chained in a Macedonian prison (in Philippi). It took courage and selfless devotion to God's purpose for the missionaries to continue to proclaim Christ in this region. **his gospel.** Paul stressed the pure, and indeed divine, source of his message and ministry. Note the emphatic use of "gospel of God" in verses 8–9. The gospel message is always carried as a trust from God himself.

2:4–6 See *WLC* 159.

2:7–11 See *WLC* 125.

2:8 Apparent throughout this section (2:17–20; 3:6–12) is Paul's deep affection for his spiritual children, who but months before had been complete strangers to him, alienated by race, culture and religion.

2:12 This verse summarizes Paul's exhortation and charge during his initial visit in Thessalonica. In contrast to the idols from which the Thessalonians had turned (1:9), the true and living God has a kingdom and glory, and in his fathomless mercy he chooses to share this kingdom with those who worship him through Jesus Christ. Called to enter this kingdom, believers know its power and enjoy its life here and now (Ro 14:17; 1Co 4:20; Col 1:13–14), even as they long for the day when they will enter its fullness.

13 And we also thank God continually[d] because, when you received the word of God,[e]
which you heard from us, you accepted it not as the word of men, but as it actually is,
the word of God, which is at work in you who believe. 14 For you, brothers, became imitators of God's churches in Judea,[f] which are in Christ Jesus: You suffered from your own
countrymen[g] the same things those churches suffered from the Jews, 15 who killed the
Lord Jesus[h] and the prophets[i] and also drove us out. They displease God and are hostile to all men 16 in their effort to keep us from speaking to the Gentiles[j] so that they may
be saved. In this way they always heap up their sins to the limit.[k] The wrath of God has
come upon them at last.[a]

Paul's Longing to See the Thessalonians

17 But, brothers, when we were torn away from you for a short time (in person, not in
thought),[l] out of our intense longing we made every effort to see you.[m] 18 For we wanted to come to you—certainly I, Paul, did, again and again—but Satan[n] stopped us.[o]
19 For what is our hope, our joy, or the crown[p] in which we will glory[q] in the presence of
our Lord Jesus when he comes?[r] Is it not you? 20 Indeed, you are our glory[s] and joy.

3 So when we could stand it no longer,[t] we thought it best to be left by ourselves in
Athens.[u] 2 We sent Timothy, who is our brother and God's fellow worker[b] in spreading the gospel of Christ, to strengthen and encourage you in your faith, 3 so that no one
would be unsettled by these trials. You know quite well that we were destined for
them.[v] 4 In fact, when we were with you, we kept telling you that we would be persecuted. And it turned out that way, as you well know.[w] 5 For this reason, when I could stand
it no longer,[x] I sent to find out about your faith. I was afraid that in some way the tempter[y] might have tempted you and our efforts might have been useless.[z]

Timothy's Encouraging Report

6 But Timothy has just now come to us from you[a] and has brought good news about
your faith and love.[b] He has told us that you always have pleasant memories of us and
that you long to see us, just as we also long to see you. 7 Therefore, brothers, in all our
distress and persecution we were encouraged about you because of your faith. 8 For now
we really live, since you are standing firm[c] in the Lord. 9 How can we thank God enough
for you[d] in return for all the joy we have in the presence of our God because of you?
10 Night and day we pray[e] most earnestly that we may see you again[f] and supply what is
lacking in your faith.

2:13 [d]1Th 1:2 [e]Heb 4:12
2:14 [f]Gal 1:22 [g]Ac 17:5; 2Th 1:4
2:15 [h]Ac 2:23 [i]Mt 5:12
2:16 [j]Ac 13:45,50 [k]Mt 23:32
2:17 [l]1Co 5:3; Col 2:5 [m]1Th 3:10
2:18 [n]Mt 4:10 [o]Ro 1:13; 15:22
2:19 [p]Php 4:1 [q]2Co 1:14 [r]Mt 16:27; 1Th 3:13
2:20 [s]2Co 1:14
3:1 [t]ver 5 [u]Ac 17:15
3:3 [v]Ac 9:16; 14:22
3:4 [w]1Th 2:14
3:5 [x]ver 1 [y]Mt 4:3 [z]Gal 2:2; Php 2:16
3:6 [a]Ac 18:5 [b]1Th 1:3
3:8 [c]1Co 16:13
3:9 [d]1Th 1:2
3:10 [e]2Ti 1:3 [f]1Th 2:17

[a] 16 Or *them fully* [b] 2 Some manuscripts *brother and fellow worker;* other manuscripts *brother and God's servant*

■ **2:13–16** *Their Reception of God's Word.* Paul returned to the faithfulness the Thessalonians had demonstrated, focusing especially on how they had responded to his preaching.
2:13 word of God. Paul characterized the message he preached among the Thessalonians as the "word of God" (to be contrasted with the "word of men"), and he encouraged them to receive it as such (see note on 4:8). **at work.** The word of God, though it comes through the agency of men, is not a message of merely human power. It is a divine message that actively and effectually works in believers through the Holy Spirit (Isa 55:11; Ac 20:32; Heb 4:12). See *WCF* 1.4; 14.2; *WLC* 160; *BC* 24.
2:14 suffered from your own countrymen. Proof of the power of God's word in them was that they, like the churches of Judea, endured faithfully and with joy in the face of fierce persecution from their kinsmen (Ac 17:5–9).
2:15–16 See *WLC* 109,151.
2:15 Just as Jesus noted the common purpose among those who had persecuted the prophets and those who were then persecuting him (Mt 23:29–32), so Paul (also Stephen; Ac 7:52) saw the same solidarity extending to those Jews (with whom he had formerly worked) who now persecuted Christ by opposing the gospel (Ac 9:4). Paul's fullest elaboration of his approach to this problem of Jewish rejection of the gospel is set forth in Romans 9–11.
2:16 The wrath of God has come upon them at last. "At last" may also be translated "to the end" (Mt 10:22; 1Co 1:8; 15:24). This may refer prophetically to the catastrophe that would overtake Jerusalem within 20 years of Paul's writing. Or it may refer to the sequence of calamities that had already begun and would reach its culmination in the momentous disaster of A.D. 70. It may also be a comment on the punitive hardening of a large segment of the children of Israel in their culpable rejection of Christ, a hardening that Jesus saw as the fulfillment of Isaiah's dire prophecy in Isaiah 6:9–10 (quoted in Mt 13:14–15). Compare a similar outworking of God's wrath upon Gentiles outlined in Romans 1:18–32. See *WLC* 113.
■ **2:17—3:10** *Paul's Absence Explained.* A second historical matter Paul had to deal with was his prolonged absence. Paul had left Thessalonica abruptly and had been unable to return. His absence raised questions about the sincerity of his love. Paul here explained the circumstances of his prolonged absence and his reasons for sending Timothy to minister among them in his stead.
2:17 torn away. The Greek word means "orphaned," and it is commonly used of parents, as well as children, who have suffered separation. Paul continued the family imagery of verses 7 and 11 in depicting his relationship with the Thessalonian congregation.
2:19 when he comes? The first of six occurrences in Paul's Thessalonian letters of the Greek word *parousia* ("coming"), as it relates to the second coming of Christ (2:19; 3:13; 4:15; 5:23; 2Th 2:1,8), all of which refer to the same event. Paul's only other use of the term in this sense occurs in 1 Corinthians 15:23. Here Christ's coming is presented as the time when the outcome of our works of faith will be disclosed. Paul's joy and crown at that day will be the presence of his beloved spiritual children, those who were converted under his ministry (2Co 1:14; Php 2:16).
3:2 See *WLC* 155.
3:3–4 we would be persecuted. Neither Paul nor Jesus himself promised Christ's followers a life of ease or public approval (see Mk 8:34; Jn 15:18–21).
3:6 Timothy has . . . come. When Paul could not personally visit Thessalonica, he sent Timothy. Paul showed great affection for the Thessalonians by sending his student and close companion.
3:8 we really live. Paul had such deep affection for the Thessalonians that he could live joyfully (v. 9) only after he had been assured of their faithfulness to Christ. Such concern exemplifies the kind of love that is proper among believers (1Co 12:26).
3:10–11 See *WLC* 155.

11 Now may our God and Father himself and our Lord Jesus clear the way for us to
come to you. 12 May the Lord make your love increase and overflow for each other[g] and
for everyone else, just as ours does for you. 13 May he strengthen your hearts so that you
will be blameless[h] and holy in the presence of our God and Father when our Lord Jesus
comes[i] with all his holy ones.

Living to Please God

4 Finally, brothers,[j] we instructed you how to live in order to please God,[k] as in fact
you are living. Now we ask you and urge you in the Lord Jesus to do this more and
more. 2 For you know what instructions we gave you by the authority of the Lord Jesus.
3 It is God's will that you should be sanctified: that you should avoid sexual immorality;[l] 4 that each of you should learn to control his own body[a][m] in a way that is holy and
honorable, 5 not in passionate lust[n] like the heathen,[o] who do not know God; 6 and that
in this matter no one should wrong his brother or take advantage of him.[p] The Lord will
punish men for all such sins,[q] as we have already told you and warned you. 7 For God did
not call us to be impure, but to live a holy life.[r] 8 Therefore, he who rejects this instruction does not reject man but God, who gives you his Holy Spirit.[s]
9 Now about brotherly love[t] we do not need to write to you,[u] for you yourselves have
been taught by God to love each other.[v] 10 And in fact, you do love all the brothers
throughout Macedonia.[w] Yet we urge you, brothers, to do so more and more.[x]
11 Make it your ambition to lead a quiet life, to mind your own business and to work
with your hands,[y] just as we told you, 12 so that your daily life may win the respect of outsiders[z] and so that you will not be dependent on anybody.

3:12 [g]1Th 4:9,10
3:13 [h]1Co 1:8 [i]1Th 2:19
4:1 [j]2Co 13:11 [k]2Co 5:9
4:3 [l]1Co 6:18
4:4 [m]1Co 7:2,9
4:5 [n]Ro 1:26 [o]Eph 4:17
4:6 [p]1Co 6:8 [q]Heb 13:4
4:7 [r]Lev 11:44; 1Pe 1:15
4:8 [s]Ro 5:5; Gal 4:6
4:9 [t]Ro 12:10 [u]1Th 5:1 [v]Jn 13:34
4:10 [w]1Th 1:7 [x]1Th 3:12
4:11 [y]Eph 4:28; 2Th 3:10-12
4:12 [z]Mk 4:11

[a] 4 *Or learn to live with his own wife; or learn to acquire a wife*

■ **3:11–13** *Paul's Prayer.* Having just mentioned that he prayed regularly for the Thessalonians (v. 10), Paul offered a prayer for them in writing.

3:11 Paul addressed God the Father and the Lord Jesus jointly in his prayer ("Introduction: Purpose and Distinctives"). The answer to this prayer for reunion came several years later (Ac 20:1). See *BC* 10.

3:13 when our Lord Jesus comes. The work of sanctification that has already begun in believers will be brought to glorious completion at the second coming of the Lord (5:23; 1Co 1:8; Php 1:6, 2Th 3:3; Jude 24). This points to a judicial scene at Christ's return. **his holy ones.** Refers to the angels who will accompany Christ at his return (Mt 13:39,48–49; 16:27; 2Th 1:7), to human saints (2Th 1:10; Rev 19:14) or to both. See *WLC* 155,195; *HC* 127.

■ **4:1—5:22** *Instructions.* Paul embarked on the second major portion of his epistle, offering instructions on several subjects: principles for Christian conduct (4:1–12); assurances and challenges regarding Christ's return (4:13—5:11); and an assortment of brief, final guidelines (5:12–22).

■ **4:1–12** *Ethical Living.* Personal and interpersonal morality were very important to Paul. Here he touched on three matters of particular significance for the Thessalonian church: sexual morality (vv. 1–8), brotherly love (vv. 9–10) and an attitude and work ethic that will gain the respect of a watching world (vv. 11–12). These instructions move from narrower to broader concerns: from one's "own body" (v. 4) to one's "brother" (v. 6) to the "brothers" in general (v. 10) and finally to "outsiders" (v. 12).

■ **4:1–8** *Sexual Morality.* The sexual mores of Hellenistic culture stood in sharp contrast to Biblical patterns. The Thessalonians probably faced many temptations to engage in culturally accepted forms of sexual immorality.

4:1 Paul praised the Thessalonians for their progress in learning how to please God but challenged them to excel further. The apostle recognized the constant need for growth and for pressing on, for "straining toward what is ahead" (Php 3:13). Spiritual complacency belies a believer's verbal confession.

4:2 Again Paul stressed that the authority underlying his instructions was not his own—not that of a mere man—but was from the risen Lord himself (2:13).

4:3–8 See *WLC* 138; *HC* 108.

4:3 God's will that you should be sanctified. Scripture generally conceives of the will of God in one of two senses. Sometimes (e.g., Eph 1:11) what is meant is the decree of God that determines history, which we cannot know except by observing its outworking or by a special revelation from God. Theologians often call this the "decretive" or "hidden" will of God. Sometimes (e.g., here and in 5:18) what is meant is a duty God has enjoined upon us through revelation—the "preceptive" or "revealed" will of God, that which he commands us to do. God's expressed will for us is that we be holy, abstaining from unchaste behavior.

4:5 like the heathen. Pagan society in Paul's day provided no inducement to sexual purity. Marital infidelity, at least for males, was the norm, and some of the pagan religions from which these Thessalonians had been liberated (one of which may have been the notorious Cabiri cult) sanctioned gross sexual defilement in their ritual. The Christian gospel brought, and continues to bring, a moral awakening and a fresh revelation of God's righteous standards.

4:6 wrong his brother. Illicit sexual involvement affects others besides the consenting parties. Spouses are wronged, and families, friends and fellow Christians are shamed. It even involves Christ (1Co 6:15). Ultimately these sins, like all others, are against the holy and righteous God, who will judge them. See *WLC* 142.

4:8 Paul claimed divine authority, not merely for his spoken proclamation, but also for his written instructions (note also his injunction in 5:27). **who gives you his Holy Spirit.** Paul pointedly reminded his readers of their renewed capacities for holiness resulting from God's continual endowment of the Holy Spirit dwelling within them (1Co 6:19; Gal 3:5). The construction in Greek emphasizes the term "holy," which is especially fitting in this context.

■ **4:9–10** *Brotherly Love.* Paul had already provided an example of fraternal love in his own ministry to the Thessalonians (2:1–12). Now he called on them to show this kind of love to each other.

4:10 more and more. Paul commended the Thessalonians for their devotion to each other and to Christians throughout Macedonia. Yet he knew that the trials facing the church required ever increasing mutual support and affection. On the importance of love among believers in Paul's writings, see 1 Corinthians 13:1–13.

■ **4:11–12** *Work Before Outsiders.* Paul's scope was broadest in this section of moral instruction. He was concerned again with the Thessalonians' work ethic and their reputation in the unbelieving community.

4:11 Make it your ambition. This phrase, just one word in Greek (*philotimeomai*), was often used to refer to attempts by the wealthy to garner civic honor and recognition through outward displays of generosity. Paul's use of the term turned it on its head: The Thessalonians should be zealous for honor that comes not through self-assertion or ostentatious shows of personal greatness, but through humble, industrious, unimpeachable behavior. This exhortation, pertinent to all Christians, had a particular urgency in Thessalonica, where the Christians had already been falsely accused of sedition (Ac 17:6–9). By living respectable and unpretentious lives, the Christians there would allay any lingering suspicions. See *WLC* 135.

4:13 [a]Eph 2:12
4:14 [b]1Co 15:18
4:15 [c]1Co 15:52
4:16 [d]Mt 24:31 [e]1Co 15:23; 2Th 2:1
4:17 [f]1Co 15:52 [g]Ac 1:9; Rev 11:12 [h]Jn 12:26
5:1 [i]Ac 1:7 [j]1Th 4:9
5:2 [k]1Co 1:8 [l]2Pe 3:10
5:4 [m]Ac 26:18; 1Jn 2:8
5:6 [n]Ro 13:11
5:7 [o]Ac 2:15; 2Pe 2:13
5:8 [p]Eph 6:14 [q]Ro 8:24 [r]Eph 6:17
5:9 [s]2Th 2:13,14
5:10 [t]2Co 5:15

The Coming of the Lord

13 Brothers, we do not want you to be ignorant about those who fall asleep, or to
grieve like the rest of men, who have no hope.[a] 14 We believe that Jesus died and rose
again and so we believe that God will bring with Jesus those who have fallen asleep in
him.[b] 15 According to the Lord's own word, we tell you that we who are still alive, who
are left till the coming of the Lord, will certainly not precede those who have fallen
asleep.[c] 16 For the Lord himself will come down from heaven, with a loud command, with
the voice of the archangel and with the trumpet call of God,[d] and the dead in Christ will
rise first.[e] 17 After that, we who are still alive and are left[f] will be caught up together with
them in the clouds[g] to meet the Lord in the air. And so we will be with the Lord[h] forever. 18 Therefore encourage each other with these words.

5 Now, brothers, about times and dates[i] we do not need to write to you,[j] 2 for you
know very well that the day of the Lord[k] will come like a thief in the night.[l] 3 While
people are saying, "Peace and safety," destruction will come on them suddenly, as labor
pains on a pregnant woman, and they will not escape.

4 But you, brothers, are not in darkness[m] so that this day should surprise you like a
thief. 5 You are all sons of the light and sons of the day. We do not belong to the night or
to the darkness. 6 So then, let us not be like others, who are asleep,[n] but let us be alert
and self-controlled. 7 For those who sleep, sleep at night, and those who get drunk, get
drunk at night.[o] 8 But since we belong to the day, let us be self-controlled, putting on faith
and love as a breastplate,[p] and the hope of salvation[q] as a helmet.[r] 9 For God did not appoint us to suffer wrath but to receive salvation through our Lord Jesus Christ.[s] 10 He died
for us so that, whether we are awake or asleep, we may live together with him.[t] 11 Therefore encourage one another and build each other up, just as in fact you are doing.

■**4:13—5:11** *The Return of Christ.* Paul's second major instructional focus was on Christ's coming return. His discussion of this matter divides into two parts: the fate of believers who die before this event (4:13–18) and preparedness for it (5:1–11).

■**4:13–18** *The Dead in Christ.* False prophets had apparently tied the hopes of the Thessalonians so tightly to an imminent return of Christ that they did not know what to think about believers who had died. Paul did not want the Thessalonians to worry about what would happen to these saints.

4:13 asleep. A standard metaphor in antiquity among pagans, as well as Jews and Christians, for death. The term had no particular reference to the state of the soul or to the consciousness of the deceased, for it was used by groups with widely diverging beliefs on this subject. For the New Testament understanding of a conscious and blessed existence between death and the resurrection, see Luke 16:19–31; 23:42–43 (see also Jn 14:1–3; 2Co 5:6–8; Php 1:23; Heb 12:22–24; Rev 6:9–11; 7:9–17; 20:4–6). **grieve.** Christ's resurrection affords Christians a deeply seated hope and assurance of never-ending fellowship with him. Therefore, their grief over departed fellow believers is softened, and they are upheld in hope.

4:14 God will bring with Jesus. This is probably to be understood as a "bringing" into God's presence (3:13) and kingdom by resurrection (1Co 6:14; 2Co 4:14), although some believe it signifies a bringing of the departed saints back to Earth when Christ returns. See *WLC* 86; *WSC* 37.

4:15–18 See *WLC* 87,90; *WSC* 38.

4:15 not precede. According to the author of 2 Esdras 13:14–20,24 (a non-canonical Jewish work written in the second century A.D.), those who survive until the coming of the glorious Messiah are more blessed than those who have died before this event. Some of the Thessalonians may have had a similar misconception. Paul, on the contrary, assured his readers that both groups will be on equal footing (1Co 15:52), as all believers will enter the fullness of the kingdom together when Jesus returns.

4:16 the dead in Christ will rise first. Those "in Christ" constitute a subcategory of those "in Adam" (the whole human race), and they comprise all who participate in salvation (1Co 15:22–23), living either before or after Christ. Therefore, this rising of the "dead in Christ" refers to a bodily resurrection (1Co 15:35–44) of all the righteous dead, not merely that of New Testament believers, at the time of Christ's return (Jn 5:28–29; 1Co 15:23). The resurrection of the unrighteous is mentioned explicitly by Paul only in Acts 24:15, although he presupposed it in his warnings of a universal judgment of individuals at the time of Christ's return (Ac 17:31; Ro 2:5–16). See *WLC* 56; *BC* 37.

4:17 caught up. This catching-up or "rapture" (from the Latin *rapere*) of the church is not portrayed here in such a way as to satisfy all our cravings for detailed knowledge of end-times chronology. For instance, we are not told whether the assembled company will descend immediately to Earth or return to heaven. What is clear is that this event will not take place until after the bodily resurrection of the dead. The doctrine is presented pastorally to comfort those grieved and confused by the deaths of beloved Christians. The assurance that all the righteous without distinction will be with the Lord forever, as well as with each other at the coming of Christ, is the burden of this passage (v. 18). Nevertheless, the phrases "loud command," "the voice of the archangel" and "the trumpet call of God" (v. 16) leave a distinct impression that the rapture will be a public, rather than a secret, event (Lk 17:24; 21:35; Rev 1:7). See note on 5:1–11. See *WCF* 32.2; *WLC* 82,90.

■**5:1–11** *The Day of the Lord.* The Thessalonians were told to prepare for the return of Christ, which will take the ungodly by surprise. Paul assumed that both Christians (in his mind, possibly the very Christians he was writing to) and non-Christians will be alive and present when this day arrives, the former being watchful and ready, the latter being startled as by a thief who strikes at night. Hence the rapture of Christians spoken of in 4:17 will occur at the same time as the sudden and inescapable destruction of the wicked (2Th 1:6–10; note on 2Th 2:1). It will be a public event that takes place at the end of creation as we know it.

5:1–2 See *BC* 37.

5:2 day of the Lord. A prominent designation of the day on which Christ returns (Mt 24:42). The term is well known from the Old Testament (e.g., Joel 2:1,31; Am 5:18; Zep 1:7,14; Mal 4:5), where it is used of God's drawing near in judgment. This association of the day of the Lord with judgment is carried on in the New Testament, where the last judgment and final rewards and punishments are in view (Ac 17:31; Ro 2:5,16; 2Co 1:14). According to 2 Peter 3:10–13, the heavens, the earth and the elements will be destroyed on that day, giving way to a new heaven and a new earth. **like a thief in the night.** See Matthew 24:43–44 (see also 2Pe 3:10; Rev 3:3; 16:15). Paul seems to have been familiar with at least some of the material that we now read in Jesus' Olivet discourse (Mt 24:3—25:46; Mk 13:3–37; Lk 21:5–36).

5:9–10 See *WCF* 3.6; *HC* 42.

5:9 God did not appoint us to suffer wrath. God has appointed his people to obtain salvation and glory in Jesus Christ (1:10; 2Th 2:14). Yet the Father has also selected innumerable Christians (including the Thessalonians) to undergo, and faithfully withstand, tribulation of every kind (3:2–4; 2Th 1:4; Jas 1:2–4; 1Pe 4:12–14; Rev 1:9). **wrath.** Refers in this context to the just condemnation and punishment that will fall upon the impenitent (Eph 5:6; Col 3:6; Rev 6:16–17; 11:18) on "the day of God's wrath" (Ro 2:5). See *WCF* 3.5; *WLC* 30.

5:11 See *WCF* 26.1.

Final Instructions

12 Now we ask you, brothers, to respect those who work hard among you, who are
over you in the Lord[u] and who admonish you. 13 Hold them in the highest regard in love
because of their work. Live in peace with each other.[v] 14 And we urge you, brothers, warn
those who are idle,[w] encourage the timid, help the weak,[x] be patient with everyone.
15 Make sure that nobody pays back wrong for wrong,[y] but always try to be kind to each
other[z] and to everyone else.
16 Be joyful always;[a] 17 pray continually; 18 give thanks in all circumstances, for this is
God's will for you in Christ Jesus.
19 Do not put out the Spirit's fire;[b] 20 do not treat prophecies[c] with contempt. 21 Test everything.[d] Hold on to the good. 22 Avoid every kind of evil.
23 May God himself, the God of peace,[e] sanctify you through and through. May your
whole spirit, soul and body be kept blameless at the coming of our Lord Jesus Christ.
24 The one who calls you is faithful[f] and he will do it.

25 Brothers, pray for us.[g] 26 Greet all the brothers with a holy kiss.[h] 27 I charge you before the Lord to have this letter read to all the brothers.[i]
28 The grace of our Lord Jesus Christ be with you.[j]

5:12 [u]1Ti 5:17; Heb 13:17
5:13 [v]Mk 9:50
5:14 [w]2Th 3:6,7,11 [x]Ro 14:1
5:15 [y]1Pe 3:9 [z]Gal 6:10; Eph 4:32
5:16 [a]Php 4:4
5:19 [b]Eph 4:30
5:20 [c]1Co 14:1-40
5:21 [d]1Co 14:29; 1Jn 4:1
5:23 [e]Ro 15:33
5:24 [f]1Co 1:9
5:25 [g]Eph 6:19
5:26 [h]Ro 16:16
5:27 [i]Col 4:16 **5:28** [j]Ro 16:20

■ **5:12–22** *Final Instructions.* Having dealt with his main concerns for the Thessalonians, Paul turned to several brief exhortations.

5:12–13 See *BC* 31.

5:12 Even at this early stage in the life of the Thessalonian congregation, leaders had of necessity been charged with spiritual care and oversight. Paul endorsed the legitimate esteem of church workers and leaders, commanding believers not only to show them respect, but also to express love for them. Some Thessalonian leaders, whom Paul named elsewhere, may have been on the apostle's mind when he wrote this: Jason (Ac 17:6–9), Aristarchus (Ac 20:4; 27:2; Col 4:10; Phm 24), Secundus (Ac 20:4) and possibly Gaius (Ac 19:29). See *WCF* 30.1; 30.4.

5:14 brothers. This address (also v. 12) indicates that the exhortations that follow enjoined a mutual responsibility for ministry upon all the congregation, not simply upon the acknowledged leaders. **those who are idle.** Although the Greek word for "idle" used here (as the related words in 2Th 3:6–7,11 reveal) has the sense of "disorderly" or "rebellious," the context shows that the form of unregulated conduct in view was an irresponsible refusal to work for a living. Many think this behavior was fed by an overripe expectancy of Christ's second coming (see "Introduction to 2 Thessalonians"). **timid.** The fainthearted or diffident need encouragement, and the weak need upholding (Ro 14:1; 15:1–2). All are to be ministered to with patience. See *WCF* 26.1; *WLC* 135; *BC* 29.

5:15 kind to each other. The Christian has a duty to seek justice for others (Isa 56:1; 58:6–8). But it is a most remarkable aspect of the Christian ethic that the believer, following the example of Christ himself (1Pe 2:21–23), is to refrain from personal retaliation on his or her own behalf (Mt 5:38–42; Ro 12:17–21; 1Co 6:7; 1Pe 3:9).

5:16–18 joyful always . . . thanks in all circumstances. Paul encouraged the Thessalonians to live lives characterized by joy and thanksgiving. He did not, however, forbid the appropriate expressions of sadness and lament. Jesus himself was not always joyful and thankful (Jn 11:35,38). As the Psalms indicate, sadness and lament are legitimate and appropriate at times (Pss 28; 38; 40; 88; 130). **God's will.** Refers here to God's prescriptive will (that which he commands), as opposed to his decretive will (that which he immutably decrees; see note on 4:3). See *HC* 116.

5:18 See *HC* 28.

5:19–21 the Spirit's fire . . . prophecies. On the one hand, Paul admonished the Thessalonians not to quench the Spirit of God by despising legitimate prophecy (both Silas and Paul were New Testament prophets; Ac 13:1, 15:32). On the other, Paul stipulated that no claim to prophecy should be accepted uncritically; all such claims must be tested for validity (1Co 14:29; 2Th 2:2).

5:21–23 See *WLC* 99; *BC* 29.

■ **5:23–28** *Concluding Prayer, Exhortations and Blessing.* Paul closed with a prayer, brief exhortations and a blessing, all in rapid succession.

5:23 sanctify. The complete mending of all human imperfections is not merely possible but certain. This restoration depends upon God, who is faithful and will accomplish it (v. 24). The time element must not be disregarded, however. Ultimate perfection, which will also include a glorified body, will be accomplished at the second coming of Jesus Christ (Php 1:6). **your whole spirit, soul and body.** Three aspects of the human person are enumerated to emphasize the wholeness of this perfection. Most often in Scripture, "spirit" and "soul" are used as virtual synonyms for the spiritual element in a person. Infrequently (here and in Heb 4:12), Scripture considers this spiritual element from different points of view, though it is difficult to tell just what shade of meaning distinguishes them. Compare the fourfold representation of "heart," "soul," "mind" and "strength" in Mark 12:30. See *WCF* 13.2; *WLC* 93,195; *HC* 127.

5:27 I charge you. The Greek verb used here is rare and emphatic, having the effect of putting the readers under oath. Paul was laying a solemn weight upon them in order to ensure the whole congregation's familiarity with the content of this epistle—so important did he deem his apostolic teaching for their spiritual good (2:13; see note on 4:2).

2 THESSALONIANS

Introduction

Overview

Author: The apostle Paul

Purpose: To follow up his previous letter (1 Thessalonians) by instructing the Thessalonians further about the return of Christ and the importance of responsible daily living

Date: A.D. 50–52

Key Truths:

- Believers are to persevere through suffering until Christ's return.
- Followers of Christ must not be misled by speculations about his coming return.
- The return of Christ will bring great judgment and reward.
- Believers are to live responsibly in their daily affairs in this world as they await Christ's return.

Author

Paul claimed authorship of this epistle (1:1; 3:17). Ignatius of Antioch, Polycarp and Justin Martyr were all apparently familiar with this letter during the first half of the second century. Despite this early attestation, 2 Thessalonians has suffered more frequent and more influential attacks on its authenticity than has 1 Thessalonians. Some scholars have seen the close similarities in subject matter and phraseology between the two letters as an indication of artificiality. But this evidence should be read another way. Who was more capable of echoing Paul's thoughts and expressions than Paul himself?

Some interpreters believe that the two letters teach competing views of the return of Christ and therefore cannot both be products of the same author. First Thessalonians is thought to teach an imminent return of Christ, whereas 2 Thessalonians insists that certain historical events will occur before Christ's return. The supposed conflict is illusory. First Thessalonians says nothing definite about the imminence of the second coming, stressing only the suddenness and unexpectedness with which the day of the Lord will overtake the unwary. Second Thessalonians specifies an order of events so as to counteract a new misunderstanding at Thessalonica that the day of the Lord had already taken place.

Moreover, 2:5 and 3:10 both present information that, had it not been legitimate, could easily have been proven spurious for at least a full generation. It is also difficult to imagine why the warning against letters falsely written in Paul's name (2:2) would have been included in a counterfeit letter. In sum, there is every reason to affirm that Paul is the author.

Time and Place of Writing

Second Thessalonians 2:15 presupposes an earlier letter from Paul, and it is highly probable that the letter being referred to is 1 Thessalonians (see "Introduction to 1 Thessalonians"). This is the most concrete internal evidence that 2 Thessalonians is indeed the later of the two Thessalonian epistles. Second Thessalonians is therefore probably to be dated a short time after 1 Thessalonians (sometime between the last months of A.D. 50 and the first months of A.D. 52). As was 1 Thessalonians, 2 Thessalonians would have been written from Corinth.

Original Audience

See "Introduction to 1 Thessalonians: Original Audience."

Purpose and Distinctives

Two major themes in this letter deserve special attention. As in 1 Thessalonians, Paul again addressed questions raised about the return of Christ. After sending 1 Thessalonians, the apostle had received further reports concerning the Thessalonian congregation. There was cause for rejoicing, for the Thessalonians continued to grow in faith, love and perseverance (1:3–4), but there was also reason for concern with regard to doctrinal and behavioral matters. Second Thessalonians was written mainly to supplement Paul's earlier teaching. In it he corrected an unsettling false belief that the day of the Lord had already taken place (2:1–11). This misguided claim may have been due in part to wrong inferences drawn from Paul's own teaching, coupled with the congregation's painful experience of persecutions presumed to indicate the coming end of the world.

Paul also dealt with chronic idleness among the Thessalonian believers (3:6–15). This misguided behavior of some within the church had continued unabated after the first letter (1Th 4:11–12; 5:14), stemming from the time the missionaries had been present (3:10–11). Paul had already given exhortations to rectify the situation, but according to fresh reports (3:11) matters had only worsened. Many scholars attribute this idleness to a feverish expectation that the Lord's return was imminent (2:1–3), along with the accompanying conclusion that continuing to work for one's daily sustenance amounted to a denial of faith. Yet it must be pointed out that Paul never explicitly stated that connection himself. Since 3:10 strongly suggests that the problem had surfaced already while the missionaries were in Thessalonica, it would seem to be unlikely that eschatological errors gave birth to the problem, though they may have provided a convenient rationale for its perpetuation.

Outline

I. Salutation (1:1–2)	*Paul greeted and blessed the church of Thessalonica.*
II. Thanksgiving and Encouragement (1:3–12)	*Paul reported that he continued to give thanks for the Thessalonians' love and endurance in the face of persecution. He reminded them of the reward to come when Christ returns in judgment, and he encouraged them to persevere until that day.*
III. Instructions (2:1—3:15) A. Return of Christ (2:1–17) B. Request for Prayer (3:1–5) C. Importance of Labor (3:6–15)	*Paul addressed several items of importance to the Thessalonians. Paul encouraged the Thessalonians to reject the false prophets who taught that Christ had already returned. He recalled his earlier teaching that rebellion and the man of lawlessness will precede Christ's return. Paul asked the Thessalonians to pray for him and his gospel ministry. Paul addressed the continuing problem of idleness. Christians should be faithful in their daily responsibilities in this life*
IV. Closing Blessing and Authentication (3:16–18)	*Paul closed with a benediction, and he authenticated this letter.*

1 Paul, Silas[a] and Timothy,[a]

To the church of the Thessalonians in God our Father and the Lord Jesus Christ:

2 Grace and peace to you from God the Father and the Lord Jesus Christ.[b]

Thanksgiving and Prayer

3 We ought always to thank God for you, brothers, and rightly so, because your faith
is growing more and more, and the love every one of you has for each other is increasing.[c] 4 Therefore, among God's churches we boast[d] about your perseverance and faith[e]
in all the persecutions and trials you are enduring.[f]
5 All this is evidence[g] that God's judgment is right, and as a result you will be counted worthy of the kingdom of God, for which you are suffering. 6 God is just: He will pay
back trouble to those who trouble you[h] 7 and give relief to you who are troubled, and to
us as well. This will happen when the Lord Jesus is revealed from heaven in blazing fire
with his powerful angels.[i] 8 He will punish those who do not know God[j] and do not obey
the gospel of our Lord Jesus.[k] 9 They will be punished with everlasting destruction[l] and

1:1 [a]Ac 16:1; 1Th 1:1
1:2 [b]Ro 1:7
1:3 [c]1Th 3:12
1:4 [d]2Co 7:14 [e]1Th 1:3 [f]1Th 2:14
1:5 [g]Php 1:28
1:6 [h]Col 3:25; Rev 6:10
1:7 [i]1Th 4:16; Jude 14
1:8 [j]Gal 4:8 [k]Ro 2:8
1:9 [l]Php 3:19; 2Pe 3:7

a *1* Greek *Silvanus,* a variant of *Silas*

■ **1:1–2** *Salutation.* Paul opened this epistle by identifying himself and those whom he was addressing.
1:1 See note on 1 Thessalonians 1:1.
■ **1:3–12** *Thanksgiving and Encouragement.* Paul expressed his gratitude for the Thessalonians' faithfulness and encouraged them to further perseverance in the faith.
1:3 growing more and more. Salvation and rewards come only through God's grace, based on the righteousness of Christ (v. 2; Tit 3:5–7). Our subsequent living through the power of the Holy Spirit conforms us to the holiness of God and confirms the genuineness of our union with Christ.
1:4 persecutions and trials. One instance of persecution is recorded in Acts 17:1–9, and the Thessalonian correspondence reveals that antagonism had not disappeared (1Th 1:6; 2:14; 3:3).
1:5–10 See *WCF* 33.2; 33.3; *WLC* 16,45,60,89; *HC* 52.
1:5 worthy of the kingdom. Paul spoke elsewhere of living lives worthy of God (1Th 2:12), of God's call (1:11; Eph 4:1), of Christ (Col 1:10) and of the gospel (Php 1:27–28). He did not mean by this that people are able to make themselves worthy of receiving these blessings. Instead, he spoke of lifestyles appropriate for recipients of God's blessing. By God's grace we are enabled to live in ways that are fitting for the people of God. In this case, Paul had in mind the ability to endure persecution. **kingdom.** Refers here to the consummation of the universal reign of God over all of the earth that will take place when Christ returns (see theological article "The Kingdom of God" at Mt 4). **for which you are suffering.** Even while enjoying the benefits of citizenship in this heavenly kingdom (see note on 1Th 2:12), Christians still suffer on its behalf (Ac 14:22), for this kingdom inevitably meets with diabolical and worldly opposition. See *BC* 37.
1:6 God is just. The believer's confidence of receiving the eternal reward offered in Christ is based on the immutable attributes of God. Here Paul focused on God's justice, which brings judgment on all who are outside Christ. **pay back trouble.** In Romans 2:9 the same Greek word for "trouble" is used for the woe brought upon the evildoer at the last judgment. Paul appears to have been speaking of the same judgment, as his next verses are concerned with ultimate bliss and woe. Paul alluded to the similar assurance given to Abraham, applying it to the Thessalonian believers, who were Abraham's descendants in Christ (Gal 3:29).
1:8 know God . . . obey the gospel. The gospel is not only a message to be received, or believed; it is also a message to be obeyed (1Pe 4:17). It carries with it the divine command for absolute surrender to God through the peace made available to believers by Jesus Christ. To obey the gospel is to know God and to have intimate fellowship with him.
1:9 everlasting destruction. The fearful doctrine of eternal punishment (Isa 66:24; Mt 25:46; Mk 9:43,48), staggering as it is,

shut out from the presence of the Lord and from the majesty of his power[m] 10on the day[n]
he comes to be glorified[o] in his holy people and to be marveled at among all those who
have believed. This includes you, because you believed our testimony to you.[p]
11With this in mind, we constantly pray for you, that our God may count you worthy[q]
of his calling, and that by his power he may fulfill every good purpose of yours and every act prompted by your faith.[r] 12We pray this so that the name of our Lord Jesus may
be glorified in you,[s] and you in him, according to the grace of our God and the Lord Jesus
Christ.[a]

The Man of Lawlessness

2 Concerning the coming of our Lord Jesus Christ and our being gathered to him,[t] we
ask you, brothers, 2not to become easily unsettled or alarmed by some prophecy,
report or letter[u] supposed to have come from us, saying that the day of the Lord[v] has already come. 3Don't let anyone deceive you[w] in any way, for ⌊that day will not come⌋ until the rebellion occurs and the man of lawlessness[b] is revealed,[x] the man doomed to destruction. 4He will oppose and will exalt himself over everything that is called God[y] or
is worshiped, so that he sets himself up in God's temple, proclaiming himself to be God.[z]
5Don't you remember that when I was with you I used to tell you these things? 6And
now you know what is holding him back, so that he may be revealed at the proper time.

[a] 12 Or *God and Lord, Jesus Christ* [b] 3 Some manuscripts *sin*

1:9 [m]2Th 2:8
1:10 [n]1Co 3:13 [o]Jn 17:10 [p]1Co 1:6
1:11 [q]ver 5 [r]1Th 1:3
1:12 [s]Php 2:9-11
2:1 [t]Mk 13:27; 1Th 4:15-17
2:2 [u]2Th 3:17 [v]1Co 1:8
2:3 [w]Eph 5:6-8 [x]Da 7:25; 8:25; 11:36; Rev 13:5,6
2:4 [y]1Co 8:5 [z]Isa 14:13,14; Eze 28:2

---

assured the hounded Thessalonian Christians of final and perfect justice. They were to refrain from taking any personal retribution (Ro 12:17–21; 1Th 5:15) for the many atrocities perpetrated against them (v. 4), but were to entrust themselves to the God who judges justly (Jer 17:10; Ac 17:31; Ro 2:6,11,16; 1Pe 2:23; Rev 22:12). See theological article "Hell" at Revelation 19. See also *WCF* 6.6; *WLC* 29.

1:10 on the day. The "day of the Lord" (2:2; 1Th 5:2). The final judgment of the ungodly will occur when Christ returns for his saints (see notes on 2:2; 1Th 5:2.

1:11 With this in mind. Realizing how important it was for the Thessalonians to endure their suffering, Paul told them of his prayers for them. He prayed that God would sustain them in their struggles. See *WLC* 191. **his calling.** See 1 Thessalonians 2:12, a passage that describes God as the caller who summons believers to his own kingdom and glory (2:14).

1:12 glorified in you, and you in him. Paul pointed to the interconnection between believers glorifying Christ and Christ glorifying believers. As believers endure, they bring much honor to God, but their endurance also leads to their glorification (see note on 2:14; see also theological article "The Glory of God" at Eze 1:28). **our God and the Lord Jesus Christ.** The Greek does not contain the second article ("the") and could therefore be translated, "our God and Lord, Jesus Christ" (see NIV text note), which would constitute a distinct use of the term "God" for Jesus Christ. Arguing against the latter translation is the relatively infrequent—though by no means nonexistent—application of the term "God" to Christ in the New Testament (cf. Ro 9:5; Tit 2:13; 2Pe 1:1). On the other hand, it should be noted that Paul habitually brought Christ and God the Father together into close unity in other formulae in these letters (e.g., 1:1–2; 2:16; 1Th 1:1; 3:11) and clearly assumed that the attributes of divinity belong to Christ. In either translation, the joint dignity of the Father and the Son is manifest. See theological article "Jesus Christ, God and Man" at John 1.

▪ **2:1—3:15** *Instructions.* At this point, Paul opened the main body of this epistle by instructing the Thessalonians on several important issues. He addressed questions about the return of Christ (2:1–17), called for prayer (3:1–5) and insisted that believers must avoid idleness based on a misapprehension of the gospel message (3:6–15).

▪ **2:1–17** *Return of Christ.* Paul countered false prophets who had announced that Christ had already returned.

2:1 Concerning the coming . . . and our being gathered to him. This refers to the "rapture" of the saints (see 1Th 4:17). Paul did not separate into multiple phases the gathering of believers to Christ, as some popular views on the second coming suggest. In this sentence Paul equated the time of Christ's coming and the rapture with the "day of the Lord." Elsewhere, the scene of all believers gathered before the Lord takes place "when he comes" (1Co 15:23; 1Th 2:19) and in "the day of the Lord" Jesus (1Th 5:2; cf. 1Co 1:7–8; 2Co 1:14; Php 2:16). Because the "rebellion" must come and the "man of lawlessness" (v. 3) must be revealed before the day of the Lord arrives, both signs must also occur before the rapture of the saints takes place. If the false teachers were claiming that the day of the Lord had already arrived (v. 2) and were thus anticipating the rapture at any moment, they could be proved wrong by the absence of these signs.

2:2 letter. It is possible that forged letters bearing Paul's name were already in existence, for pseudepigraphy was a common practice in the Mediterranean world at this time. In order to mark this letter as genuine, Paul closed it in his own handwriting (3:17–18). Paul's injunction was meant to ensure that no vehicle of instruction—even one purporting to come from him—should be heeded if it asserted that the day of the Lord had already come. See *WCF* 1.6. **day of the Lord.** In the Old Testament, the day of the Lord refers to the day on which God conclusively destroys his enemies and blesses his people (Joel 3:14–21). Although this day can be said to have begun in some sense during Christ's earthly ministry, the New Testament generally reserves the term for the day on which Christ will return, at which point this long anticipated event will be consummated in all its fullness.

2:3–4 See *WCF* 25.6.

2:3 the rebellion. This might refer to a falling away of many within the church (1Ti 4:1; 2Ti 3:1–9; Jude 17–19) or to a worldwide rebellion against God and order. This rebellion is connected to the "man of lawlessness." **man of lawlessness.** The Scriptures do not elaborate on this term, but it seems best to understand it as applying to an individual man who embodies wickedness chiefly in the sphere of religion (cf. 1Jn 2:22). He will draw away those already inclined against the true God (v. 10) and will ultimately commit the most foul sacrilege of thrusting himself upon humanity as its object of worship (v. 4). He will come by the power of Satan, as opposed to Christ, who came by the power of God (v. 9); he will work fraudulent wonders, in contrast to Christ, who worked true ones (v. 9; cf. Ac 2:22). Paul depicted this imposter as a base parody of the true Christ—as the antithesis of Christ. Although Paul did not himself use the term, "antichrist" (1Jn 2:18,22; 4:3) is a fitting synonym. The fate of this imposter is sealed; he will be destroyed at the coming of Christ.

2:4 exalt himself over everything that is called God. This description of the man of lawlessness echoes that of Daniel's little "horn" (Da 7:8,20,24; 8:9–12; cf. Da 11:31,36) and foreshadows John's description of the beast from the sea (Rev 13:1–8). See *WCF* 23.4. **he sets himself up in God's temple.** Some have concluded from this verse that the temple in Jerusalem, still standing when Paul wrote this letter but destroyed in A.D. 70, must be rebuilt prior to Christ's return in order to service the man of lawlessness, but this seems unlikely since Christ has done away with the Old Testament temple (Jn 2:19–22). Others have referred the word "temple" here to another of its New Testament meanings: the church (Eph 2:19–22; 1Pe 2:5). The reference may be hyperbolic. Just as the king of Babylon (Isa 14:13–14) aspired to set his throne in heaven (cf. the king of Tyre in Eze 28:2), so this man of lawlessness will boast that he is the possessor of God's heavenly sanctuary (Rev 13:6).

2:6 what is holding him back. Paul apparently believed that the Thessalonians understood the identity of the restrainer—perhaps he had taught them on this subject earlier. This restricting power is viewed by Paul as both impersonal in verse 6 ("what is holding him back") and as personal in verse 7 ("the one who now holds it

7For the secret power of lawlessness is already at work; but the one who now holds it
back will continue to do so till he is taken out of the way. 8And then the lawless one will
be revealed, whom the Lord Jesus will overthrow with the breath of his mouth[a] and destroy by the splendor of his coming. 9The coming of the lawless one will be in accordance
with the work of Satan displayed in all kinds of counterfeit miracles, signs and wonders,[b]
10and in every sort of evil that deceives those who are perishing.[c] They perish because
they refused to love the truth and so be saved. 11For this reason God sends them[d] a powerful delusion so that they will believe the lie 12and so that all will be condemned who
have not believed the truth but have delighted in wickedness.[e]

Stand Firm

13But we ought always to thank God for you, brothers loved by the Lord, because from
the beginning God chose you[a][f] to be saved[g] through the sanctifying work of the Spirit[h]
and through belief in the truth. 14He called you to this through our gospel, that you might
share in the glory of our Lord Jesus Christ. 15So then, brothers, stand firm[i] and hold to
the teachings[b] we passed on to you,[j] whether by word of mouth or by letter.
16May our Lord Jesus Christ himself and God our Father, who loved us[k] and by his
grace gave us eternal encouragement and good hope, 17encourage[l] your hearts and
strengthen[m] you in every good deed and word.

Request for Prayer

3 Finally, brothers,[n] pray for us[o] that the message of the Lord[p] may spread rapidly
and be honored, just as it was with you. 2And pray that we may be delivered from
wicked and evil men,[q] for not everyone has faith. 3But the Lord is faithful,[r] and he will
strengthen and protect you from the evil one.[s] 4We have confidence[t] in the Lord that you

2:8 [a]Isa 11:4; Rev 19:15
2:9 [b]Mt 24:24; Jn 4:48
2:10 [c]1Co 1:18
2:11 [d]Ro 1:28
2:12 [e]Ro 1:32
2:13 [f]Eph 1:4 [g]1Th 5:9 [h]1Pe 1:2
2:15 [i]1Co 16:13 [j]1Co 11:2
2:16 [k]Jn 3:16
2:17 [l]1Th 3:2 [m]2Th 3:3
3:1 [n]1Th 4:1 [o]1Th 5:25 [p]1Th 1:8
3:2 [q]Ro 15:31
3:3 [r]1Co 1:9 [s]Mt 5:37
3:4 [t]2Co 2:3

[a] *13* Some manuscripts *because God chose you as his firstfruits* [b] *15* Or *traditions*

back"). This variation may indicate that it is an institution that could be represented by a single person. A number of viable suggestions have been made regarding the identity of this restraining power: (1) the Roman state and its emperor; (2) the Jewish state and its high priest or another Jewish representative; (3) Seneca as the tutor of Nero, taking Nero to be the man of lawlessness; (4) the universal ministry of the gospel message and the Holy Spirit as its personal embodiment; (5) the universal ministry of the gospel message and its chief minister, Paul; or (6) an angelic being with institutions under his control (cf. Da 10:20 21). Others have suggested that the text and history are simply too vague to justify speculation. Regardless of the interpretation, God's will clearly lies behind the institution and person whose purpose it is to hold back the lawless one.

2:7 already at work. Although the man of lawlessness had not yet appeared, Paul did not want his readers left off guard, for the same satanic power that would ultimately spawn this individual was already present and exercising its influence. Paul's warning was similar to John's (1Jn 2:18). The spirit of lawlessness was at work in Paul's day, as it is in ours. That it is still being restrained is surely an urgent signal for the church to carry out its mission.

2:8–12 See *WCF* 5.6; 25.6; *WLC* 28,160; *WSC* 90; *BC* 13.

2:8 with the breath of his mouth. The imagery is from Isaiah 11:4, and it reappears in the description of the final end of the beast and his false prophet (Rev 19:15,21).

2:9 The coming of Christ is to be preceded by the "coming of the lawless one."

2:10–11 God sends them a powerful delusion. Divine sovereignty and human responsibility are both affirmed. God causes those who are perishing to have a "delusion" and "believe the lie." This language strongly asserts God's sovereignty over the wicked. But this judgment on God's part is a response to the guilt of the perishing: "They perish because they refused to love the truth and so be saved."

2:13–14 There is a wealth of theology packed into these two verses. Major elements in the Biblical doctrine of salvation—election, calling, faith, sanctification and glorification—are presented in their mutual relations. Note the harmonious working of all three persons of the Trinity: God the Father, choosing and calling; God the Son, accomplishing the Good News of the gospel and sharing his glory with his people; and God the Holy Spirit, imparting his sanctifying grace (1Pe 1:2). See *WCF* 10.1; *WLC* 13,67; *WSC* 31.

2:13 But. With this word Paul began to assure his readers of a contrast between them and those whom he had just mentioned in verses 11–12 (those who, because of their refusal to love the truth, would fall prey to deception). See *WCF* 3.6; 13.1; *WLC* 75; *WSC* 35. **God chose you.** The goal of their divine election was that they should "be saved" when Christ returns. The path that leads from election to final salvation is "the sanctifying work of the Spirit." See note on 1 Thessalonians 1:4.

2:14 He called you. On God's calling, see notes on 1:5 and 11 (see also 1Th 2:12; 1Ti 6:12). **to this.** That is, to salvation through sanctification by the Spirit and through believing the truth (v. 13). **through our gospel.** The gospel, which concerns God's Son (Ro 1:3), is the means employed by God to call sinners to glory. **share in the glory of our Lord Jesus Christ.** Another way of speaking about the salvation to which God has called believers (Ro 8:30; 1Th 2:12; 1Pe 5:10). Here Paul highlighted the fact that the blessings of salvation belong wholly to Christ and that believers partake in them only because Christ shares the blessings with them. When Christ returns, all who have followed him to the end will be exalted and glorified in the new heavens and the new earth (see theological article "The Ascension and Session of Jesus" at Heb 8).

2:15 hold to the teachings. The word translated "teachings" here and in 3:6 is, literally, "traditions." Paul used the vocabulary of "tradition" as the rabbis commonly did: to identify the body of teaching they taught their students. The Christian faith is built on the "traditions" or "teachings" of Christ and his apostles (1Co 11:2; 15:1ff.; Eph. 2:20). This terminology does not support the notion that church tradition is on an equal footing with Scripture. Paul passed on authoritative practical and doctrinal traditions, both orally and by letter (Ro 6:17; 1Co 11:2,23; 15:3; 2Ti 1:13), but only his written words have been preserved for us in Scripture. Modern claims that some still possess Paul's authoritative oral tradition are insubstantial and unsubstantiated. **letter.** The letter in view is probably 1 Thessalonians.

2:16–17 See *WLC* 191.

■ **3:1–5** *Request for Prayer.* Paul's encouragement to the Thessalonians led him to request the encouragement of prayer for himself and for others who preached the gospel.

3:1–2 pray for us. Paul faced an almost constant threat of physical danger during his years of ministry. This text (along with Ro 15:30–31; 2Co 1:11; Php 1:19) makes clear how much he relied on the prayers of God's people for the continuation of his ministry and for his own survival.

3:1 See *WLC* 190,191; *WSC* 102.

3:3 faithful. Contrasting with the faithlessness of men mentioned in the previous verse is the steadfast faithfulness of the unchanging God (Mal 3:6; 1Co 1:9; 10:13; 2Co 1:18; Jas 1:17). See *WCF* 17.2; *HC* 1.

are doing and will continue to do the things we command. **5** May the Lord direct your
hearts[u] into God's love and Christ's perseverance.

Warning Against Idleness

6 In the name of the Lord Jesus Christ,[v] we command you, brothers, to keep away
from[w] every brother who is idle[x] and does not live according to the teaching[a] you received from us.[y] **7** For you yourselves know how you ought to follow our example.[z] We
were not idle when we were with you, **8** nor did we eat anyone's food without paying for
it. On the contrary, we worked[a] night and day, laboring and toiling so that we would not
be a burden to any of you. **9** We did this, not because we do not have the right to such
help,[b] but in order to make ourselves a model for you to follow.[c] **10** For even when we
were with you,[d] we gave you this rule: "If a man will not work,[e] he shall not eat."
11 We hear that some among you are idle. They are not busy; they are busybodies.[f]
12 Such people we command and urge in the Lord Jesus Christ[g] to settle down and earn
the bread they eat.[h] **13** And as for you, brothers, never tire of doing what is right.[i]
14 If anyone does not obey our instruction in this letter, take special note of him. Do
not associate with him,[j] in order that he may feel ashamed. **15** Yet do not regard him as
an enemy, but warn him as a brother.[k]

Final Greetings

16 Now may the Lord of peace[l] himself give you peace at all times and in every way.
The Lord be with all of you.[m]
17 I, Paul, write this greeting in my own hand,[n] which is the distinguishing mark in all
my letters. This is how I write.
18 The grace of our Lord Jesus Christ be with you all.[o]

a *6* Or *tradition*

3:5 [u]1Ch 29:18
3:6 [v]1Co 5:4 [w]Ro 16:17 [x]ver 7, 11 [y]1Co 11:2
3:7 [z]1Co 4:16
3:8 [a]Ac 18:3; Eph 4:28
3:9 [b]1Co 9:4-14 [c]ver 7
3:10 [d]1Th 3:4 [e]1Th 4:11
3:11 [f]ver 6,7; 1Ti 5:13
3:12 [g]1Th 4:1 [h]1Th 4:11; Eph 4:28
3:13 [i]Gal 6:9
3:14 [j]ver 6
3:15 [k]Gal 6:1; 1Th 5:14
3:16 [l]Ro 15:33 [m]Ru 2:4
3:17 [n]1Co 16:21
3:18 [o]Ro 16:20

3:5 God's love and Christ's perseverance. Hearts should journey to these safe spiritual harbors of meditation; it is a journey directed by the Lord.

■ **3:6–15** *Importance of Labor.* Paul took firm measures against the ongoing problem of idleness and its consequences (v. 10; cf. 1Th 4:11). He regarded their offense as serious but still treated the offenders as brothers.

3:6 keep away. One understanding of this phrase is that Paul may have had in mind our Lord's instructions on church discipline recorded in Matthew 18:15–17. (Paul gave similar charges in 3:14–15; Ro 16:17; 1Co 5:9–13; 2Ti 3:1–5; Tit 3:10–11.) Alternatively, the intent of his instruction may simply have been to avoid associating with these people during their idleness in order to avoid the appearance of condoning it. See *WCF* 29.8; 30.4; *BC* 29.

3:9 the right to such help. Paul consistently taught that those who labor in the gospel deserve to be paid (1Ti 5:17–18). The apostle normally accepted support for his ministry, but when he feared his motives would be called into question or when, as in Thessalonica, a strong example needed to be set for those disinclined to work, he relinquished his right and refused any remuneration (see 1Co 9:3–18).

3:10 This verse may indicate that the problem of idleness began to surface before Paul and his companions had left the city. Even then they had felt it necessary to prod the disorderly to occupy themselves profitably. See *WLC* 135.

3:11–12 See *WLC* 135,193.

3:11 not busy; they are busybodies. The NIV translation well captures the play on words in the Greek. Without their own business to attend to, the idlers meddled in the business of others. See *WLC* 142.

3:14–15 See *WCF* 29.8; 30.4; *HC* 85.

3:14 Do not associate with him. See note on 3:6. See also *BC* 29; *WCF* 20.4. **feel ashamed.** Arousing the feeling of shame was not designed to punish but to elicit repentance and, ultimately, restoration of the church's fellowship.

■ **3:16–18** *Closing Blessing and Authentication.* Paul closed with a benediction and added a personally handwritten message to authenticate his epistle.

3:16 Lord of peace. This title was particularly important for the Thessalonians as they faced persecution. Jesus was the source of the peace within their hearts as they lived in this world (Php 4:7; Col 3:15). Moreover, he was their hope for a future world in which peace would replace all troubles, both within and without (Ro 14:17).

3:17 in my own hand. Although Paul made use of secretaries in the writing of his letters, he often penned a final greeting or benediction in his own hand. He called attention to this practice as an additional sign of authenticity to counter forgeries that had already appeared in Thessalonica or might appear there in the future (see also 1Co 16:21; Gal 6:11; Col 4:18; Phm 19). By doing so, Paul reminded his readers of his apostolic authority, which was never to be contradicted in the church (see 1Co 14:37).

1 TIMOTHY

Introduction

Overview

Author: The apostle Paul

Purpose: To guide Timothy as he opposed false teachers in Ephesus

Date: A.D. 62 64

Key Truths:

- False teaching in the church must be resisted.
- Legalistic teachings lead people away from the true gospel.
- Worship and church authority must be carefully ordered.
- Various groups within the church have special needs.
- Love for money has no place in the ministry of the gospel.

Author

According to the salutations of the Pastoral Epistles (1 and 2 Timothy and Titus), the apostle Paul is their author. In modern times, however, some interpreters have argued that Paul himself did not compose these letters but that someone else wrote under Paul's name, a practice known as pseudepigraphy. Arguments against Paul's authorship are advanced on several grounds. Some of the more significant include: (1) denials of early church knowledge of these letters; (2) the close correspondence between these letters and the Christian writings of the early second century; (3) different manners of dealing with heresy than found in Paul's other letters; (4) the difficulty of locating these letters in the known circumstances of Paul's life; (5) the differences in writing styles and vocabulary between these letters and Paul's other epistles.

In response to these objections to Paul's authorship it should be noted that Paul himself urged his readers to reject the practice of pseudepigraphy as deceptive forgery (2Th 2:2–3)—even the Pastoral Epistles contain warnings about deceivers (1Ti 4:1–2; 2Ti 3:13; Tit 1:10). This makes it unlikely that an early Christian attempt to honor Paul or to make use of his authority in order to combat heresy would have employed pseudepigraphy. Moreover, the early church refused to receive as canonical all of the gospels, apocryphal writings and acts that they knew to be pseudonymous, and there is no clear evidence that any pseudonymous epistles were ever produced in the early centuries of the church. In recorded instances in which pseudonymous writings were discovered in the early church, the writings were sometimes tolerated if their content was considered harmless, but never accorded canonical status. They were always condemned if found to teach error.

That the Pastoral Epistles were included in early lists of canonical books and ultimately affirmed as genuine strongly indicates that the early church firmly believed the Pastoral Epistles to be genuine. Some scholars, however, argue that the early church cannot be proven to have known these epistles. For example, they take issue with Polycarp's use of 1 Timothy in the *Epistle of Polycarp to the Philippians*, chapter 4, which appears to quote 1 Timothy 6:7 ("We brought nothing into the world, and we can take nothing out of it") and 10 ("The love of money is a root of all kinds of evil"). Although these formulaic statements did not originate with Paul, there is sufficient data to indicate that Polycarp's use of them depended on 1 Timothy. Specifically, both Paul and Polycarp used both these statements in close proximity to one another (within three verses in 1 Timothy, and in consecutive sentences in Polycarp's *Epistle to the Philippians*), and both included them in the context of discussing righteousness and obedience to God. Interestingly, some critical scholars have suggested that Polycarp himself wrote the Pastoral Epistles, demonstrating how close a correspondence there is between Polycarp's teaching and the content of the Pastoral Epistles. That Paul's authorship of the Pastoral Epistles has been denied both on the basis that Polycarp had no knowledge of them and on the basis that Polycarp had full knowledge of them as their author calls into serious question the means and standards by which Pauline authorship has been denied.

Similarly insubstantial are the objections to Paul's authorship based on the Pastoral Epistles' linguistic style (which may be a bit higher than that of Paul's earlier writings), approach to heresy (which appears less specific than in his earlier writings) and lack of relationship to known facts about Paul's life. Recent studies have demonstrated that the vocabulary, style and theology of the Pastoral Epistles are quite compatible with the rest of Paul's writings, and indeed that the Pastoral Epistles vary from one another as much as they vary from Paul's other writings. Paul's language and approach to dealing with heresy in these letters may differ slightly from his earlier writings, but this should not be surprising given that the Pastoral Epistles were written: (1) later in Paul's life, (2) to address different problems and (3) to individuals who were close associates of Paul rather than to churches. It should not be thought unusual that Paul would write differently at various stages in his ministry, or that he preferred one style of communication to churches and another to individuals. Moreover, Paul's less specific treatment of heresy in these letters may simply indicate that he knew that Timothy and Titus were already aware of the specifics. Finally, known facts about Paul's life at this stage are few and are not directly in conflict with any information in the Pastoral Epistles.

Time and Place of Writing

Some information in the Pastoral Epistles has led to the suggestion that these letters were written during what may have been Paul's fourth missionary journey. Acts ends not with Paul's death, but with his house arrest in Rome (Ac 28:16,30–31). While the late-first-century writing *1 Clement* suggests that Paul was martyred in Rome, it does not link his martyrdom with the imprisonment recorded in Acts 28. The fourth-century church historian Eusebius preserved a tradition that Paul was released from that imprisonment, continued his missionary labors and was martyred by Nero on his second visit to Rome. This tradition is supported by Philippians and Philemon, which, if they were written during the Roman imprisonment recorded in Acts 28, provide evidence that Paul expected to be released (Php 1:25–26; Phm 22), as well as by the Pastorals themselves. A fourth missionary journey and a second imprisonment after the one recorded in Acts 28 combine to form the most probable setting for the Pastorals.

If there were two imprisonments in Rome, Paul was released from his first around A.D. 62. According to later tradition he was martyred by Nero, who died in A.D. 68. Under this scenario, 1 Timothy, composed while Paul was still in the midst of his fourth missionary journey, was probably written during the earlier part of this period, between A.D. 62 and 64.

Paul may have written from Macedonia (1:3) in northern Greece.

Original Audience

First and Second Timothy were written to the man whose name they bear. Timothy was a native of Lystra, a Roman colony in the province of Galatia. His father was a Gentile and his mother a Jew (Ac 16:1). Little is known about his father, who apparently never became a Christian, but his mother and grandmother were probably converted to Christianity as a result of Paul's visit to Lystra on his first missionary journey (2Ti 1:5). Timothy had from his childhood been instructed in the Jewish Scriptures (2Ti 3:14–15), and these two women were undoubtedly influential in Timothy's own conversion to Christianity.

When Paul returned to Lystra on his second missionary journey, some of the Christians called his attention to a young believer named Timothy, and Paul decided to take him along on his journey (Ac 16:1–3). Since Paul would be evangelizing Jews, he circumcised Timothy according to Jewish custom (Ac 16:3). Paul and the elders of the church also laid their hands upon Timothy to set him apart and equip him for ministry (1:18; 4:14).

Timothy traveled with Paul throughout most of Paul's second and third missionary journeys (Ac 17:14–15; 18:5; 19:22; 20:4–6), and apparently for part of his fourth. He seems to have become Paul's protégé, and Paul spoke of himself as Timothy's "father" (Php 2:22) and of Timothy as his "son" (1:2,18; 1Co 4:17; 2Ti 1:2; 2:1). As Paul's coworker, Timothy served as his representative in the churches of Thessalonica (1Th 3:2,6), Corinth (1Co 4:17; 16:10), Philippi (Php 2:19,23) and Ephesus (1Ti 1:3).

If Timothy had a fault, it was that he was burdened by what Paul characterized as a "spirit of timidity" (2Ti 1:7). Paul felt it necessary to ask the church in Corinth to receive Timothy in a manner that would set him at ease (1Co 16:10–11). In his letters to Timothy, Paul exhorted him not to let anyone despise him on account of his youth (4:12), not to neglect the spiritual gift that he had received (4:14) and not to be ashamed to speak out boldly for the gospel (2Ti 1:8).

Apart from the enigmatic statement in Hebrews 13:23 that Timothy had been "released" (presumably from prison), little is known about what happened to Timothy after the writing of 2 Timothy.

Purpose and Distinctives

Paul had left Timothy in Ephesus to care for the church as his special representative (1:3), and he wrote this letter to help Timothy deal with a variety of doctrinal issues that were raised by false teachers there. Paul had established the Ephesian church early on his third missionary journey, spending about three years there (Ac 19; 20:31). At the close of that journey he had warned the Ephesian elders that false teachers, some coming from the leadership itself, would plague the church (Ac 20:29–30). This epistle indicates that his prediction had come true (1:6,19; 4:1–2; 6:3–5,10,21).

Paul described the false teaching in Ephesus as coming from within the church itself (1:6,19; 4:1; 6:10, 21; 2Ti 2:18; 4:4). It was characterized by a concern with myths (1:4; 4:7; 2Ti 4:4), genealogies (1:4), quarrels about words (6:4; 2Ti 2:14,23), controversies (1:4; 6:4), knowledge (6:20), meaningless talk (1:6) and godless chatter (6:20; 2Ti 2:16). The false doctrines included prohibitions against marriage and certain foods (4:3), as well as the belief that the resurrection had already taken place (2Ti 2:18). The false teachers wrongly interpreted Jewish law (1:7) and accordingly placed restrictions on prayer (2:1–7).

Specific leaders of the movement included Hymenaeus (1:20; 2Ti 2:17), Alexander (1:20) and Philetus (2Ti 2:17). Those who sought leadership positions in the movement apparently did so for financial gain (6:5,10). The false teachers had been divisive (6:4–5) and seem to have been particularly effective in deceiving women (2:14; 2Ti 3:6–7).

A number of these features—the specific doctrinal teachings, the interest in myths and genealogies and the concern for "knowledge" (the Greek word is *gnosis*)—suggest that the false teaching in Ephesus may have been an incipient form of Gnosticism, a heretical movement that became a strong competitor to the developing orthodox church in the second and third centuries. However, some of the more characteristic aspects of later Gnosticism are lacking here, and some assert that the movement in Ephesus can be explained in terms of Jewish and Hellenistic influences. These two suggestions need not be seen as contradictory, for Gnosticism itself was a product of both Jewish and Hellenistic ideas. But in spite of all that Paul said about the false teaching in Ephesus, its precise nature remains elusive.

First Timothy is noteworthy for its interest in church organization. It provides the longest description in the New Testament regarding the qualifications for being an overseer/elder (3:2–7). It also provides evidence for a distinction between those elders who primarily rule and those who primarily teach (5:17). It gives comments about supporting and rebuking elders (5:17–20) and includes the only explicit description in the New Testament of the qualifications for deacons (3:8–13). Paul's specific directives to Timothy also contain much practical advice on how a church leader is to function.

This epistle is also characterized by its emphasis on sound doctrine (1:9–11; 3:9; 4:6; 6:3–4), and it contains two theological meditations on the salvation God has accomplished in Jesus Christ (1:13–16; 2:3–6). These include affirmations of salvation by grace (1:13–16), Christ as the one mediator between God and humanity (2:5) and the substitutionary atonement of Christ (2:6). First Timothy also includes a meditation on the work of Christ that affirms his incarnation, resurrection and ascension (3:16), an anticipation of the second coming of Christ (6:14), a marvelous doxology (6:15–16) and evidence of the expansion of the concept of "Scripture" beyond the Old Testament to include elements of Christian tradition (5:18).

Also distinctive about 1 Timothy are its comments about women (2:9–15), including a lengthy section on proper care for widows in the church (5:3–16), and the background information it provides about Timothy, including probable references to both his baptism (6:12) and his ordination (1:18; 4:14).

Outline

I. Salutation (1:1–2)	*Paul identified himself as the author and Timothy as the main recipient of his letter.*
II. False Teaching and the Law (1:3–20) A. False Teaching (1:3–7) B. Purpose of the Law (1:8–11) C. Timothy's Responsibility (1:12–20)	*Paul challenged the legalism of the false teachers by insisting that the law was designed to condemn sinners, not followers of Christ.*
III. Conduct in the Church (2:1—3:16) A. Prayer and Worship (2:1–15) 1. Prayer for All (2:1–7) 2. Men in Worship (2:8) 3. Women in Worship (2:9–15) B. Church Leadership (3:1–13) 1. Overseers/Elders (3:1–7) 2. Deacons (3:8–13) C. Timothy's Responsibility (3:14–16)	*Paul challenged the disharmony of the false teachers by summarizing his views on prayer, modesty in worship and church leadership.*
IV. False Teaching and Asceticism (4:1—5:2) A. False Teaching (4:1–5) B. Timothy's Responsibility (4:6—5:2)	*Paul challenged the legalistic asceticism of the false teachers by explaining how all things were created for our enjoyment.*
V. Instructions Regarding Specific Groups (5:3—6:2) A. Ministering to Widows (5:3–16) B. Ministering to Elders (5:17–25) C. Ministering to Slaves (6:1–2)	*Paul explained how Timothy was to minister to different groups in the church that had become victims of the false teachers.*
VI. False Teaching and Financial Gain (6:3–19) A. False Teaching (6:3–10) B. Timothy's Responsibility (6:11–19)	*Paul challenged the financial motives of the false teachers by warning about the dangers of greed and the love of money.*
VII. Final Exhortations (6:20–21)	*Paul closed his letter with several final exhortations to Timothy.*

1:1 [a]Tit 1:3 [b]Col 1:27 **1** Paul, an apostle of Christ Jesus by the command of God[a] our Savior and of Christ
Jesus our hope,[b]
1:2 [c]Ac 16:1 [d]2Ti 1:2; Tit 1:4 2 To Timothy[c] my true son[d] in the faith:

Grace, mercy and peace from God the Father and Christ Jesus our Lord.

Warning Against False Teachers of the Law

1:3 [e]Ac 18:19 [f]Gal 1:6,7 3 As I urged you when I went into Macedonia, stay there in Ephesus[e] so that you may
1:4 command certain men not to teach false doctrines[f] any longer 4 nor to devote themselves
[g]1Ti 4:7; Tit 1:14 to myths[g] and endless genealogies. These promote controversies[h] rather than God's
[h]1Ti 6:4 work—which is by faith. 5 The goal of this command is love, which comes from a pure
1:5 [i]2Ti 2:22 [j]2Ti 1:5 heart[i] and a good conscience and a sincere faith.[j] 6 Some have wandered away from
these and turned to meaningless talk. 7 They want to be teachers of the law, but they do
not know what they are talking about or what they so confidently affirm.
1:8 [k]Ro 7:12 8 We know that the law is good[k] if one uses it properly. 9 We also know that law[a] is
1:9 made not for the righteous but for lawbreakers and rebels,[l] the ungodly and sinful, the
[l]Gal 3:19 unholy and irreligious; for those who kill their fathers or mothers, for murderers, 10 for
1:10 adulterers and perverts, for slave traders and liars and perjurers—and for whatever else
[m]2Ti 4:3; Tit 1:9 is contrary to the sound doctrine[m] 11 that conforms to the glorious gospel of the blessed
1:11 [n]Gal 2:7 God, which he entrusted to me.[n]

The Lord's Grace to Paul

1:12 [o]Php 4:13 12 I thank Christ Jesus our Lord, who has given me strength,[o] that he considered me
1:13 faithful, appointing me to his service. 13 Even though I was once a blasphemer and a per-
[p]Ac 8:3 secutor[p] and a violent man, I was shown mercy because I acted in ignorance and unbe-

[a] 9 Or *that the law*

■ **1:1–2** *Salutation.* Paul began this epistle in his usual fashion, identifying both himself and the recipient of the letter and pronouncing a blessing.

1:1 apostle of Christ Jesus. One sent out as an official representative of Christ. Paul commonly used this phrase as a self-designation in the openings of his letters. **God our Savior.** A frequent Scriptural title for God (2:3; 4:10; Tit 1:3; 2:10; 3:4). **Christ Jesus our hope.** Jesus is the basis for Christian hope, because he is the mediator of the covenant of grace (2:5).

1:2 true son. Or "genuine son" (cf. Tit 1:4). Paul viewed Timothy as his spiritual son (v. 18; 1Co 4:17; Php 2:22; 2Ti 1:2; 2:1; see "Introduction: Original Audience"). **Grace, mercy and peace.** Paul commonly substituted "grace" for the more standard salutation "greetings" (cf. Jas 1:1). He typically added the Jewish greeting "peace," meaning "health, wholeness of life." Here and in 2 Timothy 1:2 he also added "mercy."

■ **1:3–20** *False Teaching and the Law.* Paul began the body of this letter by addressing one dimension of false teaching that had risen in the church in Ephesus. Here he dealt with misconceptions about the Law of Moses; elsewhere he focused on asceticism (4:1—5:2) and financial gain (6:3–19). His discussion of the law here divides into three main parts: the false teaching itself (vv. 3–7), his corrective (vv. 8–11) and his exhortation for Timothy to deal with the false teaching (vv. 12–20).

■ **1:3–7** *False Teaching.* The false teaching was based on misinterpretation of the law and improper speculation.

1:3 not to teach false doctrines. The conflict in Ephesus centered on proper teaching (vv. 9–11; 4:1–2; 6:3–5; 2Ti 2:18). See *BC* 7.

1:4 myths. See 4:7; 2 Timothy 4:4. In Titus 1:14 Paul spoke of "Jewish myths," perhaps referring to the kinds of legends about Old Testament figures that are found in many of the non-canonical Jewish writings. **endless genealogies.** Perhaps a reference to an early form of the detailed speculations (often combined with Jewish myths) that later developed in Gnosticism concerning the origins of the world and the innumerable spiritual beings supposedly involved in creation (Tit 3:9). See *WLC* 113.

1:5 love. Paul insisted that this false teaching be corrected because of his love and concern for the people of God. See *WLC* 147; *WSC* 80; *BC* 24.

1:6–7 See *WLC* 113.

1:7 teachers of the law. These false teachers wanted to be known as experts in the Law of Moses. Paul did not forbid, but rather encouraged, a knowledge of the Mosaic Law (2Ti 3:14–17). The problem was that these false teachers did not know "what they [were] talking about"; that is, they did not interpret the law correctly. Paul explained their error in the verses that follow.

■ **1:8–11** *Purpose of the Law.* Paul's comment about the false teachers led him into a digression on the purpose of the law.

1:8 the law is good. Like Jesus himself (Mt 5:17ff.), Paul believed that the Mosaic Law in itself was a wonderful gift from God (see Ro 7:12–13,16). Yet this good gift could be abused and turned into a curse.

1:9–10 See *WLC* 96.

1:9 not for the righteous but for lawbreakers. Paul had in mind a particular use of the law. Here he presented the law as a burden—the burden of being "under the law" (Ro 2:12), striving to reach its impossible standard of perfection, which reveals sin and makes clear one's need for Christ. Elsewhere Paul made it clear that the moral standards of the Mosaic Law played an important role in guiding true believers in the ways of righteous living (see theological article "The Three Uses of the Law" at Ps 119). Apparently some false teachers in Ephesus promoted legalistic outlooks. Paul insisted that law's condemnation had ended for those who are in Christ. See *WLC* 94.

1:10 whatever else is contrary to the sound doctrine. Or "sound teaching," a running theme throughout the Pastoral Epistles (3:9; 4:6; 6:3; 2Ti 1:13–14; 2:2; 4:3; Tit 1:9,13; 2:1–2). Note that the breaking of the law (vv. 8–10) is equated with being contrary to the apostle's sound doctrine, which he also defined as the gospel (v. 11). Paul did not contrast the moral standards of the law with his own moral standards as an apostle of the gospel. See *WLC* 142.

1:11 that conforms to the glorious gospel. The Good News of what God has done in Christ is the standard by which doctrine, as well as one's understanding of the law, is judged to be sound.

■ **1:12–20** *Timothy's Responsibility.* After making his comments in opposition to false teaching about the law, Paul encouraged Timothy to resist this false teaching as he ministered in Ephesus. He introduced Timothy's responsibility by recalling his own experience of God's mercy and based his exhortation on personal experience.

1:12–14 In contrast to the legalistic teachers in Ephesus, Paul testified that divine mercy, not futile attempts to obey the law in human strength, had brought him salvation and sustained his Christian service. **a blasphemer and a persecutor and a violent man.** This refers to Paul's preconversion opposition to the church and to Christ (Ac 8:3; 9:1–5; 22:4–5; 26:9–11; Gal 1:13; Php 3:6). **because I acted in ignorance and unbelief.** Paul did not mean that his ignorance and unbelief were the grounds of God's mercy. God granted Paul what he needed, not what he deserved (cf. Ac 3:17–20). See *WCF* 15.5; *BC* 7.

lief.[q] 14 The grace of our Lord was poured out on me abundantly,[r] along with the faith
and love that are in Christ Jesus.[s]
15 Here is a trustworthy saying[t] that deserves full acceptance: Christ Jesus came into
the world to save sinners—of whom I am the worst. 16 But for that very reason I was
shown mercy[u] so that in me, the worst of sinners, Christ Jesus might display his unlimited patience as an example for those who would believe on him and receive eternal life.
17 Now to the King[v] eternal, immortal, invisible,[w] the only God, be honor and glory for
ever and ever. Amen.[x]
18 Timothy, my son, I give you this instruction in keeping with the prophecies once
made about you,[y] so that by following them you may fight the good fight,[z] 19 holding on
to faith and a good conscience. Some have rejected these and so have shipwrecked their
faith.[a] 20 Among them are Hymenaeus[b] and Alexander,[c] whom I have handed over to Satan[d] to be taught not to blaspheme.

Instructions on Worship

2 I urge, then, first of all, that requests, prayers, intercession and thanksgiving be
made for everyone— 2 for kings and all those in authority,[e] that we may live peaceful and quiet lives in all godliness and holiness. 3 This is good, and pleases God our Savior, 4 who wants[f] all men[g] to be saved and to come to a knowledge of the truth.[h] 5 For
there is one God[i] and one mediator[j] between God and men, the man Christ Jesus, 6 who
gave himself as a ransom for all men—the testimony[k] given in its proper time.[l] 7 And for

1:13 [q]Ac 26:9
1:14 [r]Ro 5:20 [s]2Ti 1:13
1:15 [t]1Ti 3:1; 2Ti 2:11; Tit 3:8
1:16 [u]ver 13
1:17 [v]Rev 15:3 [w]Col 1:15 [x]Ro 11:36
1:18 [y]1Ti 4:14 [z]2Ti 2:3
1:19 [a]1Ti 6:21
1:20 [b]2Ti 2:17 [c]2Ti 4:14 [d]1Co 5:5
2:2 [e]Ezr 6:10; Ro 13:1
2:4 [f]Eze 18:23,32 [g]Tit 2:11 [h]2Ti 2:25
2:5 [i]Ro 3:29,30 [j]Gal 3:20
2:6 [k]1Co 1:6 [l]1Ti 6:15

1:15 Here is a trustworthy saying that deserves full acceptance. This expression calls attention to the fact that Paul is about to make an important point. In the New Testament the expression is found only in the Pastoral Epistles (3:1; 4:9; 2Ti 2:11; Tit 3:8). **I am the worst.** Paul reflected not only on his pre-Christian persecution of the church (v. 12, Ac 8:1, 9:1–2,13; 1Co 15:9–10) but also on the depth of sin and opposition to God from which God had saved him. Paul is a prime example of pure grace. Although he offered his pre-Christian sin as evidence of his sinfulness (v. 13), Paul characterized himself as the "worst" of sinners in the present tense. Without the restraint and influence of the Holy Spirit, he would have returned to the same kinds of atrocities that he had performed before his conversion. This self-evaluation stood in contrast with the legalistic teachers who apparently claimed the ability to attain righteousness through their own obedience to the law. See *WCF* 15.5; *BC* 21.

1:16 worst of sinners. See note on verse 15. **unlimited patience.** Christ displayed unending patience toward Paul, both before and after his conversion. The legalistic pattern brought by the false teachers was contrary to the reality of the Christian life, which depends on the patience of Christ. **eternal life.** That which God grants to all who believe in Christ; not just everlasting life, but life in all its fullness (4:8; 6:12,19; Jn 10:10,28; 2Ti 1:1,10; Tit 1:2; 3:7).

1:17 Now to the King. Acknowledging how much Christ had done for him led Paul into an outburst of praise. See *WCF* 2.1.

1:18–20 Paul applied his own experience of God's grace to the theme of legalism (vv. 3–7). He called Timothy to faithfulness to Christ, especially in contrast to two members (perhaps leaders) of the church in Ephesus who had "shipwrecked their faith" (v. 19). See *HC* 32.

1:18 the prophecies once made about you. This refers to an event (cf. 4:14; 2Ti 1:6ff.) in which a group of elders, along with Paul, had laid hands on Timothy (perhaps when Timothy was set apart for ministry). At that time Timothy received a spiritual gift, along with a word of prophecy anointing him to service (cf. Ac 13:1–3).

1:20 Hymenaeus and Alexander. The naming of these two individuals raises the question of whether they may have been leaders in the church. Hymenaeus is later mentioned as one who had "wandered away from the truth" (2Ti 2:17–18). The relationship, if any, between the Alexander in this verse, the Alexander mentioned in Acts 19:33–34 and the Alexander mentioned in 2 Timothy 4:14–15 is unclear. It is likely that these men were proponents of the false legalistic teaching that Timothy was to oppose. **I have handed over to Satan.** This is probably a reference to placing these two individuals outside the fellowship of the church and, hence, back into the world—the domain of Satan (Jn 12:31; 14:30; 16:11; 2Co 4:4; Eph 2:2). Paul used a similar expression in 1 Corinthians 5:5 (cf. Mt 18:17). **to be taught not to blaspheme.** The purpose of this excommunication was disciplinary—that the two would recognize their errors and repent (2Ti 2:25–26; Tit 3:10). "Blaspheme" implies speech and may point to false teaching. See *WCF* 30.3; *BC* 32.

■ 2:1–3:16 *Conduct in the Church.* Paul continued to instruct Timothy on his responsibilities in Ephesus by touching on Christian life within the church community. It is likely that he continued to address matters raised by false teachers. He was particularly concerned with three matters: how prayer and worship were to be conducted (2:1–15), the qualifications of church leaders (3:1–13) and Timothy's responsibilities (3:14–16).

■ 2:1–15 *Prayer and Worship.* Paul's first concern in this section was the manner in which prayer and worship were to be offered. Apparently some confusion had arisen in the church regarding these matters. His discussion divides into three sections: offering prayer for all people (vv. 1–7), the prayers of men (v. 8) and the prayers of women (vv. 9–15).

■ 2:1–7 *Prayer for All.* Paul began with encouragement that believers offer prayers for various authorities for the sake of the gospel. This led him into an affirmation of God's act of redemption in Christ and a digression on his own call as the Apostle to the Gentiles.

2:1–2 See *WCF* 20.4; 21.4; 23.2; 23.4; 31.2; *WLC* 127,183,191; *WSC* 100; *BC* 36.

2:1 everyone. In response to the narrow perspective of the false teachers (v. 7; cf. 1:7), Paul addressed the issue of those for whom Christians should pray. As can be seen from the next expression ("for kings and all those in authority"), this does not mean for "every human being" but rather for "all types of people," whatever their station in life. See *HC* 103.

2:4 who wants all men to be saved. This does not mean that God sovereignly wills every human being to be saved. It may refer to God's general benevolence in that he takes no delight in the death of the wicked, or it may mean that God wills all types of people (see note on v. 1) to be saved (i.e., God does not exclude certain types of people from election to salvation). See theological article "The Will of God" at Ezekiel 18.

2:5–6 See *WCF* 11.3; *WLC* 71; *WSC* 21; *HC* 34,36.

2:5 there is one God. This is a fundamental affirmation of the Jewish religion (Dt 6:4; cf. Ro 3:30; 1Co 8:6; Gal 3:20; Eph 4:6). It is not the case that there is one God for the Jews and another for Gentiles; there is only one God for all types of people. **one mediator between God and men.** There is One who arbitrates between God and man and reconciles them. **the man Christ Jesus.** The full humanity of Christ is essential to his serving as mediator of the covenant of grace (Heb 2:9–18). See *WCF* 8.1; 8.2; 21.2; *WLC* 36,181; *BC* 1,18,26; *HC* 18,29.

2:6 who gave himself as a ransom. By his death on the cross, Christ paid the price necessary to free people from their sins (Mt 20:28; Mk 10:45; Tit 2:14; 1Pe 1:18–19); thus, he is the "one mediator" (v. 5). **all men.** That is, "all types of men" (see notes on vv. 1,4). Salvation is not limited to a particular ethnic group or gender or to any other subsection of humanity. That "all" is commonly used to mean "all types" can be seen clearly in 6:10, where the same Greek word is translated "all kinds." Although the value of Christ's death is infinite, his sacrifice on the cross was fully effective in winning the salvation of the elect only (see theological article "Definite Atonement" at Jn 10). See *WCF* 8.1; 11.4; *BC* 23.

2:7 [m]2Ti 1:11 [n]Ac 9:15; Eph 3:7,8
2:8 [o]Ps 134:2; Lk 24:50
2:9 [p]1Pe 3:3
2:11 [q]1Co 14:34

this purpose I was appointed a herald and an apostle—I am telling the truth, I am not
lying—and a teacher[m] of the true faith to the Gentiles.[n]
8 I want men everywhere to lift up holy hands[o] in prayer, without anger or disputing.
9 I also want women to dress modestly, with decency and propriety, not with braided hair or gold or pearls or expensive clothes,[p] 10 but with good deeds, appropriate for
women who profess to worship God.
11 A woman should learn in quietness and full submission.[q] 12 I do not permit a wom-

---

2:7 herald. Or "preacher" (2Ti 1:11). **I am telling the truth, I am not lying.** An odd statement to make to a close friend, but Paul intended for the letter to be read to the whole church (see note on 6:21). **the true faith to the Gentiles.** The false teachers with their emphasis on the law had presumably questioned Paul's call and mission. Paul insisted that God had called him for the purpose of bringing the faith of Israel to the Gentiles. His call to the Gentiles supported his exhortation for the church to pray on behalf of all kinds of people.

■ **2:8** *Men in Worship.* It is likely that Paul continued to focus on prayer and worship in the context of the legalistic false teachers and their views on Gentiles. Apparently controversy and division had grown in the church over these matters, so Paul addressed them by means of instruction on worship.

2:8 men. Here the Greek term translated "men" is gender specific (it may also mean "husbands"), in distinction from women (or "wives") in verses 9–15. Paul had in mind male believers. Paul assumed in 1 Corinthians 11:5 that women would also pray when the church met for worship. **everywhere.** Literally, "in every place." This probably refers to corporate worship. **lift up holy hands.** On this manner of prayer, see Psalms 63:4 and 141:2. **without anger or disputing.** Paul did not mandate a particular physical posture for prayer but assumed that lifting hands would be a part of both worship and prayer. His main interest was to encourage a proper attitude (1:5). Knowing that the men in Ephesus would want to pray and worship, Paul insisted that they do so without the quarreling engaged in by the false teachers. From the preceding context (vv.1–7), it appears that at least one of the central controversies that Paul addressed here was the relationship of Gentiles to the law and to Jewish believers. See *WCF* 21.6; *WLC* 112,185; *HC* 99.

■ **2:9–15** *Women in Worship.* The controversies stirred by false teachers touched the lives of women as well as of men. As with men, Paul called on women to worship in ways that brought healing and did not aggravate the divisions and quarreling.

2:9 also. Literally, "similarly" or "in the same way," thus continuing the focus on corporate worship. **with decency . . . not with . . . expensive clothes.** Paul probably had wealthy women in mind here, as they would have been most able to afford lavish attire (cf. the emphasis on financial gain at 6:5). It is likely that the false teachers encouraged the demonstration of wealth in worship, although Paul was likely more concerned with the attitude of flaunting wealth than with the clothing and jewelry themselves. See *WLC* 138.

2:11 in quietness. As 1 Corinthians 11:5 indicates, Paul did not utterly forbid all vocal participation by women in the worship service. Here, as in 1 Corinthians 14:34, he enjoined silence for the sake of unity in the church. In Corinth the main concern was regard for husbands; here the problem appears to have been regard for the

Paul's Fourth Missionary Journey

C. A.D. 62–68

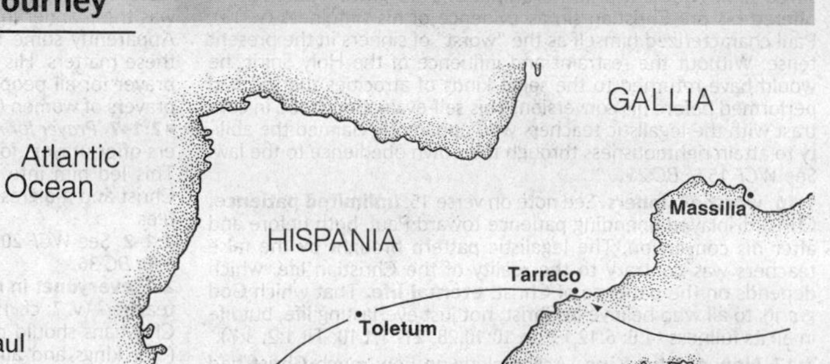

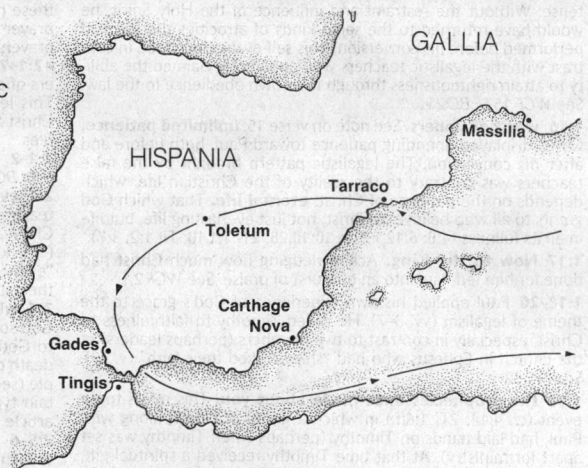

It is clear from Ac 13:1–21:17 that Paul went on three missionary journeys. There is also reason to believe that he made a fourth journey after his release from the Roman imprisonment recorded in Ac 28. The conclusion that such a journey did indeed take place is based on: (1) Paul's declared intention to go to Spain (Ro 15:24,28), (2) Eusebius's implication that Paul was released following his first Roman imprisonment (*Ecclesiastical History*, 2.22.2-3) and (3) statements in early Christian literature that he took the gospel as far as Spain (Clement of Rome, *Epistle to the Corinthians*, ch. 5; *Actus Petri Vercellenses*, chs. 1-3; Muratorian Canon, lines 34-39).

The places Paul may have visited after his release from prison are indicated by statements of intention in his earlier writings and by subsequent mention in the Pastoral Letters. The order of his travel cannot be determined with certainty, but the itinerary at the right seems likely.

1. **Rome**—released from prison in A.D. 62
2. **Spain**—62-64 (Ro 15:24,28)
3. **Crete**—64-65 (Tit 1:5)
4. **Miletus**—65 (2Ti 4:20)
5. **Colosse**—66 (Phm 22)
6. **Ephesus**—66 (1Ti 1:3)
7. **Philippi**—66 (Php 2:23-24; 1Ti 1:3)
8. **Nicopolis**—66-67 (Tit 3:12)
9. **Rome**—67 (2Ti 1:17)
10. Martyrdom—67/68 (2Ti 4:6)

an to teach or to have authority over a man; she must be silent. 13For Adam was formed
first, then Eve.[r] 14And Adam was not the one deceived; it was the woman who was deceived and became a sinner.[s] 15But women[a] will be saved[b] through childbearing—if they
continue in faith, love[t] and holiness with propriety.

2:13 [r]Ge 2:7,22; 1Co 11:8
2:14 [s]Ge 3:1-6,13; 2Co 11:3
2:15 [t]1Ti 1:14

[a] *15* Greek *she* [b] *15* Or *restored*

authoritative teaching of, and governing by, the leaders of the church (v. 12). **full submission.** Paul did not mean by this that women are to submit to the teaching of the church in all cases—the only unquestionable rule of faith is Scripture itself. Rather, he meant that they (like male laypersons) are not to usurp or rebel against properly appointed church authorities. This may well indicate that the false teachers were manipulating women in their attempt to subvert the proper church structures and teachings (cf. 2Ti 3:6).

2:12 I do not permit. Here Paul exercised his apostolic authority in restricting women from exercising a certain kind of authority and teaching. **to teach.** The structure of the Greek implies that this is not a prohibition against teaching men but simply a prohibition against "teaching" (although "teaching over a man" is a possible reading). Many other Biblical passages affirm women in various teaching roles (e.g., Jdg 4:4; 2Ki 22:14; Pr 1:8, 6:20; Ac 18:26; Tit 2:3). It is best to take this not as a prohibition against the act of teaching, but as a prohibition against improper teaching in conjunction with the improper authority some women sought and perhaps wielded in Timothy's context. The prohibition was probably against women being ordained to the teaching and ruling office of elder/overseer. **to have authority over.** This rare Greek word, which here probably refers to some level of judicial or governing authority, is used in the New Testament only here. Apparently, under the influence of the contentious attitude of the false teachers, certain women had moved into positions of governing authority within the church, which Paul prohibited (cf. 1Co 14:34). **silent.** See note on verse 11.

2:13 For Adam. Paul appealed to creation (Ge 2:7,21–22), indicating that his rationale was not based on a contemporary custom. He used a similar argument in 1 Corinthians 11:8–9, but then went on to qualify it in 1 Corinthians 11:11–12.

2:14 the woman. Again Paul alluded to Genesis, this time to the account of the fall (Ge 3:1–6). The argument may seem unfair, since both Adam and Eve had sinned. In fact Paul elsewhere had no qualms about blaming the fall on Adam (Ro 5:12–19; 1Co 15:21–22). But Paul's point is correct: Eve was the one who was "deceived" by the serpent. Paul's argument here, with its emphasis on the one who was deceived, was probably a reflection of the relative success that the false teachers in Ephesus had experienced in leading women astray (5:11–15; 2Ti 3:6–7), not an indication that he thought women were more gullible than men.

2:15 will be saved through childbearing. Probably not "brought safely," as some hold. Paul used "saved" as he normally did, meaning "redeemed from sin," thereby contrasting being deceived into sin (v. 14) with being saved from it. This allusion to Genesis highlights God's statement to Eve after the fall concerning her role in childbearing (Ge 3:16). There have been three main interpretations of this passage: (1) Women are saved through the birth of Christ; (2) women are kept safe in childbirth; and (3) Christian mothers will demonstrate saving faith by being faithful mothers. Compare Paul's words about widows and childrearing (5:10, 14). Childbearing is clearly not the basis for salvation, but it is a prime example of the godly responsibility and labor that are to

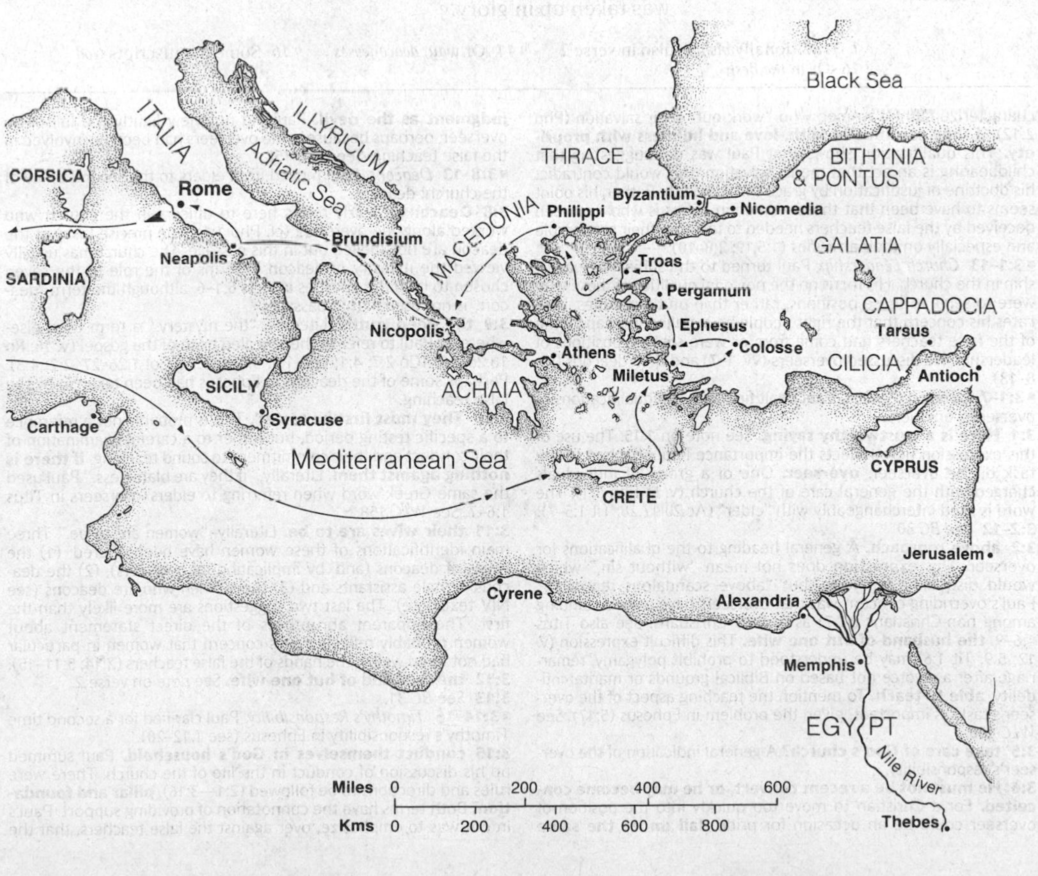

Overseers and Deacons

3 Here is a trustworthy saying:[u] If anyone sets his heart on being an overseer,[a v] he
desires a noble task. 2 Now the overseer must be above reproach,[w] the husband of
but one wife, temperate, self-controlled, respectable, hospitable,[x] able to teach,[y] 3 not
given to drunkenness, not violent but gentle, not quarrelsome,[z] not a lover of money.[a]
4 He must manage his own family well and see that his children obey him with proper respect.[b] 5 (If anyone does not know how to manage his own family, how can he take care
of God's church?)[c] 6 He must not be a recent convert, or he may become conceited[d] and
fall under the same judgment as the devil. 7 He must also have a good reputation with
outsiders, so that he will not fall into disgrace and into the devil's trap.[e]
8 Deacons,[f] likewise, are to be men worthy of respect, sincere, not indulging in much
wine,[g] and not pursuing dishonest gain. 9 They must keep hold of the deep truths of the
faith with a clear conscience.[h] 10 They must first be tested; and then if there is nothing
against them, let them serve as deacons.
11 In the same way, their wives[b] are to be women worthy of respect, not malicious talkers[i] but temperate and trustworthy in everything.
12 A deacon must be the husband of but one wife and must manage his children and
his household well.[j] 13 Those who have served well gain an excellent standing and great
assurance in their faith in Christ Jesus.
14 Although I hope to come to you soon, I am writing you these instructions so that,
15 if I am delayed, you will know how people ought to conduct themselves in God's
household, which is the church[k] of the living God, the pillar and foundation of the truth.
16 Beyond all question, the mystery[l] of godliness is great:

He[c] appeared in a body,[d m]
  was vindicated by the Spirit,
was seen by angels,
  was preached among the nations,[n]
was believed on in the world,
  was taken up in glory.[o]

3:1 [u]1Ti 1:15 [v]Ac 20:28
3:2 [w]Tit 1:6-8 [x]Ro 12:13 [y]2Ti 2:24
3:3 [z]2Ti 2:24 [a]Heb 13:5; 1Pe 5:2
3:4 [b]Tit 1:6
3:5 [c]1Co 10:32
3:6 [d]1Ti 6:4
3:7 [e]2Ti 2:26
3:8 [f]Php 1:1 [g]Tit 2:3
3:9 [h]1Ti 1:19
3:11 [i]2Ti 3:3; Tit 2:3
3:12 [j]ver 4
3:15 [k]ver 5; Eph 2:21
3:16 [l]Ro 16:25 [m]Jn 1:14 [n]Col 1:23 [o]Mk 16:19

[a] *1* Traditionally *bishop;* also in verse 2 [b] *11* Or *way, deaconesses* [c] *16* Some manuscripts *God*
[d] *16* Or *in the flesh*

---

characterize faithful women who "work out" their salvation (Php 2:12). **if they continue in faith, love and holiness with propriety.** This qualification shows that Paul was not suggesting that childbearing is an act that merits salvation; this would contradict his doctrine of justification by grace through faith. Rather, his point seems to have been that those women in Ephesus who had been deceived by the false teachers needed to focus on their proper role and especially on their attitudes (1:5,19; 2:8–10).

■ **3:1–13** *Church Leadership.* Paul turned to the subject of leadership in the church. His focus on the personal qualities of those who were to serve in these positions, rather than on their duties, indicates his concern that the right people be installed. Perhaps some of the false teachers had come from or were seeking positions of leadership. He discussed overseers (vv. 1–7) and then deacons (vv. 8–13).

■ **3:1–7** *Overseers/Elders.* Paul dealt first with the qualifications of overseers, or elders.

3:1 Here is a trustworthy saying. See note on 1:15. The use of this expression here reflects the importance Paul attached to the task of the overseer. **overseer.** One of a group of individuals charged with the general care of the church (v. 5; Php 1:1). The word is used interchangeably with "elder" (Ac 20:17,28; Tit 1:5–7).

3:2–12 See *BC* 30.

3:2 above reproach. A general heading to the qualifications for overseer. This expression does not mean "without sin," which would disqualify everyone, but "above scandalous reproach." Paul's overriding concern was that overseers have a good standing among non-Christians (v. 7) as well as Christians. See also Titus 1:6–9. **the husband of but one wife.** This difficult expression (v. 12; 5:9; Tit 1:6) may be understood to prohibit polygamy, remarriage after a divorce not based on Biblical grounds or marital infidelity. **able to teach.** To mention the teaching aspect of the overseer's tasks is important, given the problem in Ephesus (5:17). See *WLC* 158.

3:5 take care of God's church? A general indication of the overseer's responsibility.

3:6 He must not be a recent convert, or he may become conceited. For a Christian to move too quickly into the position of overseer could be an occasion for pride. **fall under the same judgment as the devil.** Paul did not view lightly the fall of an overseer, perhaps because some overseers had become involved in the false teaching. See *WLC* 158.

■ **3:8–13** *Deacons.* Paul moved from elders to the second office of the church: deacons.

3:8 Deacons. Clearly refers here to officers in the church who worked alongside overseers (cf. Php 1:1). The precise tasks of the deacon are not spelled out in this passage. The church has usually viewed the ministry of deacon in terms of the role of the seven chosen to help the apostles in Acts 6:1–6, although the term "deacon" is not used in that passage.

3:9 the deep truths. Literally, "the mystery," a term used elsewhere by Paul to refer to the revealed truth of the gospel (v. 16; Ro 16:25–26; 1Co 2:7; 4:1; Eph 1:9; 3:3–9; 6:19; Col 1:26–27; 2:2; 4:3). Perhaps some of the deacons in Ephesus had been taken in by the false teaching.

3:10 They must first be tested. This is probably not a reference to a specific testing period, but rather to a careful examination of their conduct and their commitment to sound teaching. **if there is nothing against them.** Literally, "if they are blameless." Paul used the same Greek word when referring to elders/overseers in Titus 1:6–7. See *WLC* 158.

3:11 their wives are to be. Literally, "women are to be." Three main identifications of these women have been offered: (1) the wives of deacons (and, by implication, of overseers), (2) the deacons' female assistants and (3) the women who are deacons (see NIV text note). The last two suggestions are more likely than the first. The apparent abruptness of the direct statement about women probably reflects Paul's concern that women in particular had not fared well at the hands of the false teachers (2:14; 5:11–15).

3:12 the husband of but one wife. See note on verse 2.

3:13 See *BC* 31.

■ **3:14–16** *Timothy's Responsibility.* Paul clarified for a second time Timothy's responsibility in Ephesus (see 1:12–20).

3:15 conduct themselves in God's household. Paul summed up his discussion of conduct in the life of the church. There were rules and directions to be followed (2:1—3:16). **pillar and foundation.** Both terms have the connotation of providing support. Paul's intent was to emphasize, over against the false teachers, that the

Instructions to Timothy

4 The Spirit[p] clearly says that in later times[q] some will abandon the faith and follow
deceiving spirits[r] and things taught by demons. 2 Such teachings come through hypocritical liars, whose consciences have been seared as with a hot iron.[s] 3 They forbid people to marry[t] and order them to abstain from certain foods,[u] which God created[v] to be
received with thanksgiving[w] by those who believe and who know the truth. 4 For everything God created is good,[x] and nothing is to be rejected if it is received with thanksgiving, 5 because it is consecrated by the word of God and prayer.
6 If you point these things out to the brothers, you will be a good minister of Christ
Jesus, brought up in the truths of the faith[y] and of the good teaching that you have followed. 7 Have nothing to do with godless myths and old wives' tales;[z] rather, train yourself to be godly. 8 For physical training is of some value, but godliness has value for all
things,[a] holding promise for both the present life[b] and the life to come.
9 This is a trustworthy saying[c] that deserves full acceptance 10 (and for this we labor
and strive), that we have put our hope in the living God, who is the Savior of all men, and
especially of those who believe.
11 Command and teach these things.[d] 12 Don't let anyone look down on you because
you are young, but set an example[e] for the believers in speech, in life, in love, in faith[f]
and in purity. 13 Until I come, devote yourself to the public reading of Scripture, to
preaching and to teaching. 14 Do not neglect your gift, which was given you through a
prophetic message[g] when the body of elders laid their hands on you.[h]
15 Be diligent in these matters; give yourself wholly to them, so that everyone may see
your progress. 16 Watch your life and doctrine closely. Persevere in them, because if you
do, you will save both yourself and your hearers.

4:1 [p]Jn 16:13 [q]2Ti 3:1 [r]2Th 2:3
4:2 [s]Eph 4:19
4:3 [t]Heb 13:4 [u]Col 2:16 [v]Ge 1:29 [w]Ro 14:6
4:4 [x]Ro 14:14-18
4:6 [y]1Ti 1:10
4:7 [z]2Ti 2:16
4:8 [a]1Ti 6:6 [b]Ps 37:9, 11; Mk 10:29, 30
4:9 [c]1Ti 1:15
4:11 [d]1Ti 5:7; 6:2
4:12 [e]Tit 2:7; 1Pe 5:3 [f]1Ti 1:14
4:14 [g]1Ti 1:18 [h]Ac 6:6; 2Ti 1:6

truth of the gospel is found in and supported by God's church (see note on 2Ti 2:19). See *WCF* 1.5.

3:16 mystery of godliness. See note on 3:9. What follows may be part of an early Christian hymn. **He appeared in a body.** A reference to the incarnation, with a hint at Christ's preexistence. **was vindicated by the Spirit.** A reference to Christ's resurrection (Ro 1:4). **was seen by angels.** A reference to the ascension (Ac 1:10–11). **was taken up in glory.** A reference to Christ's exaltation in glory. See *WCF* 8.2; *BC* 18.

■ **4:1—5:2** *False Teaching and Asceticism.* There were many dimensions to the false teaching in Ephesus. At this point, Paul touched on the tendency of at least some toward asceticism, the denial of physical pleasures. His discussion divides into an exposure of the false teaching (4:1–5) and Timothy's important responsibility (4:6—5:2).

■ **4:1–5** *False Teaching.* Returning to his main concern (1:3–20), Paul continued his attack on the false teachers and their teachings.

4:1 The Spirit clearly says. Probably a specific revelation the Holy Spirit granted to someone, perhaps to Paul himself (Ac 20:22–31; cf. 21:11). **in later times.** Or "in the last times." This does not refer to a period just prior to the second coming of Christ. Rather, in keeping with the overall New Testament perspective, it is the era that was inaugurated by Christ's first coming and will be completed at his second coming (Ac 2:17; Heb 1:2; 1Pe 1:20; 1Jn 2:18; cf. 2Ti 3:1; see theological article "The Plan of the Ages" at Heb 7). Paul understood that the entire New Testament age would be characterized by false teaching. **some will . . . demons.** A reference to the false teachers who had risen from within the church.

4:3–5 See *WLC* 193; *WSC* 104.

4:3 forbid people to marry and order them to abstain from certain foods. The false teachers promoted a rigorous lifestyle of self-denial (cf. Col 2:20–23). It would appear that the Ephesians had fallen under the Hellenistic teaching that since the material world is evil, the spiritual individual should avoid it. It would also appear that the false teachers distorted Old Testament law to support their views (1:7). **which.** The following argument focused on foods. Paul had already affirmed marriage in 3:2 and 12. See *WCF* 24.3; *WLC* 139; *BC* 12.

4:4 everything God created is good. Contrary to the false teachers, Paul affirmed the essential goodness of God's creation (Ge 1). The human race was designed to be part of the created physical universe, just as we were created with physical bodies. Proper enjoyment of these things is appropriate (6:17).

4:5 word of God and prayer. Paul did not believe that every possible activity in the physical world was automatically consecrated. Instead, each activity must be pronounced as such by God's Word, and it must be devoted to God by an act of prayer.

■ **4:6—5:2** *Timothy's Responsibility.* Having exposed the false teachers for what they were, Paul continued with a series of admonitions to Timothy regarding his response to this problem.

4:6 brought up. Literally, "being nourished." The "good minister" must continually be nourished by true doctrine.

4:7 godless myths and old wives' tales. See note on 1:4. **train yourself to be godly.** Throughout this section Paul intertwined personal discipline with official duties.

4:8 physical training . . . some value. This statement indicates that Paul still had in mind the asceticism of the false teachers. Discipline in godliness is of great value by comparison with any physical denial or discipline. See *WCF* 14.2.

4:9 See note on 1:15.

4:10 Savior of all men. As in 2:1,4 and 6 and 6:10, "all" here means "all kinds of." The free offer of the gospel—the call to repentance and salvation—is extended to all types of people (Mt 11:28). See theological article "Definite Atonement" at John 10. **especially of those who believe.** Paul narrowed the scope to indicate that salvation is extended effectually only to believers (Mt 22:14; Ro 8:30). See *WCF* 5.7; *WLC* 63.

4:12 Don't let anyone look down on you. The negative commands here and in verse 14 may indicate that Timothy had a tendency toward shyness or timidity. Furthermore, some in the church in Ephesus may not have accepted his authority (see "Introduction: Original Audience"). **because you are young.** Timothy was probably in his thirties and therefore younger than many of the Christians (and elders) in Ephesus. **but set an example . . . in purity.** Timothy was to establish his authority not by flaunting it, but by setting an example of godly living (Tit 2:7). See *WLC* 129.

4:13 Until I come. See 3:14–15 and "Introduction: Time and Place of Writing." **devote yourself . . . to teaching.** Positive methods for exposing the false teaching and neutralizing its impact (cf. 1:3–4). See *HC* 103.

4:14 your gift. See note on 1:18. See *WLC* 158; *BC* 31.

4:15 your progress. A reference to the advancement of Timothy's spiritual life, his ministry or both. Note that his advancement was described as "progress," not arrival.

4:16 your life and doctrine. That Paul summarized his instructions to Timothy in this manner is an indication of where the false teachers had gone astray and, hence, where Christians in general may go astray. **you will save.** God alone grants salvation (1:1; 2:3; 4:10), but he is pleased to use his people as instruments in bringing salvation to others. Salvation is not completed when one comes to faith. To be sure, faith brings justification and the assurance of salvation. But faith also begins the lifelong process of sanctification, which is not completed until the Christian's earthly life has ended. **yourself.** Sanctification is a work of God that demands the cooperative activity of the Christian (Php 2:12). See *WLC* 159.

Advice About Widows, Elders and Slaves

5 Do not rebuke an older man[i] harshly,[j] but exhort him as if he were your father.
Treat younger men[k] as brothers, [2]older women as mothers, and younger women as
sisters, with absolute purity.
[3]Give proper recognition to those widows who are really in need.[l] [4]But if a widow has
children or grandchildren, these should learn first of all to put their religion into practice by caring for their own family and so repaying their parents and grandparents,[m] for
this is pleasing to God.[n] [5]The widow who is really in need[o] and left all alone puts her
hope in God[p] and continues night and day to pray[q] and to ask God for help. [6]But the widow who lives for pleasure is dead even while she lives.[r] [7]Give the people these instructions,[s] too, so that no one may be open to blame. [8]If anyone does not provide for his relatives, and especially for his immediate family, he has denied[t] the faith and is worse than
an unbeliever.
[9]No widow may be put on the list of widows unless she is over sixty, has been faithful to her husband,[a] [10]and is well known for her good deeds,[u] such as bringing up children, showing hospitality, washing the feet[v] of the saints, helping those in trouble[w] and
devoting herself to all kinds of good deeds.
[11]As for younger widows, do not put them on such a list. For when their sensual desires overcome their dedication to Christ, they want to marry. [12]Thus they bring judgment on themselves, because they have broken their first pledge. [13]Besides, they get into
the habit of being idle and going about from house to house. And not only do they become idlers, but also gossips and busybodies,[x] saying things they ought not to. [14]So I
counsel younger widows to marry,[y] to have children, to manage their homes and to give
the enemy no opportunity for slander.[z] [15]Some have in fact already turned away to follow Satan.[a]
[16]If any woman who is a believer has widows in her family, she should help them and
not let the church be burdened with them, so that the church can help those widows who
are really in need.[b]
[17]The elders[c] who direct the affairs of the church well are worthy of double honor,[d]
especially those whose work is preaching and teaching. [18]For the Scripture says, "Do not

5:1 [i]Tit 2:2 [j]Lev 19:32 [k]Tit 2:6
5:3 [l]ver 5,16
5:4 [m]Eph 6:1,2 [n]1Ti 2:3
5:5 [o]ver 3,16 [p]1Co 7:34; 1Pe 3:5 [q]Lk 2:37
5:6 [r]Lk 15:24
5:7 [s]1Ti 4:11
5:8 [t]2Pe 2:1; Jude 4; Tit 1:16
5:10 [u]Ac 9:36; 1Ti 6:18; 1Pe 2:12 [v]Lk 7:44 [w]ver 16
5:13 [x]2Th 3:11
5:14 [y]1Co 7:9 [z]1Ti 6:1
5:15 [a]Mt 4:10
5:16 [b]ver 3-5
5:17 [c]Ac 11:30 [d]Php 2:29; 1Th 5:12

a 9 Or *has had but one husband*

5:1–2 See *WLC* 124.
5:1 Do not rebuke an older man harshly. A command that was to be balanced with 4:12. Timothy was not to abuse the authority he possessed. **exhort.** Or "encourage." A good minister makes appeals to other believers with an attitude of respect that is similar to that shown to family members.
▪ **5:3—6:2** *Instructions Regarding Specific Groups.* Paul's focus on Timothy's responsibility to counter the false asceticism in Ephesus led him to elaborate on some specific responsibilities. Paul told Timothy how to minister to three specific groups in Ephesus: widows (5:3–16), elders (5:17–25) and slaves (6:1–2).
▪ **5:3–16** *Ministering to Widows.* Paul's concern to identify needy widows and provide for their proper care forms the backdrop for a discussion of the problems of younger widows, some of whom had apparently become influenced by the false teaching in Ephesus (see "Introduction: Purpose and Distinctives").
5:3 Give proper recognition to. That is, care for. **widows who are really in need.** Literally, "those who are really widows." The care of widows, who frequently had great material needs, is a major theme in the Old Testament (Dt 24:19–21; Isa 1:17; Jer 22:3; Zec 7:9–10; Mal 3:5) and was a special concern of the early church (v. 16; Ac 6:1; Jas 1:27).
5:4 But if a widow has children or grandchildren. The truly needy widow had no family from which to receive support (vv. 8,16).
5:5 puts her hope in God. Genuine poverty often drove widows to exemplary lives of prayer and faithful dependence upon God. For such widows, the church was to be the visible "hand" of God in providing for needs.
5:6 dead. Spiritually dead.
5:7 Give the people . . . open to blame. Literally, "Command these things so that they might be blameless." Perhaps this is a reference to the widows alone, not the whole church.
5:8 See *WLC* 129,141,142; *WSC* 74.
5:9 the list of widows. Some have seen here an official order or office of widows with duties to perform (vv. 5,10); others have seen an agreement whereby some widows provided certain services for the church in exchange for material support. Most likely the list was simply one of widows who were to receive support from the church (v. 16). This list constituted a portion of the larger group of widows mentioned in verses 3–6. **over sixty.** A general expression reflecting the cultural perspective on the age after which remarriage would be most unlikely (cf. vv. 11–14). **has been faithful to her husband.** Literally, "wife of one husband." See note on 3:2.
5:10 such as bringing up children. Literally, "if she brought up children." The verbs in this verse are in the past tense. Paul's concern was not with what the widow might still do for the church, but with what she had accomplished in her life. Note the closely connected concept in 2:15 and 5:14. **washing the feet of the saints.** A humble expression of hospitality in a culture where people wore sandals and walked dusty roads (cf. Jn 13:4–5). Jesus commanded his disciples to wash each other's feet (Jn 13:14–15).
5:11 when their sensual desires overcome their dedication to Christ. Literally, "when they live sensually against Christ." **they want to marry.** A widow's desire to remarry is not in itself ungodly (v. 14). Paul's language here is somewhat unclear, but probably the fact that the widow's "dedication to Christ" was "overcome" implies a desire to marry an unbeliever, making the desire inappropriate.
5:12 have broken their first pledge. This is probably not a reference to a pledge of celibacy or of devotion to the church, but rather of basic commitment to Christ (vv. 11,15).
5:13 saying things they ought not to. This may refer to the false teachings (cf. v. 15; 1:3; 4:7) or simply to gossip and improper intrusion into the lives of others.
5:14 to have children. See note on 2:15.
5:15 to follow Satan. Paul gave much attention to widows, perhaps because some of the younger widows had come under the influence of the false teachers (2Ti 3:6–7) or been enticed by sensual desires to abandon the faith (vv. 11–12).
▪ **5:17–25** *Ministering to Elders.* As with widows, Paul addressed the issues of proper honor for elders and dealing with those who sin.
5:17–18 See *WLC* 108,127.
5:17 elders. See note on 3:1. **double honor.** The honor of the position as well as financial remuneration (v. 18). **especially . . . teaching.** This is a reference to two kinds of elders: those who govern the church and those who add to governance the more specialized ministry of preaching and teaching. See *WCF* 30.1.

muzzle the ox while it is treading out the grain,"[a][e] and "The worker deserves his wages."[b][f] 19Do not entertain an accusation against an elder[g] unless it is brought by two or
three witnesses.[h] 20Those who sin are to be rebuked[i] publicly, so that the others may
take warning.[j]

21I charge you, in the sight of God and Christ Jesus[k] and the elect angels, to keep these
instructions without partiality, and to do nothing out of favoritism.

22Do not be hasty in the laying on of hands,[l] and do not share in the sins of others.[m]
Keep yourself pure.

23Stop drinking only water, and use a little wine[n] because of your stomach and your
frequent illnesses.

24The sins of some men are obvious, reaching the place of judgment ahead of them;
the sins of others trail behind them. 25In the same way, good deeds are obvious, and even
those that are not cannot be hidden.

6 All who are under the yoke of slavery should consider their masters worthy of full respect,[o] so that God's name and our teaching may not be slandered.[p] 2Those who
have believing masters are not to show less respect for them because they are brothers.[q]
Instead, they are to serve them even better, because those who benefit from their service
are believers, and dear to them. These are the things you are to teach and urge on them.[r]

Love of Money

3If anyone teaches false doctrines[s] and does not agree to the sound instruction[t] of our
Lord Jesus Christ and to godly teaching, 4he is conceited and understands nothing. He
has an unhealthy interest in controversies and quarrels about words[u] that result in envy,
strife, malicious talk, evil suspicions 5and constant friction between men of corrupt mind,
who have been robbed of the truth[v] and who think that godliness is a means to financial gain.

6But godliness with contentment[w] is great gain.[x] 7For we brought nothing into the
world, and we can take nothing out of it.[y] 8But if we have food and clothing, we will be
content with that.[z] 9People who want to get rich[a] fall into temptation and a trap[b] and
into many foolish and harmful desires that plunge men into ruin and destruction. 10For
the love of money[c] is a root of all kinds of evil. Some people, eager for money, have wandered from the faith[d] and pierced themselves with many griefs.

Paul's Charge to Timothy

11But you, man of God,[e] flee from all this, and pursue righteousness, godliness,

[a] *18* Deut. 25:4 [b] *18* Luke 10:7

5:18 [e]Dt 25:4; 1Co 9:7-9 [f]Lk 10:7; Lev 19:13; Dt 24:14,15; Mt 10:10; 1Co 9:14
5:19 [g]Ac 11:30 [h]Mt 18:16
5:20 [i]2Ti 4:2; Tit 1:13 [j]Dt 13:11
5:21 [k]1Ti 6:13; 2Ti 4:1
5:22 [l]Ac 6:6 [m]Eph 5:11
5:23 [n]1Ti 3:8
6:1 [o]Eph 6:5; Tit 2:9; 1Pe 2:18 [p]Tit 2:5,8
6:2 [q]Phm 16 [r]1Ti 4:11
6:3 [s]1Ti 1:3 [t]1Ti 1:10
6:4 [u]2Ti 2:14
6:5 [v]Tit 1:15
6:6 [w]Php 4:11; Heb 13:5 [x]1Ti 4:8
6:7 [y]Job 1:21; Ecc 5:15
6:8 [z]Heb 13:5
6:9 [a]Pr 15:27 [b]1Ti 3:7
6:10 [c]1Ti 3:3 [d]Jas 5:19
6:11 [e]2Ti 3:17

5:18 For the Scripture says. That Paul cited both Deuteronomy 25:4 and a saying of Jesus recorded in Luke 10:7 as "Scripture" is an indication of how early the writings now included in the New Testament were placed on the same level of authority as those of the Old Testament (2Pe 3:15–16).

5:20 Those who sin. Elders who sin. Some had perhaps become involved in the false teaching, although the advice is also applicable to other severe sins that impact the church. That not all sin by elders was to be dealt with in this manner is indicated by verse 1. See *WCF* 30.3.

5:21 the elect angels. Those who will presumably serve as witnesses at the judgment (cf. Mt 25:31; Rev 14:10). See *WCF* 3.3; *WLC* 13,19.

5:22 Do not be hasty . . . others. This verse has been interpreted in a variety of ways. If "laying on of hands" refers to ordination, it may mean that to ordain an unqualified elder is to give tacit approval to, and thereby participate in, his sins. If it refers to restoring or affirming an elder who has been accused of sin (vv. 19–20), or to censured sinners in general, it may indicate that hasty restoration is a sinful form of favoritism (v. 21). **Keep yourself pure.** See 4:12 and 16. See *WLC* 99,158,173; *BC* 31.

5:23 Stop drinking only water. The practice of abstaining from wine as a matter of principle perhaps reflected the influence of the false teachers' concept of purity (4:3), or perhaps it was intended to protect weaker Christians from stumbling (Ro 14:21). **use a little wine . . . illnesses.** Paul recognized the medicinal value of wine. See *WLC* 135.

5:24 The sins . . . them. Another reference to the importance of carefully screening candidates for ordination.

■ **6:1–2** *Ministering to Slaves.* Finally, Paul addressed the problem of slaves who had not been showing proper respect for their Christian masters.

6:1 under the yoke of slavery. Paul gave more extensive instructions to slaves in his other letters (Eph 6:5–8; Col 3:22–25; Tit 2:9–10). **our teaching.** This is presumably in contrast to the false teaching that may have encouraged insubordination among some of the Christian slaves. See *WCF* 16.2.

■ **6:3–19** *False Teaching and Financial Gain.* Paul returned one last time to the problem of the false teachers, noting especially their divisiveness and greed. His handling of this matter divides into a description of the false teaching (vv. 3–10) and of Timothy's responsibility (vv. 11–19).

■ **6:3–10** *False Teaching.* The false teaching included, among other things (see "Introduction: Purpose and Distinctives"), the idea that godliness leads to financial gain.

6:3–5 See *WCF* 20.4; *WLC* 113.

6:4 controversies and quarrels about words. Contentiousness was one of the prominent characteristics of the false teachers (1:4; 2Ti 2:14,23; Tit 3:9). See *WLC* 145.

6:5 godliness is a means to financial gain. Apparently some of the false teachers (and perhaps their followers) found ways to gain wealth from their teaching (v. 10; 2Co 11:7; Tit 1:11). It is also possible that they taught that adherence to God's law would necessarily result in financial prosperity (cf. 1:7–9). Although the Scriptures promote the general principle of prosperity to those who obey the law (e.g., Ps 1:2–3), they do not draw a precise parallel between the two nor teach that God is obligated to bless financially all who keep the law. See *WLC* 142.

6:6–9 See *WLC* 141,193.

6:6 contentment. Christians can be content because their needs are met by Christ (2Co 12:9–10; Php 4:11–13). Se)e *WLC* 147; *WSC* 80.

6:10 Some people . . . faith. The false teaching evidently promised a means to financial gain that lured some away from sound teaching. See note on verse 5. See *WLC* 99,151.

■ **6:11–19** *Timothy's Responsibility.* Paul followed his comments

faith, love,[f] endurance and gentleness. 12 Fight the good fight[g] of the faith. Take hold of[h]
the eternal life to which you were called when you made your good confession in the
presence of many witnesses. 13 In the sight of God, who gives life to everything, and of
Christ Jesus, who while testifying before Pontius Pilate[i] made the good confession, I
charge you[j] 14 to keep this command without spot or blame until the appearing of our
Lord Jesus Christ, 15 which God will bring about in his own time—God, the blessed[k] and
only Ruler,[l] the King of kings and Lord of lords,[m] 16 who alone is immortal[n] and who lives
in unapproachable light, whom no one has seen or can see.[o] To him be honor and might
forever. Amen.

17 Command those who are rich in this present world not to be arrogant nor to put
their hope in wealth,[p] which is so uncertain, but to put their hope in God,[q] who richly
provides us with everything for our enjoyment.[r] 18 Command them to do good, to be rich
in good deeds,[s] and to be generous and willing to share.[t] 19 In this way they will lay up
treasure for themselves[u] as a firm foundation for the coming age, so that they may take
hold of the life that is truly life.
20 Timothy, guard what has been entrusted[v] to your care. Turn away from godless
chatter[w] and the opposing ideas of what is falsely called knowledge, 21 which some
have professed and in so doing have wandered from the faith.[x]
Grace be with you.[y]

6:11 [f]2Ti 2:22
6:12 [g]1Co 9:25,26; 1Ti 1:18 [h]Php 3:12
6:13 [i]Jn 18:33-37 [j]1Ti 5:21
6:15 [k]1Ti 1:11 [l]1Ti 1:17 [m]Rev 17:14; 19:16
6:16 [n]1Ti 1:17 [o]Jn 1:18
6:17 [p]Lk 12:20,21 [q]1Ti 4:10 [r]Ac 14:17
6:18 [s]1Ti 5:10 [t]Ro 12:8, 13
6:19 [u]Mt 6:20
6:20 [v]2Ti 1:12,14 [w]2Ti 2:16
6:21 [x]2Ti 2:18 [y]Col 4:18

---

about the false teachers with personal exhortations to Timothy, concluding with a marvelous doxology.

6:12 Fight the good fight of the faith. A metaphor for the Christian life, viewed in terms of faithfulness to Christ (2Ti 4:7). **Take hold of the eternal life.** That is, do not become complacent. While faith in Christ begins new life (4:8; 2Co 5:17), the ultimate goal of the Christian life is always future (1:16; 6:19; Php 3:12; 2Ti 4:8). **to which you were called.** Eternal life is not first something we choose, but something to which God calls us (Ro 8:30). **when.** Literally, "and." Timothy's call was not temporally connected to the incident described in the next clause. **confession in the presence of many witnesses.** This may refer to Timothy's baptism or to some other public ceremony in which he made profession. The "good confession" that one has come to faith in Christ leads naturally into the "good fight" of seeking to live in faithfulness to him.

6:13–16 See *WCF* 26.3; *WLC* 108; *BC* 1.

6:13 who while testifying before Pontius Pilate made the good confession. This probably refers to Jesus' trial before Pilate (Mt 27:11; Mk 15:2; Lk 23:3; Jn 18:33–37; 19:8–11). Some, however, translate it as "who while testifying in the time of Pontius Pilate" and take it to be a reference to Jesus' life, especially his death.

6:14 this command. Probably a reference to all that Paul had charged concerning Timothy's personal discipline and official duties. **appearing.** The second coming of Christ (2Ti 4:1, 8; Tit 2:13).

6:15 King of kings and Lord of lords. This expression is applied to Christ in Revelation 19:16 (cf. 17:14). See *WCF* 2.2; *WLC* 7.

6:17–19 rich. To clarify that he was not opposed to riches per se, Paul provided an exhortation for those who found themselves rich in this world (presumably not from greed). See *WLC* 141.

6:17 for our enjoyment. See note on 4:4. One of the great honors of being redeemed human beings is that God created the world not only for his glory, but also for our enjoyment. See *WSC* 1.

6:19 lay up treasure. See Matthew 6:20. **take hold of the life that is truly life.** See note on verse 12.

■ **6:20–21** *Final Exhortations.* Paul brought this letter to a close with one final charge to Timothy, once again set within the context of dealing with the false teachers.

6:20 what has been entrusted to your care. That is, the sound doctrine of the gospel (1:10–11; cf. 2Ti 1:14). **what is falsely called knowledge.** The false teachers emphasized "knowledge" (see "Introduction: Purpose and Distinctives"). See *WLC* 113.

6:21 Grace be with you. This abrupt conclusion, lacking Paul's usual personal greetings, suggests that Paul saw the situation in Ephesus as quite serious. The Greek word translated "you" is plural. Paul intended the letter to be read to the entire church (2Ti 4:22; Tit 3:15).

2 TIMOTHY

Introduction

Overview

Author: The apostle Paul

Purpose: To call for Timothy to visit Paul in his last days and to encourage Timothy in his ministry against false teachers in Ephesus

Date: A.D. 64 68

Key Truths:

- False teachers will always trouble the church.
- Church leaders must be courageous in their struggle against false teachers.
- Church leadership must be based on the Scriptures.
- God will keep true believers safe, but others in the church will be judged.

Author

The apostle Paul authored this letter. See "Introduction to 1 Timothy: Author."

Time and Place of Writing

Second Timothy is most likely the last of Paul's letters. It was written after what may have been his fourth missionary journey and probably dates between A.D. 64 and 68 (see "Introduction to 1 Timothy: Time and Place of Writing").

Paul wrote 2 Timothy from prison, probably during a second Roman imprisonment (1:8; 2:9; see also "Introduction to 1 Timothy: Time and Place of Writing"). Precisely why he was under arrest, or even where he was arrested, is unknown. He had been given a preliminary hearing, at which he had received no support (4:16). His trial still awaited him, but he knew that it would end in his execution (4:6). Most of Paul's friends found it convenient to be elsewhere (4:10–11). He had been troubled by the actions of Phygelus and Hermogenes (1:15–16) and of Alexander the metalworker (4:14), although a Christian named Onesiphorus had been an encouragement to him (1:16–18).

Original Audience

Paul wrote to his friend and coworker, Timothy. Timothy was still in Ephesus (4:19), where Paul had previously left him (1Ti 1:3) and where the false teaching that Paul had addressed in his first letter to Timothy continued to be a problem (2:14–18,23; 3:1–9,13). Remembering their longstanding friendship, Paul desired to see Timothy one last time before his death (1:4).

Timothy's mother, Eunice, and his grandmother, Lois, were both Christians (1:5) who had given Timothy early training in the Scriptures (3:15). The letter includes a probable reference to his ordination (1:6; cf. 2:2).

Purpose and Distinctives

Paul seems to have written 2 Timothy with two purposes in mind. First, he wanted to provide Timothy with a final letter of personal encouragement in his ministry (1:5 14; 2:1 16,22 26; 3:10 4:5). Second, he directed Timothy to come to Rome (4:9,21), providing instructions on who and what (4:11 13) to bring with him.

Like 1 Timothy, 2 Timothy exhibits a strong concern for sound doctrine (1:13–14; 2:2; 4:1–5) and contains marvelous theological meditations on the grace of God (1:8–11), the faithfulness of Christ (2:11–13) and the nature and function of Scripture (3:15–17). There are affirmations of salvation by grace (1:9), election (1:9; 2:10,19) and the divine inspiration of Scripture (3:16). Second Timothy also affirms the resurrection (2:8) and the second coming (4:1,8) of Christ. See also "Introduction to 1 Timothy: Purpose and Distinctives."

As the last of Paul's letters, 2 Timothy is especially important because it provides us with some final insights regarding the apostle Paul. His situation was bleak. No longer could he look forward to fruitful ministry (cf. Php 1:22–26). Most of his friends had left him (4:10–11). Yet Paul remained confident. He was not ashamed to suffer for the gospel (1:12) and was willing to "endure everything for the sake of the elect" (2:10). He knew that he had been faithful to Christ (4:7) and that Christ would always remain faithful (1:12; 2:13). Therefore Paul had confidence that the One who had rescued him from death in the past (3:11; 4:17) would rescue him through death into eternal life (4:8,18).

Outline

I. Salutation (1:1–2)	*Paul identified himself as the author and Timothy as the recipient of the letter.*
II. First Reflections and Exhortations (1:3–14) A. Timothy's Faith and Background (1:3–5) B. Exhortations to Timothy (1:6–14)	*Paul had great confidence in Timothy and encouraged him to stand for truth against false teachers.*
III. Second Reflections and Exhortations (1:15—2:26) A. Paul's Associates (1:15–18) B. Exhortations to Timothy (2:1–26) 1. Encouragement to Faithfulness (2:1–13) 2. Dealing With False Teachers (2:14–26)	*Paul encouraged Timothy to remain faithful in his opposition to false teachers, unlike some others who had turned away from the true faith.*
IV. Third Reflections and Exhortations (3:1—4:5) A. The Last Days (3:1–13) 1. False Teachers (3:1–9) 2. Paul's Endurance (3:10–13) B. Exhortations to Timothy (3:14—4:5)	*Paul reminded Timothy that he should expect to suffer in the last days at the hands of impostors, as he remained faithful.*
V. Fourth Reflections and Exhortations (4:6–18) A. Paul's Impending Death (4:6–8) B. Exhortations to Timothy (4:9–18)	*In light of his impending death, Paul appealed to Timothy to visit him.*
VI. Final Greetings (4:19–22)	*Paul closed his epistle with his customary greetings.*

1:1 [a]2Co 1:1 [b]Eph 3:6; 1Ti 6:19
1:2 [c]Ac 16:1 [d]1Ti 1:2
1:3 [e]Ro 1:8 [f]Ro 1:10
1:4 [g]Ac 20:37 [h]2Ti 4:9
1:5 [i]1Ti 1:5 [j]Ac 16:1
1:6 [k]1Ti 4:14
1:7 [l]Ro 8:15

1 Paul, an apostle of Christ Jesus by the will of God,[a] according to the promise of life
that is in Christ Jesus,[b]

2 To Timothy,[c] my dear son:[d]

Grace, mercy and peace from God the Father and Christ Jesus our Lord.

Encouragement to Be Faithful

3 I thank God,[e] whom I serve, as my forefathers did, with a clear conscience, as night
and day I constantly remember you in my prayers.[f] 4 Recalling your tears,[g] I long to see
you,[h] so that I may be filled with joy. 5 I have been reminded of your sincere faith,[i] which
first lived in your grandmother Lois and in your mother Eunice[j] and, I am persuaded,
now lives in you also. 6 For this reason I remind you to fan into flame the gift of God,
which is in you through the laying on of my hands.[k] 7 For God did not give us a spirit of
timidity,[l] but a spirit of power, of love and of self-discipline.

■ **1:1–2** *Salutation.* Paul began this letter in his usual way, by identifying himself and the recipient of his letter and by offering a benediction.
1:1 apostle of Christ Jesus. One sent out as an official and authoritative representative of Christ (1Ti 1:1; see note on 2Co 1:1). **by the will of God.** Paul established his authority on the basis of God's will alone (1Co 1:1; 2Co 1:1; Gal 1:1,10–16; Eph 1:1; Col 1:1). **according to the promise of life that is in Christ Jesus.** One role of the apostles was to proclaim the eternal life that is available in Christ (see note on 1Ti 1:16).
1:2 dear son. Or "beloved son" (1Co 4:17; cf. 1Ti 1:2). Paul had no known physical offspring, but here he identified Timothy as his spiritual son (cf. Gal 4:19). **Grace, mercy and peace.** See note on 1Ti 1:2.
■ **1:3–14** *First Reflections and Exhortations.* Paul began the main body of this epistle with several reflections, followed by exhortations to Timothy. In this section, Paul reported how he remembered Timothy's faith and background (vv. 3–5). Then he exhorted Timothy based on those facts (vv. 6–14).
■ **1:3–5** *Timothy's Faith and Background.* In most of his letters (except Galatians, 1 Timothy and Titus), Paul introduced his concerns with a report of his appreciation for his readers. Here he focused on his confidence in Timothy's faith and upbringing.
1:4–5 See *WLC* 144.
1:4 Recalling your tears. Probably the tears Timothy had shed the last time Paul had left him. **I long to see you.** Paul anticipated his request recorded in 4:9 and 21.
1:5 your grandmother Lois . . . your mother Eunice. Paul acknowledged the importance of Timothy's upbringing, which took place in the sanctified condition of a Christian home. Timothy was a prime example of a child who was made holy, set apart from the world, because of the faith of his parent (see 1Co 7:14). Christian parentage did not ensure Timothy's salvation, but it was the instrument God used to bring him to faith (see theological article "Infant or Believer's Baptism" at Col 2).
■ **1:6–14** *Exhortations to Timothy.* On the basis of Timothy's upbringing in the faith and his personal commitments to Christ, Paul encouraged his younger protégé to be bold as he shared with Paul in the suffering of Christian ministry.
1:6 fan into flame the gift of God. This strong expression suggests that Timothy was being less forceful than he should have been in using the spiritual gift God had given him. Paul's words to Timothy indicate that believers are responsible for nurturing and developing the work of the Spirit in their lives. Just as it is possible to quench the Spirit (1Th 5:19), it is possible to fan the Spirit's gift into flame. **which is in you through the laying on of my hands.** See note on 1 Timothy 1:18. See *WCF* 16.3.
1:7 timidity. Or "cowardice." Timothy apparently had a natural

8 So do not be ashamed[m] to testify about our Lord, or ashamed of me his prisoner.[n]
But join with me in suffering for the gospel,[o] by the power of God, 9 who has saved us and
called[p] us to a holy life—not because of anything we have done but because of his own
purpose and grace. This grace was given us in Christ Jesus before the beginning of time,
10 but it has now been revealed[q] through the appearing of our Savior, Christ Jesus, who
has destroyed death[r] and has brought life and immortality to light through the gospel.
11 And of this gospel I was appointed a herald and an apostle and a teacher.[s] 12 That is why
I am suffering as I am. Yet I am not ashamed, because I know whom I have believed, and
am convinced that he is able to guard[t] what I have entrusted to him for that day.[u]
13 What you heard from me, keep[v] as the pattern of sound teaching, with faith and
love in Christ Jesus.[w] 14 Guard the good deposit that was entrusted to you—guard it with
the help of the Holy Spirit who lives in us.[x]
15 You know that everyone in the province of Asia has deserted me,[y] including Phygelus and Hermogenes.
16 May the Lord show mercy to the household of Onesiphorus,[z] because he often refreshed me and was not ashamed of my chains. 17 On the contrary, when he was in Rome,
he searched hard for me until he found me. 18 May the Lord grant that he will find mercy from the Lord on that day! You know very well in how many ways he helped me[a] in
Ephesus.

2 You then, my son, be strong[b] in the grace that is in Christ Jesus. 2 And the things you
have heard me say[c] in the presence of many witnesses[d] entrust to reliable men who
will also be qualified to teach others. 3 Endure hardship with us like a good soldier[e] of
Christ Jesus. 4 No one serving as a soldier gets involved in civilian affairs—he wants to
please his commanding officer. 5 Similarly, if anyone competes as an athlete, he does not
receive the victor's crown[f] unless he competes according to the rules. 6 The hardwork-

1:8 [m]Mk 8:38; Ro 1:16 [n]Eph 3:1 [o]2Ti 2:3, 9; 4:5
1:9 [p]Ro 8:28
1:10 [q]Eph 1:9 [r]1Co 15:26, 54
1:11 [s]1Ti 2:7
1:12 [t]1Ti 6:20 [u]ver 18
1:13 [v]Tit 1:9 [w]1Ti 1:14
1:14 [x]Ro 8:9
1:15 [y]2Ti 4:10, 11, 16
1:16 [z]2Ti 4:19
1:18 [a]Heb 6:10
2:1 [b]Eph 6:10
2:2 [c]2Ti 1:13 [d]1Ti 6:12
2:3 [e]1Ti 1:18
2:5 [f]1Co 9:25

---

reticence toward assertiveness in his teaching. The gravity of the situation in Ephesus required strength and courage.

1:8–10 See *WCF* 10.1; *WLC* 67.

1:8 me his prisoner. This was probably the second time Paul was in prison in Rome (2:9; see "Introduction: Time and Place of Writing").

1:9 to a holy life. The goal of God's election and calling is the sanctification of his people (Eph 1:4). See theological article "Sanctification" at Titus 3. **not . . . grace.** This is a marvelous affirmation that all aspects of salvation, including sanctification, are accomplished entirely by grace, not by human merit (Eph 2:8–9). From unconditional election "before the creation of the world" (Eph 1:4) to our final glorification in Christ (Ro 8:30), salvation is entirely by the grace of God. **because of his own purpose.** God's decree of redemption is based solely on his own purpose and good pleasure. Elsewhere, this divine purpose is identified as mercy (Tit 3:5) and love (Eph 1:4–5). **before the beginning of time.** An affirmation of the eternal nature of the divine decision to redeem us through Christ (Eph 1:4; Tit 1:2; Rev 13:8). See *WCF* 3.5; 10.2; *WSC* 31; *BC* 16,22; *CD* 1.III.

1:10 our Savior, Christ Jesus. As mediator of the covenant of grace, Christ is Savior (Tit 1:4; 2:13; 3:6). **who has destroyed death and has brought life and immortality to light.** Christ opened the door to eternal life through his death and resurrection (Heb 2:14–15; Rev 1:18). Death has been destroyed insofar as it no longer holds power either over Christ (Ro 6:9) or over those who are in Christ (Ro 6:11). Death's final destruction will take place at the judgment of the world when Christ returns (1Co 15:51–57; Rev. 20:11–15).

1:11 herald. Or "preacher" (1Ti 2:7).

1:12 I am suffering. Paul was in prison (v. 8; 2:9). **I am not ashamed.** Having exhorted Timothy not to be ashamed to speak out for Christ (v. 8), Paul presented himself as a model of boldness in the face of danger and suffering (2:8–10; 3:10–11). **that day.** The day of judgment (v. 18; 4:8).

1:13 sound teaching. This theme runs throughout the Pastoral Epistles (3:9; 4:6; 6:3; 2Ti 1:13–14; 2:2; 4:3; Tit 1:9,13; 2:1–2). See *WLC* 5; *WSC* 3.

1:14 Guard the good deposit that was entrusted to you. That is, the sound doctrine of the gospel (cf. 1Ti 1:10–11; 6:20). **help of the Holy Spirit.** In the New Testament age the presence and gifting of the Spirit are much greater than they were in the Old Testament age. The Spirit's power enables believers to be faithful to the commands of God. Yet the Spirit's empowerment does not always come apart from attention to him. Paul did not simply encourage Timothy to be determined; he reminded him that (like Christian growth in general) it is impossible to mature as a leader apart from conscious dependence on the Holy Spirit (cf. Gal 5:25).

■ **1:15—2:26** *Second Reflections and Exhortations.* Paul turned to several more reflections, which led him to continue exhorting Timothy. Here the apostle directly instructed Timothy to resist the false teachers in Ephesus. This material divides into two sections: a discussion of some of Paul's other associates (1:15–18) and several exhortations to Timothy (2:1–26).

■ **1:15–18** *Paul's Associates.* Paul reminded Timothy that many of Paul's associates had deserted the apostle in his time of trial and informed him of another who had remained loyal.

1:15 everyone. Paul was probably using hyperbole (an intentional exaggeration for effect) to communicate that many people in Asia had been disloyal. Paul felt as though nearly everyone had deserted him. **the province of Asia.** The Roman province whose leading city was Ephesus, where Timothy was serving as Paul's representative at this time. **Phygelus and Hermogenes.** These people are not mentioned elsewhere in the New Testament. That Paul mentioned them here is probably an indication that he had counted on their support. Apparently Timothy knew who these people were and what they had done.

1:16 Onesiphorus. A member of the church at Ephesus who had distinguished himself through his loyalty to Paul (v. 18; cf. 4:19).

1:17 when he was in Rome. Onesiphorus probably traveled to Rome to assist Paul.

1:18 that day! The judgment day; the day of the Lord (v. 12; 4:8).

■ **2:1–26** *Exhortations to Timothy.* Having contrasted the many who had deserted him with the one who had been faithful, Paul exhorted Timothy to remain loyal as he continued to deal with the false teachers in Ephesus. Paul's discussion divides into two parts: his call for Timothy to be faithful (vv. 1–13) and his explicit order to deal with the false teachers (vv. 14–26).

■ **2:1–13** *Encouragement to Faithfulness.* Paul exhorted Timothy to faithfulness by drawing three analogies from everyday life that emphasized wholehearted devotion to a task. Paul then spoke of his own faithfulness in the situation he was facing, before concluding with a poetic meditation that affirmed Christ's faithfulness.

2:1 my son. See note on 1:2.

2:2 in the presence of many witnesses. This may refer to Timothy's ordination (cf. 1:6; 1Ti 1:18; 4:14). **reliable men who will also be qualified to teach others.** Timothy was to ordain elders in the church who would be faithful to Paul's teaching (1Ti 3:1–7; 5:17). See *HC* 103.

2:4–6 soldier . . . athlete . . . hardworking farmer. Paul used three analogies to explain why Timothy was to expect his task to require hard work. Excellent soldiers devote themselves to pleasing their commander; athletes must compete within the rules of their game; hardworking farmers should receive their reward before others. Timothy was to expect nothing less for those who were to lead the church.

ing farmer should be the first to receive a share of the crops. 7Reflect on what I am saying, for the Lord will give you insight into all this.
8Remember Jesus Christ, raised from the dead,[g] descended from David.[h] This is my
gospel,[i] 9for which I am suffering[j] even to the point of being chained like a criminal. But
God's word is not chained. 10Therefore I endure everything[k] for the sake of the elect, that
they too may obtain the salvation that is in Christ Jesus, with eternal glory.[l]
11Here is a trustworthy saying:

If we died with him,
 we will also live with him;[m]
12if we endure,
 we will also reign with him.[n]
If we disown him,
 he will also disown us;[o]
13if we are faithless,
 he will remain faithful,[p]
 for he cannot disown himself.

A Workman Approved by God

14Keep reminding them of these things. Warn them before God against quarreling
about words;[q] it is of no value, and only ruins those who listen. 15Do your best to present yourself to God as one approved, a workman who does not need to be ashamed and
who correctly handles the word of truth.[r] 16Avoid godless chatter,[s] because those who
indulge in it will become more and more ungodly. 17Their teaching will spread like gan-
grene. Among them are Hymenaeus[t] and Philetus, 18who have wandered away from the
truth. They say that the resurrection has already taken place, and they destroy the faith
of some.[u] 19Nevertheless, God's solid foundation stands firm,[v] sealed with this inscription: "The Lord knows those who are his,"[a][w] and, "Everyone who confesses the name
of the Lord[x] must turn away from wickedness."

2:8 [g]Ac 2:24 [h]Mt 1:1 [i]Ro 2:16
2:9 [j]Ac 9:16
2:10 [k]Col 1:24 [l]2Co 4:17
2:11 [m]Ro 6:2-11
2:12 [n]Ro 8:17; 1Pe 4:13 [o]Mt 10:33
2:13 [p]Nu 23:19; Ro 3:3
2:14 [q]1Ti 6:4
2:15 [r]Eph 1:13; Jas 1:18
2:16 [s]Tit 3:9
2:17 [t]1Ti 1:20
2:18 [u]1Ti 1:19
2:19 [v]Isa 28:16 [w]Jn 10:14 [x]1Co 1:2

[a] *19* Num. 16:5 (see Septuagint)

2:8 raised from the dead. The resurrection of Christ is central to Paul's theology (Ro 6:4–10; 1Co 15:12–22). Here it forms the basis for the hope expressed in verses 11–12. **descended from David.** Jesus fulfills the promise that God would grant to one of David's descendents an eternal kingship (2Sa 7:12–16; Mt 1:1; Mk 12:35–37; Lk 1:32–33; Jn 7:42; Ac 2:29–36; Rev 5:5). For the combination of Christ's resurrection and Davidic heritage, see Romans 1:3–4. See *BC* 17.
2:9 I am suffering even to the point of being chained like a criminal. See note on 1:8.
2:10 the elect. Those whom God has chosen to believe in Christ. No one knows precisely those who are among the elect, but believers all serve Christ with the confidence that his chosen people wait to be reached and led. See theological article "Predestination and Foreknowledge" at Romans 8. **the salvation that is in Christ Jesus.** The salvation that comes through union with Christ Jesus (3:15). See theological article "Union With Christ" at Galatians 6. **eternal glory.** Another metaphor for eternal life (v. 11–12; Mt 13:43). Just as Christ was resurrected in a glorified body, all believers united to Christ will receive glorified bodies on the day of resurrection (cf. 1 Co 15:12–56).
2:11 Here is a trustworthy saying. See note on 1Ti 1:15. What follows may be a part of an early Christian hymn. **If we died with him, we will also live with him.** Paul referred to his basic belief that salvation comes only to those who are united with Christ by faith. As Christ died under the judgment of sin and death, believers also die to sin and death. As Christ rose into newness of life, so also believers will walk in newness of life in the age to come (see Ro 6:1–8). See theological article "The Plan of the Ages" at Hebrews 7.
2:12 if we endure. This refers to perseverance in the face of hardship (v. 10). Although salvation is entirely by God's grace, all true believers will persevere in faithful service to Christ as a demonstration of the grace of God at work within them (see theological article "The Perseverance and Preservation of Believers" at Php 1). **we will also reign with him.** A New Testament image for the eternal glory that Christians receive through Christ. When Christ returns in glory, all those who have believed in him will reign over the new earth with him (Ro 5:17; Rev 3:21; 5:10; 20:4,6; 22:5). **If we disown him, he will also disown us.** A sober warning against apostasy (Mt 10:33). Paul had in mind here absolute apostasy, not temporary failure or backsliding. He may have been thinking particularly of those mentioned in 1:15 (see also 2:17–18). True believers will not turn away in flagrant rebellion against Christ (see theological article "The Perseverance and Preservation of Believers" at Php 1). See *WCF* 26.1; *HC* 32.
2:13 if we are faithless, he will remain faithful. Many interpreters have taken this as a wonderful affirmation that salvation does not rest ultimately on our faithfulness, but on that of Christ (v. 19; cf. Jn 10:28–29). As true as this is, the parallelism with verse 12 and the preceding context (vv. 8–11) suggests that Paul meant that God would remain faithful in the sense of remaining true to the threat of judgment: God will not fail to judge those who turn away from Christ. **for he cannot disown himself.** God will always remain true to his character. Both Christian hope and the threat of judgment are firmly rooted in the character of God (Nu 23:19; Tit 1:2). See *HC* 129.
▪ **2:14–26** *Dealing With False Teachers.* Paul turned to the matter of faithfulness in the face of false teachers, giving Timothy instructions both for the church and for himself and concluding with an exhortation to Timothy to reclaim some of those who had been led astray.
2:14 quarreling about words. One of the characteristics of false teachers is bickering over minutiae (v. 23; 1Ti 1:4; 6:4; Tit 3:9). See *WLC* 113; *BC* 7.
2:15 the word of truth. The gospel (2:8–9; 4:2). See *WLC* 159; *HC* 2.
2:17 Hymenaeus. Mentioned also in 1 Timothy 1:20 as one who had "shipwrecked" his faith (1Ti 1:19). **Philetus.** Mentioned nowhere else in Scripture.
2:18–19 See *WCF* 17.2.
2:18 the resurrection has already taken place. Apparently at least some false teachers in Ephesus denied that the bodily resurrection will take place on the coming day of final judgment, affirming instead a spiritual resurrection at conversion (1Co 15:12–14). **they destroy the faith of some.** The denial of bodily resurrection was hardly a small matter. Those who followed this teaching were headed toward full apostasy. Timothy was to warn the church against these false teachers (v. 14). See *BC* 29.
2:19 God's solid foundation. Paul used the metaphor of a building's foundation to represent the church. **The Lord knows those who are his.** Paul described the New Testament church in terms that derived from Numbers 16:5 in the Septuagint (the Greek translation of the OT): Thus he stressed the continuity between Old Testament Israel and the New Testament church. In the Old Testament context, these words indicated that God distinguished within the

20 In a large house there are articles not only of gold and silver, but also of wood and
clay; some are for noble purposes and some for ignoble.[y] 21 If a man cleanses himself
from the latter, he will be an instrument for noble purposes, made holy, useful to the
Master and prepared to do any good work.[z]
22 Flee the evil desires of youth, and pursue righteousness, faith, love[a] and peace,
along with those who call on the Lord out of a pure heart.[b] 23 Don't have anything to do
with foolish and stupid arguments, because you know they produce quarrels. 24 And the
Lord's servant must not quarrel; instead, he must be kind to everyone, able to teach, not
resentful.[c] 25 Those who oppose him he must gently instruct, in the hope that God will
grant them repentance leading them to a knowledge of the truth,[d] 26 and that they will
come to their senses and escape from the trap of the devil,[e] who has taken them captive
to do his will.

Godlessness in the Last Days

3 But mark this: There will be terrible times in the last days.[f] 2 People will be lovers
of themselves, lovers of money,[g] boastful, proud,[h] abusive, disobedient to their parents,[i] ungrateful, unholy, 3 without love, unforgiving, slanderous, without self-control,
brutal, not lovers of the good, 4 treacherous, rash, conceited,[j] lovers of pleasure rather
than lovers of God— 5 having a form of godliness but denying its power. Have nothing
to do with them.
6 They are the kind who worm their way[k] into homes and gain control over weak-
willed women, who are loaded down with sins and are swayed by all kinds of evil desires,
7 always learning but never able to acknowledge the truth. 8 Just as Jannes and Jambres
opposed Moses,[l] so also these men oppose[m] the truth—men of depraved minds,[n] who,
as far as the faith is concerned, are rejected. 9 But they will not get very far because, as
in the case of those men,[o] their folly will be clear to everyone.

Paul's Charge to Timothy

10 You, however, know all about my teaching,[p] my way of life, my purpose, faith, patience, love, endurance, 11 persecutions, sufferings—what kinds of things happened to
me in Antioch,[q] Iconium and Lystra, the persecutions I endured.[r] Yet the Lord rescued

2:20 [y]Ro 9:21
2:21 [z]2Ti 3:17
2:22 [a]1Ti 1:14; 6:11 [b]1Ti 1:5
2:24 [c]1Ti 3:2, 3
2:25 [d]1Ti 2:4
2:26 [e]1Ti 3:7
3:1 [f]1Ti 4:1
3:2 [g]1Ti 3:3 [h]Ro 1:30 [i]Ro 1:30
3:4 [j]1Ti 3:6
3:6 [k]Jude 4
3:8 [l]Ex 7:11 [m]Ac 13:8 [n]1Ti 6:5
3:9 [o]Ex 7:12
3:10 [p]1Ti 4:6
3:11 [q]Ac 13:14, 50 [r]2Co 11:23-27

---

nation of Israel between those who were true believers and those who were not. This inscription indicates that God continues to distinguish between believers and unbelievers in the New Testament church (cf. v. 20; see theological article "The Church: Visible and Invisible" at 1 Pe 4). **Everyone . . . must turn away.** Also inscribed on the church is God's call to holiness (v. 21). Just as in Old Testament Israel, true believers must distinguish themselves from others in the visible church by turning away from sin. Those whom God knows in a saving way will distinguish themselves by persevering in the faith (see theological article "The Perseverance and Preservation of Believers" at Php 1). See *WCF* 3.4; *WLC* 79,172; *BC* 27,29.

2:20 large house . . . noble . . . ignoble. Following verse 19, which refers to the visible church, "large house" most naturally continues the description of the visible church. In this context, "gold and silver" and "noble" metaphorically represent true believers, while "wood and clay" and "ignoble" represent those who do not believe. The metaphor therefore emphasizes the fact that the [visible] church contains both believers and unbelievers (see theological article "The Church: Visible and Invisible" at 1 Pe 4). Paul applied this same metaphor to the individual in verse 21, indicating that he intended the allusion to be somewhat ambiguous, referring both to the church and to the individual. See *WLC* 13; *BC* 16,29.

2:21 If a man. Paul now applied the metaphor of verse 20 to the individual. In this second sense of the symbolism, "gold and silver" and "noble" refer to good works and godly teaching, while "wood and clay" and "ignoble" refer to those things the believer must purge from his or her life. Paul may have specifically had in mind the false teachings in Ephesus as the "wood and clay" that were to be avoided. Paul also appealed to the first sense of the metaphor (see note on v. 20) by indicating that the one who cleanses himself or herself of the "ignoble" things becomes "an instrument for noble purposes."

2:22 desires of youth. This expression certainly would include sexual lusts, but the contrast with "righteousness, faith, love and peace," as well as the focus on arguments and quarrels in verses 23–24, indicates that Paul also wanted Timothy to avoid youthful propensities toward false teachings and divisiveness.

2:23 arguments . . . quarrels. See note on verse 14.

2:25–26 The Christian must never assume that those who are ensnared by the devil's false teaching are irretrievably lost. The gospel must be proclaimed to all. See *WLC* 27,76.

■ **3:1—4:5** *Third Reflections and Exhortations.* Having exhorted Timothy to resist the false teachers in Ephesus, Paul dealt with the terrible times of the last days. This section divides into two parts: a description of the last days (3:1–13) and exhortations to Timothy (3:14—4:5).

■ **3:1–13** *The Last Days.* To present a proper perspective on the challenges Timothy faced in Ephesus, Paul commented on the expectations all believers should have in the last days. Paul touched on two matters: false teachers (vv. 1–9) and his own endurance in trials (vv. 10–13).

■ **3:1–9** *False Teachers.* Paul considered it a characteristic of the last days that godless people would rise and exercise significant influence over the people of God.

3:1 the last days. Paul did not have in mind primarily the times immediately before the return of Christ. His concern was with his own day. This fit well with the New Testament perspective that the last days began with the inauguration of God's kingdom in Christ's earthly ministry (see 1Ti 4:1 and theological article "The Plan of the Ages" at Heb 7).

3:2–4 Paul listed a number of characteristics of those who trouble the church. Their problems go far beyond mere theological error. See *WCF* 16.2; *WLC* 105,132,145.

3:5 having a form of godliness but denying its power. What makes false teachers so dangerous is that they appear to be Christians (Mt 7:15,21–23). See *WLC* 113.

3:6 weak-willed women. Paul's point was not that all women are weak willed, but that in Ephesus some women had been especially vulnerable to deception. The false teachers in Ephesus may have been successful in deceiving a number of women (1Ti 2:14; 5:13–15).

3:8 Jannes and Jambres. Jewish tradition identified these names with the two Egyptian magicians who opposed Moses before Pharaoh (Ex 7–8).

3:9 their folly will be clear to everyone. Paul either had in mind here that Timothy would expose the false teachers in Ephesus or that the true character of the false teachers would be exposed at the final judgment. The latter seems more likely.

■ **3:10–13** *Paul's Endurance.* Paul continued his reflections on the false teachers of the last days by reminding Timothy that he (Paul) had also suffered at the hands of deceivers in the church.

3:11 Antioch, Iconium and Lystra. Antioch was in the Roman

3:11 [s]Ps 34:19
3:12 [t]Ac 14:22
3:13 [u]2Ti 2:16
3:14 [v]2Ti 1:13
3:15 [w]2Ti 1:5 [x]Jn 5:39 [y]Ps 119:98,99
3:16 [z]2Pe 1:20,21 [a]Ro 4:23,24
3:17 [b]1Ti 6:11 [c]2Ti 2:21
4:1 [d]Ac 10:42 [e]1Ti 5:21
4:2 [f]1Ti 4:13 [g]Gal 6:6 [h]1Ti 5:20; Tit 1:13; 2:15
4:3 [i]1Ti 1:10
4:4 [j]1Ti 1:4
4:5 [k]2Ti 1:8 [l]Ac 21:8
4:6 [m]Php 2:17 [n]Php 1:23
4:7 [o]1Ti 1:18 [p]1Co 9:24
4:8 [q]Col 1:5 [r]2Ti 1:12
4:10 [s]Col 4:14 [t]1Jn 2:15

me from all of them.[s] 12 In fact, everyone who wants to live a godly life in Christ Jesus will
be persecuted,[t] 13 while evil men and impostors will go from bad to worse,[u] deceiving and
being deceived. 14 But as for you, continue in what you have learned and have become
convinced of, because you know those from whom you learned it,[v] 15 and how from infancy[w] you have known the holy Scriptures,[x] which are able to make you wise[y] for salvation through faith in Christ Jesus. 16 All Scripture is God-breathed[z] and is useful for
teaching,[a] rebuking, correcting and training in righteousness, 17 so that the man of
God[b] may be thoroughly equipped for every good work.[c]

4 In the presence of God and of Christ Jesus, who will judge the living and the dead,[d]
and in view of his appearing and his kingdom, I give you this charge:[e] 2 Preach[f] the
Word;[g] be prepared in season and out of season; correct, rebuke[h] and encourage—with
great patience and careful instruction. 3 For the time will come when men will not put up
with sound doctrine.[i] Instead, to suit their own desires, they will gather around them a
great number of teachers to say what their itching ears want to hear. 4 They will turn their
ears away from the truth and turn aside to myths.[j] 5 But you, keep your head in all situations, endure hardship,[k] do the work of an evangelist,[l] discharge all the duties of your
ministry.
6 For I am already being poured out like a drink offering,[m] and the time has come for
my departure.[n] 7 I have fought the good fight,[o] I have finished the race,[p] I have kept the
faith. 8 Now there is in store for me[q] the crown of righteousness, which the Lord, the righteous Judge, will award to me on that day[r]—and not only to me, but also to all who have
longed for his appearing.

Personal Remarks

9 Do your best to come to me quickly, 10 for Demas,[s] because he loved this world,[t]

province of Pisidia, Iconium and Lystra in the Roman province of Galatia. Paul preached the gospel in all three of these cities during his first missionary journey (Ac 13:14—14:20) and, against significant opposition, established a church in each city (Ac 14:21–23). He mentioned these particular cities, including Timothy's hometown of Lystra, in order to appeal to the roots of Timothy's faith (vv. 14–15; 1:5). **the Lord rescued me.** See 4:18 and its note.

3:12 everyone who wants to live a godly life in Christ Jesus will be persecuted. The New Testament teaches that Christians should expect persecution (Mt 10:17–18; Jn 15:20; 1Pe 4:12; 5:9).

3:13–17 See *WCF* 1.6; *WLC* 2,3,155; *WSC* 89; *BC* 7; *HC* 98,103.

3:13 evil men and impostors. These words make it clear that Paul had in mind troubles that come from false teachers in the church (vv. 1–5).

■ **3:14—4:5** *Exhortations to Timothy.* Paul turned directly to Timothy, emphasizing his responsibility to resist false teachers and their godlessness.

3:14 those from whom you learned. A reference not only to Timothy's mother and grandmother (1:5), but also to Paul himself. Paul encouraged Timothy to have confidence in the truth of the gospel because of the character of his mother and grandmother.

3:15 from infancy. Or "from childhood." According to custom, the Jewish parent was to begin instructing a child in the law when the child reached five years of age. **you have known the holy Scriptures.** The false teachers had been misinterpreting the Old Testament (1Ti 1:7; Tit 3:9). Timothy needed to remember the proper instruction he had received at the hands of his mother and grandmother. The "Scriptures" here refer to the books of the Old Testament. The New Testament did not yet exist as a collection; indeed, some of the New Testament books had not even been written. Even so, as the New Testament literature developed, it, too, was called the "Scriptures" (see 2Pe 3:15–16). **which are able to make you wise for salvation through faith in Christ Jesus.** The Old Testament points clearly to the central role of Jesus Christ in God's overall plan for his creation. See *WCF* 1.1.

3:16 All Scripture. The Old Testament (see note on v. 15). **God-breathed.** This is one of the most important expressions in the New Testament of the doctrine of the divine inspiration of Scripture: It has been breathed out by God (cf. 2Pe 1:21). God is the source and ultimate author of Scripture. Though written by human authors, it nevertheless is breathed out by God and carries the full weight of his authority. See *WCF* 1.2; 1.4; *WLC* 3; *WSC* 2,3.

4:1 In the presence. Paul's mention of witnesses was intended to impress upon Timothy the utmost seriousness of the charge. **Christ Jesus, who will judge the living and the dead.** For Christ as judge, see verse 8 (see also Mt 25:31–46; Jn 5:22,27; Ac 10:42). **his appearing.** Christ's second coming (cf. v. 8; 1Ti 6:14; Tit 2:13). See *BC* 37.

4:2 the Word. All Scripture (3:16–17) and preeminently the gospel (cf. 2:15). **in season and out of season.** In every situation, whether good or bad, the Word is to be proclaimed. See *WCF* 21.5; *WLC* 108,159.

4:3–4 See *WLC* 113.

4:3 time will come. Paul expected his characterization of the last days to continue into the future. Timothy needed to be ready for these future challenges. **men.** Literally, "they," presumably a reference to some people associated with the church. **sound doctrine.** This theme runs throughout the Pastoral Epistles (1:13–14; 2:2; 1Ti 3:9; 4:6; 6:3; Tit 1:9,13; 2:1–2). **Instead . . . to hear.** Some people have an endless fascination with everything but the truth.

4:4 myths. See note on 1 Timothy 1:4.

4:5 A final exhortation to faithfulness, even though others were perhaps turning away.

■ **4:6–18** *Fourth Reflections and Exhortations.* Paul wrote yet another section of reflections, followed by exhortations to Timothy. This material divides into the announcement of Paul's impending death (vv. 6–8) and a number of exhortations (vv. 9–18).

■ **4:6–8** *Paul's Impending Death.* Paul's impending death provided the reason for his final appeals to Timothy.

4:6 already. Paul accepted the inevitability of his death, even though it may have been several months away. **poured out like a drink offering.** This metaphor for death (cf. Php 2:17) is taken from the language of the Old Testament sacrificial system. A drink offering of wine was poured out in the sanctuary as a sacrifice reflecting gratitude to God (Nu 15:5,7,10; 28:7). Paul understood his imminent death as an offering to Christ. Christ had done so much that Paul owed his very life in thankfulness to him. **my departure.** Another metaphor for death (Php 1:23) that, for Paul, held the hope and assurance of a destination beyond the grave (v. 18). See *WLC* 145.

4:7–8 See *HC* 63.

4:7 With these three metaphors Paul signified the end of his ministry. His concern was not that he had been a success, but rather that he had been faithful to his Lord. See *BC* 7.

4:8 the crown of righteousness. Some interpreters have understood this phrase to refer to the crown awarded for the faithful life of one who has received the righteousness of Christ through faith (Ro 3:22). More likely, this is the crown that consists of perfect righteousness (eternal life) that is given the believer as the climax of the process of sanctification (2:10; Jas 1:12; 1Pe 5:4; Rev 2:10). **the righteous Judge.** Refers to Christ in his role as the judge who brings to completion the work that he has begun in his elect. **that day.** The judgment day; the day of the Lord (1:12,18). **his appearing.** Christ's second coming (v. 1).

■ **4:9–18** *Exhortations to Timothy.* Paul wanted to see Timothy one last time. He gave Timothy various instructions regarding his jour-

has deserted me and has gone to Thessalonica. Crescens has gone to Galatia,[u] and Titus to Dalmatia. 11Only Luke[v] is with me.[w] Get Mark[x] and bring him with you, because
he is helpful to me in my ministry. 12I sent Tychicus[y] to Ephesus. 13When you come,
bring the cloak that I left with Carpus at Troas, and my scrolls, especially the parchments.
14Alexander[z] the metalworker did me a great deal of harm. The Lord will repay him
for what he has done.[a] 15You too should be on your guard against him, because he
strongly opposed our message.
16At my first defense, no one came to my support, but everyone deserted me. May it
not be held against them.[b] 17But the Lord stood at my side[c] and gave me strength, so that
through me the message might be fully proclaimed and all the Gentiles might hear it.[d]
And I was delivered from the lion's mouth. 18The Lord will rescue me from every evil attack[e] and will bring me safely to his heavenly kingdom. To him be glory for ever and ever.
Amen.[f]

Final Greetings

19Greet Priscilla[a] and Aquila[g] and the household of Onesiphorus. 20Erastus[h] stayed
in Corinth, and I left Trophimus[i] sick in Miletus. 21Do your best to get here before winter.[j] Eubulus greets you, and so do Pudens, Linus, Claudia and all the brothers.
22The Lord be with your spirit.[k] Grace be with you.[l]

4:10 [u]Ac 16:6
4:11 [v]Col 4:14 [w]2Ti 1:15 [x]Ac 12:12
4:12 [y]Ac 20:4
4:14 [z]Ac 19:33 [a]Ro 12:19
4:16 [b]Ac 7:60
4:17 [c]Ac 23:11 [d]Ac 9:15
4:18 [e]Ps 121:7 [f]Ro 11:36
4:19 [g]Ac 18:2
4:20 [h]Ac 19:22 [i]Ac 20:4
4:21 [j]ver 9
4:22 [k]Gal 6:18; Phm 25 [l]Col 4:18

[a] 19 Greek *Prisca,* a variant of *Priscilla*

---

ney to Rome, informed Timothy of his present status and concluded with a profound expression of trust in his Lord.

4:9 Do your best to come to me. Paul had hinted in 1:4 at his desire to see Timothy. **quickly.** See note on verse 21.

4:10 Demas. A coworker who had been present with Paul during his first Roman imprisonment (Col 4:14; Phm 24). **Thessalonica.** A city in the Roman province of Macedonia. Paul had established a church there on his second missionary journey (Ac 17:1–10). **Crescens.** Mentioned nowhere else in the New Testament. He was apparently another of Paul's coworkers. **Galatia.** A Roman province evangelized by Paul on his first missionary journey (see note on 3:11). **Titus.** Another of Paul's coworkers. See "Introduction to Titus: Original Audience." **Dalmatia.** Another name for the Roman province of Illyricum, the westernmost province reached by Paul on his first three missionary journeys (Ro 15:19).

4:11 Luke. The "beloved physician" who is mentioned in Colossians 4:14 and Philemon 24. He traveled with Paul throughout much of Paul's second and third missionary journeys. See "Introduction to Luke: Author." **Get Mark and bring him with you.** A beautiful example of forgiveness in Christ. John Mark's desertion of Paul and Barnabas during their first missionary journey (Ac 13:13) had resulted in the dissolution of the partnership between Paul and Barnabas (Ac 15:37–40). Later Mark regained Paul's favor (Col 4:10; Phm 24). Now, at the end of his life, Paul wanted to see him.

4:12 Tychicus. A coworker of Paul who is mentioned in Acts 20:4 (also Eph 6:21; Col 4:7; Tit 3:12). **to Ephesus.** Tychicus was to bring Timothy this letter and serve as his replacement.

4:13 cloak. A heavy woolen garment used for protection against dampness and cold. Paul was anticipating the arrival of winter (v. 21). **Carpus.** Mentioned nowhere else in the New Testament. **Troas.** A port city, linking the Roman province of Asia with that of Macedonia, through which Paul had traveled on his second and third missionary journeys (Ac 16:8,11; 20:5–6). At what point(s) on his present journey Paul was in Troas is not clear. **scrolls.** Literally, "books." **parchments.** Books made from animal skins. Their content is unknown; perhaps they were portions of the Old Testament.

4:14 Alexander the metalworker. See note on 1 Timothy 1:20. **did me a great deal of harm.** This incident is mentioned nowhere else in the New Testament. **The Lord will repay him for what he has done.** That is, on the day of final judgment (Mt 16:27; Ro 2:6; Rev 22:12).

4:16 first defense. A preliminary hearing prior to Paul's actual trial, which he was now awaiting (see "Introduction: Time and Place of Writing"). **May it not be held against them.** An expression of forgiveness in the face of death that is reminiscent of Christ (Lk 23:34) and of Stephen (Ac 7:60).

4:17 But the Lord stood at my side and gave me strength. Paul had learned long ago that he could always depend upon the power of the One who had commissioned him (2Co 12:9–10; Php 4:11–13). **through me the message might be fully proclaimed.** This probably refers to Paul's proclamation of the gospel at his preliminary hearing. **all the Gentiles might hear it.** Paul had preached the gospel in a public forum at the center of the Roman Empire. **delivered from the lion's mouth.** A metaphor for a narrow escape from death. Paul's preliminary hearing had resulted in a temporary reprieve.

4:18 will rescue me from every evil attack. Paul did not believe that Christ would prevent his physical death (v. 6), but he expressed absolute trust in the One who is ever faithful and will never abandon those who believe in him (2:13). **will bring me safely to his heavenly kingdom.** This is the ultimate hope of all those who trust in Christ. When Christ returns in glory, he will bring the wonders of our heavenly home to the new earth (Rev 21:1–5).

■ **4:19–22** *Final Greetings.* As was his custom, Paul closed his letter with personal greetings and a benediction.

4:19 Priscilla and Aquila. A married couple and longtime friends of Paul, whose acquaintance dated back to Paul's initial visit to Corinth on his second missionary journey. Like Paul, they were Jews and tentmakers (Ac 18:2–3). Having moved to Corinth from Rome, they later accompanied Paul to Ephesus (Ac 18:18–19), where they hosted a house church for several years before returning to Rome (Ro 16:3–4; 1Co 16:19). They had now apparently returned to Ephesus. **the household of Onesiphorus.** See note on 1:16. This is one of the clearest pieces of evidence that Timothy was still in Ephesus (1:18).

4:20 Erastus. Presumably the same person as Corinth's director of public works (mentioned in Ro 16:23). **Corinth.** The provincial capital of the Roman province of Achaia. Paul had visited Corinth on his second and third missionary journeys. **Trophimus.** A member of the church in Ephesus who had accompanied Paul to Jerusalem at the close of Paul's third missionary journey (Ac 20:4; 21:29). **Miletus.** A seaport just south of Ephesus. Paul had visited Miletus at the end of his third missionary journey (Ac 20:15,17). At what point(s) on this journey Paul was in Miletus is not clear.

4:21 before winter. Winter weather would eliminate the possibility of travel by ship. Paul may have felt that if Timothy waited too long, he would not arrive before Paul's execution (v. 9). In any event, Paul needed his cloak before winter (v. 13). **Eubulus . . . Pudens, Linus, Claudia.** None of these individuals, who presumably were Roman Christians, are mentioned elsewhere in the New Testament, although later Roman Catholic tradition viewed Linus as the successor to Peter as bishop of Rome.

4:22 Grace be with you. The word "you" is plural in the Greek. Presumably Paul intended the letter to be read to the entire church (1Ti 6:21; Tit 3:15).

TITUS

Introduction

Overview

Author: The apostle Paul

Purpose: To encourage Titus to complete the organization of the churches on Crete, counter the effects of false teachers there and instruct believers in proper Christian conduct

Date: A.D. 62–64

Key Truths:

- The church must be organized with qualified leaders.
- False teachers must be resisted.
- Special responsibilities exist for specific groups in the church.
- Some general responsibilities are to be shared by all believers.
- All Christian conduct must rest on God's saving work in Christ.

Author

The apostle Paul wrote Titus. See "Introduction to 1 Timothy: Author."

Time and Place of Writing

Titus was most likely composed during Paul's fourth missionary journey, which took place after his first imprisonment in Rome, and it probably dates to between A.D. 62 and 64. Paul may have been in or on his way to Nicopolis in Epirus (western Greece) when he wrote Titus (3:12). See "Introduction to 1 Timothy: Time and Place of Writing."

Original Audience

Titus was a Gentile Christian who had probably been converted by Paul (1:4). The New Testament provides little information about him, and he is not mentioned in Acts. Paul took him to Jerusalem early in his missionary labors. While in Jerusalem Paul refused to have Titus circumcised (Gal 2:1–3). Titus apparently traveled with Paul on his second and third missionary journeys and later on what may have been part of his fourth (see "Introduction to 1 Timothy: Time and Place of Writing"). Titus was Paul's trusted associate, and Paul counted on him in delicate situations, such as that in Corinth (2Co 8:6,16,23; 12:18). Titus later served as Paul's representative on the island of Crete (1:5) and in the province of Dalmatia (2Ti 4:10).

On an earlier leg of Paul's fourth missionary journey, Paul and Titus were involved in missionary activity on Crete, an island in the Mediterranean Sea whose inhabitants were known for their less-than-exemplary behavior (1:12). When Paul departed, he left Titus behind to continue the work (1:5).

Purpose and Distinctives

Paul wrote to encourage Titus to bring his ministry on Crete to a close. Specifically, Paul wanted Titus to complete the organization of the churches (1:5–9), deal with the false teachers who were present (1:10–14; 3:9–11) and give instructions to the churches on proper conduct (2:1—3:8).

Like 1 Timothy, Titus is noteworthy for its information on church organization. It provides a lengthy description of the qualifications for being an overseer/elder (1:6–9) and important evidence that the terms "overseer" and "elder" refer to one office rather than to two distinct offices (1:5–7).

Also like 1 Timothy, Titus exhibits a strong concern for sound doctrine (1:9,13; 2:1–2) and contains two theological meditations on the grace that God has extended in Jesus Christ (2:11–14; 3:4–7). These include affirmations of the second coming of Christ (2:13), Christ's substitutionary atonement (2:14), regeneration by the Holy Spirit (3:5) and justification by grace (3:5,7). Titus also affirms the deity of Christ in a striking manner: The title "Savior" is applied freely and in the same contexts to both God (1:3; 2:10; 3:4) and Christ (1:4; 2:13; 3:6), with 2:13 speaking of "our great God and Savior, Jesus Christ."

Paul's concern for sound doctrine was balanced by an emphasis on proper Christian conduct. For Paul, the two clearly went hand in hand. In particular, he stressed the quality of "self-control" (1:8; 2:2,5,6,12) and the importance of doing "what is good" (2:7,14; 3:1,8,14).

It is difficult to determine in detail the nature of the false teaching on Crete. Paul described this false teaching as something that had come from within the church (1:10,16). It concerned Jewish myths (1:14), genealogies and quarrels about the law (3:9), and about human commandments (1:14). The false teachers represented a narrow Jewish-Christian perspective (1:10) and sought leadership positions for financial gain (1:11). They had divided the churches and led a number of believers astray (1:11; 3:10).

Virtually everything that Paul wrote in Titus about the false teaching on Crete parallels what he said in 1 and 2 Timothy about that same issue in Ephesus (see "Introduction to 1 Timothy: Purpose and Distinctives"). While there is no reason to assume a direct link between the fallacious teachings in Ephesus and Crete or to assume that every idea being taught in one place was also being promoted in the other, the false teachings in the two areas may have been similar manifestations of a more general tendency to mix Christian faith with forms of Jewish syncretism. (See "Introduction: Purpose and Distinctives" for both Colossians and Ephesians.)

Outline

I. Salutation (1:1–4)	*Paul identified himself and explained his ministry as an apostle.*
II. Instructions for Titus (1:5—3:11) A. Organizing the Churches on Crete (1:5–9) 1. Titus's Organizational Responsibility (1:5) 2. Qualifications for Elders (1:6–9) B. Dealing With False Teachers (1:10–16) C. Instructions for Specific Groups (2:1–15) 1. Opening Charge to Titus (2:1) 2. Older and Younger, Men and Women (2:2–8) 3. Slaves (2:9–10) 4. The Basis of Christian Living (2:11–14) 5. Concluding Charge to Titus (2:15) D. Instructions for All Christians (3:1–8) 1. Opening Charge to Titus (3:1–2) 2. The Basis of Christian Living (3:3–7) 3. Closing Charge to Titus (3:8) E. Dealing With False Teachers (3:9–11)	*Paul gave Titus the responsibility of caring for the churches on Crete. Titus was to organize the churches by establishing qualified elders, as well as to oppose false teachers. Different groups within the church were to receive different instructions from Titus, but all Christians were to observe general instructions given by him. Titus was to avoid the divisive contentions of the false teachers.*
III. Conclusion (3:12–15)	*Paul encouraged Titus to fulfill his duties of guiding the churches on Crete, and Paul sent his greetings.*

1 Paul, a servant of God[a] and an apostle of Jesus Christ for the faith of God's elect and
the knowledge of the truth[b] that leads to godliness— 2 a faith and knowledge resting on the hope of eternal life,[c] which God, who does not lie, promised before the beginning of time,[d] 3 and at his appointed season[e] he brought his word to light[f] through the
preaching entrusted to me[g] by the command of God our Savior,[h]

4 To Titus,[i] my true son in our common faith:

Grace and peace from God the Father and Christ Jesus our Savior.

Titus's Task on Crete

5 The reason I left you in Crete[j] was that you might straighten out what was left unfinished and appoint[a] elders[k] in every town, as I directed you. 6 An elder must be blame-

1:1 [a]Ro 1:1 [b]1Ti 2:4
1:2 [c]2Ti 1:1 [d]2Ti 1:9
1:3 [e]1Ti 2:6 [f]2Ti 1:10 [g]1Ti 1:11 [h]Lk 1:47
1:4 [i]2Co 2:13
1:5 [j]Ac 27:7 [k]Ac 11:30

a 5 Or *ordain*

■ **1:1–4** *Salutation.* Paul opened his letter with an elaborate identification of himself as the author and Titus as the recipient of his letter, as well as with a benediction.
1:1 servant of God. Or "slave of God" (i.e., one who is owned by and serves God; Ro 1:1; Php 1:1). **apostle of Jesus Christ.** One sent out as an authoritative, official representative of Christ. **faith of God's elect.** As in many passages, Paul spoke of those who believed and those who would believe in the future as the ones who had been elected or chosen by God (2Ti 2:10; see theological article "Predestination and Foreknowledge" at Ro 8). **knowledge . . . that leads to godliness.** Paul's apostolic mission included more than converting the lost. He also recognized that believers must grow in their knowledge of truth in order to increase in godly living. Knowledge of truth does not always lead to godliness (1Co 13:2), but such knowledge is necessary for godliness. See *BC* 16.
1:2 the hope of eternal life. True Christian faith and knowledge are based on the hope that has been secured by Christ's death and resurrection (1Ti 1:1; 2Ti 1:1; see the note on 1Ti 1:16). **who does not lie.** An affirmation of God's complete trustworthiness. God cannot break his promises (Nu 23:19). **promised before the beginning of time.** The divine promise of salvation for the elect through the means of faith (v. 1) is eternal (2Ti 1:9).
1:3 brought . . . to light. Paul's preaching of the Christian gospel announced God's eternal promise in Christ. **God our Savior.** As author of the covenant of grace, God is Savior (2:10; 3:4; 1Ti 1:1; 2:3; 4:10; see theological article "The Covenants of Works and Grace" at Ge 6).
1:4 true son. Or "genuine son" (1Ti 1:2). This probably indicates that Titus was one of Paul's converts. There is no evidence that Paul had biological children; he considered himself the spiritual father of those he brought to Christ, and he loved them with a fatherly love. **Grace and peace.** This phrase is typical of the way Paul pronounced a benediction on believers. See note on 1 Timothy 1:2. **Christ Jesus our Savior.** As mediator of the covenant of grace, Christ is Savior (2:13; 3:6; 2Ti 1:10; see theological article "The Covenants of Works and Grace" at Ge 6). Paul used the title "Savior" interchangeably for both God and Christ throughout this letter (see note on v. 3), thereby reflecting his belief in the deity of Christ (2:13).
■ **1:5—3:11** *Instructions for Titus.* Paul moved into the body of the letter. His intention was to instruct Titus regarding how to act as his (Paul's) representative on Crete (see "Introduction: Purpose and Distinctives"). His teaching divides into five sections: organizing the church (1:5–9), false teachers (1:10–16), instructions for specific groups (2:1–15), instructions for all Christians (3:1–8) and a final word about false teachers (3:9–11).
■ **1:5–9** *Organizing the Churches on Crete.* Titus remained on Crete to organize the congregations of believers (v. 5). He did so primarily by establishing elders with proper qualifications (vv. 6–9).
■ **1:5** *Titus's Organizational Responsibility.* Paul reminded Titus that his purpose for remaining on Crete was to organize the churches.
1:5 what was left unfinished. Refers perhaps to the organization of the churches in general, but especially to the appointment

less,[l] the husband of but one wife, a man whose children believe and are not open to the
charge of being wild and disobedient. 7 Since an overseer[a][m] is entrusted with God's
work,[n] he must be blameless—not overbearing, not quick-tempered, not given to drunkenness, not violent, not pursuing dishonest gain.[o] 8 Rather he must be hospitable,[p] one
who loves what is good,[q] who is self-controlled, upright, holy and disciplined. 9 He must
hold firmly[r] to the trustworthy message as it has been taught, so that he can encourage
others by sound doctrine[s] and refute those who oppose it.

10 For there are many rebellious people, mere talkers[t] and deceivers, especially those
of the circumcision group.[u] 11 They must be silenced, because they are ruining whole
households[v] by teaching things they ought not to teach—and that for the sake of dishonest gain. 12 Even one of their own prophets[w] has said, "Cretans[x] are always liars, evil
brutes, lazy gluttons." 13 This testimony is true. Therefore, rebuke[y] them sharply, so that
they will be sound in the faith[z] 14 and will pay no attention to Jewish myths[a] or to the
commands[b] of those who reject the truth. 15 To the pure, all things are pure, but to those
who are corrupted and do not believe, nothing is pure.[c] In fact, both their minds and
consciences are corrupted. 16 They claim to know God, but by their actions they deny
him.[d] They are detestable, disobedient and unfit for doing anything good.

What Must Be Taught to Various Groups

2 You must teach what is in accord with sound doctrine.[e] 2 Teach the older men to be
temperate, worthy of respect, self-controlled, and sound in faith,[f] in love and in endurance.

3 Likewise, teach the older women to be reverent in the way they live, not to be slanderers or addicted to much wine,[g] but to teach what is good. 4 Then they can train the

1:6 [l]1Ti 3:2
1:7 [m]1Ti 3:1 [n]1Co 4:1 [o]1Ti 3:3,8
1:8 [p]1Ti 3:2 [q]2Ti 3:3
1:9 [r]1Ti 1:19 [s]1Ti 1:10
1:10 [t]1Ti 1:6 [u]Ac 11:2
1:11 [v]2Ti 3:6
1:12 [w]Ac 17:28 [x]Ac 2:11
1:13 [y]2Co 13:10 [z]Tit 2:2
1:14 [a]1Ti 1:4 [b]Col 2:22
1:15 [c]Ro 14:14,23
1:16 [d]1Jn 2:4
2:1 [e]1Ti 1:10
2:2 [f]Tit 1:13
2:3 [g]1Ti 3:8

[a] 7 Traditionally *bishop*

---

of elders. **elders.** Individuals charged with the general care of a local church (Ac 14:23; 20:17; 1Ti 5:17). As verse 7 makes clear, Paul used the term "elder" interchangeably with "overseer." In 1 Timothy 3:2–7 Paul discussed the qualifications for overseers in very similar terms. Neither list was intended to be complete; both indicate representative qualities required of those who would serve as elders. See *BC* 30; *HC* 103.

■ **1:6–9** *Qualifications for Elders.* The elders Titus was called to appoint over the churches on Crete were to meet certain qualifications.

1:6 the husband of but one wife. Probably a reference to marital fidelity (see note on 1Ti 3:2). This requirement precluded the practice of polygamy for elders. In all likelihood, Paul assumed that most, if not all, elders would be married, but there is no reason to suppose that he required elders to be married.

1:7 Since an overseer. Paul's casual shift from "elder" to "overseer" shows that he understood the two terms as referring to the same office (cf. Ac 20:17,28). He may well have seen slightly different nuances in them, perhaps with "elder" focusing on character (spiritual maturity) and "overseer" on task (cf. Ac 20:28). **dishonest gain.** One should not view church leadership as an opportunity for making money (v. 11; 1Ti 6:5,10), although Paul did sanction remuneration for pastoral ministry (1Co 9:7–9; 1Ti 2:17–18).

1:8 self-controlled. In light of the culture of Crete (vv. 12–13), it is no wonder that self-control was a major emphasis in this letter (2:2,4–6,12).

1:9 the trustworthy message as it has been taught. As in his letters to Timothy, Paul was concerned with the transmission of and commitment to sound doctrine in accordance with the gospel (see note on 1Ti 1:10). **encourage others by sound doctrine and refute those who oppose it.** Two tasks of the elder were especially relevant in view of the false teachers on Crete: teaching sound doctrine and refuting error.

■ **1:10–16** *Dealing With False Teachers.* Titus was to not only oppose and correct fallacious teaching, but also deal with the false teachers themselves.

1:10–13 See *WCF* 20.4.

1:10 those of the circumcision group. Not all Jewish Christians, but those who came from a narrow Jewish-Christian perspective (Ac 15:1,5; Gal 6:12–13; see "Introduction: Purpose and Distinctives").

1:11 ruining whole households. This may refer to the false teachers' activities either in local house churches, thus emphasizing the need for better organization (v. 5), or in individual Christian households. **things they ought not to teach.** Their teaching was not in accord with "sound doctrine" (v. 9). **dishonest gain.** See note on verse 7.

1:12 one of their own prophets. Paul quoted Epimenides, a poet and religious reformer from Knossos, Crete, who had lived during the sixth century B.C. and was known for his predictions and wisdom. Paul did not place Epimenides on the same level as the Old Testament prophets. Rather, he appealed to this philosopher because the people of ancient Crete esteemed him and because the self-deprecating nature of Epimenides's admission made the description more believable. Compare note on 2:12.

1:14 Jewish myths. The reference here is unclear. Perhaps Paul was referring to the kinds of legends about Old Testament figures that are found in many of the non-canonical Jewish writings (1Ti 1:4; 4:7; 2Ti 4:4). **commands.** These may be related to the false teachers' distinctive interpretations of the Mosaic Law (3:9; 1Ti 1:7; 4:3).

1:15 To the pure, all things are pure. The false teachers had apparently prohibited the use of certain things (see note on 1Ti 4:3). For Paul's response to similar teachings, see 1 Timothy 4:3–5. See *WCF* 6.2; 16.7.

1:16 by their actions. Paul condemned not only the doctrine of the false teachers, but also their actions (2Ti 3:2–5). Both sound doctrine and actions in accordance with a changed life are necessary for Christians. **they deny him.** A lack of actions consistent with a changed life renders one's faith in Christ suspect (Mt 7:16–20; Jas 2:14–17; 1Jn 3:17; see theological article "The Perseverance and Preservation of Believers" at Php 1). See *WLC* 105.

■ **2:1–15** *Instructions for Specific Groups.* Paul turned to the kinds of things that Titus, in contrast with the false teachers, ought to teach. Paul began and ended with an exhortation to Titus (vv. 1,15). He provided specific instructions on how older men, older women, younger women, younger men (vv. 2–8) and slaves (vv. 9–10) should live. Then he explained the basis for all Christian morality (vv. 11–14).

■ **2:1** *Opening Charge to Titus.* Paul laid the responsibility on Titus to teach "sound doctrine" (see note on 1:9) that was tailored to each specific group of people in the churches on Crete.

2:1 See *WLC* 159.

■ **2:2–8** *Older and Younger, Men and Women.* Titus was to consider the ages and genders of those whom he led, for each group had special needs (cf. 1Ti 5:1–2).

2:2 self-controlled. This quality dominates Paul's advice in this section (vv. 4–6,12; see 1:8 and its note).

2:3–5 See *WLC* 129.

2:3 to teach what is good. Literally, "teachers of what is good." This probably refers to their manner in the home, as the next verse suggests.

2:4 train. A verbal form of the adjective translated "self-controlled" throughout this section. Paul repeated it in the next verse. He probably had in mind the problems that some of the younger widows were encountering in Ephesus (1Ti 5:11–13). Note that

younger women to love their husbands and children, 5 to be self-controlled and pure, to
be busy at home, to be kind, and to be subject to their husbands,[h] so that no one will
malign the word of God.[i]
6 Similarly, encourage the young men[j] to be self-controlled. 7 In everything set them
an example[k] by doing what is good. In your teaching show integrity, seriousness 8 and
soundness of speech that cannot be condemned, so that those who oppose you may be
ashamed because they have nothing bad to say about us.[l]
9 Teach slaves to be subject to their masters in everything,[m] to try to please them, not
to talk back to them, 10 and not to steal from them, but to show that they can be fully
trusted, so that in every way they will make the teaching about God our Savior attractive.[n]
11 For the grace of God that brings salvation has appeared to all men.[o] 12 It teaches us
to say "No" to ungodliness and worldly passions,[p] and to live self-controlled, upright and
godly lives[q] in this present age, 13 while we wait for the blessed hope—the glorious appearing of our great God and Savior, Jesus Christ,[r] 14 who gave himself for us to redeem
us from all wickedness and to purify for himself a people that are his very own,[s] eager
to do what is good.[t]
15 These, then, are the things you should teach. Encourage and rebuke with all authority. Do not let anyone despise you.

Doing What Is Good

3 Remind the people to be subject to rulers and authorities,[u] to be obedient, to be
ready to do whatever is good,[v] 2 to slander no one,[w] to be peaceable and considerate, and to show true humility toward all men.
3 At one time we too were foolish, disobedient, deceived and enslaved by all kinds
of passions and pleasures. We lived in malice and envy, being hated and hating one another. 4 But when the kindness[x] and love of God our Savior appeared,[y] 5 he saved us, not

2:5 [h]Eph 5:22 [i]1Ti 6:1
2:6 [j]1Ti 5:1
2:7 [k]1Ti 4:12
2:8 [l]1Pe 2:12
2:9 [m]Eph 6:5
2:10 [n]Mt 5:16
2:11 [o]1Ti 2:4
2:12 [p]Tit 3:3 [q]2Ti 3:12
2:13 [r]2Pe 1:1
2:14 [s]Ex 19.5 [t]Eph 2:10
3:1 [u]Ro 13:1 [v]2Ti 2:21
3:2 [w]Eph 4:31; 2Ti 2:24
3:4 [x]Eph 2:7 [y]Tit 2:11

although Paul gave Titus teaching pertaining to older men, older women and young men, he instructed Titus to prepare the older women to train the younger women. Teaching the younger women indirectly rather than directly would have removed a source of temptation for Titus and made good use of the teaching gifts of older women. See *WLC* 129.

2:5 busy at home. Contrast the behavior of some of the younger widows in Ephesus (1Ti 5:13). This verse does not imply that homemaking is the only vocation permitted to a Christian woman. Rather, it instructs young, married women (likely with younger children) to attend to their responsibilities at home, rather than to be busybodies (cf. 1 Tim. 5:14). **to be subject.** See note on 1 Timothy 2:11. **so that no one will malign the word of God.** Paul's overriding concern throughout this section was that the behavior of Christians should reflect positively on the gospel (vv. 8,10). See *WCF* 16.2.

2:7 set them an example. Paul gave similar counsel to Timothy (see note on 1Ti 4:12). **doing what is good.** One of Paul's main themes in the remainder of this letter (v. 14; 3:1,8,14).

2:8 See *WLC* 159.

2:9–12 See *WCF* 16.2; 18.3; *HC* 124.

■ **2:9–10** *Slaves.* The dynamics of master-slave relations on Crete required special attention. See *WLC* 127.

2:9 slaves. Without approving of slavery (cf. 1Co 7:21; see note on 1Pe 2:18), Paul wanted Titus to encourage slaves in their hardships. Paul gave more instructions about slaves in other letters (Eph 6:5–8; Col 3:22–25; 1Ti 6:1–2).

2:10 make the teaching about God our Savior attractive. See note on verse 5. See *BC* 10.

■ **2:11–14** *The Basis of Christian Living.* These verses provide the theological basis for the practical instructions given in verses 2–10. See *WLC* 97.

2:11 the grace of God. God's unmerited compassion for sinners. **that brings salvation.** God's purpose in extending grace to sinners is their salvation (3:4–7; 2Ti 1:9). **has appeared.** That is, in Jesus Christ (3:4,6; 2Ti 1:10). **all men.** All types of people are in view, regardless of their gender, age, race or social class (vv. 2–10; 1Ti 2:1–6).

2:12 self-controlled, upright and godly. This verse provides an antidote, so to speak, to the characterization of Cretans as "liars, evil brutes, lazy gluttons" (1:12). Rather than being "liars," they were to be "godly" (Nu 23:19; cf. note on 1:2); instead of being "evil brutes," they were to be "upright"; as opposed to being "lazy gluttons," they were to be "self-controlled." See *BC* 24.

2:13–14 See *WLC* 38; *HC* 52.

2:13 the blessed hope—the glorious appearing. The second coming (1Ti 6:14; 2Ti 4:1,8). **our great God and Savior, Jesus Christ.** This is one of the clearest affirmations in the New Testament of the deity of Christ.

2:14 who gave himself for us. Christ freely gave himself as a substitute for sinners. Paul followed this by stating two purposes of Christ's death. **to redeem us from all wickedness.** Paul focused here on the individual: Christ paid the price necessary to free people from their sins (Mt 20:28; Mk 10:45; 1Ti 2.6; 1Pe 1:18 19). **to purify for himself a people that are his very own.** Paul focused here on the church: Christ purifies individuals from their sins (Heb 9:14; 1Jn 1:7,9) so that together they might constitute his special people (Eze 37:23; Eph 5:25–27). **eager to do what is good.** See note on verse 7. See *WCF* 3.6; 18.3; 20.1; *HC* 1.

■ **2:15** *Concluding Charge to Titus.* Paul completed his instructions for specific groups within the church by charging Titus a second time with his responsibilities.

2:15 Encourage and rebuke. An appropriate summation of the contrasting aspects of Paul's charge to Titus in verses 2–10 and 1:10–16. **with all authority.** Titus had significant authority because he was Paul's representative. **Do not let anyone despise you.** See verse 8; 1 Timothy 4:12. See also *WLC* 129.

■ **3:1–8** *Instructions for All Christians.* Having provided instructions for specific groups, Paul gave Titus general counsel (sandwiched around another meditation on the grace of God) on encouraging the entire church to do "whatever is good" (v. 1).

■ **3:1–2** *Opening Charge to Titus.* Titus bore the responsibility to remind the church on Crete of the need for Christian conduct in relation to believers and unbelievers alike.

3:1 rulers and authorities. On Christian submission to governing authorities, see Romans 13:1–7 (see also 1Pe 2:13–17; cf. 1Ti 2:1–2). **to do whatever is good.** The theme for this section is doing good (v. 8; see note on 2:7). See *WCF* 23.4; *BC* 36.

3:2 humility toward all men. Christians must show respect and humility to all types of people, not just to rulers and those in authority (v. 1).

■ **3:3–7** *The Basis of Christian Living.* As in 2:11–14, Paul offered a theological reflection as the basis for appropriate Christian living. See *WCF* 11.4.

3:3–7 See *WCF* 9.3; 10.2; 16.5; *WLC* 30,58,67; *WSC* 29; *BC* 9; *HC* 25,60.

3:3 This verse presents a graphic description of human depravity apart from Christ (Eph 2:1–3). See *HC* 5.

3:4 But when the kindness and love of God our Savior appeared. In keeping with verse 3, Paul's primary concern here was with the sinner's experience of God's grace rather than with the first advent of Christ (2Ti 1:10). At the same time, Paul's language highlights the fact that the sinner's experience of God's

3:5 because of righteous things we had done,[z] but because of his mercy. He saved us
3:6 through the washing of rebirth and renewal[a] by the Holy Spirit, [6]whom he poured out
on us[b] generously through Jesus Christ our Savior, [7]so that, having been justified by his

[z]Eph 2:9 [a]Ro 12:2 [b]Ro 5:5

grace involves participation in the new age and new creation that Christ inaugurated in his first advent (see note on 2Co 5:17 and theological article "The Plan of the Ages" at Heb 7). See *BC* 9,16.
3:5 he saved us. See 2 Timothy 1:9. **not because of righteous things we had done, but because of his mercy.** Salvation is by grace, not works (v. 6; Eph 2:8–9; 2Ti 1:9). **washing.** Spiritual cleansing, of which baptism is the sign and seal (1Co 6:11; Eph 5:26). **of rebirth and renewal.** Both words characterize the "washing." "Rebirth" is the new life that begins when a person comes to faith in Christ (Jn 3:3,5; 1Pe 1:3,23). Renewal is closely related to rebirth; it signifies the complete transformation of a person's life that begins when he or she is regenerated (Ro 12:2; 2Co 5:17). **by the Holy Spirit.** The Spirit applies to individuals the grace of God that is extended in Christ (Jn 3:5–6). Note the Trinitarianism of verses 4–6. See *WCF* 11.1; 27.2; 28.1; 28.6; 28.7; *WLC* 70,165,177; *BC* 9,16,22,24,34; *HC* 71,78.
3:7 justified. Declared to be righteous, that is, to have met the standard of God's justice. **by his grace.** Left to ourselves (vv. 3–4),

Sanctification: When Will I Stop Sinning?

THE term *sanctification* and associated words (*sanctified, holy, holiness, consecrated, consecration, saints*) are used many different ways in Scripture. In one sense, to be sanctified is to be set apart from the world—not for salvation, but for the special privileges and responsibilities of a covenant relationship with God (1Co 7:14; Heb 10:29). In another sense, sanctification is a state of being permanently set apart to God for salvation. This holiness flows from the cross, where God through Christ purchased and claimed us for himself (Ac 20:28; 26:18; Heb 10:10). In still another sense, sanctification is the consecration of believers whereby their lives are changed over time to conform to the likeness of Christ. This moral or progressive sanctification, as it has been called, flows from the work of the Holy Spirit. God calls all of his children to seek sanctification, and he provides the Spirit's power to fulfill this call (Ro 8:13; 12:1–2; 1Co 6:11,19–20; 2Co 3:18; Eph 4:22–24; 1Th 4:4; 5:23; 2Th 2:13; Heb 13:20–21). Such sanctification is directed toward the standard of God's moral law and expounded and modeled by Christ himself (see theological article "The Three Uses of the Law" at Ps 119).

Reformed theologians usually have this third sense in mind; when they use the term *sanctification,* they are referring to the ongoing transformation of believers that results in righteous living. Regeneration is birth; glorification is the final goal; sanctification is growth out of regeneration toward the goal of glorification. In regeneration, God implants within the believer's heart a desire for God, holiness and the hallowing and glorifying of God's name in this world. He also instills a desire to pray, worship, love, serve, honor and please God, to show love and bring benefit to others (see theological article "Regeneration and New Birth" at Jn 3). In sanctification, the Holy Spirit "works in [us] to will and to act according to [God's] good purpose" (Php 2:13), and he prompts all believers to "work out [their] salvation" (Php 2:12) by fulfilling these new desires. Christians are "predestined to be conformed to the likeness of [Christ]" (Ro 8:29), and this conformity takes place to some degree even in this earthly life. Paul described this process as "being transformed into [Christ's] likeness with ever-increasing glory" (2Co 3:18). Sanctification, therefore, is the beginning of glorification. Our physical transformation when Christ brings the new heavens and the new earth will fully complete our glorification (1Co 15:49–53; Php 3:20–21).

In traditional Reformed theology, regeneration is a momentary act of God that quickens the spiritually dead. It is God's work alone that brings about the new birth. Sanctification, however, is ongoing and requires our cooperation. It is a process in which regenerate persons, alive to God and freed from sin's dominion (Ro 6:11,14–18), are required to exert themselves in sustained obedience through conscious dependence on Christ's Spirit. Paul described sanctification both as human effort and as the work of God. For instance, Paul freely acknowledged his own efforts when he said, "I press on to take hold of that for which Christ Jesus took hold of me" (Php 3:12). Near the end of his life he asserted, "I have fought the good fight . . . finished the race . . . kept the faith" (2Ti 4:7). Yet Paul also warned the Galatians, "After beginning with the Spirit, are you now trying to attain your goal by human effort?" (Gal 3:3). He rejected any thought that human endeavor alone was sufficient for sanctification, declaring, "I no longer live, but Christ lives in me" (Gal 2:20). Knowing that without Christ's enabling we can do nothing as we should, and believing that he is ready to strengthen us for all that we have to do (Php 4:13), we must consciously depend on his Spirit to empower all of our efforts (Col 1:11; 1Ti 1:12; 2Ti 1:7; 2:1).

Despite the Spirit's leading, true believers find conflict within themselves. The Spirit sustains their regenerate desires, but their fallen human nature is not yet destroyed and constantly distracts them from doing God's will (Gal 5:16–17; Jas 1:14–15). This conflict will be with Christians as long as they are in this life. Yet by watching and praying against temptation and by cultivating virtues to aid them in their battle, they may through the Spirit's help experience many particular deliverances and victories in their confrontation with sin.

Such victories over sin are not meritorious for salvation. Our merit before God comes from our justification through faith alone through the imputation of Christ's righteousness (Ro 4:1–4). Although we must never forget that our only merit before God is the righteousness we receive from Christ, we nevertheless must "make every effort . . . to be holy; without holiness no one will see the Lord" (Heb 12:14). See *WCF* 8; *BC* 24.

grace,[c] we might become heirs[d] having the hope[e] of eternal life.[f] 8This is a trustworthy saying.[g] And I want you to stress these things, so that those who have trusted in God
may be careful to devote themselves to doing what is good.[h] These things are excellent
and profitable for everyone.
9But avoid foolish controversies and genealogies and arguments and quarrels[i] about
the law, because these are unprofitable and useless. 10Warn a divisive person once, and
then warn him a second time. After that, have nothing to do with him.[j] 11You may be sure
that such a man is warped and sinful; he is self-condemned.

Final Remarks

12As soon as I send Artemas or Tychicus[k] to you, do your best to come to me at Nicopolis, because I have decided to winter there.[l] 13Do everything you can to help Zenas
the lawyer and Apollos[m] on their way and see that they have everything they need. 14Our
people must learn to devote themselves to doing what is good,[n] in order that they may
provide for daily necessities and not live unproductive lives.
15Everyone with me sends you greetings. Greet those who love us in the faith.[o]
Grace be with you all.[p]

3:7 [c]Ro 3:24 [d]Ro 8:17 [e]Ro 8:24 [f]Tit 1:2
3:8 [g]1Ti 1:15 [h]Tit 2:14
3:9 [i]1Ti 1:4; 2Ti 2:14
3:10 [j]Ro 16:17
3:12 [k]Ac 20:4 [l]2Ti 4:9, 21
3:13 [m]Ac 18:24
3:14 [n]ver 8
3:15 [o]1Ti 1:2 [p]Col 4:18

---

we could never stand righteous before God. The point of verses 3–7 is that righteousness comes through God's grace alone (Ro 3:21–25). **heirs.** God's purpose in extending his grace to sinners is not only to save them from eternal judgment, but also to make them part of his family through adoption and thus heirs of his promises (Ro 8:17; Gal 3:29; 4:7). See *WCF* 11.1; *WLC* 70.

▪ **3:8** *Closing Charge to Titus.* Paul urged Titus to stress these teachings because they would benefit everyone.

3:8 This is a trustworthy saying. See note on 1 Timothy 1:15. The expression points back to verses 4–7. **doing what is good.** See note on verse 1. **profitable for everyone.** Those who follow the instructions of verses 1–2 will receive many benefits. See *BC* 24.

▪ **3:9–11** *Dealing With False Teachers.* By way of contrast with the instructions that he had just given, Paul returned one last time to the problem of the false teachers.

3:9 controversies. A prominent characteristic of the false teachers was their contentiousness (1Ti 1:4; 6:4). **about the law.** The Law of Moses (see note on 1:10; cf. 1Ti 1:7). **unprofitable.** To be contrasted with doing what is good and therefore "profitable" (v. 8). See *WLC* 113.

3:10–11 See *WLC* 151.

3:10 Church discipline in the case of divisiveness is to include a series of warnings (cf. Mt 18:15–17). Such warnings are also appropriate in many other cases. **divisive person.** The false teachers had caused division in the churches (1Ti 6:4–5). See *WCF* 20.4; 30.4; *WLC* 105,151; *BC* 29.

▪ **3:12–15** *Conclusion.* Paul closed this letter with personal instructions to Titus, final greetings and a benediction.

3:12 Artemas. Mentioned nowhere else in the New Testament. He was apparently one of Paul's coworkers. **Tychicus.** A coworker of Paul (Ac 20:4; Eph 6:21; Col 4:7; 2Ti 4:12). **do your best to come to me.** Titus's ministry on Crete was nearing its end (see "Introduction: Purpose and Distinctives"). **Nicopolis.** A city on the western coast of the Roman province of Epirus (western Greece). **I have decided to winter there.** Paul was in, or on his way to, Nicopolis.

3:13 Zenas . . . Apollos. Probably the bearers of this letter. Zenas is mentioned nowhere else in the New Testament. He was apparently one of Paul's coworkers. Apollos, a native of Alexandria, was noted for his eloquence (Ac 18:24–26). He is best known for his ministry in Corinth (Ac 18:27—19:1; 1Co 1:12; 3:4–22; 16:12).

3:14 doing what is good. See note on 2:7.

3:15 you all. Presumably Paul intended the letter to be read to the entire church (see 1Ti 6:21; 2Ti 4:22 and their notes). See *WCF* 16.7

PHILEMON

Introduction

Overview
Author: The apostle Paul
Purpose: To obtain forgiveness for the runaway slave Onesimus
Date: c. A.D. 60
Key Truths:
- Christians must express love and forgiveness toward one another.
- Christian obedience ought to be elicited willingly rather than forcefully.

Author
The letter to Philemon was written by the apostle Paul. The authenticity of this epistle has not been seriously challenged.

Time and Place of Writing
This letter was written while Paul was in prison in Rome (c. A.D. 60), probably at approximately the same time he wrote to the Colossians. This letter was probably delivered to Philemon along with the letter to the Colossians.

Original Audience
Paul wrote to Philemon, a Christian brother and slaveholder in Colosse. Philemon's slave Onesimus had run away and, perhaps seeking assistance, had come into contact with Paul in Rome. During this visit Onesimus had become a Christian.

Purpose and Distinctives
Paul's overriding purpose in writing this letter was to appeal to Philemon to receive Onesimus back as a Christian brother (vv. 12–16). To accomplish this purpose, Paul reminded Philemon of the brotherly relationship he and Philemon shared in Christ. Since Onesimus had become very dear to Paul (vv. 12,16), Paul encouraged Philemon to receive back his runaway slave in the same manner as he would receive Paul himself (v. 17).

Philemon provides us with a clear example of how to apply the teaching of Scripture to everyday problems. Following Christ's example, Paul acted as a mediator out of love for Onesimus, and he pointed to the unity of believers as brothers and sisters in Christ as the basis for mutual love and forgiveness.

Outline

I. Introductory Greetings (1–3)	*Paul identified himself as the author and Philemon as the primary recipient of the letter.*
II. Thanksgiving (4–7)	*Paul gave thanks for Philemon's past expressions of love toward Christians.*
III. Paul's Request for Onesimus (8–21)	*Paul requested that Philemon forgive the crime of his runaway slave, Onesimus, and receive Onesimus back as a brother in Christ.*
IV. Final Requests and Conclusion (22–25)	*Paul hoped that he would be released from prison, so he requested that Philemon prepare a room for him. He closed with final greetings.*

1 Paul, a prisoner[a] of Christ Jesus, and Timothy our brother,[b]

To Philemon our dear friend and fellow worker,[c] 2 to Apphia our sister, to Archippus[d]
our fellow soldier[e] and to the church that meets in your home:[f]

3 Grace to you and peace from God our Father and the Lord Jesus Christ.

Thanksgiving and Prayer

4 I always thank my God[g] as I remember you in my prayers, 5 because I hear about your
faith in the Lord Jesus and your love for all the saints.[h] 6 I pray that you may be active in
sharing your faith, so that you will have a full understanding of every good thing we have
in Christ. 7 Your love has given me great joy and encouragement,[i] because you, brother, have refreshed[j] the hearts of the saints.

Paul's Plea for Onesimus

8 Therefore, although in Christ I could be bold and order you to do what you ought to
do, 9 yet I appeal to you on the basis of love. I then, as Paul—an old man and now also
a prisoner[k] of Christ Jesus— 10 I appeal to you for my son[l] Onesimus,[a][m] who became my
son while I was in chains. 11 Formerly he was useless to you, but now he has become useful both to you and to me.

12 I am sending him—who is my very heart—back to you. 13 I would have liked to keep
him with me so that he could take your place in helping me while I am in chains for the
gospel. 14 But I did not want to do anything without your consent, so that any favor you
do will be spontaneous and not forced.[n] 15 Perhaps the reason he was separated from you
for a little while was that you might have him back for good— 16 no longer as a slave, but
better than a slave, as a dear brother.[o] He is very dear to me but even dearer to you, both
as a man and as a brother in the Lord.

17 So if you consider me a partner,[p] welcome him as you would welcome me. 18 If he
has done you any wrong or owes you anything, charge it to me. 19 I, Paul, am writing this

1 [a]ver 9,23; Eph 3:1 [b]2Co 1:1 [c]Php 2:25
2 [d]Col 4:17 [e]Php 2:25 [f]Ro 16:5
4 [g]Ro 1:8
5 [h]Eph 1:15; Col 1:4
7 [i]2Co 7:4,13 [j]ver 20
9 [k]ver 1,23
10 [l]1Co 4:15 [m]Col 4:9
14 [n]2Co 9:7; 1Pe 5:2
16 [o]Mt 23:8; 1Ti 6:2
17 [p]2Co 8:23

a *10 Onesimus* means *useful.*

■ **1–3** *Introductory Greetings.* Paul identified himself, along with Timothy, as the author. He addressed Philemon as the main recipient of the letter and sent greetings to many others.
1 prisoner. Paul knew that his imprisonment was due to his stand for Christ and the gospel (cf. Php 1:7). **our dear friend and fellow worker.** Paul's affection for Philemon allowed him to approach him openly about the delicate matter of Onesimus.
2 Apphia. Probably Philemon's wife. She may have had some influence regarding how Onesimus would be treated upon his return. **Archippus . . . church.** Perhaps a local pastor in Colosse. The church probably met in Archippus's house, although another possible reading is that it met in Philemon's house. That Paul intended Archippus and the church to know the letter's contents likely indicates that he hoped they would hold Philemon accountable for heeding Paul's appeal.
3 you. Plural in form, it was addressed to Philemon, Apphia, Archippus and the church.
■ **4–7** *Thanksgiving.* Paul recognized and appreciated Philemon's past loving behavior and treatment of fellow believers, especially because it gave him hope that Philemon would act in a loving manner toward Onesimus.
4 I always thank my God. In verses 4–7, Paul related by way of his prayer the basis of his joy in Philemon's friendship (i.e., the common bond of their faith in Christ). Paul's letters often contain sections of thanksgiving (Php 1:3–6; Col 1:3–6).
5 love for all the saints. Philemon's reputation for loving fellow Christians encouraged Paul to believe that Philemon would also show love and mercy to Onesimus.
7 refreshed the hearts of the saints. Philemon had been a blessing to God's people. His compassion and love were evident (cf. v. 5).
■ **8–21** *Paul's Request for Onesimus.* Paul directly requested that Philemon show mercy to his returning runaway slave. Paul appealed to Philemon to receive Onesimus as a brother in Christ and not to discipline him for his crime.
8 I could . . . order. It was within Paul's apostolic authority to demand that Philemon receive Onesimus as a brother and refrain from disciplining him. **what you ought to do.** Paul made it clear that it would be sinful for Philemon to act in a manner contrary to Paul's advice.
9-10 I appeal to you. Paul wanted Philemon to choose, rather than be compelled, to do the right thing. This was for Philemon's benefit, probably so that God would reward his loving decision (cf. 1Co 9:17). **who became my son.** Paul felt affection for Onesimus because he had given spiritual birth to him when Onesimus visited him in prison. Paul expressed such affection on other occasions as well (1Co 4:15; Gal 4:19; 1Th 2:7,11).
11 useless . . . useful. Paul employed a play on words. The name *Onesimus* means "useful." As a rebellious slave, Onesimus had not been useful, but having repented of his rebellion and become obedient to Christ, he had now become useful both to Paul and to Philemon.
12 my very heart. Paul spoke of Onesimus in the most emotional terms possible. The Greek word for "heart" points to the seat of the emotions. Paul implied that any mistreatment of Onesimus would affect himself (Paul) deeply. Upon return to their masters, runaway slaves were frequently beaten severely and/or assigned tasks that significantly reduced their life expectancy.
13–14 helping me . . . your consent. Paul requested that Philemon not only forgive Onesimus but also return him to Paul so that he might minister to Paul in his imprisonment.
14 not forced. See note on verses 9–10.
15 the reason. Paul did not excuse Onesimus's crime of running away, but he saw God's hand of providence even in Onesimus's sin (cf. Ge 45:4–9; Ac 4:27–28; Ro 8:28).
16 as a dear brother. The relationship between Philemon and Onesimus would be different now, because Onesimus was now counted as a fellow believer in Christ.
17–19 Paul came to the main point of requesting that Philemon receive Onesimus as a Christian brother. Paul knew he could appeal to Philemon's love and forgiveness because Philemon had received God's forgiveness. God's love dwelling in believers transforms their relationships. **as you would welcome me . . . charge it to me . . . I will pay it back.** Following the example of Christ and demonstrating the depth of his love for Onesimus, Paul offered himself as a substitute for Onesimus. This placed Philemon in the awkward position of having to exact punishment on the beloved apostle Paul if he were to refuse to show mercy to Onesimus. Clearly such a course of action would have been ill received by the church, leaving Philemon no alternative but to choose to do the right thing. **you owe me your very self.** Paul was evidently the one who had converted Philemon, so in a real sense Philemon owed Paul his eternal life. For the benefit of Onesimus, Paul called in this debt. The strong, persuasive tech-

with my own hand. I will pay it back—not to mention that you owe me your very self. 20 I
do wish, brother, that I may have some benefit from you in the Lord; refresh[q] my heart
in Christ. 21 Confident[r] of your obedience, I write to you, knowing that you will do even
more than I ask.

22 And one thing more: Prepare a guest room for me, because I hope to be[s] restored
to you in answer to your prayers.[t]

23 Epaphras,[u] my fellow prisoner in Christ Jesus, sends you greetings. 24 And so do
Mark,[v] Aristarchus,[w] Demas[x] and Luke, my fellow workers.
25 The grace of the Lord Jesus Christ be with your spirit.[y]

20 [q]ver 7
21 [r]2Co 2:3
22 [s]Php 1:25; 2:24 [t]2Co 1:11
23 [u]Col 1:7
24 [v]Ac 12:12 [w]Ac 19:29 [x]Col 4:14
25 [y]2Ti 4:22

niques found in these verses indicate the depth of Paul's love for Onesimus and the strength of his determination that Philemon act in a loving manner.

■ **22–25** *Final Requests and Conclusion.* Paul offered final greetings and indicated his hope of restoration to the church in Colosse.

22 a guest room. Paul anticipated being released from prison, which apparently did eventually happen. Whether he made it back to Colosse or not, we do not know.

HEBREWS

Introduction

Overview

Author: Unknown

Purpose: To encourage fidelity to Christ and the new covenant by showing that Christ is the new, final and superior high priest

Date: Before A.D. 70

Key Truths:

- Christ is superior to angels, Moses, Aaron and the Old Testament priestly ministry.
- The Old Testament admitted the temporary character of its structures, so the new covenant is not at all contrary to the old.
- Turning from Christ and back to outmoded forms of faith will lead to divine judgment.
- People of the church must persevere to the end in faithfulness to Christ or they will suffer divine judgment.

Author

The author of Hebrews was a man (he used the masculine form of a Greek verb in referring to himself in 11:32) who was skilled in Greek and in Hellenistic literary style. He was immersed in the Old Testament (especially in the Septuagint, the Greek translation of the OT) and was sensitive to the way in which salvation history culminates in Jesus. He had a pastoral concern for his original readers, knew them personally (13:22–23) and understood their background (10:32–34). Like his readers, the author came to faith not through direct contact with Jesus, but through the ministry established by the apostles (2:3–4). He was also acquainted with Timothy (13:23).

Because the epistle does not reveal the author's name, we are left with a tantalizing mystery. By the time of Clement of Alexandria (c. 150–215) and Origen (185–253), the Eastern church had attributed the epistle to Paul. In the West, Tertullian (c. 155–220) proposed Barnabas (Ac 4:36) as the author. Other early suggestions were Luke and Clement of Rome (c. 95). From the fifth to the sixteenth centuries, Pauline authorship was largely accepted both in the East and in the West. During the Reformation Luther proposed Apollos (Ac 18:24–28) as the writer. Other nominees for authorship in the modern period have included Priscilla (but cf. 11:32, where the author described his own action with a masculine verb), Epaphras (Col 1:7) and Silas (Ac 15:22,32,40; 1Pe 5:12).

While it is difficult to rule out many of these candidates, it is equally hard to mount a convincing case in favor of any one of them. From the standpoint of early tradition, the strongest argument can be made for Pauline authorship, but Calvin rightly observed that Hebrews differs from Paul's writings in its style, teaching method and in the author's inclusion of himself among the disciples of the apostolic ministry. The statement in 2:3 is "wholly different," according to John Calvin in his *Commentary on the Epistle to the Hebrews,* from Paul's claims to have received his apostolic appointment and revelation of the gospel directly from Christ (e.g., Gal 1:1,11–12).

The epistle has theological affinities with Paul's writings, but the same is true of John's "Word" Christology and the portrayal of Jesus' suffering in the Synoptic Gospels. In any case, if the author is not someone whose background or other writings we know, his identity would add little to our understanding of the epistle.

Time and Place of Writing

Apparently the temple was still standing and its sacrificial rituals being regularly performed (10:1–3,11) at the time of writing. Since the temple was destroyed in A.D. 70, this indicates a probable date of composition prior to that time. If Hebrews was written during the time of the persecutions under Nero (c. A.D. 64), the suffering mentioned in 10:32–34 could have been caused by an edict of Claudius that expelled Jews from Rome in A.D. 49 (Ac 18:2).

Original Audience

Hebrews offers a fair amount of information about the original recipients and their situation. The original readers spoke Greek and probably used the Greek translation of the Old Testament (the Septuagint). They were able to follow arguments drawn from the Old Testament and were interested in the Old Testament sanctuary, sacrificial system and priesthood. They had heard the gospel through the apostolic word (2:3) rather than directly from Jesus. In addition, they may have been undergoing a transition in church leadership (13:7,17) and therefore may have been concerned about security and permanence (6:19; 11:10; 13:8,14). In any event, they had suffered, and were currently suffering, persecution (10:32–34; 13:3). Although they had not yet been martyred, death for the cause of Christ was likely a real possibility for them (12:4). It is possible that they had also been expelled from Jewish institutions (13:12–13) and thus shamed for their confession of Jesus and stripped of the familiar and visible institutions of organized Jewish religion. Some may have been tempted to "shrink back" (10:38–39) into unbelief and so to give up their journey toward God's rest and God's city (4:1–2,11; 11:10,14–16; 13:14). Finally, they received greetings through the author from "those from Italy" (13:24).

Drawing these features together, we may conclude that the recipients were primarily Jewish Christians of the dispersion. They probably lived in Italy (13:24 is likely a greeting sent "home" by expatriates) and may have lived in Rome, where the earliest evidence of acquaintance with the epistle has been found (in the early postapostolic document known as *1 Clement*).

Purpose and Distinctives

Hebrews' high literary style and theological interests set it apart from other New Testament books. Among its greatest contributions to the New Testament revelation of Jesus Christ is its detailed disclosure of Jesus' fulfillment of the temple, sacrifices and priesthood that were established in the Law of Moses (chs. 8–9).

The author referred to his work as a "word of exhortation" (13:22). Since the same Greek expression in Acts 13:15 ("message of encouragement") refers to a synagogue speech, this term may identify this "epistle" as an expository sermon in written form. Hebrews is aptly described as a "word of exhortation" (13:22), for exhortation and encouragement are at the heart of the book's purpose (3:13; 6:17–20; 10:25; 12:5–6). Hebrews repeatedly calls its readers to an active and courageous response (e.g., 4:11,14,16; 6:1; 10:19–25).

The exhortation to persevere in the faith of the new covenant rises from the fact that the Old Testament itself testifies to the incompleteness of the covenant at Sinai and of the Old Testament sacrificial system, thereby pointing out the need for a future, superior priest. That superior priest is Jesus Christ, who far surpasses the mediators, temple and sacrifices of the old order. He is worthy of "greater honor than Moses" (3:3). The "how much more" arguments of 2:2–3, 9:13–14, 10:28–29 and 12:25 underscore the greater grace and glory—and thus the greater accountability—that have arrived in the new covenant mediated by Jesus. Jesus calls believers to worship God in reality, so they may draw near to heaven itself with clean consciences. Jesus Christ is the guarantee of this better covenant, for he links us inseparably with the God of grace.

Outline

I. Christ Is Superior to the Angels (1:1—2:18) A. God's Last and Best Word in His Son (1:1–4) B. Scriptural Testimony to the Son's Greater Honor (1:5–14) C. Exhortation to Adhere to the Son (2:1–4) D. The Son and His Brothers (2:5–18)	*Revelation given by Christ, the Son of God, is superior to the revelation given to Moses by angels.*
II. Christ Is Superior to Moses (3:1—4:13) A. The Son and the Servant (3:1–6) B. Exhortation to Reject Disbelief (3:7—4:13)	*Christ, the Son of God, must never be rejected by a return to Moses, the servant of God.*
III. Christ Is Superior to Aaron (4:14—7:28) A. Christ, the Eternal High Priest (4:14—5:10) B. Exhortation to Spiritual Maturity (5:11—6:12) C. A Priest Forever by Divine Oath (6:13–20) D. A Priest Forever After the Order of Melchizedek (7:1–28)	*Christ's eternal high priesthood is far superior to the temporary high priesthood given to Aaron and his family.*
IV. Christ Is Superior to Priestly Ministry (8:1—10:18) A. A Superior Covenant (8:1–13) B. A Superior Tabernacle (9:1–10) C. A Superior Sacrifice (9:11–28) D. Christ's Sacrifice Once for All Time (10:1–18)	*Christ is superior to the priestly worship and sacrifices of the Old Testament because of the superiority of his covenant, his tabernacle and his sacrifice.*
V. Call to Persevere in Faith (10:19—12:29) A. Superior Covenant and Greater Responsibility (10:19–39) B. Examples of the Life of Faith (11:1–40) C. True Children of God (12:1–17) D. The Heavenly Jerusalem (12:18–29)	*Responsibility to remain faithful to the end is heightened in the new covenant, even in very difficult times.*
VI. Conclusion (13:1–25) A. Final Exhortations (13:1–19) B. Benediction and Greetings (13:20–25)	*Christians must remember basic moral and ethical practices as they live for Christ.*

The Son Superior to Angels

1 In the past God spoke[a] to our forefathers through the prophets[b] at many times and
in various ways,[c] 2 but in these last days he has spoken to us by his Son, whom he
appointed heir[d] of all things, and through whom[e] he made the universe. 3 The Son is the
radiance of God's glory[f] and the exact representation of his being, sustaining all things[g]
by his powerful word. After he had provided purification for sins,[h] he sat down at the
right hand of the Majesty in heaven.[i] 4 So he became as much superior to the angels as
the name he has inherited is superior to theirs.[j]
5 For to which of the angels did God ever say,

> "You are my Son;
> today I have become your Father[a]"[b]?[k]

Or again,

> "I will be his Father,
> and he will be my Son"[c]?[l]

6 And again, when God brings his firstborn into the world,[m] he says,

> "Let all God's angels worship him."[d][n]

1:1 [a]Jn 9:29; Heb 2:2, 3 [b]Ac 2:30 [c]Nu 12:6,8
1:2 [d]Ps 2:8 [e]Jn 1:3
1:3 [f]Jn 1:14 [g]Col 1:17 [h]Heb 7:27 [i]Mk 16:19
1:4 [j]Eph 1:21; Php 2:9, 10
1:5 [k]Ps 2:7 [l]2Sa 7:14
1:6 [m]Heb 10:5 [n]Dt 32:43 (LXX and DSS); Ps 97:7

[a] 5 Or *have begotten you* [b] 5 Psalm 2:7 [c] 5 2 Samuel 7:14; 1 Chron. 17:13 [d] 6 Deut. 32:43 (see Dead Sea Scrolls and Septuagint)

▪ **1:1—2:18** *Christ Is Superior to the Angels.* The epistle opens by focusing on the ways in which Christ is greater than angels. This material divides into four main sections: the greatest revelation in God's Son (1:1–4), the Old Testament witness to the superiority of Christ (1:5–14), an exhortation to be faithful to God's Son (2:1–4) and God's Son and his brothers (2:5–18).
1:1–14 See *HC* 33.
▪ **1:1–4** *God's Last and Best Word in His Son.* The prologue declares that Christ is superior to angels because he is the final revelation of God.
1:1–2 See *WCF* 1.1; *WLC* 43; *BC* 10; *HC* 19.
1:1 God spoke. An important theme in Hebrews (2:2–3; 4:12; 6:5; 11:3; 12:25). **prophets.** The piecemeal character of prophetic revelation showed its incompleteness, just as the repetition of animal sacrifices showed that they could not remove guilt (10:1). **at many times.** The writer referred to two time periods: "the past" (v. 1) and "these last days" (v. 2). The former refers to Old Testament times; the latter to the New Testament period. As in the rest of the New Testament, Christ's coming marks our present time period as the "last days" of salvation that the prophets promised would follow the exile (9:26; see also Dt 4:30; Isa 2:2; Jer 23:20; 1Co 10:11). See theological article "The Plan of the Ages" at Hebrews 7. **in various ways.** These ways included visions, dreams and riddles (Nu 12:6–8; alluded to in 3:5).
1:2 his Son. To say that any other revelation was superior to Old Testament revelation was a radical departure from traditional Judaism of the first century. Yet even Moses, the greatest spokesman for God, was only a prophet, a mere servant in God's house. Jesus was "a son over God's house" (3:6). The Son speaks, as the prophets did, but with greater authority and finality. **heir of all things.** The Son's supremacy will be displayed at the end of history, for "all things were created by him and for him" (Col 1:16). He is the firstborn (v. 6), the preeminent heir, whose enemies will be put under his feet (v. 13, citing Ps 110:1). As God's sons through Jesus, we are also heirs (v. 14; 6:12,17; Ro 8:14–17; Gal 4:6–7). **through whom he made the universe.** The Son's supremacy was also displayed at the dawn of history, for "by him all things were created" (Col 1:16; see also Jn 1:3). **universe.** Literally, "ages" (used also in 11:3), highlighting the successive periods of history in the created order (see also vv. 10–12). See *WCF* 4.1; 8.1.
1:3 radiance of God's glory. The glory of God is his radiance; Jesus therefore is God himself, the display of his glorious divinity (see theological article "The Glory of God" at Eze 1:28). **exact representation of his being.** This verse expresses both the Son's unity of essence with the Father and the distinction of divine persons. As One whose being corresponds exactly to the Father, the Son accurately reveals the Father. Christ is the "image of the invisible God" (Col 1:15); through him we see the Father (Jn 14:9; 2Co 4:4–6). **sustaining all things by his powerful word.** The universe does not hold together by its own power or even by natural laws originally designed by God. In the complex processes of divine providence, the Son holds together the created order (Col 1:17; 2Pe 3:4–7), preserving it from destruction until that day when his voice will renew the universe and establish the universal kingdom of God and his heirs (12:26–28). **provided purification for sins.** The writer changed to the past tense because Christ had already obtained purification for sins by his atoning death. This purification is continually applied to believers through Christ's ongoing priestly intercession, which cleanses us to worship in God's presence (7:25; 9:14). **sat down at the right hand . . . in heaven.** The Son's enthronement at God's "right hand" in heaven, promised in Psalm 110:1 (cited in v. 13), reveals his superiority in two ways: (1) At the "right hand" of the Majesty, Christ ministers in the true, heavenly sanctuary, not in an earthly copy (8:1–2,5). (2) Christ "sat down" because he had died once for all time (unlike the continual offerings of Levitical priests; 10:11–12). See *WCF* 5.1; *WLC* 18,55; *WSC* 11; *BC* 8,10,13,19,26; *HC* 27,80.
1:4 superior to the angels. This is proved by the series of Old Testament quotations that follows (vv. 5–14). **the name he has inherited.** The eternal Son became a human being in order to rescue us from sin and death (2:14–15). After spending a time of humiliation on Earth, he was resurrected as Israel's Messiah and received the royal title "Son of God" in the heavenly throne room (1:5; 2:10–11; Ro 1:3–4).
▪ **1:5–14** *Scriptural Testimony to the Son's Greater Honor.* The Christian belief in the superiority of Christ over all previous revelation was anticipated by the Old Testament. The writer pointed to a number of passages that indicate that the great Son of David would be exalted above all others.
1:5–6 See *WLC* 10.
1:5 You are my Son . . . I have become your Father. Refers to Psalm 2:7, where the Davidic king of Israel is declared the royal son of God at his coronation. This coronation established a pattern that Jesus fulfilled as the final son of David. The second person of the Trinity is (and has been from eternity) the eternal Son of God; there was not a time when he *became* the Father's Son in this sense (Mk 1:11; Jn 1:1; 3:16). Yet the Father declared Jesus to be his royal Son at Jesus' baptism (Mt 3:17), at his transfiguration (Mt 17:5) and at his resurrection (Ac 13:32–35; Ro 1:4). At his ascension Jesus was enthroned in heaven (vv. 3–4; see theological article "The Ascension and Session of Jesus" at Heb 8). The enthronement announced in Psalm 2:7 was conferred upon Christ at the completion of his redemptive work. **his Father . . . my Son.** A reference to 1 Chronicles 17:13 (2Sa 7:14), where God promised to sustain his paternal relationship with David's descendant. This promise was not spoken directly of Jesus because 2 Samuel 7:14 adds the phrase "when he does wrong," which Jesus never did and could never do (see theological article "The Sinlessness of Jesus" at Heb 4). Rather, the pattern established in the Old Testament for David's sons finds ultimate fulfillment in Jesus, the great son of David. Faithful sons of David were promised the fatherly love of God. As the absolutely perfect son of David, Jesus will forever be the object of the Father's love.
1:6 brings . . . into the world. As the Son condescended to assume our human nature, angels worshiped him (Lk 2:13–14). **firstborn.** As in Psalm 89:27, the term means "of the highest rank" (i.e., above the kings of the earth, not first in order of birth). In Exodus 4:22 it means "elect" or "most desired." **Let all . . . him.** Probably from the Greek translation (Septuagint) of Deuteronomy

7 In speaking of the angels he says,

> "He makes his angels winds,
> his servants flames of fire."[a][o]

8 But about the Son he says,

> "Your throne, O God, will last for ever and ever,
> and righteousness will be the scepter of your kingdom.
> 9 You have loved righteousness and hated wickedness;
> therefore God, your God, has set you above your companions[p]
> by anointing you with the oil[q] of joy."[b]

10 He also says,

> "In the beginning, O Lord, you laid the foundations of the earth,
> and the heavens are the work of your hands.
> 11 They will perish, but you remain;
> they will all wear out like a garment.[r]
> 12 You will roll them up like a robe;
> like a garment they will be changed.
> But you remain the same,[s]
> and your years will never end."[c][t]

13 To which of the angels did God ever say,

> "Sit at my right hand
> until I make your enemies
> a footstool[u] for your feet"[d]?[v]

14 Are not all angels ministering spirits[w] sent to serve those who will inherit salvation?[x]

Warning to Pay Attention

2 We must pay more careful attention, therefore, to what we have heard, so that we
do not drift away. 2 For if the message spoken[y] by angels[z] was binding, and every
violation and disobedience received its just punishment,[a] 3 how shall we escape if we
ignore such a great salvation?[b] This salvation, which was first announced by the Lord,[c]

1:7 [o]Ps 104:4
1:9 [p]Php 2:9 [q]Isa 61:1,3
1:11 [r]Isa 34:4
1:12 [s]Heb 13:8 [t]Ps 102:25-27
1:13 [u]Jos 10:24; Heb 10:13 [v]Ps 110:1
1:14 [w]Ps 103:20 [x]Heb 5:9
2:2 [y]Heb 1:1 [z]Dt 33:2; Ac 7:53 [a]Heb 10:28
2:3 [b]Heb 10:29 [c]Heb 1:2

[a] *7* Psalm 104:4 [b] *9* Psalm 45:6,7 [c] *12* Psalm 102:25–27 [d] *13* Psalm 110:1

32:43, although it also recalls Psalm 97:7. Whatever the case, the Old Testament reference is to angels worshiping Yahweh. By applying these words to Jesus, the writer indicated that he believed in the full divinity of Christ.

1:7 He makes . . . flames of fire. A reference to Psalm 104:4. "Winds" (the Greek term may also be rendered "spirits," as in v. 14) and "flames" associate angels with the created world's mutability, in contrast to the Son's eternal permanence (vv. 10–12). The main idea is that the angels are much lower than the final, royal son of David who now sits on the throne in heaven. **servants.** In contrast to the Son's royal enthronement (vv. 8–9), the angels are merely "servants."

1:8–9 Your throne . . . oil of joy. From Psalm 45:6–7, a celebration of a royal wedding that idealized the house of David and thus anticipated the reality that would come with the final Son Jesus. The One who addresses the royal Son with the words "O God" is himself "God, your God" (see theological article "Jesus Christ, God and Man" at Jn 1). See *WCF* 26.3; *WLC* 10.

1:9 loved righteousness. On the Son's obedience and righteousness, see 4:15, 5:8 and 7:26. The perfect obedience of Jesus made him far superior not only to angels, but to all other sons of David. See *HC* 31.

1:10–12 In the beginning . . . never end. From Psalm 102:25–27, another passage (see v. 6) addressed to Yahweh that is applied to Jesus because of his full divinity.

1:10 On the Son as Creator, see verse 2 and its note.

1:11 you remain. The Son's immutability and eternal existence as God are essential to his divine character. Through him the inheritance of believers will "remain" forever (see 10:34; 12:27–28; 13:14).

1:13 To which of the angels . . . ? The Son's position of heavenly authority (v. 3; 8:1) is contrasted to the angels' role as servants to "those who will inherit salvation" (v. 14; i.e., the Son's people who share by grace in his rights as heir; vv. 2,5; 2:10; 6:12). The angels are servants to Christ, but also to Christ's people who inherit salvation from him. In this sense his people are favored above the angels (cf. 2:16; 1Co 6:3). **Sit . . . your feet.** A reference to Psalm 110:1, another royal psalm granting promises to the house of David. Jesus alone receives these promises completely because he alone is the faithful, royal Son. This psalm is quoted or alluded to numerous times in Hebrews (5:6,10; 6:20; 7:3,11,17,21; 8:1; 10:10–13; 12:2).

1:14 serve those who will inherit salvation. Not only are angels subordinate to the divine Son, but they will also serve human beings in the world to come. This fact makes it obvious that Christ is superior to the angels. See *WCF* 12; *WLC* 19; *BC* 12.

■ **2:1–4** *Exhortation to Adhere to the Son.* Having established that Christ is superior to the angels, the writer called his readers to remain faithful to Christ rather than to place their allegiance elsewhere.

2:1 We must pay more careful attention. Compare similar exhortations in 3:12–14; 4:1,11; 6:11–12; 10:22–25; 12:1–13 and especially 12:25–29, another reminder of Sinai. See *WLC* 160.

2:2–3 if the message . . . if we ignore. The argument is from the lesser to the greater, a standard rabbinical style of argumentation in which reference is made first to simpler and less-pressing situations, then to similar but more significant and important circumstances. If what the angels said was binding, then what comes from One superior to angels must be even more binding. The word "binding" is legal terminology, as is the word "testified" in verse 4.

2:2 spoken by angels. The role of the angels in the giving of the law is suggested in Deuteronomy 33:2 ("The LORD came from Sinai . . . with myriads of holy ones"). The interpretation that the law had been given through angels was widespread in Jewish communities by the first century (Ac 7:53; Gal 3:19). **just punishment.** Illustrated in 10:28–29 (cf. 6:4–6). Not all violations of Moses' covenant were of equal significance, but punishments were established appropriately for each one. See *WLC* 151.

2:3 escape. Violators of the new covenant in Christ will be even less able to escape appropriate judgment than were violators of the Old Testament law. The judgment in mind is eternal judgment. The writer did not mean by this that true believers can lose

was confirmed to us by those who heard him.[d] **4**God also testified to it by signs, wonders and various miracles,[e] and gifts of the Holy Spirit[f] distributed according to his
will.[g]

Jesus Made Like His Brothers

5It is not to angels that he has subjected the world to come, about which we are
speaking. **6**But there is a place where someone has testified:

> "What is man that you are mindful of him,
> the son of man that you care for him?[h]
> **7**You made him a little[a] lower than the angels;
> you crowned him with glory and honor
> **8** and put everything under his feet."[b i]

In putting everything under him, God left nothing that is not subject to him. Yet at present we do not see everything subject to him. **9**But we see Jesus, who was made a little
lower than the angels, now crowned with glory and honor[j] because he suffered death,[k]
so that by the grace of God he might taste death for everyone.[l]
10In bringing many sons to glory, it was fitting that God, for whom and through whom
everything exists,[m] should make the author of their salvation perfect through suffering.[n]
11Both the one who makes men holy and those who are made holy[o] are of the same family. So Jesus is not ashamed to call them brothers.[p] **12**He says,

> "I will declare your name to my brothers;
> in the presence of the congregation I will sing your praises."[c q]

2:3
[d]Lk 1:2
2:4
[e]Jn 4:48 [f]1Co 12:4
[g]Eph 1:5
2:6
[h]Job 7:17
2:8
[i]Ps 8:4-6;
1Co 15:25
2:9
[j]Ac 2:33; 3:13;
Php 2:9 [k]Php 2:7-9
[l]Jn 3:16; 2Co 5:15
2:10
[m]Ro 11:36
[n]Lk 24:26;
Heb 7:28
2:11
[o]Heb 10:10
[p]Mt 28:10;
Jn 20:17
2:12
[q]Ps 22:22

[a] 7 *Or him for a little while; also in verse 9* [b] *8* Psalm 8:4-6 [c] *12* Psalm 22:22

their salvation (see theological article "The Perseverance and Preservation of Believers" at Php 1) but that the new covenant community contains unbelievers just as the old covenant community did (see theological article "The Church: Visible and Invisible" at 1 Pe 4). Unbelievers in the new covenant community will be judged more harshly than will unbelievers in the old covenant community. **salvation.** First mentioned in 1:14, this salvation ultimately includes inheritance of the world to come (v. 5; 11:16), entry into glory as God's sons (v. 10), purification from sins (1:3; 2:11,17), freedom from the fear of death (vv. 14–15) and the privilege of drawing near to God (4:16; 10:22) to offer worship that pleases him (12:28; 13:15–16). **those who heard.** The apostles and certain others witnessed the things Jesus said and did in his ministry, death and resurrection (Ac 1:14–15,21–23; 10:39–41; 1Pe 5:1; 2Pe 1:15), with the apostles being official witnesses (Ac 1:22). The writer and his original readers had heard the gospel through the apostles or perhaps through others who had accompanied the apostles and witnessed under their authority (see "Introduction: Author").

2:4 signs, wonders and various miracles. These terms are used in the New Testament for the special miracles that God used to authenticate the Savior (Ac 2:22), the apostles and Stephen (Ac 6:8; 14:3; Ro 15:18–19; 2Co 12:12). The signs associated with the revelation of the New Testament period heightened the responsibility of those who rejected the gospel.

■ **2:5–18** *The Son and His Brothers.* Having called his readers to adhere to the Son for salvation, the writer described another amazing dimension of Christ's superiority: Christ became a human being in order to bring those who believe in him to glory.

2:5–8 not to angels . . . under his feet. The author used the contrast between angels and human beings to point to the astonishing fact that Christ, the royal Son, became a full human being (vv. 14,17) in order to restore redeemed humanity's dignity and divinely intended place in creation.

2:6 someone has testified. Such vagueness in Scriptural citation is characteristic of the author of Hebrews, who stressed the divine authorship of Scripture rather than mentioning the human authors (e.g., 1:5,7–8; 2:12; 3:7; 4:3; 5:5–6). The effectiveness of the writer's method of citing a well-known Old Testament proof text about people in creation (Ps 8:4) provides evidence for the Jewish background of the recipients.

2:8 Yet at present. Psalm 8 describes the glorious status of the human race as the pinnacle of all creation. But it is obvious that human beings are far from full enjoyment of such status. The verses that follow explain that Jesus, as humanity's forerunner, rectifies this situation for the sake of those who follow him.

2:9 But we see Jesus. Although humanity has fallen, we are not without hope. The man Jesus has the crown of glory and honor, and he will share it with those who believe in him (vv. 11–13). **a little lower.** This expression can refer to status ("a little lower") or to time (cf. "a little later" in Lk 22:58; "a little while" in Ac 5:34). If it refers to status, it indicates that because humans are a little lower than the angels, Jesus, in becoming a man, also became a little lower than the angels. If it refers to time, it indicates the temporary character of Jesus' humiliation. **taste death for everyone.** The writer did not mean that every human being has been saved by Christ's death. As in ordinary speech, terms such as "everyone" find their definitions based on the contexts in which they appear. In its immediate context, the term "everyone" refers to the "many sons" (v. 10) whom God brings to glory and whom Jesus calls "brothers" (v. 11). Those for whom Jesus tasted death are made holy and perfect once for all by his sacrifice (10:10,14), their consciences are cleansed from acts that lead to death (9:14) and they are freed from the fear of death (vv. 14–15). By contrast, there are those within the church who do not trust the Son but subject him to ridicule (6:4–6). For them, "no sacrifice for sins is left, but only a fearful expectation of judgment" (10:26–27). Thus "everyone" here includes all those—and only those—who persist in trusting Jesus (3:6,14). See *HC* 40.

2:10–18 For God's children to be restored to the glory described in Psalm 8, the unique Son had to suffer death on their behalf, destroy their enemy, free them from slavery and atone for their sins. Bonds of kinship in the eternal plan of God unite the redeemed to the "author of their salvation" (vv. 10–11).

2:10 make . . . perfect. See note on 5:9. **author.** This Greek term is rare in the New Testament (12:2; Ac 3:15; 5:31) and could also be translated "leader" or "pioneer." It is used in the Septuagint (the Greek translation of the OT) to refer to tribal and military leaders (e.g., Ex 6:14; Nu 10:4; 13:3). Jesus is our guide to glory because in his humanity he pioneered the path of suffering on our behalf.

2:11–12 See *BC* 28.

2:11 of the same family. Literally, "are of one" or "have the same origin" (i.e., God). Alternatively, some interpret this to mean "are of one nature" (i.e., human nature). **not ashamed.** In view of the Son's glory as portrayed in chapter 1, we might have expected Jesus to recoil from identification with fallen human beings, but he willingly calls us his family, his own brothers and sisters (v. 17; 5:1; 7:5).

2:12 my brothers. The writer here introduced Psalm 22:22 to draw attention to the sibling relationship shared between believers and Christ. Psalm 22:22 is the turning point in a psalm that describes the passage through suffering to deliverance. Thus, the context of the words quoted corresponds to their use in Hebrews.

2:13 [r]Isa 8:17 [s]Isa 8:18; Jn 10:29
2:14 [t]Jn 1:14 [u]1Co 15:54-57; 2Ti 1:10 [v]1Jn 3:8
2:15 [w]2Ti 1:7
2:17 [x]Php 2:7 [y]Heb 5:2 [z]Heb 4:14,15; 7:26,28 [a]Heb 5:1
2:18 [b]Heb 4:15
3:1 [c]Heb 2:11 [d]Heb 2:17 [e]Heb 4:14
3:2 [f]Nu 12:7
3:5 [g]Ex 14:31 [h]ver 2; Nu 12:7

13 And again,

> "I will put my trust in him."[a] [r]

And again he says,

> "Here am I, and the children God has given me."[b] [s]

14 Since the children have flesh and blood, he too shared in their humanity[t] so that
by his death he might destroy[u] him who holds the power of death—that is, the devil[v]—
15 and free those who all their lives were held in slavery by their fear[w] of death. 16 For surely it is not angels he helps, but Abraham's descendants. 17 For this reason he had to be
made like his brothers[x] in every way, in order that he might become a merciful[y] and
faithful high priest[z] in service to God,[a] and that he might make atonement for[c] the sins
of the people. 18 Because he himself suffered when he was tempted, he is able to help
those who are being tempted.[b]

Jesus Greater Than Moses

3 Therefore, holy brothers,[c] who share in the heavenly calling, fix your thoughts on
Jesus, the apostle and high priest[d] whom we confess.[e] 2 He was faithful to the one
who appointed him, just as Moses was faithful in all God's house.[f] 3 Jesus has been found
worthy of greater honor than Moses, just as the builder of a house has greater honor
than the house itself. 4 For every house is built by someone, but God is the builder of everything. 5 Moses was faithful as a servant[g] in all God's house,[h] testifying to what would

[a] *13* Isaiah 8:17 [b] *13* Isaiah 8:18 [c] *17* Or *and that he might turn aside God's wrath, taking away*

2:13 I will put my trust in him. This confession of faith appears in 2 Samuel 22:3, Isaiah 8:17 and Isaiah 12:2. In all three passages, a servant of God expresses trust in the face of danger. For the Son, who is "the author and perfecter of our faith" (12:2), to take these words on his lips demonstrates that he lived by faith, just as we must. **I, and the children God has given me.** The writer was referring to Isaiah 8:18, where the prophet declared that he and his children were signs of God's judgment against rebellious Judah (the rebellious were not of the children given to him). In this respect, Isaiah was a type of Christ. Christ also has a circle of "children" given to him by the Father (Jn 17:6); they stand as demonstrations of God's judgment against those who rebel against him.
2:14–18 See *WCF* 8.2; *WLC* 48,85; *BC* 26; *HC* 1,14,16,34.
2:14 flesh and blood. This is an idiomatic way of saying "human" (the same Greek phrase can be rendered "man"; Mt 16:17; Gal 1:16; cf. Eph 6:12; 1Co 15:50). It may also emphasize the limitations of the human condition. **shared in their humanity.** Literally, "shared in the same things," a phrase stressing the completeness of the Son's incarnation. Jesus Christ triumphed over death and the devil by enduring God's judgment upon sinners and by fulfilling the righteousness required of human beings. But in order for him to do this, it was necessary that he share their humanity, including flesh and blood (see theological article "The Full Humanity of Christ" at Lk 3). **him who holds the power of death.** Having tempted us to sin, the devil acts as accuser (Rev 12:10), demanding that just punishment fall on us: "The wages of sin is death" (Ro 6:23; cf. 1Co 15:56). His power to inflict death is destroyed only when our sin has been punished. Because this took place in Christ's death, his accusations have no grounds (Col 2:14–15). The devil is not rendered utterly powerless (1Pe 5:8), but the inauguration of the kingdom in Christ's earthly ministry removed his stranglehold on those who follow Christ. See *WCF* 8.2; *WLC* 39,52; *WSC* 22; *BC* 18,20; *HC* 35.
2:16 not angels. This verse resumes expression of the contrast between human beings and angels begun in verses 5–8. The background is Isaiah 41:8–14, where the people of Israel are called "descendants of Abraham" (Isa 41:8) whom the Lord "takes hold of" (Isa 41:13) and whom he promises to "help" (Isa 41:14; cf. Heb 2:18). They need not "fear" (Isa 41:10; see Heb 2:15; 13:5–6). On the topic of Abraham and his descendants, see 6:15–17 and 11:8–12 (see also Ro 4:9–18; 9:6–8; Gal 3:29). **he helps.** Some translate this phrase "he takes" or "he lays hold of," as in the incarnation. Either way, the point is the same: The sort of creatures whom God wills to save determines the sort of incarnation described in verse 14. These creatures are human beings, and Christ is therefore incarnate as a man. See *WLC* 19,39; *WSC* 22; *BC* 18.
2:17 he had to be made like his brothers. Only One who had been tested in every way as we are could be a merciful priest (4:15; 5:2). Only One who had responded to every test in perfect obedience could be a faithful priest without sin (4:15; 7:26–28) and worthy to offer himself as the unblemished sacrifice (9:14). **merciful and faithful high priest.** Echoing the prophecy that announced judgment on Eli's house (of Aaron's family) and the coming of a faithful priest who would minister always (1Sa 2:35). The faithfulness (3:6) and the mercy of Christ (5:2) are explained in what follows. **make atonement for.** By bearing God's wrath and curse against "the people" who sinned (see NIV text note; see also Ro 3:25–26). See *WLC* 44; *WSC* 25; *BC* 18,21; *HC* 15,35.
■ **3:1—4:13** *Christ Is Superior to Moses.* The writer not only asserted that the Son is greater than angels, but also that Christ is superior to Moses. His explanation divides into two main parts: the comparison between Moses as a faithful servant and Christ as the faithful Son (3:1–6) and the need to hold fast to New Testament truth about Christ (3:7—4:13).
■ **3:1–6** *The Son and the Servant.* Jesus is superior to Moses because he is the royal, divine Son of God, while Moses was but a servant of God.
3:1 holy brothers. The term "brothers," a typical title of address for those in the visible church (3:12; 10:19; Ac 1:16; 1Co 3:1), has special significance here since Jesus has made believers his "holy" (2:11) "brothers" (and sisters). **heavenly calling.** The Lord calls from heaven, summoning believers to enduring faith (12:25). He also calls Christians to the kingdom of heaven (12:26–28; i.e., the new heavens and the new earth; see theological article "The Kingdom of God" at Mt 4), which is the better country (11:16) and the eternal inheritance of those who are called (9:15). **fix your thoughts.** In view of the fact that Christ is able to deal effectively with the most significant problems believers face, Christians should be eager to give close attention to what will now be said about him. **apostle.** This title is applied to Jesus only here in the entire New Testament. The term stresses his authority and his faithful accomplishment of the mission the Father sent him to accomplish (v. 2; cf. 10:5–10; Jn 6:38; 20:21).
3:2–6 faithful . . . faithful . . . faithful. With reference to Numbers 12:7, Moses and Christ are compared favorably as to their faithfulness, but contrasted as to their honor. Though privileged to speak to God face-to-face and to see his form (Nu 12:8), Moses was still only a "servant in all God's house" (v. 5). Christ, as Creator (1:2,10; Col 1:16), deserves honor as the divine builder of all things—including the final temple of God (Jn 2:19–20)—and as the "son over God's house" (v. 6).
3:3–4 See *BC* 10,12.
3:3 the builder of a house. Here the necessary implication is that Jesus, as the builder of the house, is divine (v. 4). This passage points both to Christ's identity as God ("the builder") and to his personal distinction from the Father (v. 6).
3:5 faithful . . . in all God's house. Since the writer alludes to Numbers 12:7, the emphasis is on the distinction and status of Moses' service. Moses was the unique minister of the law, but Jesus' ministry is higher still. **what would be said in the future.**

be said in the future. 6 But Christ is faithful as a son[i] over God's house. And we are his
house,[j] if we hold on[k] to our courage and the hope[l] of which we boast.

Warning Against Unbelief

7 So, as the Holy Spirit says:[m]

"Today, if you hear his voice,
8 do not harden your hearts
as you did in the rebellion,
during the time of testing in the desert,
9 where your fathers tested and tried me
and for forty years saw what I did.[n]
10 That is why I was angry with that generation,
and I said, 'Their hearts are always going astray,
and they have not known my ways.'
11 So I declared on oath in my anger,
'They shall never enter my rest.' [o]"[a][p]

12 See to it, brothers, that none of you has a sinful, unbelieving heart that turns away
from the living God. 13 But encourage one another daily,[q] as long as it is called Today, so
that none of you may be hardened by sin's deceitfulness.[r] 14 We have come to share in
Christ if we hold firmly[s] till the end the confidence we had at first. 15 As has just been said:

"Today, if you hear his voice,
do not harden your hearts
as you did in the rebellion."[b][t]

16 Who were they who heard and rebelled? Were they not all those Moses led out of
Egypt?[u] 17 And with whom was he angry for forty years? Was it not with those who
sinned, whose bodies fell in the desert?[v] 18 And to whom did God swear that they would
never enter his rest[w] if not to those who disobeyed[c]?[x] 19 So we see that they were not able
to enter, because of their unbelief.[y]

A Sabbath-Rest for the People of God

4 Therefore, since the promise of entering his rest still stands, let us be careful that
none of you be found to have fallen short of it.[z] 2 For we also have had the gospel
preached to us, just as they did; but the message they heard was of no value to them, be-

3:6 [i]Heb 1:2 [j]1Co 3:16 [k]Ro 11:22 [l]Ro 5:2
3:7 [m]Heb 9:8
3:9 [n]Ac 7:36
3:11 [o]Heb 4:3,5 [p]Ps 95:7-11
3:13 [q]Heb 10:24,25 [r]Eph 4:22
3:14 [s]ver 6
3:15 [t]ver 7,8; Ps 95:7,8
3:16 [u]Nu 14:2
3:17 [v]Nu 14:29; Ps 106:26
3:18 [w]Nu 14:20-23 [x]Heb 4:6
3:19 [y]Jn 3:36
4:1 [z]Heb 12:15

[a] *11* Psalm 95:7–11 [b] *15* Psalm 95:7,8 [c] *18* Or *disbelieved*

Moses' ultimate ministry was to testify to Christ's coming (Jn 5:46–47). The Mosaic Law was a shadow that pointed toward the coming "good things" brought by Christ (9:11; 10:1), for in its regulations the Holy Spirit showed that access into God's presence would come only when the earthly tabernacle was replaced by something better (9:8).

3:6 over God's house. Note the preposition: Moses was "in" (v. 5) the house, but Christ is "over" the house (see also 10:21). **we are his house.** God's house consists of his people (1Sa 2:35; 2Sa 7:16; Eph 2:19–22; 1Ti 3:15; 1Pe 2:5). He is present with us and takes care of us. **If we hold on to.** This verse tells believers how to prove that they truly belong to God: Their faith must confirm itself in perseverance (v. 14; 6:11; 10:23). Its note of warning is a fitting introduction to the quotation from Psalm 95 that follows (see theological article: "The Perseverance and Preservation of Believers" at Php 1).

■ **3:7—4:13** *Exhortation to Reject Disbelief.* Mentioning the need to persevere in order to receive God's blessing led the writer to call on his readers to reject disbelief. He quoted Psalm 95:7–11 and echoed it throughout his exposition. Key words in this section include "Today" (3:13,15; 4:7) and "rest" (4:3,5–6,8–11). The treatment of "rest" is developed from the Sabbath teaching of Genesis 2:2. Corresponding to this teaching is the exhortation to "enter that rest" (4:11) and the warning not to "harden your hearts" (3:15; 4:7).

3:8 time of testing. A significant occasion of testing had occurred at Rephidim (Ex 17:1–7), where the people grumbled and Moses struck the rock to give them water. The entire 40-year period of disobedience and resistance while wandering in the desert may also be in view (vv. 9–10; Ps 78:40). As with Israel in the wilderness, the Christian life is a test of faith (2Co 13:5–7).

3:11 on oath. Numbers 14:21–30 records God's oath not to allow that generation to enter the promised land. Hebrews views the Sabbath of the promised land as an anticipation of the final, eternal Sabbath to come—a Sabbath that will be experienced in the new heavens and the new earth (4:1–11). **my rest.** See note on 4:8.

3:12 brothers. The author addressed his readers in terms of their confession of faith and their involvement in the church. Even so, he also recognized that some within the Christian fellowship had "sinful, unbelieving heart[s]" (cf. 12:15–17) that would lead them to apostasy and judgment. Christ saves completely those who come to God through him by saving faith (7:25). Yet Christians must encourage one another (10:24–25), as the author does throughout this letter (13:22), to persevere and to demonstrate their saving faith through fidelity. **unbelieving heart.** That is, unbelieving hearts like those of their "fathers" (v. 9), whose unbelief had prevented them from entering God's rest (v. 19). See *WLC* 105.

3:13 Today. See note on 4:7. **sin's deceitfulness.** The illusion that disobedience provides more security (Ex 17:3) or pleasure (11:25–26; Ex 16:3) than does the pilgrimage of faith.

3:14 share in Christ. Although the Greek term can mean "share with" (in the sense of companionship), here it points to the intimate union of the believer with Christ.

3:16–19 heard and rebelled? Neither the blessing of the exodus from Egypt nor the privilege of hearing God's voice guaranteed the generation that died in the desert entry into God's rest in the promised land (see note on 4:8). Their rebellion (v. 16), sin (v. 17) and disobedience (v. 18; 4:6) were rooted in unbelief—they failed to cling persistently to God's promise (v. 19; 4:2–3) and proved by their actions that they were not truly redeemed.

4:1 let us be careful. Literally, "let us fear." Divine judgment inspires fear (10:27,31; 12:21), but we should not fear what other people may do (11:27; 13:6).

4:2 just as they did. The way of salvation presented in both the Old and New Testaments is the same: faith in the promises of God. There is therefore a correlation between the word of God that

cause those who heard did not combine it with faith.[a a] 3Now we who have believed enter that rest, just as God has said,

> "So I declared on oath in my anger,
> 'They shall never enter my rest.' "[b b]

And yet his work has been finished since the creation of the world. 4For somewhere he
has spoken about the seventh day in these words: "And on the seventh day God rested
from all his work."[c c] 5And again in the passage above he says, "They shall never enter
my rest."[d]
6It still remains that some will enter that rest, and those who formerly had the gospel preached to them did not go in, because of their disobedience.[e] 7Therefore God again
set a certain day, calling it Today, when a long time later he spoke through David, as was
said before:

> "Today, if you hear his voice,
> do not harden your hearts."[d f]

8For if Joshua had given them rest,[g] God would not have spoken[h] later about another

4:2 [a]1Th 2:13
4:3 [b]Ps 95:11; Heb 3:11
4:4 [c]Ge 2:2,3; Ex 20:11
4:5 [d]Ps 95:11
4:6 [e]Heb 3:18
4:7 [f]Ps 95:7,8; Heb 3:7,8,15
4:8 [g]Jos 22:4 [h]Heb 1:1

[a] 2 Many manuscripts *because they did not share in the faith of those who obeyed* [b] 3 Psalm 95:11; also in verse 5 [c] 4 Gen. 2:2 [d] 7 Psalm 95:7,8

Moses delivered to the Old Testament Israelites as they moved toward the promised land and the gospel preached to believers in the New Testament era as they move toward their eternal reward in Christ. For instance, note Paul's use of Deuteronomy 30:14 in Romans 10:8. **of no value to them.** The writer did not mean that the Word given through Moses was of no value or that it was weak in itself. Rather, it was of no value because most of the Old Testament Israelites did not add faith to their hearing. By their disbelief, they negated the value of the word. This example should motivate Christians to exercise faith in conjunction with the Word of God they receive. See *WCF* 21.5; *WLC* 160; *WSC* 90.

4:3–5 rest . . . rest . . . rest. The central theme of these verses is God's "rest," which has existed from the seventh day of creation (v. 4; Ge 2:2). Israel's entry into the promised land was a major step toward God's people entering that eternal, divine rest. The ultimate fulfillment of entering God's rest will occur when believers find themselves in the new creation that Christ will bring at his return.

4:3 never enter my rest. The writer quoted Psalm 95:11 because of the theme of rest. In verse 7 he returned to Psalm 95, pointing out that this warning came long after Joshua had brought Israel into the land of Canaan. Possessing Canaan, therefore, was only a foretaste of, not the final fulfillment of, rest for the people of God.

4:7 a long time later. Referring to Psalm 95:7–8, the writer noted David's warning that hardness of heart would result in a failure to enter God's rest (see 4:3). **Today.** The readers had already learned that they lived in the time called "Today" (3:13). The writer used this term in a poignant way that roughly corresponds to the notion of "the day of the Lord," a day when there will no longer be time to delay one's response to the mercy of God because of impending judgment. Christians since the time of Christ live during a period calling for decision ("Today") because the entire present age comprises the "last days," the period when divine judgment and blessing have begun to be dispensed.

4:8 if Joshua. Another indication (cf. vv. 3–5) that the physical land of Canaan did not completely fulfill the promise of God's rest. David wrote the words of Psalm 95 approximately 400 years after Israel entered Canaan under Joshua. If the land into which Joshua had led them had completely fulfilled the promise of divine rest, then the psalm's warning to David's generation would have been pointless. The patriarchs' hope was fixed on a better, heavenly country (11:16). Note similar arguments from the Old Testament in 7:11 and 8:7.

The Sinlessness of Jesus: Did Jesus Have to Be Without Sin?

THE New Testament teaches time and again that Jesus was entirely free from sin (Jn 8:46; 2Co 5:21; Heb 4:15; 7:26; 1Pe 2:22; 1Jn 3:5). Jesus' moral nature was unaffected by Adam's fall, as was Adam's prior to his sin. Jesus loved God's law and kept it perfectly. He loved the Lord "with all [his] heart and with all [his] soul and with all [his] strength" (Dt 6:5).

Jesus had to be sinless for a number of important reasons. First, Jesus' sinlessness was necessary so that on the cross he could be a worthy substitute for sinners. Had he not been "a lamb without blemish or defect," his blood would not have been "precious" (1Pe 1:19) in the eyes of God. In that case, Jesus would have needed a savior himself, and his death could not have redeemed us from eternal judgment. His perfection qualified him to be our atoning sacrifice.

Second, by living an utterly perfect life in active conformity to God's law, Jesus earned the right to sit on David's throne forever (Pss 89; 132; Mt 1:1). In this way, Jesus secures our salvation as he reigns over all on our behalf.

Third, the active righteousness of Christ actually makes believers righteous before God. Not only are believers forgiven of their sins through Christ's atonement, but they actually become the righteousness of God (2Co 5:21) because Christ's own righteousness is reckoned to their account through faith in him. When believers are in Christ, God the Father looks on them as he looks upon sinless Jesus.

Fourth, Jesus faced and overcame temptation to become our sympathetic high priest before the Father in the heavenly places. He was "tempted in every way, just as we are," though he was without sin (Heb 4:15). This means that every type of temptation that we face also assailed him; but he yielded to none of them. Even through the agony of Gethsemane and the cross, he successfully resisted temptation (Mt 26:36ff.; Mk 14:32ff.). Jesus' sinlessness in the face of temptation formed him into our perfectly sympathetic high priest and secured his right to represent us permanently before the Father (Heb 5:9–10; 7:25—8:13).

day. 9There remains, then, a Sabbath-rest for the people of God; 10for anyone who enters God's rest also rests from his own work, just as God did from his.[i] 11Let us, therefore, make every effort to enter that rest, so that no one will fall by following their example of disobedience.[j]
12For the word of God[k] is living and active.[l] Sharper than any double-edged sword,[m]
it penetrates even to dividing soul and spirit, joints and marrow; it judges the thoughts
and attitudes of the heart.[n] 13Nothing in all creation is hidden from God's sight.[o] Everything is uncovered and laid bare before the eyes of him to whom we must give account.

Jesus the Great High Priest

14Therefore, since we have a great high priest who has gone through the heavens,[a][p]
Jesus the Son of God, let us hold firmly to the faith we profess.[q] 15For we do not have a
high priest who is unable to sympathize with our weaknesses, but we have one who has
been tempted in every way, just as we are[r]—yet was without sin.[s] 16Let us then approach
the throne of grace with confidence, so that we may receive mercy and find grace to help
us in our time of need.

5 Every high priest is selected from among men and is appointed to represent them
in matters related to God, to offer gifts and sacrifices[t] for sins.[u] 2He is able to deal
gently with those who are ignorant and are going astray,[v] since he himself is subject to
weakness.[w] 3This is why he has to offer sacrifices for his own sins, as well as for the sins
of the people.[x]
4No one takes this honor upon himself; he must be called by God, just as Aaron was.[y]

4:10 [i]ver 4
4:11 [j]Heb 3:18
4:12 [k]1Pe 1:23 [l]Jer 23:29 [m]Eph 6:17; Rev 1:16 [n]1Co 14:24,25
4:13 [o]Ps 33:13-15
4:14 [p]Heb 6:20 [q]Heb 3:1
4:15 [r]Heb 2:18 [s]2Co 5:21
5:1 [t]Heb 8:3 [u]Heb 7:27
5:2 [v]Heb 2:18 [w]Heb 7:28
5:3 [x]Heb 7:27; 9:7
5:4 [y]Ex 28:1

[a] 14 Or *gone into heaven*

4:9–11 See *HC* 103.
4:9 There remains . . . a Sabbath-rest. The final sabbath-rest celebration awaits God's people in the future.
4:10 rests from his own work. This probably does not refer to conversion, at which time we exchange trust in our own works for trust in Christ's finished work. The comparison with God resting from his work of ordering the chaotic, primeval world indicates that it is a rest from performing good works in our struggle against sin. This rest comes only with our final deliverance from suffering, testing and effort (v. 11) at the return of Christ. Those who die in the Lord "rest from their labor" (Rev 14:13).
4:11 make every effort. Although salvation is by divine grace from beginning to end, believers are to actively pour all their strength into pursuing holiness, without which salvation is impossible (12:14). This obligation indicates that the "work" of verse 10 continues for believers and that "rest" still lies in the future. See *WLC* 75.
4:12 the word of God. The preceding argument (3:7—4:11) illustrates how the word of God exposed the faithlessness of the desert generation and how Scripture (e.g., Ps 95) penetrates and judges those whom it warns about the deceitfulness of sin (3:13) and the possibility of falling short of salvation (v. 1). **dividing soul and spirit, joints and marrow.** Although some find grounds here for a threefold view of the human being as body, soul and spirit, the context stresses the power of God's Word to penetrate into the deepest recesses of a person's being. It does not emphasize a division of that being into separate, constituent parts. See *WLC* 4.
4:13 Everything is uncovered . . . we must give account. The writer warns that, because the Word of God is "living and active" (v. 12), everyone—including the church—will face final judgment. Nothing will remain hidden (Lk 12:2–5; 1Co 4:5; 2Co 5:10). This fact emphasizes how important it is to pursue God's rest diligently. See *WCF* 2.2; *WLC* 7.
■ **4:14—7:28** *Christ Is Superior to Aaron.* Having established that Christ is superior to the angels and to Moses, the writer turned to his third major concern: Christ's superiority to Aaron. This material divides into four main parts: Christ's eternal priesthood (4:14—5:10), the need for growing in the faith (5:11—6:12), the divine oath supporting Christ's priesthood (6:13–20) and the relationship between Christ and Melchizedek (7:1–28).
■ **4:14—5:10** *Christ, the Eternal High Priest.* The writer explained that Jesus far surpasses Old Testament priests in a number of ways.
4:14–16 Therefore . . . in our time of need. The sobering thought of our complete exposure before God draws us to the merciful priest who, having himself been tempted, can help us in our weakness (cf. 2:17–18). An exhortation to "hold firmly to the faith" (v. 14) caps the preceding section, and an invitation to approach God's throne introduces the discussion of Christ as the merciful high priest. See *WLC* 42,180; *BC* 26; *HC* 21.
4:14 gone through the heavens. Christ was raised, ascended and now sits at God's right hand (8:1), where he ministers as our great and eternal high priest (7:26; 9.11,24). **the Son of God.** See note on 1:5 (cf. 5:5). See *WCF* 20.1.
4:15 tempted in every way. Jesus is able to sympathize with us in our weaknesses because he lived life as a true human being. This is a vivid restatement of 2:17–18. Despite his personal knowledge of human struggles and in the face of very real temptation, Christ was still "without sin." See *WCF* 8.2; *WLC* 37,39,48; *WSC* 22; *BC* 18; *HC* 35.
4:16 Let us then approach . . . with confidence. Confident access to God is ours because Christ has gone before us and sympathetically intercedes for us. Because of his intercession on our behalf—for we have been purified from sin's pollution by Jesus' sacrifice (7:19; 10:19,22)—we may offer sacrifices of thanksgiving that are pleasing to God (12:28; 13:15–16). **mercy . . . grace to help.** Mercy points to our inability to earn our own good standing before God, and grace brings us timely support in those times when we are enduring or have succumbed to temptation (2:18).See *WCF* 20.1; *WLC* 39,55.
5:1–10 Every high priest . . . in the order of Melchizedek. As the Old Testament priests were identified with the weak and erring people whom they represented (vv. 1–3) and served at God's appointment (v. 4), so also Christ became high priest by the Father's appointment (vv. 5–6) and was identified with his people through suffering (vv. 7–10).
5:1 offer gifts and sacrifices for sins. The phrase "gifts and sacrifices" encompasses several different kinds of offerings that were made by the Old Testament priests (8:3; see also Lev 1–7). But the main interest here is in those sacrifices that were offered for sins.
5:2 able to deal gently. The Old Testament high priest's weakness in the face of his own temptations compelled him to moderate his indignation over others' sins and to "deal gently" with them. Thus his mercy may have resembled Jesus' greater sympathy. Without having succumbed to temptation (4:15), Jesus still fully identifies with the struggles of his people. **ignorant and are going astray.** The Mosaic Law (Nu 15:27–31) distinguished between sin committed out of weakness and ignorance and sin committed in defiance of the Lord's authority (10:26–27).
5:3 for his own sins. Unlike Christ, our sinless high priest (4:15; 7:26), the Old Testament high priest was himself in need of atonement and forgiveness (7:27; 9:7; Lev 16:11).
5:4–7 See *WCF* 8.1; 8.3; *WLC* 42; *WSC* 23.
5:4 called by God, just as Aaron was. The initial call of Aaron (Ex 28:1) was confirmed through the budding of Aaron's staff (Nu 17:1–10; see Heb 9:4) in response to the challenge of Korah, Dathan and Abiram (Nu 16). The priestly privilege of approaching God was by invitation only, mediated through genealogical descent for the Old Testament Levitical priests but ultimately established through the divine oath to Jesus the Son (7:11–28). See *WCF* 23.3; *WLC* 158,176; *BC* 31.

5:5 [z]Jn 8:54 [a]Heb 1:1 [b]Ps 2:7
5:6 [c]Ps 110:4; Heb 7:17,21
5:7 [d]Mt 27:46,50 [e]Mk 14:36
5:8 [f]Php 2:8
5:9 [g]Heb 2:10
5:10 [h]ver 5 [i]ver 6
5:12 [j]Heb 6:1 [k]1Co 3:2; 1Pe 2:2
5:13 [l]1Co 14:20
5:14 [m]1Co 2:6 [n]Isa 7:15
6:1 [o]Php 3:12-14 [p]Heb 5:12 [q]Heb 9:14
6:2 [r]Jn 3:25 [s]Ac 6:6 [t]Ac 17:18,32
6:3 [u]Ac 18:21
6:4 [v]Heb 10:32 [w]Eph 2:8 [x]Gal 3:2

5 So Christ also did not take upon himself the glory[z] of becoming a high priest. But God
said[a] to him,

> "You are my Son;
> today I have become your Father.[a]"[b]

6 And he says in another place,

> "You are a priest forever,
> in the order of Melchizedek."[c]

7 During the days of Jesus' life on earth, he offered up prayers and petitions with loud
cries and tears[d] to the one who could save him from death, and he was heard because
of his reverent submission.[e] 8 Although he was a son, he learned obedience from what
he suffered[f] 9 and, once made perfect,[g] he became the source of eternal salvation for all
who obey him 10 and was designated by God to be high priest[h] in the order of Melchizedek.[i]

Warning Against Falling Away

11 We have much to say about this, but it is hard to explain because you are slow to
learn. 12 In fact, though by this time you ought to be teachers, you need someone to teach
you the elementary truths[j] of God's word all over again. You need milk, not solid food![k]
13 Anyone who lives on milk, being still an infant,[l] is not acquainted with the teaching
about righteousness. 14 But solid food is for the mature,[m] who by constant use have
trained themselves to distinguish good from evil.[n]

6 Therefore let us leave[o] the elementary teachings[p] about Christ and go on to maturity, not laying again the foundation of repentance from acts that lead to death,[d][q]
and of faith in God, 2 instruction about baptisms,[r] the laying on of hands,[s] the resurrection of the dead,[t] and eternal judgment. 3 And God permitting,[u] we will do so.
4 It is impossible for those who have once been enlightened,[v] who have tasted the
heavenly gift,[w] who have shared in the Holy Spirit,[x] 5 who have tasted the goodness of

[a] 5 Or *have begotten you* [b] 5 Psalm 2:7 [c] 6 Psalm 110:4 [d] 1 Or *from useless rituals*

5:5 You are my Son. See note on 1:5.

5:6 in the order of Melchizedek. A quotation from Psalm 110:4. This mysterious figure is mentioned only twice in the Old Testament (Ge 14:18; Ps 110:4). The association of the phrase "priest forever, in the order of Melchizedek" with the words "my Son" (see note on 1:5) shows that Melchizedek was both king and priest. In his unique and unsurpassed way, Jesus too is both king and priest.

5:7–10 See *WLC* 38; *HC* 44.

5:7 loud cries and tears. Jesus' anguish at the prospect of the cross (Mk 14:33–36; Jn 12:27) demonstrates that he is not aloof from the weaknesses and fears that threaten us. **he was heard.** The psalmists praised God for hearing their cries of distress (Pss 22:24; 30:23; 116:1). Jesus' plea for salvation from death was answered not through his escape from the ordeal of the cross, but through his resurrection from death.

5:8 he learned obedience. Although entirely free from sin (4:15), Jesus' struggle against temptation was real (2:18). Having come into the world to do the Father's will (10:7), Jesus Christ successfully met each increasingly difficult challenge to his integrity. These challenges climaxed in his shameful and painful death on the cross (Php 2:8). This life of learned obedience offset the disobedience of Adam (Ro 5:19) and qualified Christ to serve as our eternal high priest (2:17–18; 4:15).

5:9 made perfect. This does not mean that Jesus finally became sinless but that he finished the course of suffering that was set before him, including his sacrificial death. Having done this, he was then "perfect," or "completely qualified," to serve as a uniquely effective high priest. **eternal salvation.** Jesus lives forever to intercede as our high priest (7:24–25).

5:10 Melchizedek. See 7:1–28. See *BC* 21.

■ **5:11—6:12** *Exhortation to Spiritual Maturity.* Christ's priestly ministry after the order of Melchizedek was "hard to explain" (5:11) because of the readers' immaturity. The writer therefore exhorted his readers to "go on to maturity" (6:1).

5:11 slow to learn. The Greek word here translated "slow" is rendered as "lazy" in 6:12, suggesting that the danger of indolence is in view throughout this section.

5:12–14 See *WCF* 14.3; *WLC* 77,159.

5:12 elementary truths of God's word. Such truths are listed in 6:1–2.

5:13 milk. Although milk is nourishing for infants (1Pe 2:2), the author desired that his readers become mature Christians, for whom solid food is appropriate (1Co 3:1–2).

5:14 The maturity that is needed in order to grasp Christ's priestly ministry includes not only intellectual sophistication but also spiritual discernment arising from consistent obedience to God's revealed will (Php 1:9–11).

6:1–2 See *BC* 34.

6:1 the elementary teachings about Christ. The fundamental tenets of the gospel and the basic instruction regarding inclusion in the church, which are briefly enumerated in verses 1–2. **repentance . . . and of faith.** See Mark 1:15 and Acts 20:21.

6:2 baptisms. The plural is unexpected; there is only one Christian baptism (Eph 4:5). Probably the author had in mind other types of "baptisms" or "washings" (e.g., temple washings and John's baptism) that were present in the early years of the church but distinct from Christian baptism (9:10; Mt 3:11; 28:19; Mk 1:4; Jn 4:1; Ac 1:5; 1Co 15:29). He may also have been referring to acts of baptism rather than to the concept of baptism itself. **laying on of hands.** In New Testament times, this action accompanied blessing, healing the sick, ordination of church officers and especially the conferring of the gift of the Spirit, which was also associated with baptism (Mt 19:13–15; Lk 4:40; Ac 6:6; 8:17; 9:17; 28:8; 1Ti 4:14).

6:3 God permitting. This conventional phrase acknowledges the need for God's help in learning and teaching Christian doctrine. Its use suggests that the material to follow is difficult, as indeed it is.

6:4–12 It is impossible. The first of two sobering warnings (10:26–29) against apostasy in the face of the great blessings and privileges of the new covenant (cf. 2:1–4; 4:1–2). Although Jesus saves completely (7:25) and has made perfect forever (10:13) those who accept his word with saving faith, all are exhorted to prove the sincerity of their faith by persevering. Even for those without saving faith, involvement in the church carries blessings in this life. Nevertheless, those in the church who never come to saving faith will be subjected to more severe judgment than will unbelievers who have never been members of the church. Verses 4–5 describe those who fall from the faith in terms of the blessings they had shared to some degree with genuine believers up to the moment of their apostasy.

6:4–7 See *WCF* 2.1; 10.4; *WLC* 68,151.

6:4 enlightened. Apprised of the knowledge of God as disclosed in the gospel message (10:26; Jn 1:9; 2Co 4:4–6). **tasted the heavenly gift.** Some see here a reference to participation in the sacra-

the word of God and the powers of the coming age, [6]if they fall away, to be brought back
to repentance,[y] because[a] to their loss they are crucifying the Son of God all over again
and subjecting him to public disgrace.
[7]Land that drinks in the rain often falling on it and that produces a crop useful to
those for whom it is farmed receives the blessing of God. [8]But land that produces thorns
and thistles is worthless and is in danger of being cursed.[z] In the end it will be burned.
[9]Even though we speak like this, dear friends,[a] we are confident of better things in
your case—things that accompany salvation. [10]God is not unjust; he will not forget your
work and the love you have shown him as you have helped his people and continue to
help them.[b] [11]We want each of you to show this same diligence to the very end, in order
to make your hope[c] sure. [12]We do not want you to become lazy, but to imitate[d] those
who through faith and patience[e] inherit what has been promised.[f]

The Certainty of God's Promise

[13]When God made his promise to Abraham, since there was no one greater for him
to swear by, he swore by himself,[g] [14]saying, "I will surely bless you and give you many
descendants."[b][h] [15]And so after waiting patiently, Abraham received what was promised.[i]
[16]Men swear by someone greater than themselves, and the oath confirms what is said
and puts an end to all argument.[j] [17]Because God wanted to make the unchanging[k] nature of his purpose very clear to the heirs of what was promised,[l] he confirmed it with
an oath. [18]God did this so that, by two unchangeable things in which it is impossible for
God to lie,[m] we who have fled to take hold of the hope[n] offered to us may be greatly en-

6:6 [y]2Pe 2:21; 1Jn 5:16
6:8 [z]Ge 3:17,18; Isa 5:6
6:9 [a]1Co 10:14
6:10 [b]Mt 10:40,42; 25:40; 1Th 1:3
6:11 [c]Heb 3:6
6:12 [d]Heb 13:7 [e]2Th 1:4; Jas 1:3; Rev 13:10 [f]Heb 10:36
6:13 [g]Ge 22:16; Lk 1:73
6:14 [h]Ge 22:17
6:15 [i]Ge 21:5
6:16 [j]Ex 22:11
6:17 [k]Ps 110:4 [l]Heb 11:9
6:18 [m]Nu 23:19; Tit 1:2 [n]Heb 3:6

[a] *6* Or *repentance while* [b] *14* Gen. 22:17

ment of the Lord's Supper. Alternatively, the phrase may perhaps be paired with "enlightened" as a broad description of apparent conversion. **shared in the Holy Spirit.** Had some experience of the Holy Spirit. Tasting "the powers of the coming age" (v. 5) is an example of this (see note on v. 5).

6:5 the powers of the coming age. The signs and wonders that accompanied the introduction of the gospel, as well as the gifts of the Holy Spirit (2:4). The Holy Spirit sometimes gifts even unbelievers or apostates in order to benefit his covenant people (e.g., Balaam; see Nu 22–24; 2Pe 2:15–17).

6:6 if they fall away, to be brought back to repentance. There is a kind or degree of falling away that is irreversible (see note on 1Jn 5:16). Only God knows with certainty when the severity of falling away reaches such a level. Such flagrant apostasy cannot be reversed. Apostates generally appear to be genuine believers until they fall away (cf. 1Jn 2:19). Judas Iscariot is the clearest Biblical example of one who participated in many blessings of the kingdom of Christ (even possessing great spiritual gifts; Mt 10:5–8) but who failed to enter the kingdom in a saving manner (Mt 26:47–49; Jn 17:12; cf. Mt 7:21–23). **crucifying the Son of God all over again.** Those who reject the blessings of being part of the church behave like those who literally crucified Christ, for they are rejecting Christ as he offers them God's blessings. **public disgrace.** The apostasy described is not a matter of private, internal doubt. It is an outspoken, complete and public rejection that dishonors Christ and his body. See *WLC* 113.

6:7–8 Land . . . burned. According to conventional imagery of the Old Testament, the ground is the people of God (Isa 5:1–7), and the rain falling on it is the word of God (Isa 55:10–11) or the Spirit of God (Isa 44:3–4). The useful crop is good works that bring God's blessing of eternal life. The thorns and thistles are the evil deeds of apostasy that lead to God's eternal judgment if repentance does not occur (Isa 5:4–6).

6:9–12 better things . . . inherit. The writer had seen evidence that gave him confidence that the original readers would continue to produce good works and receive God's blessing of salvation. Still, the readers needed to shake off their sluggishness in order to receive the inheritance promised to persevering believers. See *WCF* 14.3; 16.3; 18.3; *WLC* 75,80,144.

6:10 God is not unjust. God is not merciless; he will not forget or renounce the sincere efforts of his people. See *WCF* 16.6.

6:11 to the very end. The New Testament repeatedly makes it clear that temporary faith is not saving faith (see theological article "The Perseverance and Preservation of Believers" at Php 1). See *WCF* 18.2.

6:12 lazy. This term (rendered "slow" in 5:11) marks both the beginning and the end of the exhortation. **who through faith and patience inherit what has been promised.** Abraham is the preeminent example (vv. 15,17; 11:8–19), but Biblical history is full of witnesses who have run the course of patient faith ahead of us (11:4–38) and have now received the promised inheritance together with us through Christ's perfecting work (11:13,39–40). See *WCF* 12; *WLC* 74.

■ **6:13–20** *A Priest Forever by Divine Oath.* To support his outlook on the need to hold fast to Christ, the writer explained how Jesus' priesthood was established by divine oath. Faith can endure patiently because God's oath secures his word of promise to us, as it did to Abraham.

6:13–14 promise. The specific promise in view here is unclear. It may be the promise made in Genesis 22:16–18 at the time God swore the oath in question, so that the promise is the content ("I will surely bless you and make your descendents as numerous") and the oath is the swearing ("I swear by myself"; Ge 22:16). This accords well with the use of "oath" in verse 16. It may also be that the promise in question is one or more of God's prior promises to Abraham of descendants (e.g. Ge 15:5), of land and descendants (Ge 15; 17) or specifically of the birth of Isaac (Ge 17:19,21; 18:10–14). In this case, the oath in Genesis 22:16–18 confirms that Abraham has remained faithful to God (Ge 22:1,12) by keeping the conditions of the covenant (e.g. Ge 17:1–2,14), and thus ensures Abraham's heirs that Abraham's faithfulness has ensured that the promises have been extended to them as well. This interpretation is supported by the emphasis on Isaac as the main heir in Genesis 22 (see notes on Ge 22:17–18), and by God's purpose of assuring Abraham's heirs as stated here in verse 17. **he swore by himself.** That God, whose "word is truth" (Jn 17:17; cf. Tit 1:2), should reinforce the surety of that infallible word of promise through an oath (Ge 22:16–18) underscores the permanence and seriousness of the divine promise. While sinful and fallible human beings "swear by someone greater than themselves" (v. 16), God, the highest authority, "swore by himself" (v. 13).

6:15 after waiting patiently, Abraham received. In the birth and rescue of Isaac (Ge 21:1–3; 22:11–12), Abraham received the beginning of the promised blessing of offspring. Nevertheless, he did not see the complete fulfillment of those covenantal promises (11:39–40; cf. Ro 4:13,16–17).

6:16–19 See *WCF* 18.2; 22.2; *HC* 101.

6:17 his purpose. God's unchanging purpose was to bless the world through the seed of Abraham (Ge 22:17-8). The meaning of this was revealed in the gospel (Gal 3:6–9). **the heirs of what was promised.** God's oath-bound promise was not only for Abraham, but also for his descendants through Isaac (cf. 11:9) as the covenant head of his people (see notes on Ge 22:17–18). All who follow in Abraham's footsteps of faith are accounted members of this covenant community (1:14; 2:16; 6:12; 10:36; Ro 4:23–24). God's oath was given for the sake of the heirs of Abraham to ensure them that they would receive the blessings previously promised to Abraham. See *WCF* 3.1.

6:18 two unchangeable things. Most likely (1) the promise and (2) the oath (see note on vv. 13–14). Also possible, the two main contents of the promises made to Abraham: (1) land (11:8; Ge

6:19 [o]Lev 16:2; Heb 9:2, 3,7 **6:20** [p]Heb 4:14 [q]Heb 2:17 [r]Heb 5:6 **7:1** [s]Mk 5:7 [t]Ge 14:18–20

couraged. 19 We have this hope as an anchor for the soul, firm and secure. It enters the
inner sanctuary behind the curtain,[o] 20 where Jesus, who went before us, has entered on
our behalf.[p] He has become a high priest[q] forever, in the order of Melchizedek.[r]

Melchizedek the Priest

7 This Melchizedek was king of Salem and priest of God Most High.[s] He met Abraham
returning from the defeat of the kings and blessed him,[t] 2 and Abraham gave him

---

15:7,18–21; 17:8; 22:17) and (2) descendants (v. 14; Ge 15:5; 17:7–10,19; 22:17).

6:19 the inner sanctuary behind the curtain. Our life's anchor is secured in the innermost section of the heavenly tabernacle, the original upon which the earthly sanctuary was modeled (8:2; 9:11–12,24–25; 10:19–20).

6:20 where Jesus . . . has entered. Entrance to the inner sanctuary is impossible without Jesus. He entered first so that his people could follow. His entrance, and the means by which his people have a part in it, requires a lengthy explanation. The remainder of this verse begins the discussion of Christ's priesthood "in the order of Melchizedek," a subject first announced in 5:6. See *WLC* 53.

■ **7:1–28** *A Priest Forever After the Order of Melchizedek.* The wondrous promise in Psalm 110:4 of a royal priest like Melchizedek was ultimately fulfilled in Jesus Christ. Jesus' eternal priesthood is explained in terms of the two Old Testament texts that mention

The Plan of the Ages: Are We in the Last Days?

IN every generation Christians ask the question, "Are we in the last days?" This intense desire to see Christ return should be admired. Believers who seek the Lord's return cry with the apostle John, "Amen. Come, Lord Jesus" (Rev 22:20). They join the faithful virgins keeping their lamps trimmed in anticipation of the bridegroom's arrival (Mt 25:1–13). Yet all too often Christians become so confident of their interpretations of Biblical prophecy and their analyses of current events that they bring disrepute to the faith by their excessive claims about the last days.

Much of this problem stems from the fact that in traditional theology the doctrine of last things, or eschatology (from the Greek word *eschatos,* meaning "last" or "end"), has focused almost exclusively on the return of Christ in glory. Apart from discussions of "personal eschatology," what happens to individuals when they die, it has been widely assumed that the expression "last (or latter) days" always refers to events to take place near the second coming of Christ. As a result, the doctrine of the last days has been focused on constructing elaborate schemes for what the Bible says about events and characters such as the Great Tribulation, the Rapture, the antichrist, the beast and the Millennium.

The return of Christ is an essential Christian doctrine, but a doctrine of the last days that focuses exclusively on this event is much too narrow. During the past century it has become evident to many Reformed theologians that the last days stretch from the first coming of Christ to his return. In this sense, everything in the New Testament era is eschatological, having to do with the end of time.

This theological use of the term "last days" is rooted in early depictions of Israel's future. The Pentateuch described Israel's future in two stages (Lev 26:14–45; Dt 4:25–31; 30:1–10). First, it predicts that God's people would go through a time of sin and trouble that would eventually end with severe judgment of national exile. This exile took place in two stages: when the Assyrians defeated northern Israel in 722 B.C. (2Ki 17) and when the Babylonians later destroyed southern Judah and Jerusalem in 586 B.C. (2Ki 25). These early Old Testament books also spoke of a second stage of history that would transpire after Israel's exile. God promised that upon their repentance he would return his people to their land and bless them in greater measure than ever before (Dt 30:5). Deuteronomy 4:30 states that this age of restoration after exile will take place "in the latter days," and it is from this passage that we derive our theological term "eschatology."

Old Testament prophets followed this two-age outlook on Israel's history as they envisioned the future of God's people. Many of them announced that the judgment of exile would come upon the nation because of sin, but they also held forth the hope that this exile would be followed by a great age of blessing, which they also called "the last days" (e.g., Isa 2:2–5; Hos 3:5). They also designated this future age in a number of other ways: the reign of God (Isa 52:7), the new heavens and the new earth (Isa 65:17), the time of the new covenant (Jer 31:31) and the covenant of peace (Eze 34:25)—to name a few.

During the period between the Old and New Testaments, the Jews continued to describe history using this two-age frame of reference. On the one side, it became common to use the term "this age" to describe the age of sin and death that culminated in the exile. On the other, the phrase "the age to come" commonly designated the last days when the Messiah would bring the exile to an end and establish the kingdom of God over the earth (see theological article "The Kingdom of God" at Mt 4.)

Jesus and New Testament writers also adopted the basic twofold historical framework, but they significantly modified the scheme. The Jews to whom Jesus and his apostles ministered believed that the latter days would come suddenly and completely in the great moment when the Messiah would step onto the stage of history. Yet Jesus and his followers proclaimed that the latter days would come in another manner. The New Testament teaches that, instead of history moving simply from one age to the next, Jesus' first coming inaugurated the age to come; that this present age and the age to come overlap during the time between the first and second comings of Christ; and that the latter days, or the age to come, will arrive in their fullness at the consummation of all things when Christ returns. This is why Jesus taught that the kingdom of God is like a mustard seed that begins small and grows into the

a tenth of everything. First, his name means "king of righteousness"; then also, "king of
Salem" means "king of peace." [3]Without father or mother, without genealogy,[u] without
beginning of days or end of life, like the Son of God[v] he remains a priest forever.

7:3 [u]ver 6 [v]Mt 4:3

Melchizedek: Genesis 14:17–20 (vv. 1–10) and Psalm 110:4 (vv. 11–28).
7:1 king of Salem. The introduction of Melchizedek emphasizes that he was a king as well as a priest. As such Melchizedek was a type of Christ, whereas Jesus is the final great priest and king. Salem is likely the ancient name for Jerusalem (Ps 76:2).
7:2 "king of righteousness." In Hebrew the name Melchizedek is composed of two parts: *melek*, which means "king," and *tsedek*, which means "righteousness." Thus the name means "king of righteousness," an appropriate name for a type of Christ.
7:3 Without father or mother . . . beginning of days or end of life. While priests were normally legitimated by being located in a genealogical line, Melchizedek appears in Scripture without ancestors, progeny or notice of his birth or death. This does not mean that Melchizedek had no ancestors, nor does it imply that he was without a mother or a grave. Instead, the writer used these phrases to point out that Melchizedek had no genealogical right to be called a priest of the Lord. He was a man whom God appointed a royal priest (see note on 7:13–28). The uniqueness of Melchizedek's priesthood foreshadowed Christ and his special priesthood. See *BC* 10. **like the Son of God.** Some believe that Melchizedek was a preincarnate appearance of Christ. This is unlikely since terms of comparison and analogy are used: First, Melchizedek is described as being "like the Son of God" (a comparison of the Son with himself would be odd). Second, the Son became a priest "in the order of Melchizedek" (6:20) only later, through his incarna-

largest plant in the garden (Mt 13:31). It is why, although the new creation has begun in Jesus and in our hearts (2Co 5:17), we still await its fullness at the return of Christ (Rev 21:1–3). In a word, with Christ's first coming many dimensions of the latter days become reality, but when Christ returns we will experience them in full measure.

In this light, it is not surprising to find that the New Testament used the terminology of the last days to designate more than the second coming of Christ. It applies to events surrounding his first coming (Ac 2:17; Heb 1:2; 1Pe 1:20), the church age as a whole (2Ti 3:1) and the age after Christ's return (1Pe 1:5). The entire New Testament age is designated the "last days" because Jesus ascended to his throne and poured out great judgments and blessings when he first came to Earth. The entire history of the church is rightly designated the last days because we live in the time when the kingdom of God in Christ is expanding to the ends of the earth.

Recognizing that the New Testament speaks of the entire time from Christ's first coming to his return as the end times helps us to redirect our priorities. Rather than reading about the last days in the Old and New Testaments simply to create elaborate schemes of indicators for Christ's return, we need to learn how to see the entire New Testament age as the fulfillment of the latter days. This approach will help us to see more clearly the wonder of what Christ did in his first coming. It will also open our eyes to our responsibility to live for Christ as we enjoy God's intense blessings even while we suffer for the sake of Christ. Moreover, it will help us to avoid the danger of becoming preoccupied with speculations about the timing of Christ's return.

So, when we wonder whether we are already in the last days, the answer of the Bible is an unequivocal yes. Along with all Christians in every generation, we are in the final stage of history. God's kingdom of the last days is already here—as it has been for over two thousand years. We should rejoice in this truth, knowing that one day Christ will return to bring all things to their glorious end.

Traditional Jewish View

When the Messiah comes, the current age ends and the new age begins.

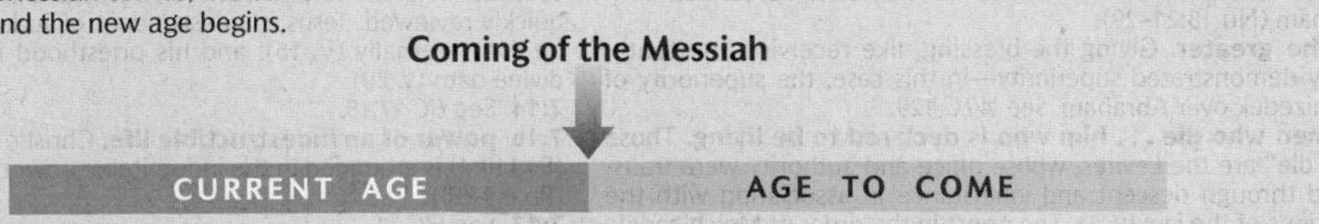

New Testament View

When the Messiah comes the first time, the age to come begins but the current age does not end; when the Messiah returns, the current age ends and the age to come continues.

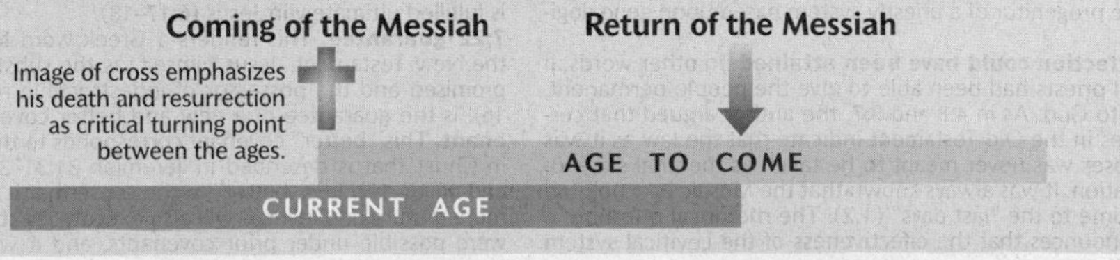

4 Just think how great he was: Even the patriarch[w] Abraham gave him a tenth of the
plunder![x] 5 Now the law requires the descendants of Levi who become priests to collect
a tenth from the people[y]—that is, their brothers—even though their brothers are descended from Abraham. 6 This man, however, did not trace his descent from Levi, yet he
collected a tenth from Abraham and blessed[z] him who had the promises.[a] 7 And without doubt the lesser person is blessed by the greater. 8 In the one case, the tenth is collected by men who die; but in the other case, by him who is declared to be living.[b] 9 One
might even say that Levi, who collects the tenth, paid the tenth through Abraham, 10 because when Melchizedek met Abraham, Levi was still in the body of his ancestor.

Jesus Like Melchizedek

11 If perfection could have been attained through the Levitical priesthood (for on the
basis of it the law was given to the people),[c] why was there still need for another priest
to come[d]—one in the order of Melchizedek,[e] not in the order of Aaron? 12 For when there
is a change of the priesthood, there must also be a change of the law. 13 He of whom these
things are said belonged to a different tribe,[f] and no one from that tribe has ever served
at the altar.[g] 14 For it is clear that our Lord descended from Judah,[h] and in regard to that
tribe Moses said nothing about priests. 15 And what we have said is even more clear if another priest like Melchizedek appears, 16 one who has become a priest not on the basis
of a regulation as to his ancestry but on the basis of the power of an indestructible life.
17 For it is declared:

> "You are a priest forever,
> in the order of Melchizedek."[a][i]

18 The former regulation is set aside because it was weak and useless[j] 19 (for the law
made nothing perfect),[k] and a better hope is introduced, by which we draw near to God.[l]
20 And it was not without an oath! Others became priests without any oath, 21 but he
became a priest with an oath when God said to him:

> "The Lord has sworn
> and will not change his mind:[m]
> 'You are a priest forever.' "[a][n]

22 Because of this oath, Jesus has become the guarantee of a better covenant.[o]

[a] *17,21* Psalm 110:4

7:4 [w]Ac 2:29 [x]Ge 14:20
7:5 [y]Nu 18:21,26
7:6 [z]Ge 14:19,20 [a]Ro 4:13
7:8 [b]Heb 5:6; 6:20
7:11 [c]ver 18,19; Heb 8:7 [d]Heb 10:1 [e]ver 17
7:13 [f]ver 11 [g]ver 14
7:14 [h]Isa 11:1; Mt 1:3; Lk 3:33
7:17 [i]Ps 110:4; ver 21; Heb 5:6
7:18 [j]Ro 8:3
7:19 [k]Ac 13:39; Ro 3:20; Heb 9:9 [l]Heb 4:16
7:21 [m]1Sa 15:29 [n]Ps 110:4
7:22 [o]Heb 8:6

---

tion, atoning death and exaltation. In addition, in Genesis 14 Melchizedek is presented as one who had a recognized political position (king of Salem).

7:4–10 how great he was . . . Levi was still. Two actions demonstrate Melchizedek's priestly superiority to Abraham's Levite descendants: Abraham gave a tenth to Melchizedek (vv. 4–6,8–10), and Melchizedek blessed Abraham (vv. 6–7).

7:5 the descendants of Levi. The Levitical priests inherited a right to tax (i.e., collect the tenth) even persons descended from Abraham (Nu 18:21–29).

7:7 the greater. Giving the blessing, like receiving the tenth, clearly demonstrated superiority—in this case, the superiority of Melchizedek over Abraham. See *WLC* 129.

7:8 men who die . . . him who is declared to be living. Those "who die" are the Levites, whose office and authority were transmitted through descent and inheritance in association with the provisions of the law (v. 5). The priest in the order of Melchizedek, however, is said to be "living." The declaration that he is living is found in Psalm 110:4, quoted in Hebrews 5:6 and returned to the foreground with the allusions in 6:20 and 7:3. The importance of this declaration, or "oath" (v. 21), is explained in verses 20–22.

7:9 paid the tenth through Abraham. The argument here does not depend simply on the genealogical relationship, as if any person could meaningfully be said to participate in the actions of all his ancestors. Rather, it depends upon Abraham's representative status as the progenitor of a priestly system based upon genealogical descent.

7:11 If perfection could have been attained. In other words, if the Levitical priests had been able to give the people permanent, free access to God. As in 4:8 and 8:7, the author argued that certain promises in the Old Testament indicate that the law as it was given to Moses was never meant to be taken as the final stage of God's revelation. It was always known that the Mosaic Law pointed forward in time to the "last days" (1:2). The rhetorical question in verse 11 announces that the effectiveness of the Levitical system will be compared with that of the "priest to come." **on the basis of it the law was given.** The Levitical priesthood, together with the Mosaic Law that provided for it, was instituted because of sin and the need for a ministry of reconciliation. The law and the priesthood are here being considered together, as one system of religious life. They were both temporary and designed for particular purposes. See theological article "The Three Uses of the Law" at Psalm 119.

7:13–28 The differences between Jesus and the Levites are now quickly reviewed: Jesus is a descendant of Judah, not Levi (v. 14); he lives eternally (v. 16); and his priesthood is founded on the divine oath (v. 20).

7:14 See *BC* 17,18.

7:16 power of an indestructible life. Christ's eternal priesthood (Ps 110:4) is grounded in the indomitable power of his resurrection (Ro 6:9–10).

7:17 See *HC* 31.

7:19 See note on verse 11. **a better hope.** This hope and the promise/oath were mentioned together in 6:17–18. Verses 20–28 continue to demonstrate the connection between our hope and the certainty of God's promise and oath. See *BC* 22.

7:21 with an oath. The divine oath expressed in Psalm 110:4 ("The LORD has sworn") demonstrates that just as David's family rules forever over the kingdom of God, the royal priesthood of David's family is also permanent. This joint royal and priestly office is fulfilled ultimately in Jesus (6:17–18).

7:22 guarantee. This renders a Greek word found only here in the New Testament. Jesus himself, as the substance of what was promised and the possessor of indestructible resurrection life (v. 16), is the guarantee of a new and better covenant. **better covenant.** This "better" covenant corresponds to the "new covenant" in Christ that is described in Jeremiah 31:31–34 (cited in 8:8–12 and 10:16–17). It is "better" in the sense that it is more complete, more mature and fuller. It will also execute greater judgments than were possible under prior covenants, and it will bestow greater

23 Now there have been many of those priests, since death prevented them from continuing in office; 24 but because Jesus lives forever, he has a permanent priesthood.[p]
25 Therefore he is able to save completely[a] those who come to God[q] through him, because
he always lives to intercede for them.[r]

26 Such a high priest meets our need—one who is holy, blameless, pure, set apart from
sinners,[s] exalted above the heavens.[t] 27 Unlike the other high priests, he does not need
to offer sacrifices[u] day after day, first for his own sins,[v] and then for the sins of the people. He sacrificed for their sins once for all[w] when he offered himself.[x] 28 For the law appoints as high priests men who are weak;[y] but the oath, which came after the law, appointed the Son,[z] who has been made perfect[a] forever.

The High Priest of a New Covenant

8 The point of what we are saying is this: We do have such a high priest,[b] who sat
down at the right hand of the throne of the Majesty in heaven, 2 and who serves in
the sanctuary, the true tabernacle[c] set up by the Lord, not by man.

3 Every high priest is appointed to offer both gifts and sacrifices,[d] and so it was necessary for this one also to have something to offer.[e] 4 If he were on earth, he would not
be a priest, for there are already men who offer the gifts prescribed by the law.[f] 5 They
serve at a sanctuary that is a copy[g] and shadow[h] of what is in heaven. This is why Moses was warned[i] when he was about to build the tabernacle: "See to it that you make everything according to the pattern shown you on the mountain."[b][j] 6 But the ministry Jesus
has received is as superior to theirs as the covenant[k] of which he is mediator[l] is superi-
or to the old one, and it is founded on better promises.

[a] 25 Or *forever* [b] 5 Exodus 25:40

7:24 [p]ver 28
7:25 [q]ver 19 [r]Ro 8:34
7:26 [s]2Co 5:21 [t]Heb 4:14
7:27 [u]Heb 5:1 [v]Heb 5:3 [w]Heb 9:12,26,28 [x]Eph 5:2; Heb 9:14,28
7:28 [y]Heb 5:2 [z]Heb 1:2 [a]Heb 2:10
8:1 [b]Heb 2:17
8:2 [c]Heb 9:11,24
8:3 [d]Heb 5:1 [e]Heb 9:14
8:4 [f]Heb 5:1
8:5 [g]Heb 9:23 [h]Col 2:17; Heb 10:1 [i]Heb 11:7; 12:25 [j]Ex 25:40
8:6 [k]Lk 22:20 [l]Heb 7:22

blessings than were previously bestowed. The idea that the final covenant would be better or greater finds its roots in Moses' announcement that after Israel's repentance in exile God would grant his people greater blessings than their fathers had enjoyed (Dt 30:5). See *WCF* 7.4; 8.3; *WLC* 71; *CD* 2.II.

7:23–28 See *WCF* 29.2; *WLC* 36,38,39,181; *WSC* 21,25; *BC* 26; *HC* 16,35,46.

7:23 many of those priests. The reference is to the many high priests who succeeded one another in office. The law of priestly succession (Ex 29:29–30) presupposed the eventual death of the priest. This lack of permanence, together with the repetition of the Old Testament sacrifices (10:11), reveals the inadequacy of the old order. See *WLC* 86.

7:25 able to save completely. Jesus' eternal life and priesthood make possible his eternal intercession for worshipers who "come to God through him," leading to their complete and eternal salvation. The word "completely" stands in contrast to the covenant with Moses that could only offer temporary relief from the consequences of sin because it merely moved the people of God forward toward the culmination in the new covenant. Thus Jesus is able to give comprehensive salvation (meeting our every need) and eternal salvation (rooted in the fact that Christ always lives to intercede for us). See *WCF* 8.4; 17.2; *WLC* 44,79; *WSC* 23; *HC* 29.

7:26 holy, blameless, pure, set apart from sinners. In 2:18 and 4:15—5:3, the author showed the importance of Jesus' identification with us in undergoing temptation. But it was also imperative that Jesus be "without sin" (4:15), a criterion that qualified him to enter the heavenly sanctuary on our behalf (8:1–2; 9:11–12,24–25). See *WCF* 8.3; *WLC* 37; *WSC* 22; *HC* 15.

7:27 Unlike. The contrast between the Levitical priests' repeated daily (and yearly) sacrifices and Jesus' once-for-all offering of himself is developed in 9:25—10:18. See *WCF* 29.2; *HC* 80.

7:28 the law . . . but the oath. This verse summarizes the contrast between the old and the new covenant priesthoods. First, the old covenant priesthood was appointed by law without a specific divine oath (v. 20), while the eternal priesthood of Christ was appointed by an oath to the house of David (v. 21). Second, the temporary appointment of weak and sinful (v. 27) priests is contrasted with the eternal appointment of the sinless "Son . . . made perfect forever."

■ **8:1—10:18** *Christ Is Superior to Priestly Ministry.* Christ's superiority to Aaron and the Levitical priesthood led the writer to give a fuller description of Jesus' unsurpassed priestly ministry. This material divides into four parts: the superiority of the New Testament covenant (8:1–13), the New Testament tabernacle (9:1–10), the New Testament sacrifice (9:11–28) and Christ's final sacrifice (10:1–18).

■ **8:1–13** *A Superior Covenant.* Jesus' magnificent priestly work is supreme because it is set within the context of the new covenant.

8:1–13 See *WCF* 7.5; *WLC* 34.

8:1 The point. The writer paused to summarize what he had said thus far: Jesus is a new high priest in the old order of Melchizedek. Before the author explained what Jesus does in this role, he paused to indicate that he knew his argument was difficult, but important, for his readers to understand. **We do have such a high priest.** Jesus' present high priesthood over New Testament believers continues the Old Testament priesthood of Melchizedek and David (see notes on 5:6; 7:21). His office as priest is not brand new; rather, it is renewed. **the throne of the Majesty in heaven.** This entire section contrasts Jesus' priestly ministry in the heavenly reality of God's throne room with the priestly ministry of the old covenant, which was an earthly replica of the heavenly throne room. See *HC* 80.

8:2 the true tabernacle. The heavenly temple of God is the original after which the earthly tent and temple were copied (v. 5). Nevertheless, they were not *merely* copies. They were also places where God chose to manifest his glorious presence (Ex 40:34–38). In many ways they were mystical places where the heavenly throne room and the earthly copy of that heavenly throne room intersected (2Ch 6:1–42; Isa 6:1–13). **not by man.** See 9:11,24. God appointed the earthly sanctuaries of the tabernacle and temple as places to be among his people, but those structures were designed as a step in bringing God's people to the final stage of history when the heavenly realities that they reflected would come into full view.

8:3 something to offer. Jesus offered himself (7:27)—his own blood (9:12) and body (10:10).

8:4 he would not be a priest. Under the provisions of the Mosaic Law that set apart the tribe of Levi as the priestly family, Jesus, as a descendant of Judah, could not be a priest (7:13). Jesus' priestly service is of a royal order far superior to the temporary Mosaic system. It is of an older, more permanent order, one stemming from the days of Abraham and established on the promises made to Abraham (6:17–18).

8:5 pattern. Literally, "type." The plan or pattern of the heavenly tabernacle was revealed to Moses, and the earthly tabernacle was built accordingly (Ex 25:40).

8:6 mediator. A legal intermediary who represents two parties and through whom a new relationship is established. Moses is described as the mediator of the law (Gal 3:19–20). Crucial to Christ's mediatorial work was his offering of himself as an atoning sacrifice for sin (9:14–15; 12:24; 1Ti 2:5–6). See *WLC* 35. **superior.** See note on 7:22. The new covenant is superior because it was made with an oath to Abraham (6:17–18) and confirmed with an oath to David (7:21–22). It rests on "better promises" as well (see 6:13–20; cited in vv. 8–12).

8:7 [7]For if there had been nothing wrong with that first covenant, no place would have
*m*Heb 7:11,18 been sought for another. *m* [8]But God found fault with the people and said[a]:

[a] 8 Some manuscripts may be translated *fault and said to the people.*

8:7 nothing wrong. Moses knew that the covenant made with him was not final (see note on 7:22), but this verse implies some kind of flaw. The fault, however, was not with the covenant itself, but with the people who failed to observe it (see v. 8). **that first covenant.** The writer described the covenant with Moses at Sinai as "first" in comparison with the "superior" covenant made with Abraham, which he referred to as the "second." Clearly these identifications as "first" and "second" are not absolute. After all, the covenants with Adam, Noah and Abraham all preceded the "first" covenant, and the covenant with David intervened between the "first" and "second" (see theological article "The Covenants of Works and Grace" at Ge 6). The writer focused on the Mosaic covenant as the "first" because it was the one that instituted the Levitical priesthood that existed when Christ came. The writer referred to the new covenant in Christ as the "second" because its priestly order (which had previously coexisted with the Levitical priesthood) finally replaced that of the first covenant. **covenant.** The promise that God would one day fulfill his covenant with Abraham

The Ascension and Session of Jesus: Why Did Jesus Go to Heaven?

JESUS' ascension was his bodily rising into heaven when the Father withdrew him from his disciples' gaze and brought him into his holy presence (Ac 1:9–11). This event took place 40 days after his resurrection (Ac 1:3). Jesus foretold the ascension (Jn 6:62; 14:2,12; 16:5,10,17,28; 17:5; 20:17), and Luke described it (Lk 24:50–53; Ac 1:6–11). Paul celebrated it and affirmed Christ's consequent lordship (Eph 1:20; 4:8–10; Php 2:9–11; 1Ti 3:16). The book of Hebrews applies this truth for encouragement of the fainthearted (Heb 1:3; 4:14; 9:24).

Christ's ascension into heaven had two distinct effects on him. In terms of his divine nature, the Father restored the glory that his divine Son had possessed before the humiliation of his incarnation, suffering and death (Jn 17:5). In terms of his human nature, Christ was glorified as no human had or has since ever been (1Co 15:20–23,35–44). When Jesus ascended into heaven, he took his throne at the right hand of God the Father (Heb 8:1; 12:2), fulfilling the promise to David that one of his sons would sit on his throne forever (2Sa 7:12–16; 1Ch 17:11–14; 2Ch 6:14–17; Pss 89:1–4; 132:11–12). From there Christ now reigns as King over all until all his enemies are put under his feet (1Co 15:25) and he returns to rule over the new heavens and the new earth.

The ascension establishes at least four important facts: First, Jesus was enthroned upon his entry into heaven in the seat of greatest honor except for the throne of his Father. To sit at the Father's right hand is to occupy the position of executive ruler on the Father's behalf. This means that Jesus has been given rightful rule over all of creation and is able therefore to secure the success of the gospel and the eventual eternal salvation of all who believe in him. Although he has not yet crushed all who oppose his reign, no power in heaven or on Earth can overrule him (Mt 28:18; 1Co 15:27; Eph 1:20–22; 1Pe 3:22). His name is above all other names (Ps 138:2; Php 2:9).

Second, when Jesus ascended into heaven, he and the Father poured out the Holy Spirit on his church (Jn 16:7–14; Ac 2:33). The Spirit of God had always been present with his people, even in the Old Testament (Ps 106:32–33; Isa 63:7–14; Hag 2:4–5). Yet with Christ's victory over death, the Spirit was poured out in anticipation of the day when the presence of God will fill the entire earth. He was sent to more people than ever before (Ac 1:8; Eph 2:17–22). The Spirit, who leads and comforts the church in Christ's absence, so perfectly joins the will of Christ that he is said to be the Spirit of Christ and Christ to be the Spirit (Ro 8:9, 2Co 3:17–18, 1Pe 1:11). These passages do not confuse the second and third persons of the Trinity (see theological article "The Trinity" at Jn 14), but refer to the harmony and identity of purpose between the Son and the Spirit. It is through the Spirit that Jesus is present with his church, even in the sacrament of the Lord's Supper.

Third, after completing his atoning work on the cross, ascending to the right hand of the Father and sending the Spirit to his church, Jesus has continued serving his followers as their royal high priest. This heavenly service is what theologians call Christ's "session." All who pray in Jesus' name find him accessible and powerful to help them (Heb 4:14,16; 7:25; 9:24; 12:22–24; 13:6–8). He ministers before the Father on our behalf, representing us and pleading sympathetically for us because he knows our temptations (Rom 8:34; Heb 2:18; 4:15). Jesus' heavenly session is part of the means by which the benefits he obtained at the cross are applied to believers, including maintaining all believers in a state of forgiveness and justification (1Jn 1:9—2:2).

Fourth, just as we (as believers) are united with Christ in his death and resurrection (Ro 6:5), we are also joined with him in his heavenly reign (Eph 1:3,20; 2:6; 3:10; 6:12). Just as Jesus' human nature reached heights of glorification when he began to reign over all as David's son and God's vice-regent, we also are promised that if we overcome, we will sit at his throne even as he sits at the throne of his heavenly Father (Rev 3:21–22). In Jesus' heavenly reign we find a portrait of what will happen to the entirety of redeemed humanity at Christ's return. Although we will always remain mere creatures, we will be like him in his humanity (1Jn 3:2). We will experience the wonder of being glorified images of God, creatures whom God has ordained from the beginning to rule over creation on his behalf (see theological article "Human Beings in God's Image" at Ge 1). The Ephesians passages suggest, moreover, that in one sense our reign with Christ is not only future, but also present. Perhaps Paul had one or both of the following ideas in mind: (1) Our future heavenly destiny is so certain that it can be spoken of as present. (2) Jesus even now is reigning on behalf of his people, which is a great comfort to us.

"The time is coming, declares the Lord,
when I will make a new covenant[n]
with the house of Israel
and with the house of Judah.
9 It will not be like the covenant
I made with their forefathers[o]
when I took them by the hand
to lead them out of Egypt,
because they did not remain faithful to my covenant,
and I turned away from them,
declares the Lord.
10 This is the covenant I will make with the house of Israel
after that time, declares the Lord.
I will put my laws in their minds
and write them on their hearts.[p]
I will be their God,
and they will be my people.[q]
11 No longer will a man teach his neighbor,
or a man his brother, saying, 'Know the Lord,'
because they will all know me,[r]
from the least of them to the greatest.
12 For I will forgive their wickedness
and will remember their sins no more."[s][a][t]

13 By calling this covenant "new," he has made the first one obsolete;[u] and what is obsolete and aging will soon disappear.

Worship in the Earthly Tabernacle

9 Now the first covenant had regulations for worship and also an earthly sanctuary.[v]
2 A tabernacle[w] was set up. In its first room were the lampstand,[x] the table[y] and the
consecrated bread;[z] this was called the Holy Place. 3 Behind the second curtain was a
room called the Most Holy Place,[a] 4 which had the golden altar of incense[b] and the gold-

8:8 [n]Jer 31:31
8:9 [o]Ex 19:5,6
8:10 [p]2Co 3:3; Heb 10:16 [q]Zec 8:8
8:11 [r]Isa 54:13; Jn 6:45
8:12 [s]Heb 10:17 [t]Ro 11:27
8:13 [u]2Co 5:17
9:1 [v]Ex 25:8
9:2 [w]Ex 25:8,9 [x]Ex 25:31-39 [y]Ex 25:23-29 [z]Lev 24:5-8
9:3 [a]Ex 26:31-33
9:4 [b]Ex 30:1-5

[a] *12* Jer. 31:31–34

in astounding proportions is a unifying theme of 8:7—10:18, where the word translated "covenant" occurs 14 times. In addition, it occurs three other places in Hebrews (7:22; 12:24; 13:20), making the word "covenant" more common in Hebrews than in the rest of the New Testament combined (the word appears 16 times elsewhere in the New Testament).
8:8 found fault with the people. The Greek text of this phrase is disputed. Either God "found fault with the people" (see NIV text) or he "found fault [i.e., with the old covenant] and said to the people" (see NIV text note). The quotation from Jeremiah 31 in verse 9 makes it clear, however, that the problem in view was the people's disobedience, which the sacrificial system of the Mosaic covenant did not have the ability to solve. The new covenant in Christ, however, permanently resolves all problems by making one atonement for sin for all time (10:12) and by installing a high priest who will never die (7:24). Although not all the promised blessings of the new covenant have been realized, they will all be fulfilled when Christ returns (9:28). **new covenant.** This verse begins an extended quote from Jeremiah 31:31–34. In its original context, Jeremiah's prophecy spoke of a time when the exiled people of Israel and Judah would be restored to the promised land and would receive the blessings of God's covenant in all their fullness. Jeremiah's offer of a "new covenant" was an offer of forgiveness for transgressions committed under the covenant as it was administered under Moses (cf. 9:15) and of restoration to God's favor under that same covenant (v. 12; Jer 31:34). Through Jeremiah, God offered to renew and restore—not replace—his covenant with his people. Although traditional translations have favored the term "new," both the Hebrew (Jer 31:31) and the Greek (v. 8) words for "new" may be translated "renewed" (see theological article "The Covenants of Works and Grace" at Ge 6).
8:9–11 See *WLC* 35; *BC* 7.
8:10 put my laws in their minds . . . hearts. Inward appropriation of the law is not unique to the covenant in Christ; it was always the ideal for God's people (Dt 6:4–9; 30:1–6,14; Pss 37:31; 40:8; 119:11). In Jeremiah's day, as in the first century, many Jews had reduced the old covenant to externalities, but Jesus and his apostles resisted this (Mt 5:17–19). When Christ returns, the new covenant will bring wholehearted obedience to God's will; this process began with the first coming of Christ. See *WCF* 19.7.
8:11 they will all know me. Under the law, access to God's presence was restricted (9:7–8). But in the New Testament, God's presence and blessings are poured out more fully upon all kinds of people (Ac 2:17–21). However, this promise will not be completely fulfilled until Christ returns. Only then will the church be composed entirely of believers (see theological articles "The Plan of the Ages" at Heb 7 and "The Church: Visible and Invisible" at 1 Pe 4).
8:12 I will . . . remember their sins no more. Like all the promises of the new covenant, the full application of forgiveness to God's people will come only when Christ returns and purifies his church. Yet the inauguration of the new covenant has brought us a step closer to this destiny. Unlike the repeated sacrifices made by the Old Testament priests—repetitions of which were an annual reminder of the people's sins (10:3)—Jesus' offering of himself has obtained forgiveness, holiness and perfection once for all time (10:10,13,18).
8:13 what is obsolete . . . will soon disappear. The covenant with Moses is not obsolete in the sense that it has no value since the inauguration of the new covenant. After all, Jesus, the One who brought the new covenant, embraced the old covenant as relevant and taught his disciples to do the same (see theological articles "The Three Uses of the Law" at Ps 119 and "The Covenants of Works and Grace" at Ge 6). It is "obsolete" in the sense that its priestly institutions have been superseded by Christ's priesthood. As a result, the faithful people of God can no longer define their relationship with God primarily in terms of the Mosaic covenant.
9:1–28 See *WCF* 7.5; 19.3; *WLC* 34.
■ **9:1–10** *A Superior Tabernacle.* The writer explained specifically how the new covenant brought with it a superior focus of worship and sacrifice.
9:1 worship . . . sanctuary. This verse begins a lengthy comparison of Old Testament sacrifice and the sacrifice of Christ. The first part summarizes the Old Testament sanctuary and its activities.
9:3 curtain. This curtain closed off the Most Holy Place, where God's presence among his people was most intensely revealed (6:19). With Jesus' death, this curtain was torn in two (10:20; Mt 27:51), enlarging the place of God's holy dwelling from one geo-

covered ark of the covenant.[c] This ark contained the gold jar of manna,[d] Aaron's staff
that had budded,[e] and the stone tablets of the covenant. 5 Above the ark were the cherubim of the Glory,[f] overshadowing the atonement cover.[a] But we cannot discuss these
things in detail now.
6 When everything had been arranged like this, the priests entered regularly[g] into the
outer room to carry on their ministry. 7 But only the high priest entered[h] the inner
room, and that only once a year,[i] and never without blood, which he offered for himself[j]
and for the sins the people had committed in ignorance. 8 The Holy Spirit was showing[k]
by this that the way[l] into the Most Holy Place had not yet been disclosed as long as the
first tabernacle was still standing. 9 This is an illustration for the present time, indicating that the gifts and sacrifices being offered[m] were not able to clear the conscience of
the worshiper. 10 They are only a matter of food[n] and drink[o] and various ceremonial
washings—external regulations[p] applying until the time of the new order.

The Blood of Christ

11 When Christ came as high priest[q] of the good things that are already here,[b][r] he
went through the greater and more perfect tabernacle[s] that is not man-made, that is to
say, not a part of this creation. 12 He did not enter by means of the blood of goats and
calves;[t] but he entered the Most Holy Place[u] once for all[v] by his own blood, having obtained eternal redemption. 13 The blood of goats and bulls and the ashes of a heifer[w]
sprinkled on those who are ceremonially unclean sanctify them so that they are outwardly clean. 14 How much more, then, will the blood of Christ, who through the eternal Spirit[x] offered himself unblemished to God, cleanse our consciences[y] from acts that lead to
death,[c][z] so that we may serve the living God!
15 For this reason Christ is the mediator[a] of a new covenant, that those who are called
may receive the promised eternal inheritance—now that he has died as a ransom to set
them free from the sins committed under the first covenant.[b]

9:4 [c]Ex 25:10-22 [d]Ex 16:32,33 [e]Nu 17:10
9:5 [f]Ex 25:17-19
9:6 [g]Nu 28:3
9:7 [h]Lev 16:11-19 [i]Lev 16:34 [j]Heb 5:2,3
9:8 [k]Heb 3:7 [l]Jn 14:6; Heb 10:19,20
9:9 [m]Heb 5:1
9:10 [n]Lev 11:2-23 [o]Col 2:16 [p]Heb 7:16
9:11 [q]Heb 2:17 [r]Heb 10:1 [s]Heb 8:2
9:12 [t]Heb 10:4 [u]ver 24 [v]Heb 7:27
9:13 [w]Nu 19:9,17,18
9:14 [x]1Pe 3:18 [y]Tit 2:14; Heb 10:2,22 [z]Heb 6:1
9:15 [a]1Ti 2:5 [b]Heb 7:22

[a] 5 Traditionally *the mercy seat* [b] 11 Some early manuscripts *are to come* [c] 14 Or *from useless rituals*

graphical location and beginning the process of the sanctification of the entire creation—a process that will be completed at Christ's return (Rev 21:1–27).
9:4 golden altar of incense. Although the incense altar was just outside the curtain (Ex 40:26), its function was so closely associated with the inner chamber and the ark within it (Ex 30:6) that it was considered to belong there (1Ki 6:22). When the high priest entered the Most Holy Place, he took the smoking incense with him. The smoke hid from view the atonement cover (on top of the ark of testimony) and shielded him from the Lord's burning purity (Lev 16:12–13). **Aaron's staff.** The staff that budded to show that priestly privilege comes only by God's appointment (Nu 17:10; see 5:4–5).
9:5 cherubim of the Glory. The "atonement cover," or lid of the ark, had on it two figures of cherubim facing each other. They were representative of God's heavenly courtiers, who serve constantly in his presence. **we cannot discuss these things in detail now.** First-century Jewish writers such as Philo gave great attention to the symbolism of the sanctuary furniture. The author of Hebrews, however, desired to address what took place in the tabernacle and said no more about the furniture, whatever symbolic value the pieces may have had.
9:6 the priests entered regularly. To replace the bread of the Presence (Ex 25:30; Lev 24:5–9), to keep the lampstand burning (Ex 27:20–21; Lev 24:1–4) and to burn fragrant incense twice daily, symbolizing the people's prayers (Ex 30:7–9; Lk 1:8–10; Rev 8:3).
9:7–8 only the high priest . . . The Holy Spirit was showing. The fact that only one person, only once a year and only with special preparation, could enter the Most Holy Place was the Holy Spirit's revelation through the law that the earthly sanctuary was only a step toward, not the fulfillment of, the extension of God's presence throughout the world so that all peoples could have open access to him. The new covenant promise that "they will all know me" (8:11) could not be fulfilled through the earthly tent.
9:7 for himself. Unlike our holy priest, Jesus (5:3; 7:26–27), Levitical priests were themselves in need of atonement. **committed in ignorance.** See note on 5:2.
9:9–10 illustration for the present time. The high priest's very limited access to the inner sanctuary revealed that his offerings did not permanently take away guilt. Although for a time they provided the means by which God was pleased to apply forgiveness to his people, they had no merit in themselves. They only reflected the merit of Christ's coming sacrifice that was to be offered in the heavenly temple. The inability of those offerings permanently to remove guilt becomes clearer when we note the writer's emphasis on how they had to be perpetually repeated (10:1). See *WCF* 28.3.
■ **9:11–28** *A Superior Sacrifice.* The writer declared Christ's sacrificial work to be better than the sacrifices of the Old Testament.
9:11–15 See *WCF* 17.2; *WLC* 38; *HC* 36.
9:11 good things that are already here. While the first covenant's sanctuary and sacrifices were in force (10:1), cleansing of conscience and confidence to draw near to God were still to come, but now they have partly arrived through Christ. The author of Hebrews viewed the blessings that will be given in fullness when Christ returns as already partially experienced by the church (6:5; 12:22–24). See theological article "The Plan of the Ages" at Heb 7. **greater and more perfect tabernacle.** The heavenly reality behind Moses' earthly copy (8:5; 9:24).
9:12 blood of goats and calves. Used by the high priest on the Day of Atonement (once a year) to cleanse the Most Holy Place (Lev 16:11–16). **once for all.** That is, once for all *time,* in contrast to the repetition of sacrifices by the Levitical priests (10:2–3,10–14). This emphatic word anticipates the climactic statement in verses 26–28. **eternal redemption.** Redemption is a purchase made by paying a price or ransom. The effect of Christ's redemption is permanent because it was accomplished by his own blood. See *WCF* 8.5; *WLC* 55,57; *BC* 21; *HC* 31,80.
9:13 ashes of a heifer. This residue was used with water to purify persons who had touched a corpse (Nu 19:9,17–18). Such persons were considered to be unclean in a ceremonial sense, not in a moral sense. **outwardly clean.** They became eligible again for their duties of worship.
9:14 How much more. As in 2:2–3, the writer used an argument from the lesser to the greater. The lesser is the blood of animals offered by the high priest on Earth; the greater is the blood shed by Christ. The lesser had ceremonial power; the greater can free the conscience of guilt. **unblemished.** A sacrifice must be without defect in order to be an atoning substitute for sinners (Nu 6:14; 1Pe 1:19). This Levitical regulation pointed toward the perfection required of the final sacrifice, Jesus himself. **acts that lead to death.** Not the works of the law that are useless for justification (Gal 3:1–14), but sinful deeds that deserve the covenant curse of death (6:1). **serve the living God!** The goal of forgiveness is not only our enjoyment, but also the glory of God (12:28; 13:15–16,21). See *WCF* 8.5; 8.7; *WLC* 38,40,44; *WSC* 25; *BC* 21,34.
9:15–17 See *WCF* 7.4; *CD* 2.II.
9:15 a ransom. A payment to release someone from captivity. A related Greek word is translated "redemption" in verse 12. Viola-

[16]In the case of a will,[a] it is necessary to prove the death of the one who made it, [17]be-
cause a will is in force only when somebody has died; it never takes effect while the one
who made it is living. [18]This is why even the first covenant was not put into effect without blood.[c] [19]When Moses had proclaimed every commandment of the law to all the people, he took the blood of calves, together with water, scarlet wool and branches of hyssop, and sprinkled the scroll and all the people.[d] [20]He said, "This is the blood of the
covenant, which God has commanded you to keep."[b][e] [21]In the same way, he sprinkled
with the blood both the tabernacle and everything used in its ceremonies. [22]In fact, the
law requires that nearly everything be cleansed with blood,[f] and without the shedding
of blood there is no forgiveness.[g]

[23]It was necessary, then, for the copies[h] of the heavenly things to be purified with
these sacrifices, but the heavenly things themselves with better sacrifices than these.
[24]For Christ did not enter a man-made sanctuary that was only a copy of the true one;[i]
he entered heaven itself, now to appear for us in God's presence. [25]Nor did he enter heav-
en to offer himself again and again, the way the high priest enters the Most Holy Place[j]
every year with blood that is not his own.[k] [26]Then Christ would have had to suffer many
times since the creation of the world.[l] But now he has appeared once for all[m] at the end
of the ages to do away with sin by the sacrifice of himself. [27]Just as man is destined to die
once,[n] and after that to face judgment,[o] [28]so Christ was sacrificed once to take away the
sins of many people; and he will appear a second time,[p] not to bear sin,[q] but to bring
salvation to those who are waiting for him.[r]

Christ's Sacrifice Once for All

10 The law is only a shadow[s] of the good things[t] that are coming—not the realities themselves.[u] For this reason it can never, by the same sacrifices repeated
endlessly year after year, make perfect[v] those who draw near to worship. [2]If it could,

9:18 [c]Ex 24:6-8
9:19 [d]Ex 24:6-8
9:20 [e]Ex 24:8; Mt 26:28
9:22 [f]Lev 8:15 [g]Lev 17:11
9:23 [h]Heb 8:5
9:24 [i]Heb 8:2
9:25 [j]Heb 10:19 [k]ver 7,8
9:26 [l]Heb 4:3 [m]Heb 7:27
9:27 [n]Ge 3:19 [o]2Co 5:10
9:28 [p]Tit 2:13 [q]1Pe 2:24 [r]1Co 1:7
10:1 [s]Heb 8:5 [t]Heb 9:11 [u]Heb 9:23 [v]Heb 7:19

[a] *16* Same Greek word as *covenant*; also in verse 17 [b] *20* Exodus 24:8

---

tion of God's covenant creates a liability to condemnation that can only be satisfied by the violator's death or by redemption through a substitute. See *WCF* 8.5; *CD* 2.II.

9:16 In the case of a will. The Greek word for "will" can also be translated "covenant" (see NIV text note). The author employed this term's dual usage to compare a will with a covenant and to underline the point that both are in some sense impacted by death. A covenant is not identical to a will, but it has force only while the parties are still alive. See *WCF* 8.5.

9:19–22 See *WCF* 28.3.

9:19 Moses . . . took the blood. The immediate reference is to Exodus 24:4–8, but the writer included things not mentioned there (e.g., hyssop). In view are the Old Testament sacrifices in general, as is evident in verse 22. Both the people and God, the author of the scroll, were sworn in this ceremony to the provisions and penalties of the covenant.

9:20 This is the blood. Referring to Exodus 24:9, when the covenant at Sinai came into force, the writer pointed out that the covenant was written down in the scroll and ratified with the offering of blood. This blood was shed not by those who might have broken the covenant, but by animals that substituted for them (cf. Ge 15:9–18; Jer 34:18–20). All of this vividly demonstrated the ultimate sanction or penalty for flagrant covenantal violation: death.

9:21–24 The sanctuary—the meeting place of the holy God with sinful humans—must itself be purified through sacrificial blood, "for without the shedding of blood there is no forgiveness" (v. 22). This was true not only of the earthly tent of the old covenant (vv. 21–22), but also of the heavenly reality (vv. 23–24), which was purified by Christ's sacrifice on the cross (see note on v. 23).

9:22 nearly everything. The tent and its furnishings were so closely identified with the worshipers who met God there that the sacrificial blood shed for the worshipers' forgiveness (10:18) was also required to cleanse the worship instruments and environment (Lev 16:16). **without the shedding of blood there is no forgiveness.** This fundamental principle (Lev 17:11) is restated after having been introduced in verses 16–18. This standard was not absolute in the law (e.g., Lev 5:11–13) but was the rule barring exception. Having established the importance of blood to forgiveness, the writer turned from the earthly to the heavenly sanctuary. See *WCF* 29.2; *WLC* 152,194.

9:23 the heavenly things themselves with better sacrifices. Human sin defiles everything on Earth, but the heavenly temple is beyond the corruption of sinful humanity. Already undefiled by sin, the heavenly sanctuary did not need purification or cleansing. It was appropriate, however, for Christ's blood to consecrate it, dedicating it to God and setting it apart for holy use. For sinful humans to be forgiven and welcomed into the presence of God, Christ's sacrificial blood had to be offered in the heavenly temple on their behalf (10:19–22; 12:24).

9:24 to appear for us in God's presence. Just as the high priest appeared for Israel on the Day of Atonement (Lev 16:32–33). See *WCF* 8.4; *WLC* 55; *BC* 26; *HC* 31,46.

9:25–28 See *WCF* 29.2; *BC* 21; *HC* 80.

9:25 again and again. This Greek word appears in verse 26 ("many times") and in 10:11. Repetition of sacrifices testified to their ineffectiveness in permanently removing guilt (10:2) and served as a recurring reminder both of sin (10:3) and of the need for an ultimate, final sacrifice. Verse 7 stressed that the Day of Atonement ceremonies took place "only" once a year; here the emphasis is on the facts that they were offered "every" year and "repeated endlessly" (10:1). **blood that is not his own.** The high priest's offering is contrasted with Christ's offering of himself. As one who himself needed atonement (v. 7), a Levitical high priest could never offer himself as an unblemished substitute for others (v. 14).

9:26 creation of the world . . . end of the ages. These phrases bracket a vast span of time, during the whole of which Christ had to offer himself only once. The "end of the ages" is the equivalent of the "last days" (1:2), a period that was ushered in by the death, resurrection and ascension of Christ (see theological article "The Plan of the Ages" at Heb 7).

9:27 to die once, and after that to face judgment. Both reincarnation and the belief that physical death is the end of existence are excluded. Christ suffered the common human destiny of death and judgment (v. 28), but for him the judgment was followed by resurrection and vindication (1Ti 3:16). This vindication will be fully manifested when he comes again (1Th 1:10). See *WLC* 84; *BC* 21,37; *HC* 10.

9:28 to take away the sins of many people. Literally, "to bear the sins of many," a direct reference to the suffering servant in Isaiah 53:12. See *WCF* 29.2; *WLC* 44; *WSC* 25.

10:1–39 See *WCF* 7.5; *WLC* 34.

■ **10:1–18** *Christ's Sacrifice Once for All Time.* The writer elaborated further on the grand importance of Christ's final sacrifice for the sins of God's people.

10:1–10 See *HC* 19.

10:1 a shadow of the good things that are coming. The "good things" were future with respect to the law, which foreshadowed them; with Christ's first coming, they became partially present, and they will be completely fulfilled at his return (9:11). **make perfect.** The worshipers could not be "cleansed once for all" time (v. 2).

would they not have stopped being offered? For the worshipers would have been
cleansed once for all, and would no longer have felt guilty for their sins. 3But those sacrifices are an annual reminder of sins,[w] 4because it is impossible for the blood of bulls
and goats[x] to take away sins.
5Therefore, when Christ came into the world,[y] he said:

> "Sacrifice and offering you did not desire,
> but a body you prepared for me;[z]
> 6with burnt offerings and sin offerings
> you were not pleased.
> 7Then I said, 'Here I am—it is written about me in the scroll[a]—
> I have come to do your will, O God.' "[a][b]

8First he said, "Sacrifices and offerings, burnt offerings and sin offerings you did not desire, nor were you pleased with them"[c] (although the law required them to be made).
9Then he said, "Here I am, I have come to do your will."[d] He sets aside the first to establish the second. 10And by that will, we have been made holy[e] through the sacrifice of the
body[f] of Jesus Christ once for all.[g]
11Day after day every priest stands and performs his religious duties; again and again
he offers the same sacrifices,[h] which can never take away sins.[i] 12But when this priest
had offered for all time one sacrifice for sins, he sat down at the right hand of God.
13Since that time he waits for his enemies to be made his footstool,[j] 14because by one sacrifice he has made perfect[k] forever those who are being made holy.
15The Holy Spirit also testifies[l] to us about this. First he says:

> 16"This is the covenant I will make with them
> after that time, says the Lord.
> I will put my laws in their hearts,
> and I will write them on their minds."[b][m]

17Then he adds:

> "Their sins and lawless acts
> I will remember no more."[c][n]

18And where these have been forgiven, there is no longer any sacrifice for sin.

10:3 [w]Heb 9:7
10:4 [x]Heb 9:12,13
10:5 [y]Heb 1:6 [z]1Pe 2:24
10:7 [a]Jer 36:2 [b]Ps 40:6-8
10:8 [c]ver 5,6; Mk 12:33
10:9 [d]ver 7
10:10 [e]Jn 17:19 [f]Heb 2:14; 1Pe 2:24 [g]Heb 7:27
10:11 [h]Heb 5:1 [i]ver 1,4
10:13 [j]Heb 1:13
10:14 [k]ver 1
10:15 [l]Heb 3:7
10:16 [m]Jer 31:33; Heb 8:10
10:17 [n]Heb 8:12

[a] *7* Psalm 40:6–8 (see Septuagint) [b] *16* Jer. 31:33 [c] *17* Jer. 31:34

The law could neither remove their guilt nor provide them permanent access to God (7:11,19; 9:9). See *WCF* 19.3; *WLC* 34.
10:3 reminder of sins. The Old Testament sacrifices were a public notice, before God and humanity, that the people were still sinners (Lev 14:12–28; Nu 5:15; Isa 53:10). In the new covenant, God will "remember their sins no more" (8:12; see 10:17). This "forgetting" takes place with respect to individuals when they come to possess saving faith in Christ, and it will take place with the people of God as a whole when Christ returns in glory.
10:4 it is impossible. The inadequacy of the Old Testament sacrifices was not a new idea but one that had been sharply expressed in several Old Testament passages (e.g., 1Sa 15:22; Isa 1:10–17; Am 5:21-24; Mic 6:6–8). The function and intent of the law were frustrated by the people's sin (8:8–12; Ro 8:3–4). See *WCF* 27.4.
10:5–7 Sacrifice . . . your will, O God. Psalm 40:6–8 recites David's commitment to obey the law of God. Jesus perfectly fulfilled this commitment. For this reason, the writer to the Hebrews understood the psalm to be an indication that Christ's obedient self-sacrifice replaced the Old Testament sacrificial system. See *WCF* 8.4.
10:5 a body you prepared for me. The Hebrew text of Psalm 40:6 reads "my ears you have pierced" (i.e., "you have made me ready to obey"; cf. Isa 50:5). In the Septuagint (the Greek translation of the OT), which Hebrews follows, this psalm speaks of the readiness of the whole person ("the body"), not just a part (the "ears") of the person. Thus, the "body prepared for me" refers to Jesus' readiness to become human and to suffer death on our behalf (2:14; 5:8). See *WSC* 22.
10:7 the scroll. Probably a reference to the scrolls of the law that the kings of Israel were to hold to express their submission to God (Dt 17:18–20; 2Ki 11:12)
10:8 Sacrifices and offerings, burnt offerings and sin offerings. These terms sum up the whole Levitical sacrificial system. Over against all of this (called "the first" in v. 9), Christ has offered another sacrifice (called "the second" in v. 9). Although instituted by God in the law (2:2; 8:9; 12:18–21,25), the Levitical system was not the means willed by God to remove his people's sin.
10:9 to do your will. Jesus was to be obedient through suffering (2:10; 5:8), to perform the ultimate act of obedience: atoning for sin through his own death (v. 10). **sets aside the first.** That is, the Levitical sacrificial system of the Old Testament (see notes on 8:7,13).
10:10–18 See *WCF* 8.5; 11.3; 11.5; 17.2; 29.2; *BC* 21; *HC* 31,37,80.
10:10 by that will. The unchanging purpose of God, which Jesus Christ willingly accomplished, brought salvation to us (see notes on vv. 7,9). **we have been made holy.** The term "holy" means "set apart" or "consecrated." Here and in verse 14 the topic is not the process of sanctification that takes place throughout life (as in 12:14), but the once-for-all-time change in our status that occurs when we are united with Christ by faith and so are separated from sin's pollution and qualified to worship God. Being "cleansed," "made holy" and "made perfect" are virtually synonymous in Hebrews. See *WCF* 11.3; 17.2; *WLC* 71; *HC* 21,66.
10:11 Day after day every priest stands. The daily sacrifices, no less than the yearly Day of Atonement offerings, announced by their repetition that they could not eradicate sin's guilt.
10:12 sat down. A further contrast (standing vs. sitting) is emblematic of the difference between the Levitical priesthood and the priesthood of Christ. In contrast to the Levitical priests, who stood because their work of offering sacrifices was never completed, Jesus finished his sacrifice and therefore "sat down at the right hand of God," as Psalm 110:1 had prophesied (1:3,13; 8:1).
10:15 The Holy Spirit also testifies. With other New Testament books, Hebrews affirms that the Spirit is the primary author of Scripture (3:7; 9:8; Ac 4:25). Quotations from Jeremiah 31 mark the beginning (8:8–12) and the end (10:16–17) of the important argument developed from Jeremiah 31.
10:16–17 The quotations from Jeremiah 31 (8:8–12; 10:16–17) demonstrate that Christ's once-for-all-time sacrifice results in both the inner transformation of the believer (sanctification; v. 16) and forgiveness of sins (justification; v. 17).

A Call to Persevere

19 Therefore, brothers, since we have confidence to enter the Most Holy Place[o] by the
blood of Jesus, 20 by a new and living way[p] opened for us through the curtain,[q] that is,
his body, 21 and since we have a great priest[r] over the house of God, 22 let us draw near
to God[s] with a sincere heart in full assurance of faith, having our hearts sprinkled to
cleanse us from a guilty conscience[t] and having our bodies washed with pure water.
23 Let us hold unswervingly to the hope[u] we profess, for he who promised is faithful.[v]
24 And let us consider how we may spur one another on toward love and good deeds.
25 Let us not give up meeting together,[w] as some are in the habit of doing, but let us encourage one another[x]—and all the more as you see the Day approaching.
26 If we deliberately keep on sinning[y] after we have received the knowledge of the
truth, no sacrifice for sins is left, 27 but only a fearful expectation of judgment and of raging fire[z] that will consume the enemies of God. 28 Anyone who rejected the law of Moses
died without mercy on the testimony of two or three witnesses.[a] 29 How much more severely do you think a man deserves to be punished who has trampled the Son of God under foot,[b] who has treated as an unholy thing the blood of the covenant[c] that sanctified
him, and who has insulted the Spirit[d] of grace?[e] 30 For we know him who said, "It is mine
to avenge; I will repay,"[a][f] and again, "The Lord will judge his people."[b][g] 31 It is a dreadful thing to fall into the hands of the living God.[h]
32 Remember those earlier days after you had received the light,[i] when you stood your
ground in a great contest in the face of suffering.[j] 33 Sometimes you were publicly exposed

10:19 [o]Eph 2:18; Heb 9:8,12,25
10:20 [p]Heb 9:8 [q]Heb 9:3
10:21 [r]Heb 2:17
10:22 [s]Heb 7:19 [t]Eze 36:25; Heb 9:14
10:23 [u]Heb 3:6 [v]1Co 1:9
10:25 [w]Ac 2:42 [x]Heb 3:13
10:26 [y]Nu 15:30; 2Pe 2:20
10:27 [z]Isa 26:11; 2Th 1:7; Heb 9:27
10:28 [a]Dt 17:6,7; Heb 2:2
10:29 [b]Heb 6:6 [c]Mt 26:28 [d]Eph 4:30; Heb 6:4 [e]Heb 2:3
10:30 [f]Dt 32:35; Ro 12:19 [g]Dt 32:36
10:31 [h]Mt 16:16
10:32 [i]Heb 6:4 [j]Php 1:29,30

[a] *30* Deut. 32:35 [b] *30* Deut. 32:36; Psalm 135:14

■ **10:19—12:29** *Call to Persevere in Faith.* The writer turned to his fifth main concern: calling for faithfulness to the end. His discussion divides into four parts: the greater responsibility of the new covenant (10:19–39), examples of faith (11:1–40), divine discipline for God's children (12:1–17) and the heavenly Jerusalem (12:18–29).

■ **10:19–39** *Superior Covenant and Greater Responsibility.* The new and superior covenant reveals more divine grace but also entails more responsibility.

10:19–22 See *WCF* 20.1; *WLC* 171.

10:19 Therefore, brothers, since we. The writer included himself with his readers in a renewed appeal for confidence, or boldness, in approaching God. This confidence is grounded not in any merits that we possess, but in the person and work of our great high priest. **to enter . . . by the blood of Jesus.** Not only Jesus on our behalf (8:3; 9:12,24), but also we ourselves enter into God's heavenly sanctuary through the merits of Jesus' sacrifice. See *BC* 26.

10:20 a new and living way . . . through the curtain, that is, his body. This phrase either compares Jesus' body to the curtain, or it proclaims that his body is the way through the curtain. If the curtain is a metaphor for Christ's body, the analogy lies in the fact that just as the veil of the temple was torn to open the way into the Most Holy Place (6:19; 9:3; Mt 27:51), so also Christ's body was torn so that his blood might be shed to open the way into the heavenly sanctuary (v. 19). The parallel is figurative and should not be pressed. If Jesus' body is identified as the "way . . . through the curtain, the phrase repeats the idea found in verse 19.See *BC* 23.

10:21 over the house of God. See note on 3:6.

10:22 draw near. See note on 4:16. **full assurance of faith.** The call for faith hints at the subject of chapter 11. **having our hearts sprinkled . . . and having our bodies washed.** The inner cleansing of conscience that makes Jesus' death superior to the sacrifices under the law (9:13–14) is visibly symbolized in baptism (Eph 5:26). As the high priest washed his body with water in preparation for entering the Most Holy Place (Ex 29:4; Lev 16:4), so purified believers may enter now as priests into God's presence. See *WCF* 14.3; *BC* 26.

10:23–25 See *WCF* 26.2; *WLC* 99; *HC* 103.

10:23 hold unswervingly to the hope we profess. In 3:1–14, another passage mentioning "God's house" (3:5; cf. v. 21), there is a similar exhortation to "hold firmly" (3:14) and a similar assurance that Christ "is faithful" (3:6; cf. v. 23). "The confidence we had at first" (3:14), like the "hope we profess" (v. 23), probably refers to the time of our baptism (note the term "water" in v. 22) and entrance into the church (v. 32).

10:24 how we may spur one another on. The duty of encouraging each other can find expression in church gatherings (v. 25). "Love" (v. 24) completes a familiar triad with "faith" (v. 22) and "hope" (v. 23). This triad seems to have played a prominent role in the teaching of the early church (1Co 13:13; Col 1:4–5; 1Th 1:3).

10:25 not give up meeting together. Since the believers had been severely persecuted (vv. 32–34), they might have been tempted to forgo their normal gatherings. See *WCF* 21.6; *BC* 20. **the Day approaching.** The day of Jesus' return to bring salvation to those who wait for him (9:28; 12:26–27). See *WLC* 171.

10:26 deliberately keep on sinning. Christians who claim to be sinless are self-deluded (1Jn 1:8,10), but those who sin should not despair, because grace and forgiveness are available (4:16; 1Jn 1:9; 2:1–2). Yet here the writer warned the entire church not to turn away from the gospel (see 6:1–8). He had in mind the most severe forms of sin—acts done "deliberately," or "defiantly" (see Nu 15:30)—as well as unrelentingly sinful lifestyles, as opposed to temporary lapses into doubt or sin. In verse 29 he referred to trampling the Son underfoot (i.e., treating his sacrificial blood as unclean and insulting God's gracious Spirit; see note on 6:6), indicating that the sin he had in mind was, or accompanied, rejection of the gospel. **no sacrifice for sins is left.** Since God has set aside the Levitical system of animal sacrifices (v. 9), those who abandon their confession of trust in Christ have nowhere else to turn for forgiveness.

10:27 enemies of God. This phrase makes it plain that the writer had more than temporary discipline in mind. He had in view God's eternal judgment. See *WLC* 83; *BC* 37.

10:28 rejected the law of Moses. Those who turned from God to idols (Dt 17:2–7).

10:29 How much more. This argument from the lesser (the law) to the greater (the gospel) is also found in 2:2–3. If contemptuous violation of the law given through Moses the servant (3:5) warranted the punishment of death, then scorn for the Son of God (1:2–3; 3:6; 6:6; 2Pe 2:1), his sacrificial blood (9:20; cf. Ex 24:8; Mk 14:24) and the Spirit of grace through whom he offered himself (9:14) deserves nothing less than "raging fire that will consume the enemies of God" (v. 27). **the blood of the covenant that sanctified.** This description indicates that apostates were counted among the people of the covenant (the church; see theological article "The Church: Visible and Invisible" at 1Pe 4) and thus were set apart by the blood of Christ—but in a non-saving way. Compare similar descriptions in 6:4–6. See *WLC* 113,151.

10:30–31 See *HC* 11.

10:30 The Lord will judge his people. The two quotations from the song of Moses (Dt 32:35–36) show that God is ready to judge those who are in covenant with him. This Old Testament principle applies to the new covenant as well. God will separate those who are truly his own from apostates (cf. 1Pe 4:17). See theological article "The Church: Visible and Invisible" at 1 Peter 4.

10:32–39 Remember . . . we are not. As in 6:9–12, the writer here balanced his severe warning with an encouraging reminder that his original readers had exhibited the fruits of grace, especially by their mutual support in the face of earlier suffering.

10:32 stood your ground. Even as new believers, these Christians suffered persecution.

10:33 publicly exposed. Public imprisonment and the seizure of

to insult and persecution;[k] at other times you stood side by side with those who were so
treated.[l] 34You sympathized with those in prison[m] and joyfully accepted the confiscation of
your property, because you knew that you yourselves had better and lasting possessions.[n]
35So do not throw away your confidence; it will be richly rewarded. 36You need to persevere[o] so that when you have done the will of God, you will receive what he has promised. 37For in just a very little while,

> "He who is coming[p] will come and will not delay.[q]
> 38 But my righteous one[a] will live by faith.[r]
> And if he shrinks back,
> I will not be pleased with him."[b]

39But we are not of those who shrink back and are destroyed, but of those who believe
and are saved.

By Faith

11 Now faith is being sure of what we hope for and certain of what we do not see.[s]
2This is what the ancients were commended for.[t]
3By faith we understand that the universe was formed at God's command,[u] so that
what is seen was not made out of what was visible.
4By faith Abel offered God a better sacrifice than Cain did. By faith he was commended as a righteous man, when God spoke well of his offerings.[v] And by faith he still speaks,
even though he is dead.[w]
5By faith Enoch was taken from this life, so that he did not experience death; he could
not be found, because God had taken him away.[x] For before he was taken, he was commended as one who pleased God. 6And without faith it is impossible to please God, because anyone who comes to him[y] must believe that he exists and that he rewards those
who earnestly seek him.
7By faith Noah, when warned about things not yet seen, in holy fear built an ark[z] to
save his family.[a] By his faith he condemned the world and became heir of the righteousness that comes by faith.
8By faith Abraham, when called to go to a place he would later receive as his inher-

10:33 [k]1Co 4:9 [l]Php 4:14; 1Th 2:14
10:34 [m]Heb 13:3 [n]Heb 11:16
10:36 [o]Lk 21:19; Heb 12:1
10:37 [p]Mt 11:3 [q]Rev 22:20
10:38 [r]Ro 1:17; Gal 3:11
11:1 [s]Ro 8:24; 2Co 4:18
11:2 [t]ver 4,39
11:3 [u]Ge 1; Jn 1:3; 2Pe 3:5
11:4 [v]Ge 4:4; 1Jn 3:12 [w]Heb 12:24
11:5 [x]Ge 5:21-24
11:6 [y]Heb 7:19
11:7 [z]Ge 6:13-22 [a]1Pe 3:20

[a] *38* One early manuscript *But the righteous* [b] *38* Hab. 2:3,4

property (but not martyrdom; 12:4) were among the forms of persecution that the original recipients had suffered. These persecutions may reflect conditions after the edict of Claudius (A.D. 49) that evicted Jews from Rome (see "Introduction: Time and Place of Writing").
10:34 You sympathized . . . joyfully accepted. Encouragement for the original readers to remember the solidarity and joy they had shared, despite persecution. **better and lasting possessions.** The heavenly city and country of God (11:10,16; 12:22) that will endure because they cannot be shaken by the trauma that will destroy the present created order (12:27–28). In comparison to this eternal inheritance (9:15), earthly property lost for Christ's sake is of no value.
10:35 richly rewarded. Like Moses, the readers were to fix their eyes on the future reward (11:26).
10:36 done the will of God. God's laws were written in their hearts (8:10; 10:16), so they were to follow in the footsteps of Jesus, who came to do God's will (vv. 9–10; 13:21). **receive what he has promised.** See note on 6:12. See also *HC* 94.
10:37–38 He who is coming. The writer referred to Habakkuk 2:34, from which he derived principles of faithful living. Chapter 11 indicates three characteristics that appeared in the lives of Old Testament people of faith—qualities that must also appear in the lives of all believers. Saving faith (1) fixes its sights on the One who is coming, hoping in his future appearing (11:1,7,10,13,20,22,27); (2) receives God's verdict of righteousness (11:4,7; 12:23); and (3) does not draw back in the face of suffering (11:24–26,35–38).
10:39 we are not. The substance of this encouragement is like that of 6:9–10. Here the writer included himself, using "we" instead of "you." See *WCF* 14.1; *WLC* 72; *WSC* 86.
■ **11:1–40** *Examples of the Life of Faith.* This well-known discourse on faithful men and women of the Old Testament begins and ends with commentary that alerts the readers to a specific aspect of Old Testament faith: the certainty of receiving what God had promised but had not yet provided (vv. 1–2,39–40).
11:1–3 See *HC* 21.
11:1 what we hope for . . . what we do not see. For the time being, only faith can see the future as it relates to receiving the promises of God.
11:2 commended. Literally, "testified." God declared them righteous by their faith (see note on v. 4), as is explicitly stated regarding Abel and Enoch (vv. 4–5; cf. v. 39).
11:3 By faith we understand. Although no human witnessed the creation, we know from Scripture that God brought the world into being through his word (Ps 33:6,9). Thus we discern that "what is seen" is not self-existent reality. See *WCF* 4.1; *WLC* 15; *WSC* 9; *BC* 10.
11:4 better sacrifice. Abel's sacrifice was better in that it was offered in sincere faith (see note on Ge 4:4). **commended . . . spoke well.** The same Greek term is used twice in this verse ("commended" and "spoke well"); it is also found in verses 2, 5 and 39. Abel is the first example of one who received the divine commendation of being a righteous person because he lived by faith (cf. 10:38; Ro 1:17). Verses 2 and 39 indicate that the entire chapter offers such examples. **he still speaks.** As one from among the "cloud of witnesses" (12:1). See *WCF* 16.6; 16.7; *BC* 24.
11:5 As one who "did not experience death" (cf. Ge 5:18–24), Enoch prefigured the deliverance from death into which Jesus leads the faithful. **pleased God.** Pleasing God is the criterion of appropriate worship (12:28; 13:16,21; Ro 12:1; Php 4:18).
11:6 impossible to please God. Faith is an absolute necessity for perceiving the things for which we should hope (v. 1), for understanding that God is the Creator of all (v. 3) and for offering acceptable worship (v. 4). See *WCF* 2.1; 16.7; *WLC* 6; *BC* 24; *HC* 63,91.
11:7 things not yet seen. The coming flood of judgment was not yet visible when God's word of warning came to Noah. Noah built the ark in reverent response to God's warning, and through his active faith his family received salvation. The unbelieving world was condemned for its preoccupation with the present, and Noah inherited the righteousness that comes by faith (10:38; Ro 4:13), not by sight. See *BC* 23.
11:8–10 Abraham's faith regarding the promise of a homeland was demonstrated when he (1) obeyed God's voice, leaving Ur for a future inheritance, the location of which he did not know (v. 8); (2) lived as a stranger in the land promised to him (vv. 9,13); and (3) looked beyond Canaan to a lasting, heavenly country and city, designed and built by God himself (vv. 10,14–16; 13:14)—that will come down to the new earth when Christ returns in glory (Rev 21:2).

itance,[b] obeyed and went,[c] even though he did not know where he was going. 9By faith
he made his home in the promised land[d] like a stranger in a foreign country; he lived in
tents,[e] as did Isaac and Jacob, who were heirs with him of the same promise.[f] 10For he
was looking forward to the city[g] with foundations,[h] whose architect and builder is God.
11By faith Abraham, even though he was past age—and Sarah herself was barren[i]—
was enabled to become a father[j] because he[a] considered him faithful who had made the
promise. 12And so from this one man, and he as good as dead,[k] came descendants as numerous as the stars in the sky and as countless as the sand on the seashore.[l]
13All these people were still living by faith when they died. They did not receive the
things promised;[m] they only saw them and welcomed them from a distance.[n] And they
admitted that they were aliens and strangers on earth.[o] 14People who say such things
show that they are looking for a country of their own. 15If they had been thinking of the
country they had left, they would have had opportunity to return.[p] 16Instead, they were
longing for a better country—a heavenly one.[q] Therefore God is not ashamed[r] to be
called their God,[s] for he has prepared a city[t] for them.
17By faith Abraham, when God tested him, offered Isaac as a sacrifice.[u] He who had
received the promises was about to sacrifice his one and only son, 18even though God
had said to him, "It is through Isaac that your offspring[b] will be reckoned."[c][v] 19Abraham
reasoned that God could raise the dead,[w] and figuratively speaking, he did receive
Isaac back from death.
20By faith Isaac blessed Jacob and Esau in regard to their future.[x]
21By faith Jacob, when he was dying, blessed each of Joseph's sons,[y] and worshiped
as he leaned on the top of his staff.
22By faith Joseph, when his end was near, spoke about the exodus of the Israelites
from Egypt and gave instructions about his bones.[z]
23By faith Moses' parents hid him for three months after he was born,[a] because they
saw he was no ordinary child, and they were not afraid of the king's edict.[b]
24By faith Moses, when he had grown up, refused to be known as the son of Pharaoh's
daughter.[c] 25He chose to be mistreated[d] along with the people of God rather than to enjoy the pleasures of sin for a short time. 26He regarded disgrace[e] for the sake of Christ
as of greater value than the treasures of Egypt, because he was looking ahead to his reward.[f] 27By faith he left Egypt,[g] not fearing the king's anger; he persevered because he

11:8 [b]Ge 12:7 [c]Ge 12:1-4; Ac 7:2-4
11:9 [d]Ac 7:5 [e]Ge 12:8; 18:1,9 [f]Heb 6:17
11:10 [g]Heb 12:22; 13:14 [h]Rev 21:2,14
11:11 [i]Ge 17:17-19; 18:11-14 [j]Ge 21:2
11:12 [k]Ro 4:19 [l]Ge 22:17
11:13 [m]ver 39 [n]Mt 13:17 [o]Ge 23:4; Ps 39:12; 1Pe 1:17
11:15 [p]Ge 24:6-8
11:16 [q]2Ti 4:18 [r]Mk 8:38 [s]Ex 3:6,15 [t]Heb 13:14
11:17 [u]Ge 22:1-10; Jas 2:21
11:18 [v]Ge 21:12; Ro 9:7
11:19 [w]Ro 4:21
11:20 [x]Ge 27:27-29,39,40
11:21 [y]Ge 48:1,8-22
11:22 [z]Ge 50:24,25; Ex 13:19
11:23 [a]Ex 2:2 [b]Ex 1:16,22
11:24 [c]Ex 2:10,11
11:25 [d]ver 37
11:26 [e]Heb 13:13 [f]Heb 10:35
11:27 [g]Ex 12:50,51

a *11* Or *By faith even Sarah, who was past age, was enabled to bear children because she* b *18* Greek *seed*
c *18* Gen. 21:12

11:11–12 past age . . . as good as dead. Abraham's faith regarding the promise of descendants was rewarded with the conception of Isaac, which was miraculous since Sarah was barren and Abraham was (with respect to the possibility of reproduction) "as good as dead" (Ro 4:19). Despite misguided alternatives (Ge 16:1–4) and perplexing doubts (Ge 17:17-18), in the end Abraham "considered him faithful who had made the promise" (v. 11).

11:13–16 All these people . . . a city for them. The inheritance on which the patriarchs' faith was fixed was invisible for two reasons: It was heavenly, not earthly, and it was future, not present. See notes on verses 8–10, 20, 21 and 22.

11:13 saw them and welcomed them from a distance. Abraham rejoiced when he foresaw the day on which Jesus the Messiah would come (Jn 8:56). **aliens and strangers on earth.** All the heirs of salvation are homeless refugees in the present world (v. 38) because, until Christ's return, they are in exile from the home they are waiting to inherit (1Pe 1:1,4–5,17; 2:11). See *WCF* 7.5; 14.2; *WLC* 34.

11:16 for a better country. Even the Old Testament believers realized that God had promised them an inheritance that exceeded the confines of Canaan.

11:17–19 God tested him . . . he did receive Isaac. The ultimate test of Abraham's faith came with the command to sacrifice Isaac. Isaac was Abraham's "one and only son" (see note on Jn 3:16) insofar as the promises were concerned (v. 19)—neither Abraham's servant Eliezer (Ge 15:2) nor his slave-son, Ishmael (Ge 17:20–21), would suffice. If Isaac were to perish without offspring, the promises of God would fail. Abraham's readiness to slay the son of promise at God's command arose from nothing less than the conviction that "God could raise the dead" (v. 19). Isaac's "resurrection" was only figurative, but believers who have died for their faith await a literal resurrection (cf. v. 35).

11:20 their future. Isaac spoke of a future in which Jacob would possess a fruitful land and have dominion over nations, including the descendants of Esau (Ge 27:27–29).

11:21 Joseph's sons. In his blessing, Jacob foresaw that the descendants of Joseph's younger son would surpass those of Joseph's older son in number and influence (Ge 48:13–20). Both Jacob and Joseph were themselves younger brothers who had been elevated over older ones.

11:22 spoke about the exodus. Joseph remembered the promise of the exodus that had first been spoken to Abraham long before Isaac's birth (Ge 15:13–14) and that would await fulfillment through four more centuries of oppression. Joseph's instructions to take his bones to the land of promise expressed faith in realities not yet seen (Ex 13:19).

11:23–28 By faith . . . Moses. Prominent aspects of the faith associated with Moses are his fearlessness (v. 27) and his willingness to suffer disgrace rather than to enjoy sin's temporary pleasures (vv. 24–26).

11:23 no ordinary child. This description is quoted from Exodus 2:2 (cf. Ac 7:20). Moses' parents understood upon seeing him that he would have a special role in God's redemptive plan.

11:25–26 pleasures of sin . . . treasures of Egypt. Moses' decision to forfeit "the treasures of Egypt" and to suffer "disgrace for the sake of Christ" should encourage believers who have lost possessions and suffered insult for their faith (10:33–34). In trials in which identification with Christ means expulsion from "the camp" (13:13), believers must be willing to bear the disgrace Christ bore (13:12–13). Moses' choice exemplified certainty of what he hoped for (v. 1), since he was looking ahead to his reward (10:35; 11:6,13). See *WLC* 99.

11:27 he left Egypt, not fearing. This is often taken to refer to the first time Moses left Egypt. But Moses, after choosing to identify himself with his own people against the Egyptians (vv. 24–25), killed an Egyptian and, because he "was afraid" (Ex 2:14), "fled from Pharaoh" (Ex 2:15). Therefore, it is more likely that this verse refers to the exodus, at which time Moses clearly was without fear. If this latter interpretation is correct, verse 27 mentions the exodus in a general way, and details such as the Passover and the parting of the Red Sea follow in verses 28–29.

saw him who is invisible. 28By faith he kept the Passover and the sprinkling of blood, so
that the destroyer of the firstborn would not touch the firstborn of Israel.[h]
29By faith the people passed through the Red Sea[a] as on dry land; but when the Egyptians tried to do so, they were drowned.[i]
30By faith the walls of Jericho fell, after the people had marched around them for sev-
en days.[j]
31By faith the prostitute Rahab, because she welcomed the spies, was not killed with
those who were disobedient.[b][k]
32And what more shall I say? I do not have time to tell about Gideon, Barak,[l] Samson,
Jephthah, David,[m] Samuel[n] and the prophets, 33who through faith conquered kingdoms,[o] administered justice, and gained what was promised; who shut the mouths of lions,[p] 34quenched the fury of the flames, and escaped the edge of the sword; whose weakness was turned to strength;[q] and who became powerful in battle and routed foreign
armies.[r] 35Women received back their dead, raised to life again.[s] Others were tortured
and refused to be released, so that they might gain a better resurrection. 36Some faced
jeers and flogging,[t] while still others were chained and put in prison.[u] 37They were
stoned[c];[v] they were sawed in two; they were put to death by the sword.[w] They went
about in sheepskins and goatskins,[x] destitute, persecuted and mistreated— 38the world
was not worthy of them. They wandered in deserts and mountains, and in caves[y] and
holes in the ground.
39These were all commended[z] for their faith, yet none of them received what had
been promised.[a] 40God had planned something better for us so that only together with
us would they be made perfect.

God Disciplines His Sons

12 Therefore, since we are surrounded by such a great cloud of witnesses, let us
throw off everything that hinders and the sin that so easily entangles, and let us
run[b] with perseverance[c] the race marked out for us. 2Let us fix our eyes on Jesus, the au-

11:28 [h]Ex 12:21-23
11:29 [i]Ex 14:21-31
11:30 [j]Jos 6:12-20
11:31 [k]Jos 2:1,9-14; 6:22-25; Jas 2:25
11:32 [l]Jdg 4-5 [m]1Sa 16:1,13 [n]1Sa 1:20
11:33 [o]2Sa 7:11; 8:1-3 [p]Da 6:22
11:34 [q]2Ki 20:7 [r]Jdg 15:8
11:35 [s]1Ki 17:22,23
11:36 [t]Jer 20:2 [u]Ge 39:20
11:37 [v]2Ch 24:21 [w]1Ki 19:10 [x]2Ki 1:8
11:38 [y]1Ki 18:4
11:39 [z]ver 2,4 [a]ver 13
12:1 [b]1Co 9:24 [c]Heb 10:36

[a] *29* That is, Sea of Reeds [b] *31* Or *unbelieving* [c] *37* Some early manuscripts *stoned; they were put to the test;*

11:28 sprinkling of blood. Moses directed that blood be sprinkled on the doorframes of Israelite homes in expectation of the coming destruction of firstborn children in the land and of the deliverance of Israelite households from this awful event (Ex 12:7,12–13). This was another act of confidence in that which was not yet seen.
11:30 walls of Jericho. The Israelites marched around Jericho seven times in obedience to the Lord's command. Their only knowledge that this would result in the defeat of the city was provided by God's assurance, "I have delivered Jericho into your hands" (Jos 6:2).
11:31 Rahab . . . was not killed. Rahab proved her allegiance to God when she protected the Israelite spies. She was justified (Jas 2:25) and became an ancestor of Jesus Christ (Mt 1:5), even though she had been a prostitute.
11:32–38 The list of accomplishments achieved by faith moves from those in which faith's victory was manifest in history (vv. 33–35a) to those in which faith entailed suffering and apparent defeat (vv. 35b–38).
11:32 And what more shall I say? A rhetorical question, for the author went on to mention many more names and acts of heroism in order to demonstrate further the power of faith (vv. 32–38).
11:33 gained what was promised. That is, they saw answers to particular promises (plural) along the way. But they still waited in faith for the "promise" (singular) of Christ's coming (v. 39). The promises made to Abraham were partly fulfilled before Christ came, as his descendants multiplied (v. 12) and lived in the promised land (vv. 9,33). But to the extent that these promises referred to the heavenly reality, "God's rest" (4:10), they could not begin to be fulfilled until Christ came, and they will not be fully consummated until he comes again.
11:35 Women received back their dead. A reference to events recorded in 1 Kings 17:22–23 and 2 Kings 4:36–37. **Others were tortured.** An apparent reference to events during the Maccabean revolt (c. 167–157 B.C.), which occurred after the close of the Old Testament but are recorded in the Apocrypha (2 Maccabees 6–7).
11:37 sawed in two. According to tradition, the prophet Isaiah, who is quoted often in Hebrews, died in this manner.
11:39 commended. See note on verse 4. **none of them received what had been promised.** Although some Old Testament promises were fulfilled, the true hope of their recipients (the promise of the coming Messiah) was yet to come (see v. 33 and its note). This verse summarizes the message of verses 13–16 and applies it to the second half of the chapter.
11:40 something better . . . together. For the meaning of "better," see note on 7:22. This verse asserts both the difference between the Old and New Testament periods and the unity of the people of God in both eras. Although the Old Testament believers lived by faith (10:38), they were not privileged to witness on Earth the fulfillment of the great promise of God. Nevertheless, they also participate in the benefits of Christ's high priestly work and "together with us" are "made perfect." Together we await the perfection that will appear only at Christ's second coming (12:26; 13:14; Ro 8:18; Eph 1:9–10).
■ **12:1–17** *True Children of God.* To encourage faithfulness, the writer explained that hardship is often divine discipline designed to test and mature God's true children.
12:1 cloud of witnesses. Believers are in effect running a race before a great crowd of people who have already finished the race with honors. They are examples from the past that encourage us and admonish us in case we should stumble. **everything that hinders and the sin that so easily entangles.** Among the encumbrances to be thrown off are fear that shrinks back in the face of suffering (10:38–39), bitter discouragement that defiles others through doubt (v. 15) and sensuality that seeks immediate gratification (v. 16). **run . . . the race.** The athletic competitions of the Greeks provided a common New Testament analogy for the Christian life (1Co 9:24–27; Php 2:16; 2Ti 2:5; 4:7–8). Like a runner, the Christian must be in constant motion toward the goal, despite opposition. This demands strenuous effort and endurance, which are attained through constant discipline. See *WLC* 78.
12:2–3 See *WLC* 48; *WSC* 27.
12:2 fix our eyes on Jesus. The cloud of Old Testament witnesses inspires us, but our principal encouragement is found in the person and work of Christ, who, having gone before us as the "author and perfecter of our faith," is the supreme example of faith in the race (v. 3). **author.** See note on 2:10. **perfecter of our faith.** Jesus has brought the faith of all who approach God through him to its intended goal: thankful worship that is acceptable to God and presented in his presence (10:14; 11:40; 12:28). **for the joy set before him.** Jesus endured the cross in anticipation of the joy of being Savior of his people once the necessary suffering was over. As Moses

thor and perfecter of our faith, who for the joy set before him endured the cross,[d] scorning its shame,[e] and sat down at the right hand of the throne of God. 3 Consider him who
endured such opposition from sinful men, so that you will not grow weary[f] and lose
heart.

4 In your struggle against sin, you have not yet resisted to the point of shedding your
blood.[g] 5 And you have forgotten that word of encouragement that addresses you as sons:

> "My son, do not make light of the Lord's discipline,
> and do not lose heart when he rebukes you,
> 6 because the Lord disciplines those he loves,[h]
> and he punishes everyone he accepts as a son."[a][i]

7 Endure hardship as discipline; God is treating you as sons.[j] For what son is not disciplined by his father? 8 If you are not disciplined (and everyone undergoes discipline),[k]
then you are illegitimate children and not true sons. 9 Moreover, we have all had human
fathers who disciplined us and we respected them for it. How much more should we submit to the Father of our spirits[l] and live![m] 10 Our fathers disciplined us for a little while
as they thought best; but God disciplines us for our good, that we may share in his holiness.[n] 11 No discipline seems pleasant at the time, but painful. Later on, however, it produces a harvest of righteousness and peace[o] for those who have been trained by it.

12 Therefore, strengthen your feeble arms and weak knees.[p] 13 "Make level paths for
your feet,"[b][q] so that the lame may not be disabled, but rather healed.[r]

Warning Against Refusing God

14 Make every effort to live in peace with all men[s] and to be holy;[t] without holiness no
one will see the Lord.[u] 15 See to it that no one misses the grace of God[v] and that no bitter
root grows up to cause trouble and defile many. 16 See that no one is sexually immoral, or
is godless like Esau, who for a single meal sold his inheritance rights as the oldest son.[w]

12:2 [d]Php 2:8,9 [e]Heb 13:13
12:3 [f]Gal 6:9
12:4 [g]Heb 10:32-34
12:6 [h]Ps 94:12; Rev 3:19 [i]Pr 3:11,12
12:7 [j]Dt 8:5
12:8 [k]1Pe 5:9
12:9 [l]Nu 16:22 [m]Isa 38:16
12:10 [n]2Pe 1:4
12:11 [o]Isa 32:17; Jas 3:17,18
12:12 [p]Isa 35:3
12:13 [q]Pr 4:26 [r]Gal 6:1
12:14 [s]Ro 14:19 [t]Ro 6:22 [u]Mt 5:8
12:15 [v]Gal 5:4; Heb 3:12
12:16 [w]Ge 25:29-34

[a] *6* Prov. 3:11,12 [b] *13* Prov. 4:26

looked forward to his reward (11:26), so Jesus was aware of his own coming reward. A less probable, though still possible, interpretation of this phrase is "in place of the joy set before him." If this reading is held, Jesus chose suffering over "joy" (i.e., instead of living an untroubled life, he chose to die), for he might have remained in heaven (Php 2:6) or at least avoided the cross on Earth (Jn 10:17–18; 12:27). **scorning its shame.** Crucifixion was so shameful a form of execution that it was forbidden for Roman citizens; in addition, the Jews believed that to be "hung on a tree" was to be cursed by God (Dt 21:23; Gal 3:13). See *WCF* 8.8; 14.3; *WLC* 49.

12:3 opposition. The Greek word may suggest hard words and mocking (Mt 27:39–44), trials with which the readers had some experience (10:33). **lose heart.** A warning from Proverbs 3:11–12 that is quoted in verses 5–6.

12:4 shedding your blood. The readers had known persecution but had endured nothing as serious as what Jesus suffered or, indeed, what was cataloged in 11:35–38. It was not time for them to think of giving up.

12:5–6 The writer drew upon Proverbs 3:11–12 to support the outlook on suffering in the Christian life that he was about to present. See *WCF* 12

12:5 sons. God's plan to lead many sons to glory meant that the author of their salvation was to be perfected through suffering (2:10), even though he was the Son who deserved no suffering (5:8). It is not surprising that the sons who follow him should be prepared to receive their inheritance through painful discipline.

12:7 hardship as discipline. When trials and sufferings come to believers, they should be viewed as God's gracious training or discipline. Discipline demonstrates God's love rather than his judgment.

12:8 illegitimate children. The writer was possibly alluding to the fact that many Roman nobles had illegitimate sons who were financially supported but left virtually without discipline. On the other hand, the son of the nobleman's legal wife, the one who would carry his father's name and inherit his father's estate, was subjected to a training regimen comparable to slavery (Gal 4:1–2).

12:9 human fathers. Literally, "fathers of our flesh," in direct contrast to "Father of our spirits." This argument from the lesser (human parenthood) to the greater (divine fatherhood) is completed in verse 10. See *WLC* 127,135.

12:10 Our fathers. The discipline of our earthly fathers is limited by time and by their fallible lack of wisdom. The heavenly Father's discipline is planned by his infinite wisdom for "our good," and it makes us holy, as he is holy (v. 14; 1Pe 1:15–16). See *WLC* 130.

12:11 righteousness and peace. This gives some idea of what holiness involves (vv. 10,14). **trained.** A return to the athletic analogy of verse 1.

12:12–13 strengthen . . . not be disabled. The race will be successfully completed only if past spiritual injuries are healed (v. 12) and future pitfalls avoided (v. 13). The context of Isaiah 35:3, from which "strengthen your feeble arms and weak knees" is taken, is one of encouragement for the fearful (Isa 35:4). Compare the author's calls for mutual encouragement (e.g., 3:13), including that which follows in 12:15, with the warning against losing heart (vv. 3,5). The context of Proverbs 4:26 (the source of "make level paths for your feet") is a call to single-minded adherence to the path of righteousness (Pr 4:25,27). The metaphor of strengthening and healing injured limbs in order to run the race is clarified by specific commands (vv. 14–17).

12:14 Make every effort to live in peace with all men. Despite the temptation when persecuted to repay evil for evil, we should live at peace with everyone "as far as it depends on [us]" (Ro 12:18), just as our Lord Jesus refused to retaliate with insults or threats (1Pe 2:23). **be holy.** Hebrews has shown how Jesus' sacrifice made us holy in status once for all time (10:10), giving us confident access to God's presence. Here, however, "holiness" refers to purity of life. It is provided by God (13:21) and guided by his discipline (v. 10). Although it is God's grace that sanctifies believers, each believer must put forth "every effort." **see the Lord.** That is, be with God, the goal of salvation (Rev 22:4). Those who now by faith see the glory of God in the face of Christ (2Co 3:18; 4:6) will indeed see the Lord and become like him (1Jn 3:2). See *WCF* 13.1.

12:15 no one misses. Believers are responsible to watch out for one another so that none of them "misses," or is found to have "fallen short" of (4:1, where the same Greek verb is used), God's grace. **bitter root.** In Deuteronomy 29:18, the "root . . . that produces such bitter poison" refers to the person who spreads doubt and disloyalty toward the Lord among the covenant people. Here, too, the "bitter root" refers to a person who may "cause trouble" and "defile" others. To sustain each other's faith, we must encourage the weak and oppose apostates, who may influence others.

12:16 Esau. Esau is presented as an example of one who despised the inheritance of God's people and whose loss was irrevocable (v. 17). Moses traded Egypt's treasures for the disgrace of Christ because he saw the reward (11:26); in contrast, Esau traded his birthright for a bowl of food because lentil stew was all he could see (Ge 25:29–34). **inheritance rights as the oldest son.** As the

17 Afterward, as you know, when he wanted to inherit this blessing, he was rejected. He
could bring about no change of mind, though he sought the blessing with tears.[x]
18 You have not come to a mountain that can be touched and that is burning with fire;
to darkness, gloom and storm;[y] 19 to a trumpet blast[z] or to such a voice speaking words
that those who heard it begged that no further word be spoken to them,[a] 20 because they
could not bear what was commanded: "If even an animal touches the mountain, it must
be stoned."[a][b] 21 The sight was so terrifying that Moses said, "I am trembling with fear."[b]
22 But you have come to Mount Zion, to the heavenly Jerusalem,[c] the city[d] of the living God. You have come to thousands upon thousands of angels in joyful assembly, 23 to
the church of the firstborn, whose names are written in heaven.[e] You have come to God,
the judge of all men,[f] to the spirits of righteous men made perfect,[g] 24 to Jesus the mediator of a new covenant, and to the sprinkled blood that speaks a better word than the
blood of Abel.[h]
25 See to it that you do not refuse him who speaks. If they did not escape when they
refused him who warned[i] them on earth, how much less will we, if we turn away from
him who warns us from heaven?[j] 26 At that time his voice shook the earth,[k] but now he
has promised, "Once more I will shake not only the earth but also the heavens."[c][l] 27 The
words "once more" indicate the removing of what can be shaken[m]—that is, created
things—so that what cannot be shaken may remain.
28 Therefore, since we are receiving a kingdom that cannot be shaken,[n] let us be
thankful, and so worship God acceptably with reverence and awe,[o] 29 for our "God is a
consuming fire."[d][p]

Concluding Exhortations

13 Keep on loving each other as brothers.[q] 2 Do not forget to entertain strangers,[r]
for by so doing some people have entertained angels without knowing it.[s] 3 Re-

12:17 [x]Ge 27:30-40
12:18 [y]Ex 19:12-22; Dt 4:11
12:19 [z]Ex 20:18 [a]Ex 20:19; Dt 5:5, 25
12:20 [b]Ex 19:12,13
12:22 [c]Gal 4:26 [d]Heb 11:10
12:23 [e]Lk 10:20 [f]Ps 94:2 [g]Php 3:12
12:24 [h]Ge 4:10; Heb 11:4
12:25 [i]Heb 8:5; 11:7 [j]Heb 2:2,3
12:26 [k]Ex 19:18 [l]Hag 2:6
12:27 [m]1Co 7:31; 2Pe 3:10
12:28 [n]Da 2:44 [o]Heb 13:15
12:29 [p]Dt 4:24
13:1 [q]Ro 12:10; 1Pe 1:22
13:2 [r]Mt 25:35 [s]Ge 18:1-33

[a] *20* Exodus 19:12,13 [b] *21* Deut. 9:19 [c] *26* Haggai 2:6 [d] *29* Deut. 4:24

firstborn son, Esau had a special "birthright" (Ge 25:31–34; 27:36). Later, under the Mosaic Law, the right of the firstborn was that of a double share of all the father possessed (Dt 21:17). Esau despised the privilege of being the expected heir of God's covenant promises. See *WLC* 105.

12:17 Afterward, as you know. A call to remember the second stage of Esau's loss: His brother Jacob usurped Esau's rightful place when their father, Isaac, gave the solemn blessing (Ge 27). This blessing included the substance of the promise made to Abraham (Ge 12:2–3; 27:29). **no change of mind.** Literally, "no repentance." This probably refers to Esau's lack of repentance rather than to a "change of mind" on the part of his father, Isaac. Although Esau mourned his loss with tears (Ge 27:38; cf. 2Co 7:10), he did not repent of the sin of despising God's promises.

▪ **12:18–29** *The Heavenly Jerusalem.* The old and new covenants are compared in terms of the mountains (Sinai and Zion) associated with each. Fear was the dominant motif at Sinai, a touchable (and thus earthly and mutable) mountain on which the law was given (vv. 18–21). Joy and confidence characterize the heavenly (and thus eternal) Zion, because the Savior is there with the blood of forgiveness (vv. 22–24).

12:18 that can be touched. Like the sanctuary established by the first covenant (9:1,11,24), the mountain on which the law was given was part of the "created things" (v. 27) that are destined to be "shaken" (v. 27) and removed by God's voice from heaven. The tangibility of Sinai testifies to the impermanence of the first covenant (8:13).

12:19 begged that no further word be spoken to them. Because they were afraid that direct contact with the Lord's awesome holiness would destroy them (Ex 20:19), the Israelites pleaded with Moses to mediate God's words to them.

12:21 terrifying . . . with fear. The giving of the law took place with an awesome demonstration of God's power. Fear was a proper reaction (cf. Isa 6:4–5; Mt 17:6; Rev 1:17).

12:22–29 See *WCF* 7.6; 19.6; *WLC* 90.

12:22 you have come. Although in our earthly pilgrimage we have not yet arrived at the abiding city (13:14), we have nevertheless arrived by faith at the heavenly Jerusalem because of Jesus our forerunner, and we may now enter into the Most Holy Place in worship (10:19–22). **angels in joyful assembly.** They always serve God's majesty (Dt 33:2; Ps 68:17; Da 7:10). Here they are assembled as for a festival or holiday celebration. See *WLC* 19.

12:23 church of the firstborn. All the firstborn in Israel were sanctified at the time of the Passover and consecrated to service in God's presence, but the Levites served the sanctuary in their place (Nu 3:11–13). In the heavenly assembly, all believers redeemed from destruction are "firstborn"; they are consecrated to God and enrolled as his priests. Unlike Esau, who scorned his inheritance rights as firstborn (v. 16), all true believers gratefully share in the inheritance of Jesus the firstborn (1:6,14; 2:11–12) and join in the worship of the heavenly assembly, whether they are in heaven or on Earth (10:19-25). **righteous men made perfect.** These are the spirits of those who have died in the Lord (2Co 5:8–10; Rev 14:13). Particularly in view are the Old Testament and intertestamental saints to whose righteousness by faith God himself testified (11:2,4–5,39) but whose righteousness was not accompanied by perfection until Jesus came (11:40). See *WCF* 9.5; 32.1; *WSC* 37.

12:24 to Jesus the mediator. Jesus' presence in the heavenly Zion explains its atmosphere of joy and confidence. The blood of Abel cried for vengeance from the ground (Ge 4:10), but the blood of Jesus, to use the same figure, "speaks a better word" of forgiveness for the children of God and judgment for the wicked (9:12–15; 10:19–22). See *WCF* 8.3; *HC* 70.

12:25–27 God's voice speaking the gospel must be listened to and obeyed with even greater attention than that given when he spoke the law at Sinai (2:1–4; 3:1–5; 10:28–29).

12:25 on earth . . . from heaven. The contrast between the Old Testament message and the message through the Son from heaven goes back to 1:1–4. By closing the circle, the writer carried his argument toward conclusion. See *WLC* 151; *WSC* 23.

12:27 the removing of what can be shaken. Christ will roll up the heavens and the earth "like a robe" (1:12), but he will remain. The passing of the first "obsolete and aging" (8:13) covenant, with its sanctuary (9:8) and sacrifices (10:9), is the foretaste of this final shaking.

12:28 worship God acceptably. Gratitude derives from knowing that our names are written in heaven (Lk 10:20) and from our experience of God's "indescribable gift" (2Co 9:15): Jesus Christ. Reverence and awe come from an appreciation of who God is (v. 29), and acceptable worship combines these motives. See *WCF* 21.3; 21.5; *WLC* 174.

12:29 a consuming fire. This quotation from Deuteronomy 4:24 provides a fitting conclusion to this exhortation, which stresses the holiness of God and the finality of his judgment upon apostates (10:27).

▪ **13:1–25** *Conclusion.* The writer closed his letter with some exhortations, a blessing and greetings. This closing divides into two

member those in prison[t] as if you were their fellow prisoners, and those who are mistreated as if you yourselves were suffering.
4 Marriage should be honored by all, and the marriage bed kept pure, for God will
judge the adulterer and all the sexually immoral.[u] 5 Keep your lives free from the love of
money and be content with what you have,[v] because God has said,

"Never will I leave you;
never will I forsake you."[a][w]

6 So we say with confidence,

"The Lord is my helper; I will not be afraid.
What can man do to me?"[b]

7 Remember your leaders,[x] who spoke the word of God to you. Consider the outcome
of their way of life and imitate[y] their faith. 8 Jesus Christ is the same yesterday and today
and forever.[z]
9 Do not be carried away by all kinds of strange teachings.[a] It is good for our hearts
to be strengthened[b] by grace, not by ceremonial foods,[c] which are of no value to those
who eat them. 10 We have an altar from which those who minister at the tabernacle have
no right to eat.[d]
11 The high priest carries the blood of animals into the Most Holy Place as a sin offering, but the bodies are burned outside the camp.[e] 12 And so Jesus also suffered outside
the city gate[f] to make the people holy through his own blood. 13 Let us, then, go to him
outside the camp, bearing the disgrace he bore.[g] 14 For here we do not have an enduring city, but we are looking for the city that is to come.[h]
15 Through Jesus, therefore, let us continually offer to God a sacrifice[i] of praise—the

13:3 [t]Mt 25:36; Col 4:18
13:4 [u]1Co 6:9
13:5 [v]Php 4:11 [w]Dt 31:6,8; Jos 1:5
13:7 [x]ver 17,24 [y]Heb 6:12
13:8 [z]Heb 1:12
13:9 [a]Eph 4:14 [b]Col 2:7 [c]Col 2:16
13:10 [d]1Co 9:13; 10:18
13:11 [e]Ex 29:14; Lev 16:27
13:12 [f]Jn 19:17
13:13 [g]Heb 11:26
13:14 [h]Php 3:20; Heb 12:22
13:15 [i]1Pe 2:5

[a] 5 Deut. 31:6 [b] 6 Psalm 118:6,7

parts: final exhortations (vv. 1–19), and benediction and greetings (vv. 20–23).

■ **13:1–19** *Final Exhortations.* His main theme having been addressed, the writer turned to a number of lesser matters that concerned him.

13:1 Keep on loving. The responsibility to guard and encourage each other's perseverance in faith takes tangible forms. It includes brotherly love to all fellow believers (Ro 12:10; 1Pe 1:22), hospitality to those needing shelter or food (11:38), identification with prisoners (10:34) and compassionate support for those mistreated because of their confession (10:33; 11:25; cf. Mt 25:35–37).

13:2 Do not forget. The pressure of suffering can drive fundamental responsibilities of love from our minds (vv. 3,7,16). **entertained angels without knowing it.** Abraham, himself a stranger (11:13), showed hospitality to "three men" (Ge 18:2), who proved to be the Lord himself and two of his supernatural messengers (Ge 18:1—19:22). Some interpreters take "angels" to mean simply human messengers who are sent from church to church.

13:3 Remember those in prison. Paul's commendation of Onesiphorus, who "was not ashamed of [Paul's] chains" (2Ti 1:16–18), reflects the importance of this type of encouragement.

13:4 Marriage should be honored. A second hint (12:16) that sexual immorality may tempt believers. The antidote to immorality is not ascetic self-denial but a proper appreciation of the honor that God has bestowed on the marriage relationship (1Co 7:3–5; Eph 5:22–33). See *WCF* 24.3; *WLC* 139; *HC* 108.

13:5–6 love of money. Those tempted by discontent and the "love of money" are people who seek their security in financial resources (Mt 6:19–21,24–34). But God's promise gives greater confidence: "Never will I leave you" (Dt 31:6). Our confident response reaffirms that the Lord our Helper (2:18; 4:16) sets us free from all kinds of fear (2:15; 11:23,27). See *WLC* 147; *WSC* 80; *HC* 125.

13:7 your leaders, who spoke the word of God. The ministry of the congregation's first generation of teachers (2:3) was complete, and the author would later exhort the original readers to submit to the new leaders, as their leaders' pastoral role required (v. 17). **imitate their faith.** We must imitate those who inherit the promises through enduring faith (6:12). See *WCF* 30.1; *WLC* 127.

13:8 Even though human leaders pass from the scene, Jesus Christ is "the same" (1:12) "yesterday" (the time during which God spoke through prophets [1:1]), "today" (as God summons us to enter his rest through faith [3:7,13; 4:7]) and "forever" (1:8; 7:16–17,21,24,28). He is the strong anchor amid sufferings and uncertainties (6:19). See *WCF* 7.6; 8.6; 11.6; *BC* 10.

13:9 strange teachings. These teachings apparently maintained that because the readers were excluded from the cultic life of the temple (v. 13), including the sacrificial feasts in which worshipers participated, they were thereby excluded from access to God. The author responded that grace, not ceremonial food, strengthens our hearts, for by grace we participate in the worship at the heavenly altar where Jesus ministers. **of no value to those who eat them.** Just as the sin offering could not secure cleansing of the conscience (9:9), so also the fellowship offering could not guarantee that the worshiper had peace and communion with God (Lev 7:11–18; 1Co 10:18).

13:10 right to eat. The Levitical priests had the right to a portion of every animal sacrificed as a fellowship offering at the Old Testament tabernacle (Lev 6:18,29; 7:6,28–36). As long as those priests and others depended on the old system of animal sacrifices for atonement and peace with God, they could not benefit from Christ's heavenly high priestly ministry.

13:11–12 blood . . . outside. The symbolism of the Day of Atonement expressed two important aspects of Christ's atoning work: (1) The blood brought into the Most Holy Place declared that only through the death of a blameless substitute could humans approach the holy God. (2) The bodies of the animals burned outside the camp indicated that the substitute became unclean as the bearer of the people's sins.

13:13 go to him outside the camp. Jesus' suffering outside the city gate symbolized not only the curse he bore as our sin-bearer, but also his rejection by the Jewish religious establishment and its leaders. The original readers were now summoned to accept with courage their own expulsion from Jewish institutions (the synagogue, the temple and perhaps their families as well). They were to look forward with confident expectation to the city that is to come (v. 14). **the disgrace he bore.** See Psalm 69:7–9 (see also Ro 15:3; Heb 11:25–26 and its note).

13:15 continually offer. The time of animal sacrifice is past, but the servants of God, like all priests, still have gifts and offerings to bring to him. These spiritual sacrifices (1Pe 2:5) include praises toward God (v. 15) and acts of love toward other people (v. 16). **a sacrifice of praise.** In the Greek translation of Leviticus 7:11–21, this phrase refers to a kind of "fellowship offering," which was an animal sacrifice. But the meaning here is closer to Psalm 50:14 and 23, where the Lord called for "thank offerings" instead of animal sacrifices. **the fruit of lips that confess his name.** In Hosea 14:12 this attractive figure of speech is used for the words that one offers to God when one's sins are forgiven. This is the "sacrifice of praise." See *WLC* 181; *BC* 26; *HC* 32.

fruit of lips[j] that confess his name. 16 And do not forget to do good and to share with others,[k] for with such sacrifices[l] God is pleased.
17 Obey your leaders and submit to their authority. They keep watch over you[m] as men
who must give an account. Obey them so that their work will be a joy, not a burden, for
that would be of no advantage to you.
18 Pray for us.[n] We are sure that we have a clear conscience[o] and desire to live honorably in every way. 19 I particularly urge you to pray so that I may be restored to you
soon.[p]
20 May the God of peace,[q] who through the blood of the eternal covenant[r] brought
back from the dead[s] our Lord Jesus, that great Shepherd of the sheep,[t] 21 equip you with
everything good for doing his will, and may he work in us[u] what is pleasing to him,[v]
through Jesus Christ, to whom be glory for ever and ever. Amen.[w]

22 Brothers, I urge you to bear with my word of exhortation, for I have written you only
a short letter.[x]
23 I want you to know that our brother Timothy[y] has been released. If he arrives soon,
I will come with him to see you.
24 Greet all your leaders[z] and all God's people. Those from Italy[a] send you their greetings.
25 Grace be with you all.[b]

13:15 [j]Hos 14:2
13:16 [k]Ro 12:13 [l]Php 4:18
13:17 [m]Isa 62:6; Ac 20:28
13:18 [n]1Th 5:25 [o]Ac 23:1
13:19 [p]Phm 22
13:20 [q]Ro 15:33 [r]Isa 55:3; Eze 37:26; Zec 9:11 [s]Ac 2:24 [t]Jn 10:11
13:21 [u]Php 2:13 [v]1Jn 3:22 [w]Ro 11:36
13:22 [x]1Pe 5:12
13:23 [y]Ac 16:1
13:24 [z]ver 7,17 [a]Ac 18:2
13:25 [b]Col 4:18

13:16 do not forget. Sacrifices of words must be accompanied by deeds of love toward others (Jas 1:27). Paul called material gifts a "fragrant offering, an acceptable sacrifice" (Php 4:18). See note on verse 2.

13:17 Obey . . . submit. Members of the new generation of leaders (v. 7) were apparently not receiving the respectful submission that their task warranted. **They keep watch.** Church leaders are like faithful shepherds (Jer 23:4; Ac 20:28; 1Pe 5:2–4) or watchmen who call out danger alarms to the city (Eze 33:6). The leaders' care is deep and genuine because leaders are appointed by God and will give account to him (cf. 4:13). Everyone suffers when the ministry of the Lord's appointed leaders is resisted. See *WCF* 20.4; 30.1; *WLC* 127; *BC* 31.

13:18 Pray for us. Believers have the privilege of acting as priests by praying for each other in reliance upon their open access to the throne of grace (4:16). **we have a clear conscience.** Perhaps the author wanted to reassure his readers that he was exercising his own leadership in a careful manner, according to the same guidelines he had just delineated (v. 17; cf. 2Co 1:12).

13:19 restored to you soon. The precise circumstances of the author are unknown. He had previously been with the group he addressed and was anxious to see its members again.

▪ 13:20–25 *Benediction and Greetings.* The writer left his readers with a benediction and several greetings.

13:20–21 See *WCF* 16.6; *WLC* 79,195.

13:20 through the blood of the eternal covenant. The sacrifice of Christ defeated death (2:14) and inaugurated the new and eternal covenant (9:12–15). Since Christ was raised, "he cannot die again" (Ro 6:9); the effects of his sacrifice are eternal. **that great Shepherd of the sheep.** The Good Shepherd leads and protects his sheep (Ps 23; Eze 34:11–16,31) and has laid down his life for them (Jn 10:11; 1Pe 2:24–25). See *WCF* 17.2.

13:21 doing his will. God has made full provision for our growth in godliness (2Pe 1:3) and is always ready to help in time of need or temptation (2:18; 4:16). **work in us what is pleasing to him.** God will help us to love him and our neighbor (vv. 15–16; Php 2:13). **through Jesus Christ.** Salvation, forgiveness of sins and renewal of life is through Jesus Christ. See *WCF* 16.1; 17.2.

13:22 word of exhortation. This sermon, which is in the form of a letter, would have taken approximately an hour to read aloud. The writer could have expanded certain sections if he had wished to do so (9:5).

13:24 Greet all your leaders. The author went out of his way to underscore appropriate recognition of the congregation's present leaders (cf. v. 17). **Those from Italy.** See "Introduction: Original Audience." See *WCF* 30.1.

JAMES

Introduction

Overview

Author: James, the brother of Jesus
Purpose: To teach wisdom from God for persevering through difficulties until the return of Christ
Date: A.D. 44–62
Key Truths:

- Believers are to gain wisdom from God to remain faithful through trials and conflicts.
- Hearing God's Word must lead to doing God's Word.
- Saving faith shows itself in the good work of caring for the poor.
- Divine wisdom teaches believers to love and serve each other.
- Harmony in the Christian community is of great importance.

Author

The author of this epistle identified himself as James. Although the New Testament church knew various men with this name, the author of this book was almost certainly James the brother of Jesus. The author assumed a position of authority in the church, which certainly was accorded James, the Lord's brother. James was a leader of the Jerusalem church and presided at the council of Jerusalem (Ac 15). He was identified in Galatians 1:19 as "the Lord's brother" and was considered one of the pillars of the church, along with Peter and John (Gal 2:9). The New Testament lists James as one of the sons of Mary, Jesus' mother (Mt 13:55; Mk 6:3). James, along with his brothers, was skeptical of Jesus during his earthly ministry (Jn 7:5), but he was converted as an eyewitness of the resurrection (1Co 15:7). The early church historian Hegesippus identified him as "James the Just," testifying to his extraordinary godliness, his zeal for the law of God and his singular devotion to prayer. It was said that James's knees became so calloused from prayer that they resembled those of a camel. Josephus recorded that James was martyred in A.D. 62. Eusebius reported that he was beaten to death with a club after having been thrown from the temple parapet. Hegesippus also stated that he was thrown from the pinnacle of the temple.

Time and Place of Writing

James was written between A.D. 44 (the year that marked the beginning of the Jewish persecution of the church; see Ac 12) and A.D. 62 (the year of James's death).

It is possible that James's treatment of faith and justification (Jas 2:14ff.) was a response to a misunderstanding of Paul's theology. If James wrote before he had the opportunity to speak with Paul on the subject at the Jerusalem council (Ac 15), this would explain why James did not address Paul's actual arguments.

Purpose and Distinctives

James wrote to Christians who had suffered persecution. He encouraged them to gain wisdom, strengthen their faith and display their faith through obedience to God, especially in their treatment of other people.

The book of James has been variously considered an epistle, a sermon (to be read aloud in the churches), a form of Wisdom Literature, a diatribe (expressing the thoughts of one person as an internal conversation) and a paraenesis (a text that strings together admonitions and exhortations of an ethical nature). These categories are not mutually exclusive, and there are elements of each of these forms in James.

The book displays a markedly Jewish flavor and contains frequent references to the Old Testament. Parallelism like that found in Biblical poetry appears (1:9–10), along with aphorisms, vivid images drawn from nature and groupings of sayings that reveal a marked similarity to the style of Jesus.

James drew attention to the need for divine wisdom, especially in times of trial and troubles. He urged his readers to pray for wisdom and to be aware of its distinguishing marks in their lives. Wisdom from God results in a life conformed to God's Word and characterized by humble service to God and others.

Outline

I. Salutation (1:1)	*James greeted his Christian readers as the spiritual descendants of Old Testament Israel.*
II. Wisdom and Its Effects in Trials (1:2—3:12) A. Asking for Wisdom From God (1:2–18) B. Hearing and Doing (1:19–27) C. Favoring the Rich (2:1–13) D. Faith and Obedience (2:14–26) E. Controlling the Tongue (3:1–12)	*James explained why divine wisdom was needed and how it would show itself in the trials facing his readers. Believers must ask for wisdom from God, who freely gives it to those who do not waver. Wisdom will teach both rich and poor how to live in harmony with each other and with God. Simply hearing or knowing the Word is not sufficient; we must also obey it. Believers are to resist the temptation to favor the rich over the poor. Claiming faith is not enough; faith must be expressed in good works, especially with regard to the poor. Believers (especially teachers) must control their speech, which has great power to create conflicts and difficulties in the church.*
III. Wisdom and Its Effects in Quarrels (3:13—5:11) A. Distinguishing Wisdom From God (3:13—4:10) B. Slander (4:11–12) C. Warnings Against Presumption (4:13–17) D. Warnings for the Rich (5:1–6) E. Patience (5:7–11)	*James explained a second time how divine wisdom was needed for the trials facing his readers, especially the trials of conflict among believers. Wisdom from God is humble, but worldly wisdom is proud and envious. Believers must avoid slandering each other because only God is our judge. Believers must also avoid pride before God, knowing that he controls our lives. The rich who oppress the poor risk the eternal judgment of God. Patience is required of all of us because we will receive our reward when Christ returns.*
IV. Final Exhortations Toward Harmony (5:12–19)	*James touched on an assortment of issues, especially those related to harmony within the church.*

1:1 [a]Ac 15:13 [b]Tit 1:1 [c]Ac 26:7 [d]Dt 32:26; Jn 7:35; 1Pe 1:1

1 James,[a] a servant of God[b] and of the Lord Jesus Christ,

To the twelve tribes[c] scattered[d] among the nations:

Greetings.

Trials and Temptations

1:2 [e]Mt 5:12; 1Pe 1:6

1:5 [f]1Ki 3:9,10; Pr 2:3-6

[2]Consider it pure joy, my brothers, whenever you face trials of many kinds,[e] [3]because
you know that the testing of your faith develops perseverance. [4]Perseverance must finish its work so that you may be mature and complete, not lacking anything. [5]If any of you
lacks wisdom, he should ask God,[f] who gives generously to all without finding fault, and

■ **1:1** *Salutation.* James identified himself and his readers.
1:1 James, a servant. James claimed to be a bond-servant, or slave, of God and of Christ. A servant is one purchased and owned by a master or "lord." This indicates not only James's humility but also the profound testimony of his faith in his earthly half brother as his Redeemer (1Co 15:3). Here servanthood is linked to both God and Jesus, a crucial theological bracketing. **twelve tribes scattered.** Two understandings of this expression are possible. First, James could have been addressing Christian Jews who were scattered among the nations. Second, James could have been addressing even Gentile believers in this manner because Jews and Gentiles have been joined together into one body in Christ along with the 12 apostles, a symbolic number recalling the 12 tribes of Israel.
■ **1:2—3:12** *Wisdom and Its Effects in Trials.* James moved immediately to his central concern: divine wisdom in the midst of trials and testing. He focused on five matters: asking God for wisdom (1:2–18), obeying the Word of God (1:19–27), declining to favor the rich (2:1–13), proving faith through obedience (2:14–26) and avoiding the damage caused by unbridled speech within the Christian community (3:1–12).
■ **1:2–18** *Asking for Wisdom From God.* James encouraged his readers to view their trials as a way in which they matured in Christ, but he also warned them not to attribute temptation toward sin to God.
1:2 Consider. What follows requires careful thinking from a theological perspective. It is a call to understand suffering from the vantage point of confidence in God's sovereignty. **pure joy.** Believers are not to have a morbid joy in their suffering but to experience joy in the midst of trials because of the positive results brought about by suffering. **brothers.** The recipients were addressed in filial terms befitting membership in the family of God, the visible church. **trials of many kinds.** Here James had in mind a broad, general category of trials. Later he would draw from the general principles set forth here for discussion of the more specific issue of conflict among believers, especially between rich and poor (see vv. 9–11).
1:3 testing. That trials are to be considered pure joy is based on the knowledge that they are designed by God for a purpose. They are tests of faith given in order to develop perseverance. In turn, perseverance produces mature Christian character (Ro 5:3–4). See *HC* 28.
1:5 wisdom. Wisdom is understood in Biblical terms as including knowledge, insight, prudence, shrewdness, wariness, learning, guidance, competence, resourcefulness, planning and even heroic strength. James especially had in mind wisdom with regard to righteousness and living in relationship with other believers. **ask God.**

it will be given to him.[g] 6But when he asks, he must believe and not doubt,[h] because he
who doubts is like a wave of the sea, blown and tossed by the wind. 7That man should
not think he will receive anything from the Lord; 8he is a double-minded man,[i] unstable in all he does.
9The brother in humble circumstances ought to take pride in his high position. 10But
the one who is rich should take pride in his low position, because he will pass away like
a wild flower.[j] 11For the sun rises with scorching heat and withers[k] the plant; its blossom falls and its beauty is destroyed.[l] In the same way, the rich man will fade away even
while he goes about his business.
12Blessed is the man who perseveres under trial, because when he has stood the test,
he will receive the crown of life[m] that God has promised to those who love him.[n]
13When tempted, no one should say, "God is tempting me." For God cannot be
tempted by evil, nor does he tempt anyone; 14but each one is tempted when, by his own
evil desire, he is dragged away and enticed. 15Then, after desire has conceived, it gives
birth to sin;[o] and sin, when it is full-grown, gives birth to death.[p]
16Don't be deceived,[q] my dear brothers.[r] 17Every good and perfect gift is from above,[s]
coming down from the Father of the heavenly lights, who does not change[t] like shifting
shadows. 18He chose to give us birth[u] through the word of truth, that we might be a kind
of firstfruits[v] of all he created.

Listening and Doing

19My dear brothers, take note of this: Everyone should be quick to listen, slow to
speak[w] and slow to become angry, 20for man's anger does not bring about the righteous
life that God desires. 21Therefore, get rid of[x] all moral filth and the evil that is so prevalent and humbly accept the word planted in you,[y] which can save you.
22Do not merely listen to the word, and so deceive yourselves. Do what it says. 23Any-
one who listens to the word but does not do what it says is like a man who looks at his
face in a mirror 24and, after looking at himself, goes away and immediately forgets what
he looks like. 25But the man who looks intently into the perfect law that gives freedom,[z]
and continues to do this, not forgetting what he has heard, but doing it—he will be
blessed in what he does.[a]
26If anyone considers himself religious and yet does not keep a tight rein on his
tongue,[b] he deceives himself and his religion is worthless. 27Religion that God our Fa-

1:5 [g]Mt 7:7
1:6 [h]Mk 11:24
1:8 [i]Jas 4:8
1:10 [j]1Co 7:31; 1Pe 1:24
1:11 [k]Ps 102:4,11 [l]Isa 40:6-8
1:12 [m]1Co 9:25 [n]Jas 2:5
1:15 [o]Job 15:35; Ps 7:14 [p]Ro 6:23
1:16 [q]1Co 6:9 [r]ver 19
1:17 [s]Jn 3:27 [t]Nu 23:19; Mal 3:6
1:18 [u]Jn 1:13 [v]Eph 1:12; Rev 14:4
1:19 [w]Pr 10:19
1:21 [x]Eph 4:22 [y]Eph 1:13
1:25 [z]Jas 2:12 [a]Jn 13:17
1:26 [b]Ps 34:13; 1Pe 3:10

God is the source of wisdom, granting it to those who sincerely seek it from him. See *HC* 117.

1:6–7 See *WCF* 21.3; *WLC* 185; *HC* 117.

1:8 double-minded man. This rare expression was possibly coined by James. It suggests a man who has two souls; he is unstable, seeking mutually exclusive and conflicting goals.

1:9–10 humble circumstances . . . rich. Here James hinted for the first time that the trials he had in mind involved conflict between the rich and the poor. Both groups are exhorted to take pride in their positions. The poor can be wealthy in spiritual treasure and enjoy high status in the kingdom of God. The rich need to recognize that their earthly wealth means little. James may have been referring to wealthy Christians who can rejoice at having learned where their true treasure is found. If he was referring to unbelievers, James's words are ironic.

1:11 See Job 14:2, Psalm 103 and Isaiah 40:6–7.

1:12 Blessed. This echoes the prophetic oracles used by Old Testament prophets and by Jesus (Mt 5:3–11).

1:13–14 See *WCF* 5.4.

1:13 tempted. There is an important difference between a test (v. 12) and a temptation (v. 14). God frequently tests his people to expose their inward qualities (Ge 22:1; Ex 15:25; 16:4; Ps 66:10), but God never tempts anyone in the sense of enticing them to sin. James understood that believers can easily attribute temptation to God because they know God is sovereign over all. In fact, Jesus taught us to pray "lead us not into temptation" (Mt 6:13) because God does permit Satan to do his evil work. James insisted, however, that it is a perverse misunderstanding to attribute evil motives, including temptation, to God. See *WCF* 3.1; *BC* 13.

1:14–15 See *WCF* 6.4; 9.1; *WLC* 25,151,195; *WSC* 4.

1:17 good and perfect gift. God does not tempt. He only gives gifts that accord with his unchanging goodness. **Father of the heavenly lights.** Nature's luminaries vary in magnitude and are subject to phases, eclipses and shadows. God is the ultimate author of light. In him there are no changes of brightness or clarity. His character is immutable, not given to fluctuations. For this reason Christians can be confident that God will not change so as to tempt them to sin or to determine any purpose for their lives contrary to their being "a kind of firstfruits" (v. 18). See *WCF* 2.1; 3.1; 5.4; *WLC* 7; *WSC* 4; *BC* 1; *HC* 94,118,125.

1:18 He chose to give us birth. This refers to the grace of regeneration by which we are adopted into God's family (1Pe 1:23). **a kind of firstfruits.** The firstfruits were not only the first, but also the best, of the harvest (Ex 23:19; 34:26; Lev 23:9–19; Eze 44:30). Redeemed humanity is the pinnacle of God's creation, regardless of when its individual members come to faith, as well as the beginning of the redemption of the whole creation (Col 1:20). See *WLC* 4.

■ **1:19–27** *Hearing and Doing.* Having established the importance of gaining divine wisdom in the trials of the Christian life, James turned attention to the fact that human anger does not accomplish the wisdom of God's design. This truth must not only be heard but also fully obeyed.

1:19 quick to listen, slow to speak . . . angry. Patience and deference in speech further peace and harmony and promote righteous living in the Christian community.

1:21–22 See *WLC* 108.

1:21 word planted in you. God's law is written in the hearts of believers (Dt 6:6). See *WLC* 160.

1:22 Do what it says. True hearing of the Word must lead to godly action. It is not enough to know that a Christian should be slow to anger. A Christian must actually become slow to anger. See *WCF* 21.5.

1:23–25 See *WCF* 19.6.

1:23 mirror. Mirrors in the ancient world were made of polished metal, not glass. Scripture is a mirror of the soul's need for grace, revealing our true character. Here, however, James warned against having sins exposed but forgetting to implement the teaching of Scripture.

1:25 perfect law. James probably used this phrase as a synonym for sacred Scripture, with particular emphasis on the law. **freedom.** In Christ, the law of God sets us free from the tyranny of human traditions and the futility of having no guidance in life (Jn 8:36; Ro 8:2; Gal 5:13). See *WCF* 19.2; *WLC* 160; *WSC* 90.

1:26 tongue. James anticipated a subject he would treat more fully in 3:1–12.

ther accepts as pure and faultless is this: to look after[c] orphans and widows[d] in their distress and to keep oneself from being polluted by the world.[e]

Favoritism Forbidden

2 My brothers, as believers in our glorious[f] Lord Jesus Christ, don't show favoritism.[g]
[2]Suppose a man comes into your meeting wearing a gold ring and fine clothes, and
a poor man in shabby clothes also comes in. [3]If you show special attention to the man
wearing fine clothes and say, "Here's a good seat for you," but say to the poor man, "You
stand there" or "Sit on the floor by my feet," [4]have you not discriminated among yourselves and become judges[h] with evil thoughts?

[5]Listen, my dear brothers:[i] Has not God chosen those who are poor in the eyes of the
world[j] to be rich in faith[k] and to inherit the kingdom he promised those who love him?[l]
[6]But you have insulted the poor.[m] Is it not the rich who are exploiting you? Are they not
the ones who are dragging you into court?[n] [7]Are they not the ones who are slandering
the noble name of him to whom you belong?

[8]If you really keep the royal law found in Scripture, "Love your neighbor as yourself,"[a][o] you are doing right. [9]But if you show favoritism,[p] you sin and are convicted by
the law as lawbreakers.[q] [10]For whoever keeps the whole law and yet stumbles at just one
point is guilty of breaking all of it.[r] [11]For he who said, "Do not commit adultery,"[b][s] also
said, "Do not murder."[c][t] If you do not commit adultery but do commit murder, you have
become a lawbreaker.

[12]Speak and act as those who are going to be judged by the law that gives freedom,[u]
[13]because judgment without mercy will be shown to anyone who has not been merciful.[v]
Mercy triumphs over judgment!

Faith and Deeds

[14]What good is it, my brothers, if a man claims to have faith but has no deeds?[w] Can
such faith save him? [15]Suppose a brother or sister is without clothes and daily food.[x] [16]If

1:27 [c]Mt 25:36 [d]Isa 1:17,23 [e]Ro 12:2
2:1 [f]1Co 2:8 [g]Lev 19:15
2:4 [h]Jn 7:24
2:5 [i]Jas 1:16,19 [j]1Co 1:26-28 [k]Lk 12:21 [l]Jas 1:12
2:6 [m]1Co 11:22 [n]Ac 8:3
2:8 [o]Lev 19:18
2:9 [p]ver 1 [q]Dt 1:17
2:10 [r]Mt 5:19; Gal 3:10
2:11 [s]Ex 20:14; Dt 5:18 [t]Ex 20:13; Dt 5:17
2:12 [u]Jas 1:25
2:13 [v]Mt 5:7; 18:32-35
2:14 [w]Mt 7:26; Jas 1:22-25
2:15 [x]Mt 25:35,36

[a] *8* Lev. 19:18 [b] *11* Exodus 20:14; Deut. 5:18 [c] *11* Exodus 20:13; Deut. 5:17

1:27 Religion . . . pure and faultless. James stressed that a concern for the plight of widows and orphans is a true measure of the kind of obedience that is pleasing to God. To live in accordance with the wisdom and Word of God is to serve others, not to be filled with pride (vv. 9–11). Attention to widows and orphans reflects the concerns of God himself (Dt 10:18; Pss 68:5; 146:9). Israel had been given this responsibility in the Old Testament (Dt 14:29; Eze 22:7).

■ **2:1–13** *Favoring the Rich.* James again explicitly referred to the theme of relations between rich and poor (see 1:9–11) because this was a crucial issue facing his readers. Here he pointed out that it is contrary to the Word of God (and thus to the wisdom of God) to show favoritism to the rich.

2:1 glorious Lord Jesus Christ. This may be rendered, "our Lord Jesus Christ, the glory." Here Jesus may be identified with the glory of God. He was the living, incarnate cloud of glory (Ex 16:10; 24:16; 40:34–35), the dwelling of God among us. **show favoritism.** This indicates a respect for persons based purely on externals. It is contrary to the behavior of God, who is no respecter of persons (Ro 2:11; Eph 6:9; Col 3:25). In the light of Christ's divine glory, it is foolish to show favoritism based on inferior levels of human glory.

2:4 discriminated. God calls us to discriminate between good and evil. Yet favoring one person above another based on mere externals such as economic status, race, ethnicity or similar criteria is evil.

2:5 chosen those . . . poor in the eyes of the world. Inheritance in the kingdom of God is based on God's sovereign election, not on human merit of any kind. Scripture reveals that God shows special attention to those who are weak and lowly according to human standards. He often chose his people from among the ranks of the poor in order to display the glory of his power to save (Lk 6:20; 1Co 1:28–29). Just as true religion pays attention to widows and orphans (1:27), it also runs contrary to showing favoritism toward the rich.

2:6 rich who are exploiting you? "Exploiting" may be rendered "oppressing." The verb is strong and elsewhere refers to the oppressive work of Satan (Ac 10:38). The rich all too frequently used political and judicial power to exploit the poor, and many still rely upon their wealth and power rather than on Christ for their salvation. James's readers showed their lack of faith by subscribing to the world's value system. They favored the rich despite the fact that the affluent mistreated believers and slandered Christ—and that God shows favor to the poor.

2:8–9 royal law. The supreme law ordained by God, the great King, for his royal images in Christ (see theological article "Human Beings in God's Image" at Ge 1). **Love your neighbor.** James regarded the sin of favoritism as a violation of the great commandment (Lev 19:18; Dt 6:5; Mt 22:36–39), making the perpetrator a lawbreaker.

2:8 See *WCF* 19.2; 19.5.

2:10–12 See *WCF* 19.2.

2:10–11 whole law . . . one point. James did not deny the clear teaching of the Old and New Testaments that some sins are more serious than others (Ex 21:12–14; Mt 11:22; Mk 3:29; 1Jn 5:16). Instead, he stressed that because God gave all the stipulations of the law, none of its requirements is insignificant (Mt 5:17–19). Because every law reflects God's perfect character in some way, every violation of the law is a transgression against him, and thus against the spirit of the whole law. James apparently believed that his readers might treat this matter lightly by excusing themselves from loving their neighbors and continuing to favor the rich. See *WCF* 19.5; 19.6; *WLC* 95,99,152; *BC* 23.

2:12 going to be judged. On the day of judgment, believers will not stand on the basis of their own merit. If we were to be judged on that basis, we would all be condemned. By God's mercy, we will be judged on the basis of Christ's merit. Because we have been judged mercifully, we are to judge other believers in the same way, showing mercy rather than discrimination.

2:13 Mercy triumphs. See Matthew 5:7; 18:21–35 (cf. Zec 7:9). Though God is never obligated to show mercy, he freely chooses to do so in abundance. He reserves the divine prerogative to show mercy upon whom he wills (Ro 9:18). By his law, however, we are commanded to temper justice with mercy. He warns that if we refuse to show mercy, we will not receive mercy from him.

■ **2:14–26** *Faith and Obedience.* Having stressed the importance of moving beyond knowing the Word of God to doing the Word of God in the area of loving our neighbors, James turned to another side of the same issue: the relationship between faith and works in the matter of taking care of fellow Christians.

2:14 Can such faith save him? It is important to remember that the New Testament uses the term "faith" in different ways. Theologians have distinguished these different meanings in a variety of ways. Here James was distinguishing "saving faith" (faith that will result in eternal salvation) from false faith. Faith that yields no good works is not saving faith.

2:15 Suppose . . . without clothes and daily food. James illustrated what he meant by faith without works. As this illustration

one of you says to him, "Go, I wish you well; keep warm and well fed," but does nothing
about his physical needs, what good is it?[y] 17 In the same way, faith by itself, if it is not
accompanied by action, is dead.
18 But someone will say, "You have faith; I have deeds."
Show me your faith without deeds,[z] and I will show you my faith by what I do.[a] 19 You
believe that there is one God.[b] Good! Even the demons believe that[c]—and shudder.
20 You foolish man, do you want evidence that faith without deeds is useless[a]?[d] 21 Was
not our ancestor Abraham considered righteous for what he did when he offered his son
Isaac on the altar?[e] 22 You see that his faith and his actions were working together,[f] and his
faith was made complete by what he did.[g] 23 And the scripture was fulfilled that says, "Abraham believed God, and it was credited to him as righteousness,"[b][h] and he was called God's
friend.[i] 24 You see that a person is justified by what he does and not by faith alone.
25 In the same way, was not even Rahab the prostitute considered righteous for what
she did when she gave lodging to the spies and sent them off in a different direction?[j]
26 As the body without the spirit is dead, so faith without deeds is dead.[k]

Taming the Tongue

3 Not many of you should presume to be teachers, my brothers, because you know
that we who teach will be judged more strictly. 2 We all stumble[l] in many ways. If
anyone is never at fault in what he says,[m] he is a perfect man,[n] able to keep his whole
body in check.[o]
3 When we put bits into the mouths of horses to make them obey us, we can turn the

[a] *20* Some early manuscripts *dead* [b] *23* Gen. 15:6

2:16 [y]1Jn 3:17,18
2:18 [z]Ro 3:28 [a]Jas 3:13
2:19 [b]Dt 6:4 [c]Mt 8:29; Lk 4:34
2:20 [d]ver 17,26
2:21 [e]Ge 22:9,12
2:22 [f]Heb 11:17 [g]1Th 1:3
2:23 [h]Ge 15:6; Ro 4:3 [i]2Ch 20:7; Isa 41:8
2:25 [j]Heb 11:31
2:26 [k]ver 17,20
3:2 [l]1Ki 8:46; Jas 2:10 [m]1Pe 3:10 [n]Mt 12:37 [o]Jas 1:26

shows, he continued to focus on showing mercy to the poor (see 2:1–13). Here, however, he pointed to the fact that faith that does not serve the poor is not saving faith. Although James's reasoning is focused narrowly, we are right to apply the same kind of thinking more broadly. If we do not manifest good works that grow out of our faith in Christ, then we do not have saving faith.

2:17 faith by itself . . . is dead. When Luther and the Reformers insisted on the formula "Justification by faith alone," their intention was to insist that justification comes by means of faith and not by means of good works. The word "alone" does not mean that saving or justifying faith exists without any subsequent fruit of obedience. Luther insisted that saving faith is a living faith. The image of dead faith refers not to a faith that has perished but to a faith that never had any true life in it. Such faith cannot be the means of justification.

2:18 Show me your faith. James challenged anyone who claimed to have faith to demonstrate it, to make it visible. The only visible evidence available to human eyes is that of the deeds of obedience. Although God can read the hearts of individuals, humanity's only view of the heart condition is the sight of outward fruit. See *WCF* 16.2; *WLC* 32.

2:19 You believe that there is one God. To believe that there is one God (indeed, that God exists) is to assent to a proposition that even the demons acknowledge. To believe "in" God, on the other hand, requires personal trust. Saving faith includes cognitive knowledge but continues beyond it to personal trust and submission. See *HC* 21.

2:20 You foolish man. This is a strong rebuke. It is a moral judgment more than an intellectual one, recalling the judgment that falls upon the fool in the Wisdom Literature of the Old Testament. **useless.** Barren of fruit.

2:21 considered righteous. Other translations (e.g., KJV, NRSV) translate this phrase as "justified." James appealed to Abraham as the chief example of a person who was justified by his works. James is not in conflict with Paul, who also appealed to Abraham—as the chief exhibit of a person who was justified by faith apart from works (e.g., Ro 4:1–25; Gal 3:6–9). The difference between Paul's and James's statements is that Paul used the word "justified" in this context to refer to the *crediting* of righteousness to Abraham (e.g., Ro 4:3,9,22; Gal 3:6), which we find recorded in Genesis 15:6. James used the word "justified" to refer to the *proof,* or vindication, of Abraham's faith that took place many years later (Ge 22:12). In James, the phrases "considered righteous" (here) and "is justified" (v. 24) do not refer to reconciliation to God but to demonstration of the truth of a prior claim. Jesus used the same verb (*dikaioô*) in this way in Luke 7:35, when he declared, "Wisdom is proved right by all her children" (i.e., wisdom is shown to be genuine wisdom by its results). Just as true wisdom is demonstrated by its fruit, Abraham's claim to faith was justified (i.e., demonstrated) by his outward obedience. Yet his works were not the meritorious cause of his salvation; they added nothing to the perfect and sufficient merit of Christ.

2:22 faith was made complete. The full outworking of faith is seen in works. True faith always produces fruit. Faith and works may be distinguished, but never separated or divorced. See *WCF* 11.2; 16.2; *WLC* 32.

2:23 the scripture was fulfilled. True faith necessarily produces good works (v. 17). Therefore, when Abraham performed the good works of Genesis 22, he fulfilled the expectations created by the pronouncement of his faith in Genesis 15:6.

2:24 not by faith alone. A person is not proven to be just by the mere profession, or even possession, of faith. A person is only shown to be just by what he or she does. None of our deeds are worthy of ultimate justification in the sight of God. Only the merit of Christ avails for that kind of justification, so that only by trusting in Christ alone can we be reckoned righteous in the sight of God. Here James attacked all forms of antinomianism that seek to have Jesus as Savior without embracing him as Lord. Just as Paul demonstrated that trusting in one's own works for salvation is deadly, so James taught that resting on empty or dead faith is equally lethal.

2:25 considered righteous. Again, this is the verb "justify" (see note on v. 21). As with Abraham, Rahab's actions demonstrated the authenticity of her faith.

2:26 See *WCF* 11.2.

■ **3:1–12** *Controlling the Tongue.* James offered yet another insight into the way of wisdom in trials and conflicts that test our faith. He pointed to the importance of controlling how we speak within the Christian community.

3:1 judged more strictly. This is a sober warning concerning the responsibility of teachers. Teachers have both the ability and the responsibility to study and know the truth. As a result, God holds them to a higher standard (cf. Lk 12:47–48) of accountability. Teachers also exert influence over trusting students, a relationship that makes the students vulnerable to serious error on the part of the teacher. This strict judgment should restrain teachers from erroneous and careless words. The early church gave high esteem to the office of teacher (Mt 5:19; 18:6). Even so, James quickly broadened his perspective beyond teachers to include all Christians.

3:2–13 See *WLC* 149; *WSC* 82.

3:2 We all stumble. James was still speaking primarily of teachers here, indicating that teaching some error is unavoidable. The strict judgment against unavoidable sin should strongly dissuade many from becoming teachers. James used this point to segue into universally applicable teachings on the use of the tongue. See *WCF* 6.5; *WLC* 149.

3:3–5 James used metaphors from common experience to illustrate his cardinal point that great results can be achieved by small means. The tongue is a small part of the body that is capable both

3:3 pPs 32:9 whole animal.[p] 4Or take ships as an example. Although they are so large and are driv-
en by strong winds, they are steered by a very small rudder wherever the pilot wants to
3:5 qPs 12:3,4 go. 5Likewise the tongue is a small part of the body, but it makes great boasts.[q] Consider what a great forest is set on fire by a small spark. 6The tongue also is a fire,[r] a world
3:6 rPr 16:27 of evil among the parts of the body. It corrupts the whole person,[s] sets the whole course
sMt 15:11,18,19 of his life on fire, and is itself set on fire by hell.
7All kinds of animals, birds, reptiles and creatures of the sea are being tamed and
3:8 tPs 140:3; Ro 3:13 have been tamed by man, 8but no man can tame the tongue. It is a restless evil, full of
deadly poison.[t]
3:9 9With the tongue we praise our Lord and Father, and with it we curse men, who have
uGe 1:26,27; been made in God's likeness.[u] 10Out of the same mouth come praise and cursing. My
1Co 11:7 brothers, this should not be. 11Can both fresh water and salt[a] water flow from the same
3:12 vMt 7:16 spring? 12My brothers, can a fig tree bear olives, or a grapevine bear figs?[v] Neither can
a salt spring produce fresh water.

Two Kinds of Wisdom

3:13 wJas 2:18 13Who is wise and understanding among you? Let him show it[w] by his good life, by
deeds done in the humility that comes from wisdom. 14But if you harbor bitter envy and
3:14 xver 16 yJas 5:19 selfish ambition[x] in your hearts, do not boast about it or deny the truth.[y] 15Such "wisdom"
3:15 zJas 1:17 a1Ti 4:1 does not come down from heaven[z] but is earthly, unspiritual, of the devil.[a] 16For where
you have envy and selfish ambition, there you find disorder and every evil practice.
3:17 b1Co 2:6 cLk 6:36 17But the wisdom that comes from heaven[b] is first of all pure; then peace-loving, con-
dRo 12:9 siderate, submissive, full of mercy[c] and good fruit, impartial and sincere.[d] 18Peacemak-
3:18 ePr 11:18; Isa 32:17 ers who sow in peace raise a harvest of righteousness.[e]

Submit Yourselves to God

4:1 fTit 3:9 gRo 7:23 4 What causes fights and quarrels[f] among you? Don't they come from your desires
that battle[g] within you? 2You want something but don't get it. You kill and covet,

a *11* Greek *bitter* (see also verse 14)

of creating enormous disasters and of providing life-enhancing guidance.

3:6 tongue . . . a fire. An unrestrained tongue is like a fire that rages out of control (Ps 120:3–4; Pr 16:27). This image highlights the incredible damage that can be done with words—not only to those whom the words target, but also to others in their wake and to those who speak them. Because evil speech can cause so much (often upredictable) harm, Christians must be especially careful of what they say. **corrupts.** Evil uses of speech (including blasphemy, gossip, slander, lying, false vows and the like) have the power to spoil, stain or corrupt the entire moral character of a person. **set on fire by hell.** Perhaps an exaggerated statement indicating the severity of the results of evil speech, or an indication that the demons themselves tempt believers to employ destructive words.

3:7 tamed. James did not have domestication in view, but subjection under humanity's dominion over the animal kingdom (Ge 1:28).

3:8 no man can tame the tongue. The tongue is harder to tame than are wild beasts; that is, verbal sin is among the most difficult to resist. **full of deadly poison.** The tongue is filled with poison more venomous than a viper's (Pss 58:4; 140:3; Ro 3:13–14). In this metaphor, James was perhaps alluding to the serpent in the Garden of Eden; its innocent-sounding words brought about the destruction of the entire human race (Ge 3). Although verbal sins are easy to commit, they can wreak terrible havoc.

3:9 praise . . . curse. James applied his principles to human relationships. His chief concern about controlling the tongue was that Christians should realize that cursing the image and likeness of God is akin to cursing God himself. Furthermore, it is entirely unacceptable for someone to make pious claims while ignoring or abusing others, especially those who are weak and helpless. Proper regard for other people as the bearers of God's image will cause us to speak to them with the dignity and honor God has granted them (see 1Jn 3:17; 4:8). See theological article "Human Beings in God's Image" at Genesis 1.

3:11–12 Note the similarity here between James's metaphors and those used by Jesus in Matthew 7:16. It is inconsistent with a believer's character and identity in Christ to use the tongue for sin.

■ **3:13—5:11** *Wisdom and Its Effects in Quarrels.* James returned explicitly to the theme of wisdom. His concerns here were similar to those expressed in the first half of his epistle, but now he focused more on wisdom manifested in the context of conflict. His discussion divides into five parts: humility and peace as the distinguishing marks of wisdom from God (3:13—4:10), the inappropriateness of slander (4:11–12), presumptuousness (4:13–17), warnings for wealthy believers (5:1–6) and the importance of patience (5:7–11).

■ **3:13—4:10** *Distinguishing Wisdom From God.* There are two kinds of wisdom: one from God, the other from the world. James advised his readers on how to distinguish between the two.

3:13 wise . . . show it. Just as James exhorts believers to demonstrate their faith through works, so he also calls for the demonstration of wisdom by godly living. **deeds done in . . . humility.** One sign of wisdom is a gentle and humble spirit. As arrogance and foolishness go together, so do humility and wisdom. Wisdom realistically assesses life and fosters humility in the wise person. While even the example of Jesus demonstrates that self-effacing passivity is not always appropriate (Jn 2:15–16), wise people for the most part understand enough about themselves and the world in which they live to serve God with a humble and gentle spirit.

3:14 bitter envy and selfish ambition. Envy and covetousness poison the spirit. They are linked to self-centered and self-serving ambition. These vices arise out of foolishness. They are contrary to true understanding and the love of one's neighbor. See *WLC* 148; *WSC* 81.

3:15 earthly, unspiritual, of the devil. Here divine wisdom is set in bold contrast with the "wisdom" of this world. The wisdom of the flesh reflects the deception of Satan and is foolishness in the sight of God (see 1Co 1:19–21).

3:16 disorder and every evil practice. Envy and selfish ambition flow from a lack of divine wisdom. Such folly leads to many different kinds of harmful sins. See *WLC* 148; *WSC* 81.

3:17 wisdom . . . from heaven. Wisdom that is a gift of God reflects the purity of God himself. Again wisdom is linked to godliness, as God himself is the source and fountainhead of true wisdom. **peace-loving.** A love of authentic peace, free of a quarrelsome attitude. **considerate.** Thoughtful and respectful of other people's feelings. **submissive.** Willing to listen and to defer to others when appropriate. **full of mercy.** Not stingy in mercy but sufficiently aware of one's own need for mercy to be "mercy-full" toward others. **impartial and sincere.** Fair and free from deception or fraud. See *WLC* 135.

3:18 harvest of righteousness. The fruit reaped by the planting of wisdom is a bountiful crop of righteousness, both in oneself and in others positively affected by one's attitudes and actions.

but you cannot have what you want. You quarrel and fight. You do not have, because you
do not ask God. [3]When you ask, you do not receive,[h] because you ask with wrong motives,[i] that you may spend what you get on your pleasures.
[4]You adulterous people, don't you know that friendship with the world[j] is hatred toward God?[k] Anyone who chooses to be a friend of the world becomes an enemy of God.[l]
[5]Or do you think Scripture says without reason that the spirit he caused to live in us envies intensely?[a] [6]But he gives us more grace. That is why Scripture says:

"God opposes the proud
but gives grace to the humble."[b][m]

[7]Submit yourselves, then, to God. Resist the devil,[n] and he will flee from you. [8]Come
near to God and he will come near to you.[o] Wash your hands,[p] you sinners, and purify your
hearts, you double-minded.[q] [9]Grieve, mourn and wail. Change your laughter to mourning
and your joy to gloom.[r] [10]Humble yourselves before the Lord, and he will lift you up.
[11]Brothers, do not slander one another.[s] Anyone who speaks against his brother or
judges him[t] speaks against the law and judges it. When you judge the law, you are not
keeping it,[u] but sitting in judgment on it. [12]There is only one Lawgiver and Judge, the one
who is able to save and destroy.[v] But you—who are you to judge your neighbor?[w]

Boasting About Tomorrow

[13]Now listen, you who say, "Today or tomorrow we will go to this or that city, spend
a year there, carry on business and make money."[x] [14]Why, you do not even know what
will happen tomorrow. What is your life? You are a mist that appears for a little while and
then vanishes.[y] [15]Instead, you ought to say, "If it is the Lord's will,[z] we will live and do
this or that." [16]As it is, you boast and brag. All such boasting is evil.[a] [17]Anyone, then, who
knows the good he ought to do and doesn't do it, sins.[b]

Warning to Rich Oppressors

5 Now listen, you rich people,[c] weep and wail because of the misery that is coming
upon you. [2]Your wealth has rotted, and moths have eaten your clothes.[d] [3]Your gold

4:3 [h]Ps 18:41 [i]1Jn 3:22; 5:14
4:4 [j]Jas 1:27 [k]1Jn 2:15 [l]Jn 15:19
4:6 [m]Ps 138:6; Pr 3:34; Mt 23:12
4:7 [n]Eph 4:27; 1Pe 5:6-9
4:8 [o]2Ch 15:2 [p]Isa 1:16 [q]Jas 1:8
4:9 [r]Lk 6:25
4:11 [s]1Pe 2:1 [t]Mt 7:1 [u]Jas 1:22
4:12 [v]Mt 10:28 [w]Ro 14:4
4:13 [x]Pr 27:1
4:14 [y]Job 7:7; Ps 102:3
4:15 [z]Ac 18:21
4:16 [a]1Co 5:6
4:17 [b]Lk 12:47; Jn 9:41
5:1 [c]Lk 6:24
5:2 [d]Job 13:28; Mt 6:19,20

[a] 5 Or *that God jealously longs for the spirit that he made to live in us*; or *that the Spirit he caused to live in us longs jealously* [b] 6 Prov. 3:34

4:1 causes fights. Evil desires are the root cause of divisions among the saints. Envy is still in view as a destructive evil desire. The tongue may be the instrument of evil in quarrels, but evil desires lie at the source.
4:2 you do not ask God. Envy is a sin against God. It flows from a lack of commitment to bringing our needs to God. James did not promise here that if we simply pray, all of our desires will be met. Prayer for our needs and desires demonstrates wisdom, but prayer is often the means by which God shapes our desires to conform to his. When we fail to approach God in prayer about our needs, we are apt to resort to worldly greed and struggle.
4:3 wrong motives. God often refuses to grant petitions that proceed from evil desires. To pray with wrong motives is to pray without faith (Ro 14:23; Heb 11:6). See *WLC* 193.
4:4 adulterous. Spiritual infidelity is in view here.
4:5 Scripture says. The text James had in mind is not known, although he may have been referring specifically to Deuteronomy 6:15 or, more generally, to Scripture in a broader sense (e.g., Ex 20:3,5; 34:14; Dt 32:21; Jos 24:19; Na 1:2). **spirit . . . envies.** God's Spirit takes up residence in believers so that they are joined with him in deepest intimacy. God therefore will not tolerate loyalties that are divided between himself and the world.
4:6 See Proverbs 3:34.
4:7–8 Submit yourselves . . . Resist . . . Come near . . . Wash . . . purify. James used Old Testament language of worship to describe how believers may gain divine wisdom and avoid quarrels and envy by submitting to God in faith and repentance, aligning themselves with God and refusing to give allegiance to Satan. James also offered assurance of forgiveness to those who honestly seek it (cf. Zec 1:3; Mal 3:7). **the devil . . . will flee.** Satan is not equal in power or authority with God. Although Satan remains powerful, he is not invincible. Christians are to resist the devil by relying on God to protect them. As God comes near to believers, the devil flees. See *WLC* 104.
4:9 Grieve, mourn and wail. Genuine repentance includes acts demonstrating contrition.
▪ **4:11–12** *Slander.* James paused to focus on the particular problem of believers who quarrel and envy.
4:11 slander. In the strictest sense, slander is reporting falsehoods about another for the purpose of damaging that person's reputation. Slander usually flows out of envy and always reflects the work of Satan. Slandering a fellow believer destroys Christian fellowship and breaks the royal law of love (2:8–9). See *WLC* 145.
4:12 judge your neighbor? In this context, the word "judge" denotes slanderous condemnation (v. 11). It is appropriate for Christians to discern between good and evil, even among their fellow Christians (e.g., 1Co 5:12). See *WCF* 20.2.
▪ **4:13–17** *Warnings Against Presumption.* Closely related to slander against others is the sin of presumption (thinking too highly of oneself). Wisdom from God is humble, not proud.
4:13–15 See *BC* 13.
4:14 know what will happen. James rebuked those who were arrogantly disregarding divine sovereignty by living their lives and making future plans without regard for the providence of God.
4:15 If it is the Lord's will. The word "if" refers to future events that are conditional or unknown. James identifies the primary consideration in all future planning as acknowledgment that the control of our lives is in the hands of God. This text has led to the customary use of the phrase "God willing" among Christians (Ac 18:21; 1Co 4:19; 16:7; Heb 6:3).
4:16 boast. Prideful boasting about one's abilities and accomplishments is evil because it demonstrates failure to recognize God's role in our accomplishments. The Christian is to boast only in the Lord (2Co 11:30; 12:5,9).
4:17 sins. This principle is broadly applicable to all areas of life. In this context, James applied it to those who refuse to accept his teaching in these matters or to alter their behavior as instructed. See *WLC* 151.
▪ **5:1–6** *Warnings for the Rich.* As elsewhere in this epistle, James applied his principles to the attitudes and behaviors of wealthy believers (see 1:10–11; 2:1–13). See *HC* 110.
5:1 rich people. The Bible nowhere condemns wealth in and of itself. Material possessions are in fact often viewed as blessings from God (Pr 10:22). However, James generalizes that the rich are susceptible to the temptation to exploit the poor or to ignore their

and silver are corroded. Their corrosion will testify against you and eat your flesh like fire.
You have hoarded wealth in the last days.[e] 4 Look! The wages you failed to pay the workmen[f] who mowed your fields are crying out against you. The cries[g] of the harvesters have
reached the ears of the Lord Almighty.[h] 5 You have lived on earth in luxury and self-indulgence. You have fattened yourselves[i] in the day of slaughter.[a][j] 6 You have condemned
and murdered innocent men,[k] who were not opposing you.

Patience in Suffering

7 Be patient, then, brothers, until the Lord's coming. See how the farmer waits for the
land to yield its valuable crop and how patient he is for the autumn and spring rains.[l]
8 You too, be patient and stand firm, because the Lord's coming is near.[m] 9 Don't grumble against each other, brothers,[n] or you will be judged. The Judge[o] is standing at the
door![p]
10 Brothers, as an example of patience in the face of suffering, take the prophets[q] who
spoke in the name of the Lord. 11 As you know, we consider blessed[r] those who have persevered. You have heard of Job's perseverance[s] and have seen what the Lord finally
brought about.[t] The Lord is full of compassion and mercy.[u]
12 Above all, my brothers, do not swear—not by heaven or by earth or by anything
else. Let your "Yes" be yes, and your "No," no, or you will be condemned.[v]

The Prayer of Faith

13 Is any one of you in trouble? He should pray.[w] Is anyone happy? Let him sing songs
of praise.[x] 14 Is any one of you sick? He should call the elders of the church to pray over
him and anoint him with oil[y] in the name of the Lord. 15 And the prayer offered in faith
will make the sick person well; the Lord will raise him up. If he has sinned, he will be forgiven. 16 Therefore confess your sins[z] to each other and pray for each other so that you
may be healed.[a] The prayer of a righteous man is powerful and effective.[b]
17 Elijah was a man just like us.[c] He prayed earnestly that it would not rain, and it did
not rain on the land for three and a half years.[d] 18 Again he prayed, and the heavens gave
rain, and the earth produced its crops.[e]

5:3 [e]ver 7,8
5:4 [f]Lev 19:13 [g]Dt 24:15 [h]Ro 9:29
5:5 [i]Am 6:1 [j]Jer 12:3; 25:34
5:6 [k]Heb 10:38
5:7 [l]Dt 11:14; Jer 5:24
5:8 [m]Ro 13:11; 1Pe 4:7
5:9 [n]Jas 4:11 [o]1Co 4:5; 1Pe 4:5 [p]Mt 24:33
5:10 [q]Mt 5:12
5:11 [r]Mt 5:10 [s]Job 1:21, 22; 2:10 [t]Job 42:10,12-17 [u]Nu 14:18
5:12 [v]Mt 5:34-37
5:13 [w]Ps 50:15 [x]Col 3:16
5:14 [y]Mk 6:13
5:16 [z]Mt 3:6 [a]1Pe 2:24 [b]Jn 9:31
5:17 [c]Ac 14:15 [d]1Ki 17:1; Lk 4:25
5:18 [e]1Ki 18:41-45

[a] 5 Or *yourselves as in a day of feasting*

legitimate needs. Those who fail to be charitable promote oppression. They will receive God's severe judgment (Lk 6:24).

5:2–3 rotted . . . eaten . . . corroded. Sinfully acquired wealth, such as that accrued by denying workers their rightful wages, is no blessing. Rather, it is a cause for God's judgment.

5:4 wages you failed to pay. This is a violation of the law of God. Wages are not only to be paid but are to be paid on time (Lev 19:13; Dt 24:14–15). See *WLC* 142.

5:5 fattened yourselves. The rich are likened to animals being fattened in preparation for slaughter. The contented livestock are oblivious to the disaster awaiting them. For the unbeliever, every blessing turns ultimately into a curse, because for each good thing received from God's providence without a response of gratitude and honor, there is a corresponding increase of guilt and judgment.

5:6 condemned and murdered. This may be taken either literally or figuratively. The unjust use of power may actually have caused the execution of innocent people. Figuratively, to deprive a man of his wages is to commit a kind of murder against him.

▪ **5:7–11** *Patience.* James called for patience as another demonstration of wisdom from God. See *WLC* 135.

5:7 patient. The saints are to exercise patience as they await God's promised vindication of his people. God promises ultimately to eradicate injustice in this world (Lk 18:1–8).

5:9 The Judge is standing at the door! This verse reflects an urgent sense of the imminence of Christ's coming. It reinforces the New Testament hope for the return of Jesus, who will come at the end of the age. James may also have had in view the radical nearness of the judgment that awaits every person, for all will stand before the Judge to give an accounting. See verse 3, where James mentioned the "last days."

▪ **5:12–19** *Final Exhortations Toward Harmony.* James closed his epistle by addressing several specific aspects of harmonious living among believers.

5:12 Above all. This emphatic exhortation signals the weighty priority James attributed to godliness. To emphasize refraining from false oaths and vows so strongly may seem strange to modern ears, but it is consistent with the Biblical concerns for covenant keeping and for maintaining the sanctity of the faith. **do not swear.** This is not a prohibition against cursing or the use of vulgarity. James's teaching obviously derived from Jesus' instruction on the subject of vows (Mt 5:33–37). Neither Jesus nor James condemned proper vows and oaths. Rather, both condemned frivolous vows (cf. Paul's teaching in 2Co 1:23; 1Th 2:10). James was especially concerned that empty oaths would destroy relationships among believers. For a discussion of the proper role of oaths in the Christian life, see *WCF* 21.5; 22.1–5. **"Yes" be yes.** The Christian is expected to be a person whose word is reliable. See *WCF* 22.2; *HC* 99,102.

5:13 See *WCF* 21.5.

5:14 sick? That the elders were to be called to the sick person and that their prayers would save the person "from death" (v. 20) probably indicate that James had in mind extreme cases of illness believed to have been caused by sin in the person's life (see note on v. 20). There are implications, however, for many other uses of intercessory prayer and confession to elders. **elders.** See Acts 14:23 and Titus 1:5. **anoint him with oil.** Olive oil had a common medicinal use in the ancient world (Mk 6:13; Lk 10:34), but here the oil had a symbolic use in reference to the healing power of God.

5:15 prayer offered in faith. This verse enjoins the Christian community to be devoutly involved with intercessory prayer for the sick as an expression of faithful dependence on God. It does not support the notion popular in some Christian circles that a special kind of "prayer of faith" invariably heals, nor does it support the Roman Catholic tradition of last rites. **If he has sinned.** Not every sickness is an expression of God's judgment or discipline against sin (Jn 9:2–3), but some instances of illness are (1Co 11:29–30).

5:16 confess your sins. James is not advocating that Christians confess their sins to one another under normal circumstances, but rather that they should confess their sins to the elders when those sins are the possible reason for their illness. **righteous man.** A godly individual who prays in faith is a just or righteous person. **powerful and effective.** In divine providence, the prayers of righteous people often direct the course of history. See *WCF* 15.6; 21.3; *WLC* 183,185.

5:17–18 See *BC* 26.

5:17 Elijah. Although Elijah held the special office of Old Testament prophet, he shares a common humanity with all believers. His effectual prayer life is a model for the saints.

[19]My brothers, if one of you should wander from the truth[f] and someone should bring
him back,[g] [20]remember this: Whoever turns a sinner from the error of his way will save[h]
him from death and cover over a multitude of sins.[i]

5:19 [f]Jas 3:14 [g]Mt 18:15
5:20 [h]Ro 11:14 [i]1Pe 4:8

5:19 wander from the truth. To stray into sinful patterns or to give evidence of the absence of a saving faith.

5:20 turns a sinner. The care of the souls within the community should be the concern of every member, not only that of the clergy or church officers. Mutual help and encouragement are required. **from death.** This may refer either to spiritual or to physical death. If spiritual death is in view, this verse pertains to the one who has wandered from true faith. If physical death is in mind, it may also apply to believers who have fallen into significant sin. James may have intended this ambiguity so that his words would be applied to both situations. **cover over.** Refers to God's covering of sins with forgiveness (Pss 32:1; 85:2).

1 PETER

Introduction

Overview

Author: The apostle Peter
Purpose: To encourage persecuted and bewildered Christians to stand fast together in their faith
Date: A.D. 60–68
Key Truths:

- Christians have a wonderful privilege of seeing God's great salvation in Christ.
- The privilege of salvation entails a number of important responsibilities.
- Christians are to be holy, deeply loving of each other and devoted to the glory of God.
- Relationships within and outside the church must be maintained according to the standards of Christ, not the standards of the world.
- Christians should face suffering as followers of Christ with the proper perspective.

Author

The author identified himself as "Peter, an apostle of Jesus Christ" (1:1). That he was the well-known apostle of the Gospels and Acts is confirmed by both internal and external evidence. The author described himself as "a witness of Christ's sufferings" (5:1), and there are numerous echoes of Jesus' teaching and deeds in this epistle (e.g., 5:2–3; cf. Jn 21:15–17). Parallels of thought and phrase between 1 Peter and Peter's speeches in Acts (e.g., 2:7–8; cf. Ac 4:10–11) lend further support to Peter's authorship.

The external attestation to 1 Peter as a genuine epistle of Peter is widespread and early. There is no evidence that this epistle was ever attributed to anyone else. Irenaeus (c. A.D. 185; *Against Heresies,* 4.9.2), Tertullian (c. A.D. 160–225), Clement of Alexandria (c. A.D. 150–215) and Origen (c. A.D. 185–253) all attributed the epistle to Peter. By the time of Eusebius (c. A.D. 265–339), there was no question of its authenticity (*Ecclesiastical History,* 3.3.1).

Although the case for Petrine authorship is strong, linguistic and historical objections have been raised during the last two centuries. The Greek of 1 Peter is said to be too polished and too influenced by the Septuagint (the Greek translation of the OT) to have come from an uneducated Galilean fisherman like Peter (cf. Ac 4:13). The persecutions alluded to in the epistle (4:12–19; 5:6–9) are alleged to reflect a situation that occurred after Peter's lifetime.

None of these objections is decisive. In response to the linguistic objection, the following points can be made: First-century Galilee was bilingual (Aramaic and Greek), the description of Peter and John as "unschooled, ordinary men" (Ac 4:13) may only refer to their lack of formal training in the Scriptures, the 30 years that elapsed between the days of Peter the fisherman and Peter the writer would have provided ample time for Peter to have improved his proficiency in Greek, and Silas's possible role as secretary (5:12) could account for the smoother style of 1 Peter compared to 2 Peter.

With regard to the historical objections, the sufferings alluded to by Peter can just as well be accounted for by citing the local, sporadic harassment that was routinely experienced by early Christians from the days of the apostles on, as by citing the official persecution in the days of Domitian (c. A.D. 95) or Trajan (c. A.D. 111).

Time and Place of Writing

According to 5:13, Peter was in "Babylon" when he wrote this epistle. Various identifications of the location have been suggested, among them (1) a military outpost in Egypt, (2) the ancient Mesopotamian city itself and (3) Rome. Several lines of evidence favor Rome. Mark, who was with Peter when he wrote this epistle (5:13), is known to have been with Paul in Rome (Col 4:10; Phm 24). Rome is called "Babylon" in Revelation (Rev 17:5). Finally, this interpretation has been generally accepted since the second century. The uniform testimony of early church history is that Peter was in Rome at the end of his life.

If Rome is the place of origin, the epistle must have been composed between A.D. 60 and 68. The earlier limit is established by Peter's familiarity with Ephesians and Colossians (cf. 2:18 and Col 3:22; cf. 3:1–6 and Eph 5:22–24); the later date, by the tradition that Peter was crucified upside down in Rome in or before A.D. 68.

Original Audience

While the introduction ("scattered throughout"; 1:1) and the frequent Old Testament quotations and allusions in the epistle might imply Jewish Christian recipients (as Calvin thought), there are stronger indications that most of the recipients were from a pagan background. The reference in 1:18, for example, to "the empty way of life handed down to you from your forefathers" hardly seems fitting for Jews. Furthermore, the sins listed in 4:3 are typically those that were committed by pagans.

Although 1 Peter has the character of a general epistle (cf. James, 2 Peter, 1 John, Jude), it differs from the other general epistles in that it specifies the areas in which the readers lived: "Pontus, Galatia, Cappadocia, Asia and Bithynia" (1:1). What is known from the epistle itself is that the readers were suffering persecution for their faith (1:6–7; 3:13–17; 4:12–19; 5:9–10).

Nothing in the epistle indicates official, legislative persecution or requires a date of composition later than the 60s. The sufferings were the trials common to first-century Christians, including insults (4:4,14) and slanderous accusations of wrongdoing (2:12; 3:16). Beatings (2:20), social ostracism, sporadic mob violence and local police action may have been involved as well.

Purpose and Distinctives

Peter wrote to encourage persecuted and bewildered Christians and to exhort them to stand fast in their faith (5:12). For that purpose he repeatedly turned their thoughts to the joys and glories of their eternal inheritance (1:3–13; 3:7; 4:13–14; 5:1,4,6,10) and instructed them about proper Christian behavior in the midst of undeserved suffering (4:12–19). While addressed primarily to persecuted Christians, the principles Peter taught apply to all Christians who suffer, regardless of the cause, provided the suffering is not occasioned by one's own sin. On the basis of this epistle, Peter has with justice been called "the apostle of hope" (cf. 1:3,13,21; 3:5,15). The hortatory thrust of the entire epistle can be summed up in the phrase "trust and obey" (see 4:19; cf. 2:23).

Outline

I. Salutation (1:1–2)	*Peter identified himself as an apostle and his readers as strangers in the world.*
II. The Christian's Sure Salvation (1:3–12)	*Peter praised God for the wondrous privilege of seeing the salvation Christ has brought to his people.*
III. The Implications of Salvation (1:13—3:12) A. Personal Holiness (1:13–16) B. Reverent Fear (1:17–21) C. Mutual Love (1:22—2:3) D. A Temple and Priesthood (2:4–10) E. Social Relationships (2:11—3:12) 1. The World in General (2:11–12) 2. Civil Authorities (2:13–17) 3. The Household (2:18—3:7) 4. Summary (3:8–12)	*Peter addressed a number of important practical implications of salvation in Christ, focusing especially on the need for holiness and godly interactions among believers and with the world.*
IV. Christian Suffering and Service (3:13—5:11) A. Suffering for Righteousness' Sake (3:13–22) B. Suffering for God's Glory (4:1–11) C. Suffering With Christ (4:12–19) D. Elders and Young Men Suffering Together (5:1–11)	*Peter provided outlooks on the persecutions and sufferings of his readers; he explained the basis, motivations and goals of suffering as a Christian.*
V. Final Greetings (5:12–14)	*Paul encouraged his readers with several personal greetings and a blessing for them.*

1 Peter, an apostle of Jesus Christ,[a]

To God's elect,[b] strangers in the world, scattered throughout Pontus, Galatia, Cappadocia, Asia and Bithynia,[c] 2 who have been chosen according to the foreknowledge[d]
of God the Father, through the sanctifying work of the Spirit,[e] for obedience to Jesus
Christ and sprinkling by his blood:[f]

Grace and peace be yours in abundance.

1:1 [a]2Pe 1:1 [b]Mt 24:22 [c]Ac 16:7
1:2 [d]Ro 8:29 [e]2Th 2:13 [f]Heb 10:22; 12:24

■ **1:1–2** *Salutation.* Peter introduced himself and identified the recipients of his letter.

1:1 Peter. The name (meaning "rock") given this apostle by Jesus (Mt 16:18; Jn 1:42) in anticipation of Peter's role in the early church. His given Hebrew name was probably Simeon (see NIV text note on Ac 15:14), the Greek equivalent of which is Simon. "Cephas" (Jn 1:42; 1Co 1:12) is the transliteration of the Aramaic word for "rock." **apostle.** See note on 2 Corinthians 1:1. **elect.** Peter reminded his readers of their privileged and secure position as the objects of God's sovereign, gracious, eternal choice of them as his people in and through Jesus Christ (2:9–10). The theme of election is developed in verse 2. **strangers in the world.** This phrase translates one Greek word (*parepidçmos*) that is also used in 2:11; it emphasizes the temporary nature of a sojourner's stay in a place. As pilgrims, Christians live in the world, but their real homeland is in heaven (Php 3:20; Heb 11:13–16), and their hope is anchored there. **scattered.** This word (Greek, *diaspora*) was a technical term among Greek-speaking Jews that was used to describe Jews who lived outside the Holy Land (Jn 7:35). Peter's readers were not entirely Jewish, so it is likely that he used the term "scattered" figuratively to describe all believers who were still waiting for their full inheritance in the new heavens and the new earth.

1:2 according to the foreknowledge. Peter did not mean that God sovereignly elected some to salvation on the basis of his knowledge of what they would choose if left to themselves. Foreknowledge here is of people, not of events; it implies his love for

1:3 [g]2Co 1:3; Eph 1:3 [h]Tit 3:5; Jas 1:18 [i]1Co 15:20
1:4 [j]Col 1:5
1:5 [k]Jn 10:28
1:6 [l]Ro 5:2 [m]1Pe 5:10 [n]Jas 1:2
1:7 [o]Job 23:10; Ps 66:10; Pr 17:3 [p]Jas 1:3 [q]Ro 2:7
1:8 [r]Jn 20:29
1:9 [s]Ro 6:22
1:10 [t]Mt 26:24 [u]Mt 13:17
1:11 [v]2Pe 1:21
1:12 [w]ver 25

Praise to God for a Living Hope

3 Praise be to the God and Father of our Lord Jesus Christ![g] In his great mercy[h] he has
given us new birth into a living hope through the resurrection of Jesus Christ from the
dead,[i] 4 and into an inheritance that can never perish, spoil or fade—kept in heaven for
you,[j] 5 who through faith are shielded by God's power[k] until the coming of the salvation
that is ready to be revealed in the last time. 6 In this you greatly rejoice,[l] though now for
a little while[m] you may have had to suffer grief in all kinds of trials.[n] 7 These have come
so that your faith—of greater worth than gold, which perishes even though refined by
fire[o]—may be proved genuine[p] and may result in praise, glory and honor when Jesus
Christ is revealed.[q] 8 Though you have not seen him, you love him; and even though you
do not see him now, you believe in him[r] and are filled with an inexpressible and glorious joy, 9 for you are receiving the goal of your faith, the salvation of your souls.[s]

10 Concerning this salvation, the prophets, who spoke[t] of the grace that was to come
to you, searched intently and with the greatest care,[u] 11 trying to find out the time and
circumstances to which the Spirit of Christ[v] in them was pointing when he predicted the
sufferings of Christ and the glories that would follow. 12 It was revealed to them that they
were not serving themselves but you, when they spoke of the things that have now been
told you by those who have preached the gospel to you[w] by the Holy Spirit sent from
heaven. Even angels long to look into these things.

Be Holy

13 Therefore, prepare your minds for action; be self-controlled; set your hope fully on
the grace to be given you when Jesus Christ is revealed. 14 As obedient children, do not

---

them before all time (see theological article "Predestination and Foreknowledge" at Ro 8). See the related verb "chosen" in 1:20. **sanctifying work of the Spirit.** Note the close connection between the Father's electing love and the Spirit's work in applying redemption to the elect (2Th 2:13). Most comprehensively, "sanctifying work" includes all of the Spirit's operations in setting sinners apart from sin (e.g., regeneration and faith) and consecrating them to God's service, including sanctification in the progressive sense (see theological article "Sanctification" at Tit 3). **obedience to Jesus Christ.** The initial act of obedience is faith in Christ (Jn 6:28–29), and the fundamental element of all obedience is continued faith. Election is "for" or "with the goal of" faith (obedience), not as a result of it (Eph 1:3–4; 2Ti 1:9). **sprinkling by his blood.** This Old Testament imagery has several possible references: (1) the transference to the elect of the merits and cleansing virtue of Christ's death (cf. Lev 16:15–16; Heb 9:13–14); (2) the sealing of the new covenant and participation in its benefits and obligations (cf. Ex 24:3–8; 1Co 11:25); (3) the consecration to priestly service (2:5,9; cf. Ex 29:21; Heb 10:19–22). **Grace and peace.** Peter's greeting was also a blessing that had special relevance for suffering Christians. Grace is God's loving favor that rests upon sinners because of their identification with Christ. Peace is the objective condition of being right with God through Christ (Ro 5:1–2), together with all that flows from that relationship. See *WCF* 3.6; 11.4; *BC* 9,16,34; *HC* 70.

■ **1:3–12** *The Christian's Sure Salvation.* Peter encouraged his persecuted readers by beginning his epistle with a description of their sure and glorious salvation in Christ.

1:3–5 *WCF* 12; *HC* 45,54.

1:3 In his great mercy. Literally, "according to his mercy," emphasizing that salvation is based entirely on God's loving initiative. **given us new birth.** Although the verb that translates this phrase occurs only here and in 1:23 in the New Testament, the thought is found frequently (e.g., Jn 1:12–13; 3:3–8; Tit 3:5; Jas 1:18). **living hope.** Hope is an important concept in this epistle (1:13,21; 3:5,15). It conveys the idea of confidence and energy that flow from the expectation of future blessing based on facts and promises. The word "living" indicates the vibrancy and experiential character of this hope. See *BC* 22.

1:4 inheritance. This term derives from the Old Testament terminology identifying the promised land as Israel's inheritance (Ex 32:13; Lev 20:24; Nu 26:53–56; Dt 3:28). The land of Canaan was a foretaste of the new heavens and the new earth that are the Christian's ultimate inheritance. As God's children by the new birth, Christians are heirs of God and coheirs with Christ (Ro 8:16–17). Their inheritance is explained in verse 5 as full salvation (cf. Heb 1:14).

1:5 who through faith are shielded by God's power. Literally, "who by God's power are being guarded through faith." This verse stresses both the priority of divine grace and the importance of the human action that results from that grace. Although faith is a gift of God, believers are still responsible for exercising faith (steadfast trust) in spiritual battle (5:8–9; Eph 6:16; Php 2:12–13). The strength of God's protection is conveyed by means of a military term ("shielded"), signifying vigilant defense of a fortress. **salvation.** Here the word connotes complete and final future deliverance from sin and full enjoyment of eternal glory (1:9; 4:13–14; 5:1,4). **the last time.** Terminology closely associated with the last, or latter, days (see theological article "The Plan of the Ages" at Heb 7). On the last day of this age, Christ will return in the final manifestation of his power and glory. See *WCF* 3.6; 17.1; *WLC* 79; *WSC* 36; *HC* 1.

1:6 may have had. Literally, "if necessary." Although God himself never tempts anyone to sin (Jas 1:13), he allows or sends trials to test and strengthen faith (v. 7).

1:7 These have come. An explicit statement of the divine purpose of trials that was implied in verse 6 (cf. Ro 5:3–4; Jas 1:2–4). **may be proved genuine.** As humans use fire to refine precious metals, so God uses trials to distinguish genuine faith from superficial profession and to simultaneously strengthen faith (Job 23:10). **may result in praise, glory and honor.** Peter may have been referring to praise, glory and honor that will come to Christ in the final day, but he more likely had in mind the final glorification of believers (5:1,4). **when Jesus Christ is revealed.** For all to see, at his second coming (v. 5; 4:13; 5:1; 1Co 4:3–5).

1:9 are receiving. Believers already enjoy many blessings of their salvation, but full possession of it awaits the return of Christ (v. 5). **souls.** Used here for the whole person; in 3:20 the same Greek word is translated "people." See *WCF* 17.1.

1:10–12 See *WLC* 43; *WSC* 24; *BC* 7.

1:10 the prophets, who spoke of the grace. Most prophets in the Old Testament spoke of the time of God's mercy after the exile of Israel and Judah. They knew that God had promised not only Israel's gracious restoration, but also the merciful inclusion of Gentiles among the people of God (e.g., Isa 2:2ff.; Isa 65; Am 9:15ff.). The prophets had not known about these events in much detail, but Peter said that they had longed to know more.

1:11 time and circumstances. The Old Testament prophets knew that salvation would come, but not precisely when or how. **the Spirit of Christ.** This phrase appears only here and in Romans 8:9 (cf. Ac 16:6–7; Gal 4:6; Php 1:19). The Holy Spirit is called the Spirit of Christ because he is sent by Christ (Jn 15:26) and because, since the time of the resurrection, Christ and the Spirit function as one in applying redemption to the believer (see notes on Ro 8:10; 1Co 15:45).

1:12 not serving themselves but you. The prophets said and wrote many things about the days of salvation after Israel's exile, things that would be understood deeply only by future generations. **the things that have now been told you.** Many details about the final stages of God's kingdom were unknown to the prophets. Those who brought the gospel during the apostolic age announced how the salvation promised by the prophets had come about. **Holy Spirit sent from heaven.** Underlines the divine origin of the gospel message. The same Spirit who inspired the prophets was directing the gospel messengers. **angels long to look.**

conform[x] to the evil desires you had when you lived in ignorance.[y] 15But just as he who
called you is holy, so be holy in all you do;[z] 16for it is written: "Be holy, because I am
holy."[a][a]

17Since you call on a Father who judges each man's work impartially,[b] live your lives
as strangers here in reverent fear.[c] 18For you know that it was not with perishable
things such as silver or gold that you were redeemed[d] from the empty way of life handed down to you from your forefathers, 19but with the precious blood of Christ, a lamb[e]
without blemish or defect.[f] 20He was chosen before the creation of the world,[g] but was
revealed in these last times[h] for your sake. 21Through him you believe in God,[i] who
raised him from the dead and glorified him, and so your faith and hope are in God.

22Now that you have purified[j] yourselves by obeying the truth so that you have sincere love for your brothers, love one another deeply,[k] from the heart.[b] 23For you have
been born again,[l] not of perishable seed, but of imperishable, through the living and enduring word of God.[m] 24For,

> "All men are like grass,
> and all their glory is like the flowers of the field;
> the grass withers and the flowers fall,
> 25 but the word of the Lord stands forever."[c][n]

And this is the word that was preached to you.

1:14 [x]Ro 12:2 [y]Eph 4:18
1:15 [z]2Co 7:1; 1Th 4:7
1:16 [a]Lev 11:44,45
1:17 [b]Ac 10:34 [c]Heb 12:28
1:18 [d]Mt 20:28; 1Co 6:20
1:19 [e]Jn 1:29 [f]Ex 12:5
1:20 [g]Eph 1:4 [h]Heb 9:26
1:21 [i]Ro 4:24
1:22 [j]Jas 4:8 [k]Jn 13:34; Heb 13:1
1:23 [l]Jn 1:13 [m]Heb 4:12
1:25 [n]Isa 40:6-8

[a] *16* Lev. 11:44,45; 19:2 [b] *22* Some early manuscripts *from a pure heart* [c] *25* Isaiah 40:6–8

Even celestial beings are intensely interested in final redemption. God's plan is made known to them through the church (Eph 3:8–10).

■ **1:13—3:12** *The Implications of Salvation.* Having described the glorious salvation that Christ had accomplished on their behalf, Peter turned to the responsibilities given to all those who follow Christ. His discussion divides into five parts: the need for personal holiness (1:13–16), the importance of reverence (1:17–21), love among Christians (1:22—2:3), living as a temple and priesthood (2:4–10) and a variety of social relationships (2:11—3:12).

■ **1:13–16** *Personal Holiness.* God has given, and will give, so much to his people in Christ that they in turn should give themselves over to personal holiness.

1:13 prepare your minds for action. Literally, "having girded up the loins of your mind." The imagery is taken from the Middle Eastern practice of gathering up the long main garment and tucking it into a belt in preparation for action, freeing the legs for rapid movement. The emphasis here is on active preparation for vigorous and sustained spiritual exertion. **on the grace to be given.** Christ's past accomplishments on behalf of his people are wondrous, but what lies ahead is even greater. When Christ returns he will bring our final reward and inheritance: eternal glory in the new heavens and the new earth.

1:15–19 See *WLC* 71,101,152; *WSC* 44; *BC* 21; *HC* 1,34,36.

1:15 called you. God's gracious initiative effectually brings people into new life.

1:16 Be holy, because I am holy. Just as Old Testament Israel was set apart by God from the surrounding nations to be holy, so also the church is to be set apart from sin to the service of God (2:9; Lev 19:2). The Christian's standard of, and motivation for, holiness is nothing less than the absolute moral perfection of God himself (v. 16; Mt 5:48; Eph 5:1).

■ **1:17–21** *Reverent Fear.* Peter encouraged his readers to remember how serious their choices were by reminding them of God's judgment.

1:17 Father who judges . . . impartially. Although Christians will not be condemned for their sins (2:24), they will be judged for their deeds as Christians and rewarded accordingly (Ro 14:10–12; 1Co 3:12–15). Beyond this, Peter also knew that not all in the churches he addressed had exercised saving faith; he warned them that they would be condemned for their sins if they did not repent (Heb 10:26–29). **strangers.** A different Greek word from that used in verse 1. This word connotes those who live in a place without holding citizenship, highlighting the Christian's pilgrim status in this world. The only way to remain faithful to Christ is to disengage our natural love for the things of this world (1Jn 2:15). **reverent fear.** Because God is both Father and Judge, believers are to approach him with humble reverence and awe (Ps 34:11; Ac 9:31). See *HC* 94.

1:18 redeemed. Freed from the bondage of sin by the payment of a price (Ro 8:2–3; 1Co 7:23; Gal 3:13; Eph 1:7). The price of redemption is the blood of Christ (v. 19). **empty way of life handed down to you.** The "emptiness" or "worthlessness" of pagan worship is a frequent theme of Biblical writers (Jer 2:5; Ac 14:15). Although there are condemnations in the New Testament of the Jewish traditions that added to the demands of the Old Testament law (Mk 7:8–13; Php 3:3–7), Peter here seems to have had Gentile paganism in view (1:14; 4:3). See "Introduction: Original Audience."

1:19–20 See *WCF* 8.1; 11.4.

1:19 lamb. The imagery is from the Old Testament sacrificial system, with special reference to the Passover (Ex 12:5; Lev 3:6–7; Isa 53:7; Jn 1:29). **without blemish or defect.** In order to be acceptable, a sacrifice had to be free from all defect (Lev 22:20–25). Christ's sinless life qualified him to die for the sins of others (Heb 7:26–27). See *HC* 98.

1:20 chosen. Literally, "foreknown" (see v. 2). **before the creation of the world.** Christ was chosen as Redeemer of the elect in eternity (Jn 17:24; Rev 13:8). **these last times.** Includes the entire period between the first and second comings of Jesus (Ac 2:17; Heb 1:2). See theological article "The Plan of the Ages" at Hebrews 7.

1:21 Through him you believed in God. As the mediator between God and man, Christ provides the only access to God (Jn 14:6). In Christ, the Father is revealed (Jn 1:18). Christ's redeeming death has opened the path of access to God (3:18).

■ **1:22—2:3** *Mutual Love.* Having been purified by faith in Christ, Peter's readers needed to display their saving faith through service and love for each other.

1:22 have sincere love. Believers' genuine and enduring love for others is possible only because of the love God has first shown to them in giving them new birth in Christ (Jn 13:35; 1Jn 4:10–12). **deeply, from the heart.** Christians are to display the kind of love for each other that God and Christ have for believers and for one another. It is not mere outward behavior that is in view, but fervent, heart-felt affection and commitment that is demonstrated in loving actions.

1:23–25 See *HC* 65.

1:23 born again. See note on 1:3. **perishable . . . imperishable.** Sincere Christian love is possible because believers no longer belong to the world of hatred and strife but to the new world of love and unity. This verse compares and contrasts human procreation with the life-giving power of God's Word (cf. Jn 1:12–13). **through the living and enduring word.** The Word of God in the gospel does not pass away, nor does the salvation it brings.

1:24–25 All men . . . word of the Lord. Peter referred to Isaiah 40:6–8, a prophecy that contrasts ordinary, transient human life with the promise of restoration after exile. This promise or word from God is eternal, and the new creation it predicts will never pass away. **the word that was preached to you.** Peter identified the Christian gospel message with the prophetic word promising the final salvation after exile. The gospel announces the Good News that the promised kingdom has come (Isa 52:7).

2

Therefore, rid yourselves[o] of all malice and all deceit, hypocrisy, envy, and slander[p]
of every kind. [2]Like newborn babies, crave pure spiritual milk,[q] so that by it you may
grow up[r] in your salvation, [3]now that you have tasted that the Lord is good.[s]

The Living Stone and a Chosen People

[4]As you come to him, the living Stone[t]—rejected by men but chosen by God and precious to him—[5]you also, like living stones, are being built[u] into a spiritual house[v] to be
a holy priesthood,[w] offering spiritual sacrifices acceptable to God through Jesus Christ.[x]
[6]For in Scripture it says:

> "See, I lay a stone in Zion,
> a chosen and precious cornerstone,[y]
> and the one who trusts in him
> will never be put to shame."[a][z]

[7]Now to you who believe, this stone is precious. But to those who do not believe,[a]

> "The stone the builders rejected
> has become the capstone,[b]"[c][b]

[8]and,

> "A stone that causes men to stumble
> and a rock that makes them fall."[d][c]

They stumble because they disobey the message—which is also what they were destined
for.[d]
[9]But you are a chosen people,[e] a royal priesthood, a holy nation,[f] a people belonging to God, that you may declare the praises of him who called you out of darkness into

2:1 [o]Eph 4:22 [p]Jas 4:11
2:2 [q]1Co 3:2 [r]Eph 4:15,16
2:3 [s]Heb 6:5
2:4 [t]ver 7
2:5 [u]1Co 3:9 [v]1Ti 3:15 [w]Isa 61:6 [x]Php 4:18; Heb 13:15
2:6 [y]Eph 2:20 [z]Isa 28:16
2:7 [a]2Co 2:16 [b]Ps 118:22
2:8 [c]Isa 8:14; 1Co 1:23 [d]Ro 9:22
2:9 [e]Dt 10:15 [f]Isa 62:12

[a] 6 Isaiah 28:16 [b] 7 Or *cornerstone* [c] 7 Psalm 118:22 [d] 8 Isaiah 8:14

2:1–2 See *WLC* 160.
2:1 Therefore, rid yourselves. Because his readers had received the enduring word that the salvation of the last days had come, they were no longer to be like people who followed the ways of the evil and hateful world. See *WSC* 90.
2:2 newborn babies. Peter continued the imagery of new birth (1:23). Believers are to show the same yearning for spiritual food that a healthy infant shows for its mother's milk. See *WCF* 14.1. **pure spiritual milk.** Although the churches to which Peter wrote no doubt included many recent converts, here "milk" does not indicate elementary Christian teaching for the spiritually immature (as it does in 1Co 3:2 and Heb 5:12–13). Rather, it indicates the appropriateness and sufficiency of pure Christian teaching (found in God's Word; 1:22–25) as spiritual food for all Christians. **grow up in your salvation.** Full salvation is the goal of Christian growth and maturity (1:5). Maturity is measured by Christlikeness (Eph 4:13–15).
2:3 See *WLC* 138.
■ **2:4–10** *A Temple and Priesthood.* Having called on his readers to mature in their faith, Peter drew a metaphorical portrait of what their lives were to be like. He urged them to live as a temple and a priesthood.
2:4 As you come. Believers are to draw near to Christ with the intent of staying close and enjoying personal fellowship. Their initial coming to Christ in repentance and faith is included, along with the act of continual coming. **living Stone.** The rock/stone imagery is common in the Old Testament (e.g., Ps 118:22; Isa 8:14; 28:16) and is applied by Jesus to himself (Mt 21:42). As the context makes clear, "living" indicates that the stone represents a person: Christ.
2:5–10 See *WCF* 5.6; *HC* 2,86.
2:5 living stones. Peter further developed the rock/stone metaphor by describing stones that form a building. By speaking of the stones as living, he once again revealed that he was talking about people. Christians are to conceive of themselves as together forming a temple for the praise of God. **spiritual house.** Not a non-physical house, but a house of the Spirit. The background of the symbolism is the Old Testament temple as the house or dwelling place of God. The church, which the Holy Spirit indwells, is the true temple of God (2Co 6:16–18; Eph 2:19–22). **holy priesthood.** Every true believer is a priest (v. 9) in the sense of: having equal and immediate access to God; serving him personally; interceding for others; and leading others to receive God's ultimate sacrifice, Jesus Christ. **spiritual sacrifices.** Not "immaterial" sacrifices, but sacrifices appropriate to the present age of the Holy Spirit. While Christ's once-for-all sacrifice of propitiation on the cross has fulfilled the Old Testament sacrificial system and rendered its continued practice obsolete (Heb 10:1–18), the appropriateness of sacrifice (the grateful response of a redeemed people) remains. Such sacrifice is seen both in the Christian's worship and in his or her pattern of living (Ro 12:1; Php 4:18; Heb 13:15; Rev 8:3–4; cf. Ps 51:16–19). **acceptable to God through Jesus Christ.** The priesthood of all believers (v. 9) depends upon the eternal high priesthood of Christ. Through his once-for-all-time sacrifice (Heb 7:27) and continued intercession (Heb 7:25), Christians and their sacrifices are acceptable to God (Heb 13:15–16). See *WCF* 16.6; 21.3; *WLC* 55; *HC* 32.
2:6 cornerstone. Peter referred to Isaiah 28:16, where the prophet spoke of God rebuilding his people as a building after the exile. It was appropriate for Peter to apply this verse to the church, because God rebuilt his people as the church after the exile. (See theological article "The Plan of the Ages" at Heb 7.) The cornerstone was a great stone laid for the foundation at the place where two walls came together. It was of particular importance for the stability of the entire building. The foundation of the church is established on the prophets and apostles, who are held together by the chief cornerstone: Christ (Eph 2:20). See *WLC* 40.
2:7 capstone. Literally, "the head of the corner" or chief cornerstone (see NIV text note). Peter drew upon Psalm 118:22, which referred to the king of Israel who was exalted by God when others had disdained him.
2:8 A stone . . . a rock. Peter referred to Isaiah 8:14, where God himself is portrayed as a rock that causes the wicked in Israel to stumble. Unbelievers stumble over the very hope of eternal salvation, namely, Christ. **what they were destined for.** This terminology is used elsewhere of God's sovereign choice in election to salvation (1Th 5:9). This verse teaches both divine sovereignty and human responsibility. People are condemned because they "disobey the message" (stumble), but their disobedience does not occur apart from God's sovereign, blameless will (Ro 9:16–24). See theological article "Predestination and Foreknowledge" at Romans 8. See also *WCF* 3.7; *WLC* 13.
2:9 But you. These two brief words mark a sharp contrast between the destiny of unbelievers (v. 8) and the status of the elect. The theme of God's sovereign choice of both Christ and the church is prominent in this passage (vv. 6,9). **a chosen people, a royal priesthood, a holy nation.** Here Peter shifted his metaphor slightly. Not only are believers living stones in a temple for God, but they are also the priests who serve in this temple. Peter's lan-

his wonderful light.[g] [10]Once you were not a people, but now you are the people of God;[h]
once you had not received mercy, but now you have received mercy.
[11]Dear friends, I urge you, as aliens and strangers in the world, to abstain from sinful desires,[i] which war against your soul.[j] [12]Live such good lives among the pagans that,
though they accuse you of doing wrong, they may see your good deeds[k] and glorify God[l]
on the day he visits us.

Submission to Rulers and Masters

[13]Submit yourselves for the Lord's sake to every authority[m] instituted among men:
whether to the king, as the supreme authority, [14]or to governors, who are sent by him
to punish those who do wrong[n] and to commend those who do right.[o] [15]For it is God's
will[p] that by doing good you should silence the ignorant talk of foolish men.[q] [16]Live as
free men,[r] but do not use your freedom as a cover-up for evil; live as servants of God.[s]
[17]Show proper respect to everyone: Love the brotherhood of believers,[t] fear God, hon-
or the king.[u]
[18]Slaves, submit yourselves to your masters with all respect,[v] not only to those who
are good and considerate,[w] but also to those who are harsh. [19]For it is commendable if
a man bears up under the pain of unjust suffering because he is conscious of God.[x] [20]But
how is it to your credit if you receive a beating for doing wrong and endure it? But if you
suffer for doing good and you endure it, this is commendable before God.[y] [21]To this[z] you
were called, because Christ suffered for you, leaving you an example,[a] that you should
follow in his steps.

> [22]"He committed no sin,
> and no deceit was found in his mouth."[a] [b]

[23]When they hurled their insults at him, he did not retaliate; when he suffered, he made
no threats.[c] Instead, he entrusted himself[d] to him who judges justly. [24]He himself bore

2:9 [g]Ac 26:18
2:10 [h]Hos 1:9,10
2:11 [i]Gal 5:16 [j]Jas 4:1
2:12 [k]Php 2:15; 1Pe 3:16 [l]Mt 5:16; 9:8
2:13 [m]Ro 13:1
2:14 [n]Ro 13:4 [o]Ro 13:3
2:15 [p]1Pe 3:17 [q]ver 12
2:16 [r]Jn 8:32 [s]Ro 6:22
2:17 [t]Ro 12:10 [u]Ro 13:7
2:18 [v]Eph 6:5 [w]Jas 3:17
2:19 [x]1Pe 3:14,17
2:20 [y]1Pe 3:17
2:21 [z]Ac 14:22 [a]Mt 16:24
2:22 [b]Isa 53:9
2:23 [c]Isa 53:7 [d]Lk 23:46

[a] *22* Isaiah 53:9

guage derives from Exodus 19:6 and Deuteronomy 7:6, where Moses called Israel these things. Thus, Peter highlighted the continuity between the church and Old Testament Israel. **that you may declare.** The praise of God is the reason believers are called to be priests. Believers both worship God and witness to the nations through their praises. See *WCF* 16.2; *HC* 32.
2:10 not a people . . . are the people of God. Continuing the application to the church of Old Testament texts dealing with Israel, Peter drew on the Septuagint texts of Hosea 1:6,9–10 and 2:23, which in their original contexts were prophecies of God's embracing of Israel after rejecting her in the exile. Both Peter and Paul (Ro 9:25–26) saw parallels between the acceptance of Israel after exile and the incorporation of Gentiles into the kingdom of God. For Jews, to become "not my people" was to have the status of Gentiles in God's eyes.
■ **2:11—3:12** *Social Relationships.* Peter focused on how salvation in Christ should influence the believer's behavior and attitudes in a number of social relationships. He mentioned the world in general (2:11–12), the civil government (2:13–17) and household relations (2:18—3:7), and he closed with a summary (3:8–12).
■ **2:11–12** *The World in General.* Peter called on his readers to avoid the ways of the pagan world around them.
2:11 sinful desires. Literally, "fleshly desires." Bodily desires are not wrong in themselves, but they are perverted by humanity's sinful nature. The expression includes more than sensual desires (Gal 5:19–21) and refers to the desires of our fallen nature. See *WCF* 13.2.
2:12 accuse you of doing wrong. Among the accusations against Christians in Peter's time were these: being disloyal to the emperor (Jn 19:12), propagating "unlawful customs" (Ac 16:16–21), defaming the gods (Ac 19:23–27) and defying authority (Ac 17:7). **glorify God on the day he visits us.** God's "visitation" is his drawing near either for judgment or for mercy. Peter had in mind either the final judgment or some special occasions when the presence of God is evident among his people. See *WCF* 16.2; *WLC* 112; *HC* 86.
■ **2:13–17** *Civil Authorities.* Peter focused on the submission believers are to render to civil authorities.
2:13–15 See *WCF* 16.2; 19.4; 20.4; 23.1; 23.4; *WLC* 127.
2:13 Submit yourselves . . . to every authority. This introduces the theme of voluntary submission and obedience to those in authority (v. 18; 3:1). **for the Lord's sake.** That is, to commend Christ to others and not to bring reproach on his name. Also, submission to others is itself service to Christ (Eph 6:7–8). **the king, as the supreme authority.** Chiefly the Roman emperor, who at that time was Nero (A.D. 54–68). The king was supreme relative to governors and other rulers. Although Peter did not discuss the origin of kingly authority (cf. Ro 13:1–7), Scripture elsewhere teaches that submission is in order as long as it does not involve violation of God's law (Mt 22:21; Ac 4:19; 5:29). See *WCF* 23.2.
2:16 Live as free men. Submission does not mean a denial of Christian freedom, but it is in fact the act of free people. **not . . . as a cover-up for evil.** Christian freedom must not be used as a license to sin (Gal 5:13; 2Pe 2:19–20). **live as servants of God.** Christian freedom does not involve escape from service; rather, it entails a change of masters (Ro 6:22). See *WCF* 20.3; 20.4; 23.4.
2:17 proper respect to everyone. An exhortation either to recognize the value of each person as an image bearer of God or to respect all those in positions of authority. **fear God.** See note on 1:17. See *WCF* 23.4; *WLC* 126,131; *WSC* 64; *BC* 36.
■ **2:18—3:7** *The Household.* Peter turned to the crucial matter of how Christians are to conduct themselves within their homes.
2:18–20 See *WLC* 127,130.
2:18 Slaves. Literally, "domestic servants." The economy of the ancient world depended on slavery for the performance of many necessary functions. Paul encouraged slaves to seek their freedom by lawful means whenever possible (1Co 7:21–24). Like other New Testament writers, however, Peter did not condemn every form of servitude. Nevertheless, the New Testament requires that slaves be treated with respect and that masters not mistreat them (Eph 6:9; Col 4:1). Furthermore, the spiritual equality of both slave and free within the church community is strongly emphasized (1Co 7:22; 12:13; Gal 3:28; Col 3:11). Such teachings, together with the general Biblical defense of the poor and oppressed (Pr 22:22–23; Lk 6:20–21), the Biblical focus on the dignity of the human race (Ge 1:26–29) and the injunction against kidnapping (Dt 24:7), served to undermine the institution of slavery as it developed in the Western world and led to slavery's eventual demise through civil legislation. See *WLC* 127; *HC* 104.
2:21 To this you were called . . . leaving you an example. Enduring suffering is a part of the Christian's calling in this life (Ro 8:17; 2Ti 3:12), just as it was part of Christ's calling (Jn 15:18–20). This call to suffering and endurance is grounded in the experience and example of Christ in that Christians are united with him both in his sufferings and in his resurrection (2Co 1:5; 4:10; Php 3:10–11). The example of Christ provides a pattern by which Christians are to understand their own lives (vv. 21–22).
2:22 See theological article "The Sinlessness of Jesus" at Hebrews 4.

2:24 [e]Heb 9:28 [f]Ro 6:2 [g]Isa 53:5; Heb 12:13; Jas 5:16
2:25 [h]Isa 53:6 [i]Jn 10:11
3:1 [j]1Pe 2:18 [k]Eph 5:22 [l]1Co 7:16; 9:19
3:3 [m]Isa 3:18-23; 1Ti 2:9
3:4 [n]Ro 7:22
3:5 [o]1Ti 5:5
3:6 [p]Ge 18:12
3:7 [q]Eph 5:25-33
3:8 [r]Ro 12:10 [s]1Pe 5:5
3:9 [t]Ro 12:17 [u]1Pe 2:23 [v]1Pe 2:21 [w]Heb 6:14

our sins[e] in his body on the tree, so that we might die to sins[f] and live for righteousness;
by his wounds you have been healed.[g] 25 For you were like sheep going astray,[h] but now
you have returned to the Shepherd[i] and Overseer of your souls.

Wives and Husbands

3 Wives, in the same way be submissive[j] to your husbands[k] so that, if any of them do
not believe the word, they may be won over[l] without words by the behavior of their
wives, 2 when they see the purity and reverence of your lives. 3 Your beauty should not
come from outward adornment, such as braided hair and the wearing of gold jewelry
and fine clothes.[m] 4 Instead, it should be that of your inner self,[n] the unfading beauty of
a gentle and quiet spirit, which is of great worth in God's sight. 5 For this is the way the
holy women of the past who put their hope in God[o] used to make themselves beautiful.
They were submissive to their own husbands, 6 like Sarah, who obeyed Abraham and
called him her master.[p] You are her daughters if you do what is right and do not give way
to fear.

7 Husbands,[q] in the same way be considerate as you live with your wives, and treat
them with respect as the weaker partner and as heirs with you of the gracious gift of life,
so that nothing will hinder your prayers.

Suffering for Doing Good

8 Finally, all of you, live in harmony with one another; be sympathetic, love as brothers,[r] be compassionate and humble.[s] 9 Do not repay evil with evil[t] or insult with insult,[u]
but with blessing, because to this[v] you were called so that you may inherit a blessing.[w]
10 For,

> "Whoever would love life
> and see good days
> must keep his tongue from evil
> and his lips from deceitful speech.
> 11 He must turn from evil and do good;
> he must seek peace and pursue it.

2:24 bore our sins. See Isaiah 53:12. Christ is more than an example; he is the sin-bearer. As the perfect sacrifice (1:19; 2:22), Jesus suffered the curse of sin, accepted the punishment that our sins deserved and provided forgiveness and freedom from the bondage of sin. **tree.** The cross (Ac 10:39). This Old Testament idiom emphasizes the curse-bearing nature of Christ's death (Dt 21:22–23; Gal 3:13). See *BC* 21,34; *HC* 37.
2:25 now you have returned. This refers to their initial conversion to Christ and suggests redirection of life and new personal attachment. **Shepherd.** Familiar Old Testament imagery for God's care of his covenant people (e.g., Ps 23:1; Eze 34; 37:24) is applied to Christ (5:4; Jn 10:1–18; Heb 13:20; Rev 7:17).
3:1–2 See *WSC* 71; *HC* 86.
3:1 in the same way be submissive. The phrase "in the same way" refers generally back to the examples of Christian submission to the civil government (2:13–17) and to masters (2:18–21), as well as to Christ's submission to the civil authorities who crucified him. It is not intended to equate the wife's submission to the husband with any of these models, but to indicate that similarities exist between these relationships. Note also that the wife's submission to the husband is reciprocated ("in the same way"; v. 7) by the special consideration that he is to give her (Eph 5:21,25). The relationship between men and women involves both spiritual equality (Gal 3:28) and some differentiation in roles and functions in the home and church (Eph 5:22–33; 1Ti 2:8–15). **without words.** In ancient Roman culture, the wife was expected to adopt the religion of her husband, and some of the Christian women in the churches of Asia Minor apparently had unbelieving spouses. Peter urged these Christian wives not to depend primarily on verbal argumentation, which might be seen as insubordination by their already suspicious husbands, but to rely primarily on behavior that could be used by God to support and prepare for the presentation of the truth. The enduring principle involved in this statement is not that women should be utterly silent about their faith before unbelieving husbands (cf. v. 15), but that they should wisely rely more on behavior than on speech to attract their unbelieving spouses to Christ. Similarly, husbands of unbelieving wives would do well to know that godly behavior can sometimes be as or more effective than words in seeking to draw the wife to Christ.
3:3–4 See *WLC* 135.
3:3 hair . . . jewelry . . . clothes. Not a blanket prohibition against adornment, but a warning against preoccupation with outward appearances (1Ti 2:9–10). Excesses in these areas are well attested in the pagan literature and art of the first century. The principle enjoined is that of modesty.
3:6 her master. A conventional Eastern expression of respect and submission (v. 1; Ge 18:12). **daughters.** Those women displaying the same submissive attitude as that of Sarah. **do not give way to fear.** In dealing with unbelieving husbands (see note on v. 1), Christian wives were to maintain their commitment to Christ while at the same time showing proper deference to their husbands. The difficulties involved in doing both could have led in some circumstances to intimidation by the husband and thus to fear by the wife. See *WLC* 127.
3:7 as the weaker partner. Probably refers to the general truth that women have less physical strength than men. There is no reason to suggest that Peter was referring to moral, spiritual or mental abilities. The discrepancy in physical strength provides one reason for the special consideration husbands are to show their wives. **as heirs with you of . . . life.** Fellowship in the faith adds another reason for showing respect. Here Peter assumed that both husband and wife in this situation were Christians (cf. v. 1). Women enjoy full spiritual equality with men (Gal 3:28). **hinder your prayers.** Estrangement from others often affects our relationship with God (Mt 5:23–24). In particular, the failure to observe God's will for the marriage relationship can disrupt a believer's spiritual relationship with God. The importance of healthy family relationships is highlighted by the typological relationship between Christ/church and husband/wife (Eph 5:23–24) and by the persistent New Testament characterization of the church as the "family" or "household" of God, with God as the Father and members of the church as his children (1:14–17; Ro 8:14–17; 1Ti 3:14–15; 5:1–2). See *WCF* 21.6; *WLC* 129,138.
▪ **3:8–12** *Summary.* Peter closed his discussion of relationships with some principles that apply to all interactions.
3:8–12 See *WCF* 19.6; *WLC* 135.
3:8–9 Note the parallel teaching in Romans 12:9–21. See *HC* 107,112.
3:9 Do not repay . . . blessing. Christians are not to retaliate in response to persecution, but are to "bless" their enemies (1Co 4:12; 1Th 5:15). Such blessing may take many forms, including prayer, lending money, and other good deeds (Mt 5:44-46; Lk 6:27,35).

> 12 For the eyes of the Lord are on the righteous
> and his ears are attentive to their prayer,
> but the face of the Lord is against those who do evil."[a][x]

13 Who is going to harm you if you are eager to do good?[y] 14 But even if you should suffer for what is right, you are blessed.[z] "Do not fear what they fear[b]; do not be frightened."[c][a] 15 But in your hearts set apart Christ as Lord. Always be prepared to give an answer[b] to everyone who asks you to give the reason for the hope that you have. But do
this with gentleness and respect, 16 keeping a clear conscience,[c] so that those who speak
maliciously against your good behavior in Christ may be ashamed of their slander.[d] 17 It
is better, if it is God's will,[e] to suffer for doing good[f] than for doing evil. 18 For Christ died
for sins[g] once for all, the righteous for the unrighteous, to bring you to God. He was put
to death in the body[h] but made alive by the Spirit,[i] 19 through whom[d] also he went and
preached to the spirits in prison[j] 20 who disobeyed long ago when God waited patiently
in the days of Noah while the ark was being built.[k] In it only a few people, eight in all,
were saved[l] through water, 21 and this water symbolizes baptism that now saves you[m]
also—not the removal of dirt from the body but the pledge[e] of a good conscience toward
God. It saves you by the resurrection of Jesus Christ,[n] 22 who has gone into heaven and
is at God's right hand[o]—with angels, authorities and powers in submission to him.[p]

Living for God

4 Therefore, since Christ suffered in his body, arm yourselves also with the same attitude, because he who has suffered in his body is done with sin. 2 As a result, he

[a] *12* Psalm 34:12–16 [b] *14* Or *not fear their threats* [c] *14* Isaiah 8:12 [d] *18,19* Or *alive in the spirit, 19through which* [e] *21* Or *response*

3:12 [x]Ps 34:12-16
3:13 [y]Pr 16:7
3:14 [z]1Pe 2:19,20; 4:15,16 [a]Isa 8:12,13
3:15 [b]Col 4:6
3:16 [c]Heb 13:18 [d]1Pe 2:12,15
3:17 [e]1Pe 2:15 [f]1Pe 2:20
3:18 [g]1Pe 2:21 [h]Col 1:22; 1Pe 4:1 [i]1Pe 4:6
3:19 [j]1Pe 4:6
3:20 [k]Ge 6:3,5,13,14 [l]Heb 11:7
3:21 [m]Tit 3:5 [n]1Pe 1:3
3:22 [o]Mk 16:19 [p]Ro 8:38

■ **3:13 5:11** *Christian Suffering and Service.* Peter's exhortation toward humility and harmony in relationships led him to focus on suffering persecution and trouble from others outside the Christian community. His attention to this subject divides into four sections: suffering because of righteousness (3:13–22), suffering for God's glory (4:1–11), suffering with Christ (4:12–19) and elders and young men suffering together (5:1–11)

■ **3:13–22** *Suffering for Righteousness' Sake.* Peter warned that when believers suffer, they should not do so because of sin.

3:13 Who is going to harm you . . . ? Peter was not denying that Christians may suffer for their faith (4:12). This statement may be interpreted either as a truism teaching that mistreatment is less likely if one's behavior is exemplary or, more likely, as a statement that no matter what happens to the Christian, no external force can cause spiritual harm (Ps 56:4; Lk 12:4–7; Ro 8:31–39).

3:14 blessed. Recalls Matthew 5:10–12 and sounds the theme of verses 13–17. Christians who suffer for the truth are blessed by God and will be rewarded by him, even if their immediate circumstances or feelings do not give evidence of such blessing.

3:15 set apart Christ as Lord. Or "regard the Lord Christ as holy." This verse affirms Christ's deity by applying to Christ language from Isaiah 8:13, which speaks of the Lord Almighty as holy. **Always be prepared.** Readiness to confess Christ is an important aspect of regarding Christ the Lord as holy. **answer.** Literally, "apology" or "defense." The word may suggest response to abusive or derisive inquiries from hostile people. Such a response includes an explanation of the main points of Christianity. See *WLC* 112.

3:16 ashamed of their slander. By their conduct Christians show that accusations against them are unfounded (2:12,15).

3:17 if it is God's will. Unjust suffering is within the providence of God and is for the good of his children, as well as for his own glory (1:6–7; 4:19).

3:18 Christ died for sins. Peter appealed to the purpose of Christ's death to justify his call to suffer for doing good. He then diverged from his main argument to offer an elaborate description of what Christ has done (vv. 19–22). **made alive by the Spirit.** See Romans 1:4; 8:9–11. See *WCF* 8.2; 8.7; *BC* 21; *HC* 16,37.

3:19 preached to the spirits in prison. Four main interpretations of verses 19–20 have been promoted. (1) The section refers to preincarnate preaching (i.e., that Christ preached through Noah [cf. 2Pe 2:5] to Noah's wicked contemporaries while they were still alive). He called them to repentance, but they disobeyed and are now imprisoned. The point of Peter's argument would then be the parallel between God's vindication of Noah in a world of unbelievers and his vindication of Christians in similar circumstances. (2) This passage refers to preresurrection preaching (i.e., preaching that occurred between Christ's death and resurrection, during a "descent into hell"). One variation of this view holds that Christ announced his victory and their doom to the spirits of Noah's wicked contemporaries in the place of the dead. (3) Another version of the preresurrection approach holds that Christ proclaimed the same message to fallen angels, who are often identified with the "sons of God" of Genesis 6:2 and 4 (cf. NIV text notes on Job 1:6; 2:1), in their place of confinement. (4) These two verses refer to postresurrection preaching (i.e., Christ proclaimed his victory to fallen angels at the time of his ascension into heaven). The point of the last three interpretations is that just as Jesus was vindicated, so God will vindicate Christians. In no case was Peter suggesting that Christ offered deceased unbelievers an opportunity to receive the gospel and thus be saved.

3:20 See *BC* 27,33.

3:21 water symbolizes baptism. In Noah's physical salvation, God carried him through the waters of the flood (Ge 7:7), prefiguring the waters of baptism and the salvation to which they point. Like baptism, which symbolizes both judgment upon sin in the death of Christ and renewal of life (Ro 6:4), the floodwaters carried out judgment against the wicked and also demonstrated God's salvation for Noah and his family as they passed through the waters. **that now saves you.** Here the emphasis is upon baptism as a sign and seal of God's grace in Jesus Christ. This startling statement that baptism "saves" underscores the close relationship between the sign and the reality it signifies. See *WCF* 27.2; 27.3; 28.6. **not the removal of dirt from the body.** Lest his readers mistakenly attribute a magical or automatic power to the sacrament of baptism, Peter stated that the means of salvation is not the performance of the external rite. Rather, baptism serves as a pledge or response (see NIV text note) of faith, which is, in turn, a means by which God saves believers through identification with Christ in his resurrection (and death, cf. 4:1). See *WCF* 27.3; *WLC* 161,163,167; *WSC* 91; *BC* 34; *HC* 69,72.

3:22 at God's right hand. The place in the universe of supreme privilege and sovereignty (Eph 1:20–23; Heb 1:3). See *WLC* 54.

■ **4:1–11** *Suffering for God's Glory.* Peter returned to his main line of thinking by pointing out that believers who have suffered with Christ should live for the honor of God.

4:1 is done with sin. The preceding reference to baptism (3:21; cf. Ro 6:1–10) indicates that Peter was here referring to the union of believers with Christ in his suffering and death, a union particularly symbolized by baptism (Ro 6:4). Although Christ remained completely sinless (2:22; 2Co 5:21; Heb 4:15), he nonetheless fully identified with sinful humanity by coming "in the likeness of sinful man" (Ro 8:3) and by being subject to temptation, suffering and death (Mk 1:12–13; Heb 2:10; 4:15). Christ "died to sin" (Ro 6:10) in the sense that after his death and resurrection, he was no longer subject to the power of sin and death. See theological article "The Sinlessness of Jesus" at Hebrews 4.

4:2 See *WCF* 22.7.

does not live the rest of his earthly life for evil human desires,[q] but rather for the will of
God. 3For you have spent enough time in the past[r] doing what pagans choose to do—
living in debauchery, lust, drunkenness, orgies, carousing and detestable idolatry. 4They
think it strange that you do not plunge with them into the same flood of dissipation, and
they heap abuse on you.[s] 5But they will have to give account to him who is ready to judge
the living and the dead.[t] 6For this is the reason the gospel was preached even to those
who are now dead,[u] so that they might be judged according to men in regard to the
body, but live according to God in regard to the spirit.
7The end of all things is near.[v] Therefore be clear minded and self-controlled so that
you can pray. 8Above all, love each other deeply,[w] because love covers over a multitude
of sins.[x] 9Offer hospitality to one another without grumbling.[y] 10Each one should use
whatever gift he has received to serve others,[z] faithfully[a] administering God's grace in
its various forms. 11If anyone speaks, he should do it as one speaking the very words of
God. If anyone serves, he should do it with the strength God provides,[b] so that in all

- **4:2** [q]Ro 6:2
- **4:3** [r]Eph 2:2
- **4:4** [s]1Pe 3:16
- **4:5** [t]Ac 10:42; 2Ti 4:1
- **4:6** [u]1Pe 3:19
- **4:7** [v]Ro 13:11
- **4:8** [w]1Pe 1:22 [x]Pr 10:12
- **4:9** [y]Php 2:14
- **4:10** [z]Ro 12:6,7 [a]1Co 4:2
- **4:11** [b]Eph 6:10

4:3 This catalog of sins closely resembles Romans 13:13 and Galatians 5:19–21 and points to the pagan background of most of Peter's audience (1:14,18; see "Introduction: Original Audience"). **debauchery.** Unrestrained indulgence of one's desires, especially for sensual pleasure (Ro 13:13; 2Co 12:21; Eph 4:19). **lust.** Almost always used in the negative sense of evil desire, often relating to sexual immorality. **orgies.** Excessive feasting, often in honor of a pagan god. **carousing.** Drinking parties, often involving excess. See *WLC* 139.

4:4–5 See *WLC* 113; *BC* 37.

4:6 this is the reason. A further development of the basic principle of a universal divine judgment given in verse 5. The reason in question is provided in verse 6. **was preached even to those who are now dead.** Although some connect this preaching with 3:19–20, it is more likely that it is unrelated. The people in question had been members of the Christian communities to which Peter wrote; they had been alive at the time of the preaching but had died by the time Peter wrote this epistle. **be judged . . . in regard to the body.** A probable reference to the physical death of the people in question. Although Christ triumphed over physical death in his death and resurrection (Ro 6:9), the full extent of that victory has not yet been manifested in the lives of God's people. As a result, physical death is still a reality Christians face (Ro 6:5–8). Nevertheless, just as believers now enjoy spiritual renewal through union with Christ, they have full assurance that Christ's victory will be extended to their physical bodies (1Co 15:25–26).

4:7 is near. From a New Testament perspective, the entire period between the resurrection of Christ and his second coming is seen as the "last days" (Ac 2:17; 1Pe 1:20; see note on 1Ti 4:1; see also theological article "The Plan of the Ages" at Heb 7).

4:8 Above all, love each other deeply. See note on 1:22. **love covers . . . sins.** Love keeps no record of wrongs but forgives in response to God's forgiveness (Pr 10:12; Mt 18:21–22; 1Co 13:5; Jas 5:20). See *WLC* 144; *HC* 112.

4:9 hospitality. One of the fruits of love (v. 8). A variety of situations necessitating hospitality may be in view, such as homelessness due to persecution, Christians traveling on business or the needs of itinerant missionaries (Ro 12:13; 3Jn 5–8).

4:10–11 See *BC* 7.

4:10 Each one should use. See Romans 12:3–8 and 1 Corinthians 12:1–27.

The Church: Visible and Invisible: Is Everyone in the Church Saved?

IT has been common in traditional theology to categorize people not only according to eternal destiny (i.e., "elect" and "reprobate"), but also according to historical experience. One way this distinction has been made relates to belief and unbelief within the church: All those who belong to the church as an organization are generally baptized and recognized as members; they constitute the "visible church." All true believers within the visible church constitute the "invisible church."

As the Westminster Confession of Faith puts it, the visible church "consists of all those throughout the world that profess the true religion; and of their children: and is the kingdom of the Lord Jesus Christ, the house and family of God, out of which there is no ordinary possibility of salvation" (*WCF* 25.2). All who make a credible profession of faith in Christ, along with their children, are members of the church, even though many of them may not now or ever be truly regenerated. Put simply, not everyone who attends church is saved (Mt 7:15–27; 12:47–50; 25:1–46; 1Co 5:11–13; 16:22; 1Jn 2:18–19). In fact, within the church it is usually impossible to distinguish true believers from those who merely claim to believe (Mt 13:24–30,36–43). Within the visible church is the group theologians call the invisible church. The invisible church is composed of all true believers throughout the ages, including those who have died (Heb 11:4–40). It "consists of the whole number of the elect, that have been, are, or shall be gathered into one, under Christ the Head thereof; and is the spouse, the body, the fullness of Him that filleth all in all" (*WCF* 25.1). In other words, only those who are truly saved are included in the invisible church. These people are kept safe from judgment and will invariably enjoy eternal life with Christ.

This distinction is important for a number of reasons. For one thing, Christians must be on guard against false teachers and false Christians in the church who would do harm to others by their teachings, actions, words or examples (Mt 7:15; Ac 20:28–31; 1Co 5:6–13; 1Jn 2:18–19). Christians need also to remember that the church itself is a mission field; therefore, it must preach and teach the gospel message in order not only to evangelize unsaved visitors but also to save its members who have not yet come to faith (Dt 6:4–7; Ps 78:5–8; 2Co 5:20). Further, Christians must not become presumptuous regarding their own salvation but must earnestly pursue holiness (Heb 12:14; 2Pe 1:3–10) and fidelity to Christ (1Co 15:2; Heb 3:14; Rev 14:12) in order to prove their faith and persevere to the end (2Co 13:5; Rev 2:7,11,17,26; 3:5,12,21; 21:7).

things God may be praised[c] through Jesus Christ. To him be the glory and the power for
ever and ever. Amen.

Suffering for Being a Christian

12 Dear friends, do not be surprised at the painful trial you are suffering,[d] as though
something strange were happening to you. 13 But rejoice that you participate in the sufferings of Christ, so that you may be overjoyed when his glory is revealed.[e] 14 If you are
insulted because of the name of Christ, you are blessed,[f] for the Spirit of glory and of God
rests on you. 15 If you suffer, it should not be as a murderer or thief or any other kind of
criminal, or even as a meddler. 16 However, if you suffer as a Christian, do not be
ashamed, but praise God that you bear that name.[g] 17 For it is time for judgment to begin with the family of God;[h] and if it begins with us, what will the outcome be for those
who do not obey the gospel of God?[i] 18 And,

> "If it is hard for the righteous to be saved,
> what will become of the ungodly and the sinner?"[a][j]

19 So then, those who suffer according to God's will should commit themselves to their
faithful Creator and continue to do good.

To Elders and Young Men

5 To the elders among you, I appeal as a fellow elder,[k] a witness[l] of Christ's sufferings and one who also will share in the glory to be revealed:[m] 2 Be shepherds of
God's flock[n] that is under your care, serving as overseers—not because you must, but
because you are willing, as God wants you to be; not greedy for money,[o] but eager to
serve; 3 not lording it over[p] those entrusted to you, but being examples[q] to the flock. 4 And
when the Chief Shepherd appears, you will receive the crown of glory[r] that will never
fade away.

4:11 [c]1Co 10:31
4:12 [d]1Pe 1:6,7
4:13 [e]Ro 8:17
4:14 [f]Mt 5:11
4:16 [g]Ac 5:41
4:17 [h]Jer 25:29 [i]2Th 1:8
4:18 [j]Pr 11:31; Lk 23:31
5:1 [k]Ac 11:30 [l]Lk 24:48 [m]1Pe 1:5,7; Rev 1:9
5:2 [n]Jn 21:16 [o]1Ti 3:3
5:3 [p]Eze 34:4 [q]Php 3:17
5:4 [r]1Co 9:25

[a] *18* Prov. 11:31

4:11 very words of God. Peter's concern in this section was that his readers live for the honor of God, as Christ himself did. **God may be praised . . . To him be the glory.** The words of those whose gifts (v. 10) involve speaking (teaching, preaching, evangelism, etc.) are granted by God, so that God receives the glory for the benefits they produce.

■ **4:12–19** *Suffering With Christ.* Having drawn close connections between Christian living and Christ's own life, Peter described Christian suffering as suffering with Christ.

4:13 But rejoice. The same paradox of exultation in suffering is found in 1:6–7. **participate in the sufferings of Christ.** Christians are the body of Christ. They therefore share in Christ's sufferings, not in the sense that they add to Christ's finished work of atonement for sin, but in that his suffering is extended to them because they are identified and united with him during the time between his first and second comings (vv. 14,16; Ro 8:17; Php 1:29; see notes on 2Co 1:5; Col 1:24).

4:14 See *HC* 53.

4:17 time for judgment . . . family of God. Suffering with Christ is one way the visible church is purified (Mal 3:1–5; Heb 12:1–13) and its faith is strengthened (1:6–7). At the judgment, the purification of the church will be finalized by the destruction of all unbelievers within its ranks. True believers in Christ need not fear God's judgment, but many in the visible church have not exercised saving faith (see theological article "The Perseverance and Preservation of Believers" at Php 1). Peter intended his words to inspire faithfulness to God, for the suffering of believers indicated that God was continuing to bring his kingdom on Earth and to refine his church. **what will the outcome be for those who do not obey . . . ?** This rhetorical question assumes that since even those in God's covenant community will be judged, certainly those outside the church will be judged as well. As a result, those who suffer in the church must not turn away from God. Only continued faithfulness to the gospel—even in the midst of suffering—will be rewarded.

4:18 hard for the righteous to be saved. Peter referred to Proverbs 11:31, which uses the terms "righteous" and "ungodly" to distinguish between those who live in basic conformity with the standards of covenant life and those who do not. Peter used this contrast to describe the general difference between the church ("righteous") and those outside the church ("ungodly"). His point was that even those in God's special covenant community are saved only with difficulty. **what will become of the ungodly . . . ?** In reasoning very similar to that found in verse 17, Peter's rhetorical question assumed that if God's special, covenant people are saved only with difficulty, there is no hope, humanly speaking, for those outside the covenant community.

4:19 commit . . . continue to do good. In light of the suffering that occurs even in the church, everyone who professes faith in Christ must persevere in faithful living (see theological article "The Perseverance and Preservation of Believers" at Php 1).

■ **5:1–11** *Elders and Young Men Suffering Together.* Apparently, conflicts had risen between elders and young men in the church as the readers suffered. Peter addressed these matters directly.

5:1 a fellow elder. Although Peter had already mentioned his office as an apostle (1:1), here he stressed his solidarity and shared authority with the leaders of the churches as an encouragement to them.

5:2 shepherds of God's flock. This phrase broadly describes the functions of elders. The shepherd imagery suggests care, protection, discipline and guidance. The word was used in the Old Testament as a metaphor for Israel's leaders (Eze 34) and by Jesus for his own care for the church (Jn 10:1–18; cf. 1Pe 2:25) and for God's gracious initiative with sinners (Lk 15:3–7). Peter's use of the term recalls the confirmation of his own commission (Jn 21:15–17). **serving as overseers.** The noun form of the Greek word translated here "serving as overseers" is *episkopos,* which has traditionally been rendered "bishops" (2:25; Ac 20:28 and NIV text note; Php 1:1; 1Ti 3:1–2). The term "overseer" is used as a synonym for "elder" (Greek, *presbyteros*) in Acts 20:28 (cf. "elders" in Ac 20:17) and Titus 1:7 (cf. "elders" in Tit 1:5; "elder" in Tit 1:6). It implies supervision, direction and guidance (see note on Tit 1:7). **not greedy.** Not a prohibition against fair remuneration but against love of gain and abuse of one's position of trust (1Co 9:14; 1Ti 5:17–18).

5:3 not lording it over . . . but being examples. Peter warned against haughty abuse of power and exhorted his audience to humble service (Mk 10:42–45; Jn 13:1–17; Php 2:5–11; 1Ti 4:12). Here as in 3:1 example is the best way of influencing the behavior of others.

5:4 Chief Shepherd. Christ (2:25). The title brings out the relationship between Christ's pastoral care and work and that of church leaders: They serve as undershepherds who are responsible to the Chief Shepherd.

5:5 [s]Eph 5:21 [t]Pr 3:34; Jas 4:6
5:6 [u]Jas 4:10
5:7 [v]Ps 37:5; Mt 6:25 [w]Heb 13:5
5:8 [x]Job 1:7
5:9 [y]Jas 4:7 [z]Col 2:5 [a]Ac 14:22
5:10 [b]2Co 4:17 [c]2Th 2:17
5:11 [d]Ro 11:36
5:12 [e]2Co 1:19 [f]Heb 13:22
5:13 [g]Ac 12:12
5:14 [h]Ro 16:16 [i]Eph 6:23

[5]Young men, in the same way be submissive[s] to those who are older. All of you, clothe
yourselves with humility toward one another, because,

> "God opposes the proud
> but gives grace to the humble."[a t]

[6]Humble yourselves, therefore, under God's mighty hand, that he may lift you up in due
time.[u] [7]Cast all your anxiety on him[v] because he cares for you.[w]
[8]Be self-controlled and alert. Your enemy the devil prowls around[x] like a roaring lion
looking for someone to devour. [9]Resist him,[y] standing firm in the faith,[z] because you know
that your brothers throughout the world are undergoing the same kind of sufferings.[a]
[10]And the God of all grace, who called you to his eternal glory[b] in Christ, after you
have suffered a little while, will himself restore you and make you strong,[c] firm and
steadfast. [11]To him be the power for ever and ever. Amen.[d]

Final Greetings

[12]With the help of Silas,[b e] whom I regard as a faithful brother, I have written to you
briefly,[f] encouraging you and testifying that this is the true grace of God. Stand fast in it.
[13]She who is in Babylon, chosen together with you, sends you her greetings, and so
does my son Mark.[g] [14]Greet one another with a kiss of love.[h]
Peace[i] to all of you who are in Christ.

[a] *5* Prov. 3:34 [b] *12* Greek *Silvanus*, a variant of *Silas*

5:5–6 See *HC* 94.
5:5 those who are older. Literally, "elders," the same Greek word used in verse 1 in the technical sense of church office holders. Here, as the NIV indicates, the word probably has a more general reference (cf. 1Ti 5:1).
5:7 See *WCF* 12.
5:8–10 See *WLC* 195.
5:8 enemy the devil. The Greek word translated "enemy" or "adversary" was used of an opponent in a lawsuit, and "devil" (Greek, *diabolos*) was used in the Septuagint (the Greek translation of the OT) to translate the Hebrew "Satan," which means "adversary," "slanderer" or "accuser" (Job 1:6–12; Zec 3:1–2; cf. Rev 12:9–10). The phrase reveals the ultimate source behind all persecution. See theological article "Demons" at 1 Co 10. **lion.** The imagery is perhaps borrowed from the Psalms, where the psalmist's enemies and the wicked are so described (e.g., Pss 7:2; 10:9–10). The metaphor conveys the devil's strength and destructiveness and accentuates the need for alertness on the part of believers. Although Christ's death and resurrection have severely limited Satan's power, he has not yet been tamed. See *HC* 127.
5:9 your brothers throughout the world. Peter hoped that his readers would not think of themselves as being alone in their suffering. Before the return of Christ, believers should expect suffering of all kinds throughout the world. Suffering is a certainty for the church (Jn 15:20; 2Ti 3:12).
5:10 God of all grace. As his thoughts turned to the return of Christ and to the great blessings that will come to the church at that time, Peter closed this section with a doxology. **called you to his eternal glory.** The goal of God's eternal and effectual plan for believers is their glorification (Ro 8:28–30; 2Co 4:17; 2Ti 2:10). **in Christ.** All the blessings of God's grace in this life and the next come to the believer through union with Christ. See theological article "Union With Christ" at Galatians 6. See *WLC* 66.
■ **5:12–14** *Final Greetings.* Peter closed his epistle by mentioning several of his friends and offering a blessing to his readers.
5:12 With the help of Silas. Literally, "by Silas," a probable reference to the Silas of Acts 15:40, Paul's companion on his second missionary journey. The phrase "by Silas" does not precisely identify Silas's role. Silas may simply have delivered the epistle, or he may have acted as a secretary, perhaps even helping Peter draft the letter (see "Introduction: Author"). See *BC* 7.
5:13 She . . . in Babylon. Probably a reference to the church in Rome (see "Introduction: Time and Place of Writing"). **my son Mark.** The John Mark of Acts (Ac 12:12,25; 13:5,13; 15:37–39). According to Papias (c. A.D. 60–130), Mark worked closely with Peter and derived much of the information for the Gospel of Mark from the apostle.
5:14 kiss of love. The kiss was, and still is, a common form of greeting in the Near East (Lk 15:20), corresponding to the modern handshake of the Western world. For these Christians, this cultural form was to be an outward sign of their love and unity. Compare Paul's "holy kiss" (Ro 16:16; 1Th 5:26).

2 PETER

Introduction

Overview

Author: The apostle Peter

Purpose: To encourage persecuted and bewildered Christians to stand fast together in their faith

Date: A.D. 65–67

Key Truths:

- Christians should move forward in spiritual growth because of their great blessings in Christ.
- The certainty of Christ's return comes from eyewitnesses of Christ and from the Scriptures.
- God will severely judge false teachers who deny that Christ will return.
- Jesus has not yet come back because God is patient toward his people.
- Christians should be patient but also seek to hasten the day of Christ's return through such means as prayer, obedience and evangelism.

Author

The author of this epistle claimed to be Simon Peter (1:1), and data in the epistle support the claim: The writer referred to his own imminent death in terms that recall Jesus' words to Peter (1:14; cf. Jn 21:18–19), claimed to have been an eyewitness of the transfiguration (1:16–18; cf. Mt 17:1–8; Mk 9:2–13; Lk 9:28–36), and implied a connection between this epistle and 1 Peter (3:1).

Indisputable references to 2 Peter do not appear in first- and early-second-century Christian writings. Origen (c. A.D. 185–254) was the first to explicitly attribute the epistle to Peter, but he recorded that others doubted its authenticity. Eusebius (c. A.D. 265–339) listed it among the disputed books, and Jerome (c. A.D. 342–420), while noting some disagreement regarding its authenticity, suggested that its stylistic differences with 1 Peter were due to Peter's use of different secretaries. The epistle was accepted as authentic and canonical by influential fourth-century church fathers such as Athanasius, Cyril of Jerusalem, Ambrose and Augustine, as well as by the late-fourth-century church councils of Hippo and Carthage, and its subsequent place in the New Testament canon was assured.

Notwithstanding the epistle's own claims, a number of objections have been raised to Petrine authorship. Among the more common objections are the lack of early attestation and slow recognition by the church, stylistic differences from 1 Peter and the apparent use of Greek religious and philosophical language. The usual alternative to the traditional view is pseudepigraphy—the idea that an unknown author wrote 2 Peter and attributed the work to Peter as a literary device to commend his message.

Marked stylistic diversity between 1 and 2 Peter must be admitted. For example, many of the favorite words and expressions in 1 Peter are absent in 2 Peter. The differences are not absolute, however, and several striking similarities do exist between the two epistles. There are also a number of parallels between 2 Peter and Peter's speeches in Acts (e.g., the use of the Greek word *eusebeia* ["godliness"] in both 2 Pe 1:3,6–7; 3:11 and Ac 3:12—a word occurring elsewhere in the New Testament only in Paul's Pastoral Letters). On purely literary grounds, 2 Peter is allied to no other New Testament writing more closely than it is to 1 Peter.

The claim that 2 Peter was falsely attributed to Peter is also weak. Genuine examples of pseudepigraphy in early Christian literature are almost invariably heretical, an indication that the device was used to commend works whose content was suspect. There is strong evidence that the church did not tolerate the practice at all, but in fact strictly rejected it (see 2Th 2:2; 3:17).

The force of these objections should not be exaggerated. None offers conclusive evidence against accepting the epistle's own claim to have come from Peter.

A comparison of 2 Peter and Jude reveals that some connection probably existed between the two books. Although actual verbal agreement is rare (2Pe 2:17; cf. Jude 13), the two books contain similar ideas, words, Old Testament illustrations and order of text (2Pe 2:1–18; cf. Jude 4–16). Several explanations are possible: 2 Peter used Jude (the scholarly consensus), Jude used 2 Peter, or both used a common source unknown to us. In any event, these matters do not significantly touch the question of authorship.

Time and Place of Writing

Peter died in A.D. 67–68, so that time frame marks the latest possible date for the writing of 2 Peter. The reference to his imminent death in 1:12–15 suggests a time near the end of his life. If 3:1 refers to 1 Peter, the date of composition must have been sometime after A.D. 63–64 (see "Introduction to 1 Peter: Time and Place of Writing"). A date between A.D. 65–67 is therefore plausible.

The place of origin of 2 Peter is uncertain. Rome is a likely suggestion, given Peter's location there in 1 Peter (see note on 1Pe 5:13) and the tradition that he was martyred there under Nero.

Original Audience

Unlike 1 Peter, there is little information in this epistle about its recipients. If 3:1 refers to 1 Peter, then Christians in Asia Minor were the recipients of both epistles. However, if 3:1 is not a reference to 1 Peter but to a lost epistle, then there is no firm data to determine Peter's intended audience.

Purpose and Distinctives

Second Peter was written to Christians being threatened by false teaching (2:1). In response to this false teaching, Peter stressed the truth and ethical implications of the gospel.

This false teaching appears to have been an early precursor of Gnosticism, a term designating a variety of heretical movements in the early Christian centuries (especially the second century) that combined ideas from Greek philosophy, oriental mysticism and Christianity. The proto-Gnosticism Peter encountered taught that salvation came through intuitive, esoteric knowledge rather than through faith in Christ.

Because they prized the mind so highly over the body, second-century Gnostics often fell into blatant immorality or rigorous asceticism. Asceticism does not appear to be addressed in 2 Peter, but immorality is clearly rebuked (2:13–19). The false teachers apparently used Christian liberty as a license to sin, especially to commit sexual immorality (2:14). In addition, they were guilty of denying the Lord (2:1), despising authority and celestial beings (2:10) and scoffing at the second coming of Christ (3:3–4).

Outline

I. Salutation (1:1–2)	*Peter greeted his readers with a blessing.*
II. Encouragement Toward Spiritual Growth (1:3–11) A. Christian Privileges (1:3–4) B. Christian Responsibilities (1:5–11)	*Peter encouraged spiritual growth in his readers as they took up their responsibilities, in light of God's mercies toward them in Christ.*
III. True Teaching (1:12–21) A. Peter's Purpose (1:12–15) B. Apostolic Testimony (1:16–18) C. Prophetic Testimony (1:19–21)	*Peter insisted that his teaching about the certainty of Christ's return was supported by his own experience of Christ and by the prophecies of Scripture.*
IV. False Teaching (2:1–22) A. Conduct of False Teachers (2:1–3) B. Judgment Against False Teachers (2:4–10a) C. Denunciation of False Teachers (2:10b–22)	*Peter exposed and condemned the false teachers who had led his readers astray.*
V. Truth About Christ's Return (3:1–16) A. Peter's Purpose Reiterated (3:1–2) B. Certainty of Christ's Return (3:3–10) C. Implications of Christ's Return (3:11–16)	*Peter explained that Jesus' return is certain, even though many claim it will not happen. God has delayed his return because of his patience, but he will not delay forever.*
VI. Conclusion (3:17–18)	*Peter concluded with some exhortations and a blessing.*

1:1 [a]Ro 1:1 [b]1Pe 1:1 [c]Ro 3:21-26 [d]Tit 2:13

1 Simon Peter, a servant[a] and apostle of Jesus Christ,[b]

To those who through the righteousness[c] of our God and Savior Jesus Christ[d] have
received a faith as precious as ours:

1:2 [e]Php 3:8

2 Grace and peace be yours in abundance through the knowledge of God and of
Jesus our Lord.[e]

Making One's Calling and Election Sure

1:3 [f]1Pe 1:5

3 His divine power[f] has given us everything we need for life and godliness through our

■ **1:1–2** *Salutation.* Peter identified himself; designated his recipients as believers and pronounced a blessing on them.

1:1 Simon Peter. Many manuscripts read "Simeon," which is the Aramaic form of "Simon." "Simeon" is used only here and in Acts 15:14 to refer to Simon Peter (see notes on 1Pe 1:1). **apostle.** See note on 2 Corinthians 1:1. **To those.** See note on 3:1. **through the righteousness.** Probably a reference to God's fairness and impartiality in bestowing the gift of faith upon all types of people, rather than a reference to the righteousness of Christ by which Christians are justified (cf. Ro 3:22; 4:6). **God and Savior Jesus Christ.** Since one definite article ("the") governs both "God" and "Savior" in the Greek, this phrase ascribes full divinity to Jesus. **a faith as precious as ours.** Though some interpret "faith" as referring to "the faith" (Jude 3) as a body of belief, it more likely refers to the subjective faith experience of believers. As an apostle writing to those who would live on after his death (vv. 13–15), Peter assured his readers that they were not second-class Christians (cf. Jn 20:29).

1:2 knowledge of God and of Jesus. Knowledge is an important theme in 2 Peter (related words occur 11 times) because the false teachers were preoccupied with esoteric knowledge. Peter affirmed here that knowledge of God and of Jesus are connected because God is known only in and through Jesus Christ (Mt 11:27; Jn 1:18). See *WLC* 194.

knowledge of him who called us[g] by his own glory and goodness. **4**Through these he has
given us his very great and precious promises,[h] so that through them you may participate in the divine nature[i] and escape the corruption in the world caused by evil desires.[j]
5For this very reason, make every effort to add to your faith goodness; and to goodness, knowledge;[k] **6**and to knowledge, self-control;[l] and to self-control, perseverance;
and to perseverance, godliness;[m] **7**and to godliness, brotherly kindness; and to brotherly kindness, love.[n] **8**For if you possess these qualities in increasing measure, they will
keep you from being ineffective and unproductive[o] in your knowledge of our Lord Jesus
Christ. **9**But if anyone does not have them, he is nearsighted and blind,[p] and has forgotten that he has been cleansed from his past sins.[q]
10Therefore, my brothers, be all the more eager to make your calling and election
sure. For if you do these things, you will never fall,[r] **11**and you will receive a rich welcome
into the eternal kingdom of our Lord and Savior Jesus Christ.

Prophecy of Scripture

12So I will always remind you of these things,[s] even though you know them and are
firmly established in the truth you now have. **13**I think it is right to refresh your memory as long as I live in the tent of this body,[t] **14**because I know that I will soon put it aside,[u]
as our Lord Jesus Christ has made clear to me.[v] **15**And I will make every effort to see that
after my departure[w] you will always be able to remember these things.
16We did not follow cleverly invented stories when we told you about the power and
coming of our Lord Jesus Christ, but we were eyewitnesses of his majesty.[x] **17**For he received honor and glory from God the Father when the voice came to him from the Majestic Glory, saying, "This is my Son, whom I love; with him I am well pleased."[a][y] **18**We

1:3 [g]1Th 2:12
1:4 [h]2Co 7:1 [i]Eph 4:24; Heb 12:10; 1Jn 3:2 [j]2Pe 2:18-20
1:5 [k]Col 2:3
1:6 [l]Ac 24:25 [m]ver 3
1:7 [n]1Th 3:12
1:8 [o]Jn 15:2; Tit 3:14
1:9 [p]1Jn 2:11 [q]Eph 5:26
1:10 [r]2Pe 3:17
1:12 [s]Php 3:1; 1Jn 2:21
1:13 [t]2Co 5:1,4
1:14 [u]2Ti 4:6 [v]Jn 21:18, 19
1:15 [w]Lk 9:31
1:16 [x]Mt 17:1-8
1:17 [y]Mt 3:17

[a] *17* Matt. 17:5; Mark 9:7; Luke 9:35

■ **1:3–11** *Encouragement Toward Spiritual Growth.* Peter began his letter with exhortations toward spiritual maturity. His handling of these matters divides into two parts: a brief description of our privileges and blessings (vv. 3–4) and a summary of our responsibilities (vv. 5–11).

■ **1:3–4** *Christian Privileges.* Believers have received wondrous blessings, forming the basis of all spiritual growth, from God in Christ.

1:3 everything we need for life and godliness. The blessings of God in Christ are sufficient for every believer's growth. Chief among these is the Holy Spirit. No one has an excuse for not living for Christ. See *WCF* 16.3.

1:4–5 See *WCF* 18.2.

1:4 participate in the divine nature. Believers are not absorbed into deity, nor do they become divine. Rather, believers receive the Holy Spirit (Ro 8:9–21) and are thereby being conformed to the likeness of Christ in true righteousness (Ro 8:29; Eph 4:24; Col 3:10).

■ **1:5–11** *Christian Responsibilities.* God's mercies toward us lead to responsibilities we are to fulfill out of gratitude for what he has done on our behalf.

1:5–11 See *WCF* 16.2; 16.3; 18.2; *WLC* 113; *HC* 86.

1:5–7 faith . . . love. The order of virtues here is not comprehensive or sequential, as if specific stages of the Christian life were being described (vv. 8–9). The various elements relate to each other in many different ways. Peter here used a rhetorical form known as "sorites," in which a series of elements builds to a climax. It is not uncommon for lists of virtues from early Christian history to begin with "faith" (the starting point of the Christian life) and end with "love" (Ro 5:1–5; cf. 1Co 13:13).

1:8 ineffective and unproductive. Christians should desire to be as effective and productive as possible for the kingdom of God.

1:9 anyone does not have them. Here (and in similar contexts; e.g., 2:20–22) we must remember that Peter was speaking to the visible church, which included many who had not exercised saving faith in Christ. See theological article "The Church: Visible and Invisible" at 1 Peter 4. **nearsighted and blind.** Literally, "blind and nearsighted." The combination of terms here is strange, since the two physical conditions are mutually exclusive. It is probable that Peter simply multiplied related terms for emphasis. The image of blindness is often used to describe the failure to comprehend spiritual truth (Isa 42:19; Jn 9:39–41; 2Co 4:4).

1:10 make your calling and election sure. Literally, "make sure for yourself your calling and election." While God's choice of the elect is firm and certain to himself (Eph 1:4–6), it is not immediately obvious to human beings. Assurance of God's call comes through the internal testimony of the Spirit in our hearts (Gal 4:6) in conjunction with the evidence of his work in our lives (vv. 5–7). See *WCF* 3.8; 17.1; 18.3. **if you do these things . . . the eternal kingdom.** God's promise of salvation is to those with a genuine, persevering faith (Mt 10:22; 24:12–13; Php 2:12–13). True faith that perseveres to the end will inevitably bear fruit (Gal 5:6,19–26) and lead to eternal life in the kingdom of God to come. See theological article "The Perseverance and Preservation of Believers" at Php 1.

■ **1:12–21** *True Teaching.* Peter briefly identified his teaching as the truth of God, in contrast with the false teachings that had entered the churches to whom he wrote. His discussion divides into three parts: his purpose (vv. 12–15), his eyewitness testimony (vv. 16–18) and the confirmation of prophecy (vv. 19–21).

■ **1:12–15** *Peter's Purpose.* Peter declared his intention to remind his readers of the truths they already knew. The context shows that he had in mind primarily his teaching about the return of Christ.

1:13 tent of this body. A phrase emphasizing the transitory nature of human life this side of Christ's return (2Co 5:1,4).

1:15 make every effort. Another reference to Peter's purpose in writing this epistle—the firm establishment of his readers in the truth of the gospel (v. 12). **departure.** Literally, "exodus." Peter viewed his death as a "going out" or "departure" from this life (see note on Lk 9:31).

■ **1:16–18** *Apostolic Testimony.* Peter reminded his readers that he did not invent his message about Jesus' return. He was an eyewitness to the transfiguration of Christ, which foreshadowed the glory of Christ's return.

1:16 We. Peter connected his message with that of the other apostles and presupposed that they all preached the same message. **stories.** Literally, "myths," a word always used in the New Testament in a negative sense and in contrast to the truth of the gospel (1Ti 1:4; 2Ti 4:4). **the power and coming of . . . Christ.** The Greek word translated "coming" is the usual New Testament term for Christ's second coming in glory (Mt 24:27; 1Th 3:13; 2Pe 3:4,12). "Power" is elsewhere associated with Christ's return (Mt 24:30), and the combination here may suggest "coming in power." **eyewitnesses of his majesty.** A reference to Peter's personal presence at Christ's transfiguration (see Mt 17:1–8; Mk 9:2–13; Lk 9:28–35). Peter stressed his apostolic, eyewitness testimony to the transfiguration in order to establish the truth of his message in general and to provide the historical basis for the apostolic expectation of Christ's return in particular. The transfiguration was understood by the apostles to have been a brief glimpse of the divine glory with which Christ will come at his return (Mt 16:27—17:8).

1:17 Majestic Glory. An indirect way, typical of Jewish speech, of referring to God himself.

ourselves heard this voice that came from heaven when we were with him on the sacred
mountain.[z]
19 And we have the word of the prophets made more certain, and you will do well to
pay attention to it, as to a light[a] shining in a dark place, until the day dawns and the
morning star[b] rises in your hearts. 20 Above all, you must understand that no prophecy
of Scripture came about by the prophet's own interpretation. 21 For prophecy never had
its origin in the will of man, but men spoke from God[c] as they were carried along by the
Holy Spirit.[d]

1:18 [z]Mt 17:6
1:19 [a]Ps 119:105 [b]Rev 22:16
1:21 [c]2Ti 3:16 [d]2Sa 23:2; Ac 1:16; 1Pe 1:11

False Teachers and Their Destruction

2 But there were also false prophets[e] among the people, just as there will be false
teachers among you.[f] They will secretly introduce destructive heresies, even denying the sovereign Lord[g] who bought them[h]—bringing swift destruction on themselves.
2 Many will follow their shameful ways and will bring the way of truth into disrepute.
3 In their greed these teachers will exploit you[i] with stories they have made up. Their
condemnation has long been hanging over them, and their destruction has not been
sleeping.
4 For if God did not spare angels when they sinned, but sent them to hell,[a] putting
them into gloomy dungeons[b] to be held for judgment;[j] 5 if he did not spare the ancient
world[k] when he brought the flood on its ungodly people, but protected Noah, a preacher of righteousness, and seven others;[l] 6 if he condemned the cities of Sodom and Gomor-

2:1 [e]Dt 13:1-3 [f]1Ti 4:1 [g]Jude 4 [h]1Co 6:20
2:3 [i]2Co 2:17; 1Th 2:5
2:4 [j]Jude 6; Rev 20:1,2
2:5 [k]2Pe 3:6 [l]Heb 11:7; 1Pe 3:20

a 4 Greek *Tartarus* b 4 Some manuscripts *into chains of darkness*

■ **1:19–21** *Prophetic Testimony* Peter turned to prophecy as testi mony supporting his teaching about Christ's glorious return.
1:19–21 See *WLC* 3,157.
1:19 we have the word of the prophets made more certain. Peter taught that the word of prophecy about the glorious return of Christ was confirmed by the transfiguration as an anticipatory fulfillment of predictions of the second coming. The Greek here is somewhat ambiguous and may also be rendered, "we have more certain the word of prophecy." The latter reading would mean that the prophetic word of Scripture is an even more certain testimony than the admittedly spectacular experience of witnessing the transfiguration. See *BC* 25; *WCF* 1.1; 1.4. **a light shining in a dark place.** The confirmed testimony of the prophets is like a light in a world of darkness, giving hope until the dawning of a new day when Christ returns in glory. **the morning star.** Likely an allusion to Numbers 24:17, a passage that predicted the rise of kingship in Israel and that applies to Jesus, the final and great son of David (Rev 2:28; 22:16). **rises in your hearts.** Peter probably was referring to the effect upon believers of the full revelation that will accompany Christ's actual return. His readers must pay attention to the sure "word of the prophets" until the day when that word will be superseded by the full revelation to come (1Co 13:8–12).
1:20–21 See *WCF* 1.9.
1:20 by the prophet's own interpretation. Although some understand this to refer to the interpretation of Old Testament prophecy by those who read Scripture, both the Greek and the immediate context indicate that Peter was speaking here of the divine origin and reliability of Scripture. Although Peter confronted the faulty interpretations of his opponents (3:16), his concern in this context was to stress the reliability and God-given character of the apostolic and prophetic witness (vv. 16–19,21). Old Testament prophecy often involved both a divinely given dream or vision and a God-given interpretation of that revelation (e.g., Da 8:1–12, 15–26; Zec 1:7–21). In their scoffing at the second coming (3:3–4), Peter's opponents may have argued that the Old Testament prophetic interpretations were not inspired.
1:21 carried along by the Holy Spirit. The Holy Spirit was the source of prophecy, enabling the prophets to speak (and write) as God's spokesmen (2Ti 3:16; 1Pe 1:10–12). Thus the prophecies of Scripture are true, reliable and authoritative. See *WCF* 1.3; 1.4; *BC* 3.
■ **2:1–22** *False Teaching.* Having affirmed the credibility of his own teaching about the return of Christ, Peter discredited the false teaching that had gained acceptance among believers. He touched on three main subjects: the conduct of the false teachers (vv. 1–3), the certainty of judgment against these individuals (vv. 4–10a) and further denunciation of them (vv. 10b–22).
■ **2:1–3** *Conduct of False Teachers.* Peter described what the false teachers had been doing.
2:1 heresies. The Greek term (*hairesis*) originally referred in a neutral sense to groups or sects and was used by Paul of divisive groups ("factions"; Gal 5.20). It soon came to denote the specific teachings of such groups that departed from the truth of the gospel. Here teachings regarding Christian conduct were probably in view—conduct that placed the teachers under eschatological judgment (v. 3). See *WCF* 23.4. **denying the sovereign Lord who bought them.** Peter did not say that those for whom Christ died could actually lose their salvation (Jn 10:28–29; Ro 8:28–39). Instead, the phrase "who bought them" refers to people in the church who had been set apart from the world by the blood of the covenant and joined to the many blessings of the covenant people of God (see Heb 6:4–9; 10:26–29). By teaching and practicing immorality (vv. 2,10,13–15,18–19), they flouted the lordship of Christ and thus belied their own spurious profession of faith (1Jn 2:3–6,19). See theological article "The Church: Visible and Invisible" at 1 Peter 4.
2:2 shameful ways. Incorrigible and reckless sensual indulgence, especially in terms of sexual immorality ("debauchery"; 1Pe 4:3). **disrepute.** Immoral behavior by those who claim to be Christians gives Christianity a bad name among unbelievers. Christians are often urged to practice exemplary behavior so that the cause of the gospel will not be hindered (1Ti 6:1; Tit 2:5,9–10).
2:3 greed. Love of gain and abuse of one's position of trust (1Co 9:14; 1Ti 5:17–18).
■ **2:4–10a** *Judgment Against False Teachers.* Peter made it clear that the false teachers would not be able to escape the judgment of God.
2:4 angels when they sinned. The meaning of this phrase is disputed. Many view this as an allusion to the sin of the "sons of God" in Genesis 6:1–4 (cf. Jude 6). From this perspective, Peter may have been assuming for illustrative purposes the elaboration of the Genesis 6 narrative in the non-canonical book of 1 Enoch (see note on Jude 14). While "sons of God" can refer to angels (e.g., see NIV text notes on Job 1:6; 2:1), this interpretation is not without difficulties (see note on Ge 6:2). Others speculate that this refers to the fall of the evil angels prior to the sin of Adam and Eve in Genesis 3 (see theological article "Demons" at 1 Co 10). Whatever the case, it is clear that if God judged evil angels, he will certainly judge ungodly people as well. See *BC* 12; *WCF* 8.4; 33.1; *WLC* 16,19,88. **sent them to hell.** Translates a verb phrase "cast into *Tartarus*" (see NIV text note). In Greek mythology *Tartarus* was the place of punishment for the departed spirits of the wicked. Just as Paul quoted an apt verse from a pagan writer for his own purposes (cf. Ac 17:28; Tit 1:12), so Peter here used Homeric imagery to convey the idea of a particular place of confinement until final judgment.
2:5 preacher of righteousness. This description of Noah is unique to 2 Peter in Scripture, but it is well known in Jewish tradition. It refers either to Noah's exhortations to righteous living unrecorded in the Old Testament or to his lifestyle that condemned sin and proclaimed righteous living to his contemporaries (Ge 6:9).

rah by burning them to ashes,[m] and made them an example[n] of what is going to happen to the ungodly; 7 and if he rescued Lot,[o] a righteous man, who was distressed by the
filthy lives of lawless men[p] 8 (for that righteous man, living among them day after day,
was tormented in his righteous soul by the lawless deeds he saw and heard)— 9 if this is
so, then the Lord knows how to rescue godly men from trials[q] and to hold the unrighteous for the day of judgment, while continuing their punishment.[a] 10 This is especially
true of those who follow the corrupt desire[r] of the sinful nature[b] and despise authority.
Bold and arrogant, these men are not afraid to slander celestial beings;[s] 11 yet even
angels, although they are stronger and more powerful, do not bring slanderous accusations against such beings in the presence of the Lord.[t] 12 But these men blaspheme in
matters they do not understand. They are like brute beasts, creatures of instinct, born
only to be caught and destroyed, and like beasts they too will perish.[u]
13 They will be paid back with harm for the harm they have done. Their idea of pleasure is to carouse in broad daylight.[v] They are blots and blemishes, reveling in their pleasures while they feast with you.[c][w] 14 With eyes full of adultery, they never stop sinning;
they seduce[x] the unstable; they are experts in greed[y]—an accursed brood![z] 15 They have
left the straight way and wandered off to follow the way of Balaam[a] son of Beor, who
loved the wages of wickedness. 16 But he was rebuked for his wrongdoing by a donkey—
a beast without speech—who spoke with a man's voice and restrained the prophet's
madness.[b]
17 These men are springs without water[c] and mists driven by a storm. Blackest darkness is reserved for them.[d] 18 For they mouth empty, boastful words[e] and, by appealing
to the lustful desires of sinful human nature, they entice people who are just escaping
from those who live in error. 19 They promise them freedom, while they themselves are
slaves of depravity—for a man is a slave to whatever has mastered him.[f] 20 If they have
escaped the corruption of the world by knowing[g] our Lord and Savior Jesus Christ and
are again entangled in it and overcome, they are worse off at the end than they were at
the beginning.[h] 21 It would have been better for them not to have known the way of righ-

2:6 [m]Ge 19:24,25 [n]Nu 26:10; Jude 7
2:7 [o]Ge 19:16 [p]2Pe 3:17
2:9 [q]1Co 10:13
2:10 [r]2Pe 3:3 [s]Jude 8
2:11 [t]Jude 9
2:12 [u]Jude 10
2:13 [v]Ro 13:13 [w]1Co 11:20,21; Jude 12
2:14 [x]ver 18 [y]ver 3 [z]Eph 2:3
2:15 [a]Nu 22:4-20; Jude 11
2:16 [b]Nu 22:21-30
2:17 [c]Jude 12 [d]Jude 13
2:18 [e]Jude 16
2:19 [f]Jn 8:34; Ro 6:16
2:20 [g]2Pe 1:2 [h]Mt 12:45

[a] 9 Or *unrighteous for punishment until the day of judgment* [b] 10 Or *the flesh* [c] 13 Some manuscripts in *their love feasts*

2:7 Lot, a righteous man. A surprising description in view of the portrait of Lot in Genesis (Ge 19:15–16,30–38). Lot's righteousness may have been inferred (either by Peter or by extrabiblical tradition) from Abraham's intercession for the righteous of Sodom and from Lot's subsequent deliverance (Ge 18:23–32; 19:16–17) or from Lot's welcoming of the angels in contrast to the Sodomites, who desired to rape the angelic visitors (Ge 19:1–9).
2:9 if this is so, then. The implication of the three examples in verses 4–8 is clear: God will surely judge the wicked and deliver the righteous. **while continuing their punishment.** Some commentators and most English translations see here a reference to preliminary punishment before the final judgment. While this is the most natural reading of the Greek grammar, many commentators understand the text to mean that God holds the unrighteous for punishment on judgment day (see NIV text note). Because Peter's concern in this passage is the certainty of final judgment, the latter view seems more appropriate to the argument than the former. See *BC* 37; *HC* 128.
▪ **2:10b–22** *Denunciation of False Teachers.* Peter continued to expose and condemn the false teachers.
2:10–11 See *WCF* 23.4.
2:10 slander celestial beings. Literally, "slander glories," a probable reference to angels, either good or evil. The statement in verse 11 that "even angels . . . do not bring slanderous accusations against such beings" (cf. Jude 9–11) indicates that evil angels are in view. When warned of the danger of being "handed over" (1Ti 1:20; cf. 1Co 5:5) to the power of the spiritual forces of evil, the false teachers apparently mocked the power and perhaps even denied the existence of the devil and his demons. Even today, a flippant attitude toward the devil and his power can lead to spiritual danger. See *BC* 36.
2:13 in their pleasures while they feast with you. Peter may have had in mind the love feasts or communal fellowship meals of the churches (see note on Jude 12) and may even have been making a pun on the similar-sounding Greek words for "pleasures" (*apatais*) and "love feasts" (*agapais*). The false teachers had turned the church's communal meals into occasions for self-indulgence. Peter here emphasized the extent of their self-indulgence.
2:14 eyes full of adultery. Literally, "eyes full of an adulterous woman," a vivid portrayal of their insatiable sensuality (see note on v. 2). See *WLC* 139. **seduce the unstable.** The word translated "seduce" is a hunting term and has the meaning "entice" or "ensnare"; it denotes deliberate deception (v. 18; Jas 1:14). In contrast to the "firmly established" believers of 1:12, the "unstable" lacked a firm foundation in the Christian faith and were easy prey to the enticements of the false teachers (v. 18; 3:16). **experts in greed.** An athletic metaphor; literally, "having a heart exercised (or trained) in greed." At least part of their purpose in making disciples was to profit financially from them (vv. 3,15).
2:15 way of Balaam. Both in his greed (Nu 22–24; Jude 11) and in his evil influence on the Israelites (Nu 31:16), Balaam typified the behavior of false teachers.
2:16 a beast without speech. Peter probably intended an ironic contrast with verse 12. While the false teachers resembled "brute beasts" and "creatures of instinct" (v. 12) in their slavery to greed, their prototype (Balaam) was himself rebuked by a beast.
2:17–19 See *BC* 7.
2:17 springs without water. Just as water sustains physical life, so true spiritual teaching nourishes spiritual life (Pr 13:14; Jn 4:13–14)—a vivid image in a culture in which water was a treasured resource. Like the dry well that only disappoints the thirsty (Jer 14:3), the false teachers could only deceive and disappoint. **mists driven by a storm.** Like a mist that is easily dispersed by the wind or threatening storm clouds that provide no refreshing rain (Jude 12), false teaching cannot provide spiritual sustenance.
2:18 entice people who are just escaping. New converts or those not yet well grounded in the faith fall prey to the lure of false teachers (see v. 14 and its note).
2:19 They promise them freedom. The false teachers may have used Paul's declaration that the Christian is not under law (3:16; cf. Gal 3:25; 5:18) as the basis for their mistaken teaching that the Christian is free from the restraint of God's moral law (cf. Ro 6:15–18; 1Co 9:21; Gal 5:13–15). **slaves of depravity.** A profound irony of sin is evident here: The quest for human autonomy from God in all of life inevitably leads only to slavery to sin and self. True freedom from sin involves joyful "slavery" to God (Ro 6:15–18). See *WCF* 20.3.
2:20–22 The false teachers, rather than the "people" of verse 18, are probably in view. These false teachers apparently professed to be Christians, but their return to their old sinful way of life showed that their knowledge of Christ and the way of righteousness was only superficial (see note on v. 1). See *WLC* 151.
2:21 better . . . not to have known the way of righteousness.

2:21 [i]Heb 6:4-6
2:22 [j]Pr 26:11
3:1 [k]2Pe 1:13
3:3 [l]1Ti 4:1 [m]2Pe 2:10; Jude 18
3:4 [n]Isa 5:19; Eze 12:22; Mt 24:48 [o]Mk 10:6
3:5 [p]Ge 1:6,9; Heb 11:3 [q]Ps 24:2
3:6 [r]Ge 7:21,22
3:7 [s]ver 10,12; 2Th 1:7
3:8 [t]Ps 90:4
3:9 [u]Hab 2:3; Heb 10:37 [v]Ro 2:4 [w]1Ti 2:4
3:10 [x]Lk 12:39; 1Th 5:2 [y]Mt 24:35; Rev 21:1

teousness, than to have known it and then to turn their backs on the sacred command
that was passed on to them.[i] 22 Of them the proverbs are true: "A dog returns to its vomit,"[a][j] and, "A sow that is washed goes back to her wallowing in the mud."

The Day of the Lord

3 Dear friends, this is now my second letter to you. I have written both of them as reminders[k] to stimulate you to wholesome thinking. 2 I want you to recall the words
spoken in the past by the holy prophets and the command given by our Lord and Savior through your apostles.
3 First of all, you must understand that in the last days[l] scoffers will come, scoffing and
following their own evil desires.[m] 4 They will say, "Where is this 'coming' he promised?[n]
Ever since our fathers died, everything goes on as it has since the beginning of creation."[o]
5 But they deliberately forget that long ago by God's word[p] the heavens existed and the
earth was formed out of water and by water.[q] 6 By these waters also the world of that time
was deluged and destroyed.[r] 7 By the same word the present heavens and earth are reserved for fire,[s] being kept for the day of judgment and destruction of ungodly men.
8 But do not forget this one thing, dear friends: With the Lord a day is like a thousand
years, and a thousand years are like a day.[t] 9 The Lord is not slow in keeping his promise,[u] as some understand slowness. He is patient[v] with you, not wanting anyone to perish, but everyone to come to repentance.[w]
10 But the day of the Lord will come like a thief.[x] The heavens will disappear with a
roar; the elements will be destroyed by fire, and the earth and everything in it will be laid
bare.[b][y]

[a] *22* Prov. 26:11 [b] *10* Some manuscripts *be burned up*

Deliberate rejection of the truth increases one's responsibility before God (Lk 12:47–48). The phrase "known the way" refers to the fact that they were part of the visible church and understood many aspects of the Christian faith (see theological article "The Church: Visible and Invisible" at 1 Pe 4). Scripture elsewhere teaches that those who are truly regenerate will persevere in the faith (Jn 10:26–30; cf. 1Jn 2:19; see theological article "The Perseverance and Preservation of Believers" at Php 1).

2:22 A dog . . . A sow. Peter likens apostates to a dog and a sow. In neither comparison does the nature of the animal change. In contrast to the modern view of a dog as "man's best friend," the ancient Jews despised the animal (Ex 22:31; Pr 26:11; cf. Rev 22:15). It is no surprise that a dog would be depicted as returning to eat its vomit. Swine were, of course, avoided as unclean (Lev 11:7; Isa 65:4). Even when they are washed on the outside, their first impulse is to return to the filth. Peter's point was that mere religious profession or outward change does not transform a person's heart. The apostasy of the false teachers revealed their true nature.

■ **3:1–16** *Truth About Christ's Return.* Peter turned to a positive presentation of certain teachings regarding the return of Christ. His discussion divides into three parts, in which he reiterated his purpose (vv. 1–2), declared the certainty of Christ's return (vv. 3–10) and explained some of the implications of that return (vv. 11–16).

■ **3:1–2** *Peter's Purpose Reiterated.* Peter revealed his intentions to remind his readers of some basic but crucial Christian teachings.

3:1 second letter. The first letter may well refer to 1 Peter. If so, the recipients of both letters were the same (see "Introduction: Original Audience"). **as reminders to stimulate you to wholesome thinking.** If 1 Peter is in view, the reminder in question was probably Peter's general concern—which is quite evident in both epistles—that his readers live holy lives worthy of the gospel (1Pe 1:13—2:12; 2Pe 2).

3:2 prophets . . . apostles. Peter recalled his discussion in 1:16–21. See *BC* 25.

■ **3:3–10** *Certainty of Christ's Return.* The false teachers called into question whether Jesus would ever return. Peter countered their views in this section.

3:3 the last days. The entire period between the first and second comings of Jesus (Ac 2:17; Heb 1:2). See theological article "The Plan of the Ages" at Hebrews 7. See *WLC* 113.

3:4 this 'coming' he promised? Based on the delay in Christ's return, the false teachers wrongly concluded that he would never come back to judge them. Peter portrayed their arguments as ironic evidence that the last days had in fact already begun (see v. 3 and its note). **since our fathers died.** Perhaps a reference to Old Testament forefathers (Jn 6:31; Ac 3:13), although many interpret this as referring to the deaths of people belonging to the first Christian generation, especially early Christian leaders such as Stephen (Heb 13:7). Whatever the case, the false teachers argued that God had never interrupted history and that we should not therefore expect him to do so in the future in the second coming of Christ.

3:5–6 Against the false teachers' denial that God would intervene in history, Peter cited creation and the flood as prime examples of God's intimate involvement and intervention in the historical process.

3:5 God's word. His creative command (Ge 1:3–30; Ps 33:6; Heb 11:3). God intervened at the very outset of history; the heavens and earth came into existence only at his command. **out of water and by water.** God created the earth by first separating the waters into two major sections (above and under the sky; Ge 1:6–7) and then by gathering together the waters under the sky (Ge 1:9–10).

3:6 world of that time. In this passage, Peter divided world history into three parts: the world at "that time" (creation to the flood), the present heavens and Earth (v. 7) and a new heaven and a new earth (v. 13). His point was that divine intervention occurred at the beginning and in the days of the flood. Therefore, we have no reason to doubt that it will take place again at Christ's return. **was deluged and destroyed.** God also intervened, in judgment, with the flood (2:5; Ge 6:5—8:19).

3:7 By the same word. The same divine word that created the world (v. 5) and brought judgment at the time of the flood (v. 6). Whether manifested by water or fire, the role of God's all-powerful word in creation, the flood and final judgment is stressed. **reserved for fire.** Peter saw Sodom and Gomorrah as the prototype of final, fiery judgment (2:6). Although this picture of an eschatological, cosmic inferno is unique to Peter, the idea of divine judgment by fire is common in the Old Testament (e.g., Dt 32:22; Isa 66:15–16; Mal 4:1) and is found in the New Testament as well (e.g., Mt 3:11–12; 1Co 3:13; 2Th 1:7–8).

3:8 a day . . . a thousand years. This passage and Psalm 90:4 (upon which it is based) are sometimes implausibly cited to support a theory that when a "day" is mentioned in Biblical prophecy, a literal thousand years is meant. But Peter's point was simply to assert God's sovereignty over time and to state that God's viewpoint on time differs radically from the human perspective.

3:9 as some understand slowness. See verse 4. **patient with you . . . everyone to come to repentance.** Peter wanted his Christian readers to realize that the delay of divine judgment was a sign of God's forbearance and mercy toward them, particularly toward the believers in their midst who had been confused and misled by the false teachers. Note that the scope of the word "everyone" (literally, "all") is qualified by the word "you." The repentance in view, for the sake of which God delays judgment, is that of God's people rather than that of the world at large. God is not willing that any of his elect should perish (Jn 10:28–29).

3:10 day of the Lord. The final Lord's day. Although the church celebrated the victory of God weekly on the Lord's Day (Ac 20:7; Rev 1:10), Peter had in mind here the time of divine, eschatological

11 Since everything will be destroyed in this way, what kind of people ought you to be?
You ought to live holy and godly lives 12 as you look forward[z] to the day of God and speed
its coming.[a][a] That day will bring about the destruction of the heavens by fire, and the
elements will melt in the heat.[b] 13 But in keeping with his promise we are looking forward
to a new heaven and a new earth,[c] the home of righteousness.
14 So then, dear friends, since you are looking forward to this, make every effort to
be found spotless, blameless[d] and at peace with him. 15 Bear in mind that our Lord's patience[e] means salvation,[f] just as our dear brother Paul also wrote you with the wisdom
that God gave him.[g] 16 He writes the same way in all his letters, speaking in them of
these matters. His letters contain some things that are hard to understand, which ignorant and unstable[h] people distort, as they do the other Scriptures,[i] to their own destruction.
17 Therefore, dear friends, since you already know this, be on your guard[j] so that you
may not be carried away by the error[k] of lawless men and fall from your secure position.[l]
18 But grow in the grace and knowledge of our Lord and Savior Jesus Christ.[m] To him be
glory both now and forever! Amen.

3:12 [z]1Co 1:7 [a]Ps 50:3 [b]ver 10
3:13 [c]Isa 65:17; 66:22; Rev 21:1
3:14 [d]1Th 3:13
3:15 [e]Ro 2:4 [f]ver 9 [g]Eph 3:3
3:16 [h]2Pe 2:14 [i]ver 2
3:17 [j]1Co 10:12 [k]2Pe 2:18 [l]Rev 2:5
3:18 [m]2Pe 1:11

[a] *12 Or as you wait eagerly for the day of God to come*

intervention and judgment (Isa 13:9–13; 1Th 5:2), when the Lord will destroy all of his enemies and reward his people in one day. See note on 2 Thessalonians 2:2. **like a thief.** A metaphor from Jesus' own teaching (Lk 12:39–40) that conveys the unexpectedness of the event. **The heavens . . . with a roar.** Language reminiscent of the Old Testament and of Jesus' words (Isa 34:4; 64:1–4; Mt 24:29,35). **elements.** Greek, *stoicheia,* a term used for: (1) the elements making up the world (according to the ancients: earth, air, fire and water), (2) heavenly bodies such as the sun, moon and stars; and (3) angelic beings with power over nature. Most interpreters favor the second view here or a combination of the second and the third. **earth . . . laid bare.** The Greek text of this phrase is uncertain. Possible interpretations include: (1) a reference to the earth and human history being "laid bare" before the eye of God's judgment, (2) a reference to the destruction of the earth by fire (see NIV text note) or (3) a statement that the earth and everything in it will be destroyed in an unspecified manner. The strong judicial note in the context favors the first view, though a combination of the first and second is also possible, especially given the common association between judgment and fire (vv. 7,11–14; cf. 1Co 3:13–15). See *BC* 37.

■ **3:11–16** *Implications of Christ's Return.* The certainty of Christ's return was not mere theory for Peter. He immediately turned to some practical implications of the teaching.

3:11 See *WCF* 33.3.

3:12 the day of God. An unusual expression (cf. Rev 16:14), equivalent to "the day of the Lord" (see note on 3:10). The phrases "day of the Lord" and "day of God" used in conjunction with Christ's second coming indicate Peter's high Christology: The coming One is none other than God himself. **speed its coming.** Though sometimes translated "eagerly awaiting," the Greek word here usually has the meaning of "hastening on." The time of Christ's coming is determined by the unchangeable, eternal decree of God, as are all things (Eph 1:11; cf. *WCF* 3.1). Nevertheless, we fall into unbiblical fatalism unless we also look at this event from the viewpoint of the interactions of creaturely second causes in God's providence (cf. *WCF* 5.2). On this level, many factors can speed up or delay the return of Christ. Peter had already explained that God's delay is merciful (see v. 9 and its note), indicating that the salvation of all of the elect is one relevant factor (Mk 13:10). Other factors include prayer (Lk 11:2; Rev 8:3–5; 22:20) and obedience (v. 11). At the return of Christ, final blessings and judgments will come. For this reason, Christians should do everything they can to hasten the coming of that day.

3:13 a new heaven and a new earth. See note on Revelation 21:1.

3:14 See *WCF* 33.3.

3:15 patience means salvation. Rather than despising the delay of Christ's return, we should honor God for his patience. See notes on verses 9 and 12. **wisdom that God gave him.** Tantamount to a claim of divine inspiration for Paul's letters (v. 16; cf. Eph 3:2–5). Paul understood and explained that the consummation of the kingdom was a separate event from the first coming of Christ. This insight came from the Holy Spirit.

3:16 other Scriptures. Peter viewed Paul's letters in the same category as the inspired, authoritative writings of the Old Testament (v. 15; 1:21) and in harmony with Paul's own claims to unique apostolic authority (Ro 1:1; Gal 1:1; 1Th 2:13). See *WCF* 1.7; *WLC* 113.

■ **3:17–18** *Conclusion.* Peter closed his epistle with a final encouragement and a blessing.

3:17 lawless men. False teachers are characterized as people who ignore all moral restraints (cf. 2:7). **fall from your secure position.** That Peter described a fall into error rather than into damnation indicates that "secure position" refers to stable grounding in sound doctrine rather than to salvation, though certainly some false doctrines, namely false gospels, lead ultimately to damnation (v. 16). By contrast, while a proper understanding of the gospel does not guarantee salvation, it is the normal means through which God works to save sinners.

3:18 grow in . . . knowledge. This knowledge is the ever-deepening experience of Christ and understanding of his truth that should characterize the entire course of the believer's life. See *BC* 25. **To him be glory.** A statement presupposing the deity of Christ (1:1; see note on 3:12). It is noteworthy for the direct ascription of glory to Christ (Rev 1:5–6). **forever!** Literally, "unto the day of eternity." Glory belongs to Christ both now and throughout the endless day that will dawn when he comes again (1:19; Isa 60:19–20). See *WCF* 13.3.

1 JOHN

Introduction

Overview

Author: The apostle John

Purpose: To warn against the false teaching that Christ had not actually come in the flesh and to encourage a lifestyle appropriate for followers of the incarnate Christ.

Date: A.D. 85–95

Key Truths:

- Receiving salvation from God results in righteous living, and especially in love for fellow believers.
- Jesus was fully human.
- Many who claim to follow Christ are not true followers.
- Believers must be ready to examine themselves to see whether their faith in Christ is genuine.
- Full assurance of salvation is appropriate for those whose lives give evidence that they are living for Christ.

Author

First John is so similar to the fourth Gospel in style, diction and content that it may almost certainly be attributed to the same author. For this reason, conclusions about the authorship of 1 John depend on the conclusions reached about the author of the fourth Gospel (see "Introduction to John: Author"). While both writings are anonymous, their traditional ascription to John, son of Zebedee, cannot be disproved. The emphasis in the opening verse on authoritative proclamation and eyewitness testimony is most naturally seen as a reflection of John's apostolic calling (Jn 19:35; 20:3–8; 21:24).

Time and Place of Writing

The recognition that 1 John may be John's apostolic legacy passed on near the end of his life (see "Purpose and Distinctives") puts its date in the last two decades of the first century (c. A.D. 85–95). A number of evidences suggest that 1 John was written after the Gospel of John. First, the density of its references to ideas that are unfolded more clearly and fully in the Gospel of John strongly suggests that the author presupposed that the readers were familiar with the Gospel of John. Second, the conflict with Docetism is absent from the Gospel of John and appears to be a later development. Third, the thematic parallels between 1 John and the Gospel of John show another significant difference: There is no hint in 1 John of the conflict with "the Jews" that pervades the first half of the Gospel of John. The Gospel of John reflects the painful separation of the Christian community as the people of God distinct from the Jewish people, but 1 John reflects a period in the life of the church after that separation had become established.

Other indications for a first-century date for 1 John come by comparison with the letters of Ignatius and the letter of Polycarp (all from the second century). These writings reflect a struggle against false teachings that are similar to, but more developed than, those addressed in 1 John. This confirms that 1 John should be dated in the first century.

Original Audience

John probably wrote to a specific group of Christians with whom he had a close relationship, but their precise identity is unknown (see "Purpose and Distinctives").

Purpose and Distinctives

In general terms, 1 John was written to hand down the fruits of a life's work to the next generation. Beyond this, 1 John's specific purpose was to warn and instruct its readers against a false teaching denying that Jesus Christ had come in the flesh (4:2–3). Several forms of this teaching, commonly known as "Docetism," existed in early Christian history. Some Docetists believed that Christ the Savior was a divine spirit that began to inhabit the man Jesus of Nazareth at his baptism but left him just before the crucifixion. Others held that Jesus himself was only a spirit who appeared to be human and to undergo human experiences (e.g., suffering and death). A wide range of additional views also existed between these two extremes.

Some scholars think that this false teaching can be identified more precisely as a variety of Gnosticism, a religious attitude that connected salvation with an experience of individual, esoteric revelation—or more precisely still, as the teaching of the late-first-century teacher Cerinthus. Cerinthus was certainly identified by later writers as both Gnostic and Docetic, but there is little in 1 John to connect the false teaching with the specific ideas attributed to Cerinthus; in fact, there is little to identify the fallacious teaching as Gnostic. Beyond the fact that John was targeting his remarks against Docetism, few details about the controversy are evident.

Although 1 John has traditionally been regarded as a letter, it lacks normal features of that genre (salutation, introductory greeting, final greeting). On the other hand, John addressed the readers as his "dear children" (2:1,13,18,28; 3:7,18; 4:4; 5:21), indicating that he was writing to a specific group of people with whom he had a close relationship. In its basic purposes of admonition and instruction, 1 John is similar to most of the New Testament letters.

It may be better to describe 1 John as John's "testament." It contains the three key elements of a testament: review of the testator's life, ethical exhortation and predictions and warnings about the future (cf. 1Sa 12; Ac 20:18–35). John's review of his life focuses on his faithfulness to his apostolic commission (Ac 20:20–21; 1Jn 1:1–3), and his distinctive use of the present tense draws the act of writing this very book into the review of his ministry (1Jn 1:4). John's exhortations include the admonition to serve the true God and to shun idolatry (1Sa 12:14–15; 1Jn 2:3–5)—especially in the light of the example of Jesus (1Jn 2:6). John highlights confession of sin and the resultant blessings (1Sa 12:10–11; 1Jn 1:9).

Outline

I. Prologue (1:1–4)	*John testified to the reality of Jesus' incarnation, which he had seen firsthand, in the hope that his readers would reaffirm this essential truth of the gospel.*
II. "God Is Light" and Its Moral Implications (1:5—2:2) A. God, the Light (1:5) B. Living in the Light (1:6—2:2) C. Obedience to Commands (2:3–6) D. The New Command (2:7–11) E. Assurances (2:12–14) F. Love for God and the World (2:15–17)	*God is pure light, and those who follow him must be pure like God, following his commandments—especially the commandment of love.*
III. "Jesus Is the Christ" and Its Moral Implications (2:18—3:24) A. Warning About Antichrist Heresy (2:18–27) B. Living as God's Children (2:28—3:24) 1. Pure and Righteous (2:28—3:10) 2. Loving One Another (3:11–24)	*Jesus the Christ was fully man, and those who deny this cardinal truth are antichrists. Those who are children of God must learn to be righteous like God, manifesting their righteousness by their love for one another.*
IV. "Christ Was Flesh" and Its Moral Implications (4:1–21) A. Discerning Spirits (4:1–6) B. Living Out the Incarnation (4:7–12) C. Confidence in the Incarnation (4:13–16a) D. Living in God's Love (4:16b–21)	*Christ was fully human, and anyone who teaches otherwise follows the spirit of antichrist. God demonstrated wondrous love for us in sending his Son to become flesh. We must learn to demonstrate the same kind of love toward each other.*
V. "Jesus Is the Christ" and Its Moral Implications (5:1–5) A. Belief and Rebirth (5:1) B. Loving God's Children (5:2—5:5)	*Experiencing a new birth from God leads to belief in Jesus as the Christ. If we are born of God, we will love others whom he loves.*
VI. The Three Witnesses (5:6–12)	*Three witnesses support John's words in this letter. The water and blood spilled at Jesus' death showed that he was truly human, and the Holy Spirit in John's ministry testified to this fact as well.*
VII. Conclusion (5:13–21)	*By understanding this letter, we may have proper assurance that we have eternal life. We can pray with confidence for others who may stray, and we can be assured of victory over the evil one.*

The Word of Life

1 That which was from the beginning,[a] which we have heard, which we have seen
with our eyes,[b] which we have looked at and our hands have touched[c]—this we
proclaim concerning the Word of life. **2**The life appeared;[d] we have seen it and testify to
it, and we proclaim to you the eternal life, which was with the Father and has appeared
to us. **3**We proclaim to you what we have seen and heard, so that you also may have fellowship with us. And our fellowship is with the Father and with his Son, Jesus Christ.[e]
4We write this[f] to make our[a] joy complete.[g]

Walking in the Light

5This is the message we have heard[h] from him and declare to you: God is light; in him
there is no darkness at all. **6**If we claim to have fellowship with him yet walk in the darkness,[i] we lie and do not live by the truth.[j] **7**But if we walk in the light, as he is in the light,
we have fellowship with one another, and the blood of Jesus, his Son, purifies us from
all[b] sin.[k]
8If we claim to be without sin,[l] we deceive ourselves and the truth is not in us.[m] **9**If
we confess our sins, he is faithful and just and will forgive us our sins[n] and purify us from
all unrighteousness. **10**If we claim we have not sinned, we make him out to be a liar[o] and
his word has no place in our lives.[p]

1:1 [a]Jn 1:2 [b]Jn 1:14; 2Pe 1:16 [c]Jn 20:27
1:2 [d]Jn 1:1-4; 1Ti 3:16
1:3 [e]1Co 1:9
1:4 [f]1Jn 2:1 [g]Jn 3:29
1:5 [h]1Jn 3:11
1:6 [i]2Co 6:14 [j]Jn 3:19-21
1:7 [k]Heb 9:14; Rev 1:5
1:8 [l]Pr 20:9; Jas 3:2 [m]1Jn 2:4
1:9 [n]Ps 32:5; 51:2
1:10 [o]1Jn 5:10 [p]1Jn 2:14

[a] *4* Some manuscripts *your* [b] *7* Or *every*

■ **1:1–4** *Prologue.* John introduced his writing by summing up the important events of his Christian life and ministry. Jesus Christ was the focal point of his life. John was one of the chosen witnesses who were privileged to see, hear and touch someone who had existed from the beginning: the Son of God, whose eternal fellowship with the Father has now been extended to others. The extension of that fellowship occurs by means of the proclamations of John and the other apostles; it is carried on by 1 John itself, which invites its readers to receive and rejoice in that proclamation.
1:1 the beginning. This verse echoes John 1:1 (which in turn echoes Ge 1:1); both passages highlight the incarnation as an event as significant as creation itself, for it is the beginning of the new creation, the re-creation of the heavens and the earth (Isa 65:17; 66:22; 2Co 5:17; Gal 6:15; Rev 21:1). **heard . . . seen . . . looked at . . . touched.** These vivid, sensory verbs defend the reality of the human nature of Christ against the Docetic speculation that Jesus was not fully human (2:22; 4:2–3; see "Introduction: Purpose and Distinctives"). **the Word of life.** The subject of John's proclamation is Jesus the incarnate Word (Jn 1:1,14). John also proclaimed the message about eternal life brought by Jesus. See *BC* 8.
1:3–4 See *WSC* 2.
1:3 seen and heard. These past-tense verbs refer back to similar words in verses 1–2 and emphasize that John's proclamation was about the incarnate Christ. **fellowship with us.** Only through hearing and believing the gospel proclamation was it possible for anyone to have fellowship or commonality with John and the other apostles. Sharing in this fellowship was important because the apostles enjoyed a close relationship with the Father and his Son. Relationship with God's people cannot be separated from relationship with God. Both are possible only through belief in the gospel. See *WCF* 26.1; *HC* 55.
1:4 to make our joy complete. John most likely was referring to himself and his company. Thus far, the readers have been referred to as "you" and "your." It is possible, however, that he had in mind not only his own joy, but also that of his readers. John indicated that, because of what he knew about his readers, he was not yet full of joy. Yet if they would understand, believe and follow his instructions, his joy would be complete. Christians should rejoice in the good of fellow believers, as well as mourn their shortcomings (1Co 12:26–27, 1Th 3:6).
■ **1:5—2:2** *"God Is Light" and Its Moral Implications.* John began to approach the problems facing his readers by drawing attention to the moral holiness of God and the implications of that holiness for believers.
■ **1:5** *God, the Light.* John described God's holiness by equating him with light.
1:5 God is light. These words recall the opening chapter of John's Gospel, in which Jesus is called "the true light" (Jn 1:9) that broke into a world of sin and darkness. Here and in his Gospel, John alluded to the primeval light that broke into the darkness of creation (Ge 1:1–4). In these passages, darkness represents sin and death; light epitomizes goodness and life. **no darkness at all.** Although light is closely associated with the glory of God (see theological article "The Glory of God" at Eze 1), here it is more closely associated with God's moral holiness and the fact that he has no connection with the darkness of evil. God is perfect, wholly without evil, and his people should seek him for that same quality. See *WCF* 3.1.
■ **1:6—2:2** *Living in the Light.* John's statement that God is light laid a foundation for his view that true believers walk in the light of God by striving to be holy, as God is holy.
1:6–7 walk in the darkness . . . walk in the light. John contrasted in absolute terms two diametrically opposed ways of living. The Greek verb translated "walk" suggests that he had in mind regular patterns of life, or consistent lifestyles. Walking in the light does not imply perfection or sinlessness. Everyone sins (vv. 8,10), and even those walking in the light sin when the goals and patterns of their lives stray into paths of darkness. This is why John warned his readers against sin (2:1). True believers are set free from the *dominion* or *domination* of sin, but not from its *influence* (see theological article "Sanctification" at Tit 3). **fellowship with one another, and the blood.** As John emphasized throughout this letter, a right relationship with God through the blood of Christ is closely joined to fellowship with other believers. Those who are forgiven of their sins will live in fellowship and love with others who are forgiven. See *WCF* 18.3.
1:7–10 See *WCF* 6.5; 11.5; *WLC* 77,149; *WSC* 82; *BC* 34; *HC* 1,5, 30,56,72,114.
1:8 claim to be without sin. Probably not a denial of sin as general guilt or an active influence, but the refusal to admit to having committed any sinful acts. John did not have in view Christians who occasionally misconstrue the sinfulness of their actions or deny their sin in order to hide it from others, but unbelievers who see themselves as sinless. **we deceive ourselves.** The Greek suggests an active rejection of the truth rather than simple misconception. **the truth is not in us.** A strong statement that those who deceive themselves in this way are not saved (cf. 2:4; 5:6). In denying their sins they also deny their need for the forgiveness found in Christ, and thus reject the truth of the gospel.
1:9 If we confess . . . forgive . . . purify. When we place our trust in Christ, we are justified and forgiven in the court of heaven (Ro 5:1; 1Jn 2:12; see theological article "Justification and Merit" at Ro 3). In this ultimate sense, the final destiny of true believers does not depend on their confessing sins day by day. Even so, we do not experience the full benefits of our justification in this life. As a result, just as true believers sin, they are in need of the experience of forgiveness from God. We enjoy God's blessing rather than his temporary discipline (Heb 12:5–11) when we readily acknowledge our sins before him. Repeated and unrelenting rebellion against God may indicate that a person does not have saving faith, but those who genuinely trust Christ for salvation will heed John's call for confession. See *WCF* 11.5; 15.6; *HC* 115.
1:10 claim we have not sinned. An explicit denial of having committed sinful acts (cf. v. 8). **his word has no place in our lives.** Another insistence that those who deny their own sins are not saved (cf. v. 8; 2:14). Just as the truth is not in those who deny their sins (v. 8), neither is God's Word. These words warn against any claim that believers are able to live without sin in this life. See *WCF* 6.5; 13.2; *WLC* 77,149; *WSC* 82; *HC* 2,5.

2 My dear children,[q] I write this to you so that you will not sin. But if anybody does
sin, we have one who speaks to the Father in our defense[r]—Jesus Christ, the Righteous One. 2 He is the atoning sacrifice for our sins,[s] and not only for ours but also for[a]
the sins of the whole world.
3 We know that we have come to know him if we obey his commands.[t] 4 The man who
says, "I know him," but does not do what he commands is a liar, and the truth is not in
him.[u] 5 But if anyone obeys his word,[v] God's love[b] is truly made complete in him.[w] This
is how we know we are in him: 6 Whoever claims to live in him must walk as Jesus did.[x]
7 Dear friends, I am not writing you a new command but an old one, which you have
had since the beginning.[y] This old command is the message you have heard. 8 Yet I am
writing you a new command;[z] its truth is seen in him and you, because the darkness is
passing[a] and the true light[b] is already shining.[c]
9 Anyone who claims to be in the light but hates his brother is still in the darkness.
10 Whoever loves his brother lives in the light,[d] and there is nothing in him[c] to make him
stumble. 11 But whoever hates his brother is in the darkness and walks around in the
darkness; he does not know where he is going, because the darkness has blinded
him.[e]

12 I write to you, dear children,
because your sins have been forgiven on account of his name.

2:1 [q]ver 12,13,28 [r]Ro 8:34; Heb 7:25
2:2 [s]Ro 3:25
2:3 [t]Jn 14:15
2:4 [u]1Jn 1:6,8
2:5 [v]Jn 14:21,23 [w]1Jn 4:12
2:6 [x]Mt 11:29; 1Pe 2:21
2:7 [y]1Jn 3:11,23; 2Jn 5,6
2:8 [z]Jn 13:34 [a]Ro 13:12 [b]Jn 1:9 [c]Eph 5:8; 1Th 5:5
2:10 [d]1Jn 3:14
2:11 [e]Jn 12:35

[a] 2 Or *He is the one who turns aside God's wrath, taking away our sins, and not only ours but also* [b] 5 Or *word, love for God* [c] 10 Or *it*

2:1–2 See *WCF* 8.8; 11.5; 18.3; *WLC* 55; *HC* 60,126.
2:1 so that you will not sin. The availability of forgiveness does not remove our obligation to obey God's commands. John's desire that his readers respond to God's mercy by living lives of obedience is pervasive in 1 John (see also 2Jn 4–6 and 3Jn 3–4). His repeated urging of faithful obedience shows his concern for those among whom he had served (cf. 1Sa 12:24). It does not provide any support for the view that the Docetic opponents lived lives of conspicuous immorality. **one who speaks . . . in our defense.** This expression translates one Greek term that is also found in the discourses of John 14–16 as a name for the Holy Spirit. The term has legal connotations that are reflected in the controversy between God and "the world" in John 14–16. In this controversy, the Spirit encourages believers and undertakes to refute "the world" (all those opposed to God; Jn 16:8–14). The Spirit is called "another Counselor" (Jn 14:16) because his work of encouragement and refutation is a continuation of Jesus' own work (Jn 15:18–25). Christ's work defending believers who sin is part of his "session" in heaven (Ro 8:34; see theological article "The Ascension and Session of Jesus" at Heb 8). This work is necessary to the application of forgiveness that believers receive when they confess. See *BC* 23,26; *HC* 49.
2:2 atoning sacrifice. Jesus received God's judgment and wrath against sin in his own person, fully absorbing that judgment by his death (1Pe 2:24). In his session, he continually pleads the cases of sinful believers based on the merit of his sacrifice (see theological article "The Ascension and Session of Jesus" at Heb 8). **for the sins of the whole world.** This does not suggest that Jesus' death atones for every person's sins. Rather, it teaches that he is the only atoning sacrifice available in the whole world—all who seek forgiveness and cleansing through confession of their sins (1:9) must approach God through Jesus (cf. vv. 22–23; 4:15; 5:1–5,12,19). That Jesus is available to everyone in the world prohibits any attitude that would view God's gracious provision as the exclusive property of any particular ethnic group. In his session, Jesus speaks to the Father on behalf of the elect from all parts of the world (see theological article "The Ascension and Session of Jesus" at Heb 8). See John 10:14–16,25–29. See also *HC* 1,37,56.
■ **2:3–6** *Obedience to Commands.* Those who truly know Christ also obey him.
2:3–4 See *WCF* 19.5.
2:3 know . . . know him. John used the same word to mean two different things. If we obey God's commandments, we "know" (in the sense of having confidence) that we "know" (in the sense of personal intimacy) Christ. **obey his commands.** Knowing Christ is the privilege of believers only, and believers obey the Lord (Jn 14:15; Eph 2:10), however imperfectly. See *WCF* 16.2; 18.1; 18.2; *WLC* 80.
2:5 God's love is . . . made complete. It is not entirely clear whether this refers to God's love for us or our love for him. If it refers to our love for him, it is "made complete" by coming to fruition in obedience. If it refers to his love for us, it is "made complete" by producing its intended result: obedience. **we know we are in him.** Obedience to God can come only through the new life believers receive when they are united to Christ; therefore, obedience assures believers of both their union with Christ and of their salvation. See *WCF* 16.2.
2:6 walk as Jesus did. John presumed that his readers had extensive knowledge about Jesus' life and purposes—the kind of knowledge provided by John's Gospel. See "Introduction: Time and Place of Writing."
■ **2:7–11** *The New Command.* John turned to a specific command of God that deeply concerned him throughout this letter: the command to love.
2:7–8 new command . . . old command . . . new command. John recalled Jesus' description of the command "Love one another" as "new" (Jn 13:34). This command is both old and new. It is old because it stems from the Law of Moses (Lev 19:18), but it is new because it has new significance and implications for those living after the first coming of Christ. **new.** Often refers to the age that Jesus inaugurated through his death and resurrection (see theological article "The Plan of the Ages" at Heb 7). Now that believers actually are the body of Christ, joined together into the holy temple of God, the command to love each other takes on new, ultimate significance. The reality of love distinguishes the realm of light from that of darkness, where hatred still rules. John speaks of love for our "brother" (v. 9), which was Jesus' command to the first Christian community (Jn 13:34; 15:17). Jesus drew a sharp contrast between the love that rules within the Christian community and the hatred that the world directs toward Christians (Jn 15:18–19). Love for one another arises from Christ's love for us (Jn 15:12); hatred from others toward Christians stems from their hatred of Christ (Jn 15:18). See *WCF* 19.5.
2:7 beginning. While John sometimes used this word to refer to the beginning of all things (1:1; 2:13–14; possibly 3:18), here he was referring to the beginning of the Christian movement in the life and teaching of Jesus (2:24; 3:11). The coming of Jesus was the critical turning point that ushered in a new epoch, the dawning of a new day (as the next verse shows).
2:9–11 hates his brother. Some within the Christian community are not believers. Their lack of love for Christians is evidence that they also lack love for Christ. See *HC* 106.
■ **2:12–14** *Assurances.* Having called on his readers to commit themselves to the law of love, John paused to assure them of his confidence in them.
2:12–14 children . . . fathers . . . young men. Although it is possible, it is unlikely that John used these terms as references to the biological ages of three different groups. He often used the term "children" to refer to all of his readers (3:7,18; 4:4; 5:21). Several other possibilities exist: (1) He may have been referring to all of his readers with each term. (2) He may have been referring to the spiritual maturity of different groups of his readers. (3) He may have used the term "children" to refer to his whole readership, while "fathers" and "young men" may have been age distinctions within that larger group. See *WLC* 77.
2:12 your sins have been forgiven on account of his name.

[13]I write to you, fathers,
because you have known him who is from the beginning.
I write to you, young men,
because you have overcome the evil one.[f]
I write to you, dear children,
because you have known the Father.
[14]I write to you, fathers,
because you have known him who is from the beginning.
I write to you, young men,
because you are strong,[g]
and the word of God lives in you,[h]
and you have overcome the evil one.[i]

Do Not Love the World

[15]Do not love the world or anything in the world.[j] If anyone loves the world, the love
of the Father is not in him.[k] [16]For everything in the world—the cravings of sinful man,[l]
the lust of his eyes[m] and the boasting of what he has and does—comes not from the Father but from the world. [17]The world and its desires pass away,[n] but the man who does
the will of God lives forever.

Warning Against Antichrists

[18]Dear children, this is the last hour; and as you have heard that the antichrist is coming,[o] even now many antichrists have come.[p] This is how we know it is the last hour.
[19]They went out from us,[q] but they did not really belong to us. For if they had belonged
to us, they would have remained with us; but their going showed that none of them belonged to us.[r]
[20]But you have an anointing[s] from the Holy One,[t] and all of you know the truth.[a][u] [21]I
do not write to you because you do not know the truth, but because you do know it[v] and

2:13 [f]ver 14
2:14 [g]Eph 6:10 [h]Jn 5:38; 1Jn 1:10 [i]ver 13
2:15 [j]Ro 12:2 [k]Jas 4:4
2:16 [l]Ro 13:14 [m]Pr 27:20
2:17 [n]1Co 7:31
2:18 [o]ver 22; 1Jn 4:3; 2Jn 7 [p]1Jn 4:1
2:19 [q]Ac 20:30 [r]1Co 11:19
2:20 [s]2Co 1:21 [t]Mk 1:24 [u]Jn 14:26
2:21 [v]2Pe 1:12; Jude 5

[a] *20* Some manuscripts *and you know all things*

The power of the name of Jesus was central in early Christian proclamations (Ac 2:38; 3:6; 4:12). The name Jesus, which was given to the Savior by God's authority, means "Yahweh saves." God's name belongs rightfully to the Son of God and indicates his divine authority and mission to save his people from their sins (Mt 1:21; Lk 1:31; 2:21).

2:13–14 you have overcome the evil one. The theme of overcoming appears again in 5:3–5, where the victory is over "the world" that opposes God. The kind of victory John described (resistance against temptation and faithfulness to God's word) contrasts with the defeat suffered by the human race at the fall (Ge 3). From John's perspective, "the true light is already shining" (v. 8); therefore, the battle against temptation has already been won (1Jn 5:4).

▪ **2:15–17** *Love for God and the World.* John's focus on love as characteristic of believers' lives raised the issue of love for the world. John insisted that love for God is incompatible with love for the world.

2:15–16 See *WLC* 105.

2:15 love the world. The admonition not to love the world is practical advice as well as a moral demand, for it is already clear that the world is passing away (v. 17). **the world.** Refers here to the system of rebellion and pride that seeks to displace God and his rule. It is this sinful system, not the created order itself, that has already been marked for judgment and destruction (Jn 12:31). But those who are not of the world—those who have received the word of the Father from Jesus (Jn 17:14)—show by their response to that word that they are marked for salvation and eternal life.

2:16 cravings . . . lust . . . boasting. These characteristics of those who love this world reflect a short-term perspective: the desire and intention to be satisfied and honored now (Lk 6:24–26). In contrast, those who love the Father have a long-term perspective and wait for God's reward (Lk 6:20–23). See *WCF* 5.4; *BC* 13.

2:17 the man who does the will of God lives forever. John was not teaching that our obedience merits eternal life. Only the perfect obedience of Jesus is worthy of eternal life, but John was contrasting the fate of the world—and, by implication, of those who love the world—with the destiny of those who love God.

▪ **2:18—3:24** *"Jesus Is the Christ" and Its Moral Implications.* Having explained how the belief that God is light leads to love for God and for our fellow Christians, John turned to another issue that troubled his readers: the influence of those who denied that the man Jesus is the Christ.

▪ **2:18–27** *Warning About Antichrist Heresy.* John openly identified a false teaching that Jesus was not the Christ, and he warned that those who followed this teaching were antichrists.

2:18 the last hour. This terminology is closely associated with the concept of "last days," which the New Testament uses to describe the entire period extending from Christ's first coming to his return (Ac 2:17; 2Ti 3:1; Heb 1:2; 1Pe 1:20). **antichrist . . . many antichrists.** John distinguished "the antichrist" (a single man) from "antichrists" (those who support the antichrist's cause prior to his appearance). Many interpreters associate the antichrist with "the man of lawlessness" (2Th 2:3) and "the beast" (Rev 13:2), but these identifications are difficult to establish with certainty. Apparently, John expected some man (perhaps a religious or political leader) to be so opposed to the church that he would be called the "antichrist." Even so, the false teachers and apostates to whom John referred here were "antichrists" in the sense that the demonic spirit of antichrist was already at work in them because of their opposition to the Christian faith (see 4:3).

2:19 They went out from us. This verse clearly explains how some who profess faith in Christ turn away from that profession and prove that they never had saving faith. Participation in the church does not guarantee salvation (see *WLC* 61; see also theological article "The Church: Visible and Invisible" at 1 Pe 4). Inward apathy or hostility to the gospel may be masked by outward conformity. Apostates reveal such inward hostility through their departure. Their going out to oppose the word of the gospel was, like Judas's going out from the Last Supper (Jn 13:30), a renunciation of the church and its message of salvation. See *WCF* 3.6; 17.2; *BC* 7.

2:20 an anointing from the Holy One. In contrast to the antichrists, believers have been anointed by the Holy Spirit and have had their hearts and minds opened to know the saving truth (see 2:27). The Spirit himself will remain with believers always and protect them from the kind of falsehood that would lead them away from Christ. The Spirit remains wherever the message of the gospel is received, and wherever the Spirit remains, the Son and the Father are present as well (see 2:24). The New Testament reveals that Christ was anointed by God directly with the Holy Spirit to be the consummate prophet, priest and king (Ac 10:38; Heb 1:1–9). In a secondary manner, believers also have prophetic, priestly and kingly responsibilities and are anointed with the Holy Spirit (2Co 1:21–22) for this work. See *WCF* 1.5; *WLC* 4.

because no lie comes from the truth. 22Who is the liar? It is the man who denies that Jesus
is the Christ. Such a man is the antichrist—he denies the Father and the Son.[w] 23No one
who denies the Son has the Father; whoever acknowledges the Son has the Father also.[x]
24See that what you have heard from the beginning remains in you. If it does, you also
will remain in the Son and in the Father.[y] 25And this is what he promised us—even eternal life.
26I am writing these things to you about those who are trying to lead you astray.[z] 27As
for you, the anointing[a] you received from him remains in you, and you do not need anyone to teach you. But as his anointing teaches you about all things and as that anointing is real, not counterfeit—just as it has taught you, remain in him.

Children of God

28And now, dear children,[b] continue in him, so that when he appears[c] we may be
confident[d] and unashamed before him at his coming.[e]
29If you know that he is righteous,[f] you know that everyone who does what is right
has been born of him.
3 How great is the love[g] the Father has lavished on us, that we should be called children
of God![h] And that is what we are! The reason the world does not know us is that it did
not know him.[i] 2Dear friends, now we are children of God, and what we will be has not yet
been made known. But we know that when he appears,[a] we shall be like him,[j] for we shall
see him as he is.[k] 3Everyone who has this hope in him purifies himself,[l] just as he is pure.
4Everyone who sins breaks the law; in fact, sin is lawlessness.[m] 5But you know that
he appeared so that he might take away our sins. And in him is no sin.[n] 6No one who
lives in him keeps on sinning.[o] No one who continues to sin has either seen him[p] or
known him.[q]
7Dear children,[r] do not let anyone lead you astray.[s] He who does what is right is righteous, just as he is righteous.[t] 8He who does what is sinful is of the devil,[u] because the
devil has been sinning from the beginning. The reason the Son of God appeared was to
destroy the devil's work. 9No one who is born of God[v] will continue to sin,[w] because

2:22 [w]2Jn 7
2:23 [x]Jn 8:19; 1Jn 4:15
2:24 [y]Jn 14:23
2:26 [z]2Jn 7
2:27 [a]ver 20
2:28 [b]ver 1 [c]1Jn 3:2 [d]1Jn 4:17 [e]1Th 2:19
2:29 [f]1Jn 3:7
3:1 [g]Jn 3:16 [h]Jn 1:12 [i]Jn 16:3
3:2 [j]Ro 8:29; 2Pe 1:4 [k]2Co 3:18
3:3 [l]2Co 7:1; 2Pe 3:13, 14
3:4 [m]1Jn 5:17
3:5 [n]2Co 5:21
3:6 [o]ver 9 [p]3Jn 11 [q]1Jn 2:4
3:7 [r]1Jn 2:1 [s]1Jn 2:26 [t]1Jn 2:29
3:8 [u]Jn 8:44
3:9 [v]Jn 1:13 [w]1Jn 5:18

[a] 2 *Or when it is made known*

2:22 denies that Jesus is the Christ. The emphasis of this false teaching appears to have been the denial that Jesus (the man) is the Christ (the Savior). The antichrist denies the full humanity of Christ. To separate Christ the Savior from the man Jesus was a hallmark of Docetism (see "Introduction: Purpose and Distinctives").
2:25 eternal life. This is the supreme gift of God that was denied to rebellious Adam and Eve after the fall (Ge 3:22) but awarded to Jesus Christ in response to his obedience (Jn 12:46) and given to us as a free gift by means of faith in Christ (Jn 3:16; 1Jn 5:11,13).
2:27 you do not need anyone to teach you. Believers are enlightened directly by God through the ministry of the Holy Spirit, who illumines the Word and protects them from dangerous deviation from the truth of the gospel. Nonetheless, Christians are obligated to listen receptively to other believers who may admonish and instruct them, for they also have the Spirit. The confusion generated by false teaching is a real danger (4:1–6). **all things.** This is not a promise that the Spirit makes us omniscient. John had in view that the Spirit was instructing his readers about the various false teachings they encountered and specifically about the deceptive claims made by those attempting to lead believers astray (see 2:26). See *WCF* 1.5; 17.2; *WLC* 4,79; *HC* 32.
■ **2:28—3:24** *Living as God's Children.* Having identified the false teachers and their error regarding the full humanity of Christ, John turned to the practical moral implications of the truth of Christ's incarnation by calling on his readers to live as children of God.
■ **2:28—3:10** *Pure and Righteous.* The first implication of being children of God is that believers must strive for purity and righteousness.
2:28 when he appears. Refers to Christ's return. Christians should strive to live in obedience to God to ensure that they need not be ashamed on the day of judgment, when each one will give an account (Ro 14:12). **at his coming.** Refers to the visible and final return of Christ at the end of the age, when he will come back as judge. Those who "continue in him" by continuing to trust in the gospel message (v. 24) need have no fear of condemnation (Jn 3:17–18).
2:29 has been born of him. John introduced the idea of living as God's children by drawing a logical conclusion from the righteous character of God. If God is righteous, then it is impossible for one to have been born of him unless that person does right (1Jn 3:7). If a person has been given new life by God, then that new life will be distinguished by righteousness. Once again, John did not mean perfect sinlessness, but a lifestyle characterized by the sanctifying work of the Spirit.
3:1–11 See *HC* 1,115.
3:1 children of God! All who receive Christ enjoy the wonder of being God's children (see Jn 1:12). See *WLC* 74; *WSC* 34.
3:2–3 we shall be like him . . . purifies himself. Because believers are God's children, they will be glorified like Christ when he returns (Ro 8:29–30). But while believers wait for that day, they must purify themselves from sin's defilement because they realize that God is pure. This theme is very similar to the earlier connection between God as light and believers living in the light (1:5–22). See *WCF* 9.5; 18.3; *WLC* 86,90; *WSC* 38; *HC* 57; *CD* 5.VIII.
3:3 this hope. The promise of Christ's appearing fills believers with confidence, not with apprehension (1Th 4:13–18).
3:4 sin is lawlessness. The basic contrast between light and darkness and between the children of God and those who are of the world is now explained as a contrast between those who obey God's law and those who break it. The moral principles of God's law still apply to believers, even though they are no longer condemned by the law (see theological article "The Three Uses of the Law" at Ps 119). See *WCF* 6.6; *WLC* 24,152; *WSC* 14.
3:5 take away our sins. Jesus took away the curse of sin, but he also removed its mastery over the lives of believers (Ro 6:6–7). As a result, believers may now live lives that are pleasing to God.
3:6 keeps on sinning . . . continues to sin. Literally, "sins . . . sins." This rendering (cf. v. 9) suggests that John had in mind the usual or characteristic behavior of an individual. According to this view, John acknowledged, but did not excuse, the possibility of sin. Several other interpretations have been suggested. For example, John's form of expression may simply indicate what Christians should not do (e.g., "Good citizens do not break traffic laws"). The significance of this interpretation for Christian living is not much different from the first interpretation. A third view, however, argues that John had in mind the specific sin of apostasy (mentioned in 2:19 and possibly alluded to in 5:16–18). If so, John meant that a true believer will not totally abandon his or her faith.
3:8 to destroy the devil's work. The opposition between Christ and Satan was foreshadowed as early as Genesis 3:15. Satan's destructive work used the righteous law of God as a tool to hold sinners captive under the fear of death and condemnation. By suf-

God's seed[x] remains in him; he cannot go on sinning, because he has been born of God.
10 This is how we know who the children of God are and who the children of the devil are:
Anyone who does not do what is right is not a child of God; nor is anyone who does not
love[y] his brother.

Love One Another

11 This is the message you heard[z] from the beginning: We should love one another.[a]
12 Do not be like Cain, who belonged to the evil one and murdered his brother.[b] And why
did he murder him? Because his own actions were evil and his brother's were righteous.
13 Do not be surprised, my brothers, if the world hates you.[c] 14 We know that we have
passed from death to life,[d] because we love our brothers. Anyone who does not love remains in death.[e] 15 Anyone who hates his brother is a murderer,[f] and you know that no
murderer has eternal life in him.[g]

16 This is how we know what love is: Jesus Christ laid down his life for us. And we
ought to lay down our lives for our brothers.[h] 17 If anyone has material possessions and
sees his brother in need but has no pity on him,[i] how can the love of God be in him?[j]
18 Dear children,[k] let us not love with words or tongue but with actions and in truth.[l]
19 This then is how we know that we belong to the truth, and how we set our hearts at
rest in his presence 20 whenever our hearts condemn us. For God is greater than our
hearts, and he knows everything.

21 Dear friends, if our hearts do not condemn us, we have confidence before God[m]
22 and receive from him anything we ask,[n] because we obey his commands and do what
pleases him.[o] 23 And this is his command: to believe[p] in the name of his Son, Jesus Christ,
and to love one another as he commanded us.[q] 24 Those who obey his commands live in
him,[r] and he in them. And this is how we know that he lives in us: We know it by the Spirit he gave us.[s]

Test the Spirits

4 Dear friends, do not believe every spirit, but test the spirits to see whether they are
from God, because many false prophets have gone out into the world.[t] 2 This is how
you can recognize the Spirit of God: Every spirit that acknowledges that Jesus Christ has
come in the flesh[u] is from God,[v] 3 but every spirit that does not acknowledge Jesus is not

3:9 [x]1Pe 1:23
3:10 [y]1Jn 4:8
3:11 [z]1Jn 1:5 [a]Jn 13:34, 35; 2Jn 5
3:12 [b]Ge 4:8
3:13 [c]Jn 15:18,19; 17:14
3:14 [d]Jn 5:24 [e]1Jn 2:9
3:15 [f]Mt 5:21,22; Jn 8:44 [g]Gal 5:20, 21
3:16 [h]Jn 15:13
3:17 [i]Dt 15:7,8 [j]1Jn 4:20
3:18 [k]1Jn 2:1 [l]Eze 33:31; Ro 12:9
3:21 [m]1Jn 5:14
3:22 [n]Mt 7:7 [o]Jn 8:29
3:23 [p]Jn 6:29 [q]Jn 13:34
3:24 [r]1Jn 2:6 [s]1Jn 4:13
4:1 [t]2Pe 2:1; 1Jn 2:18
4:2 [u]Jn 1:14; 1Jn 2:23 [v]1Co 12:3

---

fering the penalty due to sinners under that law, Christ undid Satan's work at its foundation (Heb 2:14–15). See *BC* 13; *HC* 123.
3:9 See *WCF* 17.1; 17.2; 18.4; *WLC* 75,79,81; *CD* 5.III.
3:10 This is how we know. John identified the way of confidently distinguishing between the children of God and those of the devil. His language alluded both to the distinction of Genesis 3:15, where Eve's descendants are contrasted with the descendants of the serpent, and to Jesus' declaration that the Pharisees' father was the devil (Jn 8:44). In the sense of life habits and direction in life, children of God do what is right. **not love his brother.** Mentioning righteous living in general is insufficient. As in numerous expressions in this letter, John's chief concern was to show that righteous living is demonstrated by our love for other Christians. See *WLC* 24.
▪ **3:11–24** *Loving One Another.* Having introduced the idea that children of God will be pure and righteous like God the Father and Christ, John turned to a specific application which he considered important to his readers.
3:11 from the beginning. Probably a reference to Christ's earthly ministry (see 1:1; 2:7). The law of love was not John's invention. **love one another.** The command of Christ, reinforced by his own gift of love (Jn 13:34–35).
3:12 Cain. The history of the world is a story of hatred that reaches back to the archetypal conflict between Cain and Abel (Ge 4:1–16). John traced Cain's hatred to the radical incompatibility of his motivations with those of Abel (Jn 3:19; 8:37). That incompatibility will always exist between the world and God's people (v. 13), but such animosity does not belong in the fellowship of believers. Its absence is tangible evidence that believers "have passed from death to life" (v. 14). But if such animosity should occur in the fellowship, it signifies a tacit rejection of the gospel of Christ (v. 11). See *WLC* 24,113.
3:14–21 See *WCF* 8.7; 18.1; 18.2; 26.1; 26.2; *WLC* 80,136,141,142; *HC* 54,87,106.
3:16–17 laid down his life. Here John revealed one way in which the incarnation is important to the Christian life. Jesus the man loved us so much that he gave his life for us, accepting the painful death of the cross so that we might be saved from eternal destruction (Jn 10:11–15). The love of believers for one another is to be shown in similar practical decisions, even including a willingness to die for one another. John mentioned material assistance as a less costly example (v. 17; cf. Jas 1:27).
3:19 set our hearts at rest. There are times when believers' hearts do not confirm that they are the children of God, even when their lives conform to the teaching of 1 John. John assured his readers that in these cases, they should set their "hearts at rest."
3:20 greater. The word is also used in 4:4, suggesting a real conflict in which God prevails over believers' hearts. The Word of God that acquits believers must prevail over the word of their hearts that condemns them.
3:22 anything we ask. This confidence must be grounded in the awareness that the believer's desires are attuned to God's (1Jn 5:14–15). See *WLC* 104.
3:23 this is his command. The two parts of this command reflect the two parts of the Ten Commandments, reminding believers that their relationship with God takes precedence over their relationship with their neighbor. Faith in Christ rightly orients believers to God and enables them to love one another.
3:24 Those who obey . . . by the Spirit. One aspect of the Holy Spirit's work in believers' hearts is to assure them that they are in Christ. Yet their sense of his assurance must not be divorced from his more objective work of empowering them to obey the truth. See *WCF* 18.1; *WLC* 80; *HC* 76; *CD* 5.V.
▪ **4:1–21** "*Christ Was Flesh*" *and Its Moral Implications.* John turned to yet another doctrinal perspective that had caused trouble for his readers.
▪ **4:1–6** *Discerning Spirits.* John's mention of the Holy Spirit in 3:24 brought to mind the work of other spirits in the church and the way to distinguish those associated with the Holy Spirit from those associated with the spirit of the antichrist.
4:1 every spirit. John mentioned multiple spirits in this passage. He was probably referring to the supernatural forces (angels and demons) that influenced teachers in the church. He wanted his readers to test the spirits because there were many false prophets about (cf. 1Co 12:10; 2Th 2:2). John did not see the problem of false teaching as a merely human affair. He drew attention to the supernatural influences on teachers because he realized that the church is engaged in spiritual warfare (Eph 6:10–11). See *WLC* 105; *BC* 7.
4:2–3 come in the flesh. John chose the most blatant way of

from God. This is the spirit of the antichrist,[w] which you have heard is coming and even
now is already in the world.
[4]You, dear children, are from God and have overcome them, because the one who is
in you[x] is greater than the one who is in the world.[y] [5]They are from the world[z] and therefore speak from the viewpoint of the world, and the world listens to them. [6]We are from
God, and whoever knows God listens to us; but whoever is not from God does not listen
to us.[a] This is how we recognize the Spirit[a] of truth[b] and the spirit of falsehood.

God's Love and Ours

[7]Dear friends, let us love one another,[c] for love comes from God. Everyone who loves

4:3 [w]1Jn 2:22; 2Jn 7
4:4 [x]Ro 8:31 [y]Jn 12:31
4:5 [z]Jn 15:19
4:6 [a]Jn 8:47 [b]Jn 14:17
4:7 [c]1Jn 3:11

[a] 6 Or *spirit*

expressing Jesus' full incarnation by using the word "flesh," a term often associated in the New Testament with the sinful world. Jesus was not sinful, but he became a part of this sinful world order. Although there are other criteria to be considered, the key issue in the situation that John addressed was the perspective of a teacher and his spirit on the incarnation of Christ: Only spirits who affirmed the incarnation were from God. See *BC* 29.
4:3 antichrist. See note on 2:18.
4:4 the one who is in the world. John pointed to the world in its hostility to God as pervaded by the purposes of the devil and therefore in antithesis to the purposes of God (see 2:15–17).
4:6 listens to us . . . does not listen to us. John stated plainly that one distinguishing mark of true Christians is that they submit to the teachings of the apostles. In the early church, false teachers led many to deny the authority of the apostles whom Jesus had appointed. In modern times, similar actions are proposed by those who deny the authority of the summation of the apostles' teaching in the New Testament. Following Christ means following the teachings of the authorities he appointed over the church (see 1Co 14:37). This is one of the crucial tests for distinguishing the work of the Spirit of truth from the spirit of falsehood.
■ **4:7–12** *Living Out the Incarnation.* John turned again to his chief moral concern in this book: love for one another. He built on the truth of the incarnation to provide a model for Christian love.

Divine Love: Does God Love Everyone?

GOD'S love has always played a central role in Reformed theology, but this attribute of his must be properly understood. The statement "God is love" is often explained in rather complex theological terms as a combination of two main ideas. First, the endless life of the triune God is one of mutual affection and honor (Mt 3:17; 17:5; Jn 3:35; 14:31; 16:13–14; 17:1–5,22–26). Second, God made angels and people to glorify their Maker by sharing the joyful give-and-take of this divine life according to their own creaturely mode. But when John asserted that "God is love" (1Jn 4:8), he was thinking primarily of God's love for human beings and specifically of the fact that God through Christ has actually saved us who were formerly lost sinners but who now believe. "This is how God showed his love among us: He sent his one and only Son into the world that we might live through him. This is love: not that we loved God"—we didn't—"but that he loved us and sent his Son as an atoning sacrifice for our sins" (1Jn 4:9–10).

As always in the New Testament, "us" as the objects and beneficiaries of redeeming love means "us who believe" (cf. Ro 8:39; 1Jn 4:13). Neither here nor elsewhere does "we" or "us" refer to each individual belonging to the human race. The New Testament teaching on redemption is particularistic throughout, and when "the world" is said to be loved and redeemed (Jn 3:16–17; 2Co 5:19; 1Jn 2:2), the reference is generally to the great number of God's elect scattered worldwide throughout the ungodly human community (cf. Jn 10:16; 11:51–52). This is not to say that God does not express a certain type of merciful, forbearing love toward all of humankind (Mt 5:44–45), but this love is not sufficient to motivate God to provide Jesus as the mediator and atoning sacrifice on their behalf. Never does the Bible speak of God's redemptive love applying to each and every member of the human race who did, does or will ever exist (cf. Ro 1:7).

This sovereign, redemptive love is one facet of the quality that Scripture calls God's goodness (Ps 100:5; Mk 10:18); that is, the glorious kindness and generosity that touches all his creatures (Ps 145:9,15–16) and that ought to lead all sinners to repentance (Ro 2:4). Other aspects of this goodness are the mercy, or compassion or pity, that shows kindness to persons in distress by rescuing them from trouble (Pss 107; 136), as well as the longsuffering, forbearance and slowness to anger that continue to show kindness toward persons who have persisted in sinning (Ex 34:6; Ps 78:38; Jnh 3:10—4:11; Ro 9:22; 2Pe 3:9). The supreme expression of God's goodness is still, however, the amazing grace and inexpressible love that shows kindness by saving sinners who deserve only condemnation—saving them, moreover, at the tremendous cost of Jesus' death on Calvary (Ro 3:22–24; 5:5–8; 8:32–39; Eph 2:1–10; 3:14–19; 5:25–27).

God's faithfulness to his purposes, promises and people is a further aspect of his love as expressed in goodness and praiseworthiness. Humans lie and break their word; God does neither. Even in the worst of times, it can still be said that "his compassions never fail . . . Great is your faithfulness" (La 3:22–23; see Ps 36:5; cf. Ps 89, especially vv. 1–2,14,24,33,49). Although God's ways of expressing his faithfulness are sometimes unexpected and bewildering—at times looking to the casual observer, and in the short term, more like unfaithfulness—the final testimony of those who walk with God through life's ups and downs is a resounding declaration that "every promise has been fulfilled; not one has failed" (Jos 23:14). God's fidelity, along with the other aspects of his gracious goodness as set forth in his Word, is always solid ground on which to rest our faith and hope.

has been born of God and knows God.[d] [8]Whoever does not love does not know God, because God is love.[e] [9]This is how God showed his love among us: He sent his one and only
Son[a] into the world that we might live through him.[f] [10]This is love: not that we loved God,
but that he loved us[g] and sent his Son as an atoning sacrifice for[b] our sins.[h] [11]Dear
friends, since God so loved us,[i] we also ought to love one another. [12]No one has ever seen
God;[j] but if we love one another, God lives in us and his love is made complete in us.[k]

[13]We know that we live in him and he in us, because he has given us of his Spirit.[l]
[14]And we have seen and testify[m] that the Father has sent his Son to be the Savior of the
world.[n] [15]If anyone acknowledges that Jesus is the Son of God,[o] God lives in him and he
in God. [16]And so we know and rely on the love God has for us.

God is love.[p] Whoever lives in love lives in God, and God in him.[q] [17]In this way, love
is made complete[r] among us so that we will have confidence on the day of judgment, because in this world we are like him. [18]There is no fear in love. But perfect love drives out
fear,[s] because fear has to do with punishment. The one who fears is not made perfect
in love.

[19]We love because he first loved us.[t] [20]If anyone says, "I love God," yet hates his brother,[u] he is a liar.[v] For anyone who does not love his brother, whom he has seen,[w] cannot love God, whom he has not seen.[x] [21]And he has given us this command: Whoever
loves God must also love his brother.[y]

Faith in the Son of God

5 Everyone who believes that Jesus is the Christ[z] is born of God,[a] and everyone who
loves the father loves his child as well.[b] [2]This is how we know that we love the children of God: by loving God and carrying out his commands. [3]This is love for God: to obey

4:7 [d]1Jn 2:4
4:8 [e]ver 7,16
4:9 [f]Jn 3:16,17; 1Jn 5:11
4:10 [g]Ro 5:8,10 [h]1Jn 2:2
4:11 [i]Jn 3:16
4:12 [j]Jn 1:18; 1Ti 6:16 [k]1Jn 2:5
4:13 [l]1Jn 3:24
4:14 [m]Jn 15:27 [n]Jn 3:17
4:15 [o]Ro 10:9
4:16 [p]ver 8 [q]1Jn 3:24
4:17 [r]1Jn 2:5
4:18 [s]Ro 8:15
4:19 [t]ver 10
4:20 [u]1Jn 2:9 [v]1Jn 2:4 [w]1Jn 3:17 [x]ver 12
4:21 [y]Mt 5:43
5:1 [z]1Jn 2:22 [a]Jn 1:13; 1Jn 2:23 [b]Jn 8:42

[a] 9 *Or his only begotten Son* [b] 10 *Or as the one who would turn aside his wrath, taking away*

4:8 God is love. See also 4:16. John's main concern was that his readers understand that God's act of sending his one and only Son into the world (4:9) was the supreme display of love. This act demonstrated such magnificent love that John was able to say that God *is* love, that love is such an integral part of his being that he personifies this quality. Two popular misunderstandings of this verse should be distinguished from John's intention. (1) John did not say, "Love is God" (i.e., that love and God are synonymous or interchangeable in every respect). (2) Nor did John say, "God is *only* love," (i.e., that all of God's other attributes—such as holiness, justice, power or wisdom—are unimportant or null or subcategories of his love). Nevertheless, we fail to understand the praise offered to God in this statement unless we see that John was overwhelmed with the divine love shown in the incarnation of God's Son. See *WCF* 2.1.
4:10 This is love. John argued that human love pales in significance to the love God demonstrated to and for us. **atoning sacrifice.** See note on 2:2. See *BC* 26; *HC* 37; *CD* 1.V.
4:11 we also ought to love. God's love should inspire believers to love each other. So much love has been shown to believers that they must not hesitate to demonstrate love for one another.
4:12 God lives in us. The Spirit of the God who is love lives within Christians. As a result, Christians' lives should be characterized by love for others. Christians love because the One who loves them is in them. God can be seen indirectly in the fruit of love his Spirit produces in Christians.
■ **4:13–16a** *Confidence in the Incarnation.* John assured his readers that they could trust his testimony that Jesus was indeed God in the flesh.
4:13–14 See *BC* 9.
4:13 We know. Probably a reference to John and the other apostles, as in 4:14. **his Spirit.** John knew he was in Christ because of the demonstrations of the Spirit in his life. See *WCF* 18.3; *WLC* 80; *HC* 76.
4:14 we have seen and testify. John's testimony regarding Jesus was secure because he saw Jesus during his earthly ministry. **the Savior of the world.** See note on 2:2.
4:15 Jesus is the Son of God. At least some Docetists maintained that Christ was the Son of God, but that Jesus was merely a human whom Christ the Son of God temporarily inhabited (see "Introduction: Purpose and Distinctives"). John's declaration explicitly denies this teaching.
■ **4:16b–21** *Living in God's Love.* God's love transforms those whom it indwells, creating in them love for God and for others.
4:16 God is love. See note on 4:8. **Whoever lives in love.** John did not mean by this that anyone who loves anything or anyone lives in God. Rather, John had in mind the kind of love he affirmed in 1 John: love within the Christian community. See *WCF* 2.1; *WLC* 80.
4:17 confidence on the day of judgment. Once again John emphasized how very important love is by referring to the final judgment (see 2:28). **we are like him.** Even though they are not like Christ in terms of the completeness of their obedience, believers are like him in their basic orientation, and they stand out as Christ did in contrast to the world at large (Jn 5:44; 17:16). See *BC* 37.
4:18 not made perfect in love. God's love is perfect in itself, and it is thus implicitly perfect (complete) when believers receive it (2:5; 4:12,17). Christians themselves, however, are made perfect (complete) in God's love over time (3:2). Even so, remnants of fear may temporarily coexist with love. "Perfect love" from God "drives out fear" gradually rather than instantaneously. See *WCF* 20.1.
4:20 If anyone says. John anticipated an objection to his emphasis on love among believers. Some might say that they love God despite the fact that they do not love one another. John utterly denied this possibility. His opponents failed to see that loving the invisible God is much more difficult than loving visible people. A believer's love for God inevitably overflows into love for other people. John claimed here that love for people is an essential proof of love for God.
4:21 loves God must also love his brother. John alluded to Jesus' teaching that the greatest commandment must be coupled with the second greatest commandment (see note on Mt 22:38–39). The two commands are inseparable. Proper love for others flows from love for God; love for God is evidenced by love for others.
■ **5:1–5** *"Jesus Is the Christ" and Its Moral Implications.* John returned to the doctrinal affirmations that Jesus is the Christ and the Son of God to stress the results of these beliefs in the lives of Christians.
■ **5:1** *Belief and Rebirth.* Belief that Jesus is the Christ leads to a rebirth that draws believers invariably into love for God's other children.
5:1 Jesus is the Christ. See 2:22. **born of God.** Here John referred to Jesus' teaching about rebirth from above, as John had recorded it earlier in his Gospel (Jn 3:1–18,31). **who loves the father loves his child as well.** Following the analogy of birth and parentage, John remarked that those born of God love him as their father. Moreover, if believers love God as their father, then they will love God's other children, whom he loves.
■ **5:2—5:5** *Loving God's Children.* Believers express love for God and for his children by obeying his commands.
5:2 we know that we love. Love for God's people must be clearly defined. John did this in terms of obedience to the commands of God. All of God's commands were designed to give proper honor to God and to his people. Therefore, believers are not left to speculate as to what it means to love others. Following the commands

his commands.[c] And his commands are not burdensome,[d] 4for everyone born of God
overcomes[e] the world. This is the victory that has overcome the world, even our faith.
5Who is it that overcomes the world? Only he who believes that Jesus is the Son of God.
6This is the one who came by water and blood[f]—Jesus Christ. He did not come by water only, but by water and blood. And it is the Spirit who testifies, because the Spirit is
the truth.[g] 7For there are three[h] that testify: 8the[a] Spirit, the water and the blood; and
the three are in agreement. 9We accept man's testimony,[i] but God's testimony is greater because it is the testimony of God,[j] which he has given about his Son. 10Anyone who
believes in the Son of God has this testimony in his heart.[k] Anyone who does not believe
God has made him out to be a liar,[l] because he has not believed the testimony God has
given about his Son. 11And this is the testimony: God has given us eternal life, and this
life is in his Son.[m] 12He who has the Son has life; he who does not have the Son of God
does not have life.[n]

Concluding Remarks

13I write these things to you who believe in the name of the Son of God[o] so that you
may know that you have eternal life.[p] 14This is the confidence[q] we have in approaching
God: that if we ask anything according to his will, he hears us.[r] 15And if we know that
he hears us—whatever we ask—we know[s] that we have what we asked of him.
16If anyone sees his brother commit a sin that does not lead to death, he should pray
and God will give him life.[t] I refer to those whose sin does not lead to death. There is a
sin that leads to death.[u] I am not saying that he should pray about that.[v] 17All wrongdoing is sin,[w] and there is sin that does not lead to death.[x]

5:3 [c]Jn 14:15; 2Jn 6 [d]Mt 11:30
5:4 [e]Jn 16:33
5:6 [f]Jn 19:34 [g]Jn 14:17
5:7 [h]Mt 18:16
5:9 [i]Jn 5:34 [j]Mt 3:16, 17; Jn 8:17,18
5:10 [k]Ro 8:16; Gal 4:6 [l]Jn 3:33
5:11 [m]Jn 1:4; 1Jn 2:25
5:12 [n]Jn 3:15,16,36
5:13 [o]1Jn 3:23 [p]Jn 20:31; 1Jn 1:1,2
5:14 [q]1Jn 3:21 [r]Mt 7:7
5:15 [s]ver 18,19,20
5:16 [t]Jas 5:15 [u]Heb 6:4-6; 10:26 [v]Jer 7:16
5:17 [w]1Jn 3:4 [x]1Jn 2:1

[a] *7,8* Late manuscripts of the Vulgate *testify in heaven: the Father, the Word and the Holy Spirit, and these three are one. 8And there are three that testify on earth: the* (not found in any Greek manuscript before the fourteenth century)

---

of God (e.g., keeping the Sabbath, not stealing, and so forth) is the sure way to demonstrate love for others.
5:4–5 See *WCF* 14.3.
5:4 overcomes the world? See note on 2:12–14. See *WCF* 13.3.
5:5 Son of God. See 4:15. See also *BC* 10.
■ **5:6–12** *The Three Witnesses.* John turned to a lengthy declaration of the witnesses that support the claims he made in his letter.
5:6 came by. Or possibly "came through." The meaning of this phrase depends largely on the meaning of "water and blood." It is capable of many nuances, including but not limited to "endured," "experienced" and "arrived by way of." **water and blood.** There are a number of interpretations of these words, and none is without difficulty. Some suggest that they refer to Jesus' baptism and crucifixion, which would make sense as a refutation of those Docetists who believed that the Christ was with Jesus in his baptism but not in his crucifixion (see "Introduction: Purpose and Distinctives"). The use of the compound name "Jesus Christ" also adds to this interpretation as a denial that Jesus and the Christ are separate entities. Against this view are the facts that John in his Gospel did not recount the baptism of Jesus and that "water" as a reference to baptism is somewhat vague. Others suggest that "water and blood" refer to the two sacraments of the New Testament: baptism and the Lord's Supper. This view is lacking in that John did not mention these rites in his letter or record their institution in his Gospel, and that neither "water" nor "blood" is a clear reference to the sacraments. It does, however provide a good explanation for why "water" and "blood" would be said to "testify" (vv. 7–8), since both baptism and the Lord's Supper visibly proclaim the gospel of Christ. Others believe that this saying reflects John 19:34. A key theme in John's Gospel is the testimony God bears to Jesus, his Son. The blood and water that flowed from Jesus' side after his death attested to the reality of his death; Jesus' wounded side later confirmed the reality of his bodily resurrection (Jn 20:20,25–27). In favor of this view is that John 19:34 uses both the words "water" and "blood" and that these elements can be reasonably understood as testifying to Jesus humanity and against John's opponents, who denied the true humanity of Christ (4:2). One weakness of this view is that John's emphasis on blood as a distinct element from water is not as clearly meaningful except as an additional witness to fulfill the number required by law. **the Spirit who testifies.** See 4:13. See also *BC* 34.
5:7–8 See NIV text note.
5:7-8 For there are three that testify. Old Testament law required two or three witnesses to convict a person of a crime (Dt 17:6; 19:15). John referred to three witnesses to the full humanity of Jesus. The blood and water that flowed from Jesus' pierced side when he was on the cross (see v. 6) each testified to the fact that Jesus was a man. The agency of the Spirit in the apostles' ministries also confirmed the message that Jesus was God incarnate (see v. 6). See *WCF* 2.3; *WLC* 6,9; *WSC* 6; *BC* 9,34.
5:9 God's testimony is greater. By appealing directly to God as witness, John, like Jesus, overruled all human disputes (Jn 6:33–40). See *WCF* 1.4.
5:10–12 See *WCF* 14.2; *WLC* 32; *BC* 21; *HC* 61.
5:11 eternal life . . . in his Son. The Son is both alive and the source of life for believers (cf. Gal 2:20).
5:12 does not have life. John maintained that salvation cannot be found apart from faith in Jesus as the Son of God. See *WCF* 10.3.
■ **5:13–21** *Conclusion.* John closed his letter with several summaries and some final instructions.
5:13–15 See *WCF* 21.3; 21.4; *WLC* 180,184,186; *WSC* 98,99; *BC* 12; *HC* 117.
5:13 so that you may know. John's Gospel was written to move readers to faith in Jesus (Jn 20:31); 1 John was written to give believers the ability to find assurance of their salvation. See *WCF* 18.1; 18.3; *WLC* 80,172; *WSC* 36.
5:16–18 See *CD* 5.IV.
5:16 he should pray. Four convictions combine to motivate such petitions. (1) Children of God and sinners are mutually exclusive categories (v. 18). Believers pray that their fellow believers will leave the path of sin. (2) Everyone either belongs to God or is, with the world at large, in the grip of the devil (v. 19). Believers pray that God will keep them out of the devil's hands. (3) The Son of God has come with the Good News that the true God offers eternal life (v. 20). Believers pray that this Good News will free their brothers and sisters from sin. The true God is the One who has sent his Son to free people from sin and from the evil one. (4) Jesus is the only Savior in the world (2:2). Any promise of another way of freedom or any pretense that such freedom is impossible amounts to idolatry (v. 21)—the substitution of a false god for the true God. **sin that leads to death.** Some connect this sin with the unforgivable sin mentioned in Matthew 12:31–32 (see also Mk 3:28–39; Lk 12:10; see theological article "Blasphemy Against the Holy Spirit" at Mk 3). It is more likely that John was referring to a stubborn refusal to accept the message of the gospel, as in John 8:24 (see note on 1:8). John distinguished between "sin that leads to death" and "sin that does not lead to death." For those who have not renounced the way of faith and love altogether, we can pray with assurance that God will restore them, but for those who have renounced that way, we cannot pray with such assurance. Some have also suggested that this refers to a sin that leads to the punishment of physical death, such as the flagrant violation of the Lord's Supper (1Co 11:30). See *WCF* 21.4; *WLC* 150,183; *WSC* 83.

5:18 [y]Jn 14:30
5:19 [z]1Jn 4:6 [a]Gal 1:4
5:20 [b]Lk 24:45 [c]Jn 17:3 [d]ver 11
5:21 [e]1Co 10:14; 1Th 1:9

18 We know that anyone born of God does not continue to sin; the one who was born
of God keeps him safe, and the evil one cannot harm him.[y] **19** We know that we are children of God,[z] and that the whole world is under the control of the evil one.[a] **20** We know
also that the Son of God has come and has given us understanding,[b] so that we may
know him who is true.[c] And we are in him who is true—even in his Son Jesus Christ. He
is the true God and eternal life.[d]
21 Dear children, keep yourselves from idols.[e]

5:18 does not continue to sin. See note on 3:6.
5:19 the control of the evil one. The devil has captured the human race by temptation (see notes on 3:8; 4:4), and no one can escape the cycle of temptation, sin and condemnation without divine aid. However, there can be no evasion of responsibility by blaming the evil one (Ge 3:13), for the enslavement to sin is fully voluntary (Jas 1:13–15). Only the Son of God can break this cycle and replace it with one of forgiveness, gratitude and obedience (3:8).
5:20 him who is true. The Father is referred to as the One "who is true," whose Son is Jesus Christ. This suggests that "the true God" also refers to the Father, although grammatically this could refer to the Son. See *WCF* 8.2; *WLC* 11; *HC* 35.
5:21 See *HC* 94.

2 JOHN

Introduction

Overview

Author: The apostle John

Purpose: To warn against the false teaching that Christ had not actually come in the flesh and to encourage hospitality toward preachers of the true gospel.

Date: A.D. 85–95

Key Truths:

- Love among Christians is a central moral concern for followers of Christ.
- Denying the full incarnation of Christ leads to the judgment of God.

Author

The style, diction and content of 2 John strongly suggest that the letter was written by the same person who wrote 1 John and the Gospel of John. This author has been traditionally identified as the apostle John, the son of Zebedee, and no more plausible ascription has been proposed. See "Introduction to John: Author."

Time and Place of Writing

Several parallels between passages in this letter and verses in both 1 John and the Gospel of John (e.g., v. 7 with 1Jn 4:2–3; v. 5 with Jn 13:34 and 1Jn 2:7) hint that all these works may have been written at approximately the same time: A.D. 85–95.

Original Audience

John wrote to a Christian woman and her family—either her natural family or the fellowship of believers associated with her.

Purpose and Distinctives

Second John was written to warn against the same strain of false teaching that 1 John opposed (see "Introduction to 1 John: Purpose and Distinctives"). It was probably written at about the same time, in the last two decades of the first century (c. A.D. 85–95). While it repeats ideas from 1 John, it does not presuppose that its readers had prior knowledge of 1 John or its contents.

Second John has the typical characteristics of a letter: a salutation, introductory greeting and final greeting. Like the early epistles of Paul, it is a letter of encouragement and warning to a specific fellowship for which the author felt pastoral responsibility.

Outline

I. Salutation and Greeting (1–3)	*John greeted the woman to whom he wrote and blessed her and her associates.*
II. Commendation (4)	*John commended believers for their faithfulness.*
III. Exhortation to Love (5–6)	*John exhorted believers to follow the old command to love.*
IV. Warning Against False Teaching (7–11)	*John warned against following the false teaching that denied the full incarnation of Christ.*
V. Closing Remarks and Farewell (12–13)	*John closed his letter with final greetings.*

1 The elder,[a]
To the chosen[b] lady and her children, whom I love in the truth—and not I only, but
also all who know the truth[c]— **2** because of the truth,[d] which lives in us[e] and will be with
us forever:
3 Grace, mercy and peace from God the Father and from Jesus Christ,[f] the Father's
Son, will be with us in truth and love.
4 It has given me great joy to find some of your children walking in the truth,[g] just as
the Father commanded us. **5** And now, dear lady, I am not writing you a new command
but one we have had from the beginning.[h] I ask that we love one another. **6** And this is
love:[i] that we walk in obedience to his commands. As you have heard from the beginning, his command is that you walk in love.
7 Many deceivers, who do not acknowledge Jesus Christ[j] as coming in the flesh,
have gone out into the world.[k] Any such person is the deceiver and the antichrist.[l]
8 Watch out that you do not lose what you have worked for, but that you may be rewarded fully.[m] **9** Anyone who runs ahead and does not continue in the teaching of
Christ does not have God; whoever continues in the teaching has both the Father and
the Son.[n] **10** If anyone comes to you and does not bring this teaching, do not take him
into your house or welcome him.[o] **11** Anyone who welcomes him shares[p] in his wicked work.
12 I have much to write to you, but I do not want to use paper and ink. Instead, I hope
to visit you and talk with you face to face,[q] so that our joy may be complete.
13 The children of your chosen[r] sister send their greetings.

1 [a] 3Jn 1 [b] Ro 16:13 [c] Jn 8:32
2 [d] 2Pe 1:12 [e] 1Jn 1:8
3 [f] Ro 1:7
4 [g] 3Jn 3,4
5 [h] 1Jn 2:7; 3:11
6 [i] 1Jn 2:5
7 [j] 1Jn 2:22; 4:2,3 [k] 1Jn 4:1 [l] 1Jn 2:18
8 [m] 1Co 3:8
9 [n] 1Jn 2:23
10 [o] Ro 16:17
11 [p] 1Ti 5:22
12 [q] 3Jn 13,14
13 [r] ver 1

■ **1–3** *Salutation and Greeting.* John identified himself and the recipients of his letter.

1 The elder. John also identified himself in this way in 3 John 1. He was referring either to his church office (see 1Ti 3:1) or to his biological age. There is no real difficulty with an apostle identifying himself as an elder, since the responsibilities of an apostle toward each individual congregation were precisely those of an elder (1Pe 5:1–4). **chosen lady.** Refers either to an otherwise unknown woman or speaks figuratively of a local church. The latter figurative use does not appear elsewhere, so the former seems more likely (see also 2Jn 13). John addressed this woman with much respect and love, thus indicating his pastoral interest in her. **her children.** Either the biological children of the woman or her spiritual children; that is, her followers. The former seems more likely.

■ **4** *Commendation.* John commended the woman and her household for their faithfulness. The elder and the woman shared the joy of seeing members of her household continuing to be faithful to the truth.

4 See *WLC* 144.

■ **5–6** *Exhortation to Love.* The mark of Christian faithfulness is love for one another.

5 not writing you a new command. See note on 1 John 2:7–8.

6 obedience to his commands. John explained that the definition of love among believers derives from the commands of God. Love is more than mere affection; it is living with each other in the light of God's Word. **from the beginning.** See note on 1 John 2:7.

■ **7–11** *Warning Against False Teaching.* John spoke in very strong terms against the false teaching that Jesus had not come in the flesh. This truth is so crucial that to reject it is to reject all hope of reconciliation with God, while to receive it is to receive God himself, as he offers himself in the gospel.

7 do not acknowledge Jesus Christ as coming in the flesh. The deceivers were Docetists, who denied the reality of Christ's human nature (see note on 1Jn 4:2–3; see also theological article "The Full Humanity of Christ" at Lk 3). **gone out.** See note on 1 John 2:19. **the antichrist.** See note on 1 John 2:18.

8 lose . . . rewarded fully. This is not a warning about losing salvation. Instead, John taught that those who temporarily lapsed into this false teaching might lose rewards they had stored up in heaven (cf. Mt 6:20). He may also have meant that well-intentioned Christians who offer hospitality to known false teachers will also lose such rewards because they aid and abet the Lord's enemies (vv. 10–11). In 1 John 2:19 he also warned that turning from the true gospel of Christ come in the flesh could prove a person had never exercised saving faith. **worked for.** Christians work hard for many reasons—but not to earn their salvation. Properly motivated good works bring future rewards (Mk 9:41; Lk 19:16–19). See *BC* 24.

9–11 See *WCF* 10.4.

9 runs ahead. That is, to leave the truth behind. Membership in the church does not ensure salvation; only those who have saving faith will remain true to the gospel of Christ (see theological article "The Church: Visible and Invisible" at 1 Pe 4).

10–11 See *WCF* 20.4.

10 do not take him into your house or welcome him. Itinerant teachers in the early church frequently received hospitality from local Christians (see 3Jn). The error against which John warned was so serious that he advised total separation. The rejection of fellowship with false teachers contrasts sharply with the exhortation in 3 John 5–8 and 10 to welcome believers who were proclaiming the true gospel. See *BC* 7.

11 shares in his wicked work. John instructed his readers not to enable or encourage the work of those who actively oppose the gospel.

■ **12–13** *Closing Remarks and Farewell.* John closed his letter with expressions of affection and hope.

12 paper and ink. John acknowledged that a letter is no substitute for personal fellowship. He looked forward to sharing with the lady and her household the kind of mutual encouragement that can only take place in person.

13 children of your chosen sister. See verse 1. It is most likely that John was referring to another Christian woman and her household, who were sending their greetings.

3 JOHN

Introduction

Overview

Author: The apostle John

Purpose: To encourage service toward others, especially with regard to hospitality toward those who minister the gospel

Date: A.D. 80–90

Key Truths:

- Christians who are faithful in showing goodness to others are to be commended.
- Showing hospitality to others, especially to ministers of the gospel, is an important Christian privilege and responsibility.
- Christian leaders should appreciate and support, rather than fear and abuse, each other.

Author

Third John was written by the author of 1 and 2 John, as is indicated by the many similarities of style and structure. Like the Gospel of John and 1 and 2 John, the traditional ascription of 3 John to the apostle John is more likely than any alternative (see "Introduction to John: Author").

Original Audience

John wrote to his friend Gaius. The name Gaius appears elsewhere in Scripture (Ac 19:29; 20:4; Ro 16:23; 1Co 1:14), but Gaius was a common name. It is not known whether the Gaius who received this letter can be identified with any of the other Scriptural references to the name.

Purpose and Distinctives

While 1 and 2 John celebrate truths that unite all Christians, 3 John laments the petty rivalry that sets Christians against one another. In particular, the letter was occasioned by a sharp conflict between Diotrephes (apparently an elder in a congregation under John's care) and others in the congregation over hospitality shown to traveling missionaries. It is likely that Demetrius, who was commended to Gaius by this letter, was either one who had cared for missionaries or one who was himself a traveling missionary in need of temporary lodging.

There is no trace in 3 John of the conflict over the person and work of Christ that looms large in 1 and 2 John. It may be that 3 John was written earlier than either 1 or 2 John and before this controversy rose, possibly between A.D. 80 and 90.

Third John is characterized as an epistle by its salutation, introductory greeting and final greeting. It is a letter commending Demetrius to the recipient, Gaius. The central concern of 3 John is that traveling missionaries should be offered hospitality in accordance with the principle of Christian love.

Outline

I. Salutation and Greeting (1–2)	*John greeted his beloved Gaius and wished him well.*
II. Commending Hospitality (3–10) A. Positive Encouragement (3–8) B. Negative Contrast (9–10)	*John commended Gaius for his past hospitality toward missionaries and condemned Diotrephes for mistreating fellow Christians.*
III. Exhorting Hospitality (11–12)	*John exhorted Gaius to further righteousness.*
IV. Conclusion and Farewell (13–14)	*John expressed his desire to see Gaius and offered final greetings.*

1 [a]2Jn 1
1 The elder,[a]

To my dear friend Gaius, whom I love in the truth.

2 Dear friend, I pray that you may enjoy good health and that all may go well with you,
3 [b]ver 5, 10 [c]2Jn 4 even as your soul is getting along well. 3 It gave me great joy to have some brothers[b] come
and tell about your faithfulness to the truth and how you continue to walk in the truth.[c]
4 [d]1Co 4:15; 1Jn 2:1 4 I have no greater joy than to hear that my children[d] are walking in the truth.
5 Dear friend, you are faithful in what you are doing for the brothers, even though they
5 [e]Ro 12:13; Heb 13:2 are strangers to you.[e] 6 They have told the church about your love. You will do well to
send them on their way in a manner worthy of God. 7 It was for the sake of the Name[f] that
7 [f]Jn 15:21 [g]Ac 20:33, 35 they went out, receiving no help from the pagans.[g] 8 We ought therefore to show hospitality to such men so that we may work together for the truth.
9 I wrote to the church, but Diotrephes, who loves to be first, will have nothing to do
10 [h]2Jn 12 [i]ver 5 [j]Jn 9:22, 34 with us. 10 So if I come,[h] I will call attention to what he is doing, gossiping maliciously
about us. Not satisfied with that, he refuses to welcome the brothers.[i] He also stops those
who want to do so and puts them out of the church.[j]
11 [k]Ps 37:27 [l]1Jn 2:29 [m]1Jn 3:6, 9, 10 11 Dear friend, do not imitate what is evil but what is good.[k] Anyone who does what
is good is from God.[l] Anyone who does what is evil has not seen God.[m] 12 Demetrius is
12 [n]1Ti 3:7 [o]Jn 21:24 well spoken of by everyone[n]—and even by the truth itself. We also speak well of him, and
you know that our testimony is true.[o]
13 I have much to write you, but I do not want to do so with pen and ink. 14 I hope to
14 [p]2Jn 12 [q]Jn 10:3 see you soon, and we will talk face to face.[p]

Peace to you. The friends here send their greetings. Greet the friends there by name.[q]

■ **1–2** *Salutation and Greeting.* John began this letter with a typical greeting, wishing the recipient God's blessings.
1 The elder. The author identified himself as "the elder" (as in 2Jn 1), probably as a reference to his age. **dear friend Gaius.** John had deep affection for Gaius, the primary recipient of this letter, calling him "dear friend" four times (see vv. 1,2,5,11). John also described his own company as the "friends" of Gaius (v. 14). These bonds of Christian friendship stood in sharp contrast to the actions of Diotrephes (vv. 9–10).
2 good health . . . all may go well. John did not promise Gaius that he would have good health and success. On the contrary, he simply told Gaius that he prayed for his well-being as any good friend would. Health and prosperity are not guaranteed to Christians before the return of Christ in glory.
■ **3–10** *Commending Hospitality.* John commended Gaius for his hospitality toward missionaries. He contrasted the Christian ideal with the actions of Diotrephes. This material divides into positive words toward Gaius (3–8) and condemnation of Diotrephes (9–10).
■ **3–8** *Positive Encouragement.* Gaius had been faithful up to this point in caring for Christian missionaries.
3–4 See *WLC* 144.
3 tell about your faithfulness. The verb used here means "bear witness; give testimony." It has connotations of legal controversy (indicating the seriousness of the issues in John's view) and of the joyful proclamation of the gospel (indicating that Gaius's consistent life was an outworking of the salvation effected by God in Christ). The verb is used similarly in verses 6 and 12.
4 my children. John referred to believers under his care as his children, as he did 14 times in 1 John and three times in 2 John. He revealed his paternal affection toward them as well as his pride when they did well.
5–8 doing for the brothers . . . show hospitality. John commended Gaius for receiving traveling Christian teachers with hospitality. The obligation to welcome and encourage those who proclaim the true gospel from place to place, and the joy that comes from doing so, stand in contrast to the need to avoid those who proclaim a false gospel (1Jn 4:1–3; 2Jn 10–11). Those who proclaim the true Christian message and those who encourage and support them collaborate in serving the truth. This outlook on hospitality stems from the larger Christian ethic of demonstrating love to others, as John emphasized in his other epistles.
7 the pagans. Literally, "Gentiles." John was probably referring metaphorically to unbelievers, those outside the church. The early church consisted of people from both Jewish and Gentile backgrounds. John's language here suggests that the Christian community had come to see itself as the true remnant of Israel in distinction from pagans, those outside of the Christian community.
■ **9–10** *Negative Contrast.* The cooperation and love that should be normal among Christians had been broken by the behavior of Diotrephes. He was a leader who abused his position. Evidently Diotrephes regarded other Christian teachers as threats rather than as coworkers; his selfish point of view led him to turn away traveling evangelists and to excommunicate those who welcomed them.
9 See *WLC* 132.
10 if I come. An apostle's personal presence was an extension of the presence of Christ, both for encouragement and for warning (2Co 13:1–3,10). See *WLC* 151.
■ **11–12** *Exhorting Hospitality.* Although Gaius had treated missionaries well in the past, John felt the need to exhort him to continue to do so.
11 what is evil . . . what is good. Although this principle has broad applications, John's chief concern was that Gaius and others not imitate Diotrephes's evil treatment of missionaries, but follow what they knew to be good.
12 Demetrius The body of the letter closes with a commendation of Demetrius, the bearer of the letter, as a faithful Christian. Such commendation by name, like the naming of the addressee, was necessary to ensure that the letter was neither suppressed nor misused by those who, like Diotrephes, wanted to disrupt the unity of the congregation (v. 9). Demetrius may have been a traveling teacher himself or a faithful member of the congregation. **testimony.** See note on verse 3. See *WLC* 144; *WSC* 77.
■ **13–14** *Conclusion and Farewell.* John put off writing more in the hopes of visiting personally, and offered greetings from those who were with him.
14 I hope to see you soon. John's normal desire for personal fellowship (2Jn 12) was intensified by the need to restore peace within the community of believers. Until John's arrival, Gaius was exhorted to greet at least those who were willing to receive John's goodwill. **by name.** John wanted Gaius to greet all of his friends personally on his behalf.

JUDE

Introduction

Overview

Author: Jude, the brother of Jesus

Purpose: To combat the false teaching that Christian liberty and salvation by grace give believers license to sin

Date: Before A.D. 65–67

Key Truths:

- Terrible judgment awaits those who rebel against God and Christ.
- False teachers in the church must be strongly resisted.
- Christian liberty and God's free grace do not give believers license to sin.
- Believers are responsible to actively pursue good works and spiritual growth.

Author

The author of this epistle identified himself as "Jude, a servant of Jesus Christ and a brother of James" (v. 1). Jude was a common name (Greek, "Judas"; Hebrew, "Judah") among first-century Jews. At least eight different Judases are mentioned in the New Testament (including two of Jesus' disciples; Lk 6:16). The author cannot, therefore, be identified on the basis of his name alone.

The best clue to his identity is the description "a brother of James" (v. 1). The only James known well enough in the early church to be referred to in this unqualified way was James of Jerusalem, who was a prominent church leader (Ac 12:17; 15:13), the author of the epistle that bears his name (Jas 1:1) and the half brother of Jesus (the son of Mary and Joseph, not begotten by the Holy Spirit; Mt 13:55; Mk 6:3; Gal 1:19). If this identification of James is correct, the author of this epistle is Jude, the half brother of Jesus (Mt 13:55; Mk 6:3), who along with his other brothers did not believe in Jesus as the Messiah until after Jesus' resurrection (Mk 3:21; Jn 7:5; Ac 1:14). This conclusion is strengthened by the following evidence that the author was Jewish: his many allusions to the Old Testament (although he includes no direct quotations), his familiarity with Jewish non-canonical traditions and his strong ethical concern. The only possible mention elsewhere in the New Testament of Jude's activity as a Christian is Paul's reference to the itinerant ministry of the Lord's brothers and their wives (1Co 9:5). The probable explanation for Jude's decision not to mention his familial relationship with Jesus in verse 1 is his humility (note the similar reserve in Jas 1:1).

Several objections to the authenticity of Jude have been raised, but they all rest on questionable assumptions and/or exegesis. Most are linked with postulating a date too late for Jude's lifetime (see "Introduction: Time and Place of Writing"). Some have argued that the quality of the Greek used in this epistle is better than one might expect of a Galilean author, but Galilee was bilingual (Greek and Aramaic) in the first century, and too little is known about Jude's Greek to conclude that he could not have written as this author did. There is little reason, therefore, to assume that the author is someone other than Jude, the brother of Jesus.

Despite its brevity, the epistle was widely studied in the early church because of its obvious orthodoxy and value. Questions about the epistle's canonical status arose largely because of its references of non-canonical literature (see notes on vv. 9,14,15; see also "Introduction: Purpose and Distinctives"). In addition to possible allusions to Jude in works by the Apostolic Fathers (e.g., Clement of Rome and the writers of the *Shepherd of Hermas* and the *Epistle of Barnabas*—all prior to A.D. 150), Jude was listed in the Muratorian Canon (c. 200) and was accepted as authentic by Clement of Alexandria (c. 150–c. 215), Tertullian (c. 160–c. 225), Origen (c. 185–c. 253) and Athanasius (c. 296–373).

Time and Place of Writing

Neither internal nor external evidence provides any indication of the place of origin of Jude's epistle, and the only evidences for the date of Jude are inferences from Jude's probable life span and from the heresy he combated. If Jude was the younger brother of Jesus and James (as his position in the lists of brothers in Mt 13:55 and Mk 6:3 suggests), he could easily have survived well into the last quarter of the first century. Assuming Peter's authorship and probable use of Jude in writing 2 Peter, Jude would have been written before A.D. 65–67, the likely date for 2 Peter.

Some have argued for a second-century date on the supposition that the book of Jude combats Gnosticism. While the teachings Jude opposes may well have been early precursors of Gnosticism, they cannot be identified with the fully developed Gnostic heresies of the second century (see "Introduction to 2 Peter: Purpose and Distinctives").

Original Audience

Nothing in the epistle indicates the location or specific identity of the recipients. While some believe that Jude's use of the Old Testament and Jewish non-canonical literature points to a Jewish-Christian audience, this material is more an evidence of Jude's background than of that of his readers. Perhaps Jude intended his epistle to be a circular letter to a number of churches about whose conditions he was aware due to an itinerant ministry among them (cf. 1Co 9:5).

Purpose and Distinctives

Jude's main concern in this letter was to denunciate false teachers. He confronted a threat similar to that opposed in 2 Peter: false teachers who used Christian liberty and the free grace of God as a license for immorality (v. 4; cf. notes on 2Pe 2:2,14). Most of the epistle (vv. 4–19) is devoted to stern condemnations of the false teachers in order to impress the readers with the seriousness of the threat. Jude's strategy was more than one of mere negative opposition, however. He also urged his readers to grow in their knowledge of Christian truth ("build yourselves up in your most holy faith"; v. 20), to bear a firm witness for the truth ("contend for the faith"; v. 3) and to seek to reclaim those whose faith was wavering ("snatch others from the fire"; v. 23). This prescription for confronting spiritual error is as timely and relevant today as it was when it was first written.

Jude is also noteworthy for its use of non-canonical materials. While allusion to and citation of extra-biblical materials are relatively rare in the New Testament, such occasional use is not surprising, especially given the currency of non-canonical religious works during the period and the desire of the New Testament writers to communicate the gospel message in language and terms familiar to their readers. Other examples include Peter's use of similar apocalyptic literature (2 Peter) and Paul's use of the Jewish tradition's elaboration of Exodus 7:11 in 2 Timothy 3:8, as well as his quotations of pagan poets (Ac 17:28; 1Co 15:33; Tit 1:12). The use of such materials for illustrative purposes or as a subsidiary appeal to conventional wisdom implies neither the inspiration of such non-canonical documents nor the accuracy of all the materials contained in them.

Outline

I. Salutation (1–2)	*Jude identified himself and greeted his readers.*
II. Purpose of the Letter (3–4)	*Jude wrote in order to denounce the false teachers in the church and the immoral lifestyles they promoted.*
III. Denunciation of False Teachers (5–19) A. Judgment on the Ungodly (5–10) 1. Examples of Divine Judgment on the Ungodly (5–7) 2. Application of Examples to False Teachers (8–10) B. Judgment on Those Who Lead Others Into Sin (11–13) 1. God's Past Judgment on Those Who Led Others Into Sin (11) 2. Application to False Teachers (12–13) C. Past Prophecy of Judgment (14–16) 1. Enoch's Prophecy of Judgment on the Ungodly (14–15) 2. Application to False Teachers (16) D. Apostolic Prophecies of Judgment (17–19) 1. Apostolic Prophecies of Scoffers (17–18) 2. Application to False Teachers (19)	*Jude warned against heeding the false teachers by insisting that God's judgment would come against them and those who followed them. God's past judgment on the ungodly indicated that God would punish the false teachers for their own sin. God's past judgment against those who led others into sin indicated that God would punish the false teachers for leading others into sin. Past prophecy regarding the coming last judgment warned of even greater punishments for the false teachers. Apostolic prophecies regarding the coming last judgment confirmed that even greater punishments were in store for the false teachers.*
IV. Positive Exhortations to Believers (20–23)	*Believers must not only resist false teaching, but they must also actively pursue righteous living and devotion to God.*
V. Concluding Doxology (24–25)	*Jude assured his readers that God preserves true believers in faithfulness, and he praised God for his goodness and power.*

1 Jude,[a] a servant of Jesus Christ and a brother of James,
To those who have been called,[b] who are loved by God the Father and kept by[a] Jesus
Christ:[c]
2 Mercy, peace and love be yours in abundance.[d]

The Sin and Doom of Godless Men

3 Dear friends, although I was very eager to write to you about the salvation we
share,[e] I felt I had to write and urge you to contend[f] for the faith that was once for all
entrusted to the saints. 4 For certain men whose condemnation was written about[b] long
ago have secretly slipped in among you.[g] They are godless men, who change the grace
of our God into a license for immorality and deny Jesus Christ our only Sovereign and
Lord.[h]
5 Though you already know all this, I want to remind you that the Lord[c] delivered his
people out of Egypt, but later destroyed those who did not believe.[i] 6 And the angels who
did not keep their positions of authority but abandoned their own home—these he has
kept in darkness, bound with everlasting chains for judgment on the great Day.[j] 7 In a
similar way, Sodom and Gomorrah and the surrounding towns[k] gave themselves up to
sexual immorality and perversion. They serve as an example of those who suffer the punishment of eternal fire.[l]
8 In the very same way, these dreamers pollute their own bodies, reject authority and

1 [a]Mt 13:55; Ac 1:13 [b]Ro 1:6,7 [c]Jn 17:12
2 [d]2Pe 1:2
3 [e]Tit 1:4 [f]1Ti 6:12
4 [g]Gal 2:4 [h]Tit 1:16; 2Pe 2:1
5 [i]Nu 14:29; Ps 106:26
6 [j]2Pe 2:4,9
7 [k]Dt 29:23 [l]2Pe 2:6

[a] *1* Or *for;* or *in* [b] *4* Or *men who were marked out for condemnation* [c] *5* Some early manuscripts *Jesus*

■ **1–2** *Salutation.* Jude identified himself as the author of the letter and greeted his readers.
1 Jude . . . brother of James. See "Introduction: Author." **called.** The expression of God's sovereign and gracious initiative in effectually summoning to salvation those whom he has chosen. **loved.** God's sovereign election and calling are grounded in the eternal love of the Father for the elect (Ro 8:28–39; Eph 1:4–5). **kept by Jesus Christ.** The Greek may also be rendered "kept for Jesus Christ." The elect will persevere in faith because God preserves them (v. 24; Jn 10:27–30; 1Pe 1:5).
2 Mercy, peace and love. Jude filled a traditional Jewish greeting ("mercy and peace") with profound Christian meaning by adding the word "love." The mercy of God to undeserving sinners and the peace that results are grounded in the divine love manifested in Jesus Christ (see notes on v. 1; Jn 3:16).
■ **3–4** *Purpose of the Letter.* Jude explained that he wrote in order to refute the false teaching that God's grace gives believers license to sin.
3 although . . . I felt I had to write. Instead of the letter he had intended to write (perhaps a doctrinal treatise on salvation), Jude felt compelled by circumstances to address the problem of false teachers (v. 4). We do not know whether the originally intended letter was ever written. **contend for the faith.** Here "faith" indicates the content of the message taught by the apostles and held in common by all Christians (Gal 1:23; 1Ti 3:9) rather than the personal exercise of faith and trust by the believer. To contend for the faith when it is under attack means more than simply verbally opposing false teachers; it involves a positive way of life that is faithful to the gospel message (vv. 20–23). **once for all entrusted to the saints.** Christianity involves a normative body of belief given by God to the church through the apostles (1Co 15:3–8). Together with the Old Testament (see 2Ti 3:14–17), the apostolic witness, as found in the New Testament, remains the standard for the church (2Jn 9–10).
4 certain men . . . slipped in among you. The troublemakers apparently came from outside the particular church(es) that Jude addressed, perhaps as itinerant prophets or teachers (cf. 2Co 11:1–5; 2Jn 7,9–11). **whose condemnation was written about long ago.** This difficult phrase probably refers to various prophecies of the coming condemnation of ungodly men like the false teachers, perhaps including the examples in verses 5–7 and 11, the prophecy of Enoch in verses 14–15 and the apostolic prophecies in verses 17–18. Although less likely (see NIV text note), this may refer to the fate of the wicked being written in heavenly books (cf. Jer 22:30). **godless men.** A phrase summing up Jude's indictment of the false teachers. They were guilty of practical godlessness in that they refused to recognize the lordship of Christ. **change the grace of our God into a license for immorality.** Jude's opponents were guilty of antinomianism—the belief that Christians are under no obligation to follow the moral law as a rule of life. Such teaching was a persistent problem in the early church (Ro 3:8; 6:15; 1Co 6:12–20; Gal 5:13), especially in those churches in which Paul's emphasis upon justification by grace through faith was misunderstood and perverted (2Pe 3:16). **deny . . . Sovereign and Lord.** By their godless and immoral behavior, the false teachers denied Christ. The Greek word translated "Sovereign" (*despotes*) connotes supreme power and authority and is often used of God in the Septuagint (the Greek translation of the OT). The designation of Christ as "Sovereign and Lord" equates Christ's lordship and authority with God's and thereby implies Christ's divinity (see theological article "Jesus Christ, God and Man" at Jn 1). See *WCF* 3.7; *WLC* 13,113.
■ **5–19** *Denunciation of False Teachers.* Jude condemned the false teachers and warned against believing their lies. He supported his argument with four sets of examples: (1) judgment on the ungodly (5–10); (2) judgment on those who lead others into sin (11–13); (3) past prophecy of judgment (14–16); and (4) apostolic prophecies of judgment (17–19).
■ **5–10** *Judgment on the Ungodly.* Jude began his condemnation with examples of God's past executions of judgment against the wicked (5–7). He then applied the principles demonstrated in these examples to the false teachers (8–10).
■ **5–7** *Examples of Divine Judgment on the Ungodly.* Jude drew three examples of past divine judgments from the Old Testament and the Jewish Apocrypha.
5 destroyed those who did not believe. God judged the Israelites for their unbelief when they refused to enter Canaan following the report of the spies (Nu 13:25—14:38). The consequence for their sin: 40 years of wandering in the desert. Just as judgment fell on the apostate Israelites after their deliverance from Egypt, so also it will fall on apostate church members (Heb 3:7–12).
6–7 See *WCF* 32.1; *WLC* 86,88.
6 angels. See note on 2 Peter 2:4 **did not keep their positions of authority but abandoned their own home.** The angels in question rebelled against their God-given responsibilities and abandoned their areas of ministry or residence. Some interpret this to mean that they abandoned their residences in heaven and came to Earth. The suggestion that this is a reference to the sin of the "sons of God" in Genesis 6:2 is problematic (see note on Gen 6:2). **the great Day.** The day of judgment at the second coming of Christ. See *WCF* 8.4; 33.1, *WLC* 19.
7 similar way. If verse 6 refers to traditions associated with Genesis 6:2–4, the phrase "similar way" refers to sexual immorality in general and to unnatural sexual unions in particular. Since Genesis 6:2–4 probably does not refer to angels (see notes on Ge 6:1–4), it is preferable to understand this verse as comparing the two cases by pointing to flagrancy of violation and pride in disobedience. **sexual immorality and perversion.** The sexual perversion in view is the homosexuality described in Genesis 19:4–9. **an example of . . . punishment of eternal fire.** The fiery destruction of Sodom and Gomorrah and the surrounding towns in Genesis 19 serves throughout Scripture as a paradigm of God's judgment on sin (Dt 29:23; Isa 1:9; Jer 49:17–18; Lk 17:29–30; Ro 9:29). See *WLC* 27.
8–11 See *WCF* 23.4.

slander celestial beings.[m] 9But even the archangel Michael,[n] when he was disputing
with the devil about the body of Moses, did not dare to bring a slanderous accusation
against him, but said, "The Lord rebuke you!"[o] 10Yet these men speak abusively against
whatever they do not understand; and what things they do understand by instinct, like
unreasoning animals—these are the very things that destroy them.[p]
11Woe to them! They have taken the way of Cain;[q] they have rushed for profit into Balaam's error;[r] they have been destroyed in Korah's rebellion.[s]
12These men are blemishes at your love feasts,[t] eating with you without the slightest
qualm—shepherds who feed only themselves. They are clouds without rain,[u] blown
along by the wind;[v] autumn trees, without fruit and uprooted[w]—twice dead. 13They are
wild waves of the sea,[x] foaming up their shame;[y] wandering stars, for whom blackest
darkness has been reserved forever.[z]
14Enoch,[a] the seventh from Adam, prophesied about these men: "See, the Lord is
coming with thousands upon thousands of his holy ones[b] 15to judge[c] everyone, and to
convict all the ungodly of all the ungodly acts they have done in the ungodly way, and
of all the harsh words ungodly sinners have spoken against him."[d] 16These men are
grumblers and faultfinders; they follow their own evil desires; they boast[e] about themselves and flatter others for their own advantage.

8 [m]2Pe 2:10
9 [n]Da 10:13,21 [o]Zec 3:2
10 [p]2Pe 2:12
11 [q]Ge 4:3-8; 1Jn 3:12 [r]2Pe 2:15 [s]Nu 16:1-3,31-35
12 [t]2Pe 2:13; 1Co 11:20-22 [u]Pr 25:14; 2Pe 2:17 [v]Eph 4:14 [w]Mt 15:13
13 [x]Isa 57:20 [y]Php 3:19 [z]2Pe 2:17
14 [a]Ge 5:18,21-24 [b]Dt 33:2; Da 7:10
15 [c]2Pe 2:6-9 [d]1Ti 1:9
16 [e]2Pe 2:18

■ **8–10** *Application of Examples to False Teachers.* God's past judgments on the wicked were indications that he would also bring judgment against the false teachers.

8 dreamers. A probable reference to the false teachers' claims to divine revelation through visionary experiences, claims perhaps used to justify the three actions that follow. **pollute . . . bodies.** Sexual immorality (v. 4; cf. 1Co 6:18), perhaps even homosexuality (v. 7; cf. Ro 1:26–27). **reject authority.** Although some interpret the authority in question as human or angelic, a reference to the lordship and authority of Jesus Christ is more likely (see note on v. 4). **slander celestial beings.** See note on 2 Peter 2:10. See *WLC* 151; *BC* 36.

9 Evidence indicates that this incident is based on *The Assumption of Moses,* a non-canonical Jewish work (of which only fragments have survived) that expands on the narrative of the burial of Moses in Deuteronomy 34:5–6 (see "Introduction: Purpose and Distinctives"). The story in question concerns a confrontation between the archangel Michael and the devil over possession of Moses' body. As usually interpreted, Jude's point was that the rash talk of the false teachers contrasted with the circumspection of Michael (see 2Pe 2:10 and its note). Others interpret Jude as contrasting Michael's appeal to God's authority over Satan with the false teachers' claims to spiritual authority. **archangel Michael.** Michael is one of the chief angels and the special guardian of Israel (Da 10:13,21; 12:1). In Revelation 12:7 Michael is seen leading the angelic host in war against the devil and his angels. See theological article "Angels" at Zechariah 9.

■ **11–13** *Judgment on Those Who Lead Others Into Sin.* Jude moved to examples of God's past judgments on those who had caused others to sin (11). He then applied principles from those judgments to the false teachers (12–13).

■ **11** *God's Past Judgment on Those Who Led Others Into Sin.* Jude appealed to three Old Testament examples of God's retribution against those who had motivated others to sin.

11 way of Cain. See Genesis 4:3–12 (cf. Heb 11:4; 1Jn 3:12). According to Jewish tradition, to which Jude may have been referring, Cain was the archetypal sinner and the instructor of others in sin. **Balaam's error.** See note on 2 Peter 2:15. **Korah's rebellion.** Korah, along with Dathan and Abiram, led 250 men in rebellion against the authority of Moses and Aaron (Nu 16). Korah's rebellion and the resulting divine judgment provide an apt parallel to the false teachers' rebellion against proper church authority and their dangerous ability to lead others astray. They also provide a graphic illustration of the divine judgment awaiting the false teachers (Nu 16:31–33).

■ **12–13** *Application to False Teachers.* On the basis of God's prior judgment on those who led others into sin, Jude argued that God would also judge the false teachers for leading members of the Christian church into sin.

12 blemishes. The Greek word used here can mean "reefs; hidden rocks" (which can endanger shipping) or, less often, "spot; blemish." Perhaps Jude intentionally drew on the ambiguity of the word to emphasize that the false teachers were dangerous because they defiled and led others astray. **love feasts.** See note on 2 Peter 2:13 (cf. 1Co 11:20–34). The reading "love feasts," uncertain at 2 Peter 2:13 (see NIV text note), is correct here. **eating with you without the slightest qualm.** Although the false teachers may have made the love feasts occasions for blatant immorality (cf. 2Pe 2:13, but see note on "love feasts," above), Jude may also have been concerned about their influence at such gatherings. Because teaching took place at the love feasts (Ac 20:7,11), there was opportunity for the false teachers to advance their ideas. **clouds without rain.** A form of hypocrisy that fails to produce what is promised (see note on 2Pe 2:17). **without fruit and uprooted—twice dead.** Like trees failing to bear fruit at harvest time, the lives of these people were barren, and they stood under God's judgment (Mt 7:16–20).

13 wandering stars. Meteors, shooting stars, comets or, most probably, planets. Either the opponents' teaching was ephemeral (lasting a short time, like the light of a shooting star) or untrustworthy and useless (as when an unpredictable heavenly body is used for navigation).

■ **14–16** *Past Prophecy of Judgment.* Jude moved beyond examples of past temporal judgments to a past prophecy indicating the more severe judgment that would take place on the day of the Lord.

■ **14–15** *Enoch's Prophecy of Judgment on the Ungodly.* A non-canonical prophecy stating that God will come to Earth to destroy all his enemies with utter finality.

14–15 See *WLC* 88.

14 Enoch, the seventh from Adam. The Enoch of Genesis 5:18–24 is of the seventh generation from Adam if Adam is counted as the first. In verses 14–15 Jude quoted almost verbatim from the well-known and respected non-canonical work known as the *Book of Enoch,* or *1 Enoch,* which is attributed to this Biblical figure. In doing so Jude did not imply that *1 Enoch* was divinely inspired or that it was actually written by the Biblical Enoch of Genesis 5:18–24. He was simply using a familiar source that further confirmed his theme of coming divine judgment on the ungodly. **prophesied.** In saying that Enoch "prophesied about these men," Jude appears to have confirmed that Enoch uttered this particular prophecy, though he did not state his opinion of the authorship of *1 Enoch* as a whole. The quotation from *1 Enoch* teaches, in dependence upon and consistent with a host of Old Testament prophecies (e.g., Da 7:9–10; Zec 14:5), that God will come with his heavenly hosts to judge the wicked. Jude was justified in applying the general truth of this Biblically based text to his specific situation. **holy ones.** A probable reference to the angelic host that will accompany the Lord's return (Zec 14:5; Mt 25:31).

15 ungodly. The repetition of this term is important. The same Greek word is used in verses 4 ("godless") and 18. Rebellion by the false teachers was first and foremost against God and his authority, and it would meet with God's certain judgment (see note on v. 4). See *BC* 37.

■ **16** *Application to False Teachers.* From the teaching that God will come with his heavenly hosts to destroy the wicked, Jude drew the application that terrible eternal destruction awaited the false teachers.

16 grumblers and faultfinders. Like Israel in the wilderness (v. 5; cf. 1Co 10:10), the false teachers resisted God's will, perhaps by complaining about the law's restrictions on their behavior. **boast about themselves.** Literally, "their mouths speak arrogant words." This may have involved claims to visionary experiences (v. 8), freedom from the law (vv. 4,8) and possession of the Holy Spirit (vv. 18–19). **flatter others for their own advantage.** They showed partiality to some in the church (probably the rich; cf. Jas 2:1–9)

A Call to Persevere

[17]But, dear friends, remember what the apostles of our Lord Jesus Christ foretold.[f]
[18]They said to you, "In the last times[g] there will be scoffers who will follow their own ungodly desires."[h] [19]These are the men who divide you, who follow mere natural instincts
and do not have the Spirit.[i]
[20]But you, dear friends, build yourselves up[j] in your most holy faith and pray in the
Holy Spirit.[k] [21]Keep yourselves in God's love as you wait[l] for the mercy of our Lord Jesus
Christ to bring you to eternal life.

17 [f]2Pe 3:2
18 [g]1Ti 4:1 [h]2Pe 2:1
19 [i]1Co 2:14,15
20 [j]Col 2:7 [k]Eph 6:18
21 [l]Tit 2:13; 2Pe 3:12

---

and may have adapted their teaching to please the influential in their audience. See *WLC* 145.
■ **17–19** *Apostolic Prophecies of Judgment.* Jude appealed to apostolic teaching that confirmed that God would come to destroy the wicked.
■ **17–18** *Apostolic Prophecies of Scoffers.* The apostles predicted that some would reject their teaching regarding Jesus' return.
17 remember what the apostles . . . foretold. Some have taken this as an indication that Jude was not a contemporary of the apostles, but the text makes no such claim. Jude merely stated that he himself was not an apostle.
18 last times. The entire period between the first and second comings of Jesus (Ac 2:17; Heb 1:2; see theological article "The Plan of the Ages" at Heb 7). **scoffers.** Especially at the moral law of God and the certainty of divine punishment upon the disobedient (2Pe 3:3–4).
■ **19** *Application to False Teachers.* Jude indicated that the false teachers were among the "scoffers" the apostolic prophecies condemned.
19 divide you. Division within the church was an inevitable result of the false teachers' arrogance (v. 16) and their claim, against the church leadership and ordinary Christians, to possess the Spirit. They may have been classifying people (as the later Gnostics did) as "spiritual" (the false teachers themselves) and "natural" (ordinary Christians). **follow mere natural instincts and do not have the Spirit.** Against his opponents' claims, Jude argued that the false teachers themselves were the ones who lived entirely at the level of natural, earthly life (v. 10) and that they were without the Spirit.
■ **20–23** *Positive Exhortations to Believers.* Jude turned from denunciation of the false teachers to positive exhortation of his readers. The Trinitarian form of the exhortation should be noted ("Holy Spirit" in v. 20; "God" in v. 21; "Lord Jesus Christ" in v. 21).
20–21 See *WCF* 16.3; *BC* 9.
20 build . . . holy faith. Literally, "build yourselves up on your most holy faith." Jude, like Peter (1Pe 2:5) and Paul (1Co 3:16–17), described the church using the metaphor of a building. As in verse 3, "faith" refers to the foundational message of the prophets and apostles (Gal 1:23; 1Ti 3:9). **pray in the Holy Spirit.** In contrast to the false teachers, the prayers of Jude's readers were to be controlled by the Spirit, as indeed were their whole lives (Gal 5:16–18; Eph 6:18). See *WLC* 75.
21 Keep yourselves in God's love. Believers are responsible for remaining faithful to God, and they must exert effort to do so. Although God preserves believers in faithfulness to him (cf. v. 24), he does not do so apart from the means of their earnest, godly works.

The Final Judgment: Will I Be Judged?

THE Bible clearly teaches not only that Christ brings salvation to the world, but also that he judges all people. The concept of God's final judgment on the last day is essential to understanding the Bible's message of salvation. In Christ we are saved from the condemnation that comes through the final judgment of God. Final judgment is the counterpart to the message of saving grace. It is impossible for salvation to come in its fullness without a full-scale judgment of the wicked.

Paul in particular stressed this certainty, highlighting it to the sophisticated Athenians (Ac 17:30–31) and spelling it out in detail in Romans 2:5–16. It is from "the coming wrath" (1Th 1:10) on "the day of God's wrath" (Ro 2:5) that Jesus Christ will save us (cf. Jn 3:36; Ro 5:9; Eph 5:6; Col 3:6; Rev 6:17; 19:15). Throughout Scripture, terms pointing to divine indignation, anger and fury indicate that the holy Creator personally and actively judges sin. The New Testament teaches that Jesus Christ will act as Judge on his Father's behalf (Mt 13:40–43; 25:41–46; Jn 5:22–30; Ac 10:42; 2Co 5:10; 2Ti 4:1; Heb 9:27; 10:25–31; 12:23; 2Pe 3:7; Jude 6–7; Rev 20:11–15).

When Christ comes again, all humans of all eras will appear before his judgment seat. All will give an account of their lives to God, and God through Christ "will give to each person according to what he has done" (Ro 2:6; cf. Ps 62:12; Mt 16:27; 2Co 5:10; Rev 22:12). The faithful, who have learned to love righteousness, will be acknowledged, and on the basis of Christ's atonement and merit they will be awarded the salvation they seek. The lost will receive a destiny commensurate with the godless way of life they have chosen, and that destiny will come to them on the basis of their own demerit (Ro 2:6–11). To what degree they knew of the will of God will be the standard by which their demerit is assessed (Mt 11:20–24; Lk 11:42–48; Ro 2:12).

Beyond this, the judgment will demonstrate, and so finally vindicate, the perfect justice of God. In a world of sinners in which God has overlooked sin and "let all nations go their own way" (Ac 14:16), it is no wonder that many question whether God is just. The last judgment will be God's final self-vindication against the suspicion that he has ceased to care about righteousness (Ps 50:16–21; Rev 6:10; 16:5–7; 19:1–5).

God will pay special attention to those in the visible church, reviewing their actual words and works (Mt 12:36–37) and revealing whether they are truly faithful and regenerate (Mt 12:33–35) or merely hypocrites (Mt 7:21–23). Everything about everyone will be exposed to the Lord on the judgment day (1Co 4:5), and each person will receive from God according to what he or she has done. God alone can determine the true condition of a person's heart, but the Scriptures teach in principle that those who have not brought forth evidence of true repentance in his eyes will be lost forever (Mt 18:23–35; 25:34–46; Jas 2:14–26).

Fallen angels (demons) will also be judged on the last day (Mt 8:29; Jude 6) and believers will be involved in this process (1Co 6:3), though Scripture does not reveal much detail in this regard.

23 [m]Am 4:11; Zec 3:2-5 [n]Rev 3:4
24 [o]Ro 16:25 [p]2Co 4:14 [q]Col 1:22
25 [r]Jn 5:44; 1Ti 1:17 [s]Heb 13:8 [t]Ro 11:36

22Be merciful to those who doubt; 23snatch others from the fire and save them;[m] to
others show mercy, mixed with fear—hating even the clothing stained by corrupted
flesh.[n]

Doxology

24To him who is able[o] to keep you from falling and to present you before his glorious
presence[p] without fault[q] and with great joy— 25to the only God[r] our Savior be glory, majesty, power and authority, through Jesus Christ our Lord, before all ages, now and forevermore![s] Amen.[t]

22–23 There are some variations among Greek manuscripts regarding these verses. Some have rendered verse 23 as "save others with fear, snatching them from the fire, hating even the clothing . . ." With this reading, there are two groups instead of three represented in verses 22–23. Whatever the exact textual solution, Jude clearly recognized that different pastoral strategies are to be employed with different people. Those expressing doubt (i.e., those who have not yet actively embraced unbelief) are to be gently counseled, while those adopting false doctrine require a more direct and confrontational approach. Such sinners must be "snatch[ed] . . . from the fire."

23 mixed with fear. Taking care not to fall into the same sin, knowing the damnation that awaits the unrepentant. **clothing stained by corrupted flesh.** A vivid metaphor for the contaminating influence of the false teachers, this phrase underscored the care that Jude's readers were to exercise in their contact with the false teachers and with those under their influence (1Co 5:11; 2Jn 10–11). See *WCF* 19.3; 30.3; *WLC* 173.

■ **24–25** *Concluding Doxology.* Jude concluded his epistle with a doxology (cf. Ro 16:25–27) expressing confidence in God's power to preserve his people to the end and acknowledging God's eternal greatness in his "glory, majesty, power and authority."

24 able to keep you from falling. A great assurance in light of the many threats of judgment Jude had listed against the false teachers and those who followed them. It is only through God's enabling and preserving that believers remain faithful to Christ (see theological article "The Perseverance and Preservation of Believers" at Php 1). See *WCF* 9.5; *WLC* 195.

REVELATION

Introduction

Overview

Author: The apostle John

Purpose: To encourage fidelity to Christ in the midst of suffering by affirming that God rules history and will surely bring it to a glorious consummation of judgment and blessing in Christ

Date: A.D. 66–95

Key Themes:

- The church faces much suffering in this sinful world.
- God requires sincere repentance and enduring faithfulness from his people.
- God controls history so that evil will not prevail against the church.
- Jesus will return in glory to bring final judgment on the wicked and final blessings to the righteous who overcome.

Author

The author identified himself as John (1:1,4,9; 22:8). He was well known to the churches in Asia Minor (1:9; see "Original Audience"). As early as the second century A.D., Justin Martyr, Irenaeus and others identified the author as the apostle John. In the third century, however, Dionysius, bishop of Alexandria, compared the style and themes of Revelation with the Gospel of John and concluded that the two must have had different authors. On balance it is still probable that the apostle John was the author. The different styles may be explained by the different genres in which John wrote (Gospel, epistle, apocalypse), and John's different purposes in writing these works easily account for the thematic differences. In any event, Revelation stresses that its message and content derive ultimately from Jesus Christ and from God the Father (1:1,10–11; 22:16,20), so Revelation possesses full divine authority (22:18–19).

Time and Place of Writing

John indicated that he wrote from the isle of Patmos (1:9), which is off the coast of Ephesus. The Roman authorities used this island as a place of exile.

The date of the writing of Revelation is disputed. Interpreters generally favor an early date near the end of the reign of the Roman emperor Nero (A.D. 54–68) or a later date during the reign of Domitian (A.D. 81–96). Several factors are pertinent to this issue.

The reference to "seven kings" in 17:9–11 indicates that the sixth king was in power at the time of writing. Most commentators assume that these kings refer to Roman emperors. Nero himself was the fifth emperor if Augustus is counted as the first true emperor. If Julius Caesar is accepted as the first king (even though he was not an emperor), then Nero was the sixth emperor. On the other hand, it is not entirely clear that these seven kings refer necessarily to successive kings or that the counting must begin with a particular emperor or ruler. Those who favor a date in Domitian's reign point out that Caligula was the first emperor who severely persecuted Christians and that three minor emperors (Galba, Otho, Vitellius) held extremely brief and rather inconsequential rules between the end of Nero's reign in A.D. 68 and the beginning of Vespasian's reign in A.D. 69. If Caligula is counted as the first emperor and these three others are passed over, then Domitian was the sixth emperor in the sequence.

That Revelation was written during a time of persecution is indicated by the circumstances of the author and of the churches to which he wrote (1:9; 2:10,13; 3:10), as well as by the recurrent theme of persecution throughout (6:9; 17:6; 18:24; 19:2; 20:4). Widespread persecution was more characteristic of Domitian's reign than of Nero's, although lesser degrees of persecution did take place under Nero.

The reference to the temple in 11:1–2 may indicate that it was still standing when the book was written (the temple was destroyed in A.D. 70), which conclusion would favor an early date. Those who support a later date respond that the passage may be metaphoric or may depend on a source.

Emperor worship also seems to have been an issue for the original audience (13:4,15–16; 14:9–11; 16:2; 19:20; 20:4). While such worship may have been required under Nero, there is no solid evidence verifying that speculation. Evidence does exist, however, that Domitian required emperor worship. Although inconclusive, the lack of evidence indicating the worship of Nero more strongly supports a date during Domitian's reign.

In addition, some have argued that the conditions of the seven churches addressed in chapters 2–3 are more appropriate to Domitian's reign. Others suggest that the beast who recovers from a "fatal wound" (13:12) corresponds to the first-century myth that Nero would rise from the dead and return to Rome.

Although the data is inconclusive, most scholars believe that the weight of the evidence favors a date around A.D. 95. This concurs with the indications of the second-century church fathers.

Original Audience

Revelation is addressed to seven churches in Asia Minor (1:4,11), an area now part of western Turkey. These churches received rebukes and encouragements in accordance with their conditions (2:1—3:22). Persecution had fallen on some Christians (1:9; 2:9,13), and more was coming (2:10; 13:7–10). Roman officials tried to force Christians to worship the emperor, and heretical teachings and declining fervor tempted Christians to compromise with pagan society (2:2,4,14–15,20–24; 3:1–2,15,17).

Purpose and Distinctives

Revelation assured the churches of Asia Minor that Christ knew their condition and was calling them to stand fast against all temptation. Their victory had been secured through the blood of the Lamb (5:9–10; 12:11). Christ would come soon to defeat Satan and all his agents (19:11—20:10), and Christ's people would enjoy everlasting peace in his presence (7:15–17; 21:3–4).

Revelation is apocalyptic literature. Like Ezekiel, Daniel and Zechariah, it contains visions with many symbolic elements. Using visual imagery as well as verbal promises and warnings, it weaves together into a vast poetic tapestry the themes of the whole of Scripture. Its depths are displayed through its multiple allusions, which often refer simultaneously to various Old Testament texts. It is "revelation," or disclosure, that is intended to nourish all those who are servants of Christ (1:1).

The principal theme of Revelation is that God rules history and will bring it to its consummation in Christ. At the center are the visions of Christ (1:12–16) and of God (4:1—5:14). God displays his majesty, authority and righteousness as the Ruler and Judge of the universe (1:12–20). These central visions foreshadow the consummation of history, when God's glory will fill all things (21:22–23; 22:5; see note on 4:1—5:14). Detailed elements in the visions flesh out these truths and are to be seen as part of a larger picture. Revelation is thus a picture book, a dramatic presentation that enables the reader to have a God-centered view of history. It is not a puzzle book to be used as a source of arcane calculations.

The prologue (1:1–3) explains Revelation's basic purpose. Revelation 1:4—22:21 is a letter with a greeting (1:4–5a), a body (1:5b—22:20) and a farewell (22:21). In formal features this arrangement is similar to Paul's letters. The main portion of the book (4:1—22:5) consists of seven cycles of judgments, each of which leads to a description of the second coming (4:1—8:1; 8:2—11:19; 12:1—14:20; 15:1—16:21; 17:1—19:10; 19:11–21; 20:1–15), and a final, eighth portion that presents the supreme vision of the new Jerusalem following the second coming (21:1—22:5). Each of the seven cycles of judgment is best understood as depicting the same spiritual war, but from a fresh vantage point. Later cycles concentrate progressively more on the most intense phases of conflict and on the second coming itself. The vision of the New Jerusalem presents the peace of the new heavens and the new earth after the war has ceased.

Symbolic personages are introduced into the drama one by one, with their destinies assigned later in the book in reverse order, as follows:

A. The People of God Depicted With the Imagery of Light and Creation (12:1–2)
  B. The Dragon: Satan (12:3–6)
    C. The Beast and the False Prophet (13:1–18)
      D. The Bride: The People of God in the Imagery of Sexual Purity (14:1–5)
        E. Babylon the Prostitute (17:1–6)
        E. Babylon Destroyed (17:15—18:24)
      D. The Bride Is Blessed With Marriage(19:1–10)
    C. The Beast and the False Prophet Are Destroyed (19:11–21)
  B. The Dragon Is Destroyed (20:1–10)
A. The People of God in the Imagery of Light and Creation (21:1—22:5)

Many thematic features unify the book. Repeated use of the number seven signifies completeness. God's plan and power determine the outcomes. Praise to God rises from the angels and saints (see note on 1:6). Satanic counterfeits oppose God in a spiritual war of cosmic proportions. The present struggles of the church (2:1—3:22) contrast with its final rest. The church must maintain its witness and purity. Everything moves forward to the victory of Christ at his coming.

Interpreters disagree about the time and the manner in which the visions (especially those in chapters 6–18) have been, are being or will be fulfilled. Four major views have emerged: (1) "Preterists" believe that fulfillment occurred in the fall of Jerusalem (if Revelation was written in A.D. 67–68) and/or the fall of the Roman Empire. (2) "Futurists" contend that fulfillment will occur in a period of final crisis just before the second coming. (3) "Historicists" interpret chapters 6–18 as a basically chronological outline of the course of church history from the first century (6:1) until the second coming (e.g., 19:11). (4) "Idealists" argue that the scenes of Revelation depict general principles of spiritual warfare, not specific events. These principles are operative throughout the church age and may have repeated fulfillments.

A combination of these views is probably closest to the truth. The imagery in Revelation is multifaceted and is in principle capable of multiple embodiments. Idealists maintain that general principles are expressed. If so, those principles had a particular relevance to the seven churches and their struggles in the first century (1:4; see "Original Audience"). The principles also will come to climactic expression in the final crisis of the second coming (22:20; cf. 2Th 2:1–12). Christians today are involved in the same spiritual warfare and so must apply the principles to themselves and this present time. Hence, many passages have at least three main applications: to the first century, to the final crisis and to whatever time period the readers happen to be living in.

On the other hand, preterists can easily acknowledge that the underlying principles of conflict have wider significance. Thus the practical applications they draw can be similar to those of the idealists. Patience and humility are needed when we confront disagreements on these matters. In the meantime, Revelation has broad lessons from which all can profit.

Outline

I. Introduction (1:1–8) A. Prologue (1:1–3) B. Greeting (1:4–5a) C. Praise (1:5b–8)	*John set the stage for his epistle by exalting Christ as the source of his revelation and by identifying himself and his addressees.*
II. Visions (1:9—22:5) A. Vision of Christ: The King, Priest and Judge (1:9–20) B. Exhortations to the Seven Churches (2:1—3:22) C. Heavenly Visions (4:1—22:5) 1. Cycle One: The Scroll and Its Seven Seals (4:1—8:1) a. God the King and Christ the Worthy One (4:1—5:14) b. Opening the Six Seals (6:1–17) c. Care for the Saints (7:1–17) d. Opening the Seventh Seal (8:1) 2. Cycle Two: Seven Angels With Seven Trumpets (8:2—11:19) a. Seven Angels Before God (8:2–6) b. Six Angels Blow Their Trumpets (8:7—9:21) c. Care for John and the Two Witnesses (10:1—11:14) d. The Seventh Angel Blows His Trumpet (11:15–19) 3. Cycle Three: Seven Symbolic Histories (12:1—14:20) a. Principal Personages: The People of God Versus Satan (12:1–6) b. Six Symbolic Histories (12:7—14:11) (1) The Dragon (12:7–12) (2) The Woman (12:13–17) (3) The Beast From the Sea (13:1–10) (4) The Beast From the Earth: The False Prophet (13:11–18) (5) The 144,000 (14:1–5) (6) Three Angelic Messengers (14:6–11) c. Care for the Saints (14:12–13) d. The Seventh Symbolic History: One Like a Son of Man(14:14–20) 4. Cycle Four: Seven Bowls of God's Wrath From the Temple (15:1—16:21) 5. Cycle Five: Judgment on Babylon and Vindication of the Church (17:1—19:10) 6. Cycle Six: The Final Battle (19:11–21) 7. Cycle Seven: The Reign of the Saints and the Last Judgment (20:1—21:8) 8. The New Jerusalem (21:19—22:5)	*Seven cycles of highly symbolic visions of the present and future challenges and blessings are described to encourage believers to be faithful to Christ while undergoing suffering and to warn against turning away from Christ. An eighth vision, one that describes the new Jerusalem, is also presented.*
III. Conclusion (22:6–21) A. Final Exhortations (22:6–20) B. Closing Blessing (22:21)	*John drew his letter to a conclusion with several encouragements and a blessing.*

Prologue

1:1 **1** The revelation of Jesus Christ, which God gave him to show his servants what must
[a]Rev 22:16 soon take place. He made it known by sending his angel[a] to his servant John, 2who
1:2 testifies to everything he saw—that is, the word of God and the testimony of Jesus
[b]1Co 1:6; Christ.[b] 3Blessed is the one who reads the words of this prophecy, and blessed are those
Rev 12:17 who hear it and take to heart what is written in it,[c] because the time is near.

1:3
[c]Lk 11:28

Greetings and Doxology

4John,

To the seven churches in the province of Asia:

Grace and peace to you from him who is, and who was, and who is to come, and from
1:4 [d]Rev 3:1; 4:5 the seven spirits[a][d] before his throne, 5and from Jesus Christ, who is the faithful witness,[e]
1:5 the firstborn from the dead,[f] and the ruler of the kings of the earth.[g]
[e]Rev 3:14 [f]Col 1:18
[g]Rev 17:14

To him who loves us and has freed us from our sins by his blood, 6and has made us
1:6 [h]1Pe 2:5 [i]Ro 11:36 to be a kingdom and priests[h] to serve his God and Father—to him be glory and power
for ever and ever! Amen.[i]

1:7
[j]Da 7:13
[k]Zec 12:10

> 7Look, he is coming with the clouds,[j]
> and every eye will see him,
> even those who pierced him;
> and all the peoples of the earth will mourn[k] because of him.
> So shall it be! Amen.

1:8
[l]Rev 21:6 [m]Rev 4:8

8"I am the Alpha and the Omega,"[l] says the Lord God, "who is, and who was, and who
is to come, the Almighty."[m]

1:9
[n]Php 4:14

One Like a Son of Man

9I, John, your brother and companion in the suffering[n] and kingdom and patient en-

[a] 4 Or *the sevenfold Spirit*

■ **1:1–8** *Introduction.* John began his book with a rather elaborate opening. His introduction divides into three parts: a prologue (vv. 1–3), greetings (vv. 4–5a) and praise (vv. 5b–8).
■ **1:1–3** *Prologue.* These verses orient readers to the content they may expect. Stress is placed on the divine authority of the message, its certainty (note the word "must" in v. 1) and its crucial relevance (v. 3). God made thorough provision for the communication process: The message originated with God the Father, was given to Jesus Christ and was made known to John through an angel (v. 1). John testified by writing it (v. 2), and all are encouraged to read and hear (v. 3).
1:1 soon. See 22:6, 7, 10, 12 and 20. Spiritual warfare takes place throughout the church age, and the seven churches would soon experience all dimensions of the conflict. Moreover, the "last days" of Old Testament prophecy have been inaugurated by Christ's resurrection (Ac 2:16–17). The time of waiting is ending, and God is conducting the final phase of his victorious warfare against evil. By such reckoning, today is "the last hour" (1Jn 2:18). See theological article "The Plan of the Ages" at Hebrews 7.
1:2 testimony of Jesus Christ. Because of the present reality of persecution (17:6), the theme of witness echoes throughout Revelation. Jesus Christ is the preeminent witness (1:5; 3:14; 19:11), and imitating him may include martyrdom (12:11). Revelation itself is a testimony intended to strengthen the testimony of its readers.
1:3 Blessed. Revelation pronounces not only judgment on the faithless, but also blessing on the faithful (14:13; 16:15; 19:9; 20:6; 22:7,14; see note on Mt 5:3). **prophecy.** See 22:7–10,18–19. Like much Old Testament prophecy, Revelation combines visions of the future with exhortations to faithfulness. Prophecy is a distinctive and inspired form of Christian testimony (see note on 1:2). See *WCF* 21.5; *WLC* 156. **take to heart.** Revelation is not intended to tickle one's fancy but to strengthen one's heart (see "Introduction: Purpose and Distinctives").
■ **1:4–5a** *Greeting.* This greeting follows the formal arrangement of a Greek letter: It identifies the author and the recipients.
1:4 To the seven churches. See 1:11; 2:1—3:22. Revelation is organized in sevens (see "Introduction: Outline"), the symbolic number of completeness stemming from the original week of creation (Ge 2:2–3). The choice of seven churches expresses the relevance of the message to all churches (1:1,3; 2:7,11,17,29; 3:6,13,22; 22:7,11–14,16,18–21). **Asia.** The Roman province of Asia lay in what is now western Turkey. **him who is, and who was, and who is to come.** Similar to the divine name in Exodus 3:14–15. See note on 1:8. **seven spirits.** The Holy Spirit is described in sevenfold fullness (see NIV text notes here and at 4:5; see also Zec 4:2,6). Note the origin of grace and peace from the Trinity: God the Father ("him who is . . ."), the Son (1:5) and the Spirit (cf. 2Co 13:14; 1Pe 1:1–2).
1:5a Jesus Christ . . . faithful witness . . . firstborn . . . ruler. The key roles of Jesus Christ in this book are anticipated in this description. **faithful witness.** See note on verse 2. **firstborn.** See note on verse 18. **ruler.** See note on 4:1—5:14. Because all things hold together in Christ (Col 1:17), the Trinitarian imagery of verses 4–5 and 4:1—5:14 forms a foundation for the book. Because the Trinity is deeply mysterious, the imagery of Revelation has inexhaustible profundity.
■ **1:5b–8** *Praise.* Revelation begins with praise to God, which is similar to the beginnings of most Pauline letters. The themes of God's sovereignty and redemption, as well as of Christ's second coming, recur throughout the book.
1:5b To him. The theme of worship and praise of God extends throughout the book (e.g., 4:8,11; 5:9–14; 7:12; 11:15–17; 12:10–12; 15:3–4; 19:1–8) because praise is an integral part of spiritual warfare. **has freed us.** See note on 5:1–14. See *WLC* 165; *BC* 34; *HC* 70,73.
1:6 kingdom and priests. John applied Exodus 19:6 to all believers from all nations because they collectively enjoy God's rule and as priests have intimate access to him (Heb 10:19–22; 1Pe 2:5–9). In the future, they will reign with him (2:26–27; 3:21; 5:10; 20:4,6). The purposes of redemption that were embodied in Israel's exodus from Egypt are fulfilled through Christ (5:9–10). The theme of priestly worship and access to God is complementary to the temple theme in Revelation (see note on 4:1—5:14).
1:7 mourn. The return of Christ in judgment against his enemies encouraged John and his readers during the persecution they endured (see theological article "The Final Judgment" in Jude).
1:8 the Alpha and the Omega. The first and last letters of the Greek alphabet. God is Alpha (Creator) and Omega (Consummator). He is Lord of all—past, present and future—as suggested by the attribution "who is, and who was, and who is to come" (cf. v. 4; see note on 4:1—5:14). His sovereignty in creation guarantees the fulfillment of his purposes in re-creation (Ro 8:18–25). **who is to come.** In the future God will come to consummate all his purposes (21:1—22:5; see theological article "The Kingdom of God" at Mt 4).
■ **1:9—22:5** *Visions.* In these chapters John formed the main body

durance[o] that are ours in Jesus, was on the island of Patmos because of the word of God
and the testimony of Jesus. 10On the Lord's Day I was in the Spirit,[p] and I heard behind
me a loud voice like a trumpet,[q] 11which said: "Write on a scroll what you see and send
it to the seven churches:[r] to Ephesus, Smyrna, Pergamum, Thyatira, Sardis,[s] Philadelphia and Laodicea."

12I turned around to see the voice that was speaking to me. And when I turned I saw
seven golden lampstands,[t] 13and among the lampstands was someone "like a son of
man,"[a][u] dressed in a robe reaching down to his feet and with a golden sash around his
chest.[v] 14His head and hair were white like wool, as white as snow, and his eyes were like
blazing fire.[w] 15His feet were like bronze glowing in a furnace,[x] and his voice was like the
sound of rushing waters.[y] 16In his right hand he held seven stars,[z] and out of his mouth
came a sharp double-edged sword.[a] His face was like the sun shining in all its brilliance.

17When I saw him, I fell at his feet[b] as though dead. Then he placed his right hand
on me and said: "Do not be afraid. I am the First and the Last.[c] 18I am the Living One; I
was dead,[d] and behold I am alive for ever and ever![e] And I hold the keys of death and
Hades.[f]

19"Write, therefore, what you have seen, what is now and what will take place later.
20The mystery of the seven stars that you saw in my right hand and of the seven golden
lampstands[g] is this: The seven stars are the angels[b] of the seven churches,[h] and the sev-
en lampstands are the seven churches.[i]

To the Church in Ephesus

2 "To the angel[c] of the church in Ephesus write:

These are the words of him who holds the seven stars in his right hand[j] and
walks among the seven golden lampstands:[k] 2I know your deeds,[l] your hard

1:9 [o]2Ti 2:12
1:10 [p]Rev 4:2 [q]Rev 4:1
1:11 [r]ver 4,20 [s]Rev 3:1
1:12 [t]Ex 25:31-40; Zec 4:2
1:13 [u]Eze 1:26; Da 7:13; 10:16 [v]Da 10:5; Rev 15:6
1:14 [w]Da 7:9; 10:6; Rev 19:12
1:15 [x]Da 10:6 [y]Eze 43:2; Rev 14:2
1:16 [z]Rev 2:1; 3:1 [a]Isa 49:2; Heb 4:12; Rev 2:12,16
1:17 [b]Eze 1:28; Da 8:17, 18 [c]Isa 41:4; 44:6; 48:12; Rev 22:13
1:18 [d]Ro 6:9 [e]Rev 4:9, 10 [f]Rev 20:1
1:20 [g]Zec 4:2 [h]ver 4,11 [i]Mt 5:14,15
2:1 [j]Rev 1:16 [k]Rev 1:12,13
2:2 [l]Rev 3:1,8,15

[a] *13* Daniel 7:13 [b] *20* Or *messengers* [c] *1* Or *messenger*; also in verses 8, 12 and 18

---

of his letter by reporting a number of visions he had experienced. This material divides into three main sections: a vision of Christ (1:9–20), exhortations to the seven churches (2:1—3:22) and a series of seven heavenly visions (4:1—22:5).

■ **1:9–20** *Vision of Christ: The King, Priest and Judge.* Christ appears as the majestic king and judge of the universe and ruler of the churches (vv. 12–20).

1:9 your brother and companion. John represents the whole church. **patient endurance.** The practical exhortation to endure and remain faithful in the midst of persecution runs through Revelation (2:2–3,13,19; 3:10; 6:11; 13:10; 14:12; 16:15; 18:4; 20:4; 22:7, 11,14). **Patmos.** A small island off the western coast of Asia Minor. Patmos was the site of a Roman penal settlement that was used for persons considered dangerous to good order.

1:10 the Lord's Day. Sunday, the Christian day of worship, celebrating Christ's resurrection. The Sunday celebration anticipates the celebration of God's final victory (19:1–10). **in the Spirit.** The Spirit provided John with visions and transported him to vantage points from which he could view them (4:2; 17:3; 21:10). **loud voice.** The voice of Christ. Loud voices and noises indicate the power and universal relevance of the messages and events (1:15; 4:1,5; 5:2,12; 6:1; 7:2,10; 8:5,13; 10:3; 11:12,15,19; 12:10; 14:7,9, 15,18; 19:1,3,6,17). See *WCF* 21.7; *WLC* 116,121.

1:11 seven churches. See note on 1:4.

1:12–13 lampstands. The lampstands symbolize the churches in their light- or witness-bearing function (1:20; Mt 5:14–16). Christ walks among the churches as Lord, Shepherd and Priest, just as God's cloud of glory condescended to dwell in the tabernacle and the temple, both of which had lampstands (Ex 25:31–40; 1Ki 7:49). God's character as light (1Jn 1:5) is supremely manifested in Christ (Jn 1:4–5; 8:12; 9:5; Ac 26:13), but it is also reflected in various ways in his creation: in fiery angels (10:1; Eze 1:13), in natural light (21:23; Ge 1:3), in the temple lampstands, in the churches and in each individual believer (Mt 5:14–16). Christ thus presents the pattern in which the destiny of the whole universe is summed up (Eph 1:10; Col 1:16–17).

1:13–18 Christ appears in overwhelming glory (cf. 21:22–24). The features of verses 12–16 are reminiscent of Ezeziel 1:25–28 and Daniel 7:9–10 and 10:5–6, but they also include more distant similarities to many Old Testament appearances of God. The vision shows Christ as Judge and Ruler—first of all over the churches (1:20—3:22) but also over the whole universe (1:17–18; 2:27; 3:21). His deity, authority and conquest of death guarantee final victory (vv. 17–18; 17:14; 19:11–16). This vision of God's sovereignty, exercised through Christ, is a fundamental center point to the message of Revelation. Christ's warriorlike fierceness anticipates his role in the final battle (19:11–21) but also looks backward to God's battles in the Old Testament (Ex 15:3; Dt 32:41–42; Isa 59:17–18; Zec 14:3).

1:15 sound of rushing waters. See note on 1:10.

1:17 the First and the Last. Essentially the same as "the Alpha and the Omega," a description attributed to the Father in verse 8 (see note on v. 8; cf. 2:8; 22:13; Isa 41:4; 44:6; 48:12). Revelation indicates the deity of Christ by giving him the same title as God the Father (v. 8; 22:13), by indicating in the vision of verses 13–16 that he shares the attributes of God and by showing that he shares in God's sovereignty (22:1).

1:18 Living One. Christ's resurrection and new life provide for the new life of his people (2:8; 5:9–10; 20:4–5) and the renewal of the world itself (22:1–2). **keys of death.** This phrase anticipates 20:14. See *WLC* 52.

1:19 have seen . . . is now . . . will take place later. A reference to the past, present and future. Each portion of Revelation contains significant references to all three periods.

1:20 the angels. The Greek word means "messengers." It may refer to human messengers, specifically to the pastors of the churches, or to supernatural beings. The prominence of angels in Revelation would support the latter meaning here (22:6; Da 10:10–21). Compare 2:1, 8, 12 and 18 and 3:1, 7 and 14.

■ **2:1–3:22** *Exhortations to the Seven Churches.* Christ shows care for the churches by addressing a letter to each according to its needs, including commendations or rebukes, as well as exhortations and promises. He shows detailed knowledge of their individual situations ("I know," 2:2,9,13,19; 3:1,8,15). All seven letters allude to circumstances or traditions of each particular city. At the same time, all the churches are included in a universal calling to faithfulness and endurance until the promises reach their fulfillment in the heavenly Jerusalem. Their struggles contrast with the peace and satisfaction at the end, as pictured in 21:1—22:5. Each letter's exhortations are reinforced by opening allusions to elements of the majestic vision of 1:12–20. The selection of exactly seven churches suggests the wider relevance of the message (see note on 1:4). Each message has the same basic form: (1) Addressee: "to the angel of the church in . . . write." (2) Identification of Christ, alluding back to his majesty displayed in 1:12–20: "These are the words of . . ." (3) Claim of knowledge: "I know." (4) Evaluation: rebukes and/or commendations. (5) Promise or threat: usually "I will." (6) Promise to "him who overcomes." (7) Exhortation to listen: "He who has an ear." Note that elements (6) and (7) may occur in reverse order and that (5) may be mixed with (4).

2:1–29 See *WCF* 25.4; 25.5.

2:1 angel. See note on 1:20. **church.** The visible churches in each

work and your perseverance. I know that you cannot tolerate wicked men, that
you have tested[m] those who claim to be apostles but are not, and have found them
false.[n] 3 You have persevered and have endured hardships for my name,[o] and have
not grown weary.

4 Yet I hold this against you: You have forsaken your first love.[p] 5 Remember the
height from which you have fallen! Repent[q] and do the things you did at first. If
you do not repent, I will come to you and remove your lampstand[r] from its place.
6 But you have this in your favor: You hate the practices of the Nicolaitans,[s] which
I also hate.

7 He who has an ear, let him hear[t] what the Spirit says to the churches. To him
who overcomes, I will give the right to eat from the tree of life,[u] which is in the paradise[v] of God.

To the Church in Smyrna

8 "To the angel of the church in Smyrna[w] write:

These are the words of him who is the First and the Last,[x] who died and came
to life again.[y] 9 I know your afflictions and your poverty—yet you are rich![z] I
know the slander of those who say they are Jews and are not,[a] but are a synagogue
of Satan.[b] 10 Do not be afraid of what you are about to suffer. I tell you, the devil
will put some of you in prison to test you,[c] and you will suffer persecution for ten
days.[d] Be faithful,[e] even to the point of death, and I will give you the crown of life.

11 He who has an ear, let him hear what the Spirit says to the churches. He who
overcomes will not be hurt at all by the second death.[f]

To the Church in Pergamum

12 "To the angel of the church in Pergamum[g] write:

These are the words of him who has the sharp, double-edged sword.[h] 13 I
know where you live—where Satan has his throne. Yet you remain true to my
name. You did not renounce your faith in me,[i] even in the days of Antipas, my
faithful witness, who was put to death in your city—where Satan lives.[j]

14 Nevertheless, I have a few things against you:[k] You have people there who
hold to the teaching of Balaam,[l] who taught Balak to entice the Israelites to sin
by eating food sacrificed to idols and by committing sexual immorality.[m] 15 Likewise you also have those who hold to the teaching of the Nicolaitans.[n] 16 Repent
therefore! Otherwise, I will soon come to you and will fight against them with the
sword of my mouth.[o]

17 He who has an ear, let him hear what the Spirit says to the churches. To him
who overcomes, I will give some of the hidden manna.[p] I will also give him a white
stone with a new name[q] written on it, known only to him who receives it.[r]

2:2 [m]1Jn 4:1 [n]2Co 11:13
2:3 [o]Jn 15:21
2:4 [p]Mt 24:12
2:5 [q]ver 16,22 [r]Rev 1:20
2:6 [s]ver 15
2:7 [t]Mt 11:15; Rev 3:6, 13,22 [u]Ge 2:9; Rev 22:2,14,19 [v]Lk 23:43
2:8 [w]Rev 1:11 [x]Rev 1:17 [y]Rev 1:18
2:9 [z]Jas 2:5 [a]Rev 3:9 [b]Mt 4:10
2:10 [c]Rev 3:10 [d]Da 1:12, 14 [e]ver 13
2:11 [f]Rev 20:6,14; 21:8
2:12 [g]Rev 1:11 [h]Rev 1:16
2:13 [i]Rev 14:12 [j]ver 9, 24
2:14 [k]ver 20 [l]2Pe 2:15 [m]1Co 6:13
2:15 [n]ver 6
2:16 [o]2Th 2:8; Rev 1:16
2:17 [p]Jn 6:49,50 [q]Isa 62:2 [r]Rev 19:12

location are addressed. Not all within these churches were true believers. Thus there is an emphasis on threats of judgment and the need for perseverance in all of these letters to the churches (see theological articles "The Church: Visible and Invisible" at 1Pe 4 and "The Perseverance and Preservation of Believers" at Php 1).

2:2–4 See *WCF* 17.3; 20.4; *WLC* 109.

2:5 remove your lampstand. Ephesus had previously changed its location because of the gradual silt deposits building up in its river, the Cayster. It had been "removed" from earlier locations. By analogy, Christ threatened to remove the church unless its people repented.

2:6 Nicolaitans. A heretical group, probably holding views similar to the teachings of Balaam and Jezebel (see notes on vv. 14,20).

2:7 him who overcomes. In this and parallel verses to the other churches, faithful saints are promised participation in all aspects of the new Jerusalem (vv. 11,17,26; 3:5,12,21; 21:1—22:5). The requirement of perseverance through trials does not make salvation dependent on human effort. Rather, saving faith demonstrates itself through the believer's steadfastness. See theological article "The Perseverance and Preservation of Believers" at Philippians 1. **tree of life.** See note on 22:2.

2:9 synagogue of Satan. The membership of the Jewish synagogue in Smyrna was composed of Jews who had refused the message concerning the coming of the Messiah. Although they professed to worship God, their opposition to Christians showed that they were in fact under the power of satanic darkness (2Co 4:4). See *BC* 29.

2:10 Be faithful. The city of Smyrna prided itself on its faithfulness to Rome. **crown of life.** Smyrna's goddess Cybele was pictured on coins with a crown consisting of a city battlement. The Smyrnan buildings on Mount Pagos were said to look like a crown. Over against these claims, Jesus offered to impart the true crown. See *WLC* 45.

2:11 second death. The first death is the normal experience of death in this creation, which in some sense is preliminary. At the end of the age, all who have died will be resurrected and judged (Jn 5:28–29). Unbelievers who are resurrected will be condemned as sinners and will die a second, final death. Believers will be resurrected unto life, avoiding this second death.

2:13 where Satan has his throne. Pergamum possessed the oldest temple in Asia Minor devoted to emperor worship.

2:14–15 See *WCF* 20.4; *WLC* 109.

2:14 Balaam. Balaam (Nu 22:5) gave Balak advice that led to the incident in Numbers 25:1–4. "Jezebel" (v. 20 and its note) and other professing Christians in the seven churches were indulging in pleasures offered by their pagan environment (see note on 17:1—19:10). The mention of Balaam thus introduces the general theme of the temptation to compromise with the world that results in entrapment by its idolatries.

2:15 Nicolaitans. See note on verse 6.

2:17 hidden manna. Perhaps an allusion to the manna preserved in the Most Holy Place of the tabernacle (Ex 16:33–35; Heb 9:4). Christ promised to nourish the faithful with an unfailing supply of heavenly, spiritual food (Jn 6:32–58). **new name.** Naming was an exercise of authority over the one named (e.g., Ge 2:19–20; Mt 1:25). By renaming the faithful, Jesus confirms them as his own who are under his authority. **known only.** In some instances, knowing a being's name was a way of gaining power over him or

To the Church in Thyatira

18"To the angel of the church in Thyatira[s] write:

These are the words of the Son of God, whose eyes are like blazing fire and whose
feet are like burnished bronze.[t] 19I know your deeds,[u] your love and faith, your service and perseverance, and that you are now doing more than you did at first.
20Nevertheless, I have this against you: You tolerate that woman Jezebel,[v] who
calls herself a prophetess. By her teaching she misleads my servants into sexual immorality and the eating of food sacrificed to idols. 21I have given her time[w] to repent
of her immorality, but she is unwilling.[x] 22So I will cast her on a bed of suffering, and
I will make those who commit adultery[y] with her suffer intensely, unless they repent
of her ways. 23I will strike her children dead. Then all the churches will know that I
am he who searches hearts and minds,[z] and I will repay each of you according to
your deeds. 24Now I say to the rest of you in Thyatira, to you who do not hold to her
teaching and have not learned Satan's so-called deep secrets (I will not impose any
other burden on you):[a] 25Only hold on to what you have[b] until I come.
26To him who overcomes and does my will to the end, I will give authority over
the nations[c]—

27'He will rule them with an iron scepter;[d]
he will dash them to pieces like pottery'[a][e]—

just as I have received authority from my Father. 28I will also give him the morning
star.[f] 29He who has an ear, let him hear[g] what the Spirit says to the churches.

To the Church in Sardis

3 "To the angel[b] of the church in Sardis write:

These are the words of him who holds the seven spirits[c][h] of God and the sev-
en stars.[i] I know your deeds;[j] you have a reputation of being alive, but you are

2:18 [s]Rev 1:11 [t]Rev 1:14,15
2:19 [u]ver 2
2:20 [v]1Ki 16:31; 21:25; 2Ki 9:7
2:21 [w]Ro 2:4 [x]Rev 9:20
2:22 [y]Rev 17:2; 18:9
2:23 [z]1Sa 16:7; Jer 11:20; Ac 1:24; Ro 8:27
2:24 [a]Ac 15:28
2:25 [b]Rev 3:11
2:26 [c]Ps 2:8; Rev 3:21
2:27 [d]Rev 12:5 [e]Isa 30:14; Jer 19:11
2:28 [f]Rev 22:16
2:29 [g]ver 7
3:1 [h]Rev 1:4 [i]Rev 1:16 [j]Rev 2:2

[a] 27 Psalm 2:9 [b] 1 Or *messenger*; also in verses 7 and 14 [c] 1 Or *the sevenfold Spirit*

her (see note on Mk 5:9). By keeping the new names secret, Jesus ensures that believers will never fall under the power of an enemy.
2:18 burnished bronze. Thyatira had a famous guild of bronze workers.
2:20 Jezebel. See 1 Kings 16:31, 19:1–2, 21:5–26 and 2 Kings 9:30–37. This woman was called Jezebel because, like the Old Testament figure by that name, she seduced people to sexual immorality and idolatry, two major forms of indulgence in pagan Asia Minor. See notes on 14:8 and 17:1—19:10. See also *WCF* 20.4; *WLC* 109.
2:23 See *BC* 24.
2:28 morning star. In the Bible the Greek term is used only here and in 22:16, where it refers to Jesus.
3:1–22 See *WCF* 25.4; 25.5.
3:1 See *WLC* 105.

The Seven Churches of Revelation

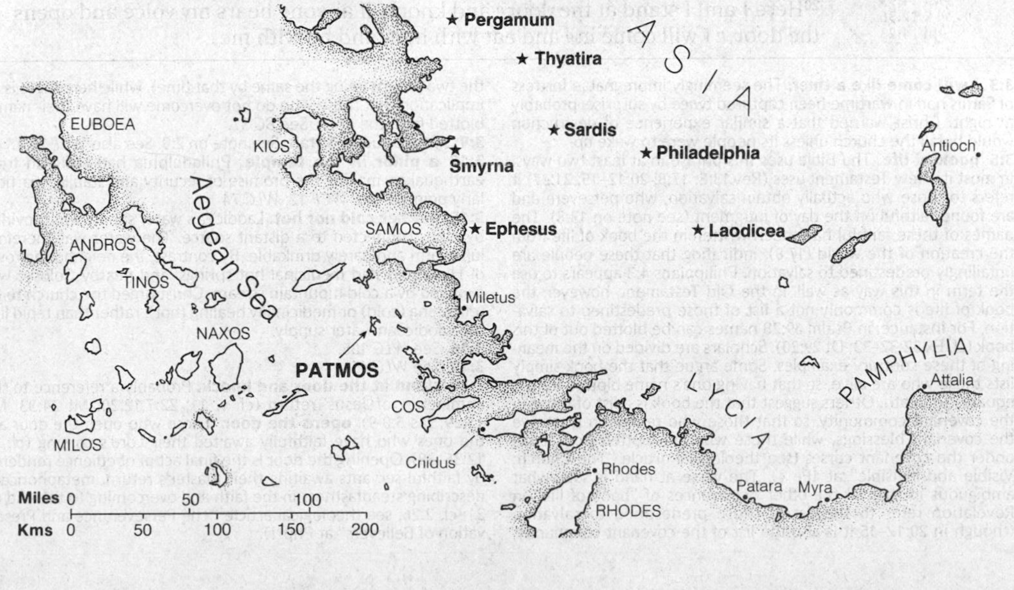

dead.[k] 2 Wake up! Strengthen what remains and is about to die, for I have not
found your deeds complete in the sight of my God. 3 Remember, therefore, what
you have received and heard; obey it, and repent.[l] But if you do not wake up, I will
come like a thief,[m] and you will not know at what time I will come to you.
4 Yet you have a few people in Sardis who have not soiled their clothes.[n] They
will walk with me, dressed in white,[o] for they are worthy. 5 He who overcomes will,
like them, be dressed in white. I will never blot out his name from the book of life,[p]
but will acknowledge his name before my Father[q] and his angels. 6 He who has an
ear, let him hear[r] what the Spirit says to the churches.

To the Church in Philadelphia

7 "To the angel of the church in Philadelphia[s] write:
These are the words of him who is holy and true,[t] who holds the key of David.[u]
What he opens no one can shut, and what he shuts no one can open. 8 I know your
deeds. See, I have placed before you an open door[v] that no one can shut. I know
that you have little strength, yet you have kept my word and have not denied my
name.[w] 9 I will make those who are of the synagogue of Satan,[x] who claim to be
Jews though they are not, but are liars—I will make them come and fall down at
your feet[y] and acknowledge that I have loved you.[z] 10 Since you have kept my command to endure patiently, I will also keep you[a] from the hour of trial that is going to come upon the whole world to test[b] those who live on the earth.[c]
11 I am coming soon. Hold on to what you have,[d] so that no one will take your
crown.[e] 12 Him who overcomes I will make a pillar[f] in the temple of my God. Never again will he leave it. I will write on him the name of my God[g] and the name of
the city of my God, the new Jerusalem,[h] which is coming down out of heaven from
my God; and I will also write on him my new name. 13 He who has an ear, let him
hear what the Spirit says to the churches.

To the Church in Laodicea

14 "To the angel of the church in Laodicea write:
These are the words of the Amen, the faithful and true witness, the ruler of
God's creation.[i] 15 I know your deeds, that you are neither cold nor hot.[j] I wish you
were either one or the other! 16 So, because you are lukewarm—neither hot nor
cold—I am about to spit you out of my mouth. 17 You say, 'I am rich; I have acquired wealth and do not need a thing.'[k] But you do not realize that you are
wretched, pitiful, poor, blind and naked. 18 I counsel you to buy from me gold refined in the fire, so you can become rich; and white clothes to wear, so you can
cover your shameful nakedness;[l] and salve to put on your eyes, so you can see.
19 Those whom I love I rebuke and discipline.[m] So be earnest, and repent.[n]
20 Here I am! I stand at the door[o] and knock. If anyone hears my voice and opens
the door,[p] I will come in[q] and eat with him, and he with me.

3:1 [k] 1Ti 5:6
3:3 [l] Rev 2:5 [m] 2Pe 3:10
3:4 [n] Jude 23 [o] Rev 4:4; 6:11; 7:9,13,14
3:5 [p] Rev 20:12 [q] Mt 10:32
3:6 [r] Rev 2:7
3:7 [s] Rev 1:11 [t] 1Jn 5:20 [u] Isa 22:22; Mt 16:19
3:8 [v] Ac 14:27 [w] Rev 2:13
3:9 [x] Rev 2:9 [y] Isa 49:23 [z] Isa 43:4
3:10 [a] 2Pe 2:9 [b] Rev 2:10 [c] Rev 6:10; 17:8
3:11 [d] Rev 2:25 [e] Rev 2:10
3:12 [f] Gal 2:9 [g] Rev 14:1; 22:4 [h] Rev 21:2,10
3:14 [i] Col 1:16,18
3:15 [j] Ro 12:11
3:17 [k] Hos 12:8; 1Co 4:8
3:18 [l] Rev 16:15
3:19 [m] Pr 3:12; Heb 12:5,6 [n] Rev 2:5
3:20 [o] Mt 24:33 [p] Lk 12:36 [q] Jn 14:23

3:3 I will come like a thief. The seemingly impregnable fortress of Sardis had in wartime been captured twice by surprise, probably at night. Christ warned that a similar experience of destruction would befall the church unless its people were to wake up.

3:5 book of life. The Bible uses this phrase in at least two ways. In most its New Testament uses (Rev.13:8; 17:8; 20:12–15; 21:27) it refers to those who actually obtain salvation, who persevere and are found faithful on the day of judgment (see note on 13:8). The names of these faithful have been written in the book of life from the creation of the world (17:8), indicating that these people are unfailingly predestined to salvation. Philippians 4:3 appears to use the term in this way as well. In the Old Testament, however, the book of life is commonly not a list of those predestined to salvation. For instance, in Psalm 69:28 names can be blotted out of this book (cf. Ex 32:32–33; Dt 29:20). Scholars are divided on the meaning of these contrary examples. Some argue that the book simply lists those who are alive, so that having one's name blotted from it equates to death. Others suggest that the book is a list of those in the covenant community, so that those who remain in it receive the covenant blessings, while those who are blotted from it fall under the covenant curses (see theological article "The Church: Visible and Invisible" at 1Pe 4). The verse at hand is somewhat ambiguous in that all the other occurrences of "book of life" in Revelation refer to the list of those predestined to salvation (though in 20:12–15 it is also the list of the covenant community, the two groups being the same by that time), while here there is an implication that those who do not overcome will have their names blotted from the book. See *BC* 37.

3:9 synagogue of Satan. See note on 2:9. See also *WCF* 20.4.

3:12 a pillar in the temple. Philadelphia had suffered from earthquakes, making the promise of security and stability particularly pointed. See *WCF* 12; *WLC* 74

3:15 neither cold nor hot. Laodicea's water supply was provided by pipes connected to a distant source. The water was therefore lukewarm and barely drinkable. By contrast, the neighboring town of Hierapolis had medicinal hot springs, and nearby Colosse was supplied by a cold mountain stream. Christ urged the church to be refreshing (cold) or medicinally healing (hot), rather than tepid like the Laodicean water supply.

3:16 See *WLC* 105.

3:19 See *WLC* 45.

3:20 stand at the door and knock. Probably a reference to the imminence of Jesus' return (cf. v. 11; 22:7,12,20; Mt 24:33; Mk 13:29; Jas 5:8-9). **opens the door.** Those who open the door are the ones who have faithfully awaited their Lord's coming (cf. Lk 12:35–38). Opening the door is the final act of obedience rendered by faithful servants awaiting their master's return, metaphorically describing steadfastness in the faith and overcoming to the end (v. 21; cf. 2:26; see theological article "The Perseverance and Preservation of Believers" at Php 1).

21 To him who overcomes, I will give the right to sit with me on my throne,[r] just
as I overcame[s] and sat down with my Father on his throne. 22 He who has an ear,
let him hear[t] what the Spirit says to the churches."

The Throne in Heaven

4 After this I looked, and there before me was a door standing open in heaven. And the
voice I had first heard speaking to me like a trumpet[u] said, "Come up here,[v] and I
will show you what must take place after this."[w] 2 At once I was in the Spirit,[x] and there
before me was a throne in heaven[y] with someone sitting on it. 3 And the one who sat there
had the appearance of jasper and carnelian. A rainbow,[z] resembling an emerald, encircled the throne. 4 Surrounding the throne were twenty-four other thrones, and seated on
them were twenty-four elders.[a] They were dressed in white[b] and had crowns of gold on
their heads. 5 From the throne came flashes of lightning, rumblings and peals of thunder.[c]
Before the throne, seven lamps[d] were blazing. These are the seven spirits[a][e] of God. 6 Also
before the throne there was what looked like a sea of glass,[f] clear as crystal.
In the center, around the throne, were four living creatures,[g] and they were covered

[a] 5 Or *the sevenfold Spirit*

3:21 [r]Mt 19:28 [s]Rev 5:5
3:22 [t]Rev 2:7
4:1 [u]Rev 1:10 [v]Rev 11:12 [w]Rev 1:19
4:2 [x]Rev 1:10 [y]Isa 6:1; Eze 1:26-28; Da 7:9
4:3 [z]Eze 1:28
4:4 [a]Rev 11:16 [b]Rev 3:4,5
4:5 [c]Rev 8:5; 16:18 [d]Zec 4:2 [e]Rev 1:4
4:6 [f]Rev 15:2 [g]Eze 1:5

■ **4:1—22:5** *Heavenly Visions.* Through Christ and his angels (22:8–9,16) John received a series of seven cycles of visions—seven seals of the scroll (4:1—8:1), seven angels and trumpets (8:2—11:19), seven symbolic histories (12:1—14:20), seven bowls of wrath (15:1—16:21), Babylon and the church (17:1—19:10), the final battle (19:11–21) and the reign of the saints and the last judgment (20:1—21:8)—followed by a vision of the new Jerusalem (21:9—22:5). These visions were intended to rebuke and encourage the churches by opening their eyes to the kingship and majesty of God, the nature of spiritual warfare, God's judgments on evil and the outcome of the conflict. God and his army must ultimately win the battle (17:14; 19:1–2), but his forces are currently opposed by Satan, the great dragon (12:3), who leads the whole world astray (12:9). Satan has two agents, the beast and the false prophet, who together with him make up a counterfeit trinity (13:1–18; 16:13; see note on 13:1–10). The beast, representing raw power and state persecution, threatens to suppress true witness and to compel people to worship him (13:7–8). The false prophet is his assistant and propagandist. Babylon, representing the worldly city and the alluring aspects of idolatrous society, threatens to seduce the saints away from spiritual purity (2:20–23; 17:1–18). In opposition to these threats the saints must maintain a true and faithful witness—even to the point of martyrdom (12:11)—as well as true spiritual purity (14:4; 19:8). In the consummation, their witness finds its fulfillment in the final light of God's truth (21:22–27), and their purity takes perfect form in the spotless bride of the Lamb (21:9).

■ **4:1—8:1** *Cycle One: The Scroll and Its Seven Seals.* Judgments from God's throne unfold as the scroll's seven seals are opened one by one. The participation of the Lamb reminds us that such judgments are based on his unique qualifications and accomplishments (5:1–14). In formal structure, 5:1—8:1 parallels 8:2—11:19. Each has an opening scene that introduces the origin of the judgments (5:1–14; 8:2–6). Six judgments follow (6:1–17; 8:7—9:21). A dramatic interlude promises care for God's people (7:1–17; 10:1—11:14). The seventh and climactic judgment follows the interlude (8:1; 11:15–19; see "Introduction: Outline"). The seven judgments move forward toward the second coming, which occurs in 6:12–17 and 11:15–19. The first four judgments of the seven have an inner unity. The description in 6:1–8 corresponds to that of the four living creatures of 4:6 and the four horsemen of Zechariah 1:8. The 8:7–12 passage concerns the four major physical features of the world (i.e., dry land, sea, fresh water and air/sky).

■ **4:1—5:14** *God the King and Christ the Worthy One.* God appears in his throne room as the King of heaven and Earth who is surrounded by angelic courtiers (1Ki 22:19; Job 1:6; 2:1; Ps 89:6–7; Eze 1; Da 7:9–10). His rule was established in creation (4:11) and through the Lamb (5:1–14; 22:1). It is exercised in the panorama of history (6:1—22:5) and celebrated in songs of praise and worship (5:12–13; cf. note on 1:6). This heavenly scene not only reflects God's present rule in heaven but also anticipates his future rule in the new heavens and the new earth (cf. Mt 6:10). For those experiencing temptation and persecution, this vision provides hope and assurance: God's power guarantees the final victory, his justice guarantees vindication of the right, his goodness and magnificence guarantee blessing and comfort, and the blood of the Lamb guarantees that final redemption will be accomplished.

4:1–11 See *WCF* 2.1; *WLC* 7,191; *WSC* 4; *HC* 117.

4:1 Come up here. Moses went up to Mount Sinai (Ex 19:3,20), and Paul was caught up to heaven (2Co 12:2) to receive special revelations. **what must take place after this.** See note on 1:19.

4:2 in the Spirit. See note on 1:10. **throne in heaven.** In the Old Testament the tabernacle (Ex 25–40) and temple (1Ki 5–7; 2Ch 2–4) were shadows of God's throne room in heaven (Ex 25:40; Heb 8:5–6; 9:1–14). John saw the heavenly original rather than an earthly copy. Revelation fittingly contains many allusions to the temple (3:12; 7:15; 11:19; 14:15,17; 15:5—16:1; 16:17; 21:22) and to elements within it. For example, there are the lamps (1:12; 4:5); the living creatures, who are like cherubim (vv. 6–9); incense and prayer (5:8); songs of praise, like those offered by the Levites (vv. 8,11; 5:9–13; cf. 1Ch 16); a sacrifice (5:6,9); the ark of the covenant (11:19); the altar (11:1); and the outer court (11:2). **someone sitting on it.** The details of God's appearance are not described, reminding us that his greatness always exceeds our grasp. See note on 1:13–18.

4:4 twenty-four elders. A class of angelic ministers (7:13) are here called elders because of their wisdom. As God's cabinet officers, they must reflect his own wisdom, which is associated with age (Da 7:9). The name "elder" also suggests an analogy with the church's elders who perform their service on Earth. Hence, some have suggested that the elders here are simply a representation of the church. A number of interpreters suggest that the number 24 signifies the 12 tribes of Israel plus the 12 apostles. If this is so, 12 is a symbolic rather than an actual number, as there were actually 14 apostles (the original Twelve plus Matthias [Ac 1:26] and Paul). There were also 14 tribal names in the Old Testament (Joseph's sons Ephraim and Manasseh are often listed as full tribes), and tribal lists varied as to which names they included. The list of the 12 tribes in 7:4–8 does not mirror any Old Testament list, omitting Dan and listing both Joseph and his son Manasseh (but not Ephraim).

4:5 lightning. God exhibits his power in a manner analogous to his revelation to Moses on Mount Sinai (Ex 19:16–19) and to other divine appearances (8:5; 11:19; 16:18; see also Ps 18:11–15; Eze 1:4). He thus reminds us of the power of his voice (1:15; see note on 1:10) and the final shaking of creation still to come (11:19; 21:1; Heb 12:25–27). **seven lamps.** See note on 1:12–13 (cf. Zec 4:2). The sevenfold light of the Holy Spirit is the original light of which the seven-branched lampstand of Exodus 25:31–40 was a copy. The similarities with 1:12 suggest that the seven churches, viewed collectively as a true temple of God, were to give out light, reflecting the very presence of God through his Spirit. **seven spirits of God.** The Holy Spirit (see note on 1:4).

4:6 sea of glass. See 15:2 and Exodus 24:10. This imagery might suggest a number of associations. (1) The parallel verse in 15:2 calls to mind the waters of the Red Sea and the defeat of Pharaoh; the pushing back of the waters foreshadows God's final victory over evil (Isa 51:9–11). If so, the sea of glass pictures waters subdued under God's power. (2) The extent and beauty of the crystal-like sea, when taken together with the precious stones in verse 3 and in 21:18–21, suggest the magnificence and preciousness of God's throne. The numerous parallels elsewhere with the temple (see note on verse 2) might suggest that this sea is the heavenly counterpart of the sea in Solomon's temple (1Ki 7:23–25). (3) The picture of heavenly water might simply suggest the fact that God faithfully supplies water from heaven (Dt 11:11). **four living creatures.** These angelic ministers of God are reminiscent of the living creatures (Eze 1), the cherubim (Eze 10) and the seraphim (Isa 6). They are guardians and bearers of the throne of God (as in Ge 3:24; Ex 25:17–22; 1Ch 28:18; Ps 18:10).

4:7 [h]Eze 1:10; 10:14
4:8 [i]Isa 6:2 [j]Isa 6:3; Rev 1:8 [k]Rev 1:4

with eyes, in front and in back. 7The first living creature was like a lion, the second was
like an ox, the third had a face like a man, the fourth was like a flying eagle.[h] 8Each of
the four living creatures had six wings[i] and was covered with eyes all around, even under his wings. Day and night they never stop saying:

"Holy, holy, holy
is the Lord God Almighty,[j]
who was, and is, and is to come."[k]

4:9 [l]Ps 47:8
4:10 [m]ver 4 [n]Rev 5:8, 14 [o]ver 2

9Whenever the living creatures give glory, honor and thanks to him who sits on the
throne[l] and who lives for ever and ever, 10the twenty-four elders[m] fall down before him[n]
who sits on the throne,[o] and worship him who lives for ever and ever. They lay their
crowns before the throne and say:

4:11 [p]Rev 5:12 [q]Rev 10:6

11"You are worthy, our Lord and God,
to receive glory and honor and power,[p]
for you created all things,
and by your will they were created
and have their being."[q]

The Scroll and the Lamb

5:1 [r]ver 7, 13 [s]Eze 2:9, 10 [t]Isa 29:11; Da 12:4

5 Then I saw in the right hand of him who sat on the throne[r] a scroll with writing on
both sides[s] and sealed[t] with seven seals. 2And I saw a mighty angel proclaiming in
a loud voice, "Who is worthy to break the seals and open the scroll?" 3But no one in heav-
en or on earth or under the earth could open the scroll or even look inside it. 4I wept and
wept because no one was found who was worthy to open the scroll or look inside.
5Then one of the elders said to me, "Do not weep! See, the Lion[u] of the tribe of Judah,
the Root of David,[v] has triumphed. He is able to open the scroll and its seven seals."
6Then I saw a Lamb,[w] looking as if it had been slain, standing in the center of the
throne, encircled by the four living creatures and the elders. He had seven horns and sev-
en eyes,[x] which are the seven spirits[a] of God sent out into all the earth. 7He came and
took the scroll from the right hand of him who sat on the throne.[y] 8And when he had tak-
en it, the four living creatures and the twenty-four elders fell down before the Lamb. Each
one had a harp[z] and they were holding golden bowls full of incense, which are the
prayers[a] of the saints. 9And they sang a new song:[b]

5:5 [u]Ge 49:9 [v]Isa 11:1, 10; Ro 15:12; Rev 22:16
5:6 [w]Jn 1:29 [x]Zec 4:10
5:7 [y]ver 1
5:8 [z]Rev 14:2 [a]Ps 141:2
5:9 [b]Ps 40:3 [c]Rev 4:11 [d]Heb 9:12 [e]1Co 6:20

"You are worthy[c] to take the scroll
and to open its seals,
because you were slain,
and with your blood[d] you purchased[e] men for God
from every tribe and language and people and nation.
10You have made them to be a kingdom and priests[f] to serve our
God,
and they will reign on the earth."

5:10 [f]1Pe 2:5

[a] 6 Or *the sevenfold Spirit*

4:10 worship. God's servants bring songs of praise as a fitting response to his glory and his wondrous deeds (Ex 15:11; Isa 6:3; see note on Rev 1:6).

4:11 you created. The praise and imagery focus on creation, asserting God's sovereignty over the universe (see note on 1:8). See *WCF* 2.2; *BC* 12.

5:1–14 Chapters 4–5 are two parts of a single vision (see note on 4:1—5:14). From creation (4:11) the action shifts to a focus on redemption and re-creation (5:1–14). God's purposes of redemption and rule can be accomplished only through One who is uniquely worthy: Jesus Christ. He is simultaneously the fierce Lion of the tribe of Judah, warring against God's enemies (19:11–21; 17:14), and the gentle Lamb that has been slain, purchasing his people with the blood of his atoning sacrifice (vv. 9–10). Each person of the Trinity contributes to fulfilling these magnificent purposes: the Father ("him who sat on the throne"; vv. 1,7); the Son ("Lamb"; vv. 6–7); and the Spirit of God (v. 6; see note on 1:4), represented by the horns and eyes of the Lamb.

5:1 scroll. The scroll might represent a number of things: God's covenant, his law, his promises, his plans or perhaps a legal will. The close parallel between this verse and Daniel 12:4 makes it likely that the scroll is a heavenly book containing God's plan and the destiny of the world.

5:2–4 open the scroll. The unsealing of the book implies the accomplishment of the things God has purposed. John wept (v. 4) because he longed for God's purposes to be accomplished (Mt 6:10), but such a thing appeared to be impossible.

5:6 as if it had been slain. The phrase "as if" is used because, although the Lamb had indeed been slain, he is now alive forever and ever (1:18). Only on the basis of the accomplished sacrifice of Christ and his resurrection can God's purposes for history be accomplished. **seven horns.** Horns in the Old Testament frequently represent power (Pss 89:17; 92:10; Da 7:8; 8:3). In this case they represent the power of Christ's Spirit-filled, eternal life (Jn 3:34; Ro 8:11; 1Co 15:45). **seven spirits of God.** See note on 1:4.

5:9 every tribe and language and people and nation. In spiritual battle, both God and Satan claim allegiances on a cosmic, universal scale (7:9; 10:11; 11:9; 12:5; 13:7; 14:6,8; 15:4; 17:15; 18:3; 19:15; 20:3). Through the merit and power of Christ's sacrifice, God's purposes will be accomplished, redeeming a whole host and fulfilling the Abrahamic promise of blessing to all nations (7:9–17; 21:24–27; Ge 18:18; 22:18; Isa 60:1–5). See *HC* 54.

5:10 kingdom and priests. See note on 1:6.

11 Then I looked and heard the voice of many angels, numbering thousands upon
thousands, and ten thousand times ten thousand.[g] They encircled the throne and the
living creatures and the elders. 12 In a loud voice they sang:

"Worthy is the Lamb, who was slain,
to receive power and wealth and wisdom and strength
and honor and glory and praise!"[h]

13 Then I heard every creature in heaven and on earth and under the earth[i] and on
the sea, and all that is in them, singing:

"To him who sits on the throne and to the Lamb[j]
be praise and honor and glory and power,
for ever and ever!"[k]

14 The four living creatures said, "Amen,"[l] and the elders fell down and worshiped.[m]

The Seals

6 I watched as the Lamb[n] opened the first of the seven seals.[o] Then I heard one of the
four living creatures[p] say in a voice like thunder,[q] "Come!" 2 I looked, and there before me was a white horse![r] Its rider held a bow, and he was given a crown,[s] and he rode
out as a conqueror bent on conquest.[t]
3 When the Lamb opened the second seal, I heard the second living creature[u] say,
"Come!" 4 Then another horse came out, a fiery red one.[v] Its rider was given power to
take peace from the earth[w] and to make men slay each other. To him was given a large
sword.
5 When the Lamb opened the third seal, I heard the third living creature[x] say, "Come!"
I looked, and there before me was a black horse![y] Its rider was holding a pair of scales
in his hand. 6 Then I heard what sounded like a voice among the four living creatures,[z]
saying, "A quart[a] of wheat for a day's wages,[b] and three quarts of barley for a day's wages,[b] and do not damage[a] the oil and the wine!"
7 When the Lamb opened the fourth seal, I heard the voice of the fourth living creature[b] say, "Come!" 8 I looked, and there before me was a pale horse![c] Its rider was
named Death, and Hades[d] was following close behind him. They were given power over
a fourth of the earth to kill by sword, famine and plague, and by the wild beasts of the
earth.[e]
9 When he opened the fifth seal, I saw under the altar[f] the souls of those who had been
slain[g] because of the word of God and the testimony they had maintained. 10 They called
out in a loud voice, "How long,[h] Sovereign Lord, holy and true,[i] until you judge the inhabitants of the earth and avenge our blood?"[j] 11 Then each of them was given a white
robe,[k] and they were told to wait a little longer, until the number of their fellow servants
and brothers who were to be killed as they had been was completed.[l]
12 I watched as he opened the sixth seal. There was a great earthquake.[m] The sun

5:11 [g]Da 7:10; Heb 12:22
5:12 [h]Rev 4:11
5:13 [i]ver 3; Php 2:10 [j]Rev 6:16 [k]1Ch 29:11
5:14 [l]Rev 4:9 [m]Rev 4:10; 19:4
6:1 [n]Rev 5:6 [o]Rev 5:1 [p]Rev 4:6,7 [q]Rev 14:2; 19:6
6:2 [r]Zec 6:3; Rev 19:11 [s]Zec 6:11; Rev 14:14 [t]Ps 45:4
6:3 [u]Rev 4:7
6:4 [v]Zec 6:2 [w]Mt 10:34
6:5 [x]Rev 4:7 [y]Zec 6:2
6:6 [z]Rev 4:6,7 [a]Rev 9:4
6:7 [b]Rev 4:7
6:8 [c]Zec 6:3 [d]Hos 13:14 [e]Jer 15:2,3; Eze 5:12,17
6:9 [f]Rev 14:18; 16:7 [g]Rev 20:4
6:10 [h]Zec 1:12 [i]Rev 3:7 [j]Rev 19:2
6:11 [k]Rev 3:4 [l]Heb 11:40
6:12 [m]Rev 16:18

[a] 6 Greek *a choinix* (probably about a liter) [b] 6 Greek *a denarius*

5:11–14 Praises that began in the inner circles of worship around the throne now extend outward until they fill the universe. See *WCF* 2.2.

■ **6:1–17** *Opening the Six Seals.* The four horsemen (vv. 1–8) represent the first four seals: conquest, war, famine and death. These calamities characterize an indefinite period before the second coming (Mk 13:6–8). Such disasters occurred in the tumults of the Roman Empire and may be expected to occur both now and immediately before the second coming. The imagery is capable of multiple embodiments (see "Introduction: Purpose and Distinctives"). The seven churches were exhorted to put their confidence not in the peace and prosperity supposedly achieved by Roman rule, but in God and his promises of a new world (2:17; 3:12; 21:4). When catastrophes occurred, they were assured that the Lamb was still in control—in fact, the tumults issued from his worthiness to break the seals and from the voice of the living creatures. Such judgments represent the chastening hand of God on a rebellious world (cf. 9:20–21). The fifth seal (vv. 9–11) represents God's justice on behalf of martyrs, and the sixth (vv. 12–17) speaks of God's judgment on the whole earth in events associated with the return of Christ.

6:2 white horse! On the basis of similarities with 19:11, some think that Christ appears here, conquering through the gospel. More probably, the white horse here symbolizes conquest as one form of earthly calamity. Thus the calamity of verses 1–2 is parallel to those of verses 3–8 (see note on 4:1—8:1).

6:6 A quart of wheat. Famine comes that is so severe that a laborer's entire wages are sufficient merely to feed himself. To feed his family, a worker is compelled to purchase barley, a lower quality food. Oil and wine are spared, which perhaps indicates that the rich are still able to indulge themselves.

6:9–11 Martyred saints cry out for justice not because of selfish desires, but because they are in tune with the justice of God's throne. They desire to see God's justice fully manifested. **the inhabitants of the earth.** Revelation shows that humanity consists of two groups: the people of God, whose citizenship is in heaven (Php 3:20), and, in opposition to them, the rebellious Earth-dwellers (v. 15; 8:13; 11:10; 13:3,8,12,14; 17:2,8). See *BC* 37.

6:12–17 All those who dwell on Earth, as well as the cosmos itself, experience God's judgment. These verses give the first of seven descriptions in Revelation of events associated with the second coming (see "Introduction: Purpose and Distinctives"). In Mark 13:24–26 and Luke 21:25–27 the coming of the Son of Man immediately follows unusual phenomena involving the sun, moon and stars. The mention of seven types of people (v. 15) suggests complete judgment, as does the characterization of "the great day of their wrath" (vv. 16–17). Since this world is to be so thoroughly shaken, saints must place their hope in God (Lk 12:32–34; 1Co 7:29–31; Heb 12:25–29).

turned black[n] like sackcloth made of goat hair, the whole moon turned blood red,
13and the stars in the sky fell to earth,[o] as late figs drop from a fig tree[p] when shaken by
a strong wind. 14The sky receded like a scroll, rolling up, and every mountain and island
was removed from its place.[q]
15Then the kings of the earth, the princes, the generals, the rich, the mighty, and every slave and every free man hid in caves and among the rocks of the mountains.[r] 16They
called to the mountains and the rocks, "Fall on us[s] and hide us from the face of him who
sits on the throne and from the wrath of the Lamb! 17For the great day[t] of their wrath
has come, and who can stand?"[u]

144,000 Sealed

7 After this I saw four angels standing at the four corners of the earth, holding back
the four winds[v] of the earth to prevent any wind from blowing on the land or on the
sea or on any tree. 2Then I saw another angel coming up from the east, having the seal
of the living God. He called out in a loud voice to the four angels who had been given
power to harm the land and the sea: 3"Do not harm[w] the land or the sea or the trees until we put a seal on the foreheads[x] of the servants of our God." 4Then I heard the number[y] of those who were sealed: 144,000[z] from all the tribes of Israel.

5From the tribe of Judah 12,000 were sealed,
from the tribe of Reuben 12,000,
from the tribe of Gad 12,000,
6from the tribe of Asher 12,000,
from the tribe of Naphtali 12,000,
from the tribe of Manasseh 12,000,
7from the tribe of Simeon 12,000,
from the tribe of Levi 12,000,
from the tribe of Issachar 12,000,
8from the tribe of Zebulun 12,000,
from the tribe of Joseph 12,000,
from the tribe of Benjamin 12,000.

The Great Multitude in White Robes

9After this I looked and there before me was a great multitude that no one could
count, from every nation, tribe, people and language,[a] standing before the throne[b] and
in front of the Lamb. They were wearing white robes and were holding palm branches
in their hands. 10And they cried out in a loud voice:

"Salvation belongs to our God,[c]
who sits on the throne,
and to the Lamb."

11All the angels were standing around the throne and around the elders[d] and the four
living creatures.[e] They fell down on their faces[f] before the throne and worshiped God,
12saying:

"Amen!
Praise and glory
and wisdom and thanks and honor
and power and strength
be to our God for ever and ever.
Amen!"[g]

13Then one of the elders asked me, "These in white robes—who are they, and where
did they come from?"

6:12 [n]Mt 24:29
6:13 [o]Mt 24:29; Rev 8:10; 9:1 [p]Isa 34:4
6:14 [q]Jer 4:24; Rev 16:20
6:15 [r]Isa 2:10,19,21
6:16 [s]Hos 10:8; Lk 23:30
6:17 [t]Zep 1:14,15; Rev 16:14 [u]Ps 76:7
7:1 [v]Da 7:2
7:3 [w]Rev 6:6 [x]Eze 9:4; Rev 22:4
7:4 [y]Rev 9:16 [z]Rev 14:1,3
7:9 [a]Rev 5:9 [b]ver 15
7:10 [c]Ps 3:8; Rev 12:10; 19:1
7:11 [d]Rev 4:4 [e]Rev 4:6 [f]Rev 4:10
7:12 [g]Rev 5:12-14

■ **7:1–17** *Care for the Saints.* The announcement of the seventh seal is dramatically delayed while the saints receive assurance that God knows and looks after them (v. 3) in the midst of the calamities depicted in 6:1–17. They are sealed from harm with a mark of ownership and protection (vv. 1–10; 9:4; cf. Eze 9:4) and given perfect rest in the end (vv. 15–17). Such promises hold for saints throughout the church age, just as they held for the seven churches in the first century.

7:3 seal. The faithful are sealed as a sign of protection and ownership (9:4; 14:1), analogous to that in Ezekiel 9:4.

7:4–8 The balanced numbering suggests that 12 is a symbolic number for the fullness of the people of God. Dan is omitted, possibly because this tribe was associated with idolatry (cf. Jdg 18 with Rev 21:8; 22:15). Some think that the number 144,000 includes only Jewish believers, but "servants of our God" in verse 3 must include Gentile saints as well. The equal status of Gentiles and Jews in the church (Ro 9:8; Eph 2:11–22) and the promises associated only with the 144,000 (9:4; 14:1–5) confirm this. According to verses 1–8, the saints are known individually by God, and none slips away from his care (Mt 10:30). According to verses 9–17, no human being can count their number.

7:9 See *WCF* 25.2; *WLC* 62.

14 I answered, "Sir, you know."
And he said, "These are they who have come out of the great tribulation; they have
washed their robes[h] and made them white in the blood of the Lamb.[i] 15 Therefore,

"they are before the throne of God[j]
and serve him[k] day and night in his temple;[l]
and he who sits on the throne will spread his tent over them.[m]
16 Never again will they hunger;
never again will they thirst.
The sun will not beat upon them,
nor any scorching heat.[n]
17 For the Lamb at the center of the throne will be their shepherd;[o]
he will lead them to springs of living water.
And God will wipe away every tear from their eyes."[p]

The Seventh Seal and the Golden Censer

8 When he opened the seventh seal,[q] there was silence in heaven for about half an
hour.
2 And I saw the seven angels[r] who stand before God, and to them were given seven
trumpets.
3 Another angel,[s] who had a golden censer, came and stood at the altar. He was giv-
en much incense to offer, with the prayers of all the saints,[t] on the golden altar[u] before
the throne. 4 The smoke of the incense, together with the prayers of the saints, went up
before God[v] from the angel's hand. 5 Then the angel took the censer, filled it with fire
from the altar,[w] and hurled it on the earth; and there came peals of thunder,[x] rumblings,
flashes of lightning and an earthquake.[y]

The Trumpets

6 Then the seven angels who had the seven trumpets[z] prepared to sound them.
7 The first angel sounded his trumpet, and there came hail and fire[a] mixed with
blood, and it was hurled down upon the earth. A third[b] of the earth was burned up, a
third of the trees were burned up, and all the green grass was burned up.[c]
8 The second angel sounded his trumpet, and something like a huge mountain,[d] all
ablaze, was thrown into the sea. A third[e] of the sea turned into blood,[f] 9 a third[g] of the
living creatures in the sea died, and a third of the ships were destroyed.
10 The third angel sounded his trumpet, and a great star, blazing like a torch, fell from
the sky[h] on a third of the rivers and on the springs of water[i]— 11 the name of the star is

7:14 [h]Rev 22:14 [i]Heb 9:14; 1Jn 1:7
7:15 [j]ver 9 [k]Rev 22:3 [l]Rev 11:19 [m]Isa 4:5,6; Rev 21:3
7:16 [n]Isa 49:10
7:17 [o]Ps 23:1; Jn 10:11 [p]Isa 25:8; Rev 21:4
8:1 [q]Rev 6:1
8:2 [r]ver 6-13; Rev 9:1, 13; 11:15
8:3 [s]Rev 7:2 [t]Rev 5:8 [u]Ex 30:1-6; Heb 9:4; Rev 9:13
8:4 [v]Ps 141:2
8:5 [w]Lev 16:12,13 [x]Rev 4:5 [y]Rev 6:12
8:6 [z]ver 2
8:7 [a]Eze 38:22 [b]ver 7-12; Rev 9:15,18; 12:4 [c]Rev 9:4
8:8 [d]Jer 51:25 [e]ver 7 [f]Rev 16:3
8:9 [g]ver 7
8:10 [h]Isa 14:12; Rev 6:13; 9:1 [i]Rev 14:7; 16:4

7:14 great tribulation. Many identify the great tribulation with a final period of persecution to take place shortly before, during or after the second coming (see theological article "The Millennium" at Rev 20). But tribulations for Christians have occurred, and will continue to occur, throughout the church age, so the whole age can be characterized as a time of tribulation (2Th 1:5–6; 2Ti 3:1,12). This verse was a relevant comfort to first-century Christians (and will be so for those in the final crisis as well). For example, the same Greek word (*thlipsis*) translated here as "tribulation" is rendered as "suffering" in 1:9, "afflictions" in 2:9, "persecution" in 2:10 and "suffer" in 2:22—all of these other meanings relate to the circumstances of the first-century audience. See note on 11:1–2. See *HC* 73.

■ **8:1** *Opening the Seventh Seal.* The next event after 6:12–17 would most naturally be the appearance of Christ himself as the final Warrior and Judge (Mk 13:24–26), but the assurances of 7:1–17 intervene. Resuming the seals, the assumption should be that Christ's return is in view.

8:1 silence in heaven. Although the text does not point explicitly to Christ's return when the seventh seal is broken, the silence may indicate that heaven stands in awe at his presence (Hab 2:20; Zep 1:7). At this early point, John was not given a fuller picture disclosing the events of final judgment and re-creation. This delay maintains the reader's interest for later cycles of judgment, during which such details are unveiled.

■ **8:2—11:19** *Cycle Two: Seven Angels With Seven Trumpets.* Seven angels blow seven trumpets. The trumpets set in motion seven judgments leading up to the second coming, depicting God's rule over history from various angles. Regarding the structure, see note on 4:1—8:1. Like the trumpets used in the battle of Jericho (Jos 6), these trumpets lead up to the fall of the worldly city (11:13) and, in the seventh trumpet, the complete victory of God. The trumpet plagues are reminiscent of the plagues on Egypt, signifying God's judgments on idolatrous power. The seven seals began with announcements of riders commissioned to bring calamities (6:1—8:1). The seven trumpets, by contrast, contain descriptions of the calamities themselves. The intensity of judgment has accelerated. Still, a part of creation is spared: Most of the trumpet plagues fall on a third of the people or land, not on all. For example, the locust plague of 9:1–12 ends after five months, and some people survive the collapse of the city in 11:13. In contrast, the later judgments with the bowls (15:1—16:21) are thoroughly devastating.

■ **8:2–6** *Seven Angels Before God.* The trumpet judgments issue from God's angels who stand before his throne (v. 2). The vision of 4:1—5:14 remains an anchor point for this new cycle of visions. Like the seal judgments of 6:1—8:1, these judgments are executed according to God's plan and his orders. The prayers of the saints play a notable part in originating the judgments (vv. 3–4).

■ **8:7—9:21** *Six Angels Blow Their Trumpets.* The first four trumpet plagues (vv. 7–12) strike the four major realms of creation: land, sea, fresh water and sky. The first four bowls affect the same four regions (16:1–9). Within the period of the early church, these visions were fulfilled both through natural calamities and through analogous spiritual calamities afflicting the souls of the wicked (in apocalyptic imagery, the natural can represent the spiritual). The general principles can be applied more broadly (see "Introduction: Purpose and Distinctives"). Both human beings and the natural world undergo stress until the time of final renewal (Ro 8:18–25).

8:7 hail and fire. Parallel to Exodus 9:23–24.

8:8 blood. Parallel to Exodus 7:14–24.

Wormwood.[a] A third[j] of the waters turned bitter, and many people died from the waters that had become bitter.[k]

12 The fourth angel sounded his trumpet, and a third of the sun was struck, a third of the moon, and a third of the stars, so that a third[l] of them turned dark.[m] A third of the day was without light, and also a third of the night.

13 As I watched, I heard an eagle that was flying in midair[n] call out in a loud voice: "Woe! Woe! Woe[o] to the inhabitants of the earth, because of the trumpet blasts about to be sounded by the other three angels!"

9 The fifth angel sounded his trumpet, and I saw a star that had fallen from the sky to the earth.[p] The star was given the key to the shaft of the Abyss.[q] 2 When he opened the Abyss, smoke rose from it like the smoke from a gigantic furnace.[r] The sun and sky were darkened[s] by the smoke from the Abyss. 3 And out of the smoke locusts[t] came down upon the earth and were given power like that of scorpions[u] of the earth. 4 They were told not to harm[v] the grass of the earth or any plant or tree,[w] but only those people who did not have the seal of God on their foreheads.[x] 5 They were not given power to kill them, but only to torture them for five months.[y] And the agony they suffered was like that of the sting of a scorpion[z] when it strikes a man. 6 During those days men will seek death, but will not find it; they will long to die, but death will elude them.[a]

7 The locusts looked like horses prepared for battle.[b] On their heads they wore something like crowns of gold, and their faces resembled human faces.[c] 8 Their hair was like women's hair, and their teeth were like lions' teeth.[d] 9 They had breastplates like breastplates of iron, and the sound of their wings was like the thundering of many horses and chariots rushing into battle.[e] 10 They had tails and stings like scorpions, and in their tails they had power to torment people for five months.[f] 11 They had as king over them the angel of the Abyss,[g] whose name in Hebrew is Abaddon, and in Greek, Apollyon.[b]

12 The first woe is past; two other woes are yet to come.[h]

13 The sixth angel sounded his trumpet, and I heard a voice coming from the horns[c][i] of the golden altar that is before God.[j] 14 It said to the sixth angel who had the trumpet, "Release the four angels who are bound at the great river Euphrates."[k] 15 And the four angels who had been kept ready for this very hour and day and month and year were released to kill a third of mankind.[l] 16 The number of the mounted troops was two hundred million. I heard their number.[m]

17 The horses and riders I saw in my vision looked like this: Their breastplates were fiery red, dark blue, and yellow as sulfur. The heads of the horses resembled the heads of lions, and out of their mouths[n] came fire, smoke and sulfur.[o] 18 A third of mankind was killed[p] by the three plagues of fire, smoke and sulfur[q] that came out of their mouths. 19 The power of the horses was in their mouths and in their tails; for their tails were like snakes, having heads with which they inflict injury.

20 The rest of mankind that were not killed by these plagues still did not repent of the work of their hands;[r] they did not stop worshiping demons,[s] and idols of gold, silver,

8:11 [j]ver 7 [k]Jer 9:15; 23:15
8:12 [l]ver 7 [m]Ex 10:21-23; Rev 6:12,13
8:13 [n]Rev 14:6; 19:17 [o]Rev 9:12; 11:14
9:1 [p]Rev 8:10 [q]ver 2, 11; Lk 8:31
9:2 [r]Ge 19:28; Ex 19:18 [s]Joel 2:2, 10
9:3 [t]Ex 10:12-15 [u]ver 5,10
9:4 [v]Rev 6:6 [w]Rev 8:7 [x]Rev 7:2,3
9:5 [y]ver 10 [z]ver 3
9:6 [a]Job 3:21; Jer 8:3; Rev 6:16
9:7 [b]Joel 2:4 [c]Da 7:8
9:8 [d]Joel 1:6
9:9 [e]Joel 2:5
9:10 [f]ver 3,5,19
9:11 [g]ver 1,2
9:12 [h]Rev 8:13
9:13 [i]Ex 30:1-3 [j]Rev 8:3
9:14 [k]Rev 16:12
9:15 [l]ver 18
9:16 [m]Rev 5:11; 7:4
9:17 [n]Rev 11:5 [o]ver 18
9:18 [p]ver 15 [q]ver 17
9:20 [r]Dt 31:29 [s]1Co 10:20

a *11* That is, Bitterness b *11* *Abaddon* and *Apollyon* mean *Destroyer.* c *13* That is, projections

8:12 turned dark. Parallel to Exodus10:21–23.
8:13 Woe! A typical beginning to a prophetic oracle (e.g., Am 5:18; 6:1). The three last trumpets are grouped together as three woes (9:12; 11:14). These plagues explicitly discriminate between the righteous and the wicked, as did the final plagues on Egypt (e.g., Ex. 9:4–6; 10:22–23; 11:1–7).
9:1–12 The fifth . . . trumpet. This blast sets in motion a horrific army of locusts that are energized by demonic sources (vv. 1–3). The imagery derives from Exodus 10:13–15 and Joel 2:1–11, where a literal locust plague foreshadows even more devastating judgment coming from a divinely commissioned army (Joel 2:11). Their terrorizing powers compare only to those of the beast (13:1–10). These infernal monsters attack only the wicked, not the saints (v. 4). The wicked sometimes suffer even in this life in a way that presages their final punishment (20:11–15). According to idealist interpreters, this vision depicts the self-defeating and tormenting nature of wickedness in the human soul. Powers from the Abyss attack not the saints, but only the wicked. Historicists have generally seen this vision as a depiction of Islamic conquest of a degenerate Western Europe (A.D. 612–762), but such an application would be only one embodiment of the principle, and an imperfect one at that. Futurists understand the vision as a supernatural plague of demonic spirits that are to be loosed on the earth shortly before the second coming. The fundamental principle is the same in all these interpretations, and multiple applications of the principle are possible (see "Introduction: Purpose and Distinctives").
9:5 five months. A normal locust swarm would move on after a few days. This demonic swarm stays for the whole period during which locusts might be seen.
9:11 Abaddon . . . Apollyon. Both names mean "destroyer." There may be an ironic allusion to Nero or Domitian, both of whom saw themselves as imitators of the Greek god Apollo.
9:13–21 The sixth . . . trumpet. The Roman Empire feared an attack by the Parthians from beyond the Euphrates (v. 14), the eastern border of the empire. But all such fears are dwarfed by what Revelation pictures. Outside threats experienced by the Roman Empire presage the final day of cosmic battle (16:14). This passage is similar to 16:14, but the consequences here are less severe, and time is allowed for repentance (vv. 18–21).
9:14 four angels. The Old Testament indicates that certain angels hold sway over worldly kingdoms and governments (Da 10:13,20–21). Such angels may be in view here, so that human military forces cause the plagues in verses 16–19. It is also possible that the armies figuratively represent either natural or supernatural calamities.
9:20 still did not repent. An indication that the calamities are inflicted with the understanding—perhaps made known through the prophetic witnesses in 10:1—11:14 (see note)—that repentance from sin may lead to the avoidance of coming calamities.

bronze, stone and wood—idols that cannot see or hear or walk.[t] 21Nor did they repent[u]
of their murders, their magic arts,[v] their sexual immorality[w] or their thefts.

The Angel and the Little Scroll

10 Then I saw another mighty angel[x] coming down from heaven. He was robed in
a cloud, with a rainbow above his head; his face was like the sun,[y] and his legs
were like fiery pillars.[z] 2He was holding a little scroll, which lay open in his hand. He
planted his right foot on the sea and his left foot on the land, 3and he gave a loud shout
like the roar of a lion. When he shouted, the voices of the seven thunders[a] spoke. 4And
when the seven thunders spoke, I was about to write; but I heard a voice from heaven
say, "Seal up what the seven thunders have said and do not write it down."[b]
5Then the angel I had seen standing on the sea and on the land raised his right hand
to heaven.[c] 6And he swore by him who lives for ever and ever, who created the heavens
and all that is in them, the earth and all that is in it, and the sea and all that is in it,[d] and
said, "There will be no more delay![e] 7But in the days when the seventh angel is about to
sound his trumpet, the mystery[f] of God will be accomplished, just as he announced to
his servants the prophets."
8Then the voice that I had heard from heaven[g] spoke to me once more: "Go, take the
scroll that lies open in the hand of the angel who is standing on the sea and on the land."
9So I went to the angel and asked him to give me the little scroll. He said to me, "Take
it and eat it. It will turn your stomach sour, but in your mouth it will be as sweet as honey."[h] 10I took the little scroll from the angel's hand and ate it. It tasted as sweet as honey in my mouth, but when I had eaten it, my stomach turned sour. 11Then I was told,
"You must prophesy[i] again about many peoples, nations, languages and kings."

The Two Witnesses

11 I was given a reed like a measuring rod[j] and was told, "Go and measure the temple of God and the altar, and count the worshipers there. 2But exclude the out-

9:20 [t]Ps 115:4-7; 135:15-17; Da 5:23
9:21 [u]Rev 2:21 [v]Rev 18:23 [w]Rev 17:2,5
10:1 [x]Rev 5:2 [y]Mt 17:2; Rev 1:16 [z]Rev 1:15
10:3 [a]Rev 4:5
10:4 [b]Da 8:26; 12:4,9; Rev 22:10
10:5 [c]Da 12:7
10:6 [d]Rev 4:11; 14:7 [e]Rev 16:17
10:7 [f]Ro 16:25
10:8 [g]ver 4
10:9 [h]Jer 15:16; Eze 2:8-3:3
10:11 [i]Eze 37:4,9
11:1 [j]Eze 40:3; Rev 21:15

▪ **10:1—11:14** *Care for John and the Two Witnesses.* Between the sixth and seventh trumpets stands an interlude (10:1—11:14) with two scenes (10:1–11 and 11:1–14). Both concern the role of God's people and their prophetic witness during the time of trial. In the first scene (10:1–11) John received prophetic messages and was commissioned to proclaim them. The second scene (11:1–14) depicts the history of the two witnesses and their larger environment.

10:1–11 This scene focuses on John's prophetic witness and has parallels to Daniel (Da 10:5–6) and to the call of Ezekiel (Eze 2:1—3:11). John received the prophetic messages of a "little scroll." Some surmise that the scroll records the contents of 12:1—22:5 and that 12:1 begins a new major division in the structure of Revelation. More likely, the vision of chapter 10 speaks in a general fashion of John's empowerment to continue to prophesy. Although John's role was unique, he was still in many ways an example and pattern for the church's witness (see note on 1:2). The church must take to heart the message of John (1:3), live by it and be ready to communicate its implications to "peoples, nations, languages and kings" (v. 11).

10:1 mighty angel. A mighty angel appears, reflecting the very glory of God and his throne room (10:1–3; cf. 1:14–16; Eze 1:27–28; Da 10:5–6). His majesty reinforces the authority and divine source of the message.

10:9–10 turn your stomach sour. The scroll contains news of suffering. Alternatively, this may indicate that the result of John's further prophesying (v. 11) would be further suffering for the people to whom he would preach, perhaps because they would reject his offer of salvation. **sweet as honey.** See Psalms 19:10, 119:103 and Ezekiel 3:3. The Word of God provides communion with God and his goodness; hence, sweetness accompanies even a message of woe. Alternatively, this image may indicate that John would be allowed to offer repentance and forgiveness by which those who received his message might escape coming calamities (see note on 9:20; cf. Eze 3:17–21).

10:11 many peoples. See note on 5:9.

11:1–14 This second part of the interlude concentrates on the story of the two witnesses. Like Moses and Elijah, these witnesses perform striking miracles (vv. 5–6). Other Old Testament references are woven into the vision: The two olive trees and lampstands (v. 4) liken the witnesses to the vision of Zechariah 4:1–14 (in which the trees probably symbolize the ruling and priestly offices of Zerubbabel and Joshua). Thus, the witnesses are prominent representatives of God. The witnesses' stand against the beast (vv. 7–10) recalls the conflicts against bestial kingdoms described in Daniel. Verse 8 is reminiscent of wicked, oppressive cities and powers: Sodom, Egypt and the Jerusalem that crucified Jesus. The resurrection in verses 11–12 recalls Christ's resurrection, but also the language of Ezekiel 37 and the rapture of Elijah (2Ki 2:11–12). As was true of John in chapter 10, the two witnesses are models for the saints. All Christians are to be faithful to the testimony of Jesus, even in the face of violent persecution from the beast. They must be willing to face martyrdom, for God guarantees their vindication (vv. 11–12). Some aspects of this vision remain difficult and controversial. It is possible that two literal, individual human beings are in view: either two Christian prophets who were martyred shortly before the fall of Jerusalem or two prophets who will appear shortly before the second coming. But their identification with two lampstands (v. 4) suggests that they are probably symbolic figures representing the witness of the lampstand-churches of 1:20. As such, they represent churches rather than specific individuals. Two rather than seven lampstands are mentioned to allude to the pattern of Zechariah 4 and of Moses and Elijah (Dt 17:6; Mt 17:3–4; cf. Lk 10:1). The image may also highlight the two "faithful" churches of the seven churches in Asia Minor (Smyrna and Philadelphia). It may also allude to the law's requirement that at least two witnesses testify to a person's guilt in court (Dt. 17:6).

11:1–2 temple . . . altar . . . outer court . . . trample. The description is reminiscent of the fall of Jerusalem in A.D. 70. Assuming that Revelation was written before A.D. 70, some interpreters see 6:1—11:19 or even larger portions of Revelation as prophecy concerning the fall of Jerusalem. But verses 1–2 may just as easily be a figurative picture of the preservation of God's people in the midst of attacks. The temple represents the presence of God on Earth, especially through his people (see note on 4:1—5:14). Measurement signifies God's knowledge and care (Eze 40:1—43:17). The altar and those who worship there represent the true worshipers of God, who are sealed and protected (7:1–17). The destruction of the outer court represents the attack of outsiders on God's people.

42 months. A time of distress and intense conflict between God's people and their opponents (13:5). This is also described as 1,260 days (v. 3; 12:6) or "a time, times and half a time" (12:14; i.e., three and one-half years). It is half of seven years, which from a symbolic point of view suggests a complete period of suffering cut short by half. The main background is found in Daniel 7:25, which in turn is related to other passages (Da 9:27; 12:7,11–12). Some futurist interpreters look for a period of time of this length shortly before the second coming. But like other numbers in Revelation, this one is probably symbolic, relating to the three and one-half days in

er court;[k] do not measure it, because it has been given to the Gentiles.[l] They will trample on the holy city[m] for 42 months.[n] 3 And I will give power to my two witnesses,[o] and
they will prophesy for 1,260 days, clothed in sackcloth."[p] 4 These are the two olive
trees[q] and the two lampstands that stand before the Lord of the earth.[r] 5 If anyone tries
to harm them, fire comes from their mouths and devours their enemies.[s] This is how anyone who wants to harm them must die.[t] 6 These men have power to shut up the sky so
that it will not rain during the time they are prophesying; and they have power to turn
the waters into blood[u] and to strike the earth with every kind of plague as often as they
want.

7 Now when they have finished their testimony, the beast[v] that comes up from the
Abyss will attack them,[w] and overpower and kill them. 8 Their bodies will lie in the street
of the great city, which is figuratively called Sodom[x] and Egypt, where also their Lord
was crucified.[y] 9 For three and a half days men from every people, tribe, language and
nation will gaze on their bodies and refuse them burial.[z] 10 The inhabitants of the earth[a]
will gloat over them and will celebrate by sending each other gifts,[b] because these two
prophets had tormented those who live on the earth.

11 But after the three and a half days a breath of life from God entered them,[c] and they
stood on their feet, and terror struck those who saw them. 12 Then they heard a loud voice
from heaven saying to them, "Come up here."[d] And they went up to heaven in a cloud,[e]
while their enemies looked on.

13 At that very hour there was a severe earthquake[f] and a tenth of the city collapsed.
Seven thousand people were killed in the earthquake, and the survivors were terrified
and gave glory[g] to the God of heaven.[h]

14 The second woe has passed; the third woe is coming soon.[i]

The Seventh Trumpet

15 The seventh angel sounded his trumpet,[j] and there were loud voices[k] in heaven,
which said:

"The kingdom of the world has become the kingdom of our Lord
and of his Christ,[l]
and he will reign for ever and ever."[m]

16 And the twenty-four elders,[n] who were seated on their thrones before God, fell on their
faces and worshiped God, 17 saying:

"We give thanks to you, Lord God Almighty,[o]
the One who is and who was,
because you have taken your great power
and have begun to reign.[p]
18 The nations were angry;[q]
and your wrath has come.
The time has come for judging the dead,
and for rewarding your servants the prophets[r]
and your saints and those who reverence your name,
both small and great[s]—
and for destroying those who destroy the earth."

19 Then God's temple[t] in heaven was opened, and within his temple was seen the ark
of his covenant. And there came flashes of lightning, rumblings, peals of thunder, an
earthquake and a great hailstorm.[u]

11:2 [k]Eze 40:17,20 [l]Lk 21:24 [m]Rev 21:2 [n]Da 7:25; Rev 13:5
11:3 [o]Rev 1:5 [p]Ge 37:34
11:4 [q]Ps 52:8; Jer 11:16; Zec 4:3, 11 [r]Zec 4:14
11:5 [s]2Ki 1:10; Jer 5:14 [t]Nu 16:29,35
11:6 [u]Ex 7:17,19
11:7 [v]Rev 13:1-4 [w]Da 7:21
11:8 [x]Isa 1:9 [y]Heb 13:12
11:9 [z]Ps 79:2,3
11:10 [a]Rev 3:10 [b]Est 9:19,22
11:11 [c]Eze 37:5,9,10,14
11:12 [d]Rev 4:1 [e]2Ki 2:11; Ac 1:9
11:13 [f]Rev 6:12 [g]Rev 14:7 [h]Rev 16:11
11:14 [i]Rev 8:13
11:15 [j]Rev 10:7 [k]Rev 16:17; 19:1 [l]Rev 12:10 [m]Da 2:44; 7:14,27
11:16 [n]Rev 4:4
11:17 [o]Rev 1:8 [p]Rev 19:6
11:18 [q]Ps 2:1 [r]Rev 10:7 [s]Rev 19:5
11:19 [t]Rev 15:5,8 [u]Rev 16:21

verses 9 and 11. In this case it designates a persecution of limited length.
11:7 the beast. See note on 13:1–10.
11:8 the great city. This verse suggests to many that ancient Jerusalem is in view throughout verses 1–19 (see note on vv. 1–2), but the symbolism has many potential applications. The city is the worldly city, representing humanity and human civilization in rebellion against God. Babel, Sodom, Egypt, Jerusalem, ancient Rome, present-day cities and a final apostasy before the second coming are all examples. See "Introduction: Purpose and Distinctives" and note on 17:1—19:10.
11:9 three and a half days. See note on verses 1–2. **people, tribe, language and nation.** See note on 5:9.
11:10 The inhabitants of the earth. See note on 6:9–11.
11:11–12 If the witnesses are symbolic of the churches, their resurrection probably symbolizes the victory of Christian witness after a time of intense persecution (6:9–11; 20:1–6). If the two witnesses are individuals, which is perhaps more likely, their resurrection should presumably be interpreted literally. See note on verses 1–14.
■ **11:15–19** *The Seventh Angel Blows His Trumpet.* The second cycle of judgments (8:2—11:19) closes with a second description of the second coming, focusing on the last judgment (v. 18) and the triumph of God's kingly rule (vv. 15,17). Final effects, touching the natural world as well as human beings, accompany the second coming (2Pe 3:10,12).
11:17 See *BC* 12.
11:19 God's temple. See note on 4:1—5:14. **ark.** The ark was the most holy object in the tabernacle (Ex 25:10–22). It was normally concealed from sight behind the tabernacle curtains. That this innermost object is no longer obscured signifies that God has fully revealed his glory, both in rewarding his people and in destroying the wicked (v. 18).

The Woman and the Dragon

12 A great and wondrous sign appeared in heaven: a woman clothed with the sun,
with the moon under her feet and a crown of twelve stars on her head. 2 She was
pregnant and cried out in pain[v] as she was about to give birth. 3 Then another sign appeared in heaven: an enormous red dragon with seven heads and ten horns[w] and sev-
en crowns[x] on his heads. 4 His tail swept a third[y] of the stars out of the sky and flung
them to the earth.[z] The dragon stood in front of the woman who was about to give birth,
so that he might devour her child[a] the moment it was born. 5 She gave birth to a son, a
male child, who will rule all the nations with an iron scepter.[b] And her child was
snatched up to God and to his throne. 6 The woman fled into the desert to a place prepared for her by God, where she might be taken care of for 1,260 days.[c]

7 And there was war in heaven. Michael and his angels fought against the dragon,[d]
and the dragon and his angels fought back. 8 But he was not strong enough, and they lost
their place in heaven. 9 The great dragon was hurled down—that ancient serpent[e] called
the devil,[f] or Satan, who leads the whole world astray.[g] He was hurled to the earth,[h] and
his angels with him.

10 Then I heard a loud voice in heaven[i] say:

"Now have come the salvation and the power and the kingdom of
our God,
and the authority of his Christ.
For the accuser of our brothers,[j]
who accuses them before our God day and night,
has been hurled down.
11 They overcame him
by the blood of the Lamb[k]
and by the word of their testimony;[l]
they did not love their lives so much
as to shrink from death.[m]
12 Therefore rejoice, you heavens[n]
and you who dwell in them!
But woe[o] to the earth and the sea,[p]
because the devil has gone down to you!
He is filled with fury,
because he knows that his time is short."

13 When the dragon[q] saw that he had been hurled to the earth, he pursued the wom-

12:2 [v]Gal 4:19
12:3 [w]Da 7:7,20; Rev 13:1 [x]Rev 19:12
12:4 [y]Rev 8:7 [z]Da 8:10 [a]Mt 2:16
12:5 [b]Ps 2:9; Rev 2:27
12:6 [c]Rev 11:2
12:7 [d]ver 3
12:9 [e]Ge 3:1-7 [f]Mt 25:41 [g]Rev 20:3,8,10 [h]Lk 10:18; Jn 12:31
12:10 [i]Rev 11:15 [j]Job 1:9-11; Zec 3:1
12:11 [k]Rev 7:14 [l]Rev 6:9 [m]Lk 14:26
12:12 [n]Ps 96:11; Isa 49:13; Rev 18:20 [o]Rev 8:13 [p]Rev 10:6
12:13 [q]ver 3

▪ **12:1—14:20** *Cycle Three: Seven Symbolic Histories.* This third cycle of visions consists primarily of histories of key symbolic characters: the dragon, the woman, the beast, the false prophet, the 144,000, angelic announcers and the Son of Man. Unlike the cycles of seven seals (5:1—8:1) and seven trumpets (8:2—11:19), these visions have no explicit numbering. But like the preceding cycles, these characters number seven and lead to a vision of Christ's return (14:14–20). The two preceding cycles focused on the judgments issuing from God's throne. This cycle depicts in depth the nature of the spiritual conflict. Characters appear in symbolic form to represent the forces on the two sides of a cosmic, spiritual war.

▪ **12:1–6** *Principal Personages: The People of God Versus Satan.* God himself has already been revealed in 4:1—5:14. Satan is here portrayed as a dragon, while later in this cycle his agents—the beast (13:1–10) and the false prophet (13:11–18; 16:13)— support his opposition to God. Here and in verses 13–17 God's people are depicted as a light-bearing woman in conflict with Satan. Later they are envisioned as a chaste, numbered and protected multitude (14:1–5). These two complementary pictures show the saints in their capacity as witnesses of God's light and as those separated from the corruption of the world. Thus the saints are exhorted to remain faithful to Christ (in opposition to the persecution of the beast) and to remain pure (in opposition to the seduction of the prostitute of ch. 17). The symbolic pictures show the two sides stripped of all inconsistency and confusion so that the nature of the believers' spiritual warfare may be better understood (Eph 6:10–20). The present conflicts will be superseded by the peace of 21:1—22:5, when the consummation of God's plans takes effect.

12:1 a woman. The imagery calls to mind Joseph's dream (Ge 37:9–10) and the picture of Jerusalem bringing forth the Messiah and his remnant (Isa 54:1–4; 66:7–13; Mic 5:3;). The Old Testament saints collectively are in view. Mary, the mother of Jesus, is included in this group, but only as an outstanding member of the whole. The later history shows that the New Testament saints are also included (vv. 13–17). The light bearing character of the woman foreshadows the glory of the new Jerusalem (21:11,22–27). In her privileges the church now already partakes of the blessings to come. But she is still buffeted by Satan (see note on 12:1—14:20).

12:3 an enormous red dragon. Identified as Satan, the devil, in verse 9. The image of a dragon depicts Satan as enormous in his power and hideous in his enmity against God. Satan has constantly opposed the plans of God and has been repeatedly defeated by the great acts of God's saving power (Ge 3:1,15; Ps 74:13–14; Isa 27:1; 51:9–10; Lk 10:18; 11:14–23; Jn 12:31; Col 2:15). He rises against the Messiah (vv. 4–5) and his servants (v. 17) but will suffer final destruction (20:10).

12:5 a son. In fulfillment of Micah 5:3–5, Christ is born, and his triumphant rule over the nations is certain to be established.

12:6 God promises protection for a persecuted church. **1,260 days.** See note on 11:1–2. See *WCF* 25.4.

▪ **12:7—14:11** *Six Symbolic Histories.* Six brief metaphoric accounts relate various aspects of the conflict between God's forces and Satan's: (1) The Dragon (12:7–12); (2) The Woman (12:13–17); (3) The Beast From the Sea (13:1–10); (4) The Beast From the Earth: The False Prophet (13:11–18); (5) The 144,000 (14:1–5); and (6) Three Angelic Messengers (14:6–11).

▪ **12:7–12** *The Dragon.* The victory of Christ (v. 5) results in sweeping consequences, beginning with the expulsion of Satan by Michael, who functions as an agent of Christ. The passage does not speak of Satan's initial fall but of his defeat at the time of Christ's crucifixion and resurrection (v. 12; Jn 12:31; Col 2:15).

12:10–11 See *WLC* 191; *HC* 31.

▪ **12:13–17** *The Woman.* Having failed to destroy Jesus (vv. 4–5), the dragon tries to annihilate Christ's people. He uses his mouth, representing deceit (vv. 9,15; 2Th 2:9–10). When deceit fails, he employs persecuting power (12:17—13:10).

an who had given birth to the male child.[r] ¹⁴The woman was given the two wings of a
great eagle,[s] so that she might fly to the place prepared for her in the desert, where she
would be taken care of for a time, times and half a time,[t] out of the serpent's reach.
[15]Then from his mouth the serpent spewed water like a river, to overtake the woman and
sweep her away with the torrent. [16]But the earth helped the woman by opening its mouth
and swallowing the river that the dragon had spewed out of his mouth. [17]Then the dragon was enraged at the woman and went off to make war[u] against the rest of her offspring[v]—those who obey God's commandments[w] and hold to the testimony of Jesus.[x]

13 [1]And the dragon[a] stood on the shore of the sea.

The Beast out of the Sea

And I saw a beast coming out of the sea.[y] He had ten horns and seven heads,[z] with
ten crowns on his horns, and on each head a blasphemous name.[a] [2]The beast I saw resembled a leopard,[b] but had feet like those of a bear[c] and a mouth like that of a lion.[d]
The dragon gave the beast his power and his throne and great authority.[e] [3]One of the
heads of the beast seemed to have had a fatal wound, but the fatal wound had been
healed.[f] The whole world was astonished[g] and followed the beast. [4]Men worshiped the
dragon because he had given authority to the beast, and they also worshiped the beast
and asked, "Who is like[h] the beast? Who can make war against him?"

[5]The beast was given a mouth to utter proud words and blasphemies[i] and to exercise
his authority for forty-two months.[j] [6]He opened his mouth to blaspheme God, and to
slander his name and his dwelling place and those who live in heaven.[k] [7]He was given
power to make war[l] against the saints and to conquer them. And he was given authority over every tribe, people, language and nation.[m] [8]All inhabitants of the earth[n] will
worship the beast—all whose names have not been written in the book of life[o] belonging to the Lamb that was slain from the creation of the world.[b][p]

12:13 [r]ver 5
12:14 [s]Ex 19:4 [t]Da 7:25
12:17 [u]Rev 11:7 [v]Ge 3:15 [w]Rev 14:12 [x]Rev 1:2
13:1 [y]Da 7:1-6; Rev 15:2 [z]Rev 12:3 [a]Da 11:36; Rev 17:3
13:2 [b]Da 7:6 [c]Da 7:5 [d]Da 7:4 [e]Rev 16:10
13:3 [f]ver 12,14 [g]Rev 17:8
13:4 [h]Ex 15:11
13:5 [i]Da 7:8,11,20,25; 11:36; 2Th 2:4 [j]Rev 11:2
13:6 [k]Rev 12:12
13:7 [l]Da 7:21; Rev 11:7 [m]Rev 5:9
13:8 [n]Rev 3:10 [o]Rev 3:5; 20:12 [p]Mt 25:34

[a] *1* Some late manuscripts *And I* [b] *8* Or *written from the creation of the world in the book of life belonging to the Lamb that was slain*

12:14 a time, times and half a time. See note on 11:1–2. See *WCF* 25.4.

■ **13:1–10** *The Beast From the Sea.* The Old Testament presents the sea as a dwelling for monsters (cf. Job 7:12; 41:1; Pss 74:13; 89:9–10; Isa 27:1). A beast rising out of the sea represents persecuting power, especially the power of a demonized state. The monstrous mixture of features shows both the fierceness and the repulsiveness of the beast. He is hideous. One might be terrorized into submission, but who would genuinely want to worship this mass of ugliness? The rebellious world is fascinated with his power (v. 4), but Christians have their eyes opened through this and other Biblical revelations.

The beast combines features from the four beasts of Daniel 7:1–8 and 17–27, which represent idolatrous kingdoms. This beast in Revelation must be a worldly kingdom that represents them all. The state persecutions of Daniel and his friends thus suggest the nature of the persecution that the seven churches must face from the Roman state (and possibly suggest persecutions of later ages). In Asia Minor, local officials threatened to kill Christians if they refused to worship the Roman emperor. A similar opposition to godly worship will occur just before Christ returns (2Th 2:4). Persecutions come sporadically between these two times (Mt 24:9; 2Ti 3:12–13; 1Pe 4:12–19). Second Thessalonians 2:7–8 appears to suggest both a repeated pattern of satanic opposition and a final, climactic outbreak. Christians must not be surprised by these pressures. They must face martyrdom, if necessary, knowing that God is in control and that his triumph is certain.

The beast is a counterfeit of Christ. Note the following parallels: (1) The beast, whom Satan brought forth, is an image of Satan (v. 1), just as Christ is the exact image of God, begotten by the Father (Ps 2:7; Col 1:15; Heb 1:3). (2) The beast has ten crowns, while Christ has many crowns (19:12). (3) The beast has blasphemous names written on him, while Christ has a worthy name, unknown to anyone else, written on him (19:12). The dragon gives the beast his power, throne and great authority (v. 2), just as Christ has been given power (5:12–13), a throne (3:21) and authority (12:10) from the Father (Jn 5:21–23). (4) The beast has a seemingly fatal wound from which he recovers—a counterfeit enactment of Christ's resurrection (v. 3). The beast's healing is one of the principal features that attract followers, just as the resurrection of Christ is one of the principal points of evangelistic proclamation. (5) Worship is directed toward both the dragon and the beast, just as Christians worship both the Father and the Son (Jn 5:23). (6) The beast attracts the worship of the whole world (v. 3), just as Christ is to be worshiped universally. (7) The beast utters blasphemies, while Christ utters the praises of God (Heb 2:12). (8) The beast makes war against the saints, while Christ makes war against the beast (19:11–21). The song of praise to the beast in verse 4 counterfeits the song to God the warrior in Exodus 15:11. The striking juxtaposition of Christ and the beast in 19:11–21 shows that they are the two main warriors in the battle. Christ is the divine warrior, fulfilling the imagery of Exodus 15:3 (see also Isa 59:16–18; 63:1–6; Hab 3:3–15; Zec 9:13–16; 14:1–5). The beast is the unholy, counterfeit warrior who fulfills the imagery of Daniel 7:1–8.

Satan himself attempts to replicate God the Father. He engages in a mock creation in which he brings forth his image out of chaotic waters (verse 1; see parallel at Ge 1:2). Similarly, the false prophet, or beast from the earth, counterfeits the work of the Holy Spirit (see note on verses 11–18).

Together Satan, the beast and the false prophet form an unholy trio (16:13), counterfeiting the holy Trinity. Satan, as a deceiver, is always trying to make his ways look attractive (2Co 11:14–15). Danger lies in the fact that his forgeries often appear close to the real thing, and believers may mistake the one for the other. But when Revelation opens believers' eyes, they see a world of difference between Satan's horrors and God's beauties. Believers can be confident because Satan is only an imitator, not a creator, and his productions are always bestial and degenerate, as he himself is. Beasts must give way before Christ the King (19:11–21). Another counterfeit figure is Babylon the prostitute, who is the imitation of the bride of Christ (see note on 17:1—19:10).

13:5 forty-two months. See note on 11:1–2.

13:6 See *WCF* 25.6.

13:7 war against the saints. The beast compels worship (v. 8), and when the saints refuse to submit they are martyred. But despite their apparent defeat, martyrs enjoy victory with Christ both immediately (6:9–11) and later, when their prayers for the final defeat of the beast are answered (19:11–21). **tribe, people, language and nation.** See note on 5:9.

13:8 book of life. See NIV text note. This book is the heavenly roster of names of those destined to new life (see note on 3:5;) through the purchase of Christ's blood (5:9). In the midst of persecution and over against the immense power of the beast, the saints may find security in God's guarantee of their heavenly citizenship (17:8; 20:12,15; 21:27). A similar guarantee is found in 7:1–17. See *WCF* 8.6.

9 He who has an ear, let him hear.[q]

> 10 If anyone is to go into captivity,
> into captivity he will go.
> If anyone is to be killed[a] with the sword,
> with the sword he will be killed.[r]

This calls for patient endurance and faithfulness[s] on the part of the saints.[t]

The Beast out of the Earth

11 Then I saw another beast, coming out of the earth. He had two horns like a lamb,
but he spoke like a dragon. 12 He exercised all the authority[u] of the first beast on his behalf,[v] and made the earth and its inhabitants worship the first beast,[w] whose fatal
wound had been healed.[x] 13 And he performed great and miraculous signs,[y] even causing fire to come down from heaven[z] to earth in full view of men. 14 Because of the signs[a]
he was given power to do on behalf of the first beast, he deceived[b] the inhabitants of the
earth. He ordered them to set up an image in honor of the beast who was wounded by
the sword and yet lived. 15 He was given power to give breath to the image of the first
beast, so that it could speak and cause all who refused to worship the image to be killed.[c]
16 He also forced everyone, small and great,[d] rich and poor, free and slave, to receive a
mark on his right hand or on his forehead,[e] 17 so that no one could buy or sell unless he
had the mark,[f] which is the name of the beast or the number of his name.[g]

18 This calls for wisdom.[h] If anyone has insight, let him calculate the number of the
beast, for it is man's number.[i] His number is 666.

The Lamb and the 144,000

14 Then I looked, and there before me was the Lamb,[j] standing on Mount Zion,[k]
and with him 144,000[l] who had his name and his Father's name[m] written on
their foreheads. 2 And I heard a sound from heaven like the roar of rushing waters[n] and
like a loud peal of thunder. The sound I heard was like that of harpists playing their
harps.[o] 3 And they sang a new song[p] before the throne and before the four living creatures and the elders. No one could learn the song except the 144,000[q] who had been redeemed from the earth. 4 These are those who did not defile themselves with women, for
they kept themselves pure.[r] They follow the Lamb wherever he goes. They were purchased from among men[s] and offered as firstfruits[t] to God and the Lamb. 5 No lie was
found in their mouths;[u] they are blameless.[v]

The Three Angels

6 Then I saw another angel flying in midair,[w] and he had the eternal gospel to proclaim to those who live on the earth[x]—to every nation, tribe, language and people.[y] 7 He
said in a loud voice, "Fear God[z] and give him glory,[a] because the hour of his judgment
has come. Worship him who made the heavens, the earth, the sea and the springs of water."[b]

13:9 [q]Rev 2:7
13:10 [r]Jer 15:2; 43:11 [s]Heb 6:12 [t]Rev 14:12
13:12 [u]ver 4 [v]ver 14 [w]Rev 14:9,11 [x]ver 3
13:13 [y]Mt 24:24 [z]1Ki 18:38; Rev 20:9
13:14 [a]2Th 2:9,10 [b]Rev 12:9
13:15 [c]Da 3:3-6
13:16 [d]Rev 19:5 [e]Rev 14:9
13:17 [f]Rev 14:9 [g]Rev 14:11; 15:2
13:18 [h]Rev 17:9 [i]Rev 15:2; 21:17
14:1 [j]Rev 5:6 [k]Ps 2:6 [l]Rev 7:4 [m]Rev 3:12
14:2 [n]Rev 1:15 [o]Rev 5:8
14:3 [p]Rev 5:9 [q]ver 1
14:4 [r]2Co 11:2; Rev 3:4 [s]Rev 5:9 [t]Jas 1:18
14:5 [u]Ps 32:2; Zep 3:13 [v]Eph 5:27
14:6 [w]Rev 8:13 [x]Rev 3:10 [y]Rev 13:7
14:7 [z]Rev 15:4 [a]Rev 11:13 [b]Rev 8:10

a 10 Some manuscripts *anyone kills*

13:10 patient endurance. See note on 1:9.

■ **13:11–18** *The Beast From the Earth: The False Prophet.* The beast from the earth, also called the false prophet (16:13; 19:20; 20:10), functions as a propagandist for the beast. His actions counterfeit the witness of the Holy Spirit (cf. note on vv. 1–10). He desires that people worship the beast, not himself, just as the Holy Spirit glorifies Christ, not himself (Jn 16:14). The false prophet works false miraculous signs, counterfeiting the miracles of the Holy Spirit (vv. 13–14). He forces a mark on his subjects (v. 16), just as Christians are sealed with the mark of the Holy Spirit (Eph 1:13). In first-century Asia Minor, the main propagandists would have been priests of the emperor cult and the "Commune of Asia," a council of distinguished city representatives promoting loyalty to the emperor. In our present day, totalitarianism also enlists propagandists. Just before Christ returns, counterfeit miracles will accompany the appearance of "the lawless one" (2Th 2:9). The false prophet embodies a repeatable pattern (see "Introduction: Purpose and Distinctives").

13:12–17 See *WCF* 20.2; 23.4.

13:16 a mark. The mark of the beast is a fakery of the seal of God's name on the saints (7:2–8; 14:1; Eze 9:4–6). The beast owns those who are marked; they are his slaves (14:9; 19:20; 20:4). Speculations about a visible mark are beside the point.

13:18 666. The number 666 falls short of the divine completeness of seven. By the time of Domitian, the earlier emperor Nero had become a traditional antichrist figure, and "666" was probably already known to be the numerical value associated with the name Nero Caesar in Hebrew. The number thus designates either Nero himself (if one accepts an early dating of Revelation) or a later figure imitating Nero's godlessness. Many have tried to identify the final antichrist on the basis of this number, but its connections with Nero and the symbolism of falling short of seven may well be its only significance. Believers must always be watchful for Christ's return without falling into the foolishness of date setting (Mt 24:36–51).

■ **14:1–5** *The 144,000.* These represent the saints in their complete number (see note on 7:4–8). They form a priestly company (5:10) consecrated to offer praise to God on Mount Zion.

14:4 pure. Sexual imagery is used to denote spiritual purity. Christ's faithful followers keep away from Babylon the prostitute and, as his pure bride, are loyal exclusively to him (19:7–8; Eph 5:26–27). Purity in sexual behavior is included as one element in this comprehensive purity (1Co 6:15–20).

■ **14:6–11** *Three Angelic Messengers.* These three angels appear in concert, conceptually forming a single, united image with a single, threefold message.

14:6 every nation, tribe, language and people. See note on 5:9.

[8]A second angel followed and said, "Fallen! Fallen is Babylon the Great,[c] which
made all the nations drink the maddening wine of her adulteries."[d]
[9]A third angel followed them and said in a loud voice: "If anyone worships the beast
and his image[e] and receives his mark on the forehead or on the hand, [10]he, too, will drink
of the wine of God's fury,[f] which has been poured full strength into the cup of his
wrath.[g] He will be tormented with burning sulfur in the presence of the holy angels and
of the Lamb. [11]And the smoke of their torment rises for ever and ever.[h] There is no rest
day or night for those who worship the beast and his image, or for anyone who receives
the mark of his name." [12]This calls for patient endurance on the part of the saints[i] who
obey God's commandments and remain faithful to Jesus.
[13]Then I heard a voice from heaven say, "Write: Blessed are the dead who die in the
Lord[j] from now on."
"Yes," says the Spirit, "they will rest from their labor, for their deeds will follow them."

The Harvest of the Earth

[14]I looked, and there before me was a white cloud, and seated on the cloud was one
"like a son of man"[a][k] with a crown[l] of gold on his head and a sharp sickle in his hand.
[15]Then another angel came out of the temple and called in a loud voice to him who was
sitting on the cloud, "Take your sickle[m] and reap, because the time to reap has come,
for the harvest[n] of the earth is ripe." [16]So he who was seated on the cloud swung his sickle over the earth, and the earth was harvested.
[17]Another angel came out of the temple in heaven, and he too had a sharp sickle.
[18]Still another angel, who had charge of the fire, came from the altar and called in a loud
voice to him who had the sharp sickle, "Take your sharp sickle and gather the clusters
of grapes from the earth's vine, because its grapes are ripe." [19]The angel swung his sickle on the earth, gathered its grapes and threw them into the great winepress of God's
wrath.[o] [20]They were trampled in the winepress[p] outside the city,[q] and blood flowed out
of the press, rising as high as the horses' bridles for a distance of 1,600 stadia.[b]

Seven Angels With Seven Plagues

15 I saw in heaven another great and marvelous sign:[r] seven angels[s] with the sev-
en last plagues[t]—last, because with them God's wrath is completed. [2]And I saw
what looked like a sea of glass[u] mixed with fire and, standing beside the sea, those who
had been victorious over the beast and his image[v] and over the number of his name.
They held harps given them by God [3]and sang the song of Moses[w] the servant of God and
the song of the Lamb:

"Great and marvelous are your deeds,[x]
Lord God Almighty.
Just and true are your ways,[y]
King of the ages.

14:8 [c]Isa 21:9; Jer 51:8 [d]Rev 17:2,4; 18:3,9
14:9 [e]Rev 13:14
14:10 [f]Isa 51:17; Jer 25:15 [g]Rev 18:6
14:11 [h]Isa 34:10; Rev 19:3
14:12 [i]Rev 13:10
14:13 [j]1Co 15:18; 1Th 4:16
14:14 [k]Da 7:13; Rev 1:13 [l]Rev 6:2
14:15 [m]Joel 3:13 [n]Jer 51:33
14:19 [o]Rev 19:15
14:20 [p]Isa 63:3 [q]Heb 13:12; Rev 11:8
15:1 [r]Rev 12:1,3 [s]Rev 16:1 [t]Lev 26:21
15:2 [u]Rev 4:6 [v]Rev 13:14
15:3 [w]Ex 15:1; Dt 32:4 [x]Ps 111:2 [y]Ps 145:17

[a] *14* Daniel 7:13 [b] *20* That is, about 180 miles (about 300 kilometers)

14:8 Babylon the Great. See note on 17:1—19:10. **wine of her adulteries.** Sexual immorality and idolatry, which is spiritual adultery, were major temptations for the seven churches (see note on 2:20). The effect of immorality and idolatry, like that of drunkenness, is shame, foolishness and disgrace (17:2,4; 18:3; 19:2; Pr 9:13–18; Jer 51:7).
14:9 the beast. See note on 13:1–10. **his mark.** See note on 13:16.
■ **14:12–13** *Care for the Saints.* Amid the warnings and judgments of the seven histories (see note on 12:1—14:20) comes this assurance of care for believers.
14:12 patient endurance. See note on 1:9.
14:13 See *WCF* 21.4; *WLC* 85,90.
■ **14:14–20** *The Seventh Symbolic History: One Like a Son of Man.* A description of the second coming as the harvest over which the Son of Man presides (Joel 3:12–16; Mt 13:36–43). The one "like a son of man" is Jesus Christ (1:13; Da 7:13–14). Two harvests are described: grain (vv. 14–16) and grapes (vv. 17–20). These are perhaps two aspects of the same event of judgment. Or the grain harvest may be the harvest of the righteous (Lk 3:17) and the grapes the harvest of the wicked.
14:17 See *BC* 37.
■ **15:1–16:21** *Cycle Four: Seven Bowls of God's Wrath From the Temple.* The opening scene of worship (15:1—16:1) calls to mind the worship around God's throne in 4:1—5:14. Those who overcome rejoice in God's presence (15:2–4). Seven resplendent angels receive bowls from the presence of God in the temple. The bowls symbolize the cup of God's wrath, which makes the nations drunk (14:10; 16:19; Isa 51:17–22; Jer 25:15–29; La 4:21; Eze 23:31–34; Hab 2:16). The bowls are poured out at God's command (16:1), resulting in seven last plagues. The plagues lead up to the second coming, since "with them God's wrath is completed" (15:1).

The seven bowls show notable similarities with the seven trumpets (8:2—11:19). The first four bowls, like the first four trumpets, result in devastation on the four major regions or realms of creation: land, sea, fresh water and sky. Like the trumpets, the bowls are reminiscent of the plagues against Egypt. But the bowls result in more severe judgments than did the trumpets. The trumpet judgments typically affected a third of the total, but the bowls affect the whole.

These bowls symbolize the judgments of God against evildoers. The general pattern may include both the judgments against the godless Roman Empire and judgments in the final crisis leading up to the second coming (see "Introduction: Purpose and Distinctives").
15:2 sea of glass. See note on 4:6. **those who had been victorious.** The saints, through their prayers, have a role to play in the judgments of God (6:9–11). As in 7:1–17, they are protected from the judgments that fall on the earth.
15:3–4 See *WLC* 7,110,112; *WSC* 4,54.
15:3 song of Moses. An allusion to Exodus 15. Like the Israelites, the saints are delivered from idolatrous oppression through plagues sent from God. **Just.** God's acts of judgment are never

4 Who will not fear you, O Lord,[z]
and bring glory to your name?
For you alone are holy.
All nations will come
and worship before you,[a]
for your righteous acts have been revealed."

5 After this I looked and in heaven the temple,[b] that is, the tabernacle of the Testimony,[c] was opened. 6 Out of the temple[d] came the seven angels with the seven plagues.[e]
They were dressed in clean, shining linen and wore golden sashes around their chests.[f]
7 Then one of the four living creatures[g] gave to the seven angels seven golden bowls filled
with the wrath of God, who lives for ever and ever. 8 And the temple was filled with
smoke[h] from the glory of God and from his power, and no one could enter the temple[i]
until the seven plagues of the seven angels were completed.

The Seven Bowls of God's Wrath

16 Then I heard a loud voice from the temple saying to the seven angels,[j] "Go, pour
out the seven bowls of God's wrath on the earth."
2 The first angel went and poured out his bowl on the land,[k] and ugly and painful
sores[l] broke out on the people who had the mark of the beast and worshiped his image.[m]
3 The second angel poured out his bowl on the sea, and it turned into blood like that
of a dead man, and every living thing in the sea died.[n]
4 The third angel poured out his bowl on the rivers and springs of water,[o] and they became blood.[p] 5 Then I heard the angel in charge of the waters say:

"You are just in these judgments,[q]
you who are and who were,[r] the Holy One,[s]
because you have so judged;
6 for they have shed the blood of your saints and prophets,
and you have given them blood to drink[t] as they deserve."

7 And I heard the altar[u] respond:

"Yes, Lord God Almighty,
true and just are your judgments."[v]

8 The fourth angel[w] poured out his bowl on the sun, and the sun was given power to
scorch people with fire.[x] 9 They were seared by the intense heat and they cursed the
name of God,[y] who had control over these plagues, but they refused to repent[z] and glorify him.[a]
10 The fifth angel poured out his bowl on the throne of the beast,[b] and his kingdom
was plunged into darkness.[c] Men gnawed their tongues in agony 11 and cursed[d] the God
of heaven[e] because of their pains and their sores,[f] but they refused to repent of what they
had done.[g]
12 The sixth angel poured out his bowl on the great river Euphrates,[h] and its water was
dried up to prepare the way for the kings from the East.[i] 13 Then I saw three evil[a] spirits
that looked like frogs; they came out of the mouth of the dragon,[j] out of the mouth of
the beast[k] and out of the mouth of the false prophet.[l] 14 They are spirits of demons[m] performing miraculous signs, and they go out to the kings of the whole world, to gather
them for the battle[n] on the great day of God Almighty.

a *13* Greek *unclean*

15:4 [z]Jer 10:7 [a]Isa 66:23
15:5 [b]Rev 11:19 [c]Nu 1:50
15:6 [d]Rev 14:15 [e]ver 1 [f]Rev 1:13
15:7 [g]Rev 4:6
15:8 [h]Isa 6:4 [i]Ex 40:34,35; 1Ki 8:10,11; 2Ch 5:13,14
16:1 [j]Rev 15:1
16:2 [k]Rev 8:7 [l]Ex 9:9-11 [m]Rev 13:15-17
16:3 [n]Ex 7:17-21; Rev 8:8,9
16:4 [o]Rev 8:10 [p]Ex 7:17-21
16:5 [q]Rev 15:3 [r]Rev 1:4 [s]Rev 15:4
16:6 [t]Isa 49:26; Rev 17:6
16:7 [u]Rev 6:9 [v]Rev 15:3; 19:2
16:8 [w]Rev 8:12 [x]Rev 14:18
16:9 [y]ver 11,21 [z]Rev 2:21 [a]Rev 11:13
16:10 [b]Rev 13:2 [c]Rev 9:2
16:11 [d]ver 9,21 [e]Rev 11:13 [f]ver 2 [g]Rev 2:21
16:12 [h]Rev 9:14 [i]Isa 41:2
16:13 [j]Rev 12:3 [k]Rev 13:1 [l]Rev 19:20
16:14 [m]1Ti 4:1 [n]Rev 17:14

arbitrary or spiteful, but they are just payment for evil deeds (v. 4; 16:5,7; 19:2,11).
15:5 the temple. The inner area of God's heavenly dwelling has already been pictured (see note on 4:1—5:14).
15:6 clean, shining linen. Old Testament priestly clothing was made of linen (Ex 28:42; Lev 16:4). The holiness of God's judgments is thereby emphasized (see note on verse 3).
15:7 four living creatures. See note on 4:6.
15:8 smoke. Smoke or a thick cloud frequently accompanies God's presence, especially when he is angry. The associations include Mount Sinai (Ex 19:9,16,18; 20:18) and the visions of Isaiah and Ezekiel (Isa 6:4; Eze 1:4; cf. Nu 12:5; Ps 18:8,11).
16:2 sores. Like the Egyptian plague of boils (Ex 9:8–12).
16:3–4 blood. Like the Egyptian plague of blood (Ex 7:14–24).
16:5 just. See note on 15:3.
16:10 darkness. Like the Egyptian plague of darkness (Ex 10:21–23).
16:14 to gather them for the battle. In the climactic battle, all the forces of wickedness are assembled to make war against the warrior Lamb (17:14). The imagery alludes to the battle between God and Pharaoh in Exodus 15:2, but the panorama is cosmic in scope. Several passages in Revelation (17:13–14; 19:11–21; 20:7–10; possibly 6:12–17) describe the battle with increasing detail and precision; all are based on the eschatological battle of Gog and Magog in Ezekiel 38–39. Throughout the church age there are times of intense confrontation between God and the forces of Satan (2:10,13), but the most intense battle will take place at the second coming (19:11–21).

[15]"Behold, I come like a thief! Blessed is he who stays awake[o] and keeps his clothes
with him, so that he may not go naked and be shamefully exposed."
[16]Then they gathered the kings together to the place that in Hebrew[p] is called Armageddon.[q]
[17]The seventh angel poured out his bowl into the air,[r] and out of the temple[s] came
a loud voice[t] from the throne, saying, "It is done!"[u] [18]Then there came flashes of lightning, rumblings, peals of thunder[v] and a severe earthquake.[w] No earthquake like it
has ever occurred since man has been on earth,[x] so tremendous was the quake.
[19]The great city[y] split into three parts, and the cities of the nations collapsed. God remembered[z] Babylon the Great[a] and gave her the cup filled with the wine of the fury
of his wrath.[b] [20]Every island fled away and the mountains could not be found.[c] [21]From
the sky huge hailstones[d] of about a hundred pounds each fell upon men. And they
cursed God on account of the plague of hail,[e] because the plague was so terrible.

The Woman on the Beast

17 One of the seven angels[f] who had the seven bowls[g] came and said to me,
"Come, I will show you the punishment[h] of the great prostitute,[i] who sits on
many waters.[j] [2]With her the kings of the earth committed adultery and the inhabitants
of the earth were intoxicated with the wine of her adulteries."[k]
[3]Then the angel carried me away in the Spirit into a desert.[l] There I saw a woman
sitting on a scarlet beast that was covered with blasphemous names[m] and had seven
heads and ten horns.[n] [4]The woman was dressed in purple and scarlet, and was glittering with gold, precious stones and pearls.[o] She held a golden cup[p] in her hand, filled
with abominable things and the filth of her adulteries. [5]This title was written on her
forehead:

16:15 [o]Lk 12:37
16:16 [p]Rev 9:11 [q]2Ki 23:29,30
16:17 [r]Eph 2:2 [s]Rev 14:15 [t]Rev 11:15 [u]Rev 21:6
16:18 [v]Rev 4:5 [w]Rev 6:12 [x]Da 12:1
16:19 [y]Rev 17:18 [z]Rev 18:5 [a]Rev 14:8 [b]Rev 14:10
16:20 [c]Rev 6:14
16:21 [d]Rev 11:19 [e]Ex 9:23-25
17:1 [f]Rev 15:1 [g]Rev 21:9 [h]Rev 16:19 [i]Rev 19:2 [j]Jer 51:13
17:2 [k]Rev 14:8; 18:3
17:3 [l]Rev 12:6,14 [m]Rev 13:1 [n]Rev 12:3
17:4 [o]Rev 18:16 [p]Jer 51:7; Rev 18:6

16:16 Armageddon. Generally thought to be "the mountain of Megiddo" from the Hebrew word for mountain (*har*) and the Greek word for Megiddo (*Magedôn*). In ancient Israel, Megiddo was a key city overseeing a major travel route between the great kingdoms of Mesopotamia and Egypt. Huge armies frequently assembled in the neighboring Plain of Esdraelon. Thus it is a fitting symbol for the location of the climactic battle. It has been suggested that Megiddo is not the appropriate location on the basis that it is not built on a mountain; Megiddo is built on a small, artificial hill or *tel.* However, the Hebrew word for mountain may also refer to a hill. By comparison, John used the Greek word for mountain to describe the seven hills on which Rome is built (17:9). The name may also simply be symbolic.
16:17–21 The seventh bowl brings the cycle of judgments to an end. Like the other cycles, this one ends with the second coming (see "Introduction: Purpose and Distinctives"), although the symbols of the second coming are not as obvious as in some other cases. Note the following features: Readers have already been told in 15:1 that the end of God's wrath would come with the seventh bowl. The removal of all islands and mountains in verse 20 corresponds to the final shaking of the earth in 6:14 and 20:11 (Heb 12:26–27). Elsewhere the fall of Babylon is immediately followed by the marriage supper of the Lamb (19:1–10). In 17:14–17 the fall of Babylon is associated with the final battle, which takes place at the second coming (19:11–21). Moreover, the final battle was imminent in verse 16. In Revelation, the imagery of the final battle is repeatedly drawn from Ezekiel 38–39 (see note on verse 14). Revelation 16:17–21 fits into this practice by grouping together an earthquake, the overturning of the mountains and hail, as in Ezekiel 38:19–23. Hence it describes the divine plague-judgments accompanying the battle. A description of other aspects of the battle is delayed until 19:11–21, in keeping with the dramatic, progressively unfolding plan of Revelation.
■ **17:1—19:10** *Cycle Five: Judgment on Babylon and Vindication of the Church.* Babylon the prostitute appears, representing the seductions of the world (17:4; 18:3). Her corruption is contrasted with the purity of the bride of the Lamb (19:7–9). Babylon encompasses the worship of the godless world. By contrast, the bride (the church) represents the worshipers of the true God. Just as Satan, the beast and the false prophet form a counterfeit trinity (see notes on 13:1–10; 13:11–18), so Babylon is a counterfeit church that seduces the world to allegiance to the counterfeit trinity. Satan attacks the saints in two main ways: (1) The beast attacks with power and persecution, endeavoring to destroy the witness of the saints and to force them to worship the beast, and (2) Babylon attacks with seduction, endeavoring to destroy the purity of the saints.
Babylon stands for the city of Rome with its immorality. For the seven churches of Revelation, Rome was the source of all manner of idolatry—not only the worship of the Roman emperor, but also the structures of an idolatrous society. The paganism of the cities of Asia Minor made each into a small manifestation of Rome. Full economic and social participation (13:17) involved attendance at idol feasts and pagan religious celebrations. Worship of the emperor was an expected expression of political allegiance. Pagans called Christians "atheists" because Christians did not worship the many gods, and they accused believers of hating humankind because Christians withdrew from compromised forms of social life (1Pe 2:12; 4:3–4). In reaction to this pressure, some professing Christians argued that participation in idolatrous feasts and sexual immorality was acceptable (2:12,20; 1Co 6:12–20). The woman Jezebel mentioned in 2:20–23 was a key seducer whose work is generalized and more deeply symbolized in Babylon the prostitute (cf. 17:2). Modern cities may also be centers of seduction to idolatry and sexual immorality. Thus, the symbolism of Babylon is capable of multiple embodiments, including a final, climactic embodiment just before the second coming (see "Introduction: Purpose and Distinctives").
Much of the imagery fits well the character of Jerusalem before its destruction. By refusing to accept the Messiah, she became a prostitute, as had happened in the Old Testament (Isa 1:21; Eze 16; 23; Hos 2). Revelation 11:8 links Jerusalem with Sodom and Egypt. A few interpreters favor identifying Babylon the prostitute with Jerusalem. But Jerusalem was only one instance of a society seducing people away from true worship. In Old Testament times ancient Babylon was another such city, and accordingly Revelation takes up the language of the Old Testament prophetic condemnations of Babylon and Tyre (Jer 50–51; Eze 27–28). Revelation 17:9 and 18 are most naturally understood as allusions to Rome, not Jerusalem.
The prostitute is borne up by a hideous beast (evidently the same beast as in 13:1–10). The beast, representing the Roman Empire, supports the city of Rome in its luxurious idolatry. It also spreads the practices of Rome throughout the empire. Eventually, however, the beast turns against the prostitute and destroys her (17:16–17). The rapacious powers of Roman government and the Roman legions destroyed prosperity, and eventually the military powers of surrounding tribes completely destroyed the city of Rome. The lesson from Roman times can be generalized: Idolatrous states end up destroying the very powers, riches, privileges and people that they start out supporting. False worship is self-destructive. When the destruction of false worship is complete (17:1—18:24), the true worshipers (the bride of the Lamb) stand out in their splendor and joy (19:1–10).
17:3 in the Spirit. See note on 1:10. See *BC* 29.
17:4 adulteries. See note on 2:20.

MYSTERY
BABYLON THE GREAT[q]
THE MOTHER OF PROSTITUTES
AND OF THE ABOMINATIONS OF THE EARTH.

6 I saw that the woman was drunk with the blood of the saints,[r] the blood of those who
bore testimony to Jesus.
When I saw her, I was greatly astonished. 7 Then the angel said to me: "Why are you astonished? I will explain to you the mystery[s] of the woman and of the beast she rides, which
has the seven heads and ten horns.[t] 8 The beast, which you saw, once was, now is not, and
will come up out of the Abyss and go to his destruction.[u] The inhabitants of the earth[v] whose
names have not been written in the book of life[w] from the creation of the world will be astonished[x] when they see the beast, because he once was, now is not, and yet will come.
9 "This calls for a mind with wisdom.[y] The seven heads are seven hills on which the
woman sits. 10 They are also seven kings. Five have fallen, one is, the other has not yet come;
but when he does come, he must remain for a little while. 11 The beast who once was, and
now is not,[z] is an eighth king. He belongs to the seven and is going to his destruction.
12 "The ten horns[a] you saw are ten kings who have not yet received a kingdom, but
who for one hour[b] will receive authority as kings along with the beast. 13 They have one
purpose and will give their power and authority to the beast.[c] 14 They will make war[d]
against the Lamb, but the Lamb will overcome them because he is Lord of lords and King
of kings[e]—and with him will be his called, chosen[f] and faithful followers."
15 Then the angel said to me, "The waters[g] you saw, where the prostitute sits, are peoples, multitudes, nations and languages.[h] 16 The beast and the ten horns you saw will
hate the prostitute. They will bring her to ruin[i] and leave her naked;[j] they will eat her
flesh[k] and burn her with fire.[l] 17 For God has put it into their hearts to accomplish his purpose by agreeing to give the beast their power to rule, until God's words are fulfilled.[m]
18 The woman you saw is the great city[n] that rules over the kings of the earth."

The Fall of Babylon

18 After this I saw another angel[o] coming down from heaven.[p] He had great authority, and the earth was illuminated by his splendor.[q] 2 With a mighty voice he
shouted:

"Fallen! Fallen is Babylon the Great![r]
She has become a home for demons
and a haunt for every evil[a] spirit,
a haunt for every unclean and detestable bird.[s]
3 For all the nations have drunk
the maddening wine of her adulteries.[t]
The kings of the earth committed adultery with her,[u]
and the merchants of the earth grew rich[v] from her excessive
luxuries."[w]

[a] 2 Greek *unclean*

17:5 [q]Rev 14:8
17:6 [r]Rev 18:24
17:7 [s]ver 5 [t]ver 3
17:8 [u]Rev 13:10 [v]Rev 3:10 [w]Rev 13:8 [x]Rev 13:3
17:9 [y]Rev 13:18
17:11 [z]ver 8
17:12 [a]Rev 12:3 [b]Rev 18:10,17,19
17:13 [c]ver 17
17:14 [d]Rev 16:14 [e]1Ti 6:15; Rev 19:16 [f]Mt 22:14
17:15 [g]Isa 8:7 [h]Rev 13:7
17:16 [i]Rev 18:17,19 [j]Eze 16:37,39 [k]Rev 19:18 [l]Rev 18:8
17:17 [m]Rev 10:7
17:18 [n]Rev 16:19
18:1 [o]Rev 17:1 [p]Rev 10:1 [q]Eze 43:2
18:2 [r]Rev 14:8 [s]Isa 13:21,22; Jer 50:39
18:3 [t]Rev 14:8 [u]Rev 17:2 [v]Eze 27:9-25 [w]ver 7,9

17:6 See *WLC* 151.
17:8 once was, now is not, and will come. The description is a counterfeit of the sovereignty of God, which is proclaimed in 1:4 and 8 and in 4:8. "Now is not" indicates that persecution is now at an ebb but that it will rise with renewed intensity in the future. The beast represents a repeated pattern of persecution, as in the four successive beasts of Daniel 7 (see note on 13:1–10). **book of life.** See note on 13:8.
17:9 seven hills. Rome was built on seven hills (see note on 17:1—19:10).
17:10 Five have fallen. See "Introduction: Time and Place of Writing" for speculations regarding the identity of these kings. It might also be that "five" simply represents an indefinite number of previous persecuting states (such as the beasts of Da 7). The presence of the sixth would then indicate in symbolic fashion that Christians are near the end, but not quite there.
17:12 ten horns. The symbolic significance of the number ten goes back to 13:1 and 17:7 and, more fundamentally, to Daniel 7:7 and 24. But the beast of Revelation cannot simply be identified with the fourth beast of Daniel. Rather, he is a composite that incorporates characteristics of all four of Daniel's beasts. In Revelation, the ten horns are kingly confederates of the beast. The political powers beyond the borders of the Roman Empire are most directly in mind (in view of 16:12,14,16; 19:19; 20:8). Barbarian tribes eventually overran Rome. But the scenario moves beyond the limitations of Rome and opens up a picture of the final battle in which the beast will enlist large-scale assistance. See *WCF* 20.4; *WLC* 109.
17:14 See *WCF* 23.2.
17:15 peoples, multitudes, nations and languages. See note on 5:9.
17:16–17 See *WCF* 20.4; *WLC* 109.
17:16 will hate the prostitute. See note on 17:1—19:10. See *WCF* 23.2.
17:17 God has put it into their hearts. In the midst of trials, the saints are assured that God is in control of even this appalling conflict.
18:1–24 Seven messages of judgment on Babylon are arranged into larger groups: three angelic messages of doom (17:7–18; 18:1–3,4–8), three laments by those committed to Babylon (vv. 9–10,11–17a,17b–19) and a climactic pronouncement of the permanence of Babylon's fall (vv. 21–24). Note also the many allusions to Jeremiah 50–51 and Ezekiel 27.
18:1 his splendor. Because of his exalted commission, the angel's splendor reflects that of God himself (10:1).
18:2 haunt. See Jeremiah 50:39. See *WCF* 25.5.
18:3 wine of her adulteries. See note on 2:20.

4 Then I heard another voice from heaven say:

"Come out of her, my people,[x]
so that you will not share in her sins,
so that you will not receive any of her plagues;
5 for her sins are piled up to heaven,[y]
and God has remembered[z] her crimes.
6 Give back to her as she has given;
pay her back[a] double for what she has done.
Mix her a double portion from her own cup.[b]
7 Give her as much torture and grief
as the glory and luxury she gave herself.[c]
In her heart she boasts,
'I sit as queen; I am not a widow,
and I will never mourn.'[d]
8 Therefore in one day[e] her plagues will overtake her:
death, mourning and famine.
She will be consumed by fire,[f]
for mighty is the Lord God who judges her.

9 "When the kings of the earth who committed adultery with her[g] and shared her luxury see the smoke of her burning,[h] they will weep and mourn over her.[i] 10 Terrified at her
torment, they will stand far off[j] and cry:

" 'Woe! Woe, O great city,[k]
O Babylon, city of power!
In one hour[l] your doom has come!'

11 "The merchants[m] of the earth will weep and mourn over her because no one buys
their cargoes any more[n]— 12 cargoes of gold, silver, precious stones and pearls; fine lin-
en, purple, silk and scarlet cloth; every sort of citron wood, and articles of every kind
made of ivory, costly wood, bronze, iron and marble;[o] 13 cargoes of cinnamon and spice,
of incense, myrrh and frankincense, of wine and olive oil, of fine flour and wheat; cattle
and sheep; horses and carriages; and bodies and souls of men.[p]
14 "They will say, 'The fruit you longed for is gone from you. All your riches and
splendor have vanished, never to be recovered.' 15 The merchants who sold these things
and gained their wealth from her[q] will stand far off, terrified at her torment. They will
weep and mourn[r] 16 and cry out:

" 'Woe! Woe, O great city,
dressed in fine linen, purple and scarlet,
and glittering with gold, precious stones and pearls![s]
17 In one hour[t] such great wealth has been brought to ruin!'[u]

"Every sea captain, and all who travel by ship, the sailors, and all who earn their living from the sea,[v] will stand far off. 18 When they see the smoke of her burning, they will
exclaim, 'Was there ever a city like this great city?'[w] 19 They will throw dust on their
heads,[x] and with weeping and mourning cry out:

" 'Woe! Woe, O great city,
where all who had ships on the sea
became rich through her wealth!
In one hour she has been brought to ruin![y]
20 Rejoice over her, O heaven![z]
Rejoice, saints and apostles and prophets!
God has judged her for the way she treated you.' "[a]

21 Then a mighty angel[b] picked up a boulder the size of a large millstone and threw
it into the sea,[c] and said:

18:4 [x]Isa 48:20; Jer 50:8; 2Co 6:17
18:5 [y]Jer 51:9 [z]Rev 16:19
18:6 [a]Ps 137:8; Jer 50:15,29 [b]Rev 14:10; 16:19
18:7 [c]Eze 28:2-8 [d]Isa 47:7,8; Zep 2:15
18:8 [e]ver 10; Isa 47:9; Jer 50:31,32 [f]Rev 17:16
18:9 [g]Rev 17:2,4 [h]ver 18; Rev 19:3 [i]Eze 26:17,18
18:10 [j]ver 15,17 [k]ver 16, 19 [l]Rev 17:12
18:11 [m]Eze 27:27 [n]ver 3
18:12 [o]Rev 17:4
18:13 [p]Eze 27:13; 1Ti 1:10
18:15 [q]ver 3 [r]Eze 27:31
18:16 [s]Rev 17:4
18:17 [t]ver 10 [u]Rev 17:16 [v]Eze 27:28-30
18:18 [w]Eze 27:32; Rev 13:4
18:19 [x]Jos 7:6; Eze 27:30 [y]Rev 17:16
18:20 [z]Jer 51:48; Rev 12:12 [a]Rev 19:2
18:21 [b]Rev 5:2 [c]Jer 51:63

18:4 Come out. See Isaiah 48:20 and 52:11 (see also Jer 50:8; 51:6,45; 2Co 6:17). See *BC* 28.
18:5 piled up to heaven. An ironic reminiscence of Jeremiah 51:9 (cf. Ge 11:4).
18:6 Give back. Judgment fits the nature of the offense (Ex 21:23–25).
18:8 consumed by fire. See Jeremiah 50:32.
18:11 buys their cargoes. Kings, merchants and sailors have been seduced to worship luxury.
18:12–13 See *WLC* 151.
18:21 The finality of Babylon's fall is depicted by the irreversible act of throwing a large stone into the sea (Jer 51:63–64; cf. Mt 18:6).

"With such violence
the great city of Babylon will be thrown down,
never to be found again.
22 The music of harpists and musicians, flute players and
trumpeters,
will never be heard in you again.[d]
No workman of any trade
will ever be found in you again.
The sound of a millstone
will never be heard in you again.[e]
23 The light of a lamp
will never shine in you again.
The voice of bridegroom and bride
will never be heard in you again.[f]
Your merchants were the world's great men.[g]
By your magic spell[h] all the nations were led astray.
24 In her was found the blood of prophets and of the saints,[i]
and of all who have been killed on the earth."[j]

Hallelujah!

19 After this I heard what sounded like the roar of a great multitude[k] in heaven shouting:

"Hallelujah!
Salvation[l] and glory and power[m] belong to our God,
2 for true and just are his judgments.
He has condemned the great prostitute
who corrupted the earth by her adulteries.
He has avenged on her the blood of his servants."[n]

3 And again they shouted:

"Hallelujah!
The smoke from her goes up for ever and ever."[o]

4 The twenty-four elders[p] and the four living creatures[q] fell down[r] and worshiped God, who was seated on the throne. And they cried:

"Amen, Hallelujah!"

5 Then a voice came from the throne, saying:

"Praise our God,
all you his servants,[s]
you who fear him,
both small and great!"[t]

6 Then I heard what sounded like a great multitude,[u] like the roar of rushing waters and like loud peals of thunder, shouting:

"Hallelujah!
For our Lord God Almighty reigns.
7 Let us rejoice and be glad
and give him glory!
For the wedding of the Lamb[v] has come,
and his bride[w] has made herself ready.
8 Fine linen, bright and clean,
was given her to wear."

(Fine linen stands for the righteous acts[x] of the saints.)

18:22 [d]Isa 24:8; Eze 26:13 [e]Jer 25:10
18:23 [f]Jer 7:34; 16:9; 25:10 [g]Isa 23:8 [h]Na 3:4
18:24 [i]Rev 16:6; 17:6 [j]Jer 51:49
19:1 [k]Rev 11:15 [l]Rev 7:10 [m]Rev 4:11
19:2 [n]Dt 32:43; Rev 6:10
19:3 [o]Isa 34:10; Rev 14:11
19:4 [p]Rev 4:4 [q]Rev 4:6 [r]Rev 5:14
19:5 [s]Ps 134:1 [t]Rev 11:18; 20:12
19:6 [u]Rev 11:15
19:7 [v]Mt 22:2; 25:10; Eph 5:32 [w]Rev 21:2,9
19:8 [x]Rev 15:4

19:1–10 The triumph of the pure bride is contrasted with the destruction of the corrupt false church (Babylon). Note the repeated hallelujahs (vv. 1,3–4,6).
19:2 just. See note on 15:3.
19:4 The twenty-four elders and the four living creatures. See notes on 4:4 and 6. The final celebration of God's victory fittingly takes place before his presence in the company of the heavenly host (Heb 12:22–24).
19:7 wedding of the Lamb. The wedding imagery expresses the intimacy, love and joy between Christ and his people. It consummates the commitments expressed earlier in Scripture (Isa 54:5–8; Hos 2:19–20; Eph 5:26–27).

9 Then the angel said to me,[y] "Write:[z] 'Blessed are those who are invited to the wedding supper of the Lamb!' "[a] And he added, "These are the true words of God."[b]
10 At this I fell at his feet to worship him.[c] But he said to me, "Do not do it! I am a fellow servant with you and with your brothers who hold to the testimony of Jesus. Worship God![d] For the testimony of Jesus[e] is the spirit of prophecy."

The Rider on the White Horse

11 I saw heaven standing open and there before me was a white horse, whose rider[f]
is called Faithful and True.[g] With justice he judges and makes war.[h] 12 His eyes are like
blazing fire,[i] and on his head are many crowns.[j] He has a name written on him that no
one knows but he himself.[k] 13 He is dressed in a robe dipped in blood,[l] and his name is
the Word of God.[m] 14 The armies of heaven were following him, riding on white horses
and dressed in fine linen,[n] white and clean. 15 Out of his mouth comes a sharp sword[o]
with which to strike down[p] the nations. "He will rule them with an iron scepter."[a][q] He
treads the winepress[r] of the fury of the wrath of God Almighty. 16 On his robe and on his
thigh he has this name written:[s]

KING OF KINGS AND LORD OF LORDS.[t]

17 And I saw an angel standing in the sun, who cried in a loud voice to all the birds[u]
flying in midair,[v] "Come,[w] gather together for the great supper of God, 18 so that you may

19:9 [y]ver 10 [z]Rev 1:19 [a]Lk 14:15 [b]Rev 21:5; 22:6
19:10 [c]Rev 22:8 [d]Ac 10:25,26; Rev 22:9 [e]Rev 12:17
19:11 [f]Rev 6:2 [g]Rev 3:14 [h]Isa 11:4
19:12 [i]Rev 1:14 [j]Rev 6:2 [k]Rev 2:17
19:13 [l]Isa 63:2,3 [m]Jn 1:1
19:14 [n]ver 8
19:15 [o]Rev 1:16 [p]Isa 11:4; 2Th 2:8 [q]Ps 2:9; Rev 2:27 [r]Rev 14:20
19:16 [s]ver 12 [t]Rev 17:14
19:17 [u]ver 21 [v]Rev 8:13 [w]Eze 39:17

a *15* Psalm 2:9

19:9 wedding supper. Note the contrasts between this blessed feast and the horrific feast of verses 17–18.
19:10 the testimony of Jesus is the spirit of prophecy. The angel is a fellow servant of the prophets (22:9). John had the Spirit of prophecy (22:6); he received the testimony (witness) that Jesus gave and presented it to the church (1:2). John's ministry compares to that of the angels. See *WCF* 21.2; *WLC* 105; *HC* 94.
■ **19:11–21** *Cycle Six: The Final Battle.* Christ appears as the divine warrior to wage final battle against all the enemies of God, who are headed up by the beast and the false prophet. Christ's holy attributes contrast markedly with the unholy, counterfeit attributes of the beast (13:1–10). This final war brings to a climax all the wars that God has waged on behalf of his people (Ex 15:2–3; Dt 20; Isa 59:16–19; Eze 38–39; Hab 3:8–15; Zec 12:1–9; 14:3–5) and consummates the triumph achieved by Christ on the cross (5:9–10; 12:10–11; Jn 12:31; Col 2:15). Some have interpreted the imagery as a reference to the spread of Christ's rule through submission to the gospel. But the parallels with 16:14 and 16, 17:14 and 20:7–10 show that the final battle is primarily in view (see notes on 16:14,17–21). In the later cycles (see "Introduction: Purpose and Distinctives"), the imagery progressively concentrates more intensively on the second coming and its immediate precursors. In this cycle, all the events are actually part of the second coming. But, as is typical of Revelation, they bring into full manifestation spiritual principles of war that have been operative throughout the church age (Eph 6:10–20; 1Jn 5:4–5). At the end, Jesus Christ is fully revealed as he who has always been and will always be (22:13; Heb 13:8).
19:11–16 See *BC* 8; *HC* 51.
19:11 heaven standing open. In contrast to 4:1, the heavenly presence of God is now revealed not merely to John the seer, but to the whole world of humanity. The appearance of the divine warrior in his majesty must mean the end of the battle and the destruction of all enemies before him.
19:17 great supper. See Ezekiel 39:4,17–20.

Hell: What Is Hell Like?

THE New Testament views hell ("Gehenna," the place of incineration; Mt 5:22; 18:9) as the final abode of those consigned to eternal punishment at the last judgment (Mt 25:41–46; Rev 20:11–15). It is described as a place of fire and darkness (Jude 7,13), of "weeping and gnashing of teeth" (Mt 8:12; 13:42,50; 22:13; 24:51; 25:30), of destruction (1Th 5:3; 2Th 1:7–9; 2Pe 3:7) and of torment (Lk 16:23; Rev 20:10). New Testament teaching about hell is meant to appall us and strike us dumb with horror, convincing us that as eternal life with God will be better than we could dream, so eternal punishment will be worse than we could conceive.

The Scriptures teach a number of specific facts about hell. First, hell is unending, conscious punishment (Jude 13; Rev 20:10). Teachings of eventual release from hell (or from purgatory) or of the annihilation of the ungodly at some stage have no Biblical basis.

Second, hell is not an experience of God's absence but an experience of his presence in displeasure and wrath. The experience of God's anger as "a consuming fire" (Heb 12:29), of his righteous condemnation and of the deprivation of all that is valuable, pleasant and worthwhile will be the nature of the experience of hell (Ro 2:8–9,12).

Third, everyone in hell is sentenced to this destiny by his or her own choice. Judgment comes upon unbelievers because they have refused to acknowledge God as their Lord, have rejected his righteousness in favor of sin and (if they have encountered the gospel) have rejected Jesus rather than coming to him (Jn 3:18–21; Ro 1:18,24,26,28,32; 2:8; 2Th 2:9–12). In this way, hell affirms the genuine significance of human choice. All people receive what they actually choose: to be with God forever, worshiping him, or to be under his wrathful condemnation forever, worshiping themselves.

The Scriptures teach about hell in order to call all people gratefully to embrace the grace of Christ that saves them from eternal punishment (Mt 5:29–30; 13:49–50). God mercifully forewarns us about the reality of hell so that we may turn to Christ and find salvation in him.

eat the flesh of kings, generals, and mighty men, of horses and their riders, and the flesh
of all people,[x] free and slave, small and great."
19Then I saw the beast and the kings of the earth[y] and their armies gathered together to make war against the rider on the horse and his army. 20But the beast was captured,
and with him the false prophet[z] who had performed the miraculous signs on his behalf.[a]
With these signs he had deluded those who had received the mark of the beast and worshiped his image. The two of them were thrown alive into the fiery lake[b] of burning sulfur.[c] 21The rest of them were killed with the sword[d] that came out of the mouth of the
rider on the horse,[e] and all the birds[f] gorged themselves on their flesh.

The Thousand Years

20 And I saw an angel coming down out of heaven,[g] having the key[h] to the Abyss
and holding in his hand a great chain. 2He seized the dragon, that ancient serpent, who is the devil, or Satan,[i] and bound him for a thousand years.[j] 3He threw him
into the Abyss, and locked and sealed[k] it over him, to keep him from deceiving the nations[l] anymore until the thousand years were ended. After that, he must be set free for
a short time.
4I saw thrones[m] on which were seated those who had been given authority to judge.
And I saw the souls of those who had been beheaded[n] because of their testimony for
Jesus and because of the word of God. They had not worshiped the beast[o] or his image
and had not received his mark on their foreheads or their hands.[p] They came to life and
reigned with Christ a thousand years. 5(The rest of the dead did not come to life until the
thousand years were ended.) This is the first resurrection.[q] 6Blessed[r] and holy are those
who have part in the first resurrection. The second death[s] has no power over them, but
they will be priests[t] of God and of Christ and will reign with him[u] for a thousand years.

Satan's Doom

7When the thousand years are over,[v] Satan will be released from his prison 8and will
go out to deceive the nations[w] in the four corners of the earth—Gog and Magog[x]—to
gather them for battle.[y] In number they are like the sand on the seashore.[z] 9They
marched across the breadth of the earth and surrounded[a] the camp of God's people, the
city he loves. But fire came down from heaven[b] and devoured them. 10And the devil, who
deceived them,[c] was thrown into the lake of burning sulfur, where the beast and the false
prophet had been thrown. They will be tormented day and night for ever and ever.[d]

The Dead Are Judged

11Then I saw a great white throne[e] and him who was seated on it. Earth and sky fled
from his presence, and there was no place for them. 12And I saw the dead, great and

19:18 [x]Eze 39:18-20
19:19 [y]Rev 16:14,16
19:20 [z]Rev 16:13 [a]Rev 13:12 [b]Da 7:11; Rev 20:10,14,15; 21:8 [c]Rev 14:10
19:21 [d]ver 15 [e]ver 11,19 [f]ver 17
20:1 [g]Rev 10:1 [h]Rev 1:18
20:2 [i]Rev 12:9 [j]2Pe 2:4
20:3 [k]Da 6:17 [l]Rev 12:9
20:4 [m]Da 7:9 [n]Rev 6:9 [o]Rev 13:12 [p]Rev 13:16
20:5 [q]Lk 14:14; Php 3:11
20:6 [r]Rev 14:13 [s]Rev 2:11 [t]Rev 1:6 [u]ver 1
20:7 [v]ver 2
20:8 [w]ver 3,10 [x]Eze 38:2; 39:1 [y]Rev 16:14 [z]Heb 11:12
20:9 [a]Eze 38:9,16 [b]Eze 38:22; 39:6
20:10 [c]Rev 19:20 [d]Rev 14:10,11
20:11 [e]Rev 4:2

19:19 beast. See note on 13:1–10. **armies gathered.** See note on 16:14.
19:20 fiery lake. Hell, the final abode of the wicked (20:10,14–15; 21:8; Isa 66:24). Fire is frequently associated with all-consuming judgment (Isa 66:15–16; Joel 2:3). See theological article "Hell" on previous page.
■ **20:1—21:8** *Cycle Seven: The Reign of the Saints and the Last Judgment.* An angel descending from heaven binds Satan for a thousand years. The faithful martyrs (20:4) come to life and reign with Christ. After the thousand years, Satan is released, gathers the nations for battle and is finally rendered powerless (20:10). The thousand-year period, commonly called the "Millennium," is variously understood (see theological article "The Millennium" on the next page). The final judgment follows the Millennium (see 20:11–15 and its note), as does the final state of restoration (21:1—22:5; see notes on 21:1–8; 21:9—22:5; 22:1–5).
20:2 bound him. Satan's power to influence the nations is suppressed. Premillennialists and some postmillennialists associate this event with the advent of an extraordinary future era of peace and prosperity, contrasting with the present era (1Th 2:18; 1Pe 5:8). Amillennialists and other postmillennialists think that the binding of Satan has already taken place through Christ's inauguration of God's kingdom on Earth (12:9; Mt 12:22–29; Mk 3:22–27; Jn 12:31; Col 2:15; see theological article "The Plan of the Ages" at Heb 7). The present spread of the gospel to the nations, as initiated in Acts, is the result of a restriction on Satan's power to deceive. Possibly this restriction on Satan's power is closely associated with the present, temporary demise of the beast (17:8). **a thousand years.** See notes on 20:1—22:5 and 20:11–15.
20:3 deceiving the nations. See 20:8,10; see also 13:14, 16:14 and 19:20.
20:4 souls. See 6:9–10. Martyrs are singled out as the most notable group of faithful witnesses, but other saints are not excluded from the privileges mentioned. **the beast.** See note on 13:1–10. **reigned.** See 2:26–27 and 3:21.
20:5–6 the first resurrection. If this refers to bodily resurrection, then it coincides with the second coming (1Co 15:51–57; 1Th 4:13–18), and the premillennialists are likely correct (see note on vv. 11–15). On the other hand, the language concerning the second death in verses 6 and 14 and 21:8 suggests a contrast between the first and the second deaths. The first death is bodily death, but it is only preliminary, not ultimate. The second death is ultimate and is spiritual in character. Likewise, the first and second resurrections may be preliminary and ultimate, respectively. The first resurrection is spiritual; the second is of the body. The first resurrection is then to be understood as coinciding either with spiritual new birth (Jn 5:24–25) or with going to be with Christ at the time of bodily death (6:9–10; 2Co 5:8; Php 1:23). In view of the concern in Revelation for vindicating martyrs (verse 4), the latter alternative seems preferable.
20:6 priests. See note on 1:6.
20:8 Gog and Magog. Names taken from Ezekiel 38–39. They represent the final enemies of God. **gather them for battle.** See 16:14.
20:11–15 God appears in a scene of final judgment. God's authority to judge has already been anticipated in 4:1—5:14. Now he executes the judgment that befits his character and power over the created universe. The vision shares features with Psalms 7:6–8 and 47:8–9, Daniel 7:9–10 and other Old Testament judgment scenes (see also Mt 25:31–46). Injustices and sufferings in history never escape God's eye. Those who persecute and practice injustice can never win. God will judge every deed, all wrongs will be righted and all attempts to dethrone God and enthrone oneself will be

The Millennium: Will Christ Reign for a Thousand Years?

CONVINCED that "all things in Scripture are not alike plain in themselves, nor alike clear unto all" (*WCF* 1.7), Reformed theologians have often acknowledged that sincere believers hold different views on a number of subjects. One issue about which there has been much friendly disagreement is that of the Millennium.

Reformed confessions and catechisms have unanimously affirmed a number of cardinal truths about Biblical eschatology, the doctrine of the last things (*WCF* 32; 33; *WLC* 84,85,86,87,88,89,90; *WSC* 38; *BC* 37; *HC* 52). The Scriptures clearly teach the following: (1) Christ will return in glory (Col 3:4). (2) The righteous and wicked will be resurrected from the dead (Jn 5:28–29). (3) A final judgment will take place (Mt 25:31ff.). (4) The righteous in Christ will be rewarded with eternal life in the new heavens and the new earth (Mk 10:29–30; Rev 21:1–5). (5) The wicked will be condemned to eternal judgment (Mt 25:41,46).

Even so, Reformed confessions and catechisms have been purposefully silent on a number of issues related to the end of time—issues on which there has been little unanimity among Reformed theologians. When will Christ return? What will be the signs of his coming? What will be the condition of the church and the world when he returns?

The question of the Millennium, Christ's one-thousand-year reign on Earth, has largely to do with the interpretation of Revelation 20. Three basic approaches have been taken toward this passage, and all are fully acceptable in Reformed theology: premillennialism, postmillennialism and amillennialism.

Premillennialists believe that the thousand years of Christ's millennial reign will follow the second coming (described in Rev 19:11–21). After the second coming, Satan is bound and Christ ushers in a prolonged period of earthly peace and prosperity. Some think of this as a literal thousand years, while others regard the number as symbolic of a very long period of time. Christians receive resurrected bodies at the beginning of the Millennium, but the resurrection of the wicked (and of those living in untransformed bodies during the Millennium), as well as the final judgment for all others, takes place at the end of the Millennium, following a rebellion led by Satan. Reformed premillennialism should be distinguished, however, from currently popular dispensational premillennialism, which adds features such as a rapture of the church before, during or after a seven-year future tribulation period that precedes Jesus' millennial reign.

Postmillennialists believe that the kingdom of Christ and the church will experience much more expansion on Earth before the second coming. The thousand years are understood by some as a final period of Christian earthly triumph following the spread of the gospel (described in Rev 19:11–21). Other postmillennialists agree with amillennialists in identifying Revelation 20:1–6 with the entire period beginning with the resurrection of Christ and ending with his return.

Amillennialists understand the Millennium to be a picture of the present reign of Christ and the saints in heaven (analogous to Rev 6:9–10) and of the inauguration of Christ's rule on Earth, especially through the church. The first resurrection is either the life of disembodied Christians with Christ in heaven or life in Christ that begins with spiritual new birth (Ro 6:8–11; Eph 2:6; Col 3:1–4). Satan has been bound through the triumph of Christ in his crucifixion and resurrection (Jn 12:31; Col 2:15). Although there are variations in details, amillennialists remain largely uncommitted to a particular scenario for the end times. The church may or may not fare well; evil may grow stronger or weaken. In the end, however, Christ will return in glory to reward his church and to judge the wicked.

The dispute among the various views partly concerns the chronological relation of Revelation 20:1–10 to Revelation 19:11–21. Premillennialists believe that Revelation 20:1–10 simply follows the second coming (depicted in Rev 19:11–21). But Revelation 20:1–15 might also represent a seventh cycle of judgments leading up to the second coming. The final battle in Revelation 20:7–10 seems to be the same as that in Revelation 16:14,16; 17:14; and 19:11–21. Similar language from Ezekiel 38–39 is used in the various descriptions. The judgment of Satan in Revelation 20:10 parallels the judgments against Babylon (Rev 17–18) and against the beast and the false prophet (Rev 19:11–21). These enemies of God are all consigned to doom, and the visions depicting their demise may be arranged thematically rather than chronologically. Certain features in Revelation 20:11–15 correspond to earlier descriptions of the second coming (Rev 6:14; 11:18). Most important, all Christ's enemies have already been destroyed in Revelation 19:11–21. If Revelation 20:1–6 represents later events, there would be no one left for Satan to deceive in Revelation 20:3, nor would Satan be around to deceive anyone.

Caution is needed because the different millennial positions depend on the interpretation of Old Testament prophetic texts as well as of Revelation 20:1–10. Moreover, like most of Revelation, Revelation 20:1–10 uses language that in principle may be capable of more than one concrete embodiment. These facts make precise interpretation difficult. The major point is that Satan will be finally defeated and that, even before that time, God takes care of his saints and allows them to enjoy the benefits of his triumphant rule. This assurance ought to comfort us, whatever our millennial position.

small, standing before the throne, and books were opened.[f] Another book was opened,
which is the book of life.[g] The dead were judged according to what they had done[h] as
recorded in the books. 13The sea gave up the dead that were in it, and death and Hades[i]
gave up the dead[j] that were in them, and each person was judged according to what he
had done. 14Then death[k] and Hades were thrown into the lake of fire. The lake of fire is
the second death. 15If anyone's name was not found written in the book of life,[l] he was
thrown into the lake of fire.

The New Jerusalem

21 Then I saw a new heaven and a new earth,[m] for the first heaven and the first
earth had passed away, and there was no longer any sea. 2I saw the Holy City,
the new Jerusalem, coming down out of heaven from God,[n] prepared as a bride beautifully dressed for her husband. 3And I heard a loud voice from the throne saying, "Now
the dwelling of God is with men, and he will live with them. They will be his people, and
God himself will be with them and be their God.[o] 4He will wipe every tear from their
eyes.[p] There will be no more death[q] or mourning or crying or pain,[r] for the old order of
things has passed away."

5He who was seated on the throne[s] said, "I am making everything new!" Then he
said, "Write this down, for these words are trustworthy and true."[t]

6He said to me: "It is done.[u] I am the Alpha and the Omega,[v] the Beginning and the
End. To him who is thirsty I will give to drink without cost from the spring of the water
of life.[w] 7He who overcomes will inherit all this, and I will be his God and he will be my
son. 8But the cowardly, the unbelieving, the vile, the murderers, the sexually immoral,
those who practice magic arts, the idolaters and all liars[x]—their place will be in the fiery lake of burning sulfur. This is the second death."[y]

9One of the seven angels who had the seven bowls full of the seven last plagues[z] came
and said to me, "Come, I will show you the bride,[a] the wife of the Lamb." 10And he car-

20:12 [f]Da 7:10 [g]Rev 3:5 [h]Jer 17:10; Mt 16:27; Rev 2:23
20:13 [i]Rev 6:8 [j]Isa 26:19
20:14 [k]1Co 15:26
20:15 [l]ver 12
21:1 [m]Isa 65:17; 2Pe 3:13
21:2 [n]Heb 11:10; 12:22; Rev 3:12
21:3 [o]2Co 6:16
21:4 [p]Rev 7:17 [q]1Co 15:26; Rev 20:14 [r]Isa 35:10; 65:19
21:5 [s]Rev 4:9; 20:11 [t]Rev 19:9
21:6 [u]Rev 16:17 [v]Rev 1:8; 22:13 [w]Jn 4:10
21:8 [x]1Co 6:9 [y]Rev 2:11
21:9 [z]Rev 15:1,6,7 [a]Rev 19:7

turned around to frustrate God's enemies completely. The prospect of final judgment ought to be a terror to God's enemies but a foundation of assurance for the saints. This judgment follows the thousand years of verses 2 and 7. Premillennialists believe that the second coming precedes the thousand years and hence must include a distinct, separate judgment of its own. They argue that at the second coming Christians receive their reward, while this later judgment is for the wicked and those living in untransformed bodies during the thousand years. Amillennialists and postmillennialists, on the other hand, have generally understood this passage as one among many references to a universal, final judgment at the second coming (see note on 21:1–8).

20:11 throne. See 4:2. **sky fled.** See 6:14. See *BC* 37.

20:12 book of life. See note on 13:8. See *BC* 37.

20:14 lake of fire. See note on 19:20 and theological article "Hell" at Revelation 19. **second death.** See note on verses 5–6.

20:15 book of life. See note on 13:8.

21:1–8 The voice of God announces the descent of the new Jerusalem against the backdrop of total renovation—a new heaven and a new earth. God is the Alpha (see note on 1:8), the Creator, whose purposes were expressed in creation from the beginning. Now he shows himself to be the Omega, the Consummator, who brings his purposes to final realization. The throne vision of 4:1–11 displayed God's glory, power and beauty within the fundamental sphere of heaven. Now the dwelling of God extends to all his people (v. 3). In contrast to the pain, suffering and struggles running through the earlier parts of Revelation, evil and pain are now abolished. The promises made to those who overcome are now fulfilled (see note on 2:7). This vision is meant to encourage faithfulness, confidence and hope in Christians, especially in those who face persecution. God will achieve his full purposes, and Christians will inherit his full blessing, however grim their circumstances might appear. Although this vision pertains to the consummation of all things, in Christ we even now receive the down payment of our future inheritance (Eph 1:14; Heb 12:18–29). Hence, Christians may receive a foretaste now of that final bliss. God's promises should stimulate our fervent devotion to Christ.

The final visions of Revelation weave into a beautiful unity a host of themes from the rest of the Bible. Note the themes of creation (v. 1); the holy city of Jerusalem (v. 2); communion with God expressed through marriage imagery (v. 2); the dwelling of God, including the tabernacle and temple (v. 3; see note on 4:1—5:14); the saints as God's own people (v. 3); the end of suffering and death (v. 4); new deeds of salvation (v. 5); the trustworthiness of God's word (v. 5); living water (v. 6); becoming a son of God (v. 7); warnings to the faithless (v. 8); and judgment (v. 8).

Revelation 21:1–8 is usually grouped with 21:9—22:5. The two passages present two aspects of the final vision of the new Jerusalem. Revelation 21:1–8 introduces many features that appear with greater elaboration in 21:9—22:5. Revelation 21:1–8 consists primarily of messages announcing the new realities, while 21:9—22:5 contains a more visionary description of these realities. But 21:1–8 also has close relations to 20:11–15. The final judgment of God in fact has two sides. The negative side (the judgment of the wicked) is expressed in 20:11–15, while the positive side (the reward for the righteous) is expressed in 21:1–8. Within the negative message of 20:11–15 is found a final exception in the mention of the book of life (20:15). Similarly, within the positive message of 21:1–8 is found a final exception in the mention of the fiery lake (v. 8). Thus 20:11–15 and 21:1–8 form two symmetric scenes depicting judgment both negatively and positively. Revelation 21:1–8 is thus a bridge between the judgment of 20:11–15 and the extended description of the new Jerusalem in 21:9—22:5.

21:1 new heaven and a new earth. Some have thought that the new universe will be an entirely new world that has no connection with the old one. But Isaiah 65:17–25 and Romans 8:21–23 indicate that a transfiguration of the old world is in view, similar to the way in which our new bodies will be transfigurations of the old ones (1Co 15:35–57). Everything is new (v. 5), which indicates the thoroughness and extensiveness of the transfiguration, but the result is redemption and not mere abolition of the old. **no longer any sea.** The salt water sea, where monsters live (see note on 13:1–10), is replaced with life-giving, fresh water (cf. v. 6; 22:1).

21:4 See *BC* 37.

21:6 water of life. See note on 22:1.

21:8 second death. See note on 20:5–6. See *BC* 37; *HC* 112.

■ **21:9—22:5** *The New Jerusalem.* The picture of the new Jerusalem is now unfolded in detail. The final dwelling place of the saints is a simultaneous fulfillment of earlier revelations that include the following: God appearing in glory and reigning in his heavenly court (21:22–23; 22:1,3; cf. 4:1–11); the holy city Jerusalem (21:10); the Garden of Eden (22:1–3); the bride, the marriage partner of the Lamb (21:9); and the temple as the dwelling place of God (21:22–23). The central figures and central blessings of the city are God himself and the Lamb (21:22–23; 22:1–5). The final revelation of God necessarily brings to a climax all earlier revelations. It completes God's purpose of bringing all things under one head, even Christ (11:15; Eph 1:10). Thus the final revelation in the end harmonizes with the creation of all things by Christ at the beginning (1:17; 4:11; Col 1:15–17) and with the redemption of all things through Christ in the middle (5:9–14; Ro 11:36; Col 1:18–20). Because of the fluid character of the

ried me away[b] in the Spirit[c] to a mountain great and high, and showed me the Holy City,
Jerusalem, coming down out of heaven from God. 11 It shone with the glory of God,[d] and
its brilliance was like that of a very precious jewel, like a jasper, clear as crystal.[e] 12 It had
a great, high wall with twelve gates, and with twelve angels at the gates. On the gates
were written the names of the twelve tribes of Israel.[f] 13 There were three gates on the
east, three on the north, three on the south and three on the west. 14 The wall of the city
had twelve foundations, and on them were the names of the twelve apostles of the Lamb.
15 The angel who talked with me had a measuring rod[g] of gold to measure the city,
its gates and its walls. 16 The city was laid out like a square, as long as it was wide. He
measured the city with the rod and found it to be 12,000 stadia[a] in length, and as wide
and high as it is long. 17 He measured its wall and it was 144 cubits[b] thick,[c] by man's measurement, which the angel was using. 18 The wall was made of jasper,[h] and the city of
pure gold, as pure as glass.[i] 19 The foundations of the city walls were decorated with every kind of precious stone.[j] The first foundation was jasper, the second sapphire, the
third chalcedony, the fourth emerald, 20 the fifth sardonyx, the sixth carnelian,[k] the seventh chrysolite, the eighth beryl, the ninth topaz, the tenth chrysoprase, the eleventh jacinth, and the twelfth amethyst.[d] 21 The twelve gates were twelve pearls, each gate
made of a single pearl. The great street of the city was of pure gold, like transparent
glass.[l]
22 I did not see a temple[m] in the city, because the Lord God Almighty[n] and the Lamb[o]
are its temple. 23 The city does not need the sun or the moon to shine on it, for the glory
of God gives it light,[p] and the Lamb is its lamp. 24 The nations will walk by its light, and
the kings of the earth will bring their splendor into it.[q] 25 On no day will its gates ever be
shut,[r] for there will be no night there.[s] 26 The glory and honor of the nations will be
brought into it. 27 Nothing impure will ever enter it, nor will anyone who does what is
shameful or deceitful,[t] but only those whose names are written in the Lamb's book of
life.

The River of Life

22 Then the angel showed me the river of the water of life, as clear as crystal,[u] flowing[v] from the throne of God and of the Lamb 2 down the middle of the great
street of the city. On each side of the river stood the tree of life,[w] bearing twelve crops
of fruit, yielding its fruit every month. And the leaves of the tree are for the healing of the
nations.[x] 3 No longer will there be any curse.[y] The throne of God and of the Lamb will
be in the city, and his servants will serve him.[z] 4 They will see his face,[a] and his name will
be on their foreheads.[b] 5 There will be no more night.[c] They will not need the light of a

21:10 [b]Rev 17:3 [c]Rev 1:10
21:11 [d]Rev 15:8; 22:5 [e]Rev 4:6
21:12 [f]Eze 48:30-34
21:15 [g]Rev 11:1
21:18 [h]ver 11 [i]ver 21
21:19 [j]Isa 54:11,12
21:20 [k]Rev 4:3
21:21 [l]ver 18
21:22 [m]Jn 4:21,23 [n]Rev 1:8 [o]Rev 5:6
21:23 [p]Isa 24:23; 60:19, 20; Rev 22:5
21:24 [q]Isa 60:3,5
21:25 [r]Isa 60:11 [s]Zec 14:7; Rev 22:5
21:27 [t]Isa 52:1; Joel 3:17; Rev 22:14,15
22:1 [u]Rev 4:6 [v]Eze 47:1; Zec 14:8
22:2 [w]Rev 2:7 [x]Eze 47:12
22:3 [y]Zec 14:11 [z]Rev 7:15
22:4 [a]Mt 5:8 [b]Rev 14:1
22:5 [c]Rev 21:25

[a] *16* That is, about 1,400 miles (about 2,200 kilometers) [b] *17* That is, about 200 feet (about 65 meters) [c] *17* Or *high* [d] *20* The precise identification of some of these precious stones is uncertain.

imagery, it is wise not to distinguish rigidly between the inhabitants of the city (the saints) and the city itself (saints together with the glorified creation).

21:9 bride. See note on 19:1–10.

21:10 in the Spirit. See note on 1:10. **mountain.** The mountain of God's special meeting place with human beings, alluding to 14:1 and other passages (e.g., Ex 15:17; 19:1–25; Pss 48:1–2; 68:15–16; Eze 28:14; Mic 4:1–2).

21:11 glory of God. Closely associated with the imagery of light, glory represents the majesty, awesomeness and beauty of God. Glory, a prominent theme in 21:9—22:5 (e.g., 15:8; 21:22–23; 22:5), is associated with the temple and the appearing of God in the Old Testament (Ex 16:10; 24:16–17; 40:34–35; Isa 6:3; 60:1–2,19–20; Hab 2:14; Zec 2:5). God's heavenly splendor, as seen in 4:1–11, now fills the new world.

21:16 wide and high. The city is a perfect cube, the same shape as the Most Holy Place in the tabernacle and the temple. Thus the whole city is not only architecturally perfect, but it has also become the most intimate dwelling place of God (vv. 22–23; 22:45).

21:17 144 cubits. The number 144 equals 12 times 12. All the dimensions of the city symbolize its associations with the 12 tribes of Israel and the 12 apostles (vv. 12,14). "Twelve" symbolically designates the people of God.

21:19 every kind of precious stone. The list of precious stones depicts the beauty and magnificence of the city and the way in which it reflects the beauty of God, who fills it with his glory (4:3). The list also corresponds roughly to the 12 precious stones of Aaron's breastpiece (Ex 28:15–21). The prerogatives that once belonged exclusively to the high priest are now reflected in the entire city.

21:22 temple. See note on 4:1—5:14.

21:23 the sun or the moon. Fulfillment of Isaiah 60:19–20.

21:24 The nations. Redeemed humanity in all its cultural diversity (Isa 60:3–12; see note on 5:9). **splendor.** See Isaiah 60:3–5 and Haggai 2:7–9.

21:25 gates ever be shut. Fulfillment of Isaiah 60:11. Ancient city gates needed to be shut in case of attack.

21:27 book of life. See note on 13:8.

22:1–5 The final description of paradise contains elements alluding to the Garden of Eden. The intimacy of God with his people (vv. 3–4) and the abundance of his blessing (vv. 1–2,5) are stressed even more here than they were in the preceding verses. The final state restores the unbroken, idyllic communion between God and human beings. But the apex of history is ever so much more magnificent than the beginning. The garden is now also a city, and the light has driven out all night. The book of Revelation is designed not only to inform and assure believers of God's final purposes, but also to increase their longing for God and for the realization of his purposes. The sureness of that final bliss comforts saints during times of temptation and persecution.

22:1 river of the water of life. Abundant supply of life-giving water comes from God. Revelation weaves together allusions to several passages (e.g., Ge 2:10–14; Ps 46:4; Eze 47:1–12; Joel 3:18; Jn 4:10–14; 7:37–39).

22:2 tree of life. Access to God's life-giving blessings, which was barred after the fall, is here renewed (2:7; 22:14,19; Ge 2:9; 3:22–24; Eze 47:12).

lamp or the light of the sun, for the Lord God will give them light.[d] And they will reign
for ever and ever.[e]
6 The angel said to me,[f] "These words are trustworthy and true.[g] The Lord, the God
of the spirits of the prophets,[h] sent his angel[i] to show his servants the things that must
soon take place."

Jesus Is Coming

7 "Behold, I am coming soon![j] Blessed[k] is he who keeps the words of the prophecy in
this book."

8 I, John, am the one who heard and saw these things.[l] And when I had heard and
seen them, I fell down to worship at the feet[m] of the angel who had been showing them
to me. 9 But he said to me, "Do not do it! I am a fellow servant with you and with your
brothers the prophets and of all who keep the words of this book.[n] Worship God!"[o]
10 Then he told me, "Do not seal up[p] the words of the prophecy of this book, because
the time is near.[q] 11 Let him who does wrong continue to do wrong; let him who is vile
continue to be vile; let him who does right continue to do right; and let him who is holy
continue to be holy."[r]

12 "Behold, I am coming soon![s] My reward is with me,[t] and I will give to everyone according to what he has done. 13 I am the Alpha and the Omega,[u] the First and the Last,[v]
the Beginning and the End.[w]
14 "Blessed are those who wash their robes, that they may have the right to the tree
of life[x] and may go through the gates[y] into the city.[z] 15 Outside[a] are the dogs,[b] those who
practice magic arts, the sexually immoral, the murderers, the idolaters and everyone
who loves and practices falsehood.
16 "I, Jesus,[c] have sent my angel to give you[a] this testimony for the churches.[d] I am the
Root[e] and the Offspring of David, and the bright Morning Star."[f]

17 The Spirit[g] and the bride say, "Come!" And let him who hears say, "Come!" Whoever is thirsty, let him come; and whoever wishes, let him take the free gift of the water
of life.

18 I warn everyone who hears the words of the prophecy of this book: If anyone adds
anything to them,[h] God will add to him the plagues described in this book.[i] 19 And if anyone takes words away[j] from this book of prophecy, God will take away from him his
share in the tree of life and in the holy city, which are described in this book.
20 He who testifies to these things[k] says, "Yes, I am coming soon."
Amen. Come, Lord Jesus.[l]
21 The grace of the Lord Jesus be with God's people.[m] Amen.

[a] *16* The Greek is plural.

22:5 [d]Rev 21:23 [e]Da 7:27; Rev 20:4
22:6 [f]Rev 1:1 [g]Rev 19:9; 21:5 [h]Heb 12:9 [i]ver 16
22:7 [j]Rev 3:11 [k]Rev 1:3
22:8 [l]Rev 1:1 [m]Rev 19:10
22:9 [n]ver 10,18,19 [o]Rev 19:10
22:10 [p]Da 8:26; Rev 10:4 [q]Rev 1:3
22:11 [r]Eze 3:27; Da 12:10
22:12 [s]ver 7,20 [t]Isa 40:10
22:13 [u]Rev 1:8 [v]Rev 1:17 [w]Rev 21:6
22:14 [x]Rev 2:7 [y]Rev 21:12 [z]Rev 21:27
22:15 [a]1Co 6:9,10; Gal 5:19-21; Col 3:5,6 [b]Php 3:2
22:16 [c]Rev 1:1 [d]Rev 1:4 [e]Rev 5:5 [f]2Pe 1:19; Rev 2:28
22:17 [g]Rev 2:7
22:18 [h]Dt 4:2; Pr 30:6 [i]Rev 15:6-16:21
22:19 [j]Dt 4:2
22:20 [k]Rev 1:2 [l]1Co 16:22
22:21 [m]Ro 16:20

■ **22:6–21** *Conclusion.* Having reported his extensive visions, John turned to several exhortations (vv. 6–20) and closed with a blessing for the readers (v. 21).
■ **22:6–20** *Final Exhortations.* The central visionary part of Revelation ends with 22:5. The book now concludes with a promise, exhortation and confirmation in order to drive home the message of the visions and to stir up hope for the coming of the Lord Jesus (v. 20). Its major themes continue to be woven into this concluding section. There are many allusions to chapter 1.
22:6 trustworthy and true. See note on 1:2.
22:7 soon! See note on 1:1. **Blessed.** See note on 1:3.
22:8–9 See *HC* 94.
22:8 worship. See 19:10.
22:10 seal up. Daniel's scroll was sealed because the time of fulfillment was distant (Da 12:4). Now "the time is near" (see note on 1:1).
22:11 See Ezekiel 3:27, Daniel 12:10 and 2 Corinthians 2:15–16. If people do not repent when they hear the word of God, the hardness of their hearts increases. If hearing the book of Revelation does not completely change one's course of life, it fixes one more firmly to one's present course, whichever side of the battle the individual may be on.
22:12 soon! See note on 1:1. **what he has done.** See 20:12. See *WLC* 45; *BC* 37.
22:13 the Alpha and the Omega. See note on 1:8.
22:14 Blessed. See note on 1:3. **tree of life.** See note on verse 2.
22:15 Outside. See 20:15, 21:8 and 27. All evildoers are banished from the holy city, not only to punish them for their evil, but also to protect the city from their contamination. We may take heart from the firmness of God's commitment to exclude evil from the final kingdom.
22:17 water of life. See note on verse 1. See *WLC* 174; *HC* 123.
22:18–19 The warning against adding to, or subtracting from, these words puts the book of Revelation on the same level as the Old Testament words of God (Dt 4:2; 12:32). The word of God is to be protected from corruption and distinguished from merely human words. See *WCF* 1.2; *WLC* 3.
22:19 tree of life. See note on verse 2.
22:20–21 See *WLC* 196; *WSC* 107.
22:20 soon. See note on 1:1. **Come, Lord Jesus.** The whole of Revelation is meant to stir believers' longing and prayers for the full realization of God's purposes that accompany the second coming. Revelation fittingly ends on this note (1Co 16:22). See *WCF* 33.3; *WLC* 191; *WSC* 102; *HC* 123.
■ **22:21** *Closing Blessing.* This rather standard blessing concludes the book of Revelation in the typical format of a letter (see "Introduction: Purpose and Distinctives").

STUDY HELPS

TABLE OF WEIGHTS AND MEASURES

	BIBLICAL UNIT	APPROXIMATE AMERICAN EQUIVALENT	APPROXIMATE METRIC EQUIVALENT
WEIGHTS	talent (60 minas)	75 pounds	34 kilograms
	mina (50 shekels)	$1^{1}/_{4}$ pounds	0.6 kilogram
	shekel (2 bekas)	$^{2}/_{5}$ ounce	11.5 grams
	pim ($^{2}/_{3}$ shekel)	$^{1}/_{3}$ ounce	7.6 grams
	beka (10 gerahs)	$^{1}/_{5}$ ounce	5.5 grams
	gerah	$^{1}/_{50}$ ounce	0.6 gram
LENGTH	cubit	18 inches	0.5 meter
	span	9 inches	23 centimeters
	handbreadth	3 inches	8 centimeters
CAPACITY			
Dry Measure	cor [homer] (10 ephahs)	6 bushels	220 liters
	lethek (5 ephahs)	3 bushels	110 liters
	ephah (10 omers)	$^{3}/_{5}$ bushel	22 liters
	seah ($^{1}/_{3}$ ephah)	7 quarts	7.3 liters
	omer ($^{1}/_{10}$ ephah)	2 quarts	2 liters
	cab ($^{1}/_{18}$ ephah)	1 quart	1 liter
Liquid Measure	bath (1 ephah)	6 gallons	22 liters
	hin ($^{1}/_{6}$ bath)	4 quarts	4 liters
	log ($^{1}/_{72}$ bath)	$^{1}/_{3}$ quart	0.3 liter

The figures of the table are calculated on the basis of a shekel equaling 11.5 grams, a cubit equaling 18 inches and an ephah equaling 22 liters. The quart referred to is either a dry quart (slightly larger than a liter) or a liquid quart (slightly smaller than a liter), whichever is applicable. The ton referred to in the footnotes is the American ton of 2,000 pounds.

This table is based upon the best available information, but it is not intended to be mathematically precise; like the measurement equivalents in the footnotes, it merely gives approximate amounts and distances. Weights and measures differed somewhat at various times and places in the ancient world. There is uncertainty particularly about the ephah and the bath; further discoveries may shed more light on these units of capacity.

NIV CONCORDANCE INTRODUCTION

The NIV Concordance, created by Edward W. Goodrick and John R. Kohlenberger III, has been developed specifically for use with the New International Version. Like all concordances, it is a special index which contains an alphabetical listing of words used in the Bible text. By looking up key words, readers can find verses and passages for which they remember a word or two but not their location.

This concordance contains 2,000 word entries, with some 13,000 Scripture references. Each word entry is followed by the Scripture references in which that particular word is found, as well as by a brief excerpt from the surrounding context. The first letter of the entry word is italicized to conserve space and to allow for a longer context excerpt. Variant spellings due to number and tense and compound forms follow the entry in parentheses, and direct the reader to check other forms of that word in locating a passage.

This concordance contains a number of "block entries," which highlight some of the key events and characteristics in the lives of certain Bible figures. The descriptive phrases replace the brief context surrounding each occurrence of the name. In those instances where more than one Bible character has the same name, that name is placed under one block entry, and each person is given a number (1), (2), etc. Insignificant names are not included.

Word or block entries marked with an asterisk (*) list every verse in the Bible in which the word appears.

This concordance is a valuable tool for Bible study. While one of its key purposes is to help the reader find forgotten references to verses, it can also be used to do word studies and to locate and trace biblical themes. Be sure to use this concordance as more than just a verse finder. Whenever you look up a verse, aim to discover the intended meaning of the verse in context. Give special attention to the flow of thought from the beginning of the passage to the end.

ABBREVIATIONS AND SYMBOLS USED IN THE NIV CONCORDANCE

Ac . . . . . Acts
Am . . . . . Amos
1Ch . . . . . 1 Chronicles
2Ch . . . . . 2 Chronicles
1Co . . . . . 1 Corinthians
2Co . . . . . 2 Corinthians
Col . . . . . Colossians
Da . . . . . Daniel
Dt . . . . . Deuteronomy
Ecc . . . . . Ecclesiastes
Eph . . . . . Ephesians
Est . . . . . Esther
Ex . . . . . Exodus
Eze . . . . . Ezekiel
Ezr . . . . . Ezra
Gal . . . . . Galatians
Ge . . . . . Genesis
Hab . . . . . Habakkuk
Hag . . . . . Haggai
Heb . . . . . Hebrews
Hos . . . . . Hosea
Isa . . . . . Isaiah
Jas . . . . . James
Jdg . . . . . Judges
Jer . . . . . Jeremiah
1Jn . . . . . 1 John
2Jn . . . . . 2 John
3Jn . . . . . 3 John
Jn . . . . . John
Jnh . . . . . Jonah
Job . . . . . Job
Joel . . . . . Joel
Jos . . . . . Joshua
Jude . . . . . Jude
1Ki . . . . . 1 Kings
2Ki . . . . . 2 Kings
La . . . . . Lamentations
Lev . . . . . Leviticus
Lk . . . . . Luke
Mal . . . . . Malachi
Mic . . . . . Micah
Mk . . . . . Mark
Mt . . . . . Matthew
Na . . . . . Nahum
Ne . . . . . Nehemiah
Nu . . . . . Numbers
Ob . . . . . Obadiah
1Pe . . . . . 1 Peter
2Pe . . . . . 2 Peter
Phm . . . . . Philemon
Php . . . . . Philippians
Pr . . . . . Proverbs
Ps . . . . . Psalms
Rev . . . . . Revelation
Ro . . . . . Romans
Ru . . . . . Ruth
1Sa . . . . . 1 Samuel
2Sa . . . . . 2 Samuel
SS . . . . . Song of Songs
1Th . . . . . 1 Thessalonians
2Th . . . . . 2 Thessalonians
1Ti . . . . . 1 Timothy
2Ti . . . . . 2 Timothy
Tit . . . . . Titus
Zec . . . . . Zechariah
Zep . . . . . Zephaniah
* . . . All NIV occurrences are listed
† . . . . . Lord or lord in the NIV
‡ . . . . . LORD (*Yahweh*) in the NIV

NIV CONCORDANCE

AARON
Priesthood of (Ex 28:1; Nu 17; Heb 5:1-4; 7), garments (Ex 28; 39), consecration (Ex 29), ordination (Lev 8).

Spokesman for Moses (Ex 4:14-16, 27-31; 7:1-2). Supported Moses' hands in battle (Ex 17:8-13). Built golden calf (Ex 32; Dt 9:20). Talked against Moses (Nu 12). Priesthood opposed (Nu 16); staff budded (Nu 17). Forbidden to enter land (Nu 20:1-12). Death (Nu 20:22-29; 33:38-39).

ABANDON
Dt 4:31 he will not *a* or destroy you
1Ti 4: 1 in later times some will *a* the faith

ABBA
Ro 8:15 And by him we cry, "*A*, Father."
Gal 4: 6 the Spirit who calls out, "*A*, Father

ABEL
Second son of Adam (Ge 4:2). Offered proper sacrifice (Ge 4:4; Heb 11:4). Murdered by Cain (Ge 4:8; Mt 23:35; Lk 11:51; 1Jn 3:12).

ABHORS
Pr 11: 1 The LORD *a* dishonest scales,

ABIGAIL
Wife of Nabal (1Sa 25:30); pled for his life with David (1Sa 25:14-35). Became David's wife (1Sa 25:36-42).

ABIJAH
Son of Rehoboam; king of Judah (1Ki 14:31-15:8; 2Ch 12:16-14:1).

ABILITY (ABLE)
Ezr 2:69 According to their *a* they gave
2Co 1: 8 far beyond our *a* to endure,
8: 3 were able, and even beyond their *a*.

ABIMELECH
1. King of Gerar who took Abraham's wife Sarah, believing her to be his sister (Ge 20). Later made a covenant with Abraham (Ge 21:22-33).

2. King of Gerar who took Isaac's wife Rebekah, believing her to be his sister (Ge 26:1-11). Later made a covenant with Isaac (Ge 26:12-31).

ABLE (ABILITY ENABLE ENABLED ENABLES)
Eze 7:19 and gold will not be *a* to save them
Da 3:17 the God we serve is *a* to save us
Ro 8:39 will be *a* to separate us
14: 4 for the Lord is *a* to make him stand
16:25 to him who is *a* to establish you
2Co 9: 8 God is *a* to make all grace abound
Eph 3:20 him who is *a* to do immeasurably
2Ti 1:12 and am convinced that he is *a*
3:15 which are *a* to make you wise
Heb 7:25 he is *a* to save completely
Jude :24 To him who is *a* to keep you
Rev 5: 5 He is *a* to open the scroll

ABOLISH
Mt 5:17 that I have come to *a* the Law

ABOMINATION
Da 11:31 set up the *a* that causes desolation.

ABOUND (ABOUNDING)
2Co 9: 8 able to make all grace *a* to you,
Php 1: 9 that your love may *a* more

ABOUNDING (ABOUND)
Ex 34: 6 slow to anger, *a* in love
Ps 86: 5 *a* in love to all who call to you.

ABRAHAM
Covenant relation with the LORD (Ge 12:1-3; 13:14-17; 15; 17; 22:15-18; Ex 2:24; Ne 9:8; Ps 105; Mic 7:20; Lk 1:68-75; Ro 4; Heb 6:13-15).

Called from Ur, via Haran, to Canaan (Ge 12:1; Ac 7:2-4; Heb 11:8-10). Moved to Egypt, nearly lost Sarah to Pharoah (Ge 12:10-20). Divided the land with Lot (Ge 13). Saved Lot from four kings (Ge 14:1-16); blessed by Melchizedek (Ge 14:17-20; Heb 7:1-20). Declared righteous by faith (Ge 15:6; Ro 4:3; Gal 3:6-9). Fathered Ishmael by Hagar (Ge 16).

Name changed from Abram (Ge 17:5; Ne 9:7). Circumcised (Ge 17; Ro 4:9-12). Entertained three visitors (Ge 18); promised a son by Sarah (Ge 18:9-15; 17:16). Moved to Gerar; nearly lost Sarah to Abimelech (Ge 20). Fathered Isaac by Sarah (Ge 21:1-7; Ac 7:8; Heb 11:11-12); sent away Hagar and Ishmael (Ge 21:8-21; Gal 4:22-30). Tested by offering Isaac (Ge 22; Heb 11:17-19; Jas 2:21-24). Sarah died; bought field of Ephron for burial (Ge 23). Secured wife for Isaac (Ge 24). Death (Ge 25:7-11).

ABSALOM
Son of David by Maacah (2Sa 3:3; 1Ch 3:2). Killed Amnon for rape of his sister Tamar; banished by David (2Sa 13). Returned to Jerusalem, reconciled to David (2Sa 14). Rebelled against David; seized kingdom (2Sa 15-17). Killed (2Sa 18).

ABSTAIN (ABSTAINS)
1Pe 2:11 to *a* from sinful desires,

ABSTAINS* (ABSTAIN)
Ro 14: 6 thanks to God; and he who *a*,

ABUNDANCE (ABUNDANT)
Lk 12:15 consist in the *a* of his possessions."
Jude : 2 peace and love be yours in *a*.

ABUNDANT (ABUNDANCE)
Dt 28:11 will grant you *a* prosperity—
Ps 145: 7 will celebrate your *a* goodness
Pr 28:19 works his land will have *a* food,
Ro 5:17 who receive God's *a* provision

ACCEPT (ACCEPTED ACCEPTS)
Ex 23: 8 "Do not *a* a bribe,
Pr 10: 8 The wise in heart *a* commands,
19:20 Listen to advice and *a* instruction,
Ro 15: 7 *A* one another, then, just
Jas 1:21 humbly *a* the word planted in you,

ACCEPTED (ACCEPT)
Lk 4:24 "no prophet is *a* in his hometown.

ACCEPTS (ACCEPT)
Ps 6: 9 the LORD *a* my prayer.
Jn 13:20 whoever *a* anyone I send *a* me;

ACCOMPANY
Mk 16:17 these signs will *a* those who believe
Heb 6: 9 your case—things that *a* salvation.

ACCOMPLISH
Isa 55:11 but will *a* what I desire

ACCORD
Nu 24:13 not do anything of my own *a*,
Jn 10:18 but I lay it down of my own *a*.
12:49 For I did not speak of my own *a*,

ACCOUNT (ACCOUNTABLE)
Mt 12:36 to give *a* on the day of judgment
Ro 14:12 each of us will give an *a* of himself
Heb 4:13 of him to whom we must give *a*.

ACCOUNTABLE (ACCOUNT)
Eze 33: 6 but I will hold the watchman *a*
Ro 3:19 and the whole world held *a* to God.

ACCUSATION (ACCUSE)
1Ti 5:19 Do not entertain an *a*

ACCUSATIONS (ACCUSE)
2Pe 2:11 do not bring slanderous *a*

ACCUSE (ACCUSATION ACCUSATIONS)
Pr 3:30 Do not *a* a man for no reason—
Lk 3:14 and don't *a* people falsely—

ACHAN*
Sin at Jericho caused defeat at Ai; stoned (Jos 7; 22:20; 1Ch 2:7).

ACHE*
Pr 14:13 Even in laughter the heart may *a*,

ACKNOWLEDGE
Mt 10:32 *a* him before my Father in heaven.
1Jn 4: 3 spirit that does not *a* Jesus is not

ACQUIT
Ex 23: 7 to death, for I will not *a* the guilty.

ACTION (ACTIONS ACTIVE ACTS)
Jas 2:17 if it is not accompanied by *a*,
1Pe 1:13 minds for *a*; be self-controlled;

ACTIONS (ACTION)
Mt 11:19 wisdom is proved right by her *a*."
Gal 6: 4 Each one should test his own *a*.
Tit 1:16 but by their *a* they deny him.

ACTIVE (ACTION)
Heb 4:12 For the word of God is living and *a*

ACTS (ACTION)
Ps 145:12 all men may know of your mighty *a*
150: 2 Praise him for his *a* of power;
Isa 64: 6 all our righteous *a* are like filthy
Mt 6: 1 not to do your '*a* of righteousness'

ADAM
First man (Ge 1:26-2:25; Ro 5:14; 1Ti 2:13). Sin of (Ge 3; Hos 6:7; Ro 5:12-21). Children of (Ge 4:1-5:5). Death of (Ge 5:5; Ro 5:12-21; 1Co 15:22).

ADD
Dt 12:32 do not *a* to it or take away from it
Pr 30: 6 Do not *a* to his words,
Lk 12:25 by worrying can *a* a single hour
Rev 22:18 God will *a* to him the plagues

ADMIRABLE*
Php 4: 8 whatever is lovely, whatever is *a*—

ADMONISH
Col 3:16 and *a* one another with all wisdom,

ADOPTED (ADOPTION)
Eph 1: 5 In love he predestined us to be *a*

ADOPTION (ADOPTED)
Ro 8:23 as we wait eagerly for our *a* as sons,

ADORE*
SS 1: 4 How right they are to *a* you!

ADORNMENT* (ADORNS)
1Pe 3: 3 should not come from outward *a*,

ADORNS (ADORNMENT)
Ps 93: 5 holiness *a* your house

ADULTERY
Ex 20:14 "You shall not commit *a*.
Mt 5:27 that it was said, 'Do not commit *a*.'
5:28 lustfully has already committed *a*
5:32 the divorced woman commits *a*.
15:19 murder, *a*, sexual immorality, theft

ADULTS*
1Co 14:20 but in your thinking be *a*.

ADVANCED
Job 32: 7 *a* years should teach wisdom.'

ADVANTAGE
Ex 22:22 "Do not take *a* of a widow
Dt 24:14 Do not take *a* of a hired man who is
1Th 4: 6 should wrong his brother or take *a*

ADVERSITY
Pr 17:17 and a brother is born for *a*.

ADVICE
1Ki 12: 8 rejected the *a* the elders
12:14 he followed the *a* of the young men
Pr 12: 5 but the *a* of the wicked is deceitful.
12:15 but a wise man listens to *a*.
19:20 Listen to *a* and accept instruction,
20:18 Make plans by seeking *a;*

AFFLICTION
Ro 12:12 patient in *a*, faithful in prayer.

AFRAID (FEAR)
Ge 26:24 Do not be *a*, for I am with you;
Ex 3: 6 because he was *a* to look at God.
Ps 27: 1 of whom shall I be *a?*
56: 3 When I am *a*, / I will trust in you.
Pr 3:24 lie down, you will not be *a;*
Jer 1: 8 Do not be *a* of them, for I am
Mt 8:26 You of little faith, why are you so *a*
10:28 be *a* of the One who can destroy
10:31 So don't be *a;* you are worth more
Mk 5:36 "Don't be *a;* just believe."
Jn 14:27 hearts be troubled and do not be *a*.
Heb 13: 6 Lord is my helper; I will not be *a*.

AGED
Job 12:12 Is not wisdom found among the *a?*
Pr 17: 6 children are a crown to the *a*,

AGREE
Mt 18:19 on earth *a* about anything you ask
Ro 7:16 want to do, I *a* that the law is good.
Php 4: 2 with Syntyche to *a* with each other

AHAB
Son of Omri; king of Israel (1Ki 16:28-22:40), husband of Jezebel (1Ki 16:31). Promoted Baal worship (1Ki 16:31-33); opposed by Elijah (1Ki 17:1; 18; 21), a prophet (1Ki 20:35-43), Micaiah (1Ki 22:1-28). Defeated Ben-Hadad (1Ki 20). Killed for failing to kill Ben-Hadad and for murder of Naboth (1Ki 20:35-21:40).

AHAZ
Son of Jotham; king of Judah, (2Ki 16; 2Ch 28; Isa 7).

AHAZIAH
1. Son of Ahab; king of Israel (1Ki 22:51-2Ki 1:18; 2Ch 20:35-37).
2. Son of Jehoram; king of Judah (2Ki 8:25-29; 9:14-29), also called Jehoahaz (2Ch 21:17-22:9; 25:23).

AIM
1Co 7:34 Her *a* is to be devoted to the Lord
2Co 13:11 *A* for perfection, listen

AIR
Mt 8:20 and birds of the *a* have nests,
1Co 9:26 not fight like a man beating the *a*.
Eph 2: 2 of the ruler of the kingdom of the *a*,
1Th 4:17 clouds to meet the Lord in the *a*.

ALABASTER
Mt 26: 7 came to him with an *a* jar

ALERT
Jos 8: 4 All of you be on the *a*.
Mk 13:33 Be *a!* You do not know
Eph 6:18 be *a* and always keep on praying
1Th 5: 6 but let us be *a* and self-controlled.

ALIEN (ALIENATED)
Ex 22:21 "Do not mistreat an *a*

ALIENATED (ALIEN)
Gal 5: 4 by law have been *a* from Christ;

ALIVE (LIVE)
Ac 1: 3 convincing proofs that he was *a*.
Ro 6:11 but *a* to God in Christ Jesus.
1Co 15:22 so in Christ all will be made *a*.

ALMIGHTY (MIGHT)
Ge 17: 1 "I am God *A;* walk before me
Job 11: 7 Can you probe the limits of the *A?*
33: 4 the breath of the *A* gives me life.
Ps 91: 1 will rest in the shadow of the *A*.
Isa 6: 3 "Holy, holy, holy is the LORD *A;*

ALTAR
Ge 22: 9 his son Isaac and laid him on the *a*,
Ex 27: 1 "Build an *a* of acacia wood,
1Ki 18:30 and he repaired the *a* of the LORD
2Ch 4: 1 made a bronze *a* twenty cubits
4:19 the golden *a;* the tables

ALWAYS
Ps 16: 8 I have set the LORD *a* before me.
51: 3 and my sin is *a* before me.
Mt 26:11 The poor you will *a* have with you,
28:20 And surely I will be with you *a*,
1Co 13: 7 *a* protects, *a* trusts, *a* hopes, *a*
Php 4: 4 Rejoice in the Lord *a*.
1Pe 3:15 *A* be prepared to give an answer

AMAZIAH
Son of Joash; king of Judah (2Ki 14; 2Ch 25).

AMBASSADORS
2Co 5:20 We are therefore Christ's *a*,

AMBITION
Ro 15:20 It has always been my *a*
1Th 4:11 Make it your *a* to lead a quiet life,

AMON
Son of Manasseh; king of Judah (2Ki 21:18-26; 1Ch 3:14; 2Ch 33:21-25).

ANANIAS
1. Husband of Sapphira; died for lying to God (Ac 5:1-11).
2. Disciple who baptized Saul (Ac 9:10-19).
3. High priest at Paul's arrest (Ac 22:30-24:1).

ANCHOR
Heb 6:19 We have this hope as an *a*

ANCIENT
Da 7: 9 and the *A* of Days took his seat.

ANDREW*
Apostle; brother of Simon Peter (Mt 4:18; 10:2; Mk 1:16-18, 29; 3:18; 13:3; Lk 6:14; Jn 1:35-44; 6:8-9; 12:22; Ac 1:13).

ANGEL (ANGELS ARCHANGEL)
Ps 34: 7 The *a* of the LORD encamps
Ac 6:15 his face was like the face of an *a*.
2Co 11:14 Satan himself masquerades as an *a*
Gal 1: 8 or an *a* from heaven should preach

ANGELS (ANGEL)
Ps 91:11 command his *a* concerning you
Mt 18:10 For I tell you that their *a*
25:41 prepared for the devil and his *a*.
Lk 20:36 for they are like the *a*.
1Co 6: 3 you not know that we will judge *a?*
Heb 1: 4 as much superior to the *a*
1:14 Are not all *a* ministering spirits
2: 7 made him a little lower than the *a;*
13: 2 some people have entertained *a*
1Pe 1:12 Even *a* long to look
2Pe 2: 4 For if God did not spare *a*

ANGER (ANGERED ANGRY)
Ex 32:10 alone so that my *a* may burn
34: 6 slow to *a*, abounding in love
Dt 29:28 In furious *a* and in great wrath
2Ki 22:13 Great is the LORD's *a* that burns
Ps 30: 5 For his *a* lasts only a moment,
Pr 15: 1 but a harsh word stirs up *a*.
29:11 A fool gives full vent to his *a*,

ANGERED (ANGER)
Pr 22:24 do not associate with one easily *a*,
1Co 13: 5 it is not easily *a*, it keeps no record

ANGRY (ANGER)
Ps 2:12 Kiss the Son, lest he be *a*
Pr 29:22 An *a* man stirs up dissension,
Jas 1:19 slow to speak and slow to become *a*

ANGUISH
Ps 118: 5 In my *a* I cried to the LORD,

ANOINT
Ps 23: 5 You *a* my head with oil;
Jas 5:14 and *a* him with oil in the name

ANT*
Pr 6: 6 Go to the *a*, you sluggard;

ANTICHRIST
1Jn 2:18 have heard that the *a* is coming,
2Jn : 7 person is the deceiver and the *a*.

ANTIOCH
Ac 11:26 were called Christians first at *A*.

ANXIETY (ANXIOUS)
1Pe 5: 7 Cast all your *a* on him

ANXIOUS (ANXIETY)
Pr 12:25 An *a* heart weighs a man down,
Php 4: 6 Do not be *a* about anything,

APOLLOS*
Christian from Alexandria, learned in the Scriptures; instructed by Aquila and Priscilla (Ac 18:24-28). Ministered at Corinth (Ac 19:1; 1Co 1:12; 3; Tit 3:13).

APOSTLES
See also Andrew, Bartholomew, James, John, Judas, Matthew, Nathanael, Paul, Peter, Philip, Simon, Thaddaeus, Thomas.
Mk 3:14 twelve—designating them *a*—
Ac 1:26 so he was added to the eleven *a*.
2:43 signs were done by the *a*.
1Co 12:28 God has appointed first of all *a*,
15: 9 For I am the least of the *a*
2Co 11:13 masquerading as *a* of Christ.
Eph 2:20 built on the foundation of the *a*

APPEAR (APPEARANCE APPEARING)
Mk 13:22 false prophets will *a* and perform
2Co 5:10 we must all *a* before the judgment
Col 3: 4 also will *a* with him in glory.
Heb 9:24 now to *a* for us in God's presence.
9:28 and he will *a* a second time,

APPEARANCE (APPEAR)
1Sa 16: 7 Man looks at the outward *a*,
Gal 2: 6 God does not judge by external *a*—

APPEARING (APPEAR)
2Ti 4: 8 to all who have longed for his *a*.
Tit 2:13 the glorious *a* of our great God

APPLY
Pr 22:17 *a* your heart to what I teach,
23:12 *A* your heart to instruction

APPROACH
Eph 3:12 in him we may *a* God with freedom
Heb 4:16 Let us then *a* the throne of grace

APPROVED
2Ti 2:15 to present yourself to God as one *a*,

AQUILA*
Husband of Priscilla; co-worker with Paul, instructor of Apollos (Ac 18; Ro 16:3; 1Co 16:19; 2Ti 4:19).

ARARAT
Ge 8: 4 came to rest on the mountains of *A*.

ARCHANGEL* (ANGEL)
1Th 4:16 with the voice of the *a*
Jude : 9 *a* Michael, when he was disputing

ARCHITECT*
Heb 11:10 whose *a* and builder is God.

ARK
Ge 6:14 So make yourself an *a*
Dt 10: 5 put the tablets in the *a* I had made,
2Ch 35: 3 "Put the sacred *a* in the temple that
Heb 9: 4 This *a* contained the gold jar

ARM (ARMY)
Nu 11:23 "Is the LORD's *a* too short?
1Pe 4: 1 *a* yourselves also with the same

ARMAGEDDON*
Rev 16:16 that in Hebrew is called *A*.

ARMOR (ARMY)
1Ki 20:11 on his *a* should not boast like one
Eph 6:11 Put on the full *a* of God
6:13 Therefore put on the full *a* of God,

ARMS (ARMY)
Dt 33:27 underneath are the everlasting *a*.
Ps 18:32 It is God who *a* me with strength
Pr 31:20 She opens her *a* to the poor
Isa 40:11 He gathers the lambs in his *a*
Mk 10:16 And he took the children in his *a*,

ARMY (ARM ARMOR ARMS)
Ps 33:16 No king is saved by the size of his *a*
Rev 19:19 the rider on the horse and his *a*.

AROMA
2Co 2:15 For we are to God the *a* of Christ

ARRAYED*
Ps 110: 3 *A* in holy majesty,
Isa 61:10 and *a* me in a robe of righteousness

ARROGANT
Ro 11:20 Do not be *a*, but be afraid.

ARROWS
Eph 6:16 you can extinguish all the flaming *a*

ASA
King of Judah (1Ki 15:8-24; 1Ch 3:10; 2Ch 14-16).

ASCENDED
Eph 4: 8 “When he *a* on high,

ASCRIBE
1Ch 16:28 *a* to the LORD glory and strength,
Job 36: 3 I will *a* justice to my Maker.
Ps 29: 2 *A* to the LORD the glory due his

ASHAMED (SHAME)
Lk 9:26 If anyone is *a* of me and my words,
Ro 1:16 I am not *a* of the gospel,
2Ti 1: 8 So do not be *a* to testify about our
2:15 who does not need to be *a*

ASSIGNED
Mk 13:34 with his *a* task, and tells the one
1Co 3: 5 as the Lord has *a* to each his task.
7:17 place in life that the Lord *a* to him

ASSOCIATE
Pr 22:24 do not *a* with one easily angered,
Ro 12:16 but be willing to *a* with people
1Co 5:11 am writing you that you must not *a*
2Th 3:14 Do not *a* with him,

ASSURANCE
Heb 10:22 with a sincere heart in full *a* of faith

ASTRAY
Pr 10:17 ignores correction leads others *a*.
Isa 53: 6 We all, like sheep, have gone *a*,
Jer 50: 6 their shepherds have led them *a*
Jn 16: 1 you so that you will not go *a*.
1Pe 2:25 For you were like sheep going *a*,
1Jn 3: 7 do not let anyone lead you *a*.

ATHALIAH
Evil queen of Judah (2Ki 11; 2Ch 23).

ATHLETE*
2Ti 2: 5 if anyone competes as an *a*,

ATONEMENT
Ex 25:17 “Make an *a* cover of pure gold—
30:10 Once a year Aaron shall make *a*
Lev 17:11 it is the blood that makes *a*
23:27 this seventh month is the Day of *A*.
Nu 25:13 and made *a* for the Israelites.”
Ro 3:25 presented him as a sacrifice of *a*,
Heb 2:17 that he might make *a* for the sins

ATTENTION
Pr 4: 1 pay *a* and gain understanding.
5: 1 My son, pay *a* to my wisdom,
22:17 Pay *a* and listen to the sayings
Tit 1:14 and will pay no *a* to Jewish myths

ATTITUDE (ATTITUDES)
Eph 4:23 new in the *a* of your minds;
Php 2: 5 Your *a* should be the same
1Pe 4: 1 yourselves also with the same *a*,

ATTITUDES (ATTITUDE)
Heb 4:12 it judges the thoughts and *a*

ATTRACTIVE
Tit 2:10 teaching about God our Savior *a*.

AUTHORITIES (AUTHORITY)
Ro 13: 5 it is necessary to submit to the *a*,
13: 6 for the *a* are God's servants,
Tit 3: 1 people to be subject to rulers and *a*,
1Pe 3:22 *a* and powers in submission to him.

AUTHORITY (AUTHORITIES)
Mt 7:29 because he taught as one who had *a*
9: 6 the Son of Man has *a* on earth
28:18 “All *a* in heaven and on earth has
Ro 13: 1 for there is no *a* except that which
13: 2 rebels against the *a* is rebelling
1Co 11:10 to have a sign of *a* on her head.
1Ti 2: 2 for kings and all those in *a*,
2:12 to teach or to have *a* over a man;
Heb 13:17 your leaders and submit to their *a*.

AVENGE (VENGEANCE)
Dt 32:35 It is mine to *a*; I will repay.

AVOID
Pr 20: 3 It is to a man's honor to *a* strife,
20:19 so *a* a man who talks too much.
1Th 4: 3 you should *a* sexual immorality;
5:22 *A* every kind of evil.
2Ti 2:16 *A* godless chatter, because those
Tit 3: 9 But *a* foolish controversies

AWAKE
Ps 17:15 when I *a*, I will be satisfied

AWE (AWESOME)
Job 25: 2 “Dominion and *a* belong to God;
Ps 119:120 I stand in *a* of your laws.
Ecc 5: 7 Therefore stand in *a* of God.
Isa 29:23 will stand in *a* of the God of Israel.
Jer 33: 9 they will be in *a* and will tremble
Hab 3: 2 I stand in *a* of your deeds,
Mal 2: 5 and stood in *a* of my name.
Mt 9: 8 they were filled with *a*;
Lk 7:16 They were all filled with *a*
Ac 2:43 Everyone was filled with *a*,
Heb 12:28 acceptably with reverence and *a*,

AWESOME (AWE)
Ge 28:17 and said, “How *a* is this place!
Ex 15:11 *a* in glory,
Dt 7:21 is among you, is a great and *a* God.
10:17 the great God, mighty and *a*,
28:58 revere this glorious and *a* name—
Jdg 13: 6 like an angel of God, very *a*.
Ne 1: 5 of heaven, the great and *a* God,
9:32 the great, mighty and *a* God,
Job 10:16 again display your *a* power
37:22 God comes in *a* majesty.
Ps 45: 4 let your right hand display *a* deeds.
47: 2 How *a* is the LORD Most High,
66: 5 how *a* his works in man's behalf!
68:35 You are *a*, O God,
89: 7 he is more *a* than all who surround
99: 3 praise your great and *a* name—
111: 9 holy and *a* is his name.
145: 6 of the power of your *a* works,
Da 9: 4 “O Lord, the great and *a* God,

BAAL
1Ki 18:25 Elijah said to the prophets of *B*

BAASHA
King of Israel (1Ki 15:16-16:7; 2Ch 16:1-6).

BABIES (BABY)
Lk 18:15 also bringing *b* to Jesus
1Pe 2: 2 Like newborn *b*, crave pure

BABY (BABIES)
Isa 49:15 “Can a mother forget the *b*
Lk 1:44 the *b* in my womb leaped for joy.
2:12 You will find a *b* wrapped in strips
Jn 16:21 but when her *b* is born she forgets

BABYLON
Ps 137: 1 By the rivers of *B* we sat and wept

BACKSLIDING
Jer 3:22 I will cure you of *b*.”
14: 7 For our *b* is great;
Eze 37:23 them from all their sinful *b*,

BALAAM
Prophet who attempted to curse Israel (Nu 22-24; Dt 23:4-5; 2Pe 2:15; Jude 11). Killed (Nu 31:8; Jos 13:22).

BALM
Jer 8:22 Is there no *b* in Gilead?

BANISH
Jer 25:10 I will *b* from them the sounds of joy

BANQUET
SS 2: 4 He has taken me to the *b* hall,
Lk 14:13 when you give a *b*, invite the poor,

BAPTIZE (BAPTIZED)
Mt 3:11 He will *b* you with the Holy Spirit
Mk 1: 8 he will *b* you with the Holy Spirit.”
1Co 1:17 For Christ did not send me to *b*,

BAPTIZED (BAPTIZE)
Mt 3: 6 they were *b* by him in the Jordan
Mk 1: 9 and was *b* by John in the Jordan.
10:38 or be *b* with the baptism I am
16:16 believes and is *b* will be saved,
Jn 4: 2 in fact it was not Jesus who *b*,
Ac 1: 5 but in a few days you will be *b*

BARABBAS
Mt 27:26 Then he released *B* to them.

BARBS*
Nu 33:55 allow to remain will become *b*

BARE
Heb 4:13 and laid *b* before the eyes of him

BARNABAS*
Disciple, originally Joseph (Ac 4:36), prophet (Ac 13:1), apostle (Ac 14:14). Brought Paul to apostles (Ac 9:27), Antioch (Ac 11:22-29; Gal 2:1-13), on the first missionary journey (Ac 13-14). Together at Jerusalem Council, they separated over John Mark (Ac 15). Later co-workers (1Co 9:6; Col 4:10).

BARREN
Ps 113: 9 He settles the *b* woman

BARTHOLOMEW*
Apostle (Mt 10:3; Mk 3:18; Lk 6:14; Ac 1:13). Possibly also known as Nathanael (Jn 1:45-49; 21:2).

BATH
Jn 13:10 person who has had a *b* needs only

BATHSHEBA
Wife of Uriah who committed adultery with and became wife of David (2Sa 11), mother of Solomon (2Sa 12:24; 1Ki 1-2; 1Ch 3:5).

BATTLE
2Ch 20:15 For the *b* is not yours, but God's.
Ps 24: 8 the LORD mighty in *b*.
Ecc 9:11 or the *b* to the strong,

BEAR (BEARING BIRTH BIRTHRIGHT BORN FIRSTBORN NEWBORN)
Ge 4:13 punishment is more than I can *b*.
Ps 38: 4 like a burden too heavy to *b*.
Isa 53:11 and he will *b* their iniquities.
Da 7: 5 beast, which looked like a *b*.
Mt 7:18 A good tree cannot *b* bad fruit,
Jn 15: 2 branch that does *b* fruit he prunes
15:16 and appointed you to go and *b* fruit—
Ro 15: 1 ought to *b* with the failings
1Co 10:13 tempted beyond what you can *b*.
Col 3:13 *B* with each other and forgive

BEARING (BEAR)
Eph 4: 2 *b* with one another in love.
Col 1:10 *b* fruit in every good work

BEAST
Rev 13:18 him calculate the number of the *b*,

BEAT (BEATING)
Isa 2: 4 They will *b* their swords
Joel 3:10 *B* your plowshares into swords
1Co 9:27 I *b* my body and make it my slave

BEATING (BEAT)
1Co 9:26 I do not fight like a man *b* the air.
1Pe 2:20 if you receive a *b* for doing wrong

BEAUTIFUL (BEAUTY)
Ge 6: 2 that the daughters of men were *b*,
12:11 “I know what a *b* woman you are.
12:14 saw that she was a very *b* woman.
24:16 The girl was very *b*, a virgin;
26: 7 of Rebekah, because she is *b*.”
29:17 Rachel was lovely in form, and *b*.
Job 38:31 “Can you bind the *b* Pleiades?
Pr 11:22 is a *b* woman who shows no
Ecc 3:11 He has made everything *b*
Isa 4: 2 of the LORD will be *b*
52: 7 How *b* on the mountains
Eze 20: 6 and honey, the most *b* of all lands.
Zec 9:17 How attractive and *b* they will be!
Mt 23:27 which look *b* on the outside
26:10 She has done a *b* thing to me.
Ro 10:15 “How *b* are the feet
1Pe 3: 5 in God used to make themselves *b*.

BEAUTY (BEAUTIFUL)
Ps 27: 4 to gaze upon the *b* of the LORD
45:11 The king is enthralled by your *b*;
Pr 31:30 is deceptive, and *b* is fleeting;
Isa 33:17 Your eyes will see the king in his *b*
53: 2 He had no *b* or majesty
61: 3 to bestow on them a crown of *b*
Eze 28:12 full of wisdom and perfect in *b*.
1Pe 3: 4 the unfading *b* of a gentle

BED
Heb 13: 4 and the marriage *b* kept pure,

BEELZEBUB
Lk 11:15 “By *B*, the prince of demons,

BEER
Pr 20: 1 Wine is a mocker and *b* a brawler;

BEERSHEBA
Jdg 20: 1 all the Israelites from Dan to *B*

BEGINNING
Ge 1: 1 In the *b* God created the heavens
Ps 102:25 In the *b* you laid the foundations
111:10 of the LORD is the *b* of wisdom;
Pr 1: 7 of the LORD is the *b* of knowledge

Jn 1: 1 In the *b* was the Word,
1Jn 1: 1 That which was from the *b*,
Rev 21: 6 and the Omega, the *B* and the End.

BEHAVE
Ro 13:13 Let us *b* decently, as in the daytime

BELIEVE (BELIEVED BELIEVER BELIEVERS BELIEVES BELIEVING)
Mt 18: 6 one of these little ones who *b* in me
21:22 If you *b*, you will receive whatever
Mk 1:15 Repent and *b* the good news!"
9:24 "I do *b;* help me overcome my
16:17 signs will accompany those who *b:*
Lk 8:50 just *b*, and she will be healed."
24:25 to *b* all that the prophets have
Jn 1: 7 that through him all men might *b*.
3:18 does not *b* stands condemned
6:29 to *b* in the one he has sent."
10:38 you do not *b* me, *b* the miracles,
11:27 "I *b* that you are the Christ,
14:11 *B* me when I say that I am
16:30 This makes us *b* that you came
16:31 "You *b* at last!" Jesus answered.
17:21 that the world may *b* that you have
20:27 Stop doubting and *b*."
20:31 written that you may *b* that Jesus is
Ac 16:31 They replied, "*B* in the Lord Jesus,
24:14 I *b* everything that agrees
Ro 3:22 faith in Jesus Christ to all who *b*.
4:11 he is the father of all who *b*
10: 9 *b* in your heart that God raised him
10:14 And how can they *b* in the one
16:26 so that all nations might *b*
1Th 4:14 We *b* that Jesus died and rose again
2Th 2:11 delusion so that they will *b* the lie
1Ti 4:10 and especially of those who *b*.
Tit 1: 6 a man whose children *b*
Heb 11: 6 comes to him must *b* that he exists
Jas 2:19 Even the demons *b* that—
1Jn 4: 1 Dear friends, do not *b* every spirit,

BELIEVED (BELIEVE)
Ge 15: 6 Abram *b* the LORD, and he
Jnh 3: 5 The Ninevites *b* God.
Jn 1:12 to those who *b* in his name,
2:22 Then they *b* the Scripture
3:18 because he has not *b* in the name
20: 8 He saw and *b*.
20:29 who have not seen and yet have *b*."
Ac 13:48 were appointed for eternal life *b*.
Ro 4: 3 Scripture say? "Abraham *b* God,
10:14 call on the one they have not *b* in?
1Co 15: 2 Otherwise, you have *b* in vain.
Gal 3: 6 Consider Abraham: "He *b* God,
2Ti 1:12 because I know whom I have *b*,
Jas 2:23 that says, "Abraham *b* God,

BELIEVER (BELIEVE)
1Co 7:12 brother has a wife who is not a *b*
2Co 6:15 What does a *b* have in common

BELIEVERS (BELIEVE)
Ac 4:32 All the *b* were one in heart
5:12 And all the *b* used to meet together
1Co 6: 5 to judge a dispute between *b?*
1Ti 4:12 set an example for the *b* in speech,
1Pe 2:17 Love the brotherhood of *b*,

BELIEVES (BELIEVE)
Pr 14:15 A simple man *b* anything,
Mk 9:23 is possible for him who *b*."
11:23 *b* that what he says will happen,
16:16 Whoever *b* and is baptized will be
Jn 3:16 that whoever *b* in him shall not
3:36 Whoever *b* in the Son has eternal
5:24 *b* him who sent me has eternal life
6:35 and he who *b* in me will never be
6:40 and *b* in him shall have eternal life,
6:47 he who *b* has everlasting life.
7:38 Whoever *b* in me, as the Scripture
11:26 and *b* in me will never die.
Ro 1:16 for the salvation of everyone who *b*
10: 4 righteousness for everyone who *b*.
1Jn 5: 1 Everyone who *b* that Jesus is
5: 5 Only he who *b* that Jesus is the Son

BELIEVING (BELIEVE)
Jn 20:31 and that by *b* you may have life

BELONG (BELONGS)
Dt 29:29 The secret things *b*
Job 25: 2 "Dominion and awe *b* to God;
Ps 47: 9 for the kings of the earth *b* to God;
95: 4 and the mountain peaks *b* to him.
Jn 8:44 You *b* to your father, the devil,
15:19 As it is, you do not *b* to the world,
Ro 1: 6 called to *b* to Jesus Christ.
7: 4 that you might *b* to another,
14: 8 we live or die, we *b* to the Lord.
Gal 5:24 Those who *b* to Christ Jesus have
1Th 5: 8 But since we *b* to the day, let us be

BELONGS (BELONG)
Job 41:11 Everything under heaven *b* to me.
Ps 111:10 To him *b* eternal praise.
Eze 18: 4 For every living soul *b* to me,
Jn 8:47 He who *b* to God hears what God
Ro 12: 5 each member *b* to all the others.

BELOVED (LOVE)
Dt 33:12 "Let the *b* of the LORD rest secure

BELT
Isa 11: 5 Righteousness will be his *b*
Eph 6:14 with the *b* of truth buckled

BENEFIT (BENEFITS)
Ro 6:22 the *b* you reap leads to holiness,
2Co 4:15 All this is for your *b*,

BENEFITS (BENEFIT)
Ps 103: 2 and forget not all his *b*.
Jn 4:38 you have reaped the *b* of their labor

BENJAMIN
Twelfth son of Jacob by Rachel (Ge 35:16-24; 46:19-21; 1Ch 2:2). Jacob refused to send him to Egypt, but relented (Ge 42-45).

BEREANS*
Ac 17:11 the *B* were of more noble character

BESTOWS
Ps 84:11 the LORD *b* favor and honor;

BETHLEHEM
Mt 2: 1 After Jesus was born in *B* in Judea,

BETRAY
Pr 25: 9 do not *b* another man's confidence,

BIND (BINDS)
Dt 6: 8 and *b* them on your foreheads.
Pr 6:21 *B* them upon your heart forever;
Isa 61: 1 me to *b* up the brokenhearted,
Mt 16:19 whatever you *b* on earth will be

BINDS (BIND)
Ps 147: 3 and *b* up their wounds.
Isa 30:26 when the LORD *b* up the bruises

BIRDS
Mt 8:20 and *b* of the air have nests,

BIRTH (BEAR)
Ps 58: 3 Even from *b* the wicked go astray;
Mt 1:18 This is how the *b* of Jesus Christ
1Pe 1: 3 great mercy he has given us new *b*

BIRTHRIGHT (BEAR)
Ge 25:34 So Esau despised his *b*.

BLAMELESS
Ge 17: 1 walk before me and be *b*.
Job 1: 1 This man was *b* and upright;
Ps 84:11 from those whose walk is *b*.
119: 1 Blessed are they whose ways are *b*,
Pr 19: 1 Better a poor man whose walk is *b*
1Co 1: 8 so that you will be *b* on the day
Eph 5:27 any other blemish, but holy and *b*.
Php 2:15 so that you may become *b* and pure
1Th 3:13 hearts so that you will be *b*
5:23 and body be kept *b* at the coming
Tit 1: 6 An elder must be *b*, the husband of
Heb 7:26 *b*, pure, set apart from sinners,
2Pe 3:14 effort to be found spotless, *b*

BLASPHEMES
Mk 3:29 whoever *b* against the Holy Spirit

BLEMISH
1Pe 1:19 a lamb without *b* or defect.

BLESS (BLESSED BLESSING BLESSINGS)
Ge 12: 3 I will *b* those who *b* you,
Ro 12:14 Bless those who persecute you; *b*

BLESSED (BLESS)
Ge 1:22 God *b* them and said, "Be fruitful
2: 3 And God *b* the seventh day
22:18 nations on earth will be *b*,
Ps 1: 1 *B* is the man
2:12 *B* are all who take refuge in him.
33:12 *B* is the nation whose God is
41: 1 *B* is he who has regard for the weak
84: 5 *B* are those whose strength is
106: 3 *B* are they who maintain justice,
112: 1 *B* is the man who fears the LORD,
118:26 *B* is he who comes in the name
Pr 29:18 but *b* is he who keeps the law.
31:28 Her children arise and call her *b;*
Mt 5: 3 saying: "*B* are the poor in spirit,
5: 4 *B* are those who mourn,
5: 5 *B* are the meek,
5: 6 *B* are those who hunger
5: 7 *B* are the merciful,
5: 8 *B* are the pure in heart,
5: 9 *B* are the peacemakers,
5:10 *B* are those who are persecuted
5:11 "*B* are you when people insult you,
Lk 1:48 on all generations will call me *b*,
Jn 12:13 "*B* is he who comes in the name
Ac 20:35 'It is more *b* to give than to receive
Tit 2:13 while we wait for the *b* hope—
Jas 1:12 *B* is the man who perseveres
Rev 1: 3 *B* is the one who reads the words
22:14 "*B* are those who wash their robes,

BLESSING (BLESS)
Eze 34:26 there will be showers of *b*.

BLESSINGS (BLESS)
Pr 10: 6 *B* crown the head of the righteous,

BLIND
Mt 15:14 a *b* man leads a *b* man, both will fall
23:16 "Woe to you, *b* guides! You say,
Jn 9:25 I was *b* but now I see!"

BLOOD
Ge 9: 6 "Whoever sheds the *b* of man,
Ex 12:13 and when I see the *b*, I will pass
24: 8 "This is the *b* of the covenant that
Lev 17:11 For the life of a creature is in the *b*,
Ps 72:14 for precious is their *b* in his sight.
Pr 6:17 hands that shed innocent *b*,
Mt 26:28 This is my *b* of the covenant,
Ro 3:25 of atonement, through faith in his *b*
5: 9 have now been justified by his *b*,
1Co 11:25 cup is the new covenant in my *b;*
Eph 1: 7 we have redemption through his *b*,
2:13 near through the *b* of Christ.
Col 1:20 by making peace through his *b*,
Heb 9:12 once for all by his own *b*,
9:22 of *b* there is no forgiveness.
1Pe 1:19 but with the precious *b* of Christ,
1Jn 1: 7 and the *b* of Jesus, his Son,
Rev 1: 5 has freed us from our sins by his *b*,
5: 9 with your *b* you purchased men
7:14 white in the *b* of the Lamb.
12:11 him by the *b* of the Lamb

BLOT (BLOTS)
Ex 32:32 then *b* me out of the book you have
Ps 51: 1 *b* out my transgressions.
Rev 3: 5 I will never *b* out his name

BLOTS (BLOT)
Isa 43:25 "I, even I, am he who *b* out

BLOWN
Eph 4:14 and *b* here and there by every wind
Jas 1: 6 doubts is like a wave of the sea, *b*

BOAST
1Ki 20:11 armor should not *b* like one who
Ps 34: 2 My soul will *b* in the LORD;
44: 8 In God we make our *b* all day long,
Pr 27: 1 Do not *b* about tomorrow,
1Co 1:31 Let him who boasts *b* in the Lord."
Gal 6:14 May I never *b* except in the cross
Eph 2: 9 not by works, so that no one can *b*.

BOAZ
Wealthy Bethlehemite who showed favor to Ruth (Ru 2), married her (Ru 4). Ancestor of David (Ru 4:18-22; 1Ch 2:12-15), Jesus (Mt 1:5-16; Lk 3:23-32).

BODIES (BODY)
Ro 12: 1 to offer your *b* as living sacrifices,
1Co 6:15 not know that your *b* are members
Eph 5:28 to love their wives as their own *b*.

BODY (BODIES)
Zec 13: 6 What are these wounds on your *b?*'
Mt 10:28 afraid of those who kill the *b*
26:26 saying, "Take and eat; this is my *b*
26:41 spirit is willing, but the *b* is weak."
Jn 13:10 wash his feet; his whole *b* is clean.
Ro 6:13 Do not offer the parts of your *b*
12: 4 us has one *b* with many members,
1Co 6:19 not know that your *b* is a temple
11:24 "This is my *b*, which is for you;
12:12 The *b* is a unit, though it is made up

Eph 5:30 for we are members of his *b*.

BOLD (BOLDNESS)
Ps 138: 3 you made me *b* and stouthearted.
Pr 21:29 A wicked man puts up a *b* front,
28: 1 but the righteous are as *b* as a lion.

BOLDNESS* (BOLD)
Ac 4:29 to speak your word with great *b*.

BONDAGE
Ezr 9: 9 God has not deserted us in our *b*.

BOOK (BOOKS)
Jos 1: 8 Do not let this *B* of the Law depart
Ne 8: 8 They read from the *B* of the Law
Jn 20:30 which are not recorded in this *b*.
Php 4: 3 whose names are in the *b* of life.
Rev 21:27 written in the Lamb's *b* of life.

BOOKS (BOOK)
Ecc 12:12 Of making many *b* there is no end,

BORN (BEAR)
Isa 9: 6 For to us a child is *b*,
Jn 3: 7 at my saying, 'You must be *b* again
1Pe 1:23 For you have been *b* again,
1Jn 4: 7 Everyone who loves has been *b*
5: 1 believes that Jesus is the Christ is *b*

BORROWER
Pr 22: 7 and the *b* is servant to the lender.

BOUGHT
Ac 20:28 which he *b* with his own blood.
1Co 6:20 You are not your own; you were *b*
7:23 You were *b* at a price; do not
2Pe 2: 1 the sovereign Lord who *b* them—

BOW
Ps 95: 6 Come, let us *b* down in worship,
Isa 45:23 Before me every knee will *b*;
Ro 14:11 'every knee will *b* before me;
Php 2:10 name of Jesus every knee should *b*,

BRANCH (BRANCHES)
Isa 4: 2 In that day the *B* of the LORD will
Jer 33:15 I will make a righteous *B* sprout

BRANCHES (BRANCH)
Jn 15: 5 "I am the vine; you are the *b*.

BRAVE
2Sa 2: 7 Now then, be strong and *b*,

BREAD
Dt 8: 3 that man does not live on *b* alone
Pr 30: 8 but give me only my daily *b*.
Ecc 11: 1 Cast your *b* upon the waters,
Isa 55: 2 Why spend money on what is not *b*
Mt 4: 4 'Man does not live on *b* alone,
6:11 Give us today our daily *b*.
Jn 6:35 Jesus declared, "I am the *b* of life.
21:13 took the *b* and gave it to them,
1Co 11:23 took *b*, and when he had given

BREAK (BREAKING BROKEN)
Nu 30: 2 he must not *b* his word
Jdg 2: 1 'I will never *b* my covenant
Isa 42: 3 A bruised reed he will not *b*,
Mt 12:20 A bruised reed he will not *b*,

BREAKING (BREAK)
Jas 2:10 at just one point is guilty of *b* all

BREASTPIECE (BREASTPLATE)
Ex 28:15 Fashion a *b* for making decisions—

BREASTPLATE* (BREASTPIECE)
Isa 59:17 He put on righteousness as his *b*,
Eph 6:14 with the *b* of righteousness in place
1Th 5: 8 putting on faith and love as a *b*,

BREATHED (GOD-BREATHED)
Ge 2: 7 *b* into his nostrils the breath of life,
Jn 20:22 And with that he *b* on them

BREEDS*
Pr 13:10 Pride only *b* quarrels,

BRIBE
Ex 23: 8 "Do not accept a *b*,
Pr 6:35 will refuse the *b*, however great it

BRIDE
Rev 19: 7 and his *b* has made herself ready,

BRIGHTER (BRIGHTNESS)
Pr 4:18 shining ever *b* till the full light

BRIGHTNESS (BRIGHTER)
2Sa 22:13 Out of the *b* of his presence
Da 12: 3 who are wise will shine like the *b*

BROAD
Mt 7:13 and *b* is the road that leads

BROKEN (BREAK)
Ps 51:17 The sacrifices of God are a *b* spirit;
Ecc 4:12 of three strands is not quickly *b*.
Jn 10:35 and the Scripture cannot be *b*—

BROKENHEARTED* (HEART)
Ps 34:18 The LORD is close to the *b*
109:16 and the needy and the *b*.
147: 3 He heals the *b*
Isa 61: 1 He has sent me to bind up the *b*,

BROTHER (BROTHER'S BROTHERS)
Pr 17:17 and a *b* is born for adversity.
18:24 a friend who sticks closer than a *b*.
27:10 neighbor nearby than a *b* far away.
Mt 5:24 and be reconciled to your *b*;
18:15 "If your *b* sins against you,
Mk 3:35 Whoever does God's will is my *b*
Lk 17: 3 "If your *b* sins, rebuke him,
1Co 8:13 if what I eat causes my *b* to fall
1Jn 2:10 Whoever loves his *b* lives
4:21 loves God must also love his *b*.

BROTHER'S (BROTHER)
Ge 4: 9 "Am I my *b* keeper?" The LORD

BROTHERS (BROTHER)
Ps 133: 1 is when *b* live together in unity!
Pr 6:19 who stirs up dissension among *b*.
Mt 25:40 one of the least of these *b* of mine,
Mk 10:29 or *b* or sisters or mother or father
Heb 13: 1 Keep on loving each other as *b*.
1Pe 3: 8 be sympathetic, love as *b*,
1Jn 3:14 death to life, because we love our *b*.

BUILD (BUILDING BUILDS BUILT)
Mt 16:18 and on this rock I will *b* my church,
Ac 20:32 which can *b* you up and give you
1Co 14:12 excel in gifts that *b* up the church.
1Th 5:11 one another and *b* each other up,

BUILDING (BUILD)
1Co 3: 9 you are God's field, God's *b*.
2Co 10: 8 us for *b* you up rather
Eph 4:29 helpful for *b* others up according

BUILDS (BUILD)
Ps 127: 1 Unless the LORD *b* the house,
1Co 3:10 one should be careful how he *b*.
8: 1 Knowledge puffs up, but love *b* up.

BUILT (BUILD)
Mt 7:24 is like a wise man who *b* his house
Eph 2:20 *b* on the foundation of the apostles
4:12 the body of Christ may be *b* up

BURDEN (BURDENED BURDENS)
Ps 38: 4 like a *b* too heavy to bear.
Mt 11:30 my yoke is easy and my *b* is light."

BURDENED (BURDEN)
Gal 5: 1 do not let yourselves be *b* again

BURDENS (BURDEN)
Ps 68:19 who daily bears our *b*.
Gal 6: 2 Carry each other's *b*,

BURIED
Ro 6: 4 *b* with him through baptism
1Co 15: 4 that he was *b*, that he was raised

BURNING
Lev 6: 9 the fire must be kept *b* on the altar.
Ro 12:20 you will heap *b* coals on his head."

BUSINESS
Da 8:27 and went about the king's *b*.
1Th 4:11 to mind your own *b* and to work

BUSY
1Ki 20:40 While your servant was *b* here
2Th 3:11 They are not *b*; they are
Tit 2: 5 to be *b* at home, to be kind,

CAESAR
Mt 22:21 "Give to *C* what is Caesar's,

CAIN
Firstborn of Adam (Ge 4:1), murdered brother Abel (Ge 4:1-16; 1Jn 3:12).

CALEB
Judahite who spied out Canaan (Nu 13:6); allowed to enter land because of faith (Nu 13:30-14:38; Dt 1:36). Possessed Hebron (Jos 14:6-15:19).

CALF
Ex 32: 4 into an idol cast in the shape of a *c*,
Lk 15:23 Bring the fattened *c* and kill it.

CALL (CALLED CALLING CALLS)
Ps 105: 1 to the LORD, *c* on his name;
145:18 near to all who *c* on him,
Pr 31:28 children arise and *c* her blessed;
Isa 5:20 Woe to those who *c* evil good
55: 6 *c* on him while he is near.
65:24 Before they *c* I will answer;
Jer 33: 3 '*C* to me and I will answer you
Mt 9:13 come to *c* the righteous,
Ro 10:12 and richly blesses all who *c* on him,
11:29 gifts and his *c* are irrevocable.
1Th 4: 7 For God did not *c* us to be impure,

CALLED (CALL)
1Sa 3: 5 and said, "Here I am; you *c* me."
2Ch 7:14 if my people, who are *c*
Ps 34: 6 This poor man *c*, and the LORD
Mt 21:13 " 'My house will be *c* a house
Ro 8:30 And those he predestined, he also *c*
1Co 7:15 God has *c* us to live in peace.
Gal 5:13 You, my brothers, were *c* to be free
1Pe 2: 9 of him who *c* you out of darkness

CALLING (CALL)
Jn 1:23 I am the voice of one *c* in the desert
Ac 22:16 wash your sins away, *c* on his name
Eph 4: 1 worthy of the *c* you have received.
2Pe 1:10 all the more eager to make your *c*

CALLS (CALL)
Joel 2:32 And everyone who *c*
Jn 10: 3 He *c* his own sheep by name
Ro 10:13 "Everyone who *c* on the name

CAMEL
Mt 19:21 it is easier for a *c* to go
23:24 strain out a gnat but swallow a *c*.

CANAAN
1Ch 16:18 "To you I will give the land of *C*

CANCELED
Lk 7:42 so he *c* the debts of both.
Col 2:14 having *c* the written code,

CAPITAL
Dt 21:22 guilty of a *c* offense is put to death

CAPSTONE (STONE)
Ps 118:22 has become the *c*;
1Pe 2: 7 has become the *c*,"

CARE (CAREFUL CARES CARING)
Ps 8: 4 the son of man that you *c* for him?
Pr 29: 7 The righteous *c* about justice
Lk 10:34 him to an inn and took *c* of him.
Jn 21:16 Jesus said, "Take *c* of my sheep."
Heb 2: 6 the son of man that you *c* for him?
1Pe 5: 2 of God's flock that is under your *c*,

CAREFUL (CARE)
Ex 23:13 "Be *c* to do everything I have said
Dt 6: 3 be *c* to obey so that it may go well
Jos 23: 6 be *c* to obey all that is written
23:11 be very *c* to love the LORD your
Pr 13:24 he who loves him is *c*
Mt 6: 1 "Be *c* not to do your 'acts
Ro 12:17 Be *c* to do what is right in the eyes
1Co 3:10 each one should be *c* how he builds
8: 9 Be *c*, however, that the exercise
Eph 5:15 Be very *c*, then, how you live—

CARELESS
Mt 12:36 for every *c* word they have spoken.

CARES (CARE)
Ps 55:22 Cast your *c* on the LORD
Na 1: 7 He *c* for those who trust in him,
Eph 5:29 but he feeds and *c* for it, just
1Pe 5: 7 on him because he *c* for you.

CARING* (CARE)
1Th 2: 7 like a mother *c* for her little
1Ti 5: 4 practice by *c* for their own family

CARRIED (CARRY)
Ex 19: 4 and how I *c* you on eagles' wings
Isa 53: 4 and *c* our sorrows,
Heb 13: 9 Do not be *c* away by all kinds
2Pe 1:21 as they were *c* along by the Holy

CARRIES (CARRY)
Dt 32:11 and *c* them on its pinions.
Isa 40:11 and *c* them close to his heart;

CARRY (CARRIED CARRIES)
Lk 14:27 anyone who does not *c* his cross
Gal 6: 2 *C* each other's burdens,
6: 5 for each one should *c* his own load.

CAST
Ps 22:18 and *c* lots for my clothing.
55:22 *C* your cares on the LORD
Ecc 11: 1 *C* your bread upon the waters,
Jn 19:24 and *c* lots for my clothing."
1Pe 5: 7 *C* all your anxiety on him

CATCH (CAUGHT)
Lk 5:10 from now on you will *c* men."

CATTLE
Ps 50:10 and the *c* on a thousand hills.

CAUGHT (CATCH)
1Th 4:17 and are left will be *c* up together

CAUSE (CAUSES)
Pr 24:28 against your neighbor without *c*,
Ecc 8: 3 Do not stand up for a bad *c*,
Mt 18: 7 of the things that *c* people to sin!
Ro 14:21 else that will *c* your brother
1Co 10:32 Do not *c* anyone to stumble,

CAUSES (CAUSE)
Isa 8:14 a stone that *c* men to stumble
Mt 18: 6 if anyone *c* one of these little ones

CAUTIOUS*
Pr 12:26 A righteous man is *c* in friendship,

CEASE
Ps 46: 9 He makes wars *c* to the ends

CENSER
Lev 16:12 is to take a *c* full of burning coals

CENTURION
Mt 8: 5 had entered Capernaum, a *c* came

CERTAIN (CERTAINTY)
2Pe 1:19 word of the prophets made more *c*,

CERTAINTY* (CERTAIN)
Lk 1: 4 so that you may know the *c*
Jn 17: 8 They knew with *c* that I came

CHAFF
Ps 1: 4 They are like *c*

CHAINED
2Ti 2: 9 But God's word is not *c*.

CHAMPION
Ps 19: 5 like a *c* rejoicing to run his course.

CHANGE (CHANGED)
1Sa 15:29 of Israel does not lie or *c* his mind;
Ps 110: 4 and will not *c* his mind:
Jer 7: 5 If you really *c* your ways
Mal 3: 6 "I the LORD do not *c*.
Mt 18: 3 unless you *c* and become like little
Heb 7:21 and will not *c* his mind:
Jas 1:17 who does not *c* like shifting

CHANGED (CHANGE)
1Co 15:51 but we will all be *c*— in a flash,

CHARACTER
Ru 3:11 that you are a woman of noble *c*.
Pr 31:10 A wife of noble *c* who can find?
Ro 5: 4 perseverance, *c*; and *c*, hope.
1Co 15:33 "Bad company corrupts good *c*."

CHARGE
Ro 8:33 Who will bring any *c*
2Co 11: 7 the gospel of God to you free of *c*?
2Ti 4: 1 I give you this *c*: Preach the Word;

CHARIOTS
2Ki 6:17 and *c* of fire all around Elisha.
Ps 20: 7 Some trust in *c* and some in horses,

CHARM
Pr 31:30 *C* is deceptive, and beauty is

CHASES
Pr 12:11 he who *c* fantasies lacks judgment.

CHATTER* (CHATTERING)
1Ti 6:20 Turn away from godless *c*
2Ti 2:16 Avoid godless *c*, because those

CHATTERING* (CHATTER)
Pr 10: 8 but a *c* fool comes to ruin.
10:10 and a *c* fool comes to ruin.

CHEAT* (CHEATED)
Mal 1:14 "Cursed is the *c* who has
1Co 6: 8 you yourselves *c* and do wrong,

CHEATED (CHEAT)
Lk 19: 8 if I have *c* anybody out of anything,
1Co 6: 7 Why not rather be *c*? Instead,

CHEEK
Mt 5:39 someone strikes you on the right *c*,

CHEERFUL* (CHEERS)
Pr 15:13 A happy heart makes the face *c*,
15:15 but the *c* heart has a continual feast
15:30 A *c* look brings joy to the heart,
17:22 A *c* heart is good medicine,
2Co 9: 7 for God loves a *c* giver.

CHEERS (CHEERFUL)
Pr 12:25 but a kind word *c* him up.

CHILD (CHILDISH CHILDREN)
Pr 20:11 Even a *c* is known by his actions,
22: 6 Train a *c* in the way he should go,
22:15 Folly is bound up in the heart of a *c*
23:13 not withhold discipline from a *c*;
29:15 *c* left to himself disgraces his mother.
Isa 7:14 The virgin will be with *c*
9: 6 For to us a *c* is born,
11: 6 and a little *c* will lead them.
66:13 As a mother comforts her *c*,
Mt 1:23 "The virgin will be with *c*
18: 2 He called a little *c* and had him
Lk 1:42 and blessed is the *c* you will bear!
1:80 And the *c* grew and became strong
1Co 13:11 When I was a *c*, I talked like a *c*,
1Jn 5: 1 who loves the father loves his *c*

CHILDISH* (CHILD)
1Co 13:11 When I became a man, I put *c* ways

CHILDREN (CHILD)
Dt 4: 9 Teach them to your *c*
11:19 them to your *c*, talking about them
Ps 8: 2 From the lips of *c* and infants
Pr 17: 6 Children's *c* are a crown
31:28 Her *c* arise and call her blessed;
Mt 7:11 how to give good gifts to your *c*,
11:25 and revealed them to little *c*.
18: 3 you change and become like little *c*
19:14 "Let the little *c* come to me,
21:16 " 'From the lips of *c* and infants
Mk 9:37 one of these little *c* in my name
10:14 "Let the little *c* come to me,
10:16 And he took the *c* in his arms,
13:12 *C* will rebel against their parents
Lk 10:21 and revealed them to little *c*.
18:16 "Let the little *c* come to me,
Ro 8:16 with our spirit that we are God's *c*.
2Co 12:14 parents, but parents for their *c*.
Eph 6: 1 *C*, obey your parents in the Lord,
6: 4 do not exasperate your *c*; instead,
Col 3:20 *C*, obey your parents in everything,
3:21 Fathers, do not embitter your *c*,
1Ti 3: 4 and see that his *c* obey him
3:12 and must manage his *c* and his
5:10 bringing up *c*, showing hospitality,
1Jn 3: 1 that we should be called *c* of God!

CHOOSE (CHOOSES CHOSE CHOSEN)
Dt 30:19 Now *c* life, so that you
Jos 24:15 then *c* for yourselves this day
Pr 8:10 *C* my instruction instead of silver,
16:16 to *c* understanding rather
Jn 15:16 You did not *c* me, but I chose you

CHOOSES (CHOOSE)
Jn 7:17 If anyone *c* to do God's will,

CHOSE (CHOOSE)
Ge 13:11 So Lot *c* for himself the whole plain
Ps 33:12 the people he *c* for his inheritance.
Jn 15:16 but I *c* you and appointed you to go
1Co 1:27 But God *c* the foolish things
Eph 1: 4 he *c* us in him before the creation
2Th 2:13 from the beginning God *c* you

CHOSEN (CHOOSE)
Isa 41: 8 Jacob, whom I have *c*,
Mt 22:14 For many are invited, but few are *c*
Lk 10:42 Mary has *c* what is better,
23:35 the Christ of God, the *C* One."
Jn 15:19 but I have *c* you out of the world.
1Pe 1:20 He was *c* before the creation
2: 9 But you are a *c* people, a royal

CHRIST (CHRIST'S CHRISTIAN CHRISTS)
Mt 1:16 was born Jesus, who is called *C*.
16:16 Peter answered, "You are the *C*,
22:42 "What do you think about the *C*?
Jn 1:41 found the Messiah" (that is, the *C*).
20:31 you may believe that Jesus is the *C*,
Ac 2:36 you crucified, both Lord and *C*."
5:42 the good news that Jesus is the *C*.
9:22 by proving that Jesus is the *C*.
17: 3 proving that the *C* had to suffer
18:28 the Scriptures that Jesus was the *C*.
26:23 that the *C* would suffer and,
Ro 3:22 comes through faith in Jesus *C*
5: 6 we were still powerless, *C* died
5: 8 While we were still sinners, *C* died
5:17 life through the one man, Jesus *C*.
6: 4 as *C* was raised from the dead
8: 1 for those who are in *C* Jesus,
8: 9 Spirit of *C*, he does not belong to *C*.
8:35 us from the love of *C*?
10: 4 *C* is the end of the law
14: 9 *C* died and returned to life
15: 3 For even *C* did not please himself
1Co 1:23 but we preach *C* crucified:
2: 2 except Jesus *C* and him crucified.
3:11 one already laid, which is Jesus *C*.
5: 7 For *C*, our Passover lamb,
8: 6 and there is but one Lord, Jesus *C*,
10: 4 them, and that rock was *C*.
11: 1 as I follow the example of *C*.
11: 3 the head of every man is *C*,
12:27 Now you are the body of *C*,
15: 3 that *C* died for our sins according
15:14 And if *C* has not been raised,
15:22 so in *C* all will be made alive.
15:57 victory through our Lord Jesus *C*.
2Co 3: 3 show that you are a letter from *C*,
4: 5 not preach ourselves, but Jesus *C*
5:10 before the judgment seat of *C*,
5:17 Therefore, if anyone is in *C*,
11: 2 you to one husband, to *C*,
Gal 2:20 I have been crucified with *C*
3:13 *C* redeemed us from the curse
6:14 in the cross of our Lord Jesus *C*,
Eph 1: 3 with every spiritual blessing in *C*.
3: 8 the unsearchable riches of *C*,
4:13 measure of the fullness of *C*.
5: 2 as *C* loved us and gave himself up
5:23 as *C* is the head of the church,
5:25 just as *C* loved the church
Php 1:21 to live is *C* and to die is gain.
1:27 worthy of the gospel of *C*.
4:19 to his glorious riches in *C* Jesus.
Col 1:27 which is *C* in you, the hope of glory
1:28 may present everyone perfect in *C*.
2: 6 as you received *C* Jesus as Lord,
2:17 the reality, however, is found in *C*.
3:15 Let the peace of *C* rule
2Th 2: 1 the coming of our Lord Jesus *C*
1Ti 1:15 *C* Jesus came into the world
2: 5 the man *C* Jesus, who gave himself
2Ti 2: 3 us like a good soldier of *C* Jesus.
3:15 salvation through faith in *C* Jesus.
Tit 2:13 our great God and Savior, Jesus *C*,
Heb 3:14 to share in *C* if we hold firmly
9:14 more, then, will the blood of *C*,
9:15 For this reason *C* is the mediator
9:28 so *C* was sacrificed once
10:10 of the body of Jesus *C* once for all.
13: 8 Jesus *C* is the same yesterday
1Pe 1:19 but with the precious blood of *C*,
2:21 because *C* suffered for you,
3:18 For *C* died for sins once for all,
4:14 insulted because of the name of *C*,
1Jn 2:22 man who denies that Jesus is the *C*.
3:16 Jesus *C* laid down his life for us.
5: 1 believes that Jesus is the *C* is born
Rev 20: 4 reigned with *C* a thousand years.

CHRIST'S (CHRIST)
2Co 5:14 For *C* love compels us,
5:20 We are therefore *C* ambassadors,
12: 9 so that *C* power may rest on me.

CHRISTIAN (CHRIST)
1Pe 4:16 as a *C*, do not be ashamed,

CHRISTS (CHRIST)
Mt 24:24 For false *C* and false prophets will

CHURCH
Mt 16:18 and on this rock I will build my *c*,
18:17 if he refuses to listen even to the *c*,
Ac 20:28 Be shepherds of the *c* of God,
1Co 5:12 of mine to judge those outside the *c*
14: 4 but he who prophesies edifies the *c*.
14:12 to excel in gifts that build up the *c*.
14:26 done for the strengthening of the *c*.
Eph 5:23 as Christ is the head of the *c*,
Col 1:24 the sake of his body, which is the *c*.

CIRCUMCISED
Ge 17:10 Every male among you shall be *c.*

CIRCUMSTANCES
Php 4:11 to be content whatever the *c.*
1Th 5:18 continually; give thanks in all *c,*

CITIZENS (CITIZENSHIP)
Eph 2:19 but fellow *c* with God's people

CITIZENSHIP (CITIZENS)
Php 3:20 But our *c* is in heaven.

CITY
Mt 5:14 A *c* on a hill cannot be hidden.
Heb 13:14 here we do not have an enduring *c,*

CIVILIAN*
2Ti 2: 4 a soldier gets involved in *c* affairs—

CLAIM (CLAIMS)
Pr 25: 6 do not *c* a place among great men,
1Jn 1: 6 If we *c* to have fellowship
1: 8 If we *c* to be without sin, we
1:10 If we *c* we have not sinned,

CLAIMS (CLAIM)
Jas 2:14 if a man *c* to have faith
1Jn 2: 6 Whoever *c* to live in him must walk
2: 9 Anyone who *c* to be in the light

CLAP
Ps 47: 1 *C* your hands, all you nations;
Isa 55:12 will *c* their hands.

CLAY
Isa 45: 9 Does the *c* say to the potter,
64: 8 We are the *c,* you are the potter;
Jer 18: 6 "Like *c* in the hand of the potter,
La 4: 2 are now considered as pots of *c,*
Da 2:33 partly of iron and partly of baked *c.*
Ro 9:21 of the same lump of *c* some pottery
2Co 4: 7 we have this treasure in jars of *c*
2Ti 2:20 and *c;* some are for noble purposes

CLEAN
Lev 16:30 you will be *c* from all your sins.
Ps 24: 4 He who has *c* hands and a pure
Mt 12:44 the house unoccupied, swept *c*
23:25 You *c* the outside of the cup
Mk 7:19 Jesus declared all foods "*c.*")
Jn 13:10 to wash his feet; his whole body is *c*
15: 3 are already *c* because of the word
Ac 10:15 impure that God has made *c.*"
Ro 14:20 All food is *c,* but it is wrong

CLING (CLINGS)
Ro 12: 9 Hate what is evil; *c* to what is good.

CLINGS (CLING)
Ps 63: 8 My soul *c* to you;

CLOAK
2Ki 4:29 "Tuck your *c* into your belt,

CLOSE (CLOSER)
Ps 34:18 LORD is *c* to the brokenhearted
Isa 40:11 and carries them *c* to his heart;
Jer 30:21 himself to be *c* to me?'

CLOSER (CLOSE)
Ex 3: 5 "Do not come any *c,*" God said.
Pr 18:24 there is a friend who sticks *c*

CLOTHE (CLOTHED CLOTHES CLOTHING)
Ps 45: 3 *c* yourself with splendor
Isa 52: 1 *c* yourself with strength.
Ro 13:14 *c* yourselves with the Lord Jesus
Col 3:12 *c* yourselves with compassion,
1Pe 5: 5 *c* yourselves with humility

CLOTHED (CLOTHE)
Ps 30:11 removed my sackcloth and *c* me
Pr 31:25 She is *c* with strength and dignity;
Lk 24:49 until you have been *c* with power

CLOTHES (CLOTHE)
Mt 6:25 the body more important than *c?*
6:28 "And why do you worry about *c?*
Jn 11:44 Take off the grave *c* and let him go

CLOTHING (CLOTHE)
Dt 22: 5 A woman must not wear men's *c,*
Mt 7:15 They come to you in sheep's *c,*

CLOUD (CLOUDS)
Ex 13:21 them in a pillar of *c* to guide them
Isa 19: 1 See, the LORD rides on a swift *c*
Lk 21:27 of Man coming in a *c* with power
Heb 12: 1 by such a great *c* of witnesses,

CLOUDS (CLOUD)
Ps 104: 3 He makes the *c* his chariot
Da 7:13 coming with the *c* of heaven.
Mk 13:26 coming in *c* with great power
1Th 4:17 with them in the *c* to meet the Lord

CO-HEIRS* (INHERIT)
Ro 8:17 heirs of God and *c* with Christ,

COALS
Pr 25:22 you will heap burning *c* on his head
Ro 12:20 you will heap burning *c* on his head

COLD
Pr 25:25 Like *c* water to a weary soul
Mt 10:42 if anyone gives even a cup of *c* water
24:12 the love of most will grow *c,*

COMFORT (COMFORTED COMFORTS)
Ps 23: 4 rod and your staff, they *c* me.
119:52 and I find *c* in them.
119:76 May your unfailing love be my *c,*
Zec 1:17 and the LORD will again *c* Zion
1Co 14: 3 encouragement and *c.*
2Co 1: 4 so that we can *c* those
2: 7 you ought to forgive and *c* him,

COMFORTED (COMFORT)
Mt 5: 4 for they will be *c.*

COMFORTS* (COMFORT)
Job 29:25 I was like one who *c* mourners.
Isa 49:13 For the LORD *c* his people
51:12 "I, even I, am he who *c* you.
66:13 As a mother *c* her child,
2Co 1: 4 who *c* us in all our troubles,
7: 6 But God, who *c* the downcast,

COMMAND (COMMANDED COMMANDING COMMANDMENT COMMANDMENTS COMMANDS)
Ex 7: 2 You are to say everything I *c* you.
Nu 24:13 to go beyond the *c* of the LORD—
Dt 4: 2 Do not add to what I *c* you
30:16 For I *c* you today to love
32:46 so that you may *c* your children
Ps 91:11 For he will *c* his angels concerning
Pr 13:13 but he who respects a *c* is rewarded
Ecc 8: 2 Obey the king's *c,* I say,
Joel 2:11 mighty are those who obey his *c.*
Jn 14:15 love me, you will obey what I *c.*
15:12 My *c* is this: Love each other
1Co 14:37 writing to you is the Lord's *c.*
Gal 5:14 law is summed up in a single *c:*
1Ti 1: 5 goal of this *c* is love, which comes
Heb 11: 3 universe was formed at God's *c,*
1Jn 3:23 this is his *c:* to believe in the name
2Jn : 6 his *c* is that you walk in love.

COMMANDED (COMMAND)
Ps 33: 9 he *c,* and it stood firm.
148: 5 for he *c* and they were created.
Mt 28:20 to obey everything I have *c* you.
1Co 9:14 Lord has *c* that those who preach
1Jn 3:23 and to love one another as he *c* us.

COMMANDING (COMMAND)
2Ti 2: 4 he wants to please his *c* officer.

COMMANDMENT (COMMAND)
Jos 22: 5 But be very careful to keep the *c*
Mt 22:38 This is the first and greatest *c.*
Jn 13:34 "A new *c* I give you: Love one
Ro 7:12 and the *c* is holy, righteous
Eph 6: 2 which is the first *c* with a promise

COMMANDMENTS (COMMAND)
Ex 20: 6 who love me and keep my *c.*
34:28 of the covenant—the Ten *C.*
Ecc 12:13 Fear God and keep his *c,*
Mt 5:19 one of the least of these *c*
22:40 the Prophets hang on these two *c.*"

COMMANDS (COMMAND)
Dt 7: 9 those who love him and keep his *c.*
11:27 the blessing if you obey the *c*
Ps 112: 1 who finds great delight in his *c.*
119:47 for I delight in your *c*
119:86 All your *c* are trustworthy;
119:98 Your *c* make me wiser
119:127 Because I love your *c*
119:143 but your *c* are my delight.
119:172 for all your *c* are righteous.
Pr 3: 1 but keep my *c* in your heart,
6:23 For these *c* are a lamp,
10: 8 The wise in heart accept *c,*
Da 9: 4 all who love him and obey his *c,*
Mt 5:19 teaches these *c* will be called great
Jn 14:21 Whoever has my *c* and obeys them,
Ac 17:30 but now he *c* all people everywhere
1Co 7:19 Keeping God's *c* is what counts.
1Jn 5: 3 And his *c* are not burdensome,
5: 3 This is love for God: to obey his *c.*

COMMEND (COMMENDED COMMENDS)
Ecc 8:15 So I *c* the enjoyment of life,
Ro 13: 3 do what is right and he will *c* you.
1Pe 2:14 and to *c* those who do right.

COMMENDED (COMMEND)
Heb 11:39 These were all *c* for their faith,

COMMENDS (COMMEND)
2Co 10:18 not the one who *c* himself who is

COMMIT (COMMITS COMMITTED)
Ex 20:14 "You shall not *c* adultery.
Ps 37: 5 *C* your way to the LORD;
Mt 5:27 that it was said, 'Do not *c* adultery.'
Lk 23:46 into your hands I *c* my spirit."
Ac 20:32 I *c* you to God and to the word
1Co 10: 8 We should not *c* sexual immorality,
1Pe 4:19 to God's will should *c* themselves

COMMITS (COMMIT)
Pr 6:32 man who *c* adultery lacks
29:22 a hot-tempered one *c* many sins
Mt 19: 9 marries another woman *c* adultery

COMMITTED (COMMIT)
Nu 5: 7 and must confess the sin he has *c.*
1Ki 8:61 But your hearts must be fully *c*
2Ch 16: 9 those whose hearts are fully *c*
Mt 5:28 lustfully has already *c* adultery
2Co 5:19 And he has *c* to us the message
1Pe 2:22 "He *c* no sin,

COMMON
Pr 22: 2 Rich and poor have this in *c:*
1Co 10:13 has seized you except what is *c*
2Co 6:14 and wickedness have in *c?*

COMPANION (COMPANIONS)
Pr 13:20 but a *c* of fools suffers harm.
28: 7 a *c* of gluttons disgraces his father.
29: 3 *c* of prostitutes squanders his

COMPANIONS (COMPANION)
Pr 18:24 A man of many *c* may come to ruin

COMPANY
Pr 24: 1 do not desire their *c;*
Jer 15:17 I never sat in the *c* of revelers,
1Co 15:33 "Bad *c* corrupts good character."

COMPARED (COMPARING)
Eze 31: 2 Who can be *c* with you in majesty?
Php 3: 8 I consider everything a loss *c*

COMPARING* (COMPARED)
Ro 8:18 present sufferings are not worth *c*
2Co 8: 8 the sincerity of your love by *c* it
Gal 6: 4 without *c* himself to somebody else

COMPASSION (COMPASSIONATE COMPASSIONS)
Ex 33:19 I will have *c* on whom I will have *c.*
Ne 9:19 of your great *c* you did not
9:28 in your *c* you delivered them time
Ps 51: 1 according to your great *c*
103: 4 and crowns you with love and *c.*
103:13 As a father has *c* on his children,
145: 9 he has *c* on all he has made.
Isa 49:13 and will have *c* on his afflicted ones
49:15 and have no *c* on the child she has
Hos 2:19 in love and *c.*
11: 8 all my *c* is aroused.
Jnh 3: 9 with *c* turn from his fierce anger
Mt 9:36 When he saw the crowds, he had *c*
Mk 8: 2 "I have *c* for these people;
Ro 9:15 and I will have *c* on whom I have *c*
Col 3:12 clothe yourselves with *c,* kindness,
Jas 5:11 The Lord is full of *c* and mercy.

COMPASSIONATE (COMPASSION)
Ne 9:17 gracious and *c,* slow to anger
Ps 103: 8 The LORD is *c* and gracious,
112: 4 the gracious and *c* and righteous
Eph 4:32 Be kind and *c* to one another,
1Pe 3: 8 love as brothers, be *c* and humble.

COMPASSIONS* (COMPASSION)
La 3:22 for his *c* never fail.

COMPELLED (COMPELS)
Ac 20:22 "And now, *c* by the Spirit,
1Co 9:16 I cannot boast, for I am *c* to preach.

COMPELS (COMPELLED)
2Co 5:14 For Christ's love *c* us, because we

COMPETENCE* (COMPETENT)
2Co 3: 5 but our *c* comes from God.

COMPETENT* (COMPETENCE)
Ro 15:14 and *c* to instruct one another.
1Co 6: 2 are you not *c* to judge trivial cases?
2Co 3: 5 Not that we are *c* in ourselves
3: 6 He has made us *c* as ministers

COMPETES*
1Co 9:25 Everyone who *c* in the games goes
2Ti 2: 5 Similarly, if anyone *c* as an athlete,
2: 5 unless he *c* according to the rules.

COMPLACENT
Am 6: 1 Woe to you who are *c* in Zion,

COMPLAINING*
Php 2:14 Do everything without *c* or arguing

COMPLETE
Jn 15:11 and that your joy may be *c*.
16:24 will receive, and your joy will be *c*.
17:23 May they be brought to *c* unity
Ac 20:24 *c* the task the Lord Jesus has given
Php 2: 2 then make my joy *c*
Col 4:17 to it that you *c* the work you have
Jas 1: 4 so that you may be mature and *c*,
2:22 his faith was made *c* by what he did

CONCEAL (CONCEALED CONCEALS)
Ps 40:10 I do not *c* your love and your truth
Pr 25: 2 It is the glory of God to *c* a matter;

CONCEALED (CONCEAL)
Jer 16:17 nor is their sin *c* from my eyes.
Mt 10:26 There is nothing *c* that will not be
Mk 4:22 and whatever is *c* is meant

CONCEALS (CONCEAL)
Pr 28:13 He who *c* his sins does not prosper,

CONCEITED
Ro 12:16 Do not be *c*.
Gal 5:26 Let us not become *c*, provoking
1Ti 6: 4 he is *c* and understands nothing.

CONCEIVED
Mt 1:20 what is *c* in her is from the Holy
1Co 2: 9 no mind has *c*

CONCERN (CONCERNED)
Eze 36:21 I had *c* for my holy name, which
1Co 7:32 I would like you to be free from *c*.
12:25 that its parts should have equal *c*
2Co 11:28 of my *c* for all the churches.

CONCERNED (CONCERN)
Jnh 4:10 "You have been *c* about this vine,
1Co 7:32 An unmarried man is *c* about

CONDEMN (CONDEMNATION CONDEMNED CONDEMNING CONDEMNS)
Job 40: 8 Would you *c* me to justify yourself?
Isa 50: 9 Who is he that will *c* me?
Lk 6:37 Do not *c*, and you will not be
Jn 3:17 Son into the world to *c* the world,
12:48 very word which I spoke will *c* him
Ro 2:27 yet obeys the law will *c* you who,
1Jn 3:20 presence whenever our hearts *c* us.

CONDEMNATION (CONDEMN)
Ro 5:18 of one trespass was *c* for all men,
8: 1 there is now no *c* for those who are

CONDEMNED (CONDEMN)
Ps 34:22 no one will be *c* who takes refuge
Mt 12:37 and by your words you will be *c*."
23:33 How will you escape being *c* to hell
Jn 3:18 Whoever believes in him is not *c*,
5:24 has eternal life and will not be *c*;
16:11 prince of this world now stands *c*.
Ro 14:23 But the man who has doubts is *c*
1Co 11:32 disciplined so that we will not be *c*
Heb 11: 7 By his faith he *c* the world

CONDEMNING (CONDEMN)
Pr 17:15 the guilty and *c* the innocent—
Ro 2: 1 judge the other, you are *c* yourself,

CONDEMNS (CONDEMN)
Ro 8:34 Who is he that *c*? Christ Jesus,
2Co 3: 9 the ministry that *c* men is glorious,

CONDUCT
Pr 10:23 A fool finds pleasure in evil *c*,
20:11 by whether his *c* is pure and right.
21: 8 but the *c* of the innocent is upright.
Ecc 6: 8 how to *c* himself before others?
Jer 4:18 "Your own *c* and actions
17:10 to reward a man according to his *c*,
Eze 7: 3 I will judge you according to your *c*
Php 1:27 *c* yourselves in a manner worthy
1Ti 3:15 to *c* themselves in God's household

CONFESS (CONFESSION)
Lev 16:21 and *c* over it all the wickedness
26:40 " 'But if they will *c* their sins
Nu 5: 7 must *c* the sin he has committed.
Ps 38:18 I *c* my iniquity;
Ro 10: 9 That if you *c* with your mouth,
Php 2:11 every tongue *c* that Jesus Christ is
Jas 5:16 Therefore *c* your sins to each other
1Jn 1: 9 If we *c* our sins, he is faithful

CONFESSION (CONFESS)
Ezr 10:11 Now make *c* to the LORD,
2Co 9:13 obedience that accompanies your *c*

CONFIDENCE
Ps 71: 5 my *c* since my youth.
Pr 3:26 for the LORD will be your *c*
11:13 A gossip betrays a *c*,
25: 9 do not betray another man's *c*,
31:11 Her husband has full *c* in her
Isa 32:17 will be quietness and *c* forever.
Jer 17: 7 whose *c* is in him.
Php 3: 3 and who put no *c* in the flesh—
Heb 3:14 till the end the *c* we had at first.
4:16 the throne of grace with *c*,
10:19 since we have *c* to enter the Most
10:35 So do not throw away your *c*;
1Jn 5:14 This is the *c* we have

CONFORM* (CONFORMED)
Ro 12: 2 Do not *c* any longer to the pattern
1Pe 1:14 do not *c* to the evil desires you had

CONFORMED (CONFORM)
Ro 8:29 predestined to be *c* to the likeness

CONQUERORS
Ro 8:37 than *c* through him who loved us.

CONSCIENCE (CONSCIENCES)
Ro 13: 5 punishment but also because of *c*.
1Co 8: 7 since their *c* is weak, it is defiled.
8:12 in this way and wound their weak *c*
10:25 without raising questions of *c*,
10:29 freedom be judged by another's *c*?
Heb 10:22 to cleanse us from a guilty *c*
1Pe 3:16 and respect, keeping a clear *c*,

CONSCIENCES* (CONSCIENCE)
Ro 2:15 their *c* also bearing witness,
1Ti 4: 2 whose *c* have been seared
Tit 1:15 their minds and *c* are corrupted.
Heb 9:14 cleanse our *c* from acts that lead

CONSCIOUS*
Ro 3:20 through the law we become *c* of sin
1Pe 2:19 of unjust suffering because he is *c*

CONSECRATE (CONSECRATED)
Ex 13: 2 "*C* to me every firstborn male.
Lev 20: 7 " '*C* yourselves and be holy,

CONSECRATED (CONSECRATE)
Ex 29:43 and the place will be *c* by my glory.
1Ti 4: 5 because it is *c* by the word of God

CONSIDER (CONSIDERATE CONSIDERED CONSIDERS)
1Sa 12:24 *c* what great things he has done
Job 37:14 stop and *c* God's wonders.
Ps 8: 3 When I *c* your heavens,
107:43 and *c* the great love of the LORD.
143: 5 and *c* what your hands have done.
Lk 12:24 *C* the ravens: They do not sow
12:27 about the rest? "*C* how the lilies
Php 2: 3 but in humility *c* others better
3: 8 I *c* everything a loss compared
Heb 10:24 And let us *c* how we may spur one
Jas 1: 2 *C* it pure joy, my brothers,

CONSIDERATE* (CONSIDER)
Tit 3: 2 to be peaceable and *c*,
Jas 3:17 then peace-loving, *c*, submissive,
1Pe 2:18 only to those who are good and *c*,
3: 7 in the same way be *c* as you live

CONSIDERED (CONSIDER)
Job 1: 8 "Have you *c* my servant Job?
2: 3 "Have you *c* my servant Job?
Ps 44:22 we are *c* as sheep to be slaughtered.
Isa 53: 4 yet we *c* him stricken by God,
Ro 8:36 we are *c* as sheep to be slaughtered

CONSIDERS (CONSIDER)
Pr 31:16 She *c* a field and buys it;
Ro 14: 5 One man *c* one day more sacred
Jas 1:26 If anyone *c* himself religious

CONSIST
Lk 12:15 a man's life does not *c*

CONSOLATION
Ps 94:19 your *c* brought joy to my soul.

CONSTRUCTIVE*
1Co 10:23 but not everything is *c*.

CONSUME (CONSUMING)
Jn 2:17 "Zeal for your house will *c* me."

CONSUMING (CONSUME)
Dt 4:24 For the LORD your God is a *c* fire,
Heb 12:29 and awe, for our "God is a *c* fire."

CONTAIN
1Ki 8:27 the highest heaven, cannot *c* you.
2Pe 3:16 His letters *c* some things that are

CONTAMINATES*
2Co 7: 1 from everything that *c* body

CONTEMPT
Pr 14:31 He who oppresses the poor shows *c*
17: 5 He who mocks the poor shows *c*
18: 3 When wickedness comes, so does *c*
Da 12: 2 others to shame and everlasting *c*.
Ro 2: 4 Or do you show *c* for the riches
Gal 4:14 you did not treat me with *c*
1Th 5:20 do not treat prophecies with *c*.

CONTEND (CONTENDING)
Jude : 3 you to *c* for the faith that was once

CONTENDING* (CONTEND)
Php 1:27 *c* as one man for the faith

CONTENT (CONTENTMENT)
Pr 13:25 The righteous eat to their hearts' *c*,
Php 4:11 to be *c* whatever the circumstances
4:12 I have learned the secret of being *c*
1Ti 6: 8 and clothing, we will be *c* with that.
Heb 13: 5 and be *c* with what you have,

CONTENTMENT (CONTENT)
1Ti 6: 6 But godliness with *c* is great gain.

CONTINUAL (CONTINUE)
Pr 15:15 but the cheerful heart has a *c* feast.

CONTINUE (CONTINUAL)
Php 2:12 *c* to work out your salvation
2Ti 3:14 *c* in what you have learned
1Jn 5:18 born of God does not *c* to sin;
Rev 22:11 and let him who is holy *c* to be holy
22:11 let him who does right *c* to do right;

CONTRITE*
Ps 51:17 a broken and *c* heart,
Isa 57:15 also with him who is *c* and lowly
57:15 and to revive the heart of the *c*.
66: 2 he who is humble and *c* in spirit,

CONTROL (CONTROLLED SELF-CONTROL SELF-CONTROLLED)
Pr 29:11 a wise man keeps himself under *c*.
1Co 7: 9 But if they cannot *c* themselves,
7:37 but has *c* over his own will,
1Th 4: 4 you should learn to *c* his own body

CONTROLLED (CONTROL)
Ps 32: 9 but must be *c* by bit and bridle
Ro 8: 6 but the mind *c* by the Spirit is life
8: 8 Those *c* by the sinful nature cannot

CONTROVERSIES
Tit 3: 9 But avoid foolish *c* and genealogies

CONVERSATION
Col 4: 6 Let your *c* be always full of grace,

CONVERT
1Ti 3: 6 He must not be a recent *c*,

CONVICT
Jn 16: 8 he will *c* the world of guilt in regard

CONVINCED (CONVINCING)
Ro 8:38 For I am *c* that neither death
2Ti 1:12 and am *c* that he is able
3:14 have learned and have become *c*

CONVINCING* (CONVINCED)
Ac 1: 3 and gave many *c* proofs that he was

CORNELIUS*
Roman to whom Peter preached; first Gentile Christian (Ac 10).

CORNERSTONE (STONE)
Isa 28:16 a precious *c* for a sure foundation;
Eph 2:20 Christ Jesus himself as the chief *c.*
1Pe 2: 6 a chosen and precious *c,*

CORRECT (CORRECTING CORRECTION CORRECTS)
2Ti 4: 2 *c,* rebuke and encourage—

CORRECTING* (CORRECT)
2Ti 3:16 *c* and training in righteousness,

CORRECTION (CORRECT)
Pr 10:17 whoever ignores *c* leads others
12: 1 but he who hates *c* is stupid.
15: 5 whoever heeds *c* shows prudence.
15:10 he who hates *c* will die.
29:15 The rod of *c* imparts wisdom,

CORRECTS* (CORRECT)
Job 5:17 "Blessed is the man whom God *c;*
Pr 9: 7 Whoever *c* a mocker invites insult;

CORRUPT (CORRUPTS)
Ge 6:11 Now the earth was *c* in God's sight

CORRUPTS* (CORRUPT)
Ecc 7: 7 and a bribe *c* the heart.
1Co 15:33 "Bad company *c* good character."
Jas 3: 6 It *c* the whole person, sets

COST
Pr 4: 7 Though it *c* all you have, get
Isa 55: 1 milk without money and without *c.*
Rev 21: 6 to drink without *c* from the spring

COUNSEL (COUNSELOR)
1Ki 22: 5 "First seek the *c* of the LORD."
Pr 15:22 Plans fail for lack of *c,*
Rev 3:18 I *c* you to buy from me gold refined

COUNSELOR (COUNSEL)
Isa 9: 6 Wonderful *C,* Mighty God,
Jn 14:16 he will give you another *C* to be
14:26 But the *C,* the Holy Spirit,

COUNT (COUNTING COUNTS)
Ro 4: 8 whose sin the Lord will never *c*
6:11 *c* yourselves dead to sin

COUNTING (COUNT)
2Co 5:19 not *c* men's sins against them.

COUNTRY
Jn 4:44 prophet has no honor in his own *c.)*

COUNTS (COUNT)
Jn 6:63 The Spirit gives life; the flesh *c*
1Co 7:19 God's commands is what *c.*
Gal 5: 6 only thing that *c* is faith expressing

COURAGE (COURAGEOUS)
Ac 23:11 "Take *c!* As you have testified
1Co 16:13 stand firm in the faith; be men of *c;*

COURAGEOUS (COURAGE)
Dt 31: 6 Be strong and *c.*
Jos 1: 6 and *c,* because you will lead these

COURSE
Ps 19: 5 a champion rejoicing to run his *c.*
Pr 15:21 of understanding keeps a straight *c.*

COURTS
Ps 84:10 Better is one day in your *c*
100: 4 and his *c* with praise;

COVENANT (COVENANTS)
Ge 9: 9 "I now establish my *c* with you
Ex 19: 5 if you obey me fully and keep my *c,*
1Ch 16:15 He remembers his *c* forever,
Job 31: 1 "I made a *c* with my eyes
Jer 31:31 "when I will make a new *c*
1Co 11:25 "This cup is the new *c* in my blood;
Gal 4:24 One *c* is from Mount Sinai
Heb 9:15 Christ is the mediator of a new *c,*

COVENANTS (COVENANT)
Ro 9: 4 theirs the divine glory, the *c,*
Gal 4:24 for the women represent two *c.*

COVER (COVER-UP COVERED COVERS)
Ps 91: 4 He will *c* you with his feathers,
Jas 5:20 and *c* over a multitude of sins.

COVER-UP (COVER)
1Pe 2:16 but do not use your freedom as a *c*

COVERED (COVER)
Ps 32: 1 whose sins are *c.*
Isa 6: 2 With two wings they *c* their faces,
Ro 4: 7 whose sins are *c.*
1Co 11: 4 with his head *c* dishonors his head.

COVERS (COVER)
Pr 10:12 but love *c* over all wrongs.
1Pe 4: 8 love *c* over a multitude of sins.

COVET
Ex 20:17 You shall not *c* your neighbor's
Ro 13: 9 "Do not steal," "Do not *c,*"

COWARDLY*
Rev 21: 8 But the *c,* the unbelieving, the vile,

CRAFTINESS (CRAFTY)
1Co 3:19 "He catches the wise in their *c*";

CRAFTY (CRAFTINESS)
Ge 3: 1 the serpent was more *c* than any
2Co 12:16 *c* fellow that I am, I caught you

CRAVE
Pr 23: 3 Do not *c* his delicacies,
1Pe 2: 2 newborn babies, *c* pure spiritual

CREATE (CREATED CREATION CREATOR)
Ps 51:10 *C* in me a pure heart, O God,
Isa 45:18 he did not *c* it to be empty,

CREATED (CREATE)
Ge 1: 1 In the beginning God *c* the heavens
1:21 God *c* the great creatures of the sea
1:27 So God *c* man in his own image,
Ps 148: 5 for he commanded and they were *c*
Isa 42: 5 he who *c* the heavens and stretched
Ro 1:25 and served *c* things rather
1Co 11: 9 neither was man *c* for woman,
Col 1:16 For by him all things were *c:*
1Ti 4: 4 For everything God *c* is good,
Rev 10: 6 who *c* the heavens and all that is

CREATION (CREATE)
Mk 16:15 and preach the good news to all *c.*
Jn 17:24 me before the *c* of the world.
Ro 8:19 The *c* waits in eager expectation
8:39 depth, nor anything else in all *c,*
2Co 5:17 he is a new *c;* the old has gone,
Col 1:15 God, the firstborn over all *c.*
1Pe 1:20 chosen before the *c* of the world,
Rev 13: 8 slain from the *c* of the world.

CREATOR (CREATE)
Ge 14:22 God Most High, *C* of heaven
Ro 1:25 created things rather than the *C*—

CREATURE (CREATURES)
Lev 17:11 For the life of a *c* is in the blood,

CREATURES (CREATURE)
Ge 6:19 bring into the ark two of all living *c,*
Ps 104:24 the earth is full of your *c.*

CREDIT (CREDITED)
Ro 4:24 to whom God will *c* righteousness
1Pe 2:20 it to your *c* if you receive a beating

CREDITED (CREDIT)
Ge 15: 6 and he *c* it to him as righteousness.
Ro 4: 5 his faith is *c* as righteousness.
Gal 3: 6 and it was *c* to him as righteousness
Jas 2:23 and it was *c* to him as righteousness

CRIED (CRY)
Ps 18: 6 I *c* to my God for help.

CRIMSON
Isa 1:18 though they are red as *c,*

CRIPPLED
Mk 9:45 better for you to enter life *c*

CRITICISM
2Co 8:20 We want to avoid any *c*

CROOKED
Pr 10: 9 he who takes *c* paths will be found
Php 2:15 children of God without fault in a *c*

CROSS
Mt 10:38 and anyone who does not take his *c*
Lk 9:23 take up his *c* daily and follow me.
Ac 2:23 to death by nailing him to the *c.*
1Co 1:17 lest the *c* of Christ be emptied
Gal 6:14 in the *c* of our Lord Jesus Christ,
Php 2: 8 even death on a *c!*
Col 1:20 through his blood, shed on the *c.*
2:14 he took it away, nailing it to the *c.*
2:15 triumphing over them by the *c.*
Heb 12: 2 set before him endured the *c,*

CROWD
Ex 23: 2 Do not follow the *c* in doing wrong.

CROWN (CROWNED CROWNS)
Pr 4: 9 present you with a *c* of splendor."
10: 6 Blessings *c* the head
12: 4 noble character is her husband's *c,*
17: 6 Children's children are a *c*
Isa 61: 3 to bestow on them a *c* of beauty
Zec 9:16 like jewels in a *c.*
Mt 27:29 then twisted together a *c* of thorns
1Co 9:25 it to get a *c* that will last forever.
2Ti 4: 8 store for me the *c* of righteousness,
Rev 2:10 and I will give you the *c* of life.

CROWNED (CROWN)
Ps 8: 5 and *c* him with glory and honor.
Pr 14:18 the prudent are *c* with knowledge.
Heb 2: 7 you *c* him with glory and honor

CROWNS (CROWN)
Rev 4:10 They lay their *c* before the throne
19:12 and on his head are many *c.*

CRUCIFIED (CRUCIFY)
Mt 20:19 to be mocked and flogged and *c.*
27:38 Two robbers were *c* with him,
Lk 24: 7 be *c* and on the third day be raised
Jn 19:18 Here they *c* him, and with him two
Ac 2:36 whom you *c,* both Lord and Christ
Ro 6: 6 For we know that our old self was *c*
1Co 1:23 but we preach Christ *c:* a stumbling
2: 2 except Jesus Christ and him *c.*
Gal 2:20 I have been *c* with Christ
5:24 Christ Jesus have *c* the sinful

CRUCIFY (CRUCIFIED CRUCIFYING)
Mt 27:22 They all answered, "*C* him!" "Why
27:31 Then they led him away to *c* him.

CRUCIFYING* (CRUCIFY)
Heb 6: 6 to their loss they are *c* the Son

CRUSH (CRUSHED)
Ge 3:15 he will *c* your head,
Isa 53:10 it was the LORD's will to *c* him
Ro 16:20 The God of peace will soon *c* Satan

CRUSHED (CRUSH)
Ps 34:18 and saves those who are *c* in spirit.
Isa 53: 5 he was *c* for our iniquities;
2Co 4: 8 not *c;* perplexed, but not in despair;

CRY (CRIED)
Ps 34:15 and his ears are attentive to their *c;*
40: 1 he turned to me and heard my *c.*
130: 1 Out of the depths I *c* to you,

CUP
Ps 23: 5 my *c* overflows.
Mt 10:42 if anyone gives even a *c* of cold water
23:25 You clean the outside of the *c*
26:39 may this *c* be taken from me.
1Co 11:25 after supper he took the *c,* saying,

CURSE (CURSED)
Dt 11:26 before you today a blessing and a *c*
21:23 hung on a tree is under God's *c.*
Lk 6:28 bless those who *c* you, pray
Gal 3:13 of the law by becoming a *c* for us,
Rev 22: 3 No longer will there be any *c.*

CURSED (CURSE)
Ge 3:17 "*C* is the ground because of you;
Dt 27:15 "*C* is the man who carves an image
27:16 "*C* is the man who dishonors his
27:17 "*C* is the man who moves his
27:18 "*C* is the man who leads the blind
27:19 *C* is the man who withholds justice
27:20 "*C* is the man who sleeps
27:21 "*C* is the man who has sexual
27:22 "*C* is the man who sleeps
27:23 "*C* is the man who sleeps
27:24 "*C* is the man who kills his
27:25 "*C* is the man who accepts a bribe
27:26 "*C* is the man who does not uphold
Ro 9: 3 I could wish that I myself were *c*
Gal 3:10 "*C* is everyone who does not

CURTAIN
Ex 26:33 The *c* will separate the Holy Place
Lk 23:45 the *c* of the temple was torn in two.
Heb 10:20 opened for us through the *c,*

CYMBAL*
1Co 13: 1 a resounding gong or a clanging *c.*

DANCE (DANCING)
Ecc 3: 4 a time to mourn and a time to *d,*
Mt 11:17 and you did not *d;*

DANCING (DANCE)
Ps 30:11 You turned my wailing into *d;*

Ps 149: 3 Let them praise his name with *d*

DANGER
Pr 27:12 The prudent see *d* and take refuge,
Ro 8:35 famine or nakedness or *d* or sword?

DANIEL
Hebrew exile to Babylon, name changed to Belteshazzar (Da 1:6-7). Refused to eat unclean food (Da 1:8-21). Interpreted Nebuchadnezzar's dreams (Da 2; 4), writing on the wall (Da 5). Thrown into lion's den (Da 6). Visions of (Da 7-12).

DARK (DARKNESS)
Job 34:22 There is no *d* place, no deep
Pr 31:15 She gets up while it is still *d;*
Ro 2:19 a light for those who are in the *d,*
2Pe 1:19 as to a light shining in a *d* place,

DARKNESS (DARK)
Ge 1: 4 he separated the light from the *d.*
2Sa 22:29 the LORD turns my *d* into light.
Jn 3:19 but men loved *d* instead of light
2Co 6:14 fellowship can light have with *d?*
Eph 5: 8 For you were once *d,* but now you
1Pe 2: 9 out of *d* into his wonderful light.
1Jn 1: 5 in him there is no *d* at all.
2: 9 but hates his brother is still in the *d.*

DAUGHTERS
Joel 2:28 sons and *d* will prophesy,

DAVID
Son of Jesse (Ru 4:17-22; 1Ch 2:13-15), ancestor of Jesus (Mt 1:1-17; Lk 3:31).

Anointed king by Samuel (1Sa 16:1-13). Musician to Saul (1Sa 16:14-23; 18:10). Killed Goliath (1Sa 17). Relation with Jonathan (1Sa 18:1-4; 19-20; 23:16-18; 2Sa 1). Disfavor of Saul (1Sa 18:6-23:29). Spared Saul's life (1Sa 24; 26). Among Philistines (1Sa 21:10-14; 27-30). Lament for Saul and Jonathan (2Sa 1).

Anointed king of Judah (2Sa 2:1-11); of Israel (2Sa 5:1-4; 1Ch 11:1-3). Promised eternal dynasty (2Sa 7; 1Ch 17; Ps 132). Adultery with Bathsheba (2Sa 11-12). Absalom's revolt (2Sa 14-18). Last words (2Sa 23:1-7). Death (1Ki 2:10-12; 1Ch 29:28).

DAWN
Ps 37: 6 your righteousness shine like the *d,*
Pr 4:18 is like the first gleam of *d,*

DAY (DAYS)
Ge 1: 5 God called the light "*d,*"
Ex 20: 8 "Remember the Sabbath *d*
Lev 23:28 because it is the *D* of Atonement,
Nu 14:14 before them in a pillar of cloud by *d*
Jos 1: 8 meditate on it *d* and night,
Ps 84:10 Better is one *d* in your courts
96: 2 proclaim his salvation *d* after *d.*
118:24 This is the *d* the LORD has made;
Pr 27: 1 not know what a *d* may bring forth.
Joel 2:31 and dreadful *d* of the LORD.
Ob :15 The *d* of the LORD is near
Lk 11: 3 Give us each *d* our daily bread.
Ac 17:11 examined the Scriptures every *d*
2Co 4:16 we are being renewed *d* by *d.*
1Th 5: 2 for you know very well that the *d*
2Pe 3: 8 With the Lord a *d* is like

DAYS (DAY)
Dt 17:19 he is to read it all the *d,* of his life
Ps 23: 6 all the *d* of my life,
90:10 The length of our *d* is seventy years
Ecc 12: 1 Creator in the *d* of your youth,
Joel 2:29 I will pour out my Spirit in those *d.*
Mic 4: 1 In the last *d*
Heb 1: 2 in these last *d* he has spoken to us
2Pe 3: 3 that in the last *d* scoffers will come,

DEACONS
1Ti 3: 8 *D,* likewise, are to be men worthy

DEAD (DIE)
Dt 18:11 or spiritist or who consults the *d.*
Mt 28: 7 'He has risen from the *d*
Ro 6:11 count yourselves *d* to sin
Eph 2: 1 you were *d* in your transgressions
1Th 4:16 and the *d* in Christ will rise first.
Jas 2:17 is not accompanied by action, is *d.*
2:26 so faith without deeds is *d.*

DEATH (DIE)
Nu 35:16 the murderer shall be put to *d.*
Ps 23: 4 the valley of the shadow of *d,*
116:15 is the *d* of his saints.
Pr 8:36 all who hate me love *d.*"
14:12 but in the end it leads to *d.*
Ecc 7: 2 for *d* is the destiny of every man;
Isa 25: 8 he will swallow up *d* forever.
53:12 he poured out his life unto *d,*
Jn 5:24 he has crossed over from *d* to life.
Ro 5:12 and in this way *d* came to all men,
6:23 For the wages of sin is *d,*
8:13 put to *d* the misdeeds of the body,
1Co 15:21 For since *d* came through a man,
15:55 Where, O *d,* is your sting?"
Rev 1:18 And I hold the keys of *d* and Hades
20: 6 The second *d* has no power
20:14 The lake of fire is the second *d.*
21: 4 There will be no more *d*

DEBAUCHERY
Ro 13:13 not in sexual immorality and *d,*
Eph 5:18 drunk on wine, which leads to *d.*

DEBORAH
Prophetess who led Israel to victory over Canaanites (Jdg 4-5).

DEBT (DEBTORS DEBTS)
Ro 13: 8 Let no *d* remain outstanding,
13: 8 continuing *d* to love one another,

DEBTORS (DEBT)
Mt 6:12 as we also have forgiven our *d.*

DEBTS (DEBT)
Dt 15: 1 seven years you must cancel *d.*
Mt 6:12 Forgive us our *d,*

DECAY
Ps 16:10 will you let your Holy One see *d.*
Ac 2:27 will you let your Holy One see *d.*

DECEIT (DECEIVE)
Mk 7:22 greed, malice, *d,* lewdness, envy,
1Pe 2: 1 yourselves of all malice and all *d,*
2:22 and no *d* was found in his mouth."

DECEITFUL (DECEIVE)
Jer 17: 9 The heart is *d* above all things
2Co 11:13 men are false apostles, *d* workmen,

DECEITFULNESS (DECEIVE)
Mk 4:19 the *d* of wealth and the desires
Heb 3:13 of you may be hardened by sin's *d.*

DECEIVE (DECEIT DECEITFUL DECEITFULNESS DECEIVED DECEIVES DECEPTIVE)
Lev 19:11 " 'Do not *d* one another.
Pr 14: 5 A truthful witness does not *d,*
Mt 24: 5 'I am the Christ,' and will *d* many.
Ro 16:18 and flattery they *d* the minds
1Co 3:18 Do not *d* yourselves.
Eph 5: 6 Let no one *d* you with empty words
Jas 1:22 to the word, and so *d* yourselves.
1Jn 1: 8 we *d* ourselves and the truth is not

DECEIVED (DECEIVE)
Ge 3:13 "The serpent *d* me, and I ate."
Gal 6: 7 Do not be *d:* God cannot be
1Ti 2:14 And Adam was not the one *d;*
2Ti 3:13 to worse, deceiving and being *d.*
Jas 1:16 Don't be *d,* my dear brothers.

DECEIVES (DECEIVE)
Gal 6: 3 when he is nothing, he *d* himself.
Jas 1:26 he *d* himself and his religion is

DECENCY*
1Ti 2: 9 women to dress modestly, with *d*

DECEPTIVE (DECEIVE)
Pr 31:30 Charm is *d,* and beauty is fleeting;
Col 2: 8 through hollow and *d* philosophy,

DECLARE (DECLARED DECLARING)
1Ch 16:24 *D* his glory among the nations,
Ps 19: 1 The heavens *d* the glory of God;
96: 3 *D* his glory among the nations,
Isa 42: 9 and new things I *d;*

DECLARED (DECLARE)
Mk 7:19 Jesus *d* all foods "clean.")
Ro 2:13 the law who will be *d* righteous.
3:20 no one will be *d* righteous

DECLARING (DECLARE)
Ps 71: 8 *d* your splendor all day long.
Ac 2:11 we hear them *d* the wonders

DECREED (DECREES)
La 3:37 happen if the Lord has not *d* it?
Lk 22:22 Son of Man will go as it has been *d,*

DECREES (DECREED)
Lev 10:11 Israelites all the *d* the LORD has
Ps 119:112 My heart is set on keeping your *d*

DEDICATE (DEDICATION)
Nu 6:12 He must *d* himself to the LORD
Pr 20:25 for a man to *d* something rashly

DEDICATION (DEDICATE)
1Ti 5:11 sensual desires overcome their *d*

DEED (DEEDS)
Col 3:17 you do, whether in word or *d,*

DEEDS (DEED)
1Sa 2: 3 and by him *d* are weighed.
Ps 65: 5 with awesome *d* of righteousness,
66: 3 "How awesome are your *d!*
78: 4 the praiseworthy *d* of the LORD,
86:10 you are great and do marvelous *d;*
92: 4 For you make me glad by your *d,*
111: 3 Glorious and majestic are his *d,*
Hab 3: 2 I stand in awe of your *d,* O LORD.
Mt 5:16 that they may see your good *d*
Ac 26:20 prove their repentance by their *d.*
Jas 2:14 claims to have faith but has no *d?*
2:20 faith without *d* is useless?
1Pe 2:12 they may see your good *d*

DEEP (DEPTH)
1Co 2:10 all things, even the *d* things
1Ti 3: 9 hold of the *d* truths of the faith

DEER
Ps 42: 1 As the *d* pants for streams of water,

DEFEND (DEFENSE)
Ps 74:22 Rise up, O God, and *d* your cause;
Pr 31: 9 *d* the rights of the poor and needy
Jer 50:34 He will vigorously *d* their cause

DEFENSE (DEFEND)
Ps 35:23 Awake, and rise to my *d!*
Php 1:16 here for the *d* of the gospel.
1Jn 2: 1 speaks to the Father in our *d*—

DEFERRED*
Pr 13:12 Hope *d* makes the heart sick,

DEFILE (DEFILED)
Da 1: 8 Daniel resolved not to *d* himself

DEFILED (DEFILE)
Isa 24: 5 The earth is *d* by its people;

DEFRAUD
Lev 19:13 Do not *d* your neighbor or rob him.

DEITY*
Col 2: 9 of the *D* lives in bodily form,

DELIGHT (DELIGHTS)
1Sa 15:22 "Does the LORD *d*
Ps 1: 2 But his *d* is in the law of the LORD
16: 3 in whom is all my *d.*
35: 9 and *d* in his salvation.
37: 4 *D* yourself in the LORD
43: 4 to God, my joy and my *d.*
51:16 You do not *d* in sacrifice,
119:77 for your law is my *d.*
Pr 29:17 he will bring *d* to your soul.
Isa 42: 1 my chosen one in whom I *d;*
55: 2 and your soul will *d* in the richest
61:10 I *d* greatly in the LORD;
Jer 9:24 for in these I *d,*"
15:16 they were my joy and my heart's *d,*
Mic 7:18 but *d* to show mercy.
Zep 3:17 He will take great *d* in you,
Mt 12:18 the one I love, in whom I *d;*
1Co 13: 6 Love does not *d* in evil
2Co 12:10 for Christ's sake, I *d* in weaknesses,

DELIGHTS (DELIGHT)
Ps 22: 8 since he *d* in him."
35:27 who *d* in the well-being
36: 8 from your river of *d.*
37:23 if the LORD *d* in a man's way,
Pr 3:12 as a father the son he *d* in.
12:22 but he *d* in men who are truthful.
23:24 he who has a wise son *d* in him.

DELILAH*
Woman who betrayed Samson (Jdg 16:4-22).

DELIVER (DELIVERANCE DELIVERED DELIVERER DELIVERS)
Ps 72:12 For he will *d* the needy who cry out
79: 9 *d* us and forgive our sins
Mt 6:13 but *d* us from the evil one.'
2Co 1:10 hope that he will continue to *d* us,

DELIVERANCE (DELIVER)
Ps 3: 8 From the LORD comes *d.*
32: 7 and surround me with songs of *d.*

Ps 33:17 A horse is a vain hope for *d;*

DELIVERED (DELIVER)
Ps 34: 4 he *d* me from all my fears.
Ro 4:25 He was *d* over to death for our sins

DELIVERER (DELIVER)
Ps 18: 2 is my rock, my fortress and my *d;*
40:17 You are my help and my *d;*
140: 7 O Sovereign LORD, my strong *d,*
144: 2 my stronghold and my *d,*

DELIVERS (DELIVER)
Ps 34:17 he *d* them from all their troubles.
34:19 but the LORD *d* him from them all
37:40 The LORD helps them and *d* them
37:40 he *d* them from the wicked

DEMANDED
Lk 12:20 This very night your life will be *d*
12:48 been given much, much will be *d;*

DEMONS
Mt 12:27 And if I drive out *d* by Beelzebub,
Mk 5:15 possessed by the legion of *d,*
Ro 8:38 neither angels nor *d,* neither
Jas 2:19 Good! Even the *d* believe that—

DEMONSTRATE (DEMONSTRATES)
Ro 3:26 he did it to *d* his justice

DEMONSTRATES* (DEMONSTRATE)
Ro 5: 8 God *d* his own love for us in this:

DEN
Da 6:16 and threw him into the lions' *d.*
Mt 21:13 you are making it a '*d* of robbers.' "

DENARIUS
Mk 12:15 Bring me a *d* and let me look at it."

DENIED (DENY)
1Ti 5: 8 he has *d* the faith and is worse

DENIES (DENY)
1Jn 2:23 No one who *d* the Son has

DENY (DENIED DENIES DENYING)
Ex 23: 6 "Do not *d* justice to your poor
Job 27: 5 till I die, I will not *d* my integrity.
La 3:35 to *d* a man his rights
Lk 9:23 he must *d* himself and take up his
Tit 1:16 but by their actions they *d* him.

DENYING* (DENY)
Eze 22:29 mistreat the alien, *d* them justice
2Ti 3: 5 a form of godliness but *d* its power.
2Pe 2: 1 *d* the sovereign Lord who bought

DEPART (DEPARTED)
Ge 49:10 The scepter will not *d* from Judah,
Job 1:21 and naked I will *d.*
Mt 25:41 '*D* from me, you who are cursed,
Php 1:23 I desire to *d* and be with Christ,

DEPARTED (DEPART)
1Sa 4:21 "The glory has *d* from Israel"—
Ps 119:102 I have not *d* from your laws,

DEPOSIT
2Co 1:22 put his Spirit in our hearts as a *d,*
5: 5 and has given us the Spirit as a *d,*
Eph 1:14 who is a *d* guaranteeing our
2Ti 1:14 Guard the good *d* that was

DEPRAVED (DEPRAVITY)
Ro 1:28 he gave them over to a *d* mind,
Php 2:15 fault in a crooked and *d* generation,

DEPRAVITY (DEPRAVED)
Ro 1:29 of wickedness, evil, greed and *d.*

DEPRIVE
Dt 24:17 Do not *d* the alien or the fatherless
Pr 18: 5 or to *d* the innocent of justice.
Isa 10: 2 to *d* the poor of their rights
29:21 with false testimony *d* the innocent
1Co 7: 5 Do not *d* each other

DEPTH (DEEP)
Ro 8:39 any powers, neither height nor *d,*
11:33 the *d* of the riches of the wisdom

DESERT
Nu 32:13 wander in the *d* forty years,
Ne 9:19 you did not abandon them in the *d.*
Ps 78:19 "Can God spread a table in the *d?*
78:52 led them like sheep through the *d.*
Mk 1:13 and he was in the *d* forty days,

DESERTED (DESERTS)
Ezr 9: 9 our God has not *d* us
Mt 26:56 all the disciples *d* him and fled.
2Ti 1:15 in the province of Asia has *d* me,

DESERTING (DESERTS)
Gal 1: 6 are so quickly *d* the one who called

DESERTS (DESERTED DESERTING)
Zec 11:17 who *d* the flock!

DESERVE (DESERVES)
Ps 103:10 he does not treat us as our sins *d*
Jer 21:14 I will punish you as your deeds *d,*
Mt 22: 8 those I invited did not *d* to come.
Ro 1:32 those who do such things *d* death,

DESERVES (DESERVE)
2Sa 12: 5 the man who did this *d* to die!
Lk 10: 7 for the worker *d* his wages.
1Ti 5:18 and "The worker *d* his wages."

DESIRABLE (DESIRE)
Pr 22: 1 A good name is more *d*

DESIRE (DESIRABLE DESIRES)
Ge 3:16 Your *d* will be for your husband,
Dt 5:21 You shall not set your *d*
1Ch 29:18 keep this *d* in the hearts
Ps 40: 6 Sacrifice and offering you did not *d*
40: 8 I *d* to do your will, O my God;
73:25 earth has nothing I *d* besides you
Pr 3:15 nothing you *d* can compare
10:24 what the righteous *d* will be
11:23 The *d* of the righteous ends only
Isa 26: 8 are the *d* of our hearts.
53: 2 appearance that we should *d* him.
55:11 but will accomplish what I *d*
Hos 6: 6 For I *d* mercy, not sacrifice,
Mt 9:13 learn what this means: 'I *d* mercy,
Ro 7:18 For I have the *d* to do what is good,
1Co 12:31 But eagerly *d* the greater gifts.
14: 1 and eagerly *d* spiritual gifts,
Php 1:23 I *d* to depart and be with Christ,
Heb 13:18 *d* to live honorably in every way.
Jas 1:15 Then, after *d* has conceived,

DESIRES (DESIRE)
Ge 4: 7 at your door; it *d* to have you,
Ps 34:12 and *d* to see many good days,
37: 4 he will give you the *d* of your heart.
103: 5 satisfies your *d* with good things,
145:19 He fulfills the *d* of those who fear
Pr 11: 6 the unfaithful are trapped by evil *d*
19:22 What a man *d* is unfailing love;
Mk 4:19 and the *d* for other things come in
Ro 8: 5 set on what that nature *d;*
13:14 to gratify the *d* of the sinful nature.
Gal 5:16 and you will not gratify the *d*
5:17 the sinful nature *d* what is contrary
1Ti 3: 1 an overseer, he *d* a noble task.
6: 9 and harmful *d* that plunge men
2Ti 2:22 Flee the evil *d* of youth,
Jas 1:20 about the righteous life that God *d.*
4: 1 from your *d* that battle within you?
1Pe 2:11 to abstain from sinful *d,* which war
1Jn 2:17 The world and its *d* pass away,

DESOLATE
Isa 54: 1 are the children of the *d* woman

DESPAIR
Isa 61: 3 instead of a spirit of *d.*
2Co 4: 8 perplexed, but not in *d;* persecuted,

DESPISE (DESPISED DESPISES)
Job 42: 6 Therefore I *d* myself
Pr 1: 7 but fools *d* wisdom and discipline.
3:11 do not *d* the LORD's discipline
23:22 do not *d* your mother
Lk 16:13 devoted to the one and *d* the other.
Tit 2:15 Do not let anyone *d* you.

DESPISED (DESPISE)
Ge 25:34 So Esau *d* his birthright.
Isa 53: 3 He was *d* and rejected by men,
1Co 1:28 of this world and the *d* things—

DESPISES (DESPISE)
Pr 14:21 He who *d* his neighbor sins,
15:20 but a foolish man *d* his mother.
15:32 who ignores discipline *d* himself,
Zec 4:10 "Who *d* the day of small things?

DESTINED (DESTINY)
Lk 2:34 "This child is *d* to cause the falling

DESTINY (DESTINED PREDESTINED)
Ps 73:17 then I understood their final *d.*
Ecc 7: 2 for death is the *d* of every man;

DESTITUTE
Pr 31: 8 for the rights of all who are *d.*
Heb 11:37 *d,* persecuted and mistreated—

DESTROY (DESTROYED DESTROYS DESTRUCTION)
Pr 1:32 complacency of fools will *d* them;
Mt 10:28 of the One who can *d* both soul

DESTROYED (DESTROY)
Job 19:26 And after my skin has been *d,*
Isa 55:13 which will not be *d.*"
1Co 8:11 for whom Christ died, is *d*
15:26 The last enemy to be *d* is death.
2Co 5: 1 if the earthly tent we live in is *d,*
Heb 10:39 of those who shrink back and are *d,*
2Pe 3:10 the elements will be *d* by fire,

DESTROYS (DESTROY)
Pr 6:32 whoever does so *d* himself.
11: 9 mouth the godless *d* his neighbor,
18: 9 is brother to one who *d.*
28:24 he is partner to him who *d.*
Ecc 9:18 but one sinner *d* much good.
1Co 3:17 If anyone *d* God's temple,

DESTRUCTION (DESTROY)
Pr 16:18 Pride goes before *d,*
Hos 13:14 Where, O grave, is your *d?*
Mt 7:13 broad is the road that leads to *d,*
Gal 6: 8 from that nature will reap *d;*
2Th 1: 9 punished with everlasting *d*
1Ti 6: 9 that plunge men into ruin and *d.*
2Pe 2: 1 bringing swift *d* on themselves.
3:16 other Scriptures, to their own *d.*

DETERMINED (DETERMINES)
Job 14: 5 Man's days are *d;*
Isa 14:26 This is the plan *d* for the whole
Da 11:36 for what has been *d* must take place
Ac 17:26 and he *d* the times set for them

DETERMINES* (DETERMINED)
Ps 147: 4 He *d* the number of the stars
Pr 16: 9 but the LORD *d* his steps.
1Co 12:11 them to each one, just as he *d.*

DETESTABLE (DETESTS)
Pr 21:27 The sacrifice of the wicked is *d*—
28: 9 even his prayers are *d.*
Isa 1:13 Your incense is *d* to me.
Lk 16:15 among men is *d* in God's sight.
Tit 1:16 They are *d,* disobedient

DETESTS (DETESTABLE)
Dt 22: 5 LORD your God *d* anyone who
23:18 the LORD your God *d* them both.
25:16 LORD your God *d* anyone who
Pr 12:22 The LORD *d* lying lips,
15: 8 The LORD *d* the sacrifice
15: 9 The LORD *d* the way
15:26 The LORD *d* the thoughts
16: 5 The LORD *d* all the proud of heart
17:15 the LORD *d* them both.
20:23 The LORD *d* differing weights,

DEVIL (DEVIL'S)
Mt 13:39 the enemy who sows them is the *d.*
25:41 the eternal fire prepared for the *d*
Lk 4: 2 forty days he was tempted by the *d.*
8:12 then the *d* comes and takes away
Eph 4:27 and do not give the *d* a foothold.
2Ti 2:26 and escape from the trap of the *d,*
Jas 4: 7 Resist the *d,* and he will flee
1Pe 5: 8 Your enemy the *d* prowls
1Jn 3: 8 who does what is sinful is of the *d,*
Rev 12: 9 that ancient serpent called the *d*

DEVIL'S* (DEVIL)
Eph 6:11 stand against the *d* schemes.
1Ti 3: 7 into disgrace and into the *d* trap.
1Jn 3: 8 was to destroy the *d* work.

DEVOTE (DEVOTED DEVOTING DEVOTION DEVOUT)
Job 11:13 "Yet if you *d* your heart to him
Jer 30:21 for who is he who will *d* himself
Col 4: 2 *D* yourselves to prayer, being
1Ti 4:13 *d* yourself to the public reading
Tit 3: 8 may be careful to *d* themselves

DEVOTED (DEVOTE)
Ezr 7:10 For Ezra had *d* himself to the study
Ac 2:42 They *d* themselves
Ro 12:10 Be *d* to one another
1Co 7:34 Her aim is to be *d* to the Lord

DEVOTING (DEVOTE)
1Ti 5:10 *d* herself to all kinds of good deeds.

DEVOTION (DEVOTE)
1Ch 28: 9 and serve him with wholehearted *d*
Eze 33:31 With their mouths they express *d,*
1Co 7:35 way in undivided *d* to the Lord.
2Co 11: 3 from your sincere and pure *d*

DEVOUR
2Sa 2:26 "Must the sword *d* forever?
Mk 12:40 They *d* widows' houses
1Pe 5: 8 lion looking for someone to *d.*

DEVOUT (DEVOTE)
Lk 2:25 Simeon, who was righteous and *d.*

DIE (DEAD DEATH DIED DIES)
Ge 2:17 when you eat of it you will surely *d*
Ex 11: 5 Every firstborn son in Egypt will *d,*
Ru 1:17 Where you *d* I will *d,* and there I
2Ki 14: 6 each is to *d* for his own sins."
Pr 5:23 He will *d* for lack of discipline,
10:21 but fools *d* for lack of judgment.
15:10 he who hates correction will *d.*
23:13 with the rod, he will not *d.*
Ecc 3: 2 a time to be born and a time to *d,*
Isa 66:24 their worm will not *d,* nor will their
Eze 3:18 that wicked man will *d* for his sin,
18: 4 soul who sins is the one who will *d.*
33: 8 'O wicked man, you will surely *d,*'
Mt 26:52 "for all who draw the sword will *d*
Jn 11:26 and believes in me will never *d.*
Ro 5: 7 Very rarely will anyone *d*
14: 8 and if we *d,* we *d* to the Lord.
1Co 15:22 in Adam all *d,* so in Christ all will
15:31 I *d* every day—I mean that,
Php 1:21 to live is Christ and to *d* is gain.
Heb 9:27 Just as man is destined to *d* once,
Rev 14:13 Blessed are the dead who *d*

DIED (DIE)
Ro 5: 6 we were still powerless, Christ *d*
6: 2 By no means! We *d* to sin;
6: 8 if we *d* with Christ, we believe that
14:15 brother for whom Christ *d.*
1Co 8:11 for whom Christ *d,* is destroyed
15: 3 that Christ *d* for our sins according
2Co 5:14 *d* for all, and therefore all *d.*
Col 3: 3 For you *d,* and your life is now
1Th 5:10 He *d* for us so that, whether we are
2Ti 2:11 If we *d* with him,
Heb 9:15 now that he has *d* as a ransom
1Pe 3:18 For Christ *d* for sins once for all,
Rev 2: 8 who *d* and came to life again.

DIES (DIE)
Job 14:14 If a man *d,* will he live again?
Pr 11: 7 a wicked man *d,* his hope perishes;
Jn 11:25 in me will live, even though he *d;*
1Co 15:36 does not come to life unless it *d.*

DIFFERENCE (DIFFERENT)
Ro 10:12 For there is no *d* between Jew

DIFFERENT (DIFFERENCE)
1Co 12: 4 There are *d* kinds of gifts,
2Co 11: 4 or a *d* gospel from the one you

DIGNITY
Pr 31:25 She is clothed with strength and *d;*

DIGS
Pr 26:27 If a man *d* a pit, he will fall into it;

DILIGENCE (DILIGENT)
Heb 6:11 to show this same *d* to the very end

DILIGENT (DILIGENCE)
Pr 21: 5 The plans of the *d* lead to profit
1Ti 4:15 Be *d* in these matters; give yourself

DIRECT (DIRECTS)
Ps 119:35 *D* me in the path of your
119:133 *D* my footsteps according
Jer 10:23 it is not for man to *d* his steps.
2Th 3: 5 May the Lord *d* your hearts

DIRECTS (DIRECT)
Ps 42: 8 By day the LORD *d* his love,
Isa 48:17 who *d* you in the way you should

DIRGE
Mt 11:17 we sang a *d,*

DISAPPEAR
Mt 5:18 will by any means *d* from the Law
Lk 16:17 earth to *d* than for the least stroke

DISAPPOINT* (DISAPPOINTED)
Ro 5: 5 And hope does not *d* us,

DISAPPOINTED (DISAPPOINT)
Ps 22: 5 in you they trusted and were not *d.*

DISASTER
Ps 57: 1 wings until the *d* has passed.
Pr 3:25 Have no fear of sudden *d*
17: 5 over *d* will not go unpunished.
Isa 45: 7 I bring prosperity and create *d;*
Eze 7: 5 An unheard-of *d* is coming.

DISCERN (DISCERNING DISCERNMENT)
Ps 19:12 Who can *d* his errors?
139: 3 You *d* my going out and my lying
Php 1:10 you may be able to *d* what is best

DISCERNING (DISCERN)
Pr 14: 6 knowledge comes easily to the *d.*
15:14 The *d* heart seeks knowledge,
17:24 A *d* man keeps wisdom in view,
17:28 and *d* if he holds his tongue.
19:25 rebuke a *d* man, and he will gain

DISCERNMENT (DISCERN)
Pr 17:10 A rebuke impresses a man of *d*
28:11 a poor man who has *d* sees

DISCIPLE (DISCIPLES)
Mt 10:42 these little ones because he is my *d,*
Lk 14:27 and follow me cannot be my *d.*

DISCIPLES (DISCIPLE)
Mt 28:19 Therefore go and make *d*
Jn 8:31 to my teaching, you are really my *d*
13:35 men will know that you are my *d*
Ac 11:26 The *d* were called Christians first

DISCIPLINE (DISCIPLINED DISCIPLINES)
Ps 38: 1 or *d* me in your wrath
39:11 You rebuke and *d* men for their sin;
94:12 Blessed is the man you *d,* O LORD
Pr 1: 7 but fools despise wisdom and *d.*
3:11 do not despise the LORD's *d*
5:12 You will say, "How I hated *d!*
5:23 He will die for lack of *d,*
6:23 and the corrections of *d*
10:17 He who heeds *d* shows the way
12: 1 Whoever loves *d* loves knowledge,
13:18 He who ignores *d* comes to poverty
13:24 who loves him is careful to *d* him.
15: 5 A fool spurns his father's *d,*
15:32 He who ignores *d* despises himself,
19:18 *D* your son, for in that there is hope
22:15 the rod of *d* will drive it far
23:13 Do not withhold *d* from a child;
29:17 *D* your son, and he will give you
Heb 12: 5 do not make light of the Lord's *d,*
12: 7 as *d;* God is treating you
12:11 No *d* seems pleasant at the time,
Rev 3:19 Those whom I love I rebuke and *d.*

DISCIPLINED (DISCIPLINE)
Pr 1: 3 for acquiring a *d* and prudent life,
Jer 31:18 'You *d* me like an unruly calf,
1Co 11:32 we are being *d* so that we will not
Tit 1: 8 upright, holy and *d.*
Heb 12: 7 For what son is not *d* by his father?

DISCIPLINES (DISCIPLINE)
Dt 8: 5 your heart that as a man *d* his son,
Pr 3:12 the LORD *d* those he loves,
Heb 12: 6 because the Lord *d* those he loves,
12:10 but God *d* us for our good,

DISCLOSED
Lk 8:17 is nothing hidden that will not be *d,*

DISCOURAGED
Jos 1: 9 Do not be terrified; do not be *d,*
10:25 "Do not be afraid; do not be *d.*
1Ch 28:20 or *d,* for the LORD God,
Isa 42: 4 he will not falter or be *d*
Col 3:21 children, or they will become *d.*

DISCREDITED
2Co 6: 3 so that our ministry will not be *d.*

DISCRETION*
1Ch 22:12 May the LORD give you *d*
Pr 1: 4 knowledge and *d* to the young—
2:11 *D* will protect you,
5: 2 that you may maintain *d*
8:12 I possess knowledge and *d.*
11:22 a beautiful woman who shows no *d.*

DISCRIMINATED*
Jas 2: 4 have you not *d* among yourselves

DISFIGURED
Isa 52:14 his appearance was so *d*

DISGRACE (DISGRACEFUL DISGRACES)
Pr 11: 2 When pride comes, then comes *d,*
14:34 but sin is a *d* to any people.
19:26 is a son who brings shame and *d.*
Ac 5:41 of suffering *d* for the Name.
Heb 13:13 the camp, bearing the *d* he bore.

DISGRACEFUL (DISGRACE)
Pr 10: 5 during harvest is a *d* son.
17: 2 wise servant will rule over a *d* son,

DISGRACES (DISGRACE)
Pr 28: 7 of gluttons *d* his father.
29:15 but a child left to itself *d* his mother

DISHONEST
Pr 11: 1 The LORD abhors *d* scales,
29:27 The righteous detest the *d;*
Lk 16:10 whoever is *d* with very little will
1Ti 3: 8 wine, and not pursuing *d* gain.

DISHONOR (DISHONORS)
Lev 18: 7 " 'Do not *d* your father
Pr 30: 9 and so *d* the name of my God.
1Co 15:43 it is sown in *d,* it is raised in glory;

DISHONORS (DISHONOR)
Dt 27:16 Cursed is the man who *d* his father

DISMAYED
Isa 28:16 the one who trusts will never be *d.*
41:10 do not be *d,* for I am your God.

DISOBEDIENCE (DISOBEY)
Ro 5:19 as through the *d* of the one man
11:32 to *d* so that he may have mercy
Heb 2: 2 and *d* received its just punishment,
4: 6 go in, because of their *d.*
4:11 fall by following their example of *d.*

DISOBEDIENT (DISOBEY)
2Ti 3: 2 proud, abusive, *d* to their parents,
Tit 1: 6 to the charge of being wild and *d.*
1:16 *d* and unfit for doing anything

DISOBEY (DISOBEDIENCE DISOBEDIENT)
Dt 11:28 the curse if you *d* the commands
2Ch 24:20 'Why do you *d* the LORD's
Ro 1:30 they *d* their parents; they are

DISORDER
1Co 14:33 For God is not a God of *d*
2Co 12:20 slander, gossip, arrogance and *d.*
Jas 3:16 there you find *d* and every evil

DISOWN
Pr 30: 9 I may have too much and *d* you
Mt 10:33 I will *d* him before my Father
26:35 to die with you, I will never *d* you."
2Ti 2:12 If we *d* him,

DISPLAY (DISPLAYS)
Eze 39:21 I will *d* my glory among the nations
1Ti 1:16 Christ Jesus might *d* his unlimited

DISPLAYS (DISPLAY)
Isa 44:23 he *d* his glory in Israel.

DISPUTE (DISPUTES)
Pr 17:14 before a *d* breaks out.
1Co 6: 1 If any of you has a *d* with another,

DISPUTES (DISPUTE)
Pr 18:18 Casting the lot settles *d*

DISQUALIFIED
1Co 9:27 I myself will not be *d* for the prize.

DISREPUTE*
2Pe 2: 2 will bring the way of truth into *d.*

DISSENSION*
Pr 6:14 he always stirs up *d.*
6:19 and a man who stirs up *d*
10:12 Hatred stirs up *d,*
15:18 A hot-tempered man stirs up *d,*
16:28 A perverse man stirs up *d,*
28:25 A greedy man stirs up *d,*
29:22 An angry man stirs up *d,*
Ro 13:13 debauchery, not in *d* and jealousy.

DISSIPATION*
Lk 21:34 will be weighed down with *d,*
1Pe 4: 4 with them into the same flood of *d,*

DISTINGUISH
1Ki 3: 9 and to *d* between right and wrong.
Heb 5:14 themselves to *d* good from evil.

DISTORT
2Co 4: 2 nor do we *d* the word of God.
2Pe 3:16 ignorant and unstable people *d*,

DISTRESS (DISTRESSED)
Ps 18: 6 In my *d* I called to the LORD;
Jnh 2: 2 "In my *d* I called to the LORD,
Jas 1:27 after orphans and widows in their *d*

DISTRESSED (DISTRESS)
Ro 14:15 If your brother is *d*

DIVIDED (DIVISION)
Mt 12:25 household *d* against itself will not
Lk 23:34 they *d* up his clothes by casting lots
1Co 1:13 Is Christ *d*? Was Paul crucified

DIVINATION
Lev 19:26 " 'Do not practice *d* or sorcery.

DIVINE
Ro 1:20 his eternal power and *d* nature—
2Co 10: 4 they have *d* power
2Pe 1: 4 you may participate in the *d* nature

DIVISION (DIVIDED DIVISIONS DIVISIVE)
Lk 12:51 on earth? No, I tell you, but *d*.
1Co 12:25 so that there should be no *d*

DIVISIONS (DIVISION)
Ro 16:17 to watch out for those who cause *d*
1Co 1:10 another so that there may be no *d*
11:18 there are *d* among you,

DIVISIVE* (DIVISION)
Tit 3:10 Warn a *d* person once,

DIVORCE
Mal 2:16 "I hate *d*," says the LORD God
Mt 19: 3 for a man to *d* his wife for any
1Co 7:11 And a husband must not *d* his wife.
7:27 Are you married? Do not seek a *d*.

DOCTOR
Mt 9:12 "It is not the healthy who need a *d*,

DOCTRINE
1Ti 4:16 Watch your life and *d* closely.
Tit 2: 1 is in accord with sound *d*.

DOMINION
Ps 22:28 for *d* belongs to the LORD

DOOR
Ps 141: 3 keep watch over the *d* of my lips.
Mt 6: 6 close the *d* and pray to your Father
7: 7 and the *d* will be opened to you.
Rev 3:20 I stand at the *d* and knock.

DOORKEEPER
Ps 84:10 I would rather be a *d* in the house

DOUBLE-EDGED
Heb 4:12 Sharper than any *d* sword,
Rev 1:16 of his mouth came a sharp *d* sword.
2:12 of him who has the sharp, *d* sword.

DOUBLE-MINDED (MIND)
Ps 119:113 I hate *d* men,
Jas 1: 8 he is a *d* man, unstable

DOUBT
Mt 14:31 he said, "why did you *d*?"
21:21 if you have faith and do not *d*,
Mk 11:23 and does not *d* in his heart
Jas 1: 6 he must believe and not *d*,
Jude :22 Be merciful to those who *d*;

DOWNCAST
Ps 42: 5 Why are you *d*, O my soul?
2Co 7: 6 But God, who comforts the *d*,

DRAW (DRAWING DRAWS)
Mt 26:52 "for all who *d* the sword will die
Jn 12:32 up from the earth, will *d* all men
Heb 10:22 let us *d* near to God

DRAWING (DRAW)
Lk 21:28 because your redemption is *d* near

DRAWS (DRAW)
Jn 6:44 the Father who sent me *d* him,

DREADFUL
Heb 10:31 It is a *d* thing to fall into the hands

DRESS
1Ti 2: 9 I also want women to *d* modestly,

DRINK (DRUNK DRUNKARDS DRUNKENNESS)
Pr 5:15 *D* water from your own cistern,
Lk 12:19 Take life easy; eat, *d* and be merry
Jn 7:37 let him come to me and *d*.
1Co 12:13 were all given the one Spirit to *d*.
Rev 21: 6 to *d* without cost from the spring

DRIVES
1Jn 4:18 But perfect love *d* out fear,

DROP
Pr 17:14 so *d* the matter before a dispute
Isa 40:15 Surely the nations are like a *d*

DRUNK (DRINK)
Eph 5:18 Do not get *d* on wine, which leads

DRUNKARDS (DRINK)
Pr 23:21 for *d* and gluttons become poor,
1Co 6:10 nor the greedy nor *d* nor slanderers

DRUNKENNESS (DRINK)
Lk 21:34 weighed down with dissipation, *d*
Ro 13:13 and *d*, not in sexual immorality
Gal 5:21 factions and envy; *d*, orgies,
1Pe 4: 3 living in debauchery, lust, *d*, orgies,

DRY
Isa 53: 2 and like a root out of *d* ground.
Eze 37: 4 '*D* bones, hear the word

DUST
Ge 2: 7 man from the *d* of the ground
Ps 103:14 he remembers that we are *d*.
Ecc 3:20 all come from *d*, and to *d* all return.

DUTY
Ecc 12:13 for this is the whole *d* of man.
Ac 23: 1 I have fulfilled my *d* to God
1Co 7: 3 husband should fulfill his marital *d*

DWELL (DWELLING)
1Ki 8:27 "But will God really *d* on earth?
Ps 23: 6 I will *d* in the house of the LORD
Isa 43:18 do not *d* on the past.
Eph 3:17 so that Christ may *d* in your hearts
Col 1:19 to have all his fullness *d* in him,
3:16 the word of Christ *d* in you richly

DWELLING (DWELL)
Eph 2:22 to become a *d* in which God lives

EAGER
Pr 31:13 and works with *e* hands.
1Pe 5: 2 greedy for money, but *e* to serve;

EAGLE'S (EAGLES)
Ps 103: 5 your youth is renewed like the *e*.

EAGLES (EAGLE'S)
Isa 40:31 They will soar on wings like *e*;

EAR (EARS)
1Co 2: 9 no *e* has heard,
12:16 if the *e* should say, "Because I am

EARNED
Pr 31:31 Give her the reward she has *e*,

EARS (EAR)
Job 42: 5 My *e* had heard of you
Ps 34:15 and his *e* are attentive to their cry;
Pr 21:13 If a man shuts his *e* to the cry
2Ti 4: 3 to say what their itching *e* want

EARTH (EARTHLY)
Ge 1: 1 God created the heavens and the *e*.
Ps 24: 1 *e* is the LORD's, and everything
108: 5 and let your glory be over all the *e*.
Isa 6: 3 the whole *e* is full of his glory."
51: 6 the *e* will wear out like a garment
55: 9 the heavens are higher than the *e*,
66: 1 and the *e* is my footstool.
Jer 23:24 "Do not I fill heaven and *e*?"
Hab 2:20 let all the *e* be silent before him."
Mt 6:10 done on *e* as it is in heaven.
16:19 bind on *e* will be bound
24:35 Heaven and *e* will pass away,
28:18 and on *e* has been given to me.
Lk 2:14 on *e* peace to men
1Co 10:26 The *e* is the Lord's, and everything
Php 2:10 in heaven and on *e* and under the *e*,
2Pe 3:13 to a new heaven and a new *e*,

EARTHLY (EARTH)
Php 3:19 Their mind is on *e* things.
Col 3: 2 on things above, not on *e* things.

EAST
Ps 103:12 as far as the *e* is from the west,

EASY
Mt 11:30 For my yoke is *e* and my burden is

EAT (EATING)
Ge 2:17 but you must not *e* from the tree
Isa 55: 1 come, buy and *e*!
65:25 and the lion will *e* straw like the ox,
Mt 26:26 "Take and *e*; this is my body."
Ro 14: 2 faith allows him to *e* everything,
1Co 8:13 if what I *e* causes my brother to fall
10:31 So whether you *e* or drink
2Th 3:10 man will not work, he shall not *e*."

EATING (EAT)
Ro 14:17 kingdom of God is not a matter of *e*

EDICT
Heb 11:23 they were not afraid of the king's *e*.

EDIFIES
1Co 14: 4 but he who prophesies *e* the church

EFFECT
Isa 32:17 *e* of righteousness will be quietness
Heb 9:18 put into *e* without blood.

EFFORT
Lk 13:24 "Make every *e* to enter
Ro 9:16 depend on man's desire or *e*,
14:19 make every *e* to do what leads
Eph 4: 3 Make every *e* to keep the unity
Heb 4:11 make every *e* to enter that rest,
12:14 Make every *e* to live in peace
2Pe 1: 5 make every *e* to add
3:14 make every *e* to be found spotless,

ELAH
Son of Baasha; king of Israel (1Ki 16:6-14).

ELDERLY* (ELDERS)
Lev 19:32 show respect for the *e*

ELDERS (ELDERLY)
1Ti 5:17 The *e* who direct the affairs

ELECTION
Ro 9:11 God's purpose in *e* might stand:
2Pe 1:10 to make your calling and *e* sure.

ELI
High priest in youth of Samuel (1Sa 1-4). Blessed Hannah (1Sa 1:12-18); raised Samuel (1Sa 2:11-26).

ELIJAH
Prophet; predicted famine in Israel (1Ki 17:1; Jas 5:17). Fed by ravens (1Ki 17:2-6). Raised Sidonian widow's son (1Ki 17:7-24). Defeated prophets of Baal at Carmel (1Ki 18:16-46). Ran from Jezebel (1Ki 19:1-9). Prophesied death of Azariah (2Ki 1). Succeeded by Elishah (1Ki 19:19-21; 2Ki 2:1-18). Taken to heaven in whirlwind (2Ki 2:11-12).

Return prophesied (Mal 4:5-6); equated with John the Baptist (Mt 17:9-13; Mk 9:9-13; Lk 1:17). Appeared with Moses in transfiguration of Jesus (Mt 17:1-8; Mk 9:1-8).

ELISHA
Prophet; successor of Elijah (1Ki 19:16-21); inherited his cloak (2Ki 2:1-18). Miracles of (2Ki 2-6).

ELIZABETH*
Mother of John the Baptist, relative of Mary (Lk 1:5-58).

EMBITTER*
Col 3:21 Fathers, do not *e* your children,

EMPTY
Eph 5: 6 no one deceive you with *e* words,
1Pe 1:18 from the *e* way of life handed

ENABLE (ABLE)
Lk 1:74 to *e* us to serve him without fear
Ac 4:29 *e* your servants to speak your word

ENABLED (ABLE)
Lev 26:13 *e* you to walk with heads held high.
Jn 6:65 unless the Father has *e* him."

ENABLES (ABLE)
Php 3:21 by the power that *e* him

ENCAMPS*
Ps 34: 7 The angel of the LORD *e*

ENCOURAGE (ENCOURAGEMENT)
Ps 10:17 you *e* them, and you listen
Isa 1:17 *e* the oppressed.
Ac 15:32 to *e* and strengthen the brothers.
Ro 12: 8 if it is encouraging, let him *e*;
1Th 4:18 Therefore *e* each other
2Ti 4: 2 rebuke and *e*— with great patience
Tit 2: 6 *e* the young men to be
Heb 3:13 But *e* one another daily, as long
10:25 but let us *e* one another—

ENCOURAGEMENT (ENCOURAGE)
Ac 4:36 Barnabas (which means Son of *E*),
Ro 15: 4 *e* of the Scriptures we might have
15: 5 and *e* give you a spirit of unity
1Co 14: 3 to men for their strengthening, *e*
Heb 12: 5 word of *e* that addresses you

END
Ps 119:33 then I will keep them to the *e*.
Pr 14:12 but in the *e* it leads to death.
19:20 and in the *e* you will be wise.
23:32 In the *e* it bites like a snake
Ecc 12:12 making many books there is no *e*,
Mt 10:22 firm to the *e* will be saved.
Lk 21: 9 but the *e* will not come right away
Ro 10: 4 Christ is the *e* of the law
1Co 15:24 the *e* will come, when he hands

ENDURANCE (ENDURE)
Ro 15: 4 through *e* and the encouragement
15: 5 May the God who gives *e*
2Co 1: 6 which produces in you patient *e*
Col 1:11 might so that you may have great *e*
1Ti 6:11 faith, love, *e* and gentleness.
Tit 2: 2 and sound in faith, in love and in *e*.

ENDURE (ENDURANCE ENDURES)
Ps 72:17 May his name *e* forever;
Pr 12:19 Truthful lips *e* forever,
27:24 for riches do not *e* forever,
Ecc 3:14 everything God does will *e* forever;
Mal 3: 2 who can *e* the day of his coming?
2Ti 2: 3 *E* hardship with us like a good
2:12 if we *e*, / we will also reign
Heb 12: 7 *E* hardship as discipline; God is
Rev 3:10 kept my command to *e* patiently,

ENDURES (ENDURE)
Ps 112: 9 his righteousness *e* forever;
136: 1 *His love e forever.*
Da 9:15 made for yourself a name that *e*

ENEMIES (ENEMY)
Ps 23: 5 in the presence of my *e*.
Mic 7: 6 a man's *e* are the members
Mt 5:44 Love your *e* and pray
Lk 20:43 hand until I make your *e*

ENEMY (ENEMIES ENMITY)
Pr 24:17 Do not gloat when your *e* falls;
25:21 If your *e* is hungry, give him food
27: 6 but an *e* multiplies kisses.
1Co 15:26 The last *e* to be destroyed is death.
1Ti 5:14 and to give the *e* no opportunity

ENJOY (JOY)
Dt 6: 2 and so that you may *e* long life.
Eph 6: 3 and that you may *e* long life
Heb 11:25 rather than to *e* the pleasures of sin

ENJOYMENT (JOY)
Ecc 4: 8 and why am I depriving myself of *e*
1Ti 6:17 us with everything for our *e*.

ENLIGHTENED* (LIGHT)
Eph 1:18 that the eyes of your heart may be *e*
Heb 6: 4 for those who have once been *e*,

ENMITY* (ENEMY)
Ge 3:15 And I will put *e*

ENOCH
Walked with God and taken by him (Ge 5:18-24; Heb 11:5). Prophet (Jude 14).

ENTANGLED (ENTANGLES)
2Pe 2:20 and are again *e* in it and overcome,

ENTANGLES* (ENTANGLED)
Heb 12: 1 and the sin that so easily *e*,

ENTER (ENTERED ENTERS ENTRANCE)
Ps 100: 4 *E* his gates with thanksgiving
Mt 5:20 will certainly not *e* the kingdom
7:13 "*E* through the narrow gate.
18: 8 It is better for you to *e* life maimed
Mk 10:15 like a little child will never *e* it."
10:23 is for the rich to *e* the kingdom

ENTERED (ENTER)
Ro 5:12 as sin *e* the world through one man,
Heb 9:12 but he *e* the Most Holy Place once

ENTERS (ENTER)
Mk 7:18 you see that nothing that *e* a man
Jn 10: 2 The man who *e* by the gate is

ENTERTAIN
1Ti 5:19 Do not *e* an accusation
Heb 13: 2 Do not forget to *e* strangers,

ENTHRALLED*
Ps 45:11 The king is *e* by your beauty;

ENTHRONED (THRONE)
1Sa 4: 4 who is *e* between the cherubim.
Ps 2: 4 The One *e* in heaven laughs;
102:12 But you, O LORD, sit *e* forever;
Isa 40:22 He sits *e* above the circle

ENTICE
Pr 1:10 My son, if sinners *e* you,
2Pe 2:18 they *e* people who are just escaping

ENTIRE
Gal 5:14 The *e* law is summed up

ENTRUSTED (TRUST)
1Ti 6:20 guard what has been *e* to your care.
2Ti 1:12 able to guard what I have *e* to him
1:14 Guard the good deposit that was *e*
Jude : 3 once for all *e* to the saints.

ENVY
Pr 3:31 Do not *e* a violent man
14:30 but *e* rots the bones.
1Co 13: 4 It does not *e*, it does not boast,

EPHRAIM
1. Second son of Joseph (Ge 41:52; 46:20). Blessed as firstborn by Jacob (Ge 48).
2. Synonymous with Northern Kingdom (Isa 7:17; Hos 5).

EQUAL
Isa 40:25 who is my *e*?" says the Holy One.
Jn 5:18 making himself *e* with God.
1Co 12:25 that its parts should have *e* concern

EQUIP* (EQUIPPED)
Heb 13:21 *e* you with everything good

EQUIPPED (EQUIP)
2Ti 3:17 man of God may be thoroughly *e*

ERROR
Jas 5:20 Whoever turns a sinner from the *e*

ESAU
Firstborn of Isaac, twin of Jacob (Ge 25:21-26). Also called Edom (Ge 25:30). Sold Jacob his birthright (Ge 25:29-34); lost blessing (Ge 27). Reconciled to Jacob (Gen 33).

ESCAPE (ESCAPING)
Ro 2: 3 think you will *e* God's judgment?
Heb 2: 3 how shall we *e* if we ignore such

ESCAPING (ESCAPE)
1Co 3:15 only as one *e* through the flames.

ESTABLISH
Ge 6:18 But I will *e* my covenant with you,
1Ch 28: 7 I will *e* his kingdom forever
Ro 10: 3 God and sought to *e* their own,

ESTEEMED
Pr 22: 1 to be *e* is better than silver or gold.
Isa 53: 3 he was despised, and we *e* him not.

ESTHER
Jewess who lived in Persia; cousin of Mordecai (Est 2:7). Chosen queen of Xerxes (Est 2:8-18). Foiled Haman's plan to exterminate the Jews (Est 3-4; 7-9).

ETERNAL (ETERNALLY ETERNITY)
Ps 16:11 with *e* pleasures at your right hand.
111:10 To him belongs *e* praise.
119:89 Your word, O LORD, is *e*;
Isa 26: 4 LORD, the LORD, is the Rock *e*.
Mt 19:16 good thing must I do to get *e* life?"
25:41 into the *e* fire prepared for the devil
25:46 they will go away to *e* punishment,
Jn 3:15 believes in him may have *e* life.
3:16 him shall not perish but have *e* life.
3:36 believes in the Son has *e* life,
4:14 spring of water welling up to *e* life."
5:24 believes him who sent me has *e* life
6:68 You have the words of *e* life.
10:28 I give them *e* life, and they shall
17: 3 this is *e* life: that they may know
Ro 1:20 his *e* power and divine nature—
6:23 but the gift of God is *e* life
2Co 4:17 for us an *e* glory that far outweighs
4:18 temporary, but what is unseen is *e*.
1Ti 1:16 believe on him and receive *e* life.
1:17 Now to the King *e*, immortal,
Heb 9:12 having obtained *e* redemption.
1Jn 5:11 God has given us *e* life,
5:13 you may know that you have *e* life.

ETERNALLY (ETERNAL)
Gal 1: 8 let him be *e* condemned! As we

ETERNITY (ETERNAL)
Ps 93: 2 you are from all *e*.
Ecc 3:11 also set *e* in the hearts of men;

ETHIOPIAN
Jer 13:23 Can the *E* change his skin

EUNUCHS
Mt 19:12 For some are *e* because they were

EVANGELIST (EVANGELISTS)
2Ti 4: 5 hardship, do the work of an *e*,

EVANGELISTS* (EVANGELIST)
Eph 4:11 some to be prophets, some to be *e*,

EVE
2Co 11: 3 as *E* was deceived by the serpent's
1Ti 2:13 For Adam was formed first, then *E*

EVEN-TEMPERED*
Pr 17:27 and a man of understanding is *e*.

EVER (EVERLASTING FOREVER)
Ex 15:18 LORD will reign for *e* and *e*."
Dt 8:19 If you *e* forget the LORD your
Ps 5:11 let them *e* sing for joy.
10:16 The LORD is King for *e* and *e*;
25: 3 will *e* be put to shame,
26: 3 for your love is *e* before me,
45: 6 O God, will last for *e* and *e*;
52: 8 God's unfailing love for *e* and *e*.
89:33 nor will I *e* betray my faithfulness.
145: 1 I will praise your name for *e* and *e*.
Pr 4:18 shining *e* brighter till the full light
5:19 may you *e* be captivated
Isa 66: 8 Who has *e* heard of such a thing?
Jer 31:36 the descendants of Israel *e* cease
Da 7:18 it forever—yes, for *e* and *e*.'
12: 3 like the stars for *e* and *e*.
Mk 4:12 *e* hearing but never understanding;
Jn 1:18 No one has *e* seen God,
Rev 1:18 and behold I am alive for *e* and *e*!
22: 5 And they will reign for *e* and *e*.

EVER-INCREASING* (INCREASE)
Ro 6:19 to impurity and to *e* wickedness,
2Co 3:18 into his likeness with *e* glory,

EVERLASTING (EVER)
Dt 33:27 and underneath are the *e* arms.
Ne 9: 5 your God, who is from *e* to *e*."
Ps 90: 2 from *e* to *e* you are God.
139:24 and lead me in the way *e*.
Isa 9: 6 *E* Father, Prince of Peace.
33:14 Who of us can dwell with *e* burning
35:10 *e* joy will crown their heads.
45:17 the LORD with an *e* salvation;
54: 8 but with *e* kindness
55: 3 I will make an *e* covenant with you,
63:12 to gain for himself *e* renown,
Jer 31: 3 "I have loved you with an *e* love;
Da 9:24 to bring in *e* righteousness,
12: 2 some to *e* life, others to shame
Jn 6:47 the truth, he who believes has *e* life.
2Th 1: 9 punished with *e* destruction
Jude : 6 bound with *e* chains for judgment

EVER-PRESENT*
Ps 46: 1 an *e* help in trouble

EVIDENCE (EVIDENT)
Jn 14:11 on the *e* of the miracles themselves.

EVIDENT (EVIDENCE)
Php 4: 5 Let your gentleness be *e* to all.

EVIL
Ge 2: 9 of the knowledge of good and *e*.
Job 1: 1 he feared God and shunned *e*.
1: 8 a man who fears God and shuns *e*."
34:10 Far be it from God to do *e*,
Ps 23: 4 I will fear no *e*,
34:14 Turn from *e* and do good;
51: 4 and done what is *e* in your sight,
97:10 those who love the LORD hate *e*,
101: 4 I will have nothing to do with *e*.
Pr 8:13 To fear the LORD is to hate *e*;
10:23 A fool finds pleasure in *e* conduct,
11:27 *e* comes to him who searches for it.
24:19 Do not fret because of *e* men
24:20 for the *e* man has no future hope,
Isa 5:20 Woe to those who call *e* good
13:11 I will punish the world for its *e*,
55: 7 and the *e* man his thoughts.
Hab 1:13 Your eyes are too pure to look on *e*;

Mt 5:45 He causes his sun to rise on the *e*
6:13 but deliver us from the *e* one.'
7:11 If you, then, though you are *e*,
12:35 and the *e* man brings *e* things out
Jn 17:15 you protect them from the *e* one.
Ro 2: 9 for every human being who does *e*:
12: 9 Hate what is *e*; cling
12:17 Do not repay anyone *e* for *e*.
16:19 and innocent about what is *e*.
1Co 13: 6 Love does not delight in *e*
14:20 In regard to *e* be infants,
Eph 6:16 all the flaming arrows of the *e* one.
1Th 5:22 Avoid every kind of *e*.
1Ti 6:10 of money is a root of all kinds of *e*.
2Ti 2:22 Flee the *e* desires of youth,
Jas 1:13 For God cannot be tempted by *e*,
1Pe 2:16 your freedom as a cover-up for *e*;
3: 9 Do not repay *e* with *e* or insult

EXACT
Heb 1: 3 the *e* representation of his being,

EXALT (EXALTED EXALTS)
Ps 30: 1 I will *e* you, O LORD,
34: 3 let us *e* his name together.
118:28 you are my God, and I will *e* you.
Isa 24:15 *e* the name of the LORD, the God

EXALTED (EXALT)
2Sa 22:47 *E* be God, the Rock, my Savior!
1Ch 29:11 you are *e* as head over all.
Ne 9: 5 and may it be *e* above all blessing
Ps 21:13 Be *e*, O LORD, in your strength;
46:10 I will be *e* among the nations,
57: 5 Be *e*, O God, above the heavens;
97: 9 you are *e* far above all gods.
99: 2 he is *e* over all the nations.
108: 5 Be *e*, O God, above the heavens,
148:13 for his name alone is *e*;
Isa 6: 1 *e*, and the train of his robe filled
12: 4 and proclaim that his name is *e*.
33: 5 The LORD is *e*, for he dwells
Eze 21:26 The lowly will be *e* and the *e* will be
Mt 23:12 whoever humbles himself will be *e*.
Php 1:20 always Christ will be *e* in my body,
2: 9 Therefore God *e* him

EXALTS (EXALT)
Ps 75: 7 He brings one down, he *e* another.
Pr 14:34 Righteousness *e* a nation,
Mt 23:12 For whoever *e* himself will be

EXAMINE (EXAMINED)
Ps 26: 2 *e* my heart and my mind;
Jer 17:10 and *e* the mind,
La 3:40 Let us *e* our ways and test them,
1Co 11:28 A man ought to *e* himself
2Co 13: 5 *E* yourselves to see whether you

EXAMINED (EXAMINE)
Ac 17:11 *e* the Scriptures every day to see

EXAMPLE (EXAMPLES)
Jn 13:15 have set you an *e* that you should
1Co 11: 1 Follow my *e*, as I follow
1Ti 4:12 set an *e* for the believers in speech,
Tit 2: 7 In everything set them an *e*
1Pe 2:21 leaving you an *e*, that you should

EXAMPLES* (EXAMPLE)
1Co 10: 6 Now these things occurred as *e*
10:11 as *e* and were written down
1Pe 5: 3 to you, but being *e* to the flock.

EXASPERATE*
Eph 6: 4 Fathers, do not *e* your children;

EXCEL (EXCELLENT)
1Co 14:12 to *e* in gifts that build up the church
2Co 8: 7 But just as you *e* in everything—

EXCELLENT (EXCEL)
1Co 12:31 now I will show you the most *e* way
Php 4: 8 if anything is *e* or praiseworthy—
1Ti 3:13 have served well gain an *e* standing
Tit 3: 8 These things are *e* and profitable

EXCHANGED
Ro 1:23 *e* the glory of the immortal God
1:25 They *e* the truth of God for a lie,

EXCUSE (EXCUSES)
Jn 15:22 they have no *e* for their sin.
Ro 1:20 so that men are without *e*.

EXCUSES* (EXCUSE)
Lk 14:18 "But they all alike began to make *e*.

EXISTS
Heb 2:10 and through whom everything *e*,
11: 6 to him must believe that he *e*

EXPECT (EXPECTATION)
Mt 24:44 at an hour when you do not *e* him.

EXPECTATION (EXPECT)
Ro 8:19 waits in eager *e* for the sons
Heb 10:27 but only a fearful *e* of judgment

EXPEL*
1Co 5:13 *E* the wicked man from among you

EXPENSIVE
1Ti 2: 9 or gold or pearls or *e* clothes,

EXPLOIT
Pr 22:22 Do not *e* the poor because they are
2Co 12:17 Did I *e* you through any

EXPOSE
1Co 4: 5 will *e* the motives of men's hearts.
Eph 5:11 of darkness, but rather *e* them.

EXTENDS
Pr 31:20 and *e* her hands to the needy.
Lk 1:50 His mercy *e* to those who fear him,

EXTINGUISHED
2Sa 21:17 the lamp of Israel will not be *e*."

EXTOL*
Job 36:24 Remember to *e* his work,
Ps 34: 1 I will *e* the LORD at all times;
68: 4 *e* him who rides on the clouds—
95: 2 and *e* him with music and song.
109:30 mouth I will greatly *e* the LORD;
111: 1 I will *e* the LORD with all my heart
115:18 it is we who *e* the LORD,
117: 1 *e* him, all you peoples.
145: 2 and *e* your name for ever and ever.
145:10 your saints will *e* you.
147:12 *E* the LORD, O Jerusalem;

EXTORT*
Lk 3:14 "Don't *e* money and don't accuse

EYE (EYES)
Ex 21:24 you are to take life for life, *e* for *e*,
Ps 94: 9 Does he who formed the *e* not see?
Mt 5:29 If your right *e* causes you to sin,
5:38 '*E* for *e*, and tooth for tooth.'
7: 3 of sawdust in your brother's *e*
1Co 2: 9 "No *e* has seen,
Col 3:22 not only when their *e* is on you
Rev 1: 7 and every *e* will see him,

EYES (EYE)
Nu 33:55 remain will become barbs in your *e*
Jos 23:13 on your backs and thorns in your *e*,
2Ch 16: 9 For the *e* of the LORD range
Job 31: 1 "I made a covenant with my *e*
36: 7 He does not take his *e*
Ps 119:18 Open my *e* that I may see
121: 1 I lift up my *e* to the hills—
141: 8 But my *e* are fixed on you,
Pr 3: 7 Do not be wise in your own *e*;
4:25 Let your *e* look straight ahead,
15: 3 The *e* of the LORD are everywhere
Isa 6: 5 and my *e* have seen the King,
Hab 1:13 Your *e* are too pure to look on evil;
Jn 4:35 open your *e* and look at the fields!
2Co 4:18 So we fix our *e* not on what is seen,
Heb 12: 2 Let us fix our *e* on Jesus, the author
Jas 2: 5 poor in the *e* of the world to be rich
1Pe 3:12 For the *e* of the Lord are
Rev 7:17 wipe away every tear from their *e*."
21: 4 He will wipe every tear from their *e*

EZEKIEL
Priest called to be prophet to the exiles (Eze 1-3).

EZRA
Priest and teacher of the Law who led a return of exiles to Israel to reestablish temple and worship (Ezr 7-8). Corrected intermarriage of priests (Ezr 9-10). Read Law at celebration of Feast of Tabernacles (Neh 8).

FACE (FACES)
Ge 32:30 "It is because I saw God *f* to *f*,
Ex 34:29 was not aware that his *f* was radiant
Nu 6:25 the LORD make his *f* shine
1Ch 16:11 seek his *f* always.
2Ch 7:14 and seek my *f* and turn
Ps 4: 6 Let the light of your *f* shine upon us
27: 8 Your *f*, LORD, I will seek.
31:16 Let your *f* shine on your servant;
105: 4 seek his *f* always.
Ps 119:135 Make your *f* shine
Isa 50: 7 Therefore have I set my *f* like flint,
Mt 17: 2 His *f* shone like the sun,
1Co 13:12 mirror; then we shall see *f* to *f*.
2Co 4: 6 the glory of God in the *f* of Christ.
1Pe 3:12 but the *f* of the Lord is
Rev 1:16 His *f* was like the sun shining

FACES (FACE)
2Co 3:18 who with unveiled *f* all reflect

FACTIONS
Gal 5:20 selfish ambition, dissensions, *f*

FADE
1Pe 5: 4 of glory that will never *f* away.

FAIL (FAILING FAILINGS FAILS)
1Ch 28:20 He will not *f* you or forsake you
2Ch 34:33 they did not *f* to follow the LORD,
Ps 89:28 my covenant with him will never *f*.
Pr 15:22 Plans *f* for lack of counsel,
Isa 51: 6 my righteousness will never *f*.
La 3:22 for his compassions never *f*.
2Co 13: 5 unless, of course, you *f* the test?

FAILING (FAIL)
1Sa 12:23 sin against the LORD by *f* to pray

FAILINGS (FAIL)
Ro 15: 1 ought to bear with the *f* of the weak

FAILS (FAIL)
1Co 13: 8 Love never *f*.

FAINT
Isa 40:31 they will walk and not be *f*.

FAIR
Pr 1: 3 doing what is right and just and *f*;
Col 4: 1 slaves with what is right and *f*,

FAITH (FAITHFUL FAITHFULLY FAITHFULNESS FAITHLESS)
2Ch 20:20 Have *f* in the LORD your God
Hab 2: 4 but the righteous will live by his *f*—
Mt 9:29 According to your *f* will it be done
17:20 if you have *f* as small as a mustard
24:10 many will turn away from the *f*
Mk 11:22 "Have *f* in God," Jesus answered.
Lk 7: 9 I have not found such great *f*
12:28 will he clothe you, O you of little *f*!
17: 5 "Increase our *f*!" He replied,
18: 8 will he find *f* on the earth?"
Ac 14: 9 saw that he had *f* to be healed
14:27 the door of *f* to the Gentiles.
Ro 1:12 encouraged by each other's *f*.
1:17 is by *f* from first to last,
1:17 "The righteous will live by *f*."
3: 3 What if some did not have *f*?
3:22 comes through *f* in Jesus Christ
3:25 a sacrifice of atonement, through *f*
4: 5 his *f* is credited as righteousness.
5: 1 we have been justified through *f*,
10:17 *f* comes from hearing the message,
14: 1 Accept him whose *f* is weak,
14:23 that does not come from *f* is sin.
1Co 13: 2 and if I have a *f* that can move
13:13 And now these three remain: *f*,
16:13 stand firm in the *f*; be men
2Co 5: 7 We live by *f*, not by sight.
13: 5 to see whether you are in the *f*;
Gal 2:16 Jesus that we may be justified by *f*
2:20 I live by *f* in the Son of God,
3:11 "The righteous will live by *f*."
3:24 that we might be justified by *f*.
Eph 2: 8 through *f*— and this not
4: 5 one Lord, one *f*, one baptism;
6:16 to all this, take up the shield of *f*,
Col 1:23 continue in your *f*, established
1Th 5: 8 on *f* and love as a breastplate,
1Ti 2:15 if they continue in *f*, love
4: 1 later times some will abandon the *f*
5: 8 he has denied the *f* and is worse
6:12 Fight the good fight of the *f*.
2Ti 3:15 wise for salvation through *f*
4: 7 finished the race, I have kept the *f*.
Phm : 6 may be active in sharing your *f*,
Heb 10:38 But my righteous one will live by *f*.
11: 1 *f* is being sure of what we hope for
11: 3 By *f* we understand that
11: 5 By *f* Enoch was taken from this life
11: 6 And without *f* it is impossible
11: 7 By *f* Noah, when warned about
11: 8 By *f* Abraham, when called to go
11:17 By *f* Abraham, when God tested
11:20 By *f* Isaac blessed Jacob

Heb 11:21 By *f* Jacob, when he was dying,
11:22 By *f* Joseph, when his end was near
11:24 By *f* Moses, when he had grown up
11:31 By *f* the prostitute Rahab,
12: 2 the author and perfecter of our *f*,
Jas 2:14 if a man claims to have *f*
2:17 In the same way, *f* by itself,
2:26 so *f* without deeds is dead.
2Pe 1: 5 effort to add to your *f* goodness;
1Jn 5: 4 overcome the world, even our *f*.
Jude : 3 to contend for the *f* that was once

FAITHFUL (FAITH)
Nu 12: 7 he is *f* in all my house.
Dt 7: 9 your God is God; he is the *f* God,
32: 4 A *f* God who does no wrong,
2Sa 22:26 "To the *f* you show yourself *f*,
Ps 25:10 of the LORD are loving and *f*
31:23 The LORD preserves the *f*,
33: 4 he is *f* in all he does.
37:28 and will not forsake his *f* ones.
97:10 for he guards the lives of his *f* ones
145:13 The LORD is *f* to all his promises
146: 6 the LORD, who remains *f* forever.
Pr 31:26 and *f* instruction is on her tongue.
Mt 25:21 'Well done, good and *f* servant!
Ro 12:12 patient in affliction, *f* in prayer.
1Co 4: 2 been given a trust must prove *f*.
10:13 And God is *f*; he will not let you be
1Th 5:24 The one who calls you is *f*
2Ti 2:13 he will remain *f*,
Heb 3: 6 But Christ is *f* as a son
10:23 for he who promised is *f*.
1Pe 4:19 themselves to their *f* Creator
1Jn 1: 9 he is *f* and just and will forgive us
Rev 1: 5 who is the *f* witness, the firstborn
2:10 Be *f*, even to the point of death,
19:11 whose rider is called *F* and True

FAITHFULLY (FAITH)
Dt 11:13 if you *f* obey the commands I am
1Sa 12:24 and serve him *f* with all your heart;
1Ki 2: 4 and if they walk *f* before me
1Pe 4:10 *f* administering God's grace

FAITHFULNESS (FAITH)
Ps 57:10 your *f* reaches to the skies.
85:10 Love and *f* meet together;
86:15 to anger, abounding in love and *f*.
89: 1 mouth I will make your *f* known
89:14 love and *f* go before you.
91: 4 his *f* will be your shield
117: 2 the *f* of the LORD endures forever.
119:75 and in *f* you have afflicted me.
Pr 3: 3 Let love and *f* never leave you;
Isa 11: 5 and *f* the sash around his waist.
La 3:23 great is your *f*.
Ro 3: 3 lack of faith nullify God's *f*?
Gal 5:22 patience, kindness, goodness, *f*,

FAITHLESS (FAITH)
Ps 119:158 I look on the *f* with loathing,
Jer 3:22 "Return, *f* people;
Ro 1:31 they are senseless, *f*, heartless,
2Ti 2:13 if we are *f*,

FALL (FALLEN FALLING FALLS)
Ps 37:24 though he stumble, he will not *f*,
55:22 he will never let the righteous *f*.
69: 9 of those who insult you *f* on me.
Pr 11:28 Whoever trusts in his riches will *f*,
Lk 11:17 a house divided against itself will *f*.
Ro 3:23 and *f* short of the glory of God,
Heb 6: 6 if they *f* away, to be brought back

FALLEN (FALL)
2Sa 1:19 How the mighty have *f*!
Isa 14:12 How you have *f* from heaven,
1Co 15:20 of those who have *f* asleep.
Gal 5: 4 you have *f* away from grace.
1Th 4:15 precede those who have *f* asleep.

FALLING (FALL)
Jude :24 able to keep you from *f*

FALLS (FALL)
Pr 24:17 Do not gloat when your enemy *f*;
Jn 12:24 a kernel of wheat *f* to the ground
Ro 14: 4 To his own master he stands or *f*.

FALSE (FALSEHOOD FALSELY)
Ex 20:16 "You shall not give *f* testimony
23: 1 "Do not spread *f* reports.
Pr 13: 5 The righteous hate what is *f*,
19: 5 A *f* witness will not go unpunished,
Mt 7:15 "Watch out for *f* prophets.
19:18 not steal, do not give *f* testimony,
24:11 and many *f* prophets will appear
Php 1:18 whether from *f* motives or true,
1Ti 1: 3 not to teach *f* doctrines any longer
2Pe 2: 1 there will be *f* teachers among you.

FALSEHOOD (FALSE)
Ps 119:163 I hate and abhor *f*
Pr 30: 8 Keep *f* and lies far from me;
Eph 4:25 each of you must put off *f*

FALSELY (FALSE)
Lev 19:12 " 'Do not swear *f* by my name
Lk 3:14 and don't accuse people *f*—
1Ti 6:20 ideas of what is *f* called knowledge,

FALTER*
Pr 24:10 If you *f* in times of trouble,
Isa 42: 4 he will not *f* or be discouraged

FAMILIES (FAMILY)
Ps 68: 6 God sets the lonely in *f*,

FAMILY (FAMILIES)
Pr 15:27 greedy man brings trouble to his *f*,
31:15 she provides food for her *f*
Lk 9:61 go back and say good-by to my *f*."
12:52 in one *f* divided against each other,
1Ti 3: 4 He must manage his own *f* well
3: 5 how to manage his own *f*,
5: 4 practice by caring for their own *f*
5: 8 and especially for his immediate *f*,

FAMINE
Ge 41:30 seven years of *f* will follow them.
Am 8:11 but a *f* of hearing the words
Ro 8:35 or persecution or *f* or nakedness

FAN*
2Ti 1: 6 you to *f* into flame the gift of God,

FAST
Dt 13: 4 serve him and hold *f* to him.
Jos 22: 5 to hold *f* to him and to serve him
23: 8 to hold *f* to the LORD your God,
Ps 119:31 I hold *f* to your statutes, O LORD;
139:10 your right hand will hold me *f*.
Mt 6:16 "When you *f*, do not look somber
1Pe 5:12 Stand *f* in it.

FATHER (FATHER'S FATHERLESS FATHERS FOREFATHERS)
Ge 2:24 this reason a man will leave his *f*
17: 4 You will be the *f* of many nations.
Ex 20:12 "Honor your *f* and your mother,
21:15 "Anyone who attacks his *f*
21:17 "Anyone who curses his *f*
Lev 18: 7 " 'Do not dishonor your *f*
19: 3 you must respect his mother and *f*,
Dt 5:16 "Honor your *f* and your mother,
21:18 son who does not obey his *f*
Ps 27:10 Though my *f* and mother forsake
68: 5 A *f* to the fatherless, a defender
Pr 10: 1 A wise son brings joy to his *f*,
17:21 there is no joy for the *f* of a fool.
23:22 Listen to your *f*, who gave you life,
23:24 *f* of a righteous man has great joy;
28: 7 of gluttons disgraces his *f*.
29: 3 loves wisdom brings joy to his *f*,
Isa 9: 6 Everlasting *F*, Prince of Peace.
Mt 6: 9 " 'Our *F* in heaven,
10:37 "Anyone who loves his *f*
15: 4 'Honor your *f* and mother'
19: 5 this reason a man will leave his *f*
Lk 12:53 *f* against son and son against *f*,
23:34 Jesus said, "*F*, forgive them,
Jn 6:44 the *F* who sent me draws him,
6:46 No one has seen the *F*
8:44 You belong to your *f*, the devil,
10:30 I and the *F* are one."
14: 6 No one comes to the *F*
14: 9 who has seen me has seen the *F*.
Ro 4:11 he is the *f* of all who believe
2Co 6:18 "I will be a *F* to you,
Eph 6: 2 "Honor your *f* and mother"—
Heb 12: 7 what son is not disciplined by his *f*?

FATHER'S (FATHER)
Pr 13: 1 A wise son heeds his *f* instruction,
15: 5 A fool spurns his *f* discipline,
19:13 A foolish son is his *f* ruin,
Lk 2:49 had to be in my *F* house?"
Jn 2:16 How dare you turn my *F* house
10:29 can snatch them out of my *F* hand.
14: 2 In my *F* house are many rooms;

FATHERLESS (FATHER)
Dt 10:18 He defends the cause of the *f*
24:17 Do not deprive the alien or the *f*
24:19 Leave it for the alien, the *f*
Ps 68: 5 A father to the *f*, a defender
Pr 23:10 or encroach on the fields of the *f*,

FATHERS (FATHER)
Ex 20: 5 for the sin of the *f* to the third
Lk 11:11 "Which of you *f*, if your son asks
Eph 6: 4 *F*, do not exasperate your children;
Col 3:21 *F*, do not embitter your children,

FATHOM*
Job 11: 7 "Can you *f* the mysteries of God?
Ps 145: 3 his greatness no one can *f*.
Ecc 3:11 yet they cannot *f* what God has
Isa 40:28 and his understanding no one can *f*
1Co 13: 2 and can *f* all mysteries and all

FAULT (FAULTS)
Mt 18:15 and show him his *f*, just
Php 2:15 of God without *f* in a crooked
Jas 1: 5 generously to all without finding *f*,
Jude :24 his glorious presence without *f*

FAULTFINDERS*
Jude :16 These men are grumblers and *f*;

FAULTS (FAULT)
Ps 19:12 Forgive my hidden *f*.

FAVORITISM*
Ex 23: 3 and do not show *f* to a poor man
Lev 19:15 to the poor or *f* to the great,
Ac 10:34 true it is that God does not show *f*
Ro 2:11 For God does not show *f*.
Eph 6: 9 and there is no *f* with him.
Col 3:25 for his wrong, and there is no *f*.
1Ti 5:21 and to do nothing out of *f*.
Jas 2: 1 Lord Jesus Christ, don't show *f*.
2: 9 But if you show *f*, you sin

FEAR (AFRAID FEARS)
Dt 6:13 *F* the LORD your God, serve him
10:12 but to *f* the LORD your God,
31:12 and learn to *f* the LORD your God
Ps 19: 9 The *f* of the LORD is pure,
23: 4 I will *f* no evil,
27: 1 whom shall I *f*?
91: 5 You will not *f* the terror of night,
111:10 *f* of the LORD is the beginning
Pr 8:13 To *f* the LORD is to hate evil;
9:10 *f* of the LORD is the beginning
10:27 The *f* of the LORD adds length
14:27 The *f* of the LORD is a fountain
15:33 *f* of the LORD teaches a man
16: 6 through the *f* of the LORD a man
19:23 The *f* of the LORD leads to life:
29:25 *F* of man will prove to be a snare,
Isa 11: 3 delight in the *f* of the LORD.
41:10 So do not *f*, for I am with you;
Lk 12: 5 I will show you whom you should *f*:
Php 2:12 to work out your salvation with *f*
1Jn 4:18 But perfect love drives out *f*,

FEARS (FEAR)
Job 1: 8 a man who *f* God and shuns evil."
Ps 34: 4 he delivered me from all my *f*.
Pr 31:30 a woman who *f* the LORD is
1Jn 4:18 The one who *f* is not made perfect

FEED
Jn 21:15 Jesus said, "*F* my lambs."
21:17 Jesus said, "*F* my sheep.
Ro 12:20 "If your enemy is hungry, *f* him;
Jude :12 shepherds who *f* only themselves.

FEET (FOOT)
Ps 8: 6 you put everything under his *f*:
22:16 have pierced my hands and my *f*.
40: 2 he set my *f* on a rock
110: 1 a footstool for your *f*."
119:105 Your word is a lamp to my *f*
Ro 10:15 "How beautiful are the *f*
1Co 12:21 And the head cannot say to the *f*,
15:25 has put all his enemies under his *f*.
Heb 12:13 "Make level paths for your *f*,"

FELLOWSHIP
2Co 6:14 what *f* can light have with darkness
13:14 and the *f* of the Holy Spirit be
Php 3:10 the *f* of sharing in his sufferings,
1Jn 1: 6 claim to have *f* with him yet walk
1: 7 we have *f* with one another,

FEMALE
Ge 1:27 male and *f* he created them.

Gal 3:28 *f*, for you are all one in Christ Jesus

FERVOR
Ro 12:11 but keep your spiritual *f*, serving

FIELD (FIELDS)
Mt 6:28 See how the lilies of the *f* grow.
13:38 *f* is the world, and the good seed
1Co 3:9 you are God's *f*, God's building.

FIELDS (FIELD)
Lk 2:8 were shepherds living out in the *f*
Jn 4:35 open your eyes and look at the *f*!

FIG (FIGS)
Ge 3:7 so they sewed *f* leaves together

FIGHT (FOUGHT)
Ex 14:14 The LORD will *f* for you; you need
Dt 1:30 going before you, will *f* for you,
3:22 the LORD your God himself will *f*
Ne 4:20 Our God will *f* for us!"
Ps 35:1 *f* against those who *f* against me.
Jn 18:36 my servants would *f*
1Co 9:26 I do not *f* like a man beating the air.
2Co 10:4 The weapons we *f*
1Ti 1:18 them you may *f* the good *f*,
6:12 Fight the good *f* of the faith.
2Ti 4:7 I have fought the good *f*, I have finished

FIGS (FIG)
Lk 6:44 People do not pick *f*

FILL (FILLED FILLS FULL FULLNESS FULLY)
Ge 1:28 and increase in number; *f* the earth
Ps 16:11 you will *f* me with joy
81:10 wide your mouth and I will *f* it.
Pr 28:19 who chases fantasies will have his *f*
Hag 2:7 and I will *f* this house with glory,'
Jn 6:26 you ate the loaves and had your *f*.
Ac 2:28 you will *f* me with joy
Ro 15:13 the God of hope *f* you with all joy

FILLED (FILL)
Ps 72:19 may the whole earth be *f*
119:64 The earth is *f* with your love,
Eze 43:5 the glory of the LORD *f* the temple
Hab 2:14 For the earth will be *f*
Lk 1:15 and he will be *f* with the Holy Spirit
1:41 and Elizabeth was *f* with the Holy
Jn 12:3 the house was *f* with the fragrance
Ac 2:4 All of them were *f*
4:8 Then Peter, *f* with the Holy Spirit,
9:17 and be *f* with the Holy Spirit."
13:9 called Paul, *f* with the Holy Spirit,
Eph 5:18 Instead, be *f* with the Spirit.
Php 1:11 *f* with the fruit of righteousness

FILLS (FILL)
Nu 14:21 of the LORD *f* the whole earth,
Ps 107:9 and *f* the hungry with good things.
Eph 1:23 fullness of him who *f* everything

FILTHY
Isa 64:6 all our righteous acts are like *f* rags;
Col 3:8 and *f* language from your lips.
2Pe 2:7 by the *f* lives of lawless men

FIND (FINDS FOUND)
Nu 32:23 be sure that your sin will *f* you out.
Dt 4:29 you will *f* him if you look for him
1Sa 23:16 and helped him *f* strength in God.
Ps 36:7 *f* refuge in the shadow
91:4 under his wings you will *f* refuge;
Pr 14:22 those who plan what is good *f* love
31:10 A wife of noble character who can *f*
Jer 6:16 and you will *f* rest for your souls.
Mt 7:7 seek and you will *f*; knock
11:29 and you will *f* rest for your souls.
16:25 loses his life for me will *f* it.
Lk 18:8 will he *f* faith on the earth?"
Jn 10:9 come in and go out, and *f* pasture.

FINDS (FIND)
Ps 62:1 My soul *f* rest in God alone;
112:1 who *f* great delight
119:162 like one who *f* great spoil.
Pr 18:22 He who *f* a wife *f* what is good
Mt 7:8 he who seeks *f*; and to him who
10:39 Whoever *f* his life will lose it,
Lk 12:37 whose master *f* them watching
15:4 go after the lost sheep until he *f* it?

FINISH (FINISHED)
Jn 4:34 him who sent me and to *f* his work.
5:36 that the Father has given me to *f*,
Ac 20:24 if only I may *f* the race
2Co 8:11 Now *f* the work, so that your eager

Jas 1:4 Perseverance must *f* its work

FINISHED (FINISH)
Ge 2:2 seventh day God had *f* the work he
Jn 19:30 the drink, Jesus said, "It is *f*."
2Ti 4:7 I have *f* the race, I have kept

FIRE
Ex 13:21 in a pillar of *f* to give them light,
Lev 6:12 *f* on the altar must be kept burning;
Isa 30:27 and his tongue is a consuming *f*.
Jer 23:29 my word like *f*," declares
Mt 3:11 you with the Holy Spirit and with *f*.
5:22 will be in danger of the *f* of hell.
25:41 into the eternal *f* prepared
Mk 9:43 where the *f* never goes out.
Ac 2:3 to be tongues of *f* that separated
1Co 3:13 It will be revealed with *f*,
1Th 5:19 Do not put out the Spirit's *f*;
Heb 12:29 for our "God is a consuming *f*."
Jas 3:5 set on *f* by a small spark.
2Pe 3:10 the elements will be destroyed by *f*,
Jude :23 snatch others from the *f*
Rev 20:14 The lake of *f* is the second death.

FIRM
Ex 14:13 Stand *f* and you will see
2Ch 20:17 stand *f* and see the deliverance
Ps 33:11 of the LORD stand *f* forever,
37:23 he makes his steps *f*;
40:2 and gave me a *f* place to stand.
89:2 that your love stands *f* forever,
119:89 it stands *f* in the heavens.
Pr 4:26 and take only ways that are *f*.
Zec 8:23 nations will take *f* hold of one Jew
Mk 13:13 he who stands *f* to the end will be
1Co 16:13 on your guard; stand *f* in the faith;
2Co 1:24 because it is by faith you stand *f*.
Eph 6:14 Stand *f* then, with the belt
Col 4:12 that you may stand *f* in all the will
2Th 2:15 stand *f* and hold to the teachings
2Ti 2:19 God's solid foundation stands *f*,
Heb 6:19 an anchor for the soul, *f* and secure
1Pe 5:9 Resist him, standing *f* in the faith,

FIRST
Isa 44:6 I am the *f* and I am the last;
48:12 I am the *f* and I am the last.
Mt 5:24 *F* go and be reconciled
6:33 But seek *f* his kingdom
7:5 *f* take the plank out
20:27 wants to be *f* must be your slave—
22:38 This is the *f* and greatest
23:26 *F* clean the inside of the cup
Mk 13:10 And the gospel must *f* be preached
Ac 11:26 disciples were called Christians *f*
Ro 1:16 *f* for the Jew, then for the Gentile.
1Co 12:28 in the church God has appointed *f*
2Co 8:5 they gave themselves *f* to the Lord
1Ti 2:13 For Adam was formed *f*, then Eve.
Jas 3:17 comes from heaven is *f* of all pure;
1Jn 4:19 We love because he *f* loved us.
3Jn :9 but Diotrephes, who loves to be *f*,
Rev 1:17 I am the *F* and the Last.
2:4 You have forsaken your *f* love.

FIRSTBORN (BEAR)
Ex 11:5 Every *f* son in Egypt will die,

FIRSTFRUITS
Ex 23:19 "Bring the best of the *f* of your soil

FISHERS
Mk 1:17 "and I will make you *f* of men."

FITTING*
Ps 33:1 it is *f* for the upright to praise him.
147:1 how pleasant and *f* to praise him!
Pr 10:32 of the righteous know what is *f*,
19:10 It is not *f* for a fool to live in luxury
26:1 honor is not *f* for a fool.
1Co 14:40 everything should be done in a *f*
Col 3:18 to your husbands, as is *f* in the Lord
Heb 2:10 sons to glory, it was *f* that God,

FIX
Dt 11:18 *F* these words of mine
Pr 4:25 *f* your gaze directly before you.
2Co 4:18 we *f* our eyes not on what is seen,
Heb 3:1 heavenly calling, *f* your thoughts
12:2 Let us *f* our eyes on Jesus,

FLAME (FLAMES FLAMING)
2Ti 1:6 you to fan into *f* the gift of God,

FLAMES (FLAME)
1Co 3:15 only as one escaping through the *f*.

1Co 13:3 and surrender my body to the *f*,

FLAMING (FLAME)
Eph 6:16 you can extinguish all the *f* arrows

FLASH
1Co 15:52 in a *f*, in the twinkling of an eye,

FLATTER (FLATTERING FLATTERY)
Job 32:21 nor will I *f* any man;
Jude :16 *f* others for their own advantage.

FLATTERING (FLATTER)
Ps 12:2 their *f* lips speak with deception.
12:3 May the LORD cut off all *f* lips
Pr 26:28 and a *f* mouth works ruin.

FLATTERY (FLATTER)
Ro 16:18 and *f* they deceive the minds
1Th 2:5 You know we never used *f*,

FLAWLESS*
2Sa 22:31 the word of the LORD is *f*.
Job 11:4 You say to God, 'My beliefs are *f*
Ps 12:6 And the words of the LORD are *f*,
18:30 the word of the LORD is *f*.
Pr 30:5 "Every word of God is *f*;
SS 5:2 my dove, my *f* one.

FLEE
Ps 139:7 Where can I *f* from your presence?
1Co 6:18 *F* from sexual immorality.
10:14 my dear friends, *f* from idolatry.
1Ti 6:11 But you, man of God, *f* from all this
2Ti 2:22 *F* the evil desires of youth,
Jas 4:7 Resist the devil, and he will *f*

FLEETING
Ps 89:47 Remember how *f* is my life.
Pr 31:30 Charm is deceptive, and beauty is *f*

FLESH
Ge 2:23 and *f* of my *f*;
2:24 and they will become one *f*.
Job 19:26 yet in my *f* I will see God;
Eze 11:19 of stone and give them a heart of *f*.
36:26 of stone and give you a heart of *f*.
Mk 10:8 and the two will become one *f*.'
Jn 1:14 The Word became *f* and made his
6:51 This bread is my *f*, which I will give
1Co 6:16 "The two will become one *f*."
Eph 5:31 and the two will become one *f*."
6:12 For our struggle is not against *f*

FLOCK (FLOCKS)
Isa 40:11 He tends his *f* like a shepherd:
Eze 34:2 not shepherds take care of the *f*?
Zec 11:17 who deserts the *f*!
Mt 26:31 the sheep of the *f* will be scattered.'
Ac 20:28 all the *f* of which the Holy Spirit
1Pe 5:2 Be shepherds of God's *f* that is

FLOCKS (FLOCK)
Lk 2:8 keeping watch over their *f* at night.

FLOG
Ac 22:25 to *f* a Roman citizen who hasn't

FLOODGATES
Mal 3:10 see if I will not throw open the *f*

FLOURISHING
Ps 52:8 *f* in the house of God;

FLOW (FLOWING)
Nu 13:27 and it does *f* with milk and honey!
Jn 7:38 streams of living water will *f*

FLOWERS
Isa 40:7 The grass withers and the *f* fall,

FLOWING (FLOW)
Ex 3:8 a land *f* with milk and honey—

FOLDING
Pr 6:10 a little *f* of the hands to rest—

FOLLOW (FOLLOWING FOLLOWS)
Ex 23:2 Do not *f* the crowd in doing wrong.
Lev 18:4 and be careful to *f* my decrees.
Dt 5:1 Learn them and be sure to *f* them.
Ps 23:6 Surely goodness and love will *f* me
Mt 16:24 and take up his cross and *f* me.
Jn 10:4 his sheep *f* him because they know
1Co 14:1 *F* the way of love and eagerly
Rev 14:4 They *f* the Lamb wherever he goes.

FOLLOWING (FOLLOW)
1Ti 1:18 by *f* them you may fight the good

FOLLOWS (FOLLOW)
Jn 8:12 Whoever *f* me will never walk

FOOD (FOODS)
Pr 20:13 you will have *f* to spare.
22: 9 for he shares his *f* with the poor.
25:21 If your enemy is hungry, give him *f*
31:15 she provides *f* for her family
Da 1: 8 to defile himself with the royal *f*
Jn 6:27 Do not work for *f* that spoils,
Ro 14:14 fully convinced that no *f* is unclean
1Co 8: 8 But *f* does not bring us near to God
1Ti 6: 8 But if we have *f* and clothing,
Jas 2:15 sister is without clothes and daily *f*.

FOODS (FOOD)
Mk 7:19 Jesus declared all *f* "clean.")

FOOL (FOOLISH FOOLISHNESS FOOLS)
Ps 14: 1 The *f* says in his heart,
Pr 15: 5 A *f* spurns his father's discipline,
17:28 Even a *f* is thought wise
18: 2 A *f* finds no pleasure
26: 5 Answer a *f* according to his folly,
28:26 He who trusts in himself is a *f*,
Mt 5:22 But anyone who says, 'You *f*!'

FOOLISH (FOOL)
Pr 10: 1 but a *f* son grief to his mother.
17:25 A *f* son brings grief to his father
Mt 7:26 practice is like a *f* man who built
25: 2 of them were *f* and five were wise.
1Co 1:27 God chose the *f* things of the world

FOOLISHNESS (FOOL)
1Co 1:18 of the cross is *f* to those who are
1:25 For the *f* of God is wiser
2:14 for they are *f* to him, and he cannot
3:19 of this world is *f* in God's sight.

FOOLS (FOOL)
Pr 14: 9 *F* mock at making amends for sin,
1Co 4:10 We are *f* for Christ, but you are

FOOT (FEET FOOTHOLD)
Jos 1: 3 every place where you set your *f*,
Isa 1: 6 From the sole of your *f* to the top
1Co 12:15 If the *f* should say, "Because I am

FOOTHOLD (FOOT)
Eph 4:27 and do not give the devil a *f*.

FORBEARANCE*
Ro 3:25 because in his *f* he had left the sins

FORBID
1Co 14:39 and do not *f* speaking in tongues.

FOREFATHERS (FATHER)
Heb 1: 1 spoke to our *f* through the prophets

FOREKNEW* (KNOW)
Ro 8:29 For those God *f* he
11: 2 not reject his people, whom he *f*.

FOREVER (EVER)
1Ch 16:15 He remembers his covenant *f*,
16:34 his love endures *f*.
Ps 9: 7 The LORD reigns *f*;
23: 6 dwell in the house of the LORD *f*.
33:11 the plans of the LORD stand firm *f*
86:12 I will glorify your name *f*.
92: 8 But you, O LORD, are exalted *f*.
110: 4 "You are a priest *f*,
119:111 Your statutes are my heritage *f*;
Jn 6:51 eats of this bread, he will live *f*.
14:16 Counselor to be with you *f*—
1Co 9:25 it to get a crown that will last *f*.
1Th 4:17 And so we will be with the Lord *f*.
Heb 13: 8 same yesterday and today and *f*.
1Pe 1:25 but the word of the Lord stands *f*."
1Jn 2:17 who does the will of God lives *f*.

FORFEIT
Lk 9:25 and yet lose or *f* his very self?

FORGAVE (FORGIVE)
Ps 32: 5 and you *f*
Eph 4:32 just as in Christ God *f* you.
Col 2:13 He *f* us all our sins, having
3:13 Forgive as the Lord *f* you.

FORGET (FORGETS FORGETTING)
Dt 6:12 that you do not *f* the LORD,
Ps 103: 2 and *f* not all his benefits.
137: 5 may my right hand *f* its skill.
Isa 49:15 "Can a mother *f* the baby
Heb 6:10 he will not *f* your work

FORGETS (FORGET)
Jn 16:21 her baby is born she *f* the anguish
Jas 1:24 immediately *f* what he looks like.

FORGETTING (FORGET)
Php 3:13 *F* what is behind and straining

FORGIVE (FORGAVE FORGIVENESS FORGIVING)
2Ch 7:14 will *f* their sin and will heal their
Ps 19:12 *F* my hidden faults.
Mt 6:12 *F* us our debts,
6:14 For if you *f* men when they sin
18:21 many times shall I *f* my brother
Mk 11:25 in heaven may *f* you your sins."
Lk 11: 4 *F* us our sins,
23:34 Jesus said, "Father, *f* them,
Col 3:13 *F* as the Lord forgave you.
1Jn 1: 9 and just and will *f* us our sins

FORGIVENESS (FORGIVE)
Ps 130: 4 But with you there is *f*;
Ac 10:43 believes in him receives *f* of sins
Eph 1: 7 through his blood, the *f* of sins,
Col 1:14 in whom we have redemption, the *f*
Heb 9:22 the shedding of blood there is no *f*.

FORGIVING (FORGIVE)
Ne 9:17 But you are a *f* God, gracious
Eph 4:32 to one another, *f* each other,

FORMED
Ge 2: 7 And the LORD God *f* man
Ps 103:14 for he knows how we are *f*,
Isa 45:18 but *f* it to be inhabited—
Ro 9:20 "Shall what is *f* say to him who *f* it,
1Ti 2:13 For Adam was *f* first, then Eve.
Heb 11: 3 understand that the universe was *f*

FORSAKE (FORSAKEN)
Jos 1: 5 I will never leave you nor *f* you.
24:16 "Far be it from us to *f* the LORD
2Ch 15: 2 but if you *f* him, he will *f* you.
Ps 27:10 Though my father and mother *f* me
Isa 55: 7 Let the wicked *f* his way
Heb 13: 5 never will I *f* you."

FORSAKEN (FORSAKE)
Ps 22: 1 my God, why have you *f* me?
37:25 I have never seen the righteous *f*
Mt 27:46 my God, why have you *f* me?"
Rev 2: 4 You have *f* your first love.

FORTRESS
Ps 18: 2 The LORD is my rock, my *f*
71: 3 for you are my rock and my *f*.

FOUGHT (FIGHT)
2Ti 4: 7 I have *f* the good fight, I have

FOUND (FIND)
1Ch 28: 9 If you seek him, he will be *f* by you;
Isa 55: 6 Seek the LORD while he may be *f*;
Da 5:27 on the scales and *f* wanting.
Lk 15: 6 with me; I have *f* my lost sheep.'
15: 9 with me; I have *f* my lost coin.'
Ac 4:12 Salvation is *f* in no one else,

FOUNDATION
Isa 28:16 a precious cornerstone for a sure *f*;
1Co 3:11 For no one can lay any *f* other
Eph 2:20 built on the *f* of the apostles
2Ti 2:19 God's solid *f* stands firm,

FOXES
Mt 8:20 "*F* have holes and birds

FRAGRANCE
2Co 2:16 of death; to the other, the *f* of life.

FREE (FREED FREEDOM FREELY)
Ps 146: 7 The LORD sets prisoners *f*,
Jn 8:32 and the truth will set you *f*."
Ro 6:18 You have been set *f* from sin
Gal 3:28 slave nor *f*, male nor female,
1Pe 2:16 *f* men, but do not use your freedom

FREED (FREE)
Rev 1: 5 has *f* us from our sins by his blood,

FREEDOM (FREE)
Ro 8:21 into the glorious *f* of the children
2Co 3:17 the Spirit of the Lord is, there is *f*.
Gal 5:13 But do not use your *f* to indulge
1Pe 2:16 but do not use your *f* as a cover-up

FREELY (FREE)
Isa 55: 7 and to our God, for he will *f* pardon
Mt 10: 8 Freely you have received, *f* give.
Ro 3:24 and are justified *f* by his grace
Eph 1: 6 which he has *f* given us

FRIEND (FRIENDS)
Ex 33:11 as a man speaks with his *f*.
Pr 17:17 A *f* loves at all times,
18:24 there is a *f* who sticks closer
27: 6 Wounds from a *f* can be trusted,
27:10 Do not forsake your *f* and the *f*
Jas 4: 4 Anyone who chooses to be a *f*

FRIENDS (FRIEND)
Pr 16:28 and a gossip separates close *f*.
Zec 13: 6 given at the house of my *f*.'
Jn 15:13 that he lay down his life for his *f*.

FRUIT (FRUITFUL)
Ps 1: 3 which yields its *f* in season
Pr 11:30 The *f* of the righteous is a tree
Mt 7:16 By their *f* you will recognize them.
Jn 15: 2 branch in me that bears no *f*,
Gal 5:22 But the *f* of the Spirit is love, joy,
Rev 22: 2 of *f*, yielding its *f* every month.

FRUITFUL (FRUIT)
Ge 1:22 "Be *f* and increase in number
Ps 128: 3 Your wife will be like a *f* vine
Jn 15: 2 prunes so that it will be even more *f*.

FULFILL (FULFILLED FULFILLMENT)
Ps 116:14 I will *f* my vows to the LORD
Mt 5:17 come to abolish them but to *f* them.
1Co 7: 3 husband should *f* his marital duty

FULFILLED (FULFILL)
Pr 13:19 A longing *f* is sweet to the soul,
Mk 14:49 But the Scriptures must be *f*."
Ro 13: 8 loves his fellowman has *f* the law.

FULFILLMENT (FULFILL)
Ro 13:10 Therefore love is the *f* of the law.

FULL (FILL)
Ps 127: 5 whose quiver is *f* of them.
Pr 31:11 Her husband has *f* confidence
Isa 6: 3 the whole earth is *f* of his glory."
11: 9 for the earth will be *f*
Jn 10:10 may have life, and have it to the *f*.
Ac 6: 3 known to be *f* of the Spirit

FULLNESS (FILL)
Col 1:19 to have all his *f* dwell in him,
2: 9 in Christ all the *f* of the Deity lives

FULLY (FILL)
1Ki 8:61 your hearts must be *f* committed
2Ch 16: 9 whose hearts are *f* committed
Ps 119: 4 that are to be *f* obeyed.
119:138 they are *f* trustworthy.
1Co 15:58 Always give yourselves *f*

FUTURE
Ps 37:37 there is a *f* for the man of peace.
Pr 23:18 There is surely a *f* hope for you,
Ro 8:38 neither the present nor the *f*,

GABRIEL*
Angel who interpreted Daniel's visions (Da 8:16-26; 9:20-27); announced births of John (Lk 1:11-20), Jesus (Lk 1:26-38).

GAIN (GAINED)
Ps 60:12 With God we will *g* the victory,
Mk 8:36 it for a man to *g* the whole world,
1Co 13: 3 but have not love, I *g* nothing.
Php 1:21 to live is Christ and to die is *g*.
3: 8 that I may *g* Christ and be found
1Ti 6: 6 with contentment is great *g*.

GAINED (GAIN)
Ro 5: 2 through whom we have *g* access

GALILEE
Isa 9: 1 but in the future he will honor *G*

GALL
Mt 27:34 mixed with *g*; but after tasting it,

GAP
Eze 22:30 stand before me in the *g* on behalf

GARDENER
Jn 15: 1 true vine, and my Father is the *g*.

GARMENT (GARMENTS)
Ps 102:26 they will all wear out like a *g*.
Mt 9:16 of unshrunk cloth on an old *g*,
Jn 19:23 This *g* was seamless, woven

GARMENTS (GARMENT)
Ge 3:21 The LORD God made *g* of skin
Isa 61:10 me with *g* of salvation
63: 1 with his *g* stained crimson?
Jn 19:24 "They divided my *g* among them

GATE (GATES)
Mt 7:13 For wide is the *g* and broad is

Jn 10: 9 I am the *g;* whoever enters

GATES (GATE)
Ps 100: 4 Enter his *g* with thanksgiving
Mt 16:18 the *g* of Hades will not overcome it

GATHER (GATHERS)
Zec 14: 2 I will *g* all the nations to Jerusalem
Mt 12:30 he who does not *g* with me scatters
23:37 longed to *g* your children together,

GATHERS (GATHER)
Isa 40:11 He *g* the lambs in his arms
Mt 23:37 a hen *g* her chicks under her wings,

GAVE (GIVE)
Ezr 2:69 According to their ability they *g*
Job 1:21 LORD *g* and the LORD has taken
Jn 3:16 so loved the world that he *g* his one
2Co 8: 5 they *g* themselves first to the Lord
Gal 2:20 who loved me and *g* himself for me
1Ti 2: 6 who *g* himself as a ransom

GAZE
Ps 27: 4 to *g* upon the beauty of the LORD
Pr 4:25 fix your *g* directly before you.

GENEALOGIES
1Ti 1: 4 themselves to myths and endless *g.*

GENERATIONS
Ps 22:30 future *g* will be told about the Lord
102:12 your renown endures through all *g.*
145:13 dominion endures through all *g.*
Lk 1:48 now on all *g* will call me blessed,
Eph 3: 5 not made known to men in other *g*

GENEROUS
Ps 112: 5 Good will come to him who is *g*
Pr 22: 9 A *g* man will himself be blessed,
2Co 9: 5 Then it will be ready as a *g* gift,
1Ti 6:18 and to be *g* and willing to share.

GENTILE (GENTILES)
Ro 1:16 first for the Jew, then for the *G.*
10:12 difference between Jew and *G*—

GENTILES (GENTILE)
Isa 42: 6 and a light for the *G,*
Ro 3: 9 and *G* alike are all under sin.
11:13 as I am the apostle to the *G,*
1Co 1:23 block to Jews and foolishness to *G,*

GENTLE (GENTLENESS)
Pr 15: 1 A *g* answer turns away wrath,
Zec 9: 9 *g* and riding on a donkey,
Mt 11:29 for I am *g* and humble in heart,
21: 5 *g* and riding on a donkey,
1Co 4:21 or in love and with a *g* spirit?
1Pe 3: 4 the unfading beauty of a *g*

GENTLENESS* (GENTLE)
2Co 10: 1 By the meekness and *g* of Christ,
Gal 5:23 faithfulness, *g* and self-control.
Php 4: 5 Let your *g* be evident to all.
Col 3:12 kindness, humility, *g* and patience.
1Ti 6:11 faith, love, endurance and *g.*
1Pe 3:15 But do this with *g* and respect,

GETHSEMANE
Mt 26:36 disciples to a place called *G,*

GIDEON*
Judge, also called Jerub-Baal; freed Israel from Midianites (Jdg 6-8; Heb 11:32). Given sign of fleece (Jdg 8:36-40).

GIFT (GIFTS)
Pr 21:14 A *g* given in secret soothes anger,
Mt 5:23 if you are offering your *g*
Ac 2:38 And you will receive the *g*
Ro 6:23 but the *g* of God is eternal life
1Co 7: 7 each man has his own *g* from God;
2Co 8:12 the *g* is acceptable according
9:15 be to God for his indescribable *g!*
Eph 2: 8 it is the *g* of God—not by works,
1Ti 4:14 not neglect your *g,* which was
2Ti 1: 6 you to fan into flame the *g* of God,
Jas 1:17 and perfect *g* is from above,
1Pe 4:10 should use whatever *g* he has

GIFTS (GIFT)
Ro 11:29 for God's *g* and his call are
12: 6 We have different *g,* according
1Co 12: 4 There are different kinds of *g,*
12:31 But eagerly desire the greater *g.*
14: 1 and eagerly desire spiritual *g,*
14:12 excel in *g* that build up the church.

GILEAD
Jer 8:22 Is there no balm in *G?*

GIVE (GAVE GIVEN GIVER GIVES GIVING)
Nu 6:26 and *g* you peace." '
1Sa 1:11 then I will *g* him to the LORD
2Ch 15: 7 be strong and do not *g* up,
Pr 21:26 but the righteous *g* without sparing
23:26 My son, *g* me your heart
30: 8 but *g* me only my daily bread.
31:31 *G* her the reward she has earned,
Isa 42: 8 I will not *g* my glory to another
Eze 36:26 I will *g* you a new heart
Mt 6:11 *G* us today our daily bread.
10: 8 Freely you have received, freely *g.*
22:21 "*G* to Caesar what is Caesar's,
Mk 8:37 Or what can a man *g* in exchange
Lk 6:38 *G,* and it will be given to you.
11:13 Father in heaven *g* the Holy Spirit
Jn 10:28 I *g* them eternal life, and they shall
13:34 "A new commandment I *g* you:
Ac 20:35 blessed to *g* than to receive.' "
Ro 12: 8 let him *g* generously;
13: 7 *G* everyone what you owe him:
14:12 each of us will *g* an account
2Co 9: 7 Each man should *g* what he has
Rev 14: 7 "Fear God and *g* him glory,

GIVEN (GIVE)
Nu 8:16 are to be *g* wholly to me.
Ps 115:16 but the earth he has *g* to man.
Isa 9: 6 to us a son is *g,*
Mt 6:33 and all these things will be *g* to you
7: 7 "Ask and it will be *g* to you;
Lk 22:19 saying, "This is my body *g* for you;
Jn 3:27 man can receive only what is *g* him
Ro 5: 5 the Holy Spirit, whom he has *g* us.
1Co 4: 2 those who have been *g* a trust must
12:13 we were all *g* the one Spirit to drink
Eph 4: 7 to each one of us grace has been *g*

GIVER* (GIVE)
Pr 18:16 A gift opens the way for the *g*
2Co 9: 7 for God loves a cheerful *g.*

GIVES (GIVE)
Ps 119:130 The unfolding of your words *g* light;
Pr 14:30 A heart at peace *g* life to the body,
15:30 good news *g* health to the bones.
28:27 He who *g* to the poor will lack
Isa 40:29 He *g* strength to the weary
Mt 10:42 if anyone *g* even a cup of cold water
Jn 6:63 The Spirit *g* life; the flesh counts
1Co 15:57 He *g* us the victory
2Co 3: 6 the letter kills, but the Spirit *g* life.

GIVING (GIVE)
Ne 8: 8 *g* the meaning so that the people
Ps 19: 8 *g* joy to the heart.
Mt 6: 4 so that your *g* may be in secret.
2Co 8: 7 also excel in this grace of *g.*

GLAD (GLADNESS)
Ps 31: 7 I will be *g* and rejoice in your love,
46: 4 whose streams make *g* the city
97: 1 LORD reigns, let the earth be *g;*
118:24 let us rejoice and be *g* in it.
Pr 23:25 May your father and mother be *g;*
Zec 2:10 and be *g,* O Daughter of Zion.
Mt 5:12 be *g,* because great is your reward

GLADNESS (GLAD)
Ps 45:15 They are led in with joy and *g;*
51: 8 Let me hear joy and *g;*
100: 2 Serve the LORD with *g;*
Jer 31:13 I will turn their mourning into *g;*

GLORIFIED (GLORY)
Jn 13:31 Son of Man *g* and God is *g* in him.
Ro 8:30 those he justified, he also *g.*
2Th 1:10 comes to be *g* in his holy people

GLORIFY (GLORY)
Ps 34: 3 *G* the LORD with me;
86:12 I will *g* your name forever.
Jn 13:32 God will *g* the Son in himself,
17: 1 *G* your Son, that your Son may

GLORIOUS (GLORY)
Ps 45:13 All *g* is the princess
111: 3 *G* and majestic are his deeds,
145: 5 of the *g* splendor of your majesty,
Isa 4: 2 the LORD will be beautiful and *g,*
12: 5 for he has done *g* things;
42:21 to make his law great and *g.*
63:15 from your lofty throne, holy and *g.*
Mt 19:28 the Son of Man sits on his *g* throne,

Lk 9:31 appeared in *g* splendor, talking
Ac 2:20 of the great and *g* day of the Lord.
2Co 3: 8 of the Spirit be even more *g?*
Php 3:21 so that they will be like his *g* body.
4:19 to his *g* riches in Christ Jesus.
Tit 2:13 the *g* appearing of our great God
Jude :24 before his *g* presence without fault

GLORY (GLORIFIED GLORIFY GLORIOUS)
Ex 15:11 awesome in *g,*
33:18 Moses said, "Now show me your *g*
1Sa 4:21 "The *g* has departed from Israel"—
1Ch 16:24 Declare his *g* among the nations,
16:28 ascribe to the LORD *g*
29:11 and the *g* and the majesty
Ps 8: 5 and crowned him with *g* and honor
19: 1 The heavens declare the *g* of God;
24: 7 that the King of *g* may come in.
29: 1 ascribe to the LORD *g*
72:19 the whole earth be filled with his *g.*
96: 3 Declare his *g* among the nations,
Pr 19:11 it is to his *g* to overlook an offense.
25: 2 It is the *g* of God to conceal
Isa 6: 3 the whole earth is full of his *g.*"
48:11 I will not yield my *g* to another.
Eze 43: 2 and the land was radiant with his *g.*
Mt 24:30 of the sky, with power and great *g.*
25:31 the Son of Man comes in his *g,*
Mk 8:38 in his Father's *g* with the holy
13:26 in clouds with great power and *g.*
Lk 2: 9 and the *g* of the Lord shone
2:14 saying, "*G* to God in the highest,
Jn 1:14 We have seen his *g,* the *g* of the One
17: 5 presence with the *g* I had with you
17:24 to see my *g,* the *g* you have given
Ac 7: 2 The God of *g* appeared
Ro 1:23 exchanged the *g* of the immortal
3:23 and fall short of the *g* of God,
8:18 with the *g* that will be revealed
9: 4 theirs the divine *g,* the covenants,
1Co 10:31 whatever you do, do it all for the *g*
11: 7 but the woman is the *g* of man.
15:43 it is raised in *g;* it is sown
2Co 3:10 comparison with the surpassing *g.*
3:18 faces all reflect the Lord's *g,*
4:17 us an eternal *g* that far outweighs
Col 1:27 Christ in you, the hope of *g.*
3: 4 also will appear with him in *g.*
1Ti 3:16 was taken up in *g.*
Heb 1: 3 The Son is the radiance of God's *g*
2: 7 you crowned him with *g* and honor
1Pe 1:24 and all their *g* is like the flowers
Rev 4:11 to receive *g* and honor and power,
21:23 for the *g* of God gives it light,

GLUTTONS
Tit 1:12 always liars, evil brutes, lazy *g.*"

GNASHING
Mt 8:12 where there will be weeping and *g*

GNAT*
Mt 23:24 You strain out a *g* but swallow

GOAL
2Co 5: 9 So we make it our *g* to please him,
Gal 3: 3 to attain your *g* by human effort?
Php 3:14 on toward the *g* to win the prize

GOAT (GOATS SCAPEGOAT)
Isa 11: 6 the leopard will lie down with the *g*

GOATS (GOAT)
Nu 7:17 five male *g* and five male lambs

GOD (GOD'S GODLINESS GODLY GODS)
Ge 1: 1 In the beginning *G* created
1: 2 and the Spirit of *G* was hovering
1:26 Then *G* said, "Let us make man
1:27 So *G* created man in his own image
1:31 *G* saw all that he had made,
2: 3 And *G* blessed the seventh day
2:22 Then the LORD *G* made a woman
3:21 The LORD *G* made garments
3:23 So the LORD *G* banished him
5:22 Enoch walked with *G* 300 years
6: 2 sons of *G* saw that the daughters
9:16 everlasting covenant between *G*
17: 1 "I am *G* Almighty; walk before me
21:33 name of the LORD, the Eternal *G.*
22: 8 "*G* himself will provide the lamb
28:12 and the angels of *G* were ascending
32:28 because you have struggled with *G*
32:30 "It is because I saw *G* face to face,
35:10 *G* said to him, "Your name is Jacob

Ge 41:51 *G* has made me forget all my
50:20 but *G* intended it for good
Ex 2:24 *G* heard their groaning
3:6 because he was afraid to look at *G.*
6:7 own people, and I will be your *G.*
8:10 is no one like the LORD our *G.*
13:18 So *G* led the people
15:2 He is my *G,* and I will praise him,
17:9 with the staff of *G* in my hands."
19:3 Then Moses went up to *G,*
20:2 the LORD your *G,* who brought
20:5 the LORD your *G,* am a jealous *G,*
20:19 But do not have *G* speak to us
22:28 "Do not blaspheme *G*
31:18 inscribed by the finger of *G.*
34:6 the compassionate and gracious *G,*
34:14 name is Jealous, is a jealous *G.*
Lev 18:21 not profane the name of your *G.*
19:2 the LORD your *G,* am holy.
26:12 walk among you and be your *G,*
Nu 22:38 I must speak only what *G* puts
23:19 *G* is not a man, that he should lie,
Dt 1:17 for judgment belongs to *G.*
3:22 LORD your *G* himself will fight
3:24 For what *g* is there in heaven
4:24 is a consuming fire, a jealous *G.*
4:31 the LORD your *G* is a merciful *G;*
4:39 heart this day that the LORD is *G*
5:11 the name of the LORD your *G,*
5:14 a Sabbath to the LORD your *G.*
5:26 of the living *G* speaking out of fire,
6:4 LORD our *G,* the LORD is one.
6:5 Love the LORD your *G*
6:13 the LORD your *G,* serve him only
6:16 Do not test the LORD your *G*
7:9 your *G* is *G;* he is the faithful *G,*
7:12 the LORD your *G* will keep his
7:21 is a great and awesome *G.*
8:5 the LORD your *G* disciplines you.
10:12 but to fear the LORD your *G,*
10:14 the LORD your *G* belong
10:17 For the LORD your *G* is *G* of gods
11:13 to love the LORD your *G*
13:3 The LORD your *G* is testing you
13:4 the LORD your *G* you must
15:6 the LORD your *G* will bless you
19:9 to love the LORD your *G*
25:16 the LORD your *G* detests anyone
29:29 belong to the LORD our *G,*
30:2 return to the LORD your *G*
30:16 today to love the LORD your *G,*
30:20 you may love the LORD your *G,*
31:6 for the LORD your *G* goes
32:3 Oh, praise the greatness of our *G!*
32:4 A faithful *G* who does no wrong,
33:27 The eternal *G* is your refuge,
Jos 1:9 for the LORD your *G* will be
14:8 the LORD my *G* wholeheartedly.
22:5 to love the LORD your *G,*
22:34 Between Us that the LORD is *G.*
23:11 careful to love the LORD your *G.*
23:14 the LORD your *G* gave you has
Jdg 16:28 O *G,* please strengthen me just
Ru 1:16 be my people and your *G* my *G.*
1Sa 2:2 there is no Rock like our *G.*
2:3 for the LORD is a *G* who knows,
2:25 another man, *G* may mediate
10:26 men whose hearts *G* had touched.
12:12 the LORD your *G* was your king.
17:26 defy the armies of the living *G?"*
17:46 world will know that there is a *G*
30:6 strength in the LORD his *G.*
2Sa 14:14 But *G* does not take away life;
22:3 my *G* is my rock, in whom I take
22:31 "As for *G,* his way is perfect;
1Ki 4:29 *G* gave Solomon wisdom
8:23 there is no *G* like you in heaven
8:27 "But will *G* really dwell on earth?
8:61 committed to the LORD our *G,*
18:21 If the LORD is *G,* follow him;
18:37 are *G,* and that you are turning
20:28 a *g* of the hills and not a *g*
2Ki 19:15 *G* of Israel, enthroned
1Ch 16:35 Cry out, "Save us, O *G* our Savior;
28:2 for the footstool of our *G,*
28:9 acknowledge the *G* of your father,
29:10 *G* of our father Israel,
29:17 my *G,* that you test the heart
2Ch 2:4 for the Name of the LORD my *G*
5:14 of the LORD filled the temple of *G*
6:18 "But will *G* really dwell on earth
18:13 I can tell him only what my *G* says
2Ch 20:6 are you not the *G* who is in heaven?
25:8 for *G* has the power to help
30:9 for the LORD your *G* is gracious
33:12 the favor of the LORD his *G*
Ezr 8:22 "The good hand of our *G* is
9:6 "O my *G,* I am too ashamed
9:13 our *G,* you have punished us less
Ne 1:5 the great and awesome *G,*
8:8 from the Book of the Law of *G,*
9:17 But you are a forgiving *G,*
9:32 the great, mighty and awesome *G,*
Job 1:1 he feared *G* and shunned evil.
2:10 Shall we accept good from *G,*
4:17 a mortal be more righteous than *G?*
5:17 is the man whom *G* corrects;
11:7 Can you fathom the mysteries of *G*
19:26 yet in my flesh I will see *G;*
22:13 Yet you say, 'What does *G* know?
25:4 can a man be righteous before *G?*
33:14 For *G* does speak—now one way,
34:12 is unthinkable that *G* would do
36:26 is *G*— beyond our understanding!
37:22 *G* comes in awesome majesty.
Ps 18:2 my *G* is my rock, in whom I take
18:28 my *G* turns my darkness into light.
19:1 The heavens declare the glory of *G;*
22:1 *G,* my *G,* why have you forsaken
29:3 the *G* of glory thunders,
31:14 I say, "You are my *G."*
40:3 a hymn of praise to our *G.*
40:8 I desire to do your will, O my *G;*
42:2 thirsts for *G,* for the living *G.*
42:11 Put your hope in *G,*
45:6 O *G,* will last for ever and ever;
46:1 *G* is our refuge and strength,
46:10 "Be still, and know that I am *G;*
47:7 For *G* is the King of all the earth;
50:3 Our *G* comes and will not be silent;
51:1 Have mercy on me, O *G,*
51:10 Create in me a pure heart, O *G,*
51:17 O *G,* you will not despise.
62:7 my honor depend on *G;*
65:5 O *G* our Savior,
66:1 Shout with joy to *G,* all the earth!
66:16 listen, all you who fear *G;*
68:6 *G* sets the lonely in families,
71:17 my youth, O *G,* you have taught
71:19 reaches to the skies, O *G,*
71:22 harp for your faithfulness, O my *G;*
73:26 but *G* is the strength of my heart
77:13 What *g* is so great as our God?
78:19 Can *G* spread a table in the desert?
81:1 Sing for joy to *G* our strength;
84:2 out for the living *G.*
84:10 a doorkeeper in the house of my *G*
86:12 O Lord my *G,* with all my heart;
89:7 of the holy ones *G* is greatly feared;
90:2 to everlasting you are *G.*
91:2 my *G,* in whom I trust."
95:7 for he is our *G*
100:3 Know that the LORD is *G.*
108:1 My heart is steadfast, O *G;*
113:5 Who is like the LORD our *G,*
139:23 Search me, O *G,* and know my
Pr 3:4 in the sight of *G* and man.
25:2 of *G* to conceal a matter;
30:5 "Every word of *G* is flawless;
Ecc 3:11 cannot fathom what *G* has done
11:5 cannot understand the work of *G,*
12:13 Fear *G* and keep his
Isa 9:6 Wonderful Counselor, Mighty *G,*
37:16 you alone are *G* over all
40:3 a highway for our *G.*
40:8 the word of our *G* stands forever."
40:28 The LORD is the everlasting *G,*
41:10 not be dismayed, for I am your *G.*
44:6 apart from me there is no *G.*
52:7 "Your *G* reigns!"
55:7 to our *G,* for he will freely pardon.
57:21 says my *G,* "for the wicked."
59:2 you from your *G;*
61:10 my soul rejoices in my *G.*
62:5 so will your *G* rejoice over you.
Jer 23:23 "Am I only a *G* nearby,"
31:33 I will be their *G,*
32:27 "I am the LORD, the *G*
Eze 28:13 the garden of *G;*
Da 3:17 the *G* we serve is able to save us
9:4 O Lord, the great and awesome *G,*
Hos 12:6 and wait for your *G* always.
Joel 2:13 Return to the LORD your *G,*
Am 4:12 prepare to meet your *G,* O Israel."
Mic 6:8 and to walk humbly with your *G.*
Na 1:2 LORD is a jealous and avenging *G;*
Zec 14:5 Then the LORD my *G* will come,
Mal 3:8 Will a man rob *G?* Yet you rob me.
Mt 1:23 which means, "*G* with us."
5:8 for they will see *G.*
6:24 You cannot serve both *G*
19:6 Therefore what *G* has joined
19:26 but with *G* all things are possible."
22:21 and to *G* what is God's."
22:37 " 'Love the Lord your *G*
27:46 which means, "My *G,* my *G,*
Mk 12:29 the Lord our *G,* the Lord is one.
16:19 and he sat at the right hand of *G.*
Lk 1:37 For nothing is impossible with *G."*
1:47 my spirit rejoices in *G* my Savior,
10:9 'The kingdom of *G* is near you.'
10:27 " 'Love the Lord your *G*
18:19 "No one is good—except *G* alone.
Jn 1:1 was with *G,* and the Word was *G.*
1:18 seen *G,* but *G* the One and Only,
3:16 "For *G* so loved the world that he
4:24 *G* is spirit, and his worshipers must
14:1 Trust in *G;* trust also in me.
20:28 "My Lord and my *G!"*
Ac 2:24 But *G* raised him from the dead,
5:4 You have not lied to men but to *G*
5:29 "We must obey *G* rather than men!
7:55 to heaven and saw the glory of *G,*
17:23 TO AN UNKNOWN *G.*
20:27 to you the whole will of *G.*
20:32 "Now I commit you to *G*
Ro 1:17 a righteousness from *G* is revealed,
2:11 For *G* does not show favoritism.
3:4 Let *G* be true, and every man a liar.
3:23 and fall short of the glory of *G,*
4:24 to whom *G* will credit
5:8 *G* demonstrates his own love for us
6:23 but the gift of *G* is eternal life
8:28 in all things *G* works for the good
11:22 the kindness and sternness of *G:*
14:12 give an account of himself to *G.*
1Co 1:20 Has not *G* made foolish
2:9 what *G* has prepared
3:6 watered it, but *G* made it grow.
6:20 Therefore honor *G* with your body.
7:24 each man, as responsible to *G,*
8:8 food does not bring us near to *G;*
10:13 *G* is faithful; he will not let you be
10:31 do it all for the glory of *G.*
14:33 For *G* is not a *G* of disorder
15:28 so that *G* may be all in all.
2Co 1:9 rely on ourselves but on *G,*
2:14 be to *G,* who always leads us
3:5 but our competence comes from *G.*
4:7 this all-surpassing power is from *G*
5:19 that *G* was reconciling the world
5:21 *G* made him who had no sin
6:16 we are the temple of the living *G.*
9:7 for *G* loves a cheerful giver.
9:8 *G* is able to make all grace abound
Gal 2:6 *G* does not judge by external
6:7 not be deceived: *G* cannot be
Eph 2:10 which *G* prepared in advance for us
4:6 one baptism; one *G* and Father
5:1 Be imitators of *G,* therefore,
Php 2:6 Who, being in very nature *G,*
4:19 And my *G* will meet all your needs
1Th 2:4 trying to please men but *G,*
4:7 For *G* did not call us to be impure,
4:9 taught by *G* to love each other.
5:9 For *G* did not appoint us
1Ti 2:5 one mediator between *G* and men,
4:4 For everything *G* created is good,
5:4 for this is pleasing to *G.*
Tit 2:13 glorious appearing of our great *G*
Heb 1:1 In the past *G* spoke
4:12 For the word of *G* is living
6:10 *G* is not unjust; he will not forget
10:31 to fall into the hands of the living *G*
11:6 faith it is impossible to please *G,*
12:10 but *G* disciplines us for our good,
12:29 for our "*G* is a consuming fire."
13:15 offer to *G* a sacrifice of praise—
Jas 1:13 For *G* cannot be tempted by evil,
2:19 You believe that there is one *G.*
2:23 "Abraham believed *G,*
4:4 the world becomes an enemy of *G.*
4:8 Come near to *G* and he will come
1Pe 4:11 it with the strength *G* provides,
2Pe 1:21 but men spoke from *G*
1Jn 1:5 *G* is light; in him there is no

1Jn 3:20 For *G* is greater than our hearts,
4: 7 for love comes from *G*.
4: 9 This is how *G* showed his love
4:11 Dear friends, since *G* so loved us,
4:12 No one has ever seen *G*;
4:16 *G* is love.
Rev 4: 8 holy is the Lord *G* Almighty,
7:17 *G* will wipe away every tear
19: 6 For our Lord *G* Almighty reigns.

GOD-BREATHED* (BREATHED)
2Ti 3:16 All Scripture is *G* and is useful

GOD'S (GOD)
2Ch 20:15 For the battle is not yours, but *G*.
Job 37:14 stop and consider *G* wonders.
Ps 52: 8 I trust in *G* unfailing love
69:30 I will praise *G* name in song
Mk 3:35 Whoever does *G* will is my brother
Jn 7:17 If anyone chooses to do *G* will,
10:36 'I am *G* Son'? Do not believe me
Ro 2: 3 think you will escape *G* judgment?
2: 4 not realizing that *G* kindness leads
3: 3 lack of faith nullify *G* faithfulness?
7:22 in my inner being I delight in *G* law
9:16 or effort, but on *G* mercy.
11:29 for *G* gifts and his call are
12: 2 and approve what *G* will is—
12:13 Share with *G* people who are
13: 6 for the authorities are *G* servants,
1Co 7:19 Keeping *G* commands is what
2Co 6: 2 now is the time of *G* favor,
Eph 1: 7 riches of *G* grace that he lavished
1Th 4: 3 It is *G* will that you should be
5:18 for this is *G* will for you
1Ti 6: 1 so that *G* name and our teaching
2Ti 2:19 *G* solid foundation stands firm,
Tit 1: 7 overseer is entrusted with *G* work,
Heb 1: 3 The Son is the radiance of *G* glory
9:24 now to appear for us in *G* presence.
11: 3 was formed at *G* command,
1Pe 2:15 For it is *G* will that
3: 4 which is of great worth in *G* sight.
1Jn 2: 5 *G* love is truly made complete

GODLINESS (GOD)
1Ti 2: 2 and quiet lives in all *g* and holiness.
4: 8 but *g* has value for all things,
6: 6 *g* with contentment is great gain.
6:11 and pursue righteousness, *g*, faith,

GODLY (GOD)
Ps 4: 3 that the LORD has set apart the *g*
2Co 7:10 *G* sorrow brings repentance that
11: 2 jealous for you with a *g* jealousy.
2Ti 3:12 everyone who wants to live a *g* life
2Pe 3:11 You ought to live holy and *g* lives

GODS (GOD)
Ex 20: 3 "You shall have no other *g*
Ac 19:26 He says that man-made *g* are no *g*

GOLD
Job 23:10 tested me, I will come forth as *g*.
Ps 19:10 They are more precious than *g*,
119:127 more than *g*, more than pure *g*,
Pr 22: 1 esteemed is better than silver or *g*.

GOLGOTHA
Jn 19:17 (which in Aramaic is called *G*).

GOLIATH
Philistine giant killed by David (1Sa 17; 21:9)

GOOD
Ge 1: 4 God saw that the light was *g*,
1:31 he had made, and it was very *g*.
2:18 "It is not *g* for the man to be alone.
50:20 but God intended it for *g*
Job 2:10 Shall we accept *g* from God,
Ps 14: 1 there is no one who does *g*.
34: 8 Taste and see that the LORD is *g*;
37: 3 Trust in the LORD and do *g*;
84:11 no *g* thing does he withhold
86: 5 You are forgiving and *g*, O Lord
103: 5 satisfies your desires with *g* things,
119:68 You are *g*, and what you do is *g*;
133: 1 How *g* and pleasant it is
147: 1 How *g* it is to sing praises
Pr 3: 4 you will win favor and a *g* name
11:27 He who seeks *g* finds *g* will,
17:22 A cheerful heart is *g* medicine,
18:22 He who finds a wife finds what is *g*
22: 1 A *g* name is more desirable
31:12 She brings him *g*, not harm,
Isa 5:20 Woe to those who call evil *g*
52: 7 the feet of those who bring *g* news,
Jer 6:16 ask where the *g* way is,
32:39 the *g* of their children after them.
Mic 6: 8 has showed you, O man, what is *g*.
Mt 5:45 sun to rise on the evil and the *g*,
7:17 Likewise every *g* tree bears *g* fruit,
12:35 The *g* man brings *g* things out
19:17 "There is only One who is *g*.
25:21 'Well done, *g* and faithful servant!
Mk 3: 4 lawful on the Sabbath: to do *g*
8:36 What *g* is it for a man
Lk 6:27 do *g* to those who hate you,
Jn 10:11 "I am the *g* shepherd.
Ro 8:28 for the *g* of those who love him,
10:15 feet of those who bring *g* news!"
12: 9 Hate what is evil; cling to what is *g*.
1Co 10:24 should seek his own *g*, but the *g*
15:33 Bad company corrupts *g* character
2Co 9: 8 you will abound in every *g* work.
Gal 6: 9 us not become weary in doing *g*,
6:10 as we have opportunity, let us do *g*
Eph 2:10 in Christ Jesus to do *g* works,
Php 1: 6 that he who began a *g* work
1Th 5:21 Hold on to the *g*.
1Ti 3: 7 have a *g* reputation with outsiders,
4: 4 For everything God created is *g*,
6:12 Fight the *g* fight of the faith.
6:18 them to do *g*, to be rich in *g* deeds,
2Ti 3:17 equipped for every *g* work.
4: 7 I have fought the *g* fight, I have
Heb 12:10 but God disciplines us for our *g*,
1Pe 2: 3 you have tasted that the Lord is *g*.
2:12 Live such *g* lives among the pagans

GOSPEL
Ro 1:16 I am not ashamed of the *g*,
15:16 duty of proclaiming the *g* of God,
1Co 1:17 to preach the *g*—not with words
9:16 Woe to me if I do not preach the *g*!
15: 1 you of the *g* I preached to you,
Gal 1: 7 a different *g*—which is really no *g*
Php 1:27 in a manner worthy of the *g*

GOSSIP
Pr 11:13 A *g* betrays a confidence,
16:28 and a *g* separates close friends.
18: 8 of a *g* are like choice morsels;
26:20 without *g* a quarrel dies down.
2Co 12:20 slander, *g*, arrogance and disorder.

GRACE (GRACIOUS)
Ps 45: 2 lips have been anointed with *g*,
Jn 1:17 *g* and truth came through Jesus
Ac 20:32 to God and to the word of his *g*,
Ro 3:24 and are justified freely by his *g*
5:15 came by the *g* of the one man,
5:17 God's abundant provision of *g*
5:20 where sin increased, *g* increased all
6:14 you are not under law, but under *g*.
11: 6 If by *g*, then it is no longer by works
2Co 6: 1 not to receive God's *g* in vain.
8: 9 For you know the *g*
9: 8 able to make all *g* abound to you,
12: 9 "My *g* is sufficient for you,
Gal 2:21 I do not set aside the *g* of God,
5: 4 you have fallen away from *g*.
Eph 1: 7 riches of God's *g* that he lavished
2: 5 it is by *g* you have been saved.
2: 7 the incomparable riches of his *g*,
2: 8 For it is by *g* you have been saved,
Php 1: 7 all of you share in God's *g* with me.
Col 4: 6 conversation be always full of *g*,
2Th 2:16 and by his *g* gave us eternal
2Ti 2: 1 be strong in the *g* that is
Tit 2:11 For the *g* of God that brings
3: 7 having been justified by his *g*,
Heb 2: 9 that by the *g* of God he might taste
4:16 find *g* to help us in our time of need
4:16 the throne of *g* with confidence,
Jas 4: 6 but gives *g* to the humble."
2Pe 3:18 But grow in the *g* and knowledge

GRACIOUS (GRACE)
Nu 6:25 and be *g* to you;
Pr 22:11 a pure heart and whose speech is *g*
Isa 30:18 Yet the LORD longs to be *g* to you

GRAIN
1Co 9: 9 ox while it is treading out the *g*."

GRANTED
Php 1:29 For it has been *g* to you on behalf

GRASS
Ps 103:15 As for man, his days are like *g*,
1Pe 1:24 "All men are like *g*,

GRAVE (GRAVES)
Pr 7:27 Her house is a highway to the *g*,
Hos 13:14 Where, O *g*, is your destruction?

GRAVES (GRAVE)
Jn 5:28 are in their *g* will hear his voice
Ro 3:13 "Their throats are open *g*;

GREAT (GREATER GREATEST GREATNESS)
Ge 12: 2 "I will make you into a *g* nation
Dt 10:17 the *g* God, mighty and awesome,
2Sa 22:36 you stoop down to make me *g*.
Ps 19:11 in keeping them there is *g* reward.
89: 1 of the LORD's *g* love forever;
103:11 so *g* is his love for those who fear
107:43 consider the *g* love of the LORD.
108: 4 For *g* is your love, higher
119:165 *G* peace have they who love your
145: 3 *G* is the LORD and most worthy
Pr 23:24 of a righteous man has *g* joy;
Isa 42:21 to make his law *g* and glorious.
La 3:23 *g* is your faithfulness.
Mk 10:43 whoever wants to become *g*
Lk 21:27 in a cloud with power and *g* glory.
1Ti 6: 6 with contentment is *g* gain.
Tit 2:13 glorious appearing of our *g* God
Heb 2: 3 if we ignore such a *g* salvation?
1Jn 3: 1 How *g* is the love the Father has

GREATER (GREAT)
Mk 12:31 There is no commandment *g*
Jn 1:50 You shall see *g* things than that."
15:13 *G* love has no one than this,
1Co 12:31 But eagerly desire the *g* gifts.
Heb 11:26 as of *g* value than the treasures
1Jn 3:20 For God is *g* than our hearts,
4: 4 is in you is *g* than the one who is

GREATEST (GREAT)
Mt 22:38 is the first and *g* commandment.
Lk 9:48 least among you all—he is the *g*."
1Co 13:13 But the *g* of these is love.

GREATNESS (GREAT)
Ps 145: 3 his *g* no one can fathom.
150: 2 praise him for his surpassing *g*.
Isa 63: 1 forward in the *g* of his strength?
Php 3: 8 compared to the surpassing *g*

GREED (GREEDY)
Lk 12:15 on your guard against all kinds of *g*
Ro 1:29 kind of wickedness, evil, *g*
Eph 5: 3 or of any kind of impurity, or of *g*,
Col 3: 5 evil desires and *g*, which is idolatry
2Pe 2:14 experts in *g*—an accursed brood!

GREEDY (GREED)
Pr 15:27 A *g* man brings trouble
1Co 6:10 nor thieves nor the *g* nor drunkards
Eph 5: 5 No immoral, impure or *g* person—
1Pe 5: 2 not *g* for money, but eager to serve;

GREEN
Ps 23: 2 makes me lie down in *g* pastures,

GREW (GROW)
Lk 2:52 And Jesus *g* in wisdom and stature,
Ac 16: 5 in the faith and *g* daily in numbers.

GRIEF (GRIEVE)
Ps 10:14 O God, do see trouble and *g*;
Pr 14:13 and joy may end in *g*.
La 3:32 Though he brings *g*, he will show
Jn 16:20 but your *g* will turn to joy.
1Pe 1: 6 had to suffer *g* in all kinds of trials.

GRIEVE (GRIEF)
Eph 4:30 do not *g* the Holy Spirit of God,
1Th 4:13 or to *g* like the rest of men,

GROUND
Ge 3:17 "Cursed is the *g* because of you;
Ex 3: 5 where you are standing is holy *g*."
Eph 6:13 you may be able to stand your *g*,

GROW (GREW)
Pr 13:11 by little makes it *g*.
1Co 3: 6 watered it, but God made it *g*.
2Pe 3:18 But *g* in the grace and knowledge

GRUMBLE (GRUMBLING)
1Co 10:10 And do not *g*, as some of them did
Jas 5: 9 Don't *g* against each other,

GRUMBLING (GRUMBLE)
Jn 6:43 "Stop *g* among yourselves,"
1Pe 4: 9 to one another without *g*.

GUARANTEE (GUARANTEEING)
Heb 7:22 Jesus has become the *g*

GUARANTEEING (GUARANTEE)
2Co 1:22 as a deposit, *g* what is to come.
Eph 1:14 who is a deposit *g* our inheritance

GUARD (GUARDS)
Ps 141: 3 Set a *g* over my mouth, O LORD;
Pr 4:23 Above all else, *g* your heart,
Isa 52:12 the God of Israel will be your rear *g*
Mk 13:33 Be on *g!* Be alert! You do not know
1Co 16:13 Be on your *g;* stand firm in the faith
Php 4: 7 will *g* your hearts and your minds
1Ti 6:20 *g* what has been entrusted

GUARDS (GUARD)
Pr 13: 3 He who *g* his lips *g* his life,
19:16 who obeys instructions *g* his life,
21:23 He who *g* his mouth and his tongue
22: 5 he who *g* his soul stays far

GUIDE
Ex 13:21 of cloud to *g* them on their way
15:13 In your strength you will *g* them
Ne 9:19 cease to *g* them on their path,
Ps 25: 5 *g* me in your truth and teach me,
43: 3 let them *g* me;
48:14 he will be our *g* even to the end.
67: 4 and *g* the nations of the earth.
73:24 You *g* me with your counsel,
139:10 even there your hand will *g* me,
Pr 4:11 I *g* you in the way of wisdom
6:22 When you walk, they will *g* you;
Isa 58:11 The LORD will *g* you always;
Jn 16:13 comes, he will *g* you into all truth.

GUILTY
Ex 34: 7 does not leave the *g* unpunished;
Jn 8:46 Can any of you prove me *g* of sin?
Heb 10:22 to cleanse us from a *g* conscience
Jas 2:10 at just one point is *g* of breaking all

HADES
Mt 16:18 the gates of *H* will not overcome it.

HAGAR
Servant of Sarah, wife of Abraham, mother of Ishmael (Ge 16:1-6; 25:12). Driven away by Sarah while pregnant (Ge 16:5-16); after birth of Isaac (Ge 21:9-21; Gal 4:21-31).

HAGGAI*
Post-exilic prophet who encouraged rebuilding of the temple (Ezr 5:1; 6:14; Hag 1-2).

HAIR (HAIRS)
Lk 21:18 But not a *h* of your head will perish
1Co 11: 6 for a woman to have her *h* cut

HAIRS (HAIR)
Mt 10:30 even the very *h* of your head are all

HALLELUJAH*
Rev 19: 1, 3, 4, 6

HALLOWED (HOLY)
Mt 6: 9 *h* be your name,

HAND (HANDS)
Ps 16: 8 Because he is at my right *h,*
37:24 the LORD upholds him with his *h.*
139:10 even there your *h* will guide me,
Ecc 9:10 Whatever your *h* finds to do,
Mt 6: 3 know what your right *h* is doing,
Jn 10:28 one can snatch them out of my *h.*
1Co 12:15 I am not a *h,* I do not belong

HANDS (HAND)
Ps 22:16 they have pierced my *h*
24: 4 He who has clean *h* and a pure
31: 5 Into your *h* I commit my spirit;
31:15 My times are in your *h;*
Pr 10: 4 Lazy *h* make a man poor,
31:20 and extends her *h* to the needy.
Isa 55:12 will clap their *h.*
65: 2 All day long I have held out my *h*
Lk 23:46 into your *h* I commit my spirit."
1Th 4:11 and to work with your *h,*
1Ti 2: 8 to lift up holy *h* in prayer,
5:22 hasty in the laying on of *h,*

HANNAH*
Wife of Elkanah, mother of Samuel (1Sa 1). Prayer at dedication of Samuel (1Sa 2:1-10). Blessed (1Sa 2:18-21).

HAPPY
Ps 68: 3 may they be *h* and joyful.
Pr 15:13 A *h* heart makes the face cheerful,
Ecc 3:12 better for men than to be *h*
Jas 5:13 Is anyone *h?* Let him sing songs

HARD (HARDEN HARDSHIP)
Ge 18:14 Is anything too *h* for the LORD?
Mt 19:23 it is *h* for a rich man
1Co 4:12 We work *h* with our own hands.
1Th 5:12 to respect those who work *h*

HARDEN (HARD)
Ro 9:18 he hardens whom he wants to *h.*
Heb 3: 8 do not *h* your hearts

HARDHEARTED* (HEART)
Dt 15: 7 do not be *h* or tightfisted

HARDSHIP (HARD)
Ro 8:35 Shall trouble or *h* or persecution
2Ti 2: 3 Endure *h* with us like a good
4: 5 endure *h,* do the work
Heb 12: 7 Endure *h* as discipline; God is

HARM
Ps 121: 6 the sun will not *h* you by day,
Pr 3:29 not plot *h* against your neighbor,
31:12 She brings him good, not *h,*
Ro 13:10 Love does no *h* to its neighbor.
1Jn 5:18 and the evil one cannot *h* him.

HARMONY
Ro 12:16 Live in *h* with one another.
2Co 6:15 What *h* is there between Christ
1Pe 3: 8 live in *h* with one another;

HARVEST
Mt 9:37 *h* is plentiful but the workers are
Jn 4:35 at the fields! They are ripe for *h.*
Gal 6: 9 at the proper time we will reap a *h*
Heb 12:11 it produces a *h* of righteousness

HASTE (HASTY)
Pr 21: 5 as surely as *h* leads to poverty.
29:20 Do you see a man who speaks in *h?*

HASTY* (HASTE)
Pr 19: 2 nor to be *h* and miss the way.
Ecc 5: 2 do not be *h* in your heart
1Ti 5:22 Do not be *h* in the laying

HATE (HATED HATES HATRED)
Lev 19:17 " 'Do not *h* your brother
Ps 5: 5 you *h* all who do wrong.
45: 7 righteousness and *h* wickedness;
97:10 those who love the LORD *h* evil,
139:21 Do I not *h* those who *h* you,
Pr 8:13 To fear the LORD is to *h* evil;
Am 5:15 *H* evil, love good;
Mal 2:16 "I *h* divorce," says the LORD God
Mt 5:43 your neighbor and *h* your enemy.'
10:22 All men will *h* you because of me,
Lk 6:27 do good to those who *h* you,
Ro 12: 9 *H* what is evil; cling to what is good

HATED (HATE)
Ro 9:13 "Jacob I loved, but Esau I *h.*"
Eph 5:29 no one ever *h* his own body,
Heb 1: 9 righteousness and *h* wickedness;

HATES (HATE)
Pr 6:16 There are six things the LORD *h,*
13:24 He who spares the rod *h* his son,
Jn 3:20 Everyone who does evil *h* the light,
1Jn 2: 9 *h* his brother is still in the darkness.

HATRED (HATE)
Pr 10:12 *H* stirs up dissension,
Jas 4: 4 with the world is *h* toward God?

HAUGHTY
Pr 16:18 a *h* spirit before a fall.

HAY
1Co 3:12 costly stones, wood, *h* or straw,

HEAD (HEADS HOTHEADED)
Ge 3:15 he will crush your *h,*
Ps 23: 5 You anoint my *h* with oil;
Pr 25:22 will heap burning coals on his *h,*
Isa 59:17 and the helmet of salvation on his *h*
Mt 8:20 of Man has no place to lay his *h.*"
Ro 12:20 will heap burning coals on his *h.*"
1Co 11: 3 and the *h* of Christ is God.
12:21 And the *h* cannot say to the feet,
Eph 5:23 For the husband is the *h* of the wife
2Ti 4: 5 keep your *h* in all situations,
Rev 19:12 and on his *h* are many crowns.

HEADS (HEAD)
Lev 26:13 you to walk with *h* held high.
Isa 35:10 everlasting joy will crown their *h.*

HEAL (HEALED HEALING HEALS)
2Ch 7:14 their sin and will *h* their land.
Ps 41: 4 *h* me, for I have sinned against you
Mt 10: 8 *H* the sick, raise the dead,
Lk 4:23 to me: 'Physician, *h* yourself!
5:17 present for him to *h* the sick.

HEALED (HEAL)
Isa 53: 5 and by his wounds we are *h.*
Mt 9:22 he said, "your faith has *h* you."
14:36 and all who touched him were *h.*
Ac 4:10 this man stands before you *h.*
14: 9 saw that he had faith to be *h*
Jas 5:16 for each other so that you may be *h*
1Pe 2:24 by his wounds you have been *h.*

HEALING (HEAL)
Eze 47:12 for food and their leaves for *h.*"
Mal 4: 2 rise with *h* in its wings.
1Co 12: 9 to another gifts of *h*
12:30 Do all have gifts of *h?* Do all speak
Rev 22: 2 are for the *h* of the nations.

HEALS (HEAL)
Ex 15:26 for I am the LORD, who *h* you."
Ps 103: 3 and *h* all your diseases;
147: 3 He *h* the brokenhearted

HEALTH (HEALTHY)
Pr 3: 8 This will bring *h* to your body
15:30 and good news gives *h* to the bones

HEALTHY (HEALTH)
Mk 2:17 "It is not the *h* who need a doctor,

HEAR (HEARD HEARING HEARS)
Dt 6: 4 *H,* O Israel: The LORD our God,
31:13 must *h* it and learn
2Ch 7:14 then will I *h* from heaven
Ps 94: 9 he who implanted the ear not *h?*
Isa 29:18 that day the deaf will *h* the words
65:24 while they are still speaking I will *h*
Mt 11:15 He who has ears, let him *h.*
Jn 8:47 reason you do not *h* is that you do
2Ti 4: 3 what their itching ears want to *h.*

HEARD (HEAR)
Job 42: 5 My ears had *h* of you
Isa 66: 8 Who has ever *h* of such a thing?
Mt 5:21 "You have *h* that it was said
5:27 "You have *h* that it was said,
5:33 you have *h* that it was said
5:38 "You have *h* that it was said,
5:43 "You have *h* that it was said,
1Co 2: 9 no ear has *h,*
1Th 2:13 word of God, which you *h* from us,
2Ti 1:13 What you *h* from me, keep
Jas 1:25 not forgetting what he has *h,*

HEARING (HEAR)
Ro 10:17 faith comes from *h* the message,

HEARS (HEAR)
Jn 5:24 whoever *h* my word and believes
1Jn 5:14 according to his will, he *h* us.
Rev 3:20 If anyone *h* my voice and opens

HEART (BROKENHEARTED HARDHEARTED HEARTS WHOLEHEARTEDLY)
Ex 25: 2 each man whose *h* prompts him
Lev 19:17 Do not hate your brother in your *h.*
Dt 4:29 if you look for him with all your *h*
6: 5 LORD your God with all your *h*
10:12 LORD your God with all your *h*
15:10 and do so without a grudging *h;*
30: 6 you may love him with all your *h*
30:10 LORD your God with all your *h*
Jos 22: 5 and to serve him with all your *h*
1Sa 13:14 sought out a man after his own *h*
16: 7 but the LORD looks at the *h.*"
2Ki 23: 3 with all his *h* and all his soul,
1Ch 28: 9 for the LORD searches every *h*
2Ch 7:16 and my *h* will always be there.
Job 22:22 and lay up his words in your *h.*
37: 1 "At this my *h* pounds
Ps 14: 1 The fool says in his *h,*
19:14 and the meditation of my *h*
37: 4 will give you the desires of your *h.*
45: 1 My *h* is stirred by a noble theme
51:10 Create in me a pure *h,* O God,
51:17 a broken and contrite *h,*
66:18 If I had cherished sin in my *h,*
86:11 give me an undivided *h,*
119:11 I have hidden your word in my *h*
119:32 for you have set my *h* free.
139:23 Search me, O God, and know my *h*
Pr 3: 5 Trust in the LORD with all your *h*

Pr 4:21 keep them within your *h;*
4:23 Above all else, guard your *h,*
7: 3 write them on the tablet of your *h.*
13:12 Hope deferred makes the *h* sick,
14:13 Even in laughter the *h* may ache,
15:30 A cheerful look brings joy to the *h,*
17:22 A cheerful *h* is good medicine,
24:17 stumbles, do not let your *h* rejoice,
27:19 so a man's *h* reflects the man.
Ecc 8: 5 wise *h* will know the proper time
SS 4: 9 You have stolen my *h,* my sister,
Isa 40:11 and carries them close to his *h;*
57:15 and to revive the *h* of the contrite.
Jer 17: 9 The *h* is deceitful above all things
29:13 when you seek me with all your *h.*
Eze 36:26 I will give you a new *h*
Mt 5: 8 Blessed are the pure in *h,*
6:21 treasure is, there your *h* will be
12:34 of the *h* the mouth speaks.
22:37 the Lord your God with all your *h*
Lk 6:45 overflow of his *h* his mouth speaks.
Ro 2:29 is circumcision of the *h,*
10:10 is with your *h* that you believe
1Co 14:25 the secrets of his *h* will be laid bare.
Eph 5:19 make music in your *h* to the Lord,
6: 6 doing the will of God from your *h.*
Col 3:23 work at it with all your *h,*
1Pe 1:22 one another deeply, from the *h.*

HEARTS (HEART)
Dt 11:18 Fix these words of mine in your *h*
1Ki 8:39 for you alone know the *h* of all men
8:61 your *h* must be fully committed
Ps 62: 8 pour out your *h* to him,
Ecc 3:11 also set eternity in the *h* of men;
Jer 31:33 and write it on their *h.*
Lk 16:15 of men, but God knows your *h.*
24:32 "Were not our *h* burning within us
Jn 14: 1 "Do not let your *h* be troubled.
Ac 15: 9 for he purified their *h* by faith.
Ro 2:15 of the law are written on their *h,*
2Co 3: 2 written on our *h,* known
3: 3 but on tablets of human *h.*
4: 6 shine in our *h* to give us the light
Eph 3:17 dwell in your *h* through faith.
Col 3: 1 set your *h* on things above,
Heb 3: 8 do not harden your *h*
10:16 I will put my laws in their *h,*
1Jn 3:20 For God is greater than our *h,*

HEAT
2Pe 3:12 and the elements will melt in the *h.*

HEAVEN (HEAVENLY HEAVENS)
Ge 14:19 Creator of *h* and earth.
1Ki 8:27 the highest *h,* cannot contain you.
2Ki 2: 1 up to *h* in a whirlwind,
2Ch 7:14 then will I hear from *h*
Isa 14:12 How you have fallen from *h,*
66: 1 "*H* is my throne,
Da 7:13 coming with the clouds of *h.*
Mt 6: 9 " 'Our Father in *h,*
6:20 up for yourselves treasures in *h,*
16:19 bind on earth will be bound in *h,*
19:23 man to enter the kingdom of *h.*
24:35 *H* and earth will pass away,
26:64 and coming on the clouds of *h.*"
28:18 "All authority in *h*
Mk 16:19 he was taken up into *h*
Lk 15: 7 in *h* over one sinner who repents
18:22 and you will have treasure in *h.*
Ro 10: 6 'Who will ascend into *h?*' " (that is,
2Co 5: 1 an eternal house in *h,* not built
12: 2 ago was caught up to the third *h.*
Php 2:10 *h* and on earth and under the earth,
3:20 But our citizenship is in *h.*
1Th 1:10 and to wait for his Son from *h,*
Heb 8: 5 and shadow of what is in *h.*
9:24 he entered *h* itself, now to appear
2Pe 3:13 we are looking forward to a new *h*
Rev 21: 1 Then I saw a new *h* and a new earth

HEAVENLY (HEAVEN)
Ps 8: 5 him a little lower than the *h* beings
2Co 5: 2 to be clothed with our *h* dwelling,
Eph 1: 3 in the *h* realms with every spiritual
1:20 at his right hand in the *h* realms,
2Ti 4:18 bring me safely to his *h* kingdom.
Heb 12:22 to the *h* Jerusalem, the city

HEAVENS (HEAVEN)
Ge 1: 1 In the beginning God created the *h*
1Ki 8:27 The *h,* even the highest heaven,
2Ch 2: 6 since the *h,* even the highest
Ps 8: 3 When I consider your *h,*
19: 1 The *h* declare the glory of God;
102:25 the *h* are the work of your hands.
108: 4 is your love, higher than the *h;*
119:89 it stands firm in the *h.*
139: 8 If I go up to the *h,* you are there;
Isa 51: 6 Lift up your eyes to the *h,*
55: 9 "As the *h* are higher than the earth,
65:17 new *h* and a new earth.
Joel 2:30 I will show wonders in the *h*
Eph 4:10 who ascended higher than all the *h,*
2Pe 3:10 The *h* will disappear with a roar;

HEBREW
Ge 14:13 and reported this to Abram the *H.*

HEEDS
Pr 13: 1 wise son *h* his father's instruction,
13:18 whoever *h* correction is honored.
15: 5 whoever *h* correction shows
15:32 whoever *h* correction gains

HEEL
Ge 3:15 and you will strike his *h.*"

HEIRS (INHERIT)
Ro 8:17 then we are *h*—*h* of God
Gal 3:29 and *h* according to the promise.
Eph 3: 6 gospel the Gentiles are *h* together
1Pe 3: 7 as *h* with you of the gracious gift

HELL
Mt 5:22 will be in danger of the fire of *h.*
Lk 16:23 In *h,* where he was in torment,
2Pe 2: 4 but sent them to *h,* putting them

HELMET
Isa 59:17 and the *h* of salvation on his head;
Eph 6:17 Take the *h* of salvation
1Th 5: 8 and the hope of salvation as a *h.*

HELP (HELPED HELPER HELPING HELPS)
Ps 10: 6 I cried to my God for *h*
30: 2 my God, I called to you for *h*
46: 1 an ever-present *h* in trouble.
79: 9 *H* us, O God our Savior,
121: 1 where does my *h* come from?
Isa 41:10 I will strengthen you and *h* you;
Jnh 2: 2 depths of the grave I called for *h,*
Mk 9:24 *h* me overcome my unbelief!"
Ac 16: 9 Come over to Macedonia and *h* us
1Co 12:28 those able to *h* others, those

HELPED (HELP)
1Sa 7:12 "Thus far has the LORD *h* us,"

HELPER (HELP)
Ge 2:18 I will make a *h* suitable for him."
Ps 10:14 you are the *h* of the fatherless.
Heb 13: 6 Lord is my *h;* I will not be afraid.

HELPING (HELP)
Ac 9:36 always doing good and *h* the poor.
1Ti 5:10 *h* those in trouble and devoting

HELPS (HELP)
Ro 8:26 the Spirit *h* us in our weakness.

HEN
Mt 23:37 as a *h* gathers her chicks

HERITAGE (INHERIT)
Ps 127: 3 Sons are a *h* from the LORD,

HEROD
1. King of Judea who tried to kill Jesus (Mt 2; Lk 1:5).
2. Son of 1. Tetrarch of Galilee who arrested and beheaded John the Baptist (Mt 14:1-12; Mk 6:14-29; Lk 3:1, 19-20; 9:7-9); tried Jesus (Lk 23:6-15).
3. Grandson of 1. King of Judea who killed James (Ac 12:2); arrested Peter (Ac 12:3-19). Death (Ac 12:19-23).

HERODIAS
Wife of Herod the Tetrarch who persuaded her daughter to ask for John the Baptist's head (Mt 14:1-12; Mk 6:14-29).

HEZEKIAH
King of Judah. Restored the temple and worship (2Ch 29-31). Sought the LORD for help against Assyria (2Ki 18-19; 2Ch 32:1-23; Isa 36-37). Illness healed (2Ki 20:1-11; 2Ch 32:24-26; Isa 38). Judged for showing Babylonians his treasures (2Ki 20:12-21; 2Ch 32:31; Isa 39).

HID (HIDE)
Ge 3: 8 and they *h* from the LORD God
Ex 2: 2 she *h* him for three months.
Jos 6:17 because she *h* the spies we sent.
Heb 11:23 By faith Moses' parents *h* him

HIDDEN (HIDE)
Ps 19:12 Forgive my *h* faults.
119:11 I have *h* your word in my heart
Pr 2: 4 and search for it as for *h* treasure,
Isa 59: 2 your sins have *h* his face from you,
Mt 5:14 A city on a hill cannot be *h.*
13:44 of heaven is like treasure *h*
Col 1:26 the mystery that has been kept *h*
2: 3 in whom are *h* all the treasures
3: 3 and your life is now *h* with Christ

HIDE (HID HIDDEN)
Ps 17: 8 *h* me in the shadow of your wings
143: 9 for I *h* myself in you.

HILL (HILLS)
Mt 5:14 A city on a *h* cannot be hidden.

HILLS (HILL)
Ps 50:10 and the cattle on a thousand *h.*
121: 1 I lift up my eyes to the *h*—

HINDER (HINDERS)
1Sa 14: 6 Nothing can *h* the LORD
Mt 19:14 come to me, and do not *h* them,
1Co 9:12 anything rather than *h* the gospel
1Pe 3: 7 so that nothing will *h* your prayers.

HINDERS (HINDER)
Heb 12: 1 let us throw off everything that *h*

HINT*
Eph 5: 3 even a *h* of sexual immorality,

HOLD
Ex 20: 7 LORD will not *h* anyone guiltless
Lev 19:13 " 'Do not *h* back the wages
Jos 22: 5 to *h* fast to him and to serve him
Ps 73:23 you *h* me by my right hand.
Pr 4: 4 "Lay *h* of my words
Isa 54: 2 do not *h* back;
Mk 11:25 if you *h* anything against anyone,
Php 2:16 as you *h* out the word of life
3:12 but I press on to take *h* of that
Col 1:17 and in him all things *h* together.
1Th 5:21 *H* on to the good.
1Ti 6:12 Take *h* of the eternal life
Heb 10:23 Let us *h* unswervingly

HOLINESS (HOLY)
Ex 15:11 majestic in *h,*
Ps 29: 2 in the splendor of his *h.*
96: 9 in the splendor of his *h;*
Ro 6:19 to righteousness leading to *h.*
2Co 7: 1 perfecting *h* out of reverence
Eph 4:24 God in true righteousness and *h.*
Heb 12:10 that we may share in his *h.*
12:14 without *h* no one will see the Lord.

HOLY (HALLOWED HOLINESS)
Ex 19: 6 kingdom of priests and a *h* nation.'
20: 8 the Sabbath day by keeping it *h.*
Lev 11:44 and be *h,* because I am *h.*
20: 7 " 'Consecrate yourselves and be *h,*
20:26 You are to be *h* to me because I,
21: 8 Consider them *h,* because I
22:32 Do not profane my *h* name.
Ps 16:10 will you let your *H* One see decay.
24: 3 Who may stand in his *h* place?
77:13 Your ways, O God, are *h.*
99: 3 he is *h.*
99: 5 he is *h.*
99: 9 for the LORD our God is *h.*
111: 9 *h* and awesome is his name.
Isa 5:16 the *h* God will show himself *h*
6: 3 *H, h, h* is the LORD Almighty;
40:25 who is my equal?" says the *H* One.
57:15 who lives forever, whose name is *h:*
Eze 28:25 I will show myself *h* among them
Da 9:24 prophecy and to anoint the most *h.*
Hab 2:20 But the LORD is in his *h* temple;
Ac 2:27 will you let your *H* One see decay.
Ro 7:12 and the commandment is *h,*
12: 1 as living sacrifices, *h* and pleasing
Eph 5: 3 improper for God's *h* people.
2Th 1:10 to be glorified in his *h* people
2Ti 1: 9 saved us and called us to a *h* life—
3:15 you have known the *h* Scriptures,
Tit 1: 8 upright, *h* and disciplined.
1Pe 1:15 But just as he who called you is *h,*
1:16 is written: "Be *h,* because I am *h.*"
2: 9 a royal priesthood, a *h* nation,
2Pe 3:11 You ought to live *h* and godly lives
Rev 4: 8 "*H, h, h* is the Lord God

HOME (HOMES)
Dt 6: 7 Talk about them when you sit at *h*
Ps 84: 3 Even the sparrow has found a *h*,
Pr 3:33 but he blesses the *h* of the righteous
Mk 10:29 "no one who has left *h* or brothers
Jn 14:23 to him and make our *h* with him.
Tit 2: 5 to be busy at *h*, to be kind,

HOMES (HOME)
Ne 4:14 daughters, your wives and your *h*."
1Ti 5:14 to manage their *h* and to give

HOMOSEXUAL*
1Co 6: 9 male prostitutes nor *h* offenders

HONEST
Lev 19:36 Use *h* scales and *h* weights,
Dt 25:15 and *h* weights and measures,
Job 31: 6 let God weigh me in *h* scales
Pr 12:17 truthful witness gives *h* testimony,

HONEY
Ex 3: 8 a land flowing with milk and *h*—
Ps 19:10 than *h* from the comb.
119:103 sweeter than *h* to my mouth!

HONOR (HONORABLE HONORABLY HONORED HONORS)
Ex 20:12 "*H* your father and your mother,
Nu 25:13 he was zealous for the *h* of his God
Dt 5:16 "*H* your father and your mother,
1Sa 2:30 Those who *h* me I will *h*,
Ps 8: 5 and crowned him with glory and *h*.
Pr 3: 9 *H* the LORD with your wealth,
15:33 and humility comes before *h*.
20: 3 It is to a man's *h* to avoid strife,
Mt 15: 4 '*H* your father and mother'
Ro 12:10 *H* one another above yourselves.
1Co 6:20 Therefore *h* God with your body.
Eph 6: 2 "*H* your father and mother"—
1Ti 5:17 well are worthy of double *h*,
Heb 2: 7 you crowned him with glory and *h*
Rev 4: 9 *h* and thanks to him who sits

HONORABLE (HONOR)
1Th 4: 4 body in a way that is holy and *h*,

HONORABLY (HONOR)
Heb 13:18 and desire to live *h* in every way.

HONORED (HONOR)
Ps 12: 8 when what is vile is *h* among men.
Pr 13:18 but whoever heeds correction is *h*.
1Co 12:26 if one part is *h*, every part rejoices
Heb 13: 4 Marriage should be *h* by all,

HONORS (HONOR)
Ps 15: 4 but *h* those who fear the LORD,
Pr 14:31 to the needy *h* God.

HOOKS
Isa 2: 4 and their spears into pruning *h*.
Joel 3:10 and your pruning *h* into spears.

HOPE (HOPES)
Job 13:15 Though he slay me, yet will I *h*
Ps 42: 5 Put your *h* in God,
62: 5 my *h* comes from him.
119:74 for I have put my *h* in your word.
130: 7 O Israel, put your *h* in the LORD,
147:11 who put their *h* in his unfailing love
Pr 13:12 *H* deferred makes the heart sick,
Isa 40:31 but those who *h* in the LORD
Ro 5: 4 character; and character, *h*.
8:24 But *h* that is seen is no *h* at all.
12:12 Be joyful in *h*, patient in affliction,
15: 4 of the Scriptures we might have *h*.
1Co 13:13 now these three remain: faith, *h*
15:19 for this life we have *h* in Christ,
Col 1:27 Christ in you, the *h* of glory.
1Th 5: 8 and the *h* of salvation as a helmet.
1Ti 6:17 but to put their *h* in God,
Tit 2:13 while we wait for the blessed *h*—
Heb 6:19 We have this *h* as an anchor
11: 1 faith is being sure of what we *h* for
1Jn 3: 3 Everyone who has this *h*

HOPES (HOPE)
1Co 13: 7 always *h*, always perseveres.

HORSE
Ps 147:10 not in the strength of the *h*,
Pr 26: 3 A whip for the *h*, a halter
Zec 1: 8 before me was a man riding a red *h*
Rev 6: 2 and there before me was a white *h*!
6: 4 Come!" Then another *h* came out,
6: 5 and there before me was a black *h*!
6: 8 and there before me was a pale *h*!
19:11 and there before me was a white *h*,

HOSANNA
Mt 21: 9 "*H* in the highest!"

HOSHEA
Last king of Israel (2Ki 15:30; 17:1-6).

HOSPITABLE* (HOSPITALITY)
1Ti 3: 2 self-controlled, respectable, *h*,
Tit 1: 8 Rather he must be *h*, one who loves

HOSPITALITY (HOSPITABLE)
Ro 12:13 Practice *h*.
1Ti 5:10 as bringing up children, showing *h*,
1Pe 4: 9 Offer *h* to one another

HOSTILE
Ro 8: 7 the sinful mind is *h* to God.

HOT
1Ti 4: 2 have been seared as with a *h* iron.
Rev 3:15 that you are neither cold nor *h*.

HOT-TEMPERED
Pr 15:18 A *h* man stirs up dissension,
19:19 A *h* man must pay the penalty;
22:24 Do not make friends with a *h* man,
29:22 and a *h* one commits many sins.

HOTHEADED (HEAD)
Pr 14:16 but a fool is *h* and reckless.

HOUR
Ecc 9:12 knows when his *h* will come:
Mt 6:27 you by worrying can add a single *h*
Lk 12:40 the Son of Man will come at an *h*
Jn 12:23 The *h* has come for the Son of Man
12:27 for this very reason I came to this *h*

HOUSE (HOUSEHOLD STOREHOUSE)
Ex 20:17 shall not covet your neighbor's *h*.
Ps 23: 6 I will dwell in the *h* of the LORD
84:10 a doorkeeper in the *h* of my God
122: 1 "Let us go to the *h* of the LORD."
127: 1 Unless the LORD builds the *h*,
Pr 7:27 Her *h* is a highway to the grave,
21: 9 than share a *h* with a quarrelsome
Isa 56: 7 a *h* of prayer for all nations."
Zec 13: 6 given at the *h* of my friends.'
Mt 7:24 is like a wise man who built his *h*
12:29 can anyone enter a strong man's *h*
21:13 My *h* will be called a *h* of prayer,'
Mk 3:25 If a *h* is divided against itself,
Lk 11:17 a *h* divided against itself will fall.
Jn 2:16 How dare you turn my Father's *h*
12: 3 the *h* was filled with the fragrance
14: 2 In my Father's *h* are many rooms;
Heb 3: 3 the builder of a *h* has greater honor

HOUSEHOLD (HOUSE)
Jos 24:15 my *h*, we will serve the LORD."
Mic 7: 6 are the members of his own *h*.
Mt 10:36 will be the members of his own *h*.'
12:25 or *h* divided against itself will not
1Ti 3:12 manage his children and his *h* well.
3:15 to conduct themselves in God's *h*,

HUMAN (HUMANITY)
Gal 3: 3 to attain your goal by *h* effort?

HUMANITY* (HUMAN)
Heb 2:14 he too shared in their *h* so that

HUMBLE (HUMBLED HUMBLES HUMILIATE HUMILITY)
2Ch 7:14 will *h* themselves and pray
Ps 25: 9 He guides the *h* in what is right
Pr 3:34 but gives grace to the *h*.
Isa 66: 2 he who is *h* and contrite in spirit,
Mt 11:29 for I am gentle and *h* in heart,
Eph 4: 2 Be completely *h* and gentle;
Jas 4:10 *H* yourselves before the Lord,
1Pe 5: 6 *H* yourselves,

HUMBLED (HUMBLE)
Mt 23:12 whoever exalts himself will be *h*,
Php 2: 8 he *h* himself

HUMBLES (HUMBLE)
Mt 18: 4 whoever *h* himself like this child is
23:12 whoever *h* himself will be exalted.

HUMILIATE* (HUMBLE)
Pr 25: 7 than for him to *h* you
1Co 11:22 and *h* those who have nothing?

HUMILITY (HUMBLE)
Pr 11: 2 but with *h* comes wisdom.
15:33 and *h* comes before honor.
Php 2: 3 but in *h* consider others better
Tit 3: 2 and to show true *h* toward all men.
1Pe 5: 5 clothe yourselves with *h*

HUNGRY
Ps 107: 9 and fills the *h* with good things.
146: 7 and gives food to the *h*.
Pr 25:21 If your enemy is *h*, give him food
Eze 18: 7 but gives his food to the *h*
Mt 25:35 For I was *h* and you gave me
Lk 1:53 He has filled the *h* with good things
Jn 6:35 comes to me will never go *h*,
Ro 12:20 "If your enemy is *h*, feed him;

HURT (HURTS)
Ecc 8: 9 it over others to his own *h*.
Mk 16:18 deadly poison, it will not *h* them
Rev 2:11 He who overcomes will not be *h*

HURTS* (HURT)
Ps 15: 4 even when it *h*,
Pr 26:28 A lying tongue hates those it *h*,

HUSBAND (HUSBAND'S HUSBANDS)
1Co 7: 3 The *h* should fulfill his marital duty
7:10 wife must not separate from her *h*.
7:11 And a *h* must not divorce his wife.
7:13 And if a woman has a *h* who is not
7:39 A woman is bound to her *h* as long
2Co 11: 2 I promised you to one *h*, to Christ,
Eph 5:23 For the *h* is the head of the wife
5:33 and the wife must respect her *h*.
1Ti 3: 2 the *h* of but one wife, temperate,

HUSBAND'S (HUSBAND)
Pr 12: 4 of noble character is her *h* crown,
1Co 7: 4 the *h* body does not belong

HUSBANDS (HUSBAND)
Eph 5:22 submit to your *h* as to the Lord.
5:25 *H*, love your wives, just
Tit 2: 4 the younger women to love their *h*
1Pe 3: 1 same way be submissive to your *h*
3: 7 *H*, in the same way be considerate

HYMN
1Co 14:26 everyone has a *h*, or a word

HYPOCRISY (HYPOCRITE HYPOCRITES)
Mt 23:28 but on the inside you are full of *h*
1Pe 2: 1 *h*, envy, and slander of every kind.

HYPOCRITE (HYPOCRISY)
Mt 7: 5 You *h*, first take the plank out

HYPOCRITES (HYPOCRISY)
Ps 26: 4 nor do I consort with *h*;
Mt 6: 5 when you pray, do not be like the *h*

HYSSOP
Ps 51: 7 with *h*, and I will be clean;

IDLE (IDLENESS)
1Th 5:14 those who are *i*, encourage
2Th 3: 6 away from every brother who is *i*
1Ti 5:13 they get into the habit of being *i*

IDLENESS* (IDLE)
Pr 31:27 and does not eat the bread of *i*.

IDOL (IDOLATRY IDOLS)
Isa 44:17 From the rest he makes a god, his *i*;
1Co 8: 4 We know that an *i* is nothing at all

IDOLATRY (IDOL)
Col 3: 5 evil desires and greed, which is *i*.

IDOLS (IDOL)
1Co 8: 1 Now about food sacrificed to *i*:

IGNORANT (IGNORE)
1Co 15:34 for there are some who are *i* of God
Heb 5: 2 to deal gently with those who are *i*
1Pe 2:15 good you should silence the *i* talk
2Pe 3:16 which *i* and unstable people distort

IGNORE (IGNORANT IGNORES)
Dt 22: 1 do not *i* it but be sure
Ps 9:12 he does not *i* the cry of the afflicted
Heb 2: 3 if we *i* such a great salvation?

IGNORES (IGNORE)
Pr 10:17 whoever *i* correction leads others
15:32 He who *i* discipline despises

ILLUMINATED*
Rev 18: 1 and the earth was *i* by his splendor.

IMAGE
Ge 1:26 "Let us make man in our *i*,
1:27 So God created man in his own *i*,
1Co 11: 7 since he is the *i* and glory of God;
Col 1:15 He is the *i* of the invisible God,

Col 3:10 in knowledge in the *i* of its Creator.

IMAGINE
Eph 3:20 more than all we ask or *i*,

IMITATE (IMITATORS)
1Co 4:16 Therefore I urge you to *i* me.
Heb 6:12 but to *i* those who through faith
13: 7 of their way of life and *i* their faith.
3Jn :11 do not *i* what is evil but what is

IMITATORS* (IMITATE)
Eph 5: 1 Be *i* of God, therefore,
1Th 1: 6 You became *i* of us and of the Lord
2:14 became *i* of God's churches

IMMANUEL
Isa 7:14 birth to a son, and will call him *I*.
Mt 1:23 and they will call him *I*"—

IMMORAL* (IMMORALITY)
Pr 6:24 keeping you from the *i* woman,
1Co 5: 9 to associate with sexually *i* people
5:10 the people of this world who are *i*,
5:11 but is sexually *i* or greedy,
6: 9 Neither the sexually *i* nor idolaters
Eph 5: 5 No *i*, impure or greedy person—
Heb 12:16 See that no one is sexually *i*,
13: 4 the adulterer and all the sexually *i*.
Rev 21: 8 the murderers, the sexually *i*,
22:15 the sexually *i*, the murderers,

IMMORALITY (IMMORAL)
1Co 6:13 The body is not meant for sexual *i*,
6:18 Flee from sexual *i*.
10: 8 We should not commit sexual *i*,
Gal 5:19 sexual *i*, impurity and debauchery;
Eph 5: 3 must not be even a hint of sexual *i*,
1Th 4: 3 that you should avoid sexual *i*;
Jude : 4 grace of our God into a license for *i*

IMMORTAL* (IMMORTALITY)
Ro 1:23 glory of the *i* God for images made
1Ti 1:17 Now to the King eternal, *i*,
6:16 who alone is *i* and who lives

IMMORTALITY (IMMORTAL)
Ro 2: 7 honor and *i*, he will give eternal life
1Co 15:53 and the mortal with *i*.
2Ti 1:10 and *i* to light through the gospel.

IMPERISHABLE
1Pe 1:23 not of perishable seed, but of *i*,

IMPORTANCE* (IMPORTANT)
1Co 15: 3 passed on to you as of first *i*:

IMPORTANT (IMPORTANCE)
Mt 6:25 Is not life more *i* than food,
23:23 have neglected the more *i* matters
Mk 12:29 "The most *i* one," answered Jesus,
12:33 as yourself is more *i* than all burnt
Php 1:18 The *i* thing is that in every way,

IMPOSSIBLE
Mt 17:20 Nothing will be *i* for you."
Lk 1:37 For nothing is *i* with God."
18:27 "What is *i* with men is possible
Heb 6:18 things in which it is *i* for God to lie,
11: 6 without faith it is *i* to please God,

IMPROPER*
Eph 5: 3 these are *i* for God's holy people.

IMPURE (IMPURITY)
Ac 10:15 not call anything *i* that God has
Eph 5: 5 No immoral, *i* or greedy person—
1Th 4: 7 For God did not call us to be *i*,
Rev 21:27 Nothing *i* will ever enter it,

IMPURITY (IMPURE)
Ro 1:24 hearts to sexual *i* for the degrading
Eph 5: 3 or of any kind of *i*, or of greed,

INCENSE
Ex 40: 5 Place the gold altar of *i* in front
Ps 141: 2 my prayer be set before you like *i*;
Mt 2:11 him with gifts of gold and of *i*

INCOME
Ecc 5:10 wealth is never satisfied with his *i*.
1Co 16: 2 sum of money in keeping with his *i*,

INCOMPARABLE*
Eph 2: 7 ages he might show the *i* riches

INCREASE (EVER-INCREASING INCREASED INCREASES INCREASING)
Ge 1:22 "Be fruitful and *i* in number
Ps 62:10 though your riches *i*,
Isa 9: 7 Of the *i* of his government
Lk 17: 5 said to the Lord, "*I* our faith!"
1Th 3:12 May the Lord make your love *i*

INCREASED (INCREASE)
Ac 6: 7 of disciples in Jerusalem *i* rapidly,
Ro 5:20 But where sin *i*, grace *i* all the more

INCREASES (INCREASE)
Pr 24: 5 and a man of knowledge *i* strength;

INCREASING (INCREASE)
Ac 6: 1 when the number of disciples was *i*,
2Th 1: 3 one of you has for each other is *i*.
2Pe 1: 8 these qualities in *i* measure,

INDEPENDENT*
1Co 11:11 however, woman is not *i* of man,
11:11 of man, nor is man *i* of woman.

INDESCRIBABLE*
2Co 9:15 Thanks be to God for his *i* gift!

INDISPENSABLE*
1Co 12:22 seem to be weaker are *i*,

INEFFECTIVE*
2Pe 1: 8 they will keep you from being *i*

INEXPRESSIBLE*
2Co 12: 4 He heard *i* things, things that man
1Pe 1: 8 are filled with an *i* and glorious joy,

INFANTS
Mt 21:16 " 'From the lips of children and *i*
1Co 14:20 In regard to evil be *i*,

INFIRMITIES
Isa 53: 4 Surely he took up our *i*

INHERIT (CO-HEIRS HEIRS HERITAGE INHERITANCE)
Ps 37:11 But the meek will *i* the land
37:29 the righteous will *i* the land
Mt 5: 5 for they will *i* the earth.
Mk 10:17 "what must I do to *i* eternal life?"
1Co 15:50 blood cannot *i* the kingdom of God

INHERITANCE (INHERIT)
Dt 4:20 to be the people of his *i*,
Pr 13:22 A good man leaves an *i*
Eph 1:14 who is a deposit guaranteeing our *i*
5: 5 has any *i* in the kingdom of Christ
Heb 9:15 receive the promised eternal *i*—
1Pe 1: 4 and into an *i* that can never perish,

INIQUITIES (INIQUITY)
Ps 78:38 he forgave their *i*
103:10 or repay us according to our *i*.
Isa 59: 2 But your *i* have separated
Mic 7:19 and hurl all our *i* into the depths

INIQUITY (INIQUITIES)
Ps 51: 2 Wash away all my *i*
Isa 53: 6 the *i* of us all.

INJUSTICE
2Ch 19: 7 the LORD our God there is no *i*

INNOCENT
Pr 17:26 It is not good to punish an *i* man,
Mt 10:16 shrewd as snakes and as *i* as doves.
27: 4 "for I have betrayed *i* blood."
1Co 4: 4 but that does not make me *i*.

INSCRIPTION
Mt 22:20 And whose *i*?" "Caesar's,"

INSOLENT
Ro 1:30 God-haters, *i*, arrogant

INSTITUTED
Ro 13: 2 rebelling against what God has *i*,
1Pe 2:13 to every authority *i* among men:

INSTRUCT (INSTRUCTION)
Ps 32: 8 I will *i* you and teach you
Pr 9: 9 *I* a wise man and he will be wiser
Ro 15:14 and competent to *i* one another.
2Ti 2:25 who oppose him he must gently *i*,

INSTRUCTION (INSTRUCT)
Pr 1: 8 Listen, my son, to your father's *i*
4: 1 Listen, my sons, to a father's *i*;
4:13 Hold on to *i*, do not let it go;
8:10 Choose my *i* instead of silver,
8:33 Listen to my *i* and be wise;
13: 1 A wise son heeds his father's *i*,
13:13 He who scorns *i* will pay for it,
16:20 Whoever gives heed to *i* prospers,
16:21 and pleasant words promote *i*.
19:20 Listen to advice and accept *i*,
23:12 Apply your heart to *i*
1Co 14: 6 or prophecy or word of *i*?
14:26 or a word of *i*, a revelation,
Eph 6: 4 up in the training and *i* of the Lord.
1Th 4: 8 he who rejects this *i* does not reject
2Th 3:14 If anyone does not obey our *i*
1Ti 1:18 I give you this *i* in keeping
6: 3 to the sound *i* of our Lord Jesus
2Ti 4: 2 with great patience and careful *i*.

INSULT
Pr 9: 7 corrects a mocker invites *i*;
12:16 but a prudent man overlooks an *i*.
Mt 5:11 Blessed are you when people *i* you,
Lk 6:22 when they exclude you and *i* you
1Pe 3: 9 evil with evil or *i* with *i*,

INTEGRITY
1Ki 9: 4 if you walk before me in *i* of heart
Job 2: 3 And he still maintains his *i*,
27: 5 till I die, I will not deny my *i*.
Pr 10: 9 The man of *i* walks securely,
11: 3 The *i* of the upright guides them,
29:10 Bloodthirsty men hate a man of *i*
Tit 2: 7 your teaching show *i*, seriousness

INTELLIGENCE
Isa 29:14 the *i* of the intelligent will vanish."
1Co 1:19 *i* of the intelligent I will frustrate."

INTELLIGIBLE
1Co 14:19 I would rather speak five *i* words

INTERCEDE (INTERCEDES INTERCESSION)
Heb 7:25 he always lives to *i* for them.

INTERCEDES (INTERCEDE)
Ro 8:26 but the Spirit himself *i* for us

INTERCESSION* (INTERCEDE)
Isa 53:12 and made *i* for the transgressors.
1Ti 2: 1 *i* and thanksgiving be made

INTERESTS
1Co 7:34 his wife—and his *i* are divided.
Php 2: 4 only to your own *i*, but also to the *i*
2:21 everyone looks out for his own *i*,

INTERMARRY (MARRY)
Dt 7: 3 Do not *i* with them.

INVENTED*
2Pe 1:16 We did not follow cleverly *i* stories

INVESTIGATED
Lk 1: 3 I myself have carefully *i* everything

INVISIBLE
Ro 1:20 of the world God's *i* qualities—
Col 1:15 He is the image of the *i* God,
1Ti 1:17 immortal, *i*, the only God,

INVITE (INVITED INVITES)
Lk 14:13 you give a banquet, *i* the poor,

INVITED (INVITE)
Mt 22:14 For many are *i*, but few are chosen
25:35 I was a stranger and you *i* me in,

INVITES (INVITE)
1Co 10:27 If some unbeliever *i* you to a meal

INVOLVED
2Ti 2: 4 a soldier gets *i* in civilian affairs—

IRON
1Ti 4: 2 have been seared as with a hot *i*.
Rev 2:27 He will rule them with an *i* scepter;

IRREVOCABLE*
Ro 11:29 for God's gifts and his call are *i*.

ISAAC
Son of Abraham by Sarah (Ge 17:19; 21:1-7; 1Ch 1:28). Offered up by Abraham (Ge 22; Heb 11:17-19). Rebekah taken as wife (Ge 24). Fathered Esau and Jacob (Ge 25:19-26; 1Ch 1:34). Tricked into blessing Jacob (Ge 27). Father of Israel (Ex 3:6; Dt 29:13; Ro 9:10).

ISAIAH
Prophet to Judah (Isa 1:1). Called by the LORD (Isa 6).

ISHMAEL
Son of Abraham by Hagar (Ge 16; 1Ch 1:28). Blessed, but not son of covenant (Ge 17:18-21; Gal 4:21-31). Sent away by Sarah (Ge 21:8-21).

ISRAEL (ISRAELITES)
1. Name given to Jacob (see JACOB).
2. Corporate name of Jacob's descendants; often specifically Northern Kingdom.
Dt 6: 4 Hear, O *I*: The LORD our God,
1Sa 4:21 "The glory has departed from *I*"—

Isa 27: 6 *I* will bud and blossom
Jer 31:10 'He who scattered *I* will gather
Eze 39:23 of *I* went into exile for their sin,
Mk 12:29 'Hear, O *I*, the Lord our God,
Lk 22:30 judging the twelve tribes of *I*.
Ro 9: 6 all who are descended from *I* are *I*.
11:26 And so all *I* will be saved,
Eph 3: 6 Gentiles are heirs together with *I*,

ISRAELITES (ISRAEL)
Ex 14:22 and the *I* went through the sea
16:35 The *I* ate manna forty years,
Hos 1:10 "Yet the *I* will be like the sand
Ro 9:27 the number of the *I* be like the sand

ITCHING*
2Ti 4: 3 to say what their *i* ears want to hear

JACOB
Second son of Isaac, twin of Esau (Ge 26:21-26; 1Ch 1:34). Bought Esau's birthright (Ge 26:29-34); tricked Isaac into blessing him (Ge 27:1-37). Abrahamic covenant perpetuated through (Ge 28:13-15; Mal 1:2). Vision at Bethel (Ge 28:10-22). Wives and children (Ge 29:1-30:24; 35:16-26; 1Ch 2-9). Wrestled with God; name changed to Israel (Ge 32:22-32). Sent sons to Egypt during famine (Ge 42-43). Settled in Egypt (Ge 46). Blessed Ephraim and Manasseh (Ge 48). Blessed sons (Ge 49:1-28; Heb 11:21). Death (Ge 49:29-33). Burial (Ge 50:1-14).

JAMES
1. Apostle; brother of John (Mt 4:21-22; 10:2; Mk 3:17; Lk 5:1-10). At transfiguration (Mt 17:1-13; Mk 9:1-13; Lk 9:28-36). Killed by Herod (Ac 12:2).
2. Apostle; son of Alphaeus (Mt 10:3; Mk 3:18; Lk 6:15).
3. Brother of Jesus (Mt 13:55; Mk 6:3; Lk 24:10; Gal 1:19) and Judas (Jude 1). With believers before Pentecost (Ac 1:13). Leader of church at Jerusalem (Ac 12:17; 15; 21:18; Gal 2:9, 12). Author of epistle (Jas 1:1).

JAPHETH
Son of Noah (Ge 5:32; 1Ch 1:4-5). Blessed (Ge 9:18-28).

JARS
2Co 4: 7 we have this treasure in *j* of clay

JEALOUS (JEALOUSY)
Ex 20: 5 the LORD your God, am a *j* God,
34:14 whose name is Jealous, is a *j* God.
Dt 4:24 God is a consuming fire, a *j* God.
Joel 2:18 the LORD will be *j* for his land
Zec 1:14 I am very *j* for Jerusalem and Zion,
2Co 11: 2 I am *j* for you with a godly jealousy

JEALOUSY (JEALOUS)
1Co 3: 3 For since there is *j* and quarreling
2Co 11: 2 I am jealous for you with a godly *j*.
Gal 5:20 hatred, discord, *j*, fits of rage,

JEHOAHAZ
1. Son of Jehu; king of Israel (2Ki 13:1-9).
2. Son of Josiah; king of Judah (2Ki 23:31-34; 2Ch 36:1-4).

JEHOASH
Son of Jehoahaz; king of Israel (2Ki 13-14; 2Ch 25).

JEHOIACHIN
Son of Jehoiakim; king of Judah exiled by Nebuchadnezzar (2Ki 24:8-17; 2Ch 36:8-10; Jer 22:24-30; 24:1). Raised from prisoner status (2Ki 25:27-30; Jer 52:31-34).

JEHOIAKIM
Son of Josiah; king of Judah (2Ki 23:34-24:6; 2Ch 36:4-8; Jer 22:18-23; 36).

JEHORAM
Son of Jehoshaphat; king of Judah (2Ki 8:16-24).

JEHOSHAPHAT
Son of Asa; king of Judah (1Ki 22:41-50; 2Ki 3; 2Ch 17-20).

JEHU
King of Israel (1Ki 19:16-19; 2Ki 9-10).

JEPHTHAH
Judge from Gilead who delivered Israel from Ammon (Jdg 10:6-12:7). Made rash vow concerning his daughter (Jdg 11:30-40).

JEREMIAH
Prophet to Judah (Jer 1:1-3). Called by the LORD (Jer 1). Put in stocks (Jer 20:1-3). Threatened for prophesying (Jer 11:18-23; 26). Opposed by Hananiah (Jer 28). Scroll burned (Jer 36). Imprisoned (Jer 37). Thrown into cistern (Jer 38). Forced to Egypt with those fleeing Babylonians (Jer 43).

JEROBOAM
1. Official of Solomon; rebelled to become first king of Israel (1Ki 11:26-40; 12:1-20; 2Ch 10). Idolatry (1Ki 12:25-33); judgment for (1Ki 13-14; 2Ch 13).
2. Son of Jehoash; king of Israel (1Ki 14:23-29).

JERUSALEM
2Ki 23:27 and I will reject *J*, the city I chose,
2Ch 6: 6 now I have chosen *J* for my Name
Ne 2:17 Come, let us rebuild the wall of *J*,
Ps 122: 6 Pray for the peace of *J*:
125: 2 As the mountains surround *J*,
137: 5 If I forget you, O *J*,
Isa 40: 9 You who bring good tidings to *J*,
65:18 for I will create *J* to be a delight
Joel 3:17 *J* will be holy;
Zep 3:16 On that day they will say to *J*,
Zec 2: 4 '*J* will be a city without walls
8: 8 I will bring them back to live in *J*;
14: 8 living water will flow out from *J*,
Mt 23:37 "O *J*, *J*, you who kill the prophets
Lk 13:34 die outside *J*! "O *J*, *J*,
21:24 *J* will be trampled
Jn 4:20 where we must worship is in *J*."
Ac 1: 8 and you will be my witnesses in *J*,
Gal 4:25 corresponds to the present city of *J*
Rev 21: 2 I saw the Holy City, the new *J*,

JESUS
LIFE: Genealogy (Mt 1:1-17; Lk 3:21-37). Birth announced (Mt 1:18-25; Lk 1:26-45). Birth (Mt 2:1-12; Lk 2:1-40). Escape to Egypt (Mt 2:13-23). As a boy in the temple (Lk 2:41-52). Baptism (Mt 3:13-17; Mk 1:9-11; Lk 3.21-22; Jn 1:32-34). Temptation (Mt 4:1-11; Mk 1:12-13; Lk 4:1-13). Ministry in Galilee (Mt 4:12-18:35; Mk 1:14-9:50; Lk 4:14-13:9; Jn 1:35-2:11; 4; 6), Transfiguration (Mt 17:1-8; Mk 9:2-8; Lk 9:28-36), on the way to Jerusalem (Mt 19-20; Mk 10; Lk 13:10-19:27), in Jerusalem (Mt 21-25; Mk 11-13; Lk 19:28-21:38; Jn 2:12-3:36; 5; 7-12). Last supper (Mt 26:17-35; Mk 14:12-31; Lk 22:1-38; Jn 13-17). Arrest and trial (Mt 26:36-27:31; Mk 14:43-15:20; Lk 22:39-23:25; Jn 18:1-19:16). Crucifixion (Mt 27:32-66; Mk 15:21-47; Lk 23:26-55; Jn 19:28-42). Resurrection and appearances (Mt 28; Mk 16; Lk 24; Jn 20-21; Ac 1:1-11; 7:56; 9:3-6; 1Co 15:1-8; Rev 1:1-20).

MIRACLES. Healings: official's son (Jn 4:43-54), demoniac in Capernaum (Mk 1:23-26; Lk 4:33-35), Peter's mother-in-law (Mt 8:14-17; Mk 1:29-31; Lk 4:38-39), leper (Mt 8:2-4; Mk 1:40-45; Lk 5:12-16), paralytic (Mt 9:1-8; Mk 2:1-12; Lk 5:17-26), cripple (Jn 5:1-9), shriveled hand (Mt 12:10-13; Mk 3:1-5; Lk 6:6-11), centurion's servant (Mt 8:5-13; Lk 7:1-10), widow's son raised (Lk 7:11-17), demoniac (Mt 12:22-23; Lk 11:14), Gadarene demoniacs (Mt 8:28-34; Mk 5:1-20; Lk 8:26-39), woman's bleeding and Jairus' daughter (Mt 9:18-26; Mk 5:21-43; Lk 8:40-56), blind man (Mt 9:27-31), mute man (Mt 9:32-33), Canaanite woman's daughter (Mt 15:21-28; Mk 7:24-30), deaf man (Mk 7:31-37), blind man (Mk 8:22-26), demoniac boy (Mt 17:14-18; Mk 9:14-29; Lk 9:37-43), ten lepers (Lk 17:11-19), man born blind (Jn 9:1-7), Lazarus raised (Jn 11), crippled woman (Lk 13:11-17), man with dropsy (Lk 14:1-6), two blind men (Mt 20:29-34; Mk 10:46-52; Lk 18:35-43), Malchus' ear (Lk 22:50-51). Other Miracles: water to wine (Jn 2:1-11), catch of fish (Lk 5:1-11), storm stilled (Mt 8:23-27; Mk 4:37-41; Lk 8:22-25), 5,000 fed (Mt 14:15-21; Mk 6:35-44; Lk 9:10-17; Jn 6:1-14), walking on water (Mt 14:25-33; Mk 6:48-52; Jn 6:15-21), 4,000 fed (Mt 15:32-39; Mk 8:1-9), money from fish (Mt 17:24-27), fig tree cursed (Mt 21:18-22; Mk 11:12-14), catch of fish (Jn 21:1-14).

MAJOR TEACHING: Sermon on the Mount (Mt 5-7; Lk 6:17-49), to Nicodemus (Jn 3), to Samaritan woman (Jn 4), Bread of Life (Jn 6:22-59), at Feast of Tabernacles (Jn 7-8), woes to Pharisees (Mt 23; Lk 11:37-54), Good Shepherd (Jn 10:1-18), Olivet Discourse (Mt 24-25; Mk 13; Lk 21:5-36), Upper Room Discourse (Jn 13-16).

PARABLES: Sower (Mt 13:3-23; Mk 4:3-25; Lk 8:5-18), seed's growth (Mk 4:26-29), wheat and weeds (Mt 13:24-30, 36-43), mustard seed (Mt 13:31-32; Mk 4:30-32), yeast (Mt 13:33; Lk 13:20-21), hidden treasure (Mt 13:44), valuable pearl (Mt 13:45-46), net (Mt 13:47-51), house owner (Mt 13:52), good Samaritan (Lk 10:25-37), unmerciful servant (Mt 18:15-35), lost sheep (Mt 18:10-14; Lk 15:4-7), lost coin (Lk 15:8-10), prodigal son (Lk 15:11-32), dishonest manager (Lk 16:1-13), rich man and Lazarus (Lk 16:19-31), persistent widow (Lk 18:1-8), Pharisee and tax collector (Lk 18:9-14), payment of workers (Mt 20:1-16), tenants and the vineyard (Mt 21:28-46; Mk 12:1-12; Lk 20:9-19), wedding banquet (Mt 22:1-14), faithful servant (Mt 24:45-51), ten virgins (Mt 25:1-13), talents (Mt 25:14-30; Lk 19:12-27).

DISCIPLES see APOSTLES. Call of (Jn 1:35-51; Mt 4:18-22; 9:9; Mk 1:16-20; 2:13-14; Lk 5:1-11, 27-28). Named Apostles (Mk 3:13-19; Lk 6:12-16). Twelve sent out (Mt 10; Mk 6:7-11; Lk 9:1-5). Seventy sent out (Lk 10:1-24). Defection of (Jn 6:60-71; Mt 26:56; Mk 14:50-52). Final commission (Mt 28:16-20; Jn 21:15-23; Ac 1:3-8).

Ac 2:32 God has raised this *J* to life,
9: 5 "I am *J*, whom you are persecuting
15:11 of our Lord *J* that we are saved,
16:31 "Believe in the Lord *J*,
Ro 3:24 redemption that came by Christ *J*.
5:17 life through the one man, *J* Christ.
8: 1 for those who are in Christ *J*,
1Co 2: 2 except *J* Christ and him crucified.
8: 6 and there is but one Lord, *J* Christ,
12: 3 and no one can say, "*J* is Lord,"
2Co 4: 5 not preach ourselves, but *J* Christ
Gal 2:16 but by faith in *J* Christ.
3:28 for you are all one in Christ *J*.
5: 6 in Christ *J* neither circumcision
Eph 2:10 created in Christ *J*
2:20 with Christ *J* himself as the chief
Php 1: 6 until the day of Christ *J*.
2: 5 be the same as that of Christ *J*:
2:10 name of *J* every knee should bow,
Col 3:17 do it all in the name of the Lord *J*,
2Th 2: 1 the coming of our Lord *J* Christ
1Ti 1:15 Christ *J* came into the world
2Ti 3.12 life in Christ *J* will be persecuted,
Tit 2:13 our great God and Savior, *J* Christ,
Heb 2: 9 But we see *J*, who was made a little
3: 1 fix your thoughts on *J*, the apostle
4:14 through the heavens, *J* the Son
7:22 *J* has become the guarantee
7:24 but because *J* lives forever,
12: 2 Let us fix our eyes on *J*, the author
2Pe 1:16 and coming of our Lord *J* Christ,
1Jn 1: 7 and the blood of *J*, his Son,
2: 1 *J* Christ, the Righteous One.
2: 6 to live in him must walk as *J* did.
4:15 anyone acknowledges that *J* is
Rev 22:20 Come, Lord *J*.

JEW (JEWS JUDAISM)
Zec 8:23 of one *J* by the edge of his robe
Ro 1:16 first for the *J*, then for the Gentile.
10:12 there is no difference between *J*
1Co 9:20 To the Jews I became like a *J*,
Gal 3:28 There is neither *J* nor Greek,

JEWELRY (JEWELS)
1Pe 3: 3 wearing of gold *j* and fine clothes.

JEWELS (JEWELRY)
Isa 61:10 as a bride adorns herself with her *j*.
Zec 9:16 like *j* in a crown.

JEWS (JEW)
Mt 2: 2 who has been born king of the *J*?
27:11 "Are you the king of the *J*?" "Yes,
Jn 4:22 for salvation is from the *J*.
Ro 3:29 Is God the God of *J* only?
1Co 1:22 *J* demand miraculous signs
9:20 To the *J* I became like a Jew,
12:13 whether *J* or Greeks, slave or free
Gal 2: 8 of Peter as an apostle to the *J*,
Rev 3: 9 claim to be *J* though they are not,

JEZEBEL
Sidonian wife of Ahab (1Ki 16:31). Promoted Baal worship (1Ki 16:32-33). Killed prophets of the LORD (1Ki 18:4, 13). Opposed Elijah (1Ki 19:1-2). Had Naboth killed (1Ki 21). Death prophesied (1Ki 21:17-24). Killed by Jehu (2Ki 9:30-37).

JOASH
Son of Ahaziah; king of Judah. Sheltered from Athaliah by Jehoiada (2Ki 11; 2Ch 22:10-23:21). Repaired temple (2Ki 12; 2Ch 24).

JOB
Wealthy man from Uz; feared God (Job 1:1-5). Righteousness tested by disaster (Job 1:6-22), personal affliction (Job 2). Maintained innocence in debate with three friends (Job 3-31), Elihu (Job 32-37). Rebuked by the LORD (Job 38-41). Vindicated and restored to greater stature by the LORD (Job 42). Example of righteousness (Eze 14:14, 20).

JOHN
1. Son of Zechariah and Elizabeth (Lk 1). Called the Baptist (Mt 3:1-12; Mk 1:2-8). Witness to Jesus (Mt 3:11-12; Mk 1:7-8; Lk 3:15-18; Jn 1:6-35; 3:27-30; 5:33-36). Doubts about Jesus (Mt 11:2-6; Lk 7:18-23). Arrest (Mt 4:12; Mk 1:14). Execution (Mt 14:1-12; Mk 6:14-29; Lk 9:7-9). Ministry compared to Elijah (Mt 11:7-19; Mk 9:11-13; Lk 7:24-35).

2. Apostle; brother of James (Mt 4:21-22; 10:2; Mk 3:17; Lk 5:1-10). At transfiguration (Mt 17:1-13; Mk 9:1-13; Lk 9:28-36). Desire to be greatest (Mk 10:35-45). Leader of church at Jerusalem (Ac 4:1-3; Gal 2:9). Elder who wrote epistles (2Jn 1; 3Jn 1). Prophet who wrote Revelation (Rev 1:1; 22:8).

3. Cousin of Barnabas, co-worker with Paul, (Ac 12:12-13:13; 15:37), see MARK.

JOIN (JOINED)
Pr 23:20 Do not *j* those who drink too much
24:21 and do not *j* with the rebellious,
Ro 15:30 to *j* me in my struggle by praying
2Ti 1: 8 *j* with me in suffering for the gospel

JOINED (JOIN)
Mt 19: 6 Therefore what God has *j* together,
Mk 10: 9 Therefore what God has *j* together,
Eph 2:21 him the whole building is *j* together
4:16 *j* and held together

JOINTS
Heb 4:12 even to dividing soul and spirit, *j*

JOKING
Eph 5: 4 or coarse *j*, which are out of place,

JONAH
Prophet in days of Jeroboam II (2Ki 14:25). Called to Nineveh; fled to Tarshish (Jnh 1:1-3). Cause of storm; thrown into sea (Jnh 1:4-16). Swallowed by fish (Jnh 1:17). Prayer (Jnh 2). Preached to Nineveh (Jnh 3). Attitude reproved by the LORD (Jnh 4). Sign of (Mt 12:39-41; Lk 11:29-32).

JONATHAN
Son of Saul (1Sa 13:16; 1Ch 8:33). Valiant warrior (1Sa 13-14). Relation to David (1Sa 18:1-4; 19-20; 23:16-18). Killed at Gilboa (1Sa 31). Mourned by David (2Sa 1)

JORAM
1. Son of Ahab; king of Israel (2Ki 3; 8-9; 2Ch 22).

JORDAN
Nu 34:12 boundary will go down along the *J*
Jos 4:22 Israel crossed the *J* on dry ground.'
Mt 3: 6 baptized by him in the *J* River.

JOSEPH
1. Son of Jacob by Rachel (Ge 30:24; 1Ch 2:2). Favored by Jacob, hated by brothers (Ge 37:3-4). Dreams (Ge 37:5-11). Sold by brothers (Ge 37:12-36). Served Potiphar; imprisoned by false accusation (Ge 39). Interpreted dreams of Pharaoh's servants (Ge 40), of Pharaoh (Ge 41:4-40). Made greatest in Egypt (Ge 41:41-57). Sold grain to brothers (Ge 42-45). Brought Jacob and sons to Egypt (Ge 46-47). Sons Ephraim and Manasseh blessed (Ge 48). Blessed (Ge 49:22-26; Dt 33:13-17). Death (Ge 50:22-26; Ex 13:19; Heb 11:22). 12,000 from (Rev 7:8).

2. Husband of Mary, mother of Jesus (Mt 1:16-24; 2:13-19; Lk 1:27; 2; Jn 1:45).

3. Disciple from Arimathea, who gave his tomb for Jesus' burial (Mt 27:57-61; Mk 15:43-47; Lk 24:50-52).

4. Original name of Barnabas (Ac 4:36).

JOSHUA
1. Son of Nun; name changed from Hoshea (Nu 13:8, 16; 1Ch 7:27). Fought Amalekites under Moses (Ex 17:9-14). Servant of Moses on Sinai (Ex 24:13; 32:17). Spied Canaan (Nu 13). With Caleb, allowed to enter land (Nu 14:6, 30). Succeeded Moses (Dt 1:38; 31:1-8; 34:9).

Charged Israel to conquer Canaan (Jos 1). Crossed Jordan (Jos 3-4). Circumcised sons of wilderness wanderings (Jos 5). Conquered Jericho (Jos 6), Ai (Jos 7-8), five kings at Gibeon (Jos 10:1-28), southern Canaan (Jos 10:29-43), northern Canaan (Jos 11-12). Defeated at Ai (Jos 7). Deceived by Gibeonites (Jos 9). Renewed covenant (Jos 8:30-35; 24:1-27). Divided land among tribes (Jos 13-22). Last words (Jos 23). Death (Jos 24:28-31).

2. High priest during rebuilding of temple (Hag 1-2; Zec 3:1-9; 6:11).

JOSIAH
Son of Amon; king of Judah (2Ki 22-23; 2Ch 34-35).

JOTHAM
Son of Azariah (Uzziah); king of Judah (2Ki 15:32-38; 2Ch 26:21-27:9).

JOY (ENJOY ENJOYMENT JOYFUL OVERJOYED REJOICE REJOICES REJOICING)
Dt 16:15 and your *j* will be complete.
1Ch 16:27 strength and *j* in his dwelling place.
Ne 8:10 for the *j* of the LORD is your
Est 9:22 their sorrow was turned into *j*
Job 38: 7 and all the angels shouted for *j*?
Ps 4: 7 have filled my heart with greater *j*
21: 6 with the *j* of your presence.
30:11 sackcloth and clothed me with *j*,
43: 4 to God, my *j* and my delight.
51:12 to me the *j* of your salvation
66: 1 Shout with *j* to God, all the earth!
96:12 the trees of the forest will sing for *j*;
107:22 and tell of his works with songs of *j*
119:111 they are the *j* of my heart.
Pr 10: 1 A wise son brings *j* to his father,
10:28 The prospect of the righteous is *j*,
12:20 but *j* for those who promote peace.
Isa 35:10 everlasting *j* will crown their heads
51:11 Gladness and *j* will overtake them,
55:12 You will go out in *j*
Lk 1:44 the baby in my womb leaped for *j*.
2:10 news of great *j* that will be
Jn 15:11 and that your *j* may be complete.
16:20 but your grief will turn to *j*.
2Co 8: 2 their overflowing *j* and their
Php 2: 2 then make my *j* complete
4: 1 and long for, my *j* and crown,
1Th 2:19 For what is our hope, our *j*,
Phm : 7 Your love has given me great *j*
Heb 12: 2 for the *j* set before him endured
Jas 1: 2 Consider it pure *j*, my brothers,
1Pe 1: 8 with an inexpressible and glorious *j*
2Jn : 4 It has given me great *j* to find some
3Jn : 4 I have no greater *j*

JOYFUL (JOY)
Ps 100: 2 come before him with *j* songs.
Hab 3:18 I will be *j* in God my Savior.
1Th 5:16 Be *j* always; pray continually;

JUDAH
1. Son of Jacob by Leah (Ge 29:35; 35:23; 1Ch 2:1). Tribe of blessed as ruling tribe (Ge 49:8-12; Dt 33:7).

2. Name used for people and land of Southern Kingdom.
Jer 13:19 All *J* will be carried into exile,
Zec 10: 4 From *J* will come the cornerstone,
Heb 7:14 that our Lord descended from *J*,

JUDAISM (JEW)
Gal 1:13 of my previous way of life in *J*,

JUDAS
1. Apostle (Lk 6:16; Jn 14:22; Ac 1:13). Probably also called Thaddaeus (Mt 10:3; Mk 3:18).

2. Brother of James and Jesus (Mt 13:55, Mk 6:3), also called Jude (Jude 1).

3. Apostle, also called Iscariot, who betrayed Jesus (Mt 10:4; 26:14-56; Mk 3:19; 14:10-50; Lk 6:16; 22:3-53; Jn 6:71; 12:4; 13:2-30; 18:2-11). Suicide of (Mt 27:3-5; Ac 1:16-25).

JUDGE (JUDGED JUDGES JUDGING JUDGMENT)
Ge 18:25 Will not the *J* of all the earth do
1Ch 16:33 for he comes to *j* the earth.
Ps 9: 8 He will *j* the world in righteousness
Joel 3:12 sit to *j* all the nations on every side.
Mt 7: 1 Do not *j*, or you too will be judged.
Jn 12:47 For I did not come to *j* the world,
Ac 17:31 a day when he will *j* the world
Ro 2:16 day when God will *j* men's secrets
1Co 4: 3 indeed, I do not even *j* myself.
6: 2 that the saints will *j* the world?
Gal 2: 6 not *j* by external appearance—
2Ti 4: 1 who will *j* the living and the dead,
4: 8 which the Lord, the righteous *J*,
Jas 4:12 There is only one Lawgiver and *J*,
4:12 who are you to *j* your neighbor?
Rev 20: 4 who had been given authority to *j*.

JUDGED (JUDGE)
Mt 7: 1 "Do not judge, or you too will be *j*.
1Co 11:31 But if we *j* ourselves, we would not
Jas 3: 1 who teach will be *j* more strictly.
Rev 20:12 The dead were *j* according

JUDGES (JUDGE)
Jdg 2:16 Then the LORD raised up *j*,
Ps 58:11 there is a God who *j* the earth."
Heb 4:12 it *j* the thoughts and attitudes
Rev 19:11 With justice he *j* and makes war.

JUDGING (JUDGE)
Mt 19:28 *j* the twelve tribes of Israel.
Jn 7:24 Stop *j* by mere appearances,

JUDGMENT (JUDGE)
Dt 1:17 of any man, for *j* belongs to God.
Ps 1: 5 the wicked will not stand in the *j*,
119:66 Teach me knowledge and good *j*,
Pr 6:32 man who commits adultery lacks *j*;
12:11 but he who chases fantasies lacks *j*.
Ecc 12:14 God will bring every deed into *j*,
Isa 66:16 the LORD will execute *j*
Mt 5:21 who murders will be subject to *j*.'
10:15 on the day of *j* than for that town.
12:36 have to give account on the day of *j*
Jn 5:22 but has entrusted all *j* to the Son,
7:24 appearances, and make a right *j*."
16: 8 to sin and righteousness and *j*:
Ro 14:10 stand before God's *j* seat.
14:13 Therefore let us stop passing *j*
1Co 11:29 body of the Lord eats and drinks *j*
2Co 5:10 appear before the *j* seat of Christ,
Heb 9:27 to die once, and after that to face *j*,
10:27 but only a fearful expectation of *j*
1Pe 4:17 For it is time for *j* to begin
Jude : 6 bound with everlasting chains for *j*

JUST (JUSTICE JUSTIFICATION JUSTIFIED JUSTIFY JUSTLY)
Dt 32: 4 and all his ways are *j*.
Ps 37:28 For the LORD loves the *j*
111: 7 of his hands are faithful and *j*;
Pr 1: 3 doing what is right and *j* and fair;
2: 8 for he guards the course of the *j*
Da 4:37 does is right and all his ways are *j*
Ro 3:26 as to be *j* and the one who justifies
Heb 2: 2 received its *j* punishment,
1Jn 1: 9 and *j* and will forgive us our sins
Rev 16: 7 true and *j* are your judgments."

JUSTICE (JUST)
Ex 23: 2 do not pervert *j* by siding
23: 6 "Do not deny *j* to your poor people
Job 37:23 in his *j* and great righteousness,
Ps 9: 8 he will govern the peoples with *j*.
9:16 The LORD is known by his *j*;
11: 7 he loves *j*;
45: 6 a scepter of *j* will be the scepter
101: 1 I will sing of your love and *j*;
106: 3 Blessed are they who maintain *j*,
Pr 21:15 When *j* is done, it brings joy
28: 5 Evil men do not understand *j*,
29: 4 By *j* a king gives a country stability
29:26 from the LORD that man gets *j*.
Isa 9: 7 it with *j* and righteousness
28:17 I will make *j* the measuring line
30:18 For the LORD is a God of *j*.
42: 1 and he will bring *j* to the nations.
42: 4 till he establishes *j* on earth.
56: 1 "Maintain *j*
61: 8 "For I, the LORD, love *j*;
Jer 30:11 I will discipline you but only with *j*;
Eze 34:16 I will shepherd the flock with *j*.
Am 5:15 maintain *j* in the courts.
5:24 But let *j* roll on like a river,
Zec 7: 9 'Administer true *j*; show mercy
Lk 11:42 you neglect *j* and the love of God.
Ro 3:25 He did this to demonstrate his *j*,

JUSTIFICATION (JUST)
Ro 4:25 and was raised to life for our *j*.
5:18 of righteousness was *j* that brings

JUSTIFIED (JUST)
Ac 13:39 him everyone who believes is *j*
Ro 3:24 and are *j* freely by his grace
3:28 For we maintain that a man is *j*
5: 1 since we have been *j* through faith,
5: 9 Since we have now been *j*
8:30 those he called, he also *j*; those he *j*,
1Co 6:11 you were *j* in the name
Gal 2:16 observing the law no one will be *j*.
3:11 Clearly no one is *j* before God
3:24 to Christ that we might be *j* by faith
Jas 2:24 You see that a person is *j*

JUSTIFY (JUST)
Gal 3: 8 that God would *j* the Gentiles

JUSTLY (JUST)
Mic 6: 8 To act *j* and to love mercy

KEEP (KEEPER KEEPING KEEPS KEPT)
Ge 31:49 "May the LORD *k* watch
Ex 20: 6 and *k* my commandments.
Nu 6:24 and *k* you;
Ps 18:28 You, O LORD, *k* my lamp burning
19:13 *K* your servant also from willful
119: 9 can a young man *k* his way pure?
121: 7 The LORD will *k* you
141: 3 *k* watch over the door of my lips.
Pr 4:24 *k* corrupt talk far from your lips.
Isa 26: 3 You will *k* in perfect peace
Mt 10:10 for the worker is worth his *k*.
Lk 12:35 and *k* your lamps burning,
Gal 5:25 let us *k* in step with the Spirit.
Eph 4: 3 Make every effort to *k* the unity
1Ti 5:22 *K* yourself pure.
2Ti 4: 5 *k* your head in all situations,
Heb 13: 5 *K* your lives free from the love
Jas 1:26 and yet does not *k* a tight rein
2: 8 If you really *k* the royal law found
Jude :24 able to *k* you from falling

KEEPER (KEEP)
Ge 4: 9 I my brother's *k*?" The LORD

KEEPING (KEEP)
Ex 20: 8 the Sabbath day by *k* it holy.
Ps 19:11 in *k* them there is great reward.
Mt 3: 8 Produce fruit in *k* with repentance.
Lk 2: 8 *k* watch over their flocks at night.
1Co 7:19 *K* God's commands is what counts.
2Pe 3: 9 Lord is not slow in *k* his promise,

KEEPS (KEEP)
Pr 17:28 a fool is thought wise if he *k* silent,
Am 5:13 Therefore the prudent man *k* quiet
1Co 13: 5 is not easily angered, it *k* no record
Jas 2:10 For whoever *k* the whole law

KEPT (KEEP)
Ps 130: 3 If you, O LORD, *k* a record of sins,
2Ti 4: 7 finished the race, I have *k* the faith.
1Pe 1: 4 spoil or fade—*k* in heaven for you,

KEYS
Mt 16:19 I will give you the *k* of the kingdom

KILL (KILLS)
Mt 17:23 They will *k* him, and on the third

KILLS (KILL)
Lev 24:21 but whoever *k* a man must be put
2Co 3: 6 for the letter *k*, but the Spirit gives

KIND (KINDNESS KINDS)
Ge 1:24 animals, each according to its *k*."
2Ch 10: 7 "If you will be *k* to these people
Pr 11:17 A *k* man benefits himself,
12:25 but a *k* word cheers him up.
14:21 blessed is he who is *k* to the needy.
14:31 whoever is *k* to the needy honors
19:17 He who is *k* to the poor lends
Da 4:27 by being *k* to the oppressed.
Lk 6:35 because he is *k* to the ungrateful
1Co 13: 4 Love is patient, love is *k*.
15:35 With what *k* of body will they
Eph 4:32 Be *k* and compassionate
1Th 5:15 but always try to be *k* to each other
2Ti 2:24 instead, he must be *k* to everyone,
Tit 2: 5 to be busy at home, to be *k*,

KINDNESS (KIND)
Ac 14:17 He has shown *k* by giving you rain
Ro 11:22 Consider therefore the *k*
Gal 5:22 peace, patience, *k*, goodness,
Eph 2: 7 expressed in his *k* to us
2Pe 1: 7 brotherly *k*; and to brotherly *k*,

KINDS (KIND)
1Co 12: 4 There are different *k* of gifts,
1Ti 6:10 of money is a root of all *k* of evil.

KING (KINGDOM KINGS)
1. Kings of Judah and Israel: see Saul, David, Solomon.

2. Kings of Judah: see Rehoboam, Abijah, Asa, Jehoshaphat, Jehoram, Ahaziah, Athaliah (Queen), Joash, Amaziah, Uzziah, Jotham, Ahaz, Hezekiah, Manasseh, Amon, Josiah, Jehoahaz, Jehoiakim, Jehoiachin, Zedekiah.

3. Kings of Israel: see Jeroboam I, Nadab, Baasha, Elah, Zimri, Tibni, Omri, Ahab, Ahaziah, Joram, Jehu, Jehoahaz, Jehoash, Jeroboam II, Zechariah, Shallum, Menahem, Pekah, Pekahiah, Hoshea.

Jdg 17: 6 In those days Israel had no *k*;
1Sa 12:12 the LORD your God was your *k*.
Ps 24: 7 that the *K* of glory may come in.
Isa 32: 1 See, a *k* will reign in righteousness
Zec 9: 9 See, your *k* comes to you,
1Ti 6:15 the *K* of kings and Lord of lords,
1Pe 2:17 of believers, fear God, honor the *k*.
Rev 19:16 *K* OF KINGS AND LORD

KINGDOM (KING)
Ex 19: 6 you will be for me a *k* of priests
1Ch 29:11 Yours, O LORD, is the *k*;
Ps 45: 6 justice will be the scepter of your *k*.
Da 4: 3 His *k* is an eternal *k*;
Mt 3: 2 Repent, for the *k* of heaven is near
5: 3 for theirs is the *k* of heaven.
6:10 your *k* come,
6:33 But seek first his *k* and his
7:21 Lord,' will enter the *k* of heaven,
11:11 least in the *k* of heaven is greater
13:24 "The *k* of heaven is like a man who
13:31 *k* of heaven is like a mustard seed,
13:33 "The *k* of heaven is like yeast that
13:44 *k* of heaven is like treasure hidden
13:45 the *k* of heaven is like a merchant
13:47 *k* of heaven is like a net that was let
16:19 the keys of the *k* of heaven;
18:23 the *k* of heaven is like a king who
19:24 for a rich man to enter the *k* of God
24: 7 rise against nation, and *k* against *k*.
24:14 gospel of the *k* will be preached
25:34 the *k* prepared for you
Mk 9:47 better for you to enter the *k* of God
10:14 for the *k* of God belongs to such
10:23 for the rich to enter the *k* of God!"
Lk 10: 9 'The *k* of God is near you.'
12:31 seek his *k*, and these things will be
17:21 because the *k* of God is within you
Jn 3: 5 no one can enter the *k* of God
18:36 "My *k* is not of this world.
1Co 6: 9 the wicked will not inherit the *k*
15:24 hands over the *k* to God the Father
Rev 1: 6 has made us to be a *k* and priests
11:15 of the world has become the *k*

KINGS (KING)
Ps 2: 2 The *k* of the earth take their stand
72:11 All *k* will bow down to him
Da 7:24 ten horns are ten *k* who will come
1Ti 2: 2 for *k* and all those in authority,
Rev 1: 5 and the ruler of the *k* of the earth.

KINSMAN-REDEEMER (REDEEM)
Ru 3: 9 over me, since you are a *k*."

KISS
Ps 2:12 *K* the Son, lest he be angry
Pr 24:26 is like a *k* on the lips.
Lk 22:48 the Son of Man with a *k*?"

KNEE (KNEES)
Isa 45:23 Before me every *k* will bow;
Ro 14:11 'every *k* will bow before me;
Php 2:10 name of Jesus every *k* should bow,

KNEES (KNEE)
Isa 35: 3 steady the *k* that give way;
Heb 12:12 your feeble arms and weak *k*.

KNEW (KNOW)
Job 23: 3 If only I *k* where to find him;
Jnh 4: 2 I *k* that you are a gracious
Mt 7:23 tell them plainly, 'I never *k* you.

KNOCK
Mt 7: 7 *k* and the door will be opened
Rev 3:20 I am! I stand at the door and *k*.

KNOW (FOREKNEW KNEW KNOWING KNOWLEDGE KNOWN KNOWS)
Dt 18:21 "How can we *k* when a message
Job 19:25 I *k* that my Redeemer lives,
42: 3 things too wonderful for me to *k*.
Ps 46:10 "Be still, and *k* that I am God;
139: 1 and you *k* me.
139:23 Search me, O God, and *k* my heart;
Pr 27: 1 for you do not *k* what a day may
Jer 24: 7 I will give them a heart to *k* me,
31:34 his brother, saying, '*K* the LORD,'
Mt 6: 3 let your left hand *k* what your right
24:42 you do not *k* on what day your
Lk 1: 4 so that you may *k* the certainty
Jn 3:11 we speak of what we *k*,
4:22 we worship what we do *k*,
9:25 One thing I do *k*.
10:14 I *k* my sheep and my sheep *k* me—
17: 3 that they may *k* you, the only true
21:24 We *k* that his testimony is true.
Ac 1: 7 "It is not for you to *k* the times
Ro 6: 6 For we *k* that our old self was
7:18 I *k* that nothing good lives in me,
8:28 we *k* that in all things God works
1Co 2: 2 For I resolved to *k* nothing
6:15 Do you not *k* that your bodies are
6:19 Do you not *k* that your body is
13:12 Now I *k* in part; then I shall *k* fully,
15:58 because you *k* that your labor
Php 3:10 I want to *k* Christ and the power
2Ti 1:12 because I *k* whom I have believed,
Jas 4:14 *k* what will happen tomorrow.
1Jn 2: 4 The man who says, "I *k* him,"
3:14 We *k* that we have passed
3:16 This is how we *k* what love is:
5: 2 This is how we *k* that we love
5:13 so that you may *k* that you have

KNOWING (KNOW)
Ge 3: 5 and you will be like God, *k* good
Php 3: 8 of *k* Christ Jesus my Lord,

KNOWLEDGE (KNOW)
Ge 2: 9 the tree of the *k* of good and evil.
Job 42: 3 obscures my counsel without *k*?'
Ps 19: 2 night after night they display *k*.
73:11 Does the Most High have *k*?"
139: 6 Such *k* is too wonderful for me,
Pr 1: 7 of the LORD is the beginning of *k*,
10:14 Wise men store up *k*,
12: 1 Whoever loves discipline loves *k*,
13:16 Every prudent man acts out of *k*,
19: 2 to have zeal without *k*,
Isa 11: 9 full of the *k* of the LORD
Hab 2:14 filled with the *k* of the glory
Ro 11:33 riches of the wisdom and *k* of God!
1Co 8: 1 *K* puffs up, but love builds up.
8:11 Christ died, is destroyed by your *k*.
13: 2 can fathom all mysteries and all *k*,
2Co 2:14 everywhere the fragrance of the *k*
4: 6 light of the *k* of the glory of God
Eph 3:19 to know this love that surpasses *k*
Col 2: 3 all the treasures of wisdom and *k*.
1Ti 6:20 ideas of what is falsely called *k*,
2Pe 3:18 grow in the grace and *k* of our Lord

KNOWN (KNOW)
Ps 16:11 You have made *k* to me the path
105: 1 make *k* among the nations what he
Isa 46:10 *k* the end from the beginning,
Mt 10:26 or hidden that will not be made *k*.
Ro 1:19 since what may be *k* about God is
11:34 "Who has *k* the mind of the Lord?
15:20 the gospel where Christ was not *k*,
2Co 3: 2 written on our hearts, *k*
2Pe 2:21 than to have *k* it and then

KNOWS (KNOW)
1Sa 2: 3 for the LORD is a God who *k*,
Job 23:10 But he *k* the way that I take;
Ps 44:21 since he *k* the secrets of the heart?
94:11 The LORD *k* the thoughts of man;
Ecc 8: 7 Since no man *k* the future,
Mt 6: 8 for your Father *k* what you need
24:36 "No one *k* about that day or hour,
Ro 8:27 who searches our hearts *k* the mind
1Co 8: 2 who thinks he *k* something does
2Ti 2:19 The Lord *k* those who are his," and

LABAN
Brother of Rebekah (Ge 24:29-51), father of Rachel and Leah (Ge 29-31).

LABOR
Ex 20: 9 Six days you shall *l* and do all your
Isa 55: 2 and your *l* on what does not satisfy
Mt 6:28 They do not *l* or spin.
1Co 3: 8 rewarded according to his own *l*.
15:58 because you know that your *l*

LACK (LACKING LACKS)
Pr 15:22 Plans fail for *l* of counsel,
Ro 3: 3 Will their *l* of faith nullify God's
Col 2:23 *l* any value in restraining sensual

LACKING (LACK)
Ro 12:11 Never be *l* in zeal, but keep your
Jas 1: 4 and complete, not *l* anything.

LACKS (LACK)
Pr 6:32 who commits adultery *l* judgment;
12:11 he who chases fantasies *l* judgment
Jas 1: 5 any of you *l* wisdom, he should ask

LAID (LAY)
Isa 53: 6 and the LORD has *l* on him
1Co 3:11 other than the one already *l*,
1Jn 3:16 Jesus Christ *l* down his life for us.

LAKE
Rev 19:20 into the fiery *l* of burning sulfur.
20:14 The *l* of fire is the second death.

LAMB (LAMB'S LAMBS)
Ge 22: 8 "God himself will provide the *l*
Ex 12:21 and slaughter the Passover *l*.
Isa 11: 6 The wolf will live with the *l*,
53: 7 he was led like a *l* to the slaughter,
Jn 1:29 *L* of God, who takes away the sin
1Co 5: 7 our Passover *l*, has been sacrificed.
1Pe 1:19 a *l* without blemish or defect.
Rev 5: 6 Then I saw a *L*, looking
5:12 "Worthy is the *L*, who was slain,
14: 4 They follow the *L* wherever he

LAMB'S (LAMB)
Rev 21:27 written in the *L* book of life.

LAMBS (LAMB)
Lk 10: 3 I am sending you out like *l*
Jn 21:15 Jesus said, "Feed my *l*."

LAMENT
2Sa 1:17 took up this *l* concerning Saul

LAMP (LAMPS)
2Sa 22:29 You are my *l*, O LORD;
Ps 18:28 You, O LORD, keep my *l* burning;
119:105 Your word is a *l* to my feet
Pr 31:18 and her *l* does not go out at night.
Lk 8:16 "No one lights a *l* and hides it
Rev 21:23 gives it light, and the Lamb is its *l*.

LAMPS (LAMP)
Mt 25: 1 be like ten virgins who took their *l*
Lk 12:35 for service and keep your *l* burning,

LAND
Ge 1:10 God called the dry ground "*l*,"
1:11 "Let the *l* produce vegetation:
12: 7 To your offspring I will give this *l*."
Ex 3: 8 a *l* flowing with milk and honey
Nu 35:33 Do not pollute the *l* where you are.
Dt 34: 1 LORD showed him the whole *l*—
Jos 13: 2 "This is the *l* that remains:
14: 4 Levites received no share of the *l*
2Ch 7:14 their sin and will heal their *l*.
7:20 then I will uproot Israel from my *l*,
Eze 36:24 and bring you back into your own *l*.

LANGUAGE
Ge 11: 1 Now the whole world had one *l*
Ps 19: 3 There is no speech or *l*
Jn 8:44 When he lies, he speaks his native *l*
Ac 2: 6 heard them speaking in his own *l*.
Col 3: 8 slander, and filthy *l* from your lips.
Rev 5: 9 from every tribe and *l* and people

LAST (LASTING LASTS LATTER)
2Sa 23: 1 These are the *l* words of David:
Isa 44: 6 I am the first and I am the *l*;
Mt 19:30 But many who are first will be *l*,
Mk 10:31 are first will be *l*, and the *l* first."
Jn 15:16 and bear fruit—fruit that will *l*.
Ro 1:17 is by faith from first to *l*,
2Ti 3: 1 will be terrible times in the *l* days.
2Pe 3: 3 in the *l* days scoffers will come,
Rev 1:17 I am the First and the *L*.
22:13 the First and the *L*, the Beginning

LASTING (LAST)
Ex 12:14 to the LORD—a *l* ordinance.
Lev 24: 8 of the Israelites, as a *l* covenant.
Nu 25:13 have a covenant of a *l* priesthood,
Heb 10:34 had better and *l* possessions.

LASTS (LAST)
Ps 30: 5 For his anger *l* only a moment,
2Co 3:11 greater is the glory of that which *l*!

LATTER (LAST)
Job 42:12 The LORD blessed the *l* part

LAUGH (LAUGHS)
Ecc 3: 4 a time to weep and a time to *l*,

LAUGHS (LAUGH)
Ps 2: 4 The One enthroned in heaven *l*;
37:13 but the Lord *l* at the wicked,

LAVISHED
Eph 1: 8 of God's grace that he *l* on us
1Jn 3: 1 great is the love the Father has *l*

LAW (LAWS)
Dt 31:11 you shall read this *l* before them
31:26 "Take this Book of the *L*
Jos 1: 8 of the *L* depart from your mouth;
Ne 8: 8 from the Book of the *L* of God,
Ps 1: 2 and on his *l* he meditates day
19: 7 The *l* of the LORD is perfect,
119:18 wonderful things in your *l*.
119:72 *l* from your mouth is more precious
119:97 Oh, how I love your *l*!
119:165 peace have they who love your *l*,
Isa 8:20 To the *l* and to the testimony!
Jer 31:33 "I will put my *l* in their minds
Mt 5:17 that I have come to abolish the *L*
7:12 sums up the *L* and the Prophets.
22:40 All the *L* and the Prophets hang
Lk 16:17 stroke of a pen to drop out of the *L*.
Jn 1:17 For the *l* was given through Moses;
Ro 2:12 All who sin apart from the *l* will
2:15 of the *l* are written on their hearts,
5:13 for before the *l* was given,
5:20 *l* was added so that the trespass
6:14 because you are not under *l*,
7: 6 released from the *l* so that we serve
7:12 *l* is holy, and the commandment is
8: 3 For what the *l* was powerless to do
10: 4 Christ is the end of the *l*
13:10 love is the fulfillment of the *l*.
Gal 3:13 curse of the *l* by becoming a curse
3:24 So the *l* was put in charge to lead us
5: 3 obligated to obey the whole *l*
5: 4 justified by *l* have been alienated
5:14 The entire *l* is summed up
Heb 7:19 (for the *l* made nothing perfect),
10: 1 The *l* is only a shadow
Jas 1:25 intently into the perfect *l* that gives
2:10 For whoever keeps the whole *l*

LAWLESSNESS*
2Th 2: 3 and the man of *l* is revealed,
2: 7 power of *l* is already at work;
1Jn 3: 4 sins breaks the law; in fact, sin is *l*.

LAWS (LAW)
Lev 25:18 and be careful to obey my *l*,
Ps 119:30 I have set my heart on your *l*.
119:120 I stand in awe of your *l*.
Heb 8:10 I will put my *l* in their minds
10:16 I will put my *l* in their hearts,

LAY (LAID LAYING)
Job 22:22 and *l* up his words in your heart.
Isa 28:16 "See, I *l* a stone in Zion,
Mt 8:20 of Man has no place to *l* his head."
Jn 10:15 and I *l* down my life for the sheep.
15:13 that he *l* down his life
1Co 3:11 no one can *l* any foundation other
1Jn 3:16 And we ought to *l* down our lives
Rev 4:10 They *l* their crowns

LAYING (LAY)
1Ti 5:22 Do not be hasty in the *l* on of hands
Heb 6: 1 not *l* again the foundation

LAZARUS
1. Poor man in Jesus' parable (Lk 16:19-31).
2. Brother of Mary and Martha whom Jesus raised from the dead (Jn 11:1-12:19).

LAZY
Pr 10: 4 *L* hands make a man poor,
Heb 6:12 We do not want you to become *l*,

LEAD (LEADERS LEADERSHIP LEADS LED)
Ex 15:13 "In your unfailing love you will *l*
Ps 27:11 *l* me in a straight path
61: 2 *l* me to the rock that is higher
139:24 and *l* me in the way everlasting.
143:10 *l* me on level ground.
Ecc 5: 6 Do not let your mouth *l* you
Isa 11: 6 and a little child will *l* them.
Da 12: 3 those who *l* many to righteousness,
Mt 6:13 And *l* us not into temptation,
1Jn 3: 7 do not let anyone *l* you astray.

LEADERS (LEAD)
Heb 13: 7 Remember your *l*, who spoke
13:17 Obey your *l* and submit

LEADERSHIP (LEAD)
Ro 12: 8 if it is *l*, let him govern diligently;

LEADS (LEAD)
Ps 23: 2 he *l* me beside quiet waters,
Pr 19:23 The fear of the LORD *l* to life:
Isa 40:11 he gently *l* those that have young.
Mt 7:13 and broad is the road that *l*
15:14 If a blind man *l* a blind man,
Jn 10: 3 sheep by name and *l* them out.
Ro 14:19 effort to do what *l* to peace
2Co 2:14 always *l* us in triumphal procession

LEAH
Wife of Jacob (Ge 29:16-30); bore six sons and one daughter (Ge 29:31-30:21; 34:1; 35:23).

LEAN
Pr 3: 5 *l* not on your own understanding;

LEARN (LEARNED LEARNING)
Isa 1:17 *l* to do right!
Mt 11:29 yoke upon you and *l* from me,

LEARNED (LEARN)
Php 4:11 for I have *l* to be content whatever
2Ti 3:14 continue in what you have *l*

LEARNING (LEARN)
Pr 1: 5 let the wise listen and add to their *l*,
2Ti 3: 7 always *l* but never able

LED (LEAD)
Ps 68:18 you *l* captives in your train;
Isa 53: 7 he was *l* like a lamb to the slaughter
Am 2:10 and I *l* you forty years in the desert
Ro 8:14 those who are *l* by the Spirit
Eph 4: 8 he *l* captives in his train

LEFT
Jos 1: 7 turn from it to the right or to the *l*,
Pr 4:27 Do not swerve to the right or the *l*;
Mt 6: 3 do not let your *l* hand know what
25:33 on his right and the goats on his *l*.

LEGION
Mk 5: 9 "My name is *L*," he replied,

LEND (LENDS)
Dt 15: 8 freely *l* him whatever he needs
Ps 37:26 are always generous and *l* freely;
Lk 6:34 if you *l* to those from whom you

LENDS (LEND)
Pr 19:17 to the poor *l* to the LORD,

LENGTH (LONG)
Ps 90:10 The *l* of our days is seventy years—
Pr 10:27 The fear of the LORD adds *l* to life

LEPROSY
2Ki 7: 3 men with *l* at the entrance

LETTER (LETTERS)
Mt 5:18 not the smallest *l*, not the least
2Co 3: 2 You yourselves are our *l*, written
3: 6 for the *l* kills, but the Spirit gives
2Th 3:14 not obey our instruction in this *l*,

LETTERS (LETTER)
2Co 3: 7 which was engraved in *l* on stone,
10:10 "His *l* are weighty and forceful,
2Pe 3:16 His *l* contain some things that are

LEVEL
Ps 143:10 lead me on *l* ground.
Pr 4:26 Make *l* paths for your feet
Isa 26: 7 The path of the righteous is *l*;
Heb 12:13 "Make *l* paths for your feet,"

LEVI (LEVITES)
1. Son of Jacob by Leah (Ge 29:34; 46:11; 1Ch 2:1). Tribe of blessed (Ge 49:5-7; Dt 33:8-11), chosen as priests (Nu 3-4), numbered (Nu 3:39; 26:62), allotted cities, but not land (Nu 18; 35; Dt 10:9; Jos 13:14; 21), land (Eze 48:8-22), 12,000 from (Rev 7:7).
2. See MATTHEW.

LEVITES (LEVI)
Nu 1:53 The *L* are to be responsible
8: 6 "Take the *L* from among the other
18:21 I give to the *L* all the tithes in Israel

LEWDNESS
Mk 7:22 malice, deceit, *l*, envy, slander,

LIAR (LIE)
Pr 19:22 better to be poor than a *l*.
Jn 8:44 for he is a *l* and the father of lies.
Ro 3: 4 Let God be true, and every man a *l*.

LIBERATED*
Ro 8:21 that the creation itself will be *l*

LIE (LIAR LIED LIES LYING)
Lev 19:11 "'Do not *l*.
Nu 23:19 God is not a man, that he should *l*,
Dt 6: 7 when you *l* down and when you get
Ps 23: 2 me *l* down in green pastures,
Isa 11: 6 leopard will *l* down with the goat,
Eze 34:14 they will *l* down in good grazing
Ro 1:25 exchanged the truth of God for a *l*,
Col 3: 9 Do not *l* to each other,
Heb 6:18 which it is impossible for God to *l*,

LIED (LIE)
Ac 5: 4 You have not *l* to men but to God."

LIES (LIE)
Ps 34:13 and your lips from speaking *l*.
Jn 8:44 for he is a liar and the father of *l*.

LIFE (LIVE)
Ge 2: 7 into his nostrils the breath of *l*,
2: 9 of the garden were the tree of *l*
9:11 Never again will all *l* be cut
Ex 21:23 you are to take *l* for *l*, eye for eye,
Lev 17:14 the *l* of every creature is its blood.
24:18 must make restitution—*l* for *l*.
Dt 30:19 Now choose *l*, so that you
Ps 16:11 known to me the path of *l*;
23: 6 all the days of my *l*,
34:12 Whoever of you loves *l*
39: 4 let me know how fleeting is my *l*.
49: 7 No man can redeem the *l*
104:33 I will sing to the LORD all my *l*;
Pr 1: 3 a disciplined and prudent *l*,
6:23 are the way to *l*,
7:23 little knowing it will cost him his *l*.
8:35 For whoever finds me finds *l*
11:30 of the righteous is a tree of *l*,
21:21 finds *l*, prosperity and honor.
Jer 10:23 that a man's *l* is not his own;
Eze 37: 5 enter you, and you will come to *l*.
Da 12: 2 some to everlasting *l*, others
Mt 6:25 Is not *l* more important than food,
7:14 and narrow the road that leads to *l*,
10:39 Whoever finds his *l* will lose it,
16:25 wants to save his *l* will lose it,
20:28 to give his *l* as a ransom for many."
Mk 10:45 to give his *l* as a ransom for many."
Lk 12:15 a man's *l* does not consist
12:22 do not worry about your *l*,
14:26 even his own *l*— he cannot be my
Jn 1: 4 In him was *l*, and that *l* was
3:15 believes in him may have eternal *l*.
3:36 believes in the Son has eternal *l*,
4:14 of water welling up to eternal *l*."
5:24 him who sent me has eternal *l*
6:35 Jesus declared, "I am the bread of *l*
6:47 he who believes has everlasting *l*.
6:68 You have the words of eternal *l*.
10:10 I have come that they may have *l*,
10:15 and I lay down my *l* for the sheep.
10:28 I give them eternal *l*, and they shall
11:25 "I am the resurrection and the *l*.
14: 6 am the way and the truth and the *l*.
15:13 lay down his *l* for his friends.
20:31 that by believing you may have *l*
Ac 13:48 appointed for eternal *l* believed.
Ro 4:25 was raised to *l* for our justification.
6:13 have been brought from death to *l*;
6:23 but the gift of God is eternal *l*
8:38 convinced that neither death nor *l*,
1Co 15:19 If only for this *l* we have hope
2Co 3: 6 letter kills, but the Spirit gives *l*.
Gal 2:20 The *l* I live in the body, I live
Eph 4: 1 I urge you to live a *l* worthy
Php 2:16 as you hold out the word of *l*—
Col 1:10 order that you may live a *l* worthy
1Th 4:12 so that your daily *l* may win
1Ti 4: 8 for both the present *l* and the *l*
4:16 Watch your *l* and doctrine closely.
6:19 hold of the *l* that is truly *l*.
2Ti 3:12 to live a godly *l* in Christ Jesus will
Jas 1:12 crown of *l* that God has promised
3:13 Let him show it by his good *l*,
1Pe 3:10 "Whoever would love *l*
2Pe 1: 3 given us everything we need for *l*
1Jn 3:14 we have passed from death to *l*,
5:11 has given us eternal *l*, and this *l* is
Rev 13: 8 written in the book of *l* belonging
20:12 was opened, which is the book of *l*.
21:27 written in the Lamb's book of *l*.
22: 2 side of the river stood the tree of *l*,

LIFT (LIFTED)
Ps 121: 1 I *l* up my eyes to the hills—
134: 2 *L* up your hands in the sanctuary
La 3:41 Let us *l* up our hearts and our
1Ti 2: 8 everywhere to *l* up holy hands

LIFTED (LIFT)
Ps 40: 2 He *l* me out of the slimy pit,
Jn 3:14 Moses *l* up the snake in the desert,
12:32 when I am *l* up from the earth,

LIGHT (ENLIGHTENED)
Ge 1: 3 "Let there be *l*," and there was *l*.
2Sa 22:29 LORD turns my darkness into *l*.
Job 38:19 "What is the way to the abode of *l*?
Ps 4: 6 Let the *l* of your face shine upon us
19: 8 giving *l* to the eyes.
27: 1 LORD is my *l* and my salvation—
56:13 God in the *l* of life.
76: 4 You are resplendent with *l*,
104: 2 He wraps himself in *l*
119:105 and a *l* for my path.
119:130 The unfolding of your words gives *l*;
Isa 2: 5 let us walk in the *l* of the LORD.
9: 2 have seen a great *l*;
49: 6 also make you a *l* for the Gentiles,
Mt 4:16 have seen a great *l*;
5:16 let your *l* shine before men,
11:30 yoke is easy and my burden is *l*."
Jn 3:19 but men loved darkness instead of *l*
8:12 he said, "I am the *l* of the world.
2Co 4: 6 made his *l* shine in our hearts
6:14 Or what fellowship can *l* have
11:14 masquerades as an angel of *l*.
1Ti 6:16 and who lives in unapproachable *l*,
1Pe 2: 9 of darkness into his wonderful *l*.
1Jn 1: 5 God is *l*; in him there is no
1: 7 But if we walk in the *l*,
Rev 21:23 for the glory of God gives it *l*,

LIGHTNING
Da 10: 6 his face like *l*, his eyes like flaming
Mt 24:27 For as the *l* that comes from the east
28: 3 His appearance was like *l*,

LIKENESS
Ge 1:26 man in our image, in our *l*,
Ps 17:15 I will be satisfied with seeing your *l*
Isa 52:14 his form marred beyond human *l*—
Ro 8: 3 Son in the *l* of sinful man
8:29 to be conformed to the *l* of his Son,
2Co 3:18 his *l* with ever-increasing glory,
Php 2: 7 being made in human *l*.
Jas 3: 9 who have been made in God's *l*.

LILIES
Lk 12:27 "Consider how the *l* grow.

LION
Isa 11: 7 and the *l* will eat straw like the ox.
1Pe 5: 8 around like a roaring *l* looking
Rev 5: 5 See, the *L* of the tribe of Judah,

LIPS
Ps 8: 2 From the *l* of children and infants
34: 1 his praise will always be on my *l*.
119:171 May my *l* overflow with praise,
Pr 13: 3 He who guards his *l* guards his life,
27: 2 someone else, and not your own *l*.
Isa 6: 5 For I am a man of unclean *l*,
Mt 21:16 " 'From the *l* of children
Col 3: 8 and filthy language from your *l*.

LISTEN (LISTENING LISTENS)
Dt 30:20 *l* to his voice, and hold fast to him.
Pr 1: 5 let the wise *l* and add
Jn 10:27 My sheep *l* to my voice; I know
Jas 1:19 Everyone should be quick to *l*,
1:22 Do not merely *l* to the word,

LISTENING (LISTEN)
1Sa 3: 9 Speak, LORD, for your servant is *l*
Pr 18:13 He who answers before *l*—

LISTENS (LISTEN)
Pr 12:15 but a wise man *l* to advice.

LIVE (ALIVE LIFE LIVES LIVING)
Ex 20:12 so that you may *l* long
33:20 for no one may see me and *l*."
Dt 8: 3 to teach you that man does not *l*
Job 14:14 If a man dies, will he *l* again?
Ps 119:175 Let me *l* that I may praise you,
Isa 55: 3 hear me, that your soul may *l*.
Eze 37: 3 can these bones *l*?" I said,
Hab 2: 4 but the righteous will *l* by his faith
Mt 4: 4 'Man does not *l* on bread alone,
Ac 17:24 does not *l* in temples built by hands
17:28 'For in him we *l* and move
Ro 1:17 "The righteous will *l* by faith."
2Co 5: 7 We *l* by faith, not by sight.
Gal 2:20 The life I *l* in the body, I *l* by faith
5:25 Since we *l* by the Spirit, let us keep
Php 1:21 to *l* is Christ and to die is gain.
1Th 5:13 *L* in peace with each other.
2Ti 3:12 who wants to *l* a godly life
Heb 12:14 Make every effort to *l* in peace
1Pe 1:17 *l* your lives as strangers here

LIVES (LIVE)
Job 19:25 I know that my Redeemer *l*,
Isa 57:15 he who *l* forever, whose name is
Da 3:28 to give up their *l* rather than serve
Jn 14:17 for he *l* with you and will be in you.
Ro 7:18 I know that nothing good *l* in me,
14: 7 For none of us *l* to himself alone
1Co 3:16 and that God's Spirit *l* in you?
Gal 2:20 I no longer live, but Christ *l* in me.
Heb 13: 5 Keep your *l* free from the love
2Pe 3:11 You ought to live holy and godly *l*
1Jn 3:16 to lay down our *l* for our brothers.
4:16 Whoever *l* in love *l* in God,

LIVING (LIVE)
Ge 2: 7 and man became a *l* being.
Jer 2:13 the spring of *l* water,
Mt 22:32 the God of the dead but of the *l*."
Jn 7:38 streams of *l* water will flow
Ro 12: 1 to offer your bodies as *l* sacrifices,
Heb 4:12 For the word of God is *l* and active.
10:31 to fall into the hands of the *l* God.
Rev 1:18 I am the *L* One; I was dead,

LOAD
Gal 6: 5 for each one should carry his own *l*.

LOCUSTS
Mt 3: 4 His food was *l* and wild honey.

LOFTY
Ps 139: 6 too *l* for me to attain.
Isa 57:15 is what the high and *l* One says—

LONELY
Ps 68: 6 God sets the *l* in families,

LONG (LENGTH LONGED LONGING LONGS)
1Ki 18:21 "How *l* will you waver
Jn 9: 4 As *l* as it is day, we must do
Eph 3:18 to grasp how wide and *l* and high
1Pe 1:12 Even angels *l* to look

LONGED (LONG)
Mt 13:17 righteous men *l* to see what you see
23:37 how often I have *l*
2Ti 4: 8 to all who have *l* for his appearing.

LONGING (LONG)
Pr 13:19 A *l* fulfilled is sweet to the soul,
2Co 5: 2 *l* to be clothed with our heavenly

LONGS (LONG)
Isa 30:18 Yet the LORD *l* to be gracious

LOOK (LOOKING LOOKS)
Dt 4:29 you will find him if you *l* for him
Job 31: 1 not to *l* lustfully at a girl.
Ps 34: 5 Those who *l* to him are radiant;
Pr 4:25 Let your eyes *l* straight ahead,
Isa 60: 5 Then you will *l* and be radiant,
Hab 1:13 Your eyes are too pure to *l* on evil;
Zec 12:10 They will *l* on me, the one they
Mk 13:21 '*L*, here is the Christ!' or, '*L*,
Lk 24:39 *L* at my hands and my feet.
Jn 1:36 he said, "*L*, the Lamb of God!"
4:35 open your eyes and *l* at the fields!
19:37 "They will *l* on the one they have
Jas 1:27 to *l* after orphans and widows
1Pe 1:12 long to *l* into these things.

LOOKING (LOOK)
2Co 10: 7 You are *l* only on the surface
Rev 5: 6 I saw a Lamb, *l* as if it had been

LOOKS (LOOK)
1Sa 16: 7 Man *l* at the outward appearance,
Lk 9:62 and *l* back is fit for service
Php 2:21 For everyone *l* out

LORD† (LORD'S† LORDING)
Ne 4:14 Remember the *L*, who is great
Job 28:28 'The fear of the *L*— that is wisdom,
Ps 54: 4 the *L* is the one who sustains me.
62:12 and that you, O *L*, are loving.
86: 5 You are forgiving and good, O *L*,
110: 1 The LORD says to my *L*:
147: 5 Great is our *L* and mighty in power
Isa 6: 1 I saw the *L* seated on a throne,
Da 9: 4 "O *L*, the great and awesome God,
Mt 3: 3 'Prepare the way for the *L*,
4: 7 'Do not put the *L* your God
7:21 "Not everyone who says to me, '*L*,
22:37 " 'Love the *L* your God
22:44 For he says, " 'The *L* said to my *L*:
Mk 12:11 the *L* has done this,
12:29 the *L* our God, the *L* is one.
Lk 2: 9 glory of the *L* shone around them,

Lk 6:46 "Why do you call me, '*L*, *L*,'
10:27 " 'Love the *L* your God
Ac 2:21 on the name of the *L* will be saved.'
16:31 replied, "Believe in the *L* Jesus,
Ro 10:9 with your mouth, "Jesus is *L*,"
10:13 on the name of the *L* will be saved
12:11 your spiritual fervor, serving the *L*.
14:8 we live to the *L*; and if we die,
1Co 1:31 Let him who boasts boast in the *L*."
3:5 the *L* has assigned to each his task.
7:34 to be devoted to the *L* in both body
10:9 We should not test the *L*,
11:23 For I received from the *L* what I
12:3 "Jesus is *L*," except by the Holy
15:57 victory through our *L* Jesus Christ.
16:22 If anyone does not love the *L*—
2Co 3:17 Now the *L* is the Spirit,
8:5 they gave themselves first to the *L*
10:17 Let him who boasts boast in the *L*."
Gal 6:14 in the cross of our *L* Jesus Christ,
Eph 4:5 one *L*, one faith, one baptism;
5:10 and find out what pleases the *L*.
5:19 make music in your heart to the *L*,
Php 2:11 confess that Jesus Christ is *L*,
3:1 my brothers, rejoice in the *L*!
4:4 Rejoice in the *L* always.
Col 2:6 as you received Christ Jesus as *L*,
3:17 do it all in the name of the *L* Jesus,
3:23 as working for the *L*, not for men,
4:17 work you have received in the *L*."
1Th 3:12 May the *L* make your love increase
5:2 day of the *L* will come like a thief
5:23 at the coming of our *L* Jesus Christ.
2Th 2:1 the coming of our *L* Jesus Christ
2Ti 2:19 "The *L* knows those who are his,"
Heb 12:14 holiness no one will see the *L*.
13:6 *L* is my helper; I will not be afraid.
Jas 4:10 Humble yourselves before the *L*,
1Pe 1:25 the word of the *L* stands forever."
2:3 you have tasted that the *L* is good.
3:15 in your hearts set apart Christ as *L*.
2Pe 1:16 and coming of our *L* Jesus Christ,
2:1 the sovereign *L* who bought
3:9 The *L* is not slow in keeping his
Jude :14 the *L* is coming with thousands
Rev 4:8 holy, holy is the *L* God Almighty,
4:11 "You are worthy, our *L* and God,
17:14 he is *L* of lords and King of kings—
22:20 Come, *L* Jesus.

LORD'S† (LORD†)
Ac 21:14 and said, "The *L* will be done."
1Co 10:26 "The earth is the *L*, and everything
11:26 you proclaim the *L* death
2Co 3:18 faces all reflect the *L* glory,
2Ti 2:24 And the *L* servant must not quarrel
Jas 4:15 you ought to say, "If it is the *L* will,

LORDING* (LORD†)
1Pe 5:3 not *l* it over those entrusted to you,

LORD‡ (LORD'S‡)
Ge 2:4 When the *L* God made the earth
2:7 the *L* God formed the man
3:21 The *L* God made garments of skin
7:16 Then the *L* shut him in.
15:6 Abram believed the *L*,
18:14 Is anything too hard for the *L*?
31:49 "May the *L* keep watch
Ex 3:2 the angel of the *L* appeared to him
9:12 the *L* hardened Pharaoh's heart
14:30 That day the *L* saved Israel
20:2 "I am the *L* your God, who
33:11 The *L* would speak to Moses face
40:34 glory of the *L* filled the tabernacle.
Lev 19:2 'Be holy because I, the *L* your God,
Nu 8:5 *L* said to Moses: "Take the Levites
14:21 glory of the *L* fills the whole earth,
Dt 2:7 forty years the *L* your God has
5:9 the *L* your God, am a jealous God,
6:4 The *L* our God, the *L* is one.
6:5 Love the *L* your God
6:16 Do not test the *L* your God
10:14 To the *L* your God belong
10:17 For the *L* your God is God of gods
11:1 Love the *L* your God and keep his
28:1 If you fully obey the *L* your God
30:16 today to love the *L* your God,
30:20 For the *L* is your life, and he will
31:6 for the *L* your God goes with you;
Jos 22:5 to love the *L* your God, to walk
24:15 my household, we will serve the *L*
1Sa 1:28 So now I give him to the *L*.
2:2 "There is no one holy like the *L*;
7:12 "Thus far has the *L* helped us."
12:22 his great name the *L* will not reject
15:22 "Does the *L* delight
2Sa 22:2 "The *L* is my rock, my fortress
1Ki 2:3 and observe what the *L* your God
8:11 the glory of the *L* filled his temple.
8:61 fully committed to the *L* our God,
18:21 If the *L* is God, follow him;
2Ki 13:23 But the *L* was gracious to them
1Ch 16:8 Give thanks to the *L*, call
16:23 Sing to the *L*, all the earth;
28:9 for the *L* searches every heart
29:11 O *L*, is the greatness and the power
2Ch 5:14 the glory of the *L* filled the temple
16:9 of the *L* range throughout the earth
19:6 judging for man but for the *L*,
30:9 for the *L* your God is gracious
Ne 1:5 Then I said: "O *L*, God of heaven,
Job 1:21 *L* gave and the *L* has taken away;
38:1 the *L* answered Job out
42:9 and the *L* accepted Job's prayer.
Ps 1:2 But his delight is in the law of the *L*
9:9 The *L* is a refuge for the oppressed,
12:6 And the words of the *L* are flawless
16:8 I have set the *L* always before me.
18:30 the word of the *L* is flawless.
19:7 The law of the *L* is perfect,
19:14 O *L*, my Rock and my Redeemer.
23:1 The *L* is my shepherd, I shall not be
23:6 I will dwell in the house of the *L*
27:1 The *L* is my light and my salvation
27:4 to gaze upon the beauty of the *L*
29:1 Ascribe to the *L*, O mighty ones,
32:2 whose sin the *L* does not count
33:12 is the nation whose God is the *L*,
33:18 But the eyes of the *L* are
34:3 Glorify the *L* with me;
34:7 The angel of the *L* encamps
34:8 Taste and see that the *L* is good;
34:18 The *L* is close to the brokenhearted
37:4 Delight yourself in the *L*
40:1 I waited patiently for the *L*;
47:2 How awesome is the *L* Most High,
48:1 Great is the *L*, and most worthy
55:22 Cast your cares on the *L*
75:8 In the hand of the *L* is a cup
84:11 For the *L* God is a sun and shield;
86:11 Teach me your way, O *L*,
89:5 heavens praise your wonders, O *L*,
91:2 I will say of the *L*, "He is my refuge
95:1 Come, let us sing for joy to the *L*;
96:1 Sing to the *L* a new song;
98:4 Shout for joy to the *L*, all the earth,
100:1 Shout for joy to the *L*, all the earth.
103:1 Praise the *L*, O my soul;
103:8 The *L* is compassionate
104:1 O *L* my God, you are very great;
107:8 to the *L* for his unfailing love
110:1 The *L* says to my Lord:
113:4 *L* is exalted over all the nations,
115:1 Not to us, O *L*, not to us
116:15 Precious in the sight of the *L*
118:1 Give thanks to the *L*, for he is good
118:24 This is the day the *L* has made;
121:2 My help comes from the *L*,
121:5 The *L* watches over you—
125:2 so the *L* surrounds his people
127:1 Unless the *L* builds the house,
127:3 Sons are a heritage from the *L*,
130:3 If you, O *L*, kept a record of sins,
135:6 The *L* does whatever pleases him,
136:1 Give thanks to the *L*, for he is good
139:1 O *L*, you have searched me
144:3 O *L*, what is man that you care
145:3 Great is the *L* and most worthy
145:18 The *L* is near to all who call on him
Pr 1:7 The fear of the *L* is the beginning
3:5 Trust in the *L* with all your heart
3:9 Honor the *L* with your wealth,
3:12 the *L* disciplines those he loves,
3:19 By wisdom the *L* laid the earth's
5:21 are in full view of the *L*,
6:16 There are six things the *L* hates,
10:27 The fear of the *L* adds length to life
11:1 The *L* abhors dishonest scales,
12:22 The *L* detests lying lips,
14:26 He who fears the *L* has a secure
15:3 The eyes of the *L* are everywhere,
16:2 but motives are weighed by the *L*.
16:4 The *L* works out everything
16:9 but the *L* determines his steps.
16:33 but its every decision is from the *L*.
18:10 The name of the *L* is a strong tower
18:22 and receives favor from the *L*.
19:14 but a prudent wife is from the *L*.
19:17 to the poor lends to the *L*,
21:3 to the *L* than sacrifice.
21:30 that can succeed against the *L*.
21:31 but victory rests with the *L*.
22:2 The *L* is the Maker of them all.
24:18 or the *L* will see and disapprove
31:30 a woman who fears the *L* is
Isa 6:3 holy, holy is the *L* Almighty;
11:2 The Spirit of the *L* will rest on him
11:9 full of the knowledge of the *L*
12:2 The *L*, the *L*, is my strength
24:1 the *L* is going to lay waste the earth
25:8 The Sovereign *L* will wipe away
29:15 to hide their plans from the *L*,
33:6 the fear of the *L* is the key
35:10 the ransomed of the *L* will return.
40:5 the glory of the *L* will be revealed,
40:7 the breath of the *L* blows on them.
40:10 the Sovereign *L* comes with power,
40:28 The *L* is the everlasting God,
40:31 but those who hope in the *L*
42:8 "I am the *L*; that is my name!
43:11 I, even I, am the *L*,
44:24 I am the *L*,
45:5 I am the *L*, and there is no other;
45:21 Was it not I, the *L*?
51:11 The ransomed of the *L* will return.
53:6 and the *L* has laid on him
53:10 and the will of the *L* will prosper
55:6 Seek the *L* while he may be found;
58:8 of the *L* will be your rear guard.
58:11 The *L* will guide you always;
59:1 the arm of the *L* is not too short
61:3 a planting of the *L*
61:10 I delight greatly in the *L*;
Jer 1:9 Then the *L* reached out his hand
9:24 I am the *L*, who exercises kindness,
16:19 O *L*, my strength and my fortress,
17:7 is the man who trusts in the *L*,
La 3:40 and let us return to the *L*.
Eze 1:28 of the likeness of the glory of the *L*.
Hos 1:7 horsemen, but by the *L* their God."
3:5 They will come trembling to the *L*
6:1 "Come, let us return to the *L*.
Joel 2:1 for the day of the *L* is coming.
2:11 The day of the *L* is great;
3:14 For the day of the *L* is near
Am 5:18 long for the day of the *L*?
Jnh 1:3 But Jonah ran away from the *L*
Mic 4:2 up to the mountain of the *L*,
6:8 And what does the *L* require of you
Na 1:2 The *L* takes vengeance on his foes
1:3 The *L* is slow to anger
Hab 2:14 knowledge of the glory of the *L*,
2:20 But the *L* is in his holy temple;
Zep 3:17 The *L* your God is with you,
Zec 1:17 and the *L* will again comfort Zion
9:16 The *L* their God will save them
14:5 Then the *L* my God will come,
14:9 The *L* will be king
Mal 4:5 and dreadful day of the *L* comes.

LORD'S‡ (LORD‡)
Ex 34:34 he entered the *L* presence
Nu 14:41 you disobeying the *L* command?
Dt 6:18 is right and good in the *L* sight,
32:9 For the *L* portion is his people,
Jos 21:45 Not one of all the *L* good promises
Ps 24:1 The earth is the *L*, and everything
32:10 but the *L* unfailing love
89:1 of the *L* great love forever;
103:17 *L* love is with those who fear him,
Pr 3:11 do not despise the *L* discipline
Isa 24:14 west they acclaim the *L* majesty.
62:3 of splendor in the *L* hand,
Jer 48:10 lax in doing the *L* work!
La 3:22 of the *L* great love we are not
Mic 4:1 of the *L* temple will be established

LOSE (LOSES LOSS LOST)
1Sa 17:32 "Let no one *l* heart on account
Mt 10:39 Whoever finds his life will *l* it,
Lk 9:25 and yet *l* or forfeit his very self?
Jn 6:39 that I shall *l* none of all that he has
Heb 12:3 will not grow weary and *l* heart.
12:5 do not *l* heart when he rebukes you

LOSES (LOSE)
Mt 5:13 But if the salt *l* its saltiness,

Lk 15: 4 you has a hundred sheep and l one
15: 8 has ten silver coins and l one.

LOSS (LOSE)
Ro 11:12 and their l means riches
1Co 3:15 he will suffer l; he himself will be
Php 3: 8 I consider everything a l compared

LOST (LOSE)
Ps 73: 2 I had nearly l my foothold.
Jer 50: 6 "My people have been l sheep;
Eze 34: 4 the strays or searched for the l.
34:16 for the l and bring back the strays.
Mt 18:14 any of these little ones should be l.
Lk 15: 4 go after the l sheep until he finds it?
15: 6 with me; I have found my l sheep.'
15: 9 with me; I have found my l coin.'
15:24 is alive again; he was l and is found
19:10 to seek and to save what was l."
Php 3: 8 for whose sake I have l all things.

LOT (LOTS)
Nephew of Abraham (Ge 11:27; 12:5). Chose to live in Sodom (Ge 13). Rescued from four kings (Ge 14). Rescued from Sodom (Ge 19:1-29; 2Pe 2:7). Fathered Moab and Ammon by his daughters (Ge 19:30-38).
Est 3: 7 the l) in the presence of Haman
9:24 the l) for their ruin and destruction.
Pr 16:33 The l is cast into the lap,
18:18 Casting the l settles disputes
Ecc 3:22 his work, because that is his l.
Ac 1:26 Then they drew lots, and the l fell

LOTS (LOT)
Ps 22:18 and cast l for my clothing.
Mt 27:35 divided up his clothes by casting l.

LOVE (BELOVED LOVED LOVELY LOVER LOVERS LOVES LOVING)
Ge 22: 2 your only son, Isaac, whom you l,
Ex 15:13 "In your unfailing l you will lead
20: 6 showing l to a thousand generations
20: 6 of those who l me
34: 6 abounding in l and faithfulness,
Lev 19:18 but l your neighbor as yourself.
19:34 L him as yourself,
Nu 14:18 abounding in l and forgiving sin
Dt 5:10 showing l to a thousand generations
5:10 of those who l me
6: 5 L the LORD your God
7:13 He will l you and bless you
10:12 to walk in all his ways, to l him,
11:13 to l the LORD your God
13: 6 wife you l, or your closest friend
30: 6 so that you may l him
Jos 22: 5 to l the LORD your God, to walk
1Ki 3: 3 Solomon showed his l
8:23 you who keep your covenant of l
2Ch 5:13 his l endures forever."
Ne 1: 5 covenant of l with those who l him
Ps 18: 1 I l you, O LORD, my strength.
23: 6 Surely goodness and l will follow
25: 6 O LORD, your great mercy and l,
31:16 save me in your unfailing l.
32:10 but the LORD's unfailing l
33: 5 the earth is full of his unfailing l.
33:18 whose hope is in his unfailing l,
36: 5 Your l, O LORD, reaches
36: 7 How priceless is your unfailing l!
45: 7 You l righteousness and hate
51: 1 according to your unfailing l;
57:10 For great is your l, reaching
63: 3 Because your l is better than life,
66:20 or withheld his l from me!
70: 4 may those who l your salvation
77: 8 Has his unfailing l vanished forever
85: 7 Show us your unfailing l, O LORD
85:10 L and faithfulness meet together;
86:13 For great is your l toward me;
89: 1 of the LORD's great l forever;
89:33 but I will not take my l from him,
92: 2 to proclaim your l in the morning
94:18 your l, O LORD, supported me.
100: 5 is good and his l endures forever;
101: 1 I will sing of your l and justice;
103: 4 crowns you with l and compassion.
103: 8 slow to anger, abounding in l.
103:11 so great is his l for those who fear
107: 8 to the LORD for his unfailing l
108: 4 For great is your l, higher
116: 1 I l the LORD, for he heard my
118: 1 his l endures forever.
119:47 because I l them.
119:64 The earth is filled with your l,
Ps 119:76 May your unfailing l be my
119:97 Oh, how I l your law!
119:119 therefore I l your statutes.
119:124 your servant according to your l
119:132 to those who l your name.
119:159 O LORD, according to your l.
119:163 but I l your law.
119:165 peace have they who l your law,
122: 6 "May those who l you be secure.
130: 7 for with the LORD is unfailing l
136: 1 His l endures forever.
143: 8 of your unfailing l,
145: 8 slow to anger and rich in l.
145:20 over all who l him,
147:11 who put their hope in his unfailing l
Pr 3: 3 Let l and faithfulness never leave
4: 6 l her, and she will watch over you.
5:19 you ever be captivated by her l.
8:17 I l those who l me,
9: 8 rebuke a wise man and he will l you
10:12 but l covers over all wrongs.
14:22 those who plan what is good find l
15:17 of vegetables where there is l
17: 9 over an offense promotes l,
19:22 What a man desires is unfailing l;
20: 6 claims to have unfailing l,
20:13 Do not l sleep or you will grow
20:28 through l his throne is made secure
21:21 who pursues righteousness and l
27: 5 rebuke than hidden l.
Ecc 9: 6 Their l, their hate
9: 9 life with your wife, whom you l,
SS 2: 4 and his banner over me is l.
8: 6 for l is as strong as death,
8: 7 Many waters cannot quench l;
8: 7 all the wealth of his house for l,
Isa 5: 1 I will sing for the one I l
16: 5 In l a throne will be established;
38:17 In your l you kept me
54:10 yet my unfailing l for you will not
55: 3 my faithful l promised to David.
61: 8 "For I, the LORD, l justice;
63: 9 In his l and mercy he redeemed
Jer 5:31 and my people l it this way.
31: 3 you with an everlasting l;
32:18 You show l to thousands
33:11 his l endures forever."
La 3:22 of the LORD's great l we are not
3:32 so great is his unfailing l.
Eze 33:32 more than one who sings l songs
Da 9: 4 covenant of l with all who l him
Hos 2:19 in l and compassion.
3: 1 Go, show your l to your wife again,
11: 4 with ties of l;
12: 6 maintain l and justice,
Joel 2:13 slow to anger and abounding in l,
Am 5:15 Hate evil, l good;
Mic 3: 2 you who hate good and l evil;
6: 8 To act justly and to l mercy
Zep 3:17 he will quiet you with his l,
Zec 8:19 Therefore l truth and peace."
Mt 3:17 "This is my Son, whom I l;
5:44 L your enemies and pray
6:24 he will hate the one and l the other,
17: 5 "This is my Son, whom I l;
19:19 and 'l your neighbor as yourself.' "
22:37 " 'L the Lord your God
Lk 6:32 Even 'sinners' l those who l them.
7:42 which of them will l him more?"
20:13 whom I l; perhaps they will respect
Jn 13:34 I give you: L one another.
13:35 disciples, if you l one another."
14:15 "If you l me, you will obey what I
15:13 Greater l has no one than this,
15:17 This is my command: L each other.
21:15 do you truly l me more than these
Ro 5: 5 because God has poured out his l
5: 8 God demonstrates his own l for us
8:28 for the good of those who l him,
8:35 us from the l of Christ?
8:39 us from the l of God that is
12: 9 L must be sincere.
12:10 to one another in brotherly l.
13: 8 continuing debt to l one another,
13: 9 "L your neighbor as yourself."
13:10 Therefore l is the fulfillment
13:10 L does no harm to its neighbor.
1Co 2: 9 prepared for those who l him"—
8: 1 Knowledge puffs up, but l builds up
13: 1 have not l, I am only a resounding
13: 2 but have not l, I am nothing.
13: 3 but have not l, I gain nothing.
1Co 13: 4 Love is patient, l is kind.
13: 4 L is patient, love is kind.
13: 6 L does not delight in evil
13: 8 L never fails.
13:13 But the greatest of these is l.
13:13 three remain: faith, hope and l.
14: 1 way of l and eagerly desire spiritual
16:14 Do everything in l.
2Co 5:14 For Christ's l compels us,
8: 8 sincerity of your l by comparing it
8:24 show these men the proof of your l
Gal 5: 6 is faith expressing itself through l.
5:13 rather, serve one another in l.
5:22 But the fruit of the Spirit is l, joy,
Eph 1: 4 In l he predestined us
2: 4 But because of his great l for us,
3:17 being rooted and established in l,
3:18 and high and deep is the l of Christ,
3:19 and to know this l that surpasses
4: 2 bearing with one another in l.
4:15 Instead, speaking the truth in l,
5: 2 loved children and live a life of l,
5:25 l your wives, just as Christ loved
5:28 husbands ought to l their wives
5:33 each one of you also must l his wife
Php 1: 9 that your l may abound more
2: 2 having the same l, being one
Col 1: 5 l that spring from the hope that is
2: 2 in heart and united in l,
3:14 And over all these virtues put on l,
3:19 l your wives and do not be harsh
1Th 1: 3 your labor prompted by l,
4: 9 taught by God to l each other.
5: 8 on faith and l as a breastplate,
2Th 3: 5 direct your hearts into God's l
1Ti 1: 5 The goal of this command is l,
2:15 l and holiness with propriety.
4:12 in life, in l, in faith and in purity.
6:10 For the l of money is a root
6:11 faith, l, endurance and gentleness.
2Ti 1: 7 of power, of l and of self-discipline.
2:22 and pursue righteousness, faith, l
3:10 faith, patience, l, endurance,
Tit 2: 4 women to l their husbands
Phm : 9 yet I appeal to you on the basis of l.
Heb 6:10 and the l you have shown him
10:24 may spur one another on toward l
13: 5 free from the l of money
Jas 1:12 promised to those who l him.
2: 5 he promised those who l him?
2: 8 "L your neighbor as yourself,"
1Pe 1:22 the truth so that you have sincere l
1:22 l one another deeply,
2:17 L the brotherhood of believers,
3: 8 be sympathetic, l as brothers,
3:10 "Whoever would l life
4: 8 Above all, l each other deeply,
4: 8 l covers over a multitude of sins.
5:14 Greet one another with a kiss of l.
2Pe 1: 7 and to brotherly kindness, l.
1:17 "This is my Son, whom I l;
1Jn 2: 5 God's l is truly made complete
2:15 Do not l the world or anything
3: 1 How great is the l the Father has
3:10 anyone who does not l his brother.
3:11 We should l one another.
3:14 Anyone who does not l remains
3:16 This is how we know what l is:
3:18 let us not l with words or tongue
3:23 to l one another as he commanded
4: 7 Dear friends, let us l one another,
4: 7 for l comes from God.
4: 8 Whoever does not l does not know
4: 9 This is how God showed his l
4:10 This is l: not that we loved God,
4:11 we also ought to l one another.
4:12 and his l is made complete in us.
4:16 God is l.
4:16 Whoever lives in l lives in God,
4:17 l is made complete among us
4:18 But perfect l drives out fear,
4:19 We l because he first loved us.
4:20 If anyone says, "I l God,"
4:21 loves God must also l his brother.
5: 2 we know that we l the children
5: 3 This is l for God: to obey his
2Jn : 5 I ask that we l one another.
: 6 his command is that you walk in l.
: 6 this is l: that we walk in obedience
Jude :12 men are blemishes at your l feasts,
:21 Keep yourselves in God's l
Rev 2: 4 You have forsaken your first l.

Rev 3:19 Those whom I *l* I rebuke
12:11 they did not *l* their lives so much

LOVED (LOVE)
Ge 24:67 she became his wife, and he *l* her;
29:30 and he *l* Rachel more than Leah.
37: 3 Now Israel *l* Joseph more than any
Dt 7: 8 But it was because the LORD *l* you
1Sa 1: 5 a double portion because he *l* her,
20:17 because he *l* him as he *l* himself.
Ps 44: 3 light of your face, for you *l* them.
Jer 2: 2 how as a bride you *l* me
31: 3 "I have *l* you with an everlasting
Hos 2:23 to the one I called 'Not my *l* one.'
3: 1 though she is *l* by another
9:10 became as vile as the thing they *l*.
11: 1 "When Israel was a child, I *l* him,
Mal 1: 2 "But you ask, 'How have you *l* us?'
Mk 12: 6 left to send, a son, whom he *l*.
Jn 3:16 so *l* the world that he gave his one
3:19 but men *l* darkness instead of light
11: 5 Jesus *l* Martha and her sister
12:43 for they *l* praise from men more
13: 1 Having *l* his own who were
13:23 the disciple whom Jesus *l*,
13:34 As I have *l* you, so you must love
14:21 He who loves me will be *l*
15: 9 the Father has *l* me, so have I *l* you.
15:12 Love each other as I have *l* you.
19:26 the disciple whom he *l* standing
Ro 8:37 conquerors through him who *l* us.
9:13 "Jacob I *l*, but Esau I hated."
9:25 her 'my *l* one' who is not my *l* one,"
11:28 they are *l* on account
Gal 2:20 who *l* me and gave himself for me.
Eph 5: 2 as Christ *l* us and gave himself up
5:25 just as Christ *l* the church
2Th 2:16 who *l* us and by his grace gave us
2Ti 4:10 for Demas, because he *l* this world,
Heb 1: 9 You have *l* righteousness
1Jn 4:10 This is love: not that we *l* God,
4:11 Dear friends, since God so *l* us,
4:19 We love because he first *l* us.

LOVELY (LOVE)
Ps 84: 1 How *l* is your dwelling place,
SS 2:14 and your face is *l*.
5:16 he is altogether *l*.
Php 4: 8 whatever is *l*, whatever is

LOVER (LOVE)
SS 2:16 *Beloved* My *l* is mine and I am his;
7:10 I belong to my *l*,
1Ti 3: 3 not quarrelsome, not a *l* of money.

LOVERS (LOVE)
2Ti 3: 2 People will be *l* of themselves,
3: 3 without self-control, brutal, not *l*
3: 4 *l* of pleasure rather than *l* of God—

LOVES (LOVE)
Ps 11: 7 he *l* justice;
33: 5 The LORD *l* righteousness
34:12 Whoever of you *l* life
91:14 Because he *l* me," says the LORD,
127: 2 for he grants sleep to those he *l*.
Pr 3:12 the LORD disciplines those he *l*,
12: 1 Whoever *l* discipline *l* knowledge,
13:24 he who *l* him is careful
17:17 A friend *l* at all times,
17:19 He who *l* a quarrel *l* sin;
22:11 He who *l* a pure heart and whose
Ecc 5:10 whoever *l* wealth is never satisfied
Mt 10:37 anyone who *l* his son or daughter
Lk 7:47 has been forgiven little *l* little."
Jn 3:35 Father *l* the Son and has placed
10:17 reason my Father *l* me is that I lay
12:25 The man who *l* his life will lose it,
14:21 obeys them, he is the one who *l* me.
14:23 Jesus replied, "If anyone *l* me,
Ro 13: 8 for he who *l* his fellowman has
2Co 9: 7 for God *l* a cheerful giver.
Eph 5:28 He who *l* his wife *l* himself.
5:33 must love his wife as he *l* himself,
Heb 12: 6 the Lord disciplines those he *l*,
1Jn 2:10 Whoever *l* his brother lives
2:15 If anyone *l* the world, the love
4: 7 Everyone who *l* has been born
4:21 Whoever *l* God must also love his
5: 1 who *l* the father *l* his child
3Jn : 9 but Diotrephes, who *l* to be first,
Rev 1: 5 To him who *l* us and has freed us

LOVING (LOVE)
Ps 25:10 All the ways of the LORD are *l*
62:12 and that you, O Lord, are *l*.
145:17 and *l* toward all he has made.
Heb 13: 1 Keep on *l* each other as brothers.
1Jn 5: 2 by *l* God and carrying out his

LOWLY
Job 5:11 The *l* he sets on high,
Pr 29:23 but a man of *l* spirit gains honor.
Isa 57:15 also with him who is contrite and *l*
Eze 21:26 *l* will be exalted and the exalted
1Co 1:28 He chose the *l* things of this world

LUKE*
Co-worker with Paul (Col 4:14; 2Ti 4:11; Phm 24).

LUKEWARM*
Rev 3:16 So, because you are *l*— neither hot

LUST
Pr 6:25 Do not *l* in your heart
Col 3: 5 sexual immorality, impurity, *l*,
1Th 4: 5 not in passionate *l* like the heathen,
1Jn 2:16 the *l* of his eyes and the boasting

LYING (LIE)
Pr 6:17 a *l* tongue,
26:28 A *l* tongue hates those it hurts,

MACEDONIA
Ac 16: 9 "Come over to *M* and help us."

MADE (MAKE)
Ge 1:16 He also *m* the stars.
1:25 God *m* the wild animals according
2:22 Then the LORD God *m* a woman
2Ki 19:15 You have *m* heaven and earth.
Ps 95: 5 The sea is his, for he *m* it,
100: 3 It is he who *m* us, and we are his;
118:24 This is the day the LORD has *m*;
139:14 I am fearfully and wonderfully *m*;
Ecc 3:11 He has *m* everything beautiful
Mk 2:27 "The Sabbath was *m* for man,
Jn 1: 3 Through him all things were *m*;
Ac 17:24 "The God who *m* the world
Heb 1: 2 through whom he *m* the universe.
Rev 14: 7 Worship him who *m* the heavens,

MAGI
Mt 2: 1 *M* from the east came to Jerusalem

MAGOG
Eze 38: 2 of the land of *M*, the chief prince
39: 6 I will send fire on *M*
Rev 20: 8 and *M*— to gather them for battle.

MAIDEN
Pr 30:19 and the way of a man with a *m*.
Isa 62: 5 As a young man marries a *m*,
Jer 2:32 Does a *m* forget her jewelry,

MAIMED
Mt 18: 8 It is better for you to enter life *m*

MAJESTIC (MAJESTY)
Ex 15: 6 was *m* in power.
15:11 *m* in holiness,
Ps 8: 1 how *m* is your name in all the earth
29: 4 the voice of the LORD is *m*.
111: 3 Glorious and *m* are his deeds,
SS 6:10 *m* as the stars in procession?
2Pe 1:17 came to him from the *M* Glory,

MAJESTY (MAJESTIC)
Ex 15: 7 In the greatness of your *m*
Dt 33:26 and on the clouds in his *m*.
1Ch 16:27 Splendor and *m* are before him;
Est 1: 4 the splendor and glory of his *m*.
Job 37:22 God comes in awesome *m*.
40:10 and clothe yourself in honor and *m*
Ps 45: 4 In your *m* ride forth victoriously
93: 1 The LORD reigns, he is robed in *m*
110: 3 Arrayed in holy *m*,
145: 5 of the glorious splendor of your *m*,
Isa 53: 2 or *m* to attract us to him,
Eze 31: 2 can be compared with you in *m*?
2Pe 1:16 but we were eyewitnesses of his *m*.
Jude :25 only God our Savior be glory, *m*,

MAKE (MADE MAKER MAKES MAKING)
Ge 1:26 "Let us *m* man in our image,
2:18 I will *m* a helper suitable for him."
12: 2 "I will *m* you into a great nation
Ex 22: 3 thief must certainly *m* restitution,
Nu 6:25 the LORD *m* his face shine
Ps 108: 1 *m* music with all my soul.
Isa 14:14 I will *m* myself like the Most High
29:16 "He did not *m* me"?
Jer 31:31 "when I will *m* a new covenant
Mt 3: 3 *m* straight paths for him.' "
28:19 and *m* disciples of all nations,
Mk 1:17 "and I will *m* you fishers of men."
Lk 13:24 "*M* every effort to enter
14:23 country lanes and *m* them come in,
Ro 14:19 *m* every effort to do what leads
2Co 5: 9 So we *m* it our goal to please him,
Eph 4: 3 *M* every effort to keep the unity
Col 4: 5 *m* the most of every opportunity.
1Th 4:11 *M* it your ambition
Heb 4:11 *m* every effort to enter that rest,
12:14 *M* every effort to live in peace
2Pe 1: 5 *m* every effort to add
3:14 *m* every effort to be found spotless,

MAKER (MAKE)
Job 4:17 Can a man be more pure than his *M*
36: 3 I will ascribe justice to my *M*.
Ps 95: 6 kneel before the LORD our *M*;
Pr 22: 2 The LORD is the *M* of them all.
Isa 45: 9 to him who quarrels with his *M*,
54: 5 For your *M* is your husband—
Jer 10:16 for he is the *M* of all things,

MAKES (MAKE)
1Co 3: 7 but only God, who *m* things grow.

MAKING (MAKE)
Ps 19: 7 *m* wise the simple.
Ecc 12:12 Of *m* many books there is no end,
Jn 5:18 *m* himself equal with God.
Eph 5:16 *m* the most of every opportunity,

MALE
Ge 1:27 *m* and female he created them.
Gal 3:28 slave nor free, *m* nor female,

MALICE (MALICIOUS)
Ro 1:29 murder, strife, deceit and *m*.
Col 3: 8 *m*, slander, and filthy language
1Pe 2: 1 rid yourselves of all *m*

MALICIOUS (MALICE)
Pr 26:24 A *m* man disguises himself
1Ti 3:11 not *m* talkers but temperate
6: 4 *m* talk, evil suspicions

MAN (MEN WOMAN WOMEN)
Ge 1:26 "Let us make *m* in our image,
2: 7 God formed the *m* from the dust
2:18 for the *m* to be alone
2:23 she was taken out of *m*.
9: 6 Whoever sheds the blood of *m*,
Dt 8: 3 *m* does not live on bread
1Sa 13:14 a *m* after his own heart
15:29 he is not a *m* that he
Job 14: 1 *M* born of woman is of few
14:14 If a *m* dies, will he live
Ps 1: 1 Blessed is the *m* who does
8: 4 what is *m* that you are
119: 9 can a young *m* keep his
127: 5 Blessed is the *m* whose quiver
Pr 14:12 that seems right to a *m*,
30:19 way of a *m* with a maiden.
Isa 53: 3 a *m* of sorrows,
Mt 19: 5 a *m* will leave his father
Mk 8:36 What good is it for a *m*
Lk 4: 4 '*M* does not live on bread
Ro 5:12 entered the world through one *m*
1Co 7: 2 each *m* should have his own
11: 3 head of every *m* is Christ,
11: 3 head of woman is *m*
13:11 When I became a *m*,
Php 2: 8 found in appearance as a *m*,
1Ti 2: 5 the *m* Christ Jesus,
2:12 have authority over a *m*;
Heb 9:27 as *m* is destined to die

MANAGE
Jer 12: 5 how will you *m* in the thickets
1Ti 3: 4 He must *m* his own family well
3:12 one wife and must *m* his children
5:14 to *m* their homes and to give

MANASSEH
1. Firstborn of Joseph (Ge 41:51; 46:20). Blessed (Ge 48).
2. Son of Hezekiah; king of Judah (2Ki 21:1-18; 2Ch 33:1-20).

MANGER
Lk 2:12 in strips of cloth and lying in a *m*."

MANNA
Ex 16:31 people of Israel called the bread *m*.
Dt 8:16 He gave you *m* to eat in the desert,
Jn 6:49 Your forefathers ate the *m*
Rev 2:17 I will give some of the hidden *m*.

MANNER
1Co 11:27 in an unworthy *m* will be guilty
Php 1:27 conduct yourselves in a *m* worthy

MARITAL* (MARRY)
Ex 21:10 of her food, clothing and *m* rights.
Mt 5:32 except for *m* unfaithfulness,
19: 9 except for *m* unfaithfulness,
1Co 7: 3 husband should fulfill his *m* duty

MARK (MARKS)
Cousin of Barnabas (Col 4:10; 2Ti 4:11; Phm 24; 1Pe 5:13), see JOHN.
Ge 4:15 Then the LORD put a *m* on Cain
Rev 13:16 to receive a *m* on his right hand

MARKS (MARK)
Jn 20:25 Unless I see the nail *m* in his hands
Gal 6:17 bear on my body the *m* of Jesus.

MARRED
Isa 52:14 his form *m* beyond human likeness

MARRIAGE (MARRY)
Mt 22:30 neither marry nor be given in *m;*
24:38 marrying and giving in *m,*
Ro 7: 2 she is released from the law of *m.*
Heb 13: 4 by all, and the *m* bed kept pure,

MARRIED (MARRY)
Ro 7: 2 by law a *m* woman is bound
1Co 7:27 Are you *m?* Do not seek a divorce.
7:33 But a *m* man is concerned about
7:36 They should get *m.*

MARRIES (MARRY)
Mt 5:32 and anyone who *m* the divorced
19: 9 and *m* another woman commits
Lk 16:18 the man who *m* a divorced woman

MARRY (INTERMARRY MARITAL MARRIAGE MARRIED MARRIES)
Mt 22:30 resurrection people will neither *m*
1Co 7: 1 It is good for a man not to *m.*
7: 9 control themselves, they should *m,*
1Ti 5:14 So I counsel younger widows to *m,*

MARTHA*
Sister of Mary and Lazarus (Lk 10:38-42; Jn 11; 12:2).

MARVELED
Lk 2:33 mother *m* at what was said about

MARY
1. Mother of Jesus (Mt 1:16-25; Lk 1:27-56; 2:1-40). With Jesus at temple (Lk 2:41-52), at the wedding in Cana (Jn 2:1-5), questioning his sanity (Mk 3:21), at the cross (Jn 19:25-27). Among disciples after Ascension (Ac 1:14).
2. Magdalene; former demoniac (Lk 8:2). Helped support Jesus' ministry (Lk 8:1-3). At the cross (Mt 27:56; Mk 15:40; Jn 19:25), burial (Mt 27:61; Mk 15:47). Saw angel after resurrection (Mt 28:1-10; Mk 16:1-9; Lk 24:1-12); also Jesus (Jn 20:1-18).
3. Sister of Martha and Lazarus (Jn 11). Washed Jesus' feet (Jn 12:1-8).

MASQUERADES*
2Co 11:14 for Satan himself *m* as an angel

MASTER (MASTERED MASTERS)
Mt 10:24 nor a servant above his *m.*
23: 8 for you have only one *M*
24:46 that servant whose *m* finds him
25:21 "His *m* replied, 'Well done,
Ro 6:14 For sin shall not be your *m,*
14: 4 To his own *m* he stands or falls.
2Ti 2:21 useful to the *M* and prepared

MASTERED* (MASTER)
1Co 6:12 but I will not be *m* by anything.
2Pe 2:19 a slave to whatever has *m* him.

MASTERS (MASTER)
Mt 6:24 "No one can serve two *m.*
Eph 6: 5 obey your earthly *m* with respect
6: 9 And *m,* treat your slaves
Tit 2: 9 subject to their *m* in everything,

MATTHEW*
Apostle; former tax collector (Mt 9:9-13; 10:3; Mk 3:18; Lk 6:15; Ac 1:13). Also called Levi (Mk 2:14-17; Lk 5:27-32).

MATURE (MATURITY)
Eph 4:13 of the Son of God and become *m,*
Php 3:15 of us who are *m* should take such
Heb 5:14 But solid food is for the *m,*
Jas 1: 4 work so that you may be *m*

MATURITY* (MATURE)
Heb 6: 1 about Christ and go on to *m,*

MEAL
Pr 15:17 Better a *m* of vegetables where
1Co 10:27 some unbeliever invites you to a *m*
Heb 12:16 for a single *m* sold his inheritance

MEANING
Ne 8: 8 and giving the *m* so that the people

MEANS
1Co 9:22 by all possible *m* I might save some

MEAT
Ro 14: 6 He who eats *m,* eats to the Lord,
14:21 It is better not to eat *m*

MEDIATOR
1Ti 2: 5 and one *m* between God and men,
Heb 8: 6 of which he is *m* is superior
9:15 For this reason Christ is the *m*
12:24 to Jesus the *m* of a new covenant,

MEDICINE*
Pr 17:22 A cheerful heart is good *m,*

MEDITATE (MEDITATES MEDITATION)
Jos 1: 8 from your mouth; *m* on it day
Ps 119:15 I *m* on your precepts
119:78 but I will *m* on your precepts.
119:97 I *m* on it all day long.
145: 5 I will *m* on your wonderful works.

MEDITATES* (MEDITATE)
Ps 1: 2 and on his law he *m* day and night.

MEDITATION* (MEDITATE)
Ps 19:14 of my mouth and the *m* of my heart
104:34 May my *m* be pleasing to him,

MEDIUM
Lev 20:27 " 'A man or woman who is a *m*

MEEK (MEEKNESS)
Ps 37:11 But the *m* will inherit the land
Mt 5: 5 Blessed are the *m,*

MEEKNESS* (MEEK)
2Co 10: 1 By the *m* and gentleness of Christ,

MEET (MEETING)
Ps 85:10 Love and faithfulness *m* together;
Am 4:12 prepare to *m* your God, O Israel."
1Th 4:17 them in the clouds to *m* the Lord

MEETING (MEET)
Heb 10:25 Let us not give up *m* together,

MELCHIZEDEK
Ge 14:18 *M* king of Salem brought out bread
Ps 110: 4 in the order of *M.*"
Heb 7:11 in the order of *M,* not in the order

MELT
2Pe 3:12 and the elements will *m* in the heat.

MEMBERS
Mic 7: 6 a man's enemies are the *m*
Ro 7:23 law at work in the *m* of my body,
12: 4 of us has one body with many *m,*
1Co 6:15 not know that your bodies are *m*
12:24 But God has combined the *m*
Eph 4:25 for we are all *m* of one body.
Col 3:15 as *m* of one body you were called

MEN (MAN)
Mt 4:19 will make you fishers of *m*
5:16 your light shine before *m*
12:36 *m* will have to give account
Jn 12:32 will draw all *m* to myself
Ac 5:29 obey God rather than *m!*
Ro 1:27 indecent acts with other *m,*
5:12 death came to all *m,*
1Co 9:22 all things to all *m*
2Co 5:11 we try to persuade *m.*
1Ti 2: 4 wants all *m* to be saved
2Ti 2: 2 entrust to reliable *m*
2Pe 1:21 but *m* spoke from God

MENAHEM
King of Israel (2Ki 15:17-22).

MERCIFUL (MERCY)
Dt 4:31 the LORD your God is a *m* God;
Ne 9:31 for you are a gracious and *m* God.
Mt 5: 7 Blessed are the *m,*
Lk 6:36 Be *m,* just as your Father is *m.*
Heb 2:17 in order that he might become a *m*
Jude :22 Be *m* to those who doubt; snatch

MERCY (MERCIFUL)
Ex 33:19 *m* on whom I will have *m,*
Ps 25: 6 O LORD, your great *m* and love,
Isa 63: 9 and *m* he redeemed them;
Hos 6: 6 For I desire *m,* not sacrifice,
Mic 6: 8 To act justly and to love *m*
Hab 3: 2 in wrath remember *m.*
Mt 12: 7 'I desire *m,* not sacrifice,' you
23:23 justice, *m* and faithfulness.
Ro 9:15 "I will have *m* on whom I have *m,*
Eph 2: 4 who is rich in *m,* made us alive
Jas 2:13 *M* triumphs over judgment!
1Pe 1: 3 In his great *m* he has given us new

MESSAGE
Isa 53: 1 Who has believed our *m*
Jn 12:38 "Lord, who has believed our *m*
Ro 10:17 faith comes from hearing the *m,*
1Co 1:18 For the *m* of the cross is
2Co 5:19 to us the *m* of reconciliation.

MESSIAH*
Jn 1:41 "We have found the *M*" (that is,
4:25 "I know that *M*" (called Christ) "is

METHUSELAH
Ge 5:27 Altogether, *M* lived 969 years,

MICHAEL
Archangel (Jude 9); warrior in angelic realm, protector of Israel (Da 10:13, 21; 12:1; Rev 12:7).

MIDWIVES
Ex 1:17 The *m,* however, feared God

MIGHT (ALMIGHTY MIGHTY)
Jdg 16:30 Then he pushed with all his *m,*
2Sa 6:14 before the LORD with all his *m,*
Ps 21:13 we will sing and praise your *m.*
Zec 4: 6 'Not by *m* nor by power,
1Ti 6:16 To him be honor and *m* forever.

MIGHTY (MIGHT)
Ex 6: 1 of my *m* hand he will drive them
Dt 7: 8 he brought you out with a *m* hand
2Sa 1:19 How the *m* have fallen!
23: 8 the names of David's *m* men:
Ps 24: 8 The LORD strong and *m,*
50: 1 The *M* One, God, the LORD,
89: 8 You are *m,* O LORD,
136:12 with a *m* hand and outstretched
147: 5 Great is our Lord and *m* in power;
Isa 9: 6 Wonderful Counselor, *M* God,
Zep 3:17 he is *m* to save.
Eph 6:10 in the Lord and in his *m* power.

MILE*
Mt 5:41 If someone forces you to go one *m,*

MILK
Ex 3: 8 a land flowing with *m* and honey—
Isa 55: 1 Come, buy wine and *m*
1Co 3: 2 I gave you *m,* not solid food,
Heb 5:12 You need *m,* not solid food!
1Pe 2: 2 babies, crave pure spiritual *m,*

MILLSTONE (STONE)
Lk 17: 2 sea with a *m* tied around his neck

MIND (DOUBLE-MINDED MINDFUL MINDS)
1Sa 15:29 Israel does not lie or change his *m;*
1Ch 28: 9 devotion and with a willing *m,*
Ps 26: 2 examine my heart and my *m;*
Isa 26: 3 him whose *m* is steadfast,
Mt 22:37 all your soul and with all your *m.'*
Ac 4:32 believers were one in heart and *m.*
Ro 7:25 I myself in my *m* am a slave
8: 7 the sinful *m* is hostile to God.
12: 2 by the renewing of your *m.*
1Co 2: 9 no *m* has conceived
14:14 spirit prays, but my *m* is unfruitful.
2Co 13:11 be of one *m,* live in peace.
Php 3:19 Their *m* is on earthly things.
1Th 4:11 to *m* your own business
Heb 7:21 and will not change his *m:*

MINDFUL* (MIND)
Ps 8: 4 what is man that you are *m* of him,
Lk 1:48 God my Savior, for he has been *m*
Heb 2: 6 What is man that you are *m* of him,

MINDS (MIND)
Ps 7: 9 who searches *m* and hearts,
Jer 31:33 "I will put my law in their *m*
Eph 4:23 new in the attitude of your *m;*
Col 3: 2 Set your *m* on things above,
Heb 8:10 I will put my laws in their *m*
Rev 2:23 I am he who searches hearts and *m,*

MINISTERING (MINISTRY)
Heb 1:14 Are not all angels *m* spirits sent

MINISTRY (MINISTERING)
Ac 6: 4 to prayer and the *m* of the word."
2Co 5:18 gave us the *m* of reconciliation:
2Ti 4: 5 discharge all the duties of your *m.*

MIRACLES (MIRACULOUS)
1Ch 16:12 his *m,* and the judgments he
Ps 77:14 You are the God who performs *m;*
Mt 11:20 most of his *m* had been performed,
11:21 If the *m* that were performed
24:24 and perform great signs and *m*
Mk 6: 2 does *m!* Isn't this the carpenter?
Jn 10:32 "I have shown you many great *m*
14:11 the evidence of the *m* themselves.
Ac 2:22 accredited by God to you by *m,*
19:11 God did extraordinary *m*
1Co 12:28 third teachers, then workers of *m,*
Heb 2: 4 it by signs, wonders and various *m,*

MIRACULOUS (MIRACLES)
Jn 3: 2 could perform the *m* signs you are
9:16 "How can a sinner do such *m* signs
20:30 Jesus did many other *m* signs
1Co 1:22 Jews demand *m* signs and Greeks

MIRE
Ps 40: 2 out of the mud and *m;*
Isa 57:20 whose waves cast up *m* and mud.

MIRIAM
Sister of Moses and Aaron (Nu 26:59). Led dancing at Red Sea (Ex 15:20-21). Struck with leprosy for criticizing Moses (Nu 12). Death (Nu 20:1).

MIRROR
Jas 1:23 a man who looks at his face in a *m*

MISERY
Ex 3: 7 "I have indeed seen the *m*
Jdg 10:16 he could bear Israel's *m* no longer.
Hos 5:15 in their *m* they will earnestly seek
Ro 3:16 ruin and *m* mark their ways,
Jas 5: 1 of the *m* that is coming upon you.

MISLED
1Co 15:33 Do not be *m:* "Bad company

MISS
Pr 19: 2 nor to be hasty and *m* the way.

MIST
Hos 6: 4 Your love is like the morning *m,*
Jas 4:14 You are a *m* that appears for a little

MISUSE*
Ex 20: 7 "You shall not *m* the name
Dt 5:11 "You shall not *m* the name
Ps 139:20 your adversaries *m* your name.

MOCK (MOCKED MOCKER MOCKERS MOCKING)
Ps 22: 7 All who see me *m* me;
Pr 14: 9 Fools *m* at making amends for sin,
Mk 10:34 who will *m* him and spit on him,

MOCKED (MOCK)
Mt 27:29 knelt in front of him and *m* him.
27:41 of the law and the elders *m* him.
Gal 6: 7 not be deceived: God cannot be *m.*

MOCKER (MOCK)
Pr 9: 7 corrects a *m* invites insult;
9:12 if you are a *m,* you alone will suffer
20: 1 Wine is a *m* and beer a brawler;
22:10 Drive out the *m,* and out goes strife

MOCKERS (MOCK)
Ps 1: 1 or sit in the seat of *m.*

MOCKING (MOCK)
Isa 50: 6 face from *m* and spitting.

MODEL*
Eze 28:12 " 'You were the *m* of perfection,
1Th 1: 7 And so you became a *m*
2Th 3: 9 to make ourselves a *m* for you

MOMENT
Job 20: 5 the joy of the godless lasts but a *m.*
Ps 30: 5 For his anger lasts only a *m,*
Isa 66: 8 or a nation be brought forth in a *m?*
Gal 2: 5 We did not give in to them for a *m,*

MONEY
Ecc 5:10 Whoever loves *m* never has *m*
Isa 55: 1 and you who have no *m,*
Mt 6:24 You cannot serve both God and *M.*
Lk 9: 3 no bread, no *m,* no extra tunic.
1Co 16: 2 set aside a sum of *m* in keeping
1Ti 3: 3 not quarrelsome, not a lover of *m.*
6:10 For the love of *m* is a root
2Ti 3: 2 lovers of *m,* boastful, proud,
Heb 13: 5 free from the love of *m*
1Pe 5: 2 not greedy for *m,* but eager to serve

MOON
Ps 121: 6 nor the *m* by night.
Joel 2:31 and the *m* to blood
1Co 15:41 *m* another and the stars another;

MORNING
Ge 1: 5 and there was *m*— the first day.
Dt 28:67 In the *m* you will say, "If only it
Ps 5: 3 In the *m,* O LORD,
2Pe 1:19 and the *m* star rises in your hearts.
Rev 22:16 of David, and the bright *M* Star."

MORTAL
1Co 15:53 and the *m* with immortality.

MOSES
Levite; brother of Aaron (Ex 6:20; 1Ch 6:3). Put in basket into Nile; discovered and raised by Pharaoh's daughter (Ex 2:1-10). Fled to Midian after killing Egyptian (Ex 2:11-15). Married to Zipporah, fathered Gershom (Ex 2:16-22).

Called by the LORD to deliver Israel (Ex 3-4). Pharaoh's resistance (Ex 5). Ten plagues (Ex 7-11). Passover and Exodus (Ex 12-13). Led Israel through Red Sea (Ex 14). Song of deliverance (Ex 15:1-21). Brought water from rock (Ex 17:1-7). Raised hands to defeat Amalekites (Ex 17:8-16). Delegated judges (Ex 18; Dt 1:9-18)

Received Law at Sinai (Ex 19-23; 25-31; Jn 1:17). Announced Law to Israel (Ex 19:7-8; 24; 35). Broke tablets because of golden calf (Ex 32; Dt 9). Saw glory of the LORD (Ex 33-34). Supervised building of tabernacle (Ex 36-40). Set apart Aaron and priests (Lev 8-9). Numbered tribes (Nu 1-4; 26). Opposed by Aaron and Miriam (Nu 12). Sent spies into Canaan (Nu 13). Announced forty years of wandering for failure to enter land (Nu 14). Opposed by Korah (Nu 16). Forbidden to enter land for striking rock (Nu 20:1-13; Dt 1:37). Lifted bronze snake for healing (Nu 21:4-9; Jn 3:14). Final address to Israel (Dt 1-33). Succeeded by Joshua (Nu 27:12-23; Dt 34). Death (Dt 34:5-12).

"Law of Moses" (1Ki 2:3; Ezr 3:2; Mk 12:26; Lk 24:44). "Book of Moses" (2Ch 25:12; Ne 13:1). "Song of Moses" (Ex 15:1-21; Rev 15:3). "Prayer of Moses" (Ps 90).

MOTH
Mt 6:19 where *m* and rust destroy,

MOTHER (MOTHER'S)
Ge 2:24 and *m* and be united to his wife,
3:20 because she would become the *m*
Ex 20:12 "Honor your father and your *m,*
Lev 20: 9 " 'If anyone curses his father or *m,*
Dt 5:16 "Honor your father and your *m,*
21:18 who does not obey his father and *m*
27:16 who dishonors his father or his *m."*
1Sa 2:19 Each year his *m* made him a little
Ps 113: 9 as a happy *m* of children.
Pr 23:25 May your father and *m* be glad;
29:15 child left to himself disgraces his *m.*
31: 1 an oracle his *m* taught him:
Isa 49:15 "Can a *m* forget the baby
66:13 As a *m* comforts her child,
Mt 10:37 or *m* more than me is not worthy
15: 4 'Honor your father and *m'*
19: 5 and *m* and be united to his wife,
Mk 7:10 'Honor your father and your *m,'*
10:19 honor your father and *m.' "*
Jn 19:27 to the disciple, "Here is your *m."*

MOTHER'S (MOTHER)
Job 1:21 "Naked I came from my *m* womb,
Pr 1: 8 and do not forsake your *m* teaching

MOTIVES*
Pr 16: 2 but *m* are weighed by the LORD.
1Co 4: 5 will expose the *m* of men's hearts.
Php 1:18 whether from false *m* or true,
1Th 2: 3 spring from error or impure *m,*
Jas 4: 3 because you ask with wrong *m,*

MOUNTAIN (MOUNTAINS)
Mic 4: 2 let us go up to the *m* of the LORD,
Mt 17:20 say to this *m,* 'Move from here

MOUNTAINS (MOUNTAIN)
Isa 52: 7 How beautiful on the *m*
55:12 the *m* and hills
1Co 13: 2 if I have a faith that can move *m,*

MOURN (MOURNING)
Ecc 3: 4 a time to *m* and a time to dance,
Isa 61: 2 to comfort all who *m,*
Mt 5: 4 Blessed are those who *m,*
Ro 12:15 *m* with those who *m.*

MOURNING (MOURN)
Jer 31:13 I will turn their *m* into gladness;
Rev 21: 4 There will be no more death or *m*

MOUTH
Jos 1: 8 of the Law depart from your *m;*
Ps 19:14 May the words of my *m*
40: 3 He put a new song in my *m,*
119:103 sweeter than honey to my *m!*
Pr 16:23 A wise man's heart guides his *m,*
27: 2 praise you, and not your own *m;*
Isa 51:16 I have put my words in your *m*
Mt 12:34 overflow of the heart the *m* speaks.
15:11 into a man's *m* does not make him
Ro 10: 9 That if you confess with your *m,*

MUD
Ps 40: 2 out of the *m* and mire;
Isa 57:20 whose waves cast up mire and *m.*
2Pe 2:22 back to her wallowing in the *m."*

MULTITUDE (MULTITUDES)
Isa 31: 1 who trust in the *m* of their chariots
1Pe 4: 8 love covers over a *m* of sins.
Rev 7: 9 me was a great *m* that no one could

MULTITUDES (MULTITUDE)
Joel 3:14 *M, m* in the valley of decision!

MURDER (MURDERER MURDERERS)
Ex 20:13 "You shall not *m.*
Mt 15:19 *m,* adultery, sexual immorality,
Ro 13: 9 "Do not *m,"* "Do not steal,"
Jas 2:11 adultery," also said, "Do not *m."*

MURDERER (MURDER)
Nu 35:16 he is a *m;* the *m* shall be put
Jn 8:44 He was a *m* from the beginning,
1Jn 3:15 who hates his brother is a *m,*

MURDERERS (MURDER)
1Ti 1: 9 for *m,* for adulterers and perverts,
Rev 21: 8 the *m,* the sexually immoral,

MUSIC
Jdg 5: 3 I will make *m* to the LORD,
Ps 27: 6 and make *m* to the LORD.
95: 2 and extol him with *m* and song.
98: 4 burst into jubilant song with *m;*
108: 1 make *m* with all my soul.
Eph 5:19 make *m* in your heart to the Lord,

MUSTARD
Mt 13:31 kingdom of heaven is like a *m* seed,
17:20 you have faith as small as a *m* seed,

MUZZLE
Dt 25: 4 Do not *m* an ox while it is treading
Ps 39: 1 I will put a *m* on my mouth
1Co 9: 9 "Do not *m* an ox while it is

MYRRH
Mt 2:11 of gold and of incense and of *m.*
Mk 15:23 offered him wine mixed with *m,*

MYSTERY
Ro 16:25 to the revelation of the *m* hidden
1Co 15:51 I tell you a *m:* We will not all sleep,
Eph 5:32 This is a profound *m*—
Col 1:26 the *m* that has been kept hidden
1Ti 3:16 the *m* of godliness is great:

MYTHS
1Ti 4: 7 Have nothing to do with godless *m*

NADAB
Son of Jeroboam I; king of Israel (1Ki 15:25-32).

NAIL* (NAILING)
Jn 20:25 "Unless I see the *n* marks

NAILING* (NAIL)
Ac 2:23 him to death by *n* him to the cross.
Col 2:14 he took it away, *n* it to the cross.

NAKED
Ge 2:25 The man and his wife were both *n,*
Job 1:21 *N* I came from my mother's womb,
Isa 58: 7 when you see the *n,* to clothe him,
2Co 5: 3 are clothed, we will not be found *n.*

NAME
Ex 3:15 This is my *n* forever, the *n*
20: 7 "You shall not misuse the *n*
Dt 5:11 "You shall not misuse the *n*

Dt 28:58 this glorious and awesome *n*—
1Ki 5: 5 will build the temple for my *N.'*
2Ch 7:14 my people, who are called by my *n,*
Ps 34: 3 let us exalt his *n* together.
103: 1 my inmost being, praise his holy *n.*
147: 4 and calls them each by *n.*
Pr 22: 1 A good *n* is more desirable
30: 4 What is his *n,* and the *n* of his son?
Isa 40:26 and calls them each by *n.*
57:15 who lives forever, whose *n* is holy:
Jer 14: 7 do something for the sake of your *n*
Da 12: 1 everyone whose *n* is found written
Joel 2:32 on the *n* of the LORD will be saved
Zec 14: 9 one LORD, and his *n* the only *n.*
Mt 1:21 and you are to give him the *n* Jesus,
6: 9 hallowed be your *n,*
18:20 or three come together in my *n,*
Jn 10: 3 He calls his own sheep by *n*
16:24 asked for anything in my *n.*
Ac 4:12 for there is no other *n*
Ro 10:13 "Everyone who calls on the *n*
Php 2: 9 him the *n* that is above every *n,*
Col 3:17 do it all in the *n* of the Lord Jesus,
Heb 1: 4 as the *n* he has inherited is superior
Rev 20:15 If anyone's *n* was not found written

NAOMI
Mother-in-law of Ruth (Ru 1). Advised Ruth to seek marriage with Boaz (Ru 2-4).

NARROW
Mt 7:13 "Enter through the *n* gate.

NATHANAEL
Apostle (Jn 1:45-49; 21:2). Probably also called Bartholomew (Mt 10:3).

NATION (NATIONS)
Ge 12: 2 "I will make you into a great *n*
Ps 33:12 Blessed is the *n* whose God is
Pr 14:34 Righteousness exalts a *n,*
Isa 65: 1 To a *n* that did not call on my name
1Pe 2: 9 a royal priesthood, a holy *n,*
Rev 7: 9 from every *n,* tribe, people

NATIONS (NATION)
Ge 17: 4 You will be the father of many *n.*
18:18 and all *n* on earth will be blessed
Ex 19: 5 of all *n* you will be my treasured
Ne 1: 8 I will scatter you among the *n,*
Ps 96: 3 Declare his glory among the *n,*
Isa 40:15 Surely the *n* are like a drop
Eze 36:23 *n* will know that I am the LORD,
Hag 2: 7 and the desired of all *n* will come,
Zec 8:23 *n* will take firm hold of one Jew
14: 2 I will gather all the *n* to Jerusalem
Mt 28:19 and make disciples of all *n,*
Rev 21:24 The *n* will walk by its light,

NATURAL (NATURE)
Ro 6:19 you are weak in your *n* selves.
1Co 15:44 If there is a *n* body, there is

NATURE (NATURAL)
Ro 8: 4 do not live according to the sinful *n*
8: 8 by the sinful *n* cannot please God.
Gal 5:19 The acts of the sinful *n* are obvious:
5:24 Jesus have crucified the sinful *n*
Php 2: 6 Who, being in very *n* God,

NAZARENE
Mt 2:23 prophets: "He will be called a *N."*

NAZIRITE
Jdg 13: 7 because the boy will be a *N* of God

NECESSARY
Ro 13: 5 it is *n* to submit to the authorities,

NEED (NEEDS NEEDY)
Ps 116: 6 when I was in great *n,* he saved me.
Mt 6: 8 for your Father knows what you *n*
Ro 12:13 with God's people who are in *n.*
1Co 12:21 say to the hand, "I don't *n* you!"
1Jn 3:17 sees his brother in *n* but has no pity

NEEDLE
Mt 19:24 go through the eye of a *n*

NEEDS (NEED)
Isa 58:11 he will satisfy your *n*
Php 4:19 God will meet all your *n* according

NEEDY (NEED)
Pr 14:21 blessed is he who is kind to the *n.*
14:31 to the *n* honors God.
31:20 and extends her hands to the *n.*
Mt 6: 2 "So when you give to the *n,*

NEGLECT (NEGLECTED)
Ne 10:39 We will not *n* the house of our God
Ps 119:16 I will not *n* your word.
Ac 6: 2 for us to *n* the ministry of the word
1Ti 4:14 Do not *n* your gift, which was

NEGLECTED (NEGLECT)
Mt 23:23 But you have *n* the more important

NEHEMIAH
Cupbearer of Artaxerxes (Ne 2:1); governor of Israel (Ne 8:9). Returned to Jerusalem to rebuild walls (Ne 2-6). With Ezra, reestablished worship (Ne 8). Prayer confessing nation's sin (Ne 9). Dedicated wall (Ne 12).

NEIGHBOR (NEIGHBOR'S)
Ex 20:16 give false testimony against your *n.*
Lev 19:13 Do not defraud your *n* or rob him.
19:18 but love your *n* as yourself.
Pr 27:10 better a *n* nearby than a brother far
Mt 19:19 and 'love your *n* as yourself.' "
Lk 10:29 who is my *n?"* In reply Jesus said:
Ro 13:10 Love does no harm to its *n.*

NEIGHBOR'S (NEIGHBOR)
Ex 20:17 You shall not covet your *n* wife,
Dt 5:21 not set your desire on your *n* house
19:14 not move your *n* boundary stone
Pr 25:17 Seldom set foot in your *n* house—

NEW
Ps 40: 3 He put a *n* song in my mouth,
Ecc 1: 9 there is nothing *n* under the sun.
Isa 65:17 *n* heavens and a *n* earth.
Jer 31:31 "when I will make a *n* covenant
Eze 36:26 give you a *n* heart and put a *n* spirit
Mt 9:17 Neither do men pour *n* wine
Lk 22:20 "This cup is the *n* covenant
2Co 5:17 he is a *n* creation; the old has gone,
Eph 4:24 and to put on the *n* self, created
2Pe 3:13 to a *n* heaven and a *n* earth,
1Jn 2: 8 Yet I am writing you a *n* command;

NEWBORN (BEAR)
1Pe 2: 2 Like *n* babies, crave pure spiritual

NEWS
Isa 52: 7 the feet of those who bring good *n,*
Mk 1:15 Repent and believe the good *n!"*
16:15 preach the good *n* to all creation.
Lk 2:10 I bring you good *n*
Ac 5:42 proclaiming the good *n* that Jesus
17:18 preaching the good *n* about Jesus
Ro 10:15 feet of those who bring good *n!"*

NICODEMUS*
Pharisee who visited Jesus at night (Jn 3). Argued fair treatment of Jesus (Jn 7:50-52). With Joseph, prepared Jesus for burial (Jn 19:38-42).

NIGHT
Job 35:10 who gives songs in the *n,*
Ps 1: 2 on his law he meditates day and *n.*
91: 5 You will not fear the terror of *n,*
Jn 3: 2 He came to Jesus at *n* and said,
1Th 5: 2 Lord will come like a thief in the *n.*
5: 5 We do not belong to the *n*
Rev 21:25 for there will be no *n* there.

NOAH
Righteous man (Eze 14:14, 20) called to build ark (Ge 6-8; Heb 11:7; 1Pe 3:20; 2Pe 2:5). God's covenant with (Ge 9:1-17). Drunkenness of (Ge 9:18-23). Blessed sons, cursed Canaan (Ge 9:24-27).

NOBLE
Ru 3:11 you are a woman of *n* character.
Ps 45: 1 My heart is stirred by a *n* theme
Pr 12: 4 of *n* character is her husband's
31:10 A wife of *n* character who can find?
31:29 "Many women do *n* things,
Isa 32: 8 But the *n* man makes *n* plans,
Lk 8:15 good soil stands for those with a *n*
Ro 9:21 of clay some pottery for *n* purposes
Php 4: 8 whatever is *n,* whatever is right,
2Ti 2:20 some are for *n* purposes

NOTHING
Ne 9:21 in the desert; they lacked *n,*
Jer 32:17 *N* is too hard for you
Jn 15: 5 apart from me you can do *n.*

NULLIFY
Ro 3:31 Do we, then, *n* the law by this faith

OATH
Dt 7: 8 and kept the *o* he swore

OBEDIENCE (OBEY)
2Ch 31:21 in *o* to the law and the commands,
Pr 30:17 that scorns *o* to a mother,
Ro 1: 5 to the *o* that comes from faith.
6:16 to *o,* which leads to righteousness?
2Jn : 6 that we walk in *o* to his commands.

OBEDIENT (OBEY)
Lk 2:51 with them and was *o* to them.
Php 2: 8 and became *o* to death—
1Pe 1:14 As *o* children, do not conform

OBEY (OBEDIENCE OBEDIENT OBEYED)
Ex 12:24 "*O* these instructions as a lasting
Dt 6: 3 careful to *o* so that it may go well
13: 4 Keep his commands and *o* him;
21:18 son who does not *o* his father
30: 2 and *o* him with all your heart
32:46 children to *o* carefully all the words
1Sa 15:22 To *o* is better than sacrifice,
Ps 119:34 and *o* it with all my heart.
Mt 28:20 to *o* everything I have commanded
Jn 14:23 loves me, he will *o* my teaching.
Ac 5:29 "We must *o* God rather than men!
Ro 6:16 slaves to the one whom you *o*—
Gal 5: 3 obligated to *o* the whole law.
Eph 6: 1 *o* your parents in the Lord,
6: 5 *o* your earthly masters with respect
Col 3:20 *o* your parents in everything,
1Ti 3: 4 and see that his children *o* him
Heb 13:17 *O* your leaders and submit
1Jn 5: 3 love for God: to *o* his commands.

OBEYED (OBEY)
Ps 119: 4 that are to be fully *o.*
Jnh 3: 3 Jonah *o* the word of the LORD
Jn 17: 6 and they have *o* your word.
Ro 6:17 you wholeheartedly *o* the form
Heb 11: 8 *o* and went, even though he did not
1Pe 3: 6 who *o* Abraham and called him her

OBLIGATED
Ro 1:14 I am *o* both to Greeks
Gal 5: 3 himself be circumcised that he is *o*

OBSCENITY
Eph 5: 4 Nor should there be *o,* foolish talk

OBSOLETE
Heb 8:13 he has made the first one *o;*

OBTAINED
Ro 9:30 not pursue righteousness, have *o* it,
Php 3:12 Not that I have already *o* all this,
Heb 9:12 having *o* eternal redemption.

OFFENDED (OFFENSE)
Pr 18:19 An *o* brother is more unyielding

OFFENSE (OFFENDED OFFENSIVE)
Pr 17: 9 over an *o* promotes love,
19:11 it is to his glory to overlook an *o.*

OFFENSIVE (OFFENSE)
Ps 139:24 See if there is any *o* way in me,

OFFER (OFFERED OFFERING OFFERINGS)
Ro 12: 1 to *o* your bodies as living sacrifices,
Heb 13:15 therefore, let us continually *o*

OFFERED (OFFER)
Heb 7:27 once for all when he *o* himself.
11: 4 By faith Abel *o* God a better

OFFERING (OFFER)
Ge 22: 8 provide the lamb for the burnt *o,*
Ps 40: 6 Sacrifice and *o* you did not desire,
Isa 53:10 the LORD makes his life a guilt *o,*
Mt 5:23 if you are *o* your gift at the altar
Eph 5: 2 as a fragrant *o* and sacrifice to God.
Heb 10: 5 "Sacrifice and *o* you did not desire,

OFFERINGS (OFFER)
Mal 3: 8 do we rob you?' "In tithes and *o.*
Mk 12:33 is more important than all burnt *o*

OFFICER
2Ti 2: 4 wants to please his commanding *o.*

OFFSPRING
Ge 3:15 and between your *o* and hers;
12: 7 "To your *o* I will give this land."

OIL
Ps 23: 5 You anoint my head with *o;*
Isa 61: 3 the *o* of gladness
Heb 1: 9 by anointing you with the *o* of joy."

OLIVE (OLIVES)
Zec 4: 3 Also there are two *o* trees by it,
Ro 11:17 and you, though a wild *o* shoot,

Rev 11: 4 These are the two *o* trees

OLIVES (OLIVE)
Jas 3:12 a fig tree bear *o*, or a grapevine bear

OMEGA
Rev 1: 8 "I am the Alpha and the *O*,"

OMRI
King of Israel (1Ki 16:21-26).

OPINIONS*
1Ki 18:21 will you waver between two *o?*
Pr 18: 2 but delights in airing his own *o*.

OPPORTUNITY
Ro 7:11 seizing the *o* afforded
Gal 6:10 as we have *o*, let us do good
Eph 5:16 making the most of every *o*,
Col 4: 5 make the most of every *o*.
1Ti 5:14 to give the enemy no *o* for slander.

OPPOSES
Jas 4: 6 "God *o* the proud
1Pe 5: 5 because, "God *o* the proud

OPPRESS (OPPRESSED)
Ex 22:21 "Do not mistreat an alien or *o* him,
Zec 7:10 Do not *o* the widow

OPPRESSED (OPPRESS)
Ps 9: 9 The LORD is a refuge for the *o*,
Isa 53: 7 He was *o* and afflicted,
Zec 10: 2 *o* for lack of a shepherd.

ORDAINED
Ps 8: 2 you have *o* praise

ORDERLY
1Co 14:40 done in a fitting and *o* way.
Col 2: 5 and delight to see how *o* you are

ORGIES*
Ro 13:13 not in *o* and drunkenness,
Gal 5:21 drunkenness, *o*, and the like.
1Pe 4: 3 *o*, carousing and detestable

ORIGIN
2Pe 1:21 For prophecy never had its *o*

ORPHANS
Jn 14:18 will not leave you as *o;* I will come
Jas 1:27 to look after *o* and widows

OUTCOME
Heb 13: 7 Consider the *o* of their way of life
1Pe 4:17 what will the *o* be for those who do

OUTSIDERS*
Col 4: 5 wise in the way you act toward *o;*
1Th 4:12 daily life may win the respect of *o*
1Ti 3: 7 also have a good reputation with *o*,

OUTSTANDING
SS 5:10 *o* among ten thousand.
Ro 13: 8 no debt remain *o*,

OUTSTRETCHED
Ex 6: 6 and will redeem you with an *o* arm
Jer 27: 5 and *o* arm I made the earth
Eze 20:33 an *o* arm and with outpoured wrath

OUTWEIGHS
2Co 4:17 an eternal glory that far *o* them all.

OVERCOME (OVERCOMES)
Mt 16:18 and the gates of Hades will not *o* it.
Mk 9:24 I do believe; help me *o* my unbelief
Jn 16:33 But take heart! I have *o* the world."
Ro 12:21 Do not be *o* by evil, but *o* evil
1Jn 5: 4 is the victory that has *o* the world,
Rev 17:14 but the Lamb will *o* them

OVERCOMES* (OVERCOME)
1Jn 5: 4 born of God *o* the world.
5: 5 Who is it that *o* the world?
Rev 2: 7 To him who *o*, I will give the right
2:11 He who *o* will not be hurt at all
2:17 To him who *o*, I will give some
2:26 To him who *o* and does my will
3: 5 He who *o* will, like them, be
3:12 Him who *o* I will make a pillar
3:21 To him who *o*, I will give the right
21: 7 He who *o* will inherit all this,

OVERFLOW (OVERFLOWS)
Ps 119:171 May my lips *o* with praise,
Lk 6:45 out of the *o* of his heart his mouth
Ro 15:13 so that you may *o* with hope
2Co 4:15 to *o* to the glory of God.
1Th 3:12 *o* for each other and for everyone

OVERFLOWS* (OVERFLOW)
Ps 23: 5 my cup *o*.
2Co 1: 5 also through Christ our comfort *o*.

OVERJOYED* (JOY)
Da 6:23 The king was *o* and gave orders
Mt 2:10 they saw the star, they were *o*.
Jn 20:20 The disciples were *o*
Ac 12:14 she was so *o* she ran back
1Pe 4:13 so that you may be *o*

OVERSEER (OVERSEERS)
1Ti 3: 1 anyone sets his heart on being an *o*,
3: 2 Now the *o* must be above reproach,
Tit 1: 7 Since an *o* is entrusted

OVERSEERS* (OVERSEER)
Ac 20:28 the Holy Spirit has made you *o*.
Php 1: 1 together with the *o* and deacons:
1Pe 5: 2 as *o*— not because you must,

OVERWHELMED
Ps 38: 4 My guilt has *o* me
65: 3 When we were *o* by sins,
Mt 26:38 "My soul is *o* with sorrow
Mk 7:37 People were *o* with amazement.

OWE
Ro 13: 7 If you *o* taxes, pay taxes; if revenue
Phm :19 to mention that you *o* me your very

OX
Dt 25: 4 Do not muzzle an *o*
Isa 11: 7 and the lion will eat straw like the *o*
1Co 9: 9 "Do not muzzle an *o*

PAGANS
Mt 5:47 Do not even *p* do that? Be perfect,
1Pe 2:12 such good lives among the *p* that,

PAIN (PAINFUL)
Ge 3:16 with *p* you will give birth
Job 33:19 may be chastened on a bed of *p*
Jn 16:21 woman giving birth to a child has *p*

PAINFUL (PAIN)
Ge 3:17 through *p* toil you will eat of it
Heb 12:11 seems pleasant at the time, but *p*.
1Pe 4:12 at the *p* trial you are suffering,

PALMS
Isa 49:16 you on the *p* of my hands;

PANTS
Ps 42: 1 As the deer *p* for streams of water,

PARADISE*
Lk 23:43 today you will be with me in *p*."
2Co 12: 4 God knows—was caught up to *p*.
Rev 2: 7 of life, which is in the *p* of God.

PARALYTIC
Mk 2: 3 bringing to him a *p*, carried by four

PARDON (PARDONS)
Isa 55: 7 and to our God, for he will freely *p*.

PARDONS* (PARDON)
Mic 7:18 who *p* sin and forgives

PARENTS
Pr 17: 6 and *p* are the pride of their children
Lk 18:29 left home or wife or brothers or *p*
21:16 You will be betrayed even by *p*,
Ro 1:30 they disobey their *p;* they are
2Co 12:14 for their *p*, but *p* for their children.
Eph 6: 1 Children, obey your *p* in the Lord,
Col 3:20 obey your *p* in everything,
2Ti 3: 2 disobedient to their *p*, ungrateful,

PARTIALITY
Dt 10:17 who shows no *p* and accepts no
2Ch 19: 7 our God there is no injustice or *p*
Lk 20:21 and that you do not show *p*

PARTICIPATION
1Co 10:16 is not the bread that we break a *p*

PASS
Ex 12:13 and when I see the blood, I will *p*
La 1:12 to you, all you who *p* by?
Lk 21:33 Heaven and earth will *p* away,
1Co 13: 8 there is knowledge, it will *p* away.

PASSION (PASSIONS)
1Co 7: 9 better to marry than to burn with *p*.

PASSIONS (PASSION)
Gal 5:24 crucified the sinful nature with its *p*
Tit 2:12 to ungodliness and worldly *p*,

PASSOVER
Ex 12:11 Eat it in haste; it is the LORD's *P*.
Dt 16: 1 celebrate the *P* of the LORD your
1Co 5: 7 our *P* lamb, has been sacrificed.

PAST
Isa 43:18 do not dwell on the *p*.
Ro 15: 4 in the *p* was written to teach us,
Heb 1: 1 In the *p* God spoke

PASTORS*
Eph 4:11 and some to be *p* and teachers,

PASTURE (PASTURES)
Ps 37: 3 dwell in the land and enjoy safe *p*.
100: 3 we are his people, the sheep of his *p*
Jer 50: 7 against the LORD, their true *p*,
Eze 34:13 I will *p* them on the mountains
Jn 10: 9 come in and go out, and find *p*.

PASTURES (PASTURE)
Ps 23: 2 He makes me lie down in green *p*,

PATCH
Mt 9:16 No one sews a *p* of unshrunk cloth

PATH (PATHS)
Ps 27:11 lead me in a straight *p*
119:105 and a light for my *p*.
Pr 15:19 the *p* of the upright is a highway.
15:24 The *p* of life leads upward
Isa 26: 7 The *p* of the righteous is level;
Lk 1:79 to guide our feet into the *p* of peace
2Co 6: 3 no stumbling block in anyone's *p*,

PATHS (PATH)
Ps 23: 3 He guides me in *p* of righteousness
25: 4 teach me your *p;*
Pr 3: 6 and he will make your *p* straight.
Ro 11:33 and his *p* beyond tracing out!
Heb 12:13 "Make level *p* for your feet,"

PATIENCE (PATIENT)
Pr 19:11 A man's wisdom gives him *p*,
2Co 6: 6 understanding, *p* and kindness;
Gal 5:22 joy, peace, *p*, kindness, goodness,
Col 1:11 may have great endurance and *p*,
3:12 humility, gentleness and *p*.

PATIENT (PATIENCE PATIENTLY)
Pr 15:18 but a *p* man calms a quarrel.
Ro 12:12 Be joyful in hope, *p* in affliction,
1Co 13: 4 Love is *p*, love is kind.
Eph 4: 2 humble and gentle; be *p*,
1Th 5:14 help the weak, be *p* with everyone.

PATIENTLY (PATIENT)
Ps 40: 1 I waited *p* for the LORD;
Ro 8:25 we do not yet have, we wait for it *p*.

PATTERN
Ro 5:14 who was a *p* of the one to come.
12: 2 longer to the *p* of this world,
2Ti 1:13 keep as the *p* of sound teaching,

PAUL
Also called Saul (Ac 13:9). Pharisee from Tarsus (Ac 9:11; Php 3:5). Apostle (Gal 1). At stoning of Stephen (Ac 8:1). Persecuted Church (Ac 9:1-2; Gal 1:13). Vision of Jesus on road to Damascus (Ac 9:4-9; 26:12-18). In Arabia (Gal 1:17). Preached in Damascus; escaped death through the wall in a basket (Ac 9:19-25). In Jerusalem; sent back to Tarsus (Ac 9:26-30).

Brought to Antioch by Barnabas (Ac 11:22-26). First missionary journey to Cyprus and Galatia (Ac 13-14). Stoned at Lystra (Ac 14:19-20). At Jerusalem council (Ac 15). Split with Barnabas over Mark (Ac 15:36-41).

Second missionary journey with Silas (Ac 16-20). Called to Macedonia (Ac 16:6-10). Freed from prison in Philippi (Ac 16:16-40). In Thessalonica (Ac 17:1-9). Speech in Athens (Ac 17:16-33). In Corinth (Ac 18). In Ephesus (Ac 19). Return to Jerusalem (Ac 20). Farewell to Ephesian elders (Ac 20:13-38). Arrival in Jerusalem (Ac 21:1-26). Arrested (Ac 21:27-36). Addressed crowds (Ac 22), Sanhedrin (Ac 23:1-11). Transferred to Caesarea (Ac 23:12-35). Trial before Felix (Ac 24), Festus (Ac 25:1-12). Before Agrippa (Ac 25:13-26:32). Voyage to Rome; shipwreck (Ac 27). Arrival in Rome (Ac 28).

PAY (REPAID REPAY)
Lev 26:43 They will *p* for their sins
Pr 22:17 *P* attention and listen
Mt 22:17 Is it right to *p* taxes to Caesar
Ro 13: 6 This is also why you *p* taxes,
2Pe 1:19 you will do well to *p* attention to it,

PEACE (PEACEMAKERS)
Nu 6:26 and give you *p*."

Ps 34:14 seek *p* and pursue it.
85:10 righteousness and *p* kiss each other
119:165 Great *p* have they who love your
122: 6 Pray for the *p* of Jerusalem:
Pr 14:30 A heart at *p* gives life to the body,
17: 1 Better a dry crust with *p* and quiet
Isa 9: 6 Everlasting Father, Prince of *P.*
26: 3 You will keep in perfect *p*
48:22 "There is no *p,*" says the LORD,
Zec 9:10 He will proclaim *p* to the nations.
Mt 10:34 I did not come to bring *p,*
Lk 2:14 on earth *p* to men on whom his
Jn 14:27 *P* I leave with you; my *p*
16:33 so that in me you may have *p.*
Ro 5: 1 we have *p* with God
1Co 7:15 God has called us to live in *p.*
14:33 a God of disorder but of *p.*
Gal 5:22 joy, *p,* patience, kindness,
Eph 2:14 he himself is our *p,* who has made
Php 4: 7 the *p* of God, which transcends all
Col 1:20 by making *p* through his blood,
3:15 Let the *p* of Christ rule
1Th 5: 3 While people are saying, "*P*
2Th 3:16 the Lord of *p* himself give you *p*
2Ti 2:22 righteousness, faith, love and *p,*
1Pe 3:11 he must seek *p* and pursue it.
Rev 6: 4 power to take *p* from the earth

PEACEMAKERS* (PEACE)
Mt 5: 9 Blessed are the *p,*
Jas 3:18 *P* who sow in peace raise a harvest

PEARL* (PEARLS)
Rev 21:21 each gate made of a single *p.*

PEARLS (PEARL)
Mt 7: 6 do not throw your *p* to pigs.
13:45 like a merchant looking for fine *p.*
1Ti 2: 9 or gold or *p* or expensive clothes,
Rev 21:21 The twelve gates were twelve *p,*

PEKAH
King of Israel (2Ki 15:25-31; Isa 7:1).

PEKAHIAH*
Son of Menahem; king of Israel (2Ki 15:22-26).

PEN
Mt 5:18 letter, not the least stroke of a *p,*

PENTECOST
Ac 2: 1 of *P* came, they were all together

PEOPLE (PEOPLES)
Dt 32: 9 the LORD's portion is his *p,*
Ru 1:16 Your *p* will be my *p*
2Ch 7:14 if my *p,* who are called
Jer 24: 7 They will be my *p,*
Zec 2:11 and will become my *p.*
Lk 2:10 joy that will be for all the *p.*
Ac 15:14 from the Gentiles a *p.*
2Co 6:16 and they will be my *p.*"
Tit 2:14 a *p* that are his very own,
1Pe 2: 9 you are a chosen *p,*
Rev 21: 3 They will be his *p,*

PEOPLES (PEOPLE)
Da 7:14 all *p,* nations and men
Mic 4: 1 and *p* will stream to it.

PERCEIVING
Isa 6: 9 be ever seeing, but never *p.*'

PERFECT (PERFECTER PERFECTION)
SS 6: 9 but my dove, my *p* one, is unique,
Isa 26: 3 You will keep in *p* peace
Mt 5:48 as your heavenly Father is *p.*
Ro 12: 2 his good, pleasing and *p* will.
2Co 12: 9 for my power is made *p*
Col 1:28 so that we may present everyone *p*
3:14 binds them all together in *p* unity.
Heb 9:11 and more *p* tabernacle that is not
10:14 he has made *p* forever those who
Jas 1:17 Every good and *p* gift is from above
1:25 into the *p* law that gives freedom,
3: 2 he is a *p* man, able
1Jn 4:18 But *p* love drives out fear,

PERFECTER* (PERFECT)
Heb 12: 2 the author and *p* of our faith,

PERFECTION (PERFECT)
Ps 119:96 To all *p* I see a limit;
2Co 13:11 Aim for *p,* listen to my appeal,
Heb 7:11 If *p* could have been attained

PERFORMS
Ps 77:14 You are the God who *p* miracles;

PERISH (PERISHABLE)
Ps 1: 6 but the way of the wicked will *p.*
102:26 They will *p,* but you remain;
Lk 13: 3 unless you repent, you too will all *p*
Jn 10:28 eternal life, and they shall never *p;*
Col 2:22 These are all destined to *p* with use,
Heb 1:11 They will *p,* but you remain;
2Pe 3: 9 not wanting anyone to *p,*

PERISHABLE (PERISH)
1Co 15:42 The body that is sown is *p,*

PERJURERS
1Ti 1:10 for slave traders and liars and *p*—

PERMISSIBLE (PERMIT)
1Co 10:23 "Everything is *p*"—but not

PERMIT (PERMISSIBLE)
1Ti 2:12 I do not *p* a woman to teach

PERSECUTE (PERSECUTED PERSECUTION)
Mt 5:11 *p* you and falsely say all kinds
Jn 15:20 they persecuted me, they will *p* you
Ac 9: 4 why do you *p* me?" "Who are you,
Ro 12:14 Bless those who *p* you; bless

PERSECUTED (PERSECUTE)
1Co 4:12 when we are *p,* we endure it;
2Ti 3:12 life in Christ Jesus will be *p,*

PERSECUTION (PERSECUTE)
Ro 8:35 or hardship or *p* or famine

PERSEVERANCE (PERSEVERE)
Ro 5: 3 we know that suffering produces *p;*
5: 4 *p,* character; and character, hope.
Heb 12: 1 run with *p* the race marked out
Jas 1: 3 the testing of your faith develops *p.*
2Pe 1: 6 *p;* and to *p,* godliness;

PERSEVERE* (PERSEVERANCE PERSEVERED PERSEVERES)
1Ti 4:16 *P* in them, because if you do,
Heb 10:36 You need to *p* so that

PERSEVERED* (PERSEVERE)
Heb 11:27 he *p* because he saw him who is
Jas 5:11 consider blessed those who have *p.*
Rev 2: 3 You have *p* and have endured

PERSEVERES* (PERSEVERE)
1Co 13: 7 trusts, always hopes, always *p.*
Jas 1:12 Blessed is the man who *p*

PERSUADE
2Co 5:11 is to fear the Lord, we try to *p* men.

PERVERSION (PERVERT)
Lev 18:23 sexual relations with it; that is a *p.*
Jude : 7 up to sexual immorality and *p.*

PERVERT (PERVERSION PERVERTS)
Gal 1: 7 are trying to *p* the gospel of Christ.

PERVERTS* (PERVERT)
1Ti 1:10 for murderers, for adulterers and *p,*

PESTILENCE
Ps 91: 6 nor the *p* that stalks in the darkness

PETER
Apostle, brother of Andrew, also called Simon (Mt 10:2; Mk 3:16; Lk 6:14; Ac 1:13), and Cephas (Jn 1:42). Confession of Christ (Mt 16:13-20; Mk 8:27-30; Lk 9:18-27). At transfiguration (Mt 17:1-8; Mk 9:2-8; Lk 9:28-36; 2Pe 1:16-18). Caught fish with coin (Mt 17:24-27). Denial of Jesus predicted (Mt 26:31-35; Mk 14:27-31; Lk 22:31-34; Jn 13:31-38). Denied Jesus (Mt 26:69-75; Mk 14:66-72; Lk 22:54-62; Jn 18:15-27). Commissioned by Jesus to shepherd his flock (Jn 21:15-23).

Speech at Pentecost (Ac 2). Healed beggar (Ac 3:1-10). Speech at temple (Ac 3:11-26), before Sanhedrin (Ac 4:1-22). In Samaria (Ac 8:14-25). Sent by vision to Cornelius (Ac 10). Announced salvation of Gentiles in Jerusalem (Ac 11; 15). Freed from prison (Ac 12). Inconsistency at Antioch (Gal 2:11-21). At Jerusalem Council (Ac 15).

PHARISEES
Mt 5:20 surpasses that of the *P*

PHILIP
1. Apostle (Mt 10:3; Mk 3:18; Lk 6:14; Jn 1:43-48; 14:8; Ac 1:13).

2. Deacon (Ac 6:1-7); evangelist in Samaria (Ac 8:4-25), to Ethiopian (Ac 8:26-40).

PHILOSOPHY*
Col 2: 8 through hollow and deceptive *p,*

PHYLACTERIES*
Mt 23: 5 They make their *p* wide

PHYSICAL
1Ti 4: 8 For *p* training is of some value,
Jas 2:16 but does nothing about his *p* needs,

PIECES
Ge 15:17 and passed between the *p.*
Jer 34:18 and then walked between its *p.*

PIERCED
Ps 22:16 they have *p* my hands and my feet.
Isa 53: 5 But he was *p* for our transgressions,
Zec 12:10 look on me, the one they have *p,*
Jn 19:37 look on the one they have *p.*"

PIGS
Mt 7: 6 do not throw your pearls to *p.*

PILATE
Governor of Judea. Questioned Jesus (Mt 27:1-26; Mk 15:15; Lk 22:66-23:25; Jn 18:28-19:16); sent him to Herod (Lk 23:6-12); consented to his crucifixion when crowds chose Barabbas (Mt 27:15-26; Mk 15:6-15; Lk 23:13-25; Jn 19:1-10).

PILLAR
Ge 19:26 and she became a *p* of salt.
Ex 13:21 ahead of them in a *p* of cloud
1Ti 3:15 the *p* and foundation of the truth.

PIT
Ps 40: 2 He lifted me out of the slimy *p,*
103: 4 who redeems your life from the *p*
Mt 15:14 a blind man, both will fall into a *p.*"

PITIED
1Co 15:19 we are to be *p* more than all men.

PLAGUE
2Ch 6:28 "When famine or *p* comes

PLAIN
Ro 1:19 what may be known about God is *p*

PLAN (PLANNED PLANS)
Job 42: 2 no *p* of yours can be thwarted.
Pr 14:22 those who *p* what is good find love
Eph 1:11 predestined according to the *p*

PLANK
Mt 7: 3 attention to the *p* in your own eye?
Lk 6:41 attention to the *p* in your own eye?

PLANNED (PLAN)
Ps 40: 5 The things you *p* for us
Isa 46:11 what I have *p,* that will I do.
Heb 11:40 God had *p* something better for us

PLANS (PLAN)
Ps 20: 4 and make all your *p* succeed.
33:11 *p* of the LORD stand firm forever,
Pr 20:18 Make *p* by seeking advice;
Isa 32: 8 But the noble man makes noble *p,*

PLANTED (PLANTS)
Ps 1: 3 He is like a tree *p* by streams
Mt 15:13 Father has not *p* will be pulled
1Co 3: 6 I *p* the seed, Apollos watered it,

PLANTS (PLANTED)
1Co 3: 7 So neither he who *p* nor he who
9: 7 Who *p* a vineyard and does not eat

PLATTER
Mk 6:25 head of John the Baptist on a *p.*"

PLAYED
Lk 7:32 " 'We *p* the flute for you,
1Co 14: 7 anyone know what tune is being *p*

PLEADED
2Co 12: 8 Three times I *p* with the Lord

PLEASANT (PLEASE)
Ps 16: 6 for me in *p* places;
133: 1 How good and *p* it is
147: 1 how *p* and fitting to praise him!
Heb 12:11 No discipline seems *p* at the time,

PLEASE (PLEASANT PLEASED PLEASES PLEASING PLEASURE PLEASURES)
Pr 20:23 and dishonest scales do not *p* him.
Jer 6:20 your sacrifices do not *p* me."
Jn 5:30 for I seek not to *p* myself
Ro 8: 8 by the sinful nature cannot *p* God.
15: 2 Each of us should *p* his neighbor
1Co 7:32 affairs—how he can *p* the Lord.
10:33 I try to *p* everybody in every way.
2Co 5: 9 So we make it our goal to *p* him,
Gal 1:10 or of God? Or am I trying to *p* men

1Th 4: 1 how to live in order to *p* God,
2Ti 2: 4 wants to *p* his commanding officer.
Heb 11: 6 faith it is impossible to *p* God,

PLEASED (PLEASE)
Mt 3:17 whom I love; with him I am well *p*
1Co 1:21 God was *p* through the foolishness
Col 1:19 For God was *p* to have all his
Heb 11: 5 commended as one who *p* God.
2Pe 1:17 whom I love; with him I am well *p*

PLEASES (PLEASE)
Ps 135: 6 The LORD does whatever *p* him,
Pr 15: 8 but the prayer of the upright *p* him.
Jn 3: 8 The wind blows wherever it *p*.
8:29 for I always do what *p* him."
Col 3:20 in everything, for this *p* the Lord.
1Ti 2: 3 This is good, and *p* God our Savior,
1Jn 3:22 his commands and do what *p* him.

PLEASING (PLEASE)
Ps 104:34 May my meditation be *p* to him,
Ro 12: 1 *p* to God—which is your spiritual
Php 4:18 an acceptable sacrifice, *p* to God.
Heb 13:21 may he work in us what is *p* to him,

PLEASURE (PLEASE)
Ps 5: 4 You are not a God who takes *p*
147:10 His *p* is not in the strength
Pr 21:17 He who loves *p* will become poor;
Eze 18:32 For I take no *p* in the death
Eph 1: 5 in accordance with his *p* and will—
1: 9 of his will according to his good *p*,
2Ti 3: 4 lovers of *p* rather than lovers

PLEASURES (PLEASE)
Ps 16:11 with eternal *p* at your right hand.
Heb 11:25 rather than to enjoy the *p* of sin
2Pe 2:13 reveling in their *p* while they feast

PLENTIFUL
Mt 9:37 harvest is *p* but the workers are

PLOW (PLOWSHARES)
Lk 9:62 "No one who puts his hand to the *p*

PLOWSHARES (PLOW)
Isa 2: 4 They will beat their swords into *p*
Joel 3:10 Beat your *p* into swords

PLUNDER
Ex 3:22 And so you will *p* the Egyptians."

POINT
Jas 2:10 yet stumbles at just one *p* is guilty

POISON
Mk 16:18 and when they drink deadly *p*,
Jas 3: 8 It is a restless evil, full of deadly *p*.

POLLUTE* (POLLUTED)
Nu 35:33 " 'Do not *p* the land where you are.
Jude : 8 these dreamers *p* their own bodies,

POLLUTED* (POLLUTE)
Ezr 9:11 entering to possess is a land *p*
Pr 25:26 Like a muddied spring or a *p* well
Ac 15:20 to abstain from food *p* by idols,
Jas 1:27 oneself from being *p* by the world.

PONDER
Ps 64: 9 and *p* what he has done.
119:95 but I will *p* your statutes.

POOR (POVERTY)
Dt 15: 4 there should be no *p* among you,
15:11 There will always be *p* people
Ps 34: 6 This *p* man called, and the LORD
82: 3 maintain the rights of the *p*
112: 9 scattered abroad his gifts to the *p*,
Pr 10: 4 Lazy hands make a man *p*,
13: 7 to be *p*, yet has great wealth.
14:31 oppresses the *p* shows contempt
19: 1 Better a *p* man whose walk is
19:17 to the *p* lends to the LORD,
22: 2 Rich and *p* have this in common:
22: 9 for he shares his food with the *p*.
28: 6 Better a *p* man whose walk is
31:20 She opens her arms to the *p*
Isa 61: 1 me to preach good news to the *p*.
Mt 5: 3 saying: "Blessed are the *p* in spirit,
11: 5 the good news is preached to the *p*.
19:21 your possessions and give to the *p*,
26:11 The *p* you will always have
Mk 12:42 But a *p* widow came and put
Ac 10: 4 and gifts to the *p* have come up
1Co 13: 3 If I give all I possess to the *p*
2Co 8: 9 yet for your sakes he became *p*,
Jas 2: 2 and a *p* man in shabby clothes

PORTION
Dt 32: 9 For the LORD's *p* is his people,
2Ki 2: 9 "Let me inherit a double *p*
La 3:24 to myself, "The LORD is my *p*;

POSSESS (POSSESSING POSSESSION POSSESSIONS)
Nu 33:53 for I have given you the land to *p*.
Jn 5:39 that by them you *p* eternal life.

POSSESSING* (POSSESS)
2Co 6:10 nothing, and yet *p* everything.

POSSESSION (POSSESS)
Ge 15: 7 to give you this land to take *p* of it
Nu 13:30 "We should go up and take *p*
Eph 1:14 of those who are God's *p*—

POSSESSIONS (POSSESS)
Lk 12:15 consist in the abundance of his *p*."
2Co 12:14 what I want is not your *p* but you.
1Jn 3:17 If anyone has material *p*

POSSIBLE
Mt 19:26 but with God all things are *p*."
Mk 9:23 "Everything is *p* for him who
10:27 all things are *p* with God."
Ro 12:18 If it is *p*, as far as it depends on you,
1Co 9:22 by all *p* means I might save some.

POT (POTSHERD POTTER POTTERY)
2Ki 4:40 there is death in the *p*!"
Jer 18: 4 But the *p* he was shaping

POTSHERD (POT)
Isa 45: 9 a *p* among the potsherds

POTTER (POT)
Isa 29:16 Can the pot say of the *p*,
45: 9 Does the clay say to the *p*,
64: 8 We are the clay, you are the *p*;
Jer 18: 6 "Like clay in the hand of the *p*,
Ro 9:21 Does not the *p* have the right

POTTERY (POT)
Ro 9:21 of clay some *p* for noble purposes

POUR (POURED)
Ps 62: 8 *p* out your hearts to him,
Joel 2:28 I will *p* out my Spirit on all people.
Mal 3:10 *p* out so much blessing that you
Ac 2:17 I will *p* out my Spirit on all people.

POURED (POUR)
Ac 10:45 of the Holy Spirit had been *p* out
Ro 5: 5 because God has *p* out his love

POVERTY (POOR)
Pr 14:23 but mere talk leads only to *p*.
21: 5 as surely as haste leads to *p*.
30: 8 give me neither *p* nor riches,
Mk 12:44 out of her *p*, put in everything—
2Co 8: 2 and their extreme *p* welled up
8: 9 through his *p* might become rich.

POWER (POWERFUL POWERS)
1Ch 29:11 LORD, is the greatness and the *p*
2Ch 32: 7 for there is a greater *p* with us
Job 36:22 "God is exalted in his *p*.
Ps 63: 2 and beheld your *p* and your glory.
68:34 Proclaim the *p* of God,
147: 5 Great is our Lord and mighty in *p*;
Pr 24: 5 A wise man has great *p*,
Isa 40:10 the Sovereign LORD comes with *p*
Zec 4: 6 nor by *p*, but by my Spirit,'
Mt 22:29 do not know the Scriptures or the *p*
24:30 on the clouds of the sky, with *p*
Ac 1: 8 you will receive *p* when the Holy
4:33 With great *p* the apostles
10:38 with the Holy Spirit and *p*,
Ro 1:16 it is the *p* of God for the salvation
1Co 1:18 to us who are being saved it is the *p*
15:56 of death is sin, and the *p*
2Co 12: 9 for my *p* is made perfect
Eph 1:19 and his incomparably great *p*
Php 3:10 and the *p* of his resurrection
Col 1:11 strengthened with all *p* according
2Ti 1: 7 but a spirit of *p*, of love
Heb 7:16 of the *p* of an indestructible life.
Rev 4:11 to receive glory and honor and *p*,
19: 1 and glory and *p* belong to our God,
20: 6 The second death has no *p*

POWERFUL (POWER)
Ps 29: 4 The voice of the LORD is *p*;
Lk 24:19 *p* in word and deed before God
2Th 1: 7 in blazing fire with his *p* angels.
Heb 1: 3 sustaining all things by his *p* word.
Jas 5:16 The prayer of a righteous man is *p*

POWERLESS
Ro 5: 6 when we were still *p*, Christ died
8: 3 For what the law was *p* to do

POWERS (POWER)
Ro 8:38 nor any *p*, neither height nor depth
1Co 12:10 to another miraculous *p*,
Col 1:16 whether thrones or *p* or rulers
2:15 And having disarmed the *p*

PRACTICE
Lev 19:26 " 'Do not *p* divination or sorcery.
Mt 23: 3 for they do not *p* what they preach.
Lk 8:21 hear God's word and put it into *p*."
Ro 12:13 *P* hospitality.
1Ti 5: 4 to put their religion into *p* by caring

PRAISE (PRAISED PRAISES PRAISING)
Ex 15: 2 He is my God, and I will *p* him,
Dt 32: 3 Oh, *p* the greatness of our God!
Ru 4:14 said to Naomi: "*P* be to the LORD,
2Sa 22:47 The LORD lives! *P* be to my Rock
1Ch 16:25 is the LORD and most worthy of *p*;
2Ch 20:21 and to *p* him for the splendor
Ps 8: 2 you have ordained *p*
33: 1 it is fitting for the upright to *p* him.
34: 1 his *p* will always be on my lips.
40: 3 a hymn of *p* to our God.
48: 1 the LORD, and most worthy of *p*,
68:19 *P* be to the Lord, to God our Savior
89: 5 The heavens *p* your wonders,
100: 4 and his courts with *p*;
105: 2 Sing to him, sing *p* to him;
106: 1 *P* the LORD.
119:175 Let me live that I may *p* you,
139:14 I *p* you because I am fearfully
145:21 Let every creature *p* his holy name
146: 1 *P* the LORD, O my soul.
150: 2 *p* him for his surpassing greatness.
150: 6 that has breath *p* the LORD.
Pr 27: 2 Let another *p* you, and not your
27:21 man is tested by the *p* he receives
31:31 let her works bring her *p*
Mt 5:16 and *p* your Father in heaven.
21:16 you have ordained *p*'?"
Jn 12:43 for they loved *p* from men more
Eph 1: 6 to the *p* of his glorious grace,
1:12 might be for the *p* of his glory.
1:14 to the *p* of his glory.
Heb 13:15 offer to God a sacrifice of *p*—
Jas 5:13 happy? Let him sing songs of *p*.

PRAISED (PRAISE)
1Ch 29:10 David *p* the LORD in the presence
Ne 8: 6 Ezra *p* the LORD, the great God;
Da 2:19 Then Daniel *p* the God of heaven
Ro 9: 5 who is God over all, forever *p*!
1Pe 4:11 that in all things God may be *p*

PRAISES (PRAISE)
2Sa 22:50 I will sing *p* to your name.
Ps 47: 6 Sing *p* to God, sing *p*;
147: 1 How good it is to sing *p* to our God,
Pr 31:28 her husband also, and he *p* her:

PRAISING (PRAISE)
Ac 10:46 speaking in tongues and *p* God.
1Co 14:16 If you are *p* God with your spirit,

PRAY (PRAYED PRAYER PRAYERS PRAYING)
Dt 4: 7 is near us whenever we *p* to him?
1Sa 12:23 the LORD by failing to *p* for you.
2Ch 7:14 will humble themselves and *p*
Job 42: 8 My servant Job will *p* for you,
Ps 122: 6 *P* for the peace of Jerusalem:
Mt 5:44 and *p* for those who persecute you,
6: 5 "And when you *p*, do not be like
6: 9 "This, then, is how you should *p*:
26:36 Sit here while I go over there and *p*
Lk 6:28 *p* for those who mistreat you.
18: 1 them that they should always *p*
22:40 "*P* that you will not fall
Ro 8:26 do not know what we ought to *p*,
1Co 14:13 in a tongue should *p* that he may
1Th 5:17 Be joyful always; *p* continually;
Jas 5:13 one of you in trouble? He should *p*.
5:16 *p* for each other so that you may be

PRAYED (PRAY)
1Sa 1:27 I *p* for this child, and the LORD
Jnh 2: 1 From inside the fish Jonah *p*
Mk 14:35 *p* that if possible the hour might

PRAYER (PRAY)
2Ch 30:27 for their *p* reached heaven,
Ezr 8:23 about this, and he answered our *p*.

Ps 6: 9 the LORD accepts my *p*.
86: 6 Hear my *p*, O LORD;
Pr 15: 8 but the *p* of the upright pleases him
Isa 56: 7 a house of *p* for all nations."
Mt 21:13 house will be called a house of *p*,'
Mk 11:24 whatever you ask for in *p*,
Jn 17:15 My *p* is not that you take them out
Ac 6: 4 and will give our attention to *p*
Php 4: 6 but in everything, by *p* and petition
Jas 5:15 *p* offered in faith will make the sick
1Pe 3:12 and his ears are attentive to their *p*,

PRAYERS (PRAY)
1Ch 5:20 He answered their *p*, because they
Mk 12:40 and for a show make lengthy *p*.
1Pe 3: 7 so that nothing will hinder your *p*.
Rev 5: 8 which are the *p* of the saints.

PRAYING (PRAY)
Mk 11:25 And when you stand *p*,
Jn 17: 9 I am not *p* for the world,
Ac 16:25 and Silas were *p* and singing hymns
Eph 6:18 always keep on *p* for all the saints.

PREACH (PREACHED PREACHING)
Mt 23: 3 they do not practice what they *p*.
Mk 16:15 and *p* the good news to all creation.
Ac 9:20 At once he began to *p*
Ro 10:15 how can they *p* unless they are sent
15:20 to *p* the gospel where Christ was
1Co 1:17 to *p* the gospel—not with words
1:23 wisdom, but we *p* Christ crucified:
9:14 that those who *p* the gospel should
9:16 Woe to me if I do not *p* the gospel!
2Co 10:16 so that we can *p* the gospel
Gal 1: 8 from heaven should *p* a gospel
2Ti 4: 2 I give you this charge: *P* the Word;

PREACHED (PREACH)
Mk 13:10 And the gospel must first be *p*
Ac 8: 4 had been scattered *p* the word
1Co 9:27 so that after I have *p* to others,
15: 1 you of the gospel I *p* to you,
2Co 11: 4 other than the Jesus we *p*,
Gal 1: 8 other than the one we *p* to you,
Php 1:18 false motives or true, Christ is *p*.
1Ti 3:16 was *p* among the nations,

PREACHING (PREACH)
Ro 10:14 hear without someone *p* to them?
1Co 9:18 in *p* the gospel I may offer it free
1Ti 4:13 the public reading of Scripture, to *p*
5:17 especially those whose work is *p*

PRECEPTS
Ps 19: 8 The *p* of the LORD are right,
111: 7 all his *p* are trustworthy.
111:10 who follow his *p* have good
119:40 How I long for your *p*!
119:69 I keep your *p* with all my heart.
119:104 I gain understanding from your *p*;
119:159 See how I love your *p*;

PRECIOUS
Ps 19:10 They are more *p* than gold,
116:15 *P* in the sight of the LORD
Pr 8:11 for wisdom is more *p* than rubies,
Isa 28:16 a *p* cornerstone for a sure
1Pe 1:19 but with the *p* blood of Christ,
2: 6 a chosen and *p* cornerstone,
2Pe 1: 4 us his very great and *p* promises,

PREDESTINED* (DESTINY)
Ro 8:29 *p* to be conformed to the likeness
8:30 And those he *p*, he also called;
Eph 1: 5 In love he *p* us to be adopted
1:11 having been *p* according

PREDICTION*
Jer 28: 9 only if his *p* comes true."

PREPARE (PREPARED)
Ps 23: 5 You *p* a table before me
Am 4:12 *p* to meet your God, O Israel."
Jn 14: 2 there to *p* a place for you.
Eph 4:12 to *p* God's people for works

PREPARED (PREPARE)
Mt 25:34 the kingdom *p* for you
1Co 2: 9 what God has *p* for those who love
Eph 2:10 which God *p* in advance for us
2Ti 4: 2 be *p* in season and out of season;
1Pe 3:15 Always be *p* to give an answer

PRESENCE (PRESENT)
Ex 25:30 Put the bread of the *P* on this table
Ezr 9:15 one of us can stand in your *p*."
Ps 31:20 the shelter of your *p* you hide them
89:15 who walk in the light of your *p*,
90: 8 our secret sins in the light of your *p*
139: 7 Where can I flee from your *p*?
Jer 5:22 "Should you not tremble in my *p*?
Heb 9:24 now to appear for us in God's *p*.
Jude :24 before his glorious *p* without fault

PRESENT (PRESENCE)
2Co 11: 2 so that I might *p* you as a pure
Eph 5:27 and to *p* her to himself
2Ti 2:15 Do your best to *p* yourself to God

PRESERVES
Ps 1 19:50 Your promise *p* my life.

PRESS (PRESSED PRESSURE)
Php 3:14 I *p* on toward the goal

PRESSED (PRESS)
Lk 6:38 *p* down, shaken together

PRESSURE (PRESS)
2Co 1: 8 We were under great *p*, far
11:28 I face daily the *p* of my concern

PREVAILS
1Sa 2: 9 "It is not by strength that one *p*;

PRICE
Job 28:18 the *p* of wisdom is beyond rubies.
1Co 6:20 your own; you were bought at a *p*.
7:23 bought at a *p*; do not become slaves

PRIDE (PROUD)
Pr 8:13 I hate *p* and arrogance,
16:18 *P* goes before destruction,
Da 4:37 And those who walk in *p* he is able
Gal 6: 4 Then he can take *p* in himself,
Jas 1: 9 ought to take *p* in his high position.

PRIEST (PRIESTHOOD PRIESTS)
Heb 4:14 have a great high *p* who has gone
4:15 do not have a high *p* who is unable
7:26 Such a high *p* meets our need—
8: 1 We do have such a high *p*,

PRIESTHOOD (PRIEST)
Heb 7:24 lives forever, he has a permanent *p*.
1Pe 2: 5 into a spiritual house to be a holy *p*,
2: 9 you are a chosen people, a royal *p*,

PRIESTS (PRIEST)
Ex 19: 6 you will be for me a kingdom of *p*
Rev 5:10 to be a kingdom and *p*

PRINCE
Isa 9: 6 Everlasting Father, *P* of Peace.
Jn 12:31 now the *p* of this world will be
Ac 5:31 as *P* and Savior that he might give

PRISON (PRISONER)
Isa 42: 7 to free captives from *p*
Mt 25:36 I was in *p* and you came to visit me
1Pe 3:19 spirits in *p* who disobeyed long ago
Rev 20: 7 Satan will be released from his *p*

PRISONER (PRISON)
Ro 7:23 and making me a *p* of the law of sin
Gal 3:22 declares that the whole world is a *p*
Eph 3: 1 the *p* of Christ Jesus for the sake

PRIVILEGE*
2Co 8: 4 pleaded with us for the *p* of sharing

PRIZE
1Co 9:24 Run in such a way as to get the *p*.
Php 3:14 on toward the goal to win the *p*

PROCLAIM (PROCLAIMED PROCLAIMING)
1Ch 16:23 *p* his salvation day after day.
Ps 19: 1 the skies *p* the work of his hands.
50: 6 the heavens *p* his righteousness,
68:34 *P* the power of God,
118:17 will *p* what the LORD has done.
Zec 9:10 He will *p* peace to the nations.
Ac 20:27 hesitated to *p* to you the whole will
1Co 11:26 you *p* the Lord's death

PROCLAIMED (PROCLAIM)
Ro 15:19 I have fully *p* the gospel of Christ.
Col 1:23 that has been *p* to every creature

PROCLAIMING (PROCLAIM)
Ro 10: 8 the word of faith we are *p*:

PRODUCE (PRODUCES)
Mt 3: 8 *P* fruit in keeping with repentance.
3:10 tree that does not *p* good fruit will

PRODUCES (PRODUCE)
Pr 30:33 so stirring up anger *p* strife."
Ro 5: 3 that suffering *p* perseverance;
Heb 12:11 it *p* a harvest of righteousness

PROFANE
Lev 22:32 Do not *p* my holy name.

PROFESS*
1Ti 2:10 for women who *p* to worship God.
Heb 4:14 let us hold firmly to the faith we *p*.
10:23 unswervingly to the hope we *p*,

PROMISE (PROMISED PROMISES)
1Ki 8:20 The LORD has kept the *p* he made
Ac 2:39 The *p* is for you and your children
Gal 3:14 that by faith we might receive the *p*
1Ti 4: 8 holding *p* for both the present life
2Pe 3: 9 Lord is not slow in keeping his *p*,

PROMISED (PROMISE)
Ex 3:17 And I have *p* to bring you up out
Dt 26:18 his treasured possession as he *p*,
Ps 119:57 I have *p* to obey your words.
Ro 4:21 power to do what he had *p*.
Heb 10:23 for he who *p* is faithful.
2Pe 3: 4 "Where is this 'coming' he *p*?

PROMISES (PROMISE)
Jos 21:45 one of all the LORD's good *p*
Ro 9: 4 the temple worship and the *p*.
2Pe 1: 4 us his very great and precious *p*,

PROMPTED
1Th 1: 3 your labor *p* by love, and your
2Th 1:11 and every act *p* by your faith.

PROPHECIES (PROPHESY)
1Co 13: 8 where there are *p*, they will cease;
1Th 5:20 do not treat *p* with contempt.

PROPHECY (PROPHESY)
1Co 14: 1 gifts, especially the gift of *p*
2Pe 1:20 you must understand that no *p*

PROPHESY (PROPHECIES PROPHECY PROPHESYING PROPHET PROPHETS)
Joel 2:28 Your sons and daughters will *p*,
Mt 7:22 Lord, did we not *p* in your name,
1Co 14:39 my brothers, be eager to *p*,

PROPHESYING (PROPHESY)
Ro 12: 6 If a man's gift is *p*, let him use it

PROPHET (PROPHESY)
Dt 18:18 up for them a *p* like you
Am 7:14 "I was neither a *p* nor a prophet's
Mt 10:41 Anyone who receives a *p*
Lk 4:24 "no *p* is accepted in his hometown.

PROPHETS (PROPHESY)
Ps 105:15 do my *p* no harm."
Mt 5:17 come to abolish the Law or the *P*;
7:12 for this sums up the Law and the *P*.
24:24 false Christs and false *p* will appear
Lk 24:25 believe all that the *p* have spoken!
Ac 10:43 All the *p* testify about him that
1Co 12:28 second *p*, third teachers, then
14:32 The spirits of *p* are subject
Eph 2:20 foundation of the apostles and *p*,
Heb 1: 1 through the *p* at many times
1Pe 1:10 Concerning this salvation, the *p*,
2Pe 1:19 word of the *p* made more certain,

PROSPER (PROSPERITY PROSPERS)
Pr 28:25 he who trusts in the LORD will *p*.

PROSPERITY (PROSPER)
Ps 73: 3 when I saw the *p* of the wicked.
Pr 13:21 but *p* is the reward of the righteous.

PROSPERS (PROSPER)
Ps 1: 3 Whatever he does *p*.

PROSTITUTE (PROSTITUTES)
1Co 6:15 of Christ and unite them with a *p*?

PROSTITUTES (PROSTITUTE)
Lk 15:30 property with *p* comes home,
1Co 6: 9 male *p* nor homosexual offenders

PROSTRATE
Dt 9:18 again I fell *p* before the LORD

PROTECT (PROTECTS)
Ps 32: 7 you will *p* me from trouble
Pr 2:11 Discretion will *p* you,
Jn 17:11 *p* them by the power of your name

PROTECTS (PROTECT)
1Co 13: 7 It always *p*, always trusts,

PROUD (PRIDE)
Pr 16: 5 The LORD detests all the *p*
Ro 12:16 Do not be *p*, but be willing

1Co 13: 4 it does not boast, it is not *p*.

PROVE
Ac 26:20 *p* their repentance by their deeds.
1Co 4: 2 been given a trust must *p* faithful.

PROVIDE (PROVIDED PROVIDES)
Ge 22: 8 "God himself will *p* the lamb
Isa 43:20 because I *p* water in the desert
1Ti 5: 8 If anyone does not *p*

PROVIDED (PROVIDE)
Jnh 1:17 But the LORD *p* a great fish
4: 6 Then the LORD God *p* a vine
4: 7 dawn the next day God *p* a worm,
4: 8 God *p* a scorching east wind,

PROVIDES (PROVIDE)
1Ti 6:17 who richly *p* us with everything
1Pe 4:11 it with the strength God *p*,

PROVOKED
Ecc 7: 9 Do not be quickly *p* in your spirit,

PRUDENT
Pr 14:15 a *p* man gives thought to his steps.
19:14 but a *p* wife is from the LORD.
Am 5:13 Therefore the *p* man keeps quiet

PRUNING
Isa 2: 4 and their spears into *p* hooks.
Joel 3:10 and your *p* hooks into spears.

PSALMS
Eph 5:19 Speak to one another with *p*,
Col 3:16 and as you sing *p*, hymns

PUBLICLY
Ac 20:20 have taught you *p* and from house
1Ti 5:20 Those who sin are to be rebuked *p*,

PUFFS
1Co 8: 1 Knowledge *p* up, but love builds up

PULLING
2Co 10: 8 building you up rather than *p* you

PUNISH (PUNISHED PUNISHES)
Ex 32:34 I will *p* them for their sin."
Pr 23:13 if you *p* him with the rod, he will
Isa 13:11 I will *p* the world for its evil,
1Pe 2:14 by him to *p* those who do wrong

PUNISHED (PUNISH)
La 3:39 complain when *p* for his sins?
2Th 1: 9 be *p* with everlasting destruction
Heb 10:29 to be *p* who has trampled the Son

PUNISHES (PUNISH)
Heb 12: 6 and he *p* everyone he accepts

PURE (PURIFIES PURIFY PURITY)
2Sa 22:27 to the *p* you show yourself *p*,
Ps 24: 4 who has clean hands and a *p* heart,
51:10 Create in me a *p* heart, O God,
119: 9 can a young man keep his way *p*?
Pr 20: 9 can say, "I have kept my heart *p*;
Isa 52:11 Come out from it and be *p*,
Hab 1:13 Your eyes are too *p* to look on evil;
Mt 5: 8 Blessed are the *p* in heart,
2Co 11: 2 I might present you as a *p* virgin
Php 4: 8 whatever is *p*, whatever is lovely,
1Ti 5:22 Keep yourself *p*.
Tit 1:15 To the *p*, all things are *p*,
2: 5 to be self-controlled and *p*,
Heb 13: 4 and the marriage bed kept *p*,
1Jn 3: 3 him purifies himself, just as he is *p*.

PURGE
Pr 20:30 and beatings *p* the inmost being.

PURIFIES* (PURE)
1Jn 1: 7 of Jesus, his Son, *p* us from all sin.
3: 3 who has this hope in him *p* himself,

PURIFY (PURE)
Tit 2:14 to *p* for himself a people that are
1Jn 1: 9 and *p* us from all unrighteousness.

PURITY (PURE)
2Co 6: 6 in *p*, understanding, patience
1Ti 4:12 in life, in love, in faith and in *p*.

PURPOSE
Pr 19:21 but it is the LORD's *p* that prevails
Isa 55:11 and achieve the *p* for which I sent it
Ro 8:28 have been called according to his *p*.
Php 2: 2 love, being one in spirit and *p*.

PURSES
Lk 12:33 Provide *p* for yourselves that will

PURSUE
Ps 34:14 seek peace and *p* it.
2Ti 2:22 and *p* righteousness, faith,
1Pe 3:11 he must seek peace and *p* it.

QUALITIES (QUALITY)
2Pe 1: 8 For if you possess these *q*

QUALITY (QUALITIES)
1Co 3:13 and the fire will test the *q*

QUARREL (QUARRELSOME)
Pr 15:18 but a patient man calms a *q*.
17:14 Starting a *q* is like breaching a dam;
17:19 He who loves a *q* loves sin;
2Ti 2:24 And the Lord's servant must not *q*;

QUARRELSOME (QUARREL)
Pr 19:13 a *q* wife is like a constant dripping.
1Ti 3: 3 not violent but gentle, not *q*,

QUICK-TEMPERED
Tit 1: 7 not *q*, not given to drunkenness,

QUIET (QUIETNESS)
Ps 23: 2 he leads me beside *q* waters,
Zep 3:17 he will *q* you with his love,
Lk 19:40 he replied, "if they keep *q*,
1Ti 2: 2 we may live peaceful and *q* lives
1Pe 3: 4 beauty of a gentle and *q* spirit,

QUIETNESS (QUIET)
Isa 30:15 in *q* and trust is your strength,
32:17 the effect of righteousness will be *q*
1Ti 2:11 A woman should learn in *q*

QUIVER
Ps 127: 5 whose *q* is full of them.

RACE
Ecc 9:11 The *r* is not to the swift
1Co 9:24 that in a *r* all the runners run,
2Ti 4: 7 I have finished the *r*, I have kept
Heb 12: 1 perseverance the *r* marked out

RACHEL
Daughter of Laban (Ge 29:16); wife of Jacob (Ge 29:28); bore two sons (Ge 30:22-24; 35:16-24; 46:19).

RADIANCE (RADIANT)
Heb 1: 3 The Son is the *r* of God's glory

RADIANT (RADIANCE)
Ex 34:29 he was not aware that his face was *r*
Ps 34: 5 Those who look to him are *r*;
SS 5:10 *Beloved* My lover is *r* and ruddy,
Isa 60: 5 Then you will look and be *r*,
Eph 5:27 her to himself as a *r* church,

RAIN (RAINBOW)
Mt 5:45 and sends *r* on the righteous

RAINBOW (RAIN)
Ge 9:13 I have set my *r* in the clouds,

RAISED (RISE)
Ro 4:25 was *r* to life for our justification.
10: 9 in your heart that God *r* him
1Co 15: 4 that he was *r* on the third day

RAN (RUN)
Jnh 1: 3 But Jonah *r* away from the LORD

RANSOM
Mt 20:28 and to give his life as a *r* for many."
Heb 9:15 as a *r* to set them free

RAVENS
1Ki 17: 6 The *r* brought him bread
Lk 12:24 Consider the *r*: They do not sow

READ (READS)
Jos 8:34 Joshua *r* all the words of the law—
Ne 8: 8 They *r* from the Book of the Law
2Co 3: 2 known and *r* by everybody.

READS (READ)
Rev 1: 3 Blessed is the one who *r* the words

REAL (REALITY)
Jn 6:55 is *r* food and my blood is *r* drink.

REALITY* (REAL)
Col 2:17 the *r*, however, is found in Christ.

REAP (REAPS)
Job 4: 8 and those who sow trouble *r* it.
2Co 9: 6 generously will also *r* generously.

REAPS (REAP)
Gal 6: 7 A man *r* what he sows.

REASON
Isa 1:18 "Come now, let us *r* together,"
1Pe 3:15 to give the *r* for the hope that you

REBEKAH
Sister of Laban, secured as bride for Isaac (Ge 24). Mother of Esau and Jacob (Ge 25:19-26). Taken by Abimelech as sister of Isaac; returned (Ge 26:1-11). Encouraged Jacob to trick Isaac out of blessing (Ge 27:1-17).

REBEL
Mt 10:21 children will *r* against their parents

REBUKE (REBUKED REBUKING)
Pr 9: 8 *r* a wise man and he will love you.
27: 5 Better is open *r*
Lk 17: 3 "If your brother sins, *r* him,
2Ti 4: 2 correct, *r* and encourage—
Rev 3:19 Those whom I love I *r*

REBUKED (REBUKE)
1Ti 5:20 Those who sin are to be *r* publicly,

REBUKING (REBUKE)
2Ti 3:16 *r*, correcting and training

RECEIVE (RECEIVED RECEIVES)
Ac 1: 8 you will *r* power when the Holy
20:35 'It is more blessed to give than to *r*
2Co 6:17 and I will *r* you."
Rev 4:11 to *r* glory and honor and power,

RECEIVED (RECEIVE)
Mt 6: 2 they have *r* their reward in full.
10: 8 Freely you have *r*, freely give.
1Co 11:23 For I *r* from the Lord what I
Col 2: 6 just as you *r* Christ Jesus as Lord,
1Pe 4:10 should use whatever gift he has *r*

RECEIVES (RECEIVE)
Mt 7: 8 everyone who asks *r*; he who seeks
10:40 he who *r* me *r* the one who sent me
Ac 10:43 believes in him *r* forgiveness of sins

RECKONING
Isa 10: 3 What will you do on the day of *r*,

RECOGNIZE (RECOGNIZED)
Mt 7:16 By their fruit you will *r* them.

RECOGNIZED (RECOGNIZE)
Mt 12:33 for a tree is *r* by its fruit.
Ro 7:13 in order that sin might be *r* as sin,

RECOMPENSE
Isa 40:10 and his *r* accompanies him.

RECONCILE (RECONCILED RECONCILIATION)
Eph 2:16 in this one body to *r* both of them

RECONCILED (RECONCILE)
Mt 5:24 First go and be *r* to your brother;
Ro 5:10 we were *r* to him through the death
2Co 5:18 who *r* us to himself through Christ

RECONCILIATION* (RECONCILE)
Ro 5:11 whom we have now received *r*.
11:15 For if their rejection is the *r*
2Co 5:18 and gave us the ministry of *r*:
5:19 committed to us the message of *r*.

RECORD
Ps 130: 3 If you, O LORD, kept a *r* of sins,

RED
Isa 1:18 though they are *r* as crimson,

REDEEM (KINSMAN-REDEEMER REDEEMED REDEEMER REDEMPTION)
2Sa 7:23 on earth that God went out to *r*
Ps 49: 7 No man can *r* the life of another
Gal 4: 5 under law, to *r* those under law,

REDEEMED (REDEEM)
Gal 3:13 Christ *r* us from the curse
1Pe 1:18 or gold that you were *r*

REDEEMER (REDEEM)
Job 19:25 I know that my *R* lives,

REDEMPTION (REDEEM)
Ps 130: 7 and with him is full *r*.
Lk 21:28 because your *r* is drawing near."
Ro 8:23 as sons, the *r* of our bodies.
Eph 1: 7 In him we have *r* through his blood
Col 1:14 in whom we have *r*, the forgiveness
Heb 9:12 having obtained eternal *r*.

REFLECT
2Co 3:18 unveiled faces all *r* the Lord's

REFUGE
Nu 35:11 towns to be your cities of *r*,

Dt 33:27 The eternal God is your *r*,
Ru 2:12 wings you have come to take *r*."
Ps 46: 1 God is our *r* and strength,
91: 2 "He is my *r* and my fortress,

REHOBOAM
Son of Solomon (1Ki 11:43; 1Ch 3:10). Harsh treatment of subjects caused divided kingdom (1Ki 12:1-24; 14:21-31; 2Ch 10-12).

REIGN
Ex 15:18 The LORD will *r*
Ro 6:12 Therefore do not let sin *r*
1Co 15:25 For he must *r* until he has put all
2Ti 2:12 we will also *r* with him.
Rev 20: 6 will *r* with him for a thousand years

REJECTED (REJECTS)
Ps 118:22 The stone the builders *r*
Isa 53: 3 He was despised and *r* by men,
1Ti 4: 4 nothing is to be *r* if it is received
1Pe 2: 4 *r* by men but chosen by God
2: 7 "The stone the builders *r*

REJECTS (REJECTED)
Lk 10:16 but he who *r* me *r* him who sent me
Jn 3:36 whoever *r* the Son will not see life,

REJOICE (JOY)
Ps 2:11 and *r* with trembling.
66: 6 come, let us *r* in him.
118:24 let us *r* and be glad in it.
Pr 5:18 may you *r* in the wife of your youth
Lk 10:20 but *r* that your names are written
15: 6 '*R* with me; I have found my lost
Ro 12:15 Rejoice with those who *r*; mourn
Php 4: 4 *R* in the Lord always.

REJOICES (JOY)
Isa 61:10 my soul *r* in my God.
Lk 1:47 and my spirit *r* in God my Savior,
1Co 12:26 if one part is honored, every part *r*
13: 6 delight in evil but *r* with the truth.

REJOICING (JOY)
Ps 30: 5 but *r* comes in the morning.
Lk 15: 7 in the same way there will be more *r*
Ac 5:41 *r* because they had been counted

RELIABLE
2Ti 2: 2 witnesses entrust to *r* men who will

RELIGION
1Ti 5: 4 all to put their *r* into practice
Jas 1:27 *R* that God our Father accepts

REMAIN (REMAINS)
Nu 33:55 allow to *r* will become barbs
Jn 15: 7 If you *r* in me and my words
Ro 13: 8 Let no debt *r* outstanding,
1Co 13:13 And now these three *r*: faith,
2Ti 2:13 he will *r* faithful,

REMAINS (REMAIN)
Ps 146: 6 the LORD, who *r* faithful forever.
Heb 7: 3 Son of God he *r* a priest forever.

REMEMBER (REMEMBERS REMEMBRANCE)
Ex 20: 8 "*R* the Sabbath day
1Ch 16:12 *R* the wonders he has done,
Ecc 12: 1 *R* your Creator
Jer 31:34 and will *r* their sins no more."
Gal 2:10 we should continue to *r* the poor,
Php 1: 3 I thank my God every time I *r* you.
Heb 8:12 and will *r* their sins no more."

REMEMBERS (REMEMBER)
Ps 103:14 he *r* that we are dust.
111: 5 he *r* his covenant forever.
Isa 43:25 and *r* your sins no more.

REMEMBRANCE (REMEMBER)
1Co 11:24 which is for you; do this in *r* of me

REMIND
Jn 14:26 will *r* you of everything I have said

REMOVED
Ps 30:11 you *r* my sackcloth and clothed me
103:12 so far has he *r* our transgressions
Jn 20: 1 and saw that the stone had been *r*

RENEW (RENEWED RENEWING)
Ps 51:10 and *r* a steadfast spirit within me.
Isa 40:31 will *r* their strength.

RENEWED (RENEW)
Ps 103: 5 that your youth is *r* like the eagle's.
2Co 4:16 yet inwardly we are being *r* day

RENEWING (RENEW)
Ro 12: 2 transformed by the *r* of your mind.

RENOUNCE (RENOUNCES)
Da 4:27 *R* your sins by doing what is right,

RENOUNCES (RENOUNCE)
Pr 28:13 confesses and *r* them finds

RENOWN
Isa 63:12 to gain for himself everlasting *r*,
Jer 32:20 have gained the *r* that is still yours.

REPAID (PAY)
Lk 14:14 you will be *r* at the resurrection
Col 3:25 Anyone who does wrong will be *r*

REPAY (PAY)
Dt 32:35 It is mine to avenge; I will *r*.
Ru 2:12 May the LORD *r* you
Ps 116:12 How can I *r* the LORD
Ro 12:19 "It is mine to avenge; I will *r*,"
1Pe 3: 9 Do not *r* evil with evil

REPENT (REPENTANCE REPENTS)
Job 42: 6 and *r* in dust and ashes."
Jer 15:19 "If you *r*, I will restore you
Mt 4:17 "*R*, for the kingdom of heaven is
Lk 13: 3 unless you *r*, you too will all perish.
Ac 2:38 Peter replied, "*R* and be baptized,
17:30 all people everywhere to *r*.

REPENTANCE (REPENT)
Lk 3: 8 Produce fruit in keeping with *r*.
5:32 call the righteous, but sinners to *r*."
Ac 26:20 and prove their *r* by their deeds.
2Co 7:10 Godly sorrow brings *r* that leads

REPENTS (REPENT)
Lk 15:10 of God over one sinner who *r*."
17: 3 rebuke him, and if he *r*, forgive him

REPROACH
1Ti 3: 2 Now the overseer must be above *r*,

REPUTATION
1Ti 3: 7 also have a good *r* with outsiders,

REQUESTS
Ps 20: 5 May the LORD grant all your *r*.
Php 4: 6 with thanksgiving, present your *r*

REQUIRE
Mic 6: 8 And what does the LORD *r* of you

RESCUE (RESCUES)
Da 6:20 been able to *r* you from the lions?"
2Pe 2: 9 how to *r* godly men from trials

RESCUES (RESCUE)
1Th 1:10 who *r* us from the coming wrath.

RESIST
Jas 4: 7 *R* the devil, and he will flee
1Pe 5: 9 *R* him, standing firm in the faith,

RESOLVED
Ps 17: 3 I have *r* that my mouth will not sin.
Da 1: 8 But Daniel *r* not to defile himself
1Co 2: 2 For I *r* to know nothing while I was

RESPECT (RESPECTABLE)
Lev 19: 3 " 'Each of you must *r* his mother
19:32 show *r* for the elderly and revere
Pr 11:16 A kindhearted woman gains *r*,
Mal 1: 6 where is the *r* due me?" says
1Th 4:12 so that your daily life may win the *r*
5:12 to *r* those who work hard
1Ti 3: 4 children obey him with proper *r*.
1Pe 2:17 Show proper *r* to everyone:
3: 7 them with *r* as the weaker partner

RESPECTABLE* (RESPECT)
1Ti 3: 2 self-controlled, *r*, hospitable,

REST
Ex 31:15 the seventh day is a Sabbath of *r*,
Ps 91: 1 will *r* in the shadow
Jer 6:16 and you will find *r* for your souls.
Mt 11:28 and burdened, and I will give you *r*.

RESTITUTION
Ex 22: 3 "A thief must certainly make *r*,
Lev 6: 5 He must make *r* in full, add a fifth

RESTORE (RESTORES)
Ps 51:12 *R* to me the joy of your salvation
Gal 6: 1 are spiritual should *r* him gently.

RESTORES (RESTORE)
Ps 23: 3 he *r* my soul.

RESURRECTION
Mt 22:30 At the *r* people will neither marry
Lk 14:14 repaid at the *r* of the righteous."
Jn 11:25 Jesus said to her, "I am the *r*
Ro 1: 4 Son of God by his *r* from the dead:
1Co 15:12 some of you say that there is no *r*
Php 3:10 power of his *r* and the fellowship
Rev 20: 5 This is the first *r*.

RETRIBUTION
Jer 51:56 For the LORD is a God of *r*;

RETURN
2Ch 30: 9 If you *r* to the LORD, then your
Ne 1: 9 but if you *r* to me and obey my
Isa 55:11 It will not *r* to me empty,
Hos 6: 1 "Come, let us *r* to the LORD.
Joel 2:12 "*r* to me with all your heart,

REVEALED (REVELATION)
Dt 29:29 but the things *r* belong to us
Isa 40: 5 the glory of the LORD will be *r*,
Mt 11:25 and *r* them to little children.
Ro 1:17 a righteousness from God is *r*,
8:18 with the glory that will be *r* in us.

REVELATION (REVEALED)
Gal 1:12 I received it by *r* from Jesus Christ.
Rev 1: 1 *r* of Jesus Christ, which God gave

REVENGE (VENGEANCE)
Lev 19:18 " 'Do not seek *r* or bear a grudge
Ro 12:19 Do not take *r*, my friends,

REVERE (REVERENCE)
Ps 33: 8 let all the people of the world *r* him

REVERENCE (REVERE)
Lev 19:30 and have *r* for my sanctuary.
Ps 5: 7 in *r* will I bow down
Col 3:22 of heart and *r* for the Lord.
1Pe 3: 2 when they see the purity and *r*

REVIVE (REVIVING)
Ps 85: 6 Will you not *r* us again,
Isa 57:15 to *r* the spirit of the lowly

REVIVING (REVIVE)
Ps 19: 7 *r* the soul.

REWARD (REWARDED)
Ps 19:11 in keeping them there is great *r*.
127: 3 children a *r* from him.
Pr 19:17 he will *r* him for what he has done.
25:22 and the LORD will *r* you.
31:31 Give her the *r* she has earned,
Jer 17:10 to *r* a man according to his conduct
Mt 5:12 because great is your *r* in heaven,
6: 5 they have received their *r* in full.
16:27 and then he will *r* each person
1Co 3:14 built survives, he will receive his *r*.
Rev 22:12 I am coming soon! My *r* is with me

REWARDED (REWARD)
Ru 2:12 May you be richly *r* by the LORD,
Ps 18:24 The LORD has *r* me according
Pr 14:14 and the good man *r* for his.
1Co 3: 8 and each will be *r* according

RICH (RICHES)
Pr 23: 4 Do not wear yourself out to get *r*;
Jer 9:23 or the *r* man boast of his riches,
Mt 19:23 it is hard for a *r* man
2Co 6:10 yet making many *r*; having nothing
8: 9 he was *r*, yet for your sakes he
1Ti 6:17 Command those who are *r*

RICHES (RICH)
Ps 119:14 as one rejoices in great *r*.
Pr 30: 8 give me neither poverty nor *r*,
Isa 10: 3 Where will you leave your *r*?
Ro 9:23 to make the *r* of his glory known
11:33 the depth of the *r* of the wisdom
Eph 2: 7 he might show the incomparable *r*
3: 8 to the Gentiles the unsearchable *r*
Col 1:27 among the Gentiles the glorious *r*

RID
Ge 21:10 "Get *r* of that slave woman
1Co 5: 7 Get *r* of the old yeast that you may
Gal 4:30 "Get *r* of the slave woman

RIGHT (RIGHTS)
Ge 18:25 the Judge of all the earth do *r*?"
Ex 15:26 and do what is *r* in his eyes,
Dt 5:32 do not turn aside to the *r*
Ps 16: 8 Because he is at my *r* hand,
19: 8 The precepts of the LORD are *r*,
63: 8 your *r* hand upholds me.

Ps 110: 1 "Sit at my *r* hand
Pr 4:27 Do not swerve to the *r* or the left;
14:12 There is a way that seems *r*
Isa 1:17 learn to do *r*!
Jer 23: 5 and do what is just and *r* in the land
Hos 14: 9 The ways of the LORD are *r*;
Mt 6: 3 know what your *r* hand is doing,
Jn 1:12 he gave the *r* to become children
Ro 9:21 Does not the potter have the *r*
12:17 careful to do what is *r* in the eyes
Eph 1:20 and seated him at his *r* hand
Php 4: 8 whatever is *r*, whatever is pure,
2Th 3:13 never tire of doing what is *r*.

RIGHTEOUS (RIGHTEOUSNESS)
Ps 34:15 The eyes of the LORD are on the *r*
37:25 yet I have never seen the *r* forsaken
119:137 *R* are you, O LORD,
143: 2 for no one living is *r* before you.
Pr 3:33 but he blesses the home of the *r*.
11:30 The fruit of the *r* is a tree of life,
18:10 the *r* run to it and are safe.
Isa 64: 6 and all our *r* acts are like filthy rags
Hab 2: 4 but the *r* will live by his faith—
Mt 5:45 rain on the *r* and the unrighteous.
9:13 For I have not come to call the *r*,
13:49 and separate the wicked from the *r*
25:46 to eternal punishment, but the *r*
Ro 1:17 as it is written: "The *r* will live
3:10 "There is no one *r*, not even one;
1Ti 1: 9 that law is made not for the *r*
1Pe 3:18 the *r* for the unrighteous,
1Jn 3: 7 does what is right is *r*, just as he is *r*.
Rev 19: 8 stands for the *r* acts of the saints.)

RIGHTEOUSNESS (RIGHTEOUS)
Ge 15: 6 and he credited it to him as *r*.
1Sa 26:23 LORD rewards every man for his *r*
Ps 9: 8 He will judge the world in *r*;
23: 3 He guides me in paths of *r*
45: 7 You love *r* and hate wickedness;
85:10 *r* and peace kiss each other.
89:14 *R* and justice are the foundation
111: 3 and his *r* endures forever.
Pr 14:34 *R* exalts a nation,
21:21 He who pursues *r* and love
Isa 5:16 will show himself holy by his *r*.
59:17 He put on *r* as his breastplate,
Eze 18:20 The *r* of the righteous man will be
Da 9:24 to bring in everlasting *r*,
12: 3 and those who lead many to *r*,
Mal 4: 2 the sun of *r* will rise with healing
Mt 5: 6 those who hunger and thirst for *r*,
5:20 unless your *r* surpasses that
6:33 But seek first his kingdom and his *r*
Ro 4: 3 and it was credited to him as *r*."
4: 9 faith was credited to him as *r*.
6:13 body to him as instruments of *r*.
2Co 5:21 that in him we might become the *r*
Gal 2:21 for if *r* could be gained
3: 6 and it was credited to him as *r*."
Eph 6:14 with the breastplate of *r* in place,
Php 3: 9 not having a *r* of my own that
2Ti 3:16 correcting and training in *r*,
4: 8 is in store for me the crown of *r*,
Heb 11: 7 became heir of the *r* that comes
2Pe 2:21 not to have known the way of *r*,

RIGHTS (RIGHT)
La 3:35 to deny a man his *r*
Gal 4: 5 that we might receive the full *r*

RISE (RAISED)
Isa 26:19 their bodies will *r*.
Mt 27:63 'After three days I will *r* again.'
Jn 5:29 those who have done good will *r*
1Th 4:16 and the dead in Christ will *r* first.

ROAD
Mt 7:13 and broad is the *r* that leads

ROBBERS
Jer 7:11 become a den of *r* to you?
Mk 15:27 They crucified two *r* with him,
Lk 19:46 but you have made it 'a den of *r*.' "
Jn 10: 8 came before me were thieves and *r*,

ROCK
Ps 18: 2 The LORD is my *r*, my fortress
40: 2 he set my feet on a *r*
Mt 7:24 man who built his house on the *r*.
16:18 and on this *r* I will build my church
Ro 9:33 and a *r* that makes them fall,
1Co 10: 4 the spiritual *r* that accompanied

ROD
Ps 23: 4 your *r* and your staff,
Pr 13:24 He who spares the *r* hates his son,
23:13 if you punish him with the *r*,

ROOM (ROOMS)
Mt 6: 6 But when you pray, go into your *r*,
Lk 2: 7 there was no *r* for them in the inn.
Jn 21:25 the whole world would not have *r*

ROOMS (ROOM)
Jn 14: 2 In my Father's house are many *r*;

ROOT
Isa 53: 2 and like a *r* out of dry ground.
1Ti 6:10 of money is a *r* of all kinds of evil.

ROYAL
Jas 2: 8 If you really keep the *r* law found
1Pe 2: 9 a *r* priesthood, a holy nation,

RUBBISH*
Php 3: 8 I consider them *r*, that I may gain

RUDE*
1Co 13: 5 It is not *r*, it is not self-seeking,

RUIN (RUINS)
Pr 18:24 many companions may come to *r*,
1Ti 6: 9 desires that plunge men into *r*

RUINS (RUIN)
Pr 19: 3 A man's own folly *r* his life,
2Ti 2:14 and only *r* those who listen.

RULE (RULER RULERS RULES)
1Sa 12:12 'No, we want a king to *r* over us'—
Ps 2: 9 You will *r* them with an iron
119:133 let no sin *r* over me.
Zec 9:10 His *r* will extend from sea to sea
Col 3:15 the peace of Christ *r* in your hearts,
Rev 2:27 He will *r* them with an iron scepter;

RULER (RULE)
Ps 8: 6 You made him *r* over the works
Eph 2: 2 of the *r* of the kingdom of the air,
1Ti 6:15 God, the blessed and only *R*,

RULERS (RULE)
Ps 2: 2 and the *r* gather together
Col 1:16 or powers or *r* or authorities;

RULES (RULE)
Ps 103:19 and his kingdom *r* over all.
Lk 22:26 one who *r* like the one who serves.
2Ti 2: 5 he competes according to the *r*.

RUMORS
Mt 24: 6 You will hear of wars and *r* of wars,

RUN (RAN)
Isa 40:31 they will *r* and not grow weary,
1Co 9:24 *R* in such a way as to get the prize.
Heb 12: 1 let us *r* with perseverance the race

RUST
Mt 6:19 where moth and *r* destroy,

RUTH*
Moabitess; widow who went to Bethlehem with mother-in-law Naomi (Ru 1). Gleaned in field of Boaz; shown favor (Ru 2). Proposed marriage to Boaz (Ru 3). Married (Ru 4:1-12); bore Obed, ancestor of David (Ru 4:13-22), Jesus (Mt 1:5).

SABBATH
Ex 20: 8 "Remember the *S* day
Dt 5:12 "Observe the *S* day
Col 2:16 a New Moon celebration or a *S* day

SACKCLOTH
Mt 11:21 would have repented long ago in *s*

SACRED
Mt 7: 6 "Do not give dogs what is *s*;
1Co 3:17 for God's temple is *s*, and you are

SACRIFICE (SACRIFICED SACRIFICES)
Ge 22: 2 *S* him there as a burnt offering
Ex 12:27 'It is the Passover *s* to the LORD,
1Sa 15:22 To obey is better than *s*,
Hos 6: 6 For I desire mercy, not *s*,
Mt 9:13 this means: 'I desire mercy, not *s*.'
Heb 9:26 away with sin by the *s* of himself.
13:15 offer to God a *s* of praise—
1Jn 2: 2 He is the atoning *s* for our sins,

SACRIFICED (SACRIFICE)
1Co 5: 7 our Passover lamb, has been *s*.
8: 1 Now about food *s* to idols:
Heb 9:28 so Christ was *s* once

SACRIFICES (SACRIFICE)
Ps 51:17 The *s* of God are a broken spirit;
Ro 12: 1 to offer your bodies as living *s*,

SADDUCEES
Mk 12:18 *S*, who say there is no resurrection,

SAFE (SAVE)
Ps 37: 3 in the land and enjoy *s* pasture.
Pr 18:10 the righteous run to it and are *s*.

SAFETY (SAVE)
Ps 4: 8 make me dwell in *s*.
1Th 5: 3 people are saying, "Peace and *s*,"

SAINTS
Ps 116:15 is the death of his *s*.
Ro 8:27 intercedes for the *s* in accordance
Eph 1:18 of his glorious inheritance in the *s*,
6:18 always keep on praying for all the *s*
Rev 5: 8 which are the prayers of the *s*.
19: 8 for the righteous acts of the *s*.)

SAKE
Ps 44:22 Yet for your *s* we face death all day
Php 3: 7 loss for the *s* of Christ.
Heb 11:26 He regarded disgrace for the *s*

SALT
Ge 19:26 and she became a pillar of *s*.
Mt 5:13 "You are the *s* of the earth.

SALVATION (SAVE)
Ex 15: 2 he has become my *s*.
1Ch 16:23 proclaim his *s* day after day.
Ps 27: 1 The LORD is my light and my *s*—
51:12 Restore to me the joy of your *s*
62: 2 He alone is my rock and my *s*;
85: 9 Surely his *s* is near those who fear
96: 2 proclaim his *s* day after day.
Isa 25: 9 let us rejoice and be glad in his *s*."
45:17 the LORD with an everlasting *s*;
51: 6 But my *s* will last forever,
59:17 and the helmet of *s* on his head;
61:10 me with garments of *s*
Jnh 2: 9 *S* comes from the LORD."
Zec 9: 9 righteous and having *s*,
Lk 2:30 For my eyes have seen your *s*,
Jn 4:22 for *s* is from the Jews.
Ac 4:12 *S* is found in no one else,
13:47 that you may bring *s* to the ends
Ro 11:11 *s* has come to the Gentiles
2Co 7:10 brings repentance that leads to *s*
Eph 6:17 Take the helmet of *s* and the sword
Php 2:12 to work out your *s* with fear
1Th 5: 8 and the hope of *s* as a helmet.
2Ti 3:15 wise for *s* through faith
Heb 2: 3 escape if we ignore such a great *s*?
6: 9 case—things that accompany *s*.
1Pe 1:10 Concerning this *s*, the prophets,
2: 2 by it you may grow up in your *s*,

SAMARITAN
Lk 10:33 But a *S*, as he traveled, came where

SAMSON
Danite judge. Birth promised (Jdg 13). Married to Philistine (Jdg 14). Vengeance on Philistines (Jdg 15). Betrayed by Delilah (Jdg 16:1-22). Death (Jdg 16:23-31). Feats of strength: killed lion (Jdg 14:6), 30 Philistines (Jdg 14:19), 1,000 Philistines with jawbone (Jdg 15:13-17), carried off gates of Gaza (Jdg 16:3), pushed down temple of Dagon (Jdg 16:25-30).

SAMUEL
Ephraimite judge and prophet (Heb 11:32). Birth prayed for (1Sa 1:10-18). Dedicated to temple by Hannah (1Sa 1:21-28). Raised by Eli (1Sa 2:11, 18-26). Called as prophet (1Sa 3). Led Israel to victory over Philistines (1Sa 7). Asked by Israel for a king (1Sa 8). Anointed Saul as king (1Sa 9-10). Farewell speech (1Sa 12). Rebuked Saul for sacrifice (1Sa 13). Announced rejection of Saul (1Sa 15). Anointed David as king (1Sa 16). Protected David from Saul (1Sa 19:18-24). Death (1Sa 25:1). Returned from dead to condemn Saul (1Sa 28).

SANCTIFIED (SANCTIFY)
Ac 20:32 among all those who are *s*.
Ro 15:16 to God, *s* by the Holy Spirit.
1Co 6:11 But you were washed, you were *s*,
7:14 and the unbelieving wife has been *s*
Heb 10:29 blood of the covenant that *s* him,

SANCTIFY (SANCTIFIED SANCTIFYING)
1Th 5:23 *s* you through and through.

SANCTIFYING (SANCTIFY)
2Th 2:13 through the *s* work of the Spirit

SANCTUARY
Ex 25: 8 "Then have them make a *s* for me,

SAND
Ge 22:17 and as the *s* on the seashore.
Mt 7:26 man who built his house on *s.*

SANDALS
Ex 3: 5 off your *s,* for the place where you
Jos 5:15 off your *s,* for the place where you

SANG (SING)
Job 38: 7 while the morning stars *s* together
Rev 5: 9 And they *s* a new song:

SARAH
Wife of Abraham, originally named Sarai; barren (Ge 11:29-31; 1Pe 3:6). Taken by Pharaoh as Abraham's sister; returned (Ge 12:10-20). Gave Hagar to Abraham; sent her away in pregnancy (Ge 16). Name changed; Isaac promised (Ge 17:15-21; 18:10-15; Heb 11:11). Taken by Abimelech as Abraham's sister; returned (Ge 20). Isaac born; Hagar and Ishmael sent away (Ge 21:1-21; Gal 4:21-31). Death (Ge 23).

SATAN
Job 1: 6 and *S* also came with them.
Zec 3: 2 said to *S,* "The LORD rebuke you,
Mk 4:15 *S* comes and takes away the word
2Co 11:14 for *S* himself masquerades
12: 7 a messenger of *S,* to torment me.
Rev 12: 9 serpent called the devil, or *S,*
20: 2 or *S,* and bound him for a thousand
20: 7 *S* will be released from his prison

SATISFIED (SATISFY)
Isa 53:11 he will see the light of life and be *s*

SATISFIES (SATISFY)
Ps 103: 5 who *s* your desires with good things,

SATISFY (SATISFIED SATISFIES)
Isa 55: 2 and your labor on what does not *s?*

SAUL
1. Benjamite; anointed by Samuel as first king of Israel (1Sa 9-10). Defeated Ammonites (1Sa 11). Rebuked for offering sacrifice (1Sa 13:1-15). Defeated Philistines (1Sa 14). Rejected as king for failing to annihilate Amalekites (1Sa 15). Soothed from evil spirit by David (1Sa 16:14-23). Sent David against Goliath (1Sa 17). Jealousy and attempted murder of David (1Sa 18:1-11). Gave David Michal as wife (1Sa 18:12-30). Second attempt to kill David (1Sa 19). Anger at Jonathan (1Sa 20:26-34). Pursued David: killed priests at Nob (1Sa 22), went to Keilah and Ziph (1Sa 23), life spared by David at En Gedi (1Sa 24) and in his tent (1Sa 26). Rebuked by Samuel's spirit for consulting witch at Endor (1Sa 28). Wounded by Philistines; took his own life (1Sa 31; 1Ch 10).
2. See PAUL

SAVE (SAFE SAFETY SALVATION SAVED SAVIOR)
Isa 63: 1 mighty to *s.*"
Da 3:17 the God we serve is able to *s* us
Zep 3:17 he is mighty to *s.*
Mt 1:21 he will *s* his people from their sins
16:25 wants to *s* his life will lose it,
Lk 19:10 to seek and to *s* what was lost."
Jn 3:17 but to *s* the world through him.
1Ti 1:15 came into the world to *s* sinners—
Jas 5:20 of his way will *s* him from death

SAVED (SAVE)
Ps 34: 6 he *s* him out of all his troubles.
Isa 45:22 "Turn to me and be *s,*
Joel 2:32 on the name of the LORD will be *s;*
Mk 13:13 firm to the end will be *s.*
16:16 believes and is baptized will be *s,*
Jn 10: 9 enters through me will be *s.*
Ac 4:12 to men by which we must be *s.*"
16:30 do to be *s?*" They replied,
Ro 9:27 only the remnant will be *s.*
10: 9 him from the dead, you will be *s.*
1Co 3:15 will suffer loss; he himself will be *s,*
15: 2 By this gospel you are *s,*
Eph 2: 5 it is by grace you have been *s.*
2: 8 For it is by grace you have been *s,*
1Ti 2: 4 who wants all men to be *s*

SAVIOR (SAVE)
Ps 89:26 my God, the Rock my *S.*'
Isa 43:11 and apart from me there is no *S.*
Hos 13: 4 no *S* except me.
Lk 1:47 and my spirit rejoices in God my *S,*
2:11 of David a *S* has been born to you;
Jn 4:42 know that this man really is the *S*
Eph 5:23 his body, of which he is the *S.*
1Ti 4:10 who is the *S* of all men,
Tit 2:10 about God our *S* attractive.
2:13 appearing of our great God and *S,*
3: 4 and love of God our *S* appeared,
1Jn 4:14 Son to be the *S* of the world.
Jude :25 to the only God our *S* be glory,

SCALES
Lev 19:36 Use honest *s* and honest weights,
Da 5:27 You have been weighed on the *s*

SCAPEGOAT (GOAT)
Lev 16:10 by sending it into the desert as a *s.*

SCARLET
Isa 1:18 "Though your sins are like *s,*

SCATTERED
Jer 31:10 'He who *s* Israel will gather them
Ac 8: 4 who had been *s* preached the word

SCEPTER
Rev 19:15 "He will rule them with an iron *s.*"

SCHEMES
2Co 2:11 For we are not unaware of his *s.*
Eph 6:11 stand against the devil's *s.*

SCOFFERS
2Pe 3: 3 that in the last days *s* will come,

SCORPION
Rev 9: 5 sting of a *s* when it strikes a man.

SCRIPTURE (SCRIPTURES)
Jn 10:35 and the *S* cannot be broken—
1Ti 4:13 yourself to the public reading of *S,*
2Ti 3:16 All *S* is God-breathed
2Pe 1:20 that no prophecy of *S* came about

SCRIPTURES (SCRIPTURE)
Lk 24:27 said in all the *S* concerning himself.
Jn 5:39 These are the *S* that testify about
Ac 17:11 examined the *S* every day to see

SCROLL
Eze 3: 1 eat what is before you, eat this *s;*

SEA
Ex 14:16 go through the *s* on dry ground.
Isa 57:20 the wicked are like the tossing *s,*
Mic 7:19 iniquities into the depths of the *s.*
Jas 1: 6 who doubts is like a wave of the *s,*
Rev 13: 1 I saw a beast coming out of the *s.*

SEAL (SEALS)
Jn 6:27 God the Father has placed his *s*
2Co 1:22 set his *s* of ownership on us,
Eph 1:13 you were marked in him with a *s,*

SEALS (SEAL)
Rev 5: 2 "Who is worthy to break the *s*
6: 1 opened the first of the seven *s.*

SEARCH (SEARCHED SEARCHES SEARCHING)
Ps 4: 4 *s* your hearts and be silent.
139:23 *S* me, O God, and know my heart;
Pr 2: 4 and *s* for it as for hidden treasure,
Jer 17:10 "I the LORD *s* the heart
Eze 34:16 I will *s* for the lost and bring back
Lk 15: 8 and *s* carefully until she finds it?

SEARCHED (SEARCH)
Ps 139: 1 O LORD, you have *s* me

SEARCHES (SEARCH)
Ro 8:27 And he who *s* our hearts knows
1Co 2:10 The Spirit *s* all things,

SEARCHING (SEARCH)
Am 8:12 *s* for the word of the LORD,

SEARED
1Ti 4: 2 whose consciences have been *s*

SEASON
2Ti 4: 2 be prepared in *s* and out of *s;*

SEAT (SEATED SEATS)
Ps 1: 1 or sit in the *s* of mockers.
Da 7: 9 and the Ancient of Days took his *s.*
2Co 5:10 before the judgment *s* of Christ,

SEATED (SEAT)
Ps 47: 8 God is *s* on his holy throne.
Isa 6: 1 I saw the Lord *s* on a throne,
Col 3: 1 where Christ is *s* at the right hand

SEATS (SEAT)
Lk 11:43 you love the most important *s*

SECRET (SECRETS)
Dt 29:29 The *s* things belong
Jdg 16: 6 Tell me the *s* of your great strength
Ps 90: 8 our *s* sins in the light
Pr 11:13 but a trustworthy man keeps a *s.*
Mt 6: 4 so that your giving may be in *s.*
2Co 4: 2 we have renounced *s* and shameful
Php 4:12 I have learned the *s*

SECRETS (SECRET)
Ps 44:21 since he knows the *s* of the heart?
1Co 14:25 the *s* of his heart will be laid bare.

SECURE (SECURITY)
Ps 112: 8 His heart is *s,* he will have no fear;
Heb 6:19 an anchor for the soul, firm and *s.*

SECURITY (SECURE)
Job 31:24 or said to pure gold, 'You are my *s,*'

SEED (SEEDS)
Lk 8:11 of the parable: The *s* is the word
1Co 3: 6 I planted the *s,* Apollos watered it,
2Co 9:10 he who supplies *s* to the sower
Gal 3:29 then you are Abraham's *s,*
1Pe 1:23 not of perishable *s,*

SEEDS (SEED)
Jn 12:24 But if it dies, it produces many *s.*
Gal 3:16 Scripture does not say "and to *s,*"

SEEK (SEEKS SELF-SEEKING)
Dt 4:29 if from there you *s* the LORD your
1Ch 28: 9 If you *s* him, he will be found
2Ch 7:14 themselves and pray and *s* my face
Ps 119:10 I *s* you with all my heart;
Isa 55: 6 *S* the LORD while he may be
65: 1 found by those who did not *s* me.
Mt 6:33 But *s* first his kingdom
Lk 19:10 For the Son of Man came to *s*
Ro 10:20 found by those who did not *s* me;
1Co 7:27 you married? Do not *s* a divorce.

SEEKS (SEEK)
Jn 4:23 the kind of worshipers the Father *s.*

SEER
1Sa 9: 9 of today used to be called a *s.*)

SELF-CONTROL (CONTROL)
1Co 7: 5 you because of your lack of *s.*
Gal 5:23 faithfulness, gentleness and *s.*
2Pe 1: 6 and to knowledge, *s;* and to *s,*

SELF-CONTROLLED* (CONTROL)
1Th 5: 6 are asleep, but let us be alert and *s.*
5: 8 let us be *s,* putting on faith and love
1Ti 3: 2 *s,* respectable, hospitable,
Tit 1: 8 who is *s,* upright, holy
2: 2 worthy of respect, *s,* and sound
2: 5 to be *s* and pure, to be busy at home
2: 6 encourage the young men to be *s.*
2:12 to live *s,* upright and godly lives
1Pe 1:13 prepare your minds for action; be *s;*
4: 7 and *s* so that you can pray.
5: 8 Be *s* and alert.

SELF-INDULGENCE
Mt 23:25 inside they are full of greed and *s.*

SELF-SEEKING (SEEK)
1Co 13: 5 it is not *s,* it is not easily angered,

SELFISH*
Ps 119:36 and not toward *s* gain.
Pr 18: 1 An unfriendly man pursues *s* ends;
Gal 5:20 fits of rage, *s* ambition, dissensions,
Php 1:17 preach Christ out of *s* ambition,
2: 3 Do nothing out of *s* ambition
Jas 3:14 and *s* ambition in your hearts,
3:16 you have envy and *s* ambition,

SEND (SENDING SENT)
Isa 6: 8 *S* me!" He said, "Go and tell this
Mt 9:38 to *s* out workers into his harvest
Jn 16: 7 but if I go, I will *s* him to you.

SENDING (SEND)
Jn 20:21 Father has sent me, I am *s* you."

SENSES*
Lk 15:17 "When he came to his *s,* he said,
1Co 15:34 Come back to your *s* as you ought,
2Ti 2:26 and that they will come to their *s*

SENSUAL
Col 2:23 value in restraining *s* indulgence.

SENT (SEND)
Isa 55:11 achieve the purpose for which I *s* it.
Mt 10:40 me receives the one who *s* me.
Jn 4:34 "is to do the will of him who *s* me
Ro 10:15 can they preach unless they are *s?*
1Jn 4:10 but that he loved us and *s* his Son

SEPARATE (SEPARATED SEPARATES)
Mt 19: 6 has joined together, let man not *s*."
Ro 8:35 Who shall *s* us from the love
1Co 7:10 wife must not *s* from her husband.
2Co 6:17 and be *s*, says the Lord.

SEPARATED (SEPARATE)
Isa 59: 2 But your iniquities have *s*

SEPARATES (SEPARATE)
Pr 16:28 and a gossip *s* close friends.

SERPENT
Ge 3: 1 the *s* was more crafty than any
Rev 12: 9 that ancient *s* called the devil

SERVANT (SERVANTS)
1Sa 3:10 "Speak, for your *s* is listening."
Mt 20:26 great among you must be your *s*,
25:21 'Well done, good and faithful *s!*
Lk 16:13 "No *s* can serve two masters.
Php 2: 7 taking the very nature of a *s*,
2Ti 2:24 And the Lord's *s* must not quarrel;

SERVANTS (SERVANT)
Lk 17:10 should say, 'We are unworthy *s;*
Jn 15:15 longer call you *s*, because a servant

SERVE (SERVICE SERVING)
Dt 10:12 to *s* the LORD your God
Jos 22: 5 and to *s* him with all your heart
24:15 this day whom you will *s*,
Mt 4:10 Lord your God, and *s* him only.'
6:24 "No one can *s* two masters.
20:28 but to *s*, and to give his life
Eph 6: 7 *S* wholeheartedly,

SERVICE (SERVE)
1Co 12: 5 There are different kinds of *s*,
Eph 4:12 God's people for works of *s*,

SERVING (SERVE)
Ro 12:11 your spiritual fervor, *s* the Lord.
Eph 6: 7 as if you were *s* the Lord, not men,
Col 3:24 It is the Lord Christ you are *s*.
2Ti 2: 4 No one *s* as a soldier gets involved

SEVEN (SEVENTH)
Ge 7: 2 Take with you *s* of every kind
Jos 6: 4 march around the city *s* times,
1Ki 19:18 Yet I reserve *s* thousand in Israel—
Pr 6:16 *s* that are detestable to him:
24:16 a righteous man falls *s* times,
Isa 4: 1 In that day *s* women
Da 9:25 comes, there will be *s* 'sevens,'
Mt 18:21 Up to *s* times?" Jesus answered,
Lk 11:26 takes *s* other spirits more wicked
Ro 11: 4 for myself *s* thousand who have not
Rev 1: 4 To the *s* churches in the province
6: 1 opened the first of the *s* seals.
8: 2 and to them were given *s* trumpets.
10: 4 And when the *s* thunders spoke,
15: 7 to the *s* angels *s* golden bowls filled

SEVENTH (SEVEN)
Ge 2: 2 By the *s* day God had finished
Ex 23:12 but on the *s* day do not work,

SEXUAL (SEXUALLY)
1Co 6:13 body is not meant for *s* immorality,
6:18 Flee from *s* immorality.
10: 8 should not commit *s* immorality,
Eph 5: 3 even a hint of *s* immorality,
1Th 4: 3 that you should avoid *s* immorality

SEXUALLY (SEXUAL)
1Co 5: 9 to associate with *s* immoral people
6:18 he who sins *s* sins against his own

SHADOW
Ps 23: 4 through the valley of the *s* of death,
36: 7 find refuge in the *s* of your wings.
Heb 10: 1 The law is only a *s*

SHALLUM
King of Israel (2Ki 15:10-16).

SHAME (ASHAMED)
Ps 34: 5 their faces are never covered with *s*
Pr 13:18 discipline comes to poverty and *s*,
Heb 12: 2 endured the cross, scorning its *s*,

SHARE (SHARED)
Ge 21:10 that slave woman's son will never *s*
Lk 3:11 "The man with two tunics should *s*
Gal 4:30 the slave woman's son will never *s*
6: 6 in the word must *s* all good things
Eph 4:28 something to *s* with those in need.
1Ti 6:18 and to be generous and willing to *s*.
Heb 12:10 that we may *s* in his holiness.
13:16 to do good and to *s* with others,

SHARED (SHARE)
Heb 2:14 he too *s* in their humanity so that

SHARON
SS 2: 1 I am a rose of *S*,

SHARPER*
Heb 4:12 *S* than any double-edged sword,

SHED (SHEDDING)
Ge 9: 6 by man shall his blood be *s;*
Col 1:20 through his blood, *s* on the cross.

SHEDDING (SHED)
Heb 9:22 without the *s* of blood there is no

SHEEP
Ps 100: 3 we are his people, the *s*
119:176 I have strayed like a lost *s*.
Isa 53: 6 We all, like *s*, have gone astray,
Jer 50: 6 "My people have been lost *s;*
Eze 34:11 I myself will search for my *s*
Mt 9:36 helpless, like *s* without a shepherd.
Jn 10: 3 He calls his own *s* by name
10:15 and I lay down my life for the *s*.
10:27 My *s* listen to my voice; I know
21:17 Jesus said, "Feed my *s*.
1Pe 2:25 For you were like *s* going astray,

SHELTER
Ps 61: 4 take refuge in the *s* of your wings.
91: 1 in the *s* of the Most High

SHEM
Son of Noah (Ge 5:32; 6:10). Blessed (Ge 9:26). Descendants (Ge 10:21-31; 11:10-32).

SHEPHERD (SHEPHERDS)
Ps 23: 1 LORD is my *s*, I shall not be in want.
Isa 40:11 He tends his flock like a *s:*
Jer 31:10 will watch over his flock like a *s*.'
Eze 34:12 As a *s* looks after his scattered
Zec 11:17 "Woe to the worthless *s*,
Mt 9:36 and helpless, like sheep without a *s*.
Jn 10:11 The good *s* lays down his life
10:16 there shall be one flock and one *s*.
1Pe 5: 4 And when the Chief *S* appears,

SHEPHERDS (SHEPHERD)
Jer 23: 1 "Woe to the *s* who are destroying
Lk 2: 8 there were *s* living out in the fields
Ac 20:28 Be *s* of the church of God,
1Pe 5: 2 Be *s* of God's flock that is

SHIELD
Ps 28: 7 LORD is my strength and my *s;*
Eph 6:16 to all this, take up the *s* of faith,

SHINE (SHONE)
Ps 4: 6 Let the light of your face *s* upon us,
80: 1 between the cherubim, *s* forth
Isa 60: 1 "Arise, *s*, for your light has come,
Da 12: 3 are wise will *s* like the brightness
Mt 5:16 let your light *s* before men,
13:43 the righteous will *s* like the sun
2Co 4: 6 made his light *s* in our hearts
Eph 5:14 and Christ will *s* on you."

SHIPWRECKED*
2Co 11:25 I was stoned, three times I was *s*,
1Ti 1:19 and so have *s* their faith.

SHONE (SHINE)
Mt 17: 2 His face *s* like the sun,
Lk 2: 9 glory of the Lord *s* around them,
Rev 21:11 It *s* with the glory of God,

SHORT
Isa 59: 1 of the LORD is not too *s* to save,
Ro 3:23 and fall *s* of the glory of God,

SHOULDERS
Isa 9: 6 and the government will be on his *s*
Lk 15: 5 he joyfully puts it on his *s*

SHOWED
1Jn 4: 9 This is how God *s* his love

SHREWD
Mt 10:16 Therefore be as *s* as snakes and

SHUN*
Job 28:28 and to *s* evil is understanding.' "
Pr 3: 7 fear the LORD and *s* evil.

SICK
Pr 13:12 Hope deferred makes the heart *s*,
Mt 9:12 who need a doctor, but the *s*.
25:36 I was *s* and you looked after me,
Jas 5:14 of you *s?* He should call the elders

SICKLE
Joel 3:13 Swing the *s*,

SIDE
Ps 91: 7 A thousand may fall at your *s*,
124: 1 If the LORD had not been on our *s*
2Ti 4:17 But the Lord stood at my *s*

SIGHT
Ps 90: 4 For a thousand years in your *s*
116:15 Precious in the *s* of the LORD
2Co 5: 7 We live by faith, not by *s*.
1Pe 3: 4 which is of great worth in God's *s*.

SIGN (SIGNS)
Isa 7:14 the Lord himself will give you a *s:*

SIGNS (SIGN)
Mk 16:17 these *s* will accompany those who
Jn 20:30 Jesus did many other miraculous *s*

SILENT
Pr 17:28 a fool is thought wise if he keeps *s*,
Isa 53: 7 as a sheep before her shearers is *s*,
Hab 2:20 let all the earth be *s* before him."
1Co 14:34 women should remain *s*
1Ti 2:12 over a man; she must be *s*.

SILVER
Pr 25:11 is like apples of gold in settings of *s*.
Hag 2: 8 'The *s* is mine and the gold is mine,'
1Co 3:12 *s*, costly stones, wood, hay or straw

SIMON
1. See PETER
2. Apostle, called the Zealot (Mt 10:4; Mk 3:18; Lk 6:15; Ac 1:13).
3. Samaritan sorcerer (Ac 8:9-24).

SIN (SINFUL SINNED SINNER SINNERS SINNING SINS)
Nu 5: 7 and must confess the *s* he has
32:23 be sure that your *s* will find you
Dt 24:16 each is to die for his own *s*.
1Ki 8:46 for there is no one who does not *s*
2Ch 7:14 and will forgive their *s* and will heal
Ps 4: 4 In your anger do not *s;*
32: 2 whose *s* the LORD does not count
32: 5 Then I acknowledged my *s* to you
51: 2 and cleanse me from my *s*.
66:18 If I had cherished *s* in my heart,
119:11 that I might not *s* against you.
119:133 let no *s* rule over me.
Isa 6: 7 is taken away and your *s* atoned
Mic 7:18 who pardons *s* and forgives
Mt 18: 6 little ones who believe in me to *s*,
Jn 1:29 who takes away the *s* of the world!
8:34 everyone who sins is a slave to *s*.
Ro 5:12 as *s* entered the world
5:20 where *s* increased, grace increased
6:11 count yourselves dead to *s*
6:23 For the wages of *s* is death,
14:23 that does not come from faith is *s*.
2Co 5:21 God made him who had no *s* to be *s*
Gal 6: 1 if someone is caught in a *s*,
Heb 9:26 to do away with *s* by the sacrifice
11:25 the pleasures of *s* for a short time.
12: 1 and the *s* that so easily entangles,
1Pe 2:22 "He committed no *s*,
1Jn 1: 8 If we claim to be without *s*,
3: 4 in fact, *s* is lawlessness.
3: 5 And in him is no *s*.
3: 9 born of God will continue to *s*,
5:18 born of God does not continue to *s;*

SINCERE
Ro 12: 9 Love must be *s*.
Heb 10:22 near to God with a *s* heart

SINFUL (SIN)
Ps 51: 5 Surely I was *s* at birth
51: 5 *s* from the time my mother
Ro 7: 5 we were controlled by the *s* nature,
8: 4 not live according to the *s* nature
8: 9 are controlled not by the *s* nature
Gal 5:19 The acts of the *s* nature are obvious
5:24 Jesus have crucified the *s* nature
1Pe 2:11 abstain from *s* desires, which war

SING (SANG SINGING SONG SONGS)
Ps 30: 4 *S* to the LORD, you saints of his;
47: 6 *S* praises to God, *s* praises;
59:16 But I will *s* of your strength,
89: 1 I will *s* of the LORD's great love
101: 1 I will *s* of your love and justice;
Eph 5:19 *S* and make music in your heart

SINGING (SING)
Ps 63: 5 with *s* lips my mouth will praise
Ac 16:25 Silas were praying and *s* hymns

SINNED (SIN)
2Sa 12:13 "I have *s* against the LORD."
Job 1: 5 "Perhaps my children have *s*
Ps 51: 4 Against you, you only, have I *s*
Da 9: 5 we have *s* and done wrong.
Mic 7: 9 Because I have *s* against him,
Lk 15:18 I have *s* against heaven
Ro 3:23 for all have *s* and fall short
1Jn 1:10 claim we have not *s*, we make him

SINNER (SIN)
Ecc 9:18 but one *s* destroys much good.
Lk 15: 7 in heaven over one *s* who repents
18:13 'God, have mercy on me, a *s*.'
1Co 14:24 convinced by all that he is a *s*
Jas 5:20 Whoever turns a *s* from the error
1Pe 4:18 become of the ungodly and the *s*?"

SINNERS (SIN)
Ps 1: 1 or stand in the way of *s*
Pr 23:17 Do not let your heart envy *s*,
Mt 9:13 come to call the righteous, but *s*."
Ro 5: 8 While we were still *s*, Christ died
1Ti 1:15 came into the world to save *s*—

SINNING (SIN)
Ex 20:20 be with you to keep you from *s*."
1Co 15:34 stop *s*; for there are some who are
Heb 10:26 If we deliberately keep on *s*
1Jn 3: 6 No one who lives in him keeps on *s*
3: 9 go on *s*, because he has been born

SINS (SIN)
2Ki 14: 6 each is to die for his own *s*."
Ezr 9: 6 our *s* are higher than our heads
Ps 19:13 your servant also from willful *s*;
32: 1 whose *s* are covered.
103: 3 who forgives all your *s*
130: 3 O LORD, kept a record of *s*,
Pr 28:13 who conceals his *s* does not
Isa 1:18 "Though your *s* are like scarlet,
43:25 and remembers your *s* no more.
59: 2 your *s* have hidden his face
Eze 18: 4 soul who *s* is the one who will die.
Mt 1:21 he will save his people from their *s*
18:15 "If your brother *s* against you,
Lk 11: 4 Forgive us our *s*,
17: 3 "If your brother *s*, rebuke him,
Ac 22:16 be baptized and wash your *s* away,
1Co 15: 3 died for our *s* according
Eph 2: 1 dead in your transgressions and *s*,
Col 2:13 us all our *s*, having canceled
Heb 1: 3 he had provided purification for *s*,
7:27 He sacrificed for their *s* once for all
8:12 and will remember their *s* no more
10:12 for all time one sacrifice for *s*,
Jas 4:17 ought to do and doesn't do it, *s*.
5:16 Therefore confess your *s*
5:20 and cover over a multitude of *s*.
1Pe 2:24 He himself bore our *s* in his body
3:18 For Christ died for *s* once for all,
1Jn 1: 9 If we confess our *s*, he is faithful
Rev 1: 5 has freed us from our *s* by his blood

SITS
Ps 99: 1 *s* enthroned between the cherubim,
Isa 40:22 He *s* enthroned above the circle
Mt 19:28 of Man *s* on his glorious throne,
Rev 4: 9 thanks to him who *s* on the throne

SKIN
Job 19:20 with only the *s* of my teeth.
19:26 And after my *s* has been destroyed,
Jer 13:23 Can the Ethiopian change his *s*

SLAIN (SLAY)
Rev 5:12 "Worthy is the Lamb, who was *s*,

SLANDER (SLANDERED SLANDERERS)
Lev 19:16 " 'Do not go about spreading *s*
1Ti 5:14 the enemy no opportunity for *s*.
Tit 3: 2 to *s* no one, to be peaceable

SLANDERED (SLANDER)
1Co 4:13 when we are *s*, we answer kindly.

SLANDERERS (SLANDER)
Ro 1:30 They are gossips, *s*, God-haters,
1Co 6:10 nor the greedy nor drunkards nor *s*
Tit 2: 3 not to be *s* or addicted

SLAUGHTER
Isa 53: 7 he was led like a lamb to the *s*,

SLAVE (SLAVERY SLAVES)
Ge 21:10 "Get rid of that *s* woman
Mt 20:27 wants to be first must be your *s*—
Jn 8:34 everyone who sins is a *s* to sin.
1Co 12:13 whether Jews or Greeks, *s* or free
Gal 3:28 *s* nor free, male nor female,
4:30 Get rid of the *s* woman and her son
2Pe 2:19 a man is a *s* to whatever has

SLAVERY (SLAVE)
Ro 6:19 parts of your body in *s* to impurity
Gal 4: 3 were in *s* under the basic principles

SLAVES (SLAVE)
Ro 6: 6 that we should no longer be *s* to sin
6:22 and have become *s* to God,

SLAY (SLAIN)
Job 13:15 Though he *s* me, yet will I hope

SLEEP (SLEEPING)
Ps 121: 4 will neither slumber nor *s*.
1Co 15:51 We will not all *s*, but we will all be

SLEEPING (SLEEP)
Mk 13:36 suddenly, do not let him find you *s*.

SLOW
Ex 34: 6 and gracious God, *s* to anger,
Jas 1:19 *s* to speak and *s* to become angry,
2Pe 3: 9 The Lord is not *s* in keeping his

SLUGGARD
Pr 6: 6 Go to the ant, you *s*;
20: 4 A *s* does not plow in season;

SLUMBER
Ps 121: 3 he who watches over you will not *s*;
Pr 6:10 A little sleep, a little *s*,
Ro 13:11 for you to wake up from your *s*,

SNAKE (SNAKES)
Nu 21: 8 "Make a *s* and put it up on a pole;
Pr 23:32 In the end it bites like a *s*
Jn 3:14 Moses lifted up the *s* in the desert,

SNAKES (SNAKE)
Mt 10:16 as shrewd as *s* and as innocent
Mk 16:18 they will pick up *s* with their hands;

SNATCH
Jn 10:28 no one can *s* them out of my hand.
Jude :23 *s* others from the fire and save

SNOW
Ps 51: 7 and I will be whiter than *s*.

SOAR
Isa 40:31 They will *s* on wings like eagles;

SODOM
Ge 19:24 rained down burning sulfur on *S*
Ro 9:29 we would have become like *S*,

SOIL
Ge 4: 2 kept flocks, and Cain worked the *s*.
Mt 13:23 on good *s* is the man who hears

SOLDIER
1Co 9: 7 as a *s* at his own expense?
2Ti 2: 3 with us like a good *s* of Christ Jesus

SOLE
Dt 28:65 place for the *s* of your foot.
Isa 1: 6 From the *s* of your foot to the top

SOLID
2Ti 2:19 God's *s* foundation stands firm,
Heb 5:12 You need milk, not *s* food!

SOLOMON
Son of David by Bathsheba; king of Judah (2Sa 12:24; 1Ch 3:5, 10). Appointed king by David (1Ki 1); adversaries Adonijah, Joab, Shimei killed by Benaiah (1Ki 2). Asked for wisdom (1Ki 3; 2Ch 1). Judged between two prostitutes (1Ki 3:16-28). Built temple (1Ki 5-7; 2Ch 2-5); prayer of dedication (1Ki 8; 2Ch 6). Visited by Queen of Sheba (1Ki 10; 2Ch 9). Wives turned his heart from God (1Ki 11:1-13). Jeroboam rebelled against (1Ki 11:26-40). Death (1Ki 11:41-43; 2Ch 9:29-31).

Proverbs of (1Ki 4:32; Pr 1:1; 10:1; 25:1); psalms of (Ps 72; 127); song of (SS 1:1).

SON (SONS)
Ge 22: 2 "Take your *s*, your only *s*, Isaac,
Ex 11: 5 Every firstborn *s* in Egypt will die,
Dt 21:18 rebellious *s* who does not obey his
Ps 2: 7 He said to me, "You are my *S*;
2:12 Kiss the *S*, lest he be angry
Pr 10: 1 A wise *s* brings joy to his father,
13:24 He who spares the rod hates his *s*,
29:17 Discipline your *s*, and he will give
Isa 7:14 with child and will give birth to a *s*,
Hos 11: 1 and out of Egypt I called my *s*.
Mt 2:15 "Out of Egypt I called my *s*."
3:17 "This is my *S*, whom I love;
11:27 one knows the *S* except the Father,
16:16 "You are the Christ, the *S*
17: 5 "This is my *S*, whom I love;
20:18 and the *S* of Man will be betrayed
24:30 They will see the *S* of Man coming
24:44 the *S* of Man will come at an hour
27:54 "Surely he was the *S* of God!"
28:19 and of the *S* and of the Holy Spirit,
Mk 10:45 even the *S* of Man did not come
14:62 you will see the *S* of Man sitting
Lk 9:58 but the *S* of Man has no place
18: 8 when the *S* of Man comes,
19:10 For the *S* of Man came to seek
Jn 3:14 so the *S* of Man must be lifted up,
3:16 that he gave his one and only *S*,
17: 1 Glorify your *S*, that your *S* may
Ro 8:29 conformed to the likeness of his *S*,
8:32 He who did not spare his own *S*,
1Co 15:28 then the *S* himself will be made
Gal 4:30 rid of the slave woman and her *s*,
1Th 1:10 and to wait for his *S* from heaven,
Heb 1: 2 days he has spoken to us by his *S*,
10:29 punished who has trampled the *S*
1Jn 1: 7 his *S*, purifies us from all sin.
4: 9 only *S* into the world that we might
5: 5 he who believes that Jesus is the *S*
5:11 eternal life, and this life is in his *S*.

SONG (SING)
Ps 40: 3 He put a new *s* in my mouth,
96: 1 Sing to the LORD a new *s*;
149: 1 Sing to the LORD a new *s*,
Isa 49:13 burst into *s*, O mountains!
55:12 will burst into *s* before you,
Rev 5: 9 And they sang a new *s*:
15: 3 and sang the *s* of Moses the servant

SONGS (SING)
Job 35:10 who gives *s* in the night,
Ps 100: 2 come before him with joyful *s*.
Eph 5:19 with psalms, hymns and spiritual *s*.
Jas 5:13 Is anyone happy? Let him sing *s*

SONS (SON)
Joel 2:28 Your *s* and daughters will prophesy
Jn 12:36 so that you may become *s* of light."
Ro 8:14 by the Spirit of God are *s* of God.
2Co 6:18 and you will be my *s* and daughters
Gal 4: 5 we might receive the full rights of *s*.
Heb 12: 7 discipline; God is treating you as *s*.

SORROW (SORROWS)
Jer 31:12 and they will *s* no more.
Ro 9: 2 I have great *s* and unceasing
2Co 7:10 Godly *s* brings repentance that

SORROWS (SORROW)
Isa 53: 3 a man of *s*, and familiar

SOUL (SOULS)
Dt 6: 5 with all your *s* and with all your
10:12 all your heart and with all your *s*,
Jos 22: 5 with all your heart and all your *s*."
Ps 23: 3 he restores my *s*.
42: 1 so my *s* pants for you, O God.
42:11 Why are you downcast, O my *s*?
103: 1 Praise the LORD, O my *s*;
Pr 13:19 A longing fulfilled is sweet to the *s*,
Isa 55: 2 your *s* will delight in the richest
Mt 10:28 kill the body but cannot kill the *s*.
16:26 yet forfeits his *s*? Or what can
22:37 with all your *s* and with all your
Heb 4:12 even to dividing *s* and spirit,

SOULS (SOUL)
Pr 11:30 and he who wins *s* is wise.
Jer 6:16 and you will find rest for your *s*.
Mt 11:29 and you will find rest for your *s*.

SOUND
1Co 14: 8 if the trumpet does not *s* a clear call
15:52 the trumpet will *s*, the dead will
2Ti 4: 3 men will not put up with *s* doctrine.

SOVEREIGN
Da 4:25 that the Most High is *s*

SOW (SOWS)
Job 4: 8 and those who *s* trouble reap it.
Mt 6:26 they do not *s* or reap or store away
2Pe 2:22 and, "A *s* that is washed goes back

SOWS (SOW)
Pr 11:18 he who *s* righteousness reaps a sure
22: 8 He who *s* wickedness reaps trouble
2Co 9: 6 Whoever *s* sparingly will
Gal 6: 7 A man reaps what he *s*.

SPARE (SPARES)
Ro 8:32 He who did not *s* his own Son,
11:21 natural branches, he will not *s* you

SPARES (SPARE)
Pr 13:24 He who *s* the rod hates his son,

SPEARS
Isa 2: 4 and their *s* into pruning hooks.
Joel 3:10 and your pruning hooks into *s*.
Mic 4: 3 and their *s* into pruning hooks.

SPECTACLE
1Co 4: 9 We have been made a *s*
Col 2:15 he made a public *s* of them,

SPIN
Mt 6:28 They do not labor or *s*.

SPIRIT (SPIRIT'S SPIRITS SPIRITUAL SPIRITUALLY)
Ge 1: 2 and the *S* of God was hovering
6: 3 "My *S* will not contend
2Ki 2: 9 inherit a double portion of your *s*,"
Job 33: 4 The *S* of God has made me;
Ps 31: 5 Into your hands I commit my *s*;
51:10 and renew a steadfast *s* within me.
51:11 or take your Holy *S* from me
51:17 sacrifices of God are a broken *s*;
139: 7 Where can I go from your *S*?
Isa 57:15 him who is contrite and lowly in *s*,
63:10 and grieved his Holy *S*.
Eze 11:19 an undivided heart and put a new *s*
36:26 you a new heart and put a new *s*
Joel 2:28 I will pour out my *S* on all people.
Zec 4: 6 but by my *S*,' says the LORD
Mt 1:18 to be with child through the Holy *S*
3:11 will baptize you with the Holy *S*
3:16 he saw the *S* of God descending
4: 1 led by the *S* into the desert
5: 3 saying: "Blessed are the poor in *s*,
26:41 *s* is willing, but the body is weak."
28:19 and of the Son and of the Holy *S*,
Lk 1:80 child grew and became strong in *s*;
11:13 Father in heaven give the Holy *S*
Jn 4:24 God is *s*, and his worshipers must
7:39 Up to that time the *S* had not been
14:26 But the Counselor, the Holy *S*,
16:13 But when he, the *S* of truth, comes,
20:22 and said, "Receive the Holy *S*.
Ac 1: 5 will be baptized with the Holy *S*."
2: 4 of them were filled with the Holy *S*
2:38 will receive the gift of the Holy *S*.
6: 3 who are known to be full of the *S*
19: 2 "Did you receive the Holy *S*
Ro 8: 9 And if anyone does not have the *S*
8:26 the *S* helps us in our weakness.
1Co 2:10 God has revealed it to us by his *S*.
2:14 man without the *S* does not accept
6:19 body is a temple of the Holy *S*,
12:13 baptized by one *S* into one body—
2Co 3: 6 the letter kills, but the *S* gives life.
5: 5 and has given us the *S* as a deposit,
Gal 5:16 by the *S*, and you will not gratify
5:22 But the fruit of the *S* is love, joy,
5:25 let us keep in step with the *S*.
Eph 1:13 with a seal, the promised Holy *S*,
4:30 do not grieve the Holy *S* of God,
5:18 Instead, be filled with the *S*.
6:17 of salvation and the sword of the *S*,
2Th 2:13 the sanctifying work of the *S*
Heb 4:12 even to dividing soul and *s*,
1Pe 3: 4 beauty of a gentle and quiet *s*,
2Pe 1:21 carried along by the Holy *S*.
1Jn 4: 1 Dear friends, do not believe every *s*

SPIRIT'S (SPIRIT)
1Th 5:19 not put out the *S* fire; do not treat

SPIRITS (SPIRIT)
1Co 12:10 to another distinguishing between *s*,
14:32 The *s* of prophets are subject
1Jn 4: 1 test the *s* to see whether they are

SPIRITUAL (SPIRIT)
Ro 12: 1 this is your *s* act of worship.
12:11 but keep your *s* fervor, serving
1Co 2:13 expressing *s* truths in *s* words.
3: 1 I could not address you as *s* but
12: 1 Now about *s* gifts, brothers,
14: 1 of love and eagerly desire *s* gifts,
15:44 a natural body, it is raised a *s* body.
Gal 6: 1 you who are *s* should restore him
Eph 1: 3 with every *s* blessing in Christ.
5:19 with psalms, hymns and *s* songs.
6:12 and against the *s* forces of evil
1Pe 2: 2 newborn babies, crave pure *s* milk,
2: 5 are being built into a *s* house

SPIRITUALLY (SPIRIT)
1Co 2:14 because they are *s* discerned.

SPLENDOR
1Ch 16:29 the LORD in the *s* of his holiness.
29:11 the glory and the majesty and the *s*,
Job 37:22 of the north he comes in golden *s*;
Ps 29: 2 in the *s* of his holiness.
45: 3 clothe yourself with *s* and majesty.
96: 6 *S* and majesty are before him;
96: 9 in the *s* of his holiness;
104: 1 you are clothed with *s* and majesty.
145: 5 of the glorious *s* of your majesty,
Isa 61: 3 the LORD for the display of his *s*.
63: 1 Who is this, robed in *s*,
Lk 9:31 appeared in glorious *s*, talking
2Th 2: 8 and destroy by the *s* of his coming.

SPOIL
Ps 119:162 like one who finds great *s*.

SPOTLESS
2Pe 3:14 make every effort to be found *s*,

SPREAD (SPREADING)
Ac 12:24 of God continued to increase and *s*.
19:20 the word of the Lord *s* widely

SPREADING (SPREAD)
1Th 3: 2 God's fellow worker in *s* the gospel

SPRING
Jer 2:13 the *s* of living water,
Jn 4:14 in him a *s* of water welling up
Jas 3:12 can a salt *s* produce fresh water.

SPUR*
Heb 10:24 how we may *s* one another

SPURNS*
Pr 15: 5 A fool *s* his father's discipline,

STAFF
Ps 23: 4 your rod and your *s*,

STAKES
Isa 54: 2 strengthen your *s*.

STAND (STANDING STANDS)
Ex 14:13 *S* firm and you will see
2Ch 20:17 *s* firm and see the deliverance
Ps 1: 5 Therefore the wicked will not *s*
40: 2 and gave me a firm place to *s*.
119:120 I *s* in awe of your laws.
Eze 22:30 *s* before me in the gap on behalf
Zec 14: 4 On that day his feet will *s*
Mt 12:25 divided against itself will not *s*.
Ro 14:10 we will all *s* before God's judgment
1Co 10:13 out so that you can *s* up under it.
15:58 Therefore, my dear brothers, *s* firm
Eph 6:14 *S* firm then, with the belt
2Th 2:15 *s* firm and hold to the teachings we
Jas 5: 8 You too, be patient and *s* firm,
Rev 3:20 Here I am! I *s* at the door

STANDING (STAND)
Ex 3: 5 where you are *s* is holy ground."
Jos 5:15 the place where you are *s* is holy."
1Pe 5: 9 Resist him, *s* firm in the faith,

STANDS (STAND)
Ps 89: 2 that your love *s* firm forever,
119:89 it *s* firm in the heavens.
Mt 10:22 but he who *s* firm to the end will be
2Ti 2:19 God's solid foundation *s* firm,
1Pe 1:25 but the word of the Lord *s* forever

STAR (STARS)
Nu 24:17 A *s* will come out of Jacob;
Rev 22:16 and the bright Morning *S*."

STARS (STAR)
Da 12: 3 like the *s* for ever and ever.
Php 2:15 in which you shine like *s*

STATURE
Lk 2:52 And Jesus grew in wisdom and *s*,

STEADFAST
Ps 51:10 and renew a *s* spirit within me.
Isa 26: 3 him whose mind is *s*,
1Pe 5:10 and make you strong, firm and *s*.

STEAL
Ex 20:15 "You shall not *s*.
Mt 19:18 do not *s*, do not give false
Eph 4:28 has been stealing must *s* no longer,

STEP (STEPS)
Gal 5:25 let us keep in *s* with the Spirit.

STEPS (STEP)
Pr 16: 9 but the LORD determines his *s*.
Jer 10:23 it is not for man to direct his *s*.
1Pe 2:21 that you should follow in his *s*.

STICKS
Pr 18:24 there is a friend who *s* closer

STIFF-NECKED
Ex 34: 9 Although this is a *s* people,

STILL
Ps 46:10 "Be *s*, and know that I am God;
Zec 2:13 Be *s* before the LORD, all mankind

STIRS
Pr 6:19 and a man who *s* up dissension
10:12 Hatred *s* up dissension,
15: 1 but a harsh word *s* up anger.
15:18 hot-tempered man *s* up dissension,
16:28 A perverse man *s* up dissension,
28:25 A greedy man *s* up dissension,
29:22 An angry man *s* up dissension,

STONE (CAPSTONE CORNERSTONE MILLSTONE)
1Sa 17:50 the Philistine with a sling and a *s*;
Isa 8:14 a *s* that causes men to stumble
Eze 11:19 remove from them their heart of *s*
Mk 16: 3 "Who will roll the *s* away
Lk 4: 3 tell this *s* to become bread."
Jn 8: 7 the first to throw a *s* at her."
2Co 3: 3 not on tablets of *s* but on tablets

STOOP
2Sa 22:36 you *s* down to make me great.

STORE
Pr 10:14 Wise men *s* up knowledge,
Mt 6:19 not *s* up for yourselves treasures

STOREHOUSE (HOUSE)
Mal 3:10 Bring the whole tithe into the *s*,

STRAIGHT
Pr 3: 6 and he will make your paths *s*.
4:25 Let your eyes look *s* ahead,
15:21 of understanding keeps a *s* course.
Jn 1:23 'Make *s* the way for the Lord.'"

STRAIN
Mt 23:24 You *s* out a gnat but swallow

STRANGER (STRANGERS)
Mt 25:35 I was a *s* and you invited me in,
Jn 10: 5 But they will never follow a *s*;

STRANGERS (STRANGER)
1Pe 2:11 as aliens and *s* in the world,

STREAMS
Ps 1: 3 He is like a tree planted by *s*
46: 4 is a river whose *s* make glad
Ecc 1: 7 All *s* flow into the sea,
Jn 7:38 *s* of living water will flow

STRENGTH (STRONG)
Ex 15: 2 The LORD is my *s* and my song;
Dt 6: 5 all your soul and with all your *s*.
2Sa 22:33 It is God who arms me with *s*
Ne 8:10 for the joy of the LORD is your *s*."
Ps 28: 7 The LORD is my *s* and my shield;
46: 1 God is our refuge and *s*,
96: 7 ascribe to the LORD glory and *s*.
118:14 The LORD is my *s* and my song;
147:10 not in the *s* of the horse,
Isa 40:31 will renew their *s*.
Mk 12:30 all your mind and with all your *s*.'
1Co 1:25 of God is stronger than man's *s*.
Php 4:13 through him who gives me *s*.
1Pe 4:11 it with the *s* God provides,

STRENGTHEN (STRONG)
2Ch 16: 9 to *s* those whose hearts are fully
Ps 119:28 *s* me according to your word.

Isa 35: 3 *S* the feeble hands,
41:10 I will *s* you and help you;
Eph 3:16 of his glorious riches he may *s* you
2Th 2:17 and *s* you in every good deed
Heb 12:12 *s* your feeble arms and weak knees.

STRENGTHENING (STRONG)
1Co 14:26 done for the *s* of the church.

STRIFE
Pr 20: 3 It is to a man's honor to avoid *s,*
22:10 out the mocker, and out goes *s;*

STRIKE (STRIKES)
Ge 3:15 and you will *s* his heel."
Zec 13: 7 "*S* the shepherd,
Mt 26:31 " 'I will *s* the shepherd,

STRIKES (STRIKE)
Mt 5:39 If someone *s* you on the right

STRONG (STRENGTH STRENGTHEN STRENGTHENING)
Dt 31: 6 Be *s* and courageous.
1Ki 2: 2 "So be *s,* show yourself a man,
Pr 18:10 The name of the LORD is a *s* tower
31:17 her arms are *s* for her tasks.
SS 8: 6 for love is as *s* as death,
Lk 2:40 And the child grew and became *s;*
Ro 15: 1 We who are *s* ought to bear
1Co 1:27 things of the world to shame the *s.*
16:13 in the faith; be men of courage; be *s*
2Co 12:10 For when I am weak, then I am *s.*
Eph 6:10 be *s* in the Lord and in his mighty

STRUGGLE
Ro 15:30 me in my *s* by praying to God
Eph 6:12 For our *s* is not against flesh
Heb 12: 4 In your *s* against sin, you have not

STUDY
Ezr 7:10 Ezra had devoted himself to the *s*
Ecc 12:12 and much *s* wearies the body.
Jn 5:39 You diligently *s* the Scriptures

STUMBLE (STUMBLING)
Ps 37:24 though he *s,* he will not fall,
119:165 and nothing can make them *s.*
Isa 8:14 a stone that causes men to *s*
Jer 31: 9 a level path where they will not *s,*
Eze 7:19 for it has made them *s* into sin.
1Co 10:32 Do not cause anyone to *s,*
1Pe 2: 8 and, "A stone that causes men to *s*

STUMBLING (STUMBLE)
Ro 14:13 up your mind not to put any *s* block
1Co 8: 9 freedom does not become a *s* block
2Co 6: 3 We put no *s* block in anyone's path,

SUBDUE
Ge 1:28 in number; fill the earth and *s* it.

SUBJECT (SUBJECTED)
1Co 14:32 of prophets are *s* to the control
15:28 then the Son himself will be made *s*
Tit 2: 5 and to be *s* to their husbands,
2: 9 slaves to be *s* to their masters
3: 1 Remind the people to be *s* to rulers

SUBJECTED (SUBJECT)
Ro 8:20 For the creation was *s*

SUBMISSION (SUBMIT)
1Co 14:34 but must be in *s,* as the Law says.
1Ti 2:11 learn in quietness and full *s.*

SUBMISSIVE (SUBMIT)
Jas 3:17 then peace-loving, considerate, *s,*
1Pe 3: 1 in the same way be *s*
5: 5 in the same way be *s*

SUBMIT (SUBMISSION SUBMISSIVE SUBMITS)
Ro 13: 1 Everyone must *s* himself
13: 5 necessary to *s* to the authorities,
1Co 16:16 to *s* to such as these
Eph 5:21 *S* to one another out of reverence
Col 3:18 Wives, *s* to your husbands,
Heb 12: 9 How much more should we *s*
13:17 Obey your leaders and *s*
Jas 4: 7 *S* yourselves, then, to God.
1Pe 2:18 *s* yourselves to your masters

SUBMITS* (SUBMIT)
Eph 5:24 Now as the church *s* to Christ,

SUCCESSFUL
Jos 1: 7 that you may be *s* wherever you go.
2Ki 18: 7 he was *s* in whatever he undertook.
2Ch 20:20 in his prophets and you will be *s.*"

SUFFER (SUFFERED SUFFERING SUFFERINGS SUFFERS)
Isa 53:10 to crush him and cause him to *s,*
Mk 8:31 the Son of Man must *s* many things
Lk 24:26 the Christ have to *s* these things
24:46 The Christ will *s* and rise
Php 1:29 to *s* for him, since you are going
1Pe 4:16 However, if you *s* as a Christian,

SUFFERED (SUFFER)
Heb 2: 9 and honor because he *s* death,
2:18 Because he himself *s*
1Pe 2:21 Christ *s* for you, leaving you

SUFFERING (SUFFER)
Isa 53: 3 of sorrows, and familiar with *s.*
Ac 5:41 worthy of *s* disgrace for the Name.
2Ti 1: 8 But join with me in *s* for the gospel,
Heb 2:10 of their salvation perfect through *s.*

SUFFERINGS (SUFFER)
Ro 8:17 share in his *s* in order that we may
8:18 that our present *s* are not worth
2Co 1: 5 as the *s* of Christ flow
Php 3:10 the fellowship of sharing in his *s,*

SUFFERS (SUFFER)
Pr 13:20 but a companion of fools *s* harm.
1Co 12:26 If one part *s,* every part *s* with it;

SUFFICIENT
2Co 12: 9 said to me, "My grace is *s* for you,

SUITABLE
Ge 2:18 I will make a helper *s* for him."

SUN
Ecc 1: 9 there is nothing new under the *s.*
Mal 4: 2 the *s* of righteousness will rise
Mt 5:45 He causes his *s* to rise on the evil
17: 2 His face shone like the *s,*
Rev 1:16 His face was like the *s* shining
21:23 The city does not need the *s*

SUPERIOR
Heb 1: 4 he became as much *s* to the angels
8: 6 ministry Jesus has received is as *s*

SUPERVISION
Gal 3:25 longer under the *s* of the law.

SUPREMACY* (SUPREME)
Col 1:18 in everything he might have the *s.*

SUPREME (SUPREMACY)
Pr 4: 7 Wisdom is *s;* therefore get wisdom.

SURE
Nu 32:23 you may be *s* that your sin will find
Dt 6:17 Be *s* to keep the commands
14:22 Be *s* to set aside a tenth
Isa 28:16 cornerstone for a *s* foundation;
Heb 11: 1 faith is being *s* of what we hope for
2Pe 1:10 to make your calling and election *s.*

SURPASS* (SURPASSES SURPASSING)
Pr 31:29 but you *s* them all."

SURPASSES (SURPASS)
Mt 5:20 unless your righteousness *s* that
Eph 3:19 to know this love that *s* knowledge

SURPASSING* (SURPASS)
Ps 150: 2 praise him for his *s* greatness.
2Co 3:10 in comparison with the *s* glory.
9:14 of the *s* grace God has given you.
Php 3: 8 the *s* greatness of knowing Christ

SURROUNDED
Heb 12: 1 since we are *s* by such a great cloud

SUSPENDS*
Job 26: 7 he *s* the earth over nothing.

SUSTAINING* (SUSTAINS)
Heb 1: 3 *s* all things by his powerful word.

SUSTAINS (SUSTAINING)
Ps 18:35 and your right hand *s* me;
146: 9 and *s* the fatherless and the widow,
147: 6 The LORD *s* the humble
Isa 50: 4 to know the word that *s* the weary.

SWALLOWED
1Co 15:54 "Death has been *s* up in victory."
2Co 5: 4 so that what is mortal may be *s* up

SWEAR
Mt 5:34 Do not *s* at all: either by heaven,

SWORD (SWORDS)
Ps 45: 3 Gird your *s* upon your side,
Pr 12:18 Reckless words pierce like a *s,*
Mt 10:34 come to bring peace, but a *s.*
26:52 all who draw the *s* will die by the *s.*
Lk 2:35 a *s* will pierce your own soul too."
Ro 13: 4 for he does not bear the *s*
Eph 6:17 of salvation and the *s* of the Spirit,
Heb 4:12 Sharper than any double-edged *s,*
Rev 1:16 came a sharp double-edged *s.*

SWORDS (SWORD)
Isa 2: 4 They will beat their *s*
Joel 3:10 Beat your plowshares into *s*

SYMPATHETIC*
1Pe 3: 8 in harmony with one another; be *s,*

SYNAGOGUE
Lk 4:16 the Sabbath day he went into the *s,*
Ac 17: 2 custom was, Paul went into the *s,*

TABERNACLE
Ex 40:34 the glory of the LORD filled the *t.*

TABLE (TABLES)
Ps 23: 5 You prepare a *t* before me

TABLES (TABLE)
Ac 6: 2 word of God in order to wait on *t.*

TABLET (TABLETS)
Pr 3: 3 write them on the *t* of your heart.
7: 3 write them on the *t* of your heart.

TABLETS (TABLET)
Ex 31:18 he gave him the two *t*
Dt 10: 5 and put the *t* in the ark I had made,
2Co 3: 3 not on *t* of stone but on *t*

TAKE (TAKEN TAKES TAKING TOOK)
Dt 12:32 do not add to it or *t* away from it.
31:26 "*T* this Book of the Law
Job 23:10 But he knows the way that I *t;*
Ps 49:17 for he will *t* nothing with him
51:11 or *t* your Holy Spirit from me.
Mt 10:38 anyone who does not *t* his cross
11:29 *T* my yoke upon you and learn
16:24 deny himself and *t* up his cross

TAKEN (TAKE)
Lev 6: 4 must return what he has stolen or *t*
Isa 6: 7 your guilt is *t* away and your sin
Mt 24:40 one will be *t* and the other left.
Mk 16:19 he was *t* up into heaven
1Ti 3:16 was *t* up in glory.

TAKES (TAKE)
1Ki 20:11 should not boast like one who *t* it
Ps 5: 4 You are not a God who *t* pleasure
Jn 1:29 who *t* away the sin of the world!
Rev 22:19 And if anyone *t* words away

TAKING (TAKE)
Ac 15:14 by *t* from the Gentiles a people
Php 2: 7 *t* the very nature of a servant,

TALENT
Mt 25:15 to another one *t,* each according

TAME*
Jas 3: 8 but no man can *t* the tongue.

TASK
Mk 13:34 each with his assigned *t,*
Ac 20:24 complete the *t* the Lord Jesus has
1Co 3: 5 the Lord has assigned to each his *t.*
2Co 2:16 And who is equal to such a *t?*

TASTE (TASTED)
Ps 34: 8 *T* and see that the LORD is good;
Col 2:21 Do not *t!* Do not touch!"?
Heb 2: 9 the grace of God he might *t* death

TASTED (TASTE)
1Pe 2: 3 now that you have *t* that the Lord

TAUGHT (TEACH)
Mt 7:29 he *t* as one who had authority,
1Co 2:13 but in words *t* by the Spirit,
Gal 1:12 nor was I *t* it; rather, I received it

TAXES
Mt 22:17 Is it right to pay *t* to Caesar or not
Ro 13: 7 If you owe *t,* pay *t;* if revenue,

TEACH (TAUGHT TEACHER TEACHERS TEACHES TEACHING)
Ex 33:13 *t* me your ways so I may know you
Dt 4: 9 *T* them to your children
8: 3 to *t* you that man does not live
11:19 *T* them to your children, talking
1Sa 12:23 I will *t* you the way that is good
Ps 32: 8 *t* you in the way you should go;
51:13 I will *t* transgressors your ways,

Ps 90:12 *T* us to number our days aright,
143:10 *T* me to do your will,
Jer 31:34 No longer will a man *t* his neighbor
Lk 11: 1 said to him, "Lord, *t* us to pray,
Jn 14:26 will *t* you all things and will remind
1Ti 2:12 I do not permit a woman to *t*
3: 2 respectable, hospitable, able to *t*,
Tit 2: 1 You must *t* what is in accord
Heb 8:11 No longer will a man *t* his neighbor
Jas 3: 1 know that we who *t* will be judged
1Jn 2:27 you do not need anyone to *t* you.

TEACHER (TEACH)
Mt 10:24 "A student is not above his *t*,
Jn 13:14 and *T*, have washed your feet,

TEACHERS (TEACH)
1Co 12:28 third *t*, then workers of miracles,
Eph 4:11 and some to be pastors and *t*,
Heb 5:12 by this time you ought to be *t*,

TEACHES (TEACH)
1Ti 6: 3 If anyone *t* false doctrines

TEACHING (TEACH)
Pr 1: 8 and do not forsake your mother's *t*.
Mt 28:20 *t* them to obey everything I have
Jn 7:17 whether my *t* comes from God or
14:23 loves me, he will obey my *t*.
1Ti 4:13 of Scripture, to preaching and to *t*.
2Ti 3:16 is God-breathed and is useful for *t*,
Tit 2: 7 In your *t* show integrity,

TEAR (TEARS)
Rev 7:17 God will wipe away every *t*

TEARS (TEAR)
Ps 126: 5 Those who sow in *t*
Php 3:18 and now say again even with *t*,

TEETH (TOOTH)
Mt 8:12 will be weeping and gnashing of *t*."

TEMPERATE*
1Ti 3: 2 *t*, self-controlled, respectable,
3:11 not malicious talkers but *t*
Tit 2: 2 Teach the older men to be *t*,

TEMPEST
Ps 55: 8 far from the *t* and storm."

TEMPLE (TEMPLES)
1Ki 8:27 How much less this *t* I have built!
Hab 2:20 But the LORD is in his holy *t*;
1Co 3:16 that you yourselves are God's *t*
6:19 you not know that your body is a *t*
2Co 6:16 For we are the *t* of the living God.

TEMPLES (TEMPLE)
Ac 17:24 does not live in *t* built by hands.

TEMPT (TEMPTATION TEMPTED)
1Co 7: 5 again so that Satan will not *t* you

TEMPTATION (TEMPT)
Mt 6:13 And lead us not into *t*,
26:41 pray so that you will not fall into *t*.
1Co 10:13 No *t* has seized you except what is

TEMPTED (TEMPT)
Mt 4: 1 into the desert to be *t* by the devil.
1Co 10:13 he will not let you be *t*
Heb 2:18 he himself suffered when he was *t*,
4:15 but we have one who has been *t*
Jas 1:13 For God cannot be *t* by evil,

TEN (TENTH TITHE TITHES)
Ex 34:28 covenant—the *T* Commandments.
Ps 91: 7 *t* thousand at your right hand,
Mt 25:28 it to the one who has the *t* talents.
Lk 15: 8 suppose a woman has *t* silver coins

TENTH (TEN)
Dt 14:22 Be sure to set aside a *t*

TERRIBLE (TERROR)
2Ti 3: 1 There will be *t* times

TERROR (TERRIBLE)
Ps 91: 5 You will not fear the *t* of night,
Lk 21:26 Men will faint from *t*, apprehensive
Ro 13: 3 For rulers hold no *t*

TEST (TESTED TESTS)
Dt 6:16 Do not *t* the LORD your God
Ps 139:23 *t* me and know my anxious
Ro 12: 2 Then you will be able to *t*
1Co 3:13 and the fire will *t* the quality
1Jn 4: 1 *t* the spirits to see whether they are

TESTED (TEST)
Ge 22: 1 Some time later God *t* Abraham.
Job 23:10 when he has *t* me, I will come forth
Pr 27:21 man is *t* by the praise he receives.
1Ti 3:10 They must first be *t*; and then

TESTIFY (TESTIMONY)
Jn 5:39 are the Scriptures that *t* about me,
2Ti 1: 8 ashamed to *t* about our Lord,

TESTIMONY (TESTIFY)
Isa 8:20 and to the *t*! If they do not speak
Lk 18:20 not give false *t*, honor your father

TESTS (TEST)
Pr 17: 3 but the LORD *t* the heart.
1Th 2: 4 but God, who *t* our hearts.

THADDAEUS
Apostle (Mt 10:3; Mk 3:18); probably also known as Judas son of James (Lk 6:16; Ac 1:13).

THANKFUL (THANKS)
Heb 12:28 let us be *t*, and so worship God

THANKS (THANKFUL THANKSGIVING)
1Ch 16: 8 Give *t* to the LORD, call
Ne 12:31 assigned two large choirs to give *t*.
Ps 100: 4 give *t* to him and praise his name.
1Co 15:57 *t* be to God! He gives us the victory
2Co 2:14 *t* be to God, who always leads us
9:15 *T* be to God for his indescribable
1Th 5:18 give *t* in all circumstances,

THANKSGIVING (THANKS)
Ps 95: 2 Let us come before him with *t*
100: 4 Enter his gates with *t*
Php 4: 6 by prayer and petition, with *t*,
1Ti 4: 3 created to be received with *t*

THIEF (THIEVES)
Ex 22: 3 A *t* must certainly make restitution
1Th 5: 2 day of the Lord will come like a *t*
Rev 16:15 I come like a *t*! Blessed is he who

THIEVES (THIEF)
1Co 6:10 nor homosexual offenders nor *t*

THINK (THOUGHT THOUGHTS)
Ro 12: 3 Do not *t* of yourself more highly
Php 4: 8 praiseworthy—*t* about such things

THIRST (THIRSTY)
Ps 69:21 and gave me vinegar for my *t*.
Mt 5: 6 Blessed are those who hunger and *t*
Jn 4:14 the water I give him will never *t*.

THIRSTY (THIRST)
Isa 55: 1 "Come, all you who are *t*,
Jn 7:37 "If anyone is *t*, let him come to me
Rev 22:17 Whoever is *t*, let him come;

THOMAS
Apostle (Mt 10:3; Mk 3:18; Lk 6:15; Jn 11:16; 14:5; 21:2; Ac 1:13). Doubted resurrection (Jn 20:24-28).

THONGS
Mk 1: 7 *t* of whose sandals I am not worthy

THORN (THORNS)
2Co 12: 7 there was given me a *t* in my flesh,

THORNS (THORN)
Nu 33:55 in your eyes and *t* in your sides.
Mt 27:29 then twisted together a crown of *t*
Heb 6: 8 But land that produces *t*

THOUGHT (THINK)
Pr 14:15 a prudent man gives *t* to his steps.
1Co 13:11 I talked like a child, I *t* like a child,

THOUGHTS (THINK)
Ps 94:11 The LORD knows the *t* of man;
139:23 test me and know my anxious *t*.
Isa 55: 8 "For my *t* are not your *t*,
Heb 4:12 it judges the *t* and attitudes

THREE
Ecc 4:12 of *t* strands is not quickly broken.
Mt 12:40 *t* nights in the belly of a huge fish,
18:20 or *t* come together in my name,
27:63 'After *t* days I will rise again.'
1Co 13:13 And now these *t* remain: faith,
14:27 or at the most *t*— should speak,
2Co 13: 1 testimony of two or *t* witnesses."

THRESHING
2Sa 24:18 an altar to the LORD on the *t* floor

THRONE (ENTHRONED)
2Sa 7:16 your *t* will be established forever
Ps 45: 6 Your *t*, O God, will last for ever
47: 8 God is seated on his holy *t*.
Isa 6: 1 I saw the Lord seated on a *t*,
Isa 66: 1 "Heaven is my *t*
Heb 4:16 Let us then approach the *t* of grace
12: 2 at the right hand of the *t* of God.
Rev 4:10 They lay their crowns before the *t*
20:11 Then I saw a great white *t*
22: 3 *t* of God and of the Lamb will be

THROW
Jn 8: 7 the first to *t* a stone at her."
Heb 10:35 So do not *t* away your confidence;
12: 1 let us *t* off everything that hinders

THWART*
Isa 14:27 has purposed, and who can *t* him?

TIBNI
King of Israel (1Ki 16:21-22).

TIME (TIMES)
Est 4:14 come to royal position for such a *t*
Da 7:25 to him for a *t*, times and half a *t*.
Hos 10:12 for it is *t* to seek the LORD,
Ro 9: 9 "At the appointed *t* I will return,
Heb 9:28 and he will appear a second *t*,
10:12 for all *t* one sacrifice for sins,
1Pe 4:17 For it is *t* for judgment to begin

TIMES (TIME)
Ps 9: 9 a stronghold in *t* of trouble.
31:15 My *t* are in your hands;
62: 8 Trust in him at all *t*, O people;
Pr 17:17 A friend loves at all *t*,
Am 5:13 for the *t* are evil.
Mt 18:21 how many *t* shall I forgive my
Ac 1: 7 "It is not for you to know the *t*
Rev 12:14 *t* and half a time, out

TIMIDITY*
2Ti 1: 7 For God did not give us a spirit of *t*

TIMOTHY
Believer from Lystra (Ac 16:1). Joined Paul on second missionary journey (Ac 16-20). Sent to settle problems at Corinth (1Co 4:17; 16:10). Led church at Ephesus (1Ti 1:3). Co-writer with Paul (1Th 1:1; 2Th 1:1; Phm 1).

TIRE (TIRED)
2Th 3:13 never *t* of doing what is right.

TIRED (TIRE)
Ex 17:12 When Moses' hands grew *t*,
Isa 40:28 He will not grow *t* or weary,

TITHE (TEN)
Lev 27:30 " 'A *t* of everything from the land,
Dt 12:17 eat in your own towns the *t*
Mal 3:10 the whole *t* into the storehouse,

TITHES (TEN)
Mal 3: 8 'How do we rob you?' "In *t*

TITUS
Gentile co-worker of Paul (Gal 2:1-3; 2Ti 4:10); sent to Corinth (2Co 2:13; 7-8; 12:18), Crete (Tit 1:4-5).

TODAY
Mt 6:11 Give us *t* our daily bread.
Lk 23:43 *t* you will be with me in paradise."
Heb 3:13 daily, as long as it is called *T*,
13: 8 Christ is the same yesterday and *t*

TOIL
Ge 3:17 through painful *t* you will eat of it

TOLERATE
Hab 1:13 you cannot *t* wrong.
Rev 2: 2 that you cannot *t* wicked men,

TOMB
Mt 27:65 make the *t* as secure as you know
Lk 24: 2 the stone rolled away from the *t*,

TOMORROW
Pr 27: 1 Do not boast about *t*,
Isa 22:13 "for *t* we die!"
Mt 6:34 Therefore do not worry about *t*,
Jas 4:13 "Today or *t* we will go to this

TONGUE (TONGUES)
Ps 39: 1 and keep my *t* from sin;
Pr 12:18 but the *t* of the wise brings healing.
1Co 14: 2 speaks in a *t* does not speak to men
14: 4 He who speaks in a *t* edifies himself
14:13 in a *t* should pray that he may
14:19 than ten thousand words in a *t*.
Php 2:11 every *t* confess that Jesus Christ is
Jas 1:26 does not keep a tight rein on his *t*,
3: 8 but no man can tame the *t*.

TONGUES (TONGUE)
Isa 28:11 with foreign lips and strange *t*
66:18 and gather all nations and *t*,
Mk 16:17 in new *t;* they will pick up snakes
Ac 2: 4 and began to speak in other *t*
10:46 For they heard them speaking in *t*
19: 6 and they spoke in *t* and prophesied
1Co 12:30 Do all speak in *t?* Do all interpret?
14:18 speak in *t* more than all of you.
14:39 and do not forbid speaking in *t.*

TOOK (TAKE)
1Co 11:23 the night he was betrayed, *t* bread,
Php 3:12 for which Christ Jesus *t* hold of me.

TOOTH (TEETH)
Ex 21:24 eye for eye, *t* for *t,* hand for hand,
Mt 5:38 'Eye for eye, and *t* for *t.*'

TORMENTED
Rev 20:10 They will be *t* day and night

TORN
Gal 4:15 you would have *t* out your eyes
Php 1:23 I do not know! I am *t*

TOUCH (TOUCHED)
Ps 105:15 "Do not *t* my anointed ones;
Lk 24:39 It is I myself! *T* me and see;
2Co 6:17 *T* no unclean thing,
Col 2:21 Do not taste! Do not *t!*"?

TOUCHED (TOUCH)
1Sa 10:26 men whose hearts God had *t.*
Mt 14:36 and all who *t* him were healed.

TOWER
Ge 11: 4 with a *t* that reaches to the heavens
Pr 18:10 of the LORD is a strong *t;*

TOWNS
Nu 35: 2 to give the Levites *t* to live
35:15 These six *t* will be a place of refuge

TRACING*
Ro 11:33 and his paths beyond *t* out!

TRADITION
Mt 15: 6 word of God for the sake of your *t.*
Col 2: 8 which depends on human *t*

TRAIN (TRAINING)
Pr 22: 6 *T* a child in the way he should go,
Eph 4: 8 he led captives in his *t*

TRAINING (TRAIN)
1Co 9:25 in the games goes into strict *t.*
2Ti 3:16 correcting and *t* in righteousness,

TRAMPLED
Lk 21:24 Jerusalem will be *t*
Heb 10:29 to be punished who has *t* the Son

TRANCE
Ac 10:10 was being prepared, he fell into a *t.*

TRANSCENDS*
Php 4: 7 which *t* all understanding,

TRANSFIGURED
Mt 17: 2 There he was *t* before them.

TRANSFORM* (TRANSFORMED)
Php 3:21 will *t* our lowly bodies

TRANSFORMED (TRANSFORM)
Ro 12: 2 be *t* by the renewing of your mind.
2Co 3:18 are being *t* into his likeness

TRANSGRESSION (TRANSGRESSIONS TRANSGRESSORS)
Isa 53: 8 for the *t* of my people he was
Ro 4:15 where there is no law there is no *t.*

TRANSGRESSIONS (TRANSGRESSION)
Ps 32: 1 whose *t* are forgiven,
51: 1 blot out my *t.*
103:12 so far has he removed our *t* from us
Isa 53: 5 But he was pierced for our *t,*
Eph 2: 1 you were dead in your *t* and sins,

TRANSGRESSORS (TRANSGRESSION)
Ps 51:13 Then I will teach *t* your ways,
Isa 53:12 and made intercession for the *t.*
53:12 and was numbered with the *t.*

TREADING
Dt 25: 4 an ox while it is *t* out the grain.
1Co 9: 9 an ox while it is *t* out the grain."

TREASURE (TREASURED TREASURES)
Isa 33: 6 of the LORD is the key to this *t.*
Mt 6:21 For where your *t* is, there your
2Co 4: 7 But we have this *t* in jars of clay

TREASURED (TREASURE)
Dt 7: 6 to be his people, his *t* possession.
Lk 2:19 But Mary *t* up all these things

TREASURES (TREASURE)
Mt 6:19 up for yourselves *t* on earth,
Col 2: 3 in whom are hidden all the *t*
Heb 11:26 of greater value than the *t* of Egypt,

TREAT
Lev 22: 2 sons to *t* with respect the sacred
1Ti 5: 1 *T* younger men as brothers,
1Pe 3: 7 and *t* them with respect

TREATY
Dt 7: 2 Make no *t* with them, and show

TREE
Ge 2: 9 and the *t* of the knowledge of good
2: 9 of the garden were the *t* of life
Dt 21:23 hung on a *t* is under God's curse.
Ps 1: 3 He is like a *t* planted by streams
Mt 3:10 every *t* that does not produce good
12:33 for a *t* is recognized by its fruit.
Gal 3:13 is everyone who is hung on a *t.*"
Rev 22:14 they may have the right to the *t*

TREMBLE (TREMBLING)
1Ch 16:30 *T* before him, all the earth!
Ps 114: 7 *T,* O earth, at the presence

TREMBLING (TREMBLE)
Ps 2:11 and rejoice with *t.*
Php 2:12 out your salvation with fear and *t,*

TRESPASS
Ro 5:17 For if, by the *t* of the one man,

TRIALS
1Th 3: 3 one would be unsettled by these *t.*
Jas 1: 2 whenever you face *t* of many kinds,
2Pe 2: 9 how to rescue godly men from *t*

TRIBES
Ge 49:28 All these are the twelve *t* of Israel,
Mt 19:28 judging the twelve *t* of Israel.

TRIBULATION*
Rev 7:14 who have come out of the great *t;*

TRIUMPHAL* (TRIUMPHING)
Isa 60:11 their kings led in *t* procession.
2Co 2:14 us in *t* procession in Christ

TRIUMPHING* (TRIUMPHAL)
Col 2:15 of them, *t* over them by the cross.

TROUBLE (TROUBLED TROUBLES)
Job 14: 1 is of few days and full of *t.*
Ps 46: 1 an ever-present help in *t.*
107:13 they cried to the LORD in their *t,*
Pr 11:29 He who brings *t* on his family will
24:10 If you falter in times of *t,*
Mt 6:34 Each day has enough *t* of its own.
Jn 16:33 In this world you will have *t.*
Ro 8:35 Shall *t* or hardship or persecution

TROUBLED (TROUBLE)
Jn 14: 1 "Do not let your hearts be *t.*
14:27 Do not let your hearts be *t*

TROUBLES (TROUBLE)
1Co 7:28 those who marry will face many *t*
2Co 1: 4 who comforts us in all our *t,*
4:17 and momentary *t* are achieving

TRUE (TRUTH)
Dt 18:22 does not take place or come *t,*
1Sa 9: 6 and everything he says comes *t.*
Ps 119:160 All your words are *t;*
Jn 17: 3 the only *t* God, and Jesus Christ,
Ro 3: 4 Let God be *t,* and every man a liar.
Php 4: 8 whatever is *t,* whatever is noble,
Rev 22: 6 These words are trustworthy and *t.*

TRUMPET
1Co 14: 8 if the *t* does not sound a clear call,
15:52 For the *t* will sound, the dead will

TRUST (ENTRUSTED TRUSTED TRUSTS TRUSTWORTHY)
Ps 20: 7 we *t* in the name of the LORD our
37: 3 *T* in the LORD and do good;
56: 4 in God I *t;* I will not be afraid.
119:42 for I *t* in your word.
Pr 3: 5 *T* in the LORD with all your heart
Isa 30:15 in quietness and *t* is your strength,
Jn 14: 1 *T* in God; *t* also in me.
1Co 4: 2 been given a *t* must prove faithful.

TRUSTED (TRUST)
Ps 26: 1 I have *t* in the LORD
Isa 25: 9 we *t* in him, and he saved us.
Da 3:28 They *t* in him and defied the king's
Lk 16:10 *t* with very little can also be *t*

TRUSTS (TRUST)
Ps 32:10 surrounds the man who *t* in him.
Pr 11:28 Whoever *t* in his riches will fall,
28:26 He who *t* in himself is a fool,
Ro 9:33 one who *t* in him will never be put

TRUSTWORTHY (TRUST)
Ps 119:138 they are fully *t.*
Pr 11:13 but a *t* man keeps a secret.
Rev 22: 6 "These words are *t* and true.

TRUTH (TRUE TRUTHFUL TRUTHS)
Ps 51: 6 Surely you desire *t*
Isa 45:19 I, the LORD, speak the *t;*
Zec 8:16 are to do: Speak the *t* to each other,
Jn 4:23 worship the Father in spirit and *t,*
8:32 Then you will know the *t,*
8:32 and the *t* will set you free."
14: 6 I am the way and the *t* and the life.
16:13 comes, he will guide you into all *t.*
18:38 "What is *t?*" Pilate asked.
Ro 1:25 They exchanged the *t* of God
1Co 13: 6 in evil but rejoices with the *t.*
2Co 13: 8 against the *t,* but only for the *t.*
Eph 4:15 Instead, speaking the *t* in love,
6:14 with the belt of *t* buckled
2Th 2:10 because they refused to love the *t*
1Ti 2: 4 to come to a knowledge of the *t.*
3:15 the pillar and foundation of the *t.*
2Ti 2:15 correctly handles the word of *t.*
3: 7 never able to acknowledge the *t.*
Heb 10:26 received the knowledge of the *t,*
1Pe 1:22 by obeying the *t* so that you have
2Pe 2: 2 the way of *t* into disrepute.
1Jn 1: 6 we lie and do not live by the *t.*
1: 8 deceive ourselves and the *t* is not

TRUTHFUL (TRUTH)
Pr 12:22 but he delights in men who are *t.*
Jn 3:33 it has certified that God is *t.*

TRUTHS (TRUTH)
1Co 2:13 expressing spiritual *t*
1Ti 3: 9 hold of the deep *t* of the faith
Heb 5:12 to teach you the elementary *t*

TRY (TRYING)
Ps 26: 2 Test me, O LORD, and *t* me,
Isa 7:13 enough to *t* the patience of men?
1Co 14:12 *t* to excel in gifts that build up
2Co 5:11 is to fear the Lord, we *t*
1Th 5:15 always *t* to be kind to each other

TRYING (TRY)
2Co 5:12 We are not *t* to commend ourselves
1Th 2: 4 We are not *t* to please men but God

TUNIC
Lk 6:29 do not stop him from taking your *t.*

TURN (TURNED TURNS)
Ex 32:12 *T* from your fierce anger; relent
Dt 5:32 do not *t* aside to the right
28:14 Do not *t* aside from any
Jos 1: 7 do not *t* from it to the right
2Ch 7:14 and *t* from their wicked ways,
30: 9 He will not *t* his face from you
Ps 78: 6 they in *t* would tell their children.
Pr 22: 6 when he is old he will not *t* from it.
Isa 29:16 You *t* things upside down,
30:21 Whether you *t* to the right
45:22 "*T* to me and be saved,
55: 7 Let him *t* to the LORD,
Eze 33:11 *T! T* from your evil ways!
Mal 4: 6 He will *t* the hearts of the fathers
Mt 5:39 you on the right cheek, *t*
10:35 For I have come to *t*
Jn 12:40 nor *t*— and I would heal them."
Ac 3:19 Repent, then, and *t* to God,
26:18 and *t* them from darkness to light,
1Ti 6:20 *T* away from godless chatter
1Pe 3:11 He must *t* from evil and do good;

TURNED (TURN)
Ps 30:11 You *t* my wailing into dancing;
40: 1 he *t* to me and heard my cry.
Isa 53: 6 each of us has *t* to his own way;
Hos 7: 8 Ephraim is a flat cake not *t* over.
Joel 2:31 The sun will be *t* to darkness
Ro 3:12 All have *t* away,

TURNS (TURN)
2Sa 22:29 the LORD *t* my darkness into light
Pr 15: 1 A gentle answer *t* away wrath,
Isa 44:25 and *t* it into nonsense,
Jas 5:20 Whoever *t* a sinner from the error

TWELVE
Ge 49:28 All these are the *t* tribes of Israel,
Mt 10: 1 He called his *t* disciples to him

TWINKLING*
1Co 15:52 in a flash, in the *t* of an eye,

UNAPPROACHABLE*
1Ti 6:16 immortal and who lives in *u* light,

UNBELIEF (UNBELIEVER UNBELIEVERS UNBELIEVING)
Mk 9:24 help me overcome my *u*!"
Ro 11:20 they were broken off because of *u*,
Heb 3:19 able to enter, because of their *u*.

UNBELIEVER* (UNBELIEF)
1Co 7:15 But if the *u* leaves, let him do so.
10:27 If some *u* invites you to a meal
14:24 if an *u* or someone who does not
2Co 6:15 have in common with an *u*?
1Ti 5: 8 the faith and is worse than an *u*.

UNBELIEVERS (UNBELIEF)
1Co 6: 6 another—and this in front of *u*!
2Co 6:14 Do not be yoked together with *u*.

UNBELIEVING (UNBELIEF)
1Co 7:14 For the *u* husband has been
Rev 21: 8 But the cowardly, the *u*, the vile,

UNCERTAIN*
1Ti 6:17 which is so *u*, but to put their hope

UNCHANGEABLE*
Heb 6:18 by two *u* things in which it is

UNCIRCUMCISED
1Sa 17:26 Who is this *u* Philistine that he
Col 3:11 circumcised or *u*, barbarian,

UNCIRCUMCISION
1Co 7:19 is nothing and *u* is nothing.
Gal 5: 6 neither circumcision nor *u* has any

UNCLEAN
Isa 6: 5 ruined! For I am a man of *u* lips,
Ro 14:14 fully convinced that no food is *u*
2Co 6:17 Touch no *u* thing,

UNCONCERNED*
Eze 16:49 were arrogant, overfed and *u*;

UNCOVERED
Heb 4:13 Everything is *u* and laid bare

UNDERSTAND (UNDERSTANDING UNDERSTANDS)
Job 42: 3 Surely I spoke of things I did not *u*,
Ps 73:16 When I tried to *u* all this,
119:125 that I may *u* your statutes.
Lk 24:45 so they could *u* the Scriptures.
Ac 8:30 "Do you *u* what you are reading?"
Ro 7:15 I do not *u* what I do.
1Co 2:14 and he cannot *u* them,
Eph 5:17 but *u* what the Lord's will is.
2Pe 3:16 some things that are hard to *u*,

UNDERSTANDING (UNDERSTAND)
Ps 119:104 I gain *u* from your precepts;
147: 5 his *u* has no limit.
Pr 3: 5 and lean not on your own *u*;
4: 7 Though it cost all you have, get *u*.
10:23 but a man of *u* delights in wisdom.
11:12 but a man of *u* holds his tongue.
15:21 a man of *u* keeps a straight course.
15:32 whoever heeds correction gains *u*.
23:23 get wisdom, discipline and *u*.
Isa 40:28 and his *u* no one can fathom.
Da 5:12 a keen mind and knowledge and *u*,
Mk 4:12 and ever hearing but never *u*;
12:33 with all your *u* and with all your
Php 4: 7 of God, which transcends all *u*,

UNDERSTANDS (UNDERSTAND)
1Ch 28: 9 and *u* every motive
1Ti 6: 4 he is conceited and *u* nothing.

UNDIVIDED*
1Ch 12:33 to help David with *u* loyalty—
Ps 86:11 give me an *u* heart,
Eze 11:19 I will give them an *u* heart
1Co 7:35 way in *u* devotion to the Lord.

UNDOING
Pr 18: 7 A fool's mouth is his *u*,

UNDYING*
Eph 6:24 Lord Jesus Christ with an *u* love.

UNFADING*
1Pe 3: 4 the *u* beauty of a gentle

UNFAILING
Ps 33: 5 the earth is full of his *u* love.
119:76 May your *u* love be my comfort,
143: 8 bring me word of your *u* love,
Pr 19:22 What a man desires is *u* love;
La 3:32 so great is his *u* love.

UNFAITHFUL (UNFAITHFULNESS)
Lev 6: 2 is *u* to the LORD by deceiving his
1Ch 10:13 because he was *u* to the LORD;
Pr 13:15 but the way of the *u* is hard.

UNFAITHFULNESS (UNFAITHFUL)
Mt 5:32 except for marital *u*, causes her
19: 9 for marital *u*, and marries another

UNFOLDING
Ps 119:130 the *u* of your words gives light;

UNGODLINESS
Tit 2:12 It teaches us to say "No" to *u*

UNIT
1Co 12:12 body is a *u*, though it is made up

UNITED (UNITY)
Ro 6: 5 If we have been *u* with him
Php 2: 1 from being *u* with Christ,
Col 2: 2 encouraged in heart and *u* in love,

UNITY (UNITED)
Ps 133: 1 is when brothers live together in *u*!
Ro 15: 5 a spirit of *u* among yourselves
Eph 4: 3 effort to keep the *u* of the Spirit
4:13 up until we all reach *u* in the faith
Col 3:14 them all together in perfect *u*.

UNIVERSE
Php 2:15 which you shine like stars in the *u*
Heb 1: 2 and through whom he made the *u*.

UNKNOWN
Ac 17:23 TO AN *U* GOD.

UNLEAVENED
Ex 12:17 "Celebrate the Feast of *U* Bread,

UNPROFITABLE
Tit 3: 9 because these are *u* and useless.

UNPUNISHED
Ex 34: 7 Yet he does not leave the guilty *u*;
Pr 19: 5 A false witness will not go *u*,

UNREPENTANT*
Ro 2: 5 stubbornness and your *u* heart,

UNRIGHTEOUS*
Zep 3: 5 yet the *u* know no shame.
Mt 5:45 rain on the righteous and the *u*.
1Pe 3:18 the righteous for the *u*, to bring you
2Pe 2: 9 and to hold the *u* for the day

UNSEARCHABLE
Ro 11:33 How *u* his judgments,
Eph 3: 8 preach to the Gentiles the *u* riches

UNSEEN
2Co 4:18 on what is seen, but on what is *u*.
4:18 temporary, but what is *u* is eternal.

UNSTABLE*
Jas 1: 8 he is a double-minded man, *u*
2Pe 2:14 they seduce the *u*; they are experts
3:16 ignorant and *u* people distort,

UNTHINKABLE*
Job 34:12 It is *u* that God would do wrong,

UNVEILED*
2Co 3:18 with *u* faces all reflect the Lord's

UNWORTHY
Job 40: 4 "I am *u*— how can I reply to you?
Lk 17:10 should say, 'We are *u* servants;

UPRIGHT
Job 1: 1 This man was blameless and *u*;
Pr 2: 7 He holds victory in store for the *u*,
15: 8 but the prayer of the *u* pleases him.
Tit 1: 8 who is self-controlled, *u*, holy
2:12 *u* and godly lives in this present

UPROOTED
Jude :12 without fruit and *u*— twice dead.

USEFUL
2Ti 2:21 *u* to the Master and prepared
3:16 Scripture is God-breathed and is *u*

USELESS
1Co 15:14 our preaching is *u*
Jas 2:20 faith without deeds is *u*?

USURY
Ne 5:10 But let the exacting of *u* stop!

UTTER
Ps 78: 2 I will *u* hidden things, things from of

UZZIAH
Son of Amaziah; king of Judah also known as Azariah (2Ki 15:1-7; 1Ch 6:24; 2Ch 26).

VAIN
Ps 33:17 A horse is a *v* hope for deliverance;
Isa 65:23 They will not toil in *v*
1Co 15: 2 Otherwise, you have believed in *v*.
15:58 labor in the Lord is not in *v*.
2Co 6: 1 not to receive God's grace in *v*.

VALLEY
Ps 23: 4 walk through the *v* of the shadow
Isa 40: 4 Every *v* shall be raised up,
Joel 3:14 multitudes in the *v* of decision!

VALUABLE (VALUE)
Lk 12:24 And how much more *v* you are

VALUE (VALUABLE)
Mt 13:46 When he found one of great *v*,
1Ti 4: 8 For physical training is of some *v*,
Heb 11:26 as of greater *v* than the treasures

VEIL
Ex 34:33 to them, he put a *v* over his face.
2Co 3:14 for to this day the same *v* remains

VENGEANCE (AVENGE REVENGE)
Isa 34: 8 For the LORD has a day of *v*,

VICTORIES (VICTORY)
Ps 18:50 He gives his king great *v*;
21: 1 great is his joy in the *v* you give!

VICTORIOUSLY* (VICTORY)
Ps 45: 4 In your majesty ride forth *v*

VICTORY (VICTORIES VICTORIOUSLY)
Ps 60:12 With God we will gain the *v*,
1Co 15:54 "Death has been swallowed up in *v*
15:57 He gives us the *v* through our Lord
1Jn 5: 4 This is the *v* that has overcome

VINDICATED
1Ti 3:16 was *v* by the Spirit,

VINE
Jn 15: 1 "I am the true *v*, and my Father is

VINEGAR
Mk 15:36 filled a sponge with wine *v*,

VIOLATION
Heb 2: 2 every *v* and disobedience received

VIOLENCE
Isa 60:18 No longer will *v* be heard
Eze 45: 9 Give up your *v* and oppression

VIPERS
Ro 3:13 "The poison of *v* is on their lips."

VIRGIN
Isa 7:14 The *v* will be with child
Mt 1:23 "The *v* will be with child
2Co 11: 2 that I might present you as a pure *v*

VIRTUES*
Col 3:14 And over all these *v* put on love,

VISION
Ac 26:19 disobedient to the *v* from heaven.

VOICE
Ps 95: 7 Today, if you hear his *v*,
Isa 30:21 your ears will hear a *v* behind you,
Jn 5:28 are in their graves will hear his *v*
10: 3 and the sheep listen to his *v*.
Heb 3: 7 "Today, if you hear his *v*,
Rev 3:20 If anyone hears my *v* and opens

VOMIT
Pr 26:11 As a dog returns to its *v*,
2Pe 2:22 "A dog returns to its *v*," and,

VOW
Nu 30: 2 When a man makes a *v*

WAGES
Lk 10: 7 for the worker deserves his *w*.

Ro 4: 4 his *w* are not credited to him
6:23 For the *w* of sin is death,

WAILING
Ps 30:11 You turned my *w* into dancing;

WAIST
2Ki 1: 8 with a leather belt around his *w.*"
Mt 3: 4 he had a leather belt around his *w.*

WAIT (WAITED WAITS)
Ps 27:14 *W* for the LORD;
130: 5 I *w* for the LORD, my soul waits,
Isa 30:18 Blessed are all who *w* for him!
Ac 1: 4 *w* for the gift my Father promised,
Ro 8:23 as we *w* eagerly for our adoption
1Th 1:10 and to *w* for his Son from heaven,
Tit 2:13 while we *w* for the blessed hope—

WAITED (WAIT)
Ps 40: 1 I *w* patiently for the LORD;

WAITS (WAIT)
Ro 8:19 creation *w* in eager expectation

WALK (WALKED WALKS)
Dt 11:19 and when you *w* along the road,
Ps 1: 1 who does not *w* in the counsel
23: 4 Even though I *w*
89:15 who *w* in the light of your presence
Isa 2: 5 let us *w* in the light of the LORD.
30:21 saying, "This is the way; *w* in it."
40:31 they will *w* and not be faint.
Jer 6:16 ask where the good way is, and *w*
Da 4:37 And those who *w* in pride he is able
Am 3: 3 Do two *w* together
Mic 6: 8 and to *w* humbly with your God.
Mk 2: 9 'Get up, take your mat and *w*'?
Jn 8:12 Whoever follows me will never *w*
1Jn 1: 7 But if we *w* in the light,
2Jn : 6 his command is that you *w* in love.

WALKED (WALK)
Ge 5:24 Enoch *w* with God; then he was no
Jos 14: 9 which your feet have *w* will be your
Mt 14:29 *w* on the water and came toward

WALKS (WALK)
Pr 13:20 He who *w* with the wise grows wise

WALL
Jos 6:20 *w* collapsed; so every man charged
Ne 2:17 let us rebuild the *w* of Jerusalem,
Rev 21:12 It had a great, high *w*

WALLOWING
2Pe 2:22 back to her *w* in the mud."

WANT (WANTED WANTING WANTS)
1Sa 8:19 "We *w* a king over us.
Ps 23: 1 is my shepherd, I shall not be in *w.*
Lk 19:14 'We don't *w* this man to be our king
Ro 7:15 For what I *w* to do I do not do,
Php 3:10 I *w* to know Christ and the power

WANTED (WANT)
1Co 12:18 of them, just as he *w* them to be.

WANTING (WANT)
Da 5:27 weighed on the scales and found *w.*
2Pe 3: 9 with you, not *w* anyone to perish,

WANTS (WANT)
Mt 20:26 whoever *w* to become great
Mk 8:35 For whoever *w* to save his life will
Ro 9:18 he hardens whom he *w* to harden.
1Ti 2: 4 who *w* all men to be saved

WAR (WARS)
Isa 2: 4 nor will they train for *w* anymore.
Da 9:26 *W* will continue until the end,
2Co 10: 3 we do not wage *w* as the world does
Rev 19:11 With justice he judges and makes *w*

WARN (WARNED WARNINGS)
Eze 3:19 But if you do *w* the wicked man
33: 9 if you do *w* the wicked man to turn

WARNED (WARN)
Ps 19:11 By them is your servant *w;*

WARNINGS (WARN)
1Co 10:11 and were written down as *w* for us,

WARS (WAR)
Ps 46: 9 He makes *w* cease to the ends
Mt 24: 6 You will hear of *w* and rumors of *w,*

WASH (WASHED WASHING)
Ps 51: 7 *w* me, and I will be whiter
Jn 13: 5 and began to *w* his disciples' feet,
Ac 22:16 be baptized and *w* your sins away,
Rev 22:14 Blessed are those who *w* their robes

WASHED (WASH)
1Co 6:11 you were *w,* you were sanctified,
Rev 7:14 they have *w* their robes

WASHING (WASH)
Eph 5:26 cleansing her by the *w* with water
Tit 3: 5 us through the *w* of rebirth

WATCH (WATCHES WATCHING WATCHMAN)
Ge 31:49 "May the LORD keep *w*
Jer 31:10 will *w* over his flock like a shepherd
Mt 24:42 "Therefore keep *w,* because you do
26:41 *W* and pray so that you will not fall
Lk 2: 8 keeping *w* over their flocks at night
1Ti 4:16 *W* your life and doctrine closely.

WATCHES (WATCH)
Ps 1: 6 For the LORD *w* over the way
121: 3 he who *w* over you will not slumber

WATCHING (WATCH)
Lk 12:37 whose master finds them *w*

WATCHMAN (WATCH)
Eze 3:17 I have made you a *w* for the house

WATER (WATERED WATERS)
Ps 1: 3 like a tree planted by streams of *w,*
22:14 I am poured out like *w,*
Pr 25:21 if he is thirsty, give him *w* to drink.
Isa 49:10 and lead them beside springs of *w.*
Jer 2:13 broken cisterns that cannot hold *w.*
Zec 14: 8 On that day living *w* will flow out
Mk 9:41 anyone who gives you a cup of *w*
Jn 4:10 he would have given you living *w.*"
7:38 streams of living *w* will flow
Eph 5:26 washing with *w* through the word,
1Pe 3:21 this *w* symbolizes baptism that now
Rev 21: 6 cost from the spring of the *w* of life.

WATERED (WATER)
1Co 3: 6 I planted the seed, Apollos *w* it,

WATERS (WATER)
Ps 23: 2 he leads me beside quiet *w,*
Ecc 11: 1 Cast your bread upon the *w,*
Isa 58:11 like a spring whose *w* never fail.
1Co 3: 7 plants nor he who *w* is anything,

WAVE (WAVES)
Jas 1: 6 he who doubts is like a *w* of the sea,

WAVES (WAVE)
Isa 57:20 whose *w* cast up mire and mud.
Mt 8:27 Even the winds and the *w* obey him
Eph 4:14 tossed back and forth by the *w,*

WAY (WAYS)
Dt 1:33 to show you the *w* you should go.
2Sa 22:31 "As for God, his *w* is perfect;
Job 23:10 But he knows the *w* that I take;
Ps 1: 1 or stand in the *w* of sinners
37: 5 Commit your *w* to the LORD;
119: 9 can a young man keep his *w* pure?
139:24 See if there is any offensive *w* in me
Pr 14:12 There is a *w* that seems right
16:17 he who guards his *w* guards his life.
22: 6 Train a child in the *w* he should go,
Isa 30:21 saying, "This is the *w;* walk in it."
53: 6 each of us has turned to his own *w;*
55: 7 Let the wicked forsake his *w*
Mt 3: 3 'Prepare the *w* for the Lord,
Jn 14: 6 "I am the *w* and the truth
1Co 10:13 also provide a *w* out so that you can
12:31 will show you the most excellent *w.*
Heb 4:15 who has been tempted in every *w,*
9: 8 was showing by this that the *w*
10:20 and living *w* opened for us

WAYS (WAY)
Ex 33:13 teach me your *w* so I may know
Ps 25:10 All the *w* of the LORD are loving
51:13 I will teach transgressors your *w,*
Pr 3: 6 in all your *w* acknowledge him,
Isa 55: 8 neither are your *w* my *w,*"
Jas 3: 2 We all stumble in many *w.*

WEAK (WEAKER WEAKNESS)
Mt 26:41 spirit is willing, but the body is *w.*"
Ro 14: 1 Accept him whose faith is *w,*
1Co 1:27 God chose the *w* things
8: 9 become a stumbling block to the *w.*
9:22 To the *w* I became *w,* to win the *w.*
2Co 12:10 For when I am *w,* then I am strong.
Heb 12:12 your feeble arms and *w* knees.

WEAKER (WEAK)
1Co 12:22 seem to be *w* are indispensable,
1Pe 3: 7 them with respect as the *w* partner

WEAKNESS (WEAK)
Ro 8:26 the Spirit helps us in our *w.*
1Co 1:25 and the *w* of God is stronger
2Co 12: 9 for my power is made perfect in *w*
Heb 5: 2 since he himself is subject to *w.*

WEALTH
Pr 3: 9 Honor the LORD with your *w,*
Mk 10:22 away sad, because he had great *w.*
Lk 15:13 and there squandered his *w*

WEAPONS
2Co 10: 4 The *w* we fight with are not

WEARIES (WEARY)
Ecc 12:12 and much study *w* the body.

WEARY (WEARIES)
Isa 40:31 they will run and not grow *w,*
Mt 11:28 all you who are *w* and burdened,
Gal 6: 9 Let us not become *w* in doing good,

WEDDING
Mt 22:11 who was not wearing *w* clothes.
Rev 19: 7 For the *w* of the Lamb has come,

WEEP (WEEPING WEPT)
Ecc 3: 4 a time to *w* and a time to laugh,
Lk 6:21 Blessed are you who *w* now,

WEEPING (WEEP)
Ps 30: 5 *w* may remain for a night,
126: 6 He who goes out *w,*
Mt 8:12 where there will be *w* and gnashing

WELCOMES
Mt 18: 5 whoever *w* a little child like this
2Jn :11 Anyone who *w* him shares

WELL
Lk 17:19 your faith has made you *w.*"
Jas 5:15 in faith will make the sick person *w*

WEPT (WEEP)
Ps 137: 1 of Babylon we sat and *w*
Jn 11:35 Jesus *w.*

WEST
Ps 103:12 as far as the east is from the *w,*

WHIRLWIND (WIND)
2Ki 2: 1 to take Elijah up to heaven in a *w,*
Hos 8: 7 and reap the *w.*
Na 1: 3 His way is in the *w* and the storm,

WHITE (WHITER)
Isa 1:18 they shall be as *w* as snow;
Da 7: 9 His clothing was as *w* as snow;
Rev 1:14 hair were *w* like wool, as *w* as snow,
3: 4 dressed in *w,* for they are worthy.
20:11 Then I saw a great *w* throne

WHITER (WHITE)
Ps 51: 7 and I will be *w* than snow.

WHOLE
Mt 16:26 for a man if he gains the *w* world,
24:14 will be preached in the *w* world
Jn 13:10 to wash his feet; his *w* body is clean
21:25 the *w* world would not have room
Ac 20:27 proclaim to you the *w* will of God.
Ro 3:19 and the *w* world held accountable
8:22 know that the *w* creation has been
Gal 3:22 declares that the *w* world is
5: 3 obligated to obey the *w* law.
Eph 4:13 attaining to the *w* measure
Jas 2:10 For whoever keeps the *w* law
1Jn 2: 2 but also for the sins of the *w* world.

WHOLEHEARTEDLY (HEART)
Dt 1:36 because he followed the LORD *w*
Eph 6: 7 Serve *w,* as if you were serving

WICKED (WICKEDNESS)
Ps 1: 1 walk in the counsel of the *w*
1: 5 Therefore the *w* will not stand
73: 3 when I saw the prosperity of the *w.*
Pr 10:20 the heart of the *w* is of little value.
11:21 The *w* will not go unpunished,
Isa 53: 9 He was assigned a grave with the *w*
55: 7 Let the *w* forsake his way
57:20 But the *w* are like the tossing sea,
Eze 3:18 that *w* man will die for his sin,
18:23 pleasure in the death of the *w?*
33:14 to the *w* man, 'You will surely die,'

WICKEDNESS (WICKED)
Eze 28:15 created till *w* was found in you.

WIDE
Isa 54: 2 stretch your tent curtains *w*,
Mt 7:13 For *w* is the gate and broad is
Eph 3:18 to grasp how *w* and long and high

WIDOW (WIDOWS)
Dt 10:18 cause of the fatherless and the *w*,
Lk 21: 2 saw a poor *w* put in two very small

WIDOWS (WIDOW)
Jas 1:27 look after orphans and *w*

WIFE (WIVES)
Ge 2:24 and mother and be united to his *w*,
24:67 she became his *w*, and he loved her;
Ex 20:17 shall not covet your neighbor's *w*,
Dt 5:21 shall not covet your neighbor's *w*.
Pr 5:18 in the *w* of your youth.
12: 4 *w* of noble character is her
18:22 He who finds a *w* finds what is
19:13 quarrelsome *w* is like a constant
31:10 *w* of noble character who can find?
Mt 19: 3 for a man to divorce his *w* for any
1Co 7: 2 each man should have his own *w*,
7:33 how he can please his *w*—
Eph 5:23 the husband is the head of the *w*
5:33 must love his *w* as he loves himself,
1Ti 3: 2 husband of but one *w*, temperate,
Rev 21: 9 I will show you the bride, the *w*

WILD
Lk 15:13 squandered his wealth in *w* living.
Ro 11:17 and you, though a *w* olive shoot,

WILL (WILLING WILLINGNESS)
Ps 40: 8 I desire to do your *w*, O my God;
143:10 Teach me to do your *w*,
Isa 53:10 Yet it was the LORD's *w*
Mt 6:10 your *w* be done
26:39 Yet not as I *w*, but as you *w*."
Jn 7:17 If anyone chooses to do God's *w*,
Ac 20:27 to you the whole *w* of God.
Ro 12: 2 and approve what God's *w* is—
1Co 7:37 but has control over his own *w*,
Eph 5:17 understand what the Lord's *w* is.
Php 2:13 for it is God who works in you to *w*
1Th 4: 3 God's *w* that you should be
5:18 for this is God's *w* for you
Heb 9:16 In the case of a *w*, it is necessary
10: 7 I have come to do your *w*, O God
Jas 4:15 "If it is the Lord's *w*,
1Jn 5:14 we ask anything according to his *w*,
Rev 4:11 and by your *w* they were created

WILLING (WILL)
Ps 51:12 grant me a *w* spirit, to sustain me.
Da 3:28 were *w* to give up their lives rather
Mt 18:14 Father in heaven is not *w* that any
23:37 her wings, but you were not *w*.
26:41 The spirit is *w*, but the body is weak

WILLINGNESS (WILL)
2Co 8:12 For if the *w* is there, the gift is

WIN (WINS)
Php 3:14 on toward the goal to *w* the prize
1Th 4:12 your daily life may *w* the respect

WIND (WHIRLWIND)
Jas 1: 6 blown and tossed by the *w*.

WINE
Pr 20: 1 *W* is a mocker and beer a brawler;
Isa 55: 1 Come, buy *w* and milk
Mt 9:17 Neither do men pour new *w*
Lk 23:36 They offered him *w* vinegar
Ro 14:21 not to eat meat or drink *w*
Eph 5:18 on *w*, which leads to debauchery.

WINESKINS
Mt 9:17 do men pour new wine into old *w*.

WINGS
Ru 2:12 under whose *w* you have come
Ps 17: 8 hide me in the shadow of your *w*
Isa 40:31 They will soar on *w* like eagles;
Mal 4: 2 rise with healing in its *w*.
Lk 13:34 hen gathers her chicks under her *w*,

WINS (WIN)
Pr 11:30 and he who *w* souls is wise.

WIPE
Rev 7:17 God will *w* away every tear

WISDOM (WISE)
1Ki 4:29 God gave Solomon *w* and very
Ps 111:10 of the LORD is the beginning of *w*;
Pr 31:26 She speaks with *w*,
Jer 10:12 he founded the world by his *w*
Mt 11:19 But *w* is proved right by her actions
Lk 2:52 And Jesus grew in *w* and stature,
Ro 11:33 the depth of the riches of the *w*
Col 2: 3 are hidden all the treasures of *w*
Jas 1: 5 of you lacks *w*, he should ask God,

WISE (WISDOM WISER)
1Ki 3:12 give you a *w* and discerning heart,
Job 5:13 He catches the *w* in their craftiness
Ps 19: 7 making *w* the simple.
Pr 3: 7 Do not be *w* in your own eyes;
9: 8 rebuke a *w* man and he will love
10: 1 A *w* son brings joy to his father,
11:30 and he who wins souls is *w*.
13:20 He who walks with the *w* grows *w*,
17:28 Even a fool is thought *w*
Da 12: 3 Those who are *w* will shine like
Mt 11:25 hidden these things from the *w*
1Co 1:27 things of the world to shame the *w*;
2Ti 3:15 able to make you *w* for salvation

WISER (WISE)
1Co 1:25 of God is *w* than man's wisdom,

WITHER (WITHERS)
Ps 1: 3 and whose leaf does not *w*.

WITHERS (WITHER)
Isa 40: 7 The grass *w* and the flowers fall,
1Pe 1:24 the grass *w* and the flowers fall,

WITHHOLD
Ps 84:11 no good thing does he *w*
Pr 23:13 Do not *w* discipline from a child;

WITNESS (WITNESSES)
Jn 1: 8 he came only as a *w* to the light.

WITNESSES (WITNESS)
Dt 19:15 by the testimony of two or three *w*.
Ac 1: 8 and you will be my *w* in Jerusalem,

WIVES (WIFE)
Eph 5:22 *W*, submit to your husbands
5:25 love your *w*, just as Christ loved
1Pe 3: 1 words by the behavior of their *w*,

WOE
Isa 6: 5 "*W* to me!" I cried.

WOLF
Isa 65:25 *w* and the lamb will feed together,

WOMAN (MAN)
Ge 2:22 God made a *w* from
3:15 between you and the *w*,
Lev 20:13 as one lies with a *w*,
Dt 22: 5 *w* must not wear men's
Ru 3:11 a *w* of noble character
Pr 31:30 a *w* who fears the LORD
Mt 5:28 looks at a *w* lustfully
Jn 8: 3 a *w* caught in adultery.
Ro 7: 2 a married *w* is bound to
1Co 11: 3 the head of the *w* is man,
11:13 a *w* to pray to God with
1Ti 2:11 A *w* should learn in

WOMEN (MAN)
Lk 1:42 Blessed are you among *w*,
1Co 14:34 *w* should remain silent in
1Ti 2: 9 want *w* to dress modestly
Tit 2: 3 teach the older *w* to be
1Pe 3: 5 the holy *w* of the past

WOMB
Job 1:21 Naked I came from my mother's *w*,
Jer 1: 5 you in the *w* I knew you,
Lk 1:44 the baby in my *w* leaped for joy.

WONDER (WONDERFUL WONDERS)
Ps 17: 7 Show the *w* of your great love,

WONDERFUL (WONDER)
Job 42: 3 things too *w* for me to know.
Ps 31:21 for he showed his *w* love to me
119:18 *w* things in your law.
119:129 Your statutes are *w*;
139: 6 Such knowledge is too *w* for me,
Isa 9: 6 *W* Counselor, Mighty God,
1Pe 2: 9 out of darkness into his *w* light.

WONDERS (WONDER)
Job 37:14 stop and consider God's *w*.
Ps 119:27 then I will meditate on your *w*.
Joel 2:30 I will show *w* in the heavens
Ac 2:19 I will show *w* in the heaven above

WOOD
Isa 44:19 Shall I bow down to a block of *w*?"
1Co 3:12 costly stones, *w*, hay or straw,

WORD (WORDS)
Dt 8: 3 but on every *w* that comes
2Sa 22:31 the *w* of the LORD is flawless.
Ps 119: 9 By living according to your *w*.
119:11 I have hidden your *w* in my heart
119:105 Your *w* is a lamp to my feet
Pr 12:25 but a kind *w* cheers him up.
25:11 A *w* aptly spoken
30: 5 "Every *w* of God is flawless;
Isa 55:11 so is my *w* that goes out
Jn 1: 1 was the *W*, and the *W* was
1:14 The *W* became flesh and made his
2Co 2:17 we do not peddle the *w* of God
4: 2 nor do we distort the *w* of God.
Eph 6:17 of the Spirit, which is the *w* of God.
Php 2:16 as you hold out the *w* of life—
Col 3:16 Let the *w* of Christ dwell
2Ti 2:15 and who correctly handles the *w*
Heb 4:12 For the *w* of God is living
Jas 1:22 Do not merely listen to the *w*,
2Pe 1:19 And we have the *w* of the prophets

WORDS (WORD)
Dt 11:18 Fix these *w* of mine in your hearts
Ps 119:103 How sweet are your *w* to my taste
119:130 The unfolding of your *w* gives light;
119:160 All your *w* are true;
Pr 30: 6 Do not add to his *w*,
Jer 15:16 When your *w* came, I ate them;
Mt 24:35 but my *w* will never pass away.
Jn 6:68 You have the *w* of eternal life.
15: 7 in me and my *w* remain in you,
1Co 14:19 rather speak five intelligible *w*
Rev 22:19 And if anyone takes *w* away

WORK (WORKER WORKERS WORKING WORKMAN WORKMANSHIP WORKS)
Ex 23:12 "Six days do your *w*,
Nu 8:11 ready to do the *w* of the LORD.
Dt 5:14 On it you shall not do any *w*,
Ecc 5:19 his lot and be happy in his *w*—
Jer 48:10 lax in doing the LORD's *w*!
Jn 6:27 Do not *w* for food that spoils,
9: 4 we must do the *w* of him who sent
1Co 3:13 test the quality of each man's *w*.
Php 1: 6 that he who began a good *w*
2:12 continue to *w* out your salvation
Col 3:23 Whatever you do, *w* at it
1Th 5:12 to respect those who *w* hard
2Th 3:10 If a man will not *w*, he shall not eat
2Ti 3:17 equipped for every good *w*.
Heb 6:10 he will not forget your *w*

WORKER (WORK)
Lk 10: 7 for the *w* deserves his wages.
1Ti 5:18 and "The *w* deserves his wages."

WORKERS (WORK)
Mt 9:37 is plentiful but the *w* are few.
1Co 3: 9 For we are God's fellow *w*;

WORKING (WORK)
Col 3:23 as *w* for the Lord, not for men,

WORKMAN (WORK)
2Ti 2:15 a *w* who does not need

WORKMANSHIP* (WORK)
Eph 2:10 For we are God's *w*, created

WORKS (WORK)
Pr 31:31 let her *w* bring her praise
Ro 8:28 in all things God *w* for the good
Eph 2: 9 not by *w*, so that no one can boast.
4:12 to prepare God's people for *w*

WORLD (WORLDLY)
Ps 50:12 for the *w* is mine, and all that is in it
Isa 13:11 I will punish the *w* for its evil,
Mt 5:14 "You are the light of the *w*.
16:26 for a man if he gains the whole *w*,
Mk 16:15 into all the *w* and preach the good
Jn 1:29 who takes away the sin of the *w*!
3:16 so loved the *w* that he gave his one
8:12 he said, "I am the light of the *w*.
15:19 As it is, you do not belong to the *w*,
16:33 In this *w* you will have trouble.
18:36 "My kingdom is not of this *w*.
Ro 3:19 and the whole *w* held accountable
1Co 3:19 the wisdom of this *w* is foolishness
2Co 5:19 that God was reconciling the *w*
10: 3 For though we live in the *w*,
1Ti 6: 7 For we brought nothing into the *w*,

1Jn 2: 2 but also for the sins of the whole *w.*
2:15 not love the *w* or anything in the *w.*
Rev 13: 8 slain from the creation of the *w.*

WORLDLY (WORLD)
Tit 2:12 to ungodliness and *w* passions,

WORM
Mk 9:48 " 'their *w* does not die,

WORRY (WORRYING)
Mt 6:25 I tell you, do not *w* about your life,
10:19 do not *w* about what to say

WORRYING (WORRY)
Mt 6:27 of you by *w* can add a single hour

WORSHIP
1Ch 16:29 *w* the LORD in the splendor
Ps 95: 6 Come, let us bow down in *w,*
Mt 2: 2 and have come to *w* him."
Jn 4:24 and his worshipers must *w* in spirit
Ro 12: 1 this is your spiritual act of *w.*

WORTH (WORTHY)
Job 28:13 Man does not comprehend its *w;*
Pr 31:10 She is *w* far more than rubies.
Mt 10:31 are *w* more than many sparrows.
Ro 8:18 sufferings are not *w* comparing
1Pe 1: 7 of greater *w* than gold,
3: 4 which is of great *w* in God's sight.

WORTHLESS
Pr 11: 4 Wealth is *w* in the day of wrath,
Jas 1:26 himself and his religion is *w.*

WORTHY (WORTH)
1Ch 16:25 For great is the LORD and most *w*
Eph 4: 1 to live a life *w* of the calling you
Php 1:27 in a manner *w* of the gospel
3Jn : 6 on their way in a manner *w* of God.
Rev 5: 2 "Who is *w* to break the seals

WOUNDS
Pr 27: 6 *W* from a friend can be trusted,
Isa 53: 5 and by his *w* we are healed.
Zec 13: 6 'What are these *w* on your body?'
1Pe 2:24 by his *w* you have been healed.

WRATH
2Ch 36:16 scoffed at his prophets until the *w*
Ps 2: 5 and terrifies them in his *w,* saying,
76:10 Surely your *w* against men brings
Pr 15: 1 A gentle answer turns away *w,*
Jer 25:15 filled with the wine of my *w*
Ro 1:18 The *w* of God is being revealed
5: 9 saved from God's *w* through him!
1Th 5: 9 God did not appoint us to suffer *w*
Rev 6:16 and from the *w* of the Lamb!

WRESTLED
Ge 32:24 and a man *w* with him till daybreak

WRITE (WRITING WRITTEN)
Dt 6: 9 *W* them on the doorframes
Pr 7: 3 *w* them on the tablet of your heart.
Heb 8:10 and *w* them on their hearts.

WRITING (WRITE)
1Co 14:37 him acknowledge that what I am *w*

WRITTEN (WRITE)
Jos 1: 8 careful to do everything *w* in it.
Da 12: 1 everyone whose name is found *w*
Lk 10:20 but rejoice that your names are *w*
Jn 20:31 these are *w* that you may believe
1Co 4: 6 "Do not go beyond what is *w.*"
2Co 3: 3 *w* not with ink but with the Spirit
Col 2:14 having canceled the *w* code,
Heb 12:23 whose names are *w* in heaven.

WRONG (WRONGDOING WRONGED WRONGS)
Ex 23: 2 Do not follow the crowd in doing *w*
Nu 5: 7 must make full restitution for his *w,*
Job 34:12 unthinkable that God would do *w,*
1Th 5:15 that nobody pays back *w* for *w,*

WRONGDOING (WRONG)
Job 1:22 sin by charging God with *w.*

WRONGED (WRONG)
1Co 6: 7 not rather be *w?* Why not rather

WRONGS (WRONG)
Pr 10:12 but love covers over all *w.*
1Co 13: 5 angered, it keeps no record of *w.*

YEARS
Ps 90: 4 For a thousand *y* in your sight
90:10 The length of our days is seventy *y*
2Pe 3: 8 the Lord a day is like a thousand *y,*
Rev 20: 2 and bound him for a thousand *y.*

YESTERDAY
Heb 13: 8 Jesus Christ is the same *y*

YOKE (YOKED)
Mt 11:29 Take my *y* upon you and learn

YOKED (YOKE)
2Co 6:14 Do not be *y* together

YOUNG (YOUTH)
Ps 119: 9 How can a *y* man keep his way
1Ti 4:12 down on you because you are *y,*

YOUTH (YOUNG)
Ps 103: 5 so that your *y* is renewed like
Ecc 12: 1 Creator in the days of your *y,*
2Ti 2:22 Flee the evil desires of *y,*

ZEAL
Pr 19: 2 to have *z* without knowledge,
Ro 12:11 Never be lacking in *z,*

ZECHARIAH
1. Son of Jeroboam II; king of Israel (2Ki 15:8-12).
2. Post-exilic prophet who encouraged rebuilding of temple (Ezr 5:1; 6:14; Zec 1:1).
3. Father of John the Baptist (Lk 1:13; 3:2).

ZEDEKIAH
Mattaniah, son of Josiah (1Ch 3:15), made king of Judah by Nebuchadnezzar (2Ki 24:17-25:7; 2Ch 36:10-14; Jer 37-39; 52:1-11).

ZERUBBABEL
Descendant of David (1Ch 3:19; Mt 1:3). Led return from exile (Ezr 2-3; Ne 7:7; Hag 1-2; Zec 4).

ZIMRI
King of Israel (1Ki 16:9-20).

ZION
Ps 137: 3 "Sing us one of the songs of *Z!*"
Jer 50: 5 They will ask the way to *Z*
Ro 9:33 I lay in *Z* a stone that causes men
11:26 "The deliverer will come from *Z;*

THE HEIDELBERG CATECHISM

The Heidelberg Catechism was composed in Heidelberg at the request of Elector Frederick III, who ruled the Palatinate, an influential German province, from 1559 to 1576. An old tradition credits Zacharius Ursinus and Caspar Olevianus with being coauthors of the new catechism. Both were certainly involved in its composition, although one of them may have had primary responsibility. All we know for sure is reported by the Elector in his preface of January 19, 1563. It was, he writes, "with the advice and cooperation of our entire theological faculty in this place, and of all superintendents and distinguished servants of the church" that he secured the preparation of the Heidelberg Catechism. The catechism was approved by a synod in Heidelberg in January 1563. A second and third German edition, each with small additions, as well as a Latin translation were published the same year in Heidelberg. Soon the catechism was divided into fifty-two sections so that one Lord's Day could be explained in preaching each Sunday of the year.

The Synod of Dort in 1618–1619 approved the Heidelberg Catechism, and it soon became the most ecumenical of the Reformed catechisms and confessions. The catechism has been translated into many European, Asian, and African languages and is the most widely used and most warmly praised catechism of the Reformation period.

The 1968 Synod of the Christian Reformed Church appointed a committee to prepare "a modern and accurate translation . . . which will serve as the official text of the Heidelberg Catechism and as a guide for catechism preaching." A translation was adopted by the Synod of 1975, and some editorial revisions were approved by the Synod of 1988.

The English translation follows the first German edition of the catechism except in two instances explained in footnotes to questions 57 and 80. The result of those inclusions is that the translation therefore actually follows the German text of the third edition as it was included in the Palatinate Church Order of November 15, 1563. This is the "received text" used throughout the world.

Biblical passages quoted in the catechism are taken from the New International Version. In the German editions, biblical quotations sometimes include additional words not found in the Greek text and therefore not included in recent translations such as the NIV. The additions from the German are indicated in footnotes in Q & A 4. 71 and 119.

LORD'S DAY 1

1. What is your only comfort in life and in death?
That I am not my own,[1] but belong—body and soul, in life and in death[2]—to my faithful Savior Jesus Christ.[3] He has fully paid for all my sins with his precious blood,[4] and has set me free from the tyranny of the devil.[5] He also watches over me in such a way[6] that not a hair can fall from my head without the will of my Father in heaven:[7] in fact, all things must work together for my salvation.[8] Because I belong to him, Christ, by his Holy Spirit, assures me of eternal life[9] and makes me wholeheartedly willing and ready from now on to live for him.[10]

1 1Co 6:19–20
2 Ro 14:7–9
3 1Co 3:23; Tit 2:14
4 1Pe 1:18–19; 1Jn 1:7–9; 2:2
5 Jn 8:34–36; Heb 2:14–15; 1Jn 3:1–11
6 Jn 6:39–40; 10:27–30; 2Th 3:3; 1Pe 1:5
7 Mt 10:29–31; Lk 21:16–18
8 Ro 8:28
9 Ro 8:15–16; 2Co 1:21–22; 5:5; Eph 1:13–14
10 Ro 8:1–17

2. What must you know to live and die in the joy of this comfort?
Three things: first, how great my sin and misery are;[1] second, how I am set free from all my sins and misery;[2] third, how I am to thank God for such deliverance.[3]

1 Ro 3:9–10; 1Jn 1:10
2 Jn 17:3; Ac 4:12; 10:43
3 Mt 5:16; Ro 6:13; Eph 5:8–10; 2Ti 2:15; 1Pe 2:9–10

PART I: HUMAN MISERY

LORD'S DAY 2

3. How do you come to know your misery?
The law of God tells me.[1]

1 Ro 3:20; 7:7–25

4. What does God's law require of us?
Christ teaches us this in summary in Matthew 22: Love the Lord your God with all your heart and with all your soul and with all your mind and with all your strength.[1] * This is the first and greatest commandment. And the second is like it: Love your neighbor as yourself.[2] All the Law and the Prophets hang on these two commandments.

1 Dt 6:5
2 Lev 19:18
* Earlier and better manuscripts of Matthew 22 omit the words "and with all your strength." They are found in Mark 12:30.

5. Can you live up to all this perfectly?
No.[1] I have a natural tendency to hate God and my neighbor.[2]

1 Ro 3:9–20,23; 1Jn 1:8,10
2 Ge 6:5; Jer 17:9; Ro 7:23–24; 8:7; Eph 2:1–3; Tit 3:3

LORD'S DAY 3

6. Did God create people so wicked and perverse?
No. God created them good[1] and in his own image,[2] that is, in true righteousness and holiness,[3] so that they might truly know God their creator,[4] love him with all their heart, and live with him in eternal happiness for his praise and glory.[5]

1 Ge 1:31
2 Ge 1:26–27
3 Eph 4:24
4 Col 3:10
5 Ps 8

7. Then where does this corrupt human nature come from?
From the fall and disobedience of our first parents, Adam and Eve, in Paradise.[1] This fall has so poisoned our nature[2] that we are born sinners—corrupt from conception on.[3]

1 Ge 3
2 Ro 5:12,18–19
3 Ps 51:5

8. But are we so corrupt that we are totally unable to do any good and inclined toward all evil?
Yes,[1] unless we are born again, by the Spirit of God.[2]

1 Ge 6:5; 8:21; Job 14:4; Isa 53:6
2 Jn 3:3–5

LORD'S DAY 4

9. But doesn't God do us an injustice by requiring in his law what we are unable to do?
No, God created humans with the ability to keep the law.[1] They, however, tempted by the devil,[2] in reckless disobedience,[3] robbed themselves and all their descendants of these gifts.[4]

1 Ge 1:31; Eph 4:24
2 Ge 3:13; Jn 8:44
3 Ge 3:6
4 Ro 5:12,18–19

10. Will God permit such disobedience and rebellion to go unpunished?
Certainly not. He is terribly angry about the sin we are born with as well as the sins we personally commit. As a just judge he punishes them now and in eternity.[1] He has declared: "Cursed is everyone who does not continue to do everything written in the Book of the Law.[2]

1 Ex 34:7; Ps 5:4–6; Na 1:2; Ro 1:18; Eph 5:6; Heb 9:27
2 Dt 27:26; Gal 3:10

11. But isn't God also merciful?
God is certainly merciful,[1] but he is also just.[2] His justice demands that sin, committed against his supreme majesty, be punished with the supreme penalty—eternal punishment of body and soul.[3]

1 Ex 34:6–7; Ps 103:8–9
2 Ex 34:7; Dt 7:9–11; Ps 5:4–6; Heb 10:30–31
3 Mt 25:35–46

PART II: DELIVERANCE

LORD'S DAY 5

12. According to God's righteous judgment we deserve punishment both in this world and forever after: How then can we escape this punishment and return to God's favor?
God requires that his justice be satisfied.[1] Therefore the claims of his justice must be paid in full, either by ourselves or another.[2]

1 Ex 23:7; Ro 2:1–11
2 Isa 53:11; Ro 8:3–4

13. Can we pay this debt ourselves?
Certainly not. Actually, we increase our guilt every day.[1]

1 Mt 6:12; Ro 2:4–5

14. Can another creature—any at all—pay this debt for us?
No. To begin with, God will not punish another creature for what a human is guilty of.[1] Besides, no mere creature can bear the weight of God's eternal anger against sin and release others from it.[2]

1 Eze 18:4,20; Heb 2:14–18
2 Ps 49:7–9; 130:3

15. What kind of mediator and deliverer should we look for then?
One who is truly human[1] and truly righteous,[2] yet more powerful than all creatures, that is, one who is also true God.[3]

1 Ro 1:3; 1Co 15:21; Heb 2:17
2 Isa 53:9; 2Co 5:21; Heb 7:26
3 Isa 7:14; 9:6; Jer 23:6; Jn 1:1

LORD'S DAY 6

16. Why must he be truly human and truly righteous?
God's justice demands that human nature, which has sinned, must pay for its sin;[1] but a sinner could never pay for others.[2]

1 Ro 5:12,15; 1Co 15:21; Heb 2:14–16
2 Heb 7:26–27; 1Pe 3:18

17. Why must he also be true God?
So that, by the power of his divinity, he might bear the weight of God's anger in his humanity and earn for us and restore to us righteousness and life.[1]

1 Isa 53; Jn 3:16; 2Co 5:21

18. And who is this mediator—true God and at the same time truly human and truly righteous?
Our Lord Jesus Christ,[1] who was given us to set us completely free and to make us right with God.[2]

1 Mt 1:21–23; Lk 2:11; 1Ti 2:5
2 1Co 1:30

19. How do you come to know this?
The holy gospel tells me. God himself began to reveal the gospel already in Paradise;[1] later, he proclaimed it by the holy patriarchs[2] and prophets,[3] and portrayed it by the sacrifices and other ceremonies of the law;[4] finally, he fulfilled it through his own dear Son.[5]

1 Ge 3:15
2 Ge 22:18; 49:10
3 Isa 53; Jer 23:5–6; Mic 7:18–20; Ac 10:43; Heb 1:1–2
4 Lev 1–7; Jn 5:46; Heb 10:1–10
5 Ro 10:4; Gal 4:4–5; Col 2:17

LORD'S DAY 7

20. Are all saved through Christ just as all were lost through Adam?
No. Only those are saved who by true faith are grafted into Christ and accept all his blessings.[1]

1 Mt 7:14; Jn 3:16,18,36; Ro 11:16–21

21. What is true faith?
True faith is not only a knowledge and conviction that everything God reveals in his Word is true;[1] it is also a deep-rooted assurance,[2] created in me by the Holy Spirit[3] through the gospel,[4] that, out of sheer grace earned for us by Christ,[5] not only others, but I too,[6] have had my sins forgiven, have been made forever right with God, and have been granted salvation.[7]

1 Jn 17:3,17; Heb 11:1–3; Jas 2:19
2 Ro 4:18–21; 5:1; 10:10; Heb 4:14–16
3 Mt 16:15–17; Jn 3:5; Ac 16:14
4 Ro 1:16; 10:17; 1Co 1:21
5 Ro 3:21–26; Gal 2:16; Eph 2:8–10
6 Gal 2:20
7 Ro 1:17; Heb 10:10

22. What then must a Christian believe?
Everything God promises us in the gospel.[1] That gospel is summarized for us in the articles of our Christian faith—a creed beyond doubt, and confessed throughout the world.

1 Mt 28:18–20; Jn 20:30–31

23. What are these articles?
I believe in God, the Father almighty, creator of heaven and earth.
I believe in Jesus Christ, his only Son, our Lord, who was conceived by the Holy Spirit and born of the virgin Mary. He suffered under Pontius Pilate, was crucified, died, and was buried; he descended to hell. The third day he rose again from the dead. He ascended to heaven and is seated at the right hand of God the Father almighty. From there he will come to judge the living and the dead.
I believe in the Holy Spirit, the holy catholic church, the communion of saints, the forgiveness of sins, the resurrection of the body, and the life everlasting. Amen.

LORD'S DAY 8

24. How are these articles divided?
Into three parts: God the Father and our creation; God the Son and our deliverance; God the Holy Spirit and our sanctification.

25. Since there is but one God,[1] why do you speak of three: Father, Son, and Holy Spirit?
Because that is how God has revealed himself in his Word:[2] these three distinct persons are one, true, eternal God.

1 Dt 6:4; 1Co 8:4,6
2 Mt 3:16–17; 28:18–19; Lk 4:18 (Isa 61:1); Jn 14:26; 15:26; 2Co 13:14; Gal 4:6; Tit 3:5–6

God the Father

LORD'S DAY 9

26. What do you believe when you say, "I believe in God, the Father almighty, creator of heaven and earth"?
That the eternal Father of our Lord Jesus Christ, who out of nothing created heaven and earth and everything in them,[1] who still upholds and rules them by his eternal counsel and providence,[2] is my God and Father because of Christ his Son.[3] I trust him so much that I do not doubt he will provide whatever I need for body and soul,[4] and he will turn to my good whatever adversity he sends me in this sad world.[5] He is able to do this because he is almighty God;[6] he desires to do this because he is a faithful Father.[7]

1 Ge 1–2; Ex 20:11; Ps 33:6; Isa 44:24; Ac 4:24; 14:15
2 Ps 104; Mt 6:30; 10:29; Eph 1:11
3 Jn 1:12–13; Ro 8:15–16; Gal 4:4–7; Eph 1:5
4 Ps 55:22; Mt 6:25–26; Lk 12:22–31
5 Ro 8:28
6 Ge 18:14; Ro 8:31–39
7 Mt 7:9–11

LORD'S DAY 10

27. What do you understand by the providence of God?
Providence is the almighty and ever present power of God[1] by which he upholds, as with his hand, heaven and earth and all creatures,[2] and so rules them that leaf and blade, rain and drought, fruitful and lean years, food and drink, health and sickness, prosperity and poverty[3]—all things, in fact, come to us not by chance[4] but from his fatherly hand.[5]

1 Jer 23:23–24; Ac 17:24–28
2 Heb 1:3
3 Pr 22:2; Jer 5:24; Ac 14:15–17; Jn 9:3
4 Pr 16:33
5 Mt 10:29

28. How does the knowledge of God's creation and providence help us?
We can be patient when things go against us,[1] thankful when things go well,[2] and for the future we can have good confidence in our faithful God and Father that nothing will separate us from his love.[3] All creatures are so completely in his hand that without his will they can neither move nor be moved.[4]

1 Job 1:21–22; Jas 1:3
2 Dt 8:10; 1Th 5:18
3 Ps 55:22; Ro 5:3–5; 8:38–39
4 Job 1:12; 2:6; Pr 21:1; Ac 17:24–28

God the Son

LORD'S DAY 11

29. Why is the Son of God called "Jesus," meaning "savior"?
Because he saves us from our sins.[1] Salvation cannot be found in anyone else; it is futile to look for any salvation elsewhere.[2]

1 Mt 1:21; Heb 7:25
2 Isa 43:11; Jn 15:5; Ac 4:11–12; 1Ti 2:5

30. Do those who look for their salvation and security in saints, in themselves, or elsewhere really believe in the only savior Jesus?
No. Although they boast of being his, by their deeds they deny the only savior and deliverer, Jesus.[1] Either Jesus is not a perfect savior, or those who in true faith accept this savior have in him all they need for their salvation.[2]

1 1Co 1:12–13; Gal 5:4
2 Col 1:19–20; 2:10; 1Jn 1:7

LORD'S DAY 12

31. Why is he called "Christ," meaning "anointed"?
Because he has been ordained by God the Father and has been anointed with the Holy Spirit[1] to be our chief prophet and teacher[2] who perfectly reveals to us the secret counsel and will of God for our deliverance;[3] our only high priest[4] who has set us free by the one sacrifice of his body,[5] and who continually pleads our cause with the Father;[6] and our eternal king[7] who governs us by his Word and Spirit, and who guards us and keeps us in the freedom he has won for us.[8]

1 Lk 3:21–22; 4:14–19 (Isa 61:1); Heb 1:9 (Ps 45:7)
2 Ac 3:22 (Dt 18:15)
3 Jn 1:18; 15:15
4 Heb 7:17 (Ps 110:4)
5 Heb 9:12; 10:11–14
6 Ro 8:34; Heb 9:24
7 Mt 21:5 (Zec 9:9)
8 Mt 28:18–20; Jn 10:28; Rev 12:10–11

32. But why are you called a Christian?
Because by faith I am a member of Christ[1] and so I share in his anointing.[2] I am anointed to confess his name,[3] to present myself to him as a living sacrifice of thanks,[4] to strive with a good conscience against sin and the devil in this life,[5] and afterward to reign with Christ over all creation for all eternity.[6]

1 1Co 12:12–27
2 Ac 2:17 (Joel 2:28); 1Jn 2:27
3 Mt 10:32; Ro 10:9–10; Heb 13:15
4 Ro 12:1; 1Pe 2:5,9
5 Gal 5:16–17; Eph 6:11; 1Ti 1:18–19
6 Mt 25:34; 2Ti 2:12

LORD'S DAY 13

33. Why is he called God's "only Son" when we also are God's children?
Because Christ alone is the eternal, natural Son of God.[1] We, however, are adopted children of God—adopted by grace through Christ.[2]

1 Jn 1:1–3,14,18; Heb 1
2 Jn 1:12; Ro 8:14–17; Eph 1:5–6

34. Why do you call him "our Lord"?
Because—not with gold or silver, but with his precious blood[1]—he has set us free from sin and from the tyranny of the devil,[2] and has bought us, body and soul, to be his very own.[3]

1 1Pe 1:18–19
2 Col 1:13–14; Heb 2:14–15
3 1Co 6:20; 1Ti 2:5–6

LORD'S DAY 14

35. What does it mean that he "was conceived by the Holy Spirit and born of the virgin Mary"?
That the eternal Son of God, who is and remains true and eternal God,[1] took to himself, through the working of the Holy Spirit,[2] from the flesh and blood of the virgin Mary,[3] a truly human

nature so that he might become David's true descendant,[4] like his brothers in every way[5] except for sin.[6]

[1] Jn 1:1; 10:30–36; Ac 13:33 (Ps 2:7); Col 1:15–17; 1Jn 5:20
[2] Lk 1:35
[3] Mt 1:18–23; Jn 1:14; Gal 4:4; Heb 2:14
[4] 2Sa 7:12–16; Ps 132:11; Mt 1:1; Ro 1:3
[5] Php 2:7; Heb 2:17
[6] Heb 4:15; 7:26–27

36. How does the holy conception and birth of Christ benefit you?
He is our mediator,[1] and with his innocence and perfect holiness he removes from God's sight my sin—mine since I was conceived.[2]

[1] 1Ti 2:5–6; Heb 9:13–15
[2] Ro 8:3–4; 2Co 5:21; Gal 4:4–5; 1Pe 1:18–19

LORD'S DAY 15

37. What do you understand by the word "suffered"?
That during his whole life on earth, but especially at the end, Christ sustained in body and soul the anger of God against the sin of the whole human race.[1] This he did in order that, by his suffering as the only atoning sacrifice,[2] he might set us free, body and soul, from eternal condemnation,[3] and gain for us God's grace, righteousness, and eternal life.[4]

[1] Isa 53; 1Pe 2:24; 3:18
[2] Ro 3:25; Heb 10:14; 1Jn 2:2; 4:10
[3] Ro 8:1–4; Gal 3:13
[4] Jn 3:16; Ro 3:24–26

38. Why did he suffer "under Pontius Pilate" as judge?
So that he, though innocent, might be condemned by a civil judge,[1] and so free us from the severe judgment of God that was to fall on us.[2]

[1] Lk 23:13–24; Jn 19:4,12–16
[2] Isa 53:4–5; 2Co 5:21; Gal 3:13

39. Is it significant that he was "crucified" instead of dying some other way?
Yes. This death convinces me that he shouldered the curse which lay on me, since death by crucifixion was accursed by God.[1]

[1] Gal 3:10–13 (Dt 21:23)

LORD'S DAY 16

40. Why did Christ have to go all the way to death?
Because God's justice and truth demand it:[1] only the death of God's Son could pay for our sin.[2]

[1] Ge 2:17
[2] Ro 8:3–4; Php 2:8; Heb 2:9

41. Why was he "buried"?
His burial testifies that he really died.[1]

[1] Isa 53:9; Jn 19:38–42; Ac 13:29; 1Co 15:3–4

42. Since Christ has died for us, why do we still have to die?
Our death does not pay the debt of our sins.[1] Rather, it puts an end to our sinning and is our entrance into eternal life.[2]

[1] Ps 49:7
[2] Jn 5:24; Php 1:21–23; 1Th 5:9–10

43. What further advantage do we receive from Christ's sacrifice and death on the cross?
Through Christ's death our old selves are crucified, put to death, and buried with him,[1] so that the evil desires of the flesh may no longer rule us,[2] but that instead we may dedicate ourselves as an offering of gratitude to him.[3]

[1] Ro 6:5–11; Col 2:11–12
[2] Ro 6:12–14
[3] Ro 12:1; Eph 5:1–2

44. Why does the creed add, "He descended to hell"?
To assure me in times of personal crisis and temptation that Christ my Lord, by suffering unspeakable anguish, pain, and terror of soul, especially on the cross but also earlier, has delivered me from the anguish and torment of hell.[1]

[1] Isa 53; Mt 26:36–46; 27:45–46; Lk 22:44; Heb 5:7–10

LORD'S DAY 17

45. How does Christ's resurrection benefit us?
First, by his resurrection he has overcome death, so that he might make us share in the righteousness he won for us by his death.[1] Second, by his power we too are already now resurrected to a new life.[2] Third, Christ's resurrection is a guarantee of our glorious resurrection.[3]

[1] Ro 4:25; 1Co 15:16–20; 1Pe 1:3–5
[2] Ro 6:5–11; Eph 2:4–6; Col 3:1–4
[3] Ro 8:11; 1Co 15:12–23; Php 3:20–21

LORD'S DAY 18

46. What do you mean by saying, "He ascended to heaven"
That Christ, while his disciples watched, was lifted up from the earth to heaven[1] and will be there for our good[2] until he comes again to judge the living and the dead.[3]

[1] Lk 24:50–51; Ac 1:9–11
[2] Ro 8:34; Eph 4:8–10; Heb 7:23–25; 9:24
[3] Ac 1:11

47. But isn't Christ with us until the end of the world as he promised us?[1]
Christ is truly human and truly God. In his human nature Christ is not now on earth;[2] but in his divinity, majesty, grace, and Spirit he is not absent from us for a moment.[3]

[1] Mt 28:20
[2] Ac 1:9–11; 3:19–21
[3] Mt 28:18–20; Jn 14:16–19

48. If his humanity is not present wherever his divinity is, then aren't the two natures of Christ separated from each other?
Certainly not. Since divinity is not limited and is present everywhere,[1] it is evident that Christ's divinity is surely beyond the bounds of the humanity he has taken on, but at the same time his divinity is in and remains personally united to his humanity.[2]

[1] Jer 23:23–24; Ac 7:48–49 (Isa 66:1)
[2] Jn 1:14; 3:13; Col 2:9

49. How does Christ's ascension to heaven benefit us?
First, he pleads our cause in heaven in the presence of his Father.[1] Second, we have our own flesh in heaven—a guarantee that Christ our head will take us, his members, to himself in heaven.[2] Third, he sends his Spirit to us on earth as a further guarantee.[3] By the Spirit's power we make the goal of our lives, not earthly things, but the things above where Christ is, sitting at God's right hand.[4]

[1] Ro 8:34; 1Jn 2:1
[2] Jn 14:2; 17:24; Eph 2:4–6
[3] Jn 14:16; 2Co 1:21–22; 5:5
[4] Col 3:1–4

LORD'S DAY 19

50. Why the next words: "and is seated at the right hand of God"?
Christ ascended to heaven, there to show that he is head of his church,[1] and that the Father rules all things through him.[2]

[1] Eph 1:20–23; Col 1:18
[2] Mt 28:18; Jn 5:22–23

51. How does this glory of Christ our head benefit us?
First, through his Holy Spirit he pours out his gifts from heaven upon us his members.[1] Second, by his power he defends us and keeps us safe from all enemies.[2]

[1] Ac 2:33; Eph 4:7–12
[2] Ps 110:1–2; Jn 10:27–30; Rev 19:11–16

52. How does Christ's return "to judge the living and the dead" comfort you?
In all my distress and persecution I turn my eyes to the heavens

and confidently await as judge the very One who has already stood trial in my place before God and so has removed the whole curse from me.[1] All his enemies and mine he will condemn to everlasting punishment: but me and all his chosen ones he will take along with him into the joy and the glory of heaven.[2]

1 Lk 21:28; Ro 8:22–25; Php 3:20–21; Tit 2:13–14
2 Mt 25:31–46; 2Th 1:6–10

God the Holy Spirit

LORD'S DAY 20

53. What do you believe concerning "the Holy Spirit"?
First, he, as well as the Father and the Son, is eternal God.[1] Second, he has been given to me personally,[2] so that, by true faith, he makes me share in Christ and all his blessings,[3] comforts me,[4] and remains with me forever.[5]

1 Ge 1:1–2; Mt 28:19; Ac 5:3–4
2 1Co 6:19; 2Co 1:21–22; Gal 4:6
3 Gal 3:14
4 Jn 15:26; Ac 9:31
5 Jn 14:16–17; 1Pe 4:14

LORD'S DAY 21

54. What do you believe concerning "the holy catholic church"?
I believe that the Son of God through his Spirit and Word,[1] out of the entire human race,[2] from the beginning of the world to its end,[3] gathers, protects, and preserves for himself a community chosen for eternal life[4] and united in true faith.[5] And of this community I am[6] and always will be[7] a living member.

1 Jn 10:14–16; Ac 20:28; Ro 10:14–17; Col 1:18
2 Ge 26:3b–4; Rev 5:9
3 Isa 59:21; 1Co 11:26
4 Mt 16:18; Jn 10:28–30; Ro 8:28–30; Eph 1:3–14
5 Ac 2:42–47; Eph 4:1–6
6 1Jn 3:14,19–21
7 Jn 10:27–28; 1Co 1:4–9; 1Pe 1:3–5

55. What do you understand by "the communion of saints"?
First, that believers one and all, as members of this community, share in Christ and in all his treasures and gifts.[1] Second, that each member should consider it a duty to use these gifts readily and cheerfully for the service and enrichment of the other members.[2]

1 Ro 8:32; 1Co 6:17; 12:4–7,12–13; 1Jn 1:3
2 Ro 12:4–8; 1Co 12:20–27; 13:1–7; Php 2:4–8

56. What do you believe concerning "the forgiveness of sins"?
I believe that God, because of Christ's atonement, will never hold against me any of my sins[1] nor my sinful nature which I need to struggle against all my life.[2] Rather, in his grace God grants me the righteousness of Christ to free me forever from judgment.[3]

1 Ps 103:3–4,10,12; Mic 7:18–19; 2Co 5:18–21; 1Jn 1:7; 2:2
2 Ro 7:21–25
3 Jn 3:17–18; Ro 8:1–2

LORD'S DAY 22

57. How does "the resurrection of the body" comfort you?
Not only my soul will be taken immediately after this life to Christ its head,[1] but even my very flesh, raised by the power of Christ, will be reunited with my soul and made like Christ's glorious* body.[2]

1 Lk 23:43; Php 1:21–23
2 1Co 15:20,42–46,54; Php 3:21; 1Jn 3:2
* The first edition had here the German word for "holy." This was later corrected to the German word for "glorious."

58. How does the article concerning "life everlasting" comfort you?
Even as I already now experience in my heart the beginning of eternal joy,[1] so after this life I will have perfect blessedness such as no eye has seen, no ear has heard, no human heart has ever imagined: a blessedness in which to praise God eternally.[2]

1 Ro 14:17
2 Jn 17:3; 1Co 2:9

LORD'S DAY 23

59. What good does it do you, however, to believe all this?
In Christ I am right with God and heir to life everlasting.[1]

1 Jn 3:36; Ro 1:17 (Hab 2:4); Ro 5:1–2

60. How are you right with God?
Only by true faith in Jesus Christ.[1] Even though my conscience accuses me of having grievously sinned against all God's commandments and of never having kept any of them,[2] and even though I am still inclined toward all evil,[3] nevertheless, without my deserving it at all,[4] out of sheer grace,[5] God grants and credits to me the perfect satisfaction, righteousness, and holiness of Christ,[6] as if I had never sinned nor been a sinner, as if I had been as perfectly obedient as Christ was obedient for me.[7] All I need to do is to accept this gift of God with a believing heart.[8]

1 Ro 3:21–28; Gal 2:16; Eph 2:8–9; Php 3:8–11
2 Ro 3:9–10
3 Ro 7:23
4 Tit 3:4–5
5 Ro 3:24; Eph 2:8
6 Ro 4:3–5 (Ge 15:6); 2Co 5:17–19; 1Jn 2:1–2
7 Ro 4:24–25; 2Co 5:21
8 Jn 3:18; Ac 16:30–31

61. Why do you say that by faith alone you are right with God?
It is not because of any value my faith has that God is pleased with me. Only Christ's satisfaction, righteousness, and holiness make me right with God.[1] And I can receive this righteousness and make it mine in no other way than by faith alone.[2]

1 1Co 1:30–31
2 Ro 10:10; 1Jn 5:10–12

LORD'S DAY 24

62. Why can't the good we do make us right with God, or at least help make us right with him?
Because the righteousness which can pass God's scrutiny must be entirely perfect and must in every way measure up to the divine law.[1] Even the very best we do in this life is imperfect and stained with sin.[2]

1 Ro 3:20; Gal 3:10 (Dt 27:26)
2 Isa 64:6

63. How can you say that the good we do doesn't earn anything when God promises to reward it in this life and the next?[1]
This reward is not earned; it is a gift of grace.[2]

1 Mt 5:12; Heb 11:6
2 Lk 17:10; 2Ti 4:7–8

64. But doesn't this teaching make people indifferent and wicked?
No. It is impossible for those grafted into Christ by true faith not to produce fruits of gratitude.[1]

1 Lk 6:43–45; Jn 15:5

The Sacraments

LORD'S DAY 25

65. It is by faith alone that we share in Christ and all his blessings: Where then does that faith come from?
The Holy Spirit produces it in our hearts[1] by the preaching of the holy gospel,[2] and confirms it through our use of the holy sacraments.[3]

1 Jn 3:5; 1Co 2:10–14; Eph 2:8
2 Ro 10:17; 1Pe 1:23–25
3 Mt 28:19–20; 1Co 10:16

66. What are sacraments?
Sacraments are holy signs and seals for us to see. They were instituted by God so that by our use of them he might make us understand more clearly the promise of the gospel, and might put his seal on that promise.[1] And this is God's gospel promise: to forgive our sins and give us eternal life by grace alone because of Christ's one sacrifice finished on the cross.[2]

[1] Ge 17:11; Dt 30:6; Ro 4:11
[2] Mt 26:27–28; Ac 2:38; Heb 10:10

67. Are both the word and the sacraments then intended to focus our faith on the sacrifice of Jesus Christ on the cross as the only ground of our salvation?
Right! In the gospel the Holy Spirit teaches us and through the holy sacraments he assures us that our entire salvation rests on Christ's one sacrifice for us on the cross.[1]

[1] Ro 6:3; 1Co 11:26; Gal 3:27

68. How many sacraments did Christ institute in the New Testament?
Two: baptism and the Lord's Supper.[1]

[1] Mt 28:19–20; 1Co 11:23–26

Baptism

LORD'S DAY 26

69. How does baptism remind you and assure you that Christ's one sacrifice on the cross is for you personally?
In this way: Christ instituted this outward washing[1] and with it gave the promise that, as surely as water washes away the dirt from the body, so certainly his blood and his Spirit wash away my soul's impurity, in other words, all my sins.[2]

[1] Ac 2:38
[2] Mt 3:11; Ro 6:3–10; 1Pe 3:21

70. What does it mean to be washed with Christ's blood and Spirit?
To be washed with Christ's blood means that God, by grace, has forgiven my sins because of Christ's blood poured out for me in his sacrifice on the cross.[1] To be washed with Christ's Spirit means that the Holy Spirit has renewed me and set me apart to be a member of Christ so that more and more I become dead to sin and increasingly live a holy and blameless life.[2]

[1] Zec 13:1; Eph 1:7–8; Heb 12:24; 1Pe 1:2; Rev 1:5
[2] Eze 36:25–27; Jn 3:5–8; Ro 6:4; 1Co 6:11; Col 2:11–12

71. Where does Christ promise that we are washed with his blood and Spirit as surely as we are washed with the water of baptism?
In the institution of baptism where he says: "Therefore go and make disciples of all nations, baptizing them in the name of the Father and of the Son and of the Holy Spirit."[1] "Whoever believes and is baptized will be saved, but whoever does not believe will be condemned."[2] * This promise is repeated when Scripture calls baptism the washing of rebirth[3] and the washing away of sins.[4]

[1] Mt 28:19
[2] Mk 16:16
[3] Tit 3:5
[4] Ac 22:16
* Earlier and better manuscripts of Mark 16 omit the words "Whoever believes and is baptized . . . condemned."

LORD'S DAY 27

72. Does this outward washing with water itself wash away sins?
No, only Jesus Christ's blood and the Holy Spirit cleanse us from all sins.[1]

[1] Mt 3:11; 1Pe 3:21; 1Jn 1:7

73. Why then does the Holy Spirit call baptism the washing of rebirth and the washing away of sins?
God has good reason for these words. He wants to teach us that the blood and Spirit of Christ wash away our sins just as water washes away dirt from our bodies.[1] But more important, he wants to assure us, by this divine pledge and sign, that the washing away of our sins spiritually is as real as physical washing with water.[2]

[1] 1Co 6:11; Rev 1:5; 7:14
[2] Ac 2:38; Ro 6:3–4; Gal 3:27

74. Should infants, too, be baptized?
Yes. Infants as well as adults are in God's covenant and are his people.[1] They, no less than adults, are promised the forgiveness of sin through Christ's blood and the Holy Spirit who produces faith.[2] Therefore, by baptism, the mark of the covenant, infants should be received into the Christian church and should be distinguished from the children of unbelievers.[3] This was done in the Old Testament by circumcision,[4] which was replaced in the New Testament by baptism.[5]

[1] Ge 17:7; Mt 19:14
[2] Isa 44:1–3; Ac 2:38–39; 16:31
[3] Ac 10:47; 1Co 7:14
[4] Ge 17:9–14
[5] Col 2:11–13

The Lord's Supper

LORD'S DAY 28

75. How does the Lord's Supper remind you and assure you that you share in Christ's one sacrifice on the cross and in all his gifts?
In this way: Christ has commanded me and all believers to eat this broken bread and to drink this cup. With this command he gave this promise:[1] First, as surely as I see with my eyes the bread of the Lord broken for me and the cup given to me, so surely his body was offered and broken for me and his blood poured out for me on the cross. Second, as surely as I receive from the hand of the one who serves, and taste with my mouth the bread and cup of the Lord, given me as sure signs of Christ's body and blood, so surely he nourishes and refreshes my soul for eternal life with his crucified body and poured-out blood.

[1] Mt 26:26–28; Mk 14:22–24; Lk 22:19–20; 1Co 11:23–25

76. What does it mean to eat the crucified body of Christ and to drink his poured-out blood?
It means to accept with a believing heart the entire suffering and death of Christ and by believing to receive forgiveness of sins and eternal life.[1] But it means more. Through the Holy Spirit, who lives both in Christ and in us, we are united more and more to Christ's blessed body.[2] And so, although he is in heaven[3] and we are on earth, we are flesh of his flesh and bone of his bone.[4] And we forever live on and are governed by one Spirit, as members of our body are by one soul.[5]

[1] Jn 6:35,40,50–54
[2] Jn 6:55–56; 1Co 12:13
[3] Ac 1:9–11; 1Co 11:26; Col 3:1
[4] 1Co 6:15–17; Eph 5:29–30; 1Jn 4:13
[5] Jn 6:56–58; 15:1–6; Eph 4:15–16; 1Jn 3:24

77. Where does Christ promise to nourish and refresh believers with his body and blood as surely as they eat this broken bread and drink this cup?
In the institution of the Lord's Supper: "The Lord Jesus, on the night he was betrayed, took bread, and when he had given thanks, he broke it and said, 'This is my body, which is for you; do this in remembrance of me.' In the same way, after supper he took the cup, saying, 'This cup is the new covenant in my blood; do this, whenever you drink it, in remembrance of me.' For whenever you eat this bread and drink this cup, you proclaim the Lord's death until he comes."[1] This promise is repeated by Paul in these words: "Is not the cup of thanksgiving for which we give thanks a participation in the blood of Christ? And is not the bread that we break a participation in the body of Christ? Because there is one loaf, we, who are many, are one body, for we all partake of the one loaf."[2]

[1] 1Co 11:23–26
[2] 1Co 10:16–17

LORD'S DAY 29

78. Are the bread and wine changed into the real body and blood of Christ?
No. Just as the water of baptism is not changed into Christ's blood and does not itself wash away sins but is simply God's sign and assurance,[1] so too the bread of the Lord's Supper is not changed into the actual body of Christ[2] even though it is called the body of Christ[3] in keeping with the nature and language of sacraments.[4]

1 Eph 5:26; Tit 3:5
2 Mt 26:26–29
3 1Co 10:16–17; 11:26–28
4 Ge 17:10–11; Ex 12:11,13; 1Co 10:1–4

79. Why then does Christ call the bread his body and the cup his blood, or the new covenant in his blood? (Paul uses the words, a participation in Christ's body and blood.)
Christ has good reason for these words. He wants to teach us that as bread and wine nourish our temporal life, so too his crucified body and poured-out blood truly nourish our souls for eternal life.[1] But more important, he wants to assure us, by this visible sign and pledge, that we, through the Holy Spirit's work, share in his true body and blood as surely as our mouths receive these holy signs in his remembrance,[2] and that all of his suffering and obedience are as definitely ours as if we personally had suffered and paid for our sins.[3]

1 Jn 6:51,55
2 1Co 10:16–17; 11:26
3 Ro 6:5–11

LORD'S DAY 30

***80. How does the Lord's Supper differ from the Roman Catholic Mass?**
The Lord's Supper declares to us that our sins have been completely forgiven through the one sacrifice of Jesus Christ which he himself finished on the cross once for all.[1] It also declares to us that the Holy Spirit grafts us into Christ,[2] who with his very body is now in heaven at the right hand of the Father[3] where he wants us to worship him.[4] But the Mass teaches that the living and the dead do not have their sins forgiven through the suffering of Christ unless Christ is still offered for them daily by the priests. It also teaches that Christ is bodily present in the form of bread and wine where Christ is therefore to be worshiped. Thus the Mass is basically nothing but a denial of the one sacrifice and suffering of Jesus Christ and a condemnable idolatry.

1 Jn 19:30; Heb 7:27; 9:12,25–26; 10:10–18
2 1Co 6:17; 10:16–17
3 Ac 7:55–56; Heb 1:3; 8:1
4 Mt 6:20–21; Jn 4:21–24; Php 3:20; Col 3:1–3
* Question and answer 80 were altogether absent from the first edition of the catechism but were present in a shorter form in the second edition. The translation here given is of the expanded text of the third edition.

81. Who are to come to the Lord's table?
Those who are displeased with themselves because of their sins, but who nevertheless trust that their sins are pardoned and that their continuing weakness is covered by the suffering and death of Christ, and who also desire more and more to strengthen their faith and to lead a better life. Hypocrites and those who are unrepentant, however, eat and drink judgment on themselves.[1]

1 1Co 10:19–22; 11:26–32

82. Are those to be admitted to the Lord's Supper who show by what they say and do that they are unbelieving and ungodly?
No, that would dishonor God's covenant and bring down God's anger upon the entire congregation.[1] Therefore, according to the instruction of Christ and his apostles, the Christian church is duty-bound to exclude such people, by the official use of the keys of the kingdom, until they reform their lives.

1 Ps 50:14–16; Isa 1:11–17; 1Co 11:17–32

LORD'S DAY 31

83. What are the keys of the kingdom?
The preaching of the holy gospel and Christian discipline toward repentance. Both preaching and discipline open the kingdom of heaven to believers and close it to unbelievers.[1]

1 Mt 16:19; Jn 20:22–23

84. How does preaching the gospel open and close the kingdom of heaven?
According to the command of Christ: The kingdom of heaven is opened by proclaiming and publicly declaring to all believers, each and every one, that, as often as they accept the gospel promise in true faith, God, because of what Christ has done, truly forgives all their sins. The kingdom of heaven is closed, however, by proclaiming and publicly declaring to unbelievers and hypocrites that, as long as they do not repent, the anger of God and eternal condemnation rest on them. God's judgment, both in this life and in the life to come, is based on this gospel testimony.[1]

1 Mt 16:19; Jn 3:31–36; 20:21–23

85. How is the kingdom of heaven closed and opened by Christian discipline?
According to the command of Christ: Those who, though called Christians, profess unchristian teachings or live unchristian lives, and after repeated and loving counsel refuse to abandon their errors and wickedness, and after being reported to the church, that is, to its officers, fail to respond also to their admonition—such persons the officers exclude from the Christian fellowship by withholding the sacraments from them, and God himself excludes them from the kingdom of Christ.[1] Such persons, when promising and demonstrating genuine reform, are received again as members of Christ and of his church.[2]

1 Mt 18:15–20; 1Co 5:3–5,11–13; 2Th 3:14–15
2 Lk 15:20–24; 2Co 2:6–11

PART III: GRATITUDE

LORD'S DAY 32

86. We have been delivered from our misery by God's grace alone through Christ and not because we have earned it: Why then must we still do good?
To be sure, Christ has redeemed us by his blood. But we do good because Christ by his Spirit is also renewing us to be like himself, so that in all our living we may show that we are thankful to God for all he has done for us,[1] and so that he may be praised through us.[2] And we do good so that we may be assured of our faith by its fruits,[3] and so that by our godly living our neighbors may be won over to Christ.[4]

1 Ro 6:13; 12:1–2; 1Pe 2:5–10
2 Mt 5:16; 1Co 6:19–20
3 Mt 7:17–18; Gal 5:22–24; 2Pe 1:10–11
4 Mt 5:14–16; Ro 14:17–19; 1Pe 2:12; 3:1–2

87. Can those be saved who do not turn to God from their ungrateful and impenitent ways?
By no means. Scripture tells us that no unchaste person, no idolater, adulterer, thief, no covetous person, no drunkard, slanderer, robber, or the like is going to inherit the kingdom of God.[1]

1 1Co 6:9–10; Gal 5:19–21; Eph 5:1–20; 1Jn 3:14

LORD'S DAY 33

88. What is involved in genuine repentance or conversion?
Two things: the dying-away of the old self, and the coming-to-life of the new.[1]

1 Ro 6:1–11; 2Co 5:17; Eph 4:22–24; Col 3:5–10

89. What is the dying-away of the old self?
It is to be genuinely sorry for sin, to hate it more and more, and to run away from it.[1]

1 Ps 51:3–4,17; Joel 2:12–13; Ro 8:12–13; 2Co 7:10

90. What is the coming-to-life of the new self?
It is wholehearted joy in God through Christ[1] and a delight to do every kind of good as God wants us to.[2]

[1] Ps 51:8,12; Isa 57:15; Ro 5:1; 14:17
[2] Ro 6:10–11; Gal 2:20

91. What do we do that is good?
Only that which arises out of true faith,[1] conforms to God's law,[2] and is done for his glory;[3] and not that which is based on what we think is right or on established human tradition.[4]

[1] Jn 15:5; Heb 11:6
[2] Lev 18:4; 1Sa 15:22; Eph 2:10
[3] 1Co 10:31
[4] Dt 12:32; Isa 29:13; Eze 20:18–19; Mt 15:7–9

LORD'S DAY 34

92. What does the Lord say in his law?
God spoke all these words:

The First Commandment
I am the Lord your God, who brought you out of Egypt, out of the land of slavery. You shall have no other gods before me.

The Second Commandment
You shall not make for yourself an idol in the form of anything in heaven above or on the earth beneath or in the waters below. You shall not bow down to them or worship them; for I, the Lord your God, am a jealous God, punishing the children for the sin of the fathers to the third and fourth generation of those who hate me, but showing love to a thousand generations of those who love me and keep my commandments.

The Third Commandment
You shall not misuse the name of the Lord your God, for the Lord will not hold anyone guiltless who misuses his name.

The Fourth Commandment
Remember the Sabbath day by keeping it holy. Six days you shall labor and do all your work, but the seventh day is a Sabbath to the Lord your God. On it you shall not do any work, neither you, nor your son or daughter, nor your manservant or maidservant, nor your animals, nor the alien within your gates. For in six days the Lord made the heavens and the earth, the sea, and all that is in them, but he rested on the seventh day. Therefore the Lord blessed the Sabbath day and made it holy.

The Fifth Commandment
Honor your father and your mother, so that you may live long in the land the Lord your God is giving you.

The Sixth Commandment
You shall not murder.

The Seventh Commandment
You shall not commit adultery.

The Eighth Commandment
You shall not steal.

The Ninth Commandment
You shall not give false testimony against your neighbor.

The Tenth Commandment
You shall not covet your neighbor's house. You shall not covet your neighbor's wife, or his manservant or maidservant, his ox or donkey, or anything that belongs to your neighbor.[1]

[1] Ex 20:1–17; Dt 5:6–21

93. How are these commandments divided?
Into two tables. The first has four commandments, teaching us what our relation to God should be. The second has six commandments, teaching us what we owe our neighbor.[1]

[1] Mt 22:37–39

94. What does the Lord require in the first commandment?
That I, not wanting to endanger my very salvation, avoid and shun all idolatry,[1] magic, superstitious rites,[2] and prayer to saints or to other creatures.[3] That I sincerely acknowledge the only true God,[4] trust him alone,[5] look to him for every good thing[6] humbly[7] and patiently,[8] love him,[9] fear him,[10] and honor him[11] with all my heart. In short, that I give up anything rather than go against his will in any way.[12]

[1] 1Co 6:9–10; 10:5–14; 1Jn 5:21
[2] Lev 19:31; Dt 18:9–12
[3] Mt 4:10; Rev 19:10; 22:8–9
[4] Jn 17:3
[5] Jer 17:5,7
[6] Ps 104:27–28; Jas 1:17
[7] 1Pe 5:5–6
[8] Col 1:11; Heb 10:36
[9] Mt 22:37 (Dt 6:5)
[10] Pr 9:10; 1Pe 1:17
[11] Mt 4:10 (Dt 6:13)
[12] Mt 5:29–30; 10:37–39

95. What is idolatry?
Idolatry is having or inventing something in which one trusts in place of or alongside of the only true God, who has revealed himself in his Word.[1]

[1] 1Ch 16:26; Gal 4:8–9; Eph 5:5; Php 3:19

LORD'S DAY 35

96. What is God's will for us in the second commandment?
That we in no way make any image of God[1] nor worship him in any other way than he has commanded in his Word.[2]

[1] Dt 4:15–19; Isa 40:18–25; Ac 17:29; Ro 1:22–23
[2] Lev 10:1–7; 1Sa 15:22–23; Jn 4:23–24

97. May we then not make any image at all?
God can not and may not be visibly portrayed in any way. Although creatures may be portrayed, yet God forbids making or having such images if one's intention is to worship them or to serve God through them.[1]

[1] Ex 34:13–14,17; 2Ki 18:4–5

98. But may not images be permitted in the churches as teaching aids for the unlearned?
No, we shouldn't try to be wiser than God. He wants his people instructed by the living preaching of his Word[1]—not by idols that cannot even talk.[2]

[1] Ro 10:14–15,17; 2Ti 3:16–17; 2Pe 1:19
[2] Jer 10:8; Hab 2:18–20

LORD'S DAY 36

99. What is God's will for us in the third commandment?
That we neither blaspheme nor misuse the name of God by cursing,[1] perjury,[2] or unnecessary oaths,[3] nor share in such horrible sins by being silent bystanders.[4] In a word, it requires that we use the holy name of God only with reverence and awe,[5] so that we may properly confess him,[6] pray to him,[7] and praise him in everything we do and say.[8]

[1] Lev 24:10–17
[2] Lev 19:12
[3] Mt 5:37; Jas 5:12
[4] Lev 5:1; Pr 29:24
[5] Ps 99:1–5; Jer 4:2
[6] Mt 10:32–33; Ro 10:9–10
[7] Ps 50:14–15; 1Ti 2:8
[8] Col 3:17

100. Is blasphemy of God's name by swearing and cursing really such serious sin that God is angry also with those who do not do all they can to help prevent it and forbid it?
Yes, indeed.[1] No sin is greater, no sin makes God more angry than blaspheming his name. That is why he commanded the death penalty for it.[2]

[1] Lev 5:1
[2] Lev 24:10–17

LORD'S DAY 37

101. But may we swear an oath in God's name if we do it reverently?
Yes, when the government demands it, or when necessity requires it, in order to maintain and promote truth and trustworthiness for God's glory and our neighbor's good. Such oaths are approved in God's Word[1] and were rightly used by Old and New Testament believers.[2]

1 Dt 6:13; 10:20; Jer 4:1–2; Heb 6:16
2 Ge 21:24; Jos 9:15; 1Ki 1:29–30; Ro 1:9; 2Co 1:23

102. May we swear by saints or other creatures?
No. A legitimate oath means calling upon God as the one who knows my heart to witness to my truthfulness and to punish me if I swear falsely.[1] No creature is worthy of such honor.[2]

1 Ro 9:1; 2Co 1:23
2 Mt 5:34–37; 23:16–22; Jas 5:12

LORD'S DAY 38

103 Q. What is God's will for you in the fourth commandment?
First, that the gospel ministry and education for it be maintained,[1] and that, especially on the festive day of rest, I regularly attend the assembly of God's people[2] to learn what God's Word teaches,[3] to participate in the sacraments,[4] to pray to God publicly,[5] and to bring Christian offerings for the poor.[6] Second, that every day of my life I rest from my evil ways, let the Lord work in me through his Spirit, and so begin already in this life the eternal Sabbath.[7]

1 Dt 6:4–9,20–25; 1Co 9:13–14; 2Ti 2:2; 3:13–17; Tit 1:5
2 Dt 12:5–12; Ps 40:9–10; 68:26; Ac 2:42–47; Heb 10:23–25
3 Ro 10:14–17; 1Co 14:31–32; 1Ti 4:13
4 1Co 11:23–25
5 Col 3:16; 1Ti 2:1
6 Ps 50:14; 1Co 16:2; 2Co 8–9
7 Isa 66:23; Heb 4:9–11

LORD'S DAY 39

104. What is God's will for you in the fifth commandment?
That I honor, love, and be loyal to my father and mother and all those in authority over me; that I obey and submit to them, as is proper, when they correct and punish me;[1] and also that I be patient with their failings[2]—for through them God chooses to rule us.[3]

1 Ex 21:17; Pr 1:8; 4:1; Ro 13:1–2; Eph 5:21–22; 6:1–9; Col 3:18–4:1
2 Pr 20:20; 23:22; 1Pe 2:18
3 Mt 22:21; Ro 13:1–8; Eph 6:1–9; Col 3:18–21

LORD'S DAY 40

105. What is God's will for you in the sixth commandment?
I am not to belittle, insult, hate, or kill my neighbor—not by my thoughts, my words, my look or gesture, and certainly not by actual deeds—and I am not to be party to this in others;[1] rather, I am to put away all desire for revenge.[2] I am not to harm or recklessly endanger myself either.[3] Prevention of murder is also why government is armed with the sword.[4]

1 Ge 9:6; Lev 19:17–18; Mt 5:21–22; 26:52
2 Pr 25:21–22; Mt 18:35; Ro 12:19; Eph 4:26
3 Mt 4:7; 26:52; Ro 13:11–14
4 Ge 9:6; Ex 21:14; Ro 13:4

106. Does this commandment refer only to killing?
By forbidding murder God teaches us that he hates the root of murder: envy, hatred, anger, vindictiveness.[1] In God's sight all such are murder.[2]

1 Pr 14:30; Ro 1:29; 12:19; Gal 5:19–21; 1Jn 2:9–11
2 1Jn 3:15

107. Is it enough then that we do not kill our neighbor in any such way?
No. By condemning envy, hatred, and anger God tells us to love our neighbors as ourselves,[1] to be patient, peace-loving, gentle, merciful, and friendly to them,[2] to protect them from harm as much as we can, and to do good even to our enemies.[3]

1 Mt 7:12; 22:39; Ro 12:10
2 Mt 5:3–12; Lk 6:36; Ro 12:10,18; Gal 6:1–2; Eph 4:2; Col 3:12; 1Pe 3:8
3 Ex 23:4–5; Mt 5:44–45; Ro 12:20–21 (Pr 25:21–22)

LORD'S DAY 41

108. What is God's will for us in the seventh commandment?
God condemns all unchastity.[1] We should therefore thoroughly detest it[2] and, married or single, live decent and chaste lives.[3]

1 Lev 18:30; Eph 5:3–5
2 Jude 22–23
3 1Co 7:1–9; 1Th 4:3–8; Heb 13:4

109. Does God, in this commandment, forbid only such scandalous sins as adultery?
We are temples of the Holy Spirit, body and soul, and God wants both to be kept clean and holy. That is why he forbids everything which incites unchastity,[1] whether it be actions, looks, talk, thoughts, or desires.[2]

1 1Co 15:33; Eph 5:18
2 Mt 5:27–29; 1Co 6:18–20; Eph 5:3–4

LORD'S DAY 42

110. What does God forbid in the eighth commandment?
He forbids not only outright theft and robbery, punishable by law.[1] But in God's sight theft also includes cheating and swindling our neighbor by schemes made to appear legitimate,[2] such as: inaccurate measurements of weight, size, or volume; fraudulent merchandising; counterfeit money; excessive interest; or any other means forbidden by God.[3] In addition he forbids all greed[4] and pointless squandering of his gifts.[5]

1 Ex 22:1; 1Co 5:9–10; 6:9–10
2 Mic 6:9–11; Lk 3:14; Jas 5:1–6
3 Dt 25:13–16; Ps 15:5; Pr 11:1; 12:22; Eze 45:9–12; Lk 6:35
4 Lk 12:15; Eph 5:5
5 Pr 21:20; 23:20–21; Lk 16:10–13

111. What does God require of you in this commandment?
That I do whatever I can for my neighbor's good, that I treat others as I would like them to treat me, and that I work faithfully so that I may share with those in need.[1]

1 Isa 58:5–10; Mt 7:12; Gal 6:9–10; Eph 4:28

LORD'S DAY 43

112. What is God's will for you in the ninth commandment?
God's will is that I never give false testimony against anyone, twist no one's words, not gossip or slander, nor join in condemning anyone without a hearing or without a just cause.[1] Rather, in court and everywhere else, I should avoid lying and deceit of every kind; these are devices the devil himself uses, and they would call down on me God's intense anger.[2] I should love the truth, speak it candidly, and openly acknowledge it.[3] And I should do what I can to guard and advance my neighbor's good name.[4]

1 Ps 15; Pr 19:5; Mt 7:1; Lk 6:37; Ro 1:28–32
2 Lev 19:11–12; Pr 12:22; 13:5; Jn 8:44; Rev 21:8
3 1Co 13:6; Eph 4:25
4 1Pe 3:8–9; 4:8

LORD'S DAY 44

113. What is God's will for you in the tenth commandment?
That not even the slightest thought or desire contrary to any one of God's commandments should ever arise in my heart. Rather, with all my heart I should always hate sin and take pleasure in whatever is right.[1]

1 Ps 19:7–14; 139:23–24; Ro 7:7–8

114. But can those converted to God obey these commandments perfectly?
No. In this life even the holiest have only a small beginning of this obedience.[1] Nevertheless, with all seriousness of purpose, they do begin to live according to all, not only some, of God's commandments.[2]

1 Ecc 7:20; Ro 7:14–15; 1Co 13:9; 1Jn 1:8–10
2 Ps 1:1–2; Ro 7:22–25; Php 3:12–16

115. No one in this life can obey the Ten Commandments perfectly: Why then does God want them preached so pointedly?
First, so that the longer we live the more we may come to know our sinfulness and the more eagerly look to Christ for forgiveness of sins and righteousness.[1] Second, so that, while praying to God for the grace of the Holy Spirit, we may never stop striving to be renewed more and more after God's image, until after this life we reach our goal: perfection.[2]

1 Ps 32:5; Ro 3:19–26; 7:7,24–25; 1Jn 1:9
2 1Co 9:24; Php 3:12–14; 1Jn 3:1–3

Prayer

LORD'S DAY 45

116. Why do Christians need to pray?
Because prayer is the most important part of the thankfulness God requires of us.[1] And also because God gives his grace and Holy Spirit only to those who pray continually and groan inwardly, asking God for these gifts and thanking him for them.[2]

1 Ps 50:14–15; 116:12–19; 1Th 5:16–18
2 Mt 7:7–8; Lk 11:9–13

117. How does God want us to pray so that he will listen to us?
First, we must pray from the heart to no other than the one true God, who has revealed himself in his Word, asking for everything he has commanded us to ask for.[1] Second, we must acknowledge our need and misery, hiding nothing, and humble ourselves in his majestic presence.[2] Third, we must rest on this unshakable foundation: even though we do not deserve it, God will surely listen to our prayer because of Christ our Lord. That is what he promised us in his Word.[3]

1 Ps 145:18–20; Jn 4:22–24; Ro 8:26–27; Jas 1:5; 1Jn 5:14–15
2 2Ch 7:14; Ps 2:11; 34:18; 62:8; Isa 66:2; Rev 4
3 Da 9:17–19; Mt 7:8; Jn 14:13–14; 16:23; Ro 10:13; Jas 1:6

118. What did God command us to pray for?
Everything we need, spiritually and physically,[1] as embraced in the prayer Christ our Lord himself taught us.

1 Mt 6:33; Jas 1:17

119. What is this prayer?
Our Father in heaven, hallowed be your name, your kingdom come, your will be done on earth as it is in heaven. Give us today our daily bread. Forgive us our debts, as we also have forgiven our debtors. And lead us not into temptation, but deliver us from the evil one. For yours is the kingdom and the power and the glory forever. Amen.[1] *

1 Mt 6:9–13; Lk 11:2–4
* Earlier and better manuscripts of Matthew 6 omit the words "For yours is . . . Amen."

LORD'S DAY 46

120. Why did Christ command us to call God "our Father"?
At the very beginning of our prayer Christ wants to kindle in us what is basic to our prayer—the childlike awe and trust that God through Christ has become our Father. Our fathers do not refuse us the things of this life; God our Father will even less refuse to give us what we ask in faith.[1]

1 Mt 7:9–11; Lk 11:11–13

121. Why the words "in heaven"?
These words teach us not to think of God's heavenly majesty as something earthly,[1] and to expect everything for body and soul from his almighty power.[2]

1 Jer 23:23–24; Ac 17:24–25
2 Mt 6:25–34; Ro 8:31–32

LORD'S DAY 47

122. What does the first request mean?
"Hallowed be your name" means, Help us to really know you,[1] to bless, worship, and praise you for all your works and for all that shines forth from them: your almighty power, wisdom, kindness, justice, mercy, and truth.[2] And it means, Help us to direct all our living—what we think, say, and do—so that your name will never be blasphemed because of us but always honored and praised.[3]

1 Jer 9:23–24; 31:33–34; Mt 16:17; Jn 17:3
2 Ex 34:5–8; Ps 145; Jer 32:16–20; Lk 1:46–55,68–75; Ro 11:33–36
3 Ps 115:1; Mt 5:16

LORD'S DAY 48

123. What does the second request mean?
"Your kingdom come" means, Rule us by your Word and Spirit in such a way that more and more we submit to you.[1] Keep your church strong, and add to it.[2] Destroy the devil's work; destroy every force which revolts against you and every conspiracy against your Word.[3] Do this until your kingdom is so complete and perfect that in it you are all in all.[4]

1 Ps 119:5,105; 143:10; Mt 6:33
2 Ps 122:6–9; Mt 16:18; Ac 2:42–47
3 Ro 16:20; 1Jn 3:8
4 Ro 8:22–23; 1Co 15:28; Rev 22:17,20

LORD'S DAY 49

124. What does the third request mean?
"Your will be done on earth as it is in heaven" means, Help us and all people to reject our own wills and to obey your will without any back talk. Your will alone is good.[1] Help us one and all to carry out the work we are called to,[2] as willingly and faithfully as the angels in heaven.[3]

1 Mt 7:21; 16:24–26; Lk 22:42; Ro 12:1–2; Tit 2:11–12
2 1Co 7:17–24; Eph 6:5–9
3 Ps 103:20–21

LORD'S DAY 50

125. What does the fourth request mean?
"Give us today our daily bread" means, Do take care of all our physical needs[1] so that we come to know that you are the only source of everything good,[2] and that neither our work and worry nor your gifts can do us any good without your blessing.[3] And so help us to give up our trust in creatures and to put trust in you alone.[4]

1 Ps 104:27–30; 145:15–16; Mt 6:25–34
2 Ac 14:17; 17:25; Jas 1:17
3 Dt 8:3; Ps 37:16; 127:1–2; 1Co 15:58
4 Ps 55:22; 62; 146; Jer 17:5–8; Heb 13:5–6

LORD'S DAY 51

126. What does the fifth request mean?
"Forgive us our debts, as we also have forgiven our debtors" means, Because of Christ's blood, do not hold against us, poor sinners that we are, any of the sins we do or the evil that constantly clings to us.[1] Forgive us just as we are fully determined, as evidence of your grace in us, to forgive our neighbors.[2]

1 Ps 51:1–7; 143:2; Ro 8:1; 1Jn 2:1–2
2 Mt 6:14–15; 18:21–35

LORD'S DAY 52

127. What does the sixth request mean?
"And lead us not into temptation, but deliver us from the evil one" means, By ourselves we are too weak to hold our own even for a moment.[1] And our sworn enemies—the devil,[2] the world,[3] and our own flesh[4]—never stop attacking us. And so, Lord, uphold us and make us strong with the strength of your Holy Spirit, so that we may not go down to defeat in this spiri-

tual struggle,[5] but may firmly resist our enemies until we finally win the complete victory.[6]

1 Ps 103:14–16; Jn 15:1–5
2 2Co 11:14; Eph 6:10–13; 1Pe 5:8
3 Jn 15:18–21
4 Ro 7:23; Gal 5:17
5 Mt 10:19–20; 26:41; Mk 13:33; Ro 5:3–5
6 1Co 10:13; 1Th 3:13; 5:23

128. What does your conclusion to this prayer mean?
"For yours is the kingdom and the power and the glory forever" means, We have made all these requests of you because, as our all-powerful king, you not only want to, but are able to give us all that is good;[1] and because your holy name, and not we ourselves, should receive all the praise, forever.[2]

1 Ro 10:11–13; 2Pe 2:9
2 Ps 115:1; Jn 14:13

129. What does that little word "Amen" express?
"Amen" means, This is sure to be! It is even more sure that God listens to my prayer, than that I really desire what I pray for.[1]

1 Isa 65:24; 2Co 1:20; 2Ti 2:13

THE BELGIC CONFESSION

One of the oldest of the doctrinal standards, particularly of the Dutch Reformed tradition, is the Confession of Faith, popularly known as the Belgic Confession, following the seventeenth-century Latin designation "Confessio Belgica." "Belgica" referred to the whole of the Netherlands, both north and south, which today is divided into the Netherlands and Belgium. The confession's chief author was Guido de Bres, a preacher of the Reformed churches of the Netherlands, who died a martyr to the faith in the year 1567. During the sixteenth century the churches in this country were exposed to the most terrible persecution by the Roman Catholic government. To protest against this cruel oppression, and to prove to the persecutors that the adherents of the Reformed faith were not rebels, as was laid to their charge, but law-abiding citizens who professed the true Christian doctrine according to the Holy Scriptures, de Bres prepared this confession in the year 1561. In the following year a copy was sent to King Philip II, together with an address in which the petitioners declared that they were ready to obey the government in all lawful things, but that they would "offer their backs to stripes, their tongues to knives, their mouths to gags, and their whole bodies to the fire," rather than deny the truth expressed in this confession.

Although the immediate purpose of securing freedom from persecution was not attained, and de Bres himself fell as one of the many thousands who sealed their faith with their lives, his work has endured and will continue to endure. In its composition the author availed himself to some extent of a confession of the Reformed churches in France, written chiefly by John Calvin, published two years earlier. The work of de Bres, however, is not a mere revision of Calvin's work, but an independent composition. In 1566 the text of this confession was revised at a synod held at Antwerp. In the Netherlands it was at once gladly received by the churches, and it was adopted by national synods held during the last three decades of the sixteenth century. The text, not the contents, was revised again at the Synod of Dort in 1618–19 and adopted as one of the doctrinal standards to which all officebearers in the Reformed churches were required to subscribe. The confession stands as one of the best symbolical statements of Reformed doctrine. The translation presented here is based on the French text of 1619.

Article 1: The Only God

We all believe in our hearts and confess with our mouths that there is a single and simple spiritual being, whom we call God—eternal, incomprehensible, invisible, unchangeable, infinite, almighty; completely wise, just, and good, and the overflowing source of all good.

Article 2: The Means by Which We Know God

We know him by two means:

First, by the creation, preservation, and government of the universe, since that universe is before our eyes like a beautiful book in which all creatures, great and small, are as letters to make us ponder the invisible things of God: his eternal power and his divinity, as the apostle Paul says in Romans 1:20. All these things are enough to convict men and to leave them without excuse.

Second, he makes himself known to us more openly by his holy and divine Word, as much as we need in this life, for his glory and for the salvation of his own.

Article 3: The Written Word of God

We confess that this Word of God was not sent nor delivered by the will of men, but that holy men of God spoke, being moved by the Holy Spirit, as Peter says.[1]

Afterwards our God—because of the special care he has for us and our salvation—commanded his servants, the prophets and apostles, to commit this revealed Word to writing. He himself wrote with his own finger the two tables of the law.

Therefore we call such writings holy and divine Scriptures.

1 2Pe 1:21

Article 4: The Canonical Books

We include in the Holy Scripture the two volumes of the Old and New Testaments. They are canonical books with which there can be no quarrel at all.

In the church of God the list is as follows:

In the Old Testament, the five books of Moses—Genesis, Exodus, Leviticus, Numbers, Deuteronomy; the books of Joshua, Judges, and Ruth; the two books of Samuel, and two of Kings; the two books of Chronicles, called Paralipomenon; the first book of Ezra; Nehemiah, Esther, Job; the Psalms of David; the three books of Solomon—Proverbs, Ecclesiastes, and the Song; the four major prophets—Isaiah, Jeremiah, Ezekiel, Daniel; and then the other twelve minor prophets—Hosea, Joel, Amos, Obadiah, Jonah, Micah, Nahum, Habakkuk, Zephaniah, Haggai, Zechariah, Malachi.

In the New Testament, the four gospels—Matthew, Mark, Luke, and John; the Acts of the Apostles; the fourteen letters of Paul—to the Romans; the two letters to the Corinthians; to the Galatians, Ephesians, Philippians, and Colossians; the two letters to the Thessalonians; the two letters to Timothy; to Titus, Philemon, and to the Hebrews; the seven letters of the other apostles—one of James; two of Peter; three of John; one of Jude; and the Revelation of the apostle John.

Article 5: The Authority of Scripture

We receive all these books and these only as holy and canonical, for the regulating, founding, and establishing of our faith.

And we believe without a doubt all things contained in them—not so much because the church receives and approves them as such but above all because the Holy Spirit testifies in our hearts that they are from God, and also because they prove themselves to be from God.

For even the blind themselves are able to see that the things predicted in them do happen.

Article 6: The Difference Between Canonical and Apocryphal Books

We distinguish between these holy books and the apocryphal ones, which are the third and fourth books of Esdras; the books of Tobit, Judith, Wisdom, Jesus Sirach, Baruch; what was added to the Story of Esther; the Song of the Three Children in the Furnace; the Story of Susannah; the Story of Bell and the Dragon; the Prayer of Manasseh; and the two books of Maccabees.

The church may certainly read these books and learn from them as far as they agree with the canonical books. But they do not have such power and virtue that one could confirm from their testimony any point of faith or of the Christian religion. Much less can they detract from the authority of the other holy books.

Article 7: The Sufficiency of Scripture

We believe that this Holy Scripture contains the will of God completely and that everything one must believe to be saved is sufficiently taught in it. For since the entire manner of service which God requires of us is described in it at great length, no one—even an apostle or an angel from heaven, as Paul says[1]—ought to teach other than what the Holy Scriptures have already taught us. For since it is forbidden to add to or subtract from the Word of God,[2] this plainly demonstrates that the teaching is perfect and complete in all respects.

Therefore we must not consider human writings—no matter how holy their authors may have been—equal to the divine writings; nor may we put custom, nor the majority, nor age, nor the passage of time or persons, nor councils, decrees, or official decisions above the truth of God, for truth is above everything else.

For all human beings are liars by nature and more vain than vanity itself.

Therefore we reject with all our hearts everything that does not agree with this infallible rule, as we are taught to do by the apostles when they say, "Test the spirits to see if they are of God,"[3] and also, "If anyone comes to you and does not bring this teaching, do not receive him into your house."[4]

1 Gal 1:8
2 Dt 12:32; Rev 22:18–19
3 1Jn 4:1
4 2Jn 10

Article 8: The Trinity

In keeping with this truth and Word of God we believe in one God, who is one single essence, in whom there are three persons, really, truly, and eternally distinct according to their incommunicable properties—namely, Father, Son, and Holy Spirit. The Father is the cause, origin, and source of all things, visible as well as invisible. The Son is the Word, the Wisdom, and the image of the Father. The Holy Spirit is the eternal power and might, proceeding from the Father and the Son.

Nevertheless, this distinction does not divide God into three, since Scripture teaches us that the Father, the Son, and the Holy Spirit each has his own subsistence distinguished by characteristics—yet in such a way that these three persons are only one God.

It is evident then that the Father is not the Son and that the Son is not the Father, and that likewise the Holy Spirit is neither the Father nor the Son.

Nevertheless, these persons, thus distinct, are neither divided nor fused or mixed together.

For the Father did not take on flesh, nor did the Spirit, but only the Son. The Father was never without his Son, nor without his Holy Spirit, since all these are equal from eternity, in one and the same essence.

There is neither a first nor a last, for all three are one in truth and power, in goodness and mercy.

Article 9: The Scriptural Witness on the Trinity

All these things we know from the testimonies of Holy Scripture as well as from the effects of the persons, especially from those we feel within ourselves.

The testimonies of the Holy Scriptures, which teach us to believe in this Holy Trinity, are written in many places of the Old Testament, which need not be enumerated but only chosen with discretion.

In the book of Genesis God says, "Let us make man in our image, according to our likeness." So "God created man in his own image"—indeed, "male and female he created them."[1] "Behold, man has become like one of us."[2]

It appears from this that there is a plurality of persons within the Deity, when he says, "Let us make man in our image"—and afterwards he indicates the unity when he says, "God created."

It is true that he does not say here how many persons there are—but what is somewhat obscure to us in the Old Testament is very clear in the New.

For when our Lord was baptized in the Jordan, the voice of the Father was heard saying, "This is my dear Son";[3] the Son was seen in the water; and the Holy Spirit appeared in the form of a dove.

So, in the baptism of all believers this form was prescribed by Christ: "Baptize all people in the name of the Father, and of the Son, and of the Holy Spirit."[4]

In the Gospel according to Luke the angel Gabriel says to Mary, the mother of our Lord: "The Holy Spirit will come upon you, and the power of the Most High will overshadow you; and therefore that holy one to be born of you shall be called the Son of God."[5]

And in another place it says: "The grace of our Lord Jesus Christ, and the love of God, and the fellowship of the Holy Spirit be with you."[6]

"There are three who bear witness in heaven—the Father, the Word, and the Holy Spirit—and these three are one."[7]

In all these passages we are fully taught that there are three persons in the one and only divine essence. And although this doctrine surpasses human understanding, we nevertheless believe it now, through the Word, waiting to know and enjoy it fully in heaven.

Furthermore, we must note the particular works and activities of these three persons in relation to us. The Father is called our Creator, by reason of his power. The Son is our Savior and Redeemer, by his blood. The Holy Spirit is our Sanctifier, by his living in our hearts.

This doctrine of the holy Trinity has always been maintained in the true church, from the time of the apostles until the present, against Jews, Muslims, and certain false Christians and heretics, such as Marcion, Mani, Praxeas, Sabellius, Paul of Samosata, Arius, and others like them, who were rightly condemned by the holy fathers.

And so, in this matter we willingly accept the three ecumenical creeds—the Apostles', Nicene, and Athanasian—as well as what the ancient fathers decided in agreement with them.

1 Ge 1:26–27
2 Ge 3:22
3 Mt 3:17
4 Mt 28:19
5 Lk 1:35
6 2Co 13:14
7 1Jn 5:7 (KJV)

Article 10: The Deity of Christ

We believe that Jesus Christ, according to his divine nature, is the only Son of God—eternally begotten, not made nor created, for then he would be a creature.

He is one in essence with the Father; coeternal; the exact image of the person of the Father and the "reflection of his glory,"[1] being in all things like him.

He is the Son of God not only from the time he assumed our nature but from all eternity, as the following testimonies teach us when they are taken together.

Moses says that God "created the world";[2] and John says that "all things were created by the Word,"[3] which he calls God. The apostle says that "God made the world by his Son."[4] He also says that "God created all things by Jesus Christ."[5]

And so it must follow that he who is called God, the Word, the Son, and Jesus Christ already existed when all things were created by him.

Therefore the prophet Micah says that his origin is "from ancient times, from eternity."[6] And the apostle says that he has "neither beginning of days nor end of life."[7]

So then, he is the true eternal God, the Almighty, whom we invoke, worship, and serve.

1 Col 1:15; Heb. 1:3
2 Ge 1:1
3 Jn 1:3
4 Heb 1:2
5 Col 1:16
6 Mic 5:2
7 Heb 7:3

Article 11: The Deity of the Holy Spirit

We believe and confess also that the Holy Spirit proceeds eternally from the Father and the Son—neither made, nor created, nor begotten, but only proceeding from the two of them. In regard to order, he is the third person of the Trinity—of one and the same essence, and majesty, and glory, with the Father and the Son.

He is true and eternal God, as the Holy Scriptures teach us.

Article 12: The Creation of All Things

We believe that the Father created heaven and earth and all other creatures from nothing, when it seemed good to him, by his Word—that is to say, by his Son.

He has given all creatures their being, form, and appearance, and their various functions for serving their Creator.

Even now he also sustains and governs them all, according to his eternal providence, and by his infinite power, that they may serve man, in order that man may serve God.

He has also created the angels good, that they might be his messengers and serve his elect.

Some of them have fallen from the excellence in which God created them into eternal perdition; and the others have persisted and remained in their orginal state, by the grace of God.

The devils and evil spirits are so corrupt that they are enemies of God and of everything good. They lie in wait for the church and every member of it like thieves, with all their power, to destroy and spoil everything by their deceptions.

So then, by their own wickedness they are condemned to everlasting damnation, daily awaiting their torments.

For that reason we detest the error of the Sadducees, who deny that there are spirits and angels, and also the error of the Manicheans, who say that the devils originated by themselves, being evil by nature, without having been corrupted.

Article 13: The Doctrine of God's Providence

We believe that this good God, after he created all things, did not abandon them to chance or fortune but leads and governs them according to his holy will, in such a way that nothing happens in this world without his orderly arrangement.

Yet God is not the author of, nor can he be charged with, the sin that occurs. For his power and goodness are so great and incomprehensible that he arranges and does his work very well and justly even when the devils and wicked men act unjustly. We do not wish to inquire with undue curiosity into what he does that surpasses human understanding and is beyond our ability to comprehend. But in all humility and reverence we adore the just judgments of God, which are hidden from us, being content to be Christ's disciples, so as to learn only what he shows us in his Word, without going beyond those limits.

This doctrine gives us unspeakable comfort since it teaches us that nothing can happen to us by chance but only by the arrangement of our gracious heavenly Father. He watches over us with fatherly care, keeping all creatures under his control, so that not one of the hairs on our heads (for they are all numbered) nor even a little bird can fall to the ground[1] without the will of our Father.

In this thought we rest, knowing that he holds in check the devils and all our enemies, who cannot hurt us without his permission and will.

For that reason we reject the damnable error of the Epicureans, who say that God involves himself in nothing and leaves everything to chance.

1 Mt 10:29–30

Article 14: The Creation and Fall of Man

We believe that God created man from the dust of the earth and made and formed him in his image and likeness—good, just, and holy; able by his own will to conform in all things to the will of God.

But when he was in honor he did not understand it[1] and did not recognize his excellence. But he subjected himself willingly to sin and consequently to death and the curse, lending his ear to the word of the devil. For he transgressed the commandment of life, which he had received, and by his sin he separated himself from God, who was his true life, having corrupted his entire nature.

So he made himself guilty and subject to physical and spiritual death, having become wicked, perverse, and corrupt in all his ways. He lost all his excellent gifts which he had received from God, and he retained none of them except for small traces which are enough to make him inexcusable.

Moreover, all the light in us is turned to darkness, as the Scripture teaches us: "The light shone in the darkness, and the darkness did not receive it."[2] Here John calls men "darkness."

Therefore we reject everything taught to the contrary concerning man's free will, since man is nothing but the slave of sin and cannot do a thing unless it is "given him from heaven."[3]

For who can boast of being able to do anything good by himself, since Christ says, "No one can come to me unless my Father who sent me draws him"?[4]

Who can glory in his own will when he understands that "the mind of the flesh is enmity against God"?[5] Who can speak of his own knowledge in view of the fact that "the natural man does not understand the things of the Spirit of God"?[6]

In short, who can produce a single thought, since he knows that we are "not able to think a thing" about ourselves, by ourselves, but that "our ability is from God"?[7]

And therefore, what the apostle says ought rightly to stand fixed and firm: "God works within us both to will and to do according to his good pleasure."[8]

For there is no understanding nor will conforming to God's understanding and will apart from Christ's involvement, as he teaches us when he says, "Without me you can do nothing."[9]

1 Ps 49:20
2 Jn 1:5
3 Jn 3:27
4 Jn 6:44
5 Ro 8:7
6 1Co 2:14
7 2Co 3:5
8 Php 2:13
9 Jn 15:5

Article 15: The Doctrine of Original Sin

We believe that by the disobedience of Adam original sin has been spread through the whole human race.

It is a corruption of all nature—an inherited depravity which even infects small infants in their mother's womb, and the root which produces in man every sort of sin. It is therefore so vile and enormous in God's sight that it is enough to condemn the human race, and it is not abolished or wholly uprooted even by baptism, seeing that sin constantly boils forth as though from a contaminated spring.

Nevertheless, it is not imputed to God's children for their condemnation but is forgiven by his grace and mercy—not to put them to sleep but so that the awareness of this corruption might often make believers groan as they long to be set free from the "body of this death."[1]

Therefore we reject the error of the Pelagians who say that this sin is nothing else than a matter of imitation.

1 Ro 7:24

Article 16: The Doctrine of Election

We believe that—all Adam's descendants having thus fallen into perdition and ruin by the sin of the first man—God showed himself to be as he is: merciful and just.

He is merciful in withdrawing and saving from this perdition those whom he, in his eternal and unchangeable counsel, has elected and chosen in Jesus Christ our Lord by his pure goodness, without any consideration of their works.

He is just in leaving the others in their ruin and fall into which they plunged themselves.

Article 17: The Recovery of Fallen Man

We believe that our good God, by his marvelous wisdom and goodness, seeing that man had plunged himself in this manner into both physical and spiritual death and made himself completely miserable, set out to find him, though man, trembling all over, was fleeing from him.

And he comforted him, promising to give him his Son, "born of a woman,"[1] to crush the head of the serpent,[2] and to make him blessed.

[1] Gal 4:4
[2] Ge 3:15

Article 18: The Incarnation

So then we confess that God fulfilled the promise which he had made to the early fathers by the mouth of his holy prophets when he sent his only and eternal Son into the world at the time set by him. The Son took the "form of a servant" and was made in the "likeness of man,"[1] truly assuming a real human nature, with all its weaknesses, except for sin; being conceived in the womb of the blessed virgin Mary by the power of the Holy Spirit, without male participation.

And he not only assumed human nature as far as the body is concerned but also a real human soul, in order that he might be a real human being. For since the soul had been lost as well as the body he had to assume them both to save them both together.

Therefore we confess, against the heresy of the Anabaptists who deny that Christ assumed human flesh from his mother, that he "shared the very flesh and blood of children";[2] that he is "fruit of the loins of David" according to the flesh;[3] "born of the seed of David" according to the flesh;[4] "fruit of the womb of the virgin Mary";[5] "born of a woman";[6] "the seed of David";[7] "a shoot from the root of Jesse";[8] "the offspring of Judah,"[9] having descended from the Jews according to the flesh; "from the seed of Abraham"—for he "assumed Abraham's seed" and was "made like his brothers except for sin."[10]

In this way he is truly our Immanuel—that is: "God with us."[11]

[1] Php 2:7
[2] Heb 2:14
[3] Ac 2:30
[4] Ro 1:3
[5] Lk 1:42
[6] Gal 4:4
[7] 2Ti 2:8
[8] Ro 15:12
[9] Heb 7:14
[10] Heb 2:17; 4:15
[11] Mt 1:23

Article 19: The Two Natures of Christ

We believe that by being thus conceived the person of the Son has been inseparably united and joined together with human nature, in such a way that there are not two Sons of God, nor two persons, but two natures united in a single person, with each nature retaining its own distinct properties.

Thus his divine nature has always remained uncreated, without beginning of days or end of life,[1] filling heaven and earth.

His human nature has not lost its properties but continues to have those of a creature—it has a beginning of days; it is of a finite nature and retains all that belongs to a real body. And even though he, by his resurrection, gave it immortality, that nonetheless did not change the reality of his human nature; for our salvation and resurrection depend also on the reality of his body.

But these two natures are so united together in one person that they are not even separated by his death.

So then, what he committed to his Father when he died was a real human spirit which left his body. But meanwhile his divine nature remained united with his human nature even when he was lying in the grave; and his deity never ceased to be in him, just as it was in him when he was a little child, though for a while it did not show itself as such.

These are the reasons why we confess him to be true God and true man—true God in order to conquer death by his power, and true man that he might die for us in the weakness of his flesh.

[1] Heb 7:3

Article 20: The Justice and Mercy of God in Christ

We believe that God—who is perfectly merciful and also very just—sent his Son to assume the nature in which the disobedience had been committed, in order to bear in it the punishment of sin by his most bitter passion and death.

So God made known his justice toward his Son, who was charged with our sin, and he poured out his goodness and mercy on us, who are guilty and worthy of damnation, giving to us his Son to die, by a most perfect love, and raising him to life for our justification, in order that by him we might have immortality and eternal life.

Article 21: The Atonement

We believe that Jesus Christ is a high priest forever according to the order of Melchizedek—made such by an oath—and that he presented himself in our name before his Father, to appease his wrath with full satisfaction by offering himself on the tree of the cross and pouring out his precious blood for the cleansing of our sins, as the prophets had predicted.

For it is written that "the chastisement of our peace" was placed on the Son of God and that "we are healed by his wounds." He was "led to death as a lamb"; he was "numbered among sinners"[1] and condemned as a criminal by Pontius Pilate, though Pilate had declared that he was innocent.

So he paid back what he had not stolen,[2] and he suffered—the "just for the unjust,"[3] in both his body and his soul—in such a way that when he senses the horrible punishment required by our sins his sweat became like "big drops of blood falling on the ground."[4] He cried, "My God, my God, why have you abandoned me?"[5]

And he endured all this for the forgiveness of our sins.

Therefore we rightly say with Paul that we "know nothing but Jesus and him crucified";[6] we consider all things as "dung for the excellence of the knowledge of our Lord Jesus Christ."[7] We find all comforts in his wounds and have no need to seek or invent any other means to reconcile ourselves with God than this one and only sacrifice, once made, which renders believers perfect forever.

This is also why the angel of God called him Jesus—that is, "Savior"—because he would save his people from their sins.[8]

[1] Isa 53:4-12
[2] Ps 69:4
[3] 1Pe 3:18
[4] Lk 22:44
[5] Mt 27:46
[6] 1Co 2:2
[7] Php 3:8
[8] Mt 1:21

Article 22: The Righteousness of Faith

We believe that for us to acquire the true knowledge of this great mystery the Holy Spirit kindles in our hearts a true faith that embraces Jesus Christ, with all his merits, and makes him its own, and no longer looks for anything apart from him.

For it must necessarily follow that either all that is required for our salvation is not in Christ or, if all is in him, then he who has Christ by faith has his salvation entirely. Therefore, to say that Christ is not enough but that something else is needed as well is a most enormous blasphemy against God—for it then would follow that Jesus Christ is only half a Savior. And therefore we justly say with Paul that we are justified "by faith alone" or by faith "apart from works."[1]

However, we do not mean, properly speaking, that it is faith itself that justifies us—for faith is only the instrument by which we embrace Christ, our righteousness.

But Jesus Christ is our righteousness in making available to us all his merits and all the holy works he has done for us and in our place. And faith is the instrument that keeps us in communion with him and with all his benefits.

When those benefits are made ours they are more than enough to absolve us of our sins.

[1] Ro 3:28

Article 23: The Justification of Sinners

We believe that our blessedness lies in the forgiveness of our sins because of Jesus Christ, and that in it our righteousness before God is contained, as David and Paul teach us when they declare that man blessed to whom God grants righteousness apart from works.[1]

And the same apostle says that we are justified "freely" or "by grace" through redemption in Jesus Christ.[2] And therefore we cling to this foundation, which is firm forever, giving all glory to God, humbling ourselves, and recognizing ourselves as we are; not claiming a thing for ourselves or our merits and leaning and resting on the sole obedience of Christ crucified, which is ours when we believe in him.

That is enough to cover all our sins and to make us confident, freeing the conscience from the fear, dread, and terror of God's approach, without doing what our first father, Adam, did, who trembled as he tried to cover himself with fig leaves.

In fact, if we had to appear before God relying—no matter how little—on ourselves or some other creature, then, alas, we would be swallowed up.

Therefore everyone must say with David: "Lord, do not enter into judgment with your servants, for before you no living person shall be justified."[3]

1 Ps 32:1; Ro 4:6
2 Ro 3:24
3 Ps 143:2

Article 24: The Sanctification of Sinners

We believe that this true faith, produced in man by the hearing of God's Word and by the work of the Holy Spirit, regenerates him and makes him a "new man,"[1] causing him to live the "new life"[2] and freeing him from the slavery of sin.

Therefore, far from making people cold toward living in a pious and holy way, this justifying faith, quite to the contrary, so works within them that apart from it they will never do a thing out of love for God but only out of love for themselves and fear of being condemned.

So then, it is impossible for this holy faith to be unfruitful in a human being, seeing that we do not speak of an empty faith but of what Scripture calls "faith working through love,"[3] which leads a man to do by himself the works that God has commanded in his Word.

These works, proceeding from the good root of faith, are good and acceptable to God, since they are all sanctified by his grace. Yet they do not count toward our justification—for by faith in Christ we are justified, even before we do good works. Otherwise they could not be good, any more than the fruit of a tree could be good if the tree is not good in the first place.

So then, we do good works, but nor for merit—for what would we merit? Rather, we are indebted to God for the good works we do, and not he to us, since it is he who "works in us both to will and do according to his good pleasure"[4]—thus keeping in mind what is written: "When you have done all that is commanded you, then you shall say, 'We are unworthy servants; we have done what it was our duty to do.' "[5]

Yet we do not wish to deny that God rewards good works—but it is by his grace that he crowns his gifts.

Moreover, although we do good works we do not base our salvation on them; for we cannot do any work that is not defiled by our flesh and also worthy of punishment. And even if we could point to one, memory of a single sin is enough for God to reject that work.

So we would always be in doubt, tossed back and forth without any certainty, and our poor consciences would be tormented constantly if they did not rest on the merit of the suffering and death of our Savior.

1 2Co 5:17
2 Ro 6:4
3 Gal 5:6
4 Php 2:13
5 Lk 17:10

Article 25: The Fulfillment of the Law

We believe that the ceremonies and symbols of the law have ended with the coming of Christ, and that all foreshadowings have come to an end, so that the use of them ought to be abolished among Christians. Yet the truth and substance of these things remain for us in Jesus Christ, in whom they have been fulfilled.

Nevertheless, we continue to use the witnesses drawn from the law and prophets to confirm us in the gospel and to regulate our lives with full integrity for the glory of God, according to his will.

Article 26: The Intercession of Christ

We believe that we have no access to God except through the one and only Mediator and Intercessor: Jesus Christ the Righteous.[1]

He therefore was made man, uniting together the divine and human natures, so that we human beings might have access to the divine Majesty. Otherwise we would have no access.

But this Mediator, whom the Father has appointed between himself and us, ought not terrify us by his greatness, so that we have to look for another one, according to our fancy. For neither in heaven nor among the creatures on earth is there anyone who loves us more than Jesus Christ does. Although he was "in the form of God," he nevertheless "emptied himself," taking the form of "a man" and "a servant" for us;[2] and he made himself "completely like his brothers."[3]

Suppose we had to find another intercessor. Who would love us more than he who gave his life for us, even though "we were his enemies"?[4] And suppose we had to find one who has prestige and power. Who has as much of these as he who is seated "at the right hand of the Father,"[5] and who has all power "in heaven and on earth"?[6] And who will be heard more readily than God's own dearly beloved Son?

So then, sheer unbelief has led to the practice of dishonoring the saints, instead of honoring them. That was something the saints never did nor asked for, but which in keeping with their duty, as appears from their writings, they consistently refused.

We should not plead here that we are unworthy—for it is not a question of offering our prayers on the basis of our own dignity but only on the basis of the excellence and dignity of Jesus Christ, whose righteousness is ours by faith.

Since the apostle for good reason wants us to get rid of this foolish fear—or rather, this unbelief—he says to us that Jesus Christ was "made like his brothers in all things," that he might be a high priest who is merciful and faithful to purify the sins of the people.[7] For since he suffered, being tempted, he is also able to help those who are tempted.[8]

And further, to encourage us more to approach him he says, "Since we have a high priest, Jesus the Son of God, who has entered into heaven, we maintain our confession. For we do not have a high priest who is unable to have compassion for our weaknesses, but one who was tempted in all things, just as we are, except for sin. Let us go then with confidence to the throne of grace that we may obtain mercy and find grace, in order to be helped."[9]

The same apostle says that we "have liberty to enter into the holy place by the blood of Jesus. Let us go, then, in the assurance of faith . . ."[10]

Likewise, "Christ's priesthood is forever. By this he is able to save completely those who draw near to God through him who always lives to intercede for them."[11]

What more do we need? For Christ himself declares: "I am the way, the truth, and the life; no one comes to my Father but by me."[12] Why should we seek another intercessor?

Since it has pleased God to give us his Son as our Intercessor, let us not leave him for another—or rather seek, without ever finding. For when God gave him to us he knew well that we were sinners.

Therefore, in following the command of Christ we call on the heavenly Father through Christ, our only Mediator, as we are taught by the Lord's Prayer, being assured that we shall obtain all we ask of the Father in his name.

1 1Jn 2:1
2 Php 2:6–8
3 Heb 2:17
4 Ro 5:10
5 Ro 8:34; Heb 1:3
6 Mt 28:18
7 Heb 2:17
8 Heb 2:18
9 Heb 4:14–16
10 Heb 10:19,22

[11] Heb 7:24–25
[12] Jn 14:6

Article 27: The Holy Catholic Church

We believe and confess one single catholic or universal church—a holy congregation and gathering of true Christian believers, awaiting their entire salvation in Jesus Christ being washed by his blood, and sanctified and sealed by the Holy Spirit.

This church has existed from the beginning of the world and will last until the end, as appears from the fact that Christ is eternal King who cannot be without subjects.

And this holy church is preserved by God against the rage of the whole world, even though for a time it may appear very small in the eyes of men—as though it were snuffed out.

For example, during the very dangerous time of Ahab the Lord preserved for himself seven thousand men who did not bend their knees to Baal.[1]

And so this holy church is not confined, bound, or limited to a certain place or certain persons. But it is spread and dispersed throughout the entire world, though still joined and united in heart and will, in one and the same Spirit, by the power of faith.

[1] 1Ki 19:18

Article 28: The Obligations of Church Members

We believe that since this holy assembly and congregation is the gathering of those who are saved and there is no salvation apart from it, no one ought to withdraw from it, content to be by himself, regardless of his status or condition.

But all people are obliged to join and unite with it, keeping the unity of the church by submitting to its instruction and discipline, by bending their necks under the yoke of Jesus Christ, and by serving to build up one another, according to the gifts God has given them as members of each other in the same body.

And to preserve this unity more effectively, it is the duty of all believers, according to God's Word, to separate themselves from those who do not belong to the church, in order to join this assembly wherever God has established it, even if civil authorities and royal decrees forbid and death and physical punishment result.

And so, all who withdraw from the church or do not join it act contrary to God's ordinance.

Article 29: The Marks of the True Church

We believe that we ought to discern diligently and very carefully, by the Word of God, what is the true church—for all sects in the world today claim for themselves the name of "the church."

We are not speaking here of the company of hypocrites who are mixed among the good in the church and who nonetheless are not part of it, even though they are physically there. But we are speaking of distinguishing the body and fellowship of the true church from all sects that call themselves "the church."

The true church can be recognized if it has the following marks: The church engages in the pure preaching of the gospel; it makes use of the pure administration of the sacraments as Christ instituted them; it practices church discipline for correcting faults. In short, it governs itself according to the pure Word of God, rejecting all things contrary to it and holding Jesus Christ as the only Head. By these marks one can be assured of recognizing the true church—and no one ought to be separated from it.

As for those who can belong to the church, we can recognize them by the distinguishing marks of Christians: namely by faith, and by their fleeing from sin and pursuing righteousness, once they have received the one and only Savior, Jesus Christ. They love the true God and their neighbors, without turning to the right or left, and they crucify the flesh and its works.

Though great weakness remains in them, they fight against it by the Spirit all the days of their lives, appealing constantly to the blood, suffering, death, and obedience of the Lord Jesus, in whom they have forgiveness of their sins, through faith in him.

As for the false church, it assigns more authority to itself and its ordinances than to the Word of God; it does not want to subject itself to the yoke of Christ; it does not administer the sacraments as Christ commanded in his Word; it rather adds to them or subtracts from them as it pleases; it bases itself on men, more than on Jesus Christ; it persecutes those who live holy lives according to the Word of God and who rebuke it for its faults, greed, and idolatry.

These two churches are easy to recognize and thus to distinguish from each other.

Article 30: The Government of the Church

We believe that this true church ought to be governed according to the spiritual order that our Lord has taught us in his Word. There should be ministers or pastors to preach the Word of God and adminster the sacraments. There should also be elders and deacons, along with the pastors, to make up the council of the church.

By this means true religion is preserved; true doctrine is able to take its course; and evil men are corrected spiritually and held in check, so that also the poor and all the afflicted may be helped and comforted according to their need.

By this means everything will be done well and in good order in the church, when such persons are elected who are faithful and are chosen according to the rule that Paul gave to Timothy.[1]

[1] 1Ti 3

Article 31: The Officers of the Church

We believe that ministers of the Word of God, elders, and deacons ought to be chosen to their offices by a legitimate election of the church, with prayer in the name of the Lord, and in good order, as the Word of God teaches.

So everyone must be careful not to push himself forward improperly, but he must wait for God's call, so that he may be assured of his calling and be certain that he is chosen by the Lord.

As for the ministers of the Word, they all have the same power and authority, no matter where they may be, since they are all servants of Jesus Christ, the only universal bishop, and the only head of the church.

Moreover, to keep God's holy order from being violated or despised, we say that everyone ought, as much as possible, to hold the ministers of the Word and elders of the church in special esteem, because of the work they do, and be at peace with them, without grumbling, quarreling, or fighting.

Article 32: The Order and Discipline of the Church

We also believe that although it is useful and good for those who govern the churches to establish and set up a certain order among themselves for maintaining the body of the church, they ought always to guard against deviating from what Christ, our only Master, has ordained for us.

Therefore we reject all human innovations and all laws imposed on us, in our worship of God, which bind and force our consciences in any way.

So we accept only what is proper to maintain harmony and unity and to keep all in obedience to God.

To that end excommunication, with all it involves, according to the Word of God, is required.

Article 33: The Sacraments

We believe that our good God, mindful of our crudeness and weakness, has ordained sacraments for us to seal his promises in us, to pledge his good will and grace toward us, and also to nourish and sustain our faith.

He has added these to the Word of the gospel to represent better to our external senses both what he enables us to understand by his Word and what he does inwardly in our hearts, confirming in us the salvation he imparts to us.

For they are visible signs and seals of something internal and invisible, by means of which God works in us through the power of the Holy Spirit. So they are not empty and hollow signs to fool and deceive us, for their truth is Jesus Christ, without whom they would be nothing.

Moreover, we are satisfied with the number of sacraments that Christ our Master has ordained for us. There are only two: the sacrament of baptism and the Holy Supper of Jesus Christ.

Article 34: The Sacrament of Baptism

We believe and confess that Jesus Christ, in whom the law is fulfilled, has by his shed blood put an end to every other shedding of blood, which anyone might do or wish to do in order to atone or satisfy for sins.

Having abolished circumcision, which was done with blood, he established in its place the sacrament of baptism. By it we are received into God's church and set apart from all other people and alien religions, that we may be dedicated entirely to him, bearing his mark and sign. It also witnesses to us that he will be our God forever, since he is our gracious Father.

Therefore he has commanded that all those who belong to him be baptized with pure water in the name of the Father, and the Son, and the Holy Spirit.[1]

In this way he signifies to us that just as water washes away the dirt of the body when it is poured on us and also is seen on the body of the baptized when it is sprinkled on him, so too the blood of Christ does the same thing internally, in the soul, by the Holy Spirit. It washes and cleanses it from its sins and transforms us from being the children of wrath into the children of God.

This does not happen by the physical water but by the sprinkling of the precious blood of the Son of God, who is our Red Sea, through which we must pass to escape the tyranny of Pharoah, who is the devil, and to enter the spiritual land of Canaan.

So ministers, as far as their work is concerned, give us the sacrament and what is visible, but our Lord gives what the sacrament signifies—namely the invisible gifts and graces, washing, purifying, and cleansing our souls of all filth and unrighteousness; renewing our hearts and filling them with all comfort; giving us true assurance of his fatherly goodness; clothing us with the "new man" and stripping off the "old," with all its works.

For this reason we believe that anyone who aspires to reach eternal life ought to be baptized only once without ever repeating it—for we cannot be born twice. Yet this baptism is profitable not only when the water is on us and when we receive it but throughout our entire lives.

For that reason we detest the error of the Anabaptists who are not content with a single baptism once received and also condemn the baptism of the children of believers. We believe our children ought to be baptized and sealed with the sign of the covenant, as little children were circumcised in Israel on the basis of the same promises made to our children.

And truly, Christ has shed his blood no less for washing the little children of believers than he did for adults.

Therefore they ought to receive the sign and sacrament of what Christ has done for them, just as the Lord commanded in the law that by offering a lamb for them the sacrament of the suffering and death of Christ would be granted them shortly after their birth. This was the sacrament of Jesus Christ.

Furthermore, baptism does for our children what circumcision did for the Jewish people. That is why Paul calls baptism the "circumcision of Christ."[2]

1 Mt 28:19
2 Col 2:11

Article 35: The Sacrament of the Lord's Supper

We believe and confess that our Savior Jesus Christ has ordained and instituted the sacrament of the Holy Supper to nourish and sustain those who are already born again and ingrafted into his family: his church.

Now those who are born again have two lives in them. The one is physical and temporal—they have it from the moment of their first birth, and it is common to all. The other is spiritual and heavenly, and is given them in their second birth; it comes through the Word of the gospel in the communion of the body of Christ; and this life is common to God's elect only.

Thus, to support the physical and earthly life God has prescribed for us an appropriate earthly and material bread, which is as common to all as life itself also is. But to maintain the spiritual and heavenly life that belongs to believers he has sent a living bread that came down from heaven: namely Jesus Christ, who nourishes and maintains the spiritual life of believers when eaten—that is, when appropriated and received spiritually by faith.

To represent to us this spiritual and heavenly bread Christ has instituted an earthly and visible bread as the sacrament of his body and wine as the sacrament of his blood. He did this to testify to us that just as truly as we take and hold the sacraments in our hands and eat and drink it in our mouths, by which our life is then sustained, so truly we receive into our souls, for our spiritual life, the true body and true blood of Christ, our only Savior. We receive these by faith, which is the hand and mouth of our souls.

Now it is certain that Jesus Christ did not prescribe his sacraments for us in vain, since he works in us all he represents by these holy signs, although the manner in which he does it goes beyond our understanding and is uncomprehensible to us, just as the operation of God's Spirit is hidden and incomprehensible.

Yet we do not go wrong when we say that what is eaten is Christ's own natural body and what is drunk is his own blood—but the manner in which we eat it is not by the mouth but by the Spirit, through faith.

In that way Jesus Christ remains always seated at the right hand of God the Father in heaven—but he never refrains on that account to communicate himself to us through faith.

This banquet is a spiritual table at which Christ communicates himself to us with all his benefits. At that table he makes us enjoy himself as much as the merits of his suffering and death, as he nourishes, strengthens, and comforts our poor, desolate souls by the eating of his flesh, and relieves and renews them by the drinking of his blood.

Moreover, though the sacraments and thing signified are joined together, not all receive both of them. The wicked person certainly takes the sacrament, to his condemnation, but does not receive the truth of the sacrament, just as Judas and Simon the Sorcerer both indeed received the sacrament, but not Christ, who was signified by it. He is communicated only to believers.

Finally, with humility and reverence we receive the holy sacrament in the gathering of God's people, as we engage together, with thanksgiving, in a holy remembrance of the death of Christ our Savior, and as we thus confess our faith and Christian religion. Therefore no one should come to this table without examining himself carefully, lest "by eating this bread and drinking this cup he eat and drink to his own judgment."[1]

In short, by the use of this holy sacrament we are moved to a fervent love of God and our neighbors.

Therefore we reject as desecrations of the sacraments all the muddled ideas and damnable inventions that men have added and mixed in with them. And we say that we should be content with the procedure that Christ and the apostles have taught us and speak of these things as they have spoken of them.

1 1Co 11:27

Article 36: The Civil Government

We believe that because of the depravity of the human race our good God has ordained kings, princes, and civil officers. He wants the world to be governed by laws and policies so that human lawlessness may be restrained and that everything may be conducted in good order among human beings.

For that purpose he has placed the sword in the hands of the government, to punish evil people and protect the good.

And being called in this manner to contribute to the advancement of a society that is pleasing to God, the civil rulers have the task, subject to God's law, of removing every obstacle to the preaching of the gospel and to every aspect of divine worship.

They should do this while completely refraining from every tendency toward exercising absolute authority, and while functioning in the sphere entrusted to them, with the means belonging to them.

They should do it in order that the Word of God may have free course; the kingdom of Jesus Christ may make progress; and every anti-Christian power may be resisted.*

* The Synod of 1958, in line with 1910 and 1938, substituted the above statement for the following (which it judged unbiblical): And the government's task is not limited to caring for and watching over the public domain but extends also to upholding the sacred ministry, with a view to removing and destroying all idolatry and false worship of the Antichrist; to promoting the kingdom of Jesus Christ; and to furthering the preaching of the gospel everywhere; to the end that God may be honored and served by everyone, as he requires in his Word.

Moreover everyone, regardless of status, condition, or rank, must be subject to the government, and pay taxes, and hold its representatives in honor and respect, and obey them in all things that are not in conflict with God's Word, praying for them that the Lord may be willing to lead them in all their ways and that we may live a peaceful and quiet life in all piety and decency.*

* The Synod of 1985 directed that the following paragraph be taken from the body of the text and be placed in a footnote: And on this matter we denounce the Anabaptists, other anarchists, and in general all those who want to reject the authorities and civil officers and to subvert justice by introducing common ownership of goods and corrupting the moral order that God has established among human beings.

Article 37: The Last Judgment

Finally we believe, according to God's Word, that when the time appointed by the Lord is come (which is unknown to all creatures) and the number of the elect is complete, our Lord Jesus Christ will come from heaven, bodily and visibly, as he ascended, with great glory and majesty, to declare himself the judge of the living and the dead. He will burn this old world, in fire and flame, in order to cleanse it.

Then all human creatures will appear in person before the great judge—men, women, and children, who have lived from the beginning until the end of the world.

They will be summoned there by the voice of the archangel and by the sound of the divine trumpet.[1]

For all those who died before that time will be raised from the earth, their spirits being joined and united with their own bodies in which they lived. And as for those who are still alive, they will not die like the others but will be changed "in the twinkling of an eye" from "corruptible to incorruptible."[2]

Then "the books" (that is, the consciences) will be opened, and the dead will be judged according to the things they did in the world,[3] whether good or evil. Indeed, all people will give account of all the idle words they have spoken,[4] which the world regards as only playing games. And then the secrets and hypocrisies of men will be publicly uncovered in the sight of all.

Therefore, with good reason the thought of this judgment is horrible and dreadful to wicked and evil people. But it is very pleasant and a great comfort to the righteous and elect, since their total redemption will then be accomplished. They will then receive the fruits of their labor and of the trouble they have suffered; their innocence will be openly recognized by all; and they will see the terrible vengeance that God will bring on the evil ones who tyrannized, oppressed, and tormented them in this world.

The evil ones will be convicted by the witness of their own consciences, and shall be made immortal—but only to be tormented in the everlasting fire prepared for the devil and his angels.[5]

In contrast, the faithful and elect will be crowned with glory and honor. The Son of God will "confess their names"[6] before God his Father and the holy and elect angels; all tears will be "wiped from their eyes";[7] and their cause—at present condemned as heretical and evil by many judges and civil officers—will be acknowledged as the "cause of the Son of God."

And as a gracious reward the Lord will make them possess a glory such as the heart of man could never imagine.

So we look forward to that great day with longing in order to enjoy fully the promises of God in Christ Jesus, our Lord.

1 1Th 4:16
2 1Co 15:51–53
3 Rev 20:12
4 Mt 12:36
5 Mt 25:14
6 Mt 10:32
7 Rev 7:17

THE CANONS OF DORT

"The Decision of the Synod of Dort on the Five Main Points of Doctrine in Dispute in the Netherlands" is popularly known as the Canons of Dort. It consists of statements of doctrine adopted by the great Synod of Dort which met in the city of Dordrecht in 1618–19. Although this was a national synod of the Reformed churches of the Netherlands, it had an international character, since it was composed not only of Dutch delegates but also of twenty-six delegates from eight foreign countries.

The Synod of Dort was held in order to settle a serious controversy in the Dutch churches initiated by the rise of Arminianism. Jacob Arminius, a theological professor at Leiden University, questioned the teaching of Calvin and his followers on a number of important points. After Arminius's death, his own followers presented their views on five of these points in the Remonstrance of 1610. In this document or in later more explicit writings, the Arminians taught election based on foreseen faith, universal atonement, partial depravity, resistible grace, and the possibility of a lapse from grace. In the Canons the Synod of Dort rejected these views and set forth the Reformed doctrine on these points, namely, unconditional election, limited atonement, total depravity, irresistible grace, and the perseverance of saints.

The Canons have a special character because of their original purpose as a judicial decision on the doctrinal points in dispute during the Arminian controversy. The original preface called them a "judgment, in which both the true view, agreeing with God's Word, concerning the aforesaid five points of doctrine is explained, and the false view, disagreeing with God's Word, is rejected." The Canons also have a limited character in that they do not cover the whole range of doctrine, but focus on the five points of doctrine in dispute.

Each of the main points consists of a positive and a negative part, the former being an exposition of the Reformed doctrine on the subject, the latter a repudiation of the corresponding errors. Although in form there are only four points, we speak properly of five points, because the Canons were structured to correspond to the five articles of the 1610 Remonstrance. Main Points 3 and 4 were combined into one, always designated as Main Point III/IV.

This translation of the Canons is based on the only extant Latin manuscript among those signed at the Synod of Dort. The biblical quotations are translations from the original Latin and so do not always correspond to current versions. Though not in the original text, subheadings have been added to the positive articles and to the conclusion in order to facilitate study of the Canons.

The Canons of Dort

Formally Titled

The Decision of the Synod of Dort
on the Five Main Points of Doctrine in Dispute
in the Netherlands

THE FIRST MAIN POINT OF DOCTRINE

Divine Election and Reprobation

The Judgment Concerning Divine Predestination
Which the Synod Declares to Be in Agreement
with the Word of God and Accepted Till Now
in the Reformed Churches,
Set Forth in Several Articles

Article 1: God's Right to Condemn All People

Since all people have sinned in Adam and have come under the sentence of the curse and eternal death, God would have done no one an injustice if it had been his will to leave the entire human race in sin and under the curse, and to condemn them on account of their sin. As the apostle says: "The whole world is liable to the condemnation of God" (Ro 3:19), "All have sinned and are deprived of the glory of God" (Ro 3:23), and "The wages of sin is death" (Ro 6:23).*

* All quotations from Scripture are translations of the original Latin manuscript.

Article 2: The Manifestation of God's Love

But this is how God showed his love: he sent his only begotten Son into the world, so that whoever believes in him should not perish but have eternal life.

Article 3: The Preaching of the Gospel

In order that people may be brought to faith, God mercifully sends proclaimers of this very joyful message to the people he wishes and at the time he wishes. By this ministry people are called to repentance and faith in Christ crucified. For "how shall they believe in him of whom they have not heard? And how shall they hear without someone preaching? And how shall they preach unless they have been sent?" (Ro 10:14–15).

Article 4: A Twofold Response to the Gospel

God's anger remains on those who do not believe this gospel. But those who do accept it and embrace Jesus the Savior with a true and living faith are delivered through him from God's anger and from destruction, and receive the gift of eternal life.

Article 5: The Sources of Unbelief and of Faith

The cause or blame for this unbelief, as well as for all other sins, is not at all in God, but in man. Faith in Jesus Christ, however, and salvation through him is a free gift of God. As Scripture says, "It is by grace you have been saved, through faith, and this not from yourselves; it is a gift of God" (Eph 2:8). Likewise: "It has been freely given to you to believe in Christ" (Php 1:29).

Article 6: God's Eternal Decision

The fact that some receive from God the gift of faith within time, and that others do not, stems from his eternal decision. For "all his works are known to God from eternity" (Ac 15:18; Eph 1:11). In accordance with this decision he graciously softens the hearts, however hard, of his chosen ones and inclines them to believe, but by his just judgment he leaves in their wickedness and hardness of heart those who have not been chosen. And in this especially is disclosed to us his act—unfathomable, and as merciful as it is just—of distinguishing between people equally lost. This is the well-known decision of election and reprobation revealed in God's Word. This decision the wicked, impure, and unstable distort to their own ruin, but it provides holy and godly souls with comfort beyond words.

Article 7: Election

Election [or choosing] is God's unchangeable purpose by which he did the following:

Before the foundation of the world, by sheer grace, according to the free good pleasure of his will, he chose in Christ to salvation a definite number of particular people out of the entire human race, which had fallen by its own fault from its original innocence into sin and ruin. Those chosen were neither better nor more deserving than the others, but lay with them in the common misery. He did this in Christ, whom he also appointed from eternity to be the mediator, the head of all those chosen, and the foundation of their salvation.

And so he decided to give the chosen ones to Christ to be saved, and to call and draw them effectively into Christ's fellowship through his Word and Spirit. In other words, he decided to grant them true faith in Christ, to justify them, to sanctify them, and finally, after powerfully preserving them in the fellowship of his Son, to glorify them.

God did all this in order to demonstrate his mercy, to the praise of the riches of his glorious grace.

As Scripture says, "God chose us in Christ, before the foundation of the world, so that we should be holy and blameless before him with love; he predestined us whom he adopted as his children through Jesus Christ, in himself, according to the good pleasure of his will, to the praise of his glorious grace, by which he freely made us pleasing to himself in his beloved" (Eph 1:4–6). And elsewhere, "Those whom he predestined, he also called; and those whom he called, he also justified; and those whom he justified, he also glorified" (Ro 8:30).

Article 8: A Single Decision of Election

This election is not of many kinds; it is one and the same election for all who were to be saved in the Old and the New Testament. For Scripture declares that there is a single good pleasure, purpose, and plan of God's will, by which he chose us from eternity both to grace and to glory, both to salvation and to the way of salvation, which he prepared in advance for us to walk in.

Article 9: Election Not Based on Foreseen Faith

This same election took place, not on the basis of foreseen faith, of the obedience of faith, of holiness, or of any other good quality and disposition, as though it were based on a prerequisite cause or condition in the person to be chosen, but rather for the purpose of faith, of the obedience of faith, of holiness, and so on. Accordingly, election is the source of each of the benefits of salvation. Faith, holiness, and the other saving gifts, and at last eternal life itself, flow forth from election as its fruits and effects. As the apostle says, "He chose us" (not because we were, but) "so that we should be holy and blameless before him in love" (Eph 1:4).

Article 10: Election Based on God's Good Pleasure

But the cause of this undeserved election is exclusively the good pleasure of God. This does not involve his choosing certain human qualities or actions from among all those possible as a condition of salvation, but rather involves his adopting certain particular persons from among the common mass of sinners as his own possession. As Scripture says, "When the children were not yet born, and had done nothing either good or bad..., she" (Rebecca)" was told, "The older will serve the younger." As it is written, "Jacob I loved, but Esau I hated" " (Ro 9:11–13). Also, "All who were appointed for eternal life believed" (Ac 13:48).

Article 11: Election Unchangeable

Just as God himself is most wise, unchangeable, all-knowing, and almighty, so the election made by him can neither be suspended nor altered, revoked, or annulled; neither can his chosen ones be cast off, nor their number reduced.

Article 12: The Assurance of Election

Assurance of this their eternal and unchangeable election to salvation is given to the chosen in due time, though by various stages and in differing measure. Such assurance comes not by inquisitive searching into the hidden and deep things of God, but by noticing within themselves, with spiritual joy and holy delight, the unmistakable fruits of election pointed out in God's Word—such as a true faith in Christ, a childlike fear of God, a godly sorrow for their sins, a hunger and thirst for righteousness, and so on.

Article 13: The Fruit of This Assurance

In their awareness and assurance of this election God's children daily find greater cause to humble themselves before God, to adore the fathomless depth of his mercies, to cleanse themselves, and to give fervent love in return to him who first so greatly loved them. This is far from saying that this teaching concerning election, and reflection upon it, make God's children lax in observing his commandments or carnally self-assured. By God's just judgment this does usually happen to those who casually take for granted the grace of election or engage in idle and brazen talk about it but are unwilling to walk in the ways of the chosen.

Article 14: Teaching Election Properly

Just as, by God's wise plan, this teaching concerning divine election has been proclaimed through the prophets, Christ himself, and the apostles, in Old and New Testament times, and has subsequently been committed to writing in the Holy Scriptures, so also today in God's church, for which it was specifically intended, this teaching must be set forth—with a spirit of discretion, in a godly and holy manner, at the appropriate time and place, without inquisitive searching into the ways of the Most High. This must be done for the glory of God's most holy name, and for the lively comfort of his people.

Article 15: Reprobation

Moreover, Holy Scripture most especially highlights this eternal and undeserved grace of our election and brings it out more clearly for us, in that it further bears witness that not all people have been chosen but that some have not been chosen or have been passed by in God's eternal election—those, that is, concerning whom God, on the basis of his entirely free, most just, irreproachable, and unchangeable good pleasure, made the following decision:

to leave them in the common misery into which, by their own fault, they have plunged themselves;

not to grant them saving faith and the grace of conversion;

but finally to condemn and eternally punish them (having been left in their own ways and under his just judgment), not only for their unbelief but also for all their other sins, in order to display his justice.

And this is the decision of reprobation, which does not at all make God the author of sin (a blasphemous thought!) but rather its fearful, irreproachable, just judge and avenger.

Article 16: Responses to the Teaching of Reprobation

Those who do not yet actively experience within themselves

a living faith in Christ or an assured confidence of heart, peace of conscience, a zeal for childlike obedience, and a glorying in God through Christ, but who nevertheless use the means by which God has promised to work these things in us—such people ought not to be alarmed at the mention of reprobation, nor to count themselves among the reprobate; rather they ought to continue diligently in the use of the means, to desire fervently a time of more abundant grace, and to wait for it in reverence and humility. On the other hand, those who seriously desire to turn to God, to be pleasing to him alone, and to be delivered from the body of death, but are not yet able to make such progress along the way of godliness and faith as they would like—such people ought much less to stand in fear of the teaching concerning reprobation, since our merciful God has promised that he will not snuff out a smoldering wick and that he will not break a bruised reed. However, those who have forgotten God and their Savior Jesus Christ and have abandoned themselves wholly to the cares of the world and the pleasures of the flesh—such people have every reason to stand in fear of this teaching, as long as they do not seriously turn to God.

Article 17: The Salvation of the Infants of Believers

Since we must make judgments about God's will from his Word, which testifies that the children of believers are holy, not by nature but by virtue of the gracious covenant in which they together with their parents are included, godly parents ought not to doubt the election and salvation of their children whom God calls out of this life in infancy.

Article 18: The Proper Attitude Toward Election and Reprobation

To those who complain about this grace of an undeserved election and about the severity of a just reprobation, we reply with the words of the apostle. "Who are you, O man, to talk back to God?" (Ro 9:20), and with the words of our Savior, "Have I no right to do what I want with my own?" (Mt 20:15). We, however, with reverent adoration of these secret things, cry out with the apostle: "Oh, the depths of the riches both of the wisdom and the knowledge of God! How unsearchable are his judgments, and his ways beyond tracing out! For who has known the mind of the Lord? Or who has been his counselor? Or who has first given to God, that God should repay him? For from him and through him and to him are all things. To him be the glory forever! Amen" (Ro 11:33–36).

Rejection of the Errors by Which the Dutch Churches Have for Some Time Been Disturbed

Having set forth the orthodox teaching concerning election and reprobation, the Synod rejects the errors of those

I

Who teach that the will of God to save those who would believe and persevere in faith and in the obedience of faith is the whole and entire decision of election to salvation, and that nothing else concerning this decision has been revealed in God's Word.

For they deceive the simple and plainly contradict Holy Scripture in its testimony that God does not only wish to save those who would believe, but that he has also from eternity chosen certain particular people to whom, rather than to others, he would within time grant faith in Christ and perseverance. As Scripture says, "I have revealed your name to those whom you gave me" (Jn 17:6). Likewise, "All who were appointed for eternal life believed" (Ac 13:48), and "He chose us before the foundation of the world so that we should be holy . . ." (Eph 1:4).

II

Who teach that God's election to eternal life is of many kinds: one general and indefinite, the other particular and definite; and the latter in turn either incomplete, revocable, nonperemptory (or conditional), or else complete, irrevocable, and peremptory (or absolute). Likewise, who teach that there is one election to faith and another to salvation, so that there can be an election to justifying faith apart from a peremptory election to salvation.

For this is an invention of the human brain, devised apart from the Scriptures, which distorts the teaching concerning election and breaks up this golden chain of salvation: "Those whom he predestined, he also called; and those whom he called, he also justified; and those whom he justified, he also glorified" (Ro 8:30).

III

Who teach that God's good pleasure and purpose, which Scripture mentions in its teaching of election, does not involve God's choosing certain particular people rather than others, but involves God's choosing, out of all possible conditions (including the works of the law) or out of the whole order of things, the intrinsically unworthy act of faith, as well as the imperfect obedience of faith, to be a condition of salvation; and it involves his graciously wishing to count this as perfect obedience and to look upon it as worthy of the reward of eternal life.

For by this pernicious error the good pleasure of God and the merit of Christ are robbed of their effectiveness and people are drawn away, by unprofitable inquiries, from the truth of undeserved justification and from the simplicity of the Scriptures. It also gives the lie to these words of the apostle: "God called us with a holy calling, not in virtue of works, but in virtue of his own purpose and the grace which was given to us in Christ Jesus before the beginning of time" (2Ti 1:9).

IV

Who teach that in election to faith a prerequisite condition is that man should rightly use the light of nature, be upright, unassuming, humble, and disposed to eternal life, as though election depended to some extent on these factors.

For this smacks of Pelagius, and it clearly calls into question the words of the apostle: "We lived at one time in the passions of our flesh, following the will of our flesh and thoughts, and we were by nature children of wrath, like everyone else. But God, who is rich in mercy, out of the great love with which he loved us, even when we were dead in transgressions, made us alive with Christ, by whose grace you have been saved. And God raised us up with him and seated us with him in heaven in Christ Jesus, in order that in the coming ages we might show the surpassing riches of his grace, according to his kindness toward us in Christ Jesus. For it is by grace you have been saved, through faith (and this not from yourselves; it is the gift of God) not by works, so that no one can boast" (Eph 2:3–9).

V

Who teach that the incomplete and nonperemptory election of particular persons to salvation occurred on the basis of a foreseen faith, repentance, holiness, and godliness, which has just begun or continued for some time; but that complete and peremptory election occurred on the basis of a foreseen perseverance to the end in faith, repentance, holiness, and godliness. And that this is the gracious and evangelical worthiness, on account of which the one who is chosen is more worthy than the one who is not chosen. And therefore that faith, the obedience of faith, holiness, godliness, and perseverance are not fruits or effects of an unchangeable election to glory, but indispensable conditions and causes, which are prerequisite in those who are to be chosen in the complete election, and which are foreseen as achieved in them.

This runs counter to the entire Scripture, which throughout impresses upon our ears and hearts these sayings among others: "Election is not by works, but by him who calls" (Ro 9:11–12); "All who were appointed for eternal life believed" (Ac 13:48); "He chose us in himself so that we should be holy" (Eph 1:4); "You did not choose me, but I chose you" (Jn 15:16); "If by grace, not by works" (Ro 11:6); "In this is love, not that we loved God, but that he loved us and sent his Son" (1Jn 4:10).

VI

Who teach that not every election to salvation is unchangeable, but that some of the chosen can perish and do in fact perish eternally, with no decision of God to prevent it.

By this gross error they make God changeable, destroy the comfort of the godly concerning the steadfastness of their election, and contradict the Holy Scriptures, which teach that "the elect cannot be led astray" (Mt 24:24), that "Christ does not lose those given to him by the Father" (Jn 6:39), and that "those whom God predestined, called, and justified, he also glorifies" (Ro 8:30).

VII

Who teach that in this life there is no fruit, no awareness, and no assurance of one's unchangeable election to glory, except as conditional upon something changeable and contingent.

For not only is it absurd to speak of an uncertain assurance, but these things also militate against the experience of the saints, who with the apostle rejoice from an awareness of their election and sing the praises of this gift of God; who, as Christ urged, "rejoice" with his disciples "that their names have been written in heaven" (Lk 10:20); and finally who hold up against the flaming arrows of the devil's temptations the awareness of their election, with the question "Who will bring any charge against those whom God has chosen?" (Ro 8:33).

VIII

Who teach that it was not on the basis of his just will alone that God decided to leave anyone in the fall of Adam and in the common state of sin and condemnation or to pass anyone by in the imparting of grace necessary for faith and conversion.

For these words stand fast: "He has mercy on whom he wishes, and he hardens whom he wishes" (Ro 9:18). And also: "To you it has been given to know the secrets of the kingdom of heaven, but to them it has not been given" (Mt 13:11). Likewise: "I give glory to you, Father, Lord of heaven and earth, that you have hidden these things from the wise and understanding, and have revealed them to little children; yes, Father, because that was your pleasure" (Mt 11:25–26).

IX

Who teach that the cause for God's sending the gospel to one people rather than to another is not merely and solely God's good pleasure, but rather that one people is better and worthier than the other to whom the gospel is not communicated.

For Moses contradicts this when he addresses the people of Israel as follows: "Behold, to Jehovah your God belong the heavens and the highest heavens, the earth and whatever is in it. But Jehovah was inclined in his affection to love your ancestors alone, and chose out their descendants after them, you above all peoples, as at this day" (Dt 10:14–15). And also Christ: "Woe to you, Korazin! Woe to you, Bethsaida! for if those mighty works done in you had been done in Tyre and Sidon, they would have repented long ago in sackcloth and ashes" (Mt 11:21).

THE SECOND MAIN POINT OF DOCTRINE

Christ's Death and Human Redemption Through It

Article 1: The Punishment Which God's Justice Requires

God is not only supremely merciful, but also supremely just. His justice requires (as he has revealed himself in the Word) that the sins we have committed against his infinite majesty be punished with both temporal and eternal punishments, of soul as well as body. We cannot escape these punishments unless satisfaction is given to God's justice.

Article 2: The Satisfaction Made by Christ

Since, however, we ourselves cannot give this satisfaction or deliver ourselves from God's anger, God in his boundless mercy has given us as a guarantee his only begotten Son, who was made to be sin and a curse for us, in our place, on the cross, in order that he might give satisfaction for us.

Article 3: The Infinite Value of Christ's Death

This death of God's Son is the only and entirely complete sacrifice and satisfaction for sins; it is of infinite value and worth, more than sufficient to atone for the sins of the whole world.

Article 4: Reasons for This Infinite Value

This death is of such great value and worth for the reason that the person who suffered it is—as was necessary to be our Savior—not only a true and perfectly holy man, but also the only begotten Son of God, of the same eternal and infinite essence with the Father and the Holy Spirit. Another reason is that this death was accompanied by the experience of God's anger and curse, which we by our sins had fully deserved.

Article 5: The Mandate to Proclaim the Gospel to All

Moreover, it is the promise of the gospel that whoever believes in Christ crucified shall not perish but have eternal life. This promise, together with the command to repent and believe, ought to be announced and declared without differentiation or discrimination to all nations and people, to whom God in his good pleasure sends the gospel.

Article 6: Unbelief Man's Responsibility

However, that many who have been called through the gospel do not repent or believe in Christ but perish in unbelief is not because the sacrifice of Christ offered on the cross is deficient or insufficient, but because they themselves are at fault.

Article 7: Faith God's Gift

But all who genuinely believe and are delivered and saved by Christ's death from their sins and from destruction receive this favor solely from God's grace—which he owes to no one—given to them in Christ from eternity.

Article 8: The Saving Effectiveness of Christ's Death

For it was the entirely free plan and very gracious will and intention of God the Father that the enlivening and saving effectiveness of his Son's costly death should work itself out in all his chosen ones, in order that he might grant justifying faith to them only and thereby lead them without fail to salvation. In other words, it was God's will that Christ through the blood of the cross (by which he confirmed the new covenant) should effectively redeem from every people, tribe, nation, and language all those and only those who were chosen from eternity to salvation and given to him by the Father; that he should grant them faith (which, like the Holy Spirit's other saving gifts, he acquired for them by his death); that he should cleanse them by his blood from all their sins, both original and actual, whether committed before or after their coming to faith; that he should faithfully preserve them to the very end; and that he should finally present them to himself, a glorious people, without spot or wrinkle.

Article 9: The Fulfillment of God's Plan

This plan, arising out of God's eternal love for his chosen ones, from the beginning of the world to the present time has been powerfully carried out and will also be carried out in the future, the gates of hell seeking vainly to prevail against it. As a result the chosen are gathered into one, all in their own time, and there is always a church of believers founded on Christ's blood, a church which steadfastly loves, persistently worships, and—here and in all eternity—praises him as her Savior who laid down his life for her on the cross, as a bridegroom for his bride.

Rejection of the Errors

Having set forth the orthodox teaching, the Synod rejects the errors of those

I

Who teach that God the Father appointed his Son to death on the cross without a fixed and definite plan to save anyone by name, so that the necessity, usefulness, and worth of what Christ's death obtained could have stood intact and altogether perfect, complete and whole, even if the redemption that was obtained had never in actual fact been applied to any individual.

For this assertion is an insult to the wisdom of God the Father and to the merit of Jesus Christ, and it is contrary to Scripture. For the Savior speaks as follows: "I lay down my life for the sheep, and I know them" (Jn 10:15,27). And Isaiah the prophet says concerning the Savior: "When he shall make himself an offering for sin, he shall see his offspring, he shall prolong his days, and the will of Jehovah shall prosper in his hand" (Isa 53:10). Finally, this undermines the article of the creed in which we confess what we believe concerning the Church.

II

Who teach that the purpose of Christ's death was not to establish in actual fact a new covenant of grace by his blood, but only to acquire for the Father the mere right to enter once more into a covenant with men, whether of grace or of works.

For this conflicts with Scripture, which teaches that Christ "has become the guarantee and mediator of a better—"that is, "a new-covenant" (Heb 7:22; 9:15), "and that a will is in force only when someone has died" (Heb 9:17).

III

Who teach that Christ, by the satisfaction which he gave, did not certainly merit for anyone salvation itself and the faith by which this satisfaction of Christ is effectively applied to salvation, but only acquired for the Father the authority or plenary will to relate in a new way with men and to impose such new conditions as he chose, and that the satisfying of these conditions depends on the free choice of man; consequently, that it was possible that either all or none would fulfill them.

For they have too low an opinion of the death of Christ, do not at all acknowledge the foremost fruit or benefit which it brings forth, and summon back from hell the Pelagian error.

IV

Who teach that what is involved in the new covenant of grace which God the Father made with men through the intervening of Christ's death is not that we are justified before God and saved through faith, insofar as it accepts Christ's merit, but rather that God, having withdrawn his demand for perfect obedience to the law, counts faith itself, and the imperfect obedience of faith, as perfect obedience to the law, and graciously looks upon this as worthy of the reward of eternal life.

For they contradict Scripture: "They are justified freely by his grace through the redemption that came by Jesus Christ, whom God presented as a sacrifice of atonement, through faith in his blood" (Ro 3:24–25). And along with the ungodly Socinus, they introduce a new and foreign justification of man before God, against the consensus of the whole church.

V

Who teach that all people have been received into the state of reconciliation and into the grace of the covenant, so that no one on account of original sin is liable to condemnation, or is to be condemned, but that all are free from the guilt of this sin.

For this opinion conflicts with Scripture which asserts that we are by nature children of wrath.

VI

Who make use of the distinction between obtaining and applying in order to instill in the unwary and inexperienced the opinion that God, as far as he is concerned, wished to bestow equally upon all people the benefits which are gained by Christ's death; but that the distinction by which some rather than others come to share in the forgiveness of sins and eternal life depends on their own free choice (which applies itself to the grace offered indiscriminately) but does not depend on the unique gift of mercy which effectively works in them, so that they, rather than others, apply that grace to themselves.

For, while pretending to set forth this distinction in an acceptable sense, they attempt to give the people the deadly poison of Pelagianism.

VII

Who teach that Christ neither could die, nor had to die, nor did die for those whom God so dearly loved and chose to eternal life, since such people do not need the death of Christ.

For they contradict the apostle, who says: "Christ loved me and gave himself up for me" (Gal 2:20), and likewise: "Who will bring any charge against those whom God has chosen? It is God who justifies. Who is he that condemns? It is Christ who died," that is, for them (Ro 8:33–34). They also contradict the Savior, who asserts: "I lay down my life for the sheep" (Jn 10:15), and "My command is this: Love one another as I have loved you. Greater love has no one than this, that one lay down his life for his friends" (Jn 15:12–13).

THE THIRD AND FOURTH MAIN POINTS OF DOCTRINE

Human Corruption, Conversion to God, and the Way It Occurs

Article 1: The Effect of the Fall on Human Nature

Man was originally created in the image of God and was furnished in his mind with a true and salutary knowledge of his Creator and things spiritual, in his will and heart with righteousness, and in all his emotions with purity; indeed, the whole man was holy. However, rebelling against God at the devil's instigation and by his own free will, he deprived himself of these outstanding gifts. Rather, in their place he brought upon himself blindness, terrible darkness, futility, and distortion of judgment in his mind; perversity, defiance, and hardness in his heart and will; and finally impurity in all his emotions.

Article 2: The Spread of Corruption

Man brought forth children of the same nature as himself after the fall. That is to say, being corrupt he brought forth corrupt children. The corruption spread, by God's just judgment, from Adam to all his descendants—except for Christ alone—not by way of imitation (as in former times the Pelagians would have it) but by way of the propagation of his perverted nature.

Article 3: Total Inability

Therefore, all people are conceived in sin and are born children of wrath, unfit for any saving good, inclined to evil, dead in their sins, and slaves to sin; without the grace of the regenerating Holy Spirit they are neither willing nor able to return to God, to reform their distorted nature, or even to dispose themselves to such reform.

Article 4: The Inadequacy of the Light of Nature

There is, to be sure, a certain light of nature remaining in man after the fall, by virtue of which he retains some notions about God, natural things, and the difference between what is moral and immoral, and demonstrates a certain eagerness for virtue and for good outward behavior. But this light of nature is far from enabling man to come to a saving knowledge of God and conversion to him—so far, in fact, that man does not use it rightly even in matters of nature and society. Instead, in various ways he completely distorts this light, whatever its precise character, and suppresses it in unrighteousness. In doing so he renders himself without excuse before God.

Article 5: The Inadequacy of the Law

In this respect, what is true of the light of nature is true also of the Ten Commandments given by God through Moses specifically to the Jews. For man cannot obtain saving grace through the Decalogue, because, although it does expose the magnitude of his sin and increasingly convict him of his guilt, yet it does not offer a remedy or enable him to escape from his misery, and, indeed, weakened as it is by the flesh, leaves the offender under the curse.

Article 6: The Saving Power of the Gospel

What, therefore, neither the light of nature nor the law can do, God accomplishes by the power of the Holy Spirit, through the Word or the ministry of reconciliation. This is the gospel about the Messiah, through which it has pleased God to save believers, in both the Old and the New Testament.

Article 7: God's Freedom in Revealing the Gospel

In the Old Testament, God revealed this secret of his will to a small number; in the New Testament (now without any distinction between peoples) he discloses it to a large number. The reason for this difference must not be ascribed to the greater worth of one nation over another, or to a better use of the light of nature, but to the free good pleasure and undeserved love of God. Therefore, those who receive so much grace, beyond and in spite of all they deserve, ought to acknowledge it with humble and thankful hearts; on the other hand, with the apostle they ought to adore (but certainly not inquisitively search into) the severity and justice of God's judgments on the others, who do not receive this grace.

Article 8: The Serious Call of the Gospel

Nevertheless, all who are called through the gospel are called seriously. For seriously and most genuinely God makes known in his Word what is pleasing to him: that those who are called should come to him. Seriously he also promises rest for their souls and eternal life to all who come to him and believe.

Article 9: Human Responsibility for Rejecting the Gospel

The fact that many who are called through the ministry of the gospel do not come and are not brought to conversion must not be blamed on the gospel, nor on Christ, who is offered through the gospel, nor on God, who calls them through the gospel and even bestows various gifts on them, but on the people themselves who are called. Some in self-assurance do not even entertain the Word of life; others do entertain it but do not take it to heart, and for that reason, after the fleeting joy of a temporary faith, they relapse; others choke the seed of the Word with the thorns of life's cares and with the pleasures of the world and bring forth no fruits. This our Savior teaches in the parable of the sower (Mt 13).

Article 10: Conversion as the Work of God

The fact that others who are called through the ministry of the gospel do come and are brought to conversion must not be credited to man, as though one distinguishes himself by free choice from others who are furnished with equal or sufficient grace for faith and conversion (as the proud heresy of Pelagius maintains). No, it must be credited to God: just as from eternity he chose his own in Christ, so within time he effectively calls them, grants them faith and repentance, and, having rescued them from the dominion of darkness, brings them into the kingdom of his Son, in order that they may declare the wonderful deeds of him who called them out of darkness into this marvelous light, and may boast not in themselves, but in the Lord, as apostolic words frequently testify in Scripture.

Article 11: The Holy Spirit's Work in Conversion

Moreover, when God carries out this good pleasure in his chosen ones, or works true conversion in them, he not only sees to it that the gospel is proclaimed to them outwardly, and enlightens their minds powerfully by the Holy Spirit so that they may rightly understand and discern the things of the Spirit of God, but, by the effective operation of the same regenerating Spirit, he also penetrates into the inmost being of man, opens the closed heart, softens the hard heart, and circumcises the heart that is uncircumcised. He infuses new qualities into the will, making the dead will alive, the evil one good, the unwilling one willing, and the stubborn one compliant; he activates and strengthens the will so that, like a good tree, it may be enabled to produce the fruits of good deeds.

Article 12: Regeneration a Supernatural Work

And this is the regeneration, the new creation, the raising from the dead, and the making alive so clearly proclaimed in the Scriptures, which God works in us without our help. But this certainly does not happen only by outward teaching, by moral persuasion, or by such a way of working that, after God has done his work, it remains in man's power whether or not to be reborn or converted. Rather, it is an entirely supernatural work, one that is at the same time most powerful and most pleasing, a marvelous, hidden, and inexpressible work, which is not lesser than or inferior in power to that of creation or of raising the dead, as Scripture (inspired by the author of this work) teaches. As a result, all those in whose hearts God works in this marvelous way are certainly, unfailingly, and effectively reborn and do actually believe. And then the will, now renewed, is not only activated and motivated by God but in being activated by God is also itself active. For this reason, man himself, by that grace which he has received, is also rightly said to believe and to repent.

Article 13: The Incomprehensible Way of Regeneration

In this life believers cannot fully understand the way this work occurs; meanwhile, they rest content with knowing and experiencing that by this grace of God they do believe with the heart and love their Savior.

Article 14: The Way God Gives Faith

In this way, therefore, faith is a gift of God, not in the sense that it is offered by God for man to choose, but that it is in actual fact bestowed on man, breathed and infused into him. Nor is it a gift in the sense that God bestows only the potential to believe, but then awaits assent—the act of believing—from man's choice; rather, it is a gift in the sense that he who works both willing and acting and, indeed, works all things in all people produces in man both the will to believe and the belief itself.

Article 15: Responses to God's Grace

God does not owe this grace to anyone. For what could God owe to one who has nothing to give that can be paid back? Indeed, what could God owe to one who has nothing of his own to give but sin and falsehood? Therefore the person who receives this grace owes and gives eternal thanks to God alone; the person who does not receive it either does not care at all about these spiritual things and is satisfied with himself in his condition, or else in self-assurance foolishly boasts about having something which he lacks. Furthermore, following the example of the apostles, we are to think and to speak in the most favorable way about those who outwardly profess their faith and better their lives, for the inner chambers of the heart are unknown to us. But for others who have not yet been called, we are to pray to the God who calls things that do not exist as though they did. In no way, however, are we to pride ourselves as better than they, as though we had distinguished ourselves from them.

Article 16: Regeneration's Effect

However, just as by the fall man did not cease to be man, endowed with intellect and will, and just as sin, which has spread through the whole human race, did not abolish the nature of the human race but distorted and spiritually killed it, so also this divine grace of regeneration does not act in people as if they were blocks and stones; nor does it abolish the will and its properties or coerce a reluctant will by force, but spiritually revives, heals, reforms, and—in a manner at once pleasing and powerful—bends it back. As a result, a ready and sincere obedience of the Spirit now begins to prevail where before the rebellion and resistance of the flesh were completely dominant. It is in this that the true and spiritual restoration and freedom of our will consists. Thus, if the marvelous Maker of every good thing were not dealing with us, man would have no hope of getting up from his fall by his free choice, by which he plunged himself into ruin when still standing upright.

Article 17: God's Use of Means in Regeneration

Just as the almighty work of God by which he brings forth and sustains our natural life does not rule out but requires the use of means, by which God, according to his infinite wisdom and goodness, has wished to exercise his power, so also the aforementioned supernatural work of God by which he regenerates us in no way rules out or cancels the use of the gospel, which God in his great wisdom has appointed to be the seed of regeneration and the food of the soul. For this reason, the apostles and the teachers who followed them taught the people in a godly manner about this grace of God, to give him the glory and to humble all pride, and yet did not neglect meanwhile to keep the people, by means of the holy admonitions of the gospel, under the administration of the Word, the sacraments, and discipline. So even today it is out of the question that the teachers or those taught in the church should presume to test God by separating what he in his good pleasure has wished to be closely joined together. For grace is bestowed through admonitions, and the more readily we perform our duty, the more lustrous the benefit of God working in us usually is and the better his work advances. To him alone, both for the means and for their saving fruit and effectiveness, all glory is owed forever. Amen.

Rejection of the Errors

Having set forth the orthodox teaching, the Synod rejects the errors of those

I

Who teach that, properly speaking, it cannot be said that original sin in itself is enough to condemn the whole human race or to warrant temporal and eternal punishments.

For they contradict the apostle when he says: "Sin entered the world through one man, and death through sin, and in this way death passed on to all men because all sinned" (Ro 5:12); also: "The guilt followed one sin and brought condemnation" (Ro 5:16); likewise: "The wages of sin is death" (Ro 6:23).

II

Who teach that the spiritual gifts or the good dispositions and virtues such as goodness, holiness, and righteousness could not have resided in man's will when he was first created, and therefore could not have been separated from the will at the fall.

For this conflicts with the apostle's description of the image of God in Ephesians 4:24, where he portrays the image in terms of righteousness and holiness, which definitely reside in the will.

III

Who teach that in spiritual death the spiritual gifts have not been separated from man's will, since the will in itself has never been corrupted but only hindered by the darkness of the mind and the unruliness of the emotions, and since the will is able to exercise its innate free capacity once these hindrances are removed, which is to say, it is able of itself to will or choose whatever good is set before it—or else not to will or choose it.

This is a novel idea and an error and has the effect of elevating the power of free choice, contrary to the words of Jeremiah the prophet: "The heart itself is deceitful above all things and wicked" (Jer 17:9); and of the words of the apostle: "All of us also lived among them" (the sons of disobedience) "at one time in the passions of our flesh, following the will of our flesh and thoughts" (Eph 2:3).

IV

Who teach that unregenerate man is not strictly or totally dead in his sins or deprived of all capacity for spiritual good but is able to hunger and thirst for righteousness or life and to offer the sacrifice of a broken and contrite spirit which is pleasing to God.

For these views are opposed to the plain testimonies of Scripture: "You were dead in your transgressions and sins" (Eph 2:1,5); "The imagination of the thoughts of man's heart is only evil all the time" (Ge 6:5; 8:21). Besides, to hunger and thirst for deliverance from misery and for life, and to offer God the sacrifice of a broken spirit is characteristic only of the regenerate and of those called blessed (Ps 51:17; Mt 5:6).

V

Who teach that corrupt and natural man can make such good use of common grace (by which they mean the light of nature)or of the gifts remaining after the fall that he is able thereby gradually to obtain a greater grace—evangelical or saving grace—as well as salvation itself; and that in this way God, for his part, shows himself ready to reveal Christ to all people, since he provides to all, to a sufficient extent and in an effective manner, the means necessary for the revealing of Christ, for faith, and for repentance.

For Scripture, not to mention the experience of all ages, testifies that this is false: "He makes known his words to Jacob, his statutes and his laws to Israel; he has done this for no other nation, and they do not know his laws" (Ps 147:19–20); "In the past God let all nations go their own way" (Ac 14:16); "They" (Paul and his companions)" were kept by the Holy Spirit from speaking God's word in Asia;" and "When they had come to Mysia, they tried to go to Bithynia, but the Spirit would not allow them to" (Ac 16:6–7).

VI

Who teach that in the true conversion of man new qualities, dispositions, or gifts cannot be infused or poured into his will by God, and indeed that the faith [or believing] by which we first come to conversion and from which we receive the name "believers" is not a quality or gift infused by God, but only an act of man, and that it cannot be called a gift except in respect to the power of attaining faith.

For these views contradict the Holy Scriptures, which testify that God does infuse or pour into our hearts the new qualities of faith, obedience, and the experiencing of his love: "I will put my law in their minds, and write it on their hearts" (Jer 31:33); "I will pour water on the thirsty land, and streams on the dry ground; I will pour out my Spirit on your offspring" (Isa 44:3); "The love of God has been poured out in our hearts by the Holy Spirit, who has been given to us" (Ro 5:5). They also conflict with the continuous practice of the Church, which prays with the prophet: "Convert me, Lord, and I shall be converted" (Jer 31:18).

VII

Who teach that the grace by which we are converted to God is nothing but a gentle persuasion, or (as others explain it) that the way of God's acting in man's conversion that is most noble and suited to human nature is that which happens by persuasion, and that nothing prevents this grace of moral suasion even by itself from making natural men spiritual; indeed, that God does not produce the assent of the will except in this manner of moral suasion, and that the effectiveness of God's work by which it surpasses the work of Satan consists in the fact that God promises eternal benefits while Satan promises temporal ones.

For this teaching is entirely Pelagian and contrary to the whole of Scripture, which recognizes besides this persuasion also another, far more effective and divine way in which the Holy Spirit acts in man's conversion. As Ezekiel 36:26 puts it: "I will give you a new heart and put a new spirit in you; and I will remove your heart of stone and give you a heart of flesh . . ."

VIII

Who teach that God in regenerating man does not bring to bear that power of his omnipotence whereby he may powerfully and unfailingly bend man's will to faith and conversion, but that even when God has accomplished all the works of grace which he uses for man's conversion, man nevertheless can, and in actual fact often does, so resist God and the Spirit in their intent and will to regenerate him, that man completely thwarts his own rebirth; and, indeed, that it remains in his own power whether or not to be reborn.

For this does away with all effective functioning of God's grace in our conversion and subjects the activity of Almighty God to the will of man; it is contrary to the apostles, who teach that "we believe by virtue of the effective working of God's mighty strength" (Eph 1:19), and that "God fulfills the undeserved good will of his kindness and the work of faith in us with power" (2Th 1:11), and likewise that "his divine power has given us everything we need for life and godliness" (2Pe 1:3).

IX

Who teach that grace and free choice are concurrent partial causes which cooperate to initiate conversion, and that grace does not precede—in the order of causality—the effective influence of the will; that is to say, that God does not effectively help man's will to come to conversion before man's will itself motivates and determines itself.

For the early church already condemned this doctrine long ago in the Pelagians, on the basis of the words of the apostle: "It does not depend on man's willing or running but on God's mercy" (Ro 9:16); also: "Who makes you different from anyone else?" and "What do you have that you did not receive?" (1Co 4:7); likewise: "It is God who works in you to will and act according to his good pleasure" (Php 2:13).

THE FIFTH MAIN POINT OF DOCTRINE

The Perseverance of the Saints

Article 1: The Regenerate Not Entirely Free from Sin

Those people whom God according to his purpose calls into fellowship with his Son Jesus Christ our Lord and regenerates by the Holy Spirit, he also sets free from the reign and slavery of sin, though in this life not entirely from the flesh and from the body of sin.

Article 2: The Believer's Reaction to Sins of Weakness

Hence daily sins of weakness arise, and blemishes cling to even the best works of God's people, giving them continual cause to humble themselves before God, to flee for refuge to Christ crucified, to put the flesh to death more and more by the Spirit of supplication and by holy exercises of godliness, and to strain toward the goal of perfection, until they are freed from this body of death and reign with the Lamb of God in heaven.

Article 3: God's Preservation of the Converted

Because of these remnants of sin dwelling in them and also because of the temptations of the world and Satan, those who have been converted could not remain standing in this grace if left to their own resources. But God is faithful, mercifully strengthening them in the grace once conferred on them and powerfully preserving them in it to the end.

Article 4: The Danger of True Believers' Falling into Serious Sins

Although that power of God strengthening and preserving true believers in grace is more than a match for the flesh, yet those converted are not always so activated and motivated by God that in certain specific actions they cannot by their own fault depart from the leading of grace, be led astray by the desires of the flesh, and give in to them. For this reason they must constantly watch and pray that they may not be led into temptations. When they fail to do this, not only can they be carried away by the flesh, the world, and Satan into sins, even serious and outrageous ones, but also by God's just permission they sometimes are so carried away—witness the sad cases, described in Scripture, of David, Peter, and other saints falling into sins.

Article 5: The Effects of Such Serious Sins

By such monstrous sins, however, they greatly offend God, deserve the sentence of death, grieve the Holy Spirit, suspend the exercise of faith, severely wound the conscience, and sometimes lose the awareness of grace for a time—until, after they have returned to the way by genuine repentance, God's fatherly face again shines upon them.

Article 6: God's Saving Intervention

For God, who is rich in mercy, according to his unchangeable purpose of election does not take his Holy Spirit from his own completely, even when they fall grievously. Neither does he let them fall down so far that they forfeit the grace of adoption and the state of justification, or commit the sin which leads to death (the sin against the Holy Spirit), and plunge themselves, entirely forsaken by him, into eternal ruin.

Article 7: Renewal to Repentance

For, in the first place, God preserves in those saints when they fall his imperishable seed from which they have been born again, lest it perish or be dislodged. Secondly, by his Word and Spirit he certainly and effectively renews them to repentance so that they have a heartfelt and godly sorrow for the sins they have committed; seek and obtain, through faith and with a contrite heart, forgiveness in the blood of the Mediator; experience again the grace of a reconciled God; through faith adore his mercies; and from then on more eagerly work out their own salvation with fear and trembling.

Article 8: The Certainty of This Preservation

So it is not by their own merits or strength but by God's undeserved mercy that they neither forfeit faith and grace totally nor remain in their downfalls to the end and are lost. With respect to themselves this not only easily could happen, but also undoubtedly would happen; but with respect to God it cannot possibly happen, since his plan cannot be changed, his promise cannot fail, the calling according to his purpose cannot be revoked, the merit of Christ as well as his interceding and preserving cannot be nullified, and the sealing of the Holy Spirit can neither be invalidated nor wiped out.

Article 9: The Assurance of This Preservation

Concerning this preservation of those chosen to salvation and concerning the perseverance of true believers in faith, believers themselves can and do become assured in accordance with the measure of their faith, by which they firmly believe that they are and always will remain true and living members of the church, and that they have the forgiveness of sins and eternal life.

Article 10: The Ground of This Assurance

Accordingly, this assurance does not derive from some private revelation beyond or outside the Word, but from faith in the promises of God which he has very plentifully revealed in his Word for our comfort, from the testimony of "the Holy Spirit testifying with our spirit that we are God's children and heirs" (Ro 8:16–17), and finally from a serious and holy pursuit of a clear conscience and of good works. And if God's chosen ones in this world did not have this well-founded comfort that the victory will be theirs and this reliable guarantee of eternal glory, they would be of all people most miserable.

Article 11: Doubts Concerning This Assurance

Meanwhile, Scripture testifies that believers have to contend in this life with various doubts of the flesh and that under severe temptation they do not always experience this full assurance of faith and certainty of perseverance. But God, the Father of all comfort, "does not let them be tempted beyond what they can bear, but with the temptation he also provides a way out" (1Co 10:13), and by the Holy Spirit revives in them the assurance of their perseverance.

Article 12: This Assurance as an Incentive to Godliness

This assurance of perseverance, however, so far from making true believers proud and carnally self-assured, is rather the true root of humility, of childlike respect, of genuine godliness, of endurance in every conflict, of fervent prayers, of steadfastness in crossbearing and in confessing the truth, and of well-founded joy in God. Reflecting on this benefit provides an incentive to a serious and continual practice of thanksgiving and good works, as is evident from the testimonies of Scripture and the examples of the saints.

Article 13: Assurance No Inducement to Carelessness

Neither does the renewed confidence of perseverance produce immorality or lack of concern for godliness in those put back on their feet after a fall, but it produces a much greater concern to observe carefully the ways of the Lord which he prepared in advance. They observe these ways in order that by walking in them they may maintain the assurance of their perseverance, lest, by their abuse of his fatherly goodness, the face of the gracious God (for the godly, looking upon his face is sweeter than life, but its withdrawal is more bitter than death) turn away from them again, with the result that they fall into greater anguish of spirit.

Article 14: God's Use of Means in Perseverance

And, just as it has pleased God to begin this work of grace in us by the proclamation of the gospel, so he preserves, continues, and completes his work by the hearing and reading of the gospel, by meditation on it, by its exhortations, threats, and promises, and also by the use of the sacraments.

Article 15: Contrasting Reactions to the Teaching of Perseverance

This teaching about the perseverance of true believers and saints, and about their assurance of it—a teaching which God has very richly revealed in his Word for the glory of his name and for the comfort of the godly and which he impresses on the hearts of believers—is something which the flesh does not understand, Satan hates, the world ridicules, the ignorant and the hypocrites abuse, and the spirits of error attack. The bride of Christ, on the other hand, has always loved this teaching very tenderly and defended it steadfastly as a priceless treasure; and God, against whom no plan can avail and no strength can prevail, will ensure that she will continue to do this. To this God alone, Father, Son, and Holy Spirit, be honor and glory forever. Amen.

Rejection of the Errors

Concerning the Teaching of the Perseverance of the Saints

Having set forth the orthodox teaching, the Synod rejects the errors of those

I

Who teach that the perseverance of true believers is not an effect of election or a gift of God produced by Christ's death, but a condition of the new covenant which man, before what they callhis "peremptory" election and justification, must fulfill by his free will.

For Holy Scripture testifies that perseverance follows from election and is granted to the chosen by virtue of Christ's death, resurrection, and intercession: "The chosen obtained it; the others were hardened" (Ro 11:7); likewise, "He who did not spare his own son, but gave him up for us all—how will he not, along with him, grant us all things? Who will bring any charge against those whom God has chosen? It is God who justifies. Who is he that condemns? It is Christ Jesus who died—more than that, who was raised—who also sits at the right hand of God, and is also interceding for us. Who shall separate us from the love of Christ?" (Ro 8:32–35).

II

Who teach that God does provide the believer with sufficient strength to persevere and is ready to preserve this strength in him if he performs his duty, but that even with all those things in place which are necessary to persevere in faith and which God is pleased to use to preserve faith, it still always depends on the choice of man's will whether or not he perseveres.

For this view is obviously Pelagian; and though it intends to make men free it makes them sacrilegious. It is against the enduring consensus of evangelical teaching which takes from man all cause for boasting and ascribes the praise for this benefit only to God's grace. It is also against the testimony of the apostle: "It is God who keeps us strong to the end, so that we will be blameless on the day of our Lord Jesus Christ" (1Co 1:8).

III

Who teach that those who truly believe and have been born again not only can forfeit justifying faith as well as grace and salvation totally and to the end, but also in actual fact do often forfeit them and are lost forever.

For this opinion nullifies the very grace of justification and regeneration as well as the continual preservation by Christ, contrary to the plain words of the apostle Paul: "If Christ died for us while we were still sinners, we will therefore much more be saved from God's wrath through him, since we have now been justified by his blood" (Ro 5:8–9); and contrary to the apostle John: "No one who is born of God is intent on sin, because God's seed remains in him, nor can he sin, because he has been born of God" (1Jn 3:9); also contrary to the words of Jesus Christ: "I give eternal life to my sheep, and they shall never perish; no one can snatch them out of my hand. My Father, who has given them to me, is greater than all; no one can snatch them out of my Father's hand" (Jn 10:28–29).

IV

Who teach that those who truly believe and have been born again can commit the sin that leads to death (the sin against the Holy Spirit).

For the same apostle John, after making mention of those who commit the sin that leads to death and forbidding prayer for them (1Jn 5:16–17), immediately adds: "We know that anyone born of God does not commit sin" (that is, that kind of sin), "but the one who was born of God keeps himself safe, and the evil one does not touch him" (v. 18).

V

Who teach that apart from a special revelation no one can have the assurance of future perseverance in this life.

For by this teaching the well-founded consolation of true believers in this life is taken away and the doubting of the Romanists is reintroduced into the church. Holy Scripture, however, in many places derives the assurance not from a special and extraordinary revelation but from the marks peculiar to God's children and from God's completely reliable promises. So especially the apostle Paul: "Nothing in all creation can separate us from the love of God that is in Christ Jesus our Lord" (Ro 8:39); and John: "They who obey his commands remain in him and he in them. And this is how we know that he remains in us: by the Spirit he gave us" (1Jn 3:24).

VI

Who teach that the teaching of the assurance of perseverance and of salvation is by its very nature and character an opiate of the flesh and is harmful to godliness, good morals, prayer, and other holy exercises, but that, on the contrary, to have doubt about this is praiseworthy.

For these people show that they do not know the effective operation of God's grace and the work of the indwelling Holy Spirit, and they contradict the apostle John, who asserts the opposite in plain words: "Dear friends, now we are children of God, but what we will be has not yet been made known. But we know that when he is made known, we shall be like him, for we shall see him as he is. Everyone who has this hope in him purifies himself, just as he is pure" (1Jn 3:2–3). Moreover, they are refuted by the examples of the saints in both the Old and the New Testament, who though assured of their perseverance and salvation yet were constant in prayer and other exercises of godliness.

VII

Who teach that the faith of those who believe only temporarily does not differ from justifying and saving faith except in duration alone.

For Christ himself in Matthew 13:20ff. and Luke 8:13ff. clearly defines these further differences between temporary and true believers: he says that the former receive the seed on rocky ground, and the latter receive it in good ground, or a good heart; the former have no root, and the latter are firmly rooted; the former have no fruit, and the latter produce fruit in varying measure, with steadfastness, or perseverance.

VIII

Who teach that it is not absurd that a person, after losing his former regeneration, should once again, indeed quite often, be reborn.

For by this teaching they deny the imperishable nature of God's seed by which we are born again, contrary to the testimony of the apostle Peter: "Born again, not of perishable seed, but of imperishable" (1Pe 1:23).

IX

Who teach that Christ nowhere prayed for an unfailing perseverance of believers in faith.

For they contradict Christ himself when he says: "I have prayed for you, Peter, that your faith may not fail" (Lk 22:32); and John the gospel writer when he testifies in John 17 that it was not only for the apostles, but also for all those who were to believe by their message that Christ prayed: "Holy Father, preserve them in your name" (v. 11); and "My prayer is not that you take them out of the world, but that you preserve them from the evil one" (v. 15).

CONCLUSION

Rejection of False Accusations

And so this is the clear, simple, and straightforward explanation of the orthodox teaching on the five articles in dispute in the Netherlands, as well as the rejection of the errors by which the Dutch churches have for some time been disturbed. This explanation and rejection the Synod declares to be derived from God's Word and in agreement with the confessions of the Reformed churches. Hence it clearly appears that those of whom one could hardly expect it have shown no truth, equity, and charity at all in wishing to make the public believe:

—that the teaching of the Reformed churches on predestination and on the points associated with it by its very nature and tendency draws the minds of people away from all godliness and religion, is an opiate of the flesh and the devil, and is a stronghold of Satan where he lies in wait for all people, wounds most of them, and fatally pierces many of them with the arrows of both despair and self-assurance;

—that this teaching makes God the author of sin, unjust, a tyrant, and a hypocrite; and is nothing but a refurbished Stoicism, Manicheism, Libertinism, and Mohammedanism;

—that this teaching makes people carnally self-assured, since it persuades them that nothing endangers the salvation of the chosen, no matter how they live, so that they may commit the most outrageous crimes with self-assurance; and that on the other hand nothing is of use to the reprobate for salvation even if they have truly performed all the works of the saints;

—that this teaching means that God predestined and created, by the bare and unqualified choice of his will, without the least regard or consideration of any sin, the greatest part of the world to eternal condemnation; that in the same manner in which election is the source and cause of faith and good works, reprobation is the cause of unbelief and ungodliness; that many infant children of believers are snatched in their innocence from their mothers' breasts and cruelly cast into hell so that neither the blood of Christ nor their baptism nor the prayers of the church at their baptism can be of any use to them; and very many other slanderous accusations of this kind which the Reformed churches not only disavow but even denounce with their whole heart.

Therefore this Synod of Dort in the name of the Lord pleads with all who devoutly call on the name of our Savior Jesus Christ to form their judgment about the faith of the Reformed churches, not on the basis of false accusations gathered from here or there, or even on the basis of the personal statements of a number of ancient and modern authorities—statements which are also often either quoted out of context or misquoted and twisted to convey a different meaning—but on the basis of the churches' own official confessions and of the present explanation of the orthodox teaching which has been endorsed by the unanimous consent of the members of the whole Synod, one and all.

Moreover, the Synod earnestly warns the false accusers themselves to consider how heavy a judgment of God awaits those who give false testimony against so many churches and their confessions, trouble the consciences of the weak, and seek to prejudice the minds of many against the fellowship of true believers.

Finally, this Synod urges all fellow ministers in the gospel of Christ to deal with this teaching in a godly and reverent manner, in the academic institutions as well as in the churches; to do so, both in their speaking and writing, with a view to the glory of God's name, holiness of life, and the comfort of anxious souls; to think and also speak with Scripture according to the analogy of faith; and, finally, to refrain from all those ways of speaking which go beyond the bounds set for us by the genuine sense of the Holy Scriptures and which could give impertinent sophists a just occasion to scoff at the teaching of the Reformed churches or even to bring false accusations against it.

May God's Son Jesus Christ, who sits at the right hand of God and gives gifts to men, sanctify us in the truth, lead to the truth those who err, silence the mouths of those who lay false accusations against sound teaching, and equip faithful ministers of his Word with a spirit of wisdom and discretion, that all they say may be to the glory of God and the building up of their hearers. Amen.

INTRODUCTION TO THE WESTMINSTER STANDARDS

The Westminster Standards include the *Confession of Faith*, the *Larger Catechism* and the *Shorter Catechism*. By order of the English Parliament these documents were drafted by the Westminster Assembly as a revision of the doctrinal standards of the Thirty-Nine Articles of the Church of England. The Assembly first met on July 1, 1643, and consisted of 151 persons appointed by Parliament: 10 land owners (Lords), 20 commoners (tradesmen) and 121 ministers (divines), including Episcopalians, Presbyterians, Independents and Erastians[1] in fair proportion. This balance changed through the years to favor the Presbyterians. The members conducted 1,163 meetings until February 22, 1649.[2]

Since their original publication these Standards have served as the basis of the confessional documents of many Presbyterian and Reformed churches throughout the world. The main version of the Standards presented here is that maintained by the Presbyterian Church in America (PCA). Chapters 34 and 35 of the Confession of Faith were not original to the Standards and are not part of the PCA version. The version of chapters 34 and 35 presented here is from the Westminster Confession of Faith in modern English by Summertown Texts. Throughout the Confession, and occasionally in the Catechisms, footnotes indicate where the version presented varies from the critical text of the Confession (abbreviated "1647")[3] as well as from the official Standards of the Evangelical Presbyterian Church (abbreviated "EPC"; the EPC's official version is the Summertown Text), the Orthodox Presbyterian Church (abbreviated "OPC") and the Associate Reformed Presbyterian Church (abbreviated "ARP").

The Scripture proofs in the footnotes are original to Standards. These proofs have also been included throughout the study notes of *The Spirit of the Reformation Study Bible*; where the Standards footnote a Scripture text, the study note for that text refers back to the appropriate section of the Standards.

Special thanks go to the Presbyterian Church in America for providing the main text of the Standards with Scripture proofs, and to Summertown Texts for providing chapters 34 and 35 of the *Confession of Faith*.

1 Erastians were Reformers who favored any church discipline be carried out with the approval of the state.

2 James Reid, *Memoirs of the Westminster Assembly of Divines* (Banner of Truth Trust, 1986).

3 Carruthers, S.W. *The Westminster Confession of Faith* (R. Aikman and Son, 1937).

THE WESTMINSTER CONFESSION OF FAITH

CHAPTER I
Of the Holy Scripture

1. Although the light of nature, and the works of creation and providence do so far manifest the goodness, wisdom, and power of God, as to leave men inexcusable;[1] yet they are not sufficient to give that knowledge of God, and of His will, which is necessary unto salvation.[2] Therefore it pleased the Lord, at sundry times, and in divers manners, to reveal Himself, and to declare that His will unto His Church;[3] and afterwards, for the better preserving and propagating of the truth, and for the more sure establishment and comfort of the Church against the corruption of the flesh, and the malice of Satan and of the world, to commit the same wholly unto writing:[4] which maketh the Holy Scripture to be most necessary,[5] those former ways of God's revealing His will unto His people being now ceased.[6]

2. Under the name of Holy Scripture, or the Word of God written, are now contained all the books of the Old and New Testaments, which are these:

OF THE OLD TESTAMENT:

Genesis	2 Chronicles	Daniel
Exodus	Ezra	Hosea
Leviticus	Nehemiah	Joel
Numbers	Esther	Amos
Deuteronomy	Job	Obadiah
Joshua	Psalms	Jonah
Judges	Proverbs	Micah
Ruth	Ecclesiastes	Nahum
1 Samuel	The Song of Songs	Habakkuk
2 Samuel	Isaiah	Zephaniah
1 Kings	Jeremiah	Haggai
2 Kings	Lamentations	Zechariah
1 Chronicles	Ezekiel	Malachi

OF THE NEW TESTAMENT:

The Gospels According to Matthew	1 Thessalonians
Mark	2 Thessalonians
Luke	1 Timothy
John	2 Timothy
The Acts of the Apostles	Titus
Paul's Epistles to the Romans	Philemon
1 Corinthians 1	The Epistle to the Hebrews
2 Corinthians 2	The Epistle of James
Galatians	The first and second Epistles of Peter
Ephesians	The first, second, and third Epistles of John
Philippians	The Epistle of Jude
Colossians	The Revelation of John[a]

All which are given by inspiration of God to be the rule of faith and life.[7]

3. The books commonly called Apocrypha, not being of divine inspiration, are no part of the canon of the Scripture, and therefore are of no authority in the Church of God, nor to be any otherwise approved, or made use of, than other human writings.[8]

4. The authority of the Holy Scripture, for which it ought to be believed, and obeyed, dependeth not upon the testimony of any man, or Church; but wholly upon God (who is truth itself) the author thereof: and therefore it is to be received, because it is the Word of God.[9]

5. We may be moved and induced by the testimony of the Church to an high and reverent esteem of the Holy Scripture.[10] And the heavenliness of the matter, the efficacy of the doctrine, the majesty of the style, the consent of all the parts, the scope of the whole (which is, to give all glory to God), the full discovery it makes of the only way of man's salvation, the many other incomparable excellencies, and the entire perfection thereof, are arguments whereby it doth abundantly evidence itself to be the Word of God: yet notwithstanding, our full persuasion and assurance of the infallible truth and divine authority thereof, is from the inward work of the Holy Spirit bearing witness by and with the Word in our hearts.[11]

6. The whole counsel of God concerning all things necessary for His own glory, man's salvation, faith and life, is either expressly set down in Scripture, or by good and necessary consequence may be deduced from Scripture: unto which nothing at any time is to be added, whether by new revelations of the Spirit or traditions of men.[12] Nevertheless, we acknowledge the inward illumination of the Spirit of God to be necessary for the saving understanding of such things as are revealed in the Word:[13] and that there are some circumstances concerning the worship of God, and government of the Church, common to human actions and societies, which are to be ordered by the light of nature, and Christian prudence, according to the general rules of the Word, which are always to be observed.[14]

7. All things in Scripture are not alike plain in themselves, nor alike clear unto all:[15] yet those things which are necessary to be known, believed, and observed for salvation, are so clearly propounded, and opened in some place of Scripture or other, that not only the learned, but the unlearned, in a due use of the ordinary means, may attain unto a sufficient understanding of them.[16]

8. The Old Testament in Hebrew (which was the native language of the people of God of old), and the New Testament in Greek (which, at the time of the writing of it, was most generally known to the nations), being immediately inspired by God, and, by His singular care and providence, kept pure in all ages, are therefore authentical;[17] so as, in all controversies of religion, the Church is finally to appeal unto them.[18] But, because these original tongues are not known to all the people of God, who have right unto, and interest in the Scriptures, and are commanded, in the fear of God, to read and search them,[19] therefore they are to be translated into the vulgar language of every nation unto which they come,[20] that, the Word of God dwelling plentifully in all, they may worship Him in an acceptable manner;[21] and, through patience and comfort of the Scriptures, may have hope.[22]

9. The infallible rule of interpretation of Scripture is the Scripture itself: and therefore, when there is a question about the true and full sense of any Scripture (which is not manifold, but one), it must be searched and known by other places that speak more clearly.[23]

10. The supreme judge by which all controversies of religion are to be determined, and all decrees of councils, opinions of ancient writers, doctrines of men, and private spirits, are to be examined, and in whose sentence we are to rest, can be no other but the Holy Spirit speaking in the Scripture.[24]

1 Ro 1:19–20,32; 2:1,14–15; Ps 19:1–3
2 1Co 1:21; 2:13–14
3 Heb 1:1
4 Pr 22:19–21; Lk 1:3–4; Ro 15:4; Mt 4:4,7,10; Isa 8:19–20
5 2Ti 3:15; 2Pe 1:19
6 Heb 1:1–2
a ARP: "The Revelation"
7 Lk 16:29,31; Eph 2:20; Rev 22:18–19; 2Ti 3:16
8 Lk 24:27,44; Ro 3:2; 2Pe 1:21
9 2Pe 1:19,21; 2Ti 3:16; 1Jn 5:9; 1Th 2:13
10 1Ti 3:15
11 1Jn 2:20; Jn 16:13–14; 1Co 2:10–12; Isa 59:21
12 2Ti 3:15–17; Gal 1:8–9; 2Th 2:2
13 Jn 6:45; 1Co 2:9–12
14 1Co 11:13–14; 14:26,40
15 2Pe 3:16
16 Ps 119:105,130
17 Mt 5:18
18 Isa 8:20; Jn 5:39,46
19 Jn 5:39
20 1Co 14:6,9,11–12,24,27–28
21 Col 3:16
22 Ro 15:4
23 2Pe 1:20–21; Ac 15:15–16
24 Mt 22:29,31; Eph 2:20; Ac 28:25

CHAPTER II
Of God, and of the Holy Trinity

1. There is but one only,[1] living, and true God,[2] who is infinite in being and perfection,[3] a most pure spirit,[4] invisible,[5] without body, parts,[6] or passions;[7] immutable,[8] immense,[9] eternal,[10] incomprehensible,[11] almighty,[12] most wise,[13] most holy,[14] most free,[15] most absolute;[16] working all things according to the counsel of His own immutable and most righteous will,[17] for His own glory;[18] most loving,[19] gracious, merciful, long-suffering, abundant in goodness and truth, forgiving iniquity, transgression, and sin;[20] the rewarder of them that diligently seek Him;[21] and withal, most just, and terrible in His judgments,[22] hating all sin,[23] and who will by no means clear the guilty.[24]

2. God hath all life,[25] glory,[26] goodness,[27] blessedness,[28] in and of Himself; and is alone in and unto Himself all-sufficient, not standing in need of any creatures which He hath made,[29] nor deriving any glory from them,[30] but only manifesting His own glory in, by, unto, and upon them. He is the alone fountain of all being, of whom, through whom, and to whom are all things[31] and hath most sovereign dominion over them, to do by them, for them, or upon them whatsoever Himself pleaseth.[32] In His sight all things are open and manifest,[33] His knowledge is infinite, infallible, and independent upon the creature,[34] so as nothing is to Him contingent, or uncertain.[35] He is most holy in all His counsels, in all His works, and in all His commands.[36] To Him is due from angels and men, and every other creature, whatsoever worship, service, or obedience He is pleased to require of them.[37]

3. In the unity of the Godhead there be three persons, of one substance, power, and eternity: God the Father, God the Son, and God the Holy Ghost:[38] the Father is of none, neither begotten, nor proceeding; the Son is eternally begotten of the Father;[39] the Holy Ghost eternally proceeding from the Father and the Son.[40]

1 Dt 6:4; 1Co 8:4–6
2 1Th 1:9; Jer 10:10
3 Job 11:7–9; 26:14
4 Jn 4:24
5 1Ti 1:17
6 Dt 4:15–16; Jn 4:24; Lk 24:39
7 Ac 14:11,15
8 Jas 1:17
9 1Ki 8:27; Jer 23:23–24
10 Ps 90:2; 1Ti 1:17
11 Ps 145:3
12 Ge 17:1; Rev 4:8
13 Ro 16:27
14 Isa 6:3; Rev 4:8
15 Ps 115:3
16 Ex 3:14
17 Eph 1:11
18 Pr 16:4; Ro 11:36
19 1Jn 4:8–16
20 Ex 34:6–7
21 Heb 11:6
22 Ne 9:32–33
23 Ps 5:5–6
24 Na 1:2–3; Ex 34:7
25 Jn 5:26
26 Ac 7:2
27 Ps 119:68
28 1Ti 6:15; Ro 9:5
29 Ac 17:24–25
30 Job 22:2–3
31 Ro 11:36
32 Rev 4:11; 1Ti 6:15; Da 4:25,35
33 Heb 4:13
34 Ro 11:33–34; Ps 147:5
35 Ac 15:18; Eze 11:5
36 Ps 145:17; Ro 7:12
37 Rev 5:12–14
38 1Jn 5:7; Mt 3:16–17; 28:19; 2Co 13:14
39 Jn 1:14,18
40 Jn 15:26

CHAPTER III
Of God's Eternal Decree

1. God, from all eternity, did, by the most wise and holy counsel of His own will, freely, and unchangeably ordain whatsoever comes to pass:[1] yet so, as thereby neither is God the author of sin,[2] nor is violence offered to the will of the creatures; nor is the liberty or contingency of second causes taken away, but rather established.[3]

2. Although God knows whatsoever may or can come to pass upon all supposed conditions,[4] yet hath He not decreed anything because He foresaw it as future, or as that which would come to pass upon such conditions.[5]

3. By the decree of God, for the manifestation of His glory, some men and angels[6] are predestinated unto everlasting life; and others foreordained to everlasting death.[7]

4. These angels and men, thus predestinated, and foreordained, are particularly and unchangeably designed, and their number so certain and definite, that it cannot be either increased or diminished.[8]

5. Those of mankind that are predestinated unto life, God, before the foundation of the world was laid, according to His eternal and immutable purpose, and the secret counsel and good pleasure of His will, hath chosen, in Christ, unto everlasting glory,[9] out of His mere free grace and love, without any foresight of faith, or good works, or perseverance in either of them, or any other thing in the creature, as conditions, or causes moving Him thereunto;[10] and all to the praise of His glorious grace.[11]

6. As God hath appointed the elect unto glory, so hath He, by the eternal and most free purpose of His will, foreordained all the means thereunto.[12] Wherefore, they who are elected being fallen in Adam, are redeemed by Christ,[13] are effectually called unto faith in Christ by His Spirit working in due season, are justified, adopted, sanctified,[14] and kept by His power, through faith, unto salvation.[15] Neither are any other redeemed by Christ, effectually called, justified, adopted, sanctified, and saved, but the elect only.[16]

7. The rest of mankind God was pleased, according to the unsearchable counsel of His own will, whereby He extendeth or withholdeth mercy, as He pleaseth, for the glory of His sovereign power over His creatures, to pass by; and to ordain them to dishonour and wrath for their sin, to the praise of His glorious justice.[17]

8. The doctrine of this high mystery of predestination is to be handled with special prudence and care,[18] that men, attending the will of God revealed in His Word, and yielding obedience thereunto, may, from the certainty of their effectual vocation, be assured of their eternal election.[19] So

shall this doctrine afford matter of praise, reverence, and admiration of God;[20] and of humility, diligence, and abundant consolation to all that sincerely obey the gospel.[21]

1 Eph 1:11; Ro 9:15,18; 11:33; Heb 6:17
2 Jas 1:13,17; 1Jn 1:5
3 Ac 2:23; 4:27–28; Mt 17:12; Jn 19:11; Pr 16:33
4 Ac 15:18; 1Sa 23:11–12; Mt 11:21,23
5 Ro 9:11,13,16,18
6 1Ti 5:21; Mt 25:41
7 Ro 9:22–23; Eph 1:5–6; Pr 16:4
8 2Ti 2:19; Jn 13:18
9 Eph 1:4,9,11; Ro 8:30; 2Ti 1:9; 1Th 5:9
10 Ro 9:11,13,16; Eph 1:4,9
11 Eph 1:6,12
12 1Pe 1:2; Eph 1:4–5; 2:10; 2Th 2:13
13 1Th 5:9–10; Tit 2:14
14 Ro 8:30; Eph 1:5; 2Th 2:13
15 1Pe 1:5
16 Jn 6:64–65; 8:47; 10:26; 17:9; Ro 8:28; 1Jn 2:19
17 Mt 11:25–26; Ro 9:17–18,21–22; 2Ti 2:19–20; Jude 4; 1Pe 2:8
18 Ro 9:20; 11:33; Dt 29:29
19 2Pe 1:10
20 Eph 1:6; Ro 11:33
21 Ro 8:33; 11:5–6,20; 2Pe 1:10; Lk 10:20

CHAPTER IV
Of Creation

1. It pleased God the Father, Son, and Holy Ghost,[1] for the manifestation of the glory of His eternal power, wisdom, and goodness,[2] in the beginning, to create, or make of nothing, the world, and all things therein whether visible or invisible, in the space of six days; and all very good.[3]

2. After God had made all other creatures, He created man male and female,[4] with reasonable and immortal souls,[5] endued with knowledge, righteousness, and true holiness, after His own image;[6] having the law of God written in their hearts,[7] and power to fulfill it:[8] and yet under a possibility of transgressing, being left to the liberty of their own will, which was subject unto change.[9] Besides this law written in their hearts, they received a command, not to eat of the tree of the knowledge of good and evil;[10] which while they kept, they were happy in their communion with God, and had dominion over the creatures.[11]

1 Heb 1:2; Jn 1:2–3; Ge 1:2; Job 26:13; 33:4
2 Ro 1:20; Jer 10:12; Ps 33:5–6; 104:24
3 Ge 1; Heb 11:3; Col 1:16; Ac 17:24
4 Ge 1:27
5 Ge 2:7; Ecc 12:7; Lk 23:43; Mt 10:28
6 Ge 1:26; Col 3:10; Eph 4:24
7 Ro 2:14–15
8 Ecc 7:29
9 Ge 3:6; Ecc 7:29
10 Ge 2:17; 3:8–11,23
11 Ge 1:26,28

CHAPTER V
Of Providence

1. God the great Creator of all things doth uphold,[1] direct, dispose, and govern all creatures, actions, and things,[2] from the greatest even to the least,[3] by His most wise and holy providence,[4] according to His infallible foreknowledge,[5] and the free and immutable counsel of His own will,[6] to the praise of the glory of His wisdom, power, justice, goodness, and mercy.[7]

2. Although, in relation to the foreknowledge and decree of God, the first Cause, all things come to pass immutably, and infallibly;[8] yet, by the same providence, He ordereth them to fall out, according to the nature of second causes, either necessarily, freely, or contingently.[9]

3. God, in His ordinary providence, maketh use of means,[10] yet is free to work without,[11] above,[12] and against them,[13] at His pleasure.

4. The almighty power, unsearchable wisdom, and infinite goodness of God so far manifest themselves in His providence, that it extendeth itself even to the first fall, and all other sins of angels and men;[14] and that not by a bare permission,[15] but such as hath joined with it a most wise and powerful bounding,[16] and otherwise ordering and governing of them, in a manifold dispensation, to His own holy ends;[17] yet so, as the sinfulness thereof proceedeth only from the creature, and not from God, who, being most holy and righteous, neither is nor can be the author or approver of sin.[18]

5. The most wise, righteous, and gracious God doth oftentimes leave, for a season, His own children to manifold temptations, and the corruption of their own hearts, to chastise them for their former sins, or to discover unto them the hidden strength of corruption and deceitfulness of their hearts, that they may be humbled;[19] and, to raise them to a more close and constant dependence for their support upon Himself, and to make them more watchful against all future occasions of sin, and for sundry other just and holy ends.[20]

6. As for those wicked and ungodly men whom God, as a righteous Judge, for former sins, doth blind and harden,[21] from them He not only withholdeth His grace whereby they might have been enlightened in their understandings, and wrought upon in their hearts;[22] but sometimes also withdraweth the gifts which they had,[23] and exposeth them to such objects as their corruption make occasion of sin;[24] and, withal, gives them over to their own lusts, the temptations of the world, and the power of Satan,[25] whereby it comes to pass that they harden themselves, even under those means which God useth for the softening of others.[26]

7. As the providence of God doth, in general, reach to all creatures; so, after a most special manner, it taketh care of His Church, and disposeth all things to the good thereof.[27]

1 Heb 1:3
2 Da 4:34–35; Ps 135:6; Ac 17:25–26,28; Job 38–41
3 Mt 10:29–31
4 Pr 15:3; Ps 104:24; 145:17
5 Ac 15:18; Ps 94:8–11
6 Eph 1:11
7 Isa 63:14; Eph 3:10; Ro 9:17; Ge 45:7; Ps 145:7
8 Ac 2:23
9 Ge 8:22; Jer 31:35; Ex 21:13; Dt 19:5; 1Ki 22:28,34; Isa 10:6–7
10 Ac 27:31,44; Isa 55:10–11
11 Hos 1:7; Mt 4:4; Job 34:20
12 Ro 9:19–21
13 2Ki 6:6; Da 3:27
14 Ro 11:32–34; 2Sa 16:10; 24:1; 1Ch 10:4,13–14; 21:1; 1Ki 22:22–23; Ac 2:23
15 Ac 14:16
16 Ps 76:10; 2Ki 19:28
17 Ge 50:20; Isa 10:6–7,12
18 Jas 1:13–14,17; 1Jn 2:16; Ps 50:21
19 2Ch 32:25–26,31; 2Sa 24:1
20 2Co 12:7–9; Ps 73; 77:1–12; Mk 14:66–72; Jn 21:15–17
21 Ro 1:24,26,28; 11:7–8
22 Dt 29:4
23 Mt 13:12; 25:29
24 Dt 2:30; 2Ki 8:12–13
25 Ps 81:11–12; 2Th 2:10–12
26 Ex 7:3; 8:15,32; 2Co 2:15–16; Isa 8:14; 1Pe 2:7–8; Isa 6:9–10; Ac 28:26–27
27 1Ti 4:10; Am 9:8–9; Ro 8:28; Isa 43:3–5,14

CHAPTER VI
Of the Fall of Man, of Sin, and of the Punishment Thereof

1. Our first parents, being seduced by the subtilty and temptation of Satan, sinned, in eating the forbidden fruit.[1] This their sin, God was pleased, according to His wise and holy counsel, to permit, having purposed to order it to His own glory.[2]

2. By this sin they fell from their original righteousness and communion with God,[3] and so became dead in sin,[4] and wholly defiled in all the parts and faculties of soul and body.[5]

3. They being the root of all mankind, the guilt of this sin was imputed;[6] and the same death in sin, and corrupted nature, conveyed to all their posterity descending from them by ordinary generation.[7]

4. From this original corruption, whereby we are utterly indis-

posed, disabled, and made opposite to all good,[8] and wholly inclined to all evil,[9] do proceed all actual transgressions.[10]

5. This corruption of nature, during this life, doth remain in those that are regenerated;[11] and although it be, through Christ, pardoned, and mortified; yet both itself, and all the motions thereof, are truly and properly sin.[12]

6. Every sin, both original and actual, being a transgression of the righteous law of God, and contrary thereunto,[13] doth, in its own nature, bring guilt upon the sinner,[14] whereby he is bound over to the wrath of God,[15] and curse of the law,[16] and so made subject to death,[17] with all miseries spiritual,[18] temporal,[19] and eternal.[20]

1 Ge 3:13; 2Co 11:3
2 Ro 11:32
3 Ge 3:6–8; Ecc 7:29; Ro 3:23
4 Ge 2:17; Eph 2:1
5 Tit 1:15; Ge 6:5; Jer 17:9; Ro 3:10–18
6 Ge 1:27–28; 2:16–17; Ac 17:26; Ro 5:12,15–19; 1Co 15:21–22,49
7 Ps 51:5; Ge 5:3; Job 14:4; 15:14
8 Ro 5:6; 7:18; 8:7; Col 1:21
9 Ge 6:5; 8:21; Ro 3:10–12
10 Jas 1:14–15; Eph 2:2–3; Mt 15:19
11 1Jn 1:8,10; Ro 7:14,17–18,23; Jas 3:2; Pr 20:9; Ecc 7:20
12 Ro 7:5–8,25; Gal 5:17
13 1Jn 3:4
14 Ro 2:15; 3:9,19
15 Eph 2:3
16 Gal 3:10
17 Ro 6:23
18 Eph 4:18
19 Ro 8:20; La 3:39
20 Mt 25:41; 2Th 1:9

CHAPTER VII
Of God's Covenant with Man

1. The distance between God and the creature is so great, that although reasonable creatures do owe obedience unto Him as their Creator, yet they could never have any fruition of Him as their blessedness and reward, but by some voluntary condescension on God's part, which He hath been pleased to express by way of covenant.[1]

2. The first covenant made with man was a covenant of works,[2] wherein life was promised to Adam; and in him to his posterity,[3] upon condition of perfect and personal obedience.[4]

3. Man, by his fall, having made himself incapable of life by that covenant, the Lord was pleased to make a second,[5] commonly called the covenant of grace; wherein[a] He freely offereth unto sinners life and salvation by Jesus Christ; requiring of them faith in Him, that they may be saved,[6] and promising to give unto all those that are ordained unto eternal life[b] His Holy Spirit, to make them willing, and able to believe.[7]

4. This covenant of grace is frequently set forth in Scripture by the name of a testament, in reference to the death of Jesus Christ the Testator, and to the everlasting inheritance, with all things belonging to it, therein bequeathed.[8]

5. This covenant was differently administered in the time of the law, and in the time of the gospel:[9] under the law it was administered by promises, prophecies, sacrifices, circumcision, the paschal lamb, and other types and ordinances delivered to the people of the Jews, all foresignifying Christ to come;[10] which were for that time, sufficient and efficacious, through the operation of the Spirit, to instruct and build up the elect in faith in the promised Messiah,[11] by whom they had full remission of sins, and eternal salvation; and is called the old Testament.[12]

6. Under the gospel, when Christ, the substance,[13] was exhibited, the ordinances in which this covenant is dispensed are the preaching of the Word, and the administration of the sacraments of Baptism and the Lord's Supper:[14] which, though fewer in number, and administered with more simplicity, and less outward glory, yet, in them, it is held forth in more fullness, evidence, and spiritual efficacy,[15] to all nations, both Jews and Gentiles;[16] and is called the new Testament.[17] There are not therefore two covenants of grace, differing in substance, but one and the same, under various dispensations.[18]

1 Isa 40:13–17; Job 9:32–33; 22:2–3; 35:7–8; 1Sa 2:25; Ps 100:2–3; 113:5–6; Lk 17:10; Ac 17:24–25
2 Gal 3:12
3 Ro 5:12–20; 10:5
4 Ge 2:17; Gal 3:10
5 Gal 3:21; Ro 3:20–21; 8:3; Ge 3:15; Isa 42:6
a ARP: "whereby"
6 Mk 16:15–16; Jn 3:16; Ro 10:6; Gal 3:11
b 1647, ARP: "ordained unto life"
7 Eze 36:26–27; Jn 6:44–45
8 Heb 7:22; 9:15–17; Lk 22:20; 1Co 11:25
9 2Co 3:6–9
10 Heb 8–10; Ro 4:11; Col 2:11–12; 1Co 5:7
11 1Co 10:1–4; Heb 11:13; Jn 8:56
12 Gal 3:7–9,14
13 Col 2:17
14 Mt 28:19–20; 1Co 11:23–25
15 Heb 12:22–28; Jer 31:33–34
16 Mt 28:19; Eph 2:15–19
17 Lk 22:20
18 Gal 3:14,16; Ro 3:21–23,30; 4:3,6,16–17,23–24; Ps 32:1; Heb 13:8

CHAPTER VIII
Of Christ the Mediator

1. It pleased God, in His eternal purpose, to choose and ordain the Lord Jesus, His only begotten Son, to be the Mediator between God and man,[1] the Prophet,[2] Priest,[3] and King,[4] the Head and Saviour of His Church,[5] the Heir of all things,[6] and Judge of the world:[7] unto whom He did from all eternity give a people, to be His seed,[8] and to be by Him in time redeemed, called, justified, sanctified, and glorified.[9]

2. The Son of God, the second person in the Trinity, being very and eternal God, of one substance and equal with the Father, did, when the fullness of time was come, take upon Him man's nature,[10] with all the essential properties, and common infirmities thereof, yet without sin;[11] being conceived by the power of the Holy Ghost, in the womb of the virgin Mary, of her substance.[12] So that two whole, perfect, and distinct natures, the Godhead and the manhood, were inseparably joined together in one person, without conversion, composition, or confusion.[13] Which person is very God, and very man, yet one Christ, the only Mediator between God and man.[14]

3. The Lord Jesus, in His human nature thus united to the divine, was sanctified, and anointed with the Holy Spirit, above measure,[15] having in Him all the treasures of wisdom and knowledge;[16] in whom it pleased the Father that all fullness should dwell;[17] to the end that, being holy, harmless, undefiled, and full of grace and truth,[18] He might be thoroughly furnished to execute the office of a mediator and surety.[19] Which office He took not unto Himself, but was thereunto called by His Father,[20] who put all power and judgment into His hand, and gave Him commandment to execute the same.[21]

4. This office the Lord Jesus did most willingly undertake;[22] which that He might[a] discharge, He was made under the law,[23] and did perfectly fulfill it;[24] endured most grievous torments immediately in His soul,[25] and most painful sufferings in His body;[26] was crucified, and died,[27] was buried, and remained under the power of death, yet saw no corruption.[28] On the third day He arose from the dead,[29] with the same body in which He suffered,[30] with which also He ascended into heaven, and there sitteth at the right hand of His Father,[31] making intercession,[32] and shall return, to judge men and angels, at the end of the world.[33]

5. The Lord Jesus, by His perfect obedience, and sacrifice of Himself, which He, through the eternal Spirit, once offered up unto God, hath fully satisfied the justice of His Father;[34] and purchased, not only reconciliation, but an everlasting inheritance in the kingdom of heaven, for all those whom the Father hath given unto Him.[35]

6. Although the work of redemption was not actually wrought by Christ till after His incarnation, yet the virtue,

efficacy, and benefits thereof were communicated unto the elect, in all ages successively from the beginning of the world, in and by those promises, types, and sacrifices, wherein He was revealed, and signified to be the seed of the woman which should bruise the serpent's head; and the Lamb slain from the beginning of the world; being yesterday and today the same, and for ever.[36]

7. Christ, in the work of mediation, acts according to both natures, by each nature doing that which is proper to itself;[37] yet, by reason of the unity of the person, that which is proper to one nature is sometimes in Scripture attributed to the person denominated by the other nature.[38]

8. To all those for whom Christ hath purchased redemption, He doth certainly and effectually apply and communicate the same;[39] making intercession for them,[40] and revealing unto them, in and by the Word, the mysteries of salvation;[41] effectively persuading them by His Spirit to believe and obey, and governing their hearts by His Word and Spirit;[42] overcoming all their enemies by His almighty power and wisdom, in such manner, and ways, as are most consonant to His wonderful and unsearchable dispensation.[43]

1 Isa 42:1; 1Pe 1:19–20; Jn 3:16; 1Ti 2:5
2 Ac 3:22
3 Heb 5:5–6
4 Ps 2:6; Lk 1:33
5 Eph 5:23
6 Heb 1:2
7 Ac 17:31
8 Jn 17:6; Ps 22:30; Isa 53:10
9 1Ti 2:6; Isa 55:4–5; 1Co 1:30
10 Jn 1:1,14; 1Jn 5:20; Php 2:6; Gal 4:4
11 Heb 2:14,16–17; 4:15
12 Lk 1:27,31,35; Gal 4:4
13 Lk 1:35; Col 2:9; Ro 9:5; 1Pe 3:18; 1Ti 3:16
14 Ro 1:3–4; 1Ti 2:5
15 Ps 45:7; Jn 3:34
16 Col 2:3
17 Col 1:19
18 Heb 7:26; Jn 1:14
19 Ac 10:38; Heb 7:22; 12:24
20 Heb 5:4–5
21 Jn 5:22,27; Mt 28:18; Ac 2:36
22 Ps 40:7–8; Heb 10:5–10; Jn 10:18; Php 2:8
a ARP: "may"
23 Gal 4:4
24 Mt 3:15; 5:17
25 Mt 26:37–38; 27:46; Lk 22:44
26 Mt 26–27
27 Php 2:8
28 Ac 2:23–24,27; 13:37; Ro 6:9
29 1Co 15:3–4
30 Jn 20:25,27
31 Mk 16:19
32 Ro 8:34; Heb 7:25; 9:24
33 Ro 14:9–10; Ac 1:11; 10:42; Mt 13:40–42; Jude 6; 2Pe 2:4
34 Ro 3:25–26; 5:19; Heb 9:14,16; 10:14; Eph 5:2
35 Da 9:24,26; Col 1:19–20; Eph 1:11,14; Jn 17:2; Heb 9:12,15
36 Gal 4:4–5; Ge 3:15; Rev 13:8; Heb 13:8
37 Heb 9:14; 1Pe 3:18
38 Ac 20:28; Jn 3:13; 1Jn 3:16
39 Jn 6:37,39; 10:15–16
40 1Jn 2:1–2; Ro 8:34
41 Jn 15:13,15; 17:6; Eph 1:7–10
42 Jn 14:16; 17:17; Heb 12:2; 2Co 4:13; Ro 8:9,14; 15:18–19
43 Ps 110:1; 1Co 15:25–26; Mal 4:2–3; Col 2:15

CHAPTER IX
Of Free-Will

1. God hath endued the will of man with that natural liberty, that it is neither forced, nor, by any absolute necessity of nature, determined to good, or evil.[1]

2. Man, in his state of innocency, had freedom, and power to will and to do that which was good and well pleasing to God;[2] but yet, mutably, so that he might fall from it.[3]

3. Man, by his fall into a state of sin, hath wholly lost all ability of will to any spiritual good accompanying salvation:[4] so as, a natural man, being altogether averse from that good,[5] and dead in sin,[6] is not able, by his own strength, to convert himself, or to prepare himself thereunto.[7]

4. When God converts a sinner, and translates him into the state of grace, He freeth him from his natural bondage under sin;[8] and, by His grace alone, enables him freely to will and to do that which is spiritually good;[9] yet so, that by reason[a] of his remaining corruption, he doth not perfectly, nor only, will that which is good, but doth also will that which is evil.[10]

5. The will of man is made perfectly and immutably free to do good alone in the state of glory only.[11]

1 Mt 17:12; Jas 1:14; Dt 30:19
2 Ecc 7:29; Ge 1:26
3 Ge 2:16–17; 3:6
4 Ro 5:6; 8:7; Jn 15:5
5 Ro 3:10,12
6 Eph 2:1,5; Col 2:13
7 Jn 6:44,65; Eph 2:2–5; 1Co 2:14; Tit 3:3–5
8 Col 1:13; Jn 8:34,36
9 Php 2:13; Ro 6:18,22
a 1647, ARP, OPC: "yet so as that by reason"
10 Gal 5:17; Ro 7:15,18–19,21,23
11 Eph 4:13; Heb 12:23; 1Jn 3:2; Jude 24

CHAPTER X
Of Effectual Calling

1. All those whom God hath predestinated unto life, and those only, He is pleased,[a] in His appointed and accepted time, effectually to call,[1] by His Word and Spirit,[2] out of that state of sin and death, in which they are by nature to grace and salvation, by Jesus Christ;[3] enlightening their minds spiritually and savingly to understand the things of God,[4] taking away their heart of stone, and giving unto them a heart of flesh;[5] renewing their wills, and, by His almighty power, determining them to that which is good,[6] and effectually drawing them to Jesus Christ:[7] yet so, as they come most freely, being made willing by His grace.[8]

2. This effectual call is of God's free and special grace alone, not from anything at all foreseen in man,[9] who is altogether passive therein, until, being quickened and renewed by the Holy Spirit,[10] he is thereby enabled to answer this call, and to embrace the grace offered and conveyed in it.[11]

3. Elect infants, dying in infancy, are regenerated, and saved by Christ, through the Spirit,[12] who worketh when, and where, and how He pleaseth:[13] so also are all other elect persons who are incapable of being outwardly called by the ministry of the Word.[14]

4. Others, not elected, although they may be called by the ministry of the Word,[15] and may have some common operations of the Spirit,[16] yet they never truly come unto Christ, and therefore cannot be saved:[17] much less can men, not professing the Christian religion, be saved in any other way whatsoever, be they never so diligent to frame their lives according to the light of nature, and the laws of that religion they do profess.[18] And to assert and maintain that they may, is very pernicious, and to be detested.[19]

a ARP: "and them only he is pleased"
1 Ro 8:30; 11:7; Eph 1:10–11
2 2Th 2:13–14; 2Co 3:3,6
3 Ro 8:2; Eph 2:1–5; 2Ti 1:9–10
4 Ac 26:18; 1Co 2:10,12; Eph 1:17–18
5 Eze 36:26
6 Eze 11:19; 36:27; Php 2:13; Dt 30:6
7 Eph 1:19; Jn 6:44–45
8 SS 1:4; Ps 110:3; Jn 6:37; Ro 6:16–18
9 2Ti 1:9; Tit 3:4–5; Eph 2:4–5,8–9; Ro 9:11
10 1Co 2:14; Ro 8:7; Eph 2:5
11 Jn 6:37; Eze 36:27; Jn 5:25
12 Lk 18:15–16; Ac 2:38–39; Jn 3:3,5; 1Jn 5:12; Ro 8:9
13 Jn 3:8
14 1Jn 5:12; Ac 4:12
15 Mt 22:14
16 Mt 7:22; 13:20–21; Heb 6:4–5
17 Jn 6:64–66; 8:24
18 Ac 4:12; Jn 4:22; 14:6; 17:3; Eph 2:12
19 2Jn 9–11; 1Co 16:22; Gal 1:6–8

CHAPTER XI
Of Justification

1. Those whom God effectually calleth, He also freely justifieth:[1] not by infusing righteousness into them, but by pardoning their sins, and by accounting and accepting their persons as righteous; not for anything wrought in them, or done by them, but for Christ's sake alone; nor by imputing faith itself, the act of believing, or any other evangelical obedience to them, as their righteousness; but by imputing the obedience and satisfaction of Christ unto them,[2] they receiving and resting on Him and His righteousness by faith; which faith they have not of themselves, it is the gift of God.[3]

2. Faith, thus receiving and resting on Christ and His righteousness, is the alone instrument of justification:[4] yet is it not alone in the person justified, but is ever accompanied with all other saving graces, and is no dead faith, but worketh by love.[5]

3. Christ, by His obedience and death, did fully discharge the debt of all those that are thus justified, and did make a proper, real, and full satisfaction to His Father's justice in their behalf.[6] Yet, inasmuch as He was given by the Father for them;[7] and His obedience and satisfaction accepted in their stead;[8] and both, freely, not for anything in them; their justification is only of free grace;[9] that both the exact justice and rich grace of God might be glorified in the justification of sinners.[10]

4. God did, from all eternity, decree to justify all the elect,[11] and Christ did, in the fullness of time, die for their sins, and rise for[a] their justification:[12] nevertheless, they are not justified, until the Holy Spirit doth, in due time, actually apply Christ unto them.[13]

5. God doth continue to forgive the sins of those that are justified;[14] and, although they can never fall from the state of justification,[15] yet they may, by their sins, fall under God's fatherly displeasure, and not have the light of His countenance restored unto them, until they humble themselves, confess their sins, beg pardon, and renew their faith and repentance.[16]

6. The justification of believers under the old testament was, in all these respects, one and the same with the justification of believers under the new testament.[17]

[1] Ro 3:24; 8:30
[2] Ro 3:22,24–25,27–28; 4:5–8; 5:17–19; 2Co 5:19,21; Tit 3:5,7; Eph 1:7; Jer 23:6; 1Co 1:30–31
[3] Ac 10:43; 13:38–39; Gal 2:16; Php 3:9; Eph 2:7–8
[4] Jn 1:12; Ro 3:28; 5:1
[5] Jas 2:17,22,26; Gal 5:6
[6] Ro 5:8–10,19; 1Ti 2:5–6; Heb 10:10,14; Da 9:24,26; Isa 53:4–6,10–12
[7] Ro 8:32
[8] 2Co 5:21; Mt 3:17; Eph 5:2
[9] Ro 3:24; Eph 1:7
[10] Ro 3:26; Eph 2:7
[11] Gal 3:8; 1Pe 1:2,19–20; Ro 8:30
[a] 1647, ARP, OPC: "and rise again for"
[12] Gal 4:4; 1Ti 2:6; Ro 4:25
[13] Col 1:21–22; Gal 2:16; Tit 3:3–7
[14] Mt 6:12; 1Jn 1:7,9; 2:1–2
[15] Lk 22:32; Jn 10:28; Heb 10:14
[16] Ps 32:5; 51:7–12; 89:31–33; Mt 26:75; 1Co 11:30,32; Lk 1:20
[17] Gal 3:9,13–14; Ro 4:22–24; Heb 13:8

CHAPTER XII
Of Adoption

1. All those that are justified, God vouchsafeth, in and for His only Son Jesus Christ, to make partakers of the grace of adoption,[1] by which they are taken into the number, and enjoy the liberties and privileges of the children of God,[2] have His name put upon them,[3] receive the spirit of adoption,[4] have access to the throne of grace with boldness,[5] are enabled to cry, Abba, Father,[6] are pitied,[7] protected,[8] provided for,[9] and chastened by Him as by a Father:[10] yet never cast off,[11] but sealed to the day of redemption;[12] and inherit the promises,[13] as heirs of everlasting salvation.[14]

[1] Eph 1:5; Gal 4:4–5
[2] Ro 8:17; Jn 1:12
[3] Jer 14:9; 2Co 6:18; Rev 3:12
[4] Ro 8:15
[5] Eph 3:12; Ro 5:2
[6] Gal 4:6
[7] Ps 103:13
[8] Pr 14:26
[9] Mt 6:30,32; 1Pe 5:7
[10] Heb 12:6
[11] La 3:31
[12] Eph 4:30
[13] Heb 6:12
[14] 1Pe 1:3–4; Heb 1:14

CHAPTER XIII
Of Sanctification

1. They, who are once effectually called, and regenerated, having a new heart, and a new spirit created in them, are further sanctified, really and personally, through the virtue of Christ's death and resurrection,[1] by His Word and Spirit dwelling in them,[2] the dominion of the whole body of sin is destroyed,[3] and the several lusts thereof are more and more weakened and mortified;[4] and they more and more quickened and strengthened in all saving graces,[5] to the practice of true holiness, without which no man shall see the Lord.[6]

2. This sanctification is throughout, in the whole man;[7] yet imperfect in this life, there abiding still some remnants of corruption in every part;[8] whence ariseth a continual and irreconcilable war, the flesh lusting against the Spirit, and the Spirit against the flesh.[9]

3. In which war, although the remaining corruption, for a time, may much prevail;[10] yet, through the continual supply of strength from the sanctifying Spirit of Christ, the regenerate part doth overcome;[11] and so, the saints grow in grace,[12] perfecting holiness in the fear of God.[13]

[1] 1Co 6:11; Ac 20:32; Php 3:10; Ro 6:5–6
[2] Jn 17:17; Eph 5:26; 2Th 2:13
[3] Ro 6:6,14
[4] Gal 5:24; Ro 8:13
[5] Col 1:11; Eph 3:16–19
[6] 2Co 7:1; Heb 12:14
[7] 1Th 5:23
[8] 1Jn 1:10; Ro 7:18,23; Php 3:12
[9] Gal 5:17; 1Pe 2:11
[10] Ro 7:23
[11] Ro 6:14; 1Jn 5:4; Eph 4:15–16
[12] 2Pe 3:18; 2Co 3:18
[13] 2Co 7:1

CHAPTER XIV
Of Saving Faith

1. The grace of faith, whereby the elect are enabled to believe to the saving of their souls,[1] is the work of the Spirit of Christ in their hearts,[2] and is ordinarily wrought by the ministry of the Word,[3] by which also, and by the administration of the sacraments, and prayer, it is increased and strengthened.[4]

2. By this faith, a Christian believeth to be true whatsoever is revealed in the Word, for the authority of God Himself speaking therein;[5] and acteth differently upon that which each particular passage thereof containeth; yielding obedience to the commands,[6] trembling at the threatenings,[7] and embracing the promises of God for this life, and that which is to come.[8] But the principal acts of saving faith are accepting, receiving, and resting upon Christ alone for justification, sanctification, and eternal life, by virtue of the covenant of grace.[9]

3. This faith is different in degrees, weak or strong;[10] may be often and many ways assailed, and weakened, but gets the victory:[11] growing up in many to the attainment of a full assurance, through Christ,[12] who is both the author and finisher of our faith.[13]

[1] Heb 10:39
[2] 2Co 4:13; Eph 1:17–19; 2:8
[3] Ro 10:14,17
[4] 1Pe 2:2; Ac 20:32; Ro 1:16–17; 4:11; Lk 17:5

5 Jn 4:42; 1Th 2:13; 1Jn 5:10; Ac 24:14
6 Ro 16:26
7 Isa 66:2
8 Heb 11:13; 1Ti 4:8
9 Jn 1:12; Ac 15:11; 16:31; Gal 2:20
10 Heb 5:13–14; Ro 4:19–20; Mt 6:30; 8:10
11 Lk 22:31–32; Eph 6:16; 1Jn 5:4–5
12 Heb 6:11–12; 10:22
13 Heb 12:2

CHAPTER XV
Of Repentance unto Life

1. Repentance unto life is an evangelical grace,[1] the doctrine whereof is to be preached by every minister of the gospel, as well as that of faith in Christ.[2]

2. By it, a sinner, out of the sight and sense not only of the danger, but also of the filthiness and odiousness of his sins, as contrary to the holy nature, and righteous law of God; and upon the apprehension of His mercy in Christ to such as are penitent, so grieves for, and hates his sins, as to turn from them all unto God,[3] purposing and endeavouring to walk with Him in all the ways of His commandments.[4]

3. Although repentance be not to be rested in, as any satisfaction for sin, or any cause of the pardon thereof,[5] which is the act of God's free grace in Christ;[6] yet it is of such necessity to all sinners, that none may expect pardon without it.[7]

4. As there is no sin so small, but it deserves damnation;[8] so there is no sin so great, that it can bring damnation upon those who truly repent.[9]

5. Men ought not to content themselves with a general repentance, but it is every man's duty to endeavour to repent of his particular sins, particularly.[10]

6. As every man is bound to make private confession of his sins to God, praying for the pardon thereof;[11] upon which, and the forsaking of them, he shall find mercy;[12] so, he that scandalizeth his brother, or the Church of Christ, ought to be willing, by a private or public confession, and sorrow for his sin, to declare his repentance to those that are offended,[13] who are thereupon to be reconciled to him, and in love to receive him.[14]

1 Zec 12:10; Ac 11:18
2 Lk 24:47; Mk 1:15; Ac 20:21
3 Eze 18:30–31; 36:31; Isa 30:22; Ps 51:4; 119:128; Jer 31:18–19; Joel 2:12–13; Am 5:15; 2Co 7.11
4 Ps 119:6,59,106; Lk 1:6; 2Ki 23:25
5 Eze 16:61–63; 36:31–32
6 Hos 14:2,4; Ro 3:24; Eph 1:7
7 Lk 13:3,5; Ac 17:30–31
8 Ro 5:12; 6:23; Mt 12:36
9 Isa 1:16,18; 55:7; Ro 8:1;
10 Ps 19:13; Lk 19:8; 1Ti 1:13,15
11 Ps 32:5–6; 51:4–5,7,9,14
12 Pr 28:13; 1Jn 1:9
13 Jas 5:16; Lk 17:3–4; Jos 7:19; Ps 51
14 2Co 2:8

CHAPTER XVI
Of Good Works

1. Good works are only such as God hath commanded in His holy Word,[1] and not such as, without the warrant thereof, are devised by men, out of blind zeal, or upon any pretence of good intention.[2]

2. These good works, done in obedience to God's commandments, are the fruits and evidences of a true and lively faith:[3] and by them believers manifest their thankfulness,[4] strengthen their assurance,[5] edify their brethren,[6] adorn the profession of the Gospel,[7] stop the mouths of the adversaries,[8] and glorify God[9] whose workmanship they are, created in Christ Jesus thereunto,[10] that, having their fruit unto holiness, they may have the end, eternal life.[11]

3. Their ability to do good works is not at all of themselves, but wholly from the Spirit of Christ.[12] And that they may be enabled thereunto, beside the graces they have already received, there is required an actual influence of the same Holy Spirit, to work in them to will, and to do, of His good pleasure:[13] yet are they not hereupon to grow negligent, as if they were not bound to perform any duty unless upon a special motion of the Spirit; but they ought to be diligent in stirring up the grace of God that is in them.[14]

4. They who, in their obedience, attain to the greatest height which is possible in this life, are so far from being able to supererogate, and to do more than God requires, as that they fall short of much which in the duty they are bound to do.[15]

5. We cannot by our best works merit pardon of sin, or eternal life at the hand of God, by reason of the great disproportion that is between them and the glory to come; and the infinite distance that is between us and God, whom, by them, we can neither profit, nor satisfy for the debt of our former sins,[16] but when we have done all we can, we have done but our duty, and are unprofitable servants:[17] and because, as they are good, they proceed from His Spirit;[18] and as they are wrought by us, they are defiled, and mixed with so much weakness and imperfection, that they cannot endure the severity of God's judgment.[19]

6. Notwithstanding,[a] the persons of believers being accepted through Christ, their good works also are accepted in Him;[20] not as though they were in this life wholly unblameable and unreproveable in God's sight;[21] but that He, looking upon them in His Son, is pleased to accept and reward that which is sincere, although accompanied with many weaknesses and imperfections.[22]

7. Works done by unregenerate men, although for the matter of them they may be things which God commands; and of good use both to themselves and others:[23] yet, because they proceed not from an heart purified by faith;[24] nor are done in a right manner, according to the Word;[25] nor to a right end, the glory of God,[26] they are therefore sinful, and cannot please God, or make a man meet to receive grace from God:[27] and yet, their neglect of them is more sinful and displeasing unto God.[28]

1 Mic 6:8; Ro 12:2; Heb 13:21
2 Mt 15:9; Isa 29:13; 1Pe 1:18; Ro 10.2; Jn 16:2; 1Sa 15:21-23
3 Jas 2.18,22
4 Ps 116:12–13; 1Pe 2:9
5 1Jn 2:3,5; 2Pe 1:5–10
6 2Co 9:2; Mt 5:16
7 Tit 2:5,9–12; 1Ti 6:1
8 1Pe 2:15
9 1Pe 2:12; Php 1:11; Jn 15:8
10 Eph 2:10
11 Ro 6:22
12 Jn 15:4–5; Eze 36:26–27
13 Php 2:13; 4:13; 2Co 3:5
14 Php 2:12; Heb 6:11–12; 2Pe 1:3,5,10–11; Isa 64:7; 2Ti 1:6; Ac 26:6–7; Jude 20, 21
15 Lk 17:10; Ne 13:22; Job 9:2–3; Gal 5:17
16 Ro 3:20; 4:2,4,6; 8:18; Eph 2:8–9; Tit 3:5–7; Ps 16:2; Job 22:2–3; 35:7–8
17 Lk 17:10
18 Gal 5:22–23
19 Isa 64:6; Gal 5:17; Ro 7:15,18; Ps 130:3; 143:2
a 1647, ARP: "Yet notwithstanding"
20 Eph 1:6; 1Pe 2:5; Ex 28:38; Ge 4:4; Heb 11:4
21 Job 9:20; Ps 143:2
22 Heb 6:10; 13:20–21; 2Co 8:12; Mt 25:21,23
23 2Ki 10:30–31; 1Ki 21:27,29; Php 1:15–16,18
24 Ge 4:5; Heb 11:4,6
25 1Co 13:3; Isa 1:12
26 Mt 6:2,5,16
27 Hag 2:14; Tit 1:15; 3:5; Am 5:21–22; Hos 1:4; Ro 9:16
28 Ps 14:4; 36:3; Job 21:14–15; Mt 25:41–43,45

CHAPTER XVII
Of the Perseverance of the Saints

1. They, whom God hath accepted in His Beloved, effectually called, and sanctified by His Spirit, can neither totally nor finally fall away from the state of grace, but shall certainly persevere therein to the end, and be eternally saved.[1]

2. This perseverance of the saints depends not upon their own free will, but upon the immutability of the decree of election, flowing from the free and unchangeable love of God the Father;[2] upon the efficacy of the merit and inter-

cession of Jesus Christ,[3] the abiding of the Spirit, and of the seed of God within them,[4] and the nature of the covenant of grace:[5] from all which ariseth also the certainty and infallibility thereof.[6]

3. Nevertheless, they may, through the temptations of Satan and of the world, the prevalency of corruption remaining in them, and the neglect of the means of their preservation, fall into grievous sins;[7] and, for a time, continue therein:[8] whereby they incur God's displeasure,[9] and grieve His Holy Spirit,[10] come to be deprived of some measure of their graces and comforts,[11] have their hearts hardened,[12] and their consciences wounded;[13] hurt and scandalize others,[14] and bring temporal judgments upon themselves.[15]

1 Php 1:6; 2Pe 1:10; Jn 10:28–29; 1Jn 3:9; 1Pe 1:5,9
2 2Ti 2:18–19; Jer 31:3
3 Heb 7:25; 9:12–15; 10:10,14; 13:20–21; Ro 8:33–39; Jn 17:11,24; Lk 22:32
4 Jn 14:16–17; 1Jn 2:27; 3:9
5 Jer 32:40
6 Jn 10:28; 2Th 3:3; 1Jn 2:19
7 Mt 26:70,72,74
8 Ps 51
9 Isa 64:5,7,9; 2Sa 11:27
10 Eph 4:30
11 Ps 51:8,10,12; Rev 2:4; SS 5:2–4,6
12 Isa 63:17; Mk 6:52; 16:14
13 Ps 32:3–4; 51:8
14 2Sa 12:14
15 Ps 89:31–32; 1Co 11:32

CHAPTER XVIII
Of the Assurance of Grace and Salvation

1. Although hypocrites and other unregenerate men may vainly deceive themselves with false hopes and carnal presumptions of being in the favour of God, and estate of salvation[1] (which hope of theirs shall perish):[2] yet such as truly believe in the Lord Jesus, and love Him in sincerity, endeavouring to walk in all good conscience before Him, may, in this life, be certainly assured that they are in the state of grace,[3] and may rejoice in the hope of the glory of God, which hope shall never make them ashamed.[4]

2. This certainty is not a bare conjectural and probable persuasion grounded upon a fallible hope;[5] but an infallible assurance of faith founded upon the divine truth of the promises of salvation,[6] the inward evidence of those graces unto which these promises are made,[7] the testimony of the Spirit of adoption witnessing with our spirits that we are the children of God,[8] which Spirit is the earnest of our inheritance, whereby we are sealed to the day of redemption.[9]

3. This infallible assurance doth not so belong to the essence of faith, but that a true believer may wait long, and conflict with many difficulties before he be partaker of it:[10] yet, being enabled by the Spirit to know the things which are freely given him of God, he may, without extraordinary revelation, in the right use of ordinary means, attain thereunto.[11] And therefore it is the duty of everyone to give all diligence to make his calling and election sure,[12] that thereby his heart may be enlarged in peace and joy in the Holy Ghost, in love and thankfulness to God, and in strength and cheerfulness in the duties of obedience,[13] the proper fruits of this assurance; so far is it from inclining men to looseness.[14]

4. True believers may have the assurance of their salvation divers ways shaken, diminished, and intermitted; as, by negligence in preserving of it, by falling into some special sin which woundeth the conscience and grieveth the Spirit; by some sudden or vehement temptation, by God's withdrawing the light of His countenance, and suffering even such as fear Him to walk in darkness and to have no light:[15] yet are they never utterly destitute of that seed of God, and life of faith, that love of Christ and the brethren, that sincerity of heart, and conscience of duty, out of which, by the operation of the Spirit, this assurance may, in due time, be revived;[16] and by the which, in the mean time, they are supported from utter despair.[17]

1 Job 8:13–14; Mic 3:11; Dt 29:19; Jn 8:41
2 Mt 7:22–23
3 1Jn 2:3; 3:14,18–19,21,24; Jn 5:13
4 Ro 5:2,5
5 Heb 6:11,19
6 Heb 6:17–18
7 2Pe 1:4-5,10–11; 1Jn 2:3; 3:14; 2Co 1:12
8 Ro 8:15–16
9 Eph 1:13–14; 4:30; 2Co 1:21–22
10 1Jn 5:13; Isa 50:10; Mk 9:24; Ps 77:1–12; 88
11 1Co 2:12; 1Jn 4:13; Heb 6:11-12; Eph 3:17–18
12 2Pe 1:10
13 Ro 5:1-2,5; 14:17; 15:13; Eph 1:3–4; Ps 4:6–7; 119:32
14 1Jn 1:6–7; 2:1–2; 3:2–3; Ro 6:1–2; 8:1,12; Tit 2:11–12,14; 2Co 7:1; Ps 130:4
15 SS 5:2–3,6; Ps 31:22; 51:8,12,14; 77:1–10; 88; Eph 4:30–31; Mt 26:69–72; Isa 50:10
16 1Jn 3:9; Lk 22:32; Job 13:15; Ps 51:8,12; 73:15; Isa 50:10
17 Mic 7:7–9; Jer 32:40; Isa 54:7–10; Ps 22:1; 88

CHAPTER XIX
Of the Law of God

1. God gave to Adam a law, as a covenant of works, by which He bound him and all his posterity to personal, entire, exact, and perpetual obedience, promised life upon the fulfilling, and threatened death upon the breach of it, and endued him with power and ability to keep it.[1]

2. This law, after his fall, continued to be a perfect rule of righteousness; and, as such, was delivered by God upon Mount Sinai, in ten commandments, and written in two tables:[2] the first four commandments containing our duty towards God; and the other six, our duty to man.[3]

3. Besides this law, commonly called moral, God was pleased to give to the people of Israel, as a church under age, ceremonial laws, containing several typical ordinances, partly of worship, prefiguring Christ, His graces, actions, sufferings, and benefits;[4] and partly of divers instructions of moral duties.[5] All which ceremonial laws are now abrogated, under the new testament.[6]

4. To them also, as a body politic, He gave sundry judicial laws, which expired together with the State of that people; not obliging any other now, further than the general equity thereof may require.[7]

5. The moral law doth for ever bind all, as well justified persons as others, to the obedience thereof;[8] and that, not only in regard of the matter contained in it, but also in respect of the authority of God the Creator, who gave it.[9] Neither doth Christ, in the Gospel, any way dissolve, but much strengthen this obligation.[10]

6. Although true believers be not under the law, as a covenant of works, to be thereby justified, or condemned;[11] yet is it of great use to them, as well as to others; in that, as a rule of life informing them of the will of God, and their duty, it directs and binds them to walk accordingly;[12] discovering also the sinful pollutions of their nature, hearts, and lives;[13] so as, examining themselves thereby, they may come to further conviction of, humiliation for, and hatred against sin,[14] together with a clearer sight of the need they have of Christ, and the perfection of His obedience.[15] It is likewise of use to the regenerate, to restrain their corruptions, in that it forbids sin:[16] and the threatenings of it serve to show what even their sins deserve; and what afflictions, in this life, they may expect for them, although freed from the curse thereof threatened in the law.[17] The promises of it, in like manner, show them God's approbation of obedience, and what blessings they may expect upon the performance thereof:[18] although not as due to them by the law as a covenant of works.[19] So as, a man's doing good, and refraining from evil, because the law encourageth to the one, and deterreth from the other, is no evidence of his being under the law; and, not under grace.[20]

7. Neither are the forementioned uses of the law contrary to the grace of the Gospel, but do sweetly comply with it;[21] the Spirit of Christ subduing and enabling the will of man to do that freely, and cheerfully, which the will of God, revealed in the law, requireth to be done.[22]

1 Ge 1:26–27; 2:17; Ro 2:14–15; 5:12,19; 10:5; Gal 3:10,12; Ecc 7:29; Job 28:28
2 Jas 1:25; 2:8,10–12; Ro 13:8–9; Dt 5:32; 10:4; Ex 34:1
3 Mt 22:37–40
4 Heb 9; 10:1; Gal 4:1–3; Col 2:17
5 1Co 5:7; 2Co 6:17; Jude 23
6 Col 2:14,16–17; Da 9:27; Eph 2:15–16
7 Ex 21; 22:1–29; Ge 49:10; 1Pe 2:13–14; Mt 5:17,38–39; 1Co 9:8–10
8 Ro 13:8–10; Eph 6:2; 1Jn 2:3–4,7–8
9 Jas 2:10–11
10 Mt 5:17–19; Jas 2:8; Ro 3:31
11 Ro 6:14; 8:1; Gal 2:16; 3:13; 4:4–5; Ac 13:39
12 Ro 7:12,22,25; Ps 119:4–6; 1Co 7:19; Gal 5:14,16,18–23
13 Ro 3:20; 7:7
14 Jas 1:23–25; Ro 7:9,14,24
15 Gal 3:24; Ro 7:24–25; 8:3–4
16 Jas 2:11; Ps 119:101,104,128
17 Ezr 9:13–14; Ps 89:30–34
18 Lev 26:1–14; 2Co 6:16; Eph 6:2-3; Ps 19:11; 37:11; Mt 5:5
19 Gal 2:16; Lk 17:10
20 Ro 6:12,14; 1Pe 3:8–12; Ps 34:12–16; Heb 12:28–29
21 Gal 3:21
22 Eze 36:27; Heb 8:10; Jer 31:33

CHAPTER XX
Of Christian Liberty, and Liberty of Conscience

1. The liberty which Christ hath purchased for believers under the Gospel consists in their freedom from the guilt of sin, the condemning wrath of God, the curse of the moral law;[1] and, in their being delivered from this present evil world, bondage to Satan, and dominion of sin;[2] from the evil of afflictions, the sting of death, the victory of the grave, and everlasting damnation;[3] as also, in their free access to God,[4] and their yielding obedience unto Him, not out of slavish fear, but a child-like love and willing mind.[5] All which were common also to believers under the law.[6] But, under the new testament, the liberty of Christians is further enlarged, in their freedom from the yoke of the ceremonial law, to which the Jewish Church was subjected;[7] and in greater boldness of access to the throne of grace,[8] and in fuller communications of the free Spirit of God, than believers under the law did ordinarily partake of.[9]

2. God alone is Lord of the conscience,[10] and hath left it free from the doctrines and commandments of men, which are, in anything, contrary to His Word; or beside it, if matters of faith,[a] or worship.[11] So that, to believe such doctrines, or to obey such commands,[b] out of conscience, is to betray true liberty of conscience:[12] and the requiring of an implicit faith, and an absolute and blind obedience, is to destroy liberty of conscience, and reason also.[13]

3. They who, upon pretence of Christian liberty, do practice any sin, or cherish any lust, do thereby destroy the end of Christian liberty, which is, that being delivered out of the hands of our enemies, we might serve the Lord without fear, in holiness and righteousness before Him, all the days of our life.[14]

4. And because the powers which God hath ordained, and the liberty which Christ hath purchased, are not intended by God to destroy, but mutually to uphold and preserve one another, they who, upon pretence of Christian liberty, shall oppose any lawful power, or the lawful exercise of it, whether it be civil or ecclesiastical, resist the ordinance of God.[15] And, for their publishing of such opinions, or maintaining of such practices, as are contrary to the light of nature, or to the known principles of Christianity (whether concerning faith, worship, or conversation), or to the power of godliness; or, such erroneous[c] opinions or practices, as either in their own nature, or in the manner of publishing or maintaining them, are destructive to the external peace[d] and order which Christ hath established in the Church, they may lawfully be called to account, and proceeded against, by the censures of the Church.[e] [16]

1 Tit 2:14; 1Th 1:10; Gal 3:13
2 Gal 1:4; Col 1:13; Ac 26:18; Ro 6:14
3 Ro 8:1,28; Ps 119:71; 1Co 15:54–57
4 Ro 5:1–2
5 Ro 8:14–15; 1Jn 4:18
6 Gal 3:9,14
7 Gal 4:1–3,6–7; 5:1; Ac 15:10–11
8 Heb 4:14,16; 10:19–22
9 Jn 7:38–39; 2Co 3:13,17–18
10 Jas 4:12; Ro 14:4
a ARP: "in matters of faith"
11 Ac 4:19; 5:29; 1Co 7:23; Mt 15:9; 23:8–10; 2Co 1:24
b ARP: "commandments"
12 Col 2:20,22–23; Gal 1:10; 2:4–5; 5:1
13 Ro 10:17; 14:23; Isa 8:20; Ac 17:11; Jn 4:22; Hos 5:11; Rev 13:12,16–17; Jer 8:9
14 Gal 5:13; 1Pe 2:16; 2Pe 2:19; Jn 8:34; Lk 1:74–75
15 Mt 12:25; 1Pe 2:13–14,16; Ro 13:1–8; Heb 13:17
c ARP: Replaces "to the power of godliness; or, such erroneous" with "the order which Christ hath established in his church, they may be lawfully called to account, and proceeded against by the censures of the church; and in proportion as their erroneous"
d ARP: Ends section 20. 4 with "external peace of the church and of civil society, they may also be proceeded against by the power of the civil magistrate."
e 1647: Ends section 20.4 with "and by the power of the civil magistrate."
16 Ro 1:32; 1Co 5:1,5,11,13; 2Jn 10–11; 2Th 3:14; 1Ti 1:19–20; 6:3–5; Tit 1:10–11,13; 3:10; Mt 18:15–17; Rev 2:2,14–15,20; 3:9

CHAPTER XXI
Of Religious Worship, and the Sabbath Day

1. The light of nature showeth that there is a God, who hath lordship and sovereignty over all, is good, and doth good unto all, and is therefore to be feared, loved, praised, called upon, trusted in, and served, with all the heart, and with all the soul, and with all the might.[1] But the acceptable way of worshipping the true God is instituted by Himself, and so limited by His own revealed will, that He may not be worshipped according to the imaginations and devices of men, or the suggestions of Satan, under any visible representation, or any other way not prescribed in the holy Scripture.[2]

2. Religious worship is to be given to God, the Father, Son, and Holy Ghost; and to Him alone;[3] not to angels, saints, or any other creature:[4] and, since the fall, not without a mediator; nor in the mediation of any other but of Christ alone.[5]

3. Prayer, with thanksgiving, being one special part of religious worship,[6] is by God required of all men:[7] and, that it may be accepted, it is to be made in the name of the Son,[8] by the help of His Spirit,[9] according to His will,[10] with understanding, reverence, humility, fervency, faith, love, and perseverance;[11] and, if vocal, in a known tongue.[12]

4. Prayer is to be made for things lawful;[13] and for all sorts of men living, or that shall live hereafter:[14] but nor for the dead,[15] nor for those of whom it may be known that they have sinned the sin unto death.[16]

5. The reading of the Scriptures with godly fear,[17] the sound preaching[18] and conscionable hearing of the Word, in obedience unto God, with understanding, faith, and reverence,[19] singing of psalms with grace in the heart;[20] as also, the due administration and worthy receiving of the sacraments instituted by Christ, are all parts of the ordinary religious worship of God:[21] beside[a] religious oaths,[22] vows,[23] solemn fastings,[24] and thanksgivings upon special occasions,[25] which are, in their several times and seasons, to be used in an holy and religious manner.[26]

6. Neither prayer, nor any other part of religious worship, is now, under the Gospel, either tied unto, or made more acceptable by any place in which it is performed, or towards which it is directed:[27] but God is to be worshipped everywhere,[28] in spirit and truth;[b] [29] as, in private families[30] daily,[31] and in secret, each one by himself;[32] so, more solemnly in the public assemblies, which are not carelessly or wilfully to be neglected, or forsaken, when God, by His Word or providence, calleth thereunto.[33]

7. As it is the law of nature, that, in general, a due proportion of time be set apart for the worship of God; so, in His Word, by a positive, moral, and perpetual commandment binding all men in all ages, He hath particularly appointed one day in seven, for a Sabbath, to be kept holy unto him:[34] which, from the beginning of the world to the resurrection of Christ, was the last day of the week; and, from the resur-

rection of Christ, was changed into the first day of the week,[35] which, in Scripture, is called the Lord's Day,[36] and is to be continued to the end of the world, as the Christian Sabbath.[37]

8. This Sabbath is then kept holy unto the Lord, when men, after a due preparing of their hearts, and ordering of their common affairs before-hand, do not only observe an holy rest, all the day, from their own works, words, and thoughts about their worldly employments and recreations,[38] but also are taken up, the whole time, in the public and private exercises of His worship, and in the duties of necessity and mercy.[39]

1 Ro 1:20; 10:12; Ac 17:24; Ps 18:3; 31:23; 62:8; 119:68; Jer 10:7; Jos 24:14; Mk 12:33
2 Dt 4:15–20; 12:32; Mt 4:9–10; 15:9; Ac 17:25; Ex 20:4-6; Col 2:23
3 Mt 4:10; Jn 5:23; 2Co 13:14
4 Col 2:18; Rev 19:10; Ro 1:25
5 Jn 14:6; 1Ti 2:5; Eph 2:18; Col 3:17
6 Php 4:6
7 Ps 65:2
8 Jn 14:13–14; 1Pe 2:5
9 Ro 8:26
10 1Jn 5:14
11 Ps 47:7; Ecc 5:1–2; Heb 12:28; Ge 18:27; Jas 1:6–7; 5:16; Mk 11:24; Mt 6:12,14–15; Col 4:2; Eph 6:18
12 1Co 14:14
13 1Jn 5:14
14 1Ti 2:1–2; Jn 17:20; 2Sa 7:29; Ru 4:12
15 2Sa 12:21–23; Lk 16:25-26; Rev 14:13
16 1Jn 5:16
17 Ac 15:21; Rev 1:3
18 2Ti 4:2;
19 Jas 1:22; Ac 10:33; Mt 13:19; Heb 4:2; Isa 66:2
20 Col 3:16; Eph 5:19; Jas 5:13
21 Mt 28:19; 1Co 11:23–29; Ac 2:42
a ARP: "besides"
22 Dt; 6:13; Ne 10:29
23 Isa 19:21; Ecc 5:4–5
24 Joel 2:12; Est 4:16; Mt 9:15; 1Co 7:5
25 Ps 107; Est 9:22
26 Heb 12:28
27 Jn 4:21
28 Mal 1:11; 1Ti 2:8
b ARP: "in spirit and in truth"
29 Jn 4:23–24
30 Jer 10:25; Dt 6:6–7; Job 1:5; 2Sa 6:18,20; 1Pe 3:7; Ac 10:2
31 Mt 6:11
32 Mt 6:6; Eph 6:18
33 Isa 56:6–7; Heb 10:25; Pr 1:20–21,24; 8:34; Ac 2:42; 13:42; Lk 4:16
34 Ex 20:8,10–11; Isa 56:2,4,6–7
35 Ge 2:2–3; 1Co 16:1; Ac 20:7
36 Rev 1:10
37 Ex 20:8,10; Mt 5:17–18
38 Ex 16:23,25–26,29–30; 20:8; 31:15–17; Isa 58:13; Ne 13:15–19,21–22
39 Isa 58:13; Mt 12:1–13

CHAPTER XXII
Of Lawful Oaths and Vows

1. A lawful oath is part of religious worship,[1] wherein, upon just occasion, the person swearing solemnly calleth God to witness what he asserteth, or promiseth, and to judge him according to the truth or falsehood of what he sweareth.[2]

2. The name of God only is that by which men ought to swear and therein it is to be used with all holy fear and reverence.[3] Therefore, to swear vainly, or rashly by that glorious and dreadful Name; or, to swear at all by any other thing, is sinful, and to be abhorred.[4] Yet, as in matters of weight and moment, an oath is warranted by the Word of God, under the new testament as well as under the old;[5] so a lawful oath, being imposed by lawful authority, in such matters, ought to be taken.[6]

3. Whosoever taketh an oath ought duly to consider the weightiness of so solemn an act, and therein to avouch nothing but what he fully persuaded is the truth:[7] neither may any man bind himself by oath to any-thing but what is good and just, and what he believeth so to be, and what he is able and resolved to perform.[a] [8]

4. An oath is to be taken in the plain and common sense of the words, without equivocation, or mental reservation.[9] It cannot oblige to sin; but in anything not sinful, being taken, it binds to performance, although to a man's own hurt.[10] Nor is it to be violated, although made to heretics, or infidels.[11]

5. A vow is of the like nature with a promissory oath, and ought to be made with the like religious care, and to be performed with the like faithfulness.[12]

6. It is not to be made to any creature, but to God alone:[13] and, that it may be accepted, it is to be made voluntarily, out of faith, and conscience of duty, in way of thankfulness for mercy received, or for the obtaining of what we want, whereby we more strictly bind ourselves to necessary duties; or, to other things, so far and so long as they may fitly conduce thereunto.[14]

7. No man may vow to do anything forbidden in the Word of God, or what would hinder any duty therein commanded, or which is not in his own power,[b] and for the performance whereof he hath no promise of ability from God.[15] In which respects, popish monastical vows of perpetual single life, professed poverty, and regular obedience, are so far from being degrees of higher perfection, that they are superstitious and sinful snares, in which no Christian may entangle himself.[16]

1 Dt 10:20
2 Ex 20:7; Lev 19:12; 2Co 1:23; 2Ch 6:22–23
3 Dt 6:13
4 Ex 20.7, Mt 5:34,37; Jas 5:12
5 Heb 6:16; 2Co 1:23; Isa 65:16
6 1Ki 8:31; Ne 13:25; Ezr 10:5
7 Ex 20:7; Jer 4:2
a The 1647 and ARP versions conclude section 22.3 with: "Yet it is a sin to refuse an oath touching anything that is good and just, being imposed by lawful authority."
8 Ge 24:2–3,5–6,8–9
9 Jer 4:2; Ps 24:4
10 1Sa 25:22,32–34; Ps 15:4
11 Eze 17:16,18–19; Jos 9:18–19; 2Sa 21:1
12 Isa 19:21; Ecc 5:4–6; Ps 66:13–14
13 Ps 76:11; Jer 44:25–26;
14 Dt 23:21–23; Ps 50:14; 66:13–14; 132:2–5;Ge 28:20–22; 1Sa 1:11
b ARP: "his power"
15 Ac 23:12,14; Mk 6:26; Nu 30:5,8,12–13
16 Mt 19:11–12; 1Co 7:2,9; Eph 4:28; 1Pe 4:2; 1Co 7:23

CHAPTER XXIII
Of the Civil Magistrate

1. God the supreme Lord and King of all the world, hath ordained civil magistrates, to be, under Him, over the people, for His own glory, and the public good: and, to this end, hath armed them with the power of the sword, for the defence and encouragement of them that are good, and for the punishment of evil doers.[1]

2. It is lawful for Christians to accept and execute the office of a magistrate, when called thereunto:[2] in the managing whereof, as they ought especially to maintain piety, justice, and peace, according to the wholesome laws of each commonwealth;[3] so, for that end, they may lawfully, now under the new testament, wage war, upon just and necessary occasion.[4]

3. Civil magistrates may not assume to themselves the administration of the Word and sacraments;[5] or the power of the keys of the kingdom of heaven;[6] or, in the least, interfere in matters of faith.[7] Yet, as nursing fathers, it is the duty of civil magistrates to protect the Church of our common Lord, without giving the preference to any denomination of Christians above the rest, in such a manner that all ecclesiastical persons whatever shall enjoy the full, free, and unquestioned liberty of discharging every part of their sacred functions, without violence or danger.[8] And, as Jesus Christ hath appointed a regular government and discipline in His Church, no law of any commonwealth should interfere with, let, or hinder, the due exercise thereof, among the voluntary members of *any* denomination of Christians, according to their own profession and belief.[9] It is the duty of civil magistrates to protect the person and good name of

all their people, in such an effectual manner as that no person be suffered, either upon pretence of religion or of infidelity, to offer any indignity, violence, abuse, or injury to any other person whatsoever: and to take order, that all religious and ecclesiastical assemblies be held without molestation or disturbance.[a] [10]

4. It is the duty of people to pray for magistrates,[11] to honour their persons,[12] to pay them tribute or other dues,[13] to obey their lawful commands, and to be subject to their authority, for conscience sake.[14] Infidelity, or difference in religion, doth not make void the magistrates' just and legal authority, nor free the people from their due obedience to them:[15] from which ecclesiastical persons are not exempted,[16] much less hath the Pope any power and jurisdiction over them in their dominions, or over any of their people; and, least of all, to deprive them of their dominions, or lives, if he shall judge them to be heretics, or upon any other pretence whatsoever.[17]

1 Ro 13:1–4; 1Pe 2:13–14
2 Pr 8:15–16; Ro 13:1–2,4
3 Ps 2:10–12; 82:3–4; 1Ti 2:2; 2Sa 23:3; 1Pe 2:13
4 Lk 3:14; Ro 13:4; Mt 8:9–10; Ac 10:1–2; Rev 17:14,16
5 2Ch 26:18
6 Mt 16:19; 18:17; 1Co 4:1–2; 12:28–29; Eph 4:11–12; Ro 10:15; Heb 5:4
7 Jn 18:36; Ac 5:29; Eph 4:11–12
8 Isa 49:23; Ro 13:1–6
9 Ps 104:15; Ac 18:14–15
a Section 23.3 of the 1647 version reads: "The civil magistrate may not assume to himself the administration of the Word and sacraments; or the power of the keys of the kingdom of heaven; yet he hath authority, and it is his duty, to take order, that unity and peace be preserved in the Church, that the truth of God be kept pure and entire; that all blasphemies and heresies be suppressed; all corruptions and abuses in worship and discipline prevented or reformed; and all the ordinances of God duly settled, administered, and observed. For the better effecting whereof, he hath power to call synods, to be present at them, and to provide that whatsoever is transacted in them be according to the mind of God." The ARP version of section 23.3 reads: "The civil magistrate may not assume to himself the administration of the Word and sacraments; or the power of the keys of the kingdom of heaven; yet, as the gospel revelation lays indispensable obligations upon all classes of people who are favored with it, magistrates as such, are bound to execute their respective offices in a subserviency thereunto; administering government on Christian principles, and ruling in the fear of God, according to the directions of his word; as those who shall give an account to the Lord Jesus, whom God hath appointed to be the judge of the world. Hence, magistrates, as such, in a Christian country, are bound to promote the Christian religion, as the most valuable interest of their subjects, by all such means as are not inconsistent with civil rights; and do not imply an interference with the policy of the church, which is the free and independent kingdom for the Redeemer; nor an assumption of dominion over conscience."
10 Ro 13:4; 1Ti 2:2
11 1Ti 2:1–2
12 1Pe 2:17
13 Ro 13:6–7
14 Ro 13:5; Tit 3:1
15 1Pe 2:13–14,16
16 Ro 13:1; 1Ki 2:35; Ac 25:9–11; 2Pe 2:1,10–11; Jude 8–11
17 2Th 2:4; Rev 13:15–17

CHAPTER XXIV
Of Marriage and Divorce

1. Marriage is to be between one man and one woman: neither is it lawful for any man to have more than one wife, nor for any woman to have more than one husband, at the same time.[a] [1]

2. Marriage was ordained for the mutual help of husband and wife,[2] for the increase of mankind with legitimate issue, and of the Church with an holy seed;[3] and for preventing of uncleanness.[b] [4]

3. It is lawful for all sorts of people to marry, who are able with judgment to give their consent.[5] Yet it is the duty of Christians to marry only in the Lord.[6] And therefore such as profess the true reformed religion should not marry with infidels, papists, or other idolaters:[c] neither should such as are godly be unequally yoked, by marrying with such as are notoriously wicked in their life, or maintain damnable heresies.[d] [7]

4. Marriage ought not to be within the degrees of consanguinity or affinity forbidden by the Word.[e] [8] Nor can such incestuous marriages ever be made lawful by any law of man or consent of parties, so as those persons may live together as man and wife.[f] [9]

5. Adultery or fornication committed after a contract, being detected before marriage, giveth just occasion to the innocent party to dissolve that contract.[10] In the case of adultery after marriage, it is lawful for the innocent party to sue out a divorce:[11] and, after the divorce, to marry another, as if the offending party were dead.[g] [12]

6. Although the corruption of man be such as is apt to study arguments unduly to put asunder those whom God hath joined together in marriage: yet, nothing but adultery, or such wilful desertion as can no way be remedied by the Church, or civil magistrate, is cause sufficient of dissolving the bond of marriage:[13] wherein, a public and orderly course of proceeding is to be observed; and the persons concerned in it not left to their own wills, and discretion, in their own case.[h] [14]

7. [Section 24.7 is found only in the EPC version] Divorced persons should give prayerful thought to discover if God's vocation for them is to remain unmarried, since one failure in this realm raises serious questions as to the rightness and wisdom of undertaking another union.

a The EPC version of section 24.1 reads: "Marriage is a union between one man and one woman, designed of God to last so long as they both shall live."
1 Ge 2:24; Mt 19:5–6; Pr 2:17
2 Ge 2:18
3 Mal 2:15
b The EPC version of section 24.2 reads: "Marriage is designed for the mutual help of husband and wife; for the safeguarding, undergirding, and development of their moral and spiritual character; for the propagation of children and the rearing of them in the discipline and instruction of the Lord."
4 1Co 7:2,9
5 Heb 13:4; 1Ti 4:3; 1Co 7:36–38; Ge 24:57
6 1Co 7:39
c ARP: "infidels or other idolaters"
d The EPC version of section 24.3 reads: "All persons who are able with judgment to give their consent may marry, except within the limits of blood relationship forbidden by Scripture, and such marriages are valid before God in the eyes of the church. But no marriage can be fully and securely Christian in spirit or in purpose unless both partners are committed to a common Christian faith and to a deeply shared intention of building a Christian home. Evangelical Christians should seek as partners in marriage only persons who hold in common a sound basis of evangelical faith."
7 Ge 34:14; Ex 34:16; Dt 7:3–4; 1Ki 11:4; Ne 13:25–27; Mal 2:11–12; 2Co 6:14
e 1647: "forbidden in the Word"; ARP: "forbidden in the word"
8 Lev 18; 1Co 5:1; Am 2:7
f The 1647 version concludes section 24.4 by adding: "The man may not marry any of his wife's kindred nearer in blood than he may of his own; nor the woman of her husband's kindred nearer in blood than of her own." The EPC version of section 24.4 reads: "Marriage for the Christian has religious as well as civil significance. The distinctive contribution of the church in performing the marriage ceremony is to affirm the divine institution of marriage; to invoke God's blessing upon those who enter into the marital relationship in accordance with his word; to hear the vows of those who desire to be married; and to assure the married partners of God's grace within their new relationship."
9 Mk 6:18; Lev 18:24–28
10 Mt 1:18–20
11 Mt 5:31–32

g The EPC version of section 24.5 reads: "It is the divine intention that persons entering the marriage covenant become inseparably united, thus allowing for no dissolution save that caused by the death of either husband or wife. However, the weaknesses of one or both partners may lead to gross and persistent denial of the marriage vows; yet only in cases of extreme, unrepented-of, and irremediable unfaithfulness (physical or spiritual) should separation or divorce be considered. Such separation or divorce is accepted as permissible only because of the failure of one or both of the partners, and does not lessen in any way the divine intention for indissoluble union."

12 Mt 19:9; Ro 7:2–3

13 Mt 19:8–9; 1Co 7:15; Mt 19:6

h The EPC version of section 24.6 reads: "The remarriage of divorced persons may be sanctioned by the church in keeping with the redemptive gospel of Christ, when sufficient penitence for sin and failure is evident, and a firm purpose of and endeavor after Christian marriage is manifested."

14 Dt 24:1–4

CHAPTER XXV
Of the Church

1. The catholic or universal Church, which is invisible, consists of the whole number of the elect, that have been, are, or shall be gathered into one, under Christ the Head thereof; and is the spouse, the body, the fulness of Him that filleth all in all.[1]

2. The visible Church, which is also catholic or universal under the Gospel (not confined to one nation, as before under the law), consists of all those throughout the world that profess the true religion;[2] and of their children:[a] [3] and is the kingdom of the Lord Jesus Christ,[4] the house and family of God,[5] out of which there is no ordinary possibility of salvation.[6]

3. Unto this catholic visible Church Christ hath given the ministry, oracles, and ordinances of God, for the gathering and perfecting of the saints, in this life, to the end of the world: and doth, by His own presence and Spirit, according to His promise, make them effectual thereunto.[7]

4. This catholic Church hath been sometimes more, sometimes less visible.[8] And particular Churches, which are members thereof, are more or less pure, according as the doctrine of the Gospel is taught and embraced, ordinances administered, and public worship performed more or less purely in them.[9]

5. The purest Churches under heaven are subject both to mixture and error;[10] and some have so degenerated as to become no Churches of Christ, but synagogues of Satan.[11] Nevertheless, there shall be always a Church on earth, to worship God according to His will.[12]

6. There is no other head of the Church but the Lord Jesus Christ.[13] Nor can the Pope of Rome, in any sense,[b] be head thereof.[c] [d] [14]

1 Eph 1:10,22–23; 5:23,27,32; Col 1:18

2 1Co 1:2; 12:12–13; Ps 2:8; Rev 7:9; Ro 15:9–12

a ARP: "together with their children"

3 1Co 7:14; Eze 16:20–21; Ro 11:16; Ge 3:15; 17:7

4 Mt 13:47; Isa 9:7

5 Eph 2:19; 3:15

6 Ac 2:47

7 1Co 12:28; Eph 4:11–13; Mt 28:19–20; Isa 59:21

8 Ro 11:3–4; Rev 12:6,14

9 Rev 2–3; 1Co 5:6–7

10 1Co 13:12; Rev 2–3; Mt 13:24–30,47

11 Rev 18:2; Ro 11:18–22

12 Mt 16:18; 28:19–20; Ps 72:17; 102:28

13 Col 1:18; Eph 1:22

b ARP: "nor can mere man in any sense"

c ARP: "be the head thereof"

d The 1647 version concludes section 25.6 with: "thereof; but is that Antichrist, that man of sin, and son of perdition, that exalteth himself, in the Church, against Christ and all that is called God."

14 Mt 23:8–10; 2Th 2:3–4,8–9; Rev 13:6

CHAPTER XXVI
Of the Communion of the Saints

1. All saints, that are united to Jesus Christ their Head, by His Spirit, and by faith, have fellowship with Him in His graces, sufferings, death, resurrection, and glory:[1] and, being united to one another in love, they have communion in each other's gifts and graces,[2] and are obliged to the performance of such duties, public and private, as do conduce to their mutual good, both in the inward and outward man.[3]

2. Saints by profession are bound to maintain an holy fellowship and communion in the worship of God, and in performing such other spiritual services as tend to their mutual edification;[4] as also in relieving each other in outward things, according to their several abilities and necessities. Which communion, as God offereth opportunity, is to be extended unto all those who, in every place, call upon the name of the Lord Jesus.[5]

3. This communion which the saints have with Christ, doth not make them in any wise partakers of the substance of His Godhead; or to be equal with Christ in any respect: either of which to affirm is impious and blasphemous.[6] Nor doth their communion one with another, as saints, take away, or infringe the title or propriety which each man hath in his goods and possessions.[7]

1 1Jn 1:3; Eph 2:5–6; 3:16–19; Jn 1:16; Php 3:10; Ro 6:5–6; 2Ti 2:12

2 Eph 4:15–16; 1Co 3:21–23; 12:7; Col 2:19

3 1Th 5:11,14; Ro 1:11–12,14; 1Jn 3:16–18; Gal 6:10

4 Heb 10:24–25; Ac 2:42,46; Isa 2:3; 1Co 11:20

5 Ac 2:44–45; 11:29–30; 1Jn 3:17; 2Co 8–9

6 Col 1:18–19; 1Co 8:6; 1Ti 6:15–16; Ps 45:7; Heb 1:8–9

7 Ex 20:15; Eph 4:28; Ac 5:4

CHAPTER XXVII
Of the Sacraments

1. Sacraments are holy signs and seals of the covenant of grace,[1] immediately instituted by God,[2] to represent Christ, and His benefits; and to confirm our interest in Him:[3] as also, to put a visible difference between those that belong unto the Church, and the rest of the world;[4] and solemnly to engage them to the service of God in Christ, according to His Word.[5]

2. There is, in every sacrament, a spiritual relation, or sacramental union, between the sign and the thing signified: whence it comes to pass, that the names and effects of the one are attributed to the other.[6]

3. The grace which is exhibited in or by the sacraments rightly used, is not conferred by any power in them; neither doth the efficacy of a sacrament depend upon the piety or intention of him that doth administer it:[7] but upon the work of the Spirit,[8] and the word of institution, which contains, together with a precept authorizing the use thereof, a promise of benefit to worthy receivers.[9]

4. There be only two sacraments ordained by Christ our Lord in the Gospel; that is to say, Baptism, and the Supper of the Lord: neither of which may be dispensed by any, but by a minister of the Word lawfully ordained.[a] [10]

5. The sacraments of the old testament, in regard of the spiritual things thereby signified and exhibited, were, for substance, the same with those of the new.[11]

1 Ro 4:11; Ge 17:7,10

2 Mt 28:19; 1Co 11:23

3 1Co 10:16; 11:25–26; Gal 3:17

4 Ro 15:8; Ex 12:48; Ge 34:14

5 Ro 6:3–4; 1Co 10:16,21

6 Ge 17:10; Mt 26:27–28; Tit 3:5

7 Ro 2:28–29; 1Pe 3:21

8 Mt 3:11; 1Co 12:13

9 Mt 26:27–28; 28:19–20

a The EPC version of section 27.4 reads: "There are only two sacraments ordained by Christ our Lord in the gospel: baptism and the Lord's supper. Ordinarily, neither of these may be administered by anyone but a lawfully ordained minister of the word."

10 Mt 28:19; 1Co 4:1; 11:20,23; Heb 5:4

11 1Co 10:1–4

CHAPTER XXVIII
Of Baptism

1. Baptism is a sacrament of the new testament, ordained by Jesus Christ,[1] not only for the solemn admission of the party baptized into the visible Church;[2] but also, to be unto him a sign and seal of the covenant of grace,[3] of his ingrafting into Christ,[4] of regeneration,[5] of remission of sins,[6] and of his giving up unto God, through Jesus Christ, to walk in newness of life.[7] Which sacrament is, by Christ's own appointment, to be continued in His Church[a] until the end of the world.[8]

2. The outward element to be used in this sacrament is water, wherewith the party is to be baptized, in the name of the Father, and of the Son, and of the Holy Ghost, by a minister of the Gospel, lawfully called thereunto.[9]

3. Dipping of the person into the water is not necessary; but Baptism is rightly administered by pouring, or sprinkling water upon the person.[10]

4. Not only those that do actually profess faith in the obedience unto Christ,[11] but also the infants of one, or both, believing parents, are to be baptized.[12]

5. Although it be a great sin to contemn or neglect this ordinance,[13] yet grace and salvation are not so inseparably annexed unto it, as that no person can be regenerated, or saved, without it;[14] or, that all that are baptized are undoubtedly regenerated.[15]

6. The efficacy of Baptism is not tied to that moment of time wherein it is administered;[16] yet, not withstanding, by the right use of this ordinance, the grace promised is not only offered, but really exhibited, and conferred, by the Holy Ghost, to such (whether of age or infants) as that grace belongeth unto, according to the counsel of God's own will, in His appointed time.[17]

7. The sacrament of Baptism is but once to be administered unto any person.[18]

1 Mt 28:19
2 1Co 12:13
3 Ro 4:11; Col 2:11–12
4 Gal 3:27; Ro 6:5
5 Tit 3:5
6 Mk 1:4
7 Ro 6:3–4
a ARP: "this church"
8 Mt 28:19–20
9 Mt 3:11; 28:19–20; Jn 1:33
10 Heb 9:10,19–22; Ac 2:41; 16:33; Mk 7:4
11 Mk 16:15–16; Ac 8:37–38
12 Ge 17:7–10; Gal 3:9,14; Col 2:11–12; Ac 2:38–39; Ro 4:11–12; 1Co 7:14; Mt 28:19; Mk 10:13–16; Lk 18:15
13 Lk 7:30; Ex 4:24–26
14 Ro 4:11; Ac 10:2,4,22,31,45,47
15 Ac 8:13,23
16 Jn 3:5,8
17 Gal 3:27; Tit 3:5; Eph 5:25–26; Ac 2:38,41
18 Tit 3:5

CHAPTER XXIX
Of the Lord's Supper

1. Our Lord Jesus, in the night wherein He was betrayed, instituted the sacrament of His body and blood, called the Lord's Supper, to be observed in His Church,[a] unto the end of the world, for the perpetual remembrance of the sacrifice of Himself in His death; the sealing all benefits thereof unto true believers, their spiritual nourishment and growth in Him, their further engagement in and to all duties which they owe unto Him; and, to be a bond and pledge of their communion with Him, and with each other, as members of His mystical body.[1]

2. In this sacrament, Christ is not offered up to His Father; nor any real sacrifice made at all, for remission of sins of the quick or dead;[2] but only a commemoration of that one offering up of Himself, by Himself, upon the cross, once for all: and a spiritual oblation of all possible praise unto God, for the same;[3] so that the popish sacrifice of the mass (as they call it) is most abominably injurious to Christ's one, only sacrifice, the alone propitiation for all the sins of His elect.[b] [4]

3. The Lord Jesus hath, in this ordinance, appointed His ministers to declare His word of institution to the people; to pray, and bless the elements of bread and wine, and thereby to set them apart from a common to an holy use; and to take and break the bread, to take the cup, and (they communicating also themselves) to give both to the communicants;[5] but to none who are not then present in the congregation.[6]

4. Private masses, or receiving this sacrament by a priest, or any other, alone;[7] as likewise, the denial of the cup to the people,[8] worshipping the elements, the lifting them up, or carrying them about, for adoration, and the reserving them for any pretended religious use; are all contrary to the nature of this sacrament, and to the institution of Christ.[9]

5. The outward elements in this sacrament, duly set apart to the uses ordained by Christ, have such relation to Him crucified, as that, truly, yet sacramentally only, they are sometimes called by the name of the things they represent, to wit, the body and blood of Christ;[10] albeit, in substance and nature, they still remain truly and only bread and wine, as they were before.[11]

6. That doctrine which maintains a change of the substance of bread and wine, into the substance of Christ's body and blood (commonly called transubstantiation) by consecration of a priest, or by any other way, is repugnant, not to Scripture alone, but even to common sense, and reason; overthroweth the nature of the sacrament, and hath been, and is, the cause of manifold superstitions; yea, of gross idolatries.[12]

7. Worthy receivers, outwardly partaking of the visible elements, in this sacrament,[13] do then also, inwardly by faith, really and indeed, yet not carnally and corporally but spiritually, receive, and feed upon, Christ crucified, and all benefits of His death: the body and blood of Christ being then, not corporally or carnally, in, with, or under the bread and wine; yet, as really, but spiritually, present to the faith of believers in that ordinance, as the elements themselves are to their outward senses.[14]

8. Although ignorant and wicked men receive the outward elements in this sacrament; yet, they receive not the thing signified thereby; but, by their unworthy coming thereunto, are guilty of the body and blood of the Lord, to their own damnation. Wherefore, all ignorant and ungodly persons, as they are unfit to enjoy communion with Him, so are they unworthy of the Lord's table; and cannot, without great sin against Christ, while they remain such, partake of these holy mysteries,[15] or be admitted thereunto.[16]

a ARP: "this church"
1 1Co 10:16–17,21; 11:23–26; 12:13
2 Heb 9:22,25–26,28
3 1Co 11:24–26; Mt 26:26–27
b ARP: "of the elect"
4 Heb 7:23–24,27; 10:11–12,14,18
5 Mt 26:26–28; Mk 14:22–24; Lk 22:19–20; 1Co 11:23–26
6 Ac 20:7; 1Co 11:20
7 1Co 10:16
8 Mk 14:23; 1Co 11:25–29
9 Mt 15:9
10 Mt 26:26–28
11 1Co 11:26–28; Mt 26:29
12 Ac 3:21; 1Co 11:24–26; Lk 24:6,39
13 1Co 11:28
14 1Co 10:16
15 1Co 11:27–29; 2Co 6:14,16
16 1Co 5:6–7,13; 2Th 3:6,14–15; Mt 7:6

CHAPTER XXX
Of Church Censures

1. The Lord Jesus, as King and Head of His Church, hath therein appointed a government, in the hand of Church officers, distinct from the civil magistrate.[1]

2. To these officers the keys of the kingdom of heaven are committed; by virtue whereof, they have power, respectively, to retain, and remit sins; to shut that kingdom

against the impenitent, both by the Word, and censures; and to open it unto penitent sinners, by the ministry of the Gospel; and by absolution from censures, as occasion shall require.[2]

3. Church censures are necessary, for the reclaiming and gaining of offending brethren, for deterring of others from the like offences, for purging out of that leaven which might infect the whole lump, for vindicating the honour of Christ, and the holy profession of the Gospel, and for preventing the wrath of God, which might justly fall upon the Church, if they should suffer His covenant, and the seals thereof, to be profaned by notorious and obstinate offenders.[3]

4. For the better attaining of these ends, the officers of the Church are to proceed by admonition; suspension from the sacrament of the Lord's Supper for a season; and by excommunication from the Church; according to the nature of the crime, and demerit of the person.[4]

[1] Isa 9:6–7; 1Ti 5:17; 1Th 5:12; Ac 20:17,28; Heb 13:7,17,24; 1Co 12:28; Mt 28:18–20
[2] Mt 16:19; 18:17–18; Jn 20:21–23; 2Co 2:6–8
[3] 1Co 5; 11:27–34; 1Ti 5:20; Mt 7:6; 1Ti 1:20; Jude 23
[4] 1Th 5:12; 2Th 3:6,14–15; 1Co 5:4–5,13; Mt 18:17; Tit 3:10

CHAPTER XXXI
Of Synods and Councils

1. For the better government, and further edification of the Church, there ought to be such assemblies as are commonly called synods or councils:[a] [1] and it belongeth to the overseers and other rulers of the particular churches, by virtue of their office, and the power which Christ hath given them for edification and not for destruction, to appoint such assemblies;[2] and to convene together in them, as often as they shall judge it expedient for the good of the Church.[3]

2. It belongeth to synods and councils, ministerially to determine controversies of faith, and cases of conscience; to set down rules and directions for the better ordering of the public worship of God, and government of His Church; to receive complaints in cases of maladministration, and authoritatively to determine the same: which decrees and determinations, if consonant to the Word of God, are to be received with reverence and submission; not only for their agreement with the Word, but also for the power whereby they are made, as being an ordinance of God appointed thereunto in His Word.[b] [4]

3. All synods or councils, since the Apostles' times, whether general or particular, may err; and many have erred. Therefore they are not to be made the rule of faith, or practice; but to be used as a help in both.[c] [5]

4. Synods and councils are to handle, or conclude nothing, but that which is ecclesiastical: and are not to intermeddle with civil affairs which concern the commonwealth, unless by way of humble petition in cases extraordinary; or, by way of advice, for satisfaction of conscience, if they be thereunto required by the civil magistrate.[d] [6]

[a] 1647, ARP: Both end section 31.1 at this point and begin a new section entitled 31.2. Section 31.2 in the 1647 version reads: "As magistrates may lawfully call a synod of ministers, and other fit persons, to consult and advise with, about matters of religion; so, if magistrates be open enemies to the Church, the ministers of Christ of themselves, by virtue of their office, or they, with other fit persons, upon delegation from their Churches, may meet together in such assemblies." Section 31.2 in the ARP version reads: "The ministers of Christ, of themselves, and by virtue of their office; or they with other fit persons, upon delegation from their churches, have the exclusive right to appoint, adjourn, or dissolve such synods or councils; though, in extraordinary cases, it may be proper for magistrates to desire the calling of a synod of ministers and other fit persons, to consult and advise with about matters of religion; and in such cases, it is the duty of churches to comply with their desire."
[1] Ac 15:2,4,6
[2] Ac 15
[3] Ac 15:22–23,25
[b] 1647, ARP: This section is numbered 31.3
[4] Ac 15:15,19,24,27–31; 16:4; Mt 18:17–20.
[c] 1647, ARP: This section is numbered 31.4
[5] Eph 2:20; Ac 17:11; 1Co 2:5; 2Co 1:24
[d] 1647, ARP: This section is numbered 31.5
[6] Lk 12:13–14; Jn 18:36

CHAPTER XXXII
Of the State of Men after Death, and of the Resurrection of the Dead

1. The bodies of men, after death, return to dust, and see corruption:[1] but their souls, which neither die nor sleep, having an immortal subsistence, immediately return to God who gave them:[2] the souls of the righteous, being then made perfect in holiness, are received into the highest heavens, where they behold the face of God, in light and glory, waiting for the full redemption of their bodies.[3] And the souls of the wicked are cast into hell, where they remain in torments and utter darkness, reserved to the judgment of the great day.[4] Beside these two places, for souls separated from their bodies, the Scripture acknowledgeth none.

2. At the last day, such as are found alive shall not die, but be changed:[5] and all the dead shall be raised up, with the selfsame bodies, and none other (although with different qualities), which shall be united again to their souls for ever.[6]

3. The bodies of the unjust shall, by the power of Christ, be raised to dishonour: the bodies of the just, by His Spirit, unto honour; and be made conformable to His own glorious body.[7]

[1] Ge 3:19; Ac 13:36
[2] Lk 23:43; Ecc 12:7
[3] Heb 12:23; 2Co 5:1,6,8; Php 1:23; Ac 3:21; Eph 4:10
[4] Lk 16:23–24; Ac 1:25; Jude 6–7; 1Pe 3:19
[5] 1Th 4:17; 1Co 15:51–52
[6] Job 19:26–27; 1Co 15:42–44
[7] Ac 24:15; Jn 5:28–29; 1Co 15:43; Php 3:21

CHAPTER XXXIII
Of the Last Judgment

1. God hath appointed a day, wherein He will judge the world, in righteousness, by Jesus Christ,[1] to whom all power and judgment is given of the Father.[2] In which day, not only the apostate angels shall be judged,[3] but likewise all persons that have lived upon earth shall appear before the tribunal of Christ, to give an account of their thoughts, words, and deeds; and to receive according to what they have done in the body, whether good or evil.[4]

2. The end of God's appointing this day is for the manifestation of the glory of His mercy, in the eternal salvation of the elect; and of His justice, in the damnation of the reprobate, who are wicked and disobedient. For then shall the righteous go into everlasting life, and receive that fulness of joy and refreshing, which shall come from the presence of the Lord; but the wicked who know not God, and obey not the Gospel of Jesus Christ, shall be cast into eternal torments, and be punished with everlasting destruction from the presence of the Lord, and from the glory of His power.[5]

3. As Christ would have us to be certainly persuaded that there shall be a day of judgment, both to deter all men from sin; and for the greater consolation of the godly in their adversity:[6] so will He have that day unknown to men, that they may shake off all carnal security, and be prepared to say, Come Lord Jesus, come quickly. Amen.[7]

[1] Ac 17:31
[2] Jn 5:22,27
[3] 1Co 6:3; Jude 6; 2Pe 2:4
[4] 2Co 5:10; Ecc 12:14; Ro 2:16; 14:10,12; Mt 12:36–37
[5] Mt 25:21,31–46; Ro 2:5–6; 9:22–23; Ac 3:19; 2Th 1:7–10
[6] 2Pe 3:11,14; 2Co 5:10–11; 2Th 1:5–7; Lk 21:27–28; Ro 8:23–25
[7] Mt 24:36,42–44; Mk 13:35–37; Lk 12:35–36; Rev 22:20

[This section is found in the ARP and EPC versions only]

CHAPTER XXXIV
Of the Holy Spirit[a]

1. The Holy Spirit, the third person in the Trinity, proceeding from the Father and the Son, of the same substance and

equal in power and glory, is, together with the Father and the Son, to be believed in, loved, obeyed, and worshipped throughout all ages.[1]

2. He is the Lord and Giver of life, everywhere present, and is the source of all good thoughts, pure desires, and holy counsels in men. By him the prophets were moved to speak the word of God, and all the writers of the Holy Scriptures inspired to record infallibly the mind and will of God. The dispensation of the gospel is especially committed to him. He prepares the way for it, accompanies it with his persuasive power, and urges its message upon the reason and conscience of men, so that they who reject its merciful offer are not only without excuse, but are also guilty of resisting the Holy Spirit.[2]

3. The Holy Spirit, whom the Father is ever willing to give to all who ask him, is the only efficient agent in the application of redemption. He regenerates men by his grace, convicts them of sin, moves them to repentance, and persuades and enables them to embrace Jesus Christ by faith. He unites all believers to Christ, dwells in them as their Comforter and Sanctifier, gives them the spirit of Adoption and Prayer, and performs all those gracious offices by which they are sanctified and sealed unto the day of redemption.[3]

4. By the indwelling of the Holy Spirit all believers are vitally united to Christ, who is the Head, are thus united one to another in the church, which is his body. He calls and anoints ministers for their holy office, qualifies all other officers in the church for their special work, and imparts various gifts and graces to its members. He gives efficacy to the word and to the ordinances of the gospel. By him the church will be preserved, increased, purified, and at last made perfectly holy in the presence of God.[4]

[a] The title of chapter 34 in the EPC version is "The Holy Spirit"

[1] 2Co 13:14; Jn 4:24; 14:26; 15:26; 16:7; 20:22; Mt 3:16–17; 28:19; Lk 1:35; Eph 2:18–20,22; 4:30; Heb 10:29; 1Co 10:10–11; Rev 22:17; Gal 4:4–6; Ac 2:33; 5:3–4; 16:6–7; Mk 3:29; Ro 8:14,26–27; 1Jn 2:20–27; 1Th 5:19

[2] Eph 4:30; 5:9; Ge 1:2; Jn 3:5,7; 16:8–11,13–15; Ac 1:8; 2:1–21; 7:51; 28:25; Gal 5:22–25; 2Pe 1:21; 2Ti 3:16; 1Co 2:9–10,13; 1Pe 1:11; 1Th 5:19; Ps 104:30; 139:7; Ro 5:5; 8:9,14–16; Tit 3:5–6; Mt 12:31–32

[3] Jn 3:1–8; Ac 2:38; Lk 11:13; 1Co 2:13–14; 3:16; 6:19; 12:3; Jn 7:37–39; 16:7–11,13; Rev 22:17; Tit 3:5–7; 2Th 2:13; Gal 4:6; 6:8; 1Jn 4:2; Ro 8:14–17,26–27; 15:16; Eph 1:13; 2:18; 4:3,30; 5:9; 1Th 1:5; Jude 20–21; Heb 10:14–15

[4] Eph 2:14–18; 4:1–6,30; 5:18; Ac 1:8; 2:4; 6:3,5–6; 13:2–3; 20:28; 1Co 2:10; 12:4–13; 2Pe 1:19–21; 1Th 1:5–6; Jn 16:13–14; 20:22–23; Mt 28:19–20; Gal 5:16,22–23; 2Ti 3:16; Rev 2:7; 22:17

[This section is found in the ARP and EPC versions only]

CHAPTER XXXV
Of the Gospel[a]

1. God in infinite and perfect love, having provided in the covenant of grace, through the mediation and sacrifice of the Lord Jesus Christ, as way of life and salvation, sufficient for and adapted to the whole lost race of man, doth freely offer this salvation to all men in the gospel.[1]

2. In the gospel God declares his love for the world and his desire that all men should be saved; reveals fully and clearly the only way of salvation; promises eternal life to all who truly repent and believe in Christ; invites and commands all to embrace the offered mercy; and by his Spirit accompanying the word pleads with men to accept his gracious invitation.[2]

3. It is the duty and privilege of everyone who hears the gospel immediately to accept its merciful provisions; and they who continue in impenitence and unbelief incur aggravated guilt and perish by their own fault.[3]

4. Since there is no other way of salvation than that revealed in the gospel, and since in the divinely established and ordinary method of grace faith cometh by hearing the word of God, Christ hath commissioned his church to go into all the world and to make disciples of all nations. All believers are, therefore, under obligation to sustain the ordinances of the Christian religion where they are already established, and to contribute by their prayers, gifts, and personal efforts to the extension of the kingdom of Christ throughout the whole earth.[4]

[a] The title of chapter 35 in the EPC version is "The Gospel of the Love of God and Missions"

[1] Rev 11:15; 22:17; Jn 3:16; 4:42; 10:10–11; 11:25; 14:6,19; 1Jn 2:1–2; 4:9,16; Ac 2:38–39; 4:12; Mt 11:28–30; 24:14; 2Co 5:14–19; 9:15; Tit 2:11; 3:4–5; Heb 2:9; 5:9; 8:10; 9:26; 12:22–24; 13:20–21; Lk 24:46–47; Jer 31:3; Eph 2:8; 1Ti 2:5-6; 1Co 15:3; Ro 1:16; 5:6,8; 6:23; Php 1:21; 2Pe 3:9

[2] Mt 11:28–30; 28:19–20; Ac 2:38; 4:12, 13:38–39,48; 16:30–31; 17:30; Jn 3:16–17; 6:37–40; 14:6; 16:13–14; 17:3; Gal 2:16–20; Ro 1:16–17; 4:5; 5:8; 10:9; 2Pe 3:9; Mk 1:14–15; Rev 22:17; Eze 33:11; Isa 1:18; 45:22; Lk 13:34; 1Jn 4:9–10; Heb 3:7–8; 4:16; 10:19–22; 1Pe 1:8–9; 2Co 6:2; 2Th 3:5; Php 2:12–13

[3] Heb 2:3; 4:16; 10:29; 12:25; Ac 13:46; Mt 10:32–33; 25:46; Lk 12:47–48; 1Th 5:9–10; Jn 1:12; Rev 22:17; 1Ti 6:12; Jn 3:18; Ro 6:23

[4] Ac 1:8; 4:12; 13:2–4; 16:31; 20:28; Mt 6:10,13; 9:36–38; 10:8; 13:38; 24:14; 28:19–20; Ro 10:13–17; 12:11; Heb 10:19–25; 13:16; Gal 3:28; 6:6; 1Co 3:9; 11:24; 16:1–2; Col 1:28–29; 3:16,23–24; Rev 11:15; 22:17; 2Ti 2:15; 3:15; Jn 5:39; 17:18; 21:15–16; 1Pe 5:2; 2Co 1:11; 9:7; Eph 6:18–19

Finis

THE LARGER CATECHISM

WITH THE SCRIPTURE PROOFS

1. What is the chief and highest end of man?
Man's chief and highest end is to glorify God,[1] and fully to enjoy him forever.[2]

1 Ro 11:36; 1Co 10:31
2 Ps 73:24–28; Jn 17:21–23

2. How doth it appear that there is a God?
The very light of nature in man, and the works of God, declare plainly that there is a God;[1] but his word and Spirit only do sufficiently and effectually reveal him unto men for their salvation.[2]

1 Ro 1:19–20; Ps 19:1–3; Ac 17:28
2 1Co 2:9–10; 2Ti 3:15–17; Isa 59:21

3. What is the word of God?
The holy scriptures of the Old and New Testament are the word of God,[1] the only rule of faith and obedience.[2]

1 2Ti 3:16; 2Pe 1:19–21
2 Eph 2:20; Rev 22:18–19; Isa 8:20; Lk 16:29,31; Gal 1:8–9; 2Ti 3:15–16

4. How doth it appear that the scriptures are of the word of God?
The scriptures manifest themselves to be the word of God, by their majesty[1] and purity;[2] by the consent of all the parts,[3] and the scope of the whole, which is to give all glory to God;[4] by their light and power to convince and convert sinners, to comfort and build up believers unto salvation:[5] but the Spirit of God bearing witness by and with the scriptures in the heart of man, is alone able fully to persuade it that they are the very word of God.[6]

1 Hos 8:12; 1Co 2:6–7,13; Ps 119:18,129
2 Ps 12:6; 119:140
3 Ac 10:43; 26:22
4 Ro 3:19,27
5 Ac 18:28; 20:32; Heb 4:12; Jas 1:18; Ps 19:7–9; Ro 15:4
6 Jn 16:13–14; 20:31; 1Jn 2:20,27

5. What do the scriptures principally teach?
The scriptures principally teach, what man is to believe concerning God, and what duty God requires of man.[1]

1 2Ti 1:13

WHAT MAN OUGHT TO BELIEVE CONCERNING GOD

6. What do the scriptures make known of God?
The scriptures make known what God is,[1] the persons in the Godhead,[2] his decrees,[3] and the execution of his decrees.[4]

1 Heb 11:6
2 1Jn 5:17
3 Ac 15:14–15,18
4 Ac 4:27–28

7. What is God?
God is a Spirit,[1] in and of himself infinite in being,[2] glory,[3] blessedness,[4] and perfection;[5] all-sufficient,[6] eternal,[7] unchangeable,[8] incomprehensible,[9] every where present,[10] almighty,[11] knowing all things,[12] most wise,[13] most holy,[14] most just,[15] most merciful and gracious, long-suffering, and abundant in goodness and truth.[16]

1 Jn 4:24
2 Ex 3:14; Job 11:7–9
3 Ac 7:2
4 1Ti 6:15
5 Mt 5:48
6 Ge 17:1
7 Ps 90:2
8 Mal 3:6; Jas 1:17
9 1Ki 8:27
10 Ps 139:1–13
11 Rev 4:8
12 Heb 4:13
13 Ro 16:27
14 Isa 6:3
15 Dt 32:4
16 Ex 34:6

8. Are there more Gods than one?
There is but one only, the living and true God.[1]

1 Dt 6:4; 1Co 8:4,6; Jer 10:10

9. How many persons are there in the Godhead?
There be three persons in the Godhead, the Father, the Son, and the Holy Ghost; and these three are one true, eternal God, the same in substance, equal in power and glory; although distinguished by their personal properties.[1]

1 1Jn 5:7; Mt 3:16–17; 28:19; 2Co 13:14; Jn 10:30

10. What are the personal properties of the three persons in the Godhead?
It is proper to the Father to beget the Son,[1] and to the Son to be begotten of the Father,[2] and to the Holy Ghost to proceed from the Father and the Son from all eternity.[3]

1 Heb 1:5–6,8
2 Jn 1:14,18
3 Jn 15:26; Gal 4:6

11. How doth it appear that the Son and the Holy Ghost are God equal with the Father?
The scriptures manifest that the Son and the Holy Ghost are God equal with the Father, ascribing unto them such names,[1] attributes,[2] works,[3] and worship,[4] as are proper to God only.

1 Isa 6:3,5,8; Jn 12:41; Ac 5:3–4; 28:25; 1Jn 5:20
2 Jn 1:1; 2:24–25; Isa 9:6; 1Co 2:10–11
3 Col 1:16; Ge 1:2
4 Mt 28:19; 2Co 8:14

12. What are the decrees of God?
God's decrees are the wise, free, and holy acts of the counsel of his will,[1] whereby, from all eternity, he hath, for his own glory, unchangeably foreordained whatsoever comes to pass in time,[2] especially concerning angels and men.

1 Eph 1:11; Ro 9:14–15,18; 11:33
2 Eph 1:4,11; Ro 9:22–23; Ps 33:11

13. What hath God especially decreed concerning angels and men?
God, by an eternal and immutable decree, out of his mere love, for the praise of his glorious grace, to be manifested in due time, hath elected some angels to glory;[1] and in Christ hath chosen some men to eternal life, and the means thereof:[2] and also, according to his sovereign power, and the unsearchable counsel of his own will, (whereby he extendeth or withholdeth favor as he pleaseth,) hath passed by and foreordained the rest

to dishonor and wrath, to be for their sin inflicted, to the praise of the glory of his justice.[3]

1 1Ti 5:21;
2 Eph 1:4–6; 2Th 2:13–14
3 Ro 9:17–18,21–22; Mt 11:25–26; 2Ti 2:20; Jude 4; 1Pe 2:8

14. How doth God execute his decrees?
God executeth his decrees in the works of creation and providence, according to his infallible foreknowledge, and the free and immutable counsel of his own will.[1]

1 Eph 1:11

15. What is the work of creation?
The work of creation is that wherein God did in the beginning, by the word of his power, make of nothing the world, and all things therein, for himself, within the space of six days, and all very good.[1]

1 Ge 1:1–31; Heb 11:3; Pr 16:4

16. How did God create angels?
God created all the angels[1] spirits,[2] immortal,[3] holy,[4] excelling in knowledge,[5] mighty in power,[6] to execute his commandments, and to praise his name,[7] yet subject to change.[8]

1 Col 1:16
2 Ps 104:4
3 Mt 22:30
4 Mt 25:31
5 2Sa 14:17; Mt 24:36
6 2Th 1:7
7 Ps 103:20–21
8 2Pe 2:4

17. How did God create man?
After God had made all other creatures, he created man male and female;[1] formed the body of the man of the dust of the ground,[2] and the woman of the rib of the man,[3] endued them with living, reasonable, and immortal souls;[4] made them after his own image,[5] in knowledge,[6] righteousness, and holiness;[7] having the law of God written in their hearts,[8] and power to fulfill it,[9] and dominion over the creatures;[10] yet subject to fall.[11]

1 Ge 1:27
2 Ge 2:7
3 Ge 2:22
4 Ge 2:7; Job 35:11; Ecc 12:7; Mt 10:28; Lk 23:43
5 Ge 1:27
6 Col 3:10
7 Eph 4:24
8 Ro 2:14–15
9 Ecc 7:29
10 Ge 1:28
11 Ge 3:6; Ecc 7:29

18. What are God's works of providence?
God's works of providence are his most holy,[1] wise,[2] and powerful preserving[3] and governing[4] all his creatures; ordering them, and all their actions,[5] to his own glory.[6]

1 Ps 145:17
2 Ps 104:24; Isa 28:29
3 Heb 1:3
4 Ps 103:19
5 Mt 10:29–31; Ge 45:7
6 Ro 11:36; Isa 63:14

19. What is God's providence towards the angels?
God by his providence permitted some of the angels, willfully and irrecoverably, to fall into sin and damnation,[1] limiting and ordering that, and all their sins, to his own glory;[2] and established the rest in holiness and happiness;[3] employing them all,[4] at his pleasure, in the administrations of his power, mercy, and justice.[5]

1 Jude 6; 2Pe 2:4; Heb 2:16; Jn 8:44
2 Job 1:12; Mt 8:31
3 1Ti 5:21; Mk 8:38; Heb 12:22
4 Ps 104:4
5 2Ki 19:35; Heb 1:14

20. What was the providence of God toward man in the estate in which he was created?
The providence of God toward man in the estate in which he was created, was the placing him in paradise, appointing him to dress it, giving him liberty to eat of the fruit of the earth;[1] putting the creatures under his dominion,[2] and ordaining marriage for his help;[3] affording him communion with himself;[4] instituting the Sabbath;[5] entering into a covenant of life with him, upon condition of personal, perfect, and perpetual obedience,[6] of which the tree of life was a pledge;[7] and forbidding to eat of the tree of knowledge of good and evil, upon the pain of death.[8]

1 Ge 2:8,15–16
2 Ge 1:28
3 Ge 2:18
4 Ge 1:26–29; 3:8
5 Ge 2:3
6 Gal 3:12; Ro 10:5
7 Ge 2:9
8 Ge 2:17

21. Did man continue in that estate wherein God at first created him?
Our first parents being left to the freedom of their own will, through the temptation of Satan, transgressed the commandment of God in eating the forbidden fruit; and thereby fell from the estate of innocency wherein they were created.[1]

1 Ge 3:6–8,13; Ecc 7:29; 2Co 11:3

22. Did all mankind fall in that first transgression?
The covenant being made with Adam as a public person, not for himself only, but for his posterity, all mankind descending from him by ordinary generation,[1] sinned in him, and fell with him in that first transgression.[2]

1 Ac 17:26
2 Ge 2:16–17; Ro 5:12–20; 1Co 15:21–22

23. Into what estate did the fall bring mankind?
The fall brought mankind into an estate of sin and misery.[1]

1 Ro 3:23; 5:12

24. What is sin?
Sin is any want of conformity unto, or transgression of, any law of God, given as a rule to the reasonable creature.[1]

1 1Jn 3:4; Gal 3:10,12

25. Wherein consisteth the sinfulness of that estate whereinto man fell?
The sinfulness of that estate whereinto man fell, consisteth in the guilt of Adam's first sin,[1] the want of that righteousness wherein he was created, and the corruption of his nature, whereby he is utterly indisposed, disabled, and made opposite unto all that is spiritually good, and wholly inclined to all evil, and that continually;[2] which is commonly called Original Sin, and from which do proceed all actual transgressions.[3]

1 Ro 5:12,19
2 Ro 3:10–19; 5:6; 8:7–8; Eph 2:1–3; Ge 6:5
3 Jas 1:14–15; Mt 15:19

26. How is original sin conveyed from our first parents unto their posterity?
Original sin is conveyed from our first parents unto their posterity by natural generation, so as all that proceed from them in that way are conceived and born in sin.[1]

1 Ps 51:5; Job 14:4; 15:14; Jn 3:6

27. What misery did the fall bring upon mankind?
The fall brought upon mankind the loss of communion with God,[1] his displeasure and curse; so as we are by nature children of wrath,[2] bond slaves to Satan,[3] and justly liable to all punishments in this world, and that which is to come.[4]

1 Ge 3:8,10,24
2 Eph 2:2–3
3 2Ti 2:26
4 Ge 2:17; La 3:39; Ro 6:23; Mt 25:41,46; Jude 7

28. What are the punishments of sin in this world?
The punishments of sin in this world are either inward, as blindness of mind,[1] a reprobate sense,[2] strong delusions,[3] hard-

ness of heart,[4] horror of conscience,[5] and vile affections;[6] or outward, as the curse of God upon the creatures of our sakes,[7] and all other evils that befall us in our bodies, names, estates, relations, and employments;[8] together with death itself.[9]

1 Eph 4:18
2 Ro 1:28
3 2Th 2:11
4 Ro 2:5
5 Isa 33:14; Ge 4:13; Mt 27:4
6 Ro 1:26
7 Ge 3:17
8 Dt 28:15–18
9 Ro 6:21,23

29. What are the punishments of sin in the world to come?
The punishments of sin in the world to come, are everlasting separation from the comfortable presence of God, and most grievous torments in soul and body, without intermission, in hell-fire for ever.[1]

1 2Th 1:9; Mk 9:43–44,46,48; Lk 16:24

30. Doth God leave all mankind to perish in the estate of sin and misery?
God doth not leave all men to perish in the estate of sin and misery,[1] into which they fell by the breach of the first covenant, commonly called the Covenant of Works;[2] but of his mere love and mercy delivereth his elect out of it, and bringeth them into an estate of salvation by the second covenant, commonly called the Covenant of Grace.[3]

1 1Th 5:9
2 Gal 3:10,12
3 Tit 3:4–7; Gal 3:21; Ro 3:20,8–9

31. With whom was the covenant of grace made?
The covenant of grace was made with Christ as the second Adam, and in him with all the elect as his seed.[1]

1 Gal 3:16; Ro 5:15–21; Isa 53:10–11

32. How is the grace of God manifested in the second covenant?
The grace of God is manifested in the second covenant, in that he freely provideth and offereth to sinners a Mediator,[1] and life and salvation by him;[2] and requiring faith as the condition to interest them in him,[3] promiseth and giveth his Holy Spirit[4] to all his elect, to work in them that faith,[5] with all other saving graces;[6] and to enable them unto all holy obedience,[7] as the evidence of the truth of their faith[8] and thankfulness to God,[9] and as the way which he hath appointed them to salvation.[10]

1 Ge 3:15; Isa 42:6; Jn 6:27
2 1Jn 5:11–12
3 Jn 1:12; 3:16
4 Pr 1:23
5 2Co 4:13
6 Gal 5:22–23
7 Eze 36:27
8 Jas 2:18,22
9 2Co 5:14–15
10 Eph 2:18

33. Was the covenant of grace always administered after one and the same manner?
The covenant of grace was not always administered after the same manner, but the administrations of it under the Old Testament were different from those under the New.[1]

1 2Co 3:6–7,21–22

34. How was the covenant of grace administered under the Old Testament?
The covenant of grace was administered under the Old Testament, by promises,[1] prophecies,[2] sacrifices,[3] circumcision,[4] the passover,[5] and other types and ordinances, which did all foresignify Christ then to come, and were for that time sufficient to build up the elect in faith in the promised Messiah,[6] by whom they then had full remission of sin, and eternal salvation.[7]

1 Ro 15:8
2 Ac 3:20,24
3 Heb 10:1
4 Ro 4:11
5 1Co 5:7
6 Heb 8—11; 13
7 Gal 3:7–9,14

35. How is the covenant of grace administered under the New Testament?
Under the New Testament, when Christ the substance was exhibited, the same covenant of grace was and still is to be administered in the preaching of the word,[1] and the administration of the sacraments of baptism[2] and the Lord's supper;[3] in which grace and salvation are held forth in more fulness, evidence, and efficacy, to all nations.[4]

1 Mk 16:15
2 Mt 28:19–20
3 1Co 11:23–25
4 2Co 3:6–9; Heb 8:6,10–11; Mt 28:19

36. Who is the Mediator of the covenant of grace?
The only Mediator of the covenant of grace is the Lord Jesus Christ,[1] who, being the eternal Son of God, of one substance and equal with the Father,[2] in the fulness of time became man,[3] and so was and continues to be God and man, in two entire distinct natures, and one person, for ever.[4]

1 1Ti 2:5
2 Jn 1:1,14; 10:30; Php 2:6
3 Gal 4:4
4 Lk 1:35; Ro 9:5; Col 2:9; Heb 7:24–25

37. How did Christ, being the Son of God, become man?
Christ the Son of God became man, by taking to himself a true body, and a reasonable soul,[1] being conceived by the power of the Holy Ghost in the womb of the Virgin Mary, of her substance, and born of her,[2] yet without sin.[3]

1 Jn 1:14; Mt 26:38
2 Lk 1:27,31,35,42; Gal 4:4
3 Heb 4:15; 7:26

38. Why was it requisite that the Mediator should be God?
It was requisite that the Mediator should be God, that he might sustain and keep the human nature from sinking under the infinite wrath of God, and the power of death,[1] give worth and efficacy to his sufferings, obedience, and intercession;[2] and to satisfy God's justice,[3] procure his favour,[4] purchase a peculiar people,[5] give his Spirit to them,[6] conquer all their enemies,[7] and bring them to everlasting salvation.[8]

1 Ac 2:24–25; Ro 1:4; 4:25; Heb 9:14
2 Ac 20:28; Heb 7:25–28; 9:14
3 Ro 3:24–26
4 Eph 1:6; Mt 3:17
5 Tit 2:13–14
6 Gal 4:6
7 Lk 1:68 69,71,74
8 Heb 5:8–9; 9:11–15

39. Why was it requisite that the Mediator should be man?
It was requisite that the Mediator should be man, that he might advance our nature,[1] perform obedience to the law,[2] suffer and make intercession for us in our nature,[3] have a fellow-feeling of our infirmities;[4] that we might receive the adoption of sons,[5] and have comfort and access with boldness unto the throne of grace.[6]

1 Heb 2:16
2 Gal 4:4
3 Heb 2:14; 7:24–25
4 Heb 4:15
5 Gal 4:5
6 Heb 4:16

40. Why was it requisite that the Mediator should be God and man in one person?
It was requisite that the Mediator, who was to reconcile God and man, should himself be both God and man, and this in one person, that the proper works of each nature might be accepted of God for us,[1] and relied on by us as the works of the whole person.[2]

1 Mt 1:21,23; 3:17; Heb 9:14
2 1Pe 2:6

41. Why was our Mediator called Jesus?
Our Mediator was called Jesus, because he saveth his people from their sins.[1]

1 Mt 1:21

42. Why was our Mediator called Christ?
Our Mediator was called Christ, because he was anointed with the Holy Ghost above measure,[1] and so set apart, and fully furnished with all authority and ability,[2] to execute the offices of prophet,[3] priest,[4] and king of his church,[5] in the estate both of his humiliation and exaltation.

1 Jn 3:34; Ps 45:7
2 Jn 6:27; Mt 28:18–20
3 Ac 3:21–22; Lk 4:18,21
4 Heb 4:14–15; 5:5–7
5 Ps 2:6; Mt 21:5; Isa 9:6–7; Php 2:8–11

43. How doth Christ execute the office of a prophet?
Christ executeth the office of a prophet, in his revealing to the church,[1] in all ages, by his Spirit and word,[2] in divers ways of administration,[3] the whole will of God,[4] in all things concerning their edification and salvation.[5]

1 Jn 1:18
2 1Pe 1:10–12
3 Heb 1:1–2
4 Jn 15:15
5 Ac 20:23; Eph 4:11–13; Jn 20:31

44. How doth Christ execute the office of a priest?
Christ executeth the office of a priest, in his once offering himself a sacrifice without spot to God,[1] to be reconciliation for the sins of his people;[2] and in making continual intercession for them.[3]

1 Heb 9:14,28
2 Heb 2:17
3 Heb 7:25

45. How doth Christ execute the office of a king?
Christ executeth the office of a king, in calling out of the world a people to himself,[1] and giving them officers,[2] laws,[3] and censures, by which he visibly governs them;[4] in bestowing saving grace upon his elect,[5] rewarding their obedience,[6] and correcting them for their sins,[7] preserving and supporting them under all their temptations and sufferings,[8] restraining and overcoming all their enemies,[9] and powerfully ordering all things for his own glory,[10] and their good;[11] and also in taking vengeance on the rest, who know not God, and obey not the gospel.[12]

1 Ac 15:14–16; Isa 55:4–5; Ge 49:10; Ps 110:3
2 Eph 4:11–12; 1Co 12:28
3 Isa 33:22
4 Mt 18:17–18; 1Co 5:4–5
5 Ac 5:31
6 Rev 2:10; 22:12
7 Rev 3:19
8 Isa 63:9
9 1Co 15:25; Ps 110:1–2
10 Ro 14:10–11
11 Ro 8:28
12 2Th 1:8–9; Ps 2:8–9

46. What was the estate of Christ's humiliation?
The estate of Christ's humiliation was that low condition, wherein he for our sakes, emptying himself of his glory, took upon him the form of a servant, in his conception and birth, life, death, and after his death, until his resurrection.[1]

1 Php 2:6–8; Lk 1:31; 2Co 8:9; Ac 2:24

47. How did Christ humble himself in his conception and birth?
Christ humbled himself in his conception and birth, in that, being from all eternity the Son of God, in the bosom of the Father, he was pleased in the fulness of time to become the son of man, made of a woman of low estate, and to be born of her; with divers circumstances of more than ordinary abasement.[1]

1 Jn 1:14,18; Gal 4:4; Lk 2:7

48. How did Christ humble himself in his life?
Christ humbled himself in his life, by subjecting himself to the law,[1] which he perfectly fulfilled;[2] and by conflicting with the indignities of the world,[3] temptations of Satan,[4] and infirmities in his flesh, whether common to the nature of man, or particularly accompanying that his low condition.[5]

1 Gal 4:4
2 Mt 5:17; Ro 5:19
3 Ps 22:6; Heb 12:2–3
4 Mt 4:1–12; Lk 4:13
5 Heb 2:17–18; 4:15; Isa 52:13–14

49. How did Christ humble himself in his death?
Christ humbled himself in his death, in that having been betrayed by Judas,[1] forsaken by his disciples,[2] scorned and rejected by the world,[3] condemned by Pilate, and tormented by his persecutors;[4] having also conflicted with the terrors of death, and the powers of darkness, felt and borne the weight of God's wrath,[5] he laid down his life an offering for sin,[6] enduring the painful, shameful, and cursed death of the cross.[7]

1 Mt 27:4
2 Mt 26:56
3 Isa 53:2–3
4 Mt 27:26–50; Jn 29:34
5 Lk 22:44; Mt 27:46
6 Isa 53:10
7 Php 2:8; Heb 12:2; Gal 3:13

50. Wherein consisted Christ's humiliation after his death?
Christ's humiliation after his death consisted in his being buried,[1] and continuing in the state of the dead, and under the power of death till the third day;[2] which hath been otherwise expressed in these words, He descended into hell.

1 1Co 15:3–4
2 Ps 16:10; Ac 2:24–27,31; Ro 6:9; Mt 12:40

51. What was the estate of Christ's exaltation?
The estate of Christ's exaltation comprehendeth his resurrection,[1] ascension,[2] sitting at the right hand of the Father,[3] and his coming again to judge the world.[4]

1 1Co 15:4
2 Mk 16:19
3 Eph 1:20
4 Ac 1:11; 17:31

52. How was Christ exalted in his resurrection?
Christ was exalted in his resurrection, in that, not having seen corruption in death, (of which it was not possible for him to be held,)[1] and having the very same body in which he suffered, with the essential properties thereof,[2] (but without mortality, and other common infirmities belonging to this life,) really united to his soul,[3] he rose again from the dead the third day by his own power;[4] whereby he declared himself to be the Son of God,[5] to have satisfied divine justice,[6] to have vanquished death, and him that had the power of it,[7] and to be Lord of quick and dead:[8] all which he did as a public person,[9] the head of his church,[10] for their justification,[11] quickening in grace,[12] support against enemies,[13] and to assure them of their resurrection from the dead at the last day.[14]

1 Ac 2:24,27
2 Lk 24:39
3 Ro 6:9; Rev 1:18
4 Jn 10:18
5 Ro 1:4
6 Ro 8:34
7 Heb 2:14
8 Ro 14:9
9 1Co 15:21–22
10 Eph 1:20–23; Col 1:18
11 Ro 4:25
12 Eph 2:1,5–6; Col 2:12
13 1Co 15:25–27
14 1Co 15:20

53. How was Christ exalted in his ascension?
Christ was exalted in his ascension, in that having after his resurrection often appeared unto and conversed with his apostles, speaking to them of the things pertaining to the kingdom of God,[1] and giving them commission to preach the gospel to all nations,[2] forty days after his resurrection, he, in our nature, and as our head,[3] triumphing over enemies,[4] visibly went up into the highest heavens, there to receive gifts for men,[5] to raise up

our affections thither,[6] and to prepare a place for us,[7] where he himself is, and shall continue till his second coming at the end of the world.[8]

1 Ac 1:2–3
2 Mt 28:19–20
3 Heb 6:20
4 Eph 4:8
5 Ac 1:9–11; Eph 4:10; Ps 68:18
6 Col 3:1–2
7 Jn 14:3
8 Ac 3:21

54. How is Christ exalted in his sitting at the right hand of God?
Christ is exalted in his sitting at the right hand of God, in that as God-man he is advanced to the highest favour with God the Father,[1] with all fulness of joy,[2] glory,[3] and power over all things in heaven and earth;[4] and does gather and defend his church, and subdue their enemies; furnishes his ministers and people with gifts and graces,[5] and makes intercession for them.[6]

1 Php 2:9
2 Ac 2:28; Ps 16:11
3 Jn 17:5
4 Eph 1:22; 1Pe 3.22
5 Eph 4:10–12; Ps 110–1
6 Ro 8:34

55. How does Christ make intercession?
Christ maketh intercession, by his appearing in our nature continually before the Father in heaven,[1] in the merit of his obedience and sacrifice on earth,[2] declaring his will to have it applied to all believers;[3] answering all accusations against them,[4] and procuring for them quiet of conscience, notwithstanding daily failings,[5] access with boldness to the throne of grace,[6] and acceptance of their persons[7] and services.[8]

1 Heb 9:12,24
2 Heb 1:3
3 Jn 3:16; 17:9,20,24
4 Ro 8:33–34
5 Ro 5:1–2; 1Jn 2:1–2
6 Heb 4:16
7 Eph 1:6
8 1Pe 2:5

56. How is Christ to be exalted in his coming again to judge the world?
Christ is to be exalted in his coming again to judge the world, in that he, who was unjustly judged and condemned by wicked men,[1] shall come again at the last day in great power,[2] and in the full manifestation of his own glory, and of his Father's, with all his holy angels,[3] with a shout, with the voice of the archangel, and with the trumpet of God,[4] to judge the world in righteousness.[5]

1 Ac 3:14–15
2 Mt 24:30
3 Lk 9:26; Mt 25:31
4 1Th 4:16
5 Ac 17:31

57. What benefits has Christ procured by his mediation?
Christ, by his mediation, has procured redemption,[1] with all other benefits of the covenant of grace.[2]

1 Heb 9:12
2 2Co 1:20

58. How do we come to be made partakers of the benefits which Christ hath procured?
We are made partakers of the benefits which Christ hath procured, by the application of them unto us,[1] which is the work especially of God the Holy Ghost.[2]

1 Jn 1:11–12
2 Tit 3:5–6

59. Who are made partakers of redemption through Christ?
Redemption is certainly applied, and effectually communicated, to all those for whom Christ hath purchased it;[1] who are in time by the Holy Ghost enabled to believe in Christ according to the gospel.[2]

1 Eph 1:13–14; Jn 6:37,39; 10:15–16
2 Eph 2:8; 2Co 4:13

60. Can they who have never heard the gospel, and so know not Jesus Christ, nor believe in him, be saved by their living according to the light of nature?
They who, having never heard the gospel,[1] know not Jesus Christ,[2] and believe not in him, cannot be saved,[3] be they never so diligent to frame their lives according to the light of nature,[4] or the laws of that religion which they profess;[5] neither is there salvation in any other, but in Christ alone,[6] who is the Savior only of his body the church.[7]

1 Ro 10:14
2 2Th 1:8–9; Eph 2:12; Jn 1:10–12
3 Jn 8:24; Mk 16:16
4 1Co 1:20–24
5 Jn 4:22; Ro 9:31–32; Php 3:4–9
6 Ac 4:12
7 Eph 5:23

61. Are all they saved who hear the gospel, and live in the church?
All that hear the gospel, and live in the visible church, are not saved; but they only who are true members of the church invisible.[1]

1 Jn 12:38–40; Ro 9:6; 11:7; Mt 22:14

62. What is the visible church?
The visible church is a society made up of all such as in all ages and places of the world do profess the true religion,[1] and of their children.[2]

1 1Co 1:2; 12:13; Ro 15:9–12; Rev 7:9; Ps 2:8; 22:27 31; 45:17; Mt 28:19–20; Isa 59:21
2 1Co 7:14; Ac 2:39; Ro 11 16, Ge 17:7

63. What are the special privileges of the visible church?
The visible church hath the privilege of being under God's special care and government;[1] of being protected and preserved in all ages, notwithstanding the opposition of all enemies;[2] and of enjoying the communion of saints, the ordinary means of salvation,[3] and offers of grace by Christ to all members of it in the ministry of the gospel, testifying, that whosoever believes in him shall be saved,[4] and excluding none that will come unto him.[5]

1 Isa 9:5–6; 1Ti 4:10
2 Ps 115:1–2,9; Isa 31:4–5; Zec 12:2–4,8–9
3 Ac 2:39,42
4 Ps 147:19–20; Ro 9:4; Eph 4:11–12; Mk 16:15–16
5 Jn 6:37

64. What is the invisible church?
The invisible church is the whole number of the elect, that have been, are, or shall be gathered into one under Christ the head.[1]

1 Eph 1:10:22–23; Jn 10:16; 11:52

65. What special benefits do the members of the invisible church enjoy by Christ?
The members of the invisible church by Christ enjoy union and communion with him in grace and glory.[1]

1 Jn 17:21,24; Eph 2:5–6

66. What is that union which the elect have with Christ?
The union which the elect have with Christ is the work of God's grace,[1] whereby they are spiritually and mystically, yet really and inseparably, joined to Christ as their head and husband;[2] which is done in their effectual calling.[3]

1 Eph 1:22; 2:6–7
2 1Co 6:17; Jn 10:28; Eph 5:23,30
3 1Pe 5:10; 1Co 1:9

67. What is effectual calling?
Effectual calling is the work of God's almighty power and grace,[1] whereby (out of his free and special love to his elect, and from nothing in them moving him thereunto)[2] he doth, in his accepted time, invite and draw them to Jesus Christ, by his word and Spirit;[3] savingly enlightening their minds,[4] renewing and powerfully determining their wills,[5] so as they (although in themselves dead in sin) are hereby made willing and able

freely to answer his call, and to accept and embrace the grace offered and conveyed therein.[6]

1 Jn 5:25; Eph 1:18–20; 2Ti 1:8–9
2 Tit 3:4–5; Eph 2:4–5,7–9; Ro 9:11
3 2Co 5:20; 6:1–2; Jn 6:44; 2Th 2:13–14
4 Ac 26:18; 1Co 2:10,12
5 Eze 11:19; 36:26–27; Jn 6:45
6 Eph 2:5; Php 2:13; Dt 30:6

68. Are the elect only effectually called?
All the elect, and they only, are effectually called:[1] although others may be, and often are, outwardly called by the ministry of the word,[2] and have some common operations of the Spirit;[3] who, for their wilful neglect and contempt of the grace offered to them, being justly left in their unbelief, do never truly come to Jesus Christ.[4]

1 Ac 13:48
2 Mt 22:14
3 Mt 7:22; 13:20–21; Heb 6:4–6
4 Jn 6:64–65; 12:38–40; Ac 28:25–27; Ps 81:11–12

69. What is the communion in grace which the members of the invisible church have with Christ?
The communion in grace which the members of the invisible church have with Christ, is their partaking of the virtue of his mediation, in their justification,[1] adoption,[2] sanctification, and whatever else, in this life, manifests their union with him.[3]

1 Ro 8:30
2 Eph 1:5
3 1Co 1:30

70. What is justification?
Justification is an act of God's free grace unto sinners,[1] in which he pardoneth all their sins, accepteth and accounteth their persons righteous in his sight;[2] not for any thing wrought in them, or done by them,[3] but only for the perfect obedience and full satisfaction of Christ, by God imputed to them,[4] and received by faith alone.[5]

1 Ro 3:22,24–25; 4:5
2 2Co 5:19,21; Ro 3:22,24–25,27–28
3 Tit 3:5,7; Eph 1:7
4 Ro 4:6–8; 5:17–19
5 Ac 10:43; Gal 2:16; Php 3:9

71. How is justification an act of God's free grace?
Although Christ, by his obedience and death, did make a proper, real, and fully satisfaction to God's justice in the behalf of them that are justified;[1] yet in as much as God accepteth the satisfaction from a surety, which he might have demanded of them, and did provide this surety, his own only Son,[2] imputing his righteousness to them,[3] and requiring nothing of them for their justification but faith,[4] which also is his gift,[5] their justification is to them of free grace.[6]

1 Ro 5:8–10,19
2 1Ti 2:5–6; Heb 7:22; 10:10; Mt 20:28; Da 9:24,26; Isa 53:4–6,10–12; Ro 8:32; 1Pe 1:18–19
3 2Co 5:21
4 Ro 3:24–25
5 Eph 2:8
6 Eph 1:17

72. What is justifying faith?
Justifying faith is a saving grace,[1] wrought in the heart of a sinner by the Spirit[2] and word of God,[3] whereby he, being convinced of his sin and misery, and of the disability in himself and all other creatures to recover him out of his lost condition,[4] not only assenteth to the truth of the promise of the gospel,[5] but received and rested upon Christ and his righteousness, therein held forth, for pardon of sin,[6] and for the accepting and accounting of his person righteous in the sight of God for salvation.[7]

1 Heb 10:39
2 2Co 4:13; Eph 1:17–19
3 Ro 10:14–17
4 Ac 2:37; 4:12; 16:30; Jn 16:8–9; Ro 6:6; Eph 2:1
5 Eph 1:13
6 Jn 1:12; Ac 10:43; 16:31
7 Php 3:9; Ac 15:11

73. How doth faith justify a sinner in the sight of God?
Faith justifies a sinner in the sight of God, not because of those other graces which do always accompany it, or of good works that are the fruits of it,[1] nor as if the grace of faith, or any act thereof, were imputed to him for his justification;[2] but only as it is an instrument by which he receiveth and applieth Christ and his righteousness.[3]

1 Gal 3:11; Ro 3:28
2 Ro 4:5; 10:10
3 Jn 1:12; Php 3:9; Gal 1:16

74. What is adoption?
Adoption is an act of the free grace of God,[1] in and for his only Son Jesus Christ,[2] whereby all those that are justified are received into the number of his children,[3] have his name put upon them,[4] the Spirit of his Son given to them,[5] are under his fatherly care and dispensations,[6] admitted to all the liberties and privileges of the sons of God, made heirs of all the promises, and fellow-heirs with Christ in glory.[7]

1 1Jn 3:1
2 Eph 1:5; Gal 4:4–5
3 Jn 1:12
4 2Co 6:18; Rev 3:12
5 Gal 4:6
6 Ps 103:13; Pr 14:26; Mt 6:32
7 Heb 6:12; Ro 8:17

75. What is sanctification?
Sanctification is a work of God's grace, whereby they whom God hath, before the foundation of the world, chosen to be holy, are in time, through the powerful operation of his Spirit[1] applying the death and resurrection of Christ unto them,[2] renewed in their whole man after the image of God;[3] having the seeds of repentance unto life, and all other saving graces, put into their hearts,[4] and those graces so stirred up, increased, and strengthened,[5] as that they more and more die unto sin, and rise unto newness of life.[6]

1 Eph 1:4; 1Co 6:11; 2Th 2:13
2 Ro 6:4–6
3 Eph 4:23–24
4 Ac 11:18; 1Jn 3:9
5 Jude 20; Heb 6:11–12; Eph 3:16–19; Col 1:10–11
6 Ro 6:4,6,14; Gal 5:24

76. What is repentance unto life?
Repentance unto life is a saving grace,[1] wrought in the heart of a sinner by the Spirit[2] and word of God,[3] whereby, out of the sight and sense, not only of the danger,[4] but also of the filthiness and odiousness of his sins,[5] and upon the apprehension of God's mercy in Christ to such as are penitent,[6] he so grieves for[7] and hates his sins,[8] as that he turns from them all to God,[9] purposing and endeavouring constantly to walk with him in all the ways of new obedience.[10]

1 2Ti 2:25
2 Zec 12:10
3 Ac 11:18,20–21
4 Eze 18:28,30,32; Lk 15:17–18; Hos 2:6–7
5 Eze 36:31; Isa 30:22
6 Joel 2:12–13
7 Jer 31:18–19
8 2Co 7:11
9 Ac 26:18; Eze 14:6; 1Ki 8:47–48
10 Ps 119:6,59,128; Lk 1:6; 2Ki 23:25

77. Wherein do justification and sanctification differ?
Although sanctification be inseparably joined with justification,[1] yet they differ, in that God in justification impureth the righteousness of Christ;[2] in sanctification of his Spirit infuseth grace, and enableth to the exercise thereof;[3] in the former, sin is pardoned;[4] in the other, it is subdued:[5] the one doth equally free all believers from the revenging wrath of God, and that perfectly in this life, that they never fall into condemnation[6] the other is neither equal in all,[7] nor in this life perfect in any,[8] but growing up to perfection.[9]

1 1Co 1:30; 6:11
2 Ro 4:6,8
3 Eze 36:27
4 Ro 3:24–25
5 Ro 6:6,14
6 Ro 8:33–34

[7] 1Jn 2:12–14; Heb 5:12–14
[8] 1Jn 1:8,10
[9] 2Co 7:1; Php 3:12–14

78. Whence ariseth the imperfection of sanctification in believers?
The imperfection of sanctification in believers ariseth from the remnants of sin abiding in every part of them, and the perpetual lustings of the flesh against the spirit; whereby they are often foiled with temptations, and fall into many sins,[1] are hindered in all their spiritual services,[2] and their best works are imperfect and defiled in the sight of God.[3]

[1] Ro 7:18,23; Mk 14:66–72; Gal 2:11–12
[2] Heb 12:1
[3] Isa 64:6; Ex 28:38

79. May not true believers, by reason of their imperfections, and the many temptations and sins they are overtaken with, fall away from the state of grace?
True believers, by reason of the unchangeable love of God,[1] and his decree and covenant to give them perseverance,[2] their inseparable union with Christ,[3] his continual intercession for them,[4] and the Spirit and seed of God abiding in them,[5] can neither totally nor finally fall away from the state of grace,[6] but are kept by the power of God through faith unto salvation.[7]

[1] Jer 31:3
[2] 2Ti 2:19; Heb 13:20–21; 2Sa 23:5
[3] 1Co 1:8–9
[4] Heb 7:25; Lk 22:32
[5] 1Jn 3:9; 1Jn 2:27
[6] Jer 32:40; Jn 10:28
[7] 1Pe 1:5

80. Can true believers be infallibly assured that they are in the estate of grace, and that they shall persevere therein unto salvation?
Such as truly believe in Christ, and endeavour to walk in all good conscience before him,[1] may, without extraordinary revelation, by faith grounded upon the truth of God's promises, and by the Spirit enabling them to discern in themselves those graces to which the promises of life are made,[2] and bearing witness with their spirits that they are the children of God,[3] be infallibly assured that they are in the estate of grace, and shall persevere therein unto salvation.[4]

[1] 1Jn 2:3
[2] 1Co 2:12; 1Jn 3:14,18–19,21,24; 4:13,16; Heb 6:11–12
[3] Ro 8:16
[4] 1Jn 5:13

81. Are all true believers at all times assured of their present being in the estate of grace, and that they shall be saved?
Assurance of grace and salvation not being of the essence of faith,[1] true believers may wait long before they obtain;[2] and, after the enjoyment thereof, may have it weakened and intermitted, through manifold distempers, sins, temptations, and desertions;[3] yet they are never left without such a presence and support of the Spirit of God as keeps them from sinking into utter despair.[4]

[1] Eph 1:13
[2] Isa 50:10; Ps 88:1–3,6–7,9–10,13–15
[3] Ps 22:1; 51:8,12; 77:1–12; SS 5:2–3,6
[4] 1Jn 3:9; Ps 73:15,23; Isa 54:7–10

82. What is the communion in glory which the members of the invisible church have with Christ?
The communion in glory which the members of the invisible church have with Christ, is in this life,[1] immediately after death,[2] and at last perfected at the resurrection and day of judgment.[3]

[1] 2Co 3:18
[2] Lk 23:43
[3] 1Th 4:17

83. What is the communion in glory with Christ which the members of the invisible church enjoy in this life?
The members of the invisible church have communicated to them in this life the first-fruits of glory with Christ, as they are members of him their head, and so in him are interested in that glory which he is fully possessed of;[1] and, as an earnest thereof, enjoy the sense of God's love,[2] peace of conscience, joy in the Holy Ghost, and hope of glory;[3] as, on the contrary, sense of God's revenging wrath, horror of conscience, and a fearful expectation, are to the wicked the beginning of their torments which they shall endure after death.[4]

[1] Eph 2:5–6
[2] Ro 5:5; 2Co 1:22
[3] Ro 5:1–2; 14:17
[4] Ge 4:13; Mt 27:4; Heb 10:27; Ro 2:9; Mk 9:44

84. Shall all men die?
Death being threatened as the wages of sin,[1] it is appointed unto all men once to die;[2] for that all have sinned.[3]

[1] Ro 6:23
[2] Heb 9:27
[3] Ro 5:12

85. Death, being the wages of sin, why are not the righteous delivered from death, seeing all their sins are forgiven in Christ?
The righteous shall be delivered from death itself at the last day, and even in death are delivered from the sting and curse of it;[1] so that, although they die, yet it is out of God's love,[2] to free them perfectly from sin and misery,[3] and to make them capable of further communion with Christ in glory, which they then enter upon.[4]

[1] 1Co 15:26,55–57; Heb 2:15
[2] Isa 57:1–2; 2Ki 22:20
[3] Rev 14:13; Eph 5:27
[4] Lk 23:43; Php 1:23

86. What is the communion in glory with Christ, which the members of the invisible church enjoy immediately after death?
The communion in glory with Christ, which the members of the invisible church enjoy immediately after death is, in that their souls are then made perfect in holiness,[1] and received into the highest heavens,[2] where they behold the face of God in light and glory,[3] waiting for the full redemption of their bodies,[4] which even in death continue united to Christ,[5] and rest in their graves as in their beds,[6] till at the last day they be again united to their souls.[7] Whereas the souls of the wicked are at their death cast into hell, where they remain in torments and utter darkness, and their bodies kept in their graves, as in their prisons, till the resurrection and judgment of the great day.[8]

[1] Heb 12:32
[2] 2Co 5:1,6,8; Php 1:23; Ac 3:21; Eph 4:10
[3] 1Jn 3:2; 1Co 13:12
[4] Ro 8:23; Ps 16:9
[5] 1Th 4:14
[6] Isa 57:2
[7] Job 19:26–27
[8] Lk 16:23–24; Ac 1:25; Jude 6–7

87. What are we to believe concerning the resurrection?
We are to believe that at the last day there shall be a general resurrection of the dead, both of the just and unjust:[1] when they that are then found alive shall in a moment be changed; and the self-same bodies of the dead which were laid in the grave, being then again united to their souls for ever, shall be raised up by the power of Christ.[2] The bodies of the just, by the Spirit of Christ, and by virtue of his resurrection as their head, shall be raised in power, spiritual, incorruptible, and made like to his glorious body;[3] and the bodies of the wicked shall be raised up in dishonour by him, as an offended judge.[4]

[1] Ac 24:15
[2] 1Co 15:51–53; 1Th 4:15–17; Jn 5:28–29
[3] 1Co 15:21–23,42–44; Php 3:21
[4] Jn 5:27–29; Mt 25:33

88. What shall immediately follow after the resurrection?
Immediately after the resurrection shall follow the general and final judgment of angels and men;[1] the day and hour whereof no man knoweth, that all may watch and pray, and be ever ready for the coming of the Lord.[2]

[1] 2Pe 2:4,6–7,14–15; Mt 25:46
[2] Mt 24:36,42,44

89. What shall be done to the wicked at the day of judgment?
At the day of judgment, the wicked shall be set on Christ's left hand,[1] and, upon clear evidence, and full conviction of their own consciences,[2] shall have the fearful but just sentence of condemnation pronounced against them;[3] and thereupon shall be cast out from the favourable presence of God, and the glorious fellowship with Christ, his saints, and all his holy angels, into hell, to be punished with unspeakable torments, both of body and soul, with the devil and his angels for ever.[4]

1 Mt 25:33
2 Ro 2:15–16
3 Mt 25:41–43
4 Lk 16:26; 2Th 1:8–9

90. What shall be done to the righteous at the day of judgment?
At the day of judgment, the righteous, being caught up to Christ in the clouds,[1] shall be set on his right hand, and there openly acknowledged and acquitted,[2] shall join with him in the judging of reprobate angels and men,[3] and shall be received into heaven,[4] where they shall be fully and for ever freed from all sin and misery;[5] filled with inconceivable joys,[6] made perfectly holy and happy both in body and soul, in the company of innumerable saints and holy angels,[7] but especially in the immediate vision and fruition of God the Father, of our Lord Jesus Christ, and of the Holy Spirit, to all eternity.[8] And this is the perfect and full communion, which the members of the invisible church shall enjoy with Christ in glory, at the resurrection and day of judgment.

1 1Th 4:17
2 Mt 10:32; 25:33
3 1Co 6:2–3
4 Mt 25:34,46
5 Eph 5:27; Rev 14:13
6 Ps 16:11
7 Heb 12:22–23
8 1Jn 3:2; 1Co 13:12; 1Th 4:17–18

HAVING SEEN WHAT THE SCRIPTURES PRINCIPALLY TEACH US TO BELIEVE CONCERNING GOD, IT FOLLOWS TO CONSIDER WHAT THEY REQUIRE AS THE DUTY OF MAN

91. What is the duty which God requireth of man?
The duty which God requireth of man, is obedience to his revealed will.[1]

1 Ro 12:1–2; Mic 6:8; 1Sa 15:22

92. What did God at first reveal unto man as the rule of his obedience?
The rule of obedience revealed to Adam in the estate of innocence, and to all mankind in him, besides a special command not to eat of the fruit of the tree knowledge of good and evil, was the moral law.[1]

1 Ge 1:26–27; Ro 2:14–15; 10:5; Ge 2:17

93. What is the moral law?
The moral law is the declaration of the will of God to mankind, direction and binding every one to personal, perfect, and perpetual conformity and obedience thereunto, in the frame and disposition of the whole man, soul and body,[1] and in performance of all those duties of holiness and righteousness which he oweth to God and man:[2] promising life upon the fulfilling, and threatening death upon the breach of it.[3]

1 Dt 5:1–3,31,33; Lk 10:26–27; Gal 3:10; 1Th 5:23
2 Lk 1:75; Ac 24:16
3 Ro 10:5; Gal 3:10,12

94. Is there any use of the moral law to man since the fall?
Although no man, since the fall, can attain to righteousness and life by the moral law:[1] yet there is great use thereof, as well common to all men, as peculiar either to the unregenerate, or the regenerate.[2]

1 Ro 8:3; Gal 2:16
2 1Ti 1:8

95. Of what use is the moral law to all men?
The moral law is of use to all men, to inform them of the holy nature and the will of God,[1] and of their duty, binding them to walk accordingly;[2] to convince them of their disability to keep it, and of the sinful pollution of their nature, hearts, and lives:[3] to humble them in the sense of their sin and misery,[4] and thereby help them to a clearer sight of the need they have of Christ,[5] and of the perfection of his obedience.[6]

1 Lev 11:44–45; 20:7–8; Ro 8:12
2 Mic 11:8; Jas 2:10–11
3 Ps 19:11–12; Ro 3:20; 7:7
4 Ro 3:9,23
5 Gal 3:21–22
6 Ro 10:4

96. What particular use is there of the moral law to unregenerate men?
The moral law is of use to unregenerate men, to awaken their consciences to flee from wrath to come,[1] and to drive them to Christ;[2] or, inexcusable,[3] and under the curse thereof.[4]

1 1Ti 1:9–10
2 Gal 3:24
3 Ro 1:20; 2:15
4 Gal 3:10

97. What special use is there of the moral law to the regenerate?
Although they that are regenerate, and believe in Christ, be delivered from the moral law as a covenant of works,[1] so as thereby they are neither justified[2] nor condemned;[3] yet, besides the general uses thereof common to them with all men, it is of special use, to show them how much they are bound to Christ for his fulfilling it, and enduring the curse thereof in their stead, and for their good;[4] and thereby to provoke them to more thankfulness,[5] and to express the same in their greater care to conform themselves thereunto as the rule to their obedience.[6]

1 Ro 6:14; 7:4,6; Gal 4:4–5
2 Ro 3:20
3 Gal 5:23; Ro 8:1
4 Ro 7:24–25; 8:3–4; Gal 3:13–14
5 Lk 1:68–69,74–75; Col 1:12–14
6 Ro 7:22; Ro 12:2; Tit 2:11–14

98. Where is the moral law summarily comprehended?
The moral law is summarily comprehended in the ten commandments, which were delivered by the voice of God upon Mount Sinai, and written by him in two tables of stone;[1] and are recorded in the twentieth chapter of Exodus. The four first commandments containing our duty to God, and the other six our duty to man.[2]

1 Dt 10:4; Ex 34:1–4
2 Mt 22:37–40

99. What rules are to be observed for the right understanding of the ten commandments?
For the right understanding of the ten commandments, these rules are to be observed:

1. That the law is perfect, and bindeth every one to full conformity in the whole man unto the righteousness thereof, and unto entire obedience for ever; so as to require the utmost perfection of every duty, and to forbid the least degree of every sin.[1]
2. That it is spiritual, and so reacheth the understanding, will, affections, and all other powers of the soul; as well as words, works, and gestures.[2]
3. That one and the same thing, in divers respects, is required or forbidden in several commandments.[3]
4. That as, where a duty is commanded, the contrary sin is forbidden;[4] and, where a sin is forbidden, the contrary duty is commanded:[5] so, where a promise is annexed, the contrary threatening is included;[6] and, where a threatening is annexed, the contrary promise is included.[7]
5. That what God forbids, is at no time to be done;[8] what he commands, is always our duty;[9] and yet every particular duty is not to be done at all times.[10]

6. That under one sin or duty, all of the same kind are forbidden or commanded; together with all the causes, means occasions, and appearances thereof, and provocations thereunto.[11]

7. That what is forbidden or commanded to ourselves, we are bound, according to our places to endeavour that it may be avoided or performed by others, according to the duty of their places.[12]

8. That in what is commanded to others, we are bound, according to our places and callings, to be helpful to them;[13] and to take heed of partaking with others in what is forbidden them.[14]

1 Ps 19:7; Jas 2:10; Mt 5:21–22
2 Ro 7:14; Dt 6:5; Mt 5:21–22,27–28,33–34,37–39,43–44; 22:37–39
3 Col 3:5; Am 8:5; Pr 1:19; 1Ti 6:10
4 Isa 58:13; Dt 6:13; Mt 4:9–10; 15:4–6
5 Mt 5:21–25; Eph 4:28
6 Ex 20:12; Pr 30:17
7 Jer 18:7–8; Ex 20:7; Ps 15:1,4–5; 24:4–5
8 Job 13:7–8; 36:21; Ro 3:8; Heb 11:25
9 Dt 4:8–9
10 Mt 12:7
11 Mt 5:21–22,27–28; 15:4–6; Heb 10:24–25; 1Th 5:22; Jude 23; Gal 5:26; Col 3:21
12 Ex 20:10; Lev 19:17; Ge 18:19; Jos 14:15; Dt 6:6–7
13 2Co 1:24
14 1Ti 5:22; Eph 5:11

100. What special things are we to consider in the ten commandments?
We are to consider in the ten commandments, the preface, the substance of the commandments themselves, and several reasons annexed to some of them, the more to enforce them.

101. What is the preface to the ten commandments?
The preface to the ten commandments is contained in these words, I am the Lord thy God, which have brought thee out of the land of Egypt, out of the house of bondage.[1] Wherein God manifesteth his sovereignty, as being JEHOVAH, the eternal, immutable, and almighty God;[2] having his being in and of himself,[3] and giving being to all his words[4] and works:[5] and that he is a God in covenant, as with Israel of old, so with all his people;[6] who, as he brought them out of their bondage in Egypt, so he delivereth us from our spiritual thraldom;[7] and that therefore we are bound to take him for our God alone, and to keep all his commandments.[8]

1 Ex 20:2
2 Isa 44:6
3 Ex 3:14
4 Ex 6:3
5 Ac 17:24,28
6 Ge 17:7; Ro 3:29
7 Lk 1:74–75
8 1Pe 1:15,17–18; Lev 18:30; 19:37

102. What is the sum of the four commandments which contain our duty to God?
The sum of the four commandments containing our duty to God is, to love the Lord our God with all our heart, and with all our soul, and with all our strength, and with all our mind.[1]

1 Lk 10:27

103. Which is the first commandment?
The first commandment is, Thou shalt have no other gods before me.[1]

1 Ex 20:3

104. What are the duties required in the first commandment?
The duties required in the first commandment are, the knowing and acknowledging of God to be the only true God, and our God;[1] and to worship and glorify him accordingly,[2] by thinking,[3] mediating,[4] remembering,[5] highly esteeming,[6] honouring,[7] adoring,[8] choosing,[9] loving,[10] desiring,[11] fearing of him;[12] believing him;[13] trusting[14] hoping,[15] delighting,[16] rejoicing in him;[17] being zealous for him;[18] calling upon him, giving all praise and thanks,[19] and yielding all obedience and submission to him with the whole man;[20] being careful in all things to please him,[21] and sorrowful when in any thing he is offended;[22] and walking humbly with him.[23]

1 1Ch 28:9; Dt 26:7; Isa 43:10; Jer 14:22
2 Ps 95:6–7; Mt 4:10; Ps 29:2
3 Mal 3:16
4 Ps 63:6
5 Ecc 12:1
6 Ps 71:19
7 Mal 1:6
8 Isa 45:23
9 Jos 24:15,22
10 Dt 6:5
11 Ps 73:25
12 Isa 8:13
13 Ex 14:31
14 Isa 26:4
15 Ps 130:7
16 Ps 37:4
17 Ps 32:11
18 Ro 12:11; Nu 25:11
19 Php 4:6
20 Jer 7:23; Jas 4:7
21 1Jn 3:22
22 Jer 31:18; Ps 119:136
23 Mic 6:8

105. What are the sins forbidden in the first commandment?
The sins forbidden in the first commandment are, Atheism, in denying or not having a God;[1] Idolatry, in having or worshipping more gods than one, or any with or instead of the true God;[2] the not having and avouching him for God, and our God;[3] the omission or neglect of any thing due to him, required in this commandment;[4] ignorance,[5] forgetfulness,[6] misapprehensions,[7] false opinions,[8] unworthy and wicked thoughts of him;[9] bold and curious searching into his secrets;[10] all profaneness,[11] hatred of God;[12] self-love,[13] self-seeking,[14] and all other inordinate and immoderate setting of our mind, will, or affections upon other things, and taking them off from him in whole or in part;[15] vain credulity,[16] unbelief,[17] heresy,[18] misbelief,[19] distrust,[20] despair,[21] incorrigibleness,[22] and insensibleness under judgments,[23] hardness of heart,[24] pride,[25] presumption,[26] carnal security,[27] tempting of God;[28] using unlawful means,[29] and trusting in lawful means;[30] carnal delights and joys;[31] corrupt, blind, and indiscreet zeal;[32] lukewarmness,[33] and deadness in the things of God;[34] estranging ourselves, and apostatizing from God;[35] praying, or giving any religious worship, to saints, angels, or any other creatures;[36] all compacts and consulting with the devil,[37] and hearkening to his suggestions;[38] making men the lords of our faith and conscience;[39] slighting and despising God and his commands;[40] resisting and grieving of his Spirit,[41] discontent and impatience at his dispensations, charging him foolishly for the evils he inflicts on us;[42] and ascribing the praise of any good we either are, have or can do, to fortune,[43] idols,[44] ourselves,[45] or any other creature.[46]

1 Ps 14:1; Eph 2:12
2 Jer 2:27–28; 1Th 1:9
3 Ps 81:11
4 Isa 43:2,23–24
5 Jer 4:22; Hos 4:1,6
6 Jer 2:32
7 Ac 17:23,29
8 Isa 40:18
9 Ps 50:21
10 Dt 29:29
11 Tit 1:16; Heb 12:16
12 Ro 1:30
13 2Ti 3:2
14 Php 2:21
15 1Jn 2:15–16; 1Sa 2:29; Col 2:2,5
16 1Jn 4:1
17 Heb 3:12
18 Gal 5:20; Tit 3:10
19 Ac 26:9
20 Ps 78:22
21 Ge 4:13
22 Jer 5:3
23 Isa 42:25
24 Ro 2:5
25 Jer 13:15
26 Ps 10:13
27 Zep 1:12

28 Mt 4:7
29 Ro 3:8
30 Jer 17:5
31 2Ti 3:4
32 Gal 4:17; Jn 16:2; Ro 10:2; Lk 9:54–55
33 Rev 3:16
34 Rev 2:1
35 Eze 14:5; Isa 1:4–5
36 Ro 1:25; 10:13–14; Hos 4:12; Ac 10:25–26; Rev 19:10; Mt 4:10; Col 2:18
37 Lev 20:6; 1Sa 28:7,11; 1Ch 10:13–14
38 Ac 5:3
39 2Co 1:24; Mt 23:9
40 Dt 32:15; 2Sa 12:9; Pr 13:13
41 Ac 7:51; Eph 4:30
42 Ps 73:2–3,13–15,22; Job 1:22
43 1Sa 6:7–9
44 Da 5:23
45 Dt 8:17; Da 4:30
46 Hab 1:16

106. What are we specially taught by these words [before me] in the first commandment?
These words [before me] or before my face, in the first commandment, teach us, that God, who seeth all things, taketh special notice of, and is much displeased with, the sin of having any other God: that so it may be an argument to dissuade from it, and to aggravate it as a most impudent provocation:[1] as also to persuade us to do as in his sight, whatever we do in his service.[2]

1 Eze 8:5–6; Ps 44:20–21
2 1Ch 28:9

107. Which is the second commandment?
The second commandment is, Thou shalt not make unto thee any graven image, or any likeness of any thing that is in heaven above, or that is in the earth beneath, or that is in the water under the earth. Thou shalt not bow down thyself to them, nor serve them: for I the Lord thy God am a jealous God, visiting the iniquity of the fathers upon the children unto the third and fourth generation of them that hate me; and showing mercy unto thousands of them that love me, and keep my commandments.[1]

1 Ex 20:4–5–6

108. What are the duties required in the second commandment?
The duties required in the second commandment are, the receiving, observing, and keeping pure and entire, all such religious worship and ordinances as God hath instituted in his word;[1] particularly prayer and thanksgiving in the name of Christ;[2] the reading, preaching, and hearing of the word;[3] the administration and receiving of the sacraments;[4] church government and discipline;[5] the ministry and maintainance thereof;[6] religious fasting;[7] swearing by the name of God;[8] and vowing unto him;[9] as also the disapproving, detesting, opposing all false worship;[10] and, according to each one's place and calling, removing it, and all monuments of idolatry.[11]

1 Dt 32:46–47; Mt 28:20; Ac 2:42; 1Ti 6:13–14
2 Php 4:6; Eph 5:20
3 Dt 17:18–19; Ac 10:33; 15:21; 2Ti 4:2; Jas 1:21–22
4 Mt 28:19; 1Co 11:23–30
5 Mt 16:19; 18:15–17; 1Co 5:1–13; 12:28
6 Eph 4:11–12; 1Ti 5:17–18; 1Co 9:7–15
7 Joel 2:12,18; 1Co 7:5
8 Dt 6:13
9 Isa 19–21; Ps 76:11
10 Ac 17:16–17; Ps 16:4
11 Dt 7:5; Isa 30:22

109. What are the sins forbidden in the second commandment?
The sins forbidden in the second commandment are, all devising,[1] counselling,[2] commanding,[3] using,[4] and any wise approving, any religious worship not instituted by God himself;[5] the making any representation of God, of all or of any of the three persons, either inwardly in our mind, or outwardly in any kind of image or likeness of any creature whatsoever;[6] all worshipping of it,[7] or God in it or by it;[8] the making of any representation of feigned deities,[9] and all worship of them, or service belonging to them,[10] all superstitious devices,[11] corrupting the worship of God,[12] adding to it, or taking from it,[13] whether invented and taken up of ourselves,[14] or received by tradition from others,[15] though under the title of antiquity,[16] custom,[17] devotion,[18] good intent, or any other pretence whatsoever;[19] simony;[20] sacrilege;[21] all neglect,[22] contempt,[23] hindering,[24] and opposing the worship and ordinances which God hath appointed.[25]

1 Nu 15:39
2 Dt 13:6–8
3 Hos 5:11; Mic 6:16
4 1Ki 11:33; 12:33
5 Dt 12:30–32
6 Dt 4:15–19; Ac 17:29; Ro 1:21–23,25
7 Da 3:18; Gal 4:8
8 Ex 32:5
9 Ex 32:8
10 1Ki 18:26,28; Isa 65:11
11 Ac 17:22; Col 2:21–23
12 Mal 1:7–8,14
13 Dt 4:2
14 Ps 106:39
15 Mt 15:9
16 1Pe 1:18
17 Jer 44:17
18 Isa 65:3–5; Gal 1:13–14
19 1Sa 13:11–12; 15:21
20 Ac 8:18
21 Ro 2:22; Mal 3:8
22 Ex 4:24–26
23 Mt 22:5; Mal 1:7,13
24 Mt 23:13
25 Ac 13:44–45; 1Th 2:15–16

110. What are the reasons annexed to the second commandment, the more to enforce it?
The reasons annexed to the second commandment, the more to enforce it, contained in these words, For I the Lord thy God am a jealous God, visiting the iniquity of the fathers upon the children unto the third and fourth generation of them that hate me; and showing mercy unto thousands of them that love me, and keep my commandments;[1] are, besides God's sovereignty over us, and propriety in us,[2] his fervent zeal for his own worship,[3] and his revengeful indignation against all false worship, as being a spiritual whoredom;[4] accounting the breakers of this commandment such as hate him, and threatening to punish them unto divers generations;[5] and esteeming the observers of it such as love him and keep his commandments, and promising mercy to them unto many generations.[6]

1 Ex 20:5–6
2 Ps 45:11; Rev 15:3–4
3 Ex 34:13–14
4 1Co 10:20–22; Dt 32:16–20
5 Hos 2:2–4
6 Dt 5:29

111. Which is the third commandment?
The third commandment is, Thou shalt not take the name of the Lord thy God in vain: for the Lord will not hold him guiltless that taketh his name in vain.[1]

1 Ex 20:7

112. What is required in the third commandment?
The third commandment requires, That the name of God, his titles, attributes,[1] ordinances,[2] the word,[3] sacraments,[4] prayer,[5] oaths,[6] vows,[7] lots,[8] his works,[9] and whatsoever else there is whereby he makes himself known, be holy and reverently used in thought,[10] meditation,[11] word,[12] and writing;[13] by an holy profession,[14] and answerable conversation,[15] to the glory of God,[16] and the good of ourselves,[17] and others.[18]

1 Mt 11:9; Dt 28:58; Ps 29:2; 68:4; Rev 15:3–4
2 Mal 1:14; Ecc 5:1
3 Ps 138:2
4 1Co 11:24–25,28–29
5 1Ti 2:8
6 Jer 4:2
7 Ecc 5:2–6
8 Ac 1:24,26
9 Job 36:24
10 Mal 3:16
11 Ps 8:1,3–4,9
12 Col 3:17; Ps 105:2,5

13 Ps 102:18
14 1Pe 3:15; Mic 4:5
15 Php 1:27
16 1Co 10:31
17 Jer 32:39
18 1Pe 2:12

113. What are the sins forbidden in the third commandment?

The sins forbidden in the third commandment are, the not using of God's name as is required;[1] and the abuse of it in an ignorant,[2] vain,[3] irreverent, profane,[4] superstitious[5] or wicked mentioning or otherwise using his titles, attributes,[6] ordinances,[7] or works,[8] by blasphemy,[9] perjury;[10] all sinful cursings,[11] oaths,[12] vows,[13] and lots;[14] violation of our oaths and vows, if lawful[15] and fulfilling them, if of things unlawful;[16] murmuring and quarrelling at,[17] curious prying into,[18] and misapplying of God's decrees[19] and providences;[20] misinterpreting,[21] misapplying,[22] or any way perverting the word, or any part of it;[23] to profane jests,[24] curious or unprofitable questions, vain janglings, or the maintaining of false doctrines;[25] abusing it, the creatures, or any thing contained under the name of God, to charms,[26] or sinful lusts and practices;[27] the maligning,[28] scorning,[29] reviling,[30] or any wise opposing of God's truth, grace, and ways;[31] making profession of religion in hypocrisy, or for sinister ends;[32] being ashamed of it,[33] or a shame to it, by unconformable,[34] unwise,[35] unfruitful,[36] and offensive walking,[37] or backsliding from it.[38]

1 Mal 2:2
2 Ac 17:23
3 Pr 30:9
4 Mal 1:6–7,12; 3:14
5 1Sa 4:3–5; Jer 7:4,9–10,14,31; Col 2:20–22
6 2Ki 18:30,35; Ex 5:2
7 Ps 50:16–17
8 Isa 5:12
9 2Ki 19:22; Lev 24:11
10 Zec 5:4; 8:17
11 1Sa 17:43; 2Sa 16:5
12 Jer 5:7; 23:10
13 Dt 23:18; Ac 23:12,14
14 Est 3:7; 9:24; Ps 22:18
15 Ps 24:4; Eze 17:16,18–19
16 Mk 6:26; 1Sa 25:22,32–34
17 Ro 9:14,19–20
18 Dt 29:29
19 Ro 3:5,7; 6:1
20 Ecc 8:11; 9:3; Ps 39
21 Mt 5:21–48
22 Eze 13:22
23 2Pe 3:16; Mt 22:24–31
24 Isa 22:13; Jer 23:34,36,38
25 1Ti 1:4,6–7; 6:4–5,20; 2Ti 2:14; Tit 3:9
26 Dt 18:10–14,11–12; Ac 19:13
27 2Ti 4:3–4; Ro 13:13–14; 1Ki 21:9–10; Jude 4
28 Ac 13:45; 1Jn 3:12
29 Ps 1:1
30 1Pe 4:4
31 Ac 4:18; 13:45–46,50; 19:9; 1Th 2:16; Heb 10:29
32 2Ti 3:5; Mt 6:1–2,5,16; 23:14
33 Mk 8:38
34 Ps 73:14–15
35 1Co 6:5–6; Eph 5:15–17
36 Isa 5:4; 2Pe 1:8–9
37 Ro 2:23–24
38 Gal 3:1,3; Heb 6:6

114. What reasons are annexed to the third commandment?

The reasons annexed to the third commandment, in these words, [The Lord thy God,] and, [For the Lord will not hold him guiltless that taketh his name in vain,][1] are, because he is the Lord and our God, therefore his name is not to be profaned, or any way abused by us;[2] especially because he will be so far from acquitting and sparing the transgressors of this commandment, as that he will not suffer them to escape his righteous judgment;[3] albeit many such escape the censures and punishments of men.[4]

1 Ex 20:7
2 Lev 19:12
3 Eze 36:21–23; Dt 28:58–59; Zec 5:2–4
4 1Sa 2:12,17,22,24; 3:13

115. Which is the fourth commandment?

The fourth commandment is, Remember the sabbath-day, to keep it holy. Six days shalt thou labour, and do all thy work; but the seventh day is the sabbath of the Lord thy God: in it thou shalt not do any work, thou, nor thy son, nor thy daughter, thy man-servant, nor thy maid-servant, nor thy cattle, nor thy stranger that is within thy gates. For in six days the Lord made heaven and earth, the sea, and all that in them is, and rested in the seventh day: wherefore the Lord blessed the sabbath-day and hallowed it.[1]

1 Ex 20:8–11

116. What is required in the fourth commandment?

The fourth commandment requireth of all men the sanctifying or keeping holy to God such set times as he hath appointed in his word, expressly one whole day in seven; which was the seventh from the beginning of the world to the resurrection of Christ, and the first day of the week ever since, and so to continue to the end of the world; which is the Christian sabbath,[1] and in the New Testament called The Lord's day.[2]

1 Dt 5:12–14; Ge 2:2–3; 1Co 16:1–2; Mt 5:17–18; Isa 56:2,4,6–7
2 Rev 1:10

117. How is the sabbath or the Lord's day to be sanctified?

The sabbath or Lord's day is to be sanctified by an holy resting all the day,[1] not only from such works as are at all times sinful, but even from such worldly employments and recreations as are on other days lawful;[2] and making it our delight to spend the whole time (except so much of it as is to be taken up in works of necessity and mercy[3]) in the public and private exercises of God's worship:[4] and, to that end, we are to prepare our hearts, and with such foresight, diligence, and moderation, to dispose and seasonably dispatch our worldly business, that we may be the more free and fit for the duties of that day.[5]

1 Ex 20:8,10
2 Ex 16:25–28; Ne 13:15–22; Jer 17:21–22
3 Mt 11:1–13
4 Isa 58:18; 66:23; Lk 4:16; Ac 20:7; 1Co 16:1–2; Ps 92; Lev 23:3
5 Ex 20:8,56; 16:22,25–26,29; Lk 23:54; Ne 13:19

118. Why is the charge of keeping the sabbath more specially directed to governors of families, and other superiors?

The charge of keeping the sabbath is more specially directed to governors of families, and other superiors, because they are bound not only to keep it themselves, but to see that it be observed by all those that are under their charge; and because they are prone ofttimes to hinder them by employments of their own.[1]

1 Ex 20:10, 23:12; Jos 24:15; Ne 13:15,17; Jer 17:20–22

119. What are the sins forbidden in the fourth commandment?

The sins forbidden in the fourth commandment are, all omissions of the duties required,[1] all careless, negligent, and unprofitable performing of them, and being weary of them;[2] all profaning the day by idleness, and doing that which is in itself sinful;[3] and by all needless works, words, and thoughts, about our worldly employments and recreations.[4]

1 Eze 22:26
2 Ac 20:7,9; Eze 33:30–32; Am 8:5; Mal 1:13
3 Eze 23:38
4 Jer 17:24,27; Isa 58:13

120. What are the reasons annexed to the fourth commandment, the more to enforce it?

The reasons annexed to the fourth commandment, the more to enforce it, are taken from the equity of it, God allowing us six days of seven for our own affairs, and reserving but one for himself in these words, Six days shalt thou labour, and do all thy work:[1] from God's challenging a special propriety in that day, The seventh day is the sabbath of the Lord thy God:[2] from the example of God, who in six days made heaven and earth, the sea, and all that in them is, and rested the seventh day: and from that blessing which God put upon that day, not only in sanctifying it to be a day for his service, but in ordaining it to be a means of blessing to us in our sanctifying it; Wherefore the Lord blessed the sabbath-day, and hallowed it.[3]

1 Ex 20:9

2 Ex 20:10
3 Ex 20:11

121. Why is the Word Remember set in the beginning of the fourth commandment?
The word Remember is set in the beginning of the fourth commandment,[1] partly, because of the great benefit of remembering it, we being thereby helped in our preparation to keep it,[2] and, in keeping it, better to keep all the rest of the commandments,[3] and to continue a thankful remembrance of the two great benefits of creation and redemption, which contain a short abridgment of religion;[4] and partly, because we are very ready to forget it,[5] for that there is less light of nature for it,[6] and yet it restraineth our natural liberty in things at other times lawful;[7] that it cometh but once in seven days, and many worldly businesses come between, and too often take off our minds from thinking of it, either to prepare for it, or to sanctify it;[8] and that Satan with his instruments labours much to blot out the glory, and even the memory of it, to bring in all irreligion and impiety.[9]

1 Ex 20:8
2 Ex 16:23; Lk 23:54,56; Mk 15:42; Ne 13:19
3 Ps 92:13–14; Eze 20:12,19–20
4 Ge 2:2–3; Ps 118:22,24; Ac 4:10–11; Rev 1:10
5 Eze 22:26
6 Ne 9:14
7 Ex 34:21
8 Dt 5:14–15; Am 8:5
9 La 1:7; Jer 17:21–23; Ne 13:15–23

122. What is the sum of the six commandments which contain our duty to man?
The sum of the six commandments which contain our duty to man, is, to love our neighbour as ourselves,[1] and to do to others what we would have them to do to us.[2]

1 Mt 22:39
2 Mt 7:12

123. Which is the fifth commandment?
The fifth commandment is, Honour thy father and thy mother: that thy days may be long upon the land which the Lord thy God giveth thee.[1]

1 Ex 20:12

124. Who are meant by father and mother in the fifth commandment?
By father and mother, in the fifth commandment, are meant, not only natural parents,[1] but all superiors in age[2] and gifts;[3] and especially such as, by God's ordinance, are over us in place of authority, whether in family,[4] church,[5] or commonwealth.[6]

1 Pr 23:22,25; Eph 6:1–2
2 1Ti 5:1–2
3 Ge 4:20–22; 45:8
4 2Ki 5:13
5 2Ki 2:12; 13:14; Gal 4:19
6 Isa 49:23

125. Why are superiors styled Father and Mother?
Superiors are styled Father and Mother, both to teach them in all duties toward their inferiors, like natural parents, to express love and tenderness to them, according to their several relations;[1] and to work inferiors to a greater willingness and cheerfulness in performing their duties to their superiors, as to their parents.[2]

1 Eph 6:4; 2Co 12:14; 1Th 2:7–8,11; Nu 11:11–12
2 1Co 4:14–16; 2Ki 5:13

126. What is the general scope of the fifth commandment?
The general scope of the fifth commandment is, the performance of those duties which we mutually owe in our several relations, as inferiors, superiors, or equals.[1]

1 Eph 5:21; 1Pe 2:17; Ro 12:10

127. What is the honour that inferiors owe to their superiors?
The honour which inferiors owe to their superiors is, all due reverence in heart,[1] word,[2] and behaviour;[3] prayer and thanksgiving for them;[4] imitation of their virtues and graces;[5] willing obedience to their lawful commands and counsels;[6] due submission to their corrections;[7] fidelity to,[8] defence,[9] and maintenance of their persons and authority, according to their several ranks, and the nature of their places;[10] bearing with their infirmities, and covering them in love,[11] that so they may be an honour to them and to their government.[12]

1 Mal 1:6; Lev 19:3
2 Pr 31:28; 1Pe 3:6
3 Lev 19:32; 1Ki 2:19
4 1Ti 2:1–2
5 Heb 13:7; Php 3:17
6 Eph 6:1–2,6–7; 1Pe 2:13–14; Ro 13:1–5; Heb 13:17; Pr 4:3–4; 23:22; Ex 18:19,24
7 Heb 12:9; 1Pe 2:18–20
8 Tit 2:9–10
9 1Sa 26:15–16; 2Sa 18:3; Est 6:2
10 Mt 22:21; Ro 13:6–7; 1Ti 5:17–18; Gal 6:6; Ge 45:11; 47:12
11 1Pe 2:18; Pr 23:22; Ge 9:23
12 Ps 127:3–5; Pr 31:23

128. What are the sins of inferiors against their superiors?
The sins of inferiors against their superiors are, all neglect of the duties required toward them;[1] envying at,[2] contempt of,[3] and rebellion[4] against, their persons[5] and places,[6] in their lawful counsels,[7] commands, and corrections;[8] cursing, mocking[9] and all such refractory and scandalous carriage, as proves a shame and dishonour to them and their government.[10]

1 Mt 15:4–6
2 Nu 11:28–29
3 1Sa 8:7; Isa 3:5
4 2Sa 15:1–12
5 Ex 24:15
6 1Sa 10:27
7 1Sa 2:25
8 Dt 21:18–21
9 Pr 30:11,17
10 Pr 19:26

129. What is required of superiors towards their inferiors?
It is required of superiors, according to that power they receive from God, and that relation wherein they stand, to love,[1] pray for,[2] and bless their inferiors;[3] to instruct,[4] counsel, and admonish them;[5] countenancing,[6] commending,[7] and rewarding such as do well;[8] and discountenancing,[9] reproving, and chastising such as do ill;[10] protecting,[11] and providing for them all things necessary for soul[12] and body:[13] and by grave, wise, holy, and exemplary carriage, to procure glory to God,[14] honour to themselves,[15] and so to preserve that authority which God hath put upon them.[16]

1 Col 3:19; Tit 2:4
2 1Sa 12:23; Job 1:5
3 1Ki 8:55–56; Heb 7:7; Ge 49:28
4 Dt 6:6–7
5 Eph 6:4
6 1Pe 3:7
7 1Pe 2:14; Ro 13:3
8 Est 6:3
9 Ro 13:3–4
10 Pr 29:15; 1Pe 2:14
11 Job 29:13–16; Isa 1:10,17
12 Eph 6:4
13 1Ti 5:8
14 1Ti 4:12; Tit 2:3–5
15 1Ki 3:28
16 Tit 2:15

130. What are the sins of superiors?
The sins of superiors are, besides the neglect of the duties required of them,[1] and inordinate seeking of themselves,[2] their own glory,[3] ease, profit, or pleasure;[4] commanding things unlawful,[5] or not in the power of inferiors to perform;[6] counseling,[7] encouraging,[8] or favouring them in that which is evil;[9] dissuading, discouraging, or discountenancing them in that which is good;[10] correcting them unduly;[11] careless exposing, or leaving them to wrong, temptation, and danger;[12] provoking them to wrath;[13] or any way dishonouring themselves, or lessening their authority, by an unjust, indiscreet, rigorous, or remiss behaviour.[14]

1 Eze 34:2–4

2 Php 2:21
3 Jn 5:44; 7:18
4 Isa 56:10–11; Dt 17:17
5 Da 3:4–6; Ac 4:17–18
6 Ex 5:10–18; Mt 23:2,4
7 Mt 14:8; Mk 6:24
8 2Sa 13:28
9 1Sa 3:13
10 Jn 7:46–49; Col 3:21; Ex 5:17
11 1Pe 2:18–20; Heb 12:10; Dt 25:3
12 Ge 38:11,26; Ac 18:17
13 Eph 6:4
14 Ge 9:21; 1Ki 1:6; 12:13–16; 1Sa 2:29–31

131. What are the duties of equals?
The duties of equals are, to regard the dignity and worth of each other,[1] in giving honour to go one before another;[2] and to rejoice in each others' gifts and advancement, as their own.[3]

1 1Pe 2:17
2 Ro 12:10
3 Ro 12:15–16; Php 2:3–4

132. What are the sins of equals?
The sins of equals are, besides the neglect of the duties required,[1] the undervaluing of the worth,[2] envying the gifts,[3] grieving at the advancement or prosperity one of another;[4] and usurping pre-eminence one over another.[5]

1 Ro 13:8
2 2Ti 3:3
3 Ac 7:9; Gal 5:26
4 Nu 12:2; Est 6:12–13
5 3Jn 9; Lk 22:24

133. What is the reason annexed to the fifth commandment, the more to enforce it?
The reason annexed to the fifth commandment, in these words, That thy days may be long upon the land which the Lord thy God giveth thee,[1] is an express promise of long life and prosperity, as far as it shall serve for God's glory and their own good, to all such as keep this commandment.[2]

1 Ex 20:12
2 Dt 5:16; 1Ki 8:25; Eph 6:2–3

134. Which is the sixth commandment?
The sixth commandment is, Thou shalt not kill.[1]

1 Ex 20:13

135. What are the duties required in the sixth commandment?
The duties required in the sixth commandment are all careful studies, and lawful endeavors, to preserve the life of ourselves[1] and others[2] by resisting all thoughts and purposes,[3] subduing all passions,[4] and avoiding all occasions,[5] temptations,[6] and practices, which tend to the unjust taking away the life of any;[7] by just defence thereof against violence,[8] patient bearing of the hand of God,[9] quietness of mind,[10] cheerfulness of spirit;[11] a sober use of meat,[12] drink,[13] physick,[14] sleep,[15] labour,[16] and recreations;[17] by charitable thoughts,[18] love,[19] compassion,[20] meekness, gentleness, kindness;[21] peaceable,[22] mild and courteous speeches and behaviour;[23] forbearance, readiness to be reconciled, patient bearing and forgiving of injuries, and requiting good for evil;[24] comforting and succouring the distressed and protecting and defending the innocent.[25]

1 Eph 5:28–29
2 1Ki 18:4
3 Jer 26:15–16; Ac 23:12,16–17,21,27
4 Eph 4:26–27
5 2Sa 2:22; Dt 22:8
6 Mt 4:6–7; Pr 1:10–11,15–16
7 1Sa 24:12; 26:9–11; Ge 37:21–22
8 Ps 82:4; Pr 24:11–12; 1Sa 14:45
9 Jas 5:7–11; Heb 12:9
10 1Th 4:11; 1Pe 3:3–4; Ps 37:8–11
11 Pr 17:22
12 Pr 25:16,27
13 1Ti 5:23
14 Isa 38:21
15 Ps 127:2
16 Ecc 5:12; 2Th 3:10,12; Pr 16:20
17 Ecc 3:4,11
18 1Sa 19:4–5; 22:13–14
19 Ro 13:10
20 Lk 10:33–34
21 Col 3:12–13
22 Jas 3:17
23 1Pe 3:8–11; Pr 15:1; Jdg 8:1–3
24 Mt 5:24; Eph 5:2,32; Ro 12:17,20
25 1Th 5:14; Job 31:19–20; Mt 25:35–36; Pr 31:8–9

136. What are the sins forbidden in the sixth commandment?
The sins forbidden in the sixth commandment are, all taking away the life of ourselves,[1] or of others,[2] except in case of public justice,[3] lawful war,[4] or necessary defence;[5] the neglecting or withdrawing the lawful and necessary means of preservation of life;[6] sinful anger,[7] hatred,[8] envy,[9] desire of revenge;[10] all excessive passions,[11] distracting cares;[12] immoderate use of meat, drink,[13] labor,[14] and recreations;[15] provoking words,[16] oppression,[17] quarreling,[18] striking, wounding,[19] and whatsoever else tends to the destruction of the life of any.[20]

1 Ac 16:28
2 Ge 9:6
3 Nu 35:31,33
4 Jer 48:10; Dt 20:1
5 Ex 22:2–3
6 Mt 25:42–43; Jas 2:15–16; Ecc 6:1–2
7 Mt 5:22
8 1Jn 3:15; Lev 19:17
9 Pr 14:30
10 Ro 12:19
11 Eph 4:31
12 Mt 6:31,34
13 Lk 21:34; Ro 13:13
14 Ecc 2:22–23; 12:12
15 Isa 5:12
16 Pr 12:18; 15:1
17 Eze 18:18; Ex 1:14
18 Gal 5:15; Pr 23:29
19 Nu 35:16–18,21
20 Ex 21:18–36

137. Which is the seventh commandment?
The seventh commandment is, Thou shalt not commit adultery.[1]

1 Ex 20:14

138. What are the duties required in the seventh commandment?
The duties required in the seventh commandment are, chastity in body, mind, affections,[1] words,[2] and behavior;[3] and the preservation of it in ourselves and others;[4] watchfulness over the eyes and all the senses;[5] temperance,[6] keeping of chaste company,[7] modesty in apparel;[8] marriage by those that have not the gift of continency,[9] conjugal love,[10] and cohabitation;[11] diligent labor in our callings;[12] shunning all occasions of uncleanliness, and resisting temptations thereunto.[13]

1 1Th 4:4; Job 31:1; 1Co 7:34
2 Col 4:6
3 1Pe 2:3
4 1Co 7:2,35–36
5 Job 31:1
6 Ac 24:24–25
7 Pr 2:16–20
8 1Ti 2:9
9 1Co 7:2,9
10 Pr 5:19–20
11 1Pe 3:7
12 Pr 3:11,27–28
13 Pr 5:8; Ge 39:8–10

139. What are the sins forbidden in the seventh commandment?
The sins forbidden in the seventh commandment, besides the neglect of the duties required,[1] are, adultery, fornication,[2] rape, incest,[3] sodomy, and all unnatural lusts;[4] all unclean imaginations, thoughts, purposes, and affections;[5] all corrupt or filthy communications, or listening thereunto;[6] wanton looks,[7] impudent or light behaviour, immodest apparel;[8] prohibiting of lawful,[9] and dispensing with unlawful marriages;[10] allowing, tolerating, keeping of stews, and resorting to them;[11] entangling vows of single life,[12] undue delay of marriage,[13] hav-

ing more wives or husbands than one at the same time;[14] unjust divorce,[15] or desertion;[16] idleness, gluttony, drunkenness,[17] unchaste company;[18] lascivious songs, books, pictures, dancings, stage plays;[19] and all other provocations to, or acts of uncleanness, either in ourselves or others.[20]

1 Pr 5:7
2 Heb 13:4; Gal 5:19
3 2Sa 13:14; 1Co 5:1
4 Ro 1:24,26–27; Lev 20:15–16
5 Mt 5:28; 15:19; Col 3:5
6 Eph 5:3–4; Pr 7:5,21–22
7 Isa 3:16; 2Pe 2:14
8 Pr 7:10,13
9 1Ti 4:3
10 Lev 18:1–21; Mk 6:18; Mal 2:11–12
11 1Ki 15:12; 2Ki 23:7; Dt 23:17–18; Lev 19:29; Jer 5:7; Pr 7:24–27
12 Mt 19:10–11
13 1Co 7:7–9; Ge 38:26
14 Mal 2:14–15; Mt 19:5
15 Mal 2:16; Mt 5:32
16 1Co 7:12–13
17 Eze 16:49; Pr 23:30–33
18 Ge 39:19; Pr 5:8
19 Eph 5:4; Eze 23:14–16; Isa 3:16; 23:15–17; Mk 6:22; Ro 13:13; 1Pe 4:3
20 2Ki 9:30; Jer 4:30; Eze 23:40

140. Which is the eighth commandment?
The eighth commandment is, Thou shalt not steal.[1]

1 Ex 20:15

141. What are the duties required in the eighth commandment?
The duties required in the eighth commandment are, truth, faithfulness, and justice in contracts and commerce between man and man;[1] restitution of goods unlawfully detained from the right owners thereof;[2] giving and lending freely, according to our abilities, and the necessities of others;[3] moderation of our judgments, wills, and affections concerning worldly goods;[4] a provident care and study to get,[5] keep, use, and dispose these things which are necessary and convenient for the sustentation of our nature, and suitable to our condition;[6] a lawful calling,[7] and diligence in it;[8] frugality;[9] avoiding unnecessary law-suits,[10] and suretiship, or other like engagements;[11] and an endeavor, by all just and lawful means, to procure, preserve, and further the wealth and outward estate of others, as well as our own.[12]

1 Ps 15:2,4; Zec 7:4,10; 8:16–17
2 Lev 6:2–5; Lk 19:8
3 Lk 6:30,38; 1Jn 3:17; Eph 4:28; Gal 6:10
4 1Ti 6:6–9; Gal 6:14
5 1Ti 5:8
6 Pr 27:23–27; Ecc 2:24; 3:12–13; 1Ti 6:17–18; Isa 38:1; Mt 11:8
7 1Co 7:20; Ge 2:15; Ge 3:19
8 Eph 4:28; Pr 10:4
9 Jn 6:12; Pr 21:20
10 1Co 6:1–9
11 Pr 6:1–6; 11:15
12 Lev 25:35; Dt 22:1–4; Ex 23:4–5; Ge 47:14,20; Php 2:4; Mt 22:39

142. What are the sins forbidden in the eighth commandment?
The sins forbidden in the eighth commandment, besides the neglect of the duties required,[1] are, theft,[2] robbery,[3] man-stealing,[4] and receiving any thing that is stolen;[5] fraudulent dealing,[6] false weights and measures,[7] removing landmarks,[8] injustice and unfaithfulness in contracts between man and man,[9] or in matters of trust;[10] oppression,[11] extortion,[12] usury,[13] bribery,[14] vexatious law-suits,[15] unjust inclosures and depopulations;[16] ingrossing commodities to enhance the price;[17] unlawful callings,[18] and all other unjust or sinful ways of taking or withholding from our neighbour what belongs to him, or of enriching ourselves;[19] covetousness;[20] inordinate prizing and affecting worldly goods;[21] distrustful and distracting cares and studies in getting, keeping, and using them;[22] envying at the prosperity of others;[23] as likewise idleness,[24] prodigality, wasteful gaming; and all other ways whereby we do unduly prejudice our own outward estate,[25] and defrauding ourselves of the due use and comfort of that estate which God hath given us.[26]

1 Jas 2:15–16; 1Jn 3:17
2 Eph 4:28
3 Ps 62:10
4 1Ti 1:10
5 Pr 29:24; Ps 50:18
6 1Th 4:6
7 Pr 11:1; 20:10
8 Dt 19:14; Pr 23:10
9 Am 8:5; Ps 37:21
10 Lk 16:10–12
11 Eze 22:29; Lev 25:17
12 Mt 23:25; Eze 22:12
13 Ps 15:5
14 Job 15:34
15 1Co 6:6–8; Pr 3:29–30
16 Isa 5:8; Mic 2:2
17 Pr 11:26
18 Ac 19:19,24–25
19 Job 20:19; Jas 5:4; Pr 21:6
20 Lk 12:15
21 1Ti 6:5; Col 3:2; Ps 62:10
22 Mt 6:25,31,34; Ecc 5:12
23 Ps 37:1,7; 73:3
24 2Th 3:11; Pr 18:9
25 Pr 21:17; 23:20–21; 28:19
26 Ecc 4:8; 6:2; 1Ti 5:8

143. Which is the ninth commandment?
The ninth commandment is, Thou shalt not bear false witness against thy neighbor.[1]

1 Ex 20:16

144. What are the duties required in the ninth commandment?
The duties required in the ninth commandment are, the preserving and promoting of truth between man and man,[1] and the good name of our neighbour, as well as our own;[2] appearing and standing for the truth;[3] and from the heart,[4] sincerely,[5] freely,[6] clearly,[7] and fully,[8] speaking the truth, and only the truth, in matters of judgment and justice,[9] and in all other things whatsoever;[10] a charitable esteem of our neighbours;[11] loving, desiring, and rejoicing in their good name;[12] sorrowing for,[13] and covering of their infirmities;[14] freely acknowledging of their gifts and graces,[15] defending their innocency;[16] a ready receiving of a good report,[17] and unwillingness to admit of an evil report,[18] concerning them; discouraging tale-bearers,[19] flatterers,[20] and slanderers;[21] love and care of our own good name, and defending it when need requireth;[22] keeping of lawful promises;[23] studying and practicing of whatsoever things are true, honest, lovely, and of good report.[24]

1 Zec 8:16
2 3Jn 12
3 Pr 31:8–9
4 Ps 15:2
5 2Ch 19:9
6 1Sa 19:4–5
7 Jos 7:19
8 2Sa 14:18–20
9 Lev 19:15; Pr 14:5,25
10 2Co 1:17–18; Eph 4:25
11 Heb 6:9; 1Co 13:7
12 Ro 1:8; 2Jn 4; 3Jn 3–4
13 2Co 2:4; 12:21
14 Pr 17:9; 1Pe 4:8
15 1Co 1:4–5,7; 2Ti 1:4–5
16 1Sa 22:14
17 1Co 13:6
18 Ps 15:3
19 Pr 25:23
20 Pr 26:24–25
21 Ps 101:5
22 Pr 22:1; Jn 8:49
23 Ps 15:4
24 Php 4:8

145. What are the sins forbidden in the ninth commandment?
The sins forbidden in the ninth commandment are, all prejudicing the truth, and the good name of our neighbours, as well as our own,[1] especially in public judicature;[2] giving false evidence,[3] suborning false witnesses,[4] wittingly appearing and pleading for an evil cause, out-facing and overbearing the truth;[5] passing unjust sentence,[6] calling evil good, and good

evil; rewarding the wicked according to the work of the righteous, and the righteous according to the work of the wicked;[7] forgery,[8] concealing the truth, undue silence in a just cause,[9] and holding our peace when iniquity calleth for either a reproof from ourselves,[10] or complaint to others;[11] speaking the truth unseasonably,[12] or maliciously to a wrong end,[13] or perverting it to a wrong meaning,[14] or in doubtful or equivocal expressions, to the prejudice of truth or justice;[15] speaking untruth,[16] lying,[17] slandering,[18] backbiting,[19] talebearing,[20] whispering,[21] scoffing,[22] reviling,[23] rash,[24] harsh,[25] and partial censuring;[26] misconstructing intentions, words, and actions;[27] flattering,[28] vain-glorious boasting;[29] thinking or speaking too highly or too meanly of ourselves or others;[30] denying the gifts and graces of God;[31] aggravating smaller faults;[32] hiding, excusing, or extenuating of sins, when called to a free confession;[33] unnecessary discovering of infirmities;[34] raising false rumors,[35] receiving and countenancing evil reports,[36] and stopping our ears against just defense;[37] evil suspicion;[38] envying or grieving at the deserved credit of any,[39] endeavoring or desiring to impair it,[40] rejoicing in their disgrace and infamy;[41] scornful contempt,[42] fond admiration;[43] breach of lawful promises;[44] neglecting such things as are of good report,[45] and practicing, or not avoiding ourselves, or not hindering what we can in others, such things as procure an ill name.[46]

1 1Sa 17:28; 2Sa 1:9–10,15–16; 16:3
2 Lev 19:15; Hab 1:4
3 Pr 6:16,19; 19:5
4 Ac 6:13
5 Jer 9:3,5; Ac 24:2,5; Ps 12:3–4; 52:1–4
6 Pr 17:15; 1Ki 21:9–14
7 Isa 5:23
8 Ps 119:69; Lk 16:5–7; 19:8
9 Lev 5:1; Dt 13:8; Ac 5:3,8–9; 2Ti 4:6
10 1Ki 1:6; Lev 19:17
11 Isa 59:4
12 Pr 29:11
13 1Sa 22:9–10; Ps 52:1–5
14 Ps 56:5; Jn 2:19; Mt 26:60–61
15 Ge 3:5; 26:7,9
16 Isa 59:13
17 Lev 19:11; Col 3:9
18 Ps 50:20
19 Jas 4:11; Jer 38:4
20 Lev 19:19
21 Ro 1:29–30
22 Ge 21:9; Gal 4:29
23 1Co 6:10
24 Mt 7:1
25 Ac 28:4
26 Ge 38:24; Ro 2:1
27 Ne 6:6–8; Ro 3:8; Ps 69:10; 1Sa 1:13–15; 2Sa 10:3
28 Ps 12:2–3
29 2Ti 3:2
30 Lk 18:9,11; Ro 12:16; 1Co 4:6; Ac 12:22; Ex 4:10–14
31 Job 4:6; 27:5,6
32 Mt 7:3–5
33 Pr 28:13; 30:20; Ge 3:12–13; 4:9; Jer 2:35; 2Ki 5:25
34 Ge 9:22; Pr 25:9–10
35 Ex 23:1
36 Pr 29:12
37 Ac 7:56–57; Job 31:13–14
38 1Co 13:5; 1Ti 6:4
39 Nu 11:29; Mt 21:15
40 Ezr 4:12–13
41 Jer 48:27
42 Ps 35:15–16,21; Mt 27:28–29
43 Jude 16; Ac 12:22
44 Ro 1:31; 2Ti 3:3
45 1Sa 2:24
46 1Sa 2:24

146. Which is the tenth commandment?
The tenth commandment is, Thou shalt not covet thy neighbour's house, thou shall not covet they neighbour's wife, nor his man-servant, nor his maid-servant, nor his ox, nor his ass, nor any thing that is thy neighbour's.[1]

1 2Sa 13:12–13; Pr 5:8–9; 6:33

147. What are the duties required in the tenth commandment?
The duties required in the tenth commandment are, such a full contentment with our own condition,[1] and such a charitable frame of the whole soul toward our neighbour, as that all our inward motions and affections touching him, tend unto, and further all that good which is his.[2]

1 Heb 13:5; 1Ti 6:6
2 Job 31:29; Ro 12:15; Ps 122:7–9; 1Ti 1:5; Est 10:3; 1Co 13:4–7

148. What are the sins forbidden in the tenth commandment?
The sins forbidden in the tenth commandment are, discontentment with our own estate;[1] envying[2] and grieving at the good of our neighbour,[3] together with all inordinate motions and affections to any thing that is his.[4]

1 1Ki 21:4; Est 5:13; 1Co 10:10
2 Gal 5:26; Jas 3:14,16
3 Ps 112:9–10; Ne 2:10
4 Ro 7:7–8; 13:9; Col 3:5; Dt 5:21

149. Is any man able perfectly to keep the commandments of God?
No man is able, either of himself,[1] or by any grace received in this life, perfectly to keep the commandments of God;[2] but doth daily break them in thought,[3] word, and deed.[4]

1 Jas 3:2; Jn 15:5; Ro 8:3
2 Ecc 7:20; 1Jn 1:8,10; Gal 5:17; Ro 7:18–19
3 Ge 6:5; 8:21
4 Ro 3:9–19; Jas 3:2–13

150. Are all transgressions of the law of God equally heinous in themselves, and in the sight of God?
All transgressions of the law of God are not equally heinous: but some sins in themselves, and by reason of several aggravations, are more heinous in the sight of God than others.[1]

1 Jn 19:11; Eze 8:6,13,15; 1Jn 5:16; Ps 73:17,32,56

151. What are those aggravations that make some sins more heinous than others?
Sins receive their aggravations,

1. From the persons offending[1] they be of riper age,[2] greater experience of grace,[3] eminent for profession,[4] gifts,[5] place,[6] office,[7] guide to others,[8] and whose example is likely to be followed by others.[9]

2. From the parties offended:[10] if immediately against God,[11] his attributes,[12] and worship;[13] against Christ, and his grace;[14] the Holy Spirit,[15] his witness,[16] and workings[17] against superiors, men of eminency,[18] and such as we stand especially related and engaged unto;[19] against any of the saints,[20] particularly weak brethren,[21] the souls of them, or any other,[22] and the common good of all or many.[23]

3. From the nature and quality of the offense:[24] if it be against the express letter of the law,[25] break many commandments, contain in it many sins:[26] if not only conceived in the heart, but breaks forth in words and actions,[27] scandalize others,[28] and admit of no reparation:[29] if against means,[30] mercies,[31] judgments,[32] light of nature,[33] conviction of conscience,[34] public or private admonition,[35] censures of the church,[36] civil punishments;[37] and our prayers, purposes, promises,[38] vows,[39] covenants,[40] and engagements to God of men:[41] if done deliberately,[42] wilfully,[43] presumptuously,[44] impudently,[45] boastingly,[46] maliciously,[47] frequently,[48] obstinately,[49] with delight,[50] continuance,[51] or relapsing after repentance.[52]

4. From circumstances of time[53] and place:[54] if on the Lord's day,[55] or other times of divine worship;[56] or immediately before[57] or after these,[58] or other helps to prevent or remedy such miscarriages;[59] if in public, or in the presence of others, who are thereby likely to be provoked or defiled.[60]

1 Jer 2:8
2 Job 32:7,9; Ecc 4:13
3 1Ki 11:4,9
4 2Sa 12:14; 1Co 5:1
5 Jas 4:17; Lk 12:47–48
6 Jer 5:4–5
7 2Sa 12:7–9; Eze 8:11–12

8 Ro 2:17–24
9 Gal 2:11–14
10 Mt 21:38–39
11 1Sa 2:25; Ac 5:4; Ps 5:4
12 Ro 2:4
13 Mal 1:8,14
14 Heb 2:2–3; Heb 7:25
15 Heb 10:29; Mt 12:31–32
16 Eph 4:30
17 Heb 6:4–6
18 Jude 8; Nu 12:8–9; Isa 3:5
19 Pr 30:17; 2Co 12:15; Ps 55:12–15
20 Zep 2:8,10–11; Mt 18:6; 1Co 6:8
21 1Co 8:11–12; Ro 14:13,15,21
22 Eze 13:19; 1Co 8:12; Rev 18:12–13; Mt 23:15
23 1Th 2:15–16; Jos 22:20
24 Pr 6:30–33
25 Ezr 9:10–12; 1Ki 11:9–10
26 Col 3:5; 1Ti 6:10; Pr 5:8–12; 6:32–33; Jos 7:21
27 Jas 1:14–15; Mt 5:22; Mic 2:1
28 Mt 18:7; Ro 2:23–24
29 Dt 22:22,28–29; Pr 7:32–35
30 Mt 11:21–24; Jn 15:22
31 Isa 1:3; Dt 32:6
32 Am 4:8–11; Jer 5:3
33 Ro 1:26–27
34 Ro 1:32; Da 5:22; Tit 3:10–11
35 Pr 29:1
36 Tit 3:10; Mt 18:17
37 Pr 23:35; 27:22
38 Ps 73:34–37; Jer 2:20; 45:5–6,20–21
39 Ecc 5:4–6; Pr 20:25
40 Lev 26:25
41 Pr 2:17; Eze 7:18–19
42 Ps 36:4
43 Jer 6:16
44 Nu 15:30; Ex 21:14
45 Jer 3:3; Pr 7:13
46 Ps 52:1
47 3Jn 10
48 Nu 15:22
49 Zec 7:11–12
50 Pr 2:14
51 Isa 57:17
52 Jer 34:8–11; 2Pe 2:20–22
53 2Ki 5:26
54 Jer 7:10; Isa 26:10
55 Eze 23:37–39
56 Isa 58:3–5; Nu 25:6–7
57 1Co 11:20–21
58 Jer 7:8–10; Pr 7:14–15; Jn 13:27,30
59 Ezr 9:13–14
60 2Sa 16:22; 1Sa 2:22–24

152. What doth every sin deserve at the hands of God?
Every sin, even the least, being against the sovereignty,[1] goodness,[2] and holiness of God,[3] and against his righteous law,[4] deserveth his wrath and curse,[5] both in this life,[6] and that which is to come;[7] and cannot be expiated but by the blood of Christ.[8]

1 Jas 2:10–11
2 Ex 20:1–2
3 Hab 1:13; Lev 10:3; 11:44–45
4 1Jn 3:4; Ro 7:12
5 Eph 5:6; Gal 3:10
6 La 3:39; Dt 20:15–20
7 Mt 25:41
8 Heb 9:22; 1Pe 1:18–19

153. What doth God require of us, that we may escape his wrath and curse due to us by reason of the transgression of the law?
That we may escape the wrath and curse of God due to us by reason of the transgression of the law, he requireth of us repentance toward God, and faith toward our Lord Jesus Christ,[1] and the diligent use of the outward means whereby Christ communicates to us the benefits of his mediation.[2]

1 Ac 16:30–31; 20:21; Mt 3:7–8; Lk 13:3,5; Jn 3:16,18
2 Pr 2:1–5; 8:33–36

154. What are the outward means whereby Christ communicates to us the benefits of his mediation?
The outward and ordinary means whereby Christ communicates to his church the benefits of his mediation, are all his ordinances; especially the word, sacraments, and prayer; all which are made effectual to the elect for their salvation.[1]

1 Mt 28:19–20; Ac 2:42,46–47

155. How is the word made effectual to salvation?
The Spirit of God maketh the reading, but especially the preaching of the word, an effectual means of enlightening,[1] convincing, and humbling sinners;[2] of driving them out of themselves, and drawing them unto Christ;[3] of conforming them to his image,[4] and subduing them to his will;[5] of strengthening them against temptations and corruptions;[6] of building them up in grace,[7] and establishing their hearts in holiness and comfort through faith unto salvation.[8]

1 Ne 8:8; Ac 26:18; Ps 19:8
2 1Co 14:24–25; 2Ch 34:18–19,26–28
3 Ac 2:37,41; 8:27–30,35–38
4 2Co 3:18
5 2Co 10:4–6; Ro 6:17
6 Mt 4:4,7,10; Eph 6:16–17; Ps 19:11; 1Co 10:11
7 Ac 20:32; 2Ti 3:15–17
8 Ro 1:16; 10:13–17; 15:4; 16:25; 1Th 3:2,10–11,13

156. Is the word of God to be read by all?
Although all are not to be permitted to read the word publicly to the congregation,[1] yet all sorts of people are bound to read it apart by themselves,[2] and with their families:[3] to which end, the holy scriptures are to be translated out of the original into vulgar languages.[4]

1 Dt 31:9,11–13; Ne 8:2–3; 9:3–5
2 Dt 17:19; Rev 1:8; Jn 5:39; Isa 34:16
3 Dt 6:6–9; Ge 18:17,19; Ps 78:5–7
4 1Co 14:6,9,11–12,15–16,24,27–28

157. How is the word of God to be read?
The holy scriptures are to be read with an high and reverent esteem of them;[1] with a firm persuasion that they are the very word of God,[2] and that he only can enable us to understand them;[3] with desire to know, believe, and obey the will of God revealed in them;[4] with diligence,[5] and attention to the matter and scope of them;[6] with meditation,[7] application,[8] self-denial,[9] and prayer.[10]

1 Ps 19:10; Ne 8:3–6,10; Ex 24:7; 2Ch 34:27; Isa 66:2
2 2Pe 1:19–21
3 Lk 24:45; 2Co 3:13–16
4 Dt 17:10,20
5 Ac 17:11
6 Ac 8:30,34; Lk 10:26–28
7 Ps 1:2; 119:97
8 2Ch 34:21
9 Pr 3:5; Dt 33:3
10 Pr 2:1–6; Ps 119:18; Ne 7:6,8

158. By whom is the word of God to be preached?
The word of God is to be preached only by such as are sufficiently gifted,[1] and also duly approved and called to that office.[2]

1 1Ti 3:2,6; Eph 4:8–11; Hos 4:6; Mal 2:7; 2Co 3:6
2 Jer 14:15; Ro 10:15; Heb 5:4; 1Co 12:28–29; 1Ti 3:10; 4:14; 5:22

159. How is the word of God to be preached by those that are called thereunto?
They that are called to labour in the ministry of the word, are to preach sound doctrine,[1] diligently,[2] in season and out of season;[3] plainly,[4] not in the enticing words of man's wisdom, but in demonstration of the Spirit, and of power;[5] faithfully,[6] making known the whole counsel of God;[7] wisely,[8] applying themselves to the necessities and capacities of the hearers;[9] zealously,[10] and fervent love to God[11] and the souls of his people;[12] sincerely,[13] aiming at his glory,[14] and their conversion,[15] edification,[16] and salvation.[17]

1 Tit 2:1,8
2 Ac 18:25
3 2Ti 4:2
4 1Co 14:19
5 1Co 2:4
6 Jer 23:28; 1Co 4:1–2

7 Ac 20:27
8 Col 1:28; 2Ti 2:15
9 1Co 3:2; Heb 5:12–14; Lk 12:42
10 Ac 18:25
11 2Co 5:13–14; Php 1:15–17
12 Col 4:12; 2Co 12:15
13 2Co 2:17; 4:2
14 1Th 2:4–6; Jn 7:18
15 1Co 9:19–22
16 2Co 12:19; Eph 4:12
17 1Ti 4:16; Ac 26:16–18

160. What is required of those that hear the word preached?
It is required of those that hear the word preached, that they attend upon it with diligence,[1] preparation,[2] and prayer;[3] examine what they hear by the scriptures;[4] receive the truth with faith,[5] love,[6] meekness,[7] and readiness of mind,[8] as the word of God;[9] meditate,[10] and confer of it;[11] hide it in their hearts,[12] and bring forth the fruit of it in their lives.[13]

1 Pr 8:34
2 1Pe 2:1–2; Lk 8:18
3 Ps 119:18; Eph 6:18–19
4 Ac 17:11
5 Heb 4:2
6 2Th 2:10
7 Jas 1:21
8 Ac 17:11
9 1Th 2:13
10 Lk 9:44; Heb 2:1
11 Lk 24:14; Dt 6:6–7
12 Pr 2:1; Ps 119:11
13 Lk 8:15; Jas 1:25

161. How do the sacraments become effectual means of salvation?
The sacraments become effectual means of salvation, not by any power in themselves, or any virtue derived from the piety or intention of him by whom they are administered, but only by the working of the Holy Ghost, and the blessing of Christ, by whom they are instituted.[1]

1 1Pe 3:21; Ac 8:13,23; 1Co 3:6–7; 12:13

162. What is a sacrament?
A sacrament is an holy ordinance instituted by Christ in his church,[1] to signify, seal, and exhibit[2] unto those that are within the covenant of grace,[3] the benefits of his mediation;[4] to strengthen and increase their faith, and all other graces;[5] to oblige them to obedience;[6] to testify and cherish their love and communion one with another;[7] and to distinguish them from those that are without.[8]

1 Ge 17:7,10; Ex 12; Mt 26:26–28; 28:19
2 Ro 4:11; 1Co 11:24–25
3 Ro 15:8; Ex 12:48
4 Ac 2:38; 1Co 10:16
5 Ro 4:11; Gal 3:27
6 Ro 6:3–4; 1Co 10:21
7 Eph 4:2–5; 1Co 12:13
8 Eph 2:11–12; Ge 34:14

163. What are the parts of the sacrament?
The parts of the sacrament are two; the one an outward and sensible sign, used according to Christ's own appointment; the other an inward and spiritual grace thereby signified.[1]

1 Mt 3:11; 1Pe 3:21; Ro 2:28–29

164. How many sacraments hath Christ instituted in his church under the New Testament?
Under the New Testament Christ hath instituted in his church only two sacraments, baptism and the Lord's supper.[1]

1 Mt 26:26–28; 28:19; 1Co 11:20,23

165. What is Baptism?
Baptism is a sacrament of the New Testament, wherein Christ hath ordained the washing with water in the name of the Father, and of the Son, and of the Holy Ghost,[1] to be a sign and seal of ingrafting into himself,[2] of remission of sins by his blood,[3] and regeneration by his Spirit;[4] of adoption,[5] and resurrection unto everlasting life;[6] and whereby the parties baptized are solemnly admitted into the visible church,[7] and enter into an open and professed engagement to be wholly and only the Lord's.[8]

1 Mt 28:19
2 Gal 3:27
3 Mk 1:4; Rev 1:5
4 Tit 3:5; Eph 5:26
5 Gal 3:26–27
6 1Co 15:29; Ro 6:5
7 1Co 12:13
8 Ro 6:4

166. Unto whom is baptism to be administered?
Baptism is not to be administered to any that are out of the visible church, and so strangers from the covenant of promise, till they profess their faith in Christ, and obedience to him,[1] but infants descending from parents, either both, or but one of them, professing faith in Christ, and obedience to him, are in that respect within the covenant, and to be baptized.[2]

1 Ac 2:38; 8:36–37
2 Ge 17:7,9; Gal 3:9; Col 2:11–12; Ac 2:38–39; Ro 4:11–12; 11:16; 1Co 7:14; Mt 28:19; Lk 18:15–16

167. How is our baptism to be improved by us?
The needful but much neglected duty of improving our baptism, is to be performed by us all our life long, especially in the time of temptation, and when we are present at the administration of it to others;[1] by serious and thankful consideration of the nature of it, and of the ends for which Christ instituted it, the privileges and benefits conferred and sealed thereby, and our solemn vow made therein;[2] by being humbled for our sinful defilement, our falling short of, and walking contrary to, the grace of baptism, and our engagements;[3] by growing up to assurance of pardon of sin, and of all other blessings sealed to us in that sacrament;[4] by drawing strength from the death and resurrection of Christ, into whom we are baptized, for the mortifying of sin, and quickening of grace;[5] and by endeavouring to live by faith,[6] to have our conversation in holiness and righteousness,[7] as those that have therein given up their names to Christ;[8] and to walk in brotherly love, as being baptized by the same Spirit into one body.[9]

1 Col 2:11–12; Ro 6:4,6,11
2 Ro 6:3–5
3 1Co 1:11–13; Ro 6:2–3
4 Ro 4:11–12; 1Pe 3:21
5 Ro 6:3–5
6 Gal 3:26–27
7 Ro 6:22
8 Ac 2:38
9 1Co 12:13,25–27

168. What is the Lord's supper?
The Lord's supper is a sacrament of the New Testament[1] wherein, by giving and receiving bread and wine according to the appointment of Jesus Christ, his death is showed forth and they that worthily communicate feed upon his body and blood, to their spiritual nourishment and growth in grace,[2] have their union and communion with him confirmed;[3] testify and renew their thankfulness,[4] and engagement to God,[5] and their mutual love and fellowship each with other, as members of the same mystical body.[6]

1 Lk 22:20
2 Mt 26:26–28; 1Co 11:23–26
3 1Co 10:16
4 1Co 11:24
5 1Co 10:14–16,21
6 1Co 10:17

169. How hath Christ appointed bread and wine to be given and received in the sacrament of the Lord's supper?
Christ hath appointed the ministers of his word,[a] in the administration of this sacrament of the Lord's supper, to set apart the bread and wine from common use, by the word of institution, thanksgiving, and prayer; to take and break the bread, and to give both the bread and the wine to the communicants: who are, by the same appointment, to take and eat the bread, and to drink the wine, in thankful remembrance that the body of Christ was broken and given, and his blood shed, for them.[1]

a The EPC version does not include the words "the ministers of his word"
1 1Co 11:23–24; Mt 26:26–28; Mk 14:22–24; Lk 22:19–20

170. How do they that worthily communicate in the Lord's supper feed upon the body and blood of Christ therein?

As the body and blood of Christ are not corporally or carnally present in, with, or under the bread and wine in the Lord's supper,[1] and yet are spiritually present to the faith of the receiver, no less truly and really than the elements themselves are to their outward senses;[2] so they that worthily communicate in the sacrament of the Lord's supper, do therein feed upon the body and blood of Christ, not after a corporal and carnal, but in a spiritual manner, yet truly and really,[3] while by faith they receive and apply unto themselves Christ crucified, and all the benefits of his death.[4]

[1] Ac 3:21
[2] Mt 26:26,28
[3] 1Co 11:24–29
[4] 1Co 10:16

171. How are they that receive the sacrament of the Lord's supper to prepare themselves before they come unto it?

They that receive the sacrament of the Lord's supper are, before they come, to prepare themselves thereunto, by examining themselves[1] of their being in Christ,[2] of their sins and wants;[3] of the truth and measure of their knowledge,[4] faith,[5] repentance;[6] love to God and the brethren,[7] charity to all men,[8] forgiving those that have done them wrong;[9] of their desires after Christ,[10] and of their new obedience,[11] and by renewing the exercise of these graces,[12] by serious meditation,[13] and fervent prayer.[14]

[1] 1Co 11:28
[2] 2Co 13:5
[3] 1Co 5:7; Ex 12:15
[4] 1Co 11:29
[5] 1Co 13:5; Mt 26:28
[6] Zec 12:10; 1Co 11:31
[7] 1Co 10:16–17; Ac 2:46–47
[8] 1Co 5:8; 11:18,20
[9] Mt 5:23–24
[10] Isa 55:1; Jn 7:37
[11] 1Co 5:7–8
[12] 1Co 11:25–26,28; Heb 10:21–22,24; Ps 26:6
[13] 1Co 11:24–25
[14] 2Ch 30:18–19; Mt 26:26

172. May one who doubteth of his being in Christ, or of his due preparation, come to the Lord's supper?

One who doubteth of his being in Christ, or of his due preparation to the sacrament of the Lord's supper, may have true interest in Christ, though he be not yet assured thereof[1] and in God's account hath it, if he be duly affected with the apprehension of the want of it,[2] and unfeignedly desires to be found in Christ,[3] and to depart from iniquity:[4] in which case (because promises are made, and this sacrament is appointed, for the relief even of weak and doubting Christians[5]) he is to bewail his unbelief,[6] and labour to have his doubts resolved;[7] and, so doing, he may and ought to come to the Lord's supper, that he may be further strengthened.[8]

[1] Isa 50:10; 1Jn 5:13; Ps 77:1–12; 88; Jnh 2:4,7
[2] Isa 54:7–10; Mt 5:3–4; Ps 31:22; 73:13,22–23
[3] Php 3:8–9; Ps 10:17; 42:1–2,5,11
[4] 2Ti 2:19; Isa 50:10; Ps 66:18–20
[5] Isa 40:11,29,31; Mt 11:28; 12:20; 26:28
[6] Mk 9:24
[7] Ac 2:37; Ac 16:30
[8] Ro 4:11; 1Co 11:28

173. May any who profess his faith, and desire to come to the Lord's supper, be kept from it?

Such as are found to be ignorant or scandalous, notwithstanding their profession of the faith, and desire to come to the Lord's supper, may and ought to be kept from that sacrament, by the power which Christ hath left in his church,[1] until they receive instruction and manifest their reformation.[2]

[1] 1Co 5:1–13; 11:27–31; Mt 7:6; Jude 23; 1Ti 5:22
[2] 2Co 2:7

174. What is required of them that receive the sacrament of the Lord's supper in the time of the administration of it?

It is required of them that receive the sacrament of the Lord's supper, that, during the time of the administration of it, with all holy reverence and attention they wait upon God in that ordinance,[1] diligently observe the sacramental elements and actions,[2] heedfully discern the Lord's body,[3] and affectionately meditate on his death and sufferings,[4] and thereby stir up themselves to a vigorous exercise of their graces;[5] in judging themselves,[6] and sorrowing for sin;[7] in earnest hungering and thirsting after Christ,[8] feeding on him by faith,[9] receiving of his fulness,[10] trusting in his merits,[11] rejoicing in his love,[12] giving thanks for his grace;[13] in renewing of their covenant with God,[14] and love to all the saints.[15]

[1] Lev 10:3; Heb 12:28; Ps 5:7; 1Co 11:17,26–27
[2] Ex 24:8; Mt 26:28
[3] 1Co 11:29
[4] Lk 22:19
[5] 1Co 10:3–5,11,14; 11:26
[6] 1Co 11:31
[7] Zec 12:10
[8] Rev 22:17
[9] Jn 6:35
[10] Jn 1:16
[11] Php 1:16
[12] Ps 63:4–5; 2Ch 30:21
[13] Ps 22:26
[14] Jer 1:5; Ps 1:5
[15] Ac 2:42

175. What is the duty of Christians, after they have received the sacrament of the Lord's supper?

The duty of Christians, after they have received the sacrament of the Lord's supper, is seriously to consider how they have behaved themselves therein, and with what success;[1] if they find quickening and comfort, to bless God for it,[2] beg the continuance of it,[3] watch against relapses,[4] fulfill their vows,[5] and encourage themselves to a frequent attendance on that ordinance:[6] but if they find no present benefit, more exactly to review their preparation to, and carriage at, the sacrament;[7] in both which, if they can approve themselves to God and their own consciences, they are to wait for the fruit of it in due time:[8] but, if they see they have failed in either, they are to be humbled,[9] and to attend upon it afterward with more care and diligence.[10]

[1] Ps 28:7; 85:8; 1Co 11:17,30–31
[2] 2Ch 30:21–23,25–26; Ac 2:42
[3] Ps 36:10; SS 3:4; 1Ch 29:18
[4] 1Co 10:3–5,12
[5] Ps 50:14
[6] 1Co 11:25–26; Ac 2:42,46
[7] SS 5:1–6; Ecc 5:1–6
[8] Ps 42:5,8; 43:3–5; 123:1–2
[9] 2Ch 30:18–19; Isa 1:16,18
[10] 2Co 7:11; 1Ch 15:12–14

176. Wherein do the sacraments of baptism and the Lord's supper agree?

The sacraments of baptism and the Lord's supper agree, in that the author of both is God;[1] the spiritual part of both is Christ and his benefits,[2] both are seals of the same covenant,[3] are to be dispensed[a] by ministers of the gospel, and by none other,[4] and to be continued in the church of Christ until his second coming.[5]

[1] Mt 28:19; 1Co 11:23
[2] Ro 6:3–4; 1Co 10:16
[3] Ro 4:11; Col 2:12; Mt 26:27–28
[a] The EPC version reads "are ordinarily to be dispensed"
[4] Jn 1:38; Mt 28:19; 1Co 4:1; 11:23; Heb 5:4
[5] Mt 28:19–20; 1Co 11:26

177. Wherein do the sacraments of baptism and the Lord's supper differ?

The sacraments of baptism and the Lord's supper differ, in that baptism is to be administered but once, with water, to be a sign and seal of our regeneration and ingrafting into Christ,[1] and that even to infants;[2] whereas the Lord's supper is to be administered often, in the elements of bread and wine, to represent and exhibit Christ as spiritual nourishment to the soul,[3] and to confirm our continuance and growth in him,[4] and that only to such as are of years and ability to examine themselves.[5]

1 Mt 3:11; Tit 3:5; Gal 3:27
2 Ge 17:7,9; Ac 2:38–39; 1Co 7:14
3 1Co 11:23–26
4 1Co 10:16
5 1Co 11:28–29

178. What is prayer?
Prayer is an offering up of our desires unto God,[1] in the name of Christ,[2] by the help of his Spirit;[3] with confession of our sins,[4] and thankful acknowledgement of his mercies.[5]

1 Ps 62:8
2 Jn 16:23
3 Ro 8:26
4 Ps 32:5–6; Da 9:4
5 Php 4:6

179. Are we to pray unto God only?
God only being able to search the hearts,[1] hear the requests,[2] pardon the sins,[3] and fulfil the desire of all;[4] and only to be believed in,[5] and worshipped with religious worship;[6] prayer, which is a special part thereof,[7] is to be made by all to him alone,[8] and to none other.[9]

1 1Ki 8:39; Ac 1:24; Ro 8:27
2 Ps 65:2
3 Mic 7:18
4 Ps 145:18–19
5 Ro 10:14
6 Mt 4:10
7 1Co 1:2
8 Ps 50:15
9 Ro 10:14

180. What is it to pray in the name of Christ?
To pray in the name of Christ is, in obedience to his command, and in confidence on his promises, to ask mercy for his sake;[1] not by bare mentioning of his name,[2] but by drawing our encouragement to pray, and our boldness, strength, and hope of acceptance in prayer, from Christ and his mediation.[3]

1 Jn 14:13–14; 16:24; Da 9:17
2 Mt 7:21
3 Heb 4:14–16; 1Jn 5:13–15

181. Why are we to pray in the name of Christ?
The sinfulness of man, and his distance from God by reason thereof, being so great, as that we can have no access into his presence without a mediator;[1] and there being none in heaven or earth appointed to, or fit for, that glorious work but Christ alone,[2] we are to pray in no other name but his only.[3]

1 Jn 14:6; Isa 59:2; Eph 3:12
2 Jn 6:27; Heb 7:25–27; 1Ti 2:5
3 Col 3:17; Heb 13:15

182. How doth the Spirit help us to pray?
We not knowing what to pray for as we ought, the Spirit helpeth our infirmities, by enabling us to understand both for whom, and what, and how prayer is to be made; and by working and quickening in our hearts (although not in all persons, nor at all times, in the same measure) those apprehensions, affections, and graces which are requisite for the right performance of that duty.[1]

1 Ro 8:26–27; Ps 10:17; Zec 12:10

183. For whom are we to pray?
We are to pray for the whole church of Christ upon earth;[1] for magistrates,[2] and ministers;[3] for ourselves,[4] our brethren,[5] yea, our enemies;[6] and for all sorts of men living,[7] or that shall live hereafter,[8] but not for the dead,[9] nor for those that are known to have sinned the sin unto death.[10]

1 Eph 6:18; Ps 28:19
2 1Ti 2:1–2
3 Col 4:3
4 Ge 32:11
5 Jas 5:16
6 Mt 5:44
7 1Ti 2:1–2
8 Jn 17:20; 2Sa 7:29
9 2Sa 12:21–23
10 1Jn 5:16

184. For what things are we to pray?
We are to pray for all things tending to the glory of God,[1] the welfare of the church,[2] our own[3] or others good;[4] but not for any thing that is unlawful.[5]

1 Mt 6:9
2 Ps 51:18; 122:6
3 Mt 7:11
4 Ps 125:4
5 1Jn 5:14

185. How are we to pray?
We are to pray with an awful apprehension of the majesty of God,[1] and deep sense of our own unworthiness,[2] necessities,[3] and sins;[4] with penitent,[5] thankful,[6] and enlarged hearts;[7] with understanding,[8] faith,[9] sincerity,[10] fervency,[11] love,[12] and perseverance,[13] waiting upon him,[14] with humble submission to his will.[15]

1 Ecc 5:1
2 Ge 18:27; 32:10
3 Lk 15:17–19
4 Lk 18:13–14
5 Ps 51:17
6 Php 4:6
7 1Sa 1:15, 2:1
8 1Co 14:15
9 Mk 11:24; Jas 1:6
10 Ps 17:1; 145:18
11 Jas 5:16
12 1Ti 2:8
13 Eph 6:18
14 Mic 7:7
15 Mt 26:39

186. What rule hath God given for our direction in the duty of prayer?
The whole word of God is of use to direct us in the duty of prayer,[1] but the special rule of direction is that form of prayer which our Saviour Christ taught his disciples, commonly called The Lord's Prayer.[2]

1 1Jn 5:14
2 Mt 6:9–13

187. How is the Lord's prayer to be used?
The Lord's prayer is not only for direction, as a pattern, according to which we are to make other prayers, but may also be used as a prayer, so that it be done with understanding, faith, reverence, and other graces necessary to the right performance of the duty of prayer.[1]

1 Mt 6:9; Lk 11:2

188. Of how many parts doth the Lord's prayer consist?
The Lord's prayer consists of three parts; a preface, petitions, and a conclusion.

189. What doth the preface of the Lord's prayer teach us?
The preface of the Lord's prayer (contained in these words, Our Father, which art in heaven,[1]) teacheth us, when we pray, to draw near to God with confidence of his fatherly goodness, and our interest therein;[2] with reverence, and all other childlike dispositions,[3] heavenly affections,[4] and due apprehensions of his sovereign power, majesty, and gracious condescension:[5] as also, to pray with and for others.[6]

1 Mt 6:9
2 Lk 11:13; Ro 8:15
3 Isa 64:9
4 Ps 123:1; La 3:41
5 Isa 63:15–16; Ne 1:4–6
6 Ac 12:5

190. What do we pray for in the first petition?
In the first petition (which is, Hallowed be thy name,[1]) acknowledging the utter inability and indisposition that is in ourselves and all men to honour God aright,[2] we pray, that God would by his grace enable and incline us and others to know, to acknowledge, and highly to esteem him,[3] his titles,[4] attributes,[5] ordinances, word,[6] works, and whatsoever he is pleased to make himself known by;[7] and to glorify him in thought, word,[8] and deed:[9] that he would prevent and remove atheism,[10] ignorance,[11] idolatry,[12] profaneness,[13] and whatso-

ever is dishonourable to him;[14] and, by his overruling providence, direct and dispose of all things to his own glory.[15]

1 Mt 6:9
2 2Co 3:5; Ps 2:15
3 Ps 67:2
4 Ps 83:18
5 Ps 86:10–15
6 2Th 3:1; Ps 138:1–3; 147:19–20; 2Co 2:14–15
7 Ps 8; 145
8 Ps 19:14; 103:1
9 Php 1:9,11
10 Ps 67:1–4
11 Eph 1:17–18
12 Ps 97:7
13 Ps 74:18,22–23
14 2Ki 19:15–16
15 2Ch 20:6,10–12; Ps 140:4,8

191. What do we pray for in the second petition?
In the second petition (which is, Thy kingdom come,1) acknowledging ourselves and all mankind to be by nature under the dominion of sin and Satan,[2] we pray, that the kingdom of sin and Satan may be destroyed,[3] the gospel propagated throughout the world,[4] the Jews called,[5] the fulness of the Gentiles brought in;[6] the church furnished with all gospel-officers and ordinances,[7] purged from corruption,[8] countenanced and maintained by the civil magistrate:[9] that the ordinances of Christ may be purely dispensed, and made effectual to the converting of those that are yet in their sins, and the confirming, comforting, and building up of those that are already converted:[10] that Christ would rule in our hearts here,[11] and hasten the time of his second coming, and our reigning with him for ever:[12] and that he would be pleased so to exercise the kingdom of his power in all the world, as may best conduce to these ends.[13]

1 Mt 6:10
2 Eph 2:2–3
3 Ps 67:1,18; Rev 12:10–11
4 2Th 3:1
5 Ro 10:1
6 Jn 17:9,20; Ro 11:25–26; Ps 67
7 Mt 9:38; 2Th 3:1
8 Mal 1:11; Zep 3:9
9 1Ti 2:1–2
10 Ac 4:29–30; Eph 6:18–20; Ro 15:29–30,32; 2Th 1:11; 2:16–17
11 Eph 3:14–20
12 Rev 22:20
13 Isa 64:1–2; Rev 4:8–11

192. What do we pray for in the third petition?
In the third petition (which is, Thy will be done in earth, as it is in heaven,1) acknowledging, that by nature we and all men are not only utterly unable and unwilling to know and do the will of God,[2] but prone to rebel against his word,[3] to repine and murmur against his providence,[4] and wholly inclined to do the will of the flesh, and of the devil:[5] we pray, that God would by his Spirit take away from ourselves and others all blindness,[6] weakness,[7] indisposedness,[8] and perverseness of heart;[9] and by his grace make us able and willing to know, do, and submit to his will in all things,[10] with the like humility,[11] cheerfulness,[12] faithfulness,[13] diligence,[14] zeal,[15] sincerity,[16] and constancy,[17] as the angels do in heaven.[18]

1 Mt 6:10
2 Ro 7:18; Job 21:14; 1Co 2:14
3 Ro 8:7
4 Ex 7:7; Nu 14:2
5 Eph 2:2
6 Eph 1:17–18
7 Eph 3:16
8 Mt 26:40–41
9 Jer 31:18–19
10 Ps 119:1,8,35–36; Ac 21:14
11 Mic 6:8
12 Ps 100:2; Job 1:21; 2Sa 15:25–26
13 Isa 38:3
14 Ps 119:4
15 Ro 12:11
16 Ps 119:80
17 Ps 119:112
18 Isa 6:2–3; Ps 103:20–21; Mt 18:10

193. What do we pray for in the fourth petition?
In the fourth petition (which is, Give us this day our daily bread,1) acknowledging, that in Adam, and by our own sin, we have forfeited our right to all the outward blessings of this life, and deserve to be wholly deprived of them by God, and to have them cursed to us in the use of them;[2] and that neither they of themselves are able to sustain us,[3] nor we to merit,[4] or by our own industry to procure them;[5] but prone to desire,[6] get,[7] and use them unlawfully:[8] we pray for ourselves and others, that both they and we, waiting upon the providence of God from day to day in the use of lawful means, may, of his free gift, and as to his fatherly wisdom shall seem best, enjoy a competent portion of them;[9] and have the same continued and blessed unto us in our holy and comfortable use of them,[10] and contentment in them;[11] and be kept from all things that are contrary to our temporal support and comfort.[12]

1 Mt 6:11
2 Ge 2:17; 3:17; Ro 8:20–22; Jer 5:25; Dt 28:15–68
3 Dt 8:3
4 Ge 32:10
5 Dt 8:17–18
6 Jer 6:13; Mk 7:21–22
7 Hos 12:7
8 Jas 4:3
9 Ge 28:20; 43:12–14; Eph 4:28; 2Th 3:11–12; Php 4:6
10 1Ti 4:3–5
11 1Ti 6:6–8
12 Pr 30:8

194. What do we pray for in the fifth petition?
In the fifth petition (which is, Forgive us our debts, as we forgive our debtors,1) acknowledging, that we and all others are guilty both of original and actual sin, and thereby become debtors to the justice of God; and that neither we, nor any other creature, can make the least satisfaction for that debt:[2] we pray for ourselves and others that God of his free grace would, through the obedience and satisfaction of Christ, apprehended and applied by faith, acquit us both from the guilt and punishment of sin,[3] accept us in his Beloved;[4] continue his favour and grace to us,[5] pardon our daily failings,[6] and fill us with peace and joy, in giving us daily more and more assurance of forgiveness;[7] which we are the rather emboldened to ask, and encouraged to expect, when we have this testimony in ourselves, that we from the heart forgive others their offences.[8]

1 Mt 6:12
2 Ro 3:9–22; Mt 18:24–25; Ps 130:3–4
3 Ro 3:24–26; Heb 9:22
4 Eph 1:6–7
5 2Pe 1:2
6 Hos 14:2; Jer 14:7
7 Ro 15:13; Ps 51:7–10,12
8 Lk 11:4; Mt 6:14–15; 18:35

195. What do we pray for in the sixth petition?
In the sixth petition (which is, And lead us not into temptation, but deliver us from evil,1) acknowledging, that the most wise, righteous, and gracious God, for divers holy and just ends, may so order things, that we may be assaulted, foiled, and for a time led captive by temptations;[2] that Satan,[3] the world,[4] and the flesh, are ready powerfully to draw us aside, and ensnare us;[5] and that we, even after the pardon of our sins, by reason of our corruption,[6] weakness, and want of watchfulness,[7] are not only subject to be tempted, and forward to expose ourselves unto temptations,[8] but also of ourselves unable and unwilling to resist them, to recover out of them, and to improve them;[9] and worthy to be left under the power of them:[10] we pray, that God would so overrule the world and all in it,[11] subdue the flesh,[12] and restrain Satan,[13] order all things,[14] bestow and bless all means of grace,[15] and quicken us to watchfulness in the use of them, that we and all his people may by his providence be kept from being tempted to sin;[16] or, if tempted, that by his Spirit we may be powerfully supported and enabled to stand in the hour of temptation:[17] or when fallen, raised again and recovered out of it,[18] and have a sanctified use and improvement thereof:[19] that our sanctification and salvation may be perfected,[20] Satan trodden under our feet,[21] and we fully freed from sin, temptation, and all evil, for ever.[22]

1 Mt 6:13
2 2Ch 32:31
3 1Ch 21:1

[4] Lk 21:34; Mk 4:19
[5] Jas 1:14
[6] Gal 5:17
[7] Mt 26:41
[8] Mt 26:69–72; Gal 2:11–14; 2Ch 18:3; 19:2
[9] Ro 7:23–24; 1Ch 21:1–4; 2Ch 16:7–10
[10] Ps 81:11–12
[11] Jn 17:15
[12] Ps 51:10; 119:133
[13] 2Co 12:7–8
[14] 1Co 10:12–13
[15] Heb 13:20–21
[16] Mt 26:41; Ps 19:13
[17] Eph 3:14–17; 1Th 3:13; Jude 24
[18] Ps 51:12
[19] 1Pe 5:8–10
[20] 2Co 13:7,9
[21] Ro 16:20; Zec 3:2; Lk 22:31–32
[22] Jn 17:15; 1Th 5:23

196. What doth the conclusion of the Lord's prayer teach us?

The conclusion of the Lord's prayer (which is, For thine is the kingdom, and the power, and the glory, for ever. Amen,[1]) teacheth us to enforce our petitions with arguments,[2] which are to be taken, not from any worthiness in ourselves, or in any other creature, but from God;[3] and with our prayers to join praises,[4] ascribing to God alone eternal sovereignty, omnipotency, and glorious excellency;[5] in regard whereof, as he is able and willing to help us,[6] so we by faith are emboldened to plead with him that he would,[7] and quietly to rely upon him, that he will fulfil our requests.[8] And, to testify this our desire and assurance, we say, Amen.[9]

[1] Mt 6:13
[2] Ro 15:30
[3] Da 9:4,7–9,16–19
[4] Php 4:6
[5] 1Ch 29:10–13
[6] Eph 3:20–21; Lk 11:13
[7] 2Ch 20:6,11
[8] 2Ch 14:11
[9] 1Co 14:16; Rev 22:20–21

THE SHORTER CATECHISM

WITH THE SCRIPTURE PROOFS

1. What is the chief end of man?
Man's chief end is to glorify God,[1] and to enjoy him for ever.[2]

1 1Co 10:31; Ro 11:36
2 Ps 73:25–28

2. What rule hath God given to direct us how we may glorify and enjoy him?
The Word of God, which is contained in the Scriptures of the Old and New Testaments,[1] is the only rule to direct us how we may glorify and enjoy him.[2]

1 2Ti 3:16; Eph 2:20
2 1Jn 1:3–4

3. What do the Scriptures principally teach?
The Scriptures principally teach what man is to believe concerning God, and what duty God requires of man.[1]

1 2Ti 1:13; 3:16

4. What is God?
God is a Spirit,[1] infinite,[2] eternal,[3] and unchangeable[4] in his being,[5] wisdom,[6] power,[7] holiness,[8] justice, goodness, and truth.[9]

1 Jn 4:24
2 Job 11:7–9
3 Ps 90:2
4 Jas 1:17
5 Ex 3:14
6 Ps 117:5
7 Rev 4:8
8 Rev 15:4
9 Ex 34:6–7

5. Are there more Gods than one?
There is but One only, the living and true God.[1]

1 Dt 6:4; Jer 10:10

6. How many persons are there in the Godhead?
There are three persons in the Godhead; the Father, the Son, and the Holy Ghost; and these three are one God, the same in substance, equal in power and glory.[1]

1 1Jn 5:7; Mt 28:9

7. What are the decrees of God?
The decrees of God are, his eternal purpose, according to the counsel of his will, whereby, for his own glory, he hath foreordained whatsoever comes to pass.[1]

1 Eph 1:4,11; Ro 9:22–23

8. How doth God execute his decrees?
God executeth his decrees in the works of creation and providence.

9. What is the work of creation?
The work of creation is, God's making all things of nothing, by the word of his power, in the space of six days, and all very good.[1]

1 Ge 1; Heb 11:3

10. How did God create man?
God created man male and female, after his own image, in knowledge, righteousness, and holiness, with dominion over the creatures.[1]

1 Ge 1:26–28; Col 3:10; Eph 4:24

11. What are God's works of providence?
God's works of providence are, his most holy,[1] wise,[2] and powerful preserving[3] and governing all his creatures, and all their actions.[4]

1 Ps 145:17
2 Ps 104:24; Isa 28:29
3 Heb 1:3
4 Ps 103:19; Mt 10:29–31

12. What special act of providence did God exercise toward man in the estate wherein he was created?
When God had created man, he entered into a covenant of life with him, upon condition of perfect obedience; forbidding him to eat of the tree of the knowledge of good and evil, upon the pain of death.[1]

1 Gal 3:12; Ge 2:17

13. Did our first parents continue in the estate wherein they were created?
Our first parents, being left to the freedom of their own will, fell from the estate wherein they were created, by sinning against God.[1]

1 Ge 3:6–8,13; Ecc 7:29

14. What is sin?
Sin is any want of conformity unto, or transgression of, the law of God.[1]

1 1Jn 3:4

15. What was the sin whereby our first parents fell from the estate wherein they were created?
The sin whereby our first parents fell from the estate wherein they were created, was their eating the forbidden fruit.[1]

1 Ge 3:6

16. Did all mankind fall in Adam's first transgression?
The covenant being made with Adam, not only for himself, but for his posterity; all mankind, descending from him by ordinary generation, sinned in him, and fell with him, in his first transgression.[1]

1 Ge 2:16–17; Ro 5:12; 1Co 15:21–22

17. Into what estate did the fall bring mankind?
The fall brought mankind into an estate of sin and misery.[1]

1 Ro 5:12

18. Wherein consists the sinfulness of that estate whereinto man fell?
The sinfulness of that estate whereinto man fell, consists in the guilt of Adam's first sin, the want of original righteousness, and the corruption of his whole nature, which is commonly called Original Sin; together with all actual transgressions which proceed from it.[1]

1 Ro 5:10–20; Eph 2:1–3; Jas 1:14–15; Mt 15:19

19. What is the misery of that estate whereinto man fell?
All mankind by their fall lost communion with God,[1] are under his wrath and curse,[2] and so made liable to all miseries in this life, to death itself, and to the pains of hell for ever.[3]

1 Ge 3:8,10,24
2 Eph 2:2–3; Gal 3:10

3 La 3:39; Ro 6:23; Mt 25:41,46

20. Did God leave all mankind to perish in the estate of sin and misery?
God having, out of his mere good pleasure, from all eternity, elected some to everlasting life,[1] did enter into a covenant of grace, to deliver them out of the estate of sin and misery, and to bring them into an estate of salvation by a Redeemer.[2]

1 Eph 1:4
2 Ro 3:20–22; Gal 3:21–22

21. Who is the Redeemer of God's elect?
The only Redeemer of God's elect is the Lord Jesus Christ,[1] who, being the eternal Son of God, became man[2] and so was, and continueth to be, God and man in two distinct natures, and one person, for ever.[3]

1 1Ti 2:5–6
2 Jn 1:14; Gal 4:4
3 Ro 9:5; Lk 1:35; Col 2:9; Heb 7:24–25

22. How did Christ, being the Son of God, become man?
Christ, the Son of God, became man, by taking to himself a true body,[1] and a reasonable soul,[2] being conceived by the power of the Holy Ghost, in the womb of the Virgin Mary, and born of her[3] yet without sin.[4]

1 Heb 2:14,16; 10:5
2 Mt 26:38
3 Lk 1:27,31,35,42; Gal 4:4
4 Heb 4:15; 7:26

23. What offices doth Christ execute as our Redeemer?
Christ, as our Redeemer, executeth the offices of a prophet, of a priest, and of a king, both in his estate of humiliation and exaltation.[1]

1 Ac 3:21–22; Heb 5:5–7; 7:25; 12:25 with 2Co 13:3; Ps 2:6; Isa 9:6–7; Mt 21:5; Ps 2:8–11

24. How doth Christ execute the office of a prophet?
Christ executeth the office of a prophet, in revealing to us, by his word and Spirit, the will of God for our salvation.[1]

1 Jn 1:18; 15:15; 20:31; 1Pe 1:10–12

25. How doth Christ execute the office of a priest?
Christ executeth the office of a priest, in his once offering up of himself a sacrifice to satisfy divine justice,[1] and reconcile us to God;[2] and in making continual intercession for us.[3]

1 Heb 9:14,28
2 Heb 2:17
3 Heb 7:24–25

26. How doth Christ execute the office of a king?
Christ executeth the office of a king, in subduing us to himself,[1] in ruling[2] and defending us,[3] and in restraining and conquering all his and our enemies.[4]

1 Ac 15:14–16
2 Isa 32:22
3 Isa 32:1–2
4 1Co 15:25; Ps 110

27. Wherein did Christ's humiliation consist?
Christ's humiliation consisted in his being born, and that in a low condition,[1] made under the law,[2] undergoing the miseries of this life,[3] the wrath of God,[4] and the cursed death of the cross;[5] in being buried,[6] and continuing under the power of death for a time.[7]

1 Lk 2:7
2 Gal 4:4
3 Heb 12:2–3; Isa 53:2–3
4 Lk 22:44; Mt 27:46
5 Php 2:8
6 1Co 15:3–4
7 Ac 2:24–27,31

28. Wherein consisteth Christ's exaltation?
Christ's exaltation consisteth in his rising again from the dead on the third day,[1] in ascending up into heaven,[2] in sitting at the right hand of God the Father,[3] and in coming to judge the world at the last day.[4]

1 1Co 15:4
2 Mk 16:19
3 Eph 1:20
4 Ac 1:11; 17:31

29. How are we made partakers of the redemption purchased by Christ?
We are made partakers of the redemption purchased by Christ, by the effectual application of it to us[1] by his Holy Spirit.[2]

1 Jn 1:11–12
2 Tit 3:5–6

30. How doth the Spirit apply to us the redemption purchased by Christ?
The Spirit applieth to us the redemption purchased by Christ, by working faith in us,[1] and thereby uniting us to Christ in our effectual calling.[2]

1 Eph 1:13–14; 2:8; Jn 6:37,39
2 Eph 3:17; 1Co 1:9

31. What is effectual calling?
Effectual calling is the work of God's Spirit,[1] whereby, convincing us of our sin and misery,[2] enlightening our minds in the knowledge of Christ,[3] and renewing our wills,[4] he doth persuade and enable us to embrace Jesus Christ, freely offered to us in the gospel.[5]

1 2Ti 1:9; 2Th 2:13–14
2 Ac 2:37
3 Ac 26:18
4 Eze 36:26–27
5 Jn 6:44–45; Php 2:13

32. What benefits do they that are effectually called partake of in this life?
They that are effectually called do in this life partake of justification,[1] adoption,[2] and sanctification, and the several benefits which in this life do either accompany or flow from them.[3]

1 Ro 8:30
2 Eph 1:5
3 1Co 1:26,30

33. What is justification?
Justification is an act of God's free grace, wherein he pardoneth all our sins,[1] and accepteth us as righteous in his sight[2] only for the righteousness of Christ imputed to us,[3] and received by faith alone.[4]

1 Ro 3:24–25; 4:6–8
2 2Co 5:19,21
3 Ro 5:17–19
4 Gal 2:16; Php 3:9

34. What is adoption?
Adoption is an act of God's free grace,[1] whereby we are received into the number, and have a right to all the privileges of the sons of God.[2]

1 1Jn 3:1
2 Jn 1:12; Ro 8:17

35. What is sanctification?
Sanctification is the work of God's free grace,[1] whereby we are renewed in the whole man after the image of God,[2] and are enabled more and more to die unto sin, and live unto righteousness.[3]

1 2Th 2:13
2 Eph 4:23–24
3 Ro 6:4,6; 8:1

36. What are the benefits which in this life do accompany or flow from justification, adoption, and sanctification?
The benefits which in this life do accompany or flow from justification, adoption, and sanctification, are, assurance of God's love, peace of conscience,[1] joy in the Holy Ghost,[2] increase of grace,[3] and perseverance therein to the end.[4]

1 Ro 5:1–2,5
2 Ro 14:17
3 Pr 4:18
4 1Jn 5:13; 1Pe 1:5

37. What benefits do believers receive from Christ at death?
The souls of believers are at their death made perfect in holiness,[1] and do immediately pass into glory;[2] and their bodies, being still united to Christ,[3] do rest in their graves[4] till the resurrection.[5]

1 Heb 12:23
2 2Co 5:1,6,8; Php 1:23; Lk 23:43
3 1Th 4:14
4 Isa 57:2
5 Job 19:26–27

38. What benefits do believers receive from Christ at the resurrection?
At the resurrection, believers being raised up in glory,[1] shall be openly acknowledged and acquitted in the day of judgment,[2] and made perfectly blessed in the full enjoying of God[3] to all eternity.[4]

1 1Co 15:43
2 Mt 10:32; 25:23
3 1Jn 3:2; 1Co 13:12
4 1Th 4:17–18

39. What is the duty which God requireth of man?
The duty which God requireth of man, is obedience to his revealed will.[1]

1 Mic 6:8; 1Sa 15:22

40. What did God at first reveal to man for the rule of his obedience?
The rule which God at first revealed to man for his obedience, was the moral law.[1]

1 Ro 2:14–15; 10:5

41. Where is the moral law summarily comprehended?
The moral law is summarily comprehended in the ten commandments.[1]

1 Dt 10:4; Mt 19:17

42. What is the sum of the ten commandments?
The sum of the ten commandments is, To love the Lord our God with all our heart, with all our soul, with all our strength, and with all our mind; and our neighbour as ourselves.[1]

1 Mt 22:37–40

43. What is the preface to the ten commandments?
The preface to the ten commandments is in these words, I am the LORD thy God, which have brought thee out of the land of Egypt, out of the house of bondage.[1]

1 Ex 20:2

44. What doth the preface to the ten commandments teach us?
The preface to the ten commandments teacheth us, That because God is the Lord, and our God, and Redeemer, therefore we are bound to keep all his commandments.[1]

1 Lk 1:74–75; 1Pe 1:15–18

45. Which is the first commandment?
The first commandment is, Thou shalt have no other gods before me.[1]

1 Ex 20:3

46. What is required in the first commandment?
The first commandment requireth us to know and acknowledge God to be the holy true God, and our God;[1] and to worship and glorify him accordingly.[2]

1 1Ch 28:9; Dt 26:17
2 Mt 4:10; Ps 29:2

47. What is forbidden in the first commandment?
The first commandment forbiddeth the denying,[1] or not worshipping and glorifying the true God as God,[2] and our God;[3] and the giving of that worship and glory to any other, which is due to him alone.[4]

1 Ps 14:1
2 Ro 1:21
3 Ps 81:10–11
4 Ro 1:25–26

48. What are we specially taught by these words [before me] in the first commandment?
These words [before me] in the first commandment teach us, That God, who seeth all things, taketh notice of, and is much displeased with, the sin of having any other God.[1]

1 Eze 8:5–6; Ps 46:20–21

49. Which is the second commandment?
The second commandment is, Thou shalt not make unto thee any graven image, or any likeness of any thing that is in heaven above, or that is in the earth beneath, or that is in the water under the earth: Thou shalt not bow down thyself to them, nor serve them: for I the LORD thy God am a jealous God, visiting the iniquity of the fathers upon the children unto the third and fourth generation of them that hate me; and showing mercy unto thousands of them that love me, and keep my commandments.[1]

1 Ex 20:4–6

50. What is required in the second commandment?
The second commandment requireth the receiving, observing, and keeping pure and entire, all such religious worship and ordinances as God hath appointed in his Word.[1]

1 Dt 32:46; Mt 28:20; Ac 2:42

51. What is forbidden in the second commandment?
The second commandment forbiddeth the worshipping of God by images,[1] or any other way not appointed in his Word.[2]

1 Dt 4:15–19; Ex 32:5,8
2 Dt 12:31–32

52. What are the reasons annexed to the second commandment?
The reasons annexed to the second commandment are, God's sovereignty over us,[1] his propriety in us,[2] and the zeal he hath to his own worship.[3]

1 Ps 95:2–3
2 Ps 45:11
3 Ex 34:13–14

53. Which is the third commandment?
The third commandment is, Thou shalt not take the name of the LORD thy God in vain; for the Lord will not hold him guiltless that taketh his name in vain.[1]

1 Ex 20:7

54. What is required in the third commandment?
The third commandment requireth the holy and reverent use of God's names,[1] titles,[2] attributes,[3] ordinances,[4] Word,[5] and works.[6]

1 Mt 6:9; Dt 28:58
2 Ps 68:4
3 Rev 15:3–4
4 Mal 1:11,14
5 Ps 138:1–2
6 Job 26:24

55. What is forbidden in the third commandment?
The third commandment forbiddeth all profaning and abusing of any thing whereby God maketh himself known.[1]

1 Mal 1:6–7,12; 2:2; 3:14

56. What is the reason annexed to the third commandment?
The reason annexed to the third commandment is, That however the breakers of this commandment may escape punishment from men, yet the Lord our God will not suffer them to escape his righteous judgment.[1]

1 1Sa 2:12,17,22,29; 3:13; Dt 28:58–59

57. Which is the fourth commandment?
The fourth commandment is, Remember the sabbath day, to keep it holy. Six days shalt thou labour, and do all thy work: but the seventh day is the sabbath of the LORD thy God: in it thou shalt not do any work, thou, nor thy son, nor thy daughter, thy manservant, nor thy maidservant, nor thy cattle, nor thy

stranger that is within thy gates: for in six days the LORD made heaven and earth, the sea, and all that in them is, and rested the seventh day: wherefore the LORD blessed the sabbath day, and hallowed it.[1]

[1] Ex 20:8–11

58. What is required in the fourth commandment?
The fourth commandment requireth the keeping holy to God such set times as he hath appointed in his Word; expressly one whole day in seven, to be a holy Sabbath to himself.[1]

[1] Dt 5:12–14

59. Which day of the seven hath God appointed to be the weekly Sabbath?
From the beginning of the world to the resurrection of Christ, God appointed the seventh day of the week to be the weekly Sabbath; and the first day of the week ever since, to continue to the end of the world, which is the Christian Sabbath.[1]

[1] Ge 2:2–3; 1Co 16:1–2; Ac 20:7

60. How is the Sabbath to be sanctified?
The Sabbath is to be sanctified by a holy resting all that day,[1] even from such worldly employments and recreations as are lawful on other days;[2] and spending the whole time in the public and private exercises of God's worship,[3] except so much as is to be taken up in the works of necessity and mercy.[4]

[1] Ex 16:25–28; 20:8,10
[2] Ne 13:15–19
[3] Lk 4:16; Ac 20:7; Ps 92 title; Isa 66:23
[4] Mt 12:1–31

61. What is forbidden in the fourth commandment?
The fourth commandment forbiddeth the omission or careless performance of the duties required,[1] and the profaning the day by idleness,[2] or doing that which is in itself sinful,[3] or by unnecessary thoughts, words, or works, about our worldly employments or recreations.[4]

[1] Eze 22:26; Am 8:5; Mal 1:13
[2] Ac 20:7,9
[3] Eze 23:38
[4] Jer 17:24–26; Isa 58:13

62. What are the reasons annexed to the fourth commandment?
The reasons annexed to the fourth commandment are, God's allowing us six days of the week for our own employments,[1] his challenging a special propriety in the seventh, his own example, and his blessing the sabbath day.[2]

[1] Ex 20:9
[2] Ex 20:11

63. Which is the fifth commandment?
The fifth commandment is, Honour thy father and thy mother: that thy days may be long upon the land which the LORD thy God giveth thee.[1]

[1] Ex 20:12

64. What is required in the fifth commandment?
The fifth commandment requireth the preserving the honor, and performing the duties, belonging to every one in their several places and relations, as superiors,[1] inferiors,[2] or equals.[3]

[1] Eph 5:21
[2] 1Pe 2:17
[3] Ro 12:10

65. What is forbidden in the fifth commandment?
The fifth commandment forbiddeth the neglecting of, or doing any thing against, the honor and duty which belongeth to every one in their several places and relations.[1]

[1] Mt 15:4–6; Eze 34:2–4; Ro 13:8

66. What is the reason annexed to the fifth commandment?
The reason annexed to the fifth commandment, is a promise of long life and prosperity (as far as it shall serve for God's glory and their own good) to all such as keep this commandment.[1]

[1] Dt 5:16; Eph 6:2–3

67. Which is the sixth commandment?
The sixth commandment is, Thou shalt not kill.[1]

[1] Ex 20:13

68. What is required in the sixth commandment?
The sixth commandment requireth all lawful endeavors to preserve our own life,[1] and the life of others.[2]

[1] Eph 5:28–29
[2] 1Ki 18:4

69. What is forbidden in the sixth commandment?
The sixth commandment forbiddeth the taking away of our own life, or the life of our neighbour unjustly, or whatsoever tendeth thereunto.[1]

[1] Ac 16:28; Ge 9:6

70. Which is the seventh commandment?
The seventh commandment is, Thou shalt not commit adultery.[1]

[1] Ex 20:14

71. What is required in the seventh commandment?
The seventh commandment requireth the preservation of our own and our neighbour's chastity, in heart, speech, and behavior.[1]

[1] 1Co 7:2–3,5,34,36; Col 4:6; 1Pe 3:2

72. What is forbidden in the seventh commandment?
The seventh commandment forbiddeth all unchaste thoughts, words, and actions.[1]

[1] Mt 5:28; 15:19; Eph 5:3–4

73. Which is the eighth commandment?
The eighth commandment is, Thou shalt not steal.[1]

[1] Ex 20:15

74. What is required in the eighth commandment?
The eighth commandment requireth the lawful procuring and furthering the wealth and outward estate of ourselves and others.[1]

[1] Ge 30:30; 47:14,20; 1Ti 5:8; Lev 25:35; Dt 22:1–5; Ex 23:4–5

75. What is forbidden in the eighth commandment?
The eighth commandment forbiddeth whatsoever doth or may unjustly hinder our own or our neighbour's wealth or outward estate.[1]

[1] Pr 21:17; 23:20–21; 28:19; Eph 4:28

76. Which is the ninth commandment?
The ninth commandment is, Thou shalt not bear false witness against thy neighbour.[1]

[1] Ex 20:16

77. What is required in the ninth commandment?
The ninth commandment requireth the maintaining and promoting of truth between man and man,[1] and of our own and our neighbour's good name,[2] especially in witness-bearing.[3]

[1] Zec 8:16
[2] 3Jn 12
[3] Pr 14:5,25

78. What is forbidden in the ninth commandment?
The ninth commandment forbiddeth whatsoever is prejudicial to truth, or injurious to our own or our neighbour's good name.[1]

[1] 1Sa 17:28; Lev 19:16; Ps 15:3

79. Which is the tenth commandment?
The tenth commandment is, Thou shalt not covet thy neighbour's house, thou shalt not covet thy neighbour's wife, nor his manservant, nor his maidservant, nor his ox, nor his ass, nor any thing that is thy neighbour's.[1]

[1] Ex 20:17

80. What is required in the tenth commandment?
The tenth commandment requireth full contentment with our

own condition,[1] with a right and charitable frame of spirit toward our neighbour, and all that is his.[2]

1 Heb 13:5; 1Ti 6:6
2 Job 31:29; Ro 12:15; 1Ti 1:5; 1Co 13:4–7

81. What is forbidden in the tenth commandment?
The tenth commandment forbiddeth all discontentment with our own estate,[1] envying or grieving at the good of our neighbour,[2] and all inordinate motions and affections to any thing that is his.[3]

1 1Ki 21:4; Est 5:13; 1Co 10:10
2 Gal 5:26; Jas 3:14,16;
3 Ro 7:7–8; 13:9; Dt 5:21

82. Is any man able perfectly to keep the commandments of God?
No mere man since the fall is able in this life perfectly to keep the commandments of God,[1] but doth daily break them in thought, word, and deed.[2]

1 Ecc 7:20; 1Jn 1:8,10; Gal 5:17
2 Ge 6:5; 8:21; Ro 3:9–21; Jas 3:2–13

83. Are all transgressions of the law equally heinous?
Some sins in themselves, and by reason of several aggravations, are more heinous in the sight of God than others.[1]

1 Eze 8:6,13,15; 1Jn 5:16; Ps 78:17,32,56

84. What doth every sin deserve?
Every sin deserveth God's wrath and curse, both in this life, and that which is to come.[1]

1 Eph 5:6; Gal 3:10; La 3:39; Mt 25:41

85. What doth God require of us, that we may escape his wrath and curse due to us for sin?
To escape the wrath and curse of God due to us for sin, God requireth of us faith in Jesus Christ, repentance unto life,[1] with the diligent use of all the outward means whereby Christ communicateth to us the benefits of redemption.[2]

1 Ac 20:21
2 Pr 2:1–5; 8:33–36; Isa 55:3

86. What is faith in Jesus Christ?
Faith in Jesus Christ is a saving grace,[1] whereby we receive and rest upon him alone for salvation as he is offered to us in the gospel.[2]

1 Heb 10:39
2 Jn 1:12; Isa 26:3–4; Php 3:9; Gal 2:16

87. What is repentance unto life?
Repentance unto life is a saving grace,[1] whereby a sinner, out of a true sense of his sin,[2] and apprehension of the mercy of God in Christ,[3] doth, with grief and hatred of his sin, turn from it unto God,[4] with full purpose of, and endeavour after, new obedience.[5]

1 Ac 11:18
2 Ac 2:37–38
3 Joel 2:12
4 Jer 31:18–19; Eze 36:31
5 2Co 7:11; Isa 1:16–17

88. What are the outward means whereby Christ communicateth to us the benefits of redemption?
The outward and ordinary means whereby Christ communicateth to us the benefits of redemption, are his ordinances, especially the Word, sacraments, and prayer; all which are made effectual to the elect for salvation.[1]

1 Mt 28:19–20; Ac 2:42,46–47

89. How is the Word made effectual to salvation?
The Spirit of God maketh the reading, but especially the preaching of the Word, an effectual means of convincing and converting sinners, and of building them up in holiness and comfort, through faith, unto salvation.[1]

1 Ne 8:8; 1Co 14:24–25; Ac 20:32; 26:18; Ps 19:8; Ro 1:16; 10:13–17; 15:4; 2Ti 3:15–17

90. How is the Word to be read and heard, that it may become effectual to salvation?
That the Word may become effectual to salvation, we must attend thereunto with diligence,[1] preparation,[2] and prayer;[3] receive it with faith and love,[4] lay it up in our hearts,[5] and practice it in our lives.[6]

1 Pr 8:34
2 1Pe 2:1–2
3 Ps 119:18
4 Heb 4:2; 2Th 2:10
5 Ps 119:11
6 Lk 8:15; Jas 1:25

91. How do the sacraments become effectual means of salvation?
The sacraments become effectual means of salvation, not from any virtue in them, or in him that doth administer them; but only by the blessing of Christ,[1] and the working of his Spirit in them that by faith receive them.[2]

1 1Pe 3:21; Mt 3:11; 1Co 3:6–7
2 1Co 12:13

92. What is a sacrament?
A sacrament is an holy ordinance instituted by Christ, wherein, by sensible signs, Christ, and the benefits of the new covenant, are represented, sealed, and applied to believers.[1]

1 Ge 17:7,10; Ex 12; 1Co 11:23,26

93. Which are the sacraments of the New Testament?
The sacraments of the New Testament are, Baptism,[1] and the Lord's Supper.[2]

1 Mt 28:19
2 Mt 26:26–28

94. What is Baptism?
Baptism is a sacrament, wherein the washing with water in the name of the Father, and of the Son, and of the Holy Ghost,[1] doth signify and seal our ingrafting into Christ, and partaking of the benefits of the covenant of grace, and our engagement to be the Lord's.[2]

1 Mt 28:19
2 Ro 6:4; Gal 3:27

95. To whom is Baptism to be administered?
Baptism is not to be administered to any that are out of the visible church, till they profess their faith in Christ, and obedience to him;[1] but the infants of such as are members of the visible church are to be baptized.[2]

1 Ac 2:38; 8:36–38
2 Ac 2:38–39; Ge 17:10 with Col 2:11–12; 1Co 7:14

96. What is the Lord's Supper?
The Lord's Supper is a sacrament, wherein, by giving and receiving bread and wine, according to Christ's appointment, his death is showed forth; and the worthy receivers are, not after a corporal and carnal manner, but by faith, made partakers of his body and blood, with all his benefits, to their spiritual nourishment, and growth in grace.[1]

1 1Co 11:23–26

97. What is required for the worthy receiving of the Lord's Supper?
It is required of them that would worthily partake of the Lord's Supper, that they examine themselves of their knowledge to discern the Lord's body,[1] of their faith to feed upon him,[2] of their repentance,[3] love,[4] and new obedience;[5] lest, coming unworthily, they eat and drink judgment to themselves.[6]

1 1Co 11:28–29
2 2Co 13:5
3 1Co 11:31
4 1Co 10:16–17
5 1Co 5:7–8
6 1Co 11:28–29

98. What is prayer?
Prayer is an offering up of our desires unto God[1] for things agreeable to his will,[2] in the name of Christ,[3] with confession of our sins,[4] and thankful acknowledgement of his mercies.[5]

1 Ps 62:8
2 1Jn 5:14
3 Jn 16:23
4 Ps 32:5–6; Da 9:4
5 Php 4:6

99. What rule hath God given for our direction in prayer?
The whole Word of God is of use to direct us in prayer;[1] but the special rule of direction is that form of prayer which Christ taught his disciples, commonly called the Lord's Prayer.[2]

1 1Jn 5:14;
2 Mt 6:9–13 with Lk 11:2–4

100. What doth the preface of the Lord's Prayer teach us?
The preface of the Lord's Prayer, which is, Our Father which art in heaven,[1] teacheth us to draw near to God with all holy reverence and confidence, as children to a father, able and ready to help us;[2] and that we should pray with and for others.[3]

1 Mt 6:9
2 Ro 8:15; Lk 11:13
3 Ac 12:5; 1Ti 2:1–2

101. What do we pray for in the first petition?
In the first petition, which is, Hallowed be thy name,[1] we pray, That God would enable us and others to glorify him in all that whereby he maketh himself known;[2] and that he would dispose all things to his own glory.[3]

1 Mt 6:9
2 Ps 67:2–3
3 Ps 83

102. What do we pray for in the second petition?
In the second petition, which is, Thy kingdom come,[1] we pray, That Satan's kingdom may be destroyed;[2] and that the kingdom of grace may be advanced,[3] ourselves and others brought into it, and kept in it;[4] and that the kingdom of glory may be hastened.[5]

1 Mt 6:10
2 Ps 68:1,18
3 Rev 12:10–11
4 2Th 3:1; Ro 10:1; Jn 17:9,20
5 Rev 22:20

103. What do we pray for in the third petition?
In the third petition, which is, Thy will be done in earth, as it is in heaven,[1] we pray, That God, by his grace, would make us able and willing to know, obey, and submit to his will in all things,[2] as the angels do in heaven.[3]

1 Mt 6:10
2 Ps 67; 119:36; Mt 26:39; 2Sa 15:25; Job 1:21
3 Ps 103:20–21

104. What do we pray for in the fourth petition?
In the fourth petition, which is, Give us this day our daily bread,[1] we pray, That of God's free gift we may receive a competent portion of the good things of this life, and enjoy his blessing with them.[2]

1 Mt 6:11
2 Pr 30:8–9; Ge 28:23; 1Ti 4:4–5

105. What do we pray for in the fifth petition?
In the fifth petition, which is, And forgive us our debts, as we forgive our debtors,[1] we pray, That God, for Christ's sake, would freely pardon all our sins;[2] which we are the rather encouraged to ask, because by his grace we are enabled from the heart to forgive others.[3]

1 Mt 6:12
2 Ps 51:1–2,7,9; Da 9:17–19
3 Lk 11:4; Mt 13:35

106. What do we pray for in the sixth petition?
In the sixth petition, which is, And lead us not into temptation, but deliver us from evil,[1] we pray, That God would either keep us from being tempted to sin,[2] or support and deliver us when we are tempted.[3]

1 Mt 6:13
2 Mt 26:41
3 2Co 12:7–8

107. What doth the conclusion of the Lord's Prayer teach us?
The conclusion of the Lord's Prayer, which is, For thine is the kingdom, and the power, and the glory, for ever. Amen,[1] teacheth us, to take our encouragement in prayer from God only,[2] and in our prayers to praise him, ascribing kingdom, power, and glory to him.[3] And, in testimony of our desire, and assurance to be heard, we say, Amen.[4]

1 Mt 6:13
2 Da 9:4,7–9,16–19
3 1Ch 29:10–13
4 1Co 14:16; Rev 22:20–21

INDEX TO COLOR MAPS

D

E

F

G

H

I

J

K

L

M

N

O

P

Q

R

SPIRIT OF THE REFORMATION STUDY BIBLE

General Editor	**Richard Pratt** (see also "Contributors" in front of this Bible)
Project Management and Editorial	**by Donna Huisjen**
Editorial Assistance	**by Amy Ballor, Natalie J. Block, Paul Brinkerhoff and Diana Wallis**
Theological Review	**by John Frame, Jordan Ballor, Andrew Kuyvenhoven and John Timmer**
Interior Proofreading	**by Peachtree Editorial and Proofreading Service, Peachtree City, GA**
Interior Typesetting	**by Blue Heron Bookcraft, Battle Ground, WA**
Interior Design	**by Sharon VanLoozenoord, Belmont, MI**
Art Direction	**by Jamie DeBruyn**
Cover Design	**by Christopher Tobias, Outerwear for Books**
Cover Photo	**by Photonica**
Production Management	**by Phil Herich**
Published in partnership with	**Excelsis (formerly Foundation for Reformation), Orlando, FL**

Guarantee
Zondervan guarantees leather Bibles unconditionally against manufacturing defects for a lifetime and hardcover, softcover and Leatherlook™ Bibles for four years. This guarantee does not apply to normal wear. Contact Zondervan Customer Service, 800-727-1309, for replacement instructions.

Care
We suggest loosening the binding of your new Bible by gently pressing on a small section of pages at a time from the center. To ensure against breakage of the spine, it is best not to bend the cover backward around the spine or to carry study notes, church bulletins, pens, and the like, inside the cover. Because a felt-tipped marker will "bleed" through the pages, we recommend use of a ball-point pen or pencil to underline favorite passages. Your Bible should not be exposed to excessive heat, cold or humidity. Protecting the gold or silver edges of the paper from moisture will avoid spotting, streaking or fading.

Map 1: **WORLD OF THE PATRIARCHS**

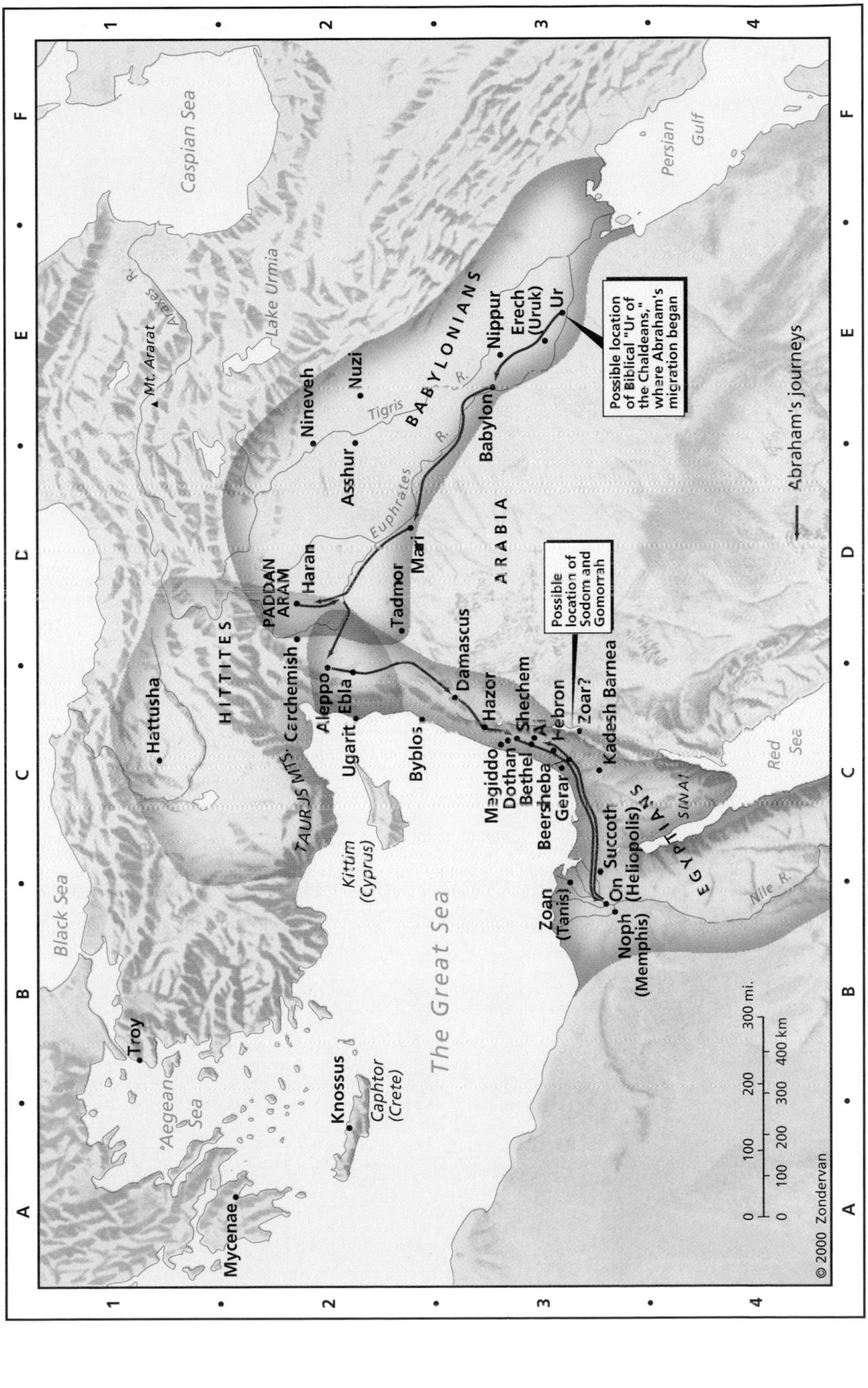

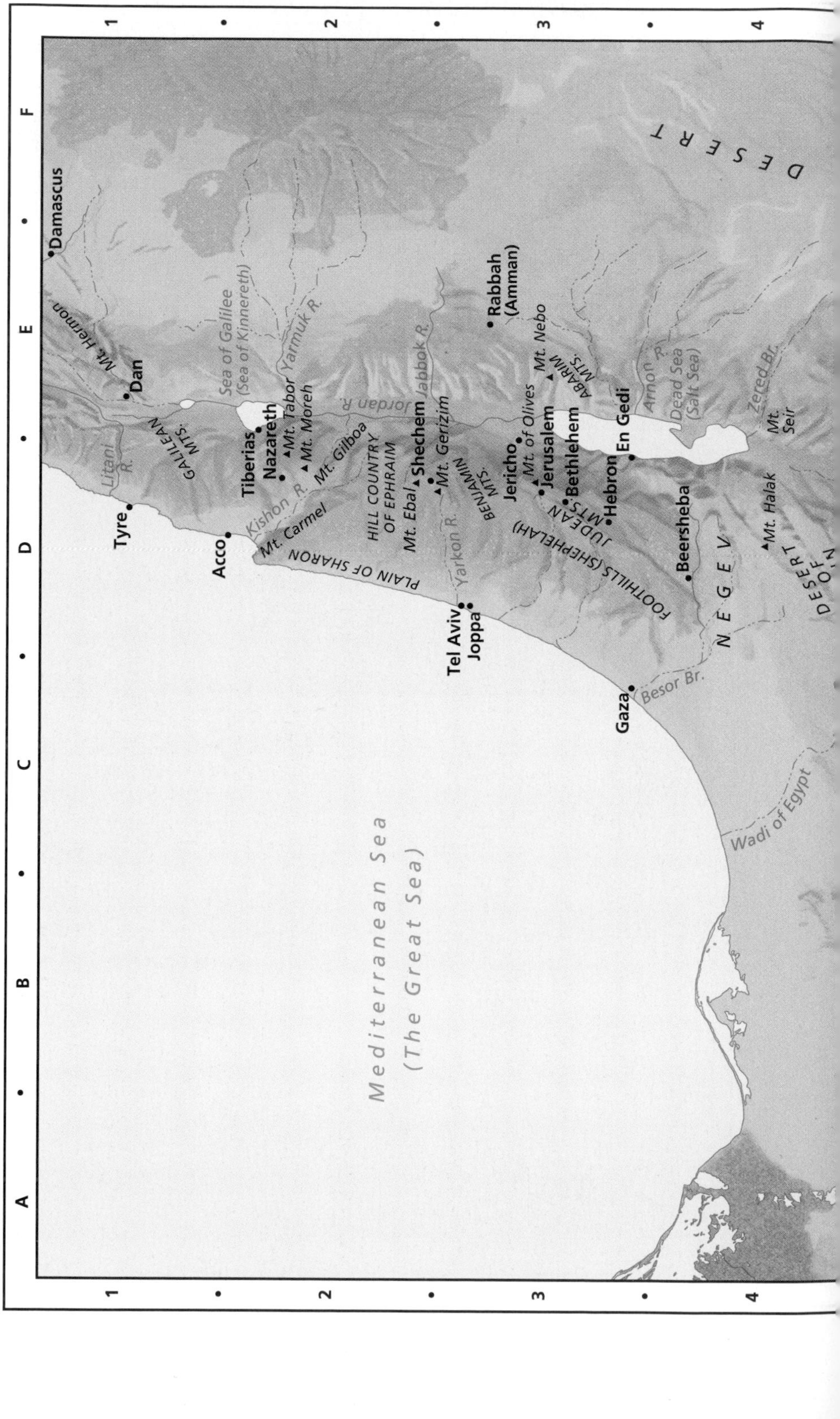
1
2
3
4
A
B
C
D
E
F
Damascus
Mt. Hermon
Dan
Tyre
Litani R.
GALILEAN MTS.
Acco
Mt. Carmel
Kishon R.
Tiberias
Nazareth
Mt. Tabor
Mt. Moreh
Mt. Gilboa
Sea of Galilee
(Sea of Kinnereth)
Yarmuk R.
Jordan R.
Jabbok R.
HILL COUNTRY
OF EPHRAIM
Mt. Ebal
Shechem
Mt. Gerizim
BENJAMIN MTS.
Yarkon R.
PLAIN OF SHARON
Tel Aviv
Joppa
Rabbah
(Amman)
Jericho
Mt. of Olives
Mt. Nebo
Jerusalem
Bethlehem
ABARIM MTS.
JUDEAN MTS.
Hebron
En Gedi
Arnon R.
Dead Sea
(Salt Sea)
FOOTHILLS (SHEPHELAH)
Beersheba
Zered Br.
Mt. Seir
Mt. Halak
NEGEV
DESERT OF ZIN
Gaza
Besor Br.
Wadi of Egypt
DESERT
Mediterranean Sea
(The Great Sea)

Map 9: HOLY LAND IN THE TIME OF JESUS

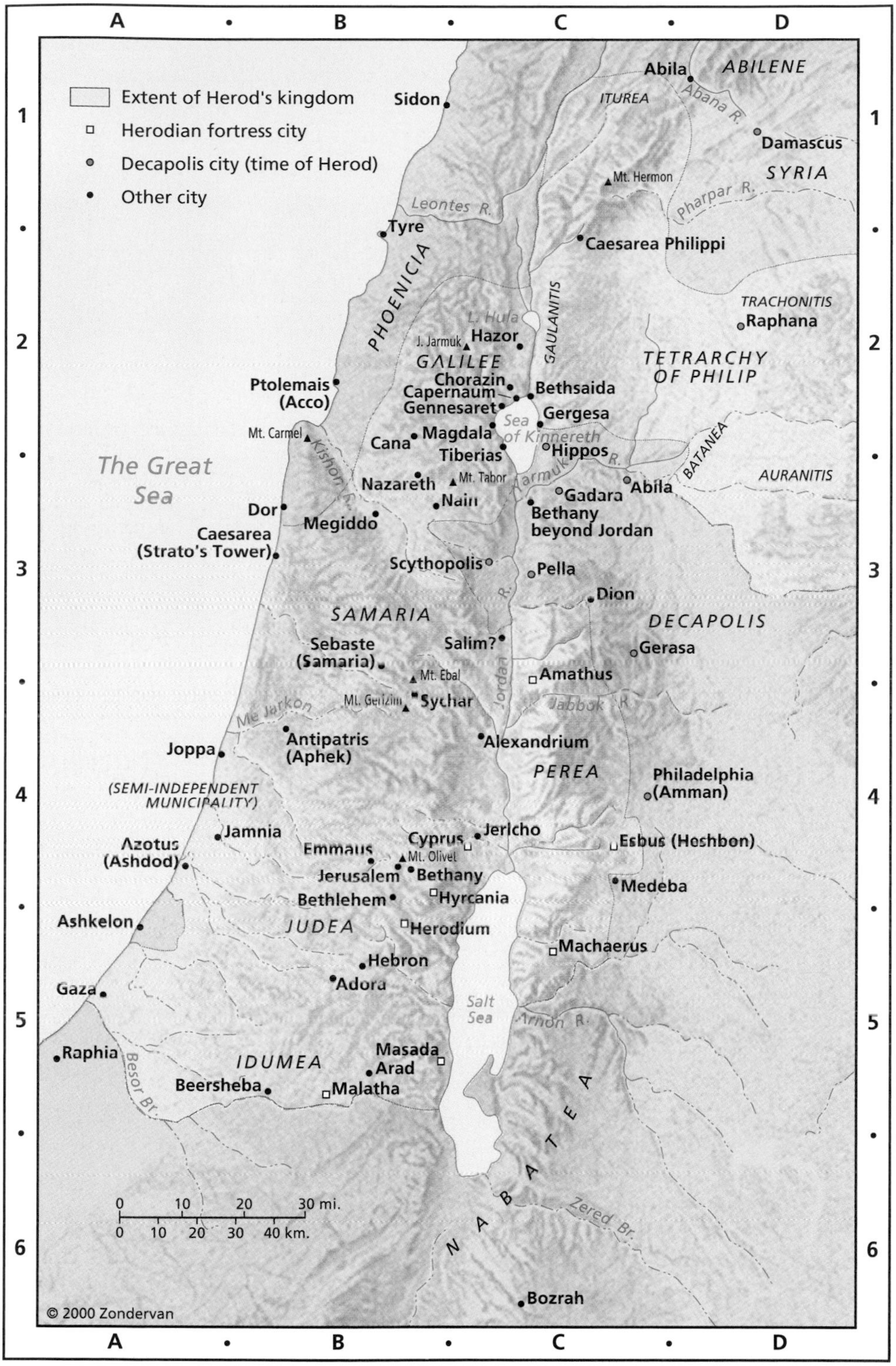

Extent of Herod's kingdom
Herodian fortress city
Decapolis city (time of Herod)
Other city
The Great Sea
Sidon
Abila
ABILENE
ITUREA
Abana R.
Damascus
SYRIA
Mt. Hermon
Pharpar R.
Leontes R.
Tyre
Caesarea Philippi
PHOENICIA
GAULANITIS
TRACHONITIS
Raphana
L. Hula
J. Jarmuk
Hazor
GALILEE
TETRARCHY OF PHILIP
Ptolemais (Acco)
Chorazin
Capernaum
Gennesaret
Bethsaida
Gergesa
Sea of Kinnereth
Mt. Carmel
Kishon R.
Cana
Magdala
Tiberias
Hippos
BATANEA
Yarmuk R.
Nazareth
Mt. Tabor
Nain
Gadara
Abila
AURANITIS
Dor
Megiddo
Bethany beyond Jordan
Caesarea (Strato's Tower)
Scythopolis
Pella
Dion
SAMARIA
DECAPOLIS
Sebaste (Samaria)
Salim?
Gerasa
Mt. Ebal
Amathus
Mt. Gerizim
Sychar
Jordan R.
Jabbok R.
Me Jarkon
Antipatris (Aphek)
Alexandrium
Joppa
PEREA
(SEMI-INDEPENDENT MUNICIPALITY)
Philadelphia (Amman)
Jamnia
Jericho
Azotus (Ashdod)
Emmaus
Cyprus
Mt. Olivet
Esbus (Heshbon)
Jerusalem
Bethany
Medeba
Bethlehem
Hyrcania
Ashkelon
JUDEA
Herodium
Machaerus
Hebron
Adora
Gaza
Salt Sea
Arnon R.
Raphia
Besor Br.
IDUMEA
Masada
Arad
Beersheba
Malatha
NABATEA
Zered Br.
0 10 20 30 mi.
0 10 20 30 40 km.
Bozrah
A B C D
1 2 3 4 5 6

Map 8: ASSYRIAN AND BABYLONIAN EMPIRES

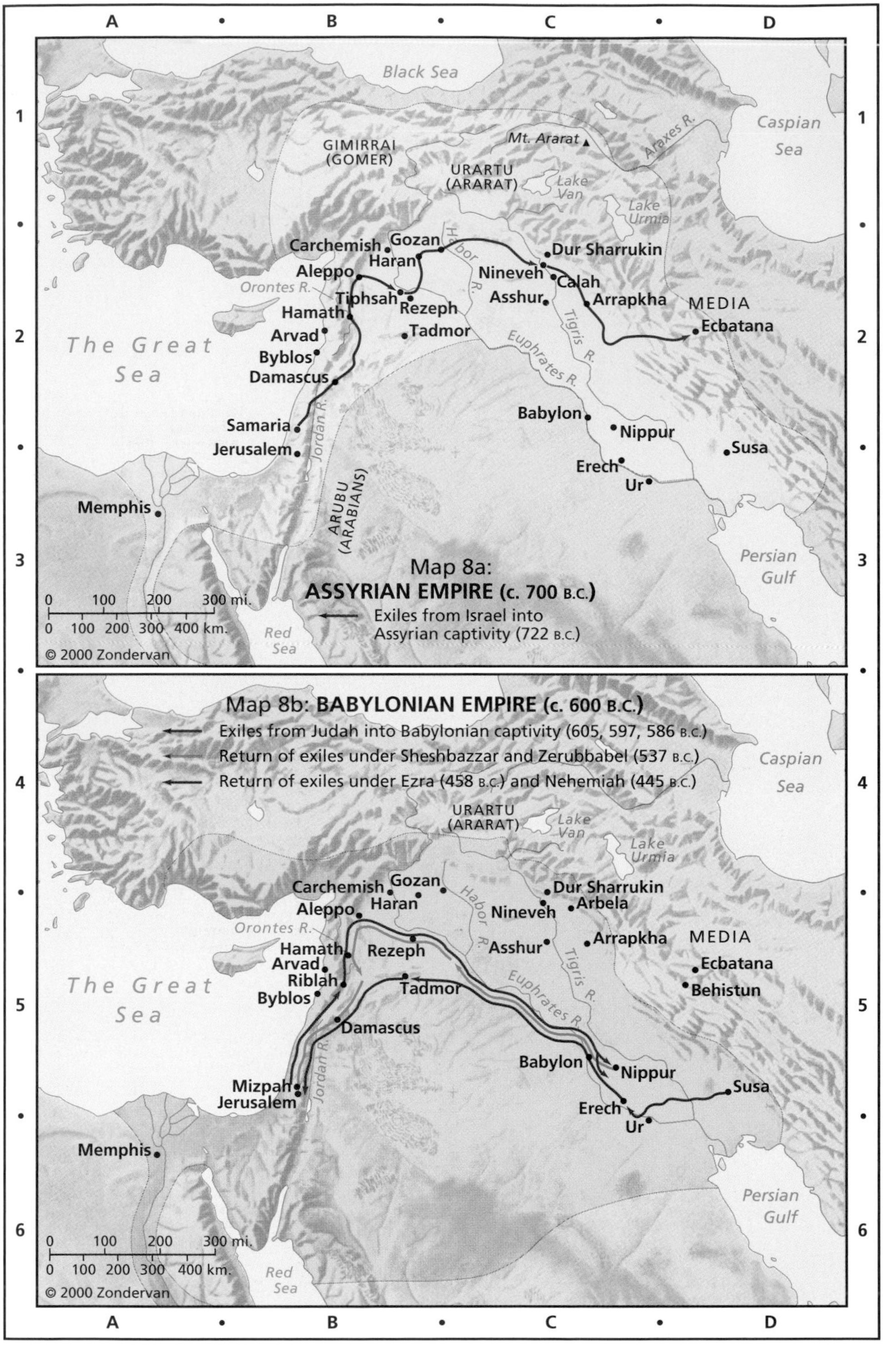

Map 7: **PROPHETS IN ISRAEL AND JUDAH**

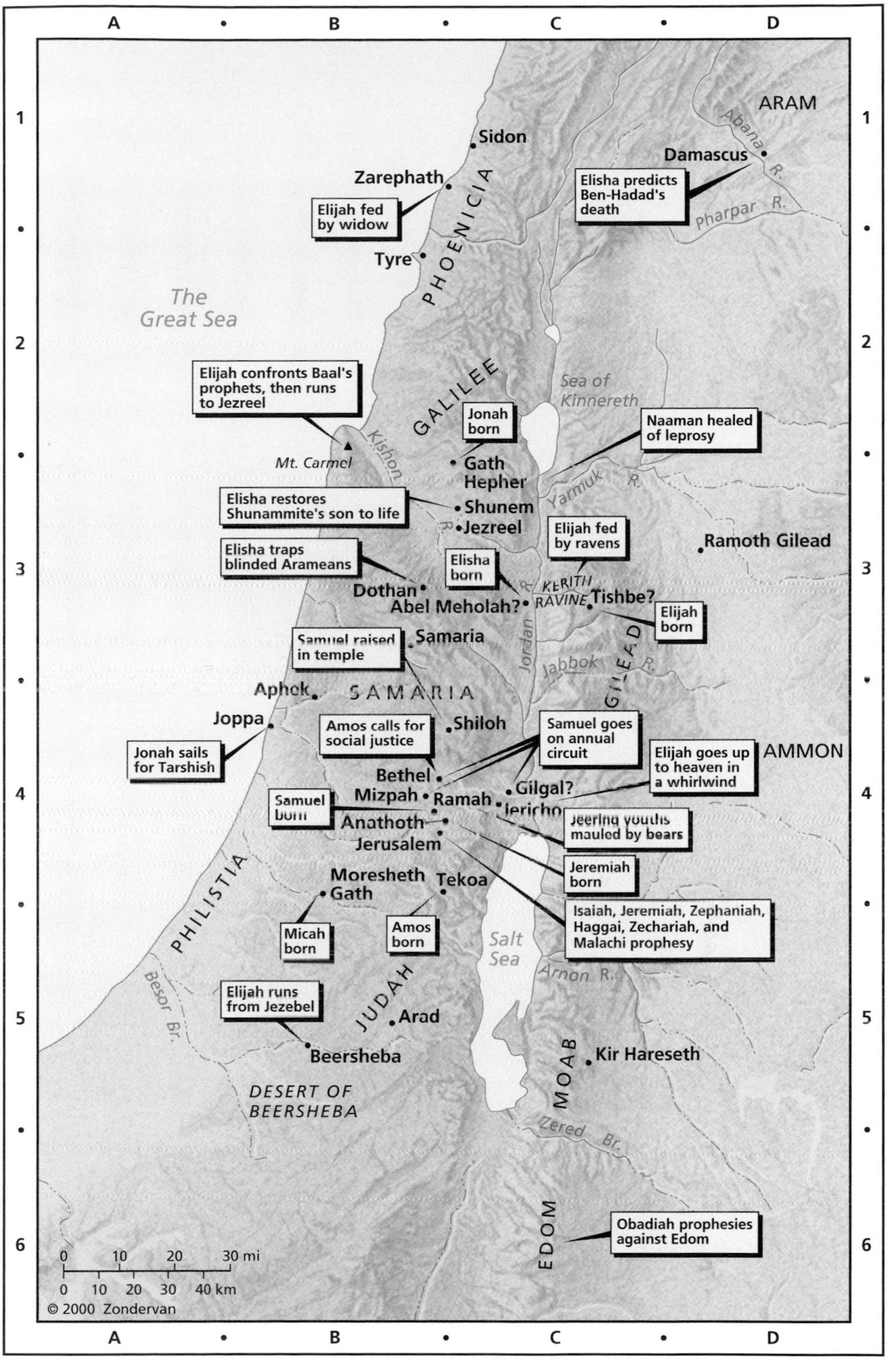
ARAM
Damascus
Abana R.
Pharpar R.
Elisha predicts Ben-Hadad's death
Sidon
Zarephath
Elijah fed by widow
PHOENICIA
Tyre
The Great Sea
Elijah confronts Baal's prophets, then runs to Jezreel
Mt. Carmel
Kishon
GALILEE
Jonah born
Gath Hepher
Sea of Kinnereth
Naaman healed of leprosy
Yarmuk R.
Elisha restores Shunammite's son to life
Shunem
Jezreel
Elijah fed by ravens
Ramoth Gilead
Elisha traps blinded Arameans
Elisha born
Dothan
Abel Meholah?
KERITH RAVINE
Tishbe?
Elijah born
Samuel raised in temple
Samaria
Jordan R.
Jabbok R.
GILEAD
Aphek
SAMARIA
Joppa
Jonah sails for Tarshish
Amos calls for social justice
Shiloh
Samuel goes on annual circuit
Elijah goes up to heaven in a whirlwind
AMMON
Bethel
Gilgal?
Mizpah
Ramah
Jericho
Samuel born
Anathoth
Jeering youths mauled by bears
Jerusalem
Jeremiah born
Moresheth Gath
Tekoa
Isaiah, Jeremiah, Zephaniah, Haggai, Zechariah, and Malachi prophesy
PHILISTIA
Micah born
Amos born
Salt Sea
Arnon R.
Besor Br.
Elijah runs from Jezebel
JUDAH
Arad
Beersheba
MOAB
Kir Hareseth
DESERT OF BEERSHEBA
Zered Br.
EDOM
Obadiah prophesies against Edom
0 10 20 30 mi
0 10 20 30 40 km
© 2000 Zondervan

Map 6: **KINGDOMS OF ISRAEL AND JUDAH**

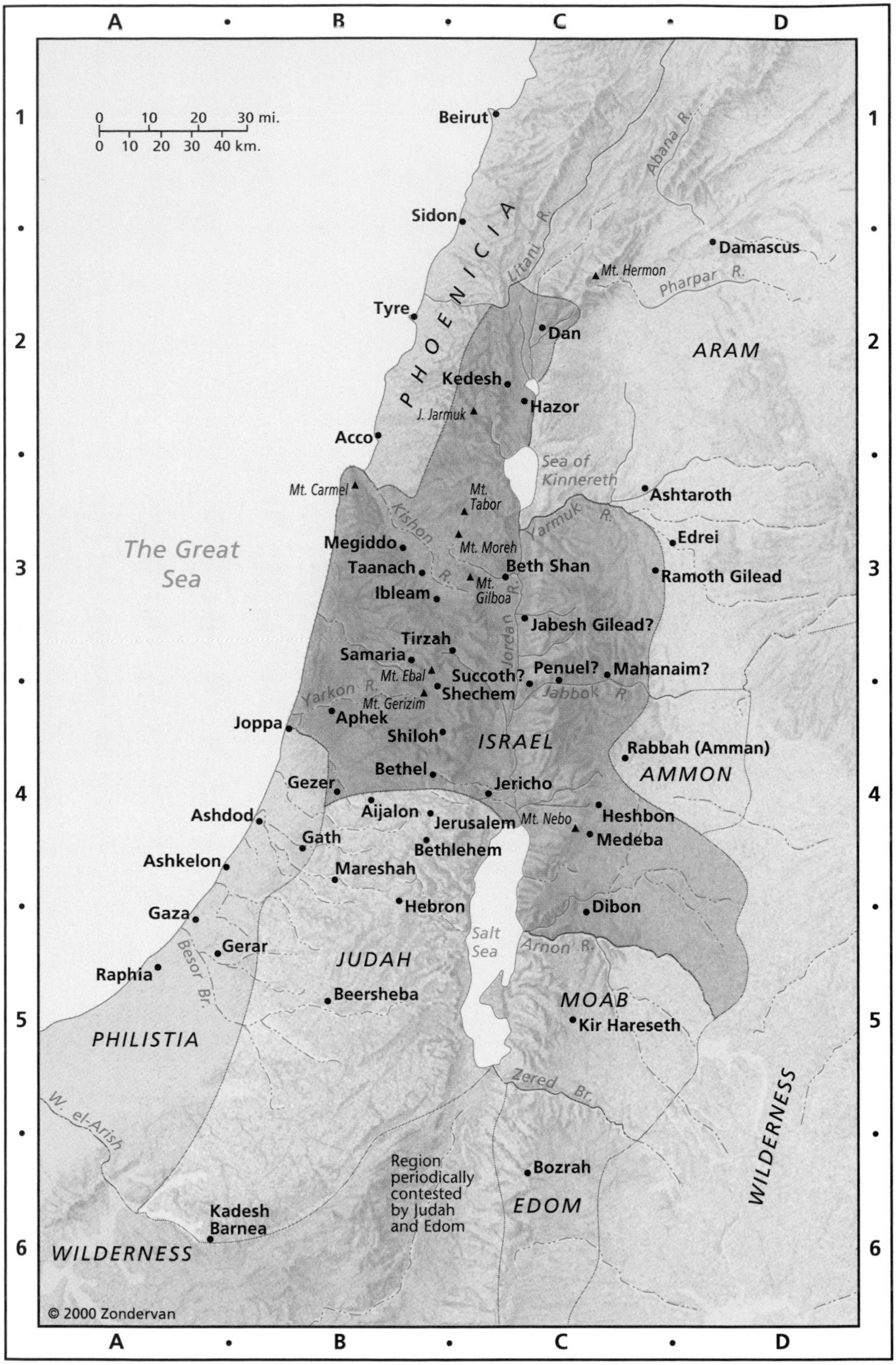
A
B
C
D
1
2
3
4
5
6
0 10 20 30 mi.
0 10 20 30 40 km.
Beirut
Sidon
Tyre
Acco
PHOENICIA
Abana R.
Litani R.
Damascus
Mt. Hermon
Pharpar R.
Dan
ARAM
Kedesh
Hazor
J. Jarmuk
Sea of Kinnereth
Mt. Carmel
Mt. Tabor
Ashtaroth
Kishon R.
Yarmuk R.
Edrei
Megiddo
Mt. Moreh
The Great Sea
Taanach
Beth Shan
Ramoth Gilead
Ibleam
Mt. Gilboa
Jordan R.
Jabesh Gilead?
Tirzah
Samaria
Mt. Ebal
Succoth?
Penuel?
Mahanaim?
Yarkon R.
Shechem
Jabbok R.
Mt. Gerizim
Aphek
Joppa
Shiloh
ISRAEL
Rabbah (Amman)
Bethel
AMMON
Gezer
Jericho
Aijalon
Heshbon
Ashdod
Jerusalem
Mt. Nebo
Gath
Medeba
Bethlehem
Ashkelon
Mareshah
Gaza
Hebron
Dibon
Salt Sea
Gerar
Arnon R.
Besor Br.
JUDAH
Raphia
Beersheba
MOAB
Kir Hareseth
PHILISTIA
Zered Br.
W. el-Arish
WILDERNESS
Bozrah
Region periodically contested by Judah and Edom
EDOM
Kadesh Barnea
WILDERNESS
© 2000 Zondervan

Map 5: KINGDOM OF DAVID AND SOLOMON

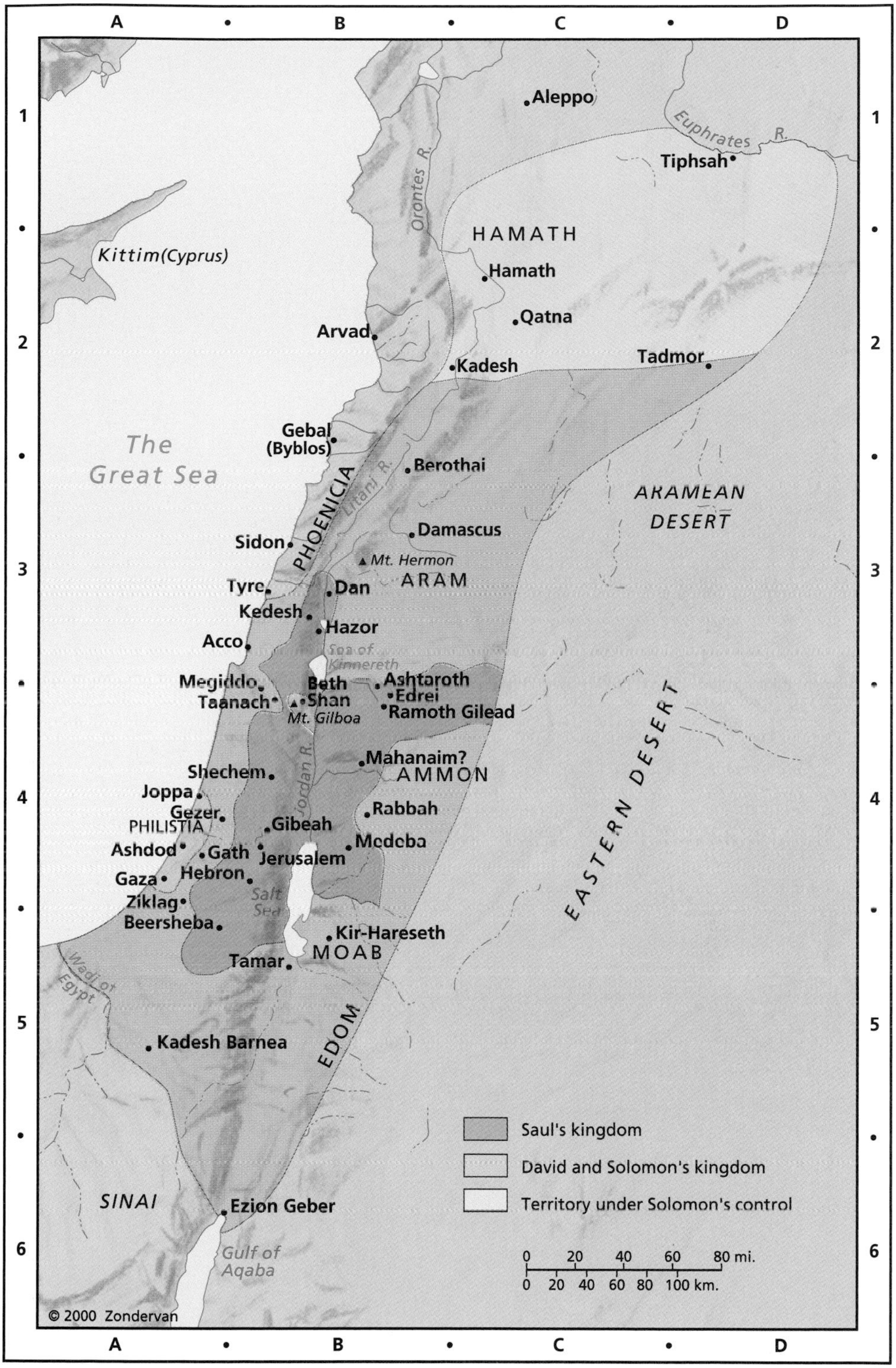
A
B
C
D
1
2
3
4
5
6
Aleppo
Euphrates R.
Tiphsah
Orontes R.
HAMATH
Hamath
Qatna
Kittim(Cyprus)
Arvad
Kadesh
Tadmor
Gebal (Byblos)
The Great Sea
Berothai
Litani R.
PHOENICIA
ARAMEAN DESERT
Damascus
Sidon
Mt. Hermon
ARAM
Tyre
Dan
Kedesh
Hazor
Acco
Sea of Kinnereth
Megiddo
Beth Shan
Ashtaroth
Edrei
Taanach
Ramoth Gilead
Mt. Gilboa
EASTERN DESERT
Jordan R.
Mahanaim?
Shechem
AMMON
Joppa
Gezer
Rabbah
PHILISTIA
Gibeah
Ashdod
Gath
Medeba
Jerusalem
Gaza
Hebron
Salt Sea
Ziklag
Beersheba
Kir-Hareseth
MOAB
Tamar
Wadi of Egypt
Kadesh Barnea
EDOM
Saul's kingdom
David and Solomon's kingdom
Territory under Solomon's control
SINAI
Ezion Geber
Gulf of Aqaba
0 20 40 60 80 mi.
0 20 40 60 80 100 km.
© 2000 Zondervan

Map 4: **LAND OF THE TWELVE TRIBES**

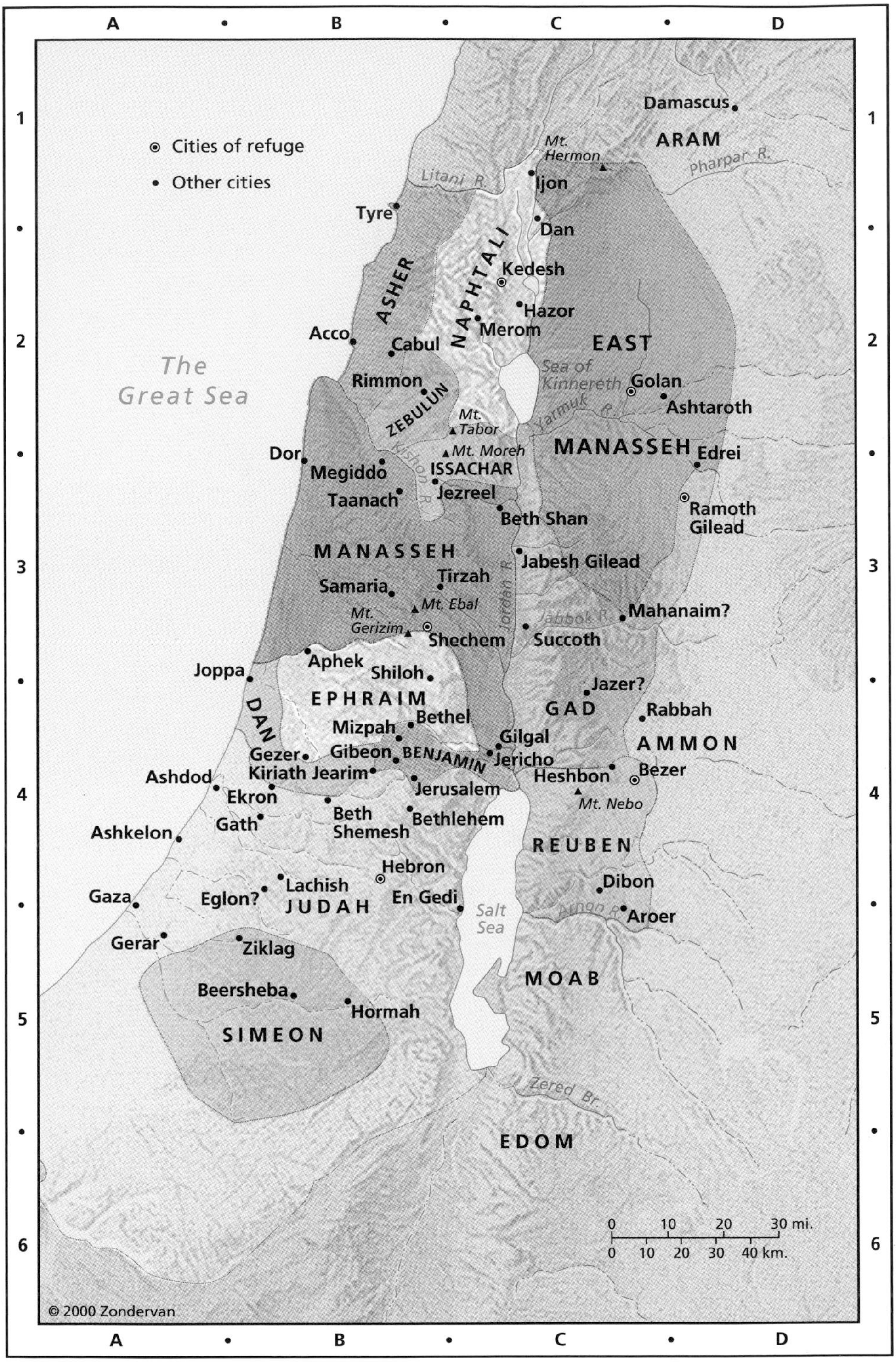

Map 3: EXODUS AND CONQUEST OF CANAAN

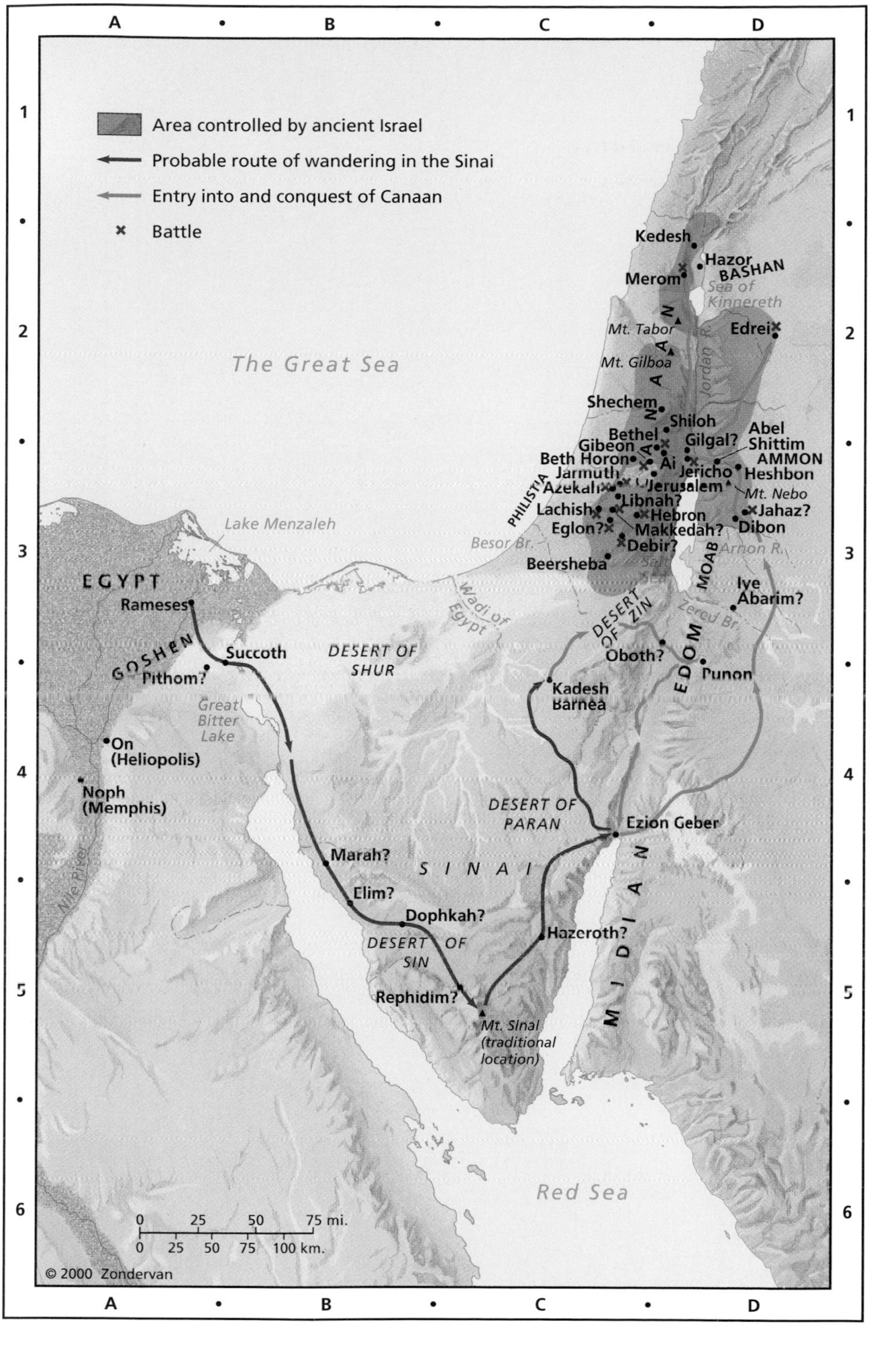

A
B
C
D
1
2
3
4
5
6
Area controlled by ancient Israel
Probable route of wandering in the Sinai
Entry into and conquest of Canaan
Battle
Kedesh
Hazor
BASHAN
Merom
Sea of Kinnereth
Mt. Tabor
Edrei
Mt. Gilboa
Jordan R.
The Great Sea
CANAAN
Shechem
Shiloh
Abel Shittim
Bethel
Gilgal?
Gibeon
AMMON
Beth Horon
Ai
Jarmuth
Jericho
Heshbon
Azekah
Jerusalem
Mt. Nebo
PHILISTIA
Libnah?
Lachish
Hebron
Jahaz?
Eglon?
Makkedah?
Dibon
Lake Menzaleh
Besor Br.
Debir?
Arnon R.
Beersheba
Salt Sea
MOAB
EGYPT
Rameses
Wadi of Egypt
DESERT OF ZIN
Iye Abarim?
Zered Br.
GOSHEN
Succoth
DESERT OF SHUR
Oboth?
EDOM
Pithom?
Punon
Kadesh Barnea
Great Bitter Lake
On (Heliopolis)
Noph (Memphis)
DESERT OF PARAN
Ezion Geber
Marah?
SINAI
Elim?
MIDIAN
Nile River
Dophkah?
DESERT OF SIN
Hazeroth?
Rephidim?
Mt. Sinai (traditional location)
Red Sea
0 25 50 75 mi.
0 25 50 75 100 km.

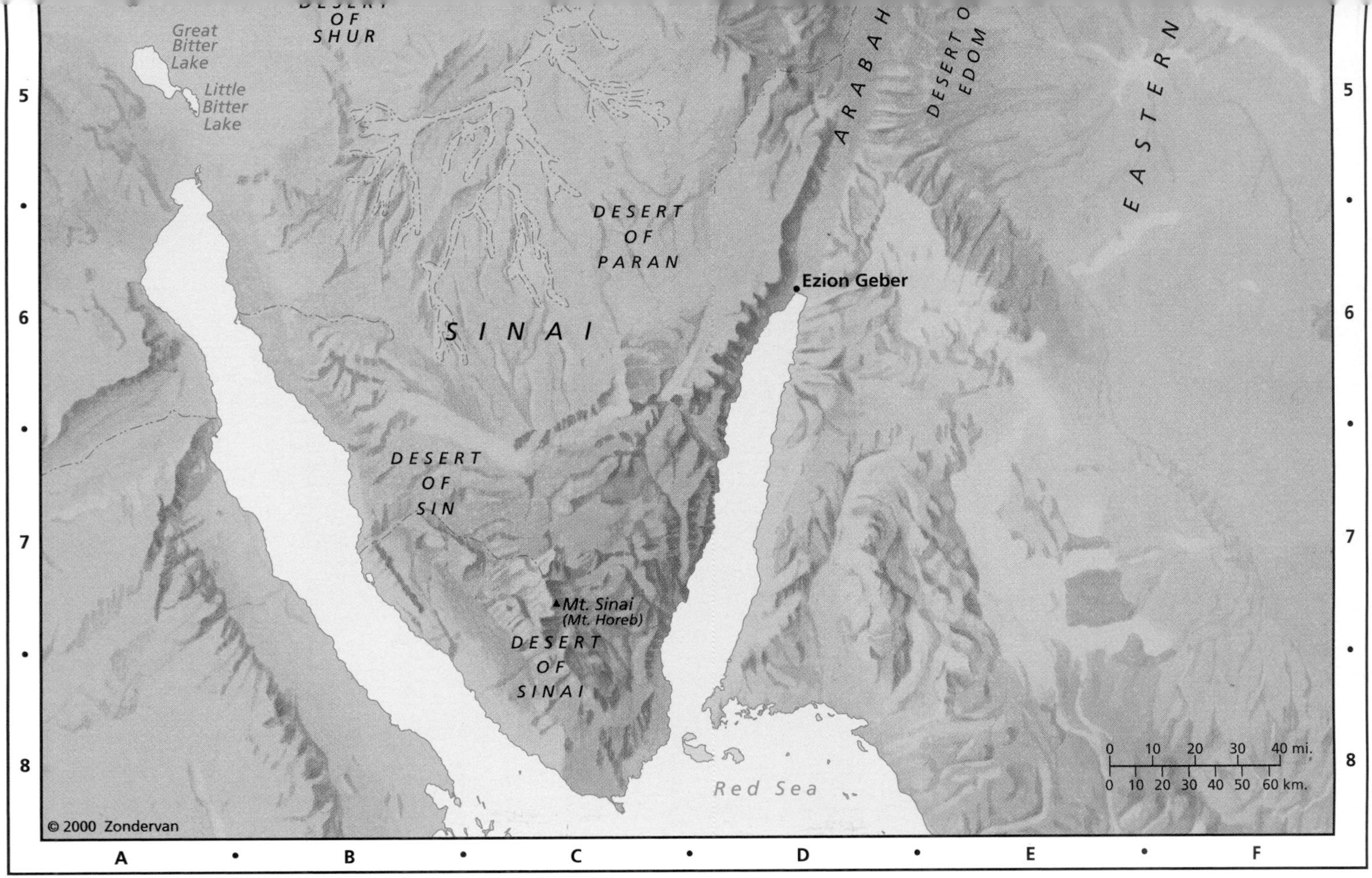
OF
SHUR
Great
Bitter
Lake
Little
Bitter
Lake
ARABAH
DESERT OF
EDOM
EASTERN
DESERT
OF
PARAN
Ezion Geber
SINAI
DESERT
OF
SIN
Mt. Sinai
(Mt. Horeb)
DESERT
OF
SINAI
Red Sea
0 10 20 30 40 mi.
0 10 20 30 40 50 60 km.
© 2000 Zondervan
A
B
C
D
E
F
5
6
7
8

Map 10: **JERUSALEM IN THE TIME OF JESUS**

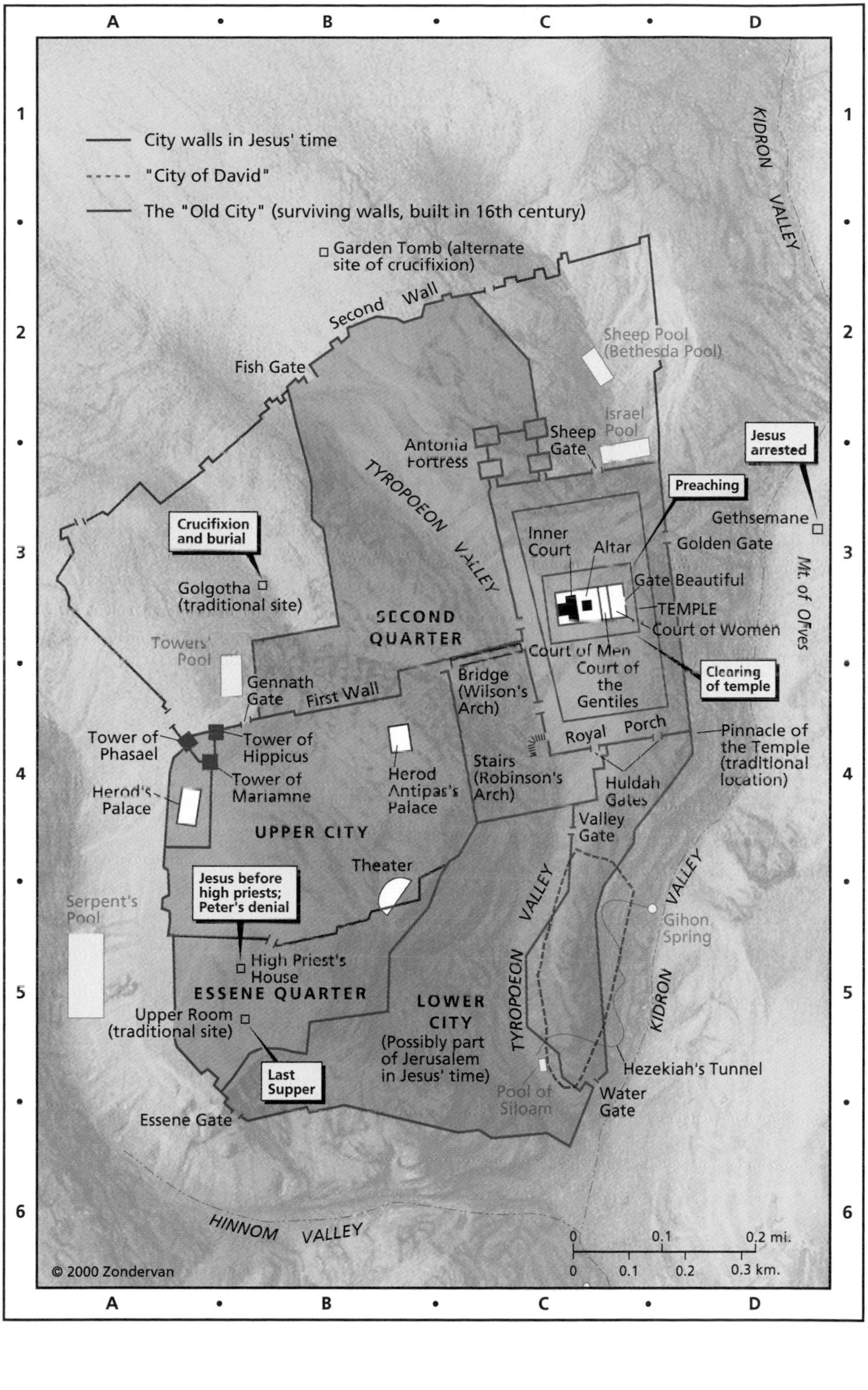

City walls in Jesus' time
"City of David"
The "Old City" (surviving walls, built in 16th century)
Garden Tomb (alternate site of crucifixion)
Second Wall
Fish Gate
Sheep Pool (Bethesda Pool)
Israel Pool
Sheep Gate
Antonia Fortress
TYROPOEON VALLEY
KIDRON VALLEY
Jesus arrested
Preaching
Gethsemane
Golden Gate
Mt. of Olives
Crucifixion and burial
Golgotha (traditional site)
Inner Court
Altar
Gate Beautiful
TEMPLE
Court of Women
SECOND QUARTER
Towers' Pool
Court of Men
Court of the Gentiles
Clearing of temple
Gennath Gate
First Wall
Bridge (Wilson's Arch)
Tower of Phasael
Tower of Hippicus
Tower of Mariamne
Royal Porch
Pinnacle of the Temple (traditional location)
Herod's Palace
Herod Antipas's Palace
Stairs (Robinson's Arch)
Huldah Gates
Valley Gate
UPPER CITY
Theater
Jesus before high priests; Peter's denial
Serpent's Pool
Gihon Spring
High Priest's House
ESSENE QUARTER
LOWER CITY (Possibly part of Jerusalem in Jesus' time)
Upper Room (traditional site)
Last Supper
Hezekiah's Tunnel
Pool of Siloam
Water Gate
Essene Gate
HINNOM VALLEY
0 0.1 0.2 mi.
0 0.1 0.2 0.3 km.
© 2000 Zondervan

Map 11: JESUS' MINISTRY

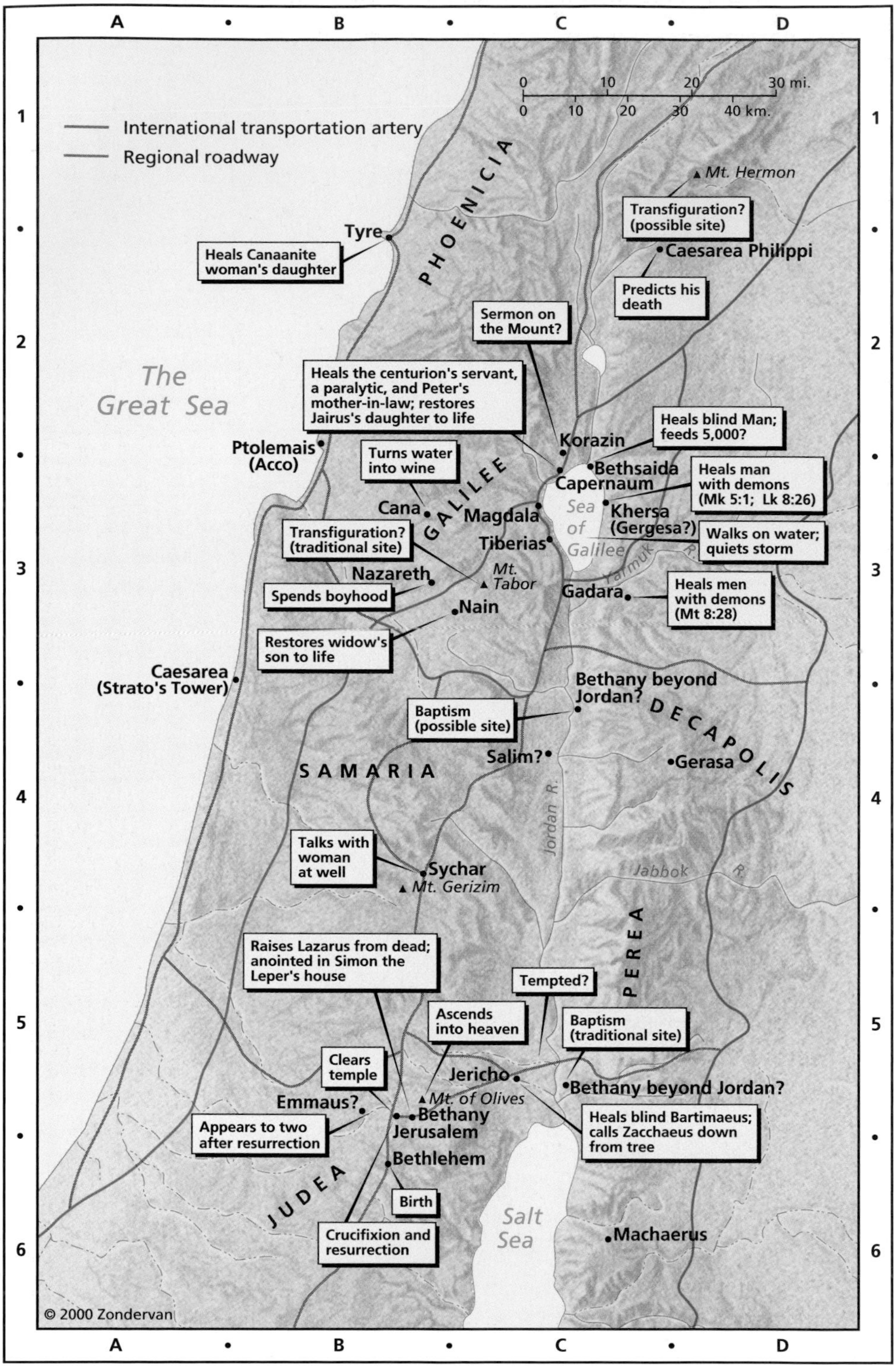

A
B
C
D
1
2
3
4
5
6
0 10 20 30 mi.
0 10 20 30 40 km.
International transportation artery
Regional roadway
PHOENICIA
Mt. Hermon
Transfiguration? (possible site)
Caesarea Philippi
Predicts his death
Tyre
Heals Canaanite woman's daughter
Sermon on the Mount?
The Great Sea
Heals the centurion's servant, a paralytic, and Peter's mother-in-law; restores Jairus's daughter to life
Heals blind Man; feeds 5,000?
Korazin
Bethsaida
Capernaum
Heals man with demons (Mk 5:1; Lk 8:26)
Ptolemais (Acco)
Turns water into wine
GALILEE
Cana
Magdala
Sea of Galilee
Khersa (Gergesa?)
Walks on water; quiets storm
Transfiguration? (traditional site)
Tiberias
Yarmuk R.
Nazareth
Mt. Tabor
Spends boyhood
Gadara
Heals men with demons (Mt 8:28)
Nain
Restores widow's son to life
Caesarea (Strato's Tower)
Bethany beyond Jordan?
DECAPOLIS
Baptism (possible site)
Salim?
Gerasa
SAMARIA
Jordan R.
Talks with woman at well
Sychar
Mt. Gerizim
Jabbok R.
PEREA
Raises Lazarus from dead; anointed in Simon the Leper's house
Tempted?
Ascends into heaven
Baptism (traditional site)
Clears temple
Jericho
Bethany beyond Jordan?
Emmaus?
Mt. of Olives
Bethany
Jerusalem
Appears to two after resurrection
Heals blind Bartimaeus; calls Zacchaeus down from tree
Bethlehem
JUDEA
Birth
Salt Sea
Machaerus
Crucifixion and resurrection
© 2000 Zondervan

Map 12: **APOSTLES' EARLY TRAVELS**

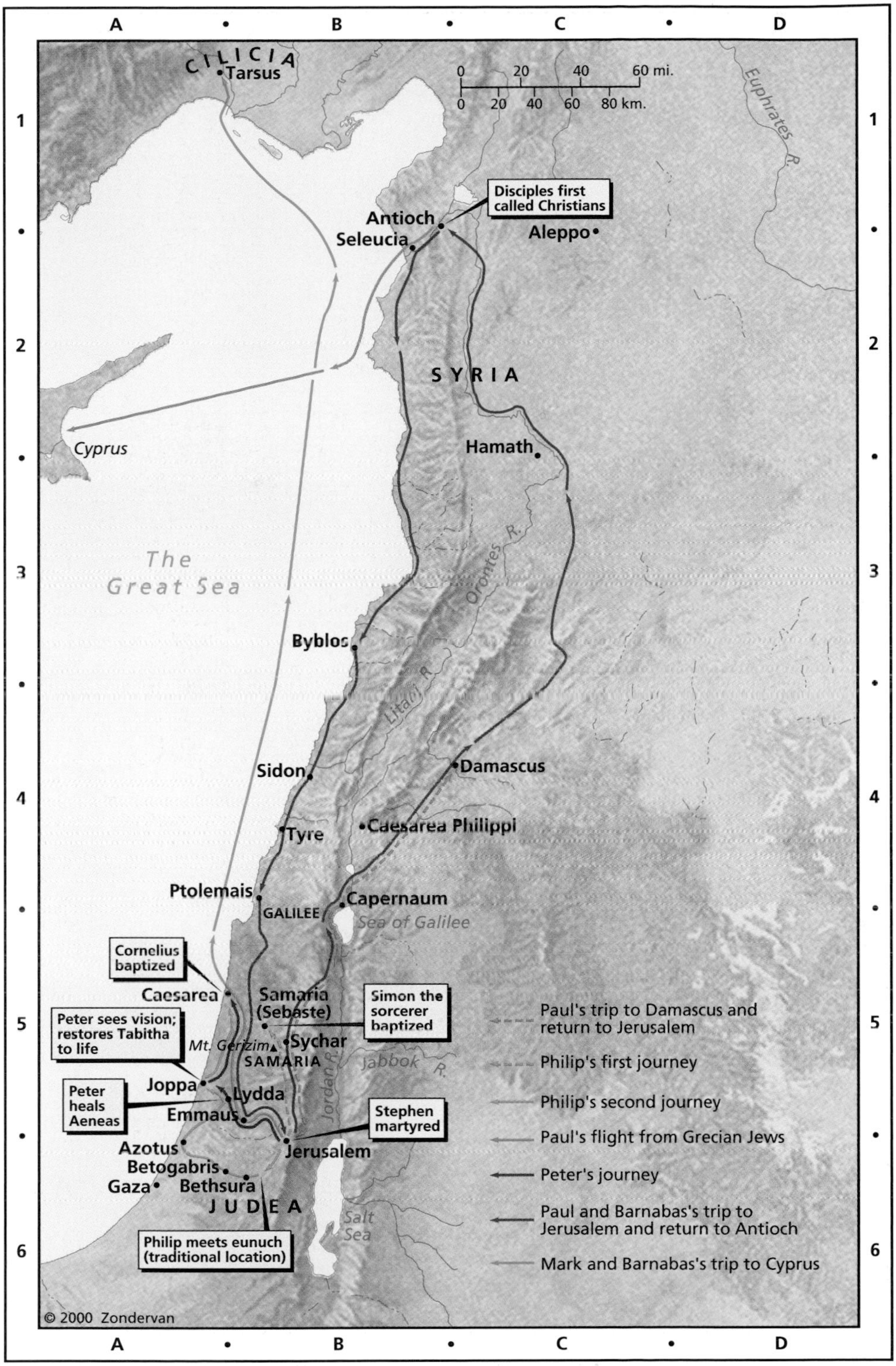

CILICIA
Tarsus
0 20 40 60 mi.
0 20 40 60 80 km.
Euphrates R.
Disciples first called Christians
Antioch
Seleucia
Aleppo
SYRIA
Cyprus
Hamath
Orontes R.
The Great Sea
Byblos
Litani R.
Sidon
Damascus
Tyre
Caesarea Philippi
Ptolemais
Capernaum
GALILEE
Sea of Galilee
Cornelius baptized
Caesarea
Samaria (Sebaste)
Simon the sorcerer baptized
Peter sees vision; restores Tabitha to life
Mt. Gerizim
Sychar
SAMARIA
Jabbok R.
Jordan R.
Joppa
Lydda
Peter heals Aeneas
Emmaus
Stephen martyred
Azotus
Jerusalem
Betogabris
Gaza
Bethsura
JUDEA
Salt Sea
Philip meets eunuch (traditional location)
Paul's trip to Damascus and return to Jerusalem
Philip's first journey
Philip's second journey
Paul's flight from Grecian Jews
Peter's journey
Paul and Barnabas's trip to Jerusalem and return to Antioch
Mark and Barnabas's trip to Cyprus
© 2000 Zondervan
A B C D
1 2 3 4 5 6

Map 13: PAUL'S MISSIONARY JOURNEYS

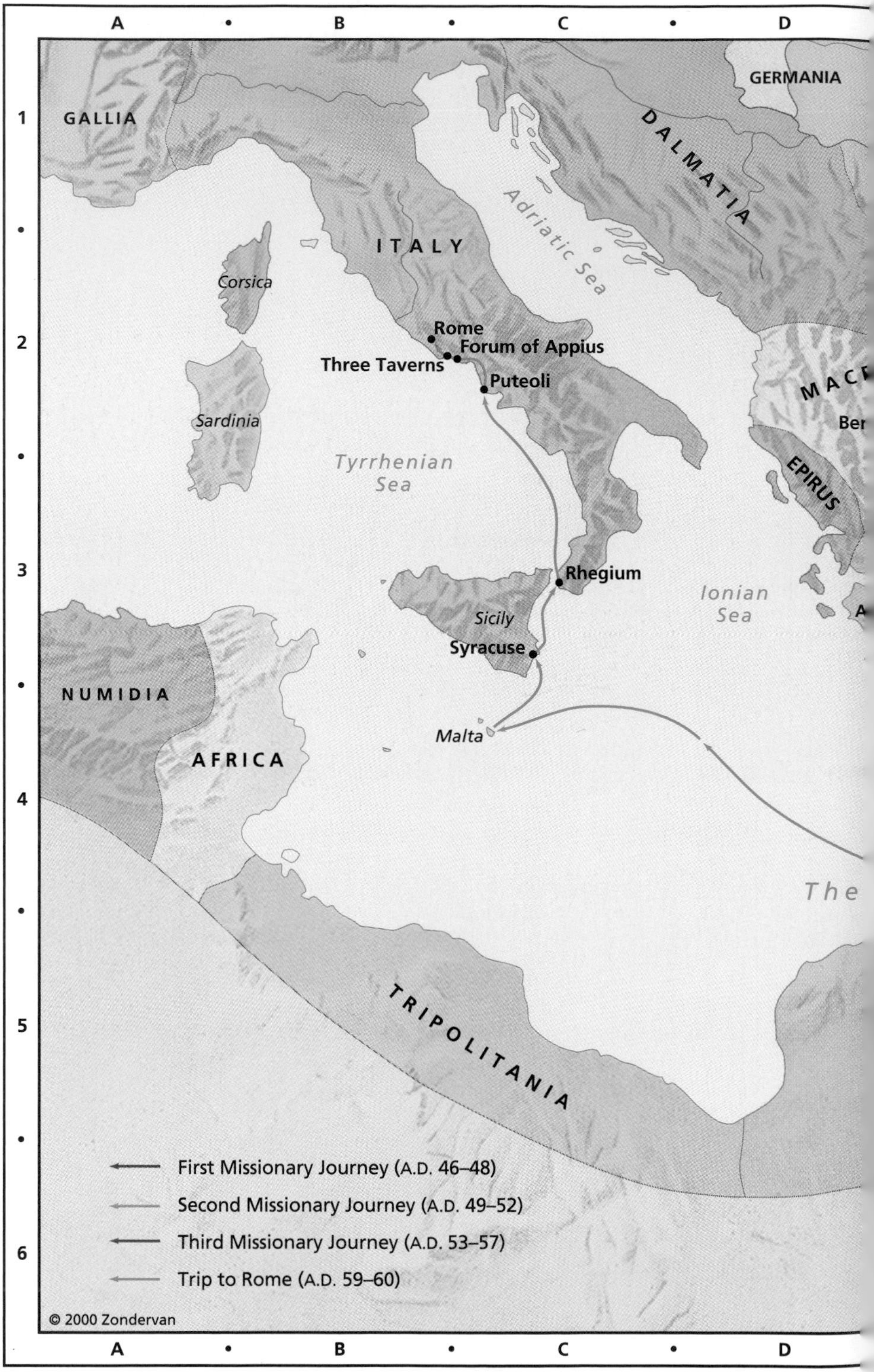
A
B
C
D
1
2
3
4
5
6
GALLIA
GERMANIA
DALMATIA
ITALY
Adriatic Sea
Corsica
Sardinia
Rome
Forum of Appius
Three Taverns
Puteoli
Tyrrhenian Sea
Rhegium
Ionian Sea
Sicily
Syracuse
EPIRUS
NUMIDIA
AFRICA
Malta
TRIPOLITANIA
First Missionary Journey (A.D. 46–48)
Second Missionary Journey (A.D. 49–52)
Third Missionary Journey (A.D. 53–57)
Trip to Rome (A.D. 59–60)
© 2000 Zondervan

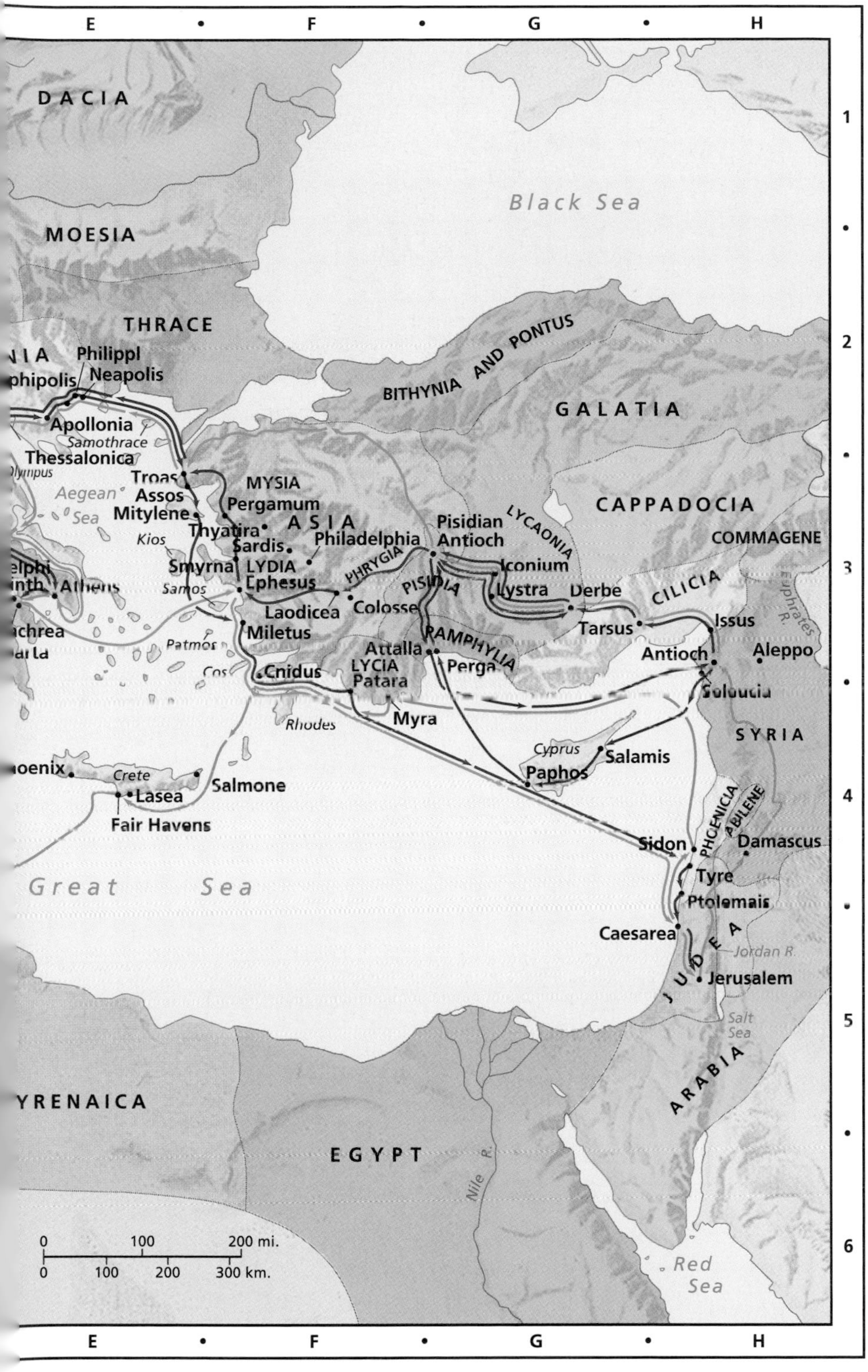

E
F
G
H
1
2
3
4
5
6
DACIA
MOESIA
THRACE
Black Sea
BITHYNIA AND PONTUS
GALATIA
CAPPADOCIA
COMMAGENE
Philippi
Neapolis
Apollonia
Samothrace
Thessalonica
Troas
Assos
Mitylene
Aegean Sea
Kios
Samos
Patmos
Cos
MYSIA
Pergamum
ASIA
Thyatira
Sardis
Philadelphia
Smyrna
LYDIA
Ephesus
Athens
Laodicea
Colosse
Miletus
PHRYGIA
PISIDIA
Pisidian Antioch
LYCAONIA
Iconium
Lystra
Derbe
CILICIA
Tarsus
Issus
Antioch
Aleppo
Euphrates R.
PAMPHYLIA
Attalla
Perga
LYCIA
Patara
Cnidus
Rhodes
Myra
Cyprus
Salamis
Paphos
SYRIA
Crete
Lasea
Fair Havens
Salmone
PHOENICIA
ABILENE
Sidon
Damascus
Tyre
Ptolemais
Caesarea
Jordan R.
JUDEA
Jerusalem
Salt Sea
ARABIA
Great Sea
YRENAICA
EGYPT
Nile R.
Red Sea
0 100 200 mi.
0 100 200 300 km.

Map 14: **ROMAN EMPIRE**

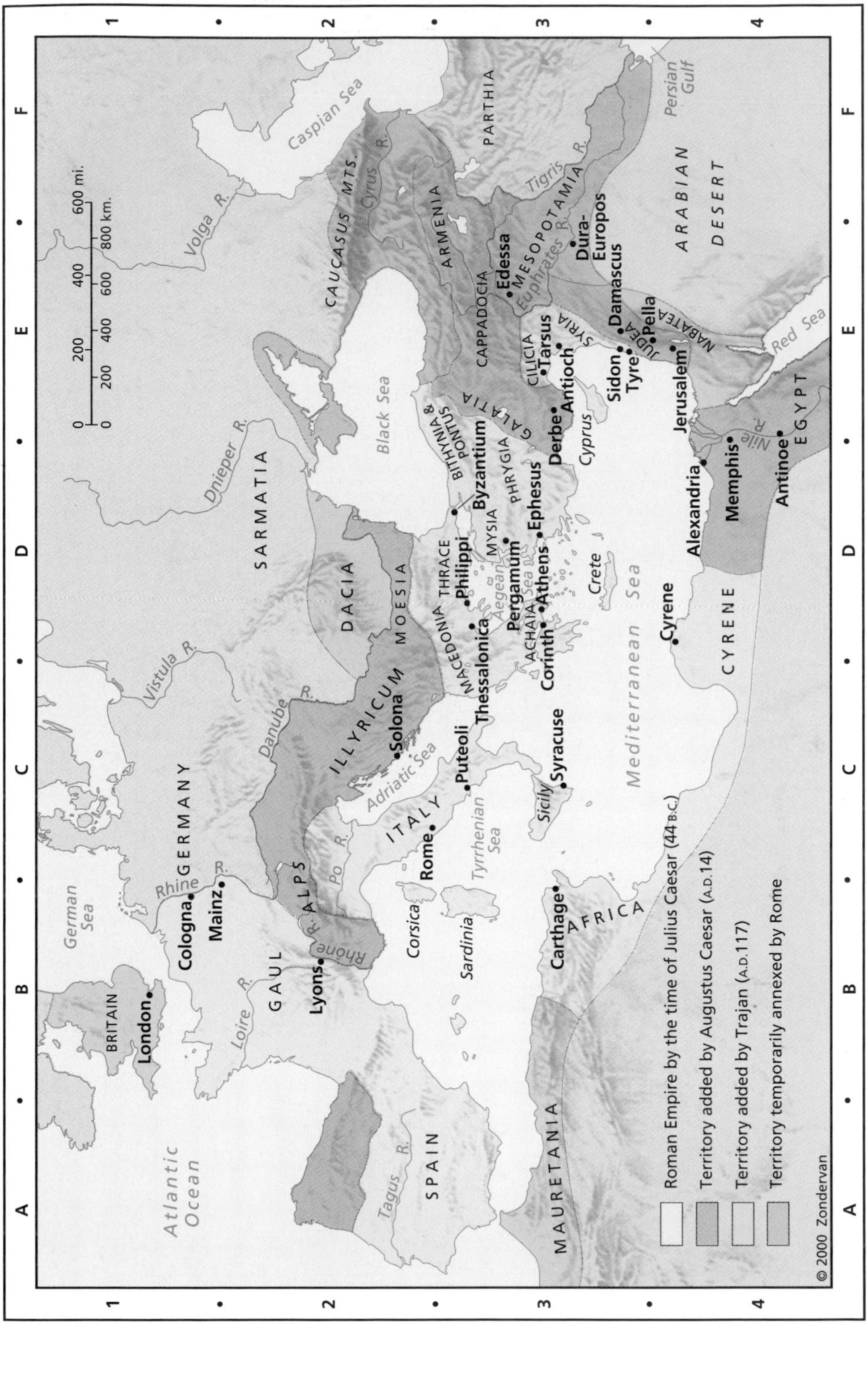